KU-778-400

PEARS

CYCLOPAEDIA

1986–87

A BOOK OF BACKGROUND INFORMATION
AND REFERENCE FOR EVERYDAY USE

EDITED BY

CHRISTOPHER COOK

M.A. Cantab., D.Phil. Oxon., F.R.Hist. S.

Ninety-fifth Edition

The Editor desires to express his gratitude to readers for their criticisms and suggestions and to all those who in one way or another have contributed to the making of this edition. Correspondence on editorial matters should be addressed to Dr. Christopher Cook, "Pears Cyclopaedia", Pelham Books Ltd., 27 Wrights Lane, Kensington, London W8 5DZ.

First published 1897

ISBN 0 7207 1665 9

© 1986 by Pelham Books Ltd.

All Rights Reserved. No part of this publication may be reproduced, stored in a retrieval system or transmitted in any form or by any means, electronic, mechanical, photocopying, recording or otherwise, without the prior permission of the Copyright owner.

Printed and Bound in Great Britain by Richard Clay (The Chaucer Press) Ltd., Bungay, Suffolk

CONTENTS

Sections are arranged alphabetically, or chronologically, or have a detailed Table of Contents.

HISTORICAL EVENTS

Chronicle of events from the earliest times to the present day. For events in pre-history the reader may also like to consult the relevant sections on geology and man's early ancestors in the Science section.

CHRONICLE OF EVENTS

Note.—*For classical history and for the past millennium most dates are well established. For other periods there is sometimes considerable uncertainty. Many of the dates in ancient history are either dubious or approximate, sometimes both. For dates on hominid evolution the reader is invited to consult* **Section F, Part V.**

B.C.

PREHISTORY

4,600,000,000	Age of Earth.
3,300,000,000	Earliest known rocks (found in Greenland).
2,000,000,000	Life appears.
600,000,000	First large-scale occurrence of fossils.
30,000,000	First old world monkeys' fossils (Oligocene period—Fayum, Egypt).
20,000,000	Early ape fossils *Dryopithecinae* (Miocene period—E. Africa, India, parts of Europe).
1,700,000	Earliest known hominids (Lower Pleistocene—*Australopithecus*, and *Homo habilis* S. Africa, E. Africa.) Oldowan culture—first stage of Palaeolithic or Old Stone Age (hunting and food-gathering) which persisted until end of Ice Age, *c. 8,000* B.C.
400,000	*Homo erectus* stage (Java, China, Africa) with crude chopping tools and early hand-axes. Heidelberg jaw, Vertezöllös remains (Europe).
180,000	Ancestors of Neanderthalers and *Homo sapiens*, with advanced hand-axes (Europe: Steinheim and Swanscombe).
70,000	Neanderthalers (Europe, Asia, N. Africa). Rhodesian Man (S. Africa). Solo Man (Java). Flake tools.
40,000	First cold phase ends. Neanderthal race becoming extinct. Second cold phase. *Homo sapiens* (modern man). Implements show significant advances: small knife-blades, engraving tools. Paintings and sculpture; magic rites and ceremonies. Cro-Magnons with Aurignacian culture.
18,000	Final culmination of last ice age. Aurignacian culture dying out to be replaced by Solutrean and then by the Magdalenian cultures. Great flowering of Palaeolithic art.
15,000	First immigrants from Asia to cross Behring Straits?
15,000	Last glaciers in Britain disappeared. Proto-Neolithic in Middle East. Agricultural settlements (*e.g.*, Jericho). Settled way of life leading eventually to such skills as weaving, metallurgy; inventions as ox-drawn plough, wheeled cart.
5,000	Britain becomes an island (land connection with continent severed by melting ice-sheets)

B.C. **CIVILISATION IN THE MIDDLE EAST**

4000	Susa founded.
3500	Sumerian civilisation flourishes. Cuneiform writing.
3100	First Egyptian Dynasty. Hieratic writing already perfected. Early Minoan Age (Crete). Pictorial writing, copper, silver, gold in use. Early Mycenaean civilisation begins.

B.C.

2980	Memphis, capital of Egypt.
2870	First settlements at Troy.
2850	Golden Age of China begins (legendary).
2700	Great Pyramid age in Egypt begins.
2400	Aryan migrations.
2371	Sargon founds Akkad: Akkadian empire.
2205	Hsia Dynasty begins in China (legendary).
2200	Middle Minoan Age: pottery, linear writing in pen and ink.
2100–1600	Building and rebuilding of Stonehenge.
1720–1550	Hyksos in Egypt. War chariots introduced. Hebrews entered Egypt (Joseph) *c.* 1600.
1751	Code of Hammurabi at Babylon.
1600	Late Minoan Age: Linear B script.
1600–1027	Shang Dynasty in China.
1546	18th Dynasty in Egypt. Civilisation at peak (under Tuthmosis III, 1490). Chronology more certain.
1500	Powerful Mitanni (Aryan) kingdom in Asia Minor. Phoenicia thriving—trade with Egypt and Babylonia. Vedic literature in India.
1450	Zenith of Minoan civilisation.
1400	Ugarit (N. Syria) culture at its zenith. Cretan civilisation ends: Knossos burnt. Temple at Luxor built.
1379	Amenhotep IV (Akhnaten), the "heretic" Pharaoh.
1350	Zenith of Hittite civilisation.
1300	Israelite oppression (Rameses II); Exodus from Egypt (Moses). Phoenician settlements—Hellas and Spain (Cadiz). Tyre flourishing.
1250	Israelites invade Palestine (Joshua).
1200	Attacks on Egypt by "Peoples of the Sea". Downfall of Hittite kingdom. Siege of Troy (Homeric). Beginning of sea-power of independent Phoenician cities. Probably all these are connected with Achaean and other migrations in Aegean area.
1115	Magnetic needle reputed in China.
1027–249	Chou Dynasty in China.
1005–925	Kingdom of David and Solomon: Jerusalem as Sanctuary.
1000	*Rig Veda* (India).
925–722	Israel and Judah divided.
893	Assyrian chronological records begin.
850	Foundation of Carthage (traditional).
781	Chinese record of an eclipse.
776	First Olympiad to be used for chronological purposes.
753	Foundation of Rome (traditional).
750	Greek colonists settling in Southern Italy.
745	Accession of Tiglath-Pileser III; Assyrian Power at its height.
722	Capture of Samaria by Sargon II: Israel deported to Nineveh.
700	Homer's poems probably written before this date. Spread of the iron-using Celtic Hallstatt culture about this time.
625	Neo-Babylonian (Chaldean) Empire (Nineveh destroyed 612).

A.D.

446 "Groans of the Britons"—last appeal to Rome (traditional).

451 Châlons: Attila the Hun repelled from Gaul by mixed Roman–Barbarian forces.

452 Attila's raid into Italy: destruction of Aquilea and foundation of Venice by refugees.

455 Rome pillaged by Vandals.

476 Romulus Augustulus, last Western Roman Emperor, deposed by Odovacar: conventionally the end of the Western Roman Empire.

481 Clovis becomes King of the Franks, who eventually conquer Gaul (d. 511).

493 Theodoric founds Ostrogothic Kingdom in Italy (d. 526).

515 Battle of Mount Badon: West Saxon advance halted by Britons, perhaps led by Arthur (?).

BYZANTIUM AND ISLAM

527 Accession of Justinian I (d. 565).

529 Code of Civil Law published by Justinian. Rule of St. Benedict put into practice at Monte Cassino (traditional).

534 Byzantines under Belisarius reconquer North Africa from Vandals.

552 Byzantine reconquest of Italy complete.

563 St. Columba founds mission in Iona.

568 Lombard Kingdom founded in Italy.

570 Birth of Mohammed.

577 Battle of Deorham: West Saxon advance resumed.

581–618 Sui Dynasty in China.

590 Gregory the Great becomes Pope.

597 St. Augustine lands in Kent.

605 Grand Canal of China constructed.

618–907 T'ang Dynasty in China: their administrative system lasts in essentials for 1,300 years.

622 Hejira or flight from Mecca to Medina of Mohammed: beginning of Mohammedan era.

627 Battle of Nineveh: Persians crushed by Byzantines under Heraclius.

632 Death of Mohammed: all Arabia now Moslem. Accession of Abu Bakr, the first Caliph.

634 Battle of Heavenfield: Oswald becomes king of Northumbria, brings in Celtic Christianity.

638 Jerusalem captured by Moslems.

641 Battle of Mehawand: Persia conquered by Moslems.

643 Alexandria taken by Moslems.

645 Downfall of Soga clan in Japan, after establishing Buddhism: beginning of period of imitation of Chinese culture.

650 Slav occupation of Balkans now complete.

663 Synod of Whitby: Roman Christianity triumphs over Celtic Christianity in England.

685 Nectansmere: end of Northumbrian dominance in England.

698 Carthage taken by Moslems.

711 Tarik leads successful Moslem invasion of Spain.

718 Failure of second and greatest Moslem attack on Constantinople. Pelayo founds Christian kingdom of Asturias in Northern Spain.

726 Byzantine Emperor Leo III begins Iconoclast movement: opposed by Pope Gregory II, and an important cause of difference between Roman and Byzantine churches.

THE HOLY ROMAN EMPIRE AND THE TRIUMPH OF CHRISTIANITY IN EUROPE: NORSEMEN AND NORMANS

732 Poitiers: Moslem western advance halted by Charles Martel.

735 Death of Bede.

750 Beginning of Abbasid Caliphate (replacing Omayyads)

A.D.

751 Pepin King of the Franks: founds Carolingian dynasty. Ravenna taken by Lombards: end of Byzantine power in the West.

754 Pepin promises central Italy to Pope: beginning of temporal power of the Papacy.

778 Roncesvalles: defeat and death of Roland.

786 Accession of Haroun-al-Rashid in Baghdad.

793 Sack of Lindisfarne: Viking attacks on Britain begin.

795 Death of Offa: end of Mercian dominance in England.

800 Coronation of Charlemagne as Emperor by Pope Leo III in Rome.

814 Death of Charlemagne: division of empire.

825 Ellandun: Egbert defeats Mercians and Wessex becomes leading kingdom in England.

827 Moslem invasion of Sicily.

840 Moslems capture Bari and occupy much of Southern Italy.

843 Treaty of Verdun: final division of Carolingian Empire, and beginning of France and Germany as separate states.

844 Kenneth MacAlpin becomes king of Picts as well as Scots: the kingdom of Alban.

862 Rurik founds Viking state in Russia: first at Novgorod, later at Kiev.

866 Fujiwara period begins in Japan. Viking "Great Army" in England: Northumbria, East Anglia and Mercia subsequently overwhelmed.

868 Earliest dated printed book in China.

872 Harold Fairhair King of Norway.

874 Iceland settled by Norsemen.

885–6 Viking attack on Paris.

893 Simeon founds first Bulgar Empire in Balkans.

896 Arpad and the Magyars in Hungary.

899 Death of Alfred the Great.

900 Ghana at the height of its power in North West Africa.

907–960 Five Dynasties in China: partition.

910 Abbey of Cluny founded: monastic reforms spread from here.

911 Rolf (or Rollo) becomes ruler of Normandy.

912 Accession of Abderrahman III: the most splendid period of the Omayyad Caliphate of Cordova (d. 961).

928 Brandenburg taken from the Slavs by Henry the Fowler, King of Germany.

929 Death of Wenceslas, Christian King of Bohemia.

937 Battle of Brunanburh: crowning victory of Athelstan. West Saxon kings now masters of England.

955 Battle of Lechfeld: Magyars finally defeated by Otto the Great and settle in Hungary.

960–1279 Sung Dynasty in China.

965 Harold Bluetooth king of Denmark, accepts Christianity.

966 Mieszko I king of Poland, accepts Christianity.

968 Fatimids begin their rule in Egypt.

982 Discovery of Greenland by Norsemen.

987 Hugh Capet king of France: founder of Capetian dynasty.

988 Vladimir of Kiev accepts Christianity.

991 Battle of Maldon: defeat of Byrhtnoth of Essex by Vikings—renewed Viking raids on England.

993 Olof Skutkonung, king of Sweden, accepts Christianity.

1000 Leif Ericsson discovers North America.

1001 Coronation of St. Stephen of Hungary with crown sent by the Pope.

1002 Massacre of St. Brice's Day: attempt by Ethelred to exterminate Danes in England.

A.D.

1014 Battle of Clontarf: victory of Irish under Brian Boru over Vikings.

1016 Canute becomes king of England; builds short-lived Danish "empire."

1018 Byzantines under Basil 11 complete subjection of Bulgars.

1040 Attempts to implement Truce of God from about this time.

1046 Normans under Robert Guiscard in southern Italy.

1054 Beginning of Almoravid (Moslem) conquests in West Africa.

1060 Normans invade Sicily.

1066 Norman conquest of England under William I.

1069 Reforms of Wang An-Shih in China.

THE CRUSADES

1071 Manzikert: Seljuk Turks destroy Byzantine army and overrun Anatolia.

1073 Hildebrand (Gregory VII) becomes Pope. Church discipline and Papal authority enforced.

1075 Seljuk Turks capture Jerusalem.

1076 Kumbi, capital of Ghana, sacked by Almoravids: subsequent break-up of Ghana Empire,

1084 Carthusians founded by St. Bruno at Chartreuse.

1086 Compilation of Domesday Book.

1094 El Cid takes Valencia.

1095 Council of Clermont: Urban II preaches First Crusade.

1098 Cistercians founded by St. Robert at Citeaux.

1099 First Crusade under Godfrey of Bouillon takes Jerusalem.

1100 Death of William Rufus in the New Forest. Baldwin I: Latin Kingdom of Jerusalem founded.

1106 Tinchebrai: Henry I of England acquires Normandy, captures his brother Robert.

1115 Abelard teaching at Paris. St. Bernard founds monastery at Clairvaux.

1119 Order of Knights Templars founded.

1120 Loss of the White Ship and heir to English throne.

1122 Concordat of Worms: Pope and Emperor compromise on the Investiture Controversy, but continue to quarrel over other matters (Guelfs and Ghibellines).

1135 Stephen takes English crown: civil wars with Matilda and anarchy ensue.

1143 Alfonso Henriques proclaimed first king of Portugal.

1144 Moslems take Christian stronghold of Edessa.

1148 Second Crusade fails to capture Damascus.

1150 Carmelites founded about this time by Berthold.

1152 Accession of Emperor Frederick Barbarossa.

1154 Henry of Anjou succeeds Stephen: first of Plantagenet kings of England.

1161 Explosives used in warfare in China.

1169 Strongbow invades Ireland: beginning of Anglo-Norman rule. Saladin ruling in Egypt.

1170 Murder of Thomas Becket in Canterbury cathedral.

1171 Spanish knightly Order of Santiago founded.

1176 Battle of Legnano: Frederick Barbarossa defeated by the Lombard League. Italian autonomy established.

1185 Kamakura Period in Japan: epoch of feudalism: until 1333.

1187 Hattin: destruction of Latin kingdom of Jerusalem by Saladin.

A.D.

1189 Third Crusade launched: leaders—Frederick Barbarossa, Philip Augustus of France, Richard Lionheart of England.

1191 Capture of Acre by Crusaders.

1192 End of Third Crusade without regaining Jerusalem. Richard I seized and held to ransom in Austria on return journey.

1198 Innocent III becomes Pope.

1202 Fourth Crusade, diverted by Venetians takes Zara from Byzantines.

1204 Fourth Crusade captures Constantinople, founds Latin Empire. King John of England loses Normandy to France.

1206 Temujin proclaimed Genghiz Khan (Very Mighty King) of all the Mongols: soon controls all of Central Asia.

1208 Albigensian Crusade launched: the first against Christians.

1212 Battle of Las Navas de Tolosa: decisive victory of Spaniards over Moors. The Children's Crusade.

THE CULMINATION OF THE MIDDLE AGES

1215 Fourth Lateran Council: the authority of the mediaeval Church and Papacy at its zenith. Dominicans recognised by the Pope. Magna Carta extorted by barons from John.

1223 Franciscans recognised by the Pope.

1229 Emperor Frederick II, through diplomacy, recognised by Moslems as King of Jerusalem.

1230 Teutonic Knights established in Prussia.

1237 Golden Horde (Mongols) begin subjugation of Russia.

1241 Mongol incursions into Central Europe.

1250 St. Louis of France captured on his Crusade in Egypt. Mamelukes become rulers of Egypt. Mandingo king declares his independence of Ghana and embraces Islam.

1256 Conference of Baltic ports; the first form of the Hanseatic League.

1258 Provisions of Oxford: barons under Simon de Montfort force reforms on Henry III of England. Baghdad destroyed by Mongols.

1264 Battle of Lewes: Montfort's party become rulers of England.

1265 Simon de Montfort's Parliament, Battle of Evesham: defeat and death of de Montfort.

1274 Death of Thomas Aquinas.

1279–1368 Mongol Dynasty in China (Kublai Khan).

1231 Repulse of Mongol attack on Japan.

1282 Sicilian Vespers: rising of Sicilians against French ruler.

1284 Completion of Edward I of England's conquest of Wales.

1290 Expulsion of Jews from England. Death of Maid of Norway: Edward I begins attempts to rule Scotland.

1291 Fall of Acre: end of Crusading in Holy Land. Everlasting League of Uri: beginnings of Swiss Confederation.

1294 Death of Roger Bacon, the founder of experimental science.

1295 "Model Parliament" of Edward I (anticipated in 1275).

1308 Death of Duns Scotus.

THE DECLINE OF THE MIDDLE AGES

1309 Papacy moves to Avignon: beginning of the Babylonish Captivity.

1312 Suppression of Templars by king of France and Pope.

1314 Battle of Bannockburn: victory of Robert Bruce secures Scottish independence.

1321 Death of Dante.

1325 Zenith of Mandingo Empire of Mali (North West Africa) under Mansa Musa; superseded at end of 15th century by Songhai empire.

1327 Deposition of Edward II; subsequently murdered.

A.D.

1336 Ashikaga Period in Japan: great feudal lords semi-independent of authority of Shogun.

1337 Death of Giotto.

1338 Beginning of Hundred Years' War between England and France.

1340 Battle of Sluys: English capture French fleet.

1344 Swabian League: weakness of Imperial authority in Germany obliges towns to form leagues for mutual protection.

1346 Battles of Crecy and Neville's Cross: spectacular English victories over French and Scots.

1347 Calais taken by Edward III of England. Cola di Rienzi attempts to reform government of Rome: killed 1354.

1348 Black Death reaches Europe (England 1349, Scotland 1350).

1351 Statute of Labourers: attempt by English Parliament to freeze wages.

1353 Statute of Praemunire: restraints placed on Papal intervention in England.

1354 Ottoman Turks make first settlement in Europe, at Gallipoli.

1355 Death of Stephen Dushan: collapse of Serbian Empire which he had built.

1356 Battle of Poitiers: capture of King John of France by Black Prince. "Golden Bull" regulates Imperial elections in such a way as to place power in the hands of the German princes: valid until 1806.

1358 The Jacquerie: rising of French peasants.

1360 Peace of Bretigny: Edward III makes great territorial gains in France.

1362 English becomes the official language in Parliament and the Law Courts.

1363 Timur (Tamerlane) begins his career of conquest in Asia.

1368–1644 Ming Dynasty in China.

1370 Bertrand du Guesclin Constable of France: regains much territory from the English. Peace of Stralsund: Hansa in complete control of Baltic Sea.

1377 Pope returns to Rome: End of Babylonish Captivity.

1378 Disputed Papal Election: Beginning of Western Schism.

1380 Battle of Chioggia: decisive victory of Venice over Genoa. Battle of Kulikovo: Dmitri Donskoi of Moscow wins first major Russian victory over Golden Horde.

1381 Peasants' Revolt in England under Wat Tyler.

1384 Death of John Wyclif.

1385 Battle of Aljubarotta: Portugal safeguards independence from Castile.

1386 Battle of Sempach: Swiss safeguard independence from Habsburgs. Jagiello (Vladislav V) unites Lithuania and Poland.

1389 Battle of Kossovo: crushing defeat of Serbs and neighbouring nations by Turks.

1396 Battle of Nicopolis: "the last crusade" annihilated by Turks.

1397 Union of Kalmar: Denmark, Norway and Sweden united under one crown: dissolved 1448.

1398 Timur invades and pillages Northern India.

1399 Richard II deposed by Henry IV: first of the Lancastrian kings of England.

1400 Owen Glendower revolts in Wales. Death of Chaucer.

1401 De Haeretico Comburendo: the burning of heretics made legal in England.

1410 Battle of Tannenberg: Poles and Lithuanians break power of Teutonic Knights.

1415 Battle of Agincourt: great success of Henry V of England in France. Council of Constance ends Western Schism, burns John Hus.

1420 Treaty of Troyes: English claims to French throne recognised. Hussite Wars begin: Bohemian heretics defend themselves successfully.

A.D.

1429 Relief of Orleans by Joan of Arc.

1431 Burning of Joan of Arc.

1433 Rounding of Cape Bojador: first great achievement in exploration ordered by Henry the Navigator.

1434 Cosimo die Medici begins his family's control of Florence.

1435 Congress of Arras: Burgundians withdraw support from England, in favour of France.

1438 Albert II became German king and began Hapsburg rule over Holy Roman Empire, 1438–1806.

1440 Death of Jan van Eyck.

1450 Rebellion of Jack Cade against government of Henry VI of England.

1453 Battle of Castillon: final English defeat and end of Hundred Years' War. Constantinople taken by Turks: end of Byzantine or Eastern Roman Empire.

RENAISSANCE, DISCOVERIES, "NEW MONARCHIES"

1454 First dated printing from movable types in Europe: Papal indulgence printed at Mainz.

1455 First battle of St. Albans: beginning of Wars of the Roses.

1458 Mathias Corvinus becomes king of Hungary. George of Podiebrad becomes king of Bohemia.

1461 Battle of Towton: Yorkist victory in a particularly bloody battle. Louis XI becomes king of France.

1467 Charles the Bold becomes Duke of Burgundy.

1469 Marriage of Ferdinand of Aragon with Isabella of Castile: union of the main kingdoms of Spain (1474). Lorenzo the Magnificent becomes ruler of Florence.

1470 Warwick ("The Kingmaker") turns Lancastrian, dethrones Edward IV.

1471 Return of Edward IV: Lancastrians crushed at Barnet and Tewkesbury. Ivan III of Moscow takes Novgorod: Muscovy rising to supremacy in Russia.

1476 Caxton sets up his press at Westminster.

1477 Battle of Nancy: defeat and death of Charles the Bold: end of the greatness of Burgundy.

1479 Pazzi conspiracy against the Medici in Florence.

1481 Inquisition becomes active in Castile (1484 in Aragon).

1485 Battle of Bosworth Field: beginning of Tudor period in England.

1487 Lambert Simnel's rising fails.

1488 Bartholomew Diaz rounds Cape of Good Hope.

1491 Brittany acquired by King of France (by marriage).

1492 Rodrigo Borgia becomes Pope Alexander VI. Granada, last Moorish foothold in Western Europe, conquered by Spain. Christopher Columbus discovers the West Indies.

1493 Sonni Ali brings Songhai Empire to height of its prestige: Timbuktu renowned centre of literary culture.

1494 Italy invaded by French led by Charles VIII: beginning of Italian Wars and "modern" European diplomacy and international relations. Treaty of Tordesillas: Spain and Portugal agree to divide unexplored part of world; subsequently approved by Pope.

1496 Hapsburg-Spanish marriages: foundation of later empires.

1497 Perkin Warbeck captured by Henry VII (hanged 1499). John Cabot discovers Newfoundland.

1498 Savonarola burned. Vasco da Gama at Calicut: the sea route to India found.

1499 Amerigo Vespucci charts part of the South American coast.

A.D.
1500 Brazil discovered by Pedro Cabral.

1503 Casa de Contratación established at Seville; beginnings of Spanish colonial government. Fall of Caesar Borgia.

1507 Alfonso de Albuquerque becomes Viceroy of Portuguese Empire in the East.

1513 Accession of Pope Leo X, zenith of Renaissance Papacy. Machiavelli writes *The Prince*. Balboa discovers the Pacific (South Sea). Battle of Flodden: James IV of Scotland defeated and killed by English.

1514 Battle of Chaldiran: Turkish victory begins long series of wars between Turkish and Persian Empires.

REFORMATION, HAPSBURG–VALOIS WARS

1515 Francis I becomes king of France: victory of Marignano ends legend of Swiss invincibility. Thomas Wolsey becomes Lord Chancellor of England and Cardinal.

1516 Algiers taken by Barbarossa; beginning of the Corsairs.

1517 Martin Luther nails up his Ninety-five Theses: beginning of the Reformation. Turks conquer Egypt.

1519 Charles V inherits Hapsburg lands and elected emperor. Magellan begins first circumnavigation of the world. Death of Leonardo da Vinci.

1520 Suleiman the Magnificent becomes Sultan; Turkish power at its height. Field of Cloth of Gold; celebrated diplomatic meeting, spectacular but with no results.

1521 Mexico conquered by Hernando Cortes. Belgrade taken by the Turks. Diet of Worms; Luther commits himself irrevocably. Charles V divides his dominions: Austrian and Spanish Hapsburgs.

1522 Rhodes taken by the Turks; Knights of St. John move to Malta. Election of Adrian VI, first non-Italian Pope since 1378.

1523 Swedes expel Danish overlords, elect Gustavus Vasa King.

1524 Peasants' War in Germany (suppressed 1525).

1525 Battle of Pavia: defeat and capture of Francis I by Imperialists.

1526 Battle of Mohács: Turkish victory ends Hungarian independence. Foundation of Danubian Hapsburg Monarchy (Hungarian and Bohemian crowns united with Austrian patrimony of Hapsburgs): Holy Roman Empire prolonged for 300 years. Battle of Panipat: Babar begins Moslem conquest of India, founds Mogul Empire.

1527 Sack of Rome by Imperialists. Italy under control of Charles V.

1529 Siege of Vienna by the Turks. Peace of Cambrai; pause in Hapsburg–Valois struggle, end of serious French intervention in Italy. Diet of Speyer: origin of the name Protestant.

1532 Peru conquered by Francisco Pizarro.

1533 Ivan IV (the Terrible) becomes Tsar. Marriage of Henry VIII and Catherine of Aragon declared null.

1534 Act of Supremacy: Henry VIII asserts control over English Church.

1535 Coverdale's English Bible printed. Execution of Thomas More and John Fisher.

1536 Execution of Anne Boleyn. Dissolution of smaller Monasteries by Henry VIII and Thomas Cromwell (remainder dissolved 1539). Pilgrimage of Grace: Northern rising because of religious grievances.

1538 Chibchas of Bogota conquered by Gonzalo de Quesada.

1540 Francisco de Coronado begins explorations in North America. Society of Jesus recognised by Pope.

1541 John Calvin regains authority in Geneva.

1542 First Portuguese reach Japan. New Laws of the Indies: first attempt to legislate for welfare of colonial natives, by Spanish government.

1543 Death of Copernicus.

1545 Opening of Council of Trent: the Counter-Reformation.

A.D.
1547 Death of Henry VIII: Somerset Protector in the name of the boy king, Edward VI.

1549 First English Book of Common Prayer. Kett's Rebellion in Norfolk, because of economic grievances.

1550 Deposition of Protector Somerset: Northumberland rules England.

1553 Lady Jane Grey proclaimed Queen by Northumberland on death of Edward VI: Mary I succeeds. Servetus burned by Calvin.

1555 Latimer and Ridley burned by Mary. Religious Peace of Augsburg: policy of *cuius regio, eius religio* accepted in Germany.

1556 Charles V abdicated imperial powers in favour of brother Ferdinand. Cranmer burned. Akbar becomes Mogul Emperor (d. 1605).

1557 Macao becomes permanent Portuguese port in China.

1558 Calais lost by English to French. Elizabeth I becomes Queen of England.

1559 Peace of Cateau-Cambrésis: end of Hapsburg–Valois duel.

RELIGIOUS WARS

1561 Mary, Queen of Scots, returns to Scotland.

1562 First War of Religion in France: wars continue intermittently until 1598.

1563 Thirty-nine Articles define Elizabethan Church settlement.

1564 Birth of Shakespeare; death of Michelangelo.

1565 Malta beats off Turks.

1567 Deposition of Mary, Queen of Scots. Alva in the Netherlands: severe rule.

1568 Flight of Mary, Queen of Scots, to England: imprisonment. San Juan de Ulua: defeat of Hawkins, and end of his slave-trading voyages. Beginning of Anglo-Spanish maritime feud. Revolt of Moriscos of Granada (suppressed 1570).

1569 Rebellion of Northern Earls (Catholic) in England.

1570 Elizabeth I anathematised by Pope.

1571 Battle of Lepanto: spectacular defeat of Turkish sea-power by Don John of Austria. Bornu (or Kanem) in Central Sudan at its zenith under Idris III.

1572 Dutch "Sea Beggars" take Brill. Massacre of St. Bartholomew in France. Polish Crown elective again, on death of Sigismund II.

1576 Catholic League formed in France, led by Guise family.

1577 Drake begins voyage round world (returns 1580).

1578 Battle of Alcazar-Quivir: death of King Sebastian of Portugal. Parma re-establishes Spanish rule in Southern Netherlands.

1579 Union of Utrecht: seven northern provinces of Netherlands form what becomes Dutch Republic. Death of Grand Vizier Sokolli: decline of Turkish power begins.

1580 Philip II of Spain becomes king of Portugal.

1582 Gregorian Calendar (or New Style) introduced by Pope Gregory XIII.

1584 Assassination of William the Silent.

1585 Hidéyoshi Dictator of Japan: unification of the country. English intervention in Spanish–Dutch War.

1587 Execution of Mary, Queen of Scots. Drake "singes King of Spain's beard." Shah Abbas I (the Great) becomes ruler of Persia (d. 1629).

1588 Spanish Armada defeated.

1589 Death of Catherine de' Medici, Queen-Mother of France.

1592 Moorish conquest of African Songhai Empire.

1593 Henry IV of France becomes Catholic.

1598 Edict of Nantes: French Protestants guaranteed liberty of worship. End of French Wars of Religion.

1600 English East India Company founded. Tokugawa Period begins in Japan (Ieyasu takes title of Shogun, 1603): lasts until 1868.

A.D.

1601 Rebellion and execution of Earl of Essex, Elizabethan Poor Law.

1602 Dutch East India Company founded.

1603 Irish revolts finally suppressed by Mountjoy. Accession of James VI of Scotland as James I of England: Union of English and Scottish Crowns.

1604 Hampton Court Conference: James I disappoints Puritans.

1605 Gunpowder Plot.

1607 Virginia colonised by London company: Jamestown founded.

1608 Quebec founded by Champlain.

1609 Twelve Years' Truce between Spain and United Provinces: Dutch independence in fact secured. Expulsion of Moriscos from Spain.

1610 Assassination of Henry IV of France.

1611 Plantation of Ulster with English and Scottish colonists. Authorised Version of the Bible in England.

1613 Michael Romanov becomes Tsar: the first of the dynasty.

1614 Napier publishes his explanation of logarithms.

1616 Death of Shakespeare and Cervantes. Edict of Inquisition against Galileo's astronomy.

1618 "Defenestration of Prague": Bohemian assertion of independence begins Thirty Years' War.

1620 Pilgrim Fathers settle in New England.

1624 "Massacre of Amboina": English driven out of spice islands by Dutch. Richelieu becomes Chief Minister in France.

1628 Murder of Duke of Buckingham. Petition of Right by Commons to Charles I. Fall of La Rochelle: French Protestants lose political power. Harvey publishes his work on the circulation of blood.

1629 Charles I begins Personal Rule.

1630 Gustavus Adolphus of Sweden enters Thirty Years' War, turns tide against Imperialists.

1631 Sack of Magdeburg, one of the worst incidents of the Thirty Years' War.

1632 Battle of Lützen: death of Gustavus Adolphus.

1633 William Laud appointed Archbishop of Canterbury. Thomas Wentworth takes up his post as Lord Deputy of Ireland.

1634 Dismissal and murder of Imperialist general Wallenstein.

1635 John Hampden refuses to pay Ship Money.

1636 Japanese forbidden to go abroad.

1637 Russian pioneers reach shores of Pacific.

1638 Covenant widely signed in Scotland.

1639 First Bishops' War: Charles I comes to terms with Scots.

1640 Second Bishops' War: Charles I defeated by Scots. Long Parliament begins: abolition of Royal prerogatives. Great Elector (Frederick William) becomes ruler of Brandenburg. Revolt of Catalonia (finally suppressed 1659). Revolt of Portugal: Duke of Braganza proclaimed king.

1641 Japanese exclude all foreigners (except for small Dutch trading fleet). Massacre of Protestants in Ireland. Wentworth (Earl of Strafford) executed. Grand Remonstrance of Commons to Charles I.

1642 Charles I attempts to arrest the Five Members. Outbreak of English Civil War: first general engagement, Edgehill. Death of Richelieu.

1643 Mazarin becomes Chief Minister of France. Battle of Rocroi: French victory, end of Spanish reputation for invincibility. English Parliament agrees to Solemn League and Covenant, secures services of Scots army.

1644 Marston Moor: decisive battle of English Civil War. North lost to Charles I. Tippemuir: Montrose begins victorious Royalist

A.D.

campaign in Scotland. 1644–1911 Manchu dynasty in China.

1645 Formation of New Model Army. Naseby: main Royalist army crushed. Battle of Philiphaugh: Montrose's army destroyed.

1646 Charles I surrenders to Scots.

1647 Charles I handed over to Parliament. Charles I seized by Army. Charles I flees to Carisbrooke Castle.

1648 Second Civil War: New Model Army defeats Scots and Royalists. "Pride's Purge": Parliament refashioned by Army. Peace of Westphalia ends Thirty Years' War.

ASCENDANCY OF FRANCE

1649 Charles I executed. England governed as Commonwealth. Cromwell in Ireland. New Code of Laws in Russia completes establishment of serfdom.

1651 Battle of Worcester: Cromwell's final victory, now master of all Britain. First English Navigation Act. Hobbes' *Leviathan* published.

1652 Foundation of Cape Colony by Dutch under Van Riebeek. First Anglo-Dutch War begins (ends 1654).

1653 Cromwell dissolves Rump, becomes Protector.

1655 Major-Generals appointed to supervise districts of England. Jamaica seized by English.

1656 Grand Vizier Kiuprili: revival of Turkish government.

1658 Death of Cromwell.

1659 Peace of the Pyrenees: France replaces Spain as greatest power in Western Europe.

1660 Restoration of monarch in Britain: Charles II. Royal Society founded.

1661 Death of Mazarin: Louis XIV now rules in person. "Clarendon Code"; beginning of persecution of Non-conformists in England.

1664 New York taken by English: Second Anglo-Dutch War ensues (ends 1667).

1665 Great Plague of London.

1666 Great Fire of London. Newton's discovery of law of gravitation.

1667 Dutch fleet in the Medway. War of Devolution begins: first of Louis XIV's aggressions.

1668 Portuguese Independence recognised by Spain.

1669 Death of Rembrandt.

1670 Secret Treaty of Dover between Charles II and Louis XIV. Revolt of peasants and Don Cossacks under Stenka Razin (suppressed 1671).

1672 Third Anglo-Dutch War begins (ends 1674). Murder of De Witt brothers: William of Orange becomes leader of Dutch against French invasion.

1673 Test Act deprives English Catholics and Non-conformists of public offices. Death of Molière.

1675 Battle of Fehrbellin: Swedes defeated by Great Elector; rise of Prussian military power. Greenwich Royal Observatory founded.

1678 "Popish Plot" of Titus Oates utilised by Shaftesbury and the Whigs to bring pressure on Charles II.

1679 Bothwell Brig: suppression of Scottish Covenanters. Habeas Corpus Act passed.

1680 Chambers of Reunion: Louis XIV uses legal arguments to complete annexation of Alsace.

1681 Oxford Parliament: Charles II overcomes his opponents, begins to rule without Parliament.

1683 Rye House Plot. Siege of Vienna by the Turks: last major Turkish attack on Europe.

1685 Sedgemoor: Monmouth's rebellion crushed by James II. Revocation of Edict of Nantes: persecution of French Protestants by Louis XIV.

A.D.

1688 Seven Bishops protest against James II's policy of toleration, and are acquitted. William of Orange lands in England: flight of James II. "The Glorious Revolution."

1689 Derry relieved: failure of James II to subdue Irish Protestants. Killiecrankie: death of Dundee and collapse of Highland rising. Bill of Rights defines liberties established by "Glorious Revolution."

1690 Locke's *Two Treatises on Government* published. Beachy Head: French victory over Anglo-Dutch fleet. Boyne: defeat of James II by William III.

1691 Capitulation of Limerick: surrender of Irish supporters of James II on conditions which are not fulfilled.

1692 Massacre of Glencoe: Government's "lesson" to Highlanders. La Hogue: Anglo-Dutch fleet regains command of the sea.

1693 National Debt of England begun.

1694 Bank of England founded.

1695 Press licensing abandoned: freedom of the press in England.

1696 Peter the Great sole Czar.

1697 Peace of Ryswyck between Louis XIV and William III. Peter journeys "incognito" to the West.

1699 Treaty of Karlowitz: great Turkish concessions to Austrians. Death of Racine.

1700 Great Northern War, involving all Baltic powers, begins (ends 1721). Battle of Narva: Russians defeated by Charles XII of Sweden. Death of Charles II of Spain: under French influence Louis XIV's grandson Philip of Anjou named successor.

1701 War of the Spanish Succession begins. Hungarian revolt led by Francis Rakoczi against Austrians. Elector of Brandenburg receives title of King of Prussia. Act of Settlement establishes Protestant Hanoverian Succession in England.

1703 Methuen Treaty between England and Portugal. St. Petersburg founded.

1704 Gibraltar taken by Rooke. Blenheim: Marlborough stops France from winning war.

1706 Ramillies: Marlborough's second great victory. Turin: Eugene defeats French in Italy.

1707 Almanza: Anglo-Austrian forces in Spain defeated by French under Berwick. Act of Union: English and Scottish Parliaments united. Death of Aurungzib, last powerful Mogul.

1708 Oudenarde: Marlborough's third great victory.

1709 Pultava: Charles XII's invasion of Russia smashed by Peter the Great. Malplaquet: Marlborough's fourth great victory—at great cost in lives.

1710 Tory government in England.

1711 Dismissal of Marlborough.

1713 Peace of Utrecht: England makes advantageous peace with Louis XIV. Bourbon king of Spain grants Asiento (monopoly of Spanish American slave trade) to England.

1714 Peace of Rastatt between France and Austria. Death of Queen Anne: accession of George I. Beginning of Hanoverian Dynasty in Britain. Whig oligarchy rules.

1715 Jacobite Rising defeated at Preston and Sheriffmuir. Death of Louis XIV. France under Regent Orleans.

ENLIGHTENED DESPOTS: FIRST BRITISH EMPIRE

1716 Septennial Act: English Parliament prolongs its life from three to seven years. Prince Eugène of Savoy defeated Turks at Petrovaradin (Yugoslavia).

1720 Collapse of Law's system of banking ("Mississippi Bubble") in France. "South Sea Bubble" in England.

A.D.

1721 Robert Walpole becomes first Prime Minister. Peace of Nystad: Sweden no longer a major power at end of Great Northern War. Russian gains.

1723 Death of Christopher Wren.

1727 First Indemnity Act for Non-conformists.

1729 Methodists begin at Oxford.

1730 Resignation from government of Townshend, who becomes agricultural pioneer.

1733 First Family Compact between Bourbon kings of France and Spain. Withdrawal of Walpole's Excise Bill. John Kay invents flying shuttle, first of the great textile inventions. Jethro Tull publishes *The Horse-Hoeing Husbandry*, advocating new agricultural methods.

1738 Lorraine ceded to France.

1739 Nadir Shah with Persian army sacks Delhi, ruins Mogul power. War of Jenkins' Ear begins between Spain and Britain.

1740 Frederick II (the Great) becomes king of Prussia. Maria Theresa succeeds to Austrian dominions. Frederick seizes Silesia, begins War of the Austrian Succession.

1742 Fall of Walpole.

1743 Dettingen: George II, last British king to command his army in the field, defeats French.

1745 Fontenoy: Duke of Cumberland defeated by Marshal Saxe. Jacobite Rebellion under Prince Charles Edward: initial success, victory of Prestonpans, march to Derby.

1746 Culloden: Jacobites destroyed by Cumberland.

1748 Treaty of Aix-la-Chapelle: Frederick retains Silesia, elsewhere status quo.

1750 Death of J. S. Bach.

1751 First volume of the *Encyclopédie* published in France. Clive takes and holds Arcot: checks plans of Dupleix in Southern India. Chinese conquest of Tibet.

1752 Britain adopts New Style calendar.

1753 British Museum begun by government purchase of Sloane's collection.

1755 Lisbon earthquake. Braddock's defeat and death at the hands of French and Indians.

1756 Diplomatic Revolution (alliance of Austria with France) achieved by Kaunitz; Britain and Prussia perforce became allies. Seven Years' War begins. Minorca taken from British by French (Byng executed 1757). Black Hole of Calcutta: suffocation of many British prisoners.

1757 Pitt Secretary of State, main influence in British government. Rossbach: one of Frederick II's numerous victories against heavy odds. Plassey: Clive conquers Bengal.

1759 "Year of Victories" for Britain: Quebec, Minden, Lagos, Quiberon Bay. James Brindley designs Worsley–Manchester Canal: the beginning of this form of transport in Britain. Voltaire publishes *Candide*. Death of Handel.

1760 Wandewash: decisive defeat of French in India, by Coote.

1761 Panipat: Mahrattas heavily defeated by Afghans. Fall of Pitt.

1762 Catherine II (the Great) becomes Czarina. Rousseau's *Social Contract* and *Emile* published.

1763 Peace of Paris: British colonial gains, First British Empire at its height. Peace of Hubertusburg: Frederick II retains his gains. Pontiac's Conspiracy: failure of Red Indian attempt to destroy British power.

1764 John Wilkes expelled from Commons. James Hargreaves invents spinning jenny.

1766 Henry Cavendish proves hydrogen to be an element.

1768 Royal Academy of Arts founded.

1769 Richard Arkwright erects spinning mill (invention of water frame).

1770 Struensee comes to power in Denmark (executed 1772). "Boston Massacre." James Cook discovers New South Wales.

1772 First Partition of Poland between Russia, Prussia and Austria.

A.D.

1773 Society of Jesus suppressed by Pope (restored 1814). Revolt led by Pugachov in Russia (suppressed 1775). "Boston Tea Party."

1774 Warren Hastings appointed first Governor-General of India. Treaty of Kutchuk Kainarji; great Turkish concessions to Russia. Karl Scheele discovers chlorine. Joseph Priestley's discovery of oxygen.

1775 Watt and Boulton in partnership at Soho Engineering Works, Birmingham. Lexington: first action in American War of Independence.

1776 American Declaration of Independence. Adam Smith's *Wealth of Nations* published.

1777 Saratoga: surrender of British army under Burgoyne to Americans.

1779 Beginning of great Franco-Spanish siege of Gibraltar (raised finally, 1783). Samuel Crompton invents spinning mule.

1780 Joseph II assumes sole power in Austria. Armed neutrality of maritime nations to restrain British interference with shipping.

1781 Joseph II introduces religious toleration, abolishes serfdom in Austria. Yorktown: surrender of British under Cornwallis to American and French forces.

1782 Battle of the Saints: Rodney's victory save British West Indies.

1783 Treaty of Versailles: American independence recognised. Pitt the Younger becomes Prime Minister of Britain. First flights in hot-air (Montgolfier) and hydrogen (Charles) balloons.

1784 Death of Dr. Samuel Johnson.

1785 Edmund Cartwright invents the power loom.

1787 American Constitution drafted.

1788 Impeachment of Warren Hastings begins (ends 1795).

FRENCH REVOLUTION AND NAPOLEON

1789 Washington first President of U.S.A. French Revolution begins. Storming of the Bastille (July 14).

1790 Civil constitution of the Clergy in France.

1791 Flight of Louis XVI and Marie Antoinette to Varennes.

1792 Battle of Valmy: French Revolution saved from intervention of European kings. Denmark becomes first country to prohibit slave trade. France becomes a Republic.

1793 Louis XVI beheaded. Second partition of Poland.

1794 "Glorious First of June." Fall of Robespierre and end of Jacobin Republic. Negro revolt in Haiti led by Toussaint L'Ouverture.

1795 The Directory established. "Whiff of Grapeshot": Napoleon Bonaparte disperses Paris mob, Oct. 5. Batavian Republic set up by France.

1796 First Italian campaign of Bonaparte: victories of Lodi, Arcola.

1797 Treaty of Campo Formio: Bonaparte compels Austria to make peace. Britain left to fight France alone.

1798 Bonaparte goes to Egypt. Battle of the Nile. Vinegar Hill rebellion in Ireland suppressed.

1799 New coalition against France: Suvorov and Russians victorious in Italy. Bonaparte returns to France. *Coup d'état* of Brumaire, Nov. 9. Consulate set up.

1800 Parliamentary Union of Great Britain and Ireland.

1801 Treaty of Lunéville: Austria makes peace; great French gains in Germany.

1802 Peace of Amiens between Britain and France. *Charlotte Dundas*, first practical steamship, on Clyde.

1803 Insurrection in Ireland under Robert Emmet. Britain again at war with France.

A.D.

1804 Bonaparte becomes Emperor. Spain declares war against Great Britain. Serbian revolt against Turks under Kara George.

1805 Battle of Trafalgar, Nelson's great victory and death, Oct.21. Battle of Austerlitz, Dec. 2.

1806 Death of Pitt, Jan. 23. Confederation of the Rhine: Napoleon's reorganisation of Germany, July 12. End of Holy Roman Empire, Aug. 6. Prussia overthrown at Jena. Napoleon declares Great Britain in a state of blockade—"Continental System."

1807 Slave trade abolished in British Empire. Treaty of Tilsit: with Alexander of Russia his friend, Napoleon controls all of Europe Occupation of Portugal by French, to enforce Continental Blockade.

1808 Occupation of Spain by French. Spanish rising: guerilla warfare. Peninsular War begins. Battle of Vimeiro (defeat of French by Wellington), Aug. 21.

1809 Battle of Corunna and death of Sir John Moore, Jan. 16. Attempted risings in Germany against Napoleon: Austria renews war. Treaty of Schönbrunn, Oct. 14.

1810 Self-government established in Argentina: first South American state to become independent of Spain.

1811 Massacre of Mamelukes at Cairo. Luddite riots.

1812 Retreat from Moscow: destruction of Napoleon's Grand Army.

1813 War of Liberation starts in Germany. Defeat of French by Wellington at Vitoria, June 21

1814 Soult defeated by Wellington at Toulouse, April 10. Abdication of Napoleon, April 11; Louis XVIII king of France. Congress of Vienna (concluded June 1815) under guidance of Metternich. Resettlement of Europe, usually by restoration of kings. Germanic Confederation under Austrian supervision. Poland ruled by Czar. Kingdom of Netherlands to include Belgium.

THE OLD ORDER RESTORED

1815 Escape of Napoleon from Elba. Battle of Waterloo, June 18. Corn Law in Britain to safeguard agricultural interests by keeping up prices. Quadruple Alliance (Austria, Russia, Prussia, Britain) to maintain Vienna settlement and hold regular meetings ("Congress System") —frequently confused with Holy Alliance, which was simply a declaration of Christian principles. Napoleon sent to St. Helena, Oct. 16.

1818 Bernadotte made king of Sweden (Charles XIV), Feb. 6.

1819 Singapore founded by Stamford Raffles. Beginning of Zollverein (Customs Union) in Germany under Prussian influence. Parliamentary reform meeting at Manchester dispersed by military ("Peterloo"), Aug. 16.

1820 Death of George III, Jan. 29.

1821 Death of Napoleon at St. Helena, May 5.

1822 Congress of Verona: congress system breaks down with refusal of Britain (Canning) to intervene against revolutions.

1823 "Monroe Doctrine" announced by U.S.A. President. Dec. 2.

1824 Repeal of Combination Acts in Britain which had forbidden Trades Unions. Charles X king of France.

1825 Independence of all Spanish American mainland now achieved. Nicholas I Czar of Russia. First railway, Stockton to Darlington, opened.

1826 First crossing of Atlantic under steam by Dutch ship *Curaçao*. Menai suspension bridge opened.

1827 Battle of Navarino, Turkish and Egyptian fleet destroyed. Death of Beethoven.

1828 Death of Chaka, great Zulu conqueror.

1829 Greece independent. Catholic Emancipation Act in Britain. Metropolitan Police established.

A.D.

1830 Death of George IV, June 26. Louis Philippe ousts Charles X. Belgium breaks away from Holland. Russian Poland revolts.

1831 First Reform Bill introduced by Lord John Russell. Leopold of Saxe-Coburg becomes king of independent Belgium. British Association founded. Faraday discovers electromagnetic induction.

1832 Reform Bill passed, June 7. Walter Scott, Jeremy Bentham, and Goethe die. Electric telegraph invented by Morse.

1833 Beginning of "Oxford Movement" in English Church. First government grant made to English schools. First British Factory Act.

1834 Poor Law Amendment Act: tightening up of relief in Britain. "Tolpuddle Martyrs" victimised to discourage British working-class movement. Carlist wars begin in Spain.

1835 Municipal Reform Act revises British local government. The word "socialism" first used. "Tamworth Manifesto" of Peel defines aims of Conservative Party.

1836 People's Charter states programme of Chartists. Great Trek of Boers from British South African territory. Texas achieves independence of Mexico.

1837 Queen Victoria succeeds to the throne.

1838 National Gallery opened.

1839 First Afghan war begins. Chartist riots at Birmingham and Newport. Anti-Corn Law League founded. Aden annexed by Britain.

1840 Penny postage instituted. Queen Victoria marries Prince Albert of Saxe-Coburg-Gotha. "Opium War" with China begins. Union Act gives Canada responsible government. Last convicts landed in New South Wales.

1841 Hong Kong acquired by Britain.

1842 Chartists present second national petition and put themselves at the head of strikes. Great potato famine in Ireland begins.

1846 Repeal of the Corn Laws. Peel resigns.

1847 British Museum opened.

REVOLUTIONS AND NEW NATIONS

1848 Monster meeting of Chartists on Kennington Common, procession abandoned, Apr. 10. General revolutionary movement throughout the Continent. Louis Philippe abdicates: French Republic proclaimed. Swiss Federal Constitution established after defeat of Sonderbund (Catholic succession movement). Rising in Vienna: flight of Metternich, accession of Francis Joseph. Nationalist risings in Bohemia and Hungary. Frankfurt Parliament: attempt to unite Germany on liberal principles. Communist Manifesto produced by Marx and Engels. U.S.A. makes great territorial gains from Mexico. Gold discovered in California.

1849 Collapse of revolutionary movements. Rome republic besieged by French (June 3), defended by Garibaldi, holds out until July 2. Austrians take Venice, Aug. 22. Repeal of old Navigation Laws. Punjab annexed by Britain.

1850 Cavour becomes Prime Minister of Sardinia. Don Pacifico affair: privileges of British citizenship at their highest defended by Palmerston.

1851 Great Exhibition in Hyde Park. First satisfactory submarine telegraph cable between Dover and Calais laid. Gold in Australia.

1852 Independence of Transvaal recognised by Britain. Napoleon III Emperor of the French.

1853 U.S. Commodore Perry lands in Japan: beginning of Western influence. Russia and Turkey at war.

1854 War declared against Russia by France and Britain. Allied armies land in Crimea, Sept. 14 (Alma, Siege of Sevastopol, Balaklava, Inkerman). Orange Free State set up.

1855 Sardinia joins Britain and France against Russia. Fall of Sevastopol and end of Crimean War. Alexander II Czar of Russia.

A.D.

1856 Peace Treaty signed at Paris. Bessemer invents process for large-scale production of steel. Livingstone completes journey across Africa.

1857 Indian Mutiny. Relief of Lucknow. Canton captured by English and French.

1858 *Great Eastern* launched. Crown assumes government of India. Treaty of Aigun, by which China cedes Amur region to Russia.

1859 Darwin publishes *Origin of Species*. French support for Piedmont in war with Austria (Magenta, Solferino). Piedmont receives Lombardy. Harper's Ferry raid: John Brown hanged, Dec. 2.

1860 Garibaldi and the Thousand Redshirts in Sicily and Naples; most of Italy united to Piedmont. Vladivostok founded; Russia strongly established on N.W. Pacific.

1861 Abraham Lincoln takes office as Pres. of U.S. American Civil War commences with 11 states breaking away to form Southern Confederacy. Bull Run (July 21) Confederate success ends Federal hopes of easy victory. Victor Emmanuel proclaimed by first Italian Parliament as king of Italy. Emancipation of Serfs in Russia. Death of Prince Albert, Dec. 14.

1862 Bismarck becomes leading minister in Prussia. Garibaldi attempts to seize Rome but wounded at Aspromonte. Aug. 29. Cotton famine in Lancashire.

1863 Polish rising against Russia (suppressed 1864). French in Mexico. Battle of Gettysburg, July 1–3. Maximilian of Austria made emperor of Mexico.

1864 Cession of Schleswig-Holstein to Prussia and Austria. First Socialist International formed. Taiping rebellion in China ended. Federal army enters Atlanta, Sept. 2: General Sherman captures Savannah ("From Atlanta to the sea"). Dec. 22. Geneva Convention originated.

1865 Death of Cobden, Apr. 2. General Lee surrenders to Grant, Apr. 9. Lincoln assassinated, Apr. 14. Thirteenth Amendment to Constitution: slavery abolished in U.S. Death of Palmerston, Oct. 18. Lister introduces antiseptic surgery in Glasgow. Tashkent becomes centre of Russian expansion in Central Asia. Mendel experiments on heredity. William Booth founds Salvation Army.

1866 Austro-Prussian War over Schleswig-Holstein ("Seven Weeks War"). Prussian victory at Sadowa (July 3). Venice secured for Italy, who had, however, been defeated by Austrians at Custozza (June 24) and Lissa (July 20). Treaty of Prague, Aug. 23.

1867 North German Confederation founded. Emperor Maximilian of Mexico shot. Dominion of Canada established. Russia sells Alaska to America for $7 million. Garibaldi makes second attempt to seize Rome, but defeated by Pope with French support at Mentana, Nov. 3. Second Parliamentary Reform Bill passed (Disraeli "dished the Whigs").

1868 Shogunate abolished in Japan: Meiji period of rapid Westernisation under Imperial leadership begins. Ten Years' War (1868–78); struggle for Cuban independence from Spain. Disraeli succeeds Derby as Prime Minister but defeated in general election by Gladstone, Nov.

1869 General Grant, Pres. of U.S. Irish Church disestablished. Suez Canal formally opened.

1870 Napoleon III declares war against Prussia. French defeated at Woerth, Gravelotte, and Sedan. Paris besieged. Rome and Papal states annexed to kingdom of Italy. Irish Land Act passed. Forster's Education Act puts elementary education within reach of all British children. Papal Infallibility announced.

1871 William I of Prussia proclaimed German emperor at Versailles, Jan. 18. Paris capitulates, Jan. 28. Commune of Paris proclaimed, Mar. 28. Peace signed at Frankfurt-on-Main, May 10. Government troops enter Paris and

A.D.

crush Communards, May 28. Thiers President of the Republic, Aug. 31. Mont Cenis tunnel opened. Trade Unions in Britain legalised.

RIVAL IMPERIAL POWERS

1872 Secret ballot introduced in Britain. Death of Mazzini, Mar. 10.

1873 Death of Livingstone, May 4. Ashanti war.

1874 Disraeli succeeds Gladstone as Prime Minister.

1875 England purchases Khedive's shares in Suez Canal, Nov.

1876 Bulgarian massacres. Serbo-Turkish war. Bell invents the telephone. Custer defeated and killed in last large-scale Red Indian success. Porfirio Diaz in power in Mexico (until 1911). Victoria declared Empress of India.

1877 Transvaal annexed to British Empire. War between Russia and Turkey. Satsuma rebellion in Japan: final unsuccessful attempt to halt new ideas.

1878 Congress of Berlin: general Balkan settlement. Cyprus leased to Britain (annexed 1914). Second war with Afghanistan (ended 1880). Edison and Swan produce first successful incandescent electric light.

1879 Dual control (Britain and France) in Egypt. Zulu War. Gladstone's Midlothian Campaign. Tay Bridge destroyed, Dec. 28.

1880 Beaconsfield ministry succeeded by second Gladstone ministry. Transvaal declared a republic.

1881 British defeat at Majuba: independence of Transvaal recognised. France occupies Tunis. Gambetta becomes Prime Minister of France. Revolt of the Mahdi in the Sudan. Pasteur's famous immunisation experiment to show that inoculated animals can survive anthrax.

1882 Lord Frederick Cavendish, Irish Secretary, assassinated in Phoenix Park, Dublin, May 6. Triple Alliance (Germany, Austria, Italy) first formed. Alexandria bombarded, July 11. Cairo occupied by British troops, Sept. 14.

1883 National Insurance begun in Germany. Death of Wagner.

1884 Wolseley heads expedition to Khartoum to rescue Gordon. French establish complete protectorate in Indo-China. Evelyn Baring takes over administration of Egypt. Russians capture Merv. Berlin Conference defines rights of European Powers in Africa. Third Parliamentary Reform Bill. Parsons invents his turbine. Greenwich meridian internationally recognised as prime meridian. Fabian Society founded.

1885 Khartoum captured; Gordon slain, Jan. 26.

1886 Upper Burma annexed by Britain. Home Rule Bill defeated in Commons. All Indians in U.S.A. now in Reservations. Daimler produces his first motor car. Completion of Canadian Pacific Railway. Gold discovered in the Transvaal.

1887 Queen Victoria's Jubilee celebration, June 21.

1888 William II German Emperor. County Councils set up in Britain.

1889 Mayerling: tragic death of Prince Rudolf of Austria, Jan. 30. Flight of General Boulanger, after attempting to become master of France. Second Socialist International set up. Great London dock strike, Aug. 15-Sept. 16. Parnell Commission concludes sittings, Nov. 23 (129th day).

1890 Parnell ruined by divorce case: Irish politicians split. Sherman Anti-Trust Law: first attempt in U.S.A. to break cartels. Opening of Forth Bridge, Mar. 4. Bismarck resigns, Mar. 17. Caprivi succeeds. Heligoland ceded to Germany.

1891 The United States of Brazil formed.

1892 Panama Canal financial scandals in France.

1893 Home Rule Bill passes third reading in Commons, Sept. 1: Lords reject Bill, Sept. 8.

1894 Opening of Manchester Ship Canal, Jan. 1.

A.D.

Gladstone resigns, Mar. 3, Lord Rosebery succeeds. Armenian massacres by Turks: repeated at intervals for next quarter of century. Japan declares war against China. Dreyfus convicted of treason.

1895 Opening of Kiel canal, June 21. Rosebery resigns, June 22; Salisbury Ministry succeeds. Treaty of Shimonoseki: Japan gets Formosa, free hand in Korea. New Cuban revolution breaks out against Spanish. Marconi sends message over a mile by wireless. Röntgen discovers X-rays. Freud publishes his first work on psycho-analysis. Jameson Raid, Dec. 29.

1896 Jameson raiders defeated by Boers, Jan. 1. Adowa: Italian disaster at hands of Abyssinians, the first major defeat of a white colonising power by "natives." Gold discovered in the Klondike.

1897 Cretan revolt leads to Greek-Turkish War. Hawaii annexed by U.S.A. Queen Victoria's Diamond Jubilee, June 22. Great Gold Rush began.

1898 Port Arthur ceded to Russia. Spanish-American War. *Maine*, U.S. warship blown up in Havana harbour. Treaty of Paris, Dec. 10: Cuba freed, Puerto Rico and Guam ceded to U.S.A., Phillippines surrendered for $20 million. Death of Gladstone, May 19. Battle of Omdurman, decisive defeat of Mahdists, Sept. 2. Empress of Austria assassinated, Sept. 10. The Curies discovered Radium.

1899 Boer War begins, Oct. 10.

1900 Boers attack Ladysmith, Jan. 6. Battle of Spion Kop, Buller repulsed with severe losses, Jan. 14. Relief of Kimberley, Feb. 15. Ladysmith relieved, Feb. 28. Mafeking relieved, May 17. Boxer outbreak in China, May. Annexation of Orange Free State, May 26. Roberts occupies Johannesburg, May 31. "Khaki Election." Annexation of the Transvaal, Oct. 25. Australian Commonwealth proclaimed, Dec. 30.

1901 Queen Victoria dies, Jan. 22. Trans-Siberian Railway opened for single-track traffic.

1902 Anglo-Japanese Alliance, Jan. 30. Death of Cecil Rhodes, Mar. 26. Treaty of Vereeniging ends Boer War, May 31.

1903 Congo scandal: celebrated case of misrule and exploitation. Royal family of Serbia assassinated, May 29. First controlled flight in heavier-than-air machine—Orville and Wilbur Wright at Kitty Hawk, U.S.A., Dec. 17.

1904 Russo-Japanese War begins, Feb. 8. Japanese victory at Yalu River, May 1. British forces under Younghusband reach Lhasa, Aug. 3. Treaty with Tibet signed at Lhasa, Sept. 7.

1905 Port Arthur falls to Japanese, Jan. 3. "Bloody Sunday" massacre at St. Petersburg, Jan. 22. Destruction of Russian fleet under Rozhdestvenski at Tsushima by Admiral Togo (May). Treaty of Portsmouth (U.S.A.) ends Russo-Japanese war. Separation of Church and State in France. Norway separates itself from Sweden.

1906 General strike in Russia. San Francisco destroyed by earthquake and fire, Apr. 18. Simplon tunnel opened for railway traffic, June 1. First Duma (Parliament with limited powers) in Russia. Liberal "landslide" majority in Britain: Labour M.P.s appear. Movement for Women's Suffrage becomes active in Britain. Algeciras Conference: Franco-German crises resolved in favour of France. Death of Ibsen. Vitamins discovered by F. G. Hopkins.

1907 New Zealand becomes a dominion.

1908 Annexation of Congo by Belgium. Young Turk revolution. Annexation of Bosnia and Herzegovina by Austria: severe rebuff for Russia. Asquith becomes Prime Minister of Britain.

1909 Old Age Pensions in Britain. Peary reaches North Pole. Blériot makes first cross-Channel flight. House of Lords rejects Lloyd George's budget. Union of South Africa formed. Henry Ford concentrates on producing Model T chassis: beginnings of cheap motors.

A.D.

1910 Accession of George V on death of Edward VII, May 6. Liberals win two General Elections. Labour Exchanges established in Britain. Death of Tolstoy and Florence Nightingale.

1911 Parliament Act: power of Lords decisively reduced. British M.P.s paid for first time. National Insurance in Britain. Great British rail strike. Tripoli taken from Turkey by Italy. Chinese Revolution. Amundsen reaches South Pole, Dec. 14.

1912 China becomes a Republic under Sun Yat Sen. *Titanic* disaster off Cape Race, Apr. 14–15. Great British coal strike. Scott's last expedition. Outbreak of Balkan Wars.

1913 Treaty of Bucharest: most of Turkey-in-Europe divided among Balkan states.

FIRST WORLD WAR

1914 Archduke Francis Ferdinand, heir to the Hapsburg thrones, assassinated at Sarajevo, June 28. Austria-Hungary declares war against Serbia, July 28. Germany declares war against Russia, Aug. 1. Germany declares war against France, Aug. 3. German invasion of Belgium: Great Britain declares war against Germany, Aug. 4. Great Britain declares war on Austria-Hungary, Aug. 12. British Expeditionary Force concentrated before Mauberge, Aug. 20. Battle of Mons; Japan declared war on Germany, Aug. 23. Battle of the Marne, Sept. 5–9. Trench warfare began on Aisne salient, Sept. 16. Three British cruisers (*Aboukir*, *Hogue*, and *Cressy*) sunk by one U-boat, Sept. 22. First Battle of Ypres, Oct. 12–Nov. 11. Raiding of German cruiser *Emden* until destroyed, Nov. 9. Battle of Coronel: German cruisers *Scharnhorst* and *Gneisenau* sink British cruisers *Good Hope* and *Monmouth*, Nov. 1. Great Britain declares war against Turkey, Nov. 5. Destruction of German squadron off Falkland Is., Dec. 8. British protectorate over Egypt proclaimed, Dec. 17. First Zeppelin appeared over British coast, Dec. 20.

1915 Turkish army defeated in Caucasus, Jan 5. Great Britain declared blockade of Germany, Mar. 1. Battle of Neuve Chapelle, Mar. 10–13. Naval attack on Dardanelles called off, Mar. 22. First landing of British, Australian, New Zealand troops on Gallipoli Peninsula, Apr. 25. Second Battle of Ypres, Apr. 22–May 25: Germans first used gas. Sinking of *Lusitania*, May 7. Battle of Aubers Ridge, May 9–25. Italy declares war on Austria, May 22. British Coalition Government formed, May 26. Italian army crosses Isonzo, June 2. Zeppelin destroyed by R. A. J. Warneford, June 7. Second landing of Allied troops at Suvla Bay. Italy declares war on Turkey, Aug. 20. Turks defeated at Kut-el-Amara, Sept 28. Serbia conquered by Austria and Bulgaria, Nov. 6. French and British troops occupy Salonika, Dec. 13. British troops withdraw from Anzac and Suvla, Dec. 20.

1916 Evacuation of Gallipoli completed, Jan 8. Opening of Battle of Verdun, Feb. 21. Republican rising in Ireland, Apr. 24. First Daylight Saving Bill passed. Fall of Kut, Apr. 29. Battle of Jutland, May 31. Brusilov's offensive in Galicia begins, June 4. Kitchener drowned when *Hampshire* struck mine, June 5. Battle of the Somme, July 1–Nov. 13: British losses: 420,000. Italians capture Gorizia, Aug. 10. Hindenburg and Ludendorff chiefs of German staff, Aug. 27. Rumania declares war against Austria and Germany, Aug. 27. Tanks first used by British, Sept. 15. Death of Francis Joseph of Austria, Nov. 21. Lloyd George forms War Cabinet, Dec. 6. Joffre replaced by Nivelle, early Dec.

1917 Unrestricted submarine warfare begins, Feb. 1. British troops occupy Baghdad, Mar. 11. Revolution in Russia, Mar. 12. U.S.A. declares war on Germany, April 6. Battle of Arras, Apr. 9–14; Vimy Ridge taken by Canadians, Apr. 10. Pétain replaced Nivelle, May 15. Messines Ridge taken by British, June 7. First American contingents arrive in France, June 26. Allenby assumes Palestine

A.D.

command, June 29. Third Battle of Ypres opened, July 31. Russia proclaimed a Republic, Sept. 15. British victory on Passchendaele Ridge, Oct. 4. French victory on the Aisne, Oct. 23. Caporetto: Italians severely defeated by Austrians. Oct. 24. Bolshevik Revolution, Nov. 7 (Oct. 25 O.S.). Passchendaele captured by British, Nov. 6. Balfour declaration recognised Palestine as "a national home" for the Jews, Nov. 8. Hindenburg Lines smashed on 10-mile front, Nov. 20. Fall of Jerusalem, Dec. 9. Russo-German armistice signed, Dec. 15.

1918 Treaty of Brest-Litovsk, Mar. 3. German offensive against British opened on Somme, Mar. 21. Battle of Arras, Mar. 21–Apr. 4. Second German offensive against British, Apr. 9–25. British naval raid on Zeebrugge and Ostend, Apr. 23. Foch appointed C.-in-C. Allied armies, Apr. 14. Peace signed between Rumania and Central Powers, May 7. *Vindictive* sunk in Ostend harbour, May 9. Last German offensive against French, July 15. British, Canadians, and Australians attack in front of Amiens, Aug. 8. Allenby destroyed last Turkish army at Megiddo, Sept. 19. Bulgarians signed armistice, Sept. 29. General Allied offensive in West began, Sept. 26. Germans accepted Wilson's Fourteen Points, Oct. 23. Great Italian advance, Oct. 24. Turkey surrenders, Oct. 30. Austria accepts imposed terms, Nov. 3. Popular government in Poland (Lublin), Nov. 7. Revolutionary movement begins in Germany, Nov. 8. Kaiser abdicates and escapes to Holland, Nov. 9. Armistice signed by Germans, Nov. 11. Proclamation of Kingdom of Serbs, Croats and Slovenes in Belgrade, Dec. 1.

THE TWENTIES AND THIRTIES

1919 Peace Conference in Paris, Jan. 18. Einstein's theory of Relativity confirmed experimentally during solar eclipse, March 29. First direct flight across Atlantic by Sir J. Alcock and Sir A. W. Brown, June 15. Interned German fleet scuttled at Scapa Flow, June 19. Treaty of Peace with Germany signed at Versailles, June 28. Treaty of St. Germain: break-up of Austrian Empire, Sept. 10.

1920 Peace Treaty ratified in Paris. First meeting of League of Nations, from which Germany, Austria, Russia, and Turkey are excluded, and at which the U.S.A. is not represented. Prohibition in U.S.A. Peace Treaty with Turkey signed at Sèvres: Ottoman Empire broken up Aug. 10. Degrees first open to women at Oxford Univ., Oct. 14.

1921 Riots in Egypt, May 23. In complete disregard of the League of Nations, Greece makes war on Turkey. Heligoland fortresses demolished, Oct. 14. Irish Free State set up by Peace Treaty with Britain, Dec. 6.

1922 Four-Power Pacific Treaty ratified by U.S. Senate, Mar. 24. Heavy fighting in Dublin, the Four Courts blown up, July 2. Defeat of Greek armies by the Turks, Aug.–Sept. Mussolini's Fascist "March on Rome," Oct. 28.

1923 French troops despatched to Ruhr, Jan. 11. Treaty of Lausanne, July 24. Earthquake in Japan, Tokio and Yokohama in ruins, Sept. 1. Rhine Republic proclaimed, Bavaria defies the Reich, Oct. 20. Turkish Republic proclaimed; Kemal Pasha, first President, Oct. 29.

1924 Lenin dies, Jan. 21. First Labour Ministry in Britain under MacDonald, Jan. 22; lasts 9 months. George II of Greece deposed and a Republic declared, Mar. 25. Dawes Plan accepted by London conference; Ruhr evacuation agreed to, Aug. 16.

1925 Hindenburg elected German President, Mar. 26. Treaty of Locarno signed in London, Dec. 1. Summer Time Act made permanent.

1926 Ibn Saud proclaimed king of the Hedjaz in Jeddah, Jan. 11. Evacuation of Cologne by British forces, Jan. 31. General strike in Britain.

1927 Lindbergh flies Atlantic alone, May 21.

1928 Earthquake in Greece, Corinth destroyed. Apr. 23. Capt. Kingsford-Smith flies the

A.D.

Pacific, June 9. General Nobile rescued by aeroplane from Arctic one month after disaster, June 24. Kellogg Pact accepted by Gt. Britain, July 18. German airship with 60 persons crosses Atlantic, Oct. 15. Women in Britain enfranchised on same basis as men.

1929 Second Labour Ministry under MacDonald. Graf Zeppelin makes numerous successful intercontinental flights. Commander Byrd flies over South Pole, Nov. 30. American slump and Wall Street crash.

1930 *R.101* destroyed in France on first flight to India, 48 lives lost, Oct. 5—end of British interest in airships.

1931 Great floods in China. Resignation of Labour Government and formation of Coalition under MacDonald. Invergordon naval mutiny.

1932 Manchuria erected into Japanese puppet state of Manchukuo, Feb. 18. Sydney Harbour Bridge opened, Mar. 19. Ottawa Imperial Conference.

1933 Hitler appointed Chancellor by Hindenburg, Jan. 30, and step by step gains supreme control. German Reichstag set on fire, Feb. 27.

1934 Dollfuss, Austrian Chancellor, murdered by Austrian Nazis, July 25. Death of Hindenburg, Aug. 2. Hitler becomes Dictator. Alexander of Yugoslavia assassinated in Marseilles, Oct. 9.

1935 Saar plebiscite for return to Germany, Jan. 13. Baldwin succeeds MacDonald as Prime Minister, June 7. War begins between Italy and Abyssinia, Oct. 3. Ineffectual economic "sanctions" by League of Nations against Italy, Nov. 11.

1936 Accession of King Edward VIII, Jan. 20. Repudiation of Locarno Treaty by Germany, Mar. 7. Remilitarisation of Rhineland, Mar. 8. Italian troops occupy Addis Ababa, May 5. Civil War breaks out in Spain, July 18. King Edward VIII abdicates after a reign of 325 days, Dec. 10. The Duke of York succeeds his brother as King George VI, Dec. 12.

1937 Coalition Ministry under Chamberlain, May 28. Japanese begin attempted conquest of China—"China incident," July 7.

1938 Austria annexed by Germany, Mar. 13. British navy mobilised, Sept. 28. Munich Agreement between Chamberlain, Daladier, Hitler, and Mussolini, Sept. 29.

1939

February 27 Great Britain recognises General Franco's Government.

March 16 Bohemia and Moravia annexed by Hitler and proclaimed a German Protectorate. **22** Memel ceded to Germany by Lithuania. **28** Anti-Polish press campaign begun by Germany.

April 1 Spanish War ends. **7** Italy seizes Albania. **14** First British talks with Russia. **27** Conscription introduced in Great Britain. **28** Hitler denounces Anglo-German Naval agreement and the Polish Non-Aggression Treaty.

May 12 Great Britain signs defensive agreement with Turkey. **22** Italy and Germany sign pact. **23** France and Turkey sign defensive agreement. **25** Anglo-Polish treaty signed in London.

July 10 Chamberlain re-affirms British pledge to Poland.

August 23 German-Soviet Pact signed by von Ribbentrop. **25** Japan breaks away from the Anti-Comintern Pact. **28** Holland mobilises. **31** British fleet mobilised.

SECOND WORLD WAR

September 1 Poland invaded by German forces. Great Britain and France mobilise. **1–4** Evacuation schemes put in motion in England and Wales: 1,200,000 persons moved. **2** Compulsory military service for all men in Britain aged 18 to 41. **3** War declared (11 a.m.) between Britain and Germany as from 5 p.m. **4** British liner *Athenia* sunk by submarine. R.A.F. raid the Kiel Canal entrance and bomb German warships. **6** First enemy air raid on Britain. **8** Russia mobilises. Russian troops on Polish border. **11** British troops on French soil. **17**

A.D.

Russian troops cross the Polish frontier along its entire length. Russian and German troops meet near Brest Litovsk. **27** Capitulation of Warsaw. **29** Nazi-Soviet pact signed in Moscow approving partition of Poland.

October 14 *Royal Oak* sunk in Scapa Flow with a loss of 810 lives.

November 8 Bomb explosion in the Bürgerbräukeller at Munich after Hitler's speech. Germans using magnetic mines. **29** Diplomatic relations between Russia and Finland severed. **30** Finland attacked by Russia.

December 11 Italy leaves the League of Nations. **13** Battle of the River Plate: engagement of German warship *Admiral Graf Spee* by H.M. cruisers *Exeter*, *Ajax*, and *Achilles*. **14** Rejection by Russia of the League of Nations' offer of mediation in the Russo-Finnish war. Russia expelled from the League of Nations. **17** *Admiral Graf Spee* scuttles herself in the entrance of Montevideo harbour.

1940

February 14 Finnish advanced posts captured by Russians. **16** 299 British prisoners taken off the German Naval Auxiliary *Altmark* in Norwegian waters. **26** Finns lose the island fortress of Kolvisto. Finns retreat from Petsamo.

March 12 British ships to be fitted with a protective device against magnetic mines. Finland concludes a peace treaty whereby she cedes to Russia the Karelian Isthmus, the town of Vipuri and a military base on Hango Peninsula.

April 9 Invasion of Denmark and Norway by Germany. **15** British troops arrive in Norway. **19** British soldiers land in the Faroes.

May 2 British troops withdrawn from Norway. **10** Holland, Belgium and Luxembourg invaded by German forces. Parachute troops landed near Rotterdam. British troops cross the Belgian border. British troops land in Iceland. Rotterdam bombed. **11** National Government formed under Churchill. **13** Queen Wilhelmina arrives in London. **14** Rotterdam captured. Holland ceases fighting. Allied troops land near Narvik. **17** Belgian Government moves to Ostend. **24** German forces enter Boulogne. **27** Belgian army capitulates on the order of King Leopold. British forces to be withdrawn from Flanders. Narvik captured by Allied forces. **29** Ostend, Ypres, Lille and other Belgian and French towns lost to the Germans.

June Evacuation of British army from Dunkirk (May 27–June 4): 299 British warships and 420 other vessels under constant attack evacuate 335,490 officers and men. **5** Hitler proclaims a war of total annihilation against his enemies. **8** German armoured forces penetrate French defences in the West near Rouen. **10** Italy declares war on Great Britain and France. **14** Paris captured by German forces. **15** Soviet troops occupy Lithuania, Latvia and Estonia. **22** French delegates accept terms for an Armistice. **25** Hostilities in France cease at 12.35 a.m.

July 1 Channel Islands occupied by Germany. **3** French naval squadron at Oran immobilised. **10** Battle of Britain began.

August 19 British withdrew from British Somaliland. **25** British began night bombing of Germany.

September 6 King Carol of Rumania abdicates in favour of his son Michael. **7** London sustains severe damage in the largest aerial attack since war commenced. **15** Battle of Britain ends with British victory: German aeroplanes destroyed, 1,733; R.A.F. losses, 915. **23** Japanese troops enter Indo-China.

October 7 German troops enter Rumania. **28** Greece rejects an Italian ultimatum.

November 1 Greeks repel Italian attacks, **5** H.M.S. *Jervis Bay* lost defending Atlantic convoy from German warship *Admiral Scheer*. **11** Italian fleet at Taranto crippled by Fleet Air Arm. **14** Coventry heavily attacked, the Cathedral destroyed. **22** Albanian town of Koritza captured by the Greeks.

December 2 Bristol heavily bombed. **11** Sidi Barrani captured by British forces: beginning

A.D.
of Wavell's destruction of Italian forces in Cyrenaica. **29** City of London severely burned by incendiary bombs: Guildhall and eight Wren Churches destroyed.

1941

January 5 Bardia captured. **22** Tobruk captured by Australian troops.

February 7 Benghazi captured. **26** Mogadishu, capital of Italian Somaliland, occupied by Imperial troops. German mechanised troops in Libya.

March 4 British raid Lofoten Islands. **11** U.S. Lease and Lend Bill signed by Roosevelt. **27** Keren—main battle in British conquest of Abyssinia and Somaliland. **28** Cape Matapan: Italian fleet routed by British. **30** Rommel opens attack in N. Africa.

April 4 Addis Ababa entered by Imperial troops. **6** Greece and Yugoslavia invaded by German troops. **8** Massawa capitulates. **11** Belgrade occupied by German forces. **13** Bardia given up by British. Tobruk holds out. **24** Empire forces withdrawing from Greece. **27** Athens captured by the Germans.

May 2 Evacuation from Greece completed. **10** Rudolf Hess descends by parachute in Scotland. **20** Crete invaded by German air-borne troops. **24** H.M.S. Hood sunk. **27** German battleship. Bismark sunk; British forces withdrawn from Crete.

June 2 Clothes rationing commences. **4** William II (ex-Kaiser of Germany) dies. **18** Treaty of friendship between Turkey and Germany signed. **22** Germany attacks Russia. **24** Russia loses Brest Litovsk.

July 3 Palmyra (Syria) surrenders to Allied forces. **7** U.S. forces arrive in Iceland. **9** General Dentz, the French High Commissioner in Syria, asks for Armistice terms. **25** Fighting round Smolensk.

August 25 British and Russian troops enter Persia. **27** The Dnepropetrovsk dam blown up by the Russians.

September 18 Crimea cut off from mainland. **19** Kiev entered by Germans.

October 6 German attack on Moscow. **16** Soviet Government leaves Moscow. Odessa occupied by German and Rumanian troops. **19** Taganrog on Sea of Azov captured by Germans. **26** Kharkov captured by the Germans.

November 14 Ark Royal sunk. **18** Libyan battle opens: Eighth Army's first offensive. **23** Bardia and Fort Capuzzo captured by British. **24** H.M.S. Dunedin torpedoed. **25** H.M.S. Barham sunk. **30** Russians re-take Rostov.

December 1 Points rationing scheme in force in Britain. **4** German attack on Moscow halted. **6** Japanese attack on Pearl Harbor. **8** Japanese forces land in Malaya. **9** British forces in Tobruk relieved. **10** H.M.S. Repulse and Prince of Wales sunk off Malaya by Japanese. Phillipines invaded by Japanese. **25** Hong-kong surrenders to Japanese.

1942

January 2 Manila and Cavite taken by Japanese. **23** Japanese forces land in New Guinea and the Solomon Islands.

February 9 Soap rationed. **12** Escape through English Channel of German ships Scharnhorst, Gneisenau, and Prinz Eugen. **15** Singapore surrenders to Japanese. **27** Battle of Java Sea.

March 9 Surrender of Java to Japanese.

April 15 George Cross awarded to the island of Malta.

May 4–8 Battle of Coral Sea. **7** Madagascar invaded by British forces. **7** U.S. forces sink 11 Japanese warships off the Solomon islands. **30** Over 1,000 bombers raid Cologne. Canterbury bombed.

June 3–7 Midway Island: U.S. naval victory turns tide in Pacific. **20** Tobruk captured by the Germans.

July 16 R.A.F. make first daylight raid on the Ruhr.

August 6 Germans advancing towards the Caucasus. **10** American forces land in the Solomon

A.D.
Islands. **11** Malta convoy action (loss of H.M.S. Eagle, Manchester, Cairo, and one destroyer). **19** Raid on Dieppe. **23–25** Battle of Solomons.

September 6 Germans halted at Stalingrad.

October 23 El Alamein: Allied offensive opens in Egypt.

November 4 Rommel's army in full retreat. **5** Red Army holding firm at Stalingrad. **7** Allied invasion of N. Africa. **27** German forces enter Toulon. French Fleet scuttled.

December 2 First self-sustained, controlled nuclear chain reaction in uranium achieved by group working under Enrico Fermi at Chicago. **24** Admiral Darlan assassinated.

1943

January 6 German armies in the Caucasus and the Don elbow in retreat. **18** Leningrad 16-month siege ended. **23** Tripoli occupied by the Eighth Army. **27** American bombers make their first attack on Germany. **31** Remnants of the German army outside Stalingrad surrender.

February 9 Guadalcanal Island cleared of Japanese troops. **16** Kharkov retaken by the Russians.

March 1–3 Battle of Bismarck Sea. **23** 8th Army penetrates the Mareth Line.

May 7 Tunis and Bizerta captured by Allies. **12** All organised German resistance in Tunisia ceases. **16** Dams in the Ruhr breached by the R.A.F. **22** Moscow dissolves the Comintern.

June 3 French Committee for National Liberation formed in Algiers.

July 10 Allied invasion of Sicily. **25** Mussolini overthrown. **28** Fascist Party in Italy dissolved.

August 17 Sicily in Allied hands.

September 3 Italian mainland invaded. **7** Italy surrenders. **9** British and American troops land near Naples. **10** Rome seized by the Germans. **14** Salamaua captured from the Japanese. **23** Tirpitz severely damaged (sunk Nov. 12, 1944). **25** Smolensk taken by the Russians.

October 1 Naples taken. **25** Russians capture Dnepropetrovsk and Dneprodzerzhinck.

November 6 Kiev taken by the Russians. **26** Second Battle of Solomons. **28** Churchill, Roosevelt, and Stalin meet in Teheran.

December 2 Men between 18 and 25 to be directed to the mining industry by ballot in Britain. **26** Sinking of German battleship Scharnhorst.

1944

January 22 Allied landings at Anzio. **28** Argentina breaks with the Axis Powers.

February 1 American forces land on the Marshall Islands. **2** Russians penetrate Estonia.

March 15 Cassino (Italy) destroyed by Allied bombers.

May 9 Sevastopol captured by Russians. **18** Capture of Cassino and Abbey by Allies. **19** 50 Allied officers shot after escaping from a German prison camp. **30** Battle for Rome commences.

June 4 Allied forces enter Rome. King of Italy signs decree transferring his powers to Prince Umberto, his son. **6** D-Day: invasion of Europe (over 4,000 ships in invasion fleet). **7** Defeat of Japanese thrust at India, outside Imphal. **9** Heavy fighting near Caen. **12** First V-1 falls on England. **18** Cherbourg peninsula cut by the Americans. Russians break through the Mannerheim Line.

July 3 Minsk captured by Russians. **9** Caen captured by Allies. **20** "Bomb plot" on Hitler's life. **21** Guam captured by Americans.

August 1 Uprising in Warsaw. **4** Myitkyina falls to Allied forces. **15** Allied forces land in southern France. Marseilles taken. Rumania surrenders. **25** Paris liberated. Rumania declares war on Germany.

September 3 Allies in Belgium. **4** Antwerp and Brussels taken by Allies. Holland entered. Finland "ceases fire." **6** Bulgaria asks for an armistice. **7** Boulogne entered by Allies. Bulgaria declares war on Germany. **8** First V-2 falls on England. **11** Allied forces fighting on

A.D.
Reich territory. **17** Allied air-borne troops land near Arnhem. **22** First Battle of Philippines.

October 3 Warsaw rising crushed by the Germans. **5** British troops land on the mainland of Greece. **14** Athens occupied by Allies. **15** Hungary asks for armistice terms. **20** Aachen captured by the Americans. **25** Battle of Leyte Gulf: end of Japanese sea-power. **28** Second Battle of Philippines.

December 6 Civil war breaks out in Athens. **16** German forces counter-attack in the Ardennes: last German offensive in the West. **26** Budapest encircled by Russians.

1945
January 5 Organized fighting in Athens ceases. **11** U.S. forces land on Island of Luzon. **17** Warsaw captured by the Russians. **21** Russian troops in Silesia. **23** Burma road to China reopened.

February 4 Yalta conference. **14** Bombing of Dresden. **19** Americans land on Iwojima Island.

March 6 Cologne captured by Allies.

April 1 U.S. Invasion of Okinawa. **5** Russian Government denounces the Soviet-Japan neutrality pact. Japanese Cabinet resigns. **11** Russian Army enters Vienna after 7-day battle. **12** Death of President Roosevelt. **25** Berlin surrounded by Russian troops. **27** Russians and Americans link up in Germany. **28** Mussolini and his mistress shot by Italian partisans. **30.** Hitler killed himself and his mistress.

May 2 German armies in Italy surrender. Berlin captured by the Russians. **3** Rangoon captured by British. **4** German forces in N.W. Germany, Holland and Denmark surrender. **8** End of World War II against Germany officially declared to be one minute past midnight (Tuesday). **28** Naval air attacks on Japan.

June 26 United Nations Charter signed at San Francisco.

July 5 Polish Government in Warsaw recognised by Allies. **26** Striking Labour victory in general election; Attlee became Prime Minister.

August 6 Atomic bomb first used against Japan: Hiroshima laid waste. **8** Russia declares war against Japan. **9** Russia advances into Manchuria. Nagasaki target for atomic bomb No. 2. **14** Japan surrenders unconditionally to the Allies. **17** Lend-Lease terminated.

September 2 Victory over Japan celebrated: end of Second World War.

"COLD WAR": AFRO-ASIAN INDEPENDENCE

October 9 U.S.A. to keep secret of manufacture of atomic bomb. **15** Laval executed.

November 20 Trial of major war criminals opens at Nuremberg.

1946
February 1 Mr. Trygve Lie elected Secretary-General of UNO.

April 19 League of Nations formally wound up.

June 30 United States atom bomb tests at Bikini.

July 13 United States House of Representatives approves loan to Britain. **22** Bread rationing in Britain. British H.Q. in Jerusalem blown up. **24** Underwater atom bomb test at Bikini.

August 1 Peace Conference opens in Paris.

September 6 United Nations F.A.O. considers establishment of World Food Board.

October 16 Nuremberg sentences on Nazis carried out, Goering commits suicide. **23** General Assembly of the United Nations opens in New York.

November 10 Communists head poll in French General Elections.

December 2 Agreement signed for economic fusion of British and American zones in Germany.

A.D.
1947
January 1 British coal industry nationalised. **14** M. Vincent-Auriol elected first President of Fourth Republic.

March 24 Netherlands Government and Indonesian Cabinet sign agreement in Batavia for a United States of Indonesia.

April 1 School leaving age raised to 15 in Great Britain.

June 5 Inauguration of "Marshall Aid".

August 3 Dutch military action in Indonesia ends. **15** India and Pakistan assume Dominion Status. Viscount Mountbatten appointed Governor-General of India and Mr. Jinnah Governor-General of Pakistan. **29** Palestine Committee agrees British Mandate should end, majority report recommends partition.

September 22 First Atlantic automatic flight by U.S. pilotless aircraft.

October 6 Cominform, new international Communist organization, set up in Belgrade.

November 20 Marriage of Princess Elizabeth. **29** Palestine Committee of U.N. Assembly votes in favour of partition of Palestine into Jewish and Arab States.

December 15 Breakdown of 4-Power Conference on Germany. **30** King Michael of Romania abdicates; Rumania becomes a People's Republic.

1948
January 1 British Railways nationalised. **4** Burma becomes independent Republic. **30** Mahatma Gandhi assassinated in New Delhi.

February 1 New Malayan federal constitution comes into force. **4** Ceylon Independence Act. **25** New Czechoslovak Government formed under Communist leadership.

April 1 British electricity industry nationalised. **5** First European Aid shipments sail from America. **16** O.E.E.C. established.

May 3 Mr. Rajagopalachari appointed Gov.-Gen. of India in succession to Earl Mountbatten. **14** British Mandate for Palestine ended at midnight. Jews proclaim new State of Israel.

June 28 Yugoslavia expelled from Cominform.

July 1 "Berlin Airlift": American, British and French zones of Berlin supplied by air. **5** Establishment of National Health Service. **29** Bread rationing in Great Britain ends.

August 15 Republic of Korea proclaimed.

September 17 Count Bernadotte, U.N. Mediator for Palestine, assassinated.

October 30 Chinese Communist forces capture Mukden.

November 3 Mr. Truman elected U.S. President. **14** Birth of a son to Princess Elizabeth.

December 21 Republic of Ireland Bill signed in Dublin.

1949
March 15 Clothes rationing ends in Great Britain. **31** Russia protests against Atlantic Pact.

April 1 Newfoundland becomes part of Canada.

May 1 Gas Industry nationalised. **3** Ten-power conference in London establishes Council of Europe. **12** Berlin blockade lifted.

August 24 North Atlantic Treaty comes into force.

September 12 Professor Theodor Heuss elected first President of West German Republic. **21** General Mao Tse-Tung proclaims People's Republic of China.

October 2 Russia recognises newly-established Chinese People's Republic. **11** Herr Wilhelm Pieck elected first President of East German Republic.

December 8 Chinese Nationalist Government leaves mainland and sets up H.Q. in Formosa. **27** United States of Indonesia come into being.

1950
January 6 Britain recognises Communist Government of China: **24** Dr. Rajendra Prasad elected first President of Indian Republic; **26** New Constitution of Indian Republic comes into force.

February 14 30-year treaty of alliance between Russia and China signed in Moscow; **23** Labour

A.D.

Party wins General Election with narrow majority.

April 1 Italy takes over from Britain administration of Somaliland; **13** First shipment of military aid to France under N.A. Pact unloaded at Cherbourg.

May 19 Points rationing ends in Britain after 8 years; **25** Middle East Tripartite Declaration by Britain, France, and U.S.A.; **26** Petrol rationing ends in Britain.

June 25 N. Korean troops advance into S. Korea; Security Council calls for cease fire; **27** Pres. Truman orders U.S. air, and sea forces to support S. Korea and protect Formosa; U.N. Commission in Korea proposes neutral mediator; military assistance to S. Korea endorsed by Security Council; **30** Pres. Truman authorizes use of American ground troops in Korea.

July 2 American troops land in S. Korea; **8** Gen. MacArthur designated C.-in-C. of U.N. forces in Korea.

August 1 Security Council meets under chairmanship of M. Malik, the Soviet delegate; **7** American forces in Korea open offensive and halt drive on Pusan; **15** Princess Elizabeth gives birth to a daughter; **17** Independence Day in Indonesia.

September 6 British troops in action in Korea; **9** Soap rationing ends in Britain.

October 9 U.N. forces across the 38th parallel in strength; **19** Pyongyang, N. Korean capital, captured by U.N. forces; **26** New Chamber of House of Commons opened at Westminster; **29** King Gustav V of Sweden dies.

December 4 Pyongyang occupied by Chinese; **19** Gen. Eisenhower appointed Supreme Commander of West European Defence Forces set up by Atlantic Powers; **25** Stone of Scone stolen from Westminster Abbey.

1951

January 30 U.N. Assembly rejects resolution of 12 Asian and Arab nations calling for 7-nation conference for peaceful settlement of Korean question; **31** Decree confiscating property of Alfred Krupp cancelled.

February 15 Vesting date for Iron and Steel.

April 11 Gen. MacArthur relieved of all his commands by Pres. Truman and replaced by Lt.-Gen. Ridgway; **13** Coronation Stone returned to Westminster Abbey.

May 2 Persian oil industry nationalized; Germany admitted to Council of Europe; **3** H.M. the King opens Festival of Britain from steps of St. Paul's.

July 1 Colombo plan comes into force; **9** State of war between Britain and Germany officially ended; **10** Armistice negotiations open at Kaesong; **17** King Leopold abdicates in favour of his son Baudouin; **20** King Abdullah of Jordan assassinated.

September 1 Tripartite Security Treaty between U.S.A., Australia and New Zealand signed in San Francisco; **8** Japanese Peace Treaty signed at San Francisco; **23** H.M. the King undergoes successful operation.

October 8 Princess Elizabeth and Duke of Edinburgh leave for Canadian tour; **15** Egyptian Parliament passes unanimously Bills abrogating Anglo-Egyptian treaty of 1936 and 1899 Sudan Condominium Agreement; **16** Assassination of Liaquat Ali Khan; **25** General Election won by Conservatives with small majority.

December 17 London foreign-exchange market re-opens after 12 years; **24** Libya becomes independent state.

1952

January 2 Mutual Security Agency replaces Economic Co-operation Administration; **31** Princess Elizabeth and Duke of Edinburgh leave London on the first stage of Commonwealth tour.

February 6 King George VI died at Sandringham aged 56; **7** Queen Elizabeth II and the Duke of

A.D.

Edinburgh arrive home by air from Kenya; **21** Identity cards abolished.

April 11 H.M. the Queen declares that she wishes her children and descendants to bear the name of Windsor; **23** Japan regains status as sovereign and independent power.

May 5 H.M. the Queen takes up residence at Buckingham Palace; **27** Treaty setting up European Defence Community signed in Paris.

June 23 Power plants along Yalu River attacked by U.S. aircraft in biggest raid of Korean war.

July 7 American ship *United States* wins Atlantic Blue Riband; **23** Military *coup d'état* takes place in Cairo.

August 1 Ratification of Bonn Agreement, by which W. Germany again becomes independent nation, and Treaty of Paris, which sets up the European Defence Community, approved by Government against Labour opposition; **16** Severe thunderstorms in Somerset and N. Devon bring devastation to Lynmouth; **26** Passive resistance campaign against racial laws in S. Africa gains momentum.

September 8 New Egyptian Cabinet appoints Gen. Neguib military Gov.-Gen. of Egypt and approves land reforms.

October 3 Britain's first atomic weapon exploded in Monte Bello Islands, off N.W. Australia; **5** Tea derationed and decontrolled; **20** State of emergency declared in Kenya as a result of Mau Mau activities.

November 1 Reported explosion of U.S. hydrogen bomb at Eniwetok atoll in mid-Pacific; **4** Gen. Eisenhower, Republican candidate, wins sweeping victory in American Presidential election.

1953

January 31 Violent N.E. gales combined with surging high tides caused extensive flooding with loss of life along coasts of eastern England, the Netherlands, and Belgium.

February 4 Sweet rationing ended; **23** War-time deserters in Britain granted amnesty.

March 6 Marshal Stalin died, aged 74; **24** Death of Queen Mary at Marlborough House, aged 85; **31** Mr. Dag Hammarskjöld elected U.N. Sec.-Gen. in succession to Mr. Trygve Lie.

April 15 Dr. Malan's National Party again returned to power in S. Africa with increased majority; **24** Mr. Churchill created a Knight of the Garter by the Queen.

May 4 Duke of Edinburgh received his pilot's "wings"; **29** E. P. Hillary and Sherpa Tenzing of the Everest Expedition led by Colonel John Hunt reached summit of Everest (29,002 ft.).

June 2 Coronation of H.M. Elizabeth II in Westminster Abbey amid scenes of magnificent pageantry; ceremony televised; **26** Republic of Egypt accorded *de facto* recognition by Britain.

July 4 German–Austrian Expedition reached summit of Nanga Parbat in the Himalayas; **13** De-nationalisation of British steel industry; **14** Royal Assent given to Central African Federation Bill; **27** Korean Armistice signed at Panmunjom.

August 9–12 Disastrous earthquakes in Greek Ionian Islands; **12** Explosion of Russian hydrogen bomb reported.

September 26 Sugar rationing ended after nearly 14 years.

October 15 Sir Winston Churchill awarded 1953 Nobel Prize for Literature.

November 11 Great bell at Notre Dame rung by electricity for first time; **21** Piltdown skull, discovered in Sussex in 1911, found by anthropologists to be partial hoax; **23** The Queen and Duke of Edinburgh began 6 months' tour of Commonwealth.

December 1 Agreement signed for laying first transatlantic telephone cable; **23** M. René Coty elected President of France at the 13th ballot; L. P. Beria, former chief of Soviet Secret Police, and six associates sentenced to death and shot; **25** The Queen gave her Christmas broadcast from Auckland; **31** Mildest December for 20 years, and before that for over 200 years.

A.D.
1954

January 9 Self-government began in the Sudan; **12** M. Le Trouquer (Socialist) elected President of French National Assembly; **16** M. René Coty became President of France in succession to M. Vincent Auriol.

February 3 First Parliament of newly formed Federation of Rhodesia and Nyasaland opened in Salisbury; **5** Britain's first "breeder" pile in operation at Harwell.

March 1 American hydrogen bomb exploded at Bikini; **22** London gold market reopened after 15 years.

April 3 Oxford won 100th Boat Race; **21** Russia joined UNESCO.

May 6 Roger Bannister ran first under 4 minute mile; **7** Fortress of Dien Bien Phu fell to Viet-Minh; **18** Liverpool Cotton Exchange reopened.

June 1 Television licence fee raised from £2 to £3 a year; **2** Mr. John A. Costello (Fine Gael) elected Prime Minister of Ireland; **17** Indo-Chinese crisis brought M. Mendès-France to power in France; **22** First all-African Cabinet in British Africa appointed in the Gold Coast; **27** First electric power station using atomic energy began working in Soviet Union; **30** Eclipse of the sun.

July 3 Food rationing officially ended in Britain; **27** Agreement reached in Cairo for withdrawal of British troops from Suez Canal Zone; **31** K2 climbed by Italian team.

August 5 Persian oil dispute settled; **11** Cessation of hostilities in Indo-China after 8 years of fighting.

September 14 Sheffield–Manchester electrified railway opened.

October 14 Mr. Anthony Eden created a Knight of the Garter; **19** Anglo-Egyptian Suez Canal Agreement.

November 1 French settlements in India passed under Indian control; **30** Sir Winston Churchill celebrated his 80th birthday.

1955

January 31 Princess Margaret left for tour of W. Indies.

February 8 Marshal Bulganin succeeded Mr. Malenkov as chairman of the Soviet Council of Ministers; **17** Britain to proceed with manufacture of hydrogen bombs; **24** Restrictions on hire purchase announced; Dr. Albert Schweitzer appointed honorary member of the Order of Merit; Turco–Iraqi pact signed at Baghdad (Britain, Pakistan, and Persia acceded later).

April 5 Sir Winston Churchill resigned as Prime Minister; **6** Sir Anthony Eden succeeded as Prime Minister; **18** Afro-Asian conference (29 nations) opened at Bandung; **20** Signor Gronchi elected President of Italy.

May 5 Ratification of London and Paris agreements completed; Germany attained full sovereignty and Western European Union came into being; **26** British general election resulted in Conservative majority of 59.

June 15 U.S. and Britain agreed to co-operate on atomic energy; **16** Revolt against the Perón government in Argentina.

July 18 First meeting in Geneva between heads of Government since Potsdam, 1945; **27** Austrian State Treaty came into force.

August 8 International conference on peaceful uses of atomic energy opened in Geneva.

September 16 Universal Copyright convention came into force; **19** General Perón resigned after rebels threatened to bombard Buenos Aires; **22** Independent television service began.

October 2 City of London became a "smokeless zone"; **12** British and Soviet warships exchanged courtesy visits; **20** Syria and Egypt signed mutual defence treaty.

November 5 Vienna State Opera House re-opened; **23** *Hamlet* played on Russian stage by British company, the first since Tsarist times.

December 7 Mr. Attlee announced his retirement and was created an earl; **12** Completion of 830-mile pipeline through Urals; **14** Mr. Hugh Gaitskell elected leader of Labour Party.

A.D.
1956

January 1 Sudan proclaimed an independent republic; **27** The Queen and the Duke of Edinburgh left for tour of Nigeria; 200th anniversary of birth of Mozart celebrated.

February 1 Britain had coldest day since 1895; **13** Referendum in Malta resulted in vote in favour of integration with Britain; **16** Bank rate increased from 4½ to 5½ per cent. (highest since 1932); **25** Khrushchev denounced Stalin.

March 2 King Hussein of Jordan discharged Lieut.-Gen. J. B. Glubb; **5** Telephone weather forecast began; **9** Archbishop Makarios with leaders of Enosis movement in Cyprus deported to the Seychelles; **23** The Queen laid foundation stone of new Coventry Cathedral; Pakistan proclaimed an Islamic republic within the Commonwealth.

April 6 Earl Attlee created Knight of the Garter; **11** Five-day week for Civil Servants announced; **18** Cease-fire between Israel and Egypt came into force; **29** French occupation of Indo-China ended after 80 years.

May 23 First atomic power station in Britain started working at Calder Hall; **24** 2,500th anniversary of the death of Buddha celebrated in India; **31** May was the sunniest month at Kew since 1922 and the driest since 1896.

June 3 Third-class travel abolished on British Railways to conform to continental practice; **13** Last British troops left Suez; **24** Col. Nasser elected Pres. of Egypt.

July 26 Pres. Nasser announced nationalisation of Suez Canal Company.

August 30 French troops arrived in Cyprus.

September 25 Submarine telephone cable linking Britain and America opened to public service.

October 3 Bolshoi Ballet danced at Covent Garden; **15** Duke of Edinburgh left on world tour; **23** Insurrection broke out in Budapest and spread throughout Hungary; **29** Israeli forces invaded Egypt and after 5 days' fighting had control of Sinai peninsula; **30** Britain and France issued 12-hour ultimatum to Israel and Egypt to cease fighting; **31** Anglo-French offensive launched against military targets in Egypt.

November 4 Soviet forces launched attack on Budapest to crush Hungarian uprising; **5** Anglo-French troops landed at Port Said; **6** Pres. Eisenhower re-elected President with Congress controlled by Democrats; Anglo-French forces ceased fire at midnight; **7** Egypt accepted cease fire on UN conditions; **15** UN Emergency Force left Naples for Suez; **16** Suez Canal blocked by 49 ships; **17** First refugees from Hungary arrived in Britain; **22** Duke of Edinburgh opened 16th Olympic Games in Melbourne; **28** Sir Anthony Eden flew to Jamaica for rest cure; **24** UN for third time called upon Britain, France, and Israel to withdraw troops from Egypt.

December 5 140 people arrested in S. Africa for alleged treason; Anglo-French forces began to leave Port Said; **19** Lord Radcliffe's proposals for a constitution for Cyprus published; **29** Suez Canal clearing operation by UN salvage fleet began.

1957

January 1 Anglo-Egyptian treaty of 1954 abrogated by Pres. Nasser as from October 31, 1956; Saar became tenth *Land* of German Federal Republic; **5** Eisenhower Doctrine for Middle East announced; **9** Resignation of Sir Anthony Eden as Prime Minister; **10** Mr. Harold Macmillan appointed Prime Minister; **20** India's first atomic reactor, *Apsara*, inaugurated; **31** Trans-Iranian oil pipeline from Abadan to Teheran (600 m.) completed.

February 15 Mr. Gromyko replaced Mr. Shepilov as Soviet Foreign Minister; **16** The Queen flew to Portugal on State visit; **22** Duke of Edinburgh granted title of Prince.

March 1 Mass protest in Tokyo against nuclear weapon tests in Pacific; **5** Fianna Fail majority in Irish general election; **6** Ghana celebrated independence; Israeli withdrawal from Sinai completed; **11** Warning by WHO of genetic effects of radiation; **21** Homicide Act in force (death penalty

A.D.

retained only for five categories of "capital murder"); **25** European Common Market and Euratom treaties signed by France, Germany, Italy, and Benelux.

April 8 The Queen and Prince Philip arrived in France on State visit; **9** Suez Canal cleared and opened to all shipping; **17** Archbishop Makarios arrived in Athens from exile.

May 14 Petrol rationing (imposed 17.12.56) ended; **15** First British H-bomb exploded in Central Pacific near Christmas I.; **16** M. Spaak succeeded Lord Ismay as NATO Sec. Gen.; **18** The Queen and Prince Philip left for State visit to Denmark.

June 1 New Copyright Act came into force; First drawing of Premium Bond prizes; **30** The IGY opened at midnight.

July 1 First Egyptian general election since revolution of 1952; **25** Tunisia declared a republic.

August 1 Sir Christopher Hinton appointed chairman of new C.E.G.B., responsible for new nuclear power stations.

September 15 German general election (Dr. Adenauer re-elected Chancellor Oct. 22); **30** Network Three introduced by B.B.C.

October 4 First earth satellite launched by Russia; **11** Radio telescope at Jodrell Bank inaugurated.

November 3 Satellite launched with dog on board.

December 4 90 killed in Lewisham rail crash; **25** Queen's Christmas broadcast televised for the first time.

CO-EXISTENCE AND REALIGNMENT: THE NEW EUROPE

1958

January 1 Treaties establishing EEC (Common Market) and EAEC (Euratom) came into force; **3** Inauguration of West Indian Federation; Sir Edmund Hillary and New Zealand party reached South Pole; **4** *Sputnik I* disintegrated after completing 1,367 circuits of the Earth and travelling 43 million miles; **7** Mr. Macmillan left for 6-week tour of Commonwealth; **31** First American earth satellite *Explorer I* launched.

February 1 Union of Egypt and Syria in the United Arab Republic; **14** Merger of Iraq and Jordan: lasted only 6 months; **25** Campaign for Nuclear Disarmament launched under presidency of Lord Russell.

March 2 IGY Commonwealth Trans-Antarctic Expedition, led by Dr. Vivian Fuchs, completed first crossing of Antarctic (2,200 miles in 99 days); **8** Federal union between UAR and Yemen; **21** Opening of London planetarium; **27** Mr. Khrushchev elected Soviet Prime Minister in succession to Mr. Bulganin.

April 4 First CND protest march from London to Aldermaston; **17** Nationalist Party of S. Africa returned with increased majority.

May 24 Nuclear reactor at Dounreay began working.

June 1 General de Gaulle became Prime Minister of France; Clean Air Act banning emission of dark smoke came into force; **9** Gatwick Airport opened by the Queen; **20** London bus strike ended after 7 weeks; **21** Greek Government rejected British plan for Cyprus.

July 1 Conference of scientists, including Russian delegation, met at Geneva to discuss ways of detecting nuclear tests; **14** Iraq monarchy overthrown. King Faisal assassinated; establishment of Republic; **15** US marines landed in Lebanon; **17** British troops flown to Jordan to restore order; **24** First life barons and baronesses under Life Peerages Act named; **26** H.M. the Queen created her son, Charles, Prince of Wales.

August 1 British Government recognised Republic of Iraq; **5** U.S. nuclear submarine *Nautilus* passed under North Pole; **17** Britain to resume nuclear tests on Christmas Island; **23** Bombardment by Chinese of Quemoy; American warships joined Seventh Fleet in Formosa Strait.

A.D.

September 1 International conference on peaceful uses of atomic energy opened in Geneva; **7** Britain successfully fired ballistic rocket (Black Knight) from Woomera; **16** Relaxations in hire-purchase; **29** Lord Goddard retired as Lord Chief Justice; succeeded by Lord Justice Parker.

October 2 French Guinea proclaimed Republic of Guinea; **8** Martial law began in Pakistan; **9** Death of Pope Pius XII; **11** US *Pioneer* successfully launched; **21** First women peers introduced to House of Lords; **28** State opening of Parliament and Queen's Speech televised; Cardinal Roncalli, Patriarch of Venice, elected as Pope John XXIII at age of 76; **31** Conference opened in Geneva (Russia, Britain, and the US) on suspension of nuclear tests.

December 18 Empire Day to be known as Commonwealth Day; **21** General de Gaulle elected President of France; **27** Partial convertibility between £ and $ announced; UAR and Russia signed agreement on Russian co-operation in Aswan high dam project; **28** General de Gaulle announced devaluation of the franc.

1959

January 1 Batista Government in Cuba overthrown by revolutionary movement under Dr. Fidel Castro; **2** Russian launched planet round the sun (*Lunik I*); **3** Alaska became 49th state of American Union.

February 1 Votes for women rejected by Swiss national poll; **21** Mr. Macmillan arrived in Moscow on official visit; **23** Archbishop Makarios returned to Cyprus after 3-year exile. Cyprus to become a republic with Greek Pres. and Turkish Vice-Pres.; **26** State of emergency declared in Southern Rhodesia; **27** Riots in Malta dockyard due to dismissal of workers.

March 3 State of emergency declared in Nyasaland; British scientists isolated basic molecule of penicillin; **17** Uprising in Lhasa against Chinese rule; Flight of Dalai Lama to India; **24** Iraq withdrew from Baghdad Pact.

April 5 Panchen Lama took over local government of Tibet.

May 15 Jodrell Bank radioed message to United States via moon; **30** Auckland Harbour Bridge officially opened.

June 17 Mr. de Valera elected Pres. of Rep. of Ireland; **26** St. Lawrence Seaway formally opened.

July 3 Tancarville suspension bridge, opened; **5** Recovery in good condition of 3 animals from outer space; **21** First nuclear merchant ship *Savannah* launched.

September 13 Russian launched *Lunik II* which landed on moon; **25** Mr. Bandaranaike, Prime Min. of Ceylon, assassinated.

October 8 General Election returned Conservatives with 100 overall majority.

November 1 Basic travel allowance for British tourists ended; **2** First section of London-Yorkshire motorway (M1) opened to traffic; **14** Dounreay fast breeder reactor went into operation.

December 1 State of emergency in Cyprus ended; Bursting of dam at Fréjus killed 384 people; **5** Opening of 400-mile Sahara pipeline by French Prime Minister; **10** Raising of school-leaving age to 16 recommended by Crowther Report; **14** Archbishop Makarios elected first Pres. of Cyprus; **26** Soviet Antarctic expedition reached South Pole.

1960

January 1 Republic of Cameroun (formerly French Cameroons) became independent. **9** Work begun on Aswan High Dam. **12** State of emergency ended in Kenya after 8 years; Army rising in Algeria.

February 3 Mr. Macmillan addressed S. African Parliament ("wind of change" speech). **13** First French atomic test in Sahara. **17** British agreement to U.S. ballistic missile early-warning system at Fylingdales Moor,

A.D.

Yorkshire. **19** Prince Andrew born. **29** Agadir destroyed by earthquake.

March 17 New £1 notes issued in Britain. **18** Last steam locomotive of British Railways named. **21** 67 shot dead by police in Sharpeville in S. Africa: State of emergency.

April 1 U.N. Security Council adopted resolution deploring shootings in S. Africa. Dr. Hastings Banda, released from detention in S. Rhodesia. **5** Pres. de Gaulle on state visit to Britain. **9** Attempt on life of Dr. Verwoerd. **27** Togoland became independent as Togo.

May 1 U.S. aircraft engaged in military reconnaissance flight over Soviet territory shot down. **6** Wedding of Princess Margaret and Mr. A. Armstrong-Jones. **7** Mr. Leonid Brezhnev became President of Soviet Union. **16** Opening and breakdown of Summit conference in Paris. **17** The Queen Mother officially opened Kariba Dam. **21** Earthquake disaster in Chile. **25** Everest climbed by 3 Chinese; Army seized control in Turkey; End of U.S. foreign aid to Cuba.

June 25 Completion of second Saharan oil pipe-line (Edjelé to La Skirra on Tunisian coast). **26** Madagascar became independent state within French Community. **29** House of Commons rejected Wolfenden Committee's recommendations on homosexuality. **30** Belgian Congo became independent as the Congo Republic.

July 1 Ghana proclaimed a Republic; Somali Republic came into being. **6** Army mutiny in Congo. **11** Ivory Coast, Dahomey, Niger, and Upper Volta became independent; M. Tshombe, Congolese provincial leader, declared Katanga independent: M. Lumumba asked for U.N. help. **12** Congo (French), Chad and Central African Rep. became independent.

August 8 Military *coup d'état* in Laos. **16** Cyprus became independent. **25** Olympic Games opened in Rome. **29** Prime Minister of Jordan assassinated.

September 5 M. Lumumba dismissed as Prime Minister of Congo.

October 1 Nigeria became independent. **21** Royal Navy's first nuclear submarine *Dreadnought* launched by the Queen.

November 9 Senator John Kennedy elected Pres. of United States. **28** Islamic Republic of Mauritania proclaimed its independence.

December 2 Archbishop of Canterbury visited the Pope at the Vatican. **14** Fighting in Laos, between right-wing and left-wing forces. **15** Marriage of King Baudouin of Belgium. **27** Union of Ghana, Guinea, and Mali. **31** Farthing ceased to be legal tender.

1961

January 18 M. Lumumba, first Prime Min. of the independent Congo, sent to Katanga for imprisonment. **20** The Queen and the Duke of Edinburgh left for tour of India, Pakistan, Nepal and Iran.

February 13 Death of M. Lumumba announced (violent demonstrations in many countries). **15** Total eclipse of the sun visible from Europe.

March 8 First Polaris submarines arrived at Holy Loch. **14** The New English Bible (New Testament) published. **25** Russian satellite with dog aboard launched and brought safely back to earth.

April 12 Major Yuri Gagarin made first flight into space and back. **17** Unsuccessful invasion of Cuba by rebel forces. **24** Census held in Great Britain. **24** Gen. de Gaulle ordered blockade of Algeria. **25** Both sides in Laos agreed to ceasefire. **26** Collapse of mutiny in Algeria. **27** Independence of Sierra Leone.

May 1 Betting and Gaming Act came into force in Britain: betting shops opened. **5** Commander Alan Shepard made first American flight

A.D.

into space; The Queen and the Duke of Edinburgh visited Pope John XXIII at the Vatican. **16** International conference on Laos opened in Geneva; Army in South Korea seized power. **17** Guildford Cathedral consecrated. **31** Gen. Trujillo, dictator of Dominican Republic, assassinated; South Africa became a Republic and withdrew from British Commonwealth.

June 3 Meeting of Pres. Kennedy and M. Khrushchev in Vienna. **27** Enthronement of Dr. Ramsey as Archbishop of Canterbury in Canterbury Cathedral.

July 21 New Runcorn–Widnes Bridge opened.

August 13 Soviet sector of Berlin sealed off from Western sectors. **14** Jomo Kenyatta freed. **15** U.N. recognised M. Adoula's government as the central government of the Congo. **16** Dr. Hastings Banda's Malawi Congress Party won control in the Nyasaland Legislative Assembly.

September 18 Mr. Hammarskjöld killed in plane crash when flying from Leopoldville, to Ndola, to arrange ceasefire between U.N. and Katanga forces. **28** Syria seceded from the United Arab Republic.

October 1 S. Cameroons gained independence as part of Cameroun. **3** Mr. A. Armstrong-Jones created Earl of Snowdon. **10** Volcanic eruption on Tristan da Cunha; whole population evacuated to Britain. **30** Russia tested a bomb of over 60 megatons amid world-wide protest. **31** Hurricane struck British Honduras, Belize devastated; Stalin's body removed from the Lenin Mausoleum in Red Square.

November 3 Birth of son to Princess Margaret and Lord Snowdon. **7** Dr. Adenauer re-elected Chancellor of Fed. German Rep. for fourth time. **8** Official negotiations for entry of Britain into Common Market opened in Brussels. **9** The Queen and the Duke of Edinburgh left for tour of Ghana, Liberia, and Sierra Leone. **20** Admission of Russian Orthodox Church to World Council of churches. **28** South Africa's apartheid policy condemned by U.N.

December 9 Tanganyika became independent sovereign state. **15** Adolf Eichmann sentenced to death by Israeli court for crimes against the Jewish people and against humanity: executed June 1962. **17** Indian troops took over Portuguese colony of Goa. **20** Mr. Adoula and Mr. Tshombe agreed on Katanga's subordinate status. **27** Belgium and the Congo resumed diplomatic relations.

1962

January 11 Smallpox outbreak in Britain.

March 7 Publication of Royal College of Physician's Report on dangers to health from cigarette smoking. **14** Opening of 17-nation disarmament conference at Geneva. **19** End of Algerian war.

April 1 Government's "pay pause" ended. **5** Completion of Gt. St. Bernard road tunnel. **13** International agreement (40 countries) to stop oil pollution of seas and beaches. **26** Britain's first satellite, *Ariel*, launched from Cape Canaveral.

May 6 Signor Segni elected Pres. of Italy. **8** Trolleybuses ran for last time in London. **13** Dr. Radhakrishnan elected Pres. of India. **25** Consecration of new Coventry Cathedral.

June 15 Nuclear power station at Berkeley, Glos., began electricity supply to national grid. **18** Conservatives (Mr. Diefenbaker) won Canadian general election by small majority. **23** Ceasefire in Laos.

July 1 Burundi and Rwanda became independent; French colonial rule in Algeria ended; Commonwealth Immigrants Act came into force. **10** First live television between U.S. and Europe via *Telstar*.

August 6 Jamaica became independent. **14** Completion of Mont Blanc tunnel (7½ m.). **21** Maiden

A.D.
voyage of *Savannah*, world's first nuclear-powered merchant ship. **31** Trinidad and Tobago became independent.

September 3 Opening of Trans-Canada highway. **27** Republic proclaimed in Yemen.

October 9 Uganda became independent. **11** 21st Oecumenical Council opened at Rome. **24** Commencement of U.S. naval quarantine of Cuba. **28** Dismantling of missile base in Cuba agreed by Russia.

November 1 Russia sent spacecraft on 7-month journey to Mars. **20** Cuba blockade ended. **21** Ceasefire declaration by China on Sino-Indian border dispute. **30** U Thant unanimously elected Sec.-Gen. of U.N.

December 5 British nuclear device exploded underground in Nevada. **9** Tanganyika became republic and Dr. Julius Nyerere its first president. **12** British troops in control of Brunei uprising. **14** N. Rhodesia's first African dominated government formed. **15** Sir Edgar Whitehead's party lost to right-wing party in S. Rhodesian general election. **25** Europe snowbound with freezing temperatures. **31** British Transport Commission replaced by British Railways Board with Dr. Beeching as chairman.

1963

January 29 Britain was refused entry to EEC.

February 1 Nyasaland became self-governing protectorate. **8** Overthrow of Iraq government and execution of Gen. Kassim. **12** Seventeen-nation disarmament conference resumed in Geneva. **14** Harold Wilson elected leader of Labour Party.

March 5–6 First frost-free night in Britain since Dec. 22. **8** Syrian government overthrown by military coup. **17** Typhoid broke out in Zermatt. **27** Publication of Beeching Report on British Railways.

April 6 Polaris missile agreement signed between U.S. and Britain. **8** Mr. Diefenbaker's Conservative Party defeated by Liberals in Canadian general election.

May 20 Life presidency for Pres. Sukarno of Indonesia.

June 3 Death of Pope John XXIII. **14–19** Bykovsky-Tereshkova space flights (first woman astronaut). **20** House of Commons censure on Mr. John Profumo, former Sec. of State for War. **30** Pope Paul VI inaugurated.

July 26 Skopje destroyed by earthquake.

August 1 Minimum prison age raised to 17. **3** First successful solo climb on north wall of Eiger by Michel Darbellay. **5** Partial nuclear-test ban treaty signed in Moscow by America, Russia, and Britain. **7** Security Council resolution to stop sale and shipment of arms to S. Africa. **8** Glasgow-London mail train robbery (£2·5 million). **21** Buddhists arrested and martial law imposed in South Vietnam. **28** Great Negro "freedom march" on Washington. **31** The "hot-line" linking Kremlin with White House went into service.

September 16 New state of Malaysia (Malaya, Singapore, North Borneo and Sarawak) came into being. **17** Malaysia broke off diplomatic relations with Indonesia; Fylingdales ballistic missile early warning station came into operation. **25** Denning report on Profumo affair published.

October 1 Nigeria became a republic within the Commonwealth. **15** Dr. Adenauer succeeded by Prof. Ludwig Erhard. **18** Mr. Macmillan resigned as Prime Minister: succeeded by the Earl of Home. **23** Robbins report on higher education published.

November 1 Diem oligarchy of S. Vietnam overthrown by military coup. **7** Sir Alec Douglas-Home elected at Kinross and W. Perthshire. **18** Opening of Dartford tunnel. **22** Assassination of

A.D.
President Kennedy in Dallas, Texas; Vice-President Lyndon Johnson sworn in as new President.

December 9 Zanzibar became independent. **12** Kenya became independent. **31** Dissolution of Federation of Rhodesia and Nyasaland.

1964

January 4–6 Pope Paul made pilgrimage to Holy Land.

February 11 Fighting between Greeks and Turks at Limassol, Cyprus.

March 10 Birth of Prince Edward. **27** U.N. peacekeeping force in Cyprus operational.

April 9 First Greater London Council election; Labour 64, Conservatives 36. **10** Mr. Macmillan declined earldom and Order of the Garter. **13** Mr. Ian Smith became Prime Minister of S. Rhodesia. **21** Opening of BBC-2. **26** Tanganyika and Zanzibar united (United Republic of Tanzania).

May 1 Birth of a daughter to Princess Margaret and Lord Snowdon. **26** Typhoid outbreak in Aberdeen. **27** Death of Jawaharlal Nehru.

June 2 Mr. Lal Bahadur Shastri elected Prime Minister of India. **5** First flight into space of Britain's *Blue Streak* rocket. **12** Life imprisonment imposed on Nelson Mandela and others in Rivonia trial, Pretoria; 20-year treaty of friendship signed between Soviet Union and E. Germany.

July 2 Enactment of U.S. Civil Rights Bill. **6** Nyasaland became independent state of Malawi. **10** M. Tshombe succeeded M. Adoula as Prime Minister of the Congo. **15** Mr. Mikoyan succeeded Mr. Brezhnev as President of the Soviet Union. **27** Last appearance of Sir Winston Churchill in House of Commons.

August 2 U.S. destroyer attacked by N. Vietnam torpedo boats off N. Vietnam. **5** Congolese rebels captured Stanleyville; U.S. air raid on N. Vietnam.

September 2 Indonesian landings in Malaya. **4** Opening of new Forth bridge. **7** People's Republic of the Congo declared by Congolese rebels. **21** Malta became independent.

October 5 The Queen and the Duke of Edinburgh in Canada on week's visit. **10** Opening of Olympic Games in Tokyo. **15** Mr. Khrushchev replaced in posts of First Secretary of the CPSU and Prime Minister by Mr. Brezhnev and Mr. Kosygin; General election in Britain; Labour won with overall majority of five. **16** Mr. Harold Wilson became Prime Minister; China exploded an atomic device. **24** Northern Rhodesia achieved independence as Republic of Zambia; S. Rhodesia became officially known as Rhodesia. **26** Government proposed 15% import surcharge and export tax rebate to deal with balance of payments crisis.

November 2 Deposition of King Saud of Saudi Arabia and accession of his brother Faisal. **3** U.S. Presidential election: sweeping victory for President Johnson over Senator Goldwater. **17** Government to ban export of arms to S. Africa. **24** Belgian paratroops landed at Stanleyville to rescue rebel-held hostages.

December 2 The Pope welcomed in Bombay. **12** Kenya became Republic within Commonwealth. **16** Statement of Intent on productivity, prices and incomes signed by Government, T.U.C. and Employers' organisations.

1965

January 21 Prime Minister of Iran assassinated. **24** Death of Sir Winston Churchill.

February 1 The Queen and Duke of Edinburgh in Ethiopia on state visit. **7** First U.S. retaliatory raids against N. Vietnam. **18** Gambia became independent. **24** U.S. jets bombed Vietcong in S. Vietnam.

A.D.
March 7 First of 3,500 American marines landed in S. Vietnam. **18** Alexei Leonov became first man to leave a spaceship and float in space. **25** Defeat of Mrs. Bandaranaike in Ceylon elections; Mr. Senanayake became Prime Minister.

April 6 Launching of *Early Bird* commercial communication satellite; Cancellation of TSR 2. **29** Australian troops to be sent to S. Vietnam.

May 11 Cyclone and tidal wave disaster in E. Pakistan killing 16,000 people. **13** Conservatives made big gains in U.K. local government elections. **18** The Queen and the Duke of Edinburgh on 10-day state visit to Fed. German Republic. **28** 267 miners killed in Indian colliery disaster.

June 1 237 miners killed in Japanese colliery explosion. **7** 128 miners killed in Yugoslav mine disaster. **19** Pres. Ben Bella of Algeria deposed by Revolutionary Council under Col. Boumedienne.

July 15 King Constantine of Greece dismissed his Prime Minister, Mr. Papandreou. **22** Sir Alec Douglas-Home resigned as leader of the Conservative Party; succeeded by Mr. Edward Heath (July 28).

August 1 Television ban on cigarette advertising. **9** Singapore seceded from Malaysia. **11** Negro riots in Los Angeles. **12** Appointment of first woman High Court judge. **24** Pres. Nasser and King Faisal signed ceasefire agreement in Yemen.

September 1 Pakistan forces crossed Kashmir ceasefire line. **12** American division 20,000 strong landed in S. Vietnam: General election in Norway: Labour Government defeated. **21** British Petroleum struck oil in North Sea.

October 1 Attempt to overthrow Pres. Sukarno of Indonesia: reprisals against communists. **8** Rhodesian independence talks failed. **13** Pres. Kasavubu of the Congo dismissed Mr. Tshombe. **17** Demonstrations throughout U.S. and in London against war in Vietnam. **22** Pakistan and India accepted ceasefire call of Security Council. **26** Dr. Horace King elected Speaker of House of Commons. **28** Parliament passed Bill abolishing death penalty for murder.

November 11 UDI in Rhodesia: Britain declared régime illegal and introduced economic sanctions. **20** Security Council called on all states to sever economic relations with Rhodesia, and urged oil embargo. **25** General Mobuto deposed Pres. Kasavubu.

December 8 The Second Vatican Council closed. **9** Mr. Mikoyan retired as President of the Soviet Union; replaced by Mr. Nikolai Podgorny. **17** Britain imposed oil embargo on Rhodesia. **22** 70 m.p.h. speed limit on British roads came into force.

1966

January 15 Army coup in Nigeria; Fed Prime Min. killed. **16** General Ironsi, C.-in-C. of Nigerian army, took over command to restore law and order. **31** U.S. bombing of N. Vietnam resumed after 37 days; British Government banned all trade with Rhodesia.

February 3 Successful soft landing on moon by *Luna 9*. **24** Army coup in Ghana while Dr. Nkrumah absent in Far East.

March 4 Britain recognised new régime in Ghana. **23** Historic meeting in Rome of Archbishop of Canterbury and the Pope. **31** British General Election: Labour victory with overall majority of 97.

May 16 Seamen's strike began (ended 1 July). **26** British Guiana became independent state of Guyana.

June 11 Commonwealth Day (the Queen's official birthday) to be observed on this date in future.

July 3 Resignation of Mr. Frank Cousins as Minister of Technology over prices and incomes policy. **6** Malawi became a Republic. **20** Prime

A.D.
Minister announced six-month freeze on wages, salaries, and prices. **21** Successful landing of *Gemini 10*: docking manœuvre and space walk. **29** Mutiny by section of Nigerian army; General Ironsi killed. **30** World Cup won by England.

August 1–2 Plenary session of Central Committee of Chinese Communist Party: Marshal Lin Piao officially recognised as Mao Tse-tung's successor. **3** Post Office to become public corporation. **4** Sir Edmund Compton named Britain's first Ombudsman. **10** Cabinet reshuffle: Mr. George Brown became Foreign Secretary. **11** Indonesian-Malaysian peace agreement signed in Djakarta. **18** Start of the "cultural revolution" in China; Earthquake in E. Turkey: over 2,000 killed.

September 5 Selective Employment Tax came into force. **6** Dr. Verwoerd assassinated in Parliament, Cape Town. **8** Opening of new Severn road bridge. **13** Mr. John Vorster chosen as S. Africa's new Prime Minister. **30** Bechuanaland became Republic of Botswana.

October 4 Basutoland became independent kingdom of Lesotho. **21** Aberfan disaster avalanche from coal tip slid down upon mining village killing 144, including 116 children.

November 23 Red Guards demanded dismissal of Liu Shao-ch'i, China's Head of State. **26** Australian General Election: Liberal–Country Party Coalition Government led by Mr. Harold Holt returned; New Zealand General Election: Mr. Keith Holyoake's National Party returned. **30** Barbados became independent.

December 1 Dr. Kiesinger took office as Chancellor of German Federal Republic. **2** Meeting of Prime Minister and Mr. Ian Smith of Rhodesia on board H.M.S. *Tiger* off Gibraltar. **5** Mr. Ian Smith rejected working document. **16** U.N. Security Council voted for British resolution for mandatory sanctions (including oil) against Rhodesia.

1967

January 18 Mr. Jeremy Thorpe, elected Leader of Liberal Party following resignation of Mr. Grimond. **27** 3 American astronauts killed in fire during ground test at Cape Kennedy.

February 9 Historic meeting between the Queen and Mr. Kosygin at Buckingham Palace. **22** Pres. Sukarno of Indonesia surrendered rule to Gen. Suharto.

March 12 Mrs. Indira Gandhi re-elected Prime Minister of India. **13** Gaullists gained bare majority in French National Assembly. **18** *Torrey Canyon* ran aground off Land's End with 120,000 tons of crude oil aboard. **22** Army in Sierra Leone seized power.

April 13 Conservatives gained landslide victory in GLC elections. **21** Army coup in Greece. **27** Opening in Montreal of Expo 67.

May 11 Britain presented application to join Common Market. **28** Francis Chichester arrived in Plymouth after solo circumnavigation of world. **30** Secession of Eastern Region (Biafra) from Nigerian Federation.

June 5 Outbreak of six-day war in Middle East: lightning attack by Israel caused severe Arab losses and capture of territory, mainly from Egypt and Jordan. **17** China exploded her first H-bomb. **28** Israel took over control of the Old City of Jerusalem.

July 1 Mr. Tshombe kidnapped in mid-flight and arrested in Algeria; Colour television began in Britain on BBC-2. **7** Francis Chichester knighted by the Queen at Greenwich. **10** Last use of steam engines on British Rail Southern Region. **12** Negro riots in Newark, N.J. **13** Public Record Act passed: public records now closed for only 30 years. **18** Defence cuts announced: withdrawal from East of Suez by mid-1970s.

August 3 Aberfan tribunal report blamed N.C.B. for the disaster; Lord Robens' resignation not

A.D.
accepted. **13** U.S. bombed N. Vietnam 10 miles from Chinese border.

September 3 Chinese Red Guards ordered to cease violence: Sweden's traffic changed from left to right. **20** Launching on Clydebank of Cunard Liner *Queen Elizabeth II*. **27** *Queen Mary* arrived at Southampton at end of her last transatlantic voyage.

October 9 Road Safety Act dealing with drink and driving came into force. **22** Big demonstrations against Vietnam war in Washington, London and other capitals. **25** Foot-and-mouth epidemic began at Oswestry. **30** Russians performed first automatic link-up and separation of unmanned spacecraft.

November 14 State visit to Malta by the Queen. **26** Lisbon area floods—464 dead. **27** End of eight-week unofficial London dock strike. **29** Aden independent as Republic of South Yemen.

December 3 First human heart transplant operation at Cape Town. **17** Mr. Harold Holt, Australian P.M., drowned in swimming accident.

1968

January 9 Senator John G. Gorton elected P.M. of Australia. **23** Seizure by N. Korea of *USS Pueblo* off N. Korean coast.

February 13 U.S. planes bombed outskirts of Saigon. **18** Introduction of British Standard Time. **19** Decision of Rann of Kutch Tribunal: nine-tenths to India and rest to Pakistan. **24** End of 25-day defence of Hué by Vietcong.

March 6 Africans in Rhodesia hanged in defiance of the Queen's reprieve. **12** Mauritius became independent. **14** Rush for gold in leading financial centres: U.S. Bank rate raised. Stock Exchange and Banks closed in Britain; Resignation of Mr. George Brown as Foreign Secretary. **17–18** Summit Meeting of Western Central Bankers: two-tier system for gold agreed.

April 4 Assassination of Martin Luther King at Memphis, Tennessee.

May 10 Violent clashes between students and security police in Paris.

June 5–6 Senator Robert Kennedy shot and died in Los Angeles. **10** National Health prescription charge introduced. **26** Pierre Trudeau's Liberal Party won Canadian election. **30** Gaullists increased their majority in French election.

July 4 Mr. Alec Rose landed at Portsmouth after sailing single-handed round the world. **29** Pope issued encyclical condemning all forms of artificial birth control.

August 20 Soviet and Warsaw Pact forces entered Czechoslovakia. **27** Death of Princess Marina, Duchess of Kent.

September 6 Swaziland independent. **11** Departure of Soviet troops from Prague. **15** Worst flooding in England since 1953. **16** Two-tier postal system began in Britain. **21–22** Clashes between students and police in Mexico City. **26** Theatres Act, abolishing censorship, in force. **27** French vetoed British entry into Common Market.

October 1 Federal Nigerian troops captured Okigwi in Biafra. **5** Clashes between police and crowds in Londonderry (beginning of disturbances in N. Ireland). **9** H.M.S. *Fearless* talks on Rhodesia failed. **12** Olympic Games in Mexico City. **16** Treaty signed providing for stationing of Soviet troops in Czechoslovakia. **27** Czechoslovakia became a two-state federation.

November 8 Mr Richard Nixon won U.S. Presidential elections.

December 28 Israeli commandos destroyed 13 Arab aircraft at Beirut after two Israeli airliners attacked by Arabs at Athens.

A.D.
1969

January 16 First manned docking operation in orbit by Soviet *Soyuz 4* and *5*.

March 2 Maiden flight of French-built *Concorde*; Mrs. Golda Meir chosen as Israel's P.M. **7** Opening of London's Victoria Line. **13** B.P. found Alaskan oil deposits.

April 9 Maiden flight of British-built *Concorde*. **14** Lin Piao declared Mao's successor. **17** Mr. Dubcek replaced as first Secretary of Czechoslovak Communist Party by Dr. Husak. **21** British Army units to guard key points in N. Ireland. **23** Biafran capital of Umuahia captured by Federal forces. **28** Gen. de Gaulle resigned as President of France after defeat on referendum.

May 1 Maj. James Chichester-Clark became P.M. of N. Ireland after resignation of Mr. Terence O'Neill. **12** Voting age became 18.

June 15 M. Georges Pompidou elected President of France. **18** Government dropped plans to put legal restraints on unofficial strikers in return for T.U.C. pledge to deal with disputes. **24** Resignation of Sir Humphrey Gibbs as Governor of Rhodesia.

July 1 Investiture of Prince Charles as 21st Prince of Wales at Caernarvon Castle. **8** Church of England rejected scheme for unity with Methodists; Methodists accepted it. **21** Armstrong and Aldrin first men to land on the Moon at 3·56 a.m. (B.S.T.). **22** Prince Juan Carlos named future King of Spain by Gen. Franco. **31** Halfpennies ceased to be legal tender in Britain.

August 12 Three-day street battle in Londonderry after apprentice boys march. **19** Army took over security and police in N. Ireland.

September 10 Barricades dismantled in Belfast and Army's "peace line" erected. **28** Herr Brandt became Chancellor of W. Germany.

October 10 Hunt Committee report on N. Ireland recommended disarming police and disbanding B specials. **14** 50p (10s.) piece introduced.

November 11 Owners of *Torrey Canyon* agreed to pay £1·5 million each to Britain and France for oil damage. **14** Colour programmes began on BBC-1 and ITV. **24** Soviet Union and U.S. ratified Nuclear Non-Proliferation Treaty. **25** U.S. renounced use of biological warfare.

December 1–2 EEC Summit Meeting at The Hague agreed on negotiations for British entry by June 1970. **16–18** Houses of Commons and Lords voted for permanent abolition of the death penalty. **27** Ruling Liberal Democratic Party won sweeping victory in Japanese General Election.

1970

January 12 Gen. Effilong proclaimed end of Biafran secession.

February 1 Pope reaffirmed celibacy as a fundamental law of the Latin church; Serious clash on Golan Heights between Israel and Syria. **5** Special Public Order Act for N. Ireland passed.

March 2 Rhodesia proclaimed a republic. **16** Publication of the complete *New English Bible*.

April 18 Splashdown of *Apollo 13* after complex rescue operation (Lovell, Halse and Swigert). **21** Pres. Nixon announced withdrawal of another 150,000 U.S. troops from Vietnam in next year. **28** ELDO decided to abandon British *Blue Streak* in favour of French rocket. **30** U.S. combat troops entered Cambodia.

May 4 4 students shot dead during demonstration at Kent state University, U.S.A. **15** S. Africa expelled from International Olympic Committee. **22** Britain cancelled S. African cricket tour.

June 4 Tonga independent. **7** Fighting between Jordan troops and Palestinian guerrillas. **11** Warmest night in Britain for a century. **18** General Election in Britain; Conservative overall majority

A.D.
of 30. **23** Arrival of steamship *Great Britain* at Bristol from Falklands. **26** Mr. Dubcek expelled from Czechoslovak Communist Party. **29** British Government to end restrictions on sale of Council houses; Britain made third application to join EEC; Circular 10/70 issued, with Conservative policy on secondary education.

July 6 Government to resume arms sales to S. Africa. **30** Damages awarded to 28 deformed thalidomide children and their parents.

August 2 Army fired rubber bullets during Belfast disturbances. **7** Ceasefire in force along Suez Canal.

September 4 World Council of Churches proposed financial aid to African guerrillas. **17** Civil War in Jordan between King Hussein's army and Palestinian guerillas. **27** Agreement to end Jordan Civil War signed in Cairo by King Hussein, guerrilla leaders and leaders of eight Arab states. **29** Death of Pres. Nasser (later succeeded by Mr. Anwar Sadat).

October 15 Canonisation of 40 English and Welsh martyrs. **24** Dr. Salvador Allende, Marxist Socialist, elected President of Chile.

November 9 Death of Gen. de Gaulle. **20** U.N. voted to admit China but without necessary two-thirds majority. **21** U.S. bombed N. Vietnam after two-year halt.

December 18 Divorce became legal in Italy.

1971

January 1 Divorce Reform Act (1969) came into force; Kentucky mine disaster. **2** Ibrox Park disaster in Glasgow. **3** Open University on the air. **10** Highest ever January temperatures recorded in London. **25** Pres. Obote of Uganda deposed by Maj. Gen. Amin, Army Commander.

February 4 Financial collapse of Rolls Royce Ltd. **7** Male referendum in Switzerland gave women right to vote in national elections. **15** Decimal Day in Britain. **24** Immigration Bill published, placing Commonwealth and alien immigrants under one system of control.

March 11 Landslide victory for Mrs. Gandhi in Indian General Election. **20** Resignation of Maj. Chichester-Clark as N. Ireland's P.M. (succeeded by Mr Brian Faulkner). **26** Civil war erupted in E. Pakistan after arrest of Sheikh Mujibar Rahman. **29** Lieut. Calley convicted of murder of 22 people in My Lai massacre in S.Vietnam. **30** Soviet Union agreed to outlaw germ warfare.

April 17 Egypt, Syria and Libya formed new Federation of Arab republics.

May 10 Flotation of Deutsche Mark and Dutch guilder following Common Market currency crisis. **20–21** Heath–Pompidou talks on Common Market in Paris. **27** 15-year treaty of friendship and co-operation signed by Egypt and Russia.

June 10 Lifting of 21-year embargo on trade with China by U.S. **21** Labour Party victory in Malta General Election, Mr. Dom Mintoff Prime Minister. **30** Russian space tragedy; 3 astronauts killed just before touchdown.

August 9 Internment without trial introduced in Northern Ireland. **22** Right wing coup in Bolivia. **23** Foreign Exchange markets reopened: sterling allowed to float upwards to new parity against the U.S. dollar.

September. 9 Parliament recalled for special debate on Northern Ireland. **24** Britain expelled 105 Russian diplomats for espionage. **27** Meeting of Prime Ministers Heath, Lynch and Faulkner at Chequers.

October 26 U.N. General Assembly voted to admit China and expel Taiwan. **28** House of Commons (and Lords) voted in favour of joining Common Market on terms presented by Government: 69

A.D.
Labour M.P.s voted with the Government. **31** Explosion at Post Office tower in London wrecked three floors.

November 16 Compton Report on Interrogation in Northern Ireland found "some ill-treatment but no brutality." **25** Terms of a Rhodesia settlement announced.

December 3 Outbreak of Indo-Pakistan war after prolonged friction and many border disputes. **17** End of Indo-Pakistan War. **18** Pres. Yahya Khan of Pakistan ousted and succeeded by Mr. Ali Bhutto; Group of Ten agreed on terms for re-alignment of currencies. **24** Signor Leone elected new President of Italy after 24 ballots. **29** British troops began withdrawal from Malta.

1972

January 9 *Queen Elizabeth* destroyed by fire in Hong Kong harbour; Miners' strike began with widespread power cuts and industrial disruption. **12** Sheikh Mujibar Rahman appointed Prime Minister of Bangladesh. **13** Dr. Busia's government in Ghana overthrown. **22** Britain, Ireland, Norway and Denmark signed European Economic Community treaty. **30** "Bloody Sunday" in Londonderry: 13 civilians killed.

February 9 State of emergency in power crisis declared and large-scale power cuts began. **15** Over 1·5 million workers laid off at height of power crisis. **17** Second reading of European Communities Bill carried by only eight votes. **18** Wilberforce Enquiry's terms for settling the miners' dispute published. **22** Seven killed in IRA bomb explosion at Aldershot. **25** Miners voted to return to work.

March 4 Belfast restaurant explosion killed two and injured 136. **29** Tutankhamun exhibition opened at the British Museum; Berlin Wall opened for the first time in six years. **30** Direct rule came into force in Northern Ireland.

April 10 46 countries signed a convention outlawing biological weapons. **18** Bangladesh admitted to the Commonwealth. **19** National Industrial Relations Court ordered 14-day cooling-off period in rail dispute.

May 3 Church of England Synod failed to reach required vote in favour of Anglican-Methodist union. **9** Black September hijackers killed at Lydda airport by Israeli soldiers. **15** The Queen began state visit to France. **22** President Nixon arrived in Moscow for talks; Ceylon became the republic of Sri Lanka. **23** Pearce Commission reported that the Rhodesians were not generally in favour of settlement proposals. **28** Duke of Windsor died in Paris.

June 6 430 killed in Wankie Colliery explosion in Rhodesia. **16** 120 killed in tunnel rail crash near Soissons, France; 5 burglars caught in Watergate building, Democratic Party's campaign H.Q. **23** Government decision to "float" the pound.

July 9 Ceasefire in Northern Ireland ended and six people were shot dead in Belfast. **28** Start of national dock strike following rejection of Jones-Aldington proposals for the modernisation of the docks.

August 4 President Amin ordered expulsion of 40,000 British Asians in Uganda. **28** Prince William of Gloucester killed in air race crash.

September 1 Iceland extended fishing limits from 12 to 50 miles. **5** Arab guerrillas held Israeli athletes hostage in Munich: the hostages, 5 guerrillas and a policeman were killed in gun battle at Fürstenfeldbruk airport. **25** Darlington conference on the future of Northern Ireland opened.

October 2 Denmark voted to join European Economic Community. **5** Congregational Church in England and Wales and Presbyterian Church of England combined to form the United Reformed Church. **10** Sir John Betjeman appointed Poet Laureate. **13** Bank rate abolished (now called minimum lending rate).

A.D.
November 6 Government imposed immediate 90-day freeze on prices, pay, rent and dividend increases. **7** President Nixon elected for a further term of office. **19** Herr Brandt re-elected in West German poll. **20** Silver Wedding anniversary of the Queen and Duke of Edinburgh.

December 2 Mr. G. Whitlam became first Labour Prime Minister in Australia since 1946. **18** United States resumed bombing of North Vietnam. **21** Treaty signed between West and East Germany. **23** Earthquake in Nicaragua devastated the capital Managua.

1973

January 1 Britain, Ireland and Denmark became members of the European Economic Community. **27** Vietnam ceasefire agreement signed.

February 1 The Common Agricultural Policy of the EEC came into operation. **5** First Protestant loyalists detained without trial in Northern Ireland. **12** First group of American prisoners released from North Vietnam. **21** Israeli fighters brought down a Libyan Boeing 727 with the loss of 104 lives.

March 1 Fine Gael and Labour Party coalition won Irish General Election: Mr. Liam Cosgrave became Prime Minister. **8** One killed and 238 injured in two bomb blasts in central London. **9** Result of Northern Ireland referendum showed 591,820 in favour of retaining links with Britain, and 6,463 for links with the Republic. **11** Gaullists and their allies won an absolute majority of seats in the French General Election. **18** Icelandic patrol vessel fired live shots across bow of a British trawler. **29** Last American soldier left Vietnam.

April 1 VAT introduced in Britain.

May 7 President Nixon denied all knowledge of Watergate. **10** Elections held for 36 new metropolitan district councils. **11** Charges dismissed in Pentagon papers case in Washington. **17** Senate Select Committee hearings on Watergate opened. **18** Royal Navy frigates sent to protect British trawlers in disputed 50-mile limit off Iceland. **25** 3 American astronauts docked with crippled Skylab. **31** Mr. Erskine Childers succeeded Mr. de Valera as President of Ireland.

June 1 Greece declared a republic. **7** Skylab astronauts freed solar panels and saved mission. **21** Mr. Brezhnev and President Nixon signed agreement on arms limitation.

July 31 First sitting of new Ulster Assembly ended in chaos.

August 2 50 killed in Summerland fire at Douglas, Isle of Man. **19** Mr. George Papadopoulos became first President of Greece.

September 3 Dr. Henry Kissinger became U.S. Secretary of State. **7** Mr. Len Murray succeeded Mr. Vic Feather as TUC General Secretary. **10** Bombs in London stations injured 13 people. **11** Allende government overthrown in Chile. **14** Death of King Gustav of Sweden. **20** Bomb exploded in Chelsea barracks. **25** Skylab astronauts returned after 59 days in space.

October 6 Start of Arab–Israeli war. **8** Britain's first commercial radio station opened. **10** Mr. Spiro Agnew resigned as Vice-President of U.S.A. **12** General Peron became President of Argentina and his wife Vice-President. **16** Government placed embargo on arms sales to Middle East. **17** Arab oil producers announced cut in oil supplies until Israel withdrew from occupied territories. **22** UN proposal for ceasefire agreed by Israel, Egypt and Jordan (marred by subsequent clashes). **31** 3 Provisional IRA leaders freed from Mountjoy prison by hijacked helicopter.

November 8 End of "cod war" between Britain and Iceland. **12** Miners started overtime ban and ambulance drivers began selective strikes. **14** Wedding of Princess Anne and Captain Mark Philips. **25** Army coup in Greece.

December 5 50 mile/h speed limit imposed to conserve fuel. **6** Mr. Gerald Ford became Vice-Presi-

A.D.
dent of U.S.A. **12** Rail drivers' union ASLEF began ban on overtime. **13** Further series of measures to conserve fuel announced: three-day working week from 31 December. **17** Emergency budget included cuts in consumer credit and reduction in public expenditure. **20** Admiral Carrero Blanco, Prime Minister of Spain, assassinated in Madrid. **23** Iran announced doubling of price of Persian Gulf oil. **28** Power engineers called off ban on out-of-hours working.

1974

January 1 Direct rule by U.K. Govt.in N. Ireland ended: New Ulster Executive took office; Mrs. Golda Meir won narrow victory in Israeli General Election. **8** Lord Carrington became Secretary for Energy at head of new department. **9** Parliament recalled for two-day debate on energy crisis. **18** Israel and Egypt signed agreement on separation of forces. **22** Loyalists expelled from N. Ireland Assembly after angry scenes.

February 4 Miners' strike ballot showed 81% in favour of strike action. **7** Prime Minister called for General Election on 28 February; Island of Grenada achieved independence. **10** Miners' strike began. **28** Election in Britain resulted in no clear majority.

March 4 Mr. Edward Heath resigned and a minority Labour Government took office. **9** Britain returned to five-day week. **11** Miners returned to work.

April 10 Resignation of Mrs. Golda Meir and her Cabinet after 5 years as Prime Minister. **14** Heaviest fighting on Golan Heights and Mount Hermon since ceasefire in Oct. 1973. **24** General election in S. Africa: Nationalist Party returned for seventh successive time; Progressive Party won 6 seats. **25** Army uprising in Portugal: authoritarian régime in power since 1926 overthrown.

May 6 Resignation of Herr Brandt on discovery of chancellery aide spying for E. Germany. **15** General Spinola became President of Portugal; In Israeli village of Ma'alot schoolchildren killed when Israeli troops stormed school where children held hostage by Arab terrorists. **16** Herr Schmidt became Chancellor of West Germany. **19** Victory for M. Giscard d'Estaing in French general election. **28** Collapse of N.I. executive. **29** Ulster Workers' Council called off strike; Assembly suspended: direct rule from Westminster resumed.

June 1 Explosion at Flixborough Nypro chemical works: 29 dead. **3** Mr. Rabin became Prime Minister of Israel; Michael Gaughan, Irish hunger striker, died at Parkhurst. **17** Bomb exploded beside Westminster Hall, injuring 11 people. **27** Foreign husbands and fiancés of British women to be allowed to live in Britain.

July 9 Canadian general election gave Trudeau overall majority of 18. **13** Final Report of Ervin Senate Watergate Committee published. **15** Coup d'etat in Cyprus: President Makarios overthrown and replaced by Nicos Sampson. **17** Bomb exploded with no warning in Tower of London: one killed, 41 injured. **18** Abolition of Pay Board and end of statutory incomes policy. **20** Turkish invasion of Cyprus. **26** Junta in Greece collapsed: Mr. Karamanlis returned to power. **24** Supreme Court ordered surrender of 64 White House tape recordings subpoenaed by Mr. Leon Jaworski, the special Watergate prosecutor. **27–30** Three articles of impeachment adopted by Judiciary Committee of the House of Representatives against President Nixon.

August 8 President Nixon resigned. **9** Mr. Gerald Ford sworn in as 38th President of USA. **14** Failure of peace talks on Cyprus: Turks renewed offensive and took control of most of north-east third of island. **26** Guinea-Bissau became independent.

September 8 President Ford granted full pardon to Richard Nixon. **12** Emperor Haile Selassie deposed by military command. **30** General Spinola

A.D.

resigned as President of Portuguese Republic: succeeded by General Francisco da Costa Gomes.

October 5 Two bombs in Guildford public houses killed five people and injured 70. **10** General Election in Britain: Labour returned with overall majority of 3. **15** Rioting in the Maze prison. **31** Hostages held for 6 days at Scheveningen gaol freed by Dutch commandos.

November 2–3 Summit meeting between President Ford and Mr. Brezhnev at Vladivostok. **7** 2 killed in bomb attack on Woolwich pubs. **17** Greece held first general elections since 1967: victory for Mr. Constantine Karamanlis. **21** 21 killed and 120 injured in bomb blasts in two Birmingham bars. **29** Anti-Terrorism Bill proscribing the IRA and giving police wider powers received Royal Assent.

December 3 Defence cuts announced: £4,700 million over next 10 years. **7** Archbishop Makarios returned to Cyprus. **9** Mr. Tanaka resigned as Prime Minister of Japan. **11** House of Commons voted against restoration of capital punishment for terrorism. **18–22** New wave of bombs in London: outside Selfridges; at Harrods; and at the home of Mr. Edward Heath. **25** Devastation of Darwin, Australia, by cyclone Tracy.

1975

January 1 Watergate defendants Mitchell, Haldeman, Ehrlichman and Mardian found guilty of conspiracy and of obstruction of justice. **24** Dr. Coggan enthroned 101st Archbishop of Canterbury. **25** End of democracy in Bangladesh: Shaikh Mujibur Rahman became President of one-party state.

February 11 Mrs. Thatcher elected leader of the Conservative Party. **13** Declaration by Turkish Cypriots of separate state in Cyprus.

March 13 Portugal's new Supreme Revolutionary Council headed by President Gomes took power. **25** Assassination of King Faisal of Saudi Arabia. **26** Evacuation of Hué by S. Vietnamese forces. **30** Da Nang abandoned by S. Vietnamese forces after panic and confusion.

April 1 Departure of Marshal Lon Nol from besieged capital Phnom Penh. **17** Phnom Penh government surrendered to Khmer Rouge. **21** President Thieu resigned as N. Vietnamese forces encircled Saigon. **23** Massive airlift of refugees from Vietnam to USA. **25** Elections in Portugal the first for 50 years: Socialist Party (PSP) 38% of votes, the largest single party. **30** End of Vietnam war.

May 30–31 Coldest May night in Britain since records began.

June 5 UK voted "Yes" by 2 to 1 majority in EEC referendum. **5** Reopening of Suez Canal to international shipping after 8 years of closure. **9** First live radio broadcast of House of Commons sitting. **12** Mrs. Gandhi convicted of illegally using Government officials in her campaign for Parliament in 1971.

July 1 Mr. S. S. Ramphal succeeded Mr. Arnold Smith as Commonwealth Secretary-General. **5** Cape Verde Islands achieved independence from Portugal. **11** £6 a week limit on pay increases till 1 Aug. 1976; Independence of Portuguese Sao Tomé and Principe. **29** Military coup in Nigeria: new head of state Brigadier Murtala Mohammed.

August 7 Hottest August day in London since records began in 1940 (32·3°C). **15** Assassination of Mujibur Rahman of Bangladesh. **27–28** Bombs at Caterham and London.

September 9 Return after 5½ years of exile of Prince Sihanouk to Cambodia as titular head of state. **16** Independence of Papua New Guinea. **24** Government announced £175m package of measures to check unemployment; Dougal Haston and Doug Scott climbed Everest by south-west face.

October 3 Dr. Herrema, a Dutch industrialist, kidnapped in Limerick: released 7 Nov. **15** Iceland unilaterally extended its fishing rights from 50 to 200 miles. **21** In Britain, unemployment rose to over one million for first time since the war. **23**

A.D.

Bomb placed under car of Mr. Hugh Fraser MP in London killed Professor Fairley, leading cancer expert. **26** In Beirut, clashes between right-wing Christian Phalangists and left-wing Muslims developed into full-scale battles.

November 3 Queen formally inaugurated the flow of North Sea oil from the BP Forties field. **10** Independence of Angola after 500 years of Portuguese rule. **11** Australia's Labour Government, led by Gough Whitlam, dismissed by the Governor-General, Sir John Kerr. **22** Prince Juan Carlos crowned King of Spain. **25** Surinam (Dutch Guiana) became independent.

December 2 BAC signed contract to supply Iran with Rapier anti-aircraft missile system. **4** End of detention without trial in N. Ireland after 4½ years. **10** First shots fired in "cod war". **11** House of Commons voted 361–232 not to restore death penalty; End of Balcombe Street siege in London: Mr. and Mrs. Matthews held in flat by IRA terrorists since 6 Dec. **14** End of Dutch train siege at Beilen; Landslide victory in Australia for Liberal Country Party. **18** Education Bill compelling comprehensive school education published. **29** Sex Discrimination and Equal Pay Acts came into force.

1976

January 19 Government majority of 158 at end of 4-day devolution debate. **21** Concorde entered supersonic passenger service.

February 11 Recognition of MPLA as legal government of Angola by OAU. **13** Assassination of General Murtala Mohammed, Nigerian head of state, in unsuccessful coup. **19** Iceland broke off diplomatic relations with Britain over fishing dispute.

March 5 Ulster Convention dissolved: direct rule from Westminster continued. **16** Resignation of Mr. Wilson as Prime Minister. **19** Official announcement of separation of Princess Margaret and Lord Snowdon. **24** Senora Perón of Argentina deposed. **25** Basil Hume installed as Archbishop of Westminster.

April 5 Mr. James Callaghan became Prime Minister. **27** Britain began exporting North Sea oil.

May 10 Resignation of Mr. Jeremy Thorpe as leader of the Liberal Party. **12** Mr. Jo Grimond agreed to resume leadership of the Liberal Party for a temporary period. **24** Concordes from England and France flew to Washington for first time. **28** Soviet-American treaty controlling underground nuclear explosions for non-military purposes signed.

June 1 Interim agreement signed in Oslo ending "cod war" between Britain and Iceland. **16** Riots began in African township of Soweto near Johannesburg. **24** Vietnam reunified: recognition by British. **27** Gen. Antonio Ramalho Eanes, Army Chief of Staff, elected President of Portugal. **29** Independence of Seychelles as republic within Commonwealth.

July 2 Government emergency powers to control water shortage in Britain. **4** Israeli attack on Entebbe airport to free 100 Israeli hostages. **7** The Queen arrived in Washington for bicentennial celebrations; Mr. David Steel elected leader of the Liberal Party. **10** Explosion at Hoffman-La Roche's Seveso plant near Milan: poisonous chemical contaminated area of 7 km radius. **14** Official handing over to Tanzania and Zambia of Chinese-built Tanzam railway (1,860 km). **21** Mr. Christopher Ewart-Biggs, British Ambassador to Irish Republic, and a member of his staff, assassinated by landmine. **28** Major earthquake destroyed Chinese mining town of Tangshan; Britain broke off diplomatic relations with Uganda.

August 1 Trinidad and Tobago became independent republic within Commonwealth. **4** Renewed violence in South African township of Soweto. **6** Drought Act 1976 came into force. **25** Resignation of M. Chirac, Prime Minister of France.

September 2 European Commission on Human

A.D.

Rights found Britain guilty of torturing detainees in Ulster. **10** Mid-air collision of 2 airliners near Zagreb: 176 killed. **20** Electoral defeat of Sweden's Social Democratic Party after 44 years in power. **24** Mr. Ian Smith announced acceptance of British and American proposals for majority rule in Rhodesia in two years.

October 3 Bishop Muzorewa returned to Rhodesia from exile. **4** British Rail's high-speed train came into service. **6** Military coup in Thailand and the end of civilian rule after 3 years. **25** Official opening of the National Theatre by the Queen. **28** Conference on future of Rhodesia, chaired by Mr. Ivor Richard, opened in Geneva. **29** Opening of world's largest mining complex at Selby, Yorks.

November 1 Mr. Jimmy Carter elected President of the USA with Democratic majorities in both Houses. **15** Formal end of civil war in Lebanon as Syrian troops (as part of Arab peacekeeping force) moved into heart of Beirut. **27** Rally in Trafalgar Square in support of N. Ireland Peace People.

December 16 Landslide victory for Mr. Michael Manley in Jamaica's general election. **17** Exchange of Vladimir Bukovsky, Soviet dissident, and Señor Corvalán, veteran leader of Chileán Communist Party.

1977

January 1 Britain together with EEC countries extended fishing limits to 200 miles offshore (with effect from 1 April). **24** Collapse of second round of Rhodesian talks: Mr. Ian Smith rejected British proposals for transition to black majority rule.

February 15 Deaths in England and Wales exceeded number of live births in 1976 (for first time since records began in 1837). **17** Uganda's Anglican archbishop and two cabinet ministers killed in mysterious circumstances while under arrest.

March 1 Mr. Callaghan's Government went into minority. **7** The Queen arrived in Australia on her Jubilee tour; Landslide victory for Mr. Bhutto in Pakistan's national assembly election. **22** Resignation of Mrs. Gandhi after loss of seat in general election and defeat of Congress Party after 30 years in power. **23** Lib-Lab pact: Conservative motion of no-confidence defeated by 322 to 298. **24** Janata Government sworn in with Mr Moraji Desai as Prime Minister of India. **27** Collision on runway of two jumbo-jets at Tenerife: 577 killed.

April 21 Imposition of martial law in Karachi, Hyderabad and Lahore following 6 weeks of political violence in Pakistan. **22** Norwegian Ekofisk Bravo oilfield disaster.

May 5 Conservative gains in local government elections in England and Wales. **13** Collapse of Ulster 11-day strike despite widespread intimidation. **17** Israeli Labour Party defeated in general election: right-wing Likud Party, led by Mr. Menachem Begin, emerged as largest party. **18** International Commission of Jurists reported to UN horrifying massacres and murders in Uganda under Amin's rule.

June 1 Change in road traffic speed limits in UK: 70 mile/h, dual roads, 60 mile/h, single. **5** Bloodless coup in the Seychelles. **7** Silver Jubilee Thanksgiving celebrations with state pageantry in London. **11** End of 11-day Dutch sieges by South Moluccan terrorists after storming of train and school by Dutch Marines and police: 2 hostages and 6 Moluccans died. **15** General election in Spain, first since 1936: victory for Union of Democratic Centre (UCD) led by Prime Minister Suarez. **16** Britain severed last diplomatic link with Uganda; Irish Republic's coalition Fine Gael-Labour government defeated in general election by Mr. Jack Lynch's Fianna Fail. **26** Independence for Djibouti (Afars and Issas).

July 5 Army took charge in Pakistan and deposed Mr. Bhutto. **11** Trade union demonstration outside Grunwick factory. **15** Pay rises in next 12 months to be limited to 10%. **21** Mrs. Bandar-

A.D.

anaike and her Sri Lanka Freedom Party suffered defeat in general election.

August 10 Conclusion of new Panama Canal Agreement: gradual takeover by Panama of the zone and canal by the year 2000. **13** National Front march in Lewisham, London, brought violent clashes. **31** Mr. Spyros Kyprianou became President of Cyprus. **25** Scarman Report on Grunwick dispute recommended company to re-employ strikers, but company rejected report.

September 1 Dr. Owen presented Mr. Ian Smith with Anglo-American proposals for a Rhodesian settlement. **25** Skytrain service to New York began.

October 16 The Queen began her Canadian Jubilee tour. **31** Effective revaluation of the £: Government allowed it to float upwards.

November 4 Mandatory arms embargo imposed by UN Security Council against S. Africa. **14** First day of firemen's strike after their claim for a 30% pay increase had been rejected: armed forces dealt with fires. **15** A son (Peter Mark Andrew) born to Princess Anne. **19** Historic meeting in Israel between President Sadat of Egypt and Prime Minister Menachem Begin of Israel; Coastal belt off Bay of Bengal hit by cyclone: estimated death toll 20,000–25,000. **29** Home Secretary granted amnesty for immigrants who had entered the country illegally before 1 Jan. 1976. **30** South African general election: Mr. Vorster's governing National Party vanquished both liberal and ultra right-wing political parties.

December 8 Fall of Dr. Soares' minority Socialist Government in Portugal. **10** Resignation of Gough Whitlam as Australia's Labour leader after general election when Malcolm Fraser's Conservative coalition was returned. **14** House of Lords dismissed appeal by Advisory, Conciliation and Arbitration Service (ACAS) in Grunwick dispute. **16** Extension of Piccadilly tube line to Heathrow opened by the Queen. **21** OPEC countries froze oil prices for next 6 months.

1978

January 1 Air India jumbo jet crashed in sea off Bombay: all 213 people on board killed. **4** Said Hammani, PLO's London representative, shot dead in Mayfair. **20** Mario Soares re-appointed Prime Minister of Portugal. **21** Special Liberal Party Assembly voted 1727–520 to continue Lib-Lab pact until July. **25** Serious Government defeats on the Scottish Devolution Bill. **29** Talks in Malta on future of Rhodesia with leaders of the Patriotic Front, Joshua Nkomo and Robert Mugabe: in Rhodesia itself, Ian Smith began negotiations for an internal settlement.

February 4 Major Ethiopian offensive launched in the Ogaden: Somalia appealed to the West for aid. **7** Government majority of 14 in Commons for its policy of sanctions against companies breaking the pay guideline (the "black list"). **19** Egyptian commandos stormed hi-jacked airliner at Larnaca airport in Cyprus: 15 commandos killed and 14 others injured. **21** All-Party Speakers' Conference recommended increased Ulster representation at Westminster: number of seats to be increased from 12 to 17.

March 3 Internal settlement agreed in Rhodesia between Ian Smith and three black Nationalist leaders: majority rule to become effective by 31 December 1978. **8** Agreement reached in Italy on formation of new government to be headed by Giulio Andreotti. **15** Massive Israeli thrust into south Lebanon. **16** Aldo Moro, five times Prime Minister of Italy, kidnapped by "Red Brigade" terrorists: body found 9 May; *Amoco Cadiz* supertanker ran aground off the Brittany coast: major pollution of Brittany coastal waters.

April 3 First regular radio broadcasts of proceedings in Parliament commenced. **9** Attempted *coup* in Somalia crushed. **10** The Transkei, the first tribal homeland in South Africa to be granted independence, severed diplomatic links with South Africa. **17** World Health Organisation

A.D.
(WHO) announced no cases of smallpox reported anywhere in the world during the previous year. **26** Arab terrorist attack on bus in Nablus in Israeli-occupied West Bank. **27** President Daoud deposed in pro-Soviet *coup* in Afghanistan.

May 1 First May Day holiday celebrated in Britain. **24** Princess Margaret obtained a divorce from Lord Snowdon. **25** David Steel, the Liberal leader announced that the Lib-Lab pact would terminate at the end of July.

June 3 Presidential election in Bangladesh resulted in easy victory for General Zia ur- Rahman. **10** Riots in Londonderry. **12** Provisional IRA leader Seamus Twomey sentenced in Dublin. **19** OPEC agreed to peg oil prices until December.

July 5 Resignation of General Acheampong, head of state in Ghana. **7** Independence of Solomon Islands. **9** Former P.M. of Iraq, General Abdul Razzale al-Naif, shot in London. **18** Talks began at Leeds Castle between Egyptian and Israeli foreign ministers and the US Secretary of State. **25** World's first "test-tube" baby born in Oldham. **26** Queen began official visit to Canada. **31** Devolution Bills for Scotland and Wales received royal assent.

August 6 Death of Pope Paul VI. **13** Bomb in PLO headquarters in Beirut killed at least 100 people. **22** Gunmen held hundreds hostage in Nicaraguan Parliament and succeeded in gaining release of 83 political prisoners. **26** Cardinal Albino Luciani of Venice elected as Pope John Paul I. **30** Case of smallpox confirmed in Birmingham: Janet Parker died on 11 September.

September 7 Prime Minister announced that he was not calling a general election in the autumn. **8** Martial law declared in Tehran and 11 Iranian cities: riots resulted in which many were killed. **11** Martial law declared in part of Nicaragua. **16** Earthquake in Tabas in north-east Iran killed 11,000. **17** Camp David talks between Sadat and Begin concluded with signing of a framework for a Middle East peace treaty. **20** P.M. of South Africa, John Vorster, resigned because of ill health. **27** Disastrous floods in India caused deaths of at least 1,200 and 43m displaced. **28** Pope John Paul I died after only 33 days as pontiff; Pieter Botha became P.M. of South Africa. **30** Ellice Islands became independent nation of Tuvalu.

October 7 Declaration of ceasefire in Lebanon. **9** Britain agreed to accept 346 Vietnamese refugees. **10** Daniel Arap Moi became President of Kenya. **12** *Christos Bitas* grounded off St. David's Head: oil slick threatened South Wales coastline. **15** Cardinal Karol Wojtyla of Cracow became first non-Italian Pope for 450 years as Pope John Paul II. **20** 4-week siege of Beirut lifted.

November 3 Dominica achieved independence from Britain. **5** Serious riots in Tehran. **25** National Party returned to power in New Zealand with reduced majority. **26** Clashes in Iran during 24-hour general strike. **27** Japanese P.M., Takeo Fukuda, resigned. **30** Publication of *The Times* suspended until agreement reached on new technology and manning levels: returned 13 Nov 1979.

December 7 Masayoshi Ohira became P.M. of Japan. **15** Government won a vote of confidence. **17** OPEC announced rise in oil prices in four stages in 1979; IRA bomb explosions in Southampton, Bristol, Manchester and Coventry. **18** Further bombs exploded or were discovered in London, Southampton and Bristol. **20** Bomb explosion in Jerusalem and Israeli attack on terrorist bases in Lebanon.

1979

January 1 Dr. Bakhtiar became new P.M. of Iran. **4** Guadeloupe summit talks held between UK, US, W. Germany and France. **7** Phnom Penh, the Cambodian capital, captured by Vietnamese and rebel forces. **14** Human rights demonstration in Peking. **15** Secondary picketing in road haulage strike caused growing problems: about 150,000 laid off as result of strike. **16** Shah left Iran amidst great rejoicing but there were demonstrations next day by troops loyal to him. **17** IRA bomb attacks on gas-holder in Greenwich and oil depot on Canvey Island; Britain to admit a further 1,500 Vietnamese refugees. **18** Code on picketing distributed to road haulage strikers: shortages continued and lay-offs mounted. **21** Government in Equatorial Guinea condemned for atrocities. **30** Rhodesian referendum among whites voted by 6:1 majority in favour of Ian Smith's proposals for transfer to majority rule. **31** Resignation of Italian government.

February 1 Muslim leader, the Ayatollah Khomeini, returned to Iran from exile in Paris. **5** Dr. Mehdi Bazargan nominated by Ayatollah Khomeini as P.M. of Iran. **6** Dr. Bhutto's appeal against the death sentence rejected by 4–3 by Pakistan Supreme Court. **11** Dr. Bakhtiar finally resigned as P.M. of Iran. **12** Remaining royalist guards surrendered to Khomeini supporters. **13** Floods in Isle of Portland, Dorset, caused by freak waves. **14** "Concordat" between government and TUC announced together with agreement on target of 5% inflation within 3 years; Rioters stoned the US embassy in Iran and in Afghanistan US ambassador killed when government troops stormed the hotel in which he was held hostage. **15** Power handed over to army in Chad. **16** Execution of pro-Shah generals in Iran. **21** Volcano erupted in Jakarta resulting in 175 deaths. **22** St. Lucia became independent. **27** Mineworkers reached pay agreement with NCB. **28** Final meeting of white Rhodesian House of Assembly.

March 1 32·5% of Scots voted in favour of devolution proposals, thus failing to reach 40% requirement; in Wales there was an overwhelming vote against devolution. **4** Trade agreement between China and Britain signed. **6** Commander of Rhodesian army dismissed. **12** Iran and Pakistan withdrew from Central Treaty Organisation. **13** Government of Sir Eric Gairy in Grenada overthrown. **22** Sir Richard Sykes, British ambassador to The Hague and a footman shot dead: IRA claimed responsibility. **26** Peace treaty between Israel and Egypt signed in Washington. **28** Government defeated by 1 vote on no confidence motion; Radiation leak at Three Mile Island nuclear power plant in Pennsylvania led to declaration of emergency. **29** Prime Minister announced general election for 3 May. **30** Assassination of Airey Neave, Conservative M.P. and Shadow Northern Ireland Secretary; Ilie Verdel became Prime Minister of Romania. **31** Final withdrawal of British navy from Malta.

April 1 Islamic Republic declared in Iran. **2** First visit of Israeli Prime Minister to Egypt; Adolfo Suarez became Spain's first elected Prime Minister for more than 40 years. **4** Former Prime Minister of Pakistan, Zulfikar Ali Bhutto, executed. **11** Kampala captured by Tanzanian troops and Ugandan exiles: Professor Yusufo Lule became new leader of Uganda. **23** Teacher killed and 300 people arrested after clashes in Southall between National Front and Anti-Nazi League. **27** Exchange of prisoners between Russia and USA: two Russian spies freed in return for 5 Russian dissidents including Alexander Ginsberg.

May 3 General Election in Britain. **4** Margaret Thatcher became first woman Prime Minister in Britain: Conservatives won election with overall majority of 43. **16** Government removed legal compulsion on LEAs to reorganise education on comprehensive lines. **17** BL announced joint plan with Honda to build new car in Britain. **21** Appointment of Sir Nicholas Henderson as ambassador to Washington. **22** Progressive Conservatives led by Mr. Joe Clark formed minority government in Canada. **23** Prof. Karl Carstens elected Federal President of West Germany. **24** Conservative team led by Lord Boyd reported that the Rhodesian elections had been fair. **25** Sinai capital of El Arish returned to Egypt. **27**

A.D.

Border between Egypt and Israel re-opened. **29** Bishop Abel Muzorewa sworn in as Zimbabwe Rhodesia's first black P.M.

June 3 Christian Democrats maintained position in Italian elections as largest single party. **4** John Vorster resigned as President of South Africa after publication of Erasmus Report on the "Muldergate" scandal; Ghanaian forces led by Flight-Lieut. Rawlings seized power. **11** Tories took 60 seats, Labour 17 and SNP 1 in European election. **16** General Acheampong, former ruler of Ghana, executed by firing squad. **18** Presidents Carter and Brezhnev signed SALT II treaty in Vienna. **20** President Lule deposed as Ugandan leader after only 2 months: succeeded by Mr. Godfrey Binaisa. **22** Jeremy Thorpe and 3 others acquitted in Old Bailey conspiracy trial.

July 11 International Whaling Conference approved an indefinite ban on offshore hunting of all but Minke whales. **12** Gilbert Islands became independent nation of Kiribati. **13** Majority of 144 on bill to tighten abortion law. **17** President Somoza of Nicaragua resigned and fled to Miami. **19** Death penalty rejected by 119 votes in Commons. **26** Government announced decision to sell off substantial part of BNOC. **31** Nigeria to nationalise all BP interests in the country.

August 1 Leaders of Lambeth, Southwark and Lewisham AHA stripped of powers after refusal to make spending cuts; Queen Mother installed as Warden of the Cinque Ports. **8** 2 North Sea divers died after being trapped in a diving bell. **9** Riots in W. Belfast on 8th anniversary of internment. **14** Gale-force winds brought havoc and 17 deaths in Fastnet yacht race. **18** Heart transplant operation carried out at Papworth Hospital near Cambridge. **19** Former Cambodian leader, Pol Pot, convicted in his absence of causing the death of 3m people. **20** Indian P.M. Charan Singh resigned after 24 days in office. **27** Earl Mountbatten, 2 relatives and a young boy killed by bomb explosion on boat in Sligo.

September 5 Zimbabwe Rhodesia launched ground and air attacks on Mozambique. **10** Zimbabwe Rhodesia constitutional talks opened in Lancaster House in London; BL announced decision to cut work force by 25,000 over 2 years. **17** Environment Secretary announced the abolition of 57 quangos. **18** ILEA voted to abolish corporal punishment in schools. **19** The 3-party non-Socialist coalition won Swedish general election. **20** Emperor Bokassa of the Central African Empire ousted in coup by the former President David Dacko. **26** Government announced abandonment of compulsory metrication orders. **29** Pope arrived in Ireland for first-ever papal visit.

October 1 Civilian rule restored in Nigeria. **16** Government to sell 5% of its holdings in BP; General Zia of Pakistan cancelled elections due to be held on 17 November. **17** Army colonels who carried out coup in El Salvador imposed martial law. **19** End of ITV strike announced after 11-week black-out; programmes resumed on 24 October. **22** Israeli court ruled that Elon Morah settlement on West Bank was illegal. **23** Exiled Shah of Iran flown to New York for cancer treatment; Government announced removal of all foreign exchange controls.

November 1 Military coup in Bolivia; BL workers overwhelmingly endorsed recovery plans for the company; BSC announced plans to cease steel making at Corby. **2** Irish security forces seized up to £500,000 weapons and ammunition in Dublin harbour. **4** Iranian students occupied US embassy in Tehran taking hostages. **6** PM Bazargan resigned in Iran. **9** Computer fault led to full-scale nuclear alert in US; BSC announced closure of Shotton steel works; UN Security Council called for release of American hostages. **12** President Carter ordered cessation of all American oil imports from Iran. **13** Commons completed all stages of bill restoring legality to Zimbabwe Rhodesia and lifting sanctions; *The Times* returned after nearly a year. **14** All Iranian assets in US frozen

A.D.

in retaliation for embassy occupation. **19** Derek Robinson, Communist convenor of shop stewards at BL's Longbridge works dismissed; immediate walkout of several thousand workers. **23** Thomas MacMahon sentenced to life imprisonment for murder of Lord Mountbatten; Ford reached agreement on 21·5% pay increase for workers. **26** Government to reintroduce political honours; Wave of bombs in Northern Ireland shops and hotels.

December 5 Jack Lynch, Irish PM, resigned. **6** Britain withdrew recognition of Pol Pot regime in Kampuchea; Dutch parliament rejected NATO plan for stationing of cruise missiles in Holland. **7** Captain Shariar Chefik, nephew of the ex-Shah, shot dead in Paris; Charles Haughey elected leader of Ireland's governing party; Lord Soames appointed governor of Rhodesia. **11** BSC announced axing of 52,000 jobs; Charles Haughey confirmed as Irish PM after bitter debate. **12** NATO approved stationing of 572 American missiles in Europe. **15** Ex-Shah given asylum in Panama. **21** Rhodesian treaty signed at Lancaster House. **27** President Hafizullah Amin of Afghanistan ousted in Soviet-backed coup. **30** Patriotic Front announced split into separate ZANU and ZAPU parties for election.

1980

January 7 Mrs. Gandhi's Congress Party won absolute majority in Indian general election; USSR blocked Security Council call for immediate Russian withdrawal from Afghanistan. **9** 63 beheaded in Saudi Arabia for attacking Grand Mosque in Mecca. **13** Joshua Nkomo returned to Rhodesia after 3½ years exile. **16** Diplomatic links with Chile restored after 4 years. **22** Dr. Andrei Sakharov, winner of 1975 Nobel Peace Prize sent into internal exile in the city of Gorky. **27** Border between Egypt and Israel in Sinai reopened; Robert Mugabe returned to Rhodesia from exile to fight election.

February 12 Publication of Brandt report "North South: a programme for survival". **13** Opening of winter Olympic Games at Lake Placid. **18** Pierre Trudeau returned to power in Canadian general election after nine months out of office. **28** 5 orchestras to be scrapped in economy package announced by BBC; Government defeated no confidence motion in Commons, majority of 59.

March 4 Robert Mugabe invited to form government in Zimbabwe Rhodesia after winning absolute majority: his ZANU(PF) party won 57 seats. **11** Zimbabwe cabinet included Joshua Nkomo and 2 white Rhodesians. **24** Archbishop Romero shot dead at altar in San Salvador. **25** Enthronement of Robert Runcie as Archbishop of Canterbury. **26** British Olympic Association voted in favour of attending Moscow Olympics. **27** The *Alexander Keilland*, an oil accommodation rig, overturned in North Sea: 124 dead. **30** 39 persons killed and 100 injured in gun battle in San Salvador during Archbishop Romero's funeral.

April 2 Rioting and street fighting in St. Pauls area of Bristol: 19 police hurt, many arrests. **3** Return to work after 13-week steel strike. **9** Israeli troops moved into Lebanon; Resignation of Belgian PM, Wilfried Martens. **13** US Olympic committee voted two-to-one to accept President Carter's boycott of games. **18** Rhodesia became independent nation of Zimbabwe, with Robert Mugabe as Prime Minister and the Rev. Canaan Banana as President. **20** 67 arrests and 4 hurt in Lewisham National Front and Anti-Nazi League marches. **25** President Carter announced unsuccessful attempt to free US hostages in Iran: 8 Americans killed in collision on ground in desert. **28** American Secretary of State, Cyrus Vance, resigned in protest against hostage mission: replaced by Edward Muskie. **30** Armed men seized Iranian Embassy in London; Queen Beatrix invested as Queen of the Netherlands: riots in Amsterdam by anti-monarchist groups.

A.D.

May 5 Following shooting of 2 hostages, SAS commandos stormed Iranian Embassy and released hostages: all but one of the gunmen killed. **11** Much damage caused by forest fires after dry weather: Forestry Commission lost at least 3000 acres. **18** Eruption of Mount St. Helens volcano began. **24** Entries for Olympic Games officially closed with 85 out of 145 accepting: 27 countries failed to reply. **27** Ex-President Obote returned to Uganda after 9 years' exile.

June 1 Start of Musicians' Union strike in protest against BBC cuts. **8** US computer sent out second false war alert in a week; Wave of bombings in Ulster. **22** Liberals won Japanese general election. **23** Sanjay Gandhi, son of Indian PM, died in plane crash. **27** All 67 British athletes selected for Moscow agreed to go. **30** Ms. Vigdis Finnbogadottir elected head of state in Iceland.

July 3 Mr. George Howard appointed chairman of BBC. **16** Government dismissed Brandt Commission's proposals. **17** Military coup in Bolivia. **19** Opening of 22nd Olympic Games in Moscow. **22** Lifting of arms embargo on Chile. **23** Dispute between Musicians' Union and BBC settled: 3 orchestras reprieved. **27** Death of deposed Shah of Iran. **30** New Hebrides became independent nation of Vanuatu.

August 4 Queen Mother's 80th birthday. **10** Violence in Ulster to mark 9th anniversary of internment. **13** 18 pickets arrested in Brixton; Start of French fishermen's blockade of Channel ports: continued until 30 August. **24** Polish PM dismissed. **31** Polish government agreed to establish independent trade unions and recognise right to strike.

September 5 Edward Gierek, Polish leader, replaced by Stanislav Kania after heart attack; Opening of 10-mile road tunnel in St. Gotthard massif. **7** Hua Guofeng resigned as Chinese leader, replaced by Zhao Ziyang. **10** Libya and Syria announced merger into unitary Arab state. **17** Ex-dictator of Nicaragua, Anastasio Somoza assassinated in Paraguay; President Husain of Iraq abrogated 1975 border agreement with Iran. **18** Environment Secretary withdrew £200m government money from local councils. **22** Outbreak of war between Iran and Iraq.

October 5 Helmut Schmidt re-elected Chancellor of West Germany. **10** Earthquakes destroyed Algerian town of El-Asnam: death toll over 4000. **14** ICI, Britain's largest industrial company, announced 4500 redundancies; Launch of new Mini Metro at Motor Show; Ivor Richard appointed as Britain's second member of European Commission. **15** James Callaghan announced retirement from leadership of Labour Party. **17** Queen met Pope in Vatican. **18** Liberal and Country coalition in Australia led by Malcolm Fraser returned to power. **22** Chief executive of Thomson announced sale of *The Times* and *Sunday Times*. **23** Alexei Kosygin resigned as Soviet PM. **24** Solidarity, Polish independent trade union, recognised by Polish authorities. **27** 7 Republican prisoners at Maze prison began hunger strike.

November 4 American Presidential election: Ronald Reagan won landslide victory. **6** Government announced 6% ceiling on pay increases in public sector. **10** Michael Foot elected new leader of Labour Party by 10 votes. **13** Labour MPs involved in clashes in Commons to prevent Black Rod proroguing Parliament: Government forced to postpone council house rent rises. **23** Violent earthquake in Southern Italy caused enormous devastation and loss of life.

December 8 Summit meeting in Dublin between Thatcher and Haughey: agreed programme for wider future cooperation. **12** 6 UDA men began hunger strike at Maze prison. **15** Dr. Milton Obote sworn in as President of Uganda. **16** 3 prisoners escaped from Brixton gaol: included Gerard Tuite, alleged IRA bomber. **17** Heseltine announced reduced rate-support grant; Prof. Alan Walters

A.D.

appointed personal economic adviser to PM at salary of £50,000. **18** IRA hunger strike called off as one of the strikers was close to death. **19** Resignations from Polish parliament included that of Edward Gierek. **21** Iran demanded £10,000m for release of hostages.

1981

January 1 Greece became 10th member of EEC. **3** Death of Princess Alice, Countess of Athlone. **4** BL workers voted to accept peace formula in Longbridge strike. **10** Dr. Francisco Pinto Balsemao became PM of Portugal. **18** 13 young people killed in fire at south London party: arson suspected. **20** US hostages finally left Iran. **21** Sir Norman Stronge and his son, both former Stormont MPs, killed by IRA. **24** Wembley Labour Party conference voted for election of party leader by electoral college with 40% votes for unions, 30% Labour MPs and 30% constituencies. **25** "Gang of Four", Roy Jenkins, Shirley Williams, William Rodgers and David Owen announced launching of a Council for Social Democracy; In China Mao's widow Jiang Qing found guilty but death penalty suspended for 2 years. **27** Joshua Nkomo appointed Minister without Portfolio in attempt to prevent confrontation in Zimbabwe.

February 3 Dr. Gro Harlem Brundtland elected Norway's first woman PM. **12** Rupert Murdoch announced purchase of *The Times* and agreement with unions about manning levels and new technology; Ian Paisley suspended from Commons for 4 days after calling N. Ireland Secretary a liar. **14** 48 young people killed in disco fire in Dublin. **15** First Sunday games in Football League. **20** Peter Sutcliffe charged with murder of 13 women in north of England. **23** Abortive military coup in Spain: right-wing guards held MPs hostage in lower house. **24** Prince Charles and Lady Diana Spencer announced engagement.

March 16 Government majority cut to 14 after backbench rebellion on petrol tax increase. **17** EEC announced £1m in food aid for China. **26** Social Democratic Party launched at public meeting. **29** First London marathon run. **30** President Reagan shot outside Hilton Hotel in Washington: gun man John Hinckley detained.

April 2 Longest Commons sitting since June 1977 on British Telecommunications Bill. **5** President Brezhnev flew to Czechoslovakia for talks on Polish crisis; Census day in Britain. **11** Start of weekend of violence in Brixton. **12** US shuttle *Columbia* successfully launched. **13** Lord Scarman to head inquiry into Brixton riots. **25** Snowy weekend in Britain: worst April blizzards this century. **27** *Now!* magazine closed after £6m losses. **28** Pope's special envoy visited hunger striker Bobby Sands in Maze prison.

May 5 Death of Bobby Sands after 66-day fast. **9** Bomb explosion at Sullom Voe oil terminal while Queen and King Olav were inaugurating the complex. **10** François Mitterrand won French presidential election: followed by panic selling on the Bourse; Government announced cut in lead content in petrol. **12** 2nd IRA hunger striker Francis Hughes died on 59th day of fast. **13** Pope John Paul shot by Turkish gunman Mehmet Ali Agca: 4½-hour operation to remove bullets; Open verdict after stormy coroner's inquest on Deptford fire. **15** Princess Anne gave birth to daughter, later named Zara Anne Elizabeth. **18** Keith Speed, junior Navy Minister, sacked for speech against reduction in Navy's capacity; Weekend referendum in Italy showed majority in favour of retaining liberal abortion laws. **22** Peter Sutcliffe sentenced to life imprisonment for Yorkshire Ripper murders. **30** Assassination of General Zia ur Rahman, President of Bangladesh.

June 1 PLO representative to Common Market shot dead in Brussels. **8** Israeli air force destroyed Iraqi nuclear reactor: widespread international condemnation. **10** Polish President Stanislav Kania survived attempt by hard-liners to remove him; 8 leading IRA prisoners made armed escape from

A.D.

Crumlin Road gaol. **13** Blanks fired at the Queen during Trooping of the Colour. **16** Working alliance between Liberals and SDP announced. **21** Socialists won general election in France. **22** President Bani-Sadr dismissed by Ayatollah Khomeni. **24** First traffic crossed new Humber Bridge. **25** Defence cuts announced in Commons: closure of Chatham dockyard; 7 BBC foreign language services axed. **30** General election in Israel: Begin secured continuation of coalition by agreement with National Religious Party; Dr Garret Fitz-Gerald elected PM of Irish Republic by 3-vote majority; End of 5½-year Nazi war crimes trial: sentences ranging from 3 years to life.

July 2 UGC announced massive cuts in university spending. **3** Riots in Southall after coaches of skinheads arrived for punk concert; Shot fired at Ian Paisley in Markets district of Belfast. **4** Weekend of serious riots in Toxteth: savage conflict between police and youths. **8** Riots in Moss Side, Manchester and Wood Green, London. **9** Lonhro announced take-over of *Observer* and launch of new London evening paper. **10** Further riots in British cities: continued until 12 July; 6 held after gun battle in Belfast following hunger striker's funeral. **14** Polish Communist Party voted to expel ex-PM Edvard Gierek and 6 close associates. **15** Early morning police raids in Brixton led to fresh rioting; Northern Ireland office asked Red Cross to mediate at the Maze. **22** Mehmet Ali Agca sentenced to life imprisonment for shooting the Pope. **23** Polish government announced increase in food prices and cut in rations: led to many protests and general strike on 5 August. **26** Further riots in Toxteth. **29** Wedding of Prince Charles and Lady Diana Spencer. **30** President of Gambia deposed whilst attending royal wedding: coup finally put down on 6 August; End of 21-week civil servants' strike.

August 8 Rioting in Northern Ireland after death of 9th hunger striker and 10 years of internment; Reagan administration announced decision to produce and stockpile neutron bomb. **15** Street violence in Liverpool during demonstration against policing methods. **20** Bank of England suspended MLR. **24** Mark David Chapman gaoled for murder of John Lennon. **25** South African troops crossed border into Angola. **29** Anti-apartheid demonstrators in Wellington, New Zealand, involved in violent protests against the Springboks' tour. **30** Iran's President and PM assassinated in bomb explosion in Tehran; Polish prices of bread and cereals trebled.

September 1 Army seized control in Bangui, capital of Central African Republic. **4** French ambassador to Lebanon assassinated in Beirut. **6** Solidarity's first national congress in Gdansk, Poland. **15** Cabinet set 4% pay guidelines for public service pay settlements. **17** Soviet Union delivered ultimatum to Polish leadership to act against Solidarity. **18** France abolished capital punishment. **21** Belize became independent. **27** Denis Healey won Labour deputy leadership election by less than 1% over Tony Benn; Major spy swap arranged between East and West Germany: Gunther Guillaume handed over to East Germany on 1 October.

October 4 Emergency Brussels meeting led to European currency revaluations; End of hunger strike at Maze prison: 10 men had died during 7-month campaign. **6** President Sadat of Egypt assassinated at a military parade; Government announced prison reforms in Northern Ireland following end of hunger strike. **10** 2 killed in IRA bomb explosion in Chelsea: aimed at Irish Guards' coach. **14** Hosni Mubarak sworn in as President of Egypt. **17** Car bomb injured Lt.-Gen. Sir Steuart Pringle, Commandant-General of the Royal Marines. **18** Left-wing victory in Greek general election; General Wojciech Jaruzelski replaced Stanislav Kania as leader of Polish Communist Party. **19** Government announced sale of state North Sea oil assets. **21** Street riots in Poland over food shortages. **26** Bomb disposal expert killed by IRA bomb in Oxford Street. **29** OPEC agreed on unified oil price structure.

A.D.

November 6 Anglo-Irish summit ended with agreement on new Anglo-Irish Intergovernmental Council. **14** Unionist MP Rev. Robert Bradford shot dead in Belfast. **15** Senegal and Gambia united to form Senegambia. **16** Uproar in Commons led to adjournment and then suspension of 3 Democratic Unionist MPs: Ian Paisley declared he would make province ungovernable. **17** Northern Ireland Secretary attacked by mob at funeral of Robert Bradford. **19** Tony Benn lost place in Shadow Cabinet election. **24** Crewmen evacuated from Transworld oil rig which broke loose in gales. **25** Scarman Report on summer riots published: Home Secretary told Commons that independent element in police complaints procedures and increase in police training period were already being considered. **30** Opening of Geneva disarmament talks between US and USSR.

December 1 180 killed in Yugoslav DC9 plane crash. **7** Lockheed announced end of TriStar production: blow to Rolls Royce who produced RB211 engine; BR launched APT, wiping an hour off Glasgow/London journey time. **8** Sudden heavy falls of snow caused chaos in Britain; Arthur Scargill elected leader of National Union of Mineworkers. **9** Labour National Executive agreed to investigate activities of Militant Tendency; After Sakharov hunger strike (begun 22 November) Kremlin agreed to visa for their daughter-in-law Liza Alexeyeva to join her husband in US. **11** Javier Perez de Cuellar chosen as Secretary General of United Nations. **13** Martial law imposed in Poland: General Jaruzelski seized emergency powers. **14** Israel annexed Golan Heights, captured from Syria during Six Day War in 1967; Dom Mintoff and Labour Party returned to power in Malta for third term. **15** Bomb in Iraqi embassy in Beirut killed at least 20 and injured 95. **17** Law Lords ruled that GLC cheap fares policy and supplementary rate were illegal; American general James Dozier kidnapped by Red Brigades in Verona. **19** Crew of Penlee lifeboat drowned during attempt to rescue crew of coaster *Union Star*. **20** US granted political asylum to Polish ambassador to Washington; 10,000 Poles in march to Polish embassy in London. **21** Environment Secretary announced strategy designed to force councils to spend less on services and more on capital investment. **31** Military coup in Ghana: Flight-Lt. Rawlings took over power and 2 days later suspended constitution and banned political parties.

1982

January 3 Torrential rain and rapid thaw caused widespread flooding. **4** EEC governments voted against following US economic sanctions against Poland and Soviet Union. **8** Blizzards swept Britain at start of weekend of chaos. **13** 81 dead after Air Florida Boeing 737 crashed into bridge in central Washington. **18** American diplomat murdered in Paris by Lebanese terrorists. **24** World Airways DC10 crashed into Boston harbour: all 208 on board rescued. **26** Unemployment reached 3m or 1:8 of working population. **27** Irish budget defeated by a single vote: PM asked for dissolution of parliament. **28** Brigadier-General James Dozier rescued from Red Brigades by Italian police: 5 guerrillas arrested.

February 1 Massive price increases in Poland. **5** Collapse of Laker Airways with debts of over £210m. **8** Japan Air Lines DC8 crashed into Tokyo Bay: 24 killed. **15** *Ocean Ranger* oil rig sank off Newfoundland: all 84 on board drowned. **17** Joshua Nkomo dropped from Zimbabwe cabinet; Settlement of rail strike: uneasy agreement reached after long negotiations; Neither main party won clear majority in Irish general election. **19** De Lorean car company in Belfast went into liquidation. **25** Scenes in Stock Market when Amersham International shares went on sale: Government accused of under-valuation; European Court of Human Rights ruled it was wrong to use corporal punishment in schools against parental wishes; Sir William Rees-Mogg appointed chairman of Arts Council. **28** Party of English cricketers arrived in South Africa to play cricket in defiance of Gleneagles agreement.

A.D.

March 1 Dylan Thomas plaque unveiled at Poets' Corner, Westminster Abbey. **3** Queen opened Barbican Centre in City of London. **4** Gerald Tuite who escaped from Brixton while waiting trial on charges of causing IRA explosions recaptured in Irish Republic. **9** Charles Haughey elected P.M. of Ireland after gaining support of left. **11** Government announced decision to buy new Trident II nuclear deterrent; Militant Protestants prevented Archbishop of Canterbury preaching in Liverpool parish church. **14** Bomb wrecked London offices of African National Congress. **16** President Brezhnev announced unilateral freeze on deployment of Soviet missiles in Europe: called on similar US action. **18** Group of Argentinians in South Georgia to dismantle whaling station raised Argentinian flag. **19** Cricketers playing in unofficial tour of South Africa banned from playing for England for 3 years. **23** Coup in Guatemala City. **24** After bloodless coup, Bangladesh under martial law for third time since independence.

April 1 2 soldiers shot dead in Northern Ireland: death toll 6 in one week. **2** Argentina invaded Falkland Islands: emergency Cabinet meeting, and humiliation for Foreign and Defence Secretaries. **3** Special Saturday sitting of Commons to discuss crisis. **5** Lord Carrington and 2 other Foreign Office ministers resigned; Francis Pym appointed Foreign Secretary; Fleet set sail from Portsmouth for the Falklands. **6** UK banned all Argentinian imports. **7** Defence Secretary announced 200-mile naval blockade of Falklands. **12** Start of British naval blockade of Falklands. **15** 5 Muslims executed for assassination of President Sadat. **25** British troops recaptured South Georgia; Israel handed over Sinai to Egypt. **28** Britain announced air blockade of Falklands.

May 1 British aircraft bombed Port Stanley airport, followed by naval bombardment. **2** Argentine cruiser *General Belgrano* sunk after British attack. **4** British destroyer *HMS Sheffield* hit by Exocet missile and abandoned after fire: 20 men lost. **7** Britain extended total exclusion zone to within 12 nautical miles of Argentine coastline; UN peace proposals under discussion by both sides. **9** British boarding party took over Argentine trawler *Narwal* believed to have been spying on fleet. **10** 23 Conservatives voted against 2nd reading of proposed new legislation for Northern Ireland. **11** Navy frigate attacked Argentine vessel between 2 main Falkland islands; MPs rejected return of death penalty by 357 votes to 195 in free vote. **12** *QE2* sailed to join task force; **12** Argentine Skyhawk jets shot down. **15** British commando raid on Argentine airstrip at Pebble Island. **18** Decision on farm prices taken by EEC on majority vote: Britain criticised unprecedented breaking of Luxembourg compromise. **21** Mass for peace at Vatican when Pope joined by British and Argentine cardinals; British forces established a bridgehead at San Carlos: 5 warships hit, *HMS Ardent* sunk with loss of 22 lives, 21 soldiers killed when Sea King helicopter crashed. **24** *HMS Antelope* sunk after fire; De Lorean car company in Belfast to suspend production. **25** *HMS Coventry* and Cunard container ship *Atlantic Conveyor* destroyed. **27** British task force began to move forward from San Carlos bridgehead. **28** Goose Green and Darwin captured by paratroops; Pope arrived in Britain at start of 6-day visit. **30** Marines captured Douglas and Teal Island.

June 3 British dropped leaflets on Port Stanley urging surrender; Israeli ambassador shot in London. **4** Israeli aircraft bombed Palestinian quarters of Beirut in retaliation. **6** British took Bluff Cove and Fitzroy; Death of 2 British climbers on Everest reported. **7** Argentine raids on *Sir Tristram* and *Sir Galahad* off Bluff Cove. **11** *QE2* returned to Southampton with survivors from 3 British warships. **14** Ceasefire agreed in Falklands as British troops reached outskirts of Port Stanley. **17** General Galtieri deposed as President of Argentina. **21** Birth of Prince William of Wales. **22** John Hinckley acquitted of attempted assassination of President Reagan by virtue of insanity. **23** Labour National Executive voted for action against Militant Tendency. **25** Alexander Haig

A.D.

replaced as US Secretary of State by George Shultz; Former Governor of Falklands returned to Stanley.

July 1 General Reynaldo Bignone installed as President of Argentina. **2** Roy Jenkins elected leader of SDP. **7** Church of England rejected proposals for covenanting with 3 Free Churches. **9** Boeing 727 crashed into residential suburb of New Orleans: 153 dead; Intruder found in Queen's bedroom at Buckingham Palace. **13** Gerard Tuite gaoled in Dublin for bomb offences committed in Britain. **20** IRA bomb explosions in Hyde Park and Regent's Park killed 11 and injured 50. **23** Senior PLO official killed by bomb in Paris. **25** 25% Zimbabwe's air force destroyed by sabotage. **26** End of hire purchase restrictions announced.

August 4 Arthritis drug Opren suspended after allegations about side effects; Israeli tanks invaded West Beirut. **12** Further ceasefire in Lebanon forced on Israel by President Reagan. **14** Barclays Bank branches opened on Saturday for the first time in 13 years. **17** Mutiny in Seychelles put down within 24 hours; US and China agreed on common policy towards Taiwan; Ruth First, prominent member of African National Congress killed by letter bomb in South Africa. **21** Evacuation of PLO fighters from Beirut began. **23** Bashire Gemayel elected President of Lebanon.

September 11 48 killed in helicopter crash near Mannheim. **14** Princess Grace of Monaco died following road accident; Lebanese leader Bashire Gemayel killed by bomb in East Beirut; Britain and Argentina ended financial sanctions. **15** Israeli troops crossed ceasefire line to bomb West Beirut. **17** Hundreds of Palestinians massacred in refugee camps in West Beirut: Israelis allowed Christian phalangist militia to enter Sabra camp: widespread international condemnation. **19** Swedish Social Democrats won general election. **23** Shirley Williams elected President of SDP; Amin Gemayel sworn in as President of Lebanon.

October 1 Helmut Kohl, leader of Christian Democrats, became Chancellor of West Germany after defeating Helmut Schmidt in no confidence vote. **2** Bomb explosion in centre of Tehran killed at least 60. **8** Polish government dissolved Solidarity, Eastern Europe's first trade union. **11** Tudor warship *Mary Rose* finally raised; Strike in Gdansk against ban on Solidarity. **21** Election for Ulster Assembly: SDLP won 14 seats and Sinn Fein 5 and both parties said they would not take up seats. **28** Socialists came to power in Spain. **31** Thames barrier raised for first time.

November 1 Opening of Channel 4 television. **3** 24 Republican seats lost in US mid-term elections. **4** Permitted weight of lorries increased to 38 tonnes; Irish government collapsed after no confidence vote. **10** Over 1,000 Soviet troops and Afghans killed in crash in tunnel north of Kabul; Geoffrey Prime gaoled for 35 years for spying; Death of Leonid Brezhnev, Soviet leader. **11** 50 Tory MPs abstained in Commons vote on immigration rules; Massive explosion at Israeli military HQ in Tyre: 89 dead; First session of Ulster Assembly. **12** Yuri Andropov became new Soviet leader. **20** Britoil shares undersubscribed. **24** El Al, Israeli national airline, put into liquidation. **25** Irish general election: neither main party had overall majority—coalition of Fine Gael and Labour formed, led by Garret FitzGerald.

December 6 Bomb killed 16 and injured 66 at Droppin Well bar in Ballykelly: INLA claimed responsibility. **8** £31m to be given in government aid to Falklands. **10** 2 Russian cosmonauts landed after record 211 days in space. **12** 30,000 women ringed perimeter of Greenham Common missile base in anti-nuclear protest. **15** Government defeated by 15 votes on proposed new immigration rules; Gibraltar's frontier with Spain opened to pedestrians after 13 years. **21** New Soviet leader Yuri Andropov offered to reduce medium range nuclear weapons by two-thirds if NATO gave up Pershing and Cruise missiles: proposal rejected by Western leaders. **30** Martial Law suspended in Poland.

A.D.
1983

January 11 Opening of public inquiry into proposed pressurised water reactor at Sizewell. **17** Start of breakfast TV in Britain. **25** EEC agreement on common fishing policy after 7 years. **27** New High Court judgement allowed GLC to cut fares. **31** Law came into force about wearing of seat belts.

February 8 Publication of report on Beirut massacre: Defence Minister Sharon later forced to resign whilst remaining in cabinet. **9** 1981 Derby winner Shergar stolen from stable in County Kildare. **13** Queen started 4-week tour of Jamaica, Mexico, US and Canada. **23** Labour NEC voted to expel 5 members of Militant Tendency.

March 1 Launch of new BL car, the Maestro. **5** Labour Party won decisive victory in Australian general election. **6** Chancellor Helmut Kohl's Christian Democrats won clear victory in West German general election. **8** Miners voted against strike action over pit closures. **14** Tadworth Hospital for children saved from closure. **18** Start of Prince and Princess of Wales' tour of Australia and New Zealand. **22** Chaim Herzog elected president of Israel in preference to PM's candidate. **28** Ian MacGregor appointed chairman of NCB. **31** 3 Russians expelled from Britain for alleged espionage.

April 4 White senator and 2 others killed by dissidents in Zimbabwe. **6** UK passport issued to Ian Smith, ex-PM of Rhodesia. **10** Relatives of Falklands casualties attended service at San Carlos. **12** British-made film Gandhi won 8 Oscars. **18** Many killed in bombing of US embassy in West Beirut; Government agreed to phasing out of lead in petrol. **21** New £1 coin came into circulation. **24** Austria's Chancellor, Dr Bruno Kreisky, resigned after 13 years in office. **25** Socialists failed to gain absolute majority in Portuguese general election. **26** 8 famine relief workers kidnapped in Ethiopia by Tigré People's Liberation Front. **28** High Court judge refused to declare Exit guide to euthanasia illegal.

May 1 Police broke up demonstrations in 20 Polish cities. **6** West German government pronounced that so-called Hitler diaries published in Stern magazine were a forgery. **8** US Secretary of State left Middle East after 2 weeks without peace deal. **13** Parliament dissolved: George Thomas retired as Speaker. **16** London police began fitting wheel clamps to illegally parked cars. **17** Israeli–Lebanon agreement signed on troop withdrawal: Syria imposed blockade in protest. **18** State of Emergency in Sri Lanka after election violence. **19** Missing barrels of Dioxin from chemical plant at Seveso found in Northern France. **20** Bomb exploded in centre of Pretoria, S. Africa; Roof-top protest at Albany gaol: ended 6 days later. **23** Retaliatory S. African raids on Maputo, Mozambique. **24** Huge bomb damaged Andersonstown police station in Belfast. **30** End of Williamsburg summit of 7 industrialised nations: reaffirmation of commitment to fight inflation.

June 9 Election Day: Conservatives had majority of 144; Foreign relief workers freed after 6 weeks as captives of Tigré liberation group in Ethiopia. **11** New Cabinet announced: Francis Pym and David Howell dismissed, hereditary peerage for William Whitelaw, Leon Brittan Home Secretary, Nigel Lawson Chancellor and Sir Geoffrey Howe Foreign Secretary. **13** Roy Jenkins resigned as leader of SDP: David Owen succeeded without election; Pioneer 10 spacecraft became first man-made object to travel beyond solar system. **14** Government 'Fortress Falklands' policy endorsed by all-party Commons defence committee. **15** Mr. Bernard Weatherill elected Speaker. **16** Mr Andropov elected President of USSR. **18** At European summit £450m budget rebate granted to Britain. **22** State opening of Parliament. **24** Syria expelled Yasser Arafat, PLO leader.

July 3 Home of former Ulster MP Gerry Fitt burnt out by IRA. **6** Chancellor announced £500m cuts in state spending. **13** Commons decisively rejected return of death penalty. **15** 6 killed by suitcase

bomb at Orly airport: Armenian extremists responsible; Backbench MPs agreed to pay increases of 5½%. **16** BA helicopter crashed near Scillies with loss of 20 lives. **19** Government agreed to stop OFT inquiry into restrictive practices of Stock Exchange. **21** Polish authorities ended Martial Law. **25** Riots in Colombo against minority Tamil community. **26** Curfew in Hebron after renewed violence; High Court ruling that under-16s were entitled to contraceptive advice without parental consent. **28** Conservatives won Penrith by-election by only 552 votes: Liberal vote increased from 28% to 44%.

August 1 12 injured in oil rig explosion in Forties field. **3** BR announced plans to close 114 miles of track; Settlement of Financial Times dispute that had halted production for 9 weeks. **4** Mr. Bettino Craxi became Italy's first socialist Prime Minister since 1946. **5** Explosion in Lebanese mosque killed 19 people. **8** Military coup in Guatemala. **11** Chad town of Faya-Largeau fell to Libyan troops. **14** French troops took up positions in north-east Chad. **15** Joshua Nkomo returned to Zimbabwe to claim seat in parliament. **21** Philippine opposition leader shot dead at Manila airport; 7 killed and over 50 injured in train crash in Irish Republic. **29** 2 US marines from international peace-keeping force killed in Beirut. **31** South Korean airliner reported missing off coast of Japan: USSR accused of shooting it down and later admitted to.

September 4 Israeli army withdrew from Chouf mountains above Beirut. **8** Rocket attack on Managua airport, Nicaragua. **12** 63 killed in South African mine disaster. **15** Cabinet announced pay target of 3% in public sector; PM Begin of Israel formally resigned amid speculation about his health. **17** US shelled artillery positions in Lebanon. **18** St. Kitts and Nevis became independent. **23** Air crash near Abu Dhabi: all 112 on board killed. **25** 38 IRA prisoners escaped from Maze Prison: prison officer stabbed to death. **26** Lebanese cabinet resigned; Australia II beat Liberty in America's Cup.

October 2 Neil Kinnock elected leader of Labour Party and Roy Hattersley deputy. **7** Government plans announced for abolition of GLC and 6 metropolitan counties. **9** South Korean deputy PM and Foreign Minister among 19 killed by bomb explosion in Rangoon. **10** Mr Yitzhak Shamir's new Israeli government took office. **14** Cecil Parkinson resigned from cabinet after further statement from his former secretary: replaced by Norman Tebbit, Tom King to Employment and Nicholas Ridley to Transport. **19** PM of Grenada, Maurice Bishop shot by troops: army commander General Hudson Austin took control. **23** Suicide bombers killed 229 US marines and 58 French paratroops in Beirut. **25** US troops invaded Grenada together with troops from 6 Caribbean states: Britain opposed to invasion. **27** Last outpost of Grenadan resistance, Fort Frederick, fell to US: Governor-General Sir Paul Scoon returned to island; European Parliament to freeze Britain's promised EEC rebate of £450m. **30** Earthquake in eastern Turkey: at least 226 killed; Raul Alfonsin, Radical Party leader won Argentine general election.

November 3 White minority in South Africa gave 2:1 endorsement to plan to give limited representation to Asians and Coloureds. **4** Dennis Nilsen sentenced to 8 life sentences for 15 killings; 60 people killed in suicide bomb attack on Israeli headquarters in Tyre; 2 RUC men killed by bomb at Ulster Polytechnic. **6** Conservative Motherland Party won election in Turkey. **10** The Queen and Duke of Edinburgh began state visit to Kenya. **12** Gerry Adams, MP for West Belfast became leader of Irish Republican movement. **14** First cruise missiles arrived at Greenham Common. **15** Turkish Cypriots declared UDI under Rauf Denktash. **16** PLO leader Yasser Arafat driven back to Tripoli. **17** Chancellor's autumn statement: cuts to keep public expenditure down, extra 1% to NHS. **18** Sextuplets born in Liverpool; Enthronement of Archbishop of York, Dr John Habgood. **20** 3 killed and 7 injured in terrorist attack in Darkley Gospel Hall in Northern Ireland. **21** Unionist Party with-

A.D.

drew from Northern Ireland Assembly in protest. **23** Soviet Union walked out of Geneva disarmament talks. **24** 6 Israelis released by PLO in return for 4,700 PLO prisoners. **26** 2-day Fleet St. newspaper strike in support of Warrington NGA; £26m gold bullion stolen from Heathrow. **27** Columbian jumbo jet crash near Madrid: 181 killed. **28** European space lab blasted off from Cape Canaveral.

December 5 14 killed in car bomb explosion in Beirut's Moslem area. **6** First heart-lung transplant operation in Britain: patient died after 2 weeks; European summit ended in total failure. **7** 2 Spanish airliners crashed in fog on runway at Madrid airport: 92 killed; Official Unionist, Mr Edgar Graham shot dead at Queen's University, Belfast. **8** US announced lifting of ban on arms sales to Argentina. **10** Bomb explosion at Woolwich RA barracks. **13** Bomb found and detonated in Kensington High St. **15** NGA industrial action called off; European Parliament blocked Britain's EEC rebate. **17** Massive bomb explosion outside Harrods: 6 killed and many injured: IRA stated bomb was 'unauthorised'; 83 died in disco fire in Madrid. **19** Britoil's cancellation of oil rig order led to crisis in Scott Lithgow yard on Clyde. **20** Yasser Arafat and 4,000 guerrillas left Tripoli by sea. **25** Small bomb exploded in Oxford St. **27** Pope met his assailant in prison; Collapse of deal between BSC and US Steel Corporation over Ravenscraig plant. **31** Military coup in Nigeria: Maj.-Gen. Mohammed Buhari new leader.

1984

January 9 Share prices exceeded 800 on FT index; Health Secretary announced extra money for health service. **11** 2 lorry drivers hijacked by French farmers in protest against foreign meat imports. **13** Civil disturbances in Hong Kong. **17** 13 Tories voted against government and 20 abstained in second reading of Rates Bill; Opening of Stockholm conference on disarmament and security in Europe. **18** 2 gunmen assassinated President of American University of Beirut. **20** £1m diamonds stolen from Christie's. **23** Further Tory revolt over government proposals to curb rate rises; 17 drowned when *Radiant Med* sank in English Channel. **24** 1-day strike and demonstrations against abolition of GLC and ILEA. **25** Government announced ban on union membership at GCHQ. **26** Maze prison governor resigned after critical Hennessy report on escape of IRA prisoners. **29** Spanish general murdered by Basque terrorists in Madrid.

February 1 General Kiessling reinstated as German NATO commander. **3** Indian diplomat Ravindra Mhatre kidnapped in Birmingham and later found dead. **5** Lebanese cabinet resigned following 4 days of bitter fighting between army and Shi'ite Moslems. **7** US Marines to be removed from Beirut to offshore ships. **8** British contingent of multinational force in Lebanon airlifted to *Reliant*. **9** Death of President Andropov of Russia: succeeded by Konstantin Chernenko; Mr Harold Macmillan awarded earldom on his 90th birthday. **14** Jayne Torvill and Christopher Dean won ice dancing gold medal at Winter Olympics. **15** Druze and Shi'ite militiamen pushed Lebanese army out of southern approaches to Beirut. **20** Italian peace-keeping contingent left Beirut. **24** French lorry drivers lifted roadblocks which had been crippling traffic in France. **26** All but 100 US marines withdrawn from Beirut. **29** Pierre Trudeau announced resignation as Canadian PM.

March 1 Tony Benn won Chesterfield by-election for Labour. **6** NCB announced loss of 20,000 jobs in mining industry and closure of 21 pits; Deputy prison governor at Maze, William McConnell, shot dead outside home. **12** First day of miners' strike against pit closures. **13** Budget included widespread tax reforms, increases in duty on petrol, beer and spirits but decrease on wine. **14** Gerry Adams, MP for West Belfast, injured in assassination attempt; High Court injunction granted to NCB to prevent flying pickets from Yorkshire. **15** Massive £5m silver robbery at Woburn Abbey. **18**

A.D.

Boat race, postponed for one day by accident to Cambridge boat, won by Oxford. **20** Collapse of EEC summit: Britain blamed for intransigence. **23** Sarah Tisdall, Foreign Office clerk, gaoled for 6 months for leaking documents to *The Guardian*: widespread protests. **25** France began withdrawing peace-keeping force from Beirut. **26** Queen in Jordan for 4-day visit: unprecedented security after bomb explosion. **28** Jardine Matheson to withdraw from Hong Kong; British diplomat shot dead in Athens; Government approved sale of Scott Lithgow shipyard to Trafalgar House. **30** Nissan to build new factory at Washington, Tyne & Wear; Rugby Union team to go to South Africa.

April 3 Coup in Guinea following death (8 days earlier) of President Sekou Touré. **4** Women evicted by bailiffs at Greenham Common. **5** BBC1 blacked out by strike; ILEA to be replaced by directly elected body, not board of nominees. **6** Zola Budd, South African athlete, granted British citizenship in record time. **8** Daughter of RC magistrate killed in IRA trap: woman later charged with murder. **10** Fire destroyed Falkland Islands' only hospital: 8 died; Shuttle crew succeeded in retrieving Solar Max satellite for repair. **11** Konstantin Chernenko approved as President of Supreme Soviet. **12** Miners' executive ruled out national ballot. **13** 5 airmen and 2 soldiers from Cyprus charged under Official Secrets Act. **16** Michael Bettaney gaoled for 23 years after conviction on espionage charges. **17** WPC Yvonne Fletcher shot dead outside Libyan embassy: embassy under siege. **22** Britain broke off diplomatic relations with Libya. **26** British diplomatic families arrived home from Libya. **27** End of siege with deportation of 30 Libyans and return of British ambassador and diplomats from Tripoli.

May 2 47 rescued after ditching of Chinook helicopter in North Sea; Queen opened Liverpool garden festival; NCB announced deal to sell 175,000 tonnes of coke to American steel works. **3** Labour won Cynon Valley by-election, Conservatives won Surrey SW and Stafford with greatly reduced majorities. **7** Napoleon Duarté, Christian Democratic candidate claimed victory in Salvadorean presidential election. **8** Russians announced boycott of Olympic Games: followed later by other Warsaw Pact countries; Commandos attacked Gadafy barracks in Tripoli. **10** Verdict of unlawful killing at inquest into death of WPC Yvonne Fletcher outside Libyan embassy. **13** 16 held hostage by rebels in Angola since February freed. **18** 4 members of security forces killed by IRA; Government to exempt listed building repairs from VAT. **23** Horrific explosion at underground pumping station in Lancs killed 15 people; Talks between NCB and NUM abandoned after 65 minutes. **24** Increase in tension in Gulf war: tanker ablaze.

June 1 President Reagan in Ireland for 3-day visit; Fresh disturbances in Punjab; PM Botha of South Africa in talks with Mrs Thatcher at Chequers amidst protests by anti-apartheid movement. **5** US announced increase in military role in Gulf with dispatch of Awacs. **6** Sikh fanatics in Golden Temple of Amritsar surrendered to Indian army: leader found dead; Celebration of 40th anniversary of D-Day. **8** 7-nation economic summit in London. **14** Elections to European Parliament: substantial gains by Labour although Tories kept majority; Alliance won Portsmouth by-election from Tories. **15** 4 killed in explosions in oil tanker at Milford Haven. **16** John Turner elected leader of Canadian Liberal Party and thus PM. **20** Education Secretary announced plans for new GCSE to replace O level and CSE in 1986. **22** Reports of massive explosion in Soviet Union naval base at Severomorsk; Inaugural flight of Virgin Atlantic, new cut price airline. **26** Agreement reached over EEC budget: Britain settled for 66% rebate; West German Economics Minister resigned after corruption charges. **28** Government defeated in Lords over paving bill for abolition of GLC and metropolitan authorities.

July 2 2,000 short-term prisoners released under new parole procedures. **5** Abducted Nigerian exile, Umaru Dikko found in crate at Stansted. **6** David Jenkins installed as Bishop of Durham. **9** Roof

A.D.

of York Minster destroyed by fire. **12** Robert Maxwell acquired Mirror Group Newspapers. **13** Labour Party won general election in New Zealand. **16** High Court ruled that government ban on unions at GCHQ was illegal; Lords finally voted to abolish GLC and other metropolitan authority elections. **17** Resignation of French government. **18** Publication of Warnock Report on Human Fertilization and Embryology. **19** Large areas of Britain struck by earthquake with epicentre at Porthmadog. **21** Amnesty for 652 political prisoners in Poland. **23** General election in Israel: inconclusive result. **24** Secretary of State for Environment announced 18 councils to have rates capped. **25** Soviet cosmonaut became first woman to walk in space. **27** European Parliament voted to withhold Britain's rebate until agreement on supplementary budget. **29** Opening of Olympic Games in Los Angeles. **30** Agreement reached with China over future of Hong Kong. **31** Air France Boeing hijacked; surrendered on 2 August after blowing up flight deck.

August 2 Bomb exploded at Madras airport. **5** Leader of Israeli Labour Party, Mr Shimon Peres asked to form coalition government. **16** De Lorean cleared of drugs charges in USA. **17** Heart transplant baby Hollie Roffey died 18 days after operation. **19** 11 killed in veteran plane crash in Staffs. **21** Widespread arrests in South Africa on eve of coloured elections which were won by Labour Party. **25** *Mont Louis* sank in English Channel on sand bank. **26** Start of outbreak of salmonella poisoning at Stanley Royde hospital in Wakefield: 26 died. **31** TUC general council agreed to back pit strike; 2 Britons detained in Libya released; Bomb explosion at Kabul airport.

September 3 29 killed in rioting in black townships in Transvaal. **4** Erich Honecker, East German PM cancelled visit to West Germany; Conservatives won enormous victory in Canadian general election: Mr Brian Mulroney became PM. **5** Israeli government of national unity agreed; TUC voted to rejoin Neddy. **10** In government re-shuffle Jim Prior returned to back benches, Douglas Hurd and Rhodes Boyson to Northern Ireland. **13** MoD official Clive Ponting charged under Official Secrets Act; 6 political fugitives took refuge in British Consulate in Durban. **14** Week of pit talks ended in failure. **15** Birth of Prince Henry to Prince and Princess of Wales. **20** US embassy in Beirut attacked by suicide bombers: 20 killed; Labour won 4 GLC by-elections in absence of Tory candidates. **26** Sino-British declaration on future of Hong Kong signed in Peking: capitalist system to be maintained until at least 2047.

October 1 Bank of England rescued leading bullion dealer Johnson Matthey; Sikh Golden Temple returned to civilian hands. **5** Agreement reached between British Airways and British Caledonian over air routes. **10** NUM fined by High Court for contempt; European Parliament paid Britain rebate frozen for 10 months. **12** IRA bomb explosion at Grand Hotel, Brighton: 4 killed, Norman Tebbit and John Wakeham injured. **15** Peace talks on mines dispute at ACAS broke down after 4 days. **23** 350 blacks arrested in SA Vaal townships after 24 hours of violence; Military blamed for murder of Philippines opposition leader. **24** Salvadorean opposition leader died in helicopter crash; Collapse of 2 British tour companies. **25** High Court ordered sequestration of NUM assets; Ethiopian government and Red Cross launched concerted attempt to airlift emergency food supplies; Speaker of Bundestag resigned after allegations of secret payments. **30** EEC announced £34m aid for Ethiopia; Kidnapped Polish priest, Father Popieluszko found dead. **31** PM of India, Mrs Indira Gandhi assassinated by Sikh members of bodyguard: 12 hours later her son Rajiv was sworn in as PM; ACAS talks between NUM and NCB broke down again.

November 1 Violence in India in reprisals against Sikh community. **2** Further riots throughout N. India: calm restored by 4/11. **4** Daniel Ortega elected President of Nicaragua. **5** Irish court froze NUM assets as drift back to work continued. **6**

A.D.

President Reagan won second term of office: Senate with smaller Republican majority and House of Representatives controlled by Democrats. **9** 2 Britons to face spying charges in Libya. **12** Autumn economic statement: commitment to spring tax cuts, phasing out of £1 note, abolition of minimum student grant. **13** Mrs Muriel McLean died as result of injuries received in Brighton bombing. **15** C of E voted to begin process to allow ordination of women; Edward du Cann replaced as chairman of Tory backbench committee after 12 years by Cranley Onslow; Proposals for new pay structure for teachers announced by employers. **18** 4, including 2 Britons detained in Cairo after unsuccessful attempt to murder former Libyan PM. **19** Anglo-Irish summit ended without any significant agreement; Over 600 killed in gas explosion in Mexico City. **21** Report recommended removal of restrictions on Sunday trading; Revolt in Commons over withholding of £15 supplementary benefit from striking miners. **22** Law Lords upheld ban on unions at GCHQ; Foreign Secretary announced cuts in BBC external services, British Council and withdrawal from UNESCO. **26** President Chernenko promised Labour leader that no missiles would be targetted on Britain if Labour scrapped independent deterrent. **27** British deputy high commissioner in Bombay, Mr Percy Norris murdered. **29** Many Tories signed Commons motion denouncing cuts in student grants. **30** Taxi driver taking miner to work killed after concrete post dropped from bridge; High Court appointed receiver to control NUM funds.

December 1 Labour Party returned with reduced majority in Australian general election. **3** Leakage of poisonous gas from pesticides factory in Bhopal, India: at least 2,500 killed and thousands blinded; British Telecom shares made massive gains in first day's trading. **4** 2 killed and 77 injured in collision between Inter-City express and fuel train in Salford; Kuwait airliner hijacked to Tehran: 2 killed and passengers tortured but finally freed on 9 Dec. after action by security forces; Herbert Blaize became PM of Grenada after Nationalist Party won 14 out of 15 seats. **5** Education Secretary capitulated on plans to increase parental contributions to student grants. **10** Inspector recommended immediate expansion of Stansted airport; South African authorities freed 11 anti-apartheid campaigners and re-arrested 6 of them. **11** Patrick Jenkin announced statutory rate limits for 18 high-spending councils; Fog crash on M25 killed 11 motorists. **12** Anti-apartheid demonstrators left British consulate in Durban: 2 arrested at once. **13** Government held Enfield Southgate by-election with greatly reduced majority. **18** Environment Secretary told local authorities to cut capital spending by at least £1 billion next year: Tory backbench revolt. **19** Anglo-Chinese agreement on Hong Kong signed in Peking; Ted Hughes appointed Poet Laureate. **20** Appeal Court ruled that under-16s should not be given contraceptive advice without parental consent; Oil tanker on derailed train exploded in Summit tunnel under Pennines. **21** Death of Marshal Dmitri Ustinov, Soviet Defence Minister announced; 4 killed in car bomb in Beirut; Christening of Prince Harry. **23** PM returned from talks with President Reagan on limiting 'Star Wars' weaponry. **25** Terry Waite, Archbishop of Canterbury's envoy met Colonel Gaddafi and received promise that release of Britons would be recommended to People's Congress. **28** Results of Indian general election gave Rajiv Gandhi massive majority.

1985

January 1 Hundreds died in pitched battle in Northern Angola. **2** Norwegian defence ministry disclosed that Soviet cruise missile had crashed in Finland. **3** News released of airlift of over 12,000 Ethiopian Jews to Israel; Opening of Australian commission hearings into British nuclear tests. **4** Baby born to Britain's first commercial surrogate mother made subject of place of safety order. **7** Start of talks between US and USSR in Geneva on arms control; Princess Margaret had part of left lung removed at

A.D.

Brompton Hospital: tissue found to be innocent; 4 charged in Liverpool with conspiring to cause an explosion. **8** Geneva talks ended in agreement on arms control negotiations to start within a month; Surrogate baby made ward of court; US Treasury Secretary, Donald Regan and White House Chief-of-Staff, James Baker to change posts. Death of Sir Robert Mayer aged 105. **10** Gas explosion in Putney block of flats killed 9 people. **11** 1% rise in base lending rate; 3 US soldiers killed in fire in Pershing missile in Heilbronn. **13** Libyan diplomat murdered in Rome. **14** Chancellor ordered 1.5% rise in clearing bank base rate in dramatic rescue attempt for pound. **15** Civilian became President of Brazil after elections. **17** Rail strike in E. Midlands and S. Yorks over harrassment of men blacking coal trains; Commons suspended for 20 minutes after left-wing protests over miners' strike; 3 shot dead in army payroll robbery in Scotland; Publication of Thomas Report on primary education in London. **18** Mortgage rate to rise; Maximum smog alert in W. German Ruhr area. **20** 36 killed by Tamil separatist bomb on Sri Lankan train; Death of Lord Balogh. **23** House of Lords debate televised live for first time. **27** Death of journalist James Cameron. **28** 2% rise in bank lending rates in attempt to save pound. **29** Oxford University refused PM an honorary degree; Preliminary talks on miners' strike broke down. **30** Larry Whitty elected general secretary of Labour Party; Tory revolt over plan to extend Stansted airport. **31** Labour censure motion on handling of economy; South African government offered to release Nelson Mandela if he renounced violence: Mandela refused.

February 3 Desmond Tutu enthroned as bishop of Johannesburg. **4** Border between Spain and Gibraltar re-opened. **5** Release of 4 Britons held hostage in Libya; Midnight military operation to clear demonstrators from Molesworth cruise missile site. **7** 4 members of Polish secret police gaoled for murder of Polish priest; National Theatre to close Cottesloe and sack 100 staff. **10** Residents returned home after bomb found in Sheffield defused; 9 killed in motorway pile up in snow.**11** Clive Ponting acquitted of breaching the Official Secrets Act; 20 servicemen from RAF band killed in bus collision in W. Germany. **15** Pit peace talks collapsed again; Commons majority in favour of Enoch Powell's bill banning all experiments on human embryos. **18** Deaths in rioting at Crossroads shanty town, South Africa. **19** Arrest of leading anti-apartheid leaders in South Africa after continuing violence. **20** Allegations made by former MI5 officers of telephone tapping of CND and NUM members; PM spoke to joint session of US Congress. **21** Social Services Secretary announced revised list of approved drugs to be prescribed by NHS. **23** 3 youths shot dead by army in N. Ireland. **25** Increase in number of miners returning to work after failure of TUC initiative; Pound reached record low against dollar; General election in Pakistan. **26** Statement from chairman of US Federal Reserve led to recovery of sterling. **28** 9 police killed in IRA mortar bomb attack on Newry police station; Meeting of NUM executive agreed to call a delegate conference to consider strike.

March 3 Miners agreed to call off strike without an agreement; RC policeman in Ulster shot outside church. **4** New Zealand PM re-affirmed his country's ban on nuclear weapons after visit to Britain; 15 killed in bombing of Shi'ite mosque in Lebanon. **6** Bridge Report into ministerial authorisation of telephone tapping cleared government of breaking rules. **7** 2 Belfast men sentenced to life imprisonment for bombings in London; Sizewell inquiry ended after 26 months. **8** Car bomb killed 80 in Beirut. **10** Lebanese car bomb killed 12 Israeli soldiers in retaliation; GLC finally approved legal budget after disarray in Labour group; Death of President Chernenko of Soviet Union: Mikhail Gorbachev named as successor. **11** Israelis killed 34 Shi'ite Muslims in further reprisals; Prescription charges to rise to £2 and increases in dental charges; Harrods and other House of Fraser stores bought by Egyptian Al Fayed company. **12** Commons statement that no breaches of guidelines over surveillance by MI5

A.D.

had taken place; Geneva arms control talks began. **13** Government to abolish BNOC; Funeral of President Chernenko used as opportunity for meetings between world leaders; Serious violence during and after Luton–Millwall soccer match. **14** Swann committee reported on education of ethnic minority children; 3 Britons freed by Angolan rebels. **15** *Rand Daily Mail*, South Africa's leading liberal newspaper to cease publication; Belgian government gave go-ahead for deployment of cruise missiles. **18** 4 blacks died in fresh violence in eastern Cape Province, SA. **19** Budget Day: alterations in NI, extension of YTS, increase in tax on cigarettes and drink and higher road tax. **20** Base rate rose to 13%. **21** SA police shot dead 19 blacks in Uitenhage on 25th anniversary of Sharpeville massacre; Pound soared as dollar fell; Death of Sir Michael Redgrave. **23** Death of Lord Beeching. **24** American army major shot dead by Russian soldier in East Germany. **26** Education white paper proposed legislation to appraise teachers. **27** Colour TV licence to rise to £58 and black and white to £18. **28** Inquiry began into death of Jasmine Beckford after father found guilty of manslaughter; Death of painter Marc Chagall. **29** Political crisis in Greece after election of president; Maori archbishop to be Governor of New Zealand. **30** 4 killed in hovercraft crash at Dover.

April 2 Federation of Conservative Students suspended in effort to curb activities of far right. **4** PM began 11-day tour of Asia. **6** President Numeiri of Sudan deposed in military coup. **7** Mr Gorbachev announced Soviet freeze in deployment of nuclear missiles in Europe for 6 months. **11** Death of Albanian leader Mr Enver Hoxha announced; 24 killed by Tamil bomb at Colombo shortly before arrival of PM in Sri Lanka. **15** South Africa announced intention to withdraw from Angola and repeal mixed marriage laws. **18** 2 Russians expelled from Britain: later expulsions of Britons from Russia in retaliation. **19** Higher inflation rate announced as interest rates fell. **21** Death of Mr Tancredo Neves, President-elect of Brazil. **22** Launch of all-party Charter for Jobs; Nissan signed agreement for single union at new Washington plant. **24** 3rd stage of Israeli withdrawal from Lebanon began. **25** TGWU ordered re-ballot of members after allegations over general secretary elections. **26** NCB announced closure of Polkemmet colliery after flooding during strike. **28** Ken Livingstone selected as prospective candidate for Brent East seat. **29** Prince and Princess of Wales had audience with Pope. **30** Britain's first black bishop, Venerable Wilfred Wood appointed.

May 1 US banned all trade with Nicaragua; Ethiopia's largest famine relief camp forcibly cleared by troops; President Reagan arrived in Germany at start of controversial tour of Europe. **2** General secretary of NCCL, Larry Gostin resigned after disagreement over attitude towards miners' strike; Gains by Alliance in county council elections: held balance of power in over half. **3** Epidemic in Stafford identified as Legionnaires' disease: 30 dead; Uproar in Commons over bill to ban research on human embryos. **6** 4 schoolboys drowned by wave at Land's End. **7** Government announced privatisation of British Gas. **8** Commemoration of 40th anniversary of VE day. **9** Vetting procedures in security services to be tightened. **10** President Reagan agreed to freeze in defence spending; Sikh bomb explosions in several North Indian cities; 12 killed in swimming pool roof collapse near Zurich. **11** Fire at Bradford City FC left 55 dead and many others seriously injured; Violence at Birmingham halted match. **12** Launch of Conservative Centre Forward group led by Francis Pym; Demonstrations against Pope in Holland; Prince Andrew opened new £276m Falklands airport. **13** Government suffered fourth defeat in Lords over GLC abolition bill. **15** Sri Lankan Tamil terrorists shot dead more than 146 people. **16** 2 miners gaoled for life for murder of taxi driver during miners' strike; Sinn Fein won number of seats in Northern Ireland local elections. **20** 3 Israeli prisoners exchanged for 1,150 Palestinians and Lebanese held by Israel; Bomb killed 4 members of RUC; Commons accepted case for Sunday trading. **21** Publication of government

A.D.

green paper on universities. **22** Massive car bomb devasted residential area of E. Beirut in week of renewed violence; Environment Secretary rejected plan for tower block opposite Mansion House. **23** Development of airport in London's docklands approved. **24** NCB announced further redundancies in Yorks; Tidal wave swamped islands off coast of Bangladesh: thousands drowned or made homeless. **26** 33 killed when 2 oil tankers exploded and caught fire in Bay of Algeciras; Death of Roy Plomley, broadcaster. **28** European Court of Human Rights ruled that British immigration rules discriminate against women. **29** 38 killed after wall collapse in soccer violence at Heysel stadium, Brussels before Liverpool v. Juventus match: British teams later banned indefinitely from European competition; 7 killed in British school coach crash in France.

June 2 Socialist Party won absolute majority in Greek general election; Chinese PM in London for 6-day visit; Death of Lord George-Brown. **3** Government announced proposed social security reforms: state earnings related pension scheme to be phased out and cuts in housing benefit. **5** Government approved development of Stansted as London's third airport. **6** Government announced pay increase for nurses, midwives and armed forces but did not alter cash limits to pay for them; Worldwide ban on English football teams imposed by Fifa. **7** Powell bill on research on human embryos 'talked out' of Commons; 700 passengers evacuated from holed British ferry *Norland*. **9** Further fighting in Sri Lanka between Sinhalese and Tamils. **10** President Reagan announced continued adherence to unratified Salt II; Israel announced completion of withdrawal from Lebanon. **11** 4 Soviet spies exchanged for 25 Western agents; Mrs Barbara Castle defeated in election for leadership of Labour group in European Parliament. **12** Mr Ron Todd won re-run election for general secretary of TGWU; Shi'ite Moslem gunmen blew up Jordanian aircraft cockpit after releasing hijack passengers and crew. **13** John Paul Getty Jnr offered £50m to the National Gallery. **14** TWA airliner hijacked after leaving Athens: 1 passenger shot, other hostages removed from airliner and eventually freed on 30 June; South African troops carried out raid into Botswana on illegal ANC bases. **17** Government gave go-ahead for closer links between Honda and BL. **18** Social Services Secretary announced rise in child benefit below inflation but uprating of other benefits; 19th policeman this year killed in Ulster. **19** Bomb explosion in departure hall at Frankfurt airport: 3 killed; Car bomb in Tripoli killed 60. **21** Forensic scientists concluded that body exhumed in São Paulo was that of Josef Mengele. **23** Air India Boeing crashed in Irish Sea killing all 329 on board; 2 freight handlers in Japan killed by bomb; Bomb found in Rubens Hotel near Buckingham Palace successfully defused: later 9 arrested and plans discovered for bombing campaign in seaside resorts. **25** Sir Kenneth Newman to head anti-terrorist operation in Britain.

July 1 7 charged in London for terrorism offences; Patrick Magee charged with Grand Hotel explosion; Bomb attacks in Madrid and Rome. **2** Mr Andrei Gromyko became President of USSR and Mr Eduard Shevardnadze, Foreign Minister; Church of England general synod approved ordination of women as deacons. **3** Notts leaders sacked from jobs by NUM; followed by withdrawal of area from NUM; Announcement of summit between President Reagan and Mr Gorbachev; Israel released 300 Lebanese prisoners from detention. **4** Alliance candidate won Brecon and Radnor by-election: Labour close second, Tory third; NUM approved new constitution which will allow Arthur Scargill to remain president until his retirement. **7** Unseeded teenager, Boris Becker won Wimbledon men's singles title; Robert Mugabe won 63 out of 79 seats in Zimbabwe election. **8** 8 killed in Paris express train crash at automatic level crossing; Britain lifted ban on trade with Argentina. **9** Violence in Kwa Thema township near Johannesburg; 2 suicide bombers killed 15 in South Lebanon. **10** 2 explosions sank Greenpeace campaign ship *Rainbow Warrior* in Auckland, NZ: 1 man on board killed. **12** Birmingham chosen to

A.D.

be Britain's nomination for 1992 Olympic Games; 6p cut in petrol prices; 23 RUC officers injured after ban on Orange Day parade through RC areas. **13** President Reagan underwent operation to remove cancerous growth from his intestines; Live Aid pop concert in Britain and America raised more than £50m for famine victims in Africa. **15** Cut of base lending rates from 12.5% to 12%; 5 ministers resigned from Belgian coalition in reaction to report on Heysel stadium tragedy: general election to be held in October. **16** Steve Cram set new world record for 1500 metres; Death of Heinrich Böll, Nobel prize-winning novelist. **17** Government announced inquiry into collapse of Johnson Matthey Bankers; Radical new plan announced for BBC. **18** Political storm after announcement of massive pay rises for top civil servants, judges and members of armed forces; New National Drugs Intelligence Unit set up headed by senior police officer. **19** 260 died in dam collapse in tourist resort of Stava, Italy: Spain agreed to new extradition treaty with Britain. **21** South African goverment declared State of Emergency after increasing unrest in black townships; Sandy Lyle became first British golfer for 16 years to win the Open. **24** France launched international campaign to organise sanctions against South Africa; Popplewell report on safety and combating violence on football grounds published; Government had a majority of only 17 on vote on top people's pay awards; Commons foreign affairs committee split over sinking of *Belgrano*. **25** Halifax and Abbey National announced cut in mortgage rate to 13.25%. **26** Transport Secretary announced routing of Okehampton bypass through Dartmoor National Park. **27** Milton Obote of Uganda overthrown in military coup; Steve Cram won world record mile in 3.463 minutes in Oslo. **29** Base rate cut by further ¼% to 11.5%. **30** BBC cancelled programme on N. Ireland: NUJ strike in protest on 7 August, programme later screened.

August 2 TriStar crash at Dallas-Fort Worth killed 133. **3** 35 killed in French rail crash. **4** Steve Cram broke 3rd world record: 200 metres in Budapest. **7** BSC announced closure of 2 steel plants. **8** South African government announced tougher emergency powers to deal with violence in black townships; Pope began tour of 7 African countries. **11** Death toll of 65 in 6 day's rioting in Durban townships; 100 yachts forced to retire from Fastnet race in bad weather. **12** Japanese Boeing 747 crashed near Tokyo: 524 killed, 4 survived; Rail disruption began over single-manning of freight trains. **13** Petrol bomb damaged home of Mrs Winnie Mandela in Brandfort, OFS. **15** South African President P. W. Botha rejected concept of overnight reform of apartheid; Mortgage rate to be cut by 1.25%; *Virgin Atlantic Challenger* sank shortly before reaching Land's End in Blue Riband attempt. **16** BR sacked 147 Glasgow guards after protests against introduction of driver-only trains. **17** 54 killed by car bomb in Christian East Beirut. **19** 29 killed in retaliation in Muslim area: led to escalation of violence with another 200 killed. **20** Moderate Sikh leader Sant Harchand Singh Longowal shot dead by extremists in Punjab. **21** Laker accepted £5.7m to end legal battle over collapse of Laker Airways. **22** 54 died and 83 escaped when Boeing 737 burst into flames at Manchester airport; Production of the *Daily Mirror* halted during dispute until 2 September. **23** Guinness took over control of Arthur Bell and Son, whisky maker; Defection of West German counter-espionage agent to East Germany. **24** 5-year-old boy accidentally shot dead by policeman in Birmingham. **26** Tricot report on sinking of Greenpeace vessel cleared French government and secret service of responsibility; Zola Budd broke world 5000 metre record. **27** South African government suspended stock market trading to protect rand; Nigeria's military government overthrown in coup. **28** BR guards rejected NUR strike call by majority of 455; 4 shot dead after march in South Africa halted: rioting spread and death toll for year reached more than 650. **29** Miss Benazir Bhutto held under house arrest after returning to Pakistan for brother's funeral. **30** 30 died in train derailment near Argenton sur Creuse in France:

A.D.

driver charged with manslaughter; Alert in USA as Hurricane Elena approached: damage less than feared.

September 1 South Africa announced suspension of repayments on foriegn debt in order to protect the rand; Riots in Cork prison destroyed much of the building. **2** Cabinet re-shuffle: Leon Brittan replaced as Home Secretary by Douglas Hurd, Norman Tebbit party chairman, Tom King to Northern Ireland; Wreck of *Titanic* found and filmed; England regained the Ashes. **3** British tourists injured in grenade attack on hotel swimming pool near Athens. **4** TUC leaders averted serious crisis over AUEW acceptance of government money for ballots; Arjun Dass of Indian Congress Party shot dead by Sikh extremists. **5** South African violence spread to white areas; High Court ordered reinstatement of Ray Honeyford, Bradford head suspended for racist remarks. **6** SA authorities in Western Cape closed many schools. **9** President Reagan announced limited sanctions against SA; Riots in Handsworth area of Birmingham: large scale disturbances, looting and arson; Attempted coup in Bangkok, Thailand quelled by government forces. **10** Scottish team manager Jock Stein collapsed and died after world cup qualifying match. **11** President P. W. Botha to restore SA citizenship to nearly 8m blacks in tribal 'homelands'; 46 killed in Portuguese train crash. **12** SA President's Council recommended abolition of pass laws; Britain expelled 25 Russians after defection of KGB double agent, Oleg Gordievsky. **14** Russia expelled 25 diplomats in retaliation: on subsequent days a further 6 from each side were expelled; Britain won £3 billion contract to supply aircraft to Saudi Arabia. **17** Defection of secretary of Chancellor Kohl to East Berlin; Death of Laura Ashley, fashion designer. **9** Massive earthquake in Mexico:: more than 4,700 killed and 30,000 injured. **20** French Defence Minister Mr Charles Hernu resigned over *Rainbow Warrior* affair: PM later admitted Hernu had ordered sinking. **22** Death of German publisher Axel Springer. **24** Indefinite strike by Liverpool's workforce called off by unions; New plan for coal delivered to NUM; 25,000 in London teachers' rally. **25** Sikh party won landslide victory in elections to Punjab assembly. **27** Americans evacuated as Hurricane Gloria pounded eastern seaboard. **28** Violent rioting in Brixton following shooting of Mrs Cherry Groce by police inspector. **30** President Botha committed government to power-sharing; 4 Soviet diplomats kidnapped in West Beirut: 1 later found dead, others released on 30 October.

October 1 Tension in Toxteth area of Liverpool; Israeli bombers launched air raid on PLO guerrilla headquarters in Tunisia: 60 killed; Death of AUEW President Terry Duffy and of Dr Charles Richter. **2** Film star Rock Hudson died of AIDS. **3** Mr Gorbachev in Paris announced Russian proposals for cuts in long range weapons and direct talks with Britain and France; Unemployment reached record 3,346,198 in September; Chairman of British Steel, Sir Robert Haslam to become chairman of NCB. **6** Policeman killed in riots on Broadwater Farm estate in Tottenham: followed collapse and death of black woman while police searched her home; Portuguese general election returned minority centre right government. **7** Italian cruise ship *Achille Lauro* hijacked by PLO group: 1 passenger killed, remainder released on 9 October. **8** Men at Cortonwood colliery accepted redundancy proposals. **10** Death of Yul Brynner and Orson Welles. **11** US F-14 fighters hijacked 4 *Achille Lauro* terrorists to Sicily as they were being flown to Tunis; Queen began tour of Caribbean in Belize; Nobel peace prize awarded to 2 professors who founded International Physicians for the Prevention of Nuclear War. **12** Guerrilla Mohammed Abbas believed to have masterminded hijack allowed to go to Yugoslavia. **13** Belgian general election: centre right coalition had slightly increased majority. **14** Death of Lord Diplock; Foreign Secretary cancelled planned talks with PLO leaders because they refused to comdemn violence. **16** Opening of Commonwealth summit meeting in Nassau. **17** Italian coalition collapsed after row over *Achille Lauro* kidnapping;

A.D.

Law Lords overturned earlier ruling that it was unlawful to give contraceptive advice to under-16s; High Court ruled that Liverpool Council acted illegally in issuing redundancy notices to teachers in attempt to solve financial crisis; Nobel prize for literature won by Claude Simon; EFU voted to allow England to stay in European soccer championships; David Hodge, freelance photographer died as result of injuries in Tottehnham riots. **18** Benjamin Moloise executed in South Africa; riots in protest in central Johannesburg; Miners in Notts and South Derbyshire voted to leave NUM and join Union of Democratic Mineworkers. **20** Commonwealth leaders agreed measures to be taken against South Africa: ban on imports of krugerrands and government funded trade missions. **21** 13 killed in coach crash on M6. **24** French commandos seized Greenpeace protest yacht *Vega*; Trading in tin suspended on London Metal Exchange. **25** Derbyshire's chief constable removed from his post; South Africa State of Emergency extended to cover Cape Town and 7 surrounding areas. **27** Prince and Princess of Wales began 10-day Australian tour; Armed gang stole Monet's painting *Impression, Sunrise* and 8 other paintings from Paris galley. **28** Cyprus spy trial ended after 119 days with the acquittal of last 2 of 7 servicemen accused: political storm, triple inquiry set up. **29** Retirement of Lester Piggott as jockey; Death of editor of *The Times*, Charles Douglas-Home: deputy editor Charles Wilson later appointed. **31** 2 Welsh miners convicted of murder of taxi driver had sentences reduced to manslaughter; Booker prize won by Keri Hulme's *The Bone People*.

November 1 Netherlands government to proceed with deployment of cruise missiles. **2** South African government banned television coverage of riots and imposed restrictions on newspaper reporters. **3** Hackney tower block left partly standing after failure of demolition explosion. **4** 'Voluntary' entrance charge introduced at Victoria and Albert museum; KGB officer who defected to US in September returned to USSR: claimed he had been abducted. **5** 14 hours of talks between US Secretary of State and Soviet leaders; US chose to buy French communications system rather than British. **6** Queen's speech: Sale of British Gas, tougher law and order measures and economic strategy geared to tax cuts, deregulation of Sunday trading. **7** Siege of Bogota's Supreme Court by Colombian left-wing guerrillas ended with death of more than 90. **8** Soccer fan given life imprisonment for riot and assault; Out-of-court settlement of compensation for victims of Manchester air disaster; 2 Sikhs charged in British Columbia with making and possessing explosives. **9** Kasparov beat Karpov to become world chess champion. **10** 8 killed in supermarket robbery in Belgium. **11** Report on Land's End drowning tragedy censured head for failure to lead trip adequately; Brian Sedgemore MP suspended from Commons for allegations over Johnson Matthey Bankers' affair. **12** Chancellor's autumn statement: increase in public expenditure, privatisation of British Gas; 2 bombs defused outside Chelsea barracks. **13** Israeli PM sacked Likud Minister of Trade, Ariel Sharon; High Court ruled Bradford Council did have right to suspend head, Ray Honeyford despite opposition of governors. **14** Eruption of long-dormant volcano in W. Colombia caused landslide: 20,000 feared dead in Armero; NUM apologised in court to end sequestration of assets. **15** Agreement on Ulster signed by PM and Dr Garret Fitzgerald: Republic given right to formal participation in Ulster affairs: Treasury Minister Ian Gow resigned in protest; Transport Minister announced fitting of governors to motorway coaches to prevent speeding. **19** Start of summit meeting between President Reagan and Mr Gorbachev: news black-out imposed. **20** Commons voted against televising of proceedings; Northern Ireland Secretary abused and attacked in Loyalist demonstration. **21** Summit ended in harmony but with few concrete proposals: acceleration of arms control negotiations, opening of consulates and increased trade and cultural exchanges; Irish parliament approved Anglo-Irish accord; 13 killed in further unrest in South Africa. **22** Loan from Swiss bankers averted Liverpool's

A.D.

financial crisis: Council to set a legal budget; Terry Waite trapped for 4 days in his Beirut hotel by fighting. **24** 60 killed when Egyptian commandos in Malta stormed hijacked Boeing; Oxfam to withdraw account from Barclays because of involvement in South Africa; State of Emergency declared in Colombia. **27** Anglo-Irish agreement approved in Commons by massive majority of 473 to 47: 2 Unionist MPs resigned at once and others said they would follow; Liverpool Labour Party activities suspended pending inquiry into Militant activities; France exploded nuclear device at Mururoa Atoll. **28** City of London police announced discovery of fraud against Johnson Matthey Bank in 1981; Guerrillas launched rocket attack on South African oil plants in E. Transvaal. **20** Seychelles resistance leader Gerard Hoareau shot in London.

December 1 Congress of South African trade unions launched at rally in Durban: federation of 34 unions representing 500,000 black workers. **2** Yelena Bonner, wife of Andrei Sakharov arrived in Italy from internal exile for medical treatment. **3** Publication of Anglican report *Faith in the City* highly critical of government policy; Blom-Cooper Report criticised many of those involved in death of Jasmine Beckford: 3 council employees subsequently dismissed; Death of poet Philip Larkin; Common Market summit marathon ended with agreement on trade barriers and reforms. **4** Admiral John Poindexter became US National Security Adviser; Northern Ireland Secretary apologised in Commons for gaffe over Anglo-Irish agreement; Accidental death verdict in inquest on death which sparked off Tottenham riots. **5** Britain announced decision to withdraw from Unesco; Labour retained seat in Tyne Bridge by-election; Tories in third place. **6** Britain signed agreement to participate in US strategic defence initiative (SDI). **7** Death of Robert Graves. **9** In Argentina 2 junta members were sentenced to life imprisonment but ex-President Galtieri acquitted on human rights charges; 50 bravery awards presented arising from Bradford fire; Commons voted for fixed Channel link; OPEC ended controls on oil production. **11** New code of conduct to be issued for RUC: 38 police officers hurt in rally of Loyalists protesting at first meeting of Anglo-Irish conference; Control of *Daily Telegraph* passed to Canadian, Conrad Black. **12** 249 US servicemen killed in DC8 crash in Newfoundland; 2 men acquitted on charge of murdering a policeman: self defence accepted. **13** Army called in to assist with Leeds water supplies after burst main; Westland helicopters announced it had agreed to a deal with US and Italian consortium: Defence Secretary against deal; Court of Appeal ruled Social Services Secretary had acted illegally over lodging rules for unemployed; Man accused of murder of Sir Norman Stronge acquitted after extradition from Republic. **14** Ray Honeyford, Bradford head to accept early retirement. **16** Social Security White Paper: SERPS retained in reduced form, cuts in rent and rates payments, new system of income support for families; 6 white people killed in landmine attack in N. Transvaal, S.A.; US Mafia boss shot dead in New York. **17** Mass resignation of Ulster Unionist MPs: January poll on Anglo-Irish agreement. **18** Shire counties to face 20% increase in rates because of changes in rate support grant; 27 Belfast men gaoled after information from informer Harry Kirkpatrick. **20** 3 gunmen surrendered after court siege at Nantes; Ostermilk products withdrawn after salmonella alert; Nigerian coup failed. **23** 7 killed in bomb explosion near Durban, S.A. **24** Fierce tribal clashes between Zulus and Pondos, S of Durban. **25** Eruption of Mount Etna. **27** Terrorist attacks at Rome and Vienna airports directed at Israeli check-in desks: 19 killed. **30** Black nationalist leader, Winnie Mandela arrested for a second time for defying ban on entering Soweto; 550 extra soldiers flown to Ulster; Military rule ended in Pakistan.

1986

January 1 2 policemen killed by IRA bomb one minute after midnight. **2** England B cricket team

A.D.

refused entry to Bangladesh: tour to Zimbabwe cancelled on 8 January; Thousands of blacks joined white mourners at funeral of Molly Blackburn, leading anti-apartheid activist; 2 BBC journalists suspended without pay for 3 months after criticism of the Rough Justice programme tactics. **3** £500m submarine order awarded by MoD to Vickers-Cammell Laird. **4** Death of Christopher Isherwood. **5** Westland to recommend US rescue plan to shareholders in preference to European option. **6** New Law Lords appointed following retirement of Lords Scarman and Roskill. **7** President Reagan broke off economic and commercial links with Libya: Britain refused to join sanctions. **8** 1% rise in bank interest rates. **9** Michael Heseltine resigned over Westland affair and accused Prime Minister of stifling debate: George Younger became Defence Secretary; Mrs Sandra Riley committed to maximum security hospital after killing the third of her sons; Militant candidate defeated in Liverpool council by-election. **10** Roskill Committee recommended Fraud Trials Tribunal for complex fraud trials rather than jury; Mrs Lynda Chalker became Minister of State at the Foreign Office. **11** 3 British explorers reached South Pole on foot. **12** Metropolitan Police report on Tottenham riots stated riot was prepared in advance; Lazard, financial advisers to Westland failed to buy out Alan Bristow the largest shareholder. **13** Leon Brittan forced to apologise to the Commons for concealing the existence of letter about Westland: meeting of shareholders postponed until Friday; South African court upheld ban on Winnie Mandela entering Soweto; 4 plotters executed for attempted coup in S. Yemen. **15** Government published spending plans for next 3 years; Government majority of 153 at end of Westland debate. **16** Publication of final report of Popplewell Inquiry; Dutch arrested 3 IRA men who escaped from Maze prison 3 years ago; Geneva arms talks resumed after new proposals by Mr Gorbachev; Christian militia leader in Syria overthrown and forced into exile. **17** Brother of Arab ambassador freed after 3m dollar ransom paid; Westland shareholders blocked US deal; 3 Spanish embassy officials kidnapped in Beirut; Royal yacht *Britannia* evacuated Britons and others from Aden. **19** Rebel forces claimed victory in Aden; Michael Cocks, former Labour Chief Whip lost re-selection battle to Bennite. **20** Anglo-French agreement on twin tunnel Channel rail link; 30 Tory MPs voted against rate support grant settlement in Commons; Claim that Russian agents had infiltrated Greenham Common peace camp; Chief Jonathan overthrown in Lesotho. **21** Inquiry into food poisoning at Stanley Royd hospital in Wakefield blamed human error; Farley baby food firm to close after salmonella outbreak; Beirut car bomb killed 27 people. **22** 3 Sikhs sentenced to death in India for part in assassination of Mrs Indira Gandhi. **23** PM statement to Commons admitted leak of letter had been authorised by No 10 and DTI; Further 2,000 refugees rescued from S. Yemen by British, French and Soviet ships. **24** Leon Brittan resigned after criticism over leaks; Ulster by-election result: 14 seats retained by Unionists, 1 won by SDLP; Teachers reached agreement at ACAS over settlement of 11-month dispute. **26** Rupert Murdoch printed *Sunday Times* and *News of the World* at Wapping despite strike action by print unions; Portuguese presidential election: second ballot necessary; National Resistance Army took control of capital of Uganda, Kampala; *Voyager II* sent back excellent pictures of Uranus. **27** Thatcher statement on Westland affair resulted in government majority. **28** *Challenger* shuttle crashed during take-off: all 7 on board killed; Publication of green paper on rate reform. **29** Yoweri Museveni sworn in as new President of Uganda. **30** Dramatic increase in unemployment to 3,400,000. **31** Violence in Haiti as President Duvalier clung to power.

February 1 Pope arrived in India for 10-day visit. **2** Government accused of planning to sell BL bus and truck divisions to General Motors; Floods in Venice and severe weather throughout Europe. **4** Israeli war planes forced Libyan jet to land; aircraft found to have only politicians on

A.D.

board; Pump price of petrol cut by 3p per gallon. **5** Amber alert at Sellafield after release of radioactive cloud; 3rd bomb explosion in Paris in 3 days injured 9; Government announced plans for water privatisation. **6** Cabinet vetoed Ford take-over of Austin-Rover. **7** Jean-Claude Duvalier left Haiti for French exile: jubilation among Haitians; Leader of opposition in South Africa resigned from parliament; Early results in Philippine election showed no clear result: serious voting and counting anomalies. **8** 50 killed in Canadian rail crash in Rocky Mountain foothills; New Haitian military rulers attempted to restore order after looting and violence against Tontons Macoutes. **10** Graham Greene, Sir Frank Whittle and Frederick Sanger received OM; Start of massive Mafia trial in Sicily; High Court ordered sequestration of Sogat 82 assets. **11** Anatoly Shcharansky and 3 others freed by Soviet Union in return for 5 Eastern bloc agents; Extra £25m for police to combat terrorism, public disorder and drug abuse. **12** Control of Westland finally passed to Sikorsky-Fiat after shareholders' vote; Channel tunnel agreement signed in Canterbury. **14** Death of Edmund Rubbra, composer. **15** President Marcos proclaimed victor in Philippines amid protests of illegality. **16** 700 saved after wreck of Soviet cruise liner off New Zealand; Philippines opposition leader called for national strike and campaign of civil disobedience; Mario Soares won Portuguese presidential election; Queen and Prince Philip in Nepal for 5-day visit. **17** 9 EEC members signed package of reforms: followed by Denmark after referendum on 2 February and Italy and Greece the next day. **18** Worsening violence in Alexandria township outside Johannesburg: Bishop Tutu attempted to quell riots. **19** Inquiry set up into safety at Sellafield after a number of radioactive leaks. **20** Soviet Union launched first stage of manned orbiting laboratory; Publication of Education Bill. **21** Scotland Yard ordered new inquiry into police assault on 5 youths: 4 policemen charged 2 days later; Radioactive gas released at Trawsfynydd, North Wales. **24** Increase of 10p in child benefit announced; Start of royal tour of New Zealand. **25** Mrs Corazon Aquino assumed power in Philippines as Marcos fled; Announcement of 3 sites for nuclear waste disposal: Bradwell, South Killingholme and Fulbeck; Northern Ireland talks between PM and Ulster Unionist leaders; Mr Gorbachev gave keynote speech to party congress: challenge to US over disarmament; IBA vetoed Rank bid for Granada. **26** Rioting in Cairo left 107 dead; Labour NEC to begin disciplinary proceedings against 16 Militants in Liverpool following inquiry; European Court ruled that retirement age should be the same for men and women; Admission charges to be imposed at 3 further national museums. **27** Customs investigators arrested 12 in raids over gold bullion. **28** Olof Palme, Swedish PM assassinated; President Aquino freed over 400 political prisoners; Defence Secretary ordered phone tapping on ministry phones; Pound dropped after oil price forecast by Sheikh Yamani.

March 1 Further radiation leak at Sellafield. **2** Mayor of Nablus on the West Bank assassinated: Iranian planes bombed Turkish tanker in the Gulf; Queen signed proclamation giving Australia legal independence; 150 foreign workers kidnapped in Angola. **3** Violence during one-day strike in Ulster against Anglo-Irish agreement; 7 Blacks killed in police ambush near Cape Town; End of teacher's strike: NUT to continue ban on extra activities. **4** South African PM announced lifting of State of Emergency; First issue of *Today* published; Death of MP for Ryedale. **5** High Court rejected plea over failure of Liverpool and Lambeth to set rate: councillors faced loss of office and surcharges; President Aquino ordered release of former communists in Philippines. **6** HQ of Release Mandela committee in South Africa gutted by fire; Government inquiry set up into Scottish teachers' pay. **7** Government approved management buyout for Vickers despite higher offer by Trafalgar House. **8** 4-man French television crew seized in Beirut by Islamic Jihad. **10** Government announced further 20p rise in prescription charges to £2·20 per item. **12** Spanish referendum voted to stay in NATO; All-party Commons committee

A.D.

recommended abandonment of new nuclear reprocessing plant at Sellafield; BA privatisation postponed; Ingvar Carlsson elected PM of Sweden. **13** Home Office figures showed alarming rise in crime figures, especially rape; Further 550 troops ordered to Northern Ireland. **14** Death of Sir Huw Wheldon and Lord Fulton. **15** Collapse of 7-storey hotel in Singapore: 33 killed. **15** Massive demonstration at Wapping: 28 arrested. **16** Move to right in French general election: Jacques Chirac later appointed Prime Minister; 75% of Swiss voters voted against joining UN; 16 South Africans died in weekend violence. **17** 176 foreign hostages in Angola handed over to Red Cross; Death of Sir John Glubb. **18** Budget Day: standard rate income tax reduced to 29%, 11p on cigarettes and 7·5p on petrol; Death of Bernard Malamud. **19** Engagement of Prince Andrew and Miss Sarah Ferguson; Banks cut base rate by 1% to 11·5%. **20** President Reagan defeated in House of Representatives on aid to Contras in Nicaragua; Bomb attack in Champs Élysées in Paris. **22** Evelyn Glenholmes freed in Dublin after errors in extradition warrant; US conducted nuclear test beneath Nevada desert. **23** Floods damaged priceless treasures at Victoria and Albert museum. **24** US fleet destroyed missile battery on Gulf of Sidra after Libya fired 6 surface to air missiles; OPEC adjourned conference after failing to reach agreement on production cuts; Hurricane force winds killed at least 8 in Britain; Further restrictions on cigarette advertising announced. **25** US stepped up attacks on Libyan forces; Dutch court refused to extradite convicted Irish bomber and escaped convict; Further South Africans, including white policeman killed in riots; Commons announcement that deal to sell part of BL to General Motors had collapsed. **26** 7 left-wing members of Labour NEC walked out, thus halting disciplinary hearing against Liverpool Militant members; Police killed 11 in Bophuthatswana; 8 killed in bomb explosion in Christian East Beirut; Police shot dead Sikh militants in Punjab. **27** 22 hurt in car bomb explosion in Melbourne, Australia. **28** 14 died in South African rail crash: sabotage feared; *Express* journalists agreed to job losses in face of threat of closure. **29** Death of film star James Cagney. **31** Loyalist riots in Portadown, Co. Armagh; South wing of Hampton Court damaged by fire; Mexican air crash: 166 killed; GLC and 6 Metropolitan councils abolished.

April 1 Oil prices fell below 10 dollars a barrel for first time in 12 years; Women to get right to continue working until 65; Prince of Wales opened Terminal 4 at Heathrow. **2** 4 killed when bomb exploded on TWA Boeing between Rome and Athens; 15 Italians killed by excess methanol in cheap red wine; NUT voted for ban on GCSE preparation. **3** Death of Sir Peter Pears; RUC announced steps to protect officers after wave of attacks; Woolworths rejected take-over bid by Dixons. **4** Murdoch offered unions Grays Inn Road print plant in attempt to settle dispute. **5** Bomb in Berlin disco killed US soldier and a civilian. **6** Continued attacks on RUC: 16 firebombs over weekend; Strike in Norway's North Sea oil industry. **7** Sinclair home computers sold to Amstrad Electronics; President Chun of South Korea in Britain at start of 10-day tour of Western Europe. **8** *HMS Coventry* launched at night in face of union protests; Base lending rate cut to 11%; 6 people killed in helicopter crash in Oxfordshire; Mrs Jennifer Guinness kidnapped in Ireland; Film star Clint Eastwood elected mayor of Carmel, California. **9** 37 Tory MPs voted against government over privatisation of airports. **10** Fulham by-election: Labour won seat with a swing of 10·9%; Miss Benazir Bhutto welcomed home to Pakistan from exile by millions; US carried out further nuclear test in Nevada. **11** USSR responded by ending self-imposed ban on tests. **13** Rising tension between US and Libya; RC Bishop of Tripoli abducted in Benghazi. **14** Death of Simone de Beauvoir; Death of Protestant youth injured by plastic bullet in Portadown riots. **15** US bombed Benghazi and Tripoli in retaliation for Libyan terrorism: planes came from British bases, widespread international protest; Government defeated by 14 votes on Second Reading of Shops Bill; Death of Jean Genet. **16** Mrs Jennifer Guinness freed after 8 day's captivity: 3 men arrested.

A.D.

17 2 British hostages killed in Lebanon in retaliation for government support for US; Bomb attack on El-Al jet from Heathrow failed. **18** Nazar Hindawi sought by police for attack arrested in West London; Guinness succeeded in take-over of Distillers; President Botha announced abolition of pass laws in South Africa and release of blacks held under them. **19** Major demonstration against US in Grosvenor Square. **20** British residents in W. Beirut moved into E. Beirut; London marathon won by Toshihiko Seko and Milk Cup by Oxford United. **21** 60th birthday of the Queen; EEC foreign ministers agreed restrictions on Libyans based in Europe; Mortgage rate fell to 11%. **22** King Juan Carlos of Spain in London for official visit; European Court ruling in favour of invalid care allowance for married women; **21** Libyan students to be expelled from Britain. **23** Death of film maker Otto Preminger and cricketer Jim Laker; King Juan Carlos addressed both Houses of Parliament. **24** Government announced that Land Rover would not be sold and that RN contract would be split between Harland and Wolff and Swan Hunter; Bomb explosion in Oxford Street; Death of Duchess of Windsor; Start of prison officers' action against staff cuts. **25** 335 Libyan aircraft engineers and trainee pilots banned from completing their courses in Britain; British head of Black and Decker in France shot dead in Lyons. **26** Seamus McElwaine, IRA escaped prisoner shot dead whilst planting a bomb near Rosslea. **28** Major nuclear power accident at Chernobyl in Soviet Union reported: caused deaths and sent cloud of radioactivity over Scandinavia; RTZ to close 3 mines in Cornwall with loss of 1000 jobs. **30** Police invaded Sikh Golden Temple at Amritsar and seized extremists who had earlier proclaimed independent state; Colonel Gadaffi ordered expulsion of 19 Britons in retaliation for British expulsions.

May 1 Night of violence in prisons as officers took industrial action: 841 gaol places destroyed in fires; Rothmans to close in Belfast with loss of 800 jobs. **2** Minority Labour government in Norway after resignation of centre right PM; Radiation from Chernobyl reached Britain; Prison officers suspended industrial action for talks with Home Office; Tanker captain killed by rocket from Iranian gunship in Gulf. **3** Fierce clashes between police and pickets at Wapping; Bomb on board Sri Lankan airliner killed 14. **4** Rocket salvo fired at palace where Tokyo economic summit was being held; Afghan leader Babrak Karmal resigned; Kurt Waldheim failed to win Austrian presidential election in first ballot; ANC rescued captured comrade under armed guard in Natal hospital. **5** Tokyo summit agreed relentless campaign against terrorism and co-ordinated course for economies. **6** Start of trial over bombing of Grand Hotel in Brighton. **7** Death of Lord Shinwell at 101; Bangladesh parliamentary election; Iraqi planes set on fire Tehran's main oil refinery. **8** Alliance won Ryedale by-election with swing of 18·9% from Tories: Tories held West Derbyshire with majority of only 100; Local elec-

A.D.

tions showed widespread losses for Tories; Privilege committee recommended banning of *Sunday Times* journalist Richard Evans for leaking committee report; Prince and Princess of Wales in Japan for official visit. **9** Death of Tenzing Norgay, conqueror of Everest. **10** Britain ordered expulsion of 3 Syrians suspected of being involved in terrorism. **11** Syria expelled 3 British diplomats in retaliation; Soviet television showed first pictures of Chernobyl. **12** Libya expelled 36 diplomats from 7 West European countries; Publication of defence estimates: first real decline since 1979. **13** Prison officers' dispute resolved; 2 killed in Falklands helicopter crash. **14** 3,500 to lose jobs at state-owned British Shipbuilders; Mr Gorbachev spoke on television to Russian people about Chernobyl; Rebellion in bantustan of Kwa Ndebele, South Africa; 86-year-old Yugoslav sentenced to death in Zagreb for war crimes. **15** Unemployment figures up and sharp rise in manufacturing output; Unemployed house owners to lose right to supplementary benefit to cover half mortgage interest. **16** Ex-President Galtieri and 2 others gaoled for negligence in conduct of Falklands war. **18** 300 whites honoured black victims in Alexandra township, SA; Sri Lankan army launched attack against Tamil guerrillas; Channel ports on alert against possible terrorist attack. **19** South African commando attacks on Zimbabwe, Zambia and Botswana. **20** BR announced 7,650 redundancies in engineering workshops over next 3 years; 2% cut in UGC funding for universities; Extra 3,200 police to be recruited. **21** Re-shuffle: Kenneth Baker to become Education Secretary, Nicholas Ridley Environment Secretary and John Moore Transport Secretary; Up to £10m worth of paintings stolen from home of Sir Alfred Beit in Ireland. **22** Neo-Fascists in South Africa disrupted a National Party meeting; Government proposed payment of pay review body increases to be delayed for 3 months; Nat West cut interest rates to 10%: followed by other banks; 2 policemen and major killed by IRA bomb near Crossmaglen; Labour National Executive adjourned after expelling 3 militants and acquitting another. **23** Car bomb explosion in East Beirut killed 9. **25** Up to 30m people in the world ran for Africa in Sport Aid's Race against Time; 7 killed by South African police in weekend of violence; Tamil guerrillas killed 20 Sinhalese villagers; PM on visit to Israel. **26** Rupert Murdoch offered 'final' package to unions in attempt to solve Wapping dispute; Death toll from Chernobyl rises to 19; Punjab cabinet minister shot in chest during Canadian tour; Helicopter snatched criminal Michael Vaujour from La Santé prison in Paris. **27** President Reagan announced abandonment of the two SALT treaties after the autumn. **28** Publication of assessment of quality of research in universities. **29** High Court injunction to force hippie convoy to leave Somerset farmer's field; Ian Botham banned from cricket for 2 months. **30** NATO divided over US threat to scrap SALT II arms treaty; Spanish authorities admitted 4 bombs had been discovered on Costa del Sol in new ETA bombing campaign; 22 killed in Tamil bombings in Sri Lanka.

PROMINENT PEOPLE

Glimpses of some of the famous people in the history of the world. See also Section E for composers; Section M for prominent English novelists; Section D for a Who's Who in British politics; and Section S for the Biblical World.

PROMINENT PEOPLE

A

Abel, Sir Frederick (1826–1902). English military chemist, an authority on explosives. He and his friend James Dewar patented the propellant cordite (*see* Section L).

Abelard, Peter (1079–1142), one of the founders of scholastic moral theology, b. at Pallet (Palais) near Nantes. He lectured in Paris, where he was sought by students, though persecuted for alleged heresy. His main achievement was to discuss where others asserted. His love for Héloïse, a woman of learning, ended in tragic separation and in a famous correspondence.

Abercrombie, Sir Patrick (1879–1957), architect and town-planner. He was consulted on the re-planning of Plymouth, Hull, Bath and other cities and produced a plan for Greater London, 1943.

Acton, 1st Baron (John Emerich Edward Dalberg Acton) (1834–1902), English historian. He planned the *Cambridge Modern History*.

Adam, Robert (1728–92), architect, one of four Scottish brothers. He developed a character-istic style in planning and decoration and his achievements in interior design include Hare-wood House, Yorks.; Osterley Park, Middlesex; Syon House, Middlesex; Kedleston Hall, Derbyshire; Luton Hoo, Bedfordshire; and Kenwood. *See* Neo-Classical Style, Section L.

Adams, John (1735–1826), succeeded Washington as president of the U.S.A. He was the first of the republic's ambassadors to England.

Adams, John Couch (1819–92), English mathe-matician and astronomer. He shared credit for the discovery of the planet Neptune (1846) with the French astronomer Leverrier, working independently.

Adams, Samuel (1722–1803), American revolution-ary statesman, b. Boston. He advocated "no taxation without representation" as early as 1765; promoted the "Boston tea-party"; and in 1776 signed the Declaration of Independence.

Adams, William (*c.* 1564–1620), navigator, b. Gillingham, Kent; the first Englishman to visit Japan. He found favour with the shogun Ieyasu, and an English and Dutch trading settlement was established till 1616.

Addams, Jane (1860–1935), American sociologist who founded Hull House, Chicago, in 1889.

Addison, Joseph (1672–1719), writer and Whig politician. He contributed to the *Tatler*, and was co-founder with Steele of the *Spectator*.

Adelard of Bath (*c.* 1090–*c.* 1150), English mathe-matician who translated into Latin the *Arith-metic* of Al-Kwarizmi and so introduced the Arabic numerals to the West (*see* L7).

Adenauer, Konrad (1876–1967), chancellor of the West German Federal Republic, 1949–63; founder and chairman of the Christian Democra-tic Party, 1945–66. To a defeated Germany he gave stable constitutional government and a place in the Western alliance. He promoted reconciliation with France but resisted accom-modation with Russia.

Adler, Alfred (1870–1937), Austrian psychiatrist, founder of the school of individual psychology. An earlier pupil of Freud, he broke away in 1911, rejecting the emphasis on sex, regarding man's main problem as a struggle for power to com-pensate for feelings of inferiority. *See* **Adlerian psychology, Section J.**

Adrian, 1st Baron (Edgar Douglas Adrian) (1889–1977), English physiologist. He shared with Sherrington the 1932 Nobel Prize for medicine for work on the electrical nature of the nerve impulse, Pres. Royal Society 1950–5; Pres. British Association 1954; Chancellor Leicester Univ. 1958–71; Chancellor Cambridge Univ. 1967–75; O.M. 1942.

Adrian IV (Nicholas Breakspear) (d. 1159), pope 1154–50, the only English pope, b. near St. Albans. He crowned Frederick Barbarossa

Holy Roman Emperor. Granted overlordship of Ireland to Henry II.

Aeschylus (524–456 B.C.), founder of Greek tragic drama. Of the many plays he wrote, only seven have come down to us, including *The Seven against Thebes, Prometheus Bound*, and a trilogy on Orestes.

Aesop (? 6th cent. B.C.), semi-legendary fabulist, originally a slave. The fables attributed to him probably have many origins.

Agassiz, Louis (1807–73), Swiss-American em-bryologist, author of *Lectures on Comparative Embryology*, intended for laymen, *Researches on Fossil Fishes*, and *Studies on Glaciers*. He was an opponent of Darwinian evolution.

Agricola, Gnaeus Julius (37–93), Roman governor of Britain, who subdued the country except for the Scottish highlands. His son-in-law Tacitus wrote his life.

Agrippa, Marcus Vipsanius (63–12 B.C.), Roman general.

Ahmad Khan, Sir Syed (1817–98), Indian educa-tionist and social reformer who founded what is now the Aligarh Muslim University.

Airy, Sir George Biddell (1801–92), English mathe-matician who was astronomer royal for over 40 years, 1835–81. He set up a magnetic observatory at Greenwich.

Akbar, Jalal-ud-din Mohammed (1542–1605), Mogul emperor of India, son of Humayun. He extended the imperial power over much of India, stabilised the administration, promoted commerce and learning; and, though a Muslim, respected Hindu culture and tolerated Christian missions. His reign saw a flowering of Mogul culture.

Akhenaten, the name adopted by the heretic pharaoh **Amenhotep IV** (d. 1362 B.C.), who in-troduced a short-lived but influential religious and artistic reformation. He sought to convert his people from their polytheistic beliefs to a more compassionate religion based on the one supreme sun-god Aten (hence his name). His pacifism caused the temporary loss of most of Egypt's overseas territories. His wife was Nefertiti and he was succeeded by Tutankha-mun, who gave in to the conservative forces of the priesthood.

Alanbrooke, 1st Viscount (Alan Francis Brooke) (1883–1963), British field-marshal; chief of the imperial general staff 1941–46. Sir Arthur Bryant's *The Turn of the Tide* and *Triumph in the West* are based on his war diaries.

Alarcón, Pedro Antonio de (1833–91), Spanish novelist. His short story, *El Sombrero de tres picos* (The Three-Cornered Hat) became the subject of Falla's ballet and of Hugo Wolf's opera *Der Corregidor*.

Alaric I (376–410), Visigothic chief who, as first auxiliary to the Roman emperor Theodosius, later attacked the empire and sacked Rome in 410.

Alban, St. (d. *c.* 303), proto-martyr of Britain, con-verted by a priest to whom he had given shelter. He suffered under Diocletian at Verulam (now St. Albans), where in the 8th cent. King Offa of Mercia founded the abbey of that name.

Albert, Prince Consort (1819–61), son of the Duke of Saxe-Coburg-Gotha, married Queen Victoria in 1840. He helped the queen with political duties, projected the international exhibition of 1851, and in 1861 in a dispute with the United States advised a conciliatory attitude which averted war. He died of typhoid fever and is commemorated by the Albert Memorial in Kensington Gardens.

Albertus Magnus (Albert the Great) (1206–80), Dominican scholastic philosopher, b. Swabia. His interest in nature as an independent obser-ver marked the awakening of the scientific spirit. Among his pupils was Thomas Aquinas.

Alcibiades (*c.* 450–404 B.C.), Athenian general and statesman. Pupil and friend of Socrates, he was an egoist whose career brought Athens disaster. He was murdered in Phrygia.

Alcott, Louisa May (1832–88), American author of books for girls, notably *Little Women*.

Alcuin (735–804), English scholar, who settled on the Continent and helped Charlemagne with the promotion of education.

Aldred (d. 1069), Saxon archbishop of York who crowned William the Conqueror.

Aldrich, Henry (1647–1710), English composer of church music, theologian and architect. He designed Peckwater quadrangle at Christ Church, the chapel of Trinity College, and All Saints' Church, Oxford, and wrote the "Bonny Christ Church bells."

Alekhine, Alexander (1892–1946), world chess champion, 1927–35, 1937–46. He was born in Moscow but later became a French citizen.

Alembert, Jean le Rond d' (1717–83), French mathematician and philosopher, one of the encyclopaedists, a leading representative of the Enlightenment.

Alexander of Tunis, Earl (Harold Leofric George Alexander) (1891–1969), British field-marshal, b. Ireland. Directed retreat at Dunkirk 1940, and Burma 1942; C.-in-C. Allied Armies in Italy 1943–4; Supreme Allied Commander, Mediterranean 1944–5, Governor-general of Canada 1946–52.

Alexander II (1818–81), reforming Tsar of Russia, succeeded his father Nicholas in 1855. In 1861 he emancipated the serfs and in 1865 established provincial elective assemblies. Later his government became reactionary; he was assassinated by Nihilists; the pogroms followed.

Alexander the Great (356–323 B.C.), Greek conqueror. Educated by Aristotle, he succeeded his father Philip as king of Macedon in 336 B.C. He led the Greek states against Persia; and, crossing the Hellespont, he defeated Darius and sacked Persepolis. He captured Egypt and founded Alexandria. He penetrated to India. D. at Babylon.

Alexandra, Queen (1844–1925), daughter of Christian IX of Denmark, married the Prince of Wales (afterwards Edward VII) 1863.

Alfieri, Vittorio, Count (1749–1803), Italian poet and dramatist.

Alfonso the Wise (1221–84), king of León and Castile, known for his code of laws and his planetary tables. He caused the first general history of Spain to be written. Dethroned 1282.

Alfred the Great (849–99), king of Wessex who became a national figure. From the outset he had to repel Danish invaders. After years of effort he won the battle of Ethandun (Edington), and subsequently, probably in 886, made peace with Guthrum, leaving to the Danes the north and east. He built ships, was an able administrator, and promoted education, his own translations from the Latin being part of the earliest English literature.

Al-Kwarizimi (fl. *c.* 830), Persian mathematician said to have given algebra its name.

Allenby, 1st Viscount (Edmund Henry Hynman Allenby) (1861–1936), British general. He served on the Western front 1914–16, commanded in Palestine 1917–18, capturing Jerusalem on 9 December 1917.

Allende, Salvador (1908–73), Chilean radical leader, a Marxist democrat, who won the presidency 1970. He tried to bring social reform by democratic means but met his death resisting the military coup in which it is alleged the American CIA played a role.

Alleyne, Edward (1566–1626), actor and founder of Dulwich College.

Al-Mamun (1813–33), caliph of Baghdad, son of Harun-al-Rashid. He built an observatory at Baghdad where observations were long recorded.

Ampère, André Marie (1775–1836), French physicist who propounded the theory that magnetism is the result of molecular electric currents. The unit of electric current is named after him.

Amundsen, Roald (1872–1928), Norwegian explorer, the first to navigate the north-west passage and to reach the south pole. Sailing in the fishing smack *Gjoa*, he made the north-west passage in 3 years, 1903–6, and in 1911 sailed to the Antarctic in the *Fram*, reaching the pole on 14 December 1911, a month before his English rival Scott. His attempt to rescue

Nobile after his crash in the airship *Italia* cost him his life.

Anacreon (*c.* 569–475 B.C.), Greek lyric poet.

Anaxagoras (488–428 B.C.), Ionian philosopher who came to Athens 464 B.C. and inspired Pericles and the poet Euripides with his love of science. His rational theories outraged religious opinion.

Anaximander (611–547 B.C.), Miletan philosopher, pupil of Thales, the first among the Greeks to make geographical maps, and to speculate on the origin of the heavenly bodies. He introduced the sundial from Babylon or Egypt.

Anaximenes (b. *c.* 570 B.C.), the last of the Miletan school founded by Thales. For him the primal substance was air. He was the first to see the differences between substances in quantitative terms.

Andersen, Hans Christian (1805–75), Danish writer, especially of fairy tales such as *The Little Mermaid* and *The Ugly Duckling*.

Anderson, Elizabeth Garrett (1836–1917), one of the first English women to enter the medical profession. She practised in London for many years and later became mayor of Aldeburgh, her native town, the first woman to hold the office of mayor. Sister of Millicent Garrett Fawcett.

Andrea del Sarto (1487–1531), Italian painter, b. Florence, the son of a tailor. Known as the "faultless painter," his chief works are the frescoes of the Annunziata at Florence and his Holy Families. He died of the plague.

Andrée, Salomon August (1854–97), Swedish explorer who attempted in 1897 to reach the north pole by balloon. In 1930 a Norwegian scientific expedition discovered the remains of the Andrée expedition on White Island.

Andrew, St., one of the apostles of Jesus, brother of Simon Peter, whose festival is observed on 30 November. He became the patron saint of Scotland in the 8th cent.

Andropov, Yuri Vladimirovich (1914–84), Russian statesman. Counsellor, subsequently Ambassador, to Hungary, 1953–7. Chairman, State Security Committee (K.G.B.), 1967–82. Succeeded Brezhnev as Secretary-General of C.P.S.U., 1982; State President, 1983–84. He tried to bring greater efficiency to Soviet life and to improve relations with China and the West but illness cut short his life after just 15 months in power. *See* **Section C.**

Angelico, Fra (1387–1455), Italian painter. An exquisite colourist, Fra Giovanni (his Dominican name) painted especially religious frescoes, mainly at Florence and Rome.

Ångström, Anders Jöns (1814–74), Swedish physicist who studied heat, magnetism, and spectroscopy; hence the ångström unit used for measuring the wavelength of light.

Anne, Queen (1665–1714), Queen of Gt. Britain and Ireland. A daughter of James II, she succeeded William III in 1702. The act of union with Scotland was passed in 1707. A well-intentioned woman without marked ability, she was influenced by favourites, at first by the Duchess of Marlborough, but in the main she was guided by Tory and high church principles (she established Queen Anne's Bounty to improve church finances). Her reign was notable for literary output (Swift, Pope, Addison, Steele, Defoe), developments in science (Newton), architecture (Wren, Vanbrugh), and for the Duke of Marlborough's victories in war.

Anouilh, Jean (b. 1910), French dramatist, whose plays with various settings—classical, historical and contemporary—include *Eurydice, Antigone, The Lark, Becket, The Fighting Cock.*

Anselm, St. (1033–1109), Italian scholar who succeeded Lanfranc as archbishop of Canterbury.

Anson, 1st Baron (George Anson) (1697–1762), English admiral who sailed round the world 1740–44, his squadron being reduced during the voyage from seven ships to one. An account was compiled by his chaplain.

Antoninus Pius (86–161), Roman emperor, successor of Hadrian. In his reign, which was peaceful, the Antonine wall between the Forth and the Clyde was built to protect Britain from northern attack.

Antonius Marcus (Mark Antony) (c. 83–30 B.C.), Roman triumvir. He supported Caesar, and after the latter's death was opposed by Brutus and Cassius, and defeated by Octavian; committed suicide. His association with the Egyptian queen Cleopatra is the subject of Shakespeare's play.

Antony, St. (c. 251–356), early promoter of the monastic life. B. in Upper Egypt, he retired into the desert, where he was tempted, but attracted disciples and founded a monastery. Took part in the Council of Nicaea 325. (From his supposed help against erysipelas derives its name of St. Antony's fire.)

Apelles, 4th cent. B.C., Greek painter whose chief paintings, which have not survived, were of Alexander the Great holding a thunderbolt and of Aphrodite rising from the sea.

Apollinaire, Guillaume (Wilhelm Apollinaris Kostrowitzi) (1880–1918), French poet representative of the restless and experimental period in the arts before the first world war. He invented the term *surrealism* (*see* **Section L**). B. Rome of Polish extraction.

Apollonius of Perga (fl. 220 B.C.), Greek mathematician of the Alexandrian school, remembered for his conic sections; introduced the terms *ellipse, parabola,* and *hyperbola.*

Apollonius Rhodius (fl. 250 B.C.), scholar and poet of Alexandria and Rhodes, librarian at Alexandria. His epic *Argonautica* is about the Argonaut heroes.

Appert, Nicholas (1752–1841), sometimes known as François Appert, invented the method of preserving animal and vegetable foods by means of hermetically sealed cans or tins, and paved the way for the creation of a vast world industry.

Appleton, Sir Edward Victor (1892–1965), English physicist, best known as the discoverer of the ionised region of the upper atmosphere which became known as the Appleton layer. His researches led to the development of radar. Nobel prizewinner 1947.

Aquinas, Thomas, St. (c. 1225–74), scholastic philosopher and Dominican friar of Italian birth, whose philosophico-theological system (called Thomism) is still accepted by Catholic ecclesiastics. He understood Aristotle well and interpreted his thought in accord with Christian teaching. His most important works are *Summa contra Gentiles* and *Summa theologica.* *See also* **God and Man, Section J.**

Arago, Dominique François Jean (1786–1853), French astronomer and physicist, remembered for his discoveries in electromagnetism and optics.

Archimedes (287–212 B.C.), Greek mathematician, b. Syracuse, son of an astronomer; remembered for his contributions to pure mathematics, mechanics, and hydrostatics, notably the Archimedean screw for raising water, the conception of specific gravity, the doctrine of levers, and the measurement of curved areas. Not less than his scientific knowledge was his practical skill. He was killed by the Romans in the siege of Syracuse.

Argand, Aimé (1755–1803), Swiss physician, inventor of the lamp bearing his name, which was the first to admit a current of air to increase the power of the flame, by use of a chimney glass and circular wick.

Ariosto, Ludovico (1474–1533), Italian poet, author of *Orlando Furioso.*

Aristides (d. c. 468 B.C.), Athenian general and statesman, called "the just"; fought at Marathon.

Aristippus (c. 435–356 B.C.), founder of the Cyrenaic school of philosophy. He taught that man should aim at pleasure, but held that the pleasant was identical with the good.

Aristophanes (c. 444–c. 385 B.C.), Greek dramatist and comic poet, who satirised Athenian life. Among his plays are *The Clouds* and *The Birds.*

Aristotle (384–322 B.C.), Greek philosopher, pupil of Plato, after whose death in 347 he left Athens to become tutor to the young prince Alexander of Macedon. Subsequently at Athens he established his famous school in the garden known as the *Lyceum,* where he lectured in the *peripatos* (cloister) which gave his school of philosophy its name *Peripatetic.* He took the whole field of knowledge as his subject, giving it unity, and providing a philosophy which held its own for 2,000 years.

Arkwright, Sir Richard (1732–92), English inventor. A native of Preston, and originally a barber, he experimented with cotton-spinning machines. His "water frame" (run by water power), patented in 1769, was an early step in the industrial revolution. In 1790 he made use of Boulton and Watt's steam-engine. Rioters sacked one of his mills in 1779.

Armstrong, Neil (b. 1930), American astronaut, the first man to set foot on the moon, 21 July 1969.

Arne, Thomas Augustine (1710–78), English composer, remembered for *Rule, Britannia!* (from a masque called *Alfred*), and for Shakespearean songs such as *Where the Bee Sucks.* He also wrote operas (women singers appeared in *Judith* in 1761) and oratorios.

Arnold, Thomas (1795–1842), English headmaster, whose influence at Rugby (1828–42) gave it a high position among public schools.

Arrhenius, Svante August (1859–1927), Swedish chemist, one of the founders of modern physical chemistry. Received 1903 Nobel prize for originating the theory of electrolytic dissociation (ionisation).

Artaxerxes, the name borne by several ancient Persian kings. The first Artaxerxes, son of Xerxes, reigned 464–424 B.C.; he was succeeded by Darius II 424–404 B.C., who was followed by Artaxerxes II, who reigned until 358 B.C. Artaxerxes III, the last to bear the name, was a cruel and treacherous man and was poisoned in 338 B.C.

Arthur (c. 500), fabled Celtic warrior, whose feats, although referred to in passing in early Celtic writings, were first narrated in Geoffrey of Monmouth's *Historia* (c. 1135). In mediaeval times his legend developed an extensive literature, woven together by Sir Thomas Malory in his *Morte d'Arthur,* printed in 1485. Excavations have recently been carried out at South Cadbury, Somerset, the supposed site of his seat, Camelot.

Arundel, Thomas (1353–1414), archbishop of Canterbury 1396, and for a time lord chancellor. An enemy of heresy, he persecuted the Lollards.

Aske, Robert, leader of the Pilgrimage of Grace 1536, directed against the Henrician Reformation; executed 1537.

Asoka (c. 269–232 B.C.), Indian emperor and upholder of Buddhism. At first he expanded his empire by conquest, but on being converted to Buddhism rejected war and aimed at the good of his people. He sent Buddhist missionaries as far as Sri Lanka and Syria. Art flourished, and many rock inscriptions commemorate his doings.

Asquith, Herbert Henry, 1st Earl of Oxford and Asquith (1852–1928), Liberal prime minister 1908–16, having previously served under Gladstone. His government enacted social reforms including old-age pensions (1908) and unemployment insurance (1911), but as a war minister he had to give way to Lloyd George. He resigned leadership of his party in 1926. His daughter Violet (1887–1969), an eloquent speaker, was created a life peeress in 1964.

Asser, a Welsh monk of the 9th cent., traditionally author of a life of King Alfred.

Astor, John Jacob (1763–1848), founder of the millionaire family, was a native of Heidelberg, emigrated to America, and made a fortune by trading in fur.

Astor, Viscountess (Nancy Witcher Astor, *née* Langhorne) (1879–1964), the first woman M.P. to take her seat in the House of Commons, an American by birth, wife of the 2nd Viscount Astor.

Atatürk, Kemal (1881–1938), builder of modern Turkey. A fine soldier, he defended the Dardanelles against the British in 1915 and drove the Greeks out of Turkey in 1922. President of the Turkish Republic, and virtually dictator, 1923–38.

Athanasius, St. (296–373), upholder of the doctrine of the Trinity against Arius, who denied the divinity of Christ. He was bishop of Alexandria. He is not now thought the author of the creed which bears his name.

Athelstan (895–940), grandson of Alfred the Great, was crowned king of England in 925, and was the first ruler of all England.

Attila (406–53), invading king of the Huns from Asia. He defeated the Roman Emperor Theodosius, and entered Gaul, but was defeated in 451 near Châlons-sur-Marne.

Attlee, 1st Earl (Clement Richard Attlee) (1883–1967), Labour prime minister 1945–51, having served as deputy to Churchill 1942–5. Called to the Bar in 1905, he lectured at the London School of Economics 1913–23, was mayor of

Stepney 1919, and parliamentary leader of his party 1935–55. His government helped to create a welfare society and granted independence to India. His writings include an autobiography, *As it Happened*, and *Empire into Commonwealth*.

Auchinleck, Sir Claude John Eyre (1884–1981), British field-marshal; G.O.C. North Norway 1940; C.-in-C. India 1941, 1943–7; Middle East 1941–2.

Auden, Wystan Hugh (1907–73), poet, b. in England and naturalised an American. Succeeded C. Day Lewis as professor of poetry at Oxford 1956–61.

Auer, Leopold (1845–1930), Hungarian violinist and teacher; Mischa Elman and Jascha Heifetz were among his pupils.

Augustine of Canterbury, St. (d. c. 605), first archbishop of Canterbury. He was sent from Rome in 597 by Gregory the Great to convert the English peoples.

Augustus, Caius Octavianus (63 B.C.–A.D. 14), first Roman emperor. Great-nephew of Julius Caesar, he was for 12 years triumvir with Mark Antony and Lepidus; then reigned alone. His reign was notable for peace, and for writers like Horace and Virgil; hence Augustan age for a great period in literature (the title Augustus was given him by the Senate).

Aurelius, Marcus Antonius. *See* **Marcus Aurelius Antoninus.**

Auriol, Vincent (1884–1966), French politician. He voted against surrender in 1940, was interned and escaped to London in 1943. President of the Fourth Republic 1947–54.

Aurangzeb (1618–1707), Mogul emperor of India. Son of Shah Jehan, he obtained power by acting against his father and brothers. In his long reign the Mogul empire reached its fullest extent; but he estranged Hindus and Sikhs; and when he died his authority was in dispute and the Mogul empire broke up.

Austen, Jane (1775–1817), author of *Emma, Mansfield Park, Northanger Abbey, Persuasion, Pride and Prejudice*, and *Sense and Sensibility*. Though confining herself to the personal relations of the English middle classes, she combined artistry, accuracy, imaginative power, satiric humour, sense, and genuine feeling with the ability to create a range of living characters. She spent the first 25 years of her life at her father's Hampshire rectory. She was unmarried.

Austin, 1st Baron (Herbert Austin) (1886–1941), English motor manufacturer, pioneer of the small car—the 7-horsepower car—which he put on the market in 1921.

Avenzoar (Ibn Zuhr) (c. 1090–1162), Arab physician, b. Seville. His chief work was the *Tasir.*

Averroës (Ibn Rushd) (1126–98), Arab philosopher, b. Córdova. He believed in the eternity of the world (not as a single act of creation as demanded by the current theology of Islam, Christianity and Judaism, but as a continuous process) and in the eternity of a universal intelligence, indivisible but shared in by all. He expounded Aristotle to his countrymen, but his teaching was modified by Neoplatonism. He was a friend of Avenzoar.

Avicenna (Ali ibn-Sina) (980–1037), Arab philosopher and physician, of Bukhara, whose influence on mediaeval Europe was chiefly through his *Canon of Medicine*, in which he attempted to systematise all the medical knowledge up to his time.

Avogadro, Amedeo (1776–1856), Italian physicist, remembered for his hypothesis, since known as Avogadro's Law, that equal volumes of gases under identical conditions of temperature and pressure contain the same number of molecules.

Avon, Earl of. *See* **Eden, Anthony.**

Ayrton, William Edward (1847–1908), English electrical engineer, inventor of a number of electrical measuring instruments. His first wife, **Matilda Chaplin Ayrton** (1846–83), was one of the first woman doctors, and his second wife, **Hertha Ayrton** (1854–1923), became known for her scientific work on the electric arc and sand ripples and for her work for woman suffrage.

Ayub Khan, Mohammed (1907–74), Pakistani military leader; president of Pakistan, 1958–69.

Azikiwe, Nnamdi (b. 1904), Nigerian statesman; president of Nigeria, 1963–6.

B

Baber, Babar or Babur (Zahir ud-din Mohammed) (1483–1530), founder of the Mogul dynasty which ruled northern India for nearly three centuries; a descendant of Tamerlane.

Bach, Johann Sebastian (1685–1750), composer. B. at Eisenach, Germany, he was successively violinist, church organist, and chief court musician. It was as organist at the Thomaskirche, Leipzig, that he composed the St. Matthew and the St. John Passion and the B minor Mass. His work was in the school of the contrapuntal style (especially the fugue and the chorale); after his day it lost favour, but during the last century it has gained ground continually. Personally he was contented and unworldly; latterly he became blind. His family was connected with music for seven generations. *See* **Section E.**

Bach, Karl Philipp Emmanuel (1714–88), 3rd son of the above, and one of the first experimenters in the symphonic and sonata forms.

Backhaus, Wilhelm (1884–1969), German pianist, gifted in interpreting classical and romantic concertos.

Bacon, Francis, Lord Verulam (1561–1626), English philosopher. He threw over Aristotelian deductive logic for the inductive method (*see* **Baconian method, Section J**); remembered for the impulse his writings gave to the foundation of the Royal Society (c. 1662). His chief work is the *Novum Organum*. His career as statesman under Elizabeth and James I was brought to an end by charges of corruption.

Bacon, Roger (c. 1219/20–94), founder of English philosophy, advocate of the value of observation and experiment in science. He first studied arts at Oxford but when he returned from lecturing in Paris he devoted himself to experimental science, especially alchemy and optics. He became a Franciscan friar in 1257. After his death he acquired a reputation for necromancy which was undeserved.

Baden-Powell, 1st Baron (Robert Stephenson Smyth Baden-Powell) (1857–1941), founder of Boy Scouts (1908) and Girl Guides (1910) to promote good citizenship in the rising generation; Chief Scout of the World 1921–41. As a young cavalry officer in the South African war he defended Mafeking.

Baer, Karl Ernst von (1792–1876), German naturalist, b. Estonia, founder of the science of embryology. He discovered the mammalian ovum (1827). An opponent of Darwin's theory.

Baffin, William (1584–1622), British navigator and explorer who in 1616 discovered the bay which separates the north-east coast of Canada from Greenland, which bears his name.

Bagehot, Walter (1826–77), English economist and journalist, editor of *The Economist*. Among his works are *The English Constitution, Physics and Politics*, and *Lombard Street*.

Baird, John Logie (1888–1946), Scottish television pioneer, inventor of the televisor and the noctovisor.

Baker, Sir Benjamin (1840–1907), English civil engineer. With Sir John Fowler he built the Forth bridge and the London Metropolitan railway. He designed the vessel which brought Cleopatra's Needle to London. In Egypt he was consulting engineer for the Aswan dam.

Baker, Sir Herbert (1862–1946), English architect who designed the Bank of England, Rhodes House, Oxford, and, with Sir E. Lutyens, New Delhi.

Bakst, Léon (1868–1924), Russian painter who designed scenery and costumes for Diaghilev's ballets.

Baldwin of Bewdley, 1st Earl (Stanley Baldwin) (1867–1947), Conservative prime minister, 1923–4, 1924–9, and 1935–7. His handling of the crisis over Edward VIII's proposed marriage ended with the king's abdication.

Balewa, Sir Abubakar Tafawa (1912–66), federal prime minister of Nigeria, 1960–6; murdered during the crisis of January 1966.

Balfour, 1st Earl (Arthur James Balfour) (1848–1930), statesman and writer. He was Conservative prime minister 1902–5. As foreign secretary under Lloyd George, he was responsible for a declaration on Palestine.

Ball, John (d. 1381), English priest and a leader of the Peasants' Revolt, after which he was executed. The couplet *When Adam delved, and Eve span, Who was then the gentleman?* is attributed to him.

Balliol, John de (d. 1269), founder of Balliol College, Oxford; a regent for Scotland; sided with Henry III against his barons.

Balliol, John de (1249–1315), king of Scotland. Son of the above, he claimed the throne against Robert Bruce and was chosen by the arbitrator, Edward I of England, whose overlordship he acknowledged. Later, on renouncing homage, he was taken captive and d. in retirement. His son Edward Balliol (d. 1363) obtained the kingdom for a time, acknowledging Edward III of England and surrendering Lothian; but retired on an annuity, 1356.

Balzac, Honoré de (1799–1850), French novelist of wide influence, and author of over eighty novels to which he gave the covering title of *La Comédie Humaine*, depicting the appetites and passions of the new social class born of the revolution and Napoleon.

Bancroft, Sir Squire (1841–1926), Victorian actor-manager.

Bandaranaike, Solomon West Ridgway Dias (1899–1959), socialist prime minister of Ceylon from 1956 until his assassination in 1959. His widow, Mrs Sirimavo Bandaranaike, (b. 1916) became the world's first woman premier, 1960–5, 1970–7.

Banks, Sir Joseph (1743–1820), an amateur scientist of wealth who accompanied Captain Cook on his expedition to the Pacific 1768–76. He left botanical collections to the British Museum.

Banting, Sir Frederick Grant (1891–1941), Canadian physician who with C. H. Best discovered insulin.

Bantock, Sir Granville (1868–1946), composer of songs, orchestral and choral music.

Barbarossa (Ital. = red beard), surname of two brothers who were Barbary pirates: **Uruz** (*c.* 1474–1518), was killed by Spaniards, and **Khaireddin** (*c.* 1483–1546) conquered Tunis for the Turks and died in Constantinople.

Barbellion, W.N.P. See under Cummings, Bruce.

Barbirolli, Sir John (1899–1970), conductor of the Hallé Orchestra 1943–70; succeeded Toscanini as conductor of the New York Philharmonic Symphony Orchestra 1937–42.

Barbusse, Henri (1874–1935), French writer, author of the war novel *Le Feu*, which portrays in a starkly vivid way the experience of the common soldier.

Barham, Richard Harris (1788–1845), English humorist, author of *The Ingoldsby Legends*, written under his pen-name of Thomas Ingoldsby. His best-known poem is *The Jackdaw of Rheims*.

Barnardo, Thomas John (1845–1905), founder of homes for orphan-waifs; devoted himself to the protection, education, and advancement of destitute children.

Barrie, Sir James Matthew (1860–1937), Scottish author and dramatist. His novels include *A Window in Thrums*. Among his plays are *Dear Brutus*, *The Admirable Crichton*, and *Peter Pan* which gained great popularity with children.

Barrow, Isaac (1630–77), divine and mathematician, tutor of Sir Isaac Newton.

Barry, Sir Charles (1795–1860), architect of the houses of parliament at Westminster, the details of which were contributed by his assistant A. W. Pugin.

Barth, Karl (1886–1968), Swiss theologian, described by the late Pope John as a Protestant St. Thomas Aquinas.

Bartók, Bela (1881–1945), Hungarian composer. From an early age he was deeply interested in folk-song which inspired his researches into Hungarian and Rumanian peasant music. He left for America in 1940, where he lived precariously and apparently unhappily until the end of the war made a return possible, regrettably too late. *See* **Section E.**

Bartolommeo, Fra (di Paolo) (1475–1517), Italian painter. At first influenced by Savonarola, he later resumed painting. Some of his best work is at Lucca.

Bartolozzi, Francesco (1725–1815), Italian engraver, who settled in England and became a founder-member of the Royal Academy; noted for his stipple engravings.

Bashkirtseva, Maria Konstantinovna (1859–84), a Russian girl, achieved eminence as a painter in Paris, author of a famous diary.

Bassi, Agostino (1773–1856), Italian amateur microscopist who first suggested that infectious diseases might be caused by the invasion of the body by micro-organisms.

Batten, Jean Gardiner (b. 1909), New Zealand airwoman who flew solo from England to Australia in 1934.

Baudelaire, Charles Pierre (1821–67), French poet of originality and sensitivity, best known for his *Les Fleurs du Mal*. His life was darkened by poverty and ill-health. He was also a talented draughtsman.

Bax, Sir Arnold (1883–1953), composer of piano compositions, songs, and chamber works.

Baxter, Richard (1615–91), noncomformist divine, b. Shropshire; author of many books on theology; imprisoned after the Restoration by Judge Jeffreys.

Bayard, Pierre de Terrail, Seigneur de (*c.* 1474–1524), French knight, known as the "chevalier sans peur et sans reproche." He fought in campaigns against Italy and fell at the battle of Romagnano.

Bayle, Pierre (1647–1706), French philosopher, author of the *Dictionnaire historique et critique* (1697). His sceptical views influenced Voltaire and the encyclopedists of the 18th cent.

Baylis, Lilian Mary (1874–1937), manager of the Old Vic theatre from 1898 and of Sadler's Wells from 1931.

Beardsley, Aubrey Vincent (1872–98), black-and-white artist, who published much work, some of it controversial (as in the *Yellow Book*).

Beatles, The (Paul McCartney (b. 1942), John Lennon (1940–80), George Harrison (b. 1943), Ringo Starr (b. 1940)), a Liverpool pop group whose highly original and melodic songs held the attention of youth all over the world, especially during the period 1963–5 when they were in their prime. They parted in 1971 and went their separate ways. Lennon was shot dead in New York in 1980.

Beatty, 1st Earl (David Beatty) (1871–1936), British admiral; succeeded Jellicoe as commander of the Grand Fleet 1916–19. Commanding the British battlecruisers, he fought the German fleet on 28 August 1914 in the Heligoland Bight, and on 31 May 1916 off Jutland.

Beaufort, Sir Francis (1774–1857), hydrographer of the navy, who introduced the wind scale (1805) which bears his name. *See* **Section N.**

Beaumont, Francis (1584–1616), and **Fletcher, John** (1579–1625), joint authors of many plays, including *The Maid's Tragedy* and *Philaster*.

Beaverbrook, 1st Baron (William Maxwell Aitken) (1879–1964), British newspaper owner and politician, a Canadian by birth. He gave energetic service as minister of aircraft production 1940–1. He controlled the *Daily Express*, *Sunday Express*, and *Evening Standard*, which sponsored his political campaigns.

Becket, Thomas (1118?–70), saint and martyr. An able chancellor, 1155–62, on becoming archbishop of Canterbury he made the position of the church his first care; and, coming into conflict with Henry II, was murdered in Canterbury cathedral. His shrine became a place of pilgrimage.

Beckett, Samuel (b. 1906), Anglo-Irish dramatist and novelist, b. Dublin. Plays include *Waiting for Godot*, *Endgame*, *Krapp's Last Tape*, *Happy Days*, *Not I*; novels include *The Nouvelles* (3 stories), the trilogy: *Molloy*, *Malone Dies*, *The Unnamable*, and *How It Is*. His work expresses man's isolation, bewilderment and suffering. Nobel Prize for Literature.

Becquerel, Antoine Henri (1852–1908), French physicist who in 1896 discovered radioactivity in uranium. Shared with the Curies the 1903 Nobel prize in physics.

Bede, the Venerable (673–735), English historian and scholar; lived at Jarrow. His chief work is his *Ecclesiastical History* to 731.

Beecham, Sir Thomas (1879–1961), English conductor and impresario. Founded the London Philharmonic Orchestra in 1931; introduced into England the operas of Richard Strauss, Russian operas, and the Diaghilev ballet; championed the music of Delius.

Beecher, Henry Ward (1813–87), American preacher whose church was at Brooklyn.

Beerbohm, Sir Max (1872–1956), critic and caricaturist, master of irony and satire. His works include *Zuleika Dobson* and *A Christmas Garland*, and he contributed to the *Saturday Review*.

Beethoven, Ludwig van (1770–1827), composer. B. at Bonn (his father being a tenor singer at the Elector's court), at 17 he went to Vienna, was recognised by Mozart, and eventually settled there; he never married; gradually he became deaf. In the development from simplicity to complexity of musical treatment, he stands midway between Mozart and Wagner; but in him were uniquely combined the power to feel and the mastery of musical resources necessary to express his feelings. Between the years 1805 and 1808 he composed some of his greatest works: the oratorio *Mount of Olives*, the opera *Fidelio*, and the *Pastoral* and *Eroica* symphonies besides a number of concertos, sonatas, and songs. The symphonies, nine in number, rank as the greatest ever written. *See* **Section E.**

Begin, Menachem (b. 1913), b. Poland; active in Zionist movement since youth; leader of Israeli *Likud* party; prime minister 1977–83. Made peace with Egypt (1979) but failed to solve Palestinian problem; took Israel into war in Lebanon (1982) which led to the end of his premiership and to renewed conflict in that country. Nobel Peace Prize 1978. *See* **Section C.**

Behring, Emil von (1854–1917), German bacteriologist, founder of the science of immunology. Nobel prizewinner 1901.

Behring, Vitus (1680–1741), Danish navigator who entered the Russian service and in 1728 discovered the strait which bears his name.

Belisarius (505–65), Roman general under Justinian who fought against the Vandals.

Bell, Alexander Graham (1847–1922), inventor, b. Edinburgh, emigrated to Canada in 1870, later becoming an American citizen. In 1876 he exhibited an invention which was developed into the telephone. He devoted attention to the education of deaf-mutes.

Bell, Gertrude Margaret Lowthian (1868–1926), the "uncrowned queen of Arabia," was a traveller in the Middle East; her knowledge proved of service to the British government in the first world war.

Bellini, family of Venetian painters: **Jacopo** (*c.* 1400–70) and his two sons, **Gentile** (1429–1507), whose works include the *Adoration of the Magi* (National Gallery); and **Giovanni** (*c.* 1429–1516), brother-in-law of Mantegna, and teacher of Giorgione and Titian.

Belloc, Hilaire (1870–1953), versatile writer whose works include *The Bad Child's Book of Beasts, The Path to Rome, Hills and the Sea, Cautionary Tales*, and historical studies of Danton, Robespierre, and Richelieu. B. in France, he became a British subject in 1902.

Bellow, Saul (b. 1915), American novelist and short-story writer, author of *Adventures of Augie March, Henderson the Rain King, Herzog, Mr. Sammler's Planet* and *Humboldt's Gift*. Nobel prizewinner 1976.

Belzoni, Giovanni Battista (1778–1823), Egyptologist. B. at Padua, he settled in England in 1803. His first interest was in hydraulics, and for this purpose he went to Egypt to Mehemet Ali. There he explored Thebes, Abu Simbel, and one of the pyramids, sending some sculptures to the British Museum.

Benavente y Martinez, Jacinto (1866–1954), Spanish dramatist, whose plays include *Los Intereses Creados* (Bonds of Interest). Nobel prizewinner 1922.

Benedict, St. (*c.* 480–*c.* 550), patriarch of western monasticism. B. at Nursia, and at first a hermit at Subiaco, he attracted numerous followers and grouped them in twelve monasteries. Later he went to Monte Cassino, where he formulated the Benedictine rule, of wide application in Western Christendom.

Beneš, Eduard (1884–1948), Czechoslovak statesman; co-worker with Thomas Masaryk of the Czech Republic after the break-up of the Austro-Hungarian monarchy (1918).

Ben Gurion, David (1886–1973), Zionist leader. He helped organise the Jewish Legion in 1918, and was prominently connected with the Labour movement in Palestine in between the world wars. Prime minister of Israel 1948–63.

Bennett, Enoch Arnold (1867–1931), English author, who wrote of the pottery towns where

he was brought up. His novels include *Clayhanger* and *Hilda Lessways*.

Bennett, James Gordon (1841–1918), proprietor of the *New York Herald*. He sent out Stanley on an expedition to find Livingstone.

Bennett, Sir William Sterndale (1816–75), English composer, pianist and teacher, best known for his oratorio *The Woman of Samaria*, songs and piano pieces. Founded the Bach Society.

Bentham, Jeremy (1748–1832), utilitarian philosopher and writer on jurisprudence. His main works are *Government* and *Principles of Morals and Legislation*.

Bentley, Richard (1662–1742), classical scholar who did pioneer work in textual criticism.

Benz, Karl (1844–1929), German engineer whose motor car produced in 1885 was one of the first to be driven by an internal combustion engine.

Beresford, 1st Viscount (William Carr Beresford) (1768–1854), British general. He fought under Wellington in the Peninsular War and reorganised the Portuguese army.

Berg, Alban (1885–1935), Austrian composer whose best-known work is the three-act opera *Wozzeck*, based upon a drama by Büchner, which has become a modern classic.

Bergson, Henri Louis (1859–1941), French philosopher, exponent of the theory of creative evolution and the life force. Nobel prizewinner 1927. *See* **Vitalism, Section J.**

Bériot, Charles Auguste de (1802–70), Belgian violinist, whose wife was the operatic contralto Malibran. His son, **Charles Wilfrid de Bériot** (1833–1914) was a pianist and the teacher of Ravel.

Berkeley, George (1685–1753), idealist philosopher and critic of Locke. His spiritual outlook led him to believe that reality exists only in the eye of God, that it is undiscoverable by science, though it can be revealed by religion. His chief work is *Alciphron*. He was a master of prose. Of Irish birth, he became bishop of Cloyne.

Berlin, Irving (b. 1888), American composer of popular songs, b. Russia; pioneer of both ragtime and jazz music. *See* **Section E, Part IV.**

Berlin, Sir Isaiah (b. 1909), British philosopher, b. Riga; Chichele Prof. of Social and Political Theory at Oxford 1957–67. His works include *Karl Marx, The Hedgehog and the Fox*, and *The Age of Enlightenment*. O.M. (1971).

Berlioz, Hector (1803–69), composer. B. near Grenoble, the son of a doctor, his romantic sensibility, taste for the grand (as in his *Requiem*), and response to literary influence made him a prime figure in the French romantic movement. His works include the symphony *Romeo and Juliet*, and the operas *Benvenuto Cellini* and *Beatrice and Benedict*. *See* **Section E.**

Bernadotte, Count Folke (1895–1948), nephew of the late King Gustav of Sweden. U.N. mediator for Palestine 1947. Assassinated by Jewish terrorists.

Bernadotte, Jean Baptiste (1764–1844), a French commander who served under Napoleon, and in 1810 was chosen heir to the throne of Sweden. In 1818 he succeeded as Charles XIV.

Bernal, John Desmond (1901–71), physicist, b. Ireland. Prof. of Physics, Birkbeck College, Univ. of London, 1937–63, Prof of Crystallography, 1963–8. Author of *The Social Functions of Science, Science in History, The Origin of Life*. Lenin peace prize 1953.

Bernard, Claude (1813–78), French physiologist whose discoveries though not of immediate application paved the way for the work of Pavlov and Hopkins.

Bernard of Menthon (923–1008), patron saint of mountaineers. He founded Alpine hospices in the passes that bear his name.

Bernard, St. (1090–1153), abbot of Clairvaux, which became a chief centre of the Cistercian order. This order aimed at seclusion and austerity, and practised manual work. His writings had wide influence in Europe.

Bernhardt, Sarah (1844–1923), French tragedienne, b. Paris, daughter of Dutch jewess. She became a member of the Comédie Française after the siege of Paris. Her first performance in London was in 1879. Her successes included *Phèdre, La Dame aux Camélias, Fédora, Théodora*, and *La Tosca*, and she produced and played in Racine and Molière.

Berthelot, Marcellin Pierre Eugène (1827–1907), French chemist and politician. He was the first to produce organic compounds synthetically.

Berzelius, Jöns Jakob (1779–1848), Swedish chemist, founder of electrochemical theory. His work was mainly concerned with the exact determination of atomic and molecular weights and he devised the system of chemical symbols in use today.

Bessemer, Sir Henry (1813–98), inventor of the process of converting cast-iron direct into steel. This revolutionised steel manufacture, reducing the cost of production and extending its use.

Best, Charles Herbert (1899–1978), Canadian physiologist, who with F. G. Banting discovered the use of insulin in the treatment of diabetes.

Betjeman, Sir John (1906–84), English poet, author and broadcaster; Poet Laureate from 1972 until his death in May 1984.

Bevan, Aneurin (1897–1960), British socialist politician, architect of the National Health Service which came into operation in 1948.

Beveridge, 1st Baron (William Henry Beveridge) (1879–1963), British economist who drew up the Beveridge Plan (1942), which formed the basis of the present social security services.

Bevin, Ernest (1881–1951), British trade union leader, who later became a forceful foreign secretary. He was assistant general secretary of the Dockers Union (his masterly advocacy of the London dockers' case in 1920 earned him the title of "the dockers' K.C."), later general secretary of the Transport and General Workers Union; Minister of Labour 1940–5, and Foreign Secretary 1945–51.

Beyle, Marie Henri. See Stendhal.

Bhave, Vinova (b. 1895), Indian reformer, leader of the Sarvodaya movement. A follower of Gandhi, in 1951 he began a walking mission to persuade landlords to help landless peasants.

Bichat, Marie François Xavier (1771–1802), French physiologist whose study of tissues founded modern histology. His theory was that life is "the sum of the forces that restrict death."

Biddle, John (1615–62), unitarian. He taught in Gloucester: was several times imprisoned for his controversial writings; and died of fever contracted in prison.

Binyon, Laurence (1869–1943), poet, art critic, and orientalist, who worked at the British Museum 1893–1933.

Birch, Samuel John Lamorna (1869–1955), English landscape painter in watercolour, known for his Cornish and Australian studies.

Birkbeck, George (1776–1841), founder of mechanics' institutes, first at Glasgow, later in London (the Birkbeck Institution developed into Birkbeck College, London University).

Birkenhead, 1st Earl of (Frederick Edwin Smith) (1872–1930), English lawyer and politician; lord chancellor 1919–22; secretary for India 1924–8.

Bishop, Sir Henry Rowley (1786–1855), English composer who wrote *Home, sweet Home*, glees, and operas.

Bismarck, Otto Eduard Leopold von, Prince Bismarck, Duke of Lauenburg (1815–98), Prusso-German diplomat and statesman, chief architect of the German empire. He was of Junker family. As Prussian ambassador at St. Petersburg (1859–62) and at Paris (1862), he learned to assess the European situation. He was recalled to Berlin by the king to become chief Prussian minister; and when the house of representatives would not pass a military bill he closed the house. He used a dispute over Schleswig-Holstein to bring about the defeat of Austria at Königgratz in 1866; and he provoked the Franco-Prussian war of 1870–1 when France was defeated at Sedan. Germany then became united under the military leadership of Prussia, with the king as emperor, instead of by the slower processes of democracy. He presided over the Berlin Congress of European powers in 1878. In 1884 he began a colonial policy. His authoritarian system, in spite of its inherent defects, was at least based on cautious and accurate assessment of power politics. This factor was not understood by William II, who succeeded as emperor in 1888, and dismissed the "iron chancellor" in 1890.

Bizet, Georges (1838–75), properly **Alexandre César Léopold**, French composer, chiefly remembered for his opera *Carmen* from the story by Mérimée.

Björnson, Björnstjerne (1832–1910), Norwegian poet, dramatist and novelist. His work provides an image of Norwegian life from the period of the sagas (*Kong Sverre*) to contemporary problems (*Over Aevne*), and he wrote the national anthem.

Black, Joseph (1728–90), Scottish chemist. A professor first at Glasgow, later at Edinburgh, he was the first to undertake a detailed study of a chemical reaction. He laid the foundation of the quantitative science of heat and his discovery of latent heat was applied by Watt in improving his steam-engine.

Blackett of Chelsea, Baron (Patrick Maynard Stuart Blackett) (1897–1974), British physicist whose work on nuclear and cosmic ray physics gained him a Nobel prize in 1948; author of *Military and Political Consequences of Atomic Energy* (1948), *Lectures on Rock Magnetism* (1956), *Studies of War* (1962). Pres. British Assoc. 1956; Pres. Royal Society 1966–70; O.M. 1967.

Blackmore, Richard Doddridge (1825–1900), English novelist and author of *Lorna Doone*.

Blackstone, Sir William (1723–80), English judge. His *Commentaries on the Laws of England* is a classic.

Blackwood, Algernon (1869–1951), English novelist and writer of short stories.

Blackwood, William (1776–1834), originator of *Blackwood's Magazine*.

Blair, Robert (1699–1746), Scottish poet, author of *The Grave*.

Blake, Robert (1599–1657), Parliamentary general and an admiral in the Cromwellian navy in the Dutch and Spanish wars.

Blake, William (1757–1827), English poet, mystic, and artist, son of a hosier in Carnaby market, Soho. A solitary and deeply religious man, he had a hatred of materialism. He produced his own books, engraving on copper plates both the text of his poems and the illustrations. His *Book of Job* is a masterpiece in line-engraving in metal, his poems range from the mystical and almost incomprehensible to the delightfully simple *Songs of Innocence*. He has been called "the great teacher of the modern western world." His art is in many ways reminiscent of that of another rebel of the same day, the Spanish painter Goya.

Blanqui, Louis Auguste (1805–81), French revolutionary leader, master of insurrection. He invented the term "dictatorship of the proletariat," and his social theories, stressing the class struggle, influenced Marx. Active in 1830, 1848, and 1871, he spent 37 years in prison.

Blériot, Louis (1872–1936), French airman; the first to fly the English Channel from Calais to Dover, on 25 July 1909.

Bligh, William (1754–1817), sailor, b. Plymouth. He accompanied Cook 1772–4, and discovered bread-fruit; but was in 1789 cast adrift from *The Bounty* by his mutinous crew. As governor of New South Wales (1806) he fought to suppress the rum traffic.

Blind, Karl (1826–1907), German agitator, b. Mannheim. He was active in the German risings of 1848, and imprisoned; but escaped and settled in England, remaining in touch with men like Mazzini and Louis Blanc.

Bliss, Sir Arthur (1891–1975), English composer; succeeded Sir Arnold Bax as Master of the Queen's Musick 1953.

Bloch, Ernest (1880–1959), composer, whose music is characterised by Jewish and oriental themes. B. in Geneva, he became a naturalised American.

Blondin, Charles (1824–97), French rope performer, who crossed the Niagara Falls on a tight-rope.

Blücher, Gebhard Leberecht von (1742–1819), Prussian general. He fought against Napoleon, especially at Lützen and Leipzig; and he completed Wellington's victory at Waterloo by his timely arrival.

Blum, Léon (1872–1950), French statesman, leader of the French Socialist Party. His efforts strengthened the growth of the Popular Front and the campaign against appeasement of Hitler. He held office only briefly and was interned in Germany 1940–5.

Blumlein, Alan Dower (1903–42), British electronics engineer and inventor, chiefly remembered for his fundamental work on stereophony.

Blunden, Edmund Charles (1896–1974), English poet and critic; professor of poetry at Oxford 1966–8.

Blunt, Wilfrid Scawen (1840–1922), English poet and political writer who championed Egyptian, Indian, and Irish independence; imprisoned in 1888 for activities in the Irish Land League.

Boadicea (Boudicca), queen of the Iceni in eastern Britain, who fought against the Roman invaders, but was defeated in A.D. 61 and killed herself. Archaeologists in 1982 tentatively identified her place at Gallows Hill, Thetford, Norfolk.

Boccaccio, Giovanni (1313–75), Italian author, father of the novel. He is chiefly known for his *Decameron* (set in the neighbourhood of Florence during the plague), and for his life of Dante.

Boccherini, Luigi (1743–1805), Italian cellist and composer of chamber music.

Bode, Johann Ehlert (1747–1826), German astronomer remembered for his theoretical calculation (known as Bode's law) of the proportionate distances of the planets from the sun.

Boethius (480–524), Roman scientific writer who translated the logical works of Aristotle and provided the dark ages with some elementary mathematical treatises.

Bohr, Niels Henrik David (1885–1962), Danish nuclear physicist whose researches into the structure of the atom gave him great authority in the world of theoretical physics. With Rutherford he applied the quantum theory to the study of atomic processes. Nobel prizewinner 1922.

Boieldieu, François Adrien (1775–1834), French composer especially of operas, including *La Dame blanche*.

Boileau-Despréaux, Nicolas (1636–1711), French literary critic and poet, best known for his *Satires*.

Boito, Arrigo (1842–1918), Italian poet and composer; he wrote the libretti of *Otello* and *Falstaff* for Verdi.

Boleyn, Anne (1507–36), queen of Henry VIII and mother of Queen Elizabeth. She was maid-in-waiting to Catherine of Aragon and her successor when Catherine's marriage was annulled. She failed to produce a male heir and was beheaded on a charge of adultery.

Bolívar, Simón (1783–1830), South American revolutionist, called the Liberator, b. Carácas. He led independence movements in the north-west of South America against Spanish rule, aiming at a South American federation. He founded Grand Colombia (now Venezuela, Colombia, Panama, Ecuador). Revered as a Latin-American hero.

Bonaventura, St. (1221–74), Franciscan theologian, b. Orvieto. His mystical theory of knowledge was in the Augustinian tradition.

Bondfield, Margaret Grace (1873–1953), as minister of Labour, 1929–31, she was the first woman to enter the cabinet and become a privy councillor.

Bondi, Sir Hermann (b. 1919), British mathematician and astronomer, b. Vienna: chief scientist to Min. of Defence, 1971–7.

Bone, Sir Muirhead (1876–1953), architectural draughtsman and etcher, b. Glasgow; excelled in dry-point and drawings of intricate scaffolding; official war artist in both world wars.

Bonheur, Rose (1822–99), French painter of animals.

Boniface, St. (680–754), apostle of Germany. B. at Crediton, Devon, his name being Wynfrith, he became a Benedictine monk, and went as missionary to Friesland, securing papal approval. He founded Fulda Abbey and became archbishop of Mainz, but was martyred.

Bonnard, Pierre (1867–1947), French painter of landscapes, still life, and nudes, a colourist and skilled draughtsman.

Booth, Edwin Thomas (1833–93), American Shakespearean actor, brother of John Wilkes Booth who assassinated President Lincoln.

Booth, William (1829–1912), founder and first general of the Salvation Army, b. Nottingham. In 1865, with the help of his wife, Catherine Booth, he began mission work in the East End of London, which led to the creation in 1878 of the Salvation Army on military lines. It developed branches in many parts of the world. His son Bramwell (d. 1929) and his daughter

Evangeline were among his successors. *See also* **Salvation Army, Section J.**

Borges, Jorge Luis (1899–1986), Argentine poet, critic, and short story writer. Some of his work has been translated into English, including *A Personal Anthology* and *Labyrinths*.

Borgia, Caesar (1476–1507), Italian general. The son of Pope Alexander VI, at 17 he was suspected of murdering his brother. He became captain-general of the church, and made himself master of Romagna, the Marches, and Umbria. Banished by Pope Julius II he met his death fighting in Spain.

Borlaug, Norman Ernest (b. 1914), American wheat scientist, responsible for the "green revolution" (*see* **Section L**) which is transforming the agricultural prospects of the less-developed countries of the world. Nobel prize for peace 1970.

Borodin, Alexander Porfyrievich (1833–87), Russian composer who taught chemistry and founded a school of medicine for women. In a busy professional life he wrote two symphonies, two string quartets, the symphonic sketch *In the Steppes of Central Asia* and the opera *Prince Igor*. *See* **Section E.**

Borrow, George Henry (1803–81), English author, for many years agent for the British and Foreign Bible Society; in the course of his wanderings he studied gypsy life and wrote of his experiences in *Lavengro*, *Romany Rye*, *Bible in Spain*.

Bose, Subhas Chandra (1897–1945), Indian nationalist leader; killed in a plane crash.

Boswell, James (1740–95), Scottish author of *The Life of Dr. Johnson*, with whom he spent some years in intimacy. His own journals and letters recently published form an extensive literary collection.

Botha, Louis (1862–1919), South African soldier and statesman. In command of Transvaal forces 1899–1902 in the Boer war, he became prime minister of the Transvaal in 1907, and first premier of the Union of South Africa in 1910. In the 1914–18 war he conquered territory then under German rule.

Bottesini, Giovanni (1821–89), Italian double-bass player.

Botticelli, Sandro (c. 1445–1510), Italian painter. He worked under Fra Lippo Lippi, and was influenced by Savonarola. His art is delicate and poetic. His *Birth of Venus* is in the Uffizi Gallery, Florence, and his *Mars and Venus* in the National Gallery. He illustrated Dante's *Inferno*.

Bottomley, Horatio (1860–1933), English politician, journalist, and notorious financier, who died in poverty after serving a prison sentence for fraud.

Botvinnik, Mikhail (b. 1911), Russian chess player: world champion 1948–57, 1958–60, 1961–3. Retired 1965.

Boughton, Rutland (1878–1960), English composer of the opera *The Immortal Hour*, and writer on the history and philosophy of music.

Boult, Sir Adrian (1889–1983), conductor of the London Philharmonic Orchestra 1950–7, and of the B.B.C. Symphony Orchestra 1930–50. Musical Director B.B.C. 1930–42.

Boulton, Matthew (1728–1809), engineer who in partnership with James Watt manufactured steam-engines at his Soho works near Birmingham. He also minted a new copper coinage for Great Britain.

Bowdler, Thomas (1754–1825), issued for family reading expurgated editions of Shakespeare and Gibbon, hence the term "bowdlerise."

Boyce, William (1710–79), London organist and composer, who also collected the works of English church composers. He was master of the orchestra of George III.

Boyd Orr, 1st Baron (John Boyd Orr) (1880–1971), British physiologist and nutritional expert. Director-general World Food and Agriculture Organisation 1945–8. Chancellor Glasgow Univ. 1946. Nobel prizewinner 1949.

Boyle, Robert (1627–91), English scientist who with Robert Hooke laid the foundations of the modern sciences of chemistry and physics. He established the law which states that the volume of a gas varies inversely as the pressure upon it, provided temperature is constant. His chief work is the *Sceptical Chymist* (1661).

Bradley, Omar Nelson (1893–1981), American general. In the second world war he commanded in Tunis, Sicily, and Normandy.

Bradman, Sir Donald George (b. 1908), Australian cricketer who captained Australia in test matches against England 1936–48.

Bragg, Sir William Henry (1862–1942), English physicist. He held the chair of physics at Adelaide, Leeds, and London, and was professor of chemistry at the Royal Institution 1923–42. Pres. Royal Society 1935–40.

Bragg, Sir William Lawrence (1890–1971), son of the above. He succeeded Rutherford at the Cavendish laboratory, Cambridge, 1938–53. Dir. Royal Institution 1954–66. Shared with his father the 1915 Nobel prize for their fundamental work on X-rays and crystal structure.

Brahe, Tycho (1546–1601), Danish astronomer. At his island observatory at Uraniborg, provided by his sovereign, he carried out systematic observations which enabled Kepler to work out his planetary laws.

Brahms, Johannes (1833–97), composer. B. in Hamburg (son of a double-bass player). He was a friend of the Schumanns. *See* **Section E.**

Braille, Louis (1809–52), French educationist, who, as teacher of the blind, perfected his system of reading and writing for the blind. As the result of an accident when he was three years old he was himself blind.

Bramah, Joseph (1749–1814), English inventor of the safety-lock and hydraulic press which bear his name. He also invented the modern water-closet (1778) and a machine for printing the serial numbers on bank-notes.

Brandes, Georg Morris Cohen (1842–1927), Danish literary critic who exerted a vitalising influence on literature and art.

Brandt, Willy (b. 1913), first social democratic chancellor of the Federal Republic of Germany, 1969–74. His main achievements have been the Moscow and Warsaw treaties (1972) the treaty between E. and W. Germany (1973) which recognised their sovereign existence and the Brandt Report setting out a world development programme. *See* **Section C, Part II.**

Brangwyn, Sir Frank (1867–1956), artist of Welsh extraction, b. Bruges; first worked for William Morris making cartoons for textiles; he excelled in murals and in etching.

Breakspear, Nicholas. *See* **Adrian IV.**

Brecht, Bertold (1898–1956), German dramatist and poet, b. Augsburg, whose brilliant experimental theatre was characteristic of the period in Germany between the two world wars. A Marxist, he left Nazi Germany in 1933 and returned after the war to direct the Berliner Ensemble in E. Berlin and develop his influential techniques of production. His plays include *The Threepenny Opera* (with music by Kurt Weill), *Mother Courage* and *The Caucasian Chalk Circle*. He may be regarded as the most original and vigorous dramatist and producer of this century.

Brennan, Louis (1853–1932), inventor, b. Ireland. His inventions include a gyro-directed torpedo and a mono-rail locomotive.

Breton, André (1896–1966), French poet, founder of the surrealist literary movement in France and a close friend of Apollinaire.

Brewster, Sir David (1781–1868), Scottish physicist, noted for his research into the polarisation of light; invented the kaleidoscope. He helped to found the British Association for the Advancement of Science.

Brezhnev, Leonid Ilyich (1906–82), succeeded Khrushchev as First Secretary of the Soviet Communist Party in 1964. Under his leadership the Soviet Union achieved strategic parity with the United States, society became more stable, education and living standards steadily improved, though the economy was put under strain with expectations not matching performance.

Bridges, Robert (1844–1930), poet laureate 1913–30. His *Testament of Beauty* (1929) has been called "a compendium of the wisdom, learning and experience of an artistic spirit."

Bridgewater, 3rd Duke of (Francis Egerton) (1736–1803), founder of British inland navigation by his canal, to the design of James Brindley (*q.v.*) from Manchester to his coal mines at Worsley, later extended to join the Mersey at Runcorn.

Bridie, James (pseudonym of Osborne Henry Mavor) (1888–1951), Scottish author and dramatist. The first of his many successful plays was *The Anatomist*, produced in 1931. Other plays include *Tobias and the Angel*, *Jonah and the Whale*, *Mr. Bolfrey*, *Dr. Angelus*.

Bright, Sir Charles Tilston (1832–88), English telegraph engineer who supervised the laying of the British telegraph network and the Atlantic cables (1856–8).

Bright, John (1811–89), radical Quaker statesman and orator, b. Rochdale; friend of Cobden, with whom he promoted the movement for free trade.

Brindley, James (1716–72), English canal builder, b. Derbyshire, of poor parents, apprenticed as a millwright. He was employed by the Duke of Bridgewater (*q.v.*) and designed and constructed the Bridgewater canal, carrying it over the R. Irwell by an aqueduct, the first of its kind. He also built the Grand Trunk canal linking the Mersey with the Trent.

Britten, Baron (Edward Benjamin Britten) (1913–76), English composer, closely associated with the Aldeburgh festival. O.M. 1965. *See* **Section E.**

Broca, Paul (1824–80), French pathologist, anthropologist and pioneer in neuro-surgery. He localised the seat of speech in the brain and originated methods for measuring brain and skull ratios.

Broch, Hermann (1886–1951), Austrian novelist, author of the trilogy *The Sleepwalkers*. Lived in U.S.A. after 1938.

Broglie, prominent family of Piedmontese origin; **Victor Maurice** (1647–1727), and **François Marie** (1671–1745) were marshals of France; **Louis Victor, Prince de Broglie** (b. 1892) received the Nobel prize for his work on quantum mechanics, and his brother **Maurice, Duc de Broglie** (1875–1960), also a physicist, is noted for his work on the ionisation of gases, radioactivity, and X-rays.

Brontë, Charlotte (1816–55), forceful novelist, daughter of an Anglican clergyman of Irish descent, incumbent of Haworth, Yorkshire. She published under a pseudonym *Jane Eyre*, which was at once successful and was followed by *Shirley* and *Villette*. Her sister **Emily** (1818–48) wrote poetry and also *Wuthering Heights*; and Anne (1820–49) wrote *Agnes Grey*.

Brooke, Rupert (1887–1915), English poet who died during the first world war, whose works, though few, showed promise and include the poems *Grantchester* and *The Soldier*.

Brougham and Vaux, 1st Baron (Henry Peter Brougham) (1778–1868), English legal reformer; advocate of Queen Caroline against George IV; helped to found London university.

Brown, Sir Arthur Whitten (1886–1948), together with Sir John Alcock (d. 1919) in 1919 made the first transatlantic flight, crossing from Newfoundland to Ireland in 16 hr. 12 min.

Brown, John (1800–59), American abolitionist. His action in inciting Negro slaves to rebel in 1859 led to the civil war. He was hanged after failing to hold the U.S. arsenal at Harper's Ferry which he had captured. Known as "Old Brown of Osawatomie" and regarded as a martyr.

Browne, Charles Farrer (1834–67), American humorist who wrote under the pseudonym of Artemus Ward.

Browne, Hablot Knight (1815–82), English artist, the "Phiz" of many book illustrations, including Dickens's *Pickwick Papers*.

Browne, Sir Thomas (1605–82), author of *Religio Medici* and *Urne-Buriall*, was born in London and practised in Norwich as a physician.

Browning, Elizabeth Barrett (1806–61), English poet. Owing to an injury in childhood, she spent her youth lying on her back, but her meeting with Robert Browning, whom she married, brought a remarkable recovery. In her lifetime her works were more read than those of her husband. They include *Cry of the Children*, *Sonnets from the Portuguese*, and *Aurora Leigh*.

Browning, Robert (1812–89), English poet. Because of his involved style his reputation grew only slowly. In *Strafford* and *The Blot on the 'Scutcheon* he attempted drama also. He married Elizabeth Barrett and lived mainly abroad. His works include *Dramatis Personae* and *The Ring and The Book*.

Bruce, Robert (1274–1329), Scottish national leader against Edward I and Edward II of England. Crowned king in 1306, after years of struggle he defeated Edward II at Bannockburn in 1314.

Bruce, William Spiers (1867–1921), Scottish polar explorer who led the Scottish national antarctic expedition in the *Scotia* 1902–4 and set up a meteorological station on the South Orkneys.

Bruch, Max (1838–1920), German composer and conductor, best known for his G minor violin concerto.

Bruckner, Anton (1824–96), Austrian composer and organist. *See* **Section E.**

Brummell, George Bryan (1778–1840), "Beau Brummell," fashion leader and friend of the Prince Regent (George IV).

Brunel, Isambard Kingdom (1806–59), English civil engineer, son of **Sir Marc Isambard Brunel** (1769–1849), whom he assisted in building the Thames (Rotherhithe) tunnel. He was engineer of the Great Western Railway and built the ocean liners, the *Great Western*, the *Great Britain* (brought back from the Falkland Is. to Bristol in 1970), and the *Great Eastern*. His other works include the Clifton suspension bridge over the R. Avon at Bristol and the Royal Albert bridge over the R. Tamar at Saltash.

Brunelleschi, Filippo (1377–1446), Italian architect, b. Florence; he adapted the ideals of the Roman period. Examples of his work in Florence include the Pitti Palace, the churches of San Lorenzo and San Spirito, and the cathedral dome.

Bruno, Giordano (1548–1600), Italian philosopher. A Dominican friar, he came to favour the astronomical views of Copernicus and was burnt at the stake.

Bruno, St. (*c.* 1032–1101), German monk, founder in 1084 of the Carthusian order at La Grande Chartreuse in the French Alps.

Brutus, Marcus Junius (85–42 B.C.), conspirator against Julius Caesar; later committed suicide.

Buchanan, George (1506–82), Scottish humanist who spent most of his life in France lecturing and writing Latin poems, plays, and treatises. Montaigne, Mary Queen of Scots, and James VI of Scotland were his pupils at various times.

Buchner, Eduard (1860–1917), German chemist, remembered for his work on the chemistry of fermentation. Nobel prizewinner 1907.

Büchner, Georg (1813–37), German dramatist. Dying at 24, his limited output (principally *Dantons Tod* and the fragment *Wozzeck*) is marked by power and maturity.

Buckle, Henry Thomas (1821–62), author of *The History of Civilisation in England.*

Buddha. *See* **Gautama, Siddhartha.**

Budge, Sir Ernest Alfred Wallis (1857–1934), archaeologist who conducted excavations in Mesopotamia and Egypt.

Buffon, Georges-Louis Leclerc, Comte de (1707–88), French naturalist, author of the *Histoire naturelle* (44 vols., 1749–1804).

Bulganin, Nikolai Alexandrovich (1895–1975), Soviet prime minister 1955–8; defence minister 1947–9, 1953–5. Retired 1960.

Bull, John (*c.* 1562–1628), English composer; possibly composer of *God save the Queen.*

Bülow, Hans Guido von (1830–94), German pianist and conductor. He married Liszt's daughter Cosima, who later left him in order to marry Wagner.

Bunsen, Robert Wilhelm (1811–99), German chemist, discoverer of the metals caesium and rubidium, and inventor of the Bunsen burner, battery, and pump. Made important observations in spectrum analysis.

Bunyan, John (1628–88), was originally a travelling tinker and is believed to have served in the Parliamentary army. He joined an Independent church in Bedford in 1655 and became a popular preacher. After the Restoration he was thrown into prison, and there wrote *The Pilgrim's Progress.* Of his 60 works, the best known after *Pilgrim's Progress* are *The Holy War, Grace Abounding,* and *Mr. Badman.*

Burckhardt, Jacob Christoph (1818–97), Swiss historian, author of *The Civilisation of the Renaissance in Italy.*

Burghley, 1st Baron (William Cecil) (1520–98), English statesman. After holding office under her two predecessors, he was Queen Elizabeth I's secretary of state, 1558–72, and lord high treasurer, 1572–98.

Burke, Edmund (1729–97), Whig writer and political philosopher. B. in Dublin, he became secretary to Lord Rockingham and entered parliament in 1765. He advocated the emancipation (though not the independence) of the American colonies; and better administration in India; but was against the French revolution.

Burnett, Gilbert (1643–1715) bishop of Salisbury, b. Edinburgh. He wrote a *History of his Own Times*, which deals with many events of which he had personal knowledge.

Burnet, Sir John James (1859–1938), architect, b. Glasgow. The north front of the British Museum (King Edward's galleries) is his most important work in London.

Burney, Fanny (Madame D'Arblay) (1752–1840), originator of the simple novel of home life. Daughter of the organist, Dr. Burney, she published *Evelina* in 1778, and this brought her into court and literary society. She also wrote *Cecilia* and *Camilla.*

Burns, Robert (1759–96), Scottish poet. The son of a cottar, his first poems published in 1786 were at once successful, and he bought a farm. The farm failed, but he had a post as exciseman, and continued to write simply with tenderness and humour. Among his best-known poems are *Auld Lang Syne, Scots wa hae, Comin' through the rye,* and *The Banks of Doon.*

Burton, Sir Richard Francis (1821–90), British explorer and orientalist, who made a pilgrimage to Mecca and Medina in 1853 disguised as a Moslem. He explored Central Africa and translated the *Arabian Nights* (16 vols.).

Burton, Robert (1577–1640), English clergyman and scholar, author of *The Anatomy of Melancholy.*

Busoni, Ferruccio Benvenuto (1866–1920), pianist and composer of three operas (the last *Dr. Faust*, unfinished at his death), much orchestral and chamber music, and works for the piano. B. in Empoli, he lived in Germany. *See* **Section E.**

Butler, Joseph (1692–1752), English bishop, remembered for his *Analogy of Religion*, published in 1736 in reply to deistic attacks.

Butler, Nicholas Murray (1862–1947), American educationist who shared with the sociologist Jane Addams the 1931 Nobel peace prize.

Butler, Baron (Richard Austen Butler) (1902–82), Conservative M.P. for Saffron Walden 1929–65. Brought in Education Act 1944; helped secure Conservative acceptance of the welfare state; held high office 1951–64 (*see* **D8**). "Butskellism" applied to Conservative social and economic policies of the '50s. Described by Sir Harold Wilson as the best prime minister we never had. Life peerage 1965; Master of Trinity College, Cambridge, 1965–78.

Butler, Samuel (1612–80), English verse-satirist, author of the poem *Hudibras* against the Puritans.

Butler, Samuel (1835–1902), English novelist and satirist, author of *Erewhon* and its sequel *Erewhon Revisited.* Other works include *The Fair Haven, Life and Habit,* and *Evolution Old and New,* in which he attacked Darwinism. His autobiographical novel *The Way of All Flesh* and his *Notebooks* were published after his death. He exhibited regularly at the Academy and was also a musician.

Butt, Clara (1872–1936), English contralto; made her début in London in 1892.

Buxton, Sir Thomas Fowell (1786–1845), English social reformer; succeeded Wilberforce as leader of the anti-slavery group in parliament.

Buys Ballot, Christoph Henrich Diedrich (1817–90), Dutch meteorologist who formulated the law which bears his name (an observer with back to wind in northern hemisphere has lower pressure to left; in southern hemisphere to right).

Byrd, Richard Evelyn (1888–1957), American rear-admiral, explorer and aviator. He flew over the north pole, 1926; and in 1929 made the first flight over the south pole. He made other polar expeditions in 1925, 1933–5, 1939 and 1946.

Byrd, William (1543–1623), English composer of church music, sacred choral music, string music, vocal and instrumental music; and a founder of the school of English madrigalists. He was organist of Lincoln cathedral at 20 and later of Queen Elizabeth's chapel royal. *See* Section E.

Byron, 6th Baron (George Gordon Byron) (1788–1824), English romantic poet who influenced European literature and thought. At 20 he published *Hours of Idleness*, which was violently attacked by the *Edinburgh Review*. This provoked his retaliatory *English Bards and Scotch Reviewers*, which caused a sensation. His *Childe Harold's Pilgrimage* appeared in 1812. His married life was unhappy. He went to help the Greeks in their struggle for independence and died at Missolonghi.

C

Cable, George Washington (1844–1925), American author and social critic, b. New Orleans, whose writings reflect the colour problems of his day: *Ole Creol Days*, *The Silent South*.

Cabot, John (1425–*c.* 1500), Genoese explorer who settled in Bristol and sailed westwards under letters-patent from Henry VII of England in 1497. Discovered Newfoundland and Nova Scotia, believing them to be part of Asia, and may have reached the mainland of America before Columbus did. His son:

Cabot, Sebastian (1474–1557), was born in Venice, and in 1509 in search of a north-west passage to Asia sailed as far as Hudson Bay. Entered Spanish service in 1512, and spent several years exploring the Plate and Paraná rivers. Re-entered English service in 1548 and organised expedition to seek a north-east passage to India, which resulted in trade with Russia. English claim to North America is founded on the voyages of the Cabots.

Cabral, Pedro Alvarez (*c.* 1467–*c.* 1520), Portuguese navigator, friend of Vasco da Gama, discovered Brazil, which he named "Terra da Santa Cruz."

Cadbury, George (1839–1922), liberal Quaker philanthropist of Cadbury Bros., mainly responsible for the pioneer garden city of Bournville.

Cadogan, Sir Alexander (1884–1968), English diplomat. He helped to draft the charter of the United Nations organisation and became Gt. Britain's representative on the Security Council.

Caedmon, the first English Christian poet, lived in the 7th cent. and, according to Bede, was first a cowherd and later a monk at Whitby. His poetry was based on the scriptures.

Caesar, Caius Julius (*c.* 101–44 B.C.), Roman general and writer. Under the declining republic, he was assigned in 61 the province of Gaul; in the course of pacifying it he invaded Britain (55 B.C.). Opposition in Rome to his career, mainly from Pompey, provoked him in 49 to the defiance of crossing the Rubicon with his army. He defeated Pompey, whom he pursued to Egypt, where he established Cleopatra as queen. At Rome he became dictator, and his reforms include the Julian calendar. He was murdered in 44. His career paved the way for Rome becoming an empire under his nephew Octavian.

Calderón de la Barca, Pedro (1600–81), Spanish dramatist, representative of contemporary Spanish thought, who also wrote court spectacles for Philip IV. Among his best-known works are *La Vida es Sueño* and *El divino Orfeo*.

Callaghan, James (b. 1912), Labour's fourth prime minister, 1976–9; parliamentary leader of the Labour Party, April 1976, following Sir Harold Wilson's resignation: elected for South Cardiff 1950; served as Chancellor of the Exchequer, Home Secretary, and Foreign Secretary in the Labour administrations, 1964–70, 1974–76. Succeeded by Michael Foot as leader, 1980.

Calvin, John (1509–64), French Protestant reformer and theologian. B. in Picardy, he broke with the Roman Catholic church about 1533, and subsequently settled in Geneva, where from 1541 he established a theocratic regime of strict morality. His theology was published in his *Institutes*; while, like Luther, he accepted justification by faith without works, he also believed in predestination. His doctrines spread on the continent, in Scotland and to some extent in England. *See* Calvinism, Section J.

Câmara, Helder Pessoa (b. 1908), Brazilian archbishop of Recife; critic of the economic imperialism of multinational companies and courageous campaigner for social reform.

Camden, William (1551–1623), English antiquary and historian. His *Britannia* appeared in 1586.

Cameron, Sir David Young (1865–1945), Scottish etcher and landscape painter.

Cameron, Richard (1648–80), Scottish preacher who revolted in defence of the Solemn League and Covenant and was killed at Airds Moss (Ayrshire).

Cameron, Verney Lovett (1844–94), English explorer, the first to cross the African continent from east to west. He surveyed Lake Tanganyika and in 1872 went out to find Livingstone.

Camillus, Marcus Furius (4th cent. B.C.), Roman general. When the Gauls attacked in 387 B.C., he was made dictator and defeated them.

Camões, Luis Vaz de (1524–80), Portuguese poet, author of *Os Lusiadas*, an epic of Portuguese history and discovery.

Campbell, Colin, 1st Baron Clyde (1792–1863), Scottish general who was commander-in-chief in India during the Mutiny.

Campbell, Sir Malcolm (1885–1948), racing driver who held the land-speed record of 301 mile/h (1935) and water-speed record of 141·7 mile/h (1939). His son **Donald** held the water-speed record of 276·33 mile/h (1964); killed in 1967 at Coniston.

Campbell, Mrs. Patrick (Beatrice Stella Tanner) (1865–1940), English actress of beauty and wit, friend of G. B. Shaw.

Campbell, Thomas (1777–1844), Scottish poet, who at 22 published *The Pleasures of Hope*. His war poems include *Ye Mariners of England* and *The Battle of the Baltic*. He was one of the founders of University College, London.

Campbell-Bannerman, Sir Henry (1836–1908), Liberal statesman, prime minister 1905–8. His ministry included Asquith, Lloyd George, and Churchill.

Camus, Albert (1913–60), French existentialist philosopher and writer, native of Algeria. Preoccupied with the themes of the Stranger and the Absurd, the works for which he is particularly remembered are the philosophical essay *Le Mythe de Sisyphe*, the plays *Caligula* and *The Price of Justice*, and the novel *L'Etranger*. Nobel prize 1957. Killed in car crash.

Canaletto (Antonio Canal) (1697–1768), Italian artist. B. at Venice, he painted views of his city. From 1746 to 1756 he worked mainly in London. Some of his work is in the National Gallery, and there is a collection at Windsor.

Canning, George (1770–1827), English statesman. He was an advocate of Catholic emancipation, and was the first to recognise the free states of South America.

Cannizzaro, Stanislao (1826–1910), Italian chemist who carried forward the work of Avogadro in distinguishing between molecular and atomic weights.

Canova, Antonio (1757–1822), Italian sculptor. B. at Venice, he infused grace into the classical style.

Canton, John (1718–72), English physicist and schoolmaster, the first to verify in England Franklin's experiments on the identity of lightning with electricity. He was the first to demonstrate that water is compressible and produced a new phosphorescent body (Canton's phosphorus) by calcining oyster shells with sulphur.

Canute (*c.* 994–1035), king of the English, Danes and Norwegians. The son of a Danish king, after some years of fighting he established himself as king of England and ruled with wisdom and firmness.

Capablanca, José Raoul (1888–1942), Cuban chess player, world champion from 1921 to 1927 when he was beaten by Alekhine.

Caractacus or **Caradoc**, a king in west Britain, who resisted the Romans in the first century. After capture he was freed by the emperor Claudius.

Carey, William (1761–1834), first Baptist missionary to India. An Oriental scholar, he published 24 translations of the scriptures.

Carissimi, Giacomo (1604–74), Italian composer, b. near Rome. He introduced more instrumental variety into the cantata and oratorio, and brought the recitative to perfection. His *Jephtha* is still in print, and there are collections of his works at Paris and Oxford. *See* **Section E.**

Carlyle, Thomas (1795–1881), Scottish author. Of peasant stock, he went to Edinburgh university, but later lived mainly in England where he lectured. He married Jane Welsh. His individual views pervade his historical writing. His best-known works include *Sartor Resartus*, *Heroes and Hero Worship*, *Cromwell's Letters and Speeches*, and the *French Revolution*.

Carnegie, Andrew (1835–1919), philanthropist b. Dunfermline; emigrated to America 1848; after early struggles established the Carnegie iron works. He made munificent gifts to Free Libraries and other educational work.

Carnot, Lazare Nicolas Marguerite (1753–1823), French military engineer, prominent in the French revolutionary wars, 1792–1802. His son, **Sadi Carnot** (1796–1832), was a physicist and engineer who worked on the motive power of heat, establishing the principle that heat and work are reversible conditions.

Caroline, Queen (1768–1821), was married to George IV when he was Prince of Wales. They soon separated, but when he became king in 1820, she tried to assert her position. The question came before parliament. In spite of some public sympathy she was unsuccessful.

Carrel, Alexis (1873–1944), American surgeon who won the Nobel prize in 1912 for his success in suturing blood vessels in transfusion and in transplantation of organs. A Frenchman by birth, he returned to France in 1939.

Carroll, Lewis. *See* Dodgson, Charles Lutwidge.

Carson, Baron (Edward Henry Carson) (1854–1935), Irish barrister, solicitor-general for Ireland 1892; attorney general 1915; first lord of the admiralty 1916–17; member of the war cabinet 1917–18. He led a semi-militant organisation against Home Rule.

Carson, Rachel (1907–64), American biologist, remembered for *The Silent Spring*.

Carter, Howard (1873–1939), Egyptologist who was associated with Lord Carnarvon in discovering in 1922 the Tomb of Tutankhamun.

Carter, James Earl (b. 1924), American Democratic President 1977–81; former Governor of Georgia. His main achievements were the treaty between Israel and Egypt, the Panama Canal treaty, Salt II (though not ratified) and the settling of the release of American hostages held captive in Iran.

Cartier, Jacques (1494–1557), French navigator, b. St. Malo, who explored Canada, especially the gulf and river of St. Lawrence.

Cartwright, Edmund (1743–1823), English inventor of the power-loom, and also of a wool-combing machine, important steps in the weaving side of the textile revolution.

Cartwright, John (1740–1824), brother of the above; reformer and agitator against slavery.

Caruso, Enrico (1873–1921), Italian tenor, b. Naples.

Carver, George Washington (1864–1943), American Negro agricultural chemist of world repute.

Casabianca, Louis de (c. 1752–98), captain of the French flagship *L'Orient* at the Battle of the Nile. He and his ten-year-old-son died together in the burning ship.

Casals, Pablo (1876–1973), Spanish cellist and conductor, son of an organist, b. Vendrell, Tarragona. He exiled himself from Spain in 1939 as a protest against dictatorship.

Casanova de Seinfalt, Giacomo (1725–98), Italian adventurer, author of licentious memoirs.

Cassini, French family of Italian origin, distinguished for work in astronomy and geography. Through four generations (1671–1793) they were heads of the Paris Observatory.

Cassius, Caius Longinus, Roman general who opposed the dictatorship of Julius Caesar, and took part in his murder. He died in 42 B.C. after being defeated by Mark Antony.

Castlereagh, Viscount (Robert Stewart Castlereagh) (1769–1822), British minister of war and foreign secretary, who took a leading part in the Napoleonic wars. He was however unpopular and committed suicide.

Castro, Fidel (b. 1927), Cuban revolutionary. After two unsuccessful attempts he succeeded in 1959 in overthrowing a police-state. He has

initiated reforms in agriculture, industry, and education, and repulsed American economic dominance. His acceptance of Russian support led to the "missiles crisis" of 1962.

Catchpool, E. St. John (1890–1971), first secretary of the English Youth Hostels Association, 1930–50; president, International Federation, 1938–50.

Catherine, St. (4th cent.). Traditionally a virgin martyr in Alexandria, though not mentioned before the 10th cent. Legend represents her as tied to a wheel.

Catherine de' Medici (1519–89), Italian-born wife of Henry II and mother of three French kings (she was regent for Charles IX). Her antagonism to the Protestants may have led to the massacre of St. Bartholomew's day. She was able, and appreciated art and literature, but was unscrupulous and cruel.

Catherine of Aragon (1485–1536), first wife of Henry VIII of England, was daughter of Ferdinand and Isabella of Spain, and mother of Mary Tudor. After the Pope had refused to release Henry VIII from the marriage an English declaration of nullity was obtained (thus precipitating a movement towards the Reformation).

Catherine the Great (1729–96), Empress Catherine II of Russia. Daughter of a German prince, she married in 1745 the future Peter III, a weakling, later deposed and murdered. Intelligent, cultivated, autocratic, she proved a capable ruler for a time but was hampered and opposed by the landed interests and, despite plans for reform, her reign was marked by imperialist expansion and extension of serfdom.

Cato, Marcus Porcius (234–149 B.C.), Roman statesman and writer. His tenure of office as censor was characterised by austerity and conservatism. He advocated opposition to Carthage. His writings deal with agriculture and history.

Catullus, Caius Valerius (c. 84–54 B.C.), Roman poet who wrote lyrics to Lesbia. His poems show sincere feeling and also Greek influence.

Cavell, Edith Louisa (1865–1915), English nurse who cared for friend and foe in Brussels in 1914–15, but was executed by the Germans for helping Allied fugitives to escape.

Cavendish, Henry (1731–1810), English scientist, a contemporary of Black, Priestley, Scheele, and Lavoisier, remembered for his investigations into the nature of gases. He discovered hydrogen and the chemical composition of water. The Cavendish Laboratory is named after him.

Cavour, Camilio Benso di (1810–61), Italian statesman, who, as premier of Sardinia, helped to bring about the unification of Italy.

Caxton, William (1422–91), the first English printer and publisher, a man of wide-ranging abilities. He probably learnt the art of printing at Cologne (1471–2), setting up his own printing press at Westminster (1476). He printed Chaucer's *Canterbury Tales*, Malory's *Le Morte d'Arthur* and Aesop's *Fables*. He was an accomplished linguist.

Cecil of Chelwood, 1st Viscount (Robert Cecil) (1864–1958), English politician who helped draft the Charter of the League of Nations. Nobel prize for peace 1937.

Cecilia, St. (2nd or 3rd cent.), patron saint of music. She is often represented playing the organ.

Cellini, Benvenuto (1500–71), Italian sculptor and goldsmith. B. at Florence, he worked for some years in Rome. His bronze statue *Perseus with the head of Medusa* is at Florence. His life was adventurous and he wrote an *Autobiography* which is revealing of himself and his time.

Celsius, Anders (1701–44), Swedish physicist and astronomer who invented the centigrade thermometer.

Ceresole, Pierre (1879–1945), Swiss founder of International Voluntary Service. He was by profession a teacher of engineering, and his pacifism led him to become a Quaker.

Cervantes, Saavedra Miguel de (1547–1616), Spanish novelist and dramatist, b. at Alcalá de Henares. He was injured at the battle of Lepanto, and thereafter struggled to earn a livelihood from literature. His *Don Quixote* describes the adventures of a poor gentleman, confused in mind, who on his horse Rosinante with his squire Sancho Panza seeks adventures; it satirised chivalry, but is also a permanent criticism of life. Of his plays only two survive.

Cézanne, Paul (1839–1906), French painter, b. in Aix-en-Provence, the son of a wealthy banker and tradesman. He developed a highly original style, using colour and tone in such a way as to increase the impression of depth. He said that he wanted "to make of Impressionism something solid and durable, like the art of the Museums." Like Giotto, six hundred years before, he more than any other artist determined the course European painting was to take. *La Veille au Chapelet* and *Les Grandes Baigneuses* are in the National Gallery. He was a friend of Zola.

Chadwick, Sir Edwin (1800–90), English social reformer whose most important work was as Secretary of the Poor Law Board.

Chadwick, Sir James (1891–1974), English physicist, one of Rutherford's collaborators in the field of atomic research. Discovered the neutron in 1932, one of the main steps in the discovery of the fission process which led to the production of the atom bomb.

Chagall, Marc (1889–1985), Russian painter, b. at Vitebsk; the forerunner of surrealism.

Chamberlain, Joseph (1836–1914), English statesman. He began with municipal work in Birmingham. At first a Liberal under Gladstone, he became Conservative. He opposed Home Rule for Ireland, and was the first advocate of a partial return to protection.

Chamberlain, Neville (1869–1940), son of Joseph. He was prime minister 1937–40, when he appeased Hitler by the Munich agreement, 1938.

Chambers, Sir William (1726–96), British architect, b. Stockholm. He rebuilt Somerset House and designed the pagoda in Kew Gardens.

Champlain, Samuel de (1567–1635), French navigator who founded Quebec (1608), and discovered the lake known by his name.

Champollion, Jean François (1790–1832), French egyptologist, who found the key to the decipherment of hieroglyphics from the Rosetta stone (**L106**).

Chantrey, Sir Francis Legatt (1781–1841), English sculptor who left a fortune to the Royal Academy for the purchase of works of British art.

Chaplin, Sir Charles Spencer (1889–1977), first international screen star, with more than 50 years' achievement. B. in London, his mother was a music-hall singer and he made his début at five. In 1910 he went to the United States; and with the Keystone Company in Los Angeles (1914–15) he made films in which his early hardships are reflected in humour and sadness. His films include *Shoulder Arms, The Kid, The Gold Rush, City Lights, The Great Dictator, Modern Times,* and *Limelight. Autobiography* (1964).

Chapman, George (1559–1634), Elizabethan poet, dramatist, and translator of the *Iliad* and *Odyssey*. His best-known play is *Bussy d'Ambois*.

Chapman, Sydney (1888–1970), English mathematician and geophysicist, noted for his work on the kinetic theory of gases, geomagnetism, and solar and ionospheric physics. He was president of the special committee of the I.G.Y., 1957–8. An upper layer of the atmosphere and a crater on the moon are named after him.

Charcot, Jean Baptiste (1867–1936), French explorer, who in 1903–5 and 1908–10 commanded expeditions to the south polar regions. Charcot Island in the Antarctic is named after him.

Chardin, Jean Baptiste Siméon (1699–1779), French painter of still life and domestic scenes.

Chares (*c.* 300 B.C.), Greek worker in bronze from Rhodes, sculptor of the Colossus of Rhodes, one of the seven wonders of the world.

Charlemagne (742–814), Charles the Great. From being King of the Franks, he came to govern an empire comprising Gaul, Italy, and large parts of Spain and Germany, and was crowned Emperor by the Pope in Rome on Christmas Day, A.D. 800. His revival of the Western Empire was the foundation of the Holy Roman Empirè (*q.v.*).

Charles, Jacques Alexandre César (1746–1823), French physicist, the first to use hydrogen gas in balloons and who anticipated Gay-Lussac's law on the expansion of gases.

Charles Edward (Stuart) (1720–88), the Young Pretender (*i.e.,* claimant of the English throne), grandson of James II, led an unsuccessful rising in 1745 and died in exile.

Charles (Philip Arthur George) (b. 1948), Prince of Wales, Duke of Cornwall and Rothesay, eldest son of Queen Elizabeth II; married Lady Diana Spencer, daughter of 8th Earl Spencer, 1981.

Charles I (1600–49), King of England, Scotland, and Ireland, succeeded his father James I in 1625. Personally sincere, and having an appreciation of art, he was yet ill-fitted to cope with the political problems of his time. His marriage with the French princess Henrietta Maria was unpopular. He supported Archbishop Laud's strict Anglicanism, and he also attempted to rule without parliament. Defeated in the Civil War which broke out in 1642, he spun out negotiations for a settlement till he was beheaded in 1649.

Charles II (1630–85), King of England, Scotland, and Ireland, son of Charles I; after the Civil War escaped to France, and returned in 1660 when the monarchy was restored. His religious sympathies were Roman Catholic and his personal life was amorous; but in political matters he was shrewd and realistic, and contrived not to "go on his travels" again. He promoted the development of the navy, but had to accept the laws enforcing religious conformity imposed by parliament.

Charles V (1500–58), Hapsburg ruler, succeeded his grandfather, Maximilian I, as emperor of the Holy Roman Empire, and as heir to Ferdinand and Isabella succeeded to the Spanish crown. His rivalry with Francis I of France led to prolonged war. He crushed a revolt of peasants in 1525. He presided in 1521 at the Diet before which Luther appeared, after which religious struggle continued in Germany till the Augsburg settlement of 1555. In that year he retired to a monastery in Spain.

Charles XII of Sweden (1682–1718), a brave but rash and ambitious general. He repelled Russian attacks at Narva in 1700, but subsequntly pursuing military adventure he was defeated by Peter the Great at Poltava in 1709; and on invading Norway was killed.

Chateaubriand, François René, Vicomte de (1768–1848), French writer and diplomat. In a varied career he was at first an emigré, and later served as diplomat under both Napoleon and Louis XVIII. He was a friend of Mme. Recamier. His writings include *Mémoires d'outre-tombe.*

Chatham, 1st Earl of (William Pitt) (1708–78), English statesman and orator. His energetic conduct of the Seven Years War was an important contribution to English victory and to acquisitions in Canada and India at the peace (1763), though by then he was out of office. In the dispute with the American colonies he upheld their right to resist imposed taxation, and collapsed while making a last speech on this dispute.

Chatterton, Thomas (1752–70), English poet who tried to pass off his writings as newly discovered ancient manuscripts. Killed himself at the age of 17.

Chaucer, Geoffrey (1340?–1400), English poet. His main work, *The Canterbury Tales,* gives a vivid picture of contemporary life.

Chekhov, Anton (1860–1904), Russian dramatist and short-story writer, whose plays include *The Cherry Orchard, Uncle Vanya,* and *The Three Sisters.* His stories include *The Steppe, The Sleepyhead, The Post, The Student,* and *The Bishop.* He was of humble origin and while a student at Moscow supported his family by writing humorous sketches and tales.

Chernenko, Konstantin Ustinovich (1911–85) Soviet politician. Succeeded Andropov (q.v.) as General Secretary of the Communist Party, February 1984. Long career as bureaucrat, serving the Praesidium of the Supreme Soviet. Widely regarded as a protégé of Brezhnev, his ineffectual rule lasted a mere 13 months.

Cherubini, Luigi (1760–1842), Italian-born musician, director of the Paris Conservatoire.

Chesterfield, 4th Earl of (Philip Dormer Stanhope) (1694–1773), English statesman, whose *Letters* to his natural son, Philip Stanhope, are full of grace, wit, and worldly wisdom.

Chesterton, Gilbert Keith (1874–1936), English essayist, novelist and poet, who also wrote studies of Charles Dickens and Robert Browning. His works include *The Napoleon of Notting Hill* and *The Ballad of the White Horse.*

Chevalier, Albert (1861–1923), English music-hall comedian known for his coster sketches.

Chiang Kai-shek (1887–1975), Chinese general. He at first fought for Sun Yat-sen. After the latter's death (1925), as commander of the

Kuomintang army, he attempted to unite China; but (involved as he was with business interests) he was more anxious to defeat the Communists than to repel the Japanese adventure in Manchuria in 1931. He was unable to establish peace and a stable, progressive régime; and in 1949 retired to Formosa after military defeat by the Communists. His widow is Mayling Soong.

Chichester, Sir Francis (1902–72), English seaman, who sailed his *Gipsy Moth IV* into Sydney harbour in 1966 after a 107-day voyage from Plymouth, and back again round the Horn.

Chippendale, Thomas (1718–79), designer of furniture, b. Otley, Yorks, son of a joiner. His designs are shown in *The Gentleman and Cabinet Maker's Director*, 1754.

Chirico, Giorgio de (1888–1978), painter associated with the surrealist school, born in Greece of Italian parents.

Chomsky, Noam (b. 1928), American theoretical linguist, professor of Linguistics, Massachusetts Institute of Technology; inventor of transformational grammar.

Chopin, Frédéric François (1810–49), Polish pianist and composer, son of a French father and Polish mother. He has been called "the poet of the piano" because of the originality and delicacy of his playing. He enjoyed Paris intellectual and musical society, was a friend of George Sand, and played in numerous concerts all over Europe. He died of consumption. *See* **Section E.**

Chou En-lai (1898–1976), Chinese revolutionary statesman, administrator and diplomat. He organised revolt in Shanghai 1927, later formed close partnership with Mao Tse-tung, took part in the "long march" 1934–5, becoming prime minister of the new China in 1949. Headed the Chinese delegation to the Geneva Conference of 1954.

Chrysostom, St. John (*c.* 347–407), preacher. Chrysostom means golden-mouthed. First at Antioch, and later as patriarch of Constantinople, he was an eloquent teacher; but by outspokenness he lost the Empress Eudoxia's favour and died from ill-treatment.

Chulalongkorn, Phra Paramindr Maha (1853–1910), Siamese reforming monarch.

Churchill, Lord Randolph Henry Spencer (1849–95), Conservative politician, who held brief office only. He was father of Winston Churchill.

Churchill, Sir Winston Leonard Spencer (1874–1965), British statesman and author, son of the last-named. He entered parliament in 1900. He served as a junior officer with the British forces abroad; and during the Boer War he acted as war correspondent. He held the following ministerial posts: Under-Secretary for the Colonies 1905–8; President of the Board of Trade 1908–10; Home Secretary 1910–11; First Lord of the Admiralty 1911–15, 1939–40; Chancellor of the Duchy of Lancaster 1915; Minister of Munitions 1917; Minister of War 1918–21; Minister of Air 1919–21; Secretary of State for the Colonies 1921–2; Chancellor of the Exchequer 1924–9; Prime Minister and Minister of Defence 1940–5; Prime Minister 1951–5. He was rector or chancellor of three universities. Cast in the heroic mould, he lived a full life. His main achievement was as leader of the British people in the second world war. His writings include a biography of his ancestor, Marlborough, and histories of the first and second world wars. He exhibited at the Royal Academy. Hon. American citizenship conferred 1963.

Cibber, Colley (1671–1757), a London actor and dramatist. His best comedies are *The Careless Husband* and *Love's Last Shift*. He wrote an autobiography.

Cicero, Marcus Tullius (106–43 B.C.), Roman orator and philosopher, many of whose letters and speeches survive. He held political office but was killed by the troops of the triumvirate.

Cid (El Campeador) (*c.* 1035–99), name given to the Spanish knight Rodrigo Diaz, a soldier of fortune who fought against Moors and Christians alike. Myth made him a national hero of knightly and Christian virtue.

Cierva, Juan de la (1895–1936), Spanish engineer who invented the autogiro.

Cimabue, Giovanni (Cenni di Pepo) (1240–1302), early Florentine painter. His only certain work is the St. John in Pisa cathedral.

Cimarosa, Domenico (1749–1801), Italian composer. His best-known opera is *Il Matrimonio Segreto*. He held revolutionary views.

Cimon (*c.* 512–449 B.C.), Athenian statesman and general, son of Miltiades. He defeated the Persian fleet at the mouth of the Eurymedon in 468. He worked for cooperation with other states, including Sparta.

Cipriani, Giambattista (1727–85), Italian painter of historical subjects who worked in London; a founder member of the Royal Academy.

Clair, René (1898–1981), French film producer, whose early films, full of wit and satire, include *Sous les Toits de Paris* and *A Nous la Liberté*.

Clare, John (1793–1864), Northamptonshire labourer who became a poet. *Poems Descriptive of Rural Life and Scenery*, and *The Village Minstrel* were among his publications. He died in the county lunatic asylum.

Clarendon, 1st Earl of (Edward Hyde) (1609–74), English statesman and historian. He was for some years chancellor to Charles II, and his daughter married the future James II, but he fell and died in exile. He wrote a *History of the Rebellion*.

Clark, Baron (Kenneth McKenzie Clark) (1903–83), English art historian. He was director of the National Gallery 1934–45, Slade professor of fine arts at Oxford 1946–50, and chairman of the Arts Council 1953–60. Life peer 1969. Chanc. York University 1969. O.M. 1976.

Clarkson, Thomas (1760–1846) devoted his life to the abolition of slavery and shares with Wilberforce credit for the passing of the Act of 1807 abolishing the British slave trade.

Claude Lorrain (Gelée) (1600–82), French landscape painter. B. near Nancy, he settled in Rome. A close student of nature, he excelled in depicting sunrise or sunset, and founded a "picturesque" tradition.

Claudius (10 B.C.–A.D. 54), Roman emperor. After the murder of Caligula, he was proclaimed emperor almost accidentally by the Praetorian Guard. He was a sensible administrator. In his time the empire was extended to include Britain, Thrace, and Mauretania. He was probably poisoned by his wife Agrippina.

Clausewitz, Karl von (1780–1831), German military expert whose *Vom Kriege*, expounding his theories on war, dominated Prussia in the 19th cent.

Clemenceau, Georges (1841–1929), French statesman of radical views; twice premier, 1906–9, 1917–20. He was a defender of Dreyfus. In old age he presided at the peace conference of 1919, where he was hostile to Germany ("the Tiger").

Cleopatra (69–30 B.C.), daughter of Ptolemy XI, the sixth queen of Egypt by that name, a brilliant, ambitious woman. In 51 she became joint sovereign with her younger brother Ptolemy XII. She was banished to Syria, but, obtaining the help of Caesar, regained the kingdom. She and Caesar became lovers, and in 47 she bore him a son Caesarion (later Ptolemy XIV). After Caesar's murder she returned to Egypt. She met the triumvir Mark Antony and bore him twins; he deserted his wife and broke with his brother-in-law Octavian (later Augustus). Antony and Cleopatra were, however, defeated in 31 B.C.; Antony fell upon his sword, and Cleopatra killed herself with an asp bite. Her life inspired Shakespeare's *Antony and Cleopatra* and Shaw's *Caesar and Cleopatra*.

Clive, 1st Baron (Robert Clive) (1725–74), English general who helped to lay the foundations of English power in India. B. near Market Drayton, he entered the service of the East India Company. He contemplated suicide, but Anglo-French rivalry, culminating in the Seven Years War, gave scope for his military powers in the siege of Arcot and the battle of Plassey. As a governor he showed administrative capacity. In his later life he was unpopular which led to his suicide.

Clovis (*c.* 465–511), Merovingian king of the Franks and a convert to Christianity. He defeated the Burgundians and West Goths, and fixed his court at Paris.

Clyde, Lord. *See* **Campbell, Colin.**

Cobbett, William (1763–1835), English controversialist. He is chiefly known for his *Rural Rides*, but also published a weekly *Political Register* from 1802.

Cobden, Richard (1804–65), English advocate of free trade. The son of a Sussex farmer, he led agitation against the laws restricting import of corn, and they were repealed in 1846. He was impoverished by his public work and was helped by subscription.

Cochrane, Thomas, 10th Earl of Dundonald (1775–1860), British seaman, who crippled a French fleet in Biscay (1809), aided the liberation of Chile and Peru from Spanish rule (1819–22), of Brazil from Portuguese rule (1823–5), and assisted the Greeks in their struggle to throw off the Turkish yoke (1827).

Cockcroft, Sir John Douglas (1897–1967), Cambridge nuclear physicist who shared with E. T. S. Walton the 1951 Nobel prize. They had worked together at Cambridge in the historic "atom-splitting" experiments beginning with the transmutation of lithium into boron. He was directly involved in Britain's first nuclear power programmes.

Cockerell, Christopher (b. 1910), English inventor of the hovercraft, which works on the aircushioning principle. *See* **Hovercraft, Section L.**

Cocteau, Jean (1891–1963), French writer and artist in widely varied forms of art.

Cody, Samuel Franklin (1861–1913), American aviator, the first man to fly in Britain (1,390 ft. on 16 Oct. 1908). He became a British subject in 1909. Killed while flying.

Cody, William Frederick (1846–1917), American showman, known as "Buffalo Bill," whose Wild West Show toured America and Europe.

Coggan, Donald (b. 1909), enthroned 101st archbishop of Canterbury, January 1975; archbishop of York 1961–74; Canterbury 1975–80.

Cohn, Ferdinand Julius (1828–98), German botanist, founder of the science of bacteriology.

Coke, Sir Edward (1552–1634), English legal author, judge, and rival of Francis Bacon. His legal works are his *Reports* and *Institutes.*

Colbert, Jean Baptiste (1619–83), French statesman under Louis XIV, who fostered new industries, encouraged commerce, reformed the finances and established the navy on a sound basis. A patron of literature, science, and art.

Cole, George Douglas Howard (1889–1959), English economist and political journalist, professor of social and political theory at Oxford, 1944–57. Among his writings are *The Intelligent Man's Guide through World Chaos,* and *A History of Socialist Thought* (5 vols.).

Coleridge, Samuel Taylor (1772–1834), English poet, critic, and friend of Wordsworth, with whom he published *Lyrical Ballads.* His poems include *The Ancient Mariner, Christabel,* and *Kubla Khan.* His literary criticism is still valuable.

Coleridge-Taylor, Samuel (1875–1912), English composer, the son of a West African doctor practising in London and an Englishwoman. He is best known for his Hiawatha trilogy.

Colet, John (c. 1467–1519), English humanist and divine, founded St. Paul's School (1512). As scholar and friend of Erasmus he helped to bring the new learning to England.

Colette (Sidonie Gabrielle Claudine Colette) (1873–1954), French author of the *Claudine* stories, *Chéri* and *La Fin de Chéri.*

Collier, John (1850–1934), English painter noted for his "problem" pictures.

Collingwood, 1st Baron (Cuthbert Collingwood) (1750–1810), British admiral whose ship, the *Royal Sovereign,* led the fleet to battle at Trafalgar, and who on Nelson's death assumed command.

Collingwood, Robin George (1889–1943), English philosopher, historian, and archaeologist, associated with Oxford from 1908 to 1941. His philosophical thought is best studied in *Speculum Mentis, Essay on Philosophical Method, Idea of Nature,* and *Idea of History.*

Collins, Michael (1890–1922), Irish politician and Sinn Fein leader. He successfully organised guerrilla warfare, and mainly negotiated the treaty with Britain in 1921, but was killed in a Republican ambush on his return.

Collins, William (1788–1847), English landscape and figure painter.

Collins, William Wilkie (1824–89), son of the above; practically the first English novelist to

deal with the detection of crime. *The Woman in White* appeared in 1860.

Colt, Samuel (1814–62), of Hartford, Connecticut, invented the revolver in 1835. It was used in the war with Mexico.

Columba, St. (521–97), founder of the monastery of Iona, b. Ireland. From the island shrine he made missionary journeys to the Highlands of Scotland.

Columbanus, St. (c. 540–615), Irish abbot who founded a number of monasteries in continental Europe. *See* **Monasticism, Section J.**

Columbus, Christopher (c. 1451–1506), Italian navigator, b. Genoa, who, prevailing upon Ferdinand and Isabella of Spain to bear the expense of an expedition, in 1492 discovered the Bahamas, Cuba, and other West Indian islands. In 1498 he landed on the lowlands of S. America.

Comenius, John Amos (1592–1670), Czech educationist and pastor, advocate of the "direct" method of teaching languages, of the use of pictures in education, and of equality of educational opportunity for girls.

Compton, Arthur Holly (1892–1962), American physicist whose work on X-rays established what is known as the Compton effect (1923). While professor of physics at the university of Chicago (1923–45) he helped to develop the atomic bomb. Nobel prizewinner 1927.

Compton, Karl Taylor (1887–1954), scientist-administrator, brother of the above. Pres. Massachusetts Institute of Technology 1930–48.

Compton-Burnett, Dame Ivy (1884–1969), English novelist whose books deal with family relationships and include *Pastors and Masters, Men and Wives, A House and Its Head, Manservant and Maidservant.*

Comte, August (1798–1857), French philosopher, founder of positivism. *See* **Positivism, Section J.**

Condé, Louis, Prince de (1621–86), French general who defeated Spain at Rocroi in 1643.

Confucius or K'ung Fu-tse (c. 551–478 B.C.), Chinese philosopher, founder of the system of cosmology, politics, and ethics known as Confucianism. He was not concerned with the supernatural, but appealed to reason and taught love and respect of one's fellows, superiority to ambition, charity, forgiveness, and repentance. *See* **Confucianism, Section J.**

Congreve, William (1670–1729). Restoration dramatist, whose witty plays include *The Way of the World* and *Love for Love.*

Conrad, Joseph (1857–1924), English novelist of Polish birth, whose parents were exiled to Russia for political reasons. He became master mariner in the British merchant service, and began to write novels after he left the sea in 1884. His novels include *Almayer's Folly, Lord Jim, Nostromo.*

Conscience, Hendrik Henri (1812–83), Flemish novelist who wrote *The Lion of Flanders.*

Constable, John (1776–1837), English landscape painter, b. East Bergholt, Suffolk. Unlike his contemporary Turner, who journeyed over the Continent with his sketchbook, he found his scenes within a few miles of his home. His work was more popular in France than in England at the time and affected the Barbizon school and Delacroix. Examples of his work are in the National Gallery (including *The Hay Wain, Flatford Mill,* and *The Cornfield*), the Victoria and Albert, and the Tate (*The Valley Farm*).

Constant, Jean Joseph Benjamin (1845–1902), French painter of portraits and Oriental subjects.

Constantine (274–338), called "the Great," the first Christian Roman emperor. He was proclaimed at York by the army in 306. He stabilised the empire after a period of decline, and founded a new capital at Constantinople. A Christian council was held under his auspices at Nicaea in 325, and he was baptised on his death-bed.

Cook, James (1728–79), English navigator, son of an agricultural labourer. He entered the Royal Navy and gained a high reputation for his scientific skill. He made voyages of discovery to New Zealand and Australia in the ships under his command, *Endeavour, Resolution,* and *Adventure.* He anchored at Botany Bay in 1770 on his first voyage and gave it that name because of the interesting plants found on its shores. He also surveyed the Newfoundland coast. In an attempt to find the north-west passage he was murdered at Hawaii.

Cooper, Sir Astley Paston (1768–1841), English surgeon and author of medical textbooks.

Cooper, James Fenimore (1789–1851), American novelist, who produced stirring stories of adventure, among them *The Spy*, *The Last of the Mohicans*, *The Pathfinder*, and *The Deerslayer*.

Cooper, Samuel (1609–72), English miniaturist, represented with his brother Alexander (d. 1660) in the Victoria and Albert Museum. Among his miniatures is a portrait of Cromwell.

Copernicus, Nicolas (1478–1543), founder of modern astronomy, b. at Torun in Poland. He studied at Cracow and at a number of Italian universities before settling at Frauenburg in 1512 where he became canon of the cathedral. More of a student than a practical astronomer, he spent most of his private life seeking a new theory of the heavenly bodies. In his *On the Revolution of the Celestial Orbs*, published after his death, he broke with the past and put forward the novel theory that the planets, including the earth, revolve round the sun.

Coppée, François Joachim (1842–1908), French poet, novelist and dramatist.

Coquelin, Benoit Constant (1841–1909), and **Coquelin, Ernest** (1848–1909), (Coquelin aîné et cadet), brothers, were leading lights of the French theatre.

Corelli, Arcangelo (1653–1713), Italian composer and violinist, who established the form of the concerto grosso. *See* **Section E.**

Corneille, Pierre (1606–84), French dramatist, who ranks with Racine as a master of classical tragedy. *Le Cid*, *Polyeucte*, and *Le Menteur* marked a new era in French dramatic production.

Cornwallis, 1st Marquess (Charles Cornwallis) (1738–1805), British general who commanded the British forces which surrendered to the Americans at Yorktown in 1781, thus ending the war of independence. He was twice governor-general of India.

Corot, Jean Baptiste (1796–1875), French landscape painter.

Correggio, Antonio Allegri da (1494–1534), Italian painter, b. Correggio. His style anticipates the baroque. His *Ecce Homo* is in the National Gallery.

Cortés, Hernando (1488–1547), Spanish adventurer, b. Medellin, Estremadura, who captured Mexico for Spain, crushing an ancient civilisation.

Coulton, George Gordon (1858–1947), scholar and historian of the Middle Ages. In his *Five Centuries of Religion* he sets forth his interpretation of monastic history in England from the Conquest to the Reformation.

Couperin, a family of French musicians who were organists at St. Gervais, Paris, from about 1650 till 1826. François Couperin (1668–1783), called "Couperin the Great," is the best known today for his harpsichord music.

Cousin, Victor (1792–1867), French educationist and philosopher, founder of the eclectic school.

Cousins, Samuel (1801–87), English mezzotint engraver of plates after Reynolds, Millais, Landseer, and Hogarth.

Cousteau, Jacques-Yves (b. 1910), French underwater explorer, pioneer of aqualung diving.

Couve de Murville, Maurice (b. 1907), French diplomat; General de Gaulle's foreign minister 1958–68.

Coverdale, Miles (1488–1568), one of the early English reformers, b. Yorkshire, later to become bishop of Exeter. He assisted Tyndale in translating the Pentateuch and completed his own translation of the Bible in 1535. The Psalms still used in the Prayer Book and many of the phrases in the authorised version of 1611 are from his translation.

Cowper, William (1731–1800), English religious poet. His work is characterised by simplicity and tenderness. His best-known poems are *John Gilpin* and *The Task*.

Cox, David (1783–1859), English landscape painter. A collection of his works is in the Birmingham Gallery and the Tate Gallery.

Crabbe, George (1754–1832), English narrative poet of grim humour; author of *The Village* and *The Borough*.

Craig, Edward Gordon (1872–1966), son of Ellen Terry, producer and author of books on stage-craft.

Cranmer, Thomas (1489–1556), archbishop of Canterbury under Henry VIII, and Edward VI; an ardent promoter of the Reformation. On Mary's accession he at first consented to return to the old faith, but when called upon to make public avowal of his recantation, refused, and was burnt at the stake. His contributions were the English Bible and Book of Common Prayer.

Crichton, James (1560–82), Scottish adventurer who for his scholarly accomplishments was called "the admirable Crichton." He was killed in a brawl.

Cripps, Sir Stafford (1889–1952), British Labour statesman. A successful barrister, he relinquished practice for public work. As chancellor of the exchequer in post-war Britain, his programme was one of austerity, but his able exposition and single-minded purpose won him general support. Ill-health terminated his career.

Crispi, Francesco (1819–1901), Italian statesman, who aided Garibaldi and was later premier.

Crispin, St. (c. 285), martyr with his brother. By tradition they were Roman and became shoemakers, hence patron saints of shoemaking.

Croce, Benedetto (1886–1952), Italian philosopher and critic. His philosophy is expounded in the four volumes of *Filosofia dello Spirito* (which has been translated into English). He founded and edited *La Critica* in 1908, a review of literature, history, and philosophy. He was strongly opposed to fascism.

Croesus (d. c. 546 B.C.), last king of Lydia, reputed to be of immense wealth. Conquered and condemned to death by Cyrus, he was reprieved when Cyrus heard him recall Solon's saying "Call no man happy till he is dead."

Crome, John (1769–1821), English landscape painter, b. Norwich.

Cromer, 1st Earl of (Evelyn Baring) (1841–1917), British diplomat who, as British comptroller-general in Egypt from 1883 to 1907, did much to maintain order, improve the finances, and promote development. His *Modern Egypt* appeared in 1908.

Crompton, Samuel (1753–1827), English inventor of the spinning-mule (1779), which substituted machinery for hand work. He was b. near Bolton, a farmer's son, and benefited little by his invention.

Cromwell, Oliver (1599–1658), Protector of the commonwealth of England, Scotland, and Ireland. B. at Huntingdon, he represented Huntingdon in parliament. When civil war broke out, he served under the Earl of Essex; and then reorganised the parliamentary army, winning victories at Marston Moor and Naseby. Tortuous negotiations with Charles I could not be brought to an end, and he promoted the king's trial and execution in 1649. He defeated the Scots at Dunbar. When continued difficulties beset government he became Protector in 1653, but was soon obliged to govern by major-generals. His handling of Ireland enhanced the difficulties of that country. An able general and a strong character, he was personally tolerant (an Independent), sincere and devout; but he found himself in the revolutionary's dilemma— that there is no easy exit from a revolutionary situation; thus paradoxically he provoked English aversion to military rule.

Cromwell, Richard (1626–1712), son of the above, and his successor in the protectorate.

Cromwell, Thomas (1485–1540), English statesman, who succeeded Wolsey in the service of Henry VIII, and carried out the dissolution of the monasteries, but on his fall from favour he was executed.

Crookes, Sir William (1832–1919), English physicist who discovered the element thallium (1861) and invented the Crookes tube (1874) which was used by J. J. Thomson and others in their researches into the conduction of electricity in gases. He was also an authority on sanitation.

Cruikshank, George (1792–1878), caricaturist and book illustrator, whose work includes illustrations to *Grimm's Fairy Tales*, and *Oliver Twist*. Collections of his work are in the British Museum and the Victoria and Albert Museum.

Cummings, Bruce Frederick (1889–1919), English

zoologist and won fame as author of *Journal of a Disappointed Man.*

Cunard, Sir Samuel (1787–1865), founder of the Cunard line of steam ships. He was born in Nova Scotia, of a Welsh family of Quakers.

Cunningham of Hyndhope, 1st Viscount (Andrew Browne Cunningham) (1883–1963). British admiral in two world wars, b. Edinburgh. He served as commander-in-chief, Mediterranean, 1939–42 and Feb.–Oct. 1943; naval commander-in-chief for the Allied assault on North Africa 1942; first sea lord 1943–6.

Curie, Marie Sklodowska (1867–1934), first great woman scientist, b. Poland. Her father was a professor of physics at Warsaw. She came to Paris to study at the Sorbonne and married **Pierre Curie** (1859–1906), professor of physics. Thus began a fruitful collaborative career that led to the discovery of radium for which they shared the 1903 Nobel prize for physics. In 1911 Mme. Curie received the Nobel prize for chemistry. Pierre Curie was killed in an accident. *See also* **Joliot-Curie.**

Curzon of Kedleston, 1st Marquess (George Nathaniel Curzon) (1859–1925), statesman and administrator; viceroy of India 1898–1905; member of Lloyd George's war cabinet 1916–18; foreign secretary 1919–24.

Cuthbert, St. (c. 635–87), Celtic monk who became prior of Old Melrose (on the Tweed) and later of Lindisfarne. For a time he lived in seclusion on one of the Farne islands. The story of his life we owe to Bede.

Cuvier, Georges (1769–1832), French naturalist, noted for his system of classification of animals and his studies in comparative anatomy. His *La Règne Animal* (1819) was a standard work for many years.

Cuyp, Albert (1620–91), Dutch landscape painter of sea and river views.

Cyprian, St. (d. 258), bishop of Carthage, and early Christian writer who was martyred.

Cyrus (559–529 B.C.), Persian emperor. He founded the Achaemenid line, having defeated the Medes. By conquering Lydia and Babylonia, he controlled Asia Minor. He was a wise and tolerant ruler, allowing the Jews to rebuild their temple.

D

Daguerre, Louis Jacques Mandé (1789–1851), French photographic pioneer, who invented the daguerrotype process. *See* **Section L.**

Daimler, Gottlieb (1834–1900), German inventor, with N. A. Otto of Cologne, of the Otto gas engine. The Mercédès car, exhibited at Paris in 1900, was named after the daughter of Emile Jellinek, Austrian banker and car enthusiast.

Dale, Sir Henry Hallett (1875–1968), English physiologist. He shared the 1936 Nobel prize for medicine for his work on the chemical transmission of nerve impulses.

Dalhousie, 1st Marquess of (James Andrew Broun Ramsay) (1812–60), governor-general of India. He annexed the Punjab and later other states; opened the civil service to Indians and acted against suttee.

Dalton, John (1766–1844), English chemist and mathematician, a Quaker teacher of Manchester. In 1808 in the first number of his *New System of Chemical Philosophy* (1808–27) the modern chemical atomic theory was first propounded by him. According to this the atoms of the chemical elements are qualitatively different from one another.

Damien, Father (1840–89), Belgian missionary priest, originally named Joseph de Veuster, who, witnessing the sufferings of the lepers confined on the Hawaiian island of Molokai, obtained permission to take charge, and remained there until he himself died of leprosy.

Damocles, 5th cent. B.C., Syracusan flatterer who pronounced the tyrant Dionysius the happiest of men. To illustrate the uncertainty of life, Dionysius invited him to a banquet, where a naked sword hung over his head by a hair. Hence the expression "Sword of Damocles" to mean impending danger or threat.

Damrosch, Walter Johannes (1862–1950), American conductor and composer, b. Breslau, Prussia. He promoted musical development in the U.S., especially while conductor of the New York Symphony Society which his father, Leopold Damrosch (1832–1885) had founded in 1878.

D'Annunzio, Gabriele (1863–1938), Italian poet, dramatist and nationalist. In 1919 he led a raid on Fiume and seized it, but was eventually forced to surrender. His bodyguard wore the black shirt which was to be the uniform of the Fascists.

Dante Alighieri (1265–1321), Italian poet, a figure of world literature. He was b. at Florence in a troubled period. Though he saw her but once or twice, he loved a lady whom he called Beatrice, who is believed to have been Bice Portinari who married Simone di Bardi; she died in 1290, after which Dante wrote his *Vita Nuova.* His next work *Convivio* was philosophical. He joined the party of the Bianchi, attained municipal office, but was imprisoned and in 1301 fled. His *Divina Commedia* is a description of hell, purgatory, and heaven, a work of moral edification, replete with symbolism. He d. at Ravenna.

Danton, Georges Jacques (1759–94), French revolutionary. To his eloquent lead in 1792 was largely due the defeat of the foreign forces attempting to quell the revolution. He was a member of the committee of public safety, and sought to modify the extremists, but was displaced by Robespierre and was subsequently executed.

D'Arblay. *See* **Burney.**

Darby, Abraham (1677–1717), member of the Quaker family of ironmasters of Coalbrookdale, Shropshire, who paved the way for the industrial revolution by developing iron metallurgy. His grandson **Abraham** (1750–91) built the first cast-iron bridge (1779) over the Severn at Coalbrookdale.

Darius I (548–486 B.C.), Persian king and founder of Persepolis. He extended the borders of the Persian empire beyond the Indus, and reorganised it into satrapies. He declared "God's plan for the earth is not turmoil but peace, prosperity and good government." On clashing with the Greeks, however, he was defeated at Marathon. **Darius II** was a natural son of Artaxerxes I and d. 405 B.C. **Darius III** (d. 331 B.C.) was the last of the Persian kings, and was defeated by Alexander and assassinated.

Darling, Grace Horsley (1815–42), English heroine who by putting off in a small boat from the lighthouse on one of the Farne islands, of which her father was keeper, saved the shipwrecked crew of the *Forfarshire.*

Darnley, Henry Stewart, Lord (1545–67), second husband of Mary, Queen of Scots (1565). He plotted the murder of her secretary Rizzio, and was subsequently himself murdered. Through his son James I he is the ancestor of the Stuart monarchs.

Darwin, Charles Robert (1809–82), English naturalist, b. Shrewsbury, one of the pioneers of experimental biology. After returning from his formative voyage round the world as naturalist on the *Beagle* (1831–6), he spent nearly twenty years building up evidence for his theory of evolution before publishing it in *The Origin of Species* (1859). In it he argued that the evolution of present-day morphology had been built up by the gradual and opportunistic mechanism of natural selection. His ideas though welcomed by biologists aroused bitter controversy.

Daudet, Alphonse (1840–97), French writer who covered a wide range and whose works include *Lettres de mon Moulin, Robert Helmont,* and *Tartarin de Tarascon.*

David I (1084–1153), King of Scotland. As uncle of Matilda, daughter of Henry I of England, he supported her claim to the English crown, but was defeated. In Scotland he promoted unity and development.

David II (1324–71), King of Scotland. He was son of Robert Bruce. In invading England he was captured at Neville's Cross, 1346.

David, Sir Edgeworth (1848–1934), Australian geologist who accompanied Shackleton's antarctic expedition, 1907–9, leading the party that reached the south magnetic pole.

David, Jacques Louis (1748–1825), French painter of classical subjects and an ardent republican.

David, St., patron saint of Wales who lived in south Wales in the 6th cent.

Davidson, 1st Baron (Randall Thomas Davidson) (1848–1930), archbishop of Canterbury, 1903–28.

Davies, Sir Walford (1869–1941), English organist, composer, and broadcaster on music.

Davies, William Henry (1871–1940), Welsh poet. He spent some years tramping in both England and America, and his work shows knowledge of and love for nature. He wrote *Autobiography of a Super-tramp*.

Da Vinci. *See* Leonardo.

Davis, Jefferson (1808–89), American civil war leader. B. in Kentucky, he was made president of the Confederate States when the civil war broke out. After the war he was tried for treason, but discharged. He wrote *The Rise and Fall of the Confederate Government*.

Davis, John (c. 1550–1605), Elizabethan explorer and discoverer of Davis's Strait, the channel between the Atlantic and Arctic oceans on the west of Greenland. Invented the backstaff, or Davis's quadrant.

Davitt, Michael (1846–1906), Irish nationalist. The son of a peasant who later came to England, he joined the Fenians, and in 1870 was sentenced to penal servitude. On his release he helped to found the Land League in 1879; was again imprisoned; and wrote *Leaves from a Prison Diary*. He was subsequently returned to parliament.

Davy, Sir Humphry (1778–1829), English chemist, b. Penzance. Much of his work found practical application, *e.g.*, the miner's safety lamp which still bears his name. His *Elements of Agricultural Chemistry* (1813) contains the first use in English of the word "element." He took Michael Faraday as his assistant at the Royal Institution.

Dawber, Sir Guy (1861–1938), English architect. As chairman of the Council for the Preservation of Rural England, he did much to bring about the restoration of buildings throughout the country.

Day Lewis, Cecil (1904–72), poet and critic; professor of poetry at Oxford from 1951–6. He succeeded Masefield as poet laureate in 1968.

Debussy, Claude Achille (1862–1918), composer and leader of the French Impressionist school in music. Among his works are *Suite bergamasque*, containing the popular *Clair de lune*; *L'après-midi d'un Faune*, inspired by the poem of Mallarmé, and *La Mer*. He also wrote an opera *Pelléas et Mélisande* based on Maeterlinck's drama. *See also* Section E.

Defoe, Daniel (1660–1731), English political writer; also author of *Robinson Crusoe*, *Moll Flanders*, and a *Tour of Gt. Britain*. His *Shortest Way with Dissenters* brought him imprisonment.

De Forest, Lee (1873–1961), American inventor who was the first to use alternating-current transmission, and improved the thermionic valve detector by which wireless and sound films were made possible.

Degas, Edgar (1834–1917), French impressionist painter and sculptor, son of a banker. He painted subjects from everyday life—dancers, café life, the racecourse.

De Gasperi, Alcide (1881–1954), Italian politician who founded the Christian Democrat Party.

de Gaulle. *See* Gaulle, Charles de.

De Havilland, Sir Geoffrey (1882–1965), pioneer of civil and military aviation in Britain; designer of the famous Moth machines. His son was killed in 1946 while testing a plane.

Delacroix, Ferdinand Victor Eugène (1798–1863), French painter of the Romantic school.

De la Mare, Walter John (1873–1956), English poet and novelist whose work has a characteristic charm. Much of it was written for children.

Delane, John Thadeus (1817–79), editor of *The Times*, 1841–77, who did much to establish that paper's standing.

Delaroche, Paul (1797–1856), French historical painter.

Delibes, Clément Philibert Léo (1836–91), French composer of much graceful music, including operas, of which *Lakmé* is the best known, and ballets, among them *Coppélia*.

Delius, Frederick (1862–1934), English composer of German parentage. His music, highly idiosyncratic in idiom, was more readily re-

ceived in Germany than in England until promoted by Sir Thomas Beecham. *See* Section E.

Democritus (c. 470–c. 400 B.C.), one of the first scientific thinkers, pupil of Leucippus (fl. c. 440 B.C.). He took an atomic view of matter, denied the existence of mind as a separate entity, and counted happiness and inner tranquility as important moral principles. His attitude was not shared by his contemporary, Socrates, nor by Plato and Aristotle, but was accepted by Epicurus. The atomic theory thus passed into the background for many centuries.

Demosthenes (384–322 B.C.), Greek orator who, by his *Philippics*, roused the Athenians to resist the growing power of Philip of Macedon.

Deng Xiaoping (b. 1904), Chinese politician, b. Szechwan; rehabilitated at Eleventh Party Congress (1977); one of the 3 vice-chairmen of the Communist Party, 1980–82.

De Quincey, Thomas (1785–1859), English essayist and critic; friend of Wordsworth and Southey. He wrote *Confessions of an English Opium-eater*.

De Reszke, Jean (1853–1925) and **De Reszke, Edouard** (1856–1917), Polish operatic singers, the first a tenor, the second a baritone.

Derwentwater, 3rd Earl of (James Radcliffe) (1689–1716), leader of the English Jacobite movement for placing the pretender on the throne. He was defeated at Preston in 1715 and beheaded.

Descartes, René (1596–1650), French mathematician, pioneer of modern philosophy. Unconvinced by scholastic tradition and theological dogma, he sought to get back to why anything can be said to be true, which turned out to be a fruitful line of thought. The basis of his Cartesian philosophy is summed up in his own words, *Cogito, ergo sum* (I think, therefore I am).

Desmoulins, Camille (1760–94), French revolutionary. He represented Paris in the National Convention, and wrote witty and sarcastic pamphlets and periodicals. He was an ally of Danton.

Deutscher, Isaac (1907–67), Marxist historian, biographer of Stalin and Trotsky. B. in Poland, he joined the outlawed Polish Communist Party but was expelled for his anti-Stalinist views. In 1939 he came to London.

De Valéra, Eamon (1882–1975), Irish statesman, b. New York, son of a Spanish father and an Irish mother. He was imprisoned for his part in the Easter rising of 1916. He opposed the treaty of 1921; and in 1926, when the republican Fianna Fáil was founded, he became its president. Fianna Fáil won the election of 1932, and he then became president of the Executive Council, 1932–7; prime minister, 1937–48, 1951–4, 1957–9; president of the republic, 1959–73. He promoted Irish neutrality in the second world war, encouraged the use of the Irish language, and in spite of early intransigence his leadership was moderate.

de Valois, Dame Ninette (b. 1898), Irish-born ballet dancer and choreographer. She toured Europe with Diaghilev, 1923–5, and in 1931 founded the Sadler's Wells Ballet School (now Royal Ballet School), of which she became director. *Autobiography* (1957).

Dewar, Sir James (1842–1923), chemist and physicist, a native of Kincardine. He succeeded in liquefying hydrogen, and invented the vacuum flask. The explosive cordite was the joint invention of himself and Sir Frederick Abel.

Dewey, John (1859–1952), American philosopher, psychologist, and educationist. A follower of William James, he was an exponent of pragmatism.

De Wit, Jan (1625–72), Dutch republican statesman, who carried on war with England and later negotiated the Triple Alliance, but was overthrown by the Orange Party and murdered.

Diaghilev, Sergei Pavlovich (1872–1929), Russian ballet impresario and founder of the Russian ballet. Among those associated with him are Anna Pavlova, Vaslav Nijinsky, Tamara Karsavina, Leonide Massine, Michel Fokine, the choreographer, L. N. Bakst, the painter, and Igor Stravinsky, the composer.

Dickens, Charles (1812–70), popular English novelist of the 19th cent., with enormous output and capacity for vivid story-telling. Of humble origin, he was extremely successful.

His best-known works are perhaps *Pickwick Papers*, *Oliver Twist*, *A Christmas Carol* (this influenced the observance of Christmas), *Dombey and Son*, *David Copperfield*, *Little Dorrit*, and *Great Expectations*. He gave public readings from his works.

Dickinson, Emily (1830–86), American poet whose writing has a mystic quality. She lived a cloistered life and published almost nothing in her lifetime.

Dickinson, Goldsworthy Lowes (1863–1932), English author, an interpreter and upholder of the Greek view of life.

Diderot, Denis (1713–84), French man of letters, critic of art and literature, and editor of the *Encyclopédie* (1713–84) to which many writers of the Englightenment contributed.

Diemen, Anthony van (1593–1645), Dutch promoter of exploration. As governor-general in the Far East, he promoted Dutch trade and influence; and despatched Abel Tasman, who in 1642 discovered New Zealand and Van Diemen's Land (now Tasmania).

Diesel, Rudolf (1858–1913), German engineer, inventor of an internal combustion engine which he patented in 1893. *See also* **L31**.

Diocletian (245–313), Roman emperor and persecutor of Christianity. He divided the empire under a system of joint rule; later abdicated; and built a palace in Dalmatia.

Diogenes (412–322 B.C.), Greek cynic philosopher who lived in a tub and told Alexander to get out of his sunshine. He sought virtue and moral freedom in liberation from desire.

Dionysius the elder and younger, tyrants of Syracuse in the 4th cent. B.C.

Dirac, Paul Adrien Maurice (1902–84), English physicist who shared with Erwin Schrödinger the 1933 Nobel prize for their work in developing Heisenberg's theory of quantum mechanics. Order of Merit (1973).

Disney, Walter Elias (1901–66), American film cartoonist, creator of Mickey Mouse. He is known for his *Silly Symphonies*, *Snow White and the Seven Dwarfs*, and *Pinocchio*.

Disraeli, Benjamin, Earl of Beaconsfield (1804–81), British statesman and novelist who helped to form modern Conservatism in England. The son of Isaac (*q.v.*), he published his first novel at 21, and later *Coningsby* and *Sibyl*, which helped to rouse the social conscience. He entered parliament in 1837 and was prime minister 1868 and 1874–80, when he arranged the purchase of shares in the Suez canal. He was rival of Gladstone and friend of Queen Victoria.

D'Israeli, Isaac (1766–1848), father of Benjamin (*q.v.*) and author of *Curiosities of Literature*.

Dobson, Austin (1840–1921), English writer of light verse and of 18th cent. biography.

Dodgson, Charles Lutwidge (1832–98), English writer. Under the pseudonym Lewis Carroll, he wrote poems and books for children, including *Alice in Wonderland*. In private life he was a lecturer in mathematics at Oxford.

Dolci, Carlo (1616–86), one of the last Florentine painters.

Dolci, Danilo (b. 1924), Italian social reformer who since 1952 has dedicated himself to the rehabilitation of the people of Sicily in their desperate poverty.

Dominic, St. (1170–1221), founder of the Friars Preachers or Black Friars. B. in Castile, he and his followers sought to teach the ignorant. In 1216 they were formed into an order and vowed to poverty. The order spread through Europe.

Domitian (Titus Flavius Domitianus) (A.D. 51–96), Roman emperor, son of Vespasian. He ruled despotically, aroused the hatred of the senate, and was assassinated as a result of a palace conspiracy.

Donatello (Donato di Niccolò) (c. 1386–1466), Italian sculptor, b. Florence, son of Niccolò di Betto di Bardo. He was the founder of modern sculpture, producing statues independent of a background, designed to stand in the open to be viewed from all angles. Among his masterpieces are the statues of *St. George* and *David* (in the Bargello, Florence) and his equestrian *Gattamelata* in Padua, the first bronze horse to be cast in the Renaissance.

Donizetti, Gaetano (1797–1848), Italian composer. The best known of his sixty operas are *Lucia*

di Lammermoor, *La Fille du Régiment*, and *Don Pasquale*. *See* **Section E.**

Donne, John (1572–1631), English metaphysical poet and preacher (dean of St. Paul's). His poems and sermons marked by passion, wit, and profundity of thought have received full publicity only in the present century. His writings include *Elegies*, *Satires*, *Songs and Sonnets*, *Problems and Paradoxes* and the *Holy Sonnets*.

Doré, Gustave (1833–83), French artist who painted scriptural subjects and illustrated Dante, Milton, and Tennyson.

Dostoyevsky, Feodor Mikhailovich (1821–81), Russian novelist, b. Moscow. As a result of his revolutionary activity he was sent to hard labour in Siberia. In his books, which include *Crime and Punishment*, *The Brothers Karamazov*, *The Idiot*, and *The Possessed*, he explored the dark places of the human spirit to a degree not previously attempted.

Douglas of Kirtleside, 1st Baron (William Sholto Douglas) (1893–1969), British airman; commanded Fighter command, 1940–2, Coastal command, 1944–5. A Labour peer.

Douglas, Norman (1868–1952), novelist and travel writer. A Scot, born in Austria, he made his home on the Mediterranean. His works include *South Wind*.

Doulton, Sir Henry (1820–97), English potter and the inventor of Doulton ware.

Dowden, Edward (1843–1913), English literary critic and Shakespearean scholar.

Dowding, 1st Baron (Hugh Caswell Tremenheere Dowding) (1882–1970), British airman; commanded Fighter command during the Battle of Britain period (1940).

Dowland, John (c. 1563–1626), English composer of songs with lute accompaniment. His son Robert succeeded him as Court lutenist to Charles I.

Doyle, Sir Arthur Conan (1859–1930), British writer, b. Edinburgh, creator of the detective Sherlock Holmes and his friend and foil, Dr. Watson. He was trained as a doctor but gave up his medical practice in 1890 to devote himself to writing.

Doyle, Richard (1824–83), humorous artist on the staff of *Punch*.

D'Oyly Carte, Richard (1844–1901), English theatrical manager, who built the Savoy theatre and there produced Gilbert and Sullivan operas.

Drake Sir Francis (c. 1540–96), English seaman. In 1577–80 he sailed round the world in the *Golden Hind*. In 1587 he destroyed a number of Spanish ships in Cadiz harbour; and under Lord Howard he helped to defeat the Spanish Armada in 1588.

Draper, John William (1811–82), American chemist, b. near Liverpool. He was the first, using Daguerre's process, to take a successful photograph of the human face (1840), and of the moon.

Dreiser, Theodore (1871–1935). American novelist of austere realism. Author of *An American Tragedy*.

Dreyfus, Alfred (1859–1935), French victim of injustice. Of Jewish parentage, in 1894 he was accused of divulging secrets to a foreign power, and was sentenced by a military secret tribunal to imprisonment for life on Devil's Island in French Guiana. At a new trial in 1899 he was again found guilty. Efforts continued to be made on his behalf, and in 1906 he was entirely exonerated, restored to his rank in the army, and made a Chevalier of the Legion of Honour.

Drinkwater, John (1882–1937), English poet and playwright. His plays include *Abraham Lincoln*, and *Oliver Cromwell*.

Drummond, William, (1585–1649), Scottish poet and Royalist pamphleteer. He was laird of Hawthornden.

Drury, Alfred (1857–1944), English sculptor, especially of statues of Queen Victoria at Bradford and Portsmouth.

Dryden, John (1631–1700), prolific English poet and dramatist, who also wrote political satire (*Absalom and Achitophel*). He was hostile to the revolution of 1688, and thereafter mainly translated classical writers, including Virgil.

Du Barry, Marie Jean Bécu, Comtesse (1746–93), mistress of Louis XV of France and guillotined by the revolutionary tribunal.

Du Chaillu, Paul Belloni (1835–1903), traveller in Africa, who in 1861 and 1867 published accounts of his explorations. A French-American.

Dufferin and Ava, 1st Marquess of (Frederick Temple Hamilton-Temple Blackwood) (1826–1902), British diplomat, writer, and governor-general of Canada and viceroy of India.

Dulles, John Foster (1888–1959), U.S. Secretary of State in the Republican administration 1953–9. His foreign policy was inflexibly opposed to negotiations with Russia and to U.S. recognition of China.

Dumas, Alexandre (1802–70), French romantic novelist, among whose many works are *The Three Musketeers*, *The Count of Monte Cristo*, and *The Black Tulip*.

Dumas, Alexandre (1824–95), French dramatist, son of the above; author of *La Dame aux Camélias*.

Du Maurier, George (1834–96), contributor to *Punch* and author of *Trilby*.

Dundee, 1st Viscount (John Graham of Claverhouse), (1648–89), Scottish soldier ("Bonnie Dundee"). Employed to suppress the covenanters, he was defeated at Drumclog, but victorious at Bothwell Brig. At the revolution of 1688 he supported James II, and was killed in the (victorious) battle of Killiecrankie.

Dundonald, Earl of. *See* **Cochrane, Thomas.**

Duns Scotus, John (*c.* 1265–1308), Scottish scholastic philosopher, b. at Maxton near Roxburgh, opponent of Thomas Aquinas. He joined the Franciscans, studied and taught at Oxford and Paris, and probably d. at Cologne. He challenged the harmony of faith and reason.

Dunstable, John (*c.* 1380–1453), the earliest English composer known by name. He was a contemporary of the Netherlands composers Dufay and Binchois. *See* **Section E.**

Dunstan, St. (908–88), reforming archbishop of Canterbury. He lived through seven reigns from Athelstan to Ethelred, and was adviser especially to Edgar. Under him Glastonbury Abbey became a centre of religious teaching.

Dupleix, Joseph François (1697–1763), French governor in India. He extended French influence and power in the Carnatic, but his plans were frustrated by his English opponent, Clive. He was recalled in 1754 and died in poverty.

Dürer, Albrecht (1471–1528), German painter and engraver. B. at Nuremberg, he was (like his Italian contemporary, Leonardo) a man of intellectual curiosity and scientific insight. His best work is in his copper engravings, woodcuts, and drawings; the former include *The Knight, Melancholia*, and *St. Jerome in his Study*. He may be regarded as the founder of the German school and a pioneer of etching. Examples of his work are in the British Museum. He was the friend of Luther and Melanchthon.

Durham, Earl of (John George Lambton) (1792–1840), served as governor-general of Canada after the disturbances of 1837, and in 1839 presented to parliament the *Durham Report*, which laid down the principle of colonial self-government.

Duse, Elenora (1861–1924), Italian tragedienne.

Duval, Claude (1643–70), notorious highwayman who came to England from Normandy and was eventually hanged at Tyburn.

Dvořák, Antonín (1841–1904), Czech composer whose music is rich in folk-song melodies of his native Bohemia. In 1884 he conducted his *Stabat Mater* in London. His *New World* symphony was composed in New York, where he was head of the National Conservatoire (1892–5). *See* **Section E.**

Dyson, Sir Frank Watson (1868–1939), English astronomer who was astronomer royal 1910–33, and astronomer royal for Scotland 1905–10.

Dyson, Sir George (1883–1964), English composer and writer. In *The New Music* he analysed the technique of modern schools of composition. He composed several choral works such as *The Canterbury Pilgrims* and *Nebuchadnezzar*.

E

Eastlake, Sir Charles Lock (1793–1865), English painter of historical and religious works.

Eastman, George (1854–1932), American inventor of the roll photographic film and the Kodak camera. His philanthropies were estimated at over $100 million.

Eck, Johann von (1486–1543), German Catholic theologian and opponent of Luther.

Eddington, Sir Arthur Stanley (1882–1944), English astronomer (Greenwich observatory 1906–13; Cambridge observatory 1914–44). His works include *The Nature of the Physical World*.

Eddy, Mrs Mary Baker (1821–1910), American founder of the Church of Christ Scientist. Her *Science and Health with Key to the Scriptures* was published in 1875. *See* **Christian Science, Section J.**

Edelinck, Gerard (1640–1707), Flemish engraver, b. Antwerp, the first to reproduce in print the colour, as well as the form, of a picture.

Eden, Robert Anthony, 1st Earl of Avon (1897–1977), British statesman. He entered parliament in 1923; became foreign secretary in 1935 (resigning in 1938 over Chamberlain's negotiation with Mussolini and rebuff to President Roosevelt); deputy prime minister in 1951; succeeded Sir Winston Churchill in 1955. His Suez policy divided the country. He resigned for health reasons in 1957. Memoirs, *Facing the Dictators*; *The Reckoning*; and *Full Circle*. Earldom conferred 1961.

Edgar (943–75), King of England 959–75. He was advised by Archbishop Dunstan.

Edgar Atheling (*c.* 1060–c. 1130), was the lawful heir of Edward the Confessor, but in the Norman invasion he was unable to maintain his claim.

Edgeworth, Maria (1767–1849), Irish novelist, whose stories include *Castle Rackrent, The Absentee*, and *Belinda*.

Edinburgh, Duke of (Philip Mountbatten) (b. 1921), consort of Queen Elizabeth II. He relinquished his right of accession to the thrones of Greece and Denmark on his naturalisation in 1947 when he took the name of Mountbatten. He is the great-great-grandson of Queen Victoria, grandson of Admiral Prince Louis of Battenberg, and nephew of the late Earl Mountbatten of Burma. Pres. British Association 1951–2.

Edison, Thomas Alva (1847–1931), American inventor of the transmitter and receiver for the automatic telegraph; the phonograph; the incandescent lamp (shared with the British inventor Swan); and many devices for the electrical distribution of light and power. From being a newsboy on the railway and later a telegraph clerk, he became a master at applying scientific principles to practical ends. He set up a research laboratory (originally a barn) at Menlo Park, New Jersey.

Edmund II (Ironside) (*c* 990–1016), the son of Ethelred, king of the English, made a compact with Canute to divide England, but soon afterwards died.

Edward the Confessor (*c.* 1004–1066), English king who preceded the Norman Conquest and founded Westminster Abbey. He was canonised in 1161.

Edward the Elder (*c.* 870–c. 924), son of Alfred, succeeded him as king of the West Saxons in 899. He overcame the Danes and reoccupied the northern counties.

Edward I (1239–1307), King of England, succeeded his father Henry in 1272. Able and energetic, his legislation influenced the development of the land law, and he summoned parliamentary assemblies. A soldier, he conquered Wales, building castles, but could not maintain his hold on Scotland.

Edward II (1284–1327), succeeded his father Edward I as king of England in 1307 and was defeated by the Scots at Bannockburn. Weak and inept, he was murdered in 1327.

Edward III (1312–77), succeeded his father Edward II as king of England in 1327. Popular and ambitious for military glory, he began the Hundred Years War with France. He fostered the woollen industry. Latterly he became senile.

Edward IV (1442–83), able but dissolute Yorkist leader whose reign (1461–70, 1471–83) brought about a revival in the power of the monarchy, in

English sea power, and in foreign trade (in which he himself took part). Spent 1470–71, in exile. Began rebuilding of St. George's chapel, Windsor. Patron of Caxton.

Edward V (1470–83), succeeded his father Edward IV at the age of 12 and was a pawn in the quarrels of baronial relatives. He and his brother were shut up in the Tower by his uncle, Richard, Duke of Gloucester, and there probably murdered, though exact proof has not been established.

Edward VI (1537–53), succeeded his father, Henry VIII, as king of England when in his tenth year. He was delicate and studious, and his government was carried on successively by the Dukes of Somerset and Northumberland; while under Archbishop Cranmer the prayer book was issued. He was induced to name Lady Jane Grey his successor.

Edward VII (1841–1910), King of Gr. Britain and Ireland. The son of Queen Victoria, he married Princess Alexandra of Denmark in 1863, and succeeded his mother in 1901. Interested mainly in social life and in international contacts, he visited India in 1875 and travelled much in Europe.

Edward VIII (1894–1972), King of Gt. Britain, succeeded his father George V 1936, and abdicated later that year because of disagreement over his proposed marriage. He was created Duke of Windsor, and was governor of the Bahamas 1940–45. The Duchess of Windsor died in 1986 in Paris.

Ehrlich, Paul (1854–1915), German bacteriologist, who at Frankfurt-on-Main carried out work in immunology. He discovered salvarsan for the treatment of syphilis. Nobel prizewinner 1908.

Eiffel, Alexandre Gustave (1832–1923), French engineer, one of the first to employ compressed air caissons in bridge building. Among his works are the Eiffel Tower (1887–9) and the Panama Canal locks.

Einstein, Albert (1879–1955), mathematical physicist whose theory of relativity superseded Newton's theory of gravitation. He was born in Ulm of Jewish parents, lived for many years in Switzerland, and held a succession of professorial chairs at Zurich, Prague, and Berlin. In 1921 he was awarded the Nobel prize for his work in quantum theory. He was driven by the Nazis to seek asylum in America and became professor at the Institute of Advanced Study at Princeton 1933–45. In August 1939 at the request of a group of scientists he wrote to President Roosevelt warning of the danger of uranium research in Germany and stressing the urgency of investigating the possible use of atomic energy in bombs. *See* **Relativity, Section F, Part II.**

Eisenhower, Dwight David (1890–1969), American general and statesman. He was C.-in-C. Allied Forces, N. Africa, 1942–3; and in the European theatre of operations, 1943–5; and was Republican President, 1953–61.

Eisenstein, Sergei Mikhailovich (1898–1948), Russian film director of *The Battleship Potemkin, Alexander Nevsky,* and *Ivan the Terrible.*

Eleanor, Queen of Edward I. After her death in 1290 the king had memorial crosses erected at the twelve places where her body rested on its way from Grantham to Westminster.

Elgar, Sir Edward (1857–1934), English composer, specially of choral-orchestral works for festivals. His oratorios include *The Kingdom, The Apostles,* and *The Dream of Gerontius;* he also wrote the *Enigma Variations,* and the tone-poem *Falstaff. See* **Section E.**

Elgin, 7th Earl of (Thomas Bruce) (1766–1841), British diplomat who, with the object of saving them, conveyed some sculptures from the Parthenon in Athens to the British Museum.

Eliot, George (1819–80), pen-name of Mary Anne (later Marion) Evans, b. Warwickshire. Her novels include *Adam Bede, The Mill on the Floss, Silas Marner, Middlemarch,* and *Daniel Deronda.* Her works show deep insight. She lived with the writer George Lewes from 1854 until his death 25 years later. (Although Lewes had been deserted by his wife it was not then possible to obtain a divorce.) She brought up his three children.

Eliot, Thomas Stearns (1888–1965), poet and critic. He was born in St. Louis, Missouri,

and became a British subject in 1927. His poems include *Prufrock and Other Observations, The Waste Land, The Hollow Men, Ash Wednesday, Four Quartets;* his verse dramas *Murder in the Cathedral* and *The Family Reunion.* He described himself as "classical in literature, royalist in politics, and Anglo-Catholic in religion". He was a Nobel prizewinner 1948.

Elizabeth (b. 1900), Queen Consort of George VI, daughter of the 14th Earl of Strathmore. Before her marriage in 1923 she was Lady Elizabeth Angela Marguerite Bowes-Lyon.

Elizabeth I (1533–1603), Queen of England, daughter of Henry VIII, succeeded her sister Mary in 1558. Politically and intellectually able and firm, though personally vain and capricious, she chose to serve her able men such as William Cecil; and her long reign was one of stability, victory over the Spanish, and adventure in the New World; while the Church of England was established, and literary output prepared the way for Shakespeare; it was however marred by the execution of Mary, Queen of Scots.

Elizabeth II (Elizabeth Alexandra Mary of Windsor) (b. 1926), Queen of Gt. Britain and N. Ireland, ascended the throne Feb. 1952 on the death of her father George VI. Her Consort, Prince Philip, Duke of Edinburgh, is the son of Prince Andrew of Greece and a descendant of the Danish royal family. They have four children: Charles, Prince of Wales (b. 1948), Princess Anne (b. 1950), Prince Andrew (b. 1960), and Prince Edward (b. 1964).

Ellis, Havelock (1859–1939), English writer whose *Studies in the Psychology of Sex* was influential in changing the public attitude towards sex. His books were published in America long before they were in England.

Emerson, Ralph Waldo (1803–82), American poet and essayist, b. Boston, member of the transcendentalist group of thinkers. Among his best-known poems are *Woodnotes, Threnody, Terminus, Brahma, The Problem.*

Emin Pasha, the name adopted by **Eduard Schnitzer** (1840–92), a German explorer associated with Gen. Charles Gordon in the Sudan as a medical officer; and governor of the Equatorial Province 1878–89, when he was menaced by the Mahdi and rescued by Stanley. He had contributed greatly to African studies.

Emmet, Robert (1778–1803), Irish patriot, led the rising of 1803, was betrayed, and executed.

Empedocles (c. 500–c. 430 B.C.), Greek philosopher, b. Agrigentum in Sicily, founder of a school of medicine which regarded the heart as the seat of life, an idea which passed to Aristotle, as did his idea that all matter was composed of four elements: earth, air, fire, and water.

Engels, Friedrich (1820–95), German socialist, son of a wealthy textile manufacturer, lifelong friend of Karl Marx, with whom he collaborated in writing the *Communist Manifesto* of 1848. Through him Marx acquired his knowledge of English labour conditions.

Epicurus of Samos (342–270 B.C.), refounded the atomic view of matter put forward by Democritus, and held that peace of mind comes through freedom from fear, the two main sources of which he regarded as religion and fear of death. The Epicureans were a rival sect to the Peripatetics and Stoics.

Epstein, Sir Jacob (1880–1959), sculptor, b. New York of Russian–Polish parents. His work includes *Rima,* in Hyde Park; *Day* and *Night* on the building of London Underground headquarters; *Genesis,* exhibited in 1931; *Lazarus,* in New College, Oxford; the *Madonna and Child* group in Cavendish Square, London; the figure of *Christ in Majesty* in aluminium in Llandaff cathedral; a sculpture for the T.U.C. headquarters in London; and a bronze group for Coventry cathedral.

Erasmus, Desiderius (1466–1536), Dutch Renaissance humanist, who spent several years in England and was the friend of Dean Colet and Sir Thomas More. He aimed at ecclesiastical reform from within and scorned the old scholastic teaching. He thus prepared the way for Luther. His *Praise of Folly* continues to be widely read.

B23

Erhard, Ludwig (1897–1977), German economist and politician; succeeded Adenauer as Chancellor of the West German Federal Republic, 1963–7.

Essex, 2nd Earl of (Robert Devereux) (1566–1601), favourite of Queen Elizabeth I in her old age. Unsuccessful as governor-general of Ireland, he returned to England against the Queen's wish; plotted; and was executed.

Ethelbert, King of Kent at the close of the 6th cent., accepted Christianity on the mission of St. Augustine.

Ethelred II (c. 968–1016), King of England. Unable to organise resistance against the Danish raids, he was called the Unready (from Old Eng. uraed = without counsel).

Etty, William (1787–1849), English artist of historical and classical subjects.

Eucken, Rudolf Christoph (1846–1926), German philosopher of activism, which puts personal ethical effort above intellectual idealism. Nobel prizewinner 1908.

Euler, Leonhard (1707–83), Swiss mathematician, remembered especially for his work in optics and on the calculus of variations. He was called by Catherine I to St. Petersburg, where he was professor, 1730–41, and by Frederick the Great to Berlin, 1741–66. He became blind but continued his work.

Euripides (480–406 B.C.), Greek tragic dramatist, who is known to have written about 80 plays of which 18 are preserved, including *Alcestis, Medea, Iphigenia,* and *Orestes.* He displayed a sceptical attitude towards the myths.

Eusebius (264–340), ecclesiastical historian. His *Ecclesiastical History* gives the history of the Christian church to 324. He also wrote a general history, *Chronicon.*

Evans, Sir Arthur John (1851–1941), English archaeologist, known for his excavations at Knossos in Crete and his discovery of the pre-Phoenician script.

Evans, Dame Edith Mary (1888–1976), versatile English actress who made her first appearance as Cressida in *Troilus and Cressida* in 1912.

Evelyn, John (1620–1706), cultured English diarist who gives brilliant portraits of contemporaries. He was a book collector and librarian and wrote *Sylva,* a manual of arboriculture. His magnificent library was sold by Christies in 1977.

Eyck, Jan van (c. 1389–1441), Flemish painter, whose best-known work is the altarpiece in Ghent cathedral. His brother Hubert (c. 1370–1426) is associated with him.

F

Fabius, the name of an ancient Roman family who over many generations played an important part in early Roman history. **Quintus Fabius Maximus Verrucosus** (d. 203 B.C.) saved Rome from Hannibal by strategic evasion of battle; hence his name *Cunctator* (delayer), and the term Fabian policy.

Fabre, Jean Henri Casimir (1823–1915), French naturalist, whose study of the habits of insects were delightfully recorded in his *Souvenirs entomologiques.*

Faed, name of two Scottish genre painters, **Thomas** (1826–1900), and **John** (1819–1902). A third brother, **James,** engraved their works.

Fahrenheit, Gabriel Daniel (1686–1736), German physicist, b. Danzig. He introduced c. 1715 the mercury thermometer and fixed thermometric standards.

Fairbairn, Sir William (1789–1874), Scottish engineer. In 1817 he took the lead in using iron in shipbuilding.

Fairfax, 3rd Baron (Thomas Fairfax) (1612–71), parliamentary general in the English civil war, and victor of Marston Moor. In 1650 he withdrew into private life.

Falconer, Hugh (1806–65), British botanist and palaeontologist, b. Forres, Scot.; physician to East India Co.; introduced tea into India.

Falla, Manuel (1876–1946), Spanish composer whose music is highly individual with a strong folk-song element. *See* **Section E.**

Faraday, Michael (1791–1867), English experimental physicist, founder of the science of electromagnetism. He was the son of a Yorkshire

blacksmith and at 13 became apprenticed to a bookseller in London. In 1813 he became laboratory assistant to Sir Humphry Davy at the Royal Institution, succeeding him as professor of chemistry in 1833. He set himself the problem of finding the connections between the forces of light, heat, electricity, and magnetism and his discoveries, translated by Maxwell (*q.v.*) into a single mathematical theory of electromagnetism, led to the modern developments in physics and electronics. He inaugurated the Christmas lectures for juvenile audiences at the Royal Institution.

Farman, Henri (1874–1958), French aviator, one of the pioneers of aviation, and a designer and builder of aeroplanes.

Farouk I (1920–65), King of Egypt, 1936–52. He was forced to abdicate as a result of the military coup of 1952.

Farrar, Frederick William (1831–1903), English clergyman, author of the schoolboy story *Eric.*

Faulkner, William (1897–1962), American novelist, whose series of novels, *The Sound and the Fury, As I Lay Dying, Light in August, Sanctuary,* depict the American South. Nobel prizewinner 1949.

Fauré, Gabriel Urbain (1845–1924), French composer and teacher. His works include chamber music, nocturnes, and barcarolles for piano, an opera *Pénélope,* some exquisite songs, and *Requiem.* Ravel was among his pupils. *See* **Section E.**

Fawcett, Millicent Garrett (1847–1929), educational reformer and leader of the movement for women's suffrage; one of the founders of Newnham College, Cambridge. She was the wife of the blind Liberal politician and economist, **Henry Fawcett** (1833–84) and sister of **Elizabeth Garrett Anderson.**

Fawkes, Guy (1570–1606), a Yorkshire catholic, who with Catesby and other conspirators planned the Gunpowder Plot. Though warned, he persisted and was captured and hanged.

Fénelon, François de Salignac de la Mothe (1651–1715), archbishop of Cambrai and author of *Telemachus.*

Ferdinand II of Aragon (1452–1516), who married Isabella of Castile, and with her reigned over Spain, saw the Moors expelled from Spain, equipped Columbus for the discoveries that led to Spain's vast colonial possessions, and instituted the Inquisition.

Ferguson, James (1710–76), Scottish astronomer who, from being a shepherd-boy, educated himself in astronomy, mathematics, and portrait painting.

Fermi, Enrico (1901–54), Italian nuclear physicist whose research contributed to the harnessing of atomic energy and the development of the atomic bomb. Nobel prizewinner 1938.

Fichte, Johann Gottlieb (1762–1814), German philosopher of the nationalistic Romantic school who prepared the way for modern totalitarianism.

Field, John (1782–1837), Irish composer of nocturnes, pupil of Clementi and teacher of Glinka. His work served as a model for Chopin.

Fielding, Henry (1707–54), English novelist, author of *Tom Jones, Joseph Andrews,* and *Amelia,* as well as plays.

Fildes, Sir Luke (1844–1927), English painter and woodcut-designer.

Finsen, Niels Ryberg (1860–1904), Danish physician who established an institute for light therapy and invented the Finsen ultra-violet lamp. Nobel prizewinner 1903.

Firdausi, *pen-name* **of Abu'l Kasim Mansur** (940–1020), Persian poet, author of the epic *Shah-Nama* or Book of Kings.

Fisher of Lambeth, Baron (Geoffrey Francis Fisher) (1887–1972), archbishop of Canterbury, 1945–61; Headmaster of Repton School, 1914–32.

Fisher, Herbert Albert Laurens (1865–1940), English historian and educational reformer; author of *A History of Europe.*

Fisher, Sir Ronald Aylmer (1890–1962), British scientist who revolutionised both genetics and the philosophy of experimentation by founding the modern corpus of mathematical statistics.

FitzGerald, Edward (1809–83), English poet who translated the *Rubaiyát* of Omar Khayyam (1859).

Fitzroy, Robert (1805–65), British meteorologist, who introduced the system of storm warnings which were the beginning of weather forecasts.

Flammarion, Camille (1842–1925), French astronomer, noted for his popular lectures and books which include *L'Astronomie Populaire*.

Flamsteed, John (1646–1719), the first English astronomer royal, for whom Charles II built an observatory at Greenwich (1675) where he worked for 44 years.

Flaubert, Gustave (1821–80), French novelist, and creator of *Madame Bovary*. Other works were *Salammbô*, *L' Education sentimentale*, and *Bouvard et Pécuchet*.

Flaxman, John (1755–1826), English sculptor, b. York, employed as modeller by Josiah Wedgwood. He then took to monumental sculpture.

Flecker, James Elroy (1884–1915), English poet whose works include *Golden Journey to Samarkand*, *Hassan* (staged in London, 1923), and *Don Juan*, as well as many lyrics.

Fleming, Sir Alexander (1881–1955), Scottish bacteriologist who discovered the antibacterial enzyme lysozyme in 1922 and penicillin in 1928. Full recognition came during the war when Florey separated the drug now used from the original penicillin. Awarded Nobel prize jointly with Florey and Chain, 1945.

Fleming, Sir Ambrose (1849–1945), British scientist whose invention of the radio valve in 1904 revolutionised radio telegraphy and solved problems of radio-telephony. This eventually made possible high quality sound transmission, and thus led to broadcasting and television.

Fletcher, John (1579–1625), English dramatist who collaborated with Francis Beaumont (*q.v.*) in writing many pieces for the stage.

Flinders, Matthew (1774–1814), English navigator and explorer who made discoveries in and around Australia. He sailed through Bass Strait, so called in honour of his surgeon.

Florey, Baron (Howard Walter Florey) (1898–1968), British pathologist, b. Australia. Shared 1945 Nobel prize with Fleming and Chain for work on penicillin.

Foch, Ferdinand (1851–1929), French general, b. Tarbes. In the first world war he halted the German advance at the Marne (1914), and was engaged in the battles of Ypres (1914 and 1915) and the Somme (1916). In 1918 he became supreme commander of the British, French, and American armies and dictated the terms of Allied victory.

Fokine, Michel (1880–1944), Russian dancer, choreographer to Diaghilev's company, and creator of *Les Sylphides*, *Prince Igor*, *Scheherazade*, *Firebird*, and *The Spectre of the Rose*.

Fokker, Anthony (1890–1939), Dutch aircraft engineer, b. Java. The Fokker factory in Germany made warplanes for the Germans in the first world war.

Fonteyn, Dame Margot (Mme. Roberto de Arias) (b. 1919), prima ballerina of the Royal Ballet and acclaimed foremost English dancer.

Foot, Michael (b. 1913), British journalist and politician; leader of the Labour Party 1980–83; pubs. inc. biography of Aneurin Bevan. *See* **Sections C & D.**

Ford, Gerald R. (b. 1913), American Republican President 1974–7; automatically succeeded Richard Nixon when he resigned.

Ford, Henry (1863–1947), founder of Ford Motor Company (1903), of which he was president until 1919, when he was succeeded by his son, Edsel B. Ford (1893–1943). He was the pioneer of the cheap motor car.

Forester, Cecil Scott (1899–1966), English novelist, author of the *Captain Hornblower* series.

Forster, Edward Morgan (1879–1970), English novelist, author of *The Longest Journey, A Room with a View, Howards End, A Passage to India*. O.M. 1969.

Foscari, Francesco (*c.* 1372–1457), Doge of Venice and victor over Milan.

Fourier, Charles (1772–1837), French socialist who propounded a system of associated enterprise which although utopian stimulated social reform.

Fourier, Jean Baptiste Joseph (1768–1830), French mathematical physicist. He played an active part in politics, holding administrative posts in Egypt and Isère, yet finding time for his own research, especially on the flow of heat.

Fowler, Sir John (1817–98), was the engineer of the first underground railway (the London Metro-

politan) and with his partner Sir Benjamin Baker, of the Forth bridge.

Fox, Charles James (1749–1806), English Whig statesman. Son of the 1st Lord Holland, he entered parliament at 19. He held office only for brief periods between 1770 and 1806, but he upheld the liberal causes of the day (American independence, the French revolution, and parliamentary reform), and was one of the impeachers of Warren Hastings.

Fox, George (1624–91), founder of the Society of Friends, son of a weaver of Fenny Drayton, Leicestershire.

Foxe, John (1516–87), English martyrologist, author of *History of the Acts and Monuments of the Church* (better known as *Foxe's Book of Martyrs*).

Frampton, Sir George James (1860–1928), English sculptor of the Peter Pan statue in Kensington Gardens and the Edith Cavell memorial.

France, Anatole (1844–1924), French writer, especially of short stories. Nobel prize 1921.

Francis I (1494–1547), King of France. Brilliant but ambitious and adventurous, he fostered learning and art, and met Henry VIII at the Field of the Cloth of Gold. His rivalry with the Emperor Charles V involved France in prolonged war, especially in Italy (he was captured at Pavia, 1525). He persecuted the Protestants.

Francis of Assisi, St. (1181/2–1226), founder of the Franciscan Order. Son of a wealthy cloth merchant, in 1208 he turned from a life of pleasure to poverty and the complete observance of Christ's teaching. He and his friars went about preaching the gospel by word and example, and the brotherhood increased rapidly. He was canonised in 1228.

Francis, Sir Philip (1740–1818), English politician, reputed author of the *Letters of Junius*.

Franck, César Auguste (1822–90), composer and organist, b. at Liège in Belgium. *See* **Section E.**

Franco, Francisco (1892–1975), Spanish general and dictator. He led the Fascist rebellion against the Republican government (1936) and with German and Italian help ended the civil war (1939), after which he ruled Spain with utter ruthlessness.

Franklin, Benjamin (1706–90), American statesman. B. at Boston, he was at first a printer and journalist. He then took an interest in electricity, explained lightning as of electrical origin, and invented the lightning conductor. He was active in promoting the Declaration of Independence in 1773; he negotiated French support; and helped to frame the American constitution.

Franklin, Sir John (1786–1847), English Arctic explorer. His expedition in the *Erebus* and the *Terror* to find the north-west passage ended disastrously, and all attempts to find survivors failed.

Franks, Baron (Oliver Shewell Franks) (b. 1905), British academic, diplomat and banker; British ambassador to U.S.A. 1948–52; provost of Worcester College, Oxford 1962–76; chosen to head Falklands inquiry 1982. O.M. 1977.

Fraunhofer, Joseph von (1787–1826), optical instrument-maker of Munich, the first to map the dark lines of the solar spectrum named after him.

Frazer, Sir James George (1854–1941), Scottish anthropologist, author of *The Golden Bough*.

Frederick I (*c.* 1123–90). Holy Roman Emperor, nicknamed Barbarossa. A strong personality, he sought to impose his will on the city-states of northern Italy and the papacy, and was defeated at Legnano in 1176 but was more successful with a conciliatory policy (1183). He had also to contend with opposition at home. He died on the third crusade.

Frederick II (1194–1250), Holy Roman Emperor, grandson of the above, and son of the heiress of Sicily. Brilliant and enlightened, he attracted to his court in Sicily Jewish, Mohammedan, and Christian scholars; founded the university of Naples; was a patron of the medical school of Salerno; wrote a treatise on falconry; and commissioned a code of laws. Politically he was less successful, having trouble with the Lombard cities, and being involved with the papacy especially as regards his delay in going on crusade; but after negotiations with the sultan of Egypt he actually was crowned king of Jerusalem.

Frederick II (the Great) (1712–86), King of Prussia. Having inherited from his father a well-drilled army, in 1740 he seized Silesia from Austria, and retained it through the resulting war and the Seven Years war. He also took part in the partition of Poland. An able administrator and and outstanding general he made Prussia powerful and strengthened its military tradition. He corresponded with Voltaire and he also played the flute.

French, Sir John, 1st Earl of Ypres (1852–1925), first British commander-in-chief in the first world war; replaced by Sir Douglas Haig in 1915.

Freud, Sigmund (1856–1939), psychiatrist and founder of psychoanalysis; b. Moravia, studied medicine in Vienna, where he lived until 1938 when the Nazi invasion of Austria sent him into exile in London where he died. His theories of the mind, based on years of investigation, illumined the way we think about ourselves, and had immense influence upon modern thought. See **Psychoanalysis, Section J.**

Friese-Greene, William (1855–1921), English inventor of the cinematograph. His first film was shown in 1890. He died in poverty.

Frobisher, Sir Martin (1535–94), first British navigator to seek the north-west passage from the Atlantic to the Pacific through the Arctic seas. He is commemorated in Frobisher's Strait. He also fought against the Spanish Armada.

Froebel, Friedrich Wilhelm August (1782–1852), German educational reformer, founder of the Kindergarten system.

Froissart, Jean (1337–1410), French author of *Chronicles* covering the history of Western Europe from 1307 to 1400, one of the chief sources for the history of the first half of the Hundred Years war.

Frost, Robert (1874–1963), American poet, author of *Stopping by Woods on a Snowy Evening, Birches, The Death of the Hired Man, After Apple-Picking.*

Froude, James Anthony (1818–94), English historian and biographer of Carlyle.

Fry, Christopher (b. 1907), English poet and dramatist of Quaker family; author of *The Lady's Not for Burning, Venus Observed, The Dark is Light Enough, Curtmantle, A Yard of Sun* and the religious play *A Sleep of Prisoners.*

Fry, Elizabeth (1780–1845), English prison reformer. She lived at Norwich and belonged to the Society of Friends.

Fry, Roger (1866–1934), English art critic and painter; introduced the work of Cézanne and the post-impressionists into England; author of *Vision and Design.*

Fuchs, Leonard (1501–66), German naturalist whose compendium of medicinal plants was for long a standard work. He was professor of medicine at Tübingen and the genus *Fuchsia* is named after him.

Fuchs, Sir Vivian Ernest (b. 1908), British geologist and explorer; leader of the British Commonwealth Trans-Antarctic Expedition 1957–8, the first to cross the Antarctic continent.

Fuller, Thomas (1608–61), English antiquarian and divine, author of *Worthies of England* and a *Church History of Britain.*

Fulton, Robert (1765–1815), American engineer who experimented in the application of steam to navigation, and in 1807 launched the *Clermont* on the Hudson.

Furniss, Harry (1854–1925), caricaturist, b. Wexford. He came to London as a young man, served on the staff of *Punch* and illustrated the works of Dickens and Thackeray.

G

Gade, Niels Vilhelm (1817–90), Danish composer. While studying at Leipzig he met Mendelssohn, whom he succeeded as conductor of the Gewandhaus orchestra.

Gagarin, Yuri Alexeyevich (1934–68), Soviet cosmonaut, the first man to be launched into space and brought safely back (12 April 1961). His flight was made in the front portion of a multi-stage rocket which made a single circuit of the earth in 108 min. Killed in an air crash.

Gainsborough, Thomas (1727–88), English landscape and portrait painter, b. at Sudbury in Suffolk. His portraits are marked by informality and grace.

Gaiseric or Genseric (c. 390–477), king of the Vandals, the ablest of the barbarian invaders of the Roman empire. He led his people from Spain into Africa, took Carthage, gained control of the Mediterranean and sacked Rome in 455.

Gaitskell, Hugh Todd Naylor (1906–63), Labour politician and economist. He represented Leeds South from 1945; was chancellor of the exchequer 1950–1; and leader of the Labour opposition 1955–63.

Galbraith, John Kenneth (b. 1908), American university professor of economics, b. Canada; author of *The Affluent Society* (1958), *The Liberal Hour* (1960), *The New Industrial State* (1967), *The Age of Uncertainty* (1977). He was ambassador to India 1961–3.

Galdós, Benito Pérez. See **Pérez Galdós.**

Galen, Claudius (131–201), physician, b. Pergamum (Asia Minor) of Greek parents. He systematised medical knowledge with his idea of purposive creation by the will of God; and thus discouraged original investigation. Many of his treatises survive, and his influence lasted for more than a thousand years.

Galileo (1564–1642), Italian scientist whose experimental-mathematical methods in the pursuit of scientific truth laid the foundations of modern science. He became professor of mathematics at Pisa university when he was 25 and lectured at Padua for 18 years. He made a number of fundamental discoveries, *e.g.*, in regard to the hydrostatic balance, thermometer, telescope, and foreshadowed Newton's laws of motion. He detected the four major satellites of Jupiter, the ring of Saturn, and the spots of the sun. He supported the superiority of the Copernican over the Ptolemaic theory, and was put under house arrest for so doing. He died the year Newton was born.

Galsworthy, John (1867–1933), English novelist and playwright, author of *The Forsyte Saga,* a series of novels dealing with the history of an upper middle-class family. Nobel prizewinner 1932.

Galton, Sir Francis (1822–1911), founder of eugenics, cousin of Darwin. His early work *Meteorographica* (1863), contains the basis of the modern weather chart. He devised a scheme for classifying finger-prints for rapid identification, and was one of the first to apply mathematics to biological problems.

Galvani, Luigi (1737–98), Italian physician and physiologist, whose experiments at Bologna demonstrated the principle of animal electricity.

Gama, Vasco da (c. 1460–1524), Portuguese navigator who discovered the sea route to India in 1498 by rounding the Cape of Good Hope.

Gandhi, Indira (1917–84), daughter of Nehru, succeeded Shastri in 1966 to become India's first woman prime minister. She suffered a defeat at the polls in 1977 but was spectacularly successful in 1980. Assassinated 1984. Succeeded by her son, Rajiv Gandhi. See **Section C, Part II.**

Gandhi, Mohandâs Karamchand (Mahatma) (1869–1948), Indian patriot, social reformer and moral teacher. From 1893 to 1914 he lived in South Africa opposing discrimination against Indians. In the movement for Indian independence after 1914 he dominated Congress, instituted civil disobedience, and advocated non-violence; and he sought to free India from caste. After independence he strove to promote the co-operation of all Indians but was assassinated on his way to a prayer meeting. His teaching of non-violence has had great influence.

Garbo, Greta (b. 1905), Swedish film actress of poetical quality. Her films included *Queen Christina* and *Ninotchka.*

García, Manuel de Popolo Vincente (1775–1832), Spanish tenor, composer, and singing master. His son **Manuel Patricio Rodriguez** (1805–1906) was tutor to Jenny Lind. Both his daughters (Mme. Malibran and Mme. Viardot) were operatic singers, and his grandson and great-grandson baritones.

Garcia Lorca, Federico. *See* **Lorca.**

Gardiner, Samuel Rawson (1890–1902), English historian of the Stuart period.

Garibaldi, Giuseppe (1807–82), Italian soldier and patriot, who with Mazzini and Cavour created a united Italy. In 1834 he was condemned to death for helping in a republican plot to seize Genoa, but escaped to S. America. He returned in 1848 to fight for Mazzini but was again forced to flee. In 1851 he returned and gave his support to Cavour, taking part in the Austrian war of 1859. In 1860 with a thousand volunteers he freed Sicily, took Naples, and handed over the Two Sicilies to Victor Emmanuel who was proclaimed king.

Garrick, David (1717–79), English actor and theatrical manager. Brought up at Lichfield, he was taught by Samuel Johnson.

Garrison, William Lloyd (1805–79), American philanthropist who worked to end slavery.

Gaskell, Mrs. Elizabeth Cleghorn (1810–65), English novelist, author of *Mary Barton*, *Cranford*, and a *Life of Charlotte Brontë*. She was brought up by an aunt in the little Cheshire town of Knutsford.

Gaulle, Charles de (1890–1970), French general and statesman, son of a headmaster of a Jesuit school; first president of the Fifth Republic 1959–69. He fought in the first world war until his capture in 1916. In the second world war he refused to surrender (1940) and raised and led the Free French forces, with headquarters in England. He came to political power in 1958; allowed Algerian independence in 1962 in face of an army and civilian revolt, initiated closer ties with West Germany (Franco-German treaty 1963), recognised Communist China, withdrew from NATO, building his own nuclear force, vetoed Britain's entry into the Common Market (1963 and 1967); and based his government on personal prestige and use of the referendum in place of parliamentary approval. He was taken by surprise by the rising of students and workers in 1968 and resigned after losing the referendum in 1969.

Gauss, Karl Friedrich (1777–1855), German mathematician. He spent most of his life at the university of Göttingen where he set up the first special observatory for terrestrial magnetism. He made major contributions to astronomy, mathematics, and physics. The unit of magnetic induction is named after him.

Gautama, Siddhartha (Buddha, the enlightened) (c. 563–c.483 B.C.). B. near Benares, a rajah's son, he gave himself up to the religious life and attracted many disciples. Concerned with man's sorrow and suffering, he planned a movement which could be universally shared, in which kindness to others, including animals, took a leading part. His teaching is summarised in the "four noble truths" and the "eightfold path" (*see* **Buddhism, Section J**). After his death his teaching spread (with the help of the King Asoka) over much of India and through eastern Asia as far as Japan, and developed varying schools of thought. Buddhism is tolerant and also maintains that the good of the part is that of the whole; hence it is wrong to harm another or take life.

Gautier, Théophile (1811–72), French poet and novelist, author of *Mademoiselle de Maupin*.

Gay, John (1685–1732), English poet, author of *The Beggar's Opera* (set to music by Pepusch) and *Polly*.

Gay-Lussac, Joseph Louis (1778–1850), French chemist, who showed that when gases combine their relative volumes bear a simple numerical relation to each other and to the volume of their product, if gaseous (1808), *e.g.*, one volume of oxygen combines with two volumes of hydrogen to form two volumes of water vapour.

Ged, William (1690–1749), Scottish printer who patented stereotyping.

Geddes, Sir Patrick (1854–1932), Scottish biologist and a pioneer in town and regional planning, who invented the term conurbation.

Geikie, Sir Archibald (1835–1924), Scottish geologist. His brother James specialised in glacial geology.

Genghis Khan (1162–1227), Mongol conqueror. After years of struggle to make good his succession to his father, he overran the greater part of Asia bringing devastation wherever he went.

Geoffrey of Monmouth (1100–54), chronicler, b. Monmouth, later bishop of St. Asaph. His chronicle drew on his creative imagination.

George I (1660–1727), became King of Great Britain in 1714 as descendant of James I. His chief minister was Sir Robert Walpole. Himself personally undistinguished, his reign saw political development; and in spite of the Jacobite threat (rising in 1715) it began a period of dynastic stability.

George II (1683–1760), son of the above, succeeded in 1727, and survived a more serious Jacobite rising in 1745. His long reign helped the development of constitutional government, for he kept within the limitations of his powers and capacity; and it saw the extension of English power in India and North America.

George III (1738–1820), grandson of George II reigned 1760–1820. Sincere and well-intentioned, but not politically able, he suffered from mental illness due to intermittent porphyria. His reign saw a clash with John Wilkes, the rise of Methodism, and agrarian and industrial revolution; also the loss of the American colonies, the extension and the questioning of English power in India (Warren Hastings), and prolonged French wars.

George IV (1762–1830), eldest son of George III, reigned 1820–30, having become Prince Regent in 1812. Styled "the first gentleman of Europe," he is remembered for his interest in art and architecture. His married life was unfortunate, and the monarchy was at a low ebb; while his reign was a time of distress and of demand for reform.

George V (1865–1936), was the second son of Edward VII and Queen Alexandra. His elder brother died in 1892 and, in 1901, on his father's accession, he became heir to the throne. He joined the Navy as a cadet in 1877. In 1893 he married Princess Mary of Teck. He succeeded in 1910 and discharged his office conscientiously. In 1932 he began the royal broadcast on Christmas Day and in 1935 celebrated his silver jubilee. His reign included the Kaiser's war, the emergence of the Irish Free State, and the first Labour government.

George VI (1895–1952), second son of George V, was called to the throne in 1936 on the abdication of his elder brother, Edward VIII. His personal qualities gained wide respect. His reign was marked by Hitler's war and rapid social change.

George, Henry (1839–97), American political economist whose "single tax" on land values as a means of solving economic problems is expounded in his *Progress and Poverty* (1879).

George, St., patron saint of England, adopted by Edward III. He is believed to have been martyred by Diocletian at Nicomedia in 303 (and not, as believed by Gibbon, to be confused with George of Cappadocia). The story of his fight with the dragon is of late date.

Gershwin, George (1898–1937). American jazz pianist and song-writer, composer of *Rhapsody in Blue* and the Negro folk-opera *Porgy and Bess*.

Gesner, Conrad (1516–65), Swiss naturalist, b. Zurich. His magnificently illustrated volumes describe animal and vegetable kingdoms.

Ghiberti, Lorenzo (1378–1455), Florentine sculptor whose bronze doors, beautifying the baptistry in Florence, were described by Michelangelo as fit for the gates of paradise.

Ghirlandaio, Domenico (1449–94), Florentine painter. Most of his frescoes are in Florence, including the cycle of the life of the Virgin and the Baptist in S. Maria Novella. Michelangelo began his apprenticeship in his workshop.

Giacometti, Alberto (1901–66), Swiss sculptor and painter, who worked mainly in Paris and produced abstract symbolic constructions.

Giap, Vo Nguyen (b. 1912), Vietnamese general who defeated the French at Dien Bien Phu (1954) and withstood American intervention in the Vietnam war which followed; replaced in 1980 as defence minister, retaining post as vice-premier.

Gibbon, Edward (1737–94), English historian of the *Decline and Fall of the Roman Empire*.

Gibbons, Grinling (1648–1720), English wood-carver and sculptor, b. Rotterdam, was brought to the notice of Charles II by Evelyn, the diarist. The choir stalls of St. Paul's and the carving in the Wren library at Trinity College, Cambridge, are his work.

Gibbons, Orlando (1583–1625), English composer

of church music. *See also* **Section E.**

Gide, André (1869–1951), French writer of many short novels in which he gives expression to his struggle to escape from his protestant upbringing (*Strait is the Gate, The Counterfeiters*). In his memoir *Si le grain ne meurt* he tells the story of his life up to his marriage. The narratives of his journeys in Africa led to a reform in French colonial policy.

Gielgud, Sir John (b. 1904), English actor and producer, grand-nephew of Ellen Terry, to whom, the Hamlet of his generation, the present popularity of Shakespeare is largely due.

Gigli, Beniamino (1890–1957), Italian operatic tenor.

Gilbert, Sir Alfred (1854–1934). English sculptor and goldsmith. His sculptures include *Eros* in Piccadilly Circus.

Gilbert, Sir Humphrey (1537–83), English navigator. He was knighted by Queen Elizabeth for service in Ireland. In 1583 he discovered Newfoundland, but was drowned the same year.

Gilbert, William (1540–1603), English physician to Queen Elizabeth. His book *On the Magnet*, published in Latin in 1600, was the first major original contribution to science published in England.

Gilbert, Sir William Schwenck (1836–1911), English humorist and librettist, of the Gilbert and Sullivan light operas. First known as author of the *Bab Ballads*, from 1871 he collaborated with Sir Arthur Sullivan, his wit and satire finding appropriate accompaniment in Sullivan's music. Their operas include *H.M.S. Pinafore, Patience, Iolanthe, The Mikado, The Gondoliers,* and *The Yeomen of the Guard.*

Gill, Eric (1882–1940), English sculptor and engraver, whose works include the *Stations of the Cross* (Westminster Cathedral), *Prospero and Ariel* (Broadcasting House), *Christ Driving the Money-changers from the Temple* (Leeds University). He also worked as a designer for printing (Gill Sans type), and the George VI stamps were his designs.

Gillray, James (1757–1815), English caricaturist who produced over a thousand political cartoons.

Giotto di Bondone (1267–1337), Florentine artist. A pupil of Cimabue, he continued the development away from Byzantine tradition towards greater naturalism. His frescoes survive in the churches of Assisi, Padua, and Florence. He designed the western front of the cathedral at Florence and the campanile.

Gissing, George Robert (1857–1903), English novelist whose works deal with the degrading effect of poverty. The best known is *New Grub Street.*

Giulio Romano or **Giulio Pippi** (*c.* 1492–1546). Italian artist, was a pupil of Raphael. He was also an engineer and architect.

Gladstone, William Ewart (1809–98), English Liberal statesman. B. at Liverpool, he entered parliament in 1832 as a Tory and held office under Peel. From 1852 he served several terms as chancellor of the exchequer and was Liberal prime minister 1868–74, when his legislation included the education act of 1870, the ballot act, the disestablishment of the Church of Ireland and an Irish land act. In 1874 when Disraeli came to power, he temporarily withdrew, but made a come-back in 1879 with his Mid-Lothian campaign. He was again prime minister 1880–5, 1886 and 1892–4; he carried a parliamentary reform act, and advocated home rule for Ireland but was not able to carry it. His long life was one of moral stature and increasing advocacy of liberal causes. He was also a classical scholar and a writer on church matters.

Glazunov, Alexander Constantinovich (1865–1936), Russian composer, pupil of Rimsky-Korsakov. The first of his eight symphonies was composed when he was 16.

Glendower, Owen (*c.* 1350–*c.* 1416), Welsh chief, who conducted guerrilla warfare on the English border, and figures in Shakespeare's *Henry IV.*

Glinka, Mikhail Ivanovich (1804–57), Russian composer, first of the national school, best known for his operas, *A Life for the Tsar*, and *Russlan and Ludmilla*, based on a poem by Pushkin. *See* **Section E.**

Gluck, Christoph Wilibald (1714–87), German composer, important in the development of opera. He studied in Prague, Vienna and Italy, and his first operas were in the Italian tradition; but with *Orfeo ed Euridice* (1762) his style became more dramatic. There followed *Alceste, Armide,* and *Iphigénie en Tauride* (his best-known work). *See* **Section E.**

Godfrey of Bouillon (*c.* 1061–1100), Crusader on the first crusade. On capturing Jerusalem declined title of "king", preferring that of protector of the Holy Sepulchre.

Godiva, Lady (1040–80), English benefactress. According to tradition, she obtained from her husband Leofric, Earl of Chester, concessions for the people of Coventry by riding naked through the town.

Godwin, Earl of the West Saxons (d. 1053), was the father of Edith, wife of King Edward the Confessor, and of Harold, last Saxon king.

Godwin William (1756–1836), English political writer and philosopher, author of *Political Justice* (which criticised many contemporary institutions) and a novel *Caleb Williams.* He married **Mary Wollstonecraft** (1759–97), author of *A Vindication of the Rights of Women*; and their daughter, **Mary Wollstonecraft Godwin** (1797–1851) wrote *Frankenstein* and married Shelley.

Goethe, Johann Wolfgang von (1749–1832), German poet and thinker. B. at Frankfurt-on-Main, his first notable work was a romantic play, *Götz von Berlichingen*, followed by a novel *Werthers Leiden.* In 1776 he became privy councillor to the Duke of Weimar, whom he served for many years. He had wide-ranging interests, and made discoveries in anatomy and in botany. Among his later writings are the play *Iphigenie* and the novel *Wilhelm Meister*, and he wrote many lyrics. His best-known work however is *Faust*, which was composed over many years; its theme is man's search for happiness. In later life he was a friend of Schiller.

Gogol, Nikolai Vasilievich (1809–52), Russian novelist and dramatist. His comedy, *The Government Inspector*, satirised provincial bureaucracy; and his novel, *Dead Souls*, deals with malpractice in the supposed purchase of dead serfs.

Goldsmith, Oliver (1728–74), Irish poet, dramatist and novelist. The son of a poor curate, he came to London in 1756, and eventually joined the circle of Dr. Johnson. He is best known for his novel *The Vicar of Wakefield* and his play *She Stoops to Conquer.*

Goncourt, Edmond Louis Antoine Huot de (1822–96) and **Jules Alfred Huot de** (1830–70), French brothers, remembered for their *Journal des Goncourts*, an intimate account of Parisian society spanning 40 years, and of documentary interest.

Góngora y Argote, Luis de (1561–1627), Spanish poet, b. Córdova. In *Polifemo* and *Soledades* he attempted to express the core of poetry in new experimental forms.

Goodyear, Charles (1800–60), American inventor who discovered the art of vulcanising rubber.

Goossens, Sir Eugene (1893–1962), English conductor and composer of Belgian descent. His compositions include the operas *Judith* and *Don Juan de Mañara*; brother of Léon, oboe virtuoso, and of Sidonie and Marie Goossens, harpists.

Gorbachev, Mikhail (b. 1931). Soviet politician. Succeeded Chernenko (*q.v.*) as General Secretary of the Communist Party, March 1985. Highly educated, he was thought to be Andropov's (*q.v.*) choice of heir. His accession marks the end of the "old-guard" leadership.

Gordon, Charles George (1833–85), Scottish soldier. After service in the Crimea and China, in 1873 he was made governor of the Equatorial provinces of Egypt; and he was a notable governor of the Sudan, 1877–80. When a rising was led by the Mahdi, he was sent out in 1884 to the garrisons in rebel territory and was killed at Khartoum.

Gordon, Lord George (1751–93), agitator, led No-Popery riots in London in 1780.

Gorky, Maxim (Alexey Maximovich Peshkov) 1868–1936), Russian writer. From the age of ten he worked at many trades from scullion on a Volga steamboat to railway guard, while learning to write: see *My Childhood.* His early work was romantic. He spent many years abroad, but returned in 1928, a supporter of the Soviet regime. His later work is marked by social realism.

Gosse, Sir Edmund (1849–1928), English poet and critic, known for his literary studies of the 17th and 18th centuries; and for his memoir *Father and Son.*

Gounod, Charles François (1818–93), French composer, known for his operas *Faust* and *Roméo et Juliette,* though his lyrical gifts are shown in earlier works, such as *Le Médicin malgré lui* and *Mireille.*

Gower, John (1325–1408), English poet of the time of Chaucer, author of *Confessio Amantis.*

Goya y Lucientes, Francisco José (1746–1828), Spanish painter and etcher b. nr. Saragossa. He became court painter to Charles III in 1786. His portraits are painted with ruthless realism; his series of satirical etchings (*Los Caprichos* and the *Disasters of War*) expose man's inhumanity and express his hatred of the cruelty and reaction of his day. His work can best be seen in Madrid.

Grace, William Gilbert (1848–1915), English cricketer who scored 54,896 runs, including 126 centuries, and took 2,876 wickets. Scored 1,000 runs in May 1895; and three times made over 300 runs in an innings.

Grahame, Kenneth (1859–1932), Scottish writer of books for children, including *The Golden Age, Dream Days,* and *Wind in the Willows.*

Grahame-White, Claude (1879–1959), aviator and engineer, the first Englishman to gain an aviator's certificate, 1909.

Grant, Ulysses Simpson (1822–85), American general of the civil war, and president of the United States from 1869 to 1876.

Granville-Barker, Harley (1877–1946), English dramatist, actor, and producer, who promoted the plays of Ibsen, Shaw, and other serious writers. His own works include *The Voysey Inheritance.*

Grattan, Henry (1746–1820), Irish statesman, who struggled for Irish legislative independence and for Catholic emancipation (though himself a Protestant) and parliamentary reform; but unsuccessfully.

Graves, Robert Ranke (1895–1985), English writer, author of *Goodbye to All That,* written after the first world war; and of *I Claudius* and *Claudius the God;* besides poetry.

Gray, Thomas (1716–71), English poet, author of *Elegy written in a Country Churchyard* and *Ode on a Distant Prospect of Eton College.*

Greeley, Horace (1811–72), American newspaper editor, founder of the New York *Tribune* (1841).

Green, John Richard (1837–83), English historian, author of *Short History of the English People.*

Greenaway, Kate (1846–1901), English artist of children, especially for book illustrations.

Greene, Graham (b. 1904), English novelist and journalist, whose novels (*The Power and the Glory, The Heart of the Matter, The End of the Affair, The Quiet American, Our Man in Havana, A Burnt-out Case, The Comedians, The Honorary Consul,* like his plays (*The Complaisant Lover*) and films (*Fallen Idol, The Third Man*) deal with moral problems in a modern setting. O.M. (1986).

Gregory, St. (c. 240–332), converted King Tiridates of Armenia and was thus founder of the Armenian church.

Gregory I (the Great), St. (c. 540–604), Pope 590–604, was the last great Latin Father and the forerunner of scholasticism. The main founder of the temporal power and the political influence of the papacy, he also maintained the spiritual claims of Rome, enforcing discipline, encouraging monasticism, defining doctrine, and adding to the music, liturgy, and canons of the Church. It was he who sent Augustine on a mission to England.

Gregory VII (Hildebrand) (c. 1020–85), Pope 1073–85. He strove for papal omnipotence within the church and for a high standard in the priesthood (especially by stamping out simony and clerical marriage). He also upheld the papacy against the Holy Roman Empire, and the emperor Henry IV did penance for three days in the snow at Canossa; but he had not quite the vision of Gregory I of an ideal theocracy embracing all states.

Gregory XIII (1502–85), Pope 1572–85; introduced the Gregorian calendar.

Gregory, James (1638–75), Scottish mathematician. He invented a reflecting telescope and was the first to show how the distance of the sun could be deduced by observations of the passage of Venus across the disc of the sun. Successive generations of the family reached distinction.

Grenville, Sir Richard (1541–91), English sea captain, who with his one ship engaged a fleet of Spanish war vessels off Flores in 1591, an exploit celebrated in Tennyson's ballad *The Revenge.*

Gresham, Sir Thomas (1519–79), English financier and founder of the Royal Exchange. Son of a Lord Mayor of London, he was an astute moneyfinder for four successive sovereigns, including Queen Elizabeth I. "Gresham's Law" is the statement that bad money drives out good.

Greuze, Jean Baptiste (1725–1805), French artist, known especially for his studies of girls. His *Girl with Doves* is in the Wallace Collection.

Grey, 2nd Earl (Charles Grey) (1764–1845), British Whig statesman under whose premiership were passed the Reform Bill of 1832, a bill abolishing slavery throughout the Empire (1833), and the Poor Law Amendment Act, 1834.

Grey, Lady Jane (1537–54), Queen of England for a few days. The daughter of the Duke of Suffolk, she was put forward as queen by protestant leaders on the death of her cousin, Edward VI; but overcome by the legal claimant, Mary Tudor, and executed.

Grieg, Edvard Hagerup (1843–1907), Norwegian composer, b. Bergen. He presented the characteristics of his country's music with strong accentuation. He is best known for his incidental music to *Peer Gynt.*

Griffin, Bernard William (1899–1956), Roman catholic archbishop of Westminster from 1944 until his death.

Griffith, Arthur (1872–1922), the first president of the Irish Free State, 1921; founder of the *Sinn Fein* movement.

Griffith, David Wark (1880–1948), American film producer, who introduced the close-up, and the flash-back, and developed leading actors. His films include *Birth of a Nation,* and *Broken Blossoms.*

Grimm, the brothers Jakob Ludwig Karl (1785–1863), and **Wilhelm Karl** (1786–1859), German philologists and folk-lorists, best known for their *Fairy Tales.* Jakob published a notable philological dictionary, *Deutsche Grammatik.* The brothers also projected the vast *Deutsches Wörtebuch* which was completed by German scholars in 1961.

Grimthorpe, 1st Baron (Edmund Beckett Denison) (1816–1905), horologist who invented the double three-legged escapement for the clock at Westminster, familiarly known as "Big Ben" (the name of the bell). For long known as Sir Edmund Beckett.

Gromyko, Andrei Andreevich (b. 1909), Russian diplomat and statesman. President, USSR, July 1985–; Foreign Minister, 1957–85; first deputy prime minister, 1983; Ambassador to Britain 1952–3.

Grossmith, George (1847–1912), English actor. With his brother, **Weedon Grossmith,** he wrote *Diary of a Nobody.* His son, **George Grossmith** (1874–1935) was a comedian and introduced revue and cabaret entertainment into England.

Grote, George (1794–1871), English historian, author of a *History of Greece.*

Grotius (Huig van Groot) (1583–1645), Dutch jurist, the founder of international law. He was condemned to life imprisonment for religious reasons, but escaped to Paris, where he wrote *De Jure Belli et Pacis.*

Grouchy, Emmanuel, Marquis de (1766–1847), French general, who served under Napoleon; after Waterloo led defeated army back to Paris.

Grove, Sir George (1820–1900), English musicologist, author of *Dictionary of Music and Musicians.* By profession he was a civil engineer.

Guedalla, Philip (1889–1944), English historian, author of *The Second Empire, Palmerston,* and *The Hundred Days.*

Guevara, Ernesto "Che" (1928–67), revolutionary hero, b. Argentina. He took part in the Cuban guerrilla war and became a minister in the Cuban government 1959–65. He was killed while leading a band of guerrillas against American-trained Bolivian troops. ("Che" is Argentine for "chum".)

Guido Reni (1575–1642), Italian painter of the Bolognese school whose works are characteristic of the Italian baroque of his period and include the *Aurora* fresco in the Rospigliosi palace at Rome, and *Crucifixion of St. Peter* (Vatican).

Gustavus Adolphus (1594–1632), King of Sweden, the "Lion of the North." After a campaign in Poland he entered the Thirty Years' war in support of Swedish interests and Protestant distress, won the battle of Breitenfeld in 1631 and was killed in action the next year.

Gutenberg, Johann (*c.* 1400–68), German printer, b. Mainz, the first European to print with movable types cast in moulds. The earliest book printed by him was the Mazarin Bible (*see* **L76**).

Guy, Thomas (1644–1724), English philanthropist. A printer, he made money by speculation; and in 1722 founded Guy's Hospital in Southwark.

Gwyn, Nell (*c.* 1650–87), English actress and mistress of Charles II by whom she had two sons (one to become Duke of St. Albans). Of Hereford origin, she sold oranges in London and became a comedienne at Drury Lane.

H

Haakon VII (1872–1957), King of Norway, was a Danish prince and elected on the separation of Norway from Sweden in 1905. He resisted the Nazi occupation.

Hadley, George (1685–1768). He developed Halley's theory of the trade winds by taking into account the effect of the earth's rotation and the displacement of air by tropical heat (1735).

Hadrian (76–138), Roman emperor. An able general, he suppressed revolts, and he was also a lover of the arts. He visited Britain *c.* A.D. 121 and built a protective wall between Wallsend-on-Tyne and Bowness-on-Solway.

Hafiz, pseudonym of **Shams ad-Din Mohammed** (d. *c.* 1388), Persian lyrical poet. His principal work is the *Divan,* a collection of short sonnets called *ghazals.* The sobriquet *Hafiz,* meaning one who remembers, is applied to anyone who has learned the Koran by heart.

Hahn, Otto (1879–1968), German chemist and physicist, chief discoverer of uranium fission, the phenomenon on which nuclear power and the atom bomb are based.

Hahnemann, Samuel Christian Friedrich (1755–1843), German physician who founded homoeopathy (treatment of disease by small doses of drugs that in health produce similar symptoms).

Haig, Douglas, 1st Earl of Bermersyde (1861–1928), British field-marshal, b. Edinburgh. He replaced French as commander-in-chief in France, 1915–19, leading the offensive in August 1918; and after the war presided over the British Legion.

Haile Selassie I (1891–1975), Emperor of Ethiopia 1930–74. He spent the years of the Italian occupation 1936–41 in England. Deposed 1974.

Hakluyt, Richard (1553–1616), English writer on maritime discovery. B. in Herefordshire, he spent some time in Paris. From 1582 (when *Divers Voyages* appeared), he devoted his life to collecting and publishing accounts of English navigators, thus giving further impetus to discovery.

Haldane, John Burdon Sanderson (1892–1964), biologist and geneticist, noted not only for his work in mathematical evolutionary theory but for explaining science to the layman. He emigrated to India in 1957. He was the son of **John Scott Haldane** (1860–1936), b. Edinburgh, who studied the effect of industrial occupations upon health.

Haldane, 1st Viscount (Richard Burdon Haldane) (1856–1928). British Liberal statesman. As war minister in 1905 he reorganised the army and founded the Territorials.

Halévy, Ludovic (1834–1903), French playwright, who collaborated with Henri Meilhac in writing libretti for Offenbach and Bizet.

Halifax, 1st Earl of (Edward Frederick Lindley Wood) (1881–1959), British Conservative politician; foreign secretary during the period of appeasement of Germany; as Lord Irwin, viceroy of India 1926–31.

Halifax, 1st Marquess of (George Savile) (1633–95), English politician of changeable views, who wrote *Character of a Trimmer.*

Hallam, Henry (1777–1859), English historian, best known for his *Constitutional History.* He

was father of Arthur Hallam, friend of Tennyson.

Hallé, Sir Charles (1819–95), German-born pianist and conductor, who settled in Manchester and organised an orchestra of high-class talent. He married the violinist Wilhelmine Neruda.

Halley, Edmond (1656–1742), English astronomer royal 1720–42. He published observations on the planets and comets, being the first to predict the return of a comet (*see* **Section L**). He furthered Newton's work on gravitation, setting aside his own researches. He made the first magnetic survey of the oceans from the naval vessel *Paramour,* 1698–1700. His meteorological observations led to his publication of the first map of the winds of the globe (1686).

Hale, George Ellery (1868–1935), American astronomer, after whom is named the 200-inch reflecting telescope on Mount Palomar.

Hals, Frans (*c.* 1580–1666), Dutch portrait painter, b. at Mechlin. He is best known for his *Laughing Cavalier* in the Wallace Collection, and for other portraits in the Louvre and at Amsterdam.

Hamilton, Alexander (1755–1804), American statesman and economist. With Madison and Jay he wrote the *Federalist* (1787). As secretary of the Treasury (1789–95) he put Washington's government on a firm financial footing and planned a national bank. He was the leader of the Federalists, a party hostile to Jefferson. He was killed in a duel.

Hamilton, Emma, Lady (*née* Lyon) (*c.* 1765–1815), a beauty of humble birth who, after several liaisons, was married in 1791 to Sir William Hamilton, British ambassador at Naples. There she met Nelson, and later bore him a child, Horatia.

Hammarskjöld, Dag (1905–61), world statesman. After an academic and political career in Sweden, in 1953 he became secretary-general of the United Nations, and aimed at extending its influence for peace, especially by initiating a U.N. emergency force in the Middle East. He was killed in an air crash while attempting to mediate in a dispute between the Congo and the secessionist province of Katanga. Posthumous Nobel peace prize.

Hammond, John Lawrence (1872–1949), English historian of social and industrial history, whose works (with his wife Barbara) include *The Town Labourer* and *The Village Labourer.*

Hampden, John (1594–1643), English parliamentarian and civil war leader. He refused to pay Charles I's ship money in 1636. When civil war broke out, he raised a regiment and was killed on Chalgrove Field.

Hamsun, Knut, pen-name of Knut Pedersen (1859–1952), Norwegian author who in his youth struggled for existence, visited America twice and earned his living by casual labour. *The Growth of the Soil* won him the Nobel prize in 1920. Other great novels are *Hunger* and *Mysteries.*

Handel, George Frederick (1685–1759), German composer, son of a barber-surgeon to the Duke of Saxony; b. Halle, the same year as Bach; spent much of his life in England composing operas and oratorios. His operas, of which there are over 40, include *Atalanta, Berenice* and *Serse,* and his oratorios, of which there are 32, include *Saul, Israel in Egypt, Samson, Messiah, Judas Maccabaeus,* and *Jephtha.* Eight years before he died he became blind and relied upon his old friend and copyist John Christopher Smith to commit his music to paper. *See* **Section E.**

Hannibal (247–182 B.C.), Carthaginian general. He fought two wars against Rome. In the first he conquered southern Spain. In the second he overran Gaul, crossed the Alps, and defeated the Romans in successive battles, especially at Cannae. Thereafter his forces were worn down by Roman delaying tactics; he was defeated by Scipio at Zama and later poisoned himself.

Harcourt, Sir William Vernon (1827–1904), Liberal politician who revised death duties.

Hardicanute (1019–42), son of Canute, and last Danish king of England.

Hardie, James Keir (1856–1915), Scottish Labour leader, one of the founders of the Labour party. He first worked in a coal-pit; in 1882 became a journalist; and in 1892 was the first socialist to be elected to the House of Commons (for

West Ham – South). He edited the *Labour Leader* 1887–1904. He was the first chairman of the parliamentary Labour party, 1906. A pacifist, he opposed the Boer war.

Hardy, Thomas (1840–1928), English novelist and poet, was trained as an architect and practised for some time, but became known in 1871 with *Desperate Remedies*. In 1874 his *Far from the Madding Crowd* was published. Following that came a series of novels, including *The Trumpet-Major*, *The Mayor of Casterbridge*, *Tess of the D'Urbervilles*, and *Jude the Obscure*. In 1908 he completed a dramatic poem, *The Dynasts*, whose central figure is Napoleon. His underlying theme is man's struggle against neutral forces, and he depicts the Wessex countryside.

Hargreaves, James (1720–78), English inventor, b. Blackburn. His spinning-jenny was invented in 1764 and became widely used, though his own was broken by spinners in 1768 and his invention brought him no profit.

Harkness, Edward Stephen (1874–1940), American banker and philanthropist, who in 1930 founded the Pilgrim Trust in Gt. Britain.

Harley, Robert, 1st Earl of Oxford and Mortimer (1661–1724), English statesman and collector of MSS. He held office under Queen Anne, and brought a European war to an end with the treaty of Utrecht. After the Hanoverian succession he lived in retirement, and formed the MSS. collection, now in the British Museum, which bears his name.

Harold II (1022–66), last Saxon king of England, was son of Earl Godwin. He was chosen king in succession to Edward the Confessor. He had at once to meet a dual invasion. He defeated the Norwegian king at Stamford Bridge; but was himself defeated by William of Normandy at the battle of Hastings (fought at Battle 1066).

Harriman, William Averell (b. 1891), American public official. He was adviser to President Roosevelt and later presidents especially on Marshall Aid and in connection with foreign affairs generally.

Harris, Joel Chandler (1848–1908), American author, creator of Uncle Remus and Brer Rabbit in Negro folk-tales.

Harrison, Frederick (1831–1923), English philosopher and lawyer, author of *The Meaning of History* and *The Philosophy of Common Sense*. He was president of the Positivist committee. *See* **Positivism, Section J.**

Harrison, John (1693–1776)—"Longitude Harrison," English inventor of the chronometer, b. near Pontefract, Yorkshire, the son of a carpenter.

Harty, Sir Hamilton (1880–1941), composer and for some years conductor of the Hallé orchestra; b. County Down.

Harun ar-Rashid (Aaron the Upright) (763–809), 5th Abbasid caliph of Baghdad. His court was a centre for art and learning, but he governed, mainly through his vizier until the latter lost favour and was executed in 803. The *Arabian Nights* associated with him are stories collected several centuries later.

Harvey, William (1578–1657), English physician and discoverer of the circulation of the blood. B. at Folkestone, he studied at Padua while Galileo was there, and was physician to James I and Charles I. His treatise on circulation was published in Latin in 1628.

Hastings, Warren (1732–1818), English administrator in India. As governor-general for the East India Company he revised the finances, improved administration and put down disorder. On his return to England he was impeached for alleged corruption, and, though acquitted, lost his fortune in his own defence. Later however he received a grant from the company. Though he suffered unduly, his trial was important for the future as setting a high standard for Indian administration.

Hauptmann, Gerhart (1862–1946), German dramatist and novelist. B. in Silesia, he lived at first in Berlin and later abroad. His play *The Weavers* deals with a revolt of 1844 and has a collective hero. Other works include *Die versunkene Glocke*, *Der arme Heinrich*, and *Rose Bernd*. Nobel prizewinner 1912.

Havelock, Sir Henry (1795–1857), British general who helped to put down the Indian mutiny.

Hawke, 1st Baron (Edward Hawke) (1705–81), English admiral, who in 1759 defeated the

French at Quiberon in a tremendous storm.

Hawkins, Sir John (1532–95), English sailor and slave-trader. In 1562 he was the first Englishman to traffic in slaves. He helped to defeat the Spanish Armada in 1588.

Hawthorne, Nathaniel (1804–64), American author. His works include *The Marble Faun*, *The Scarlet Letter*, *The House of the Seven Gables*.

Haydn, Franz Joseph (1732–1809), Austrian composer, belongs to the classical period of Bach, Handel, and Mozart. He has been given the title "father of the symphony." Much of his life was spent as musical director to the princely Hungarian house of Esterhazy. In 1791 and again in 1794 he visited London, where he conducted his Salomon symphonies. His two great oratorios, *The Creation* and *The Seasons*, were written in his old age. *See* **Section E.**

Hazlitt, William (1778–1830), English essayist and critic. His writings include *The Characters of Shakespeare's Plays*, *Table Talk*, and *The Spirit of the Age*. His grandson William Carew Hazlitt (1834–1913) was a bibliographer and writer.

Hearst, William Randolph (1863–1951), American newspaper proprietor who built up a large newspaper empire.

Heath, Edward (b. 1916), British statesman, leader of the Conservative Party 1965–75; prime minister 1970–4; leader of the opposition 1965–70, 1974–5. In 1973 his Government took Britain into the EEC. In the contest for the leadership held in 1975 he was defeated by Mrs. Thatcher.

Hedin, Sven Anders (1865–1952), Swedish explorer of Central Asia; wrote *My Life as Explorer*.

Heenan, John Carmel (1905–76). English Roman Catholic prelate, archbishop of Westminster 1963–76; member of Sacred College (1965).

Hegel, Georg Wilhelm Friedrich (1770–1831), German idealist philosopher, b. Stuttgart, whose name is associated with the dialectic method of reasoning with its sequence of thesis—antithesis—synthesis. He studied theology at Tübingen with his friend Schelling. He taught philosophy at Jena, Nuremberg, Heidelberg, and Berlin. He produced an abstract philosophical system which was influenced by his early interest in mysticism and his Prussian patriotism. His doctrines were very influential in the 19th cent. and led to modern totalitarianism. He died of cholera. *See* **Dialectical Materialism, Section J.**

Heidenstam, Verner von (1859–1940), Swedish author and poet, leader of a new romantic movement. Nobel prizewinner 1916.

Heifetz, Jascha (b. 1901), Russian-born violinist, a U.S. citizen. He was the first musician to win a reputation in England by gramophone records before a personal appearance.

Heine, Heinrich (1797–1856), German lyric poet, b. Düsseldorf of Jewish parents. He lived mostly in Paris. His poems show profound beauty and subtlety of thought, but the satire and sometimes bitterness of his writings excited antagonism.

Heisenberg, Werner (1901–76), German physicist, noted for his theory of quantum mechanics and the Uncertainty Principle. Nobel prizewinner 1932.

Helmholtz, Herman von (1821–94), German physicist and physiologist. He published his *Erhaltung der Kraft* (Conservation of Energy) in 1847, the same year that Joule gave the first clear exposition of the principle of energy. His pupil Heinrich Hertz discovered electromagnetic radiation in accordance with Maxwell's theory.

Heloïse (*c.* 1101–64), beloved of Abelard (*q.v.*). Her letters to him are extant.

Hemingway, Ernest (1898–1961), American novelist of new technique and wide influence. His works include *A Farewell to Arms*, *Death in the Afternoon*, *For Whom the Bell Tolls*, *The Old Man and the Sea*. He committed suicide. Nobel prizewinner 1954.

Henderson, Arthur (1863–1935), British Labour politician, b. Glasgow. He worked mainly for disarmament, and was president of the World Disarmament Conference, 1932–5. Nobel peace prize 1934.

Henrietta Maria (1609–69), the daughter of Henry IV of France and wife of Charles I.

B31

Henry, Joseph (1797–1878), American physicist and schoolteacher who independently of Faraday discovered the principle of the induced current. The weather-reporting system he set up at the Smithsonian Institution led to the creation of the U.S. Weather Bureau.

Henry I (1068–1135), King of England. The youngest son of William the Conqueror, he ascended the throne during the absence on crusade of his elder brother Robert of Normandy. His long reign brought order and progress, not entirely destroyed by the anarchy under his successor Stephen.

Henry II (1133–89), King of England. He was son of Matilda, daugher of Henry I, and Geoffrey Plantagenet, count of Anjou; and his lands stretched to the Pyrenees. He was a strong ruler to whom we largely owe the establishment of the common law system and permanent administrative reforms. His conflict with the Church brought about the murder of his archbishop Becket, a man of resolute character; and his later life was troubled by his unruly sons.

Henry III (1207–72), King of England, succeeded his father John in 1216. Himself devout and simple, his long reign was troubled by a partly factious baronial opposition.

Henry IV (1367–1413), grandson of Edward III and heir to the Duchy of Lancaster, became king of England in 1399. More solid and practical than his cousin Richard II, whom he had supplanted, he consolidated the government.

Henry V (1387–1422), son of Henry IV, succeeded his father as king of England in 1413. A successful commander, he renewed the French war and won the battle of Agincourt, but died young.

Henry VI (1421–71), son of Henry V, succeeded his father as king of England in 1422 as a baby. Gentle and retiring, he inherited a losing war with France. He founded Eton, and King's College, Cambridge. The Yorkist line claimed the crown from his (the Lancastrian) line, and the Wars of the Roses led to his deposition and death. Ruled 1422–61, 1470–71.

Henry VII (1457–1509) succeeded Richard III as king of England after defeating him in 1485. The first Tudor king, he was firm and shrewd, even avaricious; he built Henry VII's Chapel in Westminster Abbey, and encouraged John Cabot to sail to North America.

Henry VIII (1491–1547), King of England, succeeded his father Henry VII in 1509. A prince of the Renaissance, skilled in music and sports, he loved the sea and built up the navy. His minister Cardinal Wolsey fell when Henry, seeking divorce to obtain a legal heir, rejected papal supremacy and dissolved the monasteries. Ruthless and ostentatious, he executed Sir Thomas More, spent his father's accumulation, and in spite of six marriages left a delicate son to succeed.

Henry IV of France (Henry of Navarre) (1553–1610). Prior to becoming king, he was the leader of the Huguenots; and although on being crowned he became a Catholic, he protected the Protestants by the Edict of Nantes. He then became a national king, but was later assassinated by Ravaillac, a religious fanatic.

Henry the Navigator (1394–1460), Portuguese promoter of discovery, son of John I. His sailors discovered Madeira and the Azores.

Henschel, Sir George (1850–1934), singer, composer, and conductor. B. in Breslau, he became a naturalised Englishman in 1890. Founder and conductor of the London Symphony Concerts (1886).

Hepplewhite, George (d. 1786), English cabinetmaker whose name is identified with the style which followed the Chippendale period.

Heraclitus of Ephesus (c. 540–475 B.C.), Greek philosopher. His discovery of a changing world (he lived in an age of social revolution when the ancient tribal aristocracy was beginning to give way to democracy) influenced the philosophies of Parmenides, Democritus, Plato, and Aristotle, and later, of Hegel.

Herbert, George (1593–1633), the most purely devotional of English poets.

Hereward the Wake, the last Saxon leader to hold out against the Normans. His base in the fens was captured in 1071 but he escaped. His exploits were written up by Kingsley.

Herod the Great (c. 73–4 B.C.). At first governor of Galilee under the Romans, he obtained the title of king of Judaea in 31 B.C. The massacre of the Innocents reported in St. Matthew (though not corroborated in any contemporary or near-contemporary history) is in keeping with his historical character.

Herodotus (c. 485–425 B.C.), Greek historian, called by Cicero, the father of history. He travelled widely collecting historical evidence.

Herrick, Robert (1591–1674), English lyric poet. His poems include *Gather ye Rose Buds*, *Cherry Ripe*, and *Oberon's Feast*.

Herriot, Edouard (1872–1957), French Radical-Socialist statesman. A scholar, mayor of Lyons for more than a generation, three times prime minister, he resisted the German occupation, and was president of the National Assembly 1947–54.

Herschel, Sir John (1792–1871), British astronomer who continued his father's researches and also pioneered photography, a term introduced by him. One of his twelve children introduced fingerprints into criminology.

Herschel, Sir William (1738–1822), German-born astronomer who came to England from Hanover as a musician; father of the above. Unrivalled as an observer, and with telescopes of his own making he investigated the distribution of stars in the Milky Way and concluded that some of the nebulae he could see were separate star systems outside our own. He discovered the planet Uranus in 1781. His sister, **Caroline Lucretia** (1750–1848), compiled a catalogue of the clusters and nebulae discovered by him.

Hertz, Heinrich Rudolf (1857–95), German physicist, whose laboratory experiments confirmed Maxwell's electromagnetic theory of waves and yielded information about their behaviour.

Herzl, Theodor (1860–1904), founder of modern political Zionism, was b. Budapest. He convened a congress at Basle in 1897.

Hesiod (fl. c. 735 B.C.), Greek poet, author of *Work and Days*, which tells of life in the country.

Hill, Octavia (1838–1912), English social reformer concerned with the housing conditions of the poor, a pioneer in slum clearance in London; founder (with Sir Robert Hunter and Canon Rawnsley) of the National Trust.

Hill, Sir Rowland (1795–1879), originator of the penny postal system. He was secretary to the Postmaster-General 1846–54, then chief secretary to the Post Office until 1864.

Hindemith, Paul (1895–1963), German composer and viola player. He is associated with the movement in *Gebrauchsmusik*, which regarded music as a social expression. He incurred Nazi hostility and his later life was spent abroad. His numerous works include chamber works, songs, operas, ballet music, symphonies, and the oratorio *Das Umaufhörliche*. *See* **Section E.**

Hindenburg, Paul von (1847–1934), German field-marshal. In 1914 he defeated the Russians at Tannenberg. In his old age a national hero, he was president of the German Reich, 1925–34.

Hinshelwood, Sir Cyril Norman (1897–1967), English chemist. He shared with Prof. Semenov of Russia the 1956 Nobel prize for chemistry for researches into the mechanism of chemical reactions. Pres. Royal Society, 1955–60.

Hinton of Bankside, Baron (Christopher Hinton) (1901–83), as managing director of the industrial group of the U.K. Atomic Energy Authority he played an important part in the building of Calder Hall. O.M. 1976.

Hippocrates of Chios (fl. c. 430 B.C.), Greek mathematician, the first to compile a work on the elements of geometry.

Hippocrates of Cos (fl. c. 430 B.C.), Greek physician, whose writings are lost, but who is believed to have established medical schools in Athens and elsewhere, and to have contributed towards a scientific separation of medicine from superstition. Traditionally he is the embodiment of the ideal physician.

Hirohito, Emperor of Japan (b. 1901), acceded to the throne in 1926. In 1946 he renounced his legendary divinity. In 1971 he paid a visit to Europe.

Hitler, Adolf (1889–1945), German dictator, founder of National Socialism, b. in Austria, son of a customs official. He was in Vienna for 5 years with no regular work before going to Munich in

1913; enlisted in Bavarian infantry at outbreak of the Kaiser's war. At the end of the war conditions in Germany favoured the growth of a fascist movement and under his leadership the National Socialist (Nazi) party climbed to power. He became Reich chancellor in 1933 and on the death of Hindenburg in 1934 Führer; and commander-in-chief Wehrmacht 1935. Under his regime working class movements were ruthlessly destroyed; all opponents—communists, socialists, Jews—were persecuted and murdered. By terrorism and propaganda the German state was welded into a powerful machine for aggression. There followed the occupation of the Rhineland (1936), the annexation of Austria and Czechoslovakia (1938-9), the invasion of Poland and declaration of war by Great Britain and France (1939), the invasion of Russia (1941). Final defeat came in 1945; on 30 April he committed suicide as the Russian troops closed in on Berlin.

Hobbes, Thomas (1588-1679), English philosopher who published *Leviathan* in 1651. He favoured strong government and supported the supremacy of the state, but his arguments aroused antagonism even among royalists. He was a child of his age in his enthusiasm for scientific enquiry.

Hobhouse, Leonard Trelawney (1864-1929), English sociologist. His books include *The Theory of Knowledge, Morals in Evolution*, and *Development and Purpose.*

Ho Chi-minh (1892-1969), leader of the Vietnam revolutionary nationalist party of Indo-China, which struggled for independence from France during and after the second world war. His main purpose was to weld together the nationalistic and communistic elements in Vietnam. As president of North Vietnam he fought to extend his control over South Vietnam, defying the United States.

Hodgkin, Sir Alan (b. 1914), British biophysicist working in the field of nerve impulse conduction. During the second world war he worked on the development of radar. Pres. Royal Society, 1970-75. Nobel prizewinner, 1970; Chancellor Univ. of Leicester (1971), O.M. 1973.

Hodgkin, Dorothy Crowfoot (b. 1910), the third woman to win the Nobel prize in chemistry, awarded in 1964 for her X-ray analysis to elucidate the structure of complex molecules, notably penicillin and vitamin B-12. She and her team at the Dept. of Molecular Biophysics at Oxford succeeded in 1969 in determining the crystalline structure of insulin. Chancellor Bristol Univ.; Order of Merit (1965).

Hogarth, William (1697-1764), English engraver and painter, who satirised his time with character, humour, and power, especially in his *Harlot's Progress, Rake's Progress, Marriage à la Mode, Industry and Idleness*, and *The March to Finchley.*

Hogg, Quintin (1845-1903), educationist and philanthropist who purchased the old Polytechnic Institution in 1882 and turned it into a popular college providing education at moderate rates. His grandson, **Lord Hailsham**, was lord chancellor in the 1970-4, 1979-83, 1983-, Conservative administrations.

Hokusai, Katsushika (1760-1849), Japanese artist of the Ukiyo-e (popular school). He excelled in landscapes.

Holbein, Hans, the elder (c. 1465-1524), German painter, b. Augsburg, father of:

Holbein, Hans, the younger (1497-1543), German painter, b. Augsburg; settled in London 1532. He won the favour of Henry VIII, for whom he painted many portraits. He is also known for his series *The Dance of Death.*

Holden, Charles (1875-1960), British architect, designer of public buildings, including British Medical Asscn. Building, London; Underground Head Offices; Univ. of London Senate House.

Holden, Sir Isaac (1807-97), British inventor of woolcombing machinery.

Hölderlin, Johann Christian Friedrich (1770-1843), German poet, friend of Hegel. His works include the novel *Hyperion* and the elegy *Menon's Laments for Diotima.* In his middle years his mind became unhinged.

Holford, Baron (William Graham Holford) (1907-75), British architect and town-planner;

planned post-war redevelopment of City of London, including precincts of St. Paul's.

Holmes, Oliver Wendell (1809-94), American author. His writings include *Autocrat of the Breakfast Table, The Professor of the Breakfast Table*, and *The Poet at the Breakfast Table.*

Holst, Gustave Theodore (1874-1934), British composer of Swedish descent whose compositions include *The Planets* suite, *The Hymn of Jesus*, an opera *The Perfect Fool*, and a choral symphony. He was outstanding as a teacher. *See* Section E.

Holyoake, George Jacob (1817-1906), English social reformer and secularist. He wrote a history of the co-operative movement.

Holyoake, Keith Jacka (1904-83), New Zealand politician and farmer; prime minister 1960-72.

Homer (c. 700 B.C.), epic poet. He is supposed to have been a Greek who lived at Chios or Smyrna, and has been regarded as the author of the *Iliad* and the *Odyssey*, though this is tradition rather than ascertained fact.

Hood, 1st Viscount (Samuel Hood) (1724-1816), British admiral who in 1793 was in command of the Mediterranean fleet and occupied Toulon.

Hood, Thomas (1799-1845), English poet. His poems include *The Song of the Shirt, The Dream of Eugene Aram* and *The Bridge of Sighs.* He was also a humorist and punster.

Hooke, Robert (1635-1703), English physicist. His inventions include the balance spring of watches. He was also an architect and drew up a plan for rebuilding London after the Great Fire. His *Diary* is published.

Hooker, Richard (1554-1600), English theologian, author of *Ecclesiastical Polity.* He was Master of the Temple, 1585-91. For his choice of words he was known as "Judicious Hooker".

Hopkins, Sir Frederick Gowland (1861-1947), English biochemist, pioneer in biochemical and nutritional research. He first drew attention to the substances later known as vitamins. Pres. Royal Society 1930-5. Nobel prize 1929.

Hopkins, Gerard Manley (1844-89), English poet of religious experience and of a style new in his day.

Hopkins, Harry (1890-1946), Franklin Roosevelt's personal assistant at foreign conferences, and in the New Deal and Lend-Lease.

Hopkinson, John (1849-98), English engineer. By developing the theory of alternating current and of the magnetic current in dynamos he paved the way to the common use of electricity.

Hoppner, John (1758-1810), English portrait painter, b. Whitechapel, of German parents.

Horace (Quintus Horatius Flaccus) (65-8 B.C.), Roman satirist and poet, son of a Greek freedman. He wrote *Satires, Epodes, Odes*, and *Epistles.* He fought on the republican side at Philippi, but lived to become poet laureate to Augustus.

Horniman, Annie Elizabeth Fredericka (1860-1937), founder of the modern repertory system in England. Her father F. J. Horniman founded the Horniman Museum.

Houdini, Harry (Erich Weiss) (1874-1926), American illusionist, son of a Hungarian rabbi. Famed for his escapes from handcuffs.

Housman, Alfred Edward (1859-1936), English poet, author of *A Shropshire Lad*; he was also a classical scholar. His brother Laurence (1865-1959) was a playwright and wrote *Little Plays of St. Francis* and *Victoria Regina.*

Howard, John (1726-90), English prison reformer. Imprisoned in France in wartime, he subsequently investigated English prisons, securing reforms; and later also continental prisons, dying in Russia of gaol fever.

Howard of Effingham, 2nd Baron (Charles Howard) (1536-1624), afterwards Earl of Nottingham; commanded the fleet which defeated the Spanish Armada (1588), and took part in the capture of Cadiz (1596).

Howe, Elias (1819-67), American inventor of the sewing machine.

Howe, Julia Ward (1819-1910), American suffragette, author of *Mine eyes have seen the glory.*

Howe, 1st Earl (Richard Howe) (1726-99), British admiral whose victories over the French in two wars included that off Ushant on 1 June 1794 ("the glorious first of June").

Hua-Guofeng (b. 1922), b. Hunan, succeeded Mao Tse-tung as Chairman of the Chinese Communist Party, 1976–81. See **Section C, Part II.**

Hubble, Edwin Powell (1889–1953), American astronomer, noted for his work on extragalactic nebulae. With the 100-inch telescope on Mount Wilson he detected the Cepheid variables.

Hudson, Henry (d. 1611), English navigator credited with the discovery of the Hudson river and Hudson Bay, where mutineers turned him adrift to die. He was on a voyage to find a passage by the north pole to Japan and China.

Hudson, William Henry (1841–1922), naturalist, b. Buenos Aires of American parents, naturalised in England (1900). His books include *The Purple Land, Green Mansions,* and *Far Away and Long Ago.* Hyde Park bird sanctuary was established in his memory.

Huggins, Sir William (1824–1910), British astronomer who pioneered in spectroscopic photography.

Hughes, Ted (b. 1930), English poet. Succeeded Sir John Betjeman as Poet Laureate (*see* **L97**) in December 1984. Best known for his poetry of wild animals.

Hughes, Thomas (1822–96), English novelist, author of *Tom Brown's Schooldays,* which is based on Rugby school.

Hugo, Victor Marie (1802–85), French poet, dramatist, and novelist, who headed the Romantic movement in France in the early 19th cent. His dramas include *Hernani, Lucrèce Borgia, Ruy Blas,* and *Le Roi s'amuse.* Of his novels *Notre Dame* belongs to his early period, *Les Misérables, Les Travailleurs de la mer,* and *L'Homme qui rit* were written while he was living in exile in Guernsey.

Humboldt, Friedrich Heinrich Alexander, Baron von (1769–1859), German naturalist and explorer whose researches are recorded in *Voyage de Humboldt et Bonpland* (23 vols., 1805–34), and *Kosmos* (5 vols., 1845–62).

Hume, David (1711–76), Scottish philosopher who developed the empiricism of Locke into the scepticism inherent in it. His main works are *Treatise of Human Nature* and *Dialogues Concerning Natural Religion.* He also wrote a *History of England.*

Hunt, Holman (1827–1910), English artist, one of the founders of the Pre-Raphaelite movement. His best-known picture is *The Light of the World.*

Hunt, Baron (John Hunt) (b. 1910), leader of the 1953 British Everest Expedition when Tenzing and Hillary reached the summit.

Hunt, Leigh (1784–1859), English poet and essayist. In 1813 he was fined and imprisoned for libelling the Prince Regent in *The Examiner.* He was a friend of Keats and Shelley.

Hus, Jan (1369–1415), Bohemian religious reformer. Strongly influenced by Wyclif, he urged reform both of abuses in the church and of doctrine. Sentenced to death or recantation, he suffered martyrdom on 6 July 1415. His death caused a civil war which lasted many years.

Hutton, James (1726–97), an Edinburgh doctor who founded modern geological theory.

Huxley, Aldous (1894–1963), English novelist, author of *Brave New World.*

Huxley, Sir Julian (1887–1975), biologist and writer, grandson of T. H. Huxley and brother of Aldous; director of the London Zoo 1935–42; first director general of Unesco 1946–8; one of the founders of the international Union for the Conservation of Nature and of the World Wild Life Fund.

Huxley, Thomas Henry (1825–95), English biologist, b. Ealing. He started life as assistant-surgeon on H.M.S. *Rattlesnake* and during the voyage (1846–50) studied marine organisms. After the publication of Darwin's *Origin of Species* he became an ardent evolutionist and gave the first recognisably modern lecture on the origin of life to the British Association in 1870. He coined the term "agnostic" to distinguish a person who does not know whether God exists or not from the atheist who asserts there is no God. By his popular lectures and vigorous writings, *e.g.*, *Man's Place in Nature,* he made a real attempt to interest the public in the importance of science.

Huygens, Christian (1629–95), Dutch mathematician, physicist, and astronomer, son of the poet **Constantijn Huygens** (1596–1687); discovered the rings of Saturn, invented the pendulum clock, and developed the wave theory of light in opposition to Newton's corpuscular theory.

Hyde, Douglas (1860–1949), Irish scholar, historian, poet, and folk-lorist; first president of Eire in the 1937 constitution, 1938–45.

Hypatia of Alexandria, the only woman mathematician of antiquity. She excited the enmity of Christian fanatics, who raised an agitation against her, and she was murdered in A.D. 415.

I

Ibsen, Henrik Johan (1828–1906), Norwegian playwright and poet, who dealt with social and psychological problems and revolutionised the European theatre. His chief works are *Ghosts, The Wild Duck, The Master Builder, A Doll's House, Hedda Gabler* and the poetic drama, *Peer Gynt.*

Ingres, Jean Auguste Dominique (1780–1867), French historical and classical painter. His paintings include *La grande odalisque* in the Louvre.

Innocent III (*c.* 1160–1216), Pope 1198–1216. He asserted the power and moral force of the papacy over the Emperor Otto IV, Philip II of France, and John of England. He launched the fourth crusade, encouraged the crusade against the Albigensian heretics, and held the 4th Lateran council. His pontificate marks the zenith of the mediaeval papacy.

Inönü, Ismet (1884–1973), Turkish soldier and statesman; leader of the Republican People's Party founded by Kemal Atatürk; premier, 1923–38; president 1938–50 and 1961–5.

Ionesco, Eugene (b. 1912), French playwright of the Absurd, b. Romania, whose influential plays include *The Bald Prima Donna, The Chairs,* and *Rhinoceros.*

Iqbal, Sir Muhammad (1877–1938), poet-philosopher, b. Sialkot (Pakistan). He wrote both poetry and prose in Urdu, Persian, and English, and his work is marked by mystic nationalism.

Ireland, John (1879–1962), English composer, popularly known for his setting of Masefield's *Sea Fever,* but also a composer of chamber music and sonatas for pianoforte and violin.

Irving, Sir Henry (1838–1905), English actor. At the Lyceum theatre from 1871, later with Ellen Terry, he gave notable Shakespearean performances, especially as Shylock and Malvolio.

Irving, Washington (1783–1859), American essayist, whose works include *Tales of a Traveller* and *The Sketch Book,* also biographies.

Isabella of Castile (1451–1504), reigned jointly with her husband, Ferdinand II of Aragon, over a united Spain, from which the Moors and the Jews were expelled. During their reign the New World was discovered.

Ismail Pasha (1830–95), grandson of Mehemet Ali, was Khedive of Egypt, and became virtually independent of the Sultan. Under him the Suez canal was made, but his financial recklessness led to Anglo-French control and to his own abdication.

Ismay, 1st Baron (Hastings Lionel Ismay) (1887–1965), British general who was chief of staff to Sir Winston Churchill in the second world war, and later the first secretary-general of NATO.

Ito, Hirobumi, Prince (1841–1909), Japanese statesman, four times premier, who helped to modernise his country. He was assassinated.

Ivan the Great (1410–1505) brought the scattered provinces of Muscovy under one control and put an end to Tartar rule.

Ivan the Terrible (1530–84), crowned as first Tsar of Russia in 1547, was an autocratic ruler who consolidated and expanded Russia and entered into trading relations with Queen Elizabeth.

J

Jackson, Andrew (1767–1845), American general who was twice president of the United States.

Jackson, Thomas Jonathan (1824–63), "Stonewall Jackson," was general on the Southern side in the American Civil War; killed at Chancellorsville.

Jacobs, William Wymark (1863–1943), English

novelist, b. London, author of humorous sea and other stories.

Jacquard, Joseph Marie (1752–1834), French inventor whose loom provided an effective method of weaving designs.

Jagellons, Lithuanian–Polish dynasty, which ruled Poland 1386–1572.

Jahangir (1569–1627), 3rd Mogul emperor and patron of art.

James I (1566–1625), King of England (1603–25) and, as James VI, King of Scotland (1567–1625). He was the son of Mary Stuart and succeeded to the English throne on the death of Elizabeth I. His reign saw the Gunpowder Plot of 1605 and the publication of the Authorised Version of the Bible, but it also marked an increasingly critical attitude of the Puritans towards the established church. Personally more of a scholar than a man of action, he was described as "the wisest fool in Christendom."

James II (1633–1701), King of England and, as James VII, King of Scotland (1685–8), was the younger son of Charles I. Personally honest, and an able admiral, he lacked political understanding; and when, having put down Monmouth's rebellion, he tried and failed to obtain better conditions for his fellow Roman Catholics, he was obliged in 1688 to flee the country.

James, Henry (1843–1916), American novelist. He lived mainly in England. His work is noted for intellectual subtlety and characterisation, and includes *The American, Daisy Miller, The Portrait of a Lady, What Maisie Knew,* and *The Spoils of Poynton.*

James, William (1842–1910), American psychologist and philosopher, brother of Henry. He was a protagonist of the theory of pragmatism developed by his friend C. S. Peirce, and invented the doctrine which he called "radical empiricism." His major works are *The Principles of Psychology, The Will to Believe,* and *The Meaning of Truth.*

Janáček, Leoš (1854–1928), Czech composer and conductor, and student of folk music, b. in Moravia, son of a village schoolmaster, creator of a national style. His best-known opera is *Jenufa. See* **Section E.**

Jefferies, Richard (1848–87), English naturalist of poetic perception, b. in Wiltshire, author of *Gamekeeper at Home* and *The Life of the Fields.*

Jefferson, Thomas (1743–1826), American president, 1801–9. He created the Republican Party, by which the federalists, led by Hamilton, were overthrown, and helped to draft the Declaration of Independence. He tried unsuccessfully to bring an end to slavery.

Jeffreys, 1st Baron (George Jeffreys) (1648–89), English judge who held the "bloody assize" after Monmouth's unsuccessful rebellion. In 1686 he was sent to the Tower and there died.

Jellicoe, 1st Earl (John Rushworth Jellicoe) (1859–1935), British admiral. He fought the uncertain battle of Jutland in 1916, after which the German fleet remained in harbour. He was later governor-general of New Zealand.

Jenkins, Roy (b. 1920), British politician, b. Wales; Pres. EEC Commission 1977–80; served as Labour's Home Sec. 1965–7; Chanc. of Exchequer 1967–70. Elected M.P. for Glasgow Hillhead for Social Democrats (1982), having previously contested Warrington. Leader, SDP 1982–June 1983.

Jenner, Edward (1749–1823), English physician, b. in Gloucs., pupil of John Hunter. His discovery of vaccination against smallpox (1798) helped to lay the foundations of modern immunology.

Jerome, Jerome Klapka (1859–1927), English humorous writer, author of *Three Men in a Boat.*

Jerome, St. (c. 331–420), scholar, whose translation of the Bible into Latin (the Vulgate) became for centuries the standard use.

Jesus Christ (c. 4 B.C.–A.D. 30), founder of Christianity, the son of Mary whose husband was Joseph, was born in a critical period of Jewish history. His home was at Nazareth in Galilee, but virtually nothing is known about his early life. When he was about 30 he began the mission which he believed to have been entrusted to him, proclaiming the Kingdom of God was at hand. His teaching is summarised in the Sermon on the Mount, and its main theme is love, especially for the poor and downtrodden. He was later crucified. The main source of his life is the New Testament. The title "Christ" comes from

the Greek word *christos* = anointed, which is the Greek translation of the Hebrew title *Messiah.* Modern dating has amended the probable year of his birth. *See also* **Section S.**

Jiménez, Juan Ramón (1881–1958), Spanish lyric poet, author of *Platero y Yo.* Nobel prizewinner 1956.

Jinnah, Mohammed Ali (1876–1948), Pakistani statesman. B. at Karachi, he became president of the Muslim League, and succeeded in 1947 in establishing the Dominion of Pakistan, becoming its first governor-general.

Joachim, Joseph (1831–1907), Hungarian violinist and composer.

Joan of Arc, St. (Jeanne d'Arc) (1412–31), French patriot, called the Maid of Orleans; of peasant parentage (she was b. at Domrémy), she believed herself called to save France from English domination; and by her efforts Charles VII was crowned at Rheims in 1429. Captured by the English, she was burned as a heretic; but canonised in 1920.

Joffre, Joseph Jacques Césaire (1852–1931), French general. He was commander-in-chief of the French army in the 1914–18 war.

John, St., the Baptist (executed A.D. 28), the forerunner of Jesus Christ. *See* **Section S.**

John, St., the Evangelist, one of the twelve apostles of Jesus Christ, a Galilean fisherman, son of Zebedee and brother of James; traditionally author of the fourth Gospel. *See* **Section S.**

John (1167–1216), youngest son of Henry II, was King of England from 1199. Able but erratic and arbitrary, he lost Normandy. Baronial opposition to him, under the influence of Archbishop Stephen Langton, acquired a national character, and in 1215 he was obliged to seal Magna Carta (*see* **Section L**).

John of Gaunt (1340–99). Duke of Lancaster, son of Edward III and father of Henry IV.

John XXIII (1881–1963), elected Pope in 1958, succeeding Pius XII, was formerly Cardinal Angelo Giuseppe Roncalli, patriarch of Venice. He sought to bring the Church closer to modern needs and to promote Christian unity. His teaching is given in his encyclicals, *Mater et Magistra* and *Pacem in Terris.* He held an Ecumenical Council in 1962.

John Paul II, (b. 1920), succeeded Pope John Paul I after his sudden death in 1978; formerly Cardinal Karol Wojtyla, archbishop of Cracow; first Pope to come from Poland. Assassination attempt made 1981.

John, Augustus (1878–1961), British painter and etcher, b. in Wales; noted for his portraits, *e.g.,* Lloyd George, Bernard Shaw, T. E. Lawrence.

Johnson, Amy (1904–41), was the first woman aviator to fly solo from England to Australia. She lost her life serving in the Air Transport Auxiliary in the second world war.

Johnson, Lyndon Baines (1908–73), President of the United States, 1963–9. He became president on Kennedy's assassination and followed a progressive policy at home, but his achievements were clouded by the war in Vietnam.

Johnson, Samuel (1709–84), English lexicographer and man of letters, b. at Lichfield. His *Dictionary* was published in 1755, and was followed by *Rasselas, The Idler* (a periodical), and *Lives of the Poets.* He was a focus of London literary life of his day, and his biographer, James Boswell, has vividly portrayed his circle.

Joliot-Curie, Jean Frédéric (1900–58), and his wife Irène (1896–1956), French scientists who discovered artificial radioactivity. Nobel prizewinners 1935. Joliot-Curie was one of the discoverers of nuclear fission. Irène was the daughter of Pierre and Marie Curie. Both were communists, and both died from cancer caused by their work.

Jones, Ernest Charles (1819–69), English Chartist leader and poet.

Jones, Sir Harold Spencer (1890–1960), British astronomer royal, 1935–55. His major research was to determine the mean distance of the earth from the sun, 93,004,000 miles.

Jones, Inigo (1573–1652), architect of the English renaissance who studied in Italy and inspired the use of Palladian forms in England. His buildings include the banqueting hall in Whitehall and the queen's house at Greenwich. He also designed furniture and introduced the proscenium arch and movable scenery on the English stage.

Jonson, Ben (1573–1637), English poet and dramatist. His plays include *Every Man in his Humour*, *Volpone*, and *The Alchemist*; and his poems *Drink to me only with thine Eyes*. He also produced court masques.

Josephine, Empress (1763–1814), wife of Napoleon I, *née* de la Pagerie, she was previously married to the Vicomte de Beauharnais. She was divorced from Napoleon in 1809.

Josephus, Flavius (38–c. 100), Jewish historian, author of *History of the Jewish War*.

Joule, James Prescott (1818–89), English physicist, pupil of Dalton, who researched on electromagnetism and determined the mechanical equivalent of heat. *See* **Section L.**

Jowett, Benjamin (1817–93), English scholar. He translated Plato's *Dialogues*, and he was an influential Master of Balliol College, Oxford.

Jowitt, Earl (William Allen Jowitt) (1885–1957), British Labour politician and lord chancellor. He wrote *The Strange Case of Alger Hiss*.

Joyce, James (1882–1941), Irish author, b. Dublin. His *Ulysses* gives a microscopic picture of a day in the life of two Irishmen, and flouted the conventions of his day. Other works include *Portrait of the Artist* and *Finnegans Wake*. He spent most of his life on the Continent.

Juin, Alphonse (1888–1967), French general who took part in the Allied invasion of Tunisia and the Italian campaign in the second world war.

Julian the Apostate (331–63), Roman emperor who tried to restore paganism in the empire. He was killed in war against Persia.

Jung, Carl Gustav (1875–1961), Swiss psychiatrist. A former pupil of Freud, he later formulated his own system of analytical psychology. *See* **Section J.**

Junot, Andoche (1771–1813), French general defeated by Wellington in the Peninsular War.

Jusserand, Jean Jules (1855–1932), French author and diplomat, who wrote on English literature and wayfaring life in the Middle Ages.

Justinian I (483–565), Roman emperor in the East. He and his wife Theodora beautified Constantinople, and his general Belisarius was successful in war. He codified Roman law.

Juvenal (60–140), Roman poet and Stoic, remembered for his *Satires*.

K

Kafka, Franz (1883–1924), German-speaking Jewish writer, b. Prague, whose introspective work, the bulk of which was not published till after his early death from tuberculosis, has had a notable influence on later schools, especially the surrealists. It includes the three novels *The Trial*, *The Castle*, and *America*, and some short stories.

Kālidāsa (*c.* A.D. 400), chief figure in classic Sanskrit literature. No facts are known about his life and date, but certain evidence places him in the 5th cent. Seven of his works survive: two lyrics, *Ritu-samhara* (The Seasons), and *Megha-dūta* (Cloud Messenger); two epics, *Raghu-vamsa* (Dynasty of Raghu) and *Kumarasambhava* (Birth of the War-god); and three dramas, *Śakūntalā*, *Mālavikāgnimitra*, and *Vikramorvaśīya*.

Kant, Immanuel (1724–1804), German philosopher, author of *Critique of Pure Reason* (1781), *Critique of Practical Reason* (1788), and *Critique of Judgement* (1790). He came from a Pietist family of Königsberg, where he lectured, but the Prussian government forbade his lectures as anti-Lutheran. He was influenced by the writings of his neighbour Hamann (*see* **Romanticism, Section J**) and by Rousseau and Hume, and his own work was of immense influence in shaping future liberal thought. He believed in the freedom of man to make his own decisions and considered the exploitation of man as the worst evil. In *Perpetual Peace* he advocated a world federation of states.

Kapitza, Pyotr (1894–1984), Russian physicist who worked on atomic research with Rutherford at the Cavendish Laboratory, Cambridge, and returned to Russia in 1935. Member of the Soviet Academy of Sciences and Fellow of the Royal Society. Nobel Prize for Physics, 1978.

Kauffman, Angelica (1741–1807), Anglo-Swiss

painter, a foundation member of the Royal Academy and the first woman R.A.

Kaulbach, Wilhelm von (1805–74), German painter who illustrated the works of Goethe and Schiller.

Kaunda, Kenneth (b. 1924), African leader of international standing, son of Christian missionaries. He has been president of Zambia since independence in 1964.

Kean, Edmund (1787–1833), English tragic actor. He made his name as Shylock.

Kean, Charles John (1811–68), English actor-manager, son of Edmund. He married Ellen Tree and in the 1850s played with her in spectacular revivals at the Princess's Theatre, London.

Keats, John (1795–1821), English poet who in his short life produced poems notable for richness of imagination and beauty of thought. They include *Odes*, *Isabella*, and *The Eve of St. Agnes*.

Keble, John (1792–1866), English clergyman associated with the Tractarian movement and author of *The Christian Year*. *See* **Tractarianism, Section J.**

Keller, Helen Adams (1880–1968), American author and lecturer who overcame great physical handicaps (blind and deaf before the age of two) to live an active and useful life.

Kelvin of Largs, 1st Baron (William Thomson) (1824–1907), British mathematician and physicist, b. Belfast, known for his work on heat and thermodynamics, and contributions to electrical science and submarine telegraphy. In the domain of heat he stands to Joule as Maxwell stands to Faraday in the history of electrical science, both bringing pre-eminently mathematical minds to bear on the results of experimental discoveries. He introduced the Kelvin or Absolute scale of temperature and was one of the original members of the Order of Merit.

Kemble, Fanny (1809–93), English actress. She came of a noted theatrical family, her father and uncle respectively being the actors Charles Kemble and John Philip Kemble, and her aunt, Mrs. Siddons.

Kempenfelt, Richard (1718–82), English admiral, who sank with his ship the *Royal George* together with 600 of the ship's company off Spithead through a shifting of the guns which caused it to capsize.

Kempis, Thomas à (1380–1471), name by which the German mystic Thomas Hammerken was known, was a monk of the Augustinian order, whose life was mainly spent at a monastery near Zwolle. He was the author of *The Imitation of Christ*.

Kennedy, John Fitzgerald (1917–63), President of the U.S.A., 1961–3, the youngest and the first Roman Catholic to be elected; son of a financier. He had world-wide pre-eminence and gave the American people a sense of purpose to meet the challenges of a scientific age. He opposed racial discrimination and initiated a new era of East–West relations; but his foreign policy sowed the seeds of the Vietnam war. He and his brother Robert were assassinated, the latter while campaigning for the presidency in 1968.

Kent, William (1684–1748), English painter, furniture designer, landscape gardener, and architect, protégé of Lord Burlington, whose buildings include the great hall at Holkham and the Horse Guards, Whitehall.

Kenyatta, Jomo (1893–1978), African leader who became president of Kenya in 1964.

Kepler, Johann (1571–1630), German astronomer and mystic, for a short time assistant to Tycho Brahe whose measurements he used in working out his laws of planetary motion, which are: 1. Planets move round the sun not in circles, but in ellipses, the sun being one of the foci. 2. A planet moves not uniformly but in such a way that a line drawn from it to the sun sweeps out equal areas of the ellipse in equal times. 3. The squares of the period of revolution round the sun are proportional to the cubes of the distances. The explanation of these laws was given by Newton; they dealt a death-blow to Aristotelian cosmology.

Keyes, 1st Baron (Roger John Brownlow Keyes) (1872–1945), British admiral who led the raid on Zeebrugge in 1918.

Keynes, 1st Baron (John Maynard Keynes) (1883–

1946), British economist, who was a Treasury representative at the Versailles peace conference, and published his views in *The Economic Consequences of the Peace*. His *Treatise on Money* (1930) and *The General Theory of Employment, Interest and Money* (1936) influenced economic thought all over the world.

Khrushchev, Nikita Sergeyevich (1894–1971), Russian statesman who became leader of the Soviet Union soon after the death of Stalin; first secretary of the Soviet Communist Party, 1953–64; prime minister, 1958–64. After the harsh years of the Stalinist régime he pursued a policy of relaxation both in home and foreign affairs. Relations with America improved but those with China became strained. Advances were made in scientific achievement, notably in the field of space research. In 1964 his posts were taken over by Leonid Brezhnev (first secretary) and Alexei Kosygin (prime minister).

Kierkegaard, Sören (1813–55), Danish philosopher and religious thinker, whose views have influenced contemporary existentialism. His main work is *Either-Or*.

King, Martin Luther (1929–68), American clergyman and Negro integration leader; awarded the 1964 Nobel peace prize for his consistent support of the principle of non-violence in the coloured people's struggle for civil rights. Assassinated at Memphis, Tennessee.

King, Mackenzie (1874–1950), prime minister of Canada, 1921–5, 1926–30, and 1935–48.

Kingsley, Charles (1819–75), English clergyman and novelist, author of *Hypatia*, *Westward Ho!*, *Hereward the Wake* and *The Water Babies*.

Kipling, Rudyard (1865–1936), British writer, b. Bombay. His vivid work portrays contemporary British rule in India and includes *The Light that Failed*, *Stalky and Co.*, *Kim*, and the *Barrack Room Ballads*. Among his books for children are the *Just So Stories*, *Puck of Pook's Hill* and the *Jungle Books*. Nobel prize 1907.

Kirchhoff, Gustav Robert (1824–87), German mathematical physicist, who with R. W. Bunsen discovered that in the gaseous state each chemical substance emits its own characteristic spectrum (1859). He was able to explain Fraunhofer's map of the solar spectrum. Using the spectroscope, he and Bunsen discovered the elements caesium and rubidium.

Kissinger, Henry (b. 1923), American Secretary of State 1973–7 and special adviser on national security affairs to Richard Nixon; inventor of shuttle-service diplomacy. Played active role in peace missions to the Middle East, Vietnam and Southern Africa and in SALT negotiations with the Soviet Union. Shared Nobel peace prize for 1973 with Le Duc Tho.

Kitchener of Khartoum, 1st Earl (Horatio Herbert Kitchener) (1850–1916), English general. In 1898 he won back the Sudan for Egypt by his victory at Omdurman. He served in the South African war; and in the first world war he was secretary of war, 1914–16. He was drowned on his way to Russia.

Klee, Paul (1879–1940), Swiss artist, whose paintings, in a restless, experimental period, are small-scale, delicate dream-world fantasies of poetical content.

Klemperer, Otto (1885–1973), German-born conductor, renowned as interpreter of the Beethoven symphonies. Expelled by the Nazis he became an American citizen and returned to Europe in 1946. He had been principal conductor of the Philharmonic Orchestra since 1959.

Kneller, Sir Godfrey (1646–1723), portrait painter, b. at Lübeck, who settled in England and was patronised by English sovereigns from Charles II to George I.

Knox, John (1514–72), Scottish reformer, b. near Haddington. While in exile at Geneva he was influenced by Calvin. On return to Scotland he was a leader of the reforming party against Mary, Queen of Scots. He wrote a *History of the Reformation in Scotland*.

Koch, Robert (1843–1910), German bacteriologist who discovered the bacillus of tuberculosis, and worked on cholera and cattle diseases.

Kodály, Zoltán (1882–1967), Hungarian composer and teacher. He worked with Bartok in the collection of folk-tunes. *See* Section E.

Kokoschka, Oskar (1886–1980), Austrian portrait and landscape painter, who, after teaching in Dresden, in 1938 settled in England.

Koniev, Ivan Stepanovich (b. 1897), Russian general of the second world war and commander of the Warsaw Pact forces in the 1950s.

Korolyov, Sergei (1907–66), Russian space scientist, who designed the world's first earth satellite, the first manned spaceship and the first moon rocket.

Kosciusko, Tadeusz (1746–1817), Polish patriot. After experience gained in America in the War of Independence, he led his countrymen against Russia in 1792 and 1794 in opposition to the partition of Poland.

Kossuth, Louis (1802–94), Hungarian patriot, who in 1848 led a rising of his countrymen against the Hapsburg dynasty, but had to flee to Turkey and later to England.

Kosygin, Alexei Nikolayevich (1904–80), succeeded Nikita Khrushchev as chairman of the Council of Ministers of the U.S.S.R. (prime minister) in 1964; key technocrat and economic organiser; resigned on health grounds, 1980.

Krebs, Sir Hans (1900–81), British biochemist, b. Germany. Taught at Cambridge and Sheffield and became Professor of Biology at Oxford in 1954. Nobel prize 1953.

Kreisler, Fritz (1875–1962), Austrian violinist, who composed violin music and an operetta. He became an American citizen in 1943.

Krenek, Ernst (b. 1900), Austrian composer of partly Czech descent, whose compositions cover a wide range, including the jazz opera *Jonny spielt auf*. He settled in America in 1938.

Kropotkin, Peter, Prince (1842–1921), Russian anarchist, geographer and explorer, who was imprisoned for favouring the political action of a working men's association, but escaped to England. He wrote on socialistic and geographical subjects. Returned to Russia in 1917.

Kruger, Stephanus Johannes Paulus (1825–1904), Boer leader, who in 1881 was appointed head of the provisional government against Britain, and later president. When the war of 1899–1902 turned against the Boers, he vainly sought help in Europe.

Krupp, Alfred (1812–87), founder of the German gun factories at Essen. He installed in a disused factory left him by his father a new steam-engine from England, began to make cast steel, and from 1844 specialised in armaments. The firm's factories made the Big Bertha guns which shelled Paris in 1918. His great-grandson Alfried (b. 1907) was tried as a war criminal in 1948.

Krylov, Ivan Andreyevich (1768–1844), Russian writer of fables who has been called the Russian La Fontaine.

Kubelik, Jan (1880–1940), Czech violinist who at the age of 12 played in public. His son **Rafael** (b. 1914) was musical director of the Royal Opera House, Covent Garden, 1955–8.

Kublai Khan (1216–94), grandson of Genghis Khan, was the first Mongol emperor of China. He extended the Mongol empire by conquest, and lived in unparalleled splendour. His court was described by Marco Polo and is the subject of a poem by Coleridge.

L

La Fayette, Marie Joseph Paul Roch Yves Gilbert du Motier, Marquis de (1757–1834), French soldier and statesman. He fought for the colonists in the American War of Independence; and in the 1789 French revolution he proposed a declaration of rights and was commander of the National Guard till his moderation made him unpopular. When the monarchy was restored he was an opposition leader, and took part in the revolution of 1830.

La Fontaine, Jean de (1621–95), French poet and fabulist, b. in Champagne, a friend of Molière, Boileau, and Racine, all brilliant writers of the reign of Louis XIV.

Lagerlöf, Selma (1858–1940), Swedish novelist and first woman member of the Swedish Academy, Nobel prizewinner 1909.

Lagrange, Joseph Louis, Comte (1736–1813), French mathematician, of Turin and Paris, whose interest in astronomy led him to distinguish two types of disturbance of members of the solar system, the periodic and the secular. He was called by Frederick the Great to Berlin to succeed Euler.

Lalande, Joseph Jerome LeFrançais de (1732–1807), French astronomer, author of *Traité d'astronomie*.

Lamarck, Jean Baptiste Pierre Antoine de Monet de (1744–1829), French biologist whose explanation of evolution was that new organs are brought into being by the needs of the organism in adapting to its environment and that the new characters acquired during its life-time can be passed on to the offspring through heredity, resulting in evolutionary change. *See* **F30**.

Lamb, Charles (1775–1834), English essayist, b. London. A clerk in the East India Office, he devoted his life to his sister Mary, who was of unstable mind. He is chiefly known for his *Essays of Elia*, and his letters, which have a blend of humour and tenderness.

Lambert, Constant (1905–51), English composer and critic, and conductor of Sadler's Wells ballet. His *Rio Grande* is in jazz idiom.

Landor, Walter Savage (1775–1864), English writer, b. Warwick, remembered for his *Imaginary Conversations* and poems.

Landseer, Sir Edwin (1802–73), English animal painter, b. London. He painted the *Monarch of the Glen* and designed the lions in Trafalgar Square.

Lane, Edward William (1801–76), English Arabic scholar, translator of the *Arabian Nights*.

Lanfranc (*c.* 1005–89), ecclesiastic. B. at Pavia, he became a prior in Normandy, and in 1070 archbishop of Canterbury, in which office he was energetic.

Lang, Andrew (1844–1912), Scottish man of letters, whose output includes *Myth, Ritual and Religion*, poems, fairy-tales, and fiction.

Lang, 1st Baron (Cosmo Gordon Lang) (1864–1945), was archbishop of Canterbury, 1928–42.

Langland, William (1330?–1400?), English poet, probably educated at Malvern, author of *The Vision of Piers the Plowman*.

Langton, Stephen (1151–1228), archbishop of Canterbury, and adviser to the insurgent barons who induced King John to grant Magna Carta.

Lansbury, George (1859–1940), British Labour politician, founder of the *Daily Herald*. He improved London's amenities.

Lâo Tsze (old philosopher) (*c.* 600 B.C.), traditional founder of Taosim in China. *See* **Section J**.

Laplace, Pierre Simon, Marquis de (1749–1827), French mathematician and astronomer, author of *Celestial Mechanics* (1799–1825). He advanced the hypothesis that the solar system had condensed out of a vast rotating gaseous nebula.

La Rochefoucauld, François, Duc de (1613–80), French writer, author of *Reflections and Moral Maxims*.

Lasker, Emanuel (1868–1941), German chess player, world champion, 1894–1921.

Lassalle, Ferdinand (1825–64), German socialist who took part in the revolutionary movement of 1848 and organised workers to press for political rights.

Lassus, Orlandus (Lasso, Orlando di) (*c.* 1532–94), Flemish composer and choirmaster, contemporary of Palestrina, writer of *chansons*, madrigals, and sacred music. *See* **Section E**.

Latimer, Hugh (*c.* 1485–1555), English Protestant martyr, became bishop of Worcester in 1535, and was executed under Queen Mary.

Laud, William (1573–1645), archbishop of Canterbury and adviser to Charles I. His attempt to get conformity for his high church policy made him unpopular and he was impeached and beheaded.

Lauder, Sir Harry (1870–1950), Scottish comic singer of wide popularity. He also wrote *Roamin' in the Gloamin'*.

Laval, Pierre (1883–1945), French politician who collaborated with the German occupation in the second world war and was subsequently tried and executed.

Lavery, Sir John (1850–1941), Irish portrait painter.

Lavoisier, Antoine Laurent (1743–94), French chemist, b. Paris, was the first to establish the

fact that combustion is a form of chemical action. We owe the word *oxygen* to him. He perished in the French Revolution.

Law, Andrew Bonar (1858–1923), Conservative politician, prime minister 1922–3.

Lawrence, David Herbert (1885–1930), English poet and novelist, b. Notts., a miner's son. He tried to interpret emotion on a deeper level of consciousness. His works, which have had wide influence, include *The White Peacock*, *Sons and Lovers*, *The Rainbow*, *Women in Love*, and *Lady Chatterley's Lover*; his plays had to wait half a century before coming to the stage in the 1960's.

Lawrence, Sir Thomas (1769–1830), English portrait painter.

Lawrence, Thomas Edward (1888–1935) (Lawrence of Arabia), British soldier who led the Arabs against the Turks in the war of 1914–18, and wrote *The Seven Pillars of Wisdom*.

Leacock, Stephen (1869–1944), Canadian humorist.

Leavis, Frank Raymond (1895–1978), British critic, who edited *Scrutiny*, 1932–63, and whose works include *The Great Tradition*, *D. H. Lawrence*, *Novelist*, and "*Anna Karenina*" *and Other Essays*.

Lecky, William Edward Hartpole (1838–1903), Irish historian, author of *England in the Eighteenth Century*.

Leclerc, Jacques Philippe (Philippe, Comte de Hauteclouge) (1902–47), French general. He led a Free French force in Africa in the second world war and liberated Paris in 1944. He died in a plane crash.

Le Corbusier (1887–1965), pseudonym of Charles Édouard Jeanneret, Swiss architect, whose books and work (especially his Unité d'Habitation at Marseilles and the new Punjab capital at Chandigarh) have widely influenced town-planning.

Le Duc Tho (b. 1911), member of the Politburo of the N. Vietnamese Workers' Party who was his country's chief negotiator at the Vietnam truce talks 1970–3. He would not accept the 1973 Nobel peace prize awarded jointly with Dr. Kissinger until peace had "really been restored in S. Vietnam."

Lee of Fareham, 1st Viscount (Arthur Hamilton Lee) (1868–1947), British politician who presented Chequers Court to the nation as prime minister's residence.

Lee, Robert Edward (1807–70), American Confederate general in the Civil War, who made the surrender at Appomattox.

Lee, Sir Sidney (1859–1926), English critic, and joint editor of the *Dictionary of National Biography*.

Leech, John (1817–64), humorist artist, b. London, of Irish descent, contributed to *Punch*.

Leibnitz, Gottfried Wilhelm (1646–1716), German philosopher and mathematician, who invented the differential and integral calculus (1684) independently of Newton whose previous work on the same subject was not published until 1687. It was Leibnitz's nomenclature that was universally adopted.

Leicester, Earl of (Robert Dudley) (1533–88), English soldier, commanded English troops in the Netherlands, 1585–7, without much success, and in 1588 commanded forces assembled against the Armada. He was husband of Amy Robsart.

Leif Ericsson (fl. 1000), discover of Vinland on the north-east coast of America; b. Iceland, son of the Norse explorer, Eric the Red, who colonised Greenland.

Leighton, 1st Baron (Robert Leighton) (1830–96), English painter of wide popularity, whose works include *Paolo and Francesca*. He was also a sculptor.

Lely, Sir Peter (Pieter van der Faes) (1618–80), Dutch painter who settled in London and painted court portraits.

Lenin (Vladimir Ilyich Ulyanov) (1870–1924), Russian revolutionary leader and statesman. From 1893 to 1917 he worked underground in Russia and abroad for the revolutionary cause. During this time the Social-Democratic party was formed; within it developed an uncompromising revolutionary group, the Bolsheviks, and of this group Lenin was the leading spirit. In April 1917 he and his fellow exiles returned; after the November revolution he headed the new government having to face both war and anarchy. In 1921 his "new economic policy" somewhat modified the intensive drive towards planned industrial development. He was born in Simbirsk (now Ulyanovsk) on the middle Volga, the son of the local inspector of education. His body lies embalmed in Red Square, Moscow.

Leonardo da Vinci (1452–1519), Italian artist and man of science, son of a Florentine lawyer and a peasant. He described himself (when applying to Lodovico Sforza, Duke of Milan, for the post of city planner) as painter, architect, philosopher, poet, composer, sculptor, athlete, mathematician, inventor, and anatomist. His artistic output is small in quantity, and he is best known for his *Last Supper* in the refectory of Santa Maria delle Grazie in Milan and his *Mona Lisa* in the Louvre. He recorded his scientific work in unpublished notebooks written from right to left in mirror writing. The anatomy of the body (himself carrying out dissections), the growth of the child in the womb, the laws of waves and currents, and the laws of flight, all were studied by this astonishing man who believed nothing but had to see for himself. Although he was much admired, few people in his time had any notion of his universal genius.

Leoncavallo, Ruggiero (1858–1919), Italian composer of the opera *Pagliacci*.

Leonidas was king of Sparta at the time of the invasion of Greece by Xerxes (480 B.C.), and led the defence of the pass of Thermopylae, where he fell.

Lermontov, Mikhail Yurevich (1814–41), Russian poet and novelist, exiled to the Caucasus for a revolutionary poem addressed to Tsar Nicholas I on the death of Pushkin. He has been called the poet of the Caucasus. His novel *A Hero of Our Time* was written at St. Petersburg. He lost his life in a duel.

Le Sage, Alain René (1668–1747), French author, b. in Brittany, who wrote *Gil Blas* and *Le Diable Boiteux*. He was also a dramatist and his plays include *Turcaret*.

Lesseps, Ferdinand, Vicomte de (1805–94), French engineer who while serving as vice-consul at Alexandria conceived a scheme for a canal across the Suez isthmus; the work was completed in 1869. He also projected the original Panama canal scheme, which failed.

Lessing, Gotthold Ephraim (1729–81), German philosopher, dramatist, and critic, noted for his critical work *Laokoon* and his play *Minna von Barnhelm*.

Leucippus (fl. 440 B.C.), Greek philosopher, founder with Democritus of atomism, a theory of matter more nearly that of modern science than any put forward in ancient times. One of his sayings survives: "Naught occurs at random, but everything for a reason and of necessity."

Leverhulme, 1st Viscount (William Hesketh Lever) (1851–1925), British industrialist and philanthropist. He founded Lever Bros. which later became Unilever Ltd., and was a practical exponent of industrial partnership. He gave Lancaster House to the nation.

Leverrier, Urbain Jean Joseph (1811–77), French astronomer who, working independently of J. C. Adams of Cambridge, anticipated the existence of the planet Neptune which was later revealed by telescopic search.

Lévi-Strauss, Claude (b. 1908), French social anthropologist, b. Belgium, exponent of the theory of symbolic structures. He has written works on anthropology, religion, myths and language. The fourth and final vol. of his *Introduction to a Science of Mythology* about the myths and rituals of American Indians was published in 1981.

Lewis, Sinclair (1885–1951), American writer of novels satirising small-town life and philistinism. His works include *Main Street*, *Babbitt* and *Elmer Gantry*. Nobel prizewinner 1931.

Liaquat Ali Khan (1895–1951), leader of the Moslem League (1946) and first premier of Pakistan in 1947. He was assassinated.

Lie, Trygve (1896–1968), Norwegian politician who became secretary-general of the United Nations, 1946–52.

Li Hung Chang (1823–1901), Chinese statesman, who though enlightened, was unable to secure

much modernisation and had to cede Formosa to Japan in 1895.

Lilburne, John (1614–57), English agitator and pamphleteer, leader of the Levellers in the Civil War period.

Linacre, Thomas (*c.* 1460–1524), English humanist and physician, who translated Galen's works and founded the College of Physicians.

Lincoln, Abraham (1809–65), American president. B. in Kentucky, he became a lawyer and was returned to Congress from Illinois in 1846. He was a leader of the Republican party which was formed in 1856 to oppose slavery. He became president in 1861, in which year the Confederate States proposed to withdraw from the Union, and war broke out. The phrase "government of the people, by the people, for the people" comes from his Gettysburg speech of 1863. He was assassinated in 1865.

Lind, Jenny (1820–87), Swedish singer, popular in Europe, and known as the Swedish nightingale. She founded musical scholarships.

Linnaeus (1707–78), Swedish botanist, remembered for his system of defining living things by two Latin names, the first being its *genus*, and the second its *species*. His method is expounded in *Philosophia Botanica* (1751). In 1757 he was ennobled as Karl von Linné. He studied, taught and died at Uppsala.

Lippi, Fra Filippo (1406–69), Italian artist, b. Florence. Frescoes in Prato cathedral are his main work. His son **Filippino** (1457–1504) finished Masaccio's frescoes in the Carmine, Florence, and executed others, for instance in Santa Maria Novella.

Lippmann, Gabriel (1845–1921), French physicist who invented a capillary electrometer and was a pioneer in colour photography. Nobel prizewinner 1908.

Lippmann, Walter (1889–1974), American journalist of influence, writing for the New York *Herald Tribune*, 1931–62.

Lipton, Sir Thomas Johnstone (1850–1931), Scottish business man and philanthropist. B. Glasgow, he emigrated to America, but returned to Scotland and established extensive chainstores for groceries. He unsuccessfully competed in yachting for the America's Cup.

Lister, Baron (Joseph Lister) (1827–1912), English surgeon, son of **J. J. Lister** (1786–1869), an amateur microscopist. He founded antiseptic surgery (1865) which greatly reduced mortality in hospitals.

Liszt, Franz (1811–86), Hungarian pianist and composer. His daughter Cosima became the wife of Hans von Bülow and later of Wagner. *See* **Section E**.

Litvinov, Maxim (1876–1952), Russian diplomat, of revolutionary origin, who first as ambassador in London, then as commissar for foreign affairs, and 1941–3 ambassador to the U.S., gained respect and understanding for his country.

Livingstone, David (1813–73), Scottish explorer in Africa. He discovered the course of the Zambesi, the Victoria Falls and Lake Nyasa (now Lake Malawi), and roused opinion against the slave trade. At one time believed lost, he was found by Stanley (*q.v.*) on 10 Nov. 1871.

Lloyd-George of Dwyfor, 1st Earl (David Lloyd George) (1863–1945), Liberal statesman of Welsh origin. He was M.P. for Caernarvon, 1890–1944; and as chancellor of the exchequer he introduced social insurance, 1908–11. The war of 1914–18 obliged him to become a war premier (superseding Asquith), and he was subsequently one of the main figures at the peace conference. In 1921 he conceded the Irish Free State. His daughter, **Lady Megan Lloyd George**, was M.P. for many years, latterly for the Labour Party.

Locke, John (1632–1704), English liberal philosopher and founder of empiricism, the doctrine that all knowledge is derived from experience. His chief work in theoretical philosophy, *Essay Concerning Human Understanding*, was written just before the revolution of 1688 and published in 1690. Other writings include *Letters on Toleration*, *Treatises on Government*, and *Education*.

Lombroso, Cesare (1836–1909), Italian criminologist, whose *L'uomo delinquente* maintained the existence of a criminal type distinguishable from the normal.

Lomonosov, Mikhail Vasilievich (1711–65),

Russian philologist and poet who systematised Russian grammar and orthography.

London, Jack (1876–1916), American author of adventure tales such as *Call of the Wild*.

Longfellow, Henry Wadsworth (1807–82), American poet, popular in his lifetime, author of *The Golden Legend* and *Hiawatha*.

Lope de Vega Carpio, Félix (1562–1635), Spanish writer of immense output. First a ballad-writer, he took to play-writing and founded the Spanish drama. The number of his plays is said to have been 1,500, the earlier ones historical, the later ones dealing with everyday life; but most are lost.

Lorca, Federico Garcia (1899–1936), Spanish poet and dramatist of Andalusia. Among his works are *Llanto por Ignacio Sánchez Mejías*, an unforgettable lament on the death of a bullfighter, and *Canción de Jinete* with its haunting refrain, "Cordoba, far away and alone." He was brutally murdered by Franco sympathisers at the outbreak of the civil war.

Louis IX (1214–70), St. Louis, King of France. Of saintly character (as described in Joinville's *Memoirs*), he also carried out practical reforms. He died on crusade.

Louis XIV (1638–1715), King of France. A despotic ruler, builder of Versailles, he also dominated the Europe of his day; but he sowed the seeds of future trouble for France by his exhausting wars. He revoked the Edict of Nantes which had given religious freedom to the Huguenots since 1598. His reign, however, was a great period for literature.

Louis XV (1710–74), King of France. Extravagant and self-indulgent, his reign marked a declining period for the monarchy, but produced some fine art.

Louis XVI (1754–93), King of France. Well-meaning but incapable, this king saw the outbreak of the French revolution of 1789, in which he and his queen Marie Antoinette were executed.

Louis, Joe (Joseph Louis Barrow) (1914–81), American Negro boxer, who became world heavyweight champion in 1936, successfully defending his title 26 times.

Low, Archibald Montgomery (1888–1956), British scientist who worked in varied fields, including wireless, television, and anti-aircraft and anti-tank apparatus.

Low, Sir David (1891–1963), British cartoonist, b. New Zealand, associated with the *Evening Standard* and later the *Guardian*; creator of Colonel Blimp.

Lowell, Robert (1917–77), American poet, author of the verse play *The Old Glory*, and *Life Studies*, an autobiographical volume in verse and prose.

Loyola, St. Ignatius (1491–1556), Spanish founder of the Jesuits, a missionary order working directly under the Pope.

Lucretius (99–55 B.C.), Roman poet, author of *De rerum natura*, a long philosophical poem advocating moral truth without religious belief.

Ludendorff, Erich (1865–1937), German general who directed German strategy in the first world war.

Lugard, 1st Baron (Frederick John Dealtry Lugard) (1858–1945), British colonial administrator in Africa, especially Nigeria, and exponent of the system of indirect rule through native chiefs.

Lukács, Georg (1885–1971), Hungarian writer, Marxist thinker and literary critic. His ideas are expounded in *History and Class Consciousness* (1923), *Studies in European Realism* (1946, Eng. tr. 1950), *The Historical Novel* (1955, Eng. tr. 1962).

Luther, Martin (1483–1546), German Protestant reformer. After spending time in a monastery, he was ordained priest (1507), and lectured at Wittenberg university. In 1517 he protested against the sale of indulgences; and when summoned before the Diet of Worms made a memorable defence. He was protected by the Elector of Saxony, and translated the Bible. German Protestantism culminated in the Augsburg confession (1530). *See also* **Lutheranism, Section J.**

Luthuli, Albert (1899–1967), African non-violent resistance leader, an ex-Zulu chief. Killed in train accident. Nobel prize for peace 1960.

Lutyens, Sir Edwin Landseer (1869–1944), English architect both of country houses and public buildings; designed the cenotaph, Whitehall; city plan and viceroy's house, New Delhi, British Embassy, Washington and Liverpool Roman catholic cathedral.

Lyell, Sir Charles (1797–1875), Scottish geologist, whose *Principles of Geology* (1830–33) postulated gradual geological change and helped to shape Darwin's ideas. His terminology—Pliocene (*Greek* = more recent), Miocene (less recent) and Eocene (dawn)—is still in use.

Lysenko, Trofim (1898–1976), Russian biologist who maintained that environmental experiences can change heredity somewhat in the manner suggested by Lamarck. After the death of Stalin his novel theories were severely criticised.

Lytton, 1st Baron (Edward George Earle Lytton Bulwer-Lytton) (1803–73), English novelist and playwright, author of *The Last Days of Pompeii*.

M

Macadam, John Loudon (1756–1836), Scottish inventor of the "macadamising" system of road repair.

MacArthur, Douglas (1880–1964), American general. He defended the Philippines against the Japanese in the second world war, and was relieved of his command in 1951 in the Korean war.

Macaulay of Rothley, 1st Baron (Thomas Babington Macaulay) (1800–59), English historian, poet and Indian civil servant. His poems include *Lays of Ancient Rome*. In India he reformed the education system.

Macaulay, Zachary (1768–1838), anti-slavery agitator, father of the above.

Macbeth (d. 1057), Scottish king, married Gruoch, granddaughter of Kenneth, king of Alban. He was mormaer of Moray, succeeding Duncan in 1040 after killing him in fair fight. His reign of seventeen years was prosperous, but he was killed by Duncan's son, Malcolm, in 1057. Shakespeare's play is based on the inaccurate *Chronicle* of Holinshed.

MacDiarmid, Hugh (1892–1978), pseudonym of Christopher Murray Grieve, Scottish poet, leader of the Scottish literary renaissance; author of *A Drunk Man Looks at the Thistle*.

Macdonald, Flora (1722–90), Scottish Jacobite heroine who saved the life of Prince Charles Edward after the defeat at Culloden Moor in 1746.

Macdonald, Sir John Alexander (1815–91), Canadian statesman, first prime minister of the Dominion of Canada.

MacDonald, James Ramsay (1866–1937), Labour politician of Scottish origin, premier 1924 and 1929–31; also of a coalition 1931–5. His action over the financial crisis of 1931 divided his party.

MacDonald, Malcolm (1901–81), son of above, held positions overseas in the Commonwealth, the last as special representative in Africa.

Machiavelli, Niccolò (1467–1527), Florentine Renaissance diplomat and theorist of the modern state. His book *The Prince* (1513), dedicated to Lorenzo, Duke of Urbino, is concerned with the reality of politics—what rulers must do to retain power. His *Discourses* is more republican and liberal.

Mackail, John William (1859–1945), British classical scholar, translator of the *Odyssey*.

Mackenzie, Sir Compton (1883–1972), British writer, whose works include *Carnival*, *Sinister Street*, and a monumental autobiography.

McLuhan, Herbert Marshall (1911–80), Canadian author of a number of books on contemporary communications, including *The Gutenberg Galaxy*, *The Mechanical Bride*. *See* **Section J.**

Macmillan, Harold (b. 1894), British Conservative statesman, prime minister 1957–63; During his premiership came the crises of the Berlin Wall and the Cuban missiles (in which his personal diplomacy played an influential role), de Gaulle's veto to our entry into Europe, the signing of the Partial Test-Ban Treaty and his "wind of change" speech which hailed African independence. Chancellor of Oxford University (1960), O.M. 1976. Created Earl of Stockton, 1984.

McMillan, Margaret (1860–1931), Scottish educational reformer, b. New York, and pioneer of open-air nursery schools.

Macneice, Louis (1907–63), British poet, playwright, and translator.

Macready, William Charles (1793–1873), British actor and manager, especially associated with Shakespearean roles.

Maeterlinck, Maurice (1862–1949), Belgian man of letters, whose plays include *La Princesse Maleine*, *Pelléas et Mélisande*, and *L'Oiseau Bleu*. Nobel prizewinner 1911. He also did scientific work on bees.

Magellan, Ferdinand (*c.* 1480–1521), Portuguese navigator, and commander of the first expedition (1519) to sail round the world.

Mahler, Gustav (1860–1911), Austrian composer and conductor; a writer of symphonies and songs, a classical romantic, much influenced by Anton Bruckner and Wagner. *See* **Section E.**

Mahavira, Vardhamana Jnatriputra (6th cent. B.C.), Indian historical (as opposed to legendary) founder of Jainism, which teaches the sacredness of all life. *See* **Jainism, Section J.**

Maintenon, Françoise d'Aubigné, Marquise de (1635–1719), second wife of Louis XIV. Her first husband was the poet Scarron.

Makarios III (1913–77), Greek Orthodox archbishop and Cypriot national leader. Deported by the British to the Seychelles in 1956, he returned in 1957 to become president of the newly independent republic in 1960.

Malibran, Marie Félicité (1808–36), Spanish mezzo-soprano.

Malik, Yakov Alexandrovich (1906–80), Soviet diplomat; permanent representative at U.N. 1949–52, 1967–76; ambassador to Britain 1953–60; deputy foreign minister 1960–7.

Malory, Sir Thomas (*c.* 1430–71), English writer. From earlier sources and legends of King Arthur and the Knights of the Round Table, he compiled the *Morte d'Arthur* printed by Caxton in 1485.

Malraux, André (1895–1976), French novelist and politician. His works include *La Condition humaine*, *L'Espoir*, and *Psychologie de l'art* (tr. in 2 vols., *Museum without Walls*, and *The Creative Act*). Served under de Gaulle.

Malthus, Thomas Robert (1766–1834), English clergyman and economist who in his gloomy essay *The Principle of Population* contended that population tends to increase faster than the means of subsistence and that its growth could only be checked by moral restraint or by disease and war. *See* **Malthusianism, Section J.**

Mandela, Nelson Rolihlahia (b. 1918), South African lawyer and politician; son of chief of Tembu tribe; imprisoned on political grounds since 1964.

Manet, Edouard (1832–83), French painter. His Impressionist pictures include *Olympia* and *Un bar aux Folies-Bergères* (the latter at the Courtauld).

Mann, Thomas (1875–1955), German writer who won world recognition at the age of 25 with his novel *Buddenbrooks*. His liberal humanistic outlook had developed sufficiently by 1930 for him to expose national socialism. He left Germany in 1933 to live in Switzerland, then settled in the U.S. Other works are *The Magic Mountain*, and the *Joseph* tetralogy. Nobel prizewinner 1929.

Mann, Tom (1856–1941), British Labour leader for more than fifty years.

Manning, Henry Edward (1808–92), English cardinal; archbishop of Westminster 1865–92. He was an Anglican churchman before he entered the church of Rome.

Mansfield, Katherine (Kathleen Beauchamp) (1890–1923), short-story writer, b. Wellington, New Zealand, whose work was influenced by the short stories of Chekhov. Her second husband was John Middleton Murry, literary critic.

Manson, Sir Patrick (1844–1922), Scottish physician, the first to formulate the hypothesis that the malarial parasite was transmitted by the mosquito. His joint work with Sir Ronald Ross rendered habitable vast areas of the earth hitherto closed.

Manuzio, Aldo Pio (1450–1515), Italian printer, founder of the Aldine press in Venice, which for just over a century issued books famed for their beautiful type and bindings.

Manzoni, Alessandro (1785–1873), Italian novelist and poet, b. Milan, whose historical novel *I Promessi Sposi* (The Betrothed) won European reputation.

Mao Tse-tung (1893–1976), Chinese national and Communist leader. B. in Hunan, of rural origin. As a young man he worked as assistant librarian at Peking University. He understood how to win peasant support for a national and progressive movement. Attacked by Chiang Kai-shek, he led his followers by the "long march" to N.W. China, whence later they issued to defeat both Japanese and Chiang and proclaim a People's Republic in 1949, and later to promote the "great leap forward" of 1958–9 (the commune movement). He stood for an egalitarian democratic society, unbureaucratic, with revolutionary momentum. He was much to the fore in the "cultural revolution" which lasted from 1965 to 1969. *See* **Section C, Part II**, and **Maoism, Section J.**

Marat, Jean Paul (1743–93), French revolution leader, largely responsible for the reign of terror, and assassinated by Charlotte Corday.

Marconi, Guglielmo, Marchese (1874–1937), Italian inventor and electrical engineer who developed the use of radio waves as a practical means of communication. In 1895 he sent long-wave signals over a distance of a mile, and in 1901 received in Newfoundland the first transatlantic signals sent out by his station in Cornwall, thus making the discovery that radio waves can bend around the spherically-shaped earth. Nobel prizewinner 1909.

Marcus Aurelius Antoninus (121–180 A.D.), Roman emperor and Stoic philosopher of lofty character, whose *Meditations* are still read.

Marcuse, Herbert (1898–1979), political philosopher. B. Berlin, he emigrated to the U.S. during the Nazi regime. A critic of Western industrial society, he saw the international student protest movement as the catalyst of revolutionary change.

Maria Theresa (1717–80), Empress, daughter of the Hapsburg Charles VI. Able and of strong character, she fought unsuccessfully to save Silesia from Prussian annexation. She promoted reforms in her dominions. She married the Duke of Lorraine and had 16 children.

Marie Antoinette (1755–93), Queen of France, was daughter of the above and wife of Louis XVI; accused of treason, she and her husband were beheaded in the French revolution.

Marie Louise (1791–1847), daughter of Francis I of Austria, became the wife of Napoleon and bore him a son (Napoleon II).

Marius, Caius (157–86 B.C.), Roman general who defended Gaul from invasion; later civil war forced him to flee from Rome, and on his return he took terrible revenge.

Mark Antony. *See* **Antonius, Marcus.**

Marlborough, 1st Duke of (John Churchill) (1650–1722), English general, victor of Blenheim, Ramillies, Oudenarde and Malplaquet. His wife, Sarah Jennings, was a favourite of Queen Anne.

Marlowe, Christopher (1564–93), English dramatist and precursor of Shakespeare. His plays include *Dr. Faustus*, *Tamburlaine the Great*, *Edward II*, and *The Jew of Malta*. His early death was due to a tavern brawl.

Marryat, Frederick (1792–1848), English author of sea and adventure stories, including *Peter Simple*, *Mr. Midshipman Easy*, and *Masterman Ready*. He was a captain in the Royal Navy.

Marshall, George Catlett (1880–1959), American general. U.S. chief of staff 1939–45; originated the Marshall Aid plan for European reconstruction. Nobel prize for peace 1953.

Martial, Marcus Valerius (*c.* 40–104), Roman poet, b. in Spain, remembered for his epigrams.

Marvell, Andrew (1620–78), English poet and political writer. He was Milton's assistant and wrote mainly during the commonwealth.

Marx, Karl (1818–83), German founder of modern international communism, b. Trier of Jewish parentage. He studied law, philosophy and history at the universities of Bonn and Berlin, and later took up the study of economics. In conjunction with his friend Engels he wrote the *Communist Manifesto* of 1848 for the Communist League of which he was the leader. Because of his revolutionary activities he was forced to leave the continent and in 1849 settled in London. Here, mainly while living at 28 Dean Street, Soho, he wrote *Das Kapital*, a deep analysis of the economic laws that govern modern society. In 1864 he helped to found the first International. He ranks as one of the most original and influential thinkers of modern times. He was buried at Highgate cemetery. *See* **Marxism, Section J.**

Mary I (1516–58), Queen of England, was daughter of Henry VIII and Catherine of Aragon. A Roman Catholic, she reversed the religious changes made by her father and brother, and about 300 Protestants were put to death. She married Philip of Spain.

Mary II (1662–94), Queen of England with her husband the Dutch William III. As daughter of James II, she was invited to succeed after the revolution of 1688 and expelled her father.

Mary Stuart, Queen of Scots (1542–87), daughter of James V of Scotland and Mary of Guise, she laid claim to the English succession. She was imprisoned in England by Elizabeth and beheaded. Her husbands were the dauphin of France (d. 1560), Lord Stanley Darnley (murdered 1567) and Bothwell.

Masaryk, Jan Garrigue (1886–1948), Czech diplomat. The son of Thomas, he was Czech minister in London 1925–38, and foreign secretary while his government was in exile in London and after it returned to Prague, 1940–8.

Masaryk, Thomas Garrigue (1850–1937), Czech statesman and independence leader. He was the first president of Czechoslovakia, 1918–35.

Mascagni, Pietro (1863–1945), Italian composer of *Cavalleria Rusticana.*

Masefield, John (1878–1967), English poet. His best-known works are *Salt-Water Ballads* (as a boy he ran away to sea), and *Reynard the Fox.* He became poet laureate in 1930.

Maskelyne, John Nevil (1839–1917), English illusionist. He also exposed spiritualistic frauds.

Massenet, Jules Emile Frédéric (1842–1912), French composer of songs, orchestral suites, oratorios, and operas, among them *Manon* and *Thaïs.*

Massine, Léonide (1896–1979), Russian dancer, one of Diaghilev's choreographers. In 1944 he became a U.S. citizen.

Masters, Edgar Lee (1869–1950), American poet remembered for his *Spoon River Anthology.*

Matisse, Henri (1869–1954), French painter, member of a group known as *Les Fauves* (the wild beasts) for their use of violent colour and colour variation to express form and relief. A number of his paintings are in the Moscow Museum of Western Art.

Matsys (Massys), Quentin (1466–1530), Flemish painter, b. Louvain, settled Antwerp; he worked at a time when Italian influence was gaining ground. His *Money-changer, and his Wife* is in the Louvre.

Maugham, William Somerset (1874–1965), British writer, b. Paris. He practised as a doctor till the success of *Liza of Lambeth* (1897) followed by *Of Human Bondage.* He was a master of the short story and his work reflects his travels in the East. In both world wars he served as a British agent.

Maupassant, Guy de (1850–93), French writer whose novels and short stories show penetrating realism. His stories include *Boule de Suif, Le Maison Tellier,* and *La Parure* (The Necklace).

Mauriac, François (1885–1970), French writer whose novels deal with moral problems and include *Le Baiser au Lépreux* and the play *Asmodée.* Nobel prizewinner 1952.

Maurois, André (Emile Herzog) (1885–1967), French writer whose works include lives of Shelley and Disraeli.

Maxim, Sir Hiram Stevens (1840–1916), American inventor of the automatic quick-firing gun.

Maxton, James (1885–1946), Scottish Labour politician and pacifist; entered parliament 1922; chairman of I.L.P. 1926–31, 1934–9.

Maxwell, James Clerk (1831–79), Scottish physicist. He wrote his first scientific paper at 15, and after teaching in Aberdeen and London became first Cavendish professor of experimental physics at Cambridge. His mathematical mind, working on the discoveries of Faraday and others, gave physics a celebrated set of equations for the basic laws of electricity and magnetism. His work revolutionised fundamental physics.

Mazarin, Jules (1602–61), cardinal and minister of France was b. in Italy. In spite of opposition from the nobles, he continued Richelieu's work of building up a strong monarchy.

Mazeppa, Ivan Stepanovich (1644–1709), Cossack nobleman, b. Ukraine (then part of Poland, before E. Ukraine passed to Russia, 1667). He fought unsuccessfully for independence allying himself with Charles XII of Sweden against Peter I of Russia (Poltava, 1709). According to legend he was punished for intrigue by being tied to the back of a wild horse and sent into the steppes. Byron wrote a poem about him.

Mazzini, Giuseppe (1805–72), Italian patriot. B. Genoa, he advocated a free and united Italy, and from Marseilles he published a journal, *Young Italy.* Expelled from the Continent, he took refuge in London in 1837. In 1848 he returned to Italy, and became dictator of the short-lived Roman republic, which was put down by French forces. His contribution to Italian unity was that of preparing the way.

Mechnikov, Ilya (1845–1916), Russian biologist who discovered that by "phagocytosis" certain white blood cells are capable of ingesting harmful substances such as bacteria (*see* **Diseases of the Blood, Section P**). For his work on immunity he shared the 1908 Nobel prize for medicine.

Medawar, Sir Peter Brien (b. 1915), British zoologist, author of *The Art of the Soluble* and *The Future of Man*; president of the British Association 1969. Nobel prizewinner 1960. O.M. 1981.

Medici, Florentine family of merchants and bankers who were politically powerful and who patronised the arts. **Cosimo the Elder** (1389–1464) was for over 30 years virtual ruler of Florence. His grandson, **Lorenzo the Magnificent** (1449–92), poet, friend of artists and scholars, governed with munificence. His grandson, **Lorenzo,** was father of **Catherine de' Medici,** Queen of France (*q.v.*). A later **Cosimo** (1519–74) was an able Duke of Florence and then Grand-Duke of Tuscany, which title the Medicis held until 1737.

Méhul, Etienne Nicolas (1763–1817), French operatic composer. *Joseph* is his masterpiece.

Meir, Golda (1898–1978), leading member of the Israeli Labour Party, her premiership included the Six Day and Yom Kippur wars.

Meitner, Lise (1878–1969), co-worker of Otto Hahn (*q.v.*) who interpreted his results (1939) as a fission process.

Melanchthon, Philip (1497–1560), German religious reformer, who assisted Luther, and wrote the first Protestant theological work, *Loci communes.* He drew up the Augsburg confession (1530).

Melba, Nellie (Helen Porter Mitchell) (1861–1931), Australian soprano of international repute, b. near Melbourne.

Melbourne, 2nd Viscount (William Lamb) (1779–1848), English Whig statesman, was premier at the accession of Queen Victoria.

Mendel, Gregor Johann (1822–84), Austrian botanist. After entering the Augustinian monastery at Brünn he became abbot and taught natural history in the school. His main interest was the study of inheritance, and his elaborate observations of the common garden pea resulted in the law of heredity which bears his name. His hypothesis was published in 1866 but no attention was given to it until 1900. *See* **Section F, Part IV.**

Mendeleyev, Dmitri Ivanovich (1834–1907), Russian chemist, first to discover the critical temperatures. He formulated the periodic law of atomic weights (1869) and drew up the periodic table (*see* **Section F**), predicting the properties of elements which might fill the gaps. Element 101 is named after him.

Mendelssohn-Bartholdy, Felix (1809–47), German composer, grandson of Moses Mendelssohn, philosopher. He belongs with Chopin and Schumann to the early 19th cent. classic-romantic school, and his music has delicacy and melodic beauty. He was conductor of the Gewandhaus concerts at Leipzig for a time and often visited England. *See* **Section E.**

Mendès-France, Pierre (1907–82), French politician, premier 1954–5, but defeated on his North African policy. He was a critic of de Gaulle.

Menuhin, Sir Yehudi (b. 1916), world-famous violinist, b. New York of Russian Jewish parentage. He first appeared as soloist at the age of seven and has international repute. Founded a School for musically gifted children. Acquired British citizenship, 1985.

Menzies, Sir Robert Gordon (1894–1978), Australian Liberal statesman, P.M. 1939–41, 1949–66.

Mercator, Gerhardus (Gerhard Kremer) (1512–94), Flemish geographer who pioneered the making of accurate navigational maps. He worked out the map which bears his name in which meridians and parallels of latitude cross each other at right angles, enabling compass bearings to be drawn as straight lines.

Meredith, George (1828–1909), English writer. b. Portsmouth. His novels include *The Ordeal of Richard Feverel*, *The Egoist*, *Evan Harrington*, *Diana of the Crossways*, and *The Amazing Marriage*. His poetry has had renewed attention; the main works are *Modern Love* and *Poems and Lyrics of the Joy of Earth*.

Mesmer, Friedrich Anton (1733–1815), Austrian founder of mesmerism, or animal magnetism. *See* **Mesmerism, Section J**.

Mestrovič, Ivan (1883–1962), Yugoslav sculptor of international repute. He designed the temple at Kossovo. He later lived in England, and examples of his work are in London museums.

Metastasio, Pietro (Pietro Bonaventura Trapassi) (1698–1782), Italian librettist who lived in Vienna and provided texts for Gluck, Handel, Haydn, and Mozart.

Michelangelo (Michelagniolo Buonarroti) (1475–1564), Italian painter, sculptor and poet. Of a poor but genteel Tuscan family, his first interest in sculpture came through his nurse, wife of a stone-cutter. He was apprenticed to Domenico Ghirlandaio. Like Leonardo, he studied anatomy, but instead of spreading his talents over a wide field, he became obsessed with the problem of how to represent the human body. In him, classical idealism, mediaeval religious belief, and renaissance energy met. Perhaps his most impressive work is the ceiling of the Sistine Chapel (a surface of about 6,000 square feet), the *Last Judgement* behind the chapel altar, his marble *Pietà* (St. Peter's) the statue of *David* (Academy, Florence), the great figure of *Moses* (San Pietro in Vincoli, Rome), and the four allegorical figures *Day*, *Night*, *Dawn*, *Twilight* (intended for the tombs of the Medici family at San Lorenzo, Florence).

Michelet, Jules (1798–1874), French historian who wrote a history of France in 24 vols. and of the revolution in 7 vols.

Michelson, Albert Abraham (1852–1931), American physicist, b. Poland. He collaborated with E. W. Morley in an experiment to determine ether drift, the negative result of which was important for Einstein. Nobel prizewinner 1907.

Mickiewicz, Adam (1798–1855), Polish revolutionary poet, author of *The Ancestors* and *Pan Tadeusz*.

Mill, John Stuart (1806–73), English philosopher. A member of Bentham's utilitarian school, he later modified some of its tenets. His main work is *On Liberty*, which advocates social as well as political freedom and warns against the tyranny of the majority. *The Subjection of Women* supported women's rights. He also wrote *Principles of Political Economy*. He was godfather to Bertrand Russell.

Millais, Sir John Everett (1829–96), English artist, b. Southampton; in his earlier years a pre-Raphaelite (*Ophelia*). Later works include *The Boyhood of Raleigh* and *Bubbles*. He married Mrs. Ruskin after the annulment of her marriage.

Millet, Jean François (1814–75), French painter of rural life, sometimes in sombre mood; his works include *The Angelus*.

Millikan, Robert Andrews (1868–1954), American physicist, who determined the charge on the electron and discovered cosmic rays. Nobel prizewinner 1923.

Milne, Alan Alexander (1882–1956), English humorist and poet whose work for children is still widely read.

Milner, 1st Viscount (Alfred Milner) (1854–1925), British administrator, especially in South Africa; author of *England in Egypt*.

Miltiades (d. 489 B.C.), one of the leaders of the Athenian army against the Persians at Marathon.

Milton, John (1608–74), English poet, author of *Paradise Lost*. B. in London, he wrote while still at Cambridge *L'Allegro*, *Il Penseroso*, *Comus*, and *Lycidas*. The Civil War diverted his energies for years to the parliamentary and political struggle, but during this period he defended in *Aereopagitica* the freedom of the press. After he had become blind he wrote *Paradise Lost* and a sonnet *On His Blindness*.

Minot, George Richards (1885–1950), who with W. P. Murphy discovered the curative properties of liver in pernicious anaemia. Shared Nobel prize 1934.

Mirabeau, Gabriel, Honoré Victor Riquetti, Comte de (1749–91), French revolutionary leader. His writings and speeches contributed to the revolution of 1789.

Mistral, Frédéric (1830–1914), French poet, and founder of a Provençal renaissance. His works include *Lou Trésor dóu Félibrige* and a Provençal dictionary. Nobel prizewinner 1904.

Mithridates (c. 132–63 B.C.), King of Pontus, in Asia Minor; after early successes against the Romans was defeated by Pompey.

Mitterand, François Maurice Marie (b. 1916), French socialist politician, proclaimed fourth president of the Fifth Republic, 21 May 1981.

Modigliani, Amedeo (1884–1920), Italian painter and sculptor, b. Livorno. His portraits and figure studies tend to elongation and simplification. He lived mainly in Paris.

Moffatt, James (1870–1944), Scottish divine who translated the Bible into modern English.

Mohammed (570–632), the founder of Islam, the religion of the Moslems, received the revelation of the Koran (their sacred book), and the command to preach, at the age of 40. By his constant proclamation that there was only One God he gathered around him a loyal following, but aroused the hostility of other Meccans, who worshipped idols. The Moslems were forced to flee to Medina in 622, but grew in strength sufficiently to return to Mecca eight years later, and establish the Kaaba as the goal of the pilgrimage in Islam. Mohammed always described himself as only the messenger of God, making it clear that he did not bring a new religion, but recalled people to that announced by other prophets from Noah, through Abraham and Moses, to Jesus. *See* **Islam, Section J**.

Molière (Jean Baptiste Poquelin) (1622–73), French playwright. B. in Paris, he gained experience as a strolling player, and subsequently in Paris, partly in the king's service; he wrote an unsurpassed series of plays varying from farce as in *Les Précieuses ridicules* to high comedy. Among his plays are *Tartuffe*, *Le Misanthrope*, *Le Bourgeois gentilhomme*, *Le Malade imaginaire*, and *Le Médécin malgré lui*.

Molotov, Vyacheslav Mikhailovich (b. 1890), Russian diplomat. He succeeded Litvinov as commissar for foreign affairs, 1939–49, and was chief representative of the Soviet Union at numerous post-war conferences. Expelled from the Communist Party 1964.

Moltke, Helmuth, Count von (1800–91), Prussian general and chief of staff (1858–88) during the period when Prussia successfully united Germany.

Mond, Ludwig (1838–1909), German chemist who in 1867 settled in England as an alkali manufacturer and in partnership with John Brunner successfully manufactured soda by the Solvay process.

Monet, Claude (1840–1926), French painter, leader of the Impressionists, the term being derived in 1874 from his landscape *Impression soleil levant*. He liked painting a subject in the open air at different times of day to show variation in light.

Monier-Williams, Sir Monier (1819–99), English Sanskrit scholar whose works include grammars, dictionaries, and editions of the *Sákuntalá*.

Monk, George, 1st Duke of Albemarle (1608–69), English general and admiral, whose reputation and moderation were mainly responsible for the return of Charles II in 1660.

Monmouth, Duke of (James Scott) (1649–85), English pretender, natural son of Charles II; centre of anti-Catholic feeling against succession of Duke of York (later James II). His troops, mostly peasants, were routed at Sedgemoor (1685) by John Churchill (later Duke of Marlborough). Beheaded on Tower Hill.

Monnet, Jean (1888–1979), French political economist, "father of the Common Market." He drafted the Monnet plan for French economic recovery (1947) and the plan for the establishment of the European Coal and Steel Community, of which he was president 1952–5.

Monroe, James (1758–1831), president of the U.S. He negotiated the purchase of Louisiana from France in 1803 and propounded the doctrine that the American continent should not be colonised by a European power. (At that time however the U.S. could not have enforced it.)

Montagu, Lady Mary Wortley (1689–1762), English writer. From Constantinople where her husband was ambassador she wrote *Letters* of which a complete edition was published 1965–7. She introduced England to the idea of inoculation against smallpox.

Montaigne, Michel de (1533–92), French essayist of enquiring, sceptical and tolerant mind.

Montcalm, Louis Joseph, Marquis de (1712–59), French general, who unsuccessfully commanded the French at Quebec against Wolfe.

Montesquieu, Charles-Louis de Secondat, Baron de la Brède et de (1689–1755), French philosopher. His works include *Lettres persanes*, a satire on contemporary life; and *De l'esprit des lois* giving his political philosophy. The latter was based largely, but to some extent mistakenly, on English practice, and its influence led the U.S. constitution to separate the executive (President) from the legislature (Congress).

Montessori, Maria (1870–1952), Italian educationist, who developed an educational system based on spontaneity.

Monteverdi, Claudio (1567–1643), Italian composer who pioneered in opera. His chief dramatic work is *Orfeo* (1607). *See* **Section E.**

Montezuma II (1466–1520), Aztec emperor of Mexico when the Spanish under Cortés invaded.

Montfort, Simon de, Earl of Leicester (*c.* 1208–65), English statesman. He led the barons in revolt against the ineffective rule of Henry III, but he differed from other rebels in that he summoned a parliamentary assembly to which for the first time representatives came from the towns. He was killed at Evesham.

Montgolfier, the name of two brothers, **Joseph Michel** (1740–1810) and **Jacques Etienne** (1745–99), French aeronauts who constructed the first practical balloon, which flew 6 miles.

Montgomery of Alamein, 1st Viscount (Bernard Law Montgomery) (1887–1976), British field-marshal; commanded 8th Army in North Africa, Sicily, and Italy, 1942–4; commander-in-chief, British Group of Armies and Allied Armies in Northern France, 1944. He served as Deputy Supreme Allied Commander Europe (NATO), 1951–8. Memoirs published in 1958.

Montrose, Marquess of (James Graham) (1612–50), Scottish general. In the Civil War he raised the Highland clansmen for Charles I and won the battles of Tippermuir, Inverlochy, and Kilsyth; but was finally defeated and executed. He was also a poet.

Moody, Dwight Lyman (1837–99), American revivalist preacher, associated with Ira D. Sankey, the "American singing pilgrim."

Moore, George (1852–1933), Irish novelist, author of *Confessions of a Young Man, Esther Waters,* and *Evelyn Innes.*

Moore, Henry (b. 1898), English sculptor in semi-abstract style, son of a Yorkshire coalminer. Examples of his work are to be seen all over the world, in the Tate Gallery, St. Matthew's Church, Northampton, the Unesco building in Paris, in Kensington Gardens and on the site in Chicago where the world's first nuclear reactor was built (1942).

Moore, Sir John (1761–1809), British general, who trained the infantry for the Spanish Peninsular campaigns and conducted a brilliant retreat to Corunna, where he was mortally wounded after defeating the French under Soult.

Moore, Thomas (1779–1852), Irish poet, author of *Irish Melodies, Lalla Rookh,* and *The Epicurean* (novel). He also wrote a life of Byron.

More, Sir Thomas (1478–1535), English writer and statesman. In 1529 he succeeded Wolsey as lord chancellor, but on his refusal to recognise Henry VIII as head of the church he was executed. His *Utopia* describes an ideal state. He was canonised 1935.

Morgan, Sir Henry (*c.* 1635–88), Welsh buccaneer who operated in the Caribbean against the Spaniards, capturing and plundering Panama in 1671. Knighted by Charles II and made deputy-governor of Jamaica.

Morgan, John Pierpont (1837–1913), American financier who built the family fortunes into a vast industrial empire.

Morland, George (1763–1804), English painter of rural life.

Morley, 1st Viscount (John Morley) (1838–1923), English biographer and Liberal politician. He held political office, but is mainly remembered for his life of Gladstone. He also wrote on Voltaire, Rousseau, Burke, and Cobden.

Morley, Thomas (*c.* 1557–1603), English composer of madrigals, noted also for his settings of some of Shakespeare's songs. He was a pupil of Byrd, organist of St. Paul's cathedral, and wrote *Plaine and Easie Introduction to Practicall Music* (1597) which was used for 200 years.

Morris, William (1834–96), English poet and craftsman. His hatred of 19th-cent. ugliness, his belief in human equality, and in freedom and happiness for all, combined to make him a socialist, and he accomplished much for the improvement of domestic decoration. He was a popular lecturer, founded the Socialist League and the Kelmscott Press.

Morrison of Lambeth, Baron (Herbert Morrison) (1888–1965), British Labour statesman. From being an errand-boy, he rose to become leader of the London County Council. During the war he was Home Secretary, and he was deputy prime minister, 1945–51.

Morse, Samuel Finley Breeze (1791–1872), American pioneer in electromagnetic telegraphy and inventor of the dot-and-dash code that bears his name. He was originally an artist.

Mountbatten of Burma, 1st Earl (Louis Mountbatten) (1900–79), British admiral and statesman. In the second world war he became chief of combined operations in 1942. As last viceroy of India, he carried through the transfer of power to Indian hands in 1947 and was the first governor-general of the dominion. He became first sea lord in 1955 and was chief of defence staff 1959–65. His assassination by Irish extremists evoked world-wide horror.

Mozart, Wolfgang Amadeus (1756–91), Austrian composer. B. Salzburg, he began his career at four and toured Europe at six. In 1781 he settled in Vienna, where he became a friend of Haydn and where his best music was written. His genius lies in the effortless outpouring of all forms of music, in the ever-flowing melodies, in the consistent beauty and symmetry of his compositions, and in the exactness of his method. Among the loveliest and grandest works in instrumental music are his three great symphonies in E. flat, G minor, and C (called the "Jupiter"), all written in six weeks in 1788. Three of the greatest operas in musical history are his *Marriage of Figaro* (1786), *Don Giovanni* (1787), and *The Magic Flute* (1791). His last composition, written under the shadow of death, was the *Requiem Mass*, a work of tragic beauty. *See* **Section E.**

Mugabe, Robert Gabriel (b. 1924), first prime minister of independent Zimbabwe after his election victory in March 1980.

Müller, Sir Ferdinand (1825–96), German-born botanist who emigrated to Australia, where he was director of the Melbourne Botanical Gardens, 1857–73, and whence he introduced the eucalyptus into Europe.

Mumford, Lewis (b. 1895), American writer on town-planning and social problems. His works include a tetralogy: *Technics and Civilisation, The Culture of Cities, The Condition of Man,* and *The Conduct of Life; The Myth of the Machine,* and *The Urban Prospect.*

Munnings, Sir Alfred (1878–1959), English painter, especially of horses and sporting subjects.

Murdock, William (1754–1839), Scottish engineer and inventor, the first to make practical use of coal gas as an iluminating agent (introduced at the Soho works, Birmingham, 1800).

Murillo, Bartolomé Esteban (1617–82), Spanish painter, b. Seville, where he founded an Academy. His early works, such as *Two Peasant Boys* (Dulwich) show peasant and street life; his later paintings are religious, *e.g.,* the *Immaculate Conception* in the Prado.

Murray, Gilbert (1866–1957), classical scholar of Australian birth who settled in England. A teacher of Greek at the universities of Glasgow and Oxford, he translated Greek drama so as to bring it within the reach of the general public. His interest in the classics was begun by an English master's enthusiasm at his country school at Mittagong, New South Wales. He was a strong supporter of the League of Nations and the United Nations.

Mussolini, Benito (1883–1945), Fascist dictator of Italy 1922–43. From 1935 an aggressive foreign policy (Abyssinia and Spain) was at first successful, and in June 1940 he entered the war on the side of Hitler. Defeat in North Africa and the invasion of Sicily caused the collapse of his government. He was shot dead by partisans while attempting to escape to Switzerland.

Mussorgsky, Modest Petrovich (1839–81), Russian composer whose masterpiece is the opera *Boris Godunov* after the play by Pushkin. His piano suite *Pictures at an Exhibition* was orchestrated by Ravel. See **Section E.**

N

Nanak (1469–1538), Indian guru or teacher, who tried to put an end to religious strife, teaching that "God is one, whether he be Allah or Rama." His followers are the Sikhs. See **Sikhism, Section J.**

Nansen, Fridtjof (1861–1930), Norwegian explorer. In 1893 his north polar expedition reached the highest latitude till then attained—86° 14′. He published an account called *Farthest North.* He was active in Russian famine relief, 1921. Nobel peace prize 1922.

Napier, John (1550–1617), Scottish mathematician, b. Edinburgh, invented logarithms (published 1614) and the modern notation of fractions, improvements in the methods of mathematical expression which helped to advance cosmology and physics.

Napoleon I (Bonaparte) (1769–1821), French emperor and general, of Corsican birth (Ajaccio). Trained in French military schools, he became prominent in the early years of the revolution, with uncertainty at home and war abroad. In 1796 he became commander of the army in Italy and defeated the Austrians, so that France obtained control of Lombardy. He then led an expedition to Egypt but Nelson destroyed his fleet. After further Italian victories, he made a *coup d'état* in 1799, and in 1804 became emperor. Against continuing European opposition, he defeated the Austrians at Austerlitz, and his power in Europe was such that he made his brothers Joseph, Louis, and Jerome kings of Naples, Holland, and Westphalia; but in Spain he provoked the Peninsular War, and his armies were gradually driven back by the Spanish, helped by Wellington; while his invasion of Russia in 1812 ended in a disastrous retreat from Moscow; and in 1814 the Allies forced him to abdicate and retire to Elba. He emerged again in 1815 to be defeated at Waterloo and exiled to St. Helena. His government at home was firm and promoted some reforms (*e.g.,* legal codification), but the country was weakened by his wars. In Europe, in spite of the suffering caused by war, there was some spread of French revolutionary ideas, and equally a reaction against them on the part of authority. The imperial idea lingered in France, and Napoleon's remains were brought to Paris in 1840. He married first Josephine Beauharnais and second Marie Louise of Austria.

Napoleon II (1811–32), son of Napoleon I and Marie Louise.

Napoleon III (1808–73), son of Napoleon I's brother Louis. He returned to France in the revolution of 1848, and in 1851 came to power by a *coup d'état.* In his reign Paris was remodelled. His foreign policy was adventurous (the Crimean war, intervention in Mexico, war against Austria and Italy); but when he was manoeuvred by Bismarck into the Franco-Prussian war and defeated at Sedan he lost his throne and retired to England. His wife was the Spanish Eugénie de Montijo.

Nash, John (1752–1835), English architect who planned Regent Street, laid out Regent's Park, enlarged Buckingham Palace, and designed Marble Arch and the Brighton Pavilion.

Nash, Paul (1889–1946), English painter and designer, official war artist in both world wars. Best-known pictures are *The Menin Road* of 1918 and *Totes Meer* of 1941.

Nash, Walter (1882–1968), New Zealand Labour politician; prime minister 1957–60.

Nasmyth, James (1808–90), Scottish inventor of the steam-hammer, which became indispensable in all large iron and engineering works.

Nasser, Gamal Abdel (1918–70), leader of modern Egypt and of the Arab world. He led the 1954 coup that deposed General Neguib. He became president of the Egyptian Republic in 1956 and of the United Arab Republic in 1958. His nationalisation of the Suez Canal in 1956 precipitated a short-lived attack by Britain and France, Israeli–Arab hostility led to the June war of 1967. He carried out reforms to bring his people out of feudal backwardness, including the building (with Russian help and finance) of the Aswan High Dam.

Needham, Joseph (b. 1900), British biochemist, historian of science, orientalist, author of the monumental work of scholarship *Science and Civilisation in China* (7 vols., 1954–).

Nehru, Pandit Jawaharlal (1889–1964), Indian national leader and statesman, first prime minister and minister of foreign affairs when India became independent in 1947. He studied at Harrow and Cambridge, and was for many years a leading member of the Congress Party, during which time he was frequently imprisoned for political activity. He played a part in the final negotiations for independence. Under his leadership India made technical, industrial, and social advances. In world affairs his influence was for peace and non-alignment. His daughter Indira became India's first woman prime minister in 1966.

Nelson, 1st Viscount (Horatio Nelson) (1758–1805), English admiral. Son of a Norfolk clergyman, he went to sea at 12 and became a captain in 1793. In the French revolutionary wars he lost his right eye in 1794 and his right arm in 1797. Rear-admiral in 1797, he defeated the French at Aboukir Bay in 1798. He was also at the bombardment of Copenhagen in 1801. In 1805 he destroyed the French fleet at Trafalgar, in which battle he was killed. His daring and decision made him a notable commander. He loved Emma Hamilton.

Nenni, Pietro (1891–1980), Italian socialist politician. He became secretary-general of his party in 1944, and was deputy prime minister, 1963–8.

Nernst, Walther Hermann (1864–1941), German scientist who established the third law of thermodynamics that dealt with the behaviour of matter at temperatures approaching absolute zero. Nobel prizewinner 1920.

Nero, Claudius Caesar (A.D. 37–68), Roman emperor, the adopted son of Claudius. He was weak and licentious and persecuted Christians. In his reign occurred the fire of Rome.

Newcomen, Thomas (1663–1729), English inventor, one of the first to put a steam-engine into practical operation. In 1705 he patented his invention, which was the pumping-engine used in Cornish mines until the adoption of Watt's engine.

Newman, Ernest (1868–1959), English music critic, whose chief work is the *Life of Richard Wagner.*

Newman, John Henry (1801–90), English priest and writer, who became a cardinal of the Roman church in 1879, and was a founder of the Oxford Movement. He is best remembered by his *Apologia pro Vita Sua* in which he described the development of his religious thought. He wrote *Lead, kindly Light,* set to music 30 years later by J. B. Dykes, and *The Dream of Gerontius,* set to music of Elgar. See **J52.**

Newton, Sir Isaac (1642–1727), English scientist, b. Woolsthorpe, Lincs. (the year Galileo died). He studied at Cambridge but was at home during the plague years 1665 and 1666 when he busied himself with problems concerned with optics and gravitation. Through his tutor Isaac Barrow he was appointed to the Lucasian chair of mathematics at Cambridge in 1669 and remained there until 1696 when he was appointed Warden, and later Master of the Mint. He was a secret Unitarian and did not marry. His three great discoveries were to show that white light could be separated into a sequence of coloured components forming the visible spectrum; to use the calculus (invented by him independently of Leibnitz) to investigate the forces of nature in a quantitative way; and to show by his theory of gravitation (for which Copernicus, Kepler and Galileo had prepared the way) that the universe was regulated by simple mathematical laws. His vision was set forth in the *Philosophiae Naturalis Principia Mathematica* of 1687, usually called the *Principia*. It was not until 200 years later that Einstein showed there could be another theory of celestial mechanics.

Ney, Michel (1769–1815), French general who served under Napoleon, especially at Jena, Borodino, and Waterloo.

Nicholas II (1868–1918), last emperor and Tsar of Russia, son of Alexander III. His reign was marked by an unsuccessful war with Japan (1904–5), and by the 1914–18 war. Ineffective and lacking ability, he set up a Duma in 1906 too late for real reform. Revolution broke out in 1917 and he and his family were shot in July 1918.

Nicholson, Sir William (1872–1949), English artist known for his portraits and woodcuts. His son, **Ben Nicholson, O.M.**, (1894–1981) was noted for his abstract paintings.

Nicolson, Sir Harold (1886–1968), English diplomat, author, and critic. His works include *King George V*; and *Diaries and Letters*. His wife was the novelist **Victoria Sackville-West** (1892–1962).

Niemöller, Martin (1892–1984), German Lutheran pastor who opposed the Nazi regime and was confined in a concentration camp. He was president of the World Council of Churches in 1961.

Nietzsche, Friedrich Wilhelm (1844–1900), German philosopher, in his younger years influenced by Wagner and Schopenhauer. His teaching that only the strong ought to survive and his doctrine of the superman are expounded in *Thus spake Zarathustra*, *Beyond Good and Evil* and *The Will to Power*.

Nightingale, Florence (1820–1910), English nurse and pioneer of hospital reform, who during the Crimean war organised in face of considerable official opposition a nursing service to relieve the sufferings of the British soldiers, who called her "the lady with the lamp." Her system was adopted and developed in all parts of the world.

Nijinsky, Vaslav (1892–1950), Russian dancer, one of the company which included Pavlova, Karsavina and Fokine, brought by Diaghilev to Paris and London before the 1914–18 war. In *Les Sylphides*, *Spectre de la Rose* and *L'Après-midi d'un Faune* he won a supreme place among male dancers.

Nikisch, Arthur (1855–1922), Hungarian conductor of the Boston Symphony Orchestra, 1889–93. He was piano-accompanist to the Lieder singer, Elena Gerhardt.

Nimitz, Chester William (1885–1966), American admiral, commanded in the Pacific 1941–5; chief of naval operations 1945–7.

Nixon, Richard Milhous (b. 1913), Republican president (for two terms) of the U.S., 1969–74. In foreign affairs he negotiated the withdrawal of American troops from S. Vietnam and began a process of reconciliation with China and détente with the Soviet Union. But at home the Watergate conspiracies brought disgrace and an end to his presidency. His resignation in August 1974 rendered the impeachment process unnecessary; he accepted the pardon offered by his successor, President Ford. *See* **The United States, Section C, Part II.**

Nkrumah, Kwame (1909–72), Ghanaian leader, first premier of Ghana when his country achieved independence in 1957. Promoted the Pan-African movement; but unsound finance and dictatorial methods led to his overthrow in 1966.

Nobel, Alfred Bernhard (1833–96), Swedish inventor and philanthropist. An engineer and chemist who discovered dynamite, he amassed a fortune from the manufacture of explosives; and bequeathed a fund for annual prizes to those who had contributed most to the benefit of mankind in the fields of physics, chemistry, medicine, literature and peace.

Nolan, Sidney Robert (b. 1917), Australian artist and set designer. O.M. 1983.

North, Frederick (1732–92), favourite minister of George III who held the premiership from 1770 to 1782. (He held the courtesy title of Lord North from 1752.) The stubborn policies of George III led to the American war of independence.

Northcliffe, 1st Viscount (Alfred Charles Harmsworth) (1865–1922), British journalist and newspaper proprietor, b. near Dublin. He began *Answers* in 1888 with his brother Harold, (later Lord Rothermere). In 1894 they bought the *Evening News*, and in 1896 the *Daily Mail*. In 1908 he took over *The Times*.

Northumberland, John Dudley, Duke of (1502–53), English politician who attempted to secure for his daughter-in-law Lady Jane Grey the succession to the throne after Edward VI.

Nostradamus or **Michel de Notre Dame** (1503–66), French astrologer and physician, known for his prophecies in *Centuries*.

Novalis, the pseudonym of Baron Friedrich von Hardenberg (1772–1801), German romantic poet and novelist, whose chief work is the unfinished *Heinrich von Ofterdingen*.

Nuffield, 1st Viscount (William Richard Morris) (1877–1963), British motor-car manufacturer and philanthropist, and until he retired in 1952 chairman of Morris Motors Ltd. He provided large sums for the advancement of medicine in the university of Oxford, for Nuffield College, and in 1943 established the Nuffield Foundation, endowing it with £10 million.

Nyerere, Julius (b. 1922), Tanzanian leader. He became first premier of Tanganyika when it became independent in 1961; and president in 1962. In 1964 he negotiated its union with Zanzibar.

O

Oates, Lawrence Edward (1880–1912), English antarctic explorer. He joined Scott's expedition of 1910, and was one of the five to reach the south pole; but on the return journey, being crippled by frost-bite, he walked out into the blizzard to die.

Oates, Titus (1649–1705), English informer and agitator against Roman catholics.

O'Casey, Sean (1880–1964), Irish dramatist whose plays include *Juno and the Paycock*, *The Silver Tassie*, *Red Roses for Me*, and *Oak Leaves and Lavender*.

Occam (**Ockham**), **William of** (c. 1270–1349), English scholar and philosopher and one of the most original thinkers of all time. He belonged to the Order of Franciscans, violently opposed the temporal power of the Pope, espoused the cause of nominalism and laid the foundations of modern theories of government and theological scepticism. *See* **Occam's razor, Section J.**

O'Connell, Daniel (1775–1847), Irish national leader. A barrister, he formed the Catholic Association in 1823 to fight elections; his followers aimed at the repeal of the Act of Union with England, and formed a Repeal Association in 1840; but the formation of the Young Ireland party, the potato famine, and ill-health undermined his position and he died in exile.

O'Connor, Feargus (1794–1855), working-class leader in England, of Irish birth. He presented the Chartist petition in 1848.

O'Connor, Thomas Power (1848–1929), Irish nationalist and journalist, sat in parliament 1880–1929 and founded the *Star*.

Oersted, Hans Christian (1777–1851), Danish physicist who discovered the connection between electricity and magnetism.

Offa (d. 796), king of Mercia (mid-England), was the leading English king of his day, and built a defensive dyke (**L90**) from the Dee to the Wye.

Offenbach, Jacques (1819–80), German–Jewish composer, b. Cologne, settled at Paris, and is mainly known for his light operas, especially *Tales of Hoffmann*.

Ohm, Georg Simon (1787–1854), German physicist, professor at Munich, who in 1826 formulated the law of electric current, known as Ohm's law, one of the foundation stones in electrical science. *See* **Section L.**

Olivier, Baron (Laurence Kerr Olivier) (b. 1907), British actor and director, especially in Shakespearean roles. He has also produced, directed, and played in films, including *Henry V*, *Hamlet*, and *Richard III*, and in television drama. In

1962 he was appointed director of the National Theatre (which opened in 1976) and in 1970 received a life peerage. O.M. 1981.

Oman, Sir Charles William (1860–1946), English historian, especially of mediaeval warfare and of the Peninsular War. He also wrote memoirs.

Omar ibn al Khattab (581–644), adviser to Mahomet, succeeded Abu Bakr as 2nd caliph. In his reign Islam became an imperial power. He died at the hands of a foreign slave.

Omar Khayyám (c. 1050–1123), Persian poet and mathematician, called Khayyám (tent-maker) because of his father's occupation. His fame as a scientist has been eclipsed by his *Rubaiyat*, made known to English readers by Edward FitzGerald in 1859.

O'Neill, Eugene Gladstone (1888–1953), American playwright who, after spending his adventurous youth in sailing, gold-prospecting, and journalism, first won success in 1914 with the one-act play, *Thirst*. His later plays include *Anna Christie, Strange Interlude, Mourning Becomes Electra, The Iceman Cometh*. Nobel prizewinner 1936.

Oppenheimer, J. Robert (1904–67), American physicist who was director of atomic-energy research at Los Alamos, New Mexico, 1942–5, when the atomic bomb was developed but in 1949 he opposed work on the hydrogen bomb on moral grounds.

Orchardson, Sir William Quiller (1835–1910), Scottish painter, b. Edinburgh, best known for his *Napoleon I on board H.M.S. Bellerophon* and *Ophelia*.

Origen (c. 185–254), Christian philosopher and Biblical scholar, who taught at Alexandria and Caesarea, and was imprisoned and tortured in the persecution of Decius, 250

Orpen, Sir William (1878–1931), British painter of portraits, conversation pieces, and pictures of the 1914–18 war.

Ortega y Gasset, José (1883–1955), Spanish philosopher and essayist, known for his *Tema de Nuestro Tiempo* and *La Rebelión de Las Masas*.

Orwell, George (Eric Arthur Blair) (1903–50), English satirist, b. India, author of *Animal Farm* and *Nineteen Eighty-Four*.

Osler, Sir William (1849–1919), Canadian physician and medical historian, authority on diseases of the blood and spleen.

Ossietzky, Carl von (1889–1938), German pacifist leader after the first world war; sent by Hitler to a concentration camp. Nobel peace prize 1935.

Oswald, St (c. 605–42), won the Northumbrian throne by battle in 633 and introduced Christianity there.

Otto I (the Great) (912–73), founder of the Holy Roman Empire (he was crowned king of the Germans in 936 and emperor at Rome in 962). The son of Henry I of Germany, he built up a strong position in Italy (as regards the papacy) and in Germany where he established the East Mark (Austria).

Otto, Nikolaus August (1832–91). German engineer who built a gas engine (1878) using the four-stroke cycle that bears his name.

Ouida (Maria Louise Ramé) (1839–1908), English novelist of French extraction, whose romantic stories include *Under Two Flags*.

Ovid (43 B.C.–A.D. 18), Latin poet (Publius Ovidius Naso), chiefly remembered for his *Art of Love* and *Metamorphoses*. He died in exile.

Owen, Robert (1771–1858), Welsh pioneer socialist, b. Montgomeryshire. As manager, and later owner, of New Lanark cotton mills he tried to put his philanthropic views into effect; other communities on co-operative lines were founded in Hampshire and in America (New Harmony, Indiana) but although unsuccessful they were influential in many directions. He challenged the doctrine of *laissez-faire*, inaugurated socialism and the co-operative movement, and foresaw the problems of industrial development.

P

Pachmann, Vladimir de (1848–1933), Russian pianist gifted in the playing of Chopin.

Paderewski, Ignace Jan (1860–1941), Polish pianist and nationalist. He represented his country at Versailles and was the first premier of a reconstituted Poland. He died in exile in the second world war.

Paganini, Niccolo (1782–1840), Italian violinist and virtuoso who revolutionised violin technique.

Paine, Thomas (1737–1809), political writer, b. Norfolk, son of a Quaker. Spent 1774–87 in America supporting the revolutionary cause. On his return to England wrote *The Rights of Man* in reply to Burke's *Reflections* on the French revolution which led to his prosecution and flight to France where he entered French politics and wrote *The Age of Reason*, advocating deism. His last years were spent in America but this time in obscurity.

Palestrina, Giovanni Pierluigi da (c. 1525–94), Italian composer of unaccompanied church music and madrigals. *See* **Section E.**

Palgrave, Sir Francis (1788–1861), English historian and archivist, an early editor of record series. His son **Francis Turner Palgrave** (1824–97) was a poet and critic and edited *The Golden Treasury*; while another son, **William Gifford Palgrave** (1826–88) was a traveller and diplomat.

Palissy, Bernard (c. 1510–89), French potter who discovered the art of producing white enamel, after which he set up a porcelain factory in Paris which was patronised by royalty.

Palladio, Andrea (1508–80), Italian architect, b. Padua, whose style was modelled on ancient Roman architecture (symmetrical planning and harmonic proportions) and had wide influence; author of *I Quattro Libri dell' Architettura*.

Palmer, Samuel (1805–81), English landscape painter and etcher, follower of Blake whom he met in 1824. *Bright Cloud* and *In a Shoreham Garden* are in the Victoria and Albert Museum.

Palmerston, 3rd Viscount (Henry John Temple) (1784–1865), English Whig statesman. At first a Tory, he was later Whig foreign secretary for many years, and prime minister 1855 and 1859–65. His vigorous foreign policy wherever possible took the lead and bluntly asserted English rights.

Pancras, St. (d. 304), patron saint of children, was (according to tradition) baptised in Rome where he was put to death at the age of fourteen in the persecution under Diocletian.

Pandit, Vijaya Lakshmi (b. 1900), sister of Nehru, was India's first ambassador to the Soviet Union (1947–9), and to the U.S. (1949–51), and the first woman to be elected president of the U.N. General Assembly (1954).

Panizzi, Sir Anthony (1797–1879), Italian bibliographer and nationalist. Taking refuge in England after 1821, he became in 1856 chief librarian of the British Museum, undertook a new catalogue and designed the reading room.

Pankhurst, Emmeline (1858–1928), English suffragette who, with her daughters Christabel and Sylvia, worked for women's suffrage, organising the Women's Social and Political Union.

Papin, Denis (1647–1714), French physicist and inventor. He invented the condensing pump, and was a pioneer in the development of the steam-engine. Not being a mechanic, he made all his experiments by means of models.

Paracelsus (Theophrastus Bombastus von Hohenhelm) (1493–1541), Swiss physician whose speculations though muddled served to reform medical thought. He criticised the established authorities, Galen and Aristotle, and experimented and made new chemical compounds. His earliest printed work was *Practica* (1529).

Park, Mungo (1771–1806), Scottish explorer in west Africa, where he lost his life. He wrote *Travels in the Interior of Africa* (1799).

Parker of Waddington, Baron (Hubert Lister Parker) (1900–72) Lord Chief Justice of England 1958–70.

Parker, Joseph (1830–1902), English Congregational preacher, especially at what later became the City Temple.

Parnell, Charles Stewart (1846–91), Irish national leader. To draw attention to Ireland's problems, he used obstruction in parliament. He was president of the Land League but was not implicated in crimes committed by some members. His party supported Gladstone, who became converted to Home Rule. His citation in divorce proceedings brought his political career to an end.

Parry, Sir William Edward (1790–1855), English explorer and naval commander in the Arctic, where he was sent to protect fisheries and also tried to reach the north pole.

Parsons, Sir Charles Algernon (1854–1931),

English inventor of the steam-turbine, who built the first turbine-driven steamship in 1897.

Pascal, Blaise (1623–62). Frenchman of varied gifts, b. at Clermont-Ferrand. At first a mathematician, he patented a calculating machine. His *Lettres provinciales* influenced Voltaire. In 1654 he turned to religion, and his incomplete religious writings were published posthumously as *Pensées*. See **Jansenism, J28**(2).

Pasternak, Boris Leonidovich (1890–1960), Russian poet and writer. B. Moscow, he published his first poems in 1931. For some years his time was spent in translating foreign literature, but in 1958 his novel *Dr. Zhivago*, which describes the Russian revolution and is in the Russian narrative tradition, was published abroad, though banned in the Soviet Union. He was awarded a Nobel prize but obliged to decline it.

Pasteur, Louis (1822–95), French chemist, b. at Dôle in the Jura, whose work was inspired by an interest in the chemistry of life. His researches on fermentation led to the science of bacteriology and his investigations into infectious diseases and their prevention to the science of immunology. The pathological–bacteriological import of his researches came about mainly through his disciples (Lister, Roux, and others) and not directly, though all founded on his early non-medical investigations on organisms of fermentation, etc., which were of great importance in industry, and fundamentally. He spent most of his life as director of scientific studies at the Ecole Normale at Paris. The Institute Pasteur was founded in 1888.

Patmore, Coventry (1823–96), English poet. *The Angel in the House* deals with domesticity. Later he became a Roman catholic, and *The Unknown Eros* is characterised by erotic mysticism.

Patrick, St. (*c.* 389–*c.* 461), apostle of Ireland, was born in Britain or Gaul, and after some time on the continent (taken thither after his capture by pirates) went as missionary to Ireland, where after years of teaching and a visit to Rome he fixed his seat at Armagh. He wrote *Confessions*.

Patti, Adelina (1843–1919), coloratura soprano, b. in Madrid of Italian parents, and of international repute.

Paul, St. (*c.* A.D. 10–64), Jew to whom was mainly due the extension of Christianity in Europe. B. Tarsus (in Asia Minor), he was a Pharisee, and became converted about A.D. 37. His missionary journeys took him to the Roman provinces of Asia, Macedonia, and Greece (Rome had already had Christian teaching; and his epistles form nearly half the New Testament and were written before the gospels. He helped to develop both the organisation of the early church and its teaching. The date order of his epistles is to some extent conjectural. It is believed that he was executed in Rome. His Hebrew name was Saul. *See also* **Section S.**

Paul VI (Giovanni Battista Montini) (1897–1978), elected Pope in 1963 on the death of John XXIII. He was formerly archbishop of Milan. His encyclical *Humanae Vitae* (1968) condemned contraception.

Pauli, Wolfgang (1900–58), Austrian-born physicist who first predicted theoretically the existence of neutrinos. Nobel prize 1945.

Pavlov, Ivan Petrovich (1849–1936), Russian physiologist, known for his scientific experimental work on animal behaviour, particularly conditioned reflexes and the relation between psychological stress and brain function. Nobel prizewinner 1904. See **Q17-18.**

Pavlova, Anna (1882–1931), Russian ballerina, b. St. Petersburg, excelling in the roles of *Giselle* and the *Dying Swan.*

Peabody, George (1795–1869), American philanthropist, a successful merchant who lived mainly in London. He gave large sums to promote education and slum clearance.

Peacock, Thomas Love (1785–1866), English novelist, b. Weymouth. His work, which is mainly satirical, includes *Headlong Hall* and *Nightmare Abbey.*

Pearson, Lester Bowles (1897–1972), Canadian politician served as minister for external affairs 1948–57, and prime minister 1963-8. He supported the United Nations. Nobel peace prize 1957.

Peary, Robert Edwin (1856–1920), American arctic explorer, discoverer of the north pole (1909).

Peel, Sir Robert (1788–1850), English Conservative statesman, b. in Lancashire, son of a manufacturer. He first held office in 1811. With Wellington he enacted toleration for Roman catholics in 1829. As home secretary he re-organised London police. He developed a new policy of Conservatism, and in 1846, largely as a result of the Irish famine, he repealed the corn laws which protected English agriculture. He died from a riding accident.

Peirce, Charles Sanders (1839–1914), American physicist and philosopher of original mind, founder of the theory of pragmatism which was later developed by his friend William James. *See* **Pragmatism, Section J.**

Penfield, Wilder Graves (1891–1976), Canadian brain surgeon, author of *The Cerebral Cortex of Man, Epilepsy and the Functional Anatomy of the Human Brain.* O.M.

Penn, William (1644–1718), English Quaker and founder of Pennsylvania. The son of Admiral William Penn, he persisted in becoming a Quaker, and on receiving for his father's services a crown grant in North America he founded there Pennsylvania. He wrote *No Cross, No Crown.*

Penney, Baron (William George Penney) (b. 1909), British scientist. His nuclear research team at A.E.A. developed the advanced gas-cooled reactor (A.G.R.) chosen for the Dungeness "B" and Hinkley Point "B" power stations.

Pepys, Samuel (1633–1703), English diarist and naval administrator. His diary, 1660–69, was kept in cipher and not deciphered till 1825. It gives vivid personal details and covers the plague and fire of London. (The first complete and unexpurgated version of the diary was issued in 1970.)

Pereda, José Maria de (1833–1906), Spanish regional novelist (around his native Santander).

Pérez Galdós, Benito (1843–1920), Spanish novelist and dramatist, who has been compared to Balzac for his close study and portrayal of all social classes, especially in the series of 46 short historical novels *Episodios nacionales.* His longer novels, *Novelas españolas contemporáneas,* some of which are translated, number 31.

Pergolesi, Giovanni Battista (1710–36), Italian composer, best known for his humorous opera *La Serva Padrona* and his *Stabat Mater.*

Pericles (*c.* 490–429 B.C.), Athenian statesman, general, and orator, who raised Athens to the point of its fullest prosperity, and greatest beauty, with the Parthenon, Erechtheum, and other buildings; but he died in the plague which followed the outbreak of the Peloponnesian war.

Perkin, Sir William Henry (1838–1907), English chemist, b. London, who while seeking to make a substitute for quinine discovered in 1856 the first artificial aniline dye, mauve. His son, **W. H. Perkin** (1860–1929) was an organic chemist of note.

Perrin, Francis (b. 1901), French scientist and socialist; succeeded Joliot-Curie as High Commr. of Atomic Energy, 1951; professor of Atomic Physics, Collège de France, 1946, Nobel prizewinner 1926.

Persius Flaccus Aulus (A.D. 34–62), Roman satirist and Stoic philosopher.

Perugino, Pietro (1446–1524), Italian artist. He worked in the Sistine Chapel at Rome and he taught Raphael.

Pestalozzi, Johann Heinrich (1746–1827), Swiss educational reformer whose theories laid the foundation of modern primary education. His teaching methods were far in advance of his time. He wrote *How Gertrude Educates Her Children.*

Pétain, Henri Philippe (1856–1951), French general and later collaborator. In the first world war he was in command at Verdun, and between the wars he sponsored the Maginot line. In the second world war, when French resistance collapsed, he came to terms with Germany and headed an administration at Vichy. After the war he was sentenced to life imprisonment.

Peter I, the Great (1672–1725), emperor of Russia. Son of Alexei, he succeeded his brother after some difficulty. He reorganised the army, and, after coming to Deptford to learn shipbuilding, he created a navy. To some extent he westernised Russian social life, and created a new capital at St. Petersburg (1703). In war with Charles XII of Sweden he was at first defeated, but later victorious at Poltava (1709). He married a peasant, Catherine, who succeeded him.

Peter the Hermit (c. 1050–1115), French monk who preached the First Crusade, originated by pope Urban II at the council of Clermont. He went on the crusade himself, but gave up at Antioch.

Petrarch, Francesco (1304–78), Italian poet, son of a Florentine exile. He is chiefly remembered for his poems *To Laura*, but he was also a scholar who paved the way for the Renaissance.

Petrie, Sir Flinders (1853–1942), British egyptologist. He excavated in Britain (1875–90), Egypt (1880–1924), and Palestine 1927–38). See his *Seventy Years of Archaeology*.

Phidias (5th cent. B.C.), Greek sculptor especially in gold, ivory and bronze, worked at Athens for Pericles. No certain examples of his work are extant, but the Elgin marbles in the British Museum may be from his designs.

Philip II of France (1165–1223), son of Louis VII. He went on the Third Crusade with Richard I of England, but in France is mainly remembered for firm government, the recovery of Normandy from England, and the beautifying of Paris.

Philip II of Macedonia (382–336 B.C.), a successful commander, made his the leading military kingdom in Greece and was father of Alexander the Great.

Philip II of Spain (1527–98), succeeded his father Charles V in Spain and the Netherlands, also in Spanish interests overseas. In the Netherlands his strict Roman catholic policy provoked a revolt which ended in 1579 in the independence of the United Provinces. He married Mary Tudor of England; and after her death sent the ill-fated Armada against Elizabeth in 1588.

Philip V of Spain (1683–1746), first Bourbon king, succeeded his great-uncle Charles II and was grandson of Louis XIV. His accession provoked European war.

Phillip, Arthur (1738–1814), first governor of New South Wales. Under his command the first fleet of 717 convicts set sail from Britain to Australia, and with the founding of Sydney in 1788 colonisation of the whole country began.

Phillips, Stephen (1868–1915), English poet who wrote verse dramas, including *Paolo and Francesca*.

Piast, first Polish dynasty in Poland until the 14th cent. and until the 17th cent. in Silesia.

Piazzi, Giuseppe (1746–1826), Italian astronomer who discovered Ceres, the first of the asteroids to be seen by man.

Picasso, Pablo Ruiz (1881–1973) Spanish painter, b. Málaga; received his early training in Catalonia and settled in Paris in 1903. He and Braque were the originators of Cubism (c. 1909). His influence over contemporary art is comparable with that exercised by Cézanne (q.v.) over the artists of his time. Perhaps the best-known single work is his mural *Guernica*, painted at the time of the Spanish civil war, expressing the artist's loathing of fascism and the horrors of war. His genius also found scope in sculpture, ceramics, and the graphic arts, and he designed décor and costumes for the ballet.

Piccard, Auguste (1884–1962), Swiss physicist, noted for balloon ascents into the stratosphere and for submarine research. In 1960 his son Jacques made a descent of over 7 miles in the Marianas trench in the western Pacific in a bathyscaphe designed and built by his father.

Pilsudski, Joseph (1867–1935), Polish soldier and statesman who in 1919 attempted by force to restore Poland's 1772 frontiers but was driven back. From 1926 he was dictator.

Pindar (522–443 B.C.), Greek lyric poet.

Pinero, Sir Arthur Wing (1855–1934), English dramatist whose plays include *Dandy Dick*, *The Second Mrs. Tanqueray* and *Mid-Channel*.

Pirandello, Luigi (1867–1936), Italian dramatist and novelist whose plays include *Six Characters in Search of an Author*. Nobel prizewinner 1934.

Pissarro, Camille (1830–1903), French impressionist painter of landscapes; studied under Corot.

Pitman, Sir Isaac (1813–97) b. Trowbridge, English inventor of a system of phonographic shorthand.

Pitt, William (1759–1806), English statesman. Younger son of the Earl of Chatham, (q.v.) he entered parliament at 21 and became prime minister at 24 in 1783 when parties were divided and the American war had been lost. He rose to the position, and held office with scarcely a break till his death. An able finance minister, he introduced reforms, and would have gone further, but Napoleon's meteoric rise obliged him to lead European allies in a long struggle against France. He died worn out by his efforts.

Pius XII (1876–1958), elected pope 1939. As Eugenio Pacelli, he was papal nuncio in Germany and later papal secretary of state. It has been argued that, as pope in wartime, he could have taken a stronger line against Nazi war crimes.

Pizarro, Francisco (c. 1478–1541), Spanish adventurer, b. Trujillo. After Columbus's discoveries, he conquered Peru for Spain, overthrowing the Inca empire. He was murdered by his men.

Planck, Max (1857–1947), German mathematical physicist, b. Kiel, whose main work was on thermodynamics. In 1900 he invented a mathematical formula to account for some properties of the thermal radiation from a hot body which has since played an important role in physics. Nobel prizewinner 1918. See **Quantum theory, Section L.**

Plato (427–347 B.C.), Athenian philosopher, pupil of Socrates, teacher of Aristotle. He founded a school at Athens under the name of the Academy, where he taught philosophy and mathematics. His great work is his *Dialogues*, which includes the *Republic*, the longest and most celebrated. His known writings have come down to us and constitute one of the most influential bodies of work in history. See also **Mind and Matter, Section J.**

Playfair, 1st Baron (Lyon Playfair) (1818–98), a far-sighted Victorian who stood for the greater recognition of science in national life. He forsook his profession as professor of chemistry at Edinburgh to enter parliament. Pres. British Association 1885.

Plimsoll, Samuel (1824–98), English social reformer, b. Bristol. He realised the evil of overloading unseaworthy ships, and as M.P. for Derby he procured the passing of the Merchant Shipping Act, 1876 which imposed a line (the Plimsoll Mark) above which no ship must sink while loading.

Pliny the Elder (A.D. 23–79), Roman naturalist, author of a *Natural History*. He died of fumes and exhaustion while investigating the eruption of Vesuvius. His nephew, **Pliny the Younger** (A.D. 62–113), wrote *Letters* notable for their charm and the insight they give into Roman life.

Plotinus (c. 203–c. 262), Greek philosopher, was the founder of Neoplatonism, which had considerable influence on early Christian thought. See also **God and Man, Section J.**

Plutarch (c. 46–120), Greek biographer, whose *Lives* portray 46 leading historical figures (in pairs, a Greek and a Roman whose careers were similar). Although based on myth his *Life of Lycurgus* about life in Sparta had a profound influence on later writers, e.g., Rousseau and the romantic philosophers. He was educated at Athens but visited Rome.

Poe, Edgar Allan (1809–49), American poet and story-writer, b. Boston, Mass. His poems include *The Raven*, *To Helen*, and *Annabel Lee*, and his stories, often weird and fantastic, include *Tales of the Grotesque and Arabesque*.

Poincaré, Raymond Nicolas (1860–1934), French statesman. He was president 1913–20, and as prime minister occupied the Ruhr in 1923.

Pole, Reginald (1500–58), archbishop of Canterbury, cardinal of the Roman church and antagonist of the reformation. He opposed Henry VIII's divorce and went abroad in 1532, writing *De Unitate Ecclesiastica*; as a result of which his mother, Countess of Salisbury, and other relatives were executed. Under Queen Mary Tudor he became archbishop and died the year she did.

Pollard, Albert Frederick (1869–1948), English historian, especially of the Tudor period, and first director of the Institute of Historical Research.

Polo, Marco (1256–1323), Venetian traveller, who made journeys through China, India, and other eastern countries, visiting the court of Kubla Khan, and leaving an account of his travels.

Pompadour, Jeanne Antoine Poisson, Marquise de (1721–64), mistress of Louis XV of France, who exercised disastrous political influence.

Pompey (106–48 B.C.), Roman commander, who cleared the Mediterranean of pirates, and became triumvir with Caesar and Crassus.

Pompidou, Georges Jean Raymond (1911–74), French administrator and politician who succeeded de Gaulle as president 1969.

Pope, Alexander (1688–1744), English poet, b. London, of a Roman catholic family, and largely self-educated. His brilliant satire was frequently directed against his contemporaries. He is especially remembered for *The Rape of the Lock*, *The Dunciad*, *Essay on Criticism*, and *Essay on Man*.

Popper, Sir Karl (b. 1902), British philosopher of science, b. Vienna; author of *The Open Society and Its Enemies* (1945), *Conjectures and Refutations* (1963), *Objective Knowledge* (1972). He rejects the doctrine that all knowledge starts from perception or sensation and holds that it grows through conjecture and refutation. C.H. (1982).

Pound, Ezra Loomis (1885–1972), American poet and writer on varied subjects, a controversial figure. Noted for his translations of Provençal, Latin, Chinese, French, and Italian poets.

Poussin, Nicolas (1593–1665), French painter. He lived in Rome 1624–40, 1642–65. His *Golden Calf* is in the National Gallery.

Powys, John Cowper (1872–1964), English writer, best known for his novel *Wolf Solent* and his essays *The Meaning of Culture* and *A Philosophy of Solitude*. His brothers, **Theodore Francis** (1875–1953) and **Llewelyn** (1884–1939) were also original writers.

Prasad, Rajendra (1884–1963), Indian statesman, first president of the Republic of India, 1950–62.

Praxiteles (4th cent. B.C.), Greek sculptor, whose main surviving work is *Hermes carrying Dionysus*.

Preece, Sir William Henry (1834–1913), Welsh electrical engineer, associated with the expansion of wireless telegraphy and telephony in the United Kingdom. He was connected with Marconi and introduced the block system.

Prichard, James Cowles (1786–1848), English ethnologist who perceived that people should be studied as a whole. His works include *Researches into the Physical History of Mankind* and *The Natural History of Man*. He practised medicine.

Priestley, John Boynton (1894–1984), English critic, novelist, and playwright, b. Bradford. His works include the novels *The Good Companions*, *Angel Pavement*, and the plays *Dangerous Corner*, *Time and the Conways*, *I Have Been Here Before*, and *The Linden Tree*, O.M. 1977.

Priestley, Joseph (1733–1804), English chemist who worked on gases, and shared with Scheele the discovery of oxygen. A presbyterian minister, he was for his time an advanced thinker. In 1794 he settled in America.

Prior, Matthew (1664–1721), English poet. In early life he was a diplomat. He was a neat epigrammatist and writer of occasional pieces. His works include *The City Mouse and Country Mouse* and *Four Dialogues of the Dead*.

Prokofiev, Serge Sergeyevich (1891–1953), Russian composer, whose music has a strong folk-song element, rich in melody and invention. He has written operas; *The Love of Three Oranges*, *The Betrothal in a Nunnery*, *War and Peace*; ballets: *Romeo and Juliet*, *Cinderella*; symphonies, chamber music, and the music for Eisenstein's films *Alexander Nevsky*, *Ivan the Terrible*.

Protagoras (c. 480–411 B.C.), Greek philosopher, chief of the Sophists, noted for his scepticism and disbelief in objective truth, and for his doctrine that "man is the measure of all things."

Proudhon, Pierre Joseph (1809–65), French socialist. In 1840 he propounded the view that property is theft. His main work is *Système des contradictions économiques* (1846). He was frequently in prison.

Proust, Marcel (1871–1922), French psychological novelist, author of a series of novels known under the title of *A la recherche du temps perdu*. His works have been admirably translated into English by C. K. Scott Moncrieff.

Ptolemy of Alexandria (Claudius Ptolemaeus) (fl. A.D. 140), astronomer and founder of scientific cartography. In the *Almagest* he attempted a mathematical presentation of the paths along which the planets appear to move in the heavens. His other great work was his *Geographical Outline*.

Puccini, Giacomo (1858–1924), Italian composer, b. Lucca, whose operas include *Manon Lescaut*, *La Bohème*, *Tosca*, *Madam Butterfly*, and *Turandot* (completed by a friend).

Pupin, Michael Idvorsky (1858–1935), physicist and inventor (telephony and X-rays), b. Idvor, Hungary (now in Yugoslavia); went to America penniless 1874 to become professor of electromechanics at Columbia University.

Purcell, Henry (1659–95), English composer, b. Westminster, son of a court musician. He became organist of the chapel royal and composer to Charles II. His best works are vocal and choral. See **Section E**.

Pusey, Edward Bouverie (1800–82), English theologian, a leader of the Oxford or Tractarian movement with Keble and at first also with Newman, till the latter became Roman catholic. The movement aimed at revival.

Pushkin, Alexander (1799–1837), Russian writer, b. Moscow, whose place in Russian literature ranks with Shakespeare's in English. He wrote in many forms—lyrical poetry and narrative verse, drama, folk-tales and short stories. Musicians have used his works as plots for operas—the fairy romance *Russlan and Ludmilla* was dramatised by Glinka; the verse novel *Eugene Onegin* and the short story *The Queen of Spades* were adapted by Tchaikovsky, and the tragic drama *Boris Godunov* formed the subject of Mussorgsky's opera. Like Lermontov, who too was exiled, he was inspired by the wild beauty of the Caucasus. He was killed in a duel defending his wife's honour.

Pym, John (1584–1643), English parliamentary leader in opposition to Charles I. He promoted the impeachment of the king's advisers, Strafford and Laud. A collateral descendant is Mr. Francis Pym, Conservative Foreign Secretary, 1982–June 1983.

Pythagoras (c. 582–500 B.C.), Greek philosopher, b. on the island of Samos, off the Turkish mainland, which he left c. 530 to settle at Croton, a Greek city in southern Italy. He was a mystic and mathematician, and founded a brotherhood who saw in numbers the key to the understanding of the universe.

Q

Quasimodo, Salvatore (1901–68), Italian poet of humanity and liberal views whose works include *La vita non e sogno*. Nobel prizewinner 1959.

Quesnay, François (1694–1774), French economist, founder of the physiocratic school who believed in *laissez-faire* and influenced the thought of Adam Smith. See **Physiocrats, Section J**.

Quiller-Couch, Sir Arthur Thomas (1863–1944), English man of letters, b. Bodmin, known as "Q." He edited the *Oxford Book of English Verse* and his works include *From a Cornish Window*.

R

Rabelais, François (c. 1495–1553), French satirist. At first in religious orders, he later studied medicine and practised at Lyons. His works, mainly published under a pseudonym, are full of riotous mirth, wit and wisdom. The main ones are *Gargantua* and *Pantagruel*.

Rachel, Élisa (Élisa Felix) (1821–58), Alsatian-Jewish tragic actress. Her chief triumph was in Racine's *Phèdre*.

Rachmaninov, Sergey Vasilyevich (1873–1943), Russian composer and pianist, b. Nijni-Novgorod (now Gorki), best known for his piano music, especially his *Prelude*. After the Russian revolution he settled in America. See **Section E**.

Racine, Jean (1639–99), French tragic poet whose dramas include *Andromaque*, *Iphigénie* and *Phèdre*. An orphan, he was brought up by grandparents who sent him to Port Royal school where he acquired a love of the classics. In Paris he became a friend of Molière, whose company acted his first play, and of Boileau, with whom he became joint historiographer to Louis XIV. *Esther* and *Athalie* were written for Madame de Maintenon's schoolgirls.

Rackham, Arthur (1867–1939), English artist and book-illustrator, especially of fairy tales.

Radhakrishnan, Sir Sarvepalli (1888–1975), Indian philosopher and statesman, vice-president of India 1952–62, president 1962–7. He was at one time a professor at Oxford, and was chairman of Unesco in 1949.

Raffles, Sir Thomas Stamford (1781–1826), English colonial administrator who founded a settlement at Singapore in 1819. He was also a naturalist, and founded the London Zoo, being first president.

Raikes, Robert (1735–1811), English educational pioneer, whose lead in the teaching of children at Gloucester on Sundays led to an extensive Sunday School movement.

Raleigh, Sir Walter (1552–1618), adventurer and writer. He found favour at the court of Elizabeth I, helped to put down the Irish rebellion of 1580, and in 1584 began the colonisation of Virginia, introducing potatoes and tobacco to the British Isles. At the accession of James I he lost favour and was sent to the Tower, where he wrote his *History of the World*. Released in 1615 to lead an expedition to the Orinoco, he was executed when it failed.

Raman, Sir Chandrasekhara Venkata (1888–1970), Indian physicist whose main work has been in spectroscopy. For his research on the diffusion of light and discovery of the "Raman effect" (a phenomenon of scattered light rays) he was awarded the 1930 Nobel prize.

Rameau, Jean Philippe (1683–1764), French composer and church organist whose works on musical theory influenced musical development in the 18th cent.

Ramón y Cajal, Santiago (1852–1934), Spanish histologist who made discoveries in the structure of the nervous system. Shared 1906 Nobel prize.

Ramsay, Sir William (1852–1916), Scottish chemist, and discoverer with Lord Rayleigh of argon. Later he discovered helium and other inert gases, which he called neon, krypton, and xenon. Nobel prizewinner 1904.

Ramsey, Arthur Michael (b. 1904), archbishop of Canterbury, 1961–74. His previous career was: professor of divinity at Cambridge 1950–2; bishop of Durham 1952–6; archbishop of York 1956–61. Widely travelled, he worked hard for church unity.

Ranke, Leopold von (1795–1886), German historian, one of the first to base his work on methodical research. His chief work is a *History of the Popes*.

Raphael (Raffaello Santi) (1483–1520) of Urbino was the youngest of the three great artists of the High Renaissance. He was taught at Perugia by Perugino, and then at Florence he came under the influence of Leonardo and Michelangelo. Raphael's Madonnas, remarkable for their simplicity and grace, include the *Madonna of the Grand Duke* (Palazzo Pitti), the *Sistine Madonna* (Dresden) the *Madonna with the Goldfinch* (Uffizi), the *Madonna of Foligno* (Vatican), and the *Ansidei Madonna* (National Gallery). He painted the frescoes on the walls of the Stanza della Segnatura in the Vatican, and designed 10 cartoons for tapestries for the Sistine Chapel, 7 of which are on loan from the Royal Collection at the V. and A. After the death of Bramante he was appointed architect in charge of the rebuilding of St. Peter's.

Rasputin, Grigori Yefimovich (1871–1916), Russian peasant from Siberia, a cunning adventurer who at the court of Nicholas II exerted a malign influence over the Tsarina through his apparent ability to improve the health of the sickly Tsarevich Alexis. He was murdered by a group of nobles.

Rathbone, Eleanor (1872–1946), social reformer who championed women's pensions and in her book *The Disinherited Family* set out the case for family allowances.

Ravel, Maurice (1875–1937), French composer, pupil of Fauré, one of the leaders of the impressionist movement.

Rawlinson, Sir Henry Creswicke (1810–95), English diplomat and archaeologist. He made Assyrian collections now in the British Museum and translated the Behistun inscription of the Persian king Darius. He also wrote on cuneiform inscriptions and on Assyrian history.

Ray, John (1627–1705), English naturalist. A blacksmith's son, he went to Cambridge, travelled in Europe, and produced a classification of plants. He also wrote on zoology.

Rayleigh, 3rd Baron (John William Strutt) (1842–1919), English mathematician and physicist. He studied sound and the wave theory of light; and with Sir William Ramsay discovered argon. Nobel prizewinner 1904.

Read, Sir Herbert (1893–1968), English poet and art critic. His writings include *Collected Poems*, *The Meaning of Art*, and an autobiography, *Annals of Innocence and Experience*.

Reade, Charles (1814–84), English novelist. His chief work is *The Cloister and the Hearth*. He also wrote *Peg Woffington*, *It is Never too Late to Mend*, and *Griffith Gaunt*, aimed at social abuses.

Reagan, Ronald (b. 1911). U.S. President, 1981– ; former T.V. and film star, 1937–66. Governor of California, 1967–74. Won Republican victory, 1980. Re-elected in landslide victory, 1984. *See* **Section C, Part II.**

Réaumur, René Antoine Ferchault de (1683–1757), French naturalist who invented a thermometer of eighty degrees, using alcohol.

Récamier, Jeanne Françoise (*née* Bernard) (1777–1849), French beauty and holder of a noted salon. Her husband was a banker.

Regnault, Henry Victor (1810–78), French chemist and physicist, who worked on gases, latent heat, and steam-engines.

Reith, 1st Baron (John Charles Walsham Reith) (1889–1971), Scottish civil engineer, first director-general of the B.B.C. 1927–38

Rembrandt (Rembrandt Harmenszoon van Rijn) (1606–69), Dutch painter and etcher, b. Leiden, a miller's son, one of the most individual and prolific artists of any period. His output includes portraits, landscapes, large groups, etchings, and drawings. He settled in Amsterdam establishing his reputation with *The Anatomy Lesson*, painted in 1632. In 1634 he married Saskia, a burgomaster's daughter. *The Night Watch* was painted in 1642; it was not well received and Saskia died the same year, leaving the infant Titus. The path from relative wealth to lonely old age is depicted in his self-portraits. Caring little for convention or formal beauty, his work is characterised by bold realism and spiritual beauty, by vitality and simplicity. His understanding of the play of colour and the effects of light can give his pictures a mystical beauty, as in the atmospheric painting *The Mill*. His figures, even for religious pictures, were taken from real life, the Jews in the etching *Christ Healing* from the Jewish quarter where he lived. He met the misfortunes of later life by withdrawing from society and it was during this period of detachment that he produced his greatest works in portraiture, landscape, and biblical story.

Renan, Ernest (1823–92), French writer who, though unable to accept the orthodox viewpoint, wrote much on religious themes, especially a *Life of Jesus*.

Reni, Guido. *See* **Guido Reni.**

Rennie, John (1761–1821), Scottish civil engineer who built the old Waterloo and Southwark bridges and designed the granite London bridge which stood until recently. He also designed docks at London, Liverpool, Leith, Dublin, and Hull; constructed Plymouth breakwater; made canals and drained fens.

Renoir, Pierre Auguste (1841–1919), French impressionist painter, b. Limoges. His works include portraits, still-life, landscapes, and groups, including *La Loge*, *Les Parapluies*, *La première Sortie*, *La Place Pigalle*. He was later crippled with arthritis.

Reuter, Paul Julius, Freiherr von (1816–99), German pioneer of telegraphic press service, who in 1851 fixed his headquarters in London.

Reymont, Vladislav Stanislav (1868–1925), Polish novelist, author of *The Peasants*. Nobel prize-winner 1924.

Reynolds, Sir Joshua (1723–92), English portrait painter, b. Plympton, Devon. His portraits, which include *Mrs. Siddons*, are remarkable for expressiveness and colour and he was a sympathetic painter of children. He was first president of the R.A. from 1768 till his death.

Rhodes, Cecil John (1853–1902), English empire-builder. B. at Bishop's Stortford, he went to South Africa for health reasons and there prospered at the diamond mines. He became prime minister of what was then Cape Colony and secured British extension in what is now Zimbabwe and Zambia. He withdrew from politics after the failure of the ill-advised Jameson Raid of 1896 into the Transvaal. He bequeathed large sums to found scholarships at Oxford for overseas students.

Ricardo, David (1772–1823), English political economist of Jewish descent. By occupation a London stockbroker, he wrote a useful work, *Principles of Political Economy*.

Richard I (1157–99), succeeded his father Henry II as king of England in 1189. A patron of troubadours and a soldier (Lion-heart), he went on the third Crusade and took Acre, but could not recover Jerusalem from Saladin. On his return journey across Europe he was imprisoned and ransomed. He was killed in war with France.

Richard II (1367–1400), son of the Black Prince, succeeded his grandfather Edward III as king of England in 1377. Artistic and able, but erratic and egocentric, he personally at the age of fourteen met the Peasants' Revolt in 1381, making untenable promises. Latterly his rule became increasingly arbitrary, and he was deposed and imprisoned in 1399.

Richard III (1452–85), King of England (1483–5), younger brother of the Yorkist, Edward IV, is believed to have murdered his two nephews in the Tower. He was defeated and killed at Bosworth by the invading Earl of Richmond, who as Henry VII brought to an end the Wars of the Roses. Richard's character is disputed, but he was able and might have been a successful ruler.

Richardson, Sir Albert Edward (1880–1964), British architect, author of *Georgian Architecture*.

Richardson, Sir Owen Willans (1879–1959), English physicist who worked on thermionics, or emission of electricity from hot bodies. Nobel prizewinner 1928.

Richardson, Sir Ralph David (1902–83), English actor who worked at the Old Vic, on the West End stage, and at Stratford-on-Avon, and appeared in films, including *South Riding*, *Anna Karenina*, and *The Fallen Idol*.

Richardson, Samuel (1689–1761), English author of *Pamela*, *Clarissa*, and *The History of Sir Charles Grandison*, exercised considerable influence on the development of the novel.

Richelieu, Armand Jean du Plessis, Duc de (1585–1642), French statesman, cardinal of the Roman church. As minister to Louis XIII from 1624 till his death, he built up the power of the French crown at home in central government, and by his military preparedness and active foreign policy gave France a lead in Europe.

Ridley, Nicholas (1500–55), English Protestant martyr, bishop of Rochester and later of London, was burnt with Latimer under Queen Mary Tudor.

Rienzi, Cola di (1313–54), Italian patriot, b. Rome, led a popular rising in 1347 and for seven months reigned as tribune, but had to flee, was imprisoned, and eventually murdered.

Rilke, Rainer Maria (1872–1926), German lyric poet, b. Prague. His work, marked by beauty of style, culminated in the *Duino Elegies* and *Sonnets to Orpheus*, both written in 1922, which gave a new musicality to German verse. His visits to Russia in 1899 and 1900 and his admiration for Rodin (who had been his wife's teacher) influenced his artistic career.

Rimbaud, Jean Nicolas Arthur (1854–91), French poet, b. Charleville, on the Meuse. In his brief poetic career (4 years from about the age of 16) he prepared the way for symbolism (*Bateau ivre*, *Les Illuminations*) and anticipated Freud (*Les déserts de l'amour*). He became in-

timate with Verlaine and at 18 had completed his memoirs. *Une saison en enfer*. He died at Marseilles.

Rimsky-Korsakov, Nikolai Andreyevich (1844–1908), Russian composer whose works include the operas *The Maid of Pskov*, *The Snow Maiden*, *Le Coq d'or*, and the symphonic suite *Scheherezade*. He was a brilliant orchestrator and re-scored many works, including Borodin's *Prince Igor*.

Rizzio, David (1533?–66), Italian musician and secretary of Mary, Queen of Scots. He was murdered in her presence at Holyrood by her jealous husband, Darnley.

Robbia, Luca Della (1400–82), Florentine sculptor who introduced enamelled terra-cotta work.

Roberts of Kandahar, 1st Earl (Frederick Sleigh Roberts) (1832–1914), British general. He took part in the suppression of the Indian Mutiny, in the Afghan war (relieving Kandahar), and when put in command in South Africa in the Boer War he relieved Kimberley and advanced to Pretoria.

Robertson, Sir William (1860–1933), the only British soldier to rise from private to field-marshal. His son, **Brian Hubert, 1st Baron** (1896–1974) served in both world wars and was chairman of the British Transport Commission, 1953–61.

Robeson, Paul (1898–1976), American Negro singer, b. Princeton, especially remembered for his singing of Negro spirituals, and his appearance in works ranging from *Showboat* to *Othello*.

Robespierre, Maximilien Marie Isidoire de (1758–94), French revolutionary. A country advocate, b. Arras, he was in 1789 elected to the States General and in 1792 to the Convention. He became a leader of the Jacobins, the more extreme party which came to power under stress of war and after the king's execution in 1793. In this crisis, the Committee of Public Safety, of which he was a member and which used his reputation as a cloak, sent many to the guillotine. He opposed the cult of Reason and inaugurated the worship of the Supreme Being. In the reaction from the reign of terror he was denounced, tried to escape, but was guillotined.

Robinson, William Heath (1872–1944), English cartoonist and book-illustrator, especially known for his fantastically humorous drawings of machines.

Rob Roy (Robert McGregor) (1671–1734), Scottish freebooter who helped the poor at the expense of the rich, and played a lone hand in the troubled times of the Jacobite rising of 1715.

Robsart, Amy (1532–60), English victim (it is believed) of murder. The wife of Robert Dudley, Earl of Leicester, she was found dead at Cumnor Place. Her death was used by Scott in *Kenilworth*.

Rockefeller, John Davison (1839–1937), American philanthropist, b. Richford, N.Y. He settled in Cleveland, Ohio, and with his brother William founded the Standard Oil Company, making a fortune. His philanthropic enterprises are carried on by the Rockefeller Foundation. **Nelson Rockefeller** (1908–79), Gov. of New York 1958–73, Vice-Pres. of the United States 1974–7, was his grandson.

Rodin, Auguste (1841–1917), French sculptor, b. Paris. His best-known works include *Le Penseur*, *Les Bourgeois de Calais*, the statues of Balzac and Victor Hugo, and *La Porte d'Enfer*, a huge bronze door for the Musée des Arts Décoratifs, which was unfinished at his death.

Rodney, 1st Baron (George Rodney) (1719–92), English admiral, who served in the Seven Years War and the War of American Independence; in the latter war he defeated the French fleet under de Grasse.

Roland de la Platière, Manon Jeanne (1754–93), a leading figure in the French revolution. Her husband **Jean Marie** (1734–93), belonged to the more moderate or Girondist party, and when threatened escaped; but she was imprisoned and executed. She wrote *Letters* and *Memoirs*.

Rolland, Romain (1866–1944), French author, whose main work is a ten-volume novel, *Jean-Christophe*, the biography of a German musician, based on the life of Beethoven, and a study of contemporary French and German civilisation. Nobel prizewinner 1915.

Romilly, Sir Samuel (1757–1818), English lawyer

and law-reformer, who aimed at mitigating the severity of the criminal law.

Rommel, Erwin (1891–1944), German Field-Marshal. He took part in the 1940 invasion of France, and was later successful in commanding the Afrika Korps till 1944. He committed suicide.

Romney, George (1734–1802), English artist, b. in Lancashire. He painted chiefly portraits, especially of Lady Hamilton, and lived mainly in London, but returned to Kendal to die.

Röntgen, Wilhelm Konrad von (1845–1923), German scientist who in 1895 discovered X-rays. Nobel prizewinner 1901.

Roosevelt, Franklin Delano (1882–1945), American statesman, a distant cousin of Theodore Roosevelt. During the first world war he held office under Wilson, and though stricken with poliomyelitis in 1921 continued his political career, becoming governor of New York in 1929 and U.S. president in 1933 (the first to hold office for more than two terms), till his death. A Democrat, he met the economic crisis of 1933 with a policy for a "New Deal" (*see* **Sec. L**). He strove in vain to ward off war. Towards other American countries his attitude was that of "good neighbour." After Pearl Harbor, he energetically prosecuted the war, holding meetings with Churchill and Stalin, and adopting a "lend-lease" policy for arms. He kept contact with his people by "fireside talks." His wife **Eleanor** (1884–1962) was a public figure in her own right, and was chairman of the U.N. Human Rights Commission 1947–51.

Roosevelt, Theodore (1858–1919), American president. Popular because of his exploits in the Spanish-American war, he was appointed Republican vice-president in 1900, becoming president when McKinley was assassinated, and was re-elected 1905. He promoted the regulation of trusts; and his promotion of peace between Russia and Japan gained the Nobel prize, 1906.

Rops, Félicien (1833–98), Belgian artist, known for his often satirical lithographs and etchings.

Ross, Sir James Clark (1800–62), Scottish explorer of polar regions, who accompanied his uncle Sir John, and himself discovered the north magnetic pole in 1831. He commanded the *Erebus* and *Terror* to the antarctic (1839–43), where his discoveries included the Ross ice barrier.

Ross, Sir John (1777–1856), Scottish explorer of polar regions, uncle of the above. He searched for the north-west passage and discovered Boothia peninsula.

Ross, Sir Ronald (1857–1932), British physician, b. India, who discovered the malaria parasite. He was in the Indian medical service, and later taught tropical medicine in England. Nobel prizewinner 1902.

Rossetti, Dante Gabriel (1828–82), English poet and painter, son of **Gabriele** (1783–1852), an exiled Italian author who settled in London in 1842. With Millais, Holman Hunt and others he formed the Pre-Raphaelite brotherhood which returned to pre-Renaissance art forms. His model was often his wife, Elizabeth Siddal. His poems include *The Blessed Damozel*. His sister **Christina Georgina** (1830–94) wrote poetry, including *Goblin Market*.

Rossini, Gioacchino Antonio (1792–1868), Italian operatic composer. See **Section E**.

Rostand, Edmond (1868–1918), French dramatist, whose *Cyrano de Bergerac* created a sensation in 1898.

Rothenstein, Sir William (1872–1945), English portrait painter. His son, **Sir John** (b. 1901), is an art historian and until 1964 was director of the Tate Gallery; he has written an autobiography.

Rothschild, Meyer Amschel (1743–1812), German financier, founder of a banking family, b. Frankfurt. His five sons controlled branches at Frankfurt, Vienna, Naples, Paris and London (**Nathan Meyer**, 1777–1836). Nathan's son, **Lionel** (1808–79), was the first Jewish member of the House of Commons.

Roubiliac, Louis François (1695–1762), French sculptor who settled in London and carved a statue of Handel for Vauxhall gardens and one of Newton for Trinity College, Cambridge.

Rouget de Lisle, Claude Joseph (1760–1836), French poet, author of words and music of the *Marseillaise*, revolutionary and national anthem.

Rousseau, Henri (1844–1910), influential French "Sunday" painter, called "Le Douanier" because he was a customs official; self-taught, he was for long unrecognised as an artist of considerable talent and originality; he used the botanical gardens for his jungle scenes.

Rousseau, Jean-Jacques (1712–78), French political philosopher and educationist, b. Geneva, herald of the romantic movement. After a hard childhood he met Mme. de Warens who for some years befriended him. In 1741 he went to Paris where he met Diderot and contributed articles on music and political economy to the *Encyclopédie*. *La Nouvelle Héloïse* appeared in 1760, *Emile*, and *Le Contrat Social* in 1762. *Emile* is a treatise on education according to "natural" principles and *Le Contrat Social*, his main work, sets forth his political theory. It begins, "Man is born free and everywhere he is in chains." Both books offended the authorities and he had to flee, spending some time in England. Later he was able to return to France. His views on conduct and government did much to stimulate the movement leading to the French Revolution. *See also* **Education, Section J.**

Rubens, Sir Peter Paul (1577–1640), Flemish painter. B. in exile, his family returned to Antwerp in 1587. He studied in Italy and visited Spain. His range was wide, his compositions vigorous, and he was a remarkable colourist. *Peace and War, The Rape of the Sabines*, and *The Felt Hat* are in the National Gallery.

Rubinstein, Anton Grigorovich (1829–94), Russian pianist and composer, who helped to found the conservatoire at St. Petersburg (Leningrad); as did his brother **Nicholas** (1835–81) at Moscow.

Rücker, Sir Arthur (1848–1915), English physicist, who made two magnetic surveys of the British Isles, 1886, and 1891.

Ruisdael, Jacob van (*c.* 1628–82), Dutch painter of landscapes, b. Haarlem. Several of his works are in the National Gallery, including *Coast of Scheveningen* and *Landscape with ruins*. He was also a fine etcher.

Runcie, Robert (b. 1921), enthroned 102nd Archbishop of Canterbury in 1980; Bishop of St. Albans, 1970–80; Principal of Cuddesdon College, Oxford 1960–69.

Rupert, Prince (1619–82), general, son of Frederick of Bohemia and his wife Elizabeth, daughter of James I of England. He commanded the Royalist cavalry in the English civil war, but was too impetuous for lasting success.

Rusk, Dean (b. 1909), American politician, who has held various posts especially in connection with foreign affairs; a former Rhodes scholar.

Ruskin, John (1819–1900), English author and art critic, b. London. His *Modern Painters* in 5 volumes was issued over a period of years, the first volume having a strong defence of Turner. He helped to establish the Pre-Raphaelites. Other notable works include *The Seven Lamps of Architecture*, *The Stones of Venice* and *Praeterita*. *Unto this Last* develops his views on social problems, and he tried to use his wealth for education and for non-profitmaking enterprises. Ruskin College at Oxford, the first residential college for working people, is named after him. In 1848 he married Euphemia Gray, but in 1854 she obtained a decree of nullity and later married Millais.

Russell, 3rd Earl (Bertrand Arthur William Russell) (1872–1970), English philosopher, mathematician, and essayist, celebrated for his work in the field of logic and the theory of knowledge, and remembered for his moral courage, belief in human reason and his championship of liberal ideas. He published more than 60 books, including *The Principles of Mathematics* (1903). *Principia Mathematica* (in collaboration with A. N. Whitehead; 3 vols., 1910–13), *The Problem of Philosophy* (1912), *Mysticism and Logic* (1918), *The Analysis of Mind* (1921), *An Inquiry into Meaning and Truth* (1940), *History of Western Philosophy* (1945), and a number on ethics and social questions. His *Autobiography* (3 vols.) appeared 1967–9. He was the grandson of Lord John Russell and John Stuart Mill was his godfather. Nobel prize for literature 1950; O.M. 1949.

Russell, 1st Earl (John Russell), (1792–1878), English statesman, third son of the 6th Duke of Bedford. He had a large share in carrying the parliamentary reform bill of 1832. He was Whig prime minister 1846–52 and 1865–6. He was also a historian and biographer.

Russell of Killowen, 1st Baron (Charles Russell), (1832–1900) British lawyer, b. Ireland; lord chief justice 1894–1900. He defended Parnell.

Rutherford, 1st Baron (Ernest Rutherford) (1871–1937), British physicist, b. New Zealand, eminent in the field of atomic research. His experiments were conducted at Manchester and Cambridge and attracted young scientists from all over the world. In 1911 he announced his nuclear theory of the atom and in 1918 succeeded in splitting the atom. His work prepared the way for future nuclear research.

Ruysdael, Jacob van. *See* Ruisdael.

Ruyter, Michiel Adrianszoon de (1607–76), Dutch admiral who ranks with Nelson. He fought against England and in 1667 caused alarm by sailing up the Medway as far as Rochester and up the Thames as far as Gravesend. He was mortally wounded at Messina.

S

Sachs, Hans (1494–1576), German poet, b. Nuremberg. A shoemaker, he wrote over 6,000 pieces, some dealing with everyday life, many (including *Die Wittenbergische Nachtigall*) inspired by the Reformation.

Sachs, Julius von (1832–97), German botanist, founder of experimental plant physiology. He demonstrated that chlorophyll is formed in chloroplasts only in light.

Sadat, Mohammed Anwar El (1919–81), Egyptian statesman, President of Egypt 1970–81. His visit to Israel in Nov. 1977 was a bold and courageous move which led to the Camp David peace treaty with Israel. Assassinated 1981.

Sádi or **Saadi** (Muslih Addin) (c. 1184–1292), Persian poet, b. Shiraz, best known for his *Gulistan* (Flower Garden).

Sainte-Beuve, Charles Augustin (1804–69), French critic, b. Boulogne. He studied medicine, abandoning it for journalism, and after attempting to write poetry, turned to literary criticism. His work reveals the wide range of his intellectual experience and includes *Causeries du lundi* and *Histoire de Port-Royal*.

Saint-Just, Antoine (1767–94), French revolutionary, a follower of Robespierre.

St. Laurent, Louis Stephen (1882–1973), Canadian politician, prime minister 1948–57.

Saint-Saëns, Charles Camille (1835–1921), French composer, for 20 years organist at the Madeleine. His compositions include symphonic and chamber music and the opera *Samson et Dalila*, which was produced by Liszt at Weimar in 1877. *See* Section E.

Saint-Simon, Claude, Comte de (1760–1825), French socialist, who in his *L'Industrie* and *Nouveau christianisme* prepared the way for much later thought.

Saintsbury, George Edward (1845–1933), English critic and literary historian.

Sakharov, Andrei Dimitrievich (b. 1921), Soviet nuclear physicist and human rights campaigner. Nobel prizewinner 1975.

Sala, George Augustus (1828–95), English journalist who contributed to *Household Words* and was a notable foreign correspondent.

Saladin (el Melik an-Nasir Salah ed-Din) (1137–93), sultan of Egypt and Syria and founder of a dynasty, who in 1187 defeated the Christians near Tiberias and took Jerusalem. This gave rise to the unsuccessful Third Crusade, in which Richard I of England joined. His great qualities were admired by his opponents, and his administration left many tangible signs in such matters as roads and canals.

Salazar, Antonio d'Oliveira (1889–1970), Portuguese dictator, having first been premier in 1932, a new constitution being adopted in 1933. He gave Portugal stability, but refused to bow to nationalism in Portuguese Africa and India.

Salimbene de Adamo (1221–c. 1228), mediaeval chronicler, b. Parma, whose vivid description of life in the 13th cent. is embodied in his *Cronica*.

Salisbury, 3rd Marquess (Robert Arthur Talbot Gascoyne-Cecil (1830–1903), English Conservative

statesman, prime minister 1885–6, 1886–92, 1895–1902, mainly remembered for his conduct of foreign affairs during a critical period, culminating in the Boer War. His grandson, **Robert Arthur, 5th Marquess** (1893–1972), led the Conservative opposition in the House of Lords.

Samuel, 1st Viscount (Herbert Samuel) (1870–1963), British Liberal statesman of Jewish parentage. He published philosophical works, including *Practical Ethics*.

Sand, George (1804–76), pseudonym of the French writer Armandine Lucie Dupin. Her publications are extensive and varied, and include the novel *Mauprat*, rural studies, and an autobiography *Histoire de ma vie*. She was associated with Alfred de Musset and Chopin.

Sandow, Eugene (1867–1925), German "strong man" who opened an Institute of Health in London.

Sanger, Frederick (b. 1918), British scientist noted for his work on the chemical structure of the protein insulin. Nobel prizewinner 1958, and 1980. O.M. (1986).

Sankey, Ira David (1840–1908), American evangelist and composer, associated with Moody.

San Martin, José de (1778–1850), South American national leader in securing independence from Spanish rule to his native Argentina, Chile and Peru.

Santayana, George (1863–1952), American philosopher and poet, b. Madrid, of Spanish parentage. He was professor of philosophy at Harvard, 1907–12. His books include *The Sense of Beauty*, *The Life of Reason*, and *The Realms of Being*.

Santos-Dumont, Alberto (1873–1932), Brazilian aeronaut who in 1898 flew a cylindrical balloon with a gasoline engine. In 1909 he built a monoplane.

Sappho of Lesbos (fl. early 6th cent. B.C.), Greek poetess, of whose love poems few remain.

Sardou, Victorien (1831–1908), French dramatist popular in his day. Sarah Bernhardt created famous parts in *Fédora*, *Théodora* and *La Tosca*; *Robespierre* and *Dante* were written for Irving.

Sargent, John Singer (1856–1922), American painter, b. Florence, who worked mainly in England, especially on portraits.

Sargent, Sir Malcolm (1895–1967), popular British conductor, who conducted the Promenade Concerts from 1950 till his death, and succeeded Sir Adrian Boult as conductor of the B.B.C. Symphony Orchestra, 1950–7.

Sartre, Jean-Paul (1905–80), French existentialist philosopher, left-wing intellectual, dramatist, essayist and novelist. His major philosophical work is *L'Etre et le Néant* and his plays include *Les Mouches*, *Huis Clos*, *Crime passionel*, *La Putain respectueuse*, and *Les Séquestrés d'Altona*. He was awarded (though he declined it) the 1964 Nobel prize.

Sassoon, Siegfried (1886–1967), English poet and writer with a hatred of war. He is mainly known for *The Memoirs of a Foxhunting Man*, the first part of the *Memoirs of George Sherston*.

Savonarola, Girolamo (1452–98), Florentine preacher and reformer, a Dominican friar, who denounced vice and corruption not only in society but also in the Church itself, especially attacking Pope Alexander VI. He was excommunicated, imprisoned, and with two of his companions, hanged and burned. His passion for reform made him impatient of opposition and incapable of compromise, yet he was a notable figure and commands the respect of later ages. George Eliot's *Romola* portrays him.

Scarlatti, Alessandro (1659–1725), Italian musician who founded the Neapolitan school of opera. He composed over 100 operas, 200 masses, and over 700 cantatas and oratorios. His son **Domenico** (1685–1757) was a harpsichord virtuoso whose work influenced the evolution of the sonata. The chief years of his life were spent at the Spanish court in Madrid. *See* Section E.

Scheele, Carl Wilhelm (1742–86), Swedish chemist, discoverer of many chemical substances, including oxygen (c. 1773—but published in 1777 after the publication of Priestley's studies).

Schiaparelli, Giovanni Virginio (1835–1910), Italian astronomer, noted for having observed certain dark markings on the surface of the planet Mars which he called canals (recent close-range photographs show none).

Schiller, Johann Christoph Friedrich von (1759–1805), German dramatist and poet, b. Marbach in Württemberg, began life as a military surgeon. His play *The Robbers* with a revolutionary theme was successful in 1782 in Mannheim. After a stay at Dresden, where he wrote *Don Carlos*, and at Jena, where he wrote a history of the Thirty Years War, he became the friend of Goethe and removed to Weimar, where he wrote *Wallenstein, Mary Stuart, The Maid of Orleans* and *William Tell*. He is a leading figure in the European romantic movement.

Schirrmann, Richard (1874–1961), German originator of youth hostels. A schoolmaster, in 1907 he converted his schoolroom during holidays to a dormitory. The Verband für deutsche Jugendherbergen was founded in 1913, and the International Youth Hostels Federation in 1932, with Schirrmann as first president.

Schlegel, Friedrich von (1772–1829), German critic, b. Hanover, prominent among the founders of German romanticism, whose revolutionary and germinating ideas influenced early 19th-cent. thought. His brother, **August Wilhelm** (1767–83, 1845), made remarkable translations of Shakespeare (which established Shakespeare in Germany), Dante, Calderón, and Camões.

Schliemann, Heinrich (1822–90), German archaeologist, who conducted excavations at Troy and Mycenae. He has been the subject of numerous biographies mostly based on his own writings which are now viewed with some scepticism.

Schmidt, Helmuth (b. 1918), German social democrat (SPD) statesman; suceeded Brandt as Chancellor of the West German Federal Republic 1974–83. *See* Section C, Part II.

Schnabel, Artur (1882–1951), American pianist of Austrian birth, regarded as a leading exponent of Beethoven's pianoforte sonatas.

Schoenberg, Arnold (1874–1951), Austrian composer of Jewish parentage who in 1933 was exiled by the Nazi regime and settled in America, teaching at Boston and Los Angeles. Among his works are the choral orchestral *Gurre-Lieder* and *Pierrot Lunaire*, a cycle of 21 poems for voice and chamber music. *See* Section E.

Schopenhauer, Arthur (1788–1860), German philosopher, b. Danzig, important historically for his pessimism, and his doctrine that will is superior to knowledge. His chief work is *The World as Will and Idea*. He regarded his contemporary Hegel as a charlatan.

Schubert, Franz Peter (1797–1828), Austrian composer, b. Vienna, the son of a schoolmaster, and a contemporary of Beethoven. He wrote not only symphonies, sonatas, string quartets, choral music and masses, but also over 600 songs of unsurpassed lyrical beauty. He might almost be called the creator of the German *Lied* as known today.

Schumann, Robert Alexander (1810–56), composer of the early 19th cent. German romantic school. He wrote much chamber music, four symphonies, a piano concerto, and choral music, but it is his early piano pieces and songs that give constant delight. His wife **Clara** (1819–96) was one of the outstanding pianists of her time.

Schweitzer, Albert (1875–1965), Alsatian medical missionary, theologian, musician and philosopher, b. at Kaysersberg. After publishing learned works, he resigned a promising European career to found at Lambaréné in French Equatorial Africa a hospital to fight leprosy and sleeping sickness and made it a centre of service to Africans. His funds were raised by periodic organ recitals in Europe. His motivation was not patronage but atonement. Nobel peace prize 1952. O.M. 1955.

Scipio, Publius Cornelius (237–183 B.C.), Roman general in the second Punic War, known as Scipio Africanus the elder. **Scipio Africanus the younger** (185–129 B.C.) was an adoptive relative and an implacable opponent of Carthage (destroyed 146).

Scott, Charles Prestwich (1846–1931), English newspaper editor. Under his editorship (1872–1929) the *Manchester Guardian* (now *The Guardian*) became a leading journal.

Scott, Sir George Gilbert (1811–78), English architect in the Gothic revival. He restored many churches and designed the Albert Memorial and the Martyrs' Memorial at Oxford.

Scott, Sir Giles Gilbert (1880–1960), English architect, grandson of above, designed the Anglican cathedral at Liverpool and planned the new Waterloo Bridge.

Scott, Robert Falcon (1868–1912), English antarctic explorer. He led two expeditions; one 1901–4 which discovered King Edward VII Land; and another 1910–12 which reached the south pole and found the Amundsen records; but while returning the party was overtaken by blizzards and perished 11 miles from their base. *See also* Antarctic exploration, Sec. L. His son, **Sir Peter Scott** (b. 1909), is an artist and ornithologist.

Scott, Sir Walter (1771–1832), Scottish novelist and poet, b. Edinburgh. He was educated for the law, but came to know and love the Border country and his interests were literary; and in 1802–3 he issued a collection of ballads, *Border Minstrelsy*. Poems such as *Marmion* and *The Lady of the Lake* followed. His novels appeared anonymously, beginning with *Waverley* in 1814; and continuing with *Guy Mannering, The Antiquary, Old Mortality, Rob Roy*, and *The Heart of Midlothian*. From 1819 he turned also to English history, with *Ivanhoe* and *Kenilworth*. In 1826 he became bankrupt, largely as the fault of his publishing partner.

Scott-Paine, Hubert (1891–1954), pioneer in the design and construction of aircraft and sea-craft.

Scriabin, Alexander (1872–1915), Russian composer and pianist, who relied to some extent on extra-musical factors such as religion, and in *Prometheus* tried to unite music and philosophy. *See* Section E.

Seeley, Sir John Robert (1834–95), English historian, author of a life of Christ, *Ecce Homo*.

Segovia, Andrés (b. 1894), Spanish concert-guitarist. He has adapted works by Bach, Haydn, Mozart etc. to the guitar.

Selfridge, Harry Gordon (1858–1947), American-born merchant who in 1909 opened a new style of department store in Oxford Street.

Semmelweis, Ignaz Philipp (1818–65), Hungarian obstetrician, a pioneer in the use of antiseptic methods, thus reducing the incidence of puerperal fever.

Seneca, Lucius Annaeus (*c.* 4 B.C.–A.D. 65), Roman stoic philosopher who was a tutor to Nero, but lost favour and was sentenced to take his own life.

Senefelder, Alois (1772–1834), Bavarian inventor of lithography about 1796.

Severus, Lucius Septimius (146–211), Roman emperor, and a successful general. On a visit to Britain he suppressed a revolt, repaired Hadrian's Wall, and died at York.

Sévigné, Marie de Rabutin-Chantai, Marquise de (1626–96), French woman of letters. Her letters to her daughter Françoise written in an unaffected elegance of style give a moving picture of fashionable society in 17th cent. France.

Sgambati, Giovanni (1841–1914), Italian pianist (pupil of Liszt), composer and teacher, who revived interest in classical instrumental music in an age of opera.

Shackleton, Sir Ernest Henry (1874–1922), British explorer, who made four antarctic expeditions; that of 1909 reached within 100 miles of the south pole. He died on his last expedition.

Shaftesbury, 7th Earl of (Anthony Ashley Cooper) (1801–85), English philanthropist largely responsible for legislation reducing the misery of the industrial revolution. He was for 40 years chairman of the Ragged Schools Union.

Shakespeare, William (1564–1616), England's greatest poet and dramatist, b. Stratford-on-Avon. Little is known of his career up to his eighteenth year, when he married Anne Hathaway. He came to London at the height of the English renaissance and soon became connected with the Globe theatre as actor and playwright. Thirty-eight plays comprise the Shakespeare canon. Thirty-six were printed in the First Folio of 1623 (the first collected edition of his dramatic works), of which eighteen had been published during his lifetime in the so-called Quartos. *Love's Labour's Lost* and *The Comedy of Errors* seem to have been among the earliest, being followed by *The Two Gentlemen of Verona*, and *Romeo and Juliet*. Then followed *Henry VI, Richard III, Richard II, Titus Andronicus, The Taming of the Shrew, King John, The*

Merchant of Venice, A Midsummer Night's Dream, All's Well that Ends Well, Henry IV, The Merry Wives of Windsor, Henry V, Much Ado about Nothing, As You Like It, Twelfth Night. Then came some of his greatest plays, *Julius Caesar, Hamlet, Troilus and Cressida, Othello, Measure for Measure, Macbeth, King Lear, Timon of Athens, Pericles, Antony and Cleopatra, Coriolanus, Cymbeline, A Winter's Tale, The Tempest, Henry VIII,* and *The Two Noble Kinsmen.* In mastery of language, in understanding of character, in dramatic perception, and in skill in the use of ritual he has never been surpassed. Fresh interpretation of his work continues.

Sharp, Granville (1735–1813), English abolitionist of slavery, and founder of the colony of Sierra Leone.

Shastri, Shri Lal Bahadur (1904–66), Indian politician who became prime minister of India after the death of Nehru in 1964. He died of a heart attack at the end of the Soviet-sponsored Tashkent talks.

Shaw, George Bernard (1856–1950), Irish dramatist who conquered England by his wit and exposure of hypocrisy, cant, and national weaknesses, and whose individual opinions found expression in musical criticism, socialist pamphlets and plays. His plays include *Man and Superman, Heartbreak House, Back to Methuselah, Saint Joan, The Apple Cart,* and *Buoyant Billions,* and most have important prefaces. In 1884 he joined the newly-born Fabian Society. Nobel prizewinner 1925.

Shelley, Percy Bysshe (1792–1822), English poet, b. Horsham. He was a master of language and of literary form, and a passionate advocate of freedom and of new thought. Sent down from Oxford for his pamphlet *The Necessity of Atheism,* he came under the influence of William Godwin; and, after his first marriage came to an unhappy end, married the latter's daughter, Mary Wollstonecraft, herself a writer. In the same year began his friendship with Byron. His works include *The Revolt of Islam,* The *Masque of Anarchy* (an indictment of Castlereagh), *The Cenci* (a play on evil), and *Prometheus Unbound,* besides lyrics such as *To a Skylark* and *Ode to the West Wind.* He was accidentally drowned while sailing near Spezzia.

Sheppard, Hugh Richard (Dick) (1880–1937), Anglican divine and pacifist. He made St. Martin-in-the-Fields a centre of social service and also founded the Peace Pledge Union.

Sheraton, Thomas (1751–1806), English cabinet-maker, b. Stockton, whose *Cabinetmaker's Book* promoted neo-classical designs.

Sheridan, Richard Brinsley (1751–1816), British dramatist, b. Dublin. He was a brilliant writer of comedies, especially *The Rivals, The Duenna, The School for Scandal,* and *The Critic.* He acquired and rebuilt Drury Lane theatre, which reopened in 1794, but was burnt down in 1809; and this, with his lack of business sense, brought him to poverty, in spite of his friends' efforts to help him. He was also in parliament where he made some notable speeches.

Sherman, William Tecumseh (1820–91), American general, who served especially in the Civil War. He took part in the battles of Bull Run and Shiloh, was appointed in 1864 to the command of the southwest, and with 65,000 men marched across Georgia to the sea. In 1865 he accepted Johnston's surrender.

Sherrington, Sir Charles Scott (1875–1952), English scientist, an authority on the physiology of the nervous system. His research led to advances in brain surgery. His principal work is *Integration Action of the Nervous System* (1906). Shared with E. D. Adrian the 1932 Nobel prize.

Shirley, James (1596–1666), English dramatist. His tragedies include *The Traitor,* and his comedies *Hyde Park.* His death was hastened by the Great Fire.

Sholokhov, Mikhail Aleksandrovich (1905–84), Russian novelist, author of *And Quiet Flows the Don.* Nobel prizewinner 1965.

Shostakovich, Dimitri (1906–75), Russian composer whose music is complex, profound, and deeply significant of the Soviet age in which he lived. His works include operas, ballets, symphonies, chamber music, and music for films. Hero of Soviet Labour 1966. *See* **Section E.**

Sibelius, Jean (1865–1957), Finnish composer imbued with national feeling. His works include seven symphonies, a violin concerto, and several tone poems, notably *Finlandia,* and some based on the Finnish poem *Kalevala.* *See* **Section E.**

Sickert, Walter Richard (1860–1942), British artist, b. Munich. He was influenced by Degas, and has himself influenced later painters. His *Ennui* is in the Tate Gallery.

Siddons, Sarah (1755–1831), English actress especially in tragic parts. She was daughter of the manager Roger Kemble and her reputation was almost unbounded.

Sidgwick, Henry (1838–1900), English philosopher who wrote *Methods of Ethics,* and who also promoted women's education, especially in the foundation of Newnham and Girton colleges at Cambridge.

Sidney, Sir Philip (1554–86), English poet and writer, best remembered for his *Arcadia, Apologie for Poetrie,* and *Astrophel and Stella,* all published after his death. He was killed at the battle of Zutphen, where he passed a cup of water to another, saying "Thy necessity is greater than mine."

Siemens, Sir William (1823–83), German-born electrical engineer who settled in England and constructed many overland and submarine telegraphs. He was brother of **Werner von Siemens,** founder of the firm of Siemens-Halske.

Sienkiewicz, Henryk (1846–1916), Polish novelist and short-story writer; best known of his historical novels is *Quo Vadis?* Nobel prizewinner 1905.

Sikorski, Vladislav (1881–1943), Polish general and statesman, prime minister of the Polish government in exile (1939) and commander-in-chief of the Polish forces. Killed in an aircraft accident at Gibraltar.

Simpson, Sir James Young (1811–70), Scottish obstetrician who initiated the use of chloroform in childbirth.

Sinclair, Upton (1878–1968), American novelist whose documentary novel *The Jungle* on the Chicago slaughter yards caused a sensation in 1906.

Singer, Isaac Merritt (1811–75), American mechanical engineer who improved early forms of the sewing-machine and patented a single-thread and chain-stitch machine.

Sisley, Alfred (1839–99), French impressionist painter of English origin, who painted some enchanting landscapes, such as *Meadows in Spring* in the Tate Gallery. He was influenced by Corot and Manet.

Sitwell, Edith (1887–1964), English poet, a great experimenter in verse forms. *Gold Coast Customs, Façade* (set to music by William Walton) and *Still Falls the Rain* are probably best known. She had two brothers, **Osbert** (1892–1969) and **Sacheverell** (b. 1897), both poets and critics.

Slim, 1st Viscount (William Slim) (1891–1970), British general. He commanded the 14th Army in Burma, was chief of the Imperial General Staff 1948–52, and governor-general of Australia 1953–60.

Sloane, Sir Hans (1660–1753), British collector, b. Ireland. He practised in London as a physician. His library of 50,000 volumes and his collection of MSS. and botanical specimens were offered under his will to the nation and formed the beginning of the British Museum.

Slowacki, Julius (1809–49), Polish romantic poet, a revolutionary, he lived in exile in Paris. His work includes the poetic dramas *Kordian, Balladyna* and *Lilli Weneda,* written in the style of Shakespeare; and the unfinished poem *King Spirit* which reveals his later mystical tendencies.

Smeaton, John (1724–92), English engineer; he rebuilt Eddystone lighthouse (1756–59), improved Newcomen's steam-engine, and did important work on bridges, harbours, and canals. He also invented an improved blowing apparatus for iron-smelting.

Smetana, Bedřich (1824–84), Czech composer, creator of a national style. He was principal conductor of the Prague National Theatre, for which he wrote most of his operas, including *The Bartered Bride* and *The Kiss.* Best known of his other compositions are the cycle of symphonic poems *My Country* and the string quartets *From My Life.* He became totally deaf in 1874, suffered a mental breakdown, and died in an asylum. *See* **Section E.**

Smiles, Samuel (1812–1904), Scottish writer, *b.* Haddington, in early life a medical practitioner, remembered for *Self Help* (1859), and his biographies of engineers of the industrial revolution.

Smith, Adam (1723–90), Scottish economist, *b.* Kirkcaldy. In Edinburgh he published *Moral Sentiments.* Later he moved to London, and his *Wealth of Nations* (1776) is the first serious work in political economy.

Smith, Sir Grafton Eliot (1871–1937), Australian anatomist who did research on the structure of the mammalian brain. His works include *The Evolution of Man.*

Smith, John (1580–1631), English adventurer who in 1605 went on a colonising expedition to Virginia and was saved from death by the Red Indian Pocahontas.

Smith, Joseph (1805–44), American founder of the Mormons. He claimed that the *Book of Mormon* was revealed to him. In 1838 feeling against the Mormons culminated in a rising and Smith was murdered. He was succeeded by Brigham Young. *See* **Mormonism, Section J.**

Smith, Sydney (1771–1845), Anglican divine and journalist, who founded the *Edinburgh Review* and supported Catholic emancipation.

Smith, William (1760–1839), English surveyor and canal-maker, the first to map the rock strata of England and to identify the fossils peculiar to each layer.

Smith, Sir William Alexander (1854–1914), Scottish founder of the Boys' Brigade (1883), the oldest national organisation for boys in Britain.

Smith, William Robertson (1846–94), Scottish biblical scholar whose "Bible" contribution to the 9th edition of *The Encyclopaedia Britannica* resulted in an unsuccessful prosecution for heresy.

Smollett, Tobias George (1721–71), Scottish novelist whose work is characterised by satire and coarse humour. His main novels are *Roderick Random, Peregrine Pickle,* and *Humphrey Clinker.*

Smuts, Jan Christian (1870–1950), South African statesman and soldier. B. in Cape Colony, during the Boer War he fought on the Boer side. He was premier of the Union 1919–24, 1939–48, and worked for cooperation within the Commonwealth and in the world, but his party was defeated in 1948 by the Nationalists under Malan.

Smyth, Ethel Mary (1858–1944), English composer and suffragette. Her main works are operas (*The Wreckers* and *The Boatswain's Mate*) and a *Mass in D.* She studied at the Leipzig Conservatory.

Snow, Baron (Charles Percy Snow) (1905–80), English physicist and novelist, author of the essay *The Two Cultures of the Scientific Revolution,* and a sequence of novels *Strangers and Brothers* (11 vols.).

Snyders, Frans (1597–1657), Flemish still-life and animal painter who studied under Breughel.

Soane, Sir John (1753–1837), English architect who designed the Bank of England. He left the nation his house and library in Lincoln's Inn Fields (Soane Museum).

Sobers, Sir Garfield (b. 1936), West Indies and Nottinghamshire cricketer who ranks as one of the greatest all-rounders. Knighted 1975.

Socinus or **Sozzini Laelius** (1525–62), Italian founder of the sect of Socinians, with his nephew **Faustus** (1539–1604). Their teachings resemble those of Unitarians.

Socrates (470–399 B.C.), Greek philosopher and intellectual leader, was the son of a sculptor of Athens. He distinguished himself in three campaigns (Potidaea, Delium, and Amphipolis). Returning to Athens, he devoted himself to study and intellectual enquiry, attracting many followers; through these, especially Xenophon and Plato, we know of his teachings, for he wrote nothing. In 399 B.C. he was charged with impiety and with corrupting the young, found guilty, and accordingly died by drinking hemlock; *see* Plato's *Apology, Crito,* and *Phaedo.*

Soddy, Frederick (1877–1956), English chemist, who in Glasgow about 1912 laid the foundation of the isotope theory, before the physicists became prominent in that field. Nobel prizewinner 1921.

Solon (638–558 B.C.), Athenian lawgiver, who in a time of economic distress cancelled outstanding debts, and introduced some democratic changes.

Solzhenitsyn, Alexander, Isayevich (b. 1918), Russian novelist, b. Rostov-on-Don; author of *One Day in the Life of Ivan Denisovich,* a documentary novel depicting life in one of Stalin's prison camps where he spent many years of his life. He was expelled from the Soviet Writers' Union in 1969, and from his country in 1974. Nobel prizewinner 1970.

Somerset, Duke of (**Edward Seymour**) (1506–52), lord protector of England in the time of the young Edward VI, but he fell from power and was executed.

Sophocles (495–406 B.C.), Athenian dramatist, who was awarded the prize over Aeschylus in 468. Of over a hundred plays of his, the only extant ones are *Oedipus the King, Oedipus at Colonus Antigone, Electra, Trachiniae, Ajax, Philoctetes.*

Sorel, Georges (1847–1922), French advocate of revolutionary syndicalism, author of *Reflections on Violence* (1905). The irrational aspects of his philosophy (derived from Bergson) appealed to Mussolini and the Fascists.

Soult, Nicolas Jean de Dieu (1769–1851), French general who fought under Napoleon in Switzerland and Italy, at Austerlitz, and in the Peninsular War.

Sousa, John Philip (1854–1932), American bandmaster and composer of some stirring marches.

Southey, Robert (1774–1843), English poet and historian. In 1803 he settled near Coleridge at Keswick, and in 1813 became poet laureate. His best work was in prose: histories of Brazil and of the Peninsular War; lives of Nelson Wesley, and others.

Southwell, Robert (1561–95), English poet and Jesuit martyr, beatified 1920. His poems include *The Burning Babe.*

Spaak, Paul Henri (1899–1972), Belgian statesman, first president of the U.N. General Assembly in 1946, and of the Assembly of the Council of Europe, 1949–51; secretary-general of NATO, 1957–61.

Spartacus (d. 71 B.C.), Thracian rebel. A Roman slave and gladiator in Capua, he escaped and headed a slave insurrection, routing several Roman armies, but was defeated and killed by Crassus.

Speke, John Hanning (1827–64), British explorer. In 1858 he discovered the Victoria Nyanza; and in 1860 with J. A. Grant traced the Nile flowing out of it.

Spence, Sir Basil Urwin (1907–76), Scottish architect, mainly known for the new Coventry cathedral, and for Hampstead civic centre. He also brought a new approach to university buildings. O.M. 1962.

Spencer, Herbert (1820–1903), English philosopher. B. Derby, he was at first a civil engineer, then a journalist (sub-editor of the *Economist*), when he wrote *Social Statics.* He coined the phrase (1852) "the survival of the fittest" and his *Principles of Psychology* (1855), published four years before Darwin's *Origin of Species,* expounded doctrines of evolution. His ten-volume *Synthetic Philosophy* was issued over a period of thirty years.

Spencer, Sir Stanley (1891–1959), English artist of visionary power. His two pictures of the *Resurrection* are in the Tate Gallery. He also painted Cookham regatta.

Spengler, Oswald (1880–1936), German historicist who held that every culture is destined to a waxing and waning life cycle and that the West European culture was entering its period of decline. His principal work is *The Decline of the West.* His views prepared the way for national socialism.

Spenser, Edmund (1552–99), English poet, b. London and educated at Cambridge. His *Shepheards Calendar* appeared in 1579. In 1580 he went to Ireland as the lord deputy's secretary, and later acquired Kilcolman castle, where he wrote most of his main work, *The Faerie Queene.* His castle was burnt in an insurrection in 1598, when he returned to London. He is called "the poet's poet."

Spinoza, Baruch (1632–77), Dutch philosopher, b. Amsterdam, whose parents came to Holland from Portugal to escape the Inquisition. An independent thinker, his criticism of the Scriptures led to his being excommunicated from the synagogue. He supported himself by grinding and polishing lenses. He owed much to Descartes but was mainly concerned with religion and virtue. His philosophical theories are set out in the *Ethics* which was published posthumously. In the light of modern science his metaphysic cannot be accepted but his moral teaching has enduring validity.

Spofforth, Reginald (1770–1827), English writer of glees, including *Hail, Smiling Morn*.

Spurgeon, Charles Haddon (1834–92), English Baptist who preached at the vast Metropolitan Tabernacle, London, from 1861 (burnt down 1898).

Staël, Anne Louise, Baronne de Staël-Holstein (1766–1817), French writer. Daughter of the finance minister, Necker, she married the Swedish ambassador, and kept a salon. Her *Lettres sur Rousseau* appeared in 1788. After the revolution she lived partly abroad, partly in France, and after a visit to Italy wrote her novel *Corinne* (1807).

Stalin (Joseph Vissarionovich Djugashvili) (1879–1953), Soviet statesman who for nearly 30 years was leader of the Russian people. He originally studied at Tiflis for the priesthood, but became an active revolutionary and took part in the civil war after 1917. After Lenin's death, he ousted Trotsky and became the outstanding figure. He modernised agriculture on socialist lines by ruthless means, and his series of five-year plans from 1929 made Russia an industrial power. On the German invasion in 1941 he assumed military leadership; and later attended Allied war conferences. After his death some of his methods and the "personality cult" were denounced by Khrushchev, and this had far-reaching results in other Communist countries. In his attack on "official" Marxism, George Lukács says Stalin "turned Marxism on its head" by making it into theories and strategies which fitted his own tactics of the day.

Stanford, Sir Charles Villiers (1852–1924), Irish composer of instrumental, choral, operatic, and other music.

Stanley, Sir Henry Morton (1841–1904), British explorer, b. Denbigh. He fought for the Confederates in the American Civil War. He then became a correspondent for the *New York Herald*, was commissioned to find Livingstone, and did so in 1871 at Ujiji, and with him explored Lake Tanganyika. In 1879 he founded the Congo Free State under the Belgian king. His works include *Through the Dark Continent* and an *Autobiography*.

Stark, Freya Madeline (b. 1893), British writer and explorer of the Arab world.

Steele, Sir Richard (1672–1729), British essayist, b. Dublin. He founded the *Tatler* (1709–11), to which Addison also contributed, and later the *Spectator* (1711–12) and the *Guardian* (1713).

Steen, Jan (1626–79), Dutch genre painter, b. Leiden, son of a brewer. *The Music Lesson* and *Skittle Alley* are in the National Gallery, the *Lute Player* in the Wallace collection.

Steer, Philip Wilson (1860–1942), English painter, especially of landscapes and of portraits.

Stefansson, Vilhjalmur (1879–1962), Canadian arctic explorer of Icelandic parentage; his publications include *Unsolved Mysteries of the Arctic*.

Stein, Sir Aurel (1862–1943), British archaeologist, b. Budapest. He held archaeological posts under the Indian government and explored Chinese Turkestan.

Stendhal, pseudonym of Marie Henri Beyle (1783–1842), French novelist, b. Grenoble. He was with Napoleon's army in the Russian campaign of 1812, spent several years in Italy, and after the revolution of 1830 was appointed consul at Trieste, and afterwards at Civitavecchia. In his plots he recreates historical and social events with imaginative realism and delineates character with searching psychological insight. His main works are *Le Rouge et le Noir*, and *La Chartreuse de Parme*.

Stephen (1105–54), usurped the crown of England from Henry I's daughter in 1135; and, after anarchy, retained it till his death.

Stephen, Sir Leslie (1832–1904), English writer, critic, and biographer. He edited the *Cornhill Magazine* (1871–82), and the *Dictionary of National Biography* (1882–91), and was the father of Virginia Woolf.

Stephenson, George (1781–1848), English engineer; a locomotive designer, b. at Wylam near Newcastle, a colliery fireman's son. As enginewright at Killingworth colliery he made his first locomotive in 1814 to haul coal from mines. He and his son Robert built the *Locomotion* for the Stockton and Darlington Railway (1825), the first locomotive for a public railway. His *Rocket* at 30 miles an hour won the prize of £500 in 1829 offered by the Liverpool and Manchester Railway. He also discovered the principle on which the miners' safety lamp was based. He was the first president of the Institution of Mechanical Engineers.

Stephenson, Robert (1803–59), English engineer, son of the above, engineered railway lines in England and abroad, and built many bridges including the Menai and Conway tubular bridges.

Sterne, Laurence (1713–68), English novelist and humorist. His main works are *Tristram Shandy* and *A Sentimental Journey*. He led a wandering and unconventional life, dying in poverty. His work helped to develop the novel.

Stevenson, Adlai (1900–65), American politician, an efficient governor of Illinois, 1949–53; ambassador to the U.N., 1960–5, and unsuccessful presidential challenger to Eisenhower 1952 and 1956.

Stevenson, Robert (1772–1850), Scottish engineer and builder of lighthouses, who invented "intermittent" and "flashing" lights.

Stevenson, Robert Louis (1850–94), Scottish author, b. Edinburgh. He suffered from ill-health and eventually settled in Samoa. His main works are *Travels with a Donkey, Treasure Island, Kidnapped, Dr. Jekyll and Mr. Hyde,* and *The Master of Ballantrae.*

Stinnes, Hugo (1870–1924), German industrialist who built up a huge coalmining, iron and steel, and transport business, and later entered politics.

Stockton, Earl of. See under **Macmillan, Harold**

Stoker, Bram (Abraham Stoker) (1847–1912), Irish author of the horror story *Dracula* and *Personal Reminiscences of Henry Irving.*

Stokes, Sir George Gabriel (1819–1903), Irish mathematician and physicist to whom is due the modern theory of viscous fluids and the discovery that rays beyond the violet end of the spectrum (the ultra-violet rays) produce fluorescence in certain substances.

Stopes, Marie Carmichael (1880–1958), English pioneer advocate of birth control. Her *Married Love* appeared in 1918, and she pioneered birth control clinics.

Stowe, Harriet Beecher (1811–96), American author of *Uncle Tom's Cabin* (1852), written to expose slavery.

Strachey, John St. Loe (1901–63), English Labour politician and writer. He held office under Attlee, 1945–51.

Stradivari, Antonio (1644–1737), Italian maker of violins, b. Cremona, first in his art.

Strafford, 1st Earl of (Thomas Wentworth) (1593–1641), English statesman. He supported Charles I with a "thorough" policy, both as president of the north and as lord deputy in Ireland, where he introduced flax. His efficiency made him a special target when parliament met, and he was impeached and executed.

Strauss, David Friedrich (1808–74), German theologian, whose *Life of Jesus* attempted to prove that the gospels are based on myths.

Strauss, family of Viennese musicians. **Johann Strauss** (1804–49), the elder, was a composer of dance music, who with Joseph Lanner established the Viennese waltz tradition. His son, **Johann Strauss** (1825–99), the younger, although not so good a violinist or conductor as his father, was the composer of over 400 waltzes, which include *The Blue Danube* and *Tales from the Vienna Woods.* Two of his brothers, **Josef Strauss** (1827–70) and **Eduard Strauss** (1835–1916) were also composers and conductors.

Strauss, Richard (1864–1949), German composer and conductor, the son of a horn player in the opera orchestra at Munich. He succeeded von Bülow as court musical director at Meiningen. His works include the operas *Salome, Elektra,* and *Der Rosenkavalier,* the symphonic poems *Don Juan, Till Eulenspiegel,* and *Don Quixote,* and many songs. *See* **Section E.**

Stravinsky, Igor (1882–1971), Russian composer and conductor, pupil of Rimsky-Korsakov. His ballets. *The Fire Bird* (1910). *Petrushka*

(1911), representative of his early romantic style, and the revolutionary *The Rite of Spring*, which caused a furore in 1913, were written for the ballet impresario Diaghilev. He adopted a neo-classical style in later works, for example, in the ballets *Pulcinella* and *Apollo Musagetes* and the opera-oratorio *Oedipus Rex*. He brought new vigour and freedom to rhythm and younger composers have been much influenced by his music. He became a French citizen in 1934 and a U.S. citizen in 1945. *See* **Section E.**

Strindberg, Johan August (1840–1912), Swedish writer of intense creative energy. His work is subjective and reflects his personal conflicts. He married three times but never happily. He produced some 55 plays as well as novels, stories, poems, and critical essays. *Lucky Peter, Gustav Adolf, Till Damascus, The Father, Miss Julie* are some of his plays.

Suckling, Sir John (1609–42), English poet, author of *Why so pale and wan?* He invented cribbage.

Sudermann, Hermann (1857–1928), German writer of plays and novels, including *Frau Sorge* (translated as Dame Care).

Sulaiman the Magnificent (1494–1566), sultan of Turkey, conqueror, and patron of art and learning, who dominated the eastern Mediterranean but failed to capture Malta.

Sullivan, Sir Arthur Seymour (1842–1900), Irish composer, mainly known for the music he wrote for light operas with W. S. Gilbert as librettist, especially *The Pirates of Penzance, Patience, The Mikado, The Yeomen of the Guard* and *The Gondoliers*. He also wrote sacred music which was popular at the time. He and a friend discovered Schubert's lost *Rosamunde* music.

Sully, Maximilien de Béthune, Duc de (1560–1641), French statesman, finance minister to Henry IV. He also left *Memoirs*.

Sun Yat Sen (1867–1925), Chinese revolutionary, idealist and humanitarian. He graduated in medicine at Hong Kong, but after a rising failed in 1895 he lived abroad, planning further attempts, which succeeded in 1911 when the Manchus were overthrown and he became president. He soon resigned in favour of Yuan Shih-kai.

Sutherland, Graham Vivian (1903–80), British artist. He painted the 80th birthday portrait of Sir Winston Churchill for parliament, and designed the tapestry for Coventry cathedral. O.M. 1960.

Swan, Sir Joseph Wilson (1829–1914), British scientist who shares with Edison the invention of the incandescent electric lamp. He also invented a number of printing processes.

Swedenborg, Emanuel (1689–1772), Swedish author of *Arcana Coelestia, The Apocalypse Revealed, Four Preliminary Doctrines,* and *The True Christian Religion.* He claimed that his soul had been permitted to travel into hell, purgatory, and heaven. His works became the scriptures of the sect named Swedenborgians.

Sweelinck, Jan Pieterszoon (1562–1621), Dutch organist and composer of sacred music. In his fugues he made independent use of the pedals, and prepared the way for Bach. *See* **Section E.**

Swift, Jonathan (1667–1745), English satirist, b. Dublin of English parents. He crossed to England in 1688 to become secretary to Sir William Temple, and took Anglican orders, but did not obtain promotion. His *Tale of a Tub* and *The Battle of the Books* appeared in 1704. At first active in Whig politics, he became Tory in 1710, writing powerful tracts such as *Conduct of the Allies* (1711). In 1714 he retired to Ireland as Dean of St. Patrick's. His devoted women friends followed him—Hester Johnson (d. 1728), the Stella of his *Journal,* and Esther Vanhomrigh (d. 1723), the Vanessa of his poetry. Here he wrote his best work, including *Gulliver's Travels* (1726) and *The Drapier's Letters.*

Swinburne, Algernon Charles (1837–1909), English poet and critic. He first won attention with a play, *Atalanta in Calydon*, in 1865, followed by *Poems and Ballads.* Later followed *Songs before Sunrise, Bothwell,* and *Mary Stuart.* His criticism includes an essay on Blake.

Swithin, St. (d. 862), English saint, bishop of Winchester. Violent rain for 40 days fell in 971 when his body was to be removed to the

new cathedral; hence the superstition as to rain on 15 July.

Syme, Sir Ronald (b. 1903), Camden Professor of Ancient History at Oxford, 1949–70; an authority on Tacitus. O.M. 1976.

Symonds, John Addington (1840–93), English author who wrote on the Italian Renaissance.

Synge, John Millington (1871–1909), Irish poet and playwright, author of *Riders to the Sea* and *The Playboy of the Western World.* He was a director of the Abbey Theatre.

T

Tacitus, Gaius Cornelius (*c.* 55–120), Roman historian. His chief works are a life of his father-in-law Agricola, and his *Histories* and *Annals.*

Tagore, Sir Rabindranath (1861–1941), Indian poet and philosopher who tried to blend east and west. His works include the play *Chitra.* Nobel prize 1913 (first Asian recipient).

Talbot, William Henry Fox (1800–77), English pioneer of photography which he developed independently of Daguerre. He also deciphered the cuneiform inscriptions at Nineveh.

Talleyrand-Périgord, Charles Maurice de (1754–1838), French politician and diplomat, led a mission to England in 1792 and was foreign minister from 1797 until 1807. He represented France at the Congress of Vienna.

Tallis, Thomas (*c.* 1510–85), English musician, with Byrd joint organist to the chapel royal under Elizabeth. He composed some of the finest of our church music.

Tamerlane (Timur the Lame) (1336–1405), Mongol conqueror. Ruler of Samarkand, he conquered Iran, Transcaucasia, Iraq, Armenia, and Georgia, and invaded India and Syria. He defeated the Turks at Angora, but died marching towards China. A ruthless conqueror, he was also a patron of literature and the arts. The line of rulers descended from him are the Timurids. He is the subject of a play by Marlowe.

Tarquinius: two kings of Rome came from this Etruscan family; **Lucius the Elder** (d. 578 B.C.); and **Lucius Superbus,** or the proud, (d. 510 B.C.) whose tyranny provoked a successful rising and brought an end to the monarchy.

Tartini, Giuseppe (1692–1770), Italian violinist, who wrote *Trillo del Diavolo.* He discovered the "third sound" resulting from two notes sounded together, a scientific explanation of which was later given by Helmholtz.

Tasman, Abel Janszoon (1603–59), Dutch navigator despatched by Van Diemen. He discovered Tasmania or Van Diemen's Land, and New Zealand, in 1642.

Tasso, Torquato (1544–95), Italian epic poet, b. Sorrento, author of *Gerusalemme Liberata.* He also wrote plays, *Aminta* and *Torrismondo.*

Tawney, Richard Henry (1880–1962), British historian. b. Calcutta, pioneer of adult education, and leader of socialist thought—the first critic of the affluent society. His works include *The Acquisitive Society, Equality, Religion and the Rise of Capitalism.*

Taylor, Sir Geoffrey Ingram (1886–1975), British scientist, noted for his work on aerodynamics, hydrodynamics, and the structure of metals. O.M. 1969.

Taylor, Jeremy (1613–67), English divine, b. Cambridge, author of many religious works, of which the chief are *Holy Living* and *Holy Dying.*

Tchaikovsky, Peter Ilyich (1840–93), Russian composer. His music is melodious and emotional and he excelled in several branches of composition. Among his works are the operas *Eugene Onegin* and *The Queen of Spades* (both from stories by Pushkin), symphonies, including the *Little Russian* and the *Pathétique,* ballets, including *Swan Lake, The Sleeping Beauty,* and *The Nutcracker,* the fantasies *Romeo and Juliet,* and *Francesca da Rimini,* the piano concerto in B flat minor, the violin concerto in D, and numerous songs. *See* **Section E.**

Tedder, 1st Baron (Arthur William Tedder) (1890–1967), British air marshal. From 1940 he reorganised the Middle East Air Force and later became deputy supreme commander under

B59

Eisenhower for the invasion of Europe. He wrote an autobiography.

Teilhard de Chardin, Pierre (1881–1955), French palæontologist and religious philosopher. He went on palæontological expeditions in Asia, but his research did not conform to Jesuit orthodoxy, and his main works were published posthumously, *The Phenomenon of Man* and *Le Milieu Divin.*

Telemann, Georg Philipp (1681–1767), German composer, b. Magdeburg. His vitality and originality of form are appreciated today after a long period of neglect.

Telford, Thomas (1757–1834), Scottish engineer, originally a stonemason. He built bridges (two over the Severn and the Menai suspension bridge), canals (the Ellesmere and Caledonian canals), roads, and docks.

Tell, William, legendary Swiss patriot, reputedly required by the Austrian governor Gessler to shoot an apple from his son's head, and the subject of a play by Schiller. The story is late, but the Swiss confederation did first arise in the 14th cent. with Schwyz, Uri, and Unterwalden.

Temple, Frederick (1821–1902), English divine. He was headmaster of Rugby, 1857–69, and archbishop of Canterbury, 1897–1902.

Temple, William (1881–1944), English ecclesiastic, son of above, was a leading moral force in social matters and a worker for ecumenism. He was headmaster of Repton, 1910–14, and became archbishop of Canterbury in 1942.

Temple, Sir William (1628–99), English diplomat and writer, was instrumental in bringing about the marriage of Princess Mary with William of Orange. Swift was his secretary.

Templewood, 1st Viscount (Samuel John Gurney Hoare) (1880–1959), British Conservative politician. He piloted the India Act through the Commons while secretary for India, 1931–5; and as foreign secretary he negotiated an abortive pact with Laval.

Teniers, David, the elder (1582–1649), and **the younger** (1610–94), Flemish painters of rural life and landscape. The elder lived at Antwerp and the younger at Brussels.

Tenniel, Sir John (1820–1914), English book illustrator, especially for *Alice in Wonderland* and *Punch.*

Tennyson, 1st Baron (Alfred Tennyson) (1809–92), English poet-laureate, b. Somersby, Lincs. A master of language, his publications extended over 60 years, mirroring much of his age. *In Memoriam* reflects his grief for his friend Arthur Hallam. Apart from his lyrics, his longer works include *The Princess, Maud, Idylls of the King,* and *Enoch Arden.* Interest in his work is returning.

Terence, Publius Terentius Afer (*c.* 184–159 B.C.), a Latin poet and dramatist, an African (Berber), who rose from the position of a slave.

Teresa, St. (1515–82), influential Spanish religious reformer and writer, b. Avila, a woman of boundless energy and spiritual strength. She entered the Carmelite order about 1534, established a reformed order in 1562 (St. Joseph's, Avila), and also founded, with the help of St. John of the Cross, houses for friars. Her writings which rank high in mystical literature include *The Way of Perfection* and *The Interior Castle.*

Terry, Ellen Alice (Mrs. James Carew) (1848–1928), English actress, especially in Shakespearean parts with Sir Henry Irving, and in the plays of her friend Bernard Shaw.

Tertullian Quintus (*c.* 160–220), Carthaginian theologian whose works, especially *Apologeticum,* have profoundly influenced Christian thought.

Tesla, Nikola (1856–1943), Yugoslav physicist and inventor; went to America 1883; pioneer in high-tension electricity.

Tettrazzini, Luisa (1871–1940), Italian soprano, especially successful in *Lucia di Lammermoor.*

Tetzel, John (*c.* 1465–1519), German Dominican preacher, whose sale of indulgences for St. Peter's building fund provoked Luther.

Thackeray, William Makepeace (1811–63), English novelist, b. Calcutta, author of *Vanity Fair, Pendennis, Esmond, The Newcomes, The Virginians, Philip,* and *Lovel the Widower.* He edited the *Cornhill Magazine* from the first number in 1860, his most notable contributions being *Roundabout Papers.* He also wrote *Yellow-plush Papers, The Book of Snobs,* and *The Four Georges* (lectures given in the United States).

Thales of Miletus (*c.* 624–565 B.C.), earliest of the Greek scientists, he created a sensation by his prediction of an eclipse of the sun, which was visible at Miletus in 585 B.C. He looked upon water as the basis of all material things, and in his mathematical work was the first to enunciate natural laws. *See also* **God and Man, Section J.**

Thant, Sithu U (1909–74), Burmese diplomat; secretary-general of the United Nations 1962–1972.

Thatcher, Margaret Hilda (b. 1925), leader of the Conservative Party 1975– ; prime minister, 1979– ; first woman to lead a western democracy; secured landslide victory, June 1983; M.P. (Finchley), 1959– . Historic accord with China over Hong Kong, December 1984. *See* **Section C, Part I.**

Themistocles (*c.* 523–458 B.C.), Athenian soldier and statesman. He fortified the harbour of Piraeus and created a navy, defeating the Persians at Salamis in 480 B.C. He prepared the way for later greatness, but fell from power and died in exile.

Theocritus (*c.* 310–250 B.C.), Greek poet, especially of pastoral subjects. His short poems came to be called *Idylls.*

Theodoric the Great (455–526), King of the East Goths, who conquered Italy. Himself an Arian, he practised toleration, and his long reign was peaceful and prosperous.

Theodosius the Great (346–95), Roman emperor of the East (the Empire being divided in 364). He was baptised as a Trinitarian, issuing edicts against the Arians, and after a judicial massacre at Thessalonica he did penance to (St.) Ambrose.

Theophrastus (*c.* 372–287 B.C.), Greek philosopher, who succeeded Aristotle as teacher at Athens and inherited his library. He is best known for his botanical works and his *Characters* (moral studies).

Thibaud, Jacques (1880–1953), French violinist, killed in an air crash.

Thierry, Augustin (1795–1856), French historian, known for his *History of the Norman Conquest.*

Thiers, Louis Adolphe (1797–1877), French statesman and historian. After a varied political career, he became president in 1871, helping to revive France after defeat. He wrote a history of the Revolution.

Thomas, Dylan (1914–53), Welsh poet, whose highly individual *Eighteen Poems* (1934) brought him instant recognition. There followed *Twenty-five Poems* and *Deaths and Entrances. Under Milk Wood,* a play for voices, has more general appeal.

Thompson, Sir D'Arcy Wentworth (1860–1948), Scottish zoologist whose *On Growth and Form* (1917), written in lucid and elegant style, has influenced biological science.

Thomson, Sir George Paget (1892–1975), English physicist, son of Sir J. J. Thomson; author of *The Atom, Theory and Practice of Electron Diffraction, The Inspiration of Science.* Nobel prizewinner 1937.

Thomson, James (1700–48), Scottish poet who wrote *The Seasons* and *The Castle of Indolence.*

Thomson, James (1834–82), poet and essayist, b. near Glasgow, who wrote *The City Of Dreadful Night.*

Thomson, Sir Joseph John (1856–1940), English physicist and mathematician, leader of a group of researchers at the Cavendish laboratory, Cambridge. He established in 1897 that cathode-rays were moving particles whose speed and specific charge could be measured. He called them corpuscles but the name was changed to electrons. This work was followed up by the study of positive rays which led to the discovery of isotopes, the existence of which had earlier been suggested by Soddy. Nobel prizewinner 1906.

Thoreau, Henry David (1817–62), American essayist and nature-lover, who rebelled against society and lived for a time in a solitary hut. His chief work is *Walden.* He was a friend of Emerson.

Thorez, Maurice (1900–64), French communist leader from 1930 and especially after the second world war.

Thorndike, Dame Sybil (1882–1976), English actress. She made her début in 1904, and played in Greek tragedies, in the plays of Shakespeare and Shaw, and in Grand Guignol. Her husband was Sir Lewis Casson.

Thornycroft, Sir William Hamo (1850–1925), English sculptor, whose works include a statue of General Gordon in Trafalgar Square.

Thorpe, Sir Thomas Edward (1845–1925), English chemist who researched in inorganic chemistry and with his friend Arthur Rücker made a magnetic survey of the British Isles.

Thorwaldsen, Bertel (1770–1844), Danish sculptor whose works include the Cambridge statue of Byron.

Thucydides (c. 460–399 B.C.), Greek historian, especially of the Peloponnesian War in which he himself fought. He was not merely a chronicler, but saw the significance of events and tried to give an impartial account. The speeches attributed by him to leaders include the beautiful funeral oration of Pericles.

Tiberius, Claudius (42 B.C.–A.D. 37), Roman emperor who succeeded Augustus. His early reign was successful but his later years were marked by tragedy and perhaps insanity. His is the Tiberius of Luke 3.1.

Tillett, Benjamin (1860–1943), English trade-union leader, especially of a dockers' strike in 1889 and a transport-workers' strike in 1911.

Tillotson, John (1630–94), English divine, a noted preacher who became archbishop of Canterbury in 1691.

Tindal, Matthew (1655–1733), English deist, author of *Christianity as old as the Creation*.

Tintoretto (1518–94), Venetian painter whose aim it was to unite the colouring of Titian with the drawing of Michelangelo. His numerous paintings, mostly of religious subjects, were executed with great speed, some of them on enormous canvases. His *Origin of the Milky Way* is in the National Gallery. His name was Jacopo Robusti, and he was called Il Tintoretto (little dyer) after his father's trade.

Tippett, Sir Michael Kemp (b. 1905), English composer whose works include the operas *The Midsummer Marriage*, *King Priam*, and *Knot Garden*, and the song-cycles *Boyhood's End* and *The Heart's Assurance*. O.M. 1983. *See* **Section E.**

Titian (Tiziano Vecelli) (c. 1487–1576), Venetian painter. He studied under the Bellinis and was influenced by Giorgione, for example, in his frescoes at Padua. His mature style is one of dynamic composition and full colour, as in his *Bacchus and Ariadne* (National Gallery). Among his principal works are *Sacred and Profane Love* (Borghese Gallery, Rome), and some in the Prado, Madrid.

Tito (Josip Broz) (1892–1980), Yugoslav leader, b. Kumrovec. In 1941 he organised partisan forces against the Axis invaders, liberated his country, and carried through a communist revolution. In 1945 he became the first communist prime minister and in 1953 president. He successfully pursued an independent line for his country. Order of Lenin (1972).

Titus (A.D. 39–81), Roman emperor, son of Vespasian, brought the Jewish war to a close with the capture of Jerusalem. He completed the Colosseum.

Tizard, Sir Henry Thomas (1885–1959), English scientist and administrator. He was chairman of the Scientific Survey of Air Defence (later known as the Tizard Committee) that encouraged the birth of radar before the second world war and turned it into a successful defence weapon. He was chief scientific adviser to the government, 1947–52.

Tocqueville, Alexis, Comte de (1805–59), French liberal politician and historian, author of *Democracy in America*, still relevant reading.

Todd, 1st Baron (Alexander Robertus Todd) (b. 1907), Scottish biochemist, noted for his work on the structure of nucleic acids. Nobel prizewinner 1957; Pres. Royal Society 1975. Chancellor Univ. of Strathclyde. O.M. 1977.

Tolstoy, Leo Nikolayevich, Count (1828–1910), Russian writer and philosopher, b. Yasnaya Polyana. Of noble family, he entered the army and fought in the Crimean War. Beginning with simple, natural accounts of his early life (*Childhood* and *Boyhood*), he proceeded to articles on the war, and so eventually to perhaps his best work, the long novel *War and Peace*, followed by *Anna Karenina*. Increasingly pre-

occupied with social problems, he freed his serfs before this was done officially, and refused to take advantage of his wealth. His later works include *The Kreutzer Sonata* and *Resurrection*. By many he was regarded as a moral teacher.

Tooke, John Horne (1736–1812), English politician and pamphleteer, was a supporter of Wilkes and later of Pitt. He was tried for high treason, but was acquitted.

Torquemada, Tomas de (1420–98), first inquisitor-general of Spain.

Torricelli, Evangelista (1608–47), Italian physicist, pupil of Galileo. He invented the barometer and improved both microscope and telescope.

Toscanini, Arturo (1867–1957), Italian conductor, b. Parma. He had a remarkable musical memory, and was at the same time exacting and self-effacing. He spent the second world war in exile.

Toulouse-Lautrec, Henri de (1864–1901), French painter, whose pictures portray with stark realism certain aspects of Parisian life in the nineties, especially the *Moulin Rouge* series. Many are in the Musée Lautrec at Albi.

Tovey, Sir Donald Francis (1875–1940), English pianist and composer. His compositions include chamber music, a piano concerto, and an opera *The Bride of Dionysus*; and his writings *Essays in Musical Analysis*.

Toynbee, Arnold (1852–83), English historian and social reformer. The settlement Toynbee Hall was founded in his memory.

Toynbee, Arnold Joseph (1889–1975), nephew of above, English historian, known mainly for his 10-volume *A Study of History*, an analysis of many civilisations. He was for 30 years director of the Institute of International Affairs.

Traherne, Thomas (c. 1636–74), English religious poet, b. Hereford; author also of *Centuries of Meditations*.

Trajan (c. 53–117), Roman emperor, was a successful general and firm administrator. He was born in Spain.

Tree, Sir Herbert Beerbohm (1853–1917), English actor-manager of the Haymarket theatre until 1897 when he built His Majesty's theatre. Sir Max Beerbohm was his half-brother.

Trenchard, 1st Viscount (Hugh Montague Trenchard) (1873–1956), British air-marshal. He served with the Royal Flying Corps in the first world war and became the first air marshal of the R.A.F. He was largely responsible for the R.A.F. college at Cranwell and was also concerned in establishing Hendon police college.

Trent, 1st Baron (Jesse Boot) (1850–1931), British drug manufacturer, b. Nottingham. He built up the largest pharmaceutical retail trade in the world, and was a benefactor of Nottingham and its university.

Trevelyan, George Macaulay (1876–1962), English historian, known for his *History of England* and *English Social History*.

Trevelyan, Sir George Otto (1838–1928), English liberal politician, father of above. He wrote a life of his uncle Lord Macaulay.

Trevithick, Richard (1771–1833), English mining engineer and inventor, b. near Redruth, Cornwall. His most important invention was a high-pressure steam-engine (1801) and he is commonly acknowledged as the inventor of the steam locomotive for railways.

Trollope, Anthony (1815–82), English novelist. His early life was a struggle, the family being supported by his mother's writings. His own career was in the post office, but by strict industry he produced many novels especially portraying clerical life (the *Barchester* series) and political life (the *Phineas Finn* series).

Trotsky, Leo (Lev Davidovich Bronstein) (1879–1940), Russian revolutionary, b. of Jewish parents in the Ukraine, one of the leaders of the Bolshevik revolution. As commissar of foreign affairs under Lenin he led the Russian delegation at the Brest-Litovsk conference. He differed from Stalin on policy, believing in "permanent revolution," according to which socialism could not be achieved in Russia without revolutions elsewhere, and was dismissed from office in 1925 and expelled from the Communist party in 1927. In 1929 he took up exile in Mexico where he was assassinated.

Trudeau, Pierre Eliott (b. 1919), Liberal prime minister of Canada 1968–79, 1980–84.

Truman, Harry F. (1884–1972), U.S. President, 1945–53. He inherited the presidency on Roosevelt's death in 1945 when he took the decision to drop the first atom bomb, and he won the election of 1948. He intervened in Korea, dismissed General MacArthur, and aimed at raising standards in underdeveloped countries.

Tulsi Das (1532–1623), Indian poet whose masterpiece *Ram-Charit-Mānas* (popularly known as the *Ramayana* and based on the Sanskrit epic of Vālmiki) is venerated by all Hindus as the Bible is in the West.

Turenne, Henri de la Tour d'Auvergne, Vicomte de (1611–75), French commander who was successful in the Thirty Years' War.

Turgenev, Ivan Sergeyvich (1818–83), Russian novelist, friend of Gogol and Tolstoy, who spent part of his life in exile. His works include *Fathers and Children, Smoke,* and *Virgin Soil.*

Turner, Joseph Mallord William (1775–1851), English landscape painter, b. London, a barber's son. He entered the Royal Academy and was at first a topographical watercolourist. Later he turned to oil and became a master of light and colour, achieving magical effects, especially in depicting the reflection of light in water. His works include *Crossing the Brook, Dido building Carthage, The Fighting Temeraire, Rain, Steam and Speed.* He also made thousands of colour studies. He encountered violent criticism as his style became more abstract which led to Ruskin's passionate defence of him in *Modern Painters.* He bequeathed his work to the nation (National and Tate Galleries, and the British Museum).

Tussaud, Marie (1761–1850), Swiss modeller in wax who learnt from her uncle in Paris, married a Frenchman, and later came to England where she set up a permanent exhibition.

Tutankhamun (d. c. 1340 B.C.), Egyptian pharaoh of the 18th dynasty, son-in-law of Akhenaten, whose tomb was discovered by Howard Carter in 1922, with the mummy and gold sarcophagus intact. He died when he was 18.

Twain, Mark (Samuel Langhorne Clemens) (1835–1910), American humorist. His *Innocents Abroad* was the result of a trip to Europe. His works include *A Tramp Abroad, Tom Sawyer, Huckleberry Finn,* and *Pudd'nhead Wilson.*

Tweedsmuir, 1st Baron (John Buchan) (1875–1940), Scottish author of biographies, historical novels, and adventure stories, including *Montrose* and *Thirty-nine Steps.* He was governor-general of Canada 1935–40.

Tyler, Wat (d. 1381), English peasant leader. He was chosen leader of the Peasants' Revolt of 1381 (due to various causes), and parleyed at Smithfield with the young king Richard II, but was killed.

Tyndale, William (c. 1494–1536), English religious reformer, translator of the Bible. He had to go abroad, where he visited Luther and his New Testament was printed at Worms. When copies entered England they were suppressed by the bishops (1526). His Pentateuch was printed at Antwerp, but he did not complete the Old Testament. He was betrayed, arrested, and executed. Unlike Wyclif, who worked from Latin texts, he translated mainly from the original Hebrew and Greek and his work is later to become the basis of the Authorised Version of the Bible.

Tyndall, John (1829–93), Irish physicist whose wide interests led him to research on heat, light, and sound, and on bacteria-free air and sterilisation. He discovered why the sky is blue (Tyndall effect) and pioneered popular scientific writing, *e.g., Heat as a Mode of Motion.* A mountaineer, one of the peaks of the Matterhorn is named after him.

U

Unamuno, Miguel de (1864–1936), Spanish philosopher, poet, essayist, and novelist, author of *El Sentimiento Trágico de la Vida* (The Tragic Sense of Life).

Ulanova, Galina (b. 1910), Russian ballerina, who made her début in 1928.

Undset, Sigrid (1882–1949), Norwegian novelist, daughter of an antiquary, author of *Jenny, Kristin Lavransdatter,* and *Olav Audunsson.* Nobel prizewinner 1928.

Unwin, Sir Raymond (1863–1940), English architect of the first garden city at Letchworth.

Ursula, St., said in late legend to have been killed by Huns at Cologne with many companions while on pilgrimage. It took rise from a 4th cent. inscription which simply referred to virgin martyrs.

Usher or **Ussher, James** (1581–1656), Irish divine who in 1625 became archbishop of Armagh, and whose writings include a long-accepted chronology, which placed the creation at 4004 B.C.

V

Valentine, St., was a christian martyr of the reign of the emperor Claudius II (d. A.D. 270). The custom of sending valentines may be connected with the pagan festival of Lupercalia.

Valéry, Paul (1871–1945), French poet and essayist, strongly influenced by the symbolist leader, Mallarmé. His poems include *La jeune Parque, Charmes,* and *Le cimetière marin.*

Vanbrugh, Sir John (1664–1726), English architect and playwright. His buildings include Blenheim Palace and his plays *The Provok'd Wife.*

Vancouver, George (1758–98), British navigator who served under Captain Cook, also doing survey work, and who sailed round Vancouver island.

Vanderbilt, Cornelius (1794–1877), American merchant and railway speculator who amassed a fortune and founded a university at Nashville. His son, **William Henry Vanderbilt** (1821–85), inherited and added to it.

Van Dyck, Sir Anthony (1599–1641), Flemish painter, b. Antwerp. He studied under Rubens, travelled in Italy, and then settled in England with an annuity from Charles I. He excelled in portraits, especially of Charles I and Henrietta Maria, and of their court.

Vane, Sir Henry (1613–62), English parliamentary leader during the civil war period, though not involved in the execution of Charles I. He was executed in 1662.

Van Gogh, Vincent (1853–90), Dutch painter of some of the most colourful pictures ever created. With passionate intensity of feeling he painted without pause whatever he found around him—landscapes, still life, portraits; his was a truly personal art. His life was one of pain, sorrow, and often despair, and in the end he committed suicide.

Vauban, Sebastien de Prestre de (1633–1707), French military engineer, whose skill in siege works (*e.g.,* at Maestricht 1673) was a factor in the expansive wars of Louis XIV. He protected France with fortresses and also invented the socket bayonet.

Vaughan Williams, Ralph (1872–1958), English composer, b. Gloucestershire. After Charterhouse and Cambridge he studied music in Berlin under Max Bruch and, later in Paris, under Ravel. He wrote nine symphonies besides a number of choral and orchestral works, operas (including *Hugh the Drover, Riders to the Sea*), ballets, chamber music, and songs. He showed great interest in folk tunes. *See* **Section E.**

Velasquez, Diego (c. 1460–1524), Spanish conquistador, first governor of Cuba.

Velasquez, Diego Rodriguez de Silva y (1599–1660), Spanish painter, b. Seville, especially of portraits at the court of Philip IV, and also of classical and historical subjects. He made two visits to Italy (1629–31, 1649–51), studying the Venetian painters, especially Titian, which hastened the development of his style. Among his masterpieces are *The Maids of Honour, The Tapestry Weavers* (both in the Prado), the Rokeby Venus and a portrait of Philip IV (both in the National Gallery), the landscape views from the Villa Medici (Prado) and *Juan de Pareja* (sold in London in 1970 for £2·25 million).

Venizelos, Eleutherios (1864–1936), Greek statesman, b. Crete. He became prime minister in 1910 and held this office intermittently. He promoted the Balkan League (1912), forced the king's abdication (1917), and brought Greece into the war on the Allied side, securing territorial concessions at the peace conference, but his expansionist policy in Turkish Asia failed.

Verdi, Giuseppe (1813–1901), Italian composer, b. near Busseto in the province of Parma. His early works include *Nabucco*, *Ernani*, *I Due Foscari*, and *Macbeth*; a middle period is represented by *Rigoletto*, *Il Trovatore*, *La Traviata*, *Un Ballo in Maschera*, and *Don Carlos*; to the last period of his life belong *Aida*, *Otello*, and *Falstaff* (produced when he was 80). *See* **Section E.**

Verlaine, Paul (1844–96), French poet, one of the first of the symbolists, also known for his memoirs and confessions. His works include *Poèmes saturniens*, *Fêtes galantes*, *Sagesse*, and *Romances sans paroles*. He was imprisoned for two years in Belgium for shooting and wounding his friend Rimbaud. He died in poverty in Paris.

Vermeer, Jan (1632–75), Dutch painter, b. Delft. His main paintings are of domestic interiors, which he makes into works of art, as in *Lady at the Virginals* (National Gallery). His reputation has grown during the last century.

Verne, Jules (1828–1905), French writer of science fiction, including *Five Weeks in a Balloon*, *Twenty Thousand Leagues Under the Sea*, *Round the World in Eighty Days*.

Vernier, Pierre (1580–1637), French inventor of the small sliding scale which enables readings on a graduated scale to be taken to a fraction of a division.

Veronese, Paolo (1528–88), Italian painter of the Venetian school, whose works include *Marriage Feast at Cana in Galilee*, *The Feast in the House of Simon*, and *The Presentation of the Family of Darius to Alexander*, *His Adoration of the Magi* is in the National Gallery.

Veronica, St., legendary woman who was said to hand her kerchief to Christ on the way to Calvary, to wipe his brow, and his impression was left on the kerchief. In its present form her legend dates from the 14th cent.

Verwoerd, Hendrik Frensch (1901–66), South African politician, b. Amsterdam, exponent of the policy of apartheid; prime minister 1958–66. He was assassinated.

Vespasian, Titus Flavius (A.D. 9–79), Roman emperor. He was sent by Nero to put down the Jews and was proclaimed by the legions. He began the Colosseum.

Vespucci, Amerigo (1451–1512), Florentine explorer, naturalised in Spain, contractor at Seville for Columbus. He later explored Venezuela. The use of his name for the continent arose through a mistake.

Vico, Giambattista (1688–1744), Italian philosopher of history and of culture, b. Naples. His ideas were developed in his *Scienza nuova* (science of history) but it was not until our own day that his originality as a thinker was fully recognised.

Victor Emmanuel II (1820–78), first king of Italy. King of Sardinia, he was proclaimed king of Italy in 1861 after the Austrians had been defeated and Garibaldi had succeeded in the south. Rome was added in 1870.

Victoria (1819–1901), Queen of the United Kingdom of Gt. Britain and Ireland and Empress of India, was granddaughter of George III and succeeded an uncle in 1837. In 1840 she married Prince Albert of Saxe-Coburg-Gotha, who died in 1861. Conscientious, hard-working, and of strict moral standards, she had by the end of a long life (jubilees 1887 and 1897) won the affection and respect of her subjects in a unique degree. Her reign saw industrial expansion, growing humanitarianism, literary output, and in the main prolonged peace; and by its close the British empire and British world power had reached their highest point.

Villeneuve, Pierre de (1763–1806), French admiral defeated by Nelson at Trafalgar and captured along with his ship, the *Bucentaure*.

Villon, François (1431–?1463), French poet, b. Paris, who lived at a turbulent time at the close of the Hundred Years War. After fatally stabbing a man in 1455 he joined the *Conquillards*, a criminal organisation. They had a secret language (the *jargon*) and it was for them that he composed his ballads. His extant works consist of the *Petit Testament* (1456),

originally called *Le Lais*, and the *Grand Testament* (1461), masterpieces of mediaeval verse.

Virgil (Publius Vergilius Maro) (70–19 B.C.), Roman epic poet, b. at Andes near Mantua, he went to Rome to obtain redress for the military confiscation of his farm. He was patronised by Maecenas, and wrote his pastoral *Eclogues*, followed by his *Georgics*. His best-known work, the *Aeneid*, deals with the wanderings of Aeneas after the fall of Troy till his establishment of a kingdom in Italy.

Vivaldi, Antonio (*c.* 1675–1743), Venetian composer, violin master at the Ospedale della Pieta. His output of orchestral works was prolific and Bach arranged some of his violin pieces for the harpsichord. *See* **Section E.**

Volta, Alessandro (1745–1827), Italian physicist of Pavia, who, working on the results of Galvani, invented the voltaic pile, the first instrument for producing an electric current. It provided a new means for the decomposition of certain substances. His name was given to the volt, the unit of electrical potential difference.

Voltaire (François Marie Arouet) (1694–1778), French philosopher and writer. His first essays offended the authorities, and he spent the years 1726–9 in England, where he wrote some of his dramas. Returning to France, he published his *Philosophical Letters*, which aroused the enmity of the priesthood. At this juncture, the Marquise du Châtelet offered him the asylum of her castle of Cirey, and for the next 15 years he made this his home, writing there his *Discourses of Man*, *Essay on the Morals and Spirit of Nations*, *Age of Louis XIV*, etc. The marquise was a mathematician and taught him some science, thus helping him in his interpretation of Newton's *Principia*. To Voltaire we owe the story of the falling apple, also the dictum that Admiral Byng was shot "pour encourager les autres." He spent the years 1750–3 in Berlin at the invitation of Frederick the Great. In challenging accepted beliefs and traditions he prepared the way for the French revolution.

Vondel, Joost van don (1587–1679), Dutch poet who lived at Amsterdam. Most of his dramas are on biblical subjects, and the two most famous are *Jephtha* and *Lucifer*.

Voroshilov, Klimentiv Efremovich (1881–1969), Soviet general who commanded the Leningrad defences in 1941, and was U.S.S.R. president, 1953–60.

Vyshinsky, Andrei Yanuarievich (1883–1954), Soviet jurist and diplomat; conducted the prosecution of the Moscow treason trials, 1936–8; represented Russian interests at the U.N.

W

Wade, George (1673–1748), English general and military engineer who, after the rising of 1715, pacified the Scottish highlands, constructing military roads and bridges. In the 1745 rising Prince Charles' forces evaded him.

Wagner, Richard (1813–83), German composer, b. Leipzig. He achieved a new type of musical expression in his operas by the complete union of music and drama. He made use of the *Leitmotif* and was his own librettist. His originality and modernism aroused a good deal of opposition, and he was exiled for some years. But he was supported by loyal friends, including Liszt, the young King Ludwig of Bavaria, and the philosopher Nietzsche. He began the music of the *Ring des Nibelungen* in 1853, but it was not until 1876 that the whole of the drama (Rheingold, Valkyrie, Siegfried, Götterdämmerung) was performed at Bayreuth under the conductor Hans Richter. Other operas are *The Flying Dutchman*, *Rienzi*, *Tannhäuser*, *Lohengrin*, *Tristan und Isolde*, *Die Meistersinger von Nürnberg*, and *Parsifal*, a religious drama. He married Liszt's daughter Cosima, formerly wife of his friend Hans von Bülow.

Waldheim, Kurt (b. 1918). Austrian diplomat; succeeded U Thant as secretary-general of the United Nations. Held office, 1972–81. Elected President of Austria, 1986, amid controversy.

Waley, Arthur (1889–1966). English orientalist, known for his translations of Chinese and Japanese poetry and prose, being the first to bring the literature of those countries to the western world.

Walker, George (1618–90), hero of the siege of Londonderry in 1688, who kept the besiegers at bay for 105 days.

Wallace, Alfred Russel (1823–1913), British naturalist, b. Usk, Monmouth, joint author with Darwin of the theory of natural selection. In 1858, while down with illness in the Moluccas, he sent a draft of his theory to Darwin in England who was amazed to find that it closely agreed with his own theory of evolution which he was on the point of publishing. The result was a reading of a joint paper to the Linnean Society.

Wallace, Edgar (1875–1932), English novelist and playwright, known for his detective thrillers.

Wallace, Sir Richard (1818–90), English art collector and philanthropist. His adopted son's wife bequeathed his collection to the nation (Wallace Collection, Manchester Square, London).

Wallace, Sir William (c. 1274–1305), Scottish patriot. He withstood Edward I, at first successfully, but was defeated at Falkirk and executed.

Wallenstein, Albrecht von (1583–1634), German soldier and statesman during the Thirty Years War. An able administrator of his own estates, he sought the unity of Germany, but was distrusted and eventually assassinated.

Waller, Edmund (1606–87), English poet of polished simplicity, author of Go, lovely rose. He was able to agree with both parliamentarians and royalists.

Wallis, Sir Barnes Neville (1887–1979), British scientist and inventor whose many designs include the R100 airship, the Wellington bomber, the swing-wing aircraft, and the "bouncing bomb" that breached the Ruhr dams in 1943.

Walpole, Horace, 4th Earl of Orford (1717–97), younger son of Sir Robert Walpole, English writer, chiefly remembered for his Letters, his Castle of Otranto, and his "Gothic" house at Strawberry Hill.

Walpole, Sir Hugh Seymour (1884–1941), English novelist, b. New Zealand. His works include Fortitude, The Dark Forest, and The Herries Chronicle.

Walpole, Sir Robert, 1st Earl of Orford (1676–1745), English Whig statesman, who came to office soon after the Hanoverian succession and is considered the first prime minister—a good finance minister, a peace minister, and a "house of commons man."

Walter, Bruno (1876–1962), German-American conductor, especially of Haydn, Mozart, and Mahler.

Walter, John (1776–1847), English newspaper editor. Under him The Times, founded by his father **John Walter** (1739–1812), attained a leading position.

Walton, Izaak (1593–1683), English writer, especially remembered for The Compleat Angler. He also wrote biographies of Donne, Hooker, and George Herbert.

Walton, Sir William Turner (1902–83), English composer, whose works include concertos for string instruments, two symphonies, two coronation marches, Façade (setting to Edith Sitwell's poem), and an oratorio, Belshazzar's Feast. O.M. 1967.

Warbeck, Perkin (1474–99), Flemish impostor, b. Tournai, who claimed to be the younger son of Edward IV with French and Scottish backing, but failed and was executed.

Warwick, Earl of (Richard Neville) (c. 1428–71), "the kingmaker." At first on the Yorkist side in the Wars of the Roses, he proclaimed Edward IV king; but later changed sides and restored the Lancastrian Henry VI. He was killed at Barnet.

Washington, Booker Taliaferro (1858–1915), American Negro educationist, author of Up from Slavery. He became principal of Tuskegee Institute, Alabama.

Washington, George (1732–99), first U.S. president. B. in Virginia, of a family which originated from Northamptonshire, he served against the French in the Seven Years War. When the dispute between the British government and the Americans over taxation came to a head, he proved a successful general, and Cornwallis's surrender to him at Yorktown in 1781 virtually ended the war. In 1787 he presided over the Philadelphia convention which formulated the constitution, and was president 1789–97.

Watson, John Broadus (1878–1958), American psychologist, an exponent of behaviourism. See Behaviourism, Section J.

Watson-Watt, Sir Robert (1892–1973), Scottish physicist, who played a major part in the development of radar.

Watt, James (1736–1819), Scottish engineer and inventor, b. Greenock. He made important improvements to Newcomen's steam-engine by inventing a separate condenser (applying Black's discoveries (1761–4) on latent heat) and other devices based on scientific knowledge of the properties of steam. He was given support by Matthew Boulton, a capitalist, and settled down in Birmingham with him. He defined one horse-power as the rate at which work is done when 33,000 lb are raised one foot in one minute. . He also constructed a press for copying manuscripts. The watt as a unit of power is named after him.

Watteau, Jean Antoine (1684–1721), French painter. He painted pastoral idylls in court dress. His works include Embarquement pour Cythère in the Louvre.

Watts, Isaac (1674–1748), English hymn-writer, author of O God, our help in ages past.

Watts-Dunton, Walter Theodore (1836–1914), English poet and critic, friend of Swinburne whom he looked after until his death in 1909.

Waugh, Evelyn (1902–66), English satirical writer, author of Vile Bodies, The Loved One, Brideshead Revisited, Life of Edmund Campion, The Ordeal of Gilbert Pinfold, and an autobiography, A Little Learning.

Wavell, 1st Earl (Archibald Percival Wavell) (1883–1950), British general. He served in the first great war on Allenby's staff and in the second he commanded in the Middle East 1939–41, defeating the Italians; and in India 1941–3. He was viceroy of India 1943–7.

Webb, Matthew (1848–83), English swimmer, the first to swim the English Channel (1875).

Webb, Sidney James, Baron Passfield (1859–1947), and his wife **Beatrice**, née Potter (1858–1943), English social reformers and historians. They combined careful investigation of social problems (their books include History of Trade Unionism and English Local Government) with work for the future; they were members of the Fabian Society, launched the New Statesman, and helped to set up the London School of Economics. He held office in Labour governments.

Weber, Carl Maria Friedrich Ernst von (1786–1826), German composer, who laid the foundation of German romantic opera. His reputation rests principally on his three operas, Der Freischütz, Euryanthe, and Oberon. He was also an able pianist, conductor, and musical director. See Section E.

Webster, Daniel (1782–1852), American statesman and orator. He held office more than once and negotiated the Ashburton Treaty which settled the Maine-Canada boundary.

Webster, Noah (1758–1843), American lexicographer, who published an American dictionary of the English language.

Wedgwood, Dame Cicely Veronica (b. 1910) English historian, author of William the Silent, Thomas Wentworth, The Thirty Years' War, The King's Peace, The Trial of Charles I; a member of the Staffordshire pottery family. O.M. 1969.

Wedgwood, Josiah (1730–95), English potter, who at his Etruria works near Hanley produced from a new ware (patented 1763) pottery to classical designs by Flaxman, and gave pottery a new impetus.

Weill, Kurt (1900–50), German composer of satirical, surrealist operas, including Die Dreigroschenoper and Mahagonny (librettist Brecht). His wife, the Venetian actress Lotte Lenya (d. 1981) will be remembered for her singing of the Brecht songs and the interpretation of her husband's works. They left Europe for the United States in 1935.

Weingartner, Felix (1863–1942), Austrian conductor, also a composer and writer of a text book on conducting.

Weismann, August (1834–1914), German biologist. He worked on the question of individual variability in evolution, stressing the continuity of the germ plasm and rejecting the idea of inheritance of acquired characteristics.

Weizmann, Chaim (1874–1952), Israeli leader, b. Pinsk. He came to England in 1903 and taught biochemistry at Manchester. He helped to secure the Balfour Declaration (1917), promising a Jewish national home, and was for many years president of the Zionists. In 1948 he became first president of Israel.

Wellesley, Marquess (Richard Colley Wellesley) (1760–1842), British administrator. He was a successful governor-general of India, and was brother of the Duke of Wellington.

Wellington, 1st Duke of (Arthur Wellesley) (1769–1852), British general. B. in Ireland, he joined the army and gained experience in India. In the Peninsular War he successfully wore down and drove out the invading French. When Napoleon escaped from Elba, Wellington defeated him at Waterloo. Thereafter he took some part in politics as a Tory, but in the last resort was capable of accepting change.

Wells, Herbert George (1866–1946), English author. B. London, he was at first a teacher. He believed in progress through science, and became one of the most influential writers of his time. His long series of books includes romances of the Jules Verne variety (*The Time Machine*, *The Island of Dr. Moreau*, *The Invisible Man*), sociological autobiography (*Love and Mr. Lewisham*, *Kipps*, *Tono-Bungay*, *The History of Mr. Polly*, *Mr. Britling Sees it Through*), and popular education (*Outline of History*, *The Science of Life*, *The Work*, *Wealth and Happiness of Mankind*, *The Shape of Things to Come*, *The Fate of Homo Sapiens*). He was an early and successful educator of the common man. He was also a founder member of the Fabian Society.

Wesley, Charles (1707–88), English hymnwriter. He was the companion of his brother John, and wrote over 5,500 hymns, including *Love divine* and *Jesu, lover of my soul*.

Wesley, John (1703–91), English evangelist and founder of Methodism (at first a nickname applied to friends of himself and his brother), b. at Epworth. After a trip to Georgia and after encountering Moravian influence, he began to teach on tour, covering in over 50 years more than 200,000 miles and preaching over 40,000 sermons. He made religion a live force to many ignorant folk of humble station who could only be reached by a new and direct challenge. He made a feature of the Sunday school and increased the use of music (the brothers' first hymnbook appeared in 1739). He did not plan separation from the Anglican church, though it was implicit in his ordination of a missionary, and it took place after his death. *See also* **Methodism, Section J.**

Westermarck, Edward Alexander (1862–1939), Finnish sociologist. His works include *History of Human Marriage*, *Origin and Development of the Moral Ideas*, and *The Oedipus Complex*.

Westinghouse, George (1846–1914), American engineer who invented an air-brake for railways (1868) called by his name, and pioneered the use of high tension alternating current for the transmission of electric power.

Westmacott, Sir Richard (1775–1856), English sculptor of Achilles in Hyde Park.

Wharton, Edith (1862–1937), American novelist and friend of Henry James. Her works include *House of Mirth* and *Custom of the Country*.

Whately, Richard (1787–1863), English archbishop of Dublin. He wrote treatises on *Rhetoric* and *Logic*.

Wheatstone, Sir Charles (1802–75), English physicist, one of the first to recognise Ohm's law. In 1837 he (with W. F. Cooke) patented an electric telegraph. He also introduced the microphone.

Wheeler, Sir Charles (1892–1974), English sculptor, especially on buildings. His autobiography is *High Relief*. P.R.A., 1956–66.

Whistler, James Abbott McNeill (1834–1903), American artist. B. at Lowell, he studied in Paris and settled in England. He reacted against the conventions of his day, and Ruskin's uncomprehending criticism of his work resulted in a lawsuit. Among his main works are studies of the Thames, and a portrait of his mother, now in the Louvre.

White, Sir George Stuart (1835–1912), British general who defended Ladysmith in the South African War.

White, Patrick (b. 1912), Australian novelist whose books include *The Aunt's Story*, *Riders in the Chariot*, *The Solid Mandala* and *The Eye of the Storm*. Nobel prizeman 1973.

Whitefield, George (1714–70), English evangelist, b. Gloucester. He was at first associated with the Wesleys, but differed from them on predestination. His supporters built him a "Tabernacle" in London, and he had other chapels elsewhere, but founded no lasting sect.

Whitgift, John (1530–1604), archbishop of Canterbury in the time of Elizabeth I (from 1583). His policy helped to clarify and strengthen the Anglican church.

Whitman, Walt (1819–92), American poet, b. Long Island. He led a wandering life and did hospital work in the Civil War. He aimed at forming a new and free American outlook. His works include *Leaves of Grass*, *Drum Taps*, and *Democratic Vistas*.

Whittier, John Greenleaf (1807–92), American Quaker poet, b. Haverhill, Mass. He wrote against slavery (*Justice and Expediency*), turning to poetry after the Civil War, especially remembered for *Snow-bound*.

Whittington, Richard (c. 1358–1423), English merchant. Son of a Gloucestershire knight, he became a London mercer and was mayor of London 1398, 1406, 1419. The cat legend is part of European folklore.

Whittle, Sir Frank (b. 1907), pioneer in the field of jet propulsion. The first flights of Gloster jet propelled aeroplanes with Whittle engines took place in May 1941. O.M. (1986).

Whymper, Edward (1840–1911), English woodengraver and mountaineer. He was the first to climb the Matterhorn.

Widgery, Baron (John Passmore Widgery) (1911–81), Lord Chief Justice of England 1971–80.

Wilberforce, William (1759–1833), English philanthropist, b. Hull. He was the parliamentary leader of the campaign against the slave trade, abolished in 1807. He then worked against slavery itself, but that further step was only taken in the year of his death.

Wilcox, Ella Wheeler (1855–1919), American writer of romantic sentimental verse.

Wilde, Oscar Fingall (1854–1900), Irish author and dramatist, son of a Dublin surgeon and leader of the cult of art for art's sake. His works include poems, fairy-tales, short stories, and witty comedies—*Lady Windermere's Fan*, *A Woman of No Importance*, *An Ideal Husband*, and *The Importance of Being Earnest*. In a libel action he was convicted of homosexual practices and imprisoned for two years, when he wrote *The Ballad of Reading Gaol*.

Wilder, Thornton Niven (1897–1975), American author and playwright. Among his books are *The Bridge of San Luis Rey* and *Ides of March*.

Wilkes, John (1727–97), English politician. A Whig, he violently attacked George III in his paper the *North Briton*, and as a result of unsuccessful proceedings against him, general warrants were determined illegal. He was again in trouble for obscene libel; his defiance of authority brought him popularity, and he was four times re-elected to parliament but refused his seat, until his opponents gave way. His motives were mixed, but he helped to establish freedom of the press.

Willcocks, Sir William (1852–1932), British engineer, b. India, who carried out irrigation works in India, Egypt, South Africa, and Mesopotamia. He built the Aswan dam (1898–1902).

Willett, William (1856–1915), English advocate of "daylight savings," adopted after his death.

William I of England (1027–87), the "Conqueror," Duke of Normandy, claimed the English throne as successor to Edward the Confessor, and defeated Harold II at Hastings in 1066. An able commander and a firm ruler, he crushed Saxon resistance, especially in the north, transferred most of the land to his Norman followers, and drew England into closer relations with the continent, as did his archbishop Lanfranc. He ordered the Domesday survey.

William II of England (1056–1100), the Conqueror's son, surnamed Rufus, succeeded in 1087. Capricious and self-indulgent, his reign was troubled, and he was shot (by accident or design) while hunting in the New Forest.

William III of England (1650–1702), King of England, Scotland, and Ireland (1689–1702), son of William II of Orange and Mary, daughter of Charles I. He married Mary, daughter of the Duke of York (later James II) while stadtholder of Holland. In 1688, when James had fled the country, he was invited to succeed and he and Mary became joint king and queen. The revolution of 1688 brought to England tolerance of Protestant worship, but William was mainly concerned with war against France, brought to an end in 1697.

William IV of England (1765–1837), third son of George III, succeeded his brother George IV in 1830; called the "sailor king." The reform bill of 1832 and other reform measures were carried without obstruction from him.

William I of Germany (1797–1888), King of Prussia and first German emperor. He succeeded to the throne in 1861 and continued resistance to reform, appointing Bismarck as chief minister, and supporting him through the Austro-Prussian and Franco-Prussian wars. His personal character was simple and unassuming.

William II of Germany, the Kaiser (1859–1941), King of Prussia and German emperor from 1888, was grandson of William I and of Queen Victoria. He was intelligent but impetuous, and believed in military power. He dismissed Bismarck. In 1914 his support of Austria helped to precipitate European war, and the resulting defeat brought his abdication, after which he lived in retirement at Doorn in Holland.

William the Silent (1533–1584), Dutch national leader. Prince of Orange, he led the revolt of the Protestant Netherlands against the rule of the Spanish Philip II. The union of the northern provinces was accomplished in 1579, and Spanish rule was renounced by 1584, in which year William was assassinated.

Williams, Sir George (1821–1905), founder of the Young Men's Christian Association.

Williamson, Malcolm (b. 1931), Australian composer, pianist and organist; succeeded Sir Arthur Bliss as Master of the Queen's Musick.

Wilson, Edmund (1895–1972), American critic, author of *Axel's Castle* (1931), *The Triple Thinkers* (1938), *The Wound and the Bow* (1941), *To the Finland Station* (1940), *The Shores of Light* (1952), *The Dead Sea Scrolls* (1955).

Wilson of Rievaulx, Lord (Sir Harold Wilson) (b. 1916), British statesman, leader parl. Labour Party 1963–76; prime minister 1964–6, 1966–70, 1974–6. Entered parliament 1945 as member for Ormskirk; elected for Huyton 1950–83. Returned three times, in 1964 and a decade later, to head a government facing a formidable balance-of-payments deficit. Resigned March 1976. Founder of the Open University.

Wilson, Richard (1714–82), British landscape painter, b. Montgomeryshire. Admired by Turner and Constable.

Wilson, Thomas Woodrow (1856–1924), American statesman. He was U.S. president 1913–21, brought America into the first world war and advocated the League of Nations, but was not a successful negotiator at the peace conference and could not carry his country into the League. His administration introduced prohibition and women's suffrage.

Wingate, Orde Charles (1903–44), leader of the Chindit forces engaged behind the Japanese lines in Burma during the second world war.

Winifred, St., the 7th cent. patron saint of North Wales, said in late legend to have been killed by her rejected suitor, Prince Caradoc, but restored by her uncle.

Wiseman, Nicholas Patrick (1802–65), cardinal, b. in Spain of an Irish family. In 1850 on the restoration in England of the Roman Catholic hierarchy he became first archbishop of Westminster, and reorganised and developed his church in Great Britain.

Wittgenstein, Ludwig Josef Johann (1889–1951), Austrian linguistic philosopher whose main works were the *Tractatus Logico-Philosophicus* of his early period, much admired by Russell, and the *Philosophical Investigations*.

Wodehouse, Pelham Grenville (1881–1975), English humorist, creator of Jeeves in the Bertie Wooster stories. He became a U.S. citizen.

Wolf, Friedrich August (1759–1824), German classical scholar, a founder of scientific classical philology.

Wolf, Hugo (1860–1903), Austrian song-writer. In his settings of over 300 German lyrics, including many of Mörike and Goethe, he achieved complete union of poetry and music. *See* Section E.

Wolfe, James (1727–59), British general, b. Westerham. He showed early promise in the Seven Years' War, and was given command of the expedition against Quebec, which in spite of its strong position he captured, but lost his life.

Wolsey, Thomas (*c.* 1475–1530), English cardinal. A butcher's son at Ipswich, he entered the church, becoming archbishop of York and cardinal, while in the same year (1515) he became Henry VIII's lord chancellor. But in spite of his ability he was unable to secure papal sanction for the king's divorce from Catherine of Aragon, and fell from power and died. He was the last of the great ecclesiastical statesmen of the Middle Ages.

Wood, Sir Henry Joseph (1869–1944), English conductor, founder of the Promenade Concerts which he conducted from 1895 till his death.

Woodcock, George (1904–79), English trade union leader. T.U.C. general secretary 1960–69; first chairman of the Commission on Industrial Relations, 1969–71.

Woodsworth, James Shaver (1874–1942), Canadian politician, parliamentary leader of the Co-operative Commonwealth Federation.

Woodville, Elizabeth (1437–91), wife of Edward IV. Her daughter Elizabeth married Henry VII.

Woolf, Virginia (1882–1941), English writer, daughter of Sir Leslie Stephen and wife of Leonard Woolf with whom she founded the Hogarth Press. Her works develop the stream-of-consciousness technique and include *To the Lighthouse*, *Mrs. Dalloway*, *The Waves*, *A Room of One's Own*.

Woolley, Sir Richard van der Riet (b. 1906), succeeded Sir Harold Spencer Jones as astronomer royal (England), 1956–72.

Wootton of Abinger, Baroness (Barbara Frances Wootton) (b. 1897), English social scientist; chairman Metropolitan Juvenile Courts 1946–62; deputy speaker of the House of Lords 1966–70. Her works include *Social Science and Social Pathology*, *Crime and the Criminal Law*, and an autobiography *In a world I never made*.

Wordsworth, William (1770–1850), English poet, b. Cockermouth. He went to Cambridge, and in 1798 with Coleridge issued *Lyrical Ballads*, a return to simplicity in English poetry. He settled at Grasmere with his sister Dorothy (1771–1855), to whose insight his poems owe much. Among his best works are his sonnets and his *Ode on the Intimations of Immortality*, besides his *Prelude*.

Wren, Sir Christopher (1632–1723), English architect, b. Wiltshire. After the great fire (1666) he prepared an abortive plan for rebuilding London, but did in fact rebuild St. Paul's and more than fifty other city churches, including St. Stephen, Walbrook, and St. Mary-le-Bow. Other works include Chelsea Hospital, portions of Greenwich Hospital, the Sheldonian theatre, Oxford, and Queen's College library, Oxford. He had wide scientific interests (he was professor of mathematics at Gresham College, London, and professor of astronomy at Oxford) and helped to found the Royal Society.

Wright, Frank Lloyd (1869–1959), American architect, initiator of horizontal strip and all-glass design. His influence has spread over the world. His buildings include the Imperial Hotel, Tokyo, and the Guggenheim Museum, New York.

Wright, Orville (1871–1948), American airman who with his brother Wilbur (1867–1912) in 1903 was the first to make a controlled sustained flight in a powered heavier-than-air machine, flying a length of 852 ft. at Kitty Hawk, N.C.

Wyatt, James (1746–1813), English architect who built Fonthill Abbey.

Wyatt, Sir Thomas (1503–42), English poet who introduced the sonnet from Italy. He was also a diplomat.

Wyatt, Sir Thomas the younger (*c.* 1520–54), son of above, unsuccessfully led a revolt against Queen Mary on behalf of Lady Jane Grey.

Wycherley, William (1640–1715), English dramatist of the Restoration period. A master of satiric comedy, his plays include *Love in a Wood*, *The Plain Dealer*, and (the best known) *The Country Wife*.

Wyclif, John (*c.* 1320–84), English religious reformer. He taught at Oxford, later becoming rector of Lutterworth. He insisted on inward religion and attacked those practices which he thought had become mechanical. His followers, called Lollards, were suppressed, partly for political reasons. The Wyclif Bible, the first and literal translation of the Latin Vulgate into English, was mainly the work of his academic followers at Oxford.

Wykeham, William of (1324–1404), English churchman. He held office under Edward III and became bishop of Winchester in 1367. He founded New College, Oxford, and Winchester School, and improved Winchester cathedral.

Wyllie, William Lionel (1851–1931), English marine painter of *The Thames Below London Bridge*.

Wyspianski, Stanislav (1869–1907), Polish poet, dramatist and painter. His plays *The Wedding*, *Liberation*, and *November Night* treat of national themes.

X

Xavier, St. Francis (1506–52), "apostle of the Indies," b. at Xavero in the Basque country. He was associated with Loyola in founding the Jesuits, and undertook missionary journeys to Goa, Ceylon, and Japan. He died while planning another to China.

Xenophon (444–359 B.C.), Athenian general and historian. He commanded Greek mercenaries under the Persian Cyrus, and on the latter's death safely marched the Ten Thousand home through hostile country. His chief works are the *Anabasis*, the *Hellenica*, and *Cyropaedia*.

Xerxes (*c.* 519–465 B.C.), King of Persia, was son of the first Darius. In 481 B.C. he started on an expedition against Greece when, according to Herodotus, he had a combined army and navy of over two and a half million men. He defeated the Spartans at Thermopylae, but his fleet was overcome at Salamis. He reigned from 485 to 465 B.C. and met his death by assassination.

Ximénes de Cisneros, Francisco (1436–1517), Spanish statesman and churchman. He became cardinal in 1507; carried out monastic reforms; and directed preparation of a polyglot bible, the *Complutensian*; but as inquisitor-general he was fanatical against heresy. He was adviser to Queen Isabella; in 1506 regent for Queen Juana; and himself directed an expedition to conquer Oran and extirpate piracy.

Y

Yeats, William Butler (1865–1939), Irish lyric poet and playwright, b. near Dublin, a leader of the Irish literary revival. His plays were performed in the Abbey Theatre (which with **Lady Gregory** (1852–1932) he helped to found), and include *Cathleen Ni Houlihan*, *The Hour Glass*, and *Deirdre*. A complete edition of the *Collected Poems* appeared in 1950.

Yonge, Charlotte Mary (1823–1901), English novelist. Influenced by Keble, she wrote novels which faithfully reflect some aspects of Victorian life; one such is *The Daisy Chain*. She also wrote historical fiction such as *The Dove in the Eagle's Nest*.

Young, Brigham (1801–77), American Mormon leader, and president in 1844 after the founder's death. He was a main founder of Salt Lake City. He practised polygamy. *See also* **Mormonism, Section J.**

Young, Francis Brett (1884–1954), English novelist, author of *My Brother Jonathan* and *Dr. Bradley remembers*.

Young, James (1811–83), Scottish chemist, b. Glasgow, whose experiments led to the manufacture of paraffin oil and solid paraffin on a large scale.

Young, Thomas (1773–1829), English physicist, physician and Egyptologist, b. Somerset, of Quaker family. He established the wave theory of light and its essential principle of interference, put forward a theory of colour vision, and was the first to describe astigmatism of the eye. He was also largely responsible for deciphering the inscriptions on the Rosetta stone.

Younghusband, Sir Francis Edward (1863–1942), English explorer and religious leader. He explored Manchuria and Tibet, and wrote on India and Central Asia. He founded the World Congress of Faiths in 1936 (*see* **Section J**).

Ypres, 1st Earl of. *See* **French.**

Ysaÿe, Eugène (1858–1929), Belgian violinist and conductor, noted chiefly for his playing of the works of Bach and César Franck.

Yukawa, Hideki (b. 1907), Japanese physicist, who received the 1949 Nobel prize for predicting (1935) the existence of the meson.

Z

Zadkiel (angel in rabbinical lore), pseudonym of two astrologers: **William Lilly** (1602–81) and **Richard James Morrison** (1794–1874).

Zadkine, Ossip (b. 1890), Russian sculptor in France, who makes play with light on concave surfaces. His works include *Orpheus* and the public monument *The Destruction of Rotterdam*.

Zaharoff, Sir Basil (1849–1936), armaments magnate and financier, b. Anatolia of Greek parents. He was influential in the first world war.

Zamenhof, Ludwig Lazarus (1859–1917), Polish-Jew who invented Esperanto. He was by profession an oculist.

Zeno of Citium (?342–270 B.C.), philosopher, founder of the Stoic system. He left Cyprus to teach in Athens.

Zeppelin, Ferdinand, Count von (1838–1917), German inventor of the dirigible airship, 1897–1900. It was used in the first world war.

Zeromski, Stefan (1864–1925), Polish novelist, author of *The Homeless*, *The Ashes*, *The Fight with Satan*.

Zhukov, Georgi Konstantinovich (1896–1974), Soviet general, who led the defence of Moscow and Stalingrad and lifted the siege of Leningrad in the second world war, and accepted the German surrender in 1945. He continued to be active till 1957.

Zhukovsky, Vasily Andreyevich (1783–1852), Russian poet and translator of German and English poets. For many years he was tutor to the future Tsar Alexander II.

Zola, Emile Edouard (1840–1902), French novelist, b. Paris, of Italian descent. His series, *Les Rougon-Macquart*, portrays in a score of volumes (the best known of which are perhaps *L'Assommoir*, *Nana* and *Germinal*) the fortunes of one family in many aspects and in realistic manner. He had the moral courage to champion Dreyfus.

Zorn, Anders Leonhard (1860–1920), Swedish sculptor, etcher, and painter.

Zoroaster (Zarathustra) (fl. 6th cent. B.C.), Persian founder of the Parsee religion. He was a monotheist, and saw the world as a struggle between good (Ahura Mazda) and evil (Ahriman). *See* **Zoroastrianism, Section J.**

Zoshchenko, Mikhail (1895–1958), Russian writer of humorous short stories, which include *The Woman who could not Read and other Tales* and *The Wonderful Dog and other Stories.*

Zosimus (fl. *c.* 300), the first known alchemist. He lived in Alexandria.

Zuccarelli, Francesco (1702–88), Italian artist of fanciful landscapes. He spent many years in London and was elected a founder member of the R.A. (1768).

Zuckermann, Baron (Solly Zuckermann) (b. 1904), British biologist; chief scientific adviser to British governments; 1940–71. His publications include *Scientists and War* and *The Frontiers of Public and Private Science*. O.M. 1968.

Zwingli, Ulrich (1484–1531), Swiss religious reformer. He taught mainly at Zurich, where he issued a list of reformed doctrines, less extreme than those of Calvin.

Zwirner, Ernst Friedrich (1802–61), German architect who restored Cologne cathedral.

BACKGROUND
TO PUBLIC
AFFAIRS

This section is in three parts. The first provides an up-to-date chronicle and analysis of recent changes in Britain, intended to put into perspective current political events. The second part provides a wide-ranging guide to events and movements elsewhere in the world. The third section consists of a series of special topics.

TABLE OF CONTENTS

BACKGROUND TO PUBLIC AFFAIRS

This section is in three parts. The first outlines the political history of the United Kingdom since 1970. The second part provides a wide-ranging guide to events elsewhere in the world and takes stock of the changing patterns in international relations. The third section contains special topics on particular themes. The reader is invited to turn to Section D for further key facts and figures relating to the British political system.

I. SURVEY OF THE BRITISH POLITICAL SCENE

BRITISH POLITICAL EVENTS 1970–86

The Political Situation in 1970.

The Labour Party, which had been in office for almost six years under the leadership of Harold Wilson, approached the General Election of June 1970 with confidence. After some traumatic years both economically and politically, the Government's popularity appeared to have been restored. The outcome, however, was a 4·7% swing to the Conservatives and their return to power, led by Edward Heath, with an overall majority of 30.

A New Style of Government.

Initially, the new Government made some radical changes in policy:

(1) *Reorganisation of the Machinery of Government*, including the creation of two new giant departments (Environment, and Trade and Industry) and a new advisory unit, the Central Policy Review Staff. Between 1970 and 1974 the Government also passed legislation reforming the structure of local government (implemented in England and Wales in 1974 and Scotland in 1975), the National Health Service (implemented in 1974) and the water industry (implemented in 1974).

(2) *Cuts in Public Expenditure.*—The Conservatives believed that government was intervening too much in the life of the nation and that too high a proportion of the nation's resources were committed to public expenditure. Following a major review of government activities, the Chancellor of the Exchequer announced that the Government planned to be more selective in its approach to the social services and to withdraw generally in its relations with private industry.

(3) *Reform of Industrial Relations.*—One of the major issues of the Conservative election campaign had been the need to take stronger action to reform industrial relations. The Government published its proposals in October 1970 and, after a long and bitter parliamentary battle, the Industrial Relations Act became law in 1971. The provisions of the Act came into force during 1972. The Act was strongly opposed by an overwhelming majority of the trade unions, most of whom refused to register, as they were required by the Act in order to receive certain benefits it conferred, and initially they decided to boycott the institutions created by the Act, in particular the National Industrial Relations Court. However, following a number of controversial decisions, most unions decided that they should at least appear in order to defend themselves.

Industrial Unrest.

The first two and a half years of the Government's life were marked by widespread outbreaks of industrial unrest. This was the result of a number of factors. First, the Government's policy of confrontation as a means of limiting wage inflation led to a number of prolonged disputes, for instance, in the docks, in the electricity power industry and by local authority manual workers. Trade union opposition to the Industrial Relations Act produced a number of one-day stoppages and unofficial strikes of longer duration. These prob-

lems were aggravated by persistently high levels of unemployment especially in certain regions. Finally, after 1972, there was industrial action in protest against the Government's prices and incomes policy. In 1972 there were three serious disputes, involving the miners, the railwaymen and the dockworkers.

The Government's About-Turn.

1972 was not a happy year for the Government. We have already seen that it was a year of confrontation with the trade unions. It was also a year in which the pressure of circumstances, especially the problems of unemployment and inflation, forced the Government to abandon many of the initiatives it had started in 1970 and to adopt policies similar to those which it had attacked so vehemently when it had been in Opposition. This was particularly the case in three fields:

(1) *Regional Policy.*—Faced with the twin problems of low levels of industrial investment and persistent unemployment in the regions, the Chancellor of the Exchequer announced in his 1972 Budget that the Government was substantially increasing government assistance to private industry and that, in the development areas, investment grants were to be reintroduced.

(2) *Consumer Protection.*—Although in 1970 the Government had brought about the demise of the Consumer Council, by 1972 it had come round to the view that some form of statutory consumer protection was necessary. Consequently, a new office, that of Director-General of Fair Trading, was created in 1973 and a new committee established to protect the interests of consumers.

(3) *Prices and Incomes Policy.*—Despite its strong opposition to the Labour Government's prices and incomes legislation and its initial refusal even to contemplate such a policy, the continuing problem of inflation placed the Government under increasing pressure to introduce some kind of prices and incomes policy. During the autumn tripartite talks were held between the Government, the TUC and the CBI in the search for voluntary agreement on prices and incomes restraint, but these broke down at the beginning of November. Consequently, the Government came to the conclusion, albeit reluctantly, that they would have to introduce legislation to give effect to their proposals. A 90-day standstill was imposed on wages and salaries, dividends, rates and rents, and prices and charges for goods and services were similarly frozen. Provision was made for firms which claimed that their costs had risen so much for it to be impracticable for them to be absorbed to apply to the Government for permission to increase prices. The prices of fresh food and of imported raw materials were excluded from the freeze.

Entry into Europe.

Negotiations with the EEC started immediately after the General Election of 1970. After a long series of talks in Brussels and a summit meeting between President Pompidou and Mr. Heath in Paris in May 1971, a formula was found to which Britain and the Six could agree. On this basis the House of Commons took the decision in principle to join the EEC on 18 October 1971, when the Conservative Government, opposed by some of its back-benchers but supported by 69 Labour pro-marketeers and five of the Liberals, had a majority of 112. Legislation to give effect to this decision was passed after a long parliamentary struggle in September 1972. Thus, twelve years after the first application had been made, Britain joined the Common Market on 1 January 1973.

Phases Two and Three.

The standstill on prices and incomes was extended until the end of April 1973 when it was replaced by the second phase of the Government's counter-inflation policy. Under Phase Two wage increases were limited to £1 per week plus 4%, with an overall ceiling of £250 per annum. Prices and dividends continued to be controlled as during the standstill. To enforce these controls the Government created two new statutory bodies, the Pay Board and the Price Commission. Phase Two was opposed by the TUC, which decided not to nominate members to serve on the new controlling bodies nor to co-operate in the implementation of the Government's policy. During the summer of 1973 bilateral talks took place between the Government and both the CBI and the TUC no what measures should succeed Phase Two in November 1973. In October the Government published its plans in a Green Paper, and these were put into practice with a few modifications. On prices the basis of control was unchanged, but there was some tightening of the regulations. On incomes, however, a more complex formula was introduced permitting a choice between a 7% increase, with a maximum of £350 per year, or an increase of £2·25 per week. In addition, higher increases could be awarded by the Pay Board on various grounds such as the removal of anomalies or the necessity of working "unsocial" hours. New Year's Day was also declared to be a public holiday.

The Oil Crisis.

The implementation of Phase Two took place against a rapidly changing economic situation. In the aftermath of the Arab–Israeli war of October 1973, problems arose in the supply of oil, on which Britain depends for 50% of her energy. First, the Arab oil producers decided to boycott some countries and to restrict supplies to most others. British imports were cut by 15%. Second, all the oil exporting countries decided to increase the price of crude oil dramatically. Shortage of petrol produced panic among many motorists leading to long queues and even violent scenes at some garages. The Government took the precaution of issuing ration coupons but managed to avoid introducing rationing, relying instead on voluntary restraint.

Deepening Economic Crisis.

The increased cost of oil imports and the reduction in supplies adversely affected both the balance of payments and industrial output. The economic situation was further weakened by the decision of the National Union of Mineworkers (NUM) in November 1973 to implement a ban on overtime and weekend working in support of a pay claim in excess of Phase Three. The rapidly deteriorating fuel situation was aggravated by an out-of-hours working ban by electricity power engineers which limited the ability of the Central Electricity Generating Board to cope with shortages at various power stations. Consequently on 13 November the Government declared a State of Emergency. Orders were enacted restricting space heating by electricity, except in the home and certain other places, and prohibiting the use of electricity for advertising, displays or floodlighting. The position worsened still further following the decision of the Amalgamated Society of Locomotive Engineers and Firemen (ASLEF) to ban Sunday, overtime and rest-day working. This had the effect of disrupting the delivery of coal to power stations as well as causing a considerable amount of inconvenience to passengers, especially in the South-East. The Government refused to make an offer to the miners outside the terms of Stage Three and was therefore compelled to introduce a package of tougher measures to deal with the crisis. Most important, as from 1 January, electricity was only provided to in-

dustry on three specified days per week. In addition a 50 mile/h speed limit was introduced on all roads, a maximum heating limit was imposed on all commercial premises and offices and television was required to close down at 10.30 p.m. each evening. The Chancellor of the Exchequer also announced large cuts in public expenditure and tighter controls on consumer credit.

Miners' Strike and the February 1974 Election.

Following an overwhelming vote in a pithead ballot, the NUM decided to intensify its industrial action by calling a national strike as from 10 February. Before the strike began, however, the Prime Minister announced that he had asked the Queen to dissolve Parliament so as to hold a general election on 28 February. For the Government, the main issue of the election was the attempt by a trade union to use its industrial strength to defeat the policy of the elected government. The Labour Party, however, attempted to widen the campaign to include the Government's general record since 1970. There was also general interest in the performance of the Liberals following a series of dramatic by-election successes in 1972 and 1973.

Minority Labour Government.

At the dissolution, Mr. Heath had had an overall majority of 16 in the House of Commons. As the results came in on election night it was clear that he was going to lose this and that the result was going to be very close. Eventually the result was as follows:

Labour	301
Conservative	296
Liberal	14
Others	24

In this situation Mr. Heath did not offer his resignation immediately but entered into discussions with Mr. Jeremy Thorpe, the Leader of the Liberals, to see if the basis existed for the formation of a coalition. No agreement, however, was reached and Mr. Heath resigned on 4 March. The Queen then asked Mr. Wilson to form a government which he agreed to do without obtaining the support of any other parties. Immediate steps were taken to settle the miners' dispute and to end the three-day working week.

The Social Contract.

Although leading a minority government, Mr. Wilson knew that the other parties would be reluctant to force another election immediately. The Government was therefore able to make a start in implementing its programme. Most of its domestic policies were included in the *Social Contract*, a package of measures agreed between the Labour Party and the Trades Union Congress in 1973. Most important were the measures to control inflation. In return for the abolition of the Pay Board and all associated statutory controls on pay, which occurred in July 1974, the trade unions agreed voluntarily to restrain wage increases. Other measures included the repeal of the Industrial Relations Act 1971, the introduction of food subsidies, the strengthening of price controls and increased payments to old-age pensioners.

October 1974 Election.

Despite the Government's success in exploiting its parliamentary position, it was clear that it would seek a new mandate from the electorate at an early opportunity. Following the publication of a large number of statements of policy during the summer, the Prime Minister sought a dissolution of Parliament for polling to take place on 10 October. The Labour Party remained ahead in the opinion polls throughout the campaign and this was confirmed in the results, but its margin was rather smaller than predicted. Labour only obtained a majority of three over all other parties. However its position was in fact considerably stronger than this because of the fragmented nature of the opposition.

Conservative Leadership.

Although many Conservatives were critical of Mr. Heath's leadership, his support was not tested immediately after the February election because of the proximity of another general election. However, after the October election Mr Heath decided to establish a committee, under the chairmanship of Lord Home, to review the procedure for electing the leader of the Conservative Party. It proposed a number of changes which were adopted for the election, held in February 1975. In the first ballot, Mrs. Margaret Thatcher defeated Mr. Heath but failed to win the required majority. Mr. Heath then withdrew, announcing his intention of returning to the back-benches, and in the second ballot Mrs. Thatcher secured an overall majority.

European Renegotiation.

The Government was committed to seek a fundamental renegotiation of the terms of entry into the European Economic Community and to consult the British people as to whether the new terms should be accepted. In April 1974 Mr. Callaghan outlined to the Council of Ministers the terms which Britain wished to change, the most important of which were the contribution to the Community budget, the effects of the Common Agricultural Policy, the need to safeguard the interests of the Commonwealth and developing countries and the promotion of regional development. After concluding successful negotiations on most of these points the Cabinet voted to recommend continued membership and this view was endorsed by 67·2% of those who voted in a referendum held in June 1975.

Counter-Inflation Programme.

Despite the agreement of the trade unions voluntarily to restrain wage increases, the rate of inflation accelerated so much that by the middle of 1975 it had reached 25% per annum. In July 1975, the Government was therefore compelled to introduce a limit of £6 a week on pay settlements for people earning up to £8,500 a year, with no increase for those earning more. This policy remained voluntary but the Government announced that employers who increased pay by more than the limit would have not only the excess but the whole pay increase disallowed for the approval of price increases under the Price Code and it warned that if the limits were exceeded it would have to seek statutory powers of enforcement. The Government also undertook to maintain strict price controls and to continue and extend the payment of food subsidies.

Rising Unemployment.

The measures taken by the Government to reduce the rate of inflation, implemented during a serious world-wide recession, led to a sharp rise in unemployment such that in January 1976 1·3 million were out of work. Various steps were taken to provide additional employment but, short of major reflationary measures which were ruled out on other grounds, there was little that the Government could do. Preparations were made, however, to facilitate the development of the economy when conditions permitted. In November 1975 the Government published a new industrial strategy designed to ensure that assistance was given to those sectors of the economy with good prospects. Its difficulties, however, were highlighted in the following month when it had to launch a major rescue to avert the closure of Chrysler car production in Great Britain. Earlier in the year the Government had purchased 95% of the shares of British Leyland as part of a package of measures of financial support.

Pay and Prices.

Although the £6 limit, which was observed without exception, succeeded in reducing the rate of inflation, it was clear that further pay restraint was needed. In his 1976 Budget the Chancellor announced various tax reliefs conditional upon agreement being reached on a voluntary pay limit for another year. Such an agreement was made in May with a new limit curbing average wage increases to 4½% in the year starting in August 1976. Price controls were also maintained, but there was some relaxation to encourage industrial investment.

Resignation of Harold Wilson.

In March 1976 Harold Wilson, to everyone's surprise, announced his intention of resigning as Prime Minister. Six candidates were nominated to succeed him and, after three ballots, James Cal-

laghan was declared the winner, defeating Michael Foot by 39 votes, and he became Prime Minister on 5 April. A number of changes were made in the Cabinet and four senior ministers, including Ted Short and Barbara Castle, retired. Ted Short remained Deputy Leader of the Labour Party until October when he was succeeded by Michael Foot. Harold Wilson, who remained an M.P., received a knighthood from the Queen in recognition of his services to the country as the longest-serving Prime Minister this century.

Cuts in Public Expenditure.

During 1976 a vigorous campaign was mounted in favour of cuts in public expenditure. Concern that the Government was borrowing excessively to finance this spending also led to weakness of sterling on the foreign exchange markets. In July, to avert a further fall in the value of sterling, substantial cuts were announced in the Government's spending plans for 1977–8 and interest rates were raised to record levels. These measures were not sufficient, however, to prevent a dramatic slide in the £ during the autumn which forced the Government to seek a $3,900 million loan from the International Monetary Fund. To obtain this assistance, further cuts in public expenditure, amounting to £3,000 m. over the next two years, and increases in taxation were imposed in December. The Government also introduced new and tighter "cash limits" over public spending.

Lords v. Commons.

Despite these economic problems, the Government proceeded with one of the largest legislative programmes ever introduced in a single session. Most of it was also controversial, and strong opposition was encountered in the House of Commons, where the Government's small majority was frequently threatened, and in the House of Lords. The Lords attempted to make major changes in six bills, but the conflict eventually centred around two bills: the Dock Work Regulation Bill and the Aircraft and Shipbuilding Industries Bill. The former was returned to the Commons with its main provision transformed by the Lords, but the defection of two of its own backbenchers prevented the Government restoring its original proposal. Disagreement over the latter was not resolved by the time Parliament was prorogued and the bill to nationalise the aerospace and shipbuilding industries therefore had to be reintroduced at the beginning of the 1976–7 session. It became law in March 1977 but only after the Government had made substantial concessions.

Devolution.

In October 1974 the Scottish National Party secured 30·4% of the Scottish vote, winning 11 seats, and Plaid Cymru won 10·8% of the Welsh vote, winning 3 seats. The SNP also came second in 42 constituencies, 35 of them held by Labour. These successes brought the question of devolution to the centre of political debate and the Government announced its intention of setting up assemblies in Scotland and Wales. Both parties were split on this issue. Traditionally the Labour Party, and particularly its Scottish members, had opposed devolution, but with a few prominent exceptions in both Scotland and Wales, the Party supported the Government's proposals. The Conservatives had supported the creation of a Scottish assembly since the late 1960s, but in 1976 decided officially to oppose the Government's plans. A number of senior Conservatives, however, dissented from this apparent change of policy. In December 1976 the Scotland and Wales Bill was given a Second Reading by a majority of 45, the Government having secured the votes of most Labour MPs by promising to hold referendums before bringing the assemblies into existence. To get the Bill through its Committee Stage, which had to be taken on the floor of the House of Commons, the Government had to introduce a "guillotine" motion, but this was defeated by 29 votes in February 1977, with back-bench Labour rebels joining Conservatives and Liberals.

Lib/Lab Pact.

By-election losses meant that by 1977 the Government had lost its overall majority. Its failure to make progress with the devolution bill also meant that it could no longer count upon the support of the Nationalists. In this situation, the Conservatives in March 1977 put down a motion of no confidence in the Government. Faced with the prospect of defeat, the Government entered into an agreement with the Liberal Party, initially until the summer. It therefore succeeded in defeating the Conservative motion with a comfortable majority of 24. In July the agreement was renewed for the next session of Parliament provided that the Government maintained the fight against inflation. Under its terms both parties retained their independence for electoral purposes and in the House of Commons, but the Liberals agreed to support the Government in return for formal consultations on government policy and some specific undertakings on subjects such as direct elections to the European Parliament and devolution.

Stage Three.

One of the reasons behind Liberal support for the Government was their belief that it would be able to agree a further year of pay restraint with the TUC. Negotiations took place during the early part of the summer but the TUC refused to agree to a limit on settlements, believing that there should be an immediate return to free collective bargaining subject only to an undertaking that settlements should last for twelve months. The Government, however, announced unilaterally in July 1977 its own pay guidelines which stated that the general level of settlements should be such that the nation's earnings would increase during 1977-8 by no more than 10%. In contrast to the first two years of pay policy, these guidelines led to a considerable number of industrial disputes. Most serious was the nine-week strike of firemen between November 1977 and January 1978 during which fire services were provided by the armed forces.

Political Tension.

1977 saw violent scenes in various parts of Britain. One problem was the rise of the National Front, a party calling among other things for a halt to immigration and the repatriation of many coloured residents. Its activities in holding marches and demonstrations, particularly in areas with large coloured populations, were opposed by many groups and resulted in clashes between its supporters and those of the extreme left, for instance in Lewisham and in Birmingham during August. There were also violent scenes in north London outside the Grunwick film-processing factory as the trade union movement organised a mass picket in connection with the firm's refusal to recognise the right of its employees to belong to a trade union.

Foreign Affairs.

For the first six months of 1977 it was Britain's turn to hold the Presidency of the EEC. This burden, along with many others, was one of the causes of the sudden death of the Foreign Secretary, Anthony Crosland, in February 1977. He was succeeded by one of his junior ministers, Dr. David Owen, who at the age of 37 was the youngest person in this office since Sir Anthony Eden in the 1930s. One of the first problems he had to face was the situation in Rhodesia. Following the breakdown of constitutional talks, held between October and December 1976 in Geneva, intensive diplomatic activity led to the publication of joint Anglo-American settlement proposals in September 1977. At the same time Ian Smith, the Rhodesian Prime Minister, also announced his intention of seeking an internal settlement with moderate African leaders.

Brighter Economic News.

The harsh economic measures taken by the Government in 1976 produced results more quickly than had been expected, and by the end of 1977 most indicators pointed to a dramatic change in the financial outlook. The balance of payments in the last part of the year was in surplus on both visible and invisible accounts; the pound was strong in relation to most other currencies and there had been massive increases in

Britain's reserves; and the rate of inflation was falling steadily and was expected to be in single figures in the spring of 1978. However, unemployment remained at the very high level of 1·4 million and the growth in industrial output was still sluggish. None the less, the Chancellor of the Exchequer was able to cut taxes on two occasions during 1977 and interest rates fell progressively from their record levels of the previous year. One cause of this economic recovery was North Sea oil. The first oil was brought ashore in 1975, and by the end of 1977 50% of the country's needs were being met from this source.

Devolution: The Second Attempt.

The defeat of its guillotine motion in February 1977 prevented the Government from proceeding with its plans for Scottish and Welsh devolution in the remaining months of that session. However, suitably modified to win Liberal support, the legislation was reintroduced in November 1977, this time in the form of separate bills for Scotland and Wales. With Liberal and Nationalist support, the Government had no difficulty in obtaining a guillotine motion, but the bills still had a lengthy and stormy passage through Parliament in the face of determined opposition from the Conservatives, a number of Labour backbenchers and from members of the House of Lords. They eventually received the Royal Assent in July 1978 but with a number of amendments that had been opposed by the Government. Most important, the schemes were to be implemented only if they were endorsed by 40% of the Scottish and Welsh electorates in the referendums which the Government had decided to hold.

Rhodesia: The Internal Settlement.

Events in Rhodesia continued to play an important part in British politics during 1978. In March, Rhodesian premier Ian Smith signed an internal agreement with three moderate African leaders on the formation of a transitional government to prepare for elections and majority rule by the end of the year. This development was welcomed by the British Government only as a first step towards a settlement as it did not include the leaders of the other African group, the Patriotic Front. The Government therefore continued to press for an all-party conference based on the latest Anglo-American proposals. Two unsuccessful attempts were made to bring all the parties to the conference-table, the first by a civil servant in June, the other in December by Cledwyn Hughes, a Labour MP and close friend of the Prime Minister. Rhodesia also caused a major political storm with the publication of a report by Mr. Thomas Bingham, QC, revealing that BP and Shell had, through their subsidiaries and various swap agreements, been breaking oil sanctions. Amidst allegations that both the Wilson and the Heath Governments had been aware of this, the Government decided to institute a further inquiry to be conducted by 7 Members of Parliament under the chairmanship of a law lord.

Strains within the EEC.

Despite the vote in 1975 in favour of continued membership of the EEC, the Government, under pressure from within the Labour Party, maintained its lukewarm attitude towards many developments in the Community. Problems in various member-countries, and especially in Britain, prevented the first elections to the European Parliament being held as planned during 1978. However, the necessary legislation was passed in February 1978 and the first elections were fixed for June 1979. On other important issues, notably agriculture and fishing, the Government antagonised other member-countries by the tough line it adopted in negotiations. Further strains occurred towards the end of 1978 when it decided not to join the new European Monetary System (EMS), designed by France and Germany to promote greater economic and financial integration, on the grounds that it would damage the British economy and impair the freedom of action of British ministers.

Ending of the Lib/Lab Pact.

The poor performances of Liberal candidates in by-elections during 1977 led to mounting pressure on Liberal MPs to end their agreement to support the Government. An attempt to persuade them to do this immediately was rejected at a special conference in January 1978, but four months later Liberal MPs decided not to renew the agreement at the end of the parliamentary session. As there was no prospect of any other party entering into a formal pact with the Government, politicians and commentators were almost unanimous in predicting an autumn general election. The Government's prospects of success also looked rosier than they had for some time. The economic situation had continued to improve and in his April Budget the Chancellor of the Exchequer had been able to make substantial reductions in personal taxation. This had been reflected in a number of good by-election results for Labour, particularly in Scotland. However, to everyone's surprise, the Prime Minister announced at the beginning of September that the Government intended to soldier on. Attention therefore turned to the problems of maintaining the fight against inflation and to the Government's tactics for survival in the Commons.

Stage Four: The Winter of Discontent.

Although the average increase in earnings during Stage Three was 5% higher than the Government's norm, this was much better than had been expected in view of TUC opposition to the pay policy, and was one factor in the fall in the rate of inflation to about 8%. Encouraged by its success, the Government announced that, in the 1978–9 pay round, settlements should not exceed 5%, excluding self-financing productivity deals and with a few exceptions such as the firemen, police, armed forces and the very low-paid. Stage Four was, however, overwhelmingly rejected by both the TUC and the Labour Party at their annual conferences. The first major confrontation occurred at Ford's, where a nine-week strike was settled only with an offer of 17%. The tough line adopted initially by Ford management was influenced by the Government's threat of sanctions if the pay guidelines were broken. However, in December, Parliament refused to endorse this course of action, thus weakening the Government's ability to enforce its pay policy. It was not long before other groups secured increases in excess of the norm: among them were staff at the BBC, who had threatened to strike over the Christmas holiday, and petrol tanker drivers, whose unofficial action caused acute shortages in many parts of the country. 1979 opened with various serious industrial disputes. An official strike of lorry drivers severely interrupted the provision of essential supplies for industry, agriculture and the retail trade. At the same time the railway drivers and many manual workers in the public sector held one-day strikes in support of their pay claims. The impact of these strikes was reinforced by the worst winter for 16 years.

No Confidence in the Government.

Until March 1979 the Government was able to survive in the House of Commons by securing the support, on different occasions, of either Ulster Unionist or Nationalist MPs. The support of the former was gained by the introduction of a bill to increase the number of parliamentary constituencies in Northern Ireland from 12 to 17. The latter were wooed by the Government's decision to hold the devolution referendums on 1 March 1979. However, once the constituencies bill was on the statute-book there were no further concessions the Government was willing to offer the Unionists; and the result of the devolution referendums effectively put an end to its marriage with the Nationalists. In Wales the Government's proposals were rejected by 80% of those who voted; in Scotland they were supported by the barest of majorities and by only a third of those entitled to vote. The Government was pressed by the Nationalists to proceed with its Scottish proposals and to attempt to overturn the requirement that they should be endorsed by 40% of the Scottish electorate, but it was unwilling to do this for fear of provoking a sizeable rebellion in its own ranks. In these circumstances the Scottish Nationalists indicated that they would no longer support the Government and in a vote of confidence held on 28 March the Government was defeated by one vote, thus precipitating an immediate dissolution of Parliament.

The 1979 General Election.

Polling day was fixed for 3 May, coinciding with local government elections in most of England and Wales. The campaign was overshadowed by the murder on 30 March of Airey Neave, Opposition spokesman on Northern Ireland and one of Mrs. Thatcher's closest advisers, when a bomb planted in his car by Irish extremists exploded in the House of Commons car park. This led to a tightening of security with fewer meetings and other public appearances by leading politicians. Television thus played an even more dominant role than in recent elections with the main focus being on the party leaders. Generally it was a very quiet campaign disrupted only by various incidents involving supporters and opponents of the National Front, the most serious of which was at Southall where one person was killed and over 300 arrested. The Conservatives started the campaign with an overwhelming lead in the opinion polls, largely reflecting the winter's industrial troubles. During the campaign the gap between the parties narrowed but the Conservative lead was maintained and it was confirmed by the actual results. There was a swing of 5·2% to the Conservatives, sufficient to give them an overall majority of 44 in the House of Commons. There were, however, significant regional variations. The swing to the Conservatives was largest in southern England, it was smaller in the north, and in Scotland there was a very small swing to Labour. The most dramatic change in Scotland was the collapse of support for the Nationalists whose share of the vote was almost halved and they lost 9 of their 11 seats. The performance of the Liberals was patchy. Overall their vote fell by 1 million and they lost 3 seats but some of their MPs, including their leader David Steel, greatly increased their majorities. The National Front did very badly, all its candidates losing their deposits and securing only 0·6% of the poll. Among the casualties of the election were Shirley Williams, Labour's Education Minister, Teddy Taylor, the Conservative spokesman on Scotland, and Jeremy Thorpe, former leader of the Liberal Party.

Mrs. Thatcher's Government.

Mrs. Thatcher's arrival at 10 Downing Street attracted great interest, not only because she was the first woman Prime Minister of a Western state, but also because of the radical policies she had advocated in Opposition. Some of her closest associates were appointed to senior posts in the Cabinet, particularly on the economic side (for instance Sir Geoffrey Howe as Chancellor of the Exchequer and Sir Keith Joseph as Industry Secretary) but the Cabinet also included many who had been closely identified with the approach of her predecessor, Edward Heath. Among them were William Whitelaw (Home Secretary), Lord Carrington (Foreign Secretary), James Prior (Employment Secretary) and Peter Walker (Minister of Agriculture). However, even though he had campaigned energetically for the Conservatives during the election, no place was found in the Government for Edward Heath himself.

A Radical Programme.

The Queen's Speech for the first session of the new Parliament (lasting from May 1979 until October 1980) was an ambitious one both in its scale and in the magnitude of the changes it proposed. Among the most important measures were: the abolition of statutory price controls; changes in the law on picketing and the closed shop; repeal of the devolution legislation; granting council tenants a statutory right to purchase their homes; denationalisation of the nationalised airline and freight and aerospace industries and a reduction generally in the powers of state intervention in industry; and repeal of the requirement that local authorities introduce comprehensive education. Legislation giving effect to most of these changes was introduced in the autumn of 1979 and, although the congestion of the Parliamentary timetable led to some problems, the Government's comfortable majority ensured that it reached the statute-book by the end of the session.

Taxation and Public Spending.

During the election campaign the Conservatives attracted widespread support with their promises to cut direct taxation and eliminate wasteful public spending. Although many commentators thought that the economic situation would preclude fulfilment of public expectations immediately, the Chancellor confounded such scepticism by cutting the standard rate of income tax from 33% to 30%, with even greater reductions at higher levels, in his first Budget in June 1979. To finance these cuts he announced, as expected, reductions in public spending but he also had to increase VAT by 7% and petrol duty by 10p a gallon and to raise interest rates. These changes, however, added to the inflationary pressure already in the economy and in November the Chancellor had to raise interest rates to record levels and to make additional cuts in public spending affecting all sectors except for the armed forces and the police. These cuts were reflected in the withdrawal of some services, increased charges for others, reductions in staffing and in the winding-up of various government agencies.

The Labour Party Constitution.

As in the past, Labour's electoral defeat was followed by internal dissent, on this occasion centred upon those parts of the Party's constitution dealing with the powers of Party members to control their leaders. In October 1979, the Party Conference endorsed two changes in the constitution, requiring sitting MPs to be re-selected during the life of each Parliament and giving the final say on the election manifesto to the National Executive Committee. These decisions were referred to the committee of inquiry it also agreed to establish into the Party's organisation. Disagreement over the composition of this committee delayed the start of its work until January 1980. James Callaghan was re-elected Leader of the Party shortly after the General Election and most of the members of the outgoing Cabinet were elected to the Shadow Cabinet; one notable absentee was Tony Benn who chose to return to the backbenches in order to have greater freedom to speak on a wide range of issues.

Europe: A Fresh Start?

The campaign for the first direct elections to the European Parliament attracted little public interest, particularly as it came immediately after the General Election, and this was reflected in a very low turnout on polling day, 7 June. The result was a further victory for the Conservatives who won 60 of the 78 British seats. The new Government promised that it would be more positive than its predecessor in its attitude towards the EEC but it soon found itself in conflict with all its partners over its demand that Britain's net contribution to the EEC Budget be reduced by £1,000 million. Britain was also alone in calling for a tough response, including a boycott of the Moscow Olympics, to the Soviet invasion of Afghanistan in January 1980. Finally there were rows with particular countries, for example with France over the latter's refusal to permit imports of British lamb and with Germany over Britain's policy on North Sea oil.

Rhodesia: Return to Legality.

Elections, under the terms of the internal settlement, were held in Rhodesia in April 1979, leading to the formation in June of a coalition government led by Bishop Abel Muzorewa. Contrary to expectations, the Conservative Government did not recognise this government and continued to seek all-party agreement. The turning point occurred during the Commonwealth Conference at Lusaka in August 1979 where agreement was reached on the basic elements of a settlement. This led to three months of difficult negotiations in London, under the chairmanship of the Foreign Secretary, Lord Carrington, which culminated in the signing of a ceasefire and the lifting of sanctions in December 1979. Under its terms, a Cabinet Minister, Lord Soames, was appointed Governor for the period leading up to independence which was to be achieved following elections in February 1980. These elections, supervised by British and Commonwealth officials, resulted in a landslide victory for one of the Patriotic Front leaders, Robert Mugabe. Following the formation of a coalition government, including two whites, independence was officially achieved in April 1980, Zimbabwe becoming the 43rd member of the Commonwealth.

Trade Unions and the Law.

One consequence of the Government's tough economic policies was an increase in unemployment. In the public sector the Government's plans to cut jobs and its reluctance to support industries in financial difficulty caused widespread alarm among the trade unions. However, an early collision between the Government and the unions was not expected, partly because of the refusal of the Employment Secretary, James Prior, to be stampeded into tough action against the unions, and partly because of the reluctance of the unions to take on the Government so soon after it had received a mandate in an election in which public dislike of union power had played a major part. However, these predictions were confounded by a crisis at British Steel. The world recession and the strict limits placed by the Government on its financial support for the industry forced British Steel to announce major redundancies, with dramatic implications for the level of employment in places such as Corby and Port Talbot. British Steel was also unable to offer its employees wage increases corresponding to the rate of inflation. Tension on both issues culminated in January 1980 in the first national steel strike for over 50 years.

Growing World Tension.

The Government, and Mrs. Thatcher in particular, acquired a reputation for taking a tough stance on international issues. Its determination to resist Soviet aggression led it to allow American Cruise missiles to be stationed in Britain and to decide to replace Polaris with Trident missiles as Britain's strategic nuclear deterrent (decisions that were opposed by a revived Campaign for Nuclear Disarmament). Its attempt to organise a boycott of the Moscow Olympics in protest at the Soviet invasion of Afghanistan had only limited success and its strong recommendation against participation was heeded by only a minority of British sportsmen. Relations with Europe, however, become more cordial, assisted by the settlement, albeit on terms less favourable than the Prime Minister had hoped, of the dispute over Britain's contribution to the EEC budget. EEC governments acted in concert on various issues such as the Middle East and the American hostages in Iran. The problems of Iran spread dramatically to London at the end of April when seven gunmen seized the Iranian Embassy, taking 24 people hostage. Under the full view of TV cameras, the siege was successfully ended by the SAS a few days later.

Leadership of the Labour Party.

Constitutional questions dominated the Labour Party throughout 1980 and into 1981. The 1980 Annual Conference the earlier decision to require re-selection of sitting MPs was confirmed but the plan to give the National Executive Committee the final say on the election manifesto was reversed. The most controversial decision, however, was to take the election of the Party leader out of the hands of the Parliamentary Labour Party alone and to set up an electoral college consisting of Labour MPs, the constituency parties and the affiliated trade unions. No agreement could be reached in October on the precise composition of such a college and a special conference was convened for this purpose in January 1981. In the midst of all this uncertainty, James Callaghan announced his retirement. The election of his successor therefore took place under the old system and, on the second ballot, the PLP elected Michael Foot by a margin of ten votes over Denis Healey. Denis Healey was subsequently elected Deputy Leader.

Deepening Recession.

The Government's counter-inflation policies, implemented at a time of worldwide recession, had a severe effect upon levels of output and employment. Industry was especially hard hit by the record interest rates and by the strength of the pound. Although inflation did fall steadily, public attention switched increasingly to unemployment which early in 1981 reached 2½ million. The Government came under bitter attack from the trade unions, although the 13-week steel strike was ended without major concessions and the TUC's Day of Action in May 1980 met with only limited success, and more woundingly from the CBI and some prominent Conservative backbenchers. These problems led ministers to relax their policy of non-intervention in industry and large amounts of money were pumped into some of the major lossmakers such as British Leyland and British Steel. Despite accusations that it was making U-turns, the Government insisted that its overall economic strategy was unchanged. Confirmation of this was provided by the Chancellor of the Exchequer. Although interest rates were lowered in November 1980 and March 1981, offsetting action was taken to restrict monetary growth. In the Budget in March substantial increases in personal taxation were imposed and windfall taxes were applied to the profits of the banks and oil companies.

The Birth of the Social Democratic Party.

During 1980 various leading members of the Labour Party became increasingly critical of its decisions on its constitution and on policy (such as the support at the Annual Conference for unilateral nuclear disarmament and withdrawal from the EEC). Led by Shirley Williams, David Owen and William Rodgers (popularly known as the Gang of Three), their disillusionment was heightened by the Special Conference at Wembley in January 1981 which not only reaffirmed the decision to establish an electoral college but also decided that its composition should be: trade unions 40%, constituency parties 30% and Labour MPs 30%. A week later, the Gang of Four (having been joined by Roy Jenkins on his retirement as President of the EEC Commission) published the Limehouse Declaration announcing the formation of a Council for Social Democracy. Initially this was not a separate party but only a group to campaign for moderate left-wing policies, but in March 1981 12 Labour MPs (including David Owen and William Rodgers) resigned the Party Whip and announced that they would not be seeking re-election as Labour MPs.

On 26 March 1981, to a fanfare of publicity, the Social Democratic Party was formally launched. In the House of Commons the SDP consisted initially of 14 MPs (13 ex-Labour and 1 ex-Conservative). One of its first decisions was to negotiate an electoral alliance with the Liberals.

Healey versus Benn.

In April 1981 Tony Benn announced his intention of standing against Denis Healey for the Deputy Leadership of the Labour Party, thereby bringing into play for the first time the new procedures which had been agreed at the Wembley conference at the beginning of the year. In a bruising six months of campaigning, Benn and Healey were joined by a third candidate, John Silkin, who offered himself as a conciliator between the Party's left and right wings. At the electoral college, held the day before the Annual Conference in Brighton in October, Silkin was eliminated in the first ballot and in a photofinish, in which the abstention of a number of MPs who had supported Silkin was decisive, Healey defeated Benn by the narrowest of margins. The ensuing conference produced further victories for the parliamentary leadership, notably in the election of the National Executive Committee and on the control of the Party's election manifesto. Although there was growing pressure from within the Party for a truce, symbolised by a meeting of the NEC and trade union leaders at Bishops Stortford in January 1982, Michael Foot's problems were by no means solved. Tension persisted between Tony Benn, who failed to secure election to the Shadow Cabinet in November, and his parliamentary colleagues. Under pressure from MPs, the NEC instituted an inquiry into the influence in the constituency parties of a Trotskyite group, the Militant Tendency.

"Wets" versus "Dries".

The Chancellor's tough Budget in March 1981 brought to the surface the tensions that had existed for some time within the Government and the Conservative Party generally. In an attempt to reassert her authority, Mrs. Thatcher undertook a major ministerial reshuffle in September. Among those dismissed was one of her most outspoken critics (who became widely known as "wets"), Sir Ian Gilmour, and another, James Prior, was switched from the Department of Employment to the Northern Ireland Office. Most of those who were promoted were loyal colleagues of the Prime Minister. Particularly significant were the appointments of Norman Tebbit as Secretary of State for Employment, charged with the task of introducing new legal curbs upon the trade unions, and of Nigel Lawson as Secretary of State for Energy who lost no time in announcing the Government's intention of privatising important parts of the state-owned North Sea oil and gas industries. The reshuffle, however, failed to silence the Prime Minister's critics within the Cabinet. After a lengthy battle, they succeeded in forcing the Chancellor of the Exchequer to make some relaxations in his plans for public spending in 1982–3 although he insisted upon recouping part of the cost in increased employee national insurance contributions. Their determination to press for a more radical change in economic strategy was strengthened by the continuing rise in the level of unemployment, which in January 1982 passed the 3 million mark, and by the financial problems of many companies which resulted in a record number of bankruptcies.

Social Unrest.

The Government's economic policies were alleged to be one of the contributory factors behind the ugly street violence which broke out in Brixton in April 1981 and in various cities, notably Liverpool, Manchester and London, three months later. Following the Brixton riots, the Government appointed a distinguished judge, Lord Scarman, to inquire into their causes. His report, completed in November, concluded that there had been a breakdown of confidence between the coloured community and the police against a background of urban deprivation, racial disadvantage and a rising level of street crime. The Liverpool riots prompted the Prime Minister to send a top-level task force, led by a Cabinet minister, Michael Heseltine, to investigate the area's problems and to find ways of overcoming them. Unemployment continued to keep down the number of industrial disputes. The Government became embroiled, however, in a major dispute with its own employees. Incensed by the Government's failure to honour its agreement that civil service pay should be fixed on the basis of fair comparison with equivalent work in the private sector, civil servants began a series of selective strikes in March which lasted for 21 weeks and had a major impact upon the work of the Government, for instance seriously disrupting the collection of tax revenue.

The Liberal/SDP Alliance.

Labour's continuing problems and the Government's economic record provided fertile ground for the launching of the Liberal/SDP Alliance. Its first real test (although it was formally endorsed by the Liberal Assembly only in September) occurred at a parliamentary by-election in Warrington in July 1981 where, in a safe Labour seat of a kind generally considered to be unpromising for the SDP, Roy Jenkins almost succeeded in overturning the Labour majority. Three months later, a Liberal, who had lost his deposit in the 1979 General Election, won the Conservative marginal seat of Croydon North West. Most dramatic of all, however, was Shirley Williams' victory in the safe Conservative seat of Crosby in late November. She thus became the first MP to be elected under the SDP's colours but the 24th member of its parliamentary group, nine further Labour MPs having transferred their allegiance since the inauguration of the Party in March. The SDP did not contest the county council elections in May but it won many local by-elections and, as a result of the defection of a majority of the Labour councillors in Islington, it took control of its first council. At the end of 1981 the opinion polls predicted a decisive victory for the Alliance were there to be an immediate general election. However, its popularity began to decline during the first few months of 1982 as the SDP (by then the third largest party in the House of Commons with 27 MPs) began to finalise its constitution and policy programme and as strains emerged in its alliance with the Liberals over the distribution of seats for the next general election. Nonetheless its momentum was maintained by Roy Jenkins' victory in the Glasgow, Hillhead by-election in March 1982, although in the May local elections it secured very few successes.

The Falkland Islands Crisis.

The Argentinian invasion of the Falkland Islands, British colonial territory in the South Atlantic, at the beginning of April 1982 provoked a major political crisis in Britain. At a special session of Parliament, the first to be held on a Saturday since the Suez crisis of 1956, there was almost universal condemnation of the Government's failure to take action to defend the Falklands against Argentinian aggression. Both the Foreign Secretary, Lord Carrington, and the Defence Secretary, John Nott, offered their resignations to the Prime Minister but only the former resigned (to be replaced by Francis Pym), along with two of his ministerial colleagues at the Foreign Office. Amidst great patriotic fervour, the Government despatched a major naval task force to re-take the islands. As it sailed on its long voyage to the South Atlantic, the United States Secretary of State, Alexander Haig, shuttled back and forth between London and Buenos Aires in an attempt to find a diplomatic solution to the crisis.

War in the South Atlantic.

A month after the task force had set out, military action commenced with British aircraft bombing Port Stanley airfield and clashes in the air and at sea. Following further unsuccessful efforts to reach a negotiated settlement, this time by the Secretary-General of the United Nations, British troops landed on East Falkland and, after 3½ weeks of bitter fighting, they encircled Port Stanley and secured the surrender of the Argentinian forces. During the conflict, over 1,000 lives were lost (255 British and 720 Argentinian). Fearing further Argentinian aggression, the Government had to make arrangements for a large permanent garrison on the islands. It also established a top-level committee of inquiry, under the chairmanship of Lord Franks, to investigate the events leading up to the crisis.

The Peace Movement.

The achievements of the task force resulted in strong public support for the armed forces and there were scenes of great jubilation on their return to this country. In other respects too defence attracted considerable public attention. The Campaign for Nuclear Disarmament organised a number of major demonstrations against the Government's nuclear weapons policy and peace camps were established at some of the bases where Cruise missiles were due to be sited in the autumn of 1983, such as Greenham Common near Newbury. Unilateral nuclear disarmament was adopted by the Labour Party as official policy at its 1982 Conference and it was recommended by a committee of the Church of England, although early in 1983 this recommendation was rejected by the Church's Synod in favour of multilateral disarmament, but with the proviso that Britain should never be the first to use nuclear weapons. To counter the arguments of the peace movement, Mrs Thatcher appointed one of the Government's most effective orators, Michael Heseltine, to be Secretary of State for Defence in January 1983, replacing John Nott who some months earlier had announced his intention of retiring from politics at the next general election.

The Difficulties of the Opposition.

In some respects 1982 was an easier year for the leadership of the Labour Party. Michael Foot and Denis Healey were re-elected as Leader and Deputy Leader unopposed and they increased their control over the National Executive Committee. However, the Party's problems were by no means resolved. At a time of national crisis and patriotic fervour the task of Opposition leader is never easy and this was one factor contributing to a steady decline in the popularity of Mr. Foot among the electorate. His difficulties were exacerbated by continuing rows within the Party. Following receipt of the report into the activities of the Militant Tendency, it was decided to require all groups that wished to operate within the Party to register and to meet certain conditions laid down by the NEC. In the opinion of the NEC, Militant failed to satisfy these conditions but action to expel its leaders was delayed by legal complications. These and other problems were reflected in the Party's electoral popularity. In October 1982 it narrowly succeeded in winning the Conservative marginal seat of Birmingham, Northfield, but in February 1983 it suffered the crushing blow of losing Bermondsey, one of the safest Labour seats in the country. This setback was to some extent offset by the retention of the marginal seat of Darlington a month later.

The 1983 General Election.

Throughout most of 1982 the Government, and Mrs. Thatcher in particular, enjoyed a commanding lead in the opinion polls. This was a remarkable achievement for a government in the fourth year of its existence, particularly in view of the continuing upward trend in unemployment, and it largely reflected public approval of the Government's handling of the Falklands crisis (and it was exonerated by the Franks Committee for not having averted the Argentinian invasion). From early 1983 onwards the continuing Conservative lead in the opinion polls fuelled speculation about an early general election. The Prime Minister, who could easily have dampened such speculation, did not do so. Instead, having seen an analysis of the municipal election results in May, she decided on a snap poll on 9 June.

Potentially, the election could have been of exceptional interest. For the first time since the 1920s it was a three-horse race, with the Liberal/SDP Alliance contesting every seat in mainland Britain. The constituency map had also been extensively redrawn since 1979, with many well-known MPs having to fight new constituencies. In practice, however, it produced few excitements. The commanding lead of the Conservatives was never challenged during the campaign and interest therefore focused upon the contest between Labour and the Alliance for second place. Labour's difficulties were aggravated, in what was an increasingly presidential-style campaign, by unfavourable comparisons drawn by most voters between Mr. Foot and Mrs. Thatcher.

A Decisive Conservative Victory.

From the very first result there was no doubt about the outcome of the election. With the Labour vote in retreat everywhere and with the Alliance polling well but failing to secure a real breakthrough, the Conservatives coasted to a decisive victory, winning an overall majority of 144, only two short of the massive majority won by Labour in the landslide of 1945. (For the full results, see D3–4.) In terms of votes, however, the Conservative share of the vote (43%) had *fallen* since 1979. What had happened was that the Conservatives had won a large number of seats because the opposition was divided, with the Alliance eating seriously into the Labour vote. Labour's share of the vote (28%) was the lowest since the early 1920s and it held only two seats in southern England outside London. Elsewhere it managed to hold on to seats and, with 209 MPs, was easily the second largest party. The Alliance polled almost as many votes as Labour (26%) but because its vote was less concentrated it won many fewer seats (only 23), and had to be content with coming second in as many as 313 constituencies. The result was a particular disappointment for the SDP, most of whose leading members, apart from Roy Jenkins and David Owen, were defeated. Other prominent casualties in the election included Tony Benn, Albert Booth, Joan Lestor and David Ennals, all former Labour Ministers.

Mrs. Thatcher's Second Term.

Strengthened by her success at the polls, Mrs. Thatcher made various ministerial changes designed to increase her dominance over the Cabinet. She sacked Francis Pym, who had been Foreign Secretary since the start of the Falklands crisis but with whom she had never enjoyed an easy relationship, and replaced him with Sir Geoffrey Howe, who had been her loyal Chancellor of the Exchequer since 1979. In his place, she promoted Nigel Lawson, a keen supporter of her economic policies. As a reward for his work as Party Chairman, she appointed Cecil Parkinson to head a new department, combining

Trade and Industry. William Whitelaw left the Home Office but remained Deputy Prime Minister and was elevated to the House of Lords as a Viscount. This was the first hereditary peerage to be conferred since 1964. (However, neither he nor the second such peer, the former Speaker, George Thomas, had male heirs; the hereditary principle was to be fully restored only in 1984 when an earldom was conferred upon Harold Macmillan on the occasion of his 90th birthday.) Victory at the polls, however, did not assure Mrs. Thatcher of an easy time. On various issues, including reductions in NHS manpower, control of local authorities, fuel prices and housing benefits, there was open criticism from Conservative backbenchers, sometimes about the substance of what the Government was doing, and often about its presentation. The most serious embarrassment concerned the personal life of Cecil Parkinson. The disclosure that his former secretary was expecting his child did not lead to his immediate resignation. However, further revelations during the Party Conference, which but for this would have been a victory celebration, made his departure from the Government inevitable and resulted in the appointment of Norman Tebbit to replace him (he had earlier handed over the Party Chairmanship to John Selwyn Gummer).

New Opposition Leaders.

Shortly after the General Election, both Michael Foot and Denis Healey announced their intention of standing down as Leader and Deputy Leader of the Labour Party at the Party Conference in October 1983. Four candidates stood for the leadership, but early in the campaign it soon emerged that leftwinger, Neil Kinnock, would be the easy winner over Roy Hattersley, the leading "moderate" candidate. Interest therefore focused upon the contest for the deputy leadership where, although there were again four candidates, the race was between Hattersley (both he and Kinnock had agreed to stand for both offices and to serve under the other) and Michael Meacher, the standard bearer for the left in the absence of Tony Benn. Although there were close decisions in a number of trade unions, Hattersley emerged as a comfortable winner, thus giving the Party the so-called "dream ticket" of balanced leadership which many supporters believed was essential if it was to rebuild its electoral support. That this was going to be a lengthy process was acknowledged in the choice of a leader aged only 41. A similar development occurred also in the SDP where David Owen, aged 45, was elected unopposed to replace Roy Jenkins as leader.

The Cruise Missile Debate.

Failure to reach a negotiated arms control agreement on intermediate-range missiles led the Government to proceed with the deployment of US Cruise missiles in Britain. This decision was endorsed by the House of Commons in October 1983 which also rejected a proposal for a dual-key control system, designed to ensure that the missiles could be used only with the consent of the British Government. This decision, and that of the German Parliament to commence deployment of Pershing II missiles, resulted in a Soviet walkout from the arms control talks at Geneva. The first Cruise missiles arrived in Britain at Greenham Common, near Newbury, in November and were operational by Christmas. Demonstrations against these developments continued throughout the year and were fuelled by tensions in the Anglo-American alliance over the US invasion in October 1983 of the Caribbean island of Grenada, an independent member of the Commonwealth, despite the serious reservations of the British Government. Sir Geoffrey Howe's handling of this crisis and of the decision early in 1984 to ban trade unions from the Government Communications Centre at Cheltenham (GCHQ) was widely criticised. At the same time, however, there were signs that Western leaders' attitudes towards the Warsaw Pact were softening, symbolised by Mrs. Thatcher's visit to Hungary in February 1984, her first visit to a Communist country, by her decision to travel to Moscow for the funerals of Presidents Andropov and Chernenko, and by her warmth towards the new Soviet leader, Mr. Gorbachev, on his accession to office in March 1985.

The Government's Programme for 1984–5.

The Queen's Speech for the first session of the new Parliament contained few surprises. Various measures, such as the privatisation of British Telecom and bills on data protection and police powers, had been introduced in the last Parliament but had been lost as a result of the early dissolution; others, including the abolition of the Greater London Council and the metropolitan county councils, the creation of a quango to run London Transport, and new curbs on local authorities, had featured prominently in the Conservative Manifesto. The Government also proceeded with its plans further to regulate the activities of trade unions, introducing legislation requiring the periodic election of union officials, and the holding of secret ballots before strike action and to decide whether to maintain a fund for financing political objectives. The prospect of a further five years of Conservative rule injected a new realism in most union leaders and this, coupled with a less strident tone on the part of ministers following Tom King's appointment to replace Norman Tebbit as Secretary for State for Employment, led to concessions on the last of these proposals. Industrial relations problems, however, remained in the public eye, especially in the printing industry where there were a number of serious disputes, including a confrontation between the National Graphical Association and a Warrington newspaper publisher which led to protracted litigation and in the mining industry, where a bitter battle against pit closures developed.

Privatisation.

Privatisation—limiting the role of the state and extending the operation of market forces—was one of the hallmarks of the Government. It embarked upon the biggest change in the boundary between the public and private sectors since 1945. It encouraged the contracting out to private firms of work that previously was undertaken by public bodies (e.g. local authority cleansing and refuse collection services, NHS cleaning, laundry and catering); it relaxed statutory monopoly powers and licensing arrangements in various sectors (e.g. buses and telecommunications); and it sold all or part of a number of public enterprises. During its first term these included selling a majority stake in British Aerospace, in the oil-producing side of the British National Oil Corporation—Britoil—and in Cable and Wireless. These were dwarfed by the sale of just over 50% of British Telecom, the largest ever flotation of a company which attracted over two million applications for shares, in November 1984. Further sales, including British Airways, British Gas and the ordnance factories, are planned.

Miners' Strike.

In March 1984 the National Coal Board (NCB) announced plans to close various pits to eliminate excess capacity. This exacerbated tensions that already existed in the industry and rapidly escalated into a national strike. Given the history of relations since the early 1970s between the miners and the Conservatives, a major confrontation seemed inevitable. But few predicted its length or bitterness. The NCB, whose chairman Ian MacGregor had earlier established a reputation for toughness at British Steel, with the full backing of the Government, was determined not to surrender; its attitude was matched by that of the striking miners, led by Arthur Scargill, who were driven on by the feeling that they were defending the very existence of their communities. The NUM, however, failed to bring the economy to its knees as it had done in 1972–4. Not only was it unsuccessful in attracting effective support from the rest of the trade union movement. It also was itself divided, with about one third of its members, especially in the prosperous Nottinghamshire coalfield, refusing to join the strike. The Government too went to some lengths to ensure that alternative sources of fuel were available. The NUM's attempts to prevent working miners getting to work led to violent scenes between pickets and the large numbers of police who were deployed, often in riot gear, to restrain them. Eventually, after various abortive rounds of negotiation, striking miners, many of whom were suffering severe financial hardship, started to trickle back to work and, after almost exactly a year, the NUM decided to end the strike without reaching an agreement with the NCB. Quite apart from the damage that it did to the economy, the strike imposed major strains upon both the TUC and the Labour Party.

The Labour leadership sought to distance itself from the more extreme statements and behaviour of Arthur Scargill and his followers while supporting the miners' case. It was criticised, however, for not giving more wholehearted support by the left wing of the Party, whose ranks in Parliament had been strengthened in March 1984 by the victory of Tony Benn in a by-election at Chesterfield.

Brighton Bombing.

The Conservative Party Conference in October 1984 at Brighton was overshadowed by a bomb explosion at the Grand Hotel where most of the Cabinet was staying. Mrs. Thatcher herself had a narrow escape and, among those seriously injured were Norman Tebbit and the Chief Whip. Responsibility was claimed by the IRA. A month earlier, Jim Prior had resigned as Secretary of State for Northern Ireland, choosing to return to the back-benches, thus removing from the Cabinet yet another critic of the Government's economic strategy. Ministers continued to be embarrassed by back-bench revolts on various issues but the Government's majority in the Commons was never endangered. In the Lords, however, it was forced to amend its plans, for example over the cancellation of the GLC and metropolitan county elections in 1986. One Opposition backbencher, Tam Dalyell, had his persistence in probing the Government's account of the sinking of the Argentinian ship, the General Belgrano, during the Falklands crisis rewarded when a leak by a senior civil servant in the Ministry of Defence, Clive Ponting, revealed inconsistencies. Controversially, the Attorney-General decided to prosecute Mr. Ponting under the widely discredited Official Secrets Act and when, contrary to all expectations, he was acquitted a major political row erupted.

Close to Dollar Parity.

The damage inflicted on the economy by the miners' strike (estimated by the Chancellor of the Exchequer to have cost £2¾ billion) was one of the factors behind a slide in the exchange rate. Miscalculations by the Government, however, also contributed to the rapid decline in the dollar value of sterling. Faced with the imminent possibility of parity between the pound and the dollar, the Chancellor was forced to re-introduce minimum lending rate and to force up interest rates. This eventually succeeded in calming the nerves of the money markets. But it had an adverse effect on the prospects of economic revival. The Government was widely attacked for its failure to take direct action to alleviate the problem of unemployment not only by the Opposition but also by some of the most senior members of its own Party and by prominent members of the Church of England. One such critic was the Earl of Stockton, formerly Harold Macmillan, who took advantage of the first televised debate from the House of Lords in January 1985 to reach a wide audience for his views.

Getting the Message Across.

By the summer of 1985, the Government's popularity was at a low ebb. Continuing record levels of unemployment, cuts in many public services, and long-running industrial disputes (the year-long miners' strike was followed by an equally protracted teachers' dispute), all contributed to the worst by-election defeat for the Conservatives for many years at Brecon and Radnor in July. In an attempt to improve the Government's standing, Mrs. Thatcher made a number of important changes in the Cabinet in September. As Party Chairman she appointed her close ally, Norman Tebbit (and to assist him in getting the Government's message across she recruited best-selling author, Jeffrey Archer, as his deputy). In the sensitive area of law and order she shifted Douglas Hurd from Northern Ireland to the Home Office. His predecessor, Leon Brittan, who was generally regarded as a poor performer on TV and who had been widely criticised for putting pressure on the BBC to cancel a programme on political extremism in Northern Ireland, replaced Norman Tebbit as Secretary of State for Trade and Industry. For a few months these changes seemed to have been successful, even though the new Home Secretary was immediately embroiled in controversy over

the outbreak of rioting in Handsworth in Birmingham and in Brixton and Tottenham in London and over the tactics adopted by the police in attempting to restore order.

Stronger Leadership.

Although Labour did well in the county council elections in May 1985, it continued to share the spoils of the Government's unpopularity with the Alliance which succeeded in breaking the two-party hold on most of the counties in England and in winning the Brecon and Radnor by-election. The strains within the Labour movement caused by the miners' strike persisted as a result of the creation of a breakaway union, the Union of Democratic Miners, which successfully challenged the National Union of Mineworkers in parts of the country. In addition, the Labour leadership was challenged to support various left-wing Labour controlled local authorities in their defiance of the new financial curbs that had been imposed by the Government. At the Party's Annual Conference, Neil Kinnock answered those who had criticised him for lack of leadership by making a vigorous attack both upon Arthur Scargill and upon hard left Labour councillors, particularly in Liverpool. His stand won him support among Labour M.P.s and in the opinion polls but it did not resolve the problems facing the Labour Party. The NEC launched an inquiry into the running of the Liverpool District Party which early in 1986 recommended action which could lead to the expulsion of various leading members. Labour councillors in Liverpool and Lambeth were also confronted with bankruptcy and disqualification following court action initiated by the District Auditor over their delay in setting a rate. They and other Labour councillors facing similar penalties pressed the Labour leadership to indemnify them on Labour's return to power.

The Westland Saga.

The Government's calmed nerves were soon disturbed by an extraordinary internal battle over the fate of a West Country helicopter manufacturer, Westland plc. Throughout the Christmas recess an unusually public row simmered between two Cabinet ministers over the merits of two alternative solutions to the financial problems of the company. The Defence Secretary, Michael Heseltine, campaigned hard for a European solution whereas the Trade and Industry Secretary, Leon Brittan, with the backing of the Prime Minister, favoured leaving the decision to the company's shareholders which in effect meant that the company would be bailed out by the American firm, Sikorsky. The first casualty was Michael Heseltine who walked dramatically out of a Cabinet meeting, refusing to accept the Prime Minister's attempt to shackle his campaign. The next fortnight saw intense political controversy, fuelled by allegations first over different versions of a meeting between Leon Brittan and the chief executive of Westland and then over the unprecedented leaking of a letter to Michael Heseltine from the Solicitor-General. Although he retained the support of the Prime Minister, Leon Brittan's position became untenable and he followed his adversary onto the backbenches. Westland continued to dominate the headlines for some weeks but the focus of attention switched to the company itself and its shareholders, who eventually backed the American option. The Government, however, was immediately involved in a new political row over the future of the state-owned car firm, British Leyland, when it was disclosed that discussions had reached an advanced stage over the sale of different parts of the company to General Motors and Ford. The Government was forced to break off its negotiations with Ford over Austin-Rover and this change of course further dented the Prime Minister's reputation.

The Political Outlook.

Westland and British Leyland were not the only sources of trouble for the Government in the early months of 1986. In November 1985, Mrs. Thatcher and the Irish premier, Dr. Fitzgerald, had signed an agreement establishing an inter-governmental conference to discuss issues of common interest (see **C68**). This had provoked the resignation of all the Unionist M.P.s in protest at what they saw as the first step towards a united Ireland and their stand attracted the support of a number of senior Conservative M.P.s, one of whom, Ian Gow, who earlier had been one of Mrs. Thatcher's closest aides, resigned from the Government. All but one of the Unionists were re-elected in by-elections held in January 1986. The Government's refusal to abandon the agreement, however, led to a one-day strike in the province in February and threats of further acts of defiance. On the economic front too, the Government's hopes of major tax cuts were dashed by a dramatic collapse in oil prices which cost the Chancellor over £5 billion in tax revenue from North Sea oil. Nonetheless, in his Budget in March, he succeeded in cutting the standard rate of income tax by 1% and in providing other tax concessions, thus giving some help to his Party as it faced three difficult by-elections. Overall the political outlook for the next general election remained uncertain. The Government's image was certainly tarnished and the Prime Minister's position had been undermined not only by the Westland affair itself but also by its effect upon the composition of the Cabinet which in 1986 was less under her control than for some years. But neither Labour nor the Alliance appeared able to establish a clear ascendancy as the main challenger and both had internal problems to be overcome if either was to present itself as a credible alternative government. This was confirmed by the results of the May by-elections (the Conservatives lost two – Fulham to Labour, Ryedale spectacularly to the Alliance – and just held on to West Derbyshire) and of the local elections which produced gains for Labour and the Alliance.

Major Government Decisions, May 1979–June 1986.

Economic Affairs

Reduction in standard rate of income tax to 30% (offset by increase in VAT to 15%)

Abolition of exchange controls

Reform of system of monetary control, including abolition of Minimum Lending Rate (reintroduced as temporary crisis measure in 1985).

Introduction of various schemes to reduce unemployment including major new Youth Training Scheme

Abolition of hire purchase controls

Education

Strengthening of position of parents on school governing bodies and in choosing schools for their children

Relaxation of obligation to provide school meals and milk

Introduction of Assisted Places Scheme to give financial support to enable certain pupils to attend independent schools

Decision to replace O Level and CSE with a new examination as from 1988

Foreign Affairs and Defence

Independence granted to Zimbabwe

Decision to permit US Cruise missiles to be stationed in Britain as from 1983

Decision to replace Polaris with US Trident missiles

Defeat of Argentinian invasion of Falkland Islands

and decision to create a large permanent garrison there

Agreement with China over future of Hong Kong after expiry of British lease in 1997

Housing

Establishment of a charter for public sector tenants, including the right to buy their homes

Industrial Relations

Provision for public funds to be used to pay for secret union ballots

Changes in the law relating to the closed shop, picketing, unfair dismissal, trade union immunities, strike ballots, and election of union officials

Industry

Strengthening of Office of Fair Trading and Monopolies and Mergers Commission, including power to investigate misuse of monopoly by nationalised industries

Privatisation of public enterprises, including denationalisation of British Aerospace, Cable & Wireless, Britoil and British Telecom; introduction of competition into the bus and telecommunications industries.

Creation of enterprise zones with special tax relief and industrial benefits, and of development corporations for London and Merseyside docklands

National Health Service

Ending of withdrawal of private beds from NHS hospitals

Reorganisation of NHS, including replacement of area health authorities with a larger number of district health authorities

Social Security

Reform of supplementary benefits system, including linking of benefit rates to prices alone (rather than prices and earnings)

Limits imposed on payment of supplementary benefit to strikers' families

End of index-linking of short-term social security benefits

Introduction of new sickness benefit arrangements

Other Decisions

Changes in the financial relationship between central and local government, strengthening central control with a new system of grants and restrictions on the powers of local authorities to levy rates

Abolition of Greater London Council and metropolitan county councils

Extension of franchise to British citizens resident abroad, and of postal voting to holidaymakers, increase in deposit at parliamentary elections

Redefinition of British citizenship and nationality and changes in the provisions relating to right of abode in the UK

Establishment of 4th TV channel under the Independent Broadcasting Authority except in Wales where a special authority was created to provide programmes in Welsh

Anglo-French decision to build Channel Tunnel.

II. THE CHANGING WORLD SCENE

WESTERN EUROPE

FRANCE

France under Mitterrand.

    M. Francois Mitterrand was elected President of France when he defeated the incumbent President, Giscard d'Estaing, in the second ballot of the elections on 10 May 1981. Mitterrand thus became the first socialist President of the Fifth Republic—indeed, the first socialist President since M. Vincent Auriol who was head of state from 1947 to 1954. Mitterrand strengthened his political position very considerably a few weeks later when, in elections which he had called for the National Assembly, the Socialist Party (PS) achieved an absolute majority

May 1981
Presidential Election Results

	First Ballot	Second Ballot
Giscard (UDF)	28·3%	48·2%
Chirac (RPR)	18·0%	
Mitterrand (PS)	25·8%	51·8%
Marchais (PCF)	15·3%	
Lalonde (Ecologist)	3·9%	
Laguiller (Trotskyist)	2·3%	
Crepeau (Left Radical)	2·2%	
Debre (Ind. Gaullist)	1·7%	
Garaud (Ind. Gaullist)	1·3%	
Bouchardeau (PSU)	1·1%	

for the first time in the party's history. Not since the huge Gaullist victories in 1968 had the governing party had an absolute majority in the National Assembly. President Mitterrand followed this by bringing four Communist Party (PCF) ministers into the government headed by Pierre Mauroy on 23 June. Communists had not tasted government power since 1947, but their situation in 1981 was one of profound weakness, not strength.

The first ballot left Mitterrand in a stronger electoral position than Giscard, and with distinct tactical advantages. The fall-off in total right-wing support on the first ballot in comparison with 1974 meant that Giscard had ground to make up. But in addition, the Communist Party managed a first ballot performance of only 15·3%. For the PCF, this was an unmitigated disaster and caused a good deal of muttering and speculation about the future of Marchais as leader of the Party. But Mitterrand had broken free of the PCF's clutches and did not have the problem of staving off Communist demands for participation in any future Socialist government as the price of PCF support for Mitterrand in the second ballot. Mitterrand's position was sufficiently strong to allow him to dictate the terms of any possible future participation. Giscard's claim that a PS victory would lead either to "socialist disorder or communist order", which would have been a potent message had the PCF ran strongly on the first ballot, therefore carried little weight. In any case, opinion polls indicated that 84% of the PCF vote would go to Mitterrand in the next ballot. And, partly because of the disunity on the right, about 18% of Chirac's first-ballot vote would also go to Mitterrand. The socialist leader also picked up most of the left minor parties' votes.

So Francois Mitterrand won a remarkable victory, with a plurality of 1·066 million votes. He was inaugurated as the fourth President of the Fifth Republic at the Elysee Palace on 21 May. In his inaugural address, President Mitterrand pledged himself to build a union of socialism and liberty, declaring himself in a grand way to be "President of all the French people". Immediately after the ceremony, President Mitterrand named Pierre Mauroy as Prime Minister. Mauroy was a long-time confidant of the President, Mayor of Lille, and a member of the national secretariat of the PS.

The Assembly Elections.

The PS completely dominated the run-up to the Assembly elections which the new President called. The two rounds on 14 and 21 June left the Socialists with a large overall majority over all the other parties. Remarkably, in the space of just two months, the Right had lost all that they had had. The Communists were routed, and the Socialists in a position of commanding power. And yet, on cooler reflection, many observers of French politics realised that the Socialists had performed as well as they could possibly have done. From such heady heights, their strength could only wane. And as soon as it showed signs of doing so, Jacques Chirac would surely take advantage of it. For he had established himself as Gaullism's heir apparent and was sure to prove a powerful political opponent as Mitterrand and the other socialist leaders struggled to keep the huge, unwieldy socialist party together. It had within it powerful groups and personalities on both left and right who could certainly not be taken for granted.

Even so, Mitterrand had a surprisingly long honeymoon period which lasted at least into the first months of 1982. Even then, it was clear that the left would be returned to power if elections were held. And the decline of the Communists continued unabated. Although Marchais retained his hold on the leadership of the PCF at the 24th Congress of the Communist Party in the early weeks of 1982, the Party's standing in the opinion polls fell to only a little over 10%. This was less than half the voting support which it received at the end of the 1960s when Marchais first rose to the top of the PCF ladder. And the PCF was also caught on the horns of a dilemma in deciding when to break with the Socialist government and resign the seats which it held under Mauroy.

Mitterrand's Domestic Programme.

The Government had its difficulties, however. In January 1982, the Constitutional Council rejected parts of the law providing for nationalisation—a key part of Mitterrand's domestic programme. And in four by-elections on 17 January, the socialists were beaten by three Gaullists and one Giscardien. Some middle-class voters deserted the PS because they were disillusioned with the rapid pace of change whilst some left-wingers abstained because of what they viewed as the government's excessively moderate stance. These pressures were reflected within the socialist party, but they were for the most part successfully contained and did not seriously hamper the government's freedom of action. However, the Left suffered further serious reverses in the local elections of March 1982, with the Communists rather than the Socialists emerging as the main losers.

Mitterrand Under Pressure.

As 1982 progressed, the Mitterrand administration came under increasing pressure, most particularly on the economic front. With inflation soaring, with a sorry franc under constant pressure and with government borrowing also rapidly mounting, Mitterand entered 1983 with a crisis on his hands. It looked as if the local elections would be a first major humiliation.

However, after suffering significant reverses in the first round of municipal elections on 6 March 1983, the Left recovered strongly in the second round a week later. So marked was the recovery that the pro-socialist daily newspaper Le Matin headlined its lead story on the Monday after the second round "The Miracle."

The Left lost control of 31 major towns, many fewer than the 61 the Right lost in the 1977 municipal elections. The Opposition parties won just 49·6% of the vote in the second round; Jacques Chirac could therefore credibly claim success for the Right. But the extent of the success was certainly less than had been widely anticipated just two days before the second round of voting, and Chirac just failed in his objective to claim that the Opposition parties now constituted a majority in France.

But the local election reprieve was short-lived. With the franc still sinking, in March 1983 Mitterrand acted. The Cabinet was re-shuffled and a crisis economic package was hurriedly introduced. It comprised a 1% levy on taxable income and a special duty on cigarettes, other tobaccos and spirits. Later in 1983, as the difficulty which President Mitterrand would have in meeting his target of keeping the government deficit down to 3% of GNP became apparent, the pressure grew to cut government spending and increase taxes still further. After intense debate within the cabinet, the country and the socialist party, the highest marginal rate of tax was increased to 70% and the 1% levy retained for a further year.

Although French workers pay less income tax than their counterparts in some other European countries, notably the UK, the increases produced resentment in France, not just among the middle-class but among parts of the working-class too who saw their tax bills increase. Party political disquiet was therefore not confined to the right-wing opposition parties, but was to a degree reflected in the socialist and communist parties.

With workers voicing their discontent, and a regime of austerity under the direction of Finance Minister Jacques Delors, it was therefore all the more striking that the socialist party should have remained united. The party's triennial conference took place in a cordial atmosphere, largely free from the rancorous exchanges that might have been expected in a party which continues to be deeply factionalised. The key to tranquillity lay in Lionel Jospin's, the party secretary, success in keeping the leaders of most of the union groups in line behind the policies of financial rigour pursued by Mitterrand and Delors.

Mitterrand's support in the party was not reflected in the country where his approval rating fell to one-third, the lowest recorded for a Fifth Republic President. Indeed, it was this weakness which persuaded some of his opponents to still their criticisms at the congress for fear of damaging the President's position and that of the party further. For so long as the socialist party remained reasonably united, the Communist Party's freedom of manoeuvre continued to be very limited, and its standing in the country seemed likely to continue to decline.

The satirical weekly newspaper, Le Canard En-

chaine, revealed in June 1983, and expanded in December, details of a hoax which quickly became a celebrated scandal in French politics, damaged the political career of the former Prime Minister, Raymond Barre, and, by extension, enhanced the political prospects of M. Jacques Chirac, the leader of the RPR. The scandal concerned authorisation given by President Giscard d'Estaing to Elf-Aquitaine, the state oil company, to pay M. Aldo Bonassoli, a (fraudulent) Italian scientist and aristocratic Belgian associate Count Alain de Villagas, $65 million to develop a device which it was claimed would revolutionise the discovery of oil fields. Elf-Aquitaine and the government were the victims of an extraordinarily crude deception. Raymond Barre did his best to conceal the affair from public view by instructing the head of the audit court to omit any reference to the scheme when auditing Elf-Aquitaine's accounts in 1979. Pierre Mauroy, the socialist Prime Minister, ordered the auditor's report to be published in early January 1984, adding to Mr. Barre's discomfiture, to M. Chirac's barely-concealed pleasure and detracting, if only briefly, from the economic problems of the Mitterrand government.

The Communist Withdrawal.

On 19 July 1984, the Communists withdrew their four members from the government. The stresses and strains induced by the government's austerity programme (*riguer*). Thus the union of the left of which M. Mitterrand was the author broke apart as politicians of all parties fixed their gaze anxiously on the forthcoming assembly elections in 1986 in which the socialists run the risk of doing particularly badly—thereby greatly complicating the French President's calculations for the rest of his term as he considers the prospect of struggling with the problems of constructing a parliamentary majority. The Communist Party's problems continued and even intensified—indeed, their falling fortunes as registered in the opinion polls took on the character of a fundamental decline. Their support in the 1984 elections to the European Assembly fell to just 11%—less than half its level in 1979.

The Advent of Fabius.

In government, the twin themes of "industrial modernisation" and "liberalism" came to dominate Mitterrand's speeches and the political agenda. Their impact was sharpened by announcements on 14 July of tax cuts for 1985, and the resignation of M. Pierre Mauroy's cabinet on the following day. Mr. Laurent Fabius, just 37 years old, was named as Mauroy's successor. He had a deserved reputation for being a brilliant technocrat, tactically adept, and completely devoted to the changing policies pursued by Mitterrand since 1981 without allowing support for them to damage him politically. With Mitterrand's personal popularity at a low ebb, Fabius's tactical skills were to be much needed to win support for the socialists in 1986. For a detailed discussion of the March 1986 elections, the appointment of Chirac and the major shift in French politics, *see* **C66–8**.

THE TWO GERMANYS.

Adenauer and West Germany.

The Federal Republic of Germany, founded in 1949, had as its first Chancellor Dr. Konrad Adenauer until his retirement in 1963 at the age of 86. His Christian Democrat government produced conditions of stability and confidence in which Germany rebuilt her shattered prosperity and a viable parliamentary democracy. His work in building a special relationship with France, culminating in a treaty of friendship, was a dramatic contrast to the long tradition of enmity towards France. But while he succeeded in building his country into the Western community he remained intransigent over German reunification within the boundaries of 1937, stressing West Germany's right to speak for the whole of Germany, including the Soviet Zone. The two states drifted steadily apart, and a seal was set on their division by East Germany's building of the Berlin Wall in 1961.

Erhard and Kiesinger.

Adenauer's successor Dr. Erhard had the prestige of having as economics minister been the main architect of West Germany's "economic miracle." As Chancellor from 1963 to 1966 he was a loyal supporter of the Atlantic Alliance—indeed it was held that he encouraged ties with the United States at the expense of the Franco-German friendship treaty, which had not lived up to the hopes reposed in it. This partly accounted for the enmity of the Bavarian wing of the Christian Democrats called the Christian Social Union (CSU), the party of Franz-Josef Strauss.

In 1966 a governmental crisis caused by the resignation of the junior partners in the coalition, the Free Democrats (FDP), led to the formation under Dr Kiesinger of a Grand Coalition in which the Social Democrats (SDP) joined the CDU and so had their first taste of government on the national level since the Federal Republic's foundation. This helped to establish the SPD in the eyes of the electorate as a potential governing party.

The End of Christian Democratic Rule, 1969.

In the general election of September 1969 the SPD made significant gains in both votes and seats. Despite widespread publicity the extreme right-ring NPD (often referred to as Neo-Nazis) failed to qualify for any seats since it polled less than the necessary 5 per cent of the total votes. It is now virtually defunct. Thus the three-party system remained. Although the CDU was still the largest party, the SPD and FDP leaders agreed to form a coalition government with Herr Brandt, the SPD leader, as Chancellor and Herr Scheel the FDP leader, as Foreign Minister.

Herr Brandt's achievement in reaching the Chancellorship was considerable, in view of his unpopularity in some quarters for having fled to Norway during the war and taken out Norwegian citizenship. However he had built up his reputation as Mayor of West Berlin.

Herr Brandt's Ostpolitik.

The Brandt Government's main achievements were in the field of foreign policy. A radical development in 1970 was the two meetings between Chancellor Brandt and the East German Prime Minister, Herr Stoph. These showed that Herr Brandt had accepted the existence of two separate states within the German nation (although this fell short of East Germany's demand for complete recognition by Bonn). A treaty signed by West Germany and the Soviet Union in Moscow on 12 August stated that the borders of all European countries are inviolable, including that between the Federal and the Democratic Republics. Bonn implies that frontiers can still be changed by mutual agreement.

Bonn insisted that the ratification of the Moscow treaty and of the Warsaw treaty recognising the Oder-Neisse Line and normalising relations between West Germany and Poland depended on a satisfactory outcome of the Four-Power talks on Berlin. At last in September 1971 an agreement was signed by which the Soviet Union in turn accepted the realities which matter to the West. It recognised the rights of the Allies in Berlin and the city's special relations with the Federal Republic, which had been constantly disputed, especially by the East Germans. The free flow of traffic to and from Berlin, formerly unregulated and therefore a favourite object of disruption and escalation of tension, is now covered by an agreement for which the Soviet Union, rather than East Germany, can be held responsible. The representation abroad of West Berlin by the Federal Republic is now legally based. West Berliners can again visit the eastern part of the city and the GDR. The details of transit were left to be filled in by East and West Germany, and after the Russians had overcome East German recalcitrance the first treaty between the two German states was signed on 20 December 1971. The Brandt Government immediately initiated the ratification of the Moscow and Warsaw treaties, which was eventually achieved in May 1972 after prolonged antagonism from the opposition CDU and some former government supporters. Bonn stressed that the treaties were not an anticipation of a Peace Treaty and formed no legal basis for the existing frontiers, but this view was rejected by the USSR and Poland.

The way was now open for general agreements on traffic and for a general treaty between East and West Germany signed on 21 December 1972, which recognised the existence of two virtually sovereign German states. Though a shock for those who clung to the illusion of German unity, the treaty marked a new realism which promised greater contact between the two states and was therefore welcomed by a majority of Germans. The concessions extorted from the East Germans as a condition of signing the treaty considerably increased the numbers of West Germans and Berliners able to visit the East. The advantages gained by the GDR in terms of confirmation of its statehood and of the division of Germany for the foreseeable future are evident from the flood of countries (including Britain and France) which have recognised it since the signature of the treaty. It was quickly followed by the admission of the two German states to the United Nations. However the limits of détente were shown up by highly restrictive interpretations of the agreements by East Germany. In pursuance of the Basic Treaty, Permanent Missions were opened in Bonn and East Berlin in May 1974.

1973 also saw the conclusion of a treaty normalising relations between West Germany and Czechoslovakia, long delayed by the Czech attempt to have the Munich Agreement of 1938 declared invalid "ab initio". In 1975 agreements were signed between West Germany and Poland on the granting of credits to Poland, the payment of claims arising from the Second World War and the resettlement of ethnic Germans living in Poland. This was criticised as paying for emigration by the Opposition who blocked it with their majority in the Upper house.

The SPD/FDP Coalition.

In April 1972 a government crisis was brought about by defection from the government coalition mainly on the question of its Ostpolitik. This led to an early election in November 1972 as a result of which Chancellor Brandt's government was triumphantly returned to power. For the first time, the SPD became the largest party in the Bundestag.

In May 1974, following the arrest of Günther Guillaume, a Chancellery aide, who admitted spying for E. Germany, political responsibility for negligence was accepted by Chancellor Brandt who then resigned. His successor was the former finance minister Helmut Schmidt whose approach is marked by realism and pragmatism.

During 1974 the CDU made significant gains in elections in the Länder. Helmut Kohl, chairman of CDU, was accepted as its candidate for Federal Chancellor. In October 1976 federal elections to the Budestag were held. The SPD and the FDP lost ground (see Table below), but their governing Coalition held.

Table: German election results for the Bundestag

	1976		1972	
	Seats	%	Seats	%
SPD .	214	42·6	230	45·9
CDU .	190	38·0 } 243, 48·6	224	44·8
CSU .	53	10·6		
FDP .	39	7·9	42	8·4
NPD .	—	0·3	—	0·6
Others .	—	0·6	—	0·3

During 1976 and 1977 the Social Democrats were weakened by a number of scandals in those Länder which were governed by them. During the same period the FDP, the small coalition partner of the SPD at federal level, formed coalition governments with the Christian Democrats in the Länder of Lower Saxony and the Saar. However, the ranks of the Federal Opposition were split following their defeat in the Federal elections by quarrels between the CDU under Kohl and its Bavarian sister party led by Franz-Joseph Strauss. This disunity was largely patched up,

but Herr Kohl's position as future CDU candidate for the Chancellorship remained insecure, and the CSU continued to threaten to form a "fourth party" throughout the Federal Republic.

Chancellor Schmidt's room for manoeuvre continued to be restricted by the opposition majority in the second chamber of the Federal parliament representing the governments of the Länder, and by the need to trim Social Democratic policies to the wishes of his coalition partner. However, his position was strengthened in the autumn of 1977 as a result of the firm stand taken against the Baader-Meinhoff terrorist group which kidnapped the chairman of the German employers' association, Hanns-Martin Schleyer, and later hi-jacked a plane-load of German tourists. Although Herr Schleyer was later found murdered across the border in France, the German government was successful in a dramatic storming of the hijacked aeroplane at Mogadishu airport without loss of life among the hostages. The decisive action against the terrorists, and especially the suicide in prison of those leading Baader-Meinhoff members whose release had been demanded by the kidnappers, caused widespread anti-German demonstrations and acts of violence especially in Italy and France. But at home and in other parts of Europe Herr Schmidt's reputation was greatly enhanced.

1978 saw some de-escalation of the terrorist situation. However, the automatic political vetting of all public employees came in for much criticism.

The Filbinger Affair.

The past came back to haunt German politics in 1978 when the long-standing Christian Democratic Prime Minister of Baden-Württemberg, Herr Filbinger, was forced to resign because of death sentences which he had passed and supervised as a naval judge in Norway during the Third Reich and especially because of his persistently self-righteous defence of his actions. The CDU candidate for the next presidential election, Herr Carstens, was then shown to have been an NSDAP member, whereupon the much respected present incumbent, President Scheel, revealed that he had also been.

In the autumn of 1978 Herr Strauss gave up his seat in the Bundestag to become Prime Minister of Bavaria. But this was not to be the end of his national ambitions. In the summer of 1979, after a long campaign of steady demolition of the Opposition leader, Herr Kohl, he succeeded in getting himself nominated by the CDU as candidate for the Chancellorship—to save the unity which he alone had threatened. This nomination set the scene for a battle of the two strong men of German politics in the 1980 elections. Right-wing, hard-hitting and with a past not altogether free from scandal, Strauss was the bogey-man of the left, and his choice thus brought about a new polarisation of German politics. However, he remained very restrained during the Afghanistan crisis, when Herr Schmidt himself was clinging to détente. Meanwhile a new threat to the Social Democrats emerged in the Bremen elections of October 1979, when the "Green List", comprising representatives of environmentalist and anti-nuclear groups gained the 5% of the votes necessary for representation in the Land parliament.

The 1980 Elections.

In the General Elections to the lower house of Parliament, the Bundestag, on 5 October, the coalition of the SPD/FDP retained power, increasing its overall majority by winning 271 of the 497 seats. The SPD improved its parliamentary strength only slightly, but the junior partners in the coalition, the FDP, made significant gains, with 10·6% of the vote. The FDP won an additional 14 seats, giving it a total of 53. Indeed, the FDP did well in all 10 Länder; equally, the CDU/CSU lost ground everywhere. Support for the Ecological Party, Die Grünen, fell away in the election from the high levels it had achieved earlier in the year. This probably resulted from its adoption of a very markedly left-wing programme.

Despite an agreement between the two major party groupings in March on a code of fair practice for the elections, to be supervised—though not enforced—by an impartial body of referees, the small amount of debate on policy issues during the campaign frequently degenerated into an unedifying spectacle of mutual abuse between Chancellor Schmidt and Herr Strauss. The election results were undoubtedly a severe repudiation of Strauss's abrasively conservative leadership of the CDU/CSU, and a reaffirmation of Schmidt's cautious but skilled centrist management and leadership.

Election Results, 1980

	1980			1976		
	Seats	%	Votes	Seats	%	Vote
SPD	218	42·9	16·26m.	214	42·6	16·10m.
CDU	174	34·2	12·99m.	190	38·0	14·37m.
FDP	53	10·6	4·03m.	39	7·9	3·00m.
CSU	52	10·3	3·91m.	53	10·6	4·03m.
Die Grünen	0	1·5	0·57m.	—	—	—

Towards the end of 1981, the strains of continuing to lead West Germany seemed to tell on Helmut Schmidt, the Federal Chancellor and by some way the most experienced statesman in the West. He entered hospital for a cardiac operation which was successful.

The events of the year showed that Chancellor Schmidt's mandate did not run so far or so deep as the 1980 election results might at first have seemed to suggest. Most importantly, Schmidt's government depended upon the continuing support of the FDP under the tactically astute leadership of Herr Genscher who continued to hold the post of Foreign Minister in the coalition government. The tensions within the government were heightened by protracted negotiations over policies to counter the sharply rising trend of unemployment. But although West Germany was, by the late winter of 1981–2, in deep economic recession with unemployment climbing towards two million, an economic recovery package was eventually agreed upon and Herr Schmidt easily won a resounding vote of confidence in the Bundestag. The respite was to be short-lived and West Germany was soon to change political direction.

Background to the 1983 Elections.

On Sunday 6 March 1983, general elections took place in West Germany. Generally acknowledged as the most important in German post-war history, they were caused by the CDU Chancellor, Helmut Kohl, deliberately losing a vote of confidence in the Bundestag. Kohl had succeeded Helmut Schmidt as Chancellor after Hans-Dietrich Genscher, the leader of the FDP, had withdrawn from the governing coalition and changed his Party's allegiance to the CDU. After the SDP/FDP government fell, Schmidt stepped down as leader of the Social Democrats. Hans Jochen Vogel, a former Justice Minister, succeeded him.

The elections resulted in a substantial victory for the CDU/CSU. When the final votes were counted, they were only a shade away from gaining an overall majority. Despite the public odium heaped upon Herr Genscher for having deserted Herr Schmidt's coalition, the FDP won nearly 7% of the votes, thereby renewing their eligibility to sit in Parliament. The Greens, too, cleared the 5% hurdle, with 5·6 of the vote. The full results were as follows:

	Votes Cast	%	Seats
CDU	14,856,835	38·2	244
CSU	4,140,351	10·6	
SPD	14,866,310	38·2	193
FDP	2,705,798	6·9	34
Die Grünen	2,191,696	5·6	27

The results of the elections were greeted with scarcely-concealed relief by West Germany's allies, fearful of the consequences of a government being returned in Bonn which refused to fulfil the NATO "twin-track" agreement of December 1979. Had the SDP depended upon support from the Greens, NATO's cohesion and policy would have been under serious strain; hence Moscow's uninvited and clumsy interventions during the campaign on behalf of the SDP, and the general pleasure in the west at the result.

Helmut Kohl, in his first year after the General Election, did not make a significant impact upon European politics or upon outstanding German domestic problems. He failed in particular to establish a comparably warm and productive relationship with the French President, Francois Mitterand, as his predecessor had done with Giscard. The absence of leadership from the two most important West European leaders was keenly felt in the European Community, which drifted deeper towards budgetary crisis and political lethargy during 1983.

The Lambsdorff Scandal.

West Germany's politics in 1984 were pervaded with the smell of corruption. On 26 June, the economics minister, Count Otto Lambsdorff, resigned as magistrates decided that he should be tried on charges that he accepted money from the industrial concern, Flick, for the Free Democratic Party's funds in return for waiving a portion of Flick's tax bill. Another former economics minister, Herr Hans Friederichs, was later indicted on similar charges. In late October, the speaker of the Bundestag, Herr Rainer Barzel, also resigned when his position became untenable after allegations that he had accepted large payments from Flick. He admitted receiving a sum of more than DM1·6 million between 1973 and 1979 from a law-firm which itself had received a similar payment from Flick, but denied that the money was a bribe to him to resign from the leadership of the CDU.

Free Democrats and their problems.

The welter of accusations, enthusiastically pressed by a number of investigative journalists, had powerful implications for party government. Hans Dietrich-Genscher, the leader of the Free Democrats, announced in May that he would resign from the leadership—though not from the post of Foreign Minister—by 1986. This, it was thought, would give the Free Democrats an appropriately long period in which to find a successor who could re-establish the Party's standing among the electorate.

Yet the possibility of the elimination of the Free Democrats from the Bundestag remained, especially since the Greens remained untainted by the enveloping scandal and so in a stronger position to make advances. Nonetheless, the Greens are themselves divided on the issue of closer cooperation with the Social Democrats, as their party conference at Hamburg in December 1984 graphically showed. The agreement struck there allowed Green parties at local level to decide whether or not to form coalitions with the SPD. But many such local parties are not disposed to form alliances with the SPD—an attitude shared by many members of the SPD, dismayed at the inroads made by the Greens into the SPD's middle-class vote.

The election of the Federal Republic's sixth president brought a considerable degree of bipartisanship to one aspect of German politics in 1984: Herr Richard von Weizsacker, the first Christian Democratic Mayor of Berlin, was elected to the presidency on 23 May with support from the SPD as well as the CDU. He formally assumed office on 1 July, succeeding Karl Carstens who declined to seek re-election after his five-year term.

East German Developments.

In October 1975 a wide-ranging 25-year Treaty of Friendship, Co-operation and Mutual Assistance was signed in Moscow. In May 1976 at the Ninth Congress of the Socialist Unity Party, the E. German leader Herr Honecker presented the General Committee report which reaffirmed close ties with the Soviet Union, reviewed economic and social developments and produced a new 5-year economic plan. The aims of the plan include increased national productivity and investment and closer economic integration with the Soviet Union and other COMECON countries. Following elections to the Volkskammer in October, the 5-year plan was endorsed and unanimous approval was given to the appointments of Herr Honecker as Chairman of the Council of State, Willi Stoph as Chairman of the Council of Ministers and Horst Sindermann as president of the Volkskammer.

Although an amendment was made to the new party programme allowing references to equality of religious beliefs, the position regarding religious and intellectual freedom remains unsatisfactory. Recent examples of this include the suicide of 2 clerics and the effective exiling of folksinger Wolf Biermann and others. In 1978 the introduction of military instruction in schools provoked opposition especially from the ranks of the Protestant Church. A sign of insecurity in 1979 was a major extension and tightening up of criminal provisions for the protection of the state.

East Germany in 1982.

East Germany's peculiar position in the Eastern bloc was highlighted again in 1982. Since many East Germans can receive West German or West Berlin television broadcasts, they are especially open to the influence of Western ideas, through a common language and the medium of television news. The West European peace movement, which gained ground during 1981 in protest at the modernisation of theatre nuclear missiles by NATO and the Warsaw Pact, gained a good deal of coverage in Eastern Europe on official news outlets where it was presented as a protest movement directed purely at the West and especially the United States. But West German broadcasts beamed to the East as well as to West Germans themselves painted a broader picture and thereby sparked off the beginnings of a general "anti-nuclear" movement in East Germany. The Protestant church is reasonably strong in East Germany and provided much of the backbone for the protests against the spread of more accurate and devastating nuclear missiles in central Europe. Although tiny, the movement was an interesting pointer to the growing flickerings of pluralism in Eastern Europe.

Relations between the two Germanys.

Relations worsened considerably in early 1978, and in the summer, in response to President Carter's visit to Berlin, the GDR engaged in disruptions of traffic which amounted to a clear breach of the Transit Agreement and started a slander campaign against West Germany in the press. But before long very rapid progress was made with agreements on the building of a motorway between Hamburg and Berlin and on the reopening of the Teltow Canal in south Berlin. The relationship between the two Germanys thus remains very ambivalent. So long as Bonn pays enough Western currency it can achieve much. But as soon as the internal situation in East Germany is affected, its leadership reacts very nervously. This can be seen from the constant friction with accredited West journalists, whose reports can be seen by East Germans on West German television.

The end of détente between Washington and Moscow at the beginning of 1980 brought no rupture of relations between East and West Germany. The planned meeting between Schmidt and Honecker was postponed, clearly on Soviet insistence; but both sides clearly showed their regret, and current negotiations continued normally.

In the two weeks after the October 1980 *Bundestag* elections, relations between the two Germanys deteriorated sharply. On 11 October, East Germany announced a change of currency regulations for West Germans and West Berliners visiting the East. The amount of West German D-Marks which have to be exchanged at the border for the overvalued East German Marks was doubled for West German citizens, and quadrupled for Berliners. Herr Honecker, the East German leader, thus once again rebuffed West Germany's attempts to forge ever closer political links between the two states. The East German leadership thereby underlined the fact that for them at least, reunification of the German nation is not on the political agenda.

Helmut Schmidt was careful not to shut the door on East Germany in 1981, despite the frigid state of most East–West relations and the stern disapproval by the Reagan Administration of attempts by Western European countries to maintain normal ties with the Warsaw Pact member-states. It was therefore doubly ironic that in the course of a carefully planned visit to East Germany, Schmidt should have learned of General Jaruzelski's military takeover in Poland.

An exchange of prisoners took place two months before the meeting between Schmidt and Herr Honecker. Among those released by the West German authorities was Günther Guillaume, the spy whose discovery by West German security forces in 1975 had caused the downfall of Chancellor Willy Brandt, in whose private office Guillaume had worked.

The Deployment of American Missiles.

1983 was a year dominated in Europe by the question of the deployment of new American intermediate-range nuclear missiles; few important foreign policy questions for the major European powers were unaffected by it. With the question of inter-German relations, and the future political status and condition of each German state, still perhaps the central issue in European politics, the impact of the missile deployment upon it was intensively discussed throughout the year.

In fact, whilst the tension between East and West caused by the missile question did not leave inter-German relations unscathed, they did emerge relatively undamaged. There was no general freeze on relations with the deployment of the Pershing II weapons in West Germany from November onwards. In part, this is due to the advantage which the Soviet Union saw in retaining a channel to other Western countries through West Germany at a time of general political difficulty. But the economic relationship between the two Germanys was too strong for a complete clamp-down on political contact to be possible; that is strengthened by East Germany's external debt of $13 billion, much of which is owed to West German banks.

Herr Josef Strauss, the leader of the CSU, visited East Germany in June 1983 in an attempt, he claimed, to prepare the ground for a loan of DM1 billion from the west to the east, and guaranteed by the West German government, in July. Other West German politicians, including Herr von Weizsacker, the Mayor of West Berlin, visited East Germany in the course of the year, and Herr Kohl's government in Bonn was receptive to later enquiries from the East for further loans, the conditions of which would tie both countries closer both financially and industrially.

West Germany derived little discernible advantage from these continuing financial subventions to her neighbour. Hopes that the doubling of the hard currency exchange fee by the East in 1980 would be revoked, or at least reduced, were dashed; similarly, the dismantling of some of the East German automatic firing devices along the border reported by the western press in the late summer later proved to be only partly true. Many of the devices had been modernised; those that had been removed affected only twenty miles of the border. But Herr Kohl, anxious to portray himself to the electorate as a pan-German statesman in the tradition of Brandt and Schmidt, would perhaps be grateful that the anticipated deterioration in relations in the event of the Bundestag's approval of the American Cruise and Pershing II deployment had not been realised.

The incidents of East Germans squatting in West German embassies in Eastern Europe in 1984 came at an unfortunate time for both Germanies. The incidents themselves created political problems for East Germany in her relations with Moscow, and for the West German government in her domestic political circumstances where conservative critics are always glad of an opportunity for criticising East German government policies, and West German governments for being insufficiently vigorous in response.

Cancellation of the Honecker Visit.

The embarrassment was highlighted in the summer of 1984 by the impending visit of Herr Honecker to West Germany for talks with Herr

Kohl. As the first-ever visit of an East German leader to West Germany, the visit took on considerable symbolic political importance of the mutual desire of Berlin and Bonn to allow themselves a degree of insulation from the wider freeze which characterised East–West relations. However, on 4 September, Herr Honecker announced that the trip would not take place. The intensity of Soviet opposition proved too much for Honecker to absorb or deflect, despite the attempts of the East German party newspaper, *Neues Deutschland* before the cancellation to trumpet the merits of closer cooperation, and then afterwards to blame the change in plans on West German conservative sniping at Herr Kohl for his handling of the affair. But the cancellation is unlikely to do long-term damage to relations between the two Germanies, as is indicated by Honecker's ability to grant record numbers of exit visas to East Germans in 1984, despite Moscow's restraining hand.

The Honecker Succession.

Although his grip on power appeared to be as firm as ever, rumours grew in late 1985 that Erich Honecker would announce his retirement during 1986. The question of who would succeed him became a little clearer after two Politburo members were ousted in November. One of the two, Konrad Naumann, had long expressed conservative misgivings at Honecker's policy towards dissenters and East Germany's growing indebtedness to West German banks. Without such prominent sniping from the party's conservative wing, the prospect was that Egon Krenz, a defence expert in his mid-fifties would succeed Honecker.

The Spy Scandals.

A flurry of spy scandals in West Germany in August 1985 did remarkably little damage to relations between the two German states. The gravest of the several defections from west to east was that of Hans Joachim-Tiedge, a senior counter-espionage official in Cologne among whose tasks it was to keep track of East German spies in West Germany. The head of West German counter-intelligence paid the price of Tiedge's defection with his job.

The scandals, jarring as they were to western observers who had assumed that successive administrations in Bonn had improved security since Guillaume's defection brought down Willy Brandt in 1974, did nothing to affect the course of relations between Bonn and East Berlin, As they had chilled with the collapse of detente from the late 1970s to the end of Ronald Reagan's first term, so with the Geneva summit between Gorbachev and Reagan Honecker and Kohl found the latitude to effect their warming. Agreements were struck on matters of common concern ranging from road improvements between Bavaria and West Berlin to an increase in West German credit to the east to cover the trade deficit between the two countries. On the larger matters of arms control and the enlargement of political relations, Herr Honecker exploited the competing enthusiasm of both government and opposition in Bonn for closer contacts, Ostpolitik was no longer the policy of the Social Democrats alone, but of Herr Kohl's floundering Christian democratic government, too.

The funeral in March 1986 of the murdered Swedish Prime Minister, Olof Palme, provided a brief opportunity for Honecker and Kohl to meet. East German officials later indicated that the long-postponed official visit to West Germany would take place later in the year.

Developments in West Germany

The spy scandals of August 1985 which did so little to alter the course of relations between the two Germanies nonetheless added to the growing woes of Chancellor Kohl's government. Whilst in the early months of 1986, defeat for the Christian Democrat-led coalition in the 1987 elections still seemed improbable, the possibility was actively discussed. The causes of the change were clear enough: Chancellor Kohl's leadership of his Cabinet colleagues was uncertain, and the defection of Joachim Tiedge did nothing to enhance the government's standing within Germany or among her international partners.

Elections in Schleswig-Holstein in early March

1986 confirmed the declining popularity of the CDU and the FDP. The CDU lost its absolute majority, and saw its share of the vote fall by nearly 6% to 44% whilst the FDP slumped to a mere 4·4% of the vote. The SPD's share of the poll rose to over 40% and took control of the state's four largest cities. *Die Grünen* won a substantially increased vote, securing 7·4% of the poll.

Further, Hans-Jochen Vogel, long considered by CDU opponents to be a relatively easy opponent in the 1987 elections, relinquished the leadership of the SPD in favour of Johannes Rau, the charismatic premier of North Rhine-Westphalia. His favourable image with voters was reflected in high public opinion poll ratings (just as Chancellor Kohl's own ratings began to fall below 50%) and was supplemented by revised policies designed to appeal both to traditional SDP voters and to deflect the brunt of the electoral threat posed by *Die Grünen*.

ITALY.

Italy under Andreotti.

In July 1976, Signor Andreotti agreed to form a new minority government. Measures were taken to alleviate the economic crisis and protect the lira, including loans from the IMF and the EEC. The Communists provided tacit support for the Government, but were faced with the dilemma of either supporting measures with which they disagreed or opposing them with the clear risk of economic and political collapse.

In July 1977 all the main Italian political parties, including the Communists but not the Neofascists, presented a common programme for curing the country's ills. Signor Andreotti emphasised that this did not bring Italy closer to a "historic compromise" (meaning Communist participation in the government). However, Signor Berlinguer, Secretary-General of the PCI, later reasserted the Communists' allegiance to the idea of a "historic compromise", appealing to the evolving ideology of the European Communist Parties which is generally known as "Eurocommunism". In Moscow in November he even proclaimed—in stark contradiction to Lenin—the thesis of a "non-ideological state".

The Fall of Andreotti.

The Andreotti Government continued to steer Italy past the abyss of an economic catastrophe and bankruptcy of political confidence. But the trade unions began to protest that restraint and sacrifice had brought them no benefits, and they and the Socialist Party began to advocate an emergency government of all the parties. The Republican Party had already called for the inclusion of the Communists, and in December 1977 the latter themselves explicitly demanded participation in a government of "national solidarity".

Finally, it was the trade unions' threat of a general strike that brought about the resignation of Signor Andreotti. Italy thus found itself in a deadlocked situation in which the Christian Democrats could not govern without the Communists.

The Moro Assassination.

The assassination of Signor Aldo Moro, five times Prime Minister of Italy and one of the most respected Christian Democrats, by members of the Red Brigades in May 1978 was condemned as an act of barbarism by both Western and Communist countries. He was a serious loss to the Christian Democrats, who had, however, consistently refused to bargain with his captors. If the terrorists hoped to provoke authoritarian reactions and so weaken democracy in Italy, they in fact made the major parties come closer together, including the Communists. However, in four regional elections the electors gave the PCI no credit for the responsibility shown by its leaders during the Moro affair, and the loss of votes led to unrest within the party. In July 1978 the election of Signor Pertini of the Socialist Party to the Presidency after 16 ballots ended a period of paralysis in Italian politics after the murder of Signor Moro.

As their three-year period of parliamentary

support for the Government had brought them no advantage, the Communists returned to a clear opposition role. But in the elections of June 1979 they suffered severe losses, although the Christian Democrats did not make the expected gains and the real winners were the small parties of the centre-left.

Chamber of Deputies.

	1979		1976	
	Seats	%	Seats	%
DC	262	38·3	262	38·7
PCI	201	30·4	228	34·4
PSI	62	9·8	57	9·6
MSI	30	5·3	35	6·1
PSDI	20	3·8	15	3·4
Radical Party	18	3·4	4	1·1
PRI	16	3·0	14	3·1
PLI	9	1·9	5	1·3
Others	12	4·1	10	2·3

The result was that the coalition government of Christian Democrats, Social Democrats and Liberals under Francesco Cossiga remained dependent on Socialist abstention for a parliamentary majority. The parties of the left in fact abstained in the autumn to enable the passage of a drastic reinforcement of provisions to deal with the ever-growing terrorist threat. Such measures would previously have caused a storm of protest, and its absence now showed the extent of the fear gripping Italian society. In January 1980, however, the PSI shifted to the left and demanded Communist participation in an all-party emergency coalition to deal with terrorism and the serious economic situation. This seemed more possible because the crisis of East-West détente following the Soviet invasion of Afghanistan had made the PCI's break with Moscow even clearer. But the Christian Democrat leaders still could not bring themselves to form a coalition with the Communists.

Cossiga Tries Again.

The fall of Signor Cossiga's Government in March 1980 precipitated another political crisis. It was resolved when Cossiga formed Italy's 39th post-war Government, composed of Christian Democrats, Socialists and the small Republican Party. It commanded 340 votes in the Chamber of Deputies.

The results of the regional elections in June 1980 gave the Christian Democrats (DC) an additional 13 seats, whilst the Communists (PCI) lost 14 seats. The Socialist Party (PSI), a coalition partner of the DC and Republicans (PSI) in government since April 1980, gained 4 seats over their 1975 total.

The Downfall of Forlani.

A huge scandal which concerned the existence of a secret Masonic lodge known as "P-2" caused the downfall of the Forlani government on 26 May 1981. The government resigned after it became known that nearly 1,000 leading members of the Italian establishment were members of P-2 which was implicated in a large number and wide range of illegal activities including fraud, tax evasion and rightwing terrorism. Others who were forced to resign included the Christian Democratic Minister of Justice, Signor Sarti who was alleged to have applied for membership of P-2, and Admiral Torrisi, the Chief of the Defence Staff. The head of the military intelligence unit, the chief of the civilian intelligence unit and the civilian head of the coordinating intelligence committee all resigned when their complicity became known.

Signor Spadolini, the leader of the Italian Republican Party, formed a government and took office on 28 June heading a five-party coalition.

The Italian police scored a spectacular success in their long-running battle against the Italian "Red Brigades" when they freed Brigadier-General James Dozier, a senior American officer, from Red Brigade custody. Dozier had been captured by the Red Brigades just after Christmas, 1981. Within days of freeing the General, Italian security police arrested another 30 terrorist suspects and made significant inroads into the terrorists' organisation. But the task facing the authorities is an enormous one. Of the 20 terrorist murders carried out in 1981, 11 were by left-wing groups, and nine by right-wing.

The Return of Fanfani.

On 30 November 1982, Signor Amintore Fanfani informed President Sandro Pertini that he could form Italy's 43rd government since the Second World War. The coalition he put together was formed of the Christian Democrats, Socialists, Social Democrats and Liberals. Giovanni Spadolini, the previous Prime Minister and leader of the small Republican Party, refused Fanfani's invitation to join the coalition.

The Communist Party energetically but cynically opposed the new government's austerity programme, calculating that they would thereby win more of the left of centre vote in the general elections which were due at the latest by 1984. The strict financial measures announced by Fanfani included the raising of taxes by $8 billion in an attempt to reduce a huge government deficit which, in 1982, ran to some 15% of GDP. Were it not for the damaging electoral consequences, Signor Fanfani would certainly have included items in the package to reduce the extreme generosity of Italy's welfare and pensions payments. Italian Old Age Pensioners, on average, receive 69% of their pre-retirement earnings in pensions; munificence on such a scale is unlikely to be cut back in an election year whatever the financial need.

In April 1983 the Fanfani administration was fatally undermined when Signor Craxi, the Socialist leader, withdrew from the four-party coalition. Italy's 44th post-war administration had ended with the country due to vote on 26 June 1983 in a general election.

By Italian standards, the result of the General Election produced a sharp change: the Christian Democrats' vote fell to 33%, five points below their historic low. Increasingly, the Communists and the Christian Democrats came to appear as two fairly evenly matched parties; despite a 0.5% fall in the Communist vote in 1983, the two were separated by just 3 percentage points. The other parties mostly gained voters, although the Socialists' hopes of winning 13% were dashed: their share increased by less than 2 points over 1979 to 11.4%.

The Advent of Craxi.

Bettino Craxi, the leader of the Socialist Party told President Pertini on 4 August that he was in a position to form a government composed, besides his own party, of the Christian Democrats, Republicans, Social Democrats and Liberals. Putting the coalition together was difficult; Craxi had to accept demands, mostly from the Christian Democrats, for policies of economic retrenchment and cuts in public spending as a means of reducing the enormous burden of Italy's public sector borrowing which, in 1983, amounted to almost one-fifth of GDP. Craxi, whose political calculations had for some while been an important element in Italian politics, agreed to the conditions demanded by his major partners, and so became the first socialist Prime Minister since the war.

The Death of Berlinguer.

Enrico Berlinguer, the Communist Party leader, died in June 1984. Grief at his death was widespread, and went well beyond the Party's own ranks. One million people attended his funeral in Rome on 13 June.

Berlinguer was succeeded in the post of Party Secretary by Alessandro Natta, formerly loyal to the Party's Stalinist policy, but who in 1985 emerged as a compromise candidate between the old-guard Stalinist conservatives in the party and the newer Eurocommunists who see the Party's task as one of reaching out to disaffected middle-class voters. In his early months as leader, Natta seemed to lead the Italian Communists away from the path on which Berlinguer had been leading them: that of accomodation with the Christian Democrats. The change in policy caused discontent within the Party's ranks, but was largely explained by Natta's calculations of the Party's best electoral interests following their displacement of the Christian Democrats as Italy's largest party in the Euro-elections in June 1984. Whereas Berlinguer had come to reserve much of his criticisms of the government's performance specifically for Mr. Craxi, the Socialist Prime Minister, Natta opted to concentrate his fire on the Christian Democrats, focusing on the economic policies of deflation which the government pursued.

Mr. Craxi's five-party coalition government came within an ace of falling on 17 October 1985 when it was just four weeks away from establishing itself as the longest-lived administration in post-war Italian history. The proximate cause of the government's near-downfall was the withdrawal from the coalition of the small Republican Party at the behest of Mr. Giovanni Spadolini, the defence minister. Spadolini was angered by what he claimed was the laxness of Mr. Giulio Andreotti, the foreign minister, towards the Palestine Liberation Organisation (PLO), exemplified in the government's decision to release Abu Abbas, the Palestinian who was widely considered to have organised the armed seizure of an Italian liner, the *Achille Lauro*, in the Mediterranean.

Within a week of the government's fall, Mr. Spadolini reconsidered his decision and announced that with small (and probably insignificant) concessions to his party's views on the Middle East he would rejoin the government. The new Italian president announced that his acceptance of Mr. Craxi's resignation had only been provisional. Mr. Spadolini's re-entry made the resignation inoperative. In any case, the government was not dependent upon Republican support, and Craxi's skilful exploitation of the Socialists' pivotal place in Italian politics (by threatening to reorder the government and enter an alliance with the Communist Party, in factional disarray) enabled him to call Spadolini's bluff. Italy, for so long accurately understood as inherently unstable and difficult to govern, had by the spring of 1986 emerged full-fledged into the company of stable European democracies with a strikingly strong economy.

PORTUGAL.

A military take-over in 1926 which brought Antonio Salazar to power inaugurated nearly fifty years of authoritarian rule. In 1968 Salazar was succeeded by Marcello Caetano who, despite slightly more liberal sympathies, maintained the instruments of oppression, including the hated Political Police (PIDE).

However, the dictatorship was overthrown by an almost bloodless military coup on 25 April 1974. Although the leadership of the seven-man "Junta of National Salvation" belonged to General Spinola, who became President, the coup was largely the work of middle ranking officers whose experience in the long struggle against Nationalist forces in Portuguese Angola, Mozambique and Guinea had brought about profound dissatisfaction with the aims and methods of the Caetano government.

The new government initiated an impressive series of liberal measures, including the abolition of press censorship (later partially restored), the lifting of the ban on political parties, the abolition of the secret police, release of political prisoners and the promise of free elections. The right to strike and right of assembly were secured in August. Rapid progress was also made towards granting independence to Portugal's large African Territories. However after so many years of dictatorship it was not surprising that the preparations for democracy and the competition for power brought about a very unsettled situation. In September, after a split between left- and right-wing factions of the Junta and an alleged attempt at a counter-coup by General Spinola to reverse Portugal's leftward drift, the latter, was replaced by General Costa Gomes and other conservatives were dismissed.

The failure of an attempted *coup d'état* on 11 March 1975 resulted in General Spinola fleeing the country and the Armed Forces Movement's Revolutionary Council taking supreme power. A ban was imposed on three political parties, including the right-wing Christian Democrats, and the activities of the Popular Democrats were disrupted by left-wing elements.

The Emergence of Soares.

In elections to a Constituent Assembly held in April 1975 (the first for fifty years) the Socialists under Dr. Soares emerged as the strongest party with 37% of the vote, while the Popular Democrats received 26% and the Communists only 12%. But there were no corresponding cabinet changes and the government continued with a programme of extensive nationalisation. Tension developed between the increasingly pro-Communist Armed Forces Movement and the Socialists and Popular Democrats, with both parties temporarily withdrawing from the coalition government. There was mounting indiscipline in the armed forces and in November 1975 some extreme leftist army units unsuccessfully attempted a putsch. In its wake the government under Pinheiro de Azevedo was able increasingly to promote law and order and in February 1976 a constitutional pact was reached between the army and the main political parties to reduce the powers of the former in the Supreme Revolutionary Council. After elections to the legislative assembly in April 1976, the Socialists remained the largest party and a new constitution was promulgated. On 27 June General Antonio dos Santos Ramalho Eanes, backed by the leading parties, was elected President with 61·5% of the vote. A new government was formed by Dr. Soares. Despite continuing support from Western Europe and a massive loan from the U.S., the position of Dr. Soares and the Socialists remained tenuous because of the virtually intractable economic problems. The international credits made available to Portugal in conjunction with stabilisation were conditional upon a policy of austerity. However, the Social Democrats and the Centre finally refused to go along with Dr. Soares' economic programme, and in December 1977 his minority government was defeated. But the Social Democrats and Centre could not muster a majority on their own, while their agreement with the Communists could run no further than the defeat of the Socialist government. There was thus no solution without the Socialists, and despite Dr. Soares' evident opposition to coalition, a government was formed with the Centre in early 1978.

Meanwhile in March 1977 Portugal officially applied for membership of the EEC.

Crisis and Compromise.

By July 1978 the coalition had broken down after disagreements on agricultural and health policies. In order to teach a lesson to the other parties which had failed to compromise, President Eanes then installed a government of "personalities and technicians" under Sr. Nobre da Costa. This represented a move away from ideologies to put emphasis on urgently needed economic stabilisation. Yet 17 days later this government was toppled in turn, especially because of Socialist and Communist objections to the principle of non-party government and its risks of an authoritarian Presidential regime. Deadlock ensued, until by late October an apparent consensus had emerged that premature elections (*i.e.* before 1980) should be avoided. This paved the way for acceptance of a new independent Prime Minister, Sr. Carlos de Mota Pinto. Like his predecessor he had no stable majority, and in June 1979 he too resigned after failing to gain the confidence of either the Socialists or the Communists in Parliament. The ensuing crisis was ended unexpectedly when President Eanes dissolved Parliament prematurely.

A Shift to the Right.

The elections in December 1979 brought a clear victory for the Democratic Alliance of the Christian-Democratic centre, the Monarchists and conservative Social Democrats under Francisco Sá Carneiro. The latter had managed to drum up a majority from those who were frightened or disappointed by Portuguese socialism. After two minority governments and three presidential cabinets he became the first prime minister to have a clear legislative majority. He sought a fundamental revision of the socialist constitution (for which he himself had voted in 1976). Meanwhile the loss of 30 seats was a crushing blow for the personality cult of Dr. Soares, whereas the Communists under Alvaro Cunhal made gains in the rural south and became with 47 seats the third strongest group in Parliament.

The new government inherited serious problems of inflation and unemployment and a heavy burden of debt. Credits granted by the IMF had tough conditions attached. In these circumstances a programme of austerity was desperately needed. But under the constitution new elections had to be held as scheduled in 1980.

In the General Election of 5 October, the country swung further to the right. Sá. Carneiro's Democratic Alliance gained 47% of the popular vote, giving it a comfortable overall majority in Parliament. The Democratic Alliance made its major gains from the Communists.

But Prime Minister Carneiro was killed in an air crash on 4 December, just three days before the incumbent President Eanes was reelected with 56% of the total vote. The Prime Minister had campaigned vigorously against Eanes and in favour of General Antonio Soares Caneiro (no relation).

The Balsemao Government.

Prime Minister Carneiro was succeeded by Dr. Pinto Balsemao on 9 January 1981. But his government lasted just seven months, undermined by political rifts between the dominant party in the coalition, the conservative Social Democrats (PSD) and its two coalition partners, the Monarchists (PPM) and the Democratic Centre (CDS). The immediate cause of Dr. Balsemao's resignation was his failure to secure a unanimous vote of confidence from a PSD National Council meeting on 9 August. Most of the opposition came from conservative elements in the PSD.

After a reconvened National Council meeting on 15–16 August, however, Dr. Balsemao secured its overwhelming support and withdrew his resignation. The Prime Minister's list of ministers was submitted to President Eanes, who approved it on 2 September. Portugal's eighth constitutional government was sworn in two days later. The Government included, for the first time, the leaders of all three parties in the governing coalition.

Results of the 1983 Elections.

Amidst political chaos, the government of Mr. Balsemao resigned in December 1982 after a period of disagreement between Centre Democrats and Social Democrats, the two main parties in the coalition. Balsemao had proved a weak leader of the governing alliance. He failed to push vital economic reforms through Parliament and, as President Eanes noted, perversely resigned at the moment when a change in Portugal's constitution gave him the powers to initiate the reforms. Eanes announced on 23 January 1983 that he was dissolving Parliament in an attempt to solve the impasse created by the break-up of Balsemao's coalition. The results of the election proved inconclusive. The Socialists under Soares emerged as the largest single party, but well short of an overall majority. Whilst it was clear that Soares would return to office, it was not clear how, or with whom, he would govern.

The Return of Soares.

Dr. Soares eventually formed a coalition government with the Social Democrats on 4 June. A joint statement issued by the two parties said that the coalition agreement heralded "a majority government based on the principles of democratic socialism ready to tackle the nation's problems through reform, modernisation and social justice."

The government, the sixth since 1976, was formed of a Cabinet comprising nine socialists, seven social democrats and one independent, the Finance Minister, Sr. Ernani Lopes. Soares had campaigned on the platform of an austerity programme designed to improve the country's weak economy. The assembly passed the government's programme on 24 June; it took steps to reduce Portugal's deficit on external trade, to stabilise the currency, and to allow for the introduction of private capital into certain sectors, including banking and insurance, which had been nationalised after the 1974 revolution. Negotiations to prepare for Portugal's accession to the EEC were to be continued. Government subsidies on food were removed, resulting in large and sudden price rises. Just prior to the passage of these measures,

the escudo had again been devalued—this time by 12%.

As in Spain, Portuguese politics centred in 1984, as increasingly in years past, around an almost unchallenged Prime Minister. Mario Soares's authority was symbolised by his arrest of an armed group led Lt.-Col. Otelo, a veteran of the 1974 revolution and his pressing through Parliament (in the same week) an anti-terrorist statute which will effectively suspend civil liberties and due process for those suspected of terrorist offences.

Soares versus Eanes.

Astonishingly, Soares's administration was severely criticised by President Eanes at the beginning of 1985 for its alleged inability to improve the condition of Portugal's economy. Eanes's atack had as much to do with presidential politicking as with concern over government policy; Soares was himself openly ambitious for the presidency, elections for which were to take place at the end of 1985. His dominance of Portuguese politics seemed likely to lead him to victory, and crown his political career; Eanes was, to his frustration, unable to stand again for the presidency in 1985, but has by no means renounced political ambition.

The October 1985 Elections.

1985 and the first two months of 1986 provided sharp changes in the direction of Portuguese politics. In May 1985, Mr Cavaco Silva won the leadership of the Social Democratic Party and promptly withdrew his party from the government coalition led by Mario Soares, thereby precipitating a general election. In the election held on 6 October, the Social Democrats won 88 of the 250 seats in the Portuguese parliament. The Socialists saw their representation fall from 101 to 57, whilst the newly-formed Democratic Renewal Party, composed of President Eanes's followers, won 45 seats. The right-wing Centre Democrats slumped badly, securing just 22 seats. The Communists and their allies also failed to make any significant impression, winning 6 fewer seats than in the 1983 election to give a total of 38.

Forming a government took several weeks: on 29 October, President Eanes asked Mr. Silva to form an administration. This he did with the consent, if not quite the enthusiastic support, of the two smaller right-wing parties. This shift of fortunes for the Portuguese left owed much to the electoral unpopularity of the deflation which the socialist-led government had pursued between 1982 and 1985 in an attempt (which proved mostly successful) to control the country's problems of inflation and balance of payments deficit. It was no surprise when opinion polls in early January showed Mario Soares's presidential candidacy to be in deep trouble with a rating of 17%. Running against Mr Freitas do Amaral, Soares lost the first round and then unexpectedly secured victory with just 51·3% of the vote in the second round of balloting. The success or otherwise of Portugal's continuing economic recovery would depend on whether political stability could be built on the shaky foundations which the general and presidential elections had provided.

SPAIN.

Death of Franco.

In November 1975 the long dictatorship of General Franco finally came to an end when he died after a prolonged illness. He was succeeded, as had been planned, by Prince Juan Carlos of Bourbon. However the new king could not make any sharp break with the past. He had to try to carry the intransigent Right with him in his reform plans, since they had a majority in the Cortes, the communes and the ministries and were determined not to give up their power. Only long-term plans were announced for repeal of the anti-terrorist law, amnesty for political prisoners and changes in the electoral law. This threatened the government's credibility with the bulk of the population. However, in July 1976 a new Prime Minister, Sr. Adolfo Suárez Gonzáles, promised that the Government would be a "lawful promoter of a political process which is open to all" and an amnesty was offered for all political prisoners excluding those concerned with terrorist offences. In November the Cortes approved plans for political reform which would replace the Cortes with a two-chamber parliament and in December, a referendum gave 94·2% support to the proposals. This was the first free vote in Spain since 1936.

The 1977 Election.

On 15 June 1977 the first free parliamentary elections for 41 years were held in Spain. This was a decisive step on the road from dictatorship to democracy, and in July the new two-chamber parliament replaced the old Cortes of General Franco. The strongest group was the "Union of the Democratic Centre" led by Sr. Suárez, who formed a minority government. The Socialist Workers' Party (PSOE) came a strong second, the Communist Party a weak third. The first task of the new government and parliament was the drawing up of a new democratic constitution. On 28 July Spain submitted its application to join the EEC. A serious economic crisis had been inherited from the last years of the Franco regime and the transitional period. But the most crucial issue for the future of the Spanish state was the regional problem. This applied not only to the Basque country, where the militant separatist organisation ETA had stepped up its terrorist activities. Both there and in Catalonia systems of "pre-autonomy" in anticipation of the new constitution were introduced in late 1977, setting Spain on the road from a strictly centralist to a federal state. Initiatives for more autonomy were taken in other Spanish regions also. However during 1978 there was growing disappointment in Catalonia and the Basque Country about the extent of the powers actually granted to them. The wave of ETA murders in the Basque Country brought fears that they might damage the process of democratisation and the lack of success of the security forces led to growing impatience in the navy and elsewhere. In July brutal and unprovoked police action, apparently in revenge for the government's decision to allow the Basques to form their own police force, increased the traditional ill-feeling against them in the Basque Country. Although the main Basque parties at last publicly denounced terror and violence, the large circle of ETA sympathisers and the Koordinadora Abertzale Sozialista which acts as ETA's political wing put forward demands amounting virtually to independence. In December 1978 EEC membership was accepted in principle, with negotiations to start in 1979 and accession planned for 1983.

The New Constitution.

Spain's new democratic constitution was adopted by both houses of parliament by an overwhelming majority in the autumn of 1978 and approved, despite substantial abstentions in the Basque provinces, by 87·87% of the votes in a referendum on 6 December. The King signed the new constitution on 27 December, thus becoming a constitutional monarch. The Cortes was then dissolved and elections called for 1 March 1979 followed by the long overdue local elections on 3 April. Prime Minister Suárez's aim in the elections was to reduce the dependence of his Union of the Democratic Centre, which had only 165 of the 350 seats in the old parliament, on the votes of small autonomy parties and its consequent vulnerability to blackmail over the coming of autonomy. However, although the UDC made slight gains, in common with the Socialist Workers' Party and the Communists, and the right-wing Democratic Coalition suffered severe losses, Sr. Suárez still fell short of an absolute majority. Thus the regionalist groupings still held the balance of power. The gains of the Socialist Workers' Party were much less than had been expected, and in May Sr. Felipe González resigned as its General Secretary after being defeated in an attempt to reduce the party's Marxist orientation.

In July 1979, following skilful negotiations by the leaders of the Basque Nationalist Party, an autonomy statute was adopted providing the Basque Country with its own legislature and judiciary and wide-ranging powers including the sensitive areas of police, education and taxation.

The 1980 Election.

Elections took place in March 1980 to the Basque and Catalan Parliaments. In the Basque provinces, the moderate Basque Nationalist Party (PNV) won 37·6% of the vote. The government party, the Union of the Democratic Centre (UCD), lost considerable support compared with the 1979 General Elections. The UCD also did poorly in the Catalan elections where the moderate nationalist coalition (CIU) and the Catalan Socialist Party (PSC/PSOE) won 28% and 23% of the vote respectively.

The 1981 Attempted Coup.

Early in 1981, under pressure from the conservative element in his party, Sr. Suárez resigned. As Parliament debated his successor, a military *coup* was attempted on 23 February 1981. The resolute action of the King prevented the army joining this rash coup attempt which rapidly collapsed. The King gained enormously in popularity as a result of his unequivocal stand. But he lost support among the military.

The 1982 Socialist Victory.

In national elections on 28 October 1982, nearly 80% of Spanish voters went to the polls and handed a solid victory to the Socialist Party. Its leader, the 40-year-old Felipe Gonzalez, became Prime Minister.

The Socialists won 201 of the 350 seats in the lower house, the Congress, and 134 of the 205 seats in the Senate. The right-wing Popular Alliance won almost all the other seats: 105 in the Congress and 53 in the Senate; the centre, extremist and minor parties were effectively eliminated. The divided Centre Party was especially badly mauled; in February of 1983, it broke apart. The Prime Minister, Calvo Sotelo, and all but two of the ministers in the Centre Government which he had led, were defeated at the polls.

For the Socialist Party, it was an enormously significant victory; for Spain, the peaceful transfer of power to a left of centre political party held yet greater significance. The Socialist Party had only existed legally for six years after a 40-year ban under Franco's rule. When a socialist victory at the polls seemed likely, commentators in Spain and elsewhere wondered aloud whether the brooding military machine, smarting at their exclusion from political power and at Spain's transition to a modern liberal democracy, would stay their hand. They did so, and Spain's experiment with democracy prospered.

Gonzalez's contribution to the election result was considerable. His style and that of his Party was in striking contrast to the heavier approach of the French socialists who spring from the altogether different tradition of bureaucratic centralism. Opinion poll data showed that Gonzalez's attempt to portray himself as a "man of the people" was mostly successful.

The Socialists' policy consisted of economic growth, improvements in education, and social reform. The last ingredient posed problems for the government in its early months, and seemed likely to continue to do so: Gonzalez's declared intention to introduce a bill permitting abortion in strictly limited circumstances provoked great controversy. The easing of the law was insufficient to placate many Spaniards, including the 300,000 Spanish women who have illegal abortions every year, anxious for a more rapid move towards the European norm; yet it was too great for the Church and millions of traditional conservative Spanish voters. There was no political advantage to Gonzalez in confronting the issue, nor any easy way of avoiding it.

During 1983 and early 1984, Spain's socialist government made rather more progress with its objective of integrating the country's armed forces with those of NATO than it did with serious and growing domestic economic difficulties.

In November 1983, the government took steps to give the Prime Minister greater control over military affairs by the creation of the post of Chief of the Defence Staff who would be directly responsible to the Defence Minister, Senor Narcis Serra, an enthusiastic proponent of the plan to link Spain's military forces fully with those of NATO's integrated commands. Admiral Liberal Lucini was chosen early in 1984 as the first Chief of the Defence Staff despite having just one year before his retirement. Prompted by King Carlos's desire for the modernisation of the Spanish armed forces, the Government simultaneously replaced the heads of all three armed services. Senor Serra, after months of careful preparation, then began to reorganise the command structure of the Army and reduce its size. Spain's military regions were reduced from nine to six, and the number of lieutenant-generals, the most senior Army rank, from 19 to 14. The expunging of the Francoist legacy provided the rationale for tighter civilian control, enhanced by continuing fears of military discontent at the failure of Senor Gonzalez's government to eradicate Basque terrorism.

Elsewhere, the Socialist government moved ahead with cautious reforms. The education bill guaranteeing the right to free secular education brought the wrath of the Church down on the government, as did the bill which legalised abortion in certain cases. The granting of financial and academic autonomy to universities was intended by the government as the first step towards enlivening and advancing the cause of higher education after years of damaging neglect under Franco.

The Ascendancy of Gonzalez.

In 1984, Mr. Gonzalez surmounted the political challenge to his administration's authority posed by wide differences of views on education and defence policy. The education question in many ways resembled that in France: the government pushed through parliament in the Spring a law which requires those private schools in receipt of state subsidies to accept pupils without regard to the religious views of their parents or lose their subsidies. For many Catholics, the prospect of losing either control over their schools or state support for them was unacceptable, and national demonstrations ensued, culminating in a huge march on Madrid on 18 November. But the government, determined to improve Spain's inadequate education system, survived the challenge to the law and to its partial secularisation of Spanish society.

A month later, Gonzalez was overwhelmingly re-elected as the leader of the Spanish Socialist Party, having made his commitment to Spain's continued membership of NATO abundantly clear. The pledge to hold a referendum on the issue would, he said, be met in February 1986. But he made clear his determination to work for a vote of approval, whilst opponents to NATO within the party were hampered by the widespread acknowledgement that he was irreplaceable as Party Leader and Prime Minister.

NATO and EEC membership.

The debate about NATO membership continued throughout 1985, peaking in the weeks before the referendum on 12 March 1986 which delivered a majority of 52%–39% in favour of retaining NATO membership. The result was a surprise for many leftwing voters who were unhappy with the prospect of remaining in an alliance dominated by the United States whilst right-wing voters had been urged by Manuel Fraga to abstain.

EEC membership was a less contentious matter altogether: Spain joined, with Portugal, on 1 January 1986, just a decade after the end of dictatorship. In that time, Spain had moved some way to becoming a modern secular European society, benefitting from remarkable political stability and (a stubbornly high unemployment level apart) relative economic success. To mark the tenth anniversary of his enthronement, King Juan Carlos unveiled in November 1985 a memorial in memory of all Spain's military dead. It was a characteristically shrewd gesture of reconciliation from the King, supremely skilled in the binding of Spain's internal political wounds, conducted before veterans of both sides from the civil war.

By the international language of economic progress, too, Spain had recorded striking successes in the ten years of her democracy. Under Mr. Soares's premiership, inflation, taxation, and wage rises were all reduced sharply – but by employing economic and financial policies of a distinctly conservative kind. More striking still, economic growth was maintained at a steady, if sluggish, rate, and Spain's external trade balance moved into surplus.

SWEDEN.

The Assassination of Olof Palme.

Olof Palme, the politician associated more than any other with the implementation of Sweden's model of social democracy, was assassinated in the late evening of 28 February 1986 by a gunman who fired a 0.357 bullet into the Prime Minister's chest as he was walking home with his family from a Stockholm cinema.

The event profoundly shocked the Swedish people—the commonly-shared assumption that their advanced industrial society was peculiarly decent and peaceful was dealt a sharp blow by the murder of Palme who, according to his normal practice, had had with him no bodyguard on his family evening out. The assassination did more than deprive Sweden of their Prime Minister, for Palme had acquired international standing for his neutralist policies, an unceasing search for international peace, and an active concern for a redistribution of wealth from the developed to the third world. These activities had given him an international stature far beyond Sweden's standing in international affairs. For the Social Democratic government in Stockholm, dependent since elections in the autumn of 1985 upon Communist Party support, Palme's death set the immensely difficult task of following in the steps of one of the world's most experienced and respected leaders. Palme's successor, Ingvar Carlsson, was an old confidante and political associate, and pledged to continue Palme's legislative programme.

EASTERN MEDITERRANEAN

GREECE.

The Cyprus Problem.

The Cyprus problem has long been an emotive issue between Greece and Turkey. When Brigadier Ioannides decided to use the officers of the Greek National Guard on Cyprus in July 1975 in a coup to replace President Makarios with a régime controlled from Athens, this grossly unrealistic move was swiftly followed by the Turkish invasion of the island, and it transpired that Greece's military rulers had allowed the army to deteriorate to a point where it was unable to go to war. In this situation the President and the Armed Forces Commanders turned to the civilian politicians.

It was decided to call back the former premier, Mr. Constantine Karamanlis, to head a government of national unity. Mr. Karamanlis, who had been living in self-imposed exile in Paris since his defeat in the 1963 elections, returned to be greeted by tumultuous crowds celebrating the downfall of the junta.

The Restoration of Democracy in Greece.

Mr. Karamanlis quickly took action to free political detainees. Greek citizenship was restored to those who had been stripped of it. The junta's constitution was scrapped and the 1952 Greek Constitution reintroduced. By mid-December more than 120,000 supporters of the junta had been removed from the state services. In October, ex-President Papadopoulos and his closest associates were banished to the island of Kea.

Political parties—including the two Greek Communist parties—were allowed to operate freely again. Mr. Karamanlis set up his own New Democracy Party, while Mr. Mavros continued to lead the Centre-Union Party. The leftward leaning and volatile Mr. Andreas Papandreou, son of the now dead George Papandreou, formed PASOK—the Pan-Hellenic Socialist Union.

Only Colonel Papadopoulos was prevented from participating in the general elections which followed on 17 November 1974. Mr. Karamanlis won a crushing victory, with the New Democracy Party taking more than 54% of the votes. Mr. Mavros's Centre Union received 20%, the Pan-Hellenic Socialist Union 13% and the Communists 8%. Three weeks later in a referendum on the future of the monarchy the Greek people overwhelmingly rejected "crowned democracy" in favour of a presidential republic. Major trials of the leaders of the military junta soon followed.

A new republican constitution was adopted by the Greek parliament in June 1975 with the opposition abstaining. In ensuing Presidential elections Mr. Tsatsos, a friend of Mr. Karamanlis, was elected. In premature parliamentary elections held on 20 November 1977, Mr. Karamanlis' New Democracy Party suffered substantial losses. The strongest gains were made by the radical Pan-Hellenic Socialist Union of Mr. Andreas Papandreou, the greatest losses by the Centre Union. Amid prospects of a polarisation and radicalisation of politics, outside Parliament as well as inside, Mr. Karamanlis formed a new government coalition with a majority of 22.

Greek Foreign Policy since the Junta.

Throughout the seven years of army rule, many Greeks regarded the United States as being responsible for the junta's survival. The invasion of Cyprus by Turkey generated a futher upsurge in anti-American feeling and, on 15 August 1974, Mr. Karamanlis announced that Greece would withdraw from the military side of NATO in protest at the second Turkish military operation on the island. In December American bases and installations in the country, not belonging to NATO, were brought under "national control" though they continued to operate.

In contrast the new regime made determined efforts to restore its links with Western Europe, pressing for early acceptance as a full member of the Common Market and readmission to the Council of Europe. Despite the serious gap in NATO's southern flank which the departure of Greece created, it seemed likely that the country would maintain its pro-Western stance. In December 1978 agreement was reached in negotiations for Greece's full membership of the European Community. Relations with neighbouring Balkan states were improved following a meeting on Balkan co-operation early in 1976.

The rising Pan-Hellenic Socialist Union is opposed to full EEC membership and to any Western military bases in Greece, as well as to the Karamanlis Government's policy of a return to the military organisation of NATO after satisfactory solution of the Cyprus and Aegean questions. It favours confrontation with Turkey.

However, May 1979 saw the signature of the treaty of accession by which Greece was to become the tenth member of the European Community from 1 January 1981. The treaty provided for a transitional period of five years (seven years for the abolition of tariffs on certain agricultural products and for the free movement of labour).

On 5 May, Mr. Konstantinos Karamanlis was elected President of Greece. Having secured the required three-fifths majority on the third ballot, Mr. Karamanlis resigned as Prime Minister and from Parliament, and took office.

The New Democracy Parliamentary Group, of which Mr. Karamanlis had been the leader, elected the Minister of Foreign Affairs, Mr. George Rallis, Prime Minister. As Foreign Minister, Mr. Rallis had sought closer ties between Greece and the Soviet Union. He formed a new government which was bolstered on 24 May by a Parliamentary motion of confidence, passed by 180 votes to 115. The government's programme showed little change from that of Mr. Karamanlis.

In January 1981, Greece became the tenth member of the EEC. Opinion poll data suggested that most Greeks supported the Government's decision to enter, although the opposition socialist party was against joining.

Greece under Andreas Papandreou.

In the elections of 18 October 1981, Greece acquired its first-ever socialist government. Led by Andreas Papandreou, the Panhellenic Socialist Movement (Pasok) won almost twice the share of the vote it had done in the 1977 elections, winning 172 seats in the 300-member Parliament. George Rallis's governing party, New Democracy (ND), won only 115 seats, whilst the Communists improved only slightly on their 1977 performance and took 13 seats.

Nationalisation of major corporations, drastic decentralisation of decision-making to local government and the creation of agricultural co-operatives formed the basis of Papandreou's domestic policy.

But such were the expectations which the more militant of Pasok's supporters had of a Papandreou government that the question of whether the government could possibly avoid disappointing them was the key one. In foreign policy, too, the election rhetoric seemed unlikely to be fulfilled. There, the policy was one of broad neutrality between the two major power-blocs of NATO and the Warsaw Pact, withdrawal from the EEC, and a policy of uncompromising assertion of the Greek national interest towards Turkey. Papandreou was almost sure to discover that his freedom of manoeuvre both in domestic and foreign policy was more tightly circumscribed than he might have supposed whilst on the hustings.

Foreign Policy Problems.

Events during 1983 showed how difficult Papandreou's task of formulating a Greek foreign policy was. The election platform of neutrality was soon abandoned, to the intense and vocal displeasure of Pasok's left-wing; in September, six of their number were expelled for making too strident attacks on Papandreou's foreign policy. Greece did not withdraw from NATO. Indeed, NATO exercises took place on Greek soil two weeks after the expulsion of the radicals.

Papandreou and his colleagues did not have the political freedom, even if they wished it, to adopt a strongly pro-American policy. During an EEC meeting in Athens, the Greeks opposed the deployment of American intermediate-range nuclear missiles in Europe, and in a gesture to the party's left-wing, Greece refused to support the general condemnation of the Soviet Union for the shooting-down of the Korean airliner.

The crucial development, however, was that the government signed an agreement, later overwhelmingly ratified by the Greek Parliament, with the United States for a five-year extension of the arrangement allowing for American bases in Greece; despite claims to the contrary, the agreement contained no clause for the removal of the bases. Papandreou's decision to depart from the position he adopted during the election was influenced partly by the $500 million assistance paid by the United States to Greece in return. With the economy in a generally poor condition by late 1983, such aid was especially welcome.

Lacking striking successes in economic policy in 1984, and fully aware that new elections must take place during 1985, Mr. Papandreou attempted to win favour with the electorate by attacking American actions and refusing to take part in a major NATO exercise. At PASOK's congress in May, the Prime Minister criticised "American imperialism"; he later visited Libya at a time when that country's relations with western countries were more than usually strained following the murder of WPC Yvonne Fletcher by a Libyan diplomat in London.

The June 1985 Election.

In the approach to the June 1985 legislative elections, political manoeuvering centred around the office of President. Having publicly backed the candidacy of the incumbent Constantine Karamanlis, Prime Minister Papandreou withdrew his support when he judged that to do so might placate the left-wing members of his party dissatisfied with the lack of substantive achievement in economic or foreign policy since PASOK's victory in 1981.

The ploy worked. Papandreou's nominee for President, Christos Sartzetakis, won election to the presidency on the third ballot. Having satisfied his left wing, Papandreou campaigned by attempting to draw the starkest contrast between his own party and the New Democracy opposition, and declining to rest his case on the slender achievements of his administration.

The parliamentary elections resulted in a surprising win for PASOK, with 45.8% of the vote, and 161 seats in the 300 seat legislature. The New Democracy Party won less than 41% of the vote, and 126 seats. The Communist Party were denied the place in government for which they had hoped by the defection of communist voters to the socialist party, fearful of a victory by the right.

TURKEY.

The 1980 Military Coup.

For the third time in 20 years, the military took control of Turkey in 1980. On the night of 10 September, after a period of political violence and grave economic problems, General Kenan Evren, Chief of the General Staff, took power in the country. The breakdown of order in Turkey during the year had been so severe that by early September it was estimated that about 25% of Turkey's 450,000 strong Army was committed to internal control and security work.

Martial law was extended to all 67 provinces after the takeover. Parliament was suspended, and political leaders placed under House arrest. Political violence virtually ceased after 11 September, but widespread arrests occurred of extreme right and left-wing groups. A mixed civilian–military Cabinet was formed on 21 September, under the Premiership of Admiral Bulent Ülüsü, a former Naval Commander.

Turkey under Evren.

The military regime managed to hold on to a good deal of public support during 1981. In comparison with the corrupt civilian politicians who had held power for the few years before the military came to power, General Evren had broad public support although he incurred the wrath of trade union leaders, intellectuals and the former political leaders whom the military government wished to prevent returning to power when civilian rule was restored. In his 1982 New Year message, General Evren promised that democratic elections would be held by early 1984 at the latest. This was not wholly improbable, in principle at least. Turkey's military had handed back power to civilians before.

On 7 November 1982, General Kenan Evren was elected as President of Turkey for seven years in a nationwide poll. A new constitution, providing for a strengthening of the executive branch over the legislature, and a ten-year ban on political activity by opponents of the military regime, was approved. The General's opponents were not allowed to campaign in the election, and the Turkish press were barred from criticising Evren and from opposing the new constitution. The two main political parties, the Justice Party, and the Republican, advised their supporters to vote "no." But, officially at least, 95% of the electorate turned out and 92% approved of both Evren and the constitution. The balloting procedures were themselves heavily biased in favour of the military government.

The General adopted an especially heavy-handed approach to campaigning which his genuine popularity made quite unnecessary. Even without censorship and a less than fair election, he would almost certainly have defeated any other candidate. Evren had expressed the wish before the election that a large majority for his continued rule would silence western critics of his autocratic government. It did. In February 1983, President Reagan announced a large programme of military aid; West Germany had resumed her own bilateral aid a few weeks before. The European Community, too, seemed ready to relax the restrictions on its own aid programme to Turkey, imposed when the Generals staged their coup in 1980.

The 1983 Election.

A general election took place on 6 November 1983, but was only a qualified expression of democracy: just three of the country's political parties were permitted to participate. The high turnout of 92% was cited by both President Evren and Mr. Turgut Ozal, the leader of the victorious and conservative Motherland Party, as evidence of the enthusiasm for the restoration of democratic elections. Enthusiasm was unquestionably buttressed, however, by the compulsion to vote on pain of a fine.

President Evren and the Generals had thrown their support in the election to Turgut Sunalp's Nationalist Democracy Party (NDP). But Ozal's accomplished performances on television in the campaign, together with his emphasis upon his ability to accelerate Turkey's economic development propelled him to an overall majority over the lacklustre Sunalp and the left of centre populist party led by Mr. Nedet Calp. To the surprise of many observers, Calp's party emerged as the second largest party in Parliament.

Ozal quickly made good his relations with President Evren, who had earlier dismissed the Motherland Party leader as a "confidence trickster" and assembled a small Cabinet composed, like himself, overwhelmingly of businessmen who shared his free-market philosophy and determination to attract inward investment and promote stronger trading ties with the Arab states. Such an approach carried high risks; failure to secure the substantial economic progress he promised during the election could quickly deprive Ozal of much of his political support.

Ozal made a further promise during his campaign which attracted little attention in the West at the time; he assured voters that he would support northern Cyprus with substantial aid if elected. After his victory, he went further and said that he would support the Turkish Cypriots if they declared independence. On 15 November, the leader of the Turkish Cypriots, Raoul Denktash, announced the birth of the "Turkish Republic of Northern Cyprus". Although officially welcomed by the new government in Ankara, Denktash's move embarrassed many senior politicians and officials in Turkey and bought immediate, but ineffective, condemnation from Greece and Turkey's NATO allies.

Reshaping Turkish Politics.

1985 saw a reshaping of the party political map in Turkey, and changes in leadership. Two of the new parties lie to the left of Turkey's political centre, and two to the right. The Social Democratic Populist Party is a moderately left-wing amalgamation of two old parties, and won early popularity in the opinion polls. The former Prime Minister's wife, Mrs. Ecevit, led an incipient grouping to the left of this moderate party's left. Although the left-wing vote was thereby split just two ways instead of three, a disunited opposition to the Prime Minister was not unwelcome to him.

The Prime Minister had two main opponents on the right. The first was Mr. Ulku Soylemezoglu, elected leader of the National Democracy Party in succession to Mr. Turgut Sunalp in July 1985; the other continued to be Mr Demirel, the main figure in the True Path Party. Like Mr. Ecevit, Demirel was officially banned from politics until 1992 but continued to make his influence felt.

In February 1986, Mr. Turgut Ozal, the Turkish Prime Minister, visited Britain in an attempt to press his case for closer links with the EEC, and for increased investment in Turkey's economy. The occasion offered the enticing prospect to British defence contractors, eager to export to Turkey, but the Ankara government's continued systematic abuse of human rights (confirmed by all independent reports) lessened the chances of major changes in European policies towards Turkey.

THE SOVIET UNION

A Turning Point in Soviet History.

Stalin died in 1953 and the struggle for succession then continued for five years. A triumvirate of successors, Malenkov, Molotov, and Beria had decided to give the post of party chief to Khrushchev, then a relatively harmless outsider, or so he was deemed by them. Beria, the all powerful police chief, was executed as a spy in 1953, Malenkov was forced to give up the premiership in 1954 and three years later both he and Molotov were expelled from the Central Committee. Khrushchev thereupon emerged with supreme powers.

In 1961 Khrushchev publicly and dramatically completed the process which he had begun in 1956, of finally rejecting the cult of Stalin. De-stalinisation brought the scaling down of the secret police; the rebuilding of the administrative apparatus; and a new theory that war was not inevitable. But the Stalinist concept of the "monolithic" party was little changed.

Khrushchev was abruptly removed from power in October 1964 and replaced by Brezhnev and Kosygin.

The Collective Leadership.

A meeting of the Supreme Soviet in 1965 confirmed the principle of collective leadership, with

Kosygin as Premier and Brezhnev General Secretary. The Brezhnev era has seen no re-Stalinisation as originally forecast, but there has been a retrenchment of the restrictive power of the establishment which had been disturbed by Khrushchev. Critics of Brezhnev, included the conservative Pyotr Shelest and Voronov, were dropped from the Politburo and subsequently all the most important ministers including Andrei Gromyko (Foreign Secretary) and Marshal Grechko (Defence Minister) were brought into the Politburo. Tension between the party and state machinery was thus eased. In April 1975 Shelepin, at 56 the youngest member of the Politburo, was ousted. At the 25th Party Congress in February 1976, Brezhnev appeared fully in control and in May he was promoted to Marshal of the Soviet Union following the death of Marshal Grechko. The 5-year plan for the Soviet economy was presented in December 1975 and the disastrous agricultural situation was to be remedied by massive investment and better planning. Priority was to be given to heavy industry with the overall aim of raising the standard of living. The plan was endorsed in November by the Central Committee. In 1977 measures to promote competition were introduced as a spur to economic development.

In June 1977 Mr. Podgorny was replaced as Chairman of the Presidium of the Supreme Soviet (in practice Head of State) by Mr. Brezhnev, who combined the office with that of General Secretary of the Communist Party. This development was a blow to the principle of collective leadership. On 7 October a new Soviet constitution came into force, in time for the celebrations of the 60th anniversary of the Russian Revolution. It was presented by Mr. Brezhnev as corresponding to a developed, mature socialist society, and the first article declares the Soviet Union to be a "socialist state of the whole people", following the fulfilment of the tasks of the "dictatorship of the proletariat". The new constitution emphasizes the leading role of the Communist Party, which was not mentioned in the previous constitution.

Détente.

The historic rapprochement between the United States and China in 1971-2 met with a sharp condemnation of Chinese intentions by the Russians. But in May 1972, the first visit to Moscow of a US President (President Nixon) took place. A 12-point statement of principles to guide the future relationship between the two countries resulted in co-operation agreements were signed. Above all, agreements on the limitation of strategic nuclear weapons were also signed (the first Strategic Arms Limitation Treaty, SALT I). In June 1973 Mr. Brezhnev and other Soviet ministers visited the US. Co-operation agreements were signed and they undertook to enter into urgent consultations if relations between them or between either and another country appeared to involve the risk of nuclear conflict. The Second Strategic Arms Limitation Treaty (SALT II) was signed in June 1979 at a US-Soviet summit in Vienna, but ratification by the US Senate was still to be won.

By early 1978 détente seemed seriously threatened by Soviet/Cuban intervention in, for example, Zaire and Ethiopia and the Soviet delivery of military aircraft to Cuba. But thereafter the Russians showed, at least temporarily, rather more self-restraint. Moreover they reacted undramatically to the establishment of diplomatic relations between Washington and Peking, though putting pressure on the Western Europeans not to play the "Chinese card" and especially not to endanger détente by supplying arms.

The Afghanistan Invasion and its Aftermath.

The invasion of Aghanistan in December 1979 affected the Soviet Union's relations with the rest of the world, but had an especially damaging effect on relations with the West. Whereas Soviet military action against Hungary in 1956, and Czechoslovakia in 1968, had been directed against Warsaw Pact members, the invasion of Afghanistan was against a third world country. It was previously a non-aligned country, and many observers in the West saw the Soviet military thrust, and subsequent poli-tical and administrative support of Barbrak Karmal's Soviet-installed government as a sig-

nificant new departure in Soviet foreign policy. In the United States, President Carter's rightwing opponents charge that the Afghanistan invasion occurred largely because of what they contended was America's military decline in recent years.

The Soviet leadership had, as always, only proceeded against Afghanistan after the most careful and painstaking assessment of the West's likely response. American retaliation consisted of a grain embargo, the effective abandonment of any hope of a ratification of the SALT II treaty by the U.S. Senate, and trade sanctions. The West's response was uncoordinated, however, and the Soviets negotiated trade deals with other Western countries which often made up for the losses from the United States. For recent events in Afghanistan, see **C40**.

The Resignation of Kosygin.

The Soviet Prime Minister, Alexei Kosygin, resigned on 23 October 1980 due to ill health. There is little doubt that his retirement was solely due to his weakening physical condition, and not caused by any power shift in the Kremlin. Mr. Kosygin died of heart failure on 19 December. An urn containing his ashes was placed in the Kremlin Wall on 23 December at a large state funeral attended by thousands of Muscovites. Mr. Kosygin's successor was his former First Deputy Premier, Mr. Nikolai Tikhonov.

For the Soviet Union, 1981 was dominated by two linked problems. The first was Poland's continuing crisis, and the second the deterioration in relations with the United States and the West largely as a result of the prevalent Western view that the Russians were largely to blame for the military crackdown in Poland. The Soviet economy also came under increasing strain during the year. Economic growth faltered, and Soviet agricultural failures continued to cause precious foreign exchange reserves to be spent on importing grain from the West. Uncertainty marked both the future direction of Soviet politics and the prospects for arms and trade agreements with the West.

Meanwhile, the domestic political balance was upset at the end of January 1982 with the death of Mikhail Suslov, a senior and extremely influential neo-Stalinist ideologue in the highest reaches of the Soviet Communist Party. Only Brezhnev outranked him. His death made the question of the succession to Brezhnev even more open. On 10 November 1982, Brezhnev died and Russia had a new leader in Yuri Andropov.

Andropov's Brief Reign.

Soviet politics in 1983 and early 1984 were greatly complicated by the evident infirmity of President Andropov; his poor physical condition, evident to Soviet television viewers by mid-1983 when he had to be assisted in walking at public appearances, deteriorated quickly. From September 1983, he was not seen again in public. Absent from November celebrations in Red Square marking the anniversary of the revolution (even Brezhnev, days before his death in 1982, had attended the celebrations), he then failed to attend key meetings of the Central Committee and of the Supreme Soviet in December 1983. Soviet sources indicated that Andropov was suffering from a serious liver disorder in addition to his difficulties in walking; official Soviet press releases that he merely had a bad cold became steadily less plausible as the winter progressed. In early February 1984, Andropov died, just fifteen months after assuming power.

Andropov's funeral in Moscow was attended by many world leaders, anxious to seize the opportunity of another leadership change to argue for a new dialogue with the Soviet Union. The man the foreign leaders met was Konstantin Chernenko, chosen after an intense dispute within the Central Committee of the Communist Party as the new General Secretary.

The Chernenko Interlude.

Chernenko had narrowly lost to Andropov in the struggle for Brezhnev's succession; in the ensuing fifteen months, his power-base had been eroded by Andropov's persistent attempts to rid the party structure of those who threatened his position. But the process was insufficiently advanced to prevent the 72-year-old Chernenko winning a majority in the Central Committee against the claims of younger rivals such as Gorbachev and Romanov.

Chernenko's career was intimately associated with that of Brezhnev; he had acted in effect as Brezhnev's aide and had often been treated as such by Politburo colleagues who were nominally his equals. There is considerable evidence that Chernenko resisted Andropov's sweeping economic reforms; in May 1983, he made a careful rebuttal of many of the theoretical claims which Andropov was making in support of them. Clearly not strong enough to use this as a pretext for edging Chernenko further from the centre of Soviet politics, Andropov had to concede an invitation to Chernenko to deliver a major speech to the Central Committee in June.

Chernenko was widely expected at the time of his accession to backpedal on the Andropov drive against corruption and economic sluggishness. He had to contend with much the same formidable list of problems as Andropov. To the extent that those problems of inefficiency, high military spending, dangerously poor relations with the West, a general lack of success in foreign policy and a weakness of Soviet authority over her client states in Eastern Europe, are long-term and deeply-engrained, Chernenko's age and evidently poor health (he suffered from emphysemia) all counted against him. In opting for Chernenko as General Secretary in 1984, the Politburo declined to grasp the nettle of generational change. The error of this decision was only too apparent. The Chernenko era proved to last only 13 months. By March 1985 he was dead. Russia had a new and very different leader in Gorbachev.

The Advent of Gorbachev.

In his first year in office, Gorbachev moved quickly and deliberately to consolidate his power base, and succeeded to a degree which astonished many observers. The widely-held view that the power of General Secretaries is weak at the beginning of their period in office was not confirmed by Gorbachev's skilful political display during his first year.

Preparing for the Party Congress in February 1986, he promoted four of his supporters to the Politburo, and quickly eased out Grigori Romanov, his main rival for the post of General Secretary, Nikolai Tikhonov retired as Prime Minister, and Andrei Gromyko left the post of Foreign Minister which he had occupied for more than thirty years, to become President. Gromyko's successor was Edward Shevardnadze, a loyal supporter of Gorbachev but whose inexperience in foreign affairs allowed Gorbachev to exercise strong influence in the field. Tikhonov's successor as Prime Minister was Nikolai Ryzhkov who shared Gorbachev's enthusiasm for radical organisational reform as part of a policy to revitalise the Soviet economy. Ryzhkov lacked the power-base of Yegor Ligachev, who gained bases in both the Central Committee and the Politburo. Ligachev assumed responsibility for ideology, and in pursuing Gorbachev's campaign to reshape party membership, showed himself strikingly orthodox in his views. Economic reform was combined, in varying degrees, with ideological conservatism. The veteran Moscow party head, Viktor Grishin, was replaced in December 1985 by Boris Yeltsin.

Elsewhere, the party's Central Committee membership changed considerably at the Party Congress, having already seen three new secretaries and seven departmental heads installed within the first eight months of Gorbachev's leadership. A reshuffle on 6 March saw five newcomers in the secretariat (one of whom was Anatoly Dobrynin, Soviet ambassador to Washington since John Kennedy's presidency), the replacement of two candidate members of the Politburo, and the promotion of Lev Zaikov, a central committee member with responsibilities for defence, to full membership.

At the regional level, Gorbachev ruthlessly pursued a policy of replacing entrenched party leaders with his own people; the reforms which Andropov initiated, but which ground to a halt under Chernenko's fitful leadership, were now restarted. By early 1986, few senior party members who had been supporters of Brezhnev remained in place.

The central difficulty with which Gorbachev and his allies had to contend was the Soviet Union's continuing poor economic performance. The rate of growth in the first half of the 1980s was half that of

the 1970s which itself was half the rate of the 1960s. Without a significant improvement, the prospects of maintaining defence programmes and investing in consumer goods industries were slight. In fact, the target which Gorbachev set in late 1985 for the rest of the century was modest, envisaging an average growth rate of less than 5%. As with changes of political leadership, the pattern set in the first year was clear: he set out to achieve it by introducing high-technology into Soviet industry, relying on a streamlined bureaucracy to plan the economy, and enforcing tighter discipline both among bureaucrats (to eliminate corruption) and among workers themselves (to improve productivity).

The reforms predictably met with opposition from those who stood to lose by their implementation, leaving the question of Gorbachev's success entirely open. By the beginning of 1986, it was clear that much would depend on the extent to which the hesitant thaw in Soviet—US relations enabled the rate of increase in defence spending to be cut, thus leaving room for increased investment in consumer goods industries. As 1986 progressed two new factors appeared: the Libyan crisis (see C66) and the disaster at the Chernobyl nuclear plant (see F71-2).

EASTERN EUROPE

POLAND.

Poland's Political Crisis.

Waves of severe industrial unrest occured in Poland during the summer of 1980, throwing the country into a severe political crisis with major implications for the maintenance of Soviet domination of Eastern Europe. Following a familiar pattern in recent Polish history, Government-ordained rises in the price of meat sparked off the initial industrial disputes, but the deeper political character of the strikes soon became apparent. Both the First Secretary of the Polish United Workers Party (PUWP, the official Polish Communist Party), Mr Edward Gierek, and the Prime Minister, Mr Edward Babiuch, were forced to resign their posts in the late summer. Gierek had himself become First Secretary of the PUWP as a result of the series of major strikes over price increases in 1970. By the end of 1980, the strikes had brought about a fundamental alteration in the character of the Polish state which lent it features unique among communist states in Eastern Europe: a number of independent unions had been formed; censorship in the Polish press had been eased, and the position of the Roman Catholic Church, already immensely strong in a country where 85% of the population are practising Catholics, was given further prominence and legitimacy by the state-controlled radio and television networks. In the space of a few months, competing centres of power had arisen in a member of the Warsaw Pact, whose politics since the war had been conditioned by the geographical proximity of a military superpower and leader of the Pact, the Soviet Union. From August 1980 to December 1981, Poland enjoyed a period of liberalism without parallel in the post-war history of Eastern Europe. For all that time, Western—and most Polish—observers concentrated on the links between Poland and the Soviet Union, speculating on the limits of the elasticity in the relationship. The possibility of a Soviet clamp-down on the Polish experiment was ever-present, although periodically intensifying with the latest series of clashes between the increasingly beleaguered authorities in Warsaw and the growing stridency and power of the Solidarity trade union organisation. But, on the night of 12 December 1981, Prime Minister General Jaruzelski, who had replaced Stanislaw Kania as Party Leader in October, abruptly halted the laborious and risky negotiations with Solidarity and declared a state of martial law. The Solidarity leadership were interned along with other Poles prominent in the reform and dissident movements. For the first time in an East European country, an internal power change took power away from the ruling Communist Party and placed it in the hands of the military leadership.

Suspension of Martial Law.

Martial Law was suspended, but not abolished, in Poland, in December 1982. General Jaruszelski stayed in power, however. Lech Walesa was released from prison at the same time but the government thereafter intensified their drive against members of the banned Solidarity and the Workers' Self Defence Committee (K O R).

Seven Solidarity leaders and five K O R members were due to be prosecuted in the early Spring of 1983 under Articles 123 and 128 of the Polish Constitution—conspiring to overthrow the state by violence. The Government's case was foreshadowed by an extraordinary document published by the Communist Party's Central Committee in which the "Oppositionists" were accused of fomenting Trotskyist world revolution. The essence of the case was that the mass movement of the workers was subverted by the ringleaders and turned against the legitimate organs of state authority.

Nobel Prize for Walesa.

1983 saw the award of the Nobel Peace Prize to Lech Walesa. Wary of the danger of his not being allowed to return to his native country from the prize-giving ceremony in Oslo, the prize was accepted on his behalf by his wife and son. Walesa announced on 5 October that the prize money would be donated to a Catholic agricultural charity.

Despite the popularity of the award among many Poles, Walesa's influence within Solidarity waned somewhat during the year, partly because of the authorities' determination to take advantage of infringement of the restrictive civilian penal code which replaced the martial code in July. Finding the task of changing Solidarity from a legal mass organisation to a small extra-legal one difficult, some members of Solidarity, and others openly hostile to Jaruzelski's regime—including the Pope—began to question whether Solidarity's structure was still appropriate in view of the changed political circumstances and the rejection by Jaruzelski of the national dialogue which Pope John-Paul II pressed during his summer visit to Poland. Some degree of change seemed inevitable.

Mindful of price rises having caused the fall of his predecessors Gromulka and Gierek, Jaruzelski conducted a partial retreat early in 1984 on proposals his Government had earlier made for substantial increases in the price of food. Even the original proposals were not made in the traditionally peremptory manner; they were floated with a view to testing public reaction in a series of "social consultations". But the criticism which arose from them, even from pro-government channels such as the official trade unions, was so hostile that they had to be withdrawn. Under later revised proposals, certain staples were not to be increased at all, and bread by less than that originally suggested.

The Murder of Father Popieluszko.

Father Jerzy Popieluszko, Poland's most prominent pro-Solidarity priest, was kidnapped on 19 October 1985 and subsequently murdered. A sense of outrage swept the country which was intensified when three members of the secret police were arrested and charged with the priest's murder.

The authorities decided to open the trial to public scrutiny. In doing so, they ran two risks: firstly, that the methods of operation of the secret police might be exposed in the course of a trial; and secondly, that the widespread suspicion that senior state figures had approved or ordered the murder of Popieluszko might be confirmed. Either outcome would cause popular disquiet and, quite possibly, weaken General Jaruzelski's support within the security apparatus.

All three accused were found guilty and received heavy prison sentences. But the more important outcome of the trial was the reawakening of anti-government sentiment at a time when the Polish government could ill afford it.

Recent Events in Poland.

1985 was a year in which General Jaruzelski's attempts to normalise Poland's relations with the West met with discernible success. The government won a public victory over dissenters in persuading between 60 and 65% of eligible voters to participate in parliamentary elections in October. The government claimed that the turnout was almost 80%, but there was no convincing evidence to support their claim; even so, it was a considerable achievement for Jaruzelski. Parliamentary docility was made probable by the government's reservation of all but 15% of its seats for the communist party.

The elections safely behind him, Jaruzelski set about reshaping the government. With twelve colleagues, the Foreign Minister, Mr Stefan Olszowski was removed from his ministerial job and deprived of his place on the Politburo as part of a policy to strengthen ties with western countries upon whom Poland continued to be dependent for finance. Indeed, Jaruzelski and his new colleagues in the finance ministry made no secret of their aspiration to join the IMF in order to use its strength to overcome Poland's persisting weakness in her trading position. Even so, it was clear that the cautious rapprochement with western European states had a long way to go. Stopping off in Paris on his way to Africa, the General met President Mitterrand for talks in early December 1985. Mitterrand aroused the wrath of his opponents and caused party allies embarrassment by his action; his Prime Minister, Laurent Fabius, went so far as to dissociate himself from the president's action—an indication of the distaste with which much western public opinion and political leaders continued to regard the Polish leader.

CZECHOSLOVAKIA.

In January 1968, in a significant move, a Slovak, Alexander Dubček, was elected to replace Novotný as Party Secretary (Novotný was later replaced as President by General Svoboda), and the era opened which has since been dubbed "the Prague Spring", when an attempt was made to give Socialism "a human face". Wide-ranging reforms were mooted in the Action Programme issued in April, but the Communist Party did not envisage relinquishing its commanding position in society. Fears that this was happening, however, led the USSR first to press for the abandonment of the Programme in a number of talks with the Czechoslovak leadership between May and August, and ultimately, in concert with the other Warsaw Pact powers except Romania, to occupy Czechoslovakia on 21 August in accordance with the "Brezhnev Doctrine" of "limited sovereignty". Soviet efforts to set up a puppet government at first met with no success. The projected federalisation of the country into the twin republics of the Czech Lands and Slovakia went ahead in October, although plans for a similar federalisation of the Party were vetoed. Gradually, however, Dubček and his team were ousted from positions of influence, and Gustav Husák, a partisan of "normalisation", took over as Party Secretary in April 1969. Czechoslovakia repudiated its condemnation of the Warsaw Pact invasion in October 1969 and consented to the stationing of Soviet troops. Pro-Dubček personnel were hounded from the Party and their jobs (Dubček himself becoming a forestry official) and most of the reforms were abandoned. In May 1970 Czechoslovakia signed a 20-year treaty of friendship with the USSR. In December 1973 West Germany and Czechoslovakia signed a treaty annulling the Munich Agreement, thus normalising their relations.

Charter '77.

At the beginning of 1977, which had been heralded as "human rights year", a dissident civil rights group "Charter '77" was formed in Prague, 1978 and 1979 saw persistent attempts to crush the latter by a policy of demoralisation and official harassment. Increasing numbers were virtually driven into exile. There were also reports of inhuman conditions of imprisonment for dissidents.

The Tomin Affair.

Human rights in Eastern Europe in 1980 focused on the case of Dr. Julius Tomin, a Czech philosopher who left Czechoslovakia in September with his family after finding it impossible to continue to give his open philosophy seminars in his home country. Harassment by the secret police was an ever-present hazard for Tomin and those 15 to 20 students who attended the seminars. Tomin was not actually charged with any offence, but he, his students and his academic guests ran considerable risks. Overnight detentions by police became so frequent as an occurrence that many students and guests frequently arrived at Tomin's house with extra clothing to keep them warm in police cells. Western attention concentrated on the Tomin case after three Oxford dons were expelled from Czechoslovakia after accepting an invitation from Dr. Tomin to attend the seminars.

Economic Developments.

President Andropov's campaign against the feather-bedding of state industries in the Soviet Union began in 1983 to have an effect in the Soviet Union's partners in COMECON, the common market of East European communist states. Czechoslovak leaders pressed during 1983 for greater attention to the marketability of export products, and for the fruits of success in productivity and exports to be directed towards the managers and workers in individual enterprises. Following the Hungarian experiments with economic reform, Czech policy-makers also indicated their determination to phase-out loss-making industries.

HUNGARY.

The Achievements of Kadar.

The leader of Hungary's Communist Party, Janos Kadar, celebrated his 70th birthday in the late spring of 1982 twenty-six years after coming to power in the inauspicious circumstances of the crushing of the uprising against Party rule by Soviet armoured divisions. To have survived so long was no mean achievement in the turbulence of post-war Eastern Europe; to have achieved genuine widespread popularity among Hungarians was astonishing. Even groups critical of Communist rule readily acknowledge that Kadar would very probably emerge victorious if free elections were to be held. Despite Kadar's liberal rule, free elections will not, of course, take place. Communist rule remains unchallenged despite economic liberalism and a political pragmatism which, in 1982, constrained the government to withhold from crushing an unofficial movement within the dominant Roman Catholic Church.

Hungary's Unique Position.

Hungary's peculiar position within the Soviet-dominated Eastern bloc was highlighted in 1983 by the British government's announcement that the Prime Minister, Mrs. Thatcher, would visit Hungary in February 1984. The general level of political tensions between East and West would have made a similar visit to other East European capitals difficult if not impossible for her. Hungary, however, continued to press for closer trading arrangements with the European Community and met with sympathetic responses from West European governments anxious to loosen ties between Budapest and Moscow without giving Moscow cause for restraining her more liberal ally.

Treading a cautious path between too ambitious a policy to the west and fealty to the east, Hungary's leaders increased the pressure on liberals and dissidents in the autumn of 1983: Ferenc Kalin, a prominent liberal editor of a monthly cultural periodical, was dismissed from his post and criticised in the official press by junior government officials. Kalin's predecessor as editor had met a similar fate nearly three years before.

Hungary's Economic Experiment.

The Hungarian economic experiment moved a stage further in 1984 when, as a result of decisions taken at a Central Committee meeting in April, many firms were given more independence from ministerial and bureaucratic control. According to the size and nature of the individual enterprise, managers were in future to be elected either by the company's board or directly by the workers. Additionally, the gap between successful and unsuccessful companies was to be reflected in the size of subsidy afforded them by the state. Under the plan, lame-ducks run the risk of having their subsidies removed altogether. The theme of deregulation, an economic doctrine with powerful political implications, ran through the proposals.

The official press in Budapest reflected the continuing change: equality of opportunity, rather than equality itself, increasingly set the ideological tone. The changes illustrated once more the variation in economic organisation among COMECON countries; the extent of such variety would have seemed shocking just twenty years before. And yet the central authorities know full well the political bounds within which they work: economic reforms can be tolerated for so long as they pose no threat to Communist Party control of a kind approved by the Soviet Union. As if by way of marking their fealty to Moscow, the authorities continued their selective policy whereby noted dissidents were subject to harrassment and arrest: Gyorgy Krasso was subjected to close police control at the end of 1984 for having given an interview about the crushing of the Hungarian uprising in 1956 to an underground magazine.

ROMANIA.

Romania under Ceaucescu.

In internal affairs rigid and orthodox, Romania began to develop an independent foreign policy in Gheorghiu-Dej's last years, and Ceaucescu has continued this trend, maintaining friendly relations with China and Israel, becoming the first Soviet bloc country to recognise West Germany, and objecting to the Soviet invasion of Czechoslovakia. There are no Soviet troops in Romania. Although a full member of Comecon, Romania has blocked plans to integrate the Communist countries' economies for fear of becoming a second-class supplier of raw materials to the more industrialised members. Instead the Romanians are aiming for economic independence by pushing ahead with a massive industrialisation programme of their own. Another point at issue with the USSR is the latter's incorporation of Bessarabia, with its two-thirds Romanian population, as the Moldavian SSR. 1978 saw not only a continuation of adventurism in foreign policy but also the beginning of the internal liberalisation of a hitherto highly orthodox centralist regime. Greater autonomy was announced for local authorities and for the State firms, with the profit motive, a say in drawing up the Plan and material incentives all being introduced for the first time. This was no doubt partly an effect of the disorders and strikes in the mining industry in 1977. Corresponding changes were made in the Party and especially in the Government leadership. At the same time—under some foreign pressure—improved conditions were promised for the Hungarian and German minorities.

China and Romania.

The visit to Romania by the Chinese leader, Hua Kuo-feng, in August 1978 was a means and an opportunity of emphasising Romanian national independence. It was clearly offensive to the Soviet Union, as was Ceaucescu's declared support for the result of the Camp David negotiations between Egypt and Israel. A reaction came in November, when after the meeting of Warsaw Pact heads of government the other six member states all recalled their ambassadors from Bucharest for consultation. They also demonstratively issued a joint condemnation of the separate Egyptian–Israeli peace negotiations without Romanian participation. Apparently the Russians had put forward surprise proposals at the summit, including integration of the armed forces whereby units from member states would be placed under a joint (Soviet) command. This was refused by Ceausescu with the backing of his own party, and he made several speeches on the importance of national independence against all interference. The point of this demonstration of strength against Romania may have been to make Ceausescu nervous and more cautious. But in December he announced that since the Warsaw Pact was not seriously threatened by NATO, the military budget would not be increased but rather reduced to make possible higher family allowances. He appealed for disarmament, making concrete suggestions. In the summer of 1979 severe petrol restrictions imposed on tourists in response to the energy crisis soured relations with other Eastern European countries. Romania's continuing independent line was strikingly demonstrated when its representative failed to take part in the UN vote on the Russian invasion of Afghanistan in January 1980.

Romania's Economic Problems.

Romania's growing economic problems became acute in the autumn of 1981. On 17 October, President Ceausescu introduced food rationing, including bread. But unlike in Poland—the other East European country to have food rationing in 1981—the dissident and trade union movements in Romania are fragile and small. And the state apparatus does not have the major problem of the Polish authorities in dealing with the Roman Catholic church. So retrenchment in the Romanian economy, forced by declining domestic oil production and a large hard-currency debt, is unlikely to result in major political upheavals. Ceausescu's power is considerable, bolstered by his old tactic of switching leading government ministers and possible rivals for his job around, keeping them off-balance.

Gromyko visits Bucharest.

The Soviet foreign minister, Mr Andrei Gromyko, visited the Romanian capital of Bucharest in late January 1984 in a move designed to forestall Romanian consideration of the possibility of leaving the Warsaw Treaty Organisation in 1985, the thirtieth year of the Organisation's existence and the year of the Treaty's expiry.

There seemed little possibility that the Soviet leadership, divided and weakened as it none the less appeared to be, would countenance the withdrawal of a Treaty partner; on the contrary, it expected that all the signatories to it would renew their membership in a new agreement. It was improbable that President Ceausescu could have supposed that Romania would have been allowed to withdraw, even had he wished it. Much more likely was that he wished to use the threat of withdrawal as a bargaining counter with the Soviet Union. This was a tactic he understood and exploited well: at the Stockholm Conference early in 1984, Ceausescu made clear his willingness to act as an honest broker between the two superpowers and made strong calls for the resumption of negotiations between the Soviet Union and the Unites States.

Continuing Economic Difficulties.

The 13th Party Congress, held in November 1984, duly re-elected Ceausescu as party leader. But unanimity was more apparent than real as the full costs of the reductions of Romania's burden of external debt gradually became apparent. The reduction, from more than $10·00 billion in 1981 to around $8·00 billion three years later, entailed considerable sacrifices. Real incomes fell markedly in the same period, whilst rationing of foodstuffs and fuel increased: consumers were instructed to reduce their use of electricity by up to 50%, and street-lamps in cities were often kept off after dark. Now a net oil importer, not least because of her substantial domestic refining capacity, Romania can turn only to the Soviet Union for trading assistance. A visit to Bucharest by the Soviet Foreign Minister Andrei Gromyko in February 1984 resulted in a Soviet undertaking to supply Romania with a small quantity of oil at prices comparable to those used for trade with Russia's politically more reliable east European neighbours. Further assistance would be more readily available in the event of Ceausescu following Soviet foreign policy preferences with greater attention. But to do so would complicate Ceausescu's delicate political calculation: the Romanian population is relatively poor, and becoming poorer, and the harshness of the internal regime shows no signs of easing. A measure of independence in foreign policy is one of the few cards the Romanian President has to play.

Yet 1985 showed that Ceausescu's much-vaunted independence from Moscow was only as strong as Romania's economy allowed. The signs of weakness, publicly evident in the crisis in the power-supply industry in the winter of 1984, were reinforced in the autumn of 1985 when Ceausescu imposed military regulations on power station workers. In a demonstration of his dissatisfaction (and an implicit recognition of his dramatic policy failure) a deputy prime minister and two energy ministers were sacked. Romania's inefficient industries had for years drained her oil reserves; oil imports rose from almost zero in the mid-seventies to about 60 billion lei in 1985.

Coal production, too, slumped alarmingly below both planning targets and industry's requirements, exacerbating the country's economic difficulties, especially in export sectors. A system of punitive fines and work regimes were introduced by Ceausescu at the end of August 1985 to encourage citizens to donate 'voluntary' labour to local public works projects, and to enhance industrial productivity. Subsequent months showed little indication that such measures would impress the Soviet Union sufficiently to induce it to aid her stricken neighbour—especially since rumours of Ceausescu's ill-health abounded. The new Soviet leadership were inclined to hold their fire in order to place pressure on Ceausescu's successor, who seemed likely to be either his wife, Elena, or his youngest son, Nicu.

YUGOSLAVIA.

In August 1949 the USSR broke off state relations with Yugoslavia, and Yugoslavia launched out under Tito on a course of independent Communism, surviving by securing economic aid from the West and abolishing the command economy at home by the institution of "workers' self-management".

Tito and the Soviet Union.

In May 1955 Khrushchev made a visit to Belgrade in an attempt to win Yugoslavia back into the Soviet camp. Inter-government relations were re-established, but very much on Tito's terms: the joint "Belgrade Declaration" promised "non-interference in other countries' affairs for any reason whatever". Tito's return visit the following June re-established Party relations, and the "Moscow Declaration" issued then conceded that countries should be allowed to follow "their own roads to Socialism". Khrushchev and Tito, however, failed to reach agreement on Yugoslavia's place in the Communist community, and a growing division between them began to emerge against a background of "Titoist" nationalist disturbances in Poland and Hungary, hardening with the publication of a new Yugoslav Party Programme in April 1958, which the Soviets considered "revisionist". This hostile episode was terminated when the Soviet Union was looking around for allies at the outbreak of its dispute with China. A further inducement to the Soviet Union to mend its fences with Yugoslavia was the latter's influence among Third World countries as one of the founders of the non-alignment movement at the Belgrade Conference in September 1961. In 1965 Yugoslavia gained observer status in Comecon, and in 1967 Tito joined other Communist leaders in condemning Israel's alleged aggression against the Arabs. The drift towards closer relations with the USSR was temporarily halted by the Soviet invasion of Czechoslovakia in 1968. In the period of tension which followed there were some fears that Yugoslavia might be the next to be invaded. A territorial defence law was hurried through, and on 15 October 1968 US Secretary of State Dean Rusk reminded the USSR that the US considered Yugoslavia to be in a "grey zone" under NATO protection. These fears were shortlived: Brezhnev and Tito exchanged visits in 1971 and 1972, and in June 1976 Yugoslavia broke a long tradition by taking part in the Conference of European Communist Parties, albeit reiterating her independent stance. Soviet toleration of Yugoslavia has been made easier by the latter's recent adoption of a harder line at home. For all its democratisation of the state structure, the League of Communists retains a monopolistic grip on the levers of power. Challenging that has led to the persecution of intellectuals like Djilas, Mihajlov and the "Praxis" group of philosophers. An upsurge of Croat nationalism in the early seventies led to a widespread purge of Party and government officials. In a Yugoslavia split by ethnic dissensions after Tito's death it would be easy for the Soviet Union to re-establish its control over the area and gain access to the Adriatic, and there are some grounds for believing that discreet Soviet support has been offered to émigré Croat terrorist organisations.

Yugoslavia after Tito.

Yugoslav independence is still based on un-certainty as to how the USA would react to an attack on it. It was therefore a shock when in the 1976 election campaign Jimmy Carter openly said that Yugoslavia would be given no military help in the event of Soviet intervention. How-ever, he took this back later and instead wooed President Tito. In the face of massive Soviet pres-sure to integrate more into the Communist bloc Tito attempted to preserve Yugoslav independence by a balancing act between East and West in terms of military and economic co-operation and the search for arms and credits.

The economic crisis, the conflict between the different nationalities, and Yugoslavia's strategic position, with consequent Soviet interest, make the country exceptionally difficult to govern. Yet, in contrast to the outside world, Yugoslavia itself reacted calmly in January 1980 to the twin challenge of the East–West crisis in the wake of the Soviet invasion of Afghanistan and the serious illness of President Tito. The collective leader-ship responded by putting the army in an in-creased state of alert, short of actual mobilisation, but even this seemed rather designed to reassure its own population. Yugoslavs appeared to ex-pect an intensification of Soviet psychological pressure but no direct intervention.

The Yugoslav leadership continued during the crisis to stress the country's non-aligned status. But in practice they looked to the European Com-munity to show solidarity by speedy and generous conclusion of the treaty on trade co-operation and mutual preference. Meanwhile, after the ampu-tation of his leg, it became clear that the long era of Tito's leadership was effectively over. His funeral in May 1980 showed the stature in which he was held by the rest of the world. A system of collective leadership succeeded Tito.

The Advent of Ms Planinc.

It was announced in January 1982 that Yugo-slavia's collective presidency had nominated Ms M. Planinc, the leader of the Croatian Communist Party, to serve as the new head of the Yugoslav government. Ms Planinc is the first woman to be Yugoslavia's Prime Minister.

The political and economic problems faced by Ms. Planinc at the half-way stage of her two-year term were inextricably linked. The system of collective leadership which Tito bequeathed to his successors entrenches the power of the six republics and the two autonomous representatives (a representative from each of them, in addition to the leader of the Communist Party, comprise the leadership). When added to the practice of rotation of most senior officeholders, the result is to leave the central government with few political cards to play in a game of economic mismanagement. During 1983, pressure for change, allowing for a degree of central control without fundamentally altering the federal character of the country grew markedly.

The cost of forcing the pace of reform too rapidly, of attempting to create a more centralised system of economic decision-making is that the most fissiparous European country will again be rent by nationalist disturbances. Tito succeeded by force of character in holding the country together to a degree which even the able and popular Ms. Planinc inevitably finds much more difficult.

The Seselj Prosecution.

The observation that the federal question is never far from the surface of Yugoslavian politics was borne out again during 1984, both directly and indi-rectly. Anxious to quieten discussion of revisions in the country's federal structure, the authorities arrested a participant in a meeting at which the prin-cipal speaker was Milovan Djilas, Yugoslavia's best-known dissident. Djilas's topic was the state's policy towards ethnic and federal problems; the little-known participant in the meeting, Vojislav Seselj, was subsequently sentenced to eight years in prison for "attempted anti-constitutional change". Seselj had, claimed the prosecution, promoted the reduction of the country's six provinces to four. The government, faced with differing demands for cons-titutional reform from Kosovo and Serbia, and the overriding requirement to maintain unity among the country's six provinces, made an issue of Seselj's case as part of a general clamp-down; his was one of many prosecutions involving provincial and ethnic questions in 1984.

Indirectly, the preference for centralisation emerged strongly among Serbian party members in the results of an investigation into the state of the Yugoslavian Communist Party initiated by a Cen-tral Committee meeting in June. The investigation, by means of questionnaire, revealed widespread dis-content with corruption and inequality and wide-spread differences of opinion about the proper balance to be struck between economic liberalisa-tion and state control—a matter which has powerful implications for the extent of central control over the six provinces and the autonomous province of Kosovo.

The general and persisting problem for Yugos-lavia's politicians of relations between the centre and the provinces was highlighted again in 1985 when Serbian discontent with events in Kosovo surfaced publicly. A petition from members of the Serbian minority in the province drew attention to what they claimed were attacks from Kosovo's Albanians, and seeking greater protection from the central authorities. Towards the end of the year, a large number of Yugoslavs of Albanian extraction were arrested and charged with belonging to an ille-gal nationalist organisation. Many such groups have been set up in Yugoslavia since the 1981 riots in Kosovo, and there is little question that they com-mand considerable support from ethnic Albanians living in Yugoslavia.

The exercise of central political authority, never easy in this most fissiparous of all European coun-tries, had especially damaging implications for the government's attempts to come to grips with a wor-sening economic crisis. As real incomes continued to fall, the rate of inflation grew rapidly, approaching 100% by the year's end.

BULGARIA

On 8 September 1984, the Bulgarian government marked the fortieth anniversary of the Communist assumption of power. Mikhail Gorbachev, the rapidly-rising member of the Soviet Politburo attended the celebrations in Sofia at which Zhivkov claimed that Bulgaria was ". . . united and strong as never before". The claim had a curious ring since 1984 was marked, most unusually for an eastern European communist state, by a spate of violent incidents including a number of terrorist bombings. The authorities quickly dismissed western specula-tion that the attacks had a political purpose, whilst the state's control over news made information about them difficult to come by. It nonetheless seems probable that attacks, of varying sizes, took place in six Bulgarian cities during the year, cul-minating in the period of the fortieth anniversary celebrations.

The dullness which superficially characterises Bulgarian politics to western observers was further disturbed during 1984 by indications that the Bul-garian Industrial Association intends to expand the scheme promoting small businesses as a means of en-livening the country's economy. Financial support from the state bank was to be made available, together with foreign capital. Thus, hesitantly and belatedly, Bulgaria seemed by the end of the year ready to embrace certain aspects of the economic reforms which Hungary had begun sixteen years before.

Economic reform was nudged a little further by Mikhail Gorbachev's election as the new Soviet party leader. His penchant for bureaucratic reor-ganisation in Moscow as a means of stimulating economic growth was followed by Sofia, thereby tending to confirm Bulgaria's status as the Soviet Union's closest ally in Eastern Europe. Indeed, Gorbachev's reforms in Moscow were pursued very much more extensively in Bulgaria where three super-ministries were created in an attempt to over-come bureaucratic squabbling and to allow, in par-ticular, for more effective central planning of the economy.

The reforms provided an opportunity for the in-troduction of new blood at the highest levels of the government, and were accompanied by a reshuffle of the Politburo. Two of the newcomers, Ognyan Doynov and Chudomir Alexandrov, held Politburo seats in addition to strategic positions in the reformed government apparatus and were well-placed to succeed Todor Zhivkov. His position had been much less secure since Gorbachev's accession to power in Moscow, and active preparations were made for his retirement at the party congress in Sofia at the beginning of April.

ALBANIA.

Communism was imposed on feudal Albania by a handful of intellectuals acting in a long tradition of elitist rule. King Zog was deposed in absentia in January 1945. The wartime resistance movement had been captured by the Communists because of the support of Yugoslavia's Partisans, and Albania became a satellite of Yugoslavia until the latter's rupture with Stalin in 1948. Thereupon the Albanian leadership split into a pro-Yugoslav faction led by Koci Xoxe and a Stalinist faction under Party Secretary Enver Hoxha. The latter triumphed. Xoxe was executed and relations with Yugoslavia were broken off. Privately the Albanian leaders considered Khrushchev's debunking of Stalin and particularly his wooing of Tito as a danger to their security, and when the Soviet–Chinese quarrel broke out in 1960 they made this view public and supported the Chinese position. Relations with the Soviet Union were broken off in 1961 and Albania became a client of China. The remarkable stability of the leadership came to an end in 1974 with the sacking of the Minister of Defence Balluku, and in April 1976 two more ministers were sacked and Hoxha announced that an "anti-China group" had been smashed.

The Split with China.

However, in July 1977 the Party organ condemned the Chinese theory of the three Worlds as anti-revolutionary, contrary to the class struggle and protective of capitalism. After Chinese repudiation of this criticism it was renewed with increased vigour and there followed further signs of deteriorating relations, including the recall of Albanian students from China. Albania seems to be deliberately choosing isolation rather than accept compromises with what it sees as the new revisionism of China. In July 1978 came the formal termination of Chinese economic aid. Albania remains a spartan and economically very backward society with agricultural forced labour for all and a conscious fostering of peasant traditions, coupled with an extreme anti-religious campaign sanctioned by the new 1976 constitution. It has made cautious contacts with Greece and other European countries, presumably in order to replace China, which previously accounted for some 60% of Albania's foreign trade. But it is still highly insulated from the outside world.

The Death of Shehu.

Albania announced on the weekend of 19-20 December 1981, that the Prime Minister, Mr. Mehmet Shehu, had committed suicide. Shehu was the closest aide and ally of Hoxha, the leader of the Albanian Communist Party, and had been Prime Minister for 28 years. Remarkably, after having been a public hero for so long, Shehu's death was publicly regarded as a disgrace by the government. There were no commemoration ceremonies, and his name went unmentioned in the national press after the release of the communique announcing his death.

Albania after Hoxha.

In January, 1982, Hoxha announced that he had chosen Mr Adil Carcani as Shehu's successor. Carcani is firmly in the Hoxha mould and likely to continue the policies of resistance to borrowing abroad, and fierce isolationism. It is possible that disagreement over policy on trade with the West was a material factor in Shehu's fall from grace and "suicide". More than this, the faint signs of a power struggle behind Shehu's demise may well herald a growing power struggle among the Albanian elite.

In a sequel to the events surrounding Mehmet Shehu the previous December, Enver Hoxha announced that his former Prime Minister had been a triple spy for the Russians, the Americans and the hated Yugoslavs. Shehu's biographical details underwent an immediate, and absurd, rewriting in the annals of official Albanian history. This, however, was only to be expected. Far more important was Hoxha's sacking of most of his Cabinet, and the installation of Ramiz Alia as President. After years of stability, the ground was beginning to move beneath the Party leader's feet.

Alia's position as President gradually assumed greater importance during 1983. With no political option to that of scrupulous loyalty to Hoxha for as long as the party leader lived, he was well placed to bid for the leadership on Hoxha's death. In April 1985 Alia duly confirmed this succession on the death of Enver Hoxha.

Changes in Foreign Policy.

Hoxha retreated somewhat from the public eye during 1984; the Head of State, Ramiz Alia, took greater control of government. It was probably not coincidental that Albania's relations with some foreign countries grew distinctly warmer as the year progressed.

Trade with China resumed as the economic costs to Albania of continued separation escalated. Cultural exchanges with Italy and Austria were established and, despite the lack of formal diplomatic relations between them, Albanian and West German officials engaged in a number of contacts and working visits. The German connection was cemented further with the visit of Herr Franz Josef Strauss, the CSU Prime Minister of Bavaria, to Albania for a vacation in August; the Albanians took the opportunity of Mr. Strauss's surprising choice of holiday destination to arrange a meeting with senior government ministers.

Relations with Greece, Albania's nearest neighbour, also improved. Although the Greek government continued to express concern at the treatment accorded the Greek minority in Albania, the Greek Prime Minister, Andreas Papandreou, renounced his country's claim to that part of Albanian territory where most of the Albanian Greeks live. The renunciation made possible increased contacts between the Greek and Albanian governments which in the longer term may well make possible an easing of the problem of the Greek minority, thus opening the way to a general improvement in relations.

Albania under Alia.

Enver Hoxha died in April 1985, and was succeeded by Ramiz Alia who had been carefully groomed for the job for several years. At a funeral oration on 15 April, the new Albanian leader extolled the virtues of the dead leader, and pledged himself to continue his policies and in particular to strengthen the 'Albanian fortress'. Later the same month, Alia reiterated the message of continuity.

Yet the declared policy of continuity is open to different interpretations. A policy of isolation, once judged necessary to preserve independence, was thought by Alia and his colleagues to be insufficient to meet her changing trading and political needs. Hoxha's last years had seen a slight (though usually unacknowledged) warming of relations with foreign countries and Alia seemed likely to continue the trend. The primary motive for expanding contacts is economic: Albania is poorly-equipped to survive alone and needs to import foreign technology and, in the long term, to attract foreign capital investment, too.

The indications of his first twelve months in power were that Alia would assert ideological orthodoxy (a policy underlined by the appointment of likeminded conservatives to the Politburo) whilst cautiously opening doors to the west. Trade and cultural ties with Albania's neighbours were extended, and negotiations with other countries (including Britain), were begun with a view to establishing full diplomatic relations. Albania's fear of being undermined by foreign contacts, rooted in British and American attempts to topple Hoxha's regime, is likely to continue to colour her foreign policy. But, as Romania had shown for many years, the maintenance of tight internal party control is not necessarily inconsistent with a flexible policy towards international political and trading links.

THE MIDDLE EAST

ISRAEL.

Israel and the Arabs.

Israel was established as an independent sovereign republic by proclamation on 14 May 1948. Arab hostility to the emergence of a Jewish state led to armed conflict, in which, due to her enemy's lack of unity, Israel gained more territory than originally allocated under the partition plan for Palestine. The Arab states continued refusal to recognise Israel's right to exist brought new wars in 1956, 1967 and 1973, at the end of which Israel was still in possession of territory formerly belonging to Egypt, Jordan and Syria.

The Camp David Agreement.

General elections held in Israel in May 1977 resulted in the replacement of the long-standing Labour government by the right-wing alliance, the Likud bloc, led by Menachem Begin. There was a dramatic breakthrough in the search for peace in November 1977 when President Sadat of Egypt visited Jerusalem to address the Knesset, the Israeli parliament, on the subject of a Middle East settlement. In September 1978 Prime Minister Begin and President Sadat met for talks under the chairmanship of President Carter at Camp David, Maryland. A framework for peace was agreed and on 26 March 1979 a treaty was signed in Washington. In return for the normalisation of relations with Egypt, Israel agreed to withdraw from the Sinai peninsula, occupied in the Six-Day War of 1967. The withdrawal was completed in April 1982.

The 1982 invasion of the Lebanon.

Mr. Begin called a general election in June 1981, in which Israel's economic problems and her relations with her neighbours were the main issues. Mr. Begin's decision to launch an air strike against Iraq's Osirak nuclear plant shortly before the election was bitterly debated. At the polls both the Likud and Labour parties gained seats at the expense of the smaller groups. Mr. Begin ended with a one-seat advantage in the Knesset over Labour, and, after protracted negotiations with the smaller parties, he was able to form a new government in August 1981.

Mr. Begin now pursued more aggressive policies towards the occupied territories and neighbouring Arab states. In December 1981 Israeli law was extended to the Golan Heights, conquered from Syria in the 1967 war, in effect annexing the territory. Even the United States voted for the unanimous UN Security Council Resolution condemning this action. Then in June 1982 Mr. Begin launched a full-scale invasion of the Lebanon in order to stop the Palestinian guerrillas using the country as a base for attacks on Israel.

Beirut was surrounded and the PLO guerrillas forced to evacuate. However, as casualties mounted, Israel found it more difficult to extricate her army of occupation from Lebanon then it had been to send it in. A treaty signed in May 1983 with the United States and President Gemayel of Lebanon proved to be a dead-letter when the Syrians refused to accept it.

The General Election of 1984.

The ailing Mr. Begin resigned in September 1983. The Foreign Minister, Mr. Shamir, formed the new government and with hyper-inflation running at over 500% per annum, introduced an urgent package of austerity measures. Labour unrest grew and Mr. Shamir's government narrowly survived a no-confidence motion in the Knesset in January 1984.

General elections were held in July 1984. The result was inconclusive, with the smaller groups doing well at the expense of the two main parties. Labour won 44 seats as against the ruling Likud's 41 seats with thirteen other parties securing representation. As leader of the largest group in the Knesset, Labour's Shimon Peres was invited to attempt to form a government by President Herzog. After several weeks of negotiation, a national unity government was formed in September 1984, with Mr Peres as Prime Minister and Mr Shamir as Deputy

Prime Minister for the first 25 months, then reversing roles for the second.

In January 1985 Mr Peres' government announced its decision to carry out a unilateral withdrawal from occupied Lebanon. Over six hundred Israelis had died in Lebanon since the ill-fated invasion of 1982. Mr. Peres now sought to make progress towards a settlement of the Palestinian problem. In October 1985 he had talks with President Reagan, in which he said Israel was ready for unconditional talks with Jordan and might make 'territorial compromises' in the search for peace. In an address to the UN General Assembly Mr. Peres announced that Israel was willing to end the state of war with Jordan and negotiate with a Jordanian-Palestinian delegation within the framework of an international forum under the auspices of the UN Security Council.

A no-confidence motion in the Knesset was defeated in October 1985, but divisions began to emerge within the coalition government. In November Mr. Peres demanded the resignation of his most outspoken critic, Mr. Sharon, the Trade and Industry Minister, if he did not apologise for violent attacks on the policy of seeking to open peace talks with King Hussein. Mr. Peres finally agreed to accept a form of apology, or 'clarification', from Mr. Sharon.

Although Israel sought a Palestinian settlement under Jordanian auspices, there was no acceptance of participation by the PLO. A number of violent incidents in 1985 helped to harden this position. In September one British and two Arab gunmen killed three Israelis on board a yacht in Larnaca harbour, Cyprus, after demanding the release of certain Palestinians held in Israel. In retaliation in October Israeli planes bombed the headquarters of the PLO near Tunis, killing some sixty people. Then at the end of December guerrillas attacked El Al Israel Airlines' passengers at Rome and Vienna airports. In turn on 4 February 1986 the Israelis forced down a Libyan executive jet which was thought to be carrying Palestinian guerrilla leaders, but was found to have only Syrian and Lebanese politicians on board. Later in February the Israelis were quick to applaud when King Hussein announced his repudiation of the PLO as a partner in the search for a Middle East peace settlement.

EGYPT.

From Independence to Revolution.

Britain ended its protectorate over Egypt in February 1922 and recognised the country as an independent state. The Sultan, Fuad, took the title of King of Egypt. In July 1952 a group of young soldiers, the 'Free Officers', secured the abdication of King Farouk in favour of his infant son, who became King Fuad II. However, in June 1953 General Neguib, head of the military junta, deposed the young king and Egypt became a republic. General Neguib became President and Prime Minister, with the leader of the Free Officers, Colonel Nasser, as Deputy Prime Minister. A power struggle between Neguib and Nasser ensued, which resulted in victory for the latter in November 1954.

From Nasser to Sadat.

Nasser's period as president saw two Israeli invasions of Egyptian territory: in 1956, when British and French troops also attacked the Suez canal, and in June 1967. The Six-Day War of 1967 resulted in a disastrous defeat for Egypt and left the Sinai peninsula in Israeli hands. Nasser began the difficult task of reconstruction, but died in September 1970. He was succeeded by the Vice-President, Anwar Sadat.

In October 1973 President Sadat launched a surprise Egyptian attack across the Suez Canal on the Israeli occupying forces in the Sinai. The Yom Kippur War did much to restore Egypt's prestige and to foster serious attempts to seek a permanent peace. There was a dramatic development in November 1977 when President Sadat visited Jerusalem to address the Israeli parliament, the Knesset, on the subject of a Middle East peace settlement. In September 1978 a summit meeting took place between the United States' President, Jimmy Carter, Mr Begin of Israel and President Sadat at Camp David in Maryland. A treaty was signed on 26

March 1979 normalising relations between Egypt and Israel, with Egypt agreeing to recognise Israel in return for the restoration of the Sinai. Egypt was ostracised by the Arab world as a result of the decision to come to terms with Israel.

Sadat's Domestic Problems.

President Sadat's domestic problems mounted at the start of the 1980s. Inflation and unemployment rose whilst the government continued the economically unsound policy of paying out huge subsidies on a range of goods to prevent a recurrence of the serious riots over food and petrol price increases which took place in 1977. Economic discontent was compounded by the growth of Islamic radicalism in Egypt. In September 1981 President Sadat arrested over 1,500 Islamic militants, left-wingers and other opponents of his regime. But on 6 October Sadat was assassinated by Islamic fundamentalists while watching a military parade in Cairo.

Mubarrak in power.

President Sadat was succeeded by the Vice-President Mubarrak, a former commander of the Egyptian air force, who had been vice-president since 1975. Mubarrak broadly continued his predecessor's policies. Crucially the change of leadership did not delay the completion of the planned Israeli withdrawal from the remainder of occupied Sinai in April 1982. Mubarrak effected a reconciliation with the Palestine Liberation Organisation when he met Yasser Arafat in December 1983, and relations with Jordan, broken off after Egypt's peace with Israel, were restored in September 1984. However, the failure to deal with the economic inequalities in Egyptian society and the demands of Islamic militants resulted in outbreaks of violence. In February 1986 a mutiny by paramilitary police conscripts led to more general rioting which had to be suppressed by the army.

JORDAN AND THE PALESTINIANS.

The Creation of Jordan.

Britain recognised Transjordan as an independent state by a treaty signed in London on 22 March 1946. On 25 May 1946 Amir Abdullah assumed the title of King and in June the name of the country was changed to the Hashemite Kingdom of Jordan. Following the war with Israel in 1948 a considerable enclave of territory on the West Bank of the River Jordan remained in Jordanian hands and this was formally annexed in 1950. King Abdullah was assassinated in 1951 and in 1952 his son, King Talal, was found to be suffering from mental illness. He was therefore deposed by parliament and succeeded by his son, Hussein.

The Palestinian Problem.

In June 1967 King Hussein led the country into the Six-Day War with Israel and suffered the loss of all his territory west of the River Jordan. There was a fresh influx of Palestinian refugees from the lands occupied by Israel. These came under the wing of the Palestine Liberation Organisation (PLO), which had been formed in 1964 and included the al-Fatah guerrilla group, headed by Yasser Arafat. In 1968 Mr. Arafat became chairman of the PLO. Relations between the Palestinians and King Hussein deteriorated as the guerrillas came to represent a serious challenge to his authority. Civil war broke out in 1970 and the guerrillas were driven from the country by the Jordanian army in 1971. However, in 1974 at an Arab summit conference in Rabat King Hussein reluctantly endorsed a resolution naming the PLO as the sole legitimate representative of the Palestinian people and affirmed their right to an independent state as their homeland.

The Reagan Plan.

In September 1982 President Reagan put forward a new set of proposals for the Israeli-occupied West Bank to be constituted as a homeland for the Palestinians in association with Jordan. However, when in April 1983 King Hussein reached agreement with Mr. Arafat on the role Jordan might play in the negotiations, this was rejected by the PLO executive committee. A rebellion against Mr. Arafat's leadership by a Syrian-backed PLO faction broke out. Mr. Arafat and his supporters, driven out of Beirut by the Israelis in August 1982, were now besieged in Tripoli. The Arafat loyalists were eventually evacuated in Greek ships flying the UN flag in December 1983.

The Hussein Initiative.

In January 1984 King Hussein took the initiative in seeking a solution of the Palestinian problem by recalling the Jordanian national assembly which had not met since 1976, because elections could not be held on the West Bank. Instead deputies were now nominated to represent the Israeli-occupied territory. However, Mr. Arafat again grew in importance in November 1984 when he succeeded in assembling a quorum for the 17th Palestine National Council in Amman.

The Arafat–Hussein Accord.

In February 1985 Mr. Arafat and King Hussein reached agreement on a common approach to negotiations, advocating an international peace conference and calling for the creation of a Palestinian state in confederation with Jordan. However, the search for a settlement was complicated by an Israeli air raid on the PLO headquarters south of Tunis on 1 October 1985, followed by the hijacking of the Italian cruise ship *Achille Lauro* off the Egyptian coast by Palestinian guerrillas on 7 October. On 14 October Britain's Foreign Secretary, Sir Geoffrey Howe, cancelled a planned meeting with representatives of Jordan and the PLO when the latter refused to agree to a statement opposing terrorism and supporting a territorial settlement based on UN Security Council Resolutions 242 and 338 (which implied an acceptance of Israel's right to exist).

Mr. Arafat held further talks with King Hussein at the end of October 1985, but the relationship between the two parties was uneasy as a result of the *Achille Lauro* incident and the rapprochement which had just taken place between Jordan and Syria. (Syria supported the anti-Arafat dissidents within the PLO). In November 1985 Mr. Arafat travelled on to Egypt for talks with Mr. Mubarrak. These led to Mr Arafat's issuing the 'Cairo declaration', in which he announced his opposition to international terrorism, but maintained the right of the Palestinians to continue the armed struggle in the occupied territories. However, the response of PLO dissidents was the hijacking of an Egyptian Boeing 737 en route from Athens to Cairo on 23 November and attacks on El Al Israel Airlines' passengers at Rome and Vienna airports on 27 December. The Israelis retaliated on 4 February 1986 by forcing down a Libyan executive jet which was thought to be carrying Palestinian guerrilla leaders, but was found to have only Syrian and Lebanese politicans on board.

Rift between King Hussein and Mr. Arafat.

King Hussein and Mr. Arafat met for further talks in February 1986. The previous October the Americans and Israelis had accepted the idea of an international conference on the Palestinian problem and in January 1986 Jordan appeared to have achieved a breakthrough when the Americans agreed that the PLO should be invited to attend once it had renounced terrorism and accepted Resolutions 242 and 338. But Mr. Arafat still insisted on prior American approval for the Palestinians' right of self-determination within a Jordanian-Palestinian confederation. Finally on 19 February 1986 King Hussein announced his repudiation of the PLO as a partner in the search for a Middle East peace settlement, accusing its leadership of bad faith. He planned to strengthen the West Bank representation in the national assembly, thereby paving the way for a revival of Jordan's claim to represent the Palestinians, rather than the PLO.

LEBANON.

Origins of the Conflict.

Tensions between the Christian and Moslem communities in the Lebanon were exacerbated by an influx of Palestinian guerrillas expelled from Jordan in 1970, and this resulted in full-scale civil war in 1975. Since then there has been great loss of life and economic disruption. Intervention by Syria and other neighbours, forming the Arab 'deterrent force', brought only a brief respite in 1976. Palestinian raids led to an invasion of the south of the country by Israeli forces between March and June 1978.

The Israeli Invasion of 1982.

Attempts to establish a workable basis for government in Lebanon repeatedly foundered amid fresh outbreaks of fighting between rival Christian and Moslem militias. Following the attempted assassination of the Israeli ambassador in London, Shlomo Argov, Israel launched a full-scale invasion of the Lebanon on 6 June 1982, aimed at driving out the Palestinians. Beirut was besieged and after tense negotiations Palestinian guerrillas were evacuated from the capital at the end of August.

The Lebanese president, Mr. Sarkis, retired in July 1982 and a Christian Phalangist Party militia leader, Bashir Gemayel, was elected to succeed him. However, he was assassinated almost immediately by a bomb explosion at the Phalangist headquarters. His elder brother, Amin Gemayel, a more moderate figure, was elected in his place. The start of his presidency was marred when on 17 September 1982 massacres of several hundred Palestinian civilians were carried out by Christian militiamen who entered the Chatilla and Sabra refugee camps in Beirut.

Negotiations took place to try to end the Israeli occupation of southern Lebanon. An American-sponsored agreement between President Gemayel and the Israelis in May 1983 proved to be a dead-letter when the Syrians refused to accept continuing Israeli influence in a buffer zone in the south of Lebanon. However, in January 1985 Israel announced that it had unilaterally decided on a three-stage withdrawal from Lebanon which was completed later in the year. As a postscript to the episode, an American Trans World Airlines Boeing 707 was hijacked in June en route from Athens to Rome by Lebanese Shia Moslems demanding the release of prisoners taken by the Israelis as they withdrew. The aircraft was forced to fly to Beirut and the passengers taken to various locations in the city. After secret negotiations, Israel began to release the detainees and the hostages were set free.

Syria's Peace Plan.

Israel's withdrawal did not solve the problems of Lebanon's internal strife. Syrian efforts at mediation led to the signing in December 1985 of a new peace pact by Syria's vice-president and leaders of Christian, Druze and Shi'ite militias. This set out a plan for a cease-fire, followed by constitutional reforms reducing the power of the Christian-held presidency, with Syria policing the settlement. However, President Gemayel was not a party to the negotiations and when he visited the Syrian capital, Damascus, in January 1986, he refused to support the agreement. The pact collapsed when the Christian signatory, Elie Hobeika, was overthrown by pro-Gemayel Phalangist Party fighters and rebels in his own Lebanese Forces militia, and peace between the warring factions in the Lebanon seemed as far away as ever.

IRAN.

The Islamic Revolution.

The Islamic revolution headed by Ayatollah Khomeini drove the Shah into exile in January 1979. Dr. Mehdi Bazargan became Prime Minister but real power lay in the hands of Khomeini and the Revolutionary Council which was mainly composed of senior Shi'ite Muslim clergy. A referendum in March 1979 resulted in an overwhelming vote in favour of Iran becoming an Islamic republic. Conflict inside Iran grew as left-wing groups clashed with Muslim extremists, and guerillas from minority groups such as the Kurds sought to assert their autonomy.

The American Hostages.

On 4 November 1979 the American embassy in Tehran was occupied by militant students and its staff held hostage against the return of the Shah to stand trial in Iran. Dr. Bazargan resigned and in elections held in January 1980 Dr. Bani-Sadr became president with over 70% of the votes. He soon came into conflict with the Islamic Republic Party. The issue of the American hostages occupied the centre of the stage as President Carter launched a military rescue attempt in April. The mission was aborted and eight American servicemen were killed as they were being evacuated. The fifty-two hostages were eventually released on 20 January 1981, the same day as Ronald Reagan was sworn in as American President, following Algerian mediation over the political and financial obstacles.

In September 1980 President Saddam Hussein of Iraq, hoping to take advantage of the turmoil in Iran, abrogated the Algiers Pact of 1975 by which his country had been forced to accept joint control of the important Shatt al-Arab waterway, and invaded Iran. Despite initial Iraqi gains, any hopes of an Israeli-style *blitzkrieg* victory soon proved to be misplaced as the offensive bogged down. A turning point in the conflict came in the autumn of 1981 as the Iranians counter-attacked and raised the siege of Abadan. The rashness of President Hussein's decision to attack revolutionary Iran was now clear.

Iran began a new offensive in March 1982. By June almost all Iraqi troops had withdrawn from Iranian territory, and in July the Iranians mounted a counter-invasion of Iraq. This was checked, but fighting continued despite calls for a cease-fire.

In 1983 and 1984 Iran launched a number of major offensives, but the military situation on land remained deadlocked. Repeated air attacks by both sides on international shipping in the Gulf represented a significant escalation of the conflict. During 1984 67 vessels, ranging from supertankers to small supply ships, were damaged by the warring states.

Downfall of Dr. Bani-Sadr.

The power struggle between secular and religious political forces culminated in Dr. Bani-Sadr's dismissal from office by Ayatollah Khomeini on 22 June 1981. Violence in Tehran increased. At the end of June seventy-two leading officials were killed in an explosion at the headquarters of the Islamic Republican Party and in August an explosion at the Prime Minister's offices killed both Prime Minister and President. During July and August the Iranian authorities retaliated by executing over six hundred opponents of the regime.

Executions continued during 1982, including that of Sadeq Qotbzadeh, the former Foreign Minister, in September after he had been found guilty of attempting to overthrow the government. The search for a successor when Ayatollah Khomeini dies took a step forward in December 1982 when an Assembly of Experts was elected to decide on a new leader or a leadership council of three or five men to succeed Khomeini as the dominant force in Iranian political life.

Action against opponents of the revolution continued in 1983 with the outlawing of the communist Tudeh Party in May. At the same time 18 Soviet diplomats were expelled from Iran for interfering in internal political affairs. Iran's relations with the USSR were as bad as those with the USA.

Developments in 1985.

The war with Iraq continued during 1985, with each side launching air attacks on the other's cities. In June 1985 Iraq announced the suspension of such attacks, but Iran rejected this conciliatory gesture. Iraq resumed its attacks on Iran's off-shore oil installations in August, but Iran launched a major new offensive in February 1986.

The Emergence of Ayatollah Montazeri.

On the domestic front in August 1985 Ali Khameini, who had become President of Iran in October 1981, was re-elected for a further four-year term with a large majority. Then in November 1985 it was announced that the Assembly of Experts had nominated Ayatollah Hussein Ali Montazeri to succeed Ayatollah Khomeini when he dies or retires. The conservative minority in the ruling Islamic republican party was said to have favoured a leadership council, but no candidates of equal weight to Ayatollah Montazeri were put forward.

IRAQ AND SYRIA.

Iraq and Syria were both governed by left-wing revolutionary Arab regimes during the 1970s. Both dealt severely with their internal opponents and Iraq in particular (where the Iranian Ayatollah Khomeini had spent almost thirteen years in exile at Najaf) was strongly hostile to the Islamic upsurge. But in Syria, fierce antagonisms between the country's Sunni majority and its Shi'ite minority—represented by President Hafiz Assad himself—revived. During the summer of 1979 there were serious incidents of violence between Sunni and Shi'ite Syrians, including the massacre of 60 cadet officers. This reflected Sunni Shi'ite conflicts immediately to Syria's north in Eastern Turkey where 120 people were murdered in the town of Kahramanmaras in riots in December 1978. In 1980, Iraq went to war with Iran whilst relations between Syria and Jordan grew increasingly tense. A rapprochement took place between Jordan and Syria in October 1985 when, in the context of negotiations over the Palestinian problem, they agreed to reject 'partial and unilateral' peace settlements with Israel and to exchange ambassadors after a four-year diplomatic freeze.

SAUDI ARABIA.

Saudi Arabia—whose royal family enforced the strict tenets of the puritanical Wahabbi sect of Islam—began the 1970s as one of the principal backers of Islamic revivalism. It ended it as a country alarmed at the spread of Islamic militancy. In March 1975 King Faisal was assassinated by a mentally deranged member of the royal family and was succeeded by his half-brother Prince Khaled. King Khaled pursued policies of careful modernisation and moderation with regard to oil pricing. The worst moment in his reign came in November 1979 when a gang of Islamic fanatics seized the Great Mosque in Mecca and held it for two weeks, threatening the position of the House of Saud as guardians of Islam's holy places.

Succession of Prince Fahd.

King Khaled died of a heart attack on 13 June 1982 and was succeeded by his brother, Prince Fahd. Prince Fahd had been associated with the progressive, pro-American faction in the royal family and his succession to the throne did not bring any great changes in Saudi Arabian policy.

SOUTH YEMEN.

Post-Independence Problems.

After a protracted guerrilla war against the British colonial rulers, the People's Republic of South Yemen became independent on 30 November 1967. The country's name was changed to the People's Democratic Republic of South Yemen in 1970. In 1969 President Qahtan Al-Shayabi, who had conducted the independence negotiations, was ousted in a bloodless coup by more radical members of his party. This was the first of a series of internal conflicts, based on personal, tribal and doctrinal differences, which has divided the government of the South Yemen since independence.

The new president, Salem Rubayi Ali was himself deposed and shot in 1978 and Abdel Fattah Ismail became head of state. In 1980 he was forced into exile in the Soviet Union, which had developed close relations with South Yemen in the 1970s, and the prime minister, Ali Nasser Mohammed, assumed the presidency.

The 1986 Coup.

Abdel Fattah Ismail returned from Moscow in 1985 and was brought back into the political bureau of the Yemeni Socialist Party. This led, however, to renewed conflict within the party, since Abdel Fattah Ismail took a hard-line Marxist stance, whereas President Ali Nasser Mohammed adopted a more pragmatic approach, for example, to relations with South Yemen's conservative neighbours. Bloodshed broke out in January 1986, either as a result of an attempted coup or pre-emptive action by the President. Thousands died in extensive fighting in and around Aden, and an international

rescue of foreign nationals took place, in which the royal yacht Britannia participated. President Ali Nasser Mohammed was forced to flee the country and the prime minister, Haider Attas, who had been appointed in February 1985, took over as the country's interim head. The upheaval had a serious effect on Soviet interests in South Yemen—Russia's most important military facility in the Middle East—as over 6,000 of its 'advisers' had to be taken to safety from the fighting.

SOUTH ASIA

INDIA SINCE 1965.

In 1965 Mrs. Indira Gandhi (daughter of Jawaharlal Nehru) became Prime Minister. After a close election victory for the ruling Congress Party in 1967, Mrs. Gandhi faced the problems of opposition from the old guard of the Party in 1969 and terrorist activities in 1970. However, in 1971, the Party won a landslide election victory and plans for Socialist reforms were launched. Since the monsoon failure of 1972 and governmental attempts to remedy the severe food crisis, opposition to the government increased. An anti-corruption campaign led by Jayaprakash Narayan was in part to blame for election losses in 1974–5 and a further setback was experienced when in June 1975, the Allahabad High Court declared Mrs. Gandhi's election null and void on the grounds that government officials had been involved in electioneering; she was debarred from office for six years. Mrs. Gandhi's appeal against the decision was subsequently upheld by the Supreme Court, but meanwhile a state of emergency was declared in June 1975. Opposition both inside and outside the government increased. Fundamental rights were suspended during the early months of 1976. In November wide powers were given to the Prime Minister. The state of emergency was accompanied by thousands of arrests without trial, a rigorous press censorship and a personal cult of Mrs. Gandhi and her son Sanjay, who was obviously her chosen successor. However, Mrs. Gandhi called elections for March 1977, in which she and the Congress Party suffered a resounding defeat at the hands of the opposition Janata coalition led by Mr. Morarji Desai, who subsequently became Prime Minister. This result was greeted as a triumph for democracy in India. The new government set about restoring basic rights, ending press restrictions and pursuing a foreign policy of neutrality and genuine non-alignment. The Bokaro Steel Agreement with the Soviet Union was renounced on the grounds of the latter's lack of the necessary know-how and negotiations were started with American firms. A campaign was launched against illiteracy, while the policy of compulsory sterilisation pursued by the previous government was rejected. Mr. Desai appeared to be trying to govern India more by persuasion than by strong leadership. But the governing parties were a coalition united by little more than their opposition to Mrs. Gandhi. The lack of direction was giving rise to increasing dissatisfaction by the end of 1977. Meanwhile the shadow of Mrs. Gandhi, who was put on trial in January 1978, continued to hang over India. The elections in Karnataka state, in February 1978, in which Mrs. Gandhi's own Congress Party swept to power were a further reminder of her still powerful appeal. In July 1978 Mr. Desai finally reacted to growing criticism in his Cabinet by dismissing two of his most prominent colleagues and critics. But Mrs. Gandhi profited from electoral disappointment at government inaction and her own continuing image of protectress of the poor. A triumphant election victory in a traditionally pro-Congress part of southern India in November was seen as the signal for her comeback, and she returned to Parliament as opposition leader. The following month she was sent to prison for violations of parliamentary privilege and lost her seat in parliament. But by-elections held after her release showed that this had done her good rather than harm.

The Triumph of Indira Gandhi.

In July 1979 Mr. Desai resigned following the loss of his parliamentary majority through defections, a split in the Janata Party and the resignation of several ministers. After unsuccessful attempts by his former colleagues to form a stable government, a general election became inevitable. The Janata Coalition collapsed because of the individual ambitions of its aged leaders and the disparate interests of their various parties. It did so against a background of several good harvests but also rising unemployment and inflation and social and racial unrest. In these circumstances the appeal of a strong leader was great. Mrs. Gandhi's previous dictatorial rule was forgotten and in the elections in January 1980 a landslide victory gave her a two-thirds majority in Parliament. Even her notorious son Sanjay gained a seat. This comeback was her own personal triumph. For her Congress Party did not seem to have any coherent strategy for tackling India's permanent problems of a soaring population, poverty, illiteracy, slums and the persistent caste system.

Initially, Mrs. Gandhi's attention was inevitably distracted from internal problems by the Afghanistan crisis. She continued her delicate balancing-act between the superpowers and stressed India's non-aligned status: India did not vote to condemn the Soviet invasion in the United Nations.

Death of Sanjay Gandhi.

Mrs. Gandhi's rule was consolidated throughout 1980, with further victories for Congress (I) in State Assembly elections and also by splits in the former ruling party, Janata, and also in the Lok Dal party, during March and April. A further development was the formation of a pro-Congress (I) All-India Communist Party, a breakaway from the Communist Party of India.

During 1980 the complicated legal case against Mrs. Gandhi, her son Sanjay, and various followers continued, with the Prime Minister emerging largely unscathed. However, these events were overshadowed by the death of Sanjay Gandhi in a flying accident on 23 July, 1980. It was Sanjay who had proved the most controversial figure during the Emergency and its aftermath.

Violence in Assam and the Punjab.

The worst political violence since India's independence took place in the north-east state of Assam in February 1983. This was the culmination of three years' agitation by Hindus against the predominantly Moslem immigrants from Bangladesh, and was sparked off by Mrs. Gandhi's move to hold elections in Assam. The Congress (I) Party won a two-thirds' majority in the new state assembly, but over 4,000 people died in the savage communal fighting.

Meanwhile, violence in the Punjab by Sikhs demanding an independent state escalated, centred on the Sikhs' holiest shrine, the Golden Temple at Amritsar, and led by Jarnail Singh Bhindranwale. In June Mrs. Gandhi ordered the army to occupy the Golden Temple, which was done at the cost of ninety soldiers dead and over 700 Sikhs, including Bhindranwale. This was followed by serious mutinies in crack Sikh regiments of the Indian Army.

Mrs. Gandhi's Assassination.

Mrs. Gandhi was assassinated on 31 October 1984 by two Sikh members of her bodyguard. Rioting followed as Hindu mobs took revenge on Sikhs and some 3,000 people died. Mrs Gandhi was succeeded as Prime Minister by her son, Rajiv. He continued with the planned elections in December 1984 and, in the aftermath of his mother's death, his party won 401 of the 508 seats in parliament. Rajiv Gandhi announced that he would embark on a programme of communal reconciliation and economic reform. Earlier in the month India had experienced one of the world's worst environmental disasters. On 3 December over forty tons of poisonous Methyl Isocyanate leaked from the Union Carbide pesticides factory at Bhopal, capital of Madhya Pradesh state. Some 2,500 people died and as many as 200,000 were injured.

Moves towards Reconciliation in 1985.

Outbreaks of violence led to the introduction in

May 1985 of the Terrorist and Disruptive Activities (Prevention) Bill. But Mr Gandhi remained faithful to the path of reconciliation rather than confrontation. In July he signed an accord with the president of the Sikh Akali Dal party, Sant Harchand Singh Longowal, affording greater political and religious autonomy to the Punjab. Sant Longowal was murdered by Sikh extremists in August, but new elections for the state assembly and representatives in the national parliament went ahead in September. The Akali Dal emerged victorious in both polls. Presidential rule in the Punjab, imposed in October 1983, was finally lifted on 29 September when Surjit Singh Barnala, leader of the Akali Dal, was sworn in as chief minister.

Turning to the problems of Assam, Mr. Gandhi announced an agreement in August regarding the protection of Assamese linguistic and cultural identity against the immigrants from Bangladesh. Illegal immigrants who entered Assam between January 1966 and March 1971 were to be disenfranchised for ten years, while any who had arrived after 1971 were to be expelled. The state assembly returned in the violently-disputed 1983 elections was dissolved and new elections were held in December 1985. These resulted in a win for the Asom Gana Parishad, a party formed only two months before by Assamese students.

Congress Party Problems.

Although opposition victories in the Punjab and Assam had promoted national reconciliation, they had left the Congress Party in a state of disarray. By the end of 1985 Mr Gandhi's party was out of power in nine out of the twenty-two states and union territories. In January 1986 he announced a thorough shake-up of the party's leadership in an effort to regain the ground lost to regional parties.

Despite the agreement of July 1985, unrest continued in the Punjab, particularly when Mrs Gandhi's three Sikh assassins were sentenced to death in January 1986. In addition, a border dispute led to delays in handing over Chandigarh, the capital city the Punjab shared with neighbouring Haryana, to the Sikh state, a measure which had formed part of the July 1985 accord. Young Sikh militants responded by taking over the Golden Temple in Amritsar, posing new problems for Mr. Gandhi and the chief minister, Surjit Barnala.

SRI LANKA.

Ceylon became a self-governing member of the British Commonwealth by the Ceylon Independence Act 1947, which came into force on 4 February 1948. A new constitution was adopted in 1972 and the country was renamed the Republic of Sri Lanka. In 1977 the National State Assembly approved a constitutional amendment introducing a presidential form of government and the Prime Minister, Junius Jayawardene, became the first Executive President on 4 February 1978. In presidential elections held on 20 October 1982 President Jayawardene was returned to office for a further six years. In November 1982 the Assembly, dominated by President Jayawardene's United National Party, voted to extend for a six-year period its term which would have expired in August 1983. This was approved by a national referendum on 20 December 1982.

Communal Violence after 1983.

There has been a long history of tension and outbreaks of violence between the majority Sinhalese Buddhist population and the Tamil Moslem minority. Parliamentary and local elections in May 1983 resulted in a landslide victory for the United National Party, but they were accompanied by bomb blasts attributed to separatist guerrillas, the Tamil Tigers. The deaths of 13 soldiers in a guerrilla ambush near Jaffna in July led to serious communal violence in the capital Colombo which spread rapidly. Some 20,000 Tamils were made homeless and many were evacuated from Colombo to the area of Jaffna where the main Tamil population is located. Over 400 people were killed in the rioting. A law was passed requiring all MPs to take an oath denouncing separatism, and the Tamil United Liberation Front boycotted the National Assembly in protest. In January 1984 President Jayawardene convened all-party "amity talks", which were attended by the Tamil United Liberation Front. However, the Tamil politicians could not accept less than regional autonomy, and so, in the absence of such a political settlement, violence continued during 1984. Guerrilla attacks provoked army reprisals which further alienated the Tamil population. Sri Lanka's relations with India were strained by accusations that the guerrillas were being trained in the southern Indian state of Tamil Nadu. In November the government announced a series of wide-ranging emergency regulations, including the formation of a prohibited zone on Sri Lanka's northern coast where all movement was to be strictly controlled.

Search for a Settlement.

Following talks in New Delhi between President Jayawardene and Rajiv Gandhi in June 1985, the Sri Lankan government announced a three-month cease-fire and in July began talks with Tamil separatists in the remote capital of Bhutan, Thimbu. However, the talks broke down in August when reports were received of new killings of Tamils in Sri Lanka. Guerrilla attacks on the security forces and Sinhalese civilians continued into 1986.

PAKISTAN.

After independence, Pakistan was beset by internal and external problems. India provided a constant external threat and there was resentment by East Pakistan of the political and economic domination by the western wing. Violent struggles resulted from the attempt to impose Urdu as the national language. Moreover, disunity among the western provinces provided continuing problems for the Government. Thirteen months after independence, Mohammed Ali Jinnah, Pakistan's leader died, and during the next decade there were many changes of government. The chaos was finally ended in October 1958 by a bloodless army coup resulting in the army dictatorship of General Ayub Khan. In 1960 he was formally elected President, and with the strong powers conferred on him by a new constitution in 1962 he instituted a series of reforms. After increasing opposition to Ayub Khan's leadership during the late 1960s, promises were made for a return to democracy. Elections were finally held in 1970 but not before the country had experienced martial law under General Yahya Khan who took over from Ayub Khan in March 1969.

Civil War.

As a result of the elections in December 1970, Sheikh Mujibur Rahman of the Awami League obtained a majority in the East and Mr. Bhutto of the People's Party triumphed in the west. Due to the greater population of the East, the Awami League commanded an overall majority, and insisted on a constitution which would give East Pakistan wide-ranging autonomy. Mr. Bhutto opposed this and Civil War erupted on 26 March 1971 following the outlawing of the Awami League and the declaration of E. Pakistan as the independent republic of Bangladesh. The opposition was quickly suppressed, but involved the loss of thousands of innocent lives and created a severe refugee problem as many fled to India. Widespread disease and the cyclone disaster of November 1970 threatened a major famine in E. Pakistan. Support for the Bangladesh guerrillas (Mukti Bahini) was provided by India and war broke out between India and Pakistan in late 1971 following Mrs. Gandhi's demand for the withdrawal of Pakistani troops from Bangladesh. Bitter fighting occurred in both E. and W. Pakistan which was ended by Yahya Khan's acceptance of India's unilateral offer of a cease-fire.

The Aftermath.

On 20 December 1971 President Yahya Khan resigned and was replaced by Mr. Bhutto who released Sheikh Mujibur Rahman the following January. At the same time Pakistan left the Commonwealth as other members were about to recognise Bangladesh. (In April 1972 Bangladesh was admitted in place of Pakistan.) Peace nego-

tiations with India were initiated to deal mainly with withdrawal from areas conquered in 1971 and the exchange of prisoners. The latter was only achieved after Pakistani recognition of Bangladesh. Diplomatic relations with India were finally re-established in May 1976. Internal problems within Pakistan arose with conflict in the provinces of Sindh and Baluchistan and have continued since then. Mr. Bhutto gradually introduced economic reform but throughout 1975 and 1976 unrest in the provinces and the outlawing of the Awami League led to approval of a declaration of a state of emergency. Elections were held in March 1977. Amid accusations of election malpractice, Mr. Bhutto claimed victory. Widespread unrest followed, with organised opposition to Mr. Bhutto being answered by the arrest of leading opposition politicians. Martial law was imposed in the major cities. The opposition Pakistani National Alliance continued to demand the resignation of Mr. Bhutto and the holding of new elections. Finally, agreement was reached on new elections to be held in October, though there was still disagreement on measures for ensuring fairness. But on 5 July the army under General Mohammed Zia ul-Haq took over power, and Mr. Bhutto and other leading politicians were arrested. The General declared that his only aim was the holding of free and fair elections. These were fixed for October, and the politicians were released at the end of July. However, the expected return to democracy did not materialise.

The Execution of Bhutto.

In March 1978 Mr. Bhutto was condemned to death for implication in the murder of a political opponent. He was eventually executed on 4 April 1979. For a short time General Zia pursued a policy of conciliation, but in October 1979 he cancelled elections planned for the following month and banned all political activities and strikes.

Opposition nevertheless continued during 1980 to his regime and in February 1981 nine political parties formed an alliance known as the Movement for the Restoration of Democracy which called for the holding of elections and the lifting of martial law. However, the movement collapsed after a Pakistani airliner was hijacked in March by members of an underground organisation headed by Murtaza Bhutto, son of the executed Prime Minister.

The Policy of Islamisation.

Public outrage gave General Zia the excuse for carrying out mass arrests of his opponents, including Mr Bhutto's wife and daughter. On 24 March he promulgated an interim constitution to remain in effect until martial law could be lifted. In 1982 General Zia continued his drive to make Islamisation reach every aspect of life in Pakistan and to foster national feeling by such measures as ordering the greater use of Urdu and national dress. In August 1983 President Zia announced his plan to hold elections in March 1985, but martial law would remain in force until then and only approved candidates would be allowed to stand. Proposed constitutional changes would also increase the powers of the President. The Movement for the Restoration of Democracy announced a campaign of civil disobedience, but dozens of its members were arrested in a pre-emptive move by the military government.

In December 1984, General Zia held a referendum on his policy of Islamisation. According to official figures 60% of the population voted and 98% of these approved the policy. General Zia declared that he was therefore endorsed as president for a further five years. Shortly before the elections the government imposed strict regulations on the press, forbidding publication of the views of the opposition who were in any case barred from competing.

Elections were held at the end of February 1985. Although they were boycotted by the Movement for the Restoration of Democracy, a turnout of 53 per cent was reported. The People's Party, formerly led by Mr Bhutto, was the largest group in the new National Assembly, and five of the nine federal ministers who stood for election were defeated. Shortly after the elections, however, General Zia announced wide-ranging constitutional amendments reducing the authority of the Prime Minister and increasing his own. In March 1985 the suspended 1973 constitution was restored and the new parliament assembled.

The End of Martial Law.

General Zia announced that he was lifting martial law on 30 December 1985. Military courts were abolished and trials transferred to civilian courts, though not before many pending cases had been rushed through in December. The response of the opposition was sceptical, particularly as General Zia retained the power of veto over political parties, which have to apply for registration and submit their political programmes to an Election Commission in order to be legalised.

AFGHANISTAN.

The last King of Afghanistan, Zahir Shah, was deposed in a coup on 17 July 1973. A republic was created with General Muhammad Daud as President. A new constitution was approved by a special National Assembly in February 1977 and Daud was elected President for a six-year term. However, he began to crack down on his opponents and in April 1978 there were massive demonstrations in the capital, Kabul, after the death of the left-wing leader Mir Ali Khaibar. On 27 April a military coup took place, in which Daud and his family were killed.

The leaders of the People's Democratic Party of Afghanistan (PDPA) were released from prison and put in power by the military. The head of the PDPA, Nur Muhammad Taraki, became President of the Revolutionary Council and Prime Minister. The PDPA introduced major land reforms, but encountered opposition from tribal and religious groups. A power-struggle developed within the PDPA between the Khalq and Parcham factions. The government looked increasingly to the USSR for aid, and in November 1978 a new Afghan–Russian Treaty of Friendship and Co-operation was signed.

In September 1979 Taraki was ousted by Hafizullah Amin, but on 27 December 1979 Soviet forces invaded Afghanistan and installed a new regime under Babrak Karmal. The USSR justified the invasion on the grounds that it was at the invitation of the Afghan government to prevent interference by outside powers, but on 14 January 1980 an emergency session of the UN General Assembly called for a Russian withdrawal.

A campaign against the Russian occupying forces and the Afghan army has been waged by the Mujaheddin guerrillas since the invasion. Although President Karmal attempted to conciliate opposition groups, his regime has failed to win the support of the mass of the people on whom the guerrillas depend. It has also failed to achieve international recognition. The United Nations has been working for an agreement involving the withdrawal of Russian troops, to which Pakistan and Iran would be parties. In June 1982 peace negotiations began at Geneva in which the UN representative, Diego Cordovez, acted as intermediary between the Afghan and Pakistani foreign ministers. The UN-sponsored talks continued in 1985, but no solution was found to the problems created by the Russian invasion, including the presence of over four million Afghan refugees in Pakistan and Iran. At the start of 1986 there were still some 100,000 Soviet troops in Afghanistan, at least 9,000 having already died there. In October 1985 the American Congress had approved 300 million dollars of clandestine military aid to the Mujaheddin guerrillas over the next two years.

BANGLADESH.

After the release of Sheikh Mujibur Rahman in 1972, plans were announced to make Bangladesh a parliamentary democracy and to carry out large-scale nationalisation. In March 1973 the Awami League won all but 7 seats in the general elections. However, rising food prices, corruption among leading members of the Awami League and national disasters created widespread unrest. In 1975 a state of emergency was declared, fundamental civil rights were suspended and the parliamentary government was replaced by a presidential one party system under President Mujib. A series of radical reforms ensued causing resentment and opposition particularly from the army and in August 1975 the President and his family were

killed in a military coup. After further coups power passed to the hands of President Sayem and the chiefs of the armed services. Although steps were taken to restore normal conditions to Bangladesh and the ban on political parties was lifted in August 1976, the general elections planned for 1977 were later postponed indefinitely. In April 1977 President Sayem designated Major-General Zia ur-Rahman, the Chief Martial Law Administrator, as his successor and himself resigned. The latter released political prisoners and announced general elections for December 1978. Islam was officially made a basic principle of the state. On 30 May President Zia ur-Rahman's position was confirmed by referendum. An attempted coup in October 1977 led to the banning of several political parties and the founding of a new government-sponsored National Democratic Party. In presidential elections held in June 1978 General Zia ur-Rahman was overwhelmingly successful, reaping the benefits of his achievements in restoring order, eliminating corruption and safeguarding food supplies. He formed a new cabinet with representatives of the parties which had supported him.

The 1979 Elections.

In late 1978 the removal of most restrictions on political parties was followed by an announcement by the President that all "undemocratic provisions" of the 1975 constitutional amendment establishing presidential government had been repealed. The new Parliament was to be a sovereign body; a Prime Minister was to be appointed who commanded its confidence; and there was to be no Presidential power to veto legislation. When elections were finally held in February 1979 the Bangladesh Nationalist Party, uniting the supporters of President Zia, won a massive victory, mainly because the opposition parties were divided among themselves. President Zia then lifted martial law.

Assassination of President Zia, 1981.

President Zia was assassinated at Chittagong on 30 May 1981 during a military insurrection allegedly led by Major-General Manzur who was himself killed as the coup collapsed on 1 June. Vice-President Abdus Sattar took over as President. However, in March 1982 the army chief, Lt.-Gen. Hossain Mohammed Ershad seized power in a bloodless coup. He said that the army had taken over to save the country from social, economic and political bankruptcy. Lt.-Gen. Ershad consolidated his position during the remainder of 1982.

At the beginning of November 1983 a general strike and protest marches took place in defiance of martial law. Shortly before the arrival of Queen Elizabeth II on a state visit to Bangladesh on 14 November, Lt-Gen. Ershad announced that presidential elections would be held in May 1984 and parliamentary elections in November; free political activity would be permitted immediately. However, the two opposition alliances demanded that the parliamentary elections should be held first. When violence broke out, Lt-Gen. Ershad reimposed the ban on political activity on 28 November.

Ershad as President.

In December he announced that he was assuming the presidency. The elections were again postponed for the duration of 1984 and set instead for April 1985. The opposition alliances feared that the elections would be rigged in favour of General Ershad's Jatiya Party, and called for the lifting of martial law and the formation of a caretaker government before they took place. In December 1984 they launched a full-scale civil disobedience campaign to back these demands.

General Ershad responded by reimposing martial law early in March 1985 and cancelling the planned elections. Instead in late March a referendum was held which was claimed to have given General Ershad's rule an overwhelming vote of confidence. Rural sub-district elections went ahead in May despite a boycott organised by the main opposition parties. The universities, which had been shut down in March, were allowed to re-open in July, and in October the ban on political activity was partially lifted. Political parties were permitted to re-open their offices, but street demonstrations remained illegal.

The long-awaited parliamentary elections were held in May 1986, amid widespread violence and accusations of vote-rigging. The outcome was a comfortable majority for the pro-government Jatiya Party, whilst the leader of the opposition Awami League, Sheikh Hasina Wajed, denounced the elections as a fraud.

THE FAR EAST

CHINA.

Note

In 1979 China adopted a new phonetic alphabet for the spelling of Chinese names in foreign language publications, e.g., Hua Guofeng for Hua Kuo-feng, Deng Xiaoping for Teng Hsiao-ping.

Introduction.

On 1 October 1949, after the Communists had gained complete control of the Chinese mainland and the Nationalist forces of Chiang Kai-shek had retreated to Taiwan, the Chinese People's Republic was proclaimed under Chairman Mao Tse-tung. It claims sovereignty over one fifth of mankind, with a population of over 1,000 million (1984 est.).

The Cultural Revolution.

In 1966 Mao instigated China's remarkable "Cultural Revolution." Huge crowds of young people with red armbands thronged the streets in general excitement. Red Guards took a prominent part. A little 300-page book of Mao's selected writings, in a red plastic cover, was carried by almost everyone and universally quoted, discussed, and preached. The revolution must be uninterrupted; the class struggle continued. This revolution emphasised rejection both of western capitalist technological society exemplified by Japan, and of "revisionism" leading to "bourgeois decay" as, it was claimed, had happened to Russia. But it developed into violent struggles between revolutionaries and reactionaries and then between the revolutionaries themselves. The Prime Minister, Chou En-lai, warned that industrial production was being seriously affected. The situation remained very confused until 1968 when there was a gradual return to moderation.

The end of the Cultural Revolution was marked formally by the Ninth Congress of the Chinese Communist Party, which took place in Peking during April 1969 in conditions of great secrecy. The following years were devoted to restoring normal conditions.

Internal Political Developments.

In 1969 Defence Minister Marshal Lin Piao was formally named as Mao's successor. However, he was subsequently discredited and died in a plane crash in 1972 while trying to escape to the Soviet Union. Campaigns against Lin Piao and the philosopher Confucius began just before the Tenth Party Congress in 1973 and local political and military leaders were condemned. The Congress produced the election of 5 vice-chairmen by the Central Committee, whereas Lin Piao alone had been elected in 1969. Deng Xiaoping increasingly took over public duties from the ailing Chou En-lai. In January 1975 the National People's Congress adopted a new constitution which emphasised the role of the Communist Party and, among other things, abolished the office of President of the Republic. Command of the armed forces was transferred to the party chairman and the president's other prerogatives to the standing committee of the National People's Congress. Chou En-lai was appointed head of the new State Council, but in January 1976 he died.

He was succeeded by Hua Guofeng and not Deng Xiaoping as had been expected. It was suggested that Hua (later appointed by the Politburo to the Vice-Chairmanship of the Party in April 1970) was chosen as a compromise between the moderates and the radicals led by Zhang Chungqiao and Jiang Qing (Mao's wife), on a question of priorities. The latter stressed ideological purity and permanent revolution at the expense of internal development, while the moderates aimed at political advancement through economic progress.

China after Mao.

On 9 September 1976 after leading China since 1949, Chairman Mao died at the age of 82. He was succeeded by Hua Guofeng, who before he replaced Chou En-lai had been a security minister for one year and had previously only been known as an agricultural specialist in the southern province of Hunan. In the months after Mao's death, a vicious poster campaign was mounted against Jiang Qing (Mao's widow) and three others, Wang Hongwen, Zhang Chungqiao and Yao Wenyuan—known as the "gang of four". All four were arrested and the allegations against them included their planning to persuade the armed militia to take over the army and causing unrest by their backing of the Shanghai radicals.

Hua's colleagues were close associates of Chou En-lai and he appeared to have the support of the army. During 1977 Deng Xiaoping, who had been dismissed from his government and party posts in April 1976, was fully rehabilitated. Meanwhile, after a series of national conferences of practically all branches of the economy, new guidelines for a more pragmatic economic policy were worked out on the lines of Chou En-lai's basic programmes as previously pursued by Deng Xiaoping.

China's Change of Course.

China's change of course internally and externally was confirmed in 1978. While the Russians were still regarded as the main enemy, partly from a historically-based nationalist hostility, reconciliation was pursued with the West. This culminated in the establishment of diplomatic relations with the USA in December. China was clearly opening up to the world in search of the benefits of modernisation and looking especially to collaboration with Western Europe. At the same time internal liberalisation brought a new emphasis on democracy and equality before the law. Henceforth the courts were to decide without interference from the Party and the State, while the people's communes in the country, the managers of industrial plants, workers and peasants were to be freed from central tutelage. All this was intended to release new energies for the new modernisation programme masterminded by Deng Xiaoping, which aims to turn China from a developing country into a leading industrial nation by the end of the century. But it was not clear how the new developments were to be kept in line with the dictatorship of the proletariat and a communist-planned economy. Demonstrations for more freedom and civil rights seemed to provide a foretaste of future problems at the beginning of 1979, and later there were riots by young people in Shanghai. The result was an abrupt end to the freedom of expression at the Wall of Democracy in Peking, which had been tolerated only so long as it did not question the system itself. This was accompanied by a dampening of the initial eupho-ria of economic reform and industrialisation plans. China appeared to have suffered economically more than had been assumed from the periods of chaos under Mao. The latter's teaching was no longer treated as sacred, and on the 30th anniversary of the foundation of the People's Republic the Cultural Revolution was denounced as a dreadful disaster.

Meanwhile, the limits of Chinese foreign policy were also becoming evident. The punitive expedition launched against Vietnam in early 1979 did not succeed in removing Vietnamese pressure from Cambodia. The propaganda attacks on the Soviet Union were reduced and the first serious talks on détente took place. But these did not get very far, and China's links with the West remained more important, as was shown by the visits of Deng Xiaoping to the USA and Hua Guofeng to Western Europe in the autumn. The Soviet invasion of Afghanistan at the end of 1979 brought increased co-operation between China and the United States.

The Trial of the "Gang of Four".

China's change of course and Deng Xiaoping's rise culminated in 1980 with two events. The first of these was the Fifth Plenary Session of the Communist Party Central Committee in February. Some of Deng's leading opponents were removed while his supporters were promoted. The rehabilitation of Liu

Shaoqi, the most prominent victim of the Cultural Revolution, was a further denunciation of that phenomenon.

The show trial of Jiang Qing and the other members of the "gang of four" led to the passing of a suspended death sentence on Mao's widow in January 1981. This was commuted to life imprisonment in January 1983. Although the official Chinese press said that this should not be taken as implicit condemnation of her late husband, in June 1981 Hu Yaobang succeeded Hua Guofeng as Communist Party Chairman marking a further shift away from Mao's policies.

In external affairs, China's relations with America and the West grew firmer, as did they also with Japan.

New Party and State Constitutions, 1982.

In September 1982 a new constitution for the Communist Party was approved. This abolished the posts of Chairman and Vice-Chairman in a move to transfer power back to the party bureaucracy. Hu Yaobang had held the post of general-secretary, as well as that of Chairman, so retained his leading position, and it remained to be seen how far a more collective form of leadership would emerge. In December 1982 a new constitution for China as a whole was approved by the National People's Congress, which included increased powers for the Prime Minister, Zhao Ziyang.

Deng Xiaoping's Policies.

In June 1983 the National People's Congress met and elected the veteran politician Li Xiannian to the newly-revived post of President, with General Ulanhu as Vice-President. Deng Xiaoping was chosen as chairman of the new State Military Commission. He already headed the Communist Party's committee in charge of military affairs and therefore had both party and state control of the army in his own hands to ensure that expenditure on national defence would be kept in check.

China's Modernisation Drive.

Deng Xiaoping's national drive towards modernisation continued during 1984, despite opposition from some die-hard Maoists. In the countryside the emphasis on the collective was reversed, with the relaxation of production quotas and central price controls leading to a considerable rise in agricultural production. In industry, factories were allowed to keep their own profits and managers to exercise greater responsibility. The armed forces were also urged to support modernisation, including the opening of more ports to foreign business and investment. In May 1984 Prime Minister Zhao Ziyang undertook a six-country tour of western Europe intended to secure additional sources for new technology.

Slowing down of Reform.

The modernisation programme and reforms in the Communist Party continued in 1985. The 'rectification campaign' against corrupt officials, launched in 1983, proceeded, and it was announced in November that party members in the countryside were to have their credentials re-examined in order to root out any remaining Maoist tendencies. Younger men were introduced into the upper echelons of the party; for example, at a meeting of the Communist Party Central Committee in September 1985 ten members of the politburo were retired.

There was, however, a greater degree of caution about Deng Xiaoping's modernisation policies. In July 1985 the leadership launched a campaign to reassert party control and the number of cities open to foreign investment was greatly reduced. The five-year plan published in September announced that, although the reduction in state control of production would continue, the pace of reform would be slowed down to curb the consumer boom. It promised a better standard of living, but higher rents and fuel and shopping bills.

HONG KONG.

Historical Background.

Hong Kong was first occupied by the British as a trading post in January 1841 and China's cession of

the island to Britain was confirmed by the Treaty of Nanking in 1842. South Kowloon and Stonecutters Island were ceded by China in the Treaty of Peking in 1860, and in 1898 the New Territories, which consist of the area north of Kowloon and other islands around Hong Kong, were leased to Britain for 99 years. Hong Kong was occupied by the Japanese from 1941 to 1945. The approaching expiry of the lease on the New Territories led to the initiation of diplomatic discussions between Britain and China on the future of Hong Kong in 1979 with a visit by Sir Murray MacLehose, governor of Hong Kong, to Peking. Mrs. Thatcher herself visited Peking in 1982. Britain had initially taken the line that the 19th century "unequal treaties", as the Chinese termed them, were not invalid, but it was forced to concede that sovereignty over Hong Kong would have to be surrendered.

The 1984 Agreement.

A new phase in the negotiations began in July 1983 and by December Britain had also given up its proposal for retaining an administrative role in Hong Kong after 1997. Deng Xiaoping insisted that an agreement should be reached by September 1984, and on 26 September the Sino-British declaration on the future of Hong Kong was initialled in Peking. China will resume the exercise of sovereignty from 1 July 1997. Except in foreign and defence affairs, however, the Hong Kong Special Administrative Region will have a considerable degree of autonomy, and for at least fifty years the social and economic system and "life-style" of Hong Kong will remain unchanged.

The New Legislative Council.

In 1985 the British colonial administration began to give way to a form of representative government. In September indirect elections were held for 24 seats to represent professionals, local councils and special interest groups on the new 56-seat Legislative Council. The remaining seats were filled by government officials and appointees. The first session of the Council was held at the end of October.

The Chinese National People's Congress formally approved the 1984 agreement on the future of Hong Kong in April 1985, but the Chinese government was unhappy about the introduction of democracy into the colony. China stressed that in 1997 sovereignty passes to her and not to the people of Hong Kong, whose form of government would finally be decided by Peking. In December 1985 a senior Chinese official, Mr Ji Pengfei, visited Hong Kong but pointedly did not formally meet the Legislative Council.

JAPAN.

Japan and the World.

By the peace treaty of 1951 Japan had given up her claims to her former colonies of Korea and Formosa, to the Kurile Islands (which went to the USSR), and to the Pacific islands mandated to it by the League of Nations. Okinawa and the neighbouring islands, which had been administered as integral parts of Japan, were taken over by the United States, though recognising Japan's residual sovereignty. In the 1960s Japan pressed for restoration, but the Americans regarded Okinawa as too important for their defence commitments. Finally, however, a treaty was signed in June 1971 providing for the return of Okinawa and the other Ryukyu Islands in 1972, with the retention of the use of some bases by US forces.

Japan's close ties with the United States made it difficult to achieve better relations with the Soviet Union and Communist China. However in the wake of President Nixon's initiatives in 1972 a new Prime Minister, Mr. Tanaka, was able to make a historic visit to Peking and to achieve a rapprochement with the Soviet Union as well, though the problem of the Kurile Islands delayed the conclusion of a peace treaty.

Internal Problems.

In 1969 Japan experienced the world-wide phenomenon of left-wing student demonstrations in a particularly violent form. They were directed especially against the United States.

Elections were held for the Lower House of the Diet in December 1972, soon after Mr. Tanaka had succeeded Mr. Sato as Prime Minister. The premature dissolution was probably prompted by the success of Mr. Tanaka's overtures to China and his desire for a mandate for his plan to overcome overcrowding and pollution by spreading industry and the population more evenly throughout the country by the building of modest new cities in less developed areas. The main opposition parties were the Japan Socialist Party (JSP), the Democratic Socialist Party (an offshoot from the JSP), the Japan Communist Party and Komeito ("Clean Government Party"). The JSP and the Communists strongly attacked increasing defence expenditure and the mutual security treaty with the USA; all called for greater emphasis on welfare policies. In the event Mr. Tanaka's Liberal Democratic Party, which had had 25 years of uninterrupted power, retained a large overall majority with 271 of the 491 seats. But significant gains were made by the left-wing parties, JSP increasing its share from 87 to 118 and the Communists from 14 to 38.

Tanaka's government lasted only two years. Increasing economic difficulties and allegations of personal misconduct eventually resulted in a loss of support, and he resigned in December 1974 to be succeeded by Mr. Takeo Miki. The eruption in February 1976 of a scandal involving senior politicians, concerning massive bribes accepted from the Lockheed Aircraft Corporation of America, and the subsequent arrest of Tanaka, the former Prime Minister, had a serious effect on the political situation. There was a split in the Liberal-Democratic Party and by September Miki was under pressure to resign. A cabinet reshuffle failed to solve the crisis. In December the results of the general election, in which the Liberal-Democrat majority was substantially reduced, finally forced Miki to resign, and he was replaced Mr. Takeo Fukuda.

The conclusion of a treaty of peace and friendship with China was achieved in 1978 in the face of massive Soviet pressure. Despite this success, Fukuda remained a luckless and unpopular Prime Minister. In November 1978 he was clearly defeated in the primary election for the leadership of the Liberal-Democratic Party by its General Secretary, Masayoshi Ohira. The latter was very much more a "man of the people" like Tanaka, and he was supported by the Tanaka faction. But he did not bring major policy changes. One of his Government's major preoccupations was that as an importer of almost all its energy requirements Japan was very hard hit by the oil crisis.

In October 1979 elections to the Lower House of the Diet brought a totally unexpected reverse for the ruling LDP, which won only 248 of the 511 seats. Mr. Ohira was re-elected head of government with a narrow majority over his predecessor Fukuda, but the period of his minority government was marked by feuding within the LDP, and also by further scandals, this time when the Director-General of the Defence Agency, Mr. Kubota, was forced to resign in February 1980 after the uncovering of a major espionage affair.

The June 1980 Election.

This state of affairs continued until, on 16 May 1980, the first successful no confidence motion since 1953 was carried against the government. The general election was scheduled for 22 June, but Mr. Ohira died on 12 June and the campaign was seriously affected. However, the LDP was able to regain its majority in both Houses, winning 284 of the 511 seats in the Lower House.

Mr. Ohira's successor was Mr. Zenko Suzuki, who formed a government on 17 July. Mr. Suzuki's government included representatives of all the rival factions in the LDP, and it was hoped that they would unite in a programme of consensus and compromise. Although one of the major aims was to establish closer trading links with China, many of the contracts agreed in 1978 were suspended following the change in emphasis in Chinese economic policy away from steel and other heavy industrial production.

Mr. Suzuki Steps Down.

Despite the hopes for unity, growing discord in the LDP over economic policies led Mr. Suzuki to announce on 12 October 1982 that he would not seek re-election when his two-year term of office ended.

On 24 November Mr. Yasuhiro Nakasone was elected President of the LDP and confirmed as Prime Minister by the Upper and Lower Houses two days later. Mr. Nakasone announced that his government would give priority to improving trade and security relations with the United States, but a visit to America by the Prime Minister in January 1983 showed that the two countries were still some way from an agreement on American exports to Japan.

The December 1983 Election.

On 12 October 1983 the former Prime Minister, Mr. Tanaka, was sentenced to four years in prison for taking bribes to help the sales of the Lockheed Aircraft Corporation. He was released on bail and refused to resign his parliamentary seat. The issue of political morality therefore dominated the general election called by Mr. Nakasone for 18 December 1983. The LDP failed to gain an overall majority, winning only 250 seats, and now had to rely on the votes of one of the independent parties. Mr. Tanaka regained his seat with an increased majority and his faction comprised about a quarter of the LDP's parliamentary strength. Although Mr. Tanaka had proved an electoral handicap to the LDP, Mr. Nakasone was therefore dependent on his support.

KOREA.

In 1945 Japanese rule in Korea came to an end after 36 years when the Russians occupied the northern part of the country and the Americans the south. It was planned that the country should be reunified after free elections, but in practice rival governments were set up. The Korean War broke out in 1950, when Communist North Korea, under Kim Il-sung, invaded the South with Chinese support in an attempt to unify the country by force. South Korea was supported by a United Nations Force in what was really an American "containment" operation. In 1953 an armistice was signed and the demarcation line between North and South Korea was agreed.

In 1960 student demonstrations in the capital, Seoul, forced the resignation of the authoritarian South Korean President, Syngman Rhee. The following year Park Chung-hee took over as President after a military coup. South Korea now experienced a period of rapid growth making it one of the greatest economic success stories among developing countries. But the threat from North Korea remained, and was illustrated in 1968 when a North Korean assassination squad penetrated to within a mile of the Presidential palace.

Political Repression.

The 1970s saw increasing political repression in South Korea. After President Park had narrowly defeated an Opposition rival in the 1971 elections, the authoritarian Yushin Constitution was introduced. This approved a procedure for election of the President by electoral college in place of direct elections and established a system whereby one-third of the seats in the National Assembly were reserved for Government nominees. This new constitution provoked bitter opposition, which in turn gave rise to further repression. Martial law was declared in 1972, and in 1974 an emergency decree was passed banning all dissident movements. The following year the notorious "Emergency Measure No. 9" prohibited public criticism of the constitution and the Government. This followed an assassination attempt on the President, in which his wife was killed, and the discovery of the first of a series of North Korean tunnels under the Demilitarised Zone.

President Carter took office in 1977 committed to a substantial reduction of US forces in Korea. Relations with the United States were further soured by the "Koreagate" scandal, in which it was revealed that South Korean agents had paid substantial sums to American Congressmen in return for political support. However, after a reassessment of the build-up of North Korean military strength the phased withdrawal of US troops was frozen in 1978. When he visited Seoul in the summer of 1979 President Carter publicly criticised the repression practised by President Park's regime but reconfirmed the American commitment to maintain South Korea's integrity.

Although President Park was re-elected for another six-year term by electoral college in 1978, the elections to the National Assembly in December of that year brought severe losses for the pro-Government Democratic Republican Party and corresponding gains for the opposition New Democratic Party and independents. The following spring the newly-elected leader of the New Democrats, Kim Young-sam, began to make public demands for constitutional reform. The Government reacted by procuring a court decision declaring Mr Kim's election as leader of the New Democratic Party invalid, and in early October 1979 he was expelled from the National Assembly on nine charges of damaging the national interest. The result was dramatic. The members of the New Democratic Party resigned en masse from the Assembly and serious rioting broke out in Pusan.

The Assassination of President Park.

It was against this background that President Park Chung-hee was assassinated in late October 1979. It was believed that his murder might have resulted from a dispute between the different security services about responsibility for the breakdown of internal security. But few believed the offical version that the assassin, Kim Jae-kyu, and his five fellow-conspirators had acted on their own initiative. The General Chief of Staff was suspected of being implicated, but this could not be proved, and the military initially remained in the background. Under the new President, Choi Kyu-hah, there was an initial period of liberalisation with the release of political prisoners. In December, however, the military hawks and the supporters of ex-President Park seemed to gain the upper hand, and the style of government became more authoritarian.

The Imposition of Martial Law.

Then on 17 May 1980, following widespread civil unrest, martial law was extended throughout South Korea, with many political leaders being arrested and all political activity being banned. This led to a popular uprising in the Kwangju district which was violently suppressed by the Army, and on 31 May a Special Committee for National Security Measures was set up. This committee was controlled by the army and it carried out a massive political purge, which included the resignation of President Choi Kyu Hah on 16 August, who was succeeded by the Head of the Army Security Command, General Chun Doo Hwan on 27 August.

The problems in South Korea were intimately bound up with the country's grave economic position, but they were also exacerbated by the heavy-handedness of the military. This was shown not only in their suppression of the Kwangju uprising, but also in the execution of Kim Jae Kyu and the others who assassinated President Park, in secret on 24 May, and also the sentencing to death of the leading dissident Kim Dae Jung on 17 September, which brought the South Korean authorities into conflict with both the Carter Administration and the Japanese government. The sentence was later commuted. President Chun was re-elected for a seven-year term in February 1981 by a popularly-elected electoral college. His Democratic Justice Party gained a majority in the National Assembly after elections in March.

International Disasters.

In 1983 South Korea was involved in two serious international incidents. On 1 September a South Korean Boeing 747 civil airliner on a flight from New York to Seoul was shot down over Soviet airspace by a Russian fighter. The 240 passengers and 29 crew on board were killed. After some delay, the Soviet Union admitted responsibility but claimed that the plane was spying. Then on 9 October 21 people, including 4 Korean cabinet ministers, were killed in a bomb explosion in Rangoon, Burma. It was alleged that North Korean agents had intended to assassinate President Chun but the bomb had exploded prematurely before he arrived at the Martyr's Mausoleum.

The 1985 Elections.

There was an 84% turnout of voters in the elec-

tions held in February 1985. President Chun's ruling Democratic Justice Party maintained its position with 148 seats in the National Assembly, but the moderate opposition group, the Democratic Korea Party, gained only 35 seats, compared with 83 in 1981. It was supplanted by the newly-formed, more radical New Korea Democratic Party (NKDP), sponsored by the main opposition leader, Kim Dae Jung, and his Movement for the Restoration of Democracy. Kim Dae Jung returned from exile in the United States five days before the elections, though he was immediately placed under house-arrest. The NKDP won 67 seats, doing particularly well in the cities. The elections improved the international respectability of President Chun's regime abroad, but at home it showed that, despite considerable economic progress, the country was looking for more genuine democracy in its system of government. Nevertheless, in the autumn of 1985 it seemed that President Chun was again cracking down on the opposition, particularly on student dissent.

VIETNAM.

When Japan collapsed in 1945, the only organised troops in Vietnam were controlled by Ho Chi-minh, a Communist, who set up a Democratic Republic in the northern part of Vietnam. France was bent upon restoring her colonial empire in the south and the next year war broke out between the French and Ho Chi-minh, culminating in the dramatic siege and capture by Ho's forces of the fort of Dien Bien Phu in 1954. As a result of a 14-nation conference on Indo-China at Geneva in the same year Vietnam was partitioned after a cease-fire, the country to be united after free elections. Laos and Cambodia became independent.

Unfortunately the United States refused to sign the agreement and South Vietnam refused to hold elections, but both affirmed that they would not use force to upset the agreement. There was thus a crystallisation into two Vietnams—Ho Chi-minh's Hanoi régime in the North and that of the Catholic nationalist Ngo Dinh Diem at Saigon in the South. By 1960 the Communist guerrillas in the South, known as the Vietcong, had set up a National Liberation Front. For eight or nine years a civil war was waged in South Vietnam against a very unpopular dictatorship. All that time it received United States miltary support while the North helped the rebels in the South. The position became increasingly untenable, and in 1963 the Buddhists rioted against the ruling Roman Catholic minority. The Diem régime which had savagely persecuted the Buddhists was overthrown by the military. In August 1964 two vessels of the US fleet were alleged to have been attacked in the Gulf of Tonking (off the North Vietnam coast) and American planes bombed North Vietnam installations as retaliation. This was the first of a series of bombing raids. In June 1965 the State Department gave authority to the American military commander to use troops in offensive operations against the Vietcong.

After being advised by his officials that a military solution was impossible and that the only possible political solution was a negotiated settlement, President Johnson in March 1968 announced his partial bombing pause. Peace talks began in Paris in May, and by January 1969 the US, South Vietnam, North Vietnam, and the National Liberation Front (NLF) were sitting round a table. But little progress was made. In September Ho Chi-minh died after 24 years in power. His special achievement was the welding together of the two elements of nationalism and communism in Vietnam.

Growing opposition and disillusionment at home with the American role in the war, and the advent of Mr Nixon to the Presidency brought an increased determination to reduce and eventually end the US military commitment in S.E. Asia. To this end a programme of "Vietnamisation" was launched by which the South Vietnamese were given the means to take on progressively a greater share of the burden.

On 26 January 1972 President Nixon revealed 2½ years of secret negotiations with the North Vietnamese and American concessions. He made a new 8-point peace offer which proposed total withdrawal of troops, simultaneous release of prisoners and neutrally organised elections in S. Vietnam. The plan was flatly rejected by N. Vietnam, mainly because it failed to provide for the discarding of President Thieu.

North Vietnamese Offensive 1972.

On 30 March the North Vietnamese began a new offensive in which for the first time North Vietnamese forces fought conventionally in South Vietnam. They succeeded in taking the provincial capital Quang Tri and endangered the former imperial capital of Hué. The United States replied with ever heavier bombing of targets in N. Vietnam, supply routes and North Vietnamese units in the Demilitarised Zone and S. Vietnam. In May President Nixon announced the mining of Haiphong and other North Vietnamese ports. This brought a sharp denuciation by the Soviet Union (and China).

Negotiations and Truce.

During the summer of 1972 the N. Vietnamese offensive failed: no major towns fell and the morale of the S. Vietnamese army held. This, combined with devastating American bombing, produced a more accommodating attitude from the Vietcong and the N. Vietnamese negotiators after many fruitless meetings between President Nixon's special adviser, Dr Kissinger, and the leader of the N. Vietnamese delegation at the Paris peace talks, Le Duc Tho.

Despite set-backs, the negotiations did at last lead to the signature of a cease-fire agreement on 27 January 1973. By its terms US forces were to leave Vietnam within 60 days and there would be an exchange of prisoners of war. Vietnamese forces on both sides were to remain within their present territory. An international commission would supervise the observance of the agreement. Only vague outlines of a political settlement were included: principles for the reunification and neutrality of North and South and provisions for the people of S. Vietnam to exercise self-determination in supervised elections. The most serious omissions were its failure to mention any withdrawal of the N. Vietnamese forces in S. Vietnam, or even to define what territory was controlled by whom, and the fact that it applied only to S. Vietnam, not to Cambodia or Laos. But President Nixon claimed "peace with honour" and promised S. Vietnam continued support.

Both Vietnamese governments claimed the agreement as a victory. President Thieu gave up his objectives and expressed satisfaction that Hanoi had been forced to recognise North and South Vietnam as two independent sovereign states. But he warned that the political struggle ahead could be even more dangerous than the war.

Vietnam was now a totally devastated country. The military casualties amounted to about 1,100,000 dead Vietnamese (and an unknown number of civilians) and 46,000 Americans. The United States had poured some $120 billion into Indo-China and suffered immense damage to its international authority. Yet the basic issue of the war remained unsettled: who had the right to govern S. Vietnam?

Neither War nor Peace.

March 1973 marked the end of an era of US military presence in Vietnam. Soon Saigon was alleging large-scale infiltration of troops and munitions into S. Vietnam. The attempts of the International Commission of Control and Supervision to enforce the cease-fire were proving largely ineffective. Talks between the S. Vietnamese Government and the Provisional Revolutionary Government on a political settlement remained fruitless: President Thieu would have no truck with anything approaching coalition government, and the Communists therefore refused to agree to elections. Then in January 1974 the increasingly offensive role of the Communist forces prompted President Thieu to put his troops on a war footing again.

Communist Victory.

In March and April 1975 as a result of increasing Vietcong pressure, South Vietnamese forces were withdrawn from the Central Highlands in order to strengthen the defence of more strategic towns. After the decisive battle of Xuan Loc in April 1975 and with Saigon encircled, President Thieu resigned. By the beginning of May the Communists had triumphed. During the latter half of 1975 an estimated 230,000 refugees left S. Vietnam. On 21 January 1976 the Military Management Committee handed over government to the People's Revolutionary Committee. Following the elections in April of a National Assembly for all Vietnam, the reunification of the country was proclaimed for the first time since 1859. A government for the Socialist Republic of Vietnam was formed by Mr Phan van Dong.

During 1978 relations with China steadily worsened owing to discrimination against the Chinese in Vietnam and the expulsion or flight of large numbers of them to China. This, combined with territorial disputes, led to border clashes. In these circumstances the Vietnamese signature of a treaty of friendship with the Soviet Union in November was particularly significant. Meanwhile many ships overladen with Vietnamese refugees tried to land in Malaysia, Hong Kong and elsewhere, often without success. The plight of these "Boat People" gave rise to international humanitarian action to save the lives of as many as possible; it also brought a worldwide loss of prestige for the Vietnamese Government. This and the serious economic situation induced Hanoi in 1979 to mitigate its clumsy integration policies in South Vietnam and abate its campaign against private trade.

The China-Vietnam Conflict.

Vietnam was punished for its military interference in Cambodia by China, whose army launched an invasion across the frontier in February 1979. Bitter fighting took place, with Chinese forces penetrating several miles across the border. Both sides suffered heavy casualties and the Chinese withdrew their forces in March. The Soviet Union stepped up its military and economic aid to Vietnam, which found itself bogged down in a familiar war of attrition in Kampuchea. Conflict on the border with China, including heavy bouts of shelling, continued during 1984 and early 1985.

LAOS.

The war in Laos officially ended on 21 February 1973 with a standstill cease-fire agreement (leaving the Pathet Lao in control of two-thirds of the country). The formation of a coalition government was agreed after some US pressure on the rightists in the Vientiane Government.

In May 1975 after local fighting and left-wing demonstrations in Vientiane the right-wing ministers resigned and fled. Army units mutinied against right-wing officers and southern Laos was occupied by Pathet Lao forces. The American protégé Souvanna Phouma remained at the head of the coalition government until December when his half-brother Prince Souphanouvong proclaimed a People's Democratic Republic with a government headed by Mr Kaysone Phomvihan. Since 1975 the government has given Laos a much-needed period of peace and brought a degree of unity to this mountainous, ethnically-diverse country.

KAMPUCHEA (CAMBODIA).

In Cambodia President Lon Nol proclaimed a state of emergency in March 1973: Prince Sihanouk's predominantly Communist forces had virtually cut off all supply routes to the capital Phnom Penh. The Republican Government was saved only by greatly intensified US bombing. However, by dramatically cutting off all funds the US Congress forced an end to bombing raids on Cambodia by 15 August. Heavy fighting followed with the Sihanoukists just failing to take Kom-pong.

During 1974 the authority of the Lon Nol régime ceased to extend beyond Phnom Penh, Battambang and a few other centres. Increasing diplomatic recognition of the exiled Sihanouk régime followed. Lon Nol left the country in March 1975 and in April came surrender to the victorious Khmer Rouge Army.

All foreigners were swiftly expelled from Cambodia (renamed Kampuchea), and although information was scanty, apparently the whole population of Phnom Penh was sent to work in the fields to increase food production.

The victors were an uneasy alliance between the royalist followers of the exiled Prince Sihanouk and the Marxist Khmer Rouges. Prince Sihanouk remained as head of state with Penn Nouth as Prime Minister. After returning to Cambodia from Peking in September 1975 Sihanouk left soon afterwards on extensive travels. Elections were held on 30 March 1976 and the Prince resigned in April. Penn Nouth's Government was followed by a new Cabinet under Mr. Pol Pot. In the early months of 1976 the entire population was mobilised in order to reconstruct the economy, but reports reached the West of massive killings verging on genocide.

Conflict with Vietnam.

From September 1977 onwards several border clashes occurred between Vietnam and Cambodia and in late 1978 Hanoi appeared to have escalated the conflict into a concerted invasion. Although the Soviet Union supplied arms and aid to Vietnam, and China to Cambodia, this conflict between communists was in fact a revival of the traditional enmity between the two neighbours. The Vietnamese, much the stronger in numbers and in arms, appear to have held back, preferring to seek dominant influence rather than open conquest. However, on 4 January 1979 Radio Phnom Penh claimed that invading Vietnamese troops were advancing into Kampuchea in eight separate thrusts, supported by heavy artillery and air bombardments. The government of Pol Pot, previously noted for its isolationism, repeatedly demanded an urgent meeting of the UN Security Council to halt the Vietnamese advance. Prince Sihanouk, having a better international reputation than Pol Pot, was sent to New York to plead the Cambodian case before the UN. The Chinese made it clear that they would not intervene militarily, no doubt because of the threat of confrontation with the Soviet Union. Phnom Penh fell on 8 January, though fighting continued in the provinces. The Vietnamese still denied having intervened, but their role in installing the "Cambodian Liberation Front for National Renewal" was clearly decisive.

Starvation and Guerrilla Warfare.

The forces of Pol Pot continued to resist by guerrilla warfare in the jungle and the mountains, tacitly tolerated by the Thais and supported by the Chinese. In September 1979 the United Nations voted to allow the Pol Pot régime to keep its seat in the General Assembly, and not the government of Heng Samrin installed by the Vietnamese—even though Pol Pot was a fugitive and had been condemned to death for genocide. Meanwhile it became clear that vast numbers of Cambodians were literally dying of starvation while the Government cynically looked on. Hundreds of thousands managed to cross the border and fill ever more refugee camps in Thailand. A major international effort was launched to get food and supplies to the population, but despite the Phnom Penh government's agreement to open the Mekong River for supplies the political will to overcome the communications problem was clearly lacking. At the end of December 1979 the Khmer Rouges replaced the notorious Pol Pot as head of government by the former head of state Khieu Samphan. But this meant no real change, since the latter was also a fanatical revolutionary and Pol Pot remained commander-in-chief of the guerrilla force, estimated at some 30,000, which controlled about one-fifth of the country. Thus the announcements about respect for property, human rights and religion were no more than a transparent attempt to halt the loss of support in the West which had set in since the UN resolution in September. Meanwhile no negotiations took place and the starvation continued.

Fighting between the Heng Samrin government and the Khmer Rouge forces continued throughout 1980, but gradually the former extended its control over most of the country. The food shortages of 1979 were alleviated with massive foreign aid, and the continuing support of the Vietnamese helped to reduce the Khmer Rouge influence to a small area in the west of the country. The Vietnamese role in Kampuchea, however, continued in 1983 to cause problems with both China and Thailand.

Anti-Vietnamese Coalition Formed.

Groups opposed to the Vietnam-backed regime of Heng Samrin formed a coalition in Kuala Lumpur, Malaysia, on 22 June 1982, and announced the establishment of a rival government on Kampuchean territory held by guerrillas on 9 July. This consisted of Khieu Samphan, Khmer Rouge Prime Minister, Prince Norodom Sihanouk and Son Sann, head of the Khmer People's National Liberation Front. The coalition sought international support, but in a counter-move Vietnam announced partial troop withdrawals from Kampuchea. By mid-1984 there were still some 150,000 Vietnamese troops in the country. These forces began a major offensive in November 1984, overrunning many guerrilla bases near the Thai border. During 1985 Vietnam indicated that it expected all its troops to be withdrawn from Kampuchea by 1990, by which time the Heng Samrin government would be able to maintain itself unaided.

THE PHILIPPINES.

The Republic of the Philippines came into existence on 4 July 1946. President Ferdinand E. Marcos was elected in November 1965 and won a second term in 1969. However, violent opposition to his regime led President Marcos to declare martial law in September 1972 and to detain his political opponents. In 1973 a revised constitution was introduced and on 7 April 1978 elections were held for an interim Legislative Assembly, as the first stage to a return to parliamentary government.

In the elections President Marcos' party, the New Society Movement, defeated its main rival, the People's Power Movement, led by Benigno Aquino, but there were accusations of widespread fraud. Mr. Aquino, who had been detained on a murder charge, was released to go to the United States for heart surgery. Mr. Aquino returned to Manila on 21 August 1983, intending to play a leading role in the opposition campaign against President Marcos in the elections called for 1984, but he was assassinated as he left his plane. Serious unrest followed as the Marcos regime was suspected of collusion in the murder. In October 1983 a presidential decreee introduced a law imposing the death penalty or life imprisonment for sedition, illegal assembly or anti-government propaganda.

Aftermath of Aquino's Murder.

During 1984 President Marcos took steps to restore his government's credibility which had been badly damaged by Mr. Aquino's murder. First, National Assembly elections were held in May. Despite calls for a boycott, there was a sizeable turnout of voters. The opposition made some gains, but President Marcos' New Society Movement won 108 of the 183 elective seats. Following the elections President Marcos, under pressure from the International Monetary Fund, introduced a series of austerity measures designed to tackle the country's economic ills.

The second important act was the establishment of a five-member panel to investigate Mr. Aquino's murder. Its findings, issued in October 1984, were that he had been assassinated by the army, rather than by Rolando Galman, who was himself killed in the incident, although the panel disagreed on how far the military conspiracy extended. In January 1985, General Ver, the Chief of Staff, 24 other soldiers and one civilian were charged in connection with the deaths of Mr. Aquino and Rolando Galman. However, in December all the defendants were acquitted of any complicity in the killings and General Ver was reinstated as Chief of Staff.

The Downfall of Marcos.

Unrest continued in the Philippines throughout 1985, with greatly increased guerrilla activity by the communist-inspired New People's Army in the countryside. This situation and pressure from the Philippines' most important ally, the United States, led President Marcos to seek a new mandate by calling elections for February 1986, although his six-year term of office did not end until 1987. In December 1985 it was announced that the opposition to President Marcos would be led by Benigno Aquino's widow, Corazon Aquino, under the banner of the United Nationalist Democratic Organisation (UNIDO). The head of UNIDO, Salvador Laurel, withdrew as a presidential candidate and put himself forward as Mrs Aquino's vice-presidential running mate.

Polling took place on 7 February 1986, amidst violence and widespread evidence of intimidation and ballot-rigging, reported both by foreign observers and the citizen watchdog group, the National Movement for Free Elections (Namfrel). Mrs. Aquino took the lead in Namfrel's tally, but official vote-counting proceeded slowly, giving rise to fresh charges of fraud. On 15 February the National Assembly, dominated by Mr Marcos' New Society Movement, declared that Mr. Marcos had won by 1·5 million votes. Mrs. Aquino announced a campaign of civil disobedience and President Reagan, who had initially blamed both sides for malpractices, now said that the actions of Mr. Marcos' supporters rendered the result of the election invalid.

The Advent of Aquino.

Events moved swiftly when the Defence Minister, Juan Ponce Enrile, and the head of the Philippines Constabulary, Lt.-General Fidel Ramos, resigned, claiming they faced imminent arrest, and transferred their allegiance to Mrs. Aquino. In a display of 'people power', thousands of Mrs. Aquino's supporters blocked the way to troops loyal to Mr. Marcos. On 25 February both Mr. Marcos and Mrs. Aquino held presidential inauguration ceremonies, but later in the day Mr. Marcos finally accepted that the time had come to stand down and allowed himself and his family to be evacuated from the American Clark Air Base. Mrs. Aquino thus became the new President of the Philippines, with Mr. Laurel as her Prime Minister and Foreign Minister.

INDONESIA.

Independence under Sukarno.

Indonesia proclaimed its independence from the Netherlands in August 1945, though it was not until 27 December 1949 that the Dutch formally recognised the transfer of power. Dr. Sukarno became the country's first president. In 1957 he introduced a type of authoritarian rule known as 'guided democracy', in which the elected parliament was replaced by an appointed legislature. Sukarno laid great stress on fostering unity, using opposition to imperialism and neo-colonialism—as in the 'confrontation' with Malaysia (1963–66)—to stimulate national sentiment.

The Overthrow of Sukarno.

Following an abortive coup in September 1965, the Indonesian Communist Party was charged with plotting to destroy the power of the army. The party was banned and thousands of its members were killed. In March 1966 the army, led by General Suharto, assumed emergency powers. The following February Sukarno handed over all power to General Suharto, who was elected President by the People's Consultative Assembly in March 1968. He was re-elected in 1973, 1978 and 1983.

The Army's Role.

President Suharto introduced his 'New Order', in which the army became the dominant factor in Indonesian political life. The army regards itself as a force for stability, occupying as it does the centre ground between the communists on the left and the Islamic fundamentalists on the right. In 1983 President Suharto brought in a large number of younger men to top military posts so that there would be continuity in the army's political role.

The Indonesian army is also involved in military operations to counter separatist insurgencies in East Timor and Irian Jaya. In the former case, when Portugal withdrew from East Timor in 1975 Indonesia intervened to prevent the marxist Fretilin movement taking power. In July 1976 East Timor was formally integrated into Indonesia. There is also conflict in Irian Jaya, which was incorporated into Indonesia in 1963. Renewed fighting in 1984 led to the flight of over 11,000 refugees to Papua New Guinea, only a handful of whom have returned.

The Status of Islam.

Alongside the military there is an impressive government political apparatus centred on the official party, Golkar. It has won all three elections since President Suharto came to power. In 1982 it won 64 per cent of the total votes and two-thirds of the parliamentary seats. Although the Muslims supported the army take-over in the mid-1960s, they have still been denied any real power.

Indonesia has the world's largest Islamic population, with 90 per cent of its 160 million inhabitants belonging to the Muslim faith. However, President Suharto rejects any thought of its becoming an Islamic state. This is made easier by the fact that only a small proportion of the population are orthodox Muslims. In 1972 four Muslim parties were forced to merge into the United Development Party (PPP), but this remains deeply divided.

However, President Suharto has to take care not to alienate grass-roots Islamic sentiment by pressing too strongly the official state ideology, "Pancasila", the tenets of which are belief in God, humanitarianism, national unity, social justice and democracy. In August 1984 Suharto assured the congress of the P.P.P. that Pancasila was not intended to create a one-party state or reduce religious freedom, but there were riots and bombings in the capital, Jakarta, in September. These were blamed on militant Muslims and had to be suppressed by the army.

Nevertheless, Indonesia enjoys a far greater degree of stability than many other developing countries. It has also made reasonable economic progress, although it has felt the effects of the world recession and the fall in the price of oil, which provides 60 per cent of the government's income. There was a devaluation and rescheduling of major projects in 1983. Some of the projects have now been reinstated and recently President Suharto has tried to encourage exports by waging an anti-corruption campaign at Indonesia's ports.

AFRICA

ETHIOPIA AND SOMALIA.

The Horn of Africa occupies a key geographical position and events there have a potential significance for the economic and strategic interests both of neighbouring Middle East countries and of maritime states around the world. The revolution of 1971 which overthrew the regime of Emperor Haile Selassie in Ethiopia created severe instability in the region. A fresh impetus was given to the separatist revolt in Ethiopia's northern province of Eritrea, whilst in the south neighbouring Somalia, which claims the Ogaden desert region of Ethiopia, fostered a guerrilla movement in the area, the Western Somali Libration Front. In July 1977 Somalia invaded the Ogaden.

Rivalries within the Horn have long provided opportunities for the great powers to involve themselves in its affairs. Prior to the 1974 revolution Ethiopia had looked to the West for support, while the left-wing government in Somalia had close links with Russia. After further upheavals in Ethiopia in 1977, the Russians began to supply arms to its Marxist government. This led to a breach with their former allies, the Somalis, who expelled their Russian advisers in November 1977. During 1978 Cuban troops and massive quantities of Russian equipment were committed to a successful Ethiopian offensive in the Ogaden. In March 1978 Somalia announced that its regular troops had withdrawn from Ethiopian territory. The Ethiopians were then able to switch their forces to the north and regain much of the ground lost to the Eritrean guerrillas.

By February 1982 when the Ethiopians launched a new offensive the only town in Eritrea outside their control was the ruined town of Nacfa. Although there has been an improvement in Ethiopia's position, it is still heavily dependent on Communist-bloc support. There are reported to be over 12,000 Cubans stiffening the Ethiopian army in the Ogaden, 2,000 Russian economic and military advisers and a number of East Germans also providing technical assistance. For her part Somalia signed an agreement with the United States to permit American access to the naval base at Berbera in August 1980, in return for financial and military assistance. Increased fighting on the border between Ethiopia and Somalia in July 1982 led to emergency military supplies being sent to Somalia by the United States.

Famine in Ethiopia.

Early in 1984 Eritrean guerrillas successfully took the offensive against government forces and enlarged their area of control in the north. However, as the year progressed the conflict in Eritrea and in the adjacent province of Tigre, where a separate rebel group operated, became bound up with the impact of a drought and famine which put some six million people in danger of starvation in Ethiopia. International opinion was mobilised and emergency food supplies were sent to Ethiopia from around the world. But relief did not get through to the war zones of Tigre and Eritrea, and thousands of refugees headed for neighbouring Sudan. In July 1985 the Eritrean guerrillas resumed their offensive, capturing the town of Barentu for the first time.

LIBYA.

The Fall of King Idris.

Libya became an independent state on 24 December 1951 under King Idris of the Libyan Sanussi dynasty. He was overthrown by a small group of junior army officers on 1 September 1969. A twelve-member Revolutionary Command Council was established as Libya's supreme authority, with Colonel Moammar Gaddafi as its chairman. Although the coup had been primarily anti-royalist, the revolutionaries announced that they sought to establish "freedom, socialism and unity", ridding Libya of colonialism and economic and social backwardness.

The Jamahiriya.

Colonel Gaddafi was born in 1942, the only son of semi-nomadic parents. His revolutionary thinking was greatly influenced by President Nasser of Egypt, with strong elements of puritanism and pan-Arabism in its make-up. In 1977 his regime implemented a new system of government involving popular participation in the political processes. A form of direct democracy, the Jamahiriya (state of the masses), was introduced and the official name of the country was changed to the Socialist People's Libyan Arab Jamahiriya. At local level authority is vested in 186 Basic and 25 Municipal People's Congresses, which appoint Popular Committees to execute policy. Officials from the Congresses and Committees form at national level the General People's Congress, a body of some 1,000 delegates which normally meets for about a week twice a year.

Gaddafi's Policies.

Under the new system Colonel Gaddafi holds no formal post, but his position as leader of the revolution and his personal popularity confer great power on him within Libya. Internationally Libya's standing is the result of its role as one of the world's major oil producers. It has enormous oil reserves, estimated at over 25,000 million barrels. Revenue from oil has been used to improve the standard of living of the small population (about 3·5 million), financing civil engineering and irrigation projects. In 1984 a 120-mile pipeline to recover water from under the desert was completed at a cost of 11 billion dollars.

Oil revenue has also been used for large-scale arms buying, as militarism, with conscription and popular militias, has become a feature of Libyan life. Colonel Gaddafi has ensured Libya a place in the world's headlines over the past fifteen years by virtue of his radical and idiosyncratic foreign policy. This has seen Libyan military involvement in the affairs of neighbouring Chad and support for international terrorism.

Britain and Libya.

Britain broke off diplomatic relations with Libya in April 1984 as a result of the shooting of a policewoman, Yvonne Fletcher, from the Libyan embassy in London during an anti-Gaddafi demonstration. Following terrorist attacks at Rome and Vienna airports in December 1985, President Reagan announced a total break in economic relations with Libya and ordered all Americans to leave the country. Although Colonel Gaddafi, whom President Reagan described as "flakey" or unbalanced, denied that there were guerrilla bases in his country, the Americans continued to argue that if their European allies joined in bringing pressure to bear on Libya, this would significantly reduce terrorist activity world-wide.

American Air Strikes.

Tension steadily increased between Libya and the United States in the Spring of 1986. In March American naval exercises in the Gulf of Sirte (claimed by Colonel Gaddafi as Libyan territorial waters) led to clashes in which Libyan patrol boats and a missile site were hit. Matters came to a head when on 2 April a bomb went off in the passenger cabin of a T.W.A. jetliner over Greece, killing four Americans, and on 5 April a second device exploded in a West Berlin night club, killing two and injuring some 230. The Americans claimed that they had indisputable evidence of Libyan involvement in the latter attack. In retaliation during the night of 14/15 April American bombers from two carriers in the Mediterranean and four US bases in Britain struck at three targets in the Tripoli area and two near Benghazi. There were many civilian casualties, including two of Colonel Gaddafi's sons and his adopted daughter. Speaking after the air raids, Colonel Gaddafi said that the American attacks would not deter Libya from supporting the Palestinian cause. *See also* **C66** for the international repercussions of the 1986 Libyan crisis.

CHAD.

Chad has been in a state of civil war for most of its history since independence in 1960, originally as a result of a guerrilla campaign waged against the government by the Chad Liberation Front (FROLINAT), backed by Libya. In 1978 the Chad head of state, General Malloum, who had come to power in a military coup in 1975, announced a cease-fire with FROLINAT. In August 1978 the former rebel leader, Hissène Habré, become Prime Minister.

However, relations between the Prime Minister and President Malloum worsened. Fighting was renewed between their supporters in February 1979 and central government in Chad broke down as Habré's forces took over part of the capital, Ndjamena. Negotiations resumed and on 21 August 1979 the eleven factions fighting in Chad signed a peace agreement in Lagos, Nigeria. A Goverment of National Unity was set up with the Toubou leader, Goukouni Oueddi, as head of state and Hissène Habré as Defence Minister.

This too broke down in renewed civil strife in March 1980 and there was increasing Libyan involvement on behalf of President Oueddei. President Gaddafi sent some 4,000 Libyan troops and at least thirty Russian-built tanks to fight for the President. Although at one point in November 1980 Hissène Habré's forces controlled two-thirds of Ndjamena, he was forced to agree to a cease-fire in December.

Libyan Intervention.

President Gaddafi's intervention in Chad greatly disturbed neighbouring African states who saw the Libyan presence there as a threat to their own security. However, in November 1981 President Gaddafi announced that he had ordered the withdrawal of all Libyan soldiers from Chad. In December the Organisation of African Unity sent a 3,000-strong peace-keeping force to Chad to replace the Libyan troops. The OAU plan for a ceasefire, negotiations and new presidential elections was rejected by President Oueddei in February 1982.

Alienated by President Oueddei's refusal to negotiate, the OAU peace-keeping force remained neutral when Hissène Habré's forces retook the Chad capital on 7 June 1982. President Oueddei was driven into exile in Cameroon, and Hissène Habré established his own government in Ndjamena.

There was renewed fighting in June 1983 as Mr. Oueddei's Libyan-backed forces advanced into

Chad and captured the strategically important town of Faya-Largeau. President Habré appealed to France, and in August French troops took up front-line positions in northern Chad to prevent any further rebel advances. Fighting subsided, and the 10th Franco-African summit meeting at Vittel in France in October 1983 rejected a partition of Chad and called for reconciliation between the warring groups. However, in January 1984 negotiations between the factions held in Addis Ababa broke down when President Habré withdrew from the talks. Reconciliation talks later took place in Brazzaville, capital of the Congo, in October 1984, but made little progress.

French Troops Withdrawn.

In September 1984 it was announced that France and Libya had agreed to a mutual withdrawal of their forces from Chad, to be completed by mid-November. The French contingent flew out, but there was strong evidence of a continuing Libyan presence in the north of the country. The government of Chad issued an official complaint to the UN Security Council in June 1985. Despite attempts by Mali and Morocco to mediate a settlement, the country remained divided and continued to suffer the hardships of drought and famine.

SUDAN.

Sudan became an independent republic on 1 January 1956. Its long-serving ruler, President Numeiry, came to power in a military coup in 1969. In 1972 the sixteen-year civil war between the government and the separatist Anya Nya rebels of southern Sudan was brought to an end by the Addis Ababa agreement, which gave a measure of regional autonomy to the south. In the mid-1980s this settlement was under threat from President Numeiry's plan to turn Sudan into an Islamic Republic, which was opposed by the African, mainly Christian or Animist, south. In 1983 army mutinies in the south led to the formation of the Sudanese People's Liberation Army and renewed guerrilla attacks.

The Fall of Numeiry.

Numeiry declared an indefinite state of emergency in April 1984, but in July opposition from the south forced him to postpone a vote in the National Assembly on proposed constitutional changes. In April 1985, against a background of guerrilla warfare, a bankrupt economy and a crippling drought, the army staged a *coup d'état* while Numeiry was returning from a visit to the United States. The new ruler was the Defence Minister, General Swar el Dahab, who formed a fifteen-man Transitional Military Council. A non-party technocratic Council of Ministers was also appointed, with Dr. El Gizouli Dafalla as Prime Minister. In May 1985 the Council declared southern Sudan a disaster zone and appealed for aid. Although the new regime moderated some of the harshest aspects of Numeiry's imposition of Islamic law, the Sudanese People's Liberation Army was still active, fighting for more drastic changes in Sudan's political structure.

NIGERIA.

Tension between the main tribal groups (Hausa and Yoruba and Ibo) led to the assassination in 1966 of the Hausa Prime Minister, Sir Abubakar Tafawa Balewa. General Ironsi, an Ibo soldier, tried to impose a unitary system of government but was murdered by non-Ibo soldiers.

Civil war broke out in July 1967 after the secession of the Eastern Region under its Ibo leader, Colonel Ojukwu. This region became known as Biafra. Federal troops under the head of the new Federal Military Government, General Gowon, advanced into Biafra, cut the secessionists off from the sea and confined them to the Ibo heartland.

The end of the civil war after a period of apparent stalemate came at the beginning of 1970, Federal troops captured Owerri, headquarters of the secessionist régime, together with Uli airstrip through which relief supplies had reached Biafra. Colonel Ojukwu departed, leaving Colonel Effiong in charge of affairs. Colonel Effiong called

on his troops to stop fighting and sued for peace.

Although he had promised a return to civilian rule, General Gowon announced its deferment in 1974. The first half of 1975 saw serious industrial unrest and highly inflationary pay increases, though Nigeria had a steadily increasing trade surplus because of her oil exports. In July 1975 General Gowon was deposed in a bloodless coup. The new head of state and commander-in-chief of the armed forces was Brigadier Murtala Mohammed. All former members of the Government and all state governors were dismissed. The plans of the new government included a timetable for return to civilian rule, the drafting of a new constitution, an anti-corruption drive and reduction of the armed forces. Steps were also taken to relieve the congestion in the port of Lagos. In February 1976 an attempted coup by officers was crushed but General Mohammed was killed. He was succeeded by General Olusegun Obasanjo who proceeded with his predecessor's policies. Port congestion was reduced and a strict economic programme placing emphasis on housing, health and agriculture was mounted. A new constitution was published in October 1976 and October 1979 was the projected date for the re-establishment of full democratic government.

In September 1977 elections to a constitutive assembly were held. All the candidates were independents because since the military take-over in 1966 all political parties had been banned. Nevertheless, these elections represented the punctual fulfilment of a further point in the Government's programme for a return to civilian government. The Assembly was opened on 6 October.

During July and August, 1979, elections were held which would lead to the first civilian government since the Biafran War broke out. Those parties that wished to participate in the elections had to satisfy the military rulers of certain conditions. The military, led by General Obasanjo, wanted to be certain that none of the old tribal rivalries would be revived, and so they insisted that all parties must have a national base. The victor in the elections was Alhaji Shehu Shagari, who led the National Party of Nigeria. They took office on 1 October, 1979. New problems faced Nigeria with the glut in world oil and the fall in the price of oil. Oil revenues dwindled from $22 billion in 1980 to under $10 billion in 1983.

Mass Expulsion of Immigrants.

Nigeria's economic problems led in January 1983 to a declaration that all illegal immigrants, who had been attracted to the country by its prosperity, had a fortnight to leave Nigeria. This was probably a move aimed at creating jobs for Nigerians put out of work by the recession, in a year which would bring national and presidential elections. About a million Ghanaians and a similar number from other west African states were forced to join the mass exodus.

From Elections to Military Coup.

In the presidential election of 6 August 1983 President Shagari was elected for a second term, and in elections during August for State Governors, Senators and the House of Representatives his National Party of Nigeria gained majorities in each case. But the speed at which President Shagari looked likely to deal with the all-pervading corruption of public life was too slow for some army officers. On 31 December 1983 a military coup took place and Maj.-Gen. Mohammed Buhari seized power as head of a supreme Military Council. On 18 January 1984 a Federal Executive Council of 7 military and 11 civilian members was sworn in, charged with ridding Nigeria of corruption and putting its economy on a sounder footing.

The Dikko Affair.

In July 1984 there was an abortive bid in London to kidnap the millionaire exile, Dr. Umaru Dikko, who had been Minister of Transport in the Shagari government in order to return him to Nigeria to face a corruption tribunal. But the attempt failed when Dr. Dikko was found in a drugged condition in a crate at Stansted airport. The Nigerian high commissioner was recalled to Lagos and the British high commissioner returned to London as relations between Britain and Nigeria suffered a temporary deterioration.

The Overthrow of Buhari.

By mid-1985 it was clear that the Buhari regime had failed to deal with the country's economic problems—unemployment, inflation and an over-dependence on oil revenues. There were also accusations of bias towards northerners, failure to deal even-handedly with former officials and excessive repression. On 27 August 1985 Maj-Gen. Buhari's government was overthrown in a bloodless military coup and Maj-Gen. Ibraham Babangida took control as head of a new Armed Forces Ruling Council. A National Council of Ministers was appointed in September, with twelve military and ten civilian members.

The new government promised greater flexibility and a more liberal approach to dealing with the country's problems. In October 1985 Maj-Gen. Babangida announced that the country would be under a fifteen-month economic "state of emergency", aimed at improving productivity and national self-reliance.

UGANDA.

In August 1972 the President of Uganda, General Amin, announced that all Asians who held British passports (whose numbers were estimated at 57,000) must leave the country within 3 months. He accused them of sabotaging the economy and corruption and insisted that the economy must be in the hands of black Ugandans. Britain condemned this move as irresponsible and racist and reacted by suspending economic aid to Uganda. But she recognised her responsibility towards Asians with British passports and organised an airlift. The expulsions were soon extended to Asians with Indian, Pakistani or Bangladesh passports, but these countries refused to accept the expellees. The Asians played an indispensable role in the Ugandan economy, which must suffer from their departure, despite aid from Colonel Gaddafi in Libya.

General Amin had been strongly condemned by Presidents Nyerere of Tanzania and Kaunda of Zambia for racism of just the kind Africans deplore. There were actually brief military clashes on the Uganda–Tanzanian border in September 1972, and further allegations by Amin in 1974 that Tanzania and Zambia were planning an invasion of Uganda and supporting conspiracies by ex-President Obote.

Relations with Britain deteriorated when following British press reports of attempts to assassinate Amin and of brutal murders of prominent Ugandans, action was taken against British interests and all but 5 British diplomats were expelled in November 1974. In April 1975, General Amin said that he was ready to lift restrictions on the British High Commission. But relations were soured by the trial and sentence to death of Mr. Dennis Hills, a British lecturer, for treason and sedition. Only intense diplomatic activity including the mediation of President Mobutu of Zaïre and a visit to Kampala by Mr. Callaghan, then the British Foreign Secretary, secured a reprieve. In July 1976 a further dispute arose over the disappearance of Mrs. Dora Block, one of the hostages in the hijacked Air France airbus which landed at Entebbe airport. On 28 July Britain broke off diplomatic relations with Uganda, the first time this had been done with a Commonwealth country.

The Entebbe incident also caused friction with Kenya who had allowed Israel to use Kenyan facilities during the rescue operation.

Early in 1977 came reports of mass arrests and killings in Uganda, Amnesty International accused Uganda at the United Nations of serious breaches of human rights: the disappearance of at least 300,000 persons since 1971—including at least 50,000 murdered—torture in concentration camps, mass murders in the army and the systematic murder of Kenyan citizens in the wake of the Entebbe incident. After discovery of an alleged plot to stage a coup, Amin intensified persecution of opponents of the régime, especially among the Christian tribes of Uganda and Acholi. The arrest and murder of the Anglican Archbishop of Uganda and two Christian Ministers was greeted with particular abhorrence abroad. Meanwhile Amin proposed to assume the titles of "Emperor" and "Son of God". He offered the Soviet

Union a military base in return for installation of a nuclear reactor. The excesses of General Amin were condemned by various African countries and Ghana broke off diplomatic relations. But there has been some restraint because of a wish not to upset the illusion of African unity. However the Commonwealth Conference in London in June at which Britain had made it clear that General Amin would not be welcome, condemned the massive violations of basic human rights in Uganda. In September 1977 Amin banned all religious communities except the Anglicans, Roman Catholics, Orthodox and Moslems. A trade embargo was imposed by the USA in 1978 because of Amin's massive violation of human rights.

In 1978 Uganda invaded Tanzania and made a number of bombing raids. This proved Amin's undoing since previously his African neighbours had been restrained from intervening against him by a fear of creating a precedent by breaking the sacred principle of respect for the arbitrarily drawn colonial frontiers of Africa. By early 1979 Tanzanian forces and Ugandans in exile were advancing through southern Uganda and Amin's troops were mutinying or deserting in large numbers. In April came the fall of Kampala, ending Amin's 8-year brutal rule of terror. He himself was believed to have escaped to Libya.

The Return of Obote.

Following the coup against Amin, Professor Yusuf Lule was chosen as a neutral President, although in June he was replaced by Mr. Godfrey Binaisa. This created an unstable security situation, which was worsened in May 1980 when Mr. Binaisa was replaced by Mr. Paulo Muwanga, Chairman of the Military Commission of the Uganda National Liberation Front. Mr. Binaisa had been trying to prevent the return of former President Milton Obote, but the attitude of Tanzania was again decisive. President Nyerere supported Mr. Muwanga, whilst insisting on elections being held. Mr. Obote returned to Uganda in May 1981 and in the ensuing elections his Uganda Peoples Congress won a majority amid charges of ballot-rigging. The remaining Tanzanian troops were withdrawn from Uganda in June.

The Overthrow of Obote.

Violence persisted in Uganda between government forces and guerrillas of the National Resistance Army (NRA), led by the former defence minister, Yoweri Museveni. There were also widespread army atrocities against the civilian population. The turmoil in Uganda came to a head in July 1985 when dissension developed within the army between members of the Langi and Acholi tribes over sharing the burden of the campaign against the NRA. On 27 July Mr. Obote was overthrown and a military council formed, led by the army chief, General Tito Okello.

Museveni Comes to Power.

Negotiations with the NRA began in Nairobi and in December 1985 General Okello and Mr. Museveni reached agreement on a power-sharing government, with the latter taking the position of deputy head. However, continuing violence and indiscipline by the army in Kampala led Mr. Museveni to delay implementing the agreement. Finally, in January 1986 the NRA occupied the capital, General Okello was deposed and Mr. Museveni was sworn in as the new president. As his forces consolidated their hold on the country, President Museveni said in his inauguration address that his priorities would be the promotion of democracy and safeguarding personal security against human rights violations.

SOUTH AFRICA.

In South Africa Africans have no civil rights except in the "Bantustans". These are some 200 pieces of land, making up about 13 per cent of the country's land area, specifically designated for African use. Elsewhere in South Africa, Africans may not vote, and they have no representatives in the South African Parliament or on any of the Provincial or Local Authorities. Their right to strike is severely limited and they have no freehold rights of land or house ownership. Freedom of movement is restricted by influx-control laws governing movement between town and between town and country. Regulations require them to carry a pass at all times. African industrial wages average a sixth of those of Whites.

The Afrikaans-led Nationalist Party has been in power since 1948. In 1961 after a referendum they made South Africa a republic.

The Implementation of Apartheid.

The theory of the government's policy of "apartheid", which owes much to the late Prime Minister, Dr. Verwoerd, looks forward to the eventual partition of South Africa as the only viable alternative to integration, which most Afrikaners regard as racial suicide. In practice, however, the government's policies are adapted to making a rigid caste system based on colour compatible with industrialisation and economic growth. Hence the increasing emphasis on the migrant labour system. Africans are brought to work in industry and returned to the Reserves at the end of their contracts.

The government is unable to impose the taxes on White voters that genuine separate development would require. The Bantustans are therefore likely to remain overcrowded Labour reserves, and millions of Africans will always live and work in the "White areas".

The implementation of apartheid legislation covering employment, housing and education after 1948 led to increasing African unrest, organised especially by the African National Congress (ANC). In 1959 the Pan-Africanist Congress (PAC) broke from the ANC, and began to organise anti-pass law demonstrations. In March 1960 such a demonstration took place at the police station in the African township of Sharpeville. The police opened fire, killing 69 Africans and wounding over 180. The government declared a state of emergency and began mass arrests of African leaders. Strikes and mass marches of Africans continued for another week and the government then banned the ANC and PAC under the Suppression of Communism Act. Some African leaders went underground and organised a campaign of sabotage. But the security forces were able to infiltrate the organisations and in 1963 Nelson Mandela, the outstanding African leader, was captured with others and brought to trial. He was sentenced to life imprisonment.

Unrest among the Africans broke out again in 1973 with widespread strikes in Natal. In 1976 the worst riots since Sharpeville occurred in Soweto. The immediate cause was opposition to the compulsory use of Afrikaans as the medium of instruction in schools. The riots continued throughout the summer and spread to other areas.

In 1976 independence was granted to the Transkei, a Bantu homeland, and in 1977 Bophutatswana became the second "Bantustan", followed by Venda in 1979. However, these states have not received international recognition.

Growing Repression in South Africa.

During 1977 the South African Government was faced with challenges to the apartheid system from various quarters. The Roman Catholic church opened its schools to all races and its Bishops' Conference published a 21-point programme for improving the situation of the Blacks. Several large American firms announced their intention of ending racial segregation in their South African branches. And the European Community also laid down guidelines for firms operating in South Africa which required equality for Black workers. The reaction was mixed. In the spring, the threat of compulsory press censorship produced an agreement on voluntary self-censorship by the press. On the other hand, White political leaders in Natal announced in July that they wanted to investigate the possibility of an autonomous multi-racial government in the province. The following month plans were made for a new South African Constitution whereby significant rights and participation would be extended to the Coloureds and the Indians but not to the Blacks, on the ground that they were covered by the Bantustan policy.

Tension and violence increased following the deaths in prison of numerous Black activists who had been imprisoned without trial. Major riots were triggered off by the death of Steve Biko, the most popular Black leader, in whose case there were contradictions in the explanations given by the Minister of Justice and an inquiry showed severe headwounds. In October the police raided 17 Black nationalist organisations and the Christian Institute, which was hostile to the régime: all were banned. This action represented a short-sighted snapping of the last threads of understanding between the races. Coming in the wake of steadily worsening relations between the United States and South Africa, it probably indicated that the latter had given up the attempt to placate Western opinion. General elections held on 30 November, in which Mr. Vorster's National Party won its greatest ever electoral victory with 135 seats out of 165, also suggested that Black unrest and world indignation over developments in South Africa had produced a dangerous attitude of defiance among Whites.

Mulder and the Resignation of Vorster.

In the autumn of 1978 Mr. Vorster moved to the less strenuous office of President. He was succeeded as Prime Minister by Pieter Willem Botha. The latter was given a difficult start by the uncovering of a scandal at the Information Ministry, where it emerged that public money had disappeared into a secret fund to finance shady activities and propaganda. Leading politicians were implicated, the former Information Minister Connie Mulder had to resign and the government suffered a serious loss of popularity. Significantly this scandal rocked the government much more than the Soweto riots, since which little seemed to have changed. By mid-1979 the "Muldergate" scandal had implicated the very highest echelons of the South African Government. President Vorster resigned in June after the report of the commission of inquiry set up by the Government concluded that he must bear joint responsibility for continued irregularities of which he had been aware while Prime Minister. He was succeeded by Mr. Marais Viljoen, who had previously been President of the Senate. A traditional conservative, he was seen by some as a possible bridgebuilder between the Government and those groups which were hostile to Mr. Botha's reform plans, which were further strengthened by the government reorganisation of 26 August, 1980, with reformist ministers being placed in three key positions, including defence and education. However, Botha's plans continued to cause dismay in certain sections of his party. The election called by Botha for April 1981, though resulting in an easy victory for the ruling party, saw significant defections both to the extreme-right and to the progressives.

The Treurnicht Split.

Early 1982 was dominated by Afrikaner infighting when Dr. Andries Treurnicht (the Minister of State Administration) and his colleague Dr. Ferdi Hartzenberg (the Education Minister) resigned from the government. Although the breakaway group of ultra-conservatives was limited to 16, and the National Party with 126 seats still had a large overall majority, there was clearly substantial support, especially in the Transvaal, for the new party.

Plans for Constitutional Reform.

A bill to give a limited parliamentary voice to Asians and coloureds (but not blacks) was introduced on 5 May 1983. It proposed a three chamber parliament, with separate assemblies for whites, coloureds (mixed race) and Indians. Each race would exercise control over its own domestic affairs, while dealing in common with matters such as defence. An executive President, elected by an electoral college of the three chambers, would decide what were "common" affairs. Despite opposition from the Conservative Party, the bill was approved by parliament on 9 September 1983 by 119 votes to 35. In a referendum in November, two-thirds of the white population voted in favour of the new constitution.

The New Constitution.

Elections to the new assemblies for coloureds and Indians were held in August 1984. Violence occurred during the elections as the multi-racial United Democratic Front campaigned for a boycott. In the poll for the coloured House of Representatives there was a 30% turn-out of registered voters (some 60%

of those eligible had registered) and the Labour Party won 76 of the 80 seats; for the Indian House of Delegates there was a 20% turn-out (80% had registered) and the two biggest groups were the National People's Party with 18 seats and Solidarity with 17 in the 40-seat House. The revised constitution came into effect in September and P. W. Botha was elected to the post of executive President by an electoral college of the three assemblies. President Botha's new cabinet included one coloured and one Indian member, although neither had executive portfolios.

International Relations.

South Africa's position in the international community initially appeared to be improving at the beginning of 1984. In February and March, South African pressure led her neighbours, Mozambique and Angola, both facing grave economic and internal security problems, to come to terms in the Nkomati and Lusaka accords. In May and June P. W. Botha visited eight European countries, including Britain, for talks.

Growing Violence and Repression.

However, South Africa's efforts to improve her standing in the world in spite of apartheid were offset by rioting in black townships in September over rent increases (later suspended), continuing sabotage attacks by ANC guerrillas and the award of the Nobel Peace Prize to the anti-apartheid campaigner, Desmond Tutu, who was installed as the first black Bishop of Johannesburg in February 1985. Moreover, the full implementation of the Nkomati and Lusaka accords to bring peace to the region was still not accomplished at the beginning of 1985. During spring 1985 continued unrest, especially in the Eastern Cape black townships led to severe police repression. It was reported that between 3 September 1984 and 9 July 1985 there were 443 deaths in the townships. Finally on 20 July a state of emergency was proclaimed in 36 areas of the country. When violence continued the government imposed strict regulations on the reporting of the unrest in November 1985.

Hopes of radical changes in the system of apartheid were disappointed in August 1985 when President Botha, in a much-heralded speech to the Natal Congress of his National Party, attacked his country's critics rather than announcing reforms. As a result South Africa's foreign exchanges had to be closed for a week when the rand hit a record low against the dollar. In September the government announced a four-month freeze on foreign debt capital repayments.

President Botha adopted a more conciliatory stance in September when he proposed a restoration of South African citizenship to the five million blacks who had been assigned to the homelands in the 1970s but were still living in South Africa; he suggested negotiations regarding the five million actually in the homelands. However, he received a setback in terms of his own white support in October when the ultra-rightwing Herstigte Nasionale Party captured the parliamentary seat of Sasolburg in the Orange Free State, the first in its sixteen-year existence.

International Pressure.

Lack of progress on reform and the violent repression of unrest in the black townships led to increased international pressure on South Africa in the autumn of 1985. The EEC approved a modest package of sanctions and President Reagan imposed American trade restrictions in September, though the latter were intended to forestall more extensive sanctions under consideration by Congress. A meeting of Commonwealth leaders at Nassau in October also agreed, despite British reluctance, on limited measures, such as a ban on the import of Krugerrands.

After the negative effects of his speech in August 1985, President Botha attempted to make a fresh start in his address at the opening of parliament in January 1986. He said that South Africa had outgrown the apartheid system and that he intended to establish a national statutory council, including black representatives, to find answers to the country's problems. But the genuineness of white South Africa's desire for reform remained in doubt.

By June 1986, with a state of emergency declared prior to the tenth anniversary of the Soweto uprising, South Africa had reached a major crisis. The reality of white supremacy was now being challenged as never before.

The Future of Nelson Mandela.

In his January 1986 speech President Botha referred to the release of Nelson Mandela, the leader of the outlawed African National Congress serving a life sentence for sabotage. He linked Mr. Mandela's release to that of Soviet dissidents and Captain Wynand du Toit, a South African commando captured in 1985 by the Angolans. However, Mr. Mandela had earlier rejected President Botha's offer to set him free if he renounced violence as a political instrument, and in February 1986 his wife, Winnie Mandela, said he would only accept freedom if he was released in South Africa and not sent into exile. The first major conference of the African National Congress for sixteen years had been held in June 1985 in Kabwe in Zambia and agreed to intensify the people's war against apartheid.

See also Section G, for an assessment of the South African economy.

NAMIBIA.

Namibia (South West Africa) has been under South African control since it was wrested from Germany in the First World War. In 1920 the League of Nations mandated the territory to South Africa.

In 1964 the Odendaal Commission, set up by the SA government, recommended the effective integration of South West and South Africa with the mandated territory being divided into ten tribal Bantustans having home rule, and a White homeland consisting of 70 per cent of the land area. The response of the United Nations was a 1966 General Assembly resolution revoking South Africa's mandate on the grounds that she was extending apartheid to the territory and therefore not administering it in the interests of all its inhabitants. SA legislation in 1969 largely put the Odendaal recommendations into effect.

During the 1960s nationalist sentiment began to grow among the majority Ovambo tribe and a number of political parties were formed including the South West Africa People's Organisation (SWAPO). This party was banned and its leaders in exile have organised guerrilla infiltration of the territory. In September 1974 the South African government declared itself ready to discuss the future of S.W. Africa and at a constitutional conference at the end of 1975 a declaration was signed promising independence in 3 years. SWAPO boycotted the conference. During 1977 five Western members of the UN Security Council held talks with Mr. Vorster. They demanded the inclusion of SWAPO in the independence process, the withdrawal of South African troops, the organisation of national elections under UN supervision and the release of all political prisoners. South Africa rejected UN supervision and troop withdrawal so long as the threat remained from the MPLA and the Cubans in neighbouring Angola. However, agreement was eventually reached that South Africa should appoint a General Administrator to govern Namibia by decree until elections were held for a constituent assembly on an unrestricted party-basis. The latter, appointed in July 1977, reduced racial discrimination and other restrictions in accordance with decisions previously taken by the "Turnhalle" constitutional conference.

Background to Independence.

After a period of intensification of SWAPO guerrilla activity, a South African attack on SWAPO camps in Angola in early 1978 almost wrecked the Western Namibia plan. However, SWAPO finally agreed to it in the summer of 1978. It envisaged a carefully timed programme, with an increasing UN presence, a cease-fire and the gradual withdrawal of South African troops, leading up to elections for a constituent assembly. But South Africa persisted in organising its own elections prior to independence, and a visit of five Western foreign ministers to Pretoria in October failed to extract any compromises apart from the postponement of independence from 31 December to the summer of 1979, thus leaving time for the organisation of UN elections. South Africa remained determined to keep its troops in Namibia so long as hostilities with SWAPO continued. In the elections held in December without international recognition and without SWAPO participation, the moderate conservative Democratic Turnhalle Alliance won a large majority of the seats. In May 1979 this Constituent Assembly, with the South African Government's encouragement, established a National Assembly with legislative powers, thus flying in the face of the Western Namibia Plan. In June 1980 a Council of Ministers drawn from the National Assembly was established. SWAPO declared that this had virtually destroyed efforts to solve the problem by negotiation. A United Nations conference on Namibia ended in failure in January 1981, and initiatives by President Reagan made little progress during the remainder of the year.

Prospects for a Settlement.

Tension remained high in the area as a result of repeated South African raids into Angola to attack SWAPO bases. However, the drain on its resources led South Africa to offer at the beginning of 1984 to "disengage" its troops from the Angolan border and to propose new talks on the future of Namibia. In February Angola and South Africa signed the Lusaka accord, by which Angola undertook to control SWAPO guerrillas in return for a South African withdrawal from its territory. In May 1984 President Kaunda of Zambia again attempted to play a mediating role when he hosted talks on Namibia in Lusaka between representatives of SWAPO, South Africa and the internal Namibian parties, but no agreement was reached.

The Transitional Government.

Progress was made in 1985 towards independence of a kind. In May a transitional government was appointed by the South African authorities, comprising eight ministers and eight deputy ministers, all from the Multi-Party Conference (MPC). The MPC was a loose coalition of six Namibian political parties, which SWAPO—still recognised by the United Nations as the only legal representative of the Namibian people—refused to join. In June President Botha signed a proclamation formally establishing a "transitional government of national unity".

LESOTHO.

The Background.

Lesotho is a former British colony which became independent on 4 October 1966. It has a population of some 1,500,000 and is entirely surrounded by South African territory. In pre-independence elections Chief Leabua Jonathan's Basotho National Party won power and he became Prime Minister. However, Chief Jonathan declared the 1970 elections invalid before the results could be announced and imposed a state of emergency. Parliamentary rule, with a National Assembly of nominated members, was reintroduced in 1973. In the 1970s Chief Jonathan became increasingly hostile to the government of South Africa, which in turn gave its support to the Lesotho Liberation Army.

Chief Jonathan Overthrown.

In 1985 the unrest in South Africa led to the use of Lesotho as a haven and staging-post by a growing number of refugees. In December commandos, presumed to be South African, raided Maseru, the capital of Lesotho, and killed nine people. Then in January 1986 South Africa imposed stringent border controls on the flow of goods and people in and out of land-locked Lesotho. This quickly had the desired effect and on 20 January the army, led by Maj-Gen Justin Lekhanya, overthrew Chief Jonathan. A military council was set up but it was announced that King Moshoeshoe II would be given executive and legislative powers. With the toppling of Chief Jonathan and expulsion of at least sixty members of the African National Congress by the

new government, South Africa lifted its border blockade.

ZIMBABWE.

In Rhodesia over five million Africans remained subordinate to 250,000 Whites until 1979. The 1961 Constitution provided for progressively increasing African representation in the Rhodesian Parliament. But a new White political party, the Rhodesian Front gained power at the 1963 elections on a platform of independence from Britain, opposition to the 1961 Constitution as too liberal, and opposition to proposals to repeal the Land Apportionment Act. The dissolution in December 1963 of the Federation of Rhodesia and Nyasaland led to the independence of Northern Rhodesia (as Zambia) and of Nyasaland (as Malawi) under majority governments and left Southern Rhodesia, renamed Rhodesia, as a self-governing colony with a White minority government. The Rhodesian Front leader, Winston Field, was replaced by Ian Smith after failing to obtain independence.

Unilateral Declaration of Independence.

Protracted negotiations took place between Mr. Smith and Mr. Wilson to reach a settlement in 1965. The latter took his stand on "five principles", including the stipulation that an agreed independence constitution should guarantee unimpeded progress to majority rule. But after winning all 50 White seats at the 1965 election, Mr. Smith made the unilateral declaration of independence from Britain on 11 November 1965. The British Government was thus confronted by an act of rebellion. However, it ruled out from the start the use of force. Mr. Wilson embarked on a policy of graduated economic sanctions, including an oil embargo; the objective being the emergence, under economic hardship, of a liberal alternative to the Smith régime. The UN Security Council later made sanctions mandatory, negotiations with the Smith régime proving fruitless. The white minority had found themselves unready to give the African majority reasonable prospects of education, jobs, political and civil rights. In 1969 a referendum led to Rhodesia being declared a republic. Under the republican Constitution, Whites were assured of a perpetual majority in the Senate and Africans could not hope for more than parity of representation in the lower House, and that in the indefinite future.

Stalemate and African Resistance.

Meanwhile exiled supporters of the banned African Nationalist organisations, Zimbabwe African People's Union (ZAPU) and Zimbabwe African National Union (ZANU), whose leaders Joshua Nkomo and Ndabaningi Sithole were imprisoned in Rhodesia, began armed incursions into Rhodesia from bases in Zambia in 1967.

However sanctions were succeeding only in increasing rural unemployment and a shortage of foreign exchange and because of "leaks" through South Africa and the Portuguese territories, they were seen more as a bargaining counter than a solution. In 1971 agreement on a settlement was reached between Mr. Smith and Sir Alec Douglas-Home conditional upon the British Government being satisfied that it was acceptable to most Rhodesians. African parliamentary representation was to rise to parity with the whites and following a referendum and a Commission inquiry majority rule was expected to follow. However, a British Commission found the settlement unacceptable to the Africans. Sanctions therefore continued and guerrilla activity increased.

In 1976 Dr. Kissinger held a series of talks with all those concerned and on 24 September Mr. Smith broadcast his agreement to the "Kissinger package". He made it clear that he had no option but to accept. In essence the package provided for the establishment of an interim government, composed of a white-headed council of state and a black-led council of ministers, which would pave the way for majority rule within 2 years. In return steps would be taken to lift sanctions and end the guerrilla war. Black African leaders, including the so-called "front-line" presidents, rejected Smith's version of the agreement. But eventually a constitutional conference began in Geneva under British chairmanship. The Africans were represented by the different nationalist leaders, Bishop Muzorewa (ANC), Joshua Nkomo (ZAPU), Robert Mugabe (ZANU) and Rev. Ndabaningi Sithole (ZANU). The talks foundered on the question of a date for majority rule and by December 1976 hopes for agreement on details had faded. The "front line" presidents recognised Nkomo and Mugabe (now united as the Patriotic Front) as the representatives of Zimbabwe.

Early 1977 saw the introduction of some measures for reducing racial discrimination in Rhodesia. However, at the same time the guerrilla war continued and intensified. In May Zambia declared that it was in a state of war with Rhodesia as a result of penetration of Zambian territory by Rhodesian troops "in hot pursuit". Rhodesian troops also occupied some Mozambiquan territory for the purpose of eliminating terrorists. Meanwhile the increasingly insecure situation in Rhodesia was causing a growing exodus of whites. It became clear that Cuba was supplying arms to the Patriotic Front.

A visit to southern Africa by an Anglo-American negotiating team in July produced some progress, including an agreement on British supervision of the Rhodesian Government during a transitional period of three to six months before the holding of general elections. But a retrograde step followed when elections based on the old purely white electorate were called prematurely for 31 August. In these the Rhodesian Front won all of the 50 seats reserved to whites, and Mr. Smith said that he had a mandate to negotiate an "internal solution" with moderate black leaders. Talks later began with Bishop Muzorewa and Mr Sithole, who disputed the primacy of the Patriotic Front and its support among the population.

A New Peace Plan.

On 1 September 1977 a new Anglo-American peace plan was published in Salisbury. It received unfavourable initial reactions from both Mr. Smith and the Patriotic Front. But by December the so-called "front-line states" and the Patriotic Front under Nkomo and Mugabe agreed to negotiate with London for a peaceful transfer of power on the basis of the Anglo-American plan. They condemned the talks aimed at an "internal solution". Meanwhile Mr. Ian Smith, after accepting the principle of universal adult suffrage for Rhodesia under certain conditions, reached agreement with the three leaders of African organisations inside Rhodesia (Bishop Muzorewa, Rev. Sithole and Chief Chirau) in March 1978 on Black majority rule by the end of 1978.

The "Internal Settlement".

This far-reaching "internal solution" provided for an interracial government immediately, followed by general elections on a one-man one-vote basis. Even if the Whites were guaranteed 28% of the seats for the first ten years, this was still a major volte-face on Mr. Smith's part and opened the way to a genuine multiracial state. Yet the exclusion of the protégés of the front-line states, Nkomo and Mugabe, from the agreement led the United States and Britain to declare it unsatisfactory. They maintained sanctions against Rhodesia, thus making life difficult for the new government and playing into the hands of the guerrillas. There was now a clear power struggle between the different Black nationalists in Rhodesia in which the members of the transitional government had the majority of the population on their side while their rivals of the Patriotic Front had the weapons. Meanwhile in August it emerged that during most of the sanctions period oil had been reaching Rhodesia from Britain via South Africa, with the connivance of Government ministers.

In the autumn of 1978 elections and majority rule were postponed until 1979 because of delays in drawing up the new constitutions and likely disruption of the elections by the Patriotic Front. In reality it seemed that Mr. Smith was trying to maintain White supremacy in the army and police, thus casting doubt on his claim that he was now ready to take part in a conference of all parties, as called for by Britain and the USA, "without pre-

conditions". In any case the prospect of more peaceful conditions was also very doubtful. The bush war was becoming even more bloody, with 30 to 50 being killed daily. Despite the undoubted superiority of the Rhodesian army, the costs of the war were very high and morale was declining.

The position of the black members of the interim government was made difficult by Mr. Smith's delay in implementing majority rule and Black equality as agreed. There was an undoubted fall in their popularity. But cracks also appeared in the Patriotic Front when it transpired that Mr. Nkomo had secretly negotiated with Mr. Smith in August 1978. This was treachery in the eyes of the more radical front-line states and led to a split between him and Mr. Mugabe. There was also disunity among the front-line states themselves. Economic necessity had even forced Zambia to reopen its rail link through Rhodesia.

Muzorewa Takes Office.

In April 1979 the first one-man one-vote elections were held. Despite threats of disruption by guerrillas, turnout was relatively high. The result produced a clear victory for Bishop Abel Muzorewa who became Rhodesia's first black Prime Minister. However, the many concessions he had made to the Whites, who had a right of veto in Parliament and retained control over civil service, courts and security forces, made him appear a traitor in the eyes of many Blacks. And the exclusion of the Patriotic Front, with its some 25,000 guerrilla fighters, meant that the new government could not win international recognition. It thus appeared that the achievement of Black majority rule was now only the prelude to an even grimmer phase of the struggle.

The Lancaster House Settlement.

By September 1979, however, the British Government had succeeded in bringing both the Muzorewa Government and the Patriotic Front to the negotiating table at Lancaster House. There followed three months of tough negotiations which often seemed on the point of breaking down. However in October Mugabe and Nkomo showed a sudden readiness to compromise. They agreed that to avoid a mass exodus of Whites, whom the country would badly need, they should in future have 20% of the seats in Parliament, even though they represented only 3% of the population. But they were to have no veto power and would lose control of the armed forces and civil service. They also gave ground on their demand for confiscation of land from Whites without compensation; but the compensation was to come from an international fund.

But once the terms of the new constitution had been agreed by both the Patriotic Front and the Rhodesian Government delegation (which included Mr. Ian Smith), the transitional arrangements and ceasefire provisions remained disputed. Zimbabwe-Rhodesia was to return temporarily to the status of a British colony. But the Patriotic Front objected to the wide powers to be held by the British Governor and his advisers between the resignation of Bishop Muzorewa and the granting of legal independence. They also regarded the two-month transitional phase leading up to the elections as too short and demanded that they be supervised by a UN force. Lord Carrington was prepared to compromise on a Commonwealth force, and after further concessions, especially on the "legalisation" of the guerrilla forces during the transitional period, a ceasefire was agreed, ending the seven-year bush war in which 20,000 people had been killed. Meanwhile sanctions against Rhodesia were not renewed when they ran out in November 1979.

The success of the Lancaster House negotiations no doubt had much to do with war-weariness and with the suffering of the front-line states, on whose support the Patriotic Front depended. But it was nevertheless a remarkable achievement, even if the ceasefire remained very fragile. The British Governor, Lord Soames, proceeded to lift the ban on political activity by the two wings of the Patriotic Front, ZANU and ZAPU. The election campaign was to start at the beginning of January 1980 and election of a new Parliament and independence were to follow two months later. Both the ceasefire and the gathering of former guerrillas at the assembly points provided for them went unexpectedly well. The Patriotic Front leaders were ecstatically received when they returned to Salisbury. But Mugabe's ZANU had declared that it had no further interest in an electoral pact with Nkomo's ZAPU, and this made the election result less predictable.

The Background to the 1980 Elections.

During February animosity increased as the Marxist Mugabe and the front-line African states claimed that Lord Soames and the British officials were discriminating in favour of his opponents. Acts of terrorism became ever more frequent. It became clear that many of Mugabe's supporters had not gone to the assembly points as agreed. But some of the attacks were on the property of Mugabe himself and other ZANU leaders. Meanwhile voting for the 80 White seats took place as planned on 14 February, with all of them falling to Ian Smith's Rhodesian Front.

Mugabe's Sweeping Victory.

The elections for the 80 Black seats in the 100-member House of Assembly produced a sweeping victory for Mugabe. His ZANU (PF) Party won 57 seats and 63% of the vote. Nkomo's Party won a disappointing 20 seats, while Bishop Muzorewa's United African National Council won only a humiliating 8% of the vote and a mere 3 seats. On 17 April 1980, Zimbabwe became an independent Republic with Mugabe as Prime Minister of a coalition which included Nkomo. The Rev. Canaan Banana became the first President.

Mugabe's early period of office was made difficult by murder charges being brought against one of his Cabinet ministers, Mr. Edgar Tekere, who was subsequently acquitted. However, he was later dismissed in a Cabinet reshuffle which also saw the demotion of Joshua Nkomo. The latter's followers, who along with many whites were worried by Mugabe's assumption of control of the news media, took part in violent clashes with Mugabe supporters, and there were many casualties before order was restored. The disarming of guerrilla groups was largely completed by May 1981. In the previous month Salisbury, the capital of Zimbabwe, had been renamed Harare.

Dismissal and Exile of Mr Nkomo.

The political outlook in Zimbabwe changed considerably in February 1982 when secret stockpiles of weapons were found on farms belonging to Nkomo. He denied he had been planning a coup, but he and three other ZAPU officials were dismissed from the cabinet by Mugabe. ZAPU retained a token presence in the government but the coalition was a dead letter. Nkomo's dismissal passed off initially without bloodshed. However, later in 1982, a new threat to Zimbabwe's stability occurred. Outbreaks of violence took place in Matabeleland following harsh repressive action by the North Korean-trained Fifth Army Brigade against supporters of Nkomo. This reached a head in March 1983 when Nkomo himself fled, first to Botswana and then on to exile in London.

Nkomo returned in August 1983 when the government made moves to strip him of his parliamentary seat. However, Mugabe took another step towards making Zimbabwe a one-party state in October 1983 when he arrested Bishop Muzorewa on the grounds of his being a threat to Zimbabwe's security. Bishop Muzorewa was freed in September 1984.

Relations with Britain and America.

Zimbabwe's relations with Britain were soured in 1983 by the trial of six white air force officers begun in May for complicity in the sabotage of 13 military aircraft at Thornhill Air Base in July 1982. Evidence that their confessions had been obtained by torture led to the acquittal of the six men on 31 August, but they were immediately re-detained by the government. Three were released in September, but the others were not released until 23 December. Then at the close of 1983 the United States announced that it had cut its $75 m of aid to Zimbabwe by $35 m after Zimbabwe

had co-sponsored a UN resolution condemning the American invasion of Grenada and abstained in a Security Council vote condemning the Russian shooting down of a South Korean airliner.

Towards a One-Party State.

In August 1984 ZANU held its second national congress (the first was in 1964) in Harare, which consolidated Mr. Mugabe's position in the party and government and ZANU's national authority. Some six thousand ZANU delegates attended the five-day conference. Mr. Mugabe was made First Secretary and President of the party, and a new fifteen-member political bureau, chosen by him, was created to exercise supreme power. The congress called for the creation of the post of executive president for Zimbabwe, and also endorsed a resolution calling for the creation of a one-party state, though the timing of this would respect the Lancaster House constitution. In November, Mr. Mugabe dismissed the two remaining ZAPU ministers from his cabinet, after blaming ZAPU for the death of a member of the ZANU central committee, thus ending all co-operation between ZANU and ZAPU.

Elections were held in mid-1985. At the end of June, elections for the 20 seats reserved for whites in the House of Assembly resulted in 15 being won by Ian Smith's Conservative Alliance of Zimbabwe, to the displeasure of Mr. Mugabe's supporters. Elections for the remaining seats were held at the beginning of July. ZANU won a landslide victory with 64 seats, but Mr. Nkomo's ZAPU secured all 15 seats in Matabeleland. The country therefore seemed to be more divided than ever on racial and tribal lines.

When Mr. Mugabe announced a new cabinet after the elections, Mr. Anderson was the only white and non-ZANU member. A number of senior members of ZAPU were detained in August, but nevertheless talks in September 1985 between ZANU and ZAPU delegations reached broad agreement on a merger between the two parties.

MOZAMBIQUE.

Rebellion broke out in Mozambique in 1963 and intensified in Angola after 1966 forcing the Portuguese to pour in even more troops. However, in 1974, cease-fires were called after an appeal by the new Portuguese government to the liberation movements for a cessation of hostilities. Agreements were reached for the independence of Guinea Bissau and Mozambique after President Spinola's statement in July on the independence of Portugal's African territories.

A transitional government was installed in Mozambique in September made up of Frelimo (Front for the Liberation of Mozambique) and Portuguese elements and full independence was scheduled for July 1975. However, the agreement led to serious racial unrest with white extremists attempting to proclaim UDI and thereby provoking a Black backlash. Nevertheless independence was granted on schedule. The Marxist-oriented government under President Machel produced plans to revolutionise the state machine and improve the economy. In December an attempt to overthrow President Machel was crushed. Relations with Portugal deteriorated and in February 1976 the capital Lourenço Marques was renamed Maputo.

Despite this, the end of the guerrilla war in Zimbabwe and the need to secure economic advances saw Mozambique moving closer to the West during 1980, signified by ministerial changes in April and changes in the economy in July.

Growing Internal Resistance.

President Machel continued to face internal opposition from the so-called Mozambique National Resistance Movement which carried out widespread sabotage and terrorist attacks. The rebels were supported by South Africa as a lever to force the Mozambique government to withdraw its backing for the African National Congress, the militant black nationalist organisation banned in South Africa. In January 1981 South African forces carried out a commando raid in a suburb of Maputo against three houses occupied by the ANC.

Guerrilla warfare continued throughout 1982–3. Following a car bomb explosion in Pretoria, the South African Air Force mounted a raid on Maputo on 23 May 1983, killing five people. Representatives of Mozambique and South Africa met for talks on security problems and economic co-operation in January 1984.

The Nkomati Accord.

These talks resulted in the signing of a non-aggression pact, the Nkomati accord, by Mozambique and South Africa in March 1984. A joint commission was set up to monitor the working of the accord. After a series of negotiations, the South African foreign minister, Pik Botha, announced in Pretoria in October that the government of Mozambique and the MNRM had agreed in principle to a cease-fire. However, guerrilla warfare continued into 1985 and President Machel accused South Africa of not curbing MNRM attacks, although Mozambique had expelled many ANC members. During talks in September 1985 President Machel was able to confront the South Africans with documents captured at the MNRM headquarters at Gorongosa, proving their continuing support for the guerrillas.

ANGOLA.

Negotiations on Angola were held up because it had three rival liberation movements torn by dissension and because of serious racial violence in this the richest of the colonies, with great mineral wealth and hundreds of thousands of Portuguese settlers. However after the formation of a common front between the three liberation movements (MPLA, FNLA and UNITA) in January 1975 agreement was reached on independence in November 1975 and until then the establishment of a transitional government of all three plus representatives of the Portuguese Government.

The Civil War.

But fighting continued, particularly between the FNLA and the Marxist MPLA, despite a truce agreement in March and became increasingly intense. During the summer of 1975 the MPLA gradually took over sole control of the capital Luanda, and UNITA joined the FNLA in operations against the MPLA. The latter held a central strip from the coast to the border with Zaïre, while UNITA held most of the South, and FNLA the rest of the South and the northern provinces.

In the months before independence there was a massive departure of European settlers, leaving appalling economic problems for Angola. Meanwhile there was increasing evidence of the Soviet Union supplying the MPLA with arms. Several thousand Cuban soldiers also appeared on the MPLA side. The FNLA received support from China and initially from the USA via Zaïre. In November two separate Angolan Republics were proclaimed with rival governments being set up, by the MPLA in Luanda and by FNLA and UNITA in Huambo (formerly Nova Lisboa).

Full-scale civil war now developed. With Soviet and Cuban support, the MPLA first brought the North under control pushing the FNLA back into Zaïre. UNITA forces in the South were attacked and the South African forces which had advanced several hundred miles into Angola withdrew to patrol a 30-mile wide strip along the border. In February 1976, following the capture of Huambo, an MPLA victory was declared. UNITA forces under Dr. Jonas Savimbi and the FNLA under Mr. Holden Roberto continued guerrilla activities throughout 1976 while the MPLA attempted to bring the country back to normal. Periodic UNITA success kept President Neto dependent on the Cubans, with whom a series of agreements on co-operation had been concluded.

The Death of Neto.

In September 1979 President Neto died. Though Moscow's protégé, he kept the Russians and Cubans at a distance after gaining power and won the respect of neighbouring, and even of Western, states.

Dr. José Eduardo dos Santos was elected to succeed him.

The Lusaka Accord.

Frequent raids into Angola were mounted by South African forces hunting for South West Africa People's Organisation (SWAPO) guerrillas. A major incursion was launched in December 1983. This was followed, however, by a South African announcement of a one-month truce in February 1984. After talks in the Zambian capital, Lusaka, an accord was signed by Angola and South Africa on 16 February 1984. The cease-fire was extended, and, in return for a South African withdrawal, Angola would curb SWAPO operations into Namibia.

It was not until April 1985 that South African troops officially withdrew from Angolan territory and then fresh incursions took place in June and September. The latter came just as government forces were attempting to mount a major offensive against UNITA. The South African government admitted it was still supporting the rebels and would continue to do so until all foreign troops had been withdrawn from Angola.

The Angolan government faced fresh problems as the American Congress voted in mid-1985 to repeal the 1976 Clark amendment banning aid to the UNITA guerrillas. In July 1985 Angola announced the suspension of all contacts with the United States.

THE UNITED STATES

America since 1976.

1976 became the year in which the country finally put Watergate and associated traumas behind it. The new spirit was symbolised by the nation's celebration of 200 years of independence which reached a climax on 4 July.

The year was dominated by the Presidential elections, President Ford had announced his intention to seek election to the office he then held by appointment, but barely won the Republican nomination over Ronald Reagan, former Governor of California. The Democrats had no single, obvious candidate and a free-for-all emerged among the possible challengers. At the beginning of the long primary election procedure to select the eventual candidate, Jimmy Carter, former Governor of Georgia, was a relative unknown outside the South. But he was eventually nominated with only token opposition. In the election itself Carter's massive early lead in the polls gradually dwindled and the result was close, although Carter had a larger popular majority than either Kennedy in 1960 or Nixon in 1968. In the electoral college, which constitutionally elects the President, the result was a margin of 56 votes for Carter.

President Carter.

Carter's election was both unusual and symbolic in a number of ways. The first President from the "deep south" since before the Civil War, some viewed Carter's election as the final act of reconciliation between North and South. Rising out of obscurity and possessing relatively little political experience, and having based much of his campaign on an attack on the Washington establishment, Carter was seen by some as a genuine Washington "outsider" not tied to any entrenched group.

In picking his Cabinet, however, Carter disappointed many of his supporters while reassuring the "establishment". During his first months in office he quickly set up a Department of Energy and proposed a drastic programme for energy saving. In nuclear energy policy he introduced many restrictions and promoted a search for greater safeguards. At the same time the proliferation of nuclear capacity abroad was discouraged. President Carter also sent to Congress an anti-inflation programme, though without wage or price controls, and a new welfare programme to benefit those unable to maintain themselves by work.

In foreign policy President Carter's emphasis on human rights proved a complicating factor in relations with the Communist states and with right-wing Latin American régimes. In November 1977 he signed the Foreign Aid Act denying aid to states which violated the human rights of their citizens. In the spring of 1978 his success in gaining Senate acceptance of the treaty to transfer control of the Panama Canal to the Panamanians by the year 2000, and the US intervention in the Dominican Republic which made possible the electoral victory of the opposition raised the US image in Latin America.

The establishment of full dipomatic relations with China in December 1978 was a dramatic move, though the consequent dropping of Taiwan was a blow to America's Asian allies.

By the spring of 1979 SALT II had been negotiated and the treaty was signed at a US–Soviet summit in Vienna in June 1979. It was a modest step which did not halt the arms race but only curbed it somewhat. But it opened the way for further negotiations, not least on middle-range missiles in Europe. However the US Senate was reluctant to ratify the treaty.

Carter's Domestic Legislation.

In his domestic legislation projects, however, the President was largely baulked by a newly self-confident Congress. His relations with Congressmen were poor and his popularity was sinking fast. However, his personal success at Camp David in September 1978 in bringing Israel and Egypt on to the road to peace silenced murmurings about weak leadership, and in the mid-term Congressional elections the Democrats lost fewer seats than expected. But at the mid-term Democratic party conference there was manifest concern about President Carter's evident determination to curb inflation and the inexorable fall in the value of the dollar even at the cost of programmes for job creation, youth employment, and training assistance (though it was precisely this clear determination which finally stabilised the dollar). The Blacks and the urban poor, who had had high hopes of Carter, were clearly disappointed. During 1979 there was a further dramatic decline in confidence in President Carter's leadership, and his attempt to restore his image by forcing the collective resignation of his Cabinet in July had rather the opposite effect. Senator Edward Kennedy emerged as the spokesman of the disgruntled liberal wing of the Democrats, and in the autumn of 1979 he announced that he would stand against Carter for the Democratic nomination for the 1980 Presidential elections.

The President's predicament was partly a result of the 'damage done to the myth of the Presidency by Vietnam and Watergate. However, he was clearly unable to gain the co-operation of Congress: his vital energy programme remained bogged down in committees and subject to ever further dilution by interest groups. Yet in other respects he was not unsuccessful. This was true, for example, of his job-creation policy, and of several foreign policy achievements as seen above. But concern was caused by his handling of the Cuban crisis in the autumn of 1979 after the revelation of the presence of a Soviet brigade on the island. President Carter made tough demands for a change in the status quo without possessing any means of enforcing it, and eventual retreat was inevitable. The President's image was also tarnished by the continuing fall in the value of the dollar, which largely reflected the changed position of the United States in the world.

The Iranian and Afghanistan Crises.

President Carter's battered reputation was rapidly restored in the USA at the end of 1979 by his handling of the crisis caused by the drama of the hostages in Tehran and the Afghan invasion. These crises caused a wave of patriotic feeling which had the traditional effect of rallying the population round the incumbent President. Carter was enabled to appear at last as a decisive leader. In response to the Iranian challenge he acted coolly but firmly, even if his plans for economic sanctions had to be revised in the light of the new strategic situation caused by the Soviet intervention in neighbouring Afghanistan. But American impotence remained all too evident. Under the impact of the crisis President Carter announced a five-year plan for the modernising of

the armed forces to meet the tasks of the 1980s. He had thus come a long way from his initial intention to reduce defence expenditure and withdraw US troops from Korea. The Afghanistan crisis further hastened the end of the "Vietnam complex" in the USA and a recognition of the need to meet threats to American interests by irrational régimes and to curb Soviet designs. Carter reacted to it by an embargo on exports of grain and high technology products to the Soviet union, a call for a boycott of the Olympic Games in Moscow, substantial military aid for Pakistan and a strengthening of the American presence in the Indian Ocean and the Persian Gulf. Deficiencies in the USA's ability to react to military threats became apparent, and President Carter's new doctrine of "peace through strength" called for major increases in defence expenditure. In April, President Carter broke off diplomatic relations with Iran and imposed economic sanctions, but the failure of some of America's allies to show the expected solidarity caused widespread dissatisfaction.

On 25 April, Carter announced to a stunned world that an unsuccessful military attempt to rescue the Iran embassy hostages had ended in tragic failure. Eight American troops had been killed in a collision in a remote desert location in Iran. Shortly afterwards, US Secretary of State Cyrus Vance, who had opposed the mission, resigned and was replaced by Senator Muskie.

Reagan's Presidential Victory.

On 4 November, 1980, the Republican candidate, Ronald Reagan, a former Governor of California, was elected the 40th President of the United States by a majority of more than 8 million votes over incumbent Democratic President Jimmy Carter. And, for the first time in a generation, the Republican Party gained control of the US Senate, winning 12 seats previously held by Democrats. Although the Democrats retained control of the House of Representatives, they suffered significant losses there, having their majority cut in half. Taken as a whole, the General Election amounted at the very least to a significant shift of power in Washington, and to a severe setback for the Democratic Party. The turnout for the election was only 53%, the fifth consecutive time that the turnout for a Presidential Election had declined.

Reagan's First Months.

Ronald Reagan's first year in office demonstrated that the political skills which he had nurtured as Governor of California, and refined in his bids for the Presidency, had not deserted him. The November 1980 elections were thought to have given him a clear mandate both for his domestic economic policies and his foreign policy. The latter rested on a huge expansion of the defence budget to meet Soviet military expansion. Reagan drew heavily on the stock of political capital provided by his election victory and the Republican advances in Congress to cut severely spending on social, welfare and educational programmes in an attempt to reduce the growing Federal deficit. But, like President Carter before him, Reagan discovered by the end of his first year as President that eliminating, or even substantially reducing the Federal deficit was far from easy.

Indeed, the deficit grew substantially under the triple pressures of the cut in taxes (which Reagan skilfully piloted through Congress), the effect of the deepening recession on the total tax revenues, and the heavy increases in defence spending. By early 1982, Reagan's sure touch in front of the television cameras, and his ardent wooing of Congress (which was in any case ideologically predisposed to support him) no longer seemed sufficient to meet the mounting doubts about his fiscal and monetary policies. Interest rates remained stubbornly high, propped up by the Federal deficit, and the rate of unemployment increased. Reagan's own budget for 1982 projected a deficit of between $90 and $100bn. The Congressional Budget Office was more pessimistic, forecasting a deficit of $160bn for 1984, the year of the next Presidential elections. But there were political pressures building up in the short term, too. The approach of the mid-term elections in 1982 caused Republican Congressmen and Senators to look hesitantly at their electorate's views before supporting the President's domestic strategy.

But if doubts were raised about Reagan's policies, he continued to show deft political touches. Perhaps the most striking was his nomination of Judge Sandra Day O'Connor to be an Associate Justice of the Supreme Court. Mrs. O'Connor took the place of Justice Potter Steward who had sat on the Court for 23 years. She was an active Republican from Arizona, and an excellent jurist, but clearly not associated with the extreme right-wing of the Republican Party. The Moral Majority and other extreme groups opposed her confirmation by the Senate because of her somewhat liberal views on abortion. The Senate none the less confirmed her nomination by 99 votes to 0. President Reagan thus distanced himself from the far-right of his Party, appeased liberal and women's groups by selecting a woman, but still succeeded in selecting a moderately conservative nominee with an impeccable legal, and unassailable political, record.

1982 Congressional Elections.

The mid-term Congressional elections in November 1982 produced the customary swing to the party in opposition: the Democrats made net gains of 24 seats in the House of Representatives and seven state Governorships, but failed to alter the party balance in the Senate. The outcome was a mild rebuff to President Reagan. It would certainly make life more difficult for him on Capitol Hill. But there was no widespread revolt against the President's brand of Republicanism. High levels of unemployment and a sluggish economy had led some commentators to predict a larger swing to the Democrats.

Significantly, the New Right, who were thought so important a component of Reagan's coalition in 1980, did badly. Whereas several senior liberal Democrats had been successfully targetted for defeat in 1980 by conservative political action committees, hardly any of those similarly arraigned in 1982 were defeated.

If the Republicans were weakened by disappointment among their 1980 supporters at the lack of economic progress, the Democrats were badly handicapped by the widespread feeling that they had no coherent policy alternative to offer. Furthermore, President Reagan proved tactically more adept than many Democrats had expected and he distanced himself from his most conservative supporters.

The 1984 Presidential Elections.

Reagan's tactical adroitness was to be seen again in the 1984 Presidential elections. Ronald Reagan capitalised upon divisions in the Democratic Party and exploited his own formidable gifts of communication to capture the presidency for a second term in the November 1984 elections.

Mondale secured the Democratic nomination at a high political cost; the mauling he had received in the primaries from Senator Gary Hart, and the mostly effective and wholly novel campaign of Jesse Jackson, weakened the Party in the approach to November. Jackson's supporters (mostly black) were much less enthusiastic about supporting a white male candidate in the presidential election than they had been in backing Jackson in the primaries. Ninety per cent of those blacks who voted supported Mondale, but many abstained. A significant proportion of Hart's primary supporters switched their general election support not to Mondale but to Reagan; defections from registered Democratic voters to Reagan were high, and strikingly so among young white professionals. Such advantage as Mondale had hoped for by having Congresswoman Geraldine Ferraro on the ticket as his running-mate was dissipated by his own insipid television performances and by the whiff of scandal surrounding Mrs. Ferraro's husband's business activities.

Reagan's victory over Mondale was huge. As a percentage of the popular vote, it was not quite as large as that secured by Lyndon Johnson in his victory over Barry Goldwater in 1964, but it approached it. Reagan improved on the size of Johnson's victory in the Electoral College: he won everywhere except in Minnesota (Mondale's home state) and Washington, DC, which, with a majority black population went decisively for the democratic candidate.

The Congressional Elections.

The implications of Reagan's victory could not be considered except in the context of the congressional election results. Although Reagan's victory at the presidential level was entirely decisive, he did not have the advantage of a large intake of Republicans in the congressional elections. The Republicans lost two seats in the Senate and gained fewer than they had anticipated in the House. By the time of Reagan's inauguration in January 1985, it seemed probable that his support in Congress would be insufficient to deliver the conservative ideological majority which he had exploited to such effect in 1981. Furthermore, Democratic control of the House, as political observers in Washington noted, was certain to be strengthened at the time of the mid-term elections in 1986 and the Republicans would very probably lose control of the Senate at the same time.

The change in circumstances between 1981 and 1985 was neatly illustrated by the rebuff delivered to the president in January 1985 when Senator Robert Dole, the new Republican Majority Leader in the Senate, announced that Mr. Reagan's budget proposals had no chance of adoption by congress. Dole emphasised that congress would take the initiative in creating a budget, and hence in attempting to deal with the major political question of the day, the large, and growing, budget deficit.

Divisions among the Democrats.

As during the election campaign, so in the early weeks of Mr. Reagan's new term: the Democrats could provide no clear alternative because they were divided among themselves. The old liberal remedies of the 1950s and 1960s had less appeal to many Democratic supporters (especially those who had backed Senator Hart's candidacy in 1984) than formerly, and to a growing proportion of Democratic sympathisers lacked intellectual or political plausibility. The task for the Democratic nominee in 1988 was bound to be great. Even with the considerable burden of a large budget deficit and high interest rates, the Republicans had good reason in early 1985 for believing that the Republican presidential ascendancy would continue beyond 1988, probable congressional losses in 1986 notwithstanding.

Background to 1986 Elections.

The approach of the 1986 elections complicated politicians' calculations about both domestic and foreign policy. The budget deficit and the consequential problems of the growing trade deficit and high real interest rates provided the economic context for policy-making during 1985 and the first few months of 1986; the cautious moves towards a new round of arms control talks with the Soviet Union dominated foreign policy considerations.

The budget deficit of approximately $200,000 billion in the 1986 fiscal year did little to damage President Reagan's standing in the opinion polls. His political finesse lay in using the deficit which his tax cuts and defence spending increases of 1981 had produced to reshape the political agenda more decisively than any president since Lyndon Johnson. The size of the deficit made a coherent political response by the Democratic opposition in congress exceedingly difficult; they could propose no new spending programmes without exposing themselves to charges of irresponsibility from the president and his party allies. The discussions within congress and between congress and the president about measures to reduce the deficit resulted in a bizarre piece of legislation, the Gramm-Rudman-Hollings Act, which brought automatic spending cuts into play in the event of president and congress failing to agree upon their size and location. The problem had become so great that politicians of all ideological stripes were simultaneously anxious to condemn the size of the deficit, whilst evading responsibility for cutting it.

In foreign affairs, the summit meeting between President Reagan and Mikhail Gorbachev, the new General Secretary of the Soviet Communist Party, at Geneva signalled the end of the rhetorical hostilities and political immobilism which had characterised superpower relations since the Soviet invasion of Afghanistan six years before. Success in arms control was far from guaranteed by the relative amity displayed for the world's press at Geneva. That would depend upon the general condition of political relations between the superpowers—without a general measure of political confidence at such a level, detailed diplomatic exchange could not succeed. But the step towards a renewed dialogue had been made, and the economic interests of both countries offered at least the prospect of a negotiated settlement to the detailed questions of strategic nuclear weapons between them, and of intermediate range nuclear weapons in Europe. The eruption of the Libya crisis, (see **C66**) threw these calculations into considerable doubt.

CANADA

The relationship between the English and French speaking communities remains Canada's principal political problem. In 1970 the Quebec Liberal Party committed to federalism gained a clear majority in the elections, but the separatist Parti Québécois took 25 per cent of the vote. The kidnapping by the Front de Libération du Quévec of a British trade commissioner and the Québec Minister of Labour, Mr. Pierre Laporte (who was later found dead), prompted Mr. Pierre Trudeau, the Canadian Prime Minister, to invoke Canada's War Emergency Act. But the Quebec separatist movement had been seriously weakened by the acts of terrorism.

In 1969 the Official Languages Act provided for equality between the two languages at federal level in parliament, government, and the courts. Bilingual districts could be established wherever the minority reached 10 per cent of the population and a Commission of Official Languages was to act as watchdog. In October 1971 Mr. Trudeau declared his allegiance to a policy of "multiculturalism within a bi-lingual framework."

In Parliamentary elections in October 1972 Mr. Trudeau's Liberal Party lost its overall majority and obtained only two seats more than the Progressive Conservative Party under Robert Stanfield, although it held its own in its stronghold of Quebec. Mr. Trudeau failed partly because rising unemployment had not prevented serious increases in the price of food, partly because of the failure of the experiment of the bilingual law. However he was able to form a government again with the parliamentary support of the small New Democratic Party (a Labour Party in all but name), which had also made gains. Further elections were held in 1974 after the Liberal Government had been defeated on a motion of no confidence in respect of the Budget. Mr. Trudeau succeeded with his argument against Mr. Stanfield that inflation was an international problem about which the Canadian Government could do little by itself.

In 1976 Mr. René Lévesque, a committed separatist, was elected Premier of Quebec. He later announced that a consultative referendum would be held before 1981 on the issue of independence for the province. A law passed in August 1977 provided that French should in future be the only official language in Quebec. Mr. Trudeau then sought Federal powers to protect the position of the English-speaking minority in Quebec and the francophone minorities in the other provinces. When opening Parliament in Ottawa in October, the Queen appealed for unity and announced a proposed revision of the constitution to strengthen federalism in Canada. Mr. Trudeau proposed that a referendum on secession by Quebec should be held throughout Canada, and not merely in Quebec itself. Meanwhile the Quebec government was intensifying its relations with France, and when Mr. Lévesque visited Paris in November he was treated like a head of state.

The Elections of 1979 and 1980.

The general election held on 22 May 1979 ended the 11-year rule of Mr. Trudeau. The electorate seemed to have grown tired of the talented, worldly, but often arrogant Prime Minister. The opposition Progressive Conservative Party, headed by 39-year-old Joe Clark, formed a minority government, having just fallen short of an overall majority. It intended to set the economy free from state controls. However Mr. Clark rapidly lost

popularity, and in December, after only 7 months in office, he resigned following the rejection of his austerity budget by Parliament.

In the ensuing elections in February 1980 Mr. Clark had the disadvantage of not having had time to make an impact; while Mr. Trudeau who had recently announced his final departure from politics, had to do a rapid about-turn because of the lack of an obvious successor. This was a very unsatisfactory situation at a time when the country was faced by the challenge of Quebec's referendum in the spring on whether to go its own way. The resurgence of support for Mr. Trudeau was checked somewhat by the increase in the Government's international stature when the Canadian ambassador in Tehran smuggled 6 US diplomats out of Iran. But his Liberal Party nevertheless won a resounding electoral victory.

The Quebec Referendum.

In a referendum held on 20 May 1980, the people of Quebec voted against the proposal of the *Parti Québécois* Government to negotiate a much looser form of political association with the rest of Canada. In an 84% turnout, the vote against negotiation of political secession was almost 60%. Thus Quebec Premier René Lévesque's drive for the independence of Quebec was effectively ended. But the need for constitutional reform was generally acknowledged, and discussions were set in motion on the question within days of the "no" vote in the referendum.

The Patriation Issue.

Canadian politics in 1981 and early 1982 centred on the question of whether the constitution would be patriated or not. For some time, it seemed unlikely that Pierre Trudeau would manage to arrive at a constitutional settlement which satisfied the fears and concerns of the provinces and of the Indians. Many British M.P.s made it clear that, whatever Trudeau's wishes, they could not support the passage of a new Canada Act, and the patriation of the Canadian constitution on terms which the Provinces rejected. Eventually, however, a settlement was arrived at which, with the exception of Quebec and the Indian National Brotherhood (themselves only a minority of the Canadians), carried with it the broad support of Canadians. In early 1982 the Canada Bill came before the House of Commons in London and duly completed its passage.

The Trudeau Succession.

Party leadership was the prominent issue in Canadian politics during 1982 and the first few months of 1983. It seemed certain to continue to be so for some time. Pierre Trudeau continually affirmed his intention to step down from the Liberal leadership, to make way for a new face to lead the Party into the elections due by early 1985 at the latest. Meanwhile, Joe Clark had gradually lost his hold on the Conservative Party, and then lost the leadership on 11 June 1983 to Mr. Brian Mulroney. Mulroney makes a substantial living as a lawyer in Montreal, but lacks political experience and knowledge. Like Prime Minister Trudeau, Mulroney is from Quebec and speaks perfect French; that was a major advantage to him in the Conservative Party's drive to gain a hold in Quebec province, long a bastion of liberal strength—indeed, increasingly, the major source of liberal strength in Canada.

Pierre Trudeau visited European capitals during the latter part of 1983 as part of his campaign to bring about a disarmament conference of the five major nuclear powers; he tried to see President Andropov on the same quest. Neither of the superpowers did more than give a cautious welcome to Trudeau's proposal; Britain and France showed still less interest. Senor Perez de Cuellar, the Secretary-General of the United Nations, supported the initiative, but it seemed unlikely to gather more substantial support in the absence of warmer political relations between East and West. Then, in early 1984, Trudeau at last announced that he was standing down as Prime Minister, to be succeeded by John Turner.

The 1984 Election.

The Canadian elections of September 1984 produced a remarkable change in fortunes for the two major political parties: the Conservatives won 211 of the 282 seats in the House of Commons, whilst the Liberals, who had been in power for more than twenty of the preceding twenty-one years and for much of the century before that, won just 40 seats. Although in the weeks before the election a Conservative victory had been expected, its scale was a suprise to almost all.

Comparisons were naturally drawn with Mr. Diefenbaker's victory in 1958. But the differences between the two are considerable, and emphasise the extraordinary nature of the Conservatives' success in 1984. Diefenbaker struck an alliance with Quebec Prime Minister, M. Duplessis, in 1958 which caused 50 Union Nationale seats to be added to the Conservatives' own strength. Twenty-seven years on, the Conservatives themselves captured 58 seats in the province of Quebec—an astonishing political achievement. Those 58 actually outnumber the Conservatives' total in the four western provinces of the country which, in recent years have been the heartland of Canadian Conservative strength. The resulting geographical shift of party strength within the party may yet cause its leader political and tactical problems of a wholly unanticipated kind.

The Conservative victory in Canada, and particularly in Quebec, owed much to the distinctive leadership provided by Mr. Brian Mulroney. A rich Montreal lawyer and business executive, Mulroney displayed a remarkable campaigning ability in both English and French putting Mr. John Turner, who had suceeded Pierre Trudeau as Liberal Party leader and Prime Minister in June, in the political shade. Turner appeared both indecisive and slow in comparison with the dynamic Mulroney.

Unsurprisingly given his corporate background, Mulroney's policy appeal rested on the Conservatives' proclaimed intention to attract substantial inward investment in order to revive the economy and reduce the unemployment level which on election day stood at 11%. This found much favour with the Reagan administration in Washington, anxious to reduce the tension between the United States and Canada which Trudeau's economic nationalism had partly caused.

Progressive Conservatives in Power.

Canada's first year under the Progressive Conservatives brought no radical changes of policy. The prudent reluctance of Canadian governments to force policies upon reluctant minorities in this sensitive federal system was thus again revealed.

The nationalist sentiment which had informed Pierre Trudeau's energy policy after 1979, and the Liberal government's pursuit of increased Canadian ownership of industry, had abated thus allowing Mr. Mulroney and his colleagues to adopt a different course. His administration's aim was one of attracting inward investment in Canada. This pragmatic approach fitted well with the traditions and necessities of Canadian politics, and informed the policy of privatisation of loss-making firms.

The sheer difficulty of governing such a huge country with disparate ethnic and political cultures made Mr. Mulroney's task difficult. But his administration also encountered difficulties of a kind which could not so easily be explained away. The fisheries minister resigned after a scandal, and the communications minister became involved in a dispute over his election expenses. The two incidents, coupled with the strikingly incompetent government response to the failure of two Alberta banks, suggested that Mr. Mulroney and his colleagues would take some while to adjust to the subtleties and magnitude of governing the federation.

CENTRAL AND SOUTH AMERICA

In 1985 natural disasters for a time overshadowed the ongoing social conflicts that dominate the political life of the region. In March 1985 earthquakes in Southern Chile left 70,000 people homeless in and around Valparaiso. Worse was to follow in Mexico and Colombia.

In September 1985 earthquakes in Mexico had repercussions throughout five provinces with hundreds of thousands of people made homeless. Mexico City was worse hit; over 10,000 people were killed. Although Mexico was a recipient of international aid the earthquake's "tremors" were felt in the nation's fragile economy. The peso reached a new low in

November 1985 and oil prices were dropped in an effort to boost export earnings. Despite initial sympathy the IMF and other agencies are pressing for payments due on Mexico's $100 billion external debt. It seems likely that the US will guarantee a $4 billion loan package in 1986 which should shield the Mexican economy (and Western financial institutions) from a repeat of the 1982 Mexican financial collapse. The full extent of the social misery is still being counted.

November was a black month in Colombia. In central Bogota a bloody siege of the law courts in the "Plaza Bolivar" ended in a fierce battle between government forces and guerrillas of the M-19 movement; a bitter eruption of the latent social conflicts within the nation. A natural disaster of greater ferocity was to follow. A volcano in Western Colombia, the Nevado del Ruiz, erupted suffocating the small town of Armero. Debris from the volcano combined with the waters of swollen rivers threatened villages forty miles from the volcano and hampered rescue work. Armero suffered terribly: most of the town's inhabitants were killed in the disaster. Over 25,000 people have been killed and many more left homeless. Temporary evacuations continued into 1986 due to fears of further volcanic activity and relief and reconstruction plans are still in turmoil.

These appalling disasters have temporarily held the world's attention and sympathy but few solutions have been offered to the region's deep-rooted problems. Even the large and more developed South American countries are trapped in intractable relationships of financial "dependency" whilst most of Central America is embroiled in social conflicts that have since 1979 claimed over 200,000 lives, left 2 million people homeless or political refugees and reduced life for the majority of the people to a grim daily struggle for survival.

CENTRAL AMERICA

EL SALVADOR.

In 1979 a "young officers" coup ousted the repressive government of General Romero and led to a short-lived period of optimism in Salvadorean politics. However, by January 1980 the civilian members of the new junta had resigned in protest at the clear military obstruction of proposed reforms. The declaration of a state of siege in March 1980 was the prelude to increased official violence well symbolised by the murder of the campaigner for human rights, Archbishop Romero. Polarisation was complete when Colonel Majano, sponsor of the Agrarian Reform, was forced out of government and ultimately into exile. Over 50,000 people have been killed in the subsequent civil conflict mainly at hands of the security forces and right-wing death squads. It would be an under-estimation to say that the junta of 1979 merely ushered in "Romerismo without Romero".

Greater unity amongst opposition groups has been generated by the conflict. On a political level this is expressed by the increasing maturity of the pluralist Revolutionary Democratic Front (FDR) in its numerous international negotiations. Militarily, opposition forces have united into the "Farabundo Marti Liberation Front" (FMLN) which, like the "Sandinistas", takes its name from a national patriot of the 1930's. Since 1981 a protracted offensive by the guerrillas has ebbed and flowed with heavy fighting particularly in Chalatenango and Morazan. Successful guerrilla attacks at San Vicente and elsewhere in early 1983 and the failure of his deployment of large army columns in "big sweeps" led to the dismissal of the Defence Minister General Garcia in April 1983. His successor General Carlos Vides Casanova was entrusted with the imposition of a US plan to boost Salvadorean army manpower by 30% before the end of 1983. However, a major guerrilla offensive in September led to two months' heavy fighting and army losses of over 1,500 men. Domestic politics mirrored the military situation as an impasse in the Constituent Assembly threatened to envelop the elections of March 1984.

Despite a guerrilla offensive which prevented polling in more than forty communities the Presidential election did take place on 25 March, 1984. However, the electoral process could at best be described as chaotic. There were numerous irregularities in the new electoral register, a failure to deliver ballot boxes, and delayed opening of polling stations as well as the guerrilla campaign and death squad intimidation. Furthermore, there was a lower turn-out than at the "stalemate" election of 1982.

President Duarte won a run-off contest with the leader of the right Roberto D'Aubuisson in May but an impasse remained as Arena, D'Aubuisson's party, still dominated the Assembly in alliance with the National Conciliation Party, the second largest conservative group. These parties by agreeing to a single list of candidates appeared to be in a strong position to contest the assembly and mayoral elections in late March 1985. However, D'Aubuisson's intransigence and his unashamed links with the death squads have made him increasingly a liability rather than an asset to Arena. Divisions within the right increasingly emerged in 1985 in part as a response to US pressure upon the elite "to clean up its act". In March this resulted in a formal split from the party of a faction led by a former vice-presidential candidate, Hugo Barrera. Barrera set up "Patria Libre" an organisation which has attracted increased support in 1985 from the traditional oligarchy and the business community.

A poor showing by Arena in the Assembly elections, when the Christian Democrats obtained a narrow majority added to the pressure upon D'Aubuisson. In September 1985 Arena elected Alfredo Christiani as president with D'Aubuisson assuming an honorary presidential position within the party. Although President Duarte benefitted from the political manoeuvring within the right-wing opposition his government and the armed forces have made little headway in 1985 in attempting to bring under control the civil conflict that has cost over 50,000 lives. The five armed groups within the FMLN have taken unified action based on a variety of tactics. At times they have operated at brigade strength and on other occasions in small groups against specific urban targets. This eclectic policy has produced a number of guerrilla successes. In March 1985 they openly attacked the National Guard barracks in San Salvador and in the pre-election period captured thirteen town halls in order to destroy electoral registers. In September, in a stepped up campaign, a large guerrilla force attacked the army training centre in La Union. The most publicised action was the kidnapping and exchange for captured guerrillas of the President's daughter. However, these successes have only caused marginal erosion of the army's morale and with little progress in the way of negotiations there seems no hope of ending the bloody stalemate in El Salvador in 1986.

GUATEMALA.

Since 1954, when the elected government of Jacobo Arbenz was removed in a CIA sponsored coup, Guatemala has been ruled by a series of harsh military rulers responsible for the deaths of over 130,000 people in security operations undertaken to maintain a petrified political system. The government of General Lucas Garcia in the late 1970's surpassed its predecessors in the severity of its repression of all opposition and in the extent of atrocities committed by right-wing death squads against the civilian (and particularly the Indian) population. Twenty thousand people died at the hands of this regime. However, even Guatemala's rigid "stability" has been eroded by the pressures for social change in the region. Since 1982 guerrilla groups have re-organised and developed cooperative links particularly in the northern Indian provinces of El Quiché, Alta Verapaz and Huehuetenango.

In March 1982 a young officers coup ousted Lucas Garcia and General Efrain Rios Montt assumed the Presidency. Massacres of civilians, particularly in Peten, by government para-military forces quickly dashed guarded hopes for an improvement in human rights. Indeed, the new government streamlined its counter-insurgency policy. *Frijoles y fusiles* (beans and guns) became the watchwords of the new policy and "preventative terror" a systematic exercise in rural Indian areas. By early 1983 human rights groups estimated that the Rios Montt regime was responsible for over ten thousand deaths.

Although in January 1983 the Reagan Administration resumed arms sales to Guatemala the eccentric style of the Rios Montt leadership (directly influenced by his "born again" Christian beliefs) led to increased disquiet amongst the conservative officer corps and the traditional Catholic oligarchy. In August 1983 the Guatemalan Defence Minister

General Oscar Humberto Mejia removed Rios Montt in a near bloodless coup. General Mejia, a typical hard-line anti-communist officer, appeared well-suited to the Guatemalan political process of coup and counter-coup within a narrow political caste.

Surprisingly in February 1984 a new electoral law was passed which allowed easier registration by political parties and did offer some marginal opening up of the political process. Elections for a constituent assembly were held in July 1984. In a low poll the centrist Christian Democrats fared particularly well against the traditional right-wing parties in a contest denounced by the guerrillas. Despite the low poll they proved to be a reliable indicator to the outcome of the Presidential campaign of 1985. In the first round poll of November 1985 the Christian Democratic candidate received 39% of the vote well ahead of the other seven candidates. In the subsequent December runoff elections Cinicio Cerezo (Christian Democrat) was an easy winner over the right-wing Jorge Carpio, leader of the National Union.

It remains to be seen whether there will be a smooth transfer to civilian rule or more likely the exact nature of the political strait-jacket that the military elite will impose on Guatemala's new ruler. Cerezo himself has conceded that the military are still the fulcrum of power in the Guatemalan political system. Indeed, cynics have a variety of explanations for the keenness of the military leadership to establish a "cosmetic" democracy in 1985. Military management of the economy has been a disaster with high inflation, rationing and massive depreciation of the quetzal. There have been rumblings of discontent from the IMF and it will be left to the new government to try to renegotiate next year nearly $500 million in short term debt whilst the military wait in the wings. The military's policy of forced labour in "civil defence" using 900,000 of the Indian population and the confinement of 60,000 Indians in the notorious "model villages" has found many enemies within Guatemala and some embarrassing ones in the US Congress. The "cosmetic" democracy of 1985 will aid the passage of a huge military assistance programme through the US Congress whilst probable dependence upon the US administration to recycle foreign debts will narrowly define the limits both to economic policy and the regional foreign policy of the civilian political leadership in Guatemala.

HONDURAS.

Honduras, the poorest country in Central America, has become increasingly embroiled in the political conflict of the region. Right-wing exiled "contras" are encamped in the south near the Nicaraguan border. Furthermore, innumerable refugees have fled into Honduras from El Salvador and Guatemala. Honduran politics has been dominated by the military for the last twenty five years. In January 1982 a right-wing President, Roberto Suazo Cordova, was elected but the real strings of power remained with the armed forces. Indeed, the election in 1981 of the hard-line General Gustavo Alvarez by the "Consejo Superior" of the armed forces was for several years a greater influence upon Honduran politics.

General Alvarez personalised the decision-making process in the army, initiated the formation of paramilitary groups to operate against "subversives" and negotiated directly with the US over military aid and joint manoeuvres ignoring provisions in the Honduran constitution. Not surprisingly Honduras has become an increasingly active "proxy" for the US in its conflict with Nicaragua. A series of joint manoeuvres including simulated air and amphibious landings in the Cabo Gracias a Dios border region started in February 1983 and continued throughout 1984. Such exercises are an obvious attempt to erode the morale of the Sandinista government in Nicaragua.

However, in March 1984 elements within the officer corps disgruntled by Alvarez's abrogation of collective leadership persuaded President Suazo to oust General Alvarez who fled into exile in the US. Initially, this move promised some modification of the Honduran role in the region's military conflict. The new military leadership of General Walter Lopez whilst increasingly critical of the character and effectiveness of "contra" forces has continued to hold joint manoeuvres with the US army. Honduras is now the base for over one thousand US "advisers". In April 1985 "Operation Scorpion" included the use of US M-60 tanks within three miles of Nicaraguan territory.

Ironically, in the same month General Walter Lopez was forced to intervene in domestic politics issuing warnings to President Suazo and other civilian politicians to keep their house in order to ensure the November 1985 Presidential election. The incumbent Suazo and elements within congress were involved in two bitter disputes. The first was over nomination of members of the Supreme Court and the second but interlinked dispute stemmed from different interpretations of the constitutional provisions relating to elections. This latter intractable debate dominated the 1985 Presidential contest.

In Honduran electoral law victory goes to the top candidate of the party with the most votes. This can be a complicated procedure when for example as in 1985 a fragmented but ruling Liberal Party runs four separate Presidential candidates. In the November poll José Azcona one of the Liberal candidate was elected President even though the leading National Party candidate Rafael Callejas received a higher vote. Callejas obtained 41% of the vote and Azcona 28%. However, the combined votes of other Liberal candidates gave the party a 51–45% margin over the National Party. José Azcona, a dissident Liberal duly assumed the Presidency in January 1986 despite some National Party officials hoping to dispute the election in the courts.

NICARAGUA.

In 1967 Anastasio "Tachito" Somoza assumed power, the third member of a "dynasty" which had consolidated a system of power based upon extortion and graft and accumulated a fortune of over $500 million. General discontent increased when it became clear, in 1972–73, that misappropriation even "embraced" aid sent to earthquake victims. By 1975 the Sandinista National Liberation Front (FSLN), named after Augusto Cesar Sandino a national hero murdered by the Somoza family in the 1920's, was gaining increased support. Moderate opinion was alienated by Somoza's assassination in 1978 of Pedro Joaquin Chamarro which precipitated violent demonstrations culminating in the civil conflict of 1979. In June 1979 Somoza fled into exile (ultimately in Paraguay where he has since met his death). In July the FSLN set up government in Managua and has since attempted to share power between its factions both in the executive junta and the *direccion nacional* (DNC).

Since its inception the Sandinista government, whilst attempting to tackle problems of economic reconstruction in a country where 40,000 people died in the civil war and a further 750,000 were made homeless, has been confronted by ever more threatening external pressures. Initially, the problem was only groups of ex-Somoza National Guard operating in the border areas but since 1982 there has been a worsening problem with direct conflict at times between the Sandinistas and the Honduran army in a smouldering border war. Heavily armed US backed "contra" guerrillas operate against the Sandinistas from bases in Honduras. They have had two debilitating effects. The "contras" divert scarce manpower in the north and also by their disruption of the coffee harvest reduce Nicaraguan export earnings.

However, US hostility is the crucial pressure upon a nation psychologically under siege since March 1982 when a state of emergency was first declared. In July 1983 US warships practised a blockade of Nicaragua. Subsequently there has been a US military build up in the Honduran and Costa Rican border areas with Nicaragua. Joint military manoeuvres with their Honduran "proxies" have been stepped up and extended over a five year period. As with the "contras" such military pressures are doubly debilitating the Nicaraguan economy as increased mobilisation for and expenditure upon defence cause further dislocations in terms of labour shortage and financial constraints.

In the election of November 1984 the Sandinista candidates received 69% of the votes cast and obtained a two thirds majority in the national

assembly. The small Democratic Conservative Party and the Independent Liberal Party received 11% of the vote and the small left wing parties the remainder. The elections were boycotted by the right-wing groups associated with the "contra" guerrillas. Daniel Ortega, leader of the moderate Sandinista grouping was elected President by a considerable majority in a significantly high poll. There was an 82% turnout. However, the relentless external pressure has continued. There are now 30 US warships stationed in and around Nicaraguan waters. Despite Sandinista successes against the "contras" in May and August 1985, especially against the "Arde" forces on the Costa Rican border these rebels have gained $27 million in "non-military" aid from the US and have attacked power stations, hospitals and other institutions in Nicaragua. In October 1985 the Sandinista government was obliged to widen the area covered by State of Emergency regulations with some inevitable loss of press freedom and the right of assembly. However, it is on the economic front that the extent of this external pressure is beginning to take toll.

On 7 May, 1985 the Reagan administration instituted a trade embargo against Nicaragua. This crucially affected the supply of spare parts for the electricity system, the national oil refinery and the telephone system. It has also prompted austerity controls for the supply of agricultural and industrial goods. The "contra" insurgency has disrupted agricultural production and prompted the rural exodus to Managua that has doubled the city's population to 900,000 since 1979. Significantly, a parallel black market system (the "bisnes") has mushroomed in the last three years severely distorting the supply of goods and labour in the Nicaraguan economy. In 1985 it was necessary to devalue the national currency (the "cordoba"). It seems inevitable that the US will continue to tighten its armoury of screws against the Sandinsta government in 1986.

SOUTH AMERICA.

ARGENTINA.

A series of military dictatorships ruled Argentina from the coup of March 1976 until late 1983. The original junta led by General Jorge Rafael Videla dissolved Congress and used State of Siege legislation to justify mass arrests, torture and political murder. In 1977 "internal exile" procedures were legalised and in the continued repression an estimated 15,000 people "disappeared". General Videla's term of office ended in 1981 when General Roberto Viola assumed the Presidency amid worsening economic and social conditions only to be removed by his disgruntled fellow officers after a mere nine months. His successor General Leopoldo Galtieri then attempted to contain the increasing economic and political pressures for change.

The initially successful invasion of the Falklands (Malvinas) in April 1982 briefly united the government and generated popular support by diverting attention from domestic problems. However, the shock of subsequent defeats, coupled with the public's realisation of blatant news manipulation, redoubled the stress on the widening fissures in the political framework of military dictatorship. Amid internal military bickering over the defeat and renewed demands for an investigation of military responsibility for the innumerable "disappearances" of its own citizens Galtieri's successor, General Reynaldo Bignone, was unable to implement harsh regulation of political activities and was eventually forced to bow to popular demands for an election.

The election of October 1983 not only terminated military rule but also ended the domination of Argentinian civilian politics by the Peronist movement. The candidate of a deeply factionalised Peronist movement, Dr. Luder, was well beaten by the Radical Party candidate, Raul Alfonsin, who received over 52% of the vote. In Congress the Radicals won 131 seats compared to only 111 by the Peronists. President Alfonsin assumed power in December 1983 to the delight of a relieved populace. However, his government was soon confronted by three thorny problems; the aftermath of the "Malvinas" fiasco; the question of military responsibility for "disappearances" during the dictatorship and the deeprooted structural economic problems.

For a time in 1984 the Alfonsin government's

position over the Falklands controversy hardened in part due to the successful termination of another longstanding territorial dispute with Chile but more especially as a consequence of failure to make progress in two more central aspects of policy: the economy and the human rights questions. Diplomatic manoeuvres seemed confined to limbo when in July 1985 the right-wing opposition made political capital from the leak of a compromise on the issue formulated by the government.

Economic difficulties in rescheduling Argentina's huge foreign debt (over $48 billion) and in tackling domestic inflation (over 600% per annum in 1984) have continued to burden the government. Assistance from the IMF was only forthcoming in exchange for promised austerity measures. In June 1985 Alfonsin introduced a plan designed to dampen down inflation. This consisted in part of measures to end cheap credit and considerable curbs on public expenditure. Such policies with their inevitable consequences for living standards have so far failed to provide political ammunition to a bitterly divided Peronist opposition.

Indeed, in the mid-term congressional and provisional government elections in November 1985 President Alfonsin's Radical Party increased its Congressional majority by one seat polling 43% of the vote to the Peronists' 34%. This was notwithstanding the results of the austerity package, a half-hearted Peronist general strike in September and the government's imposition of a sixty-day State of Siege following a series of bombings by right-wing extremists in October 1985. The state of siege was quickly lifted in December on the second anniversary of President Alfonsin's government. It remains to be seen whether the legacy of the previous military terror can be as easily purged.

Investigations into the human rights abuses committed by the military dictatorship dragged on painfully throughout 1984 and 1985. In December 1985 the leader of the original junta General Videla and Admiral Massera were sentenced to life imprisonment whilst two fellow officers received sentences of seventeen and eight years from the civilian courts. The army is still smarting at this first civilian justice meted out to military leaders and was incensed by the temporary arrest of several officers under the brief State of Siege for their connections with the extremist bomb squads. General Camps is an unrepentant force within the military who detests the present civilian government. In 1986 President Alfonsin is still plagued by foreign bankers and haunted by military phantoms.

BRAZIL.

In March 1964 the civilian government of President Goulart was ousted by a military regime. For twenty years Brazil was ruled by a succession of military Presidents. General Figuerado, who assumed office in 1979, was the last of these military nominees. His "abertura" policy saw some loosening of Brazil's political strait-jacket but also initiated measures attempting to maintain the existing political structure beyond the elections of November 1982 (the first since 1962!). However, the large poll in 1982 and the defeats for the government in the major industrial states (Sao Paulo, Minas Gerais and Rio de Janeiro) were a clear indication of dissatisfaction with military rule. These popular frustrations were fuelled by the worsening foreign debt crisis, high inflation and the continued harassment of political and trade union opposition. Increased discontent found an outlet in the mass campaign for direct elections which was inaugurated in January 1984 by a spectacular demonstration by over 500,000 people in Sao Paulo and provided a unifying aim for opposition groups.

Some dissatisfied elements within the government PDS defected to this amorphous alliance due to government intransigence on the direct election issue. This compelled opposition groups to mobilise around the PMDB candidate to the electoral college, Tancredo de Almeida Neves. The veteran governor of Minas Gerais was unsullied by contact with the military regime and had two "symbolic" credentials, he was an ex-Minister of Justice under President Garga and he was leader in Congress of the ill-fated Goulart government. Crucially the PDS's nomination of the arrogant right-wing gover-

nor Paulo Maluf as the official government candidate accelerated the disintegration of the regime's electoral campaign. In January 1985 Tancredo Neves won 480 votes in the electoral college giving him a majority of 300 over the official candidate.

Hopes for an orderly transition to civilian rule were cruelly dashed when Tancredo Neves, in his seventies, died in April after a desperate series of operations. Amid considerable confusion and disgruntlement, Vice President José Sarney assumed the Presidency. José Sarney is a career politician of the old school. He was the leader of the government party during military rule and opposed direct elections until July 1984. However, in May 1985 Congress voted a constitutional amendment restoring direct Presidential elections, removing restrictions on political parties and extending the electoral franchise to Brazil's twenty million illiterates. In September 1985 President Sarney organised a committee to draw up constitutional proposals to be approved by the Congress elected in November 1986. It is hoped that a new constitution will eventually be accepted in 1987–88 finally dismantling the legal and political strait-jacket developed during the decades of military rule. A first practical aspect of the change (and test for the political alliance supporting President Sarney) was the return of mayoral elections in November 1985.

In these political contests over 18 million Brazilians were entitled to vote for mayors in 200 cities. In seventeen out of twenty-three state capitals the candidates of the Democratic Movement Party (PMDB), the major force in the government alliance, were successful. This endorsement of President Sarney's government was marred by the result in the major city of Sao Paulo. In a dirty campaign Janio Quadros, a right-wing populist and former Brazilian President gained a narrow victory over the PMDB candidate despite gaining only 37% of the vote. The good showing of the Workers Party candidate deprived the PMDB of sufficient votes to ensure Quadros victory. The underlying bitterness in Brazilian politics is well illustrated by noting the allies of Quadros in his campaign; Paulo Maluf and Delfim Neto (former Presidential candidate and finance minister for the old military regime).

A continuation of the export-led boom resulting in a $12 billion trade surplus in 1984–85 and a 12% increase in industrial output (particularly in textiles and metallurgy) in 1985 led the new Brazilian administration to combat what President Sarney described as the "dogmatic intransigence" of the IMF. Despite the excellent export performance earnings merely matched the interest payments on Brazil's massive $100 billion external debt. President Sarney influenced by forthright Finance Minister Dilson Funaro and new Central Bank Governor Fernao Bracher has resisted IMF pressure to introduce further austerity measures in an economy where inflation is running at about 200% p.a. In aiming for growth at over 5% p.a. the administration has delayed reaching any agreement on the refinancing of the $45 billion debt due by 1991 and in 1986 was pushing for a two year rescheduling of this package of loans. Brazil may well emerge in 1987 as the leader of an embryonic debtor nation alliance and the government seems determined enough to call the bluff of the international financial community.

CHILE.

In September 1973 a military junta headed by General Augusto Pinochet seized power ousting the civilian government in a bloody coup. Thousands of supporters of Popular Unity were killed including President Allende himself. State of Siege legislation was augmented by a series of decrees and "constitutional" acts to erode further the social provisions of the 1925 Constitution and establishe a complete framework of state repression. In September 1980 a farcical referendum, held "merely" under State of Emergency provisions with all political parties being banned and no electoral registers being used, adopted a new constitution which appointed President Pinochet for a renewable eight-year term.

However, Chile's political straight-jacket has not totally suffocated opposition. The collapse of the monetarist economic "miracle", with official unemployment rising to over 25% of the workforce (40% in Valparaiso) and foreign debts reaching $18 million, has added to the social frustration building up against the military regime. Indeed, by April 1984

General Pinochet felt obliged to exile some remaining opposition leaders. Jaime Insunza, General Secretary of the Popular Democratic Movement (a loose opposition coalition), and Dr. Leopoldo Ortega, a human rights activist, were expelled from the country. September protests at the new clampdown led to four civilians, including Father Andrés Jarlan, being killed by police and hundreds of people being detained. Press censorship was tightened to muzzle further expressions of discontent. However, in October 1984 a two-day protest against the government included a general strike, despite reservations by moderate groups, which was 50% successful in some sectors like textiles and construction.

On 6 November General Pinochet reintroduced State of Siege provisions suspending habeas corpus and bringing troops onto the streets of Santiago and other cities. Subsequently, several thousand people have been arrested most notoriously in a massive swoop on the working class district of La Victoria in Santiago. Protests continued in November despite the troops on the streets. The two major opposition fronts have taken heart at the number of people willing to take part in demonstrations in September and the relative success of the October strike even though the number of people arrested continued to increase.

Ironically, it was the very brutality of the regime which led to signs of division within its ranks in 1985. In March evidence linked police officers with the murder of three communist leaders. Twelve members of the police force who were implicated were forced to resign taking with them their leader General Mendoza in a crisis within the junta. Relations between the police and the army-dominated secret police (CNI) have remained frosty.

In August 1985 impatience with Pinochet's intransigence at last overcame inter-party differences and a political document was drawn up uniting political groups across the spectrum, from Socialists to right-wing members of National Unity. The Archbishop of Santiago acted as a mediator with Pinochet attempting to sponsor the group's demands for a return to full democracy. However, in September the Archbishop's independence day mass was blacked out by the government and at Christmas a brief meeting with Pinochet was useless. Left-wing groups united in the Popular Democratic Movement have grown in support and have become increasingly restive. Bombings and demonstrations have increased prompting indiscriminate repression. The President and Vice-President of the Trade Union Confederation (CNT) were arrested after street demonstrations in September.

Equally significant for the future of the Pinochet regime are the rumblings of discontent within its own ranks when added to the increasing clamour of a united opposition. Generals Gustavo Leigh and Fernando Matthei have both criticized General Pinochet's inflexibility and unwillingness to negotiate. In November 1985 an army General, Raul Benavides, was dismissed by Pinochet probably for having similar reservations about the President's position.

PERU.

Twelve years of military rule ended in 1980 when President Belaunde Terry's conservative government was elected. A combination of deepening economic crisis and protracted civil strife in interior Andean provinces caused a steady erosion of support for the Belaunde government. By 1985 Peru's foreign debt had risen to over $13 billion, inflation was running at over 200% p.a. and there was massive structural unemployment. In the Andean provinces, particularly Ayacucho, a Maoist influenced guerrilla group, Sendero Luminoso (Shining Path), has continued to operate widely despite a heavy military presence. Over 6,000 people are known to have died in this conflict whilst thousands more have "disappeared". In these circumstances the 1985 election was an unrepeatable opportunity for the APRA (American Popular Revolutionary Alliance) opposition.

APRA has always been a significant force in Peruvian politics but has suffered because of its restricted social base of support and from conflicts with the powerful military elite. Until his death in 1979 APRA was dominated by Victor Raul Haya de la Torre who founded the movement in the 1920's. After a brief internal power struggle APRA united behind Alan Marcia as their Presidential candidate. Marcia a young and forceful candidate anxious to extend the movement's support beyond the provincial lower middle class, and skilled at adapting his message of social change to suit a variety of audiences proved to be an easy winner in the April 1985 election.

Peru's 8 million disenchanted voters were called on to elect 60 senators and 180 congressmen as well as a President at this contest. Marcia's closest rival proved to be Alfonso Barrantes, the mayor of Lima and leader of the United Left (IU). Garcia polled 46% of the votes and Barrantes 23%. The IU waved their right to a run off contest and APRA's candidate was declared the winner. Support for the government had totally evaporated and the official candidate obtained less than 6% of the votes.

On 28 July, 1985 Alan Garcia assumed the Presidency of Peru to tackle deep-rooted economic problems and civil conflict at the tender age of 36. He wished to reduce waste and corruption within the state sector and used APRA's new majorities in both houses to introduce "austerity" measures designed to be progressive in nature. Embassy staffs were reduced, cuts have been made in the higher echelons of bureaucracy in the state run industries and redundancies announced in the extensive ranks of the civil service. Garcia hopes to divert resources to the deprived rural areas attempting to ease the dominance of Lima and erase the basis for social conflict at the same time.

A parallel aim of Garcia's policy is an attempt to reform and reduce the role of the armed forces particularly in the Andean provinces. To this end he was helped by the development of two scandals implicating military and police personnel. In July 1985 the "Rodriguez case" linked police and former government officials with Peru's $600 million p.a. "cocaine" industry. In a second scandal strong evidence emerged of military involvement in civilian massacres committed in Ayacucho. These events allowed Garcia to arrange for the sacking of 4,000 police officers whilst in September he felt it necessary to dismiss the head of the armed forces General Cesar Enrico who was personally responsible for the conduct of the counter-insurgency operations mounted in three southern departments since January 1983. Subsequently, General Wilfredo Mori, commander of Ayacucho, and his superior General Jarama were also dismissed. In December 1985 the government lifted the state of emergency in seven of twenty-six affected provinces and instituted a $35 million development fund.

In relation to Peru's large external debt Garcia has advocated a forthright approach with international creditors and has made hard-line responses to IMF demands. In December 1985 he appointed Leonel Figueroa, former deputy finance minister, to the important position of Central Bank President. Peru is at present in arrears by $900 million in interest payments and $27 million in arrears with the IMF. It may well prove difficult for the Garcia government to maintain momentum in the long term with powerful enemies both inside and outside Peru.

AUSTRALASIA

AUSTRALIA AND NEW ZEALAND.

In the sixties, the Liberal–Country coalition in Australia and the National Party in New Zealand were able to consolidate and extend their power at the expense of the Labour Party in each country. During 1968 and 1969 Labour opposition to participation in the Vietnam war increased in strength; this feeling combined with new leadership within each Labour Party and, in Australia in particular, a feeling that the ruling party had "lost its steam". But in the 1969 elections the ruling parties just maintained their leads.

With Britain joining the European Community, both Australia and New Zealand sought closer relations with their neighbours. New Zealand began a search for new markets for her agricultural products, especially in Japan and Latin America. Australia made an agreement with Japan on the peaceful use of atomic energy and one with Indonesia on the provision of defence and economic aid.

Both countries established diplomatic relations with China.

Elections in 1972 brought the long expected victories of the Labour Parties, under Mr. Gough Whitlam in Australia (who thus became the first Labour Prime Minister since 1949), and Mr. Kirk in New Zealand (succeeded by Mr. Rowling in 1974). Apart from a vote for new faces these victories perhaps contained some nationalist elements; old alliances were no longer found so useful. Both victors promised the end of conscription. Mr. Whitlam's government was returned with a reduced majority in 1974.

The greater participation in Asian affairs appears slowly to be moderating Australia's traditional immigration policies. Since 1945 some three million people have settled in the country of which almost half have had assisted passages. Over half have come from Britain and more than 100,000 from each of Italy, Greece, the Netherlands, and Germany. But more than 50,000 have been admitted from Asian and African countries including 16,000 Chinese and Japanese. From 1973 non-white racial characteristics no longer constituted an obstacle to immigration though in general immigration is permitted only for those with relations in Australia and for skilled workers. As from January 1975 white citizens of Britain, Ireland, Canada and Fiji require visas before visiting or settling in Australia, thus ending long-standing preferential treatment. (New Zealand had also introduced restrictions on British and Irish immigrants.)

During 1975 the opposition Liberal–Country majority in the Australian Senate blocked approval of the budget for months, thus condemning the Whitlam government to impotence. The deadlock was eventually broken by a very controversial decision of the Governor-General to dismiss the Prime Minister. The constitutional conflict which thus flared up, added to economic problems and dissension about the government's socialist measures, poisoned the atmosphere of the ensuing election campaign. The election in December 1975 was easily won by the Conservatives led by Mr. Malcolm Fraser. The Liberal–Country coalition won their largest majority in Australian political history. A similar trend was experienced in New Zealand with the decisive defeat of the Labour government by the Nationalist party led by Robert Muldoon.

In 1977 the Governor-General of Australia, Sir John Kerr, resigned in the face of mounting criticism from Labour Party supporters and constitutional lawyers who disputed the legitimacy of his dismissal of Mr. Whitlam. However, after general elections called in December 1977 had resulted in Labour winning only one-third of the seats in the House of Representatives and a gain of 7% for the governing coalition, Mr Whitlam himself retired from politics. This Liberal–Country victory was achieved despite growing unrest about unemployment.

Labour Victory.

A dramatic change in Australian politics occurred on 5 March 1983. In the General Election, the Australian Labour Party swept into power under Robert Hawke, ending the 7-year premiership of Malcolm Fraser who later announced that he was stepping down from the Liberal leadership. With a nationwide swing of 4% to Labour, Hawke achieved a resounding victory that marked a new departure for Australia.

The General Elections of 1984.

General elections took place in both Australia and New Zealand in 1984. In New Zealand the election in July resulted in a defeat for the government of Sir Robert Muldoon. In an 86% poll, the Labour Party under David Lange won 56 seats to the National Party's 37. The Social Credit Party won 2 seats. In November Sir Robert Muldoon was replaced as leader of the National Party by James McLay.

In Australia, in the election held in December, the Labour Party under Bob Hawke was returned to office but with a reduced majority. Contrary to all opinion poll forecasts, there was a 1·5% swing to the Liberal-Country opposition coalition led by Andrew Peacock, and the government's majority

was reduced. The unexpected electoral rebuff damaged Mr. Hawke's standing in the country and his party.

Mr. Hawke's position improved, however, during 1985. In South Australia's state elections in December 1985 the Liberal Party, led by John Howard, who had succeeded Andrew Peacock as leader of the party in September, did badly at the polls. The party's policies of privatisation and the deregulation of housing interest rates and the labour market suggested radical change, whilst Mr. Hawke, whose August budget emphasised economic and social responsibility, seemed to offer greater stability.

Crisis in the ANZUS Pact.

The Pacific Security Treaty, better known as the ANZUS pact, was signed by Australia, New Zealand and the United States in 1951. The American Navy patrols the Pacific with its Fifth Fleet based at Honolulu, and requires port facilities in Australia and New Zealand. However, doubt was cast on the working of the Pact by New Zealand's new Labour government's policy of declaring the country a nuclear-free zone. This led Mr. Lange to refuse port facilities to an American destroyer, USS *Buchanan*, which could have been carrying nuclear weapons. The United States raised the possibility of ending New Zealand's preferential treatment in trade and security matters, and Bob Hawke condemned Mr. Lange's stance. However, in February 1985 pressure from the left-wing of his party caused Mr. Hawke to withdraw an earlier offer of refuelling facilities for American aircraft monitoring two proposed MX missile tests in the south Pacific. At the beginning of 1985 the future of defence co-operation in the Pacific was thus called into question. In February a meeting of ANZUS communications officials in Sydney was cancelled and in March Mr. Hawke announced the indefinite suspension of the ANZUS council meeting scheduled for July.

The Rainbow Warrior Affair.

France continued its nuclear test programme at its Mururoa site in the Pacific during 1985. On 10 July two explosions in Auckland harbour sank the Greenpeace flagship, Rainbow Warrior, which was to have led a flotilla attempting to disrupt the French tests. One crew member, Fernando Pereiro, was killed. In September the French Prime Minister, Laurent Fabius, admitted that France had ordered the sinking. The French Defence Minister, Charles Hernu, and the head of the foreign intelligence service, Admiral Pierre Lacoste, were both replaced. In November 1985 two French agents were convicted of manslaughter and sentenced to ten years in prison in Auckland.

At the 16th Annual Conference of the South Pacific forum in August 1985 an agreement was reached declaring the south Pacific a nuclear-free zone. The thirteen members of the forum called on France to adhere to the pact, but President Mitterrand's visit to the Pacific test site in September indicated that there was little chance of her doing so.

NEW CALEDONIA.

New Caledonia was annexed by France in 1853, and comprises New Caledonia itself and various other islands in the south Pacific. It has a population of some 140,000, which is made up of 43% Kanaks (the original Melanesian inhabitants); 36% white settlers; and 21% immigrant Asians and Polynesians. New Caledonia has one of the largest deposits of nickel in the world, as well as chrome, iron ore and manganese. After the nearby New Hebrides were granted independence as the Republic of Vanuatu in 1980, the Kanaks began to think in similar terms for New Caledonia. The French government was favourable, but the French settlers opposed independence. In November 1984 the settlers won elections to a new national assembly, following a boycott by the Kanak Socialist National Liberation Front. Rioting followed, in which one of the Kanak leaders. Eloi Machoro, was shot dead by police. For a time the nickel mining town of Thio was held hostage by Kanak rebels until prisoners held by the police were released. In January 1985 President Mitterrand of France visited the troubled territory in an attempt to promote a peaceful settlement.

The Territorial Congress Elections.

In April 1985 France announced fresh constitutional plans in which the national assembly would be replaced by a new territorial congress, comprising representatives from four regional councils. In an 80 per cent poll in September, pro-independence parties won control in three regions—the North, Centre-South-East and Loyalty Islands. The anti-indepence Rally for Caledonia in the Republic party won the capital, Noumea and District region. The relative weighting of the different regions meant that the anti-independence parties had a majority of 29 seats to 17 in the territorial congress, but the Kanaks were given the opportunity to administer three of the regions for themselves.

III. SPECIAL TOPICS

THE LIBYAN CRISIS

Significance of the American attack.

The attack by American military aircraft on 15 April 1986 on Tripoli and Benghazi was an event of immense importance both in itself, and in what it portended for American policy towards what President Reagan and his colleagues termed "state-sponsored terrorism". British involvement in the event was intimate and highly publicised, consisting of a decision by the Prime Minister, the Foreign Secretary and Defence Secretary, to allow the United States Air Force to use F1-11 bomber aircraft based at Lakenheath and Upper Heyford in the attack. The American request for British permission referred to the long-standing agreement between the United States and the United Kingdom under which the employment for non-NATO purposes of American forces based in Britain is subject to agreement between the president and the prime minister ". . . in the light of circumstances prevailing at the time."

The Background of Terrorism.

The attack by the United States sprang from growing American popular and congressional resentment at the Libyan government's sponsorship of terrorist attacks on American citizens in Europe. In fact, Americans did not figure especially prominently in the list of gruesome deaths at the hands of international terrorists in 1985. Of the 925 terrorist acts in the world recorded in the United States State Department's own statistics, only 23 were against Americans. Nonetheless, each act gained intensive publicity, culminating in that surrounding the bombing of La Belle disco in West Berlin which resulted in the deaths of a Turkish woman and an American soldier, Sergeant Terrance Ford. The soldier's death prompted widespread feelings of outrage in the United States, which the president shared. As American intelligence sources indicated (with considerable conviction, but no publicly-available evidence) that the Berlin bombing was executed with the complicity of the Libyan leader, Colonel Gadaffi, he responded by intensifying naval manoeuvres off the Libyan coast as a demonstration of the American government's resolve.

There was little doubt among America's European allies that Colonel Gadaffi has sponsored attacks on Libyan nationals abroad whom he deems a threat to his regime, and on European nationals. His links with international terrorist networks have been, and in some cases continue to be, close. For the British government, the memory of the shooting in 1984 of WPC Yvonne Fletcher by a diplomat attached to the Libyan People's Bureau in St. James's Square in London was too fresh for a rash of Libyan protestations of innocence in the wake of the American air-raid to carry any conviction. Nor is there serious questioning among European governments of American allegations that Syria, among other nations, harbours terrorists who have committed murderous attacks upon European and American citizens. The American action, and consultations with European allies before the attack occurred, nonetheless opened deep divisions within the Atlantic Alliance about the best way to proceed. With the exception of the British government, EEC members objected to the nature of the American response because it was considered likely to intensify Middle Eastern terrorism, and not prevent it.

Predictably (because of their close links with the Arab world) the strongest disavowal came from the Greek government. The German and Spanish governments were more cautious in their response; Germany has plentiful experience of exposure to terrorism, and so is the more aware of the threats it poses to democratic societies, whilst Libya had, days before the American attack, declared Spain (together with Italy) to be a legitimate target for Libyan military attacks. France's stance was curious: having herself employed military power against Gadaffi in Chad, her government formally denounced the American action whilst later indicating that they would have preferred a stronger military strike against Libya than the Americans actually undertook. In the event, French denial of the country's airspace to the F1-11 aircraft from Britain meant that the bombers had to take a detour of 2,800 miles over the Bay of Biscay—something which did not endear the French government to the American people or their media commentators.

The Right of Self-Defence?

The American and British governments rested their defence of the raid on the "inherent right of self-defence", as provided for in Article 51 of the United Nations charter. Many international lawyers found such a defence unconvincing. In fact, the American administration acted with its domestic audience in mind, among which there were few dissenting voices. The public hostility of the Arab nations was anticipated, and mostly disregarded, despite the evident fact that President Reagan succeeded by his actions in rallying pro-western Arab nations (such as Saudi Arabia and Egypt) to the defence of Gadaffi's regime which they normally regarded with a mixture of contempt and loathing.

Through the recriminatory exchanges between the United States and most of her allies, the central question of Middle Eastern politics went unaddressed; the absence of a settlement between the Israelis and the Palestinians was the primary irritant in the region and a persisting threat to peace there and between the superpowers. Whilst few diplomats supposed that an American-brokered series of agreements would be acceptable to the most implacable of Israel's state or terrorist opponents in the Middle East, many shared the view of Senator Charles Mathias of Maryland who perceptively argued that Americans were endangered precisely because many in the Arab world perceived that the United States no longer saw any advantage in sponsoring renewed Middle Eastern peace talks.

THE FRENCH ELECTIONS OF MARCH 1986

In the French legislative elections on 16 March 1986 the conventional right-wing parties secured an overall parliamentary majority of just two seats, thus bringing to an end five years of Socialist government in France. The elections were the first to be held under the new electoral system of proportional representation, which was introduced in 1985 by the beleaguered Socialist government in an attempt to limit the predicted right-wing victory. Proportional representation, together with the better than expected performance of both the Socialist Party (PS) and the extreme right-wing National Front (FN), effectively deprived the "legitimate" Right of a more impressive victory.

Dilemma for Mitterrand.

Yet, while the Socialists have lost their Parliamentary majority, the Constitution divides executive power between a President elected every seven years by universal suffrage and a Prime Minister, who though chosen by the President, is thereafter responsible to Parliament, which is elected every five years. With the next Presidential elections scheduled for 1988, M. François Mitterrand, who in 1981 became the first Socialist President of the Fifth Republic, now becomes the first President of this Republic to face a hostile National Assembly. A major issue raised by these elections, therefore, is whether "cohabitation" between a politically astute Socialist President and an assertive Right-wing Prime Minister will prove possible. With the Presidential elections due in 1988, all leading politicians will use this interim period of cohabitation to maximize personal and party advantage.

The Election Campaign.

The introduction of proportional representation in April 1985 signalled the Socialists' determination to contain their defeat in the forthcoming legislative elections. While it would condemn the Left to losing the election, proportional representation would effectively minimise Socialist losses. Furthermore, large parties like the Socialist Party were favoured by the new system: parties had to secure 5% of the vote in order to win any seats; and small parties stood little chance of winning a seat in over a third of the constituencies which had only 2 or 3 seats and where the major parties dominated the contest.

The Left:

The Socialists' declared target was 30% of the poll. This would give them 200 of the 577 seats in the enlarged National Assembly and make them the largest single party group in the new Parliament. Given the Party's showing of 23% in the opinion polls in Autumn 1985 and the fact that its leader, François Mitterrand, was then the most unpopular President of the Fifth Republic, this was an ambitious goal. The PS strategy was threefold: to marginalize the Communist Party (PCF); to exploit the divisions within the Right-wing coalition; and to stress its own commitment to moderate social democratic policies. The campaign was energetically led by Mitterrand himself, following the slump in the popularity of the Prime Minister, Laurent Fabius. The focus was upon the social and economic achievements of the last five years: increased minimum wages and welfare benefits; inflation down from the record high of 13.2% in 1981 to 4.7% in 1985; a 3% increase in GNP in 1985—the highest growth rate for 6 years; and a dramatic improvement in the balance of payments (largely due to falling oil prices). Support for the PS increased during the campaign and the final polls gave the Party 27–30%.

The PCF, under the leadership of Georges Marchais accused the PS of betrayal and presented itself as the only genuine Left-wing force. This attack upon the Socialists confused and offended many supporters and contributed to the PCF's showing of only 12% in the polls. The PCF faced two further problems—proportional representation would eliminate the Communists in 60 of the 96 departments which had only a few seats, and some supporters were attracted to the extreme Right-wing National Front.

The Right:

The "legitimate" Right-wing opposition comprised two main elements. The largest of these was the neo-Gaullist RPR Party, led by the Mayor of Paris, Jacques Chirac, who had been Prime Minister between 1974 and 1976. The second element was the centrist UDF, a loose umbrella party headed by the former President of the Republic between 1974 and 1981, Valery Giscard d'Estaing. These two parties formed a fragile coalition and presented many joint lists. The focus of the RPR-UDF manifesto was economic liberalism. Deregulation, denationalization, increased competition, lower taxation and public expenditure cuts were promised as a means of reducing unemployment, which, the Right stressed, had risen under the Socialists from 7.4% in 1981 to 10.2% in 1985 (2,400,000). The Right also promised tougher law and order policies and tighter immigration controls. While polls indicated a slight

fall in support for the Right during the campaign from an early 45–47% to 43–46%, no one doubted that it would obtain the 42% necessary for an overall majority.

The third largest party on the Right was the virulently nationalist and racist National Front, headed by the former Poujadist deputy, Jean-Marie Le Pen. While the FN registered only 6–8% in the polls it attracted considerably more support in areas with high unemployment and large immigrant populations and under the new electoral system would definitely be represented in the new Assembly. Other Right-wing parties, however, publicly ruled out the possibility of Parliamentary cooperation with the FN.

Divisions within the Right were skillfully exploited by Mitterrand. The most embarrassing of these was the public refusal of Raymond Barre, an independent politician who enjoyed considerable support within the UDF, to countenance the possibility of cohabitation. Barre, who had been France's highly unpopular Prime Minister between 1976 and 1981 emerged during the campaign as the most popular Right-wing politician in France and the favourite choice for President. When Giscard d'Estaing and Jacques Chirac made clear their willingness to form a government under a Socialist President, Barre—with the 1988 presidential contest in mind—accused them of opportunism and reaffirmed his commitment to presidentialism.

The Election Results.

There was never any doubt that the PS would lose; the major issue was the size of the defeat. In the event, the result was a remarkably good one for the PS, which surpassed its target of 30% of the poll and proclaimed itself still the major political force in France. The collapse of the PCF vote to below 10% also represented a personal triumph for Mitterrand, whose strategy since 1972 has been to establish the PS as the major party on the Left. Calls from within the PCF for a democratic debate on the Party's worst election performance since 1932 suggest that Marchais may shortly be replaced as PCF leader. The conventional Right lost votes to the FN, which did better than predicted, particularly in the South where it won over 20% of the vote. With its 35 seats, the FN could become an embarrassing source of unsolicited support for the RPR-UDF government.

List	% vote	Seats
Extreme Left	1.53	—
PCF	9.78	35
PS	31.04	206
MRG/Centre Left	1.61	9
Ecologists	1.21	—
Regionalists	0.10	—
RPR	11.21	76
UDF	8.31	53
Union RPR-UDF	21.46	147
Other Right	3.90	14
FN	9.65	35
Other Extreme Right	0.08	—

Electorate: 37,162,020; votes cast: 29,094,929 (78.29%)

(Source: Ministry of Interior results, *Le Monde*, 20 March 1986)*

*The results for Wallis et Futuna and Saint-Pierre-et-Miquelon are not included in this table. Both of these overseas constituencies elected one deputy under the old two ballot, simple majority system thus adding one seat each to the Right and Left.

Looking ahead.

President Mitterrand, who once hinted that he might resign in the event of a decisive Right-wing victory, immediately announced his intention to remain in office and appointed the Gaullist leader, Jacques Chirac as Prime Minister. The new government is now in place and eager to implement its programme of economic liberalism, but this may prove difficult given the presence of a Socialist President. Although the Constitution says the Prime Minister conducts the politics of the nation, it also endows the President with extensive and often unspecified powers which successive Presidents—including Mitterrand—have exploited to the full. Mitterrand must now build a favourable environment for the Socialist presidential candidate—possibly himself or the popular M. Michael Rocard. As President, he is well-placed to make life difficult for the Right-wing RPR-UDF coalition government, which in any case will find unity difficult to maintain as Chirac, Giscard d'Estaing and Barre begin to compete with each other in the presidential election campaign.

THE ANGLO-IRISH AGREEMENT

The Background: The Stormont Era.

Since 1969 the problems of Northern Ireland have beset successive British governments. Nor has their impact been confined to Westminster. The life of every British citizen has been affected by the measures taken to tighten security in the wake of bombings and other terrorist outrages not only in Northern Ireland itself but also in many cities elsewhere in the United Kingdom.

These problems are not of recent origin. Following a long and bitter campaign for home rule, compounded by the determined resistance of Protestant Ulstermen against rule from Catholic-dominated Dublin, Ireland was partitioned in 1921. The "six counties" of Ulster remained part of the UK and were governed under a scheme of devolution embodied in the Government of Ireland Act 1920. This created the Northern Ireland Parliament (known as Stormont) and Government, headed by a prime minister and small cabinet, responsible for most matters internal to the province. However, the Act preserved the sovereign authority of the UK Parliament in Westminster and it excluded certain areas, such as foreign relations, defence, customs and excise and income tax, from Stormont's jurisdiction. As a result, Northern Ireland continued to elect MPs to Westminster.

Imposition of Direct Rule.

For almost fifty years, Stormont was left largely to itself. It was dominated continuously by the Unionist Party, supported by the Protestant majority community. In permanent opposition was the Catholic minority, constituting about a third of the population, many of whom favoured reunification with the rest of Ireland. Such a long period of one-party domination, coupled with Protestant fears about the future status of the province, led to widespread discrimination in housing, jobs and political rights and to the establishment of a police force, and a paramilitary reserve force, which was completely mistrusted by a large section of the Catholic community. During the 1960s the Unionists initiated a process of gradual reform but this served only to fuel expectations and the ensuing civil rights campaign led to serious rioting. The inability of the police to keep order led in August 1969 to the despatch of British troops to the province. Continuing violence, exacerbated by the introduction of internment without trial, persuaded the Heath Government in 1972 to suspend Stormont and to transfer all executive powers to a newly-appointed Secretary of State for Northern Ireland (a system known as direct rule).

UK-Ulster-Ireland.

Since 1972 successive British governments have struggled to find a means of restoring normality to life in Northern Ireland. They have searched in vain for a system of government that will satisfy both the Unionists with their passionate commitment to a Stormont-type system within the UK, and the Nationalists with an equally passionate commitment to reunification (although they differ over the means and speed of achieving this aim). The problems have been exacerbated by the fact that political divisions spill over into every aspect of life in Northern Ireland and have been heightened by sectarian violence perpetrated by extremists on both sides. To make matters worse, most of the UK's economic problems are at their worst in the province.

Power-sharing.

The Heath Government attempted to deal with the situation in 1972 in three ways. First, it organised a plebiscite on the border in which almost 60% of the electorate voted to remain part of the UK. Second, it set up a new Northern Ireland Assembly, elected by proportional representation, with an Executive composed of representatives of more than one party (known as power-sharing). After the first elections in January 1973, prolonged negotiations resulted in the creation of such an executive. However, its position was undermined by the third initiative: the signing at the end of 1973 of the Sunningdale Agreement between the UK and Irish governments which provided, among other things, for the establishment of a Council of Ireland. The fragile Executive was further undermined by the sudden UK General Election in February 1974 and was brought down by a Protestant workers' strike two months later. Since then, a number of political initiatives have been taken in an attempt to restore power-sharing. In 1975 a Constitutional Convention was elected but it was dissolved the following year when it was clear that there was no prospect of agreement between the parties. More recently, an Assembly was elected in 1982 initially as a consultative forum but with the intention that it should take over executive responsibilities if inter-party agreement could be reached. The Assembly remains in existence, although periodically boycotted by different parties, but no devolution of powers has been agreed.

Anglo-Irish Agreement.

These political initiatives have been launched against a background of increasing polarisation between the two communities in Northern Ireland, reflected in the success of extremist politicians, and of persistent, if sporadic, violence primarily in the province itself but extending also to the mainland. Growing impatience in Britain about the failure to find a solution and about the human and financial costs of keeping troops in Northern Ireland, led the Thatcher Government not only to persist in its backing of the Assembly but also to explore new links with Dublin. In 1981 an Anglo-Irish Inter-governmental Council was established to encourage contacts at both ministerial and official levels. This process was taken a stage further with the signing at Hillsborough in November 1985 of an Anglo-Irish Agreement. Both governments affirmed the status of Northern Ireland as part of the UK so long as this was the wish of the majority of its people; and they set up an inter-governmental conference to enable the Irish government to comment on certain aspects of Northern Irish affairs and to foster improved cross-border cooperation particularly on security.

The Outlook.

Dublin's acknowledgement of the present status of Northern Ireland failed to quell Unionist fury at the involvement, albeit only on a consultative basis, of the Irish government in their affairs. Having failed to persuade Mrs Thatcher to hold a referendum, all the Unionist MPs at Westminster resigned their seats to fight by-elections. This tactic backfired in that, although 14 out of 15 were returned, one seat was lost. Unionist frustration led to a one-day strike in February 1986, called by their political leaders but increasingly taken over by extra-parliamentary forces, which spilled over into violence and confrontation with the police, not only on the streets but also against individual policemen and their families. The result was a political outlook that looked even bleaker than normal. Both the UK and Irish governments reaffirmed their commitment to the Agreement but each was under serious political pressure. Unease among Conservative backbenchers, traditionally supportive of the Unionists, was growing as law and order in the province appeared to be disintegrating; and the future of the Irish Government was in doubt as its narrow majority came under threat.

POLITICAL COMPENDIUM

This compendium provides a compact reference work of key facts and figures for an understanding of modern British politics. Readers will also find that the preceding section, *Background to Public Affairs*, complements this part of the book.

TABLE OF CONTENTS

POLITICAL COMPENDIUM

A. THE MONARCHY

The Queen is a constitutional monarch. In law she is the head of the executive, an integral part of the legislature, head of the judiciary, commander-in-chief of the armed forces and temporal head of the Church of England. In practice, the Queen's role is purely formal; she reigns, but she does not rule. In all important respects she acts only on the advice of her ministers. However, she still plays an important role symbolically as Head of State and Head of the Commonwealth.

Monarchs since 1900

1837–1901	Victoria
1901–1910	Edward VII
1910–1936	George V
1936	Edward VIII
1936–1952	George VI
1952–	Elizabeth II

B. GENERAL ELECTIONS

For electoral purposes the United Kingdom is divided into 650 constituencies (an increase of fifteen since 1979) each returning one M.P. to the House of Commons. All British subjects and citizens of the Irish Republic are entitled to vote provided they are 18 years old and over and are included on the electoral register which is compiled annually. The only exceptions are members of the House of Lords and those incapacitated through insanity or imprisonment. Anyone who is entitled to vote and aged at least 21 may stand as a candidate, the only exceptions being undischarged bankrupts, clergymen in the established church and the holders of certain other public offices. All candidates have to pay a deposit of £500 (recently increased from £150), which is forfeited unless they receive 5% of the votes cast. In each constituency the winning candidate has only to obtain a simple majority.

General elections must be held every five years,

General Elections since 1918

VOTES CAST (thousands)

	Conservative	Labour	Liberal*	Communist	Plaid Cymru	SNP	Others
1918	4,166	2,546	2,753	—	—	—	1,296
1922	5,500	4,241	4,189	34	—	—	462
1923	5,538	4,438	4,311	39	—	—	260
1924	8,039	5,489	2,928	55	—	—	126
1929	8,656	8,390	5,309	51	1	—	243
1931	12,320	6,991	1,509	75	2	21	293
1935	11,810	8,465	1,422	27	3	30	273
1945	9,988	11,995	2,248	103	16	31	752
1950	12,503	13,267	2,622	92	18	10	290
1951	13,745	13,949	731	22	11	7	177
1955	13,312	12,405	722	33	45	12	313
1959	13,750	12,216	1,639	31	78	22	125
1964	12,023	12,206	3,093	46	70	64	168
1966	11,418	13,095	2,328	62	61	128	171
1970	13,145	12,198	2,117	38	175	307	384
1974 (Feb.)	11,910	11,646	6,059	33	171	632	958
1974 (Oct.)	10,501	11,457	5,347	17	166	840	897
1979	13,698	11,532	4,314	17	133	504	1,024
1983	12,991	8,437	7,775	12	125	331	952

* 1983 figures for Liberals include the SDP total (3,571,000).

The Speaker has been regarded as a candidate of the party he represented before appointment.

SEATS WON

	Conservative	Labour	Liberal*	Communist	Plaid Cymru	SNP	Others (GB)	Others (NI)	Total
1918	383	73	161	0	0	0	9	81	707
1922	344	142	115	1	0	0	10	3	615
1923	258	191	158	0	0	0	5	3	615
1924	412	151	40	1	0	0	10	1	615
1929	260	287	59	0	0	0	6	3	615
1931	521	52	37	0	0	0	3	2	615
1935	429	154	21	1	0	0	8	2	615
1945	213	393	12	2	0	0	16	4	640
1950	299	315	9	0	0	0	0	2	625
1951	321	295	6	0	0	0	0	3	625
1955	345	277	6	0	0	0	0	2	630
1959	365	258	6	0	0	0	1	0	630
1964	304	317	9	0	0	0	0	0	630
1966	253	364	12	0	0	0	0	1	630
1970	330	288	6	0	0	1	1	4	630
1974 (Feb.)	297	301	14	0	2	7	2	12	635
1974 (Oct.)	277	319	13	0	3	11	0	12	635
1979	339	269	11	0	2	2	0	12	635
1983	397	209	23	0	2	2	0	17	650

Others (NI): Ireland in 1918, Northern Ireland only 1922–79. Ulster Unionists regarded as Conservatives 1922–70.

The Speaker has been regarded as an M.P. of the party he represented before appointment.

* 1983 figures for Liberals include SDP M.P.s (6).

By-Elections 1945–86

Parliament	Government	No. of By-elections	Changes	Con. + —		Lab. + —		Lib./All.* + —		Others + —	
1945–50	Lab.	52	3	3	—	—	—	—	—	—	3
1950–51	Lab.	16	0	—	—	—	—	—	—	—	—
1951–55	Con.	48	1	1	—	—	1	—	—	—	—
1955–59	Con.	52	6	1	4	4	—	1	1	—	1
1959–64	Con.	62	9	2	7	6	2	1	—	—	—
1964–66	Lab.	13	2	1	1	—	1	1	—	—	—
1966–70	Lab.	38	16	12	1	—	15	1	—	3	—
1970–74	Con.	30	8	—	5	1	3	5	—	2	—
1974	Lab.	1	0	—	—	—	—	—	—	—	—
1974–79	Lab.	30	7	6	—	—	7	1	—	—	—
1979–83	Con.	20†	6	1	4	1	1	4	1	—	—
1983–	Con.	27†	5	—	4	1	—	3	—	1	1

* Liberal 1945–79; Alliance (Liberal and SDP) after 1979.
† Includes 15 by-elections held in Northern Ireland in January 1986 following Unionist resignations in protest at Anglo-Irish Agreement.

Run-up to the Next General Election

Date

The next election must be held by June 1988. Unless she is defeated in the House of Commons (an unlikely event in view of the size of the Conservative majority), the Prime Minister will be able to choose the date and she is likely to choose Spring or Autumn 1987 unless the prospects then look unpromising and she therefore decides to carry on into 1988.

State of the Parties

	June 1983	June 1986	
Conservative	391	391	4 by-election losses (Portsmouth S, Brecon, Fulham, Ryedale)
Labour	207	208	1 by-election gain (Fulham)
Liberal	17	19	2 by-election gains (Brecon and Ryedale)
SDP	6	7	1 by-election gain (Portsmouth S)
Nationalists	4	4	
Unionists (NI)	15	14	1 by-election loss (Newry)
SDLP (NI)	1	2	1 by-election gain (Newry)
Others (NI)	1	1	
Speaker and deputies	4	4	
	650	650	

but may occur more frequently either because no government can command a majority in the House of Commons or at the request of the Prime Minister. If a seat falls vacant between general elections a by-election is held on a date usually chosen by the party which previously held the seat. Elections are generally held on Thursdays.

TURNOUT AND PARTY SHARE OF VOTES CAST

Turnout (%)		Share of Poll (%)		
		Conservative	Labour	Liberal
1918	59	39	24	26
1922	71	38	30	29
1923	71	38	31	30
1924	77	48	33	18
1929	76	38	37	23
1931	76	59	32	7
1935	71	54	39	6
1945	73	40	48	9
1950	84	44	46	9
1951	83	48	49	3
1955	77	50	46	3
1959	79	49	44	6
1964	77	43	44	11
1966	76	42	48	9
1970	72	46	43	8
1974 (Feb.)	78	38	37	19
1974 (Oct.)	73	36	39	18
1979	76	44	37	14
1983	73	43	28	26*

* includes SDP figures

C. POLITICAL PARTIES

To understand the operation of the British system of government it is essential to appreciate the importance of the party system. Since the seventeenth century two parties have usually been predominant, at different times Tories and Whigs, Conservatives and Liberals, and since the 1930s Conservatives and Labour. Parties exist to form governments, and the path to this goal lies in the House of Commons, for the party which obtains a majority of seats has the right to have its leaders form the government. The other party forms Her Majesty's Opposition.

To this end parties in this country have been highly disciplined organisations. The opposition accepts that, unless the government's majority is very small, it is unlikely to defeat it in the Commons, and it thus sees its role as one of criticising government policy and setting forth an alternative programme.

Party Leaders

The Conservative Party leader is elected by the members of its parliamentary party. The Labour Party leader is elected by an electoral college in which affiliated trade unions have 40% of the votes, constituency parties 30% and the Parliamentary Labour Party 30%. The Liberal and Social Democratic leaders are elected by party members nationally.

Present Leaders (May 1986)

Conservative	Mrs. Margaret Thatcher
Labour	Mr. Neil Kinnock
Liberal	Mr. David Steel
Social Democratic Party	Dr. David Owen
Plaid Cymru	Mr. Dafydd Elis Thomas
Scottish National Party	Mr. Donald Stewart
Ulster Unionist	Mr. James Molyneaux

Past Leaders

Conservative Party Leaders

1900–2	Marquis of Salisbury
1902–11	A. Balfour
1911–21	A. Bonar Law
1921–22	A. Chamberlain
1922–23	A. Bonar Law
1923–37	S. Baldwin
1937–40	N. Chamberlain
1940–55	(Sir) W. Churchill
1955–57	Sir A. Eden
1957–63	H. Macmillan
1963–65	Sir A. Douglas-Home
1965–75	E. Heath
1975–	Mrs. M. Thatcher

Labour Party Leaders

1906–8	J. K. Hardie
1908–10	A. Henderson
1910–11	G. Barnes
1911–14	J. R. MacDonald
1914–17	A. Henderson
1917–21	W. Adamson
1921–22	J. Clynes
1922–31	J. R. MacDonald
1931–32	A. Henderson
1932–35	G. Lansbury
1935–55	C. Attlee
1955–63	H. Gaitskell
1963–76	H. Wilson
1976–80	J. Callaghan
1980–83	M. Foot
1983–	N. Kinnock

Liberal Party Leaders

1900–8	Sir H. Campbell-Bannerman
1908–26	H. Asquith
1926–31	D. Lloyd George
1931–35	Sir H. Samuel
1935–45	Sir A. Sinclair
1945–56	C. Davies
1956–67	J. Grimond
1967–76	J. Thorpe
1976–	D. Steel

Social Democratic Party Leaders

1981–3	R. Jenkins
1983–	D. Owen

Party Officers

Conservative Party

Chairman of the Party Organisation
(appointed by the Leader of the Party)

1959–61	R. Butler
1961–63	I. Macleod
1963	I. Macleod ⎫
	Lord Poole ⎭
1963–65	Viscount Blakenham
1965–67	E. du Cann
1967–70	A. Barber
1970–72	P. Thomas
1972–74	Lord Carrington
1974–75	W. Whitelaw
1975–81	Lord Thorneycroft
1981–83	C. Parkinson
1983–85	J. Selwyn Gummer
1985–	N. Tebbit

Chairman of Conservative (Private) Members'
Committee (or the 1922 Committee), which is the
organisation of back-bench Conservative M.P.s

1955–64	J. Morrison
1964–66	Sir W. Anstruther-Gray
1966–70	Sir A. Harvey
1970–72	Sir H. Legge-Bourke
1972–84	E. du Cann
1984–	C. Onslow

Labour Party

General Secretary (appointed by the National
Executive Committee)

1944–62	M. Phillips
1962–68	A. Williams
1968–72	Sir H. Nicholas
1972–82	R. Hayward
1982–85	J. Mortimer
1985–	L. Whitty

Chairman of the Labour Party (elected annually
by the National Executive Committee)

1980–81	A. Kitson
1981–82	Dame J. Hart
1982–83	S. McCluskie
1983–84	E. Heffer
1984–85	A. Hadden
1985–86	N. Hough

Chairman of the Parliamentary Labour Party
(until 1970 this post only existed when the
Labour Party was in government; a chairman is now
also elected when the Party is in opposition)

1970–74	D. Houghton
1974	I. Mikardo
1974–79	C. Hughes
1979–81	F. Willey
1981–	J. Dormand

Liberal Party

Head of Liberal Party Organisation

1960–61	D. Robinson
1961–65	P. Kemmis
1965–66	T. Beaumont
1966–70	P. Chitnis
1970–76	E. Wheeler
1976–83	W. N. Hugh Jones
1983–85	J. Spiller
1986–	A. Ellis

Social Democratic Party—National Secretary: R.
Newby.

Scottish National Party—National Secretary:
N. MacCallum.

Plaid Cymru—General Secretary: D. Williams.

National Front—Chairman of National Directorate: I. Anderson.

Communist Party of Great Britain—Secretary:
G. McLennan.

Green Party—General Manager: J. Bishop.

D. PARLIAMENT

Parliament consists of the Queen, the House of
Lords and the House of Commons. Over the
centuries the balance between the three parts of
the legislature has changed such that the Queen's
role is now only formal and the House of Commons
has established paramountcy over the House of
Lords. Because of the party system the initiative
in government lies not in Parliament but in the
Cabinet. But Parliament, and especially the
Commons, has important functions to play not
only as the assembly to which the government is
ultimately responsible but also in legitimising
legislation, voting money and in acting as a body in
which complaints may be raised.

House of Lords

Composition. The House of Lords comprises
about 1,200 peers, made up in 1986 as follows:

Hereditary Peers	800
Life Peers	364
Lords of Appeal	9
Archbishops and bishops	26

No new hereditary peers were created between 1964
and 1983. Since then, there have been 3 (Viscounts
Tonypandy and Whitelaw and the Earl of Stockton). Less than 300 peers attend more than one-
third of the Lords' proceedings. Figures of party
strengths in the Lords are not easy to obtain, but
one source identified 523 Conservatives, 145 Labour,
43 Liberals and 41 Social Democrats in 1986.

Functions.

(1) Legislation. Some bills on subjects which
are not matters of partisan controversy are initiated in the Lords. It also examines in detail
many bills which originated in the Commons, but
its part is limited by the Parliament Acts, under
which it cannot require the Commons to agree to
amendments nor delay a bill indefinitely.

(2) Debate. The Lords provides a forum for
men and women, distinguished in most fields of
national life, to discuss issues of importance free
from the reins of party discipline.

(3) Court of appeal. The Lords is the highest court
of appeal. Only the law lords take part in its legal
proceedings.

House of Commons

Composition. The House of Commons comprises 650
M.P.s (an increase of fifteen since 1979) elected to
represent single-member constituencies (523 in
England, 72 in Scotland, 38 in Wales and 17 in Northern Ireland). Its proceedings are presided over by
the Speaker, who is elected by M.P.s at the beginning of each session. The present Speaker is Mr.
Bernard Weatherill.

M.P.s sit on parallel rows of seats, known as
benches, with those who support the government
on one side of the chamber and the rest on the
other side. Members of the government and the
spokesmen of the Opposition are known as "front-
benchers"; other M.P.s are "backbenchers".

Functions.

(1) Legislation. There are two types of legisla-

tion—*public acts*, most of which are introduced by the government, but which can also be introduced by individual M.P.s, and *private acts*, which confer special powers on bodies such as local authorities in excess of the general law and which are subject to special procedures.

All public legislation must pass through the following stages before becoming law:

First Reading. The bill is formally introduced.

Second Reading. The general principles of the bill are debated and voted.

Committee Stage. Each clause of the bill is debated and voted.

Report Stage. The bill is considered as it was reported by the committee, and it is decided whether to make further changes in individual clauses.

Third Reading. The bill, as amended, is debated and a final vote taken.

The Other House. The bill has to pass through the same stages in the other House of Parliament.

Royal Assent. The Queen gives her assent to the bill which becomes law as an Act of Parliament.

(2) Scrutiny of government activities. There are a number of opportunities for the opposition and the government's own back-benchers to criticise government policy. They can question ministers on the floor of the House; they can table motions for debate and speak in debates initiated by the government; and they can take part in one of the select committees set up to scrutinise government activity.

Committees. The House of Commons uses committees to assist it in its work in various ways. They are of two types:

Standing Committees. A standing committee is a miniature of the House itself, reflecting its party composition, and consists of between 20 and 50 M.P.s. Its function is to examine the Committee Stage of legislation. Usually seven or eight such committees are needed.

Select Committees. A select committee is a body with special powers and privileges to which the House has delegated its authority for the purpose of discovering information, examining witnesses, sifting evidence and drawing up conclusions which are then reported to the House. A few select committees are established *ad hoc*, but the majority are semi-permanent, although the House can always wind them up at any time.

Since 1979, there have been 14 select committees, each one scrutinising the work of one or two government departments (e.g. Agriculture, Foreign Affairs, Treasury and Civil Service); and various others including the following: European Legislation, Members' Interests, Parliamentary Commissioner for Administration, Privileges, Public Accounts, and Statutory Instruments.

Her Majesty's Government (June 1986)

The Cabinet

Prime Minister, First Lord of the Treasury and Minister for the Civil Service	Mrs. Margaret Thatcher
Lord President of the Council and Leader of the House of Lords	Viscount Whitelaw
Lord Chancellor	Lord Hailsham
Secretary of State for Foreign and Commonwealth Affairs	Sir Geoffrey Howe
Chancellor of the Exchequer	Mr. Nigel Lawson
Secretary of State for the Home Department	Mr. Douglas Hurd
Secretary of State for Education and Science	Mr. Kenneth Baker
Secretary of State for Energy	Mr. Peter Walker
Secretary of State for Defence	Mr. George Younger
Secretary of State for Wales	Mr. Nicholas Edwards
Lord Privy Seal and Leader of the House of Commons	Mr. John Biffen
Secretary of State for Social Services	Mr. Norman Fowler
Chancellor of the Duchy of Lancaster	Mr. Norman Tebbit
Secretary of State for Northern Ireland	Mr. Tom King
Minister of Agriculture, Fisheries and Food	Mr. Michael Jopling
Secretary of State for Transport	Mr. John Moore
Secretary of State for Employment	Lord Young
Secretary of State for the Environment	Mr. Nicholas Ridley
Paymaster General and Minister for Employment	Mr. Kenneth Clarke
Chief Secretary to the Treasury	Mr. John MacGregor
Secretary of State for Scotland	Mr. Malcolm Rifkind
Secretary of State for Trade and Industry	Mr. Paul Channon

Ministers not in the Cabinet

Ministers of State, Ministry of Agriculture	Lord Belstead
	Mr. John Gummer
Ministers of State, Ministry of Defence	Mr. John Stanley
	Lord Trefgarne
Minister of State, Department of Education and Science	Mr. Christopher Patten
Minister of State, Department of Energy	Mr. Alick Buchanan-Smith
Ministers of State, Department of the Environment	Lord Elton
	Mr. William Waldegrave
	Mr. John Patten
Ministers of State, Foreign and Commonwealth Office	Lady Young
	Mr. Timothy Renton
	Mrs. Lynda Chalker
	Mr. Timothy Raison
Ministers of State, Department of Health and Social Security	Mr. Barney Hayhoe
	Mr. Anthony Newton
Ministers of State, Home Office	Mr. David Waddington
	Mr. Giles Shaw
Minister of State, Northern Ireland Office	Dr. Rhodes Boyson
Minister of State, Privy Council Office (Minister for the Arts)	Mr. Richard Luce
Minister of State, Scottish Office	Lord Gray
Ministers of State, Department of Trade and Industry	Mr. Alan Clark
	Mr. Geoffrey Pattie
	Mr. Peter Morrison
Minister of State, Department of Transport	Mr. David Mitchell
Financial Secretary to the Treasury	Mr. Norman Lamont
Economic Secretary to the Treasury	Mr. Ian Stewart
Minister of State, Treasury	Mr. Peter Brooke
Parliamentary Secretary, Treasury (Chief Whip)	Mr. John Wakeham
Attorney-General	Sir Michael Havers
Solicitor-General	Sir Patrick Mayhew
Lord Advocate	Lord Cameron
Solicitor-General for Scotland	Mr. Peter Fraser

Principal Ministers 1900-86

	Prime Minister	Chancellor of the Exchequer	Foreign Secretary	Home Secretary	Leader of the House of Commons
1900–2	Marquis of Salisbury	Sir M. Hicks-Beach	Marquis of Salisbury Marquis of Lansdowne	Sir M. White-Ridley C. Ritchie	A. Balfour
1902–5	A. Balfour	C. Ritchie A. Chamberlain	Marquis of Lansdowne	A. Akers-Douglas	A. Balfour
1905–8	Sir H. Campbell-Bannerman	H. Asquith	Sir E. Grey	H. Gladstone	Sir H. Campbell-Bannerman
1908–16	H. Asquith	D. Lloyd George R. McKenna	Sir E. Grey	H. Gladstone W. Churchill R. McKenna Sir J. Simon Sir H. Samuel	H. Asquith
1916–22	D. Lloyd George	A. Bonar Law A. Chamberlain Sir R. Horne	A. Balfour Earl Curzon	Sir G. Cave E. Shortt	A. Bonar Law A. Chamberlain
1922–23	A. Bonar Law	S. Baldwin	Earl Curzon	W. Bridgeman	A. Bonar Law
1923–24	S. Baldwin	N. Chamberlain	Earl Curzon	W. Bridgeman	S. Baldwin
1924	J. R. MacDonald	P. Snowden	J. R. MacDonald	A. Henderson	J. R. MacDonald
1924–29	S. Baldwin	W. Churchill	(Sir) A. Chamberlain	Sir W. Joynson-Hicks	S. Baldwin
1929–35	J. R. MacDonald	P. Snowden N. Chamberlain	A. Henderson Marquis of Reading Sir J. Simon	J. Clynes Sir H. Samuel Sir J. Gilmour	J. R. MacDonald
1935–37	S. Baldwin	N. Chamberlain	Sir S. Hoare A. Eden	Sir J. Simon	S. Baldwin
1937–40	N. Chamberlain	Sir J. Simon	A. Eden Viscount Halifax	Sir S. Hoare Sir J. Anderson	N. Chamberlain
1940–45	W. Churchill	Sir K. Wood Sir J. Anderson	A. Eden	H. Morrison Sir D. Somervell	C. Attlee Sir S. Cripps A. Eden

Principal Ministers 1900–86

Prime Minister	Chancellor of the Exchequer	Foreign Secretary	Home Secretary	Leader of the House of Commons
1945–51 C. Attlee	H. Dalton Sir S. Cripps H. Gaitskell	E. Bevin H. Morrison	C. Ede	H. Morrison C. Ede
1951–55 Sir W. Churchill	R. Butler	Sir A. Eden	Sir D. Maxwell-Fyfe G. Lloyd George	H. Crookshank
1955–57 Sir A. Eden	R. Butler H. Macmillan	H. Macmillan S. Lloyd	G. Lloyd George	R. Butler
1957–63 H. Macmillan	P. Thorneycroft D. Heathcoat Amory S. Lloyd R. Maudling	S. Lloyd Earl of Home	R. Butler H. Brooke	R. Butler I. Macleod
1963–64 Sir A. Douglas-Home	R. Maudling	R. Butler	H. Brooke	S. Lloyd
1964–70 H. Wilson	J. Callaghan R. Jenkins	P. Gordon Walker M. Stewart G. Brown M. Stewart	Sir F. Soskice R. Jenkins J. Callaghan	H. Bowden R. Crossman F. Peart
1970–74 E. Heath	I. Macleod A. Barber	Sir A. Douglas-Home	R. Maudling R. Carr	W. Whitelaw R. Carr J. Prior
1974–76 H. Wilson	D. Healey	J. Callaghan	R. Jenkins	E. Short
1976–79 J. Callaghan	D. Healey	A. Crosland D. Owen	R. Jenkins M. Rees	M. Foot
1979– Mrs. M. Thatcher	Sir G. Howe N. Lawson	Lord Carrington F. Pym Sir G. Howe	W. Whitelaw L. Brittan D. Hurd	N. St John-Stevas F. Pym J. Biffen

E. CENTRAL GOVERNMENT

The executive work of central government is performed by the Prime Minister and the other ministers of the Crown. The power of executive action is not given to a government department as a corporate body but to the minister individually, who is responsible for the exercise of his duties legally to the Queen and politically to Parliament. For this reason, all ministers must be members of either the Commons or the Lords.

At the head of the government structure is the Cabinet, which consists of the leading members of the majority party in the Commons, selected by the Prime Minister. Most Cabinet ministers are the heads of government departments, which are staffed by civil servants, but there are usually some without departmental responsibilities. Although legally ministers are individually responsible for the exercise of government powers, politically it is accepted that the Cabinet is collectively responsible for government policy. It thus acts as one man, and a minister who disagrees with the Cabinet must either resign or remain silent.

Size of the Government 1945–86

	Cabinet Ministers	Non-Cabinet Ministers	Junior Ministers	Total
1945	20	20	49	89
1950	18	22	44	84
1960	20	23	45	88
1965	23	33	55	111
1970	17	26	41	84
1975	24	31	54	109
1986	22	33	50	105

F. HER MAJESTY'S OPPOSITION

The leader of the largest party opposed to the government is designated Leader of Her Majesty's Opposition and receives an official salary. The leading spokesmen of the Opposition meet together as a committee and are generally known as the Shadow Cabinet. A Conservative Shadow Cabinet, officially known as the Leader's Consultative Committee, is selected by the leader of the party. Labour Shadow Cabinets, officially known as the Parliamentary Committee, are elected by the Parliamentary Labour Party, but the leader retains the right to invite members to take charge of particular subjects.

Principal Opposition Spokesmen (June 1986)

Parliamentary Committee* (elected 1985)

Leader of the Opposition	Mr. Neil Kinnock
Deputy Leader, Treasury and Economic Affairs	Mr. Roy Hattersley
Opposition Chief Whip	Mr. Derek Foster
Chairman of the Parliamentary Labour Party	Mr. Jack Dormand
Home Affairs	Mr. Gerald Kaufman
Energy	Mr. Stanley Orme
Foreign and Commonwealth Affairs	Mr. Denis Healey
Employment	Mr. John Prescott
Campaigns Coordinator	Mr. Robin Cook
Leader of the House of Commons	Mr. Peter Shore
Trade and Industry	Mr. John Smith
Education	Mr. Giles Radice
Environment	Dr. John Cunningham
Northern Ireland	Mr. Peter Archer
Wales	Mr. Barry Jones
Health and Social Security	Mr. Michael Meacher
Defence and Disarmament	Mr. Denzil Davies
Scotland	Mr. Donald Dewar
Transport	Mr. Bob Hughes

Others

Agriculture, Fisheries and Food	Mr. Brynmor John
Arts	Mr. Norman Buchan
Disabled People's Rights	Mr. Alfred Morris
European and Community Affairs	Mr. George Foulkes
Health	Mr. Frank Dobson
Legal Affairs	Mr. John Morris
Overseas Development and Cooperation	Mr. Stuart Holland
Science and Technology	Dr. Jeremy Bray
Women's Rights	Ms Jo Richardson

*The Parliamentary Committee also includes three Labour peers.

G. OTHER EXECUTIVE BODIES

A large number of semi-autonomous agencies have been established to carry out functions on behalf of the government, usually because a particular function is considered to be unsuitable for a normal government department. In this category are bodies such as the British Broadcasting Corporation and the Commission for Racial Equality which need to be insulated from the political process, and the nationalised industries, most of which are managed by public corporations so as to secure managerial flexibility. Some public control over these bodies is maintained by means of various powers which ministers possess.

National Health Service

The National Health Service was created in 1948. Overall responsibility for the NHS rests with the Secretary of State for Social Services and the Secretaries of State for Scotland and Wales. Managerial and operational responsibility, however, is delegated to various health authorities appointed by central government in consultation with local authorities and the health service professions. In England there are two tiers of authorities: 14 Regional Health Authorities and 191 District Health Authorities. In Scotland and Wales the Scottish and Welsh Offices act as the regional tier and there are 14 Health Boards and 9 Health Authorities respectively.

H. THE CIVIL SERVICE

The civil service is the body of permanent officials who, working in the various departments, administer the policy of central government. It consists of some 596,000 people (2·5% of the working population), of whom 496,000 are non-industrial civil servants and the rest industrial workers in places such as the ordnance factories and naval dockyards. Over 70% of the civil service work outside Greater London, mainly in the regional and local offices of departments such as Health and Social Security, Employment and the Inland Revenue.

The political head of each department is a minister, but, as he often has no previous experience of the field to which he is appointed and his tenure of office may be fairly short-lived, great responsibility falls on the shoulders of the permanent civil servants in his department. Civil servants remain largely anonymous and their relationship with their minister is a confidential one. They are non-political in the sense that they serve both political parties impartially.

Major Nationalised Industries	*Chairman*
British Airways Board	Lord King
British Gas Corporation	Sir Denis Rooke
British Railways Board	Sir Bob Reid
British Steel Corporation	Mr. Bob Scholey
Electricity Council	Sir Philip Jones
Central Electricity Generating Board	Lord Marshall
British Coal	Sir Robert Haslam
Post Office	Sir Ron Dearing

Other Public Bodies	*Chairman*
Arts Council	Sir William Rees-Mogg
Bank of England	Mr. Robin Leigh-Pemberton
Advisory Conciliation and Arbitration Service	Sir Pat Lowry
British Broadcasting Corporation	Mr. Stuart Young
Civil Aviation Authority	Sir John Dent
Commission for Racial Equality	Mr. Peter Newsam
Equal Opportunities Commission	Lady Platt
Independent Broadcasting Authority	Lord Thomson
Health and Safety Commission	Dr. John Cullen
London Regional Transport	Dr. Keith Bright
Manpower Services Commission	Mr. Bryan Nicholson
Monopolies and Mergers Commission	Sir Godfrey Le Quesne

Civil Service Numbers

	Total	Industrial	Non-Industrial
1914	779,000	497,000	282,000
1938	581,000	204,000	377,000
1950	972,000	397,000	575,000
1960	996,000	359,000	637,000
1970	702,000	209,000	493,000
1985	596,000	100,000	496,000

Note: The drop in numbers between 1960 and 1970 is the result of the exclusion of Post Office staff, who ceased to be civil servants in 1969. Otherwise the size of the civil service grew by more than 50,000 between 1960 and 1970.

Senior Civil Servants

Head of the Home Civil Service

1945–56	Sir E. Bridges
1956–63	Sir N. Brook
1963–68	Sir L. Helsby
1968–74	Sir W. Armstrong
1974–78	Sir D. Allen
1978–81	Sir I. Bancroft
1981–83	{ Sir R. Armstrong { Sir D. Wass
1983–	Sir R. Armstrong

Head of the Diplomatic Service

1945–46	Sir A. Cadogan
1946–49	Sir O. Sargent
1949–53	Sir W. Strang
1953–57	Sir I. Kirkpatrick
1957–62	Sir F. Hoyer Millar
1962–65	Sir H. Caccia
1965–68	Sir S. Garner
1968–69	Sir P. Gore-Booth
1969–73	Sir D. Greenhill
1973–75	Sir T. Brimelow
1975–82	Sir M. Palliser
1982–86	Sir A. Acland
1986–	Sir P. Wright

Permanent Secretary to the Treasury

1945–56	Sir E. Bridges
1956–60	{ Sir N. Brook { Sir R. Makins
1960–62	{ Sir N. Brook { Sir F. Lee
1962–63	{ Sir N. Brook { Sir W. Armstrong
1963–68	{ Sir L. Helsby { (Sir) W. Armstrong
1968	{ Sir W. Armstrong { Sir D. Allen
1968–74	Sir D. Allen
1974–83	Sir D. Wass
1983–	Sir P. Middleton

Secretary to the Cabinet

1938–47	Sir E. Bridges
1947–63	Sir N. Brook
1963–73	Sir B. Trend
1973–79	Sir J. Hunt
1979–	Sir R. Armstrong

Other Public Servants

The civil service constitutes only 10% of the public service. The remainder work as follows:

Local Government	40%
National Health Service	15%
Nationalised industries and other public bodies	35%

In all there are 7 million employees in the public sector (about 25% of the total working population).

I. LOCAL GOVERNMENT

Local government in the United Kingdom is the creation of Parliament. Its structure is laid down by Parliament, and local authorities may only exercise those powers which Parliament either commands or permits them to exercise. Their functions include responsibility for all education services, except the universities, most personal welfare services, housing, public health, environmental planning, traffic management and transport, in each case subject to some central government control.

The structure of local government varies in different parts of the country. In non-metropolitan England (often known as the shire counties), Scotland and Wales there is a two-tier system. In London and the six metropolitan areas there has, since April 1986 (when the Greater London Council and the metropolitan county councils were abolished), been a single-tier system with a few special bodies undertaking county-wide functions.

Next Elections

England

County Councils 1989*

Metropolitan District Councils, 1987 (when a third of each council retires)

Non-metropolitan District Councils, 1987 (in districts in which a third of the council retire each year and in those in which all councillors retire together)

London Borough Councils, 1990

Wales

County Councils, 1989

District Councils, 1987

Scotland

Regional (and Islands) Councils, 1990

District Councils, 1988

First-tier Authorities

ENGLAND	Name	Population in 1983	Political control in 1986	Number of districts	Administrative capital
Non-Metropolitan Counties	Avon	935,900	NOM.	6	Bristol
	Bedfordshire	512,900	NOM.	4	Bedford
	Berkshire	706,900	Con.	6	Reading
	Buckinghamshire	580,100	Con.	5	Aylesbury
	Cambridgeshire	601,400	NOM.	6	Cambridge
	Cheshire	933,200	NOM.	8	Chester
	Cleveland	564,800	Lab.	4	Middlesbrough
	Cornwall	430,200	NOM.	6	Truro
	Cumbria	483,000	NOM.	6	Carlisle
	Derbyshire	911,100	Lab.	9	Matlock
	Devon	973,000	NOM.	10	Exeter
	Dorset	609,100	Con.	8	Dorchester
	Durham	606,800	Lab.	8	Durham
	East Sussex	673,800	Con.	7	Lewes
	Essex	1,491,700	NOM.	14	Chelmsford
	Gloucestershire	506,100	NOM.	6	Gloucester
	Hampshire	1,499,400	Con.	13	Winchester
	Hereford and Worcester	640,400	Con.	9	Worcester
	Hertfordshire	975,400	NOM.	10	Hertford
	Humberside	854,000	NOM.	9	Hull
	Isle of Wight	119,800	Lib.	2	Newport
	Kent	1,486,300	Con.	14	Maidstone
	Lancashire	1,377,600	NOM.	14	Preston
	Leicestershire	863,700	NOM.	9	Leicester
	Lincolnshire	554,300	Con.	7	Lincoln
	Norfolk	711,300	Con.	7	Norwich
	Northamptonshire	538,500	Con.	7	Northampton
	Northumberland	300,200	NOM.	6	Newcastle-upon-Tyne
	North Yorkshire	684,700	NOM.	8	Northallerton
	Nottinghamshire	992,200	Lab.	8	Nottingham
	Oxfordshire	550,300	NOM.	5	Oxford
	Shropshire	382,500	NOM.	6	Shrewsbury
	Somerset	435,700	NOM.	5	Taunton
	Staffordshire	1,018,000	Lab.	9	Stafford
	Suffolk	612,500	Con.	7	Ipswich
	Surrey	1,011,800	Con.	11	Kingston-upon-Thames
	Warwickshire	477,800	NOM.	5	Warwick
	West Sussex	678,900	Con.	7	Chichester
	Wiltshire	532,100	NOM.	5	Trowbridge
WALES					
Counties	Clwyd	395,300	NOM.	6	Mold
	Dyfed	335,300	NOM.	6	Carmarthen
	Gwent	439,900	Lab.	5	Cwmbran
	Gwynedd	232,000	NP.	5	Caernarfon
	Mid Glamorgan	536,400	Lab.	6	Cardiff
	Powys	110,600	Ind.	3	Llandrindod Wells
	South Glamorgan	391,700	Lab.	2	Cardiff
	West Glamorgan	366,600	Lab.	4	Swansea
SCOTLAND					
Regions	Borders	100,500	Ind.	4	Newton St. Boswells
	Central	272,600	Lab.	3	Stirling
	Dumfries and Galloway	146,100	Ind.	4	Dumfries
	Fife	342,800	Lab.	3	Cupar
	Grampian	494,000	NOM.	5	Aberdeen
	Highland	196,000	Ind.	8	Inverness
	Lothian	744,800	Lab.	4	Edinburgh
	Strathclyde	2,338,000	Lab.	19	Glasgow
	Tayside	395,000	NOM.	3	Dundee
Islands Councils	Orkney	19,200	NP.	—	Kirkwall
	Shetland	23,400	NP.	—	Lerwick
	Western Isles	31,500	NP.	—	Stornoway

NOM.—No overall majority.   NP.—Non-party

Second-tier Authorities

	Number	Range of population	Party Control
England Non-Metropolitan District Councils	296	24,000—416,000	Con. 113, Lab. 65, Lib. 2, Other 41, NOM 64.
Wales District Councils	37	20,000—282,000	Con. 3, Lab. 14, Other 9, NOM 11.
Scotland District Councils	53	9,000—856,000	Con. 4, Lab. 25, Other 10, NOM 3, NP 11.

NOM—No overall majority.   NP—Non-party.

Metropolitan Councils in England

	Name	Population in 1983	Political control in 1986
London	Barking & Dagenham	150,100	Lab.
	Barnet	294,400	Con.
	Bexley	217,900	Con.
	Brent	254,000	Lab.
	Bromley	299,200	Con.
	Camden	175,500	Lab.
	Croydon	320,600	Con.
	Ealing	283,900	Lab.
	Enfield	263,100	Con.
	Greenwich	216,100	Lab.
	Hackney	186,700	Lab.
	Hammersmith and Fulham	150,300	Lab.
	Haringey	204,700	Lab.
	Harrow	199,400	Con.
	Havering	240,300	NOM.
	Hillingdon	234,200	NOM.
	Hounslow	200,900	Lab.
	Islington	162,700	Lab.
	Kensington and Chelsea	134,100	Con.
	Kingston-on-Thames	133,600	NOM.
	Lambeth	245,000	Lab.
	Lewisham	231,900	Lab.
	Merton	165,400	Con.
	Newham	210,300	Lab.
	Redbridge	227,000	Con.
	Richmond-on-Thames	160,900	All.
	Southwark	215,400	Lab.
	Sutton	169,700	NOM.
	Tower Hamlets	144,000	All.
	Waltham Forest	215,200	Lab.
	Wandsworth	258,400	Con.
	Westminster	184,100	Con.
Greater Manchester	Bolton	261,800	Lab.
	Bury	174,800	Lab.
	Manchester	457,500	Lab.
	Oldham	220,900	Lab.
	Rochdale	206,400	Lab.
	Salford	245,000	Lab.
	Stockport	288,900	NOM.
	Tameside	216,300	Lab.
	Trafford	218,700	NOM.
	Wigan	308,200	Lab.
Merseyside	Knowsley	170,800	Lab.
	Liverpool	502,500	Lab.
	St. Helens	189,200	Lab.
	Sefton	299,800	NOM.
	Wirral	338,500	NOM.
South Yorkshire	Barnsley	224,800	Lab.
	Doncaster	289,800	Lab.
	Rotherham	253,200	Lab.
	Sheffield	542,700	Lab.
Tyne & Wear	Gateshead	210,200	Lab.
	Newcastle-upon-Tyne	281,200	Lab.
	North Tyneside	195,000	NOM.
	South Tyneside	159,500	Lab.
	Sunderland	299,400	Lab.
West Midlands	Birmingham	1,012,900	Lab.
	Coventry	315,900	Lab.
	Dudley	300,900	Lab.
	Sandwell	307,300	Lab.
	Solihull	199,900	Con.
	Walsall	265,300	NOM.
	Wolverhampton	255,400	Lab.
West Yorkshire	Bradford	463,900	Lab.
	Calderdale	192,000	NOM.
	Kirklees	377,300	Lab.
	Leeds	714,100	Lab.
	Wakefield	312,100	Lab.

Local Government Structure (showing numbers of authorities of each type)

	England			Wales	Scotland	
1st Tier	Metropolitan District Councils 36	Non-Metropolitan County Councils 39	London Borough Councils* 32	County Councils 8	Regional Councils 9	Islands Councils 3
2nd Tier		Non-Metropolitan District Councils 296		District Councils 37	District Councils 53	
3rd Tier	Parish Councils 221	Parish Councils 8,919		Community Councils	Community Councils	Community Councils

*Excluding the City of London.

Table derived from J. Stanyer and B. C. Smith, *Administering Britain* (Martin Robertson, 1980), p. 119.

Local Government—Division of Functions

Service	England and Wales			Scotland
	Metropolitan areas	Non-Metropolitan areas	Greater London	
Education	District	County	Borough (except in inner London)[1]	Region
Personal social services	District	County	Borough	Region
Police and fire services	Joint boards[2]	County	Home Secretary/Joint Board[2]	Region
Planning	District	Shared	Borough	Shared
Highways	District[3]	Shared	Borough[3]	Shared
Environmental Health	District	District	Borough	District
Housing	District	District	Borough	District

Notes:

1. In Inner London a special body, the Inner London Education Authority, runs the education service. As from May 1986 it has been directly elected.

2. Joint boards are composed of borough and district councillors, appointed by the councils within the metropolitan area or Greater London.

3. In the metropolitan areas except London, passenger transport services are run by joint boards; London Regional Transport has, since 1984, been appointed by central government.

J. REDRESS OF GRIEVANCES

In the first instance most citizens who are aggrieved by the decision of a public body take up their complaint with the body concerned, either personally or in writing. If this does not satisfy them they have a number of options which vary according to the type of body and the nature of their complaint.

Central Government

1. *M.P.s.* M.P.s may be contacted by letter, and many of them hold regular surgeries in their constituencies. On receipt of a complaint they can write to the minister in charge of the department concerned or ask a question in Parliament. If the complainant alleges maladministration (*e.g.*, arbitrary action, undue delay) this can be referred to the *Parliamentary Commissioner for Administration* (usually known as the Ombudsman) who is empowered to investigate complaints and report his findings to Parliament.

2. *Tribunals and inquiries.* In certain areas of government (*e.g.*, social security), special tribunals exist to adjudicate on disputes between citizens and government. In others (*e.g.*, planning) an inquiry can be set up. In both cases the machinery is less formal and more flexible than the ordinary courts.

3. *Courts of law.* On certain restricted matters (*e.g.*, that a public body has acted outside its lawful powers), citizens have recourse to the ordinary courts.

Local Government

1. *Councillors.* Local councillors can be contacted in the same way as M.P.s. They can also refer complaints of maladministration to a *Commissioner for Local Administration* (or local Ombudsman). There are five commissioners, three in England and one each in Scotland and Wales, each investigating complaints in a particular part of the country.

2. *Tribunals and inquiries* (as above).

3. *Courts of law* (as above).

Other Public Bodies

1. *National Health Service.* Each health authority has its own complaints procedure subject to a national code of practice. Complaints, other than those involving the exercise of clinical judgement, may be taken to the *Health Service Commissioner.* Special procedures exist for complaints against doctors.

2. *Nationalised Industries.* Each industry has a consumer council which exists both to take up individual complaints and to represent the views of consumers to the board of management for the industry (*e.g.*, The Post Office Users National Council, the Transport Users Consultative Committees).

Parliamentary Commissioner for Administration

(and Health Service Commissioner since 1973)

1967–71	Sir Edmund Compton
1971–76	Sir Alan Marre
1976–78	Sir Idwal Pugh
1979–85	Sir Cecil Clothier
1985–	Mr. A. Barrowclough

K. PRESSURE GROUPS

Large numbers of groups exist to exert pressure on government by direct consultation with ministers and civil servants, lobbying Parliament and general publicity campaigns. Some exist to defend interests such as labour, business or consumers; others promote particular causes such as the prevention of cruelty to children or the banning of blood sports. Of great importance in contemporary politics are the groups representing labour and business.

Trade Unions

About 50% of the working population belong to a trade union. The 10 largest unions are:

Transport and General Workers' Union
Amalgamated Engineering Union
General, Municipal, Boilermakers' and Allied Trades Union
National and Local Government Officers Association
National Union of Public Employees
Union of Shop, Distributive and Allied Workers
Association of Scientific, Technical and Managerial Staffs
Electrical, Electronic, Telecommunication and Plumbing Union
Union of Construction, Allied Trades and Technicians
Confederation of Health Service Employees.

Union	Members	Principal Officer
TGWU	1,490,000	R. Todd
AEU	1,220,000	W. Jordan
GMBATU	847,000	J. Edmonds
NALGO	766,000	J. Daly
NUPE	673,000	R. Bickerstaffe
USDAW	392,000	W. Whatley
ASTMS	400,000	C. Jenkins
EETPU	394,000	E. Hammond
UCATT	250,000	G. Smith
COHSE	214,000	D. Williams

91 trade unions, representing 95% of total union membership, are affiliated to the *Trades Union Congress*, which is the federal body of the trade union movement, representing its views to government and others, and giving assistance on questions relating to particular trades and industries.

TUC General Secretaries since 1946

1946–60	(Sir) V. Tewson
1960–70	G. Woodcock
1970–74	V. Feather
1974–84	L. Murray
1984–	N. Willis

Business

The peak organisation representing British business is the *Confederation of British Industry*, formed in 1965. Its members comprise (1983) over 11,000 individual enterprises (mainly in the private sector but also including most nationalised industries) and over 200 representative organisations (employers' organisations, trade associations etc.).

Director-Generals of the CBI

1965–69	J. Davies
1969–76	(Sir) C. Adamson
1976–80	(Sir) J. Methven
1980–	(Sir) T. Beckett

Business is also represented by large numbers of associations which promote the interests of individual industries and sectors (*e.g.*, the Society of Motor Manufacturers and Traders, the Retail Consortium, the Association of Independent Businesses).

Other major groups

	Principal Officer
Amnesty International	J. Johnstone
Campaign for Nuclear Disarmament	M. Beresford
Consumers Association	P. Goldman
European Movement	E. Wistrich
Joint Council for the Welfare of Immigrants	A. Owers
National Society for the Prevention of Cruelty to Children	A. Gilmour
Royal Society for the Prevention of Accidents	R. M. Warburton
Royal Society for the Prevention of Cruelty to Animals	F. Dixon Ward
Royal Society for the Protection of Birds	I. Prestt
Shelter (National Campaign for the Homeless)	S. McKechnie

Some of the largest groups (e.g. the Automobile Association, the National Federation of Women's Institutes) exist primarily to provide services for their members but also exert pressure upon government on issues within their field of interest.

L. THE MEDIA

1. Principal Newspapers

The principal national dailies, with their proprietors and circulation, are set out on **D15**.

There are also a number of provincial morning daily newspapers in England (e.g., *The Birmingham Post and Gazette*, *The Liverpool Daily Post*, *The Yorkshire Post*). Scotland has five morning dailies, of which the most important are *The Scotsman*, *The Glasgow Herald* and *The Daily Record*. Wales has one, *The Western Mail*, and Northern Ireland two, *The News-Letter* and *Irish News*.

2. Broadcasting

British Broadcasting Corporation

Established in 1926 as a public service body and financed by licence fees paid by all owners of TV sets. It is directed by a board of governors appointed by the government.

Services: Radio—4 national networks; 29 local radio stations. TV—2 channels.

Chairman of the Board of Governors, 1983– Mr. Stuart Young

Director-General, 1982– Mr. Alasdair Milne

Independent Broadcasting Authority

Established in 1954 to license programme contracting companies and to regulate their output. In 1972 its functions were extended to include local sound broadcasting. Independent broadcasting is financed by advertising revenue.

Services: TV—One channel, operated by 15 regional companies, and a second (Channel 4) run by two organisations (one for England and Scotland, the other for Wales). A common news service is provided for all the companies by Independent Television News Ltd. Radio—47 local radio stations.

Chairman of IBA, 1981– Lord Thomson

Director-General, 1982– Mr. John Whitney

Editorially all broadcasting authorities are expected to show political balance. Both the BBC and the IBA have bodies with whom individuals and organisations may raise complaints.

M. SCOTLAND, WALES AND NORTHERN IRELAND

The structure of government in Scotland, Wales and Northern Ireland differs from that in England.

Scotland

Most central government functions in Scotland are the responsibility of a single department, the Scottish Office, based in Edinburgh and represented in the Cabinet by the Secretary of State for Scotland. On many matters special Scottish legislation is enacted by Parliament and administrative structure (*e.g.* the local government system—*see* **D12**) and practice (*e.g.* the educational system) differ from that in England.

Wales

The Welsh Office, based in Cardiff and represented in the Cabinet by the Secretary of State for Wales, performs many central government functions in Wales but its responsibilities are narrower than its Scottish counterpart. In other respects too government in Wales resembles more closely that in England.

Paper	Proprietors	Circulation in 1985 (millions)	General political stance
National Dailies			
Daily Express	United Newspapers	1·9	Con.
Daily Mail	Associated Newspapers	1·8	Con.
Daily Mirror	Pergamon Press	3·2	Lab.
Daily Star	United Newspapers	1·5	Con.
Daily Telegraph	Telegraph Newspaper Trust	1·2	Con.
Financial Times	Pearson Longman	0·2	Con.
Guardian	Guardian and Manchester Evening News	0·5	Lib./SDP
Morning Star	Morning Star Co-op Society	0·03	Comm.
Sun	News International	4·1	Con.
The Times	News International	0·5	Con.
National Sundays			
Mail on Sunday	Associated Newspapers	1·6	Con.
News of the World	News International	5·0	Con.
Observer	Lonrho Group	0·7	Lib/SDP
Sunday Express	United Newspapers	2·5	Con.
Sunday Mirror	Pergamon Press	3·2	Lab.
Sunday People	Pergamon Press	3·1	Lab.
Sunday Telegraph	Telegraph Newspaper Trust	0·7	Con.
Sunday Times	News International	1·3	Con.
London Evening			
The Standard	Associated Newspapers	0·5	Con.

Northern Ireland

From 1921 until 1972 Northern Ireland was governed under the scheme of devolution embodied in the Government of Northern Ireland Act 1920. This created the Northern Ireland Parliament, generally known as Stormont after its eventual location. Executive powers were formally vested in the Governor of Northern Ireland, but were in effect performed by a Prime Minister and small cabinet, responsible to Stormont.

The recent troubles in the province led the UK Government in 1972 to suspend the Government of Northern Ireland Act. Since then, apart from a period of four months in 1974, Northern Ireland has been ruled direct from Westminster, the powers of government being vested in the Secretary of State for Northern Ireland. Most local government functions in the province are performed either by the Secretary of State or by special boards. There are, however, 26 elected district councils with limited functions, mainly in the environmental field. In October 1982 a new Assembly was elected, initially to act as a monitoring and deliberative body and eventually, subject to certain conditions, to take over responsibility for many of the functions currently undertaken by the Secretary of State. Under the terms of the Anglo-Irish agreement, signed in November 1985, the Republic of Ireland has been granted consultative status on certain issues.

N. BRITAIN IN EUROPE

Since joining the European Economic Community in 1973, the United Kingdom has participated in the principal Community institutions as follows:

Council of Ministers

The Council of Ministers is the main decision-making body within the Community, consisting of representatives of the member states, each government delegating one of its ministers according to the business under discussion. The principal U.K. delegate is the Secretary of State for Foreign and Commonwealth Affairs (Sir Geoffrey Howe).

Commission

The Commission heads a large bureaucracy in Brussels which submits proposals to the Council of Ministers, implements its decisions, and has powers of its own to promote the Community's interests. It consists of 17 members, appointed by agreement among the member states for 4-year renewable terms. Members are pledged to independence of national interests.

President of the Commission: Mr. Jacques Delors (France)

U.K. members:
Lord Cockfield (responsible for internal market, tax law and customs).
Mr. Stanley Clinton Davis (responsible for transport, environment and nuclear safety).

European Parliament

Apart from general powers of supervision and consultation, the Parliament, which meets in Luxembourg and Strasbourg, can dismiss the Commission and has some control over the Community Budget. Until 1979 it consisted of members nominated by the national parliaments of the member states. The first direct elections were held in June 1979 and the second in June 1984.

Seats Won

	1979	1984
Conservative	60	45
Labour	17	32
Scottish Nationalist	1	1
Democratic Unionist	1	1
Official Unionist	1	1
Social Democratic and Labour	1	1

Conservative Leader   Sir Henry Plumb
Labour Leader   Mr. Alf Lomas

European Court of Justice

The European Court is responsible for interpreting and applying the Community treaties. Its decisions are binding in the member countries. It consists of nine judges, appointed by the member governments for 6-year renewable terms.

U.K. members: Lord Mackenzie Stuart, Sir Gordon Slynn

O. BRITAIN AND THE U.N.

Britain was one of the founding members of the United Nations Organization which was created in 1945. The U.N. now has 157 member states. Its principal organs, with headquarters in New York, are:

the General Assembly in which each member state has one vote and which normally meets once a year in September;

the Security Council which has five permanent members (China, France, U.K., U.S.A., U.S.S.R.) and ten non-permanent members elected for a two-year term.

Also linked with the U.N. are various international organizations, including the International Court of Justice (based in the Hague), the International Labour Organization (based in Geneva), the

Food and Agriculture Organization (based in Rome), the UN Educational, Scientific and Cultural Organization (based in Paris) and the World Health Organization (based in Geneva).

U.N. Secretary-General: Mr. Javier Perez de Cuellar (Peru).

U.K. Permanent Representative to the U.N. and Representative on the Security Council: Sir John Thomson.

P. WHO'S WHO IN BRITISH POLITICS
(for M.P.s, present constituency only is indicated)

Armstrong, Sir Robert, b. 1927; entered civil service in 1950, Treasury 1950–64 and 1967–70, Cabinet Office 1964–6, Principal Private Secretary to Prime Minister 1970–5, Home Office 1975–9, Secretary of the Cabinet since 1979 and Head of the Home Civil Service since 1981.

Barrowclough, Anthony, b. 1924; Barrister since 1949, QC 1974; Parliamentary Commissioner for Administration and Health Service Commissioner since 1984.

Beckett, Sir Terence, b. 1923; Ford Motor Co. Ltd. 1950–80, Managing Director 1974–80, Chairman 1976–80; Director-General, Confederation of British Industry since 1980.

Benn, Anthony Wedgwood, b. 1925; M.P. (Lab.) 1950–83 (except for short period between father's death and renunciation of the family peerage) and since 1984 (Chesterfield); Minister of Technology 1966–70, Secretary of State for Industry 1974–5 and for Energy 1975–9; Member Labour Party NEC 1959–60 and since 1962.

Biffen, John, b. 1930; M.P. (Con.) since 1961 (Shropshire North); Chief Secretary to the Treasury 1979–81, Secretary of State for Trade 1981–2; Leader of the House of Commons since 1982, also Lord President of the Council 1982–3, and Lord Privy Seal since 1983.

Brittan, Leon, b. 1939; M.P. (Con.) since Feb. 1974 (Richmond); Minister of State, Home Office 1979–81, Chief Secretary to the Treasury 1981–3, Secretary of State for Home Department 1983–5, and for Trade and Industry 1985–6 (resigned over Westland affair).

Callaghan, James, b. 1912; M.P. (Lab.) since 1945 (Cardiff South and Penarth); Chancellor of the Exchequer 1964–7, Home Secretary 1967–70, Foreign Secretary 1974–6, Prime Minister 1976–9; Leader of Labour Party 1976–80; 'Father of The House' since June 1983.

Carrington, Lord, b. 1919; Member of House of Lords since 1938; Leader of Opposition in the Lords 1964–70 and 1974–9; Secretary of State for Defence 1970–4, for Energy 1974, and for Foreign and Commonwealth Affairs, 1979–82; Secretary-General of NATO since 1984; Chairman Conservative Party Organisation 1972–4.

Cunningham, John, b. 1939; M.P. (Lab.) since 1970 (Copeland); Shadow spokesman on the environment since 1983.

Donaldson, Sir John, b. 1920; Barrister since 1946, QC 1961; High Court Judge 1966–79, President, National Industrial Relations Court 1971–4; Lord Justice of Appeal 1979–82; Master of the Rolls since 1982.

Edmonds, John, b. 1944; National Industrial Officer, General and Municipal Workers Union (later General, Municipal, Boilermakers and Allied Trades Union) 1972–85, General Secretary since 1985.

Evans, Mostyn, b. 1925; successively district, regional and national organiser, Transport and General Workers' Union since 1956, General Secretary TGWU 1978–1985.

Foot, Michael, b. 1913; M.P. (Lab.) 1945–55 and since 1960 (Blaenau Gwent); Secretary of State for Employment 1974–6, Lord President of the Council and Leader of the Commons 1976–9; Member Labour Party NEC since 1971, Deputy Leader 1976–80, Leader, 1980–3.

Fowler, Norman, b. 1938; M.P. (Con.) since 1970 (Sutton Coldfield); Secretary of State for Transport 1979–81 and for Social Services since 1981.

Hailsham, Lord, b. 1907; Member of House of Lords 1950–63 (disclaimed hereditary title) and since 1970 (life peer); M.P. (Con.) 1938–50 and 1963–70; holder of various Cabinet posts 1959–64, Lord Chancellor 1970–4 and since 1979; Chairman Conservative Party Organisation 1957–9.

Hattersley, Roy, b. 1932; M.P. (Lab.) since 1964 (Birmingham Sparkbrook); Secretary of State for Prices and Consumer Protection 1976–9; Shadow Chancellor since 1983; Member Labour Party NEC and Deputy Leader since 1983.

Healey, Denis, b. 1917; M.P. (Lab.) since 1952 (Leeds East); Secretary of State for Defence 1964–70, Chancellor of the Exchequer 1974–9; Shadow Foreign Secretary since 1980; Member Labour Party NEC 1970–5 and 1980–3, Deputy Leader 1980–3.

Heath, Edward, b. 1916; M.P. (Con.) since 1950 (Old Bexley and Sidcup); Chief Whip 1955–9, Minister of Labour 1959–60, Lord Privy Seal 1960–3, Secretary of State for Industry, Trade and Regional Development 1963–4, Prime Minister 1970–4; Leader of the Opposition 1965–70 and 1974–5; Leader Conservative Party 1965–75.

Heseltine, Michael, b. 1933; M.P. (Con.) since 1966 (Henley); Secretary of State for the Environment 1979–83 and for Defence 1983–6 (resigned over Westland affair).

Howe, Sir Geoffrey, b. 1926; M.P. (Con.) 1964–6 and since 1970 (Surrey East); Solicitor-General 1970–2, Minister for Trade and Consumer Affairs 1972–4, Chancellor of the Exchequer 1979–83, Secretary of State for Foreign and Commonwealth Affairs since 1983.

Hurd, Douglas, b. 1930; M.P. (Con.) since 1974 (Witney); Minister of State, Foreign Office 1979–83, Home Office 1983–4, Secretary of State for Northern Ireland 1984–5 and for Home Department since 1985.

Jenkins, Roy, b. 1920; M.P. (Lab.) 1948–76, (SDP) since 1982 (Glasgow Hillhead); Home Secretary 1965–7 and 1974–6, Chancellor of the Exchequer 1967–70; Deputy Leader of Labour Party 1970–2; President, EEC Commission 1977–80; co-founder of Social Democratic Party 1981 and Leader, 1982–3.

Joseph, Sir Keith, b. 1918; M.P. (Con.) since 1956 (Leeds North East); Minister of Housing and Local Government 1962–4, Secretary of State for Social Services 1970–4, for Industry 1979-81 and for Education and Science 1981–6.

Kaufman, Gerald, b. 1930; M.P. (Lab.) since 1970 (Manchester Gorton); Minister of State, Department of Industry 1975–9; Shadow Home Secretary since 1983.

King, Tom, b. 1933; M.P. (Con.) since 1970 (Bridgwater); Minister for Local Government 1979–83, Secretary of State for the Environment Jan.–June 1983, for Transport June–Oct. 1983, for Employment 1983–5 and for Northern Ireland since 1985.

Kinnock, Neil, b. 1942; M.P. (Lab.) since 1970 (Islwyn); Leader of the Opposition since 1983; Member Labour Party NEC since 1978, Leader since 1983.

Lane, Lord, b. 1918; member of House of Lords since 1979; Barrister since 1946, QC 1962; High Court Judge 1966–74, Lord Justice of Appeal 1974–9, Lord of Appeal 1979–80, Lord Chief Justice since 1980.

Lawson, Nigel, b. 1932; M.P. (Con.) since Feb. 1974 (Blaby); Editor, *The Spectator*, 1966–70; Financial Secretary to the Treasury 1979–81, Secretary of State for Energy 1981–3, Chancellor of the Exchequer since 1983.

Lomas, Alf, b. 1928; M.E.P. (Lab.) since 1979 (London NE); Leader, Labour Group European Parliament since 1985.

Meacher, Michael, b. 1939; M.P. (Lab.) since 1970 (Oldham West); Shadow spokesman on health and social security since 1983; Member Labour Party NEC since 1983.

Middleton, Sir Peter, b. 1934; entered civil service in 1960, Treasury since 1960, Deputy Secretary 1980–3, Permanent Secretary since 1983.

Orme, Stanley, b. 1923; M.P. (Lab.) since 1964 (Salford East); Minister for Social Security 1976–9; Shadow spokesman on energy since 1983.

Owen, David, b. 1938; M.P. (Lab.) 1966–81, (SDP) since 1981 (Plymouth Devonport); Secretary of State for Foreign and Commonwealth Affairs 1977–9; co-founder of Social Democratic Party 1981 and Leader since 1983.

Paisley, Rev. Ian, b. 1926; M.P. (Protestant Unionist 1970–4, Democratic Unionist since 1974) since 1970 (Antrim North); M.E.P. since 1979; member of Stormont 1970–2, NI Assembly 1973–5, NI Constitutional Convention 1975–6, NI Assembly since 1982; minister, Martyrs Memorial Free Presbyterian Church, Belfast since 1946.

Plumb, Sir Henry, b. 1925; M.E.P. (Con.) since 1979 (The Cotswolds); President National Farmers Union 1970–9; Leader, Conservative Group European Parliament since 1982.

Powell, Enoch, b. 1912; M.P. (Con. and later UU) since 1950 (except for 7 months in 1974) (Down South); Minister of Health 1960–3; resigned from Conservative Party in 1974, joining Ulster Unionists.

Prior, James, b. 1927; M.P. (Con.) since 1959 (Waveney); Minister of Agriculture 1970–2, Lord President of the Council and Leader of the Commons 1972–4, Secretary of State for Employment 1979–81 and for Northern Ireland 1981–4.

Shore, Peter, b. 1924; M.P. (Lab.) since 1964 (Bethnal Green and Stepney); Secretary of State for Economic Affairs 1967–9, Minister without Portfolio 1969–70, Secretary of State for Trade 1974–6 and for the Environment 1976–9; Shadow Leader of the House since 1983.

Smith, John, b. 1938; M.P. (Lab.) since 1970 (Monklands East); Secretary of State for Trade 1978–9; Shadow spokesman on Trade and Industry since 1985.

Steel, David, b. 1938; M.P. (Lib.) since 1965 (Tweeddale, Etterick and Lauderdale); Leader Liberal Party since 1976.

Tebbit, Norman, b. 1931; M.P. (Con.) since 1970 (Chingford); Secretary of State for Employment 1981–3, for Trade and Industry 1983–5, Chancellor of the Duchy of Lancaster and Chairman of the Conservative Party since 1985.

Thatcher, Margaret, b. 1925; M.P. (Con.) since 1959 (Finchley); Secretary of State for Education and Science 1970–4, Prime Minister since 1979; Leader of the Conservative Party since 1975.

Todd, Ron, b. 1927; Ford Motor Co. 1954–66; full-time official of Transport and General Workers' Union since 1966, National Organiser 1978–85, General Secretary since 1985.

Walker, Peter, b. 1932; M.P. (Con.) since 1961 (Worcester); Secretary of State for the Environment 1970–2 and for Trade and Industry 1972–4, Minister of Agriculture 1979–83, Secretary of State for Energy since 1983.

Weatherill, Bernard, b. 1920; M.P. (Con.) since 1964 (Croydon North East); Conservative Party Whip 1970–9; Deputy Speaker 1979–83, Speaker since 1983.

Whitelaw, Viscount, b. 1918; M.P. (Con.) 1955–83; Lord President of the Council and Leader of the

Commons 1970–2, Secretary of State for Northern Ireland 1972–3, for Employment 1973–4 and Home Secretary 1979–83, Lord President of the Council and Leader of the House of Lords since 1983; Chairman Conservative Party Organisation 1974–5.

Williams, Shirley, b. 1930; M.P. (Lab.) 1964–79, (SDP) 1981–3; Secretary of State for Prices and Consumer Protection 1974–6 and for Education and Science 1976–9; Member Labour Party NEC 1970–81; co-founder of Social Democratic Party 1981 and President since 1982; SDP candidate for Cambridge.

Willis, Norman, b. 1933; official of Trades Union Congress since 1959, Deputy General Secretary 1977–84, General Secretary since 1984.

Wilson, Lord, b. 1916; M.P. (Lab.) 1945–83; President of Board of Trade 1947–51; Prime Minister 1964–70 and 1974–6; Leader of Labour Party 1963–76.

Wright, Sir Patrick, b. 1931; entered Diplomatic Service in 1955, Deputy Under Secretary, Foreign and Commonwealth Office 1982–4, Ambassador to Saudi Arabia 1984–6, Permanent Under Secretary since 1986.

Younger, George, b. 1931; M.P. (Con.) since 1964 (Ayr); Secretary of State for Scotland 1979–86 and for Defence since 1986.

Q. GLOSSARY OF POLITICAL PLACES AND TERMS

Political Places

Cathays Park	Location of Welsh Office in Cardiff
Chequers	Country house of Prime Ministers in Buckinghamshire
Congress House	Headquarters of TUC in London
Downing Street	The heart of government: No. 10 is the Prime Minister's official residence; No. 11, that of the Chancellor of the Exchequer; and No. 12, the offices of the Government Chief Whip
Fleet Street	Traditional home of the main national newspapers (most of which have now moved elsewhere)
St. Andrew's House	Location of the Scottish Office in Edinburgh
Smith Square	Location of Conservative Party headquarters (formerly Labour Party also)
Stormont	Location of Northern Ireland Parliament until 1972; now NI Assembly and Northern Ireland Office
Transport House	Former headquarters of Labour Party (shared with Transport and General Workers' Union) in Smith Square
Walworth Road	Current headquarters of Labour Party

Political Terms

Backbencher	An M.P. who is neither a member of the Government nor an official Opposition spokesman
Chiltern Hundreds	A fictional office of profit under the Crown, acceptance of which requires an M.P. to vacate his seat (*i.e.* the means by which an M.P. can resign)
Crossbencher	A member of the House of Lords who does not take a Party whip (see below)
Frontbencher	An M.P. who is a member of the Government or an official Opposition spokesman
Guillotine	A means of curtailing debate on parliamentary legislation
Hansard	The official report of debates in both houses of Parliament
Hung Parliament	A Parliament in which no party has an overall majority (also known as a balanced Parliament)
PLP	Parliamentary Labour Party

PR	Proportional representation (an alternative electoral system favoured by the Alliance)
Shadow Cabinet	The official Opposition's counterpart to the Cabinet (hence Shadow Chancellor etc)
Tactical voting	Voting behaviour determined by calculation of which party has the best chance of winning in a particular constituency
Tories	Abbreviation for Conservatives
Whips	Name given to the party managers in Parliament and to the written instructions they issue to M.P.s, the urgency of which is denoted by the number of times they are underlined (*e.g.* three-lined whip = extremely important)
1922 Committee	Conservative backbenchers' committee

THE
WORLD OF
MUSIC

The art of music as it has developed in the Western world, with a glossary of musical terms and an index to composers. A newly-revised section in this edition looks at contemporary music, particularly the period since 1945.

TABLE OF CONTENTS

THE WORLD OF MUSIC

In writing this section no special knowledge on the part of the reader is assumed; it is for those who want to know about the history of music, how different styles evolved, and how one composer influenced another. It is a background to music as the science section is a background to science, and just as the latter cannot show the reader the colours of the spectrum but only tell of Newton's experiments and of the relationship between colour and wavelength, so in this section we can only describe man's achievements in the world of sound. But knowing something about a composer, his work, and when he lived can help to bring fuller understanding and enjoyment when listening to his music.

The section is in four parts:

I. Historical Narrative and Discussion
II. Glossary of Musical Terms
III. Index to Composers
IV. Special Topics

I. HISTORICAL NARRATIVE AND DISCUSSION

The history of music, like that of any people or art, is not one of uninterrupted progress towards some ideal perfection. For five centuries or more music in the West has achieved peaks of accomplishment in one style or another before society has dictated or composers have felt the need for something new and different. Thus Wagner's music-drama *Parsifal*, lasting five hours, is not necessarily a more rewarding work than what Monteverdi achieved in *Orfeo* 250 years earlier. More complex yes, more rewarding—well, that is for the listener to judge.

We must keep this in mind when considering the development of music from a starting point of, say, Gregorian chant down to the complicated structures of a Schoenberg in our own day. In this development there is no true dividing line between one period and another, nor must simplifying terms such as "classical" or "romantic" be taken too literally.

The earliest history of Western music as we know it today is closely bound up with the Church, for music had to be provided for services. The earliest Christian music was influenced by Greek songs, few of which unfortunately have survived, and by the music of synagogues, where the art of chanting originated. The modal system of the ancient Greeks was highly organised. The earliest Greek scale was from A to A and the four descending notes A,G,F,E became the basis of their musical theory, and it is from them that Western music learned to call notes after the letters of the alphabet. A scale can begin on any note and always includes two semitones upon which much of the character of a melody depends.

The Greek modes were based on the white notes only; the Dorian, Phrygian, Lydian, and Mixolydian began respectively on E,D,C, and B. Their character was thus decided by the position of the semitones, and they formed the basis, often corrupted, of the mediaeval modes. This system was transmitted through Latin writers such as Boethius and Cassiodorus, and through Arabic writers. The eight Church modes were not established until the 8th or 9th cent. Their four plagal modes, as they are called, started in each case, for technical reasons, a fourth below the authentic modes.

By the end of the 6th cent. Gregorian chant had developed so far that some sort of permanent record was required. *Neumes*, signs placed over the Latin text, were the earliest attempt at musical notation. Gradually lines came into use until a four-line stave was established, probably in the 11th and 12th cent., and with them came clef signs, although the treble clef as we know it today did not appear until the 13th cent.

And what is this music—plainchant—like? It is an unaccompanied, single line of melody, which, when we have become used to its "antique" flavour is heard to have a wide range of spiritual and emotional expression, not excluding word painting. The texts used came from the Liturgy. These beautiful, extended lines of flowing, flexible melody can still be heard on Sundays in Roman Catholic cathedrals and churches.

Polyphony is Born.

The 10th cent. saw the appearance of a book called *Musica Enchiriadis* (whose authorship is disputed) which introduced theories about unison singing in which the melody is doubled at the fourth or fifth. Organum, or diaphony, is used to describe this method of writing, a term which confusingly could also be used for a kind of singing where melismatic melody was heard over a drone note on the organ. Rules came into fashion defining which intervals were allowed and which parts of the church services could be sung in more than one part. By the time of Guido d'Arezzo (*c.* 990–1050), a Benedictine monk who helped advance notation, contrary motion was permitted as the cadence was approached, another technical advance. Gradually the voices became more and more independent, and the third, so long considered a discord, came into use. Pérotin, of Notre Dame, was the first composer to write for three and four voices, and he and his great predecessor Léonin were the great masters of early polyphony. The proximity and spikiness of Pérotin's harmony is almost modern-sounding, and as with Gregorian chant, once we have adjusted ourselves to the sound, this music can be a rewarding experience.

Early Secular Music.

In mediaeval France, towards the end of the 11th cent., there developed what has become known as the age of the troubadours, poet-musicians. They were the successors to the *jongleurs*, or jugglers, and minstrels about whom we know little as practically none of their music has survived. The troubadours hymned the beauty of spring and of ladies. Contemporary with them in Germany were the Minnesingers. Their songs were mostly set in three modes. Adam de la Halle (d. 1287), because so much of his music survives, is perhaps the best known of the troubadours. He was a notable composer of *rondels*, an early form of round, of which the English *Sumer is icumen in*, written by a monk of Reading *c.* 1226, is a fine example. In that modes were used, the troubadours' music remained definitely akin to that of ecclesiastical hymns, although there is an undoubted feeling of our modern major scale in some of the songs.

Ars Nova and Early Renaissance.

The term *ars nova* derives partly from writings of Philippe de Vitry (1291–1361) who codified the rules of the old and the new music in a valuable treatise. This *new art* represented a freeing of music from organum and rhythmic modes, and an increase in the shape and form of melodic line. France was the centre of music during the 14th cent. and apart from Philippe de Vitry the leading composer was Guillaume de Machaut (1300–77), who wrote many secular works as well as a polyphonic setting of the Mass. His music is notable for its vigour and tenderness as well as for its technical expertise. Meanwhile in 14th-cent. Italy a quite separate branch of *ars nova* was developing. Imitation and canon were to be noted in the music of Italian composers, and vocal forms such as the Ballata, Madrigal (which often included instrumental accompaniment) and Caccia (a two-voice hunting song in canon) were common. The greatest Italian composer of this period was the blind organist and lutenist Francesco di Landini (*c.* 1325–97). Italian pieces of the time, as compared with their French counterparts, are notable for their sensual rather than their intellectual qualities, a difference—it has been noted—between The Southern and The Northern New Art.

England was less affected by *ars nova*, but surviving music shows the influence of the Continent. Not until the 15th cent. did she begin to make a significant contribution to the history of music. Both John Dunstable (*c.* 1380–1453), who was no less eminent as a mathematician and an astronomer than as a musician, and his contemporary Lional Power advanced the technique of music by their method of composition (use of the triad, for instance) and mellifluous style. Their musicianship was much appreciated on the Continent. Dunstable depended less upon the use of *cantus firmus*—a fixed melody—and increased the use of free composition.

After Dunstable the next great figure in European music was Guillaume Dufay (*c.* 1400–74), the most celebrated composer of the Burgundian school. His music is distinguished for its blend of flowing melody, cleverly wrought counterpoint and tender expressiveness. Much travelled, Dufay was a man of catholic outlook. Together with Dunstable and the Burgundian Gilles Binchois he bridged the gap between 14th cent. *ars nova* and the fully developed polyphony of the 15th cent.

Composers of the 14th and 15th cents. also showed an interest in secular music, and many of their songs (those of Binchois particularly) have been preserved.

The results of Dufay's good work can be heard in the flowering of the Franco-Netherland school later in the 15th cent. Its two most notable representatives are Ockeghem (*c.* 1420–95) and his pupil Josquin des Prés (*c.* 1450–1521), who carried musical expressiveness even further than Dufay; their work can also be grand and majestic. Indeed Josquin's wide range, from the humorous to the dignified, partially accounts for his justly deserved high reputation. He was a master of counterpoint but tempered his mechanical ingenuity with imaginative insight.

Throughout the Renaissance choral music was breaking away, as we have seen, from its earlier bonds. The mediaeval tradition of having the *cantus firmus* in the tenor went by the board; the use of dissonance, when only two voices were used in mediaeval times, was abandoned in favour of euphony; and all the voices, democratically, came to share the musical lines. Composers also began to respect their texts; where words were previously fitted to the music, the reverse was now the case. In Josquin's music, indeed, we have the first attempts at symbolism: matching verbal ideas with musical ones. The importance of this musical renaissance has been realised only over the past thirty years. At last the Renaissance composers are coming to be seen not merely as historical figures relevant only in so far as their work culminated in the great classical composers, but as masters in their own right, whose music should be nearly as familiar to us as is that of a Mozart or a Beethoven.

With the exception of Dufay, little is known of the lives of the musicians so far mentioned. Most of them were in the service of royal or ducal households where they were in charge of the chapel choir, or else they worked in or around the great cathedrals, teaching at choir-schools. They were well rewarded for their services and their social position was probably high.

During recent years there has been an appreciable revival of interest in mediaeval music. Numerous ensembles have emerged with their own ideas about how it should be performed—an indication that it is alive and not just part of the history of music. It can communicate just as well as the music of later eras. (*See* **Special Topic**, The Early Music Revival, **E39**.)

The Sixteenth Century.

By the 16th cent. music in England was a steadily expanding art and much encouraged. Music-making in the home was becoming quite the fashion in social circles. The Chapels Royal remained the chief musical centres but the music was changing with the development of new secular forms so that it was not so much religious as a part of life. Composers began their lives as choirboys and received a thoroughgoing education, both theoretical and practical.

Carrying on from where Josquin and his contemporaries left off, Palestrina in Italy, Victoria in Spain, Lassus in the Netherlands, and Byrd in England brought the polyphonic style to its zenith. At the same time came the rise of the madrigalists, first in Italy, then in the Netherlands; and then the beginnings of instrumental music as it came to be known in the succeeding centuries.

The vocal composers began to use chordal (homophonic) as well as contrapuntal (polyphonic) methods of writing—examples are Victoria's *Ave Verum Corpus* and Palestrina's *Stabat Mater*—but polyphony was still the fullest most magnificent instrument of composition, as for instance in Byrd's *O Quam Gloriosum* which shows an eager response to the mood and to the inflection of the words in a kind of vocal orchestration. A feature of all these composers' music, but more especially that of Victoria (*c.* 1535–1611) and Palestrina (1525–94), is its serene simplicity and fervour of utterance. Palestrina was perhaps more spacious in his effects, Victoria the more passionate. How well we can imagine—and sometimes hear—their music resounding down the naves of the great cathedrals of Europe.

The music of Lassus (*c.* 1532–94) is distinguished both in sheer amount and in vitality. His mastery in the field of motets was unrivalled, encompassing a wide range of subject and mood. He and his fellow Flemish composers, Willaert, de Monte and Arcadelt, were also expert in the Madrigal, a form popular in Italy and England as well. The Madrigal was a contrapuntal setting of a poem, usually not longer than twelve lines, in five or six parts. The subject (of the poetry) was usually amorous or pastoral. It was a short-lived, but highly prolific vogue. Orlando Gibbons (1583–1625), Thomas Weelkes (*c.* 1573–1623), and John Wilbye (1574–1638) were the most prominent English exponents.

Instrumental Music.

By the end of the 14th cent. instrumental music began to become something more than mere anonymous dance tunes or primitive organ music. Instruments often accompanied voices, or even replaced them, so that the recorder, lute, viol, and spinet indoors, and sackbuts and shawms outdoors, had already been developed by the time instrumental music came to be written down. Gradually a distinction grew up between what was appropriate to the voice and what was suitable for instruments, Byrd, Gibbons, and Giles Farnaby in England, the great blind keyboard player, Cabezón (1510–66) in Spain, and Frescobaldi (1583–1643) in Italy produced valuable instrumental works. Perhaps the *Parthenia* and the *Fitzwilliam Virginal Book*, collections of Early English Keyboard music, give as fair a representative idea as any of the development of instrumental form at this time.

In chamber music musicians often played collections of dance tunes strung together to make a whole; or they chose fantasies (or "fancies"), where a composer altered a tune as he wished. Then there were sets of variations on a ground, that is a simple tune played over and over again on a bass viol.

As far as brass instruments are concerned, they were often used on festive occasions in spacious halls or in cathedrals. The Venetian composer Andrea Gabrieli (c. 1510–86) was the first to combine voice and instruments and his nephew Giovanni Gabrieli (1557–1612) carried the process further to produce sacred symphonies, often using antiphonal effects.

Drama in Music.

Not until the end of the 16th cent. did anyone begin to think about combining drama and music, and so "invent" the new art we know today as opera. A group of artistic intelligentsia met together in Florence and conceived the idea of reviving the ancient declamation of Greek tragedy. They took Greek mythological subjects, cast them in dramatic form, and set them to music, not in the choral polyphonic style of the Madrigal, but with single voices declaiming dialogue in music. The earliest examples of what was called *Dramma per Musica* were Peri's *Dafne* in 1597 (now lost) and his *Euridice*, in which he co-operated with Caccini. The new style came to its full flowering with the appearance of Monteverdi (1567–1643), whose genius would surely have shone in any age.

Monteverdi's first opera, *Orfeo*, produced in 1607, is a landmark of dramatic expression, and it is nothing less than a catastrophe that so many of his later operas have been lost. His *Orfeo* provides the basic ground work for the operas of the next two centuries: recitative, accompanied recitative, and aria. His last opera *L'Incoronazione di Poppea*, written when he was at the great age (for those days) of 75, succeeds in its aim of creating a free, fluid form, slipping easily from recitative to arioso and even aria without the strict, closed forms that were to be used in the 17th and 18th cent. He focuses attention to an almost unbelievable extent on character rather than situation. He creates real people with all their faults and foibles—the kittenish, sexually attractive Poppaea, the power-drunk, infatuated Nero, the noble Seneca, and the dignified, rejected empress Octavia. As recent productions have shown these characters leap from the musical page as if they had just been created, each unerringly delineated in musical terms. Only the vocal line, the continuo, and the very incomplete instrumental ritornelli parts have been preserved, but in sensitive, knowledgeable hands tonal variety in the shape of wind and string parts can be added, as we know certain instruments were available to the composer.

Monteverdi's successors were Cavalli (1602–76), Cesti (1623–69) and Stradella (1642–82), who gave the solo voice more and more prominence encouraged by the advent of the castrati's brilliant voices. These artificially created singers had a vogue and popularity similar to "pop" singers of today, fêted wherever they appeared. The aria became more extended and ornate, and dramatic verisimilitude gradually but inexorably took second place to vocal display. An aria was nearly always in *da capo* form, the first section being repeated after a contrasting middle one.

Sixteenth- and Seventeenth-century Church Music.

Of course, the invention of a new dramatic style affected church music too. The concentration on

the vertical aspect of music (homophony) as opposed to the horizontal (polyphony) led to the increasing importance of the voice in religious music. In Italy, it is true, there was the late-flowering, great madrigalist Carlo Gesualdo (1560–1614), whose harmonic daring still astonishes us today, but by 1600 the cantata was coming to replace older forms in church music. In its simplest form this was a story told in accompanied recitative, Giacomo Carissimi (c. 1604–74) was one of the first significant composers of this new form. He too was in on the birth of the oratorio, whose forerunner was the *sacra rappresentazione* (mystery or miracle play) of early 16th-cent. Florence. Then in the mid-16th cent. St. Philip Neri brought in elements from popular plays on sacred subjects in his services in Rome, designed to hold the attention of youth—rather as certain parsons have tried with "pop" services today. Emilio del Cavalieri (c. 1550–1602) and Carissimi developed the form adding arias and choral movements, omitting actual representation. Alessandro Scarlatti (1660–1725), whose oratorios bear a close resemblance to his operas, brought oratorio to its zenith in Italy.

Heinrich Schütz (1585–1672), Bach's great predecessor, was the founder of German church music. His historical place has never been called into question but only in recent times have the intrinsic merits of his own music come to be recognised. He studied with Giovanni Gabrieli in his youth and later came under the influence of Monteverdi, so it was not surprising that he brought Italian ideas across the Alps to Germany and wrote the first German opera *Daphne*, now sadly lost. He also introduced his country to the Italian declamatory style and to the new kind of concertato instrumental writing. But his dramatic religious works were his greatest contribution to musical development. He wrote with a devout intensity, bringing to life the scriptural texts by closely allying his urgent music to the words. His three settings of the Passions—Matthew, Luke, and John—paved the way for Bach's even more remarkable works in this genre. Two contemporaries of Schütz, Johann Herman Schein (1586–1630) and Samuel Scheidt (1587–1654), were both important figures in German Reformation music.

Lully, Purcell, and Seventeenth-century Opera.

France resisted the tide of Italian opera, although paradoxically it was an Italian, Jean-Baptiste Lully (c. 1632–87), who charted the different course of French opera which was from the beginning associated with the court ballet. His musical monopoly during the reign of Louis XIV was put to good use. In his thirteen operas the libretto, usually on classical, allegorical themes, plays a vital part in the composition, which is therefore less clearly divided between recitative and aria than in Italian opera. The orchestration and the ballets assume greater importance than in the traditional Italian form. It was, in short, a more realistic, less stylised art.

In England, opera developed out of the entertainment known as the Masque, a succession of dances, accompanied by voices and instruments and often incorporated in a drama or spectacle. Henry Lawes's (1596–1662) setting of Milton's *Comus* is probably the most famous of these entertainments. The *Venus and Adonis* of John Blow (1649–1708) can be called the first English opera because here the music is gradually gaining the ascendancy over the spoken word. However, it was Purcell (c. 1659–95), Blow's pupil, with *Dido and Aeneas*, who really gave dramatic life to the new medium by giving his characters a true musical personality that was subtler than anything the mere spoken word could achieve. The grief-laden lament of the dying Dido "When I am laid in earth" has an expressive power, achieved by extraordinarily bold harmonic effects, never before and seldom since achieved. The opera was in fact written for a young ladies' boarding school. Purcell followed it with several outstanding semi-operas—such as *The Fairy Queen* (to Dryden's text). His untimely death at the age of 36 probably robbed us of several full-length operas—and perhaps a consequence of this was that English music after him did not develop as it should have done.

His verse anthems and much of his instrumental music, especially the Fantasias, are also rich in imaginative mastery through his original use of harmony and counterpoint. However, a large number of his pieces were written for a specific occasion and many of the odes are set to impossibly trite texts. At least his genius was partly acknowledged in his own day, and he was appointed organist in Westminster Abbey where he was buried with due pomp. He is said to have died through catching cold when locked out of his own house at night.

Vivaldi and the Rise of Instrumental Music.

Out of the dance suites popular in the 16th cent. and the beginning of the 17th (known in Italy as the *Sonata da Camera*) developed the concerto. This began as two groups of instrumentalists compared and contrasted with each other as in Giovanni Gabrieli's *Sonata piano e forte*. With Arcangelo Corelli (1653–1713) the concerto grosso took a more definite shape, alternating a solo group of instruments with the main body of strings in three or more contrasting movements. Guiseppe Torelli (1658–1709), Francesco Geminiani (1687–1762) and Tommaso Albinoni (1671–1750) were other notable contributors to the form, but none of the composers so far mentioned has today achieved the popularity of the priest Antonio Vivaldi (*c.* 1678–1741), himself a violinist, who had at his disposal the orchestra at the Ospedale della Pieta in Venice. The young women at this music school also contributed the vocal side of the concerts there of which there are many descriptions. One says: "They sing like angels, play the violin, flute, organ, oboe, cello, bassoon—in short no instrument is large enough to frighten them ... I swear nothing is so charming than to see a young and pretty nun, dressed in white, a sprig of pomegranate blossom behind one ear, leading the orchestra, and beating time with all the grace and precision imaginable." For this body, Vivaldi wrote about 500 concertos which maintain a remarkably even quality, but "The Four Seasons" are perhaps the most felicitous.

Meanwhile organ music was advancing rapidly in technique. Girolamo Frescobaldi (1583–1643) and Jan Pieterszoon Sweelinck (1562–1621) wrote works that provided the foundation of the Italian and Northern German schools of organ music. Their ricercares gradually developed into the fugue, a vein so richly mined by Bach. Among their successors the most notable figure before Bach was Johann Pachelbel (1653–1706).

Other keyboard music, especially for the harpsichord, was the particular province of France; and Jean-Philippe Rameau (1683–1764) and François Couperin (1668–1733) were both masters of keyboard style and harmonic invention. They wrote many pieces of subtle charm and exquisite craftsmanship.

Bach (1685–1750).

The two giant figures of Bach and Handel bestride the first half of the 18th cent. Their differences are perhaps greater than their similarities. Bach wrote essentially for himself (although of course, he had to satisfy his employers at Cöthen and Leipzig) while Handel was composing to please his wide public. Bach was a provincial, always remaining in central Germany; Handel was widely travelled. Bach was devoutly religious, almost ascetic; Handel was more a man of the world. They never met.

To summarise Bach's vast output in a short space is virtually impossible. One can only try to distil the flavour of his music. He brought the art of polyphony to the highest pitch of mastery that has ever been achieved or is ever likely to be achieved. In his famous "Forty-Eight" and "the Art of the Fugue" he explored all the fugal permutations of the major and minor keys. At the same time his music rose above technical brilliance to achieve, especially in his organ music,

the two Passions, many of the church cantatas, and the B minor Mass, intense emotional and expressive power. The cantatas, from his Leipzig appointment (1723) onwards, were integrated into the services. They consisted usually of a chorus based on a Lutheran hymn tune, recitatives, several extended arias, and a concluding chorus usually a straightforward version of the hymn tune in which the congregation joined. There are some two hundred of these works and they contain a wealth of comparatively unknown and sometimes even unrecognised beauties. The St. John and the St. Matthew Passion extend these procedures to a grand scale, an Evangelist telling the new Testament story in vivid recitative, the chorus taking the part of the crowd, soloists pondering in arias on the meaning of the Gospel, and Jesus's words being sung by a bass. Anyone who has heard either of these works well performed cannot help but dismiss from his mind any idea of Bach as a mere dry-as-dust musical mathematician. In the St. Matthew Passion, every suggestion in the text that can possibly be illustrated by a musical equivalent is so illustrated. The Old Testament Pharasaic law is represented by strict musical forms such as the canon; Christ's sayings are given noble arioso life; and the arias reflect truly the New Testament's compassionate message. Technically the work is a marvel; expressively it is eloquent. The B minor Mass, although it contains borrowings from many of his own works, still stands as a satisfying monumental whole in which Bach's choral writing achieved a new richness, the adaptations being in accord with their new setting.

Bach's instrumental music, especially the violin concertos and the unaccompanied works for violin and cello, not only show the immense range of his powers but also contain many of his deeper thoughts, whereas the orchestral suites and the Brandenburg concertos are more extrovert, particularly the rhythmically exuberant fast movements.

Bach closes an era—that of the later contrapuntalists—by achieving the *ne plus ultra* in fugal composition; his last, incomplete work, The Art of the Fugue, is evidence of that. In recent years there has been a trend towards playing Bach's music on original instruments of his time (or replicas) and singing it with appropriately sized, sometimes all-male choirs.

Handel (1685–1759).

During his lifetime Handel was far more widely recognised as a great composer than Bach, and his music, unlike Bach's, maintained its place in popular esteem until the re-discovery of Bach and the dominance of the symphony placed Handel somewhat in the background.

During the latter part of the 19th cent. Handel's name was mainly associated with mammoth, anachronistic performances of a small sample of his oratorios at the Crystal Palace and elsewhere in England. In his lifetime these works, and all his other pieces in the genre, were sung by a small choir who were outnumbered by the instrumental players. Over the past few years authentic-sized performances of his oratorios and a revival of interest in his operas have revealed the real Handel, unknown to our grandparents.

The operas were neglected partly because the vocal prowess they required—and which the castrati so brilliantly supplied—was no longer available and because their dramatic life, at least according to 19th- and early 20th-cent. tenets, hardly existed. Now it is realised that this neglect has deprived us of an unending stream of glorious melody and of much daring harmony. But perhaps it is in the hitherto disregarded oratorios, such as *Semele*, that Handel's innate dramatic sense and musical range are to be heard gloriously fulfilled, and the pastoral serenade *Acis and Galatea* is surely one of the most delightful scores ever composed.

Handel was a colourful, imaginative orchestrator, and this can be heard both in his accompaniment to vocal music and in his concerti grossi, op. 3 and 6, the earlier set exploiting a diversity of interesting string and wind combination. In his writing he was at home in a polyphonic or homophonic style as his superb choruses show. His organ concertos, of which he was the "inventor" (to quote a contemporary source), were often played between the acts of his oratorios. They are alternately expressive and exuberant pieces calling for some virtuosity from the player. His occasional works, such as the Water Music and Fireworks Music show his ingenuity in extending the range of the typical 17th cent. suite to serve a particular occasion.

Handel's working life was mostly spent in England where his Italian operas were acclaimed. In the years between his arrival here in 1711 and 1729 he wrote nearly thirty operas. It was only when the public tired of these and his reputation slumped that he turned to oratorio with equal success.

Bach and Handel between them crowned the age of polyphony that had lasted for two hundred years or more. After them, it is hardly surprising that composers began looking for a new style, already anticipated in the music of Rameau and particularly Dominico Scarlatti (1685–1737), whose harpsichord sonatas foreshadowed the classical sonata form that was to dominate music for the next two hundred years. The change in musical style about 1750 was partly the result of a change in musical patronage. Bach was the last great composer to earn his living through being employed by the church. The new patrons were the nobility who liked to have a composer on hand to write for the various evening entertainments of the time. For this purpose the princes and dukes had their own orchestras and their own small opera houses. The music required had to be elegant, formal, *galant*. Haydn was exceptionally fortunate in having an employer, Prince Nicholas of Esterhazy, who allowed him to write more or less as he wished so that he was able to develop symphonic form into something more than a pleasing way of passing an evening.

The early symphonists, culminating in Haydn, broke away from Bach's contrapuntal treatment of the orchestra. Instruments now came to be treated in a more colourful manner according to their particular timbre. The court of Mannheim had an orchestra of a standard unheard hitherto, and Johann Stamitz (1717–57) and his son Karl (1745–1801) influenced the great composers who were to follow in their footsteps. The composition of their orchestra was flexible, oboes, flutes, and horns often being added to the standard string section. Bach's son Carl Philipp Emanuel (1714–88) added to and developed symphonic and sonata form, especially as regards keys and subjects.

Haydn and Mozart.

These two figures dominate the second half of the 18th cent. as Bach and Handel do the first. In a brief space only a general picture can be presented of their huge output and influence. Of Haydn's 104 symphonies (there may even be others) nearly all are worthy of study and hearing. The craftsmanship is always remarkable, the invention ever new. Indeed without Haydn's harmonic daring or his melodic ingenuity, the even greater symphonic thought of Beethoven would have been impossible: Haydn laid the groundwork on which his successor built towering edifices. A work such as the 93rd symphony in D is typical of his mature style with its searching introduction, powerfully wrought, earnestly argued first movement, beautiful *Largo* and resourceful bustling finale. Haydn did not fight shy of contrapuntal writing: the development section of this symphony's first movement and the finale are evidence of that, but it was only as an integral part of a predominantly homophonic technique.

Mozart's symphonies are not so different in form from Haydn's but—and this must be a subjective judgment—he put more emotional feeling into his. Nobody could listen to the heart-searching first movement of his 40th symphony without being deeply moved. It was in his final three works in the medium that Mozart brought his symphonic art to perfection, and these obviously had an effect on Haydn's later symphonies written after them. For passion and tenderness contained within a classical form these late symphonies, and many other of Mozart's works, have yet to be surpassed.

Haydn, who has been rightly termed "the Father of the Symphony", was also the founder of the string quartet—perhaps the most perfect, because the most exactly balanced, form of musical expression. The four instruments—two violins, viola, and cello—discuss, argue, commune with each other over the whole gamut of feeling. In his quartets Haydn's mastery of structure is even more amazing than in his symphonies. Mozart's quartets (especially the six devoted to Haydn) and even more his quintets achieve miracles of beauty in sound, nowhere more so than in the first movement of the G minor (his most personal key) quintet. The two late piano quartets show how the piano *can* be ideally combined with strings. His clarinet quintet is also a masterly work.

Haydn did not leave any concertos of consequence. Mozart's, especially those for piano, are among his greatest works. As a brilliant clavier player himself, he showed a consummate skill in writing for the keyboard. Although the instrument he knew was slightly less advanced than the piano today, his concertos call for virtuosity in execution, yet they are as searching in emotional content as the late symphonies and quartets. Indeed the C major concero (K. 467) and the C minor (K. 491) may be said to hold the quintessential Mozart. As well as twenty (mature) piano concertos, Mozart wrote six for the violin, four for the horn, and eighteen others, but none of these, delightful as they are, can be placed in quite the same class.

Of their church music, Haydn's sixteen masses and his oratorios—*The Creation* and *The Seasons* (both late works)—are perhaps more worthy of attention than Mozart's various masses, but we must not forget Mozart's final work—the Requiem or the serene late Motet *Ave Verum Corpus*.

Eighteenth-century Opera.

Mozart—for many the first great opera composer—did not, of course, create his masterpieces out of nothing. In France, Lully was followed by Rameau (1683–1764), who carried on his tradition of using classical themes but developed a more flexible style of recitative and greatly increased vividness of expression. But it was Gluck (1714–87) who more than anyone broke out of the straitjacket of the now ossified Italian form of opera—dominated by the singer—and showed just what could be achieved in moving human terms. Drama in music really came of age with his *Orfeo e Euridice* (1762), *Alceste* (1767) and *Iphigénie en Tauride* (1779). His simplicity and poignancy of expression were not lost on Mozart.

Meanwhile in Germany a kind of opera called *Singspiel* appeared during the 18th cent. Breaking away from classical themes, mundane stories were told in dialogue and music.

Until quite recently Haydn's operas were dismissed as unworthy representations of his genius but, chiefly through the enlightening efforts of the Haydn scholar, H. C. Robbins Landon, some of his fifteen surviving works in the medium have been successfully revived. They have proved to be perfectly viable for the stage and, especially in the ensembles, full of that delightful invention to be found in the rest of his opus, if on a less fully developed scale. Still as musical drama they inevitably fall far short of Mozart's achievements, for the younger composer seems to have had an instinctive feeling for the stage. Into his operas he poured his most intense, personal music. He vividly portrays the foibles, desires, loves, and aspirations of mankind.

The earlier, immature stage pieces of his youth led to such works as *Lucio Silla* (1772) and *La*

Finta Giardiniera (1775) with their first glimpses of the glories to come. His first indubitably great opera is *Idomeneo* (1781). Despite its unpromisingly static plot, *Idomeneo* reveals Mozart's stature through its ability to breathe new life into a conventional *opera seria* form. Though influenced by Gluck it is yet more human and touching in its musical expression. To succeed this Mozart wrote a more frivolous piece *Die Entführung aus dem Serail*. Stemming from the *Singspiel* tradition, it none the less creates real-life characters who have much charming music to sing.

After three lesser pieces Mozart embarked on his four masterpieces—*Le Nozze di Figaro* (1786), *Don Giovanni* (1787), *Cosi fan tutte* (1790), and *Die Zauberflote* (1791).

Figaro, as well as being a delightful comedy, explores more fully than any previous opera situation and character, which find expression in beautiful arias and in two finales of symphonic proportion. In *Don Giovanni*, less satisfactory as a dramatic structure, the range of musical characterisation and insight into human motives is widened still further. *Cosi* lyrically but humorously expresses the follies of love. Mozart could not help but love his characters and his music for them is at one and the same time amusing and heartfelt, *Die Zauberflöte*—The Magic Flute—displays Mozart's deep-felt concern for his fellow men and for truth in an opera of great spiritual strength. Nor has opera any more loveable personality than the birdcatcher Papageno. Mozart's final opera *La Clemenza di Tito*, extolling imperial magnanimity, has never achieved the success or popularity of his other maturer stage works, though it contains much excellent music, and has recently been revived with honour in several opera houses.

Beethoven.

Mozart was the last major composer to depend, to any large extent, on private patronage for his living, and even he left the service of the Archbishop of Salzburg because he could not stand the restrictions imposed on his freedom. Henceforth composers would have to stand on their own two feet with all the advantages (liberty) and disadvantages (lack of security) that implied. Beethoven (1770–1827) was the first such composer of importance.

Although his work is usually divided into three periods, that division is somewhat too arbitrary, for no other composer in history, with the possible exception of Wagner, has shown such a continual development of his genius. Coming at just the right moment in musical history, he crowned the achievements of Haydn and Mozart with music of the utmost profundity of thought and feeling that looks back to its classical heritage and forward to the romantic movement of the 19th cent. His influence on musical thinking and writing is incalculable.

His first period shows his strong melodic gifts and the beginning of his individuality in developing form and structure to suit his own ends and match his particular genius. Unusual keys are explored, unusual harmonic procedures employed. With the "Eroica" (his third symphony) he established his position as a great composer. The unity of purpose he here achieved within a long and diverse structure is truly staggering, even today. In the first movement alone the formal invention and cogency went far beyond what even Mozart had achieved in his "Jupiter" symphony, and the second movement—a vast funeral March —has an overwhelmingly tragic emotional content. But the "Eroica" was followed by six equally great symphonies, each one as varied, as inventive, as unified as the others. The ninth symphony is significant both for its length and its finale. Here Beethoven crowns three superb instrumental movements with a choral movement that, as well as summing up all that has gone before, expresses in music the joy in existence more ecstatically than any other work.

The burning intensity of Beethoven's genius is just as evident in his chamber music. His quartets are the product of a revolutionary age in which the social graces and formal restraint of the 18th cent. were thrown off in a search for a more personal mode of expression. The early op. 18 set, and the Razoumovsky quartets, op. 59, go even beyond the range of Haydn's and Mozart's works in the medium but it was in his late quartets, his final musical testament, that Beethoven refined and distilled his art for posterity. No words can possibly describe their unique quality, but any and every chance should be taken to make their acquaintance; the effort required will be more than amply rewarded.

The early piano concertos do not reach quite that level of attainment, but the last three, together with the violin concerto, are on a par with the finest of the symphonies and quartets, as well as being considerable tests of the performers' technique. The Triple Concerto for piano, violin, and cello is an unusual and rewarding work.

Beethoven's grandest choral work—and one of the most noble in existence—is the Mass in D (*Missa Solemnis*). Its vast scale and sublime utterance often defeat performers, but when it is successfully done there is no more spiritually uplifting experience for the listener, except perhaps Beethoven's only opera, *Fidelio*. This simple escape story was transformed by Beethoven's creative fire into a universal symbol of liberty, the composer identifying himself with the struggle for freedom from tyranny and release from darkness.

Beethoven lived in a period of war and revolution. A passionate believer in the brotherhood of man and in liberty, he was shocked to find his ideals thrown over by revolutionaries-turned-dictators. His own tragedy of deafness, which came upon him at the moment of his triumph, nearly submerged him, but in the end he won through and produced the string of masterpieces from the "Eroica" onwards. Hope springing from despair, love from hatred, victory over defeat, these are the unquenchable legacies left by Beethoven.

The Romantic Movement.

Inevitably, the Romantic movement in literature that burst forth about 1800 was bound to have its counterpart in music. And so it was. Breaking the classical bonds, composers such as Schubert, Schumann, Liszt, and Berlioz sought a new freedom in musical expression. Form became of less importance than content; and that content often had literary connections. For their purposes a larger orchestra was needed and supplied, but the miniature, the song especially, because of its very personal connotation, was also a favourite form.

Schubert (1797–1828)—described by Liszt as "the most poetic of musicians"—is perhaps the greatest lyrical genius in musical history. In him the Viennese tradition and influence of Haydn, Mozart, and Beethoven reached its zenith. The song was always Schubert's starting point, so it is hardly surprising that his reputation as a song writer has never been impaired but in his symphonic and instrumental works too it is always his inexhaustible fund of melody that first calls for attention. Nobody could listen to his "Trout" quintet, for piano and strings, his octet, his fifth symphony, or his song cycle *Die Schöne Müllerin* without being enchanted and invigorated by the sheer tunefulness of the music. But there is much more to Schubert than this: his understanding of the possibilities of harmonic change, his grasp of orchestral coloration (in the great C major symphony, for instance), his free use of sonata structure.

Although Mozart, Haydn, and Beethoven had all contributed to the song as an art form, it was with Schubert that it achieved its first full flowering. If he had written nothing but his songs, his place in the musical firmament would be assured. With his *Erlkönig* in 1815 the German *Lied* came of age and from then until the end of his life he wrote more than six hundred songs, hardly a dud among them. Whether it is the charm of *Heiden-röslein*, the drama of *Der Doppelgänger* or the numbed intensity of the *Winterreise* cycle, Schubert unerringly went to the heart of a poet's meaning; indeed he often raised poor verses to an inspired level by his settings. And for the first time the pianist shares a place of equal importance with the singer.

There is only room to mention one or two other composers, some of them wrongly neglected, who were roughly contemporaries of Beethoven and Schubert: the Czech Dussek (1760–1812), who like Beethoven bridges the classical–romantic gulf, Boccherini (1743–1805), the two Italian opera composers Cimarosa (1749–1801) and Paisiello (1740–1816), the Frenchman Méhul (1763–1817) and the German Hummel (1778–1837).

Weber (1786–1826) lacked Beethoven's energy and constructive powers and Schubert's sheer lyrical profundity, but he is an important figure, especially in the field of opera, where his *Der Freischütz* and *Oberon* led the way to a more flexible, dramatically realistic form of opera. His vivid imagination exactly fitted the new romantic mood abroad. The sheer beauty in the melodic shape of his music is also not to be denied. His instrumental works are attractive but insubstantial.

Mendelssohn and Schumann.

Mendelssohn (1809–47) was the civilised craftsman among the Romantic composers. A boy genius—many of his finest works were written before he was twenty—he maintained the importance of classical form while imbuing it with his own affectionate brand of poetic sensibility. His third and fourth symphonies—the "Scottish" and "The Italian"—(and possibly the fifth "The Reformation"), his string quartets (some of which go deeper than the rest of his music), octet, violin concerto, first piano concerto, and of course, the incidental music to "A Midsummer Night's Dream" represent his tidy yet effervescent style at its most winning.

Schumann (1810–56) is less easy to categorise. His early romantic flame was burnt out by some flaw in his intellectual and/or emotional make-up, and his inspiration seems to have declined in later years. No matter, by then he had given us the marvellous song cycles of 1840, an ever fresh piano concerto, many fine piano solos, including the mercurial, popular *Carnaval* and four symphonies, which, if not structurally perfect, contain much lovely music. The joys and sorrows of love and the feeling for natural beauty are all perfectly mirrored in these charming, lyrical works, and in the genial piano quintet.

Romantic Giants.

Berlioz (1803–69) and Liszt (1811–86) are the two most typical representative composers of the Romantic era. Both have always been controversial figures, with ardent advocates and opponents either unduly enthusiastic or unfairly derogatory. Berlioz might be termed the perfect painter in music. With an uncanny mastery of orchestral sound he could conjure up the countryside, the supernatural and the historical with the utmost ease. He based his music on the "direct reaction to feeling" and a desire to illustrate literature by musical means. That his technical expertise was not always the equal of his undoubted genius, can be heard in many of his larger works such as the dramatic cantata *The Damnation of Faust* and the dramatic symphony *Romeo and Juliet*, yet most people are willing to overlook the occasional vulgarity for the ineffable beauty of his many fine pages, but brutal cuts in his music, such as are often made in, for instance, his epic opera *The Trojans* only have the effect of reducing the stature of his works. We must accept him, warts and all. Anyone who has seen the two parts of *The Trojans*, presented complete in one evening at Covent Garden, will realise that Berlioz knew what he was about.

His output is not quantitatively large but includes several monumental works, as well as The Trojans, The *Requiem* ("Grand Messe des Morts") requires a tenor solo, huge chorus and orchestra, and brass bands, although Berlioz uses these forces fastidiously. The *Symphonie funèbre et triomphale* calls in its original form, for choir brass, and strings. But Berlioz was just as happy writing on a smaller scale as his exquisite song cycle, to words of Théophile Gautier, *Nuits d'Eté*, shows. Gautier perhaps summed up better than anyone Berlioz's singular talent: "In that renaissance of the 1830s Berlioz represents the romantic musical idea, the breaking up of old moulds, the substitution of new forms for unvaried square rhythms, a complex and competent richness of orchestration, truth of local colour, unexpected effects in sound, tumultuous and Shakespearian depth of passion, amorous or melancholy dreaminess, longings and questionings of the soul, infinite and mysterious sentiments not to be rendered in words, and that something more than all which escapes language but may be divined in music."

During his lifetime Liszt was fêted and honoured not only by his musical colleagues but by the world at large, which idolised him and his piano. Then his reputation took a plunge from which it has only recently recovered. To be sure much of his early music is glitter and gloss, but his symphonies and tone poems—especially the Faust Symphony, the Dante Symphony (both, of course, inspired by literature), and *Orpheus* and *Prometheus*—and his late piano works show that he was an extraordinary harmonic innovator. The piano sonata in B minor brings his romantic, wilful temperament within a reasonably stable, pianistic form, and as such is a landmark in the repertory of the instrument. Liszt's output was prodigious, but the inquiring listener should explore the more original of his compositions already mentioned to form a true picture of his fertile genius.

Chopin.

Chopin (1810–49) was the master of the keyboard, par excellence. His development of the technical and expressive capabilities of the piano is unique in musical history. His inventive powers were poured out with nervous passionate energy and in a highly individual style through twenty astonishing, possibly agonised years of creative activity before his early death. A Chopin melody, limpid, transparent, singing, can be recognised easily by anyone, but his style gradually developed into something more subtle, more satisfying than pure melody. He took the greatest care of every detail so that any alteration, however small, upsets the perfect balance of his work. His poetic sensibility can be found in any of his works; for his constructive ability we must turn to the Ballades, the B minor Sonata, and the Barcarolle, while the Preludes and Studies blend technical powers and emotional expressiveness in ideal proportions.

Nineteenth-century Opera.

After Mozart's operas and Beethoven's *Fidelio* the medium might have been expected to decline. Instead it took on a new, if different, lease of life that culminated in Verdi's extraordinary output.

Rossini (1792–1868) created a world of exuberant high spirits in his operatic works that are as cheerful and heart-warming today as they were a hundred or more years ago.

He always worked in and around the lyric theatres of Italy and between 1810 and 1830 poured out a stream of works, not all of which can be expected to be masterpieces. However, *Il Barbiere di Siviglia*, *L'Italiana in Algieri*, *La Cenerentola* and *Le Comte Ory* will always delight audiences as long as opera houses exist. Although these works are difficult to sing really well, their vitality and charm can never be submerged even by poor voices or indifferent staging.

His German contemporaries were critical of his confidence and frivolity, but his works show a consistency of invention and an irresistible tunefulness that anyone might envy. In recent years, there has also been a renewed interest in his more serious operas—*Otello* (1816), *La Gazza Ladra* (1817), *Semiramide* (1823), *La Siège de Corinthe* (1820), and *Guillaume Tell* (1829)—which were certainly surpassed in dramatic power by his successors but which nevertheless are not to be despised or neglected.

William Tell, to give it its most popular title, was his last work for the stage although he lived on for nearly forty years in retirement in Paris, scene of many of his greatest successes. There he enjoyed good living, dispensing *bons mots*, and occasionally composing trifles. An exception is the unpretentious *Petite Messe Solennelle*, written originally for soloists, chorus, a harmonium, and two pianos. Rossini later orchestrated it, but he would not allow it to be performed during his lifetime. The first public performance was on 28 February 1869, as near as possible to the 78th anniversary of the composer's birth on Leap Year Day 1792.

In contrast to the mercurial Rossini, Vincenzo Bellini (1801–85) was an exquisite, romantic figure dealing with exquisite, romantic stories, an operatic equivalent to Chopin, who much admired him. His delicate, sinuous vocal line (in the arias) and brilliant acrobatics in the final sections (cabalettas) require singers of the utmost accomplishment to do them justice, although his music is never as florid as Rossini's. His most typical and popular works are probably *La Sonnambula* (1831), *Norma* (1831) and *I Puritani* (1835). The first is a tender, homely country story, the second an almost heroic lyrical drama of sacrifice, and the third a rather unsatisfactory historical story redeemed by its appealing music. In our own day singers of the calibre of Maria Callas, Joan Sutherland, Guiletta Simionato, and Marilyn Horne have brought Bellini's operas a popularity almost equal to that they enjoyed at the time they were written.

Gaetano Donizetti (1797–1848) was an even more prolific operatic composer than Rossini. He wrote at least 75 works, mostly for the Italian stage, several of which, such as *Alfredo il Grande* or *Emilia di Liverpool*, are never likely to be revived, but during the past few years, with the renewed interest in what are called the *Ottocento* operas, many of his serious operas have been resuscitated and found as enjoyable in performance as his more frequently heard comedies.

He was a well-grounded musician and although his invention is often criticised for being too tied to the conventions of his day performances often belie this reputation, his dramatic instinct proving sure. *Lucia di Lammermoor*, because of the chances it offers to a coloratura soprano with tragic pretensions, has always held the stage and of late, *Lucrezia Borgia*, *Anna Bolena*, *La Favorita*, and *Poliuto* have all been successfully revived. Of his lighter works, the comedies *L'Elixir d'Amore* and *Don Pasquale* have never declined in popularity. One of his last works was *Linda di Chamounix* (1842) which he wrote for Vienna where it aroused such enthusiasm that the Emperor appointed him Court Composer and Master of the Imperial Chapel.

French Opera.

The taste in Paris was for more and more lavish productions. Following Spontini (1774–1851), whose works were comparatively austere, came Halévy (1799–1862) and Giacomo Meyerbeer (1791–1864) whose operas contain all the ingredients that came to be expected of "Grand Opera"—spectacle, huge ensembles, showpieces for the soloists, and extended, if superfluous ballet. Drawing from Italian, German, and French traditions Meyerbeer's works contained everything the public wanted, yet today they are seldom revived, perhaps because his creative powers were essentially derivative, yet when they *are* given, operas like *Les Huguenots*, *Le Prophète*, and *L'Africaine* still have the power to fascinate and his influence on his successors, notably Wagner, was considerable.

Verdi.

Italian opera in the 19th cent. culminated in the works of Giuseppe Verdi (1813–1901), who rose from a peasant background to become his country's most noted composer, as well as something of a natural hero during the period of the Risorgimento. His earliest works, indeed, often roused his hearers to patriotic fervour. For instance, *Nabucco* (1841), with its theme of an oppressed people seeking deliverance, was treated as a symbol of the Italians' fight for freedom.

Musically, Verdi developed out of all recognition during the course of his long career. The continuously flowing structure of his last two operas *Otello* and *Falstaff* is very far removed from the start–stop formulas, inherited from his predecessors, of his first works, yet even they are touched, in harmonic subtleties, orchestral felicities, and a sense of drama, by a spark of genius, a burning inspiration that sets him apart from all other operatic composers. *Ernani* (1844), *I due Foscari* (1844), and *Luisa Miller* (1849) all have foretastes of glories to come even if as a whole they are flawed dramas, and these "galley years", as Verdi himself later described them, gave him the essential know-how to produce his later, greater operas, as well as establishing him incontrovertibly as the most popular Italian composer of the time.

However, it was with *Rigoletto* (1851), *Il Trovatore* (1853), and *La Traviata* (1853) that Verdi first really staked his claim to immortality. In these pieces his increasing dramatic mastery is married to a wonderful flow of lyrical melody, at the same time controlled by a fine musical sensibility. They were followed by four operas— *Simon Boccanegra* (1857), *Un Ballo in Maschera* (1858), *La Forza del Destino* (1862), and *Macbeth* (revised version, 1865)—in which Verdi overcame complexities of story line by his continually developing musical powers. This period is crowned by *Don Carlos* (written for the Paris Opéra, 1867) a masterly exercise in combining private and public situations in a single, grand, and characterful work. In some respects Verdi never surpassed the subtlety of his writing in this opera. *Aïda* (1871) carried on the process but the characterisation in this ever-popular piece is less refined than in *Don Carlos*, if the grandeur of the design is more spectacular.

The success of *Otello* (1887) owes nearly as much to the skill of Boito whose literary ability combined with musical knowledge (he was himself a composer) presented Verdi with an ideal libretto for his seamless music in which the drama moves inevitably to its tragic end. Recitative, aria, ensemble are fused in a single, swiftly moving music-drama, which in its very different way equals that of Wagner. *Falstaff* (1893) achieves the same success in the field of comic opera, a brilliant, mercurial ending to a distinguished career. If Verdi had written only these two final masterpieces his place in musical history would have been assured.

Brahms.

Brahms (1833–97) has justly been described as "a romantic spirit controlled by a classical intellect," for while complying with most of the formal regulations of sonata form he imbued them with an emotional content that accorded with his time. Indeed Schumann declared that he was the "one man who would be singled out to make articulate in an ideal way the highest expression of our time."

Perhaps in his chamber music will be found the quintessence of his art. The piano and clarinet quintets, the two string sextets, the horn trio, and the violin sonatas all are designed on a large scale yet the expression remains intimate, the design and structure clear.

The symphonies and concertos, though, remain his most popular works; they are part of the solid repertory of every orchestra and most piano and violin players in the world. Their high seriousness, constant lyrical beauty, and control of form are deeply satisfying. They do not provide the extremes of passion and excitement provided by his contemporaries, but their study provides continuous absorption and delight. The double concerto for violin and cello deserves a mention as a unique work in music.

Brahms wrote more than two hundred songs in which the desire for melodic beauty takes precedence over the words and meaning. Many are set to poor poetry, but hidden away are still some unexplored treasures, and the Four Serious Songs, at least, are tragic masterpieces. In a lighter vein the two sets of *Liebeslieder Walzer* for four voices are irresistible. The choral Requiem, too, is a fine work.

Bruckner.

In recent years Bruckner's reputation *vis-à-vis* his great contemporary Brahms has been enhanced in England. The old conception of him as a naïve Austrian unable to grasp the fundamentals of symphonic architecture has died hard, and the prevailing popularity of his grandest works is at last gaining him his rightful place in the 19th-cent. firmament. The nine symphonies and the masses are his chief claim to immortality. They contain melodies of unforgettable beauty, symphonic paragraphs of unparalleled grandeur, and an appreciation of formal development that, though different, is equally as valid as that of Brahms. The movements of his symphonies are long and he often pauses, as if for breath and to admire the scenery, before he reaches the climactic peak of his musical journey. His idiom is best approached by a newcomer to his work through the fourth and seventh symphonies as they are perhaps the easiest to understand, but the fifth, sixth, eighth, and ninth (unfinished) are just as beautiful—and cogently argued—once one has acquired the knack, so to speak, of listening to his music. Most of these works are now to be heard in their original form, stripped of the veneer of "improvements" suggested to the diffident composer by his friends.

The masses, which translate Bruckner's symphonic ideas to the choral plain, and Bruckner's delightful string quintet are worth investigating.

Wagner.

Praised only this side of idolatry by his admirers, unmercifully criticised by his detractors, Richard Wagner (1813–83) is perhaps the most controversial composer in musical history. And so it was bound to be with such a revolutionary figure, whose writings, other than his music, contain, to say the least, dubious theories and whose operas, composed to his own libretti, broke the bonds of the form as known until his time. He regarded music-drama as a fusion of all the arts—music, literature, painting—in one unity. With *The Ring of the Nibelungs* he achieved his purpose; no other work of art has ever tried to encompass the whole of existence. Today, and surely forever, musicians, philosophers, and writers will argue over its meaning, and each age will reinterpret it according to its own lights.

But before he reached this pinnacle of achievement, Wagner gradually transformed opera—through *Rienzi*, *The Flying Dutchman*, *Tannhäuser*, and *Lohengrin*—so that a new mould was fashioned to take what he wanted to pour into it. He introduced the *Leitmotiv*, a musical theme that could be associated with a particular person, situation, or idea, each time it occurred. Slowly he developed the musical form so that the drama could unfold continuously without breaks for arias. By the time he began to write *Tristan and Isolde* and *Die Meistersinger*, he had perfected his methods and had he never undertaken *The Ring* that tragedy and that comedy would have assured him his place in the musical firmament. Indeed, *Die Meistersinger* is considered a masterpiece even by those who are not willing or prepared to accept the rest of the Wagnerian ethos.

The length and complexity of these operas, and of *Parsifal*, a work of unique beauty in spite of certain *longueurs*, means that it is almost essential to prepare oneself by homework, with libretti and records, before attempting to assimilate them in the opera house. The added effort is well worth while for the ultimate musical satisfaction they bring because Wagner was more than an operatic reformer; he opened up a new harmonic language (especially in the use of chromaticism) that was logically to develop into the atonality of the 20th cent.

Wolf.

As Wagner was the culmination of the 19th cent. symphonic and operatic tradition, so Hugo Wolf (1860–1903) summed up, if he did not surpass, the achievements in song-writing of Schubert, Schumann, and Loewe (1796–1869).

Wolf was a lonely, pathetic man. He lived much of his life in poverty, and eventually lost his reason and died of an incurable disease. These circumstances account perhaps for his almost feverish bursts of creative activity, which were also the outward sign of his burning genius. His greatest contributions to the art of *Lieder* were his extraordinary insight into the poet's meaning and the harmonic means by which he heightened the expression of the words. He raised the importance of the piano part even higher than had Schumann, and in some of his songs the vocal part takes the form of a free declamation over a repeated idea in the piano. However, in the main the vocal and piano parts are interweaved with great subtlety, and he unerringly matched the very varied moods of the poems he chose to set. His greatest creative period was between early 1888 and early 1890 when songs poured from his pen daily—more than 50 settings of the German poet Mörike, 20 of Eichendorff, more than 50 of Goethe, and more than 40 of Heyse and Geibel (the Spanish Song-book). Later he composed songs from Heyse's Italian Song-book and the three Michelangelo sonnets. And the range of his creative understanding was wide, taking in the almost wild passion of the Spanish songs, the humanity and humour of the Italian love-songs, the titanic power of *Prometheus* (Goethe), the varying moods of the Mörike book, and the intangible power of the Michelangelo sonnets. There are almost inexhaustible riches here for the inquiring mind to discover. Outside *Lieder*, Wolf's output is small, but it includes a sadly neglected opera, *Der Corregidor*, the Italian Serenade for string quartet (alternatively for small orchestra) and a tone poem *Penthesilea*.

Ernest Newman, his greatest champion, summed up his work most aptly: "Wolf practically never repeats himself in the songs; every character is drawn from the living model. It is a positively Shakespearian imagination that is at work—Protean in its creativeness, inexhaustibly fecund and always functioning from the inside of the character or the scene, not merely making an inventory from the outside."

National Movements.

During the course of the 19th cent., alongside the emergence of national political identity, came the rise of nationalism in music, fertilising traditional Western—that is basically German—musical forms with folk material. Of these groups the Russian is certainly the most important, if not the most vital.

Glinka (1804–57) was the first important Russian composer of the national school and, although his two operas *A Life for the Tsar* (sometimes called *Ivan Susanin*) and *Russlan and Ludmilla* are strongly influenced by Italian models, they do introduce Russian song and harmony into the texture. He undoubtedly influenced Borodin (1833–87), Cui (1835–1918), Balakireff (1837–1910), Mussorgsky (1839–81) and Rimsky-Korsakov (1844–1908)—the so-called "Five" of 19th-cent. Russian music. However, each was very much of an individualist too. Borodin was a lecturer in chemistry who wrote in his spare time. His two symphonies, two string quartets led up to his most notable work, the opera *Prince Igor*, left incomplete at his death. Balakireff, friend and adviser to the rest of the group, wrote little himself, but his orchestral works and the piano fantasia, *Islamey*, are worthy of investigation.

Modest Mussorgsky (1839–81) is today seen as the most important and inspired of "The Five." More than the others he used Russian song and Russian speech as the basis of his operas in which he portrayed the lives and destinies of his own people. Although his capacities were seriously impaired by an uncongenial job, poverty, and drinking, he produced two great operas, *Boris Godunov* and *Khovanshchina*, and another *Sorochintsy Fair* that is immensely enjoyable. *Boris* should be given in its original, with spare orchestration, but more often than not it is heard in Rimsky-Korsakov's more elaborate revision. In any case the opera exists in various versions, none of them necessarily the right one; what is important is to hear it in one or the other because of its great portrayal of Boris's personality set against the background of the Russian people, unforgettably presented in choral outbursts. *Khovanshchina* was completed by Rimsky-Korsakov, *Sorochintsy Fair* by Tcherepnin (although other versions also exist). Mussorgsky's songs explore a new vein of naturalistic vocal declamation. Each of the four *Songs and Dances of Death* is a miniature drama worthy of Wolf, although of course in a quite other idiom. The *Nursery* songs miraculously conjure up a child's world as seen from a child's point of view. Many of the individual songs, the *Sunless* cycle too, should be investigated.

Rimsky-Korsakov (1844–1908) is perhaps a less attractive figure because so much of his music seems heartless or merely decorative, but this judgment is probably made on the strength of hearing *Shéhérazade* and the *Capriccio Espagnol* a few too many times. Such of his 15 operas as are played evince a (literally) fantastic mind and lyrical vein, and it is a pity that *Sadko*, *The Snow Maiden*, and *The Tsar's Bride*, at least, are not heard more often.

Tchaikovsky.

Peter Ilyich Tchaikovsky (1840–93) is a more universally admired figure than any of "The Five" and his music is indubitably closer to the mainstream than theirs in that it adheres more nearly to Western European forms. His popularity is due to his unhesitating appeal to the emotions and to his tender, often pathetic melodic expression. His lyrical gift is stronger than his sense of architecture, as he himself admitted. Yet his later symphonies—the fourth, fifth, and sixth (the *Pathétique*)—are all cogently enough argued and invigorating, as can be heard in the hands of a conductor willing to emphasise their formal power rather than their tendency towards sentimentality; the orchestral craftsmanship is also superb. The three piano concertos and the violin concerto offer rare opportunities for virtuoso display within a reasonably dramatic structure and his various overtures are always exciting to hear.

The three ballets—*The Sleeping Beauty*, *Swan Lake*, and *Nutcracker* show Tchaikovsky's skill on a smaller and perhaps more congenial scale, but only two of his operas—*Eugene Onegin* and *The Queen of Spades*—survive in regular performance. They demonstrate his ability to delineate character and his always eloquent melodic invention. His songs often felicitously capture a passing mood or emotion.

Bohemia (Czechoslovakia).

The Czech national school is dominated by two composers—Smetana (1824–84) and Dvořák (1841–1904). In his own country Smetana holds a unique position as the father of his country's music—which is remarkable when you consider that he lived in a country that was then under Austrian rule and never spoke the Czech language perfectly. Yet his music is filled with the spirit of Czech history and national life, and many of his operas, his most important contribution, deal purely with national subjects. The reawakening of interest in things national, after Austria's defeat by Italy in 1859, led to the establishment of a Provisional Theatre in 1862 and Smetana's first opera *The Brandenburgers in Bohemia* was produced there in 1866, but its success was eclipsed by the enormous popularity of *The Bartered Bride*, which appeared the same year. Its melodic charm, lively characterisation and cosy humour have carried it round the world and it is the one Smetana opera to be in the repertory of most opera houses. However, his next opera *Dalibor* (1868) is considered by some authorities as his masterpiece. It is conceived on a heroic scale, and frequently rises to great dramatic heights. His later operas include *Libuše* (1872) a solemn festival tableau, *The Two Widows* (1874), a delightful comedy, *The Kiss* (1876), *The Secret* (1878), and *The Devil's Wall* (1882).

His main orchestral work *Má Vlast* (My Country), written between 1874 and 1879, is a cycle of six symphonic poems nobly depicting the life and legends of his country. He composed only three mature chamber works—an elegiac piano trio, written in 1855 in memory of the death of his eldest daughter, and two string quartets, both autobiographical. The first in E minor (1876)—"From My Life"—tells of his youth and aspirations until a terrible, screeching E in *altissimo* describes the onset of deafness; the second in D minor, sadly neglected, was described by the composer as an attempt to explain the "whirlwind of music in the head of one, who has lost his hearing," and was probably influenced by Beethoven's later music.

Dvořák combined a fecund melodic gift with an intelligent grasp of structure. His symphonies and chamber music are mostly written in classical form, yet the works are imbued with a spontaneity and freshness that have not lost one whit of their charm over the years.

He wrote nine symphonies and, although only the last three or four are regularly performed, they are mostly mature works, several of which, for instance No. 7 in D minor (formerly known as No. 2) reach a tragic grandeur at times. They are all orchestrated in a masterly way and are full of delightful detail. Dvořák wanted to show that a Brahms could come out of Bohemia—and he succeeded in doing so while maintaining a definitely individual flavour, strongly influenced by natural rhythms.

He wrote three concertos, one each for piano, violin, and cello. The earlier ones are interesting without being quite in the first flight of the composer's output, but the cello concerto of 1895 is perhaps the composer's crowning achievement—warm, mellifluous, romantic.

He wrote chamber music throughout his long creative life. Some of the early works are weak and derivative, but the later string quartets, the "Dumky" trio, and the piano quartet and quintet are expressive and full of unforced invention. Dvořák felt himself somewhat hampered when setting words, nevertheless his *Stabat Mater* and *Te Deum* are both deeply felt choral works and he wrote songs throughout his career, many of them very fine indeed. He wrote ten operas, but only *Rusalka* (1901) has gained a foothold outside Czechoslovakia.

Janáček.

The Moravian composer Leoš Janáček (1858–1928) spent most of his life in Brno as a working musician. His music has recently come to be recognised as some of the most original written in the past hundred years. His operas, in which he closely followed the inflection of the speech of his native land, are his finest works. Over the score of his last opera, *From the House of the Dead*, he wrote the words "In every human being there is a divine spark", and it is this deep love of humanity that permeates all his works. Of his operas *Kátya Kabanová* (1921) and *The Cunning Little Vixen*

(1924), the *Makropoulos Affair* (1926), and *From the House of the Dead* (adapted from a Dostoyevsky novel, 1928) are the most important and they have all been produced in Britain in recent years. His original genius is self-evident in all of them.

Among his orchestral works *Taras Bulba* and *Sinfonietta* should be noted, and his two string quartets, very difficult to play, should be better known. The song cycle, *Diary of one who has disappeared*, for tenor, contralto, and three female voices with piano, and the Glagolithic Mass contain music of much expressive beauty.

Hungary.

The Hungarian musical outburst came somewhat later than that of other countries. Its great figure is Bela Bartók (1881–1945) who, as well as being a national figure, has proved an influential composer in the whole of 20th-cent. music. His mind was full of folk music, but it was transmuted by his strongly personal style and powerful intellect into something highly original. His music is tense and volatile but this restlessness is sometimes relieved by a kind of other-wordly, ethereal lyricism, as in the lovely slow movements of his quartets.

Bartók was affected as much by the musical innovations of Debussy and Stravinsky (see below) as by East European, notably Magyar, folk music and many of his works are an attempt to meld the two.

The most important part of his output is undoubtedly his string quartets which cover most of his creative life. To this intimate form he confided his personal innermost thoughts and in it conducted his most far-reaching musical experiments, thereby extending its boundaries beyond anything previously known. As with Beethoven's late quartets many of Bartók's rely on organic or cyclic development while remaining just within the laws of classical form. As Mosco Carner puts it, "For profundity of thought, imaginative power, logic of structure, diversity of formal details, and enlargement of the technical scope, they stand unrivalled in the field of modern chamber music."

The most important of his orchestral works are the three piano concertos, of which the first two are harsh and uncompromising, and fiendishly difficult to play, while the third, written in 1945, is mellower and more diatonic. The second violin concerto (1937–8) shows the various elements of Bartók's style in full flower, by turns exuberant, passionate, and brilliant. The *Music for Strings, Percussion and Celesta* (1937) is remarkable for its strange sonorities and its fascinating texture. The *Concerto for Orchestra* (1944) is more immediately appealing and again shows the composer in complete command of a large canvas. Of the piano works *Mikrokosmos* (1935) and the sonata for two pianos and percussion (1937) are worth investigating.

His chief stage pieces are *The Miraculous Mandarin* (1919), a harsh, cruel ballet which drew appropriately dramatic music from the composer, and the opera *Duke Bluebeard's Castle* (1911), a luscious, original score that makes one regret that he wrote no more operas later in his career.

Kodály (1882–1967) was from early years closely associated with Bartók and with him collected Hungarian folk melodies using many of them in his music. He worked in many forms and the more important of his works are the *Peacock Variations* for orchestra, the choral *Psalmus Hungaricus* and *Te Deum*, The *Dances of Galánta*, and the opera *Háry János*, and the sonatas for cello and for unaccompanied cello.

Sibelius, Nielsen and Grieg.

Among Scandinavian composers the Finn Jean Sibelius (1865–1957) and the Dane Carl Nielsen (1865–1931) are outstanding. Sibelius is a lone northern figure ploughing his own furrow oblivious or, at any rate, ignoring the unusual developments that were taking place in Central Europe, yet his seven symphonies are strong as granite, honest, rugged works that will undoubtedly stand the test of time. They are not by any means all similar in mood, or even form. The first is very much influenced by Tchaikovsky and Borodin, the second and third show a more personal style developing, the fourth is terse and tragic, the fifth lyrical, bright, and lucid; the sixth is perhaps most typically Sibelian in its evocation of primeval nature, and the seventh—in one continuous movement—is a more purely abstract piece, notable for its structural logic and the grandness of its themes. The violin concerto is the most easily understood of the composer's main works and has a grateful part for the soloist.

The tone poems *The Swan of Tuonela, Pohjola's Daughter, En Saga, Night Ride and Sunrise, The Bard*, and *Tapiola* uncannily evoke the icy words of the legends of the far north, and the primeval forces of nature. Sibelius's one string quartet *Voces Intimae* and many of his songs are worth hearing too. His music, reviled in some quarters during the 1950s, has since been restored to favour, and seems to be enjoyed again by critics and the general public alike.

Carl Nielsen (1965–1931) is another individualist. His six symphonies, like Sibelius's seven, are the most important part of his output, but whereas Sibelius was dealing with a huge, uninhabited northern landscape, Nielsen is more friendly and serene in his music, which is seldom forbidding, always inventive, throwing a new light, through unusual ideas about harmony, structure and tonality, on traditional forms. He also wrote highly individual concertos for the flute and clarinet, four string quartets and two operas—the dramatic, rather Brahmsian *Saul and David* (1902) and a delightful comedy, *Maskarade* (1906), full of lyrical music.

The Norwegian composer Edvard Grieg (1843–1907) was essentially a miniaturist whose range of feeling was not wide but whose music is always gentle and appealing. His most notable works are the romantic piano concerto, the atmospheric incidental music to Ibsen's play *Peer Gynt*, the charming Lyric Suite, and the small piano pieces. Not an important composer, then, but always an attractive one.

Elgar and the English Revival.

After the death of Purcell there is hardly a name in English music worth speaking of until the 19th cent. when Hubert Parry (1848–1918) and Charles Villiers Stanford (1852–1924), actually an Irishman, led a revival. Their music is seldom heard today, but their pioneer work paved the way for Edward Elgar (1857–1934). Although all were influenced by Brahms they nevertheless managed to establish a new English tradition that has been carried on in our own day. Elgar's symphonies are laid out on a grand, leisurely scale and they are both eloquent and exhilarating. His violin concerto has an elegiac slow movement as has the glorious cello concerto and both contain many fine opportunities for the soloist. The cello concerto is as appealing a work as any by Elgar expressing his innermost thoughts. His *Enigma Variations* are a series of portraits in sound of his friends, but there is another overall theme to go with them that has never been identified. This has not prevented the work from becoming Elgar's most popular, not surprisingly when one considers its charm and melodiousness. Three other orchestral pieces that should not be neglected are his symphonic study *Falstaff*, a many-sided musical picture of the Fat Knight, and the overtures *Cockaigne*, a happy evocation of London, and *In the South*, inspired by a visit to Italy. His three late chamber works, written when he was 61, are reticent, economic pieces that remove any misconception of Elgar as a bombastic composer. His songs are mostly feeble, but the oratorios, notably *The Dream of Gerontius*, show the composer's ability to control a large canvas. The composer himself wrote over the score of *Gerontius*,

"This is the best of me"—a verdict with which we can readily agree.

French Music.

César Franck (1822–90) was the main figure in mid-19th-cent. musical France and his influence spread even wider than his music of which only the D minor Symphony, the Symphonic Variations for piano and orchestra, the piano quintet, and the violin sonata are likely to be encountered today. The leading French opera composers of that time were Gounod (1818–93), Bizet (1838–75) and Massenet (1842–1912). Gounod's *Faust*, Bizet's *Carmen* (composed just before his untimely death when he caught cold after a swim) and Massenet's *Manon* all retain a deserved place in the repertory; each is a well-judged mini-drama unafraid of romantic ardour and forceful, histrionic strokes. Some of Massenet's other numerous operas, such as *Werther* and *Don Quichotte*, have enjoyed a revival in recent years.

Concurrently with similar movements in French painting and poetry came the French Impressionist composers at the end of the 19th cent. Their leader—and one of the great seminal forces of modern music—was Claude Debussy (1862–1918). His aim was to capture a mood or sensation, and he did that by more or less inventing a fresh system of harmony using a whole-tone scale, unusual chords, and by creating in the orchestra new, highly personal textures—there is no mistaking the Debussy idiom once you have heard at least one piece by him. His impressionistic style did not lead him, however, to abandon form as some have suggested, and his main works are just as closely organised as those by classical German composers. His music is sensuous and poetic yet nearly always structurally satisfying as well.

His reputation, at least with the general musical public, rests largely on his orchestral music, a few piano pieces and his only opera *Pelléas et Mélisande*. *La Mer* is a scintillating evocation of the sea in all its moods; *Nocturnes*, *Images*, and *Prélude à l'Après-midi d'un Faune* exactly suggest different places, times, moods—the "Iberia" and "Gigues" sections of *Images*, calling to mind respectively the spirit of Spain and the flickering light of a rainy English night. *Pelléas*, based on a Symbolist drama by Maeterlinck, tells a story of love, jealousy, and murder in predominantly restrained yet emotionally loaded terms. It is an elusive original work that has no predecessor or successor. Intensely atmospheric, rivetingly beautiful, it weaves an irresistible spell over the listener.

Debussy's chamber music is unjustly neglected. His string quartet (1893) was one of the first works in which he displayed his new and strange world of sound, and the three late sonatas, one for violin, one for cello, and the third for flute, viola, and harp are elliptical, compressed pieces which seem to be questing disjointedly into new regions of sound. His songs too, are worthy of investigation, and his piano music, especially the twenty-four Preludes and some of the shorter pieces, contain some of his most imaginative and original ideas and thoughts.

Gabriel Fauré (1845–1924) is a difficult figure to place. He lived through all kinds of musical revolutions yet they seemed to affect the character of his work very little. He has never been, and is never likely to be, a widely known or popular composer, yet his music has a reticence and delicacy that is very appealing. Despite his dreamy, retiring art he was not a recluse, but a very sociable man.

He was content with forms as he found them, but he imbued them with a very personal, human style. Perhaps his art is best heard in his songs. They are not overtly passionate or dramatic but the long, sinuous melodies and subtle harmonies are exquisitely wrought. Of the song-cycles, *La Bonne Chanson*, *Cinq Mélodies* (Verlaine), *Le Chanson d'Eve*, and *L'Horizon Chimérique* are best known. The last written in 1922, when the composer was seventy-seven, is a beautiful setting of words by a soldier killed in the first World War. There are also many remarkable single songs, many of them settings of poems by Verlaine. His opera *Pénélope*, based on the classical heroine, is unjustly neglected.

He wrote few orchestral pieces, but the *Ballade* for piano and orchestra and the *Pavane* are among his most typical, and delicate compositions, and his outstanding piano music, modelled on Chopin's, includes Nocturnes, Impromptus, and Barcarolles. His chamber music covers more than half a century from the violin sonata of 1876 to the string quartet written the year he died. In that period he composed two piano quartets, two piano quintets, another violin sonata and two cello sonatas, the later works failing to show quite the unforced lyrical grace of the earlier ones. Perhaps Fauré is best approached with the first piano quartet, a charming, easily assimilated work, and the beautiful choral *Requiem*.

Saint-Saëns (1835–1921), an accomplished, cultivated musician, has had a "bad press" but his craftsmanship, as displayed in his symphonies, concertos, and *Samson et Dalila* (one among his 12 operas) is not to be despised.

Henri Duparc (1844–1933), despite a very long life, is known today only for a group of songs he wrote before he was forty. They are among the most emotionally direct yet tasteful melodies ever written. Paul Dukas (1865–1935) is another figure off the beaten track, as it were. He, too, is known only for a handful of compositions. He was strongly influenced by Vincent d'Indy (1851–1931) and the school who strongly opposed Debussy's new ideas, yet he could not help but come under Debussy's spell. Dukas's one great work is his opera *Ariane et Barbe-Bleue*, the text adapted from a Maeterlinck play written with the composer in mind.

Maurice Ravel (1875–1937), a pupil of Fauré, followed in Debussy's footsteps, although his later pieces were more ascetic. Indeed, he was one of the most fastidious of composers, always seeking, and often finding, artistic perfection. The works he wrote before 1918 are definitely of the Impressionist School and it would be difficult to imagine more beautiful sounds than are to be found in the ballet *Daphnis el Chloé*, in the song-cycle *Shéhérazade*, and the piano fantasy *Gaspard de la Nuit*. His first style was summed up in the A minor piano trio (1915). In his later music Ravel was struggling, not always successfully, to keep up with new developments such as jazz and atonality. The piano concerto, for instance, shows very strongly the influence of jazz.

Outstanding orchestral works of his, other than *Daphnis* are *Rapsodie espagnole* (1907), *La Valse* (1920), a sumptuous evocation of the Vienna waltz, and the ever-popular *Boléro*. Two chamber works, besides the trio, are masterpieces—the string quartet (1902–3) and the Introduction and Allegro for Harp, String Quartet, Flute, and Clarinet. This Septet composed in 1906, ravishes the senses with magical sound.

Ravel's piano pieces are perhaps his most notable contribution to music, combining an extraordinary feeling for the instrument's technical possibilities with the sensibility of a Chopin, and in this field *Jeux d'eau*, *Miroirs*, and *Ma Mère l'Oye*, all written just after the turn of the century, come very close to the perfection of *Gaspard de la Nuit*. His songs show his unusual appreciation of the need to fuse poetic and musical values, and he set exotic poems for preference. His output in this field includes the cycle *Histoires naturelles* (1906), acutely observed settings of five poems about birds and animals; *Cinq Mélodies populaires grecques* (1907), charming settings of Greek folk songs; *Trois Poèmes de Mallarmé* (1913); and *Chansons madécasses* (1926), suitably exotic settings of three poems by an 18th-cent. Creole poet called Parny. Finally in 1932 came *Don Quichotte à Dulcinée*, three poems by Paul Morand, Ravel's last composition.

Ravel wrote two operas—the slight but moderately amusing *L'Heure espagnole* (1907), nicely orchestrated in a faintly and appropriately Spanish style and *L'Enfant et les Sortilèges* (1925) to a story by Colette, a delicious fantasy about a naughty child who gets his due punishment for tormenting animals and destroying furniture.

French music after Debussy and Ravel was dominated by the slighter composers known as *Les Six*, the most important of whom were Arthur Honegger (1892–1955, Swiss born), Darius Milhaud (1892–1974) and Francis Poulenc (1890–1963). Each has contributed music of some wit and charm to the repertory. They were influenced by Erik Satie (1866–1925), an eccentric but interesting figure who wrote works with odd titles such as *Three Pear Shaped Pieces*. His music is entirely unsentimental, often ironic.

Spain.

Felipe Pedrell (1841–1922) has been aptly described as the midwife of Spanish nationalist music. As a musicologist and teacher he strongly influenced the two main composers of the school, Manuel de Falla (1876–1946) and Enrique Granados (1867–1916). Falla's output was not large and most of it was written around the years of the first world war. The pre-war years were spent in Paris where Falla came under the influence of Debussy. However his style is individual and evokes all the passion and gaiety of his native land. Perhaps his most typical works are in two ballets *Love the Magician* (1915) and *The Three-Cornered Hat* (1919). The opera *La Vida Breve* (1905) despite its weak libretto also has much appeal. The vivacity and smouldering passion at the heart of the country's character is conjured up by the *Seven Popular Songs* (1914) and the *Nights in the Gardens of Spain* (1916) for piano and orchestra. His later works, especially the harpsichord concerto of 1926, show Falla tending towards a less ebullient, more restrained style. The second opera, *Master Peter's Puppet Show* (1923) is a miniaturist work, refined and intense. His third opera *Atlantida*, left unfinished at his death, was completed by his pupil Ernesto Halffter and first staged in 1962.

Granados was perhaps a more restrictedly Spanish composer than Falla, but his music is unfailingly attractive and deserves to be better known. The opera *Goyescas* (1916) is most famous for the second interlude and opening of Act III—*La Maja y el Ruiseñor* (The Lover and the Nightingale), a haunting, sinuous melody for soprano, generally heard in its original form as a piano solo.

The chief claim to fame of Albéniz (1860–1909) is *Ibéria*, masterly descriptive pieces for piano. Many of his other piano works are now more well known in the form of very effective guitar arrangements. Turina (1882–1949), attempted a more cosmopolitan style, but his most often heard music is typically Spanish.

The Late German Romantics.

While composers such as Debussy, Sibelius, Stravinsky and Schoenberg (see below for the latter pair) were striking out along new paths, Richard Strauss (1864–1949) continued in the trend of 19th-cent. German composers; he was the tradition's last great figure. At least two of his operas—*Salome* and *Elektra*—were considered shocking at the time, but today we can hear that they are essentially big-scale, romantic works—natural successors to Wagner's—however startling the harmonies may once have seemed.

If Strauss did not achieve the granite intellectual greatness of Beethoven or Wagner, there is no denying his melodic genius and powers of fertile invention which overlaid the streak of vulgarity and inflation in his musical make-up. His first outstanding achievement was in the field of the symphonic poem, where he carried the work of composers such as Liszt and Berlioz to its logical conclusion. Starting with *Don Juan* in 1888 and ending with *Sinfonia Domestica* in 1903 he wrote a series of kaleidoscopic works, full of enormous vitality, endless melody, and fascinating orchestration. The most easily assimilated—and the most popular—are *Don Juan* and *Till Eulenspiegel* but some of the longer works, notably *Also Sprach Zarathustra* (based on Nietzsche's

prose poem) and *Don Quixote* (based, of course, on Cervantes's great work) will reward the persistent, inquiring mind with long hours of enthralled listening. Other works sound somewhat dated in their bombastic over-confidence, though Strauss's skill in composition seldom flagged at this stage of his long creative career. The symphonic poems all tell something of a story usually based on a literary source, but it is not essential to the enjoyment of the music to know what this is, although it may be helpful.

Strauss's reputation is even more solidly based on his fifteen operas, the earliest of which *Guntram* was first performed in 1894, the last, *Capriccio*, in 1942. During these years the essentials of Strauss's style changed little, though it became very much more refined as the years passed. His first operatic period ended with the violent, sensual tragedies *Salome* (1905) and *Elektra* (1909), the latter being his first collaboration with his chief librettist, Hugo von Hofmannsthal. Then came their unique *Der Rosenkavalier* (1911), which filters the charm and the decadence of 18th-cent. Vienna through early 20th-cent. eyes. This was followed by *Ariadne auf Naxos* (1912). Originally intended to be given after Molière's *Le Bourgeois Gentilhomme*, it was later presented (1916) without the play but with an amusing Prologue, written by von Hofmannsthal. *Die Frau ohne Schatten* is the most grandiose result of the Strauss–Hofmannsthal partnership. It is a complex psychological allegory, but Strauss's contribution is not on as consistently lofty a level as is his librettist's. *Intermezzo* (1924), which has a libretto by Strauss himself, is a largely autobiographical domestic comedy, which has lately gained in reputation as a compact, charming piece. With *Die Aegyptische Helena* (1928), an opera on a mythical theme, and *Arabella* (1933), another sensuous Viennese comedy, the Strauss–Hofmannsthal collaboration ended on account of the librettist's death. Strauss then wrote *Die Schweigsame Frau* (1935) to a libretto by Stefan Zweig, based on a play by Ben Jonson, and *Friedenstag* (1938), *Daphne* (1938)—a beautiful opera—and *Die Liebe der Danae* (written 1938–40) with Josef Gregor as librettist. His swan-song was *Capriccio*, a dramatisation of the old argument about the relative importance of words and music in opera. The libretto is by the conductor Clemens Krauss and the opera, a serene, melodious work, was a fit end to a great operatic career.

However, Strauss went on composing till nearly the end of his life, adding a group of late orchestral pieces to his already large catalogue of works. The *Metamorphosen* for 23 solo string instruments, is probably the best of these. During his long creative career he wrote numerous songs, many of them, such as *Morgen*, *Wiegenlied* and *Ruhe, meine Seele* of surpassing beauty.

Other notable figures in German music at this time were Max Reger (1873–1916), a somewhat ponderous but highly accomplished composer who, in a quarter of a century of creative life, wrote more than 150 works, of which his sets of variations, his piano concerto, and chamber music are probably the most impressive. Hans Pfitzner (1869–1949), another German traditionalist, is chiefly remembered today for his opera *Palestrina*, about events, now known to be spurious, in the life of the 16th-cent. Italian composer.

Twentieth-century Music.

Gustav Mahler (1860–1911), the Austrian Jewish composer, is one of the most important figures in 20th-cent. music. In a sense he bridges the gulf between the late Romantics, who were tending more and more towards chromaticism and away from established key relationships, and the atonalists, who abandoned the key system entirely. His detractors maintain that his inflation of allegedly banal Viennese beer-house music to unheard-of lengths rules him out of court as a serious writer. His admirers would claim that his music encompasses the whole of life in enormous, valid structures. The truth, if truth there be, perhaps lies somewhere in between: if his material does not always justify the length of his symphonies, and if there are occasional imperfections and *longueurs*, these shortcomings are worth enduring for the sake of the depth of utterance, the humanity and the poetry of the great pages. He admitted himself that "I cannot do without trivialities," but it is out of these impurities that he forged his titanic victories.

His music is undoubtedly best approached through his songs, where the words force him to discipline his wide-ranging vision. *Lieder eines fahrenden Gesellen* (1884), to his own words, *Kindertotenlieder* (1901–4), to poems by Rückert, and some individual songs perfectly relate words to music, and are all of a poignant loveliness. Similarly *Das Lied von der Erde* (1908), especially the last of the six songs, is a touching farewell to the world, nobly expressed.

The ten symphonies, however, are Mahler's most impressive legacy to posterity. They are almost impossible to characterise briefly so vast are they in terms of both length and variety. The first, fourth and ninth are probably the easiest to grasp but the fifth, sixth and seventh, despite flaws, contain some of his most awe-inspiring conceptions. The second and third, both of which use soloists and chorus, are revolutionary in orchestration and structure; they both try, inevitably without complete success, to carry out the composer's dictum, "a symphony should be like the world—it must contain everything." The eighth is even more gargantuan, but as in all Mahler's work size does not mean loss of clarity or an overloading of the structure. Part one—a mighty choral invocation—is a visionary setting of the mediaeval hymn *Veni Creator Spiritus*. Part two, which incorporates adagio, scherzo, and finale in one, is a setting of the final scene of Goethe's *Faust*. Until recently all of Mahler's unfinished tenth symphony that was ever performed was the Adagio, but the musicologist and Mahler scholar, the late Deryck Cooke, provided a performing version of the symphony to critical and popular acclaim during the 1960s and thus added a noble, and also optimistic epilogue to the Mahler opus. The debate over the quality of Mahler's music is likely to continue; one fact, however, that cannot be gain-said is his popularity with an ever-increasing audience, largely made up of young people. There must be something in his uncertainty and intense self-inquiry that accords with the mood of the youthful mind.

Schoenberg and the Second Viennese School.

Arnold Schoenberg (1874–1951) revolutionised Western music by his twelve-note method—a system which uses all the notes of the chromatic scale "and denies the supremacy of a tonal centre," as Schoenberg himself puts it. This serial technique of composition, as it is commonly called, naturally sounds strange to an ear acclimatised to music written, as it were, with a home base, but Schoenberg and his disciples Berg and Webern showed that the system could produce works that were something more than mere intellectual exercises. None of the more recent advances in music would have been possible, even thinkable, without Schoenberg's pioneer work.

Schoenberg always considered himself as much as a composer as a theorist or teacher, and his works are supposed to appeal as much to the emotions as to the intellect, although to be understood they do, of course, require the listener's concentrated attention. To appreciate how his ideas developed it is necessary to hear first his pre-atonal music, such as the *Gurrelieder* (1900–1) and *Verklärte Nacht* (1899), in which he carried Wagnerian chromaticism to extreme lengths. The *Gurrelieder*, in particular, is a luxuriant, overblown work that shows the Wagnerian idiom in an advanced stage of decay, in spite of many beautiful pages of music. In his succeeding works the feeling of tonality began to disappear until in the Three Piano Pieces (opus 11), of 1909, he finally rejected tonality, although the new 12-note scheme is not yet evident; traces of the old order can still be heard. The succeeding works were mostly short, highly compressed, and very expressive. Schoenberg was reaching out for a new system,

which would "justify the dissonant character of these harmonies and determine their successions." By 1923 he had formulated his 12-note system and the Five Piano Pieces (opus 23), and the Serenade (opus 24) of that year, can thus be considered the first works that used a note-row as the fundamental basis of their composition. Between 1910 and 1915, however, the Russian composer Alexander Skryabin (1872–1915) had attempted to define a new method of composition of his own employing the "mystic chord" of ascending fourths, but his scheme proved comparatively abortive when compared with Schoenberg's. Josef Hauer (1883–1959) also developed a 12-note system which he propounded in 1919 and he always considered himself, rather than Schoenberg, as the true founder of the system. He later worked out a system of tropes (*i.e.*, half-series of six notes).

To return to Schoenberg, in later works he shows much more freedom and assurance in the use of his system. The wind quintet (1924), the Variations for Orchestra, opus 31 (1927–8), the third (1926), and fourth (1936) string quartets, and the string trio (1946) are modern classics of their kind; they require concentrated listening and a degree of understanding of the unfamiliar style of composition. The set of songs with piano *Das Buch der hängenden Gärten* (opus 15), written in 1908, *Pierrot Lunaire*, opus 21 (1912) and the Four Songs, opus 22 (1913–14) provide a kind of bridge between tonality and atonality that the adventurous mind should cross. The monodrama *Erwartung* (1909) is another fascinating work, but perhaps the unfinished *Moses and Aaron* (1932) is Schoenberg's masterpiece as its production at Covent Garden in 1965 showed. Here, for certain, the composer matched his obvious intellectual capacities with an evident emotional content and managed to combine *Sprechgesang* (speech-song) and singing with a real degree of success.

It is only in recent years that Schoenberg's music has had a real chance to make its mark through the essential prerequisite of frequent performance. If his idiom now seems approachable, and a reasonably natural outcome of late 19th-cent. developments, it is perhaps because other, more recent composers have extended the boundaries of sound much further.

Schoenberg's two most respected disciples were Anton Webern (1883–1945) and Alban Berg (1885–1935). Webern's output is small, reaching only to opus 31, and many of his works are very brief. They are exquisitely precise, and delicate almost to a fault. He was trying to distil the essence of each note and in so doing carried the 12-note system to its most extreme and cerebral limit. His music has often been described as pointillist in the sense that one note is entirely separated from the next, there being little discernible melody. Beyond Webern's music, there is indeed the sound of nothingness, and he was rightly described during his lifetime as the "composer of the *pianissimo espressivo*". In his later works, Webern tended towards a strict, and often ingenious use of form and the Variations for Orchestra of 1940 are a good example of this and of his delicacy of orchestration. Webern's influence has perhaps been greater than the impact of his own music, even though he has had no direct successor.

Berg's music is much more accessible. Like Webern his total output was not large, but nearly all his works are substantial additions to the repertory. He is also the directest link between Mahler and the second Viennese School, as Mahler's music influenced him strongly. He studied with Schoenberg from 1904 to 1910. His music is more intense, more lyrical, and less attenuated in sound than Schoenberg's or Webern's. His humanity and abiding compassion can be heard most strongly in his finest opera *Wozzeck* (1925) and his violin concerto (1935), written as an elegy on the death of Manon Gropius, a beautiful 18-year-old girl. Both works are very carefully designed yet formal considerations are never allowed to submerge feeling, and the note-row is fully integrated into the structure.

Both *Wozzeck* and the unfinished but rewarding

Lulu are concerned with society's outcasts who are treated with great tenderness in both operas. The later work is entirely dodecaphonic, all the opera's episodes being based on a theme associated with Lulu. Between these operas Berg wrote the highly complex Chamber Concerto for piano, violin, and thirteen wind instruments (1925) and the expressive *Lyric Suite* (1926). Among his other works the *Seven Early Songs* (1908–9) and the concert aria *Der Wein* (1929) are notable.

Stravinsky.

Igor Stravinsky (1882–1971) was another vital figure in 20th-cent. music. If his influence has been in quite another and perhaps less drastic direction than Schoenberg's it is hardly less important. Indeed, future musical historians may consider his achievement the more significant. He has been compared with the painter Picasso in his almost hectic desire to keep up with the times, yet, although he wrote in a number of very different styles over a period of fifty years, every work of his is stamped with his own definitive musical personality. His most revolutionary and seminal work is undoubtedly *The Rite of Spring* (written for the ballet impresario Diaghilev), which caused a furore when it first appeared in 1913, and although it no longer shocks, the rhythmical energy, the fierce angular thematic material, and the sheer virtuosity of the orchestration will always have the power to excite new audiences. Before *The Rite* Stravinsky had written two ballets for Diaghilev—*The Firebird* and *Petrushka*—that are no less filled with vitality and new, albeit not so violent, sounds. During the next thirty years Stravinsky wrote a series of ballet works, gradually becoming more austere and refined in composition. *Apollo* (1928) and *Orpheus* (1947) belong among his most attractive scores.

Stravinsky did not confine himself in stage works to the ballet. *The Nightingale* (1914) is a charming, early opera; *The Soldiers Tale* (1918) is a witty combination of narration, mime, and dance; *Les Noces* (1923) is a concise, original choreographic cantata for soloists and chorus; *Oedipus Rex* (1927) is a dignified version of the Sophocles play, which can be staged or given on the concert platform; either way it is a moving experience. *Perséphone* (1934), a melodrama for reciter, tenor, chorus, and orchestra is an appealing, lucid score. After the war his most important stage work by far was *The Rake's Progress* (1951), with a libretto by W. H. Auden and Chester Kallman. This fascinating opera is deliberately based on 18th-cent. forms and the music itself is neo-classical, always attractive, sometimes haunting.

Stravinsky was no laggard in writing for the concert-platform either. The finest of his orchestral pieces are probably the fervent choral *Symphony of Psalms* (1930), the violin concerto (1931) and the aggressive compact *Symphony* in Three Movements (1945). Of his chamber music the octet (1923), a duo concertant (1932), and septet (1952) are probably the most important, but no piece, even the dryest and most pedantic, is without redeeming features.

Stravinsky is often thought of as an aloof, detached figure. He has been castigated for his lack of lyrical warmth. But in spite of his own professed desire to drain his music of specific emotion, craftsmanship and originality, often with a strange other-worldly beauty added, are unmistakably there throughout his many scores. Quirky and annoying he may be, dull never.

Busoni and Puccini.

Italian music in the early part of the century was dominated by two very different composers— Ferruccio Busoni (1866–1924) and Giacomo Puccini (1858–1924). Busoni is a difficult figure to place. His austere, intellectual power is never called in question, but he seldom, if ever, succeeded

in translating his technical prowess into altogether successful compositions. We can admire the strength, honesty, and often beauty of such works as his huge piano concerto (1903–4), *Fantasia Contrappuntistica* (1912)—for piano solo—and his unfinished opera *Doktor Faust* without ever capitulating to them entirely. None the less, it has to be admitted that those who have studied his music closely have always fallen completely under his spell. In style his music is anti-Romantic and often neo-Classical yet he was an ardent admirer of Liszt and more especially of Liszt's realisation of the possibilities of the pianoforte. Busoni, himself a great pianist, carried on where Liszt had left off in his own piano music, in which form and expression often find their perfect balance. *Doktor Faust* is undoubtedly his most important opera but *Die Brautwahl* (1908–10) and *Turandot* (1917) have many points of interest too.

Puccini's *Turandot*—his last opera—is a much grander version of the same Gozzi fable and the culmination of this great opera composer's work. His achievement is at an almost directly opposite pole to Busoni's. Not for him the severity or intellectuality of his contemporary. He sought and found an almost ideal fusion of straight-forward lyricism and dramatic truth. His music unerringly follows the pathos and passion of the stories he sets and all his characters "live" as human beings. That, and his abundant flow of easy, soaring melody, are the reasons for his immense popular success, unequalled by any other 20th-cent. composer. Whether it is the pathetic Mimi (*La Bohème*—1896) and Cio-Cio-San, (*Madam Butterfly*—1904), the evil Scarpia (*Tosca* —1900), the cunning Schicchi (*Gianni Schicchi*— 1918), the ardent Rodolfo (*La Bohème*) and Cavaradossi (*Tosca*), or the ice-cold Turandot (*Turandot*—1926). Puccini's musical characterisation is unfailing. And he backs his *verismo* vocal writing with an orchestral tissue that faithfully reflects the milieu of each opera, for instance, Japanese for *Butterfly*, Chinese for *Turandot*, while never losing his particular brand of Italian warmth. His orchestration is always subtle and luminous.

Other Italian composers who wrote operas in the *verismo* style of Puccini were Leoncavallo (1858– 1919), Mascagni (1865–1945), and Giordano (1867– 1948). Mascagni's *Cavalleria Rusticana* and Leoncavallo's *Pagliacci* have formed an inseparable bill and a regular part of the repertory in most opera houses.

Prokofiev, Shostakovich, and Rachmaninov.

Sergey Prokofiev (1891–1953) spent part of his creative life in his native Russia, part of it (1918– 34) abroad, mostly in Paris. His early music, apart from the popular Classical Symphony (1916– 17) tended to be acid and harsh, but on his return to Russia his style, though still frequently satirical, became warmer, more Romantic. The third piano concerto (1917) and the second symphony (1924) are good examples of the former period, the ballets *Romeo and Juliet* (1935) and *Cinderella* (1941–4) and the fifth (1944) and sixth (1946) symphonies of the latter. His music gives the impression of immense rhythmical energy, as in the outer movements of several of his nine piano sonatas, but this fierce drive is often leavened by the soft, wistful lights of his slow movements. His second string quartet (1941), perhaps, presents all the elements of his music in the kindest light.

His strong leaning towards fantasy and mordant parody is felt in his earlier operas *The Love of the Three Oranges* (1921) and *The Fiery Angel* (1922–5). Towards the end of his life much of Prokofiev's music fell into official disfavour.

Dmitri Shostakovich (1906–75) also suffered from attacks on his style. He had to conform to Stalin's requirements for writing music, but he survived and continued to produce music of universal appeal, as, for example, his later string quartets. Like Prokofiev, his music falls into two very distinct styles: one humorous and spiky, the other intense, very personal and often large-scale in its implications. Not all his symphonies reach the expressive depths of numbers one, five, six, eight, ten and fourteen, but they all have rewarding passages, and his violin and cello concertos are of high quality. He also wrote fifteen string quartets, a piano quintet (an attractive piece) and two operas: the satirical *The Nose* (1930) and *Katrina Ismailova* (1934, revised 1959), originally known as "Lady Macbeth of Mtsensk."

Although Sergey Rachmaninov (1873–1943) was born in Russia, he left his home country in 1918, disliking the Soviet régime, and lived mostly in Switzerland and the United States. His music is chiefly notable for its Romanticism, nostalgic melody, nervous energy and, in the piano works, its opportunities for displays of virtuosity. The first three piano concertos, the third symphony, the piano preludes, and the Rhapsody on a theme of Paganini, are his most typical and attractive works, and many of his songs are touching and beautiful. He wrote three operas.

Weill and Hindemith.

Kurt Weill (1900–50) is chiefly known for his sociopolitically pointed operas, such as *Die Dreigroschenoper* (1929), *Mahagonny* (1929), *Der Jasager* (1930) and *Happy End* (1929), all effective works on the stage, and for his particular brand of brittle, yet fundamentally romantic music. His influence on later composers has been considerable.

Paul Hindemith (1895–1963) in his later years wrote in a strictly tonal, often neo-classical idiom, after being one of the most advanced intellectuals of his time. As well as many chamber and orchestral works, he wrote three formidable operas: *Die Harmonie der Welt*, *Cardillac* and *Mathis der Maler*.

Ives and Copland.

Charles Ives (1874–1954) is generally recognised as the first American composer of major stature. Most of his works were composed before about 1920, while he was pursuing a successful career in insurance. Ives' music is noted for its thorough-going eclecticism and his refusal to be bound by rules and conventions. His work anticipates many 20th century techniques, such as polytonality and polyrhythm, which he seems to have arrived at independently of others. Folk music, hymn tunes, dance music and the sound of the brass band all appear in his compositions, many of which are evocative of his New England background (*e.g.* *Three Places in New England*, the *Holidays Symphony*, the *Concord* Sonata). It was not until the 1930s that Ives began to achieve recognition, but his influence on later American composers can hardly be exaggerated.

Aaron Copland (b. 1900) is a composer who has absorbed a variety of influences—from his Jewish background, contemporary Europe, American folk music and jazz, Latin American music—while writing music which is instantly recognisable as his own in its clean textures and taut rhythms. Early works such as the Piano Concerto (1927) show the use of jazz styles, while the Piano Variations (1930) combine inventiveness and technical discipline in a tough, concentrated and highly dissonant piece. A move towards a simpler, more immediately appealing idiom is evident in pieces like *El Salón México* (1936), and the ballets *Billy the Kid* (1938), *Rodeo* (1938) and *Appalachian Spring* (1944) and the Third Symphony (1946). These works remain Copland's most popular and frequently performed pieces. A number of works from the 1950s and 1960s experiment with serial techniques, while retaining his individual voice.

Vaughan Williams, Holst and Delius.

The twentieth century revival of music in England owes much to Ralph Vaughan Williams (1872–1958) and Gustav Holst (1874–1934). The English folk song revival, associated with Cecil Sharp, was in full swing during their formative years, and both composers produced arrangements of folk songs as well as assimilating the folk idiom into their own styles. The influence of 16th century polyphony is also strong in Vaughan Williams' music, the most obvious example being the *Fantasia on a Theme by Thomas Tallis* (1909). Vaughan Williams' strongest works (*e.g.* the first, fourth, fifth and sixth sym-

phonies, the ballet *Job*, the choral *Dona Nobis Pacem*) show his characteristic alternation of the forceful and the contemplative.

Holst was a more enigmatic figure. Only his suite *The Planets* and the choral work *The Hymn of Jesus* have established themselves in the regular repertory, but his bold harmonic experiments and the austerity, even mysticism, of his style as heard in the opera *Savitri* and the orchestral piece *Egdon Heath* are perhaps more typical of this meditative, original composer.

Frederick Delius (1862–1934) was the major English composer to fall under the sway of French impressionism, though his English (north country) background, his friendship with Grieg, and the time he spent in America all contributed to the formation of his musical style. He lived in France from 1888 onwards. His most important works are the atmospheric tone-poems for orchestra, such as *Brigg Fair*, the vocal and orchestral *A Mass of Life*, *Sea Drift* and *Appalachia*, and the opera *A Village Romeo and Juliet*.

Walton, Britten and Tippett.

Sir William Walton (1902–83) became known as an *enfant terrible* with the witty and irreverent *Façade* (1923) for speaker and chamber orchestra (with words by Edith Sitwell). The poetic Viola Concerto (1929) shows another side of his musical character. His First Symphony (1934–5) is an arresting, dramatic score and the colourful oratorio *Belshazzar's Feast* (1931) is a landmark in choral music. Walton's rhythms show the influence of jazz and of Stravinsky but he is generally felt to be a quintessentially English composer. An Elgarian element is clear in such occasional pieces as the coronation marches *Crown Imperial* (1937) and *Orb and Sceptre* (1953).

Benjamin Britten (1913–76) did as much as anyone to establish English music on the forefront of the international stage. Much of his music seems to have an immediate appeal to large audiences and certainly his many stage works earned him quite exceptional prestige both at home and abroad. *Peter Grimes* (1945), *Billy Budd* (1951), *Gloriana* (1953), *A Midsummer Night's Dream* (1960) all show his mastery of stage technique and the first two are also moving human documents. On a smaller scale he has achieved as much with his chamber operas—*The Rape of Lucretia* (1946), *Albert Herring* (1947), *The Turn of the Screw* (1954)—and the three Parables for Church Performance—*Curlew River* (1964), *The Burning Fiery Furnace* (1966) and *The Prodigal Son* (1968). His operatic output was crowned by *Death in Venice* (1973). If he had written nothing else, these dramatic works would have marked him out as a composer of outstanding imaginative gifts. In addition to these, however, the choral works culminating in the *War Requiem* (1962), the various song cycles written, like so much else, for his friend Peter Pears, the *Serenade* for tenor, horn and strings, *Nocturne* for tenor and orchestra, the three *Canticles*, and the *Spring Symphony* are further evidence of both his intense emotional commitment and his technical skill. Despite the strong influence of such composers as Purcell, Schubert, Verdi, Mahler and Berg, his style is entirely his own; his musical personality combines, it has been said, "a deep nostalgia for the innocence of childhood, a mercurial sense of humour and a passionate sympathy with the victims of prejudice and misunderstanding."

This last quality is also evident in the emotional make up of Sir Michael Tippett (b. 1905), as expressed in such works as the oratorio *A Child of our Time* (1941) one of his earliest successes, which shows both his compassion and his ability to write on a large scale. This and the Concerto for Double String Orchestra (1939) remain his most popular works. Tippett has been open to a wide range of influences, both musical (from English Madrigals, Monteverdi and Beethoven to Negro spirituals and jazz) and non-musical (*e.g.* the ideas of Jung). His early style—often richly lyrical and affirmative of the continued power of tonality—reached its culmination in his allegorical opera *The Midsummer Marriage* (1952), the Piano Concerto (1955) and the Second Symphony (1957). A new style, spare and incisive, with structure arising from the juxtaposition of contrasting ideas rather than from a process of development, is evident in his second opera, *King Priam* (1961) and its offshoots, the Second Piano Sonata (1962) and the Concerto for Orchestra (1963). The mystical, ecstatic *The Vision of St. Augustine* (1965), a complex, difficult but rewarding work, is one of his finest from this period. The opera *The Knot Garden* (1970) exemplifies again Tippett's concern with human relationships and the need for self-knowledge. Tippett has never ceased to explore and experiment; his inspiration now seems as fresh as ever. His most recent works, *The Mask of Time*—a huge choral piece—and the Fourth Piano Sonata (1984) have something of the quality of summarising statements about the musical and non-musical concerns of a lifetime.

Olivier Messiaen and Elliott Carter.

Amongst the many schools and groups of composers in the twentieth century, two major figures stand apart, Olivier Messiaen and Elliott Carter. Both born in 1908, each is an individualist of great influence and stature who has pursued his own path to a personal style of composition.

A devout Catholic, Messiaen views himself as a theological composer and music as a medium for a profound communication, celebration and contemplation of the love and mystery of God. Few of his works are liturgical but most have religious and doctrinal themes, for example *La Nativité du Seigneur* (1935) for organ and *Vingt Regards sur l'Enfant-Jésus* (1944) for piano. Messiaen was inspired to compose by hearing the music of Debussy. This influence can be particularly seen in Messiaen's flexible rhythms, sensitive scoring and use of timbre. Indeed, he identifies sounds with colours and views composition as painting. The other major early influence was that of the East, particularly Indian music. Messiaen often uses Hindu rhythmic patterns alongside Greek poetic metres, plainsong and other medieval techniques and Stravinskian devices. The sum of these can be seen in *Quatuor pour la fin du temps* for violin, clarinet, cello and piano which he composed in a prisoner of war camp in 1940. A very complex work, it reflects the primacy Messiaen gives to rhythmic control. Its overwhelming impression however is of lush and exotic sounds and textures. Similarly, the vibrant colours and rhythms of the massive *Turangalila-symphonie* (1946–8) for orchestra effectively realise the ideas of life and vitality embodied in the Sanskrit title.

After *Turangalila*, Messiaen adopted a less luxurious style. It was works such as the *Livre d'orgue* (1951) which profoundly influenced many young composers of post-war years in the use of systematic transformations of rhythm and dynamics using a system of modes in a quasi-serial fashion. For Messiaen it is the seven harmonic modes, inspired by Debussy, Liszt and the Russian "Five", which are perhaps more important because they give his music its unique sound quality.

The 1950s saw the integration of the final element crucial to Messiaen's music; birdsong. A keen ornithologist, he collected and accurately notated the songs of many birds for incorporation into compositions. *Catalogue d'oiseaux* (1951–8) is a collection of thirteen piano pieces featuring French bird songs. For Messiaen birdsong represented, "the true lost face of music", and it provided a source of inspiration for many of his major post-war works. Since 1960, his style has become simpler and less complex to the ear. To encounter the many elements of his music one can do little better than to listen to *La Transfiguration de Notre Seigneur Jésus-Christ* (1963–9) for one hundred voices, seven instrumental soloists and a large orchestra. Its subject is the mystery of God, his relationship with man and nature as a revelation of God. Messiaen draws upon all his compositional techniques in a spellbinding and overwhelming work that is a profound affirmation of faith. It is fitting that his most recent work is a vast opera (1973–83), *St François d'Assise* about the saint who is best known for his great spirituality and for gaining inspiration and insight from nature.

Carter's reputation is based on a small number of works. He has concentrated on problems of language and structure in a dramatic context unlike Messiaen's preoccupations with colour and the communication of religious truths. Carter's early works reflect a variety of influences: Stravinsky, Hindemith and the English Virginalists. He con-

sciously aimed at a simple, lyrical, accessible style, for example, in the ballet, *Pocahontas* (1938–9) and *Holiday Overture* (1944). During those war years however there occurred a change of direction. The Piano Sonata (1945–6) saw the start of a compositional style where instruments were endowed with personalities who act as protagonists in a drama. His ideas crystallised in the *String Quartet No. 1* (1950–1) after an absorbing study of the music of Ives, Cowell and African and Oriental music. It led to the use of very complex rhythmic relationships and a very tightly-knit pitch structure that could be traced back to a simple and small source, in this case a four-note chord. After this Carter refined his portrayal of his dramatis personae such that in *String Quartet No. 2* (1959) his players each have a separate personality defined by melodic material, gestures and rhythms. They converse, argue and enact that work's dramatic programme. *String Quartet No. 3* (1971) marked a shift in approach. Although the players were still "personalities", the work relied heavily on the use of contrast between strict and flexible writing between members of two duos. The *Symphony of Three Orchestras* (1975–7) and *Triple Duo* (1983) continue to explore the possibilities of simultaneous presentation of independent and sometimes unrelated processes. Carter's music makes rewarding, though not always easy, listening.

MUSIC SINCE 1945—THE AVANT GARDE

Serialism.

The early post-war years saw a renewed interest in "twelve-note techniques" otherwise known as "serialism". Composers like Stravinsky and Dallapiccola (1904–75), who had shunned serialism in earlier years, began to experiment and absorb serial techniques into their musical style. Stravinsky, for example, in works such as *Threni* (1957–8) explored ideas of varied repetition both of small ideas and large sections, in a serial context. A clear example to listen to is the fifteen-minute *Requiem Canticles* (1964–6). During the progression from its Prelude to Postlude, one can hear the piece subtly develop. The succeeding movements, and phrases within movements, slightly alter that which has gone before, evolving into something fresh.

This period also saw the emergence of a new generation of composers, keen to jettison the past and begin anew. Serialism was a favoured tool, its revival stemming from Paris, where Webern's pupil René Leibowitz was teaching, and the USA where Schoenberg had fled from Nazi Germany. The American Milton Babbitt (b. 1916) was much concerned with codifying serial techniques. His younger European contemporaries Pierre Boulez (b. 1925) and Karlheinz Stockhausen (b. 1928) sought to increase the number of musical elements that could be controlled by a predetermined method. They sought to emulate the rigorous methods of Webern, hoping to control not only pitch, but also rhythm, timbre and intensity of attack. In doing so they hoped to create an impersonal, emotionally restrained music.

Attention went first to controlling rhythm. Forerunners of this control can be seen in movement three of Berg's *Lyric Suite* and in Webern's Op.30 Variations. However, the catalyst came from Messiaen. He inspired his pupil Boulez to explore the possibilities of rhythmic and dynamic serialism in his Second Piano Sonata (1951). The performance of Messiaen's *Modes de valeurs et d'intensités* (1949) at the Darmstadt Summer School proved decisive for Stockhausen. Although not serial, the piece established scales of pitch, length of note (duration), loudness and attack. The 1950s were to see this potential for serialism taken to extremes. Boulez reached "total serialism" in *Structures 1a* for piano. However, having attained it he soon became frustrated with its restrictions. Some of the more fantastic and exotic elements of earlier works were allowed to reappear. *Le Marteau sans Maître* (1952–4) for mezzo-soprano and six instruments is a masterly setting of three surreal poems by René Char, with instrumental interludes. For the listener it is the contrasts of timbres, of flexible and regular pulsing rhythms, of sound and silence that are spellbinding. The virtuosic serial workings are hidden.

Stockhausen reached total serialism in *Kreuzspiel*

(1951) for oboe, bass clarinet, piano and percussion. Each note's pitch, length, dynamic and timbre are part of a predetermined plan. All are concerned with "Kreuzspiel" or "crossplay". Its various processes reverse or change over throughout so that at the end we have returned full circle. The effect is of clearcut lines where each note is weighted. However, despite the intention of the composer, the effect is not unemotional, especially with the insistent throbbing of the percussion, and the piece builds to a series of climaxes before dying away. *Punkte* (points) (1952) for orchestra finds each note being treated as an isolated point of sound. It illustrates some of the problems of total serialism; often very difficult to play, it can be monotonous or lack focal points, appearing to be random rather than rigorously controlled. Stockhausen therefore transferred his attention to using not points but bursts of sound and moved towards possibly his most significant contribution to music, "moment form". There, different aspects of a note, chord or sound are suspended in eternity for contemplation and re-examination. Works became longer, slower and had a greater emphasis on colour and the effects of spatial separation, both between sounds and between their sources. *Carré* (1959–60) uses four orchestras between which chords move and evolve. Stockhausen wrote "you can confidently stop listening for a moment . . . each moment can stand on its own and at the same time is related to all the other moments". Although unifying principles in pitch content *etc.* might be present, "strict" serialism had been gently left behind, until *Mantra* (1970). This work for two pianos, percussion and two electronic ring modulators is totally based on a thirteen-note row, the mantra, with a different duration, mode of attack and dynamic for each note. These permeate the whole piece. For example, each of the thirteen sections is dominated by one of the thirteen types of attack. The work's climax is the coda where the 156 versions of the mantra used are rushed through in a few minutes. The work is important, not only as marking a return to serialism and notated music, but also in its rediscovery of melody—something unthinkable twenty years earlier.

Mathematics and Music.

The younger generation of composers have often used mathematical systems for composing which are not necessarily serial. A good example is Peter Maxwell Davies (b. 1934). The use of durational ratios, ciphers and magic squares features prominently in his work, partly reflecting his interest in medieval music. A magic square is a number square where the sum of any line is the same. This becomes the basis for a composition by assigning notes to the numbers—a technique that Davies has often used since the mid-1970s. For example, in *Ave Maris Stella* (1975), each of the nine movements uses a different transformation of the square and follows a characteristic route through the square. The work is governed by the square at all levels: it even determines the precise length of each movement. Far from being a mathematical exercise however the piece shows masterly control which is particularly revealed in its drama and the beauty of its colours.

Mathematical processes of a different type have been taken up by the Greek, Xenakis (b. 1922), possibly because of his original training as an engineer and architect in France. His rejection of serialism led to the use of "stochastic" principles, derived from the mathematical laws governing probability. He also applied mathematical set theory to composition. The use of these ideas however is not audible. In *Nomos Alpha* (1965) for solo cello, for example, it is the use of contrasts, of texture, dynamic, register and timbre which give shape and form for the listener.

Chance.

Although for many serialism represented the way of reviving music after the excesses of romanticism, some looked beyond Europe to the East. John Cage (b. 1912) found inspiration there, studying Zen Buddhism in the early 1950s. By using the "chance operations" of the Chinese *I Ching* ('Book of Changes) Cage brought a new radical approach to Western music. *Music of Changes* (1951) for piano is

fully notated but its content is the result of operations where chance has a role. The use of "indeterminacy" or "chance" gave the performer an active role in determining the course of a piece. This might come about by providing "graphic notation"—an artist's impression of what the piece might sound like. Thus Earle Brown's *December 1952* is a visual design to be realised on any instrument as the performer sees fit. Alternatively the composer could give the performer control over the order of sections or their content. *Twenty-five pages* (1953) by Brown is for one to twenty-five pianos. Each person has twenty-five pages and may arrange them in any order before commencing. Thus music was no longer to be necessarily a progression of fixed and immutable steps to an endpoint. This and other traditional assumptions about music were challenged in Cage's most well-known outrage, *4' 33"*. The performer does not play any notes at all. The music consists of the sounds in the environment that occur during a period of four minutes and thirty-three seconds.

In 1957, both Stockhausen and Boulez took to chance having realised that total control was an impossibility. The more rigorous the control of musical elements, the more impossible it became to realise it accurately. Stockhausen's first experiment with chance techniques was Piano Piece XI which is a single page with nineteen fragments of music. They may be played in any order but the tempo, dynamic and attack must be that shown at the end of the previous fragment. After one fragment has been played three times the work ends. Boulez's Third Piano Sonata was less free. There the choices are in the nature of varying routes through the piece. Boulez saw his music as using a form of control that is not random but akin to throwing a dice. Limited choices in the combination of instruments and their choice of lines form the basis of *Pli selon pli* (1957–65) for soprano and orchestra, offering Boulez a way "to fix the infinite".

For Stockhausen, chance has been a way to encourage performer participation and the development of "intuitive music-making". In *Prozession* (1967) for example, performers react to what is going on guided by plus or minus signs in the score which denote whether the response should be positive or negative. It has worked well in combination with the ideas behind moment form. *Stimmung* (1968) is a 45 minute meditation on one chord whose parts and overtones emerge and merge into the whole, punctuated by erotic poems, magic numbers and words which are delivered in response to chance operations. The culmination of these ideas may be seen in *Aus den Sieben Tagen* (1968) where the score for each of the seven movements is a short poem.

Use of indeterminacy does not necessarily have to be so extreme. For György Ligeti (b. 1923) and Witold Lutoslawski (b. 1913) use of controlled chance techniques has provided a way for composing atonal music without embracing serialism. During 1955–60 Lutoslawski evolved a harmonic language which used twelve-note chords for expression and colour. In 1960 he heard a performance of Cage's Piano Concerto and realised that he could use chance techniques to add a rhythmic freedom and new types of texture to his music. The exact combination of sounds at any given moment is often a matter of chance but the overall effect is planned. Textures are created by the constant repetition of small melodic ideas and simple rhythms in different parts, creating a kaleidoscope of sound, and by lines of counterpoint set off against each other, often sliding from one note to another blurring the transition between chords. The music of Lutoslawski is a fine example of the use of chance as a tool in compositions which still have strong links to tradition. The direction and drama of works such as *Mi-Parti* (1976) and his Third Symphony (1983) are firmly in the composer's hands, relying heavily on his skilful sense of harmonic movement, use of colour and proportion. Only small rhythmic details are left to chance.

Ligeti has also made use of textures created by chance operations. The contrast of such sections with fixed areas has been a way of creating large structures as in his *Requiem* (1963–5). The idea of clocks and clouds underlies several of his works of the late 1960s and 1970s: in the Double Concerto for flute, harp and orchestra (1972) we hear the transition from dense clusters or clouds of notes to regular clock-like single notes. Chance techniques have been an important element in creating these.

Electronic Music.

An important part of the post-war struggle with musical language has been the development of electronic means to generate, manipulate and record sounds. Its pioneer was the Frenchman Edgard Varèse (1883–1965). Before the war he had been an independent and radical composer much concerned with the exploration of new sounds. This had led to an emphasis on the exploitation of percussion effects in works such as *Intégrales* (1924–5) and *Ionisation* (1933). The following work *Ecuatorial* (1934) explored further, using primitive electrically generated sounds produced by two Ondes Martenot. However the catalyst for further development was the invention of the tape recorder which provided an easy means to store sounds that could then be rearranged by cutting and rejoining the tape in different ways. Varèse explored these possibilities in *Déserts* (1949–54) which alternated recorded and instrumental sounds in an atmospheric work which really seems to conjure up the aridity and emptiness of the desert. Recorded sound offered the possibility of creating illusions of aural space by technical manipulation and by judicious positioning and control of loudspeakers. This is a fundamental part of Varèse's great masterpiece, *Poème Electronique* (1958) which used soprano, chorus, bells, organs and artificial sounds. Its spatial effects were achieved by using many loudspeakers positioned around a specially designed pavilion at the 1958 Brussels Exhibition.

Generally, electronic music-making required a studio and the 1950s saw the setting up of important studios in Paris and Cologne. In Paris Pierre Schaeffer (b. 1910) pioneered "musique concrète" which used altered and rearranged natural sounds, for example, the sound of a steam train, to create a musical piece. At Cologne where Stockhausen worked, the emphasis was on creating new synthetic sounds.

Electronic music had the potential to generate complex, accurate serial structures through precise electronic operations. Boulez's studies in this however did not satisfy him and he neglected the medium until 1970 when he became Director of IRCAM (*Institut de Recherche et de Coordination Acoustique/Musique*). Stockhausen however found electronic music an ideal medium to create a musical unity far beyond that of serialism; pitch, timbre, rhythm and form could be seen as different aspects of the same thing—vibration. He did not restrict himself to pure synthetic sounds and in 1955–6 created perhaps his most well-known electronic work, *Gesang der Jünglinge*. This combines synthetic sounds with a recorded boy's voice to portray the three boys in the fiery furnace from the Book of Daniel.

With *Kontakte* (1958–60) for piano, percussion and tape, Stockhausen began an exploration of the interplay between live performers and electronic sound which still preoccupies him today. The work explores "contact" between real and artificial sounds and between the elements of music. Compared to pure electronic music, the presence of the live performers made it easier to listen to, providing a visual focus and making each performance unique. The next step was to create "live" electronic music where performers created their electronic sounds on stage. Cage had already begun this in 1960 with *Cartridge Music*. Unlike Stockhausen's first attempt, *Mikrophonie I* (1964–5), *Cartridge Music* gives much freedom to the performer in creating the electronic effects. A desire to create a world music led to one of the most vast electronic works to date, *Hymnen* (1966–7), a two-hour work for quadraphonic tape or tapes, soloists and optional symphony orchestra. Stockhausen constructed it out of national anthems from all over the world. Inspired by the occult *Urantian Book*, he became more ambitious still, seeking a galactic music. *Sirius* (1977) for four soloists and electronic music deals with the arrival on earth of four visitors from the star Sirius.

In America, developments have followed a different course. There, the use of computer synthesised sounds has been the main interest because of the computer's superior control and accuracy. It has allowed the continuation of abstract composition where complicated operations are achieved simply and effectively. Computer synthesis can also be applied to existing material. For example, *Chronometer* (1971) by Harrison Birtwistle (b. 1934) (an English composer working at that time in New York) is based on clock sounds.

Minimalism.

The transformation of existing material on tape has been a crucial part of an American movement dating from the 1960s known as 'Minimalism'. Its chief exponents are Steve Reich (b. 1936), Philip Glass (b. 1937), Terry Riley (b. 1935) and La Monte Young (b. 1935). Minimal music uses material which is limited in pitch, rhythm and timbres; the elements are subjected to simple transformations relying heavily on repetition. Of great importance are the subtle evolution from one idea to another as repetitions are modified, and the use of "phasing" techniques. Phasing is the effect of altering the rate of repetition between parts repeating the same material so that it is no longer synchronised. The effect of works such as *Drumming* (1971) by Reich may appear long and non-dramatic. However, the listener is not expected to concentrate all the time but to become aware of a piece's various elements and processes. The music's patterns will change as the listener's attention shifts from one aspect to another. As in moment form, minimalist works owe much to Indian concepts of time as a circular rather than linear phenomenon. In recent years, the minimalists have developed their style and there are greater differences between the four. Philip Glass has written three operas, *Einstein on the Beach* (1975), *Satyagraha* (1980) and *Akhnaten* (1983) while recent works by Reich such as *Desert Music* (1983) are less monochrome, exploiting bright sound colours and far from minimal forces.

Music Theatre.

During the early post-war years many composers were grappling with the tools of composition. Only more "traditional" writers such as Britten, Tippett and Hans Werner Henze (b. 1926) were engaged in writing opera. By 1970 however, most composers were including elements of theatre in their work even if they were not necessarily engaged in writing full-scale operas.

One of the major composers of "traditional" opera has been Henze. His first three operas draw heavily on the past. For example, *Boulevard Solitude* (1952) updates the story of Manon, a nineteenth-century favourite. After moving to Italy in 1953, Henze's stance appeared more traditional still as lyrical elements became more dominant in contrast to the abstract athematic style of contemporaries such as Stockhausen. Increasingly Henze's operas began to reflect his preoccupation with socialism. The *Bassarids* (1966), for example, examines through a mythological guise the precipitation of social upheaval and disruption. The oratorio *Das Floss der "Medusa"* (1968) is dedicated to Che Guevara and provoked such struggles between police and left-wing students at its premiere that Henze went to Cuba for a year. There he was inspired to write *El Cimarrón* (1969–70), a vocal monologue portraying a Cuban runaway slave accompanied by flute, guitar and percussion. For a while, Henze continued to reject the traditional opera format because of its bourgeois overtones, preferring a more intimate, chamber style. But in 1976 Henze returned to opera with *We come to the River*. It reflected a renewal of Italianate lyricism, the exploitation of opera's full potential and a less overt political message.

Luigi Nono (b. 1924) also exploited theatre for political ends, beginning with *Intolleranza* (1960). However he found greater resource than Henze in contemporary developments, taking full advantage of the opportunities offered by electronics. *Contrappunto dialettico della mente* (1967–8) includes the sounds of political demonstrations. Like Henze, Nono also returned to the opera house after a long break from large-scale opera with *Al gran sole carico d'amore* (1972–4), which consolidated the techniques he had developed in the previous decade.

"Theatre" became a dominant characteristic in the works of Luciano Berio (b. 1925). One of his most famous works is *Circles* (1960) for female voice, harp and percussion. The virtuosic technique used there and in other works was inspired by the phenomenal vocal elasticity of his then wife, Cathy Berberian. 'Circles' are depicted at many different levels in the work's structure and content. More importantly, these are underlined by the singer moving about the stage during the performance. Berio's next few works became overtly political, culminating in *Laborintus II* (1965) which was intended as an attack on capitalism via a musical collage and extracts from Dante's *Inferno*. Many of Berio's larger scale works since *Laborintus II* have been theatrical in their virtuosity and instrumental technique. For example, *Sequenza IV* (1965) demands a pianist with very agile feet. This type of dramatic gesture is much seen in Stockhausen's work, particularly those written for his own music ensemble, for example, *Solo* (1966). Since *Alphabet für Liege* (1972) his work has become increasingly theatrical and from 1978, Stockhausen has been working on an opera project *Licht*. Twenty years earlier, such a project would have been unthinkable.

The small-scale synthesis of text, music and gesture characteristic of Berio has greatly influenced British work in music theatre, notably the work of Peter Maxwell Davies and Harrison Birtwistle. Davies' work is very powerful particularly through its use of parody and wild use of outrageous gesture. *Vesalii Icones* (1969) uses a naked male dancer portraying parts of the Stations of the Cross and scenes from the anatomy text by Vesalius. It is a good example of parody, particularly of what Davies views as nineteenth-century grossness—it includes a vile distortion of a Victorian hymn tune which turns into a foxtrot, both played on a honky-tonk piano. Many of his works feature a single vocal soloist, with instrumental back up, who plays the part of a crazed, obsessive individual. For example, *Eight Songs for a Mad King* (1969) features the instrumentalists in giant bird cages who must suffer the mad ravings of George III played by the singer.

Davies has written two full-scale operas to date, *Taverner* (1962–8) and *The Martyrdom of St. Magnus* (1976) and is currently working on a third, *Resurrection*. *Taverner* deals with two fundamental preoccupations of Davies—the nature of faith and betrayal—and uses both musical and dramatic parody to convey its message. *St. Magnus* was written after Davies moved to Orkney. It reflects a change in style, uses only a small orchestra and is for production "in the round".

Birtwistle's first major dramatic work was a chamber opera, *Punch and Judy* (1966) which uses grotesque and violent gestures. However, while Davies' roots may lie with early Schoenberg, Birtwistle has found inspiration in the clear-cut lines and ritualism of Stravinsky. Possibly his most significant work to date is *The Mask of Orpheus* (1973–5 and 1981–3). This deals with Birtwistle's central dramatic concern, the conflicts between the individual ego and the collective unconscious. An important aspect of the work is the use of electronics, developed at IRCAM to create atmospheric "auras", for example, "cloud" music, and six mime interludes. Crucially, Apollo gives utterance to his commands through electronic fragments which vary in length from a second to almost a minute.

The Contemporary Music Scene.

While earlier sections have already covered part of the 1980s, little mention has been made of some younger composers. It is difficult to stand back from the music of the present, but here is a brief survey of some British composers working now who deserve attention.

Brian Ferneyhough (b. 1943) is continuing to expand the chamber music repertoire using traditional structures as a framework for music in which micro-tones play an increasingly important part. He is currently working on a seven-part cycle of chamber works of which three are complete; *Superscripto* for solo piccolo (1981), *Carceri d'Invenzione I* (1982) and *Carceri d'Invenzione II* (1985) for chamber orchestra (II with solo flute). Robin Holloway (b. 1943) has also been active in composing smaller scale works, often lyrical, of which recent examples are his *Viola Concerto* (1985) and the bleak *Ballad* for harp and chamber orchestra (1985). Nigel Osborne (b. 1948) has used electronic and non-Western music in his work, gravitating recently towards vocal works. 1986 saw the premiere of his theatre piece, *Hells Angels*. Other recent operas are *Where the Wild Things Are* (1984) and *Higglety, Pigglety Pop!* (1985) by Oliver Knussen (b. 1952) which attracted acclaim for a young composer already noted for his symphonies, vocal and chamber work. Tim Souster (b. 1943) has been active in composing and promoting electronic music of all types, some influenced by rock music. A recent example is his *Quartet with Tape* (1985). Meanwhile choral music is flourishing with new works by Paul Patterson (b. 1947) which often involve new types of notation and vocal technique, and several ritualistic works by John Tavener (b. 1948), inspired by his Eastern Orthodox faith. For example *Doxa* (1982) sets a single word from the Eastern liturgy. A meteoric rise to fame has been achieved by George Benjamin (b. 1960) starting with *Ringed by the Flat Horizon* (1980) written while still at Cambridge.

The contemporary scene is varied, exciting and constantly changing. It is well worth exploring both for itself and because it speaks to us as the music of our time.

II. GLOSSARY OF MUSICAL TERMS

A. Note of scale, commonly used for tuning instruments.

Absolute Music. Music without any literary descriptive or other kind of reference.

A Capella. Literally "in the church style." Unaccompanied.

Accelerando. Quickening of the pace.

Accidental. The sign which alters the pitch of a note; ♯ (sharp) raises and a ♭ (flat) lowers note by one semitone, ✕ (double sharp) and ♭♭ (double flat) alter by two semitones.

Accompaniment. Instrumental or piano part forming background to a solo voice or instrument that has the melody.

Ad lib. (L. *ad libitum*). Direction on music that strict time need not be observed.

Adagio. A slow movement or piece.

Aeolian mode. One of the scales in mediaeval music, represented by the white keys of the piano from A to A.

Air. A simple tune for voice or instrument.

Alberti Bass. Characteristic 18th century keyboard figuration derived by splitting chord(s) of an accompanying part. Tradition credits Alberti as its inventor.

Allegretto. Not quite so fast as *Allegro.*

Allegro. Fast, but not too fast.

Alto. An unusually high type of male voice; also the vocal part sung by women and boys with a low range.

Ambrosian Chant. Plainsong introduced into church music by St. Ambrose, bishop of Milan (d. 397), and differing from Gregorian chant.

Andante. At a walking pace, not so slow as *Adagio* nor as fast as *Allegretto.*

Animato. Lively.

Answer. Entry in a fugue or invention which imitates or "answers" the theme at a different pitch.

Anthem. Composition for use in church during a service by a choir with or without soloists.

Antiphonal. Using groups of instruments or singers placed apart.

Appoggiatura. An ornament consisting of a short note just above or below a note forming part of a chord.

Arabesque. Usually a short piece, highly decorated.

Arco. Direction for string instruments to play with bow.

Aria. Vocal solo, usually in opera or oratorio, often in three sections with the third part being a repeat of the first. An *Arietta* is a shorter, lighter kind of aria.

Arioso. In the style of an aria; halfway between aria and recitative.

Arpeggio. Notes of a chord played in a broken, spread-out manner, as on a harp.

Ars antiqua. The old mediaeval music, based on organum and plainsong, before the introduction of *Ars nova* in 14th cent.

Ars Nova. New style of composition in 14th century France and Italy. It has greater variety in rhythm and independence in part-writing.

Atonal. Not in any key; hence *Atonality.*

Aubade. Morning song.

Augmentation. The enlargement of a melody by lengthening the musical value of its notes.

Ayre. Old spelling of *air.*

B. Note of scale, represented in Germany by *H.*

Bagatelle. A short, generally light piece of music. Beethoven wrote 26 Bagatelles.

Ballad. Either a narrative song or an 18th-cent. drawing-room song.

Ballade. A substantial and dramatic work, often for piano. Notable examples are by Chopin and Brahms.

Ballet. Stage entertainment requiring intrumental accompaniment; originated at French court in 16th and 17th cent.

Bar. A metrical division of music; the perpendicular line in musical notation to indicate this.

Barcarolle. A boating-song, in particular one associated with Venetian gondoliers.

Baritone. A male voice, between tenor and bass.

Baroque. A term applied, loosely, to music written in the 17th and 18th cent., roughly corresponding to baroque in architecture.

Bass. The lowest male voice; lowest part of a composition.

Bass Drum. Largest of the drum family, placed upright and struck on the side.

Bassoon. The lowest of the woodwind instruments, uses double reed.

Beat. Music's rhythmic pulse.

Bel canto. Literally "beautiful singing"—in the old Italian style with pure tone and exact phrasing.

Berceuse. Cradle song.

Binary. A piece in two sections is said to be binary in form. The balance is obtained by a second phrase (or section) answering the first.

Bitonality. Use of two keys at once.

Bow. Stick with horsehair stretched across it for playing string instruments.

Brass. Used as a collective noun for all brass or metal instruments.

Breve. Note, rarely used nowadays, with time value of two semibreves.

Bridge. Wood support over which strings are stretched on a violin, cello, guitar, etc.

Buffo(a). Comic, as in *buffo bass* or *opera buffa.*

C. Note of scale.

Cabaletta. Final, quick section of an aria or duet.

Cadence. A closing phrase of a composition or a passage, coming to rest on tonic (key note).

Cadenza. Solo vocal or instrumental passage, either written or improvised, giving soloist chance to display technical skill to audience.

Calando. Becoming quieter and slower.

Canon. A piece or section of music resulting from one line of music being repeated imitatively in the other parts which enter in succession.

Cantabile. Song-like, therefore flowing and expressive.

Cantata. Vocal work for chorus and/or choir.

Cantilena. Sustained, smooth melodic line.

Cantus firmus. Literally "fixed song." Basic melody from 14th to 17th cent., around which other voices wove contrapuntal parts.

Canzonet. Light songs written in England *c.* 1600.

Carillon. A set of bells in tower of church, played from a keyboard below.

Carol. Christmas song.

Castrato. Artificially-created male soprano and alto, fashionable in 17th and 18th cent. (The castration of vocally gifted boys prevailed in Italy until the 19th cent.)

Catch. A part-song like a round, in vogue in England from 16th to 19th cent.

Cavatina. An operatic song in one section, or a slow song-like instrumental movement.

Celesta. Keyboard instrument with metal bars struck by hammers.

Cello. Four-stringed instrument, played with bow, with a bass range. Comes between viola and double bass in string family.

Cembalo. Originally the Italian name for the dulcimer, but sometimes applied to the harpsichord.

Chaconne. Vocal or instrumental piece with unvaried bass.

Chamber Music. Music originally intended to be played in a room for three or more players.

Chanson. Type of part-song current in France from 14th to 16th cent.

Chant. Singing of psalms, masses, etc., in plainsong to Latin words in church.

Choir. Body of singers, used either in church or at concerts.

Chorales. German hymn tunes, often made use of by Bach.

Chord. Any combination of notes heard together. *See also* Triad.

Chording. Spacing of intervals in a chord.

Chorus. Substantial body of singers, usually singing in four parts.

Chromatic. Using a scale of nothing but semitones.

Clarinet. Woodwind instrument with single reed in use since mid-18th cent.

Clavichord. Keyboard instrument having strings struck by metal tangents, much in use during 17th and 18th cent. as solo instrument.

Clavier. Used in German (*Klavier*) for piano, in England for any stringed keyboard instrument.

Clef. Sign in stave that fixes place of each note.

Coda. Closing section of movement in Sonata form.

Coloratura. Term to denote florid singing.

Common chord. *See* Triad.

Common Time. Four crotchets to the bar, 4/4 time.

Compass. Range of notes covered by voice or instruments.

Composition. Piece of music, originated by a composer's own imagination; act of writing such a piece.

Compound Time. Metre where beats are subdivided into threes rather than twos.

Con Brio. With dash.

Concert. Public performance of any music.

Concertato. Writing for several solo instruments to be played together.

Concerto. Work for one or more solo instruments and orchestra.

Concerto grosso. Orchestral work common in 17th and 18th cent. with prominent parts for small groups of instruments.

Concord. Opposite of discord, *i.e.*, notes that when sounded together satisfy the ear. (Conventional term in that its application varies according to the age in which one lives.)

Conduct. To direct a concert with a baton.

Consecutive. Progression of harmonic intervals of like kind.

Consonance. Like Concord.

Continuo. Bass line in 17th and 18th century music. Played by a bass instrument and keyboard, the latter improvising on the indicated harmonies.

Contralto. A woman's voice with a low range.

Counterpoint. Simultaneous combination of two or more melodies to create a satisfying musical texture. Where one melody is added to another, one is called the other's counterpoint. The adjective of counterpoint is contrapuntal.

Counter-tenor. Another name for male alto.

Courante. A dance in triple time.

Crescendo. Getting louder.

Crook. Detachable section of tubing on brass instruments that change the tuning.

Crotchet. Note that equals two quavers in time value.

Cycle. Set of works, especially songs, intended to be sung as group.

Cyclic form. Form of work in two or more movements in which the same musical themes recur.

Cymbal. Percussion instrument; two plates struck against each other.

D. Note of scale.

Da Capo (abbr. D.C.). A *Da Capo* aria is one in which the whole first section is repeated after a contrasting middle section.

Descant. Additional part (sometimes improvised) sung against a melody.

Development. Working-out section of movement in sonata form. *See* Sonata.

Diatonic. Opposite of chromatic; using proper notes of a major or minor scale.

Diminished. Lessened version of perfect interval, e.g., semitone less than a perfect fifth is a diminished fifth.

Diminuendo. Lessening.

Diminution. Reducing a phrase of melody by shortening time value of notes.

Discord. Opposite of concord, *i.e.*, notes that sounded together produce a clash of harmonies.

Dissonance. Like discord.

Divertimento. A piece, usually orchestral, in several movements; like a suite.

Dodecaphonic. Pertaining to 12-note method of composition.

Dominant. Fifth note of major or minor scale above tonic (key) note.

Dorian Mode. One of the scales in mediaeval music, represented by the white keys on the piano from D to D.

Dot. Placed over note indicates staccato; placed after note indicates time value to be increased by half.

Double bar. Two upright lines marking the end of a composition or a section of it.

Double bass. Largest and lowest instrument of violin family; played with bow.

Drone bass. Unvarying sustained bass, similar to the permanent bass note of a bagpipe.

Drum. Variety of percussion instruments on which sound is produced by hitting a skin stretched tightly over a hollow cylinder or hemisphere.

Duet. Combination of two performers; composition for such a combination.

Duple Time. Metre in which there are two beats to a bar.

Dynamics. Gradations of loudness or softness in music.

E. Note of scale.

Electronic. Term used to describe use of electronic sounds in music.

Encore. Request from audience for repeat of work, or extra item in a programme.

English horn (*Cor anglais*). Woodwind instrument with double reed of oboe family.

Enharmonic. Refers to use of different letter names for the same note, *e.g.* F and E♯. Often exploited to achieve modulation between distantly related keys.

Ensemble. Teamwork in performance; item in opera for several singers with or without chorus; a group of performers of no fixed number.

Episode. Section in composition usually divorced from main argument.

Exposition. Setting out of thematic material in a sonata-form composition.

Expression marks. Indication by composer of how he wants his music performed.

F. Note of scale.

False relation. A clash of harmony produced when two notes, such as A natural and A flat, are played simultaneously or immediately following one another.

Falsetto. The kind of singing by male voices above normal register and sounding like an unbroken voice.

Fanfare. Flourish of trumpets.

Fantasy. A piece suggesting free play of composer's imagination, or a piece based on known tunes (folk, operatic, etc.).

Fermata. Pause indicated by sign prolonging note beyond its normal length.

Fifth. Interval taking five steps in the scale. A perfect fifth (say, C to G) includes three whole tones and a semitone; a diminished fifth is a semitone less, an augmented fifth a semitone more.

Figure. A short phrase, especially one that is repeated.

Fingering. Use of fingers to play instrument, or the indication above notes to show what fingers should be used.

Flat. Term indicating a lowering of pitch by a semitone, or to describe a performer playing under the note.

Florid. Term used to describe decorative passages.

Flute. Woodwind instrument, blown sideways. It is played through a hole, not a reed. Nowadays, sometimes made of metal.

Folksong. Traditional tune, often in different versions, handed down aurally from generation to generation.

Form. Course or layout of a composition, especially when in various sections.

Fourth. Interval taking four steps in scale. A perfect fourth (say, C to F) includes two whole tones and a semitone. If either note is sharpened or flattened the result is an augmented fourth or a diminished fourth.

Fugato. In the manner of a fugue.

Fugue. Contrapuntal composition for various parts based on one or more subjects treated imitatively but not strictly.

G. Note of scale.

Galant. Used to designate elegant style of 18th-cent. music.

Galliard. Lively dance dating back to 15th cent. or before.

Gavotte. Dance in 4/4 time, beginning on third beat in bar.

Giusto. Strict, proper.

Glee. Short part-song.

Glissando. Rapid sliding scales up and down piano or other instruments.

Glockenspiel. Percussion instrument consisting of tuned steel bars and played with two hammers or keyboard.

Grace note. See Ornament.

Grave. In slow tempo.

Grazioso. Gracefully.

Gregorian Chant. Plainsong collected and supervised mainly by Pope Gregory (d. 604).

Ground Bass. A bass part that is repeated throughout a piece with varying material on top.

Guitar. Plucked string instrument of Spanish origin, having six strings of three-octave compass.

H. German note-symbol for *B.*

Harmony. Simultaneous sounding of notes so as to make musical sense.

Harp. Plucked string instrument of ancient origin, the strings stretched parallel across its frame. The basic scale of C flat major is altered by a set of pedals.

Harpsichord. Keyboard stringed instrument played by means of keyboard similar to a piano but producing its notes by a plucking, rather than a striking action.

Homophonic. Opposite of polyphonic, *i.e.,* indicated parts move together in a composition, a single melody being accompanied by block chords, as distinct from the contrapuntal movement of different melodies.

Horn. Brass instrument with coiled tubes. Valves introduced in 19th cent. made full chromatic use of instrument possible.

Hymn. Song of praise, especially in church.

Imitation. Repetition, exactly, or at least recognisably, of a previously heard figure.

Impromptu. A short, seemingly improvised piece of music, especially by Schubert or Chopin.

Improvise. To perform according to fancy or imagination, sometimes on a given theme.

In alt. The octave above the treble clef; *in altissimo,* octave above that.

Instrumentation. Writing music for particular instruments, using the composer's knowledge of what sounds well on different instruments.

Interlude. Piece played between two sections of a composition.

Intermezzo. Formerly meant interlude, now often used for pieces played between acts of operas.

Interval. Distance in pitch between notes.

Ionian mode. One of the scales in mediaeval music, represented on piano by white keys between C and C, identical therefore to modern C major scale.

Isorhythmic. Medieval technique using repetitions of a rhythm but with different notes. Much used in 15th century motets.

Jig. Old dance usually in 6/8 or 12/8 time.

Kettledrum (It. pl. *Timpani*). Drum with skin drawn over a cauldron-shaped receptacle, can be tuned to definite pitch by turning handles on rim, thus tightening or relaxing skin.

Key. Lever by means of which piano, organ, etc., produces note; classification, in relatively modern times, of notes of a scale. Any piece of music in major or minor is in the *key* of its tonic or keynote.

Keyboard. Term used to describe instruments with a continuous row of keys.

Key-signature. Indication on written music, usually at the beginning of each line, of the number of flats or sharps in the key of a composition.

Kitchen Department. Humorous term for percussion section of an orchestra.

Lament. Musical piece of sad or deathly significance.

Largamente. Spaciously.

Largo. Slow.

Leading-motive (Ger. *Leitmotiv*). Short theme, suggesting person, idea, or image, quoted throughout composition to indicate that person, etc.

Legato. In a smooth style (of performance, etc.).

Lento. Slow.

Libretto. Text of an opera.

Lied (pl. *Lieder*). Song, with special reference to songs by Schubert, Schumann, Brahms, and Wolf.

Lute. String instrument plucked with fingers, used in 15th- and 16th-cent. music especially.

Lydian mode. One of the scales in mediaeval music, represented by white keys of piano between F and F.

Lyre. Ancient Greek plucked string instrument.

Madrigal. Contrapuntal composition for several voices, especially prominent from 15th to 17th cent.

Maestoso. Stately.

Major. One of the two main scales of the tonal system with semitones between the third and fourth, and the seventh and eighth notes. Identical with 16th-cent. Ionian mode.

Mandolin(e). Plucked string instrument of Italian origin.

Manual. A keyboard for the hands, used mostly in connection with the organ.

Master of the King's (or Queen's) Musick. Title of British court appointment, with no precise duties.

Melisma. Group of notes sung to a single syllable.

Mélodie. Literally a melody or tune; has come to mean a French song (cf. German *Lied*).

Metronome. Small machine in use since the beginning of the 18th cent., to determine the pace of any composition by the beats of the music, *e.g.*, = 60 at the head of the music indicates sixty crotchets to the minute.

Mezzo, Mezza. (It. = "half") *Mezza voce* means using the half voice (a tone between normal singing and whispering). *Mezzo-soprano*, voice between soprano and contralto.

Minim. Note that equals two crotchets in time value.

Minor. One of the two main scales of the tonal system (cf. major), identical with 16th-cent. Aeolian mode. It has two forms—the harmonic and melodic, the former having a sharpened seventh note, the latter having the sixth and seventh note sharpened.

Minuet. Originally French 18th-cent. dance in triple time, then the usual third movement in symphonic form (with a contrasting trio section) until succeeded by scherzo.

Mixolydian mode. One of the mediaeval scales represented by the white keys on the piano from G to G.

Modes. Scales prevalent in the Middle Ages. *See* Aeolian, Dorian, Ionian, Lydian, Mixolydian, Phrygian.

Modulate. Changing from key to key in a composition, not directly but according to musical "grammar".

Molto. Much, very; thus *allegro molto.*

Motet. Sacred, polyphonic vocal composition. More loosely, any choral composition for use in church but not set to words of the liturgy.

Motive, motif. Short, easily recognised melodic figure.

Motto. Short, well-defined theme recurring throughout a composition, cf. *Idée fixe* in Berlioz's *Symphonie Fantastique.*

Movement. Separate sections of a large-scale composition, each in its own form.

Music drama. Term used to describe Wagner's, and sometimes other large-scale operas.

Mutes. Devices used to damp the sound of various instruments.

Natural (of a note or key). Not sharp or flat.

Neoclassical. Clear-cut style, originating during 1920s, that uses 17th and 18th century forms and styles. It constituted a reaction to the excesses of romanticism.

Ninth. Interval taking nine steps, *e.g.*, from C upwards an octave and a whole tone to D.

Nocturne. Literally a "night-piece" hence usually of lyrical character.

Nonet. Composition for nine instruments.

Notation. Act of writing down music.

Note. Single sound of specified pitch and duration; symbol to represent this.

Obbligato. Instrumental part having a special or essential rôle in a piece.

Oboe. Woodwind instrument with double reed, descended from hautboy; as such, in use since 16th cent., in modern form since 18th cent.

Octave. Interval taking eight steps of scale, with top and bottom notes having same "name"; C to C is an octave.

Octet. Composition for eight instruments or voices.

Ondes Martenol. Belongs to a class of melodic instruments in which the tone is produced by electrical vibrations controlled by the movement of the hands not touching the instrument.

Opera. Musical work for the stage with singing characters, originated *c.* 1600 in Italy.

Opera buffa (It.), *Opéra bouffe* (Fr.). Comic opera (in the English sense), *not* to be confused with *Opéra comique* (Fr.) which is opera with spoken dialogue and need not be humorous.

Opera seria. Chief operatic form of 17th and 18th cent., usually set to very formal librettos, concerning gods or heroes of ancient history.

Operetta. Lighter type of opera.

Opus (abbr. *Op.*). With number following *opus* indicates order of a composer's composition.

Oratorio. Vocal work, usually for soloists and choir with instrumental accompaniment, generally with setting of a religious text.

Orchestra. Term to designate large, or largish, body of instrumentalists originated in 17th cent.

Orchestration. Art of setting out work for instruments of an orchestra. To be distinguished from *Instrumentation* (*q.v.*).

Organ. Elaborate keyboard instrument in which air is blown through pipes by bellows to sound notes. Tone is altered by selection of various stops and, since the 16th cent., a pedal keyboard has also been incorporated.

Organum. In mediaeval music a part sung as an accompaniment below or above the melody of plainsong, usually at the interval of a fourth or fifth; also, loosely, this method of singing in parts.

Ornament. Notes that are added to a given melody by composer or performer as an embellishment.

Overture. Instrumental introduction or prelude to larger work, usually opera. Concert overtures are simply that: *i.e.*, work to be played at start of a concert.

Part. Music of one performer in an ensemble; single strand in a composition.

Part-song. Vocal composition in several parts.

Passacaglia. Composition in which a tune is constantly repeated, usually in the bass.

Passage. Section of a composition.

Passion. Musical setting of the New Testament story of Christ's trial and crucifixion.

Pastiche. Piece deliberately written in another composer's style.

Pavan(e). Moderately paced dance dating from 16th cent. or earlier.

Pedal. Held note in bass of composition.

Pentatonic. Scale of five consecutive notes, *e.g.*, the black keys of the piano.

Percussion. Collective title for instruments of the orchestra that are sounded by being struck by hand or stick.

Phrygian Mode. One of the scales of mediaeval music, represented by the white keys on piano from E to E.

Piano. Soft, abbr. *p*; *pp* = *pianissimo*, very soft; instrument, invented in 18th cent., having strings struck by hammer, as opposed to the earlier harpsichord where they are plucked. The modern piano has 88 keys and can be either "upright" (vertical) or "grand" (horizontal).

Pianoforte. Almost obsolete full Italian name for the piano.

Pitch. Exact height or depth of a particular musical sound or note.

Pizzicato. Direction for stringed instruments, that the strings should be plucked instead of bowed.

Plainchant, Plainsong. Mediaeval church music

consisting of single line of melody without harmony or definite rhythm.

Polka. Dance in 2/4 time originating in 19th cent. Bohemia.

Polonaise. Polish dance generally in 3/4 time.

Polyphony. Combination of two or more musical lines as in *counterpoint.*

Polytonality. Simultaneous use of several keys.

Postlude. Closing piece, opposite of Prelude.

Prelude. Introductory piece.

Presto. Very fast. *Prestissimo.* Still faster.

Progression. Movement from one chord to next to make musical sense.

Quartet. Work written for four instruments or voices; group to play or sing such a work.

Quaver. Note that equals two semiquavers or half a crotchet.

Quintet. Work written for five instruments or voices; group to play or sing such a work.

Rallentando. Slowing down.

Recapitulation. Section of composition that repeats original material in something like its original form.

Recitative. Term used for declamation in singing written in ordinary notation but allowing rhythmical licence.

Recorder. Woodwind instrument, forerunner of flute.

Reed. Vibrating tongue of woodwind instruments.

Register. Set of organ pipes controlled by a particular stop; used in reference to different ranges of instrument or voice (*e.g.,* chest register).

Relative. Term used to indicate common key signature of a major and minor key.

Répétiteur. Member of opera house's musical staff who coaches singers in their parts.

Rest. Notation of pauses for instrument in composition, having a definite length like a note.

Retrograde. Term used to describe a melody played backwards.

Rhapsody. Work of no definite kind with a degree of romantic content.

Rhythm. Everything concerned with the time of music (*i.e.,* beats, accent, metre, etc.) as opposed to the pitch side.

Ritornello. Passage, usually instrumental, that recurs in a piece.

Romance, Romanza. Title for piece of vague song-like character.

Romantic. Term used vaguely to describe music of 19th cent. that has other than purely musical source of inspiration.

Rondo. Form in which one section keeps on recurring.

Rubato. Manner of performing a piece without keeping strictly to time.

Sackbut. Early English name for trombone.

Saxophone. Classified as wind instrument, although made of brass, because it uses a reed.

Scale. Progression of adjoining notes upwards or downwards.

Scherzo. Literally "a joke". Often used as a light movement in the middle of a sonata type work.

Score. Copy of any music written in several parts.

Second. Interval taking two steps in scale, *e.g.,* C to D flat, or to D.

Semibreve. Note that equals two minims or half a breve.

Semiquaver. Note that equals half a quaver.

Semitone. Smallest interval commonly used in Western music.

Septet. Composition for seven instruments or voices.

Sequence. Repetition of phrase at a higher or lower pitch.

Serenade. Usually an evening song or instrumental work.

Seventh. Interval taking seven steps in the scale.

Sextet. Composition for six instruments or voices.

Sharp. Term indicating a raising of pitch by a semitone.

Shawm. Primitive woodwind instrument, forerunner of oboe.

Simple time. Division of music into two or four beats.

Sinfonietta. Small symphony.

Sixth. Interval taking six steps in the scale.

Solo. Piece or part of a piece for one performer playing or singing alone.

Sonata. Term to denote a musical form and a type of composition. In *sonata form* a composition is divided into exposition, development and recapitulation. A *sonata* is a piece, usually for one or more players following that form.

Song. Any short vocal composition.

Soprano. Highest female voice.

Sostenuto. Sustained, broadly.

Sotto voce. Whispered, scarcely audible, applied to vocal as well as instrumental music.

Sprechgesang. (Ger. Speech-song.) Vocal utterance somewhere between speech and song.

Staccato. Perform music in short, detached manner.

Staff. Horizontal lines on which music is usually written.

Stop. Lever by which organ registration can be altered.

String(s). Strands of gut or metal set in vibration to produce musical sounds on string or keyboard instruments. Plural refers to violins, violas, cellos, and basses of orchestra.

Study. Instrumental piece, usually one used for technical exercise or to display technical skills, but often having artistic merits as well (*e.g.,* Chopin's).

Subject(s). Theme or group of notes that forms principal idea or ideas in composition.

Suite. Common name for piece in several movements.

Symphony. Orchestral work of serious purpose usually in four movements, occasionally given name (*e.g.,* Beethoven's "Choral" symphony).

Syncopation. Displacement of musical accent.

Tempo. Pace, speed of music.

Tenor. Highest normal male voice.

Ternary. A piece in three sections is said to be in ternary form. The balance is obtained by repeating the first phrase or section (though it need not be exact or complete) after a second of equal importance.

Tessitura. Compass into which voice or instrument comfortably falls.

Theme. Same as *subject* but can also be used for a whole musical statement as in "theme and variations."

Third. Interval taking three steps in scale.

Time. Rhythmical division of music.

Timpani. See Kettledrum.

Toccata. Instrumental piece usually needing rapid, brilliant execution.

Tonality. Key, or feeling for a definite key.

Tone. Quality of musical sound; interval of two semitones.

Tonic Sol-fa. System of musical notation to simplify sight-reading.

Transcribe. Arrange piece for different medium, instrument, or voice than that originally intended.

Transition. Passage that joins two themes or sections of a composition.

Transpose. To move a musical idea, theme or piece to a different key from its original.

Treble. Highest part in vocal composition; high boy's voice.

Triad. Three note chord. Usually consists of a note and those a third and fifth above.

Trio. Work written for three instruments or voices; group to play or sing such a work.

Trombone. Brass instrument with slide adjusting length of tube.

Trumpet. Metal instrument of considerable antiquity; modern version has three valves to make it into a chromatic instrument.

Tuba. Deepest-toned brass instrument with three or four valves.

Twelve-note. Technique of composition using full chromatic scale with each note having equal importance. Notes are placed in particular order as the thematic basis of works.

Unison. Two notes sung or played together at same pitch.

Valve. Mechanism, invented in early 19th cent. to add to brass instruments allowing them to play full chromatic scale.

Variation. Varied passage of original theme. Such variations may be closely allied to or depart widely from the theme.

Verismo. Term to describe Italian operas written in "realist" style at the turn of this century.

Vibrato. Rapid fluctuation in pitch of voice or instrument. Exaggerated it is referred to as a "wobble" (of singers) or tremolo.

Viol. String instrument of various sizes in vogue until end of 17th cent.

Viola. Tenor instrument of violin family.

Violin. Musical four-string instrument, played with bow, of violin family, which superseded viol at beginning of 18th cent.

Virginals. English keyboard instrument, similar to harpsichord of 17th and 18th cent.

Vivace. Lively.

Voluntary. Organ piece for church use, but not during service.

Waltz. Dance in triple time, fashionable in 19th cent.

Whole-tone scale. Scale progressing by whole tones. Only two are possible, one beginning on C, the other on C sharp.

Xylophone. Percussion instrument with series of wood bars tuned in a chromatic scale and played with sticks.

Zither. String instrument laid on knees and plucked. Common in Central-European folk music.

III. INDEX TO COMPOSERS

IV. SPECIAL TOPICS

TWENTIETH-CENTURY POPULAR MUSIC

INTRODUCTION

"Classical" music of the European tradition has often borrowed the melodies, styles, and instruments of popular songs, and in this century the influence of "low brow" music, in particular jazz, has been considerable. As a musical form of particular identity and technique, jazz deserves serious attention, as do the many other distinct forms of popular music, including rock, since they are an important phenomenon of mass culture.

America, and particularly black America, has dominated 20th-cent. popular music in the Western World. Jazz is a rhythmic, syncopated style of music, created at the end of the 19th cent. by black Americans out of their religious and secular (gospel and blues) songs. Its birth place was New Orleans, but jazz was played elsewhere and spread by the 1920s to black communities in the north, and especially Chicago where the best performers assembled and soon began to influence white musicians.

The top American bands—mainly white, but some black—adopted and adapted jazz to bring themselves huge commercial success and immense popularity for their music, which evolved into 1930s' swing. This stamped an indelible impression on all dance music and popular songs.

Music Hall and vaudeville, and the "musicals" of Broadway, London's West End and Hollywood, now reflected the influence of jazz. Country music, later called country and western, was the only distinctly white American style which flourished through these times, as it does today.

After World War II, jazz and popular music, though inextricably intertwined, went in different directions. Black musicians, tired of swing which watered down their jazz, produced a more sophisticated style called bebop. Then some musicians, black and white, launched a revival of the original New Orleans jazz sounds, and "trad" boomed in American and Britain in the 1950s. This emphasis faced a strong challenge from the performers and fans of a new "modern jazz". By the 1960s, however, this was appreciated only amongst a minority.

Popular music meets the demands of a mass audience, and since the War has reflected more and more the needs of commerce and a large-scale record industry. Ballad singers and

crooners were big business after the War, a time when America's black communities produced rhythm-and-blues. Mixed with aspects of country music, this became rock'n'roll, the 1950s' sensation for the white community.

Here was a watershed: rock in its various forms sprang from rock'n'roll and now dominates the music scene, "pop" is its mass market manifestation, and the divisions between black music and that favoured by white audiences have gradually broken down. During the 1960s and 1970s, rock incorporated folk, and, through a blues revival, helped create soul and the modern-day disco phenomenon. It has also expressed in music the "underground", drug culture, the civil rights movement, and anti-war campaigns. The initiative in popular music's development, so long the preserve of Americans, passed briefly to British artists when Beatlemania swept the world after 1963. Since then the music scene has been kaleidoscopic, fashions come and go, but most styles of jazz, rock, or soul have their fans.

The following glossary and biographical notes are intended to help the general reader:

Acid Rock.

1960s hyper-amplified music, featuring improvisation and distorted electronic effects, it reflected the "underground" and the craze for drugs, especially LSD, which bring mind expansion (see **J52**). Artists, many based in San Francisco, include Jefferson Airplane and The Grateful Dead.

Armstrong, (Daniel) Louis (1900–71).

US jazz trumpeter, singer, and bandleader, called "Satchmo". The great exponent of New Orleans jazz, he became the supreme soloist and showman of jazz.

Bacharach, Burt (1928–).

US singer, pianist, songwriter, arranger, and record producer. His work since the mid-1950s (often with Hal David) includes pop, rock, and soul compositions, and the music for many Broadway shows and films, e.g., What's New Pussycat (1964) and Alfie (1967).

Ballads.

Simple narrative or sentimental songs, a form of popular poetry. They were a familiar feature of folk music, and were much loved in music hall. In pop music, the term ballad signifies a slow, down-beat song rather than a rock number.

Band.

A group of musicians, who feature wind and percussion instruments rather than strings. Military or marching bands have a long tradition, borrowed by the first jazz groups. The jazz line-up varies, but originally had wind instruments playing melody over a rhythm section. Big bands, formed in the 1920s, had sixteen musicians in four sections, usually for dancing. "Modern jazz" bands are much smaller. The rock band consists of electric guitar, bass guitar, and drums with additional singers and features instruments, like keyboards and saxophone.

Basie, Count (1904–84).

US jazz musician, big-band leader from 1935, pianist, and composer. A great favourite in the swing era, he remained popular in later years.

Beach Boys.

US vocal and instrumental pop group of five, originally including Brian, Dennis, and Carl Wilson. America's challenge to the Beatle craze, they pioneered the early 1960s' West Coast surfing beat, with hits like *Surfin' Safari* (1962), *Fun Fun Fun*, *California Girls* and *Good Vibrations* (1966).

Beat.

The term signifies the swing of jazz and popular music, not just the number of beats to the bar but the pulse created within and around those bars.

Beatles.

British vocal and instrumental group, of John Lennon, Paul McCartney, George Harrison, and Ringo Starr (Richard Starkey). The most successful pop group of all time, the Beatles made Liverpool the temporary capital of rock music. Their style was rhythm-and-blues, with attractive harmonies, their songs had simple themes and fresh lyrics. Lennon and McCartney were superb songwriters, and the group's material, performances, records, and films caused Beatlemania across the world. The hits began in 1963 with *Please Please Me* and *She Loves You*, and later featured the more sophisticated, drugs-influenced, *Sergeant Pepper's Lonely Hearts Club Band* (1967). The group disbanded in 1971; John Lennon was murdered in 1980.

Bebop/Bop.

A style of jazz developed in the late 1940s by Dizzy Gillespie, Charlie Parker, and others to get away from the set arrangements of swing and to feature more subtlety, sophistication, and improvisation. The style borrowed much from European musicology and from Latin America's musical tradition. The balance inside a band's rhythm section changed, so that the bass now provided a constant rhythm and the drums could be used for accentuation or even solos.

Bee Gees.

Anglo-Australian vocal and instrumental group, featuring brothers Barry, Robin, and Maurice Gibb, who won great popularity in Australia and then Britain in the 1960s with hits like *Massachusetts*. After a temporary break-up, they shot into the superstar league, following the phenomenal success of their music in the disco film, *Saturday Night Fever* (1978).

Beiderbecke, (Leon) Bix (1903–31).

US jazz trumpeter and pianist. His roots were in white Dixieland (*q.v.*) and he became one of the most distinguished white performers.

Berlin, Irving (1888–   ).

US composer of over 800 popular songs, such as *Alexander's Ragtime Band* and *White Christmas*; Broadway musicals like *Annie Get Your Gun* (1946) and *Call me Madam* (1950); and film scores.

Berry, (Charles Edward Anderson) Chuck (1926–   ).

US blues and rock singer and guitarist, this black songwriter composed the best early rock'n'-roll and rhythm-and-blues. His 1950s hits, such as *Maybellene* (1955), *Roll Over Beethoven* (1956), and *Sweet Little Sixteen* (1958) were later revived by the Beatles, Rolling Stones, and others.

Blue Beat.

West Indian pop music style, a forerunner of reggae (*q.v.*) and reaching Britain in the 1960s.

Blues

The secular music of black America developed in the 19th cent. alongside gospel (*q.v.*) when slaves adapted African rhythms and a musical tradition based on a five-note scale to European melodies based on a seven-note scale. The classical blues featured a three-line verse, in which the first line is repeated and rhymes with the third, sung over a twelve-bar sequence (sometimes eight or sixteen bars). "Blue notes" are created by lowering a semitone the third and seventh degrees of the scale.

After emancipation, Afro-Americans continued to express in song their hardship and the injustices they suffered, and the mixture of spirituals (gospel) and worksongs became blues. This music is an emotional release, expressing despondency and tales of loneliness, bad luck or betrayal. Touring "country blues" artists like W. C. Handy were popular before World War I. Later singers like Sonny Boy Williamson added sophistication to the style and female stars of the 1920s and 30s including Ma Rainey and Bessie Smith sang the blues with small jazz groups.

Musicians, such as Louis Armstrong, incorporated the harmonic sequence of the blues as a favourite basis for jazz improvisation. Blues made a similar contribution to popular music, when after World War II urban blacks revived the classic style and created rhythm-and-blues, the forerunner of rock and soul.

Bolden, Buddy (fl. 1895–1907).

US jazz musician and cornet player. He was the original "King" of New Orleans jazz, a legend in his time who left no recordings of his work and who died in a psychiatric hospital.

Boogie/Boogie Woogie.

The jazz style by which blues was best played on piano. Over a consistently repeated bass motif, a melody is played with great swing to avoid monotony. The music was popular in the 1920s, mainly in bars where the heavy bass, hard and forceful sounds matched the surroundings and atmosphere. The name was coined by pianist and composer Clarence "Pinetop" Smith in his *Pinetop's Boogie Woogie*.

Bowie, David (1947–   ).

British pop singer, born David Jones, who reached 1970s' stardom by fusing "progressive" pop music with sexual ambiguity and bizarre theatricality, as in the creation of *Ziggy Stardust* (1972).

Brubeck, Dave (1920–   ).

US "modern jazz" pianist and composer, born David Warren, who formed the Dave Brubeck Quartet in 1951, winning considerable acclaim and lasting international popularity. His most famous number is *Take Five* but other material includes cantatas and orchestral works.

Bubble Gum.

Pop music, rock in its most commercialised

form, produced from the late 1960s for the sub-teen audience and record-buying public. Artists and material include the 1910 Fruitgum Company, Ohio Express with *Yummy, Yummy, Yummy*, the Osmonds, the Archies, the Monkees, and David Cassidy. Also called Teenybop music.

Calypso.

West Indian folk-song style, originally sung by African slaves on the plantations. Highly rhythmic, hypnotic, and with strong lyrics, the traditional calypso is a major ingredient of the present-day reggae style. A watered-down commercial version of the calypso was popular with 1950s' white audiences in Britain.

Carmichael, Hoagy (1910–1982).

US composer of popular music, often adopted by jazz artists. Songs include *Georgia on My Mind*, *Lazy River*, and *Riverboat Shuffle*.

Chicago, Illinois.

The jazz capital moved from New Orleans (*q.v.*) to Chicago, the home of many illustrious musicians between World War I and the Depression. Here jazz evolved and found imitators among white artists such as Bix Beiderbecke, whose music was called the Chicago Style. Black musicians followed their people to northern cities in search of work, and found jobs in "speak easies" of the prohibition era. Jazz changed to meet the demands of white audiences, stars emerged like King Oliver and Louis Armstrong, and white musicians tried hard to re-create the jazz sound.

In Chicago jazz toughened up, it took in new sounds such as the saxophone, and a new emphasis on the clarinet. The city also saw the 1920s' development of the blues into boogie woogie.

Clapton, Eric (1945–).

British rock guitarist, much admired since the late 1960s. He played with Cream (1966–8) and Derek and the Dominoes, and his records include *Wheels of Fire* (1968) and *Layla* (1970).

Coleman, Ornette (1930–).

US jazz musician, alto saxophonist, and composer. A great name in "modern jazz", he developed a controversial, original style, ignoring chords to play free melodic lines.

Coltrane, John William (1926–67).

US jazz saxophonist. One of the leading innovators in the 1950s and 60s, he was an outstanding musician, played with Coleman, Gillespie, and Davis.

Country and Western.

Popular music originally associated with rural white "hillbilly" communities in the mountainous areas of south-eastern USA. Based on European folk music, this was the music of America's frontier, borrowing from Negro blues and attaining a particular identity in each locality. Popularised nationwide through records and the radio from the 1920s, and by travelling artists like Woody Guthrie, country music absorbed other influences, including the "cowboy" music of America's south-west. Country and western was thus born, less folksy but still featuring sentimental lyrics and instrumental accompaniment on banjo, guitar, or fiddle. Nashville, Tennessee, is the capital of country and western, which has become a great commercial success.

Rock'n'roll of the mid-1950s derived from a blending of country and western with rhythm-and-blues, and like country the new style appealed mainly to white audiences. Country and western was eclipsed for several years, but a revival in the 1960s brought success to Glen Campbell, Roger Miller, George Hamilton IV, and other artists, many of whom produced a new "up town" commercialised country and western sound, popular music using country instruments and styles.

Crooning.

The singing style of male and female popular vocalists in the 1930s and 1940s. Coined in America, the term referred to songs sung in a low, smooth voice. The crooners included Rosemary Clooney, Perry Como, Bing Crosby, Doris Day, Peggy Lee, Dean Martin, and Frank Sinatra, and in Britain Al Bowley before the War and later Vera Lynn.

Crosby, (Harry Lillis) Bing (1904–77).

US pop singer and actor. One of the most successful crooners, with big bands, on records and in films from *c*. 1930. He won an Academy Award (1942) and his *White Christmas* is the world's best selling record of all time.

Dance.

Most dances of this century, apart from folk, old time, and classical ballroom routines, are accompanied by jazz-based music, and most rock and popular music is designed for dancing. This reflects the Afro-American tradition where music and dancing are but two facets of the same art.

The cakewalk, performed by southern blacks at the turn of the century, was adapted to produce the Charleston of 1920s, popular with whites as well as blacks and typifying the "Jazz Age". A similar dance was the Black Bottom, demonstrated by Ann Pennington in the film *Scandals of 1926*. These routines were forerunners of the jitterbug, often called the Lindy Hop by blacks, which involved complex acrobatics, twisting, and whirling. Although anti-social in crowded dance halls, it was the favourite dance of jazz fans in the 1940s and 1950s. A more restrained version adopted by rock'n'rollers was the jive. Ballroom dancers borrowed jazz styles, and had their own fashions for the tango, fox-trot, quick step, etc., which they danced to jazz-influenced popular music and swing. In the 1940s there was a new Latin-American flavour, and a four-four rhythm which were incorporated in the mambo, and for the 1950s, the Cha-Cha.

These styles allowed the dancers to improvise, as did the jive which could be danced in pairs or solo. From the early 1960s solo dancing, "doing one's own thing", became more and more the norm, as fashion passed through the twist, the shuffle, the hustle, and the bump of today's disco dancing.

Davis, Miles (1926–).

US jazz trumpeter, who helped develop bebop in the 1940s, and was later known for an introspective style, his fine recordings with small groups, and a blending of rock with jazz. He is considered one of the most influential "modern jazz" musicians.

Detroit, *see* Motown.

Disc.

Popular name for the gramophone record, which is a grooved vinyl pressing containing recorded sound. The lateral disc dates from 1887, and the 78 r.p.m. shellac record from 1900, but the music industry was revolutionised by the introduction of 33 r.p.m. vinyl discs in 1948. Stereophonic sound followed in 1956, and quadrophonic about 1970. The record industry is not only the vehicle of popular music, but also the determinant of its trends and fashions.

Disco.

Discotheques—from the French *disc* (record) and *bibliotheque* (library)—are the late 1970s' entertainment sensation, the venue for a dancing craze unparalleled since the 1920s and 30s. The music is heavy soul on record, a hypnotic, almost computerised sound not easily created live, and the accent is on decor and special effects, mirrors, lasers, films, etc., to create extravagant environments.

The roots go back to youth club dance sessions of the 1960s mod era, then came mobile discos in parties, pubs, and then clubs, the disc jockey emerged as a distinct ingredient in the disco experience, much live rock music became less geared to dancing, and audiences (especially on the Northern Soul scene) rediscovered old recordings of r.-&-b., soul, and rock'n'roll. The final boost was given by films like *Thank God It's Friday, Car Wash*, and *Saturday Night Fever*. Discos in London and New York are now big business. They range from back room bars to slick, sophisticated establishments like the famous Studio 54 in New York. All depend on high-powered electronic equipment and the DJ with an endless supply of records—whether soul, reggae, or fashionable novelties like disco arrangements of 1940s swing and Broadway musical numbers. The dance routines change rapidly with fashion, some echo old ballroom classics, others break new ground—*e.g.* disco on roller skates. Whatever the style, the music is a solid wave of pounding sound, with an accent on the melody, simple lyrics, beat, and rhythm.

Dixieland.

The term refers to the jazz style, born in New Orleans in the 1900s and made famous across America by the 1920s (*see* Jazz). But the Dixieland label often indicates the white version of New Orleans jazz, as produced by Nick La Rocca's Original Dixieland Jazz Band and others, popular among fashionable whites of the "Jazz Age" and immortalised by Scott Fitzgerald. The first "jazz" to be recorded was in fact white Dixieland played by the Original Dixieland Jazz Band in 1917.

Domino, (Antoine) Fats (1928–).

US pianist, composer, and singer of rhythm-and-blues. His record sales of 23 million copies between 1949 and 1960 were exceeded only by Elvis Presley and the Beatles.

Dorsey, Jimmy (1904–57) and Tommy (1905–56).

US musicians and bandleaders. The brothers formed two of the most successful big bands, joining together in 1953 for the Fabulous Dorseys Big Band.

Dylan, Bob (1941–).

US singer, guitarist, pianist, and composer, born Robert Zimmerman. Among the most creative and influential rock performers and writers, he helped originate folk rock, with songs like *Blowin' in the Wind* and *Times They are a Changin'*, but his work ranges over a wide field. A cult figure in the 1960s for the generation of civil rights marchers and anti-war protesters, he became a legend in his lifetime. His music also includes *Just Like a Woman, Like a Rolling Stone, Lay Lady Lay*, and the albums *Nashville Skyline* and *John Wesley Harding*.

Ellington, (Edward Kennedy) Duke (1899–1974).

US jazz pianist, composer, and bandleader from 1918. In the forefront of the jazz scene until his death, as a writer, arranger, and performer, Ellington produced the best in big-band jazz, the finest orchestrations of the blues, as well as classic songs (*e.g. Mood Indigo, I Got it Bad*) and piano suites.

Fitzgerald, Ella (1918–).

US jazz singer, famous for a smooth and relaxed style. Her repertoire ranges through jazz, pop, blues, and jazz versions of old masters.

Folk.

The traditional music of a particular community, ethnic or national culture, usually songs of uncertain origin, open to variation and improvisation, but expressing usually the history of a people or customs of that people. After World War II, folk became fashionable, as many sought alternatives to materialism and technology. Folk music itself, however, also became big business (*see* **Country and Western**).

Folk has often been incorporated into "classical" compositions, as by Bartók, Britten, Grieg, and Dvořák, and in the 1950s American "country" folk was blended with music of the black folk tradition to produce rock'n'roll. In the 1960s rock composers, such as Bob Dylan, adopted folk and incorporated it into "progressive" rock.

Folk Rock.

An aspect of the increasingly sophisticated rock music in the 1960s, created by Bob Dylan (*q.v.*) and others out of the then folk revival. A product of white artists, folk rock remixed folk with blues, producing a softer, less strident sound of folk-style melodies and lyrics over a rock beat. Dylan, The Byrds, Peter Paul and Mary, Joan Baez, and Donovan in Britain were practitioners of the style.

Gershwin, George (1898–1937).

US composer of orchestral works, stage shows such as *Porgy and Bess* (1935) and *Lady Be Good* (1924), and many popular songs, for which his brother Ira wrote lyrics. Among mainstream composers he was one of the first to absorb jazz, as in the immortal *Rhapsody in Blue* (1923), originally for piano and jazz band but later orchestrated. *The Man I Love, I Got Rhythm* (1930), *Let's Call the Whole Thing Off*, and *They Can't Take That Away from Me* are among the most memorable songs.

Getz, Stan (1927–).

US jazz saxophonist. He played with Woody Herman in the 1940s, then formed his own group. He managed to win wide popularity whilst remaining a creative stylist.

Gillespie, (John Birks) Dizzy (1917–).

US jazz trumpeter and big-band leader. With Charlie Parker, he created bebop in the 1940s, his arrangements bearing much influence on other musicians.

Goodman, Benny (1909–).

US jazz clarinettist and big-band leader, from 1934. One of the great white jazz artists, he developed swing, achieving enormous commercial success and popularity. A sign of the times, his band of white players got better bookings and greater publicity than the best black bands. Goodman's work relied on arrangements supplied by black musicians such as Fletcher Henderson, and the best was produced in the small jazz groups in which Goodman mixed black and white players.

Gospel.

Often called "Negro Spirituals", this is Afro-American vocal church music. It draws from the African musical tradition of a five-note scale and retains the "call and response" verse pattern, but gospel evolved when slaves, taught to sing hymns of European style and harmonies, fused the new with their old traditions. Gospel songs reflect not only religious faith but also the protest of black Americans as slaves, *e.g. Go Down Moses*. The Bible provides the symbols for an oppressed people. Gospel continues in black churches, and developed in secular form as blues and soul.

Guthrie, Woody (1912–67).

US folk singer, most popular of the white country artists in the 1930s and 40s, and famous for his concert tours as well as records. Songs include the Dust Bowl ballads, and *This Land is My Land*. Bob Dylan is his most illustrious disciple.

Hampton, Lionel (1913–).

US jazz vibraphonist, drummer, and bandleader. One of the great black artists who played with Benny Goodman (1936–40) and later led his own band and small groups.

Hard Rock.

An element of the sophisticated "progressive" music, developed since the 1960s. This rock music features strongly emphasised beat, hyper-amplification, electronic effects, an absence of sweet sounding melodies. Leading performers in this style included Cream and Led Zeppelin.

Holliday, Billie "Lady Day" (b. 1915).

US jazz and blues singer, well known from the mid-1930s for her work on stage and record with Teddy Wilson, Count Basie, and Artie Shaw. Her tragic life was later immortalised in the film *Lady Sings the Blues* (1972).

Honky Tonk.

This was the slang name originally given to music of New Orleans' black night spots of the 1900s. Often of ill-repute, they featured piano, dancing, and a back room for girls.

Hooker, John Lee (1915–   ).

US blues singer, well known from 1949 as an exponent of old time blues which he sang whilst accompanying himself on electric guitar. The style was strongly dramatic, and the swing forceful.

Jazz.

Jazz is the late 19th-cent. creation of black Americans, originally the music of African slaves (*see* **Gospel** and **Blues**), which provided "blue notes", antiphony, emotional strength, and the twelve-bar blues set, synthesised with ragtime (*q.v.*) beat and melody, and using brass instruments as in the traditional marching bands of America's southern blacks. Into this black creation was also mixed aspects of European folk music, and white America's popular songs.

The new sound, spreading from New Orleans (*q.v.*), was fresh, melodic, rhythmic (usually four beats to the bar), and emotional. Essentially it is firstly an art of performance, a style of playing or singing rather than a formal composition, though the best jazz comes from accomplished writers like Jelly Roll Morton, Duke Ellington, or Charlie Mingus more recently. They provide a structure, but the style, emphasis, and nuances depend on the performer. Secondly, jazz relies on improvisation, the spontaneity, and freshness of each performance. Thirdly, the music is melodic. Fourthly, jazz adapts vocal techniques to brass and reed instruments, so that they convey the inflexions and contrasts of the human voice. Fifthly, jazz provided a musical response to social changes and economic pressures of the day.

New Orleans from the 1890s produced jazz, embracing ragtime, the later work of "classic blues" artists like Ma Rainey and Bessie Smith, and Dixieland (*q.v.*) as the first white spin off. The music was spread via riverboat and railway by blacks seeking jobs in northern cities. After 1917 Chicago, Kansas City (*qq.v.*), and New York became centres of a "jazz age", when King Oliver and Louis Armstrong won fame and fortune. As soloists and bandleaders, they represented the best in jazz, imitated and commercialised by others as popular entertainment for a growing and increasingly white audience. More and more white musicians (like Bix Beiderbecke, Artie Shaw, and Benny Goodman) adopted jazz, and in the Depression of the early 1930s many jazz musicians joined dance bands. Popular music thus absorbed jazz, and big bands—black and white—produced swing (*q.v.*).

By then New York big business had cashed in on jazz, producing a commercial network of records, concerts, films, dance halls, and clubs. White society cashed in on black music, so that white impresarios, bands, and artists got the best bookings and most success. But from Broadway to Harlem, jazz musicians made a living. In the 1940s some blacks including Charlie Parker, Dizzy Gillespie, and Miles Davis, tired of watered down and "arranged" jazz, developed a more sophisticated bebop (*q.v.*) style.

After World War II, jazz divided into two. The revivalist trend originated on America's West Coast, where oldtime New Orleans performers (like Bunk Johnson and George Lewis) were rediscovered, classic recordings reissued, and almost-forgotten numbers recorded. The craze spread even to Britain where the "trad" bands of Humphrey Lyttleton, Chris Barber, and others enjoyed tremendous following until the early 1960s.

"Modern jazz" was the rival trend, developed out of bebop, pioneered by the Miles Davis Group in 1948, using greater improvisation and unorthodox instrumentation (*e.g.* flute, cello, and oboe) and moving the emphasis away from declaration to understatement—from "hot" to "cool". Stan Getz, Stan Kenton, Dave Brubeck, and Gerry Mulligan, mainly West Coasters and many of them white, belonged to this trend. The work of Davis, John Coltrane, and Ornette Coleman, superb in experimentation, stressed consciousness, pride, and the roots of black music. In this jazz linked back to developments in blues, soul, and pop music.

The popularity of jazz, however, decreased in the 1960s, as it became more complex, more expressive, but more an art form than a popular accompaniment for dancing. Nonetheless Jazz is *the* music of the 20th cent., an influence on "classical" composers like Ravel on the one hand, and on the other the vital ingredient of popular music and rock, the pre-eminent form and vehicle of big business-orientated mass culture in western society.

Jesus Rock.

Late 1960s' rock music, adopting Biblical themes. Many songs and full musicals especially *Jesus Christ Superstar* and *Godspell*, attained international success.

John (Reginald Dwight) Elton (1947–   ).

British rock singer, pianist, and composer of numerous songs (lyrics by Bernie Taupin), which won world-wide acclaim and sold millions of records. Albums include *Elton John* (1970), *Goodbye Yellow Brick Road* (1973), *Rock of the Westies* (1975), and *Blue Moves* (1976).

Jolson, Al (1886–1950).

US singer and comedian in vaudeville and Broadway. He is best known for his blacked-up "minstrel" style, as filmed in *The Jazz Singer* (1927), the first talking movie, and for songs like *Swanee* and *Mammy*.

Joplin, Scott (1868–1917).

US composer and pianist, principal exponent of ragtime (*q.v.*). His music became popular again in the 1970s.

Kansas City, Missouri.

One of the 1920s centres of jazz. This was a time when the city authorities were corrupt; gambling and nightlife thrived, creating a mecca for jazz musicians. The distinctive characteristics of Kansas City jazz were firstly the continuously repeated "riff" (a one- or two-bar phrase), either backing a soloist or to build up excitement, and secondly the chase chorus, in which two soloists alternated. Performers included Bennie Moten's Kansas City Orchestra, and Count Basie started here.

Kenton, (Stanley Newcomb) Stan (1912–79).

US jazz musician, composer, and bandleader from 1941. Well known for his theme *Artistry in Rhythm* (1945) and for his patronage of other musicians.

Kern, Jerome (1885–1945).

US songwriter and composer for stage musicals. His work includes *Sally* (1920) and *Showboat* (1927) and songs like *Smoke Gets in Your Eyes* and *Ol' Man River*.

King, Carole (1942–).

US songwriter and singer, born Carole Klein. She and her then husband Gerry Goffin wrote some of the best 1960s' pop songs, *e.g. Up on the Roof*, and *It Might as Well Rain Until September*. Her album *Tapestry* (1971) sold more than 10m copies.

Liverpool, *see* **Merseybeat.**

Marley, Bob (1946–1981).

Jamaican musician and singer. With his group The Wailers, he is the best-known reggae (*q.v.*) artist. Died of cancer May 1981.

Memphis, Tennessee.

The base for Stax/Atlantic records which in the 1960s produced a distinctive heavy soul (*q.v.*) sound, *e.g.* records by Otis Reading, Sam and Dave.

Merseybeat.

A generalisation, relating to Liverpool artists, principally The Beatles, who dominated early 1960s' rock. White performers from a British culture created a new hybrid out of black Americans' rhythm-and-blues. Other British musicians, not from Liverpool, like the Rolling Stones, The Animals, and The Who, continued this development.

Miller, (Alton) Glenn (1905–44).

US jazz trombonist and leader of the most popular dance band of World War II and of all time. His "swing" sounds were distinctively reedy, and his theme tune *Moonlight Serenade* (1939) is immortal.

Mingus, Charles (1922–).

Us jazz composer, bass player, and bandleader from the 1950s. His "modern jazz" experiments with atonal sounds and impressionism produced work like *The Black Saint* and *The Sinner Lady* (1963).

Minstrel.

A mediaeval term, referring to itinerant musicians and professional entertainers, it was applied in this century to white singers and banjo players who blacked their faces and mimicked aspects of Afro-American music.

Mod.

The term refers to an early 1960s' cult among young people in Britain, which involved particular fashions in music as well as clothes, transport, etc. A mod revival in the late 1970s, a reaction against punk (*q.v.*), brought a new interest in simple rhythm-and-blues.

Morton, Jelly Roll (1885–1941).

US jazz pianist, composer, and bandleader, born Ferdinand Joseph La Menthe. A pioneer of New Orleans jazz, with Creole origins, he began recording in 1923 with a group called Morton's Red Hot Peppers.

Motown.

The term refers to Detroit, the base for Tamla Motown records which developed and produced the most successful 1960s soul (*q.v.*), by Stevie Wonder, The Supremes, The Four Tops, The Temptations, Smokey Robinson and the Miracles.

Musicals.

The theatrical vehicle for popular music, songs, and dancing, developed in the late 19th cent. from the best in light opera, review, and music hall. Devised in London's West End and on Broadway, New York, musicals were later adapted or specially written for the cinema. The style dates from London's *In Town* (1892), but the best work came from Broadway, written by George Gershwin, Cole Porter, Jerome Kern, Rodgers and Hart, Rodgers and Hammerstein, Lerner and Lowe, Jule Styne, and Stephen Sondheim.

For Hollywood, Busby Berkeley shared responsibility for classic 1930s' musical films like *Forty Second Street* (1933), and Stanley Donen achieved near perfection wtih *Singin' in the Rain* (1952).

In Britain, Ivor Novello and Noel Coward were the leading lights. More recent musicals from Britain include Lionel Bart's *Oliver* (1960), and Tim Rice and Andrew Lloyd Webber's *Jesus Christ Superstar* and *Evita*.

In America the recent best includes Leonard Bernstein's *West Side Story* (1957), also *Hair* (1967), *My Fair Lady* (1956), *Fiddler on the Roof* (1964), *Hello Dolly* (1964), and *Grease* (1972).

The musical content of these shows has reflected the fashions of the time. So jazz (in a watered down version) was absorbed in Broadway's heyday, and today's rather different musicals or "rock operas" present some of the best in pop.

Music Hall.

Known in the United States as vaudeville (or where striptease was involved, as burlesque), this was the theatrical medium for popular music and variety. A late Victorian and Edwardian phenomenon, music hall declined with the advent of the radio and cinema.

New Orleans, Louisiana.

Commonly acknowledged as the birthplace of jazz, although the same music could be heard elsewhere in the same years of the late 19th cent. However, New Orleans as a port had a bustling red light district, Storeyville, with bars and brothels where black musicians worked. The city's culture was also enriched by French influence and its Creole people, and this was reflected in jazz. The legalised brothels were closed down in 1917, and the jazz scene moved north.

Northern Soul.

A phenomenon of the British pop scene after the late 1960s, its success owing nothing to music industry manipulation but contributing in time to the growth of disco (*q.v.*). Young people in Northern England wanted to dance, rejected "progressive" rock, and in their clubs and dance halls created big hits out of the most obscure recordings of American rhythm-and-blues and early soul (*qq.v.*). The dancing craze, skilful, acrobatic, and featuring all-night and all-day marathons, produced new fashions in clothes and music, which the record industry sought to exploit. Eventually the fans drifted back to mainstream soul.

Oliver, (Joseph) King (1885–1938).

US jazz cornettist, composer, and pioneer jazz-band leader. With his Creole Jazz Band (1922), he launched the career of Louis Armstrong.

Parker, (Charles Christopher) Charlie "Bird" (1920–55).

US jazz alto sax player. He recorded with Dizzy Gillespie in the 1940s, and their work in producing bebop (*q.v.*) opened up new harmonic and rhythmic possibilities for musicians.

Pink Floyd.

British pop group of the 1960s psychedelic era of "underground" (q.v.) culture, drug taking, multi-media experiments, and light shows. Starting with rhythm-and-blues, Pink Floyd later produced complex symphonic music using electronic effects.

Pop Music.

The term coined in the early 1950s indicates a development from popular music to a distinct musical medium for the age of consumerism and "Never Had It So Good", an age of big-business record promotion, radio, television, and advertising, when young people had money to spend. Pop is the music of mass culture, created and marketed to reach most people who are not themselves involved in its creation but merely absorb it.

Porter, Cole (1892–1964).

US composer and songwriter. His work for stage and film musicals included *Gay Divorcee* (1932), *Anything Goes* (1934), *Kiss Me Kate* (1948), and *High Society* (1956).

Presley, Elvis (1935–77).

US pop singer, pre-eminent in rock'n'roll (q.v.) from 1953 to 1963, and still "The King" when he died. His music fused blues with country and folk, he had an assured vocal technique, and his records sold over 28m. The first white artist to reproduce the wildness of black music, he was condemned by the Establishment for his sexy delivery and pelvic gyrations. *Jailhouse Rock*, *Hound Dog*, *Heartbreak Hotel*, and *Love Me Tender* were his most successful songs, and of his many films *Flaming Star* (1960) brought out his best performance.

Punk.

The rebel cult of 1976–8 among young people in Britain, originally whites in deprived urban areas. Musically, punk meant a return to primitive rock, but with more cacophony, obscenities, and angry themes. The Sex Pistols became stars but shocked society.

Ragtime.

Syncopated piano music, a forerunner of jazz, most popular in the 1890s and 1900s and revived in the 1970s. Outside the mainstream of Afro-American music, ragtime belonged to the tradition of Minstrel shows, "coon" songs, and blacks playing to white audiences. Formal in structure rather than open to improvisation, the best rags were written by Scott Joplin (q.v.), e.g. original rags (1899), *Maple Leaf Rag* (1900), and *The Entertainer* (1902).

Reggae.

West Indian pop music, originally played on makeshift instruments and associated with Jamaica's Rastafarian sect, but increasingly popular in Britain in the 1970s. The music borrows from the calypso and rhythm-and-blues (qq.v.), and is related to other West Indian forms like blue beat, ska, and rock steady. Reggae puts a blend of folk and rock against a hypnotically repetitive beat, with a strong bass and a between-beat type of drumming. Since the early successes of Millie Small, Desmond Decker, and Bob Marley, innumerable reggae artists have become prominent, and many performers from other traditions have added reggae flavour to their material.

Reinhardt, (Jean Baptiste) Django (1910–53).

Belgian jazz guitarist. Representative of the best of European musicians who took up jazz, this gypsy added folk to jazz and developed guitar improvisation. In the 1930s he formed a jazz quintent with violinist Stephane Grappelli.

Rhythm-and-Blues.

Pop music developed by America's urban blacks, out of blues and swing (qq.v.), after World War II. Its exponents adopted pianos, saxophone, drums, and later electric guitars to supplement traditional instruments, and produced a more insistent rhythm as in jazz. A raw, energetic, but simple music, r-&-b was the basis of the rock revolution from rock'n'roll, to more sophisticated soul (qq.v.), and much in British pop of the 1960s. The best performers from early days included Howlin' Wolf, John Lee Hooker, Ray Charles, Chuck Berry, and Fats Domino, black artists often "covered" on record by white stars.

Richard, Cliff (1940–).

British pop singer, born Harold Webb. Well acclaimed by 1959 with *Living Doll*, a million-selling disc, he remains at the top of his profession, though latterly more of a family entertainer than a wild rock artist.

Rock'n'Roll/rock.

The dominant pop music trend since 1954. Bill Haley and the Comets' *Rock Around the Clock* (1955) established rock'n'roll as an international sensation appealing to white audiences who found rock's forerunner, black rhythm-and-blues (q.v.) too raw and inaccessible. The music belonged to black America, hit songs by whites often originating with black artists, but rock'n'roll incorporated aspects of country music to give it mass appeal. Its image, created in the film *Blackboard Jungle* (1955), was that of rebellion and overt sexuality. Gene Vincent's *Be Bop a Lula* and the Jerry Lee Lewis–Elvis Presley style gave teenagers a chance to let off steam.

The term rock'n'roll, coined by disc jockey Alan Freed, in time became plain rock, still characterised by amplified guitars, driving rhythm, and a vocal lead but taking in new fashions and reflecting social and political concerns.

The early 1960s were dominated by the Beatles and Rolling Stones, with their British-style r-&-b (q.v.). From America came surf sounds, soul, Phil Spector, and most especially folk rock (qq.v.), as produced by Bob Dylan, an intelligent rock associated with social consciousness and protest. 1960s material, by the Beatles, Dylan, or others, was often softer and usually more subtle in lyrics and music than the old rock'n'roll. Eric Clapton and Jimi Hendrix revamped the blues (q.v.).

Drug taking among artists led to considerable experimentation and a vogue for mind-expanding and psychedelic music (e.g. Pink Floyd). This "underground" produced acid rock, hard rock (qq.v.) and progressive pop, all of which involved improvisation and proved less and less suitable for dancing. Like folk rock, this music was "intellectual" in its anti-war and anti-establishment themes.

After Beatlemania, United States trend-setting was no longer assured, and constant interplay between British and American artists has occurred. The 1970s has seen a free-for-all of passing fashions and competing fads, but with a basic diet of mindless commercial pop, as a reaction against heavy rock.

Rock Steady.

West Indian pop music style, a forerunner of reggae (q.v.).

Rodgers, Jimmie (1897–1933).

US country singer, guitarist, and songwriter. He stands first in the Country Music Hall of Fame.

Rodgers and Hammerstein.

Richard Charles Rodgers (1902–80) and Oscar Hammerstein II wrote many successful musicals (q.v.), including *Oklahoma* (1943), *Carousel* (1945),

South Pacific (1949), *The King and I* (1951), and *The Sound of Music* (1959). *Oh, What a Beautiful Morning, Surrey With A Fringe on Top, Some Enchanted Evening, Getting to Know You, Shall We Dance, Edelweiss,* and *My Favourite Things* are among their most memorable songs. Rodgers previously partnered Lorenz Hart.

Rolling Stones.

British rock group of 1960s and 1970s, originally Mick Jagger, Charlie Watts, Bill Wyman, Keith Richard, and Brian Jones (d. 1969). Less wholesome in image than the Beatles, the Stones' rhythm-and-blues-based music was loud, angry, sexual, and aggressive, often expressing young people's fantasies and frustrations, *e.g. I Can't Get No Satisfaction* (1965), *Paint it Black* (1966), and *Little Red Rooster* (1963).

Simon, Paul (1942–   ).

US songwriter and singer, famous as part of the Simon and Garfunkel duo (with Art Garfunkel) in the 1960s, who were among the most successful recording artists. Simon's work is mainly smooth, folksy rock but more recently has jazz or reggae flavours. The best material includes *Sounds of Silence* (1966), *Bridge Over Troubled Water* (1970), and *America.*

Sinatra, (Francis Albert) Frank (1915–   ).

US pop singer and film actor. From his work with Tommy Dorsey's big band in the 1940s, Sinatra achieved enormous acclaim, becoming an idol for young people.

Skiffle.

A form of jazz, originally the music of so-called "spasm bands", in 1920s' America. These were small groups of black musicians in deprived areas, using makeshift instruments and domestic utensils, such as washboards and jugs. A British version evolved after World War II, reaching great popularity 1956–8 in work by Lonnie Donegan, Johnny Duncan, and Ken Colyer.

Smith, Bessie (*c.* 1895–1937).

US blues and jazz singer. Starting to record in 1928, she reached peak popularity between 1924 and the Depression. Her mournful style and powerful renderings, mostly about men, money, and drink, became part of jazz history.

Sondheim, Stephen.

US lyricist for musicals, including *West Side Story, Company,* and *A Little Night Music.*

Songwriters.

See Burt Bacharach, Beatles (for John Lennon and Paul McCartney), Irving Berlin, Chuck Berry, David Bowie, Hoagy Carmichael, Bob Dylan, George (and Ira) Gershwin, Woody Guthrie, Elton John, Jerome Kern, Carole King, Musicals, Cole Porter, Paul Simon, Stephen Sondheim.

The list includes some, but by no means all the best composers of 20th-cent. popular songs. Many of the great jazz writers and other specialists are excluded, as are notable Britons, *vis.* Ivor Novello (1893–1951), actor, playwright, and composer for *Glamorous Night* (1935), *Careless Rapture* (1936), and *The Dancing Years* (1939); also Lionel Bart (*Oliver*), Rice and Lloyd Webber (*Evita*).

The list also neglects the early American songwriting teams of Bud de Sylva, Lew Brown and Ray Henderson (*Black Bottom, Birth of the Blues, The Best Things in Life are Free, Together, Sonny Boy,* and *Seventh Heaven,* 1920s); Al Dubin and Harry Warren (*Forty Second Street, We're in the Money, Lullaby of Broadway,* and *September in the Rain,* 1930s); also Sammy Kahn (*Bye Bye Black-bird*).

Soul.

Black American pop music, derived from gospel blended with rhythm-and-blues (*qq.v.*) in the 1960s. Sophisticated sound depending on multitracking, electronic mixing, etc., soul was mass marketed by Tamla Motown in Detroit and as Memphis Sound by Stax/Atlantic. Its worldwide popularity ensured for black artists a large, lucrative, and vital share in mainstream pop. Soul singers include Ray Charles, James Brown, the Righteous Brothers, the Supremes, and others.

Spector, Phil (1940–   ).

US record company executive, producer, and songwriter. He created the early 1960s multitracked wall of sound for The Crystals (*He's a Rebel* (1962), *Da Doo Ron Ron, And Then I Kissed Him*), The Ronettes (*Baby I love You, Be My Baby,* 1963), and the Righteous Brothers (*You've Lost That Lovin' Feelin',* 1965).

Surf Sound.

Rock music of the early 1960s, associated with West Coast surf riding, popularised most by the Beach Boys (*q.v.*) and featuring melodies of traditional ballads (rather than blues) and more complex chord progressions than early rock. Other songs not on surfing themes continued to use the surfing beat.

Swing.

The popular dance music style of the 1930s and 1940s, the days after prohibition in America when the Depression relaxed and a time of dancing fever. Featuring the four even beats to the bar of New Orleans music and the characteristic riffs of Kansas City (*qq.v.*) jazz, popularised in New York by Count Basie, the music was developed as a new commercialised jazz by the big bands. Benny Goodman's success was followed by that of Artie Shaw, Tommy Dorsey, and others, all white bands. Duke Ellington and Basie, though successful, had nothing like the same popularity or the same financial rewards.

Tamla Motown, *see* Motown.

Like *Bubble Gum* (*q.v.*), pop music produced and marketed for the sub-teen audience. The Monkees (1967) were the first artists created and promoted by TV for this audience.

Underground.

Pop Music (*e.g.* early Pink Floyd) associated with the counter-culture arts movement in the US and Britain in the 1960s, when many artists, film makers, actors, and writers rejected the conventional structure of artistic success and used their work to advocate such things as revolution, anarchy, and drug taking.

Waller, (Thomas) Fats (1904–43).

US jazz and blues pianist and composer. He was a great showman and comedian, but also wrote hit songs like *Honeysuckle Rose* and *Aint Misbehavin'.*

West Coast Sound.

The soft rock of Crosby, Stills, Nash, and Young, Buffalo Springfield, The Byrds, Joni Mitchell, and the Eagles. Owing much to Bob Dylan but also to the Beach Boys' surfing sounds, the music features close harmony voices, proficient guitar playing, and lyrics which are often about protest, peace, and justice.

The Who.

British rock group, pre-eminent among "mod" groups in the mid-1960s but consistently popular ever since. Their best work includes *My Generation* (1965), *Substitute* (1966), the rock opera *Tommy* (1968), and *Quadrophenia* (1974).

INSTRUMENTS OF THE ORCHESTRA

INTRODUCTION

This article deals with all those instruments which have a regular place in the orchestra. It also deals with two keyboard instruments, the piano and organ, which are not regular members of the orchestra but which are often invited to join the orchestra as solo instruments. Other instruments which play in bands are also briefly discussed. They have evolved over a period of a few centuries after much experiment and many blind alleys and are still in the process of development. For example, violins have been made of leather or with a horn through the neck to throw out more sound. Many instruments, such as the lute, have been superseded by others, although nowadays there is interest in reviving and improving some of these instruments. Works of the time of Bach and Handel were written for instruments unlike those that are used to play them nowadays and some musicians are interested in the older versions of instruments such as the oboe and achieving the sounds that those composers intended.

The orchestra is not of a fixed size and generally speaking, the works of earlier composers such as Mozart require a far smaller orchestra than the works of Mahler or Strauss, for example. The string section of a large modern orchestra would typically have the following composition: 16 1st Violins, 16 2nd Violins, 12 Violas, 12 Cellos and 8 Double Basses. The woodwind section would contain 1 Piccolo, 3 Flutes, 3 Oboes, 1 Cor Anglais, 3 Bassoons and 3 Clarinets. The brass section might contain 8 Horns, 5 Trumpets, 3 Trombones and 2 Tubas and the percussion section 5 Timpani, a Bass Drum, Cymbals and various others. The strings sit closest to the conductor as their tone is less penetrating than the others. The woodwind sit behind the strings and behind them sit the powerful brass and percussion instruments. Of the players the leader of the first violins has an especially important role in interpreting the conductor's wishes and he is known as the leader of the orchestra. The compass (*i.e.* range of notes of each instrument) is set out in TABLE 1.

Theory of Sound.

Sound consists of vibrations which travel through the air. These vibrations can be detected by the human ear and are perceived as sound (**Q13**). The *loudness* of the sound is determined by the size of the vibrations and the *pitch*, how high or low a note

is, is determined by the *frequency, i.e.* the number of vibrations per second. When an instrument plays a note sounds of many frequencies are transmitted, all multiples of some particular frequency, called the *fundamental*. For example, when the oboe plays the A to which all the instruments tune it produces a fundamental of 440 vibrations per second, denoted 440 Hz, but in addition it produces tones of 2×440 Hz, 3×440 Hz, 4×440 Hz, etc. These extra tones are called the second, third and fourth harmonics, etc., respectively. Because different instruments produce these harmonics in different proportions they sound different even when playing a note of the same pitch and it is said they have different *timbres*. Another important reason why two instruments sound different is due to the way in which they begin a note, the short-lived overtones at the beginning, known as the *transient harmonics*. It has been shown that different instruments with similar timbres can sound different if the transient harmonics are different.

Transposing Instruments.

Many instruments are known as *transposing instruments* because they do not play the same note the player reads from the music. For example, when someone plays the note he reads as C from the music on the B♭ clarinet the actual pitch of the note played is B♭. The B♭ clarinet transposes the music the player reads down by one tone—hence the term transposing instrument. One reason for transposing instruments is that there is also an A clarinet, a semitone lower. When someone playing either the B♭ or the A clarinet reads the note C he presses the same set of keys. However on the B♭ clarinet the note played will be B♭ and on the A clarinet it will be A. If there were no transposition the player would have to remember a different set of fingerings on each clarinet. Because the piccolo is so high the music written for it is an octave lower than the notes played. As the change is an octave the piccolo is not normally called a transposing instrument.

TABLE 2 gives the *clefs* from which the music is read for the most important instruments. It also gives the transposition and a 1984 price, usually taken from one of Boosey and Hawkes cheaper ranges for each new instrument.

TABLE 1

Table 1 gives the compass of each instrument, that is the range of notes it can play. The full line down the centre is middle C on the piano. The dashed lines represent other C's, separated by octaves, above and below. The full compass can often only be achieved by an experienced player.

	CCCC	CCC	CC	C	Middle C	C¹	C²	C³	C⁴
Violin									
Viola									
Cello									
Double Bass									
Harp									
Piccolo									
Flute									
Clarinet B♭									
Oboe									
Cor Anglais									
Bassoon									
Double Bassoon									
Trumpet									
Horn									
Bass Tuba									
Tenor Trombone									
Bass Trombone									
Kettledrums									
Piano and Organ									
Harpsichord									
Soprano Voice									
Contralto Voice									
Tenor Voice									
Bass Voice									

TABLE 2: *Instruments and Musical Clefs*

Instrument	Clef	Transposition	Price £
Violin	Treble	None	80
Viola	Alto and Treble	None	120
Cello	Bass, Tenor and Treble	None	250
Double Bass	Bass and Tenor	An octave lower	400
Piccolo	Treble	An octave higher	200
Flute	Treble	None	150
Clarinet	Treble	A tone or minor third lower	170
Oboe	Treble	None	400
Cor Anglais	Treble	A fifth lower	
Bassoon	Bass and Tenor	None	1,750
Double bassoon	Bass	An octave lower	
B♭ Trumpet	Treble	None or a tone lower	200
Horn	Bass and Treble	A fifth or a tone lower	500
Trombones	Bass and Tenor	None	200
Tuba	Bass	None	600
Piano	Treble and Bass	None	1,000

THE VIOLIN FAMILY

The main stringed instruments belong to the violin family which consists of the violin, viola, cello and double bass. They are all similar in construction although the lower pitched instruments are much larger. They are usually played by drawing a bow across metal or gut strings which causes them to vibrate. The bow consists of horse hair stretched across a curved stick. Resin is rubbed on to the horse hair in order to enable it to grip the string and set it in vibration. The tension in the hair can be adjusted by turning a screw.

The vibrations of the string are transmitted by the bridge to the *belly* of the instrument which is the upper surface of a box with curved sides. The box has natural resonances of its own which depend on its size, shape, wood, etc. and it is designed so that no one note is more resonant than any other. It determines the quality of the tone of the instrument. The resonance of the violin is reduced by inserting a short stick called the sound post between the belly and the back. Very little sound is transferred directly to the air from the string because the surface area of the string is very small. So without the resonating box the violin would make little sound. The vibrating string causes the bridge to rock about an axis parallel to the strings. When a mute or any other solid object is placed on the bridge this makes the bridge heavier and less able to rock. The high frequency harmonics are most affected so muting a violin affects its tonal qualities and reduces its harmonic content giving a darker, less brilliant sound.

The player can play different notes by playing on one of the four different strings or by using the fingers of his left hand to shorten the vibrating part of the strings while he moves the bow with his right. Reducing the length of a string raises the frequency of vibration and hence the pitch of the note played. The strings are tuned by turning the *pegs* which alters their tension. The strings of the violin, viola and cello are tuned in fifths and the strings of the double bass are tuned in fourths (*i.e.* the next higher string of a double bass is the fourth note of a scale higher than the previous string). Members of this family can play more softly than any other instruments, the dynamic range being from almost nothing to about the loudness of the woodwind instruments. Unlike the wind instruments, they can play chords by bowing two or three strings simultaneously, known as *double* or *treble* stopping. A player can change the tone considerably by varying the speed of the bow, the pressure exerted by the bow, its position on the string and which part of the bow is used. These instruments can also be played by plucking the strings with the fingers, known as pizzicato. In the hands of a skilled performer the higher members of this family can perform feats of great musical agility.

These instruments developed *c.* 1550 out of the fidel and rebec and other instruments used for dancing to. Early violins were also used as a substitute for the human voice. The viols are a family of instruments similar to the violins but they are not really ancestors of the violins, although the double bass is similar to a large viol. Violin making reached its peak round about the time of Stradivari (1644–1737), the most famous of all violin makers (*see* **B57**). Stradivari violins are not however quite the same now as when they were made as they have been adapted to take the longer and higher tension strings which are used nowadays to produce a bigger sound.

The Harp.

The orchestral harp is not a regular member of the orchestra but makes an appearance occasionally. It stands over six feet high and its strings are stretched from the top of the frame down to a resonant sound board close to the player. It is played by plucking the strings with the fingers. It is tuned *diatonically*, which means that if a player runs his fingers across it he plays a scale, unlike some other harps which are tuned *chromatically*, that is a string for each semitone. Each string is capable of being made sharper by one or two semitones by means of seven pedals which can shorten the strings. Thus if one pedal is pressed to one position all the Cps are raised to C. If the same pedal is pressed further the Cs are raised to C♯. By using the pedals one can play a scale in any key one likes.

Primitive harps have existed since the beginning of mankind, along with the lyres, a different family of plucked instruments, to which the guitar belongs, with strings passing over a bridge. Harps existed in ancient Egypt, were heard by the Greeks and were popular in Europe in the Dark and Middle Ages. The harp described above is the double action pedal harp and was developed by Erard in about 1810.

The Guitar.

The guitar, along with the lute, mandolin and banjo is played by plucking the strings with the fingers and thumb of the right hand while the left hand controls the pitch. It is somewhat similar to the violin in shape but unlike the violin its belly and back are flat, not curved, and it has no soundpost between them. Unlike the violin it has *frets*, that is metal ribs on the finger board placed at intervals of a semitone. This means that the player does not have to judge the positions of the fingers of the left hand by ear and cannot play out of tune unless the strings are incorrectly tuned. It normally has six strings, tuned in fourths apart from one interval of a major third and is capable of playing chords. It was originally brought to Spain by the Moors in the Middle Ages and is often used as an accompaniment to the human voice. Quite a lot of serious music has been written for it and it is nowadays one of the most popular of all instruments.

THE WOODWIND INSTRUMENTS

The wind instruments make a sound by causing a column of air in a tube to vibrate. The woodwind instruments have holes in their sides and by opening and closing the right holes it is possible to play different notes. The holes are not always closed directly by the fingers but by *keys* with pads on them attached to a complicated set of levers, operated by the fingers.

The Flute Family.

The flute belongs to a family of instruments which is as old as mankind. Vibrations are caused by blowing air on to the edge of a hole in a tube. In the case of the orchestral flute, the player blows sideways to the length of the tube and by controlling the direction of the jet with his lips he can make fine alterations to the pitch of the note played. The whistles and recorders also belong to the flute family but here the player blows along the length of the tube through a funnel which directs the jet on to the edge. This means these instruments are easier to play than the flute but the pitch tends to rise as the player blows harder to make a louder sound. Since the recorder player cannot direct the jet he cannot control the pitch as the flute player can and he cannot avoid going out of tune when playing loud. This is one of the reasons why the flute has superseded the recorder. The flute is also louder and has a greater compass.

The modern flute is largely due to Boehm (c. 1793–1881) who invented the Boehm system of fingering, enlarged the holes and fitted them with keys and pads as they became too big to be closed by the fingers. The tube of the flute is not perfectly cylindrical, being slightly wider at the middle than at the ends. The piccolo is a small flute about an octave higher. The flute and piccolo are the most agile of the wind instruments. They are nowadays usually made of metal, unlike the other woodwind instruments which are usually made of wood.

The Clarinet.

The clarinet is known as a single reed instrument because attached to the mouthpiece is a single cane reed. When the player blows, air is forced between the reed and the mouthpiece into a hole in the mouthpiece. This causes the reed to beat against the mouthpiece and vibrations are set up in the air inside the clarinet. The frequency of these vibrations is controlled by the fingers operating the keys. The pitch can be made higher or lower by tightening or relaxing the lips for fine control. The clarinet has a cylindrical bore and behaves acoustically like a stopped pipe, which means that the odd harmonics are not present in its tone. It produces a rich, creamy tone but there are four different regions in its compass, each with a different tonal quality. It is capable of a greater variation in loudness and softness than any other woodwind instrument.

The clarinet is a relative newcomer to the orchestra, being little used until Mozart wrote outstanding parts for it. The B♭ clarinet is the one most used in the orchestra but the A clarinet is sometimes found. There are several other clarinets, some high, some lower in pitch, which are little used nowadays.

The Oboe Family.

The oboe is the highest member of the family of double reed instruments which also includes the cor anglais, basoon and double bassoon. The mouthpiece of these instruments, called the reed, consists of two cane reeds slightly apart bound round a small metal tube with a piece of cork round it. The player puts his lips round the two reeds which vibrate against each other when he blows, to produce vibrations in the air column. As in the case of the clarinet, the pitch is controlled by which keys are open and fine control of the pitch is achieved by tightening and relaxing the lips. The oboe has a conical bore with a bell at the bottom. While the flute player is apt to run out of breath on a long passage the oboist's problem is that the oboe requires very little breath and he cannot breathe out while playing.

The oboe is of ancient origin and was a very important instrument at the time of Bach and Handel and a lot of music was written for it then. Its tone is penetrating and reedy. The cor anglais, which is neither a horn nor English, is tuned a fifth below the oboe and has a pleasant horn-like tone. It is not often played but when it does appear, it is usually played by an oboist. The bassoon is two octaves in tone below the oboe and to achieve this low pitch a long tube is required which has to be bent back on itself to facilitate easy fingering. It is often used to supply comical effects. The double bassoon is an octave below the bassoon and is only occasionally used.

The Saxophone Family.

This family of instruments of varying size and pitch were invented by A. Sax in 1846 and although rarely found in an orchestra they are very popular in dance and other bands. The mouthpiece has a single reed and is very similar to that of a clarinet. The saxophone has keys like the woodwind instruments, the bore is conical like that of an oboe and the tube is made of metal.

THE BRASS INSTRUMENTS

The brass instruments are sometimes called *lip reed* instruments because instead of a reed the player uses his lips as vibrators. The fundamental note of a tube depends on the length of the tube, the pitch getting lower as the length increases. It is however possible to sound the higher harmonics without sounding the fundamental. In fact, if the tube is very narrow it may be difficult or impossible to sound the fundamental. The skilled player by tightening his lips to sound the higher harmonics can obtain the second harmonic which is an octave above the fundamental, the third harmonic which is a fifth above the second harmonic, the fourth harmonic which is two octaves above the fundamental and so on. A natural horn or natural trumpet is played by sounding the different harmonics of a very long tube. The high harmonics are very much closer together in pitch than the lower harmonics. However there are not usually enough harmonics to play the full chromatic range of notes and additional ways have been found for playing different notes in modern instruments.

Unlike the woodwind instruments the brass instruments do not have holes in their sides to control the pitch. Instead they have ways of changing the length of the tube. In the trombone this is done by means of a *slide*. Part of the tube slides out of the rest, thereby changing its length. In the other brass the length is changed by means of *valves*. When a valve is pressed the air has to pass through an extra length of tubing. Most instruments have three valves, one lowers the pitch by a semitone, another lowers the pitch by a tone and the third lowers the pitch by three semitones. By pressing valves simultaneously it is possible to lower the pitch by any number of semitones up to six. This means the instrument has seven fundamentals altogether. Since the third harmonic of the lowest fundamental is only a semitone higher than the second harmonic of the highest fundamental it is possible to play a chromatic scale upwards from the second harmonic of the lowest fundamental. It is not easy to obtain perfectly accurate pitch by means of valves and fine control over pitch has to be achieved by the lips of the player.

For convenience sake the brass instruments do not have straight tubes but are coiled. It is possible to change their timbre by inserting a mute into the bell at the end of the instrument. More than one type of mute is usually available. The timbre of the instrument is affected by the shape of the mouthpiece. A cup shaped mouthpiece is used on the trumpet, tuba and trombone and this gives a bright tone with a lot of high harmonics. A funnel shaped mouthpiece is used with the horn as this produces a more mellow tone. Most of the brass instruments are made in several sizes and are not standardised. For orchestral purposes only one or two sizes are used and these are described in more detail below.

The lip reed instruments are of ancient origin and have been made of bone, horn and pottery. Metal trumpets appear to have existed in ancient Egypt since 1400 B.C. Trumpets were used in ceremonials and for war by the ancient Greeks, Romans and Jews. Their powerful tone made them useful for issuing instructions during battle.

The B♭ Trumpet.

The trumpet has a narrow cylindrical bore for three quarters of its length which then widens to a bell. It has a brilliant tone which made it popular as a solo instrument by early composers such as Bach.

The Horn (French).

The horn has a tube of about twelve feet long, about ¼ inch in diameter at the mouthpiece end, widening continuously and finally ending in a large bell. Like the trumpet it has three valves and has too narrow a bore to sound the fundamentals. Horns are made in F and B♭ but are often combined in a single instrument called a double horn with a fourth valve. It is the brass instrument which plays most regularly with the orchestra and several concertos have been written for it. The horn is a very difficult instrument to play.

The Bass Tuba.

The tuba has a widening tube like the horn but the bore is much wider, enabling the player to sound the fundamental. In order to play a chromatic scale upwards from the fundamentals a fourth valve must be added which lowers the pitch by five semitones.

The Tenor Trombone in B♭.

Like the trumpet most of the bore of the trombone is cylindrical but it has a larger mouthpiece, giving it a more solemn tone. Although valve trombones exist the trombone normally changes its fundamental by moving the slide. The player has to judge the correct position of the slide by ear and there are seven basic positions, each a semitone apart, corresponding to the seven fundamentals of the trumpet. Unlike the trumpet, the trombone can sound its fundamentals and these are called *pedal notes*. The bass trombone is also used in the orchestra.

THE PERCUSSION SECTION

The most important percussion instrument that plays in the orchestra is the kettle drum (timpani). A kettledrum consists of a large copper bowl over which is spread a membrane of calf skin or plastic called the *head*. To change the note the kettledrum has to be retuned. This is done by changing the tension of the head and in older instruments this was achieved by turning several taps round the perimeter of the head. Tuning the kettledrums by ear while the orchestra is playing is a skilful business. In modern instruments the tuning is done by means of a foot pedal which allows a quick change between several notes. The player in a large orchestra sits on a swivel chair and may have up to five kettledrums of different sizes round him. He has a choice of several sticks with heads of felt, wood, cork, rubber or plastic for different tone colours and strikes the head fairly near the perimeter.

The percussionist will be a master of many instruments of which there are almost enough to fill a dictionary. The cymbals are brass plates which are clashed together. The bass drum and the triangle are instruments without a definite pitch which are often found in an orchestra.

THE KEYBOARD INSTRUMENTS

The Piano.

The modern piano has an iron or steel frame across which steel strings are strung. When a key is pressed a hammer is caused to strike one or more strings tuned to the same pitch and a note is produced. The harder the key is struck with the finger the faster the hammer moves and the louder the note is. The name "piano" is short for pianoforte which is Italian for soft–loud. One reason why the piano was invented was the need for a keyboard instrument which could vary its loudness in this way, unlike the harpsichord or organ.

Although various keyboard instruments in which strings were struck with hammers already existed, Cristofori is usually credited with the invention of the piano in *c.* 1709. He invented the escapement mechanism whereby the hammer leaves the string as soon as it has struck it, leaving the string free to vibrate. He also provided *dampers* so that as soon as the finger releases the key the damper presses against the string and stops any further resonance. The early pianos had wooden frames and gut strings and the sound was much weaker than that of the present piano, not unlike that of a small harpsichord. The old wooden frames would collapse under the tension of the modern strings which is about 18 tons altogether so nowadays metal is used. Just as in the case of the violin, the strings of the piano pass over a bridge which is attached to an arched sheet of wood called the *soundboard* and which is caused to vibrate when the strings vibrate. Unlike the violins which improve with age, the pressure of the bridge causes the soundboard to deteriorate with time. Another factor which has ruined many pianos is central heating which if excessive may cause the soundboard to dry out and warp. Nowadays the soundboard is usually sealed in an attempt to prevent this from happening.

Pianos are equipped with two or three pedals. The right-hand pedal is the *sustaining pedal*, sometimes called the loud pedal, and pressing this causes the dampers to lift off the strings so that if a key is pressed and then released that note continues to sound until it dies away or the pedal is released. The left-hand pedal causes the piano to play more softly and the middle pedal of the grand piano is the *sostenuto pedal*. If it is pressed while certain keys are pressed the dampers which belong to these keys do not fall when the keys are released and their notes continue to sound. Keys pressed after the sostenuto pedal has been pressed behave in the normal way. Pianos are made either *upright* with the strings in a vertical plane or *grand* with the strings horizontal. The upright piano takes up less space but the grand is able to throw out more sound and has a better action. The grand piano is nowadays fitted with *double escapement* action, allowing faster repetition of the same note. Both upright and grand pianos made nowadays are *overstrung*, which means the strings are not all parallel but cross each other making longer strings and a bigger sound possible.

The Organ.

The pipe organ produces sound by using an electric motor to blow air through pipes. When a key is pressed air is blown through a pipe or set of pipes until that key is released. Like the harpsichord, the organ does not play louder when the key is pressed harder. Each pipe can only produce a note at one particular pitch and for each note there are a large number of *stops*, that is to say pipes capable of playing the same note with different timbres and loudnesses. For example, one stop may produce a sound resembling a flute while another stop produces a sound resembling a clarinet. The stops are divided into two broad categories, the *flues* and the *reeds*. The flues are similar in principle to the recorders and air is blown through a funnel onto an edge. The reeds have a metal reed which helps to set up vibrations in the pipe. The pipes can be tuned by making small alterations in their length and also by adjusting the reed. The timbre is affected by the bore, the shape of the pipe which is sometimes cylindrical and sometimes conical, the metal or wood of which it is made and the material of the reed. In some stops several pipes with pitches corresponding to the harmonics of the fundamental sound simultaneously when a single key is pressed and this gives power and brilliancy to the note.

Unlike the piano the organ does not just have one keyboard but several. These are called *manuals* and are arranged one above the other. The most important manual is the *great organ* and this has the loudest stops and typical organ tone. The next most important manual is the *swell organ* whose pipes lie inside the *swell box*. This has shutters which can be opened or closed by means of a special pedal in order to allow more or less sound out of the box and create crescendo or diminuendo effects. Another manual is the *choir organ* which has sweet-toned and softer stops and is used for the purpose of accompanying a choir. In addition to the manuals is the pedal organ, where the keys are operated by the feet. The pedal organ contains the lowest notes, giving dignity to the sound. Two manuals can be connected by *couplers* so that playing on one keyboard has the effect of playing on two.

The manuals, pedalboard and stops are placed together within easy reach of the player and housed in a bay which together form the *console*. Pressing a key causes a hinged lid called a *pallet* to open and allow air to pass through the appropriate pipe or set of pipes. In old organs the key was coupled to the pallet by a system of levers, called *tracker action* and although tracker action is still used nowadays it has often been replaced by *electro-pneumatic* action. Here pressing the key closes an electric circuit which releases air somewhere and the fall in pressure causes a pallet to open.

As can be imagined a pipe organ is very expensive, both to buy and maintain and where the best quality cannot be afforded it has often been replaced by an electronic organ. Since at present the demand for electronic organs both in the home and for churches is strong it seems likely there will be further improvements in them.

THE EARLY MUSIC REVIVAL

Introduction

One of the most exciting developments in live and recorded music in recent years has been the revival of interest in early music. The term "early music" is nowadays a broad and rather vague one: it refers to the music of the Middle Ages and Renaissance, but many features of the "early music revival" have applications to a wider range of music than this, and the phrase is often extended to include Baroque music (*i.e.* that of the 17th and early 18th cents.).

There are two aspects to this revival: the actual retrieval and performance of early music; and a concern with *authentic* performance—with present- ing the music as it would originally have been performed. This latter aspect—the "authenticity" movement—is not restricted to early music in the narrow sense. Baroque music, including familiar works by composers like Bach and Handel, has received much attention in this respect; even the performance of Classical and early Romantic music—Haydn, Mozart, Beethoven, Schubert—is also being considered afresh.

So the music-lover today has a much greater var- iety of music readily available, than, say, twenty years ago, played by performers who are attempting to recapture the authentic sounds of the past; and he has the op- portunity to hear even well-known masterpieces presented in a new way. For example, the BBC Proms have in recent years included, alongside the more usual repertoire, sacred and secular music from the 13th and 14th cents.; music by the 15th- cent. composer Dufay and his contemporaries; Monteverdi's *Vespers* of 1610 (two performances in three years); 17th-cent. English and Italian mad- rigals; the opera *Hippolyte et Aricie* by the 18th- cent. French composer Rameau, in a concert per- formance; many choral and orchestral works by Bach and Handel performed in authentic fashion; and in 1984, for the first time at a Prom, a Beethoven symphony played on instruments of Beethoven's time (or reproductions of them).

The Scholarly Background

The development of the discipline of musicology— the scholarly study of music—in the second half of the 19th cent. laid the foundations for the revival of early music. From the 1850s onwards large collected editions of the works of past composers began to be published, many of them in Germany. The complete edition of Bach's music started publication in 1851, and was followed over the next fifty years by edi- tions of Handel, Palestrina, Schütz, Lassus, Schein and Victoria, to name only composers of pre-clas- sical times. These editions differed from earlier col- lections in attempting to reproduce what the com- poser wrote and distinguish this from the additions and alterations of later editors and arrangers. In the 20th cent. many of these editions have been revised, or completely new editions started (*e.g.* of Bach, 1954). The collections of national music, *Denkmäler deutscher Tonkunst* (begun 1892) and *Denkmäler der Tonkunst in Österreich* (begun 1894), are examples of a different type of publication, which made avail- able music by many composers of various periods who were natives of and/or worked in Germany and Austria respectively.

If the lead in producing scholarly editions of old music was taken by Germany and Austria, it was followed in other countries. In England interest in such music had never altogether died: the tradition of English church music and the influence of Handel ensured some continuity with the past through the later 18th and 19th cents. The Purcell Society, founded in 1876, began publication of a complete edition of Purcell's music in 1878. Interest in earlier music is shown by the foundation of the Plainsong and Mediaeval Music Society in 1888, which began producing publications in 1891, and by J. Stainer's collection of mediaeval music *Dufay and his Con- temporaries* (1898). In the 20th cent. knowledge of the Elizabethan and Jacobean "golden age" of

English music was spread by such publications as E. H. Fellowes's *English Madrigal School* (1913–24) and *English School of Lutenist Song-writers* (1920– 32); the collection *Tudor Church Music* (1922–29); and Fellowes's edition of the works of William Byrd (1937–50). Two later series of importance are: *Musica Britannica*, begun in 1951 under the auspices of the Royal Musical Association—an equi- valent of the German and Austrian *Denkmäler*, con- taining music of the British Isles from the Middle Ages to the 19th cent., and including complete works such as those of the 15th-cent. composer John Dunstable; and *Early English Church Music*, begun in 1963 for the British Academy, containing church music by British composers from the Norman Con- quest to the Commonwealth period "in a form both scholarly and practical".

France, Italy and the Low Countries have also produced editions of their early composers. In the U.S.A., where many scholars from Germany and Austria took refuge in the 1930s, historical mus- icology flourishes. A notable contribution to the study of early music has been the series *Corpus Mensurabilis Musicae*, begun in 1947, published by the American Institute of Musicology—a collection of mediaeval and Renaissance music which includes such major items as the complete works of Dufay.

Some Forerunners of the Early Music Revival

Although the music of Bach and Handel was per- formed and appreciated in the 19th cent. there was little attempt to judge it on its own terms or to per- form it in a manner appropriate to the period of its composition—and this applies even more to music before Bach, which tended to be seen from an evo- lutionary standpoint, in the light of what it was supposedly leading towards, rather than being con- sidered in its own right. It is only since the end of the 19th cent. that a serious and sustained effort has been made to approach pre-classical music without preconceptions—not to judge, say, early polyphony from the viewpoint of Bach, and not to assume that modern instruments are necessarily superior to older ones for the performance of older music.

In England much of the foundation work was done by Arnold Dolmetsch (1858–1940). His book *The Interpretation of the Music of the XVII and XVIII Centuries* (1915) was a pioneering study of "performance practice" in the Baroque period, using the writings of musicians of the time for in- formation on matters of interpretation. Dolmetsch restored old instruments (*e.g.* lutes, clavichords, harpsichords) and, from the 1890s on, manufactured reproductions; it is to him that we owe the revival of the recorder in this country—an instrument vir- tually forgotten for more than a century, now a regular part of music teaching in schools as well as having its share of highly accomplished professional players (among whom is Dolmetsch's son Carl). He edited and performed early instrumental music. The Haslemere Festival, which he founded in 1925, still continues; the Dolmetsch Foundation, established in 1929, supports the study and performance of early music.

As the 20th cent. progressed interest grew among professional musicians and enthusiastic amateurs in playing early music, and among instrument makers in restoring and copying old instruments. Through artists like Wanda Landowska (1879–1959), Ralph Kirkpatrick (1911–84) and Thurston Dart (1921–71) the sound of the harpsichord became familiar throughout the musical world. In England early opera received attention. It was a specialism of the influential teacher E. J. Dent, Professor of Music at Cambridge from 1926. At Oxford the first modern complete production of Monteverdi's *Orfeo* took place in 1925, in a version prepared by Jack Wes- trup while still an undergraduate; this, and pre- sentations of other works, did a great deal to stim- ulate interest in Italian Baroque opera. From 1947 onwards Anthony Lewis, Westrup's successor as Professor at Birmingham University, was re- sponsible for revivals of Baroque opera; he also directed the first recordings of such works as Monteverdi's *Vespers* and Purcell's *Fairy Queen* and *King Arthur*. The beginning of the BBC Third Programme after the war provided a stimulus to early music, with an adventurous policy of presenting unfamiliar music. The musicologist Denis Stevens worked in the music department from 1949 to 1954, and was responsible for radio opera performances of *Orfeo* and Charpentier's *Médée*.

The foundation of organisations like the Lute Society (1948) and the Viola da Gamba Society (1956) encouraged the development of interest in these old instruments and their repertoire. English consort music of the 16th and 17th cents. was revived by groups like the English Consort of Viols (founded in 1935), the Julian Bream Consort (1959) and the Jaye Consort of Viols (1960). The countertenor voice became familiar again through the singer Alfred Deller, whose collaboration with the lutenist Desmond Dupré helped to popularise the Elizabethan and Jacobean lute-song in the 1950s (as did the partnership of Julian Bream and Peter Pears at the same time).

Among developments abroad should be mentioned the work of the New York Pro Musica (founded in 1952) under Noah Greenberg, whose performances and recordings, especially of mediaeval liturgical drama, made a considerable impact.

Early Music since 1960

Nevertheless, for the general musical public of the first six decades of the 20th cent. it is probably fair to say that opera still began with Mozart rather than Monteverdi, and that Handel's *Fireworks Music* and *Water Music* were more likely to be heard in the arrangements by Hamilton Harty than in any version that Handel himself might have recognised. With some exceptions, the music of the 17th cent. and earlier tended to be a specialist interest, for both performer and listener.

It was in the 1960s that the early music revival "took off". In this country two ensembles in particular proved to be important popularisers. Musica Reservata, formed in the 1950s by Michael Morrow to perform mediaeval and Renaissance music, gave its first public concert in 1960; its extrovert, sometimes harsh, style of performance contrasted strongly with that generally adopted by early music performers at this time, and was influenced by folk and non-European musical cultures. This latter influence was also evident in the work of the Early Music Consort of London, founded by David Munrow in 1967, which perhaps did even more to bring early music before a wider audience. Munrow's death in 1976 deprived the musical world of a versatile musician and skilled communicator, who did much to make early music, from the 12th to the 17th cent., accessible while retaining his musical and scholarly integrity. The work of Munrow and the Consort ranged from major recording projects like *The Art of Courtly Love* and *Music of the Gothic Era* to the provision of music for television and films (*e.g. The Six Wives of Henry VIII, The Devils*).

Other groups formed in the 1960s which continue to flourish include the Monteverdi Choir (begun at Cambridge for a performance of Monteverdi's *Vespers* in 1964), Pro Cantione Antiqua (1968, specialising in mediaeval and Renaissance choral music), and the Consort of Musicke (1969, exploring initially the music of the English "golden age"). The 1960s and early 1970s also saw productions of early Italian opera at Glyndebourne in versions by Raymond Leppard, beginning with Monteverdi's *L'Incoronazione di Poppea* in 1962. These versions have been criticised for taking too great liberties with the original texts, but they introduced many opera-lovers for the first time to an important part of the repertoire.

By the 1970s early music could not be ignored by the serious music-lover, and performing groups multiplied. The *Directory of British Early Music Groups* (1981) lists 111 ensembles, of which 93 were established in 1970 or later. In the mediaeval and Renaissance fields there has been in some cases a trend towards greater specialisation; early music is

now sufficiently well established for groups like the Medieval Ensemble of London or the Martin Best Medieval Ensemble to concentrate on particular areas in depth.

If the 1960s were crucial for public awareness of music before about 1650, the 1970s saw a renewed interest in the authentic performance of middle and late Baroque music, with the formation of such ensembles as the Academy of Ancient Music and the English Consort, both founded in 1973 to specialise in the music of this period. It was also in 1973 that the journal *Early Music* was begun—a venture which, its editor suggested in the first issue, would have been impossible ten years previously. It continues to flourish; its articles, reviews and advertisements testify to the role of early music in British musical life. Early music in fact is now established at all levels. For the record collector the *Gramophone* magazine carries regular features on recordings of early music. A number of the music colleges, trainers of future generations of performers, offer early music courses. In 1976 the Early Music Centre opened, with the aim of encouraging the study and performance of early music. Its educational activities include full-time courses and evening classes, conferences, master classes, children's classes and summer schools. It organises concerts throughout the country and in London, and publishes a newsletter *Early Music News*. The Centre administers the Early Music Network, set up in 1978 to provide an administrative and information service and organise concert tours each year by British and foreign ensembles. There are also nine regional Early Music Forums—eight in England, one in Scotland—providing a channel of communication for players and listeners in the regions, arranging courses and concerts and publishing newsletters.

A complete survey would of course need to consider developments abroad—to cover, for example, the work of Nikolaus Harnoncourt and the Vienna Concentus Musicus, of Sigiswald Kuijken and La Petite Bande, of the recorder-player Frans Brüggen and the harpsichordist Gustav Leonhardt in the field of Baroque music; of the Munich Capella Antiqua in music ranging from Gregorian Chant to the late Renaissance. But the U.K. is at present in the forefront of the early music revival, and an account based on this country does not give a false impression of the main trends. There is naturally a constant cross-fertilisation of ideas between performers here and abroad.

Problems of Performance

The performance of early music raises many practical problems, whether the music in question be familiar or only recently revived. There is a widespread assumption that performances should set out to be 'authentic'—that is, should reflect as faithfully as possible the composer's intention in terms of the sound and the way the music is played or sung. This assumption is one which would scarcely be conceivable before the 20th cent. The 19th-cent. attitude is well illustrated by a critic who wrote in 1849: "How differently is the *Messiah* now performed—how much is it improved from the work which the Composer left!" This attitude persisted in many circles well into the 20th cent., and there are still plenty of good performances of Baroque music to be heard which make no particular claim to authenticity (though few performers would now attempt a wholesale "improvement" of the original). Authenticity is no substitute for musicality, and there is a constant danger of turning compositions of the past into museum pieces by too rigid an insistence on authenticity. However, many of the liveliest and freshest performances are precisely those which have tried to shed the weight of 200 years of tradition: a good performance of *Messiah* in Baroque style with relatively small forces and period instruments strikes the listener by its cleanness and clarity of texture and its rhythmic life; it is likely to sound much less like a museum piece than many a performance on a grander scale.

Recreating the sound of early music involves not only using early instruments or replicas but learning an idiomatic technique for playing them: such matters as bowing, fingering, the use of vibrato have to be radically rethought by the player accustomed to mid-20th-cent. techniques. It also involves, for example, finding styles of singing suitable for mediaeval, Renaissance or Baroque music. The number of performers is an important consideration (a recent prize-winning recording of Bach's *B minor Mass* even goes so far as to dispense with a choir and use single voices for each line). In earlier music the performer himself often has to choose whether particular parts in an ensemble work are to be played or sung: knowledge of the historical background and insight into style are indispensable here. The actual choice of pitch and the system of tuning to be used are also issues which modern performers of early music are increasingly taking into account.

The search for the right sound has not stopped at the Baroque period. Music of the Classical period has in recent years been played and recorded on period instruments—the complete Mozart symphonies, for example, have been recorded by the Academy of Ancient Music—and the early piano is undergoing a revival.

Even when he has achieved the right sound the performer has to interpret the notes of the score. Composers before the 19th cent. gave the performer less information than in more recent scores about *how* he was to play, and in some respects left him with a good deal more freedom of choice. Speed and dynamics, for instance, are only intermittently indicated in Baroque music; before the 17th cent., not at all. A performer of the time would know what speed was appropriate for a piece of a particular type; this is a sense which the present-day performer has to develop. Furthermore, even precisely notated music was not necessarily expected or intended to be performed as written. During the Baroque period there were certain conventions whereby some kinds of rhythm were not to be played exactly as notated. Scholars and performers today do not all agree on the meaning and application of these conventions. Again, the Baroque composer would often expect performers to ornament and decorate the written music—an art which would be second nature to the musician of the time, but which modern performers have to learn anew.

Since Dolmetsch the literature on the performance of early music has grown considerably; writers like Thurston Dart, Robert Donington and Frederick Neumann have examined the treatises of earlier musicians to arrive at conclusions about performance practice. There are many areas of debate and disagreement, but scholarship in this field is becoming increasingly sophisticated and critical.

Conclusion

There is no doubt that "early music" is here to stay. The frontiers of musical experience have been decisively extended, and the view that musical history is a matter of evolutionary progress towards the major figures of the 18th and 19th cents. is now no longer tenable. Composers like Machaut, Dufay, Josquin, Monteverdi, and Schütz are now appreciated for their own sake, not judged for what they did not try to do. The ears of the musical public have also been opened to new—or rather, old—sounds and styles in the performance of music which that public perhaps thought it knew well. The tercentenary of Bach, Handel and D. Scarlatti in 1985 provided a further stimulus to audiences and performers alike.

In the long run, however, we can look forward to a time when "early music" (a label disliked by some of its practitioners) no longer exists as somehow special or different. Already its boundaries have been pushed forward into the 19th cent. Ultimately there is only music, and the question: how is this particular piece of music best and most appropriately performed? This question may be more or less difficult to answer for the music of different periods, but it exists for the music of all periods. There is not some common factor that brings together a Machaut motet, a Monteverdi madrigal and a Scarlatti sonata as being "early" and thereby distinct from a Brahms symphony or a Bartók quartet. The interpretative and aesthetic questions involved are, at the most basic level, the same for all of them. It may therefore be significant that the Nov. 1984 issue of *Early Music* carried an article on—of all things—"The recordings of Edward Elgar (1857–1934): authenticity and performance practice".

THE WORLD OF SCIENCE

A contemporary picture of scientific discovery, designed to explain some of the most important ideas in astronomy, physics, chemistry, biology, physical and social anthropology, and to give some account of recent research in various fields. A special article in this edition explains the main units and measures encountered in the scientific world. Other special topics focus on space exploration, the evolution of the eye and the Chernobyl catastrophe.

TABLE OF CONTENTS

THE WORLD OF SCIENCE

In Parts I, II, and III the inanimate universe is described. This is the domain of cosmology, astronomy, geology, physics, and chemistry. There are already many interesting links which join this realm to that of the living and make it difficult to say where the boundary lies. Nevertheless it is still convenient to accord to the biological and social sciences two separate chapters, IV and V. In Part VI our intention is to give some short accounts of recent developments in both science and technology. They are usually contributed by scientists actively engaged in these, their own special fields. Readers may also wish to consult **Section V, Introduction to Computing**.

I. ASTRONOMY AND COSMOLOGY—THE NATURE OF THE UNIVERSE

The universe includes everything from the smallest sub-atomic particle to the mightiest system of stars. The scientific view of the universe (not the only view but the one we are concerned with here) is a remarkable achievement of the human mind, and it is worth considering at the outset what a "scientific view" is, and what is remarkable about it.

A scientific view of something is always an intimate mixture of theories and observed facts, and not an inert mixture but a seething and growing one. The theories are broad general ideas together with arguments based on them. The arguments are designed to show that, if the general ideas are accepted, then this, or the other thing ought to be observed. If this, that, or the other actually are observed, then the theory is a good one; if not, then the theoreticians have to think again. Thus theoretical ideas and arguments are continually subjected to the severe test of comparison with the facts, and scientists are proud of the rigour with which this is done. On the other hand, theories often suggest new things to look for, i.e., theories lead to predictions. These predictions are frequently successful, and scientists are entitled to be proud of that too. But it follows that no theory is immutable; any scientific view of any subject may, in principle, be invalidated at any time by the discovery of new facts, though some theories are so soundly based that their overthrow does not seem imminent.

A remarkable aspect of the scientific view of the universe is that the same principles are supposed to operate throughout the whole vastness of space. Thus the matter and radiation in stars are not different from the matter and radiation on earth, and their laws of behaviour are the same. Therefore theories hard won by studies in terrestrial physics and chemistry laboratories are applied at once to the whole cosmos. Astronomy and cosmology are spectacular extensions of ordinary mechanics and physics.

LOOKING AT THE UNIVERSE

The universe is observable because signals from it reach us and some manage to penetrate our atmosphere.

First, there are waves of visible light together with invisible rays of somewhat longer (infra-red) and somewhat shorter (ultra-violet) wavelengths. These waves show us the bright astronomical objects and, to make use of them, astronomers have constructed telescopes of great power and precision backed up with cameras, spectroscopes, and numerous auxiliaries. The biggest telescope in the world is at Mt. Pastukhov in the northern Caucasus. The earth's atmosphere acts as a distorting and only partially transparent curtain and the erection of telescopes on satellites is beginning to extend optical telescope performance significantly.

Secondly, there are radio waves of much longer wavelength than light. Radiotelescopes are sensitive radio receivers with specialised aerial systems. The scientific stature of modern radioastronomy was emphasised by the award in 1974 of the Nobel Physics Prize to two Cambridge radioastronomers, Ryle and Hewish.

Other types of radiation reach the earth from outer space. Cosmic radiation consists of fundamental particles, including protons (**F16**) of extremely high energy, moving at velocities very close to that of light. These particles can be detected by Geiger counters and by their tracks on photographic plates. X-rays and neutrinos (**F16**) are also generated by certain interesting classes of astronomical objects (**F5**). With the recent advent of satellite-borne detectors and apparatus buried in deep mines, new facets of cosmic-ray astronomy, X-ray astronomy, and neutrino astronomy are now rapidly deepening our knowledge of the nature of the universe and of the violent processes by which galaxies as well as individual stars and planetary systems evolve (**F6, F7**).

Great Distances and Large Numbers

To visualise the immense scale of the universe is almost as much a problem for the scientist as for the layman. The conventional shorthand is to express 1,000 as 10^3; 1,000,000 as 10^6. On this scale the earth is $1·496 \times 10^8$ km away from the sun. Concorde, for example, the world's fastest airliner, took about $3\frac{1}{2}$ hours to travel 5,000 km from London to New York. The "Viking" spacecraft in 1976 took just over a year to travel the 200 million km to Mars. These distances, however, are minute by comparison with the distance even to the nearest star, Proxima Centauri, some 4×10^{13} km away. This distance is more conveniently expressed in terms of the travel time of light itself. With a velocity of nearly 300,000 km per second, in a year light travels about $9·46 \times 10^{12}$ km. The distance to Proxima Centauri is therefore $4·2$ light years. Even this distance, enormous on our terrestrial scale, is a small cosmic distance. The diameter of our galaxy is about 10^5 light years, while the most distant objects yet observed are an incredible $1·4 \times 10^{10}$ light years distant.

PLANETS, STARS AND GALAXIES

The Solar System

The earth is the third, counting outward of nine planets revolving in nearly circular orbits round the sun. Some of their particulars are given in the Table (**F8**). The sun and its planets are the main bodies of the solar system. Mainly between the orbits of Mars and Jupiter revolve numerous small bodies—the minor planets or asteroids, the largest of which, Ceres, is only 800 km in diameter. Apart from these, the solar system is tenuously populated with particles varying in size from about a micron (10^{-6} m) to hundreds of metres in diameter. Some of these objects collide with the earth's atmosphere. The smaller fragments (micro-meteors) are too small to be visible. Large particles (meteors), about 1 mm up to tens of cm, cause the phenomena known as "shooting stars" when they burn up at about 100 km altitude. Even larger chunks, of rocky or iron composition, cause the rare and brilliant fireballs, some of which survive their high-speed flight through the earth's atmosphere and may later be recovered. Such objects (meteorites) are very important, providing examples of extraterrestrial rocks, and thus giving the composition of some of the most primitive material left in the solar system. Collisions with very large meteorites (or small asteroids) are now, fortunately, very rare. However, the large meteorite crater in Arizona is one recent reminder that such collisions still occur, although much less frequently now than earlier in the history of the planetary system. The surfaces of Mercury, the Moon, Mars, and Venus still show the scars from collisions with a multitude of objects of up to tens of km in diameter.

Comets are still enigmatic objects which, from time to time, provide a spectacular sight. Probably, they consist of a small nucleus (1–10 km diameter) of a compact, frozen conglomerate of dust and the so-called "icy" materials—H_2O, NH_3, CH_4, CO_2, etc. In their highly elliptical orbits, they spend most of their life at great distances from the sun, where the temperature is very low because of the feeble solar radiation, so that all the "icy" materials are solid. Periodically, when each comet returns to the inner parts of the solar system, the increasing solar radiation heats the surface layers, evaporating the volatile ices, which carry the surface dust away from the comet nucleus. After this heating and evaporation process, the ultra-violet component of sunlight further breaks down the parent "icy" molecules, a process known as photo-dissociation, and many molecules become ionised. Solar-radiation pressure, acting on the dust constituents, and the solar wind acting on the ionised constituents, form the gigantic cometary tails which may reach 2×10^8 km in length—larger than the radius of the earth's orbit. *See also* **L28.**

The sun itself is a dense, roughly spherical mass of glowing matter, 1,392,000 km across. Its heat is so intense that the atoms are split into separated electrons and nuclei (**F11**) and matter in such a state is called plasma. At the sun's centre the temperature has the unimaginable value of about 13 million degrees Centigrade (a coal fire is about 800°C). Under such conditions the atomic nuclei frequently collide with one another at great speeds and reactions occur between them. The sun consists largely of hydrogen and, in the very hot plasma, the nuclei of hydrogen atoms interact by a series of reactions whose net result is to turn hydrogen into helium. This is a process which releases energy just as burning does, only these nuclear processes are incomparably more energetic than ordinary burning. In fact, the energy released is great enough to be the source of all the light and heat which the sun has been pouring into space for thousands of millions of years.

Emerging from the sun and streaming past the earth is a "solar wind" of fast-moving electrons and protons (**F11**) whose motion is closely linked with the behaviour of an extensive magnetic field based on the sun. In fact, the region round the sun and extending far into space past the earth is full of complex, fluctuating particle streams and magnetic fields which interact with planetary atmospheres causing, among other things, auroras and magnetic storms.

Stars

In colour, brightness, age, and size the sun is typical of vast numbers of other stars. Only from the human point of view is there anything special about the sun—it is near enough to give us life. Even the possession of a system of revolving planets is not, according to some modern views, very unusual.

No star can radiate energy at the rate the sun does without undergoing internal changes in the course of time. Consequently stars evolve and old processes in them give rise to new. The exact nature of stellar evolution—so far as it is at present understood—would be too complex to describe here in any detail. It involves expansion and contraction, changes of temperature, changes of colour, and changes in chemical compositon as the nuclear processes gradually generate new chemical elements by reactions such as the conversion of hydrogen to helium, helium to neon, neon to magnesium, and so on. The speed of evolution changes from time to time, but is in any case very slow compared with the pace of terrestrial life; nothing very dramatic may occur for hundreds of millions of years. Evidence for the various phases of evolution is therefore obtained by studying many stars, each at a different stage of its life. Thus astronomers recognise many types with charmingly descriptive names, such as blue giants, sub-giants, red and white dwarfs, supergiants.

The path of stellar evolution may be marked by various explosive events. One of these, which occurs in sufficiently large stars, is an enormous explosion in which a substantial amount of the star is blown away into space in the form of high-speed streams of gas. For about a fortnight, such an exploding star will radiate energy 200 million times as fast as the sun. Japanese and Chinese (but not Western) astronomers recorded such an occurrence in A.D. 1054, and the exploding gases, now called the Crab nebula, can still be seen in powerful telescopes and form a cloud six or seven light-years across. While it lasts, the explosion shows up as an abnormally bright star and is called a *supernova*.

Groups of Stars

It is not surprising that ancient peoples saw pictures in the sky. The constellations, however, are not physically connected groups of stars but just happen to be patterns visible from earth. A conspicuous exception to this is the Milky Way, which a telescope resolves into many millions of separate stars. If we could view the Milky Way from a vast distance and see it as a whole we should observe a rather flat wheel of stars with spiral arms something like the sparks of a rotating Catherine wheel. This system of stars is physically connected by gravitational forces and moves through space as a whole; it is called a *galaxy*.

The galaxy is about 10^5 light-years across and contains roughly 10^{11} stars. An inconspicuous one of these stars near the edge of the wheel is our sun; the prominent stars in our night sky are members of the galaxy that happen to be rather near us. Sirius, the brightest, is only 8·6 light-years away, a trivial distance, astronomically speaking.

The galaxy does not contain stars only, there are also clouds of gas and dust, particularly in the plane of the galaxy. Much of the gas is hydrogen, and its detection is difficult. However, gaseous hydrogen gives out radio waves with a wavelength of 21 cm. Radio telescopes are just the instruments to receive these, and workers in Holland, America, and Australia detected the gas clouds by this means. In 1952 they found that the hydrogen clouds lie in the spiral arms of the galaxy, and this is some of the strongest evidence for the spiral form.

Another important feature of the galactic scene is the weak but enormously extensive magnetic field. This is believed to have an intimate connection with the spiral structure.

Around the spiral arms, and forming part of the galaxy, are numerous globular clusters of stars. These are roughly spherical, abnormally densely packed, collections of stars with many thousands of members. Because of its form and density, a globular cluster may be assumed to have been formed in one process, not star by star. Thus all its stars are the same age. This is of great interest to astronomers, because they can study differences between stars of similar age but different sizes.

Galaxies

One might be forgiven for assuming that such a vast system as the galaxy is in fact the universe; but this is not so. In the constellation of Andromeda is a famous object which, on close examination, turns out to be another galaxy of size and structure similar to our own. Its distance is given in the table (**F8**). The Milky Way, the Andromeda nebula, and a few other smaller galaxies form a cluster of galaxies called the Local Group. It is indeed a fact that the universe is populated with *groups*, or *clusters*, of *galaxies*. A cluster may contain two or three galaxies, but some contain thousands.

Some recent developments

By about 1920 it was known that there were at least half a million galaxies, and with the advent of the 100-in. Mt. Wilson telescope this number rose to 10^8 and has been increased further by the 254-cm telescope which can see out to a distance of 7×10^9 light-years. Through the powerful telescopes the nearer galaxies reveal their inner structures. Photographs of galaxies are among the most beautiful and fascinating photographs ever taken, and readers who have never seen one should hasten to the nearest illustrated astronomy book. Most galaxies have a spiral or elliptical structure but about 2 per cent have peculiar wisps and appendages. Some galaxies are strong emitters of radio waves.

The Expanding Universe

Two discoveries about galaxies are of the utmost importance. One is that, by and large, clusters of galaxies are uniformly distributed through the universe. The other is that the distant galaxies are receding from us.

How is this known? Many readers may be familiar with the Doppler effect first discovered in 1842. Suppose a stationary body emits waves of any kind and we measure their wavelength, finding it to be L cm. Now suppose the body approaches us; the waves are thereby crowded together in the intervening space and the wavelength appears less than L; if the body recedes the wavelength appears greater than L. The Austrian physicist, J. Doppler (1803–53), discovered the well-known change of pitch of a train whistle as it approaches and passes us. The same principle applies to the light. Every atom emits light of definite wavelengths which appear in a spectroscope as a series of coloured lines—a different series for each atom. If the atom is in a receding body all the lines have slightly longer wavelengths than usual, and the amount of the change depends uniquely on the speed. Longer wavelengths mean that the light is redder than usual, so that a light from a receding body shows what is called a "red shift". The speed of recession can be calculated from the amount of red shift.

It was the American astronomer, V. M. Slipher, who first showed (in 1914) that some galaxies emitted light with a red shift. In the 1920s and 1930s the famous astronomer E. Hubble (1889–1953) measured both the distances and red shift of many galaxies and proved what is now known as Hubble's Law about which there is now some controversy. This states that the speed of recession of galaxies is proportional to their distance from us. This does not apply to our neighbours in the Local Group, we and they are keeping together. Hubble's Law has been tested and found to hold for the farthest detectable galaxies; they are about 7×10^9 light-years away and are receding with a speed approaching that of light.

The expansion of the universe does not imply that the Local Group is the centre of the universe —from any other viewpoint in the universe Hubble's Law would also be valid, and the distant galaxies would, similarly, all appear to be rapidly receding.

One possible implication of this most exciting scientific discovery is that, if the galaxies have always been receding, at an early time they must have been closer together. We can calculate that about 10^{10} years ago all the matter of the universe could have been densely packed. The truth or otherwise of this hypothesis is the most fundamental question of cosmology, and its testing still drives the quest to explore the universe, by larger and more sensitive telescopes, to the greatest possible distances.

Quasars, Pulsars and Black Holes

In November 1962 Australian radio astronomers located a strong radio emitter with sufficient precision for the Mt. Palomar optical astronomers to identify it on photographs and examine the nature of its light. The red shift was so great that the object must be exceedingly distant; on the other hand it looked star-like, much smaller than a galaxy. By the beginning of 1967 over a hundred of these objects had been discovered and other characteristics established, such as strong ultraviolet radiation and inconstancy, in some cases, of the rate at which radiation is emitted. Not all of these so-called quasars are strong radio emitters; some show all the other characteristics except radio emission. It has been estimated that the "quiet" kind are about a hundred times more numerous than the radio kind. One great problem here is: how can such relatively small objects generate such inconceivably great amounts of energy that they appear bright at such huge distances? One new idea is that they are the central visible part of an otherwise undetected galaxy.

Late in 1967, while investigating quasars, Cambridge radio astronomers discovered pulsars, a new type of heavenly body. Their characteristic is the emission of regular pulses of radio waves every second or so. A pulsar in the Crab nebula has a repetition rate even faster—about 1/30 sec—and it follows that pulsars must be very small bodies little if at all bigger than the Earth.

The existence of such small bodies raises again the problem of the ultimate fate of evolving stars. Much depends on their mass because this determines how strong the inward pull of gravity is. For a star to be at least temporarily stable the inward pull must be balanced by an outward pressure. In the sun this is the pressure of the burning hydrogen (**F6**) and the resulting average density is about 1·4 times that of water (**Table, F8**). In some stars the inward pressure is so great that collapse proceeds until it is balanced by a different type of outward pressure that sets in when electrons and atomic nuclei are forced into proximity. Stars so formed are the "white dwarfs". They are millions of times denser than the sun—"a matchbox of their matter would weigh a ton"—and they are very small though not small enough to be pulsars. The latter are now generally thought to be a million times denser even than white dwarfs and to consist largely of tightly packed neutrons (*see* **F11**). Such bodies are called neutron stars.

Could the tendency of a massive star to fall inwards ever be so great that no outward pressure known to physics would suffice to balance it? Apparently it could! Many astrophysicists now hold on theoretical grounds that such a gravitational collapse could create a high density object whose gravitational field would be too strong to allow anything—including light waves—ever to leave the body. Such hypothetical objects are called "black holes" because, light and other signals being unable to emerge from them, their matter has literally disappeared from view. Black holes could be detected by the disturbance their gravitational attraction causes to neighbouring visible stars and also because atoms attracted by the black hole should emit intense X-rays before falling so far in that they too disappear into the black hole. Both of these detection methods have led some astronomers to conjecture (by 1973) that there is a black hole in the constellation Cygnus. The theory of gravitational collapse raises profound and unresolved problems about our physical concepts.

Very recently, it has been conjectured that

black holes, formed by the "death" of individual stars, and perhaps even on a massive scale at the centre of large and dense galaxies, have been responsible for "devouring" a very significant proportion of the total mass of the universe. Since this "devoured" mass is invisible by direct observation, we may have considerably underestimated the average density, and thus the total gravitational field of the universe.

THE ORIGIN AND DEVELOPMENT OF THE UNIVERSE

Scientists can only attempt to explain the universe by relating its observable structure to the features predicted by alternative theories of its origin and development. The time span of all our observations of the Cosmos is so small by comparison with the lifetime of the universe (more than 10^{10} years). Also, contrary to many other scientific disciplines, it is impossible to repeat the "experiment", under controlled conditions. We must, therefore, explore the evolution of the universe by using the fact that light from the most distant galaxies has taken about 10^{10} years to reach us, thus providing us with a crucial, if tantalisingly remote and thus indistinct, view of the universe at a much earlier epoch.

Evolutionary Theories

Several models of the universe have been based on Einstein's theory of General Relativity (**F17**). Einstein's equations may be solved to predict the evolution of the universe. However, there is a spectrum of solutions which vary from a continuous and indefinite expansion at the present rate to an eventual slowing and subsequent contraction to a dense state, again in the distant future, which hints at a "pulsating" universe.

The Steady-State Theory

As an alternative to the Evolutionary theory, Bondi, Gold, and Hoyle (1948) suggested the so-called "Steady-State" theory. This theory has no initial dense state or "origin" and, on a large scale, the density of galaxies and stars is always as at present. To permit this possibility, they supposed that matter—hydrogen atoms—is continuously created throughout space at a rate sufficient to compensate for the present observed expansion of the universe. Thus the average density of matter would always remain constant.

The Formation of Galaxies and Stars

On any theory of the universe, some explanation has to be found for the existence of clusters of galaxies. In all theories galaxies condense out from dispersed masses of gas, principally hydrogen. It is believed on theoretical grounds each galaxy could not condense into one enormous star but must form many fragments which shrink separately into clusters of stars. In these clusters many stars, perhaps hundreds or thousands or even millions, are born. A small cluster, visible to the naked eye, is the Pleiades. The Orion nebula, visible as a hazy blob of glowing gas in the sword of Orion, is the scene of much star-forming activity at present.

According to the Evolutionary theory the "initial dense state" consisted of very hot plasma in a state of overall expansion. The expanding plasma was both cooling and swirling about. The random swirling produces irregularities in the distribution of the hot gas—here it would be rather denser, there rather less dense. If a sufficiently large mass of denser gas happened to occur, then the gravitational attraction between its own particles would hold it together and

maintain its permanent identity, even though the rest of the gas continued to swirl and expand. Such a large mass would gradually condense into fragments to become a cluster of galaxies.

The Changing Scene

The 1960s witnessed revolutionary developments in both observational and theoretical astronomy. For example, it now seems agreed that remote sources of radio waves are more abundant the weaker their intensity. This strongly suggests that they are more abundant at greater distances. Thus the universe is not *uniform* as the original steady-state theory prescribed. Since greater distances correspond to earlier times, any extra abundance of objects observed at the greater distance means that the universe was denser in its younger days than now. This favours an evolutionary theory of the universe.

The same theory requires that the initial dense state of the universe—aptly christened "the primaeval fireball"—should contain intense electromagnetic radiation with a distribution of wavelengths characteristic of the high temperature. As the fireball, i.e., the universe, expanded over a period of about 10^{10} years it cooled, and one feature of this process is that the wavelengths of the radiation increase and their distribution becomes characteristic of a much lower temperature. In fact, the wavelengths should now be concentrated round about 1 mm to 1 cm (corresponding to about $-270°$ C) and the radiation should approach the earth uniformly from all directions. Radiation just like this was detected in the 1960s by extremely sensitive instruments both at ground-based observatories and flown from balloon payloads high in the earth's atmosphere—above most of the water vapour and other constituents which interfere with such delicate observations. This "microwave background" radiation appears to be "cosmological", and thus supports strongly the evolutionary or "Big Bang" theory as opposed to the "Steady-State" theory, which cannot rationally explain the radiation.

The Formation of the Chemical Elements

A stable nucleus is one that lasts indefinitely because it is not radioactive. There are 274 known kinds of stable atomic nuclei and little likelihood of any more being found. These nuclei are the isotopes (**F12**) of 81 different chemical elements; the other elements, including, for example, uranium and radium are always radioactive. Some elements are rare, others abundant. The most common ones on earth are oxygen, silicon, aluminium, and iron. However, the earth is rather atypical. It is especially deficient in hydrogen, because the gravitational attraction of our small planet was not strong enough to prevent this very light gas from escaping into space.

It is possible to examine the chemical constituents of meteorites and to infer the composition of the sun and other stars from the spectrum of the light they emit. By such means, the conclusion has been reached that 93% of the atoms in our galaxy are hydrogen, 7% are helium; all the other elements together account for about one in a thousand atoms. A glance at the Table of Elements (*see* end of Sec.) will show that hydrogen and helium are two of the lightest elements: they are in fact the two simplest. The problem is to explain how the heavier chemical elements appear in the universe at all. It is here that a fascinating combination of astronomy and nuclear physics is required.

We have already referred to the fact that the energy radiated from the sun originates in nuclear reactions which turn hydrogen into helium. Why is energy given out? To answer this question we note that nuclei are made up of protons and neutrons (**F11**). These particles attract one another strongly—that is why a nucleus holds together. To separate the particles, energy would have to be supplied to overcome the attractive forces. This amount of energy is called *binding energy* and is a definite quantity for every kind of nucleus. Conversely, when the particles are brought together to form a nucleus the binding energy is *released* in the form of radiations and heat. Different nuclei consist of different numbers of particles, therefore the relevant quantity to consider is the *binding energy per particle.* Let us call this B. Then if elements of *high* B are formed out of those of *low* B there is a *release* of energy. *See also* **Nuclear Energy, L88.**

Now B is small (relatively) for light elements like lithium, helium, and carbon; it rises to a maximum for elements of middling atomic weight like iron; it falls again for really heavy elements like lead, bismuth, and uranium. Consequently, energy is released by forming middleweight elements either by splitting up heavy nuclei ("nuclear fission") or by joining up light ones ("nuclear fusion"). *See also* **L88.**

It is the latter process, fusion, that is going on in stars. The fusion processes can be studied in physics laboratories by using large accelerating machines to hurl nuclei at one another to make them coalesce. In stars the necessary high velocity of impact occurs because the plasma is so hot. Gradually the hydrogen is turned into helium, and helium into heavier and heavier elements. This supplies the energy that the stars radiate and simultaneously generates the chemical elements.

The Heaviest Elements

The very heavy elements present a problem. To form them from middleweight elements, energy has to be *supplied.* Since there is plenty of energy inside a star, a certain small number of heavy nuclei will indeed form, but they will continually undergo fission again under the prevailing intense conditions. How do they ever get away to form cool ordinary elements, like lead and bismuth, in the earth? One view links them with the highly explosive supernovae, to which we have already referred (**F4(2)**). If the heavy elements occur in these stars the force of the explosion disperses them into cool outer space before they have time to undergo the fission that would otherwise have been their fate. The heavy elements are thus seen as the dust and debris of stellar catastrophes. The view is in line with the steady-state theory, because supernovae are always occurring and keeping up the supply of heavy elements. In the evolutionary theory some of the generation of elements is supposed to go on in the very early stages of the initial dense state and to continue in the stars that evolve in the fullness of time. It cannot be claimed that the origin of the chemical elements is completely known, but we have said enough to show that there are plausible theories. Time and more facts will choose between them.

The Formation of the Planets

Precisely how the planetary system was formed is still not understood in detail. From extremely precise observations of the movements of some nearby stars, it seems certain that other planetary systems occur among our stellar neighbours. By inference, it is thus probable that among certain classes of stars, planetary systems are very common throughout the universe.

Two other facts are crucial for any theory of planetary system formation. First, all the planetary orbits lie nearly in the plane perpendicular to the axis of rotation of the sun. The planets' rotations about the sun are all in the same direction and their axes of rotation, with two exceptions (Venus and Uranus), are close to the polar axis of their orbit planes, and in the same sense as their orbital rotation about the sun. Secondly, there is a very strong inverse correlation between planetary distance from the sun and the planet's mean density, particularly if the correct allowance is made for the effects of gravitational compression in the deep interiors of planets (greater in large than in small planets).

Rather than theories which would place planetary formation as either the random collection of pre-formed planets by the sun in its path through the galaxy or as the consequence of a very near encounter between our sun and another star, it is now generally believed that the origin of the planetary system (and most of the satellites, etc.) was a direct consequence of the process which originally formed the sun.

As the primaeval solar nebula contracted, to conserve angular momentum, its rotation rate increased, and a diffuse equatorial disk of dust and gas formed. In the cold outer region (10–$20°$ K) of this disk, all materials except helium and possibly hydrogen could readily condense on dust particles. Near the centre the temperature was higher, increasingly so as the proto-sun heated up, initially by the energy released by its gravitational contraction and, later, by the thermonuclear processes (**F4(1)**).

The Process of Accretion

Within this rotating and swirling disk of gas and dust, the process of accretion proceeded. Low-velocity collision between dust particles from time to time allowed larger particles to be created, composed of a mixture of the heavier elements and also the "icy" materials, particularly so in the colder outer regions where more of the "ices" were in a frozen state. Virtually our only information on the composition of such particles comes from detailed study of meteorites and from spectroscopic observation of comets. Eventually rocks of the size of centimetres, metres, and even kilometres were built up in this way. The build-up, controlled by low-velocity collisions, particularly of "sticky" materials, and also by electrostatic charges, was, at all times, however, moderated by occasional destructive high-velocity collisions. The relatively high viscosity of the dust and gas mixture throughout the disk must have been very important in producing a relatively uniform, rotational motion throughout the disk.

When "rocks" a few kilometres in size had been created new factors became important. Gravitational forces firstly increased the capacity of the larger "rocks" to accrete additional dust and smaller particles and, secondly, allowed some retention of material after even high-velocity collisions which would have destroyed smaller pieces.

The next stage is possibly the most difficult to model. Within a relatively uniform disk containing large numbers of rocks up to a few kilometres in diameter mixed within the residual dust and a large amount of gas, and extending to well outside Pluto's orbit, a small number of massive planets were formed. Some debris now remains as the comets and asteroids; however this debris and all the major planets, including the massive Jupiter, represent in total only a very small percentage of the original material of the solar nebula which was not condensed to form the sun.

It would appear that relatively quickly, during a period of 10^7 or 10^8 years, the large numbers of kilometre-sized objects, by collision and mutual gravitational attraction, formed the nuclei of the present planets and probably, in most cases, their major satellites also, in orbits relatively similar to their present ones. The planet-building process was most efficient at distances from the sun corresponding to the present orbits of Jupiter or Saturn, a compromise between temperature decreasing with distance from the sun, allowing a greater percentage of the total material to be solid and thus available for accretion, and density of material being greater closer to the sun.

The Jovian Planets

The outer or "Jovian" planets must have grown quickly, sweeping up hydrogen and helium gas as well as solid particles. Closer to the sun, the "icy" materials, still mainly in gaseous form, could not contribute very significantly to the initial accretion process, so that only smaller planets could form. Owing to their smaller mass, gravitational field and thus lower "escape velocity," they were only able to accrete a small proportion of the heavier gas present within the inner part of the solar system. Thus, at present, these

THE SOLAR SYSTEM

	Mean distance from Sun (millions of km)	Diameter km	Period of Revolution	Average density (water = 1)	Number of Satellites
Sun	—	1,392,000			
Mercury	57·9	4,880	88 days	5·4	0
Venus	108·2	12,104	224·7 days	5·2	0
Earth	149·6	12,756	365·26 days	5·5	1
Mars	227·9	6,787	687 days	3·9	2
Jupiter	778·3	142,800	11·86 years	1·3	14
Saturn	1,427	120,000	29·46 years	0·7	17
Uranus	2,869·6	51,800	84·01 years	1·2	5
Neptune	4,496·6	49,500	164·8 years	1·7	2
Pluto	5,900	3,500	247·7 years	0·6	1

Note: Chiron, an object recently discovered orbiting the sun between Saturn and Uranus has not been given "planet" status due to its small size.

"terrestrial" planets are much denser than the outer "Jovian" planets, much smaller in size, and contain very little hydrogen or helium. The planet-building process was probably ended by two factors: the gravitational disruptive effect of the planets already formed and the enhanced "solar wind" of the young sun, which swept much of the residual dust and gas out of the solar system.

Before the process was complete, however, the gravitational energy released by the material falling onto the proto-planets plus the radioactive heating of short-lived isotopes present at the time of planetary formation were responsible for melting most of the bodies of the planets and probably all the larger satellites and asteroids. This process allowed gravitational segregation of denser and lighter materials within the planets, and the production of the core, mantle and crustal regions of each of the terrestrial planets. Long after the dust and gas were driven from the solar system and the planet surfaces cooled and solidified, the residual larger rocks and asteroids, of which enormous numbers were originally still present, continued to be swept up by each of the planets. The record of this violent stage of the solar system's development can still be seen in the saturation cratering observed on the Moon, Mercury, and Mars.

In the past decade, direct space exploration, using automated space probes (and manned spacecraft in the case of the Moon) has enormously increased our knowledge of the solar system. Notable have been the Mars "Viking" project, the Venus probes, the later Pioneer probes with Pioneer 11 flying on from Jupiter to Saturn, and the Voyagers 1 and 2, the latter to visit no less than four planets. Important discoveries have continued to be made by ground-based telescopes such as a new ring system of Uranus, the object Chiron, and the radar investigation of the terrain of Venus. Space-borne optical telescopes orbiting the earth may be expected to produce exciting new results.

sphere, with an equatorial radius of 6,378 km and a polar radius 21 km less. Its mass can be calculated from Newton's Law of Gravitation and from measurements of the acceleration due to gravity, and is $5·97 \times 10^{24}$ kg. The average density follows from these two figures and is about 5·5 grams per cubic centimetre. This is nearly twice the density of typical rocks at the surface, so there must be very much denser material somewhere inside, and the earth must have a definite internal structure.

This structure can be investigated using shock waves from earthquakes or large explosions. These are received at recording stations at different distances from their source, having penetrated to varying depths within the earth, and their relative times of arrival and characteristic forms enable the deep structure to be worked out. This consists of three main units, a core at the centre with a radius about half that of the earth, the mantle outside this, and the thin crust, about 35 km thick under the continents and 5 km thick under the oceans, forming a skin surrounding the mantle.

The composition of these three units can be deduced by observation and inference. For example, meteorites which arrive at the earth's surface from other parts of the solar system consist of three main types, composed of iron-nickel alloy, stony silicates, and a mixture of iron and silicates. Could these have originated from the break-up of some planet like the earth? If so, then perhaps the core of the earth is made up of iron-nickel alloy and the mantle of magnesium-rich silicates. Experiments on the physical properties of these materials at high pressures show strong similarities with the measured properties of the earth's interior. In addition, rocks composed of magnesium-rich silicates are found at the earth's surface in places where material seems to have come from great depth, such as in the debris from volcanic explosions. These may be direct samples of the earth's mantle.

THE EARTH

Structure

The earth has the shape of a slightly flattened

Core, Mantle and Crust

By these arguments, and by many others, a picture can be built up of the internal structure of the earth. The core is composed of iron–nickel

SOME ASTRONOMICAL DISTANCES

(1 light-year = $9·46 \times 10^{12}$ km).

Object	Distance from Earth (light-years)	Velocity of recession (km per second)	Object	Distance from Earth (light-years)	Velocity of recession (km per second)
Sun	$1·6 \times 10^{-5}$	—	Andromeda Galaxy	$1·5 \times 10^6$	—
Nearest star (Proxima Centauri)	4·2	—	Galaxy in Virgo.	$7·5 \times 10^7$	1,200
Brightest star (Sirius)	8·6	—	Galaxy in Gt. Bear	10^9	14,900
Pleiades	340	—	Galaxy in Corona Borealis	$1·3 \times 10^9$	21,600
Centre of Milky Way	$2·6 \times 10^4$	—	Galaxy in Bootes	$4·5 \times 10^9$	39,300
Magellanic clouds (the nearest galaxies)	$1·6 \times 10^5$	—	Very remote quasi-stellar object	$\sim 1·5 \times 10^{10}$	$\sim 240,000$

alloy. It is liquid at the outside, but contains a solid inner core of radius about one-fifth of that of the earth. Convection currents flowing in the liquid part give rise to the earth's magnetic field. Outside this the mantle is solid, and is made up mainly of magnesium–iron silicates of various kinds. By studying its physical properties through earthquake wave observations, the mantle may be divided into several zones, of which the most important is the asthenosphere. This is the part of the mantle between 70 and 300 km depth in which volcanic lavas are formed. In this region the mantle is everywhere quite near to the temperature at which it begins to melt, and is thus rather soft compared with the rest of the mantle. The presence of a soft asthenosphere accounts for many of the surface features of the earth, mountain belts and ocean basins, that make it so very different from cratered planets such as the Moon and Mars.

The sharp boundary between mantle and crust is called the Mohorovicic Discontinuity. Above it, the crust is different under continents and oceans. The thick continental crust has a composition that can broadly be called granitic, while the thin oceanic crust is poorer in silicon, sodium, and potassium and richer in calcium, iron, and magnesium. The continental crust has been built up over thousands of millions of years by welding together mountain belts of different ages, while the oceanic crust is made up of basalt lavas and is nowhere older than 250 million years.

Rocks

Rocks are naturally occurring pieces of the solid earth. If you take a rock and break it up into grains, then separate the grains into different heaps of like grains, each heap will consist of grains of the same *mineral*. For example, the kind of rock called granite can be divided into glassy grains of the mineral quartz, milky white or pink grains of the mineral feldspar, shiny black flakes of the mineral biotite, and shiny colourless flakes of the mineral muscovite. Both biotite and muscovite belong to the mica group of minerals. Each different mineral has a well-defined composition or range of composition, and a definite and characteristic arrangement of the atoms that compose it. There are several thousand known kinds of minerals, but only fifty or so are at all common.

There are three main kinds of rock; igneous rocks, formed by the solidification of molten lava; sedimentary rocks, formed from material laid down under gravity on the earth's surface; and metamorphic rocks, formed by heating or reheating of either of the other kind of rock. Each of these broad groups may be further subdivided. When *igneous rocks* solidify deep inside the earth, they cool slowly and large crystals have time to form. Coarse-grained igneous rocks such as granites are known as plutonic igneous rocks. Conversely the rapidly cooled fine-grained igneous rocks that form the volcanic lavas, such as basalts and rhyolites, are called volcanic igneous rocks. *Sedimentary rocks* can be divided into three kinds: Clastic sediments are those formed from mechanically abraded and transported fragments of pre-existing rocks and include sandstone, mudstone, and clay. Organic sediments are those composed, as are most limestones, of fragments of organically produced material such as shells, wood, and bone. Chemical sediments are formed by direct chemical action and include, most typically, salt deposits formed by evaporation of sea water. *Metamorphic rocks* are more difficult to subdivide. They are usually classified on the basis of their original composition and/or the maximum pressure and temperature to which they have been subjected. Chemical reactions in metamorphic rocks give rise to successions of minerals as the pressure and temperature change, so that examination of a metamorphic rock will often allow one to say how deeply it was buried and how hot it was.

Age of Rocks

There are two distinct ways of estimating the age of rocks. The first gives the *relative age*. It is based on the principle that in a sequence of sediments, older rocks lie underneath and younger ones above, that igneous rocks are younger than the rocks they intrude, and that folded rocks are formed earlier than the earth movements that fold them. Correlation of a sequence of rocks in one place with those in another is made by fossil faunas and floras. Thus a complete scale of relative ages can be built up, stretching back to the first rocks containing fossils (see the table in Part IV). The *age in years* can, on the other hand, be measured by using radioactive elements (Part II) contained in rocks. If the amount of a radioactive element present is measured, and the amount of the product of radioactive decay can also be found, then, using the known rates of decay, the time since the product started to accumulate (defined for this purpose as the age in years) can be measured. This method is particularly useful for studying rocks that do not contain fossils (igneous and metamorphic rocks, or those too old to contain fossils). By similar methods, the *age of the earth* can be obtained. This turns out to be about $4 \cdot 6 \times 10^9$ years. The rocks containing the first fossils are $2 \cdot 5 - 3 \times 10^9$ years old, while organised life in abundance first appeared about $0 \cdot 6 \times 10^9$ years ago.

The Continents and the Ocean Floor

The outer part of the earth, namely, the asthenosphere and the solid mantle and crust overlying it, the lithosphere, is in a state of restless movement, and it is this movement that gives rise to the formation of oceans, continents, and mountain belts. The surface of the earth can be divided into a number of rigid plates of lithosphere, which move apart, or together, or slide past one another. Some of these plates are very large, such as the one which contains all of North America, all of South America, and about half of the Atlantic Ocean. Others are no more than a few thousand square kilometres in size. But they are all moving about relative to one another like ice floes in pack-ice. Where two plates move apart, hot material rises from the asthenosphere to fill the gap, partly melts, and gives rise to a chain of volcanoes and a thin volcanic crust. This is how ocean basins form and grow larger. In the Atlantic, the Mid-Atlantic Ridge marks the line along which plates are moving apart, and where new ocean is being formed. Long narrow pieces of ocean such as the Red Sea and the Gulf of California mark where a continent has just begun to split apart, and a new ocean is forming. Where two plates slide past one another, a great tear fault results. Such a fault is the San Andreas fault which runs from the Gulf of California to San Francisco. Jerky movement on this fault gave rise to the great San Francisco earthquake of 1906 and could give rise to another earthquake there at any time.

Where two plates move together, the result depends on the nature of the crust forming the plates. If at least one of the plates is oceanic, the oceanic crust dips down into the mantle and slides away to great depths until it eventually merges with the asthenosphere. Along this dipping sheet of crust, strong earthquakes occur and frictional heating of the sheet leads to melting and the production of quantities of lava. Examples of such boundaries are the Andes, where the Pacific Ocean bed dips beneath South America, and Indonesia, where the Indian Ocean bed dips below Asia. When both plates are continental, on the other hand, the crust is too thick and buoyant to slide into the mantle, and a collision results, giving rise to a fold mountain chain. Eventually the movement grinds to a halt, the plates weld together, and the fold mountains become dormant. The Himalayas were formed in this way from the recent collision of India and Asia. The evidence that has led to these conclusions is too complex to summarise here. It comes from a study of rock magnetism, earthquakes, the flow of heat from inside the earth and even from the shapes of the continents, that must match across the oceans by which they have been split apart. Confirmation has come from a series of holes drilled in the ocean which has shown how the crust becomes younger towards the centres of the oceans.

Rates of movement of plates have been calculated, ranging from a few millimetres a year to ten centimetres a year. The faster movements can be measured directly on the ground by such simple techniques as looking at the displacement of railway lines, walls, and roads, but the slower ones, and those beneath the oceans must be measured by more indirect geophysical methods. The mechanism by which this movement takes place is still unknown. Are the plates pulled by their sinking edges, or pushed by their rising edges, or moved by some other means? But it cannot be doubted that the movement does happen, and that it holds the key to the development of the earth's crust since the time it was first formed.

The Rest

There is a lot more to the study of the earth than has been possible to set down here. The oceans, the atmosphere, and the rocks of the crust all interact with one another in their development in a complex way. The surface of the earth has gradually changed as life has evolved over thousands of millions of years and ice ages have come and gone, changing the surface again and again. Just as important is the economic potential of the earth, on which we depend for all of our energy and all raw materials. This section has given the basic framework within which such further investigations are carried out, to help the reader understand as he reads more widely.

II. PHYSICS—THE FUNDAMENTAL SCIENCE OF MATTER

WHAT PHYSICS IS ABOUT

Anyone compelled by curiosity or professional interest to look into contemporary journals of pure physics research is soon struck by the fact that the old test-book division of physics into "heat, light, sound, electricity, and magnetism" has become very blurred.

Two different, though complementary, sections can be distinguished. First, there is the physics concerned with the properties of matter in bulk, with solids, liquids, and gases, and with those odd but very important substances, such as paints, plastic solutions, and jelly-like material, which are neither properly solid nor liquid. In this vast domain of physics questions like this are asked: Why is iron magnetic, copper not? What happens when solids melt? Why do some liquids flow more easily than others? Why do some things conduct electricity well, others badly, some not at all? During the last century, particularly the last few decades, it has become clear that such questions can be answered only by raising and solving others first. In particular, we must ask: (i) Of what nature are the invisible particles of which matter is composed? and (ii) How are those particles arranged in bulk matter?

The first of these two questions has generated the second major category of modern physics: this is the physics of particles and of the forces that particles exert on each other. In this field which represents science at its most fundamental questions like this are asked: If matter is composed of small units or particles, what are they like? How many kinds of particle are there? Do the particles possess mass? electric charge? magnetism? How do the particles influence each other? How can their motion be described and predicted?

The discussion which follows has been divided into two main parts (1) Particles and Forces, and (2) The Properties of Matter in Bulk, with part (1) describing the microscopic structure of matter and part (2) its macroscopic properties.

PARTICLES AND FORCES

Aristotle to Newton

The inference that matter should be composed of small particles or atoms originated, it is true, in classical times. The atomic idea was an attempt to solve the age-old problem of matter and its peculiar properties. The ancients had provided themselves with two solutions to the problem of matter:

(i) The theory of the four elements (earth, water, fire, air), from which all different forms of matter were composed by selecting different ratios of the four ingredients. This approach had been used by traditional philosophy and was adopted by Aristotle.
(ii) The theory of atomism which postulated the existence of atoms and empty space.

Atomism remained very much in the background in the development of Western Science and persisted even longer in the Arab world. The idea that matter is composed of "small units" was in reality forced into the mental development of mankind by the repeated application of the process of dimension halving. By the time of Newton atomism had come to the fore and Newton considered that God had made the Universe from "small indivisible grains" of matter. Nevertheless, the search for the "philosopher's stone" was still, in the seventeenth century, the main pursuit of many scientists, but the new chemistry of the seventeenth century made use of atomistic concepts. Newton's physics was a mechanics concerning particles in a vacuum and when Boyle described his gas law (i.e., Pressure × Volume is constant at a fixed temperature) he visualised matter as composed of particles with specific qualitative properties. It was, of course, the advance of experimental techniques which enabled scientists to test ideas and theories on the nature of matter.

Dalton and Atomic Theory

The modern view of atomism need be traced no farther than the beginning of the nineteenth century when Dalton and his contemporaries were studying the laws of chemical combination using precise weighing techniques. By that time the distinctions between elements, compounds, and mixtures were already made. Compounds and mixtures are substances which can be separated into smaller amounts of chemically distinguishable constituents. Elements (see end of Sec.) cannot be so divided. In a mixture the components may be mixed in any proportion and sorted out again by non-chemical means. In a compound the elements are combined in fixed proportions by weight. This last fact gives the clue to atomic theory.

Dalton pointed out that the fixed combining weights of elements could easily be explained if the elements consisted of atoms which combined in simple numerical ratios, e.g., 1 atom of element A with one of B, or one of B with two of C, and so on. For instance, 35·5 g of chlorine combine with 23·0 g of sodium to make 58·5 g of ordinary salt. If we assume one atom of chlorine links with one of sodium, then the atoms themselves must have weights in the ratio 35·5 to 23·0. This turns out to be consistent with the combining weights of chlorine and sodium in all other compounds in which they both take part. Sometimes two elements combine in several different proportions by weight. But this is easily explained by assuming that the atoms link up in a variety of ways e.g., one iron atom with one oxygen, or two irons with three oxygens, or three irons with four oxygens. Then the three different combining proportions arise from the three different numbers of atoms, using in each case the same ratio of oxygen atom weight to iron atom weight.

Atomic Weight

Over the century and a half since Dalton, these ideas have been repeatedly tested by chemical experiments No. one now doubts that every chemical element has atoms of characteristic weight. The atomic weight or more properly the relative atomic mass, of an element is by international agreement expressed relative to one isotope (see below) of carbon, namely carbon-12 which is given the relative mass of twelve. These numbers are only ratios; the real weight of one single oxygen atom is $2·7 \times 10^{-23}$ g.

Valency

That the combinations of atoms in definite proportions was necessary, to produce compounds, or more correctly molecules, was known from 1808. The reason why only one atom of sodium and one of chlorine was required to produce one molecule of salt was unknown. Further the seemingly odd combinations of two atoms of hydrogen (H) with one of oxygen (O) to give water (H_2O), while only one atom of hydrogen could combine with chlorine to give hydrogen chloride /(HCl) could not be explained. This situation was not resolved until around 1860, when the chemical formulae of many molecules were known. It was then discovered that homologies existed in the elements, for example the series Na, K, Rb, Cs, or Fl, Cl, Br, I, and this culminated in the Periodic Table of the elements (see end Sec.). The valency of an atom was determined by its position in the periodic table and determined by the number of electrons (see below) which the atom has orbiting its nucleus. Atoms combined to form molecules in a manner which maintained the number of "valence" electrons in a stable grouping of 2, 8, or 18 (see **F24**). For example, sodium has one valence electron and chlorine seven, therefore the combination NaCl gives the stable grouping of eight; hydrogen has one and oxygen six, hence it requires two atoms of hydrogen and one of oxygen to give one stable molecule, H_2O. Other more complicated molecular structures and types of bonding between atoms are dealt with in the chemistry section. This discovery of particles smaller than the atom itself was necessary to fully comprehend the nature of valency in atomic combinations.

J. J. Thomson and the Electron

Matter is electrically uncharged in its normal state, but there exist many well-known ways of producing electric charges and currents—rubbing amber, or rotating dynamos, for example. It is therefore necessary to have some theory of electricity linked to the theory of matter. The fundamental experiment in this field was made by J. J. Thomson when, in 1897, he discovered the electron.

If you take two metal electrodes sealed inside a glass vessel and if the pressure of the air is reduced from atmospheric pressure, 76 cm of mercury, to 1 mm of mercury by mechanical pumping and then a high voltage, several kilo-volts, is applied to the electrodes, the negative electrode emits a "radiation" which causes the walls of the tube to glow. The rays are called *cathode rays*. The discovery of the electron was essentially a clarification of the nature of cathode rays. Thomson showed that they were streams of particles with mass and negative electric charge and a general behaviour unlike any other atomic particle known at that time. The importance of this discovery for the world of science cannot be overestimated, and its technical progeny are in every home and factory in X-ray machines, television tubes, and all electronic devices.

Rutherford–Bohr Atom

Since the electrons emerge from matter, they are presumably parts of atoms. The relation between the negative electrons and the positively charged constituents of matter was elucidated by the great experimenter Rutherford and the great theoretician Bohr. Their work, just before the First World War, showed that the positive charge, together with almost all the mass, is concentrated in the central core or nucleus of the atom about which the very light-weight electrons revolve. The diameter of an atom is about 10^{-8} cm, roughly one three-hundred-millionth part of an inch. The central nucleus has a diameter about 10,000 times smaller still. The nucleus and the electrons hold together because of the electric attraction between them.

The positive charge of the nucleus is responsible for holding the electron in the region of space around the nucleus. The electrostatic Coulomb force, if left on its own would quickly attract the electrons into the nucleus but since the electrons move in orbits, circular and elliptical, they experience an outward centrifugal force which balances the inward electrostatic force. The mechanism is similar to that which holds the earth in orbit around the sun, only here a gravitational force replaces the effect of the Coulomb force. Modern theories of the electronic structure of atoms are quantum mechanical (see below).

At this stage work could, and did, go on separately along several different lines:

(i) Electrons could be studied on their own. Nowadays the handling of beams of electrons of all sizes and intensities has become a major branch of technology.

(ii) The nucleus could be treated as a special problem, and this led to the mid-century flowering of nuclear physics, to the atomic bomb, and to nuclear power.

(iii) The behaviour of electrons in the atom could be analysed; this is the great domain of atomic physics which spreads into many other sciences as well.

Volumes have been written about each of these three fields, but we can spare only a few lines for each.

The Electron

Electrons are expelled from solids by light, heat, electric fields, and other influences. It has therefore been possible to study beams of electrons on their own *in vacuo*. Electrons inside matter, either as constituents, or temporarily in transit, can also be observed by their innumerable effects. These observations all show the particles to be indistinguishable one from another; all electrons are the same wherever they come from. They have a definite mass ($9·11 \times 10^{-28}$ g), a negative electric charge, a magnetic moment, and a "spin" (intrinsic rotatory motion). No one has ever subdivided an electron or obtained an electric charge smaller than that on one electron. The electronic charge is therefore used as a basic unit of charge in atomic physics. The electron has come to be the best known of all the "fundamental particles." It is now used in research as probe for studying the structure of matter, for which it is ideally suited, since it is very much smaller than an atom. A whole field of electron-scattering research which studies the nature and structure of solids, liquids, and gases is being actively conducted in many laboratories.

The Nucleus

The early research programmes in nuclear physics were greatly facilitated by the occurrence in nature of certain unstable (radioactive) nuclei which emit fast-moving fragments. The latter can be used as projectiles to aim at other nuclei as targets; the resulting impacts yield much valuable information. This technique still dominates nuclear physics, though nowadays the projectiles are artificially accelerated by one or other of the large costly machines designed for the purpose.

The most important early discovery was that the nucleus consists of two types of fundamental particle—the positively charged *proton* and the electrically neutral *neutron*. These two are of nearly equal mass (about 1,800 times that of the electron), and like electrons, have a magnetic moment and spin. The proton charge is equal to the electron charge, though opposite in sign. Consider a moderately complex nucleus like that of iron. This usually has 30 neutrons and 26 protons. Its atomic weight therefore depends on the total number of neutrons plus protons, but the total charge depends only on the number of protons—called the *atomic number*. The latter is denoted by Z while the total number of neutrons plus protons is called the *mass number* and denoted by M. A species of nucleus with given values of Z and M is called a *nuclide*. Z is also the number of electrons in the atom, since the atom as a whole is electrically neutral. The atomic number determines the chemical nature of the atom (see below), so that by altering the number of *neutrons* in a nucleus we do not change the chemical species. It is therefore possible to find—and nowadays to make—nuclei of the same element which nevertheless differ slightly in weight because they have different numbers of neutrons. These are called *isotopes*. Iron isotopes are known with 26, 27, 28, 29, 30, 31, 32, and 33 neutrons, but all have 26 protons. Thus a set of isotopes consists of the various nuclides that have the same Z but different M's.

When the atomic properties of isotopes are measured it is found that small, hyperfine differences in the motions of the electrons around the respective nuclei exist. These result from the different total spin of the isotopes and its effect on the orbiting electrons. This influence of atomic properties by nuclear effects is important in that it provides a link between different fields of research.

Stable Nuclides

The protons and neutrons in a nucleus are bound together by strong forces called *nuclear forces*. In many cases, the forces are so strong that no particles ever escape and the nucleus preserves its identity. There are two hundred and seventy-four different combinations of neutrons and protons of this kind, and they are called the *stable nuclides*. The earth is largely composed of such stable nuclides, because any unstable ones have, in the course of time, spontaneously broken up into stable residues.

Nevertheless, there are some unstable nuclei left on earth. They give rise to the phenomenon of radioactivity which was discovered by Becquerel in 1893.

Unstable Nuclides: Radioactivity

Becquerel found that certain chemicals containing uranium gave off rays capable of blackening a photographic plate, and shortly afterwards Marie and Pierre Curie discovered more substances, including radium, which produce similar but stronger effects. By now, about fifty chemical elements having radioactive properties are known to exist on earth, some, like radium, being strongly radioactive, others, like potassium, being so weak that the radiations are difficult to detect. These are called the *natural radioactive nuclides*.

The main facts about radioactivity are as follows: it is a *nuclear* phenomenon and (with minor exceptions) proceeds quite independently of whatever the electrons in the atom may be doing. Thus, the radioactivity of an atom is not affected by the chemical combination of the atom with other atoms, nor by ordinary physical influences like temperature and pressure. The radioactivity consists of the emission by the substance of certain kinds of rays. The early workers, Rutherford being the giant among them, distinguished three kinds of rays labelled a, β, and γ. These are described below. Whatever kind of ray is examined, it is found that the radiation from a given sample decreases gradually with time according to a definite law which states that the intensity of radiation decreases by half every T seconds. The number T, called the half-life, is constant for each radioactive material, but varies enormously from substance to substance. For instance, radium decreases its activity by a half every 1,622 years, whereas the half-life of one of the polonium isotopes is about 0.3×10^{-6} sec.

a-, β-, and γ-rays

The three most well-known types of radioactive emission are quite distinct from one another.

(i) a-rays or a-particles consist of two protons and two neutrons bound together. They are ejected from the radioactive nucleus with one of several well-defined speeds. These speeds are high, often of the order 10^9 cm per sec. Two protons and two neutrons are the constituents of the nucleus of helium, and a-particles are thus fast-moving helium nuclei.

(ii) β-rays are moving electrons. They may emerge from their parent nucleus with any speed from zero to a definite maximum. The maximum speed often approaches that of light, and is different for each isotope. The electron has a

positively charged counterpart, the positron (see below), and β-rays are sometimes positrons. To distinguish the two cases, the symbols β^- and β^+ are used. The naturally occurring β-radiations are almost all β^-.

(iii) γ-rays travel with the speed of light because they are in fact electromagnetic waves differing from light only in the extreme shortness of their wavelength. They have no electric charge.

It is unusual, though not unheard of, for the same radioactive substance to emit both a- and β-rays. On the other hand, γ-rays frequently accompany either a- or β-rays.

γ-rays pass through matter easily; in fact, they are extra penetrating X-rays. a-rays can be stopped by thin sheets of tissue paper. a-rays brought to rest pick up a pair of electrons from the surrounding matter and become neutral helium atoms, and helium gas from this source is consequently found imprisoned in certain radioactive rocks. β-rays are intermediate in penetrating power between a- and γ-rays.

We must now try to interpret these observations.

Radioactive Disintegration

A nucleus is a collection of neutrons and protons interacting with each other and possessing collectively a certain amount of energy. Just as some human organisations lose their coherence if they accept too many members, so nuclei can remain stable only if (i) the total number of particles is not too great, and (ii) neutrons and protons are there in suitable proportions. Radioactive nuclei are the ones for which either or both these conditions do not hold. Sooner or later such nuclei eject a fragment, thus getting rid of some energy they cannot contain. This is called a *radioactive disintegration*, and the fragments are the a-, β-, and γ-rays. a-emission relieves a nucleus of two neutrons and two protons and some energy; γ-emission simply carries off excess energy without altering the number or kind of particles left behind. β-emission is more complicated. There are no electrons normally present in a nucleus, but they are suddenly created and explosively emitted if a neutron changes into a proton; positive electrons are similarly generated if a proton changes into a neutron. β-emission is therefore a mechanism for changing the ratio of protons to neutrons without altering the total number of particles.

Both a- and β-emission change the Z of a nucleus, and the product, or daughter nucleus, is a different chemical element. a-emission also changes the M. It might happen that the daughter nucleus is unstable, in which case it too will disintegrate. Successive generations are produced until a stable one is reached. Part of such a family tree is shown below. The symbols above the arrows show the kind of rays emitted at each stage, the figures are the mass numbers, M, and the names and symbols of chemical elements can be found at the end of the Section.

$$U^{238} \xrightarrow{a} Th^{234} \xrightarrow{\beta} Pa^{234} \xrightarrow{\beta} U^{234} \xrightarrow{a} Th^{230} \xrightarrow{a}$$

$$Ra^{226} \xrightarrow{a} Rn^{222} \xrightarrow{a} Po^{218} \xrightarrow{a} Pb^{214} \xrightarrow{\beta} Bi^{214} \xrightarrow{\beta}$$

$$Po^{214} \xrightarrow{a} Pb^{210} \xrightarrow{\beta} Bi^{210} \xrightarrow{\beta} Po^{210} \xrightarrow{a} Pb^{206}$$

(Pb^{206} is stable lead).

This family exists naturally on earth, because the head of the family, U^{238}, has so long a half-life (4.5×10^9 years) that there has not yet been time enough since its formation for it to have disappeared.

Artificial Radioactivity

Nowadays many new radioactive isotopes can be man-made. All that is required is to alter the M or Z (or both) of a stable isotope to a value which is incompatible with stability. The means for doing this is *bombardment*, i.e., stable nuclei are exposed to the impacts of atomic particles such as streams of protons from an accelerator, the neutrons in an atomic reactor, or simply the a-particles from another radioactive substance.

The new material is called an *artificially radio-active isotope*. Artificial radioactivity is not different in kind from that of the naturally radio-active substances, but the half-lives are usually on the short side. Indeed, the isotopes in question would exist in nature but for the fact that their short half-lives ensured their disappearance from the earth long ago.

Suppose a piece of copper is exposed to the intense neutron radiation in an atomic reactor at Harwell.

The more abundant of the two stable isotopes of ordinary copper has thirty-four neutrons and twenty-nine protons (*i.e.*, $Z = 29$, $M = 63$). In the reactor many (not all) of these nuclei absorb a neutron, giving an unstable copper nucleus with $Z = 29$, $M = 64$. When removed from the reactor the specimen is observed to be radioactive with a half-life of $12 \cdot 8$ hours. It is somewhat unusual in that it gives out both β^- and β^+ rays. Some nuclei emit electrons, leaving a daughter nucleus with one more positive charge than copper, *i.e.*, a zinc nucleus ($Z = 30$, $M = 64$). One neutron has become a proton, and the re-sulting zinc nucleus is stable. The others emit positrons, leaving behind a nucleus in which a proton has been turned into a neutron ($Z = 28$, $M = 64$); this is a stable nickel nucleus. The overall process is one example of the artificial transmutation of the chemical elements which is now a commonplace of nuclear physics. It was first discovered by Irene and Frederick Joliot-Curie in 1934.

Lack of a Complete Theory

Consider now a collection of, say, one million radioactive nuclei of the same kind. It is im-possible to tell exactly when any one of them will disintegrate; it is a matter of chance which ones break up first. All we know is that, after a time equal to the half-life, only a half a million will survive unchanged. In general, the more excess energy a nucleus has, the more likely it is to break up, and therefore the shorter the half-life of that particular nuclear species. In principle, to cal-culate the half-life theoretically, one would have to have a reliable theory of nuclear forces and energies. This is still being sought after, so it is probably fair to say that while the laws of behaviour of radioactive isotopes are well and accurately known, the *explanation* of this behaviour in terms of the properties of protons and neutrons is by no means complete.

Nuclear Fission—Chain Reaction

A discovery important not just for nuclear physics but for the whole of mankind was made by Hahn and Strassman in 1939. This was the dis-covery of nuclear fission in uranium. One of the natural isotopes of uranium is an unstable one, U^{235}, with 143 neutrons and 92 protons. It norm-ally shows its instability by emitting a- and γ-rays. If uranium is bombarded with neutrons, some U^{235} nuclei temporarily gain an extra neutron, which makes them even less stable. This they show by splitting into two roughly equal parts, called fission fragments, together with two or three neutrons. There are two highly important things about this disintegration. One is that the two or three neutrons can promote further disintegrations in other uranium nuclei, and the process can therefore be self-propagating: it is then called a *chain re-action*. The other is that the total mass of the fission products is less than that of the original nucleus. This mass difference does not disappear without trace; it turns into energy according to a formula referred to in a paragraph below (**F18(1)**).

Nuclear Fusion

The ability of two light nuclei to combine and form a heavier nucleus is called fusion. A reac-tion of this nature does not form a chain process but proceeds in singly induced reactions. A typical fusion reaction is the formation of a helium nucleus (mass 3) from two deuterium nuclei which are made to collide at an energy of 60 keV (speed of $2 \cdot 410^6$ m/s)

i.e., $^2D_1 + {}^2D_1 \rightarrow {}^3He_2$ ($0 \cdot 82$ meV) + n($2 \cdot 45$ meV)

where the $^3He_2$ particle has kinetic energy of $0 \cdot 82$ meV and the free neutron has free kinetic energy of $2 \cdot 45$ meV. This type of reaction is exo-energetic, the additional kinetic energy coming from the tighter binding of the nucleus in ^3He than in the two separate deuterium nuclei. The energy released in this form of nuclear reaction is much more than that in a fission process and is respon-sible for the emitted energy of the sun which burns hydrogen to form helium.

Applications of Nuclear Reactions

The world has two uses for the energy released in nuclear reactions:

(1) nuclear weapons;
(2) nuclear power plants.

The only nuclear bombs to be used in anger employed the fission chain reaction proceeding at a rapid rate which quickly becomes uncontrollable and produces a tremendous explosion. The second generation of nuclear warhead uses the fusion reaction, which is initiated by a fission-reacting detonator to produce an even more des-tructive blast. The third generation of nuclear warhead uses the large flux of very energetic neutrons to kill biological material, but the blast effect is essentially zero, hence attacks with neutron bombs leave most non-biological material and structures intact.

In the second application the nuclear fission process is controlled to provide a constant source of energy to drive turbines which produce electri-city.

Both uses represent epoch-making technical achievements, but mankind has yet to show itself capable of bearing sanely the burden of respon-sibility which nuclear physicists have laid upon it. One thing is certain: the discoveries will not cease. Already, other fissionable elements have been made and used; new chemical elements have been created; nuclear plants ("atomic piles") have stimulated great demands for new materials that will stand the heat and radiation inside the reactor, and this promotes research in other fields of science; irradiation inside an atomic pile gives new, and potentially useful properties to old materials; nuclear power drives ships and submarines. It is difficult to write even briefly about contemporary nuclear physics without feel-ing keenly the ambiguity of its powerful promises.

Atoms

A nucleus surrounded by its full complement of electrons is an electrically neutral system called an atom. Neither the atom as a whole, nor its nucleus, counts as a "fundamental particle" because either can be subdivided into more elementary parts, thus:

atom $\longrightarrow$ electrons + nucleus $\longrightarrow$ electrons + neutrons + protons

The chemical identity of the atoms of a given element, which was Dalton's key idea, depends entirely on the number and motion of the elec-trons. For example, the simplest element, hydrogen, has one proton for a nucleus, and one electron. The latter is comparatively easily detached or disturbed by the electric forces exerted by neighbouring atoms, consequently hydrogen is reactive chemically, *i.e.*, it readily lends its electron to build chemical structures with other equally co-operative elements. The second element, helium, has a nucleus of two protons and two neutrons; outside are two electrons in a particularly stable arrangement. Both electrons orbit the nucleus in the same spacial orbit, but with their spin directions oppo-site and at 90° to the plane through the nucleus and the electrons. This pair of electrons is so difficult to disarrange that the special name of closed shells has been coined to cover such cases. The fact that two electrons can be present in the same orbit is only possible if their spins are anti-parallel (Pauli Exclusion Principle). In the case of a stable group of eight electrons they arrange themselves in groups of two and their spins antiparallel. Helium with its closed shell will not react chemically, whereas hydrogen, which has an open shell of only one electron, will react very quickly with other atoms.

As the nuclear charge increases, different electron arrangements of greater or lesser stability succeed one another, with every so often a closed shell corresponding to one of the chemically inert gases neon, argon, xenon, krypton.

Such considerations, pursued in sufficient detail, enable atomic physics to account for all the differences and similarities among the chemical elements and, in principle at least, for all other facts of chemistry as well.

Ions

Changes in the atomic properties of an atom are accomplished by altering the position of any electron from one orbit to another. In the limit when an electron is completely removed from the atom, leaving it positively charged, the atom is said to be ionised and is called a positive ion. An atom can be singly or multiply ionised up to a level equal to the number of electrons existing in the neutral atom. In addition, atoms can, through distortion of the existing electrons, accept an additional electron and become negative ions. These can be formed in a resonance scattering process and exist only for life-times of only 10^{-14}s or be formed by chemical reactions. The roles played by negative and positive ions in the upper atmosphere of the earth and stellar atmospheres have been of special interest to atomic physicists since the 1930s.

Maxwell and Electromagnetic Waves

Atoms are held together by the electric attraction of the nucleus for the electrons. Finer details of atomic behaviour depend on the magnetic moments of the particles. Any moving charged particle gives rise to magnetic effects, and in the dynamo a coil moving in a magnet produces an electric current. It can be seen therefore that electric and magnetic phenomena are intimately linked. Any region of space subject to electric and magnetic influences is called an *electromagnetic field*.

In 1862, before the discovery of the electron, Maxwell, while still in his twenties, had perfected a general theory of the electro-magnetic field. This theory today still describes correctly almost all electro-magnetic phenomena. The elegance of this theory is difficult to appreciate, but it alone was the only theory of pre-twentieth century physics which satisfied the prerequisites of Einstein's relativity theory (1905), *i.e.*, inherent in its structure was the concept of relativistic invariance. *Inter alia*, he proved that disturbances in the electric and magnetic conditions at one place could be propagated to another place through empty space, with a definite velocity, just as sound waves are propagated through air. Such electromagnetic disturbances in transit are called *electromagnetic waves*, and their velocity turned out experimentally to be the same as that of light and radio waves—which was a decisive argument to show that both of these phenomena are themselves electro-magnetic waves.

Einstein and Photons

In the years between about 1900 and 1920 this view was upset by Planck, Einstein, Millikan, and others, who focused attention on phenomena (radiant heat, photoelectricity) in which light behaves like a stream of particles and not at all like waves. A wave and a particle are two quite different things, as anyone will admit after a moment's contemplation of, say, the ripples on a pond and a floating tennis ball. The acute question was: is light like waves or particles?

Theoretical physicists have devised means of having it both ways. To say that light behaves as particles means that the waves of the electromagnetic field cannot have their energy sub-divided indefinitely. For waves of a given frequency, there is a certain irreducible quantity of energy that must be involved whenever light interacts with anything. This quantity is the product hv where v is the frequency and h is a constant named after Planck. Each such unit

is called a *quantum of the electromagnetic field* or a *photon* and is counted as one of the fundamental particles. Frequencies and wavelengths vary widely. Typical wavelengths are: radio—hundreds or thousands of metres; radar—a few centimetres; visible light—5×10^{-5} cm; X-rays—10^{-8} cm.

De Broglie and Particles

Since it seemed possible to attribute particle properties to electro-magnetic waves, then why not associate wave properties with particles. If an electron (mass m) is travelling with a velocity of v cm/s, then De Broglie (1923) suggested that its characteristic wavelength would be given by the relation $mv \ \lambda = h$; for example if $v = 10^8$ cm/s, $m = 9 \times 10^{-28}$ g, $h = 6\cdot 610^{-27}$ erg-seconds, then $\lambda = 7,500$ Å, which is the same wavelength as red light. This proposal was confirmed in 1927 by Davisson and Germer when they showed that electrons could produce diffraction, a property until then only associated with light. These wave-like properties are now known to exist for all particles, and we now consider a particle with momentum mv to behave like a wave of wavelength $\lambda = h/mv$.

De Broglie made his revolutionary assertion in his doctoral thesis, and his examiners were so uneasy about the validity of the hypothesis that they were prepared to fail the young man in his examination. Happily for De Broglie, Einstein was visiting that particular university and he was asked his opinion of the idea; his reply ensured success for De Broglie and saved the examiners from future embarrassment.

Molecules

Electrical attractions and interactions of various kinds can cause atoms to combine with each other or themselves to form molecules. Two similar atoms, say hydrogen, combining to form the homonuclear diatomic molecule H_2, while two different atoms, hydrogen and chlorine, will form a heteronuclear diatomic molecule HCl. Molecules have a wide range of complexity, from simple pairs of atoms to highly intricate spirals and chains composed of thousands of atoms. The biological basis of all life is, of course, molecular in both origin and function.

Excited Atoms

Like nuclei, atoms, when given excess energy (insufficient to ionise them), will absorb the energy in one of the electrons, which is then displaced from its equilibrium state to a state (or orbit) of higher energy. It will remain there for typically 10^{-8} seconds before returning to its equilibrium position with the excess energy being emitted as light. The time an atom remains in its excited state can exceed 10^{-8} seconds; lifetimes of $0\cdot1$ second are known, and these metastable states are prevented by the atomic properties of the atom from decaying quickly to their equilibrium states. The colour of the light emitted is characteristic of the atom involved, with the more energetic transitions giving blue light while the less energetic transitions give red light. Hence the emitted colour (or wavelength) of the light can be used as a tool for chemical identification and study of the various transition probabilities in atoms.

Herein lies the explanation of innumerable natural and technical phenomena, such as the colours of glowing gases whether they exist in the sun and stars, in aurora, or in street-lamps and neon signs. Herein also lies the reason for the importance of spectroscopy, which is the study of the characteristic radiation from excited states for spectroscopy is not only a useful tool for the chemical identification of substances ("spectroscopic analysis") but was one of the main routes along which twentieth-century physicists broke through to a knowledge of the inner nature of the atom.

Forces in Nature

Nature uses four, possibly five, apparently different forces to make one particle interact with another. The weakest force is **gravity** which although present at all particle interactions, is insignificant in atomic and nuclear interactions. Gravity controls the mass distribution in the universe and the force has an infinite range of interaction.

The **electric force** which also has an infinite range of interaction is much stronger than the gravitational force and is responsible for the binding forces inside atoms by the attraction of nuclei for electrons.

Inside the nucleus two types of interaction take place which require different forces for their existence:

(1) the forces which hold neutrons and protons together in the nucleus and this is the **strong force**, and

(2) the **weak force** which controls the changes in charge state of nucleons, e.g., the β-decay process when a neutron in a nucleus changes into a proton with the ejection of an electron is controlled by the weak force.

Both these nuclear forces are short-range with their radius of influence approximately 10^{-13} cm, with the weak force acting on all matter and the strong force acting on nucleons only. In today's parlance the strong force will act only on particles which are single multiples of quarks (see later). Since quarks exist (or more precisely, since their existence has been deduced), then it is necessary to have a force through which they can interact.

The fifth force of the universe is postulated to be the **colour force** which operates only on quark particles and has a mode of interaction which prevents a normal range restriction being placed on it. The proton, i.e., the nucleus of atomic hydrogen, is composed of three quarks which move about freely within the shell of the proton; only when one quark tries to escape across the boundary of the proton does it experience the colour force which rebinds into the proton. Before we discuss further the interactions of these forces we must describe the range of particles which exist in physics.

Elementary Particles

When considering the word elementary in this context the reader must be wary of thinking that it implies some degree of absoluteness. The elementary mass of any particular particle is always highly qualified and subject to change. When a particle is discovered physicists measure its properties, i.e., mass, electric charge, and spin, and determine which of the five forces to which it is subject. In addition, its life-time must be determined to see if the particle is stable or only a transient particle which will break up into other particles. The life-times of unstable particles are extremely short, ranging from 10^{-17}s to 10^{-21}s, and it is debatable if a particle which lasts only for 10^{-21}s should be called a particle. Generally now such short-lived particles are called resonances which are produced in an interaction which is only a step to the final product.

The rudimentary classification of particles is into four groups:

(1) photons
(2) leptons
(3) mesons
(4) baryons

All particles have an anti-particle which has the same mass but opposite charge as the real particle, the only exception being the photon, which is its own anti-particle and forms a group on its own. The leptons (electron, muon, and neutrino) form a stable group of particles and do not react to the strong or colour forces. This group of particles, and the photon, are perhaps the most fundamental of all particles. The mesons are unstable particles and (as will be seen later) exist only to act as a means which enables nucleons to interact with each other. They are subjected to the strong nuclear force. All particles heavier than the proton are called baryons, every one of them, except the proton, is unstable in some degree, and a vast number of them are known. Only a few are listed in the Table on page **F16**.

Mesons and baryons are collectively called hadrons. All of these unstable particles have been detected either in the cosmic flux falling on the earth or produced in the very high energy accelerating machines in Europe, the USA, and the USSR.

Strangeness

Some particles have long life-times $\sim 10^{-9}$ s, which is much larger than that encountered normally. Particles which possessed these long life-times were called "strange". Strangeness describes not a new property of matter but a different quality of matter which persists long enough to enable that particle to engage in strong nuclear-force interactions. Hence strangeness does not persist indefinitely. The decay of a strange particle into other particles with the abolition of strangeness proceeds via the weak nuclear force. The strange (and doubly strange) particles form highly symmetrised shapes when combined with non-strange particles. The pattern itself does not explain anything, but the underlying theory, known as Group Theory, does indicate by symmetry arguments which particle should be necessary to form a complete group. This mathematical procedure had a resounding success in 1964 when it predicted the existence of a triply strange particle known as "omega minus". The organisation of particles according to their properties of mass, spin, and strangeness in groups is now only an organisation exercise, and it will not tell us anything about the composition of nucleons.

Interactions of Particles

The method by which atomic, nuclear, and sub-nuclear particles interact is via the exchange of energy which can be considered as a particle exchange. The interaction between electric charges proceeds by the exchange of photons. For example, two charges feel each other by one charge emitting a photon which interacts with the second charge. Since the electric force has infinite range, its force-carrying particle has zero mass. The same criteria apply in the gravitational force, where the graviton is the particle which carries the force effect between particles of matter. Since the weak, strong, and colour forces are short-range, then their force-carrying particles have finite masses. The weak force is transmitted by W and Z particles and the strong force can be considered as transmitted by mesons. The quarks interact via the colour force, which is carried by gluons (mass at present unknown), which also feel the force themselves. The colour force does not distinguish between or acknowledge the existence of strangeness and charm.

A theory which combines the electric and weak forces into a single interaction has predicted the masses of the W and Z particles to be around 80 and 90 GeV respectively. In early 1983 experimental evidence was found by international groups at $CERN$ for the existence of the W particle with the predicted mass thereby giving considerable support to this theory. A long term aim is to unify all the known forces of nature into a single interaction.

Quarks

The stability of the leptons contrasts sharply with the instability of the hadrons (excepting the proton), and this as well as other things had led physicists to consider that all hadrons were composed from different combinations of yet undiscovered particles. Gellmann has postulated the existence of three particles from which the nucleons, mesons, and hence all hadrons are composed. These "new" particles are attributed with fractional electric charges of $+\frac{2}{3}$, $-\frac{1}{3}$, and $-\frac{1}{3}$ of the electron charge. The particles were called quarks. The name quark was taken from the novel *Finnegans Wake* by James Joyce, the meaning of which is obscure, which is perhaps appropriate, but as students of Joyce will know, quark means "non sense", and other interpretations as to its meaning, such as the "sound of seagulls" or "quarts" are wrong. The three

SOME MEMBERS OF THE ATOMIC FAMILY

The numbers in brackets after the name denote first the electric charge and second, the mass. The charge on an electron is counted as -1 unit and the electron mass as $+1$ unit. Thus $(+1,207)$ means the particle has a positive charge of 1 unit and a mass 207 times that of the electron.

The mass energy of an electron is 0·51 MeV, hence conversion to mass energies can be made by multiplying the given mass by 0·51. Thus the muon has a mass energy of 106 MeV. Note: the letter M is used to denote quantities of millions and the letter G to denote quantities of thousand of millions.

Photon (0, 0)	A quantum of electromagnetic radiation, *e.g.*, light, X-rays, γ-rays. The concept was introduced by M. Planck in 1900 when he described the emission of light as taking place in "packets" rather than in a steady stream. The energy of a photon is proportional to the frequency of the radiation and inversely proportional to the wavelength.

Leptons

Electron $(-1, 1)$	Discovered by J. J. Thomson in 1897. The number of orbital electrons in an atom determines its chemical properties. Actual rest mass $= 9\cdot1 \times 10^{-28}$ g. Emitted as β-rays by some radioactive nuclei. A stable particle.
Positron $(+1, 1)$	Positive counterpart or, "anti-particle", to the electron. Predicted theoretically by P. A. M. Dirac in 1928 and first discovered in cosmic rays by C. D. Anderson in 1932. Emitted as β-rays by some radioactive nuclei. When positrons and electrons collide they usually annihilate each other and turn into γ-rays; consequently, positrons only last about 10^{-10} sec. within ordinary matter, but are stable in isolation.
Neutrino (0, 0) and Anti-neutrino (0, 0)	These particles travel with the speed of light and are distinguished from one another by the relation of their spin to their direction of motion. A neutrino is emitted with the positron during positive β-decay; and an anti-neutrino with the electron during negative β-decay. Their interaction with matter is extremely slight. First postulated by Pauli in 1933 and detected in 1956. π-meson decay also produces neutrinos and anti-neutrinos but in 1962 it was proved experimentally that these are a different species. Thus there are two kinds of neutrino each with an anti-neutrino. All these particles are distinguished from photons by having different spin.
Muon $(\pm 1, 207)$	Similar to, but heavier than, the electron and positron; disintegrates into electron (or positron if positive) + neutrino + anti-neutrino.

Mesons

Pion $(\pm 1, 273)$ or (0, 264)	The π-meson. Charged pions decay either into muons and neutrinos or into electrons and neutrinos. Neutral pions decay into γ-rays, into "positron-electron pairs", or both. Pions are intimately connected with nuclear forces, *i.e.*, with the "strong" interaction.
Kaon $(\pm 1, 966)$ or (0, 974)	The K-mesons. These decay in many different ways producing other mesons, electrons, and neutrinos.

Baryons

Proton $(+1, 1836\cdot1)$	The positively-charged constituent of nuclei; the hydrogen nucleus is one proton. Fast-moving protons occur in cosmic rays. Does not spontaneously disintegrate.
Anti-proton $(-1, 1836\cdot1)$	Negative anti-particle of the proton. Its existence was long suspected. Artificially produced and detected for the first time in 1955. Will react with the proton to produce pions or kaons.
Neutron (0, 1838·6)	Discovered by J. Chadwick in 1932. The neutral constituent of nuclei. When free it spontaneously disintegrates into a proton, an electron, and an anti-neutrino, after an average lifetime of about 18 minutes. Passes through matter much more easily than charged particles.
Anti-neutron (0, 1838·6)	The anti-particle of the neutron from which it is distinguished by properties connected with its magnetic moment and spin. Will react with neutron to produce pions or kaons.
Lambda Particle (0, 2183)	Discovered in 1947. Decays into proton plus pion.
Sigma Particle (0 or ± 1; about 2330)	Various modes of disintegration, producing neutrons, protons, mesons and lambda particles.
Omega Particle $(\pm 1, 3272)$	Predicted by recent theory and discovered at Brookhaven, New York, in 1964.
Psi Particle (0, about 6100)	Discovered independently by two laboratories in the USA 1974. Still under intensive study.

quarks were called up, down, and strange and have the properties given in the Table below:

Name	charge	spin	mass-energy (MeV)
up	$+\frac{2}{3}$	$\frac{1}{2}$	336
down	$-\frac{1}{3}$	$\frac{1}{2}$	338
strange	$-\frac{1}{3}$	$\frac{1}{2}$	540

These particles interact with each other via the colour force. Hence it can be seen that by taking different combinations of quarks, different hadrons can be built up. For example, the proton is two up quarks and one down, the neutron is two down and one up. The simplicity of this system can be appreciated, but the only experimental evidence to support the existence of quarks is indirect. No one has yet isolated a single quark! Many scientists are seeking ways to produce and detect them, but as yet (1982) no claims have stood the test of scrutiny. Of course as well as the three quarks up, down, and strange, there are the corresponding anti-quarks.

The K-mesons, for example, are composed of a quark and an anti-quark either with the spins of the two quarks aligned parallel to give a net spin of one, or aligned antiparallel to give a net spin of zero. The charges $+1$, -1, and 0 are simply determined by selecting the correct combination of up and down quarks.

Charm

In the quest to unite the weak and electric forces, theoreticians were forced to introduce yet another new particle into the quark family. This was a charmed quark with charge $+\frac{2}{3}$. The four members of the quark family seemed now to be symmetrical with the four members of the lepton group (electron, muon, and two neutrinos). Since the charmed quark had charge $+\frac{2}{3}$ and mass of 1,500 MeV, it could simply replace the up quark as a building brick in nucleons to produce charmed matter. For example, by replacing the up quark in a proton and a meson by a charmed quark we get a charmed proton and a charmed meson. The first experimental evidence of the existence of charm was obtained by the high-energy physics group at University College, London, working at CERN laboratory, when they established the existence of "a neutral current interaction" in neutrino scattering experiments. Although "naked" charm has never been detected, charmed mesons (masses of 1,865 and 2,020) have been detected by the SPEAR laboratory in USA and charmed anti-protons have also been detected with masses of 2,260 MeV. The experimentally determined masses are in sufficient agreement with theory to confirm the existence of the charmed quark. If a charmed quark combined with an anti-charmed quark it would form a particle of mass 3,000 MeV (3 GeV) and this has been given the name of the Gipsy particle. Several laboratories in 1976 reported the possible existence of a particle of this mass energy, and called it either a J particle or psi particle. The uncertainty has now been resolved and the existence of the Gipsy has been confirmed. It can exist in an excited state of 3·7 GeV, from which it decays by gamma-ray emission to a value of 3·1 GeV, the predicted value. It can further change its spin state and decay to a mass energy value of 2·8 GeV. The building bricks of matter now seemed complete!

Quarks and Pre-Quarks (Preons)

The final picture of the structure of matter is not yet complete, and indeed theorists have added two further quarks to the family of four called truth and beauty, although to date (1982) no experimental evidence of their existence is available. It is further postulated that even the quarks are composed of only two different particles called preons. All of this is only theoretical, and we must wait for the definite isolation of a single quark to settle the matter.

QUANTUM THEORY AND RELATIVITY

Quantum Theory

In our discussion of the nature of the various particles in physics we have alluded to them as being classified with well-defined sizes and weights. Of course, once we consider the physics of matter on a scale which is smaller than that of our everyday comprehension, then the classical physics of Newton is insufficient and we must use quantum physics. In the atomic region of reality we are again faced with the problem of indivisibility where the Greeks stopped their thinking and called the smallest particles of the universe atoms. Today we know that each separate particle is composed of a definite amount of energy, and the larger the particle, i.e., the more energy it is composed of, the easier it is to detect. We also know that the exchange of force between nucleons is carried by particles and that this inchangeability between mass and energy is a reality of quantum theory. To see this more fully we must realise that quantum theory rests on the theory of measurement! If a particle, of any type or structure, is composed of an amount of energy ΔE, then it is necessary to make measurements on it for a certain minimum time before it is detected. This minimum time Δt is given by the equation $\Delta E \times \Delta t \geqslant \hbar$, where $\hbar$ is Planck's constant divided by 2π; hence it can be seen that the smaller ΔE, then the longer a measurement must be made to detect the particle. Correspondingly, the time of measurement itself introduces an uncertainty, ΔE, in the energy of the particle. As well as the parameters ΔE and Δt, a particular physical event can be expressed in terms of its momentum p and position q, and these can also be expressed in a relationship as $\Delta p \times \Delta q \geqslant \hbar$. Hence one can ask at what position in space, q, is a particular particle with momentum p? Or what exactly is the wavelength of a wave? It may be thought that the first question cannot reasonably be asked of a wave nor the second of a particle, but bearing in mind the dual roles of particles and waves discussed earlier, then these questions can be interchanged. We know that electrons behave both as particles and waves. Since electrons have something in common with both, one question cannot be answered precisely for electrons without ignoring the other; alternatively, both questions can be given an imprecise answer. As the wavelength of electrons is intimately connected with their speed, one has to accept an accurate knowledge of the speed (wavelength) and ignorance of position, or the converse, or inaccurate knowledge of both. This is the famous Heisenberg UncertaiPrinciple. Quantum theory is a set of mathematical rules for calculating the behaviour of fundamental particles in accordance with the Uncertainty Principle. In spite of its equivocal-sounding name, the principle has led to an enormous increase in the accuracy with which physical phenomena can be described and predicted. Quantum theory includes all that previous theories did and more.

Quantum theory grew up in the same epoch as the Theory of Relativity. Heroic attempts have been made to combine the two, but with only partial success so far. Relativity is concerned with all motion and all physical laws, but its characteristic manifestations occur only when something is moving with nearly the velocity of light. Quantum theory is likewise all-embracing, but its typical phenomena almost always occur when something on the minute atomic scale is in question. Co. Consequently, the vast majority of everyday mechanics needs no more than the classical theory laid down by Newton, which is neither relativistic nor quantum.

Relativity

Historically, relativity grew out of attempts to measure the speed with which the earth moved through that hypothetical medium called the ether, which was supposed at that time to be the bearer of light waves. To take a simple analogy: sound waves travel through still air with a certain definite speed, v. If you move through the air with speed v' towards oncoming sound waves, they will pass you at the speed $v + v'$. Michelson and Morley, in their celebrated experiment of 1887, failed to find the corresponding behaviour on the part of light. This is so important an experiment that it has been repeated, and repeatedly discussed ever since. In Octobe58 the latest and most accurate confirmation of the Michelson–Morley result was announced. It seems as if light always travels with the same speed relative to an observer, however fast he moves relative to anything else. Einstein put it this way: two observers moving with any constant velocity relative to each other will always agree that light travels past them at the same speed; this speed is denoted by c, and is approximately 186,000 miles per second.

It should be remembered that the limiting value of the velocity of light in relativity is a postulate introduced by Einstein not a conclusion which the theory provides. There may exist forms of matter which can travel faster than light!

Nevertheless, the postulate that the maximum velocity encountered in the universe is c, logically developed, leads to remarkable conclusions. For instance: if you walk from tail to nose of an aircraft at 4 m.p.h. and the plane is receding from me at 300 m.p.h., then you recede from me at 304 m.p.h. "Common sense", Newton, and Einstein would all agree on this. But if you could walk at $0.25c$ and the plane moved at $0.5c$, the Newtonian mechanics would give your recession speed as $0.75c$, whereas Einsteinian relativity would give about $0.67c$. Although at the everyday speed of 300 m.p.h., the disagreement, though present in principle, is absolutely negligible, at speeds near that of light it becomes very pronounced. Many experiments show that the relativity answer is right.

Equivalence of Mass and Energy

The most famous consequence of relativity theory from which we derive benefit is the knowledge that mass can be converted into energy. The amount of energy, E, which can be derived from a given mass, m, of any type of material is given by the celebrated equation $E = mc^2$. If we take one gram of ash and convert it into the free energy of which it is composed we would get 10^8 kilowatts of power, sufficient to heat 15 houses for a year. The heat provided by the material which produced the ash is equivalent to that obtained from burning a single match. The massive energy released by $E = mc^2$ has been demonstrated in the power of nuclear weapons, but this energy has also been put to peaceful uses in nuclear-powered electricity generating stations.

In fundamental particle physics the masses of particles were always expressed in units of mass energy using $E = mc^2$ as the conversion equation. This is a matter of convenience from the realisation that mass is simply a condensed form of energy. The mesons which are the force-exchanging particles in the strong interaction have a mass energy of approximately 130 MeV, which is equivalent to a real mass of only 210^{-26} grams. The energy of the sun is provided by the conversion of real mass into light energy through thermonuclear fusion processes.

Mass and Rest Mass

The concept of mass is not a simple idea to grasp, for as we have seen, the mass of a body which is at rest is equivalent to its inherent latent energy. Further complications and interpretations arise when the body starts moving and its mass is no longer necessarily a constant quantity.

A stationary body can be observed to have a mass called its *rest mass*. If the body moves, it has energy of motion and therefore, according to Einstein's mass-energy equation, it increases its mass. Mass thus depends on speed, but in such a way that there is very little change unless the speed approaches that of light. Many experiments on atomic particles demonstrate this. The interesting question now arises: do all fundamental particles have rest mass? or do some have mass derived solely from their energy? The answer appears to be that photons and neutrinos have no rest mass; all other particles have. The Table on **F16** gives their rest masses.

Special Theory of Relativity

The mathematical development of Einstein's ideas, leading to the conclusions just referred to, constitutes the Special Theory of Relativity.

Stated more generally, the theory raises the question whether two observers in uniform relative motion could ever detect, as a result of their relative speed, any difference in the physical laws governing matter, motion, and light. To this, Special Relativity answers: No. The detailed theory involves special consideration of the results the two observers would obtain when measuring (i) the spatial distance, and (ii) the time interval, between the same two events. It turns out that they would not agree on these two points. They would agree, however, on the value of a certain quantity made up jointly of the spatial distance and the time interval in a somewhat complex combination. The intimate mixture of space and time in this quantity has led to the treatment of the three space dimensions and time on an equivalent footing. Hence the frequent references to time as the "fourth dimension". Minkowski devised an extremely elegant presentation of relativity theory by using an extension of ordinary geometry to four dimensions. A line drawn in his four-dimensional space represents the path of a particle in space and time, i.e., the whole history of the particle. Thus the movement of particles in the ordinary world is turned into the geometry of lines in Minkowski's four-dimensional world of "space-time".

General Relativity and Gravitation

In 1915, 10 years after the publication of the Special Theory of Relativity, Einstein published his theory of General Relativity. This apparently innocuous extension of the ideas of special relativity to include accelerated relative motion opened up new and difficult fields of mathematical complexity which, when solved, enabled Einstein to include gravitation in the theory. In discussing the physics of atomic, nuclear, and sub-nuclear particles, we did not include the effect of the gravitational force, since in relation to the Electric, Weak, Strong, and Colour forces it is extremely small and can be neglected in the discussion of the structure of matter but not in the discussion of astronomical problems and the movements of large-scale electrically uncharged bodies.

It has been usual, ever since Newton, to say that two bodies of mass m_1 and m_2, separated by a distance r attract one another with a force proportional to $m_1 m_2 / r^2$. This is Newton's inverse square law of gravitation which explains the movements of planets and comets and the falling to earth of an apple from a tree.

The apple's fall is accelerated, and we observe this by noting its position relative to certain marks fixed with respect to us, and by timing it with some sort of clock. This system of location in space and time may be called our "frame of reference". We therefore assert that, in our frame of reference, the apple falls down with an acceleration which Newton saw no alternative but to attribute to a thing called gravitational attraction. Galileo had shown that *all* bodies fall with the same acceleration at all points, and we can now rephrase this by saying that in our frame of reference there is a constant gravitational attraction or *uniform gravitational field*. (This last statement and Galileo's demonstration only refer strictly to points fairly near the earth's surface; at greater distances the gravitational field decreases and is therefore not uniform.)

Now suppose a collection of falling bodies is observed by us and an intelligent creature, designated C, inhabits one of them. C has his own frame of reference fixed relative to him and we have ours fixed relative to us. In C's frame neither his own body, nor any of the others, is accelerated, and therefore he has no reason to suppose a gravitational force is acting on them. We have, therefore, the following situation:

(i) in our frame, fixed relative to us, we find all the bodies falling subject to a gravitational pull;

(ii) in C's frame, undergoing accelerated fall relative to us, no gravitational field is apparent to C.

It looks, therefore, as if one has only to choose the correct frame of reference for the measurements in order to remove the need for any assumptions about the existence of gravitational fields. This is a simple illustration of the connection between gravitation and frames of reference for the measurement of space and time. Einstein's General Theory of Relativity extends this to cover non-uniform gravitational fields and shows that what Newton taught us to call the gravitational field of material bodies is better thought of as a peculiarity of the space and time in the neighbourhood of such bodies. Since space–time, as we mentioned above, can be expressed in geometrical terms, Einstein has transformed the theory of gravitation into an exercise (a difficult one) in the geometry of space–time. Other physicists, in Einstein's tradition, are trying to turn *all* physics into geometry, but no one knows whether this is really feasible.

All this abstruse work is much more than a demonstration of mathematical power and elegance. Observable phenomena which fall outside the scope of Newton's theory of gravitation are accounted for by relativity. One is the small but definite discrepancy between the actual orbit of the planet Mercury and the predictions of Newton's theory. Another is the effect of a gravitational field on the wavelength of light emitted by atoms. Similar atoms in different places in a gravitational field emit radiations with slightly different wavelengths. For example, the light from an atom in the intense field of a star should have slightly longer wavelength than the corresponding light from an atom on earth. This effect has always proved very difficult to detect with certainty. However, Einstein's prediction was verified with moderate accuracy in 1960 by a very subtle method which was purely terrestrial in its operation. The atoms being compared were placed at the top and bottom of a water tower and the difference in their emission was detected by means that belong rather to nuclear physics than to astronomy.

Quantum Theory and Relativity Combined

The atomic family table refers to "antiparticles". The theory which first introduced such things in 1934 is due to the Cambridge physicist Dirac and was epoch-making. Dirac conceived an equation to describe the motion of electrons subject to the laws of both quantum theory and relativity. His achievement was thus to synthesise these two great ideas. The spin of the electron was originally a supposition that helped to make sense of spectroscopic observations of light emitted from atoms. Dirac's equation made spin a logical consequence of the union of relativity and quantum theory. Perhaps even more important was the brilliant inference that the equation for the electron implied the existence of another particle having the same mass and spin but with a positive instead of a negative electric charge. This object is called the electron's antiparticle and is now well known as a positron.

Every particle is now believed to imply an antiparticle, so it is conceivable that the universe could have been (but isn't) an anti-universe, *i.e.*, all the electrons and protons might have been positrons and antiprotons and so on. The laws of physics would still have been applicable, however.

The gravitational force has an infinite range and therefore its force-carrying particles must travel at the speed of light. The graviton is the name of the particle which transmits the gravitational force between bodies with mass. To date (1983) no experiment has detected the existence of gravitons which are the postulated quanta of gravitational waves. There is an exact analogy between photons, the quanta of electro-magnetic radiation, and gravitons.

Conservation Laws

If charged particles interact, then it is found that the amount of electric charge existing after the reaction is the same as that which existed before the event. This is called the law of conservation of charge. Many other conservation laws exist in physics, *e.g.*, conservation of mass

energy, angular momentum, linear momentum, and other more abstruse conservation laws exist in particle physics, *e.g.*, conservation of baryons, leptons, strangeness, isotopic spin, and parity. The last three conservation laws listed have been found to have a limited jurisdiction, and the violation of parity in the weak interaction was a great surprise to physicists.

Any reader who looks in a mirror knows that the left- and right-hand sides of his face are interchanged in the image. Fortunately mirrors do not also turn the image upside down, but, if they did, the face would then have undergone what is called "a parity transformation". A screwdriver driving a right-handed screw downwards becomes, on parity transformation, a screwdriver driving a left-handed screw upwards. The law of conservation of parity is a way of asserting that any physical process that goes on in the world could equally well go on—obeying the same laws—in a parity transformed world. There is nothing left-handed that does not in principle have a right-handed counterpart.

For many years this belief was strongly held. It came as something of a shock when, in 1957, after theoretical proposals by Lee and Yang in America, Wu and co-workers proved that parity was not always conserved. To understand Wu's experiment, we must recall that nuclei can have intrinsic spin. Suppose the axis of spin were downwards into the page and the rotation were suitable for driving an ordinary screw into the page. Then Wu showed that beta-rays from such a nucleus are emitted *preferentially upwards*, *i.e.*, against the direction of travel of the screw. The parity transformed version of this would have the beta-rays preferentially emitted in the same direction as the travel of the screw and, if parity is conserved, this process would happen too. But it does not. If the beta-rays in the experiment had been emitted in equal numbers up and down, then the parity transformed version would have had this feature too, and thus parity would have been conserved.

Modern research on elementary particles is greatly concerned to find out which types of process obey which conservation laws. The parity surprise is only one of the stimulating shocks that this type of work is heir to.

Conclusion

Over a century's development of the atomic ideas has brought a progressive, if jerky, increase in the mathematical precision of the theories. In some fields of particle physics, observations to one part in a million, or even better, can be explained, to that level of accuracy, by the existing theories. At the same time, however, the theories have lost visual definition. An atom as an invisible but none the less solid billiard ball was easy enough; so was a light wave conceived like a sound wave in air. Even after Rutherford, an atom consisting of a miniature solar system merely exchanged the solid billiard ball for a system of revolving billiard balls and was no great obstacle to visualisation. But since quantum theory and the Uncertainty Principle, every unambiguous visualisation of fundamental wave-particles leaves out half the picture, and although the electrons are in the atom, we can no longer represent them in definite orbits. The moral seems to be that visualisation is unnecessary, or at best a partial aid to thought.

THE PROPERTIES OF MATTER IN BULK

One of the most obvious and at the same time most wonderful things about the properties of matter is their great variety. Think of air, diamond, mercury, rubber, snow, gold, pitch, asbestos.... Even the differences of state of the same chemical substance are remarkable enough, ice, water, and steam, for example. One of the aims of physics is to reach an understanding of all these different properties by explaining them in terms of the behaviour of the particles discussed in the previous section (**F10–19**). The widespread success with which this imposing programme has been carried out indicates the maturity of physics. It is difficult to think of any major property of matter in bulk for which there is not some attempted theoretical explanation, though future physicists will no doubt regard some present-day theories as rudimentary or incorrect.

Physics, Statistics, and Thermodynamics

Take a number equal to the population of London, multiply it by itself, and multiply the product by another million. The answer is about the number of molecules in 1 cubic centimetre of ordinary air. They are constantly moving about and colliding with one another. Even if the nature of the molecules and their laws of motion were perfectly understood, it would clearly be impracticable to calculate the exact paths described by each particle of so vast an assembly. This difficulty brought into being a whole branch of physics concerned with calculating the overall or average properties of large numbers of particles. Just as statisticians will provide the average height, income, expectation of life, and so on, of the population of London, without knowing everything about every individual, so statistical physicists can work out average properties of molecules or atoms in large groups. This important branch of physics is called *Statistical Mechanics*. It was founded in the nineteenth century by Maxwell, Boltzmann, and Gibbs and is still being actively developed.

Consider now all the molecules in 1 cubic centimetre of air contained in a small box. They are continually bombarding the walls of the box and bouncing off. This hail of impacts (it is actually about 10^{23} impacts per square centimetre per second) is the cause of the pressure which the gas exerts against the walls of the box. Now suppose we pump air in until there is twice as much as before, though the box is still the same size and at the same temperature. This means that the density of the gas (*i.e.*, the mass of 1 unit of volume) has doubled. We should now expect twice as many impacts per second on the walls as before, and consequently twice the pressure. We therefore arrive at a conclusion that, if the volume and temperature are constant, the pressure of a gas is proportional to its density. This is one of the simplest statistical arguments that can be checked against observation; in fact, it stands the test very well.

Heat, Temperature, and Energy

The proviso about the temperature remaining the same is an important one for the following reason. In the nineteenth century there was much discussion about the nature of heat. To Joule we owe the now well-established view that heat is equivalent to mechanical work. In one of his experiments, in the 1840s, the work necessary to rotate paddle wheels against the resistance of water in a tank generated heat that caused a slight rise in the temperature of the water. Joule found out exactly how much work was equivalent to a given quantity of heat. However, one can do other things with work besides generate heat; in particular, work creates motion, as when one pushes a car. Bodies in motion possess a special form of energy, called kinetic energy, which is equal to the work done in accelerating them from a state of rest. We have, then, three closely connected ideas: work, heat, and kinetic energy. Now according to the views of the nineteenth century, which are still accepted, any heat given to a gas simply increases the kinetic energy of its molecules; the hotter the gas, the faster its molecules are moving. If, therefore, the gas in our box is allowed to get hotter, there is an increase in molecular speed, and the impacts on the walls become correspondingly more violent. But this means the pressure increases, so we have another law: if the density remains the same, the pressure increases if the temperature does.

Laws of Thermodynamics

Such considerations as these have been pursued with great elaboration and subtlety. The notions

of heat, temperature, energy, and work—familiar but vague in everyday life—have been given precise definitions, and the relations between them have been enshrined in the Laws of Thermodynamics. Enshrined is perhaps a suitable word, because these laws are so soundly and widely based on experimental results that they have greater prestige than any others in physics. If any proposed physical law comes in conflict with thermodynamics then so much the worse for that law—it has to be revised. It is sometimes asserted that no one is properly educated who does not understand the Second Law of thermodynamics. We cannot, therefore, leave this section without at least stating the two best known thermodynamic laws:

First Law: *If any physical system is given a quantity of heat, and if the system performs some work, then the energy of the system increases by an amount equal to the excess of heat given over work done.* This law asserts that heat, energy, and work are convertible one into the other, and that all such transactions balance exactly. This is one form of a principle accepted as fundamental in all science, *viz.*, the Principle of the Conservation of Energy, according to which energy can never be created or destroyed, but only changed from one form to another.

Second Law: *It is impossible to make an engine which will continuously take heat from a heat source and, by itself, turn it all into an equivalent amount of mechanical work.* In fact, all engines which produce work from heat—steam engines for example—always use only a fraction of the heat they take in and give up the rest to some relatively cool part of the machine. The Second Law makes this obligatory on all work-from-heat devices. This statement of the Second Law has an engineering ring about and, indeed, it arose from the work of the nineteenth-century French engineer Carnot. Nevertheless, it can be rephrased in terms of the concept of entropy, and has been applied with unbroken success to all fields of science involving the transfer of heat and allied matters. It sets a definite limit to the kinds of physical and chemical process that can be conceived to take place. Nothing has been known to contravene it.

The States of Matter

The molecular motion in gases has been referred to in the previous section. Tacitly it was assumed that each molecule acted independently of all others, except that collisions occurred between them. In reality, molecules exert attractive forces on one another and, if a gas is cooled so that molecular movements become relatively sluggish, a time comes when the attractive forces succeed in drawing the molecules close together to form a liquid. This process is called condensation.

The molecules in a liquid are packed tightly together and they impede each other's movements. On the other hand, movement still persists, and the molecules struggle about like people in a milling crowd. Besides wandering about, the molecules vibrate. These motions represent the energy contained in the liquid.

The fact that the molecules, though irregularly packed, can still slip past one another and move from place to place, explains the essential property of liquids that distinguishes them from solids—ability to flow. As a matter of fact, although the rather vague assertion that in a liquid molecules are irregularly packed would be generally accepted, there is no agreed opinion on what the irregularity is actually like. Indeed, not only the precise structure of liquids, but the theory of liquids in general, is fraught with such considerable mathematical difficulties that the liquid state is much less well understood than the solid or gaseous.

Most solids are crystals. The popular idea of a crystal is of something which has a more or less regular geometrical form with faces that shut in the light—like snowflakes or gems. However, crystallinity really depends on a regular inner pattern of the atoms, and may or may not show itself on the visible surface. A lump of lead, for example, is crystalline, despite its appearance.

The actual arrangement of the atoms in a crystal can be extremely complex. Some are quite simple, however. The largest model of a crystal structure must surely be the 400-ft. "Atomium" building in the 1958 Brussels Exhibition. This consisted of eight balls, representing atoms, situated at the corners of a cube, and one more ball exactly in the middle. Imagine this repeated in all directions so that every ball is the centre of a cube whose corners are the eight neighbouring balls. This is known to crystallographers and physicists as the "body-centred cubic structure"; it is the actual arrangement of atoms in iron, sodium, chromium, and some other metals. If every ball, instead of being the centre of a cube, were the centre of a regular tetrahedron (a solid figure with four equal triangular faces), and had its four neighbours at the corners of the tetrahedron, then we should have the "diamond structure". This is how the carbon atoms are arranged in diamonds.

In crystals the atoms are locked into a regular ordered structure by attractive forces which give the solid its rigidity and prevent it from flowing. The atoms are so close together that any attempt to press them closer involves crushing or distorting the atoms—a process they resist strongly. This explains why solids (and liquids too) are so difficult to compress. Gases can easily be compressed because there is so much space between the molecules.

The distinction between solid and liquid is not so sharp as is commonly supposed. A lump of dough will not bounce, but is plastic; a steel ball-bearing is very elastic and bounces excellently, but one cannot mould it in the fingers. Neither dough nor steel qualifies for description as a liquid. There are, however, substances which can be moulded like plasticine into a ball that will then bounce very well on the floor like an elastic solid, and finally, if left on a flat table, will spread into a pool and drip off the edge like a liquid. There is no point in trying to force such things into rigid categories. One may say instead that for short, sharp impacts the material behaves like an elastic solid, but under long-sustained forces it flows like a liquid. The properties of these, and many other anomalous materials, are increasingly engaging the attention of those who study the science of flow—*rheology*. It is interesting to see how many familiar and important materials exhibit peculiar rheological behaviour—paint, dough, ball-pen ink, cheese, unset cement, and solutions of nylon and other plastics are only a few examples.

Inside a Crystalline Solid

We now return to our wallpaper analogy of crystal structure and give some free play to our visual imagination.

Suppose we have walls papered with a regular pattern of, say, roses, fuchsias, and green leaves. These represent the different kinds of atoms in the solid. Careful observation shows that the whole pattern is shimmering. The flowers and leaves are not stationary, but are undergoing slight random oscillations about their proper positions. In a crystal these movements are called thermal vibrations, and are never absent. The hotter the crystal, the more the vibration, and at a high enough temperature the vibrations become so great that the atoms get right out of position and the pattern disappears altogether, *i.e.*, the crystal melts. Thermal vibrations are essential to the theory of solids, and are responsible for numerous physical properties.

Next we note something extraordinary about some of the papered walls. On these the paper has been hung in irregular patches fitted together like a not very well-made jig-saw puzzle. Lines of roses which should be vertical are horizontal in some patches, oblique in others. This represents the situation in most ordinary solids, for they consist of many small pieces of crystal irregularly packed together. Such material is called *poly-crystalline*, and the small pieces are *crystal grains*. Crystal grains may be almost any size, sometimes visible to the naked eye, as often on galvanised iron.

However, on one wall, we see excellent regularity and no obvious patches at all. The physicist would call this a *single crystal*, and several techniques exist for preparing them. Natural single crystals can be found, and there are some beautiful large single crystals of rock salt. But on examining the single crystal wall closely, we find a number of places where the paperhanger has failed to make adjacent pieces register perfectly—there is a slight disjointedness. This occurs in real single crystals, and the line along which the structure fails to register is called a *dislocation*. These are much studied by physicists because of their bearing on the mechanical properties of solids, on the yielding of metals under strong stress, for instance.

This by no means exhausts the possibilities of the wallpaper analogy; several other phenomena can be found. For example, in a place where there should be a fuchsia there is actually a daffodil—something completely foreign to the pattern. Or perhaps a small wrongly shaped leaf is jammed between the proper leaves in a place that should really be blank. These represent chemical impurity atoms. The first is called *substitutional*, because it occupies the position of an atom that should be there, the second is called *interstitial*, because it does not. Substitutional impurities of indium metal, deliberately added to the semi-conductor silicon, make possible the manufacture of transistors (*see* **Section L**). Some steels derive their valuable properties from interstitial carbon atoms within the iron pattern.

What physicists call a vacancy would occur if a flower or leaf were simply missing. Remembering that all the atoms are vibrating, we should not be surprised if occasionally an atom jumps into a neighbouring vacancy if there happens to be one, *i.e.*, the atom and the vacancy change places. Later this may occur again. In the course of time, a rose which was near the ceiling may make its way to the floor by jumping into vacant rose positions when they occur near enough. This process, which the physicist calls *diffusion*, is also analogous to the game in which numbers or letters can be moved about in a flat box because there is one vacant space to permit adjustment. The more vacancies there are in a crystal, the faster diffusion occurs. It is, in fact, very slow in solids, but is nevertheless evidence that apparently quiescent materials are really internally active.

Metals, Electricity, and Heat

There is ample evidence that inside metals there are large numbers of free electrons. To illuminate this statement let us take sodium metal as an example. One single sodium atom has a nucleus with eleven protons; there are therefore eleven electrons in the atom. The outermost one is easily detached, leaving a positively charged sodium ion behind. We may think of these ions arranged in the three-dimensional pattern characteristic of sodium crystals. It is the same as the iron structure previously described. The detached electrons, one per atom, occupy the spaces in between. The usual metaphor is that the structure of ions is permeated by a "gas" of electrons. Like all visualisations of fundamental particles, this must be taken as a rough approximation. The important point is that the electrons in the gas are not bound to individual atoms but may wander freely about the crystal, hindered only by the collisions they make with the vibrating ions.

This is the picture as it appeared to physicists of the first decade of this century, and we can explain many properties of metals with it. Naturally the theory has developed greatly since then, thanks to the great work of Lorentz, Sommerfeld, and Bloch; it now relies heavily on quantum theory, but it is surprising how little violence is done to modern ideas by the simple picture we are using.

The free electrons move randomly in all directions at thousands of miles per hour. If the metal is connected across a battery it experiences an electric field. Electrons are negatively charged particles, and are therefore attracted to the electrically positive end of the metal. They can move through the metal because they are free; this flow is not possible to those electrons which remain bound to the ions. The function of the battery is to keep the flow going and, for as long as it is going, it is the electric current.

The flow of electrons is not unimpeded. They

constantly collide with the ions and are deflected from the path of flow. This hindrance is what the electrician calls *electrical resistance*. The electric force, due to the battery or a dynamo, accelerates the electrons, thus giving them extra energy; but they lose this to the ions at collisions because the ions recoil and vibrate more than before. The net effect of innumerable collisions is to increase the thermal vibrations of the ions, *i.e.*, to make the metal hotter. This is the explanation of the fact well known to every user of electric irons; that electric current heats the conductor. If a strong current is passed through a wire, the heating is so great the wire glows, as in electric-light bulbs, or melts and breaks, as in blown fuses.

If one end of a metal rod is heated we soon feel the heat at the other end; metals are excellent thermal conductors. This is because the mobile free electrons carry the heat energy down the rod, passing it on to the ions by colliding with them. Substances without free electrons cannot do this, nor can they conduct electricity well; we we have, in the free electrons, an explanation of the fact that the good electrical conductors are the good heat conductors. For technical purposes, it would be useful to have electrical insulators that would conduct heat well, and *vice versa*; but this is almost a contradiction in terms, and one can only compromise.

Non-conductors and Semi-conductors

There are some elements, and numerous compounds in which all the electrons are so tightly bound to their parent atoms that free electron flow is impossible. These materials are electrical and thermal insulators.

Let us return to our sodium atom. It readily loses its outer electron, forming a positive ion. The ion is very stable; indeed, its electron arrangement resembles the "closed shell" belonging to the inert gas neon. The chlorine atom, on the other hand, would have a very stable structure, resembling the inert gas argon, if only it could be given one extra electron to complete the closed shell. If the outer sodium electron were given to a chlorine atom we should have two stable ions, one positive and one negative. These would then attract each other and form a compound. This is just how common salt, sodium chloride, is formed, and its crystals consist of a regular network of alternate sodium and chlorine ions. As all the electrons are bound to ions, it is not surprising that salt will not conduct electricity or heat to any appreciable extent. Not all insulating compounds are built on this pattern, but all have structures which bind the electrons tightly.

We have seen (**F20**) that Nature does not permit a hard-and-fast distinction between solids and liquids; nor does she between conductors and insulators. Over a hundred years ago, Faraday knew of substances which would conduct electricity, but rather badly. A common one is the graphite in pencils. Others are the elements selenium, germanium, and silicon, and a considerable number of compounds. Such substances are called semi-conductors.

Semi-conductors conduct badly because they have so few free electrons, many thousands of times fewer than metals. In very cold germanium—say, 200 degrees below freezing—all the electrons are tightly bound to atoms and the substance is an insulator. It differs from normal insulators in that, on warming it, the gradually increasing thermal vibration of the crystal detaches some of the electrons, for they are only moderately tightly bound. The warmer the crystal becomes, the more of its electrons become detached and the better it conducts electricity. By about the temperature of boiling water, there are so many freed electrons that conduction is moderately good, though less good than in metals. This is basic semi-conductor behaviour. Because transistors were made of germanium, and because they are of such great technical importance, more knowledge has accumulated about germanium than about any other material. *See also* **Transistor, Section L.**

Magnetism

The most important thing about magnetism is that it is inseparably connected with electricity. Oersted showed this in July 1820, when he deflected a magnetic compass needle by passing an electric current through a wire near it. Since then, many experiments have shown that wherever a current flows there will certainly be a magnetic field in the surrounding space. The laws of this are very well known now—they are the Maxwell equations previously referred to (**F14**). However, most people first meet magnetism when, as children, they pick up pins with a magnet. Where is the electricity here? and what is a magnet?

The explanation of magnetism exemplifies beautifully the technique of explaining the bulk properties of matter in terms of fundamental particles. In the atoms the electrons are moving, and a moving electric charge constitutes an electric current. Therefore each moving electron is a tiny source of magnetism. It does not immediately follow that every atom is a source of magnetism because it might—and often does—happen that the magnetic effect of different electrons in the atom cancel out. In helium atoms, for example, the two electrons have equal but opposed magnetic effects. Nevertheless, some atoms and ions have a net effect called their *magnetic moment*. This simply means they behave like tiny magnets. Crystals containing such atoms will be magnetic, though the magnetism is much weaker than in ordinary magnets because the different atoms largely annul one another's effects. In a very limited number of crystals, however, the magnetic ions act on one another in a special way which forces all the atomic magnets to point in the same direction. The total effect of many co-operating atoms is very strong and the crystal becomes what we normally call a magnet. Iron acts like this, so do cobalt and nickel, the rarer elements gadolinium and dysprosium, and a fair number of alloys. On the whole, this behaviour, which is called *ferromagnetism*, is very rare. The reason for the co-operation of all the atomic magnets is not explained to everyone's satisfaction yet, though the key idea was given by Heisenberg in 1928.

In the section dealing with the electron it was pointed out that every electron has an *intrinsic* magnetic moment. This is in addition to any effect simply due to the electron's motion round a nucleus. The net effects of ions are therefore partly due to the intrinsic magnetism of electrons. In the ferromagnetic metals the latter is by far the most important contribution. Thus we pick up pins, and benefit from magnets in other ways, because innumerable fundamental particles act in co-operation for reasons that are still somewhat obscure. It is interesting to ask whether the electrons responsible for magnetism are the same free electrons that allow the metals to conduct electricity. It is thought not.

We are accustomed to think of magnets as metallic. Actually the magnet originally discovered by the Chinese was the mineral lodestone, which is a non-metallic oxide of iron. Nowadays a number of non-metallic magnets are made. They are called *ferrites*, and some are insulators and some are semi-conductors. The combination of magnetism and insulation is technically very valuable in radio, radar, and other applications. The explanation of ferrite behaviour is related to that of metallic ferromagnetism, but is not the same.

Conclusion

The aim of the second part of this account of physics is to show how our conception of fundamental particles allows us to build theories of the properties of matter. This very aim shows that the two "major divisions" of physics referred to at the beginning (**F10**) are divided only in the way that labour is divided by co-operating workers to lighten the task. For the task of physics is a very great one—no less than to explain the behaviour of matter; and since the universe, living and inanimate, is made of matter, physics must necessarily underlie all the other sciences.

III. THE WORLD OF THE CHEMISTS

WHAT CHEMISTRY IS ABOUT

Chemistry is the scientific study of the preparation, composition and architecture of chemical compounds, and of the modes and mechanisms of their transformations or reactions. Natural (and other) processes can be classified as *physical*, in which no chemical reactions occur, for example water running down a hill, and *chemical* if changes occur in the chemical compounds involved. Common examples are the burning of fuel, whether in a biological cell, an internal combustion engine, or a lowly domestic grate. Biological changes at the molecular level in plants and animals generally consist of many chemical reactions, as do some geological changes in rocks and deposits. Chemistry therefore is rooted in physics and interpenetrates biology (biochemistry) and geology (geochemistry). Some of the main sub-divisions of chemistry are delineated in the Table. Chemists not only aim to discover new reactions by trial and error, but by seeking to understand chemical change aspire to design new compounds and reactions. New reactions can be used to produce useful physical *effects* in new ways—like light from the cold chemical candle (chemiluminescence) as the firefly does, and electricity from more efficient batteries and from fuel cells—or to produce new *synthetic products*. These can be faithful copies of compounds like penicillin which have been discovered first in nature, or completely new, invented, compounds like the sulphonamide drugs.

This research activity, which is mainly centred in the Universities, is the basis of a large chemical industry, one of the major manufacturing industries. Other branches which deal with more restrictive topics or use combinations of the above for specific goals have names which are self-explanatory, for example:—analytical chemistry, colloid chemistry, pharmaceutical chemistry, chemistry of dyes, petroleum chemistry, polymer chemistry, environmental chemistry, medicinal chemistry.

Main Divisions of Chemistry

	Elements, Compounds and reactions involved	Examples
Organic Chemistry	Carbon in combination mainly with H, O, N.	Natural products Carbohydrates Steroids Proteins
Inorganic Chemistry	All elements and compounds not covered in organic chemistry. Minerals and salts.	Inorganic polymers (*e.g.*, silicones) Transition metal complexes Organometallic compounds
Physical Chemistry	Mathematical and physical descriptions of organic and inorganic compounds and reactions.	Electrochemistry Chemical thermodynamics Molecular spectroscopy Photochemistry
Biochemistry	The chemistry of biological systems	Enzymes Biosynthesis.

ELEMENTS AND COMPOUNDS

Elements

The reader will find a description of the formation of chemical elements in Part I (**F6**). They are listed alphabetically in the Table of Elements (with their chemical symbols) and in order of atomic number (*see* **F11**) in the Periodic Table. Other details may be found in Section L. They vary widely in natural abundance terrestrially. In the earth's crust the most abundant elements are oxygen (O), silicon (Si), aluminium (Al), and iron (Fe). Our familiarity with them varies too, not only because of the rarity of some (thulium, Tm, and radium, Ra) and the artificiality of a few (plutonium, Pu) but because we meet some only in combination with other elements and not in their elemental state, for example, fluorine (F) in fluorides. The most familiar non-metallic elements besides oxygen and nitrogen in their gaseous molecular states (O_2 and N_2) are probably carbon (C), as graphite (or diamond!) and sulphur (S). Among the metallic elements most people know aluminium (Al), tin (Sn) and lead (Pb) from the main groups of the Periodic Table, and the transition metals: iron (Fe), chromium (Cr), nickel (Ni) as well as copper (Cu) and the precious metals silver (Ag), gold (Au) and platinum (Pt). Increasingly familiar because of their use in semi-conductors are the metalloids silicon (Si) and germanium (Ge).

Compounds

Most terrestrial matter as we know it can be classified in terms of the chemical compounds it contains, *i.e.*, is a mixture of compounds. Each compound consists of chemical elements in combination, the relative amount of each being characteristic and definite (Law of Constant Composition). Compounds vary not only in the number of elements combined but also in their proportions: carbon dioxide has twice as much oxygen per carbon as carbon monoxide (*see* atoms and molecules).

The properties of a compound can be, and normally are, very different from the properties of the elements it contains, a fact not commonly recognised in the popular imagination, witness phrases like—"it's good for you, it's got iron in it". This does not mean that elemental metallic iron is present but rather that some seemingly beneficial compound of iron is present. The ambiguity is that although iron is essential to human life in the form of haemoglobin in the blood, it also can form highly poisonous compounds. Similarly arsenic (As), although notoriously poisonous as the element and in some of its compounds, was nevertheless contained in one of the first chemotherapeutic drugs ever produced, salvarsan. The point can be further illustrated by sodium chloride, a water-soluble white crystalline solid, which is a compound of the very reactive metal sodium (capable of reacting violently with water), and of chlorine (known as a poisonous green gas). Similarly diamond (a particular elemental form, or allotrope, of carbon) is one of the hardest known substances but may be combined with hydrogen (the highly inflammable gas which can combine with oxygen gas to give water), to give thousands of different derivatives which include benzene (a liquid), methane (a gas) and various hydrocarbon waxes and polishes.

ATOMS AND MOLECULES

Atoms vary in weight, structure and size from one element to the next (*see* **Part II, F10**). Molecules are made from whole numbers of atoms in combination. A particular molecule is characterised by the number of atoms of each of its constituent elements. It has a characteristic weight called its *molecular weight* (the sum of the weights of the atoms in it), and a characteristic three dimensional structure (*see below*).

An aggregate of molecules of the same type is a chemical compound, so that the molecule is to a compound as the atom is to an element.

The Mole

It is frequently very useful to know when the amounts of two compounds are the same, not in terms of their masses but in terms of the number of molecules each contains, since chemical reactions occur at the molecular level and involve small relative numbers of molecules of the reacting species at each step. Avogadro (*see* **B5**) suggested that equal volumes of gases under identical conditions contained equal molecular numbers (*see* **L12**) and it followed that if the weights of two substances were in the ratio of their relative molecular masses (molecular weights) then they too contained equal numbers of molecules. The approximate molecular weights of water (H_2O) and ethanol or ethylalcohol (C_2H_5OH) are 18 and 46 respectively and so 18 g of water for example contain the same number of molecules as 46 g of ethanol.

The amount of substance referred to in each case is called 1 mole. For any compound the weight of 1 mole is equal to the gramme molecular weight. Molecular weights (or relative molecular masses) are now referred to the carbon-12 atomic scale (*see* **F10**). The modern definition of the mole therefore is that it is the amount of substance which contains the same number of elementary particles as there are atoms in twelve grammes of carbon-12. This number, called Avogadro's number, is $6 \cdot 022\,169 \times 10^{23}$.

Molecular Structure and Isomers

Modern spectroscopic and diffraction methods have enabled the details of molecular structures to be accurately determined not only with respect to the distances between atoms (normally in the range 1–5 Å, *i.e.*, 100–150 pm for adjacent atoms) and the angles which define the structure, but also with respect to the various internal motions (vibrations and rotations).

Sometimes two (or more) different compounds have the same molecular weight (and are called, therefore, *isomers*) but have different molecular structures in which the same atoms are arranged in different relative positions, and hence have different properties. If two isomeric structures are related as left and right hands are related, the isomers are stereoisomers of a particular class called enantiomers. An example is glucose. Even such subtle variation as this produces differences in properties which can be crucial in biological function or drug metabolism.

A familiar simple example of *structural* isomers are ethylalcohol (or ethanol) and dimethyl ether of formula C_2H_6O. They each can be represented by the structural formulae

$$CH_3 - CH_2 - OH \text{ and } \begin{matrix} CH_3 \\ \diagdown \\ O \\ \diagup \\ CH_3 \end{matrix}$$

in which the lines represent some of the *covalent chemical bonds* (*see below*). It is these interatomic forces which hold the atoms in specific spatial arrangements. Some examples are shown in Fig. 1.

CHEMICAL BONDING

The number of possible arrangements of a given set of atoms is limited since each type of atom (each element) is capable of forming only a limited number of bonds, equal to its *valency*. The valency varies from element to element; hydrogen has a valency of one (exceptionally two); oxygen, two; nitrogen, three; and carbon four (hence the molecular formulae H_2, H_2O, NH_3 and CH_4 for hydrogen, water, ammonia and methane respectively).

In some compounds two atoms may be joined by a *multiple bond* so that the valency number may be reached. Examples are the double and triple bonds in ethylene (ethene) and acetylene (ethyne respectively:

$$CH_2 = CH_2 \text{ and } CH \equiv CH$$

The modern theory of chemical bonding is electronic. Bonds are formed:

(i) by the sharing of electrons in pairs between two bonded atoms (*covalent* bonding); or

(ii) by the transfer of an electron from one atom to another to form oppositely charged ions (*ionic* bonding).

The ionic situation is electrically *polar* whereas pure covalent bonds have no polarity. If, however, the shared electrons are not shared equally between the bound atoms some effective electron transfer occurs and the bond has some polar character. Covalent bonds between *dissimilar* atoms are generally polar. If one of the two atoms provides *both* the shared electrons, the polarity is particularly high and the bond is called *dative covalent*.

VALENCIES OF THE ELEMENTS

Electronic Theory of Valency

These ideas of the chemical bond lead to a ready explanation of the valencies of the elements (which are periodic if the elements are arranged in order of atomic number) when combined with knowledge of the electronic structure of atoms.

In the original Bohr theory the electrons of atoms move in well defined orbits arranged in shells. The known elements use seven shells, and each element has its unique number of electrons equal to the atomic number, Z (*see* **F11**) ranging from 1 in hydrogen to 103 in lawrencium. Each element also has its unique arrangement of its electrons in these shells. The build-up of electrons in the above sequence follows well-defined rules. The resulting electron configuration of the elements (*see* **F73**) is an important starting point for a discussion of valency. The shells each have a limited capacity and the numbers of electrons that can be accommodated in the first four labelled 1, 2, 3, 4 (or sometimes K, L, M, N) are 2, 8, 18, 32 respectively. Each of these shells has sub-shells of which there are four main types designated s, p, d and f which can contain 2, 6, 10 and 14 electrons respectively. If all the orbits in a shell have electrons actually present in them the shell is filled or closed and this confers on the shell an unusual stability or inertness. Conversely, unfilled shells lead to activity and the electrons in the incompletely filled shells largely determine the chemical and physical properties of the element and are responsible for the combination of atoms to form molecules. These electrons are referred to as *valence electrons*. The inner shell, *i.e.*, the one nearest the nucleus, can accommodate only two electrons (the element helium has just that number) and the next two shells can hold eight each. Large atoms, *e.g.*, lead, radium, have many filled shells and, subject to special exceptions, the general rule is that the inner shells are the filled ones and the outer shell may be incomplete. Elements which have equal numbers of electrons in their outer shell resemble each other and come in the same Group of the Periodic Table. Thus the elements with complete electronic shells are chemically unreactive gases, *e.g.*, argon and neon (minor constituents of the atmosphere). Elements with just one electron in the outer shell are highly reactive metals, *e.g.*, sodium and potassium which lose this electron readily to give monopositive ions, *e.g.*, Na^+. These elements are called electropositive. Contrariwise elements with just one electron too few are electronegative and readily gain one electron either by sharing, or by capture (to form anions, *e.g.*, Cl^-).

More generally, at least for the light elements of Periods 2 and 3 of the Periodic Table, the valence of an element is given by the Group Number, N, *i.e.*, the number of valence electrons which must be lost by the electropositive metals, or by $8-N$, the number of electrons which electronegative elements need to gain.

The covalence of an electronegative element is increased by one if it loses one electron to form a positive ion, and decreased by one if it gains an electron. Thus nitrogen with a covalence 3 can give either N^+ which can form 4 covalent bonds (in the ammonium ion, NH_4^+) or the N^- ion with

Valence Electrons (N) and Valency (V)

N = 1	2	3	4	5	6	7	8
V = 1	2	3	4	3	2	1	0
Hydrogen							Helium
Sodium	Magnesium	Aluminium	Carbon	Nitrogen	Oxygen	Flourine	Neon
Potassium	Calcium	Gallium	Silicon	Phosphorus	Sulphur	Chlorine	Argon
			Germanium	Arsenic		Bromine	
			Tin			Iodine	
	Barium		Lead				

←————————Metals————————→ ←—————————————→ Non-metals:
            Positive ions   Covalent   Negative ions
                                             compounds   or covalent compounds

a covalency of 2 (*e.g.*, NH_3^-). Similarly oxygen can give H_3O^+, the hydroxonium ion (the acid principle in water), H_2O (water itself), and OH^- (the hydroxyl ion).

IONIC BONDS, SALTS AND ACIDS

These bonds are normally formed between electropositive elements (at the left of the Periodic Table, *e.g.*, sodium and potassium) and electronegative elements (at the right of the Periodic Table, *e.g.*, oxygen, fluorine, chlorine). The ionic charge may be determined from the valency: Na^+, Mg^{++}, Al^{+++}; $O^=$, Cl^-.

Ions may contain a number of atoms, as shown by many of the common anions: hydroxyl, OH^-; nitrate, NO_3^-; sulphate, $SO_4^=$; carbonate $CO_3^=$. Ionic solids formed from a metal ion and one of these anions are called *salts* and are derived from the parent *acid* in which the anion is bound to a *hydrogen ion* (or ions): HNO_3, nitric acid; H_2SO_4, sulphuric acid. Sulphuric acid can form two series of salts, one called *normal* based upon the $SO_4^=$ ion and a second (called acid salts since they contain a hydrogen) based upon the HSO_4^- ion. Phosphoric acid, H_3PO_4, has three series of salts. A substance which reacts with an acid to form a salt and water as the only products is called a *base*. An example is sodium hydroxide, $NaOH$ (caustic soda). The Lewis definitions of acid and base are given below.

The ionic forces are less directional in character than covalent bonds are, but in solids the ions are in regular fixed arrangements (*see* **Part II**). Each anion is surrounded by cations and is attracted to them by electrostatic Coulomb forces. These are of long range and so the anion is attracted not only to the closest cations. Additionally each cation is surrounded by anions so that the bonding is not localised. The whole solid therefore is like a giant molecule and is not easily broken down by melting. This contrasts with covalent compounds in which the forces between molecules are small, the main attractions being within the molecule.

The structures adopted depend upon the relative numbers of the anions and cations (which are determined by ionic charges) and by the relative ionic sizes, which have been deduced from X-ray diffraction measurements.

COVALENT BONDS

In the simple theory the shared electron pairs are localised between two atoms. Multiple bonds result when there are more pairs shared. The multiplicity (or *bond order*) is then integral. The theory may be extended by admitting that an electron pair may be shared between more than two atoms in *delocalised bonding* which can then give rise to fractional bond orders. The best example is benzene (and graphite) where nine pairs of electrons are shared between six carbon-carbon bonds giving a bond order of 1·5.

Modern Theories

Modern theories of valency make use of the concepts of quantum mechanics (*see* **F17**) in which each of the well-defined electron orbits of the s, p, d and f electrons in the Bohr theory is replaced by the idea of the electron cloud with a spatial electron density and distribution. Each of these electron clouds (now called an orbital) has a definite shape depending upon the type of electrons. The orbitals of s electrons are of spherical shape with a density that falls off with the distance from the nucleus. The peak density occurs at the old Bohr radius. Electrons of the p type have orbitals with double lobes giving the figure of eight or dumbell shape. There are three such orbitals in every shell except the first and they are arranged mutually at right angles. Each one can contain two electrons giving a total of six. The d orbitals are five in number. Each again can contain two electrons giving a total of ten. Four of these d orbitals have shapes like four-leaf clovers, whereas the fifth has two lobes, rather like the p orbitals but with the addition of a torus or doughnut. The shapes of the f orbitals are even more complicated. It is the shape of these orbitals and their relative spatial arrangement which gives the covalent bond its directional character. The idea of electron sharing between two atoms becomes the notion of overlap of an orbital on one atom with an orbital on another to give a bonding *molecular orbital* which can contain the pair of shared electrons. The bond energy is a maximum when this overlap is optimum and this occurs when the atoms are in certain definite positions thus giving the molecule its own characteristic shape.

Molecular shape

For elements from the second row of the Periodic Table the number of electrons in the valence shell can be eight arranged in four pairs of orbitals (one 2s and three 2p orbitals). These orbitals can be combined or *hybridised* to give the basic tetrahedral shape (*see* Fig. 1). Each of these can overlap with say an orbital of a hydrogen atom (the 1s) to give a bonding orbital which can accommodate two electrons. Alternatively each orbital can, if the atom has enough electrons, contain two non-bonding electrons called a *lone pair*. The basic molecular shapes of methane (CH_4), ammonia (NH_3), and water (H_2O) may then be rationalised as in Fig. 1.

The bond angle in methane is the tetrahedral angle (109° 28'). The angles in ammonia (107° 18') and water (104° 30') are smaller probably because the lone pair orbital is slightly more repulsive than the bonding orbital is. This closes down the angles between the bonds.

The lone pairs may be used to bind the hydrogen ions from acids to give tetrahedral NH_4^+ and pyramidal H_3O^+. It is the lone pairs therefore which give ammonia and water their basicity. In the modern concept of acids and bases due to Lewis, a base is an electron donor and an acid becomes an electron acceptor. This definition of an acid includes the older idea of it as a hydrogen ion producer in that the hydrogen ion is an electron acceptor but it is more general—a Lewis acid need not be a protic acid.

Bond Lengths

Many covalent bond distances have been

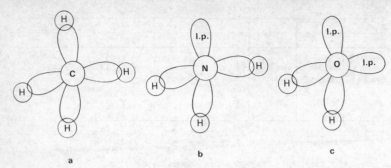

Fig. 1. The spatial arrangements of the atoms and orbitals in (a) methane (CH_4), (b) ammonia (NH_3) and (c) water (H_2O). The basic shape is tetrahedral and the hybridised orbitals are lone pair orbitals (l.p.) and bonding orbitals.

measured and each may be apportioned between the bound atoms to give a self-consistent set of covalent bond-radii for each element which can be used in predictions of molecular structures. These radii vary inversely with the bond order involved. Thus the carbon-carbon bond length varies from 154 pm (*i.e.*, 10^{12}m) for $C-C$ to 135 pm for $C=C$.

Bond Energies

Bonds differ in their strength depending upon the atoms and the bond order. A double bond between two given atoms is stronger than a single bond but generally not as strong as two single bonds. Thus "unsaturated" compounds, which contain multiple bonds, will tend to form "saturated" compounds containing only single bonds since the energetics are favourable.

Functional Groups

Compounds may be further classified according to certain persistent groups of atoms which have a residual valency and can combine with other groups. Thus the methyl group (CH_3) related to methane (CH_4) by the removal of a hydrogen atom can combine with other atoms or groups of valency one: methyl chloride (chloromethane), CH_3Cl; methyl alcohol (methanol), CH_3OH; dimethyl ether, CH_3OCH_3. Common functional groups are shown in the table.

CHEMICAL ENERGETICS

Chemical reactions are accompanied by energy changes which can be utilised as heat (in fires) or mechanical work (in explosions or rockets), or to produce electric current in batteries. Chemical compounds can therefore be said to store energy and to possess "internal energy". The energy can be thought of as being stored in the chemical bonds. The energy change (at constant volume) in a reaction is then a result of changes (denoted ΔU) in the nett internal energy of the reactants and products by the law of the conservation of energy. If the conditions are those of constant pressure, the energy change is due to overall changes in a closely related properly called enthalpy (ΔH).

It was at one time thought that reactions would proceed only if energy was given out (*exothermic* processes). Although this is now known to be true at the lowest temperature, in other cases a second consideration, the entropy term, needs to be considered, the existence of *endo*thermic changes confirms. A new "energy" term defined to contain the entropy consideration and called the Gibbs Free Energy, G, may then be used. Natural or "spontaneous" processes are accompanied by a decrease in the nett value of G, and systems tend to assume whichever state has the lowest value of G.

Chemical Equilibrium

Certain chemical changes, like physical changes

Some Classes of Simple Organic Compounds

Name	General Description and Formula	Examples
Alkanes (or paraffins)	"Saturated" hydrocarbons of the general formula C_nH_{2n+2} Contain single bonds only	methane (CH_4) butane (C_4H_{10})
Alkenes (olefins)	"Unsaturated" hydrocarbons of general formula C_nH_{2n} Contain double bonds	ethylene (C_2H_4) styrene ($C_6H_5.C_2H_3$)
Alkynes (acetylenes)	"Unsaturated" hydrocarbon of general formula C_nH_{2n-2} Contain triple bonds	acetylene (C_2H_2)
Enols (alcohols)	Contain the OH group, bound for example to an alkyl group $C_nH_{2n+1}OH$	methylalcohol (CH_3OH) ethylalcohol (C_2H_5OH)
Ketones	Contain the $C=O$ group $C_nH_{2n+1}C=O$	acetone ($CH_3)_2CO$
Aldehydes	Contain the CHO group	formaldehyde (HCHO) acetaldehyde (CH_3CHO)
Aromatic hydrocarbons	Ring compounds with reactions similiar to the proto-type, benzene (C_6H_6)	napthalene ($C_{10}H_8$) anthracene ($C_{14}H_{10}$)
Phenyl compounds	Derivatives of the phenyl group, C_6H_5	phenol (C_6H_5OH) aniline ($C_6H_5NH_2$)
Heterocyclic compounds	Ring compounds containing mainly carbon atoms and one or more other atoms, *e.g.*, nitrogen	pyridine (C_5H_5N) thiophene (C_4H_4S)

such as raising and lowering weights, or freezing and melting water, may be easily reversed. The forward and backward reactions which are proceeding continuously can then be made to balance out, given enough time, and the system is said to be in equilibrium.

Suppose that X and Y when mixed are partially converted to Z and an equilibrium mixture is obtained under certain defined conditions. The relative amounts $[X]$, $[Y]$, *etc.*, are then definite and governed by the equilibrium constant defined as

$$K = \frac{[Z]}{[X][Y]}$$

Putting it in another way, if we know K we can predict the relative amounts of products and reactants, *i.e.*, the extent to which the reaction proceeds. K in turn depends upon the change in Gibbs Free Energy for the reaction:

$$\Delta G = - RT \ln K$$

where R is the gas constant, and T the absolute temperature, and ln denotes the natural logarithm.

The efficiency of a reaction therefore can be predicted theoretically since values for ΔG can frequently be calculated from tabulated values of ΔH and ΔS. Such studies constitute *chemical thermodynamics*, the branch of thermodynamics (*see* **F20**) applied to chemical reactions. It is an essential consideration in industrial processes.

Bond Enthalpies

The enthalpy (**L40**) of a molecule can be thought of as the sum of the enthalpies associated with each covalent bond, for each of which there is a characteristic value. Determination and tabulation of these bond energies helps in the prediction of enthalpy changes in new reactions involving covalent molecules. Similarly for ionic solids.

THE SPEED OF REACTIONS—CATALYSIS

A good analogy to illustrate the difference between chemical thermodynamics and kinetics is the downhill flow of water. The water will seek the lowest point where it has the lowest potential energy, and in an analogous way a reaction will try to proceed to the state with the lowest Gibbs Free Energy. However, the speed of both water flow and reaction will depend upon a large number of factors, particularly the available *pathway* (or reaction mechanism). Indeed water at the top of a mountain or in a domestic bath may not flow down at all if a suitable path is blocked say by a hillock (or bath plug). The unblocking may involve the expenditure of energy, for example to lift the water over the dam (or pull out the plug). In reactions this type of energy is called the *activation energy*. It can be supplied in a number of ways (*see below*) such as heating. Sometimes it is small and (thankfully) at other times it is large enough that thermodynamically feasible reactions do not occur at all quickly. Each of us is, in fact, *thermodynamically* unstable with respect to our combustion products, mainly CO_2 and H_2O, *i.e.*, we should burn (!), but fortunately we are *kinetically stable*.

A *catalyst* is a substance which will provide an alternative reaction pathway of low activation energy, *i.e.*, it can speed up a reaction, without itself being consumed in the process. The analogy for the water flow would be a tunnel through the hillock. Catalysts are very important industrially, for example, in the manufacture of sulphuric acid (using platinised asbestos or vanadium pentoxide), in the Haber process for ammonia used for fertilisers (iron derivatives), and in the "cracking" of crude oil to give lighter oils (aluminium oxide). Natural catalysts are called *enzymes* (*see* **F31**(2)).

CLASSIFICATION OF REACTIONS

Chemical change can be brought about by a variety of techniques used separately or together:

mixing of single substances
heating single substances or mixtures
electrolysing solutions
exposure to light or radiation
addition of catalysts.

The changes can be classified according to the results produced:

Dissociation—breakdown into simpler substances or ions
Addition—in which one type of molecule or ion is added to another
Polymerisation—reaction of a substance (monomer) with itself to produce larger molecules of the same composition (polymer)
Substitution—in which one particular group in a molecule is replaced by another
Elimination—in which one particular group in a molecule is lost
Exchange—in which two groups are mutually substituted one by the other
Oxidation—removal of electrons (increase of oxidation number), *e.g.*, Fe^{++} ferrous ion is oxidised to ferric, Fe^{+++}
Reduction—the converse of oxidation

More significantly modern classifications are based upon the precise *molecular mechanism* employed. Examples are

Nucleophilic attack—where an electron-rich reagent attacks a position of low electron density in a molecule
Electrophilic attack—where an electron-depleted reagent—an electrophile (for example, a positive ion)—attacks a position of high electron density
Bimolecular reaction—one which involves two molecules unlike a monomolecular reaction which involves only one in each step

Precise descriptions can be built up: substitution, nucleophilic, bimolecular.

ELECTROLYTES, ELECTROLYSIS AND ELECTROCHEMICAL CELLS

Electrolytic Solutions

Ionic solids can dissolve in some solvents especially if each has a high dielectric constant to cut down the force of attraction between oppositely charged ions. The process can be assisted by solvation of the ions and also by the entropy changes which favour the less ordered state of affairs—the liquid rather than the ordered solid.

Electrolysis

The oppositely charged ions are capable of independent movement and the application of an electric potential from an external battery or source of direct current to electrodes in the solution will cause the ions to move. The positive ions (cations) will move to the negatively charged electrode (the cathode) and the negatively charged ions (anions) to the positively charged anode. At the electrodes chemical changes occur and ions may be converted to uncharged species and deposited: for example, sodium ions (Na^+) to sodium metal, Na. This process is referred to as electrolysis. Faraday discovered two laws of electrolysis: (i) the amount of any substance deposited (or dissolved) is proportional to the amount of electricity used; (ii) the relative amounts of substances deposited by the same quantity of electricity are in the ratio of their *equivalent weights*.

For any ion discharged below a certain value of the applied voltage the *discharge voltage* is small. In an electrolyte containing many different ionic species therefore, each ionic discharge will occur only as the appropriate potential is reached. For solutions of acids, hydrogen (formed from H^+ ions) is discharged at the cathode, and oxygen (formed from OH^- ions) at the anode. Electrolysis is important commercially for the refining of metals, electroplating, and in the production of many basic chemicals.

Electrochemical Cells

Ever since 1800 when Volta produced an electric battery consisting of alternate plates of silver and zinc separated by cloth impregnated with salt, the search for new batteries has been continuous. In each new battery a different chemical process is harnessed to produce electrical energy. The battery must not only be feasible according to the laws of thermodynamics, but must be practicable and cheap for widespread consumer use.

The voltages developed in any battery can be predicted from a knowledge of the two processes occurring: one at the cathode and the other at the anode. Voltages can be ascribed to each of these "half cells" according to the chemical reaction which occurs and the condition used, for example concentrations of the reactants (the so-called "standard electrode potentials"). The voltage of any combination of two half cells is the sum of the half-cell voltages. Furthermore each of these voltages is related to the change in the Gibbs Free Energy for its reaction and can, in theory, therefore be predicted thermodynamically.

CHEMISTRY IN MODERN LIFE

Chemistry plays a crucial role in modern life, not least in the third world, as well as in the more developed nations. In the U.K. chemistry has been studied, developed and put to practical use as well as anywhere in the world in modern times. It is no accident that the largest specialised scientific society in the U.K. is the Royal Society of Chemistry (R.S.C.) which has 40,000 members, and that its forerunner, The Chemical Society, lays claim to being the oldest in the world. The high quality of chemical science at the crucial level of basic research is indicated by the remarkable frequency with which the Nobel Prize in Chemistry has come to the U.K. The success is not confined to academic activity but, surely as a consequence, it extends to the economic life of the nation.

The U.K. chemical industry is among the largest in the world and one of the most successful. In national statistics it is included in the manufacturing sector alongside other sectors which have a high chemical component such as petroleum and petroleum products. Its output covers a very wide range. Firstly there are the so called "basic chemicals", such as sulphuric acid, which are utilised in the manufacturing processes of other sectors.

In agriculture chemicals are not only important in the form of bulk products such as fertilizer, without which modern agriculture could not operate efficiently, but also for the 'finer' chemicals such as herbicides and insecticides. Manufactured synthetic polymers and plastics are omnipresent in modern life, for example in architecture and building as well as in many familiar household products and uses. The list here is long and includes moulded casings for televisions and other electronic and electrical products, kitchen utensils, all forms of coverings from paints and varnishes to fabrics. Then there are the "fine" chemicals: cosmetics and pharmaceuticals, ranging from vanity products to the birth control pill and life-saving synthetic drugs. Petroleum products from oil cover an extremely wide range. Petroleum is a most valuable "feed stock" for other products and in this use it is arguably more unique and precious than as a fuel or energy source.

The economic statistics are impressive. The U.K. chemical industry accounts for 9% of manufacturing industry's "gross value added" output. The chemical industry provides for 6% of the employment in the manufacturing industry as well as directly supporting several hundred thousand additional jobs throughout the economy. Over the last decade the industry has accounted for 15% of industry's new capital spending. In 1984 for example the gross fixed capital investment in chemical and allied industry was £804m in comparison with £663m in food, £230m in metals and £672m in vehicles. It exports around 40% of its output. Comparative figures for the value of exports in 1984 are chemicals £6929m, food £2748m, petroleum and products £12,525m. Most importantly it is also profitable. In 1984 it achieved a net positive balance of payments surplus of £1·8 billion in contrast with a deficit of £6·9 billion for the rest of the British manufacturing industry.

Nevertheless, chemistry has had as bad a press recently as other basic physical sciences have had, with the consequence that young people turned away at the turn of the decade from studying the sciences. In the popular mind, chemistry has become associated with pollution resulting from the manufacturing, use and misuse of synthetic chemicals, as well as industrial accidents. Indeed, the word "chemical" has been used increasingly in a pejorative way, even in informed broadcasting and reportage. Thus chemical fertilizers (meaning synthetic fertilizers) are distinguished falsely from organic fertilizers. This sort of practice ignores the fact that we ourselves consist of, use, rely on, are surrounded by naturally occurring chemicals, organic and inorganic, as well as the useful man-made synthetics.

The word *chemist* fares no better. Whereas the terms physicist, biologist, mathematician and scientist are generally used unambiguously, the word chemist is commonly used for the pharmacist or apothecary, at least in the U.K. if not generally in the rest of the world.

IV. BIOLOGY—THE SCIENCE OF LIFE

WHAT BIOLOGY IS ABOUT

Biology embraces the study of all living things which exist on earth at the present time and also the recognisable remains of those that are extinct. Living things or organisms range from the apparently simple micro-organisms such as viruses and bacteria to the largest animals and plants.

Living Processes

The enormous variation and complexity of living processes make the task of understanding and defining life a very difficult one. Every living organism undergoes continual physical and chemical changes which, in spite of their diversity, are referred to as the metabolism of the organism. Metabolism involves the processing of food materials, the production of waste products, and all the intermediate stages between these whereby energy and matter are provided for the operation, maintenance, and growth of the organism. These reactions are under very exact chemical or nervous control at every stage and can be slowed down or speeded up as the need arises. Thus the organism can react to changes in the environment in which it lives, adjusting its activities in relation to the external changes. Finally, organisms can reproduce either in an identical or very slightly modified form. In this process new individuals are produced and the species continues to survive. Differences between offspring and parents can, under certain circumstances, act cumulatively over many generations and so form the basis of evolutionary change in which new species of organism are ultimately formed.

Molecular Biology

It has been evident for many years that the most fundamental aspects of these living processes occur in basic structural units known as cells. The study of living processes at the molecular and cell level has been given a tremendous impetus in recent years by the advent of new techniques which enable microscopic and submicroscopic parts of cell to be examined. Physicists, chemists, and mathematicians have found themselves working alongside biologists in this field and several of the very notable advances have been made by physical scientists. Molecular biology is a term frequently used in describing this rapidly expanding and fascinating field of research.

EVOLUTION

Introduction.—The idea that species of living organisms could change over long periods of time was considered by some Greek writers and, much later, by the Frenchmen Buffon and Lamarck at the end of the 18th cent. Further, the work of the 18th cent. geologists such as James Hutton and William Smith provided a basis without which the major contribution of Darwin, the great 19th cent. naturalist, would have been impossible. Hutton showed that the earth's surface had undergone prolonged upheavals and volcanic eruptions with consequent changes in sea level. This implied that the earth was much older than had previously been supposed. Smith developed a method of dating the geological strata by means of the fossils found in them and demonstrated that widely different types of animals and plants existed at different periods of the earth's history. Later in this section (**F47–8**) a general picture is presented of the evolution of organisms from the simple to the complex and from the aquatic to the terrestrial environment.

These discoveries were in conflict with the Biblical account in the book of Genesis and, although various attempts were made to explain them away or discredit them, it became abundantly clear that through millions of years life has been continually changing, with new species constantly arising and many dying out.

The Evidence for Evolution

1. *The Geological Record.*—It has already been pointed out that successively younger rocks contain fossil remains of different and relatively more complex organisms. The spore-bearing plants preceded the gymnosperms and the angiosperms arose much later. Similarly in the vertebrate series the fish appeared before the amphibia which were followed by the reptiles and later by the air breathing, warm-blooded birds and mammals. On a more restricted level the evolution of the horse has been worked out in great detail from the small Eohippus which was about a foot high and had four digits on the forefeet and three on the hind-feet to the large one-toed animal living today. However, such complete series are rare and the geological record is very incomplete. There are a number of gaps, particularly between the major groups of organisms. No satisfactory fossil evidence is known of the ancestors of the angiosperms (**F43**) so perhaps they did not grow in conditions which favoured their preservation as fossils. On the other hand, Archæopteryx provides an indisputable link between the reptiles and the birds.

Although we talk about the age of fishes, the age of reptiles and so on it must be emphasised that these are the periods during which particular groups were abundant or even dominant. Each group probably originated many millions of years before it became widespread. Further, some groups, such as the giant reptiles and the seed-ferns, died out completely whereas others, the fishes and true ferns for example, are still common today although many fishes and ferns that exist today are very different from those of the Devonian and Carboniferous periods (**F48**). On the other hand some species, for example the Maidenhair tree, have remained unaltered for many millions of years.

2. *Geographical Distribution.*—Nearly all the marsupials or pouched mammals are found in the Australian continent which was cut off from the mainland about 60 million years ago. All the fossil evidence indicates that at that time the eutherian or placental mammals did not yet exist. The marsupials are the only naturally occurring mammals in Australia (**F37(1)**) but since the isolation of the continent the group has given rise to a large number of species very similar in appearance to those which evolved elsewhere in the world among the eutherian mammals. There are marsupials which look like wolves, dogs, cats and squirrels; yet they have no close biological relationships to these animals. Further, some marsupials such as the kangaroos have evolved which are unlike any other creatures in the rest of the world. Quite clearly the isolation of Australia so long ago has resulted in the evolution of these distinct types, just as Darwin found in the Galapagos islands where each has its own distinct flora and fauna which differ also from those of the S. American mainland.

3. *Anatomy.*—The comparative study of the development and mature structure of the mammalian body provides much evidence that all the species have evolved from a single ancestral stock.

Although the arm of an ape, the leg of a dog, the flipper of a whale and the wing of a a bat appear very different externally they are all built on the same skeletal plan. It would be difficult to explain such similarities unless they had all evolved from a common type. There is also evidence that the early development of an animal recapitulates its biological history to a certain extent. For example, the gill slits found in fish are formed during the early stages in the development of a mammal although later they disappear. Finally, apparently useless vestigial structures sometimes occur which would be inexplicable unless regarded in the light of an evolutionary history. In man a small appendix and vestiges of a third eyelid occur but these are functionless although in other animals such structures are well developed and functional, *e.g.*, the appendix in the rabbit.

4. *Human Selection.*—During his brief history on earth modern man has continually selected and bred animals and plants for his own use. We have only to look at the various breeds of dogs which have been developed from a single wild type to see that under certain circumstances great structural divergence can occur in a species even in a relatively short time.

The Darwinian Theory of Evolution.—Darwin amassed a great deal of information such as that outlined above which convinced him that evolution of life had taken place over millions of years. His was the first real attempt to collect all the evidence scientifically and no other satisfactory alternative explanation of all the facts he presented has been proposed. Perhaps even more important was his attempt to explain *how* evolution had actually occurred. He published his theory after many years of work in his book *The Origin of Species by Means of Natural Selection* in 1859. Some of his ideas have since been modified owing to our increased knowledge of genetics but they are so important that it is worth while recounting the main points of his theory.

1. *The Struggle for Existence.*—It is clear that in nature there is a severe struggle for existence in all animals and plants. Over a period of time the number of individuals of a species in a given community does not vary greatly. This implies that the number of progeny which survive to become mature breeding individuals more or less replaces the number of mature ones that die. Generally speaking the reproductive output of a species is much greater than this. For example, a single large foxglove plant may produce half a million seeds each one of which is potentially capable of giving rise to a new individual. Obviously nearly all the progeny die before reaching maturity and the chance of any single one surviving is very remote.

2. *Variation.*—The individuals of any generation of human beings obviously differ from one another and such differences are found in other organisms. It is clear that they vary considerably in structure, colour, activity and so on. Darwin also pointed out that generally these variations were passed on from one generation to the next, for example, the children of tall parents tend to grow tall.

3. *Survival of the Fittest.*—If there is an intense struggle for existence in their natural environment among individuals of a species having different characteristics, those which are best "fitted" to a given set of conditions are most likely to survive to maturity. These will reproduce and the features which enabled them to survive will be passed on to their offspring. This process is liable to continue and a species will become better adapted to its environment.

4. *Natural Selection.*—Over a long period of time the environment of a given species is never stable but will change in various ways. As it does so the characters which best fit the individuals to the changed environment will be selected (not consciously of course) and the species will change. The environment may change only in part of the range of the species and thus lead to divergence and the production of a new species alongside the old one.

Darwin and Lamarck.—Darwin pictured evolution as a slow continuous process with natural selection operating on the small inheritable variations found between the individuals of a species which were undergoing intense competition. This neglects the important effect of the environment on the growth and structure of the individual. It is obvious that external conditions will affect the development of an organism, for example the effect of various soil conditions on the growth of a plant or the amount of food material available to an animal. Lamarck maintained that the characters acquired by an individual owing to the effect of its environment could be passed on to its offspring. Undoubtedly characters are acquired by the individual during its growth but in spite of many attempts to prove otherwise no experiments have been done which prove conclusively that these are inherited by the offspring. Thus Lamarck's theory that evolution has occurred by the inheritance of acquired characters is not generally acceptable today.

Neodarwinism

Darwinism received something of a setback during the early years of modern genetics. There did not seem to be much in common between the large mutations studied by geneticists and the small continuous variations which Darwin thought were the basic material upon which selection acted. With time, it became evident that not all mutations are large in their effects and that much of the continuous variation which occurs does indeed have a genetic basis. Mathematicians such as J. B. S. Haldane and Sewall Wright showed that even very small selective advantages would cause genes to spread throughout populations as the generations passed by. Experiments and observations on natural populations showed that evolution—seen as progressive, adaptive genetic change—does indeed occur today. For example, the proportion of dark-coloured moths has greatly increased in many areas where smoke pollution occurs, as a result of predation by birds on the now more obvious light forms. Again, many pest insects have evolved genetic resistance to the insecticides used to attack them.

GENETICS

Mendelism

Genetics is the study of the mechanisms of the hereditary process. Modern genetics began with the experiments of Gregor Mendel, an Austrian monk in 1865. He studied the inheritance of different factors in peas by crossing different strains and counting the numbers of plants with different characters in the succeeding generations.

In one experiment Mendel crossed peas with round seeds with peas having wrinkled seeds. All of the offspring (known as the "first filial" or F1 generation) had round seeds. Mendel allowed these plants to pollinate themselves, and then measured the characteristics of their offspring (the F2 generation). There were 5,474 round-seeded plants and 1,850 wrinkled-seeded plants in the F2 generation, a ratio of very nearly three to one. The character of roundness can be described as being "dominant" over the "recessive" character of wrinkledness.

In order to explain his results Mendel suggested that the characters of roundness and wrinkledness were determined by particulate factors (now called *genes*), and that each plant possessed two genes for each feature. Suppose the gene for roundness is A and that for wrinkledness is a. Then the parental plants in Mendel's experiment will be represented by AA (round seeds) and aa (wrinkled seeds). The gametes (the ovules and the sperm nuclei of the pollen grains) will be A and a respectively. When these combine to form the F1 generation they will produce plants with the genetic constitution Aa. Both male and female gametes of the F1 generation are then of the two types A and a, and these can combine, on self-pollination, in four different ways:

F1	male gamete	female gamete	F2
	A	A	AA
Aa	A	a	Aa
	a	A	
	a	a	aa

The individuals of the F2 generation will thus have genetic constitutions of AA, Aa and aa in the approximate proportions 1:2:1. Since both AA and Aa individuals have round seeds, the ratio of round-seeded plants to wrinkled-seeded plants will be about three to one, which indeed it is.

Mendel's results were ignored for many years until their rediscovery at the beginning of this century. Mendelian ratios were then found to govern inheritance in a large number of other cases, such as coat colour in rabbits and cattle, and white eyes and other characteristics in the fruit fly *Drosophila*. In other cases characteristics are governed by more than one set of genes so the simple mathematical relationships are obscured. This occurs in quantitative features, such as yield in crop plants and weight in animals.

Chromosome Theory

The chromosomes are dark-staining filaments which, as we shall see later, can be observed in the nucleus at cell division. Their behaviour was described in the nineteenth century, but it was not clear what their function was. After the rediscovery of Mendel's work, Sutton suggested that the genes are carried on chromosomes, since the observed behaviour of the chromosomes corresponded very well with the theoretical behaviour of Mendel's factors.

Further evidence for the chromosome theory of inheritance came from study of the phenomenon known as sex-linkage, in which the expression of a gene depends upon the sex of the individual in which it is found. Haemophilia in man, for example, is a hereditary disease which is normally found only in males, although it is clear that females can act as carriers (Queen Victoria was one, since one of her sons, three of her grandsons and seven of her greatgrandsons were haemophiliacs). Cytological study shows that there is one pair of chromosomes which differ in the two sexes. In the female (in man and most animals) the two chromosomes of this pair are similar and are known as the X chromosomes. In the male one of these is replaced by a much smaller Y chromosome. Hence recessive genes which are found on only one X chromosome are expressed in the male, since there is no other dominant gene present. A female haemophiliac would have haemophilia genes on both X chromosomes; this could only arise from a carrier mother and a haemophiliac father, a very rare occurrence.

In recent years it has become clear that chromosomes are composed largely of the DNA molecules of the cell nucleus, to be discussed later (**F33–4**). And since it has become evident that genes are DNA molecules, we now have a firm chemical basis for the assumption that genes are carried on chromosomes. Genetics has thus to some extent become a branch of molecular biology.

Mutations

Sometimes a DNA molecule may not replicate itself exactly during the process of cell division.

When this happens the gene which it constitutes has changed its character so as to produce a difference effect when expressed in the individual organism. Such a change is known as a gene mutation. It seems likely, for example, that Queen Victoria's haemophilia gene arose as a mutation in herself or in her mother. Mutations, as we shall see, are of vital importance in providing the genetic variation upon which evolutionary selection can act.

The frequency with which mutations occur is increased by certain chemicals and by ionising radiation. Hence the need for caution in exposing the body to X-rays and to radioactive materials, and the concern over the possible genetic effects of radioactive waste from power stations and from military testing programmes.

THE CELL

Cells were first seen in 1665 by Robert Hooke when he looked at a piece of cork under his primitive microscope. It was not until 1839, however, that Schlieden and Schwann produced the cell doctrine which visualised the cell as both the structural and functional unit of living organisation. Exceptions may be found to the cell doctrine. For example, some protozoa, algae, and fungi show very complex internal organisation but are not divided into cells; they are usually called acellular organisms. The viruses also constitute a difficulty since in many ways they are intermediate between living and dead matter. They are absolutely dependent on cells of other organisms for their continued existence. Outside living cells they are inert molecules which may take a crystalline form. Inside a host cell, however, they become disease-producing parasites which multiply and show many of the other properties of living organisms. They are minute and lack the complex organisation usually associated with cells. Notwithstanding their somewhat ambiguous position, the viruses are often treated as though they were single cells or parts of cells and their extreme simplicity has made them ideal material for many types of research at this level. The bacteria also lack some of the properties of cells but the differences are not so clearly defined as they are in the case of viruses.

Structure and Function of Cells

Though the constituent cells of a multicellular organism are usually specialised to perform particular functions, they have a great many features in common. The cell is often said to be made up of a substance called protoplasm, a term for the fundamental material of life which dates from the 19th cent. Protoplasm has two main constituents, the cytoplasm and the nucleus, and is bounded on the outside by a cell or plasma membrane. Plant cells generally have an additional wall composed primarily of cellulose and used for support. The nucleus is the controlling centre of the cell and has rather limited metabolic capabilities. The cytoplasm contains various subunits which operate to produce energy and new cell structure during the normal metabolism of the cell.

Cells take up the raw materials for metabolism through the cell membrane from extracellular fluid which surrounds them. The nutrients include carbohydrates, fats, proteins, minerals, vitamins, and water. Fats and carbohydrates are important principally as sources of energy, though both types of compound are found in permanent cell structure. Proteins are complex substances of high molecular weight which contain nitrogen in addition to the carbon, hydrogen, and oxygen found in the other compounds. They are of fundamental importance in the structure and function of the cell and are built up of a number of simple nitrogen-containing organic molecules called amino acids. There are twenty amino acids occurring commonly in nature so that the number of possible combinations in large protein molecules is quite clearly enormous. A group of proteins whose significance is well established are the enzymes which are the catalysts of chemical reactions in living cells. Each enzyme will control and speed up a specific reaction even though it is present in very small amounts and is usually unchanged at the end of the process. A large number of inorganic mineral salts are essential for cells to function normally. Some, such as sodium, potassium, and calcium salts, are needed in considerable quantity; others are required only in trace amounts and these include iron, copper, and manganese. The trace elements are usually important constituents of enzyme systems. Vitamins are also necessary in very small amounts and it seems reasonable to conclude that their function is also a catalytic one in parts of some enzyme systems.

I. CYTOPLASM

For a long time cytoplasm was thought to be a homogeneous and structureless substrate in which enzymes occurred as part of a general colloidal system. With the refinement of techniques such as electron microscopy and ultracentrifugation, more and more identifiable components have been found within the cytoplasm. It now seems certain that the material other than these recognisable particles is not a structureless matrix but a highly organised and variable complex.

Mitochondria and Oxidation

Mitochondria vary in shape from cylindrical rods to spheres and in size from 0·2 to 3·0 microns. When seen in the living cell they are in constant motion. The whole structure is enclosed within a thin double membrane, the inner layer of which is thrown into folds extending across the central cavity of the mitochondrion and dividing it into small chambers. The function of mitochondria is to provide energy for the reactions of the rest of the cell. Almost the whole machinery for the oxidation of foodstuffs is to be found in the mitochondria. Slight damage to the mitochondrion will render it unable to carry out a complete cycle of oxidative processes. Destruction of parts of the double membrane system prevents the production of energy-rich phosphate bonds in adenosine triphosphate (ATP) in which energy is stored and transported about the cell.

Chloroplasts and Photosynthesis

Chloroplasts are particles found in cells in the green parts of plants, in fact they contain the green pigment which is called chlorophyll. They are involved in the process known as photosynthesis in which energy absorbed from light is used to synthesise carbohydrates from carbon dioxide and water, oxygen being formed as a byproduct.

Chloroplasts are disc-shaped or flat ellipsoids from 2 to 20 microns across, possessing a complex structure which in many ways is reminiscent of that found in mitochondria. A typical double membrane surrounds the structure and the inside is made up very largely of a stack of discs consisting of paired membranes connected at their ends to form closed systems. This seems to be a further development of the type of lamellated structure seen dividing the central cavity of a mitochondrion. The chlorophylls and other pigments, such as the orange yellow carotenoids, seem to be arranged in layers a single molecule thick in the chloroplast discs so that they are maximally exposed to light.

The importance of this process whereby plants can make use of the energy in sunlight to fix carbon dioxide and produce carbohydrates is quite clear. The whole animal population of the world, including man, is dependent on plants for food since even the meat-eating carnivores prey upon herbivores. Although scientists continue to make efforts to produce adequate food materials from simple compounds, there is still no better machinery known for doing this than the plant cell. Man is dependent on photosynthesis not only for his supplies of food but also for much of his fuel, since much of the combustible material removed from the earth is of plant origin.

Endoplasmic Reticulum, Ribosomes, and Protein Synthesis.

A network of elaborate and oriented double membranes existing within parts of the cytoplasm can be seen in the electron microscope. In the space between the pairs of double membranes small granules are visible, either free in the space or attached to a membrane. The whole system is called the endoplasmic reticulum. When the cell is homogenised and centrifuged the endoplasmic reticulum appears as the microsomal fraction. Biochemical analysis after separation of the membranous from the granular components reveals that the former is composed largely of phospholipids and cholesterol, which are compounds closely related to fats, and the latter of ribonucleic acid (RNA).

Nucleic Acids

The term nucleic acid covers a class of substances, usually of great complexity, built up from smaller units called nucleotides. Each nucleotide consists of a base, united to a sugar, in turn united to phosphoric acid. Nucleotides are joined together in a linear fashion by means of the phosphoric acid residues to form a chain from which the bases project at right angles. Two types of sugar are found in naturally occurring nucleic acids and these are the ribose of RNA and the deoxyribose of desoxyribonucleic acids (DNA). We shall return to the latter when the nucleus is considered. Four nitrogen-containing bases occur in nucleic acids and in RNA—adenine, cytosine, guanine, and uracil. In DNA the uracil is replaced by thymine.

Protein Synthesis

There is good evidence that RNA is manufactured exclusively within the nucleus and subsequently moves out into the cytoplasm. Some of it, called ribosomal RNA, unites with protein to form the granules, or ribosomes, of the endoplasmic reticulum. Another form, called messenger RNA, also migrates from the nucleus to associated with ribosomes but does not become incorporated into their permanent structure. It is also well established that the ribosomes are closely linked with protein synthesis in the cell because radioactive amino acids, when fed to an animal, are always found first in the ribosomes before any other cell structure. The specificiation for a particular protein is not carried on the ribosome which is merely the factory for making these complex molecules. It is thought that messenger RNA carries instructions from the nucleus which specify exactly the protein to be synthesised at a ribosome. This is done by means of a code in which a "triplet" of three nucleotide bases codes one amino acid (Fig. 1). Thus on a long molecule of RNA, three adjacent uracil bases would specify an amino acid called phenylalanine. If these were followed on the RNA molecule by one uracil and two guanines then the amino acid tryptophan would be specified and this would be joined to the phenylalanine. In this way complex protein molecules can be built up according to instructions emanating from the nucleus for each of the 20 different amino acids.

This system is responsible for building and maintaining much of the organisation of the cytoplasm. All the enzymes, for example catalysing every reaction within the cell will be specified and built up on the appropriate RNA template. The understanding of protein synthesis is of fundamental importance to the whole of biology and has particular significance in studies on cancer where cell growth becomes abnormal.

The Golgi Apparatus

The characteristic features of the Golgi apparatus are numbers of large vacuoles or spaces bordered by closely packed layers of double membranes. The latter look very much like the

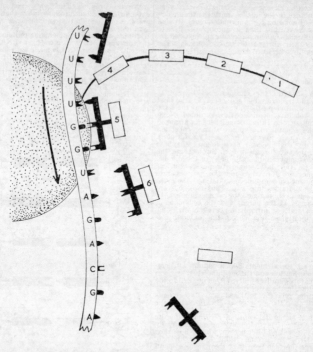

Fig. 1. This shows a portion of a molecule of messenger RNA, associated with a ribosome and synthesising a protein. Adenine specifies Uracil (U), Cytosine specifies Guanine (G), Thymine specifies Adenine (A), and Guanine specifies Cytosine (C). The ribosome is moving down the messenger RNA strand "reading" the triplet code. Amino acid 4, which is phenylalanine specified by UUU, has just been joined to three other amino acids and its carrier RNA released to the cytoplasm. Amino acid 5, tryptophan specified by UGG, is attached to its carrier RNA and in position ready to be joined to the protein chain by the ribosome. Amino acid 6, methionine specified by UAG is attached to its carrier RNA but has not been brought into position on the messenger RNA strand. Other amino acids and carrier RNA molecules exist free in the cytoplasm and have not yet associated.

membranes of the endoplasmic reticulum but do not have the ribosome particles along their edge. They are therefore known as "smooth" membranes in contrast to the "rough" membranes of endoplasmic reticulum. The function of the Golgi apparatus may be associated with secretory activity of the cell.

Cell Membrane

Though the cell membrane plays a most vital part in regulating what can enter and leave the cell, it remains rather poorly understood. It is thought to consist of a double layer of lipid molecules with a layer of protein probably outside the lipid. Fairly large molecules seem to be able to penetrate the membrane in relation to their fat solubility, which would support the hypothesis of its lipid framework. Small molecules and ions appear to penetrate in relation to their size, the smaller ones getting through more readily than the larger. This suggests that pores of a certain size exist in the membrane.

The cell membrane has mechanisms which can move ions and other substances against concentration differences either into or out of the cell. A fine microelectrode can be pushed into a cell and the electrical potential of the inside determined with respect to the outside. In all the cells studied so far there is a potential difference across the membrane which is produced by the non-uniform distribution on either side of ions, particularly those of sodium, potassium, and chloride.

Though these potentials have been studied in animal and plant cells generally, they are best known from the work on nerve cells where sudden changes in the membrane potential are the basis of nerve impulses. The basic process which produces the nerve impulse in any region of the nerve fibre has been shown to be a sudden increase in permeability of the membrane to sodium ions in that region. Transmission from one nerve cell to the next takes place at a special region called a synapse and when an impulse reaches this region it causes the release of a small amount of chemical transmitter substance which diffuses to the membrane of the adjacent cell. There it combines with the membrane in such a way as to change its permeability to ions and so produce a response in the second cell. A number of transmitter substances have now been identified and many of them are related chemically to tranquillisers and other drugs affecting the nervous system.

II. NUCLEUS

The main regions of the nucleus are the surrounding nuclear membrane, a mass of material known as chromatin, and a small sphere called the nucleolus. The nuclear membrane is a double structure very much like the membranes of the cell surface and endoplasmic reticulum. Suggestions have been made that these membranes are continuous at some regions within the cell. The status of chromatin was in doubt for many years. Light microscope studies reveal very little structure in the nucleus until the time when the cell is preparing for, and undergoing, division or mitosis. At this time a number of discrete double strands, the chromosomes, are revealed by virtue of their chromatin content—the material stains heavily with basic dyes.

Cell Division

During division the chromosomes behave in regular and recognisable sequence. In the first stage called prophase they appear and at the same time the nuclear membrane breaks down. Next, in metaphase, the chromosomes become arranged across the equator of a spindle-shaped collection of fibrils which appears in the area formerly outlined by the nucleus. Then follows anaphase in which the two threads of each chromosome, the chromatids, move to opposite poles of the spindle. Finally in the last stage, telophase, nuclear membranes are formed round the two separate collections of chromosome material and the cytoplasm itself divides into two. Thus two cells are formed each containing the same number of chromosomes as the parent and the cells enter a period of rest, or interphase, between divisions. During interphase the chromatin material disappears.

Genes

These are the elements which contain all hereditary information and the medium whereby hereditary features are transmitted from one cell to the next, either in the same organism or from parents to offspring via the fertilised egg. Experiments indicated that the same genes always occupy the same position on chromosomes and this really demands a structural continuity through the life of the cell. The chromosomes undoubtedly persist, but it is still not certain why or how they change so as to become visible during division. One suggestion has been that the nucleic acids of which they are very largely made up condense during the period of prophase. In the resting nucleus the chromosomes may be much more swollen and occupy much of the nucleus.

The problem that has attracted the most attention and is possibly the most fundamental that biology has to offer is that of the nature of the genes. The important material of the genes is known to be deoxyribonucleic acid (DNA), made up of nucleotides as is RNA, though in this case the bases are adenine, cytosine, guanine, and thymine. The DNA molecule is large and complex. Two long chains of nucleotides are known to coil round in a double helix with the pairs of bases on each helix directed towards one another and linked by means of hydrogen bonds (Fig. 2). Furthermore, if adenine is the base on one chain, thymine must be its partner on the other and similarly guanine can link only with cytosine. Because of this pairing off of bases there is sufficient information in a single chain of nucleotides to resynthesise the double helix once more. Thus if we examine a section of a single strand of the helix and find bases in the order adenine, thymine, guanine, adenine, cytosine, we can predict that in similar positions on the other strand we shall find thymine, adenine, cytosine, thymine, guanine. The capacity of one half of a DNA molecule to specify the other half exactly, enables the system to be self-replicating in a way that is essential in a hereditary transmitter and fits in well with what is known of chromosome behaviour during cell division.

Transmission of Genetic Information

Long before the structure and significance of the DNA molecules was known, geneticists were finding that alterations in a gene, known as a mutation, usually affected a particular chemical reaction and this in turn caused the changes seen in the organism as a whole. The effect was due to the failure to synthesise a necessary enzyme and so the hypothesis "one gene = one enzyme"

gathered currency. This view has now been extended to include proteins other than enzymes and it is now certain that specific genes control the synthesis of specific proteins. The DNA of the genes transmits the instructions about protein synthesis to the ribosomes via messenger RNA. In the nucleus, messenger RNA is made with specific base sequences in its molecule by using DNA as the template; thus a group of three adjacent adenine bases in DNA would produce a group of three adjacent uracil bases in the synthesised RNA and this would lead to the specification of phenylalanine at the ribosome as we have seen. Only one of the two strands in the DNA double helix participates in the production of RNA.

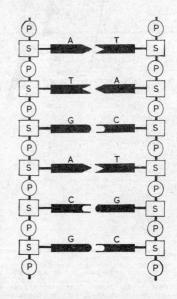

Fig. 2. A portion of a DNA molecule showing how it is made up of two strands of nucleotides. Each nucleotide consists of a base, which may be Adenine (A), Thymine (T), Guanine (G), or Cytosine (C), united to the Pentose Sugar, Desoxyribose (S), in turn joined to Phosphoric Acid (P). The nucleotides are linked through the phosphoric acid groups. The two strands are held together by hydrogen bonds between bases, adenine linking only with thymine, and guanine only with cyto-sine. They are twisted round each other so that the molecule is in the form of a double helix.

The processes involved in nuclear control and the transmission of information from cell to cell is summarised in the aphorism "DNA makes RNA and RNA makes protein." The system of carrying that information in the base sequences of DNA molecules has become known as the "genetic code." A remarkable landmark in the study of DNA occurred when, towards the end of 1967, Kornberg and his colleagues managed to synthesise a virus DNA in a test tube. The synthesised molecules proved to be capable of infecting bacteria in the same way that the naturally occurring virus would. The DNA was synthesised using an extracted virus DNA molecule as template and attaching nucleotides by means of appropriate enzymes. The newly made molecules were then separated from the template. It can hardly be claimed that this is the creation of life in a test tube since the template was extracted from a living virus. The experiment suggests many possibilities in experimental modification of the genetic constitution of an organism with all the far-reaching ethical consequences.

MULTICELLULAR ORGANISATION

It is axiomatic, if evolutionary theory is accepted, that in the course of very long periods of time there has been a general change in multicellular organisation from the simple aggregation of cells with little individual differentiation, to the highly specialised and differentiated cells and tissues seen in complex animals and plants.

Furthermore the complex organisation must be built up in the lifetime of each animal or plant from the single-celled stage of the fertilised egg. The essential problems in development are: (1) how is the smooth succession of shape changes produced during cell division so that an appropriate and recognisable end product is reached?; (2) how do the cells *differentiate* during this temporal sequence so that those which form part of the eye, say, are different from those of liver and blood?

Method of Development

There are some important differences in the method of development in animals and plants. In animals there tends to be a relatively short period during which the basic structure is produced and after which growth, repair, and replacement may cause adjustment rather than major change. In higher plants, on the other hand, the apical regions of both roots and shoots remain in a permanently embryonic state and add material, which then differentiates, in a continuous process throughout the life of the plant. In spite of these differences—and in any case there are many exceptions—the two main problems in development are essentially similar in both animals and plants.

A great deal of work has been done on animal development since this takes place in a fairly stereotyped way during a short period of time. The fertilised egg of an animal divides in such a way as to form a hollow ball of cells, the blastula, which folds in on itself to produce a two-layered sac, the gastrula. A third layer, the mesoderm, is now added between the two layers, known as ectoderm on the outside, and endoderm on the inside. At this stage much of the animal's basic structure is established. Many aspects of this orderly sequence can be explained in terms of specific adhesive properties of cells, so that a cell will stick to others of the same type but not to unrelated types. Other mechanical properties such as elasticity, particularly in surface layers, are important in maintaining shape and producing appropriate changes during processes when one layer is folded in on another. Why cells should have the different physical properties necessary to produce an integrated whole embryo is not known, but certainly it cannot be thought that every cell has an absolutely fixed constitution and therefore a predetermined role in development. Large parts of developing embryos can be removed in early stages and their places taken by remaining cells so that intact organisms are still produced.

Formation of Specialised Tissues

This is essentially a problem in the regulation of gene activity since we know that each cell division produces daughter cells which are genetically identical. It seems likely therefore that instructions are carried on the chromosomes to cope with all requirements of the organism, but that in specialised cells only a small fraction of this full potential is realised. For a long time embryologists have known that egg cytoplasm shows regional differences which make identical nuclei behave differently, and it is thought that regional cytoplasm can in some way control gene activity. Techniques for the transplantation of nuclei in developing frog embryos have been perfected and it has been possible to put a nucleus from an intestinal cell of a tadpole into an enucleate egg. The egg will go on to develop normally even though its nucleus came from a fully specialised cell derived from endoderm. The embryo will form blood and muscle from the mesodermal layer and all the other components of an organism, under the influence of a nucleus which normally would have produced none of these things. One can conclude that all the genes are present, even in the nuclei of specialised cells, but that they have to be placed in a suitable cytoplasmic environment in order to be activated. Similar nuclear transplantation experiments indicate that genes can be "turned off" as well as "turned on" by an appropriate cytoplasmic environment, even though the nuclei come from cells which are so specialised as to stop dividing. The components of cytoplasm which control gene activity are still quite unknown.

A study of cell differentiation and the development of multicellular organisation leads us to the view that, important though the nucleus and its genes are in controlling cell activity, an integrated organism is the result of complex interactions between its constituent cells and between the cytoplasm of those cells and their nuclei.

THE CLASSIFICATION OF ORGANISMS

It was clear to the biologists of the 17th cent. that animals and plants could be fitted into different groups or species. John Ray, a leading biologist of the day, defined a species as a group of individuals capable of interbreeding within the group. This criterion, with its corollary that a species is reproductively isolated from organisms outside the group, has survived more or less unchanged to the present day. The early workers also saw that some species were very similar to one another while others were obviously dissimilar. Systems of classification based on the similarities and differences were drawn up so that all organisms could be fitted into an orderly scheme and species could be given names in accordance with the scheme. The most famous collector and classifier was the Swede, Linnaeus, who established his reputation in the 1730s. A very large number of animals and plants are known by the names given to them by Linnaeus.

Systematics, as this type of study is called, acquired a new significance after Darwin and the Theory of Evolution. The most satisfactory classification became one which reflected the evolution of the organisms classified, a so-called natural classification. It is not always easy to produce because ancestral types tend to become extinct and the problem then becomes one of reconstructing a whole branching system when only the ends of the branches are known. A great deal of the work on systematics has, of necessity, to be done on museum specimens which may be fossils or material preserved in some way by the collectors. The biological criterion of reproductive isolation cannot be used to define a species when the only available representatives are in a preserved state. In this case the scientist must resort to an assessment of structural differences in an attempt to decide whether two organisms are of different species. In recent years computer techniques have been used to compare large numbers of structural differences between groups of animals or plants, as well as physiological and biochemical characteristics. All these techniques have led to the realisation that even the species cannot be regarded as a static point in an evolutionary pattern. Some species die out and others arise as conditions in the environment slowly change.

When the systematist shifts his attention to the higher levels of classification the problems are just as great as at the species level. Different species having features in common can be grouped together into genera, genera into families, families into orders, orders into classes, and classes into phyla. The dividing lines between different groups at all levels is always difficult and in the final analysis somewhat arbitrary since at these levels we do not have any biological criterion such as exists for the species. The evolutionary status of the larger groups is also poorly defined. Many are now recognised to be polyphyletic, which is to say that there are several main evolutionary lines running right through the group.

THE ANIMAL KINGDOM

The animal kingdom is divided into about 24 large groups or phyla though the number varies between different classifications. Ten of the more important phyla are listed below.

1. Protozoa.—Microscopic, unicellular forms of great variety. Some may have more than one nucleus and others form colonies. Many are able to swim by waving hair-like flagella or cilia. Others move by putting out extensions of the body or pseudopodia into which the rest of the body then flows. Protozoa are found in the sea, in fresh water and in the soil. Some are parasitic and cause important diseases in animals and man such as sleeping sickness and malaria.

2. Porifera.—Sponges. Very primitive, multicellular animals whose cells display considerable independence of one another. Largely marine. The body which may become branched and plant-like is supported by a framework of spicules and fibres. The bath sponge is the fibrous skeleton of certain species.

3. Coelenterates.—Hydra, jellyfish, sea anemones, corals. Simple animals which have a body only two cells thick surrounding a gut cavity with a single opening to the outside. Largely marine. Many are colonial. Coral reefs are formed from the calcareous skeletons of these animals.

4. Platyhelminths.—Flatworms, which are free living in water, and liver flukes and tapeworms, which are parasitic. A third, solid block of cells, the mesoderm, has been developed between the two layers of cells seen in the coelenterates. A simple gut may be developed and the reproductive system is complex especially in the parasitic forms.

5. Nematodes.—Roundworms. The body is smooth and pointed at each end. Some of the most numerous and widespread of all animals. Free living in all environments and parasitic in practically all groups of plants and animals. At the same level of complexity as the Platyhelminths.

6. Annelids.—Segmented worms such as earthworms, marine worms and leeches. A system of spaces, the body cavity, is developed in the mesoderm so that movements of the main body of the animal and movements of the gut become more or less independent. Digestive, excretory, circulatory, nervous and reproductive systems are all well developed.

7. Arthropods.—A very large, diverse and important group of animals which includes crustaceans such as crabs, shrimps and water fleas; myriapods, such as centipedes and millepedes; insects; and arachnids, such as spiders and scorpions. The arthropods show many of the developments seen in annelids and in addition they possess a jointed, hard exoskeleton. Paired appendages grow out from the segments of the body and form antennae, mouth parts, walking legs, etc. The muscles within the skeleton are able to exert a fine control over the movement of the appendage. In order to grow these animals have to shed the exoskeleton periodically.

8. Molluscs.—Mussels, clams, oysters, squids, octopods and snails. Complex body form but somewhat different from annelid-arthropod type. Unsegmented body protected by shell which is variously developed in different types. It forms two valves in mussels and oysters, a spiral structure in snails, is reduced and internal in squids and completely lost in octopods.

9. Echinoderms.—Starfish, brittle stars, sea cucumbers, sea urchins, and sea lilies. All marine and all radially symmetrical, usually with five radii. Completely unlike the other advanced, major groups. Circulatory, excretory and nervous systems differently developed. Locomotion and feeding by means of hundreds of tube feet projecting from under surface.

10. Chordates.—Sea squirts, Amphioxus, fish, amphibia, reptiles, birds and mammals. Segmented animals which at some stage in their life have gill slits leading from pharynx to the outside and a supporting notochord from which, in all chordates except sea squirts and Amphioxus, is developed a vertebral column or backbone. Those animals with a backbone are commonly referred to as vertebrates, *all* those without as invertebrates. These are obviously names of convenience having no phylogenetic significance since they lump together totally unrelated phyla in one case and align these with a part of a single phylum in the other. The vertebrates have been investigated more completely than any other animals because of their direct structural and functional relationship with man himself. There are five well defined classes which are listed below. The first vertebrates were the fish and from them came the amphibia. The amphibia gave rise to the reptiles and both birds and mammals evolved from different reptilian stock.

(a) Fish

Cold blooded, aquatic animals breathing by means of gills. Sharks, rays and dogfish belong to a group known as the elasmobranchs characterised by a skeleton made of cartilage. Bony fish, most of them in a group called the teleosts, include almost all the fresh water fish and the common marine fish such as cod, mackerel, plaice, herring, etc.

(b) Amphibia

Cold blooded, more or less terrestrial animals which have to return to water to breed. Five fingered limbs are developed in place of the fins of fish. The egg hatches into a tadpole larva which is aquatic and breathes by gills. At metamorphosis the larva changes into the terrestrial adult which possesses lungs. Some amphibia such as the axolotl may become sexually mature as a larva and so never metamorphose into the adult. The class includes newts, salamanders, frogs and toads.

(c) Reptiles

Cold blooded and terrestrial. These animals do not return to water to breed because they have an egg with a relatively impermeable shell containing the food and water requirements of the developing embryo. There is no larval stage. Present day reptiles such as lizards, snakes and crocodiles are all that remains of a tremendous radiation of dinosaur-like creatures which occurred in the Mesozoic (**F48**).

(d) Birds

Warm blooded and adapted for aerial life. The characteristic feathers are both to insulate the body against heat loss and to provide the airfoil surfaces necessary for flight. The birds are an astonishingly uniform group and show less diversity of structure than much lower classification categories (*e.g.*, the teleosts) in other classes. The relationships of the 8,000 or more species of bird are difficult to establish because of this uniformity. It is clear that the flightless forms such as the ostrich are primitive and that the penguins are also in a separate category but the typical modern birds are classified in a large number of rather arbitrary orders. About half of all the known species are placed in one enormous order called the Passeriformes or perching birds.

(e) Mammals

Warm blooded animals which have been successful in a tremendous variety of habitats. Mammals are insulated from the environment by the characteristically hairy and waterproofed skin. They are, with two exceptions, viviparous which means that their young are born alive and in typical mammals at an advanced stage of development. In the marsupials of Australia the young are born at an early stage and transferred to a pouch where they develop further. The two exceptions referred to are primitive monotreme mammals known as the duck-billed platypus and spiny ant-eater and these animals lay eggs. The young of mammals are suckled by means of the milk producing mammary glands. The mammals include aquatic whales and dolphins, hoofed ungulates, flesh eating carnivores, rodents and insectivores, the aerial bats, and the tree climbing primates to which man himself belongs.

THE PHYSIOLOGY OF ANIMALS

In multicellular animals cells are of various types, constituting distinct tissues and organs which perform special functions in the body. Although each cell has its own complex metabolism there must be coordination between cells forming special tissues and between the tissues which form the whole organism in order for the body to function efficiently. The study of these functional interrelationships at the tissue and organism level of organisation is the province of the physiologist.

1. Movement, Fibrils and Skeletons

(a) **Muscles.**—The prime movers in almost all animal movement are large protein molecules in the form of microscopic fibrillar threads. In some way not yet fully understood these fibrils can convert the chemical energy stored in the high energy phosphate bonds of ATP into mechanical energy. In the long, thin cells forming the muscles of animals, it has been discovered that there are two sets of fibrils, one formed of a protein called myosin, the other of actin, arranged in a regular, interdigitating fashion. When the muscle contracts the fibrils slide past one another so that, although the fibrils themselves do not change in length, the muscle as a whole develops tension and shortens. Fine bridges extend from the myosin fibrils to attach on to the actin and it is here that the conversion of chemical to mechanical energy goes on.

(b) **Skeletons.**—In order for muscles to work effectively it is necessary for them to operate in some sort of skeletal system. Contraction but not relaxation is an active process; muscles must be arranged in antagonistic pairs so that one muscle can extend the other. A skeleton also provides a system of levers so that the muscles can do work against the environment in an efficient manner. A simple type of skeleton found in fairly primitive animals is the hydrostatic system of coelenterates and worms. Here the animal can be thought of as a fluid-filled bag or tube which can change shape but whose volume remains constant. By contraction of circular muscles the tube will become long and thin and conversely contraction of longitudinal muscles makes the tube short and fat. Examination of an earthworm will demonstrate how alternating waves of activity of this type passing from head to tail can move the animal over the ground. The earthworm shows an advance over

the simplest systems because the hydrostatic tube is broken up into small units by the segmentation of the body. This makes local responses possible. The next advance to be seen is the development in animals such as arthropods and vertebrates of a firm skeleton to which muscles are directly attached. The skeleton can then be used to support the body and to engage the environment. It seems to matter little whether an endoskeleton (vertebrates) or exoskeleton (arthropods) is developed since in both cases a tremendous radiation of fins for swimming, legs for walking and wings for flying can be seen. However in other respects these two types of skeleton show significant differences. The exoskeleton for example offers more protection than the endoskeleton while apparently setting an upper size limit. All the really big animals have endoskeletons.

(c) **Filia.**—Fibrillar systems are also seen in the hair-like cilia which project from the surface of some cells. Cilia are important in a number of ways. They are the organelles of movement in many Protozoa, they are used to produce water currents past the bodies of some aquatic animals, and they are of great importance in moving fluid within the body of almost all animals. They beat in a regular fashion, the effective stroke being accomplished with the cilium held straight out from the surface and the recovery stroke with the cilium flexed at the base.

2. Feeding

All animals require complex organic substances, proteins, fats and carbohydrates, together with small amounts of salts and vitamins. These materials are obtained by eating the dead bodies of plants and other animals. They are taken into the alimentary canal and there broken down or digested by enzymes into simpler, soluble amino acids, sugars and fatty acids. These substances are absorbed and distributed to various parts of the body where they are used in cell metabolism (**F31–2**) or stored for future use.

Many animals, called macrophagous feeders, take in relatively large masses of food. Some such as frogs and snakes swallow their food whole, but many break it up first. Arthropods have modified appendages arranged round the mouth for cutting, some molluscs have a rasp-like radula with which to scrape off particles, and many mammals break up their food with jaws and teeth. The teeth are usually well adapted to the type of food. Carnivores have large, sharp canines, premolars and molars with which to tear the flesh of the prey, fish-eating seals have small peg-like teeth to grip the fish and herbivorous ungulates have flat grinding teeth with which they break up hard plant material.

In contrast, microphagous feeders collect small particles of food material from the environment by continuous filtration. In bivalve molluscs and many marine worms water currents are produced by beating cilia. Food is trapped within the confined space through which the water flows by means of a plentiful supply of sticky mucus in the filtering region. Some crustacea use fine hairs to sieve off food material, often from water currents created by the swimming movements. The most startling of filter feeders is the whalebone whale. As the whale swims forward a stream of water flows in at the front of the mouth and out at the sides via sheets of whalebone which filter off the organisms on which the animal feeds. Though macrophagy seems to favour the attainment of larger size there are exceptions! Another type of particulate feeding is seen in those animals which eat deposits of detritus as do many worms. Finally some animals take in only soluble food materials. These fluid feeders include internal parasites like the tapeworm which absorb substances over the surface of the body, and insects such as the aphid with sucking mouth parts.

3. Respiration. Gills, Lungs and Tracheae

All living cells respire and remain alive only if supplied with oxygen. In a multicellular body, however, many cells are remote from the oxygen of the environment and the need arises for an efficient respiratory system by which oxygen can be taken up and carbon dioxide released. In addition a circulatory system is necessary to transport the oxygen to and from the respiring cells.

(a) Simple Gas Exchange Systems

Animals such as protozoa do not need special structure for gas exchange. Diffusion over the whole body surface ensures an adequate supply of oxygen. Much larger animals such as earthworms also find it possible to rely on diffusion alone, partly because their consumption of oxygen is fairly low, and partly because their bodies are permeable all over. For various reasons most animals restrict the permeability of the outer layers of the body and under these conditions special respiratory areas have to be developed.

(b) Gas Exchange in Water

Aquatic animals, except those such as whales breathing at the surface, have to obtain their oxygen from the supplies which are dissolved in the water. This presents several problems because water is a dense medium, there is not a lot of oxygen in solution, and its diffusion rate is low. For these reasons there is a surprisingly functional uniformity in gill systems and they are very different from lungs. Gills are fine, finger-like processes with a good blood supply which are held out in a water stream. The water current is brought very close to the gill filaments so that the length of diffusion pathway for oxygen is minimal. There is a "counter current" flow of water and blood so that the water containing most oxygen comes into contact with the blood just leaving the gill. This ensures that most of the oxygen can be transferred from water to blood through the thin gill cells. The efficiency of "counter current" systems is well known to the engineer but they were invented by aquatic animals long before they were by man. These features can be seen in the gills of molluscs, crustacea and fish. The pumping devices which maintain the water currents also operate economically. Flow is maintained in crustacea by appendages modified to form beating paddles, in many molluscs by ciliary movement, and in fish by the operation of a double pump in mouth and opercular cavities. In almost all cases there is a continuous current over the gills, the water coming in one way and going out another. Thus the animal avoids reversing the flow with the consequent waste of energy in accelerating and decelerating a large mass of water. Fish, for example, take water in at the mouth and force it out through the gill slits (sharks) or operculum (teleosts).

(c) Gas Exchange in Air

Air breathing animals do not encounter these problems since the medium is less dense, contains a great deal (20%) of oxygen and diffusion rates are high. Lungs are therefore in the form of sacs whose walls are well supplied with blood. The area of the walls may be increased by folding so that the lung becomes spongy and full of minute air spaces called alveoli where the gas exchange goes on. Only the main airways receive fresh air as the lung expands; oxygen is renewed in the alveoli by diffusion. Ventilation of the lung is accomplished by a tidal flow of air in and out of the same tubular opening known as the trachea. The actual ventilating mechanism varies in different animals. In the amphibia for example air is forced into the lungs when the floor of the mouth is raised with the mouth and nostrils shut. The lungs are emptied by elastic recoil and by lowering the floor of the mouth. Higher vertebrates use a costal pump which changes the volume of chest and lungs by movements of the ribs. This change in volume is further assisted in mammals by the diaphragm, a sheet of muscle which lies beneath the lungs and separates thorax and abdomen. In many animals sound producing organs are associated with the lungs and trachea. The larynx is a vocal organ in frogs, some lizards, and most notably mammals. In birds voice production takes place in the syrinx situated further down at the base of the trachea.

A completely different gas exchanging system is seen in insects. Branching tubes, known as tracheae, run throughout the body and carry oxygen directly to the cells without the intervention of a blood system. The tracheae communicate with the outside world via a series of holes called spiracles. Although the main tubes may be actively ventilated, diffusion in the system accounts for a large part of the movement of oxygen between the outside world and cells.

4. Circulation

In the larger animals a transport system is necessary to convey materials about the body and in many, but not all, it is in the form of a blood system. Blood systems are of two types, closed and open.

(a) Open Systems

In an open circulatory system blood is pumped from the heart into a few major arteries but these very quickly give way to large tissue spaces or sinuses so that the tissues and organs of the body are directly bathed in blood. Blood flows slowly from the sinuses back to the heart. Both mollusc and arthropods possess an open system.

(b) Closed Systems

In a closed system blood is pumped round the body in a branching network of arteries and comes into contact with tissues and cells via very thin walled vessels called capillaries. Substances diffuse into and out of the blood through capillary walls. From capillaries, blood enters the veins and so returns to the heart. Blood flow in the tubes of a closed system is much more brisk and blood pressures tend to be higher than in an open system. In annelids the closed system is fairly simple with a vessel above the gut in which blood moves forward connecting to one below in which blood moves backwards. The blood is pumped by peristaltic contraction of the vessels and this system must be regarded as the precursor of a localised pump. Simple hearts are in fact seen in some annelids.

In vertebrates a well defined heart is always present, situated ventrally at the level of the forelimbs. In fish there is a single auricle and ventricle and the latter pumps blood directly to the gills. From the gills the blood is collected into a dorsal aorta which then branches to serve the rest of the body. Associated with the development of lungs and loss of gills in the tetrapods, we see a progressive modification of this simple pattern. The most posterior gill vessel is taken over as the lung or pulmonary artery and slowly a completely separate circuit evolves. This involves the division of the single heart into right and left sides, the former pumping blood to the lungs and the latter to the body. In the birds and mammals where the division is complete the system can be seen to be functionally satisfactory. Blood flows along the following route: left auricle to left ventricle, to body, to right auricle, to right ventricle, to lungs, to left auricle, and so on. Thus blood charged with oxygen in the lungs returns to the heart before being pumped to the body.

(c) Function of the Blood

Most of the materials transported by the blood such as nutrients, waste materials and hormones are carried in solution in the plasma. The respiratory gases, oxygen and carbon dioxide, are present in greater quantity than would be possible if they were in simple solution. Carbon dioxide is carried in the form of bicarbonate and oxygen combines with blood pigment. The best known blood pigment is haemoglobin which is found in a variety of animals and gives the red colour to blood. When oxygen is present in high concentration, as it is in the lungs, combination occurs to give oxyhaemoglobin. If the concentration of oxygen is low, as it is in the tissues, dissociation occurs and oxygen is given off leaving reduced haemoglobin. Carbon monoxide will combine more readily than oxygen with haemoglobin so that in carbon monoxide poisoning the blood cannot transport oxygen. The haemoglobin of vertebrates is contained in high concentration in red blood corpuscles. The amount of haemoglobin and, hence, oxygen carried is greater than if the pigment is not in corpuscles. In mammals the oxygen carrying capacity of blood is thirty times that of a similar quantity of water. Other blood pigments are the blue haemocyanin found in crustacea and molluscs, and the violet haemerythrin found in some worms. Also present in the blood are various types of white corpuscle which are part of the defence mechanism of the body and ingest invading bacteria. Special blood proteins such as fibrinogen, causing clot formation, and antibodies effective against foreign substances occur in the plasma.

5. Excretion, Ionic Regulation and Kidney Tubules

As the chemical reactions included under the term metabolism proceed, so numerous waste products accumulate. The most important of these are compounds containing nitrogen, such as ammonia, urea and uric acid, arising from the use of protein as an energy source. In terrestrial animals they are removed from the blood by the kidney. The basic unit of a kidney is the tubule; in worms these tubules are not concentrated into a solid kidney but occur, a pair in every segment, right down the body. The kidney tubule begins with an end sac, corpuscle or funnel which is closely associated with the body cavity or the blood system. Fluid is filtered from the body cavity or blood into the corpuscle whence it passes to the tubule proper. During passage down the tubule, useful materials are reabsorbed through the tubule cells into the blood whereas unwanted materials remain and pass to the outside world.

Although it is usual to think of kidney function being primarily one of nitrogenous excretion, it is quite common to find that in aquatic animals the kidneys are hardly used for this purpose. In these animals the tubules are primarily concerned in regulating the salt and water levels in the body, nitrogenous wastes being eliminated by diffusion through any permeable surface. In fresh water for example all animals have osmotic problems since the body fluids have a much greater osmotic pressure than the environment. Water tends to enter the body and salts tend to leave. Fresh water animals produce large quantities of very dilute urine, filtering off a lot of blood plasma into the tubules but reabsorbing all wanted materials including the invaluable salts. Fresh water crustacea, molluscs and fish all possess tubules of different morphology which show very similar functional properties.

Different environmental conditions impose different demands on the osmotic and ionic regulating machinery. In very dry conditions, such as in deserts, it is obviously of advantage to reabsorb as much water from the tubule as possible. All animals do this but it is interesting that only birds and mammals have discovered the secret of so concentrating the urine that its salt concentration is higher than that in the blood. This is done by means of a hairpin-like loop in the tubule called the Loop of Henle, another example of a counter current device.

6. Co-ordinating Systems

Overall co-ordination of the animal's body, so that it functions as a whole and reacts appropriately to environmental changes, is largely the province of two systems, one chemical or hormonal, the other nervous. In one respect these are systems for homeostasis, that is for preserving the *status quo*, in spite of considerable environmental fluctuation. Paradoxically they can also initiate change as, for example, one can see in the daily repertoire of complicated behaviour patterns produced by almost any animal.

(a) Nervous Systems

(i) *Sensory Information*

Before appropriate reactions can be produced to any stimulus it is necessary to measure its intensity, position, duration and, most important, character. This is done by sense organs which are usually specialised to receive stimuli of a single modality or character. Thus photoreceptors detect light, mechanoreceptors detect mechanical disturbance and chemoreceptors detect specific chemicals. In all cases the sense organs produce a message about the stimulus in the form of nerve impulses (*see* **F33**—Cell Membrane) which travel up the nerve from the sense organ to the rest of the nervous system. Change of stimulus intensity is usually signalled as a change in frequency of nerve impulses. The position of the sense organ which is active indicates the position of the stimulus within or without the body. The duration of the repeated discharge of nerve impulses indicates the duration of the stimulus.

(ii) *Simple Networks*

The simplest type of nervous system is the network of interconnected nerve cells (neurones) found in the coelenterates. Branching processes of the nerve cells communicate with neighbouring processes at special regions called synapses (**F33**). Quite complicated behaviour is possible even with this relatively simple system. If a sea anemone is prodded violently it will close up equally violently, showing that activity has spread throughout the network. If it is tickled gently it will respond with local contractions around the site of stimulation. The movements of feeding and locomotion are very delicately performed at appropriate times.

(iii) *Central Nervous Systems*

In the majority of animals all the nerve cells tend to become collected into a solid mass of tissue referred to as a central nervous system (C.N.S.). Within the mass the nerve cells are interconnected via synapses in the same way as in a nerve net. The connexions with sense organs and muscles are made via long processes called axons. Numbers of axons are usually bound together with connective tissue to form a nerve trunk. In annelids and arthropods the C.N.S. is seen as a ventral cord lying beneath the gut with a swelling or ganglion in each segment of the body. In molluscs, the ganglia are usually more closely grouped around the oesophagus, with the possible provision of a pair of ganglia further back in the viscera. Vertebrates possess a dorsal nerve cord which is uniform in diameter and not ganglionated, though nerves emerge from it in a segmental fashion. The segmental nerves arise in two separate bundles or roots. The dorsal root is made up entirely of sensory nerves conveying information to the C.N.S. The ventral root consists of motor nerves which convey nerve impulses to the muscles of limbs and alimentary canal together with other effector organs such as glands.

(iv) *Reflexes*

A reflex, in which stimulation of a sense organ or sensory nerve results in the almost immediate contraction of a muscle, is the simplest type of C.N.S. activity. Reflexes have been studied in all animals but the best known ones can be seen in frogs, cats, dogs, and sometimes humans. The very simplest is the stretch reflex, in which a stretched muscle is made to contract by activity coming into the C.N.S. from stretch receptors in the muscle. The activity is relayed directly to the motor neurones of the muscle concerned, making them active and thus causing the muscle to contract. This reflex is monosynaptic, *i.e.* there is only the single synaptic connexion between sensory nerve and motor neurone. The knee jerk in humans is a stretch reflex, the stretch being caused by hitting the muscle tendon as it passes over the knee. Much of the recent work on reflexes has been done on this simple system, notably by Eccles. The flexor reflex, which is seen as the sudden withdrawal of a limb from any painful stimulus, is more complicated. Although the stimuli may vary, the withdrawal response is always accomplished by contraction of flexor muscles which bring the limb in towards the body. The reflex is polysynaptic, *i.e.* several intermediate neurones connect the sensory nerves through to the motor neurones. More complicated still is the scratch reflex in which an animal is made to scratch its flank in response to an irritation or tickling in that region. This reflex demonstrates some of the more involved properties of the C.N.S. For example a dog will continue to scratch for a time after the tickling has stopped, so that the C.N.S. must continue to be active in the absence of sensory stimulation. This has been called after-discharge.

(v) *The Brain*

The C.N.S. functions in a more complicated way than is suggested by study of the reflexes and most of these higher activities are co-ordinated by the brain. A greater condensation of neurones is seen at the front end of the C.N.S. of all animals because of the larger numbers of sense organs in that region. Brains, which become the dominant part of the C.N.S., can be seen in arthropods, molluscs and vertebrates. The close association with sense organs is illustrated by the vertebrate brain which is divided into three regions: (a) forebrain (nose), (b) midbrain (eye) and (c) hindbrain (ear and taste). However, the brain is much more than a relay station for these stimulus modalities and it receives information from other parts of the body via the spinal cord. All this information is correlated and activity patterns initiated and transmitted to appropriate regions. In lower vertebrates, the roof of the midbrain (the optic tectum) is the important correlation centre and its effectiveness has been well established in studies on instinct and learning in fish. Another region of the brain of importance in all vertebrates is a dorsal upgrowth of the hindbrain called the cerebellum. This is a motor co-ordinating centre which ensures that all activities are performed in a smooth and well balanced way by the muscles and limbs of the body. In reptiles, the forebrain begins to take over the correlation role and in mammals this development reaches its peak in the cerebral cortex. In man the cortex overshadows the rest of the brain and contains some 1,000,000,000 neurones. It is easy to see the magnitude of the problem of understanding a system of this complexity. The bee's brain with far, far fewer cells can initiate complicated behaviour such as the hive dances. The possibilities offered by the human cortex seem vastly greater, though they are often realised in ways which give cause for concern. At the moment it would be quite impossible to build a computer with the properties of the human brain. To do this in the future would depend on major advances in computer technology and even greater advances in the knowledge of central nervous systems.

(b) Hormonal Regulation

Many aspects of an animal's metabolism are regulated, not by the nervous system, but by specific chemical signals known as hormones which are circulated in the blood stream. Growth, carbohydrate metabolism, salt balance, activity of ovaries and testes and their associated structures, and colour change are all regulated in some way by hormones. The substances are secreted by endocrine glands or ductless glands as they are often called. The important endocrine glands in vertebrates are the thyroid, parathyroid, adrenal, pancreas, the sex glands, and the pituitary.

In the past the endocrine and nervous systems were regarded as exerting an independent control in slightly different functional areas of the body. It is clear now that the integration of the two systems is much greater than was formerly envisaged and in vertebrates is accomplished through the pituitary gland. Secretions of this gland regulate almost all other endocrine glands and the secretions of the pituitary are either produced in the C.N.S. with which it is directly connected or are controlled by C.N.S. secretions. An astonishing, parallel development of other neurosecretory systems, such as those of the pituitary, has been found in a variety of animals and in all types the neurosecretory organ complex is the dominant endocrine gland of the body. In crustacea the so-called X organ complex found within the eyestalk, and in insects neurosecretory cells connecting to the corpora cardiaca glands, occupy the functional position of the vertebrate pituitary. They all regulate growth, metabolism and reproductive physiology, either directly or through the medication of other endocrine glands.

7. Animal Behaviour

In discussing the nervous system we have already dealt with simple mechanisms such as the reflex. Very much more complicated are the instinctive and learned patterns of behaviour which are studied by animal psychologists and ethologists such as Lorenz and Tinbergen.

(a) Instinct

Instinct is inborn behaviour which does not have to be learnt and is usually performed in a stereotyped way. For example a gull will retrieve an egg taken out of its nest by shovelling it back with the underside of its beak. The gull will never replace an egg in its nest in any other way, for example by using a wing or leg, and once it has begun a retrieval it will usually continue the movements back to the nest even though the egg is taken away. An instinctive behaviour pattern is triggered off by a particular stimulus or "releaser" which may be a very small part of the total environment. A male stickleback will attack a very crude model with a red belly but will not attack an exact model without it. The red underside appears to be a much more important stimulus than general shape. A particular instinctive pattern cannot always be elicited and the reaction of an animal very largely depends on when the behaviour was last produced. The longer the time that elapses, the easier it is to trigger off the instinctive pattern until eventually it may appear in the absence of an appropriate set of environmental circumstances.

(b) Learning

Learning is that behaviour acquired during the organism's lifetime as a result of experience. Evidence of learning has been seen in many animals from worms upwards though, as might be expected, the more complicated types of learning are found only in those animals with elaborate nervous systems. A simple type of learning is seen when an animal, upon repeated exposure to a stimulus, gradually decreases the normal response which is usually one of flight, until eventually the response may disappear completely. This process is called habituation. More complex are the conditioned reflexes, which were first discovered by Pavlov. In these an animal can in some way connect a conditioned stimulus such as a bell, with an unconditioned stimulus such as meat, so that eventually it salivates when the bell is rung. Trial and error learning of the type needed to be successful in running a maze is more complicated still. In this there is a retrospective element because the reward at the end of the maze comes after all the responses. Many animals can run mazes but the white rat has been extensively used in experiments of this nature and there is a huge literature on this one animal. A final category of learning can be called insight learning; in this an animal shows evidence of resolving a new problem without trial and error. This type of learning involves the perception of relations between different parts of the environment and though there may be examples in arthropods and molluscs the clearest evidence of it is seen in the behaviour of birds and mammals.

8. Reproduction

A single animal may live for a short or long time, but eventually it dies, and the continuance of the species is dependent upon reproduction. Some protozoa, such as *Amoeba*, reproduce asexually by the simple division of the cell to produce two new individuals. Asexual reproduction also occurs in some coelenterates, such as jelly-fish, in which there is an alternation of sexual and asexual generations. However, the vast majority of animals only reproduce sexually.

This involves the fusion of two cells, the gametes, produced by adult individuals, and each zygote thus formed develops into an individual of the next generation. The gametes are of two kinds, the large, spherical, immobile ova produced by the female gonad or ovary and the much smaller motile sperms produced by the male gonad or testis. The motility of the sperms helps them to reach the passive ovum, which contains food reserves to support the early development of the embryo.

Worms.—The flat worms, particularly parasitic forms, have complicated life cycles, and many are hermaphrodite, *i.e.*, each individual has both male and female organs. Cross-fertilisation usually occurs, the sperms from one worm being introduced into the female duct of another. The round worms are unisexual, and internal fertilisation also occurs. Of the annelids the polychaete worms are unisexual, but the ova and sperms are shed into the sea, where fertilisation takes place. However, *Lumbricus* and the leeches are hermaphrodite, cross-fertilisation takes place and the eggs are laid in cocoons.

Arthropods.—Many crustacea are unisexual, though the sedentary barnacles are hermaphrodite. Internal fertilisation may occur, but in the crabs and crayfish pairing takes place and the sperms are deposited on the tail of the female. When the eggs are shed they become fertilised and remain attached to the abdominal appendages. Most crustacea have motile larval stages into which the eggs first develop. In *Daphnia*, the water-flea, parthenogenesis sometimes occurs, *i.e.*, the eggs develop without being fertilised. The sexes are separate in the arachnida and there are usually no larval stages except in the primitive king-crabs. The insects are also unisexual, and the fertilised eggs are laid after copulation. In some, *e.g.*, dragon-flies, an immature nymph similar to the adult is formed, but in flies, beetles, moths, and many others the egg hatches into a larval form. This then develops into a pupa, from which the final adult or imago is produced. In the social ant's nest the workers are sterile females with large heads, reduced eyes, and no wings. The males and queens are winged, and insemination of the latter occurs during the "nuptial" flight.

Molluscs and Echinoderms.—Most lamellibranchs are unisexual, although some species of scallops and oysters are hermaphrodite. There are motile larval forms, and in the swan mussel, *Anodonta*, the larvae develop in the mantle cavity of the parent and when liberated become attached to the gills or fins of fish, where they remain parasitic for some time. Some gastropods are unisexual, but the slugs and snails are hermaphrodite. In the latter cross-fertilisation occurs, the two approaching snails being stimulated to copulate by firing small sharp darts of calcium carbonate into each other. The echinoderms are unisexual, and fertilisation takes place in the sea. The egg first develops into a ciliated larval form.

Vertebrates.—The sexes are always separate in the vertebrates. In some cartilaginous fish, *e.g.*, dogfish, internal fertilisation occurs and the eggs are laid in protective sacs. In contrast, the bony fish shed ova and sperms into the water, where fertilisation takes place. Although pairing may take place in amphibia, fertilisation occurs in water, and there is usually an aquatic larval stage. The reptiles, birds, and mammals are independent of water for fertilisation, as copulation takes place and the sperms from the male are introduced directly into the female. Most reptiles and all birds lay eggs with hard shells. Development of the embryo in marsupial mammals begins in the female uterus, but is continued in a ventral pouch which surrounds the teat of the mammary gland. In the two living species of monotreme mammals the eggs are incubated in a similar pouch. Finally, in the eutherian mammals the embryo develops in the female uterus and is born at an advanced stage.

Diversity of Sexual Reproduction.—This brief survey will give some idea of the diversity of sexual reproduction in animals. External fertilisation is very much a matter of chance, and large numbers of gametes are produced which offset the great losses of gametes and embryos that this method involves. Internal fertilisation is more certain, and is also independent of external water—an important factor in land animals. In vertebrates particularly there is increase in the care of the young by the parents, involving the development of characters of behaviour as well as those of structure. Some fish lay their eggs in holes or nests which are protected by the male. Similarly, a few frogs build nests, while others carry the eggs about. The eggs of birds require a constant high temperature for their development, and they are usually incubated by the parents. After hatching the young are fed and guarded by the parents until they can leave the nest and fend for themselves. In the eutherian mammals the embryos are attached to the uterus wall by the placenta, *via* which food materials pass from the mother. The period of gestation is long, and after birth the young are supplied with milk from the mother until they are weaned and can feed themselves. Another feature in mammals is the period of "childhood" during which they play and learn and are protected and fed by their parents. The internal fertilisation, internal development, and care and protection of the young after birth which is so conspicuous in the higher vertebrates results in the reduction of losses during the vulnerable embryonic and young stages, and in consequence relatively few progeny are produced by a pair of individuals.

THE PLANT KINGDOM

There are various ways in which the main classes of the plant kingdom can be grouped, but a simple, up-to-date arrangement is given in the chart. Vascular plants are often known as the *Tracheophyta* because they all possess woody conducting elements. These are absent in non-vascular plants, and the bacteria, fungi, and algæ are often called *Thallophyta*, *i.e.*, they have a relatively simple plant body or thallus. Many of the bryophytes also possess a thallus, but in some there is a stem bearing leaves, although a true vascular system is absent. Many thallophytes are aquatic, whereas the tracheophytes are mostly land plants in which the development of woody tissues can be related to the attainment of the land habit as the plant kingdom evolved. However, the chart should not be taken as indicating the evolutionary relationships of the various groups. It is more a convenient arrangement which reflects the relative complexity of the plant body.

1. Bacteria.—This is a vast group of minute organisms of very simple structure. They are spherical or rod shaped and may exist as separate cells, some species being motile, or as long chains or irregular masses. Their minute size makes the elucidation of their structure very difficult. There is a wall of complex composition, and cytoplasm which contains glycogen and fat. Electron-microscope studies have revealed the presence of structures which appear to consist of nuclear material. Multiplication is by simple division, which may take place very rapidly. For example, *Bacillus subtilis* can divide every 20 minutes, so that in 8 hours a single cell may give rise to 16 millions. Recent research indicates that a sexual process may also occur. Bacteria can survive unfavourable conditions by producing a resistant spore within the cell. They do not possess chlorophyll, though a few are pigmented. Most obtain their food already formed, and are thus either saprophytes or parasites. The saprophytic bacteria occupy a vital position in the living world. They are responsible for most of the decay of dead organic matter, and it has been truly said that without them the surface of the earth would soon become completely covered with the dead bodies of animals and plants. Bacteria also play a vital part in the circulation of nitrogen in nature. By breaking down organic material, ammonia is released and ammonium carbonate is formed in the soil. This is oxidised by other bacteria to form nitrates, which can be absorbed

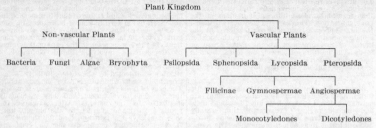

by plants again. Yet other bacteria can "fix" atmospheric nitrogen, and one species, *Rhizobium leguminosum*, occurs in the root nodules of the pea plant. Such plants are often grown on poor soils and ploughed in, thus improving the fertility of the soil. The parasitic bacteria are also of great importance, as they are responsible for many diseases of plants, animals, and man.

2. Fungi.—This is a large group of plants, none of which contain chlorophyll. Hence, like the bacteria, they are either parasites on other living plants and animals or saprophytes which live on dead organic matter. Some are unicellular aquatic plants, but many have a body called a mycelium composed of many branched threads or hyphæ. In the higher fungi (*e.g.*, toadstools, bracket fungi, and puff-balls) complex reproductive structures are formed. All fungi produce spores. In the aquatic species these may be motile, but the majority form minute, airborne spores. The spore output is often very great, and a single mushroom may produce, 1,800 million spores. Some fungi are serious diseases of crop plants, such as potato blight and wheat rust.

3. Algae.—These are essentially aquatic plants which contain chlorophyll. They range from microscopic forms to the large seaweeds. The green algae (Chlorophyceae) live mostly in fresh water and may be unicellular, motile or non-motile, or filamentous, though a few found in tropical seas are more complex. The brown algae (Phaeophyceae) are mostly seaweeds which possess a brown pigment, fucoxanthin, which masks the green chlorophyll. They include the bladder-wracks (*Fucus*) and kelps (*Laminaria*) of our coasts and the seaweeds which form dense floating masses over hundreds of square miles of the Sargasso Sea. Other groups are the red algae (Rhodophyceae), mostly seaweeds of delicate form, the unicellular motile diatoms (Bacillariophyceae), and the blue-green algae (Cyanophyceae). All algae possess unicellular reproductive organs. Various types of life cycle occur, the most complex being found in the red algae.

4. Bryophyta.—These are the liverworts (Hepaticae) and the mosses (*Muscineae*). They are all small plants characterised by a sharply defined life-cycle. This consists of an alternation of generations, the "plant" being a gametophyte bearing sex organs. The latter are multicellular, the female archegonium containing a single stationary ovum and the male antheridium producing many motile sperms. The latter are released and swim in water to the archegonium, where fertilisation takes place. After this a sporophyte is formed which is always dependent on the gametophyte and never becomes free living. The sporophyte usually consists of an absorbing foot buried in the tissue of the gametophyte and a stalk or seta bearing at the top a single sporangium. In many mosses this is a complex structure with hygroscopic teeth which move apart only when dry, thus releasing the minute spores only when conditions are suitable for their dissemination in the air. The bryophytes are of little economic importance, and may be looked upon as an evolutionary side-line. However, they occupy suitable "niches" in many plant communities, and species of the bog-moss *Sphagnum* cover large areas where rainfall is high.

5. Psilopsida.—This is a small group of primitive, vascular, spore-bearing plants. Its only living representatives are two rare genera of the Southern Hemisphere. However, a number of fossil forms are known from the Devonian period. The best known are those found in the chert at Rhynie in Scotland. The plants are excellently preserved, and their internal structure can be easily seen. They were probably marsh plants with prostrate and erect leafless stems, although *Asteroxylon* had simple leaves.

6. Sphenopsida.—The only living members of this group are about twenty-five species of horsetails (*Equisetum*). In the Carboniferous period many tree forms existed (*e.g.*, *Calamites*), the remains of which are very common in coal deposits.

7. Lycopsida.—In the Carboniferous period the tree clubmosses were also prominent members of the forests (*e.g.*, *Lepidodendron*). They often reached 30m in height, were branched or unbranched, and had large simple leaves. They also had extensive root systems. The only living members belong to a few genera of small herbaceous clubmosses, such as *Lycopodium* and *Selaginella*. Like the true mosses, they have an alternation of generations, but the elaborate plant with stem, leaves, and roots is the sporophyte, and the gametophyte is very small. In *Lycopodium* only one kind of spore is produced, and the resultant gametophyte is bisexual. *Selaginella* produces numerous small microspores which give rise to the very reduced male gametophytes and motile sperms and the few large megaspores which produce the female gametophytes. The latter are formed within the megaspore wall, which splits to allow the sperms to reach the small archegonia.

8. Filicinae.—These are the true ferns, which in some classifications are put with the horsetails and clubmosses in the Pteridophyta or vascular cryptogams (*i.e.*, vascular plants without seeds). The ferns have a long fossil history, and remains very similar to the living Royal ferns (*Osmunda*) are known from the Carboniferous. The ferns are widespread and particularly abundant in tropical forests. The majority are herbaceous perennial plants, but a few are aquatic, and there are some tree ferns, which may reach 6 m in height. Most ferns possess a stem bearing roots and large leaves or fronds. The plant is the sporophyte and produces numerous spores in sporangia borne on the fronds. Each spore gives rise to a minute green free-living gametophyte known as the prothallus, which bears the archegonia and antheridia. After fertilisation a young sporophyte develops, which at first draws nourishment from the prothallus. Thus, as in the Bryophyta, external water is essential for the motile sperms to swim, and there is a clearly defined alternation of generations, but the sporophyte is a complex independent plant, and the gametophyte is reduced though free-living.

9. Gymnospermae.—These were the dominant land plants in the Mesozoic era, although fossil remains are found as far back as the Devonian. The living members still form large forests in the North Temperate regions. They are mostly tall evergreen trees with roots, stems, and small leaves. The conifers include the pines (*Pinus*), larches (*Larix*), and yews (*Taxus*). The cycads are a relic group of tropical plants with thick, unbranched trunks and large fern-like leaves. The maiden-hair tree of Japan (*Ginkgo biloba*) has also had a long geological history. Another intresting Gymnosperm is *Metasequoia*, a genus well known to palaeobotanists. In 1948 a few living specimens were found in a remote area of China. Seeds were collected and plants are now being grown in botanical gardens all over the world. The Gymnosperms are characterised by the production of "naked" seeds, which are usually born on cones. The male pollen grains, which are equivalent to the microspores of *Selaginella*, are carried by wind to the ovule of the female cone. The pollen germinates and the pollen tube carries the male gametes to the reduced archegonia borne on the female prothallus, which, unlike those of the ferns, is retained within the ovule on the parent plant. After fertilisation an embryo is formed, the prothallus becomes the food store or endosperm, and the outer part of the ovule becomes the seed coat. The cycads and *Ginkgo* retain a primitive feature in that the male gametes are motile and they swim to the archegonia from the pollen tube.

10. Angiospermae.—The apparent sudden rise of the Angiosperms in the Cretaceous period is still the "abominable mystery" it was to Darwin. Various suggestions have been put forward, but nothing definite is known about the origin of the group. The Angiosperms or flowering plants are now the dominant group over most of the land surface of the earth, and at least 250,000 species are known. Apart from the natural vegetation, the majority of our crop and garden plants are Angiosperms. They occur in every type of habitat and range in form from gigantic trees to minute plants, such as the duck-weeds. Some are climbers, others succulents, and a number have reverted to the aquatic habit. Although most possess chlorophyll, a few are partial (*e.g.*, Mistletoe) or complete parasites (*e.g.*, Dodder).

Flower, Fruit and Seeds.—The diagnostic feature of the group is the production of seeds, which are completely enclosed within the female part of the flower, the ovary. Basically a flower is a short reproductive shoot which bears several whorls of lateral organs. At the base are several, often green, protective sepals forming the calyx, and above this are the often brightly coloured petals of the corolla. Within this are the stamens of the androecium or male part of the flower. Centrally is the female gynoecium of one or more carpels containing the ovules. The parts of the flower may be free, as in the buttercup, or fused together. In many species the petals are fused (sympetalous), the stamens are borne on the corolla (epipetalous), and the carpels are fused to form a compound gynoecium (syncarpous). The stamens possess anthers, which produce pollen grains. These are shed and carried by insects or wind to the receptive stigmas of the carpels. Each produces a tube which grows down the style to the ovary and enters an ovule. The ovule is a complex structure containing an ovum and a primary endosperm nucleus. Two male nuclei are discharged from the pollen tube, one fuses with the ovum and the other fuses with the primary endosperm nucleus. After this "double fertilisation" an embryo is formed which is embedded in the nutritive endosperm and the outer tissues of the ovule form the seed coat or testa. The ovary of the carpel develops into the fruit containing the seeds. Fruits are of various kinds, being either dehiscent and opening when mature to release the seeds or indehiscent, with a succulent or dry wall. The indehiscent fruits are shed as a whole, and often contain only a single seed. Seeds and fruits show great variation in structure, and often have adaptations assisting dispersal. Some have hairs or wings which aid wind dispersal, whereas others have hooks or are sticky and are transported by animals. Some have flotation devices and may be carried a great distance from the parent plant by water. Seeds vary in size from the microscopic seeds of orchids to those of the double coconut, which may weigh 18 kg. Only about 10% of the weight of a seed is water, and the embryo, although alive, is dormant. The bulk of a seed consists of stored food material, commonly fats or starch and proteins, which may be contained in the endosperm surrounding the embryo, although in some species the endosperm is absorbed during seed development and the food is stored in the one or two swollen seed leaves or cotyledons of the embryo.

Classification of Flowering Plants.—John Ray (1627–1705) was the first botanist to recognise the two great divisions of the Angiosperms—the dicotyledons with two seed leaves and the monocotyledons with only one. This primary division of the flowering plants has stood the test of time and is still recognised. Other differences are also found between the two groups. The dicotyledons usually have net-veined leaves and the floral parts are in fours or fives, whereas the monocotyledons usually have leaves with parallel veins and the floral parts are in threes.

THE PHYSIOLOGY OF PLANTS

Some of the fundamental differences between animals and plants can be ascribed to the ways in which the two groups of living organisms satisfy their requirements for food material. In a simple way at least, an animal can be thought of as a mobile gastro-intestinal tract which is highly specialised to search out and receive food in convenient, concentrated packets. In typical land plants, however, a quite different organisation exists because the organic nutrition is based on the process of photosynthesis in which carbon dioxide from the air is combined with water from the soil to form simple carbohydrates. An expanded foliage system is necessary to absorb carbon dioxide and to expose the photosynthetic pigment, chlorophyll, to sunlight. Similarly, an expanded root system is needed to absorb the other ingredients of nutrition, water and mineral salts, from the soil.

The work of the plant physiologist is devoted to understanding the functional relationships between these two expanded systems of root and shoot. The production of carbohydrates by photosynthesis has already been discussed (**F32**).

The Spread of Roots

In addition, the physiologist is concerned with the progressive elaboration of root and shoot as the plant grows. Plants show much less specialisation of their cells into discrete tissues and organs than do animals and they also retain special areas, at root and shoot tips for example, where new cells are added to the structure throughout the life of the plant. In some cases whole plants can be regenerated from very few cells taken almost anywhere from a growing plant body. The orderly regulation of growth and differentiation is thus a basic property of much plant tissue.

1. Movement of Solutes and Water

The movement of water and inorganic solutes in a plant is primarily upwards from the roots where they are absorbed, to the leaves or growing regions where evaporation of water or the use of both water and salts occurs. Water and inorganic ions permeate freely through the cell walls and air spaces of the more peripheral cells of the roots. Equilibrium is established between the insides of cells in this region and the water and salts outside, water tending to enter by osmosis and the salts by diffusion or active transport. Increase in cell volume which would be caused by continual influx of materials is, of course, restricted by the inextensible cell wall. In the centre of the root is a region packed with the specialised conducting tissues called xylem and phloem. These form continuous channels through the root and into the shoot and clearly serve for the conduction of water and substances in solution. In the root this central region is separated from the more peripheral tissue by a single layer of cells, the endodermis. The endodermal layer can actively pump water and salts from the outer regions through into the longitudinal conducting strands of, in this case, the xylem. Evidence for this pumping activity can be seen in the exudation of liquid from the base of a plant stem cut close to ground level. In some cases pressures of 8 to 10 atmospheres have been generated in roots as a result of the pumping action of the endodermal cells.

Water is also moved up a plant by forces generated in the leaves. Constant evaporation from the walls of leaf cells, both on the surface and within the substance of the leaf, causes loss of water from the plant. The process is called transpiration and, within limits, the plant can control transpiration rate by regulating the ease with which water-saturated air passes to the exterior through perforations in the leaf surface called stomata. The diameter of these apertures can be regulated by movements of guard cells surrounding the stomatal openings. Loss of water from the leaf cells is made good by with-drawing more water from the xylem elements within the leaves and stem of the plant. Cohesive forces between water molecules prevent the continuous water columns within the xylem from breaking. The net result is that water is drawn up the stem as transpiration occurs in the leaves. Considerable suction pressures have been measured by suitable manometer systems at-tached to the cut stems of actively transpiring plants. In addition materials such as dyes or radioactive isotopes have been followed as they move up the conducting xylem vessels at rates which can usually be related to the rate of trans-piration.

2. Movement of Organic Substances

The organic substances, whose site of manu-facture is primarily in the leaves, have to be distributed to the rest of the plant body. It is thought that a second conducting tissue, the phloem, is mainly responsible for the distribution of these materials in solution. Ploem is found as a layer of tissue to the outside of the xylem vessels in a plant stem. It consists of conducting cells which are rather different from those of the xylem, which serve, as we have seen, mainly in the transport of water and salts. Whereas xylem tissues are composed of dead cells whose cell walls form effective longitudinal conducting channels, phloem is made up mainly of living cells. Elements called sieve tubes are the most important conducting cells in phloem and, during the initial stages of differentiation, a sieve tube has a full complement of cytoplasm and cell organelles. Later differentiation sees the pro-toplasmic structures break down, but even in mature sieve tubes protoplasmic strands join through the perforated ends of adjacent cells and may extend longitudinally through the conducting elements.

Ringing experiments in which a complete ring of phloem is cut from the outside of a plant, provide evidence of the tissue's function in longitudinal conduction of carbohydrates. Sugars accumulate above such a ring but not below it. Samples of fluid taken from sieve tubes have also revealed high concentrations of carbo-hydrates in the sap. The method used to obtain such samples is very ingenious. Several aphids (insects such as green fly) are known which parasitise the phloem translocation chan-nels of plants. The aphid is allowed to insert its stylet tip into the phloem vessels and is then anaesthetised and cut off the inserted stylet. Sap exudes from the stylet stump and can be col-lected and analysed.

3. Growth

Growth is usually, but not always, thought of as involving increase of size as measured by length, volume, or weight. In these terms any unit in a plant, whether root, shoot or fruit would follow a sigmoid growth curve with growth starting slowly, then speeding up, before finally slowing down at maturity leading on to death. Growth may also be considered as an increase in the number of cells, an increase in substances such as water, protein or DNA in the growing system, or an increase in complexity of organisa-tion.

The organisation of growth, no matter how it is measured, presents a number of interesting problems. In the first divisions of a fertilised egg, all cells divide. Very soon this property becomes localised, polarity is established, and the young embryo develops a shoot tip and a root tip. These have then become discrete regions of cell division. The cells behind them cease active division, enlarge by developing large vacuoles and form mature plant tissue. A circular strand of dividing tissue, called the cambium, is left in the stem between differen-tiated xylem and phloem. The cambium is responsible for growth in girth. The acquisition of polarity has far-reaching consequences, for the behaviour of a shoot tip is very different from that of a root. The shoot tip, for example, gives rise to leaf cells with photosynthesising chloroplasts and it grows upwards away from gravity and towards light. The root tip gives rise to cells which absorb salt and water, and it grows towards gravity and away from light.

Quite a lot is known about the mechanisms which regulate growth by cell enlargement in the regions behind the actively dividing tips. Cell enlargement is achieved by the secretion of water and solutes to form a substantial vacuole within the cell, thus causing an overall increase of volume and expansion of the cell wall. The degree of enlargement is affected by external stimuli such as light and gravity, producing the differential growth patterns seen when plants orientate to these stimuli. Substances, called plant hormones or auxins, are now known to be produced at the growing apex and to move back causing vacuole formation in the actively elongating region. The distribution of auxin is affected by light or gravity so that the plant will turn towards or away from the stimulus. Indoleacetic acid is the active growth substance occurring naturally in many plants. Several man-made substances are also effective and are widely used as weedkillers. Evidence is also accumulating to show that a group of substances exists in plants to control cell division, just as auxins regulate cell enlargement.

ECOLOGY—THE STUDY OF LIVING ORGANISMS IN THEIR ENVIRONMENT

The important branch of biology which deals with the relationship between living organisms and their environment must now be considered. Living organisms and the physical environment in which they exist form what is termed an eco-system. Obviously it would be possible to regard the whole world as a giant ecosystem, though for purposes of study it would be extremely un-rewarding and impractical. A pond, a rocky or sandy shore, a forest, and a peat bog are examples of ecosystems on a somewhat smaller scale, possessing different properties and containing populations of animals and plants that are dif-ferent both in number of individuals and in species represented. The ecologist seeks to understand why a particular species is present in certain numbers in an ecosystem in terms of that species' interaction with all other living organisms (biotic factors) and with the physical (abiotic) factors of the ecosystem.

1. Abiotic Factors

All living organisms will show ranges of toler-ance for abiotic factors such as temperature, humidity, salinity, oxygen levels, amount of light, etc. Clearly, if any factor in the environment moves outside the range of tolerance of a species, it becomes limiting for that particular species which is then excluded from the environment. Within the range of tolerance there will be an optimum value for each abiotic factor at which a species will survive best.

There is not a firm line separating suitable and unsuitable environments, but rather a steady shift from optimum values into conditions in which an organism finds it more and more difficult to survive.

One of the most important abiotic factors in an environment is the nature of the substrate upon or within which an organism moves and settles.

(a) **The Terrestrial Environment.**—Soil is the commonest substrate for terrestrial organisms. Particle sizes, ranging from the coarsest gravel soils, through sands and silts to the finely textured clays, have extensive effects on the flora and fauna of any area. Coarsely textured soils are obviously penetrated most easily both by roots and by soil animals. Soils of this type also allow the rapid movement of water and soil gases, but they have the serious disadvantage of poor water retention. The level at which water saturation occurs is known as the water table and is an important abiotic factor. The terrestrial environment tends on the whole to dehydrate organisms and there is always a marked dependence on water supplies.

Soil characteristics also vary with depth. A vertical section through any soil is referred to as its profile and has considerable bearing on the ecosystems in which the soil is involved. The layers, or horizons, of a soil profile vary enormously from one soil to another. Below a surface layer of organic debris one can, in general terms, distinguish a layer of soil from which substances have been leached (A horizon), soil containing the leached-out substances from the layer above (B horizon), the weathered parent material (C horizon), and finally the parent rock or some other stratum beneath the soil (D horizon).

Humus

Humus, which is formed from animal and plant remains and is located in the lower parts of the A profile, is of great importance in providing food for soil organisms and chemical elements such as nitrogen, phosphorus, and calcium for plant growth. It is also important in maintaining good soil structure and, though inorganic fertilisers can supply chemical elements, they have little or no effect on structure. Soil requires careful cultivation, and structure is easily disturbed by such things as heavy farm machinery, which can lead to the creation of impermeable layers with the disastrous exclusion of oxygen and oxygen-consuming organisms.

(b) **The Aquatic Environments.**—Marine and freshwater environments together cover more than 75 per cent of the earth's surface and, since they can be occupied throughout their entire depth, offer a much greater volume of living space than does the land. There is only a slight difference between the density of water and of living tissues, so that the bodies of aquatic organisms are very largely supported by the environment and do not need strong woody stems or powerfully muscled limbs to hold them up. Water has a high specific heat, which means that large amounts of heat are needed to raise its temperature. The result is that aquatic environments tend to show much smaller fluctuations in temperature than the terrestrial ones. In general, the larger the volume of water the smaller are the fluctuations in temperature, and so the fauna and flora of the oceans will not show wide temperature tolerance, whereas that of small pools will, but in neither case will the tolerance be so great as that shown by many terrestrial forms. Oxygen and carbon dioxide concentrations are very different in water and in air and are also variable from one aquatic environment to another, making them suitable for the support of different fauna and flora.

An important difference between the sea and freshwater is seen when their salt concentrations are determined.

Osmotic and ionic regulation

Organisms living in fresh or in sea water face quite dissimilar problems in osmotic and ionic

regulation. Life evolved originally in the sea and the salt concentration in the blood of marine molluscs, crustaceans, and echinoderms, for example, is about the same as in sea water itself. Marine organisms have, on several occasions in the course of their evolution, moved into freshwater. Representatives of the worms, crustaceans, molluscs, and vertebrates have all independently invaded this very dilute habitat. What is more, all these animals show approximately the same types of modification to cope with the change. Their outer layers, in the main, become impermeable and the salt concentration of their blood is reduced considerably and to a spectacularly low level in the freshwater mussel. The kidneys become enlarged and produce a large volume of dilute urine. By these means freshwater animals can cut down loss of their salts (*see* **F39**). It is interesting that all terrestrial vertebrates, including the mammals have retained a salt concentration in their blood of about half the seawater level and this is partly attributable to their freshwater ancestry. The ultimate development of salinity tolerance is seen in such animals as the salmon and eel which move from fresh to salt water and back again during their life cycle.

2. Biotic Factors

(a) **Associations between Organisms.**—No organism can be considered to be independent of any other organism in an ecosystem but in some cases close associations of various types can be developed between different species or different members of the same species.

Commensalism is an association which benefits one member but has little effect on the other. Small organisms can live within the protective covering offered by a larger individual, as, for example, commensal crabs living within the shell of some species of oyster.

Symbiosis is a somewhat closer association in which both members benefit, as do certain species of green algae and the coelenterates in whose body tissues they live. The algae are protected and the coelenterates benefit from the food produced by the photosynthetic plant. Some symbiotic organisms are unable to survive outside the association. The lichens which are associations of algae and fungi, are examples of this type of symbiosis, as are some of the food-processing micro-organisms together with the animals in whose intestinal tracts they live.

Social animals. In some cases animals of the same species form social groups in which co-operative effort and division of labour makes them more successful in exploiting a particular environment. Social development is most obvious among certain insects such as termites, ants, wasps, and bees, and among the vertebrates. Social organisation in these groups may lead to the development of different behaviour patterns and ultimately, as in ants and bees, for example, to the evolution of a variety of structural modifications so that different castes are recognisable.

Parasitism. Not all associations are of mutual benefit and when one organism becomes sufficiently specialised so that it can live successfully on materials extracted from another, the latter is always adversely affected. Parasites, by causing disease in, and sometimes the death of, the host, can influence population growth and size. Important groups are bacteria, protozoa, fungi, nematodes (roundworms), and platyhelminths (tapeworms and liver flukes). Viruses are also important disease-producing agents which are incapable of an independent existence outside the cells of the host and utilise the host cell's metabolic pathways directly to synthesise new virus material.

Control of Parasites

Many parasites (and other pests which may disturb the comfort and health of man) can now be controlled to some extent, and, for a variety of reasons, such control procedures have extensive effects on the ecosystems involved. The regulation of some bacterial parasites by means of antibiotics, and control of the insect vectors of organisms such as the malaria parasite by means of insecticides, have both been important factors in the increase in human population. Though the beneficial effects of pest control of all types are clear, the process is not without its difficulties and dangers. Indiscriminate use of many chemical agents has led to the development of resistant strains. In any group of organisms, some will naturally be more resistant to a pesticide or antibiotic than others and these will be the survivors of any treatment that is less than totally effective. They will form the breeding stock for subsequent generations and so progressively more and more resistant types will evolve. Thus, there are now many strains of bacteria resistant to penicillin and other antibiotics. Even more alarming is the recent discovery that this resistance can be transferred in an infective way between bacteria of different species. Another complication associated with chemical control is that the agent concerned frequently affects a wide spectrum of organisms, including those that are in no sense injurious to man or his crops. Thus DDT kills bees and other pollinating insects unless its application to a crop is very precisely timed. In addition, the accumulation of quantities of chlorinated hydrocarbons such as DDT in the environment is known to have an injurious effect on organisms other than insects. Because these chemicals are broken down very slowly they now form a serious problem in environmental pollution.

Predation. A less direct association than that between parasite and host is the one which exists between predators and the prey which they capture and kill. However, interactions in both parasitism and predation have features in common particularly those affecting population numbers.

(b) **The Food Factor.**—Plants are the ultimate source of organic food for all animals. The most important food plants are those capable of photosynthesis (**F32**) in which organic material is synthesised from carbon dioxide and water, using radiant energy from the sun to drive the reaction.

Food Chains. Plants are eaten by herbivores which in turn are eaten by carnivores. It is possible to see many such sequences, called food chains, in all ecosystems. For example, in the open sea, green algae are the important photosynthetic organisms; these are eaten by a small crustacean, *Calanus*, which in turn forms a large part of the diet of the herring. Feeding relationships are usually of much greater complexity than is suggested by a simple food chain. Thus, *Calanus* represents about 20 per cent of the herring's diet but it is also eaten by many other marine animals as well. For example, it forms about 70 per cent of the total diet of larval sand eels. The larval eels are eaten in turn by the herring and may form 40 per cent of its diet. Because an animal's diet is usually quite varied and one species of animal or plant may be part of the food of a wide range of different animals, interactions are set up which are referred to as food webs. However, for general comparative purposes it is possible to disregard the detail of species and to group together all organisms with similar food habits. When this is done a relationship known as pyramid of numbers often appears in which organisms at the base of a food chain (the primary producers) are extremely abundant, while those at the apex (the final consumers) are relatively few in number.

Productivity. The validity of using numbers of individuals in such an analysis is often open to question, especially when ecosystems are to be compared. For example, a comparison between numbers of herring and numbers of whales as final consumers in two pyramidal systems is not very informative. This difficulty is partially overcome by using estimates of the total weight (biomass) of organisms at each level rather than their number. Even this has disadvantages because determinations of biomass give a measure of the amount of material present at any one time (the standing crop) but give no indication of the amount of material being produced or the rate of its production (the productivity). In some parts of the sea, for example, the biomass of small animals forming the zooplankton is greater than that of the plant life or phytoplankton on which it depends for food. This seems to contravene the pyramid concept. However, the rate of production of new material by the phytoplankton is very much greater than by the zooplankton so that, if taken over a year, the total amount of plant material produced would far exceed the total production of animal material. Productivity is a concept of great practical and theoretical importance. It may be determined in terms of the actual organic material produced in an area over a set period of time or, more usefully, in terms of the amounts of energy transferred and stored at each food level, again over a set period of time.

Photosynthetic efficiency

Under natural conditions only 1 to 5 per cent of the light falling on a plant is converted by its photosynthetic system into chemical energy contained in the material of its tissues. Similarly herbivores which consume plants will pass on to their predators only some 10 per cent of the energy contained in the plant material they eat. These low values for photosynthetic efficiency and ecological efficiency respectively are due to the fact that most of the energy appears as heat during the metabolic reactions needed to sustain life and only a small amount is incorporated into new tissue. It is easy to see that the form of a pyramid of numbers can be explained in terms of low ecological efficiency, as can the observation that a food chain rarely has more than five links. The loss of energy at each stage must mean that each succeeding stage becomes smaller and smaller in number and that the number of stages is severely limited.

Human Population and Food. The present very large increase in human population and the predicted rise from 4,124 million in 1977 to 6,000 million in the year 2000 has led to a pressing need for the controlled exploitation of food resources in the world. Consideration of the processes of energy transfer suggests that man should be mainly herbivorous. They also suggest that present agricultural crops, with the possible exception of sugar cane, do not achieve as high a primary productivity as that encountered in some natural ecosystems. Crops rarely achieve complete plant cover of the land throughout the growing season so as to trap the maximum amount of sunlight. It would be necessary to mix crops to do this effectively and there would then be complicated harvesting problems.

If man remains an omnivore, as he almost certainly will, then his domestic food animals will continue to be herbivorous as they are at present, though whether they will be the same herbivores is less easy to predict. Beef cattle raised on grassland convert only 4 per cent of the energy in the plants of their environment into similar chemical energy in their tissues. At the present time intensive farming practices are being employed to improve conversion, usually by harvesting plant material, processing it, and bringing it to the animals which are housed in special buildings. This cuts down on the wastage of plant food because it can be grown under better conditions and less of it is consumed by animals other than the cattle. Careful breeding and the limitation of the period over which livestock is raised to that of maximum growth efficiency have also contributed to conversions of some 35 per cent, achieved in the case of broiler chickens and calves. The moral problems raised by these methods and the circumstances which make them necessary give rise to widespread concern.

Fish are also an important part of man's diet. Many populations have been overfished so that returns have gone down in spite of intensified fishing effort. The fisheries scientist is concerned to discover the limit at which the maximum number of fish can be taken without depleting the population year by year. Research is also going on into possible methods of enclosing and farming areas of the sea or estuaries.

Population Dynamics

Study of the numbers of organisms in a population, together with their change and regulation, forms a branch of the subject of considerable practical importance known as population dynamics.

Numbers of animals and plants tend to increase up to the capacity of the environment. The rate of increase will be determined by the balance between reproduction rate and mortality. As Malthus appreciated, adults of any organism tend to replace themselves by a greater number of progeny and, in the absence of losses by mortality and other factors, there is a vast potential for increase in all populations. If an organism doubles its number in a year, there will be a 1,000-fold increase in 10 years, and a 10 million-fold increase in 20 years. Increase of this type soon leads to shortages and overcrowding so that mortality goes up, the net rate of increase diminishes, and finally an equilibrium is reached with no further increase in number. The change with the passage of time follows and S-shaped curve. At equilibrium, the numbers are kept at a steady level by factors such as competition for food, refuge, or space.

Human population is increasing rapidly at the present time, mainly because of the fall in death-rate. Food production is also increasing, but in some areas the world supply and requirement are so evenly matched that drought or war are inevitably followed by a famine. Though the human population has not yet reached the stage of equilibrium, it is clear that ultimately it must be subject to forces of regulation similar to those that control populations of other organisms. Birth-rate cannot exceed death-rate indefinitely in any living organism. By limiting the size of families it is possible for man to achieve a population equilibrium at levels lower than those at which regulative factors such as famine or aggression must begin to operate. Rational control of birth-rate seems to offer the best chance of averting a global population disaster.

THE GEOLOGICAL RECORD

The various stages in the history of the earth can be read by the geologists in the strata or layers of rock laid down since the planet began to solidify, and it is in these rocks, too, that the record of life upon earth may be traced.

No Life Rocks.—The earliest rocks in the record are known as the Azoic (no life) rocks, because they show no trace of living things, and these layers are of such thickness that they occupy more than half of the whole record. That is to say, for more than half the earth's history nothing living existed upon any part of the globe. For millions of years the surface of our planet was nothing but bare rock without soil or sand, swept by hot winds exceeding in violence the wildest tornadoes of today, and drenched by torrential downpours of tropical rain which, as we have seen elsewhere, gradually tore away the surface to form sandy sediments at the bottom of the seas. In such ancient rocks pushed above the surface by later upheavals we can still trace the marks of primeval oceans as they rippled upon the barren shores or of raindrops which left their imprint perhaps 1,500 million years ago.

Primitive Sea-life.—As we move upwards through the strata, however, traces of life begin to appear and steadily increase as we come to the more recent levels. The earliest signs appear in what is known as the Early Palaeozoic Age (or by some writers as the Proterozoic Age), when we find the fossilised remains of small shellfish, sea-weeds, and trilobites—the latter were creatures somewhat like the plant-lice of modern times. All these primitive animals and plants lived in the shallow tidal waters of ancient seas; for as yet life had not invaded either the dry land or the deep oceans. It is, of course, clear that these creatures of Early Palaeozoic times were not the first living things; they were merely the first creatures capable of leaving fossilised remains, and without doubt must have had more primitive ancestors—amoebic-like forms, jellyfish, bacteria, and so on whose bodies were too soft to leave any traces in the record of the rocks.

The Age of Fishes.—Towards the end of the Early Palaeozoic Era, in what we now know as the Silurian period, there arose a new form of life: the first backboned animals, primitive fishes somewhat similar to the sharks of today; and in the division of the Upper Palaeozoic Era known as the Devonian, they had come to multiply so greatly that this is frequently described as the Age of Fishes.

First Land Animals and Plants.—It is from this time, too, that we find traces of animal and plant life upon the dry land. Both animals and plants had acute problems to solve before it became possible for them to live out of water; for both animals and plants had hitherto been supported by the surrounding water and respired by removing oxygen dissolved in the water. In land animals this problem was solved by a long series of adaptations from gills to lungs. Plants were able to invade the land because of the evolution of an impermeable outer cuticle which prevented water loss and also the development of woody tissues which provided support and a water-conducting system for the whole plant body.

Amphibia and Spore-bearing Trees.—The first type of vertebrates (backboned animals) to live upon dry land was the group of amphibia in the Carboniferous Age, which is today represented by the newts, frogs, toads, and salamanders. In all these forms the eggs give rise to a tadpole stage with gills which lives for some time entirely in water. Later the gills give place to a primitive form of lung which enables the animal to live upon land. Even so, amphibia are restricted more or less to swampy or marshy land, and without a damp environment they would dry up and shrivel to death. The most abundant forms of plant life in the Carboniferous period were the tree-like horsetails, clubmosses, and ferns, the fossilised tissues of which are found in the coal measures and are burned as household coal. But these plants also, as in the case of the amphibia, could exist only amongst the swamps and marshes, and life, although it had freed itself from the necessity of existence in the waters of the earth, still had to return to the water in order to reproduce itself. The highlands and the deeper waters of the planet were still empty of living things. Although the Carboniferous period had been a period of warmth and abundance, the Palaeozoic Era came to an end with a long cycle of dry and bitterly cold ages. Such long-term climatic changes were due, it is now supposed, to such factors as changes in the earth's orbit, the shifting of its axis of rotation, changes in the shape of the land masses, and so on. Long before the Ice Ages of more recent times, there are records in the rocks of alternating periods of warmth and cold as far back as the Azoic and Early Palaeozoic Eras. This long cold spell at the close of the Palaeozoic era came to an end about 220 million years ago, and was succeeded by a long era of widely spread warm conditions—the Mesozoic Era, the so-called Age of Reptiles.

The Mesozoic Era.—The reptiles first appeared in the Permian, but it was during the Mesozoic era that they became the dominant group of animals. The giant reptiles included the stegosaurus, the gigantosaurus, the diplodocus, and many other kinds which were far larger than any land animals living today. Some, for example the diplodocus, were 100 ft. long, although they were vegetarian in habit and were preyed upon by other almost equally huge flesh-eating reptiles. Some species, such as the plesiosaurs and ichthyosaurs, became secondarily aquatic, while the pterodactyl possessed wings with which it could glide and perhaps fly short distances. However, they all differed from the amphibia in that they had hard, dry skins, their lungs were more efficient, fertilisation was internal due to the development of copulatory organs, and they laid eggs with hard, protective shells.

It was also during the Mesozoic era that the warm-blooded birds arose. The birds, like the reptiles, lay eggs with hard shells, and they have several internal features found in the reptiles. The fossil bird Archaeopteryx, three specimens of which have been found in Germany, lived in the Jurassic period. Although it was obviously a bird, it retained many reptilian features. Earliest mammals are recognised in rocks of the late Palaeozoic but in the Mesozoic considerable evolution of the group took place. The fossil Trituberculata which are also found in the Jurassic, are believed to be related to forms from which both the marsupial and placental mammals arose. Although insects were present as far back as the Carboniferous, it was in the Mesozoic that many of the groups we know today first appeared.

Great changes also took place in the plant cover of the land during this era. The spore-bearing giant horsetails and tree clubmosses declined and were replaced by gymnosperms—trees bearing naked seeds. One large group of these, the cycadeoids, has become extinct, but the conifers and a few of the once abundant cycads still remain. The flowering plants or angiosperms also made their appearance, and towards the end of the Cretaceous their evolution was extremely rapid. In fact, many of the fossil leaves found in rocks of Cretaceous age are indistinguishable from those of some present-day flowering plants.

A New Era.—But, perhaps 150 million years later, all this seemingly everlasting warmth and sunshine, the lush tropical life, the giant reptiles who had ruled the world, were wiped out by a new period of bitter cold which only the hardy species could survive. A new Era known as the Caenozoic was beginning, ushered in by a period of upheaval and volcanic activity, following which the map of the world came to resemble more closely the picture we know today. The old period may have lasted several million years, and the main species to survive it were those which had come into existence towards the end of the Mesozoic Era, the seed-bearing flowering plants, the birds, and the mammals. The once all-powerful reptiles from this time onwards are represented only by the comparatively few and relatively small reptilian species of today: the snakes, lizards, crocodiles, and alligators. It was at this time, too, that, long after the creation of the mountains of Scotland and Norway (the so-called Caledonian revolution), or even of the Appalachian mountains (the Appalachian revolution), there arose the great masses of the Alps, the Himalayas, the Rocky Mountains, and the Andes. These are the mountain chains of the most recent, the Caenozoic revolution. Initially, as we have seen, the climate of the Caenozoic Era was cold, but the weather grew generally warmer until a new period of abundance was reached, only to be followed at the end of the Pliocene by a period of glacial ages generally known as the First, Second, Third, and Fourth Ice Ages.

THE GEOLOGICAL TIME SCALE

ERAS	PERIODS	AGE	LIFE
		(millions of years)	
	Pleistocene	1	Man
CAENOZOIC	Pliocene		
	Miocene	25	Birds, Mammals and modern plants
	Oligocene		
	Eocene	70	
MESOZOIC	Cretaceous	135	Dinosaurs, Cycads; Earliest Birds; Ammonites and Sea-urchins
	Jurassic	180	
	Triassic	225	
PALAEOZOIC	Permian	270	First mammals; Early reptiles
	Carboniferous	350	Amphibians, tree-ferns, first insects
	Devonian	400	Fishes, first land plants
	Silurian	440	Mainly invertebrate animals; no life on land. Trilobites and graptolites
	Ordovician	500	
	Cambrian	600	

PRE-CAMBRIAN (also PROTEROZOIC, ARCHAEOZOIC) 2,000 Life emerges
4,600 Age of Earth

V. SCIENCES OF MAN

PHYSICAL ANTHROPOLOGY

MAN'S EARLY ANCESTORS

In the early Tertiary the earth's climate was generally warmer than it is today and extensive tropical forests covered much of North America and Europe as well as Africa and Asia. It is from geological deposits in these northern latitudes that the earliest fossil remains clearly attributable to the Primate order of mammals have been found. Three Families are represented in the Palaeocene period: the Carpolestidae, the Phenacolemuridae and the Plesiadipidae; the first two exclusively North American but the third known also from Europe. Most of the remains are of teeth and pieces of jaw but other parts of the skull and even bones from the rest of the skeleton have been preserved of some species. All the forms show many primitive characteristics as is to be expected in such early forms; more surprisingly they show little similarity in their special characteristics with later families, but they are judged to be Primate on the basis of the morphology of their molar teeth. By the next geological period, the Eocene, however, fossils are to be found which are fairly certainly the ancestors of present-day Primates. The Families known from the Eocene are the Adapidae, from which the Lemurs were probably descended, the Tarsiidae, containing the ancestor of the present-day *Tarsius*, the Anaptomorphidae which seem to have become extinct at the end of the Eocene and the Omomyidae, representatives of which seem to have given rise to the higher primates or Anthropoidea. The Palaeocene and Eocene primates along with the extant lemurs, lorises and tarsiers are referred to taxonomically as "prosimians". Little is known of their evolution after the Eocene until the Pleistocene, partly because of poor conditions for fossilisation where they lived, but partly also because they experienced a marked reduction in numbers following competition with evolving rodents and their own anthropoid descendants. Today the lemurs are confined to the island of Madagascar where they escaped this competition; the lorises have a restricted distribution in tropical Africa and Asia and are nocturnal in habit and the tarsier is confined to some of the islands in the East Indies.

The first definite anthropoids are known from the Oligocene period, mainly from deposits of a former swamp in the Fayum of Egypt. Among the fossils here have been identified the first Old World Monkeys (Cercopithecoidea) in *Parapithecus* and *Apidium*; the first gibbons (Hylobatidae) in *Aeolopithecus*; and the earliest ancestor of the Great Apes (Pongidae) in *Aegyptopithecus*. It has also been suggested that a form known only from a few teeth and a lower jaw *Propliopithecus* might represent the origin of the lineage giving rise to man, but this is now thought to be unlikely. Some Oligocene fossils are also known from South America and appear to be the beginnings of the New World Monkeys (Ceboidea) which are probably descended from New World prosimians and have evolved quite separately from Old World anthropoids.

From the Miocene, which follows the Oligocene, remains of a number of different apes have been found in East Africa, India (the Siwalik hills) and parts of Europe. Most are collectively referred to as the *Dryopithecinae* and still retain many monkey-like characteristics. Their skeleton indicates that they ran and jumped through the branches of trees, as most monkeys tend to do, but intermittently they probably moved by swinging from their arms; a mode of locomotion termed semi-brachiation. Present-day apes, the Orang, the Chimpanzee and the Gorilla are almost certainly descended from the Dryopithecinae. The group, however, is also seen as containing the ancestors of the human or hominid lineage. With regard to the early divergence of this lineage a fossil, known as *Ramapithecus* and found in both India, East Africa (where it was first called Kenyapithecus), Turkey and Europe is important. It is known only from teeth and jaws, but in contrast with apes these show a rounded shape to the dental arcade, small canine teeth and spatulate shaped incisors; all of which are hominid characters. It is surmised that *Ramapithecus* lived on seeds and had probably given up an arboreal life for a terrestrial one, and what is more, in becoming terrestrial had adopted an erect bipedal mode of locomotion. The fossil is dated to *c.* 14–10 million years ago. Mention should also be made here of another fossil anthropoid known best from Pliocene deposits in Italy: *Oreopithecus*. This, in a well-preserved skeleton, shows many features of bipedalism, but other characteristics, particularly of the teeth indicate that it is not closely related to man but is rather an aberrant ape.

Major Features of Primate and Human Evolution

The distinctive characteristics of Primates arise from the fact that all species in the group either themselves live in trees or have had ancestors which were tree-living. They, therefore, show, though to varying degrees, a number of arboreal adaptations.

1. Special development of the limbs

The arboreal environment is characterised by being irregular and precarious. Animals in it therefore require special mechanisms for hanging on to branches and moving through trees. Primates have adapted to these needs by evolving thumbs and big toes which are opposable to the other digits so as to form grasping organs. Associated with this is the tendency to replace claws with nails and the development of friction pads on the palmar surface of hands and feet. A considerable flexibility and wide range of movement is evolved in the forelimb and primates have the ability to sit back on their haunches and explore the irregularity in their environment with their hands thus emancipating the forelimb from a solely locomotor function. The grasping hand can also be used for collecting food and transferring it to the mouth.

2. Development of special senses

Unlike terrestrial environments the world of the trees is not a world of smells and the sense of olfaction tends to be poor in Primates. Concomitantly there is a reduction in the snout, also made possible by the development of the hand. On the other hand, vision becomes an increasingly important sense and the eyes of Primates tend not only to be large but also to move from a lateral position on the skull on to the front of the face. Eventually there is overlapping in visual fields and the evolution of stereoscopy. In higher Primates colour vision arises. Tactile sense is also increased and balance and fine movement are improved. These changes in the senses are reflected in brain structure and size and Primates tend characteristically to have large brains for their body size.

3. Reduction in offspring number

The arboreal environment because of its precarious nature puts a premium on parental care and if there are many offspring to be cared for dissipation of parental effort may lead to none surviving. The arboreal environment is thus one of the few where animals who reduce their litter size can have a higher reproductive fitness than those with large litters. Primates typically give birth to only one or two offspring at any one time. This also means that there is little or no competition between offspring and therefore no premium for rapid development. Primates tend to be characterised by slow maturation and a long dependence on parents.

Clearly many of the features we see in man are an extension of his Primate heritage. But man, of course, has his own very distinctive characteristics. Anatomically these are to be seen particularly in his adaptations to a terrestrial bipedal existence, his much reduced face and jaws and his greatly enlarged brain. In evolution it would seem that it was the acquisition of the bipedalism which was critical. Why man's ancestors abandoned an arboreal habit is obscure, though there must have been a particular terrestrial ecological niche available, perhaps grain eating. Why in becoming terrestrial these same ancestors became bipedal is also unknown. Other Primates, such as the baboons and their relatives on re-colonising the ground continued to be quadrupedal. But whatever the explanation bipedalism, superimposed upon a Primate heritage, offered important evolutionary opportunities. This is not because bipedalism itself is a particularly effective means of locomotion but rather that it emancipates the forelimbs from locomotor function. They could therefore be used for many other purposes. One of the most important of these was tool use and subsequently tool-making. When early hominids colonised the terrestrial habitat they had few inbuilt defence mechanisms and the ability to use stones, sticks and bones to ward off carnivores and other predators must have been of considerable survival value, as has been shown by observation of present-day chimpanzees when they are on the ground. The ability was enhanced and extended as it became possible to fashion these natural objects into shapes for particular purposes, and throughout the later stages of hominid evolution there is evidence of increasing refinement of the use of stone and flints in the making of tools. Initially of use in defence, the tools became of value in offence, and there is evidence quite early in hominid evolution of a lineage changing from the traditional herbivorous diet of Primates to a carnivorous one, indicating the adoption of a hunting mode of life. Tool making must have been one of the practices which favoured the development of language, and, since it came to require fine manipulative skill, hand and brain evolved together; particularly those parts of the brain concerned with precise motor control and tactile sensation. Man is sometimes defined as the tool-making animal and although other creatures use tools and some fashion them at least occasionally, only man makes tools of a consistent and repeated pattern. Another consequence of freeing of the forelimbs through bipedalism was that carrying became so much easier. Thus food and other materials could be carried over considerable distances and this facilitated the establishment of a home base. Perhaps even more importantly the human infant could be carried in its mother's arms and held close to her body, allowing a much closer and intimate relationship between mother and child than is possible in other animals. The human infant is born in a very immature state; in part because of the limitations to the size of the birth canal imposed by the demands of bipedalism. It is therefore long dependent on maternal care. This raises problems in a hunting economy where nursing mothers become dependent upon males for the catching and providing of food. It has been argued that the evolution of the particular form of reproductive cycle found in man, in which the female is receptive to the male throughout most of her menstrual cycle should be seen as a means of ensuring that a hunting male will provide for his female and offspring. Certainly the type of behaviour found in many monkeys in which a female in heat abandons her offspring to consort with dominant males would not be compatible with survival of the human baby.

In recent years a great deal of attention has been devoted by physical anthropologists to studying the behaviour and ecology of many different Primates, especially Old World Monkeys and Apes. One of the aims of this has been to try and understand the origins of human sociality. Except in the most general of terms little can be said definitively about this, mainly, of course, because the non-human Primates have themselves evolved since the time they shared common ancestry with man. And even among quite closely related forms an immense diversity of social structures exists. But these new ethological studies have added a fascinating dimension to physical anthropology and allow a much more functional interpretation of Primate variety than was possible before.

THE HOMINID LINEAGE

Australopithecinae

This group of creatures are presumed to be descended from a form like *Ramapithecus* and lived during Pliocene and Lower Pleistocene periods. They are well known from many finds made by R. Dart, R. Brown and J. T. Robinson in South Africa and more recently from East Africa, where L. S. B. Leakey and his family have been the main discoverers. For a number of years controversy raged as to whether they were apes or hominids: the brain size is small, in most cases well within the ape range, and they have heavy projecting jaws and large teeth. However, they also show a number of human characteristics; their canine teeth were not projecting dagger-like structures; their jaw movement was a rotatory grinding one not just directly up and down as in apes and most importantly, as evidenced from their post-cranial skeleton, they were terrestrial bipeds. In East Africa at least, there is also evidence that they made stone tools.

The taxonomy of the Australopithecines has been a source of great confusion. In South Africa the fossils were recovered from various former caves in Botswana and the Transvaal and those from a particular cave were given a distinct scientific name: *Australopithecus africanus* from Taung, *Australopithecus prometheus* from Makapansgat, *Plesianthropus transvaalensis* from Sterkfontein, *Paranthropus robustus* from Kromdrai and *Paranthropus crassidens* from Swartkrans. Today it is generally agreed that only two forms are represented and that they are probably distinct only at the species level. They are known as *Australopithecus robustus* representing the forms previously known as *Paranthropus* and *Australopithecus africanus* the rest. The former, as its scientific name suggests, was a heavy rugged creature and, on the evidence of its extremely large premolar and molar teeth, was probably herbivorous. *A. africanus* was a much more gracile creature and, it is surmised, may well have been an active hunter.

A major problem in discussing the evolutionary significance of the South African australopithecines has been the difficulty in establishing accurately their age, since they were found in limestone breccias which cannot be geologically dated with present techniques. The situation is much better in East Africa where the fossils are found in or nearby igneous rocks which can be dated, particularly by the potassium/argon method. This indicates that australopithecine forms existed as long as 5 million years ago and occupied the region till 1·5 million years ago. The major sites from which specimens have been recovered are Olduvai Gorge in Tanzania, East of Lake Rudolph in Kenya and Omo and Afar in Ethiopia. Again there is evidence of two distinct forms as in South Africa; one robust, such as the well-represented "Nutcracker man" *Zinjanthropus boisei* (now known as *A. boisei* or *A. robustus boisei*) from Bed I at Olduvai Gorge; and the other gracile and comparable to *A. africanus*. At Olduvai Gorge, where it occurs in Bed I and the lower part of Bed II with dates ranging from 1·9 million—1·6 million the gracile form is more advanced than in South Africa with a larger braincase and more human teeth and has been termed *H. habilis*. It was almost certainly the maker of the Olduvan pebble culture and its advance on the South African form is probably because it was later in time. However, an anomaly which has not yet been explained is the discovery at East Rudolph of a form known as ER 1470 which appears more advanced, particularly in its large cranial capacity, than any other australopithecine and yet has a date of around 2·5–2 million years.

Homo erectus

Although evolution along a lineage is a process of slow and gradual change, it is necessary taxonomically to divide the continuum into stages. When the fossil record is incomplete the gaps in it it are used for separating the stages, but as these gaps are filled by further discovery the divisions become increasingly arbitrary. Bearing this difficulty in mind we can refer the stage of human evolution after the australopithecines (probably from a form like. *A. africanus*) to *Homo erectus*. Most of the finds of this species are dated to the upper part of the Lower Pleistocene and to the Middle Pleistocene period. *H. erectus* is characterised by very thick skull bones, the development of heavy bony ridges, particularly above the eye region, and neither chin nor forehead. However the brain is much larger than in australopithecines and with a cranial capacity of 1,000 cc or more, *H. erectus* is intermediate between australopithecines and *H. sapiens*. Further the post-cranial skeleton is essentially indistinguishable from modern man and *H. erectus* was fully bipedal and made complex stone tools.

The first finds of *H. erectus* were made in middle Pleistocene river terrace deposits in Java at the end of the last century by E. Dubois. They were named *Pithecanthropus erectus*. Subsequently further fossils of the same form were recovered in the region, and some remains showing particularly primitive features were recovered from Lower Pleistocene strata. Most of the latter were originally named *P. robustus* but a particularly massive jaw fragment termed *Meganthropus palaeojavanicus* shows australopithecine features.

In 1927 and 1929 the first remains of Pekin Man (long known as *Sinanthropus pekinensis*) were found in Chou kou Tien cave near Pekin. These remains tend to show some advances on the Javanese fossils such as larger cranial capacities but otherwise are very similar. Although the first finds of *H. erectus* were in Asia it is now known that the species had a wide distribution in the Old World and remains now attributed to it have been recovered in Europe, at Heidelberg, Germany; Vertesszöllös, Hungary and Petrolona, Greece, and in Africa at Ternifine, Algeria; Sidi Abderrahman, Morocco (both initially called *Athanthropus mauritanicus*) and Olduvai Gorge, Tanzania. Some very recent discoveries in East Africa also indicate that *H. erectus* may have evolved much earlier than was formerly thought and been present 1·75 million years ago. It may thus be contemporaneous with late australopithecines.

Prior to the Middle Pleistocene all the varieties of primates, including hominids, had been confined to the tropical parts of the world. Now with cultural advances including knowledge of fire, man was able to leave the tropical areas and to utilise the space and resources of the more northerly parts of the Old World. Both at Chou kou Tien and Vertesszöllös there is clear evidence of the use of fire.

GEOLOGICAL DATING

It is evident that establishing the geological age of a fossil is critical to understanding fully the evolutionary significance of the remains. Most desirable is an ageing in years, termed absolute dating, where the results of tests are expressed as years "before present" or "b.p.", where "present" is taken as the year A.D. 1950. Where absolute dating is not possible, it is often still useful to know whether a particular fossil is older, younger or contemporaneous with other fossils. Establishing this is known as relative dating. (*See* **F9**.)

Radiometric Methods

The main methods of absolute dating are radiometric and depend upon the fact that radioactive elements break down at a constant and known rate to other non-radioactive elements. The potassium-argon method, which has been associated with the East African hominids, depends upon the fact that the radioactive isotope of potassium K-40, which occurs in rocks of igneous origin, decays to the gas argon 40 and has a half-life of $1·3 × 10^9$ years. It has been used for the absolute dating of deposits between 230,000 and 26 million

years old. For more recent fossils, up to about 50,000 years, the carbon-14 method can be used. This depends upon the constant rate of decay of the rare radioactive isotope of carbon, C-14, to normal carbon, C-12, and since bone contains carbon, it is possible to date the actual fossil rather than the deposits in which the remains have been found.

Fluorine Method

One method of relative dating is called the fluorine method, depending as it does on the fact that bone progressively takes up fluorine from the waters percolating through deposits. The rate depends upon the concentration of fluorine in these waters, but if in one particular place some bones have high fluorine contents and others low, the former are likely to be older. Relative dating may also be deduced from the depths at which fossil bones are found in undisturbed strata. An extension of this principle has been much used in the relative dating of fossil hominids in northern Eurasia, which in the second half of the Pleistocene was subjected, like North America, to a series of ice ages interrupted by periods when conditions became milder and at times even tropical. There were four major advances of the ice, often named from the Alpine ice sheets as Günz (the first), Mindel, Riss and Würm, and three major interglacials. Further, conditions ameliorated once during the course of the first three ice ages and twice during the Würm to form the so-called interstadial periods. The sequence is well represented in the geology of many regions and forms a framework for the relative dating of various fossils.

NEANDERTHAL MAN

The most distinctive forms of Neanderthal Man, often known as classical Neanderthal Man, have been recovered from deposits in Europe and surrounding regions dated to the time of the Würm I glaciation. Gibraltar was the site of the first discovery, but it was the skull fragment recovered from the Neander valley in Germany which gave the group its name. Other important sites of discovery are Spy (Belgium), La Chapelle-aux-Saints, La Ferrassie, Le Moustier and La Quina (France), Monte Circeo (Italy), Shanidar (Iraq), Mt. Carmel and Amud (Israel) and Teshik Tash (Uzbekistan). The main features of classical Neanderthal man are a long, narrow, low braincase, with a sloping forehead and a heavy bar of bone above the orbits; heavy faces with poor development of a cheek region, and the absence of a chin. However, although the general appearance of the skull has been described as "brutish", the cranial capacity of classical Neanderthal man was at least as large as that of modern man, and the post-cranial skeleton is completely modern in its anatomy. The bony remains are typically found associated with a distinctive flint industry, known as the Mousterian industry, which occurs widely in Europe, the Near East and North Africa.

Progressive Neanderthal Man

The forms that precede classical Neanderthal man in the region show to varying degrees neanderthaloid features, but these, surprisingly, tend to be less extremely developed, and most of the skulls look more like modern man than do the classical neanderthals. Important examples from the last interglacial are Ehringsdorf (Germany), Saccopastore (Italy), Fontechevade (France) and from the second or Great Interglacial, Steinheim (Germany) and Swanscombe (England). Although only the parietal and occipital bones of Swanscombe man are known, they are almost indistinguishable from modern man. This group of fossils is often referred to as Progressive Neanderthal man. The paradox of early forms being more advanced than later forms has not been satisfactorily explained. The most widely held view is that there was a reversal of an evolutionary trend in Europe, under the influence of the cold of the Würm I glaciation and the isolation of the region which occurred with the expansion of the ice sheets. But as already noted classical neanderthalers are not confined to Europe, and the features of the group do not appear to be cold adaptations. Perhaps more likely in the view that there were two (and possibly more) linkages from *Homo erectus*; a southern one evolving rapidly towards modern man, which only moved into Europe when the climate was warm, and a northerly linkage, evolving more slowly, which occupied the colder regions of Eurasia. In support of this view is the fact that not only do the remains from the Würm I glaciation appear primitive but also do those few which are known from the Riss glacial period at Abri-Suard and Arago in France. Further, more or less contemporaneous with classical Neanderthal man, on the southern border of Europe were forms, like those recovered at Jebel Ighoud (Morocco), Jebel Quafza (Palestine) and the Skhul cave at Mount Carmel (Israel), which appeal to represent the final transformation of progressive Neanderthal man into modern man as we know him.

Rhodesian Man

Although not particularly neanderthaloid, two other types of remains should be mentioned here. Rhodesian man was first known from a completely preserved cranium found at Broken Hill, Zambia. It is remarkable in that whereas the skull is quite modern there are enormous brow ridges, comparable with an ape, and an extremely receding forehead region. Whilst only one specimen was known, some suggested it might be pathological, but an almost identical skull was later found at Saldanha Bay in South Africa. Until recently, Rhodesian man was thought to be about 40,000 years old and thus younger than the European neanderthals; it is now thought, however, to be considerably older.

Solo Man

Solo man is known from a number of crania from the later river terraces of the Solo river in Java. Apart from having larger cranial capacities, the remains are not unlike Javanese *Homo erectus*, and Solo man may well be the direct descendant of *Homo erectus* in the region.

MODERN MAN

With the retreat of the ice at the end of the Würm I glaciation, men, indistinguishable skeletally from present-day man, appear to have moved into Europe and replaced the classical neanderthalers. Whether there was any intermixture is uncertain; it is customary nowadays to include modern man and all the various forms of Neanderthal man in the single species *Homo sapiens*, which would imply that intermixture would be possible. But if this happened it must have been on a small scale, since there is little evidence of any neanderthal features in the men of the Upper Palaeolithic: the latter derive their name from their stone tools which are infinitely superior to the Mousterian flakes of the neanderthalers. In the stone industries of the Upper Palaeolithic—the Aurignacian, Solutrean, Magdalenian and others—one finds delicately constructed knife blades, arrow heads and engraving tools. This is also the time of the first cave paintings and clear evidence of the development of artistic tendencies. It is the first time too when the dead were buried. The economy, however, was still based on the hunting and gathering of foodstuffs, and crop cultivation and animal domestication were unknown.

Important Sites

A number of sites have been discovered in Europe which have yielded skeletal remains from this period. Among the more important are Combe-Capelle in the French Dordogne, which provides the earliest known skull (approximately 34,000 years B.P.); Cro-Magnon and Chancelade also in the Dordogne: Oberkassel in Germany, Brünn in Czechoslovakia and Paviland near Swansea in Wales.

Remains of modern man also begin appearing around this time in other parts of the Old World. The oldest comes from the Niah cave in Sarawak with a C-14 date of 40,000 B.P. The upper cave at Chou kon Tien near Pekin has yielded a number of skulls. Then from Africa, mainly east and south, come a host of remains; the dating of many of these is not certain but most if not all are probably contemporaneous with the men of European Upper Palaeolithic. Important sites from Southern Africa are Boskop, Cape Flats, Fish Hoek, Florisbad, Matjes River and Springbok Flats and from Eastern Africa, Elmenteita, Kanam, Kanjera and Omo. Interestingly none of the remains of this period in Africa show features like modern Negroes. The earliest remains from Australia have recently been recovered from Lake Mungo in New South Wales with a date of about 25,000 years B.P. Other, but less old, Australian sites are Kow Swamp and Keilor and the remains from these at least are clearly like modern aborigines in form. The earliest known skeletal remains from the New World date about 12,000 B.P., *e.g.*, Tepexpan, Mexico, but from the finds of stone tools it is estimated that man first started occupying the Americas some 15,000–20,000 years ago, and that he came in a series of migrations from North East Asia across the Bering Straits.

Mesolithic Period

The Palaeolithic or Old Stone Age of Europe and many other parts of the world gradually gave way to the Mesolithic, from which there is evidence of domestication of the dog and the making of basketry; and this, in its turn, is transformed in the Neolithic or New Stone Age, when man first began cultivating plants and domesticating animals for food and transport, thus freeing his nutrition from the restrictions of the natural environment. In the Old World the Neolithic started in the Middle East some 10,000 years ago and rapidly spread in all directions. It developed again separately, however, in the New World. Until the Neolithic, man was a rare species; despite the fact that for many thousands of years he had been anatomically indistinguishable from present-day man. With the Neolithic, however, there began a dramatic increase in human numbers.

THE RACES OF MAN

The species *Homo sapiens*, like most other biological species, shows not only temporal variation, but at any one time, spatial or geographical variation as well. And much of this variation is hereditary in nature. Many attempts have been made to classify present-day mankind into races on the basis of this hereditary variation. In the past these attempts tended to be based on readily visible external features such as head shape, hair form and skin colour, but these characters are often affected by the environment in which individuals grow and develop, and even the hereditary component to their variation is complex and in no case fully understood. Typically, within any one population these characters show quantitative variation of a Normal or Gaussian form and it is not possible to place individuals into discrete categories, such as tall and short; the majority of a population are intermediate. When two populations are compared in such characters they usually show considerable overlap in their distributions and refined statistical methods may be necessary to reveal differences.

Racial Classifications

In recent years racial classification have more commonly been based upon biochemical characters, often of the blood, since this tissue is most easily obtained, which show discrete rather than quantitative variation. The genetics of these characters is often relatively simple and has been determined, and differences in the environment in which people develop can be ignored. Populations are characterised in terms of the frequencies with which particular genes occur in them. There can be no doubt that classifications of mankind into races on the basis of either type of character express real features of human geographical variation, but inevitably they do so in a somewhat artificial if not misleading manner; they create the impression that the species is naturally partitioned into discontinuous groups, whereas changes from one region to another are often gradual rather than abrupt transitions. Further there is little precise concordance between the geographical distribution of different hereditary characters, and often distributions show no similarity with one another. Classifications based upon just a few characteristics are therefore likely to be quite different; and in racial taxonomy it is necessary to consider as much of the hereditary variation as possible. Bearing all these difficulties in mind, racial classifications can be useful, particularly in communication, but race is best seen as a phenomenon which needs to be explained, rather than as an explanation for other things.

Mendelian Population

Race is most accurately defined in population terms. A Mendelian population is a reproductive community of individuals who share in a common gene pool. Races are Mendelian populations which differ in the composition of their gene pools. More classically, race has been defined as a group of people who have the majority of their physical attributes in common. Three levels of differentiation of Mendelian populations or races are sometimes distinguished: (1) Geographical, (2) Local and (3) Micro-geographical.

Geographical Races

This is a collection of Mendelian populations such as occupy whole continents or large islands and are separated from one another by major geographical barriers to movement such as mountains, deserts and seas. Examples are the Negroes of Africa, the Caucasians of Europe, India and the Middle East, the Mongoloids of Eastern and S.E. Asia, the Australoids of Australia and neighbouring islands and the Amerindians of the New World.

Local Races

These are sub-populations within Geographical Races, frequently corresponding with particularly isolated and distinct breeding populations. Examples include the tribes within the Amerindian Geographical Race, and such groups as the Basques, the Ainu and Gypsies.

Micro-Races

These are the numerous distinct populations which are not clearly bounded breeding populations and can be distinguished only statistically. Much of the variation within the British Isles falls into this category.

ANTHROPOMETRY

Both individuals and populations of individuals vary in their size and shape, and anthropometry represents the different measuring techniques, usually made with calipers, which are used to analyse this physical variation as it occurs both in the living body and in the skeleton. From the early 19th cent. anthropometry has been a mainstay of physical anthropology, and particular attention has been devoted to the skeleton, since one of the main problems has been in establishing the evolutionary descent of the different races and skeletal remains constitute the most direct evidence of earlier populations. Many measurements have been devised, but the ones most commonly taken are of stature, head length and head breadth. For many years the latter two were especially favoured and used to calculate the cranial index (on the skull) or the cephalic index (on the living) by expressing the breadth as a percentage of the length. Long heads, with low cephalic indices (below 75) are termed dolichocephalic, while round heads with high indices (above 81) are termed brachycephalic. The intermediates are said to be mesocephalic.

Differing Features

Anthropometric features vary widely among the world's populations. Thus while the Nilotes of the Sudan have an average stature of 1·78 m, the African pygmies average only 1·36 m. There is little systematic pattern to the geographical distribution of stature itself, but it is a component determining the relationship between body volume and skin surface area, which shows a very distinct distribution. In people in cold regions, skin surface area is low in relation to volume, whereas in hot regions it tends to be high. This is explained by the need to conserve body heat in arctic environments and to dissipate heat in the tropics. Because he follows this pattern man is said to observe the ecological rules of Bergmann and Allen. The causes for the variation in head shape are not known, though there is evidence that brachycephaly has been increasing in frequency since Upper Palaeolithic times. Nowadays, dolichocephalic heads are prevalent among Australian Aborigines while brachycephal is extremely prevalent among mongoloid peoples.

Although there is a heritable component to most anthropometric variation, the nature of the environment in which an individual grows and develops can also be important. This has been shown by comparing migrants to new environments and their offspring, with parental populations.

PIGMENTATION

Variation in the colour of hair, skin and eyes is mainly due to differences in the amount and distribution of the black pigment melanin, which even causes the "blueness" of eyes when overlain with unpigmented tissues which diffract light. The variation typically has a strong hereditary component, especially in eyes, but immediate environmental experience can have an important effect, as for example in skin tanning on exposure to ultra-violet radiation. Traditionally colour differences were described either in subjective terms or else by reference to matching standards. Both procedures presented serious limitations in reliability and in comparability of results. Recent years have witnessed the use of much more satisfactory objective procedures, involving spectrophotometers in hair and skin colour studies. These instruments record the percentage of light of a number of known specified wavelengths reflected from a surface relative to the reflectance from a pure white surface. In general, the darker the specimen, say of hair, the lower the percentage of light which it reflects. Using such instruments, precise and reliable quantitative estimations of hair and skin colour are possible and the genetic basis of the traits may be clarified and comprehended. There is some evidence that the skin colour differences between Europeans and Africans are due to three or four pairs of major genes. Dark skins confer advantages in sunny areas, since they protect the body against the harmful effects of ultraviolet radiation, minimising sunburn and the incidence of skin cancer. Light skins are advantageous in cloudy areas with low insolation, since they facilitate the body's synthesis of Vitamin D, thus reducing the incidence of rickets. The correlation between dark pigmentation and high levels of solar radiation is high, but it is impossible to state how much of the geographical distribution of skin colour mirrors the spread of dark- and light-skinned peoples from one or two sources and how much of the patterning is due to independent adaptations in many human groups in the past.

PHYSIOMETRIC OBSERVATIONS

These cover a diversity of phenomena, ranging from characters like colour blindness, ability to taste phenylthiocarbamide and fingerprints, whose variation is entirely or almost entirely hereditary, to characters like heat and cold tolerance and physiological adaptations to high altitude whose state is very largely a function of the environment in which an individual is living.

Red–green colour blindness is a sex-linked recessive character; males being far more commonly affected than females. Within Britain percentages of colour-blind males (which represent the frequency of this colour-blind gene) range from 5·4 in N.E. Scotland to 9·5 in S.W. England. Traditional societies, and particularly those still practising a hunter–gatherer economy, show much lower frequencies; and it may be presumed that colour blindness is a severe handicap under such a life-style. It has, in fact, been shown that red–green colour-blind individuals have difficulty in following a blood spoor on grass.

The tasting of P.T.C. is controlled by two genes T and t, the former being dominant. TT and Tt individuals normally experience a bitter taste sensation when they sip P.T.C. solution; tt individuals either cannot taste the substance at all or else only in very strong concentrations. The tt individuals are termed Non-tasters; TT and Tt individuals are termed Tasters. High frequencies of Non-tasters (exceeding 38%) occur in parts of Wales and Orkney, while low values (approximately 24%) occur in North Lancashire and Northumberland. A clue to the selective significance of this trait is provided by the excess of Non-tasters among individuals with nodular goitres (thyroid abnormalities). Non-European populations usually have lower percentages of Non-tasters than the British figures quoted. Thus, for example, the Jivaro Indians in the Amazonian lowlands of Ecuador contain but 1-2% of Non-tasters, as do the Chinese and many African Negro groups.

Finger-prints are one form of dermatoglyphic variation which also occurs on the palms of the hands, the soles of the feet and the toes. They arise as a series of epidermal ridges which form patterns on the surface of the stratum corneum of the skin. There is a strong genetic determination of these patterns, but the precise mode of inheritance is not known. Nor is it known why individuals and populations show this variation, or indeed why different patterns are found on the different fingers. In some pathologies, however, e.g., Down's syndrome, there is marked abnormality of the dermatoglyphics.

The physiological variations in heat, cold and altitude adaptation tell us little or nothing about race, but they do indicate how remarkably adaptable the human being is, and help to explain why man has been able to colonise every type of terrestrial environment on earth.

BLOOD GROUPS

Attributes of the blood have increasingly been used in anthropological genetics because their mode of inheritance is relatively simple. One such set of attributes comprises the blood groups, which are complex chemical substances found in the wall of the red blood cell. These substances are antigenic and can be detected through their reactions with antibodies. A number of quite different blood group systems are now known. The first to be discovered, and still the most important in blood transfusion, is the ABO system. Whereas the antibodies to the other systems are only obtainable through immunisations, those to the ABO system are naturally occurring in human blood serum. The ABO system basically involves three genes, A, B and O (though there are sub-types of A). Every individual inherits two of these genes from parents, and so the genotype (genetic constitution) must be one of the following: AA, AO, BB, BO, AB, or OO. O is recessive to both A and B, and thus there are four possible phenotypes (genetic constitutions detectable by blood grouping): A, B, AB and O.

The ABO genes constitute a polymorphic system, that is several genes occur with frequencies such that the least frequent of them occurs with a frequency exceeding that due to mutation alone. Certain selective advantages and disadvantages of the ABO genes in human populations are known. Thus stomach cancers are more frequent among individuals of group A than they are in the population at large. Again, duodenal ulcers are almost 40% more common among persons of blood group O than in individuals of the other ABO groups.

Both on a global and on a local scale, the ABO genes display marked racial variation. Within Britain A varies from 31 to 53%, increasing in frequency from North to South; O varies from 38 to 54%, increasing in frequency from South to North. B shows less variation, though it is most prevalent in the Celtic areas. The regional fluctuations are not random but systematic and statistically highly significant despite the enormous migration within Britain during the last few hundred years, which might well have masked or minimised the underlying variability.

Globally the ABO variation is also striking. Thus the percentage of the blood group B exceeds 30 among the Mongoloids of Central and East Asia, but the B gene is virtually absent in the Australian Aborigines, the American Indians and in the Basques. Many Amerindian tribes are 100% O; some others have very high A frequencies.

The Rhesus blood group system is more complicated and involves a number of closely linked genes. One pair of genes in this series determines whether an individual is rhesus positive, Rh + (DD or Dd), or rhesus negative, Rh − (dd). The system is important in pregnancy, since if a mother is Rh − and her baby Rh +, any blood of the baby which crosses into the mother's blood stream can lead her to synthesise anti-Rh + antibody. This will then cross the placenta and cause the baby's blood to haemolise; a condition known as erythroblastos foetalis and often fatal. First pregnancies are rarely affected, but subsequent ones often are, though in the last decade effective treatment has been discovered. Prior to this there was strong natural selection against the Dd heterozygote which should lead to the least frequent of the two genes in a population being eliminated. Nevertheless, many populations are polymorphic for these rhesus characteristics. In many parts of North West Europe and Africa the Rh − frequency is around 15%, and among the Basques it rises towards 40%. It is absent, however, from Amerindians, Australian Aborigines and most Eastern Asians.

An examination of the occurrence of the M and N genes of the MNS blood group system shows that most populations have an M frequency of 0·5-0·6. However, a higher frequency is found among North East Asia; while N is higher in Australian Aborigines, New Guineans and Melanesians. In fact, there is a gradient of gene frequency known as a cline, around the Pacific. On the other hand, the S-linked gene is very rare among the aboriginal people of Australia, but it occurs at a frequency of some 20% in the native population of New Guinea.

Anthropologically the Diego system is of special interest, because it indicates affinity between Amerindian populations and the peoples of Eastern Asia. Other blood group systems include Kell, Duffy, Kidd, Lutheran, P, Xg: the last of these being a sex-linked character.

HAEMOGLOBIN

Haemoglobin, the red respiratory pigment of the red blood cell, exists in alternative forms in man, and these are genetically controlled. The frequencies of some of the genes which control haemoglobins vary markedly among human populations. The principal technique used to show variant haemoglobins is electrophoresis—the movement of charged particles in an electric field.

Normal human haemoglobin comprises two different haemoglobins, A and A2. An interesting variant of A is haemoglobin S. This may be indicated by electrophoresis and also by a sickling test. Red cells containing haemoglobin S placed in an oxygen-free atmosphere assume sickle shapes. It should be noted that major advances have recently been made in the treatment of sickle-cell disease which give ground for much increased optimism. Some abnormal haemoglobins including S, E and C have high frequencies and their existence, since all of them are deleterious to some extent, provides opportunities for viewing the action of natural selection and gene flow in human populations. Haemoglobin S reaches very high frequencies among some populations in southern Asia and particularly in much of tropical Africa (10-40%), despite its severe effect on individual viability and fertility. Haemoglobin C is most prevalent in northern Ghana and contiguous areas, while Haemoglobin E is found principally in South East Asia, with frequencies as high as 27% in Cambodia.

Homozygous SS individuals may well live to transmit the S gene, but without a compensatory effect the gene would be totally lost except for certain cases possibly occurring as mutations. Compensation is through positive selection in favour of AS individuals who are more resistant to and so protected from falciparum malaria. Again AS females might be more fertile than AA females in certain populations, and this again would help to maintain the high S frequencies.

In addition to the genes which affect the chemical structure of the protein chains in haemoglobin, there are others which determine the rate of synthesis of those chains. These are the so-called thalassemia genes, and some of them also reach polymorphic proportions despite disadvantage in the homozygous state. Cooley's anaemia, which is common in certain Mediterranean countries, is an example. It would appear that this variation is also due to malaria; in Sardinia Cooley's anaemia is confined to lowland villages and does not occur in the mountains, where anopheline mosquitoes cannot breed.

OTHER SEROLOGICAL ATTRIBUTES

In addition to the blood groups and haemoglobin examples, many other polymorphisms are now known from human blood, and all of these show variation between populations as well as within them. In the serum of the blood are found the haptoglobins (proteins that bind the haemoglobin of old and broken-down red blood cells), transferrins (proteins in the blood sera used in transporting iron within the body) and the Gm groups (inherited variety within the structure of antibody molecules). The white blood cells carry the HLa antigens, so important in tissue and organ transplantation, and within the red blood cells a large number of genetically determined differences in enzyme structure have been discovered; examples include phosphoglumutase, adenylate kinase, acid phosphatase and glucose-6-phosphate dehydrogenase (which is particularly interesting, since it is a sex-linked character which, like the haemoglobins, appears to be important in resistance to malaria).

The extent of this variety is remarkable. It is now estimated that the average individual is heterozygous at 16% of his genetic loci (i.e., sites of the genes). Taking the very conservative estimate that there are only 50,000 genes in man (a gene for this purpose being defined as a segment of DNA coding for a protein), this means that on average 8,000 gene loci carry different genes. With this level of variety the probability of two individuals being genetically alike, apart from identical twins, is astronomically low.

Analysing the causes for this incredible genetic variety is one of the central problems in anthropological genetics today. The factors which can determine the frequency of genes in populations are mutation, natural selection, movement and gene flow, genetic drift and founder effects. Further, differences between populations will only arise if they are to some extent geographically or socio-culturally isolated from each other. Gene mutation is a point change in the DNA code, and it constitutes the most fundamental factor acting upon gene frequencies. The mutation rate, or the rate of this alteration in the basic chemical structure of the gene, is evidently the same in all human populations. Whether or not a new gene remains in the population after its initial appearance depends upon the action of other evolutionary agencies. Thus, for example, natural selection, which is any environmental force that promotes the reproduction of certain members of the population who carry certain genes, at the expense of all the other members. Natural selection favours those genes which place their possessors at a reproductive advantage and tend to eliminate those genes that place the individual at an initial or long-term disadvantage. An example as simple as the amount of melanin present in the skin is entirely appropriate. High melanin concentrations inhibit the natural production of vitamin D by irradiation, and thus brings about vitamin D deficiency rickets and subsequent pelvic disproportions which may adversely interfere with pregnancy and a normal delivery.

Without doubt many of the characteristics used to identify groups of people or races have come into being through the forces of natural selection. A population whose members have shared the same gene pool for many generations and who are all descendants of a common ancestry has more than likely occupied the same geographical area and has thus responded to the same environment for a long period of time. If the environment has changed over the generations it may be assumed that natural selection has been at work, retaining some mutations, eliminating others and in any event changing the gene frequencies. Thus many genes now in the pool of a particular population were established through natural selection many generations ago. Unfavourable genes in an individual cannot be modified or corrected, and it is unlikely, especially if their effects are major, that they will be transmitted to the next generation. Rather, carriers of these inbuilt genetic errors will have a lower probability of reproducing than those without them, so that the next generation will have a higher proportion of individuals without that an even higher proportion and so on. Population survival depending on genetic adaptation can only be effected through differential reproduction of genetically different individuals over the course of a number of generations.

The physical constitution of a population can also be influenced by gene flow which occurs when genes are transferred from one population to another. The carriers of these genes may arrive in great numbers and inundate the previously existing gene pool. On the other hand, the rate of genetic transfer may be slow but persistent over a protracted period. It is very unlikely that any human population ever remains totally genetically isolated over many generations despite geographical and/or socio-cultural barriers.

Recently there has been a striking increase in mobility, almost worldwide. Movement is the great homogenising force in evolution, for although it increases the variety within populations, it decreases the differences between populations. And the bicycle as well as the motor car and aeroplane can be shown to have had an effect. Racial and social barriers are also breaking down; in Brazil, for example, almost half the genes in the so-called Black group are of European origin, and in American Blacks the proportion is nearly a quarter.

Unless mutation, natural selection and gene flow are operating on a population, the gene frequencies within it will remain unchanged through successive generations, at least in large populations. On small populations, on the other hand— the situation prevailing during most of man's evolution—the genetic state of affairs is quite different, since the changes of gene frequencies may have nothing to do with selective advantages and disadvantages. In such populations the gene frequencies may oscillate due to random factors, such as the greater fertility, by chance, of one or two females, or disasters killing many men from one kin group, and the like. Similarly, only a small and unrepresentative sample of people may be involved in the founding of a new population. When this happens the genetic difference is said to have arisen from "founder effect". In this context it is necessary to refer to the effective size of a population, that is, the percentage of the total population actually carrying out reproduction. In any human population many individuals are either too old or too young to be involved in reproduction, and many who are of the appropriate biological and cultural age may not be reproducing. It has, for instance, been estimated that about 60% of the population of the U.S.A. will reproduce the entire next generation. In hunter-gatherer and simple agricultural societies the effective population is frequently below 100, and drift can produce marked changes in gene frequency in a single generation. Whether or not it does act, however, depends also on whether the genetic alternatives affect the probabilities of survival and reproduction, i.e., whether there is any natural selection. There is much debate at the moment on the extent to which neutral genes occur.

HUMAN ECOLOGY

While the main concerns of physical anthropologists are still the unravelling of the course of human evolution and explaining the patterns of present-day hereditary variation, recently, considerable attention has also been devoted to analysing the nature of all the interactions between man and his environment, whether they are genetically determined or not. This is broadly the field of human ecology and is as much concerned with the effects of the environment of man in industrial societies as in traditional societies. Much has been established of the ways human beings adapt physiologically to heat, cold, altitude; react to noise, pollution, crowding and stress; meet their nutritional requirements with different economies; and cope, culturally as well as biologically, with disease and other hazards in their environments. Even without his unique cultural and technical skills the human organism is remarkably adaptable; man's heat tolerance, for example, exceeding that of most tropical mammals, perhaps because for much of his evolution he was a tropical daylight hunter. But there is evidence that some of the diseases that appear to be increasingly common in modern industrial societies may be due to the fact that the environment has changed too much and too rapidly from that which prevailed throughout most of human existence. The flight/fight stress hormone response, for example, so adaptive in the context of a hunter-gatherer lifestyle, is probably contributing considerably to the increase in coronary heart disease in the sedentary urban man.

Human ecologists have also approached the problem of how whole communities interact with their environment. A study of energy flow through a Quechua Indian community in the Andes revealed that it was most economical to have large numbers of children. They could tend the flocks of animals, on which the community primarily depends for its food, as well as adults, but expended less energy in undertaking these tasks. Analysing the economy of energy, care and reproduction, risk and change is likely to be one of the major interests of future physical anthropologists.

THE STUDY OF SOCIAL ANTHROPOLOGY

What the Subject is About

Social anthropology is concerned with the way men live as members of ordered societies. It has been described as a branch of sociology, or as the sociology of the simpler peoples. Neither description is wholly correct. A social anthropologist seeks to identify the *structure* of the society he studies and the *processes* of social interaction within it. His method is direct contact—what has been called "participant observation." Therefore he must deal with a unit small enough to be manageable with this technique. Nation-states, such as sociologists commonly work among, are too large. Most social anthropologists have done their work in what we call "small-scale" societies; that is, peoples who lacked such media of communication as writing or money, let alone mechanical means of transport, until these were brought to them from Europe. A social anthropologist may choose to work in some section of a society that possesses those techniques—in the ancient countries of the East or in Europe or America. In that case he confines himself to a microcosm such as a village or a factory. When he is writing of societies alien to his own and that of most of his readers he is obliged to describe their *culture* as well as their social relationships, since without such a description his readers would not be able to picture, or even understand, the social rules that are his main subject of study; this would be superfluous for a sociologist taking modern machine society for granted. Culture has been called the raw material out of which the anthropologist makes his analysis of social structure. It is the sum total of standardised ways of behaving, of lore and technique, of belief and symbolism, characteristic of any given society. The founders of social anthropology as now practised in Britain were B. Malinowski and A. R. Radcliffe-Brown.

The Notion of Roles

All the world, as Shakespeare said, is a stage, and this is a key metaphor for social anthropologists. Every individual does indeed play many parts, not consecutively but all together; for every social relationship carries with it the expectation of society that the parties to it will behave in approved ways. Father and children, ruler and subject, buyer and seller, husband and wife; every one of these words is the name of a *role* to be played by the person it describes. The playing of roles involves the recognition of claims and obligations as well as appropriate modes of behaviour in personal contacts. All these rules are called *norms*; when they are concerned with rights and obligations they are *jural norms*. A social norm is what people think ought to happen; unlike a statistical norm, it may or may not be what happens in the majority of cases.

Kinship and Marriage

In societies of simple technology most roles are *ascribed*; that is, the parts people will play in life are given them at birth by the fact of their parentage and of the group of which this makes them members. In other words, the most important principle of organisation is *kinship*. W. H. R. Rivers called this "the social recognition of biological ties." The ties in question can be called genealogical; they all derive from the recognition of common ancestry. Such ties may be fictitious, as when a child is adopted. But in the vast majority of cases the relationships that are recognised are actually biological.

No man can recognise for social purposes all the individuals with whom he has a common ancestor somewhere in the past, or even know of their existence; their number increases with every generation. In every society a selection is made, from the whole universe of genealogically related persons, of certain categories towards which an individual recognises specific obligations and on whom he can make specific claims. Such *corporate groups* of kin have a permanent existence; they recruit new members in each generation in accordance with recognised rules. Kin groups are concerned largely with the transmission of property, and for this and other purposes they recognise the common authority of a senior man; they are also religious groups, performing together rituals directed to their common ancestors.

The common patrimony of a kin group normally consists in land or livestock; in societies of more advanced technology it may be a boat, as in Hong Kong, or even, as in Japan, a family business. It may have non-material resources too, such as the right to supply chiefs or priests for the society as a whole; this may be put conversely as the right to hold political or religious office. Those who share a common patrimony have a common interest in preserving and increasing it. Wrongs done by their members to outsiders are compensated from their collective resources, and they have joint responsibility for seeking compensation if one of their own members is injured, particularly in the case of homicide.

Descent

Kin groups may be recruited according to a number of principles. A principle widely followed in small-scale societies is that of *unilineal descent*; that is, group membership is derived from one parent only, either the father (*patrilineal* or *agnatic*) or the mother (*matrilineal*). Property is *administered* by men in either system, but in the matrilineal system it is *inherited* from the mother; hence its control passes from a man to the sons of his sisters. In a unilineal system every individual recognises kin linked to him through the parent from whom he does not trace his descent; this is the principle of *complementary filiation*. The complementary kin are *matrilateral* where the descent rule is patrilineal, *patrilateral* where it is matrilineal. A unilineal descent group is called a *lineage*.

Descent can also be traced *cognatically*; that is, all descendants of a common ancestral pair may be recognised as forming one *kindred*. In such a system there is no permanent group patrimony; people inherit a share of the property of both their parents, and this is often conferred upon them when they marry, while their parents are still living. Or all the inhabitants of a village may share rights in its rice-fields or fishing ponds; a man chooses among what kin he will live, but he can have rights in one village only. In such a system there are no continuing groups defined by descent; the permanent group is territorial, consisting of the inhabitants of the village.

Marriage

Kinship status is defined by legitimate birth, and this in its turn by legal marriage. There are always rules against marriage with specified categories of kin, though these are not necessarily near kin. Some societies consider that the ideal marriage is that between the children of a brother and a sister; if such marriages are repeated through the generations they create a permanent link between two lineages. Marriage between members of the same lineage is nearly always forbidden; this is expressed in the term *lineage exogamy*. The general effect of the prohibitions is to spread widely through a society the links created by marriage, links that impose an obligation of friendship on groups that without them would be mutually hostile.

In a matrilineal system women bear children for their own lineage; it is expected that they should be fathered by a man who has married their mother according to the approval procedure, but a child's lineage membership is not affected by the marriage of its mother. But in a patrilineal society wives must be brought from outside to bear children for the group. Associated with this fact is the payment of *bridewealth*, which used to be mistakenly interpreted as the purchase of wives. This payment is what fixes the status of a woman's children; all those she bears while the bridewealth is with her lineage are reckoned as the children of the man on whose behalf it was paid, even if he is dead and she is living with another partner. In a matrilineal society the making of gifts is part of the marriage procedure, but they are of slight economic value in comparison with bridewealth. The difference is correlated with the difference in what the husband acquires by the marriage; in both cases he gains the right to his wife's domestic services and sexual fidelity, but where bridewealth is paid he can also count her children as his descendants and call on their labour when he needs it.

In societies where most roles are ascribed by the fact of birth, marriage is the most important field in which there is freedom of choice. But the choice is commonly exercised not by the couple but by their lineage seniors, who are more concerned with alliances between lineages than with the personal feelings of the pair. *Polygamy*, or the simultaneous marriage of a man to more than one woman, is permitted in lineage-based societies; indeed it is the ideal, though only a minority of men attain it. One reason why it is valued is that it enables a man who has the resources necessary for successive bridewealth payments to build up a network of alliances.

Authority Systems

Every society has some arrangements for the maintenance of order, in the sense that force may be used against those who infringe legitimate rights. In every society theft, adultery, and homicide are treated as offences. Where no individual has authority to punish these on behalf of the community, *self-help* is the approved course. Lineage membership is significant here; a man who is wronged will go with his kin to seek redress (for a theft or adultery) or vengeance (for the homicide of a kinsman). Vengeance can be bought off by the payment of compensation; but because the taking of life is a serious matter in the most turbulent of societies, there must also be a solemn reconciliation, with a sacrifice to the ancestral spirits, between the lineages of killer and victim. The recognition of an appropriate method of dealing with injuries has been described as "the rule of law" in its simplest form.

Within a lineage the senior man is expected to settle quarrels, and the ancestral spirits are believed to punish with sickness juniors who do not listen to him. When quarrels break out between members of different lineages, their elders may meet and seek a solution. Where there is no hereditary authority individuals may attain positions of leadership in virtue of their powers of mediation by persuasion.

In addition to the maintenance of rights, most societies require at some time arrangements for the organisation of collective activities. It is possible for there to be no ascribed role of organ-

iser; in such a case leadership is a matter of competition. Competitive leadership in economic activities is characteristic particularly of the very small societies of New Guinea. What is needed here is not only powers of persuasion but resources to reward the participants. The very important principle, to be discussed later, that every gift ought at some time to be returned, is the basis of their position. A man who can put others in his debt can call upon their labour. It may take a long time to build up the necessary resources for acknowledged leadership, and leadership may be lost to a rival and is not necessarily passed to an heir.

Responsibility both for law and order and for collective activities may be shared on recognised principles among the whole adult male population. This is done where society is organised on the basis of *age*, a system widely found in east and west Africa. In such a system all adult men pass through a series of stages at each of which appropriate tasks are allotted to them. In its simplest form the division is made into "warriors" and "elders". This principle may be complicated in various ways, but the essence of it is that men in their prime are responsible for activities requiring physical strength, impetuosity, and courage, while their elders have the task of mediating in disputes, discussing public affairs, and performing sacrifices to the ancestors. Men in the warrior grade are the fighting force, and may also have the police functions of summoning disputants and witnesses before the elders, and seizing property from a man who has been adjudged to pay compensation and does not do so voluntarily. Sometimes specific public works are allotted to them, such as rounding up stray cattle or clearing weeds from paths or springs. It is also possible for community responsibilities to be shared in more complicated ways, as for example among the Yakö of Nigeria, where the adherents of particular religious cults are believed to call on the spirit which they worship to punish persons guilty of particular offences.

Where there are hereditary chiefs, both public works and the maintenance of law and order are the responsibility of the chief and his subordinate officials. Resources are accumulated for public purposes by the collection of tribute, and labour is obtained for public works by the recognition of the principle that persons in authority can claim the labour of those subject to them. Expectations are attached to the role of chief as to any other. Chiefs are expected to dispense justice fairly, to be generous to the poor, to reward loyalty, and to be successful in war, and they are reminded of these expectations in the course of the elaborate rituals performed at their accession. The prosperity of the whole land is commonly held to be bound up with the health of the chief and the favourable attitude towards him of supernatural beings. He may be obliged to obey all kinds of ritual restrictions to this end; for example it was believed of the ruler of Ruanda, in east Africa, that he must not bend his knee lest the country be conquered. Chiefs are either themselves responsible for the performance of ritual on behalf of the whole populace or must maintain priests to do this.

Social anthropologists have recently turned their attention to the process of competition for the commanding roles which any society offers. Some would claim to have discarded the idea of structure altogether in favour of that of process; yet the structure must be taken into account as the set of rules in accordance with which the game is played. There are societies where it is the rule that on the death of a chief his sons must fight for the succession, to test who is the strongest and has the largest following. There are others where the rule of succession may seem to be clear, and yet there can always be dispute as to who fits it best. Sometimes people pursue the struggle for power by accusing their rivals of witchcraft; sometimes by massing their followers behind them in a show of strength before which their adversaries retire; the first is the method of the Ndembu in western Zambia, the second that of the Pathans in the Swat Valley in Pakistan. Such confrontations occur at moments of crisis, but the process of building up support is going on all the time. The study of these processes is among the most interesting new developments in social anthropology.

Economic Systems

The typical methods of subsistence in societies of simple technology are food-gathering (hunting and collecting roots and berries), herding, and agriculture. The domestication of animals and plants came relatively late in man's history; without it there could have been no permanent settlement, no cities, no civilisation. But the life of those food-gatherers who still exist is not a hard one; they can get an adequate diet in a very short working week. The three modes of subsistence should not be thought of as forming a historical series; moreover, there are many varieties of each, depending on the nature of the environment and the techniques used.

We shall never know what brought about the "agricultural revolution" or why the greater number of our ancestors chose the harder, but more productive, life of cultivators. This may have been somehow made necessary by the pressure of population in certain areas. Nor shall we know when and how trade and exchange began. We can reject the argument of Adam Smith that people first provided themselves with enough to eat and then began to exchange the products of specialists for surplus food. Exchanges are made among and between peoples who suffer from periodic famines, and the objects which are most valued are not exchanged for food.

These exchanges are not conducted, however, through the medium of a currency which enables people to calculate the relative value of goods of different kinds, as does money in a commercial society. Certain goods can be exchanged only for certain others—in the highlands of New Guinea, for example, shells and the plumes of rare birds. This has led to much controversy on the question whether primitive peoples can be said to have money. Of course, if money is defined as a universal medium of exchange, they do not. But some modern anthropologists find that too strict a definition, and prefer to say that, whereas modern currencies are "general-purpose money," societies of simple technology have different kinds of "special-purpose money"—strings of shells, hoe-blades, iron bars and the like, which are used only in a limited range of transactions.

It is certainly true, however, that money of this kind cannot be made the means of very exact calculations of profit and loss. It is often assumed that where there is no such common medium of exchange people do not make any economic calculations, and dispose of their property in ways that are the reverse of business-like. The principal reason why this assumption is made is the great importance attached to the making of gifts. The essential difference between a gift and a commercial exchange is that no return is stipulated. In the commercial world goods are sold, services hired, at a price, and anyone who fails to pay has broken a contract and is liable to be punished. The obligation to return a gift is a moral one. Moreover, to compete in the giving of gifts seems at first sight the very opposite of competition in the acquisition of wealth. But in most societies people who have a surplus of wealth like to have a reputation for generosity; only in the affluent world of machine production people feel the need to have many more material possessions before they begin to think in terms of surplus.

The exchange of gifts plays a particularly large part in the societies of Melanesia, where men form partnerships for the express purpose of giving and receiving valuable objects, and earn prestige at least as much by giving as by receiving. This exchange of valuables, mostly shell ornaments, is so important that it has a name in the language of each society. The first such exchange system to be described by an anthropologist was the *kula* of the Trobriand Islands, observed by Malinowski. An important man had a partner in an island on either side of his own home; from one he received armbands and returned necklaces, from the other he received necklaces and returned armbands. These objects did not become part of a store of wealth for any man; nobody could hold one long before it was time to pass it on to his partner. To receive his gift a man sailed by canoe to his partner's home; he was there welcomed peaceably, and while he was making his formal visit the crew were bartering their goods on the shore with the local populace. Thus the *kula* partnership had the nature of a political alliance; it was a means of maintaining peaceful relations between populations which would otherwise have been hostile.

In the highland area of New Guinea identical objects are exchanged, so that the relative value of amounts given and received can be calculated. In some parts the ideal is that a return gift should be twice the original one. Naturally it is no small achievement to carry on a prolonged series of exchanges at such a rate. Very few men manage it, and those who do are the acknowledged leaders of their community. For each large gift he has made a man wears a little bamboo stick hung round his neck; thus his munificence is publicly proclaimed. A new partnership is initiated by making the minimum gift. Men make these partnerships with others not bound to them by kinship, notably with their relatives by marriage. Each partnership extends the range within which a man can count on friendly treatment. So widespread is the idea that gifts should be repaid, and services rewarded, after some delay, and at the discretion of the man making the return, that where the highland people have taken to growing coffee for sale, the large-scale planters do not pay wages but employ young men for planting who get their return by coming to them later for help in difficulties. Of course the young men would stop giving their work if they judged that the return was not adequate.

Gift-giving, then, is an investment, but not one that produces a direct material return. One anthropologist, R. F. Salisbury, has called it an investment in power. The second classic example of the uneconomic use of goods is the *potlatch* practised by the Kwakiutl and kindred tribes of the northwest coast of America. This was a public distribution of goods at which the recipients had to be given their gifts in strict order of rank. The giver earned prestige and power by the scale of his gifts, by his knowledge of the correct rank order, and by the famous deeds (*potlatches* and others) which he was able to claim as feats of himself and his ancestors. Rivals for precedence would assert their claim by vying with each other in the amounts they distributed. The Kwakiutl way of avenging an insult was what has been called the "rivalry gesture." The man who thought he had been insulted actually destroyed valuable property by throwing it on a fire, or into the sea, and his enemy had to match him in destruction or be humiliated.

Certainly this is not turning resources to material advantage. No more is the giving of a very expensive dinner-party in London or New York. But equally certainly, it is not done without calculation. In the affluent society people display their superior affluence because this demonstrates their prestige rating, just as in the *potlatch*; and they keep on good terms, through the hospitality they offer, with people from whom they may later seek a return in professional dealings, rather as in the Melanesian gift-exchanges. In fact a substantial proportion of the incomes of people in European societies who are by no means affluent goes into the making of gifts—to parents, to kin, to friends, to persons who have helped one or given one hospitality; gifts which are given as a matter of moral obligation. The difference between the uses to which resources are put in societies of simple and of complex technology is one only of degree. The proportion that is devoted to securing non-material advantages is higher in the small-scale societies, and so is the proportion of gift-giving to commercial exchange. In gift-giving there is no bargaining, but there is a clear expectation of return. The initiation of new social relationships by the making of gifts is not by any means confined to New Guinea. Bride-wealth which legitimises children is the most widespread example. Pastoral peoples in East Africa also make gifts of stock to selected friends in distant parts. The friend on his home ground is a sponsor for his partner, and he is expected to make return gifts from time to time, and may be asked for a beast if his partner is in difficulties. One could think of such an arrangement as a type of insurance.

A small number of social anthropologists have

specialised in the study of the economic systems of small-scale societies, and have asked whether the concepts devised for the analysis of monetary economies—such notions, for example, as capital and credit—can be applied to people who gain their livelihood directly from the resources of their immediate environment. Starting from the assumption that there is always some choice in the allocation of resources, they have observed how these choices are actually made in the societies where they have worked. They have asked how the value of such goods as are obtained by barter is measured; how labour is obtained, how directed and how rewarded for such enterprises as the building of a canoe or a temple, which call for the co-operation of large numbers. They have examined the use of media of exchange, asking how far any of these fulfil the functions that we associate with money.

The general conclusion of these studies is that peoples of simple technology are perfectly capable of rational calculation in the allocation of their resources, even though their calculations are rough by comparison with those of the entrepreneur in an industrial society. They know what to regard as an adequate return when they are bartering goods. They withhold goods from consumption when they are planning an enterprise; that is to say, a man who proposes to initiate such an activity as canoe-building, arranges to be able to feed his labour force.

Religion

At a time when people questioned whether "primitive" societies could be said to have religion, E. B. Tylor offered as a "minimum" definition of religion "the belief in spiritual beings." All societies of simple technology have such beliefs, and think that unseen personalised beings influence the course of nature by direct intervention, causing rain to fall if they are pleased with the actions of men and withholding it if they are angry, sending sickness as a punishment and so forth. In the great majority of such societies the most important spirits to be worshipped are those of dead ancestors. But there may also be a belief in gods responsible for particular aspects of the world, to whom offerings are made for protection or success in their special fields. Many preliterate peoples believe in a "high god" from whom all other spirits derive their power, and one school of anthropology sees this as evidence of an original state of higher religious consciousness from which man has declined; but this view is not widely held.

Rituals involving groups of people are commonly performed on occasions when changes of status are to be signalised. A child becomes a member of society not by being born, but at a naming or showing ceremony. A youth or girl becomes adult at initiation. Marriage, which makes a couple into potential parents and links their kin groups, is another such ritual.

In funerary rites the dead person is made into an ancestor, and his heir adopts his social personality and his responsibilities. The accession of a man to political office is surrounded by ritual, and chiefs frequently observe annual rites at the time of harvest, when it is the season, not the person, that is changing. These are *confirmatory* rituals, designed to keep society and the world on an even course. When something goes wrong, a drought or epidemic or an individual sickness, *piacular* rituals are performed to make peace with the spirits responsible for the disaster.

An essential aspect of many of these religions is the belief in witchcraft—that is that it is possible for humans to harm others merely by hating them. Witchcraft supplies an explanation of an undeserved misfortune. Diviners employ a multitude of techniques (which anthropologists rather inaccurately call oracles) to detect whether a disaster is a merited punishment or is due to witchcraft.

Every small-scale society has its myths—stories which tell how the word as people know it came to be. Sometimes their ritual re-enacts the myth; often the myth tells how the ritual was first performed and thereby gives a reason for its continuance. Then there are myths telling how death and evil came into the world. Some myths lend authority to the existing social order, and

particularly to the claims of ruling groups, by telling how the social structure was divinely ordained. Under the influence of the French anthropologist Lévi-Strauss, many anthropologists are beginning to see both myths and the symbolism of ritual as man's earliest attempt to order intellectually the world of his experience.

The existence of ultra-human beings on whom the affairs of men depended was universally taken for granted until a very short time ago. As long as this belief was held, the established order in any society was supported by the tenets of religion. But there are also revolutionary religions. In recent years anthropologists have been inspired by the many new religions that have arisen in developing territories to give more attention to this side of the subject. Notably in Melanesia, a succession of prophets have appeared with a message announcing the imminent coming of an ideal world from which all hardships would be banished, including the subjection of the indigenous peoples to colonial rulers. These events turned the attention of anthropologists, along with sociologists and historians, to the study of similar movements in the past, and we now have a considerable body of literature on such subjects as "the religions of the oppressed."

Closer study of traditional religions from this point of view has shown that they also often include symbolic reversals as part of their regular ritual. The high are brought low and the humble exalted. In his ritual installation a chief may be beaten and abused by his subjects, or a rite that confirms his authority may include a simulated rebellion. Women may assume for a day the garb and authority of men. There is a temporary suspension of the rules and cultural forms which differentiate the members of the ritual congregation. This may go as far as "ritual licence", in which actions that at other times are offences liable to punishment, notably sexual promiscuity, are permitted and must not be made a reason for quarrels. Or it may be simply that the participants are masked, stripped naked, or dressed identically. Such rituals affirm their common membership, or communitas, as it has been called, and where they express not merely unity and equality, but the reversal of high and low, they remind the powerful that they must not abuse their power. Rites of this kind form a phase in complex rituals. They are followed by a re-affirmation of the accepted order in its ideal form, where hierarchical relations maintain order without promoting injustice. This theory would interpret the new "subversive" religions as the response to situations in which the injustices of the powerful have gone too far for the re-assertion of communitas to be possible.

Social Change

No doubt all the societies that anthropologists have studied have been gradually changing throughout the centuries when their history was not recorded. But they experienced nothing like the rapidity of the changes that came to them when they were brought under the rule of European nations and introduced to mass production and a money economy. The effect of this has been in essence to widen the range of choice in the relationships that people can form. A man may choose to be dependent on an employer rather than on work in co-operation with his kin or village mates. He is more likely to rise in the world by going to school and getting a city job than by earning the respect of the villagers or the approval of a chief. Small-scale societies are now becoming merged in larger ones and the close ties of the isolated village are loosened. In the newly created industrial areas new specialised associations are formed to pursue professional and other interests. The social insurance that kinship provided is lacking, and it has not as yet been replaced by what the state offers in the highly industrialised societies. The minority that has whole-heartedly adopted the values of the industrialised world now produces the political rulers of new states. They are impatient to carry the majority along the same road, but there are profound conflicts of value between them and the still largely illiterate masses.

The first studies of this type of social change

were mainly interested in the effects of intrusive influence on traditional institutions in rural areas. Later, attention was turned to social relationships in the cities which have come into being, or greatly increased in size and population, as a result of the development of commerce and industry. Recent work is largely concerned with the extent to which immigrants to the cities preserve their sense of a distinctive home origin. Immigrant populations which have abandoned all their traditional customs often preserve a strong sense of a common identity which differentiates them from their neighbours, and sometimes they even create a myth of the possession of "special customs" that has no foundation in fact. This sense of a particularly close relationship between people from the same place of origin is called *ethnicity*. It has been argued that when the members of an *ethnic group* are in a privileged position they appeal to the sense of ethnicity to close the ranks against outsiders. The less fortunate might be more likely to unite on a non-ethnic basis to improve their position. Divisions based on ethnicity cut across those based on social class. This is a field in which the interests of social anthropologists and sociologists overlap. The conclusions drawn from studies in African cities could be, and no doubt will be, tested against work among immigrant populations in Europe and America.

Recent Trends in Social Anthropology

Structural Anthropology, as it has been developed in France by Lévi-Strauss, has the aim of establishing the universal characteristics of cultural, that is rule-governed, human behaviour, as opposed to the natural, instinctive behaviour of non-human species. Lévi-Strauss finds the distinguishing feature of man in communication by symbols, and holds that the way in which symbols are constructed reflects the structure of the human brain. As he uses the term social structure, it means the system of symbols by which a given society comprehends the world of its experience.

According to Lévi-Strauss communication is an exchange, and for him all exchange is communication. The prohibition of incest, which represents to him man's first move from natural to cultural life, obliges men to exchange their sisters, giving them to other men as wives. Then they exchange goods for goods or services. But for Lévi-Strauss the most important exchange is that of messages, and his central interest is in the codes in which the messages are embodied. Every code is an arbitrary set of symbols, the meaning of which depends on the way in which they are related. A code is based on a logical structure, so that social structure is the structure of a socially accepted code. It should be noted that the existence of the structure is not demonstrated independently of the code, but deduced from it, while the nature of the code is deduced from the supposed nature of the structure.

For the principles of structure Lévi-Strauss turns to the linguists, notably Roman Jakobson, according to whom all speech-sounds can be analysed into pairs of opposites; it is by recognising these opposites that children learn to speak and to distinguish meaning. Lévi-Strauss argues that the structure of the human brain leads men to classify the objects of their experience into opposites, then finding mediating terms to link the opposites. The recognition of differences is in his view the basis of classification, more important than the recognition of similarities. In totemism, a phenomenon which many anthropologists have tried to explain, awareness of differences between social groups is expressed by associating them with different animals. Exogamous descent groups, the groups which exchange sisters, are commonly called by the names of animal species. Each group has its totem animal, and they often believe that they must not eat this animal. The rules attached to these animal names form a code which can be decoded as: "We, Elephants, are different from them, Lions", not because either group is *like* elephants or lions, but because the groups differ as species differ. Any contrasting species would do; there is no intrinsic relation between Elephants and elephants just as there is

none between the sounds of a word and its meaning. Totemism, then, is an arbitrary code to express the principles on which a society is organised.

Lévi-Strauss' most massive work is devoted to the interpretation of myth. In his view the material of myth comes from the unconscious. He has made an extensive study of the myths of Amerindian peoples, and has found that stories in which the incidents are superficially dissimilar lead to the same conclusion (convey the same message), and on the way deal with oppositions (or contradictions) between rules or necessary facts of life and human wishes. The episodes of myths are the symbols of the code, and they can be combined in many different ways, but always according to an underlying, unconscious logic (structure). To explain this logic he draws comparisons with music and with mathematics. A musical note has no meaning in itself, only as an element in a melody or a chord. A musical composition plays with modifications or transformations of themes or harmonies, and just as a theme can be transposed into a different key, so a message can be conveyed in images that may refer to the objects of all the different senses; sight (light and darkness), taste (cooking—the first volume of his great book on myths is called *The Raw and the Cooked*), hearing (noise and silence) and so on. Note that all these codes are concerned with contrasts. From mathematics Lévi-Strauss takes the idea of a system of algebraic signs which can be combined in many permutations. Ultimately the theory of myth tells us that the important socially prescribed relations between persons of different status can be represented as relations between animal species, between kinds of food, between kinds of sound and silence, smells and tastes, aspects of landscape or any of these in combination.

According to Lévi-Strauss, although the deep structure of thought is unconscious, the classification of observed phenomena is conscious, and is the first activity of the human mind. Hence he rejects the view that peoples of simple technology are interested in natural phenomena only in so far as these have practical uses.

Cognitive Anthropology was first taken up as a special field in America, where its pioneers were Ward Goodenough, Charles E. Frake and Harold Conklin. It has much in common with the structuralism of Lévi-Strauss, but its practitioners are not interested in myths, and the majority make less extensive claims than he does. Some of them do believe that studies of the way in which different peoples classify the objects of their experience should lead to the discovery of universal cognitive principles, but they do not seek to reduce all categories to binary oppositions; rather they talk of *contrast sets*.

Studies in cognitive anthropology began with the examination of kinship terms by the method known as *componential analysis*. Instead of asking what relatives are grouped together under a designation found in English kinship, such as "father" or "brother", cognitive anthropologists looked for the essential *components* of any kin term, and found these to be sex, generation, and lineal or non-lineal relationship to the speaker or the person referred to by the term. This method was considered to give a truer picture of the principles according to which people group their relatives.

Cognitive anthropology has also been directed to other *domains* of experience, that is fields to which a distinguishable vocabulary is observed to apply; for example, to the classification of colours or of disease, but most of all to that of flora and fauna, or folk taxonomy, as this is called. These studies elucidate not only the principles according to which people group and distinguish the objects of their environment but also the factual knowledge they have of them.

Marxist anthropology has developed along with a general revival of interest in Marxist theory largely inspired by the new interpretation of Marxism introduced by the French writer Louis Althusser, not himself an anthropologist. The leading anthropological theorist in this field is Maurice Godelier, also in France. Like Lévi-Strauss, Marxists look for the unperceived structural laws on which all society rests, but they look in another direction. They find their answer in the *relations of production*, that is in the manner in which production is organised, and in particular the distribution of the resources which make production possible. They apply to the study of pre-capitalist societies the analysis which Marx himself made of capitalism, and seek to place the primitive and peasant societies of today, and also some vanished societies of which there are records, in their place in a line of developing social formations, each a transformation of its predecessor. Thus Marxist anthropology is in a sense an historical study, and can be contrasted with functional analysis in which societies are taken as they are when the observer sees them and treated, as Malinowski put it, as "going concerns". A functionalist study asks what keeps a society going; hence Marxists regard such studies as essentially conservative.

For Marxists a *social formation* is a combination of the forces of production and the relations of production. The forces of production consist in labour power and technical knowledge, and in the way production is organised. The relations of production are the relations between those who control the means of production—land or machines —and those who supply their labour power. Those who control the means of production are able to determine what share of the product shall go to the workers, and invariably they take more than a fair share. The state exists to practise this *extraction of surplus value*, as it is technically called. Accepted religious beliefs and other systems of ideas are not, as Lévi-Strauss and the cognitive anthrpologists would have it, attempts to organise experience; they are delusions which conceal from the workers the way in which they are exploited. One social formation gives way to another when its *internal contradictions*—conflicts, incompatibilities—become too acute to be contained within the existing system. All aspects of a society are linked to the relations of production. Hence Marxist anthropologists do not admit the validity of cross-cultural comparisons between different institutions, such as kinship, economics, politics or religion, and argue that only social formations can be compared.

Thus they have given much more attention than earlier anthropologists to societies of hunters and gatherers, where nobody is dependent on others for the weapons that are the sole means of production. As soon as the means of production are appropriated by one section of society, the opposition of classes is observed. This change took place in the Neolithic period, when the invention of agriculture led to the recognition of rights in land. Even in those systems in which land is regarded as the common property of a group, the senior man or men who control its use are in a position to exploit juniors, so that there are class divisions among kinsmen. It is also sometimes argued that where people believe that specialists in magic can influence the weather, or promote the growth of crops as the Trobriand magicians observed by Malinowski do, their knowledge is indispensable to production, and so they, too, make the workers dependent on them and can exploit them.

Marxist anthropologists make use of the ethnographic work of Malinowski and his pupils, who looked, as Malinowski had taught them, for the importance of reciprocity in exchange. Lévi-Strauss also discusses this in his theory of the exchange of women as the basis of kinship systems. But Marxists are concerned with inequalities rather than reciprocities in exchange, inequalities that those who own the means of production can impose. Thus they would not agree with Malinowski's followers, that there is any reciprocity in a state between rulers and ruled, that subjects pay tribute and rulers make their return both by maintaining order and in direct economic terms by the redistribution of wealth.

The study of **ecology** combines the work of anthropologists with that of human geographers and many natural scientists. It is associated with the name of the American anthropologist Julian Steward. Ecologists study the relations between society, technology and environment. They differ from the biologists who invented the term "ecology" in that they examine man's modification of his environment as well as his adaptation to it. Early ecological work concentrated on food-gathering populations who modify their environment very little, but it was soon extended to societies of pastoralists and cultivators.

Ecological studies have practical implications in various directions. They throw light on the success or failure of policies that are intended to raise standards of living, for example by persuading or compelling nomad pastoralists to become settled cultivators. A type of enforced change which has become widespread is the resettlement of populations whose homes have been flooded by the damming of rivers for hydro-electric projects; here the alteration in the environment is sudden and dramatic, quite unlike the effects of the unplanned changes of the past. It is usually accompanied by attempts to create a new environment that will make higher standards of living available, through housing schemes, new educational facilities, the introduction of new crops or farming methods, and so on. The proliferation of such schemes has been said to provide the anthropologist with a "laboratory situation" in which both policies and reactions can be compared. By combining ecological with medical studies it is possible to consider the prevalence of malnutrition or parasitic diseases in relation not only to the non-human environment but also to social groupings and norms which render certain populations, and particular categories within such populations, more vulnerable than others to these health hazards.

Another meeting-ground between anthropology and the natural sciences is in the new interest of sociologists in **ethology**, the study of the evolution of social behaviour. The classical exponents of this study have been Tinbergen in Holland and Lorenz in Austria. Close observation of the interaction between individuals and groups among non-human species has led many ethologists to conclude that animal populations may appropriately be regarded as societies. They hope to learn what tendencies among humans are genetically determined and so may not be amenable to deliberate attempts at social change. A subdivision of this study, human ethology, concentrates on minute details of behaviour with the aim of identifying gestures, facial expressions and the like that are found in all cultures, and so may be supposed to spring from affective systems common to all humanity. Yet a narrower subdivision is child ethology. Some anthropologists believe that these studies offer the key to the question What is Man? What are the characteristics that distinguish him from other animals, and how in fact did natural selection enable him to develop them?

These studies are still in their infancy, and in their present state they are vulnerable to some dangers. It is difficult, perhaps impossible, to use in the description of behaviour language which does not assume that what is described is social, the very question that the ethologists are asking. The assumption may be made unconsciously, but if it is consciously recognised it is possible to guard against it. The language used may also lead to the attribution to non-human animals of reactions that are specifically human (*anthropomorphism*). Zoologists may too readily assume that all human behaviour can be reduced to those reactions which are transmitted in our evolutionary heredity, forgetting that the processes of social conditioning are much more elaborate in man than in other animals. Anthropologists on their side may be too ready to seek the kind of interpretation of non-human behaviour that supports their *a priori* idea of the nature of man, *e.g.*, whether he is essentially aggressive or pacific, competitive or co-operative.

DEVELOPMENT ANTHROPOLOGY

Introduction

The word development became a technical term in colonial administration with the implementation in the British territories of the Colonial

Development and Welfare Act of 1940. With the passing of this measure Britain abandoned the principle that colonial territories should be self-supporting, and made available from British revenues grants for projects expected to improve the standard of living of the local populations. "Welfare" implied the expansion of social services: "development" was investment calculated to increase productivity. After the Second World War a similar policy was introduced in France, and as former colonial territories became independent the United States and the United Nations also contributed funds for their development; the United Nations proclaimed a "development decade" in 1960. The motives behind these policies were various; governments sought to extend their political influence, their trading relations and opportunities for their nationals, but a humanitarian element was also present. The development of resources had always been the aim of colonial powers, but now the emphasis was on the development of peoples.

The Problems of Development

In a sense anthropologists have been interested in problems of development from the time when, under the influence of Malinowski, British anthropologists turned from the reconstruction of the past to what he called "the anthropology of the changing African". African was taken as the type because it was the International African Institute, supported by large American grants, which supplied the bulk of the funds made available for research in anthropology in the period between the two world wars. Malinowski's pupils observed the effects that European penetration had had on African and other populations, and tended to concentrate on those which had been adverse. For a time they deplored economic development altogether, but they came to realise that the changes introduced by colonial rule were irreversible. They also had to recognise the fact that Western science and technology could and should be used for the benefit of non-Western peoples, particularly to raise standards of health and nutrition. Their attention was now focused on small-scale innovations with these aims, such as had of course always been attempted under colonial rule. The "community development" projects which had some vogue in West Africa in the period just before independence aimed at making much improvements through the efforts of the people expected to benefit from them, with some assistance from governments. Independent India adopted a community development policy which involved the division of the whole country into development areas under officials of the central government. Since the improvements sought were of a kind that any anthropologist would approve, it now became our task to explain the indifference or resistance which they so often encountered. Some also looked critically at the explanations in terms of "peasant conservatism" that were offered by people who were interested in development but not versed in anthropological theory.

The Awareness of Poverty

The interest in development which was manifested after the Second World War arose from a new awareness of the poverty of many millions of people in those newly independent countries that began to be called "under-developed", and later from the recognition that population was increasing faster than natural resources. These poorer countries were contrasted with the highly industrialised ones, which were assumed to be "developed", and it was further assumed that their problem was simply that too little capital had been invested in industry. Hence external finance was offered for development programmes which aimed at rapid industrialisation, and the next assumption made was that this would increase national productivity, as it often did, and thus would automatically raise standards of living. It proved, however, to do little to alleviate the poverty of the peasant majorities of the populations concerned.

Food Production

Attention then turned to the possibility of increasing food production and peasant incomes along with it, by introducing more efficient methods of farming. Since most anthropologists have worked among rural populations, it is here that they might be expected to have something to contribute, and that their advice has in fact sometimes been sought. An anthropologist may, for example, be appointed as a member of a UN development team; or a private company may engage one as consultant, as was done when copper was discovered on the island of Bougainville and the inhabitants were not satisfied with the compensation they were offered for the expropriation of their land. Sometimes one has been asked to comment on an elaborate multiple project such as the damming of a river for a hydro-electric scheme and the resettlement of the people whose homes would be flooded, and has been able to indicate situations that would have to be taken into account and persuade the planners to work to a slower timetable.

But more often anthropologists have come to the scene after a plan has been carried through, and have been able to see the various ways in which the results have differed from what was expected, and sometimes reasons why it has failed altogether—if, for example, a farm project does not attract or hold settlers.

The Colson–Scudder Survey

A well-known example of a study which was begun before the change that was planned and continued after it, is that made by Elizabeth Colson and the ecologist Thayer Scudder of the 56,000 Gwembe Tonga who were moved from their homes when the Kariba Dam was built on the Zambezi River. They made a detailed study of the Gwembe social organisation and adaptation to the environment in their traditional homes, and returned when the move was still a recent drama in most people's lives, and at intervals in later years. Their final study contrasted the adaptation to the move made by two village communities whose home environments had been very different and who had been moved to new sites only a few miles apart.

In their study of the resettlement process they called attention to the hardships that had been caused by requirements of technicians which were allowed to override consideration for human values. The height of the dam was raised after the preparations for resettlement had begun, so that the area to which many people had agreed to move was flooded and they had to be sent elsewhere. Those who had furthest to go had to be moved *en bloc* in a single day because the Public Works Department could only release the number of lorries needed for one day. New sites were not provided with water in time for the move, as had been promised.

This list of grievances illustrates both a failure to co-ordinate the activities of different technical departments of government and a lack of imaginative sympathy. But it also indicates that the agents of change must work within the limits of their technical resources. It would have been quite impracticable in this case, for example, for Public Works to transport several thousand people over 100 miles by a shuttle service, picking up families or even whole villages as and when they were ready to move. After all, the Kariba Dam had not been conceived as an operation to benefit the Gwembe Tonga. Anyone who is convinced that a project must go through can argue that the people who are affected will settle down after a temporary upset; and in a sense they do, as they come to take their new circumstances for granted.

Nevertheless, if those in authority think it important not to impose unnecessary hardships on those who are subject to their decisions, this detailed account of an exercise which is likely to be repeated in some form where dams are built, populations moved from disaster areas, refugees settled and so on, is a record to which they can look to see what mistakes they might avoid.

The Weinrich Study

A comparable study is that made by Dr. A. H. K. Weinrich (Sister Mary Aquina) of the African response to the various policies pursued by the government of Rhodesia (before independence) with the aim of improving African farming. Certain areas of land were earmarked for purchase by Africans who were required to show that they were efficient farmers. Others were irrigated and offered on lease to farmers who had to follow a closely controlled programme of work. The largest proportion of the area of land allotted to African occupation was "tribal trust land", where, after an attempt to enforce fixed standards of cultivation, the authorities fell back on the educational work of missionaries and extension officers. Dr. Weinrich investigated communities holding land in each of these three ways, and concluded that no great improvement in cultivation could be observed in any, except in the case of a minority of men and women who had followed courses of training to qualify as "master farmers". Her own conclusions were drastic: that *all* rights to agricultural land, including those of Europeans, should be conditional on efficient cultivation, and that every African cultivator should be held individually responsible for a specified area of land. Much more attention should be given to the education of peasant farmers in place of attempts at coercion, and farming communities should be given a say in the management of their own affairs. At the time when her findings were published, Zimbabwe had not achieved independence but whatever the type of government, it will have to deal with the problems that she has analysed.

These two examples are of action taken in territories where policy was dominated by European settler interests. Few such territories remain today, and it is the professed aim of the rulers of all the new states to seek the welfare of the indigenous populations. In such a context an anthropologist could be in a stronger position. If his views were asked in advance, he might be able to say that an apparently beneficial scheme would not really be so; or that it would need to overcome specific difficulties arising from existing power structures or modes of co-operation; or that the benefits would be lost if they were not accompanied by technical instruction (for instance, in the control of irrigated water supplies or the maintenance of pumps).

A difficulty in organising co-operation between anthropologists and development agents lies in the different time-scales with which they work. An anthropologist does not expect to speak with confidence about the people he studies until he has worked with them for at least a year. No doubt a development plan takes a year to complete, but once it has been adopted it is expected to be put into operation as soon as possible. Time-tables are drawn up, and even if deadlines are seldom met, there must be an attempt to meet them. In any event, decisions have to be taken at the moment when problems arise. Occasionally an anthropologist has actually been put in charge of a small-scale project and has had to face this dilemma.

Some would say, then, that the studies made after the event to explain failure or disappointment form the most valuable contribution of social anthropology; they are there as warnings or lessons for future planners, provided the planners will read them—but this is a risky assumption. Others would say that development agents should learn the elements of social anthropology as part of their training, and if they did, "village level" or "rural development" workers would certainly be more sensitive to the reception of their activities by villagers.

Intermediate Technology

Where there are the best prospects for fruitful co-operation is in the introduction of small-scale improvements such as are sometimes called "intermediate technology". Such improvements can sometimes be made by people who have made no academic study of anthropology at all, if they have enough local knowledge. It was an anthropologist working with a WHO team who pointed out that apparently simple additions to children's diet were far beyond the means of urban workers in Jakarta, but it was a doctor in India who discovered how to make existing food sources far more nutritious.

A field that anthropologists are only now beginning to enter is that of the traditional contribution of women to the farm and household economy. The exhortations and demonstrations of agronomists have commonly been directed to men, and men have been persuaded—sometimes—that methods involving harder work will bring in higher returns; it is not often noticed that the women may be doing the harder work while the men get the price of the crop. A move is now being made to train women for anthropological fieldwork among their own compatriots. They will have the general knowledge of social structure that must be the basis of any research, but they will concentrate their attention on women and on those aspects of co-operation in the household that have generally been taken for granted in the past. What are the chores that occupy a woman's day and how could they be lightened by the adoption of simple labour-saving devices? What are their ideas on the health and feeding of children and on the treatment, or recourse for aid, in sickness? How much independence of decision do they have, and in what contexts? One outcome of these studies is expected to be a fuller understanding of women's attitudes towards child-bearing and their receptiveness or resistance to the idea of family planning which is now beginning to be considered so urgently important in heavily populated countries.

The Anthropology of Development

A distinction has been drawn between "development anthropology", that is anthropology in the service of development and "the anthropology of development", or the study of interactions between all persons concerned in development, those who intend to bring benefits as well as the supposed beneficiaries. Studies of the latter type would depart from that focus on the reaction of intended beneficiaries which has been the main interest of anthropologists up to now, and would examine not only the motives of development planners but the interactions between the representatives of different interests engaged in planning. In the two African examples cited here, the benefit of the peasant cultivators was not the primary aim; the Kariba Dam was intended to provide electric power for industry, the various Rhodesian land policies, as Dr. Weinrich repeatedly emphasises, to enable an African population to subsist within limits set by the interests of a European one. Other plans are forced on governments by one crisis or another. But in addition, closer analysis would show how the competing interests of different technical agencies may influence the content of any development scheme and will certainly influence the allocation of resources within it. Governments are not the only empire-builders; divisions within them also seek to extend their power, and every expert thinks the most important benefits are those that depend on his own expertise (anthropologists are no exception). The most effective study of this kind that has been made is the work not of an anthropologist but of a political scientist, Robert Chambers, who followed in detail the history of the Mwea land settlement that was initiated in Kenya just before independence. He, however, was not solely interested in description as opposed to prescription; he travelled through Africa looking at settlement schemes, and concluded that the most important prerequisite for success was to keep government provision to the minimum and rely on self-help. But, brilliant as his analysis of the planning process is, it does not tell anyone how to plan better. It just throws light on human weakness and suggests the impossibility of making a perfect plan. A good many anthropologists would hope to offer more, even if they had to confine themselves to limited aspects of a plan.

VI. SPECIAL TOPICS

MEASURES, UNITS AND METROLOGY

Before any quantity can be measured one must decide on the *units* used for measurement. For example, a 2 lb loaf of bread when weighed in ounces will give 32, *i.e.* 2 × 16. This is because there are 16 oz in a pound. It would be incorrect to say the weight of the loaf is 2 or 32. We say it is 2 lb or 32 oz and we can convert from one unit to another by knowing the ratio of their sizes.

If a standard pound is kept somewhere this can be used to calibrate other standard weights using accurate scales. These in turn can be used to calibrate other weights which in turn can be compared with the loaf with scales in order to weigh the bread. Nowadays, for scientific purposes, weights are compared with that of the *international prototype kilogram* (**L70**), kept at Sèvres in France. For a long time the length of an object was obtained by making a comparison, direct or indirect, with the standard metre if using the metric system or the standard yard if using the Imperial system. The standard metre was the length between two notches on a metal rod, kept at a controlled temperature, at Sèvres. Time is measured in seconds, which at one time was defined as a certain fraction of the tropical year.

Definitions of this kind are unsatisfactory for two reasons. First, the tropical year is not constant and even the most carefully kept metal rods are liable to change their dimensions over a long period of time. Secondly, it is not always convenient to do a comparison with an object kept in France. Nowadays every effort is made to define units in terms of some fundamental property of matter which is reproducible everywhere and does not require comparison with one particular object. The second is now defined using an atomic clock and can be measured to an accuracy of 1 part in 10^{12}. Variations in the rotation of the earth are far greater than this. The metre is nowadays defined in terms of the distance light travels in one second (**L82**). Although the kilogram could likewise be defined in terms of some fundamental quantity of matter, such as insisting the mass of an electron is 9.1083×10^{-31} kilogram, this quantity is only known to about 2 parts in 10^{6}. Comparisons with the standard kilogram can lead to an accuracy of the order 10^{-9}, so at present this definition of the kilogram stands.

The scientist nowadays mainly uses the S.I. system of units. SI is short for "Système International d'Unités" and it is a system of metric units now coming into international use through the agency of such bodies as the General Conference of

the International Bureau of Weights and Measures and the International Organisation for Standardisation (ISO) in whose work Britain participates. Information about SI units is available in booklets published by the British Standards Institution, Sales Branch, 101–113 Pentonville Road, London, N.1.

Definitions of the Base Units

The system uses the seven *base quantities* listed below:

Quantity	Name of unit	Symbol of unit
Length	metre	m
Mass	kilogram	kg
Time	second	s
Electric current	ampere	A
Thermodynamic temperature	kelvin	K
Luminous intensity	candela	cd
Amount of substance	mole	mol

The seven S.I. base units are defined as follows:

The *metre* is the length travelled by light in a vacuum in 1/299 792 458 sec (**L82**).

The *kilogram* is the mass of the international prototype of the kilogram (**L70**). Scientists use the word "mass" where the layman would say "weight". Strictly speaking, weight is not a base quantity and is a measure of *force*.

The *second* is the duration of 9 192 631 770 periods of the radiation corresponding to the transition between the two hyperfine levels of the ground state of the caesium-133 atom (see **Clock L26**).

The *ampère* is that constant current which, if maintained in two straight parallel conductors of infinite length, of negligible circular cross-section, and placed 1 metre apart in vacuum, would produce between these conductors a force equal to 2×10^{-7} newton per metre of length.

The *Kelvin*, unit of thermodynamic temperature, is 1/273·16 of the thermodynamic temperature of the triple point of water (*see* **Absolute Temperature L3**).

The *Candela* is the luminous intensity, in the perpendicular direction, of a surface of 1/600 000 square metre of a black body at the temperature of freezing plantinum under a pressure of 101 325 newtons per square metre. Luminous intensity is a property of a *source* and is the amount of luminous flux (light) it throws out per steradian.

TABLE I

quantity	Name of SI unit	Symbol	SI unit in terms of base units or derived units
frequency	hertz	Hz	$1\ \text{Hz} = 1\ \text{s}^{-1}$
volume	stere	st	$1\ \text{st} = 1\ \text{m}^{3}$
density	kilogram per cubic metre		kg m^{-3}
velocity	metre per second		m s^{-1}
force	newton	N	$1\ \text{N} = 1\ \text{kg m s}^{-2}$
pressure, stress	pascal	Pa	$1\ \text{Pa} = 1\ \text{N m}^{-2}$
viscosity (dynamic)	pascal second		Pa s
work, energy, quantity of heat	joule	J	$1\ \text{J} = 1\ \text{N m}$
power	watt	W	$1\ \text{W} = 1\ \text{J s}^{-1}$
quantity of electricity	coulomb	C	$1\ \text{C} = 1\ \text{A s}$
electric potential, EMF	volt	V	$1\ \text{V} = 1\ \text{W A}^{-1}$
electric field	volt per metre		V m^{-1}
electric capacitance	farad	F	$1\ \text{F} = 1\ \text{C V}^{-1}$
electric resistance	ohm	Ω	$1\ \Omega = 1\ \text{V A}^{-1}$
electric conductance	siemens	S	$1\ \text{S} = 1\ \Omega^{-1}$
magnetic flux	weber	Wb	$1\ \text{Wb} = 1\ \text{V s}^{-1}$
magnetic flux density	tesla	T	$1\ \text{T} = 1\ \text{Wb m}^{-2}$
inductance	henry	H	$1\ \text{H} = 1\ \text{V s A}^{-1}$
magnetic field	ampère per metre		A m^{-1}
luminous flux	lumen	lm	$1\ \text{lm} = 1\ \text{cd sr}$
luminance	candela per square metre		cd m^{-2}
illuminance	lux	lx	$1\ \text{lx} = 1\ \text{lm m}^{-2}$
heat flux density, irradiance	watt per square metre		W m^{-2}
heat capacity	joule per kelvin		J K^{-1}
specific heat capacity	joule per kelvin per kilogram		$\text{J kg}^{-1}\ \text{K}^{-1}$
thermal conductivity	watt per metre per kelvin		$\text{W m}^{-1}\ \text{K}^{-1}$

The *mole* is the amount of substance of a system which contains as many elementary entities as there are atoms in 0·012 kilogram of carbon 12. Since this number is approximately 6·022 17 × 10²³ a mole of hydrogen molecules, for example, is approximately this number of hydrogen molecules.

In addition to the base units, two SI *supplementary units* are listed below:

Quantity	Name of unit	Symbol of unit
Plane angle	radian	rad
Solid angle	steradian	sr

They are defined as follows:

The *radian* is the plane angle between two radii of a circle which cut off on the circumference an arc equal in length to the radius.

The *steradian* is the solid angle which, having its vertex in the centre of a sphere, cuts off an area of the surface of the sphere equal to that of a square with sides of length equal to the radius of the sphere.

Derived Units

Most quantities that occur in nature are *derived quantities* and are measured in *derived units*. Speed is a derived quantity which can be measured in metres/sec, so that the units of speed involve the definition of two base units, *i.e.* metres and seconds. It is said that speed has the dimensions of [length]/[time], also written $[L][T]^{-1}$, since the metre is a measure of length and the second is a measure of time. In any equation in science the dimensions of both sides must always be the same and this is often a useful check of whether the equation is correct. If a mile = 1609·3 metre and an hour = 3600 sec, one mile/hr = 1609·3/3600 m s⁻¹. Conversions between any unit and any other unit which measures the same quantity can be similarly obtained.

Table I gives a list of some important derived quantities that occur in nature and in the fourth column the SI unit that is used to measure it. Some of these derived units have a name (usually that of a famous scientist) and a symbol which are given in the second and third columns. Thus for example, the SI unit of force is a kilogram metre sec⁻², but this unit is also given the name of a newton. A force of 5 kg m s⁻² is 5 newton, which is sometimes written "5N".

Multiples and Fractions of Units

Within the SI system there are special prefixes for forming multiples and sub-multiples of its units.

Factor by which the unit is multiplied	Prefix	Symbol
10¹²	tera	T
10⁹	giga	G
10⁶	mega	M
10³	kilo	k
10²	hecto	h
10	deca	da
10⁻¹	deci	d
10⁻²	centi	c
10⁻³	milli	m
10⁻⁶	micro	μ
10⁻⁹	nano	n
10⁻¹²	pico	p
10⁻¹⁵	femto	f
10⁻¹⁸	atto	a

Examples: one thousandth of a metre is one millimetre (1 mm); one million volts is one megavolt (1 MV). These prefixes are *recommended* but other multiples and sub-multiples will be used when convenient, *e.g.*, the centimetre (cm), the cubic decimetre (dm³).

The following is a selection of special points to note:

(i) The name litre now means 1 cubic decimetre or 10⁻³m³ and is a measure of volume.

(ii) Days, hours, and minutes are still used to measure time, though some scientists may prefer to use kiloseconds, etc.

(iii) The SI unit of plane angle is the radian (rad), but degrees, minutes and seconds are still used as well. $1° = \frac{\pi}{180}$rad.; 1 rad = 57·295 78° = 57° 7′ 44·81″

(iv) A Celsius temperature, say 15 degrees, is written 15°C; note that 15C would mean 15 coulombs.

The Imperial System of Units

The SI system is not the only system of units in use today, although it is the one most favoured by scientists. The Imperial system is widely used in the U.K. and other English speaking countries and some Imperial weights and measures are given below:

Length.

1 nail	= 2¼ in	
1 link	= 7·92 in	
12 in	= 1 ft	
3 ft	= 1 yd	
22 yd	= 1 chain	
10 chains	= 1 furlong	
8 furlongs	= 1 mile = 1760 yd = 5280 ft

Area.

$$1210 \text{ yd}^2 = 1 \text{ rood}$$
$$4 \text{ roods} = 1 \text{ acre} = 4840 \text{ yd}^2$$
$$640 \text{ acres} = 1 \text{ mile}^2$$

Volume.

$$1728 \text{ in}^3 = 1 \text{ ft}^3$$
$$27 \text{ ft}^3 = 1 \text{ yd}^3$$

Capacity.

4 gills	= 1 pint
2 pints	= 1 quart
4 quarts	= 1 gallon
2 gallons	= 1 peck
4 pecks	= 1 bushel
8 bushels	= 1 quarter
36 bushels	= 1 chaldron

The gallon, as the capacity standard, is based upon the pound.

$$1 \text{ gal} = 277·274 \text{ in}^3$$

Weight (Avoirdupois).
(System used in commerce)

1 dram	= 27·343 75 grains
16 drams	= 1 oz = 437·5 grains
16 oz	= 1 lb = 7000 grains
14 lb	= 1 stone
28 lb	= 1 quarter
4 quarters	= 1 cwt = 112 lb
20 cwt	= ton = 2240 lb

Troy Weight.

1 pennyweight	= 24 grains
480 grains	= 1 ounce

The only unit of troy weight which is legal for use in trade in Britain is the ounce Troy, and weighings of precious metal are made in multiples and decimals of this unit.

The term *carat* is not a unit of weight for precious metals, but is used to denote the quality of gold plate, etc., and is a figure indicating the number of 24ths of pure gold in the alloy, *e.g.*, a 9 carat gold ring consists of nine parts of pure gold and fifteen parts of base metals.

Nautical Measures.

1 nautical mile = 6080 ft = 1853·18 m
1 knot = 1 nautical mile per hour = 1·151 mile/h

Note.—In future the international nautical mile of 1852 m will be used.

Note.—The British Pharmaceutical Code and the

British National Formulary—the official works of medicinal reference—no longer contain the apothecaries' units of measurement since medicine is now measured in metric units. Prescriptions are in 5 millilitre (*ml*) units; medicine bottles are in six sizes from 50 to 500 m*l*.

Selected Conversions between Units

Length

1 inch	= 2·54 cm
1 foot	= 30·48 cm
1 yard	= 0·9144 m
1 mile	= 1609·344 m
1 fathom	= 6 feet
1 nautical mile	= 1852 m
1 fermi	= 1 fm (femtometre)
1 X unit	= 0·1002 pm (pico-metre)
1 angstrom	= 100 pm
1 micron	= 1 μ m
1 astronomical unit	= 149·6 Gm
1 light year	= 9460·70 Tm
1 parsec	= 30,857 Tm
	= 3·26 light years

For Angstrom, Light year, Parsec, Astronomical Unit *see* **Section L**.

Area.

1 hectare (ha)	= 10⁴ m² = 2·471 acre
1 acre	= 0·404686 ha
1 acre	= 4840 yd² which is approximately 70 yards square
1 mile²	= 258·999 ha = 2·58999 km²
1 barn	= 10⁻²⁸m² (measure of nuclear cross-section)

Volume.

1 litre (l)	= 0·001 m³
1 gallon UK	= 4·546 092 l
1 gallon UK is the volume of 10 lb water at 62 ° F	
1 pint	= 0·568 l which is approximately 4/7 l
1 gallon US	= 0·8327 gallon UK

Mass and Weight

1 oz	= 28·35 kg
1 lb	= 0·453 592 37 kg
1 cwt	= 50·80 kg
1 ton	= 2240 lb = 1016 kg = 1·016 tonne
1 tonne	= 1000 kg

Angle

	degree	*minute*	*second*	*radian*	*revolution*
1 degree	= 1	60	3600	1·745 × 10⁻²	2·778 × 10⁻³
1 minute	= 1·667 × 10⁻²	1	60	2·909 × 10⁻⁴	4·630 × 10⁻⁵
1 second	= 2·778 × 10⁻⁴	1·667 × 10⁻²	1	4·848 × 10⁻⁶	7·716 × 10⁻⁷
1 radian	= 57·30	3438	2·063 × 10⁵	1	0·1592
1 revolution	= 360	2·16 × 10⁴	1·296 × 10⁶	6·283	1

1 rt angle = 90°   1 grade = 0·01 rt angle

Time

	second	*minute*	*hour*	*solar day*	*year*
1 second	= 1	1·667 × 10⁻²	2·778 × 10⁻⁴	1·157 × 10⁻⁵	3·169 × 10⁻⁸
1 minute	= 60	1	1·667 × 10⁻²	6·944 × 10⁻⁴	1·901 × 10⁻⁶
1 hour	= 3600	60	1	4·167 × 10⁻²	1·141 × 10⁻⁴
1 solar day	= 86400	1440	24	1	2·738 × 10⁻³
1 year	= 3·156 × 10⁷	525,900	8766	365·24	1

Force

	newton	*dyne*	*poundal*	*kg force*	*pound force*
1 newton	= 1	10⁵	7·233	0·1020	0·2248
1 dyne	= 10⁻⁵	1	7·233 × 10⁻⁵	1·020 × 10⁻⁶	2·248 × 10⁻⁶
1 poundal	= 0·1383	13830	1	0·01410	0·03108
1 kg force	= 9·807	980700	70·93	1	2·205
1 lb force	= 4·448	4·448 × 10⁵	32·17	0·4536	1

Energy, Work, Heat

	joule	*kW . hr*	*ft lb*	*calory*	*B.t.u*
1 joule	= 1	2·778 × 10⁻⁷	0·7376	0·2389	9·478 × 10⁻⁴
1 kW. hr	= 3·600 × 10⁶	1	2·655 × 10⁶	8·598 × 10⁵	3412
1 ft lb	= 1·356	3·766 × 10⁻⁷	1	0·3238	1·285 × 10⁻³
1 calory	= 4·187	1·163 × 10⁻⁶	3·088	1	3·968 × 10⁻³
1 B.t.u.	= 1055	2·931 × 10⁻⁴	778·2	252	1

1 kW. hr (kilowatt hour) is 1 unit (Board of Trade unit) as measured by the electricity meter.
1 B.t.u. is a British thermal unit and is the amount of heat required to raise the temperature of 1 lb of water by 1° Fahrenheit.
1 Therm is 100 000 B.t.u. and is equivalent to the heat generated by 29·3 units of electricity.
1 calory is the heat required to raise the temperature of 1 gm of water by 1° C. The calory as used by weightwatchers is actually 1000 calories as defined above.
1 erg is 10⁻⁷ joule.
1 electron volt (eV) is 1·6 × 10⁻¹⁹ joule.

Pressure

		pascal	millibar	atmosphere	torr	lb/sq in
1 pascal	= 1		0·01	$9·869 \times 10^{-6}$	$7·501 \times 10^{-3}$	$1·450 \times 10^{-4}$
1 millibar	= 100		1	$9·869 \times 10^{-4}$	0·7501	0·01450
1 atmosphere	= 101 300		1013	1	760	14·7
1 torr	= 133·3		1·333	$1·316 \times 10^{-3}$	1	0·01934
1 lb/sq in	= 6895		68·95	0·06805	51·72	1

1 pascal = 1 newton/sq metre = 10 dyne/sq cm
1 torr is the pressure due to 1 mm of mercury.
By atmosphere is meant "standard atmosphere" which is 760 mm or 29·92 inches of mercury.

Temperature

The Celsius scale is the same as the Centigrade scale. To convert from degrees Fahrenheit (°F) to degrees Celsius (°C), subtract 32 from the temperature in Fahrenheit and multiply by 5/9. To convert from Celsius to Fahrenheit multiply the temperature in Celsius by 9/5 and add 32. Applying this rule we obtain:

0° C = 32° F	20° C = 68° F
5° C = 41° F	25° C = 77° F
10° C = 50° F	30° C = 86° F
15° C = 59° F	35° C = 95° F

37° C (normal body temperature) is 98·6 ° F, − 40° C = − 40° F.

The absolute zero temperature (lowest possible temperature) is − 273·15° C.
To convert from ° C to degrees Kelvin (° K) add 273·15 to the temperature in Celsius so that the absolute zero is 0° K.
To obtain the temperature according to the Rankine scale add 459·69 to the temperature in Fahrenheit. 0° Rankine is the absolute zero.

The c.g.s System in Electromagnetism

The centimetre gram second (c.g.s.) system of units is favoured by some scientists (notably theoretical physicists). There are in fact two sets of c.g.s. units: electrostatic units (e.s.u.) and electromagnetic units (e.m.u.). Electrostatic units are sometimes given the prefix *stat* and electromagnetic units sometimes given the prefix *ab*. Thus voltage can be measured in statvolts (e.s.u.) or abvolts (e.m.u.) as well as in volts (S.I.).

These two systems do not normally treat charge or current as base quantities as the S.I. system does but as derived quantities. In the electrostatic system the unit of electric charge, the statcoulomb is defined so that one statcoulomb of charge placed at a distance of 1 cm from another statcoulomb of electric charge in a vacuum repels it with a force of 1 dyne. In the electromagnetic system the abampere is such that if two parallel wires in a vacuum 1 cm apart both carry a current of 1 abampere the force between them is 2 dynes per cm length of wire. Also the force between two magnetic poles of unit strength one centimetre apart in a vacuum is one dyne. These two systems usually treat permittivity and permeability as dimensionless quantities, unlike the S.I. system.

In the table below $c = 2·997 925 \times 10^{10}$ and is the speed of light in cm s⁻¹.
The symbol "$\simeq$" means "is approximately equal to".
Thus $c \simeq 3 \times 10^{10}$ cm s⁻¹.

Quantity	S.I. Unit		e.m.u.	e.s.u.
Current	ampere	A	1 abampere = 10A	1 statampere = 1 abamp/c
				1 amp $\simeq 3 \times 10^9$ statamp
Charge	coulomb	C	1 abcoulomb = 10 C	1 statcoulomb = 1 abcoulomb/c
EMF	volt	V	1 abvolt = 10^{-8} V	1 statvolt = c abvolt $\simeq$ 300 V
Capacitance	farad	F	1 abfarad = 10^9 F	1 statfarad = 1 abfarad $\times$ c⁻²
				1 F $\simeq 9 \times 10^{11}$ statfarad
Permittivity	F m⁻¹			1 e.s.u./1 S.I.U. = $10^{11}/(4\pi \, c^2)$. Since the permittivity of a vacuum in e.s.u. is 1 this is equivalent to saying the permittivity of a vacuum in S.I. units = $10^{11}/(4\pi c^2) \simeq 1/(36\pi \times 10^9$.
Magnetic field	A m⁻¹		1 oersted (e.m.u.) = $10^3/(4\pi)$ Am⁻¹	
Magnetic flux density	tesla	T	1 gauss (e.m.u.) = 10^{-4} tesla. 1 gauss is equivalent to a magnetic field of 1 oersted in a vacuum	
Magnetic flux	weber	Wb	1 maxwell (e.m.u.) = 10^{-8} Wb	
Inductance (self or mutual)	henry	H	1 abhenry = 10^{-9}H	
Permeability	H m⁻¹		1 e.m.u./1 S.I.U. = $4\pi \times 10^{-7}$. Since the permeability of a vacuum in e.m.u. is 1, this equivalent to saying the permeability of a vacuum in SI units = $4\pi \times 10^{-7}$.	

THE EVOLUTION OF THE EYE

Evolution

The origins of the eye lie far back in evolutionary time beginning with light sensitive pigments in single cell organisms probably similar to the euglenoids (simple, single-cell organisms) of today.

As single cells grouped together in organised communities this light-sensitivity became diffused over the surface of the organism and the sea urchins (*echinoderms*) retain such a characteristic. Although this type of phenomenon bears little relationship to an eye, and indeed plants are light-sensitive but could not be said to "see", it represents the first and essential step towards the development of the eye. And here we arrive at a dilemma. The eye has evolved twice in the course of evolutionary history by quite distinct processes and along different branches of the evolutionary tree. The common antecedent is a group of animals, the *coelenterates* (*e.g.* sponges, hydra) which possess light-sensitive pigmented cells. Evolution produced two major branches at this point, one of which went on to become the vertebrates (animals with backbones) and the other the invertebrates (animals without backbones). While the eyes that developed in these two groups are very similar there are nonetheless critical differences.

The evolutionary history of the invertebrate eye is readily accessible both in the fossil record and in species alive today that represent stages of the evolutionary process fixed in time. So, for example, from existing species it is possible to observe the grouping of photosensitive cells on the surface of the animal (annelid worms), the cupping of these cells to form a cupulate eye (the limpet) which then forms a deeper cup and sends nerves to a central ganglion (ear shell, Haliotis). Each of these animals represents a step up the evolutionary ladder and by the time we reach Nautilus the optic cup is almost closed and focussing is achieved by the same principle as the pin-hole camera. In fact the optic cup never fully closes, and even in the most fully developed of the invertebrate eyes (the sea-dwelling *cephalopods*) the inside of the eye is open to sea water via a small hole. At the development of a connection between the eye and the central nervous system we observe one of the important differences between the vertebrate and invertebrate eye. The retina of the invertebrates is derived from surface (ectodermal) cells whereas that of the vertebrates is an outgrowth of the brain which grows out to meet the focussing apparatus, the lens and cornea. This fact makes the phenomenon of the evolution of the vertebrate eye hard to explain. If the light-sensitive cells are derived from the brain (*i.e.* central nervous tissue) how did the vertebrate eye develop from the common ancestor possessing surface light-sensitive pigments? The fossil record is of no assistance since no intermediate step has ever been found. There appears to be not one but several "missing-links".

The Vertebrate Eye.

While the invertebrate eye continued to evolve by gradual and observable stages through to the final stage represented by the eyes of the squid and the octopus, that of the vertebrates suddenly appears, more or less fully formed, in the *proto-chordates* (distant relations of the lamprey). Because of the differences, in particular the derivation of the retina, no inferences as to the evolution of the vertebrate eye can be made from that of the invertebrate eye. Thus the dilemma remains, although theories abound. One of the more plausible of which suggests that the focussing apparatus (the cornea and lens) developed independently of the retina and that the lens is the product of the depigmentation of the early surface light-sensitive cells. The lens has, of course, lost any light-sensitivity but the pigmented iris might be the vestigial remains of the early visual apparatus. Were this to be the case it is difficult to imagine how the intermediate steps were of selective advantage and how therefore the two independent systems joined to form the complex structure of the eye. But this is true of all the theories, each one fails to describe intermediate steps that would have conferred some advantage to their possessor and therefore become adopted by the evolutionary process.

Anatomy and function

The *cornea* is situated at the front of the eye and performs most (70%) of the focussing for the eye. It is composed of three cell types; *epithelial* cells, *endothelial* cells and *keratocytes*. Its strength derives from the proteins keratin and collagen in the layer of stromal keratocytes just beneath the outer layer of epithelial cells. The cornea is covered by a tear film made up of a saline solution produced by the lacrimal gland and contributed to by the fluid transporting function of the epithelial cells, lipids produced by Meibomian glands and mucus produced by goblet cells. These latter two are situated on the inner surface of the eyelids. The cornea contains nerves but no blood vessels and must therefore rely on the endothelial and epithelial cells for a supply of oxygen and metabolites. These two layers of cells transport substances from the aqueous humour, a clear fluid filling the anterior chamber of the eye. The aqueous humour is partly a filtrate of blood and partly a secretion of the ciliary body (a tissue lying behind the iris). It is produced at a rate of 2–3mm^3 (microlitres, u1) per minute and bathes the lens, the back surface of the cornea (the endothelium) and drains through the trabecular meshwork, in the corner formed where the cornea meets the iris, into the canal of Schlemm and from there into the veins. Aqueous outflow does not quite equal inflow thus giving rise to the intraocular pressure. The average normal intraocular pressure is 16mm Hg.

The Iris

The *iris* forms the back of the anterior chamber and is a pigmented tissue in the centre of which is an aperture, the pupil. It is the iris that gives the eye its characteristic colour. Muscles in the iris contract or relax to alter the size of the pupil and in bright light the circular muscles contract, reducing the size of the pupil thus allowing through less light. Dilated pupils (large opening) make it easier to see into the eye with an ophthalmoscope and so ophthalmologists use the drug atropine to cause the radial muscles to contract (these muscles act in opposition to the circular muscles) thus enlarging the pupil. The ancient Egyptians also used atropine in this way but not for the same purpose. Cleopatra used it to enhance her beauty. Behind the iris and supported by the ciliary body is the lens. The *lens* is cellular, transparent and compressible. When the eye gazes into the distance the lens is the shape of a flattened doughnut. It is the action of the ciliary muscles around the edge of the lens that cause it to become fatter, a process known as accommodation, thus increasing its refractive power. Since the cornea performs most of the refraction, 30% is left to the lens and it is the function of the lens to accommodate to allow for close-up vision (*e.g.* reading).

The *vitreous humour* fills the large chamber behind the lens and in front of the retina. It is a gel similar in composition to the aqueous humour but with the addition of microscopic fibres (composed of protein and carbohydrate molecules). The vitreous is attached to the edge of the retina and the back of the ciliary body.

The *retina* is the tissue that converts photons of light into electrical impulses that travel along the optic nerve to the brain and allow us to see. It has nine distinct layers most of which are of neuronal origin. One curious fact is that the mammalian retina is inverted, that is, the light sensitive cells (the rods and cones) lie behind the blood supply and the electrical wiring. Thus light has to travel through these layers before being detected. The rods, so called because of their shape, are responsible for vision in low light intensity (black and white vision) whereas the cones are responsible for colour vision.

Medical Aspects of the Eye

Refractive Errors

Short sight (myopia) is the result of the eyeball being physically too long for the refractive system (the cornea and lens). Consequently, parallel rays of light from a distant object are brought to focus in front of the retina. Such people will not see distant objects in focus but will have a near point closer than the average. To correct this concave lenses are prescribed. In hypermetropia the eye is too short and parallel light rays are brought to a focus behind the retina. The refractive system of the eye is insufficient and an additional lens (concave) is required to see both near and far objects in focus.

If the surface of the cornea is not perfectly spherical a distortion of the image occurs. This is known as *astigmatism*, and cylindrical lenses are used to correct this condition.

Glaucoma

In glaucoma the *intraocular* pressure (inside the eye) rises from the normal 16mm Hg to above 24mm and can result in loss of sight if uncontrolled. The increased pressure is due to inadequate or defective drainage of the aqueous humour. It is often caused by pathological changes in the trabecular meshwork or the canal of Schlemm. The condition can be controlled by drugs which suppress the production of aqueous humour or by surgery to create a channel through the trabecular meshwork for the drainage to occur. Recent advances in surgical techniques using lasers allow the operation to be performed without opening up the eye.

Cataract

The lens is transparent and anything that results in *opacification* (*i.e.* loss of optical clarity) of the lens is referred to as cataract. This can result from many different conditions; physical injury, diabetes, steroids and old age, to give a few examples. Vision becomes blurred, particularly in bright point sources of light (for example car headlights) and eventually is lost completely. Sight can be restored only be removing the lens surgically. This is now a minor operation and in some places the operation is done on an out-patient basis.

Retinal detachment

The most common form results from a hole or a tear in the retina which allows fluid to accumulate behind the tissue. This is often caused by shrinkage of the vitreous humour which can occur with age or be associated with degenerative myopia. The earliest symptom may be flashes or twinkling lights due to mechanical stimulation of the retina as it floats or moves. As the detachment progresses the patient notices a black cloud usually starting from below and spreading towards the centre of his vision. If caught early enough retinal detachment is readily treatable by surgery. The retina is "stuck" back either by using a cryoprobe (a freezing metal probe) or a laser.

Floaters

One of the most common visual defects is the appearance of light coloured spots drifting about in the visual field, particularly noticeable when looking at the sky. These are known as vitreous floaters and are the result of degenerative changes in the vitreous humour. Fine fibrils of collagen present in the matrix of the vitreous coagulate to form particles large enough to scatter light and thereby become visible. There is nothing one should do about them unless they become progressively more numerous when they may be symptomatic of inflammation or haemorrhage of the retina.

THE EXPLORATION OF THE OUTER PLANETS

Background to the Voyager Missions

Galileo discovered Saturn's rings and Jupiter's moons in 1610, but the existence of the planet Uranus was not established until more than a century and a half later, by William Herschel in 1781. In contrast the ten year period up to the end of January 1986 saw more information gained about these three largest of our planets than had been known before. The reason was the spectacular success of the two Voyager missions which cumulated with Voyager 2's encounter with Uranus (*see* TABLE 1). Voyager 2 has become the deepest space shot to send information to earth. Its signals from Uranus, even though travelling at the speed of light, took 2 hours to traverse the 2940 million km (1840 million miles) to earth.

An important feature of these space shots has been the way each subsequent mission has built on those which have gone before in terms of the detailed programme eventually assigned to it. Pioneer 11, for example, was the first probe to penetrate the Saturnian rings, just as Pioneer 10 had shown that the asteroid belt could be safely traversed. The likelihood of Voyager 2 maintaining its ongoing flight to Uranus and Neptune was assured by the success Voyager 1 had in surveying Saturn's largest moon, Titan. This option was taken before Voyager 1 reached Saturn and takes advantage of an alignment of Saturn, Uranus and Neptune which occurs only every 175 years. At each planet the gravitational pull is used in 'sling-shot' fashion to accelerate the probe to its next destination. Voyager 2 was directed by the Uranian gravity field to Neptune with an increase in speed of about 4000 miles per hour.

Voyager 2 was launched by Titan Centaur rocket about 15 days before Voyager 1 in 1977, but on a slower trajectory, so that it became five months behind Voyager 1 at Jupiter and ten months behind at Saturn (*see* TABLE 1). Each Voyager spacecraft weighed about 1979 lb (815 kg) and is rather heavier and more sophisticated than Pioneer 11, which weighed 550 lb. Power is provided by radio-isotope generators giving several hundred watts. Each Voyager carries a variety of instruments and experiments, including, for example; an ultraviolet spectrometer, a plasma experiment, an infrared spectrometer and radiometer, a low energy charged-particle experiment, and a cosmic ray experiment as well as two TV cameras. These instruments are carried on a scanning platform attached to the main body which also had a boom extending to 40 feet, at the top of which is mounted the magentometer. Radio signals are received by a 12-foot diameter parabolic dish which always points to earth.

The missions have been amazingly trouble free, and most instruments functioned well except that Voyager 1's photopolarimeter had to be switched off. Voyager 2's radio receiver gave a little trouble and for a short time its scanning platform jammed. This success is all the more amazing since design specification was for a 5-year operation. Nevertheless Voyager 2 operated beautifully on its Uranus encounter 8½ years after its launch.

Jupiter's Magnetosphere

Jupiter has an immense magnetic field generated by the metallic liquid hydrogen in its interior which is rendered metallic by the tremendous pressure which surrounds the planet's core. This field extends for nearly ten million kilometres and is larger even than the sun itself. The field is not spherical, but is distorted into a pear shape by the solar wind which is travelling at nearly a million and a half kilometres per hour. A bow shock-wave is produced where the two meet and Voyager 1 encountered it in February 1979. The magnetosphere contains many millions of trapped high energy particles and frequently gives off bursts of cosmic rays. The Gallilean satellites are heavily bombarded by these trapped ions. The closest of Jupiter's large moons, Io, is continuously giving out charged particles. These trail behind it forming a doughnut shaped tube, or torus, around the planet. From Jupiter a huge electric current, measured at five million amperes by Voyager 1, flows up from one pole, threads around the torus, passes through Io and circles back to Jupiter's other pole.

TABLE 1. DATES FOR PIONEER 11 AND THE VOYAGERS

	Pioneer 11	Voyager 1	Voyager 2
Earth launch	April 1973	5 September 1977	20 August 1977
Jupiter encounter	December 1974	5 March 1979	9 July 1979
Saturn encounter	1 September 1979	12 November 1980	26 August 1981
Uranus encounter	—	—	24 January 1986
Neptune encounter	—	—	24 August 1989

The Jovian Surface

Jupiter is the largest of the planets, but it is a low density world mainly of hydrogen and helium gases with a core probably consisting of molten silicates and metals. Covering all this are the Jovian clouds which form distinct bands observable from Earth. Some travel eastwards and others westwards with relative velocities of up to 600 km/hr. They contain huge stationary features like the Great Red Spot which is large enough to contain two earths and which was first observed as long as three hundred years ago when it was rather larger than it is now. Near it are the relatively new white oval formations which were seen forming about forty years ago. The persistence of these Jovian features arises because of the lack of a solid Jovian surface to break them up and because the surface temperature is very low at about −120° C. The main flow patterns are rather more predictable than earth's storm clouds, but whereas earth has only the single troposphere in which water is the main agent, Jupiter has three regions which involve water, ammonia and ammonium hydrogen sulphide, respectively. Voyager 1 discovered bright auroral displays in the Jovian clouds, mainly at the poles, and also lightning flashes which can trigger chemical reactions to produce the elementary compounds from which life on earth started.

Jupiter's Ring

Each probe has made its own surprising discoveries. One of Voyager 1's was the observation of a ring around Jupiter, the presence of which was confirmed later by Voyager 2. The ring is 58,000 km above the Jovian clouds and Voyager 2's pictures, taken with backlighting of the ring by the sun, showed that it is composed of very small particles which have probably been emitted by Io's volcanoes. Jupiter's fourteenth moon was later discovered by Voyager 2 at the edge of the ring, and may have the function of stabilising the ring by gravitational effects—in the same way as postulated for Saturn's complex ring system and many moons.

Jupiter's Moons

Jupiter's main moons—Io, Europa, Ganymede and Callisto—were the first heavenly bodies to be discovered by telescope—by Gallileo in 1610. Now, the two Voyagers have revealed much of their geology and probable composition by approaching them closely (see TABLE 2).

Io gave the first major surprise when Voyager 1's pictures were analysed long after the closest approach to within 20,000 kms was over. The first extraterrestrial active volcanoes, as many as eight at once, were seen, with plumes as high as 300 km. Some plumes are sulphur-rich silicate eruptions, whereas others are thought to be sulphur dioxide gas. Io has no meteoritic craters so its surface is geologically young, having been smoothed by vulcanism and eroded by the radiation of Jupiter's magnetosphere. Sulphur particles from Io find their way out to the bow shock wave, but many are concentrated into the torus with which Io has encircled Jupiter. Io orbits twice as quickly as Europa and they pass once every forty-eight hours. The pulsating gravitational forces so exerted have combined with those of Jupiter and Ganymede to crack Io's surface and they continuously heat Io's interior like a tennis ball constantly squeezed.

If Io was Voyager's moon, Europa was Voyager 2's. Europa is probably the smoothest body in the solar system with an ice surface that is extensively lined, probably by filled in fissures. Tidal heating, as on Io, probably kept the surface relatively plastic. There are few impact craters so a relatively young surface is indicated. Ganymede, larger than the planet Mercury, was found to be slightly larger than Titan, one of Saturn's moons and previously thought to be the largest in the solar system. Ganymede has an ice crust and a mantle of water and ice over a silicate core. The surface is heavily cratered, dark in the oldest places and light in others from relatively new ice produced by meteoritic impacts. The surface has stripes of parallel ridges and valleys consistent with tectonic movements of ice plates. Callisto's surface is one of the most heavily cratered yet seen. Like Ganymede's it is an ice crust. It has not been smoothed and re-worked but is continuously battered. Jupiter's moon count was increased to 14 by the Voyagers and includes Amalthea, a small inner irregular satellite which Voyager 2 approached to within 560,000 km.

Saturn and Its Rings

Voyager 1 first entered the Saturnian magnetosphere on 11 November 1980 at a distance of 26·2 Saturn radii (R_s). It crossed it a number of times, since the magnetosphere pulsates in the solar wind, and finally left it at 22·9 R_s. The magnetosphere deflects the wind away from Titan, Saturn's largest moon, orbiting at 20·3 R_s, and protects its unique atmosphere. Saturn's magnetosphere is intermediate in size between Earth's and Jupiter's and its magnetic field is between 3 and 5 times smaller than the Jovian.

Observation of Saturn's rings, which were crossed on 12 November 1980, drastically changed our knowledge of them. Before Voyager five or six rings were known (see TABLE 3). A and B are the brightest and are easily observed from Earth; F had been discovered by Pioneer 11 in 1979 whereas D was still controversial. Voyager 1 showed that there were hundreds of rings which increasingly gave an overall appearance like a gramophone record. Very small particles of material were discovered inside ring C, as expected for the controversial ring D, which extended down to Saturn's cloud tops. Voyager also discovered rings within the Cassini division, which divides the A and B rings and confirmed Pioneer's 11's discovery of the narrow ring F. Just as important scientifically were the new and completely unexpected structural features which Voyager 1 revealed. Ring F not only consisted of three components, but two of these are apparently braided like a rope, a difficult problem for the theorists. When Voyager 2 arrived the braiding had dis-

TABLE 2. DISTANCES (in kms) FOR JOVIAN MOONS

	Average Distance from Jupiter	Diameter	Voyager 1 Approach	Voyager 2 Approach
Io	421,600	3,640	20,000	1,130,000
Europa	670,900	3,130	734,000	206,000
Ganymede	1,070,000	5,270	115,000	62,000
Callisto	1,880,000	4,850	126,000	215,000

TABLE 3. SATURN'S RINGS BEFORE VOYAGER 1

Ring	Distance from Saturn (in Saturn radii, R_s)	Voyager 1
D	Controversial in Existence	Confirms some material inside ring C
C	1·22–1·50	Finds eccentric ring
B	1·53–1·90	Discovers spokes
	Cassini division	Discovers rings; one eccentric
A	2·03–2·37	Bounded by new satellite S28
	Pioneer division	
F	2·33 (narrow)	Finds 3 rings; 2 braided, bounded by S26 and S27
E	Extends to 5 or 6 R_s	

appeared. The ring has bright sections and dark regions suggestive of an uneven distribution of large (1 m) and small particles. A similar shading structure was found in the brightest ring, B, which assumed a spoke-like appearance. The spokes look either light or dark depending upon whether Voyager was either above or below the rings in relation to the sun, and this behaviour suggests that they are the result of particles of very small size. Equally surprising was the discovery of two eccentric rings, one in ring C and the other in the Cassini division.

Speculation concerning these new structural ring features centres on whether they result from gravitational effects alone or whether other forces such as magnetic ones contribute. Crucial to the pattern of the gravitation field has been the discovery of new satellites, bringing Saturn's total up to 15. Ring A may be controlled by Saturn's newest and closest satellite, S28, which orbits only 8 km outside its edge. Ring F is 'shepherded' by S26 on the outside and by S27 inside.

Saturn's Moons

Voyager 1 discovered three new small moons and passed Mimas, Dione, Rhea, Tethys, Encaledus as well as approaching Titan to within 7,000 km. Voyager 2 came close to Iapetus, Hyperion and Phoebe as well as transmitting information about Tethys and Encaledus.

The two small moons S1 and S3 travel in nearly the same orbit at slightly different velocities which slowly increase and decrease such that the moons overtake each other in turn about once every four hours. The controversial moon Janus claimed by observation from earth in 1966 is probably the two moons S1 and S3. Moons S13 and S25 are co-orbital with Tethys, the first 60° ahead and the second 60° behind. These are positions of dynamical stability as calculated as long ago as 1772 by Lagrange. S6 is also a Lagrangian moon leading Dione by 60°. All the moons present the same face to Saturn except Phoebe and possibly Hyperion which is very close to Titan. All but two orbit in circular paths in the equatorial plane of Saturn, except Iapetus whose plane is inclined at 14·7° and Phoebe at 150°. Phoebe is exceptional also in orbiting in a direction opposite to those of the others. Phoebe is the farthest moon from Saturn (at about 210R_s) and because of its peculiarities, which include a very low reflecting power (albedo) of only 5%, some think that it is a captured asteroid.

All the large moons have cratered surfaces. Rhea (diameter 1,500 km) is the most heavily cratered and appears to have one of the most ancient surfaces in the solar system. Dione (diameter 1,100 km) shows evidence of surface cracks as well as craters and Tethys (diameter 1,020 km) has a large circular feature 200 km on one face and a massive crack 750 km long on the opposite side as if it had been hit by a large body. Mimas (diameter 375 km) has a crater which is as large as half the moon's radius. Iapetus (diameter 1,000 km) has one side which is five times darker than the other, maybe because of accumulated space debris. Encaledus (diameter 520 km) appeared to have a smooth surface until Voyager 2's pictures showed a varied surface with small craters on the leading side. With an albedo of nearly 100% Encaledus probably has a surface of clean ice.

The largest moon Titan (diameter 4,820 km) is second in size only to Jupiter's Ganymede, and before the Voyager missions was the last candidate in the solar system for extraterrestrial life support since it was the only moon known to have an atmosphere. Voyager 1 showed that this atmosphere is mainly nitrogen gas ($\sim 90\%$) and argon ($\sim 12\%$) with smaller amounts of methane as well as other organic molecules such as ethane, acetylene and also hydrogen cyanide. The atmospheric pressure is 1½ times that of the earth's and the surface temperature is so low at $-175°$ C that the surface may be covered in a sea of liquid methane topped by methane clouds. The atmospheric chemistry of Titan is very rich. Many reactions can result from bombardment of the components of the atmosphere by solar ultraviolet radiation and by high energy electrons. There is an aerosal layer surrounding Titan up to about 230 kilometers.

Uranus

On 24 January 1986 Voyager 2 came as close as 50,679 miles (about 81,000 km) to the blue green planet Uranus, arriving within a minute of its schedule at a speed of 42,143 mph (about 67,200 km per hr) after its eventful journey of 8½ years from earth. Before Voyager's arrival Uranus was known to have 5 moons and 9 rings but after its departure the moon count had risen to 15 and one more faint ring had been discovered. The planet itself was shown to have cloud formations which were timed as they passed over the middle latitudes confirming that the Uranian day is about 16 hours long. The atmosphere is mainly hydrogen with about 10% helium. Most importantly a magnetic field was detected. It has about the same strength as Saturn's which is about one third of earth's. There is an amazing 55 degree angular difference between the magnetic and geographical axes. The geographical or rotational axis itself was known to be unusual being nearly in the solar equatorial plane and not at right angles to it. The magnetic field of Uranus is probably caused by a liquid core of hydrogen. The Uranian surface has a temperature of about $-210°$ C and the equator is colder than the sunlit south pole. The new ring was detected between rings ε and δ. ε is the thickest ring and consists of particles about 1 meter in size. It has a small satellite on each side like the F ring of Saturn. The Uranian rings appear to have far less dust than Saturn's. Voyager 2 unlocked some of the secrets of Uranus's large moons which appear only as featureless spots from earth. Some detail was revealed on Miranda the smallest of the moons and the closest to the planet. Ariel was shown to rotate synchronously with Uranus. Considerable detail was seen on both Titania and the farthest moon Oberon, each about 1000 km in diameter. The surface of each of these moons is pocked with white spots as if meteorites had powdered the grey surface leaving radial white streaks, probably of new ice. Oberon has a mountainous peak which is nearly 5 km high.

Now Voyager 2 is set on its 3½ year journey from Uranus to Neptune from which, if all goes well, it will transmit more new information in August 1989.

THE CHERNOBYL CATASTROPHE

A chemical explosion and serious fire at Chernobyl nuclear power plant, near Kiev in the Soviet Ukraine on Saturday 26 April 1986 proved to be a major catastrophe in two senses. Long-term, a heavy toll in human life was expected. An unofficial preliminary estimate within the UK National Radiological Protection Board, quoted by Nature (8 May 1986), was that deaths within a few weeks would be counted in hundreds; but that longer term consequences—excess cancer deaths—would be much greater in number. The other aspect was that public confidence in the safety of the nuclear power industry was severely damaged throughout the world.

The power station had four RBMK reactors with a fifth under construction. The explosion blew open the roof of one reactor building (but not the reactor itself) discharging radioactive particles that formed a "cloud". Driven by winds, this moved around Europe shedding radioactive fallout in several other countries as well as in the Soviet Union itself. The Soviet authorities, after an initial period of a few days in which they tried to play down the significance of this major accident, eventually acknowledged that they at first "did not have a true assessment" of its severity. They then began to disclose more information and invited representatives of the International Atomic Energy Agency (IAEA).

Throughout East and West Europe the authorities started intensive measurements of air, water and foodstuffs for radioactive contamination. There was intense public concern and several European countries warned people temporarily not to drink fresh milk or rain water. The European Commission tried to introduce a ban on importing fresh foodstuffs from Eastern Europe. But this attempt met with considerable opposition.

It was reported that about 50,000 people were evacuated from a 30 km radius around the plant. But expert opinion tended to indicate that there would be little significant immediate risk to people elsewhere in Europe, though the increased levels of radiation would undoubtedly cause some relatively small number of increased cancer deaths in coming decades.

According to a review in the New Scientist, 8 May 1986, the Soviet RBMK-1000 reactor involved has these four main features:

Direct cycle: water is boiled directly within the core of the reactor and led off to drive the turbine-generator;

Pressure tubes: instead of a single large pressure vessel to contain both fuel and coolant, it has more than 1600 separate pressure tubes;

Ordinary light water is used as a coolant;

Graphite is used as a moderator.

The graphite is operated at about 700° C. UK reactor designers consider this to be a source of risk since it is above its ignition temperature in air.

In the first few days after this accident, much play was made by government leaders in the UK and the USA with the idea that the Soviet Union had tried to keep the incident secret (though this had proved impossible), while "Western" societies believed in full disclosure. These government claims had to be toned down as the responsible press in the UK and elsewhere drew attention to several cases where similar secrecy had been attempted for example by UK authorities over details of the Windscale and other nuclear accidents, or their full severity.

Inevitably the accident sharpened the difference of opinion between the supporters and opponents of nuclear power, reviving heated public debate on the issue. The former noted the anticipated need in future for all forms of energy source since oil and gas are likely to be exhausted in a couple of decades. Supporters of nuclear power add that all human activities are liable to exact a toll of human life; air and car travel, for example, are not brought to a standstill despite heavy casualty figures. Public policy on these issues is to continue activities thought to be useful and to take action to make them safer.

Against nuclear power, it is argued that sufficient energy can be supplied in future by greater efforts in conservation, energy efficiency, and development of renewable forms (*e.g.* sun, wind, wave, tidal, geothermal). Also, nuclear accidents—it is argued—are far-reaching, international and long-lasting in their effects, with a potentially heavy toll of human and other life. Nuclear power is furthermore associated with providing plutonium for nuclear arms, with all the fear and abhorrence they provoke. For these reasons, nuclear power is said to be unnecessary and dangerous.

This debate continues, but generally governments have adopted the view that nuclear energy is needed and must be made safer.

On Friday 9 May, officers of the IAEA announced that the fire was out, radiation levels were falling, and a permanent IAEA radiation monitoring station was being set up 40 miles southeast of Chernobyl. A new international early warning system is planned on radiation release, and international exchange of technical data to help cope with nuclear emergencies.

ELEMENTS

Element (Symbol)	Atomic Number	Atomic Weight	Valency	Element (Symbol)	Atomic Number	Atomic Weight	Valency
actinium (Ac)*	89	227		molybdenum (Mo)	42	95·94	3, 4, 6
aluminium (Al)	13	26·9815	3				
americium (Am)*	95	243	3, 4, 5, 6	neodymium (Nd)	60	144·24	3
antimony (Sb)	51	121·75	3, 5	neon (Ne)	10	20·17	0
argon (A)	18	39·948	0	neptunium (Np)*	93	237	4, 5, 6
arsenic (As)	33	74·9216	3, 5	nickel (Ni)	28	58·71	2, 3
astatine (At)*	85	210	1, 3, 5, 7	niobium (Nn)	41	92·906	3, 5
				nitrogen (N)	7	14·0067	3, 5
barium (Ba)	56	137·34	2	nobelium (No)*	102	254	
berkelium (Bk)*	97	247	3, 4				
beryllium (Be)	4	9·0122	2	osmium (Os)	76	190·2	2, 3, 4, 8
bismuth (Bi)	83	208·980	3, 5	oxygen (O)	8	15·9994	2
boron (B)	5	10·811	3				
bromine (Br)	35	79·904	1, 3, 5, 7	palladium (Pd)	46	106·4	2, 4, 6
				phosphorus (P)	15	30·9378	3, 5
cadmium (Cd)	48	112·40	2	platinum (Pt)	78	195·09	2, 4
calcium (Ca)	20	40·08	2	plutonium (Pu)*	94	244	3, 4, 5, 6
californium (Cf)*	98	251		polonium (Po)*	84	210	
carbon (C)	6	12·0111	2, 4	potassium (K)	19	39·102	1
cerium (Ce)	58	140·12	3, 4	praseodymium (Pr)	59	140·907	3
caesium (Cs)	55	132·905	1	promethium (Pm)*	61	145	3
chlorine (Cl)	17	35·453	1, 3, 5, 7	protactinium (Pa)*	91	231	
chromium (Cr)	24	51·996	2, 3, 6				
cobalt (Co)	27	58·9332	2, 3	radium (Ra)*	88	226	2
copper (Cu)	29	63·546	1, 2	radon (Rn)*	86	222	0
curium (Cm)*	96	247	3	rhenium (Re)	75	186·2	
				rhodium (Rh)	45	102·905	3
dysprosium (Dy)	66	162·50	3	rubidium (Rb)	37	85·47	1
				ruthenium (Ru)	44	101·07	3, 4, 6, 8
einsteinium (Es)*	99	254					
erbium (Er)	68	167·26	3	samarium (Sm)	62	150·35	2, 3
europium (Eu)	63	151·96	2, 3	scandium (Sc)	21	44·956	3
				selenium (Se)	34	78·96	2, 4, 6
fermium (Fm)*	100	253		silicon (Si)	14	28·086	4
fluorine (F)	9	18·9984	1	silver (Ag)	47	107·870	1
francium (Fr)*	87	223	1	sodium (Na)	11	22·9898	1
				strontium (Sr)	38	87·62	2
gadolinium (Gd)	64	157·25	3	sulphur (S)	16	32·064	2, 4, 6
gallium (Ga)	31	69·72	2, 3				
germanium (Ge)	32	72·59	4	tantalum (Ta)	73	180·947	5
gold (Au)	79	196·967	1, 3	technetium (Tc)*	43	99	6, 7
				tellurium (Te)	52	127·60	2, 4, 6
hafnium (Hf)	72	178·49	4	terbium (Tb)	65	158·925	3
helium (He)	2	4·0026	0	thallium (Tl)	81	204·37	1, 3
holmium (Ho)	67	164·930	3	thorium (Th)	90	232·038	4
hydrogen (H)	1	1·00797	1	thulium (Tm)	69	168·934	3
				tin (Sn)	50	118·69	2, 4
indium (In)	49	114·82	3	titanium (Ti)	22	47·90	3, 4
iodine (I)	53	126·904	1, 3, 5, 7	tungsten (see wolfram)			
iridium (Ir)	77	192·2	3, 4				
iron (Fe)	26	55·847	2, 3	uranium (U)	92	238·03	4, 6
krypton (Kr)	36	83·8	0	vanadium (V)	23	50·942	3, 5
lanthanum (La)	57	138·01	3				
lawrencium (Lr)*	103	257		wolfram (W)	74	183·85	6
lead (Pb)	82	207·19	2, 4				
lithium (Li)	3	6·941	1	xenon (Xe)	54	131·30	0
lutetium (Lu)	71	174·97	3				
				ytterbium (Yb)	70	173·04	2, 3
magnesium (Mg)	12	24·305	2	yttrium (Y)	39	88·905	3
manganese (Mn)	25	54·9380	2, 3, 4, 6, 7				
mendeleevium (Md)*	101	256		zinc (Zn)	30	65·37	2
mercury (Hg)	80	200·59	1, 2	zirconium (Zr)	40	91·22	4

* In the cases of these elements, which are very rare or not found in nature, but have been artificially prepared, atomic weight in the chemical sense is meaningless; the integral mass of the most stable isotope known is given.

Note: In 1961 the isotope of carbon-12 replaced oxygen as a standard, the weight of its atom being taken as 12. This change of standard has meant a slight adjustment in atomic weights from the old chemical scale.

The new elements with an atomic number higher than that of uranium 238 (element 92) are termed Transuranics.

GAS LAWS

The Perfect or Ideal Gas Law: $pV = nRT$
where n is the number of moles in volume V at pressure p and absolute temperature T, and R is a universal constant.

Van der Waals' equation: $\left(p + \dfrac{a}{V^2}\right)(V - b) = nRT$

where a and b are constants, different for each gas.

PERIODIC TABLE OF THE ELEMENTS

Electronic Configurations. See **F71–2**

Key to Chart

Atomic Number → 5
Symbol → B
Atomic Weight → 10.811

* Lanthanides (see **L72**)

† Actinides (see **L3**)

GROUP / Period	1A Alkali metals	2A Alkaline earth metals	3B	4B	5B	6B	7B	8	8	8	1B Noble metals	2B	3A	4A	5A	6A	7A	0 Inert gases
1	1 **H** 1·00797																	2 **He** 4·0026
2	3 Li 6·941	4 Be 9·0122											5 **B** 10·811	6 **C** 12·0111	7 **N** 14·0067	8 **O** 15·9994	9 **F** 18·9984	10 **Ne** 20·179
3	11 Na 22·9898	12 **Mg** 24·305											13 Al 26·9815	14 *Si* 28·086	15 **P** 30·9738	16 **S** 32·064	17 **Cl** 35·453	18 **Ar** 39·948
4	19 K 39·102	20 Ca 40·08	21 Sc 44·9559	22 Ti 47·90	23 V 50·942	24 Cr 51·996	25 Mn 54·938	26 Fe 55·847	27 Co 58·933	28 Ni 58·71	29 Cu 63·546	30 Zn 65·37	31 Ga 69·72	32 *Ge* 72·59	33 As 74·9216	34 Se 78·96	35 **Br** 79·904	36 **Kr** 83·80
5	37 Rb 85·4678	38 Sr 87·62	39 Y 88·9059	40 Zr 91·22	41 Nb 92·9064	42 Mo 95·94	43 Tc 99	44 Ru 101·07	45 Rh 102·905	46 Pd 106·4	47 Ag 107·870	48 Cd 112·40	49 In 114·82	50 Sn 118·69	51 *Sb* 121·75	52 *Te* 127·60	53 **I** 126·904	54 **Xe** 131·30
6	55 Cs 132·905	56 Ba 137·34	57 La* 138·91	72 Hf 178·49	73 Ta 180·947	74 W 183·85	75 Re 186·2	76 Os 190·2	77 Ir 192·2	78 Pt 195·09	79 Au 196·967	80 Hg 200·59	81 Tl 204·37	82 Pb 207·19	83 Bi 208·980	84 Po 210	85 **At** 210	86 **Rn** 222
7	87 Fr 223	88 Ra 226	89 Ac† 227															

Transition metals (groups 3B through 8, 1B, 2B)

* Lanthanides

				5B	6B	7B	8	8	8	1B	2B	3A	4A	5A	6A	7A	0
				58 Ce 140·12	59 Pr 140·907	60 Nd 144·24	61 Pm 145	62 Sm 150·35	63 Eu 151·96	64 Gd 157·25	65 Tb 158·925	66 Dy 162·50	67 Ho 164·930	68 Er 167·26	69 Tm 168·934	70 Yb 173·04	71 Lu 174·97

† Actinides

				5B	6B	7B	8	8	8	1B	2B	3A	4A	5A	6A	7A	0
				90 Th 232·038	91 Pa 231	92 U 238·03	93 Np 237	94 Pu 244	95 Am 243	96 Cm 247	97 Bk 247	98 Cf 251	99 Es 254	100 Fm 253	101 Md 256	102 No 254	103 Lr 257

Roman type—metals
Italic type—semiconductors
Bold type—non-metals

These designations refer to the normal materials usually at room temperature. Processes like heating or compressing can turn metals into insulators and vice versa.

Note: It may be possible by artificial methods such as bombardment by other nuclei to produce elements with atomic numbers greater than 103. However all the very heavy elements are unstable and decay spontaneously into lighter elements. Because the lifetime of such elements is short no element with an atomic number greater than Uranium (92) occurs naturally on earth.

BACKGROUND TO ECONOMIC EVENTS

The aim of this section is to help the ordinary reader to follow economic events as they happen, and to understand the controversies that accompany them. Special articles in this year's *Pears* examine the South African sanctions debate, the decline of Britain's manufacturing industry and the Channel Tunnel project.

TABLE OF CONTENTS

BACKGROUND TO ECONOMIC EVENTS

This section is divided into five parts. Part I gives a brief description of the most important problems of economic policy. Part II is concerned with a more detailed survey of the British economy and the way in which it operates. In the course of this survey, the specialised terms used by economists are explained, and the attempt is made to present an intelligible summary of the information, facts and figures relevant to an understanding of economic events. There are five main sub-sections: International Trade and Payments; Employment, Production, and Industry; Incomes, Wages, and Prices; Money, Banking, and Finance; and Economic Aspects of the Public Services. Part III outlines the main economic problems faced by the less developed countries, and the economic policies of Britain and other developed countries towards the less developed world. Some suggestions for further reading are given at the end of Parts II and III. Part IV is written as shortly before publication as possible, and contains a survey of recent developments in the British economy. Part V consists of Special Topics on the sanctions debate over South Africa, the Channel Tunnel project and the decline of British manufacturing industry.

I. CENTRAL PROBLEMS OF ECONOMIC POLICY

Why Economists Disagree.

On many of the most important issues Economics is in a state of disarray. Economic problems are in general as serious as they have ever been, yet the economics profession is more divided now than ever on the diagnosis of the problems and on the prescriptions for economic policy. Why is this the case?

It is important to distinguish between *positive* and *normative* economics, *i.e.*, between consideration of how the economy actually works and of how it ought to be made to work. Even if economists were unanimous in their understanding of the economy, different economists might nevertheless prescribe conflicting policies because they made different moral or political judgements. For instance, macroeconomic policy prescriptions might depend crucially on the relative strength of one's dislike for the two evils, inflation and unemployment. But disagreement among economists is not only about goals and objectives. In macroeconomics, the "Keynesian consensus" which held sway in the 1950s and 1960s gave way in the 1970s and 1980s to a variety of different schools of thought. This development reflected changes in the economy and the emergence of new and more pressing economic problems: a rise in the rates of inflation and unemployment and a fall in the rate of economic growth. The accepted analysis and prescriptions were found wanting. At the simplest level, the disputing schools divide into the *New Keynesians*, on the one hand, and the *Monetarists*, or *New Classical* school, on the other.

The two major political parties in Britain have, in the 1980s, been committed to extreme and radically different approaches to the solution of Britain's economic problems. The Conservative Government, in office since 1979, has placed its faith in *laissez faire* economics, in the efficient operation of market forces, and in Monetarist policies. The Labour Party does not accept that the uncontrolled play of market forces would be beneficial, and it has favoured Keynesian reflation and a major expansion of state activity and state control. In part, these different approaches are based on differences in economic analysis. For instance, the parties might disagree on what would be the consequences of import controls, or of incomes policy, or of running a budget deficit, or of reducing unemployment benefits. However, much of the disagreement is really based on differences in objectives, or on ideological considerations. Policies based on ideology or slogans can be dangerous. A great disservice is done by those who claim to have simple answers to what in reality are complex problems.

Economic relationships are complicated and changeable, and normally difficult to measure. Economists cannot conduct rigorous experiments in the way that natural scientists do. Everything is happening at once in an economy, and the influence of any one variable is not easy to isolate, even with the use of sophisticated statistical techniques. This is another reason why economists disagree, and why they should always bear in mind the limitations of their knowledge.

Are Economists Useful?

Given their disagreements and the limitations of their knowledge, can economists perform a useful function? In the 1985 Reith Lectures, concerned with the influence of economic ideas on economic policy, David Henderson complained about the influence of what he called *do-it-yourself economics*. Over wide areas of policy the judgements of politicians and their officials, as also public opinion in general, are guided by beliefs and perceptions about the workings of the economy which owe little or nothing to the economics profession. The amateurs have not been driven from the field, and they are often in control of policy.

According to Henderson, do-it-yourself economics is based on peoples' intuitions and tends to be interventionist: politicians like to be active and to be seen to be active. These intuitions rarely extend beyond the immediate effects of the intervention, whereas professional economists analyse the less obvious, indirect and often unintended effects of interventions, which take place through the response of market forces. To give a simple example, rent controls appear to tackle the ill-effects of housing shortage but, by deterring investment in housing, they may exacerbate the shortage. Or mortgage interest tax relief may be electorally popular, but the economist's approach is to trace its consequences through to the end of the chain—higher house prices, losers as well as gainers, and less resources for non-housing. The professional approach is generally more quantitative than that of the amateur. Economists *can* often be useful, but their advice is ignored more frequently by policy-makers than that of, say, lawyers or engineers.

The Objectives of Economic Policy.

The central issues of economic policy concern certain desirable objectives. One important objective is the avoidance of unemployment. Between the wars, mass unemployment was Britain's most urgent problem: unemployment caused waste, hardship and poverty. After 1945, the maintenance of full unemployment was accepted as a primary objective of economic policy by all political parties. Until the late 1960s less than 2 per cent of the labour force was unemployed.

Unemployment can be either *cyclical* or *structural*. Cyclical unemployment, arising from a lack of demand in the economy, can be tackled by Government measures to increase total spending in the economy. Structural unemployment arises from a misallocation of resources. In the 1970s and 1980s structural unemployment grew as redundancies rocketed in the increasingly uncompetitive manufacturing sector, *e.g.*, motor and engineering industries, and in declining industries such as steel and coal. Moreover, cyclical unemployment grew as world economic recession set in and deflationary policies were introduced at home.

With the emergence during the last decade of new and greater problems of inflation, the commitment to full employment first faltered and then was withdrawn. The concern that has daunted Governments in recent years is that expansionary policies to eliminate cyclical unemployment might fuel a spiral of inflation. By the start of 1986 unemployment had exceeded the figure of 3 million, or 13 per cent of the labour force. The spectre of the 1930s loomed again.

A second objective of economic policy has been the cure of inflation. Between 1960 and 1970 retail prices increased on average by 4·4 per cent per annum; between 1970 and 1980 the inflation rate averaged no less than 14 per cent per annum. Inflation can be harmful in various ways. It is associated with an arbitrary redistribution of purchasing power. Prices rise for everyone but some groups in society are better able to protect themselves against inflation. The feeling that particular groups are falling behind is a source of much unrest and discontent. Moreover, the general economic uncertainty that inflation brings can become a threat to economic prosperity.

Two main explanations have been advanced to account for inflation. The first stresses the role of excess demand or spending power in the economy—of too much money chasing too few goods. Such *demand-pull* theories are put forward by Monetarists, who point to increases in the money supply in generating demand, and by Keynesians who recommend restrictive monetary and fiscal policies to curb excess demand, when it arises. The second explanation stresses the role of excessive increases in costs, *e.g.*, wage costs or imported raw material costs, in raising prices. Such *cost-push* theories imply, for instance, that policies are needed to restrain the power of trade unions to raise wages. Neither explanation precludes the other: both demand-pull and cost-push factors are likely to have contributed—with different strengths at different times—to inflation. Moreover, adherents of both views recognise that, once expectations of continued inflation become entrenched, these expectations themselves sustain and fuel the inflation.

A third objective of economic policy is the fostering of economic growth. Successive British Governments in the post-war period have tried to raise the growth rate—the most important long run determinant of the standard of living. Britain's living standards have until recently been rising: output per head of population increased annually by 2 per cent between 1960 and 1970 and by 1·5 per cent between 1970 and 1980. Nevertheless, the British growth rate compares unfavourably with that achieved by most other industrial countries.

The determinants of economic growth are not well understood, but most economists would agree that in order to raise the growth rate it is necessary to encourage the community to save, and businessmen to invest, a higher proportion of the national income. In a fully employed economy the source of increased output is higher productivity, *i.e.*, output per worker. There is a danger, however, that higher productivity growth will be achieved only at the expense of employment, as has been the case in Britain since 1980.

A constraint on the achievement of the above objectives has been the need to maintain balance in international payments. The British balance of payments position has been precarious, so that unfavourable turns of events have precipitated economic crises. Indeed, concern about the balance of payments so dominated economic policy-making at times during the post-war period that improvement in the balance of payments became a major objective of policy. The objective has normally been to achieve a surplus in order to pay off international debts, build up external assets by investing abroad, and provide development aid to less developed countries.

The expansion in the late 1970s of North Sea oil production, and the resulting confidence of foreign investors, has transformed the British balance of payments. But this has created new problems, particularly the adverse effect of the ensuing high exchange rate on manufacturing, our traditional export sector and an important employer of labour.

The Inter-relationship of Economic Problems.

The achievement of each of the objectives briefly described above is extremely complex. The difficulties are further aggravated by the fact that the problems are inter-related in such a way that measures which are helpful for one objective can make others more difficult to achieve. For example, a reduction of purchasing power might be considered helpful in the control of inflation, and might ease balance of payments problems by reducing—or slowing down the increase of—imports. But it could also lead to an increase in unemployment, and to a slowing down in the rate of growth of the economy. Many economic commentators now hold that it is no longer possible to keep unemployment down to the levels of the 1950s and 1960s without unleashing cumulative inflation, and that the control of inflation must now have the highest priority. This must be the rationale for the economic policies of the Conservative Government in office since 1979, as it has paid little heed to the short run effects of its policies on unemployment and economic growth. In 1980 the Government faced an inflation rate of 18 per cent and an unemployment rate of 6 per cent. By 1985 it had got inflation down, to 6 per cent, but unemployment has risen to 13 per cent.

There are other examples of a conflict in policy objectives. For instance, while the advent in the 1970s of a floating exchange rate helps to correct the balance of payments, a depreciating pound can in turn fuel inflation. If import controls were introduced to protect the manufacturing sector, this in turn would be liable to harm developing countries.

The Worsening Economic Climate.

In the mid-1970s, after 30 years of rapid growth and unprecedented prosperity for the major Western economies, the prospects for continued growth became much less favourable. This resulted partly from the acceleration of inflation in many countries, bringing with it insecurity and militancy in industrial relations. However, the main cause was the remarkable increase in the price of oil in 1973 and again in 1979, a fuel on which the Western economies had become heavily dependent. This produced a strong burst of inflation; and, because much of the oil revenue accruing to producers could not be spent, gave rise to an unprecedented balance of payments problem and severe world recession. There was a danger that, through a lack of international co-ordination and of business confidence and through misplaced attempts by countries to cure their immediate economic problems by means of deflation, mass unemployment on the scale of the 1930s would again appear. The international infectiousness of high interest rates, economic recession and rapid inflation made it hard for any one country to avoid these ills. In the changing situation both the problems of economic policy and the inter-relationships between them became more difficult.

II. SURVEY OF THE BRITISH ECONOMY

1. INTERNATIONAL TRADE AND PAYMENTS

International Trade.

(i) Imports and Exports.

In 1984 the United Kingdom bought from abroad goods to the value of £78·7 billion (thousand million), or about £1,400 per head. Food was a large item on this bill, accounting for 11 per cent of the total. Fuel, largely oil, cost about 13 per cent, basic materials for industry 7 per cent, and manufactured goods (including a large number of semi-manufactured goods bought for further processing) 67 per cent. This last category of imports has increased sharply in recent years. In 1954 it represented only 20 per cent in an import bill of only £3·4 billion. All this can be seen in the table, which compares 1954 with the most recent year, 1984.

There are three main determinants of the level of British imports. One is the competitiveness of British with foreign producers. Britain imports those commodities which—at the ruling exchange rate between the pound and foreign currencies—can be bought more cheaply from foreign than from home producers. Secondly, the level of imports depends on the extent to which free trade is prevented by tariffs on imported goods or by other devices. Thirdly, as total incomes in the economy expand, there is a general increase in the demand for goods and services including imports. Therefore imports can be expected to vary with the total incomes in the country, known as the *national income*.

Whereas in 1954 imports amounted to 23 per cent of national income, in 1984 the proportion was 33 per cent. One reason for this rise is the liberalisation of trade among the industrialised

UNITED KINGDOM IMPORTS AND EXPORTS

Imports of goods (c.i.f.)	£ million.		Percentage of total.	
	1954.	1984.	1954.	1984.
Food, drink, and tobacco	1.314	8,936	39	11
Basic materials	1,015	5,420	30	7
Fuels and lubricants	329	10,193	10	13
Semi-manufactures	513	19,762	15	25
Finished manufactures	174	33,124	5	42
TOTAL*	3,359	78,706	100	100
Exports of goods (f.o.b.)				
Food, drink, and tobacco	154	4,693	6	7
Basic materials	101	1,989	4	3
Fuels and lubricants	151	15,367	6	22
Engineering products	1,007	21,485	38	30
Other manufactured goods	490	25,483	18	36
TOTAL*	2,650	70,511	100	100

*The column figures do not add up to the totals because the former exclude postal packages.

countries during the post-war period, and the tendency for trade in manufactures among these countries to increase. An example is the formation of the *European Economic Community* in 1956

and Britain's entry to it in January 1973. Another reason is the great increase in the price of oil which occurred in the 1970s. Britain's oil import bill rose from £900 million in 1970 to £5·6 billion in 1976. Since then, however, North Sea oil has transformed the oil picture. Imports have fallen in volume, although they still amounted to nearly £8.1 billion in 1984, and exports have risen, to £14·9 billion. By the 1980s, Britain had become a net exporter of oil.

Since the exports of one country must be the imports of another, the same factors in reverse, foreign competitiveness, access to foreign markets, and the level of foreign incomes determine the level of British exports. In 1984 these amounted to over £70·5 billion of which no less than 66 per cent were manufactures, mainly engineering products. In 1954 it was true to say that Britain gained from trade by exporting manufactures, in which she had a *comparative advantage*, in return for food and raw materials, which she was not suited to produce. This is still partly true; but increasingly—with the growth of trade and specialisation among the major economies—Britain gains from trade by exporting those manufactures in which her producers specialise and importing other manufactures. Among the main manufacturing exports are cars and commercial vehicles, tractors, aircraft and aircraft engines, finished steel, various forms of machinery, woollen fabrics, man-made fibres, and chemicals; among the main manufactured imports are wood products, aluminium, newsprint, cars, and aircraft. With the expansion of British oil production, the pattern of trade continued to show rapid change.

(ii) **The Terms of Trade.**

The value of trade increased twenty-fold between 1954 and 1984. This increase can be separated into two components, price and volume, of which price has been the more important. The ratio of the average price of exports to that of imports is known as the *terms of trade*; and a rise in the price of exports relative to imports indicates an improvement in the terms of trade. Thus, when we note in the table that the terms of trade improved by some 20 per cent between 1954 and 1970 we mean that, in 1970, 20 per cent less exports by volume would have been needed to buy the same amount of imports as in 1954. This improvement in the terms of trade reflects the fact that the prices of many primary products —food and raw materials such as wool, cocoa, rubber, tea, and oil—tended to stagnate in world markets over this period (*see* **Part III**). The subsequent worsening of the terms of trade reflected the commodity boom and the oil price increase which occurred in the 1970s.

VISIBLE TRADE: VOLUME AND PRICES

	1970 = 100	
	1954	1984
Value		
Imports	37	892
Exports	33	863
Volume		
Imports	47	174
Exports	52	174
Price		
Imports	79	615
Exports	63	520
Terms of trade	80	93

(iii) **The Volume of Trade.**

Superficially it would appear that any improvement in the terms of trade raises the value of British exports relative to imports. However, this is not always true: faster inflation in Britain, leading to a more rapid increase in export prices, would harm rather than help the balance of payments. If the prices of our export goods rise faster than the prices of our competitors in overseas markets it becomes progressively more difficult to sell our exports. Conversely, inflation in Britain makes it progressively more difficult to compete with imports. Growth in the volume of imports exceeded that in exports during the period 1954–70. The trade balance may well be harmed by a rise in the price of imported primary products (as it was after 1970); but the balance of trade in manufactures is worsened by an improvement in their terms of trade (as happened before 1970).

In the post-war period there was a considerable fall in Britain's share of world exports; from 20 per cent of exports of manufactures in 1954 to 16 per cent in 1961, to 12 per cent in 1967, the year of sterling devaluation, and to the figure of 8 per cent in 1984. Britain's main competitors in export markets—and particularly Germany and Japan, with 18 and 20 per cent respectively in 1984—were more successful in expanding their exports. Britain's competitive position in manufacturing has been persistently eroded over the years.

The Balance of Payments.

The *balance of payments* is an account of the total transactions of one country with the rest of the world. To illustrate the balance of payments and its components, the British accounts are presented in the table: accounts for a good year, 1983, and for a bad year 1976. A detailed examination of recent movements in the British balance of payments is made in **Part IV**.

(i) The Balance of Visible Trade.

The *balance of (visible) trade* is the difference between exports and imports of goods. It is said to be in *surplus* if exports exceed imports and in *deficit* if imports exceed exports. In estimating the balance of trade it is important that imports and exports be valued on the same basis. The normal method in the trade returns is to measure imports *c.i.f.* (cost, insurance, and freight) and exports *f.o.b.* (free on board). In other words import prices are shown to

BALANCE OF PAYMENTS OF THE
UNITED KINGDOM, 1976 AND 1983
(£ billion)

	1976	1983
Exports (f.o.b.).	25·2	60·6
Imports (f.o.b.).	29·1	61·3
Visible balance .	−3·9	−0·7
Invisible balance	+3·1	+3·6
of which:		
private sector services .	+3·2	+4·7
interest profits and dividends	+1·4	+2·0
general government transfers	−0·8	−2·0
Current balance	−0·8	+2·9
Overseas investment in U.K.	+2·1	+5·4
U.K. private investment overseas .	−2·3	−10·6
Official long term capital	+0·2	−0·4
Other capital flows .	−3·0	+2·0
Total autonomous capital flows	−3.0	−3·6
Balance for official financing.	−3·8	−0·7
Net borrowing from I.M.F.	+1·0	0·0
Net borrowing from other monetary authorities .	+1·8	−0·2
Drawings on (+) or additions to (−) reserves	+0·8	+0·6
Total official financing .	+3·6	+0·8
Balancing item .	+0·2	−0·1

include the cost of transporting them to Britain, and exports are valued at the prices when loaded in British ports. Our table shows both imports and exports *f.o.b.*

Britain's visible balance is normally in deficit. The trade balance in 1983 was relatively small. On the other hand, the year 1976 produced the second largest deficit (after 1974) ever recorded. In that year Britain's trade was heavily in deficit to her EEC partners, to the United States, and to the oil-exporting countries.

(ii) Patterns of British Trade.

The United States and West Germany are Britain's largest trading partners, both with 13 per cent of total British trade (exports plus imports) in 1984, followed by the Netherlands and France (both 8 per cent), Belgium and Italy (both 5 per cent). Britain's EEC partners as a group accounted for no less than 45 per cent of her trade, and the rest of Western Europe for 15 per cent. The oil exporting countries as a group accounted for 6 per cent, and other less developed countries for 11 per cent of British trade in that year.

PATTERNS OF BRITISH TRADE, 1984

	British exports to: (£ billion)	British imports from: (£ billion)	Exports plus imports as a percentage of the total
European Community	31·6	35·2	44·8
of which:			
France	7·1	5·9	8·7
Netherlands	6·1	6·1	8·2
Belgium	3·1	3·7	4·6
Germany	7·5	11·1	12·5
Italy	2·9	3·8	4·5
Ireland	3·4	2·6	4·0
Denmark	1·2	1·7	1·9
Rest of Western Europe	8·7	13·2	14·7
of which:			
Sweden	2·9	2·4	3·6
Norway	1·0	3·9	3·3
Switzerland	1·5	2·5	2·7
Spain	1·2	1·6	1·9
United States	10·1	9·4	13·1
Canada	1·2	1·6	1·9
Japan	0·9	3·8	3·2
Australia	1·2	0·6	1·2
South Africa	1·2	0·7	1·3
Oil exporting countries	5·8	2·9	5·8
of which:			
Saudia Arabia	1·4	0·5	1·3
Nigeria	0·8	0·4	0·8
Other developing countries	7·5	8·6	10·8
of which:			
Hong Kong	0·9	1·3	1·5
India	0·8	0·6	0·9
Centrally planned economies	1·6	2·0	2·4
of which:			
USSR	0·7	0·7	0·9
TOTAL	70·5	78·7	100·0

(iii) The Balance on Current Account.

The chronic deficit in the balance of visible trade has in normal years been offset by a surplus in the *balance of invisible trade*. This relates to international transactions in services as opposed to goods. The main components are: receipts from non-residents *less* payments to non-residents for services such as shipping, civil aviation, tourism, insurance, and financial services; receipts from foreign governments in respect of military bases in the country *less* payments by this country in respect of military bases abroad; receipts of gifts and grants made to this country, *less* gifts and grants made by this country; all receipts of interest, dividends, and profits earned on overseas investment *less* interest, dividends, and profits paid out on foreign investment in this country.

The *balance on current account* is the sum of the balances on visible and invisible trade. We see that in 1983 there was a surplus and in 1976 a deficit.

(iv) Capital Flow.

It is not sufficient simply to avoid deficits on current account. It has been the Government's objective to earn a surplus in order to finance investment abroad and at times to repay foreign debts previously incurred and to build up reserves of gold and foreign exchange.

The capital account of the balance of payments contains net official long-term capital movements (*e.g.*, inter-government loans to less developed countries), net private investment abroad (being the difference between investment abroad by United Kingdom residents and investment by foreigners in the United Kingdom). Both these items are normally in deficit and tend to be long-term movements.

There are also large, short-term capital flows, sometimes referred to as *monetary movements*. These include trade credits, changes in sterling reserves held by foreign governments, and Eurodollar transactions. Such funds can be highly volatile, moving out of a currency if there is a risk of its depreciation and into it if there is a chance of appreciation or if other currencies are suspect. Therefore, monetary movements often accentuate a surplus or deficit in the other items of the balance of payments; as happened in 1976. They are also dependent on relative rates of interest at home and abroad, being attracted to financial centres which offer high interest rates.

(v) Balance for Official Financing.

The book-keeping identity of international payments and receipts may be illustrated by reference to the year 1976. In that year the United Kingdom had a record deficit on current and capital account of no less than £3·8 billion. In other words, there was a net demand to transfer funds from sterling into other currencies. In theory, the supply and demand for foreign exchange could be equated in the market provided that the monetary authorities made no attempt to regulate the exchange rate (*see* **G8**). But an excess demand for foreign exchange of this magnitude would have involved an unprecedented fall in the value of sterling. Indeed, the monetary authorities did permit the market price for sterling to fall—from $2·0 to the pound in January 1976 to $1·7 in December—and yet a deficit of £3·8 billion had still to be financed from official sources. Total net official financing recorded was in fact £3·6 billion, so that there must have been an unrecorded capital inflow of £200 million, known as the *balancing item*.

(vi) Foreign Exchange Reserves.

A deficit can be financed through an increase in liabilities, *i.e.* by government borrowing from abroad, or by a reduction in assets, *e.g.*, a depletion of the official gold and foreign-exchange reserves. The gold and foreign-exchange reserves are used to finance payments abroad which cannot be financed in any other way: they are a last line of defence in international trade. We see that the imbalance in 1976 was financed partly through borrowing from the International Monetary Fund, partly through foreign currency borrowing by nationalised industries, and only partly by running down the reserves.

The official reserves of gold and foreign currencies amounted to £2·4 billion at the end of 1976. There are bound to be imbalances in international trade and payments, and the function of these reserves is to tide over temporary imbalances by increasing reserves in favourable periods and running down reserves in unfavourable periods. If reserves are not sufficient to withstand temporary pressures, measures to protect the reserves will have to be taken—*e.g.*, rising interest rates and tightening up monetary policies generally—and these measures may create unemployment and recession, and restrict the growth of the economy.

Correcting a Deficit.

If an imbalance in international payments persists, the deficit cannot be met indefinitely from official financing. At some stage the Government must take action to remove the deficit. What action can it take? There are a number of alternatives available, each with its advantages and disadvantages, and economic opinion is by no means unanimous on the choice of policy. Let us consider each of these alternatives in turn.

(i) Variation of the Exchange Rate.

The *exchange rate* is the ruling official rate of exchange of pounds for dollars or other currencies. It determines the value of British goods in relation to foreign goods. Under the post-war Bretton Woods arrangements (*see* **G9**), Britain and other countries maintained a constant value of their currencies in terms of gold, permitting only very minor fluctuations of the exchange rate about its par value. However, persistent balance of payments deficits or surpluses caused occasional adjustments of the official exchange rate, the response to persistent deficit being *devaluation* and to persistent surplus *upvaluation*. In 1972 the major countries adopted a system of fluctuating exchange rates. However, exchange rates are not permitted to fluctuate entirely freely, *i.e.*, so that the market supply and demand for foreign exchange are continuously equated. While the monetary authorities permit the foreign-exchange market to influence the exchange rate, they are prepared in the national interest to intervene in the market (by buying or selling their currency) and so to keep the exchange rate within bounds. Given some flexibility in the exchange rate, a tendency for a deficit to arise is thus met by a *depreciation* of sterling, and an incipient surplus by *appreciation*.

If the pound is devalued or if it depreciates in terms of other currencies, British exports (which are paid for in pounds) become cheaper to foreigners and British imports (paid for by purchasing foreign currency) become more expensive to holders of pounds. In this way a fall in the value of the pound can improve the British balance of payments position by encouraging exports and discouraging imports.

But there are certain disadvantages attached to devaluation (or depreciation). The prospect of devaluation results in a speculative outflow of capital funds: and one fall may be taken as a sign that there will be a further in the future. Moreover, the rise in the price of imports of raw materials and consumption goods results in higher costs and prices and then in wage demands to maintain the British standard of living. It is possible that inflation will in this way neutralise the beneficial effects of devaluation.

The probable effect of a devaluation in Britain is initially to *worsen* the balance of trade, because the sterling price of imports is likely to be raised by more than that of exports. After about six months the effect of the devaluation on quantities —curbing imports and expanding the volume of exports—dominates, and the balance of trade improves. However, the improvement is maintained only if fiscal and monetary or incomes policies can prevent the devaluation from feeding through to domestic prices and costs and so both neutralising the gain in competitiveness and exacerbating inflation.

The pound was devalued in 1949, when an official exchange rate of £1 = $2·8 was established, and again in 1967, to a rate of £1 = $2·4. After the devaluation of the dollar in December 1971, the exchange rate with dollars became £1 = $2·6. After June 1972 the value of sterling in relation to other currencies was allowed to *float*. With widespread floating, an *effective exchange rate* is now calculated, which shows the value of sterling in relation to a bundle of other currencies, with each currency receiving a weight according to the extent of trade with Britain. This rate has fluctuated from month to month, but with a strong downward tendency until 1977, followed by a recovery until 1981 due mainly to the advent of North Sea oil. With the exchange rate equal to 100 in 1975, the weighted average value of sterling moved as follows:

1972	1974	1976	1977	1978	1979
123·3	108·3	85·7	81·2	81·5	87·3

1980	1981	1982	1983	1984	1985
96·1	95·3	90·7	83·3	78·8	78·4

(ii) Exchange Controls and Convertibility.

A currency is fully *convertible* if it can be freely exchanged for any other currency, or for gold, at the ruling rates of exchange. Exchange controls impose restrictions on convertibility by limiting the powers of holders of a currency to exchange their holdings for other currencies or gold. In the early post-war period there was a world-wide shortage of dollars: if sterling had been convertible, there would have been a rush to obtain dollars, with the consequence that Britain's reserves would soon have been exhausted.

Exchange controls on residents can be enforced by requiring that earnings of foreign currencies (*e.g.*, the proceeds from the sale of exports) be handed over to the exchange control authority—the Bank of England acts as the Government's agent—in exchange for sterling; and by permitting the exchange of sterling for foreign currencies (*e.g.*, to enable the purchase of imports) only for transactions approved by the exchange control authority.

By restricting convertibility the Government can make it more difficult for funds to move into or out of sterling. In this way the Government can impede capital movements, *e.g.*, British private investment abroad, or it can restrict current spending abroad, *e.g.*, on foreign holidays.

(iii) Import Controls and Tariffs.

Import controls impose limitations on the quantity or value of goods which are permitted to enter a country; tariffs are duties levied on imported goods so that the price of those goods to consumers in a country is higher than the price received by the foreigners supplying the goods. In the early post-war years. Britain maintained strict import controls over a wide range of goods. These were gradually dismantled during the 1950s.

All countries impose tariffs. Some tariffs are primarily intended to raise revenue for the Government, and others are primarily intended to protect home industries by raising the price of competing goods from abroad. The rights of countries to raise tariffs, or to operate tariffs in a discriminatory way (*i.e.*, to offer lower tariffs on goods from some sources than on similar goods from other sources), are closely circumscribed by the rules of the *General Agreement on Tariffs and Trade* (GATT). The object of the GATT is to work towards free trade, especially through a reduction in tariffs. In the post-war period GATT held several major conferences, at which bargaining to reduce tariffs was attended by modest success. The significant moves towards free trade in this period were on a regional basis.

The disadvantage of introducing import controls or tariffs to correct a deficit in the balance of payments is that the benefits of free trade are lost. Moreover, there is always the possibility of retaliation by Britain's trading partners. Yet, import controls or tariffs may well be preferable to another measure which has been used to correct a deficit, deflation. Britain's powers to impose tariffs and quotas on imports were greatly circumscribed in 1973 by her accession to the European Economic Community, since this requires free trade within the community and a common external tariff.

(iv) Deflation.

Until the late 1970s the U.K. balance of payments was far from secure. As a result, domestic economic policies were much influenced by balance of payments considerations. Devaluation was turned to only as a last resort. The movement in the 1950s and 1960s was towards greater freedom of trade. By ruling out devaluation and trade restrictions, the authorities had to fall back on *deflation* of the economy to correct periodic deficits. In other words, the Government took measures to discourage demand and so cut back incomes and employment. By reducing demand in general, the authorities secured a fall in demand for imports. However, it was necessary to cut back national income by many times the ensuing fall in imports. Deflation is a painful method of correcting a deficit: not only does it have a direct effect on the level of incomes and employment, but it is also liable to slow down the rate of growth of the economy. This can happen because deflation can weaken the incentive to expand productive capacity by investing.

(v) International Trade Flows

We can divide the world into four trading groups: the industrial countries (mainly OECD), the oil-producing developing countries (OPEC), the other developing countries, and the communist countries. In 1980 the industrial countries accounted for 61 per cent of total world exports, 43 per cent being exports to countries within that group, 5 per cent to oil producers, 9 per cent to developing countries, and 3 per cent to communist countries. Over two-thirds of the industrial countries' exports were manufactured products. The oil exports of the oil producers amounted to 15 per cent of world exports, 11 per cent going to the industrial countries. Nearly two-thirds of the exports of the other developing countries were primary products. Their exports amounted to 12 per cent of the world total, most going to the industrial countries. The communist group exported 9 per cent of the world total, half of which was traded within the group. Of the total world exports, 56 per cent were manufactures, 24 per cent fuels and 20 per cent primary products.

This pattern of world trade produced the following world current account balance for 1980. Assisted by the high price of oil at that time, the oil producers ran a surplus of $115 billion. The corresponding deficit for the rest of the world was essentially financed by OPEC lending its surplus. The main deficit regions were the industrial countries and the other developing countries (with deficits of $75b. and $58b. respectively).

The International Monetary System.

(i) International Liquidity.

Imbalance in payments between countries is financed by transfers of gold or foreign-exchange reserves. These reserves are known as *international liquidity*. Their basic characteristic is general acceptability: they can perform their function only if they retain the confidence of those engaged in international transactions. Near the end of 1985 gold, when valued at the free market price, accounted for 47 per cent of total international liquidity, foreign-exchange reserves for 46 per cent, drawing rights on the International Monetary Fund (IMF) for 5 per cent, and special drawing rights on the IMF for 2 per cent. Each of these will be described below.

(ii) The International Monetary Fund.

The *International Monetary Fund* was set up at Bretton Woods in 1944 with the object of working towards free trade at stable exchange rates. Under the original agreement establishing the Fund, members agreed to make their currencies convertible into other currencies and gold at fixed rates of exchange, and agreed not to impose exchange or import controls without the permission of the Fund.

The function of the Fund is to make foreign-exchange resources available to members which run into balance of payments difficulties. Each member country has a deposit (called its quota), paid partly in gold and partly in its own currency, with the Fund. The size of the deposit is fixed in relation to the country's share in world trade. In return, it is granted certain automatic drawing rights, which entitle it to borrow foreign currencies from the Fund. The Fund has power to make larger loans, and to grant standby credits to be drawn on if required. Before the Fund will make such loans and credits available it has to be satisfied that the borrowing country is taking appropriate action to correct the balance-of-payments disequilibrium.

(iii) Gold.

Gold played a central role in the international monetary system during the 1950s and 1960s. Central banks were prepared to buy and sell gold at a fixed price in terms of their currencies, and gold was exchanged among them in settlement of imbalances. The price of gold was held for many years at $35 per fine ounce. However, this fixed price in the face of rising costs of gold production meant that gold supply could not increase rapidly enough to provide the international liquidity needed to finance expanding world trade.

It was not clear, however, that an increased price of gold was the best solution to this problem. First, it would help those countries most which needed help least—those with large gold reserves. It would represent a victory for gold hoarders and speculators, and so act as a stimulus to further hoarding and speculation in the future; the United States had no incentive to help in particular the gold-producing countries Russia and South Africa; and finally, it would represent a sheer waste of economic resources: gold had no intrinsic value. The attempts since 1968 to *demonetise* gold are described in **Part IV**.

(iv) An International Currency?

The domestic currency of the United Kingdom is not backed by gold: on a one-pound note the Governor of the Bank of England promises to pay the bearer on demand the sum of one pound—another pound note! Yet, within Britain, there is complete confidence in the currency, because it is generally acceptable and so convertible into goods and services. Just as gold no longer backs the domestic currency, there is no need for gold in settlement of international payments. All we need is a generally acceptable international currency, *i.e.*, one in which all countries have confidence.

Such a currency could be created by an international authority constituted for this purpose; and it could be made available to deficit countries, which could then pay their creditors in the new currency. In this way the shortage of international liquidity could be made good, and indeed gold—Keynes' "barbarous relic"—could be supplanted. There are various difficulties with such a scheme. It involves some loss of national autonomy and the vesting of considerable power in the international authority issuing the paper currency. Decisions have to be made as to which countries should receive the new currency, and in what quantities. And there is a fear that it will enable reckless governments to pursue inflationary policies without the discipline imposed by shortage of reserves, and that their inflation will be infectious. Many variations on the basic scheme have been devised in an attempt to surmount these—largely political—objections.

The first, very limited, steps towards the creation of an international currency—the issue by the IMF of small quantities of *special drawing rights* —are described in **Part IV**.

(v) Foreign Exchange Reserves.

Two national currencies have been widely used in settlement of international payments: the pound and the dollar. The pound performed this function after the First World War, but the dollar has become the main reserve currency since the Second World War. Surplus countries are prepared to hold short-term debt in pounds or dollars—so earning a rate of interest—confident that their future trading deficits can be financed by payment of these currencies. These holdings are known as the *dollar* and *sterling balances*. They can perform their function only if there is confidence that they can be converted into other currencies and hence into goods and services at current exchange rates.

The United States ran a large and persistent payments deficit during the 1950s and 1960s, made possible by the willingness of the creditor countries to build up their dollar balances. Indeed, this increase in dollar balances was the main source of new international liquidity during that period. But there is necessarily a limit to such a process. The weakness in the U.S. balance of payments in fact added to the problem of international liquidity. The deficits produced periodic fears that the dollar would be devalued; and this resulted in speculation against the dollar, and contributed to the breakdown of the Bretton Woods system. The problems which have beset the dollar in recent years are explained in **Part IV**.

(vi) The Sterling Balances.

Governments and individuals may hold balances in sterling (*e.g.*, Treasury bills, Government stocks, and bank accounts) for many reasons. Some countries reckon to keep a high proportion of their reserves in the form of sterling balances. It is convenient to hold sterling to finance trading transactions because sterling is widely acceptable in settlement of trading debts. Sterling balances are also held privately to the extent that they are considered a safe way of holding liquid assets. It is profitable to hold sterling if the rate of interest paid on balances in London is higher than that paid in other financial centres, provided that the interest-rate differential is not offset by an expectation that sterling will be depreciated in terms of other currencies.

Near the end of 1985, the sterling balances totalled £40 billion—more than the official reserves, which stood at £16 billion. £8 billion was held by central banks, with the oil-exporting countries accounting for nearly a third.

An increase in the sterling balances enables Britain to finance an adverse balance of payments without reducing her gold and dollar reserves. Conversely, a reduction in sterling balances can impose a drain on reserves even if there is no adverse balance. The fear that the pound would depreciate in value makes it unlikely that Britain would be able to finance a persistent payments deficit through an increase in the sterling balances. The sterling balances thus tend to move perversely, so accentuating movements in the reserves. British Governments have been concerned to reduce the size of the sterling balances in recent years, and in this they have had the support of the international community. Attempts to run down the sterling balances and to make them less volatile are described in **Part IV**.

(vii) The Eurocurrency Market.

The Eurocurrency market is a market for bank deposits which are denominated in foreign currencies. It derives its name from the fact that most of the banks which accept these foreign currency deposits are in Europe (including Britain) and most of the deposits are denominated in U.S. dollars. The Eurodollar market has grown at remarkable speed since the 1960s. The reason for that growth was the profitability of Eurodollar transactions. Banks found that, particularly if only large units of money were handled, they could profitably borrow funds in country A and lend in country B, while paying interest rates higher than those paid in country A and charging rates lower than those charged in country B. Its growth was helped by the continuous deficit in the United States balance of payments, since this meant that banks and institutions received dollars which they were willing to hold and lend. OPEC funds obtained from their trade surpluses after 1973 tended to make their way into the market (as *petro-dollars*).

London is the largest international banking centre in the world, accounting for over a quarter of the lending market: in late 1985 the external liabilities of UK banks totalled $580 billion. Such large balances can create problems for the regulation of economic activity. Movements in the market affect interest rates, credit and exchange rates in different countries, and they can thwart domestic monetary policies.

2. EMPLOYMENT, PRODUCTION, AND INDUSTRY

Population.

In 1984 the population of the United Kingdom was estimated to be 56·5 million—49·8 m. in England and Wales, 5·1 m. in Scotland, and 1·6 m. in Northern Ireland. Since 1971 the population has increased by only 1 per cent. This slow increase is accounted for by the birth rate (the number of live births per 100 people) of 1·3 exceeding the crude death rate of 1·2. Partially offsetting this is the fact that more people migrated from the United Kingdom than have migrated to this country.

The official estimate of the population of the United Kingdom in the year 2001 is 57·7 million. But prediction of future trends is difficult. For instance, it depends on immigration and emigration policies, the effect of improving medical services on the average length of life, trends in the age at which people marry, advances in techniques of birth control, and attitudes towards desirable family size. This projection is based on the belief that there will be a continued small outward migration from Britain, and that the birth rate will slightly exceed the death rate.

The Labour Force.

Of the total population only some are of *working age, i.e.,* between the minimum school leaving age of 16 (15 before 1973) and retiring age—65 years for men and 60 for women. Of course, not all those of working age do work and not all those above working age have retired. In 1985 the labour force was 27·4 million. Of males who were aged 16 or over, nearly three quarters were in the labour force, compared with less than half of females. The labour force is defined to include not only those who are gainfully employed (as employees or self-employed) but also the unemployed who are looking for work. Students and housewives are excluded unless they do some work for cash. One feature of the past decade or so has been a slight fall in the number of adult males going out to work, a fall which it is expected will continue through the 1980s. It is caused by an increasing number of students and by more people retiring early. Those factors also affected the number of women going out to work, but they have been more than offset by a rising participation of married women, particularly in part-time work. This increasing trend is again expected to continue in the late 1980s.

Most of the labour force work for wages and salaries as employees. Of the total for the United Kingdom in June 1985 of 27·4 million, 2·6 m. were employers or self-employed. 0·3 m. were in the Forces, 21·3 m. were employees and 3·2 m. were recorded as unemployed. So less than half the population who are at work have to produce not only for themselves but also for the rest of the population who are either not in the labour force or who are unemployed.

The table shows the industries in which people work. As an economy develops there is a tendency for employment in the primary sector to decline at the expense of the production industries. At high levels of income a large proportion of income is spent on services, and employment in services expands as a proportion of the total. Thus, in 1955 services accounted for only 36 per cent of total employment; whereas by 1985 the proportion had risen to 65 per cent.

Employment and Unemployment.

In 1985 an average of 3,166,700 persons—13·1 per cent of the labour force—were unemployed in the U.K. This figure excludes school-leavers. In most post-war years until the late 1960's the average was lower than 1·5 per cent. Even in January 1959, the worst month of the 1950s, the rate rose to less than 3 per cent, and in February 1963—an exceptional month owing to weather—to less than 4 per cent. These contrast with an average figure in 1937, the best year of the 1930s, of 11 per cent, and with a figure of 22 per cent at the bottom of the slump in 1932. The low unemployment of the post-war years was not maintained from the late 1960s. Unemployment grew to reach almost one million in early 1972. It then started to fall back with the general economic recovery, only to start rising again from late 1974 as the economy moved back into recession.

Until the late 1960s 1–1·5 per cent unemployment was somewhere near the practicable minimum; for some unemployment is more or less inevitable. A seasonal rise in unemployment in the winter must be expected, *e.g.*, in seaside towns, and for this reason unemployment in January is half a per cent or so higher than in June. Moreover, some unemployment is bound to be involved in job-changing and as the demands

DISTRIBUTION OF WORKING POPULATION, GREAT BRITAIN, JUNE 1985
(Thousands)

Agriculture, forestry, and fishing	329
Coal, oil and natural gas extraction and processing	271
Electricity, gas, other energy and water supply	325
Manufacturing industries	5,370
Construction	933
Wholesale distribution and repairs	1,176
Retail distribution	2,153
Hotels and catering	1,041
Transport	847
Postal services and telecommunications	419
Banking, finance and insurance	1,932
Public administration	1,814
Education	1,537
Medical and other health services	1,317
Other services	1,372
GRAND TOTAL	20,836

of industries change. "Full employment" means that there should be about as many jobs vacant as there are workers looking for jobs. A large excess of vacancies is evidence of inflationary pressure in the labour market, for it means that the employers needing workers to meet the demands for their products will have to compete with each other by bidding up wages.

Most commentators feel that the practicable minimum level of unemployment has increased since the late 1960s. One explanation of this is that as the fixed costs (like National Insurance contributions) of employing workers have gone up, so employers have been more careful to economise on labour. Another possible explanation is that workers who were unemployed took longer to find a new job, because they may have drawn redundancy pay (since the Redundancy Payments Act of 1965) or they may have drawn earnings-related unemployment benefit, the earnings-related supplement having been introduced in 1966 (but withdrawn in 1982). A more general argument is that level of social security benefits as a whole is too high, causing people to demand an unrealistically high wage before accepting a job. It is likely that many of the unemployed have skills which are redundant in an economy where the structure of industry is changing. High real wages may have inclined investment to be of the labour-saving variety, whilst technological advance has reduced the need for labour in some firms. Amongst this range of potential explanations, the most convincing is that over a period of time, a high real wage has caused employers to try to produce a given amount of output with smaller quantities of labour. An increasing burden of labour taxes on employers, largely through national insurance contributions, also played a role. Also of great importance is the stance of the Government. If trade unions push up wages, employers may respond by putting up prices; unions then push up wages again in an attempt to obtain an increase in their living standards. Thus a wage-price spiral may cause increasing inflation. Governments concerned about inflation may therefore be forced to run the economy at lower levels of demand. There is evidence that the wage-price spiral has worsened, thereby necessitating harsher government action and higher unemployment at full employment. Whatever the relative importance of these explanations, there is little doubt that the major cause of the rise in unemployment in the 1980s is deficiency of aggregate demand for British goods. This in turn is partly the consequence of restrictive government fiscal policies, partly of declining world trade, and partly of our loss of international competitiveness.

To some extent official unemployment figures are misleading, in that certain individuals may not record themselves as being out of work and will thus appear to drop out of the working population. Until 1982 the official unemployment figure was calculated on the number registered as available for work. Registration was a prerequisite for claiming unemployment benefit. Individuals not eligible for such benefits—particularly married women—often did not register as unemployed even if they still wished to work. Their only incentive for doing so

UNEMPLOYMENT AND VACANCIES
(United Kingdom, thousands)

	Unemploy-ment.† (Annual Average)	Vacancies. (Annual Average)	Unemploy-ment as a percentage of total labour force
1932*	2,829	n.a.	22·1
1937*	1,482	n.a.	10·9
1968	574	190	2·4
1970	602	188	2·6
1972	787	147	3·5
1974	559	298	2·4
1976	1,193	122	5·0
1978	1,253	210	5·2
1980	1,487	136	6·1
1982	2,669	117	11·1
1984	3,047	154	12·6
1985	3,167	162	13·1

* Figures relate only to population insured against unemployment.

† Excluding school-leavers. From 1971 figures are based on claimants at unemployment benefit offices. Prior to 1971 they were based on registrations at employment offices.

was if they felt that the authorities would help them find a job. Further, the count did not include those who were temporarily stopped or working short time. Since late 1982 the official unemployment figures have been calculated according to the number actually claiming benefit, for which registering as available for work is no longer essential. It is estimated that 300–500,000 people may be on the work register who are not eligible for benefit. This, together with the hidden unemployment mentioned above, means that the true number of unemployed is close to 4,000,000.

Regional Unemployment.

Extreme variations in regional unemployment were not a general feature of the post-war period: until recently only in Northern Ireland was unemployment persistently very high. Between 1954 and 1986 unemployment there ranged between 5 and 21 per cent. Nevertheless, regional inequalities exist and have been magnified by the current recession.

PERCENTAGE OF WORKERS
UNEMPLOYED, BY REGIONS

	Annual average* 1965	Annual average* 1985
North	2·4	18·1
Yorkshire and Humberside	1·0	14·4
East Midlands	0·8	12·3
East Anglia	1·2	10·4
South East	0·8	9·7
South West	1·5	11·7
Wales	2·5	16·3
West Midlands	0·6	14·9
North West	1·5	15·7
Scotland	2·8	14·9
Northern Ireland	5·9	21·0

* Excluding school-leavers.

In 1985 the proportion of all workers unemployed in the U.K. was 13·1. But the table shows a lower proportion was unemployed in the South East, East Anglia, the East Midlands and the South West, and that there was a much higher proportion unemployed in the North, North West, West Midlands, Wales, Scotland, and Northern Ireland. Even within the more fortunate regions there are pockets of high unemployment. These are concentrated particularly in the inner areas of large cities, but also elsewhere. For example, in the South-East, Clacton had an unemployment rate of 20·1 per cent in early 1986, whilst in the South West, Redruth

had 23·0 per cent. This does not compare, however, with the 38·9 per cent rate in Strabane, Northern Ireland.

One of the main reasons for the regional pattern of unemployment used to be that certain industries and services, in which big changes have been taking place, tend to be grouped in specific regions. Most of our early industrial centres had to be established close to coal, iron ore, and adequate water supplies. But employment in many long-established industries has recently been declining. Such industries include textiles, mining and quarrying, shipbuilding, and agriculture. On the other hand new and growing industries, and their related offices, were concentrated in Greater London, the South East, and the Midlands. The growth of services, too, has centred on the areas where industry is booming and population is increasing. In the absence of government intervention, the process would tend to become cumulative, and regional inequalities would grow rather than diminish. The 1970s saw an interesting change. The West Midlands, traditionally after the South-East, the most prosperous area of the country, was severely hit by the particular impact of the recession on engineering. Thus it now appears as one of the regions with higher than average unemployment. Disparities in unemployment rates experienced in the 1970s and 1980s are the consequence of an additional factor— the relative concentration of unemployment in inner city areas in particular regions. Unemployment in the inner cities has grown more rapidly than elsewhere since the 1960s, and seems to be the result of limited growth of firms there together with only a slow emergence of new enterprise. It is thought that this largely reflects physical limits to expansion.

Regional Planning.

There are essentially two ways of tackling the problem of regional imbalances; taking jobs to the people or bringing people to the jobs. In so far as the latter alternative is chosen, the Government should encourage the mobility of labour, e.g., through retraining schemes or rehousing subsidies. However, the migration of population may damage community life in the denuded areas, and cause congestion, housing shortages, and overcrowding in the booming regions. The Government can create employment opportunities in the relatively depressed regions in various ways. It can try to induce expanding industries to set up new plants in these regions by offering tax incentives or grants; it can authorise additional expenditure on public works—e.g., by accelerating road-building programmes—to provide additional employment; it can place orders for the goods it needs—e.g., defence contracts—where work is required. It can also use physical controls on expansion in the better-off areas; between 1947 and 1981 factory building over a particular size, which was changed from time to time, required the granting of an *Industrial Development Certificate*.

(i) Labour's Policy.

On taking office in October 1964, the Labour Government made regional planning the responsibility of its Department of Economic Affairs. Britain was divided into eight regions, with the intention of producing a plan for each region.

Labour Government policy to cure regional unemployment took the following forms. Fiscal incentives to locate industry in the depressed regions were given, e.g., the cash grants provided in 1966 for new plants and machinery in manufacturing were at twice the national rate in the Development Areas. Buildings also received cash grants in Development Areas, in Intermediate Areas (where regional depression existed but in not such an acute form), and in Special Development Areas (where depression was most acute). By contrast, office building in the main conurbations, London and Birmingham, was strictly limited. To encourage the mobility of labour, the Government introduced redundancy compensation and achieved some expansion in both public and private training facilities. In 1967 regional differentials in the selective employment tax were also introduced. Under this scheme manufacturers in Development Areas were paid a weekly subsidy for each full-time adult male employee and lower amounts in respect of other workers, so giving the Development Areas a wage cost advantage in manufacturing. This was known as the Regional Employment Premium.

(ii) Policy since 1970.

In 1970 the incentive to invest in the Development Areas was affected by the Conservative Government's replacement of cash grants (except on buildings) by a system of initial allowances against tax. Whereas cash grants had been 40 per cent of investment in plant and machinery in Development Areas and 20 per cent in other areas, there was now a 100 per cent initial allowance in Development Areas and 60 per cent initial allowance in other areas. The system of initial allowances is explained on page **G14**.

Early in 1972 unemployment rates in Northern Ireland, Scotland, Wales and Northern England had reached high levels. The Government introduced 100 per cent allowances throughout the country on all investment in plant and machinery (*see* **Part IV**); the preferential treatment of investment in Development Areas was therefore ended. Instead *regional development grants*, in the form of cash payments towards investment in plant, machinery and buildings, were introduced. These were made by *regional industrial development boards*, at rates equal to 22 per cent of investment expenditure in Special Development Areas and 20 per cent in Development Areas and Intermediate Areas (on buildings only). The Government also proposed in four years to triple expenditure on retraining facilities, and to pay a worker who had undergone retraining a housing grant if he moved house to take a new job; and also a grant to any worker in an assisted area who moved house to take a new job. It should be remembered, however, that strong measures were necessary merely to replace the Labour Government's system of cash grants, and the Regional Employment Premium which it was planned to phase out in 1974. Though REP was retained by the incoming Labour Government, it was finally replaced by more selective measures in 1977.

In July 1979 the new Conservative Government announced some changes to be introduced over the 1979–83 period. The extent of the assisted areas would be gradually reduced, so as to cover 25 per cent instead of 40 per cent of the employed population. Some areas were "down-graded" immediately, others from 1980 and yet others from 1982. Regional development grants remained at 22 per cent in Special Development Areas, but from August 1980 the grant in Development Areas was reduced to 15 per cent and abolished altogether in Intermediate Areas. Industrial Development Certificate procedures were abolished in 1981.

In 1983 the Government introduced a Green Paper on regional policy. The suggestion was for a tighter and more selective approach, with aid being directed more at job creation, at small firms and at the services. But even this non-interventionist Government concluded that "wage adjustments and labour mobility cannot be relied upon to correct regional imbalance in employment opportunities".

Despite the Conservative Government's scepticism about the value of regional policy, expenditure on regional support in 1983/4 stood at £643 million. However, this does represent a dramatic decline from, for instance, £920 million in the previous year. The real value of expenditure on all regional incentives is less than half the levels of the early 1970's. But at the same time spending on both employment schemes and urban aid has increased.

Though regional problems remain, studies have shown that IDC's, financial incentives and REP, but particularly cash grants, have to a limited extent mitigated them. However, it was felt by many that the instruments were too blunt and insufficiently selective. It was also felt that in a slack labour market, regional policy was more likely to reallocate a given number of jobs rather than increase them in net terms. Alongside regional policy, therefore, were introduced measures on inner city decay (a problem even in non-assisted areas such as the South East), rural development and derelict land. In his March 1980 Budget the Chancellor announced proposals to establish about half a dozen "Enterprise Zones". These were small sites (of no more than 500 acres) with problems of economic and physical decay. The Zones were an experiment to test how far industrial and commercial activity could be encouraged by the removal of certain fiscal burdens, and by the removal or streamlined administration of statutory or administrative controls. By early 1985 there were 25 such zones. An additional measure, announced in the 1983 Budget, was the establishment of a number of 'freeports' which would enjoy similar relief from fiscal burdens, in particular local authority rates. By early 1985 there were 6 of these.

National Income.

Gross domestic income (GDI) is the sum total of incomes received for the services of labour, land, or capital in a country. Gross domestic product (GDP) is the money value of all the goods and services produced in the country. So as to avoid double-counting, only the *value added* at each stage of production is included: firms' purchases of goods and services from other firms are excluded. The revenue from selling the GDP is either paid out to the hired factors of production—labour, land, and capital—or retained in the form of profits. Therefore, provided it is calculated net of taxes on goods produced, GDP must equal GDI. To estimate gross national income (GNI) from GDI it is necessary to add the net income—such as profits and interest—received from abroad. If an allowance is made for wear and tear of the nation's capital equipment, *i.e.*, for *capital consumption*, we arrive at net national income, better known as the *national income*.

In 1984 the gross national income of the United Kingdom was £277,877 million, implying a national income per head of about £4,900. In 1954 the cor-responding figure had been £330 per head. However, only part of the increase in value was due to an increase in the quantity of goods and services produced; some of the increase simply reflected a rise in prices. It is important to calculate changes in the volume of output—known as *real output*—as well as changes in its value. Real output is calculated by the statistical device of constructing an index number. This is done by calculating the volume of goods and services provided in each year and then valuing these goods and services at the prices found in one particular year. Thus between 1954 and 1984 the money value of gross national product per head rose by 1,619 per cent, whereas real incomes increased by only about 75 per cent, and the difference represented a rise in prices.

The Quality of Life.

In real terms national income per head rose by about 75 per cent between 1954 and 1984, or by just over 1 per cent per annum. National income per head is an indicator of the standard of living. However, this measure is necessarily a crude one. For instance, it cannot take into account new and better products, *e.g.*, television, man-made fibres, faster flight, long-playing records, or the lowly plastic bucket; nor does it indicate changes in the distribution of income between rich and poor; nor in the length of the working week.

Data of national income per head may also conceal important changes in the "quality of life", *e.g.*, in our physical environment. This is affected by such things as traffic congestion, noise, water- and air-pollution. Between 1961 and 1984 the number of cars on British roads almost tripled, from 6·3 million to 16·5 million; the number of road goods vehicles growing more than ten-fold over the same period. Movement of civil aircraft over Britain doubled during the 1960s and increased by another 50 per cent in the 1970s, whilst some aircraft tended to become noisier. On the other hand, air in London and other major cities has become cleaner. This reflects a reduction of smoke pollution since the 1950s, and to a lesser extent of sulphur dioxide pollution. Complaints about noise pollution increased four-fold between the early 1970s and early 1980s.

Industrial Production.

It is fairly easy to measure output in the main manufacturing industries, and in many of the

AN INTERNATIONAL GROWTH LEAGUE TABLE

| | Percentage change per annum, 1960 to 1980 | | | | |
	Output	Employment.	Output per head.	Fixed investment as percentage of GDP, average, 1960-80	GDP per head, 1980 £.
Japan . .	7·7	1·1	6·5	32·5	3,858
France . .	4·6	0·5	4·1	22·7	5,276
W. Germany .	3·7	− 0·1	3·8	23·9	5,785
Italy . .	4·4	0·2	4·3	20·8	3,003
U.S.A. . .	3·5	2·0	1·5	18·2	4,941
U.K. . .	2·3	0·1	2·2	18·3	4,059

other industries producing goods. It is much more difficult to do so for the service industries: the output of a doctor or a teacher is not easily measured. So each month the Central Statistical Office calculates the *index of industrial production* covering the main production industries. Industrial production is thus an early indicator of economic trends (*see* **Part IV**), but it is prone to fluctuate more than the other components of GDP.

Manufacturing industry accounts for just under 70 per cent of industrial production. Within manufacturing the following industries have expanded rapidly since World War II—chemicals, including drugs, plastics, cosmetics and detergents, coal and petroleum products, including oil refining, and instrument and electrical engineering. The slowest growing manufacturing industries are textiles, clothing, leather and shipbuilding, which are losing their markets to cheaper competitors. Those industries in which demand has stagnated tend to be the industries in which output per employee, *i.e.*, productivity, has stagnated.

International Comparisons.

In recent years Britain's GDP has grown less rapidly than that of almost any other major Western country. The British economy is also characterised by a relatively slow growth of output per head, *i.e.*, productivity. Britain has fallen behind many of the European countries in terms of income per head. Some comparisons with other countries are made in the table. However, these may be misleading because incomes are converted into pounds at official exchange rates, and these need not reflect relative costs of living.

Many explanations of Britain's poor performance have been suggested, and there is by no means agreement on this matter among economists. It has been argued that the U.K.—like the U.S.A.—has a highly advanced economy in which there is a relatively high demand for services; and that it is difficult to raise productivity in the large services sector. Another argument is that Britain used to be hampered by its slowly growing labour force, which restricted growth not only in output but also in output per man. The reason given is that an expanding labour force needs to be equipped with additional plant and machinery so that its capital equipment tends to be newer on average than that used by a static labour force, and thus more up-to-date and efficient.

Some commentators have put the blame on the inefficiency of our business management; some on our educational system, biased towards the humanities; some on the social milieu which looks down on money-making as a career; some on over-manning and other restrictive practices of trade unions. A good deal of attention has also been paid to the proportion of output which different countries devote to *investment*, *i.e.*, expenditure on commodities—such as plant and machinery—for use in future production. These investment ratios are shown in the table. With the exception of the U.S.A., all countries have investment ratios considerably higher than in the U.K., with correspondingly higher growth rates of output and productivity. Since investment in dwellings contributes very little to growth, it may be appropriate to exclude this; however, similar results are obtained. This leads to the hypothesis

that Britain's growth rate could be raised if a higher proportion of output were devoted to investment, particularly in plant and machinery. There is probably some truth in many of these explanations, and it is unlikely that any one remedy will be sufficient to raise the British growth rate.

Recent theories and policies concerning Britain's growth performance are discussed in Part IV.

Investment.

In 1984 gross investment in capital assets amounted to £55,319 million in the United Kingdom. This was 20 per cent of the GNP. The net addition to the nation's stock of capital assets was only 30 per cent of total investment, the rest being needed to offset the wastage of assets already in use, *i.e.*, to make good the *capital consumption*.

There are four main kinds of investment: plant and machinery, vehicles, dwellings, and other new buildings and works. In 1984 the four categories accounted for 36·3, 10·5, 21·6, and 31·6 per cent respectively. Investment may also be analysed by the purpose for which it is used. Social services such as education and health take a surprisingly small proportion of total investment. Distribution and other service industries and public corporations take a large proportion: investment in oil, electricity, gas, and water alone accounts for over 12 per cent of the total. It is clear that some sectors of the economy are more capital-intensive than others. Manufacturing investment accounts for 13 per cent of the total. This is small in relation to the contribution of manufacturing to output, and has declined in recent years. Manufacturing investment has fallen more than any other form of investment in the current recession. However, many of the fast-growing manufacturing industries—*e.g.*, chemicals and electronics—use much machinery and equipment per unit of output produced. These capital-intensive plants cannot pay unless they are worked at near full capacity. With the growing capitalisation of industry it is increasingly necessary to introduce shift work.

Increasing Investment.

The proportion of total output invested—the *investment ratio*—is lower in Britain than in other countries with faster growth rates of output and productivity; and there is reason to believe that a higher proportion would improve the growth rate to a certain extent. But in a fully employed economy it is not possible to increase investment expenditures without curtailing other forms of expenditure, notably private and public consumption. This curtailment would have to be brought about by increasing taxation or encouraging people to save or by pruning public services. Yet the very act of restricting private consumption may induce private firms to *reduce* their investment expenditures.

In 1984, 74·6 per cent of total investment in the United Kingdom was carried out in the private sector, 11·8 per cent by public authorities and 13·6 per cent by the public corporations. The Government has more control over investment in the public sector than in the private sector. Governments do possess various policy measures by which to influence private investment (*see also* **Part IV**) but private investment is volatile and highly dependent on businessmen's expectations, especially their expectations about the future growth of their markets. It is no easy matter to raise the British investment ratio.

If a higher investment ratio could be achieved, a faster rate of economic growth—and therefore higher consumption in the future—would involve a sacrifice in current consumption. A choice must be made between the loss in current consumption and the ensuing gain in future consumption. Of course not all consumption expenditure is equally important to the standard of living: some would argue that if British defence expenditure was pruned to permit more investment, there would be no loss to set against the future gain.

The Finance of Investment.

Any business is allowed to charge as a cost the depreciation of its assets. Normal depreciation allowances used to be based on the original cost of the asset and on its expected useful life. In a time of price inflation depreciation allowances will not provide sufficient finance to permit the replacement of assets at higher prices, and accountants have been slowly moving towards the concept of depreciation allowances being based on replacement costs.

Governments have, however, adopted certain fiscal devices to encourage replacement and net investment. Soon after the war initial allowances were introduced. Under this system firms were permitted to charge against profits in the first year of its life 20, or at times 40, per cent of the cost of any new equipment, and the system amounted to a loan of the tax saved in the first year, repaid over the life of the asset. In 1954 initial allowances for machinery were replaced by a system of investment allowances, under which a firm could charge against profits 20 per cent of the cost of any new machine, with the difference that all ordinary depreciation allowances were still chargeable. So the investment allowance was a grant, not a loan, of the saved tax. In 1966, initial and investment allowances on new plant and machinery in three sectors—manufacturing, mining, and shipping—were replaced by cash grants. Other plant and machinery and industrial building received higher initial allowances. In 1970 the Conservative Government reintroduced initial allowances in place of investment grants but in 1972 tried to encourage investment by granting free depreciation; i.e. 100 per cent allowance in the first year. The details of capital allowances changed from time to time over the following decade, but in the 1984 Budget a more radical change was announced. By 1986 first year allowances would be scrapped, to be replaced by an annual allowance of 25 per cent and lower rates of corporation tax.

Depreciation allowances and government allowances and grants for investment have been sufficient to cover a major proportion of investment (excluding dwellings) by the private sector, and to cover a minor part of investment by the public corporations. The residue of investment, and house-building, had to be provided from other sources of funds. Companies rely mainly on retained profits, which are often larger, taking companies as a whole, than their net investment. Other sources of company finance are borrowing in financial markets and the issue of company shares. Much public investment must be financed by the Treasury, except for relatively small amounts raised by public corporations on the financial markets. The 1979 Conservative Government announced its intention to seek private capital for some investment projects, e.g. roadbuilding. The new Government also maintained a new stress on helping small firms. This had been given particular impetus by the report of the Wilson Committee and by the Budgets of 1980, 1981, 1982 and 1983. In the last, for instance, it took the forms of Corporation Tax relief and start-up grants. Traditionally investment measures are concerned with reducing the cost of capital. Many people believe that investment could be increased more effectively if more steps were taken to encourage a high and stable demand for output. Certainly under the conditions of the mid 1980s it is as likely that low demand as much as the high cost of capital is constraining investment.

Labour Subsidies.

Initially Government subsidies were employed primarily as incentives for investment, particularly in a regional context. A 1972 Act, however, gave wide powers to the Government to offer financial assistance in almost any form to almost any enterprise, provided the assistance was "in the public interest". The Labour Government in 1974 greatly increased subsidisation, aimed chiefly at maintaining employment. These subsidies consisted chiefly of direct assistance to industries both within and outside the assisted areas and labour subsidies in the form of temporary employment and job creation schemes, aimed particularly at young people. Thus there was a new emphasis on subsidies which cheapened the cost of labour. Some of the schemes, like the Temporary Employment Subsidy, were pure subsidies in this sense. Others combined the subsidy element with measures to increase either the mobility or training of workers, the Youth Opportunities Programme, for instance. The new Conservative Government cut back on such schemes soon after its election in 1979, but did continue an emphasis on training, particularly with the Youth Training Scheme, which was significantly extended in 1986..

Two other major subsidies were in force in early 1986. The Community Programme encouraged sponsoring agencies or individuals to set up projects of community value to utilise unemployed labour. The Government provided a cash grant for each person employed, and paid their wage which was supposed to be equivalent to the going rate for the job in the area. A second subsidy was the Enterprise Allowance Scheme, which provided a small weekly payment to help the unemployed set up their own business. Until 1985 the Government had a fourth scheme called the Young Workers Scheme, which paid employers to take on youths, in order to help them gain work experience.

Recently the Government has turned back more overtly to an element of "pure" subsidies. In early 1986 the Job Start Schemes was being piloted. Under this, an unemployed person who takes a job paying less than £80 per week is given a £20 weekly handout by the State. In the 1986 Budget, a New Workers' Scheme was announced. This pays employers a subsidy for taking on 18–20 year olds at a low rate of pay. The focus of these initiatives is that of encouraging employment at the low-paid end of the labour market.

Training

This emphasis on training is an important part of the Government's supply strategy for the labour market, as set out in the 1985 White Paper on unemployment, *The Challenge to the Nation*. There had long been criticism of the British training effort. It was said that the school system was ill attuned to the needs of industry, that not enough young people continued with education or full-time training after the minimum school-leaving age. The old apprenticeship system was justly accused of being too rigid and of forming skills which were not capable of being modified to meet changing technology. Financing of industrial training was thought to be insufficient. There was inadequate provision for the retraining of adults—so necessary if sufficient occupational flexibility was to be assured in a changing world.

In some respects matters had been getting worse. The recession, for example, had decimated training recruitment. Many of the old Industrial Training Boards were disappearing, without adequate substitutes being found. Yet at the same time, official thinking on training had become more sophisticated since the mid 1970s. The present Government has issued many documents on the subject, perhaps the most significant being *The New Training Initiative*. This covers all of the points mentioned in the previous paragraph. Yet in substantive terms little has been done on adult training, on the apprenticeship system and on the financing of training. Most emphasis has been put on youth training, and on the educational system, through projects like the Technical and Vocational Education Initiative. The precise worth of these policies has yet to be seen. The cynic might argue that measures such as the YTS are a cosmetic to cover up unemployment. A more measured commentator would have to agree that it is hard to discern how much is cosmetic and how much is real. In stressing the desirability of employers financing a higher proportion of training expenditure, there is a potential inconsistency in Government attitudes. Unless an employer can guarantee that an employee stays with him for the whole of his working life, then that employer's return from the training is lower than society's return. Therefore, there is a strong argument for a proportion of training costs being financed by the Government.

Monopoly and Competition.

A trend to increasing size and increasing capitalisation has been going on now for many decades, and in the process it has changed the face of British industry. In the early 19th century the typical firm was the owner-managed textile mill. Then in the 1860s and 1870s came the discovery of cheap methods of making steel, with the consequential immense growth in the engineering industries. Most of the chemical industry is still newer, and there are a number of entirely 20th century industries such as aircraft and electronics.

In the capital-intensive industries the big firm predominates. In some it has become almost a monopoly; in others the pattern is of a few firms, all large. In 1986 the top British companies included oil firms (British Petroleum and Shell), tobacco firms (British American Tobacco and Imperial Tobacco), chemical firms (Imperial Chemical Industries and Unilever) and one in the motor industry (British Leyland Motor Corporation). There is evidence that the extent of *concentration* of British industry—according to measures such as the proportion of the output of an industry produced by the largest three firms—has increased since 1945. Concentration increased particularly rapidly in the 1960s. There are two possible reasons for such an increase. The first is the natural growth of already large firms; the second is because of merger activity. This latter factor has been the more important in Britain. Although evidence is scanty, there is some suggestion that for a while in the mid 1970s, concentration has stopped increasing, and it may have fallen a little. Early 1986 was witnessing an increase in merger activity.

Competition goes on, but it has changed its form. Competition used to be largely by price. Now it is largely by advertising and by variations in the quality and other features of the product—detergents and motor cars being good examples. In many industries, groups of firms producing similar products entered into agreements which had the effect of restricting competition, for example through schemes for price-fixing. The effect is to increase the price to the consumer and to reduce the amount of output available. Some authorities have estimated that the total "welfare" loss because of this is relatively small, and have argued that our major concern should be over the dangers of large corporations having substantial political power because of their size, and over their using this power to force the Government into unwise decisions about, for example, subsidising inefficient management.

Domestic monopolies are also limited by foreign competition, and by the discipline of "potential cross entry"—that is, the possibility that a powerful firm may be attracted into a new sector by the sight of very high profits. The British industrial scene has nevertheless changed substantially, not only with the emergence of very large and powerful domestic firms, but also with the extensive presence of foreign-owned multinationals. Finally, however, it is worth remembering the words of the Nobel Prize winning economist, Sir John Hicks, that the greatest return to a monopolistic existence is a quiet life. In other words, firms will try not to make "too large" profits for fear of attracting new competition.

Regulation of Competition and Monopoly.

(i) Restrictive Practices Court.

The Restrictive Trade Practices Acts of 1956 and 1968 outlawed many of the main forms of restrictive agreements preventing competition. Collective price-fixing was declared to be illegal unless an industry could show that the practice brought substantial benefit to the public. Collective price-fixing was the system under which a central association for the industry laid down minimum prices at which members might sell. Usually such a system was backed by arrangements for collective boycotts, under which members of the association would refuse to sell goods to wholesalers or retailers who broke the rules. Collective boycotts were also found in industries without collective price-fixing, one common purpose being to make sure that retailers did not sell a manufacturer's products below his recommended price. This form of collective resale price maintenance was also outlawed by the Acts.

Under the Acts any restrictive agreements of several specified kinds had to be registered with the Registrar of Restrictive Practices. He then had to decide whether there was a *prima facie* case for the discontinuation of the agreement, and, if he thought there was, the case was referred to a Restrictive Practices Court, containing both judicial and lay members. For an agreement to be upheld, the agreeing parties had to prove to the Court that the agreement conferred some substantial benefit on the public which outweighed any injury it did to the public. A 1976 Act extended this legislation to cover service agreements.

(ii) Resale Prices Act.

The Act of 1956 permitted individual manufacturers to enforce *resale price maintenance* (r.p.m.) for their own products. Few suppliers would want the publicity of enforcing r.p.m. through the courts, but individual suppliers could still put some commercial pressure on pricecutters, *e.g.*, by offering less favourable terms or by refusing them supplies. The Resale Prices Act of 1964 prohibited all methods of enforcing minimum resale prices. However, goods which had been registered in due time with the Registrar of Restrictive Practices or had been approved by the Restrictive Practices Court, were exempted, temporarily in the former case and permanently in the latter. For r.p.m. to be approved by the Court, it had to be shown that some ensuing benefit to customers (*e.g.*, of increased quality or more retail outlets) outweighed any detriment. It was also lawful to withhold supplies to retailers selling goods at a loss to attract customers.

As a result of the Act r.p.m. has ceased to be a common practice, and has largely been replaced by "recommended" retail prices, which are in effect maximum prices. This practice has been investigated by the Monopolies Commission, which found that it was not always against the public interest.

(iii) The Monopolies Commission.

The Restrictive Practices Acts left untouched those industries in which one firm is dominant: these remained the responsibility of the Monopolies Commission. This is an independent administrative tribunal, established in 1948, with powers to investigate and decide whether a monopoly (defined in terms of market share) is contrary to the "public interest."

The Monopolies and Mergers Act of 1965 strengthened control over monopolies and mergers. With regard to monopolies, the Government wished to provide itself with legal powers of enforcement: previously monopolies had been expected to comply voluntarily with the findings of the Monopolies Commission. The Act also permitted the Government to refer a merger or a porposed merger to the Monopolies Commission in cases where the merger would lead to monopoly (defined as control of at least one third of the market) or would increase the power of an existing monopoly, or where the value of the assets taken over exceeded £5 million. The 1965 Act was repealed in 1973 and replaced by the Fair Trading Act. The rules governing referral to the Monopolies Commission were changed in this later Act. At the moment, referral can take place either if the gross assets acquired exceed a specified amount, or if the combined market share is greater than or equal to 25 per cent. Should the former criterion hold, "all aspects" of the merger may be investigated, whereas if only the latter holds, then the Commission may simply look at the consequences of the larger market share.

In interpreting the public interest, the Monopolies Commission has criticised monopolies for various practices, *e.g.*, if they attempt to deter entry to the industry, or earn abnormally high profit rates, or show weakness in research and innovation. The Commission has a difficult task in attempting to protect the consumers' interests, and also to avoid inhibiting the growth of firms, since evidence suggests that it is the large firms which are able to compete effectively abroad.

(iv) The Fair Trading Act.

The 1973 Fair Trading Act placed the previously dispersed responsibilities for overseeing competition policies in the hands of a civil servant—the Director General of Fair Trading. The Monopolies Acts of 1948 and 1965 were repealed and replaced by rather more comprehensive rules. Monopoly was now defined as control of one quarter of the market instead of one third. For the first time local monopolies were made subject to control. Also "complex monopolies" were made subject to investigation—that is situations where no one firm had 25 per cent of the market, but where several of the collaborated to restrict competition. The Director General of Fair Trading—as well as the Department of Trade and Industry—was enabled to refer monopoly situations to the Monopolies Commission; though it was still only the Department which could make references on mergers. Additionally the Director General took over the functions of the Registrar of Restrictive Practices and responsibility for general consumer protection, and set up a new body to assist in that aim—the Consumer Protection Advisory Committee. In 1978 the Labour Government published a review of its general policy. There were two main conclusions. The first was to recommend a more neutral policy towards mergers and to put greater stress on the importance of competition. The second was to suggest that the gross assets criterion for referable mergers should be increased from £5m to £8m (£30m in 1985).

In 1980 the new Conservative Government introduced a Competition Act which strengthened the powers of the authorities to deal with practices which limited competition in both the public and private sectors. Procedures were also speeded up considerably. There was a new power to refer nationalised industries and other public bodies for investigation of their efficiency, costs, services to consumers, and possible abuse of monopoly position. Perhaps the most celebrated case of applying the authorities' new legislation involves the UK Stock Exchange. In return for a pledge from the Government not to prosecute, the Stock Exchange agreed to abolish by 1986 the restrictive practices which govern entry into the stockbroking profession, and separate the broking from the market-making functions in the stock market. Also relevant are EEC provisions, Articles 85 and 86, which relate to anti-competitive practices which affect trade between member states.

(v) Industrial Structure.

Mergers may lead to monopoly and to the abuse of monopoly power. But it would be wrong to presume that mergers are always bad: mergers—by facilitating research and other economies of large-scale production—may increase industrial efficiency. For this reason the *Industrial Reorganisation Corporation* (IRC) was set up in 1966 under Government auspices. Its functions were to promote industrial reorganisation in the interests of industrial efficiency, *e.g.*, by enabling industries to achieve economies of scale or by reorganising inefficiently managed firms. It assisted firms in agreed regroupings and could intervene to encourage a particular takeover which, in its estimation, was in the public interest. However its objective in making loans was to "prod" and not to "prop" inefficient firms. It supported mergers in electronics, trawling, nuclear power, mechanical engineering, and other industries. In 1970 the Conservative Government decided to wind up the IRC. However, some of the proposed functions of the National Enterprise Board, set up in 1975, were similar to those performed by the IRC (*see* **Part IV**). The 1979 Conservative Government's streamlining of the NEB, and its subsequent amalgamation with the

National Research and Development Corporation to form the British Technology Group, means that there is no statutory body which can examine industrial structure.

Nationalised Industries.

The Nationalised Industries still account for about 10 per cent of British production. Local authorities also run some services, *e.g.*, bus transport and water provision. In many cases—*e.g.*, the railways, gas, electricity, and postal services—these industries are natural monopolies, in which the provision of competing services would obviously be wasteful. They were thus obvious candidates for public ownership. With the exception of steel—de-nationalised 1951–53 and re-nationalised in 1967—nationalisation was for a long time not extended into manufacturing industry. The post-1974 Labour Government nationalised the shipbuilding and aerospace industries, and established the British National Oil Corporation and the National Enterprise Board with wide powers to take holdings in private industry. Under the 1979 Conservative Government the post-war trend towards greater public ownership of industry was reversed (*see* **Part IV**).

A 1967 White Paper dictated that as well as achieving specified financial targets, nationalised industries should earn a target rate of return on their investments and price according to the marginal cost of a service. With respect to investment, each individual investment project was to be evaluated using a test rate of discount. This was initially 8 per cent and subsequently raised to 10 per cent, and was meant to approximate the return on low risk projects in the private sector.

With respect to marginal cost pricing, a hypothetical example will illustrate the principle. Once all gas production equipment and gas pipe have been installed the cost incurred in supplying additional gas is low; thus consumers are charged a low price per unit of gas consumed and, to avoid a financial loss, the Gas Boards make a standing charge to cover overheads. It is government policy that subsidies can be made for some services which are justified on social grounds, *e.g.*, grants to British Rail to continue unremunerative rail services. Cross-subsidisation of non-commercial services by commercial services within a nationalised industry is discouraged.

A new White Paper in 1978 changed the emphasis of government policy. Although the TDR and the principle of marginal cost pricing were retained, primary emphasis was moved from efficient decisions at the margin to a reasonable average performance, in terms of return on capital.

The nationalised industries are voracious users of capital, as they are nearly all highly-capitalised industries. Until 1956 they raised new capital, when they wanted it, by borrowing on the Stock Exchange; this fixed interest stock being guaranteed by the Treasury. Subsequently the nationalised industries drew directly on the Exchequer, through the National Loans Funds, for most of their capital investment which could not be financed from internally generated funds. This system was criticised. The advocates of equity issue pointed to the strain it put on the Exchequer and the possibility of nationalised industries cutting investment when surpluses fell or became deficits because of the ensuing difficulties in meeting interest obligations. It is also said that nationalised industries suffered from their dependence on the Exchequer, and particularly after the introduction of cash limits. In times of balance of payments crises the nationalised industries have been forced by the Government to cut back their planned expansion, sometimes at serious cost of disorganisation. It is probable that the attempts of both the 1974 Labour and post-1979 Conservative Governments to control total public expenditure have in fact resulted in an artificial squeeze on nationalised industry investment.

3. INCOMES, WAGES, AND PRICES

Personal Income.

National income is a measure of the total income accruing to the residents in a country in return for services rendered (see **G13**). It therefore consists of the sum of wages, salaries, profits, and rents having allowed for depreciation. But not all this income accrues to persons, e.g., companies do not distribute all their profits to shareholders and some nationalised industries earn profits. This is part of national income but not of *personal income*. On the other hand, some personal incomes are not payments for services rendered. Such incomes are called *transfer incomes* to emphasise that their payment does not add to the national income, but only transfers income from one agent to another. Included in this category are retirement pensions, family allowances, and student grants. In the United Kingdom in 1984 central and local government made transfer payments to the personal sector to the extent that personal income before tax (£279,556 million) was slightly higher than gross national income (£227,877 million).

Personal Disposable Income.

Not all personal income is available for spending. In 1984 the State took 15 per cent of personal income in *direct taxation*, and 4 per cent went as National Insurance contributions, which being compulsory are in effect a form of tax. Another 2 per cent went in contributions to pension schemes. The remaining 79 per cent of personal income—called *personal disposable income*—was available for spending. However, not all disposable income need be spent on consumer goods and services; income can instead be saved. There are many possible motives for saving, e.g., to meet future contingencies, for a future purchase such as a house or car, for retirement, or for the income to be derived from saving. Saving as a fraction of personal disposable income fluctuated from 7 to 10 per cent between 1960 and 1971. In 1972 it started to rise, reaching 12.8 in 1975. It remained high thereafter, and was at a peak of 15·0 in 1980. Since then it has generally fallen, and was 12·3 per cent in 1984.

Types of Personal Income.

The table shows the sources of household income. In 1984, the share of income from employment was 61 per cent. This rose considerably in the post Second World War period. The share of salaries grew relative to that of wages, not because average salaries rose faster than average wages but because the number of salaried workers expanded rapidly. With the development of the Welfare State there was an increase in the percentage of incomes derived from public grants—pensions, social security payments, student grants, etc.

SOURCES OF HOUSEHOLD INCOME, 1975 AND 1984

(As percentage of total)

	1975	1984
Wages and salaries	69	61
Self employment	8	9
Investments and rents	6	7
Annuities and pensions (other than social security benefits)	5	7
Social security benefits	10	13
Other sources	2	3

The types of income which fell as a percentage of the total in the post-war period as a whole were incomes of self-employed persons—a diminishing group—and incomes from property. During the war and for several years afterwards property incomes changed little—the effects of rent control, excess profits tax, and low interest rates were such that these incomes did not rise, while other incomes increased sharply. Subsequently there was a rise, as rent control on some property was lifted and as interest rates increased. In the latter part of the 1960s there was a growing recession in the economy. There was also an acceleration in the rate of wage increases but often prices could not be raised correspondingly because of the need to keep British products competitive with those of other countries. These developments contributed to a squeezing of the share of profits in national income. The major differences between 1975 and 1984 reflect the impact of unemployment. The share of wages and salaries has fallen, that of social security benefits has increased.

Inequality of Income.

In 1983, the top 20 per cent of income receivers (defined as households rather than individuals), received 48 per cent of total income, whilst the bottom 20 per cent obtained only 0·3 per cent. Thus Britain is far from being an egalitarian society, but discrepancies have narrowed since before the war, though with a subsequent widening in the last decade.

Taxes on income are of course highly progressive, rising sharply as income increases. Those with no incomes pay no income tax, and in so far as they are pensioners, no compulsory contributions either. The table (**G19**) shows the shares of disposable income. This is original income minus direct taxes and plus cash benefits. We can see that both are redistributive. In 1983 the share of the top 20 per cent fell to 39·6 per cent after allowing for these two items, whilst the share of the bottom 20 per cent rose to 6·9 per cent. Allowing for the effects of indirect taxation and benefits in kind yields final income. As the table shows, these two latter effects tend to be offsetting.

Thus the direct tax burden somewhat squeezes the distribution of incomes. But until the mid 1970s the narrowing dispersion of incomes before tax was of greater importance in making Britain rather more egalitarian than taxation policy. Since the late 1970s, however, inequality of pre-tax incomes has increased, whilst the tax system has become no more redistributive.

WEALTH OF INDIVIDUALS IN BRITAIN, 1983

Percentage of wealth owned by:			
Most wealthy	1 per cent of population		20
"	"	2 " " " "	27
"	"	5 " " " "	40
"	"	10 " " " "	54
"	"	25 " " " "	78
"	"	50 " " " "	96

Income and Spending Power.

In various ways figures for incomes alone underestimate the degree of inequality in British society. First, incomes are incomes as defined for income tax purposes. Any allowed expenses are excluded; and for the self-employed and the higher ranks of management the expense allowance now adds substantially to spending power. Second, if one buys an asset which then rises in value one gains extra spending power. Such capital gains can be very important to the wealthy in periods of boom in ordinary share prices, land prices and house prices—as experienced in Britain in the 1950s and 1960s. Yet only in 1965 did capital gains become taxable and even then the rate of tax on capital gains was low in relation to the rate on additional income.

Inequality of Wealth.

Spending power depends not only on income and capital gains but also on the sheer amount of capital owned. Data on the ownership of capital in Britain have to be estimated indirectly from information arising in connection with the payment of death duties, supplemented by information from capital transfer tax (from 1986 inheritance tax) returns and therefore cannot always be relied upon. An alternative method is to estimate the stock of wealth by working back from information on investment income, but this approach is also prone to error. It appears from the table that the most wealthy 1 per cent of the population own 20 per cent of all wealth, whilst 54 per cent of all wealth is owned by the richest 10 per cent. Even more strikingly, the poorer half of the population own only 4 per cent of total wealth. It should be emphasised, however, that the data refer to *individuals* rather than to *households*: this can give a misleading impression if, for example, the assets of married couples are generally registered in the name of one of the marriage partners rather than as jointly-owned assets. Nevertheless, it is fair to conclude from the data that the disparity of wealth is considerably greater than that of income. Moreover, there is a natural tendency for the inequality of wealth to grow because the higher income groups tend to save a higher proportion of their income and so to accumulate capital more readily. The Government by capital transfer tax has tried but largely failed to neutralise this tendency. Between 1971 and 1983 the share of the wealthiest 1 per cent fell from 31 to 20 per cent of total wealth. But this represents a minor change, particularly since much of what the top 1 per cent has lost has been redistributed to the rest of the top decile.

The capital transfer tax (CTT) was introduced in 1974. Until then only transfers of wealth on death or shortly before death were taxable. The CTT had many loopholes, but did something to redistribute wealth. The 1986 Budget effectively abolished CTT for gifts *inter vivos*, the tax (renamed inheritance tax) applying on death or transfers made in the 7 years preceding death.

Wages and Salaries.

In 1984 61 per cent of personal income was paid in the form of wages and salaries. The distinction between the two is very much a matter of convention; many salary-earners now earn less than wage-earners, and a more important

GROSS WEEKLY EARNINGS,
GREAT BRITAIN

(Average earnings, adults, April 1985)

	Manual	Non-Manual
Men	£163·6	£225.0
Women	£101·3	£133·8

division is between those salary-earners who are paid monthly and the rest. Even though monthly paid staff do not now earn more than wage-earners, they may still in effect be better off; for they generally work shorter hours, are more likely to be covered by private superannuation schemes, and work in better conditions. The table shows the earnings of manual and non-manual workers.

Earnings by Occupation.

Different occupations command different pay, as the table shows. The figures are of average earnings. The structure of pay reflects in part the amount of responsibility which the different jobs entail. The differentials reflect also the ease of entry into various occupations. This in turn depends on the degree of specialised knowledge, skill or talent required, and in a few cases it depends on the extent to which artificial barriers to entry have created scarcity. The

structure of pay is also influenced, of course, by the degree of organisation and bargaining strength of workers in different occupations. Finally, the relative strengths of demand for different types of worker is important, as is the force of custom.

Within the manual occupations the difference between skilled, semi-skilled and unskilled pay has narrowed over the post-war years. This was most marked during the war, in the years immediately after the war and between 1970 and 1976 when skilled workers were often granted the same flat rate advances as unskilled. The 1980's may well be seeing a reversal of such narrowing; but as yet it is too early to make a full assessment.

Occupational differentials have been a major source of industrial strife in some industries. In engineering, for instance, there has been continued conflict between unions with membership largely among the skilled and those with membership largely among the less skilled, over what forms demands for wage increases should take. On the railways there has been similar strife. Because of the importance placed on occupational differentials in collective bargaining there exist powerful rigidities in the structure of earnings in Britain.

AVERAGE GROSS WEEKLY EARNINGS
OF FULL-TIME ADULT MALE
EMPLOYEES, BY SELECTED
OCCUPATIONS, APRIL 1985

	£ per week
Medical practitioner. . . .	408·1
Finance, insurance specialist . .	379·1
University teacher	307·7
Office manager	281.8
Accountant	252·4
Production manager	250.9
Scientist	248·6
Policeman (below Sergeant) . .	244·8
Engineer, civil or structural . .	244·8
Primary teacher	203·6
Telephone fitter	194·6
Electrician.	193·8
Train driver	191·7
Maintenance fitter	191·1
Heavy goods driver	177.2
Plumber	173·5
Postman	165.9
Bricklayer	145·4
Painter, decorator	144·5
General clerk	142·7
Dustman	138·8
Unskilled building worker . .	131·6
Hospital porter.	125·3
Butcher	122·4
General farm worker . . .	116·3
Total workers	192·4
of which: Manual . . .	163·6
Non-manual . .	225·0

DISTRIBUTION OF ORIGINAL, DISPOSABLE AND FINAL HOUSEHOLD INCOME

	Quintile groups of households				
	Bottom Fifth	Next Fifth	Middle Fifth	Next Fifth	Top Fifth
Original Income					
1976	0·8	9·4	18·8	26·6	44·4
1981	0·6	8·1	18·0	26·9	46·4
1982	0·4	7·1	18·2	27·2	47·1
1983	0·3	6·7	17·7	27·2	48·0
Disposable Income					
1976	7·0	12·6	18·2	24·1	38·1
1981	6·7	12·1	17·7	24·1	39·4
1982	6·8	11·8	17·6	24·2	39·6
1983	6·9	11·9	17·6	24·0	39·6
Final Income					
1976	7·4	12·7	18·0	24·0	37·9
1981	7·1	12·4	17·9	24·0	38·6
1982	6·9	12·0	17·6	24·1	39·4
1983	6·9	12·2	17·6	24·0	39·3

Earnings by Industry.

Even within the manual occupations there are significant differences in earnings among industries. These are associated with the bargaining strength of different groups of workers, with the prosperity of the industry, and with the average skill levels required in production. Manufacturing industries as a whole pay relatively well. Public administration (including local government, roadmen and the like) is a low-wage sector.

Earnings by Sex.

The table also shows very significant earnings differences within each industry between men and women. There are two possible reasons why women are paid less than men. One is that they are crowded into lower-paying occupations. The second is that they may have lower pay than men within the same occupation. Either form of disadvantage could be the result of discrimination or of women possessing inferior productive characteristics. In practice it is a very difficult distinction to make. Equal opportunities and equal pay legislation attempts to reduce discrimination. The Equal Pay Act (1970) obliged a firm to pay men and women, who are doing the same job, the same wage by the end of 1975. In 1972 women in manual occupations had median earnings which were about half those of men. By 1978 this figure had risen to over 60 per cent, though by the early 1980s this improvement had slowed down, and was 62 per cent in 1985. Women in non-manual occupations had median earnings which were about 60 per cent of their male counterparts'. These changes are explained by the impact of the Act, by flat rate general increases agreed under incomes policies, and by trade union bargaining policy under inflation. Recently there have been renewed initiatives against sexual discrimination. In particular, in 1984 an amendment to the Equal Pay Act insisted that as well as paying men and women doing the same job the same rate of pay, parity of pay should also apply to jobs of equal value. The Equal Opportunities Commission has issued a Code of Practice which suggests positive actions which employers might take to improve the lot of women in employment.

Overtime and short-time.

The earnings of any individual worker depend on many factors, and are usually well above the basic wage rate payable for a *standard working week*. They include overtime earnings; and overtime working is common for men. In most weeks in the 1970s about 1–2 million operatives in manufacturing—about a third of the total—worked overtime to the extent of 8 to 9 hours. Even in 1985—a year of very high unemployment—34·9 per cent of operatives worked an average of 9 hours overtime each. Nor is overtime confined to male manual employment; it is found, for example, in office work and even in some of the professions like medicine and accountancy. The working week is composed of standard hours and overtime hours. Its length has diminished since before the war, although the standard week has been more significantly reduced.

AVERAGE WEEKLY EARNINGS OF MANUAL WORKERS IN CERTAIN INDUSTRIES (£p)
(April 1985)

	Men	Women
Mineral oil refining . .	243·3	—†
Printing and publishing .	222·3	121·4
Chemicals . . .	187·1	114·3
Motor vehicles . .	186·9	125·5
Textiles . . .	142·3	94·7
All manufacturing* . .	*172·6*	*104·5*
Transport and communication . .	179·4	138·0
Public administration . .	139·8	109·1
Retail distribution . .	130·5	94·3
All industries* . .	*163·6*	*101·3*

*Including industries not listed.
†Too small a number of women in this category to be recorded.

In most industries, for manual workers it was cut from 48 to 44 hours soon after the war. A 42-hour week was introduced between 1960 and 1962, and there was a movement towards a 40-hour standard working-week in the late 1960s. More recently there have been pressures from unions in several industries to reduce the standard week below 40 hours, and indeed this has happened in many sectors. In much of the Chemical industry, for example, it is often as low as 35 hours. The standard working week tends to be slightly less for white collar workers than for manual workers.

Short-time, the working of less than the standard week, has not been common since the war. It has been important in particular industries at particular times; but even at the beginning of 1986—with a national rate of unemployment of over 13 per cent—it was far smaller than overtime. Then 26,000 operatives in manufacturing were on an average short-time of 16·3 hours a week—a total 0·4 million hours lost as against 10·4 million hours of overtime in the same week.

Earnings and Rates.

Overtime is not, however, the main reason why earnings exceed minimum wage-rates; for most workers earn very much more than the minimum in the standard working-week. One reason is payment by results, the system of payment under which the worker's wage depends partly on output or performance. A common form is still the piecework system, under which pieceworkers are paid a fixed low rate per hour for each hour worked plus a fixed piecework price for each operation performed; but increasingly employers tend to prefer, as a more effective incentive, some scheme under which the bonus payment is related to the output of a larger group or to that of a whole factory. With such incentive schemes, earnings rise as productivity rises, and, as usually such workers also participate in advances in wage-rates negotiated between employers and unions, the gap between earnings and wage-rates tends to widen for them. So workers not paid on incentive systems press for similar advances for themselves, and in times of booming trade get them under a wide variety of names and forms—merit payments, lieu rates, compensation bonuses etc.

Wage Negotiation.

In Britain there were 11·1 million trade union members in 371 unions at the end of 1984. Most of these unions are very small, 252 having less than 2,500 members, but 21 have a membership of over 100,000. The main job of unions is collective bargaining with employers, and in most industries most employers also belong to associations which bargain collectively on their behalf. Some big firms, however, prefer to remain outside the associations, and strike their own bargain with the unions. Before the war many firms tried to encourage the formation of Company Unions, *i.e.*, of unions confined to employees of a single firm; but this is now uncommon. In some lowly paid trades minimum wages are fixed by Wages Councils set up by the Department of Employment: and representatives of the workers and employers, and independent members, meet together to reach agreement on the settlement to be recommended to the Minister. But over most of industry the aim of collective bargaining is to reach voluntary agreement, and the Department of Employment intervenes only when no agreement is reached. In 1974 the Labour Government set up the *Advisory Conciliation and Arbitration Service* (A.C.A.S.) to provide independent mediation and arbitration services.

The usual pattern of negotiation is like this. First, the union puts in a claim for an all-round increase, usually much larger than it expects to get. Then after a time the employers reply, often offering a much smaller increase, and sometimes none at all. They then argue round a table until either they reach agreement or they definitely fail to reach agreement. If the latter happens the next step varies considerably from industry to industry. Many industries have their own "conciliation" machinery, in which outsiders try to help the two sides to reach agreement. Some, though not many, also have their own "arbitration" machinery, in which outsiders can recommend a solution of the dispute, which is sometimes binding and sometimes not. It depends on what

WAGES AND PRICES
(1955 = 100)

	Weekly earnings.	Index of retail prices.	Real earnings.
1955 . . .	100	100	100
1960 . . .	130	114	114
1965 . . .	175	136	129
1970 . . .	250	169	148
1975 . . .	540	313	173
1980 . . .	997	611	163
1985 . . .	1,537	865	178

the two sides have agreed on in advance. Many industries have no machinery of their own and until 1974 depended on the general facilities the Minister responsible could offer. Since then they have relied on the services of A.C.A.S. Just as neither unions nor employers were obliged to call in the Minister, so now they are under no obligation to call in A.C.A.S.; the unions may opt to put pressure on the employers immediately either by strike action, or by banning overtime or piecework, or by other action.

After the Second World War plant bargaining developed as an increasingly important supplement to industry-wide bargaining in many sectors of the economy. Initially this was largely informal bargaining, with shop-stewards (unpaid lay trade union officials at the plant level) negotiating with management about, for example, special rates for working new machines. It is this which to a large degree was responsible for the growing gap between wage rates and earnings. The Donovan Commission, which was set up to inquire into the state of industrial relations and which reported in 1968, also saw it as the major cause of many of Britain's industrial relations problems, such as a high level of strike activity. Realising that it was impossible to put the clock back, the Commission recommended that plant bargaining procedures should be formalised, giving, for instance, proper channels for the resolution of wage disputes. Since then there has indeed been an increase in *formal* plant negotiations, with many plants now setting their own wage rates and using national agreements purely as a minimum benchmark. This development has probably improved the climate of industrial relations. Recently some manufacturing companies, concerned about the administrative cost as well as about the leapfrogging effects of plant agreements, have moved to single company bargains. As yet it is too early to discern whether this will be an extensive or permanent development. However, it is safe to say that today Britain has two systems of industrial relations. In large companies, especially in manufacturing, there is single employer bargaining whether this be at the establishment or company level. In small organisations, especially outside manufacturing, multi-employer industry-wide bargaining is still surprisingly important.

Such developments, however, have done little to increase the Government's power to control wages directly or to impose agreements—if anything quite the reverse. The recent attempts to introduce compulsion in wage-determination are described in **Part IV**.

Strikes.

The strike is the unions' weapon of last resort. Most unions maintain strike funds in order to support their members when they call them out on strike; but these funds are small, and strike pay is usually very much below normal wages. So unions cannot afford to call strikes irresponsibly, and major official strikes are relatively uncommon. Nevertheless, the big strikes are important; for the success or failure of one big strike can affect the results of all the other collective bargaining under way at the time.

Most strikes are neither large nor official. An official strike is one called by a union, usually by decision of the national executive, and is typically the result of collective bargaining about wages. But unofficial strikes called by local leaders are often about other matters. Few of the big unofficial strikes which plagued the docks were about wages; rather they reflected job insecurity and the poor state of labour relations in that industry. Much the same may be said about the continual strikes in ship-building, many of them caused by demarcation disputes concerning which jobs should be done by which type of skilled worker. Other strike-prone industries are mining and vehicles. In most industries there are very few strikes, and they tend to be concentrated in the larger plants.

From the mid-1950s the number of strikes in Britain tended to increase, except in coal mining. In 1969 and 1970 there was a huge jump in both the number of stoppages and working days lost. After that industrial disputes fell to a more normal level, and indeed by the early 1980s were at an historically very low intensity. Partly this reflects the impact of unemployment, but might also represent a more permanent improvement in Britain's strike record. But is Britain particularly strike prone compared with other countries? Making allowances for the size of their labour forces, Sweden and West Germany have fewer strikes and lose fewer working days than Britain. The United States has less strikes, but the ones they have are very large, and thus they lose more working days than the U.K. The

INDEX OF RETAIL PRICES
(1956 = 100)

	1956 Weight*.	1985 Weight*.	Monthly average index.						
			1956	1960	1965	1970	1975	1980	1985
Food . . .	350	190	100	105	121	152	313	601	790
Drink . . .	71	75	100	97	125	153	239	463	729
Tobacco . .	80	37	100	108	140	162	250	491	901
Housing . .	87	153	100	128	162	206	368	790	1,326
Fuel and light .	55	65	100	116	148	188	359	763	1,216
Durable household goods . .	66	65	100	97	107	129	212	366	427
Clothing and footwear	106	75	100	103	112	130	220	359	390
Transport and vehicles	68	156	100	116	132	163	311	624	848
Services . . .	58	62	100	116	148	202	379	735	1,067
Other goods .	59	77	100	112	136	178	315	629	891
Meals bought outside the home . .	—	45	—	—	—	160	209	458	653
All items . . .	*1000*	*1000*	*100*	*109*	*130*	*163*	*301*	*589*	*834*

* *i.e.*, proportionate importance of items in total expenditure in 1956 and in 1985.

strike records of Australia and France are most comparable with the U.K.'s.

In its Industrial Relations Act of 1971 the Conservative Government laid down new laws for the regulation of industrial relations and for the curbing of strikes. However, the Act was repealed by the incoming Labour Government in 1974, which itself brought in several new pieces of legislation, including the Trade Unions and Labour Relations Act, the Employment Protection Act, and the Trade Unions and Labour Relations (Amendment) Act. As well as increasing legal protection for the individual employee and extending trade union immunities and rights, this legislation was concerned to improve industrial relations practice. The belief behind the legislation was that this could be done by machinery which ensured, for example, that employers formally recognised unions for collective bargaining purposes and that unions had greater access to information to enable them to negotiate about issues (such as a firm's investment plans) which previously ignorance had precluded them from doing.

With the election of a Conservative Government in 1979, the direction of legislation altered again. The 1980 Employment Act introduced measures to moderate the closed shop, provide funds for secret union ballots about important issues such as industrial action, and to limit picketing to only the establishments at which strikes were taking place. A further Act in 1982 intensified pressure on the unions. In particular it introduced further measures against existing closed shops and increased the liability of unions for the actions of their members. In 1984 came the Trade Union Act concerned with union democracy. In this unions were denied immunity if strikes took place without ballots, voting members of union executives had to be elected, and periodic ballots on the political use of union funds were required.

Prices and Real Incomes.

The aim of a trade union is to get for its members a higher standard of living, and its success depends on the extent to which wage advances exceed the rise in the cost of living. Prices rose very rapidly (by over 30 per cent) between 1949 and 1953, and earnings only just kept ahead in this period. But after that *real earnings* (*i.e.*, the command which money earnings have over goods and services) rose steadily until the early 1970s. Since then real earnings have increased more spasmodically (*see* **Part IV**).

Price Changes.

In the calculation of real wages it is usual to make use of the *index of retail prices*, commonly called the cost-of-living index. The index is calculated monthly by the Department of Employment, and it naturally has an influence on the course of wage negotiations.

The table shows how consumers allocate their expenditure among different commodities in Britain, and how the prices of these commodities have moved over time. Nearly one fifth of expenditure in 1985 was on food; and housing, fuel and light between them accounted for 21·8 per cent. Drink and tobacco represented 11 per cent; and expenditure on transport and vehicles no less than 15·6 per cent. Comparing the allocation of expenditure in 1956 and in 1985, we see in particular the growing importance of housing and transport and vehicles and the declining importance of food in household budgets. As people grow richer they choose to spend less of their income on food.

Price changes have not been the same for all types of goods. For instance between 1956 and 1985, when the total index rose by 734 per cent, housing went up by 1,226 per cent and fuel and light by 1,116 per cent; but the prices of drink, and especially clothing and durable household goods rose less than the average.

The general retail price index is calculated by weighting each of the commodity price indexes by the proportionate importance of that commodity in total expenditure in a particular year, and then summing all the indexes, *i.e.*, the general index is a *weighted average* of its constituent indexes. A different pattern of expenditure would mean a different set of weights, and hence a different cost-of-living index. For instance, the

poor—and particularly pensioners—spend a higher proportion on the basic necessities; food, fuel and light, and housing. It is possible that the cost-of-living rose more for the poor than for the rich over these years.

The cost-of-living index has not risen evenly in Britain. There were spurts of rapid inflation in the periods 1950–52 and 1954–56, followed by a decade of relatively little inflation (averaging under 3 per cent per annum). After 1967, however, the rate of inflation accelerated, rising progressively from 2·5 per cent per annum between 1966 and 1967 to 7·0 per cent between 1971 and 1972. For more recent developments *see* **Part IV**.

The Causes of Inflation.

(i) Import Prices.

Prices charged in the shops are determined by a great many factors, over many of which the Government has little or no control. First among these is the price of imports. Prices of imported food and raw materials are determined in the world markets, in which Britain is only one of many purchasers. In the raw material markets the U.S.A. is usually the dominant purchaser, and prices depend greatly on the level of economic activity there. In the food markets British purchases are more important, since the U.S.A. grows most of its own food, and is a large exporter of some foods. Prices in raw material markets are continually changing, and can fluctuate wildly. Big increases in commodity prices occurred during the Korean war, in the early 1970's and in 1979 (*see* **Part IV**). The sharp increases in the prices of primary commodities contributed to British inflation at these and other times, but for most of the post-war period the rise in import prices has been less rapid than domestic inflation. Imports cannot be primarily blamed for the continuing inflation, nor for the acceleration of inflation after 1967. This is allowing for unfavourable exchange rate movements which push up the price of imports in sterling terms.

The source of domestic inflation has to be looked for in the tendency of wages, salaries, profits, and other incomes to rise faster than real output; and this they have done in almost every year since the war.

(ii) Demand-Pull Inflation.

An explanation of domestically generated inflation is that it arises not so much from increased costs as from demand pressures increasing prices and profits. If there is an increase in aggregate demand for goods and services in the economy, how does the economy respond? If it is operating at less than full employment, producers are able to expand their production to meet the additional demand. But if full employment has already been achieved, it is the price level and not production which rises. Given an excess demand for goods and services, there is competitive bidding for the limited supplies and producers are able to sell at higher prices. A more sophisticated version of this argument recognises that full employment cannot be precisely defined: rather, there are degrees of less or more unemployment. Bottlenecks appear in different firms and industries at different stages; so that any increase in demand is met by an increase in both prices and production. But the lower the rate of unemployment, the more does the response take the form of price increases.

A variant of the demand-pull theory is the so-called *quantity theory of money*, in which inflation is seen as a response to an increase in the supply of money; there is too much money chasing too few goods. The theory dates back at least to David Hume, but it was generally discredited as a result of the writings of Maynard Keynes in the 1930s. However, it was revived by Milton Friedman and has received some measure of acceptance among economists, especially in the United States.

The evidence for the demand-pull theory of inflation in Britain is very slight, at least in more recent times and especially since the mid-1960s. No doubt there are times at which demand contributes to inflation in the economy as a whole or in particular sectors. Thus, for instance, the great shortages during and immediately after the war would no doubt have generated rapid demand inflation had it not been for rationing and price controls; and the spurt of inflation between 1954 and 1956 was associated with a very high pressure of demand. On the other hand, inflation has occurred even in periods of relatively high unemployment. Moreover, the method by which most firms price their products is on the basis of their costs; so that most prices are not directly sensitive to the pressure of demand. A more plausible mechanism by which demand might influence prices indirectly is through its effect on wages. In fact, there has been a lively debate as to the extent to which wages are influenced by the pressure of demand as opposed to being relatively independent of it. There is, however, general agreement that wages are the main driving force behind prices.

(iii) Wages and Inflation.

When a trade union negotiates a wage increase for all or most employees in an industry, firms will immediately consider whether they should increase their prices to cover their increased wage-costs. As it is common practice for firms to fix the selling prices of their products by first calculating the direct cost of labour and of materials, and then adding on a percentage to cover overhead costs and profits, they will tend to want to raise their prices not only to cover the cost of the wage advance, but also to cover their percentage addition. Moreover, in deciding whether or not their customers will stand for such increases, firms will be influenced by the knowledge that their competitors have to pay the increased wages too, and will probably therefore be raising their prices. So industry-wide wage advances—and changes in costs of materials—are particularly likely to be passed on to the consumer; and, as wage-earners are also consumers, to generate further demands for wage advances to cover the increased prices.

Once this spiral gets going, it is very hard to stop it. In general, the requirement is that wage earnings should not rise faster than productivity (output per man). But as in some industries productivity is very slow to rise, and as it would be unfair and impracticable to exclude their workers from participating in any general rise in the standard of living, this requirement means that in industries with a rapid growth of productivity wage advances should be kept well below the rate of rise of productivity. For two reasons this is rather difficult. First, rising productivity often raises the wages of some workers in these industries automatically, because they are paid by results or through some incentive scheme. The rise of wages from this source takes the form of a tendency on the part of earnings in these industries to rise faster than wage-rates; but that does not mean that all employees benefit, or that the unions in these industries will not press for the same rate of increase in wage-rates as is achieved in the slowly-growing industries. Second, employers in the rapidly-growing industries have far less reason to resist demands for wage increases than those in slowly-growing industries. Indeed, they are quite likely to bid up wages in order to get the labour they need, rather than to try to hold down wages.

There are therefore major problems in preventing a faster rise in wages than in productivity, with its consequence of rising prices. And once a wage-price spiral has started, the problems become more acute because unions and employers become accustomed to substantial annual advances in money wages. A main source of continuing price inflation has been the tendency of money wages to continue to advance at a rate that was appropriate when the cost-of-living was going up sharply, but ceased to be appropriate in later years.

(iv) The Phillips Curve.

Even if wage behaviour is primarily responsible for inflation, the pressure of demand may still be important. If unemployment is low and unfilled vacancies high, there is competitive bidding among employers to obtain or retain their workers. Moreover, with the economy booming the bargaining strength of trade unions increases: employers are more willing to concede wage demands. These possibilities have led economists to postulate—and indeed to measure—the so-called

Phillips Curve relationship: the lower the level of unemployment, the faster the rate of increase in money wages. Such a relationship has been found to exist in the British economy over some periods. But events after 1967 reveal the danger of postulating "general laws" in economics: inflation accelerated despite high and growing unemployment. Clearly, changes in the cost-of-living, expectations for the future, Government policies and the degree of militancy of trade unionists can all have a significant influence on wage behaviour; and the level of demand may at times be relatively unimportant.

There are many schools of thought attempting to explain developments since the late 1960s, but it is possible to discern two general approaches. The first is that trade unions behave reactively. In other words, they respond in their wage demands to their expectations about prices and Government policies. A restrictive monetary policy might help moderate inflation, in that it might directly reduce prices and it might affect expectations. The second school of thought is that unions, as well as responding to their perception of the events they face, act in a more initiatory way—to fulfil, for example, aspirations (developed perhaps over a long period of time) about what their real earnings, and therefore their share of the national cake, should be. In striving to realise these aspirations, they may be relatively unaffected by concern over rising unemployment. Most of the evidence indicates that until recently this was in fact the case. A likely explanation is that unions felt unconcerned about relatively minor variations in the unemployment rate, safe in the knowledge that Government was committed to the maintenance of full employment. In the mid-1970s such a commitment was quite explicitly abandoned. That, together with the current experience of very high unemployment, might tighten the demand constraint in more prosperous future times. No longer, it is argued, will unions be able to count on being "protected from the consequences of their own actions".

The Effects of Inflation.

British Governments have been concerned about inflation mainly because of its effects on British competitiveness, and hence on the balance of payments. If our costs rise relative to competitors' costs, British exporters find it more difficult to compete in foreign markets if they raise their prices; and if they keep prices down in order to compete, this implies their having to accept lower profit margins on exports than on sales in the home market, and so discourages exporting. Alternatively, this lack of competitiveness might be reflected in falling exchange rates. This by itself is not necessarily a bad thing, but the danger is that it can start a spiral. An initial depreciation causes price inflation to increase at home, which causes further wage increases, which leads to further depreciation, and so on. The result could be hyperinflation. This clearly has a major efficiency cost, since it will cause people to economise on the use of money in conducting their transactions.

Inflation can have other harmful consequences. It often produces a redistribution of income, with the strong gaining at the expense of the weak, *i.e.*, the poorly organised workers and the pensioners. In inflationary conditions income gains can appear to result not so much from work or sacrifice as from ingenuity and speculation and the exercise of economic and political power. Inflation can breed insecurity and industrial unrest. Among businessmen it increases uncertainty, reduces investment and hence growth. Finally, it causes a redistribution of income away from lenders to borrowers.

Government Policy against Inflation.

There are several possible methods of attack on the inflationary spiral of wages and prices. Their usefulness will depend on the causes of the inflation.

One policy appropriate to most inflations, and also helpful to other objectives of economic policy is to achieve a faster rate of productivity growth. The faster the growth of average productivity the faster can average incomes rise without an increase in average prices. Comprehensive and detailed government control of wages except as an emergency policy was thought for a long time to be impractical for political and institutional reasons, as was comprehensive and detailed control of prices. Experience suggested that such detailed policy, except as a temporary general "freeze", would be very difficult to operate and, if successful, would involve a major loss of flexibility in the economy. At the other extreme, general exhortations to unions to exercise restraint on wages, and to manufacturers to exercise restraint on prices, were thought to have little effect. After 1974 more people began to think that a semi-permanent incomes policy might in fact be a viable policy tool. This development is discussed in **Part IV.**

The Government can attempt to regulate inflation by controlling purchasing power through its monetary and fiscal policies, the nature of which will be examined below. There is a danger that curbing demand also curbs the growth of output and productivity in the economy; so conflicting with other objectives of economic policy. Moreover, there is no certainty that inflation is sensitive to the rate of unemployment over the politically acceptable range of unemployment.

There is no easy solution—difficulties and disadvantages are attached to every measure for controlling inflation. In **Part IV** we shall discuss the solutions which have been attempted since 1960.

4. MONEY, BANKING AND FINANCE

Economic Objectives and Demand Management.

The various economic objectives—full employment, balance of payments equilibrium, the control of inflation, *etc.*—which, as mentioned in **Part I,** have been shared by all post-war British Governments, are all to a greater or a lesser extent dependent for their attainment upon the type of *demand management* policy pursued by the government. By this is meant the policy, or set of policies, with which the government seeks to regulate the total level of expenditure on goods and services. The latter is the sum of consumption and investment expenditure by both the private sector (firms and consumers) and the public sector (the government and the nationalised industries). If the resulting level of aggregate demand for output is greater than the amount which can be produced with the economy's resources the result will be shortages leading to inflation and/or an increased demand for imports. If the level of demand is not high enough, on the other hand, the result will be a waste of resources, *i.e.*, workers will be unemployed and capital equipment will be underutilised. Hence it is crucial for the government to keep the pressure of demand at an appropriate level by regulating the various types of expenditure making up the total.

Fiscal and Monetary Policy.

One way in which the government can attempt to regulate demand is by fiscal policy, *i.e.*, the regulation of taxes and public expenditure (*see* **Part IV**). If the government believes, for example, that the level of demand is too high, it may seek to reduce it by raising taxes whilst leaving public expenditure unchanged, thereby reducing its *budget deficit* (*i.e.*, the excess of public spending over tax revenue). Since the private sector's expenditure plans are financed partly out of its after-tax income and partly out of borrowing, an increase in taxes will generally reduce private sector expenditure, so that total expenditure then falls if public expenditure is held constant. Conversely, the government can cut taxes or increase public spending if it wants to expand the economy by increasing total expenditure.

However, fiscal policy of this type is not independent of *monetary policy*, *i.e.*, the regulation of interest rates or the stock of money in the economy. For example, if the government increases public spending it has to pay for the various resources which this involves. The finance may come from additional taxes, but if the government does not raise taxes the extra expenditure then has to be paid for in one of two ways: either the government increases its borrowing from the private sector by issuing government stock in return for money to pay for public expenditure; or the government prints new money for this purpose.

In the latter case the supply of money is increased; in the former case interest rates will generally be increased, since the private sector will probably require higher interest rates if it is to be induced to lend extra funds to the government.

Economic Controversies.

Thus changes in the government's "fiscal stance" (*i.e.*, the size of its budget deficit) necessarily involve monetary changes in the form of interest rate and/or money supply changes. There is a great deal of controversy amongst economists about what sort of monetary policy the government should follow—*i.e.*, how it should finance its budget deficit—and about the importance of monetary policy as an influence upon the level of demand for output. Broadly speaking, the so-called "monetarist" school of economists, the leading exponent of which is Professor Milton Friedman, believes that the supply of money (and its rate of increase) is the main determinant of the level of demand. They therefore argue that the government must control the rate of growth of the money supply: if it grows too fast, so will aggregate demand, with consequent inflationary and balance of payments problems. The implication is that a large budget deficit must be financed by borrowing—even if this causes a large rise in interest rates—rather than by a rapid expansion of the money supply. In contrast, the so-called "Keynesian" school of economists, following the lead of the late J. M. Keynes, does not believe that changes in the money supply necessarily have a very large or predictable impact upon aggregate demand, and they are therefore less concerned than monetarists about financing a budget deficit by expanding the money supply. They tend to stress the harm that might result from allowing interest rates to rise.

This argument spills over into a related disagreement about the budget deficit itself. Many monetarists believe that high budget deficits are harmful regardless of whether they are financed by borrowing or by monetary expansion, and since the late 1970s this school of thought has urged a progressive reduction in the size of the budget deficit, and in some cases its eventual elimination. In contrast, Keynesians tend to see budget deficits as a necessary part of economic policy, particularly in times of high unemployment when, as already mentioned, higher public spending and lower taxes—and in consequence an increased budget deficit—are seen by Keynesians as a way of combating unemployment.

The remainder of this Section describes the working of Britain's monetary system, discusses the various types of monetary policy followed since the war and their interaction with fiscal policy, and shows why there is so much controversy amongst economists and policy-makers about these aspects of economic policy.

The Definition of "Money".

Although most people probably have a clear idea of what they understand by "money", it is in fact an extremely difficult concept to define with precision. Economists tend to define it as anything which is readily acceptable as a means of payment. Evidently "money" in this sense constitutes "cash"—banknotes and coins—and also current account bank deposits, since possession of the latter allows the drawing of cheques which, normally, are a universally acceptable means of payment. The total of cash and current account deposits at any given time is one possible definition of the supply of money existing at that time: it is known as "M1", and also as the "narrowly-defined" money supply, since an alternative definition—known as "M3"—embraces other types of bank accounts (deposit accounts, foreign currency accounts, and public sector accounts) as well as the components of M1. The argument in favour of M3 is that cheques can in practice be drawn on the additional types of account which it includes and that these accounts should therefore be classed as "money" when the latter is defined as a means of payment.

The competing claims of M1 and M3 as the appropriate definition of money were recognised when monetary targets were adopted as an important part of economic policy making in Britain in the late 1970s (*see* **Part IV**). Separate targets were set for the growth of M1 and M3, and for a time it was not clear which was regarded as more important by policy-makers. In the early 1980s, however, M3 came to be regarded as the main target, and in 1984 M1 was abandoned as a formal policy target. It was replaced by MO, the so-called "monetary base", defined as notes and coins in circulation plus banks' deposits held at the Bank of England. The argument in favour of MO was that a growing proportion of M1 was made up of interest-bearing deposits and that it therefore increasingly represented peoples' savings decisions; hence it no longer provided a good guide to the amount of money available to finance current demands for goods and services. In contrast, because notes and coins constituted about 90 per cent of MO, the latter was a reliable indicator of current demand pressure.

Whatever the merits of MO as an indicator of demand pressure, it should be noted that it does not correspond to the definition of "money" as a means of payment because it excludes all current and deposit bank accounts, essentially on the grounds that holders of such accounts might choose to regard them as vehicles for savings rather than for financing current spending. It therefore narrows the definition of money beyond the "narrowly defined" M1 by including only those elements for which there is no plausible demand other than as a means of payment.

Liquidity.

In contrast, many people have criticised even the "wide" definition of money, M3, on the grounds that it excludes accounts at institutions other than banks. This is potentially important since total deposits with the banks are less than total deposits with non-bank institutions. If the government controls M1 (or M3) as a means of controlling aggregate demand, therefore its policy may be circumvented if, say, people run down building society accounts in order to increase their current expenditure. Many Keynesians regard this as a crucial objection to the idea of controlling aggregate demand by controlling the money supply (whether M1 or M3). They argue that what matters for the control of aggregate demand is not "money" but the economy's stock of *liquid assets*, *i.e.*, assets which can readily be converted into "money", and hence into potential expenditure on current output. This argument has led to attention being given to wider measures of monetary aggregates than either M1 or M3. Two measures of *private sector liquidity* (PSL) now receive considerable attention from policy makers. PSL1 is M3 minus foreign currency and public sector bank deposits, but with the addition of money market instruments (*e.g.* Treasury bills and local authority deposits) and certificates of tax deposit. PSL2 is an even broader measure: it adds to PSL1 private sector ordinary share accounts in building societies, net of building society holdings of money market instruments.

The traditional argument for concentrating on measures like M1 or M3 rather than on wider measures of liquidity was that building society accounts, and similar assets, could not be used directly as means of payment: it was necessary first to withdraw cash from a building society account before making a purchase. However, at the start of the 1980s this position changed as the banks and building societies started to compete more closely. The banks moved increasingly into the business of lending for home purchase; and several of the building societies began exploring the possibility of issuing cheque books to their account holders, the implication being that if such cheques became accepted as a means of payment, building society accounts would then take on all the essential characteristics of "money".

The Choice of Targets.

The fact that "money" can be defined in so many different ways, each having some plausible justification, poses an obvious problem for monetarists: if it is important to control the money supply, which measure is the one to be controlled? This is of some practical importance since the various monetary aggregates often grow at very different rates. In 1972 and 1973, for example, M3 grew much more

rapidly than M1; in 1975 and 1977 the position was reversed. Over the longer term, moreover, M1 has been steadily falling in size relative to M3: the ratio of M1 to M3 was about 2/3 in 1963 but less than 1/2 in the early 1980s. Similar variations also occur as between the various other possible measures of money supply and liquidity. The table illustrates the range of growth rates of the various measures in 1984–85.

Annual growth rates,
November 1984–November 1985

MO	M1	M3	PSL1	PSL2
0·6	5·3	3·4	3·2	2·8

The Liquidity Spectrum.

By definition "money" is completely liquid. Building society accounts are clearly highly liquid assets. Other types of financial assets—*e.g.*, long-dated government stock, known as *gilt-edged securities*—are less liquid, since although the owner of such assets can easily exchange them for money, he cannot confidently predict the *price* at which he can do so. For example, he may have to sell at a time when the market price of government stock is unusually low, so that he realises relatively little money from the sale. Thus "liquidity" refers not only to the speed with which assets can be sold, but also to the predictability of the amount of money which the sale will realise. In practice, there is a *liquidity spectrum*, *i.e.*, a whole range of different types of asset, each possessing a different degree of liquidity. The spectrum includes not only financial assets but also real assets—houses, capital equipment, etc.—the latter being highly illiquid, *e.g.*, selling a house takes a long time, involves high transactions costs, and the sale price is unpredictable.

Liquidity and Expenditure.

There is a crucial difference between Keynesians and monetarists about the working of the liquidity spectrum. Keynesians believe that firms and consumers regard "money" and non-money liquid assets as good alternatives to one another in as much as both provide security, predictability, etc. That is, there is on the Keynesian view a high degree of *substitutability* between money and other liquid financial assets; and, in contrast, a relatively low degree of substitutability between money and real assets. Monetarists, on the other hand, assume the reverse: relatively high substitutability between money and real assets, relatively low substitutability between money and other financial assets. These different assumptions imply different effects if the government increases the money supply. Monetarists argue that much of the extra money is spent directly on real assets, *i.e.*, there is a strong effect upon aggregate demand for real output. Keynesians argue, in contrast, that much of the extra money is spent on acquiring other financial assets, *i.e.*, the direct effect upon aggregate demand for real output is relatively low. This is not the end of the matter in the Keynesian viewpoint, however; for the increase in demand for financial assets will tend to push up their prices where these are determined in the markets, as in the case of gilt-edged securities, and this will tend to lower interest rates. (This happens because gilt-edged securities pay a fixed sum of money each year as interest; hence their proportional interest *rate* falls as their price rises, and this tends to push down interest rates elsewhere.) When interest rates fall this increases aggregate demand for real output because borrowing—which, as noted above, finances part of private expenditure—now becomes more attractive. Hence an increase in the money supply eventually increases demand for real output in the Keynesian approach; however, the mechanism is less direct than the monetarist one, and the size of the eventual increase in demand is likely to be smaller if, as many Keynesians argue, the demand for output is not very responsive to changes in interest rates.

In the monetarist view, then, changes in the money supply have a strong, direct impact upon aggregate demand; in the Keynesian view the impact is mainly indirect—being exerted through interest rate changes—and probably weaker. Thus monetarists stress the need to control the money supply regardless of what then happens to interest rates; Keynesians, at least until recently, have tended to argue for stabilising interest rates, regardless of what this implies for the money supply, since this makes it easier for the government to manage the National Debt and the interest charges involved.

The National Debt and Government Borrowing.

The *National Debt* is a measure of the total indebtedness of the government, excluding local authorities. The accompanying table shows how it has varied over time. Although the absolute size of the National Debt has risen steadily, this simply reflects inflation: as a proportion of national income the National Debt has fluctuated, rising sharply after each of the two World Wars—both of which saw borrowing on a massive scale by the government to finance the war effort—but falling slowly but steadily for 20 years up to 1975. Since 1975 the proportion has risen slowly from year to year.

THE NATIONAL DEBT IN SELECTED YEARS

	The National Debt (£bn.)	The National Debt as a percentage of national income
1900	0.6	31.9
1914	0.7	25.6
1921	7.6	147.7
1938	7.8	150.6
1946	23.0	259.6
1975	46.4	49.0
1985	158.3	52·5

The government borrows in several different ways. First, the issue of new bank-notes is a form of borrowing: as seen above it can be used to finance a budget deficit. Second, it borrows from foreign governments (*see* **G9**). Third, it borrows from companies through tax reserve certificates, whereby company taxes are paid at the later date when the taxes become legally due. Fourth, it borrows from private individuals through the various forms of national savings, *e.g.*, Post Office accounts.

These four types of borrowing result in *non-marketable debt*, *i.e.*, an individual who has a Post Office account cannot sell it in the market to another individual. Two other types of borrowing—gilt-edged securities and Treasury Bills—result in *marketable debt*, *i.e.*, an individual who owns gilt-edged securities can sell them in the market to someone else. In practice, most gilt-edged and all Treasury Bills are held by institutions—banks, discount houses, etc.—rather than by private individuals. However, whereas Treasury Bills, representing short-term (usually three months) loans to the government are liquid assets (*i.e.*, they can quickly be cashed at a predictable price), gilt-edged are illiquid. They represent promises to repay a certain sum of money at a specified date, *e.g.*, government stock outstanding in 1985 had an average remaining life of 10·4 years, with significant redemptions due in each of the next five years. Occasionally stock is issued without a repayment date. Owners of such stock are in effect promised a fixed annual interest payment for ever. At any time prior to repayment gilt-edged can be traded, and there is a large market for such trading in which the market price (as opposed to the fixed repayment price) varies widely.

Interest Rates and Debt Financing.

As already seen, such variations in gilt-edged market prices cause changes in interest rates on all financial assets. Aside from the effects on aggregate demand, interest rate changes themselves have a large impact upon the financing of the National Debt, and hence upon overall public expenditure. For example, if restrictions on the growth of the money supply cause interest rates to rise, this increases the interest charges which the government has to pay on its existing debts. Furthermore, the accompanying fall in the market price of government stock may cause potential buyers of new issues of stock to anticipate further falls (*i.e.*, further increases in interest rates), in which case they will be reluctant to purchase the stock—and the government will be unable to finance its budget deficit—unless and until these further changes occur. When they do, the interest charges on the National Debt are further in-creased; and the market may still be unsettled, expecting yet further changes.

It is problems of this sort which lead many Keynesians to advocate a policy of promoting stable (or at least slowly changing) interest rates—an "orderly market" for financial assets—rather than a predetermined growth rate of the money supply. In other words, Keynesians see monetary policy mainly as a means of easing the financing of the National Debt rather than as a means of controlling aggregate demand. Monetarists object on the grounds that the government cannot in practice stabilise interest rates in this manner. They argue that although the government may be able to stabilise or even reduce interest rates in the short run by a rapid expansion of the money supply, this expansion will itself *increase* interest rates in the longer run. This is because, on the monetarist approach, the monetary expansion increases demand for real output, which in turn generally increases the rate of inflation. If this causes people to expect a higher future rate of inflation, gilt-edged stock then becomes less attractive to investors because of the associated decline in the anticipated real value of its fixed interest payments. The demand for gilt-edged stock therefore falls, which pushes its price down and thus its effective interest rate up. This continues until the effective interest rate has risen sufficiently to offset the higher expected inflation. Interest rates elsewhere tend to get bid up at the same time, since banks, building societies, etc., have to protect their own reserves.

Monetarists therefore distinguish between the *nominal* interest rate, *i.e.*, the current money value of the interest rate, and the *real* interest rate, *i.e.*, the nominal rate minus the expected rate of price inflation on real output. They argue that firms and consumers are concerned about the real, not the nominal, interest rate; in this case nominal rates must inevitably rise if inflation increases—which it will do, on the monetarist argument, if the government, in pursuing a Keynesian policy of stabilising interest rates, over-expands the money supply. Hence the monetarists produce a paradox; a monetary policy which seeks to hold interest rates down may instead cause them to rise.

The Trend of Interest Rates in Britain.

It is difficult to deny that some element of the

BRITISH RETAIL BANKS, October 1985 (£ million)

LIABILITIES		ASSETS	
Eligible liabilities	83,375	Notes and coins	2,052
		Balances with Bank of England	440
		Market loans	24,153
		Bills	6,132
		Advances	78,165
		Investments	7,945
		Foreign currency assets	48,740
		Miscellaneous	9,788
Total Liabilities	177,415	*Total Assets*	177,415

monetarist view of interest rates has operated in the post-war period, especially in more recent years. The accompanying table shows the course of (nominal) interest rates and yields on certain types of financial assets since the war. It can be seen that with the exception of the yield on Ordinary Shares—which is considered later—all rates have shown a trend increase. Since inflation and therefore, in all probability, inflationary expectations have shown a similar trend increase, the rise in nominal interest rates is broadly consistent with the monetarist position. Furthermore, there was a tendency for all rates to rise in 1975–6, decline in 1977–8, and rise again in 1979–80. Since inflation and therefore, presumably, inflation expectations followed a similar pattern, the general argument seems consistent with recent developments. Note also that the 15 per cent Minimum Lending Rate announced in October 1976, although at the time a post-war record in nominal terms, was probably equivalent to a substantially *negative real* interest rate, given the high inflation rate then operating. The very high interest rates of 1979–81 are discussed in **Part IV**.

Although the broad trend of interest rates is consistent with the monetarist view, more detailed examination of the evidence also gives some support to the Keynesian approach. For it appears that interest rates adjust relatively slowly to changes in inflationary expectations; moreover, the latter are by no means the only influence on nominal rates. These points are illustrated by the experience of the 1980s. Inflation fell sharply from around 20 per cent in 1980 to around 5 per cent in 1984, but the table indicates that there was no corresponding fall in nominal interest rates. Indeed, in early 1985 they *rose* sharply, and the resulting combination of nominal rates of around 15 per cent and inflation at 5 per cent produced historically high real interest rates of around 10 per cent. The absence of any fall in nominal rates as inflation fell in the early 1980s to some extent indicates their tendency to lag behind changes in inflation—just as interest rates rose less fast than inflation in the mid-1970s—but another important point is the influence of factors beyond the direct control of the British Government. In particular, the rises in interest rates early in 1985 were as much a reflection of events in the American economy as in Britain (*see* **G49**). A large American budget deficit and high interest rates in the United States were attracting large flows of funds out of other currencies, including sterling, and into dollars. To prevent the resulting fall in the value of the pound, the Chancellor was forced to allow British interest rates to rise sharply, so stemming the outflow of funds. Moreover, the fear in early 1985 that world oil prices might fall weakened international confidence in the British economy and hence in the ability of the pound to maintain current exchange rates against other currencies. This factor, too, was outside the control of the British Government, indicating the extent to which British interest rates can be influenced by international events as well as by domestic inflation.

There may thus be a good deal of scope for a Keynesian policy of stabilising interest rates in the short and medium term; over a longer period, however, there are reasonable grounds for believing that attention also needs to be paid to controlling the money supply—something which is now accepted, to a greater or a lesser degree, by nearly all Keynesians.

The Commercial Banks.

If the government does adopt the monetarist approach of seeking to control the money supply rather than interest rates, its main need is to find ways of influencing the behaviour of the commercial banks, known in England as the clearing banks. For as seen above, the main component of the money supply is the deposits of the clearing banks, regardless of whether M1 or M3 is the chosen definition.

In Britain there are four main banks with one or more branches in every town. Each of them earns profits by borrowing at low or zero rates of interest—anyone holding a bank account is in effect making a loan to his bank—and lending out part of the resulting funds at higher interest rates. In normal circumstances—*i.e.*, unless there is a run on the banks—not all deposits will be withdrawn

PERCENTAGE YIELD ON FINANCIAL ASSETS
(Range during period)

	Treasury Bill rate	Long-dated government stock	Industrial ordinary shares dividend yield
1945–50	½	2–3	3½–5¼
1951–55	1–4	3½–5¼	4½–7
1956–60	3–6½	5–6	4–7
1961–65	3½–7	5–7	4–6
1966–70	5½–8	6½–10	3–6
1971–75	5½–11½	7½–17½	3–12
1976–78	4½–14½	10½–16	5–8
1979–81	11–17	11–16	4½–8
1982–83	8½–14½	10–13½	5–7½
1984–85	8½–14	10–12	4–5

at once; therefore the banks need keep only a small proportion of their deposits in the form of cash. This proportion is known as the *cash ratio* and until 1971 the Bank of England required it to be at least 8 per cent. Also, between 1951 and 1971 the Bank of England requested that the banks held liquid assets—Treasury Bills, commercial bills, and money at call and short notice as well as cash—equal to at least 30 per cent of deposits. This was known as the *liquidity ratio*.

The commercial banks can "create" money because of their ability to accept deposits far in excess of their cash and liquid asset holdings; as economists would say, because they operate under a *fractional reserve system*. If a bank provides an overdraft facility to a customer who then draws cheques on the facility, the recipients of these cheques pay the proceeds into their bank accounts which are thereby enlarged; and this represents an increase in the money supply, since the enlarged accounts can be used to finance additional transactions. Thus any increase in the banks' cash and liquid asset holdings allows them to expand loans, overdrafts, etc.—and thereby the money supply—by a multiple amount.

Controlling the Commercial Banks.

The government can control the money supply by controlling the components of banks' cash and liquid asset holdings. A reduction in the latter can be engineered in various ways. *Open market operations* involve the Bank of England's selling more gilt-edged than it otherwise would; this reduces the banks' liquidity, since, as already seen, gilt-edged are not regarded as liquid assets, so that their purchase involves a drain of liquidity from the banks. At the same time, as already seen, it will generally involve a rise in interest rates.

Another technique of monetary control is known as *Special Deposits*, which were introduced in 1960. The idea is that banks are required to place deposits with the Bank of England which, although they earn interest, do not count as liquid assets. Thus the banks' liquidity position is threatened and they may have to reduce advances to preserve their required reserve ratio. For example, in 1979 Special Deposits together with Supplementary Deposits were 0.7 per cent of total assets.

A fourth method of control is often called "*moral suasion*", and was much used in the 1960s. The government issues direct requests to banks about both the amount of advances to make to customers and their direction (*e.g.*, giving priority to exporting firms over domestic consumers).

In 1971 the government introduced a new policy, generally known as *Competition and Credit Control*, which redefined the liquidity ratio and lowered it to 12½ per cent, this being the banks' required ratio between what were defined as *eligible reserve assets* and *eligible liabilities*. The former comprised balances with the Bank of England, Treasury Bills, some commercial bills and local authority bills, and gilt-edged stock with less than one year to maturity. Eligible liabilities are, after various minor adjustments, sterling deposits.

The 1971 changes put far less stress on direct controls and placed the emphasis of policy upon controlling credit through the redefined reserve ratio. It also imposed this reserve ratio on *all* banks—not just on the clearing banks, as had previously been the case—and also on Finance Houses; special deposits could now also be called from these institutions as well as from the clearing banks. There were two reasons for this widening of controls. First, it was felt unfair to the clearing banks to subject them to controls which did not apply to potential competitors. Second, it was seen as a means of rationalising and obtaining greater control over, an increasingly complicated market for credit: in the previous two decades institutions other than clearing banks had grown in importance as sources of credit, and it had become increasingly anomalous not to seek to influence the whole of the market.

Current controls

In 1981 further changes in monetary control techniques were made. In August the reserve assets ratio was abolished. Instead, the banks undertook to keep an average of 6 per cent, and never normally less than 4 per cent, of their eligible liabilities as secured money with members of the London Discount Market Association and/or with money brokers and gilt-edged jobbers. They were also required to keep cash balances equal to ½ per cent of eligible liabilities in non-interest bearing accounts at the Bank of England. At the same time the Government abolished Minimum Lending Rate. It intended instead to set short term interest rates within an undisclosed band, thus abandoning its previous ability to influence the general level of interest rates by announcing a change in MLR. The accompanying table shows the balance sheet of the "retail banks"—*i.e.* banks in which a large proportion of their business involves dealing with individuals, as opposed to, *e.g.*, merchant banks which deal mainly with companies—in October 1985, operating under the 1981 rules.

The main idea behind these changes was to attempt to introduce a greater role for "market forces" in the determination of interest rates. Connected with this was the possibility that the government might eventually move to a system of *monetary base control*, in which it would control the reserve base of the banking system and renounce all attempts directly to influence interest rates, leaving them entirely to market forces. In practice, however, it was not clear to what extent the new system represented a change of substance rather than merely of form. In the remainder of 1981 the government twice intervened to influence the level of interest rates—in September to force them up; in November to prevent them from falling too fast—in a manner substantially very similar to its behaviour under the previous monetary control regime.

The Stock Exchange.

Whilst short-term credit is mostly provided by banks and Finance Houses, long-term borrowing by companies is undertaken through the Stock Exchange. Firms in the private sector of the economy issue three main types of security on the Stock Exchange. *Debenture Stock* is simply a fixed-interest loan. *Preference Stock* is a fixed-interest loan with provisions for waiving the interest if no profits are earned. The most important type, representing the great majority of holdings, are *Ordinary Shares*. The owner of an Ordinary Share is, legally, a part-owner of the company concerned, with a right to participate in any net profits which it makes (though he has no legal right to any particular level of dividend or interest payment).

In contrast to government stock, a significant proportion of Ordinary Shares is owned by private individuals. However, an increasing proportion is owned by insurance companies and pension funds, which have grown in importance as private superannuation schemes have become more widespread. It is likely that the market for Ordinary Shares, like that for government stock, will eventually be completely dominated by such large institutional investors.

The attraction of Ordinary Shares to the investor wanting an outlet for his savings is that because they represent a part ownership of the firm concerned, their prices and dividends are likely to rise as the value of the firm increases. This is so whether the firm's value increases in real terms, because it is expanding, or simply in money terms, because of general inflation. Thus Ordinary Shares generally represent a reasonable "hedge" against inflation—unlike fixed-interest securities such as gilt-edged. It is for this reason that, as seen in the earlier table, the dividend yield on Ordinary Shares does not tend to rise with inflation: the demand for Ordinary Shares does not necessarily fall if inflation increases, so that their prices and yields are not affected in the same way as those of gilt-edged and other fixed-interest securities by changes in inflation rates.

The one major deviation of dividend yields and share prices in the post-war period occurred in 1974, when Ordinary Share prices were for a time so depressed that dividend yields rose to 12 per cent (see earlier table). However, this almost certainly reflected the crisis of profitability and also liquidity in British industry in 1974 rather than the rapid inflation of that year; though the latter was in part responsible in a more indirect manner, since it helped to create the liquidity crisis. Apart from 1974, however, dividend yields were virtually no higher in the 1970s than in the 1950s or 1960s, despite much higher inflation rates.

Monetary Policy in Britain.

(i) The Keynesian Era.

Until 1968 British monetary policy was in practice strongly Keynesian in the sense described earlier. That is, the government was mainly concerned with attempting to stabilise interest rates in order to facilitate the management of the National Debt. For although successive governments several times embarked on a policy designed to reduce the rate of growth of the money supply by squeezing banks' liquidity, each such phase of policy was ended when the government concerned found itself unable to countenance the resulting rise in interest rates. This occurred when the banks sought to replenish their liquid assets by selling their gilt-edged holdings, particularly those nearing maturity; the banks preferred to do this rather than call in advances, since the latter were generally more profitable. In practice, it was usually the Bank of England which bought the gilt-edged being unloaded by the banks, thereby undoing the effects of its own monetary squeeze.

In effect, therefore, the Bank of England's priority was to support gilt-edged prices and keep interest rates down, without worrying too much about money supply. Such a policy is often called "permissive" monetary policy, *i.e.*, the government supplies whatever amount of money will permit trading to take place at a given set of interest rates, as opposed to laying down a target rate of monetary growth and sticking to it. In adopting a "permissive" monetary policy successive governments were reflecting the intellectual spirit of the times. In the twenty years after the war Keynesian ideas were dominant: the money supply was regarded as a relatively unimportant influence upon aggregate demand, which was best regulated by fiscal methods. Thus large Budget deficits were financed by rapid monetary growth. The high point of Keynesian influence was probably marked by the publication in 1959 of the Report of the Radcliffe Committee on the working of the monetary system. This took a strongly Keynesian line, emphasising the importance of liquidity and suggesting that "money" as such was not merely unimportant as an influence on economic activity, but more or less incapable of precise definition.

(ii) The Monetarist Revival.

Keynesian ideas began to come under increasingly strong intellectual challenge from monetarists in the 1960s, and this has been reflected in the gradual change of policy to a pre-

THE COST OF PUBLIC SERVICES
(£ million)

Expenditure.	1977.	1984.	Percentage increase 1977-84.	Percentage of total 1984.
Defence	6,863	17,046	148	11·6
Education	8,341	17,064	105	11·7
Health	6,815	16,822	147	11·5
Social Security benefits	15,009	42,414	183	29·0
Housing and community amenities	5,450	7,239	33	4·9
Agriculture, forestry and fishing	1,059	2,218	109	1·5
Transport and communication	2,428	3,448	42	2·4
Public order and safety	2,132	5,893	176	4·0
General public services	3,222	6,242	94	4·3
Other expenditure	10,433	27,956	168	19·1
Total expenditure	61,752	146,342	137	100·0

dominantly monetarist stance. The first hint of this came in 1968, when the Chancellor of the Exchequer, expressed in a "Letter of Intent" to Britain's creditor, the International Monetary Fund, the intention of controlling the growth of the money supply in order to control aggregate demand and thereby help to push the balance of payments into surplus following the 1967 devaluation. The fact that an explicitly monetarist approach was thus made the centre-piece of policy for the first time reflected not only the growing intellectual influence of such ideas in Britain, but also (and probably more importantly) their influence in the I.M.F., which has traditionally favoured the setting of monetary targets.

This trend towards monetarism appeared to have been strengthened by the 1971 measures described earlier: these removed support from the gilt-edged market in order to focus attention upon the control of money and credit. In practice, however, these measures were followed in 1972–73 by a vast expansion of the money supply —M3 rose at an annual rate of nearly 30 per cent— which was the reverse of the policy advocated by monetarists (or indeed by most Keynesians). Other measures adopted at this time—moral suasion in an attempt to limit lending for property development; subsidies to building societies to hold down their interest rates—were also incompatible with the monetarist view that the market should operate freely within a framework of monetary control. Thus in the period 1972–73 policy may have become more monetarist in form, but it was certainly not monetarist in substance.

In the second half of the 1970s, however, monetarist ideas became increasingly the dominant influence upon policy making. This happened in two stages. The first occurred in the autumn of 1976 when Britain applied to the I.M.F. for large credit facilities. One of the requirements which the I.M.F. imposed as a condition of granting these facilities was that the Government should lay down, and stick to annual *monetary targets*, *i.e.*, target annual growth rates in sterling M3. The Government has followed this policy ever since: the target for fiscal year 1984–5 was to keep the growth of M3 within a range of 4 to 8 per cent.

The adoption of monetary targets in turn meant that the *public sector borrowing requirement* (p.s.b.r.) became a target, rather than a consequence, of policy. The p.s.b.r. is the combined deficit of the central government, local authorities and public corporations. It has to be financed by a combination of borrowing (from the private sector or from abroad) and increasing the money supply. Since domestic borrowing will push up interest rates, any government which has a monetary target and which is also unwilling to tolerate rises beyond a certain point in interest rates, will be compelled to limit the size of the p.s.b.r. This has to be done by a combination of tax rises and cuts in public spending. Thus targets for monetary growth carry implications for the government's tax and expenditure policies.

The second, and decisive, stage in the growth of monetarist influence was the election of a Conservative government in May 1979. The new government came into office committed to a monetarist approach to economic policy; several of its leading members declared themselves converts, to a greater or lesser extent, to the teachings of Professor Friedman, and rejected the Keynesianism of earlier post-war years.

Early in its term of office, therefore, the new government published its medium-term financial strategy, designed to operate over the period 1980–84. It aimed to secure steady cuts from year to year over this period in both the monetary growth rate, and the p.s.b.r. as a proportion of national income. The government took the view that the scale of past government borrowing had contributed a great deal to the rapid inflation rates of the 1970s. Whether or not this was true, however, the actual burden of public debt had tended to fall during this period, as the accompanying table shows. Although total public sector indebtedness rose during the 1970s, this simply reflected inflation; indebtedness as a percentage of national income fell quite sharply. This was because the nominal interest rates paid by the government on its borrowing were below the inflation rate. Consequently, the government was effectively borrowing at negative rates of interest. Ironically, net indebtedness as a proportion of national income has tended to rise, albeit slowly, in the 1980s.

PUBLIC SECTOR NET INDEBTEDNESS

	Value of net indebtedness (£bn)	Net indebtedness as a percentage of national income
1970	38.0	86
1975	52.9	56
1981	108.5	51
1984	158·3	52·5

A further important contribution to the growth of monetarist influence at the end of the 1970s was that many of the most influential people in financial markets—the policy-makers of large institutional investors; academic economists with good connections in the City; financial journalists —had become monetarists. In this sense the "financial markets became monetarist". This caused some changes in their working, most of which had the effect of making interest rates more sensitive to short run variations in monetary policy. For reasons discussed in **Part IV**, this tended to make it more difficult for governments to adopt non-monetarist policies, even if they had wanted to. **Part IV** also provides a much more detailed account of policy making and the growth of monetarism during the 1970s and 1980s.

(iii) Doubts about Monetarism.

By the end of 1981 the experience since 1976, and more especially since 1979, had begun to erode support for monetarist ideas, at least in their simple form. One area of doubt concerned the actual ability of the government to control money supply, however defined; this led to the 1981 changes in monetary control techniques mentioned above. A second argument revived the traditional Keynesian emphasis upon wider measures of liquidity: some economists, led by Nobel prize winner Professor James Meade, argued that the government should abandon monetary targets and instead set targets for the growth of *money national income*—the volume of output multiplied by its average price level—and should use a variety of fiscal instruments for this purpose, with monetary policy being used mainly to influence interest rates and the exchange rate. A third criticism of monetarism, also associated with Professor Meade and consistently advanced by another Nobel prize-winner, James Tobin of Yale University, and also many politicians, was that deflation had mainly reduced output and employment rather than inflation, and that this would always be the case unless the government returned to some form of *incomes policy* (*see* **G68**). However, most monetarists remained hostile to the idea of incomes policy, and this therefore remained an intensely controversial question. These issues are considered further in **Part IV**.

5. ECONOMIC ASPECTS OF THE PUBLIC SERVICES

The Cost of Public Services.

In 1984, total public expenditure was £146,342 million, £2,590 per head. Of this total, 70 per cent is spent by central government, and just over a quarter by local authorities. The remainder is accounted for by the investment programmes of the nationalised industries. Total public expenditure increased more than sixteenfold in the period 1960–84, and rose as a proportion of GNP from 34 to 45 per cent.

Central Government collects in revenue considerably more than it spends itself, but transfers funds to the local authorities, to the National Insurance Fund, and to the nationalised industries. The expenditure of the public sector as a whole generally exceeds its revenue, and the difference is met by net borrowing.

A breakdown of public expenditure is shown in the table on **G29**. Not all categories of public expenditure have expanded at the same rate. Over the period from 1977, for example, expenditure on public order and safety, social security, defence and health increased faster than the total; expenditure on housing, community amenities, education, agriculture and transport fell behind the total.

Council Housing.

Expenditure on council housing (net of sales) amounted to 2.0 per cent of public expenditure in 1984. Housing expenditure consists of two quite different items. There is the capital cost of building new council houses. This is financed out of borrowing by local authorities, both from the Government and from the market. There is also a recurrent cost, in the form of subsidies on council housing. This represents the difference between the cost of housing, including the cost of borrowing, and rents received.

Up to 1957 the Government contracted to pay a flat subsidy per year on every council house built. From 1957, government subsidies were no longer paid on new council houses, but in 1961 were reintroduced, in a form intended to encourage councils to charge higher rents on their existing houses. The Labour Government substantially increased the subsidy in 1967.

The 1972 Housing Finance Act made major changes to the system of council housing finance. Councils were required to charge "fair rents"—the likely market rent for a dwelling if supply and demand for rented accommodation were in balance. The Government also financed a rent rebate scheme whereby people in need, both council tenants and private tenants, could claim a rebate according to a formula based on family size and income. A slum clearance subsidy was also paid to councils and—to encourage housebuilding—a "rising costs" subsidy whereby the additional costs resulting from council house building were subsidised. The system of "fair rents" was ended by the Housing Rents and Subsidies Act of 1975. Under this Act most Government help went to new building, the acquisition of land and housing and improving the stock of council housing. This Act was replaced by the 1980 Housing Act. Since then, council house subsidies have been substantially reduced. Central government now calculates the amount by which it will finance housing subsidies on the assumption that local authorities

charge council house tenants a "fair" or "market" rent. The result is that council rents have risen substantially in real terms. At the same time, private ownership has been encouraged *e.g.* through the sale of council houses. Between 1980 and 1984 750,000 council houses are estimated to have been sold for around £5,000 million.

The Housing Market.

Government housing policy must be seen in terms of the housing market as a whole. In 1985 there were over 22 million dwellings in the United Kingdom, 60 per cent being owner-occupied, 31 per cent being council houses, and the remaining 11 per cent privately rented. The importance of owner-occupation has grown and that of private renting has declined: in 1960 they had accounted for 42 per cent and 32 per cent of the total respectively. Of the privately rented accommodation today, around one third is military and company owned property let free to employees. On an international comparison, the private rented sector in the early 1980s, as a percentage of total housing stock, was about 60 per cent in Switzerland, 50 per cent in Holland, 40 per cent in the USA, and 18 per cent in France.

The switch to owner-occupation in the U.K. is largely the result of Government policy. Rent controls have meant that there is little incentive to build houses for renting, nor even to maintain existing rented houses. On the other hand, Government has given considerable tax advantages to owner-occupiers. Owner-occupied houses are exempt from the capital gains tax introduced in 1964, and owner-occupiers can also obtain tax relief on mortgage-interest payments on a principal of up to £30,000. Since the abolition of the Schedule A tax in 1961—whereby owner-occupiers paid tax on the rental income imputed to their houses—this tax relief on interest payments must be justified as an inducement to home-ownership; but it is also a considerable subsidy to owner-occupiers, who tend to be the relatively well-off. The trend towards owner-occupation was further encouraged by the 1980 Housing Act which also gives local authority and new town tenants a legal right to buy their homes. It also introduced measures to encourage letting in the private rented sector. In 1984, the Housing Minister suggested that the Government was planning to remove all new letters from rent restrictions and security of tenure laws.

The year 1953 was a peak for public sector housebuilding in the United Kingdom when 262,000 council dwellings were completed. There was a trough in 1961 (122,000), a peak in 1967 (211,000) and a subsequent fall to 113,000 in 1973. Since the mid 1970s there has been a steady decline in the construction of public dwellings. In 1984 only 54,000 new houses were completed. By contrast, the number of private dwellings completed rose steadily from 65,000 in 1953 to a peak of 226,000 in 1968. Thereafter the number fell back to an annual average of slightly less than 200,000 in the early 1970s, and still further to an average of about 120,000 in the early 1980's, rising again in 1983 and 1984 to about 150,000. The total number of dwellings completed reached a peak of 436,000 in 1968, and fell to 279,000 in 1974. Since then, the best year has been 1976 (338,000), the worst 1982 (159,000), while 212,000 dwellings were completed in 1984.

Over the 15 years 1955–70 the rate of inflation in the price of modern existing houses averaged 5 per cent per annum: somewhat faster than the rise in the cost of living. After 1970 there was a great surge in house prices: between December 1970 and December 1972 the average rise was no less than 30 per cent per annum. There are various reasons for this remarkable inflation. Partly it reflected the rapid acceleration of general inflation; in such times it is sensible to hold one's wealth in the form of assets which will appreciate in value. It also reflected the decline in housebuilding after 1968, and a slowing-down in the rate at which building land became available. The precise timing of the inflation resulted from the sudden and large increase in the availability of building society mortgages. And as the inflation grew, so optimistic expectations helped to raise house prices still further. By 1974 the rate of increase had slowed down considerably. It slowed even further in 1975 and 1976. In 1978 and 1979 prices started to accelerate again, slackening off in 1980, only to start accelerating again in 1982.

Education.

Educational expenditure accounted for 11·7 per cent of public expenditure in 1984. It had increased rapidly over the previous 25 years for two reasons. First the number of full-time pupils had grown. Second the more expensive sectors—secondary schools and universities—expanded most rapidly. For example, in 1984 there were 4·8 million students in secondary schools as opposed to 3·2 million in 1961. In the thirteen years to 1984, the number of full-time students in higher education increased from 432,000 to 581,000. However, falling birth rates are likely to reduce school rolls by about 15 per cent from now until the mid-1990's

In December 1972 the Conservative Government published a White Paper setting out plans for the expansion of education over the next decade. More emphasis was to be placed on nursery schooling for the 3- and 4-year-olds: within 10 years it would be available to all children whose parents wanted them to attend. There would be a school building programme to replace old school buildings. Teacher training would be expanded to reduce pupil-teacher ratios further. Higher education would be expanded less rapidly than in the previous decade, and the emphasis would be placed on polytechnics and other non-university colleges.

Unfortunately many of these plans were thwarted, largely as a result of cut-backs in total public expenditure. It is, however, generally recognised that education can be an economic investment for the future just as much as capital formation in, say, machinery or roads. There is a "private return" on "investment in education", which takes the form of higher earnings over the lifetime of the person educated; and there is a "social return" on public resources devoted to education being the greater contribution to the national product which trained and educated people can make. Although many of the 1972 White Paper plans have not been implemented, both the 1974 Labour and 1979 Conservative Governments have considered longer term policies for education. The key theme of a consultative White Paper in 1977 was the need to attune school curricula to the employment needs of school-leavers, and to encourage stronger ties between schools and industry. This has been a recurrent theme. Questions about longer term educational requirements have been subsumed under the present Conservative Government by debate on the relative merits of private and public sector education. There was also a renewed emphasis on making the later years of school education more directly related to labour market requirements, represented, for example, by the increased involvement of the Manpower Services Commission in school programmes, such as the Technical and Vocational Education Initiative. In 1986 a new school curriculum was being devised to make secondary education more broad-based for a longer period.

Social Security.

There are two forms of social security: *National Insurance* and *Supplementary Benefits*. The former are non-means tested. They were designed to be exactly what the name indicated—insurance for when an individual met circumstances implying a loss of income, be that circumstance old age, unemployment or sickness. By contrast the latter are means tested, and are designed to keep people out of poverty. As such under the original Beveridge scheme, they were meant to be a safety net for the unfortunate few. The majority were to be covered by the insurance element. Formidable financing difficulties meant that this ideal was never achieved, and supplementary benefits attained an unwanted prominence in the British social security system.

(i) National Insurance.

Under this scheme employees receive rights to unemployment benefit, sickness benefit, retirement pensions, widows' benefits, injury and disablement benefits, etc. In 1985-6, 9·3 million pensioners received National Insurance pensions. There were 1·9 million national insurance recipients amongst those below pensionable age, among whom the largest single group were 0·98 million unemployed. Weekly rates are laid down for each benefit, *e.g.*, in late 1985 a weekly rate of £30·45 was paid to a single person receiving unemployment benefit. The basic rate was increased according to the number of dependants: £18.80 for one adult, and extra still for each child. In 1966 an earnings-related supplement was introduced for benefits paid to persons between 18 and 65 (men) or 60 (women): the supplement being related to earnings in the previous tax year. The maximum total benefit, including increases for dependants, amounted to 85 per cent of earnings. This, together with tax rebates, meant a higher income out of work for a very few people. In the March 1980 Budget, the Chancellor announced that from 1982 the earnings-related unemployment supplement would be withdrawn, whilst unemployment benefit would become taxable.

By far the most important benefit is the retirement pension, paid as of right to contributors on retirement. Individuals may increase their rate of pension by staying on at work after the minimum retiring age of 65 for men and 60 for women. In late 1985 basic retirement pensions were £38·30 per week for single persons and £61·30 for a married couple.

Social Security benefits were up-dated in November each year, to account for inflation in the year to the previous May. Under the Government's social security reforms (*see* **G32**), in 1986 the uprating took place in July, and in subsequent years in April.

(ii) The Financing of National Insurance.

The main source of finance for National Insurance payments is the National Insurance Fund. These funds are built up largely from the compulsory weekly National Insurance contributions which most of the adult population have to pay. For employees, both employer and employee pay a contribution. The self-employed also pay contributions of smaller size than the sum of the employer's and employee's contribution, but they are not entitled to unemployment benefit. Weekly contributions include a contribution to the cost of the National Health Service. As a result of the 1985 Budget, employers' and employees' national insurance contributions were cut for the lowest paid workers, in order to increase the incentives to work and to hire more labour. At the same time, while a maximum earnings limit for employees contributions remains, the upper-earnings limit on employer's contributions was abolished.

The National Insurance Scheme is an odd mixture of insurance and tax. The levels of contributions, when the scheme started in 1948, were fixed on the actuarial principle that contributions by or on behalf of an individual plus a specified State contribution should on average suffice to pay for the benefits to which he was entitled. But the scheme did not allow for inflation and a rising standard of living. In particular a succession of increases granted in the rate of pensions has put an end to this actuarial probity. Instead the principle became established that the rate of contributions in each year, together with a transfer from the Government, should equal the total benefits paid out in that year. Expenditure on non-contributory benefits is covered by general revenues.

(iii) Reform of Pensions.

There are more than nine million pensioners in Britain. 20 per cent of these are kept out of poverty only by receiving a supplementary pension: it is estimated that another 10 per cent are entitled to a supplementary pension, but do not draw it. Many of the remainder find their living standards considerably reduced from when they were working. This is because the existing state retirement pension is inadequate. There are some occupational pension schemes which offer a better income, but these are rather restricted in their coverage, being available to many more non-manual than manual workers. Like personal savings, many of them also tend to have only limited safeguards against inflation unless they are index-linked. In an era of rapidly rising prices, the pensioner is at a particular disadvantage. Widows form the poorest groups among them, with over half of them needing to draw a supplementary pension.

A scheme for graduated pensions was introduced for employees in 1961. Under the scheme there were two kinds of employees—*ordinary* and *contracted-out*. In the case of contracted-out workers, their employer (on whom the decision whether to contract out rested) had to institute a private superannuation scheme that gave at least as favourable terms as the new State scheme, including the provision that rights under the scheme should be transferable up to the limits of the State scheme. Transferability was the guarantee that the individual did not lose his pension rights when he changed his job. In practise transferability was never really achieved.

In 1969 the Labour Government made proposals in a White Paper to replace the National Insurance Scheme by a new scheme of superannuation and social insurance, in which both contributions and benefits would be related to the earnings of the individual. It argued that the existing scheme failed to provide security in old age. The new earnings-related contributions would be mostly higher than contributions under the existing scheme, especially among higher earners; and in return higher pensions and other benefits would be paid.

An important feature of the proposed scheme was that benefits were to take into account both changes in prices and in general living standards. Thus, for instance, a contributor who received earnings equal to the national average throughout his working life would receive a pension calculated on the national average earnings at the time he reached pension age, not on the money he received over his working life. Some two-thirds of employed men were contracted out, *i.e.*, in occupational pensions schemes, in 1970. The Government intended that these schemes should continue to exist together with the State scheme, and it proposed to allow for partial contracting out of the State scheme.

These plans lapsed with the change of Government in 1970. The Conservative Government announced its proposals for reform in a White Paper published in 1971. It considered that the costs of earnings-related benefits would be too great; instead it favoured earnings-related contributions for basically flat-rate pensions. In addition it wished to encourage contracting out, so that almost all employees would also be members of a private occupational pension scheme, in which pensions would be related to past contributions. The Government recognised that it would have to ensure that occupational pension rights were transferable between jobs. Like the previous Government, it envisaged a legal guarantee that State pensions would be revised every two years. It also envisaged that the share which the State provides from taxation for National Insurance—about 18 per cent of contributions in 1970—would be maintained. Again the plan lapsed with the change of government.

Meanwhile the Government had become aware of the need for a frequent adjustment of pension rates in an era of high inflation. In early 1975 the full pension entitlement was £10 for a single person and £16 for a married couple. In November 1985 the rates stood at £38·30 for a single person and £61·30 for a married couple. Over the period as a whole this represents a faster increase than the rate of inflation. The real need, however, was for fundamental reform. Yet another new scheme went before Parliament in February 1975, and to some extent the scheme has been implemented. The idea was for a two-tier pension. The bottom tier was a common flat-rate for everyone. The top tier was earnings-related—that is, a fixed proportion of the pensioner's previous earnings. Because of the flat-rate element, a low earner would be able to expect a pension which was a higher percentage of his working income than that obtained by a higher earner. Contributions to the scheme would be earnings related. The pensions would be fully protected against inflation, and women would enter the scheme on the same footing as men. There was an obvious emphasis on the need to protect women from poverty in retirement, after the death of the husband. There would be a maximum pension entitlement and a maximum contribution. For this reason among others, the Government planned to encourage new and improved occupational schemes, to exist alongside the state scheme. It was hoped that the scheme will come to full maturity by 1998, this long delay reflecting the formidable difficulties in financing the

plan. In the meantime fully earnings-related contributions started in 1975, and minor earnings related benefit in 1979. These replaced flat-rate National Insurance payments and graduated pension contributions.

A renewed concern in the early 1980's was with a particular aspect of occupational pensions—their transferability from job to job. Until the present, someone who left an occupational scheme had the choice of either leaving his pension rights at his old employer, and receiving a deferred pension at retirement age, usually unadjusted for inflation between his departure and retirement; or, if his old and new employers both agreed; transferring the fund, from which effectively the pension is paid, to his new employer, usually at great loss to himself.

(iv) Poverty in Britain.

Despite the existence of National Insurance there are many people in Britain whose income falls below that which the Government regards as adequate. These people are supported from Government revenues by means of *supplementary benefits*, before 1966 known as *National Assistance*. It is a fault of the National Insurance Scheme that so many have required this assistance. About 1·75 million people receive supplementary pensions, and a further 2·5 million pensioners get help with their rents and rates. Of families whose head is in work, 200,000 receive Family Income Supplement, whilst over 60 per cent of the unemployed are wholly dependent on supplementary benefit. Anyone who is out of work for more than a year loses entitlement to unemployment benefit and becomes reliant on supplementary payments; but in addition over 25 per cent of those actually receiving unemployment compensation are "topped up" by such payments. At present, the minimum living income per week, according to the DHSS, is £29·30 for a single person, £47·85 for a couple, with extra added for children according to their age. For longer term disadvantage the corresponding rates are £37.50 and £60.00. Despite these provisions some 1·3 million households are below the official poverty line, of whom about 40 per cent are over pension age. A major fault with the supplementary benefits scheme was that they could not be paid to those in employment whose earnings were below the benefit level, and if such persons became unemployed they could claim benefits only up to their normal earnings level. The *Family Income Supplement* was introduced in 1971 to alleviate hardship amongst low earners, but it has been estimated that only half of those eligible have claimed F.I.S. As for Supplementary Benefit, it is estimated that only three quarters of those entitled to it are in fact making claims.

(v) Proposals for Reform

In 1985 the Government issued a White Paper detailing reforms of the whole social security system. The basis of dissatisfaction was three-fold. First, the system was a complex and costly one to run. Second, it worked in such a way as to help some who, on official definitions of poverty, did not need assistance; whilst, conversely, it failed to provide it for some who did. Third, it created unemployment benefit traps, supplementary benefit traps and poverty traps. These imply that people who are unemployed or employed on low pay might be deterred from taking employment or taking jobs with higher pay, because the combined effects of the tax and benefit system mean that the consequential increase in their net income is negligible. Behind their proposed reforms was the concern about future financing difficulties, and a wish to make the system simpler.

On pensions, it was originally proposed to retain basic pensions, but to abolish earnings related pensions (SERPS). Instead, greater stress was to be placed on occupational pension schemes. Substantial political pressures caused a change of mind, and SERPS will be retained, albeit in modified form. Universal child benefit will be retained. But for low earnings families, FIS will be replaced by Family Credit, to be paid through the pay packet. As compared to FIS it will allow a smoother tapering of payments as original income increases. For those not in work, supplementary benefits will be replaced by "income support", which is intended to be

SOURCES OF PUBLIC REVENUE

Revenue.	1960. £m	1984. £m	Percentage increase 1960–84.	Percentage of total revenue 1984.
Taxes on income	*3,626*	*69,119*	*1,806*	*50·8*
of which paid by:				
personal sector	1,991	34,724	1,644	25·5
companies	612	7,775	1,170	5·7
national insurance contributions	913	22,484	2,363	16·5
Taxes on capital	*236*	*1,661*	*604*	*1·2*
of which:				
capital gains tax	—	925	—	0·7
Taxes on expenditure	*3,391*	*52,578*	*1,451*	*38·7*
of which levied on:				
alcohol	400	5,531	1,283	4·1
tobacco	818	4,896	499	3·6
rates	771	13,074	1,596	9·6
Other revenues	*1,435*	*12,590*	*777*	*9·3*
Total revenue	8,688	135,948	1,465	100·0
Net borrowing	712	10,394		
Total expenditure	9,400	146,342		

simpler and to involve a smaller range of payments. Benefits will be at a lower rate for the under-25s and at a higher rate for pensioners. An additional sum will be paid for each dependent child, as it will for single parents and the long-term sick and disabled. Beyond these, there will be no additional payments. There will, however, be a new Social Fund "to provide for exceptional circumstances and emergencies". Recipients of income support will still be entitled to free school meals and free welfare foods, unlike those getting family credit. There will also be a new simplified scheme for housing benefits. Unemployment benefit, the maternity allowance (in revised form) and sickness benefit will remain, but maternity and death grants will be abolished. Substantial changes will be made in provisions for widowhood.

The Government's catchphrase for these reforms has been "the twin pillars", state help combined with encouragement for private provision. Returning to the three major complaints about the present system, certainly the revised one should be cheaper to administer. It probably will target the benefits more accurately. It will also alleviate the worst traps, but in substantially improving the lot of some in this respect, it will slightly worsen it for more. Indeed, the new scheme is not a major departure, and falls far short of the more radical proposals of (for example) the Institute for Fiscal Studies, who proposed a combined tax and benefit credit system.

Public Revenue.

In the table above we show the sources of revenue. No less than 50·8 per cent of the total public revenue in 1984 came from taxes on income; more than half of this being personal income tax. Taxation of profits amounted to only 5·7 per cent of total public revenue. Taxes on expenditure accounted for 38·7 per cent of the total. It is interesting to note the increased importance of *direct taxation* (taxes on income) relative to *indirect taxation* (taxes on expenditure on goods and services) over the period. The present Government believes that this trend should be halted.

Two commodities in particular were heavily taxed: alcoholic drink and tobacco. Together they accounted for over 7 per cent of public revenue. These commodities are singled out partly for social reasons and partly because—in economists' jargon—the demand for them is *inelastic*; *i.e.*, the public reduces its consumption of drink and tobacco only slightly in response to a rise in their price. Indirect taxation—taking the form of excise duties and purchase taxes (value added tax after 1973)—used to be spread very unevenly over the different sorts of expenditure. The introduction of Value Added Tax in 1973 tended to even out the incidence of indirect taxes on different goods and services, though tobacco, drink and motoring continued to be hit heavily.

The Budget.

Each year in the Spring the Chancellor of the Exchequer announces his Budget for the coming fiscal year. The most important and most difficult task in drawing up the Budget is to decide on the size of deficit to aim for. The deficit is the excess of public expenditure over public revenue; and it has to be financed by borrowing from the private sector. A large deficit is normally reflationary; sometimes that may be required to get the economy out of recession. A small deficit—and even more, a surplus—is deflationary, and is a means of holding a demand-pull inflation in check.

In 1970 there was a small surplus, and thus the net borrowing requirement was negative. Since then the borrowing requirement has become large and positive. This does not itself imply that governments have pursued increasingly expansionary policies. If the size of the deficit in 1984 is adjusted for the effects of inflation, and for the current high level of unemployment to make it comparable with the 1970 figure, the 1984 Budget was in fact in surplus.

The calculation of the precise deficit or surplus needed is a chancy business; for the level that is required depends on the amount of saving and on the amount of spending out of credit that people intend to do—and this is not easily predictable. It also depends on the change in the foreign balance. Nor can the Chancellor be sure his figures are right: estimating next year's revenue, and even next year's expenditure, by the Government is difficult enough, but he needs to estimate also the likely trends of private income and expenditure, without really reliable information as to what they were in the past year. The introduction of advance *cash limits* on a large proportion of expenditure in 1976 was meant to give the Government greater control over projected spending. Prior to that the general rule had been to estimate public expenditure for the following year on the basis of its volume. If inflation was higher than predicted, then the tendency was to preserve volume by increasing the value of expenditure. Cash limits altered this, and in 1982 cash planning institutionalised this change. Henceforth a large proportion of government spending would be fixed in value terms, and if inflation exceeded the predicted rate, then volume would suffer.

Nevertheless, fiscal policy—running large deficits when economic activity is low, and small ones when it seems to be excessively high—is the most important action through which the economy can be kept on an even keel. Monetary policy may help; but the Budget decision of the Chancellor on changes in taxation and public expenditure is the key one.

6. SOURCES OF STATISTICS: SOME SUGGESTIONS FOR FURTHER READING

The non-specialist will find that most of the statistics he needs are given in the *Annual Abstract of Statistics*, published every year by Her Majesty's Stationery Office. This comprehensive document includes figures on population, social conditions, education, labour, production, trade and balance of payments, national income and expenditure, wages and prices, and many other topics. For more up-to-date information, reference should be made to the *Monthly Digest of Statistics* which has a similar coverage and gives month-by-month figures. A selection of the more important series, presented in a manner which can more easily be understood by the layman, is given in another Stationery Office publication, *Economic Trends*, also issued monthly.

Fuller information on labour problems is given in the *Department of Employment Gazette*, on trade in *Trade and Industry*, and on financial matters in the *Bank of England Quarterly Bulletin*. These three periodicals include discussions on the statistics presented. *Social Trends* contains articles and detailed statistics on social and economic conditions in Britain.

For an analysis of developments in the economy see the *National Institute Economic Review*, a private publication issued by the National Institute for Economic and Social Research. To explain economic events and policy, the Treasury publishes a monthly *Economic Progress Report*. The periodic *British Economic Survey* (Oxford University Press) contains up-to-date articles on aspects of the economy.

For a comprehensive and systematic introduction to the British economy the reader is referred to A. R. Prest and D. J. Coppock, *The U.K. Economy: a Survey of Applied Economics* (Weidenfeld and Nicolson). Other introductory texts include J. Black, *The Economics of Modern Britain* (Martin Robertson), M. Stewart, *Keynes and After* (Penguin), and D. Morris (ed), *The Economic System in the UK* (Oxford).

Interesting books on particular topics include J. A. Trevithick, *Inflation* (Penguin), A. B. Atkinson, *The Economics of Inequality* (Oxford). A sourcebook on the EEC is *The Economy of the European Community* (Office for Official Publications of the European Communities). A recent view of the international debt crisis is given by H. Lever and C. Huhne, *Debt and Danger* (Penguin).

III.   THE LESS DEVELOPED ECONOMIES

Income Levels.

Two-thirds of the world's population live in dire poverty—a poverty which can scarcely be imagined by those accustomed to the standards of living attained in the relatively few developed countries of the world. The orders of world inequality may be seen from the table comparing annual gross national products per capita by region, converted into pounds sterling at official exchange rates. These figures are only very approximate because exchange rates are misleading indicators of purchasing power and because the averages conceal considerable income inequalities within some regions and countries. Nevertheless, it is clear that poverty is widespread in the world. The alleviation of this poverty is widely recognised as the most important economic—and indeed political—task of the remainder of the twentieth century. The 33 low-income developing countries referred to in the table have an average income per capita of just over £100 per annum, and contain 2,100 million people; 1,900 million in 12 Asian countries and nearly 200 million in 20 African countries.

According to a World Bank estimate, a third of the population of all developing countries in 1980 had a calorie intake below 90 per cent of the requirement laid down by the Food and Agricultural Organisation and the World Health Organisation; this meant that they did not get enough calories for an active working life. A sixth (340 million) had a calorie intake below 80 per cent: they did not get enough calories to prevent stunted growth and serious health risks. The areas particularly affected were South Asia and sub-Saharan Africa.

What is a Less Developed Country?

There are no less than 140 countries comprising the so-called "Third World," known variously as "less developed" or "developing" or "underdeveloped" or "poor" countries. There is a great diversity among them, and yet they have a number of features in common. Foremost among these is their poverty, but even poverty is not universal: some of the oil-producing countries such as Saudi Arabia, Kuwait and Libya have achieved very high levels of income per capita while retaining many of the other characteristics of less developed countries.

Most of the developing countries are primarily agricultural economies, with the bulk of the population engaged in *subsistence agriculture*. For many millions of peasant farmers the primary objective is to produce enough food for their family to subsist. India is a classic example, with no less than 70 per cent of its 700 million people dependent on agriculture for a living. Most less developed countries have only a small industrial sector as yet: it is rare for the output of the manufacturing sector to exceed 20 per cent of the gross domestic product. The main exceptions to this rule are the successful exporters of labour-intensive manufacturing goods, such as Hong Kong, Singapore, Taiwan and South Korea. Many of the less developed countries lack the necessary ingredients for successful industrialisation—capital, skills and entrepreneurship.

The developing countries vary enormously in size—from the teeming masses of India and China to scores of countries with less than a million people, including Bahrain, Botswana, Fiji, Gabon, Mauritius and many West Indian islands. The development problems and possibilities facing

GROSS NATIONAL PRODUCT PER CAPITA BY GROUPS OF COUNTRY AND SELECTED COUNTRIES, 1980

	(£ p.a.)
33 low-income developing countries	113
of which: Bangladesh	57
India	104
Sri Lanka	117
Tanzania	122
China	126
63 middle-income developing countries	609
of which: Egypt	252
Thailand	291
South Korea	661
Brazil	891
Mexico	909
19 industrialised countries	4,487
of which: Spain	2,348
U.K.	3,443
Japan	4,300
U.S.A.	4,939
W. Germany	5,909
4 high-income oil exporters	5,491
of which: Saudi Arabia	4,896
6 centrally planned economies	2,017
of which: Poland	1,696
U.S.S.R.	1,978

large and small countries are very different. The small size of most developing economies forces them to concentrate on the production of one or two primary products for world markets. Their high degree of specialisation and heavy dependence on exports and imports makes these economies dangerously vulnerable to the vagaries of world trade and the world economy.

Enough has been said to show that, apart from their poverty, the less developed countries have other economic characteristics and problems in common. However, it is dangerous to generalise because there are also important differences. In particular, they vary in their degree of development and in their potential for development. A semi-industrialised, urbanised country such as Argentina has little in common with an utterly backward country such as Chad, and the economic prospects for an oil-rich country such as Indonesia are far brighter than for a country with few natural resources such as Tanzania.

Population Growth.

Many underdeveloped countries are experiencing an unprecedented population explosion: annual rates of increase of between 2 and 3 per cent—which double population in as little as 35 and 24 years respectively—are common. This is a phenomenon of the last four decades. Death rates have fallen sharply in response to improved health services and modern methods of control, *e.g.*, the eradication of malaria through DDT spraying. On the other hand, birth rates have been kept up by such factors as tradition, social prestige, religion, the need for security in old age and a lack of facilities for family planning.

POPULATION SIZE, GROWTH AND DENSITY BY REGION

	Population 1980 (m).	Growth rate 1975–80 (% p.a.).	Density 1980 (per sq km).
North America .	248	1·0	12
Europe .	484	0·4	98
U.S.S.R. .	265	0·9	12
Oceania .	23	1·5	3
Africa .	470	2·9	15
Latin America .	364	2·5	18
China .	995	1·4	104
Other Asia .	1,584	2·1	88
World Total .	4,432	1·7	33

The table indicates that over half the world's population lives in Asia, and that the developed regions account for under a third of the total. Apart from Australasia (into which immigration is high) the developed countries show slower rates of population growth than Africa, Latin America and Asia. The figures of population density may easily be misleading, since they take no account of the nature of the area, *e.g.*, deserts are included. But it is clear that Asia is more densely populated than Africa or Latin America.

Life Expectancy.

Although death rates have fallen in the developing countries, especially infant mortality, life expectancy is generally low in the poorest countries. Thus, for instance, the male expectation of life at birth in 1980 was below 40 years in many countries of Africa, including Angola, Ethiopia, Nigeria and Sierra Leone, and some in Asia, including Afghanistan and Kampuchea. Life in these countries is all too short.

Life expectancy is related to income per head. In most of the developed countries male life expectancy at birth is about 70 years, being 68 in the United Kingdom, 70 in West Germany, 71 in the United States and 74 in Japan in 1980. However, the average length of life depends also on the quantity and quality of medical provision and the degree of income inequality about the mean: male life expectancy exceeded 60 years in some of the poorest countries, including China and Sri Lanka. Life expectancy is an important but neglected indicator of the "quality of life".

The Population Problem.

In many developing countries there is population pressure on the land, and many people want more land for farming. Population density is a hindrance in agricultural economies, but not necessarily in industrial economies: because it is

industrialised and has accumulated much capital, Europe can support at a high standard of living a population more concentrated even than that of Asia.

As a result of rapid population growth the pressure of population on the land has increased. The consequences have been far more serious in countries such as Bangladesh (with a population density of 616 people per square kilometre in 1980) or India (202 per sq km) than in Zambia (8 per sq km) or Brazil (14 per sq km). In those countries with abundant land the expanding population can spread into unused areas; but as land becomes increasingly scarce, less and less productive land must be brought into cultivation and soil erosion and loss of fertility become major problems. A substantial increase in output is required to prevent a fall in per capita income as population grows, and an even greater increase is required if living standards are to be improved. Between 1970 and 1982 food production in the developing countries as a group increased by 38 per cent and per capita food production rose only 3 per cent.

Even in those countries with plenty of land a rapid increase in population can have harmful effects. For instance, it diverts scarce investment resources away from directly productive investments such as factories and irrigation projects so as to meet the needs of the expanding population for more schools, hospitals, housing, cities and other public services.

Family Planning Programmes.

In many African and Latin American countries the rate of population growth appears to be constant or even rising, but in parts of Asia there are signs that the growth rate has peaked and is now declining. The different experiences may reflect differences in government policies: in 1980 a quarter of less developed countries had no official family planning programme. The success stories include India, where in 1980, 23 per cent of married women used contraceptives and the birth rate fell from 4·4 to 3·6 per cent per annum between 1960 and 1980, Colombia (46 per cent contraceptive use and a fall from 4·6 to 3·0 per cent) and South Korea (52 per cent contraceptive use and a fall from 4·3 to 2·4 per cent). The successful cases show what can be done, but private incentives and attitudes still favour large families in many poor societies: simply providing facilities for family planning may not be enough.

China's Population Policy.

An extreme form of family planning is the "one-child" policy in China. In the 1970s China—with its population of over a billion people and great shortage of arable land—overcame its Marxist ideological antipathy to population policy and introduced a programme to encourage later marriage, longer spacing between births, and fewer children. In the early 1980s a one-child norm was generally introduced, and financial incentives and penalties were used to persuade couples to have no more than one child. Early results of the one-child policy seem impressive. The birth rate in 1983 was down to 1·9 per cent. Nevertheless, resistance can be expected in the rural areas where children remain the main source of security in old age, and a preference for sons may have revived the practice of female infanticide. Population policies as draconian as China's, however, are unlikely to be possible in more democratic and less controlled developing countries.

Problems of Agriculture.

There are many millions of peasant farmers throughout the Third World eking out a subsistence from the soil. The margin between what can be produced and what is required to support life is narrow: the failure of crops because of drought, floods or pests can lead to famine unless food is quickly supplied from outside the area affected. For instance, relief action by the international community was too slow to prevent the drought which struck the Sahel area of Africa in 1973 and 1974 from claiming some 100,000 lives, endangering future income by destroying seeds and livestock, and breaking up rural communities. Relief was again slow and patchy in response to the more widespread and severe African famines of 1984 and 1985.

Agricultural production may be held back by a shortage of land, or by the use of primitive tools and methods of cultivation (which may in turn be due to a lack of farming knowledge and skills or to a lack of funds for investment in land improvement or equipment), or by an unjust system of land tenure which deprives the farmer of incentive to raise his production. Perhaps all these problems must be tackled simultaneously.

The Green Revolution.

A technology is being introduced which can increase the yields from foodgrains by 50 per cent or more in tropical areas. This new technology is commonly thought to have caused a *green revolution*. It consists of new high-yielding seeds, largely for wheat and rice. Not only are the yields per acre higher but also shorter cropping cycles permit multiple cropping. The new technology economises on land and, being labour-intensive, provides more farm employment. The introduction of high-yielding cereals is probably the most decisive single factor in the emergence of India and Pakistan into the ranks of solid economic achievers.

However, we cannot assume that it is going to solve the problem of foodgrain shortage in the underdeveloped countries. As yet, the new seeds are less resistant to drought, floods and disease. To be effective, they require substantial inputs of fertiliser and of water; in many areas expensive irrigation will be essential to their success. Moreover, the fact that fertiliser and water are complementary inputs has meant that the green revolution has caught on—and been encouraged by governments—among the larger, more prosperous farmers in the better-watered, more prosperous regions. This is true of, *e.g.*, Mexico, Pakistan and the Philippines. Unless governments ensure that the benefits of the green revolution are widely spread, the effect might even be to harm small peasant farmers by increasing the competition from large farmers.

Land Reform.

There are many forms of land tenure in less developed countries. In black Africa communal or tribal ownership of land is common, with members of the community or tribe receiving rights to use the land individually. In parts of Asia and Latin America, there is private ownership of land, which—particularly where the land is densely populated—has often led to great inequality of land ownership. In some cases land tenure is characterised by absentee landlords and share-cropping tenants. The development of large estates produces a class of landless labourers.

The need for land reform varies according to the circumstances. In most cases the main argument is for greater social justice. In some cases it may be possible also to expand production by redistributing land more evenly or by giving land to share-cropping tenants and so improving their incentives. On the other hand, large farmers may have access to technology, skills and capital which small farmers lack: there is a danger that greater equity will be achieved only at the expense of efficiency. Hence the need to ensure that land reform is accompanied by a package of measures, *e.g.*, education, training and advice, and credit for fertiliser, tools and land improvements. Few governments have succeeded in implementing serious land reform programmes. The main reason is that the system of land tenure in a country often reflects the balance of political power: land reform invariably faces political opposition from entrenched interests. By the same token, a successful land reform may alter the balance of political power so as to facilitate broad-based development.

Exports of Primary Products.

Almost all the underdeveloped countries export primary products (foodstuffs, industrial raw materials or minerals) and import manufactured goods, especially the capital goods (plant, machinery and vehicles) required for development. This international division of labour has recently operated to the disadvantage of the under-developed countries. The world demand for their primary products has increased only very slowly. This is because people spend just a small part of their additional income on food (*e.g.*, tea, coffee, cocoa), because synthetic substitutes have been developed for many raw materials (*e.g.*, rubber, cotton, jute), because developed countries protect their own agriculture (*e.g.*, sugar) and because demand in the developed countries has moved towards commodities with low raw material content (*e.g.*, from heavy industries to services).

In consequence, the general trend has been for the prices of primary products to fall in relation to those of manufactured goods. This was an important cause of the improvement in Britain's terms of trade (*see* **G6**). The reverse of the coin was a deterioration in the terms of trade of many underdeveloped countries, *i.e.*, they could now buy fewer imports for a given quantity of exports. Primary commodities exported by developing countries actually decreased in price on average by 10 per cent over the period 1957–70. Most poor countries benefited from the soaring prices of various commodities in world markets during 1972 and 1973. These were years of world economic boom, food shortage and speculative purchasing of primary commodities. However, the non-oil-producing developing countries suffered as a result of the oil prices rise after October 1973. The subsequent world recession depressed primary commodity prices, and inflation in developed countries increased the price of manufactured imports (*see* **Part IV**). When fuels are excluded, the terms of trade of the developing countries with the developed countries fell by 4 per cent between 1970 and 1980.

Unsatisfactory prices of primary commodities have contributed to the shortage of foreign exchange which restricts investment expenditure in many less developed countries. This was particularly marked in the early 1980s. World recession and tardy growth depressed primary product prices and sales. The purchasing power of exports from the developing countries fell by 13 per cent between 1980 and 1983: oil-exporting countries and African countries were the most badly affected.

Case-study of Deteriorating Terms of Trade.

Sri Lanka's main exports are tea, rubber and coconut—products whose relative prices have fallen almost continuously for years. In terms of the quantity of goods produced, per capita GDP increased by 2·6 per cent per annum between 1960 and 1980. However, once allowance is made for the declining import-purchasing power of exports, per capita real income in Sri Lanka increased by only 1·1 per cent per annum.

Sri Lanka represents an extreme but not a unique case of the harm that terms of trade loss can inflict on a specialised, raw-material-exporting country. The resulting persistent balance of payments difficulties led to the erection of a very restrictive exchange and trade control system with a bias against exports.

Economic Instability

Volatility of export prices is also a problem for Sri Lanka. Comparing the first quarter of 1984 with 1980 as a whole, we find that the dollar prices of tea and coconut oil soared by 75 and 66 per cent respectively, and that of rubber sank by 22 per cent. The prices of various primary products tend to fluctuate violently from one year to another. Many developing economies depend heavily on the exports of one or two commodities. For instance, coffee is the most important product in Brazil, cotton in Egypt, copper in Zambia, sugar in Cuba, cocoa in Ghana and rice in Burma. Fluctuations in the world price of its main export cause instability in the export revenues of a country, and this in turn can produce fluctuations in income throughout its domestic economy.

Even the oil-producing developing countries, whose problems are in many ways quite different, have faced problems of economic instability. The governments of these countries have had to decide how best to use their vastly increased oil revenues so as to promote economic and social development without overturning their societies. Recent political events in Iran were closely related to the economic boom which oil produced. The effects of political instability in Saudi Arabia on the world economy would be incalculable.

Oil versus Agriculture: a Case-study of Nigeria.

Not only Britain has discovered that oil production can be a mixed blessing. Oil has become Nigeria's main foreign exchange earner. Prior to the oil boom, Nigeria exported cash crops including groundnuts, palm oil and cocoa. In the 1970s agriculture—accounting for more than two-thirds of the Nigerian population—contracted as oil expanded, agricultural exports were halved, and Nigeria became a net importer of food. Oil was mainly responsible for this. The appreciation of the Nigerian currency made export crops unprofitable, while food imports became more competitive and domestic per capita food production fell. The urban boom attracted young people to the towns, leaving an ageing labour force on the farms. Oil revenues did not much help the rural areas, partly because of the lack of trained manpower available for development projects. The impressive rate of growth of GDP during the 1970s (averaging 6·5 per cent per annum) was thus accompanied by a worsening distribution of income. Nigeria also became highly dependent on oil. When the oil price fell in the 1980s, GDP contracted and investment slumped.

Problems of Industrialisation.

In those underdeveloped countries where there is population pressure on the land, alternative employment has to be created in industry or services. Even in countries with a surplus of land, if there is heavy dependence on one or two primary products, industrialisation provides a means of diversifying the economy.

But industrialisation is not an easy course. Because the margin between agricultural production and food consumption is narrow, the surplus from the agricultural sector exchangeable for the products of other sectors e.g., industry and services—is small; i.e., the demand for the goods and services produced by other sectors is low. A second constraint on industrialisation is imposed by competition from abroad; new industries in an underdeveloped country have to compete with established industries in developed countries, which have the advantage of experience, a trained labour force and markets big enough for them to reap all the potential economies of large-scale production.

Industrialisation Strategies.

One means of overcoming the small size of market is to export manufactures to the developed countries. Developing countries with cheap labour are likely to have a comparative advantage in the manufacture of relatively labour-intensive commodities. A number of less developed countries have had remarkable success in following this strategy, e.g., Hong Kong, Taiwan, South Korea, Mexico and Puerto Rico. Among their successful activities are textiles, clothing and labour-intensive components of electronic equipment. However, the developed countries often impose protective tariffs. Another form of manufacturing is the processing of primary products before exporting them. Here developing countries sometimes face the problem that tariffs are higher on the processed than on the unprocessed products.

A means of overcoming competition from the industries of the developed countries is by nurturing an infant industrial sector behind tariff walls—which is how the United States and Germany developed their industries in the face of British competition in the nineteenth century. A number of developing countries have adopted this strategy. However, it has its drawbacks. Sometimes the "infants" never grow up, and vested interests press for continued protection. Import-substituted industrialisation often means that raw materials or semi-processed goods are imported for local processing. There is a danger that fluctuations in export proceeds will periodically curtail imports of necessary intermediate goods. The under-utilisation of capital in the manufacturing sector because of foreign exchange shortages has frequently occurred in countries such as India, Sri Lanka, Tanzania and Ghana.

The Newly Industrialising Countries.

The remarkable success of a handful of developing countries—the *newly industrialising countries* (NICs)—in exporting manufactured goods raises the questions: why were they successful, and can others do the same?

South Korea is perhaps the most successful of the NICs. After a period in which government pursued a policy of industrialisation through import substitution, the policy was changed in the 1960s to one of promoting exports of labour intensive manufactures. This was achieved by devaluing the currency in order to encourage export industries in which the country would have a competitive advantage, and liberalising imports to discourage inefficient industrial production. In 1962 South Korea exported manufactures worth $10 million; in 1982 their value was $19,237 million. Between 1962 and 1982 the proportion of the labour force employed in industry rose from 10 to 30 per cent, manufacturing production rose by 17 per cent per annum, and GNP per capita rose by 7 per cent per annum. The labour-intensive nature of industrialisation, as well as its speed, helped to alleviate poverty through the market: first employment and later, as labour became less abundant, also real wages rose rapidly.

South Korea benefited from its trading relationships with Japan and its close ties with the United States in finding markets for its products. It has a well educated labour force: 89 per cent of the relevant age group in 1982 were enrolled in secondary school, which is higher than any other developing country. Industrialisation may also have benefited from stable autocratic government and a beleaguered sense of national purpose. In part the Korean success represents the harnessing of cheap labour in almost free trade conditions for exporters. However, the government also played an active role, e.g. it both generated high savings and successfully directed savings into the favoured sectors. It will take much more than policies of *laissez faire* for other developing countries to be able to emulate South Korea. Moreover, since the world market for labour-intensive products is limited, only a minority of developing countries can take the Korean path.

Other NICs include Taiwan, Hong Kong, Singapore and Brazil. As a group the NICs exported manufactures worth $70 billion in 1982.

Outward-Oriented Industrialisation Policies.

The success of the NICs has led many policy advisers to press for more outward-oriented industrialisation policies. The policy advice is gradually to dismantle the system of protection of import-substituting industries and to devalue the currency in order to provide incentives to export manufactures. It is argued that competition in world markets will act as a spur to domestic efficiency and help to divorce economic activities from domestic political processes.

The traditional view has been that few developing countries could succeed in breaking into world markets for manufactures. However, despite the resurgence of protectionism in the 1980s (*see* **G53**), potential access to the markets of industrialised countries is better than it used to be, and broadly-based progress has been made. In 1960 manufactures accounted for less than 10 per cent of the exports of the developing countries, but in 1980 for more than 20 per cent. If the NICs constitute the "first division", a "second division" of countries have expanded manufacturing exports rapidly, including India, China, Pakistan, the Philippines, Thailand, Turkey, Malaysia and Mexico. In 1982 manufacturing accounted for a third of the exports of low-income developing countries, for less than 5 per cent in the case of the oil-exporters, and for half of the total in the case of the middle-income, non-oil exporting developing countries.

Unemployment and Underemployment.

Unemployment and underemployment occur on a very considerable scale in both the rural and the urban areas of developing countries. Consider first the rural case. Because farm work is normally shared, underemployment—disguised unemployment—is more common than open unemployment. People work for only a part of the day or year. Where land is scarce, underemployment is chronic: people would like to work more if only they had more land. Unless the yield from the land can be raised, growth in population causes greater underemployment and reduces income per head on the land. Where land is abundant, underemployment is a seasonal phenomenon. People are fully employed in the busy season—harvesting and planting—but underemployed at other times of the year.

In the towns open unemployment is common with people queueing for *modern sector* jobs at the labour exchanges and at the factory gates. Rates of urban open unemployment in excess of 10 per cent are frequently recorded, *e.g.*, in Ghana, Colombia, Puerto Rico, Trinidad, Sri Lanka and the Philippines. Few developing countries can afford unemployment benefits, so that job-seekers remain openly unemployed only until their savings are used up or support by their relations is withdrawn. Then they have to scrape out a subsistence in the urban *traditional sector* while waiting and hoping for something better. Underemployment is rife in the easily entered traditional sector activities such as petty trading, hawking, beer brewing, fetching and carrying. A shoeshiner may be on the streets for ten hours a day but have only a couple of customers. The more people enter these activities, the further average income per worker is depressed. In many less developed countries this self-employment in the traditional sector accounts for the majority of urban workers.

URBAN POPULATION AS A PERCENTAGE
OF TOTAL POPULATION IN SELECTED
DEVELOPING COUNTRIES, 1960 AND 1983

	1960	1983
34 low-income developing countries	17	22
of which: Ethiopia	6	15
China	18	21
Tanzania	5	14
Ghana	23	38
60 middle-income developing countries	33	48
of which: Zambia	23	47
Peru	46	67
Brazil	45	71
Iran	34	53
Jamaica	34	52
5 high-income oil exporters	28	68
of which: Libya	23	61

Migration to the Cities.

Urbanisation is proceeding at an unprecedented pace in much of the Third World. Over the decade 1970–80 the total urban population of the developing countries as a whole grew by no less than 48 per cent. The table illustrates the pace of urbanisation in a number of developing countries.

Rural people are being drawn to the cities at a rate well in excess of the capacity of the cities to absorb them productively. The reason for this migration might be economic or social. The economic explanation runs in terms of an income differential between the urban and the rural areas. Relatively unskilled wages in the modern sector of the economy—often governed by minimum wage legislation or trade union bargaining—can be well above the incomes to be derived from peasant agriculture. People go to the town in search of modern sector wage jobs, although they may actually end up underemployed in the low-income traditional sector. Rural–urban migration may be a social phenomenon: rural people are attracted by the facilities and "bright lights" of the cities. The recent expansion of education in many countries may also play a part, since a high proportion of the migrants are school leavers.

Whatever the reasons the consequences are socially harmful and politically explosive. Shanty towns and slums proliferate in the cities and their outskirts; poverty, disease and crime flourish.

In 1950 there were only two urban agglomerations in the world with more than 10 million inhabitants, New York and London. On present trends, there will by the year 2000 be 25 such cities, of which 20 will be in the third world and the largest will be Mexico City with a forecast population of 31 million.

Employment Creation.

As recognition has grown that unemployment, in its open and disguised forms, is both high and rising in many of the developing countries, so the objective of creating productive employment has received higher priority. For various reasons the growth of modern sector employment has been tardy and has lagged behind the growth of output. One reason is that the modern sector normally uses capital equipment and technology which is imported from the developed countries. This means that, even in countries with cheap and abundant labour, the most profitable techniques of production are often highly capital-intensive, so that the amount of scarce investment funds required to equip a worker is high. Hence the case for developing an *intermediate technology* which is both profitable and suited to the needs of the underdeveloped countries.

There is some danger that the establishment of capital-intensive factories may actually harm existing labour-intensive production. For instance, sandals can be made by small cobblers using local leather (or old car tyres) or by a large plant using imported plastic materials: a new factory employing a few machine operators might displace many more traditional craftsmen who have no alternative employment opportunities.

Governments, by encouraging or discouraging particular forms and areas of investment, have the power to influence the growth of employment. In the rural areas the encouragment and organisation of labour-intensive developmental or community projects can assist in harnessing the one abundant resource which almost all developing countries possess: unskilled labour.

Educated Manpower.

Many underdeveloped countries are faced with the dual problem of unskilled labour surpluses and scarcities of skilled and educated manpower. The problem is particularly acute in some of the recently independent countries of Africa. To give an extreme example: at the time of its independence in 1964, Zambia had only 100 Zambian university graduates and 1,200 secondary school graduates in a population of 3·5 million. In such countries the great shortage of educated and skilled people enables them to earn high incomes—with the result that there is a very unequal distribution of income. And even in countries where surpluses have developed, the existence of an international market for professional people such as doctors and engineers helps to keep up their earnings: these countries suffer from a "brain drain" to the developed world.

In sub-Saharan Africa in 1980 64 per cent of children of the relevant age were at primary school, 14 per cent at secondary school and only one per cent in higher education; fewer than a third of adults were literate. The provision of education on this meagre scale nevertheless took up 16 per cent of government budgets. A reason for the expensiveness of education is the cost of scarce teachers: a primary school teacher's salary averaged 7 times the GNP per capita in Africa. In such circumstances it is not easy to meet the demand for universal primary education; especially if the sort of education provided does not enable those who receive it to become better farmers. The demand for education is generally strong and unsatisfied in Africa; often it is perceived as the passport to a good urban job.

Economic development is not just a matter of capital accumulation: it requires also an increase in educated manpower. Not only more knowledge but also new habits and attitudes—*e.g.*, attitudes towards risk-taking, hard work and thrift. Education—of the right sort and with suitable content—is generally acknowledged to be important for development, although the benefits of education cannot be quantified at all satisfactorily.

On the other hand, there are developing countries whose problem is now surplus rather than shortage of educated manpower. Such cases are common in Asia, *e.g.*, India, Sri Lanka and the Philippines. In the Philippines, for instance, in 1982 there was universal primary education, no less than 64 per cent of children in the relevant age-group were in secondary school, and 27 per cent of the relevant age-group were in higher education, much of it in private institutions of poor quality. The high financial returns accruing to the educated have generated powerful pressures for the expansion of state education, to which governments have acceded. Rapid expansion in quantity has frequently been accompanied by decline in quality of education. Some governments have found that it is easier to expand an educational system than it is to expand an economy, and shortages have given way to surpluses. The response to surplus may take various forms: unemployment of the educated, or displacement of the less educated from their jobs, so pushing the unemployment down the educational ladder, or pressures on government to create unnecessary jobs for the educated in the public service. In this last case—true of Egypt—scarce resources are doubly wasted.

Case-study of Human Resource Development.

Sri Lanka is one of the poorest less developed countries (with a GNP per capita of only about £120 in 1980), and yet it has an impressive record in the development of its human resources. Emphasis has been placed on education, health and nutrition. For instance, in 1980 life expectancy at birth was 66 years, the adult literacy rate 85 per cent, and 53 per cent of children of relevant age were enrolled in secondary school. Between 1960 and 1980 the rate of natural increase in population had fallen from 2·7 per cent to 2·1 per cent per annum, reflecting a public birth control programme: more than 50 per cent of married women used contraceptives. Moreover, government food subsidies have improved the nutrition of the poorer section of the population. However, social welfare expenditures on this lavish scale inevitably involved a cost. The growth in GNP per capita in Sri Lanka of only 2·6 per cent per annum between 1960 and 1980 might well have been higher had more resources been available instead for physical investment.

Economic Aid.

The gap between living standards in the underdeveloped areas of the world and in the areas already developed has tended to widen in recent years. In the 1950s real income per capita rose in the developed countries by 2·7 per cent per annum on average, and in the less developed countries by 2·3 per cent per annum. It was through a growing world recognition of the situation that the 1960s were designated "The United Nations Development Decade." But between 1960 and 1970 these rates of growth widened to 3·8 and 3·0 per cent per annum respectively. World inequalities continued to increase: hence the "Second United Nations Development Decade" in the 1970s. A World Bank estimate for the 1970s has the annual average per capita growth of developing countries (2·8 per cent) exceeding that of developed countries (2·4 per cent). However, when developing countries were divided into 33 low-income and 63 middle-income countries (the dividing line being per capita income of £180 in 1980) the low-income group was found to average less than 2 per cent per annum.

Over the period of world economic recession 1980–1984, GNP per capita in the industrialised economies grew by 5.5 per cent whereas the developing economies managed only 2.1 per cent over the four years. This masked wide variation in performance: GNP per capita in sub-Saharan Africa fell by over 10 per cent whereas it rose by over 14 per cent in East Asia and the Pacific developing countries.

The main industrial countries—organised as a 17-member *Development Assistance Committee* (DAC)—have provided economic aid to the de-

veloping countries. The total net flow of economic assistance from the DAC countries was $84 billion in 1984. Roughly $46 billion of this was net private investment and $29 billion official aid from governments. Over a quarter of the net *official development assistance* (ODA) was contributed by the United States; the other principal donors were Japan, France, West Germany, Canada and Britain in that order.

The DAC nations have accepted three aid targets. One is that the net flow of private and official resources combined should exceed 1 per cent of each country's gross national product. In 1984, 9 of the 17 countries had achieved this percentage. The second target is that net ODA should exceed 0·7 per cent of GNP; only 5 countries managed this in 1984. The third target, more generally achieved, concerns the "grant element"—the extent to which ODA contains an element of grant as opposed to commercial loans.

Although the money value of ODA increased between 1963 and 1973, in real terms it remained roughly constant. As a proportion of the combined GNP of the DAC countries, it fell from 0·51 per cent to 0·35 per cent over the decade. By their own standards the countries of the First World were failing to assist the Third World on an adequate scale. Yet, with the oil crisis and world recession, the situation worsened. Many of the developing countries were in greater need of assistance, and in the developed countries the stagnation in real incomes made the provision of aid more difficult. Nevertheless, some improvement in the flow of aid did occur between 1973 and 1984. The total net flow of resources from DAC countries to developing countries increased from 0·79 to 1·06 per cent of GNP, and net ODA rose to 0.36 per cent of GNP. In real terms the flow of ODA rose by 3·5 per cent per annum over the period.

Forms of Aid.

Aid to the developing countries takes many forms, it serves many purposes and it is given for many reasons. Underdeveloped countries need aid to provide finance for development projects; to provide foreign exchange with which imports for development purposes can be bought; and to provide the trained manpower and technical knowledge they lack. The motives of the donor are not always humanitarian. "Aid" can take a military form; it can be used to prop up an incompetent or unjust government, or to buy support in the cold war. Nor is aid always beneficial to the recipient country. It may be wasted on ill-conceived or prestige projects, or cause the government simply to relax its own efforts. Sometimes schools or hospitals are built with aid but there is a lack of local revenues with which to staff and run these institutions. Concern over donor's motives and instances of waste has led some people to react against aid-giving. However, the correct remedy is not to cut off aid but rather to prevent its misuse.

Donor governments may finance specific projects, or they may contribute to the general pool of funds available for expenditure by the governments of underdeveloped countries. But financial aid is not always enough. Many developing countries need technical assistance in planning their development, to ensure that development possibilities are exploited and that scarce resources are used to best advantage. Hence the many schemes for providing experts by individual countries and by the technical agencies of the United Nations, such as the Food and Agriculture Organisation (FAO), the World Health Organisation (WHO), the International Labour Organisation (ILO), the United Nations Educational, Scientific and Cultural Organisation (UNESCO), and so on. Hence also the schemes for educating and training people from the developing countries.

Foreign Private Investment.

One possible form of aid is private investment by firms from developed countries. These investments—setting up branch factories, for example—are concentrated in those projects which appear profitable to the investor. However, it is a characteristic of underdevelopment that there are few openings for profitable investment. Most of the U.K. private investment overseas, for ex-

FINANCIAL FLOWS FROM BRITAIN TO DEVELOPING COUNTRIES, 1964–1982

	Net total flows, official and private.		Net official development assistance.		
	£m.	% of GNP.	£m.	% of GNP.	£m. (1970 prices).
1964	328	0·98	176	0·53	201
1970	520	1·02	86	0·36	186
1975	1,062*	1·03*	389	0·39	197
1980	2,353*	1·04*	797	0·35	221
1984	2,839*	0·89*	1,061	0·35	220

*Excluding considerable long-term foreign currency lending by British banks.

ample, has been concentrated in relatively highly developed countries of the world. Private investment cannot be relied upon to provide an adequate flow of resources.

Indeed, it has been questioned whether private investment constitutes aid to less developed countries at all. Its opponents argue that the benefits are often small or even negative: foreign-owned firms repatriate high profits and avoid tax by means of royalty payments to the parent company or unrealistic pricing of their transactions with the parent company; and these firms deter local enterprise. Supporters of foreign investment point to the high political risks which necessitate high profits in order to attract investors to developing countries, and question whether resources are available for any alternative path to development. A form of compromise which has become common in the Third World is a partnership arrangement between multinational companies and the host country's government.

Of the total stock of direct investment in developing countries by companies based in developed countries in 1975, 23 per cent was invested in OPEC countries, 13 per cent was in tax havens, and 64 per cent in the other developing countries. There was considerable concentration in the more successful developing countries, e.g. Brazil with 13 per cent and Mexico with 7 per cent. The least developed countries—those with GNP per capita under $200—accounted for under 7 per cent of the total.

British Aid.

The table above shows how British assistance to developing countries has grown over the years, and how it has measured up to the international aid targets now accepted by the British Government. The first target is that the total net financial flow to developing countries should exceed 1 per cent of GNP. The large but fluctuating flows of private capital meant that this target was achieved in 1970 and from 1975 onwards. The second target is for a net official development assistance (ODA) in excess of 0·7 per cent of GNP. We see that British ODA as a percentage of GNP was only half of the officially accepted target in 1984, and was lower than it had been in the sixties. The table also shows that ODA has grown in value; in 1984 it equalled £19 per head of British population. However, if we allow for inflation by expressing official aid in real terms, we see that the volume of aid has risen little.

Government aid may be divided into multilateral aid and bilateral aid. Multilateral aid is given through the medium of the international development institutions: bilateral aid is given directly to the developing countries. Multilateral aid constituted 40 per cent of total British aid in 1984. Some 90 per cent of British ODA in 1984 took the form of grants, and the rest was loans. Most of the loans were fairly "soft" with long maturities and low rates of interest. Roughly half of bilateral financial aid is formally tied to the purchase of British goods and services. Other aid is not tied formally, and may be used directly to finance local expenditure; but when it is used to finance imports directly, it has to be spent on British goods if these are available on competitive terms. Most multilateral aid is untied. The tying of aid tends to raise the costs to developing countries; but it also enables countries with precarious foreign balances to be more generous.

Aid takes the form not only of financial but also of technical assistance. Government expenditure on technical assistance amounted to a third of bilateral aid in 1984. At the end of 1984 British technical assistance personnel overseas totalled 2,500 (not counting 1,000 volunteers recruited by voluntary agencies); including 1,000 teachers, 450 agricultural advisers and 200 doctors and medical workers.

All British official aid is channelled and co-ordinated by the Overseas Development Administration (ODA). In addition there are various private associations concerned with promoting development, such as Oxfam, War on Want and World Development Movement.

The World Bank.

The International Bank for Reconstruction and Development (IBRD) known as the *International Bank* or as the *World Bank*, is an agency of the United Nations established in 1945. It has the primary function of making funds available to assist developing countries. Member nations agreed to subscribe quotas—fixed in much the same way as the quotas for the IMF—to the Bank. In fact, only a small proportion of the quotas has been called up by the Bank; the major part of the Bank's resources are borrowed—on the security of the remainder of the quotas—in financial centres.

Usually, loans are made to finance specific projects of investment in underdeveloped countries; and the Bank will normally make a loan only if it is satisfied that the investment will yield a revenue sufficient to enable the payment of interest on the loan, and the repayment of the sum lent. In 1984 the Bank made loans to the value of $9,300 million. Thus a sizeable amount of lending is channelled through the Bank, but it is clear that some projects of great value to underdeveloped countries cannot be financed in this way, because they would not yield returns quickly or large enough to meet the Bank's requirements for interest and repayment. Accordingly a new institution, the *International Development Association*, was set up in 1960 with the power to make loans at low rates of interest and with more generous repayment conditions. The IDA contributes towards the development of education and agriculture ($3,200 million in 1984).

UNCTAD.

In 1964 the first United Nations Conference on Trade and Development (UNCTAD) was held. For the first time the poorer nations of the world—77 were represented—came together to act as a pressure group on trading matters. The Conference made the following recommendations. Developing countries should be given free access to world markets for their manufactures and semi-manufactures by the elimination of quotas and tariffs. International *commodity agreements* should be made for each major primary commodity in world trade, to stabilise commodity prices. Compensation schemes—whereby countries are compensated for the declining prices of their primary products—were recommended for consideration. The Conference also resolved that the developed countries should aim to provide at least 1 per cent of their national income as aid for the underdeveloped countries.

Subsequent sessions of the Conference have been held at four-year intervals. Little positive action has resulted from what have at times been political tournaments. However, UNCTAD has helped to modify international thinking. The developed countries have accepted more firmly the principle of discrimination in favour of developing countries, and the notion that aid should reach a target level.

Stabilising Export Earnings.

Two international facilities exist to help stabilise the export earnings of developing countries. One is the IMF's *Compensatory Financing Facility*. A country in balance of payments difficulty is eligible to draw up to 100 per cent of its quota with the IMF if exports fall below a defined trend for reasons generally beyond its control. The other is the EEC's *Stabex scheme*. It covers the 58 African, Caribbean and Pacific countries that are members of the Lomé agreement. Under the second Lomé agreement 44 primary products are eligible for support. These countries receive grants (if one of the 35 *least* developed countries) or interest-free loans if export earnings from a qualifying product fall below average earnings over the four preceding years by a certain percentage.

Thirdly, there is the UNCTAD *Common Fund*—agreed on in principle but still to be set up. The idea is that a central fund will finance buffer stocks under separate international commodity agreements, and will thereby stabilise commodity prices. By January 1986 90 countries had ratified the agreement for establishing a Common Fund although their pledged contribution did not yet add up to the capital required for its launching.

Case-study of a Commodity Agreement: Tin.

We take the case of tin as an example of the objectives and the working of commodity agreements, and of the difficulties that are encountered. Tin is unusual among primary commodities in having been the subject of a continuous intergovernmental commodity scheme for three decades. It was extreme instability in the tin market which led to the establishment of the International Tin Council (ITC) in London in the 1950s. The ITC is made up of most producing and consuming country governments. The four main producers of tin, accounting for 86 per cent of world production in 1980, are Malaysia (42 per cent), Thailand, Indonesia and Bolivia. The main consumers (excluding the communist countries) are the United States and the EEC, both accounting for a quarter of consumption, and Japan (18 per cent).

The ITC has two main methods of control: export quotas and a buffer stock. Quotas on tin exports of producing countries have been used at times to prevent significant imbalance between production and demand. The objective of the buffer stock scheme is to stabilise the market price. The manager of the ITC scheme uses its funds, provided by member countries and banks, to buy tin when the demand is low relative to the supply, and so keep up the price, or to sell tin when the demand is high relative to supply, and so prevent it from falling. The ITC has thus provided a "floor" price and a "ceiling" price for tin.

Crisis in the Tin Market.

The danger with a buffer stock scheme is that the manager will try to stabilise the price at too high a level. This will require persistent stock building and take up more and more funds. That is what happened to the tin buffer stock in the 1980s. The dollar price of tin peaked in the London Metal Exchange (LME) in 1980, and thereafter fell on account of the world recession, along with the prices of many other primary commodities. In 1983 the dollar price was only 77 per cent of its 1980 level and in 1985 73 per cent. However, the market price would have been even lower in the absence of intervention by the ITC.

The ITC became trapped, with no room for manoeuvre. Export quotas, imposed since 1982, kept a third of members' production off the market but these curbs were inadequate because Bolivia and new producers were outside the cartel arrangement. When ITC stocks reached 40,000 tons, the funds available for the buffer stock were depleted.

Nor was it possible for the manager to allow the price to fall because the ITC needed to maintain the value of tin held as collateral against commercial borrowing.

In October 1985 the manager suspended his operations because he could no longer support the agreed price. This led instantly to the closure of dealings in tin on the principal world market, the LME. The ITC had outstanding debts to banks and brokers of some £340 million and contractual commitments for future purchases at high prices. Thus a substantial drop in the price of tin would bankrupt the ITC and with it some tin brokers. Prices for small lots of tin traded elsewhere were about 40 per cent below the previous LME price. Talks among member countries, intended to rescue the ITC, collapsed in March 1986. The issue was the extent of responsibility of the 22 member governments for the debts of the ITC.

The impending demise of the Tin Council cast a shadow over the other commodity agreements: cocoa, jute, rubber, olive oil, sugar, tropical timber, wheat and coffee. The collapse of the tin cartel occurred at a time when the oil cartel was also collapsing (*see* **G52**).

The Impact of the Oil Price Rise.

In October 1973, during the Arab–Israeli war, the members of the Organisation of Petroleum Exporting Countries (OPEC) cut supplies of oil and increased their prices drastically. The price of oil subsequently rose fourfold above its initial level. By acting as a cartel to control supplies the OPEC countries were able to maintain the higher prices without surpluses accumulating and a competitive price war breaking out. The impact on all countries was great; indeed on a number of less developed countries it was disastrous.

Some idea of the magnitude of the problem can be given by expressing the *additional* oil bill in 1974 as a percentage of the total import bill and of the GNP in 1973 of various countries. For Uruguay the figures were 39 and 4·9 per cent respectively, for Thailand 26 and 5·4, for South Korea 20 and 9·0, and for Turkey 19 and 3·3 per cent. The bout of inflation in the industrial countries resulting from the oil crisis meant that the developing countries also had to pay more for their other imports. They were further hit by the world recession generated by the oil crisis, because the resultant fall in world demand produced a slump in the prices of primary commodities. Between June 1974 and June 1975 the primary commodity exports (other than oil) of developing countries fell in price by nearly 40 per cent, and their imports of manufactures rose in price by 40 per cent. The developing countries had to cut back on the volume of their imports, to the detriment of development programmes. However, they were partly cushioned by the emergency loans provided through the *oil facility* scheme introduced by the IMF.

Of course, a number of less developed countries benefited from the oil price increases. These included the five oil countries (Saudi Arabia, Kuwait, Qatar, Abu Dhabi and Libya) whose levels of income per capita now exceeded those in the industrial countries. Their use of the new revenues is limited by the ability of their economies to absorb them: for that reason they continue to need technical assistance. How they use their unabsorbed oil revenues can greatly affect the economies of both developed and developing countries. Other, less wealthy, oil-producing countries—including Iran, Iraq, Venezuela, Indonesia and Nigeria—have much larger populations and more absorptive capacity. They had an opportunity to transform their economies with the oil revenues.

Reappraisal of Development and Aid Policies.

By the mid-1970s it was generally recognised that there was a case for a drastic reappraisal of development policies and of aid priorities. One of the important considerations was the new situation created by the increased price of oil. Many developing countries would require substantially more aid to offset its various adverse effects. The success of OPEC in raising the oil price aroused the hopes and expectations of developing countries producing other primary commodities that they too could improve their terms of trade with the developed world. A "New International Economic Order" was envisaged by the General Assembly of the United Nations, in which the formation of producers' associations and new commodity agreements could play a part. These were the main issues debated, but with little agreement being reached, in the fourth session of UNCTAD held in 1976.

Other factors calling for a reappraisal of policies included a growing recognition of the precarious food situation in many developing countries, and an increased awareness of large and growing income inequalities both within and among the developing countries.

Growing Indebtedness.

The external indebtedness of the developing countries grew alarmingly in the years after 1973. In nominal terms debt grew at 20 per cent per annum. Debt servicing obligations increased from $10 billion in 1971 to $141 billion in 1985. For non-oil developing countries as a whole, external debt amounted to 36 per cent of GDP in 1986, and debt service payments to 26 per cent of their exports. World inflation tempers the story in two ways. First, the increase in indebtedness was much less rapid in real than in nominal terms. Secondly, with interest rates being low in the mid-1970s, inflation meant that real rates of interest on much developing country debt were actually negative. Nevertheless, many developing countries failed to adjust fully to the worsened economic and trading conditions after 1973.

The Tokyo Round.

The latest round of multilateral trade negotiations was completed in Tokyo in 1979. It provided a legal basis within GATT for preferential treatment for developing countries, and offered them some trade liberalisation. The industrialised countries agreed to reduce tariffs generally, and by an average of 25 per cent for industrial and 7 per cent for agricultural products conventionally exported by developing countries. The extent to which developing countries will actually gain, however, depends on whether developed countries make use of the *safeguard clause* which permits emergency protection on the grounds of serious injury to domestic industry: safeguard measures have frequently been invoked against imports from developing countries. Nevertheless, the prospects for success of export-based industrialisation in developing countries (*see* **G37**) are better than in the past.

The Food Crisis.

In the last couple of decades food production in the developing countries has done little more than keep pace with the growth of population. F.A.O. projections of demand and supply over the decade 1975–85 indicated no increase in food production per capita in the developing countries. Many developing countries have become net food importers, and this trend is likely to continue. In 1982 food imports represented no less than 17 per cent of the total merchandise imports of the 35 low-income developing countries and 12 per cent in the case of the 59 middle-income developing countries.

The years 1972–74 were ones of poor harvests in various parts of the developed and developing world. Famines occurred in the Sahel areas of Africa, in Bangladesh and in parts of India. In response to vast imports of grain by the Soviet Union and many other countries, world grain stocks were reduced to very low levels and the price of grain rocketed. At the same time an acute shortage of fertiliser emerged, and its price also soared. These circumstances led to the calling of a World Food Conference in 1974.

The Conference foresaw the possibility of inadequate food supplies and famines in the developing countries in future years. It called for a building up of world food stocks and increased emergency *food aid*—aid provided in the form of foodstuffs. However, the long-run solution was seen to come from a fundamental attack on the problems of agricultural development. In response, most of the DAC donor countries decided to increase very substantially their aid to agriculture in the recipient countries.

An International Emergency Food Reserve was established in 1976 and has been built up, and an IMF Food Facility was set up in 1981 to provide financial assistance to offset fluctuations in countries' food import bills. Total bilateral and multilateral ODA earmarked for agriculture more than doubled in real terms between 1973 and 1983.

The Causes of Famine.

Famine is by no means always simply the result of a fall in food production which affects all people in the area uniformly. In the 1974 Bangladesh famine and the recent Ethiopian famines, those who suffered most were respectively the landless, who normally exchange labour for food, and pastoralists, who normally exchange cattle for food grains. The landless, losing their source of earnings because farmers no longer hired labourers, and pastoralists, seeing the prices of their emaciated beasts fall as more and more were marketed, could no longer buy food: these were the people who starved.

Inequality Within Countries.

The growth performance of the less developed countries taken together—growth of GNP per capita of 2·3 per cent per annum in the 1950s, 3·0 per cent per annum in the 1960s and 3·1 per cent per annum in the 1970s—is good by the standards of the past. However, in some less developed countries these growth rates have been achieved without any apparent improvement in the lot of the masses.

The majority of the people are engaged in agriculture in the rural areas, whereas much of the development has taken place in industry and services in the urban areas. A minority of people have benefited—industrialists, bureaucrats, educated and skilled workers, organised labour in the modern sector of the economy— but the poor living in the urban slums, often in open or disguised unemployment, and the enormous numbers in the rural areas have been little affected by development. In many countries the fruits of development have not been widely spread. It is a growing criticism that development policies have been biased towards industry and towards the cities, and that rural people in agriculture have been neglected. This outcome may be a reflection of the uneven distribution of political power within a developing country.

Increasingly, the growth of GNP per capita as a goal of development has been questioned, both within the less developed countries and among national and international aid agencies. Both recipient and donor governments have recently shown a greater concern for poverty, employment creation and social equity. Many donors have modified their aid policies to try to reach the poor. Of course, this redirection coincides to a considerable extent with the increased concern for agricultural development.

Basic Needs.

A direction in which international thinking has moved is towards the acceptance of a *Basic Needs* strategy of development. Essentially the aim is to alleviate absolute poverty, *i.e.*, to meet minimum standards of food, shelter, clothing and safe drinking water, and to satisfy certain other basic human needs. It is proposed that these standards be reached not so much by means of welfare transfers as by enabling the poor to help themselves through productive employment. The minimum standards are inevitably subjective, there are economic and political obstacles to the fulfilment of basic needs, and the approach does not translate easily into specific policies. Nevertheless, the basic needs strategy may have an impact on the priorities both of aid agencies and of recipient governments.

Case Study of "Trickle Down".

Two types of strategy for the alleviation of poverty are possible. One is direct government

GROWTH OF INCOME PER HEAD 1970–1980 AND LEVEL OF INCOME PER HEAD 1980
IN DEVELOPING COUNTRIES

Group	No. of countries	Income per head ($)	Growth of income per head (% p.a.)
Least developed	31	210	0·2
Low income	35	290	2·8
Middle income	70	1,150	3·0
Newly industrialising	11	2,540	3·8
OPEC	11	3,760	3·8
Total	158	750	3·2

intervention to assist the poor and to meet basic needs: Sri Lanka provides an example of this approach (see **G39**). The other is to promote rapid growth, the benefits from which will *trickle down* to the poor: Brazil's is such a case. Between 1965 and 1980, its GDP grew annually in real terms by no less than 8.5 per cent (despite an annual inflation of 33 per cent), and GDP per capita by 5·7 per cent. In 1980 national income per capita ($1,940) was high by comparison with other developing countries. Yet inequality was also very high: the richest 10 per cent of families received 50 per cent of income, and the poorest 40 per cent received well under 10 per cent: their annual average income per head was only $560, and many lived in conditions comparable to those in countries with much lower per capita incomes.

The pattern of growth in Brazil has favoured the rich, the educated, and the skilled. The emphasis has been on capital-intensive, high-technology industrialization at the maximum rate, to the neglect of policies directed at poverty. Although their relative position has worsened, the real incomes of the poor have nevertheless improved in absolute terms, and various social indicators also reflect progress. For instance, between 1960 and 1980, life expectancy at birth rose from 55 to 64 years, the population living in homes with a sanitary device rose from 49 to 75 per cent, and primary school enrolment rose from 57 to 94 per cent. Most developing countries would reject Brazil's approach, however, because the trickle-down effects of economic growth at the growth rates of which they are capable would simply be too weak. When Brazilian growth halted in the 1980s there were no benefits of growth to trickle down.

Inequality Among Countries.

Not all less developed countries have fared equally well in recent years. In particular there appears to be a tendency for disparities among less developed countries to widen. When, in the table, developing countries are divided into five groups on the basis of income per head, it is found that the growth of income per head is slowest for the poorest group and fastest for the least poor group. The countries which have performed well tend to be semi-industrialised and able to respond to opportunities for exporting manufactures to the developed countries, or to be well endowed with mineral or oil resources. Recent growth success stories include Brazil, Colombia, South Korea, Taiwan, Mexico and Singapore. Some of these are on the way to becoming self-reliant economically: they are known as the *newly industrialising countries* (NICs).

The poorest countries—31 of which have been designated the *least developed countries* (LLDCs)—are experiencing the greatest difficulty in escaping from the vicious circle of poverty. A growing recognition of their problem has led the DAC countries to reallocate aid in favour of the least developed countries, and to offer aid on more concessionary terms to these countries.

Revision of British Aid Policies.

The revision of DAC aid policies mentioned above also occurred in the British aid programme. In 1974 the British Government began to direct more of its aid towards the poorest developing countries, and all future ODA to countries with a GNP per capita of less than $200 (£85) per annum was to take the form of outright grants. Aid for famiy planning was stepped up. Increasing weight was placed on rural development

and the expansion of agricultural production, in particular on helping the poor in rural areas, *e.g.*, small farmers and landless labourers. The proportion of net bilateral ODA disbursed which went to the poorest 50 countries was 64 per cent in 1984. In 1978 the Government announced that the debt owed by 16 of the poorest countries would be cancelled; over the ensuing years much of their debt was cancelled. British food aid and disaster relief increased sharply in the 1980s.

The Brandt Report.

In 1980 the independent commission on international development issues, under the chairmanship of Willy Brandt, published its report on relations between the North and the South. It regarded such relations as *the* great social challenge of our time, and saw its task as being to bring understanding and to change attitudes in the rich countries of the North, and to contribute to the development of "worldwide moral values". However, Brandt also appealed to the self-interests of the North: it was in the North's long run interests that poverty and hunger should not linger and spread in the countries of the South. But many people in the North were likely to be unreceptive to this view in the worsened economic climate of the time.

The commission made various general recommendations, *e.g.*, that priority be given to the poorest countries and to the elimination of hunger. Its most challenging proposal was that all countries except the poorest should contribute development finance on an automatic sliding scale related to national income—a sort of international progressive income tax. Recognising that the obstacles to action are frequently political, it recommended greater power-sharing between North and South in international economic bodies.

Public Attitudes to Aid.

A recurring theme is the need to build public support for development efforts: aid is widely seen as having no political constituency. An opinion poll carried out in Britain in 1983 at the Government's request showed that 60 per cent of respondents were in favour of British aid to the poorest countries; a similar figure had been found in 1969. The proportion of respondents who wanted aid to be increased rose from 16 to 37 per cent once they were told what the aid level was in relation to other expenditures.

Aid to Africa.

Of all the less developed regions, Africa has done least well in recent years. For instance, food production per capita in the developing countries of Africa was 10 per cent lower in 1980 than it had been 10 years before. In 1981 the World Bank undertook a study of the problem at the request of African governments. The ensuing report argued for a near doubling of external aid for these countries, even though they were already dependent on aid: aid to the sub-Saharan region was almost 40 per cent of its total imports and over half its total investment in 1981. The report also argued for policy changes by their governments, if a further fall in living standards was to be averted. The policy changes recommended generally involved less state intervention in the economy and more rein to individual incentives and to the market. The report also recognised the constraint on development imposed by a lack of trained manpower and of good management.

One problem will not be easy to deal with: the lack of political stability widely found in Africa, and in other parts of the Third World, is inimical to economic development. Violent changes of government are common, and there were in 1980 some 3 million African refugees who had fled from their own to neighbouring countries. The main "culprits" were Ethiopia, Angola, Rwanda, Burundi, Equatorial Guinea, Uganda and Chad.

Crisis and Response in Africa.

In 1983 and 1984 drought drove millions of Africans deeper into poverty. With the recurring drought and dismal statistics came vivid photographs of human suffering, conveying to the world an image of continent-wide disaster. The drought particularly affected countries in south eastern Africa, such as Mozambique, and the Sahel belt below the Sahara, e.g., Ethiopia, Sudan, and Chad. In 1983 cereal imports amounted to over a third of cereal production in two dozen affected African countries, and a FAO estimate of their cereal import requirements for 1984/5 came to more than half their 1983 production.

A number of African governments had by 1984 accepted the need for measures to stimulate agricultural production, such as the raising of prices paid to producers for their crops and a transfer of investment priorities towards agriculture. Aid donors also responded to the crisis, giving short term assistance in the form of food aid and longer term assistance in the form of increased development aid. Sub-Saharan Africa received 33 per cent of ODA in 1983 compared wiht 25 per cent in 1975.

In 1985 it was apparent that the drought-stricken African countries would be unable to make scheduled payments of interest and principal on their debts, including their obligations to the IMF. Without additional aid from the developed countries or a rescheduling of payments, a number of countries would have to default on their debts.

Income per head in sub-Saharan African fell sharply in the early 1980s. With the World Bank forecasting a further fall in the decade 1986–1995, Africa is set to become the focus of aid-donors' attention.

The Second Oil Price Rise.

In the wake of the second sharp increase in the price of oil in 1979, the world economy went into a prolonged recession. With growth in the volume of world trade falling to zero in 1981 and becoming negative in 1982, the growth in GDP of the oil-importing developing countries fell to below 2 per cent per annum, and their exports fell in value between 1980 and 1983. Over this period their current account deficits represented a quarter of their total value of exports. Many developing countries were squeezed between stagnating foreign exchange earnings and heavy foreign exchange commitments. This precipitated two problems: a *debt crisis* for certain heavily indebted developing countries and the need for *stabilization policies* among a broader group of developing countries.

The Debt Crisis.

The debt position deteriorated at the turn of the decade. Most developing countries had to go further into debt in response to the renewed increase in the oil price. With nominal interest rates now very high and real rates positive, the burden of debt servicing became more onerous. Donor countries received burgeoning requests for debt relief or the rescheduling of repayments. Private debt had also increased during the 1970s. By 1983 the total of commercial bank claims on developing countries exceeded $225 billion. It was the more successful developing countries which attracted private funds: Brazil and Mexico together accounted for 60 per cent of this total. Nevertheless, as in the case of Poland, the risk of default had become serious.

The world recession exacerbated problems of indebtedness. In 1985 the debt servicing (interest and amortisation) payments of the developing countries amounted to 26 per cent of their exports, having been 17 per cent in 1980. Countries with particularly high percentages included some newly industrialising countries with large oil imports

whose export markets had contracted (e.g. Brazil and Korea), some low income countries whose export prices fell in the world recession (e.g. Bolivia and Zaïre), and some oil exporting countries whose export earnings collapsed (e.g. Mexico and Nigeria).

At the end of 1983, it was estimated that Mexico had a total external debt of $95 billion outstanding, Brazil $95 b., Argentina $44 b., Venezuela $34 b., and Poland $28 b. In all the major cases a rescheduling of debt repayments had been arranged or was being negotiated, usually in conjunction with IMF programmes.

The IMF and Stabilization Policies.

Many developing countries ran into serious balance of payments problems in the early 1980s. The current account deficit of the developing countries taken as a whole, at $49 billion in 1985, was equivalent to 7 per cent of exports. Many sought temporary financial assistance from the International Monetary Fund (see **G9**).

As a condition of its larger loans the IMF generally requires a country to accept a series of *stabilization* measures. The typical stabilization package contains the following policies: a devaluation to assist the balance of payments, monetary and credit restrictions and reduced government budget deficits to reduce demand and curb inflation, and, more generally, the elimination of restrictions such as import controls and interest rate regulations in order to harness market forces.

The wisdom of such a package in a developing country is much disputed among economists. It is most obviously the correct remedy when the problem is one of general excess demand in the economy. However, when the problem arises from an extraneous shock, such as a fall in the world price of a major export or a rise in the price of imported oil, the IMF's remedies may prove to be inappropriate. Credit restrictions and cuts in government spending may depress the economy, reducing output and employment. This may temporarily alleviate the immediate problems of inflation and balance of payments deficit, but the effect on long run economic growth may be negative.

It is for these reasons that critics accuse the IMF of doctrinairely and narrowly focussing on monetary variables and ignoring structural problems and developmental objectives. The IMF, on the other hand, often sees itself as a handy scapegoat for unpopular measures made inescapable by domestic economic mismanagement.

A Case Study of Stabilization.

Kenya, one of the most successful of the African economies, first resorted to borrowing from the IMF under the Fund's *Extended Financing Facility* in the period 1975–7, to cope with the imbalance generated by the first oil price rise. As a condition for the loan, the Kenya government embarked on a medium term structural adjustment programme, which included, but went beyond, the usual credit and government borrowing ceilings. The serious balance of payments crisis in Kenya after the second oil price increase required IMF short term credits in 1979–81. The conditions imposed by the Fund were tougher than in 1975: tax revenues would have to be raised, government spending cut, bank credit restricted, and real wages depressed. Access to this credit was suspended in 1982 because bank credit to the government had exceeded the agreed ceiling.

Kenya was also the recipient of a large *Structural Adjustment Loan* from the World Bank in 1980. This too involved conditions: Kenya was required to make a major policy shift towards economic liberalization. Import controls were relaxed in conjunction with a devaluation of the currency, intended to provide export incentives for farmers. These conditions were in line with the prevailing view in the World Bank that government intervention in markets, however well intentioned, often gives rise to inefficiency, and that the most successful developing countries have permitted market forces to operate.

Some Suggestions for Further Reading.

For an introduction to the subject the reader is referred to Jagdish Bhagwati, *The Economics of*

Underdeveloped Countries (World University Library) or to Walter Elkan, *An Introduction to Development Economics* (Penguin). Ian Little, in *Economic Development* (Basic Books) assesses the development record and the way in which ideas and policies have evolved. A book concerned with international disparities, and addressed to the general reader, is *Development in a Divided World*, edited by Seers and Joy (Pelican). On Asia the reader may wish to dip into three volumes of Gunnar Myrdal entitled *Asian Drama: An Enquiry into the Poverty of Nations* (Allen Lane, The Penguin Press). On South America there is Celso Furtado, *Economic Development of Latin America* (Cambridge University Press). Michael Lipton's book *Why Poor People Stay Poor* (Temple Smith) throws light on the "urban bias" in development policies. Introductory books on particular topics include G. K. Helleiner, *International Trade and*

Economic Development and Peter Dorner, *Land Reform and Economic Development* (both Penguins).

The Overseas Development Administration has compiled a handbook of *British Aid Statistics* (H.M.S.O.), The World Bank produces an annual *World Development Report*. The Organisation for Economic Co-operation and Development, comprising all the major non-communist developed countries, publishes an Annual Review of aid and development entitled *Development Cooperation* (O.E.C.D.). The report of the Brandt Commission is available in paperback as *North–South: a Programme for Survival* (Pan Books).

An interesting quarterly publication of the I.M.F. and the World Bank, *Finance and Development*, is available free of charge: applications should be sent to *Finance and Development*, I.M.F. Building, Washington, D.C. 20431, U.S.A.

IV. RECENT DEVELOPMENTS IN THE BRITISH ECONOMY

1. INTERNATIONAL DEVELOPMENTS

The Balance of Payments.

The balance of payments problem has dominated events in the British economy until recent years. It is therefore important to analyse the balance of payments in some detail; to understand why the balance of payments has been a problem; and to see its effects on economic policy. The balance of payments and its components are explained in detail on **G6–8**. The balance of payments in each year from 1974 to 1985 is shown in the table below.

The 1960s.

The late 1950s and the early 1960s saw a decline in British competitiveness. The British share in world exports of manufactures fell steadily, and there was a rapid increase in imports of manufactured goods. The balance of payments deteriorated during an economic upswing, such as that generated by the pre-election boom of 1964. The current account deficit in turn would then increase expectations of devaluation and so generate an outflow of short term capital and precipitate a *sterling crisis*. To prevent the price of sterling from falling below the official minimum limit to the exchange rate of £1 = \$2.78 (*i.e.* to support sterling) the Bank of England was forced to buy pounds. To do this the Bank had to draw on the country's reserves of gold and foreign exchange. The typical response to such a crisis was for the Government to raise interest rates and deflate the economy, as happened, for instance, in the "July measures" of 1966.

Speculation against sterling nevertheless continued periodically until, in November 1967, the Government devalued the pound by 14·3 per cent, from \$2·8 to \$2·4 to the £. At the same time it was agreed among central bankers that Britain should be given credit in order to protect the reserves against speculation; but it would have to be paid back out of the balance of payments surpluses over the next few years. The devaluation was accompanied by a series of deflationary measures in order to release resources into the now profitable exporting and import substituting industries.

After slow initial progress the balance of payments improved strongly during 1969, and in 1971, most unusually for Britain, the visible balance showed a surplus. The total currency flow was transformed from an enormous deficit in 1968 to a huge surplus in 1971, some of which represented short term capital flight from the dollar.

At the end of 1968 the British Government had short- and medium-term debts outstanding to central banks and the IMF of no less than £3·4 billion. This represented about 10 per cent of the national income in 1968 and compared with gold and foreign exchange reserves of only £1·0 billion. The continued improvement in the balance of payments and the first allocation of Special Drawing Rights duly enabled the steady reduction of

outstanding debts. The vast balance of payments surplus of 1971 eliminated almost all of these debts, and by the end of 1972 the official short- and medium-term indebtedness was nil.

Floating of the Pound.

The competitive position of the United Kingdom was weakened after 1971 by an inflation more rapid than in other countries and also by the dollar devaluation of 1971. There were sharp increases in demand for such consumer goods as cars and colour television sets—no doubt set off by the abolition of hire-purchase restrictions in 1971—and the inability of domestic producers to expand their production correspondingly both constrained exports and accelerated imports. The trade balance deteriorated from a surplus in 1971 to a record deficit in 1972. There was a large outflow of short-term funds in mid-1972, which culminated in a sterling crisis and a floating of the pound in June. That was the first time that sterling had been allowed to float since a period in the 1930s, and it represented a contravention of the increasingly criticised Bretton Woods system (*see* **G9**). The pound then floated downwards after June, from about \$2·60 = £1 on an average value of roughly \$ 2·40 during 1973, \$2·30 in 1974 and \$2·20 in 1975. The downward slide continued, and in March 1976 the pound fell below \$2·00 for the first time. Sterling depreciated even further in relation to such currencies as the mark, the franc and the yen, as the dollar was itself devalued in 1971 and 1973.

The falling value of the pound was of no immediate assistance to the balance of payments: experience suggests that the improvement occurs only after a lag of a year or two. In the meantime the depreciation pushed up the domestic price of imports of raw materials and foodstuffs, so raising both the costs of production and the cost of living. The downward floating of the pound made a counter-inflation policy both more difficult and more important.

Inflation in Commodity Markets.

The current account of the balance of payments deteriorated sharply in 1973, to reach a deficit of £1·0 billion. Exports did reasonably well, rising by 25 per cent in value. However, the import bill soared, increasing by no less than 41 per cent. Import volume increased by 14 per cent, reflecting the rapid upsurge of the economy. More important was the higher price of imports: up by an average of 26 per cent between 1972 and 1973. This period witnessed a remarkable inflation in the prices of various primary products in world markets. To give some examples, between the first quarter of 1972 and the last quarter of 1973 average price increases in major world markets were as follows: cocoa 173 per cent, copper 115 per cent, cotton 127 per cent, rubber 123 per cent, wool 138 per cent and zinc 308 per cent.

This unprecedented jump in primary commodity prices stemmed from the sharp and well-synchronised expansion of the major industrial economies during 1972 and 1973, and it was assisted by some speculative buying as a hedge against inflation. Commodity prices generally reached their peak in the second quarter of 1974. Food prices continued to rise after this, while the prices of other commodities, especially fibres and metals, fell as the world economy moved into recession.

The Oil Crisis.

An event of great importance to Britain and to other industrial countries was the decision of the Arab oil-producing states, taken in October 1973, to restrict oil supplies and to raise oil prices. The restriction of supplies was initiated as a short-run political weapon in the Arab–Israeli conflict; but it revealed a potential for obtaining higher prices which had not previously been exploited by the Organisation of Petroleum Exporting Countries (OPEC). In the past the world demand for oil had grown very rapidly—by about 8 per cent per annum between 1960 and 1973—but it had been successfully met by expansion of production. A slower growth of oil supply in relation to demand produces scarcity and a rocketing of price. Alternative sources of energy cannot be developed—and thus the demand for oil cannot be curtailed or even its growth retarded—for many years. However, maintenance of high prices depends on the ability of the OPEC group to restrict oil supplies to the market despite the incentive of each individual country to take advantage of the high prices by expanding its sales.

Between September 1973 and January 1974 the oil-producing governments raised their "take" on a barrel of crude oil from $1·75 to $7·00, and the import price was increased from $3·45 to $8·70 a barrel, i.e., an increase of 150 per cent. Comparing 1974 with 1973, the price of oil imported into Britain almost trebled.

Oil and the Balance-of-Payments.

Largely because of higher import prices Britain's current balance deteriorated sharply in 1974. The value of imports rose by about 50 per cent. This was all accounted for by price increases, and not only oil prices: imported basic materials, semi-manufactures and food also rose sharply. Meanwhile the price of exports increased by 30 per cent but, because of world inflation, this involved little loss of competitiveness. In 1974 Britain recorded her worst ever current account deficit; no less than £3·3 billion. It represented a worsening of over £2·3 billion; in fact the additional oil bill amounted to £2·8 billion. The deficit was of an order of magnitude—no

less than 5 per cent of GDP—which made the deficits of previous crisis years appear puny.

In the wake of the oil crisis the world economy duly moved into severe recession. To this the British economy was no exception: real GDP stagnated in 1974 and fell in 1975. The domestic recession reduced the demand for imports, which fell in volume by 8 per cent in 1975. The world recession made it difficult for OPEC to raise oil prices still further; and the already depressed state of world demand caused the prices of primary commodities actually to fall. Britain therefore benefited from a 6 per cent improvement in the terms of trade. Moreover, the British share of world exports of manufactures rose slightly, against the long-run trend. The net result of these changes was that the current account deficit of the balance of payments was halved, to £1·5 billion, in 1975.

In 1976 the world economy began to emerge from its severe recession, and output of the OECD countries grew by 5 per cent on average. This helped the British balance of payments. Exports rose by 8 per cent in volume; they were assisted by the depreciation of sterling and by the domestic price controls which encouraged producers to switch to foreign markets. However, the volume of imports was up by a similar percentage. There was a particularly large increase in imports of cars: British producers appeared unable to expand production to meet the demand. Although the current account improved in 1976, the deficit in total currency flow rose to no less than £3·8 billion. To understand the reason we must examine the way in which the oil deficits have been financed, and movements of the exchange rate.

Financing the Deficit.

In 1974 the oil exporting countries financed the largest part of the current account deficit by adding £2·2 billion to their sterling balances. The reduced deficit of 1975 actually posed a greater problem of financing, because the oil producers were less willing to accumulate balances in sterling. Britain's foreign exchange reserves fell, the Government borrowed in the Eurodollar market and announced that it would borrow from the IMF in 1976.

Interest rates were kept high in London during 1975 to attract short-term capital and to discourage its withdrawal. However, during 1975 the rate of inflation in Britain was some 15 per cent above the average for the OECD countries; it became increasingly clear that sterling would have to be depreciated further. Speculative outflows of funds forced the authorities to intervene strongly in the foreign exchange market by selling foreign exchange, and even then the pound depreciated substantially to a new low level. The

THE UK BALANCE OF PAYMENTS

	1974	1975	1976	1977	1978
Exports (f.o.b.)	16·4	19·3	25·2	31·7	35·1
Imports (f.o.b.)	21·7	22·7	29·1	34·0	36·6
Visible balance	− 5·4	− 3·3	− 3·9	− 2·3	− 1·5
Invisible balance	+ 2·0	+ 1·8	+ 3·0	+ 2·2	+ 2·5
Current balance .	− 3·3	− 1·6	− 0·9	− 0·1	+ 1·0
Overseas investment in UK .	+ 2·2	+ 1·5	+ 2·1	+ 4·4	+ 1·9
UK private investment overseas	− 1·1	− 1·4	− 2·3	− 2·3	− 4·6
Official long term capital . .	− 0·3	− 0·3	− 0·2	− 0·3	− 0·3
Total investment and other capital transactions. .	+ 1·6	+ 0·2	− 3·0	+ 4·2	− 4·1
Allocation of SDRs .					
Net borrowing from IMF .			+ 1·0	+ 1·1	− 1·0
Other net borrowing . .	+ 1·8	+ 0·8	+ 1·8	+ 1·1	− 0·2
Change in reserves* . . .	− 0·1	+ 0·7	+ 0·9	− 9·6	+ 2·3
Total official financing . .	+ 1·6	+ 1·5	+ 3·6	− 7·4	+ 1·1
Balancing item	+ 0·1		+ 0·3	+ 3·3	+ 2·0

* A positive sign denotes drawings on and a negative sign additions to the reserves.

British economy had again become precariously dependent on creditors and speculators.

In March 1976 the value of the pound fell below $2·00: in the space of two months it depreciated by 9 per cent. The pound slipped further with large withdrawals of officially-held sterling balances, until it was checked in June by the announced agreement of a $5·3 billion standby credit facility made available to the Bank of England by the "Group of Ten" countries. With the trade returns worsening, sterling came under pressure again, the exchange rate slid to a low point of $1·57 in October, and the Bank of England's minimum lending rate (see G27) was raised to the unprecedented level of 15 per cent. The Government applied to the IMF to draw on the United Kingdom's credit tranche of $3·9 billion. The successful conclusion of these negotiations in January 1977, and the borrowing of more than £1 billion from the IMF, helped to restore confidence. However, the terms of the agreement involved some loss of control over domestic affairs: in his Letter of Intent to the IMF, the Chancellor agreed to restrictions on the rate of *domestic credit expansion* (DCE) and on the *public sector borrowing requirement* (PSBR).

Over the year 1976 the pound depreciated by some 15 per cent against other currencies. However, with the British rate of inflation running at 16 per cent and well above that in the other major countries, the ensuing gain in competitiveness was small.

The Sterling Balances.

The official sterling holdings (see G10) rose sharply after the oil crisis, as oil funds were invested in Britain; early in 1975 they amounted to £4·9 billion. In 1976, however, much of the oil money was withdrawn during the bouts of speculation against the pound, and the sterling balances fell, to reach £2·6 billion in December. It had become increasingly necessary to reduce the vulnerability of the British economy to fluctuations of this sort.

The IMF agreement of January 1977 was followed by the successful negotiation of a "safety net" for the officially held sterling balances. The new facility, for an amount of $3 billion, was to operate with the support of various major central banks. Under the scheme, the British Government offered official holders of sterling the opportunity to convert all or part of their holdings into medium-term foreign currency bonds. But in addition, the UK was able to draw on the credit facility in respect of any other net reductions in the official sterling holdings.

North Sea Oil.

The table shows how the "oil deficit" in the balance of payments, huge in 1974, gradually declined

as North Sea oil production expanded, disappeared in the course of 1980, and was transformed into an "oil surplus", becoming as large as £8·2 billion in 1985.

THE UK BALANCE OF TRADE IN OIL, 1974–1985 (£ BILLION)

1974	− 3·8
1975	− 3·4
1976	− 4·4
1977	− 3·1
1978	− 2·3
1979	− 1·1
1980	+ 0·1
1981	+ 2·9
1982	+ 4·4
1983	+ 6·8
1984	+ 6·8
1985	+ 8·2

The future course of the British balance of payments depends considerably on the rate of expansion of British oil production. The sharp build-up in production from almost nil in 1975 had arrived at about 100 million tonnes in 1980, roughly equal to U.K. net consumption of oil. Oil continues to be both exported and imported because of differences in quality: the United Kingdom exports a higher quality than it imports. British production of petroleum and natural gas amounted to 6 per cent of GDP in 1982. The value of North Sea oil to Britain in the future depends on many imponderables, including the price of oil itself. This depends on the ability of the OPEC cartel to survive and on the growth of the world economy (influenced by the pace of inflation) in relation to the supply (influenced by the development of new fields such as the North Sea, Alaska and Mexico, and by the political stability of major producers such as Iran and Saudi Arabia).

The exploitation of North Sea oil has been a mixed blessing. Through its strengthening of the balance of payments and consequent raising of the exchange rate, it has harmed the manufacturing sector. The problems of structural adjustment, of which rising unemployment is a symptom, have brought a social cost. The precise extent to which manufacturing has suffered as a result of North Sea oil has been debated among economists. Some argue that North Sea oil raised the exchange rate in real terms by more than 20 per cent above what it would have been; others that the attributable increase was only 10 per cent and that the strength of sterling had more to do with the relatively high interest rates in London and the preference of OPEC countries for holding sterling. Some economists attribute much of the slump in manufacturing—by 10 per cent between early 1979 and early 1982—to the 25 per cent rise in the ex-

---

1974–85 (£ BILLION)

1979	1980	1981	1982	1983	1984	1985 †
40·7	47·4	51·0	55·6	60·8	70·4	78·1
44·1	46·1	47·6	53·2	61·6	74·5	80·1
− 3·4	+ 1·4	+ 3·4	+ 2·3	− 0·8	− 4·1	− 2·0
+ 2·7	+ 1·7	+ 3·2	+ 2·3	+ 4·0	+ 5·0	+ 5·0
− 0·7	+ 3·1	+ 6·5	+ 4·7	+ 3·2	+ 0·9	+ 3·0
+ 4·3	+ 5·2	+ 3·4	+ 3·5	+ 5·2	+ 3·6	+ 7·5
− 6·8	− 8·1	− 10·2	− 10·4	− 11·2	− 14·6	− 22·2
− 0·4	− 0·1	− 0·3	− 0·3	− 0·4	− 0·4	− 0·3
+ 1·9	− 1·5	− 3·2	− 3·2	− 4·9	− 3·3	− 2·9
+ 0·2	+ 0·2	+ 0·2				
− 0·6	− 0·1	− 0·1	− 0·2	+ 0·2	+ 0·4	+ 0·5
− 0·3	− 0·9	− 1·6		+ 0·6	+ 0·9	− 1·8
− 1·1	− 0·3	+ 2·4	+ 1·4			
− 1·9	− 1·4	0·7	+ 1·3	+ 0·8	+ 1·3	− 0·9
+ 0·6	− 0·4	− 0·4	− 2·7	+ 0·9	+ 1·0	+ 0·8

† Preliminary.

change rate over the same period; others put most of the blame on the Government's deflationary monetary and fiscal policies. It is generally agreed, however, that if it had not been for North Sea oil, Britain in the post-1973 era would have had to devote additional resources to the production of manufactures for export simply to pay for more expensive oil.

Recovery in the Late 1970s.

There are four main reasons for the elimination of the huge current account deficit by the year 1977. One was the declining "oil deficit," discussed above. The second was the state of recession into which the economy moved. This curbed the demand for imports. Thirdly, the world recession reduced the general demand for primary commodities and so had a depressing effect on their prices. This improved the British terms of trade and helped to keep down the import bill. Finally, the sharp downward floating of the pound improved British competitiveness. Between 1974 and 1976 the value of sterling depreciated by over 20 per cent against a basket of other currencies. In 1977 the volume of manufactured exports rose rapidly.

The improvement in the current account, assisted by high interest rates in London and speculation against the dollar, produced a heavy demand for sterling in late 1977. There was a large increase in short-term sterling balances. The demand for sterling was met in part by the willingness of the monetary authorities to let the exchange rate rise. From its lowest level of £1 = $1·58 in October 1976, it rose to average $1·75 in 1977, $1·92 in 1978, $2·12 in 1979 and $2·33 in 1980, reaching a peak of $2·44 in October of that year. The heavy balance of payments deficit of the United States and continued speculation against the dollar was partly responsible. However, sterling rose steeply against other currencies as well. This was partly due to North Sea oil production, its direct effect on the balance of payments and its indirect effect on foreign confidence in the British economy. Also important were the high interest rates engendered by the government's restrictive monetary policy and the low level of demand for imports caused by the recession in the domestic economy.

The appreciation of sterling helped to curb domestic inflation by keeping down the price of imported goods, but it also had a harmful impact on the manufacturing sector and on competitiveness. In 1979 the current account moved into a deficit of £0·5 billion, mainly owing to a rapid increase in the volume of imports compared with exports. Britain was still a net oil importer and the doubling in the price of OPEC oil in 1979 also worsened the trade balance. However, a substantial capital inflow completely offset the current account deficit. Part of the explanation for the capital inflow must be sought in the relatively high interest rates: some of the sharply increased revenues of the oil-exporting countries were invested in Britain in 1979.

Balance of Payments Surplus in the 1980s.

With the economy slumping in 1980, the trade balance moved into surplus for the first time in many years. In 1981 the trade balance was in even greater surplus (£3·4 billion), reflecting the growth of North Sea oil revenues and the deeper recession in the UK than abroad, and the current account exceeded £6 billion. The strength of the balance of payments raised the exchange rate well above its 1979 level, so putting the manufacturing sector under extreme competitive pressure.

Total export volume stagnated in the world recession of 1982, while imports—mainly of manufactures—grew in volume by 5·5 per cent. The trade surplus remained high, however, because of oil, and the current account surplus was £5 billion. The current account surplus fell to £3 billion in 1983, and the trade balance moved into deficit despite an increase in the oil surplus of over £2 billion. Net trade in manufactures deteriorated by over £4·5 billion. This reflected a lagged adjustment to the unfavourable competitiveness of British products, despite a competitive gain after 1981. The worsening trade balance made domestic recovery more difficult.

Decline in the Exchange Rate.

The effective weighted exchange rate of sterling against the currencies of Britain's trading partners (with 1975 = 100) peaked at just over 100 in late 1980. The fall in 1981 was mainly due to a depreciation against the dollar, in turn attributable to the tight monetary policy and high interest rates prevailing in the United States. The effective rate was stable at 90 during much of 1982 but in November it began to fall. Despite the strength of the balance of payments, the relatively low British inflation rate and Bank of England intervention to support sterling, the pound dropped to an effective exchange rate of 85 in December and went below 80 in March 1983.

The 1982–3 depreciation of sterling was due to two main factors. First, expectations were aroused that the authorities might attempt to improve British competitiveness in the run-up to a General Election, and the publication of the Labour Party's economic programme calling for "a substantial drop in the exchange rate" unsettled the market. Secondly, the fall in the world price of oil and the rumoured break-up of OPEC generated speculation against sterling.

Repayments of Debts.

The United Kingdom incurred large overseas debts to finance balance of payments deficits in the years 1973–76, and the facilities arranged to provide such finance continued to be drawn on even in 1977. In consequence, the total official foreign borrowing outstanding, which (excluding $5 billion of long-term post-war debts) had been negligible at the end of 1972, rose to over $18 billion at the end of 1977. By then, however, the recovery in the balance of payments and the flight from the dollar enabled the British Government to begin early repayments. In September 1985 total official short-term and medium-term borrowing from abroad stood at $9·1 billion, of which $8·4 billion represented borrowing under the exchange cover scheme.

The End of Exchange Controls

In October 1979 the Conservative Government announced the immediate lifting of all remaining exchange control restrictions. Exchange controls had been in force in the United Kingdom for more than 40 years, but the tightness and effect of these controls had varied considerably over time. The announcement meant that it was now possible for residents to obtain foreign exchange for outward portfolio investment or the purchase of holiday homes abroad without the payment of a premium, and to acquire unrestricted access to foreign exchange for direct investment abroad.

The effect was to induce a capital outflow which helped to keep the exchange rate from rising further. There was a strong outflow of portfolio investment: in 1980 the outflow was £3·2 billion, and it rose in the subsequent years to £8·9 billion in 1984. However, this was probably not against the national interest: the alternative methods of financing the massive current account surpluses— a buildup of foreign exchange reserves or a further appreciation of the exchange rate—were less attractive.

Balance of Payments, 1984

Sterling fell sharply in 1984, mainly as a result of the appreciation of the dollar against all currencies. From an average of £1 = $1.52 in 1983 and a value of $1.46 in March 1984, the pound collapsed to $1.22 in October and to a low of $1.05 in March 1985. However, sterling depreciated against other currencies as well. The trade-weighted exchange rate index fell from 81 in March 1984 to 76 in October and to a floor of 71 in March 1985.

The reason for the particular weakness of sterling appeared to be market fears about oil. There were doubts about the level of official oil prices, which had been raised by the appreciation of the dollar, and about the sustainability of OPEC pricing and output arrangements. Because Britain is a net oil exporter these jitters depressed sterling. There may also have been concern in the foreign exchange markets about the coal miners' strike and its possible repercussions on the balance of payments and the economy, and about signs that Government monetary and fiscal policies were being relaxed.

The flight of capital from sterling to the dollar and the collapse of sterling forced the Government to take undesired corrective action. Between December and March, the authorities intervened to make a series of three interest rate increases, totally 4·5 per cent. In March the treasury bill rate reached 14 per cent, well above the US rate of 9 per cent.

The depreciation of sterling helped to improve British trade competitiveness. Although changes in competitiveness affect trade only with a significant lag, a continued improvement in the trade balance could be expected for that reason. Indeed, exports increased in volume by over 10 per cent in 1984, assisted also by economic expansion in other industrial countries. However, imports rose even more rapidly, and the trade deficit deteriorated sharply, to over £4 billion, while the surplus on current account fell to £1 billion. The trade balance was adversely affected by the coal miners' strike, which brought about a reduction in net oil exports and an increase in net coal imports.

Balance of Payments, 1985.

In 1985 the trade deficit fell to $2 billion and the current account surplus rose to £3·5 billion, mainly because the miners' strike ended in March. However, exports did well, rising by 6 per cent over 1984. The effects of the improved competitiveness of 1984 were still being felt, even though competitiveness declined after February 1985. The effective exchange rate rose by 17 per cent from February to July, partly because of the fall in the dollar (*see* **G**54) but also because a tightening of domestic monetary policies raised UK interest rates while foreign interest rates were falling, and so attracted funds from abroad. When the expectation grew that the oil price would fall, the pound came under pressure, depreciating by 10 per cent in the second half of the year.

Is a Lower Oil Price Good for Britain?

The market price of oil collapsed early in 1986 (*see* **G**52). Should this be a matter for concern, Britain being a net oil exporter? There are advantages as well as disadvantages, and Britain is on balance likely to be a beneficiary.

The obvious ill-effects are on the balance of payments and on North Sea oil tax revenues. The Government estimated that, if the price were $15 a barrel, oil would yield it £6 billion in 1986–7 instead of the £11·5 billion of 1985–6; and that each fall of one dollar in the price per barrel would reduce its revenue by £400 million. Moreover, if the pound came under speculative pressure it might be necessary to maintain high domestic interest rates, with adverse effects on investment and spending.

Some fall in sterling would be beneficial. The depreciation required by the worsened balance of payments on current account would improve competitiveness, expand manufacturing and reduce unemployment. The loss of tax revenue from a fall of one dollar in the price per barrel could be offset by a six per cent depreciation of the pound against the dollar. The expansion of the economy would also increase tax revenue, and should not cause inflation because the lower oil price would tend to neutralise any inflationary pressures. Most important, the boost to economic growth in oil-importing countries and to world trade would be good for Britain.

Balance of Payments Prospects.

It is important to realise that the balance of payments in recent years would have been a good deal worse had the British economy not been in serious recession. Any measures to expand the economy are therefore likely to require measures to improve the balance of payments. Hence the debate between those economists who favour import controls and those who favour depreciation of the exchange rate. There is a possibility, however, that North Sea oil will provide sufficient revenue to secure the balance of payments in the 1980s. If this proves to be the case, Government must guard against the danger that a serious structural problem will develop.

Between 1975 and 1984 employment in the manufacturing sector fell by over 2 million jobs, from 7·5 to 5·5 million. Yet in 1984 the North Sea oil industry employed only 33,000 people. A strong balance of payments could keep the exchange rate at a level too high for the manufacturing sector to remain competitive: it would thus contribute to the *deindustrialization* of Britain. The appropriate policy response would then be to reflate the economy and so both reduce unemployment and depreciate the exchange rate, but this in turn would involve the risk of generating inflation.

The Competitiveness of Manufactured Products.

In which products has British manufacturing been losing competitiveness, and in which has it been gaining? This question can be answered by examining the degree of import penetration (imports expressed as a percentage of home demand) and the export sales ratio (manufacturers' exports as a percentage of their sales), and their movements over time. These are shown in the table for selected industries for the years 1975 and 1984. The first thing to note is that the import share and the export share were very similar in 1975, and that both rose over the next decade, the former more rapidly than the latter. This trend reflects the general increase in trade among nations, associated with the decline in trade barriers, the growth in importance of multinational companies and the United Kingdom's entry to the European Economic Community. In most of the industries listed both the import share and the export share increased. Nevertheless, the high exchange rate in the wake of North Sea oil and high interest rates weakened the competitive position of British manufactures: import share has increased more than export share in most industries, and especially in motor vehicles, textiles, clothing and footwear.

UK IMPORT PENETRATION AND
EXPORT SALES RATIOS IN
MANUFACTURING, 1975 AND 1984

	Imports as a percentage of home demand	
	1975	1984
Chemicals	23	39
Mechanical engineering	26	35
Electrical and electronic engineering	25	44
Office machinery and data processing equipment	71	105
Motor vehicles	26	51
Instrument engineering	47	57
Metals	32	43
Food, drink and tobacco	18	18
Textiles	22	44
Clothing and footwear	21	36
Paper, printing and publishing	20	21
Total manufacturing *	23	33

	Exports as a percentage of manufacturers' sales	
	1975	1984
Chemicals	32	45
Mechanical engineering	43	42
Electrical and electronic engineering	33	39
Office machinery and data processing equipment	69	107
Motor vehicles	43	37
Instrument engineering	48	52
Metals	21	32
Food, drink and tobacco	8	10
Textiles	22	30
Clothing and footwear	11	18
Paper, printing and publishing	9	11
Total manufacturing *	24	28

* Includes some industries not listed.

Britain's traditional manufacturing strengths were in all forms of engineering, chemicals and vehicles. Some of these sectors came under pressure. In the case of vehicles, for instance, the export share fell from 43 to 37 per cent, but the import share rose sharply, from 26 to 51 per cent. There are more foreign cars on the roads in every country, but the international competitiveness of British car and truck production has nevertheless declined. The demise of the British motor cycle industry is an example of this trend. Britain improved or maintained her competitive position in food and drink, office machinery, chemicals and paper, printing and publishing. The growing industries in a manufacturing sector which stagnated over the decade were pharmaceuticals, plastic products, scientific instruments, electronics and computers. It is high-technology, growth industries such as these that offer the best prospects for exporting into the 1990s.

Should Imports be Controlled?

In the wake of the oil crisis of 1973, pressure was brought to bear on the British Government to ease the balance of payments and unemployment problems by imposing import duties or quotas. The Government acceded to these pressures in a selective and minor way. However, in 1976, the Chancellor rejected general and semi-permanent controls on manufactured goods: they would infringe treaty obligations to the GATT and the EEC, and he feared that they would lead to retaliation and the danger of an international trade war. That remained the policy of the Labour Government, and also of the Conservative Government returned in 1979. However, the competitive squeeze on the manufacturing sector and the rise in unemployment, and support for import controls by the Labour Party while in opposition, meant that import controls continued to be a live political issue.

The economics profession, as on so many issues, is by no means in agreement on the relative merits of devaluation (or depreciation) and import controls for remedying a balance of payments deficit. The protagonists of import controls point to their scope for selectivity, *e.g.*, permitting concentration on manufactures and excluding raw materials and food, to the possibility of using price increases in the sheltered industries, and to the avoidance of financial crises which would result from the prospect of devaluation. The imposition of tariffs could ensure that the benefits of any price increases accrued to the Government, which could then use the tariff revenues to subsidise commodities important to wage-earners' living standards. The devaluationists, on the other hand, argue that import controls are more likely to provoke retaliation by other countries, that controls breed inefficiency in production, that selective controls need to be very substantial to have the same impact as devaluation, and that controls may have to be progressively intensified.

Foreign Investment.

One of the more successful items in the UK balance of payments has been net interest, profit, and dividends from private sources. In 1976 the net figure was a £2·2 billion surplus. Much of this is made up of the overseas earnings of British companies. The net figure then fell drastically, to almost zero in 1980, reflecting the increasing payments to foreigners of profits and dividends on North Sea oil and interest on sterling balances.

In the years 1980–84 United Kingdom private investment overseas averaged £11 billion per annum and overseas investment in the United Kingdom averaged less than half of the outflow. This net acquisition of assets abroad and the movement of short term funds out of sterling and into the appreciating dollar helped to raise private sector net interest, profits and dividends to £4·6 billion in 1984.

Should the British Government discourage or encourage direct private investment abroad? An economic study has suggested that for every £100 of British direct investment abroad, British exports immediately increase by about £11, *i.e.*, there is an initial drain on the balance of payments of £89. The average rate of profit on capital overseas is thereafter about £8 per annum, or only £5

if capital appreciation is allowed for. The short-term balance of payments loss must therefore be weighed against the long-term gain. However, the effects of investment abroad will vary from one case to another. There will be some instances in which investment abroad is at the expense of production and jobs at home, and others in which foreign and domestic production are complementary.

The Rise of Multinational Companies.

The remarkable expansion since 1960 of international investment, both by foreign companies in the United Kingdom and by British companies abroad, reflects the growing importance of *multinational companies* in the world economy. Some 165 multinationals account for 80 per cent of British private investment abroad. The multinationals tend to dominate the world markets for technologically advanced products. They account for no less than 60 per cent of trade in manufactures in the developed world. Their financial and market power, their global investment strategies, and their ability to avoid national taxation pose a challenge to the economic sovereignty of national governments.

In 1950 a sample of the largest US-based multinationals had 2,200 foreign subsidiaries (276 in the UK) whereas in 1976 the figure had risen to 11,200 (1,084 in the UK). The same proliferation of foreign affiliates occurred among the largest British firms. In 1978 the world's 831 largest industrial companies made sales totalling $2,250 billion, of which 370 were US companies with sales of $1,140 billion and 75 were British companies with sales of $164 billion. The world's 50 largest industrial companies in that year contained the following British firms: Shell (oil), BP (oil), Unilever (food), ICI (chemicals) and BAT (tobacco). The total number of British multinationals (*i.e.* with the parent company based in Britain) in 1973 was 1,600, 36 per cent of which had affiliates in one other country, 50 per cent in 2–9 countries, and 14 per cent in 10 or more countries. In 1975, 74 per cent of direct investment abroad by the OECD countries was invested within the OECD group, 6 per cent in OPEC countries, 3 per cent in tax havens (*e.g.* the Bahamas, Bermuda and the Cayman Islands) and 17 per cent in the other developing countries.

Multinationals in Britain

Just as many British companies operate abroad, so many foreign companies have subsidiaries and affiliates in Britain. Some household names—including the oil companies Esso, Mobil and Texaco, the motor companies Ford, Vauxhall, Nissan and Talbot, the electrical companies Phillips and Hoover, and new technology companies like I.B.M., Kodak and Rank Xerox—are foreign-based. Events in 1986, such as the takeover of Westland helicopters and the possible sale of British Leyland, brought the issue of foreign ownership into public debate.

Opponents of foreign takeovers may be motivated by crude nationalism or by a concern that production would become internationally more footloose. Although particular cases may require scrutiny, the liberal policies which British Governments have adopted towards both inward and outward foreign investment make sense. Countries which cut themselves off from the technological and other skills of multinational companies would find it difficult to compete internationally in the long run.

The International Economic System.

The international monetary system and international liquidity are explained on **G9–10**. The main problem facing the international economic system during the 1960s was an increasing shortage of international liquidity in the face of expanding world trade. This threatened the continuation of free trade. In the 1970s the focus moved to the problems of world inflation and to the international imbalance caused by the increased price of oil, and the resultant threat to economic growth. We trace the issues and events as they unfolded.

The Group of Ten.

The main function of the IMF has been to provide deficit countries with loans, to be repaid over a certain period (*see* **G9–10**). The amount of these credit facilities has been increased over time, but the level has remained low in relation to needs, and the IMF facility has therefore been supplemented in various ways. In order to increase the resources available to neutralise the movements of short-term funds which so disrupted the balance of payments at that time, the IMF initiated a scheme for a "Lenders' Club" in 1961. According to the scheme, the main trading countries—the *Group of Ten*—undertake (subject to some control by lending countries over the use of the funds) to make available substantial loans to the IMF for re-lending to countries of the Group suffering an outflow of short-term funds. The Group of Ten has played an important role in coping with the flows of funds which have grown vastly in scale in the 1970s and 1980s.

Special Drawing Rights.

In 1967 the members of the IMF agreed in principle to a scheme according *special drawing rights* (SDRs) to member countries, and in 1970 the scheme came into operation. SDRs were distributed to all members in proportion to their quotas with the IMF. They are generally accepted as a means of payment. Thus a deficit country can use its SDRs to buy the currency of the countries with which it has a deficit, and the surplus countries, in accumulating SDRs, earn a rate of interest on them. This is a movement towards an international paper currency, since the SDRs, unlike IMF loans, do not have to be repaid: they are a permanent addition to international reserves. Allocations were made in 1970, 1971, and 1972, and again in 1979, 1980 and 1981. The scheme was launched on a scale which is minute in relation to the size of the problem: the value of SDRs amounted to 17·9 billion, or 2·4 per cent of total world reserves, at the end of 1985. The IMF, in its statistics, now values all reserves in terms of SDRs.

The Gold Crisis.

The United States ran a large and persistent payments deficit in the 1950s and 1960s. This was initially financed through the willingness of foreigners to run up dollar balances. However, distrust of the dollar grew, and between 1960 and 1967 U.S. gold reserves were run down, from $19·5 billion to $12·1 billion. Speculation against the dollar grew, and since many speculators expected the devaluation of the dollar in terms of gold to be followed by a corresponding devaluation of other currencies, there was a growing demand for gold.

The central bankers gathered for a crisis meeting in 1968, and decided to introduce two markets for gold, with private transactions taking place in the free market at a price determined by supply and demand, and transactions among central banks taking place in the official market at the official gold price. The United States was now prepared to convert dollars into gold only for central banks, *i.e.*, to finance a deficit only on its current plus long-term capital account.

The Dollar Crisis.

In 1970 the deficit in the United States balance of payments rose to a record level. This was financed by creditor countries increasing their dollar balances. They had little choice: a large-scale conversion of dollar balances would force the United States to renounce its obligation to supply gold to central banks at $35 per ounce. It became increasingly clear that if the United States failed to reduce its deficit, the creditor countries would either have to go on financing American deficits by accumulating dollars or allow their currencies to appreciate in terms of the dollar.

In May 1971, in response to speculative capital movements mainly to West Germany, the deutschmark was allowed to float upwards, *i.e.*, the authorities allowed its price to rise above the official ceiling. But massive speculation against the dollar continued and in August the United States Government suspended the convertibility of dollars into gold. Currencies of the major trading countries were then allowed to float upwards against the dollar by varying amounts.

Introduction of Flexible Exchange Rates.

The Smithsonian Agreement of December 1971 set the seal on the biggest realignment of exchange rates for nearly a quarter of a century. After negotiations among the Group of Ten it was agreed that the United States would devalue the dollar against gold if other countries would revalue upwards or at least not devalue. The year 1972 saw a rise in the free market price of gold to almost $70 per fine ounce—well above the new official rate of $38. This development reflected the doubts of speculators that the new exchange rates would be permanent.

The U.S. balance of payments on current account actually deteriorated in 1972. Speculation against the dollar broke out early in 1973: the West German central bank was believed to have taken in no less than $6 billion in ten days despite its capital controls. The chief foreign exchange markets were closed, and in February the dollar was devalued by 10 per cent and the Japanese yen—the strongest currency—was allowed to float upwards. In March the EEC countries agreed that their currencies would float jointly against the dollar, but with the currencies of Britain, Ireland and Italy—then in balance of payments difficulties—temporarily floating independently.

The international monetary system had entered a new era of flexible exchange rates. The Bretton Woods system, which had operated throughout the post-war period, had come to an end. No longer would countries be required to maintain fixed exchange rates subject only to periodic realignment in response to fundamental disequilibrium in their balance of payments. Although governments might wish to intervene to stop their currencies changing too rapidly and too far, most chose to unpeg their currencies.

The system had broken down because it could no longer perform its function. The imbalance between the United States and the other major countries was the immediate cause of the breakdown. Perhaps the more basic reasons, however, were the growing shortage of international reserves, the growing volume of internationally mobile short-term funds, and the more rapid and divergent national rates of inflation.

The First Oil Crisis.

In 1973 the oil-producing countries exported oil worth $27 billion and their surplus on current account was $13 billion. Their surplus for 1974 was estimated at $59 billion. This surplus involved a corresponding deficit for the oil-importing countries as a group. Such a transformation in the international balance of payments was unprecedented in its scale and speed. It involved a massive transfer of purchasing power from consumers to producers of oil. Since only a small part of the additional oil revenue was spent, this had a severe deflationary effect on the world economy. This effect was not remedied, and it was even compounded by the restrictive monetary and fiscal policies introduced by many of the major countries to stem their oil-induced inflation and balance of payments deficits.

The oil-producing countries had to invest their surplus funds abroad, so that there was a corresponding surplus on the capital account of the oil importing group of countries. However, it is unlikely that the current account deficit of each individual country will be offset by a corresponding capital inflow. There is a danger that these funds will be highly mobile between recipient countries, thus introducing considerable instability in the currency flows of the western oil consumers.

The Response to Oil Deficits.

Faced with these problems, the major industrial countries agreed in 1974 that capital transfers among themselves should be used to overcome individual imbalances. Despite this, many governments took restrictive measures to combat both domestic inflation and their balance of payments deficits. In 1974 and 1975 the industrial countries experienced the worst economic recession of the post-war period. For instance, the level of industrial production in the OECD group of countries was 10 per cent lower at the end of 1975 than it had been at the end of 1973.

The economic recession meant that the price of primary products fell and the price of oil could not be raised much further. As a result, the terms of trade of the developed countries improved. The recession also brought a sharp fall in their imports while the OPEC countries increased their imports very rapidly. The net effect was that the OECD countries returned to near balance on current account in 1975. The leaders of the six major non-communist countries held a summit meeting in France and agreed to various forms of economic co-ordination and co-operation, *e.g.*, rejecting protectionist, retaliatory beggar-my-neighbour trade policies.

WORLD CURRENT ACCOUNT (\$ BILLION)*

	OECD	Oil exporting countries	Non-oil developing countries
1974	− 27	59	− 24
1975	0	27	− 38
1976	− 19	37	− 26
1977	− 2	29	− 30
1978	33	6	− 43
1979	− 5	62	− 63
1980	− 38	110	− 89
1981	5	54	− 109
1982	3	− 13	− 86
1983	3	− 17	− 53
1984	35	− 3	− 39
1985	− 52	− 8	− 41

* The normally negative sum of these balances reflects the omission of some countries and the under-recording of credits, probably in the oil-exporting or OECD countries.

Financing the Oil Deficits.

The OPEC group ran a surplus of \$59 billion in 1974 and of \$27 billion in 1975. The U.S. and U.K. attracted some of the OPEC funds, but many countries, including the less developed countries, could not attract funds. Yet we see that the less developed countries sustained large deficits in the wake of the oil price increase. Their needs were met in part through the producers' financing of the IMF's *oil facility*: a loan fund intended to help countries cope with their oil deficits. In 1975 the OECD group formally established a *recycling* fund which would be used to help member countries in balance of payments difficulties; since most of the oil surpluses are invested within the OECD group inter-governmental transfers of funds are possible. In January 1976 the IMF agreed to give all its member countries a temporary increase in borrowing rights of 45 per cent. These various methods of financing oil deficits provided a temporary accommodation but they did not obviate the need for a long-run correction of the new imbalance in world trade and payments.

In 1976 the world economy began to recover from the recession. Unemployment remained high, but was lowest in those countries (*e.g.*, West Germany) which were able to "export" their unemployment by repatriating migrant workers. The recovery was tardy: the growth rate of the OECD countries averaged 3·6 per cent per annum over the three years to 1979.

The Second Oil Crisis.

Events in 1979 reopened the imbalance between the OECD and OPEC. The price of oil doubled over the course of the year, rising from \$13 to \$25 a barrel. This was due to the halving of Iranian oil production after the revolution in Iran, and to a scramble for oil stocks by the consuming countries. In 1980, assisted by the outbreak of war between Iran and Iraq, the OPEC oil price averaged \$32 a barrel.

These factors combined to cause an actual fall in industrial production in OECD countries during 1980; their GDP rose on average by only one per

cent. The higher oil price led again to higher inflation (13 per cent in 1980) and an increased balance of payments deficit (\$38 billion) in the industrialised countries. Unusually, Japan and West Germany were running the biggest deficits, Britain being cushioned by her domestic oil supplies.

The high inflation rates ensured that nominal interest rates would be high in the major countries, but one of the consequences of the restrictive monetary policies generally being pursued was to raise interest rates in real terms as well. For instance, the Eurodollar rate in London—over 17 per cent in late 1980 and early 1981—was well above inflation rates at that time. Both the restrictive policies and the high interest rates which they generated had a depressing effect on the major economies: OECD output again rose by only one per cent during 1981.

World Oil Prices.

The table shows how average world prices of oil have moved since 1973, both in nominal terms and in real terms (nominal prices being deflated by the price of world exports of manufactures). The two great increases occurred in 1973–4 and 1979–80; both involved a more than doubling of the purchasing power of oil. Despite the apparent glut of 1985, the oil price was in real terms well over four times the level of 1973.

WORLD PRICE AND PRODUCTION OF OIL, 1973–1985

	Price (OPEC average)		Production (billion barrels)	
	Nominal (\$ per barrel)	Real (1973 = 100)	OPEC	World
1973	3·5	100	11·3	21·2
1974	9·6	228	11·2	21·2
1975	10·7	225	9·9	20·1
1976	11·9	249	11·3	21·9
1977	12·8	249	11·4	22·6
1978	13·1	222	10·9	23·1
1979	19·0	283	11·3	24·0
1980	31·9	428	9·8	23·1
1981	35·9	512	8·2	21·6
1982	34·4	502	6·9	20·6
1983	29·9	456	6·3	20·6
1984	28·6	451	6·3	21·1
1985	28·0	442	5·8	20·8

The Collapse of OPEC.

The year 1982 was characterised by oil price cutting below the OPEC reference price of \$34 a barrel. In part this reflected the weakness of world demand, and in part the waning position of OPEC in the market. In March 1983 the OPEC countries tried to stabilise the market by agreeing both to curb production and to reduce the OPEC price. The new reference price was set at \$29 a barrel. This was held for more than two years: the average OPEC price stayed at about \$28 a barrel until the end of 1985.

The table shows the world production of crude oil (including communist production of 5·3 billion barrels) in 1985 was at the same level (21 billion barrels) as it had been in 1974. However, OPEC production was down to below 6 billion barrels. In particular, Saudi Arabia, which alone had produced over 3 billion barrels in 1974, was producing only half that amount a decade later. In 1974 OPEC had produced more than half of world production; now it produced only a third.

Meeting in January 1985 the OPEC members agreed to cut production down to their new, lower quotas. However, world production actually rose during 1985, whereas world demand failed to increase. Saudi Arabia was unwilling to continue withholding production so that other members—such as expansionist Libya, war-torn Iran and Iraq and heavily indebted Nigeria—could exceed their quotas: Saudi production expanded rapidly from September onwards. At its December meeting, OPEC decided on a new strategy: it would threaten a price war against outside producers in order to persuade them to curb production. It was hoped that Britain, as a high-cost producer, would be one of the countries amenable to such pressure, but the British Government responded that it had neither the power nor the purpose to limit North Sea production. A fall in the oil price would have benefits as well as costs for Britain (*see* **G**49).

The oil-dependent OPEC economies were generally more vulnerable to a fall in the oil price than the producers outside the cartel. OPEC's bluff was therefore called. With world production continuing at 52 million barrels a day (mbd), equivalent to 19·0 billion barrels a year, and world demand at 46 mbd (16.8 billion barrels a year), market forces took over. The spot price of oil plummetted, from just under $30 a barrel at the beginning of December to $10 a barrel at the beginning of April. For the time being, at any rate, the cartel had fallen apart.

World Recession, 1982.

Weaknesses in the world economy which had been apparent for almost a decade reached an alarming crescendo in 1982, as the world recession deepened. Industrial production in the OECD countries fell by 4 per cent during 1982 and real GNP by half a per cent. Unemployment reached the remarkable level of 8·5 per cent, representing over 30 million workers in the 24 OECD countries. Yet inflation was still running at an annual rate of about 8 per cent, and interest rates, although falling, were generally still in double figures. The balance of payments difficulties of heavily indebted countries raised the possibility of widespread default, with the concomitant danger of bank failures in the West.

The New Protectionism.

The rise in unemployment led to intensified protectionist measures in many countries, aimed at preserving jobs by keeping out imports, whether from other industrial countries or from developing countries. An example of this was the curbs placed by various countries on imports from Japan of cars and other "threatening" products such as television sets and videos. By 1982 the restrictions affected virtually all Japanese exports of cars to industrial countries. Another example was the import restrictions imposed in October 1982 by the United States—complaining of European subsidies of steel production—on steel from the EEC. In December 1981 the Multifibre Agreement—which authorises countries to restrict imports of textiles—was extended to 1986. These restrictions commonly take the form of bilateral export restraint agreements.

Western Europe and America have found increasing difficulty in competing in two areas: labour-intensive manufactures, such as textiles and clothing, and certain engineering products, such as cars and consumer electronics. The competiton has come from low-wage countries, in the former case, and from Japan, in the latter. In 1985 Japan had a current account surplus of over $50 billion, and the United States ran a huge trade deficit (over $40 billion) with Japan. In 1985, despite the economic recovery in industrial countries, there were considerable pressures for more protection, particularly against Japan, and governments brought concurrent pressure on Japan to open its markets to Western goods.

World Imbalance in Trade and Payments.

The current account deficit of the OECD countries as a group fell from the huge level of 1980 to approximate balance. Between 1979 and 1982, the non-oil developing countries suffered a 21 per cent worsening of their terms of trade, reflecting the rise in the oil price and the drop in world demand for other primary products. This group of countries thus continued to maintain a large current account deficit. They were in general not prepared to take the harsh measures needed to control their deficits, so long as they could obtain finance from somewhere. Although this response of the poor countries was understandable, it contributed to the growing problem of international indebtedness. The total external debt of the non-oil developing countries rose from $400 billion at the end of 1979 to some $650 billion at the end of 1982 and to $770 billion at the end of 1985.

Crisis in the Banking System.

The difficulties experienced by the international banks were partly beyond their control, being due, for instance, to the rise in interest rates produced by restrictive monetary policies, and partly to their own lack of caution. Perhaps they were too much swayed by the competitive pressures to make loans from the additional deposits being made from the OPEC surplus, and complacently confident that "the authorities" would rescue banks which got into difficulties.

The Mexican debt crisis of late 1982 brought out the precariousness of the international banking system. After that, one substantial debtor country after another sought debt rescheduling or a standstill on repayments of principal. Stop-gap credits had to be cobbled together, and in addition the IMF emergency lending facility was enlarged, and agreement was reached to expand the IMF quota resources by about half.

The debt crisis was eased as the world economy recovered during 1984. At the London summit meeting of the seven major industrial countries in June, it was agreed to extend the rescheduling of debts in cases where debtor countries were themselves making successful adjustment efforts. Substantive agreements with Argentina and the Philippines took shape, and a multi-year rescheduling of Mexico's debt was agreed in principle. Both Mexico and Brazil, the two largest troubled debtors, achieved great improvements in their balance of payments. The atmosphere of foreboding was less in evidence, and international bank lending began to pick up; but risks undoubtedly remained.

World Recovery, 1983–84.

The world economy began to recover in 1983. In the course of the year GNP in the industrial countries expanded by 2·6 per cent on average, the United States setting the pace with an even higher growth rate. The inflation rate continued to fall, however, averaging 5 per cent over the year, so making it less likely that world recovery would be pinched in the bud by fears of renewed inflation.

The recovery initiated in 1983 continued at a greater pace in 1984. The increase in GDP in the industrial countries averaged no less than 4·9 per cent, the United States leading with a remarkable 7·3 per cent. Reflecting the considerable slack in the international economy, inflation did not accelerate in response to the recovery but actually fell slightly, to under 5 per cent.

The Rise of the Dollar.

The United States recovery occurred despite a rising dollar. The effective exchange rate of the dollar against other currencies rose by 20 per cent in the 15 months up to March 1985. The reason for this appreciation is rather a puzzle. It was certainly not due to the strength of the current account. On the contrary, with rapid economic recovery the record American current account deficit of $35 billion in 1983 gave way to a new record deficit of no less than $80 billion in 1984! Rather, the relentless rise of the dollar has to be explained mainly in terms of developments in financial markets. Interest rates in the United States were high, and well above those in other countries. This was due to the strength of economic expansion and the consequent demand for funds, and to the vast Federal Government budget deficit which, on account of the restrictive monetary policy, was financed by debt issue. These high rates of interest, together with the anticipated profitability of the booming economy and the widespread sentiment that the dollar would continue to rise, attracted funds from abroad. By 1985 the loss of funds to the United States was putting authorities in other countries under pressure to raise interest rates in a way not required by domestic considerations.

Prospects for the World Economy.

The rise of the dollar and high rates of interest combined to slow down sharply the growth of the United States economy in 1985. This contributed to a general slowdown in OECD growth, which averaged under 3 per cent over the year. However, the long-expected depreciation of the dollar eventually began in March: it had fallen 19 per cent against other currencies by the end of the year. This fall would assist the United States economy, although with a time lag.

There was, however, a more important reason why the prospects in 1986 were for faster world economic growth. The most promising international development was the remarkable fall in the price of oil early in 1986 (*see* **G52**). This would have a variety of beneficial effects. Just as the two oil crises had produced bouts of stagflation so the lower oil price, if it were sustained, should achieve the reverse. First, the additional purchasing power of oil-consuming countries was itself a net force for expansion. Secondly, the fall in the oil price would help to bring down inflation in the world economy, and so permit governments to be more expansionist in their economic policies. With falling inflation, rates of interest should decline in sympathy and encourage investment.

The collapse of the oil market would of course hurt particular countries: the oil-dependent OPEC countries, the Soviet Union (the world's biggest producer of oil, oil accounting for two-thirds of Soviet hard currency sales abroad), and heavily indebted Mexico. This increased the danger that Mexico would default on its debt and interest payments. However, the international debt crisis may on balance have been eased because other debtors, such as Brazil, would be assisted to repay their debts by lower oil import bills and interest payments, and by world economic recovery.

SDRs and Gold.

Originally the SDR (*see* **G51**) had been set equal to the par value of the U.S. dollar, but when the dollar was devalued the SDR maintained its value in terms of gold (SDR1 = 0·889 grammes of fine gold). With the general floating of exchange rates after March 1973, the volatility of the SDR in terms of currencies conflicted with the aim of developing it as the principal reserve asset of a reformed international monetary system, and its adoption as the unit of account for all IMF transactions. The IMF therefore introduced, as from July 1974, a new system of valuation based on the value of a group of 17 major currencies in specified proportions. The number of currencies was reduced to 5 in 1981. These are the dollar, the mark, the franc, the yen, and the pound.

The rapid inflation and great uncertainty in the world economy, contributed to the speculative demand for gold; this raised its price many times over in the free market. In December 1974 the London gold price was $187 per fine ounce. However, the IMF in 1975 decided that the official price of gold should be abolished, and that it would auction 25 million oz (equivalent to a year's production) over a period of 4 years. The effect was to depress the free market price of gold, which fell to under $130 in April 1976. It was agreed that central banks should be allowed to buy and sell gold among themselves and on the open market at free market prices, as opposed to the old official price, provided that there is no net accrual of gold by the countries concerned.

The price of gold rose during 1978, assisted by speculation against the dollar and fears of another oil price increase. Political events in the Middle East caused further speculation during 1979, and the instability after the Soviet invasion of Afghanistan catapulted the gold price to $700 in September 1980. Gold flourishes in times of uncertainty and expected inflation. The price of gold subsequently declined as inflation rates began to diminish and as real rates of interest rose.

LONDON GOLD PRICE
(U.S. $ per fine ounce, end-year)

1974	187	1981	398
1976	135	1982	444
1978	226	1983	382
1979	524	1984	308
1980	590	1985	330

Exchange Rate Arrangements.

Towards the end of 1985 the following exchange rate arrangements were in operation. Sixteen currencies, including the dollar, the pound and the yen, were independently floating. Another 25 currencies had "managed floats", *i.e.*, floating subject to a policy of periodic government intervention. Eight members of the EEC other than Britain maintained a co-operation arrangement to float together under the European Monetary System. Most developing countries pegged their currencies to those of major trading partners, 31 to the dollar, 14 to the French franc, 12 to the SDR, and 32 to some currency composite of their own choice.

Experience of Exchange-rate Flexibility.

One of the advantages claimed for greater flexibility in exchange rates is that it diminishes the need for international liquidity. Variations in exchange rates should reduce the size of imbalances and therefore the resources required to tide over deficits.

However, it is not clear from recent experience that greater exchange-rate flexibility can produce equilibrium in international payments. It seems that the balance of payments takes a long time—perhaps two or three years—to adjust to a depreciation of the exchange rate. In the meantime there might be wage increases to compensate for the increase in the cost of living brought about by the depreciation, which in turn tend to neutralise the depreciation. For instance, the table indicates that, between 1975 and April 1986 the pound had depreciated against a basket of other

EXCHANGE RATES, 1975* AND 1986†

	Exchange rate against sterling (£1 =)	Index of effective exchange rate, 1986 (1975 = 100)
Sterling	1·00	76·4
U.S. dollars	1·06	121·5
French franc	11·08	68·5
Italian lira	2,264·7	44·8
Deutschmark	3·63	132·0
Japanese yen	279·2	195·7

* 1975 average. † 4 April 1986.

currencies by 24 per cent and the lira by 55 per cent, the dollar had appreciated by 22 per cent and the yen by 96 per cent. Yet because of their different rates of inflation, the signs were that the competitiveness of British goods was no stronger than it had been in 1975. A worrying feature of the flexible exchange rate system is that it not only permits but also generates a far wider spread of inflation rates among the major countries.

Reform of the IMF.

A major amendment of the IMF's Articles of Agreement was proposed in 1976, and accepted in 1978, formalising the end of the Bretton Woods system. The new arrangements formally permit member countries freedom to choose their exchange-rate arrangements, including floating, so departing from the par value system. In line with the objective of reducing the role of gold in the international monetary system, the amendment abolished an official price for gold and its use as a denominator in exchange arrangements, it eliminated obligations to transfer or receive gold under the Articles, and allowed for the disposal of part of the Fund's holdings of gold. The objective is to make the SDR the principal reserve asset of the international monetary system. In pursuit of this, the Fund embarked on a programme of further allocation of SDRs.

The Integration of Financial Markets.

There is a growing worldwide integration of financial markets. Financial intermediation has become a footloose industry with only limited ties to particular national markets or stock exchanges. Borrowers and lenders in different countries are brought together often by intermediaries based in a third country. The major currencies are traded in most financial centres and dealing continues around the clock. There are now over 250 companies whose equity is traded around the world.

Much of this change is due to technological innovations in communications. The declining cost of communication has meant that arbitrage is now possible at only very small price differentials, and companies throughout the world are alive to the advantages of scanning money and currency markets on a worldwide basis to meet their requirements at least cost. The consequent competitive pressures have meant that those markets have become more integrated.

The Need for Further Reform.

The movements in the 1970s towards greater control of "hot money" flows, greater flexibility of exchange rates, and increased international liquidity helped to correct international imbalances. But there were various reasons for believing that they would not provide a permanent solution. Reasons have been given above for questioning whether exchange-rate flexibility can cope with the international imbalances of the 1980s. Moreover, the amount of short-term funds and the scope for speculation with them is greater than ever. The surpluses of the OPEC countries —with their *increase* in funds totalling $350 billion in the seven years 1974–80–present a considerable problem. Towards the end of 1984 the OPEC countries had a stock of external assets of nearly $400 billion, of which $55 billion was held in the United Kingdom, mainly in Eurocurrency bank deposits. International companies, with structures that span the remaining exchange control barriers, have accumulated vast sums which they move about in search of security and profit.

The burgeoning and integration of financial markets epitomised by the growth of the Eurocurrency market (*see* **G10**), make control of short term capital flows very difficult and give rise to the possibility of exaggerated and destabilising movements in international exchange rates. For instance, the large differences in interest rates between financial centres in the early 1980s, arising because of different inflation rates and monetary policies, stimulated huge and destabilising capital flows across the exchanges. The ensuing exchange rate fluctuations were detrimental to both private and public decision-taking. Exchange rates have become more responsive to expectations about currency revaluation and to interest rate arbitrage than to underlying current account imbalances. The need for greater exchange rate stability has become more apparent.

The European Economic Community.

The *European Economic Community* (EEC), otherwise known as the Common Market, was set up by the Treaty of Rome, ratified in 1958. It consisted of six full members—Belgium, France, Holland, Italy, Luxembourg, and Western Germany. Britain had participated in the negotiations which led up to its formation, and had argued in favour of a looser "free trade area" without a common external tariff, and excluding trade in agricultural products. No compromise acceptable to the Six was found, and Britain joined with six other European countries—Austria, Denmark, Norway, Portugal, Sweden, and Switzerland—in forming the *European Free Trade Area* (EFTA).

Economic Arrangements of the EEC.

The EEC forms a common market with no tariffs or trade controls within it and a Common External Tariff (CET). There is a Common Agricultural Policy (CAP), which is maintained by a system of variable import levies setting *threshold prices* on imports of agricultural products from outside the Community, and by means of *intervention prices* at which agricultural products of the Community are purchased. The intervention price is slightly higher than the threshold price of a product. The EEC has a large Budget required mainly for supporting the CAP, *i.e.*, for subsidising Common Market farmers. There is free movement of both capital and labour within the Community, and a certain degree of fiscal harmonisation.

Accession to the Community 1973.

The United Kingdom acceded as a full member of the EEC on 1 January 1973. Two of Britain's EFTA partners—Ireland and Denmark—joined on the same date, so forming an expanded Community of nine countries. The economic ties with the Sterling Area were weakened and those with the Community strenthened. In 1972 trade with the original six members of the EEC accounted for about 23 per cent of total British trade, trade with the EFTA partners about 13 per cent, and with the Commonwealth 19 per cent. After accession, trade with the EEC expanded sharply and the proportion of trade with the former EFTA countries and the Commonwealth fell. Excluding trade with the oil-exporting countries, British trade with the original EEC countries rose from 25 per cent of the total in 1972 to 30 per cent in 1974. In 1984 no less than 45 per cent of British trade was with the EEC.

The Referendum.

The Labour Party in opposition had criticised the terms of British entry to the EEC negotiated by the Conservative Government. When it came to power in 1974 the Labour Government was determined to renegotiate terms. The Government wanted major changes in the CAP and in the method of financing the Community Budget, and other safeguards of British and Commonwealth interests. Some concessions were negotiated. It was left to the British electorate to vote in a referendum in June 1975 on the renegotiated terms. There was an overwhelming vote in favour of the United Kingdom remaining a member of the EEC: 67 per cent voted "yes" and 33 per cent "no."

In the 1980s, with the Labour Party in opposition coming out against Britain's continued membership of the EEC, the question of membership was liable to recur as a live issue in British politics.

The EEC Budget.

It is in the British interest that the CAP—with its heavy support of Common Market farmers—be reformed. Community funds are available to protect farmers by buying excess food and building up stocks of food if the free market price falls below the intervention price. As a result "food mountains" have developed.

Nevertheless, the British contribution to the EEC Budget was initially much smaller than expected. The *net* contribution (payments *less* benefits) was £104 million in 1973, £31 million in 1974, and there was a net gain of £54 million in 1975. Britain gained from "monetary compensation amounts," *i.e.*, refunds associated with the difference between the values of the pound in the foreign exchange markets and the *green pound*. The green pound is the agreed exchange rate between the pound and the other Community currencies which is used in calculating contributions to the Budget.

Britain's net contribution to the EEC budget was £180 million in 1976, £390 m. in 1977, £790 m. in 1978, £900 m. in 1979, and would have been no less than £1·2 b. in 1980. Britain would have been responsible for about 60 per cent of the total net contributions to the Community budget in 1980! Yet, as the table shows, Britain's GNP per head was the third lowest of the Nine. The high level of Britain's net contribution reflects her heavy dependence on imported food: she has only a small agricultural sector whereas most of the Community budget is used for farm support.

GNP PER HEAD OF EEC MEMBER
COUNTRIES 1983 (AVERAGE = 100)*

Denmark	118
German Federal Republic	114
Belgium	105
Luxembourg	116
Netherlands	102
France	111
United Kingdom	95
Italy	87
Ireland	63

*Comparisons are based on purchasing power parities.

Negotiating Britain's Budget Contribution.

In 1980 the British Government determined to negotiate a reduction in its contribution. After much bitter wrangling, the EEC governments agreed on a formula to limit the U.K.'s net contributi on to £370 million in 1980 and £440 million in 1981. Without the refund, in 1981 Britain—accounting for 18 per cent of the GNP of the Community—would have received only 10 per cent of the budget and paid 21 per cent into the budget. However, this was only a temporary solution, and the British Government entered further negotiations to secure repayments. It went so far as to veto CAP farm price rises as a lever to obtain a higher budget rebate, but this was overruled by an unprecedented majority decision. The budget refunds negotiated for 1982 and 1983 were—as in 1980 and 1981—roughly two-thirds of Britain's unadjusted net contribution. Total refunds negotiated for the four-year period amounted to more than £2·5 b.

These negotiations were *ad hoc*: the British Government also pressed for new financial arrangements for the Community, based on more equitable principles. Since two-thirds of the budget goes to finance the CAP, a permanent solution satisfactory to Britain would involve changes in the CAP itself. British interests would be served by a relative decline in CAP expenditure, and by country contributions being calculated as a percentage of GDP, that percentage rising as a country's GDP per head rose in relation to mean GDP per head of the Community.

Negotiations on refunds to the United Kingdom were successfully concluded at Fontainebleau in June 1984. The agreement secured a refund of £590 million in 1984 and—more important—made automatic arrangements for the future. The United Kingdom would receive a refund each year equal to two-thirds of the difference between its share of VAT payments to the Community (each country pays VAT to the Community at the rate of 1·4 per cent of value added) and its share in expenditure from the Community budget. The British Government claimed that the deal was a great success.

Reforming the CAP.

In 1984, perhaps for the first time in the history of the CAP, EEC farm ministers agreed to cut subsidies and freeze prices. The system of openended guarantees was to be largely discontinued in an effort to halt the growth of agricultural surpluses. For instance, the production of milk was subjected to restricted quotas, with adverse effects for British dairy farmers. Another aspect of the agricultural agreement was the decision to phase out the monetary compensation amounts, *i.e.*, the border taxes which iron out the effects of national currency fluctuations.

Prospects for Economic Union.

In 1970 the Commission of the European Economic Community published the Werner Plan, a report on the establishment of economic and monetary union of the EEC. The plan aimed at transferring the principal economic decisions from the national to the Community level, and at establishing within the Community complete freedom of movement of goods, services, persons and capital, with fixed and constant rates of exchange between national currencies or, preferably, a common currency. A centre of decision for economic policy would be established and made responsible to a European parliament.

These proposals have far-reaching economic and political implications, since they involve a considerable reduction of national sovereignty. For instance, the loss of power to correct balance of payments deficits by means of trade controls or variation in the exchange rate implies either that the deficit country's currency should be generally acceptable to its creditors (so that the country within the Community—like a region within a country—simply cannot have a balance of payments problem), or the country must resort to deflation. And even if there is a common currency, it is very likely that resources will concentrate in some regions of the Community to the neglect of the other regions, possibly those far from the main centres of

production and consumption. Complete mobility of resources is likely to produce a regional problem within the Community just as it can produce a regional problem within a country. But the Community may not, to the same extent as a country, possess the political power and determination required to remedy the problem. It is not surprising that the Werner Plan has been pursued in only limited respects and that its eventual implementation is uncertain; economic union cannot precede political union.

Regional differences within the Community increased with the joining of Greece in 1981, and of Spain and Portugal in 1986. The Community now united 320 million Europeans, but there were large differences in their incomes.

Towards Monetary Union.

It was on the issue of monetary union that the first major economic problem for Britain arose after entry. In conformity with the Werner Plan, the Community agreed in March 1973 to fix the exchange rates between member currencies and to float them together against the dollar. This important arrangement was known as the *snake in the tunnel*. Britain and Italy—then in balance of payments difficulties—insisted that they be permitted temporarily to float independently.

There is a danger that the right to vary exchange rates be withdrawn from member countries without there being uniformity in other policies. If there is to be a monetary union, there should also be uniformity in other economic policies, even industrial relations and incomes policies! For if inflation is more rapid in Britain than in her partner countries, and if Britain is prevented from adjusting the exchange rates or imposing import restrictions against her partners to correct the ensuing balance of payments deficit, the Government might see no alternative but to deflate the economy: stagnation could ensue.

The European Monetary System.

A modification of the snake, the *European Monetary System* was introduced in March 1979. A currency is permitted to float within a 2¼ per cent band on either side of the par rate between the currency and any other member's currency. Central bank intervention is required to keep the currency within the band. The participating currencies are defined in *European Currency Units*, issued against the deposit of 20 per cent of national gold and foreign exchange reserves and used to settle intervention debts. There is a system of central bank "swaps" and short- and medium-term credit.

For some, the EMS is the response to a growing disillusionment with the operation of floating exchange rates and a strong desire to move towards greater exchange rate stability among close trading partners. For others, the EMS represents an early step on the path to European monetary union. The restriction on national sovereignty under the EMS is not large: it probably means that exchange rate adjustments will be in discrete steps rather than by continuous and perhaps erratic floating. Nevertheless, the British Government chose not to join the EMS.

The difference in inflation rates among countries in the EMS necessitated periodic currency realignments, in October 1981, June 1982, March 1983 and April 1986. In each case the deutschemark was upvalued and the French franc devalued: the combined result of these realignments was that the franc fell by 32 per cent against the mark.

Should Britain Join the EMS?

Early in 1986 four EEC countries had not entered the EMS: Britain, Greece, Spain and Portugal. Britain had resisted the blandishments of EMS members to join them. This was partly because of the large and unpredictable flows of funds in and out of sterling on account of London's role as a financial centre. However, the main reason was that, Britain being a net oil exporter, the British balance of payments is likely to move inversely to that of other EEC countries as the world price of oil fluctuates. With the oil price falling sharply in 1986, Britain needed the power to permit a depreciation of sterling in order to maintain balance in payments.

Price Differentials within the EEC.

The EEC is supposed to be a common market. Why, then, does a £9,000 car in Britain cost £6,000 in Belgium? A 1981 study showed that if the price of a car was 100 in the United Kingdom, it sold net-of-tax in Ireland, 72 in France, 70 in West Germany and 66 in the "Benelux" countries. It has become profitable for specialist companies to arrange for British customers to go and buy their cars in other countries; but this occurs only on a small scale.

There are various possible explanations for the price differences. One is that prices are set by the degree of Japanese penetration, which is greatest in the Benelux countries. More plausible is the view that price differences result from collusive policies on the part of manufacturers, assisted by the difficulty of buying a car in one country for use in another and the "drive on the left" rule in Britain. It is possible that the British government has not discouraged the collusion—e.g. by not making transfers simpler—because of the adverse effect that would have on the ailing domestic car producer, British Leyland; but the policy implies a hidden subsidy not only to BL but also to foreign manufacturers, paid by British car buyers.

2. INTERNAL DEVELOPMENTS

Trends in Post-war Economic Policy.

Since the end of the Second World War in 1945, economic policy making in Britain can be loosely divided into several phases: the *Keynesian era* from 1945 to the mid-1960s, the era of *doubts about Keynesianism* from the mid-1960s to 1976, and since 1976 the *monetarist era*. Many economists would add a fourth phase, an era of *doubts about monetarism*, dating from the early 1980s. It should be emphasised that this division of the post-war period into these various phases is intended to provide only a very rough guide to broad trends in policy making. Further discussion of some of these trends, and of the contrast between Keynesian and monetarist policies is to be found in **Part II**.

The Keynesian Era.

For some twenty years after 1945 successive Governments were committed to "Keynesian" economic policy measures. The main aim of policy was to prevent any return to the mass unemployment of the 1920s and 1930s, and this was successfully achieved: the accompanying table indicates that up to 1965 average unemployment rates were below 2 per cent, and indeed over the whole period unemployment never rose significantly above 2·5 per cent except for very short periods of time. Other aspects of the economy also showed a marked improvement on earlier times: for example, the growth rate of real national income (and therefore of living standards) was significantly faster than it had been since the latter part of the nineteenth century. In many respects, then, the Keynesian era was one of unprecedented economic success for Britain, as indeed it was for most other industrialised countries.

POSTWAR BRITISH ECONOMIC EXPERIENCE

| | Average annual rates of: | | |
	Unemployment	Inflation	Growth of Gross National Product
1945–64	1·9	3·4	2·4
1965–69	2·1	4·3	2·5
1970–74	3·0	11·0	1·6
1975–79	5·5	14·1	1·7
1980	6·4	18·1	− 2·5
1981	9·9	11·9	− 1·4
1982	11·5	8·7	1·9
1983	12·3	4·6	3·0
1984	12·7	5·0	2·1
1985	13·1	6·1	3·4

There were nonetheless three reasons for dissatisfaction. First, the rate of improvement in living standards, although faster than before the war, was slower than the rates achieved by most competitor countries. Secondly, the economy kept running into balance of payments deficits, causing successive Governments temporarily to restrict demand in order to check the growth of imports. This became labelled 'stop go' policy, with each 'go' phase of rapid expansion and low unemployment being followed by a 'stop' phase of contraction and temporarily higher unemployment. The third source of worry was inflation. For most of the 1920s and 1930s there had been no persistent tendency for prices to rise, but after 1945 things changed: prices now began to rise continuously, and as it became clear that this was not just a temporary phenomenon, so concern began to grow about the possible adverse effects of continuing inflation.

Doubts About Keynesianism.

Worries about the balance of payments and inflation started to become widespread in the 1960s and led to the emergence of serious doubts about Keynesian policies, despite their success in preventing a return to high unemployment. The critics arued that policy-makers tended to stimulate demand too much, leading to shortages of goods which in turn produced both balance of payments and inflation problems. These doubts received powerful intellectual support from the growing number of monetarist economists led by Professor Milton Friedman (*see also* **Part II**). The monetarists argued that there were limits to the ability of governments to lower unemployment by stimulating demand, and that attempts to go beyond these limits would lead not just to inflation but to progressively *rising* inflation—in rather the same way that users of stimulant drugs often find that their bodies eventually adapt to a particular level of use so that higher levels are thereafter needed in order to maintain the same degree of stimulation.

This idea that Keynesian expansion risked ever-worsening inflation found an increasingly sympathetic audience from the late 1960s onwards, for as the table shows, it was just at that time that Britain (and most other industrialised countries) experienced a sharp rise in inflation. In an attempt to combat this the British Government allowed unemployment to rise sharply in 1970 and 1971. This represented the first time since the war that any British Government had given top priority for any significant time to an objective other than the Keynesian one of maintaining low unemployment.

The policy was reversed at the beginning of 1972 when the Government decided that unemployment levels had become unacceptably high. However, the subsequent expansion proved to be ill-judged. Demand was expanded far beyond the ability of domestic output to meet it, leading inevitably to balance of payments and inflation problems. At the same time the effects on unemployment were disappointing. This experience significantly strengthened support for the monetarist critique of Keynesian policy-making: it seemed that the latter was now producing inflation and import problems without even achieving the desired result of low unemployment. Moreover, although with the benefit of hindsight it is clear that the expansion was ill-judged—it was delayed too long, and then proceeded too rapidly—this was not clear at the time: in 1972 most economic forecasters broadly approved the strategy. This seemed to confirm another monetarist objection to Keynesian policy, namely its reliance upon short run forecasts as a basis for *fine tuning* the economy, i.e., making frequent adjustments to monetary and fiscal policies in the light of such forecasts. Monetarists argued that such forecasts were too inaccurate to provide a basis for detailed policy adjustments, and that fine tuning should therefore be abandoned. They advocated instead *fixed rule* policies, in which the main lines of monetary and fiscal policies are laid down for 4 to 5 years in advance, and are therefore not substantially altered in response to short term events.

In retrospect it is clear that many of the problems which emerged in 1972–73 and thereafter could not be blamed on the over-expansionary Keynesian policies of 1972–73 but were instead the product of international economic disturbances on a scale much bigger than anything previously experienced since 1945. There were very large rises in the prices of many raw materials and commodities, particularly in world oil prices. Since Britain was at the time a large net oil importer, this rise was bound to have a serious adverse effect on the balance of payments; similarly, the rise in import prices contributed substantially to inflationary pressure in the economy. Moreover, the large rise in oil prices and consequently in energy costs helped to explain why unemployment did not fall as much as expected in the face of expansion, and why it subsequently started to rise rapidly. Higher energy costs reduced industry's profits and this in turn meant that manufacturing firms—the main oil users—could no longer afford to employ as many people unless they could cut their labour costs, which required cuts in real wages. In practice unions and their members largely resisted such cuts, with the result that large numbers of jobs were lost in the manufacturing sector.

The combined effect of these problems was a large rise in unemployment during 1974 and 1975, and an even steeper rise in inflation, which by mid-1975 reached 25 per cent—by far the highest rate since 1945. At this point the government introduced an incomes policy which succeeded in halting and reversing the rise in inflation over the following three years. However, the government faced a major dilemma in trying to reduce the level of unemployment. In the past it would have responded by expanding aggregate demand, but fears of triggering off a fresh inflation crisis made it reluctant to consider such a course.

The Monetarist Era.

In the event the government's problem was resolved, though not in a way which it would itself have chosen. In the autumn of 1976 a loss of international confidence in the government's economic policy led to speculation against the pound and to a sharp fall in its international value. The government had to apply to the International Monetary Fund for a loan. The latter was granted, but only on condition that the government introduced *monetary targets*, i.e. specified annual growth rates of the money supply. The emergence of monetarism in Britain really dates from this time.

To meet these targets the Government was faced with an unpleasant choice. Since the p.s.b.r. could no longer be financed by uncontrolled monetary expansion, either it would have to be reduced—by tax increases and/or public spending cuts—or, if this was unacceptable, it would have to be financed by much heavier borrowing, requiring higher interest rates.

The Government judged that the electorate would not tolerate further tax increases—the tax burden had been raised during 1974–75—and it was reluctant to see interest rates, already at a record level, rise any further. It therefore opted for public spending cuts. This was anathema to many of its supporters, and it therefore ran into considerable political difficulties. The 1976–77 phase of policy was the most difficult. During this time unemployment was rising steadily, leading to pressure for increases rather than cuts in public expenditure. Nevertheless the Government stuck to its policy and by 1978 had achieved some successes, with falling inflation and a balance of payments surplus. However, these were outweighed by the collapse of its incomes policy in the second half of 1978. A series of disruptive strikes and inflationary wage increases followed which destroyed the Government's political credibility and paved the way for a Conservative victory in the May 1979 General Election. The new Government was headed by Margaret Thatcher, with Sir Geoffrey Howe as Chancellor.

Monetarism in Action, 1979–1983.

In some respects the new Government's economic policy was little more than a continuation of the Labour Government's policy since 1976. The centrepiece of economic policy was the *Medium Term Financial Strategy*, which involved laying down targets for monetary growth and the p.s.b.r. for 3 to 4 years ahead, and which thus embraced the 'fixed rule' monetarist idea discussed earlier. This policy was not substantially different in principle from that followed between 1976 and 1979.

Economic policy nonetheless differed in some important respects from that of the previous Labour Government, and indeed of all previous Governments since 1945. To begin with, it was clear that Mrs. Thatcher and Sir Geoffrey Howe were enthusiastic supporters of monetarism, whereas the feeling had existed that the previous Labour Government had only reluctantly embraced monetary targets and that it would change course if the opportunity arose. This was evidenced by attitudes towards unemployment. Within months of Mrs. Thatcher's accession to power unemployment began to rise at an unprecedented rate, far exceeding the rate of rise under Labour, though this had itself been much higher than anything previously seen since 1945. However, whereas the Labour Government had clearly been dismayed by the rise, the Conservative Government seemed to take a different view, arguing that the rise was necessary if inflation was to be reduced, that there was little that the Government could or should do to prevent it, and that the main responsibility for the rise lay with the trade unions who, it was argued, could prevent it by accepting smaller pay increases.

THE PUBLIC SECTOR BORROWING REQUIREMENT

	£billion	as a percentage of gross domestic product
1969–70	− 0·5	− 1·1
1970–71	0·8	1·4
1971–72	1·0	1·8
1972–73	2·5	3·7
1973–74	4·5	6·0
1974–75	8·0	9·1
1975–76	1·6	9·5
1976–77	8·5	6·5
1977–78	5·5	3·6
1978–79	9·2	5·3
1979–80	9·9	4·8
1980–81	13·2	5·6
1981–82	8·8	3·4
1982–83	9·2	3·2

A negative sign indicates a public sector surplus

As much as anything, therefore, the change brought about by Mrs. Thatcher's Government was a change of attitudes towards economic policy, with the Keynesian priority of low unemployment finally giving way to the monetarist priority of low inflation. The consequences are clear from the table. The two years 1980 and 1981 saw the sharpest recession for 50 years, with substantial falls in output and huge rises in unemployment. The gains, in terms of lower inflation, appeared from 1982 onwards, by which time it was clear that the "inflation psychology" of the 1970s—in which people had come to regard high and rising inflation rates as the normal state of affairs—had been broken: by 1982 few people anticipated a return to high inflation.

The Government introduced other important changes in economic policy. One was its refusal to countenance the sort of formal incomes policy to which every Government since the early 1960s had been forced to turn in attempts to control inflation. The Conservatives argued that the evidence showed such policies to be at best short term expedients, failing to secure lasting reductions in inflation. However, critics of the Government argued that it was, in reality, operating a sort of incomes policy—directly holding down the pay of its own public sector employees, and relying on high unemployment to do the same thing in the private sector—and that a return to a more systematic and formal incomes policy would allow the same degree of control over pay increases to be achieved at lower levels of unemployment.

The other main economic policy change was the Government's long term commitment to securing reductions in public spending, in taxes, and in the p.s.b.r. These objectives—like the opposition to formal incomes policy—reflected its conviction that Government intervention was in general harmful to the economy, and that long term economic gains would follow if the extent of such intervention could be reduced. The table shows that the aim of a reduced p.s.b.r. was indeed achieved by 1982–83. However, this aim was controversial. In part, criticism reflected the view that the p.s.b.r. is not an appropriate policy target since it is unpredictable in the short run: it is, in effect, simply the difference between two very large magnitudes, namely total public spending and total public sector receipts, and small proportionate variations in either can therefore produce large proportionate variations in the p.s.b.r. More fundamentally, Keynesians objected to cuts in the p.s.b.r. on the grounds that a recession should be combated by raising, not lowering, public sector borrowing. The crucial point came in 1981, when with unemployment rising very fast and output falling the Chancellor rejected Keynesian arguments for additional borrowing and moved in the opposite direction, producing a very tough monetarist Budget which increases taxes in order to maintain the Government's borrowing targets.

Yet these policies highlighted an inconsistency in the Government's approach. Its p.s.b.r. targets were under pressure by 1981 largely because of the very rise in unemployment to which its own policies were contributing. First, rising unemployment causes increased public spending (on unemployment benefits, social security payments and the like); and second, it lowers tax revenues because there are fewer people earning incomes and therefore the tax base falls. This combination of increased public outlays and lower tax revenues threatened the Government's borrowing targets. Its response was partly to seek offsetting cuts in other items of public spending—leading to squeezes on health, education, and housing expenditure—and partly to abandon its earlier hopes of securing overall reductions in the tax burden. Indeed, by 1983 it was calculated that Government policies had in fact *increased* the overall tax burden for everyone except the small minority of people earning more than around four times the national average. (The gains to high income earners reflected the sharp reductions in the higher rates of income tax on high incomes which Sir Geoffrey Howe had introduced in his first Budget in 1979.) Neither had the overall level of public spending fallen as a share of national income: rising expenditure on unemployment benefits had offset cuts in other areas of spending.

This emphasised another objection to using the p.s.b.r. as a policy target. With strict controls on most items of public spending, and a higher tax burden on most people, the Government's fiscal stance was clearly a very tight one; yet the table shows that even by 1982–83 the p.s.b.r. as a proportion of national income had not been reduced to its level at the start of the 1970s, when fiscal policy was less tight. Some economists calculated that if unemployment were still at its 1979 levels the p.s.b.r. would have disappeared altogether by 1982–83, turning instead into a *surplus* of the sort last seen in 1969–70. In other words, the actual p.s.b.r. substantially understated the severity of the Government's fiscal stance, and was therefore arguably unsuitable as a policy objective.

Another substantial difficulty which the Government faced was the effect of North Sea oil. By the early 1980s Britain was self-sufficient in oil, and the resulting large drop in our import bill was one factor behind the very large rise in the exchange rate in 1979–81. Another was the Government's own restrictive monetary and fiscal policies. This rise in the exchange rate substantially weakened the international competitiveness of the economy's trading sector, predominantly manufacturing industry. The latter therefore faced increased import penetration, and lost export markets, and the overall effect contributed a good deal to rising unemployment. A further and continuing factor was the effect, already mentioned, of higher energy prices upon the demand for labour in the energy-using sector, predominantly manufacturing industry. There was a further large rise in real oil prices in 1978–79—to add to the one in 1973—and this further eroded profits and employment in manufacturing.

In May 1983 the Prime Minister called a General Election for 9 June. The economic policies pursued since 1979 were a principal issue in the campaign. The opposition parties—Labour and the SDP–Liberal Alliance—argued for more expansionary monetary and fiscal policies, and increased public spending, in order to stimulate output and reduce unemployment. The Government rejected these proposals and made clear that it intended to continue with unchanged policies if re-elected. In the event the Government lost some support compared with the 1979 election but nevertheless secured a vastly increased Parliamentary majority: this contradictory result reflected the split in the opposition vote between Labour and the Alliance.

The Second Conservative Government.

After the election Sir Geoffrey Howe was replaced as Chancellor by Nigel Lawson. Mr Lawson confirmed that the basis of the Government's macroeconomic policies was unchanged: it remained committed to controlling the public sector borrowing requirement, to securing further reductions in inflation, and if possible to cutting both taxes and public expenditure. However, an important new aspect of government policy soon appeared: the *privatisation* of large parts of the public sector. Under this policy the government committed itself to selling shares in existing public enterprises to the private sector. The Government had two motives for this policy. First, it anticipated raising some £2 billion per year through such sales, and this was intended to help finance the p.s.b.r. Secondly, it argued that most economic activity was more efficiently carried out by the private sector, and that privatisation would therefore ultimately raise the economy's overall level of efficiency and productivity.

Both these arguments were strongly attacked. Critics pointed out that there was no evidence from international comparisons of different countries to support the view that the size of the public sector had any appreciable effect upon economic performance. There was also concern about the proposal to rely upon revenue from the sale of assets—a once-for-all event—to finance public spending on continuing projects.

Unemployment continued to rise during the first half of 1983 but thereafter stabilised at around the 3 million mark, reflecting the relatively rapid growth of output—nearly 3 per cent—during the year. The main sources of extra demand were stock-building and consumer spending, the latter boosted by the fall in inflation and nominal interest rates, and easier consumer credit. There was also some increase in investment, mainly in housebuilding and the service sector: manufacturing investment remained depressed. The steady fall of inflation since 1980 stopped in 1983 and indeed it rose slightly, to around 5·2 per cent, at the end of the year. This reflected the fact that wage settlements were no longer falling in size, perhaps because unemployment had stopped rising.

The 1984 Budget.

The new Chancellor presented his first budget in March. This combined a continuation of the broad macroeconomic principles of the previous four years with some significant changes in the structure of taxes and subsidies. The most important change concerned company taxation, where he announced the phased withdrawal, by April 1986, of tax reliefs on investment and stock appreciation, and the simultaneous phased reduction of corporation tax from 50 per cent in 1983–84 to 35 per cent by April 1986. This represented a radical break from the policies of the previous two decades, which had sought to encourage investment by generous tax allowances on the cost of new plant and machinery. The result had been that, despite a 50 per cent corporation tax rate, many companies paid little or nothing in taxes because much or all of their profits could be offset in investment allowances. The Chancellor argued that this system tended to encourage too much relatively unproductive investment by companies seeking to offset profits with tax allowances, and that it did not necessarily encourage the creation of new jobs. His new approach, offsetting the lost allowances with a much lower tax rate, was designed to encourage more investment in projects offering a high rate of return, in the hope that the spur to efficiency would ultimately create more jobs.

Another important change affecting business was the abolition, from 1 October, of the National Insurance Surcharge—the so-called "tax on jobs" which had been widely criticised. This further reduced the level of business taxation. The net effect of all these changes was a sizeable cut in business taxes both immediately and in the longer term. Perhaps partly for this reason, stock market prices rose sharply immediately after the Budget.

The Chancellor also attempted to reduce the tax burden on individuals. Basic tax thresholds were raised by 12·5 per cent, whereas only a 5·5 per cent rise would have been needed to index them against price rises; the extra rise removed an extra 400,000 people from the tax net. The Chancellor also abolished the investment income surcharge (a 15 per cent extra tax payable on investment incomes in excess of £7,100); reduced the top rates of capital transfer tax; and raised capital gains tax allowances.

The other main theme of the Budget—its macroeconomic strategy—involved no significant change from previous policies. The Chancellor announced p.s.b.r. and money supply targets for the year ahead which represented a slight tightening of previous targets. His medium term plans were very stringent: he intended to hold the p.s.b.r. to £7 billion per year from 1985–86 through to 1988–89, which with continuing inflation would inevitably mean a progressive further fall as a percentage of national income.

CONTRIBUTIONS TO THE ANNUAL GROWTH OF GROSS DOMESTIC PRODUCT

	1982	1983	1984
Exports	0·3	0·3	2·4
Consumer spending	0·7	2·9	1·5
Current government spending	0·2	0·7	0·1
Gross fixed investment	1·3	0·8	1·2
Change in stockbuilding	0·8	0·7	−0·6
Imports	−1·1	−1·6	−2·6
Residual	−0·3	−0·8	0·1
GDP (factor cost)	1·9	3·0	2·1

A major feature of 1984 was a strike by the National Union of Mineworkers. This began in March in protest against proposals by the National Coal Board to close down some unprofitable pits, continued throughout the year and only finally came to an end in March 1985, a year after it had started. It thus became easily the longest major dispute in British industrial history. The coal strike was also the bitterest dispute seen in Britain since the war. Bitterness resulted partly from a split in the union—some miners refused to join the strike—partly from violent confrontations between pickets and police, but perhaps most fundamentally because the strike's underlying issue—the loss of jobs—encapsulated much of the controversy surrounding the Government's economic policies. The dispute also had an adverse effect on the Government's economic strategy. Tentative estimates suggested that it had added some £2 billion to the p.s.b.r. during 1984. The main elements of this were the loss of revenue to the National Coal Board (partly offset by its savings on miners' pay) and the additional costs to the Central Electricity Generating Board of having to switch to more expensive oil as a source of power when coal stocks fell. Other sources of increases in the p.s.b.r. included the loss of tax revenue from miners, extra social security payments, and extra police pay associated with controlling mass pickets.

Despite the controversy surrounding the miners' strike, the major economic problem of 1984, as in preceding years, was unemployment. The earlier table indicated that after the dramatic rises of 1979–82, unemployment had risen only slowly in 1983; this continued to be the case in 1984. Nevertheless, many people argued that the official figures understated the true amount of unemployment in the economy. One reason was the growth of various *special schemes* whereby the Government subsidised a variety of short term work opportunities for people who did not have jobs, thus taking them off the official unemployment register. The accompanying table suggests that in the absence of such schemes total unemployment by the end of 1985 would have been over 600,000 above

the official figure; also, unemployment would have risen more rapidly since 1982. A further reason for believing that the official figures understated "true" unemployment was the strong probability that many people who had become discouraged by repeated failures to obtain jobs had simply dropped out of the labour force altogether. Adding these to the numbers on special schemes suggested a total "jobs gap" of over 4 million by the end of 1984.

Just as worrying as this huge total was the high incidence of long term unemployment: by January 1986 no less than 1,350,000 (40 per cent) of those officially registered as unemployed had been out of work for over a year, with a further 650,000 out of work for more than 6 months. By contrast, in January 1980 the long term unemployed (unemployed for over a year) numbered 355,000 (24 per cent of the total).

NUMBERS IN SPECIAL EMPLOYMENT SCHEMES ('000s)

	1983	1984	1985
Youth Training Scheme	198	350	357
Young Workers' Scheme	102	70	50
Community Programmes	97	123	151
Job Release	85	86	54
Enterprise Allowance	8	39	49
Other Schemes	123	21	10
TOTAL	613	689	671

Two factors made these gloomy statistics particularly disturbing. First, the consensus of economic forecasts was that if economic policies remained unchanged there was no likelihood of any significant fall in unemployment over the rest of the 1980s. Secondly, the fact that unemployment had continued to rise since 1982 despite the reasonable rates of economic growth achieved over the same period drew attention to the fact that with the labour force growing—a combination of demographic trends and increased participation by married women—a significant number of new jobs needed to be generated each year simply to prevent further rises in unemployment: to *reduce* unemployment would need faster economic growth than anything experienced for many years.

The growing perception that on existing trends there was no realistic prospect of a significant fall in unemployment, and indeed a chance of further increases, raised new voices against the Government's economic strategy. Many of the criticisms which the opposition Labour and Alliance parties had been making were now increasingly echoed by some of the Government's own supporters such as the Confederation of British Industry and—perhaps more significantly—a growing number of MPs and other leading figures in the Conservative Party. There was a widespread feeling that the Government should relax its p.s.b.r. targets and allow increased public sector borrowing as a means of financing extra public spending on *infrastructure* investment, *i.e.*, on projects such as house building and repair, road construction, maintenance and improvement of public sector capital assets such as school and hospital buildings, and the like. The critics had two reasons for proposing such action. First, they argued on traditional Keynesian lines that it represented the most effective way of reducing unemployment. Second, they argued that the squeeze on such spending in recent years had led to a serious deterioration in the infrastructure which would ultimately have to be reversed, and that the cost of doing so would increase the longer it was delayed. This latter point was supported by a series of reports into the state of various parts of the country's infrastructure from the National Economic Development Office and other bodies.

The 1985 Budget.

The Chancellor therefore had to prepare his 1985 budget in the face of growing opposition to his monetarist strategy. He was also faced early in 1985 by the need to raise interest rates—threatening a slowing of economic activity, and consequently a further rise in unemployment—as a result of the falling value of sterling. This loss of confidence in the pound, combined with the increased p.s.b.r. resulting from the miners' strike, as discussed earlier, meant that the Chancellor's scope within the terms of his own strategy for making the tax cuts which he had hoped was relatively small. The question was therefore whether or not he would alter the strategy.

In the event he refused to do so. He announced a p.s.b.r. target for 1985–86 of £7 billion, equal to just over 2 per cent of national income. This represented a further tightening of borrowing targets compared with those planned for 1984–85 (as already explained, the actual level of borrowing over the latter period far exceeded the planned level because of the miners' strike). Similarly, the monetary growth targets were lowered by 1 percentage point: 5–9 per cent for sterling M3 and 3–7 per cent for M0.

The Chancellor responded to his critics by proposing an alternative strategy to reduce unemployment. His analysis was that much unemployment, especially among relatively low-paid workers, resulted from labour costs being too high, so discouraging firms from taking on extra workers. He also argued that legislation on unfair dismissals, by making it difficult for firms to get rid of employees, tended to deter firms from hiring people in the first place. Finally, he argued that for many low-paid workers the incentive to take a job instead of remaining unemployed was not great. He therefore proposed several related measures. First, National Insurance payments for both employers and employees were reformed: he introduced lower rates for relatively low incomes and, by abolishing the upper earnings limit on employers' contributions, raised the amounts payable by firms on higher paid employees. Secondly, he raised the basic income tax thresholds by 10 per cent, twice the amount needed to index them against inflation, and so removed a number of low-paid workers from tax payments. Finally, he extended exemption from unfair dismissals claims regarding employees with less than two years of service to all firms; he also announced an enquiry into the working of Wages Councils, which set minimum wages for low-paid occupations. Mr. Lawson argued that these various measures would make unemployed people keener to seek jobs at relatively low pay and would simultaneously increase the number of such jobs on offer.

This package of proposals raised some criticisms. One objection was that the increased tax thresholds would mainly benefit secondary workers—pensioners, young people such as students, and married women—and would have only a small impact upon unemployed primary breadwinners, especially those with dependent children: but these latter, the critics argued, were the people most in need of help. Secondly, the new National Insurance arrangements still contained an anomaly, since employee contributions would continue to be levied not just on the amount of income above a threshold but—once the threshold was exceeded—on all income below it as well. For example, the lower threshold was fixed at £35.50 per week for 1985–86, with no payments below it and a 5 per cent rate above it. Consequently, someone earning £35 per week would pay nothing, but someone earning £36 per week would pay 5 per cent on the entire amount, so ending up with a lower net pay. Hence, it was argued, people currently earning at just below such a threshold would have no incentive to seek a better paid job, or more overtime. The same anomaly would also apply at the thresholds for higher contribution rates. The Chancellor might have been able to avoid such anomalies, but only at the cost of sacrificing a good deal of revenue.

An important feature of the budget was the announcement of various additional items of expenditure on special employment and training schemes. The Youth Training Scheme was to be extended from one to two years starting in 1986–87, and it was hoped to extend it to offer places to employees as well as the unemployed. The community programme scheme was also extended. The Chancellor announced a variety of other measures. Excise duties on beer, wine and cigarettes were raised by more than the rate of inflation (and on spirits by less); the car licence was raised from £90 to £100; and petrol tax was raised in line with inflation. Inflation-indexing for capital gains was extended, and the thresholds for payment of capital gains and capital transfer taxes were also raised in line with inflation.

Not surprisingly, the budget did not satisfy his critics, since it refused to alter the Government's basic strategy. Most of the critics rejected the Chancellor's strategy for jobs, arguing that the package of tax and National Insurance measures would have a negligible impact on unemployment, especially amongst the long term unemployed.

Another area of growing controversy in early 1985 was dissatisfaction over pay by many groups of workers in the public sector. These groups argued that the Government had persistently held their annual pay rises below those in the private sector, and that the cumulative effect of this over several years had now become unacceptable.

Public Sector Pay.

Feelings were strongest amongst school teachers, and just as the miners' strike finally drew to an end, so teachers in England and Wales embarked on a programme of disruption; teachers in Scotland had already been taking similar action for many months. The teachers did not stage a full strike as the miners had done, but instead refused to undertake what they regarded as voluntary duties and stuck strictly to what they interpreted as their contractual duties. The results of this were not so immediately damaging to the economy as the miners' strike had been, but the effects were substantially more disruptive to society at large: the education of many children suffered, and both children and parents found difficulty in coping with constant uncertainty as school were sometimes shut down at short notice. The dispute continued throughout 1985 and into 1986. The teachers argued that they were no longer being paid salaries appropriate to their levels of training and to the difficulty and responsibility of their jobs. In addition they argued that the government had persistently under-funded schools, so that many school buildings needed extensive renovation and many schools had insufficient text books. In this way the dispute encapsulated two separate controversies: an argument about public sector pay levels, and the separate argument by the government's critics that in squeezing public spending it had short-sightedly cut back on essential investments in education and other fields. Not surprisingly, therefore, the dispute in the schools produced, in its own way, as much bitterness as that resulting from the miners' strike during the previous year.

The Economy in 1985.

During the year national income rose by 3·5 per cent. However, most of this was concentrated in the first half of the year, with little expansion of activity during the summer and autumn. As in 1984, exports were the most important source of growth, though consumers' expenditure also grew faster than during 1984. On the other hand, fixed investment grew more slowly. This expansion of output led to a continued growth in the level of employment. As in 1983 and 1984, however, the growth in the number of people seeking work was even faster, so that total unemployment continued to rise slowly. Moreover, many of the new jobs created were part-time jobs, whereas most of the jobs lost between 1979 and 1982 were full-time jobs. The new jobs also reflected changes in the structure of the economy: most of the growth in employment was in the services sector, whereas most of the jobs lost during the period 1979–1982 had been in manufacturing. Those who were worried about the continued erosion of the economy's manufacturing base therefore found little consolation in the expansion of employment.

During 1985 the underlying growth in earnings remained at almost exactly the same level as in the previous two years, as the accompanying table indicates. With a rather slower growth in output per person employed, 1985 therefore saw an increased rate of rise of unit labour costs. However, this was offset by the fact that import prices rose much more slowly in 1985 than in 1983 or 1984, mainly as the result of a virtual standstill on import prices in the second half of the year. As a result the combined costs per unit of output rose at a slower rate in 1985. The movement in costs was nevertheless worrying, since the favourable movement in import prices could not be expected to repeat itself in future years. The main problem was the lack of any tendency for underlying earnings growth to fall, despite very high unemployment levels. In combination with continued relatively low growth of productivity, this made it difficult for the economy to avoid continued increases in unit labour costs at a rate faster than in most competitor countries.

COST AND PRODUCTIVITY INCREASES
(Percentage changes on the previous year)

	1982	1983	1984	1985
Average earnings	9·6	7·7	7·6	7·5
Output per employee	4·1	4·1	3·5	2·6
Import prices	6·8	7·7	8·8	3·7

1985 saw considerable fluctuations in some key economic variables. The sterling exchange rate fell at the beginning of the year, forcing the Chancellor to raise interest rates sharply. Both changes were reversed during the year. Interest rates fell gradually in the second half of the year, and the pound also rose. The domestic inflation rate showed a similar volatility: it rose from an annual rate of under 5 per cent at the start of the year to 7 per cent by the summer before falling back to just over 5 per cent by the year-end. This movement was itself connected to interest rate changes: higher interest rates at the start of the year forced up mortgage interest rates which in turn contributed to higher inflation; as rates drifted down later in the year, so did the inflation rate. This indicated another policy difficulty: higher interest rates to defend the sterling exchange rate had adverse effects on domestic inflation, but if instead the exchange rate had not been defended the resulting extra pressure on import costs would itself have caused inflation problems, albeit through a different route. The Chancellor's basic difficulty was that there was virtually no way of insulating the economy from the adverse effects of high American interest rates. Even with the large increase in British interest rates early in the year, average real interest rates over the year were still lower in Britain than in America.

Public Spending.

In November the Chancellor's annual autumn statement of public spending and borrowing plans announced constant real public spending targets between 1986 and 1989, together with a target for the public sector borrowing requirement equal to 2 per cent of national income. However, these figures were potentially misleading because of the effect of the government's privatisation programmes. When the government sold shares in public enterprises to the private sector these were officially counted as negative public spending, whereas in reality there was general agreement that the revenue obtained from such sales was a way of *financing* such spending. This meant that the government's official targets for spending and borrowing were lowered—by the amount of privatisation revenue—in what most people regarded as an artificial manner. Between 1983 and 1985 the government had aimed for annual revenue of £2·5 billion from asset sales, but in his autumn statement Mr. Lawson announced a new annual target from 1986 onwards of £4·75 billion. Most commentators therefore revised upwards by this amount both the public spending and the borrowing targets. A similar adjustment for continued council house sales added nearly another £2 billion. The result was that Mr. Lawson's official borrowing target of £7·5 billion was interpreted by most commentators as a "true" target of around £14 billion. This significantly affected judgements of the government's overall fiscal stance. On Mr. Lawson's official figures the stance was a tight one; on the reinterpreted figures it was much less so. Indeed, some people argued that the government was in some respects doing what its critics had been demanding—relaxing its borrowing targets—but using asset sales rather than the issue of new debt as a means of finance. On the other hand, the spending plans did not meet the critics' continued demands for higher expenditure on key infrastructure items. For example, estimates by local authorities and the Department of the Environment had suggested that

around £19 billion might be needed to renovate local council housing stocks throughout the country. The government's public spending plans included increases of £0·4 billion spread over 2 years—only about 2 per cent of the amount apparently needed. Government critics continued to argue, therefore, that with so many construction workers unemployed and so much construction work requiring to be done it made sense from every point of view to increase expenditure on these and similar items.

The autumn statement also included a new "job start" scheme under which any worker who had been unemployed for a year or more and who took a job at £80 or less per week would be paid an additional £20 per week for 6 months from government funds. The idea was two-fold. On the one hand, it sought to avoid the "poverty trap" problem whereby some unemployed people who could get jobs only at low wages were financially as well off by remaining unemployed. On the other hand, by aiming to get long-term unemployed people back into work it hoped to remove one of their main handicaps in seeking jobs—their lack of recent work experience. The hope was that after 6 months of work the people concerned would be retained by their new employers, who might even pay them the extra £20 per week themselves to reflect increases in productivity gained through renewed work experience.

The 1986 Budget.

At the start of 1986 the government was therefore faced with a mixed set of economic indicators. On the one hand, output and labour productivity had both been rising at reasonable rates for the past three years, and so had employment, albeit much of the increase in part-time rather than full-time jobs. On the other hand, the even faster rise in the labour force meant that unemployment was continuing to rise slowly; and inflation showed no tendency to fall significantly below 5 per cent.

The early part of the year saw a drastic fall in oil prices. Such a change had mixed implications for the economy. On the one hand, it benefited the oil-using sector of the economy, particularly manufacturing firms. On the other hand, it reduced the revenue available to the Chancellor from taxes on oil production, and this meant that he had less scope to make tax cuts in his Budget. In the longer term, oil at $10 per barrel threatened to make much of the North Sea's oil production uneconomic; however, the government's forecasts were for the price to climb back to $15 during the year.

The March Budget contained one surprise on which attention initially focused: a reduction in the standard rate of income tax from 30 to 29 per cent. Few people had predicted such a change beforehand. The Chancellor hinted that he hoped for a further and more substantial reduction, perhaps to 25 per cent, in his next Budget. Tax thresholds were increased in line with inflation, so that in real terms they remained unchanged. The combination of a reduced standard rate and unchanged real tax allowances represented a reversal of the policy of the previous four years, during which tax rates had been held constant whilst tax thresholds had been increased by more than the rise in prices, so increasing their real value. The switch of emphasis partly reflected the fact that, in international terms, Britain's tax thresholds were already relatively high, whilst the tax rate once the threshold was passed was higher than in other countries. Also, increases in thresholds had lost favour as a way of easing the "poverty trap" in which people on low incomes faced very high marginal tax rates: most of the people removed from the tax net by increases in thresholds over the previous three years had turned out to be married women and pensioners in part-time jobs, rather than heads of households with dependants.

Mr. Lawson followed his reforms of company taxation in the 1984 Budget with proposals for changes in personal taxation. The main proposal concerned tax allowances for married couples. The Chancellor proposed to abolish the additional allowance given to married men and to give every individual, whether male or female, married or single, the same allowance. He further proposed to make these allowances *transferable* between married couples, so that, for example, a wife looking after young children and not earning would be allowed to transfer her unused allowance to be added on to her husband's. The effect would be to benefit single-earner households at the expense of two-earner households. Critics of this approach argued that it would provide a disincentive for married women to work, since once they entered a job and claimed their tax allowance against their own earnings, their husbands would then lose the second allowance and see their take-home pay reduced. The Chancellor's counter-argument was that Denmark, which uses transferable allowances, has the highest rate of labour force participation by married women of any country in the Common Market. Other critics of the Chancellor's proposals accepted the need to abolish the married man's additional allowance but argued that the money saved would be better spent on increased child benefits—concentrating help on households with dependent children where much of the country's worst poverty was to be found—rather than on financing transferable allowances, the benefit of which would partly go to more affluent childless households. Whatever the outcome of this debate, it was unlikely that any changes would be introduced before the full computerisation of the tax system at the end of the 1980s.

Among other tax changes, Mr. Lawson raised duty on cigarettes by more than twice the rate of inflation, but several other duties—on cigar and pipe tobacco, and on all forms of alcohol—were unchanged. The Chancellor raised petrol duty slightly more than needed to keep in line with inflation, but left the cost of the road fund licence unchanged. Charities benefited in several ways: companies and individuals were given tax relief on certain charitable donations, and charities' use of transport equipment was given relief from value added tax payments. Stamp duty on share purchases was cut from 1 per cent to 0·5 per cent, but its range was extended to include purchases connected with company take-overs. Capital transfer tax was altered so that transfers of wealth were in future to be taxed only on death or, at a reduced rate, in the seven years before death. Critics objected that this gave unnecessary tax relief to wealthy individuals and their heirs.

A theme of the Budget was the aim of expanding the proportion of the population directly owning shares. To this end the Chancellor proposed a Personal Equity Plan under which individuals would be able to pay up to £200 per month into a fund to buy shares quoted on the Stock Exchange. All resulting dividends and capital gains would be tax-free provided that the original investment was not withdrawn for a year.

On broader macroeconomic issues the Budget repeated the Government's continuing strategy. The public spending and borrowing targets announced in the autumn statement were confirmed. However, the Budget also confirmed what had already become obvious: that monetary targets were no longer central to economic policy making as they had been during Sir Geoffrey Howe's period as Chancellor in 1979–83. Mr. Lawson announced an 11 to 15 per cent growth rate target for sterling M3 for 1986–87 but dropped the practice of publishing targets for future years. This reflected the fact that sterling M3 had persistently grown faster than its official targets over the previous three years. The Chancellor maintained medium range targets for the "narrow" measure of money, M0. However, financial markets seemed to have stopped regarding monetary targets of any sort as the best indicator of government policy intentions, focusing instead upon the borrowing requirement.

The immediate response to the Budget was encouraging from the Government's viewpoint: interest rates quickly fell by one percentage point, and there appeared to be reasonable prospects of further falls later in the year. At the same time uncertainty about variables outside the Chancellor's control—such as oil prices and the course of American interest rates—continued to run at a higher than normal level, making it very difficult to predict the course of the economy over the rest of the year with any confidence. Most forecasters were, however, agreed on two partly related matters: first, that the rate of increase in earnings and in unit labour costs was unlikely to fall over the coming year; and second, that there was no realistic prospect of any significant fall during the year in the level of unemployment.

Prospects for Economic Growth.

There has not only been dissatisfaction with the uneven way in which the economy has grown. There has also been increasing dissatisfaction with the rate of growth achieved in the economy since the war. The economies of most other industrial countries have expanded at a much faster rate (see **G14**). To try to improve our growth performance, the Labour Government introduced the National Plan in 1965. By setting a target annual rate of growth until 1970, it aimed to bolster firms' expectations and hence their investment and to co-ordinate their decisions. Unanticipated balance of payments difficulties meant that the Plan was short-lived, but some of the institutions associated with the Plan survived. The National Economic Development Council had been established in 1962 to stimulate a more systematic study of the problems involved in securing a faster rate of growth. Twenty-one Economic Development Committees for different industries were set up under its umbrella.

(i) Pressures on the Industrial Sector.

Between 1963 and 1985 the total employed labour force in the UK fell by about 1·5 per cent. Within this total, however, employment in the manufacturing sector fell by about 35 per cent, having been particularly badly hit by the rise in the value of the pound on the foreign exchange market between 1978 and 1981, and by a simultaneous recession. Employment has increased in private and public service industries and in the utilities. This larger non-industrial sector imposed extra demands on industrial production. Capital goods for investment in services had to be provided from the output of the industrial sector, whilst industrial production was also needed for consumers employed in the services and elsewhere. Thus less was left over for investments in industry itself and for industrial exports. This meant an inadequate growth of industrial capacity. Thus when the Government attempted to stimulate the economy, bottlenecks quickly developed and imports of consumer goods increased rapidly. The result was balance of payments difficulties, which were only partially alleviated by increasing exports of services like insurance, and therefore the government took deflationary action. This vicious circle could only be broken by an upsurge in industrial investment, which was prevented by declining profitability.

Some commentators have argued that the problem was a direct result of the growth in public sector employment. This had to be paid for either by workers or private employers, and trade unions made sure that it was the employers; if, for example, income tax was raised, this was passed on in successful wage demands. The result was declining profitability. This analysis is at best speculative. It is not, for example, at all evident that public sector employment has grown nearly as rapidly as implied. In certain activities such as local government there was a very rapid growth, but overall the ratio of public sector to total employment increased only modestly—from 23·9 per cent in 1961 to 27·2 per cent in 1974. Similarly over the same period public sector spending on goods and services increased only from 21·5 per cent to 26·8 per cent of gross domestic product. It was argued that such figures understated the true change: the spending figures are in constant prices; in current money terms the change was more striking because of the *relative price effect, i.e.*, items like teachers' and civil servants' salaries rising faster than the general price level. The figures also exclude transfers from people who produce to those who do not, such as pensioners, though this may be justifiable since such *transfer payments* do not represent final claims on resources by the public sector. It was argued that the claim of the public sector on output which could be sold increased by almost 50 per cent between 1961 and 1974 thus reducing the resources available for industrial investment. The present Conservative government, subscribing to this view, is committed to reducing the share of public expenditure in GDP, believing that this is necessary to reduce taxes on both persons and companies. This, they believe, would restore work and profit incentives, although there is scant evidence in support of this view. Since 1979 the share of public expenditure has in fact not fallen significantly mainly because of much greater demands on the social security system. If the arguments mentioned above gain force, then it is possible that the whole method of providing health care, education etc. will be called into question. This would be particularly sad if, as some of the points made above suggest, it is based on fallacious economic reasoning.

This is only one school of thought among those economists who are concerned that Britain is becoming *de-industrialised*. Another group of economists, also concerned with de-industrialisation, rejects the argument that it is the consequence of the expansion of the public sector. They stress the inability of British industry to maintain its share of world trade in manufactures, a share which fell from almost 13 per cent in the early 1970's, to under 8 per cent in 1985 . The forces causing this failure cannot be arrested by a once-and-for-all devaluation. On the demand side the conditions for an expansion of British exports are unfavourable; an important reason for this being that Britain tends to specialise in products for which demand tends to rise relatively slowly in response to increases in the standard of living. On the supply side there is a vicious circle of declining market share, declining profits and investment and declining competitive power. Some members of this group then point to the need for demand expansion, in order to stimulate output growth, and ultimately, higher productivity growth, which is the key to international competitiveness. The problem in Britain, though, appears to be in stimulating supply in an effective manner. This is clearly seen in the activities of apparently one of the most efficiently run, and best-known British companies: GEC. It has been very profitable and had a "cash mountain" of between £1,000 million and £2,000 million over a recent three year period, but could not find suitable projects/ventures in the U.K. in which to invest the funds. Yet other economists have argued that Britain's industrial structure, similar as it is to that of Germany, cannot account for our problems. Rather it is that Britain has narrowed the technological gap between herself and the US—the technical leader—more slowly than have her major competitors, thus failing to exploit the opportunities for unusually rapid growth.

Whatever disagreement exists about causes, there is basic agreement that Britain does have an industrial problem. Not least is the question of which new activities—be they in industry and services—will replace those activities in which we were once strong but no longer are. A recent House of Lords Select Committee documented the decline of manufacturing, accelerated as it was by the general recession after 1979. To many it was too messianic in tone, both in regard to its view of the inevitability of manufacturing's demise and the lack of new activities to take its place. Be that as it may, it is worrying that Britain still lags in international competitiveness.

(ii) The National Enterprise Board.

In 1974 the Labour Government published a White Paper entitled *The Regeneration of British Industry*, setting out the ideas which found their legislative expression in the *Industry Act* of 1975. Underlying this Act was the feeling that private enterprise, on its own, had not done enough to stimulate a high rate of growth. The Act aimed to remedy this by setting up the *National Enterprise Board*. Its functions were to assist the establishment, development or maintenance of any industrial enterprise or industry, to extend public ownership into profitable areas of manufacturing, to promote industrial democracy in undertakings controlled by it, and to hold and manage the securities of any other property in public ownership. The Board's borrowing capability was very modest in relation to the market value of the share capital of major British firms. Funds for aid could also be dispensed by the Board. Both the Minister for Industry and the Treasury had a responsibility to ensure that the Board earned an "adequate" return on capital employed. The Act also contained provisions for the compulsory disclosure of information by firms both to the Minister and to trade unions. It also introduced the idea of voluntary *planning agreements*, which private companies might enter into with the Government. In return such companies would be assured of regional development

grants at the rates prevailing at the time the agreement was made. By early 1979, only one planning agreement—with Chrysler—had been concluded.

Critics argued both that the Act was doctrinaire socialism and that it was not proved that such state intervention would have more favourable effects than the workings of free private enterprise. It was clear that the National Enterprise Board could not proceed far with the extension of public ownership, since it had available only small funds. Guidelines issued in early 1976 further restricted its ability to act without reference to the Secretary of State for Industry. Some measure of greater independence was given to the NEB in December 1976, when it was allowed to make loans or guarantees or engage in joint ventures without informing the Secretary of State, where the cost was small, and where no new significant policy issues arose. From February 1978 the NEB was allowed to sell off investments up to the value of £1 million without the Secretary of State's permission, and in early 1979 it was given additional spending power. When the Conservatives won the 1979 General Election there was some expectation that the National Enterprise Board would be abolished. Though this did not happen, it soon became plain that the new Government did not intend to allow the Board any role other than that of overseeing a limited number of companies in need of temporary assistance. It was certainly not going to be allowed to extend the area of public ownership. Subsequently the NEB was merged with the National Research and Development Corporation to form the British Technology Group.

Even before the NEB was effectively operational, state acquisitions in the private sector had proceeded apace. Normally the Government had provided help to ailing companies on condition of taking a shareholding, under the provisions of the Conservatives' 1972 Industry Act. State holdings in eight companies were handed over to the NEB at its inception. These companies were British Leyland, Rolls-Royce, Cambridge Instruments, Ferranti, Herbert, Brown-Boveri-Kent, Dunford and Elliott, and ICL. The NEB acquired shareholdings in another twenty-eight companies by early 1978.

Soon after taking office, the new Conservative Government announced its intention to sell off a portion of official holdings in several sectors—British Airways, British Aerospace, shipbuilding, freight, and British Petroleum. By early 1985 privitization had proceeded apace and was continuing, the most notable case being British Telecom, which was sold for £3·9 billion. In 1984–5 alone, as well as British Telecom, the following were sold to the private sector; the Government's remaining minority stakes in British Aerospace and Britoil, Jaguar, Sealink, certain parts of British Shipbuilders, the NEB's holdings in INMOS, assets of the Forestry Commission. Between 1979 and 1984 almost £3bn of state assets were sold. In early 1986 plans for the future included the National Bus Company, British Gas, the British Airports Authority, British Airways, and water supply.

(iii) An Approach to Industrial Strategy.

In 1975 a White Paper, entitled *An Approach to Industrial Strategy*, set out the Government's general views on planning for growth. The strategy was based on the fact that despite Britain's overall poor performance, some sectors had done very well. There was therefore a need to identify specific problems which had held back particular industries as well as a need to identify general problems. Some 40 sectoral working parties were established and were composed of representatives of management, workers and the Government. Their task was to analyse their own industry in detail and to agree a programme of action designed to improve competitive performance, and to make Britain a high-output, high-wage economy. Specifically they were asked to consider the following: how to get more out of existing investment and manpower in order to improve productivity; how to increase the level and quality of investment; how to improve non-price competitiveness; how to ensure that their sectors concentrate on the "correct" export markets; how to provide a sufficient supply of skilled workers. In 1978 the working parties presented their first reports. They were full of suggestions, particularly on how to improve export performance. The planning provisions of the 1975 Industry Act were abandoned by the Conservative Government, but the NEDC Sector Working Parties continue to operate, though they were subsequently re-titled Economic Development Councils. It is difficult to quantify their precise effects upon sectoral performance.

One area where the 1975 Industry Act had practical consequences was in the introduction of schemes of financial assistance to industry. By mid-1978 these schemes had run their course in six sectors and were working in eight others (including paper and board, electronic components, wool textiles, non-ferrous foundries, instrumentation and automation, and footwear). Other sectors have received funds since then. The assistance has been directed towards increases in productivity (e.g. by re-equipment), or to increases in product relevance to export markets, to improving non-price competitiveness and to improving marketing. In addition there is a selective investment scheme (before that the accelerated projects scheme) to provide funds for particular projects, there is an export market entry guarantee scheme to cover the risks of entering new markets, and there has been substantial training expenditure. Nevertheless, the crucial question remains not just whether the performance of particular sectors can be improved, but whether it can be ensured that Britain produces the right mix of products to meet the threat to employment and to our trading balance of both technological change and foreign competition. On these issues, the present Government believes firmly that if Britain is to succeed, the impetus is most likely to come from risk-taking individual entrepreneurs, and companies.

(iv) British Oil Production.

The discovery of oil in British waters has implications for Britain's long-term growth prospects. The oil crisis of 1973 and the subsequent rocketing of the price of oil drove the economy into recession and engendered concern about Britain's medium-term growth rate. Whilst these early fears may have been somewhat exaggerated, so also were expectations of a bonanza in the late 1970s from oil production in British waters. Though by early 1976 extraction of British oil had fallen behind schedule, by 1981 the UK was self-sufficient. But there were a number of doubts about the costs of exploitation and about the extent to which the Government would have already mortgaged future returns by heavy borrowing abroad. It is uncertain how long the U.K. will continue to be self-sufficient. The U.K. is likely to become dependent on imports once again in the 1990s. As oil prices plummeted in 1986, the prospects for future production weakened, since the incentive for further exploration and investment was lessened.

Meanwhile the Government tried to ensure that the state got a substantial share of the returns from offshore oil extraction. A major worry was the large degree of foreign ownership of the oil companies involved in the operations. In February 1975, therefore, a Bill was introduced into Parliament, which proposed a *petroleum revenue tax* of 45 per cent and royalties of 12½ per cent. Corporation tax was to be deducted from the residue at the standard rate. It was envisaged that this would allow the oil companies an adequate return on capital. Concern had been expressed that such a tax system would discourage exploitation of the "marginal fields", that is the smaller oil-fields which might not justify the huge initial expenditure needed to make them productive. Several safeguards were, therefore, proposed. No petroleum revenue tax would be levied until a field had earned back 175 per cent of its capital outlay. Fields returning less than 30 per cent on investment after paying p.r.t. would have the tax refunded. There was also to be discretionary provision to return all or part of the 12½ per cent royalties. The Government reiterated its intention to press for 51 per cent state participation in the oil-fields, which it proceeded to do through the agency of the British National Oil Corporation. Since January 1979 the rate of petroleum revenue tax, and associated tax relief, has been altered from time to time. The Government has had to ensure that further exploration is not discouraged by the tax system.

In March 1978 the Government published a White Paper, *The Challenge of North Sea Oil*. In this it was

estimated that by the mid-1980s North Sea Oil would increase national income by £6 billion per year and improve the balance of payments to the tune of £8 billion per year. Perhaps a more crucial aspect of the White Paper was that the annual benefit to government revenue was expected to be £4 billion. This estimate has, however, proved wide of the mark, mainly on account of exchange-rate fluctuations, but most recently because of the fall in the world price of oil. Revenue is expected to be £11·5 billion in 1985/86, but only £6 billion in 1986/7. As a percentage of government revenue, this figure is at a peak of 9 per cent estimated to fall in succeeding years. The figure of 9 per cent in 1985/6 for Britain may be compared with those of other major oil producers: Canada—11·4 per cent, Norway—17·6 per cent and Saudi Arabia—75·8 per cent. Since there is a delay between the actual oil production in the North Sea, and the collection of tax revenue, output is thought to have peaked sometime in 1983/84. The crucial issue however was how the extra revenue was to be used. The White Paper designated four priorities: more resources for industrial investment; funds for energy conservation and new energy investment; the reduction of the level of personal taxation; the improvement of certain essential services. It was clear that the Government believed that North Sea oil provided it with an opportunity to stimulate sustained growth, and the first two of the four priorities were obviously designed with this in mind. However, the election of a Conservative Government in 1979 signalled a change of emphasis. In September of that year proposals were published to reduce BNOC's role. Its preferential position in future licensing was ended, as were special access to official finance through the National Oil Account and its statutory role as adviser to the Government. Effectively its role in exploration and production activities was abandoned. In early 1985, the Conservative government announced that BNOC was to be abolished, and that oil prices would be much more closely related to market developments.

In the 1980 Budget it was implied that henceforth the oil tax revenue would be used almost exclusively to reduce the size of the public sector borrowing requirement and the scale of personal and corporate taxation. Five years on, even the Government would admit that success in these objectives has proved more difficult to achieve than originally imagined. On the balance of payments front, North Sea Oil has provided an invaluable cushion, as is evident from the fact that a petroleum-sufficient Britain is running a trade deficit. However, on the current account, Britain is more or less in balance. This leads to the question of what happens when Britain has to start importing oil again.

The Government's answer is that the country has net overseas assets in the region of £40 billion, which

RETAIL PRICES, AVERAGE WEEKLY
EARNINGS, REAL WEEKLY EARNINGS
AND REAL DISPOSABLE INCOMES
1970 = 100

	Retail prices	Weekly earnings	Real weekly earnings	Real disposable incomes
1970	100·0	100·0	100·0	100·0
1971	109·4	111·2	101·6	101·3
1972	117·3	125·5	107·0	110·0
1973	128·0	142·5	111·3	117·9
1974	148·4	167·8	113·1	116·8
1975	184·5	212·3	115·1	117·2
1976	215·2	245·3	114·0	116·5
1977	249·1	270·2	108·5	114·7
1978	269·7	309·3	114·7	123·1
1979	306·2	357·6	116·9	130·1
1980	361·1	424·8	117·6	131·4
1981	404·1	479·7	118·7	128·8
1982	438·8	524·7	119·6	129·2
1983	459·0	568·9	123·9	132·4
1984	481·8	603·7	125·3	135·4
1985	511·1	656·2	128·4	138·2

may be tapped as appropriate. This sanguine view overlooks the point that it is individuals and institutions which own these assets, not the government. The re-imposition of strict exchange controls in the 1990s is likely to prove immensely difficult.

The authorities' other main energy worry was the fast rate of extraction of North Sea gas. Many people felt that this meant that gas was being sold too cheaply, and thus was threatening the market for coal and nuclear power, which were the two fuels on which medium-term energy policy was based. As a result, the cost of gas for domestic consumers was raised gradually in the early 1980's to bring it into line with the price paid for electricity.

(v) A Productivity Breakthrough?

One cause of our poor relative growth rates has been lower productivity increases than achieved in other countries; and as in other countries this growth slowed down in the 1970s. For example, in manufacturing between 1963 and 1973 the average annual growth rate was 4·2 per cent, and for the overall economy, productivity grew at 3·1 per cent per annum between 1966 and 1973. For the economy as a whole, productivity fell in the early 1970s in response to the first oil-price rise. Then, it grew at an average rate of 2·3 per cent per annum between 1976 and 1979, and the rate of increase from the cyclical low in 1980 to 1983 was 2·5 per cent per annum. Rapidly rising North Sea oil output increased the 1976–79 figure; excluding oil, the productivity growth rate for that period was 1·2 per cent per annum.

However, in manufacturing productivity grew at an annual rate of over 5 per cent between 1980 and 1983. Some commentators believe that this represents a breakthrough and that we can expect a better productivity performance in the long-run. This is because it is believed that the last few years have induced a greater realism amongst both managers and workers, whilst the power of trade unions has been reduced. This has led, it is argued, to a substantial improvement in working practices.

Others have argued that there is no reason to expect a long-run improvement. They argue that at a time of record bankruptcies and liquidations, it would be reasonable to expect the less productive companies to be the ones which disappeared from the scene—with a consequential effect on aggregate productivity. Further, although there has undoubtedly been some improvement in working practices, there is no reason to expect continuing improvement in these practices. On balance it seems reasonable to conclude that the best which can be hoped for is a return to the productivity performance of the late 1960s. This suspicion seems confirmed by a slowing down of productivity growth in manufacturing in 1984 and 1985.

Inflation.

(i) Wages and Prices.

Retail prices continued to edge upwards during the 1960s and 1970s. In 1985 they were 590 per cent higher than in 1963. Only a part of this increase can be attributed to an increase in import prices. To explain the inflation we must look at the behaviour of labour costs. Between 1963 and 1985 weekly earnings—including overtime payments and payments negotiated on the factory floor—rose by 920 per cent. Since the increase in productivity during this period was slow, earnings per unit of output (indicating labour costs per unit of output) rose by rather less than 500 per cent. These increased costs were passed on to the public in the form of increased prices, so that real earnings rose by about 50 per cent. The table shows annual average prices, earnings, real earnings, and also real disposable incomes (*i.e.* the purchasing power of total personal incomes after income tax), all as indexes with 1970 = 100.

(ii) The Growing Inflation.

Between the late 1960s and the mid 1970s there was a growing rate of inflation. Between 1969 and 1970 retail prices rose by 6 per cent, between 1970 and 1971 by 9¼ per cent, between 1971 and 1972 by 7 per cent, between 1972 and 1973 by 9 per cent, between 1973 and 1974 by 16 per cent and between 1974 and 1975 by 24 per cent. The increase in average weekly earnings also accelerated.

Why was there this acceleration in the rate of inflation? In 1968 and 1969, it resulted partly

from the increase in import prices consequent upon the devaluation of the pound in November 1967, partly as well from the increase in indirect taxes introduced after devaluation in order to free resources for exports, and also partly from the spurt in money wages when the Government's incomes policy weakened. But in 1970 the blame could be placed squarely on the "wage explosion". Normally money wages rise more rapidly the greater the pressure of demand in the labour market. But with unemployment relatively high in 1970, pressure of demand for labour could not be the explanation. Rather, the wage explosion appeared to reflect a general increase in militancy by trade unionists angered by the near-stagnation of real earnings and real disposable incomes after 1967 and possibly influenced by events in other countries (*see* below). Once begun it was maintained by expectations that prices would continue to rise rapidly.

In 1970 there was a sharp increase in real earnings, implying a decline in the share of profits. This share (gross trading profits as a proportion of domestic income) is normally low during a recession, but the share in 1970 dropped to 10 per cent compared with 14 per cent in the recession of 1962. The share rose in 1971 when the increase in labour costs had a delayed effect on prices. This added further to the spurt of inflation in 1972. Both wage and price increases accelerated, and the Government was forced to intervene in November by introducing a pay and price standstill.

The inflation of 1972 was caused mainly by increased wage payments, although the effective devaluation of the pound in June and the rising world prices of food and raw materials also contributed, both directly to prices and indirectly through their effects on wage demands. The rising price of imports was mainly responsible for the inflation during 1973, but labour costs also rose markedly. There was a temporary slowdown in the rate of inflation following the July 1974 budget, but apart from this it accelerated fairly steadily through 1974 as a whole. Whilst import prices, particularly oil, had been the fastest growing item of costs for the two years up to the middle of 1974, by then domestic wage and salary costs had taken over this role. Average earnings increased by 25 per cent between the fourth quarters of 1973 and 1974. Since productivity growth was very slow, this meant a 23 per cent rise in labour costs. Government policy had some effect in dampening down the rate of inflation, both through the operation of the Price Code and through increased subsidies.

(iii) The Attack on Inflation.

1975 saw an even higher rate of inflation than 1974. Average weekly earnings rose by nearly 27 per cent. Productivity fell and prices rose by about 24 per cent. Import prices made a smaller contribution to inflation than in the previous two years. Real earnings rose by 2 per cent, implying a further drop in the share of profits in domestic income. But through 1975 inflation moderated. Average earnings increases started to slow down in the second quarter, and wholesale and retail prices followed with a lag. By the third quarter they were all increasing at about 15 per cent. The slowdown of average earnings in fact started before the imposition of the £6 limit, and it has been suggested that this was caused by growing unemployment. Such an effect was, however, small compared with the direct impact of the £6 rule.

Domestic inflation moderated still further in 1976, retail prices being 16 per cent higher than in 1975. The main contributor to this was the deceleration in the rate of increase in labour costs. Average weekly earnings were 15 per cent higher than in 1975. Real earnings were therefore slightly lower than in the previous year, implying some recovery in the share of profits in domestic income. By far the largest influence on the deceleration of wage inflation was the voluntary incomes policy, first the £6 limit and from August its successor, which aimed at a 4½ per cent increase in basic wage rates. However, in the last few months of the year price inflation showed a small increase. This upturn is explained by the sharp fall in the value of the pound during the year putting up the cost of raw materials and fuel purchased by British industry.

Retail prices were nearly 16 per cent higher in 1977

RISE IN CONSUMER PRICES

	1959–1980*	1980–1981	1981–1982	1982–1983	1983–1984	1984–1985
U.S.	5·0	10·4	6·1	3·2	4·3	3·6
Japan . . .	7·1	4·9	2·7	1·9	2·2	2·1
France . . .	6·4	13·4	11·8	9·6	7·4	5·8
W. Germany .	3·7	6·3	5·3	3·3	2·4	2·2
Italy	8·1	17·8	16·6	14·6	10·8	9·2
U.K.	8·2	11·9	8·6	4·6	5·3	6·1

* Annual average.

than in 1976, whilst earnings were only 10 per cent higher. Real earnings, therefore, fell by nearly 5 per cent, and this meant some further recovery in the share of profits in national income. Real disposable income fell by the smaller amount of 1½ per cent, because of the reduction of taxes in the April and October budgets. Productivity improved hardly at all during the year, and so the earnings increases meant a similar increase in labour costs per unit of output, these costs feeding through to prices.

There was a considerable contrast between the two halves of 1977. In the year to July 1977 prices rose at the rate of about 17 per cent, inflation being exacerbated by the depreciation of sterling in 1976, and further fed by the delayed impact of earnings increases of 14 per cent during Stage I of incomes policy, which ended in July 1976. Since by early 1977 Stage II of the incomes policy was holding earnings increases down to 10 per cent, real personal income was badly squeezed in the first half of the year. These lower increases in earnings together with the appreciation of sterling had their effect on retail prices in the second half of the year. By early 1978 price inflation had fallen below 10%. At the same time earnings had begun to increase at the rate of about 15 per cent per annum. This, together with the 1977 tax cuts, meant an appreciable recovery in real personal income.

Thus by early 1978 price inflation had fallen back into single figures, and it continued to fall steadily until the middle of the year. From then inflation started to increase again, so that by the spring of 1979 was going back into double figures.

Stage III of the incomes policy, which ran for the year ending July 1978, was looser than Stage II, and was accompanied by earnings increases of nearly 15 per cent. This was beginning to feed through to prices by the middle of 1978, and was the cause of the acceleration of inflation. By early 1979 earnings were rising at an annual rate of 14 per cent, and this despite continued low rates of increase of import prices and a renewed squeeze on profits, implied a likely further increase in price inflation. Real personal disposable income continued its recovery of late 1977. With earnings rising faster than prices and with only a modest increase in direct tax payments, r.p.d.i. improved substantially during 1978.

In early 1979, then, price inflation was starting to increase slowly but was still within single figures (at annual rates). Two important wage settlements following strikes—the lorry drivers and local authority manual workers—set the pace for a higher rate of increase of earnings. By the end of 1979 they were rising at nearly 20 per cent per annum compared to about 14 per cent a year earlier. In December 1979 retail prices were going up at a rate of 17 per cent per annum. An increase in indirect taxation contributed 3 per cent to price inflation. But pay remained the main force driving prices. The Conservative Government was elected in May 1979 with the defeat of inflation a central plank of its economic policy. Despite a deflationary fiscal and monetary policy, retail prices continued to rise, reaching a year on year increase of over 20 per cent in the second quarter of 1980. Much of this was due to the effects of higher indirect taxes and continued wage pressure, and was despite an appreciation in the value of sterling. Towards the end of 1980 the rate of inflation began to fall. This was partly a consequence of the recession, both at home and abroad, making it difficult for firms to mark up over costs. Real wages rose, albeit slowly, implying a further squeeze on profits.

Inflation continued to fall in 1981, as pressure on wages eased and the recession became deeper. The year on year increase in retail prices was 12 per cent. Real personal disposable income fell by 2 per cent mainly because of the Chancellor's failure to index income tax allowances and bands in the 1981 Budget. The squeeze on disposable incomes continued into 1982 as the real burden of taxation rose further.

The fall in inflation continued in 1982 and into 1983, when the annual rates were 8·6 per cent and 4·6 per cent respectively. This was despite a declining effective exchange rate. The recession and international competition were important influences making British industrialists very wary of putting up prices. At the same time earnings inflation was falling, being 9·4 per cent in 1982 and 8·4 per cent in 1983, whilst productivity was still increasing very strongly.

Since 1983 until early 1985 price inflation was pretty stable, at between 4 and 5 per cent. Once the figures are corrected for distortions such as the miners' strike, the underlying rate of increase of earnings was also stable. Profits recovered strongly in 1984. However, import prices rose more rapidly in that year. This reflected a fall in the effective sterling exchange rate. More worrying, productivity slowed in 1984. Thus our unit labour costs rose more rapidly. Indeed, taking the 1980s as a whole, although our productivity performance improved and earnings inflation decreased, our unit labour costs continued to rise faster than those of our major competitors. In other words, they did even better on these critical variables than we did.

In this context, a remarkable fact is that throughout the early 1980s the real earnings of those in work continued to increase, as did real personal disposable, which also incorporates the income of those not working.

In early 1986 earnings inflation showed little sign of slowing down, running as it was in the 7–8 per cent range. The unemployed have not bid down pay. Rather it has been forced up by high company profits, skill shortages, and the need of employers—as they see it—to attract good workers and to motivate their existing employees. By contrast, retail price inflation was dipping in early 1986, and by the second quarter of the year was around 3 per cent per annum. This reflected the recovery of sterling in 1985 together with the dramatic fall in oil prices. Further impetus was added by the slight drop in interest rates and consequently in mortgage rates in early 1986. Prospects were for price inflation to move back to the 4–5 per cent range, as rising unit labour costs and declining sterling started to have an impact.

(iv) International Inflation.

Inflation since the late 1960's has generally been more rapid in the United Kingdom than in other developed countries. But the acceleration from that period was common to most of them.

Was this the result of a series of coincidences; did the inflations have a common cause; or were they "contagious"? Both France and Italy had major strikes and subsequent "wage explosions"; Britain's inflation too was "cost-push" not "demand pull" in character (*see* **G22**): Japan and W. Germany experienced strong demand pressures; and in the United States the price increases could be explained as a lagged reaction to the demand pressure of 1966–69. Nevertheless, it is likely that inflation was to some extent transmitted from one country to another—particularly from the United States and particularly to small, trading countries—through its effects on the prices of imports and exports, and possibly through its effects on workers' expectations. In all countries, whatever the initial impetus to the inflation, expectations came to play an important role in sustaining it.

Policies against inflation were also similar. Heartened by the apparent success of the statutory wages and prices policies introduced in the United States in August 1971, a growing number of European countries, including the United Kingdom, introduced or tightened direct controls on pay and prices. But these policies did not prevent inflation from accelerating. The sharp increase in inflation experienced by all the major economies in 1973 reflected the rising prices of primary products in world markets. World inflation accelerated further during 1974 as the increased oil price had its full effect on costs and prices in the industrial countries. The high price of oil meant a transfer of purchasing power from its consumers to its producers, and therefore a fall in effective demand in industrialised countries. Many foreign countries exacerbated the consequent recession by much more restrictive fiscal and monetary policies than those employed by the British Government. The result was a fall in their inflation rates in the first half of 1975; and, though there was a renewed rise in the second half of the year, the rise of consumer prices in 1975 as a whole was somewhat lower than in 1974. Britain is the only one of the countries listed in the table whose inflation rate increased in 1975. In all major trading countries the inflation rate fell in 1976. In 1977 the inflation rate continued to fall in Japan and Germany; it rose in the United States and Italy, and remained more or less unchanged in Britain and France. Whilst inflation accelerated in the United States and Germany during 1978, it fell back in the other countries. From then until 1980 it accelerated worldwide, but in the following year decreased in all the listed countries except West Germany. Traditionally Britain was at or near the top of the international inflation league, in the late 1970s, for example, being beaten only by Italy. By 1985, Britain was still ranking relatively high in the inflation league table, despite the success of the Government's anti-inflation strategy. France and Italy were experiencing higher inflation, but we were still ahead of the United States, Japan and Germany.

Incomes Policy.

Britain's competitive position in world trade has deteriorated in relation to that of her main rivals the United States, West Germany, and France; this is one major reason for her recurrent balance of payments difficulties. The British share in total world exports of manufactures fell from 17·7 per cent to 12·3 per cent between 1959 and 1967. It fell further to 10·0 per cent by 1972 and to 8·6 per cent in 1976. Thereafter it recovered back to approximately its 1972 level, only to fall back again in the early 1980s. There are essentially two methods of remedying this situation. Either there must be a depreciation of the pound in terms of other currencies, or we must have a policy to limit the increase in British costs. Up to 1967 the Government concentrated on the latter alternative, either by restrictive budgetary policies or by *incomes policy*. In 1967 the pound was devalued, and from 1972 it was allowed to float, though the Government from time to time stepped in to prevent it floating freely. However, incomes policy was still needed if any depreciation was to be successful, and if harshly restrictive monetary and fiscal policies were to be avoided.

Other harmful effects of inflation, giving rise to the need for some form of incomes policy, are discussed in **Part II.**

(i) The Pay Pause.

In July 1961 the Chancellor of the Exchequer called for a "pause" in wages, salaries, and dividend payments. Exhortations for restraint had been a familiar feature of ministerial statements for many years, but on this occasion the Government soon made it clear that it intended to use such power as it has to influence the amount and timing of wage and salary awards. It had the power to decide when the pay awards recommended by the Wages Councils—which fix minimum wages in some low paid industries—should be implemented. The Government's power is strongest over workers which it directly or indirectly employs, *e.g.*, civil servants, teachers, and Post Office workers. Their pay awards were cut back. The Government also had a limited influence on awards made in nationalised industries.

The "pay pause" came to an end in April 1962. It was envisaged as a temporary policy, and its effects are difficult to assess. It certainly postponed some wage awards which would otherwise have been made, and it may have contributed to a stiffening of employer resistance to wage claims. But because the pause affected some groups of people more severely than others, this form of incomes policy was seen to be discriminatory.

(ii) The National Incomes Commission.

In February 1962 the Government issued a White Paper which outlined its incomes policy for the period after the pause. It stated that "the objective must be to keep the rate of increase in incomes within the long-term rate of growth of national production." The Government stressed that most of the arguments which had in the past been advanced in justification of wages and salary claims—*e.g.*, increases in the cost of living, trends in productivity or profits in particular industries, and comparisons with levels or trends in other employments—should be given less weight; and that "general economic considerations"—*i.e.*, the increases which the economy can afford given the prospective rate of increase in national production—should be given more weight.

Late in 1962 the Government set up the *National Incomes Commission* (NIC). However, the powers of this body were limited. It had, for example, no power to cancel or modify a wage agreement on which it reported. NIC produced only 4 reports, and was wound up after the change of Government.

(iii) The National Board for Prices and Incomes.

In October 1964 the Labour Government's new Department of Economic Affairs was made responsible for achieving an incomes policy. The lessons of the past had been learned; the Government recognised that a successful incomes policy would require the support of both sides of industry. Its first objective was to achieve a "Joint Statement of Intent on Productivity, Prices and Incomes"; this was signed in December 1964. In this document the T.U.C. and the employers' organisations undertook to co-operate with the Government in producing an effective machinery for the implementing of an incomes policy.

It was Government policy that growth in earnings per employee should equal the planned growth in national output per employee of 3–3½ per cent per annum. Thus, in those industries (*e.g.*, engineering) in which productivity growth exceeded this "norm", earnings should rise less rapidly than productivity, and in those industries in which productivity growth fell short of the norm, earnings could rise more rapidly than productivity. Growth in earnings per employee should exceed the norm only in exceptional cases; *i.e.*, as a reward for increasing productivity by eliminating restrictive working practices; if necessary to transfer labour from one industry to another; if earnings were too low to maintain a reasonable standard of living; or if a group of workers had fallen seriously out of line with earnings for similar work.

To make specific recommendations on the basis of this policy, the Government set up a *National Board for Prices and Incomes.* The Prices Review Division of the Board was to investigate prices, and the Incomes Review Division had power to investigate all claims and settlements relating to wages, salaries and other incomes. The Board produced over 150 reports.

There was no statutory authority to enforce its recommendations: reliance was placed on voluntary methods and the power of persuasion and public opinion. However, in late 1965 the Government introduced a compulsory "Early Warning" system, where by it was notified in advance of any intended increase in incomes or in certain prices. As a result, the Government and the Board had time to consider increases before they were put into effect.

(iv) The Prices and Incomes Standstill.

A voluntary incomes policy is very difficult to implement, since it depends on co-operation among Government, workers, and employers; moreover, co-operation among representatives at the top may be undermined by "wage-drift" at the factory level. Thus the annual average of weekly wage-rates rose by 5 percentage points between 1965 and 1966. In fact all of this increase took place in the period before July 1966. Clearly the voluntary incomes policy was meeting with little success.

Therefore, as part of the July measures taken to deal with the balance of payments problem, the Government introduced a "prices and incomes standstill." Increases in prices and incomes were as far as possible to be avoided altogether until the end of 1966. Increases already negotiated but not yet implemented were deferred for 6 months. The first half of 1967 was a period of "severe restraint." Any price increases were carefully examined, and the norm for income increases was zero. Any increase in earnings had to be justified by one of the four conditions for exception, referred to above. To enforce its "freeze" the Government took the unprecedented step of asking Parliament for reserve powers (including penalties for offenders), which were to be used only if the need should arise. For the most part, there was a voluntary observation of the standstill; but from October 1966 the Government found it necessary to exercise its powers of compulsion in a few cases. These powers lapsed in August 1967.

There then followed a year in which there was to be a "nil norm" except where increases in incomes could be justified by one of the four exceptional criteria. The Government could no longer legally enforce its policy, but it did retain the power to delay price and pay increases, Whereas the Government succeeded in slowing down the rise in wages and prices during the year in which it took compulsory powers, in the second half of 1967 weekly wage rates rose at an annual rate of 6 per cent. The advantage gained from the previous restraint was reduced but not entirely lost.

(v) Incomes Policy after Devaluation.

Incomes policy was made both more difficult and more important by the devaluation of the pound: more difficult in that devaluation involved a cut in the standard of living, and more important in that it was important that the trading benefit from devaluation should not be neutralised by inflation.

In April 1968 the Government published a White Paper outlining its policy for the period until the end of 1969. Wage increases had still to be justified by the four criteria, and there was a "ceiling" to increases in income of 3½ per cent per annum except for "productivity agreements" and low-paid workers. Price increases were permitted only as a result of unavoidable increases in cost per unit of output, and price reductions were required when these fell. The Government intended to rely on the voluntary cooperation of unions and employers over pay; but it decided to lengthen its delaying powers for pay and price increases up to 12 months, and take powers to enforce price reductions recommended by the Board.

Between November 1967 and November 1968 the retail price index rose by about 5·2 per cent, mainly due to the effect of devaluation on import prices. In the face of this rise in the cost of living the incomes policy met with firm resistance. In practice the ceiling of 3½ per cent per annum rapidly became the normal increase. In the first year after devaluation average earnings rose by 7·5 per cent. Workers were thus able to protect themselves against price inflation and to increase slightly their real incomes.

During 1969 the process of wage and price inflation accelerated. In December the Government published a White Paper on its incomes

policy for the period after 1969. It laid down a norm for wage increases of 2·5 to 4·5 per cent per annum: increases were to exceed the upper limit only in exceptional circumstances. Comparisons with other workers were not to be used, except in the case of public servants (e.g., teachers and nurses) whose productivity could not easily be measured. The Government's powers to delay the implementation of proposed wage and price increases were reduced. However, the incomes policy laid down in the White Paper was tempered by the imminence of a General Election and the recent cost of living increases; and it did not prevent a "wage explosion" occurring in 1970.

(vi) Conservative Policy.

On taking office in June 1970 the Conservative Government eschewed its predecessor's approach to incomes policy and disbanded the National Board for Prices and Incomes. To curb the inflation it maintained the economy in recession and squeezed company liquidity, hoping in this way to weaken wage pressures and strengthen the resistances of employers. In addition it attempted to resist demands for wage increases in the public sector, at the cost of prolonging strikes, e.g., in electricity supply, postal services and coal mining. In the former two cases it met with some success; in the case of the coal miners' strike early in 1972 the Government was unable to enforce its policy. In any event this form of incomes policy—like the "pay pause" of 1961—was both partial and discriminatory. The Government also intervened to curb price rises in the nationalised industries, e.g., postal charges and steel prices. The main initiative on prices came from the Confederation of British Industry (CBI): in July 1971, it asked its members to avoid price increases over the next twelve months or to limit them to 5 per cent or less in unavoidable increases. Over 170 leading British companies agreed to comply.

The Government measures were by no means a sure remedy for the inflation spiral. Moreover, even its apparent strategy of deterring wage demands by maintaining high unemployment was dropped in the reflationary budget of 1972. The Government appeared to be placing its faith in its Industrial Relations Act to solve the problem of wage inflation in the long run.

(vii) The Pay and Price Standstill.

In 1972 wage demands became more difficult to contain because of the increase in the cost-of-living resulting from the effective devaluation of the pound in June and the rise in world food prices during the year. There was a marked increase in the number and seriousness of strikes (see **G21**). The principal cause was a sharp rise in disagreements over pay claims. In the six months between the first and third quarters of 1972 average weekly earnings rose by no less than 7 per cent. It was inevitable that the Government would intervene. The expectation of an impending freeze encouraged further wage and price increases, especially after the CBI's period of voluntary restraint had elapsed.

The Government first tried to achieve a tri-partite voluntary agreement with the CBI and the TUC. After this attempt had failed, in November the Conservative Government reversed its previous policy on inflation and introduced a statutory Prices and Pay standstill. In effect there was a standstill on all prices of goods and services other than imports and fresh foods, a standstill on rents, on dividends, and on all wages and salaries including those previously negotiated but not yet in operation. Offenders were liable to be fined.

(viii) The Price Commission and the Pay Board.

In early 1973 the Government formulated its policy for after the standstill in a series of documents, culminating in a Price and Pay Code. Two new agencies—a *Price Commission* and a *Pay Board*—were established to regulate prices, dividends, rent, and pay in accordance with the Price and Pay Code.

In Stage Two of the policy—lasting from the end of the pay standstill on 31 March until the autumn—the following criteria on pay applied. The total annual pay increase for any group of employees should not exceed £1 a week plus 4 per cent of the current pay bill excluding overtime. There was flexibility for negotiation of increases within a group: emphasis was to be on the lower paid and the maximum allowable increase was £250 a year. Exceptions to the limit were made for, *e.g.*, movement towards equal pay between the sexes, personal increments and promotion, and some improved pension benefits. The Pay Board had to be notified of all settlements involving less than 1,000 employees but settlements involving more than 1,000 employees required its prior approval. It became an offence to strike or threaten to strike to force an employer to contravene an order of the Pay Board.

Prices in Stage Two could be increased only to take account of *allowable* cost increases, and were to reflect only the percentage increases in these costs per unit of output since 1 October 1972. Moreover to allow for productivity growth, firms were permitted to pass on as price increases only a fraction of the increase in the wage costs allowed by the Code. Prices were also limited by the requirement that net profit margins should not exceed the average percentage level of the best two of the last five years. Exceptions were made for companies which could show that without higher profits their investment would be held back. Large firms had to give prior notice of price increases to the Price Commission, medium sized firms had to report regularly on prices, and small firms had to keep price records. Imports, fresh foods, auctioned goods, secondhand goods and interest charges were among the exemptions from the controls. Dividends could not be raised by more than 5 per cent over the previous year.

One of the problems facing the policy was the continued sharp rise in world food prices after the standstill was declared. This made public acceptance of the Government policy more difficult to achieve.

(ix) Stage Three.

Stage Three of the counter-inflation policy was introduced in October 1973. Price controls were similar to those under Stage Two. Wage increases negotiated for any group of workers were statutorily limited to an average of either £2·25 a week per head, or if preferred, 7 per cent per head, with a limit of £350 a year on the amount to be received by any one individual. However, further increases were permitted beyond these limits, to deal with certain specific matters: changes in pay structures, better use of manpower, efficiency schemes, "unsocial" hours, and progress towards equal pay for women. A novel aspect of the pay policy was the *threshold agreement* to safeguard against increases in the cost of living. It was possible for wage negotiators to bargain for a pay increase of up to 40p a week, payable if the retail price index reached 7 per cent above its level at the beginning of Stage Three, with up to another 40p a week for each percentage point it rose thereafter until the end of Stage Three in November 1974. In Britain many people claimed that these agreements were responsible for a large part of the wage and price inflation of 1974. Indeed in a purely statistical sense this was correct. The threshold was triggered eleven times, which meant an extra £4.40 per week for anyone under the scheme. It was estimated that 10 million workers were covered by such arrangements by October 1974. The idea behind thresholds was that unions, when negotiating wage increases, might have unduly pessimistic expectations about inflation. By introducing automatic compensation, such expectations would be taken out of the bargaining situation. Without this compensation, it might be argued, many groups would have refused to settle under Stage Three terms, and their pay increases would have been just as large or even larger than the ones which they actually obtained.

(x) The Miners' Strike.

An increasing number of settlements were made under the Stage Three provisions; the number of workers covered rising to over 6 million by the end of February 1974. The National Union of Mineworkers, however, feeling strongly that their relative pay had fallen and recognising their new bargaining powers resulting from the oil crisis, refused to settle under Stage Three. A national overtime ban was begun in November which in January 1974 became a national strike. In November the Government declared a State of Emergency and in January introduced a three-day week for industry in order to conserve coal and electricity (which depended on coal). It was unwilling to waive the Stage Three legislation in the miners' case, despite a declaration by the Trade Union Congress that its member unions would not invoke a settlement of the miners' dispute in support of their own claims. The Government referred the NUM claim to the Pay Board, for the Board to determine whether the miners constituted a special case which justified a further increase in their relative pay. The Government then called a General Election. The Pay Board reported just after the election, and recommended that an additional increase be paid, on the grounds that the long-run contraction of the industry would in future be reversed and that higher relative pay would be necessary to recruit and retain sufficient mineworkers. The incoming Labour Government settled with the miners on terms very similar to those recommended by the Pay Board.

(xi) The Social Contract.

The Labour Party came to power pledged to deal firmly with prices but to abandon statutory wage controls. It took early action on house rents and food prices, by means of controls and subsidies. The Pay Board was abolished and the policy of compulsory wage restraint thus finally ended in July 1974. The Price Code and the Price Commission were, however, retained.

During the February 1974 general election campaign an agreement between the TUC and the Labour Party was announced. This became known as the *social contract*, and formed the backbone of the Labour Government's attempts to stem wage inflation. The hope was that, in return for the repeal of the Industrial Relations Act, the introduction of a measure of industrial democracy and various other concessions, the TUC would be able to persuade its members to co-operate in a programme of voluntary wage restraint. In this way it was hoped to avoid the strains caused by formal incomes policies, which have always appeared to trade unionists to leave them without any role to play. Under a voluntary system they could still do their job—that is bargain about wage rates. The terms of the contract were that there should be a twelve-month interval between wage settlements; and that negotiated increases should be confined either to compensating for price increases since the last settlement, or for anticipated future price increases before the next settlement. It is hardly surprising that most negotiators took the latter option. An attempt by the TUC to exclude this had failed.

(xii) Voluntary Restraint.

By early 1975 it was evident that this policy had failed. Some wage settlements were of the order of 30 per cent. In July 1975 the Government announced that there would be a limit of £6 per week on pay increases, £6 representing 10% of average earnings. There were to be no exceptions to this, and those earning more than £8,500 a year were to get nothing at all. The Government had the prior agreement of the TUC, which agreed to try to persuade its members to comply. The policy was voluntary to the extent that there were no legal sanctions against individual unions, but in another sense there were very powerful sanctions. These operated through the Price Code. No firms could pass on in price rises any part of a pay settlement above the limit.

The £6 limit was due to lapse in July 1976, and the April 1976 Budget gave the first indications of a possible successor. The Chancellor announced that he would make cuts in the effective amount of tax paid by private individuals, if he could secure trade union agreement to a second year of pay restraint. This would allow an increase in take-home pay with the employers bearing less than half the cost. Therefore prices would rise more slowly and our competitive position deteriorate move slowly than if the whole increase had been achieved by putting up money wages. There were, however, those who felt that the integrity of

Parliament was threatened by making taxation decisions conditional on trade union agreement. Be that as it may, agreement was reached with the TUC. From August 1976 more severe limits on pay operated than under the £6 limit. For those earning less than £50 a week, wage increases were limited to £2.50; for those earning between £50 and £80 the limit was 5 per cent, whilst those earning more than £80 could get no more than a £4 per week increase. Average earnings in August were about £75 per week, and the implied overall limit was about 4½ per cent.

There is no doubt that the pay policy was successful in holding down earnings. During the £6 policy, earnings rose by 14 per cent—a dramatic fall from the near- 30 per cent rise in the previous year. An all-round increase of £6 would have meant a 10 per cent rise. Another 2 per cent can be explained by the implementation of agreements made before August 1975, by moves towards equal pay, and by increased overtime earnings. This leaves only 2 per cent unaccounted for. Some of this "slippage" was no doubt evasion of the limits. There is no reason to think that there was any greater slippage from the 4½ per cent policy, and during the year of its operation (until August 1977) earnings rose by only 9 per cent. It is unclear whether the success of the policy was due as much to the threat of Price Code sanctions and to the recession in the economy as to the voluntary co-operation of the trade unions.

The 4½ per cent policy was due to lapse at the end of July 1977, and in the March 1977 Budget the Chancellor again offered the prospect of tax cuts if trade union agreement to a new stage could be reached. In the event the TUC agreed to continue its support for the 12-month rule, whereby no union should attempt more than one settlement in a year. It could not, however, agree to a limit of a specific amount. In return the Government gave a modest reduction in income tax, and introduced a "voluntary" policy of its own. This new Stage III policy was to last until the end of July 1978 and aimed for a national earnings increase of no more than 10 per cent during this time. No specific limit was to be put on individual negotiations, but the Government reserved the right to impose sanctions on firms whose settlements appeared inconsistent with the national target. These sanctions might be exercised through the Price Commission's controls on profit margins (though it was expected that these would lapse in July 1978), through public purchasing policy and the placing of contracts, and through consideration of industrial assistance. The Government did stress, however, the possibility that larger increases could be obtained by self-financing productivity deals.

By the spring of 1978 it seemed that earnings increases during this stage of policy would turn out to be as high as 14 per cent. The Government was reasonably successful in holding the public sector down to near 10 per cent, though there were some costly productivity deals, particularly in coal mining. But the main problem was in the private sector. Though the majority of wage-rate increases were at about 10 per cent, earnings drift together with consolidation of the previous two years' increases in rates worked out for overtime, piece rates or shiftwork were pushing earnings increases way above 10 per cent. In addition, productivity deals were incorporated in about 30 per cent of agreements, in each case adding between 6 per cent and 10 per cent to pay. It is unclear how many of these deals involved genuine cost saving, or how sanctions discouraged false deals of this sort.

In the early summer the Government announced its plans for the 1978–79 pay round. Its objective was to limit the growth in national earnings to around 5 per cent, and it was soon clear that its tactics were very similar to those it had employed in support of its 10 per cent target during the 1977–78 pay round: seeking to keep as many groups of workers as possible to settlements at or very near to the target figure by direct negotiations in the public sector and by the renewed threat of sanctions in the private sector; allowing additional increases for self-financing productivity deals; and using promises of additional increases in subsequent pay rounds in order to induce groups regarding themselves as "special cases" to settle for 5 per cent in the current round.

(xiii) Conflict with the Unions.

A serious problem, however, was the TUC's hostility to the policy. Although the TUC had not supported the Government's 10 per cent target of the previous year, it had in practice helped the Government by putting pressure on unions to settle for increases which were not too obviously out of line with its policy. This time the TUC was not prepared to do this. Its reluctance stemmed partly from the opposition of some union leaders to continued pay controls but much more from the view that even if official union policy was to observe the 5 per cent guide-lines, the frustration apparently felt by many workers after three years of pay controls would lead to widespread unofficial strikes which would undermine union leaders' authority.

The Government therefore had to enforce its policy without TUC help. In the early autumn of 1978 it seemed to be having some success as several groups settled for not much more than the limit, but the policy was severely undermined by a two-month strike at Ford's which ended with a settlement of around 17 per cent. Subsequently Parliament refused to support the Government's proposed use of sanctions against Ford and other firms breaching the guidelines, so that the Government was left without any effective incomes policy in the private sector. As a result other groups of workers in the private sector felt free to ignore the guidelines: the most spectacular breach of the policy was an increase of over 20 per cent for road haulage drivers after a disruptive strike in January 1979.

Such settlements in the private sector naturally made public sector workers unwilling to accept 5 per cent increases. The Government therefore offered 9 per cent more to most groups. However, this did not satisfy some of the lower-paid, public sector employees, particularly ambulance drivers and manual workers in hospitals and local authorities. They mounted a series of strikes, some of which—withdrawal of emergency ambulance services and disruption of hospitals—caused widespread concern and led to a growing public debate about the extent and the use of trade union power.

To deal with these problems the Government set up a new body, the Comparability Commission, to review the pay of those public sector workers who claimed that they had fallen behind comparable groups in the private sector: health and local authority workers were among the first to have their pay referred to the Commission.

(xiv) Reluctant Union Acquiescence.

The new Conservative Government, which took office in May 1979, allowed the work of the Comparability Commission to continue until the end of 1980. Otherwise it eschewed a formal incomes policy. Its policy to control earnings inflation consisted of two strands. The first was to use cash limits in the public sector and a tight monetary policy in the private. This might moderate settlements. If it did not, it was argued, it would at least make unions aware that high settlements had an unemployment cost. The second strand of policy was to reform the structure of bargaining, so as to redistribute the balance of power between union and employer. By the early autumn of 1980, the Government had moved in the direction of declaring specific limits in the public sector. Whilst they were managing to keep their settlements low in public services, they were less successful in nationalised industries. It was certainly hard to argue that pay inflation in the public sector as a whole was noticeably less than in the recession-hit private sector.

There was a muted union reaction to this policy of direct control in public sector jobs and through tight money in the private sector. Though 1979 saw the largest number of working days lost through strikes in any year since 1926, by early 1981 working days lost, like the number of stoppages, were at a very low level, and thereafter on both measures, industrial strife remained very low. By early 1982 the Government's policies were having some measure of success. In the nationalised industries even the miners were held to just over 9 per cent. In the civil service, the government launched a sustained attack on automatic comparability-based pay determination, arguing that market forces should play a role. Thus grades—like computer staff—for whom demand was high were offered greater pay increases than others, whilst new entrants—of whom there was excess supply—were offered no pay increases at all. The Megaw Committee, the Government hoped, would permanently revise methods of pay determination in the Civil Service. In the weaker tax-dependent sections of the public sector—*e.g.* teachers—the Government was ruthless in enforcing very low pay settlements. Meanwhile the recession kept settlements in the private sector at small levels. Through 1982 and into 1983 there was a further gradual reduction in pay inflation. In 1984 the policy was under some—albeit not serious—threat. There was evidence that the Government was finding it more difficult to hold the line in the public sector—a number of comparability deals were threatening. In the private sector, better economic fortunes were starting to result in some pay pressures. 1985 saw a continuation of these tensions in the public sector. Apart from the miners' strike, the Government faced severe difficulties from the civil servants and teachers. Yet, though it failed to hold public sector pay down to the 3 per cent cash limit, it was still managing to impose significantly lower settlements than in the private sector.

(xv) Making the Labour Market Work.

Incomes policies are often criticised on two grounds. The first is that, at best, they work for only a short time. The second is that they cause distortions in relative pay and prices. Hindsight might tell us that their success is no more short-run than is the impact of savage budgetary policies. It might also tell us that whatever allocative inefficiencies are involved, such inefficiencies are minor when compared with the vast waste of resources and personal anguish caused by very high levels of unemployment.

The Conservative Government seemed to believe that structural reform of the labour market was the only real alternative to incomes policies of the conventional kind. If there were features of the labour market which tended to produce infla-

tionary pressures, better, it was argued, to root these out at source rather than tinker with them as an incomes policy would do. Thus the emphasis on trade union reform and on the recession producing permanent changes in attitudes. This concern also explains the emphasis on reducing the real value of social security benefits as a percentage of income in work. Thereby people would have a greater incentive to work and to demand reasonable wage settlements. This approach was confirmed in the 1985 White Paper, *The Challenge to the Nation.* Three desiderata were mentioned: individuals pricing themselves into jobs; flexibility in the face of change; freedom from regulation. In this spirit, the Government reformed Wages Councils in 1986, in particular totally removing juveniles from their orbit. It also further weakened employment protection legislation. Whether this "strategy" will work or not is a vital, but undecided, question. Certainly the UK's failure to improve more significantly its relative unit labour cost performance casts some shadows of doubt. Yet many who are sceptical, now accept that our labour market problems are so deep-seated as to require structural action. They do not regard conventional incomes policies as sufficient. Rather they are seeking more permanent policies of this kind. Amongst an array of suggestions are three which have received much attention. The first is a tax-based incomes policy, which imposes, as part of the tax system, penalties on companies who pay over a declared maximum. The second involves various ideas of compulsory arbitration, in the hope that such arbitration can be arranged to moderate pay outcomes. The third, and most radical, involves changing the system of pay, such that a significant component takes the form of a profit share. The hope is that this would make it easier to obtain pay reductions in a recession, and moderate individual pay increases as the economy expands. All these schemes are untested in Britain, and they have many faults. But further productive thought along these lines is essential, if any Government is going to be able to safely run the economy at higher levels of demand.

V.   SPECIAL TOPICS

THE SOUTH AFRICAN
SANCTIONS DEBATE

The Background.

Because of the increased and continuing protest among blacks in South Africa, the tide of world opinion turned against its government in 1985. There were calls for economic sanctions against South Africa as a means of forcing it to change its policies or its government. The unrest is unlikely to die down rapidly, and the issue of sanctions promises to remain a live one. Here we discuss the case for and against a policy of economic sanctions.

The South African Economy.

South Africa, with a GNP per capita in 1983 of $2,500, falls squarely into the group of some 21 countries which the World Bank categorises as "upper middle income developing countries". The group also includes, for instance, Algeria, Argentina, Brazil, Iran, South Korea and Mexico. Its growth of income per capita, at 2·1 per cent per annum over the period 1960–82, is lower than that of the group (4·1 per cent), partly because the apartheid policies retarded the development of skills and partly because its rate of population growth (2·6 per cent per annum and rising) was somewhat higher than that of the group (2·4 per cent and falling). In its structure of production, with agriculture representing 7 per cent of GDP (but a third of the labour force) and manufacturing 23 per cent in 1981, South Africa is representative of the group. More than most of these countries, however, South Africa is "resource-rich", and has a large mining sector, producing gold, diamonds, uranium, coal, *etc.*

The problem of creating incomes and employment for its rapidly growing labour force is one which would face any South African government, whatever its complexion, for years to come. To solve this

problem, a high rate of capital accumulation is needed. The countries in this relatively successful and dynamic group generally have high saving and investment ratios, but South Africa's is among the highest (investing 29 per cent of GDP in 1981). Capital accumulation is assisted by the large proportion of GDP accruing as profits, and by foreign capital inflows.

The Structure of Trade.

In 1980 gold, then at a high price, comprised 60 per cent of the value of South African exports, diamonds 6 per cent, other minerals 12 per cent, agricultural products 8 per cent, and manufactures—largely basic goods like iron and steel—14 per cent. Setting aside gold, South Africa's main customers were the United States (15 per cent of exports), followed in order by West Germany, the United Kingdom and Japan. The EEC as a whole took almost half of total exports, and the developing countries 20 per cent; this included 10 per cent to African countries, mainly those in the South African sphere of influence.

Its heavy dependence on gold and other minerals makes South Africa vulnerable to fluctuations in the world price of one or two commodities. The sharp fall in the price of gold in the 1980s (the market price averaged $590 per ounce in 1980 and was $340 in mid-1986) contributed to the onset of South Africa's worst economic recession since the 1930s.

South Africa imports mainly industrial supplies (a third of recorded imports in 1980) machinery (another third), transport equipment (20 per cent), and only a small amount of final consumer goods (10 per cent). Oil is imported but, because of its strategic importance, oil imports are kept a state secret. South Africa's main suppliers were the United States, with 18 per cent of the market, the United Kingdom and Japan, but the EEC as a group supplied over half of South African imports.

The Efficacy of Sanctions in General.

The rhetoric accompanying economic sanctions asserts confident belief in their efficacy. Yet the various attempts at using economic sanctions against countries have not been noteworthy for their success in bringing about their declared objectives. Although economic sanctions *can* have effects, often they are unforeseen and unintended.

These points can be illustrated even by reference to existing international sanctions against South Africa. There is a United Nations embargo on the supply of military equipment and spares to South Africa. If the objective was not only to express diplomatic disapproval but also to weaken South Africa militarily, the embargo has not been effective. There are countries or dealers willing to engage in clandestine trade. The main consequence of the ban is that South Africa has developed its own armaments industry and is now more self-reliant and an exporter of military equipment. South Africa's "Achilles' heel" is its lack of oil resources. Yet an OPEC boycott on the supply of oil to South Africa, imposed over a decade ago, has been rendered ineffective through profitable secret trade, the building up of a large oil stock in disused coal mines, and the rapid expansion in production of oil from coal, coal being abundant in South Africa.

Partial sanctions of this sort are of course different from the mandatory, universal and comprehensive sanctions for which many opponents of apartheid continue to press. Such sanctions were attempted by the UN against Rhodesia after UDI in 1965. However, South Africa and Zambia continued to trade with Rhodesia, and many other countries made the right gestures but turned a blind eye. As a result of import substitution, the Rhodesian economy actually prospered in the first decade of UDI, and the government ensured that the costs of sanctions were borne mainly by the black population. Black majority rule, when it came, was not primarily the result of the sanctions policy.

The record is therefore not promising for a successful sanctions policy. It is true that Rhodesia had a larger neighbour—in the form of South Africa—to turn to, whereas South Africa does not. What would sanctions against South Africa achieve?

Unilateral Sanctions Against South Africa.

Some countries—mostly those, such as Sweden, with weak economic relations with South Africa—have already introduced economic sanctions. However, the effect of unilateral sanctions is no more than token. If South Africa cannot trade with one country, it can substitute others. If foreign firms from one country withdraw, others can step in. For instance, some American companies, under pressure from shareholders or fearing chaos, have chosen to get out. Employment in South Africa provided by US companies fell by 20,000 between 1980 and 1985. However, local firms and other multinationals have bought up their investments at bargain prices. West German investment in South Africa grew by 40 per cent, and employment by 20,000, over the same period. Britain is the largest foreign investor in South Africa: over 200 British companies have invested $7 billion in the country, compared with a total foreign investment there of over $20 billion. Although a British withdrawal would do economic harm to South Africa as well as to Britain, it would have greater economic effects if it were part of a comprehensive withdrawal.

Comprehensive Sanctions Against South Africa?

Let us assume that effective universal and comprehensive sanctions can be instituted against South Africa. What would be the economic effects? Trade is very important to the South African economy: exports represented no less than 36 per cent of GDP in 1981. The country benefits greatly from producing minerals for export while importing raw materials which she lacks and technology-intensive machinery and industrial components. The considerable presence of multinational companies in South Africa provides access to technology and managerial skills. A drastic diminution of trade and the withdrawal of multinational companies would be likely to initiate a sharp cut in real income and to result in economic stagnation rather than the

growth of GDP at 4 or 5 per cent per annum which might otherwise be expected.

The economy would not collapse: although there would be transitional problems, South Africa has the resources to move towards a "laager" (*i.e.* siege) economy. But there would be an economic price to pay. Those with political power would wish those without power to pay as much of that price as possible. Thus the South African government would try to shift the burden onto the black community and onto the poorer and dependent neighbouring economies, such as Botswana, Lesotho, Mozambique, Swaziland and Zimbabwe. For instance, as employment in the mines fell, so black migrant workers would be returned to the South African 'homelands' (effectively labour reserves) and to neighbouring countries.

Potential Retaliation.

The prospect of future economic benefits is an important factor in ensuring good behaviour in all economic relationships. Comprehensive sanctions would wipe out such prospects for South Africa. There would be no point in preserving reputation with international banks, and the government could renege on its debt servicing and capital repayments without doing itself future harm. It could also, by means of exchange controls, prevent the withdrawal of capital by foreigners. Termination of technology licensing agreements could be ignored.

A high proportion of OECD imports of certain strategic materials—notably manganese, chromium, silicon and vanadium—emanate from South Africa. A boycott of these commodities could not be sustained for any length of time. The South African government could use the threat of witholding such supplies as a bargaining weapon.

Comprehensive sanctions require strong international co-operation for their enforcement. Profitable incentives could be offered for clandestine trade. If other sanctions experience is taken as a guide, sanctions are likely to weaken and break down with the passage of time.

The Ethics of Sanctions.

South Africa is by no means unique among developing countries in having an authoritarian government, unresponsive to populist demands, and an extremely unequal distribution of income. Indeed, these features are common among the relatively successful developing economies with which South Africa can be grouped. What makes South Africa unique is its degree of institutionalised racial discrimination. Moral abhorrence of this practice is at the heart of the sanctions debate. But if it were the case that blacks would suffer for a long period should comprehensive sanctions be introduced, and suffer more than whites, the ethical issues would be clouded.

Will Economic Growth Destroy Apartheid?

There is a view, common among liberal-minded South Africans and business lobbies, that economic growth and prosperity will itself destroy apartheid. The argument is that economic growth improves the economic position of blacks and consequently their bargaining power. Economic growth requires that government expands black education. With rapid growth, blacks acquire more vocational skills and are less easily replaceable by employers. As their pay improves, so they can afford to organise in trade unions and go on strike. As black incomes rise, so their expectations rise as well. In the period 1979–1984, average black wages increased in real terms by 4·3 per cent per annum, nearly double the rate of increase for whites. Yet black discontent appears generally to have grown in the 1980s, despite greater prosperity for many, because aspirations have risen more rapidly than achievements. The relationship is a complicated one, however, because the rising unemployment in the black townships, which accompanied economic recession, also fomented insurgency.

The changes which stem from economic growth do not pose a revolutionary threat to the existing order, but they involve a gradual movement towards racial power-sharing. If sanctions were to slow down economic growth, they would retard this process by which blacks acquire more political say. That is an argument which has been used against sanctions. However, it is unlikely to persuade those who regard the recent pace of reform as being far too slow.

Political Consequences of Economic Sanctions.

If comprehensive sanctions were imposed, would the increased hardship and unemployment of blacks promote instability and insurrection in South Africa, and hence secure the violent overthrow of the existing order? Would sanctions put pressure on the government and the electorate to speed up the process of relatively non-violent reform? We cannot be sure that either of these objectives would be achieved, or precluded, by a policy of comprehensive sanctions.

On the one hand, if the "price" that the electorate has to pay for apartheid is increased, that should hasten its demise. On the other hand, in the face of a revolutionary threat the electorate may value a return to old-style repressive apartheid more highly than it does economic prosperity. Universally applied but selective sanctions of particular sorts, imposing recognised costs but not constituting a general threat, might be more effective than comprehensive sanctions in eliciting the reformist rather than the repressive response.

Forecasting the future of South Africa involves assigning probabilities to various possible outcomes. Consider three such outcomes: relatively non-violent reform and power-sharing, violent and revolutionary change leading to black rule, and reversion to old-style white domination. Given present policies the country appears to be on a tardy course towards the reformist outcome. However, the pace of reform permitted by White politics may prove too tardy to prevent escalating violence and revolutionary change. The balance of internal power is such that the government is not afraid of revolution in the foreseeable future. For instance, even if some townships become ungovernable "no go" areas, this will not pose a serious threat to the South African state. It is therefore unlikely that comprehensive sanctions will themselves precipitate cataclysmic change. The government may well perceive the greater danger to emanate from forces to its right: it is this threat which appears to determine the "two steps forward—one step back" pace of reform.

It is nevertheless arguable that economic stagnation over a prolonged period, as opposed to continued economic growth, would have a polarising effect. In other words, it would raise somewhat the probability that at the end of that period there would be majority rule after violent change and also the probability that there would be continued white domination, and lower somewhat the probability of relatively non-violent reform and power-sharing.

The imposition of sanctions involves an act of faith. This faith may be born of moral convictions or political necessities, but not of economic and political certainties.

Recent Developments.

Spurred by heightened and continuing black protest and township violence during 1985, a number of important governments each decided to introduce limited economic sanctions against South Africa, including France, Canada, Australia and Japan. The sanctions were generally mild, varying in severity from the French case (which included a ban on new investment) to gestures of disapproval from the United States, Britain and the EEC. These countries have preferred to use their influence as major investors by requiring their nationals operating in South Africa to observe codes of good employment practice. At the Commonwealth Conference in October, Britain stood out against the imposition by the Commonwealth of sanctions other than symbols.

The violence seen on television screens, the talk of sanctions and disappointed expectations of reform combined in mid-1985 to produce a capital flight from South Africa, a calling in of loans by international banks, and the collapse of the rand. Whereas the rand had averaged $1·34 in 1980, it was worth $0·38 in October 1985. The government responded by reintroducing exchange controls to stop the drain of funds, and refusing to meet its considerable ($14 billion) short term debt repayment obligations. Political factors had become dominant in the economy for the foreseeable future.

The Eminent Persons Group.

As a result of the Commonwealth Conference a Group of Eminent Persons (EPG) was established to have discussions with the contenders in South Africa and to report back. *Mission to South Africa. The Commonwealth Report* was published in June 1986. The EPG concluded that the South African government was not willing to end apartheid and to negotiate a transfer of power to black rule. It noted that the South African government was itself worried about the adoption of effective economic sanctions. The EPG considered that the absence of such measures deterred change and that concerted measures by the Commonwealth might avert a bloodbath.

A criticism made of the report was that it did not explain why and how the economic isolation of South Africa would cause its government to yield power and avoid confrontation rather than to assert its power and attempt to repress opposition. Nevertheless, the report made it more likely that the Commonwealth countries would agree to further economic sanctions against South Africa. It was important that these sanctions should be carefully chosen to elicit a reformist rather than a repressive response.

THE CHANNEL TUNNEL PROPOSALS

The announcement in January 1986 of the intention by Britain and France to construct a 31-mile tunnel under the Channel between Cheriton, Kent and Frethun in northern France has brought the idea of a Channel Tunnel very close to realisation. According to the plans by 1993 a direct "fixed link" will be available for travellers to and from the continent.

The Historical Background.

The idea of a Channel Tunnel has captured the imagination of the public for nearly two hundred years. Allegedly it was Napoleon who first mooted the idea of a tunnel linking Britain with mainland Europe. Later in the nineteenth century some excavation work was started near Dover although serious consideration of the project has had to wait until the late twentieth century. By 1974 the growth in Britain's trade with Europe following our entry into the EEC in 1973, together with increasing tourist travel across the Channel and improvements in technology which made the project feasible, encouraged the Wilson Government to embark upon a publicly financed construction of a tunnel. However work was very quickly abandoned in the wake of protests from environmentalists and, more tellingly, the strain created on government finances.

In the 1980s plans for a cross channel fixed link began to surface again although, after the experiences of 1974, it was stated clearly that the project would have to be entirely financed from private capital. The British and French Governments called for the submission of plans for a fixed link by November 1985, stating that the selection of the winning proposal would be made in January 1986. The rapidity of the decision-making process raised many eyebrows amongst engineers who questioned whether three months was long enough for a proper technical appraisal of the plans submitted. However political factors motivated a quick decision with the French Government aware of the public relations potential of an announcement prior to the French General Election in March 1986 and with the British Government anxious for the job-creating effects of construction to be evident before the next General Election in this country.

Four serious candidates for a fixed link were submitted, with mixtures of financial backers and ideas about how best to join Britain to Europe.

On 8 January 1986 in the Northern French town of Lille, President Mitterrand and Margaret Thatcher announced that the Channel Tunnel Group, together with their French partners, France-Manche had been selected to provide the fixed link. The decision was, at least on Britain's part, a partial compromise since the Government was wary about having a rail-only link that could be susceptible to strike action by trades unions. However a road link posed certain problems—particularly the question of whether technology was sufficiently advanced to deal with the exhaust fumes emitted by traffic driving under the Channel. Doubts were also expressed about the ability of Eurobridge and Euroroute to finance their expensive schemes whilst many considered that Channel Expressway had underestimated the cost of their proposals. Thus technological and financial prudence, together with a certain amount of pressure from the French who were keen to have a rail link which would harness their advanced rail system, led to Britain agreeing to select the most feasible, if least imaginative, proposals of the Channel Tunnel Group. To placate the road lobby it was also announced that proposals for a road link would hopefully be submitted by the year 2000, although construction of this second fixed link will be unlikely to commence until the next century. However, those favouring a road link saw the chosen alternative as a poor compromise.

The Detailed Proposals.

Channel Tunnel Group's (CTG) proposals actually involve the construction of three tunnels: an ordinary rail tunnel enabling the trip from London to Paris to be done in three hours; a "shuttle" tunnel for special trains to convey vehicles under the Channel at 100 m.p.h. in thirty minutes; and a service tunnel running between the other two. The tunnels would be 31 miles in length with 23 miles being underneath the Channel, 120 feet beneath the sea bed. Construction will start in 1987 with completion planned for 1993. Despite the problems that will always arise from constructing tunnels of this length, technicians have spoken confidently about the mining conditions they expect under the Channel. The chalk rock through which the tunnel will be bored provides an ideal medium since it can be readily extracted.

It is the shuttle element of the fixed link which has attracted most attention since it is the substitute for the road links proposed for vehicles in the unsuccessful schemes and since it will provide direct competition with the ferry and hovercraft services currently provided for those taking vehicles into Europe. The special drive-on double decker shuttle trains are planned for every three minutes at peak periods and will be able to convey 4,000 vehicles under the Channel every hour. Critics have argued that this provides little more than the ferry service currently available over the water and that, with the journey time estimated at 30 minutes, the trip will be no faster than that provided by hovercrafts. Despite the tunnel's novelty factor, that will inevitably attract demand, and its lack of vulnerability to adverse weather conditions the cross channel ferry companies confidently expect to be able to compete with CTG for the vehicles trade. Nevertheless CTG expects to attract nearly half of the estimated 67 million cross channel travellers when it opens the tunnels in 1993 (currently around 50 million cross channel trips are made per year).

The capital cost of CTG's proposals are estimated at £2·6bn consisting of £2·3bn for construction and over £200 million for land acquisition, insurances and marketing. However allowances for interest and contingencies (including delays in construction) make the likely final bill around £5·3bn. To meet these costs equity of up to £1bn will be raised in Britain and overseas and £4·3bn will be raised in development loans. To enable these costs to be recouped and to offer financial backers an acceptable return on their investments CTG will have exclusive rights to operate the fixed link until 2020 and would charge prices for tunnel users at around 10 per cent below ferry fares. Nevertheless the very real prospect of a price war between the ferry services and CTG threatens to reduce the profits of both to the obvious advantage of the traveller when the fixed link becomes a reality.

The Economic Consequences.

CTG's scheme will have a tremendous impact on the local economies around the tunnel's termini and upon the national economies of Britain and France. CTG and France-Manche plan to spend £700m in each country on materials and equipment generating 60,000 jobs. It is estimated that the actual construction will create some 5,000 jobs during the seven year tunnelling period and 5,500 long term jobs will be created at the British Terminus at Cheriton. British Rail plans to spend up to £200m on new station facilities at Waterloo and Ashford and in tracks and signalling equipment. It will also spend another £200m as its half share of a fleet of 40 trains for passenger services to and from the continent. New motorway links will be built between the tunnel and the M20 which joins with the M25, London's orbital motorway. Besides the jobs created directly by the tunnel's construction and operation, including those jobs emerging in Customs and Excise and the customer services and duty free facilities within the tunnels, other jobs will be created indirectly by the spending power of the tunnel's employees. Such spending and job creation will provide a much needed fillip to British industry and employment levels. Indeed the announcement of the selection of CTG's proposals came only two weeks before the announcement of record unemployment levels in Britain of 3·4 million in January 1986. The faster travel to and from Europe and the technologies that will have to be developed in the construction of the tunnel will also provide spin off economic benefits to Britain and France.

There is though a debit side to the tunnel's economic effects. Jobs will certainly be lost in the ferry termini and the local economies in and around Dover and Calais could be devastated since, in each case, the location of the tunnel's termini will mean that cross channel traffic will pass them by. Jobs could also be lost in other channel ports along the south coast with holiday and commercial traffic being drawn to the fixed link route to the continent. The National Union of Seamen are predicting that the fixed link will lead to the loss of 5,000 British seamen's jobs. In addition jobs could be lost in the air and the shipbuilding industries if the fixed link becomes very popular. These forecasts are backed up by the Government's White Paper on the Channel Tunnel published in February 1986. It stated that whilst around 10,000 long term jobs would be created by the tunnel, some 5,600 ferry jobs would be likely to disappear by 1993 along with some 1,600 jobs in Dover. In the longer term economic disruption could envelop Kent and Northern France when the fixed link is completed since, unless there is an immediate move to start construction of a road link, construction workers and employees in the supplying industries will be laid off. This could create particular problems in the construction areas with sig-

Channel Tunnel Schemes.

Name	Cost	Construction	Main UK Backers
Channel Tunnel Group and France-Manche	£2·6bn	twin-bore rail tunnel (with shuttle service for vehicles)	Midland Bank, Costain Granada Group, Tarmac Balfour Beatty, Wimpey Taylor Woodrow, and National Westminster Bank.
Channel Expressway	£2·5bn	twin-bore motorway tunnel, with separate twin-rail tunnel	James Sherwood of Sea Containers, Credit du Nord and First National Bank of Boston.
Euro Route	£5·6bn	bridges and tunnel (for mid Channel) system for road traffic, plus two separate rail tunnels.	Trafalgar House, British Steel, British Telecom, British Shipbuilders, Barclays Bank.
Eurobridge Studies	£5·9bn	Motorway road bridge	Laing, Brown and Root, ICI Fibres.

nificant structural unemployment. It is also argued that during the construction period tourism in Kent will be discouraged with consequent job and income losses.

The economic boost given by the construction of the fixed link is wholly consistent with regional policy in France. Northern France is a depressed area with high unemployment and is already attracting financial aid from the French Government. The decision to build the tunnel has been followed by the announcement of a large regional development programme in the Nord-Par de Calais, Picardy and Normandy areas. It will include a £258m road building scheme, electrification of the railway network and measures to help those districts whose economic future is threatened by the fixed link. The position of Kent is entirely different since it is already a prosperous area of the country with above average incomes and an unemployment rate of 10% compared with the national average of 14%. That this part of Britain will gain so much economically from the fixed link, at least during the construction period, seems iniquitous to many observers who claim that it will sharpen further the economic divisions between the prosperous south-east and the depressed Midlands and North. Certainly land and property prices—with the exception of houses in the immediate vicinity of the terminus—will be pushed upwards. There is, however, nothing that can be done about the regional imbalances created by the fixed link in Britain since the location of the Channel Tunnel is determined by the geographic facts of life rather than what may be desirable in terms of the balanced economic development of the country.

The Environmental Threat.

There is no question that the fixed link will change the environments of Kent and Northern France. Realising the threats to the "Garden of England", environmentalist groups including the Town and Country Planning Association, the Kent Trust for Nature Conservation, the Council for the Protection of Rural England and the Friends of the Earth have started to campaign against the CTG proposals—although they admit that CTG's plans are the least disruptive to the environment of all the schemes submitted for consideration. The environmental implications include the effects on the landscape and wildlife, the disruption during the building period and the impact of the fixed link on travel and settlement patterns in the south-east. The tunnelling will result in the need to dispose of 4 million tons of material and the construction will require vast amounts of aggregate to be taken from areas in Kent. Dungeness, which is a site of scientific and biological interest, has already been mentioned as a possible site for both dumping material and gathering construction aggregate. The fixed link terminus will itself occupy 350 acres with its attendant extensive warehousing facilities, and the road and rail developments will absorb further land in Kent besides attracting a greater flow of tourist and commercial traffic in the longer term. In addition there are fears that the tunnel will more readily enable rabies to enter the country as well as facilitating the easier import and export of dangerous drugs—both of which would adversely affect the quality of life in this country.

With such potential problems and disruption the environmentalists have called for a full Public Inquiry to be held on the fixed link proposals. As a bare minimum, proper planning controls and the control of the pollution and ecological effects of the tunnel have been demanded.

The Government has resisted pressure for a Public Inquiry and has drawn up a Parliamentary Bill to give the fixed link the legislative green light. It has been pointed out that some of the environmental problems, including the rabies threat, had been considered in the evaluation of the various projects submitted for the fixed link in 1985. To deal with local objections in Kent the Government has set up a committee of transport and environment officials and representatives from local authorities and CTG to examine the areas of concern. In the White Paper on the Channel Tunnel the Government recognised the potential problems that could result from the dumping of material extracted during tunnelling and requested that CTG consider the full environmental impact of their plans.

Although major construction projects, including earlier attempts at building the Channel Tunnel itself, have very often met with long delays and cancellation it does seem now that both Britain and France are intent upon the realisation of the fixed link. In Canterbury on 12 February 1986 the Foreign Ministers of Britain and France signed the treaty committing themselves to the Channel Tunnel. Both Governments hope to have completed the required legislation by early 1987 to enable construction to commence in Summer 1987. By the end of the century the Channel Tunnel will be a reality instead of a pipe dream.

THE DECLINE OF BRITISH MANUFACTURING INDUSTRY

The Background.

The publicity surrounding "Industry Year" in 1986 has focussed the public's attention on the demise of many sectors of Britain's industrial sector since the Second World War. The current state of industry, the decline in the share of export markets and the loss of home markets to overseas competition present a picture in sharp contrast to Britain's pre-eminent industrial position last century. when this country was the "workshop of the world", the first industrialised nation and the world's leader in manufactured exports. The decline from this position of world leader has really been occuring gradually since the middle of the last century when Germany and the United States emerged as industrial rivals to Britain. The destabilising impact of two World Wars and the loss of an empire with its relatively secure markets for our goods hastened the process of decline. However the last two decades have seen a crippling slump in output and employment in manufacturing industry in this country and the loss of entire industrial sectors (e.g. motor cycle production) which were once hallmarks of Britain's prowess in innovation and production.

The Debate.

The causes and implications of this decline and the resultant "deindustrialisation" of Britain have been examined and debated in many quarters. The

TABLE 1   *Output and Employment in Manufacturing Industry: Great Britain**

	1973	1975	1979	1981	1984
Employment (1975 = 100)	105	100	95	81	72
Production (1975 = 100)	109	100	105	89	97 (est)

* *Sources*: Economic Trends CSO department of Employment Gazette.

TABLE 2   *Unemployment in Selected Regions**
(Seasonally Adjusted: Excluding school leavers)

	1977 (3rd Quarter)	1979 (3rd Quarter)	1981 (3rd Quarter)	1985 (Oct)	% Growth 1977–1985
South East	4·4	3·5	8·0	9·7	120
West Midlands	5·4	5·1	13·4	15·0	178
North West	6·9	6·5	13·5	15·7	128
North	7·7	7·9	14·6	18·1	135
Great Britain	5·7	5·1	10·9	12·9	126

* *Source*: Economic Trends CSO. Department of Employment Gazette.

TABLE 4   *U.K. trade in manufactured goods*
Ratio of Export Value to Import Value

	1963	1968	1973	1978	1979	1980	1981	1982	1983
World	219	143	115	115	104	112	109	101	89
EEC	164	121	88	83	80	89	81	74	66
USA	98	95	110	94	85	70	76	75	84
Japan	149	107	53	35	33	29	23	21	18

Source: House of Lords Select Committe on Overseas Trade: 238-I, July 1985.

debate came to a head in July 1985 when the Report of the House of Lords Select Committee on Overseas Trade, which examined the plight of manufacturing industry, was published. Noting that Britain's share of world manufacturing production had fallen from 14% in 1964 to 8% in 1983 the Report concluded that, unless the decline of the manufacturing sector was reversed, there would be "a grave threat to the standard of living and to the economic and political stability of the nation".

TABLE 3   *U.K. share of exports of manufactured goods to the eleven main industrial countries.*

	Per cent
1899	33.2
1929	22.9
1950	25.4
1959	17.7
1969	11.2
1979	9.1
1984	7.6

Source: House of Lords Select Committee on Overseas Trade: 238-I, July 1985.

The Evidence of Decline.

Statistical evidence can depict the nature, extent and timing of the decline of Britain's industrial sector.

The impact of this decline has not been spread evenly throughout the country. Regions which had a concentration of industrial activity have clearly been those who have been relatively harder hit by industrial decline—in particular the North and, during the last decade, the West Midlands which has suffered as a result of the contraction in the British motor industry.

The most telling statistics are those which depict the impact of decline in Britain's trade in manufactured goods. These emphasise the degree and the rapidity with which British goods have been squeezed out of both export and domestic markets.

TABLE 5   *Imports as a percentage of the Home Market*

	1978 %	1983 %
Metal Manufacturing	25	31
Manmade Fibres	41	68
Electrical Engineering	31	43
Motor Vehicles	35	51
Textiles	31	41
Leather Goods	34	44
Footwear/clothing	26	34

Source: Department of Trade and Industry

TABLE 6   *Exports as a percentage of Home Demand*

	1978 %	1983 %
Chemicals	54	45
Mechanical Engineering	54	46
Motor Vehicles	39	28
Textiles	25	23
Footwear/clothing	18	15

Source: Department of Trade and Industry.

Hidden within these statistics are stories of extraordinary decline amongst certain industrial sectors including the virtually total demise of the British office machinery and machine tool sectors and the rapid contraction of the car industry, which experienced a halving in the level of production between

1973 and 1982. The statistics provide a gloomy review of recent industrial history and a grim prognosis for the future of manufacturing in this country.

What has caused industrial decline in Britain?

There is no unique explanation for Britain's rapid deindustrialisation. Some analysts have pointed to specific factors like the exchange rate for sterling in the late 1970s, others have taken a longer term view about the causes of decline focussing on such matters as the nature of British education and the social structure of the country. At the heart of all the explanations is a clear observation—in recent decades British goods have become unattractive and uncompetitive in domestic and overseas markets and consequently demand for our goods has fallen and the industrial sector contracted. What are the alternative explanations for this decline in competitiveness and the parallel contraction in Britain's industrial base?

(a) Insufficient Investment

The rate of investment in the manufacturing sector has lagged behind that of our competitors in recent decades.

TABLE 7   *Gross Investment as a percentage of Gross Domestic Product*

	1963	1973	1983
Canada	20·5	22·4	19.4
USA	17·9	19.1	16.9
Japan	31·5	36·4	28.5
Germany	25·6	23·9	20.8
France	22·1	23·8	19.6
UK	16·8	20·8	16.5

Source: House of Lords Select Committee on Overseas Trade: 238-I, July 1985.

The low rate of investment has reflected poor economic expectations, uncertainty about (and changes in) governmental industrial policy, high capital taxation and high interest rates. The consequence of low investment has been limitations in the ability to contain the unit costs of production and hence the price levels of products, as well as an inability to develop quickly the most up to date goods. The result is the loss of markets which in turn reduces the earnings needed to finance further investment. In this manner the interplay between lack of investment and diminishing market shares becomes an increasingly vicious circle.

(b) Government Policy and the Public Sector

Various facets of government policy have been blamed for the decline of industry and many of the arguments here revolve around the growth of the public sector in this country. Between 1958 and 1982 the proportion of Gross Domestic Product accounted for by the public sector rose from 28% to 46%, in the wake of the expansion of social security, public services and education expenditure. Why should this expansion in public services adversely affect the industrial sector? The explanation of the link focusses on a theory called "Crowding Out" first developed by Bacon and Eltis in 1974. The theory states that the expansion of the public sector has drawn resources from the private manufacturing sector. This has happened via "real resource crowding out" where physical resources including labour have been attracted into the public sector and "financial crowding out" where the financing of the public sector has affected industry's costs and competitiveness. In the latter respect it is argued that the higher taxes needed to finance government

TABLE 8 *Exchange Rate and Industrial Production*

Year	Sterling Trade Weighted Index (1975 = 100) (yearly average)	Sterling-Dollar Exchange Rate (yearly average)	Annual Growth in Industrial Production %
1977	81·2	$1·75	+ 3·8
1978	81·5	$1·92	+ 3·7
1979	87·3	$2·12	+ 2·6
1980	96·1	$2·32	− 6·5
1981	94·9	$2·03	− 5·3
1982	90·7	$1·75	+ 1·8

Source: Economic Trends C.S.O.

spending and the high interest rates resulting from the sale of government debt to finance public sector investment have enhanced costs and prices and squeezed profits in industry, as well as depriving industry of the capital required for reinvestment programmes. The "Crowding Out thesis" was further developed during the late 1970s and examined the delineation of the economy between the marketed sector (*i.e.* private sector plus those parts of the public sector which sell their output) and the non-marketed sector (*i.e.* the parts of the public sector with no sold output). Again it was argued that the high taxes needed to fund the non-marketed sector acted to fuel wage demands and costs in the marketed sector, raising prices and reducing market shares domestically and overseas. The argument brought with it the view that public sector trades unions in the 1960s and 1970s were particularly potent in the ability to pursue and achieve high wage settlements. The Conservative Government elected in 1979 was convinced of the validity of the "Crowding Out" argument, stating in their 1979 White Paper on Public Spending that "Public Expenditure is at the heart of Britain's economic difficulties".

In certain respects the "Crowding Out thesis" is supported by facts; for example there is evidence that public sector pay awards in the early 1970s did "lead" private sector pay awards and certainly aspects of governmental fiscal policy in the 1970s, including the introduction of the National Insurance Surcharge, did add to industry's costs. In addition high interest rates during the 1970s and 1980s undoubtedly deterred investment by industry—although these high rates were caused by the need to contain money supply growth and regulate the exchange rate rather than by the sale of government debt to finance public sector spending. However elsewhere the thesis does not stand up to close examination. There was, for example, no shortage of labour in the 1970s and the growth of public sector employment was undertaken very largely via the recruitment of females into the labour force to fill administration posts; this process was hardly depriving the private sector of the skilled manual labour it required. Evidence also suggests that external factors like the rise in oil prices in 1973/4 and 1978/9 had a far greater effect on British industry's costs than high taxation and interest rates.

Whilst the validity of the "Crowding Out" argument is in question one aspect of government policy during the past three decades has clearly had a detrimental impact on industry. This has been the "stop-go" policies used by government to alternately inflate and deflate the economy in the pursuit of the twin, and apparently competing, objectives of low inflation and full employment. Such rapid changes in policy that were integral to "stop-go" hardly created the ideal conditions for planning, investment and growth in the manufacturing sector and probably added pace to industry's decline.

(c) *The role of the exchange rate and the terms of trade*
Of critical importance in the determination of export sales and the degree of import penetration is the rate of exchange between currencies and the terms of trade—the ratio of export prices to import prices. These will dictate the selling prices of exported and imported goods and will therefore have a significant impact on the demand for these goods. The decline in Britain's share of overseas markets and the growth in import penetration owes much to the terms of trade and the high level of the exchange rate during periods in the last thirty years. In the 1960s, until the devaluation of November 1967, the pound was overvalued on the foreign ex-

change markets at the fixed rate of £1 = $2·80. The high value of the pound led to a deterioration in the balance of trade and a sharp increase in import penetration. The problem of a high sterling value re-emerged in the late 1970s when under a floating exchange rate system the pound rose to $2·44. In this instance the causes were twofold. Firstly, high interest rates in the U.K., that were aimed at reducing monetary growth, had the side effect of attracting foreign funds and boosting the demand for, and value of, the pound; secondly, the rise in revenues resulting from North Sea oil affected the balance of goods trade and enhanced the value of sterling. The impact on industry was devastating, with import penetration increasing sharply since the high value of the pound made overseas goods attractive in price. By contrast exports of British manufactured goods slumped. Although relatively short-lived, the high value of sterling during the period 1979–1981 had a marked effect in accelerating Britain's industrial decline

(d) *Protectionism and Free Trade*
A further reason for decline frequently cited by industry has been the exposure of British firms to unfair trading conditions. Certain overseas markets have been effectively closed off to British goods by the application of protectionist policies by foreign governments. Specific examples of countries applying protectionist policies against British goods include Spain, with their strict quotas on British car imports, and Japan. In the latter instance Japan's protectionist methods are slightly more subtle than mere tariffs or quotas on imported goods; techniques such as safety or design regulations are applied to overseas goods as a means of curbing penetration of domestic markets. Calls for Britain to retaliate against such unfair trading conditions have been met by deaf ears since the British Government has been intent upon maintaining a policy of free trade and not applying protectionist policies to protect domestic firms. Another trading factor which has had a clear impact on British industry has been the membership of the European Economic Community. When Britain entered the Community in 1973 it was argued that unhindered access to the European markets would boost British industry and provide the size of markets needed to justify investment and modernisation by firms. Regrettably this has not occurred; entry into the Community has opened British market to inroads by the firms of our European partners and has contributed to the demise of certain of our industries. The car industry in particular has witnessed a major growth in the share of the domestic market being taken by European firms since 1973. Generally since the end of the 1970s the trading effects of membership of the Community have had an adverse effect on British industry—possibly because the final removal of trading barriers exposed the lack of competitiveness of British industry.

TABLE 9 *Britain and EEC Trade*

Year	Exports	Imports	Balance of Visible Trade (£m)
1980	20,427	19,655	773
1981	20,861	20,849	12
1982	22,997	24,218	(1,221)
1983	26,453	28,859	(2,407)
1984	31,451	33,936	(2,485)

N.B. Figures for all years include transactions with Greece.
Source: United Kingdom Balance of Payments C.S.O.

(e) *The Product Life Cycle and the New Industrial Countries*

Many economists have stressed that Britain's process of deindustrialisation is not unique. Other economies including the USA, West Germany and France have also seen a decline in the proportion of the Gross Domestic Product accounted for by manufacturing industry.

TABLE 10   *Value added in manufacturing as a percentage of GDP*

Year	USA	Japan	Germany	France	UK	Italy
1960	28·6	33·9	40·3	29·1	32·1	28·6
1971	24·9	35·2	37·0	28·5	27·4	28·4
1979	23·8	30·1	34·1	27·0	24·9	30·6
1983	21·1	30·5	31.8	25·3	21·0	27·1

Source: OECD.

Consequently a more generic explanation is needed to explain why deindustrialisation occurs. This is provided by the theory of the Product Life Cycle which argues that countries which industrialise first, becoming net exporters of manufacturing goods, will eventually, after many decades, find that their industries decline and that they become net importers of the goods which initially they innovated! Once again the obvious example of this occurring is the way that Britain and other European countries are now net importers of motor bikes (largely from Japan) whereas initially Europe was the world's centre for motor bike production. The key factor which causes the Product Life Cycle to occur is the cost of inputs—particularly wage costs. The early industrial nations become prosperous and wages rise pushing up costs. Consequently countries industrialising later have the benefits of lower wage costs, of being able to harness the technological developments made by the first wave of industrial nations and of being able to avoid the errors made by the innovators. In these circumstances those countries industrialising in later decades are able to offer a cheaper, often more advanced, product to the world markets. The outcome is a change in the balance of trade in these products with the innovating countries becoming net importers of the goods they originally developed. Certainly the characteristics of the Newly Industrialised Countries, such as South Korea and Brazil fit into the pattern of the Product Life Cycle most vividly developed by Japan—they are low wage, low cost economies which have shown a willingness to apply the most recent technology to production methods. The result has been the start of a shift in the world production of manufactured goods to these new industrial centres.

(f) *Education, Cultural and Societal factors*

The House of Lords' report on manufacturing industry expressed the view that Britain's industrial decline could be partly ascribed to the educational system in the country. Arguably the system has not been geared towards producing managers, technicians and engineers needed to generate efficiency in industry. In addition it was stated that education does not sufficiently nurture the view that industry is important to the wellbeing and prosperity of the nation. Certainly the view that the structure and organisation of society and education have been in some way unhelpful or even antipathetic to industry is held widely. However it is difficult to pinpoint tangible evidence of the impact of these factors on industry's decline in this country.

(g) *Conclusions*

It is clear from the examination of the likely causes of Britain's industrial decline that both specific factors relating to certain discrete periods and longer term underlying factors have played a role in the deindustrialisation process. The Product Life Cycle, the educational system and the lack of investment in industry may have been the root causes of decline; whilst government policy, trading policy and the exchange rate have provided the more immediate causes of decline. Indeed the decline in industry is so well established it is difficult at this stage to foresee a turnaround in the performance of the manufacturing sector *as a whole* in future years—although an ability to respond to change will

always mean that some of Britain's more innovative firms will be able to withstand the rigours of international competition.

Does the decline in the manufacturing sector matter?

Why should we be concerned about the decline of industry in this country? It can, after all, be pointed out that Britain withstood and benefitted from the transition from an agricultural to an industrial economy in the late 18th century. Consequently need the long term effects of a move from an industrial to a service based economy be problematic? Since industrialisation eventually brought a boost to living standards, should not the post-industrial development of the economy bring similar progress to the quality of life? Unfortunately a number of factors suggest that deindustrialisation will lead to economic problems and a decline in living standards.

Firstly, a service based economy will not absorb the jobs lost in the manufacturing sector through deindustrialisation. Many areas of the service sector are not labour intensive due to the use of new technology. There is a limited demand for unskilled or semi-skilled labour that used to be engaged in certain sectors of industry. Many jobs in the service sector are part-time only. The loss of manufacturing industry implies the need for Britain to live with permanently high levels of unemployment.

Secondly, the decline of the manufacturing sector will eventually lead to severe problems in Britain's balance of payments. Until the end of the 1970's the balance of payments had been greatly assisted by the surplus on Britain's trade in manufactured goods. The surplus had offset, partly or wholly, the deficit created on other trade, particularly in food and fuel. Currently, however, manufacturing trade is running in deficit and the balance of payments is only kept in surplus via earnings from oil exports (and the effect of North Sea oil on the need to import oil) and income from services. Once the earnings from oil start to decline in the 1990s the impact of the imbalance on manufacturing trade will be exposed (particularly as earnings from the service sector will also be likely to decline in the next decade) and Britain will experience a severe balance of payments crisis. The crisis will almost inevitably lead to deflationary policies by the government and a decline in living standards.

Thirdly, the prosperity and development of the service sector in Britain are heavily dependent on the health of the manufacturing sector. If activity declines in these industries jobs will soon be lost in the services and the crisis brought about by the contraction of the manufacturing sector will be accentuated.

Fourthly, deindustrialisation could lead to increases in taxes since the loss of industry will narrow the tax base for government to raise revenues. In addition the growth in the public sector that may emerge from demographic change and the further shift of economic activity away from manufacturing will further enlarge the government's need to finance public services.

Finally, the loss of jobs and prosperity resulting from the contraction of manufacturing industry is concentrated in certain areas of Britain—particularly the Midlands—whilst the gain in jobs in the service sector is very largely concentrated in the South East. Deindustrialisation will therefore sharpen the economic divisions within the country that have already opened up over the past decade.

Consequently, the impact of deindustrialisation, as the Lords Report stresses, is of great importance to everyone—whether or not they are employed in the manufacturing sector.

What can be done to regenerate industry?

The Lords Report offered plenty of ideas about how the decline of industry could be halted and reversed. Changes in the education system to accord "manufacturing industry and trade the esteem they merit" are called for, together with improvements in productivity and "non-price competitiveness" (including quality, design and service). Industrial policy, particularly towards Research and Development, should be more co-ordinated and pursued more effectively. Greater stability in the exchange rate and lower interest rates would help to stabilise trading conditions and cut costs. Greater investment, improved management and an easier tax regime would help industrial expansion, whilst export promotion, enhanced substitution of imports by British goods and a fairer international policy towards protectionism would improve the balance of manufacturing trade.

However it has been argued that such measures would be insufficient to prevent industry's decline. Consequently some calls have been made in the last decade for Selective Import Controls against goods or trading rivals which are most threatening to key sectors of British industry. In the 1970s the Cambridge Economic Policy Group went further, calling for Universal Import Controls, in harness with a programme of reflation by the Government. Reflation would boost demand for industrial goods; the import controls would ensure that the demand generated did not extend significantly to imported goods; retaliation would be avoided since overseas countries would find that the loss of demand generated via import controls was offset by their limited share of the demand created by reflation.

The current government shows no sign of adopting any protectionist policy in its moves to regenerate industry. Industrial policy is largely based on the notion that free competition should be encouraged since, in the long term, only truly competitive firms will survive in the international economy.

Whatever views that are held about the most effective form of industrial policy, it is clear that the standard of living of the community as a whole over the next decade will be materially affected by the ability of the manufacturing sector to reverse its long run pattern of contraction and submission to overseas competition.

MONEY MATTERS

This popular section, specially devised for readers of Pears, provides a concise but authoritative introduction to the complex problems of money, investment and taxation. There are sections covering such everyday problems as buying a house, insurance, income tax and ways of saving. This latest edition includes a special topic on Social Security in the United Kingdom.

TABLE OF CONTENTS

MONEY MATTERS

I. MONEY

1. SPENDING

Planning a Budget.

Most of us need some form of financial planning. Wages and salaries are usually paid in regular weekly or monthly instalments. The flow of expenditure, on the other hand, is normally much less even. Bills often seem to get lonely and like to arrive in batches. The way to deal with this problem is to work out an annual budget consisting of your major expenditures. An example is given in Table 1.

TABLE 1.   *An Example of an Annual Budget*

	£
General and water rate	300
Mortgage or rent	1,000
House and contents insurance	100
Gas	100
Electricity	200
Telephone	150
Road tax	90
Car insurance	100
Television rental and licence	200
Life assurance	100
Holidays	500
Christmas expenses	200
Annual subscriptions	60
Clothing	300
Season ticket	—
	3,400
Allowance for price increases (say 5% of 3,400)	170
Estimated total bills	3,570
Monthly average	297·50

List the amounts you spent last year under each of the headings. As prices are likely to continue to rise, it is worth adding on a little extra to be on the safe side. In the example, average price increases of 5 per cent are allowed for. It is also sensible to add a small amount for unforeseen expenditure. Having calculated your estimated total bills for the forthcoming year, you can then calculate how much money has to be reserved each month or each week for these items. In the example, this works out at £297·50 per month, or £68·65 per week on average.

Preparing a budget like this has a number of advantages. First of all, by planning in this way you can save money. For example, it is cheaper to pay car tax once a year rather than every six months. Annual season tickets are cheaper than monthly or quarterly ones. Also, it is usually cheaper to pay your insurance premiums in one go, rather than by instalments. A second advantage is that you have a clear idea of your major expenses, so you know how much money there is left over for day-to-day expenses. Thirdly, because the money can be put aside when your are paid, the cash is usually ready when the bills come in.

It is also possible to arrange this through a bank with a budget account. What happens is that you calculate your monthly expenses as above. The bank then transfers that amount each month from your current account (more on this below) to a separate budget account. A separate cheque book is provided for this account. When the bills come in, you simply write out a cheque for them. Using a bank in this way does have an advantage in that you can overdraw on the budget account if a lot of bills come in early in the year. The bank will, however, expect the account to run mainly in credit. There is also a charge for this service.

2. SPENDING ECONOMICALLY

Many forms of expenditure are almost unavoidable. Rent or mortgage payments, rates and water rates cannot usually be altered unless you move home. Nevertheless, in many other areas savings can be made.

As a general guide, the Consumers' Association publishes a monthly magazine *Which?* This provides a great deal of information about the price and quality of different products. Information about subscriptions to this magazine can be obtained from *Which?*, Castlemead, Gascoigne Way, Hertford SG14 1LH. Alternatively, it is available at libraries.

Food.

There are several points to remember when buying food. First of all, larger shops often sell goods at lower prices than smaller shops. As most people know, supermarkets often sell their own brands of many products. "Own brands" are, on average, cheaper than the brands of leading manufacturers. For example, on items such as peas, baked beans, soup and soap powder, own brands can be up to 15 per cent cheaper. On some lines, such as washing-up liquid, the savings can be even greater. There is no reason to suppose that own brands are inferior. They are commonly produced in the same place as the branded products. Often, the only difference is the packaging—and the price.

Other savings can be made with stores' special offers. Things like washing powder and toothpaste will be needed sooner or later; so it can make sense to buy these items when an offer is on, rather than waiting until you have run out.

When comparing prices, it is worth bearing in mind that the quantity varies as well. It is, therefore, better to compare the *unit cost* of products. This is the cost per ounce or pound. Packaging can easily make something look larger than it actually is.

Domestic Appliances.

Like food, the price of domestic appliances varies. Much of the variation depends on the number of extras. For example, a basic gas or electric cooker costs something in the region of £300. Such a cooker would serve a family quite adequately. If, however, you want a model with extras, then the cost can be £500 or more. A second important factor is where the appliance is sold. The price of the same model can vary considerably from place to place, so it is very worthwhile shopping around. There may also be a delivery charge. Discount warehouses are usually the cheapest place to buy appliances. The sales can also make a substantial difference to the price. Most appliances are likely to be cheaper in both winter and summer sales. Fridges are often particularly good bargains in winter sales, for obvious reasons. There is nothing inferior about domestic appliances sold in sales. Traders usually want to clear their premises for new lines. They also realise that January and the summer would otherwise be very lean times for them.

A particular question often arises as to whether to rent or to buy a television set. The advantages of renting are that repairs and service calls are included in the rent. If the set breaks down it is also likely to be repaired more quickly than if you owned a set. And if it cannot be fixed straight-away the rental company will provide a substitute until the original is repaired. On the other hand, it is generally true that it is cheaper to buy in the long run. This is true even if you buy the set on hire purchase. And if you decide to dispose of the set, you can always sell it. (Provided, of course, that any HP payments have been completed.)

Cars.

Cars are very expensive to buy and to run. It is quite common for the annual cost of running a car (including the drop in its secondhand value) to exceed £2,000. So it is worth thinking care-fully about whether or not to buy a car. It may be cheaper to use taxis. They also have the advantage of removing any worries about parking, maintenance and drunken driving.

If you do decide to buy a car, the initial invest-ment can be greatly reduced by buying a second-hand car. The value of most cars drops con-siderably in their first year. There are other advantages in buying second hand. A used car will have been run in and the teething troubles ironed out. However, if the car is more than three years old it must have an MOT (Ministry of Transport) test every year. The test is now very tough, so cars should be checked carefully before purchase.

If you do not get a guarantee from a reputable dealer you should consider having it examined by the A.A. or the R.A.C. They charge a fee for the service, but it may avoid a purchase you later regret. Alternatively, if faults are discovered it may enable you to negotiate a lower price.

Before setting out to buy a secondhand car it is sensible to study the market. Car price guides are widely available. They provide useful infor-mation on cars of different ages and condition. The two major sources of secondhand cars are professional dealers and private sellers. You are unlikely to get a bargain if you buy from a dealer, since they are very familiar with the value of used cars. If you buy privately you avoid the mark-up of the dealer, and so can expect to pay less. Even if you buy a new car, it can pay to ask for a dis-count, especially if you are paying cash. Dealers receive a sizeable discount on new cars. You may be able to persuade one to pass some of it on to you. Whatever sort of car you buy, new or old, you should give it a test drive. Even new cars are not immune from faults.

3. BORROWING

Under certain circumstances, it can be advan-tageous to borrow money. The biggest example in many peoples' lives is buying a house with the aid of a mortgage (see **H11**). On a much smaller scale most goods can be bought with the aid of credit. This does enable you to enjoy something without having to wait while you accumulate the cash to buy it outright. As prices rise, you may also be able to buy goods more cheaply through buying straightaway. And you save money buy-ing things like season tickets annually. But there are some disadvantages with borrowing. Some people might find easy credit too much of a tempt-ation and spend more than they can afford.

In addition, borrowing usually costs money. How much it costs depends on where the loan comes from. At the cheapest end of the scale are first mortgages and bank overdrafts. At the beginning of 1986 mortgage interest rates varied around 12 per cent and overdraft rates varied from 14 to 18 per cent. At the other end of the scale are second mortgages, some hire-purchase

arrangements and check trading. The rates of interest at the top end can be 30 per cent per year or even more. There are many sources of credit, so only the main ones will be discussed here.

Banks.

Banks offer three main types of loan: over-drafts, ordinary loans and personal loans. In recent years they have also increased their lending for house purchase. An overdraft is simply an agree-ment with your bank manager allowing you to overdraw on your account up to an agreed figure. There is no formal arrangement about the timing of repayments, though the agreement will normally be for a specified period. Ordinary and personal loans, on the other hand, are repaid on a regular basis.

Credit Cards.

Banks also provide credit cards. Barclays Bank operate the *Barclaycard* credit card system. The four other main banks, Lloyds, Midland, National Westminister and The Royal Bank of Scotland have their own credit card—*Access*. The Trustee Savings Banks issue their *Trustcard*. Credit cards are very simple to use. When you buy something on credit the retailer makes out a sales voucher which you check and sign. The retailer then gives you a copy. You can also draw cash from a bank displaying the appropriate sign. Every month you are sent a statement showing how much you owe. You then have to repay a certain minimum amount. If you wish to pay more, or clear all the debt completely, you can.

There is no charge for obtaining an Access, Barclaycard or Trustcard. Nor is any interest charged if the full amount is repaid within 25 days of the date of the statement. If only part payment is made then the period of free credit is from the date of the purchase until the date of the state-ment. After that interest is charged on a daily basis on the outstanding balance. The arrange-ments for amounts drawn in cash differ. Barclay-card and Trustcard have a 1·5 per cent handling charge, but the 25 days free credit is still allowed. Access does not impose a handling charge, but charge interest from the date the cash was drawn.

The rate of interest charged has fluctuated in recent years between 1·5 and 2·25 per cent. These rates are equivalent to annual rates of interest as follows:

Rate per month %	Equivalent rate per year %
1·50	19·5
1·75	23·1
2·00	26·8
2·25	30·6

However, if the interest-free period is taken into account the annual rate of interest is lower. How much lower depends on when you made the pur-chase. If the purchase was made just before the statement you may only get about 30 to 35 days free credit in all. If, however, the purchase was made, say, three weeks before the statement, you would get up to 56 days free credit. If the retailer is slow in sending details of the purchase to the credit card centre the interest-free period may be even longer. For this reason, it can be useful to have both an Access and a Barclaycard or Trust-card. If your statement dates differ, you can then use the card with the statement date furthest away. Credit cards can also be used overseas.

If you lose a credit card, or have it stolen, you should inform the credit centre at once. You are liable if anyone dishonestly obtains goods with the card until the credit card centre is told of the loss of the card. However, provided the card-holder acts in good faith, Access, Barclaycard and Trustcard limit this liability to £25.

Other Cards.

There are several other cards. Two of the main ones are *American Express* and *Diners Club*. They have longer free credit periods than Access and Barclaycard, but they are accepted by fewer outlets in Britain. They also charge for the card itself. A number of other organisations operate credit card schemes. These include major department stores.

Hire Purchase.

The rates of interest on hire-purchase agreements are generally higher than those charged on bank or credit-card loans. To see this clearly, we should describe two ways of quoting interest rates. Salesmen sometimes quote "flat" rates of interest. This refers to the difference between the cash price and the cost if bought on credit. For example, suppose you could buy a cooker for £100 cash, or £125 payable in monthly instalments for one year. The extra cost of buying on credit is £25. This gives an annual flat rate of interest of 25 per cent on the £100 borrowed. But this is not the real rate of interest. The reason is that from the first month some of the capital has been repaid. In fact, the average amount borrowed throughout the year is just over £50. The true rate of interest on the balance outstanding (rather than the original loan) is over 40 per cent in this example.

Insurance Companies.

If you have an insurance policy you may be able to borrow money from the insurance company on the strength of it. The policy would have to have a cash-in, or surrender value. The interest charged on such loans is often lower than other rates.

4. SAVING

There are several reasons why people save. They include the need to meet unforeseen expenditures, to provide for retirement or simply to buy large items such as a car. It is normally cheaper to pay cash rather than to buy on hire purchase. Although many people save only when they have money left over from their various outgoings, it is better to plan savings. That is, budget your income and expenditure and to regard savings as part of your regular outgoings. This allows capital to be built up on a regular basis.

Before deciding where to invest these savings there are factors that you should consider. The first is whether to invest for short or long periods of time. It is generally true that long-term savings attract a higher rate of interest. However, there are usually financial penalties or constraints that will restrict your ability to draw on the money when required. This loss of *liquidity* is important, since you may require money immediately to meet unforeseen expenditures.

You must also consider how taxation affects the income from your investments. This is considered in the section on taxation. Nevertheless, it is important to establish the tax position of different investments. For instance, the rates of interest offered by building societies are free of income tax at the basic rate. These rates may appear low in comparison with other rates, but if you are paying tax at the basic rate they can be quite advantageous. If you do not pay tax, then there are normally better investments, since you cannot claim back the tax already paid by the building society. From 6 April 1985 this system of taxing interest has been extended to banks, but National Savings still offer a range of investments which are either tax free, or taxable but tax is not deducted at source.

Another consideration is the rate at which prices are increasing; that is the rate of inflation. The saver is particularly concerned with what goods or services money will buy in the future. The important rate of return of an investment is not the nominal or money rate of interest but the real rate of interest. If, for example, an investment offers a return of 7 per cent per annum and the rate of inflation is 5 per cent per annum, the real rate of interest is 2 per cent per annum. The individual requires 5 per cent per annum merely to maintain the purchasing power of his capital.

The real rate of interest is very important during periods of inflation because it may well be negative. For example, if the nominal rate of interest is 7 per cent per annum and the rate of inflation rises again, to say, 10 per cent per annum the real rate of interest is minus 3 per cent per annum. This means that when the saver withdraws money in the

future, it will not buy the same quantity of goods or services it would have when the investments were made.

Having considered these general points, we can now look at the specific forms of investment open to the saver.

National Savings.

These are schemes provided by the Government. They include The National Savings Bank, Savings Certificates, Premium Bonds and the Save-As-You-Earn Scheme.

The National Savings Bank.

This was formerly known as the Post Office Savings Bank. There are over 20,000 post offices in the U.K. where you can deposit or withdraw money. There are two types of account available:

Ordinary Accounts.

Ordinary accounts can be opened with as little as £1. They can also be opened for young children, but withdrawals are not allowed until the child reaches seven years of age. The rate of interest is 6 per cent on balances of £500 or more which are maintained for the whole year. If the balance falls below £500, but not below £100 during the year interest is still 6 per cent for those calendar months when the balance exceeds £500. For other months, and if the balance never exceeds £500, the rate of interest is 3 per cent. The first £70 of interest is tax free.

Interest is calculated on each complete £1 deposited for a full calendar month. The money begins to earn interest from the first day of the month after it is deposited. It does not earn interest on the month in which it is withdrawn. You should therefore try to deposit money towards the end of the month and withdraw at the beginning of the month.

Up to £100 a day can be drawn on demand from your account. The bank book will be retained if the withdrawal exceeds £50. If you require more than £100 you will have to allow a few days before you get your money. This is because you must apply in writing. Greater flexibility in withdrawing money can be achieved by having more than one account. For example, if you have two accounts you can draw up to £200 on demand. If you have a 'Regular Customer Account', you can withdraw up to £250 a day at your chosen post office and still retain your bank book. The £250 can also be drawn in Thomas Cook travellers cheques.

Ordinary accounts also have a 'Paybill' service. This allows you to pay bills directly from your account. You can pay one or more at a time provided their total value is not over £250. This service covers bills which can normally be paid through the Post Office, such as electricity, gas, rates and the TV licence. The payment of regular fixed amounts can be arranged, as long as the payments are not more frequent than once a month.

The advantage of the system is its accessibility, since there are post offices in almost every town and village, and they are open six days a week. It is cheap, since there are no bank charges and money earns interest. Also, money is available on demand. The tax-free elements make ordinary accounts particularly attractive to high tax payers.

So, National Savings accounts are a good place to keep small amounts of money to meet unforeseen expenditures. On the other hand, the services offered are still limited, when compared with banks for example.

Investment Accounts.

Like ordinary accounts, anyone over the age of seven can open an account. Children under seven can have one opened on their behalf. The minimum sum required to open an account is £5. The rate of interest is higher than an ordinary account and is liable to tax, but tax is not withheld at source. The upper limit on deposits is £50,000. In 1984 the method of calculating interest on investment accounts was changed. Previously interest had been calculated in the same way as for ordinary accounts. From 1 January 1984 interest is calculated on a daily basis. This means that interest is earned on each whole pound for every day it is in the account.

There is no limit on the amount of money that can be withdrawn. However, notice of one month is required. Investment accounts are better for long-term savers, although higher rates of interest can be obtained elsewhere. The rate of interest is more attractive to non-tax payers when compared with the rates offered by building societies and banks, which are tax paid.

National Savings Certificates.

There have been thirty-one issues of these, but only one is on sale at any particular time. At the time of writing the 31st issue was on sale. The minimum investment is £25, and an individual can invest up to £5,000 (in addition to any holdings of other National Savings Certificates). Instead of earning interest, the value of the certificate rises at an accelerating rate. With the 31st issue this is equivalent to a compound rate of interest of 7·85 per cent per annum. This is free of tax. If allowance is made for the basic rate of income tax, this is equivalent to 11·06 per cent gross. Table 2 shows how the value and yield (or interest) builds up.

TABLE 2. *The Value and Yield of the 31st Issue of Savings Certificates. (£25 units)*

Years after purchase	Value at end of year £	Yield for year %
1	26·44	5·76
2	28·20	6·66
3	30·40	7·80
4	33·12	8·95
5	36·48	10·14

The certificates are issued in units of twenty-five pounds and multiples thereof. Thus, at the end of five years each unit becomes £36·48 (column 2). This is equivalent to a compound rate of interest of 7·75 per cent. So, for example, if you invest £250 (10 units) this becomes £364·80 in five years. To cash certificates you have to give eight working days notice. If you do this before they mature, then the rate of interest or yield is considerably reduced. For example, if you cash them in at the end of one year the rate of interest is only 5·76 per cent.

You need not cash in certificates when they reach maturity. In most cases, however, it will pay to do so. The rates of interest currently paid on matured certificates can be obtained from most large post offices. Again, anybody can hold certificates, including children under seven.

Index-linked National Savings Certificates.

These were originally known as 'granny bonds' because when index-linked certificates were first issued they were only available to people over a certain age. This restriction no longer applies and the version currently available is the Third Issue. Provided the certificates are held for at least a year, their value is linked to increases in prices. Interest is also paid and the rate increases every year, from 2·50 per cent after the first year up to a maximum of 5·25 per cent after five years. If the certificates are held for five years the overall return is 3·54 per cent. (This is in addition to the increase in their value to match inflation and, once the interest is added to the capital, it is index-linked as well.) The repayments are also tax free.

The certificates are available in units of £25. You may buy up to £5,000 of the Third Issue in addition to any holdings you may have from the two previous issues.

Indexed-income Bonds.

The capital invested in these bonds is not index-linked but the income is. The income is paid on the 20th of each month and is taxable, though tax is not deducted at source. With the First Issue of these bonds (there might be other issues later) the rate of interest in the first year is 8 per cent. On the first anniversary of your investment, your income is increased by the amount of the increase in prices during the previous year. After the end of each of the following years (up to 10 years altogether) the income is increased to match the increase in prices.

This means that these bonds offer a stable real return whatever happens to interest rates in general, or to the rate of inflation.

The minimum investment in these bonds is £5,000 and extra amounts can be invested in units of £1,000 up a maximum of £50,000. Repayments may be obtained by giving three months' notice, but if repayment is made during the first year, the bond will only earn interest at half the normal rate.

The Yearly Plan.

This scheme is designed for regular investment. The saver agrees to make monthly payments by standing order for one year. The payments must be at least £20 per month and higher amounts in multiples of £5 up to a maximum of £100. At the end of the first year a Yearly Plan Certificate is issued to the value of the payments and the interest they have earned so far. The maximum rate of interest is earned if the Certificate is then held for four full years.

Once a plan has been taken out, the rate of interest in force at the time is guaranteed for the five years. However no interest is payable if the monthly payments are withdrawn in the first year. The payments can be continued beyond the first year if desired. The saver simply continues his payments and each extra year's payments gain another certificate. The returns on the Yearly Plan scheme are tax free.

Premium Savings Bonds.

Premium Bonds are one of the most popular forms of national savings. No interest is earned as such on the bonds. Instead, you have a regular chance to win a cash prize each week and month. The monthly prize fund is set by calculating one month's interest at the rate of 7·75 per cent per year on all bonds eligible for the draw.

All the prizes are tax free. However, before a bond is included in the draw it has to be held for three calendar months following the month in which it was bought. The winning numbers are generated by ERNIE (Electronic Random Number Indicator Equipment). The winning numbers are drawn entirely at random so that each bond has an equal chance of winning.

The size of the prizes varies from £50 to £250,000. Prizewinners are notified by post, so it is important to notify the Bonds and Stock Office of any change of address. The numbers of prize-winning bonds are published in the London Gazette Supplement which can be consulted at major post offices. In addition most daily newspapers publish the numbers of bonds which have won the larger prizes. If you fail to claim a prize at the time of the draw, this can be done later.

Premium Bonds can be bought at post offices and banks. Any person over the age of 16 can buy bonds. A parent or guardian can buy bonds on behalf of their children. Bonds are available in units of £1, but are sold only in multiples of £5. The minimum purchase is £10 and the maximum holding is £10,000. The bonds can be cashed by completing a withdrawal form available at post offices. Although bondholders can always realise the amount they invested originally, it should be remembered that there is no interest and as inflation continues, the real value of Premium Bonds falls.

National Savings Deposit Bonds.

Deposit bonds were designed for people who wish to invest lump sums for at least a year. Repayments can be made at any time, provided three months written notice is given. However, if the bond is cashed within a year of purchase, it will attract only half the relevant rate of interest. If it is held for more than a year, all the interest is paid in full. Interest is calculated on a daily basis, and the current rate is displayed at post offices. The interest is taxable but tax is not deducted at source. The minimum purchase is £100. Larger amounts may be brought in multiples of £50, and the maximum investment is £50,000.

National Savings Income Bonds.

These bonds provide a regular income from capital. The minimum investment is £2,000. Extra amounts can be invested in multiples of £1000 up to a maximum of £50,000. The interest is paid on the fifth of each month and tax is not withheld at source. Repayments may be obtained by giving three months' notice, but if repayment is made in the first year the bond will earn only half the published rate of interest. The interest rate is adjusted from time to time and full details are available at post offices.

Building Societies.

There are many building societies in the United Kingdom. Some of these are national, others local. All building societies are 'mutual' organisations set up for the benefit of their investing and borrowing members. There is no difference in the security of your money as between the small and large societies. If you want to be absolutely sure, you should choose one that has Trustee Status and is a member of the Building Societies Association.

Interest rates quoted by building societies are tax-paid at the basic rate, but non-taxpayers cannot claim back tax paid on interest. Interest rates tend to be higher for regular savings and the longer you are prepared to commit your money. The most popular way of saving with a building society has been through a share account. It tends to earn a higher rate of interest than deposit accounts, usually 0·25 per cent more. This is because, in the unlikely situation of a building society failure, deposit account holders have a prior claim on the assets of the society. The maximum that can be deposited is £30,000. Building societies do not normally require notice before withdrawing from share or deposit accounts unless the amounts are large. Interest is calculated daily and credited half-yearly.

Building societies now offer a wide variety of investments, in addition to share accounts. These do differ between different building societies and go by names such as higher interest accounts, term shares, capital bonds, bonus accounts and subscription shares. It is therefore worth shopping around to find those that are nearest your requirements. A final consideration is that those who have invested in a building society may get preferential treatment when it comes to getting a mortgage.

Banks.

Banks offer two main types of account, current and deposit. Current accounts are for everyday transactions, and they do not earn interest. These are discussed in the section on Banking. Deposit accounts earn interest.

The rates of interest offered on deposit accounts do tend to change more quickly than those offered by other schemes. This is because the deposit rate is based on each bank's base rate which change as interest rates generally change. The deposit rate is usually between 4½ and 3 per cent below the base rate. The current rate offered by the various banks is usually on display at the bank branches. Interest is calculated on a daily basis. The interest is taxable, but in the past tax has not been deducted at source. However, from 6 April 1985, bank interest has been paid in the same way as building society interest. This means that the interest is 'tax-paid' at the basic rate, but that tax cannot be reclaimed by non-taxpayers. There is no minimum or maximum amount that can be deposited. Although seven days notice of withdrawal is technically required, in practice you can withdraw fairly substantial sums on demand. If you do, you will usually lose seven days interest. You can only withdraw money at the branch at which you have an account. If you want ready access to your savings, deposit accounts can be attractive for small amounts of money. But you should look at the rates offered by National Savings, and Building Societies before choosing a deposit account with a bank.

Local Authority Loans.

Local authorities not only raise money through rates but also by borrowing from the public. They do this by advertising in the Press for loans or issuing loan stock quoted on the Stock Exchange. Loans are at a fixed rate of interest. The length of the loan is generally from two to five years, although you can sometimes lend for a year or less. The minimum that you can invest varies from authority to authority and is usually at least £1,000.

Different local authorities pay different rates of interest. It is therefore important to watch the newspapers carefully and not just consider investing in your own local authority. The rate of interest tends to be very attractive, especially to non-tax payers. However, tax at the basic rate is deducted from interest payments, and this must be claimed back by non-taxpayers. Interest is normally paid every six months. Generally, interest rates will be higher the longer the loans run for and the greater the minimum investment. Some of the smaller local authorities offer higher rates of interest. There is no difference in the security of such loans, since all loans are guaranteed.

It is important to bear in mind when considering whether to invest in local authority loans that you cannot normally regain your capital until the end of the investment period. Thus, local authority loans are excellent for long-term savers. They are not for short-term savers.

Gilt Edged Securities.

As well as raising taxes to finance its expenditure, the Government borrows from the general public. It does this by issuing gilt-edged stock. There are basically two types of stock, redeemable and irredeemable. Redeemable or dated stocks are those that the Government has agreed to repurchase on a certain date. Usually, two dates are given. This means that the Government cannot redeem them before the first date, but it must redeem them on or before the last date. Each stock has a par or face value of £100. This is the amount that will be repaid on redemption. An example of a redeemable stock is the 8½ per cent Treasury Stock 1987–1990. Stocks that the Government is not committed to redeem are called irredeemable or undated stocks. The 2½ per cent consol introduced after the Second World War is an example.

The cost of buying or selling securities will depend on whether you go through a stockbroker or through the Department for National Savings, Bonds and Stock Office. It is cheaper to use the National Savings Stock Office, although you can only deal in stocks that are on the National Stock Register. In addition, not more than £10,000 nominal value of any particular stock can be purchased in any one day. There is no limit to the total amount you may hold. Application forms may be obtained from Post Offices.

The interest or *coupon rate* on a stock is normally paid half-yearly. Some pay quarterly, which is particularly useful for old-age pensioners, for example. This is based on the nominal or par value. For example, the 8½ per cent Treasury Stocks pays £8·25 per year. However, the price that you pay for the stock will probably be less than par. The effective rate of interest or *running yield* will therefore be greater than 8½ per cent.

Prices of stocks fluctuate so that their yield keeps in line with interest rates generally. This presents the possibility of a capital gain or loss. However, it is generally true that as the stock approaches redemption, the closer the price will be to par, and the smaller the capital gain. The further away redemption is, the lower the price of the stock, and hence the greater will be the capital gain if the stock is held to redemption. Government securities are a very marketable investment. They can be sold quickly if need be. Also, stocks are free of capital-gains tax if in your possession for more than one year. For larger sums of money, gilt-edged stock provides a good alternative to local authority loans.

Shares.

For the more adventurous, there is the possibility of investing in shares on the stock market. If you invest in shares it is advisable to "spread your risk." This means that you must have a varied and balanced collection of shares in your portfolio. To do this will require a lot of capital and knowledge of the market. So it is best to seek professional advice from a stockbroker or your bank manager. People with more limited means will be better advised to participate indirectly in the stock market by holding units in a unit trust.

Unit Trusts

Unit trusts sell 'units' to investors and use the proceeds to buy shares. This allows the investor to spread the risk of his investment over all the shares the trust owns. Unit trusts are run by professional managers who can be expected to know more than many investors about the merits of different securities. The value of the units of a trust are worked out each day in line with the value of the fund's stock market investments. Two prices are quoted. The 'offer' price is the price at which investors can buy units. The 'bid' price is the price at which the managers will repurchase units. The offer price is higher than the bid price and the difference contributes towards the cost of running the trust. In addition, there is usually a small half-yearly or yearly charge. Units can be bought and sold directly from the managers.

Life Assurance as Saving.

Life assurance policies provide an alternative method of saving regular amounts for long periods of time. The various policies are considered in the section on insurance.

5. BANKS

Most people are familiar with the high street banks. These are the clearing banks and are known as the Big Four. They are the National Westminster, Midland, Barclays and Lloyds. In addition, there are a number of smaller banks, such as the Co-operative Bank. There are also the National Girobank and the Trustee Savings Banks. Banks offer a variety of services, and we begin by considering current accounts.

Current Accounts.

A current account is a safe and easy way of making and receiving payments. Many people automatically assume that they require a current account. If you make only a few payments each week or month and you are paid in cash it will probably be better to keep your money in an account with the National Savings Bank or a building society (see the section on Saving). This is because money in current accounts, except those of the Co-operative Bank, does not earn interest. Indeed, as we will see later, you may have to pay in one way or another for the services provided.

Opening a Bank Account.

Opening an account is straightforward. You simply go into the local branch of the bank of your choice and tell the cashier or enquiries clerk that you want to open an account. The bank will want samples of your signature, and you will have to fill in a form giving your name and address. Finally, it will require you to give two references. These could be your employer and a friend with a bank account. You can open an account with as little as £1. To pay further amounts into your account, you simply fill in a form provided by the bank.

Making Payments.

With a current account you will receive a cheque book. This is used in making cash withdrawals from the bank or in making payments without using cash. A cheque is not money. It is merely a written instruction to the bank to pay an amount out of your account, to the person(s) named on the cheque. Cash can be obtained from your local branch. If you require cash from another you must make special arrangements or use a cheque card.

Cheque Cards.

Most retailers are reluctant to accept an unsupported cheque. This is because they do not know if you have sufficient money in your account for the bank to honour the cheque. And, of course, the cheque book may have been stolen. This problem is overcome by a cheque card. The card guarantees that the bank will honour cheques up to £50 regardless of the state of the customer's account. You have to be a reliable and well-established customer before your bank will give you a cheque card. A cheque drawn on a cheque card cannot be stopped or cancelled.

Cash Cards.

A major problem with people who work is access to the banks. Banks are only open between 9.30 a.m. and 3.30 p.m. from Monday to Friday. The major banks have various schemes whereby sums of money can be automatically dispensed outside the branch, twenty-four hours a day. The problem is that not all branches have these installed.

Standing Orders.

There are other ways of making payments apart from cheques. If asked, the bank will automatically make regular payments from your account. These "standing orders" are useful for paying such things as insurance premiums, subscriptions and mortgage repayments. The banks offer an alternative to standing orders, a bank budget account (see the section on Spending).

Direct Debiting.

Direct debits are slightly different from standing orders. In both cases you give your bank a written instruction to meet payments as they fall due. However, with direct debiting the recipient approaches your bank which then deducts the payment from your account. This can be convenient where the amount varies. The recipient has to tell you beforehand of the date and amount of payment.

Cost of a Bank Account.

Charges are made for clearing cheques and putting through transactions on accounts. The rules are complicated and vary from bank to bank. Generally, if you keep a sizeable balance in your account you will escape charges. If not, the charge for each cheque is about 30p, depending on the bank. With a current account you get a regular statement. This shows the amounts paid into your account (credits) and amounts paid out (debits).

Borrowing from your Bank.

You can borrow from your bank by either having an overdraft or a personal loan. An overdraft simply means that your current account is allowed to go from credit to debit, according to the amount agreed by your bank manager. This type of loan is usually for short periods and is the cheapest way of borrowing. However, banks prefer to lend you money by means of a personal loan. You get a lump sum and pay it off in fixed instalments. The interest charged tends to be higher than that charged on an overdraft. In addition to the services mentioned, banks provide a whole range of other services. These include deposit accounts (considered in the section on Saving), travel facilities, advice on investment, insurance and taxation, safe custody of items and many more. For further information on the additional services banks offer, contact your nearest branch.

The National Girobank.

The National Giro was set up by the Government to provide a low-cost current-account bank service. When Giro started it was considerably cheaper to run compared with a current account at a bank. However, the difference is now small. Giro can be opened via the post or through the 21,000 Post Offices in the U.K. These are generally open six days a week. You therefore have access to your account for more days and for longer hours than you do with the commercial banks. Up to £50 can be withdrawn on demand every other business day at either of two post offices nominated by you. For larger sums, prior arrangements have to be made. Money can be transferred by means of a Giro transfer free to other Giro account holders. Also standing orders and statements are free. The problem with Giro is that it does not provide overdrafts, although there are arrangements for personal loans.

Trustee Savings Bank.

Trustee Savings Banks have gradually taken on the identity of a clearing bank. They offer cheque accounts which are similar to current accounts. Trustee Savings Banks also issue their own "Trustcard". This can be used both as a credit card and as a cheque guarantee card for cheques up to £50.

Trustee Savings Banks also have many other services similar to those offered by the banks. These include deposit accounts, term deposits, personal loans, unit trusts and the selling of Government stocks at low rates of commission. They thus offer a very competitive alternative to the clearing banks.

6. INSURANCE

Insurance is a contract to pay a premium in return for which the insurer will pay compensation in certain eventualities, for example, fire or theft. In effect, insurance is a means of sharing certain risks. The traditional forms of insurance are general insurance and life assurance. The latter is usually called "assurance" because the cover is given against the occurrence of an event which is inevitable.

Life Assurance.

Life assurance provides a capital sum to your estate in the event of your death. Some policies also combine a savings element so that you receive a lump sum if you survive the period. These are called endowment policies. As a general point, it is just as important that you do not overburden yourself with life assurance as it is to have some form of cover. If you have to give up or surrender your policy before it matures there are usually severe financial penalties. There are three main types of life assurance: term assurance, whole-life assurance and endowment assurance. All forms of life assurance used to attract tax relief. However, this was changed in the Budget of 13 March 1984 so that the tax relief does not apply to policies taken out after that date.

Term Assurance.

This type of policy provides life assurance for a fixed period of time. Should you die during the term of the policy your estate will receive the sum assured. However, if you survive the period you receive nothing. There are variations on the basic type of term policy. A *decreasing term* policy, for example, is often necessary if you have a mortgage. The sum assured decreases as you pay off the mortgage.

Other types of policies include level and convertible term policies. With *level term* policies the sum assured remains fixed throughout the term of the policy A *convertible term* policy has the additional option of being able to convert it to another kind of policy later on, if you so desire. Term policies provide the cheapest form of life cover.

Whole-Life Assurance.

With this type of policy you are normally required to pay the premiums for the whole of your life-time. Like term assurance, the sum assured is paid out to your estate only on your death. Whole-life policies can either be with or without profits. A with-profits policy will be more expensive, since the sum received on your death will be the sum assured plus a share in the profits made by the company. Having to keep up the premiums after your retirement can be a problem, so *limited payment* policies are available. Premiums are paid until you reach a specific age,

although life cover continues until your death. The premiums will be higher than for a straight whole-life policy.

Endowment Assurance.

Both whole-life and term policies provide benefit only on your death. With an endowment policy, benefit is still provided should you die before the maturity date of the policy. But if you survive this period you will receive the sum assured. Like whole-life policies, these policies can be with or without profits. Although the more expensive, with-profits endowment policies are the most popular form of life assurance in this country. However, the proportion of the premium used to provide death cover is small. This is because the chances of dying before the maturity date are usually low. Thus, the bulk of the premiums is used by the company to build up the capital sum on maturity.

Endowment policies are often used in conjunction with loans for house purchase, school fees and for providing for retirement. As well as with-profits investment policies, life assurance companies offer other investment policies. These include equity linked contracts, property bonds and policies linked to building societies. With equity contracts the bulk of the premium is used to purchase units in a unit trust. Property bonds are very similar, except the investment is in property.

General Insurance.

As mentioned earlier, this provides cover for an eventuality that may never happen. The types of general insurance considered here are for house and possessions, motor vehicles, sickness and medical insurance.

Insuring your House.

If you are buying a house on a mortgage the building society will insist that it is insured. The sum that you will have to insure your house for will probably be more than what you paid for it. This is because the insurance value will be related to the cost of rebuilding the house. It is therefore important to adjust the amount for which the house is insured periodically to keep pace with inflation. Alternatively, you can take out policies which are "index-linked." Although most policies give the same kind of cover, there is no standard house insurance. So you should check to see if your policy covers all eventualities. This is particularly important if your area is prone to such events as flooding or subsidence.

Insuring your Possessions.

Unless you have a combined policy, the contents of your home and other possessions will not be covered by your house insurance. In the past insurance companies have reimbursed the purchase cost of articles, less a charge for wear-and-tear. However, you can get policies that do not make this deduction.

House and Possessions.

If you are a tenant living in rented accommodation you should only buy policies that cover the contents of the house and leave the landlord to buy insurance for the buildings. For owner-occupiers, it is best to buy a combined policy of house and possessions. This has the advantage that it will be generally cheaper than buying two separate policies.

Motor Insurance.

Motor insurance is compulsory by law. However, only a basic minimum is compulsory, and many people prefer to take out more comprehensive policies. Insurance companies offer two main types of policy; third party and fully comprehensive insurance.

Third-Party Motor Insurance.

The additional cover provided by this type of policy is the cost of repairing the other driver's car. Also, if you incur legal costs in dealing with a claim, these will be reimbursed if your insurer approves your actions. Since third-party insurance does not cover damage to your car, it is only suitable if your car is fairly old.

Comprehensive Motor Insurance.

If your car is relatively new and hence more valuable, then you should consider a comprehensive policy. The most important additional benefit of such a policy is cover for loss or accidental damage to your car.

Sickness and Medical Insurance.

If you consider the benefits provided by the National Insurance schemes and the National Health Service to be inadequate, you can take out insurance that provides for you when ill. There are several schemes. *Hospital risk insurance* provides a sum only for the period you are in hospital. You may consider it best to have a *permanent health insurance*. This provides cover for the total period you are ill. In addition to providing an income for yourself when ill, there are schemes that provide for private medical treatment. The most well-known is the British United Provident Association (B.U.P.A.).

Buying Insurance.

Because of the bewildering variety of policies available it is often best to seek professional advice when buying insurance. This can be obtained from an insurance broker or your bank manager.

7. BUYING A HOUSE

Buying a house is very often preferable to renting a home. Your own house provides you and your family with a secure home. A house is also one of the soundest investments available to most people. The general tendency is for house prices to rise, and it is unusual for someone to lose money on a house, unless he or she sells it fairly quickly. In addition, a house can be a very useful asset. For example, if you wish to move elsewhere the house can always be sold and the proceeds used to buy a home elsewhere. A house can be particularly valuable on retirement. With the mortgage paid off the retired owner can choose from a number of possible courses of action. He could continue living in it rent free. If the house proved too large for retirement part of it could always be let out to provide some additional income. Alternatively, the owner could move to a smaller home and the difference in the value of the two houses would provide a useful capital sum.

For many people there is no satisfactory alternative to buying a home. Most people are unlikely to be offered council accommodation. Furthermore, a home owner is likely to find it much easier to move than a council tenant. Councils are often reluctant or unable to offer new accommodation when their tenants wish to move; whereas an owner occupier can always sell his house and buy another elsewhere.

Accommodation rented privately also has its disadvantages. Reasonably priced rented accommodation is becoming increasingly difficult to find. Tenants sometimes pay nearly as much, or even more, in rent than they would have to pay for a mortgage on similar property. And mortgage interest normally attracts tax relief whereas rent does not. Finally, rents are likely to rise as inflation continues. Mortgage repayments on the other hand, although they fluctuate from time to time, are related to the original loan and not to the current value of the property.

The basic drawback of buying a house is the cost of buying and selling. The costs can include solicitor's and surveyor's fees and (in the case of selling) an estate agent's fee. Normally there will be the costs of fitting out a new home—the cost of curtains is one example. These costs clearly mean that it is not advantageous to buy a home if you expect to move in the near future.

An obstacle for many people is cash. One hundred per cent mortgages are uncommon, and the buyer has to find the difference between the mortgage offered and the price of the house. There are also the other fees mentioned above. The position may be illustrated with an example. Mr. and Mrs. Smith agree to buy a house for £28,000. The Smiths' building society is prepared to lend them 95 per cent of the value of the property. In this case, the loan would be £26,600 which leaves the Smiths £1,400 to find. On top of the £1,400, the Smiths have to pay a valuation fee to the building society of, say, £50. The valuation fee is related to the value of the property so that the higher the value, the higher the fee. If the price of the house exceeds £30,000 stamp duty also has to be paid. The rate of the stamp duty is currently 1 per cent of the value of the house. Note that duty is levied on the total price of the house, and not just the excess over £30,000. So, for example, the stamp duty on a £50,000 house would be £500. The Smiths also decide to have a professional survey of the house done in order to see if there are any defects in the property. The surveyor's fee depends on how detailed the buyer wishes the survey to be. In this example the fee is £120. Finally, the Smiths receive a solicitor's bill for £350. The solicitor's charge will depend partly on the value of the house, and partly on how much work the solicitor has to do to transfer the house from the seller to the buyer.

Cost of the house	£28,000
Mortgage	£26,600
	1,400
Valuation fee	50
Survey fee	120
Solicitor's fee	350
	£1,920

In this example, therefore, the Smiths need at least £1,920 of their own money. Frequently the amount of money needed will be greater than this. For example, if the Smiths' mortgage were limited to 90 per cent of the value of the house they may have had to find at least £3,320.

It should also be borne in mind that more money is needed to furnish the house. A first-time buyer needs almost everything from curtains to a cooker, and from doormats to a dinner service. Not all of these things need to be bought straight away of course. Nevertheless, some items, such as something to sleep on, and to eat off, will be needed almost immediately.

So it can be seen that, unless one is likely to move in the near future, buying a house can be a sensible decision. The key thing is to save up a reasonable sum of money towards the various costs. The next step is choosing a home.

Choosing a House.

Given the price of houses, selecting your future home is clearly not a decision to be rushed. Possibly the first thing to do is to work out how much you can afford to pay. If you need a mortgage, building societies will give you a rough indication of the maximum amount they will lend. They cannot give a precise figure, however, because the amount a society will lend depends not only on your income but also the house itself. There is more on this below. The next stage is to decide where you would like to live. If you are not familiar with the area it pays to spend time studying a map in detail. That way you soon get an idea of the proximity of each area to your work, to the nearest shopping centre and so on. It is also worth thinking carefully about the type of house you want. You may, of course, be influenced by what is available. Nevertheless, if you have a fairly clear idea of what you want a lot of time can be saved by eliminating houses that are obviously unsuitable. Features to think about include whether you want a house, bungalow or flat; the number of bedrooms you require and whether you want a large, medium or small garden.

The next move is to find out as much as possible about the current state of the home market. Estate agents are always delighted to deluge prospective home buyers with details of many properties. Many of them might be unsuitable for you, but they will begin to give you an idea of the value of different houses. You may also change your mind about the sort of house you want. Estate agents are not the only source of information about houses for sale. Houses are often advertised privately, usually in the local newspaper. And because the seller will be saving hundreds of pounds in estate agent's fees, you might be able to buy a house advertised privately for a bit less than it it were handled by an agent.

There are several other considerations that should be borne in mind. For example, if you are likely to have to move within a few years you may wish to buy a house which is relatively easy to resell. Such a house might be a fairly modern three-bedroomed semi-detached house which is close to shops and schools: rather than a "character" property in a remote area.

Buying a House.

The process of buying a house should not be rushed either. In fact, at this stage it is well to have two or three properties in mind. This reduces the disappointment should you fail to get your first choice. It also puts you in a better bargaining position over the price of the house. There is nothing sacred about the asking price. Sellers will often ask for a bit more than they think they will probably get. So, depending on the state of the market, it can often pay to offer less than the advertised price.

When a price is agreed, make it "subject to contract." Neither party is formally bound to the agreement until the contracts are actually signed. Before that happens there are a number of things to be done. First of all you will probably want a solicitor. It is not absolutely necessary to use a solicitor, but unless you are familiar with the procedure it is usually advisable to do so. If you need a mortgage the next thing to do is to give full details of the house you intend to buy to your building society manager. He will then arrange to have the property surveyed and valued. The purpose of this is to safeguard the building society's money by making sure that the house is a good investment. When the building society is ready it will inform you how much it is prepared to lend on the house. Your solicitor should then be instructed to complete the remaining formalities.

As soon as the solicitors are satisfied about the technicalities of the purchase the next stage is the signing and exchange of contracts. The contract is usually prepared in duplicate with one copy to be signed by the buyer and one by the seller. The buyer is normally expected to pay a deposit of 10 per cent of the purchase price when contracts are exchanged. The exchange of contracts legally commits both parties to the purchase. This commitment stands regardless of what happens thereafter. This is why it is important for you or your solicitor or both to find out as much as possible about the property before the contract is signed. The contract will contain a number of details, including the date on which the deal will be completed. The date is usually a few weeks ahead and allows both parties to make final arrangements before the house is actually handed over. On the completion date the balance of the purchase money is paid, and the purchaser can take possession of the house.

The length of time between finding a house of your choice and taking possession can vary considerably. It depends on the number of complications involved. If everything goes well it would probably take between eight and ten weeks to buy the house. Such is the process of buying a home. However for many people the major consideration is the mortgage. It is therefore worth describing mortgages in greater detail.

Mortgages.

A "mortgage" is a technical term meaning that certain rights over one's property are given to someone else as security for a loan. In other words, if you buy a house with a loan you give a mortgage as security. In everyday usage, however, a mortgage refers just to the loan, even though the property is still used as security. Even if you can afford to pay cash, it is often worthwhile buying a house with the aid of a mort-

gage. There are several reasons for this. First of all, if the house is to be your main residence the mortgage interest on the first £30,000 borrowed qualifies for tax relief. Secondly, as inflation continues the value of money declines, and so the real value of the mortgage also declines. As a result, the mortgage repayments will not tend to rise in line with inflation.

It is true that interest rates fluctuate and that when they rise your mortgage repayments will rise as well. But sooner or later the rate of interest will fall again. In the meantime, higher interest payments are mitigated by higher tax relief. In addition, when interest rates rise it is sometimes possible to extend the repayment period, rather than increase the monthly repayments. The most common types of mortgage are repayment mortgages and endowment mortgages.

Repayment Mortgages.

Repayment mortgages are usually the most straightforward. They are repaid in equal monthly instalments. Each payment consists partly of interest and partly of a repayment of capital. In the early years the repayments consist almost entirely of interest. As the loan is paid off, the interest element declines.

It should be noted that in April 1983 the method of giving tax relief on mortgages changed. Previously the taxpayers received the relief directly through a reduction in their tax payments. Now, for most mortgages, the Inland Revenue gives the relief directly to the lenders and the borrowers pay the lenders less instead. With these arrangements there is no longer a need for the old "option mortgage" scheme, which has now been discontinued. Loans within that scheme have been incorporated into the new arrangements.

Endowment Mortgages.

An "endowment mortgage" is a mortgage linked to an insurance policy. When the policy matures it pays off the mortgage. In the meantime you only pay interest on the loan. If you die before the end of the agreement the insurance policy would pay off the mortgage. Endowment mortgages usually cost more than repayment mortgages because of the premium for the insurance policy. However, there is the advantage that as with other insurance policies, it is possible to have a "with-profits" element in an endowment policy. This costs more, but it means that the insurance company not only guarantees to provide a minimum sum but also adds "bonuses" each year. The size of the bonus depends on the investment position of the company. When the policy matures the pay-out (including bonuses) will cover the mortgage and leave you with a substantial sum as well.

Where to Get a Mortgage.

The majority of mortgages are supplied by building societies and in recent years banks have become an important source of mortgages. Local councils can also provide mortgages. But councils often limit their lending to people in certain categories, such as council tenants or those recognised as having a particular housing need. In addition, councils often charge higher rates of interest than building societies. So, clearly, the first place for most people to look for a mortgage is a building society or a bank. Councils, however, will sometimes lend money on property that building societies are reluctant to consider. This is particularly true of older houses. The reason is that many councils take the view that it is better to modernise many older properties rather than to demolish them. Some insurance companies also provide mortgages, but this is only a minor source of loans. Some employers, such as banks and building societies, will provide their employees with loans at favourable rates.

Getting a Mortgage.

The first thing to do is to plan ahead. As we have seen, you will probably need to put up a substantial sum of money of your own, so you should start saving as soon as possible. It can be advantageous to save by investing in a building society. When mortgage funds are in short supply societies are likely to consider their own investors before casual applicants. Building societies have fairly strong preferences about the sort of property they are prepared to lend on. For example, they are often very reluctant to lend on older property. In such cases local councils will often take a more liberal attitude. Many building societies are also reluctant to lend on flats. Nevertheless, the lending policies of building societies differ, so if you are turned down by one society, try another. It can also help to ask people who are likely to have close contacts with building societies. Estate agents, your solicitor or bank manager may each be able to suggest a possible source. If you are still unsuccessful, try the local authority.

How Much Can Be Borrowed?

The final question to be dealt with in this section is how much an individual will be allowed to borrow. As stated above, this partly depends on the value of the house concerned. But it also depends on the financial status of the borrower. Building societies have to safeguard their investors' money. Societies are careful not to lend more to anyone than they are likely to be able to repay. A person with a secure career may therefore be treated more favourably than a person whose future earnings are uncertain. Again, different societies have different policies. None the less, it is very rare for building societies to lend more than two and a half or three times your annual income. Most building societies will also take a spouse's income into account, but for a smaller proportion.

For example, suppose you went to a building society which was prepared to lend up to two and a half times your annual earnings plus an amount equal to your wife's annual income. If you earn £8,000 and your wife £5,000, the society would then be prepared to lend you up to £25,000:

Your income	£8,000	Maximum loan	£20,000
Wife's income	£5,000	Maximum loan	£ 5,000
		Combined Limit	£25,000

The extent to which your wife's income is taken into account depends on the lender. It can be as low as a quarter of her annual income.

II. TAXES

Taxation permeates almost every aspect of financial life. In addition, the entire subject is exceedingly complex, and the tax system is altered or amended at least once a year. All that will be attempted here, therefore, is a description of some of the most common situations faced by taxpayers. If your circumstances are more complicated you should consult your tax office, or take professional advice, or both.

For reasons which are largely historical, taxes are often divided into *direct* and *indirect* taxes. Direct taxes are paid to the Inland Revenue. There are four main types of direct taxation:

1. Income tax
2. Capital gains tax
3. Inheritance tax (formerly Capital transfer tax)
4. Corporation tax

Indirect taxes are collected mainly by the Customs and Excise. They include:

1. Value added tax
2. Customs and excise duties
3. Car tax
4. Stamp duties

Stamp duties are, however, the responsibility of the Inland Revenue.

In terms of the amount of revenue raised, income tax is by far the most important tax. It is also the tax most likely to affect the average taxpayer directly.

8. INCOME TAX

If you are resident in the United Kingdom tax is levied on your income whether it originates in the UK or from overseas. Even if you are not resident, tax is still levied on any income you have which originates in the UK. Tax is charged for each year of assessment; that is the year from 6 April to the following 5 April.

Income Subject to Tax.

Most types of income are taxable, including the following:

Income from employment. This includes wages, bonuses, commission, tips and benefits in kind, such as the private use of the company's car.

Income from self-employment, business, professions and vocations.

Interest, dividends and annuities.

Rent.

Pensions.

Income not Subject to Tax.

A few types of income are not subject to tax. The main groups are:

The first £70 of interest per person received from ordinary deposit accounts in the National Savings Bank.

Interest on National Savings Certificates and increases in the value of Index-Linked National Insurance Certificates. Also, interest from the Save-As-You-Earn scheme is exempt.

Sickness benefit (but not statutory sick pay), attendance allowance, mobility allowance, maternity benefit, death grant and family income supplement, child benefit, supplementary benefits paid under the Supplementary Benefits Acts, invalidity benefit and non-contributory invalidity pension.

TABLE 3. *Allowances Against Gross Income in 1985–86 and 1986–87*

	1985–86	1986–87
	£	£
Single person's allowance	2,205	2,335
Married allowance	3,455	3,655
Wife's earned income allowance (maximum)	2,205	2,335
Age allowance—single person (maximum)	2,690	2,850
Age allowance—married couple (maximum)	4,255	4,505
Additional personal allowance	1,250	1,320
Widow's bereavement allowance	1,250	1,320
Dependent relative allowance	100	100
Son's or daughter's services allowance	55	55
Blind person's allowance (each)	360	360

Educational grants and awards.

Compensation for loss of employment—up to £25,000. Some tax is payable on amounts over £25,000 and anything over £75,000 is taxed in full.

War and disability pensions.

Any wins from gambling, including Premium Bond prizes.

The capital element of annuity payments.

Luncheon vouchers (up to 15p a day).

Housing improvement grants from local authorities.

Allowances and Rates of Tax.

As most people know, there are allowances which may be deducted before tax is levied on the remainder of a person's income. The allowances for 1985/86 and 1986/87 are shown in Table 3. The age allowance is reduced if total income exceeds a certain limit, £9,400 for 1986/87. The age allowance is reduced by £2 for every £3 that limit is exceeded until it reaches the normal single or married allowance. The widow's bereavement allowance applies only to the tax year in which the husband died, and the tax year following the bereavement. After these allowances have been deducted from gross income, the remaining taxable income is subject to the rates of tax shown in Table 4.

TABLE 4. *Rates of Tax on Taxable Income for 1986/87*

Rate of tax %	Slice of taxable income £
29 the "basic rate"	0–17,200
40	17,201–20,200
45	20,201–25,400
50	25,401–33,300
55	33,301–41,200
60	over 41,200

Investment Income Surcharge.

Investment income surcharge was abolished in 1984. Before April 1984, it was levied on investment income in addition to the normal rates of income tax. For 1983/84 it was levied at a rate of 15 per cent on investment income over £7,100.

9. ASSESSMENT AND COLLECTION

The administration of income tax is the responsibility of the Inland Revenue. In practice, the job is divided into two parts: assessment and collection. The "assessments" for tax are the responsibility of inspectors of taxes in over 750 tax offices spread throughout the country. When an individual's tax has been assessed the information is then passed to a collector of taxes who actually sends out the bill. If you receive a tax bill which you think is wrong you should contact the inspector. The collector has no power to amend the bill, his job is simply to collect the amounts decided between you and the inspector.

The Tax Schedules.

For historical reasons, income is divided into six groups known as "schedules." These are:

1. *Schedule A:* Income from property.

2. *Schedule B:* Income from commercial woodlands.

3. *Schedule C:* Certain interest and annuities paid out of public revenue.

4. *Schedule D:* Income from trades, businesses and professions. Also included are interest, rents and income not covered by other schedules.

5. *Schedule E:* This is the schedule that affects most people as it covers wages and salaries. It also deals with pensions.

6. *Schedule F:* Dividends and other distributions made by companies.

Pay-As-You-Earn.

By far the largest schedule is Schedule E. Nearly all Schedule E income is taxed through the Pay-As-You-Earn (PAYE) system. PAYE is the method used to deduct tax from wages, salaries and some pensions. In order to keep the deductions as accurate as possible, PAYE is operated on a cumulative basis. This means that your earnings, tax paid and so on are accumulated throughout the tax year. This is how it works. At the beginning, or before the start of the tax year, your tax-free allowances are added up. The total is then converted into a code number. For example, if your allowances came to £4,000 and you are married, then your code number would be 400H. The H suffix denotes that you are entitled to the married man's allowance. (The H stands for the "higher" allowance.) If you are single or a working wife the suffix would be L (representing the "lower" single person's or wife's earned income allowance). If there are special circumstances, for example if you had a second job, the suffix would probably be T. There are also special suffixes for pensioners. The main ones are P for single people, and V for married pensioners. If your current code number is different from the previous one the tax office will send you a "Notice of Coding." This will show the allowances the tax office has taken into account and how your code number has been calculated. If you do not receive a notice of coding you may request one. You should always check to see that you have received your full entitlement to allowances. Your code number is also sent to your employer so he knows how much tax to deduct from your earnings. It is worth noting that the higher your code, the lower the tax deducted from your pay.

It may be of interest to work through a simple example of PAYE operating. Suppose that a person's allowances for the year amount to £5,200, and the appropriate code is issued to his employer. The principle is that the annual allowances are divided by the number of pay periods in the year. If an individual is paid weekly, therefore, his allowances are divided by 52. In our example the individual would be granted £100 worth of allowances each week. This weekly allowance is then accumulated as the tax year progresses. Hence in, say, week 26 of the tax year the individual would be entitled to £2,600 worth of allowances. At the same time, the PAYE system accumulates the amount of earnings received. This enables the amount of tax to be deducted to be calculated accurately. Suppose the individual in our example earned £140 in Week 1 of the tax year. The employer knows from the code number that the person's allowances for that week amount to £100. The employer then deducts this £100 from the £140 gross pay, which leaves £40 of "taxable pay." The next stage is to calculate the tax due on the £40.

To assist him in this process, the employer has two sets of tax tables. The first table converts code numbers into weekly or monthly allowances. After these allowances have been deducted from gross pay the second set of tables is used to calculate the tax due on the remaining pay. In the example, there is £40 of taxable pay, so with a tax rate of, say, 30 per cent, £12 would be deducted in tax. Suppose that the wage in the second week was also £140. Because of the cumulative feature, the value of the allowances would now be £200. (£100 for the second week, plus £100 for the first week). Cumulative pay would now be £280. After deducting the allowances, taxable pay is now £80. The second set of tables would now show a total of £24 due in tax. However, £12 ("cumulative tax paid") was deducted in week 1. The amount of tax due in week 2, therefore, is a further £12 (£24 minus £12 deducted in week 1). This process then continues for the rest of the tax year.

PAYE has a number of advantages. These include accurate deductions of tax. The system can also repay tax during the year if the employee's pay falls substantially. Repayments occur when the value of the allowances accumulates faster than gross pay. The system does not always work in this way. For example, suppose you fail to send your tax return back to the tax office. You may find that you are then put on the Emergency Code (E). This code only gives you allowances equal to the single person's allowance, so if you are entitled to more you will have too much tax deducted. This, of course, provides you with an incentive to sort out your tax affairs with the Inland Revenue. In addition, from July 1982 a taxpayer who becomes unemployed will not normally receive any rebate due until after either he or she ceases to claim unemployment or supplementary benefit, or the end of the tax year. Also, from 1982, rebates cannot usually be paid while a person is on strike.

Sometimes you may find that you have been put on what is known as a "week 1" basis. This means that tax is being deducted from your pay on a *non-cumulative* basis. In other words, every week is treated as though it were the first week of the tax year. One of the main results of the "week 1" basis is that it prevents tax repayments being made automatically if, say, your income falls through unemployment.

How to Check your Code Number.

As you can see from the above explanation, your code number is the factor that determines the amount of tax that is deducted from your pay. You can check your code number by examining your Notice of Coding. You should compare the allowances and expenses you claimed on your tax return with the ones listed on the Notice. One item which might appear on the Notice of Coding is "Tax unpaid for earlier years." This is to enable the tax office to collect outstanding tax by lowering the value of your code. The tax will then be collected slowly over the tax year rather than in one lump sum.

Appeals.

When your tax for the year is assessed you will be sent a Notice of Assessment. This is often not considered necessary if you are taxed under PAYE and your tax situation is straightforward, though you can still ask for one.

If you receive a Notice of Assessment which you think is wrong you must appeal within 30 days of the date appearing on the Notice. Appeals made after 30 days are normally allowed only if you can provide a satisfactory explanation such as being in hospital or abroad, and can show that the appeal was made without unreasonable delay. Most appeals are settled directly with the inspector. If you and the inspector cannot agree, then the case goes before the Commissioners of Income Tax. There are two types of Commissioners: the General Commissioners and the Special Commissioners. The General Commissioners are unpaid and recruited from members of the public. They sit with a clerk who provides advice on tax law. The Special Commissioners are professional civil servants who are experts in tax matters. It is often said that if your appeal is based on common sense, rather than the intricacies of tax law, you may do better to go to the General Commissioners. Each party pays its own costs for hearings before the Commissioners. If, however, the case is taken on to the High Court, or further, the loser usually pays the costs.

Taxation and Marriage.

When a couple marry, the wife continues to be treated by the tax office as a single person until the end of the tax year. The husband gets the full married allowance only if the wedding takes place between the beginning of the tax year (6 April) and 5 May. For weddings later in the year, the married man's allowance is reduced. The amount of the reduction depends on the number of complete months between the start of the tax year and the date of the wedding. For each complete month the allowance is reduced by 1/12th of the difference between the single person's and the married man's allowances.

After the end of the tax year the couple are normally treated as a single person (the husband). The husband is then responsible for completing the tax return in which he must include both his own income and his wife's. This arrangement means that many married couples are taxed more

favourably than if they were single. The reason is that the husband gets the married allowance instead of the single person's allowance. The wife also loses her single person's allowance but, if she works, she is entitled to the wife's earned income allowance.

The situation in 1986/87 is shown below:

Unmarried couple

Man	£2,335	single person's allowance
Woman	£2,335	„ „ „
Total	£4,670	

Married couple

Husband	£3,655	married allowance
Wife	£2,335	wife's earned income allowance
Total	£5,990	

If the wife has no earned income the husband cannot, of course, claim the wife's earned income allowance; just the married allowance of £3,655. On the other hand, if the wife works and the husband has no taxable income the couple are treated more favourably. This is because both the married man's allowance and the wife's earned income allowance can be set against the wife's earnings.

However, for couples with high incomes marriage can mean that they pay more tax than if they were single. The reason is that a married couple's incomes are added together. This means that they face a lower threshold for higher-rate tax than if they were single. Single people can earn up to £17,200 of *taxable income* before they become liable to higher rates of tax. The same thresholds apply to married couples who are assessed jointly.

To reduce the problems of joint assessment, there are two sets of provisions for couples to be treated separately. The first is the *separate taxation* of the wife's earnings. The second is *separate assessment*. The two provisions are quite different and should not be confused.

Separate Taxation of Wife's Earnings.

Separate taxation applies only to the wife's earnings. Couples cannot choose to have the wife's investment income taxed separately. The only way to achieve that would be permanent separation. Separate taxation often involves both gains and losses. The gains arise because the couple may reduce their liability to higher rates of tax. The losses arise because the couple will lose the married man's allowance. It is difficult to be precise about the level of earnings at which it becomes worthwhile to choose separate taxation. It depends on the individual circumstances. Clearly you have to be paying tax at higher rates before any gains can be made. Usually both you and your wife have to have a substantial income before separate taxation leads to net gains. Further information is available in the Inland Revenue's pamphlet IR 13, *Wife's Earnings Election*.

Separate Assessment.

Separate assessment does *not* affect the total amount of tax a couple has to pay. All that happens is that husband and wife get separate tax bills. Separate assessment may also be claimed for capital gains tax. It is also possible to be separately assessed *and* to have the wife's earnings taxed separately at the same time.

10. HOW TO COMPLETE A TAX RETURN

There are four main types of tax return:

1. *Form P1.* This form is mainly for people who earn a salary or a wage and do not have complicated tax problems. For example, if your main source of income is your job, and you have small amounts of interest from your savings but no other income you will probably receive form P1. (The "P" prefix, incidentally, stands for "Pay-As-You-Earn.")

The form P1 is simpler than some of the other forms and a completely redesigned version was introduced in 1984. Most people who receive form P1 do not get one every year. When this happens, the reason is that the tax office is pretty sure that it has enough information to ensure you pay the right amount of tax without having to fill in a return every year. But, remember, it is your responsibility to tell the tax office if your tax liability changes as a result of a change in your circumstances.

For example, if you become entitled to a new allowance because, say, you get married, you should tell the inspector. Nobody else will. Alternatively, if you begin to receive a new source of income you should also tell the inspector. He may well find out anyway. For instance, banks must inform the Inland Revenue of the interest they pay to depositors. Concealing income can lead to demands for back tax plus interest. You may also be liable to penalties.

2. *Form 11P*. This form is designed for people with more complicated circumstances. For example, if you have a job and some other outside earnings you will probably be sent form 11P.

3. *Form 11*. This form is for the self-employed.

4. *Form 1*. Form 1 is designed for a number of categories of tax-payer. Most of the form is specifically designed for trustees, personal representatives and partnerships.

General Points.

It is very worthwhile keeping a tax file containing all the information relevant to your tax affairs. The whole process of completing a tax return is much simpler if you keep all the relevant documents close together. These documents include items such as: P60 (from your employer); dividend advice slips; receipts for expenses. You may also be asked by the inspector to submit detailed records supporting expense claims. A second point is to keep a copy of your return. A photocopy is perhaps the best method of doing this. Alternatively, you can keep a separate record of what you put in the return as you go along.

Keeping a copy of your return has two advantages. First of all it will help you deal with any questions the inspector may have about your return. Secondly, it will enable you to complete your next return more easily. The tax office usually compares your latest tax return with your previous one to see if you have forgotten something. So it is better if you spot any omissions first. If you get into difficulties with your return, you can always telephone or write to the tax office whose address appears on the front of the form. If you wish to call personally, most tax offices are open for public enquiries between 10 am and 4 pm. But remember to take your tax file with you. It does not matter if you wish to make a personal call and your tax office is hundreds of miles away. This is often the case with Londoners and people who work for large nationwide companies. You can always call at a local office and in London there are special PAYE enquiry offices. (Their addresses are in the telephone directory.) Most enquiries can be handled without recourse to your official file. If the file is needed, the Inland Revenue can arrange to have it sent to a local office.

The Return Itself.

As stated above, there are four main types of return, and there are some other variations. Most returns cover two years. They ask for details of your income and capital gains in the previous tax year, and have room for claims for allowances in the current year. Whichever return you receive you should always read the accompanying notes. The different returns sometimes ask different questions and are set out in a different way, but most include the following headings:

INCOME.

Employments or Offices.

If you are an employee, you will receive a form P60 from your employer after 5 April each year.

The P60 will show your total earnings and tax deducted under PAYE. It will do this even if you changed your job during the year. You should enter the total figure on the return, plus any bonuses, tips and so on. You should also enter any earnings from spare-time jobs. The same information should be entered for your wife.

The tax treatment of overseas earnings is unusually complicated—even by income-tax standards! If you are going to work abroad you should enquire about the tax implications. One place to start is with the Inland Revenue's leaflets IR6, IR20 and IR25.

Trade, Profession or Vocation.

Any profits you make from self-employment should be entered here. This section covers both partnerships and sole traders. The figure required is your net profit for your accounting year which ended in the twelve months to 5 April 1986. The figure should be supported by a statement of account. If you do not know what your profits are when you complete the return you should write "per accounts to be submitted." Your accounts should then be sent to the Inspector as soon as possible.

Social Security Pensions and Benefits.

Some pensions and most social security benefits are tax-free and do not have to be entered on the tax return. Further details of these are given in the notes accompanying the return. "Retirement pension or old people's pension" refers to the state retirement pension, and this must be entered. If you are approaching retirement you should inform the tax office. This will help the Revenue make sure that your tax affairs are kept up to date when you retire. Otherwise, it is possible that you many pay too much (or too little) tax until your affairs are sorted out.

Other Pensions.

If a pension is paid by a former employer it will usually be taxed through the PAYE system. At the end of the tax year, therefore, you should receive a form P60 showing the gross pension paid during the year. This section also covers pensions from abroad. Normally overseas pensions are taxed on a preceding year basis. In other words, your current tax bill will be based on the pension you received during the previous tax year.

Property.

Rent can be treated in one of two ways. If the accommodation is furnished *and* the rent covers services such as meals and cleaning the income will be treated as *earned* income. If the accommodation is unfurnished *or* it is furnished and the rent does not cover services the rent will be treated as *investment* income. The figures required are those for total income, expenses and net income. It is only the last of these, the net income, that is taxable, and included in the taxpayer's total income. The details of property income should be presented in a separate statement.

The expenses that may be claimed include:

Rates.

Repairs and maintenance.

Insurance for the structure and its contents (but not insurance against loss of rent).

Costs of providing services to tenants.

Wear and tear for furniture and fittings. The allowance is usually 10 per cent of the rent receivable.

Management expenses. This includes items such as agents' commission for letting the property or collecting the rent.

Dividends from United Kingdom Companies, etc.

Because dividends from UK companies and distributions from unit trusts are accompanied by a "tax credit," you do not have to pay basic-rate tax on them. However, you still have to enter the dividends and tax credits from each company or unit trust, in case you are liable to higher-rate tax or are entitled to a rebate. The necessary information will be shown on your dividend slips. If you do not have enough room, make out a separate list and submit it with the return. The totals should be entered on the return itself. One point should be made about unit trusts. Part of the first distribution you receive will be called *equalisation*. This is part of your capital, and *so should not* be entered on the return.

Other Dividends, etc.

This section requires you to enter the gross (before tax) amount of income from each source. Where tax has already been deducted from foreign income you should give the details.

Interest not Taxed before Receipt.

The first £70 of interest received from ordinary (but *not* investment) accounts with the National Savings Banks is exempt from tax. Your husband or wife is also entitled to a £70 exemption. You should still enter the total amount on the return. Interest from bank desposits accounts should also be entered. Provided it is over a certain minimum amount, banks are required to report to the Inland Revenue the amount of interest they have paid or credited to you. Bank interest is often overlooked by tax-payers and normally results in an enquiry from the Inland Revenue. Bank interest is usually credited twice a year and, of course, you should enter the total of these two payments. Note that since 20 November 1979, all the interest from Trustee Savings Banks has been taxable.

Untaxed Income from Abroad.

This section refers only to unearned income from overseas. (Foreign earnings, business income and pensions are dealt with in earlier sections.) You should enter the total amounts involved, whether or not they were actually remitted to the UK. You may deduct expenses incurred. If the income has already been taxed overseas you may be entitled to relief. Details are given in the Inland Revenue's booklet IR6.

Interest from UK Building Societies.

Building society interest is "tax paid"—but this only saves you from tax at the basic rate. If you are liable to higher rates of tax you will have to pay more tax on the interest. The Inland Revenue will calculate the additional amount of tax payable. For this purpose, the interest payment will be *grossed up* to include tax at the basic rate.

Any Other Profits or Income.

As you can guess, this section is for any source of income not covered elsewhere.

Alterations in Untaxed Income, etc.

The Inspector needs to know about changes in your untaxed income and your outgoings so that he can, if necessary, adjust your code number. This will enable your deductions of tax to be kept up to date. Such a change may, of course, also affect an assessment on other income.

OUTGOINGS.

Expenses in Employment.

The basic rule covering claims for employment expenses is that they must be incurred wholly, exclusively and necessarily in the performance of the duties of that employment. The rule is usually applied quite strictly. Thus, for example, travel expenses to and from work are not normally allowable because they are not incurred *in the performance* of the duties of the employment. Travelling expenses may be allowed, but only if incurred in the course of the employment.

Nevertheless, there are several types of expenditure which may be claimed. They include subscriptions to professional bodies, tools and some types of industrial clothing. Trade Unions often agree a fixed allowance with the tax office, but you can still claim for actual expenses if they exceed the agreed figure.

Interest on Loans.

Tax relief on interest paid is now very limited. Loans from a Building Society or a Local Authority for the purchase of your main residence qualify for relief. You do not have to enter the amount of interest paid to these organisations, as they will inform the tax office themselves. The only thing you need to do is to enter the name of the building society or local authority and your account number. Bank overdrafts do not qualify for tax relief. Nor do loans obtained with credit cards. However, the interest from a bank loan which is used to buy or improve your only (or main) residence does qualify for relief.

Capital Gains.

You should give details of the assets you have bought and sold during the tax year. Capital gains tax and how to calculate your gain or loss are discussed in greater detail in a separate section below.

Allowances.

Unlike the income part of the return, which refers to income received in the previous year, the allowances section refers to your entitlement in the current year. Compared to some aspects of income tax, the allowances are relatively straightforward. You should be able to establish your entitlement by reading the official notes carefully. If not, ask at the tax office.

11. CAPITAL GAINS TAX

When you dispose of an asset or possession you may make a capital gains or a capital loss. An asset is property of any kind. It includes both property in the United Kingdom and property overseas. You are considered to have disposed of an asset if you sell it, lose it, exchange it or give it away. However, the transfer of a possession between a husband and wife who are not separated is not considered to be a disposal.

Tax-free Gains.

The following assets are exempt from capital gains tax:

Your home (but see below).

Personal possessions, household goods and other chattels, provided that each item is worth £3,000 or less at the time of the disposal. A set of goods, for example a pair of vases, is counted as one item. (*Chattels* means tangible, movable property.)

Animals, private cars, caravans and boats. Also other chattels which are wasting assets; that is assets expected to last 50 years or less.

Life assurance policies.

National Savings Certificates, British Savings Bonds and Save-As-You-Earn.

British government stocks if owned for more than one year or inherited. This exemption has been extended to corporate bonds (*e.g.* debentures) which are issued after 13 March 1984 and which are held for at least twelve months.

British money.

Foreign currency obtained for personal or family expenditure.

Winnings from betting or from Premium Bonds.

Gifts to charities.

Gifts to certain institutions such as the National Trust and the British Museum.

Your Own Home.

When you sell your house any capital gains you make will normally be exempt from tax. From 1980/81 onwards this exemption also applies (within certain limits) if you let part of your home. However, there are a number of circumstances in which you may get only partial exemption. For example, if you use part of your home for business you may not be allowed full exemption from capital gains tax. These circumstances are described in more detail in the Inland Revenue leaflet CGT4, *Capital Gains Tax—Owner-occupied houses*. You should enter any gains from the disposal of your house on your tax return in case they are not wholly exempt.

Capital Losses.

Your capital gains can be reduced by deducting allowable losses. An allowable capital loss is usually one which would have been taxable if it had been a gain. For example, a loss on an item which is exempt, such as your car, would *not* be considered an allowable loss. If your losses exceed your gains in the tax year you can carry the balance forward to set against gains in future years. You can also deduct allowable expenditure from your capital gains (or add them to your capital losses). Allowable expenditure includes the costs of acquiring or disposing of an asset; for example, commission, conveyancing costs and advertising. It also includes expenditure which increases the value of the asset, such as improvements to property.

Working Out Your Gain.

Normally your capital gain (or loss) is the amount you receive when disposing of the asset *minus* the original amount you paid for it. If you give the asset away, the market value at the time of disposal is used instead. The same method is used if you were originally given the asset, or if you inherited it. There are special rules for assets which you owned before 6 April 1965. (This was the date that capital gains tax was introduced.) These rules usually mean that it is only the gain or loss since that date which counts.

Shares.

If you buy batches of the same share at different prices the cost of each share is considered to be the average cost. For example, suppose you purchase 100 shares in a company for £200. Three months later you buy a further 100 of the same shares for £300. You would then have a total of 200 shares which cost you £500. The average cost is, therefore, £2·50 per share. When you come to sell all or some of these shares the calculation of your gain or loss will be based on this average cost.

The Rates of Capital Gains Tax.

Since 1965 net capital gains have been taxed at a flat rate of 30 per cent. There have, however, always been provisions for relief on smaller gains. Up to the tax year 1977/78, capital gains tax was payable only if the *proceeds* (not the gain) from the sale of an individual's assets exceeded £1,000 in any tax year. For this purpose the proceeds from the sale of a husband and wife's assets were aggregated. In addition, although the main rate of tax is 30 per cent, there was an alternative method of calculating the tax. By this method half an individual's gains up to a maximum of £2,500 were ignored, and the rest were taxed as investment income. For most taxpayers, this alternative method of charging capitals gains tax was the most favourable. It meant that most people who paid the tax did so at 17 per cent, as half the gain was treated as tax-free, and the other half was taxed at the basic rate of 34 per cent.

From 1977 until 1980 a different system applied. An individual's *gains* up to £1,000 in any tax year were exempt and gains between £1,000 and £5,000 were taxed at 15 per cent, that is at half the full rate. There were also marginal provisions so that the full rate of tax applied only to gains of £9,500 or more. The way it worked was that gains

between £5,000 and £9,500 were taxed at a rate of 50 per cent on the part of the gain which exceeded £5,000.

In the March 1980 budget the system was changed again. For 1980/81 onwards the first £3,000 of capital gains were exempt and any gains over £3,000 were taxed at the flat rate of 30 per cent. This threshold was increased to £5,000 for 1982/83, £5,300 for 1983/84, £5,600 for 1984/85, £5,900 for 1985/86 and £6,300 for 1986/87. Capital gains are to be adjusted for inflation since March 1982.

12. INHERITANCE TAX
(Formerly CAPITAL TRANSFER TAX)

Inheritance tax emerged from the remains of the previous capital transfer tax in March 1986. Capital transfer tax applied to transfers of capital made both during life and on a person's death. However, since its introduction in 1975 the scope of the tax had been steadily reduced so that the number of people actually paying capital transfer tax fell from 61,000 in 1976/77 to 28,000 by 1982/83.

Capital transfer tax had replaced the old estate duty which was imposed on property passing at death, and gifts made within 7 years before death. The position has now turned full circle because, essentially, inheritance tax, like the old estate duty, is levied on transfers between individuals made on the death of the donor, or up to 7 years before his or her death.

The Tax.

Inheritance tax is payable on transfers made on or after 18 March 1986 on transfers made at death or in the years preceding death. Certain gifts, most of which are listed below, are exempt from tax. All other gifts which are not exempt and which are made within 7 years of death are taxable as soon as the total amount of taxable transfers exceeds the threshold for tax (£71,000 from March 1986).

Furthermore, there are rules, similar to those operated under estate duty, which apply where the donor continues to enjoy some benefit from a gift even after it has been 'given away'. For example, this might apply where a person gives his or her home to the children, but continues to live in it. If this happens, for the purpose of inheritance tax, the gift will normally be treated as if it had been given on the date such enjoyment finally ceases.

The method of valuing assets largely continues on from the previous capital transfer tax and estate duty. Assets are usually valued at the price they would fetch on the open market at the time of the transfer.

The value of the estate on death will be taxed as the top slice of cumulative transfers in the 7 years before death. (For capital transfer tax the cumulation period was 10 years.)

The rates of tax are shown in Table 5 and apply from 18 March 1986. However, where gifts are made between individuals more than 3 years before the death of the donor the rate of tax is reduced by the relevant percentage given in Table 6. Different rules apply to gifts into and out of trust, discretionary trust charges and gifts involving companies.

TABLE 5.   *The Rates of Inheritance Tax*

0 to	71,000	Nil
71,000	95,000	30
95,001	129,000	35
129,001	164,000	40
164,001	206,000	45
206,001	257,000	50
257,001	317,000	55
over	317,000	60

TABLE 6.   *Relief for Lifetime Transfers*

Years between gift and death	Percentage of full charge
0–3	100
3–4	80
4–5	60
5–6	40
6–7	20
Over 7	0

Exempt Transfers

Certain transfers are eligible for exemption in much the same way as they were under capital transfer tax, including the following:

Transfers up to £3,000 in any one year (unused relief may be carried forward for one year only).

Small gifts of up to £250 to any one recipient in any tax year.

Gifts made as part of normal expenditure.

Marriage gifts as follows:

Parents	£5,000 each
Grandparents	£2,500 each
Bride and groom	£2,500 to each other
Other people	£1,000 each

Transfers between husband and wife if the recipient is domiciled in the United Kingdom.

Gifts to charities and political parties (unless made within one year of death, in which case the exemption is limited to £100,000). A 'political party' is defined for this purpose as one with two M.P.s, or one M.P. and not less than 150,000 votes for its candidates at the last general election.

Gifts for national purposes, *etc.* For example, gifts to the National Trust, National Gallery, universities and museums are exempt.

Other Relief.

There is also some relief for business assets, agricultural land and shares which represent a controlling interest in a company. In addition, a certain amount of relief is available for minority shareholdings in unquoted companies.

Administration and Collection.

The responsibility for the administration of inheritance tax lies with the Inland Revenue, and the procedures for assessment, appeals and penalties are similar to those for income tax. As with the previous capital transfer tax, the responsibility for dealing with Inland Revenue enquiries about transfers made before death lies with the personal representatives of the deceased. Where a person's death creates tax liability on gifts previously made, the main responsibility for the tax falls on the recipient, but with recourse to the donor's estate if necessary.

13. VALUE ADDED TAX

Value Added Tax (VAT) was introduced in the United Kingdom on 1 April 1973, and replaced the old Purchase Tax and Selective Employment Tax. One of the main reasons for changing the system was to harmonise the UK's indirect tax system with those of the other members of the Common Market, each of which now has some kind of value added tax.

As its name suggests, VAT is levied on the goods and services you buy. In the budget of June 1979, the standard and higher rates of VAT were amalgamated into a single rate of 15 per cent. The government, however, has the power to vary the rates of VAT by up to a quarter during the year in the interests of economic management. Some goods and services are "zero-rated" and others are "exempted" from VAT, a distinction which is explained shortly.

Anyone who has a business with a turnover of £19,500 per year or more must register with the Customs and Excise. In some circumstances it can be advantageous to register even if you have a business with a turnover below this level (*see* "Registration" below).

How VAT Works.

VAT is payable at every stage of production when goods and services are supplied either to another business or to the final consumer. VAT is also payable on imported goods (and some imported services). The tax is charged by the supplier, who then pays it over to the Customs and Excise. For example, a simple VAT invoice for a good would show:

	£
Goods supplied	100
VAT at 15%	15
Total payable	£115

When a business calculates how much VAT is payable to the Customs and Excise it can deduct any VAT it has been *charged* on the goods and services it has purchased itself. For instance, suppose a firm buys some wood for £100 (plus £15 VAT) which it turns into furniture and sells for £200 (plus £30 VAT). The tax position would then be as follows:

	£	£
Receipts for furniture	200	
VAT charged to customer		30
Cost of wood	100	
VAT charged by supplier		15
VAT payable to Customs & Excise		£15

The final customer is charged £30 VAT and the Customs and Excise receives £30 in VAT (£15 from the furniture maker and £15 from the wood supplier).

In principle, each business pays tax on only the *value* it has *added* to its output. In our example above, the firm took £100 worth of wood and turned it into £200 worth of furniture. It could be said, therefore, that the firm has increased the value of the wood by £100. Accordingly, £15 VAT is payable to the Customs and Excise. Since each firm is taxed on its "value added," and charges the tax to its customer, the eventual VAT bill is related to the final value of the product and is paid by the final customer.

The way VAT is operated can be further illustrated by tracing the production of a good from the raw material stage through to the sale to the final customer. This is done in the Table on page **H19**.

Zero-rated Supplies.

Goods and services that are "zero-rated" are in principle subject to VAT, but the rate applying to them is zero. This means that while VAT is not charged on these goods, businesses can still recover VAT paid on their own purchases. The effect of this arrangement is that zero-rated goods and services should be entirely free of VAT. For example, exports are relieved of VAT in this way.

Goods and services which are zero-rated may be summarised as follows:

Food—but not items such as pet foods, ice cream, soft drinks, alcoholic drinks, "meals out," and hot takeaway food and drink.

Water—except distilled water and bottled water.

Books—including newspapers, periodicals, music and maps (stationery is taxable).

Talking books and wireless for the blind.

News services.

Fuel and Power—but not petrol and petrol substitutes.

Construction—of buildings.

Transport—except taxis, hired cars and boats and aircraft used for recreation.

Caravans—provided they are too large to be used as trailers on the roads. Houseboats are also zero-rated.

Gold and banknotes—but not gold coins or jewellery.

Drugs, medicines, medical and surgical appliances—provided they are purchased on a prescription.

Exports.

Charities.

Clothing and Footwear—for young children, industrial protective clothing and crash helmets.

Exempt Supplies.

Exempt goods and services are not subject to VAT, even in principle. A business cannot take any credit for VAT paid on the supplies used to produce exempt goods. Exemption is therefore less advantageous than zero-rating, but if a good falls into both categories it is zero-rated. Exempt items include:

Land.
Insurance including brokers' services.
Postal services, but not telephones.
Betting, gaming and lotteries.
Finance such as banking.
Education—including incidental services.
Health—goods provided by opticians, etc.
Burial and cremation services.
Trade Unions and Professional Bodies

The Tax Point.

The tax point is the date on which liability to VAT arises. There are rigid rules for fixing the tax point. This is to prevent businesses from gaining an unfair advantage from manipulating the date of transactions, either to delay the payment of VAT, or to take advantage of changes in the rates of tax.

Basically the tax point is the date when goods are despatched or made available to the customer. There are, however, two main exceptions to this. First, if an invoice is issued within 14 days of this time, the date of the invoice becomes the tax point. Secondly, if payment is made in advance, the date of payment becomes the tax point. It is also possible for particular businesses to make special arrangements with the Customs and Excise regarding the tax point.

Registration.

As already stated, anyone who has a business which has a taxable turnover of £20,500 or more a year must register with the Customs and Excise. For this purpose a "business" means any trade, profession or vocation. This includes partnerships, one-man businesses and free-lance work. It also includes clubs and associations such as sports clubs, but it does not include trade unions.

Businesses with a turnover of less than £20,500 a year are not liable to register, but it might be in their interests to do so. Where a trader pays more VAT for his supplies than he receives from his customers, he may be entitled to a rebate. This is most likely to happen where a business makes or supplies mainly items that are zero-rated or exported, but it may also happen with a new business. Rebates can be claimed only by registered traders.

To register for VAT, you simply contact the local VAT office (the address will be in the local telephone directory under "Customs and Excise"). You will then be sent form VAT 1, which you will have to complete and return. If a person wishes to de-register he may do so if he can satisfy the Customs and Excise that his taxable turnover (including the VAT) of all his business activities in the next 12 months will be £19,500 or less. You can also, of course, de-register if you sell, cease trading or retire from your business.

VAT Records.

Businesses which are not exempt from VAT are required to keep certain records of their purchases and sales and the VAT relating to them. Furthermore, a *tax account* must be kept. This should contain a summary of the VAT totals from the

main records and also VAT payments made to the Customs, or any repayments received.

Most businesses also have to issue *tax invoices* when making sales. Exceptions are retail businesses and sales of zero-rated goods and services. A tax invoice has to include the business's VAT registration number, the invoice number, the tax point and the tax charged.

Returns and Payment.

Traders registered for VAT have to make a return every three months. Some traders who are likely to receive rebates may be allowed to submit returns every month. The return must be made within 30 days of the end of the period to which it relates, and any VAT due should be paid at the same time.

Essentially, the return requires the trader to calculate the value of his sales and the VAT charged thereon. He must also add up all the purchases of his business and the VAT paid on these inputs. The basic calculation will then look something like this:

Total sales for the period	£10,000	
VAT received		£1,500
Total inputs (purchases) for the period	£8,000	
VAT paid		£1,200
Balance payable to the Customs & Excise		£300

Appeals.

There are independent VAT tribunals to deal with appeals over a wide range of issues. This includes whether or not a trader should be registered and, if so, what the effective date of registration is; the amount of VAT payable; the amount of credit that can be taken for VAT paid on a business's purchases; and the value of goods and services supplied. From the tribunal there is an appeal to the High Court and from there to the Court of Appeal on a point of law (but not questions of fact). In Scotland such appeals go to the Court of Session. There are time limits for submitting appeals, and the procedure for appealing to the VAT Tribunals is described in a booklet available from the local VAT office.

Retailers.

Retailers are in a special position because they are usually unable to record each sale separately. Retailers are not required to issue tax invoices unless asked by customers, and there are several special schemes for calculating the amount of VAT payable. Retailers usually charge a price which is inclusive of VAT, and the amount of VAT can be calculated by using the appropriate fractions. With the rate of 15 per cent the relevant fraction is 3/23rds of the gross price. For example, the amount of VAT payable on an article with a gross price of £46 would be £46 × 3/23 = £6.

Bad Debts.

Where goods or services have been supplied by a trader and VAT paid to the Customs and Excise, but the purchaser then fails to pay, relief can be obtained for the VAT paid. The relief is subject

	Basic Price £	VAT £	Amount Received by Customs and Excise (C & E) £
Manufacturer imports raw materials	1,000	150	
Manufacturer pays VAT to C & E			+ 150
Manufacturer sells goods to wholesaler	2,000	300	
Manufacturer pays VAT to C & E			+ 150 (£300 minus £150)
Wholesaler sells goods to retailers	3,000	450	
Wholesaler pays VAT to C & E			+ 150 (£450 minus £300)
Retailers sell goods to customers	5,000	750	
Retailers pay VAT to C & E			+ 300 (£750 minus £450)
Customers pay	5,000 plus 750 VAT		
Customs and Excise receive total			£750

to certain conditions. First of all, the purchaser must be insolvent and the insolvency must have occurred after 1 October 1978. Secondly, the seller must obtain an acknowledgement of a claim for debt from the person acting in the insolvency, for example, the liquidator. Thirdly, the claim must not include the amount of VAT included in the debt, and the price of the goods must not have been greater than the market value. The relief takes the form of a refund of the VAT originally paid on the bad debt.

Further Information.

The Customs and Excise provide a series of detailed leaflets which cover all aspects of VAT, and which are available free of charge from any VAT office.

III. SPECIAL TOPICS

GLOSSARY OF BUSINESS TERMS AND ABBREVIATIONS

A/C. Account.

A.C.A. Associate of the Institute of Chartered Accountants in England and Wales.

A.C.C.A. Associate of the Association of Certified Accountants.

Acct. Account; accountant.

Ack. Acknowledge.

A.C.M.A. Associate Member of the Institute of Cost and Management Accountants.

ACT. Advance Corporation Tax.

Act of God. A result of natural forces, such as an earthquake, which is beyond the control of man. Therefore it cannot form a basis for legal liability.

Ad Val. Ad valorem: according to the value.

Advice Note. A document sent to a customer advising him that his order has been received or that the goods have been despatched. See also *Delivery Note.*

Agent. A person with the authority to act on behalf of another person.

Amortization 1. To pay off a debt in instalments, usually through a sinking fund.
2. See *Depreciation.*

Articles of Association. These are the rules which govern the internal workings of a company. For example, they specify what the powers of the directors are.

Assets. The resources of a business or other organisation. Current (or "circulating") assets are those which are constantly turning over and are used up in producing the output of the business. They include raw materials, stocks and money owed to the business. Fixed (or "capital") assets are those which are normally kept for longer periods in the business and are used to produce the output. Examples include land, buildings, machinery and vehicles. "Intangible" assets describes items such as patents and goodwill.

Audit. An examination of the books and accounts of a business by an independent and qualified person. See also *Internal Audit.*

Bad Debts. Debts which are unlikely to be paid and are therefore written off as losses.

Balance Sheet. A statement of the assets and liabilities of a business.

Banker's Draft. A draft, similar to a cheque but drawn on or behalf of a bank itself. As a result it is often more acceptable than a cheque.

Bankruptcy. The state of being declared by a court to be insolvent, that is unable to pay debts.

B/d. Brought down (in accounts).

B.E. Bill of Exchange.

B/f. Brought forward (in accounts).

Bill of Exchange. A written order signed by the drawer requiring the drawee to pay the amount stated to the person named. A cheque is a bill drawn on a bank.

Bill of Lading. A document issued by a ship's captain which is regarded as a contract to deliver the goods in question and which gives proof of the ownership of the goods.

B/L. Bill of lading.

Bonded Warehouse. A warehouse in which imported goods can be stored until either customs duties are paid or the goods are re-exported.

B.O.T.B. British Overseas Trade Board.

Bridging Loan. A loan made for a short period to allow the lender to make a purchase before he receives some anticipated funds.

British Overseas Trade Board. A Government organisation which provides assistance to business exporting their products.

Broker. A person who undertakes commercial transactions between two or more parties.

Brokerage. The commission charged by a broker.

Bros. Brothers.

B.S. Balance sheet; British standard.

B/S. Balance sheet; Bill of sale.

B.S.I. British Standards Institution.

Buyers' Market. A market where the amount people wish to sell exceeds the amount others wish to buy at prevailing prices. Buyers can often, therefore, obtain more favourable terms.

C.A. Chartered accountant; member of the Institute of Chartered Accountants in Scotland.

Carr. pd. carriage paid.

Cash Flow. The flow of cash in and out of a business. This is an important item for the management of a business. Even an interprise which is basically very profitable can fail if there is not enough cash available to meet commitments as they arise.

Caveat Emptor. Let the buyer beware.

C.B.I. Confederation of British Industry.

C/d. Carried down (in accounts).

C/f. Carried forward (in accounts).

C & F. Cost and freight.

c.f.i. Cost, freight and insurance.

Chamber of Commerce. An association of local manufacturers and traders.

Cheque. A bill of exchange payable on demand and drawn on a banker. In other words, it is a written instruction to the customer's bank to pay the amount specified. A crossed cheque, that is one with two parallel lines on it, can only be paid through a bank account. See also *Cheque Card.*

Cheque Card. This guarantees that the bank will honour a cheque not exceeding £50, provided the procedure on the back of the card is followed. Otherwise the cheque might not be honoured if there were insufficient funds in the customer's account or if the customer "stopped" it.

Chq. Cheque.

c.i.f. Cost, insurance and freight.

c.i.f.c. Cost, insurance, freight and commission.

Co. Company.

C.O.D. Cash on delivery.

Collateral Security. Security, such as shares, which is given to the lender to support the loan.

Company. A number of people associated for the purpose of trading for profit. A limited company is a separate legal entity from its owners. This means that the company can sue or be sued in its own right. It is taxed separately. It has an infinite life of its own though, of course, its owners may change. The owners are the shareholders, whose liability for the debts of the company is limited to the amount they paid for its shares—hence the term "limited liability".

Consignment. A shipment of goods.

Contract. A document recording an agreement enforceable by law.

Corporation Tax. A tax on company profits.

CoSIRA. Council for Small Industries in Rural Areas: provides help for business in rural areas and country towns.

C.P. Carriage paid.

Cr. Credit; creditor.

Credit Card. When a purchase is made with a credit card, the retailer is paid by the credit card company. A charge is levied on the retailer for each transaction. The charge varies between about 2 to 5 per cent of the value of the sale, depending on the trade.

Credit Note. A statement informing a person that his account has been credited with the amount shown.

C.T. Commercial traveller.

Customs and Excise. The department responsible for collecting taxes such as value added tax, and taxes on alcohol, oil and tobacco. It also enforces regulations applying to imports and exports.

C.W.O. Cash with order.

Day Book. A record of all the transactions of an enterprise, each one being entered individually on the day they took place. The entries are then transferred to the appropriate ledger.

Debit Note. or supplementary invoice. A document sent to inform the recipient that his account has been debited by the amount shown. It may be sent where a purchaser has been undercharged.

Delivery Note. A document that accompanies the delivery of goods and which gives details of the goods supplied. The supplier will often ask the customer to sign a copy of the note as evidence that the goods have been supplied.

Depreciation. An estimate of the amount by which different assets decline in value over time. The book values of the assets are then reduced accordingly.

Directors. Individuals responsible for the running of a company.

dis. Discount.

Dividend. That part of a company's profit which is distributed to shareholders. An interim dividend can be paid out at any time as part payment of the final dividend which covers the whole financial year.

Dr. Debtor; drawer.

E. and O.E. Errors and omissions excepted. This is sometimes included in documents such as invoices in case of clerical errors.

E.C.G.D. Export Credits Guarantee Department.

Endorse. To sign, usually on the back, a bill of exchange or a cheque to transfer it to another person.

Enterprise Zones. Areas in which business benefit from substantial tax concessions and a relaxation of planning controls.

Entrepreneur. A person who organises a business.

Export Credits Guarantee Department. Government department which provides insurance against bad debts incurred by exporters and can give guarantees to the businesses' bank in respect of finance used for exports.

F.A.Q. Fair average quality.

F.A.S. Free alongside ship, in other words the seller is responsible for the cost of transporting the goods to the side of the ship but not loading them aboard.

F.C.A. Fellow of the Institute of Chartered Accountants in England and Wales.

F.A.C.A. Fellow of the Association of Certified Accountants.

F.C.M.A. Fellow of the Institute of Cost and Management Accountants.

f.o.b. Free on board.

f.o.r. Free on rail.

Franchise. A licence to make or sell an established product or service.

Fringe Benefits. Benefits given by an employer to an employee, other than cash, *e.g.* luncheon vouchers.

Futures. Transactions made in a *Futures Market*.

Futures Market. Also known as a forward market. A market where commodities, securities or currencies are bought and sold for delivery at some future date.

Goodwill. The value of an enterprise over and above the value of its assets. It might be described as the intangible value of a going concern as opposed to the value of a collection of assets. It is sometimes referred to as an "intangible asset".

Gross. 1. The total amount before deductions.
   2. Twelve dozen, *i.e.* 144.

H.P. Hire purchase.

I.C.F.C. Industrial and Commercial Finance Corporation.

I.C.M.A. Institute of Cost and Management Accountants.

Inc. Incorporated—US term.

Industrial and Commercial Finance Corporation. Organisation set up to provide long term capital for small or medium sized British based firms.

Inland Revenue, Board of. The body responsible for collecting taxes such as income tax, capital gains tax, capital transfer tax and some types of National Insurance contribution.

Insolvency. The position of being unable to pay one's debts.

Inst. Of the present month.

Interest. The payment made by a borrower to a lender as a price for the loan. It is usually expressed as an annual percentage. For example, if a business borrowed £1,000 for a year at a rate of 10 per cent, the interest due would be £100.

Internal Audit. An audit carried out by staff within the business.

Inv. Invoice.

Inventory. A list of stocks.

Invoice. A list of goods and services supplied and their prices. It may also be regarded as a demand for payment.

I.O.U. I owe you.

Lease. A contract by which a person is granted the use of an asset for a fixed period of time in return for payment.

Ledger. A book in which a business enters its accounts. There may be separate ledgers, *e.g.* sales ledger and purchase ledger.

Limited Liability. See *Companies*.

Liquidation. The winding up of a company. A liquidator is appointed who disposes of the assets.

List Price. The price of a good before any discount is allowed.

Loan Guarantee Scheme. A scheme jointly operated by the Government and the banks to provide loans to small business for viable projects.

Ltd. Limited, *i.e.* limited liability. See *Companies*.

Markup. The amount a trader adds to the cost he pays for a product to give the price at which he sells.

Messrs. More than one Mr.

Misc. Miscellaneous.

M.O. Money order.

National Insurance Contributions. In the UK there are four types. Class 1 is paid by employees and employers, Classes 2 and 4 by the self-employed and Class 3 is voluntary.

Net or nett. The amount left after the appropriate deductions have been made.

o/a. On account.

O/D. Overdrawn; overdraft.

O.H.M.S. On Her/His Majesty's Service.

Overdraft. An arrangement with a bank by which a customer can overdraw his account up to an agreed limit. Interest is calculated on a daily basis on the amount overdrawn.

p.a. Per annum—yearly; personal assistant.

Partnership. Two or more people who own and control a business. The partners share the profits and are also responsible for any losses.

Patent. This is short for *letters patent*, and gives a person the exclusive rights to an invention for a period of years.

Payback period. An estimate of the length of time needed for an investment to cover its original cost.

P.A.Y.E. Pay-As-You-Earn: the system through which employers are legally required to withhold income tax from their employees' wages and salaries (and once known as Pay-*ALL*-You-Earn!)

p.c. Per cent.

Per. By.

pfd. Preferred.

P.L.C. Public limited company.

p.p. On behalf of.

pp. Pages.

Price War. Competition where two or more businesses continue to reduce their prices to undercut or keep in line with the others.

Pro forma. As a matter of form.

Pro rata. In proportion.

Pro tem. For the time being.

q.v. Which see.

R.D. Refer to the drawer (of a cheque which the bank will not meet).

Regional Development Grants. Grants given by the Government to manufacturers towards the cost of new building and machinery for use in the Development and Special Development Areas.

Rep. Representative.

Sale or Return. Goods accepted on a "sale or return" basis may be returned to the supplier if unsold.

Sgd. Signed.

Shares. The unit of ownership in a company which entitles the shareholder to a share in the profits. If the company goes into liquidation the shareholders receive any surplus capital after the company's liabilities have been met.

Small Firms Service. A service run by the Department of Industry and which provides a range of free booklets and advice for those intending to start a business and those running small businesses.

Sole Trader. This term refers to a person who owns and runs a business and who receives all the profits and is responsible for any losses. He or she may also employ people, but as long as there is only one owner, he or she remains a sole trader. See also *Partnership*.

Stamp Duties. A form of taxation on the transfer of property—such as houses, land and shares.

Tax Point. The date on which liability to value added tax arises. This is usually when goods are despatched or made available to the customer.

Ult. In the preceeding month.

Value Added Tax (VAT). An indirect tax levied on goods and services at every stage of production. Goods which are "zero-rated" are subject to VAT in principle, but at a zero rate. "Exempt" goods are not subject to VAT, even in principle. (See "Valued Adeed Tax"—section 13 above.)

Via. By way of.

Vice. In place of.

Viz. Namely.

w/e. Week ending.

W.e.f. With effect from.

SOCIAL SECURITY IN THE UNITED KINGDOM

The Green Paper

In June 1985 the Government published its plans for the future of the UK social security system in the Green Paper entitled *Reform of Social Security*. This special topic is divided into two parts. The first describes the system and its background in general terms in the light of the Government's proposals. The second goes on to provide a more detailed description of the system as it is currently operated.

Historical Background

Although other forms of social assistance had existed before, the Poor Relief Act of 1601 introduced more systematic arrangements for helping the poor. Under this Act money was raised by a compulsory poor rate levied on local property. The money was used to provide relief for the poor and also materials such as hemp and wool to give work to the unemployed. The provisions of the Poor Relief Act were enforced by the local Justices of the Peace who in turn were supervised by the Privy Council. In Scotland relief for the poor remained the responsibility of the Church and no compulsory rate was levied.

Many more developments occurred over the years. After 1795 the 'Speenhamland system', so named after a meeting of Berkshire J.P.s at Speenhamland, Newbury, enabled magistrates to supplement low wages out of the local rates. In 1832 the Royal Commission on the Poor Law was set up and concluded that relief should only be given in the workhouse and that conditions in the workhouse should be worse than employment outside. These principles were implemented by the Poor Law Amendment Act of 1834.

In the twentieth century the system changed more rapidly. Non-contributory pensions for those over seventy and on low incomes were introduced in 1908. By 1925, contributory social insurance benefits had been extended to those aged 65 to 70, the unemployed, the sick and widows. The Great Depression of the 1930s raised severe problems for the system. In particular, many workers were unemployed for so long that they exhausted their entitlement to insurance benefit. As a consequence, in 1931 a system of transitional payments was set up to provide assistance for the longer term unemployed. These payments were subject to a means test which aroused considerable resentment.

The Beveridge Report

The Second World War also had a strong influence on attitudes towards social provision and a number of developments followed. One was the publication of the Beveridge Report in 1942 entitled *Social Insurance and Allied Services*. The Report presented a plan for social security of which the main feature was a system of social insurance. Under this system, contributions would be paid and these would confer an entitlement to benefits when needed and without a means test. A Ministry of National Insurance was set up in 1944, and the years immediately after the war saw the introduction of family allowances, a much more comprehensive social insurance scheme, national assistance (later called supplementary benefit) and an industrial injuries scheme.

The Present Social Security System

A variety of changes and additions have been made since the 1940s until at the present time the entire system is not only very extensive but is also very complicated. As already stated, a more detailed description of the current system is given in the second part of this special topic. The concern here is with the overall picture.

Social security now accounts for about a third of all public expenditure, around £40 billion in 1986. About half of this money comes from National Insurance contributions and the other half from general taxation. Pensioners receive something in the region of 50 per cent of all social security spending. Another 20 per cent goes to families with children, 17 per cent for unemployment and 13 per cent for the sick and disabled. The starting point of the Government's review was that the basic system had been set up some 40 years ago and had since been subjected to a series of individual, but not necessarily co-ordinated, developments. The result was a system which is unnecessarily complicated and which is not always aimed at people most in need. In its Green Paper, the Government presented three objectives which it believed should be the basis of the reform of social security.

The first was that the system has to be able to meet genuine need. This includes not only present needs, but also that the system must be capable of meeting changing needs and recognising that the groups of people most in need change over time.

The second objective was that 'the social security system must be consistent with the Government's overall objectives for the economy'. Here two main areas were identified. One was that increased spending could reduce economic growth, and that the total amount which could be spent on social security would depend on the level of economic output. The other area was that the system should not interfere with employment. For example, where the rules of pension funds work to the disadvantage of those who leave, this may well discourage individuals from changing to better jobs.

Thirdly it is important that the system is easy to understand and to administer. At the present time the system is so complicated that the guide for social security staff consists of two volumes and 16,000 paragraphs. Furthermore different benefits are operated in different ways, for instance in the way they measure the income of the recipients. The result has been a great deal of confusion and misunderstanding.

The Changing Background

In pursuing these objectives the Government also has to consider likely future changes in society, and probably the most important of these concerns demographic changes. It has already been pointed out that about half of all social security spending goes to pensioners. In recent years the number of pensioners has increased substantially. Furthermore, as a result of the increase in the birth rate from the mid-1950s and through the 1960s, the number of individuals of pensionable age will increase again rapidly at the beginning of the next century.

Currently there are about 9.3 million pensioners and the Government Actuary has estimated that this figure will grow as follows:

1985—	9.3 million
1995—	9.8 million
2005—	10.0 million
2015—	11.1 million
2025—	12.3 million
2035—	13.2 million

These figures are likely to be highly accurate since, of course, everyone who will reach retirement age over the next 60 years is alive already. These figures could be even higher if the state retirement age of 65 for men were reduced (it is currently 60 for women).

A further consideration is that state pensions are not 'funded' in the sense that individuals pay into a special fund which is invested and from which their pensions will eventually be paid. Private pension schemes are 'funded' in that way, but the state system is operated on a 'Pay As You Go' basis. This means that current pensions are paid from the contributions of the present working population. When the current contributors retire, the hope must be that future generations will pay for their pensions.

The main concern is that, unless the birth rate increases substantially and the level of unemployment falls, the number of people contributing to state pensions will not increase in anything like the same way as the number of pensioners will. In 1986 there are 2.3 contributors for every pensioner. The Government Actuary has estimated that this figure will fall to 2.0 in the year 2015, and by the year 2035 there might be only 1.6 contributors for each pensioner.

SERPS

Added to all of this is the State Earnings-Related Pension Scheme (SERPS) which was introduced in 1978. The entitlement to this earnings-related pension is based on the recipient's National Insurance contributions, and the maximum payments can only be achieved by people who have made contributions to the scheme for at least 20 years. The cost of SERPS will therefore build up considerably in the future and the Government has estimated that its annual cost could increase from about £4 billion in the year 2,000 to about £25 billion in the year 2,033.

The Government Green Paper went on to point out that increasing numbers of elderly people will also result in a large increase in the demands made on the National Health Service and on personal social services. In addition it has been estimated that social security spending will in any case increase by between £5 billion and £8 billion in real terms if present policies are maintained.

The proposal in the Green Paper (which was subsequently modified) was that SERPS should be phased out over a three year period for men under the age of 50 and women under 45. The intention was to replace it with a system which would have given everyone who would previously have been included in SERPS a personal or an occupational pension.

The White Paper

Following the Green Paper and a certain amount of public discussion, the Government published its White Paper *Reform of Social Security: Programme for Action* in December 1985. Although some of the ideas presented in the Green Paper had been altered, the Government's aims were still as follows: 'We want to see a simpler system of social security. We want to see more effective help going to those who most need it. We want to see a system which is financially secure. And we want to see more people looking forward to greater independence in retirement.'

Clearly many detailed changes have yet to be worked out and, in any case, some of the main proposals may be further modified before they are implemented. Nevertheless a large part of the proposals can be summarised under the following headings: Retirement, the income support scheme, family credit and the social fund.

Retirement

In the White Paper the Government proposed to modify rather than to abolish SERPS. The modified scheme will not affect anyone who is retiring or who becomes widowed before the end of this century.

The main purpose of the changes was, as already indicated, to avoid the large increases in cost which would otherwise build up in the next century. The proposed modifications include basing the pension on a person's earnings over his or her lifetime, rather than on their best 20 years' earnings. Also, the SERPS pension would be based on 20 per cent of earnings rather than 25 per cent and widows and widowers over 65 would inherit half, rather than all, of their spouses' SERPS rights.

There were also proposals designed to encourage the spread of occupational pensions from employment and also personal pensions. For instance the Government proposed to make it easier for employers to set up their own pension schemes, or to adopt 'ready-made' schemes devised by other institutions.

Income Support Scheme

The present system of supplementary benefit, Family Income Supplement and housing benefit is complicated and causes confusion. For example, the amounts of Family Income Supplement and housing benefit currently paid depend on the *gross* income of the recipient. The amounts of supplementary benefit paid depend on the income *net* of tax and National Insurance contributions.

Also of considerable importance is that these and other income-related benefits are reduced when income rises. The result is that in some circumstances individuals can actually make themselves worse off by taking a job because they lose benefit as well as paying tax and National Insurance contributions. This can also happen sometimes when a person moves to a better paid job. Among the proposals is that different parts of the overall system will use the same income measure and this would be net income. This would not only simplify the system, but it should avoid situations where an increase in earnings can actually make people worse off.

It is proposed that supplementary benefit be replaced by the income support scheme. This will consist of weekly payments which are to be 'on as clear and simple a footing as possible and paid as of right'. It would be based on straightforward factors such as age. There would be a basic personal allowance together with a family supplement for dependent children. There would also be premiums for those over 60 and a higher one for those over 80. Disabled claimants and single parent families would also benefit from extra payments. The income support scheme would not cover those in full time work (defined as 24 hours a week or more) or those in full time education. The change from supplementary benefit to income support will be made in April 1988.

Family Credit

For those in full time work, again defined as 24 hours a week or more, Family Credit will replace Family Income Supplement in April 1988. This will be available to people who have children and the basis of assessment will be the same as for income support and housing benefit. The maximum credit will be arranged so that families are generally better off working than they would be on income support. It is also proposed to pay the credit through wage packets.

Social Fund

The proposed social fund is to provide extra help for special needs. This is already done, for example with mobility allowance. However, the aim here is to make the system more flexible in responding to different special needs, not all of which can be anticipated by a system of complex rules. It is intended that decisions about payments from the social fund will be made by specialist officers locally and with the minimum of formality.

There will be four elements to the social fund. The first is help with maternity and funeral payments. The second is to make loans where these would appear helpful. The third is to meet community care needs, and the fourth to tide people over financial crisis. The fund will start with maternity needs and funeral expenses in April 1987 and will be fully set up by April 1988.

THE PRESENT SYSTEM OF SOCIAL SECURITY

As already pointed out the present social security arrangements in the UK are complicated. The purpose of this special topic is therefore to provide a general description of the main benefits and who is entitled to receive them.

Types of Benefit

There are many different benefits available but they can be classified into 3 main categories. The first consists of National Insurance benefits. Entitlements to these is based on the National Insurance contributions paid, and does not depend on your income. The second are known as 'means-tested' benefits. Whether you qualify for these depends on how much income you have and other circumstances, but National Insurance contributions are not needed. Thirdly there are 'non-contributory' benefits which depend only on your circumstances. You do not need National Insurance contributions for these benefits; nor is there a means test.

In addition to these 3 categories, benefits can be either taxable or non-taxable. If they are taxable they are included in your income and might be subject to income tax if your income exceeds your personal allowances. These tax allowances are listed in the Income Tax section of 'Money Matters' (**H12**).

There are many different benefits for different circumstances and they will be described under the following general headings:

    Cash Help
    Children
    Retirement
    Widowhood
    Unemployment
    Housing
    Health and illness
    Injuries
    Disablement and handicap

CASH HELP

There are two main sources of cash help for individuals who have no income or a very low income. These are *Family Income Supplement* (FIS) and *Supplementary Benefit*. If you are entitled to either of these you will also be entitled to free dental treatment from the National Health Service, free prescriptions, free milk and vitamins for expectant and nursing mothers and children under five and free school meals.

Family Income Supplement

Family Income Supplement is tax free and is given to people with children who are in full-time employment (or self-employment) but who have low earnings. Full-time employment in this context means at least 30 hours a week, though for a single parent 24 hours a week is enough. Family Income Supplement can be claimed if the income of the family is below a certain level. This level depends on the number of children. The amount of supplement paid is half the difference between this level and the family's income.

More information about Family Income Supplement is given in leaflet FIS 1 which is available from social security offices and some post offices. This leaflet also contains a claim form.

Supplementary Benefit

Supplementary benefit is also a tax-free means-tested benefit. It is given to people who are out of work and who do not have enough to live on. Supplementary allowance is given to people under state pension age and supplementary pension is given to those over pension age. More information on this benefit is given in leaflet SB 1.

CHILDREN

A woman expecting a baby or who has had a baby in the previous year is entitled to free prescriptions,

dental treatment, milk and vitamins and further details of these benefits are described below in the section on Health and Illness. In addition, children under 16 get free prescriptions and dental treatment.

Mothers-to-be may also be entitled to maternity leave, maternity grant and maternity allowance.

Maternity Leave

Paid maternity leave is a non-contributory benefit paid by the employer who can then reclaim the money from the Department of Employment. It is available to a woman who has worked for the same employer for at least two years and stops work to have a baby.

Maternity Grant

This is a non-contributory benefit and currently consists of one payment of £25 for each baby. Claims for this grant should be made during the period between 14 weeks before the expected birth and 3 months after it. This should be done using a form which is available from social security offices and maternity clinics.

Maternity Allowance

This is a National Insurance benefit and is claimed on the contributions of the mother. The benefit is paid at a flat rate for up to 18 weeks. The claim should be made between the 14th and 11th week before the baby is due, using the form available from social security offices and maternity clinics. Both the maternity grant and the maternity allowance are not taxable.

Child Benefit

Child benefit is payable to anyone who is responsible for one or more children. It is a non-contributory tax-free benefit and is paid in respect of each child. To qualify the child has to be under 16, or under 19 if he or she is still in full time education. Claims should usually be made by the mother and claim forms can be obtained from local social security offices.

Guardian's Allowance

This allowance is non-contributory and is not taxable. It is paid in respect of an orphaned child taken into the family. It can also be paid in some cases if the child is illegitimate and the mother has died, or if the surviving parent is serving a long prison sentence or cannot be traced. In addition it can sometimes be paid where one parent is dead but the parents were divorced. Claims can be made on a form available from the social security office and this should be done within three months from the time the child joins the family.

Free School Meals etc.

Free school meals are provided by local authorities for children whose parents are receiving Family Income Supplement or Supplementary Benefit. Some education authorities will also provide free meals for other children whose parents are on low incomes. Free school milk is provided by some education authorities for children up to a certain age.

Free transport to and from school is usually available for children who live more than 3 miles from the nearest suitable school, or 2 miles if the child is under 8. Sometimes other children may benefit from subsidised transport but the rules relating to this benefit vary between education authorities.

Some education authorities provide grants towards the cost of the school uniform for children of parents on low incomes. Also, some authorities make grants for children who stay on at school after 16 and whose parents are on low incomes. The amount paid depends on the income of the parents.

Further information on these benefits is available at your local education office or from the Education Welfare Officer.

Students Grants and Allowances

There are two types of grant, mandatory and discretionary. Mandatory grants are those which local authorities are required to pay to students who are on 'designated' courses which are first degree and comparable courses and students undertaking teacher training. Discretionary grants, as the term suggests, are grants which are made according to the policy of each local authority. Further information is given in the booklet 'Grants to Students: A Brief Guide' which is available from local education authorities or from the Department of Education and Science, Room 2/11, Elizabeth House, York Road, London SE1 7PH. In Scotland the booklet 'Guide to Students' Allowances' is available from the Scottish Education Department, Awards Branch, Haymarket House, Clifton Terrace, Edinburgh, EH12 5DT.

RETIREMENT

Several different pensions are paid and these include the National Insurance Retirement Pension, the Additional Pension, the Graduated Pension, the Over 80 Pension and the Supplementary Pension.

The National Insurance Retirement Pension

This is also known as the 'state pension' or the 'old age' pension. It is payable to people who have reached retirement age, which is 65 for men and 60 for women. Also, they must have retired from regular work and satisfy the required National Insurance contribution conditions. A married woman who does not qualify for a pension by her own contributions may qualify on the basis of her husband's contributions when he draws his pension provided she is over 60 and has retired from regular work. There are also special arrangements for people who have been divorced or widowed.

A person's pension can be adjusted for a number of reasons. The earnings rule means that the pension will be reduced if the recipient earns more than a certain amount. However, if a person chooses not to draw his or her pension on reaching retirement age, the amount of pension that is eventually paid will be increased. In addition, no further contributions are payable by individuals after retirement age. When a man reaches 70, or a woman 65, the pension is not increased any further and is payable whether or not the person is still working and regardless of how much is earned. An additional 25 pence a week extra is payable to pensioners who are over 80.

The Department of Health and Social Security (DHSS) usually writes to people who are likely to be entitled to a pension enclosing a claim form about four months before they reach retirement age. If you have not heard from the DHSS by 3 months before your 65th birthday (men) or 60th (women) you should contact your local social security office.

The State Earnings-Related Pension Scheme

The State Earnings-Related Pension Scheme, or SERPS for short, is sometimes referred to as the additional pension. It was introduced in April 1978 and, unlike the flat rate basic pension described above, the additional pension is related to earnings. The additional pension does not cover people who retired before April 1979 because it is designed to benefit only those who have contributed to the scheme. It is payable to those who retired since then and is calculated on the basis of National Insurance Contributions paid as an employee since April 1978.

The additional pension scheme is complicated but in principle works as follows. On top of the basic pension, a person will receive the additional element which is related to earnings between certain limits. These limits are reviewed every year and from October 1985 the lower limit is £35.50 per week and the upper limit £265.00. The value of the additional pension is calculated as 1/80th of the earnings between these limits for each year up to a maximum of 20/80ths (one-quarter) of these earnings. This maximum can therefore be achieved only by people who will have contributed to the scheme for 20 years. However, people who retire before that time will benefit proportionately.

If an employer runs a good occupational pension scheme his employees can be contracted-out of the additional part of the state pension scheme. They will then pay lower National Insurance contributions and will, in effect, receive their 'additional pensions' from their employer's scheme. If an employer runs a pension scheme which is not contracted-out from the state scheme, National Insurance contributions are not reduced and the benefits of the scheme are payable on top of both the basic and additional parts of the state scheme.

Graduated Pension

This is also sometimes known as 'graduated retirement benefit'. This scheme was introduced in 1965 and ended in 1975, though the graduated pension rights earned during these years remain valid. Graduated pension is payable to people over pensionable age who have retired. It is also payable to men who have reached 70 and women who have reached 65 whether or not they are still working. It is payable on top of the National Insurance Retirement pension described above. However, since this scheme was in operation for only a relatively short time, the benefits payable under it are also relatively small.

Over 80 Pension

This is a non-contributory benefit for people aged 80 or more and who are not entitled to a National Insurance retirement pension or who are entitled only to a small one. The person must have lived in the United Kingdom for at least 10 years since the age of 60 to qualify. This pension is separate from the extra 25 pence a week paid in addition to the National Insurance retirement pension to those over 80.

Supplementary Pension

This is a means-tested benefit which is designed for people who are over the state pension retirement age and who do not have enough to live on. The arrangements for supplementary pension and the additional benefits that go with it are the same as for supplementary benefit and are described under 'Cash Help' above.

The Job Release Scheme

This scheme is non-contributory and is designed to make jobs available for the unemployed. Full time employees who are nearing state pension retirement age can give up their jobs in return for an allowance, provided that their employer agrees to replace them with an unemployed person. Further information and application forms are available from employment offices and jobcentres.

WIDOWHOOD

There are three different benefits specifically available for widows: widow's allowance, widowed mother's allowance and widow's pension. Entitlement to each of these benefits depends on the husband having paid sufficient National Insurance contributions. Furthermore, these benefits are withdrawn if a widow remarries or lives with a man as his wife. Claims for widow's benefits should be made to the local Social Security office within three months of bereavement. The widow's bereavement tax allowance is described in the Income Tax section of 'Money Matters' above.

Widow's Allowance

This allowance is paid for the first 26 weeks of bereavement. It is payable to widows who are under 60 when their husbands die, and to widows over 60 if their husbands were not drawing a retirement pension. There is an additional allowance for each dependent child.

Widowed Mother's Allowance

This is paid to widows with one or more dependent children. It is also paid to a widow expecting a child by her late husband. Payments should begin when the widow's allowance stops. If it does not, an enquiry should be made at the local social security office.

Widow's Pension

The widow's pension is payable to widows who are not entitled to the widowed mother's allowance, and who are 40 or over at the time of the husband's death. It should begin when the 26 weeks widow's allowance period ends. It is also payable to widows who are 40 or over when their entitlement to widowed mother's allowance ends. The rate of widow's pension is based on the widow's age at the time of her bereavement or on her age when her entitlement to widowed mother's allowance ended. The lowest rate is paid when this age is 40, and the highest rate is paid when the relevant age is 50 or over.

War Widow's or Dependant's Pension

This is a non-contributory tax-free benefit. It is payable to widows and orphaned children of a person who has died as a result of service in the armed forces. The amount of pension is calculated according to the rank of the deceased and the age of the widow. Pensions are also payable to widowers and near relatives depending on their financial circumstances.

UNEMPLOYMENT

Unemployment Benefit

This is a National Insurance benefit and is taxable. It is intended for people who would normally be employees but who have lost their jobs. To qualify, people also have to be available for work. No benefit is payable for the first three days, but after that benefit can be paid for up to a year of unemployment. Once this year has passed benefit is not payable again until the person has been employed for 13 weeks. After unemployment benefit has run out, the recipient may be entitled to Supplementary Benefit described above under 'Cash Help'. If a person has voluntarily left a job without a good reason or has been sacked for misbehaviour, unemployment benefit will not be paid for up to the first six weeks of unemployment.

Claims should be made at the local unemployment benefit office on the first day of unemployment. You should take the Form P45 with you. The P45 should be issued by your last employer, but do not delay your claim if a P45 has not been issued. You should also register for work at a jobcentre of the local employment office straightaway.

It may also be possible to get some help towards getting another job, for example with the costs of finding and moving to a job elsewhere. If you want cash help in this way you should discuss the matter at the employment office or jobcentre first.

HOUSING

The Housing Benefit Scheme

This benefit is means-tested and is calculated on the basis of income, the size of the family and the amount of rent and rates payable. It covers the rent and rates payments of tenants and the rates payments of owner-occupiers. Further information is given in the leaflet RR 1 'Who Pays Less Rent and Rates', which is available from local authorities.

HEALTH AND ILLNESS

Free Prescriptions

Free National Health Service prescriptions are available as of right to people on Family Income Supplement and Supplementary Benefit. They are also available to children under 16 and people who have reached the age of 65 (for men) or 60 (women). Expectant mothers and women who have had a baby in the last year also qualify, and so do people with certain medical conditions. People on low incomes may also qualify. Further details are contained in leaflet P 11 'NHS Prescriptions' available from Social Security offices.

Dental Treatment

Several types of dental treatment such as check-ups and action to stop bleeding are free for everyone. Other types of treatment are free for certain people. These include people receiving Family Income Supplement, Supplementary Benefit and other people on low incomes. In addition, children under 18 get free treatment except where a patient is over 16 and not in full time education. In this case he or she has to pay for dentures and bridges but other forms of treatment are still free.

To claim you should tell the dentist you want free treatment. Those on low incomes (other than patients receiving Family Income Supplement and Supplementary Benefit) should get Form F1D from the dentist and send it to the local social security office. This office will then tell you whether you are entitled to free treatment.

Milk and Vitamins

Free milk and vitamins are available to expectant and nursing mothers and children under 5 years of age in families receiving Family Income Supplement or Supplementary Benefit. Others may also qualify if they have low incomes. People on Family Income Supplement or Supplementary Benefit do not normally need to claim, but those claiming on the grounds of low income should complete the form attached to leaflet MV 11 which is available at post offices and social security offices.

Statutory Sick Pay

For up to 28 weeks of sickness, most employees will receive statutory sick pay from their employers. Statutory sick pay is non-contributory and the employers reclaim the payments from their National Insurance contributions. Statutory sick pay is taxed through the Pay-As-You-Earn system and is also subject to National Insurance contributions. Other individuals can claim sickness benefit instead. Further information is given in the leaflet NI 244 'Check Your Right to Statutory Sick Pay' available from social security offices.

Sickness Benefit

Entitlement to this benefit depends on a person's National Insurance contributions record and is available to individuals who cannot work because of illness or disablement. Sickness benefit is not taxable, and is not paid to those in receipt of statutory sick pay. Further information is given in the leaflet NI 16 'SSP and Sickness Benefit'.

Invalidity Benefit

Invalidity benefit is a contributory benefit and consists of invalidity pension and invalidity allowance. For men who were under 60 and women under 55 when their illness began, invalidity allowance is paid in addition to invalidity pension.

Severe Disablement Allowance

This allowance is a non-contributory benefit and is payable to those of working age who do not qualify for invalidity benefit and are severely disabled and have been unable to work for at least 28 weeks.

INJURIES, DISABLEMENT AND HANDICAP

A variety of benefits and payments can be claimed. In this complicated area, the following leaflets may be of value: NI 10, Industrial Death Benefits for Widows and Other Dependants; WSI, Workmens' Compensation Supplement; PN I, The Pneumoconiosis, Byssinosis and Miscellaneous Diseases Benefit Scheme; NI 205, Attendance Allowance and NI 212, Invalid Care Allowance.

CLASSICAL MYTHOLOGY

The purpose of this section is to give brief accounts of the myths and legends of Greece and Rome in an easily referable form. Great artists and writers throughout the ages have enriched their work by reference to these ancient tales of the classical world and some knowledge of them is indispensable to the full appreciation of our art and literature.

INTRODUCTION TO
CLASSICAL MYTHOLOGY

A

Abas. In Greek mythology either (1) the son of Celeus and Metanira. His mockery of Demeter (*q.v.*) as she drank resulted in his being turned into a lizard, or (2) the twelfth king of Argolis who owned a magic shield from which he derived authority. He was the father of Acrisius (*q.v.*) and Proetus (*q.v.*).

Abderus. The friend of Heracles (*q.v.*) in whose care Heracles left the mares of Diomedes (*q.v.*). The horses ate him and Heracles founded Abdera, a coastal town in Thrace, in his honour.

Absyrtus (or **Apsyrtus**). Half brother of the sorceress Medea (*q.v.*). When Aëtes pursued Jason (*q.v.*) and Medea, in order to recover the golden fleece, Medea slew the boy, cut his corpse into pieces and tossed the pieces into the sea. Because Aëtes stopped his ship to collect the pieces of his son for burial Jason and Medea were able to escape.

Abyla. See "Pillars of Hercules".

Acamas. Son of Theseus (*q.v.*) and Phaedra (*q.v.*), brother of Demophon (*q.v.*). He went to Troy (*q.v.*) with Diomedes (*q.v.*) to demand the return of Helen (*q.v.*). He and his brother also rescued their grandmother Aethra, who had been Helen's slave, when Troy fell.

Acastus. Son of Pelias King of Iolcos and one of the Argonauts (*q.v.*). When Medea (*q.v.*) caused his father's death he banished her and Jason (*q.v.*). Showed hospitality to Peleus (*q.v.*) but suspecting him of advances towards his wife he left Peleus to die at the hands of the Centaurs (*q.v.*). Later Peleus returned to slay the couple. Acastus was the father of Laodamia (*q.v.*).

Acestes. In Roman mythology a chieftain of Trojan descent who had settled in Sicily prior to the arrival of Aeneas (*q.v.*).

Achelous. A great river god, the son of Oceanus (*q.v.*) and Tethys (*q.v.*). By defeating Achelous Heracles (*q.v.*) won the hand of Deianeira (*q.v.*) daughter of Oeneus (*q.v.*).

Acheron. A real river of Epirus flowing into the Ionian Sea. Part of it runs underground which may account for its position in Greek mythology. Here it is the "river of grief" which flows in the underworld of the dead.

Achilles. A Greek warrior who is the principal character of the *Iliad*. The son of Peleus (*q.v.*) King of the Myrmidones at Phthia in Thessaly and Thetis (*q.v.*) one of the Nereides (*q.v.*). As a baby his mother dipped him in the Styx (*q.v.*) making him invulnerable save for his heel, by which she held him. He was educated in the arts of war and hunting, and in morality, by Cheiron (*q.v.*). His mother, knowing that he would die at Troy (*q.v.*) tried to prevent him joining the Greek expedition there by disguising him as a girl and sending him to the court of Lycomedes, King of Scyros. Here Lycomedes' daughter Deidamia, bore him a son, Neoptolemus (*q.v.*). Odysseus (*q.v.*) learned of this subterfuge and visited Lycomedes' court disguised as a merchant. While the king's daughters and the disguised Achilles were surveying his wares he suddenly produced swords which Achilles eagerly clasped, thus revealing himself. Achilles proved himself the most formidable warrior at Troy. At Tenedos on the way to Troy he killed King Tenes and his father Cyncus and by raiding Aeneas' (*q.v.*) cattle prompted him to join the Trojan forces. In the tenth year of the war Achilles quarrelled with Agamemnon (*q.v.*) over the captive girl Briseis and withdrew from the fighting. However he loaned his armour to Patroclus, his cousin and friend who was slain by Hector (*q.v.*). His death prompted Achilles to cease sulking in his tent and to return to the fray. Thetis gave him new armour made by Hephaestus (*q.v.*) and wearing this he slew Hector. He also killed Penthesilea (*q.v.*) and the Greek Thersites

(*q.v.*). After killing Memnon (*q.v.*) Achilles was shot in his vulnerable ankle at a battle near the Scaean gate (*q.v.*) Odysseus and Ajax (*q.v.*) recovered his body and argued over his armour.

Acis. In later Greek legend the young son of Faunus (*q.v.*) and a river nymph. He loved the sea-nymph Galatea (*q.v.*) and was killed by his jealous rival Polyphemus (*q.v.*). According to Sicilian tradition he was then turned into the river of the same name which runs at the foot of Mount Etna. This tradition first appears in the writing of Theocritus (*q.v.*) and later in Ovid's (*q.v.*) "Metamorphoses". It inspired paintings by Poussin and Claude and the opera *Acis and Galatea* by Handel.

Acrisius. Son of Abas (*q.v.*), twin brother of Proetus (*q.v.*) and King of Argos. Warned by an oracle that the son of his daughter Danaë (*q.v.*) would kill him he had her locked up in a brazen tower. But this was to no avail because Zeus (*q.v.*) visited her and fathered Perseus (*q.v.*), Acrisius then cast mother and son adrift on the sea, locked in a chest. Years later Perseus returned to Argos causing Acrisius to flee to Larissa. However Perseus, visiting Larissa to take part in the games, accidentally killed him with a discus.

Acropolis. In general terms a high citadel found in all Greek cities. The best known acropolis is that at Athens which was first inhabited around 2000 B.C. From time immemorial it was dedicated to Athene (*q.v.*).

Actaeon. Mythical huntsman and grandson of Cadmus (*q.v.*) of Thebes. Artemis (*q.v.*) turned him into a stag, torn to pieces by his own hounds because he inadvertently spied her bathing. The story is recounted in Ovid's (*q.v.*) "Metamorphoses" and recalled in the works of Titian, Veronese, Poussin, Rembrandt, Gainsborough and Parmigiano.

Admetus. King of Pherae in Thessaly and husband of the beautiful Alcestis (*q.v.*). Apollo (*q.v.*) offered to allow Admetus to avoid death if one of his family would die in his place. Alcestis offered herself but according to legend either Persephone (*q.v.*) refused the self-sacrifice or Heracles (*q.v.*) rescued Alcestis from Hades (*q.v.*). This forms the theme of one of Euripedes' best known plays and Gluck's opera *Alceste* (in which Apollo not Heracles saves her).

Adonis. A Syrian deity associated with the mystery of vegetation. He was a beautiful Cypriot youth, the son of Myrrha and her father. For this incest Myrrha was turned into a tree. Nine months later Adonis was born from the bark of the tree, taken up by Aphrodite (*q.v.*) and placed in the care of Persephone (*q.v.*). He spent alternate parts of the year with Persephone and Aphrodite who loved him. He was killed by a boar sent by Artemis (*q.v.*). Shakespeare's *Venus and Adonis* is based on Ovid's (*q.v.*) version of the tale while Shelley's elegy on the death of Keats, *Adonais*, derives its title from Bion's *Lament for Adonis*. Adonis was painted by Titian, Veronese and Poussin.

Adrastus. Son of Talaus and King of Argos. An oracle told him that his offspring would be a lion and a boar and in accordance with this he gave his daughter Argia to Polynices (*q.v.*) and her sister to Tydeus (*q.v.*) who bore images of these animals on their shields. He attempted to restore Polynices to his throne at Thebes (*see* **Seven against Thebes**). He survived this adventure—some say due to his magic horse Arion (*q.v.*)—and led a second expedition (of the Epigoni, *q.v.*) against Thebes, dying of grief when he heard that his son Aegialeus had fallen in the attack.

Aeacides. The descendants of Aeacus (*q.v.*).

Aeacus. Son of Zeus and Aegina and King of the Myrmidones. The Myrmidones were originally ants, transformed into men by Zeus at the request of Aeacus. He aided Poseidon (*q.v.*) and Apollo (*q.v.*) in the construction of the walls of Troy. He had two sons, Peleus (*q.v.*) and Telamon (*q.v.*) by his wife Endeis. He was also the father of Phocus (q.v.) by a Nereid. Aeacus later exiled Peleus (future father of Achilles) for the murder of Phocus. A model of virtue and piety, Aeacus was made one of the three judges of the Underworld.

Aeaea. In the Odyssey the island home of Circe (q.v.).

Aedon. In Greek mythology the wife of Zethus, king of Thebes. She was jealous of Niobe, wife of Zethus' brother Amphion (q.v.). In trying to murder Niobe's son she killed her own son Itylus by mistake. In pity Zeus (q.v.) turned her into a nightingale whose song still mourns Itylus.

Aegaeon. Alternative name for Briareus (q.v.).

Aegeus. King of Athens and father of Theseus (q.v.) by Aethra (q.v.) daughter of Pittheus king of Troezen. She brought Theseus up secretly at her father's court, during which time Aegeus married Medea (q.v.). When Theseus finally returned to his father's court Medea fled. Before Theseus went to slay the Minotaur (q.v.) he and Aegeus agreed that he would hoist a white sail when returning to Athens to signal his success. On returning Theseus forgot to do this and Aegeus seeing a black sail on his son's ship supposed him dead and, in grief threw himself into the sea, henceforth called the Aegean.

Aegisthus. The son of Thyestes (q.v.) by his daughter Pelopia. Pelopia exposed the baby but it was rescued by her husband Atreus (q.v.) who believed it to be his own son. Atreus was king of Mycenae and when Thyestes, an enemy, returned in later years he ordered Aegisthus to kill him. But father and son recognised each other and Aegisthus killed Atreus. Thyestes became king of Mycenae but Atreus had had two sons by Aerope, Menelaus (q.v.) and Agamemnon (q.v.). Agamemnon expelled Thyestes and reclaimed his father's throne. While Agamemnon was at Troy (q.v.) Aegisthus seduced his wife Clytemnestra (q.v.) and helped her murder him on his return. These two murderers of Agamemnon now ruled Mycenae. But at the urging of his sister Electra (q.v.) (whom Aegisthus would have liked to kill and whom he forced to marry a peasant) Agamemnon's son Orestes (q.v.) and his friend Pylades (q.v.) returned from exile in Phocis and with Electra's help avenged their father, slaying Aegisthus and Clytemnestra.

Aeneas. The Trojan hero regarded by the Romans as their ancestor. The son of Anchises (q.v.) and Aphrodite (q.v.). Led the survivors of the Trojan War to Italy. The lover of Dido. See under **Aeneid**.

Aeneid. Virgil's (q.v.) unfinished epic poem. In 12 volumes, it is written to honour Rome, to increase the prestige of Augustus (by recalling the deeds of his supposed ancestor) and to foretell prosperity to come. It describes Aeneas' (q.v.) wanderings after Troy fell, recounting his stay in Carthage and love for Dido (q.v.), the funeral games of his father Anchises (q.v.) in Sicily, a journey to the Underworld to visit his dead father's spirit and his arrival at the mouth of the Tiber where he landed on the Latin shore. Here he fought wars with the Latins and their allies before finally defeating Turnus the Rutulian prince and uniting the races by marrying Lavinia the Latin princess. He founded Lavinium, named in her honour.

Aeolian Isles. The present Aeolian Isles are off the North East of Sicily, forming part of the Liparia group. They are mentioned in the Odyssey.

Aeolus. In Greek mythology (1) the son of Helen and ruler of Thessaly, believed to be the brother of Dorus and Xuthus (q.v.) and the ancestor of the Aeolians or Aeolic Greeks, i.e. those inhabiting Aeolis.
(2) The son of Poseidon (q.v.) and ruler of the Aeolian isles (q.v.). Zeus (q.v.) made him guardian of the winds. He gave Odysseus (q.v.) a bag of winds which his men let loose and which blew the ship off course.

Aeschylus. See B2.

Aetolus. Legendary conqueror of Aetolia. The son of Endymion (q.v.) king of Elis, he was banished across the Corinthian Gulf after accidentally killing Apis in a chariot race.

Agamemnon. Son of Atreus (q.v.) and Aerope, brother of Menelaus (q.v.) and king of Mycenae. He married Helen's (q.v.) half-sister Clytemnestra (q.v.) and commanded the Greek forces at Troy (q.v.). Before the Greek fleet could leave Aulis to sail for Troy he had to sacrifice his daughter Iphigenia (q.v.). At Troy he quarrelled with Achilles (q.v.) when he seized Briseis from Achilles. He did this because Apollo (q.v.) had forced him to return Chryseis to her father, the Trojan Chryses (q.v.).

On his return to Mycenae he was murdered by Aegisthus (q.v.) and Clytemnestra. Clytemnestra attacked him with an axe while he was bathing. This occurred despite the warning given to Agamemnon by Cassandra (q.v.) whom he had brought back from Troy as his mistress. He was avenged by his children Orestes (q.v.) and Electra (q.v.). The story inspired Aeschylus' (q.v.) trilogy Orestia.

Aganippe. A fountain at the foot of Mt. Helicon, sacred to the Muses (q.v.) who are sometimes called Aganippides. It inspired those who drank from it. The fountain of Hippocrene, also sacred to the Muses, was known as Aganippis.

Agathyrsans. In the Aeneid (q.v.) a tribe in Thrace.

Aglaia. "The bright one": one of the Graces (q.v.).

Aides or **Aidoneus.** Hades (q.v.).

Ajax. (Greek Aias) In Greek legend two Ajaxes appear. The first was the son of King Telamon of Salamis. He killed Teuthras King of Teuthrania, an ally of Troy (q.v.) and took his daughter Tecmessa. At Troy he fought all day with Hector (q.v.) and at the end of the duel they exchanged gifts, Hector giving him a sword. With Menelaus (q.v.) he rescued the body of Patroclus (q.v.) and with Odysseus (q.v.) killed Glaucus and rescued the body of Achilles. Homer (q.v.) says the pair quarrelled over the armour and that Odysseus killed him. Later, when Odysseus summoned the spirits of the dead Ajax held aloof. But Sophocles (q.v.) in his Ajax calls on another tradition in which Ajax, disappointed at not being given the Palladium (q.v.) of Troy when the city fell, went mad, killing the Greek sheep under the delusion they were his rivals before impaling himself on the sword Hector had given him. The other Ajax was the son of Oileus, king of the Locrians. He was courageous but blasphemous. When Troy was sacked he dragged Cassandra (q.v.) from the altar of Athene (q.v.) where she sought refuge and gave her to Agamemnon (q.v.). On his return to Greece Poseidon (q.v.) saved him from shipwreck in a storm sent by Athene. Taking shelter on a rock he boasted himself more powerful than the goddess. She commanded Poseidon to crack the reef with his trident and Ajax drowned.

Alba Longa. The Latin city founded by Ascanius (q.v.) in the Alban Hills. In fact, as well as legend, Alba was the mother city of Rome which was probably founded as one of her western outposts. Alba was capital of the Latin League, a confederation of Latin states, but was eventually supplanted by Rome.

Alcaeus. See Alcmene.

Alcestis. Daughter of Pelias (q.v.) and the only one of his daughters not to follow Medea's (q.v.) advice and boil him alive. Married Admetus (q.v.) and was devoted to him.

Alcides. Another name for Heracles (q.v.) whose grandfather was reputed to be Alcaeus.

Alcinous. King of the mythical Phaeacians of the isle of Scheria. A grandson of Poseidon (q.v.), he married Arete his own sister. Father of the beautiful Nausicaa (q.v.). He entertained Odysseus and gave him a ship. He was also said to have entertained the Argonauts and refused to return Medea to her father. Scheria has been identified with Corfu.

Alcmaeon. In myth the son of Amphiaraus (q.v.) and Eriphyle (q.v.). One of the Epigoni (q.v.).

Alcmene. The wife of Amphitrion (q.v.) son of Alcaeus. Her brothers had been slain by the Taphians and she would not consummate her marriage until Amphitrion avenged them. While he was away warring with the Taphians Zeus (q.v.) appeared in his likeness and fathered Heracles (q.v.) upon her. Hermes (q.v.) was ordered to delay the dawn in order that Zeus might take his time— an amusing situation which has appealed to Plautus, Molière and Dryden. Later that night the real Amphitrion returned and fathered Iphicles (q.v.). In his Amphitryon 38 Jean Giraudoux claims 37 versions of the tale have preceded him. On the death of Amphitrion Alcmene married Rhadamanthus (q.v.).

Alcyone or Halcyone. (1) Leader of the Pleiades (q.v.), daughter of Atlas (q.v.) and Pleione.
(2) The daughter of Aeolus (q.v.) and wife of Ceyx. When Ceyx was lost at sea she drowned herself in sorrow. The sympathetic gods turned the pair to kingfishers which supposedly bred during the winter solstice. Then Aeolus forbids the wind to blow leaving the Aegean calm while they build and sit on their nest. This is the time of year

called the "Halcyon days". The story is told in Ovid's (q.v.) "Metamorphoses" and Chaucer's "Book of the Duchess".

Alecto. One of the Erinnyes (q.v.).

Alexander the Great. See B3

Amalthea. The she-goat which nursed the infant Zeus in the Dictaean cave in Crete. As a reward she was placed among the stars as Capricorn while one of her horns which had broken off became the Cornucopia, or horn of plenty.

Amazons. Mythical race of female warriors at one time believed by the Greeks to live in Thrace or Asia Minor. As the Greeks' knowledge of the world grew, so the homeland of the Amazons was held to be more distant. In the *Iliad* (q.v.) Priam (q.v.) is said to have warred with them, though they came to the aid of Troy (q.v.). Achilles (q.v.) slew their queen Penthesilea (q.v.). Heracles (q.v.) fought with them and seized the girdle of the queen Hippolyte (q.v.) while Theseus (q.v.) carried off either Hippolyte or Antiope (q.v.). Theseus' act caused the Amazons to invade Attica but Theseus defeated them in the streets of Athens. In antiquity it was thought they amputated their right breast (Greek *mazos*) in order to hold a bow better.

Ambrosia. The food of the Olympians which gave immortality.

Ammon. The Egyptian god Amun was known to the Greeks from the 7th century B.C. when they came into contact with his cult at the Siwa oasis. They identified him with Zeus. Alexander the Great consulted the oracle of Zeus and Ammon and was recognised as the son of Zeus by the priests of the oracle. A legend grew up that Alexander was begotten by Ammon in the form of a snake.

Amphiaraus. See **Seven Against Thebes.**

Amphion. Twin brother of Zethus, sons of Zeus (q.v.) and Antiope (q.v.). Antiope was married to Lycus King of Thebes who divorced her. She was cruelly treated by his second wife Dirce. The twins were raised by herdsmen on Mt. Cithaeron. When they reached manhood they avenged their mother by killing Zethus and tying Dirce to the horns of a wild bull. The fountain into which her body was thrown henceforth bore her name. The twins now took possession of Thebes and built the fortifications below the Cadmea. Amphion, who had been given a lyre by Hermes (q.v.) played so skilfully that the stones moved into place of their own accord. They ruled jointly, Zethus marrying Thebe who gave her name to the city, and Amphion marrying Niobe (q.v.).

Amphitrion. Son of Alcaeus, husband of Alcmene (q.v.) and father of Iphicles (q.v.). Foster father of Heracles (q.v.). When Heracles killed his teacher Linus with Linus' own lyre, Amphitrion sent him away to keep cattle. Later Amphitrion was killed helping Heracles defeat the Minyans.

Amphitrite. The daughter of Nereus (q.v.) leader of the Nereids (q.v.). Persuaded by Delphinos to accept Poseidon (q.v.) (Delphinos was rewarded by having her image placed amongst the stars as the Dolphin). By Poseidon she was mother of Triton (q.v.). Her hatred of Scylla (q.v.), Poseidon's daughter by another, led her to turn Scylla into a monster with six barking heads and twelve feet.

Amphitroniades. Another name for Heracles (q.v.) whose putative father was Amphitrion (q.v.).

Amyclae. One of the most sacred sites in the Peloponnese, a sanctuary a few miles from Sparta consecrated to Hyacinthus (q.v.).

Anchises. A cousin of Priam (q.v.). For his piety he was allowed to sleep with Aphrodite (q.v.) who bore him Aeneas. When Troy (q.v.) fell Aeneas carried his father (now blind) to safety through the Dardanian gate of the city. He died in Sicily and was buried at Eryx. In the *Aeneid* (q.v.) he appears among the blessed spirits of the dead to foretell Rome's greatness. *Aeneas carrying his Father* is an early work of Bernini.

Ancus Martius. The legendary fourth king of Rome who succeeded Tullus Hostilius. A grandson of Numa Pompilius (q.v.) he ruled from 640 to 616 B.C. He was very religious but also succeeded in defeating the Latins. He was succeeded by Tarquin the Elder.

Andromache. A Trojan princess, wife of Hector (q.v.) and by him mother of Astyanax. When Troy fell her son was thrown from the city walls, despite her spirited defence of him with a pestle. She was carried off to Epirus by Neoptolemus (q.v.) and here married his brother in law Hellenus and

became joint ruler. She also had a son by Neoptolemus and was threatened by his jealous wife Hermione (*see* Racine's *Andromaque*). Her days were ended at Pergamum, the city founded by her and Neoptolemus' son, Molossus. In historic times the Molossi claimed descent from Molossus and Neoptolemus.

Andromeda. See **Cassiopeia.**

Antaeus. A Libyan giant, son of Poseidon (q.v.) and Ge (q.v.). An invincible wrestler until Heracles (q.v.), realising he drew his strength from his mother, held him in the air and squeezed him to death. He is featured in a painting by Pollaiuolo in Florence.

Antenor. The wisest of the Trojans. Priam (q.v.) sent him to reclaim Hesione from Telamon after Heracles (q.v.) sacked Troy (q.v.). He advised the Trojans to return Helen (q.v.) to Menelaus (q.v.) but they refused. His hatred for Deiphobus (q.v.) led him to help the Greeks steal the Palladium (q.v.). The husband of Theano and father of Laocoön (q.v.). After Troy fell he and his wife went to Italy and founded either Venice or Padua.

Antigone. Daughter of Oedipus (q.v.) and Jocasta (q.v.) she accompanied her father into exile (recalled in Sophocles' *Oedipus at Colonus*). After his death she returned to Thebes where her brother Eteocles (q.v.) and Polynices (q.v.) were warring on each other. Both perished in battle and her uncle Creon (q.v.) seized power. Because Polynices had fought against his own country Creon refused him burial. Antigone defied Creon and buried her brother with full rites and was imprisoned in a cave for doing so. Here she hung herself, and her betrothed, Creon's son Haemon, committed suicide in despair. The story and the ethical principles it raises are the basis of Sophocles' *Antigone*. In his work of the same name Cocteau reconsiders the arguments involved.

Antilochus. Son of Nestor (q.v.) a valiant Greek warrior at Troy (q.v.). Too young to sail from Aulis when the expedition began he arrived later. Slain by Memnon (q.v.) while defending his father.

Antinous. See **Odysseus.**

Antiope. (1) An Amazon, sister of Hippolyte (q.v.). According to some legends she was carried off by Theseus (q.v.), perhaps with the aid of Heracles (q.v.) and bore him Hippolytus (q.v.).

(2) A Theban princess who bore Amphion (q.v.) and Zethus to Zeus (q.v.) who visited her in the form of a satyr (q.v.). Her father exposed the children on Mt. Cithaeron. She was badly treated and imprisoned by Lycus and his wife Dirce (Lycus was either her husband, who divorced her to marry Dirce, or her uncle). She was later freed and avenged by her twin sons. Titian, Correggio and Watteau have all painted Zeus visiting Antiope as a satyr.

Aphaia. A goddess worshipped in Aegina and identified with the Cretan Britomartis.

Aphrodite. The goddess of love, desire and procreation, known to the Romans as Venus. She sprang from the seed of Uranus (q.v.), rising naked from the sea at Paphos in Cyprus. However, Homer (q.v.) holds her to be the daughter of Zeus (q.v.) and Dione, and makes her the wife of Hephaestus (q.v.). She was not faithful to Hephaestus, but bore children by Ares (q.v.), Poseidon (q.v.), Dionysus (q.v.), and Hermes (q.v.), She loved the mortals Adonis (q.v.) and Anchises (q.v.) by whom she bore Aeneas (q.v.), and tempted Paris (q.v.) to desert Oenone. It was to her that Paris gave the golden apple of discord, she being the "fairest" goddess. In return she promised him the most beautiful woman in the world. Around her waist she wore a magic girdle which made her beautiful and irresistibly desirable.

Apis. The sacred bull of Memphis which the Egyptians worshipped as a god.

Apollo. Son of Zeus (q.v.) and the mortal Leto; twin brother of Artemis (q.v.). As a child he killed the she-dragon Python on Mt. Parnassus and took over her role as the oracle at Delphi. Hence he was sometimes known as the Pythian or as Loxias "the Ambiguous". He was also a symbol of light and was known as Phoebus or "shining". Apart from being god of prophecy he was a god of song and music, having been given the lyre by Hermes (q.v.). He was the leader of the Muses (q.v.) and was sometimes called Musagetes. He could be a destroyer (he is always portrayed with bow and arrows) and sent plagues amongst the Greeks at Troy, but was also protective against evil and was father of Asclepius (q.v.). When Zeus slew Asclepius he retaliated by slaying the Cyclopes (q.v.)

and was punished by being sent as a servant to Admetus (q.v.) of Pherae in Thessaly. Prior to this Zeus had sent him as a bondsman to King Laomedan whom he helped to build the walls of Troy. This was punishment for his part in a conspiracy (led by Hera, Poseidon and himself) against Zeus. He loved Hestia (q.v.) but also seduced the nymph Dryope and attempted to seduce Daphne. When Daphne protested she was turned into a laurel tree. Amongst mortal women he at one time loved Cassandra (q.v.). With his sister Artemis he shot the giant Tityus, whom the jealous Hera sent to violate Leto; it was he who shot the vulture which tormented Prometheus and he also helped Paris (q.v.) shoot Achilles (q.v.). He was identified with the sun-god by later writers but in Homer (q.v.) he and Helios (q.v.) are quite distinct.

Arachne. A Lydian maiden who competed with Athene (q.v.) at a weaving contest. When she won the angry goddess forced her to hang herself before turning her into a spider and her weaving into a cobweb.

Arcadia. Green but mountainous region, isolated in the centre of the Peloponnese. Its inhabitants were primitive shepherds and peasants.

Arcas. The son of Zeus (q.v.) and Callisto (q.v.) who gave his name to Arcadia (q.v.).

Ares. The son of Zeus (q.v.) and Hera (q.v.) and the god of war. Associated with Mars, by the Romans. He was disliked by all the gods save Hades (q.v.) and Eris (q.v.) because of his love of battle for its own sake. He loved Aphrodite (q.v.), and Hephaestus (q.v.) once caught the pair in an invisible net exposing them to the ridicule of the other gods. The father of Penthesilea (q.v.) by Otrere. He was once defeated by Heracles (q.v.), was wounded by Diomedes (q.v.) and imprisoned for 13 months (till Hermes (q.v.) released him) in a brazen vessel by the Aloeidae (q.v.). Athene (q.v.) got the better of him on several occasions. He once stood trial on the site of the Areopagus.

Arethusa. A river and a river goddess of southern Greece. She was pursued under the sea to Sicily by the river god Alpheus. In Sicily she was identified with Artemis and a cult of Artemis Arethusa flourished at Syracuse.

Argo. A fifty-oared ship built for Jason (q.v.) by Argus. In its prow Athene (q.v.) fitted an oracular beam.

Argonauts. The heroes who sailed with Jason (q.v.) in the Argo (q.v.) to fetch the golden fleece from Colchis. Their ranks included Heracles (q.v.), Orpheus (q.v.) Castor and Polydeuces (q.v.) Echion, Idas (q.v.) and Lynceus (q.v.). The voyage was an adventurous one and after dallying at Lemnos they passed through the Hellespont and reached Mysia. Here Hylas (q.v.) was lost and Heracles stayed to look for him. At some point the Sirens (q.v.) were passed with the help of Orpheus (q.v.) and at Bebrycos Polydeuces (see **Castor**) slew Amycus. In Thrace they rid Phineus (q.v.) of the Harpies (q.v.) and in return were told how to navigate the Symplegades (q.v.).

Argus. (1) The builder of the Argo (q.v.).
(2) A hundred-eyed giant set by Hera (q.v.) to watch Io (q.v.).
(3) The faithful hound of Odysseus (q.v.).

Ariadne. The daughter of Minos (q.v.) and Pasiphae (q.v.). She helped Theseus (q.v.) but he abandoned her at Naxos when Dionysus (q.v.) fell in love with her. He married her and gave her a crown of seven stars which became a constellation after her death.

Arimaspi. A mythical people of the Scythian steppes said to be neighbours of the Hyperboreans. They had one eye and constantly fought a group of griffins for the gold they guarded. Herodotus (q.v.) tells of a poem by Aristeas, a priest of Hyperborean Apollo, about them. Aristeas is clearly a *shaman*, able to separate body and soul and to be in two places at once. Aeschylus (q.v.) refers to them when describing Io's (q.v.) wanderings.

Arion. A fabulous horse, the offspring of Demeter (q.v.) and Zeus (q.v.). Demeter had taken the form of a mare and Zeus raped her in the form of a horse. She also gave birth to the nymph Despoena and possibly Persephone (q.v.) at the same time as Arion. He saved Adrastus (q.v.) at the siege of Thebes.

Aristaeus. The son of Apollo (q.v.) and a Lapith (see Lapithae) girl Cyrene. A minor deity, the protector of cattle, fruit trees and bee-keepers. Virgil (q.v.) makes Cyrene a nymph and says that Aristaeus fell in love with Eurydice who died of a snake bite she received while fleeing from him. In

punishment all his bees were killed. Cyrene sought the advice of Proteus (q.v.) and Aristaeus made sacrifices of cattle to placate the nymphs. Nine days later he found fresh swarms in the carcasses.

Aristophanes. See **B4**.

Artemis. The daughter of Zeus (q.v.) and Leto (q.v.) twin sister of Apollo (q.v.). Her Roman counterpart was Diana. She was often conflated with Hecate (q.v.) and Selene (q.v.), the moon goddess. A goddess of the chase and protectoress of children and young animals. She was also treated as a mother or earth goddess in the Asian tradition and was worshipped orgiastically at Ephesus. She was generally portrayed with a bow and arrow, made by Hephaestus (q.v.) and like Apollo could spread the plague and death. With her arrows she punished impiety (e.g. Niobe). A virgin who sternly protected her own chastity, she was known to punish unchastity in others e.g. Callisto (q.v.).

Ascanius. The son of Aeneas (q.v.) and Creusa, who escaped from Troy (q.v.) with his father. Another tradition makes his mother the Latin princess Lavinia. He succeeded his father as king and made Alba Longa (q.v.) his capital.

Asclepius or **Aesculapius.** The son of Apollo (q.v.) and Coronis, a god of healing whose worship spread to Rome after a plague in 293 B.C. He was taught healing by Cheiron the centaur (q.v.). Once he brought a dead man back to life and Zeus (q.v.) punished him, killing him with a thunderbolt. At Apollo's request he was placed among the stars.

Asopus. A river god, the son of Oceanus (q.v.) and Tethys (q.v.). The father of Evadne, Euboea and Aegina.

Astraeus. A Titan (q.v.) and by Eos the father of the beneficent winds. According to other traditions he also fathered the stars.

Astyanax. The son of Hector (q.v.) and Andromache (q.v.). He was a sensitive child frightened by the plume of his father's helmet. When Troy (q.v.) fell Andromache struggled to protect him but Neoptolemus (q.v.) threw him from the city walls. Another tradition says she took him to Neoptolemus' court in Epirus.

Atalanta. The Boeotian Atalanta was the daughter of Schoeneus and wife of Hippomenes, the Arcadian Atalanta, the daughter of Iasus and Clymene and wife of Milanion. Similar tales were told of her in both traditions. She was exposed by her father and suckled by a bear sent by Artemis (q.v.) with whom she was sometimes identified. She became a famous huntress and hunted the Calydonian Boar (q.v.). Though vowed to virginity she bore Meleager (q.v.) a son. She refused to marry any suitor except he who beat her in a foot race. Hippomenes (or Milanion) did this by placing three golden apples, gifts from Aphrodite (q.v.) in her path, causing her to stop and collect them.

Athamas. The son of Aeolus and king of Orchomenus in Boeotia. He loved Ino (q.v.) who bore him Learchus and Melicertes, but Hera (q.v.) forced him to marry Nephele who bore him Phrixus and Helle (q.v.). Hera drove him mad because he sheltered Dionysus (q.v.) and he killed Learchus. Ino flung herself into the sea with Melicertes and both became sea deities. Ino became Leucothea and Melicertes became Palaemon. Athamas fled to Thessaly.

Athene or **Athena.** Identified with Minerva by the Romans. The daughter of Zeus (q.v.) and Metis (q.v.). Though it was foretold she would be a girl, an oracle said that if Metis bore another child it would be a son who would depose Zeus. He then swallowed Metis and later suffered a terrible headache near Lake Triton. Hermes (q.v.) knew the cause and persuaded Hephaestus (q.v.) to cleave Zeus' skull. Out sprang Athene fully armed. She was the goddess of wisdom and patron of arts and crafts, a protectress of agriculture and also a warrior. Moreover, she was a virgin (see Pallas). She disputed possession of Athens with Poseidon (q.v.); he offered the city the horse, Athene the olive which was judged to be the better gift. Henceforth she was patron of the city which was a centre of her cult. Her epithet "glaucopis" meant "bright-eyed" or "owl-faced" and in the Odyssey (q.v.) she assumed the form of a bird. Athenian coins bore an owl and the saying "Owls to Athens" meant the same as "Coals to Newcastle". She was worshipped on the Acropolis. A defender of all heroes who worked for the good of mankind, e.g. Heracles (q.v.).

Atlantiades. Another name for Hermes (q.v.) whose mother Maia was the daughter of Atlas (q.v.).

Atlantis. A legendary island said to be to the west of the Pillars of Hercules (q.v.). Its inhabitants, once powerful and virtuous, became wealthy and degenerate and were conquered by the Athenians. Later the island sank beneath the ocean in a day and a night. It may be that the island Plato speaks of in *Timaeus* was part of Crete or some other island which suffered when a volcano on Suntorini (ancient Thera) erupted.

Atlas. A Titan (q.v.) the son of Iapetus and Clymene and brother of Prometheus (q.v.) and Epimetheus. For his part in the Titanomachia (q.v.) he was condemned to carry the sky on his shoulders and stood holding it far to the west of the Pillars of Hercules (q.v.). For a brief time Heracles (q.v.) shouldered his burden. It is said Perseus (q.v.) turned him to stone with Medusa's (q.v.) head and he was identified with Mt. Atlas in North-West Africa. The father of Calypso (q.v.) and the Pleiades (q.v.).

Atreus. See **Thyestes.**

Attis. A god of vegetation whose cult originated in Phrygia and involved a festival of death and resurrection in the Spring. A consort of Cybele (q.v.) according to one tradition he castrated himself in a religious frenzy and became head of her college of eunuch priests.

Augias. A king of Elis with more sheep and cattle than any other man. Heracles (q.v.) was given the task of cleansing his filthy stables which had not been cleared for many years. Heracles promised to cleanse them in a day in return for one tenth of the cattle. He did so by diverting the rivers Peneius and Alphaeus through them but Augias refused to pay him. Heracles later invaded Elis, killed Augias, his sons and their allies the Moliones and destroyed the city of Pylus which had also helped Augias. One tradition says he spared Augias.

Aurora. The Roman goddess of the dawn, associated with the Greek Eos (q.v.).

Autolycus. The son of Hermes (q.v.) and Chione, father of Anticleia and thus grandfather of Odysseus (q.v.). Also grandfather of Sinon (q.v.). He was renowned for trickery, cunning and theft.

Aventine. One of the hills of Rome and the southernmost. It was close to the Tiber, was outside the pomerium and was associated with the "plebians".

Avernus, Lake. The modern Lago di Averno near Naples, thought to be an entrance to the Underworld. This is how Aeneas (q.v.) was told to enter Hades (q.v.). Agrippa linked it with the Lucrine Lake while building the harbour of Portus Julius.

B

Bacchae. The female followers of the cult of Bacchus or Dionysus whose worship was characterised by wine-induced frenzies of a mystic nature. At the height of such frenzies they believed themselves to be at one with the god. Also known as Bacchantes, Maenads and Thyiads.

Bacchoi. Male equivalent of the Bacchae.

Bacchus. Latin name for Dionysus (q.v.).

Bassaris. A Bacchante (See **Bacchae**).

Baucis. See **Philemon.**

Bellerophon. Son of Glaucus (q.v.) King of Corinth. He killed one Bellerus and fled to Tiryns where Anteia, wife of the King Proetus falsely accused him of trying to seduce her. Proetus sent him to his father-in-law Iobates with a letter requesting Iobates to kill the bearer of it. Reluctant to kill a guest Iobates sent him to kill the Chimaera (q.v.). Capturing Pegasus (q.v.) with a golden bridle given to him by Athene (q.v.) he was able to accomplish the task. He was then sent to fight the Amazons (q.v.) and again triumphed. On his return to Tiryns he survived an ambush set by Iobates and finally persuaded the king of his innocence. Iobates made him his heir. One tradition says Bellerophon presumed to rise to Olympus on Pegasus but Zeus sent a gadfly which stung the horse. Pegasus threw Bellerophon to earth but itself entered Olympus.

Belus. One of Poseidon's (q.v.) sons and father of Danaus (q.v.), Cepheus (q.v.) and Aegyptus.

Biton and Cleobis. Sons of a priestess of Hera (q.v.) in Argos who drew their mother's chariot several miles to the goddess's temple when no oxen could be found. Their mother asked Hera to bestow on them the best of gifts for mortals, and they died in their sleep in the temple.

Boeotia. Region of northern Greece; the capital city was Thebes.

Bona Dea. A Roman fertility goddess. Only women worshipped her. Cicero (q.v.) recounts an occasion when his opponent Clodius (q.v.), disguised as a woman, entered an annual nocturnal ceremony of her worshippers over which the chief magistrate's wife presided.

Boreas. The Roman Aquilo; the north wind in Greek mythology. Son of Astraeus (q.v.) and Eos (q.v.) and brother of the other beneficent winds Zephyrus (q.v.), Notus (q.v.) and Eurus (q.v.). A friend of Athens who destroyed Xerxes' (q.v.) fleet. He carried off Oreithyia, daughter of Erechtheus king of Athens who bore him two sons Zetes (q.v.) and Calais (q.v.) and two daughters, Chione and Cleopatra, wife of Phineus.

Brauron. Site on the east coast of Attica. Centre of a cult of Artemis (q.v.). It was believed the locals had killed a she-bear, an animal sacred to the goddess, and that she demanded they worship her on the site, and that girls between the ages of 7 and 11 serve her and live in her temple. Also believed to be the burial place of Iphigenia (q.v.) after her sacrifice at Aulis.

Briareus or **Aegaeon.** One of the Hecatoncheires (q.v.).

Briseis. See **Achilles.**

Brontes. One of the Cyclopes (q.v.).

Brutus, Lucius Junius. According to a Roman tradition accepted by Livy (q.v.) the liberator of Rome from the Etruscan kings following the rape of Lucretia (q.v.). Also the first Roman consul in 509 B.C. He ordered the execution of his own sons when they became involved in a conspiracy to restore the monarchy.

C

Cacus. In Roman tradition this fire-breathing giant and his sister Caca were children of Vulcan (q.v.) who lived on the Palatine hill (q.v.), although Virgil in book 8 of the *Aeneid* (q.v.) makes it the Aventine (q.v.). Virgil tells how Cacus stole the cattle of Geryon (q.v.) from Hercules (q.v.) who pursued Cacus back to his cave, tracking him by the cattle's mooing. There he slew Cacus. This event has been portrayed in a painting by Poussin and a statue by Bandinelli in the Signoria, Florence.

Cadmus. Son of Agenor, king of Phoenicia and grandson of Poseidon (q.v.). When Zeus (q.v.) carried off his sister Europa (q.v.) he went to look for her but was told by the Delphic oracle (*see* Apollo) to relinquish the search and to follow a magical cow. Where the cow lay down he was to found a city. The place where it sank became the site of the Cadmea, the citadel of Thebes. Here Cadmus slew the dragon guarding the spring of Ares and on her advice sowed its teeth. The Sparti (q.v.) sprang up. Cadmus married Harmonia (q.v.) and their wedding was attended by the gods. Their children included Autonoe, Ino, Semele (q.v.) Agave Polydoros (q.v.) and Illyrius. In old age Cadmus, who had introduced the use of letters to Greece from Phoenicia, gave up his throne to his grandson Pentheus and went to reign in Illyria. Later he and Harmonia were received into Elysium (q.v.) in the form of serpents.

Caeneus. Originally the nymph Caenis turned into a man at her own request by Poseidon (q.v.). Accompanied the Argonauts (q.v.) and hunted the Calydonian Boar (q.v.). Invulnerable to normal blows he was killed by the Centaurs (q.v.) in their battle with the Lapithae (q.v.) when they buried him beneath a pile of trees. His soul left the body as a bird and in the Underworld again became female.

Calais. Twin brother of Zetes. Winged sons of Boreas (q.v.) and Oreithyia, they accompanied the Argonauts (q.v.) and drove off the Harpies (q.v.), tormenting Phineus (q.v.) husband of their sister Cleopatra.

Calchas. A renegade Trojan seer who helped the Greeks at Troy (q.v.). He foretold that Troy would not fall without Achilles' (q.v.) presence and that the sacrifice of Iphigenia (q.v.) was necessary to secure a favourable wind. It was he who advised Agamemnon to return the girl Chryseis to her father the Trojan priest Chryses. This caused Agamemnon to seize Briseis and sparked the quarrel with Achilles. Calchas later died of grief when surpassed in prophecy by Mopsus, a mysterious mythical figure who was also said to have sailed with the Argonauts (q.v.).

Calipe. See **Pillars of Hercules.**

Calliope. See **Muses.**

Callirhoë. Daughter of the river god Achelous (q.v.) and wife of Alcmaeon (q.v.). Alcmaeon gave her the necklace and robe of Harmonia (q.v.).

Callisto. Daughter of Lycaon (q.v.). One of Artemis' (q.v.) huntresses. She bore Arcas (q.v.) to Zeus (q.v.) who sought to conceal their affair from Hera (q.v.) by turning Callisto into a bear. Realising the ruse Hera had the bear hunted down but Zeus saved her and placed her amongst the stars as Arctos. Others say that Artemis turned her into a bear and Arcas hunted her. In this version Callisto became the Great Bear constellation and Arcas the Little Bear.

Calydonian Boar. A savage boar which Artemis (q.v.) sent to ravage Calydon because its king, Oeneus (q.v.) had not offered her proper sacrifice (see also Atalanta and Meleager). Pausanias (q.v.) tells of a story of long tusks found at Tegea, seen by Augustus and taken to Rome.

Calypso. A nymph of Ogygia who tended Odysseus (q.v.) there for eight years until Zeus (q.v.) ordered her to send him home to Ithaca. The name means "hidden" and she may have been a death goddess. At one point she offers the hero eternal youth, but he refuses, preferring real life. She bore him two sons.

Camilla. The Roman equivalent of an Amazon (q.v.) —a female warrior.

Capaneus. See **"Seven Against Thebes".**

Capricorn. See **Amalthea.**

Cassandra. Daughter of Priam (q.v.) and Hecuba and twin of Helenus. She was given the gift of prophecy by Apollo (q.v.) but when she disappointed him he decreed that no one would ever believe her prophecies. Several times her important warnings went unheeded, e.g. against Paris (q.v.) going to Sparta, and against the wooden horse (q.v.). She was taken as a slave by Agamemnon (q.v.) when Troy (q.v.) fell and became his mistress. She was murdered with him by Clytemnestra (q.v.).

Cassiopeia. The wife of Cepheus and mother of Andromeda. Her boast that Andromeda was more beautiful than the Nereids (q.v.) caused Poseidon (q.v.) to send a monster to ravage the kingdom. Only the sacrifice of Andromeda could prevent this. Perseus (q.v.), who found her chained naked to a rock by the sea, offered to save her if she would become his wife. Cepheus and Cassiopeia agreed to this and Perseus slew the beast. Her parents then attempted to renege on their promise, claiming Andromeda was promised to another. At her wedding to Perseus the other suitor and his followers attempted to seize the bride but Perseus turned them all to stone with the head of Medusa (q.v.). The images of Cepheus and Cassiopeia were set amongst the stars by Poseidon.

Castalian Spring. Sacred spring on Mt. Parnassus, near the site of the Delphic oracle. Here the young girl Castalia drowned herself to avoid Apollo's (q.v.) advances.

Castalides. A name for the Muses (q.v.).

Castor and Polydeuces. (Latin **"Pollux"**) The "Dioscuri". The twin "Sons of Zeus", brothers of Helen (q.v.) and the sons of Leda (q.v.) the wife of Tyndareus of Sparta. One tradition says that they were born from an egg, like Helen, after Zeus had visited Leda in the form of a swan. Others say only Polydeuces was Zeus' son and that Castor being the son of Tyndareus was a mere mortal. Castor was a famous horse tamer and Polydeuces a great boxer. Sailing with the Argonauts (q.v.) Polydeuces slew Amycus son of Poseidon (q.v.) who lived on the isle of Bebrycos. Amycus was a renowned boxer who killed travellers by challenging them to a boxing match. They also hunted the Calydonian boar (q.v.). The Dioscuri fought a mortal battle with their cousins the twins Idas and Lynceus. Idas Zeus then killed Idas but Polydeuces begged to die with his brother. However Zeus decided they should live alternate days with the gods and under the earth. Their image was placed amongst the stars as Gemini. Poseidon gave them power over the wind and waves and they became protectors of seafarers. They were said to have appeared on horseback to help the Romans against the Latins in the battle of Lake Regillus in 484 B.C., after which their cult was adopted at Rome.

Centaurs. A race of savage creatures, half-man, half-horse which inhabited the woodlands and mountains, particularly those of Thessaly. They were the offspring of Ixion and a cloud. In Homer (q.v.) the centaurs appear as representatives of primitive desires, fighting, drinking and womanising, but later they are only portrayed as turning to violence when drunk. When they tried to abduct Deidamia (q.v.) from her wedding, they became involved in a famous battle with their neighbours the Lapithae (q.v.).

Centimani. See **Hecatoncheires.**

Cephalus. Husband of Procris who was carried off by Eos (q.v.). Eos released him but Procris, suspicious of the time he spent hunting, followed him into the woods. Hearing him praying for a breeze she supposed it to be his mistress (the Roman equivalent of Eos was Aurora, the Latin for breeze aura). Moving closer she was struck by his spear, which never missed, and killed. The story is told by Hesiod and Ovid and inspired paintings by Poussin and Claude.

Cepheus. King of Tegea and one of the Argonauts (q.v.). He and most of his 20 sons were killed helping Heracles (q.v.) fight Hippocoon.

Cerberus. A huge and savage dog, the offspring of Echidne (q.v.) and Typhon (q.v.) which guarded the entrance to Hades (q.v.). He is usually said to have had three heads, but Hesiod gives him fifty. His back was covered with serpents' heads and he had a snake for a tail. Heracles (q.v.) dragged him from the Underworld; Orpheus (q.v.) charmed him with music when seeking Eurydice while Aeneas (q.v.) drugged him with a cake of honey and narcotics, hence "a sop to Cerberus".

Cercyon. A son of Hephaestus (q.v.) reigning near Eleusis. Here he challenged all travellers to a wrestling match and killed them, until he challenged Theseus (q.v.) and was killed himself.

Ceres. Ancient Italian corn-goddess worshipped in a temple on the Aventine. Games and a spring festival, the Ceriala, were held in her honour. She was associated with Demeter (q.v.) from an early date and her daughter Proserpina with Persephone (q.v.).

Ceryneian Hind. A creature with brazen feet and golden antlers. One of Heracles' (q.v.) tasks was to catch it alive. He pursued it for a year and caught it without shedding blood by pinning its forelegs together with an arrow.

Chalybes. Mythical inhabitants of north Asia Minor said by some traditions to have invented iron working.

Chaos. In Greek creation myth Chaos was the infinite space existing before creation. From Chaos sprang Ge (q.v.), the Earth.

Charities. Also called the Gratiae or Graces by the Romans. They were originally divinities of nature. In the Iliad (q.v.) only one Charity is personified, Charis, wife of Hephaestus (q.v.). Later the three Graces appear, Aglaia, Thalia and Euphrosyne, friends of the Muses (q.v.) with whom they inhabited Mt. Olympus.

Charon. The surly ferryman who transported the dead across the Styx (q.v.) to Hades (q.v.). He only transported them if they had received the correct funeral rite and if their relatives had placed a small coin, his fare, under the tongues. However Heracles (q.v.) forced his passage and Orpheus (q.v.) charmed his with his lyre. Amongst the Etruscans (q.v.), as in modern Greek folklore, he was regarded as a synonym or figure of death. Virgil (q.v.) portrays him with unkempt white hair and eyes of fire in the 6th book of the Aeneid.

Charybdis and Scylla. Two monsters guarding the Straits of Messina. Charybdis swallowed the sea and vessels on it, three times a day, regurgitating what she swallowed each time. Opposite was Scylla, the daughter of Poseidon (q.v.) by a mortal, whom the jealous Amphitrite (q.v.) turned into a monster with six barking heads and twelve feet. Odysseus (q.v.) was forced to pass between the two evils and the equally undesirable choice between the pair has become proverbial.

Cheiron. Also called Chiron. A centaur (q.v.). A son of Cronus (q.v.) and Philyra, hence he is sometimes referred to as Philyrides. Unlike his fellow centaurs a wise and kindly being who learnt music, medicine, hunting and prophecy from Apollo (q.v.) and Artemis (q.v.). This learning he imparted to numerous heroes including Achilles (q.v.), the Dioscuri (q.v.), Jason (q.v.) and Peleus (q.v.). An immortal, he was accidentally wounded by the poisoned arrow of his friend Heracles (q.v.). In pain he longed for death. By surrendering his immortality he was relieved of life and suffering and placed among the stars as Sagittarius.

Chimeira. A monster with a lion's head, goat's body and a serpent for a tail. It could breathe fire. The offspring of Echidne (q.v.) and Typhon (q.v.), though some say it was begot by the Sphinx (q.v.) and Orthrus (q.v.). It was killed by Bellerophon (q.v.) while ravaging Lycia. The beast gave us the word "chimera" or fanciful notion.

Chryseis. (Cressida) Daughter of the Trojan seer and priest of Apollo (q.v.). Chryseis was captured by Agamemnon (q.v.) who refused to ransom her. Apollo then sent a plague on the Greek camp and when Calchas (q.v.) explained the cause Agamemnon released her. He then seized Briseis thus causing the quarrel with Achilles (q.v.). The medieval *Roman de Troie* tells how Troilus loved her, but she left him for Diomedes (q.v.). This is the basis of Chaucer's *Troilus and Criseyde* and Shakespeare's *Troilus and Cressida*.

Chrysippus. The son of Pelops (q.v.), murdered by his half-brother Atreus (q.v.) and Thyestes (q.v.) at the instigation of his step-mother Hippodameia (q.v.).

Chthonius. *See* **Spartii.**

Circe The daughter of Helios (q.v.) and Perse. A sorceress living on the island of Aeaea (Virgil (q.v.) identifies it with Circeii in Campania (q.v.). She turned Odysseus' (q.v.) men into swine but he resisted by use of the herb "moly" given to him by Hermes (q.v.). Having forced her to restore his men he stayed a year with her and she advised him on his trip to the Underworld and return to Ithaca. She had a son, Telegonus by him and later married his son by Penelope (q.v.), Telemachus (q.v.). In the *Argonautica* of Apollonius of Rhodes she purifies Jason (q.v.) and Medea (q.v.) of murder on their return from Colchis. She was worshipped in Campania in the form of Feronia.

Cisseus. Father of Hecabe (q.v.).

Claros. Site of a shrine and oracle of Apollo (q.v.) to the south of Smyrna.

Cleobis. *See* **Biton.**

Clio. *See* **Muses.**

Cloacina. Ancient Roman divinity of "purification", later identified with Venus.

Cloelia. A Roman girl, legendary for having escaped from Porsenna (q.v.) when taken hostage and swimming back to Rome across the Tiber.

Clotho. One of the Fates (q.v.). She pulled the limbs of Pelops (q.v.) from the cauldron in which they were to be boiled, thus enabling his restoration to life.

Clytemnestra. Daughter of Tyndareus (q.v.) and a half-sister of Helen (q.v.) and Castor and Polydeuces (q.v.). Wife of Agamemnon (q.v.) by whom she bore Orestes (q.v.), Iphigenia (q.v.) and Electra (q.v.). While Agamemnon was at Troy (q.v.) she began an affair with Aegisthus (q.v.) and on his return the pair murdered him. She was killed by Orestes. Her murder of Agamemnon should be seen in the context of his infidelity with Cassandra (q.v.) and others and his sacrifice of Iphigenia. This is how Strauss views the matter in his opera *Elektra*.

Cocles. The "one-eyed", a nickname of Horatius (q.v.) who kept the bridge across the Tiber.

Cocytus. The river of wailing in Hades (q.v.).

Coeus. One of the Titans (q.v.).

Cornelia. Mother of the "Gracchi", daughter of Scipio Africanus and a model of what Romans of the Republic thought a matron should be. On the deaths of her sons she withdrew to Misenum and her home became a centre of culture. She appears in Plutarch's (q.v.) *Lives* of her sons and he tells us that when a visitor asked to see her jewels she presented her sons saying "These are my jewels".

Coronis. Thessalian princess made pregnant by Apollo (q.v.) but who fell in love with an Arcadian youth. Learning of this from a crow, Apollo sent Artemis (q.v.) to kill her. The unborn child was snatched from her and given to Cheiron (q.v.) to rear. The child was Asclepius (q.v.).

Corybantes. Priests of Rhea (q.v.) or Cybele (q.v.) in Phrygia and Asia Minor. Known for their dancing and performance of wild rites to the sound of drums and cymbals.

Corydon. Common Arcadian shepherd's name but in Virgil's (q.v.) second *Eclogue* the shepherd

Corydon laments his "faithless Alexis". From this Corydon has become a symbol of homosexual love.

Creon. A "ruler" or "prince" and the name often given to subsidiary characters in Greek legend, e.g. the brother of Jocasta (q.v.) who succeeds Oedipus (q.v.). *See also* **Jason.**

Cretan Bull. A magnificent white bull sent by Poseidon (q.v.) to Minos (q.v.) for sacrifice. Minos' wife Pasiphaë (q.v.) so admired the bull she had Daedalus (q.v.) construct a hollow cow for her to get inside. She then mated with the bull and later bore the Minotaur (q.v.). Minos also admired the bull and rather than sacrifice it, substituted another bull. The original bull escaped to ravage Crete until captured by Heracles (q.v.) and taken to Eurystheus (q.v.). Eurystheus freed it and it ravaged Greece until captured by Theseus (q.v.) at Marathon (q.v.) and sacrificed to Athene (q.v.).

Creusa. Feminine equivalent of Creon. The most famous is the daughter of Priam (q.v.), first wife of Aeneas (q.v.) and mother of Ascanius. She was lost in the escape from Troy (q.v.) when the city fell. When Aeneas looked for her he met only her ghost who bid him go forward to meet his destiny.

Croesus. Last king of Lydia who in the mid-6th century B.C. amassed a great fortune. His wealth is proverbial. Regarded as a model of piety for his gold offerings to Apollo (q.v.) at Delphi (q.v.). He met Solon and tried to persuade him to admit that Croesus was the happiest of men. Solon refused, saying that no man could be considered happy till his life had ended. The Delphic oracle told him that a great empire would fall if he invaded Persia. His own did. The Persian king Cyrus ordered him to be burnt alive but he called on Solon's name and told Cyrus of Solon's sayings. Cyrus pardoned him and made him an adviser. A later tradition says Apollo saved him and carried him to the land of the Hyperboreans.

Crommyum, Sow of. Wild sow slain by Theseus (q.v.).

Cronus. The son of Uranus (q.v.) and Ge (q.v.). The youngest of the twelve Titans (q.v.). When Ge stirred the Titans to revolt against Uranus she gave Cronus a flint sickle with which he castrated his father. Having deposed Uranus, Cronus reigned supreme and consigned the Cyclopes (q.v.) and the Hecatoncheires (q.v.) to Tartarus (q.v.). He married his sister Rhea (q.v.) and by her was father of Hestia (q.v.), Demeter (q.v.), Hera (q.v.), Poseidon (q.v.), Hades (q.v.) and Zeus (q.v.). Mindful of a curse by Uranus and Ge that he too be deposed by his own son, he swallowed each child at birth. But Rhea gave him a stone to swallow instead of Zeus and later gave him an emetic forcing him to regurgitate his other children. They now joined Zeus in a war on Cronus and the Titans. The Cyclopes aided them and gave Zeus the thunderbolt, Poseidon the trident and Hades a helmet of darkness or invisibility. Cronus was defeated and the Titans were consigned to Tartarus.

Cupid or **Amor.** Roman god of love, identified with the Greek Eros (q.v.).

Curetes. Priests of Rhea (q.v.) who drowned the cries of the infant Zeus (q.v.) as he lay in the Dictaean Cave by the clashing of their weapons. This prevented Cronus (q.v.) finding and devouring him. They were half-divine and in later times were conflated with the Corybantes (q.v.) who were also believed to be half-divine. All became part of Dionysus' ritual.

Cybele. The mother goddess of Phrygia where she and her lover Attis (q.v.) were worshipped in orgiastic rites and purification ceremonies including bathing in the blood of a sacrificed bull. Her symbol was a black stone and this was brought to Rome from Pessinus in 204 B.C. However it was only during the reign of Claudius that Roman citizens were allowed to serve as her priests and the oriental eunuchs serving her cult were always frowned upon. Her worship is described by Lucretius (q.v.) in book 2 and Catullus in his *Attis*. The artists of the classical world portray her with a crown of towers, a libation dish and tambourine, flanked by lions to show her control of wild nature.

Cyclops. Generally known to the Greeks as one-eyed giants living in a distant country, perhaps Sicily. In Homer (q.v.) the Cyclops Polyphemus is a man-eating son of Poseidon (q.v.), made drunk and blinded by Odysseus (q.v.) and his men whom he had captured and meant to eat. Hesiod (q.v.) refers to three Cyclops but describes them as Titans (q.v.). The three (Brontes, Steropes and Arges) were sons of Ge (q.v.) and Uranus (q.v.) who made weapons for Zeus (q.v.), Poseidon and Hades (q.v.) (see **Cronus**). Other traditions make them skilled craftsmen helping Hephaestus (q.v.) at his Sicilian forge. They were also builders of cities including Athens and the walls of Tiryns.

Cyllenius. Another name for Hermes (q.v.) who was said to have been born on Mt. Cyllene in southern Greece.

Cyncus. "The Swan", a mythical king of Liguria who loved Phaeton (q.v.) and was turned into a swan.

Cynthia. A name given to Artemis (q.v.). She and Apollo (q.v.) were thought to have been born on Mt. Cynthus in Delos and were thus referred to as Cynthia and Cynthus.

Cyrene. In myth the mother of Aristaeus (q.v.) by Apollo (q.v.) who carried her to Libya where he gave her name to the city of Cyrene.

Cythera. An island off the south-east coast of Greece noted for its sanctuary of Aphrodite (q.v.). She was thus referred to as "the Cytherean".

D

Dactyli. Greek equivalent of the Roman Chalybes (q.v.) the mythical beings who lived on Mt. Ida in northern Asia Minor and invented iron-working.

Daedalus. Mythical Athenian craftsman. His jealousy of his nephew Perdix of Talos, who was said to have invented the saw, caused him to throw Perdix from Athene's (q.v.) temple on the Acropolis (q.v.). Having thus committed murder he fled to Crete. Here he arranged the liaison between Pasiphaë (q.v.) and the Cretan Bull (q.v.) which produced the Minotaur (q.v.). Then, to conceal what had transpired from Minos (q.v.) he built the famous labyrinth to hide the Minotaur. When Minos discovered the truth he imprisoned Daedalus and his son Icarus in the labyrinth. Pasiphaë released them and Daedalus invented wings which, when attached to their shoulders by wax, enabled him and his son to fly. However Icarus flew too near to the sun, the wax melted, and he fell to his doom in the Icarian sea. Daedalus reached Cumae and then went to Sicily. Here King Cocalus welcomed him and when Minos arrived in pursuit Cocalus' daughters helped Daedalus kill him. In Sicily Daedalus was credited with many wonderful buildings including a honeycomb of gold for Aphrodite's (q.v.) temple on Mt. Eryx. His name has become synonymous with ingenuity and skill, hence "Daedal" and "daedalian" in the English language.

Damocles. Member of the court of Dionysius I, tyrant of Syracuse. Cicero tells how the tyrant had him eat a sumptuous dinner while a sword was suspended by a hair over his head. This illustrated the luxurious but precarious life style of the tyrant and "the sword of Damocles" has become proverbial.

Danaë. A princess of Argos, daughter of King Acrisius (q.v.). An oracle told the king that Danaë's son would kill him so he imprisoned her in a brazen tower. Zeus (q.v.) visited her in a shower of gold and fathered Perseus (q.v.). Acrisius cast them adrift in a box and they came to Seriphos. They were found by the fisherman Dictys and taken to the king Polydectes. He wished to marry Danaë and so, to get Perseus out of the way, sent him to fetch the head of Medusa (q.v.). Danaë was saved from Polydectes' advances when Perseus returned and, showing the head, turned him to stone.

Danai. A general name used by Homer for the Greeks assembled at Troy. It was meant to perpetuate the memory of a common ancestor, Danaus (q.v.).

Danaus. A king of Libya and the father of 50 daughters, the "Danaïdes". His brother Aegyptus, who had 50 sons, wanted a mass marriage, but Danaus fled with his daughters to Argos where he became king. Eventually Aegyptus' sons followed and demanded the "Danaïdes". Danaus agreed but gave each daughter a weapon with which they slew their husbands on the wedding night. All, that is, save Hypermestra who spared Lynceus. Lynceus killed Danaus and became king of Argos. In the Underworld the Danaïdes were condemned to carry water in sieves for ever. The story is told

by Pindar (q.v.) and the Danaïdes form the chorus in Aeschylos' (q.v.) Suppliants.

Daphne. The daughter of the river god Peneus or Ladon. A nymph pursued by Apollo (q.v.). To escape him she prayed either to her father or to the Earth to be turned into a laurel tree, which she was. Apollo made himself a laurel wreath as consolation and it became the prize at the Pythian Games held in his honour.

Daphnis. The son of Hermes (q.v.) and a nymph. She abandoned the infant but he was raised by Sicilian shepherds. Pan (q.v.) taught him the pipes and he was the originator of pastoral poetry. Later he was unfaithful to a nymph who loved him and in revenge she blinded him. His father ordered forth the fountain of Daphnis near Syracuse in his honour.

Dardanus. The son of Zeus (q.v.) and the Pleiad (q.v.) Electra. He founded Dardania on land given to him by Teucer. He was grandfather of Tros, great grandfather of Ilus (q.v.) and Ganymede (q.v.). Hence an ancestor of the Trojans who were sometimes called Dardanids, Dardans or Dardonians. Roman legend sometimes envisages him migrating to Dardania from Italy.

Deianeira. The daughter of Oeneus, king of Calydon and the wife of Heracles (q.v.) who won her hand by defeating the river god Achelous (q.v.). She bore him a son Hyllus. After accidentally killing Eunomus, Heracles took her and Hyllus into voluntary exile. When they came to cross the River Evenus the centaur (q.v.) Nessus offered to transport her on his back. However he tried to rape her and was killed by Heracles. As he lay dying he told her to take his blood as it was a charm which would keep Heracles in love with her. Later Heracles won Iole, daughter of Eurytus King of Oechalia, in an archery contest. When Eurytus refused to surrender Iole Heracles invaded Oechalia and defeated him. He then ordered Deianeira to send him a white shirt which he was to wear at a thanksgiving sacrifice to Zeus (q.v.). Deianeira, jealous of Iole, dipped the shirt in the blood of Nessus. But the blood was poisonous and when Heracles donned the shirt it burned his body and attempts to pull it off tore pieces of flesh from the hero. In agony he ordered Hyllus to build a funeral pyre on which he would find quick death and release from the pain. He also had Hyllus marry Iola. Deianeira, horrified at the result of her action, hanged herself. The story forms the plot of Sophocles' Women of Trachis.

Deidamia. The maiden who fell in love with Achilles (q.v.) and bore him Neoptolemus (q.v.).

Deiphobus. See **Helen** and **Helenus.**

Delis, Delius. Epithets of Artemis (q.v.) and Apollo (q.v.) who were born on Delos (q.v.).

Delos. Site of the important Ionian shrine of Apollo (q.v.). Here he was known as Phoebus ("the shining") or Lycius. When the jealous Hera (q.v.) pursued Leto (q.v.) she sought asylum where she could give birth to Apollo, her son by Zeus (q.v.). Delos, which was so poor it could lose nothing to Hera's wrath, accepted her.

Delphi. Site of Apollo's (q.v.) Dorian shrine and the most famous centre of his worship. Here he took his prophetic role having replaced Python. The oracle, located near the Castalian spring, was supposed to contain the omphalos or navel store of the Earth. A priestess, the Pythia, sat on a tripod chewing the intoxicating laurel leaf and voicing his utterances. Intoxicating vapours also issued from a chasm in the shrine. In this role Apollo was known as Loxias "the Ambiguous". (See **Croesus**). The priests of the shrine were not incorruptible and were known to take sides, e.g. with Sparta against Athens and with Philip of Macedon against Greece. The oracle had greatest influence during the period of overseas colonisation when its advice on location of colonies was always sought. The oracle encouraged Rome to defy Hannibal but was looted by Sulla. Nero visited it and Hadrian tried in vain to revive its prestige. Its decline came with the advance of Christianity and the growing interest in astrology as a means of prophecy. The temples at Delphi were sacked by Alaric in A.D. 396. Apollo's temple with its inscribed maxims "Know thyself" and "Nothing in excess" had stood on the highest point of Mt. Parnassus and had housed the sepulchre of Bacchus (q.v.) who was also worshipped at Delphi.

Demeter. The counterpart of the Roman Ceres, a

Greek corn-goddess responsible for the fertility of the earth. The daughter of Cronus (q.v.) and Rhea (q.v.) she became mother of Persephone (q.v.) or Kore ("the maiden") by her brother Zeus (q.v.). A 7th century B.C. Homeric *Hymn to Demeter* tells how Hades (q.v.) carried off Persephone from Eleusis twelve miles from Athens (Ovid says she was taken while gathering poppies in Sicily). Demeter scoured the earth for her until Helios (q.v.) told her what had occurred. She then shunned Olympus (q.v.) and wandered the earth, forbidding it to bring forth fruit and therefore threatening famine. Zeus finally agreed that Persephone could leave Hades provided she had not eaten in the Underworld. Hades agreed to let her go but tempted her into eating a pomegranate. She thus had to spend half a year with him in the Underworld and half with Demeter. Demeter again made the earth fertile but turned Ascalaphus, who had seen and reported Persephone eating the pomegranate, into an owl. She punished those who had been unkind to her during her wandering (see **Abas**) but rewarded those who had treated her hospitably. She taught Triptolemus, another son of Celeus (q.v.) the art of agriculture and gave him an ear of corn whose virtues he revealed to his fellow men. The Eleusian Festival was held in Demeter's honour from the 6th century B.C. and there was an annual procession from Eleusis to Athens. Those who spoke Greek were initiated into the mysteries of her cult. The Thesmophoria, a celebration of the foundation of laws, was held in her honour in many cities.

Demophon (1) The son of Theseus (q.v.) and Phaedra (q.v.) brother of Acamas (q.v.). He helped rescue his grandmother Aethra who had been Helen's (q.v.) slave, when Troy (q.v.) fell. Phyllis, a Thracian princess, loved him and committed suicide when he left her to visit Athens. She was then transformed into a tree.

(2) The son of Celeus and Metaneira. Demeter (q.v.) tried to reward the pair for their kindness to her by making Demophon immortal. To achieve this he had to be suspended above a fire, but Metaneira cried out thus breaking the spell and he perished.

Deucalion. The son of Prometheus (q.v.), husband of Pyrrha and father of Hellen. He was thus the ancestor of the Greeks. When Zeus (q.v.) decided to flood the earth in order to destroy mankind they escaped in an ark which finally made land on Mt. Parnassus. The couple prayed to Themis (q.v.) that mankind be restored and were told to scatter their mother's bones behind them. They took this to mean stones, the skeleton of Mother Earth. The rocks Deucalion scattered became men; those Pyrrha scattered became women.

Diana. Italian goddess of woods, women, childbirth and later, by association with the Greek Artemis (q.v.), the moon. Her cult was originally centred on the volcanic Lake Nemi at Aricia. The lake was known as Diana's mirror. The priest here, known as the rex, was always a runaway slave who had murdered his predecessor. A temple of Diana, said to have been founded by Servius Tullius also stood on the Aventine.

Dictaean Cave. A cave on Mt. Dicte in Crete, the reputed childhood home of Zeus (q.v.). Hence he was known as Dictaeus.

Dictys. (1) The sailor who found Perseus (q.v.) and his mother Danaë (q.v.) adrift at sea in a chest.

(2) A Cretan said to have accompanied Idomeneus (q.v.) to the Trojan war. His diary of the war was supposedly buried near Cnossos and found in the reign of Nero.

Dido. A daughter of the king of Tyre originally called Elissa. Her husband Sychaeus was murdered but with a few followers she escaped to Libya and founded Carthage (**K31**). Local legend said she burnt herself on a funeral pyre to avoid marrying Iarbas, a native king. The Roman version, given in the *Aeneid* takes Aeneas (q.v.) to Carthage where Dido's unrequited love for him results in her death. Aeneas abandons her to fulfil his destiny as ancestor of Rome.

Didyma. A great sanctuary of Apollo (q.v.) at Miletus.

Dindyma. Mountain in Asia Minor and a centre of the Cybele's (q.v.) cult.

Diomedes. (1) A king of the Bistones in Thrace who possessed man-eating mares. A labour of Heracles (q.v.) was to bring them to Eurystheus (q.v.). This he did by stealing them and beating off his pur-

suers. But while he was busy fighting, the mares devoured his friend Abderus. Heracles founded the city of Abdera in his honour. Eurystheus freed the horses on Mt. Olympus (q.v.) where wild beasts devoured them.

(2) The son of Tydeus, king of Argos. One of the Epigoni (q.v.). He also went to Troy (q.v.) and was a companion of Odysseus (q.v.). With Odysseus he sailed to fetch Achilles (q.v.) and later Neoptolemus (q.v.). He encouraged Agamemnon (q.v.) to sacrifice Iphigenia (q.v.) and helped Odysseus capture the Trojan spy Dolon. He wounded Aeneas (q.v.) and Aphrodite (q.v.) as she saved the Trojan. He also wounded Ares. He returned from Troy to find his wife had been unfaithful and went to settle in Daunia in Italy. Here he married Euippe, daughter of king Daunus. He was buried on one of the Diomedan islands.

Dionysus. The Roman Bacchus. Also called Bromius "the Boisterous". The son of Zeus (q.v.) and Semele, a mortal, Zeus visited her in the guise of a mortal but when she was six months pregnant the jealous Hera (q.v.) came to her as an old woman. She advised Semele to demand her lover appear in his true form. Zeus unwillingly agreed to do so and Semele was consumed by fire. The unborn child was sewn up in Zeus' thigh to be born as Dionysus. The child was given into the care of Athamas and Ino. He was disguised as a girl but Hera learned the truth and drove Athamas mad, causing him to kill his own son. Hermes (q.v.) then took Dionysus to Mt. Nysa in India where he was raised by nymphs. Zeus placed their images in the stars as the Hyades. Here he was taught the use of the vine by his tutor Silenus and his satyrs and here he invented wine. As an adult he journeyed through India, Egypt, Syria and Asia accompanied by a wild following of Maenads or Bacchae and Satyrs. As he went he founded cities and taught cultivation of the vine. When he reached Thrace, Lycurgus, king of the Edones, opposed him but was driven mad by Rhea (q.v.) and slew his own son. His people then had him torn apart by horses. King Pentheus of Thebes also opposed Dionysus and was torn apart by crazed Bacchae whose ranks included his mother and sisters. Entranced they took him for a wild animal. Sailing to Naxos Dionysus was captured by pirates for sale as a slave. He became a lion and turned the oars to serpents. Ivy grew on the mast. The terrified pirates jumped overboard and became dolphins. At Naxos he married Ariadne (q.v.) whom Theseus (q.v.) had deserted. He was eventually received into Olympus as a god, replacing Hestia (q.v.). He fetched his mother to Olympus from the Underworld and she was henceforth known as Thyone. Dionysus was the god of wine and intoxicating herbs like ivy and laurel. He was also the god of tillage and law giving. He was worshipped at Delphi (q.v.) and in the spring festival, the Great Dionysia. In Rome the mysteries of his cult were a closely guarded secret. His followers worshipped him in communal wine-induced frenzies and the ritual involved sacrifice of animals, flagellation and a mystical marriage of novices with the god.

Dioscuri. See **Castor and Polydeuces.**

Dirce. See **Antiope.**

Dis or **Orcus.** Hades (q.v.).

Dodona. Site of an oracle of Zeus (q.v.) in north west Greece near modern Janina. It was associated with the union of Zeus and Dione, a minor goddess. The oracle centred on an oak and messages were transmitted by the rustling branches and cooing of pigeons nesting in it. The priests were "Selloi" who slept on the ground and walked barefoot. It was visited by Croesus (q.v.) and Alexander the Great offered the sanctuary a large sum of money.

Dryope. The daughter of King Dryops. Apollo (q.v.) seduced her and she was carried off by the Hamadryads (nymphs of trees).

E

Echidne. A mythical creature, half-woman, half-serpent. Mother by Typhon (q.v.) of the Chimaera (q.v.), Sphinx (q.v.), Cerberus (q.v.), Hydra (q.v.), Nemean Lion, Orthrus (q.v.), and Ladon. Slain by Argus.

Echion. A son of Hermes (q.v.). An Argonaut (q.v.) who took part in the hunt of the Calydonian boar (q.v.).

Echo. A nymph who occupied Hera's (q.v.) attention by incessant talk while Zeus (q.v.) enjoyed himself with the other nymphs. In punishment Hera deprived her of the power of speech except to repeat the words of others. Echo loved Narcissus who refused her. Heart-broken she pined away to nothing, only her voice remaining. Artemis (q.v.) punished Narcissus for his heartlessness by making him fall in love with his own reflection. Despairingly he committed suicide and was turned into a flower.

Egeria. An Italian goddess or nymph whose worship was connected with that of Diana (q.v.). She was associated with water. It was believed she advised Numa Pompilius (q.v.) especially on religious matters and Livy tells us they met in a sacred grove near Rome.

Eileithyia. A goddess of childbirth whom the Greeks associated with Artemis (q.v.) and the Romans with Juno (q.v.).

Elatus. The father of Caeneus and one of the Lapithae (q.v.).

Electra. (1) A Pleiad (q.v.).
(2) The daughter of Agamemnon (q.v.) and Clytemnestra (q.v.). Treated as a slave by her mother and Aegisthus (q.v.) she later helped her brother Orestes (q.v.) and his friend Pylades (q.v.) avenge their father and married Pylades. This is the basis of Euripedes' *Electra* and Strauss's *Elektra*. Freud gave the name "Electra complex" to female fixation on the father, the opposite of the "Oedipus complex".

Electryon. The son of Perseus (q.v.) and Andromeda (q.v.). King of Mycenae and father of Alcmene (q.v.) wife of Amphitrion (q.v.).

Eleusis. A sacred site twelve miles west of Athens facing Salamis. Here Celeus received Demeter (q.v.). Games and an oracle were found there. A cult involving "Mysteries" was centred there and administered by two families, the Eumolpidae and Kerykes. Ceremonies were held twice a year in Spring and Autumn and initiation to the mysteries, of which we know little, was open to all men, Greek or not, free or slave, who had not committed murder.

Elissa. *See* Dido.

Elpenor. One of Odysseus' (q.v.) crew who fell off the roof of Circe's (q.v.) palace while sleep-walking and broke his neck. When Odysseus visited the Underworld his shade begged for cremation and a burial mound in which his ear was to be planted.

Elysium. A blessed abode of the dead, placed by Homer near the Underworld but not in Hades (q.v.). The virtuous went here after death. It was a land of warmth never knowing cold or snow. Later it was associated with "Fortunate Isles" holding "Elysian Fields" which were believed to be far to the west, beyond the Pillars of Hercules (q.v.).

Empusae. Daughters of Hecate (q.v.). They were demons with the haunches of an ass who wore brazen slippers. Able to turn themselves into cows, bitches or young maidens, as the latter they lay with young men and sucked their blood as they slept.

Enceladus. A son of Ge (q.v.). One of 24 giants (q.v.) with serpents' tails whom Alcyoneus led in an assault on Olympus (q.v.). Buried under Mt. Etna in Sicily as a punishment.

Endymion. Either a shepherd of Caria or an Aeolian youth who became king of Elis. As he slept in a cave Selene (q.v.) the moon saw him and descended to kiss him. Captivated by his looks she made him fall into a dreamless everlasting sleep so that she could always gaze upon him. His son Aetolus conquered Aetolia.

Enipeus. A river god, beloved of Tyro (q.v.).

Eos. The goddess of the dawn, the Romans identified her with Aurora (q.v.). The daughter of Hyperion (q.v.) and Theira and sister of Helios (q.v.). She drove the chariot of Helios each morning to announce his arrival and traversed the sky with him as Hemera before landing in the west as Hespera. The wife of Astraeus and by him mother of the stars and all the winds save the east. She carried off several handsome youths including Orion (q.v.), Cephalus (q.v.), and Tithonus to whom she bore Memnon (q.v.). She requested Zeus (q.v.) to make Tithonus immortal but forgot to ask for eternal youth and as he aged he shrank to a cicada.

Epaphus. The son of Zeus (q.v.) and Io who ruled Egypt and was said by some to be the sacred bull of Egypt, Apis (q.v.).

Epeius. A cowardly son of Panopeus who built the Trojan Horse.

Ephialtes. One of the 24 giants (q.v.) led by Alcyoneus. (*See also* Otus).

Epidaurus. Site of a famous sanctuary of Asclepius (q.v.) built in the 6th century B.C. Here pilgrims could see the tomb of the god.

Epigoni. Descendants of the "Seven against Thebes" (q.v.) who also attacked the city ten years after their fathers had done so. They were assembled by Adrastus (q.v.) and their ranks included his own son Aegialeus, Diomedes son of Tydeus, Sthenelus son of Capaneus and Eradne and Therseander. Like his father Polynices (q.v.) Therseander bribed Eriphyle (q.v.) into persuading Alcmaeon into joining the assault on Thebes. Aegialeus died at the walls of the city but the Theban prophet Teiresias advised the citizens to leave the city at night as he had foreseen the Argives (i.e. the Epigoni), capturing an empty city. He died next morning drinking from the well of Tilphussa. Adrastus died of grief hearing of his son's death while the remaining Epigoni were left holding an empty city. Alcmaeon went home to take revenge on Eriphyle (q.v.).

Erebos. A deep chasm in the Underworld.

Erebus. "Darkness", the son of Chaos (q.v.) and father of Aether and Hemera by "Night", his sister. Some traditions hold that the Fates (q.v.) were daughters of Erebus and Night and that they held sway even over Zeus (q.v.).

Erechtheus. Son of Pandion and grandson of Erichthonius (q.v.) with whom he is sometimes confused or identified. Both were reared by Athene (q.v.) and were associated with serpents. Both were mythical kings of Athens. When the Eleusians led by Eumolpus, a son of Poseidon (q.v.), invaded Athens, Erechtheus was told by an oracle to sacrifice his daughter Otonia. He did so and her sisters Protogonia and Panora also sacrificed themselves. He slew Eumolpus and was slain by lightning from either Poseidon or Zeus (q.v.).

Erichthonius. A son of Hephaestus (q.v.) by Athene (q.v.). The child was concealed in a chest by the normally chaste Athene and entrusted to the daughters of Cecrops of Athens who were forbidden to open it. However they did so and finding the serpent inside went mad and leaped to their death from the Acropolis (q.v.). Erichthonius eventually succeeded Cecrops as King of Athens and was grandfather of Erechtheus. It was said Erichthonius was the founder of the Panathenaean games in honour of Athene and that he was the first man to harness a team of four horses to a single chariot.

Eridanus. An Italian river god, later thought to be the River Po.

Erigone. The daughter of Icarius. Led to her father's grave by his faithful pet hound Maera, she hanged herself from the tree beneath which she lay.

Erinnyes. Three daughters of Mother Earth whom she conceived by the blood of Uranus (q.v.) when Cronus (q.v.) castrated him. They personified the conscience and were powerful divinities who punished crimes of sacrilege, especially matricide. They pursued Alcmaeon (q.v.) and drove Orestes (q.v.) mad and into exile. These winged creatures had serpent hair and lived in the Underworld. Their names were Alecto, Magaera and Tisiphone. Orestes was acquitted by Athene (q.v.) of matricide following his defence by Apollo (q.v.). To pacify the Erinnyes Athene gave them a grotto at Athens where they received libations and sacrifices. Henceforth they were euphemistically referred to as the Eumenides or "kindly ones".

Eriphyle. The sister of Adrastus (q.v.) and wife of the seer Amphiarus. Mother of Alcmaeon (q.v.). Polynices (q.v.) bribed her into persuading Amphiarus into joining the Seven Against Thebes (q.v.) despite the seer's prophecy that only Adrastus would survive their expedition. She received the necklace of Harmonia (q.v.) for this. Later Thersander bribed her with the magic robe of Harmonia into persuading Alcmaeon to join the Epigoni (q.v.). On returning from Thebes Alcmaeon slew her for her selfish deceit.

Eris. A female divinity personifying Quarrels and Strife for the Greeks.

Eros. The Greek god of love, identified with the Roman Cupid (q.v.) or Amor. A son of Aphrodite (q.v.), whom he often accompanied, by either her father Zeus (q.v.) or Hermes (q.v.). His half-brother was Anteros, son of Aphrodite and Ares (q.v.) who personified mutual love. It was only from the 4th century B.C. onwards that he came to be represented as a winged boy firing arrows of love which could wound both men and gods. (See **Psyche**).

Erymanthian Boar. A giant wild boar from Mt. Erymanthus which was ravaging the region of Psophis until captured by Heracles (q.v.). Whilst performing this task he was given wine made by Dionysus (q.v.) by the centaur Pholus. A dispute broke out with other centaurs, eager as ever for their share of the drink, and in the resulting battle Heracles accidentally wounded his friend Cheiron (q.v.). He caught and chained the boar in a snow drift and delivered it to Eurystheus (q.v.) before going to join the Argonauts (q.v.).

Erysichthon. Son of Triopas. He was punished with an insatiable hunger by the goddess Demeter (q.v.) for felling trees in one of her sacred groves.

Eryx. Mythical Sicilian hero. A son of Venus (q.v.) and a renowned boxer. The mountain near modern Trapani is named after him.

Eteocles. See **Seven Against Thebes**.

Etruscans. See **L41**.

Eumaeus. Born of royal birth but given to Phoenician slave traders, Eumaeus' story is told in Book 15 of the *Odyssey*. He became Odysseus' (q.v.) faithful swineherd.

Eumolpus. "The good singer", son of Poseidon (q.v.) and Chione. Chione threw him into the sea at birth but Poseidon saved him and he was raised at the court of King Tegyrius of Thrace before becoming a priest of Demeter (q.v.) and Persephone (q.v.) at Eleusis. Here he initiated Heracles (q.v.) into the mysteries and taught the hero the lyre. He later made war on Athens and was slain by Erechtheus (q.v.). His descendants became hereditary priests of the Eleusian mysteries.

Euphorbus. Son of Panthous, a Trojan who wounded Patroclus (q.v.) before he was slain by Hector (q.v.).

Euphrosyne. One of the Charities or Graces (q.v.).

Euripides. See **B23**.

Europa. Daughter of Agenor and Telephassa and a grand-daughter of Poseidon (q.v.). While she was on the sea-shore Zeus (q.v.) appeared in the form of a white bull and when she jumped on his back carried her off to Crete where he fathered three sons on her, Minos (q.v.), Rhadamanthus (q.v.) and Sarpedon (q.v.). The Cretan king married her and adopted the children. Zeus gave her a necklace fashioned by Hephaestus (q.v.) which rendered the wearer irresistibly beautiful.

Eurystheus. A grandson of Perseus (q.v.). He was conceived shortly after Heracles (q.v.) but when Zeus (q.v.) boasted that Heracles would rule the House of Perseus, Hera (q.v.) in her jealousy extracted a promise from Zeus that the next son born to the House of Perseus would be its ruler. She then delayed the birth of Heracles until after that of Eurystheus. Later, after Heracles had slain his children in a fit of madness he was told by the oracle to serve Eurystheus in order to be cleansed of guilt. Eurystheus, a cowardly and contemptible creature, set him twelve labours. After Heracles' death he decided to expel the Heracleidae (q.v.) or descendants of Heracles from Greece but they sheltered at Athens. Eurystheus attacked the city but was resisted by Theseus (q.v.), Iolaus (q.v.) and Hyllus (q.v.). An oracle demanded the sacrifice of one of Heracles' children and Macaria slew herself. Eurystheus was then defeated and slain by Alcmene.

Eurus. The South-East wind, son of Astraeus (q.v.) and Eos.

Euryale. One of the Gorgons (q.v.).

Eurydice. The wife of Orpheus (q.v.). She died from a snake bite and Orpheus followed her to the Underworld. Hades (q.v.) delighted by Orpheus' lyre playing allowed him to take her back to life provided he did not look back. Unfortunately at the gates of the Underworld the anxious Orpheus could no longer resist the temptation to gaze on her beauty nor acquiesce in her accusations of indifference. He turned round to see her and she was lost to him.

Eurytus. See **Deianeira**.

Euterpe. Muse of music and lyric poetry.

Evadne. The daughter of Iphis and wife of Capaneus

who killed herself on the funeral pyre of the Seven against Thebes (q.v.).

Evander. A mythical king of Arcadia who settled in Italy on the future site of Rome.

Evenus. The father of Marpessa. When Idas carried her off he drowned himself in the river which henceforth bore his name.

F

Fates. The personifications of impersonal destiny who sometimes seem to control even Zeus (q.v.), at others merely to perform his will. The concept developed of three Moirae (*Latin* Parcae) daughters of Zeus and Themis (q.v.), or of Erebus (q.v.) and Night. The first, Clotho, spans the thread of life, Lachesis who measured it, and Atropus who cut it. With Hermes (q.v.) they composed the Alphabet.

Faunus. An Italian god of the flocks, herds and wild countryside, later identified with Pan (q.v.). In this context he was half-human, half-goat and lived in Arcadia (q.v.). He had a shrine on the Palatine Hill. He is sometimes regarded not as one god but as numerous spirits of the woods or "fauns".

Faustulus. A kindly shepherd who, with his wife Acca Larentia, raised Romulus (q.v.) and Remus (q.v.). His name relates to Faunus (q.v.) and his wife's to Lares (q.v.) respectively the pastoral god of Latium and the tutelary deities of the Roman home. Up to Cicero's time Romans proudly pointed to a hut on the Palatine which was said to be that where Faustulus raised Romulus but, embarrassingly, a hut with similar claims also stood on the Capitol.

Fidius. Dius Fidius was a name for Jupiter (q.v.) as guarantor of Good Faith.

Flora. Italian goddess of flowers and the spring, worshipped at Rome from the mid 3rd century B.C. Ovid tells us the April festival in her honour, "Ludi Florales" was one of drunken boisterousness. As an earth nymph called Chloris she was pursued by Zephyr (q.v.) and changed into Flora whose breath spread flowers across the fields. The scene has been a subject for Botticelli, Titian and Poussin.

Fortuna. Roman goddess identified with Tyche (q.v.).

Fortunate Isles. See **Elysium**.

G

Gaea or Ge. The "Earth" who sprang from Chaos (q.v.). She was mother of Uranus (q.v.), the heavens, and Pontus the sea. By Uranus she was mother of the Hecatoncheires (q.v.), the Cyclopes (q.v.), the Titans (q.v.) and Themis (q.v.). When Uranus condemned the Cyclopes to Tartarus (q.v.) she instigated rebellion by the Titans and gave Cronus (q.v.) the flint sickle with which he castrated Uranus. From the blood which fell on her she bore Erinnyes (q.v.) and from the blood which fell into the sea came Aphrodite (q.v.). By Tartarus she was mother of Typhon (q.v.). She gave Hera (q.v.) a tree of golden apples which was guarded by the Hesperides (q.v.). The Romans identified her with their own earth goddess Tellus.

Gaetulians. A mythical savage tribe which the Romans placed in North Africa.

Galatea. (1) A sea nymph who loved the Sicilian shepherd Acis (q.v.). She was pursued by the Cyclops Polyphemus and to escape him threw herself into the sea off Sicily. She turned Acis into a river.

(2) See **Pygmalion**.

Ganymede. The most handsome of youths, the son of Tros (q.v.) and Callirhoë. Zeus (q.v.) loved the youth and taking the form of an eagle carried him off to become cup-bearer of the gods, leaving Tros two white horses in compensation. A subject for Correggio, Rubens, and Rembrandt.

Garamantians. Mythical North African tribe appearing in the *Aenead* (q.v.).

Ge. See **Gaea**.

Geryon. A three-bodied monster living on the island of Erythia far to the west of the known world.

|13

Here he kept cattle guarded by Eurytion, son of Ares (q.v.) and Orthrus (q.v.). Heracles (q.v.) was sent to steal the cattle by Eurystheus (q.v.) and on his way to Erythia erected the "Pillars of Hercules" (q.v.), before sailing, on a boat provided by Helios (q.v.) to the island. He overcame Eurytion, Orthrus and Geryon and fetched the cattle to Eurystheus.

Giants (Gigantes). (1) The sons of Ge (q.v.) and Uranus (q.v.), twenty-four giants with serpents' tails who, to avenge the imprisonment of their brothers the Titans (q.v.), attacked the gods on Mt. Olympus (q.v.). Their leader was Alcyoneus and their ranks included Porphyrion, Ephialtes, Pallas, Minas, Enceladus and Polybotes. The gods finally triumphed due to the help of Heracles (q.v.) and the giants were buried under various volcanoes in punishment.

(2) In another version two giants, Ephialtes and Otus, the sons of Iphimedeia and Poseidon (q.v.), but called the Aloeidae after the name of Iphimedeia's husband Aloeus, attacked Olympus. At an early age the two imprisoned Ares (q.v.), then swearing to rape Hera (q.v.) and Artemis (q.v.) they stacked Mt. Pelion on top of Mt. Ossa in order to climb to the heavens. But Artemis lured them to Naxos and disguised as a doe leapt between them and they slew each other by accident. In Hades (q.v.) they were tied by vipers to a pillar back to back.

Glauce. Or Creusa, daughter of Creon. For her Jason (q.v.) forsook Medea (q.v.) and in revenge the sorceress sent Glauce a garment which enveloped her in flames and also killed Creon.

Glaucus. (1) King of Corinth, son of Sisyphus and Merope and father of Bellerophon (q.v.). He fed his horses on human flesh but Aphrodite (q.v.) caused them to devour Glaucus himself because he mocked her.

(2) His great-grandson, the grandson of Bellerophon who fought for the Trojans and was slain by Ajax (q.v.).

(3) The son of Minos (q.v.) and Pasiphaë (q.v.) who was drowned in a barrel of honey. The seer Polyides found the corpse and was entombed with the boy for failing to restore him. Both were saved when a serpent revealed a magic herb which resurrected Glaucus.

(4) A Boeotian fisherman who pursued Scylla (q.v.) and was turned into a sea god on eating a magic herb.

Golden Age. A concept of Hesiod's who lists four ages of man in his *Works and Days*: golden, silver, bronze and iron. Horace, Virgil, and Ovid also refer to it. A tranquil time when Cronus (q.v.) ruled as the ideal king.

Golden Bough. A gift Aeneas (q.v.) had to take to Proserpina (q.v.) before he could enter the Underworld. Also associated with the cult of Diana (q.v.) at Aricia where a runaway slave had to break the bough from a sacred tree before killing the priest and taking his place. Subject of a painting by J. W. M. Turner.

Gordian Knot. Gordius was a peasant who was acclaimed king of Phrygia by the inhabitants when he appeared in a wagon. An oracle had prophesied that the new king would appear thus. In thanksgiving he dedicated the cart to Zeus (q.v.) in the acropolis of Gordium. An oracle prophesied that he who untied the complex knot joining the yoke and pole would rule all Asia. It was eventually severed by Alexander the Great.

Gorgons or **Gorgones.** Three beautiful sisters, Medusa (q.v.), Stheno and Euryale, daughters of Phorcys and Ceto. Medusa slept with Poseidon (q.v.) in a temple of Athene (q.v.) and was transformed into a winged monster with serpent hair and brazen claws by the goddess as punishment. She could turn those who looked on her to stone. The Gorgons were sisters of the Graeae (q.v.). *See also* **Perseus.**

Graces (also **Gratiae**). *See* **Charities.**

Graeae. Sisters of the Gorgons (q.v.) who lived on Mt. Atlas. The three old women possessed only one eye and one tooth which they shared, passing them from one to the other. Perseus (q.v.) stole the eye and thus forced them to reveal the whereabouts of Medusa (q.v.) and also of the Stygian nymphs who gave him the winged sandals, magic wallet and helmet of Hades which Hermes (q.v.) said he needed in order to slay Medusa.

Gyes or **Gyges.** One of the Hecatoncheires (q.v.).

H

Hades. (1) The son of Cronus (q.v.) and Rhea (q.v.) brother of Zeus (q.v.) and Poseidon (q.v.). The Cyclopes (q.v.) gave him a helmet of darkness which made him invisible. When he and his brothers threw lots for their kingdoms Hades won the Underworld, home of the dead. His name was later extended to his realm itself. He was one of the few gods to like Ares (q.v.) and Hermes (q.v.) was his herald, conducting the shades of the dead to the Underworld. Because his name was too dread to mention he was often called "Pluto" (q.v.). No favours were expected of him so no temples were dedicated to him. He abducted Persephone (q.v.) and also chased the nymph Minthe (whom the jealous Persephone turned into a mint plant) and Leuce, who was turned into the white poplar.

(2) His realm, the Underworld, land of the dead. Its deepest reaches were called Tartarus (q.v.). Hades and Persephone ruled over it. Persephone was accompanied by Hecate (q.v.). There were five rivers in Hades, the Styx, Acheron, river of woe, Phlegethon, river of flame, Lethe, river of forgetfulness and Cocytus river of wailing. Three judges Minos (q.v.), Aeacus (q.v.) and Rhadamanthus (q.v.) decided on what would happen to souls, sending the evil for punishment, the virtuous to Elysium (q.v.) and those who had led indifferent lives to the drab asphodel fields.

Harmonia. The daughter of Ares (q.v.) and Aphrodite (q.v.) and the wife of Cadmus (q.v.). The gods attended their wedding and Aphrodite gave her the necklace which Zeus (q.v.) had given to Europa (q.v.). It had been made by Hephaestus (q.v.) and conferred irresistible beauty on the wearer. Athene (q.v.) gave her a robe which conferred divine dignity on its possessor. The couple had three children, Autonoe, Ino and Semele (q.v.). After Cadmus had resigned his throne to Pentheus (q.v.) the couple left Thebes and were eventually, in the form of serpents, received in Elysia (q.v.). The necklace and robe were later used to bribe Eriphyle.

Harpalyce. A mythical princess of Thrace, a fierce warrior and huntress.

Harpies (Greek "snatchers"). Originally spirits of the wind, in Homer they appear to carry people off to their death. Later they are portrayed as winged monsters with women's heads and claws, sent by the gods to torment mortals. They snatched and carried off people for their food.

Hebe. A personification of the Greek word for youth, the daughter of Zeus (q.v.) and Hera (q.v.). She was cupbearer to the gods until replaced by Ganymede (q.v.). Her Roman counterpart was Juventas. She married Heracles (q.v.) after his apotheosis.

Hecabe or **Hecuba.** The second wife of Priam (q.v.) who bore him 19 sons including Hector (q.v.) and Paris (q.v.). By Apollo (q.v.) the mother of Troilus (q.v.). Taken as a slave by Odysseus (q.v.) when Troy (q.v.) fell. Priam had entrusted their youngest son Polydorus, plus much gold, to Polymester, king of the Thracian Chersonese. He had murdered Polydorus and thrown his body into the sea. When Odysseus took her to the Thracian Chersonese she found the body, killed Polymester and his two sons, and escaped in the form of a bitch, Maera.

Hecate. An ancient goddess, later closely associated with Artemis (q.v.). Originally she was venerated by women, she was powerful in Heaven, Earth and the Underworld. But primarily she was seen as a goddess of the Underworld and companion of Persephone (q.v.). She was represented holding torches and accompanied by wolves. She was most formidable at the full moon with which she was associated. A practitioner of sorcery her image was worshipped at crossroads where she was portrayed with three heads or three bodies.

Hecatoncheires. The sons of Ge (q.v.) and Uranus (q.v.), three 100-handed giants called Cottus, Gyes or Gyges and Briareus or Aegaeon.

Hector. The eldest son of Priam (q.v.), Trojan hero of the Trojan War. Husband of Andromache (q.v.) and father of Astynax. He fought the great Ajax (q.v.) until nightfall when the two exchanged gifts. He slew Patroclus and in turn was slain by Achilles (q.v.) who dragged his body round the walls of Troy (q.v.). Priam begged for the corpse and his funeral is the closing scene of Homer's *Iliad*. A chivalrous warrior.

Helen. The daughter of Leda (*q.v.*) by Zeus (*q.v.*), hatched from an egg, and the sister of Clytemnestra (*q.v.*), Castor and Polydeuces (*q.v.*) (known as the Dioscuri). She was raised at the court of Leda's husband, Tyndareus of Sparta. As a child she was abducted by Theseus (*q.v.*) and Pirithous (*q.v.*) but being too young to marry, was left with Theseus' mother Aethra. The Dioscuri rescued her and Aethra became her slave. The most beautiful of women she had many suitors who swore to defend her chosen husband, Menelaus (*q.v.*). She was taken by Paris (*q.v.*) to Troy (*q.v.*) thus causing the Trojan war (*q.v.*) and "launching a thousand ships" (of the Greeks who went to reclaim her). When Paris died Helenus (*q.v.*) and Deiphobus quarrelled for her, the latter forcibly marrying her. By then she was homesick for Sparta and when Odysseus (*q.v.*) entered Troy in disguise told him so and gave him information useful to the Greek cause. When Troy fell Deiphobus was killed and mangled by Odysseus and Menelaus, but when Menelaus chased her, sword drawn, to punish her, she calmed him by baring her breast. In the *Odyssey* she was reconciled to Menelaus and became a domesticated and faithful wife. She bore him a daughter, Hermione. It appears that Helen may have been a pre-Greek goddess associated with birds and trees. Various tales are told of her. Stesichorus says that only her phantom went to Troy: the real Helen went to Egypt. Another legend says that at her death she was carried off to live eternally with Achilles (*q.v.*) on a "white isle". Others suggest that her mother was not Leda but Nemesis (*q.v.*).

Helenus. The son of Priam (*q.v.*) and Hecabe (*q.v.*), twin of Cassandra (*q.v.*) and a prophet. He quarrelled with his brother Deiphobus over Helen (*q.v.*) and when the latter forcibly married her fled Troy (*q.v.*) and was captured by Odysseus (*q.v.*). Calchas (*q.v.*) had said that only Helenus knew the secret oracles of how Troy would fall. He told Odysseus that the city would be taken in the summer if a bone of Pelops (*q.v.*) were brought to the Greeks, if Neoptolemus (*q.v.*) joined them, and if the Palladium (*q.v.*) were stolen. These things were done. After the war he was taken by Neoptolemus and prophesied a safe route home for him. When Neoptolemus settled in Epirus he gave part of the kingdom to Helenus who married Andromache (*q.v.*).

Helicon. A mountain in Boeotia (*q.v.*) sacred to Apollo (*q.v.*) and inhabited by the Muses (*q.v.*) who were thus called respectively Heliconiades and Heliconides.

Helios. The Roman "Sol". A Titan (*q.v.*) later identified with Hyperion and Apollo (*q.v.*), though some traditions make him the son of Hyperion and Theia. A sun-god, his chariot was drawn across the sky each day by four horses and at night he returned to the east floating on the stream of Ocean, which surrounded the earth, in a large cup. The husband of Rhode by whom he had seven sons and a daughter, Pasiphaë. He was father of Phaeton (*q.v.*) by Clymene and of Circe (*q.v.*) by Perse. He reputedly saw all, but missed Odysseus' (*q.v.*) men stealing his cattle. When he shone too brightly Odysseus (*q.v.*) fired an arrow at him. Admiring the hero's boldness he lent him his cup or boat with which to travel to Erythia. It was he who told Demeter (*q.v.*) that Hades (*q.v.*) had abducted Persephone (*q.v.*).

Hellas, Hellenes, Hellenism. The Greeks of the classical period termed themselves Hellenes and their country Hellas (in contrast to Homer's "Achaeans"). They traced their common descent from Hellen (*q.v.*) an eponymous hero. In modern times Hellenism refers to the culture flourishing in Greece, the Aegean isles, the Ionian coast of Asia Minor and Magna Graecia between the first Olympiad in 776 B.C. and the death of Alexander the Great in 323 B.C.

Hellen. Eponymous ancestor of the Greeks or Hellenes (*q.v.*), the son of Pyrrha and Deucalion (*q.v.*). His sons were Aeolus, Dorus and Xuthus.

Hephaestus. One of the Olympian gods, the son of Zeus (*q.v.*) and Hera (*q.v.*). The god of fire and metal work, known to the Romans as Vulcan (*q.v.*). He was hated by Hera because he was lame and she threw him down from Olympus and he landed in the sea where Thetis (*q.v.*) and Eurynome cared for him. Nine years later Hera accepted him back but Zeus, angry with him for taking Hera's side in a quarrel, again cast him down. He was a day falling and landed on Lemnos. On returning to Olympus he sought to keep the peace between Zeus and Hera. The other gods always laughed at his lameness. His workshop was said to be on Olympus or else in Sicily, where the Cyclopes (*q.v.*) helped him in his labours. He made palaces for all the gods, the necklace of Harmonia (*q.v.*), the armour of Achilles (*q.v.*) and a wide variety of other wonderful articles. He was married either to Charis or to Aphrodite (*q.v.*) who deceived him with Ares (*q.v.*).

Hera. The Roman Juno, daughter of Cronus (*q.v.*) and Rhea (*q.v.*), sister and wife of Zeus (*q.v.*). A pre-Hellenic goddess, originally having power over all living things and vegetable life, she gradually lost these functions and eventually was only the goddess of marriage and childbirth. She was the mother of Ares (*q.v.*), Hephaestus (*q.v.*), Hebe (*q.v.*) and Ilythia (*q.v.*) by Zeus. Her virginity was renewed annually by bathing in a magical spring near Argos. Though she was the goddess of marital fidelity she had difficulty controlling the amorous adventures of her own husband (who had wooed her in the form of a cuckoo) and was violently jealous of his many affairs and cruel to her rivals and their offspring, *e.g.* Semele, Leto, Alcmene and Heracles. She once led a conspiracy against Zeus in which Poseidon (*q.v.*) and Apollo (*q.v.*) participated. Zeus was enchained and when he was freed he punished her by suspending her from the sky by the wrists with an anvil on each ankle. She helped Jason (*q.v.*) but was opposed to the Trojans because Paris (*q.v.*) did not give her the apple of discord. Her name means simply "lady".

Heracleidae. The children of Heracles (*q.v.*). Eurystheus (*q.v.*) attempted to expel them from Greece but failed.

Heracles. A hero who later became a god, a figure popular all over Greece and in Italy where the Romans knew him as Hercules. The son of Alcmene (*q.v.*) and Zeus (*q.v.*) and half-brother of Iphicles (*q.v.*). Alcmene fearing Hera's (*q.v.*) jealousy exposed him but by mistake Hera nursed him. After he had been returned to his mother Hera sent two snakes to kill him in his cradle, but he strangled them. He was taught to fight by Castor (*q.v.*), to play the lyre by Eumalpus, to wrestle by Autolycus (*q.v.*) and the art of archery by Eurytus. Linus also tried to teach him to play the lyre but, when he censured his awkward pupil, Heracles killed him with his own instrument. Amphitrion (*q.v.*) then sent him to keep cattle. At the age of 18, after a 50-day chase, he killed a huge lion on Mt. Cithaeron because it had been ravaging the herds of Amphitrion and Thespius. He did this with a wild olive club and later wore the pelt everywhere, though some other sources say he wore the pelt of the Nemean lion. In reward Thespius gave him his 50 daughters. At Thebes he defeated the Minyan heralds of Orchomenus who had come to demand tribute. Creon, king of Thebes, rewarded him by giving him his daughter Megara or Megera who bore him several children. His half-brother Iphicles married Creon's youngest daughter. Hera now made him mad and he killed his own children and two of Iphicles'. At Delphi the Pythia (*q.v.*), calling him Heracles for the first time, sent him to serve, for 12 years, his wretched cousin Eurystheus (*q.v.*) in order to purify himself of the murder. At the end of that time he would become immortal. With his nephew Iolaus (*q.v.*) as companion he embarked on 12 labours set by Eurystheus. These were to fetch the pelt of the Nemean lion, to kill the Hydra of Lerna (*q.v.*), to capture alive the Ceryneian Hind (*q.v.*), to capture alive the Erymanthian Boar (*q.v.*), to cleanse the stables of Augias (*q.v.*), to drive off the Stymphalian Birds (*q.v.*), to capture the Cretan Bull (*q.v.*), to fetch the horses of Diomedes (*q.v.*), to fetch the girdle of Hippolyte (*q.v.*), to steal the cattle of Geryon (*q.v.*), to fetch the golden apples of the Hesperides (*q.v.*) and to bring back Cerberus (*q.v.*). After capturing the Erymanthian Boar he had joined the Argonauts (*q.v.*) but his squire Hylas was spirited off by the Naiads (*q.v.*) while fetching water at Cios in Mysia and Heracles left the expedition to search for him. Having completed his service for Eurystheus he returned to Thebes and here gave Megara to Iolaus. But Hera again drove him mad and he killed Megara and her children. Some traditions say he also killed himself and his family. He now desired to marry Iole daughter of his friend Eurytus of Oechalia and won her in an archery contest. But Eurytus refused to surrender her because Heracles had slain his own children. The incident ended in Heracles killing Iphitus (q.v.) but he later seized Iole. To purify himself of this murder he went to serve Omphale (q.v.). After serving her he and Telamon saved Hesione, daughter of Laomedon (q.v.) and sacked Troy (q.v.). Heracles gave Hesione to Telamon and ransomed Priam (q.v.). Next he made war on Augias and Neleus (q.v.) and then on Hippocoon who had helped Neleus. In this he was assisted by Cepheus (q.v.) and he restored Tyndareus (q.v.). At this time he seduced the priestess Auge, daughter of Aleus king of Tegea, who bore him a son, Telephus. Now he married Deianeira (q.v.) who inadvertently caused his death. As Heracles ascended his funeral pyre, to be burned alive he gave his bow and quiver to Philoctetes (q.v.) who kindled the flame but thunderbolts demolished the pyre and he was carried on a cloud to Olympus. Here he was reconciled to Hera and married Hebe (q.v.), himself becoming an immortal. Numerous other legends concerning Heracles exist. We are told he rescued Alcestis (q.v.), helped the gods defeat the Giants (q.v.), defeated Antaeus (q.v.) and, when the Delphic Oracle would not give him an answer seized the sacred tripod and struggled with Apollo (q.v.) for it. Xenophon tells us that before beginning his adventures Heracles was confronted by two beautiful women, one offering a life of ease, the other of service to mankind and he had to choose between the two. Other writers tell of him having to choose between two roads offering similar alternatives to the women. From a mighty and boisterous hero the picture of Heracles gradually developed into a morality tale of selfless service and fortitude eventually rewarded and for this reason the Stoic philosophers of Rome idealised him.

Hercules. See **Heracles.**

Hermaphroditus. The son of Hermes (q.v.) and Aphrodite (q.v.) who refused the advances of the nymph Salmacis. Her request that their bodies be joined in one was then granted by the gods. The name gives us the word "hermaphrodite", a being with the characteristics of both sexes.

Hermes. The Roman Mercury. Originally a god of fertility. The son of Zeus (q.v.) and Maia, daughter of Atlas (q.v.). He was born on Mt. Cyllene (hence he was sometimes referred to as Cyllenius). While still hours old he left the cradle and stole Apollo's (q.v.) cattle. He invented the lyre by stringing a tortoise shell with cow-gut and gave it to Apollo. This calmed Apollo's wrath and the two became friends. Zeus made him messenger of the gods and gave him his winged sandals (the Alipes), broad-brimmed hat (the Petasus) and herald's staff (caduceus) originally entwined with two white ribbons, later represented as entwined snakes. He conducted the souls of the dead to Hades (q.v.) and in this role was known as Psychopompus. The patron of travellers, traders and thieves and the father of Autolycus the thief, by Chione, and of Echion herald of the Argonauts (q.v.). He was the father of Pan (q.v.) by Penelope (q.v.) and a companion of the Muses (q.v.). He helped the Fates compose the alphabet, invented the musical scale, weights and measures and olive cultivation. A god of dice games. As herald he was eloquent and in Acts ch. XIV St. Paul, who spoke in tongues more than any man, is mistaken for him.

Hermione. The daughter of Helen (q.v.) and Menelaus (q.v.). Betrothed by Tyndareus (q.v.) to Orestes (q.v.) but given to Neoptolemus (q.v.) by Menelaus.

Hero. A priestess of Aphrodite (q.v.) at Sestos. Her lover Leander (q.v.) used to swim the Hellespont each night to see her but drowned when a storm extinguished the light she used to guide him. She then drowned herself. The subject of a play by Marlowe and paintings by Rubens and Turner.

Herodotus. See **B31.**

Heroes. To the Greeks a hero was the son of a mortal or divinity who was essentially superior to other men. They were venerated and received sacrifices because they were believed to help the living. Thus Theseus (q.v.) was supposed to have helped the Athenians at Marathon. "Heroic poetry" was epic poetry, telling of their deeds.

Hesiod. See **B31.**

Hesperides. "The daughters of evening" who lived in a land at the end of the world, far to the west. These maidens guarded a tree belonging to Hera (q.v.) which bore golden apples. They were assisted by a dragon, Ladon. Ge (q.v.) had given the tree to Hera on her wedding day. On the advice of Prometheus (q.v.) Heracles (q.v.) (who had been sent to get the apples by Eurystheus (q.v.)) persuaded Atlas (q.v.) to fetch three apples while he shouldered Atlas' burden. Atlas then refused to take the sky back on his shoulders but Heracles tricked him into doing so. On his return journey Heracles slew Antaeus (q.v.). Eurystheus gave the apples back to Heracles and he passed them to Athene to return to the Hesperides.

Hesperus. The evening star, the Greek form of the Latin vesper or evening.

Hestia. The sister of Zeus (q.v.) and Hera (q.v.), the goddess of the hearth worshipped by every family. Though Poseidon (q.v.) and Apollo (q.v.) tried to seduce her she swore to Zeus always to remain a virgin. The Romans worshipped her counterpart, the goddess Vesta (q.v.).

Hippodamia. (1) The daughter of Oenomaus, king of Elis. An oracle said he would die at the hands of his son-in-law so he challenged all her suitors to a chariot race. Victory meant they could marry Hippodamia, defeat meant death. His horses were the gifts of his father Ares (q.v.). However Pelops (q.v.) engineered his death and married Hippodamia.
(2) The wife of Pirithous (q.v.). When a drunken centaur (q.v.) abducted her on her wedding day the battle between the Lapithae (q.v.) and Centaurs occurred.

Hippolyte. A queen of the Amazons (q.v.) and sister of Antiope. Heracles (q.v.) had to fetch her golden girdle for Eurystheus. At first he was well received but Hera (q.v.) stirred the Amazons against him and in the fight he slew Hippolyte and took the girdle. Returning home he saved Laomedon's (q.v.) daughter Hesione. Another legend says Theseus (q.v.) abducted Hippolyte who bore him the son Hippolytus (q.v.).

Hippolytus. The son of Theseus (q.v.) and the Amazon Hippolyte (q.v.) or her sister Antiope (q.v.). When Theseus married again to Phaedra (q.v.), sister of Ariadne (q.v.), Phaedra fell in love with her stepson and committed suicide when he refused her. She left a note falsely accusing Hippolytus. Theseus prayed to Poseidon (q.v.) who was under an obligation to him, that Hippolytus would die the same day. Poseidon then sent a sea-monster which scared the youth's horses and he was dragged to death behind his chariot.

Homer. See **B32.**

Horae. The "hours", three daughters of Zeus (q.v.) and Themis (q.v.) and tutelary goddesses of nature and the seasons. They were bound to the soil and promoted fertility. Thus they were important and are involved in solemn oaths. However they rarely appear except in attendance on other gods and have no "adventures".

Horatii. Three Roman brothers whose tale is told by Livy. In the mid 7th century B.C. while Rome was ruled by Tullus Hostilius the city of Alba Longa (q.v.) was destroyed and its population transferred to Rome. According to legend the Horatii challenged the three Alban champions, the Curatii, to a sword battle. Two Horatii were killed but the third slew all the Curatii. On returning to Rome he met his sister, who had been engaged to one of the Curatii, weeping. He stabbed her to death. After ceremonies of expiation Tullus acquitted him of murder.

Horatius Cocles. Another of the Horatii family, the "one-eyed" (Cocles). In the 6th century B.C. he held the Etruscans at bay on the wooden Sublican bridge into Rome until it was pulled down beneath him. He then swam the Tiber to safety. The subject of a Lay by Macaulay.

Hyacinthus. A Peloponnesian youth loved by Apollo (q.v.) who was killed when the jealous Zephyrus (q.v.) diverted a discus to hit him. From his blood sprang the "hyacinth" flower. He had a shrine at Amyclae in Laconia and a three-day festival, the Hyacinthia, was held in his honour at Sparta.

Hyades. Nymphs who cared for Dionysus (q.v.) as a child on Mt. Nysa. Zeus (q.v.) placed their images in the sky as the "rain stars", part of the constellation of Taurus which rises at midnight in the rainy season.

Hydra of Lerna. The "water snake", offspring of Echidne (q.v.) and Typhon (q.v.) and raised by

Hera (q.v.). It was a monster with the body of a dog and 9 serpent heads. Heracles (q.v.) was sent to kill it by Eurystheus (q.v.). It lived at the source of the River Amymone in the swamp of Lerna. As Heracles lopped off a head two more grew. He also had to crush a giant crab which Hera placed among the signs of the zodiac. Finally he crushed the Hydra's heads with his club and Iolaus (q.v.) burned them to stop them regrowing. He dipped his arrows in the beast's blood thereby making them poisonous.

Hygeia. The wife or daughter of Asclepius (q.v.), a goddess of health.

Hylas. See **Heracles**.

Hyllus. The son of Heracles (q.v.) and Deianeira (q.v.). He conducted Heracles to his funeral pyre. Either he or Iolaus (q.v.) defeated Eurystheus (q.v.). Eventually he was slain by Echemus, king of Tegea.

Hymen. God of weddings.

Hyperboreans. A mythical race living far to the north, behind Boreas (q.v.) i.e. at the place where the north wind originates. Apollo (q.v.) spent time with them before going to Delphi and spent the winter months with them. A Hyperborean soothsayer, Olen, installed Apollo's oracle at Delphi. Their land was supposed to have perpetual sunshine and was a land of plenty, an earthly paradise where men lived in peace and ease on the fruits of the earth. Herodotus (**B31**) tells us that one of their priests, Aburis, travelled the world on a golden arrow and never needed to eat. He places their land in Southern Russia.

Hypenor. One of the Spartil (q.v.).

Hyperion. A Titan (q.v.) and sun-god, father of Helios (q.v.), Selene (q.v.) and Eos (q.v.), the sun, moon and dawn. In Keats' poem he is the last of the old gods to be deposed, the young Apollo (q.v.) taking his place.

Hypermestra. See **Danaus**.

Hypnus. The god of sleep.

I

Iacchus. Alternative name for Dionysus (q.v.) used in the Eleusian mysteries where he was regarded as the son of Zeus (q.v.) and Demeter (q.v.), not Semele (q.v.).

Iapetus. A Titan (q.v.), father of Prometheus (q.v.), Atlas (q.v.) and Epimetheus.

Iasion. Or Iasius or Iasus, the son of Zeus (q.v.) and Electra (q.v.), lover of Demeter (q.v.) who bore him a son Pluton. Zeus in his jealousy slew him with a thunderbolt.

Icarius. Father of Erigone. An Athenian to whom Dionysus (q.v.) taught cultivation of the vine and who gave wine to a band of shepherds. Mistaking drunkenness for witchcraft they slew him.

Icarus. See **Daedalus**.

Idaea. A nymph, mother of Teucer (q.v.) by Scamander (q.v.) of Crete.

Idas. The twin of Lynceus and a son of Poseidon (q.v.). He abducted Marpessa in a chariot given to him by Poseidon and fought Apollo (q.v.) for possession of her. Given the choice by Zeus (q.v.) she chose Idas. He and Lynceus took part in the voyage of the Argonauts (q.v.) and the hunt of the Calydonian boar (q.v.) and were killed in battle with their cousins the Dioscuri (q.v.).

Idomeneus. King of Crete who contributed 100 ships to the expedition against Troy (q.v.). Virgil adds that on his return from Troy he was caught in a storm and vowed to sacrifice the first person he met to Poseidon (q.v.) in return for safe passage. This proved to be his son and the sacrifice brought a pestilence on Crete. Idomeneus was banished to Calabria in Italy.

Ilia. A priestess of Vesta (q.v.) also called Rhea Silvia. The mother of Romulus (q.v.) and Remus.

Iliad. Homer's epic poem on the siege of Troy (q.v.). Although it hints at earlier and later events it covers only a period of weeks in the tenth year of the war, recounting Achilles' (q.v.) quarrel with Agamemnon (q.v.), the death of Patroclus (q.v.) and the death of Hector (q.v.). It ends with Achilles returning Hector's (q.v.) body to Priam (q.v.). Although many gods and heroes appear, Achilles and Hector are the main protagonists.

Ilioneus. An old and venerated Trojan who accompanied Aeneas (q.v.).

Ilithyiae. Daughters of Hera (q.v.) who helped women in childbirth. Later only one goddess, Ilithyia, is mentioned in this connection.

Ilus. (1) The son of Tros (q.v.) and father of Laomedon (q.v.). An ancestor of the Trojans.
(2) Original name of Ascanius (q.v.) son of Aeneas (q.v.) and Creusa.

Inachus. The first king of Argos, son of Oceanus (q.v.) and Tethys. A river was named after him.

Ino. The daughter of Cadmus (q.v.) and Harmonia (q.v.), sister of Autonoe, Agave, Polydoras, Illyrus and Semele. She helped to rear Dionysus (q.v.) and her husband Athamas (q.v.) was punished for it by Hera (q.v.) who drove him into madness and the murder of his own children. Ino, Autonoe and Agave were Bacchae (q.v.) and they slew Pentheus, the son of Agave and heir to Cadmus, for opposing the worship of Dionysus. Ino committed suicide (see **Athamas**) and became a sea deity.

Io. The daughter of Inachus. Zeus (q.v.) loved her and turned her into a white heifer to deceive the jealous Hera (q.v.). He did not succeed in this and Hera set the hundred-eyed Argus to watch the heifer. But Hermes (q.v.) at Zeus' command cut off his head and placed his eyes in the tail of the peacock. He also sent a gadfly whose sting caused Io to wander the earth till she reached Egypt. On her wanderings she gave her name to the Ionian sea and to the Bosphorus ("ford of the cow"). In Egypt Zeus restored her to human form and she bore him a son, Epaphus, an ancestor of Danaus (q.v.).

Iobates. See **Bellerophon**.

Iolaus. Son of Iphicles (q.v.) and nephew of Heracles (q.v.) to whom he was charioteer and constant companion. He helped Heracles kill the Hydra (q.v.) and perform his other labours and in return Heracles gave him his wife Megara. He also sent Iolaus as the leader of his sons by the daughters of Thespius to settle in Sardinia.

Iolcus. The kingdom of Jason's (q.v.) father Aeson, usurped by his half brothers Pelias and Neleus.

Iole. See **Deianeira**.

Ion. The son of Xuthus and Creusa, brother of Achaeus. In Euripides' play Ion he is the son of Creusa and Apollo (q.v.) who is carried off to Delphi (q.v.), as a baby but is eventually restored to Creusa and adopted by Xuthus. The eponymous ancestor of the Ionian Greeks.

Iphicles. (1) One of the Argonauts (q.v.).
(2) The son of Amphitrion (q.v.) and Alcmene (q.v.) a night younger than Heracles (q.r.). The father of Iolaus (q.v.). He married the youngest daughter of Creon of Thebes when Heracles married Megara.

Iphigenia. The daughter of Agamemnon (q.v.) and Clytemnestra (q.v.), sacrificed by her father at Aulis to get a favourable wind for the Greek fleet sailing to Troy (q.v.). Euripides cites another tradition in which Artemis (q.v.) substituted a doe for Iphigenia at the last moment and carried her off to Tauris. Later Orestes (q.v.) found Iphigenia on the Tauric Chersonese and brought her home to Greece.

Iphitus. A son of Eurytus who argued that his father should deliver Iole (see **Deianeira**) to Heracles (q.v.). But in a rage Heracles slew him and though purified of the murder was told by an oracle to sell himself into slavery and give the proceeds to Iphitus' family.

Irene. The daughter of Zeus (q.v.) and Themis (q.v.), goddess of peace and one of the Horae (q.v.). The Romans identified her with Pax.

Iris. The personification of the rainbow and, in later myth, a messenger of the gods, particularly Hera (q.v.).

Isis. An Egyptian goddess, wife of Osiris and mother of Horus. In Hellenistic times she became one of the most important deities of the Mediterranean world, her cult arriving in Rome by the time of Augustus. Here the features of her worship, Egyptian priests, processions, initiation ceremonies etc. were described by Apuleius in his Golden Ass. One of her temples is preserved at Pompeii.

Ismene. The daughter of Oedipus (q.v.) and Jocasta (q.v.). She followed her father and her sister Antigone (q.v.) into exile.

Issa. The daughter of Macareus and his sister Canace, beloved by Apollo (q.v.).

Isthmian Games. Quadrennial games held at Corinth in honour of Poseidon (q.v.).

Ithaca. The island home of Odysseus (q.v.), one of the Ionian islands.

Itys, Itylus. *See* **Procne**.

Iulus. A name used for Ascanius (*q.v.*) by Virgil to indicate the descent of the Julian clan from Aeneas (*q.v.*).

J

Janus. A god of beginnings or new ventures, worshipped at Rome. He had a flamen (sacred priest) and was very important but the origin and nature of his worship is obscure. He had two faces and may represent the assimilation of an eastern god and an Etruscan (*see* **L41**) deity. Also associated with doorways and thresholds.

Jason. Son of Aeson, rightful king of Iolcus who was usurped by his half-brothers, Pelias and Neleus. The infant Jason was smuggled out of Iolcus and reared by Cheiron (*q.v.*) while Pelias expelled Neleus and ruled alone. When Jason returned to claim his birthright Pelias sent him to fetch the Golden Fleece from Colchis. This was the fleece of the ram on which Phrixus (*q.v.*) had escaped and which he had given to Aëtes, king of Colchis. Its presence was the cause of Colchis' prosperity and it hung from an oak tree in the grove of Ares (*q.v.*) where a dragon guarded it. After numerous adventures Jason and his Argonauts (*q.v.*) arrived at Colchis and Aëtes promised Jason the fleece if he could yoke two fire-breathing bulls with brazen feet made by Hephaestus (*q.v.*), and sow the grove of Ares with dragons' teeth left by Cadmus of Thebes (*q.v.*). Medea (*q.v.*) the sorceress gave him a fire-proof lotion which allowed him to complete the task and when her father Aëtes refused to give up the fleece, charmed the dragon to sleep while Jason stole it. Pursued by Aëtes the couple escaped when Medea murdered her half-brother Absyrtus and dropped pieces of his corpse into the sea, causing Aëtes to stop and collect them. They were purified of the murder by Circe (*q.v.*). At Iolchus Pelias had forced Aeson to commit suicide and in revenge Medea persuaded Pelias' daughters to boil their father alive pretending it would restore his youth. The couple were banished because of this and went to Corinth. Here Jason abandoned Medea for Glauce (*q.v.*) whom Medea killed. Jason took his own life though one tradition holds he was killed by the falling prow of the Argo (*q.v.*).

Jocasta. Daughter of Menoeceus, wife of Laius king of Thebes and mother of Oedipus (*q.v.*). When her unwitting incest with Oedipus brought a plague on Thebes Menoeceus sacrificed himself in answer to an oracle demanding the life of one of the Sparti (*q.v.*) *i.e.* a descendant of the "sown men". Jocasta hanged herself when she learned the truth of her marriage to Oedipus.

Jove. Alternative name for Jupiter (*q.v.*).

Juno. Italian goddess of womanhood and childbirth, associated by the Romans with the Greek Hera (*q.v.*) and regarded as the consort of Jupiter (*q.v.*).

Jupiter. Originally an Italian sky-god, later regarded by the Romans as *Dies Pater*—"Father Day", god of the day. Later still identified with Zeus (*q.v.*). His cult was introduced to Rome by the Etruscans and the temple to Jupiter Optimus Maximus (Best and Most High) stood on the Capitol. His *flamen*, the *flamen Dialis* was the most important of the college. He was guarantor of the *imperium* and city of Rome and triumphs were an act of Jupiter worship. Worshipped in various capacities as *Stator* (he who founds or maintains), *Teretrius* (he who strikes), *Ultor* ("Avenger") and *Tonans* ("Thunderer").

Juturna. (1) An Italian goddess of springs and streams.

(2) The sister of Turnus (*q.v.*).

Juventas. Italian goddess identified with Hebe (*q.v.*).

L

Labdacus. Mythical king of Thebes; a descendant of Cadmus (*q.v.*) and an ancestor of Oedipus (*q.v.*).

Lachesis. One of the Fates (*q.v.*).

Laelaps. A fleet-footed hound given to Procris by Cephalus (*q.v.*).

Laertes. The king of Ithaca, father of Odysseus (*q.v.*)

by Anticleia, daughter of the thief Autolycus. While Odysseus was at Troy (*q.v.*) Penelope's (*q.v.*) suitors forced him to retire to the country.

Laestrygones. A race of giant cannibals ruled by Lamus. At Telepylos, their capital city, Odysseus (*q.v.*) lost all but one of his twelve ships to them. Homer says their summer nights were so short that shepherds going out with their flocks in the morning met those returning at sunset. Traditionally located in eastern Sicily or at Formiae in central Italy.

Laius. *See* **Oedipus**.

Lamia. One of the Empusae (*q.v.*), daughter of Belus.

Lamus. *See* **Laestrygones**.

Laocoön. A Trojan prophet, son of Antenor and a priest of Apollo (*q.v.*) and Poseidon (*q.v.*). He warned the Trojans against the Wooden Horse (*q.v.*) and flung a spear at it. However he had angered Apollo by breaking his vows of celibacy and the god now sent two sea serpents which crushed him and his two sons. A famous group of statues depicting the scene, carved in Rhodes *c.* 25 B.C., now stands in the Vatican museum. The Trojans disastrously drew the wrong conclusion *viz.* that his death was punishment for striking the horse.

Laodamia. The daughter of Acastus and wife of Protesilaus of Thessaly, the first Greek ashore at Troy (*q.v.*) though he knew from an oracle the first Greek to land would die. Homer says he left his wife mourning and his house unfinished but Catullus, Virgil and Ovid follow another tradition in which she begged the gods that Protesilaus might return to life for three hours. When he died a second time she committed suicide. Wordsworth's poem *Laodamia* takes the tale as its subject.

Laodice. (1) A daughter of Priam (*q.v.*), sister of Cassandra (*q.v.*) and wife of Helicaon. When Troy (*q.v.*) fell the earth swallowed her.

(2) Alternative name for Electra (*q.v.*), Agamemnon's (*q.v.*) daughter.

Laomedon. The son of Ilus (*q.v.*), king of Troy (*q.v.*) and father of Hesione and Priam (*q.v.*). Apollo (*q.v.*) and Poseidon (*q.v.*) helped him build the walls of Troy and he refused to pay them. Poseidon then sent a sea monster to devour Hesione but Heracles (*q.v.*) saved her. Laomedon then refused to pay Heracles the agreed white horses left by Zeus (*q.v.*) in exchange for Ganymede (*q.v.*). Heracles and Telamon then sacked Troy and slew Laomedon and all his sons save Priam (*q.v.*).

Lapis Niger. Black marble paving in the Roman Forum said to cover the tomb of Romulus (*q.v.*).

Lapithae or Lapiths. Mythical tribe of Thessaly, governed by Pirithous, son of Ixion (*q.v.*) and thus half-brothers to the Centaurs (*q.v.*). At the wedding of Pirithous and Hippodamia, attended by Theseus (*q.v.*) a centaur tried to abduct the bride and a famous battle between the Lapithae and Centaurs ensued. It is described by Ovid and is depicted in the Parthenon and the frieze of Apollo's (*q.v.*) temple at Bassae. It is also the subject of a sculptured frieze by Michelangelo.

Lares. Originally fertility gods, worshipped by the Romans privately in the home and semi-publicly at crossroads. They were represented as youths with handfuls of fruit who wandered the farmstead incessantly whirling round and round. They kept away maleficent demons and ensured the prosperity of the family home. Each month they received offerings of oat cakes, milk, honey and flowers. Generally associated with the Penates, the spirits who guarded the household stores. Together the guardians of the hearth and home.

Larissa. A city in Thessaly near modern Volos. Reputed birthplace of Achilles (*q.v.*) hence his nickname "the Larissaen".

Lars Porsenna. Legendary Etruscan chief whom Livy tells us besieged Rome on behalf of the exiled Tarquinius Superbus. Lars means "overlord" and he is probably a symbol of Etruscan suzerainty over Rome. (*See* **Horatius Cocles**).

Latinus. Eponymous king of the Latini or Latins in Italy. Hesiod makes him the son of Odysseus (*q.v.*) and Circe (*q.v.*). Virgil makes him the son of Faunus (*q.v.*). Livy and Virgil portray him as opposing the settlement of Aeneas (*q.v.*) and the Trojans in Italy but then agreeing Aeneas should marry his daughter Lavinia. He next helps Aeneas fight Turnus king of the Rutuli, to whom Lavinia had been promised. Livy says he died in battle and Aeneas became king of the Latins; Virgil that he survived to celebrate the marriage and uniting of Latins and Trojans.

Leander. Mythical youth who drowned while swimming to meet Hero (q.v.).

Leda. Daughter of Thestius and wife of Tyndareus king of Sparta. Seduced by Zeus (q.v.) in the form of a swan she gave birth to two eggs, from one of which hatched Helen (q.v.) and Polydeuces (q.v.) from the other, Castor (q.v.) and Clytemnestra (q.v.). One tradition says that Helen was the daughter of Nemesis (q.v.) who left the egg for Leda to incubate.

Lemnos. A small island at the mouth of the Hellespont, home at one time of a primitive people known to the Greeks as the Pelasgi. Hephaestus (q.v.) was said to have landed on the island when Zeus (q.v.) hurled him out of heaven and supposedly had a forge here.

Lethe. "Forgetfulness", one of the rivers of the Underworld whose waters induced amnesia in those who drank of them. Virgil holds that here souls forgot their past prior to reincarnation and Ovid says that it flowed round the "cave of sleep".

Leto. Known to the Romans as Latona. The daughter of the Titans (q.v.) Coeus and Phoebe and the mother of Apollo (q.v.) and Artemis (q.v.) by Zeus (q.v.). While she carried the unborn gods the jealous Hera (q.v.) forced her to wander the earth until she finally gave birth to them at Ortygia, henceforth called Delos (q.v.). Hera sent the giant Tityus (q.v.) to rape her but her children slew him with their arrows. See also **Niobe**.

Leuce. A nymph loved by Hades (q.v.) who turned her into a white poplar tree.

Leucippus. (1) King of Messenia whose daughters Hilaera and Phoebe were abducted by the Dioscuri (q.v.) and whose brothers Idas (q.v.) and Lynceus (q.v.) fought to save them.

(2) The son of Oenomaus who loved Artemis (q.v.) To be near her he disguised himself as a nymph but when Apollo (q.v.) advised the nymphs to bathe naked he was discovered and torn to pieces by them.

Leucothea. Originally Ino, daughter of Cadmus (q.v.) and wife of Athamas who helped Zeus (q.v.) save Dionysus (q.v.) at the death of Semele (q.v.). In revenge Hera (q.v.) drove her mad and she leapt into the foaming sea to become the sea deity Leucothea—"the white goddess". In this role she helped Odysseus (q.v.) land on Scheria. Her son was Palaemon, a minor sea god.

Liber Pater. An ancient Italian god of the vine, early identified with Bacchus (q.v.) by the Romans.

Lichas. The herald of Heracles (q.v.) who took the shirt of Deineira (q.v.) to him. In his agony Heracles took him by the ankle, swung him round three times and threw him into the Euboean Sea where he became a rock of human shape which henceforth bore his name.

Linus. (1) The son of Psamathe of Argos and Apollo (q.v.). Fearful lest her father learn of her liaison with the god she exposed the baby who was reared by shepherds but later killed by her father's hounds. When her distress revealed her secret her father condemned her to death but Apollo sent a plague to the city which only abated when the Argives propitiated mother and son with dirges called linoi.

(2) The son of a Muse who was so gifted musically that the jealous Apollo killed him.

(3) Heracles' (q.v.) music tutor whom Heracles slew in a rage with his own lyre.

Lotophagi. ("The Lotus eaters"). A mythical people living on lotus fruit which induced trances and forgetfulness and made the eater lose any desire to return home. They gave the fruit to Odysseus' (q.v.) men. Herodotus placed them in western Libya, possibly the island of Jerba.

Luceres. One of the original three tribes into which Rome was divided and which were believed to date back to Romulus (q.v.). The other tribes were the Ramnes and Tities.

Lucifer. The "light bringer", the name given to the planet Venus which can be seen before dawn. In the evening sky the Greeks called it Hesperus.

Lucretia. Wife of Tarquinius Collatinus whose rape by Sextus, son of Tarquinius Superbus led her to stab herself in shame. Junius Brutus then swore by her spirit to expel the Tarquins which he did. The story is told by Livy and Ovid and inspired Shakespeare's poem The Rape of Lucrece and Brit-

ten's opera The Rape of Lucretia. A subject also for Titian, Botticelli, Tintoretto and Veronese.

Lucretius. See **B39**.

Lycaon. A mythical character who tricked Zeus (q.v.) by feeding him human flesh. Zeus killed him and all his sons save Nyctinus by lightning or turned them into wolves, hence Lycanthropy.

Lycomedes. The king of Scyros who murdered Theseus (q.v.). It was to his court that Thetis (q.v.) sent Achilles (q.v.), and Lycomedes' daughter Deidamia bore Achilles his son Neoptolemus (q.v.).

Lycurgus (1) Mythical king of Thrace who was made blind and mad for opposing the worship of Dionysus (q.v.).

(2) Mythical founder of the Spartan constitution and military regime, first mentioned by Herodotus and subject of a Life by Plutarch. Some traditions say the Pythia at Delphi gave him the constitution, others that he devised it while in Crete. In Sparta he was worshipped as a god.

Lynceus. (1) See **Danaus**.

(2) Twin of Idas (q.v.) noted for his keen eyesight.

Lyrnessus. City near Troy (q.v.) sacked by Achilles (q.v.).

M

Macareus. See **Issa**.

Macaria. See **Eurystheus**.

Machaon. The son of Asclepius the physician (q.v.).

Maenads. See **Bacchae**.

Maia. The daughter of Atlas (q.v.) and Pleione, eldest of the Pleiades (q.v.) and the most beautiful. By Zeus (q.v.) the mother of Hermes (q.v.). The Romans identified her with spring and as a nature goddess gave her name to the month of May.

Manes. "The good ones", the Roman name for the spirits of the dead, regarded as a collective divinity, Di Manes. On certain days they could leave the Underworld and were capable of great mischief. Thus they demanded propitiatory ceremonies at funerals and on set days when the head of the house, the paterfamilias, would go into the night and cast boiled beans to them. The Roman poets applied the term also to the gods of the Underworld and to the Underworld itself.

Marpessa. See **Idas**. The daughter of the river god Evenus.

Mars. Roman god of war, at one time also associated with agriculture. Later completely identified with Ares (q.v.).

Marsyas. A Phrygian, in some traditions a silenus (q.v.), who found the flute invented and discarded by Athene (q.v.). He challenged Apollo (q.v.) to a music contest, judged by the Muses (q.v.). Apollo won and had him flayed alive. The tears of the woodland spirits and animals which wept for him formed the river Meander.

Medea. The niece of Circe (q.v.) and daughter of Aëtes of Colchis some say by Hecate (q.v.). She loved Jason (q.v.) and helped him steal the Golden Fleece, murdering her half-brother in their escape. Having cut a goat in pieces, boiled them and pulled forth a lamb she persuaded the daughters of Pelias to boil him, causing his death. When Jason left her for Glauce (q.v.) she caused her death and slew her sons by Jason. She then escaped in a chariot drawn by winged serpents to Athens. Here she married Aegeus (q.v.). When Theseus (q.v.) returned she tried to poison him to secure the succession of her own son Medus (q.v.) but Aegeus recognised Theseus and saved him. She fled to wander the earth: some say she returned to Colchis and was reconciled to her father, others that she went to Asia Minor where her son gave his name to the Medes. She became an immortal.

Medus. Son of Medea (q.v.) and Aegeus (q.v.) eponymous ancestor of the Medes.

Medusa. See **Gorgons**. Slain and beheaded by Perseus (q.v.) as she slept. From her corpse sprang forth the fully grown Pegasus (q.v.) and the warrior Chrysaor.

Megaera. One of the Erinnyes (q.v.).

Megara or **Megaera**. The eldest daughter of Creon of Thebes. Wife of Heracles (q.v.) and bore him several children. Later married Iolaus (q.v.) though one tradition says Eurystheus tried to kill her and Heracles instead killed Eurystheus. In revenge Hera (q.v.) drove Heracles mad and he killed Megara and his children.

Melampus. Son of Amythaon, a seer who introduced the worship of Dionysus (q.v.) to Greece. He and his brother Bias cured the women of Argos (including the daughter of the king, Proetus) of madness and received two thirds of his kingdom in reward.

Meleager. The son of Oeneus and Althaea. The Fates (q.v.) told his mother he would only die when a certain brand, which was on the fire, was burned. She extinguished and hid it. Meleager was one of the Argonauts (q.v.) and organised the hunt of the Calydonian Boar (q.v.). He fell in love with Atalanta who joined the hunt and having killed the boar himself gave her the hide on the pretext she had touched it first. This set the hunters quarrelling and in the dispute he killed his uncles, brothers of Althaea. She cursed their murderer, not realising the truth, and when she learned the Erinnyes (q.v.) were persecuting him because of the curse burned the brand and committed suicide. Her daughters (save Gorge and Deianeira) were turned into guinea-hens by Artemis. The son of Meleager and Atlanta was Parthenopaeus.

Melpomene. The Muse of Tragedy.

Memnon. The son of Eos (q.v.) and Tithonus, half-brother of Priam (q.v.). The king of Ethiopia who helped the Trojans and killed many Greeks. Achilles (q.v.) met him in single combat while Zeus (q.v.) weighed their fates in the balance. Achilles slew him but Zeus answered his mother's request that he be honoured by having the birds called Memnonides rise above his funeral pyre, then fall as a sacrifice. They annually visited his tomb on the Hellespont though one tradition says he survived the war and ruled five generations in Ethiopia before becoming an immortal. The Greeks assumed many monuments, which they called Memnonia, were dedicated to him including a huge statue in Egyptian Thebes.

Menelaus. Son of Atreus, younger brother of Agamemnon (q.v.) and husband of Helen (q.v.). When her father chose him from amongst many suitors he made the others swear to help him in any misfortune. He was thus able to summon the Greek forces for the war on Troy (q.v.). At one stage in the war he fought a duel with Paris (q.v.) to decide the war and was winning until Aphrodite (q.v.) carried Paris off. Because he failed to sacrifice to Athene (q.v.) he took eight years to return from Troy to Sparta.

Menoeceus. (1) See **Jocasta**.

(2) See **Seven against Thebes**.

Mentor. Friend and adviser of Odysseus (q.v.) who was too old to go to Troy (q.v.) and remained at Ithaca to watch over Odysseus' interests. Athene (q.v.) took his form to guide Telemachus' (q.v.) search for his father. The name is now synonymous with a trusted counsellor.

Mercury. The Roman equivalent of Hermes (q.v.).

Merope. A Pleiad. Wife of Sisyphus.

Metis. Counsellor of the young Zeus (q.v.) and his first wife. Mother of Athene (q.v.). Herself the daughter of Oceanus (q.v.) and Tethys.

Midas. Son of Gordius. See **Gordian Knot**. His hospitality to Silenus (q.v.) led Dionysus (q.v.) to grant him any wish: he wished that all he touched would turn to gold. When even his food became gold he begged to be relieved of his gift—and was—by bathing in the River Pactolus which was henceforth rich in gold. When he judged Pan (q.v.) a better musician than Apollo (q.v.) the latter gave him asses' ears which he hid under his hat. Only his barber knew, but when his barber told a hole in the ground, reeds grew from it which, via the wind, revealed his secret to the world.

Milanion. Husband of Atalanta (q.v.).

Miletus of Crete. The son of Aria and Apollo (q.v.), a beautiful youth over whom Minos (q.v.) and his brothers Rhadamanthus (q.v.) and Sarpedon quarrelled. Miletus chose Sarpedon and to escape Minos' jealousy they fled to Asia Minor where Miletus founded the city Miletus which bore his name.

Minerva. Etruscan goddess of wisdom, the arts and crafts. The Romans identified her with Athene (q.v.).

Minos. The son of Zeus (q.v.) and Europa (q.v.), brother of Rhadamanthus (q.v.) and Sarpedon (q.v.). Ruler of Crete and supported in this by Poseidon (q.v.) who gave him a magnificent white bull. See **Cretan Bull**. He gave Crete her laws and defended the island with the aid of Talos, a brazen

giant with a bull's head. He pursued the nymph Britomartis for nine months but she leapt into the sea. Artemis (q.v.) deified her and the two shared the epithet Dictynna. While besieging Nisa, the port of Megara, Scylla, the daughter of the king Nisus fell in love with Minos and cropped her hair on which Nisus' life depended. She let Minos into the city but he was repulsed by her parricide and deserted the girl who swam after his ship. According to one tradition her father's spirit in the form of an eagle seized her and she was transformed into the Ciris bird; according to another tradition Minos drowned her and she became a fish. Minos married Pasiphaë (q.v.) who bore him Ariadne (q.v.), Androgeos and Phaedra. When Androgeos won all the events at the Panathenaic games Aegeus (q.v.) had him murdered and in revenge Minos extracted a tribute of seven Athenian youths and maidens who were devoured by the Minotaur (q.v.). He was killed by the daughters of Cocalus of Sicily while pursuing Daedalus (q.v.) and became one of the three judges of the Underworld.

Minotaur. Offspring of Pasiphaë (q.v.) and the Cretan Bull (q.v.) which had the head of a bull and body of a man. It lived in a labyrinth devised by Daedalus (q.v.) where it devoured the maidens and youths of Athens delivered in tribute to Minos (q.v.). It was slain by Theseus (q.v.).

Minyans or Minyae. Prehistoric inhabitants of Boeotia (q.v.) and Thessaly whose reputed ancestor was Minyas.

Misenus. Trumpeter of Aeneas (q.v.) who was drowned by a Triton (q.v.) and buried in the Bay of Naples at the port which then bore the name Misenum (the modern Capo Miseno). From the time of Agrippa Misenum was a major Roman naval station.

Mithras. An Iranian deity whose worship was developed in Persia and spread throughout the Middle East. Known to the Greeks from the time of Herodotus his worship spread to Rome under the Republic and from the 2nd century A.D. spread throughout the empire. Mithras was linked with astrology and appears to have been linked with the sun following a fight with the sun-god. But the core of his cult was that man or the soul had fallen from grace and that Mithras could bring redemption and thus eternal life. Very popular with the Roman legions. Mithras was the one serious contender with Christianity for religious supremacy. His ritual involved seven stages of initiation and secret ceremonies conducted in underground caves or artificial subterranean chambers such as that found in London. These temples were called mithraea. See also **J35**.

Mnemosyne. "Memory", the daughter of Uranus (q.v.) and by Zeus (q.v.) the mother of the Muses (q.v.).

Moirae or Moerae. See **Fates**.

Monoecus. "The lone dweller", Latin name for Heracles (q.v.) who was said to have dwelt alone for a time in the region of modern Monte Carlo.

Mopsus. The son of Apollo (q.v.) and Manto, daughter of Teiresias. When he beat Calchas (q.v.) in prophecy Calchas died of grief.

Morpheus. The Greek Hypnos. The son of the god of "Sleep". A god who sends dreams and visions of human form. In Ovid's Metamorphoses, Sleep sends him to Alcyone (q.v.) in the form of her dead husband.

Musaeus. A mythical poet who succeeded Orpheus (q.v.), the first poet.

Muses or Musae. The daughters of Zeus (q.v.) and Mnemosyne (q.v.) who presided over the arts and sciences. Originally three in number, Hesiod later names nine. Clio was muse of history, Euterpe of lyric poetry and music, Thalia of comedy, Melpomene of tragedy, Terpsichore of song and dance, Erato of mime, Polyhymnia or Polymnia of the hymn, Calliope of epic poetry and Urania of astronomy, though the attributions vary.

Myrmidons or Myrmidones. Tribe of southern Thessaly which provided Achilles' (q.v.) contingent at Troy.

Myrtilus. The son of Hermes (q.v.). The charioteer of Oenomaus whose death he caused by removing the lynch pin of his chariot and substituting a wax replica. He did this because Pelops (q.v.) had bribed him with the promise of half his kingdom, but instead Pelops flung him into the sea. He cursed the House of Pelops as he died and his father placed him amongst the stars.

N

Naiads or **Naiades.** Fresh-water nymphs in Greek mythology. They carried off Hylas (*q.v.*).

Narcissus. See **Echo.**

Nauplius. A king of Euboea who lured ships returning from Troy (*q.v.*) to their doom on the promontory of Caphareus by lighting misleading fires.

Nausicaa. Daughter of Alcinous, king of the Phaeacians who found Odysseus (*q.v.*) after a shipwreck while playing ball with her friends on the beach. She looked after him and her father gave him a ship.

Nectar. The drink of the Greek gods which conferred immortality.

Neleus. Twin of Pelias (*q.v.*), sons of Poseidon (*q.v.*) and the nymph Tyro. The twins were exposed by their mother but reared by a horse breeder. When Tyro married Cretheus, king of Iolcus, he adopted the boys who were thus half-brothers of Aeson. Pelias then later seized the kingdom, imprisoned Aeson and expelled Neleus who went to Pylus with Bias and Melampus and became its king. He and all twelve of his sons bar Nestor (*q.v.*) were killed by Heracles (*q.v.*) for aiding Augias (*q.v.*) in his war against Heracles.

Nemesis. Greek goddess, daughter of Oceanus. Originally she was envisaged as allotting to men their share of happiness and unhappiness, thereby chastening the over-fortunate. Later she was portrayed as the punisher of crime, the goddess of retribution. Some say she laid the egg from which Helen (*q.v.*), Clytemnestra (*q.v.*) and the Dioscuri (*q.v.*) were born. She had a sanctuary at Rhamnus from around 430 B.C.

Nemi. A lake in the Alban mountains, site of a sanctuary and sacred wood of Diana (*q.v.*).

Neoptolemus. Also called Pyrrhus, a son of Achilles (*q.v.*) and Deidamia. Odysseus (*q.v.*) and Diomedes (*q.v.*) persuaded his grandfather Lycomedes to let him go to Troy (*q.v.*) after his father's death. He was one of the Greeks inside the Wooden Horse. He slew Polites, the son of Priam (*q.v.*) and Hecuba (*q.v.*) before their eyes. He killed Priam at the altar of Zeus, smashed the skull of Astyanax (*q.v.*), Hector's (*q.v.*) child, and sacrificed Polyxena, Priam's daughter, on his father's tomb. He was given Andromache (*q.v.*) but back in Greece married Hermione (*q.v.*) with the blessing of Menelaus (*q.v.*) despite her prior betrothal to Orestes (*q.v.*). When their marriage proved barren he went to Delphi (*q.v.*) to consult the oracle and was slain either by Orestes or the priests of Apollo (*q.v.*).

Nephele. A phantom conjured up by Zeus (*q.v.*) to deceive Ixion. She later married Athamas.

Neptune. Italian sea-god whom the Romans identified with Poseidon (*q.v.*).

Nereids or **Nereides.** Fifty beautiful sea nymphs, the daughters of Nereus (*q.v.*) and Doris, of whom the most famous were Amphitrite (*q.v.*) and Thetis (*q.v.*).

Nereus. An ancient and benevolent sea god, the son of Pontus (the sea) and Ge (*q.v.*). Husband of Doris, the daughter of Oceanus (*q.v.*) by whom he was father of the Nereids (*q.v.*).

Nero. See **B44.**

Nessus. See **Deianeira.**

Nestor. King of Pylos, only one of Neleus' (*q.v.*) twelve sons spared by Heracles. He participated in the Calydonian Boar (*q.v.*) hunt and the battle of Lapithae (*q.v.*) and Centaurs (*q.v.*). The oldest of the Greeks at Troy (*q.v.*) he was famous for his eloquence and wisdom. The father of Antilochus, a friend of Achilles (*q.v.*) and one of the bravest Greeks at Troy. Nestor was the only Greek to return home without mishap.

Nike. Goddess of Victory, not only in war but in musical and athletic competitions in Hesiod's *Theogony*, the daughter of the Titan Pallas and Styx. A minor deity, later envisaged not as one goddess but as several spirits, represented as young girls with wings who flew across the heavens to carry the crown to the victor. Zeus honoured Nike for helping the Olympian gods in the Titanomachia (*q.v.*). She was sometimes identified with Athene (*q.v.*).

Niobe. Daughter of Tantalus, sister of Pelops (*q.v.*) and wife of Amphion (*q.v.*) by whom she had seven sons and seven daughters (according to Ovid, Homer makes it six of each). She boasted of being superior to Leto (*q.v.*) who only had two children and in revenge Apollo (*q.v.*) slew her sons and Artemis (*q.v.*) her daughters. She wept for nine days and nights and Zeus (*q.v.*) then turned her into a stone on Mt. Sipylus.

Nisus. See **Minos.**

Nomius. "The pasturer", a name given to Pan (*q.v.*), Apollo (*q.v.*) and Hermes (*q.v.*) in their roles as protectors of flocks and pastures.

Notus. The south-west wind, known to the Romans as Auster. The son of Astraeus (*q.v.*) and Eos (*q.v.*).

Numa. The name of two Italian warriors in the *Aeneid*.

Numa Pompilius. Legendary king of Rome. The second king, successor of Romulus (*q.v.*) he was said to have ruled between 717 and 673 B.C. Said to be of Sabine (*q.v.*) origin he reorganised Roman religion under the guidance of Egeria (*q.v.*). He was said to have been initiated into the mysteries of Pythagoras, an obvious anachronism as he predates Pythagoras' 6th century visit to Italy, but his reputed religious reforms signify a new strand in Roman religion, a disinterested search for knowledge as opposed to inspired action. He founded the cult of Janus (*q.v.*), organised the priests in *collegia* and established the flamens, and reorganised the Salii whose war dances in honour of Mars (*q.v.*) reflected a very ancient Italic rite. He also appointed the Pontifex Maximus, a high priest with responsibility for ensuring religious rites were properly performed and for preventing the growth of undesirable foreign cults. He also reformed the Roman calendar to achieve the maximum coincidence of lunar and solar cycles.

Numicius. A sacred river in Latium between Ardea and Lavinium.

Numitor. The grandfather of Romulus (*q.v.*) and Remus (*q.v.*).

Nymphae or **Nymphs.** Minor deities, the spirits of nature. These daughters of Zeus (*q.v.*) were semi-mortal and were generally benevolent, though they could be malevolent particularly to unresponsive lovers. Each was the tutelary deity of a rock, tree, cave or fountain and was better known to the local peasants than the great gods of Olympus (*q.v.*). Lavishly decorated monumental fountains (a "*nymphaeum*") were dedicated to the nymphs by both Greeks and Romans.

Nysa, Mt. Mountain in Libya where, according to tradition, Dionysus (*q.v.*) was raised.

O

Oceanides. Sea nymphs (*q.v.*) of the ocean, daughters of Oceanus (*q.v.*). Hesiod says they were 40 in number.

Oceanus. One of the Titans (*q.v.*), the son of Ge (*q.v.*) and Uranus (*q.v.*). The only Titan not to revolt against Uranus (*q.v.*). In Aeschylus' *Prometheus Bound* he preaches submission to the authority of Zeus (*q.v.*). He was seen originally as the river encircling the world from which all rivers and seas sprang. He is thus depicted as the rim on Achilles' (*q.v.*) shield. The husband of Tethys and by her father of, among others, Metis.

Odysseus. The hero of Homer's Odyssey, itself the model for James Joyce's *Ulysses*, Ulysses being the Roman name for him. The son of Laertes, king of Ithaca, and Anticleia, daughter of the wily thief Autolycus. However, one tradition makes him the son of Sisyphus (*q.v.*) he married Penelope (*q.v.*). Warned by an oracle not to go to Troy (*q.v.*) he feigned madness when the heralds arrived by sowing salt, but when Palamedes placed his son Telemachus (*q.v.*) before the plough he was forced to disclose his sanity and join the expedition. Later, at Troy, he avenged himself by having a letter signed in Priam's (*q.v.*) hand placed in Palamedes' tent. The letter was found and Palamedes was stoned to death. But Odysseus himself tricked Achilles (*q.v.*) into revealing his true identity and joining the expedition. At Troy Odysseus and Diomedes (*q.v.*) entered the city at night to kill Rhesus the Thracian and steal his white horses, because it was prophesied that if they drank of the Scamander (*q.v.*) Troy would not fall. He quarrelled with Ajax (*q.v.*) over the armour of Achilles and some say he killed him. He captured Helenus and from him learned the secret oracles which told how Troy would fall. In accordance with these he stole the Palladium of Athene (*q.v.*). It was also Odysseus who devised the stratagem of the Wooden Horse. When Troy fell he took Hecuba (*q.v.*) as a slave. His journey home lasted ten years and involved many adventures. He first went to Cicones to procure jars of sweet wine and then visited the Lotophagi (*q.v.*). After leaving them he landed in Sicily where he blinded Polyphemus the Cyclops (*q.v.*). Next he visited Aeolus (*q.v.*) and as a result was blown off course and lost all his ships save one at Telepylos. In this he reached Aeaea, land of Circe (*q.v.*) and on her advice sought the aid of Teiresias, a dead seer in the Underworld. In the land of the Cimmerians he summoned Teiresias' shade, and also those of his mother and former comrades, though Ajax (*q.v.*) held aloof. Then, with Circe's counsel he navigated the Scylla and Charybdis (*q.v.*) and neutralised the spell of the Sirens (*q.v.*) by blocking his crew's ears with wax but having himself tied to the mast that he might hear their song. At Thrinacia his men slaughtered the cattle of Helios (*q.v.*) and were punished by Zeus (*q.v.*), all but Odysseus dying in a subsequent shipwreck. He drifted to Ogygia in flotsam, where he spent eight years with the nymph Calypso (*q.v.*). On a raft he made land at Scheria, was found by Nausicaa (*q.v.*) and given a ship to Ithaca (*q.v.*). Here he was recognised by Eumaeus (*q.v.*) despite his disguise as a beggar. He found Laertes (*q.v.*) in the country and Penelope (*q.v.*) besieged by suitors. This drunken and unruly crew were headed by one Alcinous, their most persistent member. Penelope had kept them at bay by promising to marry one of them when she had finished weaving a robe for Laertes: a robe she unpicked each night. But betrayed by her servants she was now being forced to choose a husband. Meanwhile Telemachus (*q.v.*) who had sailed away to find Odysseus returned to find him with Laertes and they plotted revenge. Still dressed as a beggar Odysseus entered the palace and was recognised only by his nurse Eurycleia and his faithful hound Argus which died on seeing his long lost master. Penelope now announced she would marry the suitor who could fire Odysseus' bow. Only he was able to bend and string it. The suitors having failed Odysseus strung the bow and with Telemachus slew the suitors. The *Odyssey* ends when Athene (*q.v.*) reconciles the hero and the kinsmen of the suitors who were seeking revenge. Teiresias had prophesied that Odysseus had to set out on another journey to appease Poseidon (*q.v.*) for the blinding of his son Polyphemus and would then live to an old age until death came from the sea. One tradition tells how Telegonus, Odysseus' son by Circe came looking for his father, landed and began plundering for supplies. Odysseus and Telemachus gave battle and Telegonus killed Odysseus, not recognising his father. He also took Telemachus and Penelope to Aeaca where Circe married Telemachus and he himself married Penelope.

Odyssey. *See under* **Odysseus.**

Oedipus ("Swollen-foot"). The son of Laius, king of Thebes, and Jocasta (*q.v.*). The Delphic oracle said Laius would be killed by his son so he had the baby exposed on Mt. Cithaeron with a nail driven through its feet—hence "Oedipus". But he was found by a shepherd and raised by Polybus, king of Corinth, as his own son. As an adult Oedipus learned from the oracle that he would kill his own father and marry his own mother and believing himself the son of Polybus, left Corinth. He met Laius on the road and killed him in a quarrel. Laius had been on his way to Delphi to seek advice on ridding Thebes of the Sphinx (*q.v.*). This Oedipus did and was made king by the Thebans. He married Jocasta and they had four children, Eteocles (*q.v.*), Polynices (*q.v.*), Antigone (*q.v.*) and Ismene (*q.v.*). When Thebes suffered a plague because of their incest Oedipus contacted the seer Teiresias and learned whose son he was. When she heard the truth Jocasta hanged herself and Oedipus blinded himself with the pins from her dress. With Antigone and later Ismene he went into exile at the grove of the Eumenides (*see* **Erinnyes**) at Colonos in Attica. Here he was received by the gods, having first cursed the sons who had neglected him, saying they would divide their kingdom by the sword.

Oeneus. King of Pleuron and Calydon, husband of

Althaea and father of Tydeus (*q.v.*), Meleager (*q.v.*), Gorge and Deineira (*q.v.*). His realm was seized by his nephews but his grandson Diomedes (*q.v.*) avenged him and put Andraemon, husband of Gorge, on the throne. He accompanied Diomedes to the Peleponnesus where he was killed by two nephews who had escaped Diomedes. Deineira (*q.v.*) married Heracles (*q.v.*).

Oenomaus. A son of Ares (*q.v.*), king of Elis. An oracle said he would be killed by his son-in-law. Therefore he challenged all his daughter's suitors to a chariot race and if they won they would marry his daughter Hippodameia: if they lost they were put to death. His own chariot was drawn by wind-born horses, a gift from Ares. But he was murdered by Myrtilus at the instigation of Pelops (*q.v.*).

Oenone. A nymph who loved Paris (*q.v.*). He deserted her for Helen (*q.v.*) and when he was wounded by Philoctetes (*q.v.*) she refused to help him. Then, in remorse at his death, she committed suicide.

Oileus. One of the Argonauts (*q.v.*), and father of Ajax (*q.v.*).

Olympia. A small province in the western Peloponnesus, isolated from the centre and east of the Peloponnesus by high mountains. The site of a major sanctuary of Zeus (*q.v.*) whose worship replaced that of an early female divinity in the 9th century B.C. However, it was not till about 470 B.C. that a magnificent temple was built to Zeus. From 776 B.C. though, the Olympic games had been celebrated at Olympia in honour of Zeus. These quadrennial contests were international in character and an international truce accompanied their celebration. The prestige of the games was great and from 776 Greek chronology was based on the games, an "Olympiad" being a four-year cycle. Hence Olympiad 12, 1 denoted the 1st year in a four-year period after 11 previous Olympiads. If the number of Olympiads is multiplied by 4 and deducted from 776 we have our date *e.g.* $11 \times 4 = 44$, subtracted from 776 is 732 B.C.

Olympius. A term for any deity or muse inhabiting Olympus and not the Underworld.

Olympus Mt. The highest peak in Greece on the borders of Thessaly and Macedonia. Its 2975 m are almost inaccessible and it was not climbed until 1913. It was believed to be the home of the twelve Olympian gods.

Omphale. Queen of Lydia and widow of Tmolus who purchased Heracles (*q.v.*) as a slave. He served her for three years and one tradition says he dressed as a woman and swapped clothes with Omphale during this period.

Ops. Roman goddess of plenty, a consort of Saturn (*q.v.*) and the personification of abundance.

Orcus. The Roman name for Hades (*q.v.*) and for his realm.

Orestes. The son of Clytemnestra (*q.v.*) and Agamemnon (*q.v.*). As a child he was smuggled out of Mycenae by his sister Electra (*q.v.*) when Clytemnestra and Aegisthus (*q.v.*) seized power. He took refuge at the court of king Strophius in Phocis, becoming a close friend of Pylades (*q.v.*), the king's son. When of age he, Pylades and Electra killed Aegisthus and Clytemnestra, and Orestes was punished for his matricide by the Erinnyes (*q.v.*). He fled to the Acropolis of Athens and embraced the image of the goddess. Athene (*q.v.*) then summoned the Areopagus to judge his case. Apollo (*q.v.*), whose oracle had encouraged his crime, defended him on the grounds that fatherhood was more important than motherhood. Athene's casting vote found him innocent. Another tradition says Apollo told him he could be free of the Erinnyes by fetching the statue of Artemis (*q.v.*) from the Tauric Chersonese. Orestes and Pylades went to Tauris and were seized by the natives for sacrifice to Artemis. But it transpired that his sister Iphigenia (*q.v.*) was the priestess and she helped them steal the statue and return to Greece. They met Electra and went on to Mycenae where Orestes killed Aegisthus' son and became king. Later he slew his rival Neoptolemus (*q.v.*) and married his cousin Hermione.

Oreithyia. *See* **Boreas.** He turned her into a wind.

Orion. A giant, son of Poseidon (*q.v.*) who was a renowned hunter and very handsome. He loved Merope, daughter of Oenopion of Chios and was promised her hand in return for ridding Chios of wild animals. This he did but Oenopion would not give up Merope which led Orion to seduce her. Oenopion, with the help of his father Dionysus, blinded Orion who was told by the oracle he could only recover his sight by going to the east and gazing on the sun as it rose. This he did with the help of Hephaestus (q.v.) and once there Eos (q.v.) fell in love with him and Helios (q.v.) restored his sight. Later he joined Artemis (q.v.) in a hunt. Apollo (q.v.) angry at his boasting that he would kill all the wild beasts and afraid he would seduce Artemis contrived his death at the unwitting hands of Artemis. She placed his image in the stars, his constellation rising with the sun at the autumnal equinox.

Orpheus. The son of king Oeagrus of Thrace and Calliope (q.v.). The Greeks regarded him as the first great poet. He could enchant the beasts and trees with his lyre, a gift from Apollo (q.v.). After returning from the voyage of the Argonauts (q.v.) he married Eurydice (q.v.). His grief at losing her after redeeming her from Hades (q.v.) led to a failure to honour Dionysus (q.v.) at a Bacchanalia and he was torn to pieces by Bacchae (q.v.). The muses buried the pieces at the foot of Mt. Olympus (q.v.) save his head which was thrown into the River Hebrus still singing. The head and his lyre eventually floated to Lesbos (q.v.) and were finally placed amongst the stars at the request of Apollo and the Muses. *See also* **Orphism J38.**

Orthrus. A giant two-headed dog, the offspring of Typhon (q.v.) and Echidne (q.v.) and, some say, the father of the Sphinx (q.v.) and Chimaera (q.v.). It was set to watch the oxen of Geryon (q.v.) and was slain by Heracles (q.v.).

Ortygia (1) Port of Syracuse in Sicily.
  (2) Port of Delos (q.v.), birthplace of Artemis (q.v.).

Otus and **Ephialtes.** Twin sons of Iphimedeia and Poseidon (q.v.), named Aloeidae after their mother's later husband Aloeus. At an early age they imprisoned Ares (q.v.) and later swore to rape Hera (q.v.) and Artemis (q.v.). In a vain effort to achieve this they placed Mt. Pelion on top of Mt. Ossa and attacked Heaven. But Artemis induced them to seek her at Naxos. Here she leapt between them in the form of a doe and they accidentally slew each other. In Tartarus (q.v.) their shades were tied back to back by bonds of vipers.

Ovid. *See* **B46.**

P

Palaemon. A sea god, the son of Athamas and Ino who was originally named Melicertes.

Palamedes. *See* **Odysseus.**

Pales. Italic deity of flocks and herds, worshipped on the Palatine.

Palicus. An obscure god or hero worshipped in Sicily and mentioned in the *Aeneid* (q.v.).

Palinurus. "Wind Astern", the helmsman of Aeneas. He managed the ship between the Scylla and Charybdis (q.v.) and in the storm off the coast of Carthage but later fell asleep and into the sea. He was cast ashore but murdered by local tribesmen. His shade begged Aeneas for carriage across the Styx (q.v.) so it could be at rest, but the Sybil refused as he had not been properly buried. However she promised him a shrine, Capo Pulinuro in Lucania near modern Salerno.

Palladium. A mythical statue of Athene given to Dardanus (q.v.) by Zeus (q.v.) to ensure the protection of Troy. By one tradition it was stolen by Odysseus (q.v.) and Diomedes (q.v.). By another Aeneas (q.v.) saved it and brought it to Rome where it saved the city several times in its early years.

Pallas. (1) A title of Athene (q.v.) given to her by the Achaens. Pallas, Kore and Parthenos signify a virgin, maiden or girl.
  (2) One of the 24 Giants (q.v.) who rebelled against Zeus (q.v.).
  (3) A brother of Aegeus (q.v.). *See also* **Theseus.**
  (4) An ancestor of Evander (q.v.).
  (5) Evander's son who went to follow Aeneas (q.v.).

Pan. A god, half-man, half-goat, said by some to be a son of Zeus (q.v.) by others to be the son of Hermes (q.v.) and Penelope with whom he inhabited Arcadia. He was a patron of shepherds and herdsmen and a lover of mischief. When not frolicking with the nymphs he liked to startle peasants and flocks inspiring "panic". He loved and

pursued Syrinx whose flight from him resulted in her being transformed into a reed from which he made a seven-piped flute, the syrinx. He also seduced Selene (q.v.). Sometimes identified with the Roman Faunus (q.v.).

Pandarus. A Trojan archer who broke a truce by shooting at the Greeks. In Chaucer's *Troilus and Criseyde* and Shakespeare's *Troilus and Cressida* he is Cressida's uncle and the lovers' go-between. The word "pandar" is derived from his name for this reason.

Pandora. "All gifts", the first woman fashioned and given life by Hephaestus (q.v.) and Athene (q.v.). Zeus (q.v.) sent her to punish man after Prometheus (q.v.) had given him fire. She married the brother of Prometheus, Epimetheus. Her curiosity led her to open a box which it was forbidden to touch, and from it sprang all the evils and diseases which beset mankind. Only hope was left at the bottom of the box.

Parcae. The Roman equivalent of the "Fates" or Horae.

Paris. Son of Priam (q.v.) and Hecuba (q.v.) who dreamed during her pregnancy that she would bring forth a blazing firebrand. As a child he was exposed on Mt. Ida. Raised by shepherds he was named Paris or sometimes Alexander ("defender of men") because of his courage. He loved and deserted Oenone (q.v.) which eventually caused his death. Promised the fairest of women by Aphrodite (q.v.) if he gave her the apple of discord, he did as she bade. Reunited with his parents he then left for Sparta whence he seduced Helen (q.v.) thus starting the Trojan War. At one point in the war Aphrodite saved him from death in a duel with Menelaus. He shot the arrow which slew Achilles (q.v.) at the Scaean Gate but was himself mortally wounded by Philoctetes (q.v.).

Parnassus, Mt. 2461 m peak in the Pindus range, north-east of Delphi (q.v.). Home of Apollo (q.v.) and the Muses (q.v.) hence the name "Montparnasse" for the hill in Paris on which centred the university and cultural life of that city. On the original's slopes was also the Corycian Cave, a centre of the Bacchae (q.v.).

Parthenon. *See* **L94.**

Parthenope. A nymph whose body was said to have washed up at Neapolis (Naples) around 600 B.C. She gave her name to the short-lived Parthenopean Republic of Naples established by Napoleon in 1799.

Parthenopeus. *See* **Seven Against Thebes.**

Parthenos. *See* **Pallas.**

Pasiphaë. Daughter of Helios (q.v.) and Persë, and wife of Minos (q.v.). Mother of the Minotaur (q.v.) by the Cretan Bull (q.v.) and of many children, including Ariadne (q.v.), Glaucus and Phaedra, by Minos.

Patroclus. Cousin and bosom companion of Achilles (q.v.) whom he met at the court of Peleus (q.v.) while in exile for an accidental murder. Slain by Hector (q.v.) while wearing Achilles' armour, his death persuaded Achilles to re-enter the Trojan War.

Pausanias. Spartan king who intervened to moderate Lysander's arrogant attitude towards Athens and other Greek cities after the Peloponnesian War.

Pegasus. Winged horse, offspring of Poseidon (q.v.) and Medusa (q.v.). It was captured by Bellerophon (q.v.) at the fountain of Pirene and helped him slay the Chimaera (q.v.). It struck Mt. Helicon with its hoof and brought forth the spring of Hippocrene, sacred to the Muses.

Peleus. The son of Aeacus, king of Aegina. With his brother Telamon he killed their half-brother Phocus and the two were expelled to Phthia in Thessaly by Aeacus. Here Eurytion purified them of murder. They took part in the Calydonian Hunt when they accidentally killed Eurytion. They then fled to the court of Acastus (q.v.) of Iolcis. Zeus (q.v.) married him to Thetis (q.v.) though he himself loved Thetis. This was because the oracle foretold that her son would be greater than his father. Their son was Achilles (q.v.). All the gods save Eris (q.v.) were invited to the wedding and in revenge she cast the Apple of Discord. Peleus later ruled the Myrmidones at Phthia.

Pelias. *See* **Jason.**

Pelicles. Son of Peleus *i.e.* Achilles (q.v.).

Peloponnesus. The "island of Pelops" (q.v.), the large southern peninsular of mainland Greece, attached to northern Greece by the Corinthian isthmus.

Pelops. Son of Tantalus (q.v.) king of Lydia. Tantalus cut him in pieces and served him to the gods at a meal. Only Demeter (q.v.) grieving for Persephone (q.v.) did not realise and she ate Pelops' shoulder. Zeus (q.v.) restored him to life by having Hermes (q.v.) boil him in a pot. Demeter gave him an ivory shoulder, said to be the birthmark of his descendants. His shoulder blade was later taken to Troy (q.v.) by the Greeks as the oracle said this was necessary if the city were to fall. He married Hippodamia.

Pelorus. One of the Sparti (q.v.).

Penates. Roman deities of the home, confused from early times with the *genius* and the Lares. Eventually a wide variety of deities, *e.g.* Mars, Mercury, Venus, were regarded as "*di Penates*" that is, "guardians of the hearth".

Penelope. The wife of Odysseus (q.v.), usually seen as a symbol of fidelity. One tradition in the Peloponnesus made her adulterous and the mother of Pan (q.v.) by Hermes (q.v.) or by all of her many suitors.

Peneus. The son of Oceanus (q.v.) and Tethys. A river god and father of Daphne (q.v.) and Cyrene (q.v.). Identified with the River Peneus in Thessaly.

Penthesilea. Daughter of Otrere and Ares (q.v.), queen of the Amazons (q.v.) who helped the Trojans. Slain by Achilles (q.v.) they fell in love as she died and he later mourned her. When the wretched Thersites mocked his grief Achilles slew him which caused his kinsman Diomedes (q.v.) to throw her corpse into the Scamander. It was retrieved and honourably buried.

Pentheus. Grandson of Cadmus (q.v.) and king of Thebes. The subject of Euripides' *Bacchae*. He refused to allow Dionysus (q.v.) into the city but the god, in disguise, persuaded him to dress as one of the Bacchae (q.v.) and watch their orgies. He was then torn to pieces by the Bacchae, led by his own mother who was in a trance.

Perdix (or **Talos**). *See* **Daedalus.**

Periclymenus. The son of Neleus (q.v.) and brother of Nestor (q.v.). An Argonaut (q.v.) he could assume any form he chose. Slain by Heracles (q.v.).

Periphetes. A giant residing at Epidaurus who murdered travellers with an iron club. Slain by Theseus (q.v.) who henceforth carried his club.

Perse. The daughter of Oceanus (q.v.). Wife of Helios (q.v.) to whom she bore Circe (q.v.), Pasiphaë (q.v.), Aeetes and Perses (q.v.).

Persephone. Daughter of Zeus (q.v.) and Demeter (q.v.). She spent the winter months with Hades (q.v.) when nothing grew and with Demeter she spent the fertile months. Thus she was a goddess of vegetation. She was also queen of the Underworld and was a symbol of death. Known to the Romans as Proserpina. Her companion in the Underworld was Hecate (q.v.).

Perses. The son of Helios (q.v.) and Perse (q.v.) father of Hecate (q.v.).

Perseus. Grandson of Acrisius (q.v.) king of Argos and the son of Zeus (q.v.) and Danae (q.v.). Raised at the court of Polydectes who sent him to fetch the head of Medusa (q.v.). Hermes (q.v.) gave him a sickle with which to do this and told him how, via the Graeae (q.v.) he could procure Hades' (q.v.) helmet of invisibility, winged sandals and a magic wallet to help him in the task. Once he had the head he petrified the Titan Atlas (q.v.) with it. He then flew to Aethiopia where he found Andromeda (*see* **Cassiopeia**). Returning to Seriphos he slew Polydectes, made Dictys (q.v.) king and returned to Argos. He later exchanged the kingdom of Argos for that of his cousin Megaperthes of Tiryns.

Phaebus ("Shining"). A name used for Apollo (q.v.) at Delos (q.v.) where he was associated with Artemis (q.v.).

Phaedra. The daughter of Minos (q.v.) and wife of Theseus (q.v.) to whom she bore Acamas and Demophon. *See also* **Hippolytus.**

Phaeton. The son of Helios (q.v.) and Clymene. Helios let him drive the chariot of the sun across the sky but he lost control of it and was killed by a thunderbolt from Zeus (q.v.) for almost setting the world on fire. He fell into the River Po and his sisters who mourned him were turned into poplar or alder trees and their tears into amber.

Phalanthus. Mythical founder of Tarentum in Italy.

Phaon. *See* **Sappho.**

Philemon. The husband of Baucis. This old Phrygian couple once received Zeus (q.v.) and Hermes (q.v.) with great hospitality.

Philoctetes. The son of Poecas, nephew of Protesilaus, and companion of Heracles (q.v.). He lit Heracles funeral pyre and received his bow and arrows. On the way to Troy (q.v.) one of the poisoned arrows wounded him, or he was bitten by a snake on the island of Tenedos. The smell of the wound became so offensive that on the advice of Odysseus (q.v.) he was left on Lemnos. Later an oracle revealed that Troy would not fall till the bow and arrows of Heracles were brought to the Greeks and Odysseus and Diomedes (q.v.) fetched him to Troy. Here either Machaon or Podalirius, the sons of Asclepius (q.v.) cured him of his wound. He slew Paris (q.v.) and later settled in Italy.

Philomela. *See* **Procne.**

Phineus. King of Salmydessus in Thrace and the son of Agenor. He first married Cleopatra, then Idaca who falsely accused her stepsons of improper advances. Phineus imprisoned them and was made blind and pursued by the Harpies (q.v.). Eventually the Argonauts (q.v.) whose ranks included Zetes and Calais, Cleopatra's brothers, slew the Harpies. Phineus freed the stepsons and told Jason (q.v.) what course to set.

Phlegethon ("Blazing"). A river of the Underworld called the "river of flames" by Plato. The shades of those who had committed crimes of violence against their kin were roasted in it until they received forgiveness.

Phlegyas. A king of the Lapithae (q.v.) who burnt Apollo's (q.v.) shrine at Delphi and was punished for it in the Underworld by having to sit beneath a huge rock which was liable to fall at any time.

Phocis. Small mountainous province of northern Greece which held the oracle of Delphi.

Phocus. *See* **Peleus.**

Phoebe ("Bright"). In early myth the daughter of Heaven and Earth and mother of Leto (q.v.). Later identified with Artemis (q.v.) the moon-goddess.

Phoenix ("Red"). (1) Companion and tutor of Achilles (q.v.) who tried to reconcile him with Agamemnon (q.v.).

(2) The brother of Cadmus (q.v.) and Europa (q.v.), eponymous ancestor of the Phoenicians.

(3) A mythological Egyptian bird which died on a funeral pyre every 500 years before rising again from the ashes.

Phorcys. A sea-god, the father of Echidne (q.v.), Ladon, the Gorgons (q.v.) and the Graeae (q.v.).

Phrixus and **Helle.** Brother and sister, the children of Athamas king of Aeolia. Their stepmother, Ino (q.v.), had engineered their sacrifice by Athamas out of jealousy but they escaped on a flying ram with a golden fleece sent by Zeus (q.v.). Helle fell off into what was henceforth the Hellespont, but Phrixus reached Colchis and sacrificed the ram to Zeus (*see* **Jason**). The ram's image was placed amongst the stars as Aries.

Phyllis. *See* **Demophon.**

Picus. An ancient Italian god represented as a woodpecker *i.e.* '*picus*'.

Pierides. A name applied to the Muses (q.v.). It was derived from the inhabitants of Pieria, on the south coast of Macedonia, who were noted for their worship of the Muses.

Also a name for nine daughters of Pierus king of Macedonia who were defeated in a contest by the Muses and turned into birds.

Pillars of Hercules. Two pillars, Calpe and Abyla, erected on either side of the straits of Gibraltar by Heracles (q.v.).

Pilumnus. An ancient minor Italian god, "the spearman".

Pindar. *See* **B48.**

Pirithous. Son of Ixion (q.v.) and Dia, companion of Theseus (q.v.) and king of the Lapithae (q.v.). He led the fight on the Centaurs (q.v.). On the death of his wife Hippodamia he and Theseus abducted the young Helen (q.v.) of Troy. She fell by lot to Theseus who, in return and despite misgivings, promised to help Pirithous abduct a daughter of Zeus (q.v.) for himself. They attempted to abduct Persephone (q.v.) from the Underworld but Hades (q.v.) chained them to a rock. Heracles (q.v.) later freed Theseus but Pirithous was left to suffer torment for his sins.

Pleiades. The seven daughters of Atlas (q.v.) and Pleione and companions of Artemis (q.v.). Zeus (q.v.) turned them into doves and placed their image in the stars to save them from the attentions of Orion (q.v.) who pursued them for five years. A group of seven poets in 3rd century B.C. Alexandria also called themselves the Pleiad.

Plutarch. *See* **B48.**

Pluto. (1) A Roman name for Hades (q.v.), "the rich one" who owns the riches of the earth itself.

(2) A nymph who was mother of Tantalus (*q.v.*) by Zeus (*q.v.*).

Podarces. (1) *See* **Priam.**

(2) Son of Iphiclus, leader of the Thessalians who fought at Troy (*q.v.*).

Polites. A son of Priam (*q.v.*) and Hecabe (*q.v.*), slain before their eyes by Neoptolemus (*q.v.*).

Pollux. The Roman name for Polydeuces. *See* **Castor.**

Polydeuces. *See* **Castor.**

Polydorus. (1) The son of Cadmus (*q.v.*) and Harmonia and ancestor of Oedipus (*q.v.*) and other great Theban kings.

(2) The youngest son of Priam (*q.v.*) and Hecabe (*q.v.*).

Polymnia. *See* **Muses.**

Polynices. The son of Jocasta and Oedipus (*q.v.*), brother of Eteocles (*q.v.*), Antigone (*q.v.*) and Ismene (*q.v.*). *See also* **Seven Against Thebes.** When Creon refused to allow his burial Antigone (*q.v.*) disregarded the order and buried the corpse.

Polypemon. Also known as Procrustes, 'the stretcher'. A robber who tied travellers to a bed and if they were too tall he cut off their legs; if too short he put them on a rack. Theseus (*q.v.*) did the same to him.

Polyphemus. *See* **Cyclopes and Galatea.**

Polyxena. The daughter of Priam (*q.v.*) and Hecuba (*q.v.*) beloved by Achilles (*q.v.*) whose shade requested her sacrifice by Neoptolemus (*q.v.*) after Troy's (*q.v.*) fall. This is the theme of Euripides' *Hecabe*.

Pomona. An Italian goddess of tree-fruits (*poma*) e.g. apples. She was a minor deity but had her own priest and sanctuary near Rome. Ovid links her with Vertumnus, an Etruscan god with the power to change his shape. He was god of the changing seasons and the ripening fruits of autumn, and also of money changing. *Vertere* means "change" in Latin. He loved Pomona and pursued her disguised as a harvester, vine-dresser, herdsman and old woman, but only won her when he appeared as himself. His statue stood in the Vicus Tuscus, a busy street of brothels and shops named after him as an Etruscan.

Pontus. The sea, offspring of Ge (*q.v.*) the earth.

Pontus Euxinus. The "Hospitable Sea", the Greek name for the Black Sea. The name was an attempt to flatter and placate a hostile sea which was much feared by sailors.

Porphyrion. *See* **Giants.**

Porsenna. *See* **Lars Porsenna.**

Portunus. A Roman sea-deity associated with harbours.

Poseidon. The Roman Neptune, a god of earthquakes, and later of the sea. The eldest son of Cronus (*q.v.*) and Rhea. When he and Zeus (*q.v.*) and Hades (*q.v.*) cast lots for their realms he won the sea and had an underwater palace near Aegae in Euboea. Here he kept horses with brazen hoofs and gold manes who drew his chariot across the sea. Its passage calmed the sea. Poseidon created the horse and invented the bridle. As a horse he raped Demeter (*q.v.*) who was disguised as a mare. Their offspring was the horse Arion and the nymph Despoena and, some say, Persephone (*q.v.*). He resented Zeus (*q.v.*) and helped Hera (*q.v.*) and Apollo (*q.v.*) enchain him. In punishment Zeus made him a servant of Laomedon (*q.v.*) and he built the Neptunilia Pergama, the walls of Troy. He helped the Greeks at Troy but hated Odysseus (*q.v.*) who blinded Polyphemus (*q.v.*). He disputed the possession of Athens with Athene (*q.v.*) and lost, but Zeus gave him the Isthmus of Corinth instead. Here the Isthmian games were held in his honour. He married Amphitrite (*q.v.*). By mortal women he had many children including Pegasus (*q.v.*) and the Aloeidae (*q.v.*). He is usually portrayed with a trident which he used to shake the earth.

Priam. The son of Laomedon (*q.v.*) and husband of Hecuba (*q.v.*). Originally called Podarces his name was changed to Priam i.e. "ransomed" because Heracles (*q.v.*) spared him and sold him to Hesione (*q.v.*) his sister. He had fifty sons and fifty daughters, nineteen of whom were by Hecuba and included Hector (*q.v.*), Paris (*q.v.*), Helenus (*q.v.*) and Cassandra (*q.v.*). He begged Achilles (*q.v.*) to return Hector's body. Eventually slain at the altar of Zeus (*q.v.*) by Neoptolemus (*q.v.*).

Priapus. The son of Dionysus (*q.v.*) and Aphrodite (*q.v.*). A fertility god whose worship spread from the Hellespont to Greece and later Rome, though he was never taken seriously. He was often por-

trayed in the form of a red-faced scarecrow with a large detachable phallus and in this role was used to scare birds. The phallus became a truncheon to ward off other intruders. He was also a protector of cultivated gardens and a god of sailors. In Petronius' *Satyricon* he pursues the hero Encolpius and makes him impotent. Horace and Martial write of him lightheartedly and 85 obscene poems about him – *'priapeia'* – exist of unknown authorship. His sacrificial animal was the donkey, a symbol of lust.

Procne. The daughter of Pandion, king of Athens. Pandion gave her to Tereus in return for his assistance and they had a son Itys. But Tereus wanted her sister Philomela. He made Procne a slave and tore out her tongue, then seduced Philomela saying Procne was dead. Procne could only alert her sister and be free by stitching a message to her robe. Once free she slew Itys, cooked pieces of the corpse and fed it to Tereus. When Tereus learnt what had happened he chased the sisters with an axe but the gods turned him into a hawk, Procne into a swallow and Philomela a nightingale though some traditions say it was Philomela who lost her tongue and became a swallow.

Procris. Daughter of Erectheus of Athens and the wife of Cephalus. Eos (*q.v.*) who also loved Cephalus showed him that Procris was easily seduced in return for gold. Procris then fled to Crete and lived for a time with Minos (*q.v.*). On returning to Athens disguised as a youth she brought with her a hound and spear, gifts from Artemis (*q.v.*), which never missed their quarry. Cephalus so wanted the gifts that the couple were reconciled. But Procris suspected Cephalus of having an affair with Eos and followed him on a hunt where he accidentally killed her with the spear.

Procrustes. *See* **Polypemon.**

Proetus. The son of Abas (*q.v.*) king of Argolis. His twin brother Acrisius (*q.v.*) expelled him and he fled to Lydia where he married Anteia (also called Stheneboea) daughter of king Iobates (*see* **Bellerophon**). He later returned to Argolis and forced Acrisius to give him half the kingdom. He ruled from Tiryns whose huge walls he built with the aid of the Cyclopes (*q.v.*). Eventually gave two thirds of his kingdom to Melampus (*q.v.*) and Bias.

Prometheus. A Titan (*q.v.*) and the brother of Epimetheus (*q.v.*) or "afterthought" and Atlas (*q.v.*). Sometimes said to be the maker of mankind. He supported Zeus (*q.v.*) against his brother Titans but stole fire from Olympus and gave it to men. This angered Zeus who took revenge on man through Pandora (*q.v.*) and punished Prometheus by chaining him to a rock in the Caucasus. Here an eagle tore at his liver each day. The liver was renewed daily and Prometheus suffered this torment until Heracles (*q.v.*) rescued him.

Proserpina. Roman counterpart of Persephone (*q.v.*).

Proteus. A sea god and a subject of Poseidon (*q.v.*). He had the power of prophecy and could change his form. He would avoid prophecy by changing form until tightly gripped; then he appeared in his true shape and spoke the truth. Said to live on the isle of Pharos in the Nile Delta. Menelaus (*q.v.*) mastered him while returning from Troy (*q.v.*) and forced him to reveal the way to Sparta.

Psyche. In Greek literature, the "soul" personified, often portrayed as a butterfly. As the centre of emotion she was tormented by "*eros*". Her beauty made Aphrodite (*q.v.*) jealous and she sent Eros (*q.v.*) to torment her. Instead he fell in love with her though he would not let her see him or disclose his identity. But at the bidding of her two sisters she sought to discover who he was. For the first time she saw him, holding a candle above him as he slept, but hot wax fell on him. He woke and left her to seek him. After many trials she found him, became immortal and was united with Eros for ever.

Pygmalion. (1) The king of Tyre and brother of Dido (*q.v.*).

(2) The king of Cyprus who made and fell in love with a maiden's statue. Aphrodite (*q.v.*) answered his prayers and gave the statue life as the girl Galatea. They married and had two sons, Paphus and Metharme. In some versions the tale he is a sculptor. The basis of Shaw's *Pygmalion* and the musical *My Fair Lady*.

Pylades. Husband of Electra (*q.v.*). *See also* **Orestes.**

Pyramus and Thisbe. The lovers in a tale by Ovid which he heard in the East. Living in Babylon they are forbidden to meet but converse through a chink in a wall. They arrange a meeting at the tomb of Ninus but Thisbe, arriving first, was chased away by a lion and dropped her veil. Finding this, Pyramus thought her dead and committed suicide. She returned and slew herself on his sword. Since that time the nearby mulberry has borne fruit the colour of blood. This is the basis of Bottom's tale in Shakespeare's *A Midsummer Night's Dream.*

Pyrrhus. Another name for Neoptolemus.

Pythia. The priestess of Apollo (*q.v.*) at Delphi (*q.v.*).

Python. A she-dragon of Mt. Parnassus who controlled the oracle at Delphi (*q.v.*). The boy Apollo (*q.v.*) slew her and the Pythia (*q.v.*) took over her task of giving voice to oracles.

Q

Quirinus. A very ancient Roman deity whose cult was centred on the Quirinal. The Romans eventually forgot his original character and he was identified with Mars (*q.v.*) in classical times, though Romulus (*q.v.*) was also supposed to have adopted the name after his deification.

R

Rape of the Sabine Women. An episode recounted by Livy and Ovid to explain the intermarriage of the Roman settlers and natives. Romulus (*q.v.*) and his followers invited the surrounding tribes to celebrate a festival in the Circus Maximus then carried off the native girls. War broke out but the Sabine women, who had been well treated, intervened to restore peace. The event has been the subject of paintings by Poussin and Rubens and of a group of statues by Giovanni da Bologna.

Remus. *See* **Romulus.**

Rhadamanthus. The son of Zeus (*q.v.*) and Europa (*q.v.*), brother of Minos (*q.v.*) and Sarpedon (*q.v.*). Once the ruler of part of Crete but Minos forced him to flee to Boeotia (*q.v.*). Famed for his wisdom and justice he was made one of the judges of the Underworld after his death. He married Alcmene (*q.v.*) on the death of Amphitrion (*q.v.*).

Rhea. (1) A Titaness, daughter of Ge (*q.v.*) and Uranus (*q.v.*). *See* **Cronus.**

(2) *See* **Romulus.**

Rhesus. A Thracian king who helped the Trojans. An oracle said that if his magnificent snow-white horses ate the grass of the Trojan plain and drank of the River Scamander Troy would not fall. Diomedes (*q.v.*) and Odysseus (*q.v.*) raided his camp, slew him, and stole the horses.

Rhodos/Rhode. The daughter of Poseidon (*q.v.*), wife of Helios (*q.v.*).

Rome. The "eternal city" sited on the banks of the Tiber. Traditionally founded in 753 B.C. (year 1 of the Roman calendar) by Romulus (*q.v.*). It only really became a city in the 6th century under the Tarquins. Under the Republic it had a population of two or three hundred thousand, of 450,000 by the time of Augustus and 1,000,000 under the Antonines, though the population was occasionally reduced by wars, fires and plagues.

Romulus. The legendary founder of Rome (*q.v.*), twin brother of Remus and together the sons of Rhea or Rhea Silvia. She was the daughter of Numitor, king of Alba Longa (*q.v.*) who was deposed by his brother. Her uncle compelled her to become a Vestal Virgin (*q.v.*) but she bore Romulus and Remus, according to her, by Mars (*q.v.*). Her uncle then imprisoned her and threw the babies into the Tiber. The shepherd Faustulus (*q.v.*) found a wolf suckling them and reared them. When they reached manhood they returned to Alba Longa, restored Numitor to the throne and set off to found a city of their own. They went to the site of Rome and decided to consult the gods. Romulus chose the Palatine Hill, his childhood home, as the centre of the city, Remus the Aventine (*q.v.*). The gods favoured Romulus, sending him an extraordinary omen of twelve vultures, Remus only six. Thus Romulus was given the honour of founding Rome which he did by ploughing a furrow around the Palatine. As he commenced building the city wall Remus derisively jumped over it, a quarrel ensued and Romulus slew him. Romulus took in fugitives in order to populate the city, found them wives by the "Rape of the Sabine women" (*q.v.*) and reigned for forty years before disappearing in a whirlwind on the Campus Martius. He was deified and identified with the Sabine god Quirinus (*q.v.*).

Rubicon. *See* **L107.**

S

Sabines. A branch of the Samnite race and one of the Sabellian peoples who occupied the Etruscanised area on the middle valley of the Tiber around Falerii. To the south of Rome they held the mountainous land between Rome and Campania. They were a constant threat to early Rome and the tradition that one Titus Tatius, a Sabine prince, was offered joint rule by Romulus (*q.v.*) may indicate a period of Sabine occupation or domination of Rome.

Sabinus. A mythical Sabine king.

Salmoneus. The son of Aeolus (*q.v.*) and brother of Sisyphus (*q.v.*). The founder of Salmone. His pride led him to emulate the thunder and lightning of Zeus (*q.v.*) who slew him and crushed his city with a thunderbolt.

Sarpedon. The son of Zeus (*q.v.*) and Europa (*q.v.*), brother of Minos (*q.v.*) and Rhadamanthus (*q.v.*). The three brothers quarrelled over the love of the youth Miletus (*q.v.*). Sarpedon went to Asia Minor and became king of the Lycians after helping king Cilix of Cilicia defeat them. Zeus allowed him to live three generations and he helped Troy (*q.v.*) in the Trojan war. Patroclus (*q.v.*) slew him.

Saturn. From *Satus i.e.* "sown". Ancient Mediterranean god of agriculture, possibly of Ligurian origin and particularly revered in Sardinia (*q.v.*) and Africa (*q.v.*). Later identified with Cronus (*q.v.*) who supposedly emigrated to Italy after being deposed by Zeus (*q.v.*). Here he presided over a mythical "Golden Age". His temple in Rome was consecrated in 497 B.C. and housed the state treasury. His festival, the Saturnalia, was celebrated near the winter solstice, originally on 17 December but from the 4th century A.D. on New Year's Day. During the celebrations complete licence was given, slaves took the place of their masters, presents were given, a "Lord of Misrule" appointed and merrymaking and disorder of every kind was rife. It may be that in primitive times his worship involved the sacrifice of humans because in classical times rush dummies in human shape (*argei*) were flung into the Tiber each year on 15 May in his honour.

Satyrs. Young spirits of wildlife, the woods and hillsides. Sons of Hermes (*q.v.*) closely associated with Dionysus (*q.v.*). They were possessed by lechery and a love of wine and embodied the fertile force of nature. Usually they were personified with pointed ears, horns and a tail like Pan's (*q.v.*).

Scaean Gate. The "left hand", the gate in the walls of Troy (*q.v.*) where Achilles (*q.v.*) fell.

Scamander, River. River in Asia Minor near Troy (*q.v.*), originally called the Xanthus. Its name was changed when the mythical Scamander (*q.v.*) of Crete founded a colony in Phrygia and jumped into the river.

Scamander. One-time king of Crete, father of Teucer (*q.v.*) by the nymph Idaea and therefore an ancestor of the Trojans.

Sciron. A robber who dwelt on the border of Attica and Megara. He preyed on travellers and forced them to wash his feet on the Scironian rock. He then kicked them off the rock into the sea to be eaten by a giant turtle. Theseus (*q.v.*) slew him.

Scylla. (1) *See* **Minos.**

(2) *See* **Charybdis.**

Scyrus. Aegean isle, half-way between Lesbos and Euboea and off the major trade routes. It was of no importance save in legend: here Achilles (*q.v.*) was hidden by Lycomedes. It was also here that Lycomedes threw Theseus (*q.v.*) from a rock while the hero was in voluntary exile from Athens after giving the city its first constitution. In 470 B.C. Cimon expelled the local populace in order to install Athenian colonists. At the same time he found the reputed body of Theseus and took it back to Athens amidst great pomp.

Selene. Eastern goddess whom the Greeks identified with Artemis (q.v.) and the Romans with Diana (q.v.) or the older moon goddess Luna. Both also identified her with Hecate (q.v.) and thus the moon became associated with sorcery.

Semele. See Dionysus.

Semiramis. The wife of Ninus. These two were the mythical founders of Ninus or Nineveh.

Seven Against Thebes. Oedipus (q.v.) cursed his sons for neglecting him, saying they would divide their kingdom by the sword. To avoid this Eteocles and Polynices agreed to rule in turn but Eteocles then refused to give up the throne when his term expired. Polynices sought the help of Adrastus (q.v.) king of Argos and married his daughter Argia while her sister married Tydeus son of Oeneus of Calydon who was in exile because of a murder he had committed. Amphiaraus the seer (brother-in-law of Adrastus) prophesied death for all who marched on Thebes save Adrastus. But on the advice of Tydeus, Polynices bribed Eriphyle into persuading Amphiaraus to join them. These four were joined by Capaneus, Hippomedon and Parthenopaeus. The seven were initially successful but Teiresias (q.v.) prophesied that a Theban royal prince must sacrifice himself to save the city and Menoeceus did so. The fortunes of the seven now waned. Zeus (q.v.) killed Capaneus with a thunderbolt as he stormed the city walls. Tydeus was wounded by Melanippus but Athene (q.v.) intended to save him with an elixir from Zeus. But Amphiaraus, who had a grudge against him, persuaded him to drink the brains of Melanippus which so disgusted Athene she let him die. Hippomedon and Parthenopaeus were also slain. Polynices now fought a duel with Eteocles to settle the matter and both were mortally wounded. Amphiaraus was swallowed up by the earth and only Adrastus survived. See also **Antigone** and **Epigoni.**

Seven Hills of Rome. The Quirinal, Viminal, Esquiline, Caelian, Capitoline, Palatine and Aventine.

Seven Kings of Rome. Traditionally said to be Romulus, Numa Pompilius, Tullus Hostilius, Ancus Martius, Tarquinius Priscus, Servius Tullius and Tarquinius Superbus.

Seven Sages of Greece. Usually held to be Thales of Miletus, Bias of Priene, Solon, Chilo of Sparta who brought the bones of Orestes (q.v.) to Sparta, Periander of Corinth, Pittacus of Mytilene, a democrat, contemporary of Solon and opponent of Alcaeus, and Cleobulus of Rhodes.

Sibyl (Sibylla). A priestess and prophetess who uttered oracles. Localised in several places the term came to be used generically of many sibyls and Varro lists ten. The most famous was at Cumae in Campania and she told Aeneas (q.v.) how to enter the Underworld. Ovid says she was seven generations old when Aeneas met her and that Apollo (q.v.) had granted her request to live as many years as there were grains in a handful of sand. But she had forgotten to seek eternal youth and was now withered with age. In Petronius' *Satyricon* she hangs in a bottle and when asked what she wants replies "I want to die".

Sibylline Books. A Roman tradition tells how a sibyl (q.v.) offered Tarquinius Priscus nine prophetic books which he refused to buy at the price. She destroyed three and he still refused them; she burnt three more and he took the remaining three at the price demanded for the nine. Special priests kept them and they were consulted only when the Senate authorised it in time of need. In 83 B.C. the originals were destroyed by fire but replaced by new ones. Many later additions were made including Jewish and Christian forgeries and fourteen still exist. They were last consulted in the 4th century A.D. and shortly afterwards Stilicho had them burnt. The original books instructed the Romans to convey the sacred stone of Cybele to Rome.

Sigeum. Part of Troy (q.v.). Hence the Dardanelles were known as the "straits of Sigeum".

Sileni, Silenus. Scholars distinguish between *sileni* and satyrs (q.v.) but the two are very similar and the Greeks themselves seem to have made no distinction. They are regarded as companions of Dionysus (q.v.) and have pointed ears, flat noses and the tail of a horse or goat. By the 6th century B.C. one of their number, Silenus, stands out from his fellows for his wisdom and is sometimes said to have been the tutor of Dionysus. His special knowledge comes from wine drinking and like his fellows he is usually drunk. An old man with horse-ears and tail he proves a good raconteur when captured, though something of a comic drunkard.

Silvanus. Ancient Italian god, a protector of uncultivated land.

Sinis or **Sinnis.** A robber of the Corinthian Isthmus who killed travellers by tying them to the tops of fir trees tied to the ground and then releasing the trees. Theseus (q.v.) slew him in the same fashion.

Sinon. A cousin of Odysseus (q.v.) and grandson of Autolycus the thief. When the Greeks pretended to leave Troy (q.v.) he remained in camp and persuaded the Trojans that the wooden horse was a gift in atonement for the theft of Athene's Palladium (q.v.). Once the horse was inside Troy he signalled the Greek fleet to return.

Sirens. In Homer two sisters who lure sailors to their death by their singing. Odysseus (q.v.) and the Argonauts (q.v.) withstood their fatal charms, the latter because Orpheus (q.v.) outsang them. They have been associated with the modern Galli islands. In non-Homeric tradition their number varies and they are portrayed as having the bodies of birds and heads of either sex. Some say they were daughters of Ge (q.v.) and companions of Persephone (q.v.) who escorted the dead to the Underworld. They were said to feed on the dead. Later they are given the heads of beautiful women and sing to console the dead they escort. Finally they lose their funerary and evil nature and develop fishes' tails like mermaids.

Sisyphus. The son of Aeolus and husband of the Pleiad Merope who bore him Glaucus. He was an ancestor of Bellerophon (q.v.) and also seduced Anticleia, mother of Odysseus (q.v.) and may have been his father. The founder of Ephyra (later Corinth) and an infamous rogue and knave he was condemned in the Underworld perpetually to push a large stone, uphill, only to see it always roll down, hence the term 'labour of Sisyphus' to denote a futile task.

Sophocles. See **B56.**

Spartii. "The sown men" who sprang up when Cadmus (q.v.) sewed the dragon's teeth. They were fully armed and fought amongst themselves until only five remained, Echion, Udaeus, Chthonius, Hyperenor and Pelorus. These helped Cadmus build the Cadmea, citadel of Thebes, and were ancestors of the Thebans. The title was also given to their descendants. Cadmus saved some of the teeth and Jason (q.v.) had to sow these to get the Golden Fleece.

Sphinx. A fabulous monster with a human head and the body of a lion. In Egyptian mythology where it originates it could be of either sex but in Greek myth is a female and lives north of Thebes. It was the offspring of Echidne (q.v.) and Typhon (q.v.) or possibly Orthrus (q.v.) and the Chimaera (q.v.) and plagued Thebes by strangling and devouring all who could not answer her riddle: what walks on four legs at dawn, two at noon and three in the evening? Oedipus (q.v.) answered correctly that it was man who first crawls, then walks upright and finally uses a stick in old age. The sphinx then leapt from her rock and was dashed to pieces.

Stentor. Greek herald in the Trojan war who supposedly had a voice equal to that of fifty men. He died after Hermes (q.v.) beat him in a shouting match. His name gives us the word 'stentorian' meaning extremely loud.

Steropes. One of the Cyclopes (q.v.).

Sthenoboea. Another name for Anteia. See **Bellerophon.**

Sthenelus. (1) A king of Mycenae, the son of Perseus (q.v.) and Andromeda (q.v.). The husband of Nicippe by whom he was the father of Alcinoe, Medusa (q.v.) and Eurystheus (q.v.).
(2) The son of Capaneus and Evadne, a companion of Diomedes (q.v.) and one of the Epigoni (q.v.). One of the Greeks in the Wooden Horse (q.v.).
(3) A Trojan and companion of Aeneas (q.v.).

Stheno. One of the Gorgones (q.v.).

Strymon. River in Thrace, believed by the Greeks to be the home of the crane.

Stymphalian Birds. Monsters inhabiting Lake Stymphalus, a marshy area in northern Arcadia. They were huge birds with bronze beaks and claws that ate human flesh. They used their feathers as arrows. The birds were sacred to Ares (q.v.) but Heracles (q.v.) startled them with bronze castanets provided by Athene (q.v.) and shot them. Some say they flew to the Black Sea and were found there by the Argonauts (q.v.).

Styx. The river of "hate" in the Underworld and flowing several times around its perimeter. When dipped in it Achilles (q.v.) was made invulnerable. Ghosts could only cross it if they paid Charon (q.v.) to ferry them across and for this purpose a coin was placed beneath the tongue of corpses. On its far bank was Cerberus (q.v.). Aristophanes (q.v.) and others describe it as a marsh rather than a river though Herodotus (q.v.) identifies it with a trickle from the rock near Pheneus. Generally it was associated with the cascade on Mt. Chelmos further west whose cold waters stain the rock black. Plutarch and Arrian say Alexander the Great was poisoned by water from here brought to him in a mule's hoof.

Sul or Sulis. A Celtic deity identified with Minerva (q.v.) by the Romans. The patron of Aquae Sulis.

Symplegades. Floating islands, like icebergs, at the entrance to the Bosphorus. They clashed together and crushed ships. Jason (q.v.), on the advice of Phineus, let loose a dove which made them recoil and as they did so the Argo (q.v.) slipped between them. Henceforth they remained stationary.

Syrinx. An Arcadian nymph. *See* **Pan.**

T

Talaus. The father of Adrastus (q.v.).

Talos. (1) A mythical brazen giant with a bull's head said to protect Crete.

(2) *See* **Daedalus.** Another name for Perdix.

Tantalus. A wealthy king, the son of Zeus (q.v.) and the nymph Pluto. The father of Pelops, Broteas and Niobe. He was favoured by Zeus and was invited to Olympian banquets but stole nectar (q.v.) and ambrosia (q.v.) and revealed Zeus' secrets. He received the golden dog made by Hephaestus (q.v.) for Rhea (q.v.) (which had watched Zeus' cradle) from Pandareus. This incensed the gods but Tantalus denied having seen it. Pandareus was then put to a miserable death and his daughters were abducted by the Harpies (q.v.). His numerous other crimes included serving Pelops (q.v.) as a meal to the gods. For this he was punished in the Underworld, either by being placed beneath a huge rock which constantly threatened to fall and crush him or by being placed in a lake the waters of which receded whenever he tried to drink, while above his head were boughs of fruit "tantalisingly" behind his reach.

Tarchon. Legendary ancestor of the Etruscan "Tarquins" who lead a group of emigrants from Lydia to Italy and there founded Tarquinii and other Etruscan cities. He became an ally of Aeneas (q.v.).

Tarpeia. The daughter of Tarpeius, commander of the Roman garrison on the Capitol during the Sabine (q.v.) wars shortly after Rome's foundation. Her story is told by Livy. She treacherously offered to show the way into the citadel if the Sabine chief Tatius would give her that which his men "wore on their shield arms". By this she meant gold torques but instead the Sabines crushed her to death with their shields. The tale is an attempt to account for the name of the Tarpeian Rock (q.v.).

Tarpeian Rock. A precipice on the south-west corner of the Capitol from which traitors and other condemned criminals were thrown to their death. The last victim was an equestrian implicated in a conspiracy against Claudius in 43 A.D.

Tartarus. (1) Another name for Hades (q.v.) though in Homer it refers to the deepest reaches of the Underworld, a place of punishment to which the Titans (q.v.) and Centimani (q.v.) were consigned by Cronus (q.v.).

(2) Also the name of a son of Ge (q.v.) who was father, by his mother, of the monster Typhon (q.v.).

Teiresias or Tiresias. A blind Theban prophet, who, while young, had come upon Athene (q.v.) bathing in the nude. She had therefore blinded him but in compensation gave him the gift of prophecy. He revealed to Oedipus (q.v.) the truth of his incest. He helped Thebes against the Seven (q.v.) then died after drinking from the well of Tilphussa.

Odysseus (q.v.) consulted his shade in the land of the Cimmerians.

Telamon. The son of Aeacus and brother of Peleus (q.v.). After he had murdered their half-brother Phocus, his father expelled him to Salamis where he married Glauce and later succeeded her father as king. Next he married Periboea of Athens and she bore him Ajax (q.v.). A friend of Heracles (q.v.) and with him sacked Troy (q.v.). He carried off Hesione who bore him Teucer and his refusal to return her to her brother Priam (q.v.) was one cause of the Trojan war.

Telchines. Mythical beings, artists in metal work who made a sickle for Cronus (q.v.) and the trident for Poseidon (q.v.). They raised the infant Poseidon. At times they were destructive and interfered with the weather. They annoyed Zeus (q.v.) who drowned a number of them in a flood, and Apollo (q.v.) who took the form of a wolf to savage them.

Telemachus. *See* **Odysseus.**

Telephassa. The mother of Europa (q.v.) and Cadmus (q.v.) by Agenor.

Telephus. The son of Heracles (q.v.) and Auge (a priestess and daughter of Aleus, king of Tegea). Abandoned as a child, the Delphic oracle later directed him to the court of king Teuthras in Mysia where he found his mother married to Teuthras. He later succeeded Teuthras and married Laodice, daughter of Priam (q.v.). When the Greeks on their way to Troy (q.v.) landed in Mysia he repulsed them, but Dionysus (q.v.) caused him to trip on a vine and Achilles (q.v.) wounded him. An oracle told him he could only be cured by the one who wounded him while the Greeks were told they could not take Troy without his help. He therefore went to Achilles who cured the wound with rust from his spear and in return Telephus showed the Greeks the route to Troy.

Tempe. A vale in Thessaly where Apollo (q.v.) pursued Daphne (q.v.) and was purified of the killing of Python.

Tenedos. Small island off the coast of Asia Minor, south west of Troy (q.v.). Here Achilles (q.v.) slew king Tenes (q.v.) and his father Cyncus and here Philoctetes (q.v.) was wounded.

Tenes. The son of Apollo (q.v.) though reputed to be son of Cycnus, king of Colonae in Troas. His stepmother attempted to seduce him and, when he refused her, made false accusations against him. Cycnus then put Tenes and his sister Hemithea into a chest and cast it adrift at sea. It washed up on the isle of Leucophrys where Tenes became king and gave his name to the island, Tenedos (q.v.).

Tereus. *See* **Procne.**

Terpsichore. The muse of song and choral dance, portrayed with a lyre and plectrum.

Teucer. (1) The son of Scamander (q.v.) and the nymph Idaea. He gave the land to Dardanus (q.v.) on which Dardanus built Dardania. An ancestor of the Trojans.

(2) The son of Hesione and Telamon, half brother of Ajax (q.v.) behind whose shield he fought at Troy (q.v.).

Teucri. Name for the Trojans derived from that of their ancestor Teucer (q.v.).

Teuthras. *See* **Telephus.** The father of the girl Tecmessa. Ajax (q.v.) raided the Thracian Chersonese, slew him and abducted Tecmessa.

Tethys. A Titaness, mother of Oceanus (q.v.) of Metis.

Thalia. (1) Muse of comedy.

(2) One of the Charities (q.v.).

Thebe. The wife of Zethus, who gave her name to Thebes.

Themis. A Titaness, the daughter of Ge (q.v.) and Uranus (q.v.) and sister of Cronus (q.v.). The wife of Zeus (q.v.) before Hera (q.v.), she bore him the Horae (q.v.) and Moerae (q.v.). She determined religious rites, instituted laws and was the first to distinguish between that which was permitted and that which offended the divine order. Hence she became the personification of justice and represented the incarnation of divine law.

Therseander. *See* **Epigoni.**

Theocritus. *See* **B59.**

Thersites. A low-minded, ugly and mean spirited wretch amongst the Greek forces at Troy (q.v.). He accused Agamemnon (q.v.) of prolonging the war to serve his own interest until Odysseus (q.v.) beat him into silence.

Theseus. The son of Aethra, a princess of Troezen, by Aegeus (q.v.) though one tradition says Poseidon (q.v.) fathered him in the form of a bull.

Aegeus left her after seducing her but showed her a rock under which he had hidden his sword and sandals. Theseus was raised secretly by his mother at her father's court, and when he reached adolescence lifted the rock to claim Aegeus' sword and sandals. With these he set off for Athens and on the way had many adventures, slaying the wild sow of Crommyum, Sciron (*q.v.*), Periphetes (*q.v.*), Cercyon and Procrustes (*q.v.*). Arriving at Athens Aegeus recognised the sword and sandals and accepted him as his son despite the plots of Medea (*q.v.*). Theseus then scattered the Pallantides, fifty nephews of Aegeus and the sons of Pallas who hoped to claim the throne themselves. Next he captured the Cretan Bull (*q.v.*). But his greatest task was to go voluntarily to Crete to slay the Minotaur (*q.v.*). As one of the tribute demanded by Minos (*q.v.*) he was to be sacrificed to the monster but Minos' daughter Ariadne fell in love with him and gave him a sword with which to slay the beast and a thread by which he could retrace his steps through the massive labyrinth in which it lived. The couple then fled to Naxos where he left Ariadne and where she was loved by Dionysus (*q.v.*) whose sacred island it was. Aegeus tragically killed himself on Theseus' return and the hero then became king of Athens. Either alone or with Heracles (*q.v.*) he invaded the land of the Amazons and carried off either Antiope or Hippolyte. The Amazons attacked Athens but Theseus defeated them in the middle of Athens. By the Amazon queen he became father of Hippolytus (*q.v.*). Later he married Phaedra and was father by her of Acamas and Demophon (*q.v.*). A close friend of Pirithous (*q.v.*), the two shared many adventures. Eventually he returned again to Athens but was ousted by Menestheus and retired to Scyros where, for some reason he was murdered by Lycomedes. Unlike Heracles, Theseus was not worshipped throughout the Hellenistic world but was very much an Athenian hero and his reputed bones were brought to the city from Scyros in historical times. He is said to have gathered the villages of Attica into one state by the process of *synoecismus*.

Thetis. A Nereid (*q.v.*) who was raised by Hera (*q.v.*) and remained attached to her. Zeus (*q.v.*) and Poseidon (*q.v.*) desired her but it was foretold that her son would be greater than his father. She was thus forced to marry a mortal, Peleus (*q.v.*), but only after she had tried to avoid him by changing her shape, becoming various animals including a lion. Their wedding on Mt. Pelion was attended by all the gods save Eris (*q.v.*). They had a number of children who were killed when Thetis tried to make them immortal by throwing them into the fire. Peleus snatched their seventh child, Achilles (*q.v.*), from her as she tried yet again. Instead she dipped him in the Styx (*q.v.*). Angry at not giving birth to an immortal she left Peleus to live with her sister Neireids. She cared for Hephaestus (*q.v.*) when Zeus threw him into the sea, and for Dionysus (*q.v.*) though she and Briareus (*q.v.*) freed Zeus when the other gods enchained him.

Thoas. The son of Andraemon king of Calydon who took forty ships to Troy (*q.v.*) and was one of the Greeks in the Wooden Horse (*q.v.*).

Thyades. *See* **Thyia.**

Thyestes. The son of Pelops (*q.v.*) and Hippodamia and brother of Atreus, ancestor of the illustrious Atridae family. He and Atreus murdered their half-brother Chrysippus and fled to Mycenae. Here Atreus seized the kingdom and banished Thyestes. Thyestes had seduced Atreus' second wife Aerope and he now tricked Atreus into killing Pleisthenes, his son by his first wife. In revenge Atreus lured Thyestes to Mycenae, slew his three sons and served them to him. Thyestes unknowingly ate them. Not surprisingly he cursed the house of Atreus on learning the truth. The Delphic oracle told Thyestes he could get revenge by fathering a son on his own daughter Pelopia, a priestess at the court of Threspotus of Sicyon. He raped her and Atreus later married her, believing her to be the daughter of Threspotus. He raised Thyestes' son Aegisthus (*q.v.*) as his own.

Thyia. The first woman to worship and sacrifice to Dionysus (*q.v.*). She gave her name to the Attic women who participated in the orgies of Dionysus at Parnassus, the Thyiades. These women were also called Thyades, "raging women", a similar name but of different origin.

Thyone. *See* **Semele.**

Thyrsus. A wand carried by the Maenads, covered with ivy wreaths and surmounted by a fir cone.

Tiryns. City reputedly founded by Proetus (*q.v.*) and built with the help of the Cyclopes (*q.v.*). The actual site is a mound 300 yd long on the Gulf of Argolis. It was first inhabited in the 3rd millennium B.C. and held a chief's residence and town. Around 1600 B.C. a larger palace was built and ramparts constructed. In the 14th and 13th centuries the rampart was rebuilt and enlarged. Its impressive ruins remain.

Tisiphone. One of the Eumenides (*q.v.*).

Titanesses. Sisters of the Titans (*q.v.*), daughters of Ge (*q.v.*) and Uranus (*q.v.*). Their numbers included Rhea (*q.v.*), Themis (*q.v.*), Tethys and Mnemosyne.

Titanomachia. The ten-year war, waged in Thessaly by Zeus (*q.v.*) and the Olympian gods against Cronos (*q.v.*) and the Titans (*q.v.*) led by Atlas (*q.v.*). Ge (*q.v.*) promised Zeus (who had usurped his Titan father Cronos) victory if he would free the Cyclopes (*q.v.*) and Hecatoncheires (*q.v.*) from Tartarus (*q.v.*). He did and the Cyclopes gave him the thunderbolt, Hades (*q.v.*) a helmet which conferred invisibility and Poseidon a trident. The three overcame Cronos and the Hecatoncheires stoned the other Titans who were defeated and consigned either to Tartarus or an island far to the west. Here the Hecatoncheires guarded them. Atlas was made to carry the sky as punishment but the Titanesses (*q.v.*) were spared. The war is the basis of Keats' *Hyperion*.

Titans. The sons of Ge (*q.v.*) and Uranus (*q.v.*). There were twelve of them though the lists given of their names are inconsistent. The most often named are Cronus (*q.v.*), Oceanus (*q.v.*), Hyperion, Iapetus and Atlas (*q.v.*). Brothers of the Titanesses (*q.v.*). When Uranus consigned the Cyclopes (*q.v.*) to Tartarus (*q.v.*) Ge persuaded Cronos and his brother Titans to depose Uranus. The Titans were in turn deposed in the Titanomachia (*q.v.*).

Tithonus. The son of Laomedon and Strymon and a half-brother of Priam (*q.v.*). By Eos (*q.v.*) the father of Memnon (*q.v.*). Eos begged Zeus (*q.v.*) to make him immortal, which he did, but forgot to ask for perpetual youth. Tithonus grew older and older until Eos tired of looking on him, turned him into a cicada and locked him in a cage.

Tities. One of the three primitive tribes of Rome.

Tityus. A giant son of Ge (*q.v.*) sent by Hera (*q.v.*) to violate Leto (*q.v.*) but Artemis (*q.v.*) and Apollo (*q.v.*) slew him with their arrows. In Hades (*q.v.*) he was pegged to the ground (he covered nine acres) while two vultures picked at his liver.

Tleopolemus. A son of Heracles (*q.v.*) who settled in Argos and later Rhodes.

Triptolemus. *See* **Demeter.**

Triton. The son of Poseidon (*q.v.*) and Amphitrite (*q.v.*) though sometimes several tritons are spoken of. He was a merman, his upper body being human, the lower fish. He blew a shell-trumpet, the concha, to calm the waves and Ovid tells us that he blew the concha to order the waters to recede after the Flood. (*See* **Deucalion**).

Troilus. A young son of Priam (*q.v.*) slain by Achilles (*q.v.*). His romance with Cressida is a medieval invention.

Trojan War. The ten-year siege of Troy (*q.v.*) and its eventual sack by Greek forces under Agamemnon (*q.v.*). The combined forces sought to restore Helen (*q.v.*) to Menelaus (*q.v.*). The story of the war is told in Homer's *Iliad* where Achilles (*q.v.*) is the major hero of the Greeks and Hector (*q.v.*) of the Trojans. According to Homer the war was ended by the Wooden Horse (*q.v.*) concocted by Odysseus (*q.v.*). The war is usually placed by tradition as occurring in the 12th century B.C. The war is not a purely mythical episode. Archaeological evidence from the site of Troy shows that the city occupying the seventh stratigraphical layer was destroyed by fire, though probably in the 14th century B.C. Archaeology also confirms the *Iliad's* description of the main towns in Trojan civilisation together with its picture of the Greek people and army.

Trophonius and Agamedes. Sons of Erginus who built a temple for Apollo (*q.v.*) at Delphi. They were rewarded by living merrily for six days and dying in their sleep on the seventh. Trophonius later had an oracle of his own at Lebadeia in Boeotia. Here, according to Pausanias, the questioner underwent a complex initiation, was dressed as a sacrificial victim and (carrying a honey-cake to placate the Underworld divinities) descended into a pot-hole. An underground stream swept him along some distance before he was returned to the light having heard invisible speakers in the cavern. Not surprisingly the questioner would look dazed and dejected and it became common to speak of a gloomy person as one who had been consulting Trophonius.

Tros. (1) The grandson of Dardanus (*q.v.*) and father of Ilus (*q.v.*) and Ganymede (*q.v.*). An ancestor of the Trojans, he gave his name to Troy (*q.v.*).

(2) A small town absorbed by the city of Troy (*q.v.*).

Troy. Also called Ilium, a city of Asia Minor near the sea not far from the straits of the Dardanelles. From its position the inhabitants could watch the sea traffic between the Aegean and Sea of Marmara. Many traders off-loaded cargo and used the land route to bypass the dangerous straits. Hence in the late 3rd millennium B.C. Troy became very prosperous from trade, a prosperity which returned at various periods in the 2nd millennium. In 1870 the German Heinrich Schliemann, an amateur archaeologist, sought the site near modern Hissarlik in Turkey. He found it and later excavations have distinguished nine strata of occupations, the richest dating from 2200 B.C. and the 7th showing signs of destruction by fire (*See* **Trojan War**). From the 14th century B.C. the site was of little importance until the Roman occupation when, as Ilium Nevum, it played a large part in provincial life. Homer's Troy had probably absorbed three neighbouring towns, Tros (*q.v.*), Dardania and Ilium and the names of three tribes, Ilians, Trojans and Dardanians are represented in the myths of its foundation.

Tyche or **Tuche.** The Roman "Fortuna", and always more popular in Rome. A daughter of Zeus (*q.v.*) and the goddess of luck who bestowed or denied gifts to men according to her whims. She often accompanied Pluto (*q.v.*). She is portrayed juggling a ball, symbolising the instability of fate, or with a rudder to guide men's affairs.

Tydeus. Son of Oeneus and Calydon, husband of Deipyle. After committing a murder in his youth he fled to the court of Adrastus (*q.v.*). *See* **Seven Against Thebes.**

Tyndareus. The brother of Hippocoon who deposed him as king of Sparta, but Heracles (*q.v.*) reinstated him. Helen (*q.v.*) was brought up at his court (she was his wife Leda's (*q.v.*) child by Zeus (*q.v.*)). Helen married Menelaus (*q.v.*) who succeeded Tyndareus. Tyndareus had had all the Greek nobles who sought Helen's hand swear an oath to defend her chosen husband. This was the reason why the Greeks allied in support of Menelaus in the Trojan War (*q.v.*). Tyndareus also helped Agamemnon (*q.v.*) expel Thyestes (*q.v.*) and regain his throne.

Typhon. The monstrous offspring of Ge (*q.v.*) and Tartarus (*q.v.*), whose eyes could expel fire and whose limbs ended in snakes' heads. He attacked Olympus and the gods fled to Egypt disguised as animals, Zeus (*q.v.*) as a ram, Apollo (*q.v.*) as a cow, Dionysus (*q.v.*) as a goat, Hera (*q.v.*) as a white cow, Artemis (*q.v.*) as a cat, Aphrodite (*q.v.*) as a fish, Ares (*q.v.*) as a boar and Hermes (*q.v.*) as an ibis. Athene (*q.v.*) did not flee and persuaded Zeus to fight. In a great struggle Zeus was saved by Hermes and Pan (*q.v.*) and then defeated Typhon with his thunderbolts. He was then buried under Mt. Etna. By Echidne (*q.v.*) Typhon was father of a variety of monsters.

Tyro. A nymph, the mother of Pelias (*q.v.*) and Neleus (*q.v.*) by Zeus (*q.v.*) and of Aeson by Cretheus. The grandmother of Jason (*q.v.*).

U

Udaeus. One of the Spartii (*q.v.*).

Ulysses. The Roman name for Odysseus (*q.v.*).

Urania. The Muse of Astronomy.

Uranus. The Sky, offspring of Ge (*q.v.*) the earth and brother of Pontus, the sea. The father by Ge of the Hecatoncheires (*q.v.*), the Cyclopes (*q.v.*) and the Titans (*q.v.*). He threw the rebellious Cyclopes into Tartarus (*q.v.*). Ge then persuaded the Titans to rise against their father and avenge their brothers. She gave Cronos (*q.v.*) a flint sickle with which he castrated Uranus. The blood of Uranus which fell to earth produced the Erinyes and the blood which fell into the sea produced Aphrodite (*q.v.*). Uranus was deposed but cursed Cronos that his own children depose him.

V

Venus. Originally an Italian deity whose name meant "beauty" or "charm", she was a goddess of vegetable rather than animal fertility. She became identified with Aphrodite (*q.v.*) by way of Aphrodite's cult at Mt. Eryx in Sicily, said to have been founded by Aeneas (*q.v.*) on the death of Anchises (*q.v.*). In 217 B.C. Venus Erycina was given a temple at Rome and became completely associated with Aphrodite taking on her functions and attributes. She was patron goddess of Sulla and Pompey. In the imperial cult she played a very important role as the Julian family claimed descent from Aeneas and therefore Aphrodite. In this context she was Venus Genetrix, creator of all things, the universal mother and life giver.

Vesta. A primitive Roman goddess of the hearth, the counterpart of Hestia (*q.v.*). She was worshipped in each Roman house and officially in a circular temple in the Forum. The temple held a fire, said to have come from Troy (*q.v.*) which could never be allowed to go out. It was tended by the Vestal Virgins (*q.v.*). Her cult was purely Italian and never spread to the provinces.

Vestal Virgins. A college of priestesses of the cult of Vesta (*q.v.*). There were originally four of them, later six and finally seven. Candidates for the college were chosen at between six and ten years of age; both their parents had to be alive and they underwent a prolonged special training. They served for thirty years under the control of the Pontifex Maximus and during all this period had to remain virgins. The punishment for unchastity was burial alive. However they were highly honoured and had great privileges. For instance they could save from execution any criminal they met on the way to his death. They lived in a large residence near the temple of Vesta. The sacred fire of Vesta was tended by Vestal Virgins up to the 4th century A.D.

Virgil. *See* **B62.**

Victoria. The Roman goddess of victory, corresponding to the Greek *Nike* (*q.v.*).

Vulcan. The Roman god of fire, identified with Hephaestus (*q.v.*) and sometimes called Mulciber, "the smelter". His name gives us the word "volcano".

W

Wooden Horse of Troy. The "Trojan Horse", a stratagem devised by Odysseus (*q.v.*) which ended the Trojan War (*q.v.*). The Greeks had Epeius, son of Panopeus, build a large wooden horse. Athene (*q.v.*) helped him and it bore an inscription dedicated to her. Then twenty-three or more Greeks including Odysseus, Neoptolemus (*q.v.*), Sthenelus and Thoas hid inside it. The rest of the Greek force then burnt their camp and put to sea leaving only the wily Sinon (*q.v.*) to trick the Trojans into dragging the horse into Troy. (*See also* **Laocöon**). Inside the city Helen (*q.v.*) patted the horse and called out the names of those she suspected were inside it, but she was accompanied by the Trojan prince Deiphobus and Odysseus stopped the Greeks answering. At night the Greek fleet returned, Sinon let the men out of the horse, the gates of Troy were opened and the city was sacked.

X

Xenophon. *See* **B66.**

Xuthus. The son of Hellen and husband of Creusa, the daughter of Erectheus, king of Athens. By her the father of Achaeus and Ion. On the death of

Erectheus Xuthus was asked to determine which of the king's sons should succeed him. He chose Cecrops and was expelled to Achaia by the other heirs. Euripedes (*q.v.*) makes Ion the son of Apollo (*q.v.*) and Creusa.

Z

Zagreus. A son of Zeus (*q.v.*). He was torn apart and eaten by Titans (*q.v.*) except for his heart which Athene (*q.v.*) saved. He is sometimes identified with Dionysus (*q.v.*).

Zephyrus. The son of Astraeus and Eus. He was the west wind, originally imagined, like all winds, in the form of a horse. The father of Xanthus and Balius, the talking horses of Achilles (*q.v.*) which Poseidon (*q.v.*) had given to Peleus (*q.v.*) as a wedding gift. The husband of Iris (*q.v.*). He deflected the discus which killed Hyacinthus (*q.v.*). His Roman counterpart was Favonius.

Zetes. *See* **Calais.**

Zethus. *See* **Amphion.**

Zeus. The son of Cronos (*q.v.*) and Rhea (*q.v.*). He deposed his father and defeated the Titans (*q.v.*). Then he and his brothers Hades (*q.v.*) and Poseidon (*q.v.*) cast lots for their kingdoms and Zeus won the sky. The earth was common to all. Zeus was the king of the gods and was identified with Jupiter by the Romans. He was the father of men. In early legend his consort is Dione, but his consort on Mt. Olympus (*q.v.*) is the jealous Hera (*q.v.*). He first married Hetis who bore him Athene (*q.v.*) and his second wife was Themis (*q.v.*) who bore him the Horae and Maerae. Hera bore him Ares (*q.v.*), Hebe (*q.v.*) and Hephaestus (*q.v.*). His sister Demeter (*q.v.*) bore him Persephone (*q.v.*) and Eurynome bore him the Charities (*q.v.*) while by Mnemosyne he was father of the Muses (*q.v.*). By mortal women he was father of Hermes (*q.v.*), Apollo (*q.v.*) and Artemis (*q.v.*) and Dionysus (*q.v.*). Given the thunderbolt by the Cyclopes (*q.v.*) he was known as the thunderer.

IDEAS &
BELIEFS

This section explains many of the ideas and beliefs that have dominated men's minds during the centuries. The arrangement is alphabetical and the subjects fall broadly into four groups: religious, philosophical, political, and offbeat cults and ideas.

IDEAS AND BELIEFS

THIS section explains many of the ideas and beliefs which people have held at different periods in history. Beliefs may be true or false, meaningful or totally meaningless, regardless of the degree of conviction with which they are held. Since man has been moved to action so often by his beliefs they are worth serious study. The section throws a vivid light on human history.

Man has always felt a deep need for emotional security, a sense of "belonging". This need has found expression in the framing of innumerable religious systems, nearly all of which have been concerned with man's relation to a divine ruling power. In the past, people have been accustomed to think of their own religion as true and of all others as false. Latterly we have come to realise that in man's religious strivings there is common ground, for our need in the world today is a morality whereby human beings may live together in harmony.

There is also to be found in man an irresistible curiosity which demands an explanation of the world in which he finds himself. This urge to make the world intelligible takes him into the realm of science where the unknown is the constant challenge. Science is a creative process, always in the making, since the scientist's conjectures are constantly being submitted to severe critical tests. Basic scientific ideas are discussed in **Section F**.

A

Activists, those in a political movement who insist on taking active steps towards their objectives rather than merely putting forward a programme. Lately activism has become an increasingly common facet of political life. This is probably because the undeniably rapid social changes which are taking place across the world at the moment are not generally being followed by appropriate shifts in political structures and ideals.

Acupuncture, a quasi-medical system originating in China and based on the supposedly therapeutic effects of implanting fine gold needles in the spinal cord and other specific parts of the body. The site of needle implantation is decided according to traditional texts. The apparent lack of any logical relationship between the implantation sites and any known physiological or anatomical systems within the body has caused acupuncture to be held in low regard by Western medicine. Indeed it is certainly true that acupuncture and other similar practices tend to flourish in parts of the world where orthodox medicine has made little progress or where doctors and trained staff are scarce.

Recent years however have seen a curious and unexpected revival of interest in acupuncture in Europe and America, prompted in large part by the considerable press publicity which has surrounded a number of major surgical operations performed without anaesthesia upon human patients and which have been witnessed by sceptical Western specialists. Considerable controversy still surrounds acupuncture and is likely to continue for many years—possibly because it is hard to envisage a theory to explain its effects which is consistent with orthodox medicine. No doubt the immensely powerful effects of suggestion and hypnosis need to be taken into account. Some recent discoveries on the psychology and physiology of pain which show that severe wound pain may be alleviated by electrical stimulation of the nerve endings in the site of the wound may also have some relevance. It is tempting to take the line that acupuncture is based on some "forgotten" or "hidden" medical system and to assume that it is only because Western scientists are blinkered and hide-bound that it is not being incorporated in a big way into European and American hospitals. But there are always two sides to an argument; whereas the first reports from Western specialists visiting China were filled with grudging acceptance and genuine puzzlement, more recent visitors have brought back a subtly different story. One of the world's leading experts on pain, for example, who has himself witnessed acupuncture-based surgery, reports four significant findings: (1) contrary to earlier reports, patients *are* sedated, sometimes heavily so, before surgery;(2) those patients who do go for surgery using acupuncture are only chosen after a fairly rigorous selection procedure to see whether they have complete faith in the method; (3) acupuncture does not appear to

work with children; and (4) its use appears to be on the decline in the major hospitals in China. Despite this rather sceptical analysis, it is clear that the full story about acupuncture, its nature and its practical value has not yet been told.

Adlerian Psychology. In 1911 the Viennese psychoanalyst Alfred Adler (1870–1937) together with his colleague Carl Gustav Jung broke with their friend Sigmund Freud over disputes concerning the latter's theoretic approach to psychoanalysis. Jung and Adler were themselves shortly also to part company, each to set up and develop his own "school" of psychoanalysis. Adler's system of psychotherapy is based on the idea, not of sex as a driving force as in the case of Freud, but on the concept of "compensation" or a drive for power in an attempt to overcome the "inferiority complex" which he held to be universal in human beings. The child naturally feels inferior to adults, but bullying, making him feel insignificant or guilty or contemptible, even spoiling, which makes him feel important within the family but relatively unimportant outside, increases this feeling. Or the child may have physical defects: he may be small or underweight, have to wear glasses, become lame, be constantly ill, or stupid at school. In these ways he develops a sense of inferiority which for the rest of his life he develops a technique to overcome.

This may be done in several ways: he may try to become capable in the very respects in which he feels incompetent—hence many great orators have originally had speech defects; many painters poor eyesight; many musicians have been partially deaf; like Nietzsche, the weakling, he may write about the superman, or like Sandow, the strong man, be born with poor health.

On the other hand he may overdo his attempt and overcompensate. Hence we have the bully who is really a coward, the small man who is self-assertive to an objectionable degree (Hitler, Napoleon, Stalin, and Mussolini were all small men) or the foreigner who like three of these men wanted to be the hero of his adopted country—Hitler the Austrian, Napoleon the Italian, Stalin the Georgian.

But what about the man who can do none of these things, who continues to fail to compensate? He, says Adler, becomes a neurotic because neurosis is an excuse which means "I could have done so-and-so but ..." It is the unconscious flight into illness—the desire to be ill. Adler's treatment involves disclosing these subterfuges we play on ourselves so that we can deal with the real situation in a more realistic way. Adlerian psychoanalysis still attracts supporters, but its golden days were when the founder was at the head of the movement in the U.S.A., when his views were considered to provide a more "acceptable" theory of the mind than the enormously controversial theories of Freud with their strong sexual orientation.

Adventists, a group of American religious sects, the most familiar being the Seventh-Day Adventist Church, which observes Saturday as the true Sabbath. With more than a million members throughout the world, it shares with other Adventists a belief in the imminent second coming of Christ (a doctrine fairly widespread in the U.S.A. during the early decades of the 19th cent. when the end of the world was predicted by William Miller for 1843, then for 1844). Modern Adventists content themselves with the conviction that the "signs" of the Advent are multiplying, the "blessed event" which will solve the world's ills. Believers will be saved, but the sects differ as to whether the unjust will be tortured in hell, annihilated, or merely remain asleep eternally.

Agnosticism. See **God and Man.**

Albigenses, also known as Cathari. French heretical sect (named after the town of Albi in Provence) which appeared in the 11th cent. to challenge the Catholic Church on the way true Christians should lead their lives. They followed a life of extreme asceticism in contrast to the local clergy and their faith was adopted by the mass of the population, especially in Toulouse. Condemned as heretics by Pope Innocent III, the sect was exterminated in the savage Albigensian Crusade (1208–29), initially led by Simon de Montfort. (In his thoroughness, de Montfort also succeeded in destroying the high culture of the Troubadours.)

Alchemy, ancient art associated with magic and astrology in which modern chemistry has its roots. The earliest mention of alchemy comes from ancient Egypt but its later practitioners attributed its origins to such varied sources as the fallen angels of the Bible, to Moses and Aaron, but most commonly to Hermes Trismegistus, often identified with the Egyptian god Thoth, whose knowledge of the divine art was handed down only to the sons of kings (cf. the phrase "hermetically sealed"). Its main object was the transmutation of metals. Egyptian speculation concerning this reached its height during the 6th cent. in the Alexandrian period. Brought to Western Europe by the Moslems, one of its most famous Arab exponents was Jabir (c. 760–c. 815), known to the Latins as Geber, who had a laboratory at Kufa on the Tigris. One school of early Greek philosophy held that there was ultimately only one elemental matter of which everything was composed. Such men as Albertus Magnus (1206–80) and Roger Bacon (1214–94) assumed that, by removing impurities, this *materia prima* could be obtained. Although Bacon's ideas were in many ways ahead of his time, he firmly believed in the philosopher's stone, which could turn base metals into gold, and in an elixir of life which would give eternal youth. Modern science has, of course, shown in its researches into radioactivity, the possibility of transmutation of certain elements, but this phenomenon has little bearing on either the methods of the alchemist or the mysteries with which he surrounded them. In line with the current considerable revival of interest in the occult, alchemy appears to be staging a comeback, at least as a literary if not an experimental topic.

Anabaptists. See **Baptists.**

Analytical Psychology, the name given by Carl Gustav Jung (1875–1961) of Zürich to his system of psychology, which, like Adler's (see **Adlerian Psychology**), took its origin from Freud's psychoanalysis from which both diverged in 1911. Briefly, Jung differed from Freud: (1) in believing that the latter had laid too much emphasis on the sexual drive as the basic one in man and replacing it with the concept of *libido* or life energy of which sex forms a part; (2) in his theory of types: men are either extrovert or introvert (*i.e.* their interest is turned primarily outwards to the world or inwards to the self), and they apprehend experience in four main ways, one or other of which is predominant in any given individual— sensing, feeling, thinking, or intuiting; (3) in his belief that the individual's unconscious mind contains not only repressed materials which, as Freud maintained, were too unpleasant to be allowed into awareness, but also faculties which had not been allowed to develop—*e.g.,* the emotional side of the too rational man, the feminine side of the too masculine one; (4) in the importance he attaches to the existence of a

collective unconscious at a still deeper level which contains traces of ancient ways of thought which mankind has inherited over the centuries. These are the *archetypes* and include primitive notions of magic, spirits and witches, birth and death, gods, virgin mothers, resurrection, etc. In the treatment of the neuroses Jung believed in the importance of (a) the present situation which the patient refuses to face; (b) the bringing together of conscious and unconscious and integrating them.

In the 1940s and 50s interest in Jung's ideas waned, at least in academic circles, as the emphasis among experimental psychologists shifted closer and closer to the "hard" scientific line. This was also true in the field of psychoanalysis where the Jungian as opposed to the Freudian point of view became progressively less popular. At the present time this trend is beginning to reverse, and while Jung's offbeat views on astrology, telepathy, etc., are still unfashionable, a reappraisal of the significance of his views on the nature of the unconscious is taking place and many psychologists feel that his contribution to our understanding of the nature of human mental processes has been greatly underrated. See also **Psychoanalysis.**

Anarchism, a political philosophy which holds, in the words of the American anarchist Josiah Warren (1798–1874), an early follower of Robert Owen, that "every man should be his own government, his own law, his own church." The idea that governmental interference or even the mere existence of authority is inherently bad is as old as Zeno, the Greek Stoic philosopher, who believed that compulsion perverts the normal nature of man. William Godwin's *Enquiry Concerning Political Justice* (1793) was the first systematic exposition of the doctrine. Godwin (father-in-law of Shelley) claimed that man is by nature sociable, co-operative, rational, and good when given the choice to act freely; that under such conditions men will form voluntary groups to work in complete social harmony. Such groups or communities would be based on equality of income, no state control, and no property: this state of affairs would be brought about by rational discussion and persuasion rather than by revolution.

The French economist Proudhon (1809–65) was the first to bring anarchism to the status of a mass movement. In his book *What is Property?* he stated bluntly that "property is theft" and "governments are the scourge of God". He urged the formation of co-operative credit banks where money could be had without interest and goods would be exchanged at cost value at a rate representing the hours of work needed to produce each commodity. Like Godwin, he disapproved of violence but, unlike Marx, disapproved of trade unions as representing organised groups.

In communistic anarchism these ideas were combined with a revolutionary philosophy, primarily by the Russians Michael Bakunin (1814–76) and Peter Kropotkin (1842–1921) who favoured training workers in the technique of "direct action" to overthrow the state by all possible means, including political assassination. In 1868 anarchists joined the First International which broke up a few years later after a bitter struggle between Bakuninists and Marxists. Subsequently small anarchist groups murdered such political figures as Tsar Alexander II of Russia, King Humbert of Italy, Presidents Carnot of France and MacKinley of America, and the Empress Elizabeth of Austria.

Anarchism and communism differ in three main ways: (1) anarchism forms no political party, rejects all relationship with established authority, and regards democratic reform as a setback; (2) communism is against capitalism, anarchism against the state as such; (3) both have the final goal of a classless society, but anarchism rejects the idea of an intermediate period of socialist state control accepted by communism. Philosophical anarchists, such as the American writer Henry David Thoreau (1817–62), were primarily individualists who believed in a return to nature, the non-payment of taxes, and passive resistance to state control;

in these respects Thoreau strongly influenced Gandhi as did the Christian anarchist Tolstoy.

Anarchism has traditionally been criticised as being impractical—*e.g.*, in a non-authoritarian society, who is going to look after the sewers or clean the streets?—and there is a good deal of force to this argument. In fact anarchistic ideas became progressively less fashionable in the first half of this century. A curious and probably significant revival of interest has taken place in the past decade, however, probably because of a growing sense of disillusion, particularly on the part of young people, with the progress of orthodox political systems. *See also* **Syndicalism.**

Anglicanism, adherence to the doctrine and discipline of the Anglican Church, as the genuine representative of the Catholic Church. *See* **Church of England.**

Anglo-Catholicism. To Queen Elizabeth I the Church of England was that of the "middle way" in which human reason and commonsense took their place beside Scripture and Church authority. The extent to which these various factors are stressed creates the distinctions between "high" and "low" church. Anglo-Catholics tend to reject the term "Protestant" and stress the term "Catholic" and, although few accept the infallibility of the Pope some Anglo-Catholic churches have introduced much or all of the Roman ritual and teach Roman dogmas. *See* **Catholicism, Tractarianism.**

Animism. To early man and in primitive societies the distinction between animate and inanimate objects was not always obvious—it is not enough to say that living things move and non-living things do not, for leaves blow about in the wind and streams flow down a hillside. In the religions of early societies, therefore, we find a tendency to believe that life exists in all objects from rocks and pools to seas and mountains. This belief is technically known as *animatism*, which differs from *animism*, a somewhat more sophisticated view which holds that natural objects have no life in themselves but may be the abode of dead people, spirits, or gods who occasionally give them the appearance of life. The classic example of this, of course, is the assumption that an erupting volcano is an expression of anger on the part of the god who resides in it. Such beliefs may seem absurd today, but it is worth realising that we are not entirely free of them ourselves when we ascribe "personalities" of a limited kind to motor cars, boats, dolls, or models which incur our pleasure or anger depending upon how well they "behave".

Anthropomorphism, the atttibution of human form, thoughts or motives to non-human entities or life forms from gods to animals. At one end this can be summed up in the once widespread image of God as a "white-bearded old gentleman sitting on a cloud." At the other end is the very common tendency to invest domestic animals and pets with man-like wishes and personalities. At both extremes the belief could be seriously misleading. Firstly, it could be very unwise to assume that God, if he exists, necessarily thinks as humans do and has human interests at heart. Secondly, we shall learn very little about animal behaviour if we look upon them as mere extensions of our own personality, and we do them less than justice if we see them simply as human beings of diminutive intelligence.

Anthroposophy, a school of religious and philosophical thought based on the work of the German educationist and mystic Rudolf Steiner (1861–1925). Steiner was originally an adherent of Madame Blavatsky's theosophical movement (*cf* Theosophy) but in 1913 broke away to form his own splinter group, the Anthroposophical Society, following ideological disputes over the alleged "divinity" of the Indian boy Krishnamurti. Steiner was much influenced by the German poet and scientist, Goethe, and believed that an appreciation and love for art was one of the keys to spiritual development. One of the first tasks of his new movement was the construction of a vast temple of arts and sciences, known as the Goetheanum, to act as the headquarters of the society. This structure, which was of striking and revolutionary architectural style, was unfortunately burnt down in 1922 to be replaced by an even more imaginative one which today is one of the most interesting buildings of its kind in the world. Anthroposophy, which ceased to expand greatly following its founder's death, is nevertheless well-established in various parts of the world with specialised, and often very well equipped, schools and clinics which propagate the educational and therapeutic theories of the movement. These, which include the allegedly beneficial powers of music, coloured lights, etc., have made little impact on modern educational ideas, but the schools have acquired a reputation for success in the training of mentally handicapped children, though one suspects that these successes are due to the patience and tolerance exercised in these establishments rather than to the curative value of colour or music "therapy" itself. Despite its apparent eccentricities, anthroposophy has made its mark on art and architecture, the outstanding modern painter Kandinsky, for example, being particularly influenced by Steiner's ideas and teachings.

Anticlericalism, resentment of priestly powers and privileges, traceable in England to Wyclif's insistence in the 14th cent. on the right of all men to have access to the Scriptures. The translation of the Bible into the common tongue was a great landmark in the history of the Bible and the English language. Wyclif's principles were condemned by the Roman Church of his time but were readily accepted during the Reformation. Tudor anticlericalism arose from motives ranging from a greedy desire to plunder the riches of the Church to a genuine dislike of the powers of the priesthood whose spiritual courts still had the right to decide on points of doctrine or morals in an age when the layman felt he was well able to decide for himself. In innumerable ways the Church was permitted to extort money from the laity. It is generally agreed, says Trevelyan, that the final submission of church to state in England was motivated quite as much by anticlericalism as by Protestantism. The rise of the Reformed churches in England satisfied the people generally and anticlericalism never became the fixed principle of permanent parties as happened in France and Italy from the time of Voltaire onwards.

Antisemitism, a term first applied about the middle of the last century to those who were anti-Jewish in their outlook. Although this attitude was prevalent for religious reasons throughout the Middle Ages, modern antisemitism differed (*a*) in being largely motivated by economic or political conditions, and (*b*) in being doctrinaire with a pseudo-scientific rationale presented by such men as Gobineau (1816–82) and Houston Stewart Chamberlain (1855–1927), and later by the Nazi and Fascist "philosophers". Beginning in Russia and Hungary with the pogroms of 1882 it gradually spread south and westwards where, in France, the Dreyfus case provided an unsavoury example in 1894. Thousands of Jews from Eastern Europe fled to Britain and America during this period; for in these countries antisemitism has rarely been more than a personal eccentricity. During the last war the murder of six million Jews by the Nazis and their accomplices led to a further exodus to various parts of the world and finally to the creation of the state of Israel.

The individual Jew-hater makes unconscious use of the psychological processes of projection and displacement: his greed or sexual guilt is projected on to the Jew (or Negro or Catholic) because he cannot bear to accept them as his own emotions, and his sense of failure in life is blamed on his chosen scapegoat rather than on his own inadequacy.

But there are social causes too and politicians in some lands are well versed in the technique of blaming unsatisfactory conditions (which they themselves may have in part produced) upon minority groups and persuading others to do the same. Historically, the Jew is ideally suited for this role of scapegoat; (1) in the Middle Ages when usury was forbidden to Christians but not to Jews, the latter often became moneylenders incurring the opprobrium generally associated with this trade (*e.g.*, to the simple-minded Russian peasant the Jew often represented, not only the "Christ-killer", but also the moneylender or small shopkeeper to whom he owed money); (2) many trades being closed to Jews, it was natural that they concentrated in others, thus arousing suspicions of "influence" (*i.e.* Jews are felt to occupy a place in certain trades and professions which far exceeds their numerical proportion to the population as a whole); (3) even with the ending of ghetto life, Jews often occupy *en masse* some parts of cities rather than others and this may lead to resentment on the part of the original inhabitants who begin to feel themselves dispossessed; (4) Jews tend to form a closed society and incur the suspicions attached to all closed societies within which social contacts are largely limited to members; marriage outside the group is forbidden or strongly disapproved of, and the preservation, among the orthodox, of cultural and religious barriers tends to isolate them from their fellow citizens. Discrimination is a common phenomenon. There is often prejudice against minority groups if they are perceived as 'exclusive' or 'foreign'. *See* **Racism, Zionism, Judaism.**

Anti-vivisection, opposition to scientific experimentation upon live animals based, according to its supporters, both on the moral grounds of the suffering imposed, and on the less secure claim that many doctors and scientists of repute have rejected the value of information gained in this way. It is true that the protagonists of the movement during its early days in the mid-19th cent. included a number of eminent physicians and surgeons, but few today—whatever their moral scruples—would deny the value of the results obtained. Without animal experiments we would be unable to test out new drugs for safety before using them on human beings. There are in Britain two or three large national anti-vivisection societies and several smaller ones. Much of their work is co-ordinated through the British Council of Anti-Vivisection Societies. Animal experimentation is controlled by Act of Parliament which makes obligatory the possession of licences by experimenters, inspection of laboratories by the Home Office, and the issue of annual returns of experiments. Many people would like the number of experiments on animals reduced and the law changed to prohibit any experiments in which there is any risk of inflicting suffering. A recent opinion survey showed that while the public approves of medical experiment it strongly disapproves of animals being used for the testing of cosmetics and other chemicals which have nothing to do with medical research. Reform of the Cruelty to Animals Act 1876 has been called for in view of the enormous increase in the number and variety of live animal experiments.

Apartheid, an Afrikaans word meaning "apartness," referred to by South African Government spokesmen as "separate development" or "self-development". To others it means the system of total racial discrimination between black and white South Africans—the permanent inhabitants of the country—as enforced by the National Party since it came to power in 1948. Some degree of racial segregation has existed in South Aifrica since the earliest days of colonialism in the mid-17th cent. and the policy was continued by the United Party under Smuts and Hertzog from 1934 onwards though it was never a political issue. This changed when the National Party gained power and oppressive measures against the non-white segment of the population have grown steadily under Malan, Strydom, Verwoerd, and Vorster. *Apartheid* involves the beliefs in racial purity and *baaskap*, or white supremacy. It means keeping vast African populations in a condition of helotry. Thousands of families are broken up by the pass laws. The official policy of the South African Government is to create separate self-governing black states in which the Africans would be guided to self-government and, it is claimed, eventually to independence. The first so-called Bantu reserve was set up in the Transkei in 1962. But Africans with 70 per cent of the population would have only about 13 percent of the land, and the poorest land at that: cities and mineral areas would remain the reserve of the whites. Total *apartheid* or complete separation of the black and white races in South Africa remains unlikely to be realised since mining, the main industry of the country, is based on low-paid African labour.

The sports boycott, the conflict between the churches and the government, and the economic need to make more use of African labour, could bring an impetus for change. The increasing economic power of some of the black African states—Nigeria for example, is rich in oil resources—and the elimination of "Europeanism" from the Arab cultures of the North, have led to a steady erosion of the power-base of the white dominant countries such as South Africa. Inevitably, *apartheid* has shown signs of reaction in response to these external pressures. In 1985, the laws prohibiting inter-racial sex and marriage were abolished. However the harsh suppression of disturbances in the troubled Eastern Cape has increasingly isolated South Africa. *See also* **Africa, Section C, Part II.**

Aquarius, one of the twelve "signs of the Zodiac". This has recently achieved special significance in the mythology of our time because of the pronouncements of astrologers that the world is shifting out of the 2000-years-old cycle of the Age of Pisces, the fish, into that of Aquarius the water-carrier. The exact date of the transition is a matter of astrological controversy, but the consensus is that it began in 1960 and will be completed sometime in the 24th century. The Aquarian Age is predicted to be one of peace and harmony, replacing the era of strife which, ironically, has marked the dominance of the Christian symbol of the fish. Such speculations are totally without scientific backing and are mentioned here only to draw attention to the grip which astrological and other mythical concepts still have on human thinking. One of the first spaceships to carry man to the moon, for example, was named Aquarius by its crew. *See also* **Astrology.**

Arianism, formed the subject of the first great controversy within the Christian Church over the doctrine of Arius of Alexandria (d. 336) who denied the divinity of Christ. The doctrine, although at first influential, was condemned at the Council of Nicaea (325), called by the Emperor Constantine, at which Arius was opposed by Athanasius, also of Alexandria, who maintained the now orthodox view that the Son is of one substance with the Father. Arius was banished but the heresy persisted until the 7th cent., especially among the barbarians, the Goths, Vandals and Lombards. Disbelief in the divinity of Christ has formed part of the doctrine of many minor sects since, notably in **Unitarianism** (*q.v.*).

Assassins, a sect of Moslem Shi'ites, founded by the Persian Hasan i Sabbah (*c.* 1090), which for more than two centuries established a rule of terror all over Persia and Syria. The coming of the Mongols in 1256 destroyed them in Persia and the Syrian branch suffered a similar fate at the hands of the then Mamluk sultan of Egypt, *c.* 1270. It was a secret order, ruled over by a grand master, under whom the members were strictly organised into classes, according to the degree of initiation into the secrets of the order. The devotees, belonging to one of the lower groups, carried out the actual assassinations under strict laws of obedience, and total ignorance of the objects and ritual of the society. It is believed that the latter were given ecstatic visions under the influence of hashish, whence the term *hashshashin*, which became corrupted to "assassin".

Associationism. In psychology, the Associationist school of the 19th cent. accepted the association of ideas as the fundamental principle in mental life. It was represented in Britain by the two Mills and Herbert Spencer, in Germany by J. F. Herbart (1776–1841). To these, mental activity was nothing but the association of "ideas" conceived of as units of both thought and feeling—the emotion of anger or the perception of a chair were both "ideas"—and apart from them the self did not exist. Personality was simply a series of these units coming and going, adding to or cancelling each other out, in accordance with rigid and mechanistic scientific laws.

Astrology was once the best available theory for explaining the course of human life and bears much the same historical relationship to astronomy as alchemy does to chemistry. Originally it was divided into the two branches of Natural Astrology which dealt with the movements of the heavenly bodies and their calculations, and Judicial Astrology which studied the alleged influence of the stars and the planets on human life and fate. It was the former that developed into modern astronomy; the latter was, and remains, a primitive myth.

Astrology owes most to the early Babylonians (or Chaldeans) who, being largely nomadic in an environment which permitted an unobstructed view of the sky, readily accepted the idea that divine energy is manifested in the movements of the sun and planets. Gradually this concept became enlarged and the relative positions of the planets both in relation to each other and to the fixed stars became important together with the idea of omens—that, if a particular event occurred whilst the planets were in a particular position, the recurrence of that position heralded a recurrence of the same sort of event. Soon the planets became associated with almost every aspect of human life. They were bound up with the emotions, with parts of the body, so that astrology played quite a large part in medicine up to late mediaeval times. Not only was the position of the planet to be considered but also the particular sign of the zodiac (or house of heaven) it was occupying, and it was believed possible to foretell the destiny of an individual by calculating which star was in the ascendant (*i.e.* the sign of the zodiac nearest the eastern horizon and the star which arose at that precise moment) at the time of his birth. Astrology was popular among the Egyptians, the Romans (whose authorities found the Chaldean astrologers a nuisance and expelled them from time to time), and during the Middle Ages when astrologers were often highly respected.

Despite the apparent absurdity of astrological beliefs—for example, how could the pattern of light from stars billions of miles away possibly influence the temperament of single individuals on earth—a substantial number of intelligent and well-educated people take its study in all seriousness. The most interesting "convert" was the psychologist and philosopher, Carl Jung, who conducted a complex experiment in which he compared the "birth signs" of happily married and divorced couples and claimed to find that those most favourably matched in astrological terms were also those more likely to have permanent wedded bliss. Jung's findings were subsequently shown to have been based on a simple statistical fallacy, which did not prevent the brilliant but eccentric psychologist from offering them up as evidence in support of his own theory of "synchronicity" (**J51**), an involved and vaguely metaphysical notion which suggests that events in the universe may be significantly related in a "non-causal" fashion. To add fuel to the controversy however, the French mathematician, Michel Gauquelin, has recently offered up fresh data which apparently supports the general astrological view. In a carefully controlled study he noticed statistically significant correspondences between certain astrological signs and the professions of a large number of Frenchmen whose birth time and date were accurately recorded. Gauquelin claims to have repeated his study on a second large sample of his fellow countrymen, though he has been unable to use English people as the exact times of birth are not recorded on their birth certificates! This apparent shot in the arm for astrology is still a matter of great scientific controversy, though Gauquelin's work has been given support from the distinguished British psychologist, H. J. Eysenck, who has pronounced his statistical data to to be incontrovertible. Both scientists, however, carefully refrain from discussing the implications of these curious findings, and the controversy will no doubt increase rather than decrease in the near future.

Atheism. *See* **God and Man.**

Atlantis, a mythical continent supposed to have lain somewhere between Europe and America and a centre of advanced civilisation before it was inundated by some great natural catastrophe in pre-Christian times. There is little, if any, serious historical or archaeological evidence for its existence, but the legend of the Golden Land destroyed when the waters of the Atlantic closed over it has remarkable staying power and is believed by large numbers of people. Plato wrote convincingly about the wonders of Atlantis in his dialogues *Timaeus* and *Critias,* while other writers have suggested that the biblical story of the Flood is based on fragmentary accounts of the Atlantean deluge. The lost continent is also of occult significance, largely as the result of the writings of W. Scott-Elliott whose book, *The Story of Atlantis* (recently re-published by the Theosophical Society), alleged that by clairvoyance he had been able to contact the spirits of Atlanteans who had been destroyed because of their addiction to black magic. There even exists in Britain today a minor but ardent religious group, the "Atlanteans", who hold that Atlantis still exists today, but on a different metaphysical plane, and that it is possible to communicate with it via individuals with supposedly mediumistic powers (*see* **Spiritualism**). Members of the Atlanteans meet regularly to hear "trance addresses" by one of the high priests of Atlantis, Helio-Arconaphus. Such beliefs are essentially harmless and merely reflect the great variety of religious attitudes which human beings enjoy.

Atomism. In philosophy, the atomists were a group of early Greek thinkers, the most important of whom were Leucippus (fl. *c.* 440 B.C.) and his younger contemporary Democritus (*c.* 460–370 B.C.). Prior to these men, although it had been agreed that matter must be composed of tiny ultimate particles and that change must be due to the manner in which these mingled or separated from each other, it was supposed that there existed different types of particle for each material—*e.g.* for flesh, wood, hair, bone. The atomists taught that atoms were all made of a single substance and differed only in the connections (pictured as hooks, grooves, points, etc.) which enabled them to join each other in characteristic ways. Theirs was the first move towards modern atomic theory and a predecessor of the modern concept of chemical linkages.

Authoritarianism, a dictatorial form of government as contrasted with a democratic one based on popular sovereignty. Its alleged advantages are the avoidance of the delays and inefficiency said to be characteristic of the latter.

Automatism, the production of material, written or spoken in "automatic" fashion—*i.e.*, apparently not under the conscious or volitional control of the individual. This psychologically perplexing phenomenon has occurred from time to time throughout the history of literature and art, and while it has occasionally produced work of great merit (much of William Blake's poetry, Coleridge's "Kubla Khan", etc.) the bulk of it is indifferent and often simply rubbish. Spiritualists claim that the work is produced under the direct guidances of the spirit world, and their argument has attracted considerable attention through the compositions of the pianist Rosemary Brown who, with little or no academic background in musical theory, has produced a number of "original" piano pieces allegedly composed by Beethoven, Mozart, etc., from the astral plane. While few music critics doubt Mrs. Brown's honesty and integrity, most consider her work to be clever pastiche and barely comparable in quality to the masterworks of the dead composers. Nevertheless automatism wants some explaining, and most psychologists today defer judgement, taking the view that it serves to remind us of the fund of material which lies in the unconscious mind, and which is prone to pop up from time to time without warning. Rather similar is the case of Matthew Manning, a young English student who produced clever and artistically intriguing drawings and sketches, allegedly guided by the hands of famous dead artists.

B

Baconian Method, the use of the inductive (as opposed to the deductive or Aristotelian) method of reasoning as proposed by Francis Bacon in the 17th cent. and J. S. Mill in the 19th cent. Deduction argues from supposedly certain first principles (such as the existence of God or Descartes's "I think, therefore I am") what the nature of the universe and its laws *must* be, whereas the only means of obtaining true knowledge of the universe, in Bacon's view, was by the amassing of facts and observations so that when enough were obtained the certain truth would be known in the same way that a child's numbered dots in a playbook joined together by a pencilled line create a picture. However, this is not the way science progresses in practice (*see* **F3(1)**). Bacon underrated the importance of hypothesis and theory and overrated the reliability of the senses. In discussing the scientific tradition, Sir Karl Popper in his book, *Conjecture and Refutations,* says: "The most important function of observation and reasoning, and even of intuition and imagination, is to help us in the critical examination of those bold conjectures which are the means by which we probe into the unknown." Two of the greatest men who clearly saw that there was no such thing as an inductive procedure were Galileo and Einstein.

Bahá'í Faith, a faith which teaches the unity of all religions and the unity of mankind. It arose in Iran from the teachings of the Bab (Mirza Ali Mohammed, 1820–50) and the Bahá'u'lláh (Mirza Husain Ali, 1817–92), thought to be manifestations of God, who in his essence is unknowable. Emphasis is laid on service to others. It has communities in many states and is surprisingly strong in England with a substantial following among university students. Its aims—universal peace, love, fellowship, sexual equality, etc.—are so laudable that it is hard to disagree with anything in the movement. Since the ruling Ayatollah Khomeini's fundamentalist Islamic regime came to power in Iran in 1979 members of the faith have been persecuted and a number of women who refused to recant were executed in 1983. The movement is now guided and administered by an elected order, "The Universal House of Justice".

Baptists, a Christian denomination whose distinctive doctrines are that members can only be received by baptism "upon the confession of their faith and sins" and that "baptism is no wise appertaineth to infants." Baptism is therefore by total immersion of adults. Modern Baptists base their doctrines upon the teaching of the Apostles and some hold that the Albigenses (*q.v.*) maintained the true belief through what they regarded as the corruption of the Roman Church in mediaeval times. On the other hand any connection with the Anabaptist movement during the Reformation is rejected and the beginning of the modern Church is traced to John Smyth, a minister of the Church of England who in Amsterdam came under the influence of the Arminians (*q.v.*) and Mennonites. Smyth died in 1612 when the first Baptist church in England was built at Newgate. This, the "General" Baptist Church, rejected Calvinistic beliefs and held the Arminian doctrine of redemption open to all, but some years later a split occurred with the formation of the "Particular" Baptist Church which was Calvinist in doctrine. In 1891 the two bodies were united in the Baptist Union and today the sect is spread throughout the world, notably in the United States.

The Anabaptist movements of Germany, Switzerland, and Holland also practised adult baptism in addition to a primitive communism and demanded social reforms. Persecuted by both Catholics and Protestants, their leader, Thomas Münzer, and many others were burned at the stake (1525). However, this sect was noted for its violence under a religious guise, and its taking over of the state of Münster in 1533 was characterised by wild licentiousness, since, as Antinomians, they believed that the "elect" could do no wrong. A revival begun by Menno Simons (d. 1561), a Dutch religious reformer, led to the formation of the Mennonite

sect which, whilst rejecting infant baptism, gave up the objectionable features of the Anabaptists. This reformed sect still exists as small agricultural groups in the original strongholds of the movement and in the United States.

Beat Generation, a term first used by the American writer Jack Kerouac (d. 1969), author of *The Town and the City* and *On the Road,* to define various groups spread across the face of the country, but notably in New York and San Francisco, who, belonging to the post-war generation, represented a complex of attitudes. Briefly, these were: rejection of the values of the past and lack of conviction in the possibility of a future for humanity—hence an acceptance of nothing but the immediate present in terms of experience and sensations; rebellion against organised authority, not out of any political conviction (as in the case of anarchism), but rather from lack of any interest or desire to control events, nature, or people; contempt for the "Square"—the orthodox individual who, stuck firmly in his rut, "plays it safe" and remains confident of the rightness and decency of his moral values.

The Beat Generation of the 1940s and 50s gave way to the Love generation or Flower people, with their flowers, beads, and cowbells. Their social philosophy was the same—living in the present, unconventionally, seeking personal freedom, believing drugs to be essential, claiming to be acting against the rat race, dissociating themselves from politics, taking a superficial interest in the religions of the East, borrowing much of their language, music, and ideas on dress from the American *"hippy"*; yet believing in the creation of a new and gentler society based on different forms and values.

Both the Beat and Love generations were forerunners in America of an increasing and certainly welcome social awareness on the part of American students. This led in turn to the "campus revolutions" which were disruptive in their early stages but were also influential as part of the wave of public protest against the American involvement in Vietnam.

Behaviourism, a school of psychology founded in 1914 by J. B. Watson (1878–1958), an animal psychologist at Johns Hopkins University, Baltimore. Its main tenet was that the method of introspection and the study of mental states were unscientific and should be replaced by the study of behaviour. When animals or human beings were exposed to specific stimuli and their responses objectively recorded, or when the development of a child, as seen in its changing behaviour, was noted, these alone were methods which were truly scientific. Watson contributed an important idea to psychology and did a great deal towards ridding it of the largely philosophical speculations of the past. But he also went to absurd extremes, as in his view that thought is nothing but subvocal speech, consisting of almost imperceptible movements of the tongue, throat, and larynx (*i.e.,* when we think, we are really talking to ourselves), and his further opinion that heredity is, except in grossly abnormal cases, of no importance. He claimed that by "conditioning", the ordinary individual could be made into any desired type, regardless of his or her inheritance.

The work of Ivan Pavlov had begun about 1901, but was unknown in America until about ten years later, and it was through another Russian, Vladimir Bekhterev, that the concept of "conditioning" was introduced into the country. Bekhterev's book *Objective Psychology,* describing his new science of "reflexology". was translated in 1913 and played a great part in the development of Behaviourist ideas. The conditioned reflex became central to Watson's theory of learning and habit, formation (*e.g.,* he showed that a year-old child, at first unafraid of white rats, became afraid of them when they came to be associated with a loud noise behind the head). Finally all behaviour, including abnormal behaviour, came to be explained in terms of conditioned responses; these were built up by association on the infant's three innate emotions of fear, rage, and love, of which the original stimuli were, for the first, loud noises and the fear of falling; for the second, interference with freedom of movement; and for the third, patting and stroking.

Because of its considerable theoretical simplicity and its implicit suggestion that human behaviour could be easily described (and even modified or controlled), Pavlovian psychology appeared very attractive to the Communist regime in Russia, and before long it became the "official" dogma in universities and research laboratories. Whereas in America and Western Europe its severe limitations became gradually apparent, in Russia these were ignored or disguised for ideological reasons with the inevitable outcome that Soviet psychology failed to evolve and, at one stage, seemed to be no more than a pallid offshoot of physiology. The recent liberalisation which has been taking place throughout Soviet society has led to a considerable broadening of scientific horizons and Pavlovian ideas are no longer looked upon with such unquestioning reverence. In non-Communist countries simple Watsonian behaviourism has evolved into more sophisticated studies of animal learning, largely pioneered by the Harvard psychologist, Skinner. These techniques, which have shown that animals, from monkeys to rats, may be taught to solve a remarkable range of physical problems (such as pressing complex sequences of buttons or levers to escape from a cage) have themselves turned out to be rather disappointing in terms of advancing our general understanding of the workings of the human and animal brain. There is a growing feeling among psychologists that the real keys to the understanding of mankind will only be found through the study of man himself, and not his simpler animal cousins. *See also* **Gestalt Psychology** and **Q18-20**.

Benthamism. *See* **Utilitarianism**.

Black Power. The division of the world's population into races is now generally agreed by scientists to have arisen as the result of climatic and environmental pressures—the darker, more highly pigmented peoples tending to be better equipped to withstand higher solar output than the fairer, more northerly based types. For various reasons, again largely climatic and environmental, the first great advances in civilisation came from the temporary ascendancy over the black or near-black. Until quite recently—not much more than century ago—the technological gulf between white and black was so vast that the negroid races were often held in slavery by the Europeans and while such a thought might be repugnant to most today, attitudes to coloured people still reflect a notion of inherent white "superiority" which it is easy to deny intellectually but difficult to shake off emotionally. In the U.S.A., the most advanced and at the same time the most tormented multi-racial society in the world, the role of the substantial negroid population has changed dramatically in the last hundred years, shifting from that of slave to friendly servant, and then to near, or theoretical, equal. With this shift has come a corresponding change in the black community's view of itself, from relief at being no longer slaves, to gratitude at being allowed to do the menial jobs in the American society. More recently, with advances in educational opportunity and increasing political liberalisation, the attitude of the Negro in the U.S.A. has shifted yet again—from subservience to intellectual and physical equality, and even, perhaps, to inherent superiority. This new stand, rare at first, but spreading rapidly across America and other parts of the world throughout the 1960s, has crystallised in the concept and ideology of "Black Power". a movement of growing significance and importance in modern society. It is hard to trace the moment at which this formally emerged but one of its first expressions was the use by Negroes of the phrase "Black is beautiful", an apparent wakening of the belief that their colour, physique, features, hair, etc., were in no way aesthetically inferior to those of Europeans. Suddenly, in Negro communities it became no longer fashionable to straighten hair artificially, to bleach the skin or even to copy white American clothing, social habits, speech, and mannerisms. Alongside this highly important

psychological jump—a rejection of the white man's social patterns—came an increasing rejection of his political machinery as well, a belief that the black races should have political autonomy and power of their own and not as part of an integrationist evolution of Caucasian societies.

In the late 60s when the Black Power movement was in its most aggressive phase of expansion, there were real fears that open conflict, almost of civil war dimensions, might break out in American cities, but increasing liberalisation and better opportunities for social advancement and education for Negroes has slightly dulled its sense of purpose. The 70s in fact saw a dramatic change in the state of the American Negro, with blacks penetrating middle-class and professional strata of society—medicine, law, politics, business, science, etc.—at a rate which would have seemed incredible 20 years ago. Urban ghettoes, however, still exist and provide numerous flashpoints for black-white conflict—the city of Boston is a particularly good example—but most observers (black and white) now view the future with more optimism than pessimism. However, the fact that America is fast becoming the best integrated country in the world is at least partly due to the conflicts and injustices which launched Black Power into being. With the death of its leaders, George Jackson, Michael X, Malcolm X, Black Power in Britain has since the 1970s given way to Rastafarianism (*q.v.*).

Bolshevism, an alternative name for **Communism** (*q.v.*), usually used in the West in a derogatory sense. When the Russian Social Democratic Party at a conference held in London in 1903 split over the issue of radicalism or moderation, it was the radical faction headed by Lenin (who subsequently led the 1917 Revolution and became first Head of State of the Soviet Union) which polled the majority of votes. The Russian for majority is *bolshinstvo* and for minority *menshinstvo*; hence the radicals became known as Bolsheviki and the moderates as Mensheviki, anglicised as Bolsheviks and Mensheviks. *See* **Communism**, **Marxism**.

British Israelites, a religious group who hold the race-theory that the English-speaking peoples (of the White Race) are the lineal descendants of the "lost Ten Tribes" of Israel (deported by Sargon of Assyria on the fall of Samaria in 721 B.C.). They believe the Anglo-Saxons to be God's "Chosen People" in the literal sense of the term as it is used in the Old Testament by whom the world will be brought in readiness for the Millennium. The official organisation is the British-Israel World Federation of which the official journal is the *National Message*. Some British Israelites have the notion that the future can be foretold by the measurements of the Great Pyramid.

Buchmanism. *See* **Moral Re-Armament**.

Buddhism, one of the great Oriental religions. It arose against the background of Hinduism in north India in the 6th cent. B.C., its founder (real or legendary) being the Hindu prince Siddhartha Gautama, known as the Buddha or "Enlightened One". Distressed by the problem of human suffering from which even death allowed no escape—since Buddha accepted the Hindu doctrine of a cycle of lives—he left his palace and his beloved wife and child to become a religious mendicant and ascetic, studying without success for six years the beliefs of Brahmin hermits and self-torturing recluses. After this fruitless search he sat down under a tree (the Bo-tree) and finally came to understand the cause and cure of suffering. The result of his meditations are enshrined in the "four noble truths" which are: (1) that existence is unhappiness; (2) that unhappiness is caused by selfish desire or craving; (3) that desire can be destroyed; (4) that it can be destroyed by following the "noble eightfold path" whose steps are: right views; right desires; right speech, plain and truthful; right conduct, including abstinence not only from immorality but also from taking life, whether human or animal; right livelihood, harming no one; right effort, always pressing on; right awareness of the past, the present, and the future; and lastly, right contemplation or meditation. The more man acquires merit by following these rules in his chain of lives, the sooner is *Nirvana* attained; he loses his individuality, not by annihilation, but "as the dewdrop slips into the shining sea," by merging with the universal life.

Buddhism teaches the way of liberation through ethics and discipline. A universal God plays no part in this religion, and in many Buddhist nations no word exists for the concept which was neither affirmed not denied by Buddha himself but simply ignored. Nor did Buddha claim to be other than a man, although much superstition entered the religion at a later date; prayers were made to Buddha, ritual developed, sacred relics preserved under stupas, and the belief in a succession of Buddhas introduced; the sacred writings (*Tripitaka*) are divided into three parts; for the layman, the monks, the philosophers. They were produced by devotees at three councils—the first held immediately after the death of Buddha at the age of 80, the last at the order of King Asoka in 244 B.C. The founder himself wrote nothing.

Buddhism spread to Sri Lanka, Nepal, Tibet, Mongolia, Indo-China, Burma, Siam, China, and Japan, although on the whole losing influence in India. In Tibet, Buddhism developed into Lamaism (*q.v.*). In Sri Lanka and Burma it persisted in its pure form (the Hinayana), while in China and Japan it developed into the Mahayana with its bodhisattvas and avatars.

Bushido, the traditional code of honour of the Samurai or Japanese military caste corresponding to the European concept of knighthood and chivalry from which it took its separate origin in the 12th cent. Even today it is a potent influence among the upper classes, being based on the principles of simplicity, honesty, courage, and justice which together form a man's idea of personal honour.

C

Cabala, originally a collection of Jewish doctrines about the nature of the Universe, supposedly handed down by Moses to the Rabbis, which evolved into a kind of mystical interpretation of the Old Testament. Students of the history of religious belief have found its origins to be in fact extremely obscure, and some aspects appear to have been lifted from ancient Egyptian sources. Skilled Cabalists hold that the system contains a key to biblical interpretation based on the numerical values of the words and letters of the Scriptures which reveal hidden depths of meaning behind the allegorical Old Testament stories.

Calvinism, the branch of Protestantism founded basically (although preceded by Zwingli and others) by Jean Chauvin (1509–64), who was born in Noyon in Picardy. John Calvin, as he is usually called, from the Latin form of his name, Calvinius, provided in his *Institutions of the Christian Religion* the first logical definition and justification of Protestantism, thus becoming the intellectual leader of the Reformation as the older Martin Luther was its emotional instigator. The distinctive doctrine of Calvinism is its dogma of predestination which states that God has unalterably destined some souls to salvation to whom "efficacious grace and the gift of perseverance" is granted and others to eternal damnation. Calvinism, as defined in the Westminster Confession, is established in the Reformed or Presbyterian churches of France, Holland, Scotland, etc., as contrasted with the Lutheran churches, and its harsh but logical beliefs inspired the French Huguenots, the Dutch in their fight against Spanish Catholic domination, and the English Puritans. The rule set up under Calvin's influence in Geneva was marred by the burning at the stake of the anatomist Servetus for the heresy of "pantheism", or, as we should say, Unitarianism.

Perhaps its greatest single influence outside the Church was the result of Calvinist belief that

to labour industriously was one of God's commands. This changed the mediaeval notions of the blessedness of poverty and the wickedness of usury, proclaimed that men should shun luxury and be thrifty, yet implied that financial success was a mark of God's favour. In this way it was related to the rise of capitalism either as cause or effect. Max Weber, the German sociologist, believed that Calvinism was a powerful incentive to, or even cause of, the rise of **capitalism** (*q.v.*); Marx, Sombart, and in England, Tawney, have asserted the reverse view—that Calvinism was a result of developing capitalism, being its ideological justification.

Capitalism is an economic system under which the means of production and distribution are owned by a relatively small section of society which runs them at its own discretion for private profit. There exists, on the other hand, a propertyless class of those who exist by the sale of their labour power. Caplitalism arose towards the end of the 18th cent. in England where the early factory owners working with small-scale units naturally approved of free enterprise and free trade. But free enterprise has no necessary connection with capitalism; by the beginning of this century monopolies were developing and state protection against foreign competition was demanded. Capitalism is opposed by those who believe in socialism (*q.v.*), first, for the moral reasons that it leads to economic inequality and the exploitation of labour and the consuming public, and that public welfare rather than private profit should motivate the economic system; secondly, for the practical reason that capitalism leads to recurrent economic crises. The recent world economic crisis has led to great hopes on the part of Marxists and Communists that capitalism is now involved in its final death throes. It is worth commenting however, that the European war of the 1940s, the great depression of the 30s, the first world war and the Russian Revolution were also, in their turn, confidently held up by Communists as heralding capitalism's imminent collapse.

Cartomancy, the art of fortunes or predicting the future by playing cards or by the Tarot pack. The elegant Tarot cards number 78 in all and are probably mediaeval in origin. They are rich in symbolism and include trump cards depicting the devil, the pope, death, the moon, the wheel of fortune, etc., and are an interesting part of our cultural mythology. There is no evidence whatsoever that they can be used in any objective way to divine the future, and professional fortune tellers and clairvoyants who use them almost certainly rely on a little native, basic psychology to achieve their results.

Catholicism. For those who are not Roman Catholics the term "Catholic" has two separate meanings. The more general refers to the whole body of Christians throughout the world, the more specific refers to a particular view of Christianity. In this latter sense the Church of England, the Orthodox Eastern Churches, and others consider themselves "Catholic" meaning that (*a*) they belong to Christ's Church as organised on an accepted basis of faith and order; (*b*) they insist on the necessity of "liturgical" worship through established forms (*e.g.*, baptism, holy communion); (*c*) they emphasise the continuity of Christian tradition by the use of ancient creeds (*e.g.*, the Apostles' Creed, the Nicene Creed) and regard the ministry as a succession (Apostolic succession) deriving from early practice. In this sense there is thought to be no necessary contradiction between Catholicism and Protestantism regarded as a renewal of the Church in the 16th cent. by an appeal to the Scriptures as interpreted by the early Fathers of the Church. This definition obviously excludes Quakers, Christian Scientists, and many Nonconformist sects.

The Roman Catholic Church is the religious organisation of all those who acknowledge the bishop of Rome as head of the Christian Church, recognising him as the lawful successor of St. Peter, who was the apostle appointed by Christ to be the head of the Church.

Whereas in the Protestant Churches prayer and preaching play a central part (each individual soul seeking direct communication with God), in Roman Catholic worship the central service is the Mass, or Holy Eucharist, the seven sacraments (baptism, confirmation, eucharist, penance, extreme unction, orders, and marriage) being administered by a special priesthood. Church discipline and organisation are strong and authoritarian. See **Papal Infallibility**.

Characterology, the attempt made over many centuries to classify people into personality types on the basis of physical or psychological characteristics. The first attempt was made by Hippocrates in the 5th cent. B.C. who classified temperaments into the *sanguine* (or optimistic), the *melancholic*, the *choleric* (or aggressive), and the *phlegmatic* (or placid); these were supposed to result from the predominance of the following "humours" in the body: red blood, black bile, yellow bile, or phlegm respectively. Theophrastus, a pupil of Aristotle, described, with examples, thirty extreme types of personality (*e.g.* the talkative, the boorish, the miserly, etc.); these were basically literary and imaginative but about the same time "physiognomy" arose which attempted to interpret character from the face. Physiognomy became of importance again during the Renaissance and there are still those today who believe in it in spite of the fact that, broadly speaking, there is no connection whatever between facial features and personality (i.e. although it may be possible to tell from the features that a man is an idiot or some extreme abnormal type and some idea of character may be obtained from an individual's characteristic facial expressions, it is not possible to tell (as Johann Lavater, the best-known physiognomist of the late 18th cent. believed) from the shape of the nose, height of the brow, or dominance of the lower jaw, whether anyone is weak, intellectual or determined). The contention of the 19th cent. Italian criminologist Cesare Lombroso that criminals show typical facial characteristics—prominent cheekbones and jaw, slanting eyes, receding brow, large ears of a particular shape—was disproved by Karl Pearson early this century when he found that 3,000 criminals showed no significant differences of features, carefully measured from a similar number of students at Oxford and Cambridge.

It has, however, been noted that people in general tend to be intellectual or emotional, inward- or outward-looking, and this observation is reflected in the classification of the Scottish psychologist, Alexander Bain (d. 1903), into intellectual, artistic, and practical; Nietzsche's Apollonian and Dionysian types; William James's "tender" and "toughminded"; and C. G. Jung's introvert and extrovert. Careful experiments have shown that these are not clear-cut and that most individuals fall in between the extremes.

Some connection has been found between temperament and body-build. The German psychiatrist Ernst Kretschmer (b. 1888) showed that manic-depressive patients and normal people who are extroverted and tend to alternate in mood (as do manic-depressives to an exaggerated degree) were usually short and stout or thick-set in build; schizophrenics and normal people, who both show shyness, serious or introverted reactions, were usually tall and slender. The former of "pyknic" body-build are "cyclothyme" in temperament, the latter with "schizothyme" temperament are of two bodily types—the tall and thin or "asthenic" and the muscularly well-proportioned or "athletic". The American Sheldon has confirmed these observations on the whole and gone into further details. According to him the basic body types are: (1) *endomorphic* (rounded build), corresponding to Kretschmer's pyknic, normally associated with the *viscerotonic* temperament (relaxed, sociable); (2) *mesomorphic* (squarish, athletic build), normally associated with the *somatotonic* temperament (energetic, assertive); and (3) *ectomorphic* (linear build) normally associated with the *cerebrotonic* temperament (anxious, submissive, restless).

Glandular and metabolic factors have considerable effect on human personality and also, to some extent, on physique. It is not too surprising, therefore, to find an association between body build (or "somatotype" as Sheldon termed it) and general mood. However, Sheldon's original clear-cut and oversimplified categories of body-type are no longer looked upon as reliable indicators of personality.

Chartism, a socialistic movement in England (1837–55) which attempted to better the conditions of the working classes. Named after "The People's Charter" of Francis Place (1838), its programme demanded: (1) universal manhood suffrage; (2) vote by ballot; (3) equal electoral districts; (4) annual parliament; (5) payment of members; (6) abolition of their property qualifications. Chartism was supported by the Christian socialists (*q.v.*), J. F. D. Maurice (1805–72), and Charles Kingsley (1819–75) with certain qualifications. The movement, the first mass organisation of the industrial working class, had considerable influence on the evolution of socialist ideas in England. It is worth noting that its demands—with the exception of the unworkable "annual parliament"—have largely been met today, though at the time they were thought by many to be both outrageous and impossible.

Chauvinism, a term applied to any excessive devotion to cause, particularly a patriotic or military one. The word is derived from Nicholas Chauvin whose excessive devotion to Napoleon made him a laughing-stock.

Chirognomy, the attempt to read character from the lines in the hand (as contrasted with chiromancy or palmistry, in which an attempt is made to tell the future in the same way) is an ancient practice which, like astrology (*q.v.*) has no discernible scientific basis but a very considerable popular following. As with astrology, where it is hard to see what kind of link could exist between the constellations and human behaviour, so it is equally hard to see how the configuration of lines on the hand could be paralleled by psychological attributes. This argument might be thought of as irrelevant if palmistry, etc. actually had predictive power, but the plain fact is that when put to a scientific test, practitioners of these arts turn out to show no abilities beyond those with which a normally perceptive individual is equipped.

Chiropractice, the art of manipulation of the joints, in particular the spine, as a means of curing disease, is a slightly fashionable quasi-medical practice. Few qualified doctors employ its questionable principles though, as with its near-neighbour osteopathy, it seems on occasions to be a useful complement to medical treatment. Much controversy surrounds the status of practitioners of fringe medicine of this kind. In America osteopathy (bone manipulation), which seems to be beneficial in many cases for the condition known as prolapsed or "slipped" disc, is becoming gradually merged into orthodox medical practice.

Christadelphians, a religious denomination formed in the U.S.A. in the late 1840s by John Thomas, an Englishman from London. They claim to represent the simple apostolic faith of the 1st cent., and, in common with many other sects, hold that they alone interpret the Scriptures truly. They believe that Christ will return soon to set up the Kingdom of God with Jerusalem as its capital. In social life Christadelphians keep to themselves and hold aloof from organisational activities, though they do take an interest in political events if only from the point of view of their belief in biblical prophecy.

Christianity, the religion founded by Jesus Christ whose teaching is found in the New Testament's four Gospels. Simple as His creed may seem it soon became complicated by the various ways in which Christians interpreted it, and the differences within the early Church are reflected in the numerous Councils held to define truth from heresy. The Eastern Church of the Byzantine Empire from the 5th cent. onwards had differed in various ways from the See of Rome and by 1054 the breach became permanent. The 16th cent. Reformation was the other great break in the unity of the Church and once Protestantism had given in effect the right to each man to interpret the Scriptures in his own way, the tendency to fragmentation increased so that, by 1650, there were no fewer than 180 sects, mostly dogmatic and intolerant towards each other. Today there are many more, some of which are mentioned in this section under the appropriate headings. Nevertheless there are signs today that the trend of disunity is being reversed. The modern ecumenical movement, which has its roots in the great missionary movement of the 19th cent., aims to bring about a reunion of Christendom by uniting Christians throughout the world on the simple basis of the acceptance of Jesus Christ as God and Saviour, *i.e.*, on the basis of Christian fellowship. The movement finds expression in the World Council of Churches (*q.v.*). The Christian life is expressed in the words of Christ: "Thou shalt love the Lord thy God with all thy heart and thy neighbour as thyself." For many it is the humanitarian side of Christianity that has meaning today; to accept responsibility for others, as well as for oneself. *See chart, below.*

Christian Science claims that it is a religion based on the words and works of Christ Jesus. It draws its authority from the Bible, and its teachings are set forth in *Science and Health with Key to the Scriptures* by Mary Baker Eddy (1821–1910) the discoverer and founder of Christian Science. A distinctive part of Christian Science is its healing of physical disease as well as sin by spiritual means alone.

The Church of Christ, Scientist, was founded in 1879 when 15 students of Mrs Eddy met with their teacher and voted to organize the words and works of the Master, which should reinstate primitive Christianity and its lost element of healing.

A few years later the church took its present and permanent form as The Mother Church, The First Church of Christ, Scientist, in Boston, Massachusetts, which together with its branch churches and societies throughout the world, constitutes the Christian Science denomination. Less than 100 years after its founding there were some 3,300 branches in 58 countries, as well as numerous informal groups not yet organized and about 500 organizations at universities and colleges.

Christian Socialism, a movement launched in 1848, a year of revolutions throughout the continent, by a group in England designed to commit the church to a programme of social reform. The leaders, notably J. F. D. Maurice, Charles Kingsley (both Anglican clergymen), and John Ludlow were deeply moved by the wretched conditions of the British working class and the two priests had, indeed, given active support to the Chartist movement (*q.v.*). However, all insisted that socialism in its existing forms ignored the spiritual needs of mankind and must be tempered with Christianity. Tracts were written to expose the sweated industries, the consequences of unrestrained competition and the evils following the enclosure system; but, more concretely, Christian socialism fostered co-operative workshops and distributive societies based on those of the Rochdale pioneers, organised a working-man's college, and set up elementary classes for education. It also supported the trade-union movement's right to organise and bargain for its members.

The traditions of Christian socialism have

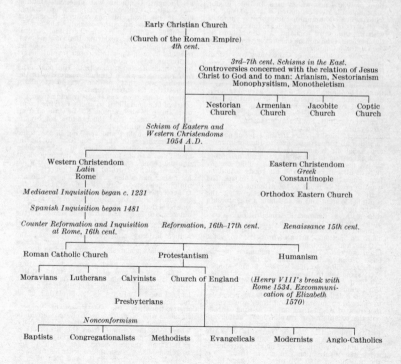

Early Christian Church

(Church of the Roman Empire)
4th cent.

3rd–7th cent. Schisms in the East.
Controversies concerned with the relation of Jesus
Christ to God and to man: Arianism, Nestorianism
Monophysitism, Monotheletism

| Nestorian Church | Armenian Church | Jacobite Church | Coptic Church |

*Schism of Eastern and
Western Christendoms
1054 A.D.*

Western Christendom
Latin
Rome

Eastern Christendom
Greek
Constantinople

Mediaeval Inquisition began c. 1231

Orthodox Eastern Church

Spanish Inquisition began 1481

*Counter Reformation and Inquisition
at Rome, 16th cent.*   Reformation, 16th–17th cent.   Renaissance 15th cent.

Roman Catholic Church   Protestantism   Humanism

Moravians   Lutherans   Calvinists   Church of England   (*Henry VIII's break with
Rome 1534. Excommunication
of Elizabeth
1570*)

Presbyterians

Nonconformism

Baptists   Congregationalists   Methodists   Evangelicals   Modernists   Anglo-Catholics been carried on by the Fabian Society, by adherents of Guild Socialism, and by individuals who reject Marx's teaching of revolutionary change, and seek to bring it about by the methods of action through political parties, education, and encouragement of the unions. They believe that Christ's teachings can only be fully realised in a new society since Christianity implies social responsibility, and material factors are admitted to have an important bearing on the ability to lead a truly religious life. See also **Fabian Society, Guild Socialism**.

Church of England. There is some evidence of possible continuity with the Christianity of Roman Britain, but in the main the Church derives from the fusion of the ancient Celtic church with the missionary church of St. Augustine, who founded the See of Canterbury in A.D. 597. To archbishop Theodore in 673 is ascribed its organisation in dioceses with settled boundaries, and in parishes. St. Augustine's church was in communion with Rome from the first, but the Church of England was not brought within papal jurisdiction until after the Norman conquest, and was at no time under the complete domination of Rome. It remains the Catholic Church of England without break of continuity, but during the Reformation the royal supremacy was accepted and that of the pope repudiated. It is the Established Church (*i.e.*, the official church of the realm), crowns the sovereign, and its archbishops and bishops in the House of Lords can act as a kind of "conscience of the state" at every stage of legislation. The Church is organised in two ecclesiastical provinces (Canterbury and York) and 43 dioceses. Its traditional forms of worship are embodied in the Book of Common Prayer, but the Alternative Service Book of 1980 is now widely used. In 1985, Easter communicants were estimated at *c* 1,650,000.

The Anglican Communion comprises the churches in all parts of the world which are in communion with the Church of England. All the bishops of the Anglican Communion meet every ten years in the Lambeth Conference (first held in 1867), over which the Archbishop of Canterbury by custom presides as *primus inter pares*. At the 1968 Conference observers and laymen were admitted for the first time. The last Conference was held in 1978. The next will meet in 1988.

Church of Scotland, the established national church of Scotland, presbyterian in constitution, and governed by a hierarchy of courts—the kirksessions, the presbyteries, the synods, and the General Assembly. See **Presbyterianism**.

Clairvoyance. See **Telepathy**.

Communism, ideally refers to the type of society in which all property belongs to the community and social life is based on the principle "from each according to his ability, to each according to his needs." There would be public ownership of all enterprises and all goods would be free. Since no such society as yet exists, the word in practice refers to the attempt to achieve such a society by initially overthrowing the capitalist system and establishing a dictatorship of the proletariat (Marx identified the dictatorship with a democratic constitution). Communists believe that their first task is the establishment of socialism under which there remain class distinctions, private property to some extent, and differences between manual and brain workers. The state is regulated on the basis "from each according to his ability, to each according to his work". Lenin applied Marx's analysis to the new conditions which had arisen in 20th-cent. capitalist society. Marxism–Leninism develops continuously with practice since failure to apply its basic principles to changed circumstances and times would result in errors of dogmatism. Mao Tse-tung worked out the techniques of revolutionary action appropriate to China; Che Guevara the guerrilla tactics appropriate to the peasants of Latin America. His counsel "It is not necessary to wait until conditions for making revolution exist; the insurrection can create them", was the opposite of Mao Tse-tung's "Engage in no battle you are not sure of winning", and Lenin's "Never play with insurrection". Two fundamental principles of communism are (1) peaceful co-existence between countries of different social systems, and (2) the class struggle between oppressed and oppressing classes and between oppressed and oppressor nations. Maoism, for example, holds that it is a mistake to lay one-sided stress on peaceful transition towards socialism otherwise the revolutionary will of the proletariat becomes passive and unprepared politically and organisationally for the tasks ahead.

In Russia the civil war developed *after* the revolution; in China the communists fought their civil war *before* they seized power: the Yugoslav partisans won their own guerrilla war *during* their stand against the fascist powers—differences which had important political consequences. Russia suffered three decades of isolationism and totalitarian suppression ("an isolated and besieged fortress") before the death of Stalin. Then came a marked, if zigzagging shift towards "liberalisation." Mao Tse-tung held to the orthodox Leninist view about capitalism and communism, regarded détente as a dangerous illusion, and compromise and "revisionism" as a fatal error. The ideological dispute between these two great communist powers which lasted from the '60s to the '80s is ending with the improvement in inter-party relations and today a movement towards détente is taking place. Communist parties in some countries, *e.g.*, Italy, are taking the democratic road to socialism and believe that a communist government should be installed by the ballot box. See also **Maoism, Marxism, Trotskyism, and Section C, Part II**.

Confucianism. Confucius (Latinised form of K'ung-Fo-tzu) was born in 551 B.C. in the feudal state of Lu in modern Shantung province. He was thus a contemporary of Buddha, although nobody could have been more dissimilar. Where Buddha was metaphysical in his thought, Confucius was practical; Buddha was original, Confucius had hardly an original idea in his head; Buddha wanted to convert individuals to an other-worldly philosophy. Confucius wanted to reform the feudal governments of his time, believing that in this way their subjects would be made happier. Other religions have in their time, been revolutionary; Confucius was a conservative who wanted to bring back a golden age from the past. The only respect in which Confucius agreed with the Buddha was that neither was particularly interested in the supernatural.

Much of his time was spent in going from the court of one feudal lord to another trying to impress them by his example. For he suffered from the curious belief that the example set by the ruler influences his subjects. He made much of etiquette, trembling and speaking in low tones and behaving with "lofty courtesy" to his inferiors. Promoting the idea of "the golden mean", he was not impressed by heroic deeds or unusual people, and was greatly displeased when he heard that a truthful son had reported that his father had stolen a sheep: "Those who are upright", he said, "are different from this; the father conceals the misconduct of the son, and the son conceals the misconduct of the father." One feels that Confucius would have felt not at all out of place in an English public school. Virtue brings its own reward in this world, ceremonial is important, politeness when universal would reduce jealousy and quarrels; "reverence the spirits but keep them far off." Destiny decides to what class a man shall belong, and as destiny is but another name for Nature prayer is unnecessary, for once having received his destiny, a man can demand and obtain from Nature what he chooses—his own will determines all things. Chinese philosophy students in Mao's day looked upon Confucius as "a forefather of all reactionaries".

Congregationalists, the oldest sect of Nonconformists who hold that each church should be independent of external ecclesiastical authority. They took their origin from the Brownists of Elizabeth's days. Robert Browne (*c.* 1550–*c.* 1633), an Anglican clergyman, who had come to reject bishops, was forced with his followers to seek refuge, first in Holland and then in Scotland where he was imprisoned by the Kirk. In later life he changed his views and is disowned by Congregationalists because of his reversion to Anglicanism. His former views were spread by Henry Barrow and John Greenwood who, under an Act passed in 1592 "for the punishment of persons obstinately refusing to come to church" (and largely designed for the suppression of this sect), were hanged at Tyburn. They had preached (a) that the only head of the church is Jesus Christ; (b) that, contrary to Elizabethan doctrine, the church had no relationship to the state; (c) that the only statute-book was the Bible whereas the Articles of Religion and Book of Common Prayer were mere Acts of Parliament; (d) that each congregation of believers was independent and had the power of choosing its own ministers. The body fled once more to Holland and were among the Pilgrims who set sail in the *Mayflower* for America in 1620 whilst those who remained were joined by Puritans fleeing from Charles I. They became free once more to live in England under the Commonwealth only to be repressed again under Charles II. Finally full liberty of worship was granted under William III. In 1833 the Congregational Union of England and Wales was formed which had no legislative power. It had issued a Declaration of Faith by which no minister was bound; he was responsible to his own church and to nobody else. The sect is widespread both in Britain and the U.S.A. where it is held in special honour because of its connection with the Pilgrim Fathers. In 1972 the Congregational Church in England and Wales and the Presbyterian Church of England decided to unite to form the United Reformed Church. The majority of members who did not join comprise the Congregational Federation.

Conservatism. The term "Conservative" came into general use after 1834 in place of the older name of "Tory". The modern Conservative Party has its origins in the period of "Tory Democracy" introduced by Disraeli between 1874 and 1880. Originally the party of church, aristocracy and landed gentry, Conservatism has been increasingly supported since the turn of the century by large business interests. Under Baldwin, Conservative-dominated administration held office for much of the inter-war period. The 1945 Labour victory caused the Conservative Party to undertake a basic review of its philosophy. From 1951 to 1964, Conservatives held office continuously, reaching a peak in Harold Macmillan's 1959 election victory. Though defeated by Labour in 1964 and 1966, the party regained power in 1970 under Edward Heath. The subsequent troubled administration, plagued with problems on the industrial front, ended with the February 1974 election. The subsequent defeat in October 1974, followed by the battle for the Conservative leadership, again caused the party to seek to review its philosophy as it had developed in recent years. Since the clear victories of the party in the 1979 and 1983 elections, the Conservatives have rejected government intervention in industry and relied on market forces and a rigid monetarist policy which has run into difficulties.

On the continent, Conservatism has generally adopted a more right-wing stance, being identified with the established order and fearing most forms of social change. *See also* **Section C, Part I.**

Coptic Church, the sect of Egyptian Christians who, holding "Monophysite" opinions (*i.e.,* refusing to grant the two natures, God and Man, of Christ), were declared heretical by the Council of Chalcedon in 451. They practise circumcision and have dietary laws. Their language is a direct descendant of ancient Egyptian. Like the Armenians, they are regarded as an heretical branch of Eastern Christianity. Their religious head is the patriarch of Alexandria.

Cynics, a school of philosophy founded in the time of Alexander the Great by Diogenes. Choosing to live like a dog by rejecting all conventions of religion, manners, or decency, and allegedly living in a tub, Diogenes unwittingly brought on his school the title "Cynic", meaning not "cynical", as the word is understood today, but "canine". His teacher, Antisthenes, who had been a disciple of Socrates, decided, after the latter's death, that all philosophy was useless quibbling and man's sole aim should be simple goodness. He believed in a return to nature, despised luxury, wanted no government, no private property, and associated with working men and slaves. Far from being cynics in the modern sense, Diogenes and Antisthenes were virtuous anarchists rather like old Tolstoy (except that in the practice of their beliefs they were more consistent).

D

Deism. *See* **God and Man.**

Demonism, Demons, and the Devil. Demons are ethereal beings of various degrees of significance and power which are believed to be implicated in men's good, but especially evil, fortune. They are common to most cultures. From the anthropological point of view the demon arose as a widespread concept in the following ways: (1) as a psychological projection into the outer world of man's own good or evil emotions and thoughts; (2) as a survival of primitive animism (*q.v.*), thus spirits are believed to haunt places, trees, stones, and other natural objects; (3) when by warlike invasion the gods of the vanquished become the devils of the conquerors (as when the Jews occupied Canaan); (4) as a primitive belief that spirits of the dead continue after death to hover near their former habitation, and not always entirely welcome to the living; (5) the conception of a supreme source of evil (the Devil or Satan) which took shape among the Jews during their sojourn in Babylon under the influence of Zoroastrianism (*q.v.*), a religion in which the struggle between the two spirits, Good and Evil, reached its height in the imagination of the ancient world. The Satan of the Old Testament was first regarded as one of God's servants (in the Book of Job he goes up and down the earth to see whether God's commands are obeyed), but when the Jews returned from their captivity he had become identified with Ahriman, the spirit of evil, who was in continual conflict with Ahursa Mazda, the spirit of good. As Dr. Margaret Murray has pointed out, the primitive mind ascribed both good and evil to one power alone; the division into God and the Devil, priest and witch, belongs to a higher stage of civilisation. The worship of evil itself, or of its personification in Satan, is a curious practice which seems to have developed hand-in-hand with Christianity and to have received steady support from a small but measurable minority. Many of the ceremonies involved in Satanism or in the so-called Black Mass appear to have been no more than opportunities for sexual excesses of one kind or another—such indulgences being traditionally barred to devout Christians. The alleged power of sex as a form of magic was propagated by the talented but rather mad poet, Aleister Crowley (1875–1947), who scandalised pre-war Europe with his very well-publicised dabblings into Satanism. The self-styled "wickedest man in the world", Crowley was a pathetic rather than shocking figure and died a drug addict. He can hardly be said to have significantly advanced the cause of Demonology, though it has to be admitted that he tried very hard.

Determinism and Free-will. The question of whether man is, or is not, free to mould his own destiny is one which has exercised the minds of philosophers since Greek mythology conceived of the Fates as weaving a web of destiny from which no man can free himself. Socrates emphasised that man could through knowledge influence his destiny whilst ignorance made him the plaything of fate; Plato went further in pointing out that man can, and does, defeat the purposes of the universe and its divine Creator. It is our duty to live a good life, but we can live a foolish and wicked one if we chose. Aristotle wrote "Virtue is a disposition or habit involving deliberate purpose or choice". If this were not so morality would be a sham.

The Problem for Theology. The last of the great philosophers of Antiquity and one of the great influences in moulding Catholic theology was Plotinus (c. 204–70). Soul, he taught, is free, but once enmeshed in the body loses its freedom in the life of sense. Nevertheless, man is free to turn away from sensuality and towards God who is perfect freedom; for even when incarnated in matter the soul does not entirely lose the ability to rescue itself. This conception was carried over into the beliefs of the early Christian Apologists because it appeared to be in line with the teaching of Jesus that He had come to save man from sin. Sin implies guilt, and guilt implies the freedom to act otherwise; furthermore an all-good God cannot be responsible for the sin in the world which must be man's responsiblity and this again implies freedom. Pelagius (c. 355–c. 425), a Welsh priest, not only believed in free-will but questioning the doctrine of original sin, said that when men act righteously it is through their own moral effort, and God rewards them for their virtues in heaven. This belief became fairly widespread and was declared a heresy by the Church, being attacked notably by St. Augustine (354–430), a contemporary of Pelagius, who believed in predestination—that, since the sin of Adam, God had chosen who in all future history would be saved and who damned. This represents one tradition in Christianity: the determinism which leads to Calvinism (q.v.). St. Thomas Aquinas (1227–74), the greatest figure of scholasticism and one of the principal saints in the Roman Catholic Church, compromised between the two positions in the sense that, believing man to be free, he yet held that Adam's sin was transmitted to all mankind and only divine grace can bring salvation. But even when God wishes to bestow this salvation, the human will must co-operate. God foresees that some will not accept the offer of grace and predestines them to eternal punishment.

The Problem for Philosophy. With the Renaissance, thinkers began to free themselves from the domination of the Church and so study the world objectively and freely without preconceptions. But the more man turned to science, the more he discovered that the world was ruled by apparently inexorable laws and, since the scientist must believe that every event has a cause, he was led back to determinism. Man as part of the universe was subject to law too and all that existed was a vast machine. Francis Bacon (1561–1626) separated the fields of religion and science but left man subject completely to the will of God. Thomas Hobbes (1588–1679) was a rigid determinist and materialist although, having had trouble with the church in France whence, as a royalist, he had fled, he took care to announce that the Christian God is the Prime Mover.

Modern philosophy begins with René Descartes (1596–1650), a Frenchman who tried to reconcile the mechanical scientific universe of his time with the spiritual need for freedom. He did this by separating completely mind and body; the former, he said, is free, the latter completely determined. But, by admitting that the will can produce certain states of body, he was left with the problem of how this could happen—a problem which the so-called Occasionists solved to their own satisfaction by stating that the will is free and God so arranges the universe that what a person wills happens. Baruch Spinoza (1632–77), a Dutch Jew whose independence of thought led to his excommunication from the Amsterdam Synagogue in 1656, was a complete determinist. He asserted that God and Nature are one, everything that happens is a manifestation of God's inscrutable nature, and it is logically impossible that things could be other than they are. Thus both Hobbes and Spinoza were determinists for entirely opposed reasons. The former as a materialist, the latter because he believed in the absolute perfection and universality of God. Yet the great religious mystic and mathematician Blaise Pascal (1623–62) held that, no matter what reason and cold logic may indicate we *know* from direct religious experience that we are free. John Calvin (1509–64) and Martin Luther (1483–1546) were both determinists. *See* **Calvinism, Lutheranism.**

To the more practical British philosophers, John Locke (1632–1704) and David Hume (1711–76), free-will was related to personality. Locke believed that God had implanted in each individual certain desires and these determine the will; the desires are already there, but we use our will to satisfy them. Hume argued that a man's behaviour is the necessary result of his character and if he had a different character he would act otherwise. Accordingly, when a man's actions arise from his own nature and desires he is free. He is not free when external events compel him to act otherwise (e.g., if he strikes another because his own nature is such he is free as he is not if he is compelled to do so against his desire). Leibnitz (1646–1716), although as a German metaphysical philosopher holding very different general views, said much the same thing—that choice is simply selecting the desire that is strongest. But most of the 18th cent. thinkers after Voltaire, with the great exceptions of Rousseau and the later German philosophers Kant, Fichte, Schopenhauer, and Hegel, who were initially influenced by him, accepted determinism. Rousseau (1712–78) began to stem the tide by his declaration that man is a free soul striving to remain free and only prevented from being so by society and the cold science which stifles his feeling heart. Once again the will became important as Kant (1724–1804) asserted that belief in freedom is a moral necessity although it cannot be proved by reason; the moral nature of man shows that there is a "transcendental" world beyond the senses where freedom applies. Fichte and Schelling found freedom in the Absolute ego or God, of whom each individual was part and thus also free. Hegel (1770–1831) saw the whole universe as evolving towards self-awareness and freedom in man although this could only be fully realised in a society that makes for freedom. Even God himself only attains full consciousness and self-realisation through the minds of such individuals as are free. This is the goal of the dialectical process. (*See* **Dialectical Materialism.**)

The Scientist's View. For the scientist the law of cause and effect is a useful hypothesis since, by and large, it is necessary for him to assume that all events are caused. Nevertheless the modern tendency is to think in terms of statistical probability rather than relentless mechanistic causality, and, although the free-will problem does not concern the scientist as such, it is clear that freedom and determinism (assuming the terms to have any meaning at all) are not necessarily opposed. In sociology, for example, we *know* that certain actions will produce certain results upon the behaviour of people in general, e.g., that raising the bank rate will discourage business expansion. But this does not mean that Mr. Brown who decides in his factory is not using his free-will. Even in the case of atoms, as Dr. Bronowski has pointed out, the observed results of allowing gas under pressure in a cylinder to rush out occur because most of the atoms are "obeying" the scientific "law" relating to such situations. But this does not mean that some atoms are not busy rushing across the stream or even against it—they are, but the general tendency is outwards and that is what we note. Lastly, the modern philosophical school of Logical Analysis would probably ask, not whether Free-will or Determinism is the true belief, but whether the question has any meaning. For what scientific experiment could we set up to prove one or the other true? The reader will note that some of the philosophers mentioned above are using the words to mean quite different concepts.

Dialectical Materialism, the combination of Hegel's dialectic method with a materialist philosophy produced by Karl Marx (1818–83) and his friend Friedrich Engels (1820–95). It is the philosophical basis of **Marxism** (q.v.) and **Communism** (q.v.). "Dialectic" to the ancient Greek philosophers meant a kind of dialogue or conversation, as used particularly by Socrates, in which philosophical disputes were resolved by a series of successive contradictions: a thesis is put forward and the opposing side holds its contradiction or antithesis until in the course of argument a synthesis is reached in which the conflicting ideas are resolved.

From Thesis through Antithesis to Synthesis. Hegel in the 19th cent. put forward the view that this process applies to the course of nature and history as they strive towards the perfect state. But to him, as to the Greeks, the conflict was in the field of ideas. The "universal reason" behind events works through the ideas held by a particular society until they are challenged by those of another which supersedes them and in turn, usually by war, becomes the agent of universal reason until the arrival of a new challenger. Hegel therefore regarded war as an instrument of progress and his Prussian compatriots found no difficulty in identifying their own state as the new agent of progress by universal conquest. Feuerbach, Lassalle, and other early socialists were impressed by some of Hegel's ideas: *e.g.*, that societies evolved (with the assumption that finally their own ideal society would be achieved) and that truth, morals, and concepts were relative so that a type of society that was "good" at one time was not necessarily so at another. But Marx and Engels in effect turned Hegel upside-down, accepted his dialectic but rejected his belief that ideas were the motive force. On the contrary, they said, ideas are determined by social and economic change as a result of materialistic forces. (*See* **Calvinism**, where it is pointed out that the Marxist view is not that Calvin changed men's economic ideas but rather that a developing capitalism unconsciously changed his.) The historical materialism of Marxism purports to show that the inexorable dialectic determines that feudalism is displaced by capitalism and capitalism by creating a proletariat (its antithesis) inevitably leads to socialism and a classless society. The state, as a tool of the dominant class, withers away. Dialectical materialism is applied in all spheres. As a philosophy there is little to be said for it save that it has shown us the close dependence of man's thoughts upon current material and social conditions. But as a battle-cry or a rationalisation of Marxism it wields immense power over the minds of men. *See* **Marxism**.

Dianetics. *See* **Scientology**.

Diggers, one of the many sects which flourished under the Commonwealth (others were the Muggletonians, the Levellers, the Millennarians, and the Fifth Monarchy Men), so-called because they attempted to dig (*i.e.* cultivate) untilled land. Gerrard Winstanley, a profoundly religious man, and leader of the Diggers, believed in the economic and social equality of man and castigated the clergy for upholding the class structure of society. In his book *The True Leveller's Standard Advanced* (1649) he wrote: "Every day poor people are forced to work for fourpence a day, though corn is dear. And yet the tithing priest stops their mouth and tells them that 'inward satisfaction of mind' was meant by the declaration 'the poor shall inherit the earth'. I tell you, the Scripture is to be really and materially fulfilled. You jeer at the name 'Leveller'; I tell you Jesus Christ is the Head Leveller".

Doukhobors, a religious sect of Russian origin, founded by a Prussian sergeant at Kharkov in the middle of the 18th cent., and now mainly settled in Canada. Like many other sects they belong to that type of Christianity which seeks direct communication with God and such bodies tend to have certain traits in common, such as belief in the "inner light", opposition to war and authority in general, and often ecstasies which show themselves in physical ways such as shaking, speaking in strange tongues (glossolalia), and other forms of what to the unbeliever seem mass hysteria. Liturgy, ritual, or ceremony is non-existent. The Doukhobors were persecuted in Tsarist Russia, but in 1898 Tolstoy used his influence to have them removed to Canada where the government granted them uninhabited land in what is now Saskatchewan and seven or eight thousand settled down in peace which they enjoyed for many years. Recently, however, their practices have caused difficulties once more; for even the most tolerant government which is prepared to accept pacifism, total dependence on communally-owned agriculture, refusal to engage in commerce, non-payment of taxes, rejection of the marriage ceremony and separation "when love ceases", finds it difficult to tolerate, as civilisation advances ever closer to Doukhobor communities, their proneness to "put off these troublesome disguises which we wear"—*i.e.*, to walk about naked in the communities of their more orthodox

neighbours. What the future of the Doukhobors in their various sects (for even they have their differences) will be it is impossible to say, but it is difficult to believe that these simple people can long resist the pressure of modern civilisation.

Dowsing. *See* **Radiesthesia**.

Druidism, the religion of Celtic Britain and Gaul of which Druids were the priesthood. They were finally wiped out by the Roman general Suetonius Paulinus about A.D. 58 in their last stronghold, the island of Anglesey. There are two sources of our present beliefs in Druidism: (1) the brief and factual records of the Romans, notably Pliny and Julius Caesar, which tell us that they worshipped in sacred oak groves and presumably practised a religion doing reverence to the powers of nature which must have had its roots in early stone age times and had many cruel rites, *e.g.*, human sacrifice; (2) the beliefs put forward by William Stukeley, an amateur antiquarian who from 1718 did valuable work by his studies of the stone circles at Stonehenge and Avebury. However, influenced by the Romantic movement, he later put forward the most extravagant theories which unfortunately are those popularly accepted by those without archaeological knowledge today. Stonehenge and Avebury were depicted as the temples of the "white-haired Druid bard sublime" and an attempt was made to tie up Druidism with early Christianity, above all with the concept of the Trinity. In fact, these circles have no connection with the Druids. They may have made ceremonial use of them but recent evidence suggests that the megalithic stones at Stonehenge belong to a Bronze Age culture (2100–1600 B.C.). Nor have Druidism and Christianity any relationship. Almost nothing is known of the religion. Yet such were its romantic associations that, even today, one hears of "Druidic" ceremonies practised at the appropriate time of year on Primrose Hill in the heart of London (though whether seriously or with tongue in cheek, one does not know). In Wales the name Druid survives as the title for the semi-religious leaders of the annual festivals of Celtic poetry, drama, and music known as Eisteddfods. Lingering, but now tenuous, druidic connections are to be found in all Celtic parts including Cornwall and Brittany where Eisteddfods are also held.

Dualism, any philosophical or theological theory which implies that the universe has a double nature, notably Plato's distinction between appearance and reality, soul and body, ideas and material objects, reason and the evidence of the senses, which infers that behind the world as we perceive it there lies an "ideal" world which is more "real" than that of mere appearance. In religions such as Zoroastrianism or the Gnostic and Manichaeism heresies, it was believed that the universe was ruled by good and evil "principles"—in effect that there was a good God and a bad one. In psychology, dualism refers to the philosophical theories which believe mind and body to be separate entities. The opposite of dualism is monism which asserts the essential unity of the substance of the universe.

An essential problem in the dualistic view lies in the question as to how and where the two separate and distinct properties of the universe interact. Where, for example, does the "mind" actually mesh with the physical mechanics of the brain and body—where does the ghost sit in his machine? Descartes decided that mind and body must interact somewhere and he selected the pineal gland (an apparently functionless part of the brain) as the spot. But this did nothing to explain how two *totally different* aspects of nature can possibly influence each other, and today most philosophers and psychologists reject dualistic views of life and personality as posing more problems than they solve. *See also* **Psychology, Occam's Razor**.

E

Ecomovement. In the early 1970s widespread publicity was for the first time given to the urgent warnings of ecologists that the current exponential increase in (a) world population, (b) depletion of natural resources, and (c) pollution of the environment could not continue without global catastrophe. The most significant single event in the evolution of what is now being known as the "ecomovement" was probably the publication of the Club of Rome's paper on *The Limits to Growth*. From this sprang a movement, unfortunately initially drawn only from the middle class and better educated, which aimed to reduce environmental pollution, the extravagances of advertising and needless waste of natural resources. Its first campaigns were directed against such obvious targets as disposable glass bottles and unnecessary packaging and wrapping in shops and supermarkets. The ecomovement also protests against industrial firms which pollute rivers and seas against aircraft noise and waste in general. Its early campaigns were greeted with some derision but have achieved dramatic point with the world energy and economic crisis which developed towards the end of 1973. *See also* **Ecology, Section F**.

Ecumenism, a world movement which springs from the Christian belief that all men are brothers and that the Christian Church should be re-structured to give reality to the belief. Christ's church exists not to serve its own members, but for the service of the whole world. Some see the answer in a united church of a federal type (unity in diversity), others in an organic structure with one set of rules. The period since the convening of the Second Vatican Council by Pope John has been one of fervent discussion among Christian theologians with the aim of promoting Christian unity. *See* **World Council of Churches**.

Education. Education was no great problem to primitive man, but as societies became more complex people began to ask themselves such questions as: *What* should young people be taught? *How* should they be taught? Should the aim of their education be to bring out their individual qualities or rather to make them good servants of the state?

The first teachers were priests who knew most about the traditions, customs, and lore of their societies and thus the first schools were in religious meeting places. This was notably true of the Jews who learned from the rabbis in the synagogue.

The Greeks. We begin, as always, with the Greeks whose city-states, based on slavery, educated men (not women) for the sort of life described in Plato's *Dialogues*—the leisured life of gentlemen arguing the problems of the universe at their banquets or in the market-place. This made it necessary to learn debate and oratory (or rhetoric) especially for those who proposed to take up politics. The Sophist philosophy taught the need to build up convincing arguments in a persuasive manner, to learn the rules of logic and master the laws and customs of the Athenians, and to know the literature of the past so that illustrations might be drawn from it. These strolling philosophers who taught for a fee were individualists showing the student how to advance himself at all costs within his community.

Socrates had a more ethical approach, believing that education was good in itself, made a man happier and a better citizen, and emphasised his position as a member of a group. His method of teaching, the dialectic or "Socratic" method, involved argument and discussion rather than overwhelming others by rhetoric and is briefly mentioned under **Dialectical Materialism** (*q.v.*). Today this method is increasingly used in adult education where a lecture is followed by a period of discussion in which both lecturer and audience participate; for psychologists have shown that people accept ideas more readily when conviction arises through their own arguments than when they are passively thrust down their throats.

Socrates' pupil Plato produced in his book *The Republic* one of the first comprehensive systems of education and vocational selection. Believing that essentially men have very different and unequal abilities he considered that in an idealistic or utopian society they should be put into social classes corresponding to these differences, and suggested the following method: (1) For the first 18 years of a boy's life he should be taught gymnastics and sports, playing and singing music, reading and writing, a knowledge of literature, and if he passed this course sent on to the next stage; those who failed were to become tradesmen and merchants. (2) From 18–20 those successful in the first course were to be given two years of cadet training, the ones thought incapable of further education being placed in the military class as soldiers. (3) The remainder, who were to become the leaders of society, proceeded with advanced studies in philosophy, mathematics, science, and art. Such education was to be a state concern, state supported and controlled, selecting men and training them for service in the state according to their abilities.

Plato's pupil Aristotle even suggested that the state should determine shortly after birth which children should be allowed to live and destroy the physically or mentally handicapped; that marriage should be state-controlled to ensure desirable offspring. However, in their time the leisured and individualistic Sophists held the field and few accepted the educational views of Plato or his pupil.

Rome. The Romans were not philosophers and most of their culture came from Greece. Administration was their chief aptitude and Quintilian (A.D. *c*. 35–*c*. 95) based his higher education on the earlier classical tuition in public speaking, but he is important for emphasising the training of character and for his humanistic approach to the method of teaching that caused his *Institutio oratoria* to be influential for centuries later—indeed one might almost say up to the time of the great Dr. Arnold of Rugby. Education, he believed, should begin early but one must "take care that the child not old enough to love his studies does not come to hate them" by premature forcing; studies must be made pleasant and interesting and students encouraged by praise rather than discouraged when they sometimes fail; play is to be approved of as a sign of a lively disposition and because gloomy, depressed children are not likely to be good students; corporal punishment should never be used because "it is an insult as you will realise if you imagine it yourself". The world became interested not in *what* he taught but *how* he taught it; he was the pioneer of humanistic education and character-training from Vittorino d. Feltre (1378–1446) of Mantua, through Milton and Pope who commended his works to the modern educationists who have studied their pupils as well as their books.

The Middle Ages: The Religious View. With the development of Christianity education once more became a religious problem. The earliest converts had to be taught Christian doctrine and were given instruction in "catechumenal" schools before admission to the group, but as the religion came increasingly into contact with other religions or heresies a more serious training was necessary, and from these newer "catechetical" schools, where the method used was the catechism (*i.e.*, question and answer as known to all Presbyterian children today), the Apologists arose among whom were Clement of Alexandria and the great Origen. From this time education became an instrument of the church and in 529 the Emperor Justinian ordered all pagan schools to be closed.

As typical of the best in mediaeval education whilst the lamp of civilisation burned low during the Dark Ages, after the fall of Roman power, and survived only in the monasteries, we may mention St. Benedict (*c*. 480–*c*. 547) of Monte Cassino. There, in southern Italy, a rule was established which became a part of monastic life in general. Monastic schools were originally intended for the training of would-be monks, but later others were admitted who simply wanted some education; thus two types of school developed one for the *interni* and the other for *externi* or external pupils. Originally studies were merely reading in order to study the Bible, writing to copy the sacred books, and sufficient calculation to be able to work out the advent of holy days or festivals. But by the end of the 6th cent. the "seven liberal arts" (grammar, rhetoric, dialectic, arithmetic, geometry, music, and astronomy) were added.

The Renaissance. The close of the Middle Ages saw the development of two types of secular school. One came with the rise of the new merchant class and the skilled trader whose "guilds" or early trade unions established schools to train young men for their trades but ultimately gave rise to burgher or town schools; the other was the court school founded and supported by the wealthy rulers of the Italian cities—Vittorio da Feltre (mentioned above) presided over the most famous at Mantua.

These Renaissance developments are parallelled in northern Europe by the Protestant reformers who, having with Martin Luther held that everyone should know how to read his Bible in order to interpret it in his own way, were logically committed to popular education, compulsory and universal. In theory this was intended for biblical study, but writing, arithmetic, and other elementary subjects were taught and Luther said that, even if heaven and hell did not exist, education was important. Universal education is a Protestant conception.

Views of Philosophers. From this period onwards people were free to put forward any ideas about education, foolish or otherwise, and to create their own types of school. Of English philosophers who theorised about, but did not practise, education we may mention the rationalist Francis Bacon (1561–1626) who saw learning as the dissipation of all prejudices and the collection of concrete facts; the materialist and totalitarian Hobbes (1588–1679) who, as a royalist, believed that the right to determine the kind of education fit for his subjects is one of the absolute rights of the sovereign power or ruler; the gentlemanly Locke (1632–1704) whose ideal was a sound mind in a sound body to be attained by hard physical exercise, wide experience of the world, and enough knowledge to meet the requirements of the pupil's environment. The end result would be one able to get on with his fellows, pious but wise in the ways of the world, independent and able to look after himself, informed but reticent about his knowledge. Classics and religious study were not to be carried to excess, since Locke held that these subjects had been overrated in the past. Locke's pupil was the well-to-do, civilised young man of the 17th cent. who knew how to behave in society.

Jean-Jacques Rousseau (1712–78), a forerunner of the Romantic movement (*q.v.*), which despised society and its institutions, put emotion at a higher level than reason. His book *Emile* describes the education of a boy which is natural and spontaneous. Society, he holds, warps the growing mind and therefore the child should be protected from its influences until his development in accordance with his own nature is so complete that he cannot be harmed by it. During the first 4 years the body should be developed by physical training; from 5 to 12 the child would live in a state of nature such that he could develop his powers of observation and his senses; from 13 books would be used and intellectual training introduced, although only in line with the child's own interests, and he would be given instruction only as he came to ask for it. Moral training and contact with his fellows to learn the principles of sympathy, kindness, and helpfulness to mankind would be given between 15 and 20. Girls, however, should be educated to serve men in a spirit of modesty and restraint. His own five children he deposited in a foundling hospital.

Summary. Broadly speaking, then, there have been four main attitudes to education: (1) religious, with a view to a life beyond death; (2) state-controlled education, with a view to uniform subservience to authority; (3) "gentlemanly" education, with a view to social graces and easy congress in company; (4) the "child-centred" education, which attempts to follow the pupil's inner nature. It is unnecessary to mention the ordinary method of attempting to instil facts without any considerable degree of co-operation between pupil and teacher in order that the former may, with or without interest, follow some occupation in adult life; for this the philosophers did not consider. Today there

remain the two fundamental principles: education for the advantage of the state and its ideology or education for individual development and freedom.

Four educationists of the modern period who have influenced us in the direction of freedom were Johann Pestalozzi of Switzerland (1746–1827) who, by trying to understand children, taught the "natural, progressive, and harmonious development of all the powers and capacities of the human being"; Friedrich Froebel (1782–1852) of Germany, the founder of the Kindergarten who, like Pestalozzi, was influenced by Rousseau but realised the need to combine complete personal development with social adjustment; Maria Montessori (1869–1952) whose free methods have revolutionised infant teaching; John Dewey (1859–1952) who held that the best interests of the group are served when the individual develops his own particular talents and nature.

Eleatics, the philosophers of Elea in ancient Greece who, at the time when Heraclitus (*c.* 535–475 B.C.) was teaching that change is all that exists and nothing is permanent, were asserting that change is an illusion. Of the three leaders of this school, Xenophanes asserted that the universe was a solid immovable mass forever the same; Parmenides explained away change as an inconceivable process, its appearance being due to the fact that what we see is unreal; and Zeno (the best-known today) illustrated the same thesis with his famous argument of the arrow which, at any given moment of its flight, must be where it is since it cannot be where it is not. But if it is where it is, it cannot move, this is based, of course, on the delusion that motion is discontinuous. The Eleatics were contemporaries of Socrates.

Empiricism. While not a single school of philosophy, empiricism is an approach to knowledge which holds that if a man wants to know what the universe is like the only correct way to do so is to go and look for himself, to collect facts which come to him through his senses. It is, in essence, the method of science as contrasted with rationalism (*q.v.*) which in philosophy implies that thinking or reasoning without necessarily referring to external observations can arrive at truth. Empiricism is typically an English attitude, for among the greatest empirical philosophers were John Locke, George Berkeley, and David Hume. *See* Rationalism.

Epicureanism. The two great schools of the Hellenistic period (*i.e.* the late Greek period beginning with the empire of Alexander the Great) were the Stoics and Epicureans, the former founded by Zeno of Citium (not to be confused with Zeno the Eleatic) (*q.v.*), the latter by Epicurus, born in Samos in 342 B.C. Both schools settled in Athens, where Epicurus taught that "pleasure is the beginning and end of a happy life." However, he was no sensualist and emphasised the importance of moderation in all things because excesses would lead to pain instead of pleasure and the best of all pleasures were mental ones. Pleasures could be active or passive but the former contain an element of pain since they are the process of satisfying desire not yet satiated. The latter involving the absence of desire are the more pleasant. In fact, Epicurus in his personal life was more stoical than many Stoics and wrote "when I live on bread and water I spit on luxurious pleasures." He disapproved of sexual enjoyment and thought friendship one of the highest of all joys. A materialist who accepted the atomic theory of Democritus, he was not a determinist, and if he did not disbelieve in the gods he regarded religion and the fear of death as the two primary sources of unhappiness.

Epiphenomenalism. *See* **Mind and Body.**

Erastianism, the theory that the state has the right to decide the religion of its members, wrongly attributed to Erastus of Switzerland (1524–83) who was believed to have held this doctrine. The term has usually been made use of in a derogatory sense—*e.g.,* by the Scottish churches which held that the "call" of the congregation was the only way to elect ministers at a time when, about the turn of the 17th and 18th cent., they felt that Episcopalianism was being foisted on them. "Episcopalianism" (*i.e.* Anglicanism) with its state church, ecclesiastical hierarchy, and system of livings presented by patrons was to them "Erastian" in addition to its other "unscriptural practices."

Essenes, a Jewish sect which, during the oppressive rule of Herod (d. 4 B.C.), set up monastic communities in the region of the Dead Sea. They refused to be bound by the scriptural interpretations of the Pharisees and adhered rigorously to the letter of Holy Writ, although with additions of their own which cause them by orthodox Jews today to be regarded as a break-away from Judaism. Among their practices and beliefs were purification through baptism, renunciation of sexual pleasures, scrupulous cleanliness, strict observance of the Mosaic law, communal possession, asceticism. Akin in spirit, although not necessarily identical with them, were the writers of Apocalyptic literature preaching that the evils of the present would shortly be terminated by a new supernatural order heralded by a Messiah who would reign over a restored Israel. The casting out of demons and spiritual healing formed part of these general beliefs which were in the air at that time. The sect has an importance far beyond its size or what has been known about it in the past since the discovery from 1947 onwards of the Dead Sea Scrolls (*see* **Section L**) of the Qumran community occupying a monastery in the same area as the Essenes and holding the same type of belief. These scrolls with their references to a "Teacher of Righteousness" preceding the Messiah have obvious relevance to the sources of early Christianity and have given rise to speculations as to whether Jesus might have been influenced by views which, like His own, were unacceptable to orthodox Jews but in line with those of the Dead Sea communities. They seem to show that early Christianity was not a sudden development but a gradual one which had its predecessors.

Ethical Church, a movement typical of 19th cent. rationalism which attempted to combine atheism (or at any rate the absence of any belief in a God which was inconsistent with reason or based on revelation) with the inculcation of moral principles. Prayers were not used and ordinarily the service consisted in the singing of edifying compositions interspersed with readings from poems or prose of a similar nature by great writers holding appropriate views. It terminated in a talk on an ethical or scientific theme. Conway Hall (built 1929) in Red Lion Square, London, belongs to the South Place Ethical Society, founded by Moncure Conway who preached at their Unitarian chapel in South Place, Finsbury, 1864–97.

Ethnocentrism, the exaggerated tendency to think the characteristics of one's own group or race superior to those of any others.

Eugenics, a 19th-cent. movement largely instigated by the British scientist and mathematician, Sir Francis Galton. Galton argued that many of the most satisfactory attributes of mankind—intelligence, physical strength, resistance to disease, etc.—were genetically determined and thus handed down in the normal process of inheritance. From this he reasoned that selective mating of physical "superior" individuals, and its converse, the controlled limitation on the breeding of criminals or the insane, would lead inevitably to a progressive improvement in the overall standards of the human race. In their simplest form these proposals are incontestable, though they do of course introduce marked restrictions on the choice of the individual for marriage and procreation. Worse yet is the way in which the argument can be misapplied or elaborated—as it was in Nazi Germany—to include the sterilisation of alcoholics, confirmed criminals and even epileptics. Nevertheless there remains the feeling that there are some aspects of eugenics which intuitively at any rate make good sense and of course the widespread application of birth control is itself an enactment of eugenic principles.

Evangelicalism, the belief of those Protestant sects which hold that the essence of the Gospel consists in the doctrine of salvation by faith in the atoning death of Christ and not by good works or the sacraments; that worship should be "free" rather than liturgical through established forms; that ritual is unacceptable and superstitious. Evangelicals are Low Churchmen.

Evangelism, the preaching of the Gospel, emphasising the necessity for a new birth or conversion. The evangelistic fervour of John Wesley and George Whitefield (*see* Methodism) aroused the great missionary spirit of the late 18th and 19th cent. George Fox, founder of the Society of Friends (*q.v.*), was also an evangelist. Evangelists can be Low, High, or Middle Churchmen.

Existentialism, a highly subjective philosophy which many people connect with such names as Jean-Paul Sartre (1905–80) or Albert Camus (1913–60) and assume to be a post-war movement associated with disillusion and a sordid view of life. However, existentialism stems from Sören Kierkegaard (1813–55), the Danish "religious writer"—his own description of himself—in such works as *Either/Or, Fear and Trembling,* and *Concluding Unscientific Postscript.* Between the two wars translations of Kierkegaard into German influenced Martin Heidegger's great work *Being and Time* and the other great existentialist Karl Jaspers; it has strongly influenced modern Protestant theology notably in Karl Barth, Reinhold Niebuhr, and Paul Tillich and beyond that field the French philosopher Gabriel Marcel, the Spanish writer Unamuno in his well-known *The Tragic Sense of Life,* and Martin Buber of Israel in his *I and Thou.* We have it on Heidegger's authority that "Sartre is no philosopher" even if it is to his works that modern existentialists often turn.

Existentialism is extremely difficult for the non-metaphysically-minded to understand, it deals, not with the nature of the universe or what are ordinarily thought of as philosophical problems but describes an attitude to life or God held by the individual. Briefly, its main essentials are: (1) it distinguishes between *essence, i.e.,* that aspect of an entity which can be observed and known—and its *existence*—the fact of its having a place in a changing and dangerous world which is what really matters; (2) existence being basic, each self-aware individual can grasp his own existence on reflection in his own immediate experience of himself and his situation as a free being in the world; what he finds is not merely a knowing self but a self that fears, hopes, believes, wills, and is aware of its need to find a purpose, plan, and destiny in life; (3) but we cannot grasp our existence by thought alone; thus the fact "all men must die" relates to the essence of man but it is necessary to be involved, to draw the conclusion as a person that "I too must die" and experience its impact on our own individual existence; (4) because of the preceding, it is necessary to abandon our attitude of objectivity and theoretical detachment when faced by the problems relating to the ultimate purpose of our own life and the basis of our own conduct; life remains closed to those who take no part in it because it can have no significance; (5) it follows that the existentialist cannot be rationalist in his outlook for this is merely an escape into thought from the serious problems of existence; none of the important aspects of life—failure, evil, sin, folly—nor (in the view of Kierkegaard) even the existence of God or the truth of Christianity—can be proved by reason. "God does not exist; He is eternal," was how he expressed it; (6) life is short and limited in space and time, therefore it is foolish to discuss in a leisurely fashion matters of life and death as if there were all eternity to argue them in. It is necessary to make a leap into the unknown, *e.g.,* accepting Christ (in the case of the Christian existentialist) by faith in the sense of giving and risking the self utterly. This means complete commitment, not a dependence on arguments as to whether certain historical events did, or did not, happen.

To summarise: existentialism of whatever type seems to the outsider to be an attitude to life concerning itself with the individual's ultimate problems (mine, not yours); to be anti-rationalist and anti-idealist (in the sense of being, as it seems to the believer, practical)—in effect it seems to say "life is too short to fool about with argument, you must dive in and become committed" to something. Sartre who called himself an "atheist existentialist" was apparently committed to the belief that "hell is other people," but for most critics the main argument against existentialist philosophy is that it often rests on a highly specialised personal experience and, as such, is incommunicable.

Existential Psychology, a new if rather diffuse movement in modern psychology with no specific founder but with a number of figures who have, perhaps against their will, acquired leader status. One of the key figures is the British psychiatrist, R. D. Laing, whose radical views on psychotherapy are counted as being heretical by the vast majority of his medical colleagues. Laing holds that many so-called neurotic and psychotic conditions are essentially not "abnormal" and merely represent extreme strategies by which an individual may adjust to environmental and personal stress. Instead of attempting to suppress or eliminate the psychosis in the traditional manner, one should lead the patient through it thus allowing the individual's "unconscious plan" for his own adjustment to be fulfilled.

Exorcism, the removal or ejection of an evil spirit by a ritual or prayer. It is easy to forget that the concept of insanity as representing a disorder of the brain, analogous to physical sickness of the body, is fairly recent in origin. Barely two centuries ago it was considered to be appropriate treatment to put lunatics into chains and beat them daily in the hope that the malevolent beings inhabiting them might be persuaded to depart. Tragically, many of the symptoms of severe forms of mental disorder induce such an apparent change in the personality of the individual as to suggest that an alien individual has indeed taken over their body, and this belief is still common in many parts of the world. Most religious systems have developed some ritual or set of rituals for expelling these demons, and while, not surprisingly, the practice of exorcism by the clergy has declined dramatically in the past century, it is still brought into play now and again in such circumstances as alleged hauntings, poltergeist phenomena, etc. From a scientific point of view, exorcism must be counted as a superstitious rite, but its suggestive power in cases of hysteria, and perhaps even more serious mental illnesses, cannot be completely ruled out. General interest in the topic has been stimulated in part by the resurgence of the practice of Black Magic and witchcraft, largely in the form of experimental dabbling by young people, who no doubt become disillusioned when it fails to live up to its promise. Testimony to the pulling-power of this remnant of our superstitious past is the fact that a sensational and terrifying novel, *The Exorcist,* which its author claimed was based on fact, topped the best-seller lists in 1972, and the even more horrific movie-version became one of the most successful (in box office terms) films of all time. The Church of England, incidentally, takes anything but a dismissive line on the matter, and in fact employs a number of ordained priests as "licensed exorcists". These services are apparently much in demand.

F

Fabian Society. In 1848 (the year of *The Communist Manifesto* by Marx and Engels) Europe was in revolt. In most countries the workers and intellectuals started bloody revolutions against the feudal ruling classes which were no less violently suppressed; hence on the continent socialism took on a Marxist tinge which to some extent it still retains. But at the same time England was undergoing a slow but non-violent transition in her political and industrial life which led the workers in general to look forward to progress through evolution. Marxism never became an important movement in England even though it took its origin here.

There were many reasons for this: the agitation of the Chartists (*q.v.*); the writings of Mill, Ruskin, and Carlyle; the reforms of Robert Owen; the religious movement led by the Wesleys; the Co-operative societies; the Christian socialists. Furthermore legislation stimulated by these bodies had led to an extension of the franchise to include a considerable number of wage-earners, remedial measures to correct some of the worst abuses of the factory system, recognition of the trade unions, etc.

This was the background against which the Fabian Society was founded in 1884 with the conviction that social change could be brought about by gradual parliamentary means. (The name is derived from Quintus Fabius Maximus, the Roman general nicknamed "Cunctator," the delayer, who achieved his successes in defending Rome against Hannibal by refusing to give direct battle.) It was a movement of brilliant intellectuals, chief among whom were Sidney and Beatrice Webb, H. G. Wells, G. B. Shaw, Graham Wallas, Sidney Olivier, and Edward Pease. The Society itself was basically a research institution which furnished the intellectual information for social reform and supported all contributing to the gradual attainment by parliamentary means of socialism.

The Webbs's analysis of society emphasised that individualist enterprise in capitalism was a hang-over from early days and was bound to defeat itself since socialism is the inevitable accompaniment of modern industrialism; the necessary result of popular government is control of their economic system by the people themselves. Utopian schemes had been doomed to failure because they were based on the fallacy that society is static and that islands of utopias could be formed in the midst of an unchanging and antagonistic environment. On the contrary, it was pointed out, society develops: "The new becomes old, often before it is consciously regarded as new." Social reorganisation cannot usefully be hastened by violent means but only through methods consonant with this natural historical progression—gradual, peaceful, and democratic. The Fabians were convinced that men are rational enough to accept in their common interest developments which can be demonstrated as necessary; thus public opinion will come to see that socialisation of the land and industries is essential in the same way that they came to accept the already-existing acts in respect of housing, insurance, medical care, and conditions of work.

The Society collaborated first in the formation of the Independent Labour Party and then with the more moderate Labour Party and the trade unions and Co-operative movement. But in general it disapproved of independent trade union action since change should come from the government and take political form. The class-war of Marx was rejected and so too was the idea of the exclusive role of the working class —reform must come from the enlightened co-operation of all classes—not from their opposition.

Faith Healing, the belief and practice of curing physical and mental ills by faith in some supernatural power, either allegedly latent in the individual (as with Christian Science) or drawn in some way from God. It is a characteristic of faith healing that it is supposed to be publicly demonstrable—*i.e.*, a "healer" will hold public meetings and invite sick people to come up to be cured on the platform. In the emotionally charged atmosphere which the healer generates, it is not unusual for people to show immediate and striking improvement in their illness, but the almost invariable rule is for relapses to occur within days or hours after the event. When remission is more permanent, the illness is generally hysterical in origin and will often return to the individual in some other form. Spiritualists claim that the healing in such cases is done not by "faith" but by direct intervention of the spirits of doctors, etc., who have died and passed on to another world. Perhaps the world's most famous faith healer in recent years was Harry Edwards (d. 1976), who had literally millions of letters from all parts of the world asking for the healing attention of his spirit guides. Many doctors, while remaining immensely sceptical about the origins and extent of this kind of therapy, are inclined to admit that it might have benefits when the sickness is mildly hysterical in origin. The real danger, of course, comes when patients seek unorthodox therapy before consulting their doctor.

Falangists. The Fascist Party of Spain founded in 1933 by José Antonio Primo de Rivera, son of the man who was dictator of the country from 1923 to 1930; he was shot by the Republicans. In 1937 the falangists who had shown unwelcome signs of social radicalism were merged with the other right-wing political groups to form the *Falange Española Tradicionalista y de las Juntas de Ofensive Nacional Sindicalistas* which replaced the Cortes (*i.e.* the Government) between 1939 and 1942 when the Cortes was reinstituted. The Falange was the only political party allowed in Spain during the Franco era. *See* **Fascism**.

Fascism. From the end of mediaeval times with the opening up of the world, the liberation of the mind and the release of business enterprise, a new spirit arose in Europe exemplified in such movements as the Renaissance, the Reformation, the struggle for democracy, the rise of capitalism, and the Industrial Revolution. With these movements there developed a certain tradition, which, in spite of hindrances and disagreement or failures, was universally held by both right- and left-wing parties however strongly they might fail to agree on the best means of attaining what was felt to be a universal ideal. The hard core of this tradition involved: belief in reason and the possibility of human progress; the essential sanctity and dignity of human life; tolerance of widely different religious and political views; reliance on popular government and the responsibility of the rulers to the ruled; freedom of thought and criticism; the necessity of universal education; impartial justice and the rule of law; the desirability of universal peace. Fascism was the negation of every aspect of this tradition and took pride in being so. Emotion took the place of reason, the "immutable, beneficial, and fruitful inequality of classes" and the right of a self-constituted élite to rule them replaced universal suffrage because absolute authority "quick, sure, unanimous" led to action rather than talk. Contrary opinions are not allowed and justice is in the service of the state; war is desirable to advance the power of the state; and racial inequality made a dogma. Those who belong to the "wrong" religion, political party, or race are outside the law.

The attacks on liberalism and exaltation of the state derive largely from Hegel and his German followers; the mystical irrationalism from such 19th cent. philosophers as Schopenhauer Nietzsche, and Bergson; from Sorel (*see* **Syndicalism**) came the idea of the "myth", and an image which would have the power to arouse the emotions of the masses and from Sorel also the rationale of violence and justification of force. But these philosophical justifications of fascism do not explain why it arose at all and why it arose where it did—in Italy, Germany, and Spain. These countries had one thing in common—disillusionment. Germany had lost the 1914–18 war, Italy had been on the winning side but was resentful about her small gains. Spain had sunk to the level of a third-rate power, and people were becoming increasingly restive under the reactionary powers of the Catholic Church, the landed aristocracy, and the army. In Marxist theory, fascism is the last fling of the ruling class and the bourgeoisie in their attempt to hold down the workers.

Italian Fascism. The corporate state set up by Benito Mussolini in Italy claimed to be neither capitalist nor socialist, and after its inception in 1922 the Fascist Party became the only recognised one. Its members wore black shirts, were organised in military formations, used the Roman greeting of the outstretched arm, and adopted as their slogan "Mussolini is always right". Membership of the Party was not allowed to exceed a number thought to be suited to the optimum size of a governing class and new candidates were drawn, after strict examinations, from the youth organisations.

The Blackshirts, a fascista militia, existed separately from the army and were ruled by Fascist Headquarters.

At the head of government was Mussolini. "Il Duce" himself, a cabinet of fourteen ministers selected by him and approved by the King to supervise the various functions of government, and the Grand Council or directorate of the Fascist Party, all the members of which were chosen by the Duce. Parliament, which was not allowed to initiate legislation but only to approve decrees from above, consisted of a Senate with life-membership and a Chamber of Fasci and Corporations composed of nominated members of the Party, the National Council of Corporations, and selected representatives of the employers' and employees' confederations. Private enterprise was encouraged and protected but rigidly controlled; strikes were forbidden, but a Charter of Labour enforced the collaboration of workers and employers whose disputes were settled in labour courts presided over by the Party. All decisions relating to industry were government-controlled (*e.g.*, wages, prices, conditions of employment and dismissal, the expansion or limitation of production), and some industries such as mining, shipping, and armaments were largely stateowned.

Italian fascism served as a model in other countries, notably for the German National Socialist Party, in Spain and Japan, and most European nations between the wars had their small Fascist parties, the British version led by Sir Oswald Mosley being known as the British Union which relied on "strong-arm tactics", marches and violence. The Public Order Act of 1936 was passed to deal with it. Although fascism in all countries has certain recognisable characteristics, it would be wrong to think of it as an international movement taking fixed forms and with a clearly thought-out rationale as in the case of communism. While there have been minor revivals of interest in Fascism in Italy—presumably as a counter-move against the considerable inroads being made by the Communist party in that country—Fascism's final remaining bastion in Europe—Spain—began to crumble with the death of its dictator, General Franco, in 1975.

See **Falange, Nazism**.

Fatalism. *See* **Determinism**.

Feedback Cult is the name given to a curious fad which began in America in 1970 and which is interesting because it incorporates complicated scientific equipment and experimental psychological methods into its practice. The basis of the cult is as follows: for nearly fifty years it has been known that the brain is the source of varied electrical signals of very low power which can be detected by attaching electrodes to the scalp and amplifying the pulses emitted. Much scientific controversy has surrounded these pulses, and their interpretation by skilled clinicians can lead to the detection of hidden cerebral disorders such as tumours, epileptic foci, etc. The presence of one particular rhythm, the so-called alpha wave, which beats at 14 cycles per second—is believed to be dependent upon whether or not the individual is "attending" to something, particularly in the visual field. It is this alpha rhythm, or rather its control, that is the basis of the feedback cult.

Within the past decade it has been discovered that when some people are connected to an electroencephalograph (the device which records brain rhythms) and are shown the recorded tracings of their own brain waves as they actually occur, they find it possible to modify and control the nature of the waves—the alpha in particular. This, a scientific curiosity rather than a major discovery, soon caught the attention of followers of yoga and other systems seeking enhanced relaxation, "mental discipline," etc. The argument was advanced that for centuries man had been seeking to exercise control over his own mental activities, without however having much opportunity to assess his success—or lack of it. The use of the EEG with the individual's brain waves "fed back" to him for inspection would remedy this. The result has been a sudden surge of lay interest in electroencephalography and a boom in the sale of small, portable EEG machines. Followers of the cult, who may sit for hours inspecting the output from their own brains and attempting to modify it, at will, claim that the activity promotes mental "relaxation" and a greater and deeper understanding of their own personal problems. Psychologists are extremely dubious about the reality of this as mental therapy, and the feedback cult will probably die away as soon as some new and equally attractive scientific toy is developed.

Fetichism, originally a practice of the natives of West Africa and elsewhere of attributing magical properties to an object which was used as an amulet, for putting spells on others, or regarded as possessing dangerous powers. In psychology the term refers to a sexual perversion in which objects such as shoes, brassières, hair, etc., arouse sexual excitement.

Feudalism. The feudal system took its origins from Saxon times and broadly speaking lasted until the end of the 13th cent. It was a military and political organisation based on land tenure, for, of course, society throughout this period was based almost entirely on agriculture. The activities of men divided them into three classes or estates. The First Estate was the clergy, responsible for man's spiritual needs; the Second was the nobility, including kings and emperor as well as the lesser nobles; the Third was composed of all those who had to do with the economic and mainly agricultural life of Europe. The praying men, the fighting men and administrators, and the toilers were all held to be dependent on each other in a web of mutual responsibilities.

The theory of feudalism, although it by no means always worked out in practice, was as follows: the earth was God's and therefore no man owned land in the modern sense of the word. God had given the pope spiritual charge of men, and secular power over them to the emperor from whom kings held their kingdoms, and in turn the dukes and counts received the land over which they held sway from the king. Members of the Second Estate held their lands on the condition of fulfilling certain obligations to their overlord and to the people living under them, so when a noble received a fief or piece of land he became the vassal of the man who bestowed it. To him he owed military service for a specified period of the year, attendance at court, and giving his lord counsel. He undertook to ransom his lord when he fell into enemy hands and to contribute to his daughter's dowry and at the knighting of his son. In return the lord offered his vassal protection and justice, received the vassal's sons into his household and educated them for knighthood.

The system was complicated by the fact that large fiefs might be subdivided and abbots often governed church lands held in fief from nobles. The serf or toiling man dwelt on the land of a feudal noble or churchman where he rendered service by tilling the soil or carrying out his craft for his manorial lord in return for protection, justice, and the security of his life and land. He was given a share in the common lands or pastures from which he provided for his own needs. In the modern sense he was not free (although at a later stage he could buy his freedom) since he was attached to the soil and could not leave without the lord's permission. On the other hand he could neither be deprived of his land nor lose his livelihood. Feudal tenures were abolished in England by statute in 1660, although they had for long been inoperative. In Japan a feudal system existed up to 1871, in Russia until 1917, and many relics of it still linger on (e.g. the mezzadria system of land tenure in parts of Italy).

Flying Saucers. In June 1947 an American private pilot, Kenneth Arnold, saw a series of wingless objects flying through the air at a speed which he estimated at thousands of miles an hour. He later told the press that the objects "flew as a saucer would if you skipped it across the water," and the phrase "flying saucers" was erroneously born. What Arnold actually saw has never been satisfactorily explained—it was probably a flight of jet fighters reflecting the sun's rays in a way that made them appear as discs—but since that date literally hundreds of thousands of people all over the world have reported the sighting of strange objects in the sky, coming in a bewildering range of shapes and sizes. Initially the American Air Force launched an official enquiry—Project Bluebook—to attempt to solve the mystery of these "unidentified flying objects" or "U.F.O.s," which finally folded in 1969 after concluding that the bulk of the sightings were probably misinterpretations of natural phenomena and that there was no evidence for the commonly held view that earth was being visited by spacecraft from some other planetary system. A rather similar conclusion was arrived at by the famous University of Colorado project—the Condon Committee—which published its findings in 1968. Despite this clear-cut official attitude, belief in the existence of flying saucers and their origin as alien space vehicles is exceedingly widespread and is held very strongly by people in all walks of life. In 1959 this striking social phenomenon attracted the attention of the psychologist C. G. Jung. He noticed that the press were inclined to report statements that saucers existed when made by prominent people and not publish contrary statements made by equally prominent people. He concluded that flying saucers were in some way welcome phenomena and in his brilliant little book. *Flying Saucers—a modern myth,* he hypothesised that the U.F.O.s were the modern equivalent of "signs in the skies." It was Jung's contention that the saucers were looked upon as the harbingers of advanced alien civilisations who had come to save the world from its descent into nuclear catastrophe—archangels in modern dress in fact.

Whatever the validity of this imaginative view of U.F.O.s, it is undeniably true that they exercise a great fascination for millions of people, some of whom invest them with definite religious significance. The best example of the open incorporation of flying saucers into a religious belief system is to be found in the Aetherius Society, an international organisation with headquarters in Los Angeles but founded by a former London clerk, George King. Mr. King, who claims to be the mediumistic link between earth and the largely benevolent beings from outer space, regularly relays messages—notably from a Venusian known as Aetherius—to enthusiastic congregations at religious meetings. The sect, which is entirely sincere and dedicated in its beliefs, also makes pilgrimages to the tops of various mountains which have been "spiritually charged" with the aid of the spacebeings in their flying saucers.

Odd though such ideas may seem to most people, they can be readily understood within the context of the very marked decline in orthodox religious belief which we have seen in the past two decades. To an increasing number of people, many of whom feel a desperate need for spiritual guidance and enlightenment, the concepts of the traditionally Western religions seem somehow unsatisfactory. Many therefore turn to cults and splinter groups which use ideas and terminology which to them seem more at home in the twentieth century than those that sprung to life thousands of years ago. To members of the Aetherius Society, for example, the idea that Jesus Christ lives on Venus and rides around in a flying saucer is neither blasphemous nor ludicrous. As long as empty churches testify to the growing, if perhaps only temporary loss of contact between orthodox religions and the man-in-the-street, then one can expect such offbeat ideas as the cults surrounding flying saucers, and the science-fiction-like cult of Scientology (q.v.) to expand and flourish.

Fourierism *See* **Utopianism.**

Freemasonry, a widespread, influential secret organisation of English origin. Although it can be traced back to the Middle Ages when itinerant working masons in England and Scotland were organised in lodges with secret signs for the recognition of fellow-members, modern freemasonry first arose in England in the early decades of the 18th cent. The first Grand Lodge was founded in London in 1716 and Freemasons' Hall was opened in 1776. With its clubs for discussion and social enjoyment (women were excluded) it met a need and became a well-known feature of English life. The movement quickly spread abroad to places which had direct trade links with England. The graded lodge structure, the social prestige conferred by membership, the symbolism, ritual and ceremony, and the emphasis on mutual help have had a lasting appeal. Interest in the occult had more appeal on the Continent than in England. Until a decade or so ago, membership conferred definite business and social advantages, particularly in small communities where the leading middleclass figures were generally members. Recently this advantage has markedly declined and freemason lodges nowadays tend to be little more than worthy charitable organisations. Fear of secret societies has given freemasonry many opponents; it was condemned by the Roman Catholic Church, banned by Fascist dictators, and denounced by the Comintern. A statement from the congregation for the doctrine of the faith in 1981 reminded Catholics that under Article 2335 of the Code of Canon Law they are forbidden under pain of excommunication from joining masonic or similar associations.

Freudian theory. *See* **Psychoanalysis.**

Friends, The Society of. *See* **Quakers.**

Fundamentalism is a term covering a number of religious movements which adhere with the utmost rigidity to orthodox tenets; for example the Old Testament statement that the earth was created by God in six days and six nights would be held to be factual rather than allegorical or symbolic. Although the holding of rigid beliefs in the literal truth of the Bible might seem to be frequently contrary to modern scientific findings, the fundamentalists at least do not have the problems of compromise and interpretation to face, and to some people this is no doubt a great attraction. A factor influencing the present troubles in Northern Ireland is the narrow and intolerant form of fundamentalism represented by the extreme brand of Presbyterianism practised there.

G

Game Theory, an approach to understanding human and animal behaviour which takes the view that psychological insight is best gained by studying the decisions which all living things make constantly and which govern the course of their lives. It proposes that life is basically a strategic game following complex rules which can probably only be understood by a study of the "decision units" as and when they occur. Because one is dealing with highly variable animals controlled by highly complex brains, and not with simple clockwork or electro-mechanical systems, the study of the rules which operate in the game of life is enormously complicated and thus game theory has quickly taken off into advanced mathematics. Game theory, incidentally, can be used to apply to individual action or to the behaviour of groups. Little of any predictive value has been put forward by the protagonists of this approach, but the use of computers to tackle the complex mathematics involved may well lead to some interesting advances.

Gestalt Psychology. In the latter half of the 19th cent. it became evident to psychologists that in principle there was no good reason why "mental" events should not be just as measurable and manageable as "physical" ones. Intensive studies of learning, memory, perception, and so on were therefore undertaken and the beginnings of an empirical science of psychology were underway. In the early part of the 20th cent. the experiments of Pavlov (*see* **Behaviourism**) and his co-workers suggested that the behaviour of an animal, or even men, might ultimately be reduced to a descriptive account of the activities of nervous reflex loops—the so-called conditioned reflexes. With the publication of Watson's important book on Behaviourism in 1914 it looked as though the transfer of psychological studies from the field of philosophy to that of science could now take place. Actually the over-simplified picture of cerebral and mental pictures which Behaviourism offered

was rather comparable to the billiard ball view of the universe so fashionable in Victorian science. Just as Behaviourism implied that there was a fundamental building block (the conditioned reflex) from which all mental events could be constructed, so Victorian physics assumed that the entire universe could be described in terms of a vast collection of atoms pushing each other around like billiard balls. The development of nuclear physics was to shatter the latter dream and at the same time a challenge to the naïve "reflex psychology" came from the Gestalt experimental school.

The founders of this school were Max Wertheimer, Kurt Koffka and Wolfgang Köhler, three young psychologists who in 1912 were conducting experiments—notably in vision—which seemed to expose the inadequacies of the behaviourist position. The Pavlov-Watson view, as we have said, implied that complex sensory events were no more than a numerical sum of individual nervous impulses. Wertheimer's group proposed that certain facts of perceptual experiences (ruled out of court as subjective and therefore unreliable by Watson) implied that the whole (*Gestalt*) was something more than simply the sum of its parts. For example, the presentation of a number of photographs, each slightly different, in rapid series gives rise to cinematographic motion. In basic terms, the eye has received a number of discrete, "still" photographs, and yet "motion" is perceived. What, they asked, was the sensory input corresponding to this motion? Some processes within the brain clearly *added* something to the total input as defined in behaviourist terms. An obvious alternative—in a different sense modality—is that of the arrangement of musical notes. A cluster of notes played one way might be called a tune; played backwards they may form another tune, or may be meaningless. Yet in all cases the constituent parts are the same, and yet their relationship to one another is evidently vital. Once again the whole is something more than the simple sum of the parts.

The implications of all this appeared to be that the brain was equipped with the capacity to organise sensory input in certain well-defined ways, and that far from being misleading and scientifically unjustifiable, human subjective studies of visual experience might reveal the very principles of organisation which the brain employs. Take a field of dots, more or less randomly distributed; inspection of the field will soon reveal certain patterns or clusters standing out—the constellations in the night sky are a good illustration. There are many other examples, and Wertheimer and his colleagues in a famous series of experiments made some effort to catalogue them and reduce them to a finite number of "Laws of Perceptual Organisation" which are still much quoted today. *See* **Q19, Q21.**

Ghosts, belief in ghosts is one of the most common features of supernatural and mystical philosophy. At its roots it is based on the assumption that Man is essentially an individual created of two separate and distinct substances, mind and body. Most religious systems hold to this dualistic view (*see* **Dualism**), arguing that whereas the body is transient and destructible, the mind or spirit is permanent and survives the death of its physical host. The discarnate spirit is normally assumed to progress to some other realm ("Heaven," "Nirvana," "The Spirit World," etc.) whereupon it loses contact with the mortal world. Occasionally, however, for one reason or another, the spirits may not progress and may become trapped and unable to escape the material world. Traditionally this is supposed to occur when the death of the individual is precipitated by some great tragedy —murder, suicide, etc.—when the site of the tragedy is supposed to be haunted by the earthbound spirit. Although the library of the Society for Psychical Research is crammed with supposedly authentic accounts of hauntings of this kind, scientific interest in ghosts has been waning rapidly in recent years. At one time, in particular in the latter part of the 19th cent., with the upsurge of scientific interest in Spiritualism (*q.v.*), there were even attempts to call up ghosts in the laboratory. These led to spectacular opportunities for fraud on the part of Spiritualist mediums and the like, but in the long run added little to the cause of science. As we have said, belief in ghosts is largely dependent upon a parallel belief that the mind or soul of man is something essentially separate from the body. With the decline in belief of this notion (it is now almost totally dismissed by most scientists and philosophers) has come an inevitable decline in belief in ghosts.

Gnosticism. Among the many heresies of early Christianity, especially during its first two centuries, was a group which came under the heading of Gnosticism. This was a system or set of systems which attempted to combine Christian beliefs with others derived from Oriental and Greek sources, especially those which were of a mystical and metaphysical nature, such as the doctrines of Plato and Pythagoras. There were many Gnostic sects, the most celebrated being the Alexandrian school of Valentius (fl. *c.* 136–*c.* 160). "Gnosis" was understood not as meaning "knowledge" or "understanding" as we understand these words, but "revelation." As in other mystical religions, the ultimate object was individual salvation; sacraments took the most varied forms. Many who professed themselves Christians accepted Gnostic doctrines and even orthodox Christianity contains some elements of Gnostic mysticism. It was left to the bishops and theologians to decide at what point Gnosticism ceased to be orthodox and a difficult task this proved to be. Two of the greatest, Clement of Alexandria and his pupil Origen, unwittingly slipped into heresy when they tried to show that such men as Socrates and Plato, who were in quest of truth, were Christian in intention, and by their lives and works had prepared the way for Christ. Thus they contradicted Church doctrine which specifically said *Extra ecclesiam nulla salus*—outside the Church there is no salvation.

God and Man. The idea of gods came before the idea of God and even earlier in the evolution of religious thought there existed belief in spirits (*see* **Animism**). It was only as a result of a long period of development that the notion of a universal "God" arose, a development particularly well documented in the Old Testament. Here we are concerned only with the views of philosophers, the views of specific religious bodies being given under the appropriate headings. First, however, some definitions.

Atheism is the positive disbelief in the existence of a God. **Agnosticism** (a term coined by T. H. Huxley, the 19th cent. biologist and contemporary of Darwin) signifies that one cannot know whether God exists or not. **Deism** is the acceptance of the existence of God, not through revelation, but as a hypothesis required by reason. **Theism** also accepts the existence of God, but, unlike Deism, does not reject the evidence of revelation (*e.g.,* in the Bible or in the lives of the saints). **Pantheism** is the identification of God with all that exists (*i.e.,* with the whole universe). **Monotheism** is the belief in one God, **Polytheism** the belief in many (*see also* **Dualism**).

Early Greek Views. Among the early Greek philosophers, Thales (*c.* 624–565 B.C.) of Miletus, in Asia Minor, Anaximander (611–547 B.C.), his pupil, and Anaximenes (b. *c.* 570 B.C.), another Miletan, were men of scientific curiosity and their speculations about the origin of the universe were untouched by religious thought. They founded the scientific tradition of critical discussion. Heraclitus of Ephesus (*c.* 540–475 B.C.), was concerned with the problem of change. How does a thing change and yet remain itself? For him all things are flames—processes. "Everything is in flux, and nothing is at rest." Empedocles of Agrigentum in Sicily (*c.* 500–*c.* 430 B.C.) introduced the idea of opposition and affinity. All matter is composed of the so-called four elements—*earth, water, air,* and *fire*—which are in opposition or alliance with each other. All these were materialist philosophers who sought to explain the working of the universe without recourse to the gods.

Socrates, Plato, and Aristotle. Socrates (470–399 B.C.) was primarily concerned with ethical matters and conduct rather than the nature of the universe. For him goodness and virtue come from knowledge. He obeyed an "inner voice" and suffered death rather than give up his philosophy. He believed in the persistence of life after death and was essentially a monotheist. Plato (427–347 B.C.) was chiefly concerned with the nature of reality and thought in terms of absolute truths which were unchanging, logical, and mathematical. (*See* **Mind and Matter.**) Aristotle (384–322 B.C.) took his views of matter not from Democritus (atomic view) but from Empedocles (doctrine of four elements), a view which came to fit in well with orthodox mediaeval theology. Matter is conceived of as potentially alive and striving to attain its particular form, being moved by divine spirit or mind (*nous*). (An acorn, for example, is matter which contains the form "oak-tree" towards which it strives.) Thus there is a whole series from the simplest level of matter to the perfect living individual. But there must be a supreme source of all movement upon which the whole of Nature depends, a Being that Aristotle describes as the "Unmoved Mover", the ultimate cause of all becoming in the universe. This Being is pure intelligence, a philosopher's God, not a personal one. Unlike Plato, Aristotle did not believe in survival after death, holding that the divine, that is the immortal element in man, is mind.

Among the later Greek thinkers the Epicureans were polytheists whose gods, however, were denied supernatural powers. The Stoics built up a materialist theory of the universe, based on the Aristotelian model. To them God was an all-pervading force, related to the world as the soul is related to the body, but they conceived of it as material. They developed the mystical side of Plato's idealism and were much attracted by the astrology coming from Babylonia. They were pantheists. The Sceptics were agnostics.

From *Pagan to Christian Thought.* Philo, "the Jew of Alexandria," who was about 20 years older than Jesus, tried to show that the Jewish scriptures were in line with the best in Greek thought. He introduced the *Logos* as a bridge between the two systems. Philo's God is remote from the world, above and beyond all thought and being, and as His perfection does not permit direct contact with matter the divine *Logos* acts as intermediary between God and man. Plotinus (204–70), a Roman, and the founder of Neoplatonism, was the last of the great pagan philosophers. Like Philo, he believed that God had created the world indirectly through emanations—beings coming from Him but not of Him. The world needs God but God does not need the world. Creation is a fall from God, especially the human soul when enmeshed in the body and the world of the senses, yet (*see* **Determinism**) man has the ability to free himself from sense domination and turn towards God. Neoplatonism was the final stage of Greek thought drawing inspiration from the mystical side of Plato's idealism and its ethics from Stoicism.

Christianity: The Fathers and the Schoolmen. It was mainly through St. Augustine (354–430), Bishop of Hippo in North Africa, that certain of the doctrines of Neoplatonism found their way into Christianity. Augustine also emphasised the concept of God as all good, all wise, all knowing, transcendent, the Creator of the universe out of nothing. But, he added, since God knows everything, everything is determined by Him forever. This is the doctrine of predestination and its subsequent history is discussed under **Determinism.**

In the early centuries of Christianity, as we have seen, some found it difficult to reconcile God's perfection with His creation of the universe and introduced the concept of the *Logos* which many identified with Christ. Further, it came to be held that a power of divine origin permeated the universe, namely the Holy Spirit or Holy Ghost. Some theory had to be worked out to explain the relationships of these three entities whence arose the conception of the Trinity. God is One; but He is also Three: Father, Son (the *Logos* or Christ), and Holy Ghost.

This doctrine was argued by the Apologists and the Modalists. The former maintained that the *Logos* and the Holy Spirit were emanations from God and that Jesus was the *Logos* in the form of a man. The Modalists held that all three Persons of the Trinity were God in three forms or modes: the *Logos* is God creating, the Holy Spirit God reasoning, and God is God being. This led to a long discussion as to whether the *Logos* was an emanation from God or God in another form; was the *Logos* of like *nature* with God or of the same *substance*? This was resolved at the Council of Nicaea (325) when Athanasius formulated the orthodox doctrine against Arius (*q.v.*): that the one God is a Trinity of the same substance, three Persons of the same nature—Father, Son, and Holy Ghost.

St. Thomas Aquinas (1227–74), influenced greatly by Aristotle's doctrines, set the pattern for all subsequent Catholic belief even to the present time. He produced rational arguments for God's existence: *e.g.*, Aristotle's argument that, since movement exists, there must be a prime mover, the Unmoved Mover or God; further, we can see that things in the universe are related in a scale from the less to the more complex, from the less to the more perfect, and this leads us to suppose that at the peak there must be a Being with absolute perfection. God is the first and final cause of the universe, absolutely perfect, the Creator of everything out of nothing. He reveals Himself in his Creation and rules the universe through His perfect will. How Aquinas dealt with the problem of predestination is told under **Determinism**.

Break with Mediaeval Thought. Renaissance thinkers, free to think for themselves, doubted the validity of the arguments of the Schoolmen but most were unwilling to give up the idea of God (nor would it have been safe to do so). Mystics (*see* **Mysticism**) or near-mystics such as Nicholas of Cusa (*c.* 1401–64) and Jacob Boehme (1575–1624) taught that God was not to be found by reason but was a fact of the immediate intuition of the mystical experience, Giordano Bruno held that God was immanent in the infinite universe. He is the unity of all opposites, a unity without opposites, which the human mind cannot grasp. Bruno was burned at the stake in 1600 at the instigation of the Inquisition (a body which, so we are told, never caused pain to anyone since it was the civil power, not the Inquisition, that carried out the unpleasant sentences) for his heresy.

Francis Bacon, who died in 1626, separated, as was the tendency of that time, science from religion. The latter he divided into the two categories of natural and revealed theology. The former, through the study of nature, may give convincing proof of the existence of a God but nothing more. Of revealed theology he said: "we must quit the small vessel of human reason ... as we are obliged to obey the divine law, though our will murmurs against it, so we are obliged to believe in the word of God, though our reason is shocked at it." Hobbes (d. 1679) was a complete materialist and one feels that his obeisance to the notion was politic rather than from conviction. However, he does mention God as starting the universe in motion; infers that God is corporeal but denies that His nature can be known.

From Descartes Onwards. Descartes (1596–1650) separated mind and body as different entities but believed that the existence of God could be deduced by the fact that the idea of him existed in the mind. Whatever God puts into man, including his ideas, must be real. God is self-caused, omniscient, omnipotent, eternal, all goodness and truth. But Descartes neglected to explain how mind separate from body can influence body, or God separate from the world can influence matter.

Spinoza (1632–77) declared that all existence is embraced in one substance—God, the all-in-all. He was a pantheist and as such was rejected by his Jewish brethren. But Spinoza's God has neither personality nor consciousness, intelligence nor purpose, although all things follow in strict law from His nature. All the thoughts of everyone in the world, make up God's thoughts.

Bishop Berkeley (1685–1753) took the view that things exist only when they are perceived, and this naturally implies that a tree, for example, ceases to exist when nobody is looking at it. This problem was solved to his own satisfaction by assuming that God, seeing everything, prevented objects from disappearing when we were not present. The world is a creation of God but it is a spiritual or mental world, not a material one.

Hume (1711–76), who was a sceptic, held that human reason cannot demonstrate the existence of God and all past arguments to show that it could were fallacious. Yet we must believe in God since the basis of all hope, morality, and society is based upon the belief. Kant (1724–1804) held a theory similar to that of Hume. We cannot know by reason that God exists, nor can we prove on the basis of argument anything about God. But we can form an idea of the whole of the universe, the one Absolute Whole, and personify it. We need the idea of God on which to base our moral life, although this idea of God is transcendent, *i.e.*, goes beyond experience.

William James (1842–1910), the American philosopher (*see* **Pragmatism**), held much the same view: God cannot be proved to exist, but we have a will to believe which must be satisfied, and the idea works in practice. Hegel (1770–1831) thought of God as a developing process, beginning with "the Absolute" or First Cause and finding its highest expression in man's mind, or reason. It is in man that God most clearly becomes aware of Himself. Finally Comte (1798–1857), the positivist, held that religion belongs to a more primitive state of society and, like many modern philosophers, turned the problem over to believers as being none of the business of science.

Golden Dawn, Order of, a strange but intellectually influential secret society founded in 1887 by three former Rosicrucians (*q.v.*). The Society, which was but one of the large number of occult organisations which flourished in the latter half of the 19th cent., was particularly interesting because it attracted so many scholarly eccentrics to its ranks. These included the poet W. B. Yeats, the actress Florence Farr, the writers Arthur Machen and Algernon Blackwood and the poetess Dion Fortune. A member with a less savoury reputation was the notorious Aleister Crowley who was ultimately expelled from the order for practising Black Magic. Essentially the movement, like others of its kind, professed to offer important secrets of occult knowledge, and taught its followers the basic principles of White, as opposed to Black Magic. Mainly harmless in their aims and activities, societies such as this served largely as pastimes for individuals of intellectual and academic standing who found the concepts and rituals of the Established Church too dull for their inquisitive minds. Most members of the Order of the Golden Dawn, either became disillusioned when the white magic, which they had so arduously studied, failed to provide any genuine supernatural results and gave up in disgust, or broke away to form their own rival groups. Though these often had equally glamorous names and rituals, they tended to be no more successful and themselves vanished into the mists of obscurity. Today so-called White Magic has become fashionable with many young people, no doubt as the result of the almost total collapse of the authority of orthodox religion, but it is noticeable that such interest is generally to be found among the less well-educated and intelligent. White Magic had its intellectual heyday in the 19th cent. and it is unlikely ever to attract such sustained academic interest again.

Good and Evil

Early Philosophers' Views. The early Greek philosophers were chiefly concerned with the laws of the universe, consequently it was common belief that knowledge of these laws, and living according to them, constituted the supreme good. Heraclitus, for example, who taught that all things carried with them their opposites, held that good and evil were like two notes in a harmony, necessary to each other. "It is the opposite which is good for us". Democritus, like Epicurus (q.v.), held that the main goal of life is happiness, but happiness in moderation. The good man is not merely the one who *does* good but who always *wants* to do so: "You can tell the good man not by his deeds alone but by his desires." Such goodness brings happiness, the ultimate goal. On the other hand, many of the wandering Sophist teachers taught that good was merely social convention, that there are no absolute principles of right and wrong, that each man should live according to his desires and make his own moral code. To Socrates knowledge was the highest good because doing wrong is the result of ignorance: "no man is voluntarily bad." Plato and Aristotle, differing in many other respects, drew attention to the fact that man is composed of three parts: his desires and appetites, his will, and his reason. A man whose reason rules his will and appetites is not only a good but a happy man; for happiness is not an aim in itself but a by-product of the good life. Aristotle, however, emphasised the goal of self-realisation, and thought that if the goal of life is (as Plato had said) a rational attitude towards the feelings and desires, it needs to be further defined. Aristotle defined it as the "Golden Mean"—the good man is one who does not go to extremes but balances one extreme against another. Thus courage is a mean between cowardice and foolhardiness. The later philosophers Philo and Plotinus held that evil was in the very nature of the body and its senses. Goodness could only be achieved by giving up the life of the senses and, freed from the domination of the body, turning to God, the source of goodness.

Christian Views. St. Augustine taught that everything in the universe is good. Even those things which appear evil are good in that they fit with the harmony of the universe like shadows in a painting. Man should turn his back on the pleasures of the world and turn to the love of God. Peter Abelard (1079–1142) made the more sophisticated distinction when he suggested that the wrongness of an act lies not in the act itself, but in the intention of the doer: "God considers not what is done but in what spirit it is done; and the merit or praise of the agent lies not in the deed but in the intention." If we do what we believe to be right, we may err, but we do not sin. The only sinful man is he who deliberately sets out to do what he knows to be wrong. St. Thomas Aquinas agreed with Aristotle in that he believed the highest good to be realisation of self as God has ordained, and he also agreed with Abelard that intention is important. Even a good act is not good unless the doer intended it to have good consequences. Intention will not make a bad act good, but it is the only thing that will make a good act genuinely good.

In general, Christianity has had difficulties in solving the problem of the existence of evil; for even when one accepts that the evil men do is somehow tied up with the body, it is still difficult to answer the question: how could an all-good God create evil? This is answered in one of two ways: (a) that Adam was given free-will and chose to sin (an answer which still does not explain how sin could exist anywhere in the universe of a God who created everything); (b) by denying the reality of evil as some Christians have chosen to do (e.g., Christian Science q.v.). The Eastern religions, on the other hand (see Zoroastrianism), solved the problem in a more realistic way by a dualism which denied that their gods were the creators of the whole universe and allowed the existence of at least two gods, one good and one evil. In Christianity there is, of course, a Devil, but it is not explained whence his evil nature came.

Later Philosophic Views. Hobbes equated good with pleasure, evil with pain. They are relative to the individual man in the sense that "one man's meat is another man's poison." Descartes believed that the power to distinguish between good and evil given by God to man is not complete, so that man does evil through ignorance. We act with insufficient knowledge and on inadequate evidence. Locke, believing that at birth the mind is a blank slate, held

that men get their opinions of right and wrong from their parents. By and large, happiness is good and pain is evil. But men do not always agree over what is pleasurable and what not. Hence laws exist and these fall into three categories: (1) the divine law; (2) civil laws; (3) matters of opinion or reputation which are enforced by the fact that men do not like to incur the disapproval of their friends. We learn by experience that evil brings pain and good acts bring pleasure and, basically, one is good because not to be so would bring discomfort.

Kant (see **God and Man**) found moral beliefs to be inherent in man whether or not they can be proved by reason. There is a categorical imperative which makes us realise the validity of two universal laws: (1) "always act in such a way that the maxim determining your conduct might well become a universal law; act so that you can will that everybody shall follow the principle of your action; (2) "always act so as to treat humanity, whether in thine own person or in that of another, in every case as an end and never as a means."

Schopenhauer (1788–1860) was influenced by Buddhism and saw the will as a blind impelling striving, and desire as the cause of all suffering. The remedy is to regard sympathy and pity as the basis of all morality and to deny one's individual will. This is made easier if we realise that everyone is part of the Universal Will and therefore the one against whom we are struggling is part of the same whole as ourselves.

John Stuart Mill and Jeremy Bentham were both representatives of the Utilitarian school, believing that good is the greatest good (happiness) of the greatest number (see **Utilitarianism**). Lastly, there is the view held mostly by political thinkers that good is what is good for the state or society in general (see **State and Man**).

Graphology, the study of the analysis of human handwriting. There are two approaches to this topic and it is important to separate them clearly. The first involves the attempt on the part of an expert to decide from looking at a signature (a) to whom it belongs, and (b) whether or not it is forgery. This art is a legitimate, though tricky area of study, and graphologists have been called in as expert witnesses in courts of law. The second approach involves attempts to detect such tenuous variables as character from a study of an individual's handwriting, and the facts here are altogether less clear. Psychologists find it difficult enough to assess character or personality in a face-to-face interview and even when they are equipped with a range of special tests. The general opinion here would seem to be that some slight information might be revealed by a careful study of handwriting, but that the overall effect would be too unreliable for this kind of graphology to be of practical value.

Greater World Spiritualists. Spiritualism, as an organised religion, holds the view that the human personality survives death, and that it is possible to communicate with the spirits of those who have died in the physical sense. Relatively little importance is attached to the divinity of Jesus Christ, which is of course the cornerstone of the Christian faith. Some Spiritualists, however, hold a kind of halfway house position, believing both that Jesus was the son of God, and also that communication with the spirit world is not only possible but also a "lost aspect" of Christian teachings. The most significant group holding this view are the Greater World Christian Spiritualists' Association founded in 1931. Their teachings are based on trance addresses received through the mediumship of Winifred Moyes. Despite the fact that her control in the spirit world was named "Zodiac," Christian Spiritualists claim that their philosophy is closer to the original teachings of Jesus than that of the orthodox Church today.

Guild Socialism, a British form of syndicalism (q.v.) created in 1906 by an architect, A. J. Penty, who was soon joined by A. R. Orage, S. G. Hobson, and G. D. H. Cole. The background to the movement was the situation that, although at that time the Labour Party had 29 members in the House of Commons, a period of severe economic crisis had shown the government unwilling and the Labourites unable to do anything about it; the workers were resorting again to direct action to secure their demands and the democratic and constitutional methods to which the Fabians had partly persuaded them seemed to have failed. The guild socialists advocated a restoration of the mediaeval guild system as was being recommended by the French syndicalists whose programme involved a return to direct economic action, a functional industrial structure, return of craftsmanship, and distrust of the state. Guild socialists believed that value was created by society as a whole rather than by individuals singly, and that capitalist economists had recommended the acquisition of wealth without emphasising the social responsibilities which wealth should bring. The trade unions were to be organised to take over and run their own industries after nationalisation. Thus guild socialists were not only against capitalism but also against state socialism in which the state took over the control of industry. Political authority was held to be uncongenial to human freedom and therefore nothing was to be gained by the substitution of state bureaucracy for capitalist control. The National Guilds League, formed in 1915, advocated abolition of the wages system, self-government in industry and control by a system of national guilds acting in conjunction with other functional democratic organisations in the community. This body was dissolved in 1925, but the theories of guild socialism have undoubtedly influenced British socialism.

Gurdjieff, Russian–Greek mystic who set up an occult commune near Paris in the 1930s, to which were attracted a host of the intellectual and literary avant-garde of the time. His teachings, which are immensely obscure, are presented in allegorical form in a lengthy philosophical novel, *All and Everything,* which has the peculiar sub-title "Beelzebub's Tales to his Grandson." Opinions as to the merits of Gurdjieff's ideas are strikingly varied: some commentators hold that he was one of the century's leading philosophers, others that he was a brazen confidence trickster with a vivid personality and the gift of making trivial observations sound pregnant with meaning. The truth probably lies somewhere in between the two extremes and, despite the fact that a number of highly intelligent individuals still espouse his cause two decades after his death, most people continue to find his books largely unreadable and his philosophy muddled and pretentious.

H

Heresy, originally meant a sect or school of thought holding views different from others (*e.g.,* Pharisees and Sadducees within Judaism). Later it came to mean beliefs contrary to orthodox teaching (*e.g.,* Arianism, Apollinarianism, Nestorianism).

Hinduism, the religion and social institutions of the great majority of the people of India. Hinduism has no fixed scriptural canon but its doctrines are to be found in certain ancient works, notably the *Veda,* the *Brahmanas,* the *Upanishads,* and the *Bhagavad-gita.* The dark-skinned Dravidians invaded India between about 3250 and 2750 B.C. and established a civilisation in the Indus valley. They were polytheists who worshipped a number of nature-gods; some elements of their beliefs persisted into Hinduism. They were subdued by a light-skinned Nordic people who invaded from Asia Minor and Iran about 1500 B.C. The language of these Aryan people was Vedic, parent of Sanskit in which their religious literature (the Vedas) came to be written after many centuries of oral transmission.

The *Veda* or Sacred Lore has come down to us in the form of mantras or hymns of which there are four great collections, the best-known being the *Rig-Veda.* These Vedic Aryans worshipped nature-deities, their favourites being Indra (rain), Agni (fire), and Surya (the sun). Their

religion contained no idolatry but became contaminated by the more primitive beliefs of the conquered Dravidians. Sacrifice and ritual became predominant in a ceremonial religion.

As a reaction a more philosophic form arose (*c.* 500 B.C.) with its scriptures in the *Upanishads.* At its highest level known as Brahmanism belief is in a subtle and sophisticated form of monotheism (Brahman is an impersonal, all-embracing spirit), but there is a tolerant acceptance of more primitive beliefs. Thus Vishnu (a conservative principle) and Siva (a destructive principle) grew out of Vedic conceptions. The two great doctrines of Hinduism are *karma* and transmigration. The universal desire to be reunited with the absolute (*atman* or Brahman) can be satisfied by following the path of knowledge. Life is a cycle of lives (*samsara*) in which man's destiny is determined by his deeds (*karma*) from which he may seek release (*moksa*) through ascetic practices or the discipline of Yoga (*q.v.*). Failure to achieve release means reincarnation—migration to a higher or lower form of life after death—until the ultimate goal of absorption in the absolute is reached.

In the great Sanskrit epic poems *Ramayana* and *Mahabharata* the deity takes three forms, represented by the divine personalities of Brahma, Vishnu, and Siva. There are also lower gods, demi-gods, supernatural beings, and members of the trinity may even become incarnate, as Vishnu became identified with Krishna, one of the heroes of the *Mahabharata* and the well-known *Bhagavad-gita.*

The ritual and legalistic side of Brahmanism is the caste system based on the elaborate codes of the *Law of Manu,* according to which God created distinct orders of men as He created distinct species of animals and plants. Men are born to be Brahmans, soldiers, agriculturists, or servants, but since a Brahman may marry a woman from any of these castes, an endless number of sub-castes arise.

Hinduism has always shown great tolerance for varieties of belief and practice. Ideas pleasant and unpleasant have been assimilated: fetishism, demon-cults, animal-worship, sexual-cults (such as the rites of *Kali* in Calcutta). Today, as would be expected in a country which is in the throes of vast social change, Hinduism itself is changing. Under the impact of modern conditions new ideas are destroying old beliefs and customs. *See also* **Jainism, Sikhism.**

Holy Rollers. Contrary to general belief there is no single individual religious group calling themselves Holy Rollers; rather this is a generic term referring to a number of minor revivalist groups whose members work themselves into an ecstatic frenzy in the course of religious worship. Swooning and fainting are probably the most popular methods of expressing this kind of religious ecstasy, but "speaking with tongues" (*i.e.,* babbling nonsense), snake handling (many believers die from snake venom as a consequence) and uncontrolled dancing are also featured. Athletic religious worship of this kind is of course of great interest to psychologists. Anthropologists are equally interested, for they see in such behaviour patterns vivid reminders—if such are needed—that mankind has a history that predates our present culture by millions and not just by thousands of years.

Homoeopathy, a branch of fringe medicine whose motto *Similia Similibus Curantur* (like cures like) sums up its controversial approach to therapy. In essence the homoeopathists claim that a disease can be treated by administering quite minute doses of a substance which produce symptoms (in the healthy person) similar to those induced by the disease itself. The founder and populariser of this unusual approach to medicine was the German Samuel Hahnemann who was born in 1775, a friend of the physician Mesmer who propagated hypnotherapy. Hahnemann lived to see his ideas spread across the civilised world and despite the grave theoretical difficulties implicit in the question of how the very minute dosages actually achieve any result at all, it remained a respectable approach of medicine until the latter half of the last century. Even today a number of qualified doctors still employ homoeopathic ideas within the framework of the national health service, and the late King George V was treated by the eminent homoeopathist, Sir John Weir, but it seems nevertheless to be in slow but steady decline. This is probably due not to any revealed deficiences in homoeopathy itself, but rather to the extraordinary advances which have been made in orthodox medicine in the last few decades.

Humanism, the term applied to (1) a system of education based on the Greek and Latin classics; and (2) the vigorous attitudes that accompanied the end of the Middle Ages and were represented at different periods by the Renaissance, the Reformation, the Industrial Revolution, and the struggle for democracy. These include: release from ecclesiastical authority, the liberation of the intellect, faith in progress, the belief that man himself can improve his own conditions without supernatural help and, indeed has a duty to do so. "Man is the measure of all things" is the keynote of humanism. The humanist has faith in man's intellectual and spiritual resources not only to bring knowledge and understanding of the world but to solve the moral problems of how to use that knowledge. That man should show respect to man irrespective of class, race or creed is fundamental to the humanist attitude to life. Among the fundamental moral principles he would count those of freedom, justice, tolerance and happiness.

Today the idea that people can live an honest, meaningful life without following a formal religious creed of some kind does not seem particularly shocking. It is an interesting gauge of the rapid change in social attitudes to religion that when, less then thirty years ago, the psychologist Margaret Knight tentatively advanced this thesis in a short B.B.C. talk, public opinion seemed to be outraged and both Mrs. Knight and the B.B.C. were openly attacked by the popular press for immoral and seditious teachings.

Hussites, the followers of John Hus, the most famous pupil of John Wyclif. He was the rector of Prague University and, although it is now by no means certain that his beliefs were heretical, he was condemned to death for heresy and burnt at the stake in 1415 at Constance whence he had come with a safe conduct issued by the Emperor Sigismund of Hungary. The latter based his action on the doctrine that no faith need be kept with heretics, but it is obvious that the main objection to Hus was his contempt for authority of any kind. After their leader's death, the Hussites became a formidable body in Bohemia and Moravia. They took up arms on behalf of their faith, their religion being strongly imbued with political feeling (hostility to Germanism and to the supremacy of the Roman Church). Their religious struggles for reform led to the Hussite Wars during which the movement splintered into several groups.

I

I Ching, the Chinese "Book of Changes" which is supposed to provide a practical demonstration of the truths of ancient Chinese philosophy.The method consists of casting forty-nine sticks into two random heaps, or more simply, of tossing three coins to see if there is a preponderance of heads or tails. The coins are cast six times whereupon the head-tail sequence achieved is referred to a coded series of phrases in the book, which are supposed to relate in some way to the question held in the mind when the sticks or coins are being cast. The phrases are without exception vague, and platitudinous remarks such as "Evil people do not further the perseverance of the superior man," etc., abound. Consequently it is not difficult to read into such amorphous stuff a suitable "interpretation" or answer to one's unspoken question. The I Ching might well be looked upon as an entertaining parlour game, but it is currently a great fad in Europe and America and is taken with great seriousness by an astonishing number of people.

Idealism, in a philosophical sense, the belief that there is no matter in the universe, that all that exists is mind or spirit. See **Mind and Matter** and **Realism.**

Illuminati, a secret society founded in 1776 by Adam Weishaupt, a Bavarian professor of canon law at Ingolstadt, in an attempt to combat superstition and ignorance by founding an association for rational enlightenment and the regeneration of the world. "He tried to give the social ideals of the Enlightenment realisation by conspiratorial means" (J. M. Roberts, *The Mythology of the Secret Societies,* 1972). Under conditions of secrecy it sought to penetrate and control the masonic lodges for subversive purposes. Among its members were Goethe and Schiller. The Order spread to Austria, Italy and Hungary but was condemned by the Roman Catholic Church and dissolved in 1785 by the Bavarian government.

Immortality. The belief in a life after death has been widely held since the earliest times. It has certainly not been universal, nor has it always taken a form which everyone would find satisfying. In the early stages of human history or prehistory everything contained a spirit (*see* **Animism**) and it is obvious from the objects left in early graves that the dead were expected to exist in some form after death. The experience of dreams, too, seemed to suggest to the unsophisticated that there was a part of man which could leave his body and wander elsewhere during sleep. In order to save space, it will be helpful to classify the various types of belief which have existed in philosophical thought regarding this problem: (1) There is the idea that, although *something* survives bodily death, it is not necessarily eternal. Thus most primitive peoples were prepared to believe that man's spirit haunted the place around his grave and that food and drink should be set out for it, but that this spirit did not go on forever and gradually faded away. (2) The ancient Greeks and Hebrews believed for the most part that the souls of the dead went to a place of shades there to pine for the world of men. Their whining ghosts spent eternity in a dark, uninviting region in misery and remorse. (3) Other people, and there were many more of these, believed in the transmigration of souls with the former life of the individual determining whether his next life would be at a higher or lower level. Sometimes this process seems to have been thought of as simply going on and on, by others (*e.g.,* in Hinduism and Buddhism) as terminating in either non-sentience or union with God but in any case in annihilation of the self as self. Believers in this theory were the Greek philosophers Pythagoras, Empedocles, Plato (who believed that soul comes from God and strives to return to God, according to his own rather confused notions of the deity. If it fails to free itself completely from the body it will sink lower and lower from one body to another.) Plotinus held similar views to Plato, and many other religious sects in addition to those mentioned have believed in transmigration. (4) The belief of Plato and Aristotle that if souls continue to exist after death there is no reason why they should not have existed before birth (this in part is covered by (3)), but some have pointed out that eternity does not mean "from now on," but the whole of the time before and after "now"—nobody, however, so far as one knows, held that *individual* souls so exist. (5) The theory that the soul does not exist at all and therefore immortality is meaningless: this was held by Anaximenes in early Greek times; by Leucippus, Democritus, and the other Greek atomists; by the Epicureans from the Greek Epicurus to the Roman Lucretius; by the British Hobbes and Hume; by Comte of France; and William James and John Dewey of America. (6) The thesis, held notably by Locke and Kant, that although we cannot prove the reality of soul and immortality by pure reason, belief in them should be held for moral ends. (For the orthodox Christian view *see* **God and Man, Determinism and Free-will.**) From this summary we can see that many philosophies and religions (with the important exceptions of Islam and Christianity) without denying a future life do deny the permanence of the individual soul in anything resembling its earthly form (*see* **Spiritualism, Psychic Research**).

Imperialism, the practice by a country, which has become a nation and embarked upon commercial and industrial expansion, of acquiring and administering territories, inhabited by peoples usually at a lower stage of development, as colonies or dependencies. Thus the "typical" imperialist powers of the 19th cent. and earlier were Britain, Belgium, Holland, Spain, and Portugal, whilst Germany, Italy, and Japan, which either did not have unity during this period or adequate industrial expansion, tried to make good their lacks in this direction by war in the 20th cent. The term "imperialism" is not easy to define today (although often enough used as a term of abuse). There is economic imperialism exerted, not through armies, but through economic penetration. There is what may be described as ideological imperialism, *e.g.*, the anti-communist crusade that led America (in the name of freedom) into acts of appalling inhumanity in Vietnam; the dogmatism that led the Soviet Union into the invasion of Czechoslovakia and Israel into occupying neighbouring territories. The Afrikaners in South Africa pass laws to permit the exploitation of the black and coloured peoples in their midst. Imperialism is a dangerous word and, before using it, we would do well to remember the retort of a British statesman who, when lecturing in America prior to Indian independence, was asked by an elderly matron "What are you going to do about the Indians?" "Which Indians, madam —ours or yours?"

Irrationalism. An attitude that puts emotion and passion before reason, and which can be exploited for dubious ends.

Islam, the religion of the Arabic and Iranian world of which Mohammed (570–632) was the prophet, the word signifying submission to the will of God. It is one of the most widespread of religions. Its adherents are called Moslems or Muslims. Islam came later than the other great monotheistic religions (Judaism and Christianity) and drew its inspiration mainly from Judaism and Nestorianism. Mohammed accepted the inspiration of the Old Testament and claimed to be a successor to Moses, but recognised Jesus only as a prophet.

The sacred book of Islam is the Koran. Its revelations are contained in 114 *suras* or chapters: all but one begin with the words: "In the name of Allah, the Merciful, the Compassionate." It is written in classical Arabic, and Moslems memorise much or all of it. Its ethical teachings are high. Like orthodox Judaism Islam is a literal-minded religion lived in everyday life. No Moslem is in any doubt as to exactly how he should carry on in the events of his day. He has five duties: (1) Once in his life he must say with absolute conviction: "There is no God but Allah, and Mohammed is His Prophet". (2) Prayer preceded by ablution must be five times daily—on rising, at noon, in mid-afternoon, after sunset, and before retiring. The face of the worshipper is turned in the direction of Mecca. (3) The giving of alms generously, including provisions for the poor. (4) The keeping of the fast of Ramadan, the holy month, during which believers in good health may neither eat nor drink nor indulge in wordly pleasures between sunrise and sunset. (5) Once in his life a Moslem, if he can, must make the pilgrimage to Mecca. In addition, drinking, gambling, and the eating of pork are forbidden and circumcision is practised. Polygamy is permitted, although decreasing; sexual relations outside marriage are disapproved of; marriage is only with the wife's consent; and divorce may be initiated by either husband or wife. A great advantage in the spread of Islam has been its lack of race prejudice.

Mohammed's main achievements were the destruction of idolatry, the welding of warring tribes into one community, the progress of a conquest which led after his death to the great and cultured empire which spread throughout the Middle East into north Africa, north India, and ultimately to Spain. That it did not spread all over Europe was due to the Muslim defeat by Charles Martel at Poitiers in 732.

J

Jainism. The Jains are a small Indian sect, largely in commerce and finance, numbering about 2 million. Their movement founded by Vardhamana, called Mahavira (the great hero), in the 6th cent. B.C. arose rather earlier than Buddhism in revolt against the ritualism and impersonality of **Hinduism** (*q.v.*). It rejects the authority of the early Hindu Vedas and does away with many of the Hindu deities whose place is largely taken by Jainism's twenty-four immortal saints; it despises caste distinctions and modifies the two great Hindu doctrines of *karma* and transmigration. Jain philosophy is based on *ahimsa*, the sacredness of all life, regarding even plants as the brethren of mankind, and refusing to kill even the smallest insect.

Jansenism, the name given by the Roman Catholic Church to the heresy of Cornelius Jansen (1585–1638), a Dutch-born professor of theology at Louvain, derived from his work *Augustinus*, published after his death.

Jehovah's Witnesses, a religious body who consider themselves to be the present-day representatives of a religious movement which has existed since Abel "offered unto God a more excellent sacrifice than Cain, by which he obtained witness that he was righteous." Abel was the first "witness," and amongst others were Enoch, Noah, Abraham, Moses, Jeremiah, and John the Baptist. Pre-eminent among witnesses, of course, was Jesus Christ who is described in the Book of Revelation as "the faithful and true witness." Thus they see themselves as "the Lord's organisation," in the long line of those who through the ages have preserved on earth the true and pure worship of God or, as the Witnesses prefer to call Him, "Jehovah-God."

So far as other people are aware, the movement was founded by Charles Taze Russell (Pastor Russell) of Allegany, Pittsburgh, Pennsylvania, U.S.A. in 1881 under the name, adopted in 1896, of the Watch Tower Bible and Tract Society, which has continued as the controlling organisation of Jehovah's Witnesses. Its magazine, *The Watch Tower Announcing Jehovah's Kingdom*, first published in 1879, and other publications are distributed by the zealous members who carry out the house-to-house canvassing. The movement has a strong leadership.

Their teaching centres upon the early establishment of God's new world on earth, preceded by the second coming of Christ. Witnesses believe this has already happened and that Armageddon "will come as soon as the Witness is completed." The millenial period will give sinners a second chance of salvation and "millions now living will never die" (the title of one of their pamphlets).

The dead will progressively be raised to the new earth until all the vacant places left after Armageddon are filled. There is, however, some doubt about the "goatish souls" who have made themselves unpleasant to the Witnesses, those who have accepted (or permitted to be accepted) a blood-transfusion contrary to the Scriptures, and others who have committed grave sins.

Every belief held by the movement, it is asserted, can be upheld, chapter and verse, by reference to the Scriptures. Witnesses regard the doctrine of the Trinity as devised by Satan. In both wars Witnesses have been in trouble for their refusal to take part in war and it is only fair to add that six thousand suffered for the same reason in German concentration camps.

Jensenism, name given to the minority group of psychologists and educationalists who, in general, support the view of the American professor, Arthur Jensen. The latter's studies of individual variation in learning and of the genetic factor in mental ability has led him to argue that heredity is more crucial in determining intellectual ability than environment. By implication this has put him and his colleagues at the centre of a divisive "race and intelligence" controversy which has acquired some political overtones. In 1978 Professor H. J. Eysenck was physically assaulted by students at a university lecture because he was reputed to be supporting the Jensenist position.

Jesus People, naïve and exhibitionist revival of interest in the teaching and personality of Jesus Christ which has recently featured as part of the American "Hippy" scene. The Jesus people or Jesus Freaks, as they are sometimes called, are generally white but not necessarily of an orthodox Christian background. The cult, like so many others of its kind seems to have developed in California and its adherents adopt the regimental attire (colourful costumes, long hair, beards, etc.) of the modern American Hippy, who is himself a descendant of the Beatnik (*see* **Beat Generation**). Apart from the fact that the long hair and beards are vaguely reminiscent of the Victorian pictorial representation of Jesus, the followers of the present-day cult would seem to have little genuinely in common with the ethos of Christianity, and the movement and its ideals appear to be superficial and probably transitory. A recent highly successful rock musical, "Jesus Christ, Superstar," blatantly cashes in on the Jesus Freak vogue.

Judaism, the religion of the Jews, the oldest of the great monotheist religions, parent of Christianity and Islam, the development of which is presented in the Old Testament. The creed of Judaism is based on the concept of a transcendent and omnipotent One True God, the revelation of His will in the *Torah*, and the special relation between God and His "Chosen People." The idea of Incarnation is rejected, Jesus is not recognised as the Messiah. The *Torah* is the Hebrew name for the Law of Moses (the Pentateuch) which, Judaism holds, was divinely revealed to Moses on Mount Sinai soon after the exodus of the Israelites from Egypt (1230 B.C.). Many critics deny the Mosaic authorship of the first five books of the Bible and believe them to be a compilation from four main sources known as J (Jahvist), E (Elohist), D (Deuteronomist) and P (Priestly Code), distinguished from each other by the name used for God, language, style, and internal evidence. From the historical point of view an important influence on Judaism may have been the monotheism of Akhenaten, the "heretic" Pharaoh (note, for example, the striking resemblance between Psalm 104 and Akhenaten's "Hymn to the Sun").

The Talmud is a book containing the civil and canonical laws of the Jews and includes the Mishna, a compilation from oral tradition written in Hebrew, and the Gemara, a collection of comments and criticisms by the Jewish rabbis, written in Aramaic. There are in fact two Talmuds: the one made in Palestine (the Jerusalem Talmud), finished at the beginning of the 5th cent., and the other made in Babylon, completed at the end of the 6th cent.

Judaism at the beginning of the Christian era had a number of sects: (1) the Pharisees (whose views include the first clear statement of the resurrection of the just to eternal life and the future punishment of the wicked) who held to the *Torah* and the universality of God; (2) the Sadducees, the upper class of priests and wealthy landowners, to whom God was essentially a national God and who placed the interests of the state before the *Torah*; they rejected ideas of resurrection and eternal life; (3) the Essenes (*q.v.*) who were regarded as a puritanical break-away movement by both parties. The views of the Pharisees prevailed.

Jewish writing continued through the years and some books were added to the *Torah*, among them the Three Major Prophets and certain books of the Twelve Minor Prophets. There were also the Apocalyptic writers who were unorthodox in their preaching of a divinely planned catastrophic end to the world with a "new Heaven and a new earth," preceded by a divine Messiah, and a future life—all of which beliefs influenced early Christianity. Judah Halevi of Toledo (*c.* 1085–*c.* 1140) and Moses Maimonides of Cordova (1135–1204) were the great Jewish philosophers.

Modern movements in Judaism stem from the Enlightenment, notably with Moses Mendelssohn in the 18th cent. who accepted, as was the tendency of the period, only that which could be proved by reason. He translated the Pentateuch into German thus encouraging German Jews to give up Yiddish and Hebrew for the language of the land and thereby preparing them for their vast contribution to Western civilisation. One of his disciples, David Friedländer (d. 1834) instituted "reform" Judaism. He wanted to eliminate anything that would hamper the relationships of Jews with their neighbours or tend to cast in doubt their loyalty to their adopted state. A similar movement in America (1885) called for the rejection of dietary laws, the inauguration of Sunday services, and the repudiation of Jewish nationalism. Between "reform" and orthodoxy there arose the conservative movement which, in England, includes prayers in English in the service, does not segregate men and woman in the synagogue, and translates the Law in a more liberal way.

Judaism is essentially a social and family religion which, more than almost any other concerns itself with the observances of every aspect of daily life. As in Islam (*q.v.*) details are laid down in the most minute way for the behaviour of the orthodox.

The home is the main Jewish institution and Jews, like Catholics, cannot surrender their religion. Circumcision takes place eight days after birth, and a boy becomes a man for religious purposes at his Bar Mitzvah at the age of thirteen. Women are spared most of this because their place in the home is considered sufficiently sacred. Among festivals are Passover, recalling the Exodus; Rosh Hashanah (the Jewish New Year), the anniversary of the Creation and the beginning of ten days of penitence ending with Yom Kippur (the Day of Atonement), a day of fasting spent in the synagogue; Purim, celebrating the deliverance of the Jews from Haman; and Chanukah, celebrating their victory against the Syrians under their leader Judas Maccabeus. A new and semi-religious festival is the Yom Haatzmaut, the anniversary of the birth of the new Jewish state of Israel.

K

Kabbala. *See* Cabala.

Ku Klux Klan. After the American Civil War (1861–65) southern conservatives and ex-Confederate leaders began to fear (as they had every reason to do) both Negro and poor White rule. Taxes were rising owing to radical legislation and the tax-burdened and disenfranchised planters finally took to illegal means to achieve their ends by trying to effect an alliance with the poor White and small farmer through appealing to his anti-Negro prejudice.

Hence the Ku Klux Klan was formed in 1866 as a secret society by a small group of Confederate veterans in Tennessee with the intention of frightening Negroes by dressing in ghostly white robes in the guise of the spirits of dead soldiers. But the movement spread like wild-fire throughout the South encouraged by small farmers and planters alike. General Nathan Bedford Forrest was appointed "Grand Wizard" of the Klan "empire" and in every community armed Klansmen riding at night horsewhipped "uppity" Negroes, beat Union soldiers, and threatened carpet-bag politicians (*i.e.*, fortune-hunters from the North). Soon several similar organisations arose, many of which did not stop at torture, burning property, and murder. In fact, although claiming to be a "holy crusade" the Klan was a vicious and contemptible organisation in which former Southern leaders trying to regain control deliberately set poor and middle-class Whites against the Negroes by appeal to race prejudice. Congress struck back with laws and intervention of Federal troops, and after a large number of convictions in South Carolina much of the violence stopped even if the feelings continued.

After the 1914–18 war the movement, dormant since 1900, revived as a sadistic anti-Negro, anti-Jewish, anti-Catholic society, spreading to the north as well as the south. By 1926, with its white-gowned hooligans and fiery crosses, the Klan began to subside once more. While it revived again in the mid-60s, the Klan suffered a loss of support in the 70s as the notion of the essential inferiority of black people wilted among the new generations of America. However, the present climate is allowing this lunatic fringe movement with its fascist-like character to reappear once more.

Kuomintang, a Chinese Nationalist party founded in 1891 by Sun Yat Sen. It took part in the first Chinese revolution of 1911 and led the second the following year, dominating south China by 1930 and, under Chiang Kai-shek, who succeeded Sun Yat Sen on his death in 1925, conducted China's defence against Japanese invasion from 1937–45. Sun Yat Sen had attempted to found a democratic republic based on Western parliamentary democracy and in his famous *Testament* laid down the principles upon which the constitution of China should be based. In 1946, Sun Fo, the son of Sun Yat Sen, deplored the party's departure from the principles of social democracy and the welfare of the people in which his father had believed. Beginning as a movement largely inspired by Russia, the Kuomintang under Chiang Kai-shek degenerated into a reactionary and corrupt military oligarchy which, collapsing in 1949, was replaced by the Communist Party, leaving Chiang and his followers to rule Formosa (Taiwan) with American aid.

L

Lamaism, the religion of Tibet. Its beliefs and worship derive from the Mahayana form of Buddhism which was introduced into Tibet in 749. The emphasis laid by its founder on the necessity for self-discipline and conversion through meditation and the study of philosophy deteriorated into formal monasticism and ritualism. The Dalai Lama, as the reincarnated Buddha, was both king and high priest, a sort of pope and emperor rolled into one. Under him was a hierarchy of officials in which the lowest order was that of the monks who became as numerous as one man in every six or seven of the population. The main work carried out by this vast church-state was the collection of taxes to maintain the monasteries and other religious offices. Second in power to the Dalai Lama was the Panchen or Tashi Lama believed to be a reincarnation of Amitabha, another Buddha. The last Dalai Lama fled to India in 1959 when the Chinese entered his country. For a brief period following his departure, the Panchen Lama surprised the Western world by publicly welcoming the Communist invasion, but he later renounced the regime and the suppression of Lamaism in Tibet continued unchecked.

Levellers, an English military-politico-religious party prominent in the Parliamentary Army about 1647 which stood for the rights of the people. *See* Diggers.

Liberalism. The Liberal Party is the successor to the Whigs (a nickname derived from *Whiggamore*, used in the 17th cent. for Scottish dissenters) of the 18th and 19th cents. Under Gladstone's two great ministries (1868–74; and 1880–85), and again under Campbell-Bannerman and Asquith (1906–14) much reforming legislation was enacted. The Asquith–Lloyd George split of 1916, and the advent of Labour as a major party after 1918, have caused the Liberals to be relegated as a smaller, third party. In the decade after 1945, there were times when the Liberal Party barely survived. But revivals have since occurred (*see* **D3**) under the leadership of Grimond (1962), Thorpe (1974) and David Steel (1979).

Liberal philosophy is moderately radical and progressive in terms of social reform. But the party strongly disapproves of state control or any form of monopoly, private or public. The main proposals favoured by the party are co-ownership in industry, proportional representation, greater protection of individual liberties, and separate Parliaments for Wales and Scotland. Many younger members of the party hold views

to the Left of official party policy. The phenomenon of "community politics" has owed much to these younger, radical Liberals. In the 1983 general election the Liberals in alliance with the Social Democrats were both fighting for the centre vote.

Logical Positivism, a school of philosophy founded in Vienna in the 1920s by a group known as "the Vienna circle": their work was based on that of Ernst Mach, but dates in essentials as far back as Hume. Of the leaders of the group, Schlick was murdered by a student, Wittgenstein came to Britain, and Carnap went to America following the entry of the Nazis. Briefly the philosophy differs from all others in that, while most people have believed that a statement might be (*a*) true, or (*b*) false, logical positivists consider there to be a third category; a statement may be meaningless. There are only two types of statement which can be said to have meaning: (1) those which are tautological, *i.e.*, those in which the statement is merely a definition of the subject, such as "a triangle is a three-sided plane figure" ("triangle" and "three-sided plane figure" are the same thing); and (2) those which can be tested by sense experience. This definition of meaningfulness excludes a great deal of what has previously been thought to be the field of philosophy; in particular it excludes the possibility of metaphysics. Thus the question as to whether there is a God or whether free-will exists is strictly meaningless for it is neither a tautological statement nor can it be tested by sense experience.

Lollards, a body of religious reformers and followers of Wyclif who were reviled and persecuted in the reign of Richard II. The name "Lollard" comes from a Flemish word meaning "mutterer"—a term of contempt used to describe the sect. After his accession Henry IV renewed persecution of the group even condemning the Lollard leader Sir John Oldcastle, to be burnt at the stake.

Luddites, a group of peasants and working men who deliberately destroyed spinning and farm machinery in England in the early part of the 19th cent., fearing that such devices would destroy their livelihood. Their name was taken from the eccentric Ned Lud who had done the same in a less organised way two or three decades earlier. The Luddites' worst fears were of course not realised, for far from putting human beings out of work the industrial revolution created jobs for a vastly increased population. Luddism, dormant for over a century, is beginning to appear again, if in muted form. Public anxiety about the rapid growth in computer technology is manifesting itself in the form of such groups as the Society for the Abolition of Data Processing Machines, which while not of course dedicated to the physical destruction of computers, urge for social and even governmental checks on the development of such things as "data banks." These are vast computer memory stores listing comprehensive records concerning all the people living in a city or country and able to cross-reference them in a way that has never previously been possible. The arguments for and against such data banks and other developments in computer technology are beyond the scope of this section, but the rise of this 20th-cent. Luddism is of considerable historical and social significance.

Lutheranism. The Reformation had a long history before it became, under Luther and Calvin, an accepted fact. The mediaeval Church had held (as the Catholic Church holds today) that the sacraments were the indispensable means of salvation. Since these were exclusively administered by the clergy, any movement which attacked clerical abuses was forced by sheer necessity to deny the Church's exclusive control of the means of salvation, before it could become free from dependence on a corrupt priesthood. Hence the Albigenses and the Waldenses (*qq.v.*), the followers of John Hus and Wycliff (*see* **Anticlericalism**), were bound to deny the authority of the Church and emphasise that of the Bible. Luther began his movement primarily in order to reform the Church from its gross abuses and the famous ninety-five theses nailed to the door of the Church at Wittenberg in 1517 were not primarily theological but moral complaints dealing with the actual behaviour of the clergy rather than Church beliefs. But, unlike the earlier reformers, Luther had arrived at the right moment in history when economic individualism and the force of nationalism were bound, sooner or later, to cause the authorities in Germany to line up on his side. Thus he began with the support of the peasants who were genuinely shocked at the abuse of indulgences and other matters, but ended up by being supported by the noblemen who wanted to destroy the power of the pope over the German states and looked forward to confiscating the lands and property of the Church. When the peasants wanted the reform of actual economic abuses relating to the feudal system, Luther took the side of the nobles against them. The contemporary movement in Switzerland led by Ulrich Zwingli had no such secular support, and Zwingli was killed in 1531.

Martin Luther (1483–1546) was the son of a miner in Eisleben in Saxony, entered the order of Austin Friars in 1505, and later taught at the newly founded university of Wittenberg. After the publication of the theses the real issue so far as the Church was concerned was whether he was willing or not to submit to the authority of his superiors; Luther refused to compromise with his conscience in the famous words: "Here I stand; I can do no other." In a further statement Luther recommended the formation of a German national church, the abolition of indulgences and other means whereby Rome obtained money from Germany, and an end to the celibacy of the clergy. For this he was naturally excommunicated. His teaching was based on the German translation of the Bible, but he was by no means a fundamentalist: e.g., he denied that the Book of Hebrews was written by Paul, would have nothing to do with the Apocrypha, and regarded the letter of James as "an epistle of straw." The Scriptures were open to all and could be interpreted by private judgment enlightened by the Spirit of God. Like Calvin, Luther was a predestinarian and determinist, but he was also a conservative and soon became alarmed about the position taken by many extremists once the Reformation was under way. He had really wanted the Church to reform itself, but when he alienated Rome he had perforce to rely more and more on the secular powers which finally resulted in the state-church form which became pronounced in Prussia and later elsewhere. Whereas Calvin wished the Church to be at least the equal of the State and in some respects its superior, Luther's rebellion resulted in the reverse, a state-controlled episcopalianism. See **Calvinism, Presbyterianism**.

Lycanthropy, the belief that men may, by the exercise of magical powers or because of some inherited affliction, occasionally transform into wolves. The so-called werewolf is an important feature of mid-European folklore and much the same can be said of the were-tigers and were-bears of Africa and the Far East. There is, needless to say, no such thing as a genuine werewolf known to biology, but it is not hard to see how legends of their existence could arise. There are a number of mental illnesses in which men may deliberately or unconsciously mimic the actions of animals and there are a number of endocrinological disorders which may cause gross changes in the features of the individuals, including the excessive growth of hair. In times when the physiological bases of such afflictions were not properly understood, sufferers from such complaints could easily be persuaded, either by themselves or others, that they were in fact wolfmen. Once the mythology of lycanthropy is established in a society, then of course it will be used by unscrupulous individuals for their own ends —for example revenge killings by people dressed as animals—thus helping to perpetuate the legend.

M

McLuhanism. According to Marshall McLuhan (1911–80), a Canadian, and former professor of English at Toronto, the *way* people com-

municate is more important than *what* they communicate: hence his famous slogan, "the medium is the message." There have been two great landmarks in human understanding since we learnt to speak and write: the invention of the printed book and the present electronic revolution. The printed word took us step by step along the linear, logical path to understanding; television comes at us from all directions at once. "Electronic circuitry has overthrown the regime of 'time' and 'space' ... Its message is Total Change." Thus the spectacle of the Chicago police force clubbing people outside the Democratic Convention in August 1968 was described by Alistair Cooke in a despatch to *The Guardian*, as "a terrifying demonstration of McLuhanism: the millions frozen with terror in front of their television screens." In his essay, "On Reading Marshall McLuhan," Dr. George Steiner (one of the first critics in England to understand him) writes: "Marshall McLuhan posits that Western civilisation has entered, or is about to enter an era of electromagnetic technology. This technology will radically alter the milieu of human perception, the reality co-ordinates within which we apprehend and order sense data. Experience will not present itself serially, in atomized or linear patterns of causal sequence, but in 'fields' of simultaneous interaction." McLuhan's importance lies in alerting us to the present clash between two great technologies, the literate and the electromagnetic, and in his vision, beyond the present chaos, of a world drawn tighter together in a "global village" where identity will merge in collectivity and we shall all be able to co-operate for the common good instead of being split up into warring nations.

Magic, a form of belief originating in very early days and based on the primitive's inability to distinguish between similarity and identity. The simplest example would perhaps be the fertility rites in which it is believed that a ceremony involving sexual relations between men and women will bring about fertility in the harvest. Or the idea that sticking pins in an image of an individual will bring about harm or even death to the real person. Magic is regarded by some as a form of early science in that man in his efforts to control Nature had recourse to magical practices when the only methods he knew had failed to bring the desired results. It filled a gap. By others magic is regarded as an elementary stage in the evolution of religion. It can be said to have served a purpose there too. Yet magic differs from religion, however closely at times it may come to be related with it in this important respect: religion depends upon a power *outside and beyond* human beings, whereas magic depends upon nothing but the casting of a spell or the performance of a ceremony—the result follows automatically.

The idea that "like produces like" is at the roots of imitative magic, and it is interesting to note that in some languages (e.g., Hebrew and Arabic) there is no word for "resembles" or "similar to." Hence one says "All thy garments are myrrh" instead of "are *like* myrrh." It follows that an event can be compelled by imitating it. One engages in swinging, not for pleasure, but to produce a wind as the swing does; ball games are played to get rainy weather because the black ball represents dark rainclouds; other ball games, in which one attempts to catch the ball in a cup or hit it with a stick, represent the sexual act (as some gentlemen at Lords may be distressed to hear) and bring about fertility; in medicine until a few centuries ago herbs were chosen to cure a disease because in some respects their leaves or other parts looked like the part of the body affected (e.g., the common wildflower still known as "eyebright" was used in bathing the eyes because the flower looks like a tiny eye). See **Witchcraft, Demonism.**

Malthusianism, the theory about population growth put forward by the Rev. Thomas Malthus (1766–1834) in *An Essay on Population* (1798). His three main propositions were (1) "Population is necessarily limited by means of subsistence." (2) "Population invariably increases where means of subsistence increase unless prevented by some very powerful and obvious checks." (3) "These checks, and the checks which repress the superior power of population, and keep its effects on a level with the means of subsistence, are all resolvable into moral restraint, vice and misery." In other words, no matter how great the food supply may become, human reproductive power will always adjust itself so that food will always be scarce in relation to population; the only means to deal with this is by "moral restraint" (*i.e.*, chastity or not marrying), "vice" (*i.e.*, birth-control methods), or misery (*i.e.*, starvation). More specifically, Malthus claimed that while food increases by arithmetical progression, population increases by geometrical progression. It is true that these gloomy predictions did not take place in Malthus's time largely owing to the opening up of new areas of land outside Europe, the development of new techniques in agriculture, the growth of international trade to poorer areas, the increased knowledge of birth-control, and developments in medical science which reduced the misery he had predicted. Furthermore, we now know that as a society becomes industrialised its birth-rate tends to fall. Growth in the world's population has increased from about 465 million in 1650 to over 4,500 million in 1982.

Manichaeism, an Asiatic religion which developed from Zoroastrianism (*q.v.*) and shows the influence of Buddhism (*q.v.*) and Gnosticism (*q.v.*), being founded by Mani, a Persian who was born in Babylonia, *c.* 216 A.D. Mani presented himself to Shapur I as the founder of a new religion which was to be to Babylonia what Buddhism was to India or Christianity to the West. His aspiration was to convert the East and he himself made no attempt to interfere directly with Christianity although he represented himself as the Paraclete (the Holy Ghost or "Comforter") and, like Jesus, had twelve disciples. His success in Persia aroused the fury of the Zoroastrian priests who objected to his reforming zeal towards their religion and in 276 Mani was taken prisoner and crucified.

Of Mani's complicated system little can be said here, save that it is based on the struggle of two eternal conflicting principles, God and matter, or light and darkness. Although its founder had no intention of interfering with the West, after his death his followers soon spread the religion from Persia and Mesopotamia to India and China. (Manichaeism flourished in China until the 11th cent.) It reached as far as Spain and Gaul and influenced many of the bishops in Alexandria and in Carthage where for a time St. Augustine accepted Manichaeism. Soon the toleration accorded it under Constantine ended and it was treated as a heresy and violently suppressed. Yet it later influenced many heresies, and even had some influence on orthodox Catholicism which had a genius for picking up elements in other religions which had been shown to appeal to worshippers provided they did not conflict unduly with fundamental beliefs.

Maoism is the branch of communism in China that was shaped by one of the most remarkable statesmen of modern times, Mao Tse-tung (1893–1976). He set the pattern of revolution for poor peasant societies and restored pride and confidence to his fellow countrymen after years of turmoil and brutality. Although Marxist theory guided the Chinese communists in their struggle for liberation from the old, bourgeois and feudal China, it was interpreted in a manner peculiar to China and developed to fit into the Chinese way of life and the "thoughts" of Chairman Mao. As early as 1926 Mao had pointed out that the Chinese proletariat had in the peasantry its staunchest and most numerous ally. "A rural revolution," he said, "is a revolution by which the peasantry overthrows the authority of the feudal landlord class." The struggles of 1925–49 (the Long March of the Red Army, the Anti-Japanese War, the Civil War against Chiang Kai-shek) were the foundations on which present-day China has been built. Maoism is against authoritarianism and for self-reliance; against bureaucracy and for revolutionary momentum; against rivalry

between individuals and for common effort. A great achievement has been the removal of poverty, ignorance, corruption and disease from China. Mao taught that struggle is necessary for the revolution to endure. "Running water does not go stale and door-hinges do not become worm-eaten," Mao reminded his comrades. "We must," he said, "make every comrade understand that the highest criterion for judging the words and deeds of the communists is whether they conform with the best interests and win the support of the broadest masses of the people." The effect of the death of Mao Tse-tung on Chinese communism has been a political direction towards the modernisation of China and away from Marxism and "continuous revolution". Mao's personally chosen successor, Hua Guofeng, was replaced as Chairman in 1981. *See also* **China, Section C, Part II.**

Marxism. The sociological theories founded by Karl Marx and Friedrich Engels on which modern communist thought is based. Marx and Engels lived in a period of unrestrained capitalism when exploitation and misery were the lot of the industrial working classes, and it was their humanitarianism and concern for social justice which inspired their work. Marx wrote his *Communist Manifesto* in Brussels in 1848 and in his great work, *Das Kapital* (1867), he worked out a new theory of society. Marx showed that all social systems are economically motivated and change as a result of technical and economic changes in methods of production. The driving force of social change Marx found to be in the struggle which the oppressed classes wage to secure a better future. Thus in his celebrated theory of historical materialism he interpreted history in terms of economics and explained the evolution of society in terms of class struggle. (*See* **Dialectical Materialism.**) "In the social production of their means of existence," he wrote, "men enter into definite and unavoidable relations which are independent of their will. These productive relationships correspond to the particular stage in the development of their material productive forces." Marx's theory of historical materialism implies that history is propelled by class struggle with communism and the classless society as the final stage when man will have emancipated himself from the productive process. Marx was the first to put socialism on a rational and scientific basis, and he foretold that socialism would inevitably replace capitalism. His prophecy, however, came to realisation not in the advanced countries as he had envisaged but in backward Russia and China. *See also* **Communism.**

Mesmerism, a rapidly vanishing name to denote the practice of hypnosis, which owes its popularity, though not its discovery, to the Austrian physician, Anton Mesmer (1733–1815). Mesmer's contribution was the realisation that a large number of what we would today call psychosomatic or hysterical conditions could be cured (or at least temporarily alleviated) by one or another form of suggestion. Mesmer himself relied on the idea of what he called "animal magnetism," a supposedly potent therapeutic force emanating from the living body which could be controlled by the trained individual. Mesmer used wands and impressive gadgetry to dispense the marvellous force and he effected a remarkable number of cures of complaints, hitherto looked upon as incurable or totally mysterious in origin—the most typical of these being hysterical blindness, paralysis or deafness, nervous skin conditions, and so on. Hypnosis, which is a valid if very poorly understood psychological phenomenon even today, would probably have been developed much further had not efficient general anaesthetics such as ether, nitrous oxide, etc., been discovered, thus greatly diminishing its role as a pain reliever in surgery. Mesmer, who was three parts charlatan, never really troubled to think deeply about the cause of his undoubted success. The first man to treat hysteria as a formal class of illness and who made a scientific attempt to treat it with hypnosis was Ambrose Liébeault (1823–1904). He and his colleagues Hippolyte Bernheim (1840–1919) believed: (*a*) that hysteria was produced by suggestion, and particularly by autosuggestion on the part of the patient, and (b) that suggestion was a normal trait found in varying degrees in everyone. These conclusions are true, but as Freud showed later are far from being the whole truth.

Messianism. Most varieties of religious belief rely on the assumption that the deity is a supernatural being either permeating the universe or dwelling in some other sphere, and normally inaccessible to man. Where divine intervention is necessary, the deity is traditionally believed to nominate a human being—in the case of Christianity, for example, Jesus is believed to be the actual son of God. Messianic cults introduce a novel variant on the traditional theme. In these a human being is held to be God himself. He may either nominate himself for this role, relying on his own personality or native talent to acquire the necessary following, or for one reason or another large numbers of people may alight on one individual and declare him the Messiah. While it might seem that beliefs of this kind would be confined to earlier epochs in man's recorded history, this is in fact not the case. In the past century, and even within recent decades, a number of individuals have been held by groups to be actually divine. Among these were the Dutchman Lourens van Voorthuizen, a former fisherman who declared himself to be God in 1950 and got large numbers to accept his claim; the Anglican priest Henry James Prince, who did much the same thing in 1850; and of course the famous Negro George Baker, who convinced hundreds of thousands of other Negroes that he was "Father Divine." To simple people the idea that God is to be found on earth and that one may even be personally introduced to him, is an obviously attractive one. The trouble is that all self-styled gods to this present date have sooner or later seriously disappointed their supporters by performing that most human of acts—dying.

Metapsychology. Not to be confused with parapsychology (q.v.). The branch or off-shoot of psychology which goes beyond empirical and experimental studies to consider such philosophical matters as the nature of mind, the reality of free-will and the mind/body problem. It was originally used by Freud as a blanket descriptive term denoting all mental processes, but this usage is now obsolete.

Methodism, the religious movement founded by John Wesley in 1738, at a time when the Anglican Church was in one of its periodic phases of spiritual torpor, with the simple aim of spreading "scriptural holiness" throughout the land. Up to that time Wesley had been a High Churchman but on a visit to Georgia in the United States he was much impressed by the group known as Moravians (q.v.), and on his return to this country was introduced by his brother Charles, who had already become an adherent, to Peter Böhler, a Moravian minister in England. Passing through a period of spiritual commotion following the meeting, he first saw the light at a small service in Aldersgate in May 1738 "where one was reading Luther's preface to the Epistle to the Romans" and from this time forth all Wesley's energies were devoted to the single object of saving souls. He did this for fifty years and at the end of his life confessed that he had wasted fifteen minutes in that time by reading a worthless book. Even when he was over eighty he still rose at 4 a.m. and toiled all day long.

Soon Whitefield, a follower with Calvinist views, was preaching throughout the country and Charles Wesley was composing his well-known hymns; John's abilities at this time were taken up in organising the movement described as "People called Methodists." They were to be arranged in "societies" which were united into "circuits" under a minister, the circuits into "districts" and all knit together into a single body under a conference of ministers which has met annually since 1744. Local lay preachers were also employed and to maintain interest the ministers were moved from circuit to circuit each year. These chapel services were not originally meant to conflict with the Church of England of which Wesley still considered himself a member. They were purely supplementary, and it used to be the custom (before the

Methodists began to count themselves as Nonconformists) for Methodists to attend Church in the morning and Chapel in the evening.

The class-meeting was the unit of the organisation where members met regularly under a chosen leader to tell their "experiences" upon which they were often subjected to severe cross-examination. At the end of every quarter, provided their attendances were regular, they received a ticket of membership which entitled them to come to monthly sacramental services. If attendance was inadequate the name was removed from the list, without appearance on which nobody was deemed a member. The price of the ticket was "a penny a week and a shilling a quarter" but Wesley was not interested in receiving money from anyone who was not utterly devoted to the cause.

John Wesley introduced four other innovations, some of which were regarded by Churchmen who had previously been willing to commend his efforts in bringing religion to the poorer classes as dangerous: (1) He started the Sunday-school scheme and afterwards enthusiastically supported that of John Raikes, often regarded as the founder of the idea; this was of immense importance in the days before the Education Acts. (2) He reintroduced the Agapae or "love feasts" of the early Church which were fellowship meetings deepening the sense of brotherhood of the society. (3) He began to copy the open-air meetings of the eloquent Whitefield and soon unwittingly produced the most extraordinary results, finding that his sermons led to groans, tears, fainting-fits, and all sorts of emotional expression. Even his open-air lay speakers produced like results and these came to be associated with Methodism and gave significance to the proud Anglican claim that *their* services would be "without enthusiasm." (4) After some hesitation he ventured to consecrate Dr. Thomas Coke, who was being sent as a missionary to America, as a bishop of his church. In addition to Wesley's religious work he was a great educator of the common man. Thus he introduced the cheap book and the church magazine, publishing books of any sort which he thought would edify and not harm even when the views expressed were different from his own—e.g., Thomas à Kempis's *Imitation of Christ* and works of history, biography, science, and medicine in some cases written by himself. In this way the movement with its cheap books and reading rooms had an influence far beyond its actual membership. Both the Anglican Church and the Evangelical movement of Wilberforce and others profited from Wesley's work. Some social historians, rightly or wrongly, have claimed that it was Wesley's influence among the working classes that spared England the revolutionary activity which characterised most other European countries during the first quarter of the 19th cent.

Methodism, especially after Wesley's death in 1791, began, like other movements, to develop schisms. These were the long-standing differences which the Baptist movement (q.v.) had shown too between Arminian and Calvinist sections—i.e., between those who did and those who did not accept the doctrine of predestination. In the case of the Methodists, this led to a complete break in 1811. Then there were differences associated with the status of the laity, or the relationship of the movement with the Anglican Church. The "Methodist New Connection" of 1797 differed only in giving the laity equal representation with the ministers but the more important break of the Primitive Methodists in 1810 gave still more power to the laity and reintroduced the "camp-meeting" type of service. In 1815 the Bryanites or "Bible Christians" were formed, and a further schism which was even brought before the law courts was ostensibly over the foundation of a theological college. The real reason, of course, was that the ministers were becoming more Tory, whilst the laity were becoming more Radical. Finally in 1932, at a conference in the Albert Hall in London, the Wesleyan Methodists, the Primitive Methodists, and the United Methodists became one Church, the Methodist Church.

Mind and Matter.

Early Greek Views: Idealism and Dualism.
Primitive peoples could see that there is a
distinction between those things which move
and do things by themselves and others, such as
stones, which do not. Following the early state
of **Animism** (*q.v.*), in which spirits were believed
to have their abode in everything, they began
to differentiate between matter or substance
and a force which seems to move it and shape it
into objects and things. Thus to the Greek
Parmenides (fl. *c.* 475 B.C.), who was a philosopher of pure reason, thought or mind was the
creator of what we observe and in some way not
quite clear to himself it seemed that mind was
the cause of everything. This is perhaps the
first expression of the movement known as
Idealism which says, in effect, that the whole
universe is mental—a creation either of our own
minds or the mind of God. But from Anaxa-
gorus (488-428 B.C.) we have the clearer statement that mind or *nous* causes all movement
but is distinct from the substance it moves.
He does not, however, think in terms of individual minds but rather of a kind of generalised
mind throughout the universe which can be
used as an explanation of anything which cannot be explained otherwise. This is the position
known as Dualism (*q.v.*) which holds that both
mind and matter exist and interact but are
separate entities.

Most people in practice are dualists since,
rightly or wrongly, mind and body are thought
of as two different things: it is the "common-
sense" (although not necessarily the true) point
of view. Plato in a much more complex way
was also a dualist although he held that the
world of matter we observe is in some sense not
the genuine world. The real world is the world
of ideas and the tree we see is not real but
simply matter upon which mind or soul has
imprinted the idea of a tree. Everything that
exists has its corresponding form in the world of
ideas and imprints its pattern upon matter.
Mind has always existed and, having become
entangled with matter, is constantly seeking to
free itself and return to God.

Plato's pupil Aristotle had a much more
scientific outlook and held that, although it was
mind which gave matter its form, mind is not
outside matter, as Plato had thought, but *inside*
it as its formative principle. Therefore there
could be no mind without matter and no matter
without mind; for even the lowest forms of
matter have some degree of mind which increases in quantity and quality as we move up
the scale to more complex things.

So far, nobody had explained how two such
different substances as matter and mind could
influence each other in any way, and this remains, in spite of attempts to be mentioned
later, a basic problem in philosophy.

Two later ideas, one of them rather foolish
and the other simply refusing to answer the question, are typified by the Stoics and some members of the Sceptic school. The first is that only
matter exists and what we call mind is merely
matter of a finer texture, a view which as an
explanation is unlikely to satisfy anyone; the
other, that of some Sceptics, is that we can know
nothing except the fleeting images or thoughts
that flicker through our consciousness. Of
either mind or matter we know nothing.

Renaissance Attitude. Christian doctrines
have already been dealt with (*see* **God and
Man, Determinism and Free-will**), and the past
and future of the soul is dealt with under
Immortality. Nor need we mention the Renaissance philosophers who were really much more
concerned about how to use mind than about its
nature. When they did consider the subject
they usually dealt with it, as did Francis Bacon,
by separating the sphere of science from that of
religion and giving the orthodox view of the
latter because there were still good reasons for
not wishing to annoy the Church.

*17th-cent. Views: Hobbes, Descartes, Guelincx,
Spinoza, Locke, Berkeley.* Thomas Hobbes in
the 17th cent. was really one of the first to
attempt a modern explanation of mind and
matter even if his attempt was crude. As a
materialist he held that all that exists is matter
and hence our thoughts, ideas, images, and

actions are really a form of motion taking place
within the brain and nerves. This is the
materialist theory which states that mind does
not exist.

Thus there are three basic theories of the
nature of mind and body: idealism, dualism,
and materialism, and we may accept any one of
the three. But, if we accept dualism, we shall
have to explain precisely the relationship between body and mind. In some of his later
writings Hobbes seems to suggest that mental
processes are the effects of motion rather than
motion itself; *i.e.*, they exist, but only as a
result of physical processes just as a flame does
on a candle. This theory of the relationship is
known as *epiphenomenalism.*

Descartes, the great French contemporary of
Hobbes, was a dualist who believed that mind
and matter both exist and are entirely different
entities; therefore he had to ask himself how,
for example, the desire to walk leads to the
physical motion of walking. His unsatisfactory
answer was that, although animals are pure
automatons, man is different in that he has a
soul which resides in the pineal gland (a tiny
structure in the brain which today we know to
be a relic of evolution with no present function
whatever). In this gland the mind comes in
contact with the "vital spirits" of the body
and thus there is interaction between the two.
This theory is known as *interactionism*, and
since we do not accept its basis in the function
of the pineal gland, we are simply left with the
notion of interaction but without the explanation of how it takes place.

One of Descartes's successors, Arnold
Guelincx, produced the even more improbable
theory of *psychophysical parallelism* sometimes
known as the theory of the "two clocks".
Imagine you have two clocks, each keeping perfect time, then supposing you saw one and
heard the other, every time one points to the
hour the other will strike, giving the impression
that the first event causes the second, although
in fact they are quite unrelated. So it is with
the body and mind in Guelincx's view, each is
"wound up" by God in the beginning in such
a way as to keep time with the other so that
when I have the desire to walk, purely unrelated
physical events in my legs cause them to move
at the same time. A variety of this theory is
occasionism, which says that whenever something happens in the physical world, God affects
us so that we *think* we are being affected by the
happening.

The trouble about all these theories is (*a*) that
they really explain nothing, and (*b*) that they
give us a very peculiar view of God as a celestial
showman treating us as puppets when it would
surely have been easier to create a world in
which mind and matter simply interacted by
their very nature. Spinoza, too, believed in a
sort of psychophysical parallelism in that he did
not think that mind and body interacted. But
since in his theory everything is God, mind
and matter are simply two sides of the same
penny.

John Locke, another contemporary, thought
of the mind as a blank slate upon which the
world writes in the form of sensations, for we have
no innate or inborn ideas and mind and matter
do interact although he does not tell us how.
All we know are sensations—*i.e.*, sense impressions. Bishop Berkeley carried this idea to
its logical conclusion: if we know nothing but
sensations, we have no reason to suppose that
matter exists at all. He was, therefore, an
idealist.

18th cent. Views: Hume, Kant. David
Hume went further still and pointed out that,
if all we know are sensations, we cannot prove
the existence of matter but we cannot prove the
existence of mind either. All we can ever know
is that ideas, impressions, thoughts, follow each
other. We do not even experience a self or
personality because every time we look into our
"minds" all we really experience are thoughts
and impressions. Hume was quick to point out
that this was not the same as saying that the
self did not exist; it only proved that we cannot
know that it does.

Kant made it clear that, although there is a
world outside ourselves, we can never know

what it is really like. The mind receives impressions and forms them into patterns which conform not to the thing-in-itself but to the nature of mind. Space and time, for example, are not realities but only the form into which our mind fits its sensations. In other words our mind shapes impressions which are no more like the thing in itself than the map of a battlefield with pins showing the position of various army groups at any given moment is like the battlefield. This, of course, is true. From physics and physiology we know that the sounds we hear are "really" waves in the air, the sights we see "really" electromagnetic waves. What guarantee do we have that the source is "really" like the impression received in our brain? Kant was the leader of the great German Idealist movement of the 18th cent. which in effect said: "why bother about matter when all we can ever know is mental?"

19th and 20th cent. Views. The Englishman Bradley, and the Frenchman Henri Bergson in the 19th and early 20th cent. both held in one form or another the belief that mind in some way creates matter and were, therefore, idealists, whereas Comte, the positivist (*q.v.*), and the Americans William James and John Dewey, held that mind is a form of behaviour. Certain acts (*e.g.*, reflexes) are "mindless" because they are deliberate; others which are intended may be described for the sake of convenience as "minded" (*i.e.*, purposeful). But like the majority of modern psychologists—insofar as they take any interest in the subject—they regarded mind as a process going on in the living body. Is there any reason, many now ask, why we should think of mind as being any different in nature from digestion? Both are processes going on in the body, the one in the brain the other in the stomach and intestines. Why should we regard them as "things"? *See also* **J43-4** and **Section Q.**

Mithraism, a sun-religion which originated in Persia with the worship of the mythical Mithra, the god of light and of truth. It was for two centuries one of early Christianity's most formidable rivals, particularly in the West since the more philosophical Hellenic Christianity of the East had little to fear from it. (Arnold Toynbee has described Mithraism as "a pre-Zoroastrian Iranian paganism—in a Hellenic dress"; Manichaeism as "Zoroastrianism—in a Christian dress".) Mithraism was a mystery-faith with secret rites known only to devotees. It appealed to the soldiers of the Roman Army which explains its spread to the farthest limits of the Roman empire and its decline as the Romans retreated. The religion resembled Zoroastrianism (*q.v.*) in that it laid stress on the constant struggle between good and evil and there are a number of parallels with Christianity. *e.g.*, a miraculous birth, death, and a glorious resurrection, a belief in heaven and hell and the immortality of the soul, a last judgment. Both religions held Sunday as the holy day of the week, celebrated 25 December (date of the pagan winter solstice festival) as the birthday of the founder; both celebrated Easter, and in their ceremonies made use of bell, holy water, and the candle. Mithraism reached its height about 275 A.D. and afterwards declined both for the reason given above and, perhaps, because it excluded women, was emotional rather than philosophical, and had no general organisation to direct its course. Yet even today, from the Euphrates to the Tyne, traces of the religion remain and antiquarians are familiar with the image of the sun-god and the inscription *Deo Soli Mithrae, Invicto, Seculari* (dedicated to the sun-god of Mithra, the unconquered). Mithraism enjoyed a brief revival of popular interest in the mid-1950s when workers excavating the foundations of the skyscraper, Bucklersbury House in the City of London, found the well-preserved remains of a Roman Mithraic temple. A campaign to save the temple as a national monument resulted in its now being on open display on a site in front of the skyscraper.

Mohammedanism. *See* **Islam.**

Monasticism. When in the 4th cent. A.D. Constantine in effect united state and church there were naturally many who hastened to become Christians for the worldly benefits they expected it to bring in view of the new situation. But there were others who, in their efforts to escape from wordly involvement, went into the deserts of North Africa and Syria to live as hermits and so in these regions there grew up large communities of monks whose lives of renunciation made a considerable impression on the Christian world. They were men of all types but the two main groups were those who preferred to live alone and those who preferred a community life. Among the first must be included St. Anthony, the earliest of the hermits, who was born in Egypt *c.* 250 and who lived alone in a hut near his home for fifteen years and then in the desert for a further twenty. As his fame spread Anthony came forth to teach and advocate a life of extreme austerity, until by the end of his life the Thebaid (the desert around Thebes) was full of hermits following his example. (Not unnaturally, he was constantly assailed by lustful visions which he thoughtfully attributed to Satan.) In the Syrian desert St. Simeon Stylites and others were stimulated to even greater austerities and Simeon himself spent many years on the top of a pillar in a space so small that it was only possible to sit or stand. With some of these men it is obvious that ascetic discipline had become perverted into an unpleasant form of exhibitionism.

The first monastery was founded by Pachomius of Egypt *c.* 315 and here the monks had a common life with communal meals, worship, and work mainly of agricultural type. In the Eastern part of the Empire St. Basil (*c.* 360) tried to check the growth of the extreme and spectacular practices of the hermits by organising monasteries in which the ascetic disciplines of fasting, meditation, and prayer, would be balanced by useful and healthy activities. His monasteries had orphanages and schools for boys—not only those who were intended for a monkish life. But the Eastern Church in general continued to favour the hermit life and ascetic extremes. Originally a spontaneous movement, the monastic life was introduced to the West by St. Athanasius in 339 who obtained its recognition from the Church of Rome and St. Augustine introduced it into North Africa beyond Egypt. The movement was promoted also by St. Jerome, St. Martin of Tours, who introduced it into France, and St. Patrick into Ireland. The monastery of Iona was founded by St. Colomba in 566. But it must be remembered that the Celtic Church had a life of its own which owed more to the Egyptian tradition than to Rome. Unlike the more elaborate monasteries of the Continent those of the early Celtic Church were often little more than a cluster of stone bee-hive huts, an oratory, and a stone cross. It had its own religious ceremonies and its own art (notably its beautifully carved crosses and the illuminated manuscripts such as the Lindisfarne Gospel (*c.* 700) and the Irish Book of Kells dating from about the same time). The Scottish St. Ninian played a major part in introducing Egyptian texts and art to Britain where, mixed with Byzantine influences and the art of the Vikings, it produced a typical culture of its own. Strangely enough, it was the relatively primitive Celts who played almost as large a part in preserving civilisation in Europe during the Dark Ages as the Italians have since. It was St. Columbanus (*c.* 540-615) who founded the great monasteries of Annegray, Luxeuil, and Fontaine in the Vosges country, St. Gall in Switzerland, and Bobbio in the Apennines. So, too, it was the Anglo-Saxon Alcuin (*c.* 735-804) who was called from York by Charlemagne to set up a system of education throughout his empire; the most famous of the monastic schools he founded was at Tours. Among those influenced by him was the philosopher John Scotus Erigena.

Meanwhile from the south, as the disintegrating Roman empire became increasingly corrupt, St. Benedict of Nursia (*c.* 480-*c.* 543) fled the pleasures of Rome to lead a hermit's life near Subiaco. Here he founded some small monasteries, but *c.* 520 made a new settlement, the great monastery of Monte Cassino in southern Italy, where he established a "Rule" for the government of monks. This included both study and work and emphasised that education was necessary for the continuance of Christianity. As his influence spread his Rule was adopted by other monasteries, and schools became part of monastic life. It is not possible to describe the many different orders of monks and nuns formed since, nor the mendicant orders of friars (*e.g.*, Franciscans, Dominicans, Carmelites, Augustinians). Outside the Roman Catholic Church, both Eastern Orthodox and Anglican Christians owe much to the monastic movement. Monasticism, of course, is not peculiar to Christianity and forms a major aspect of Buddhism, especially in the form of Lamaism in Tibet (*q.v.*).

Monophysitism, a heresy of the 5th cent. which grew out of a reaction against Nestorianism (*q.v.*). The majority of Egyptian Christians were Monophysites (Mono-physite = one nature)—*i.e.* they declared Christ's human and divine nature to be one and the same. This view was condemned at the Council of Chalcedon (A.D. 451) which pronounced that Jesus Christ, true God and true man, has two natures, at once perfectly distinct and inseparably joined in one person and partaking of the one divine substance. However, many continued to hold Monophysite opinions, including the Coptic Church (*q.v.*), declaring the Council to be unoecumenical (*i.e.* not holding the views of the true and universal Christian Church).

Montanism, a Phrygian form of primitive Puritanism with many peculiar tenets into which the early Christian theologian Tertullian (*c.* 150–*c.* 230) was driven by his extremist views that the Christian should keep himself aloof from the world and hold no social intercourse whatever with pagans. The sect had immediate expectation of Christ's second coming and indulged in prophetic utterance which they held to be inspired by the Holy Ghost but which their enemies put down to the work of the Devil.

Moral Re-Armament, a campaign launched in 1938 by an American evangelist of Lutheran background, Frank N. D. Buchman (1878–1961), founder of the Oxford Group Movement, and at first associated with the First Century Church Fellowship, a fundamentalist Protestant revivalist movement. On a visit to England in 1920 Buchman preached "world-changing through life-changing" to undergraduates at Oxford, hence the name Oxford Group. This revivalist movement was based on Buchman's conviction that world civilisation was breaking down and a change had to be effected in the minds of men.

Two of the Group's most typical practices were group confession of sins openly and the "quiet time" set aside during the day to receive messages from the Almighty as to behaviour and current problems. In the eyes of non-Groupers the confession (often of trivial sins) appeared to be exhibitionist and there was felt to be a certain snobbery about the movement which made it strongly conscious of the social status of its converts.

The Oxford Group gave way to Moral Re-Armament, the third phase of Buchmanism. M.R.A. men and women lay stress on the four moral absolutes of honesty, purity, love, and unselfishness. They believe they have the ideas to set the pattern for the changing world and, indeed, claim to have aided in solving many international disputes—political, industrial, and racial. Theologians complained of the Groups that their movement lacked doctrine and intellectual content; M.R.A. is no different in this respect.

The peak of public interest in M.R.A. was probably reached in the 1950s. Like so many movements of its kind it relied heavily for its motive force on the dynamism of its founder and leader. With the death of Dr. Buchman and the unexpected demise at an early age of his most promising protégé and successor-designate, the journalist Peter Howard, the movement began to lose its public impact. The phrase "moral rearmament" was coined by the English scientist W. H. Bragg and appropriated by Buchman.

Moravian Church, a revival of the Church of the "Bohemian Brethren" which originated (1457) among some of the followers of John Hus. It developed a kind of Quakerism that rejected the use of force, refused to take oaths, and had no hierarchy. It appears to have been sympathetic towards Calvinism but made unsuccessful approaches to Luther. As a Protestant sect it was ruthlessly persecuted by Ferdinand II and barely managed to survive. However, in the 18th cent. the body was re-established by Count Zinzendorf who offered it a place of safety in Saxony where a town called Herrnhut (God's protection) was built and this became the centre from which Moravian doctrine was spread by missionaries all over the world. Their chief belief (which had a fundamental influence on John Wesley—*see* **Methodism**) was that faith is a direct illumination from God which assures us beyond all possibility of doubt that we are saved, and that no goodness of behaviour, piety, or orthodoxy is of any use without this "sufficient sovereign, saving grace".

Mormons, or **Latter-day Saints,** one of the very numerous American religious sects; founded in 1830 by Joseph Smith, the son of a Vermont farmer, who, as a youth, had been influenced by a local religious revival though confused by the conflicting beliefs of the various denominations. He said that while praying for guidance he had been confronted by two heavenly messengers who forbade him to join any existing church but prepare to become the prophet of a new one. Soon, in a series of visions, he was told of a revelation written on golden plates concealed in a nearby hillside. These he unearthed in 1827 and with the help of "Urim and Thummin" translated the "reformed Egyptian" characters into English. Described as the *Book of Mormon*, this was published in 1830 and at the same time a little church of those few who accepted his testimony was founded in Fayette, N.Y. In addition the first of Joseph Smith's "miracles"—the casting out of a devil—was performed. The *Book of Mormon* purports to be a record of early American history and religion, the American Indians being identified as the ten Lost Tribes of Israel, whose fate has never failed to attract the attention of those who prefer myth to fact (cf. British Israelites). Jesus Christ is alleged to have appeared in America after His ascension. Yet Smith's eloquence was able to influence quite educated people, including Sidney Rigdon with whom he went into business for a time. *Doctrine and Covenants* is the title of another book dealing with the revelations Smith claimed to have received. Soon the sect was in trouble with the community both because its members insisted on describing themselves as the Chosen People and others as Gentiles and because they took part in politics, voting as Smith ordered them to. Smith was constantly in trouble with the police. Therefore they were turned out from one city after another until they found themselves a dwelling-place at Nauvoo, Illinois, on the Mississippi.

That would probably have been the end of the story had not Smith been murdered in 1844 and thereby made to appear a martyr, and had there not appeared Brigham Young, a quite extraordinary leader, who stamped out warring factions and drove out the recalcitrant. While persecutions continued Brigham Young announced that it had been revealed that he must lead the faithful to Salt Lake, then outside the area of the United States. There followed the famous trek of more than a thousand miles across desert country in which he led the way, reaching his journey's end in the forbidding valley of the Great Salt Lake on 24 July 1847. By 1851 30,000 Mormons had reached the Promised Land. Here they held their own in a hostile environment and under the practical genius of their leader carried through a vast irrigation scheme and built Salt Lake City which still serves as the headquarters of their sect. In 1850 their pioneer settlement was made Utah Territory, and in 1896 incorporated in the Union. The church was strictly ruled by its leader who also looked after affairs of state for thirty years until his death in 1877.

Polygamy, although opposed by some Mormons, and only sanctioned by Brigham Young when Salt Lake City had been built, is the best-known of Mormon doctrines. It brought the sect into much disrepute and was renounced in 1880. Mormons are millenarians, believing that some time Christ will appear and rule for a thousand years.

Members of the Church of Jesus Christ of Latter-day Saints now number over three million in congregations throughout the world.

The Reorganised Church of Jesus Christ of Latter-day Saints with its headquarters at Independence, Missouri, has been separate and distinct since 1852.

Muggletonians, one of the many sects which arose during the Commonwealth but, unlike most of the others (**Levellers** (q.v.), **Diggers** (q.v., Fifth Monarchy Men, and the Millenarians) which tended to have a strongly political aspect, this was purely religious. Founded by two journeymen tailors, Lodowick Muggleton and John Reeve, who interpreted the Book of Revelation in their own peculiar way, it was decided that Reeve represented Moses, and Muggleton, Aaron. They also believed that the Father, not the Son, had died on the cross (an ancient heresy) but added the strange statement that He left Elijah in control during His period on earth. Rejecting the doctrine of the Trinity, they also asserted that God has a human body. Nevertheless, for a time, they had a large number of followers.

Mysticism, a religious attitude which concerns itself with direct relationship with God, "reality" as contrasted with appearance or the "ultimate" in one form or another. All the higher religions have had their mystics who have not always been regarded without suspicion by their more orthodox members, and, as Bertrand Russell points out, there has been a remarkable unity of opinion among mystics which almost transcends their religious differences. Thus, characteristic of the mystical experience in general, have been the following features; (1) a belief in insight as opposed to analytical knowledge which is accompanied in the actual experience by the sense of a mystery unveiled, a hidden wisdom become certain beyond the possibility of doubt; this is often preceded by a period of utter hopelessness and isolation described as "the dark night of the soul"; (2) a belief in unity and a refusal to admit opposition or division anywhere; this sometimes appears in the form of what seem to be contradictory statements: "the way up and the way down is one and the same" (Heraclitus). There is no distinction between subject and object, the act of perception and the thing perceived; (3) a denial of the reality of time, since if all is one the distinction of past and future must be illusory; (4) a denial of the reality of evil (which does not maintain, e.g., that cruelty is good but that it does not exist in the world of reality as opposed to the world of phantoms from which we are liberated by the insight of the vision). Among the great mystics have been Meister Eckhart and Jakob Boehme, the German religious mystics of the 13th and 16th cent. respectively, Acharya Sankara of India, and St. Theresa and St. John of the Cross of Spain. Mystical movements within the great religions have been: the Zen (q.v.) movement within Buddhism; Taoism in China; the Cabalists and Hasidim in Judaism; the Sufis within Islam; some of the Quakers within Christianity.

Mystery Religions. See **Orphism.**

N

Natural Law, the specifically Roman Catholic doctrine that there is a natural moral law, irrespective of time and place, which man can know through his own reason. Originally a product of early rational philosophy, the Christian form of the doctrine is basically due to St. Thomas Aquinas who defined natural law in relation to eternal law, holding that the eternal law is God's reason which governs the relations of all things in the universe to each other. The natural law is that part of the eternal law which relates to man's behaviour. Catholic natural law assumes that the human reason is capable of deriving ultimate rules for right behaviour, since there are in man and his institutions certain stable structures produced by God's reason which man's reason can know to be correct and true. Thus, the basis of marriage, property, the state, and the contents of justice are held to be available to man's natural reason. The rules of positive morality

and civil law are held to be valid only insofar as they conform to the natural law, which man is not only capable of knowing but also of obeying.

Protestant theologians criticise this notion. Thus Karl Barth and many others hold that sinful and fallen man cannot have any direct knowledge of God or His reason or will without the aid of revelation. Another theologian Niebuhr points out that the principles of the doctrines are too inflexible and that although they are the product of a particular time and circumstance, they are regarded as if they were absolute and eternal. In fact, as most social scientists would also agree, there is no law which can be regarded as "natural" for all men at all times. Nor does it seem sensible to suppose that all or even many men possess either the reason to discern natural law or the ability to obey it; whether or not we accept man's free-will (and all Protestant sects do not), we know as a fact of science that people are not always fully responsible for their actions and some not at all.

Nazism, the term commonly used for the political and social ideology of the German National Socialist Party inspired and led by Hitler. The term *Nazi* was an abbreviation of Nazional-socialistische Deutsche Arbeiterpartei. Those in the Federal Republic today sympathetic to National Socialist aims are known as neo-Nazis. See **Fascism.**

Neoplatonism. See **Determinism and Free-will** and **God and Man.**

Nestorian heresy. The 5th cent. of the Christian Church saw a battle of personalities and opinions waged with fanatical fury between St. Cyril, the patriarch of Alexandria, and Nestorius, patriarch of Constantinople. Nestorius maintained that Mary should not be called the mother of God, as she was only the mother of the human and not of the divine nature of Jesus. This view was contradicted by Cyril (one of the most unpleasant saints who ever lived) who held the orthodox view. In addition to his utter destruction of Nestorius by stealthy and unremitting animosity Cyril was also responsible for the lynching of Hypatia, a distinguished mathematician and saintly woman, head of the Neoplatonist school at Alexandria. She was dragged from her chariot, stripped naked, butchered and torn to pieces in the church, and her remains burned. As if this were not enough Cyril took pains to stir up pogroms against the very large Jewish colony of Alexandria. At the Council of Ephesus (A.D. 431) the Western Bishops quickly decided for Cyril. This Council (reinforced by the Council of Chalcedon in 451) clarified orthodox Catholic doctrine (see **Monophysitism**). Nestorius became a heretic, was banished to Antioch where he had a short respite of peace, but later, and in spite of his weakness and age, was dragged about from one place to another on the borders of Egypt. We are assured that his tongue was eaten by worms in punishment for the wicked words he had spoken, but later the Nestorian church flourished in Syria and Persia under the protection of the rulers of Persia and missions were sent to India and China.

Nihilism, the name commonly given to the earliest Russian form of revolutionary anarchism. It originated in the early years of Tsar Alexander II (1818–81), the liberator of the serfs, who, during his attempts to bring about a constitutional monarchy, was killed by a bomb. The term "nihilist", however, was first used in 1862 by Turgenev in his novel *Fathers and Children.* See **Anarchism.**

Nominalism. Early mediaeval thinkers were divided into two schools, those who regarded "universals" or abstract concepts as mere names without any corresponding realities (Nominalists), and those who held the opposite doctrine (**Realism**) that general concepts have an existence independent of individual things. The relation between universals and particulars was a subject of philosophical dispute all through the Middle Ages.

The first person to hold the nominalist doctrine was probably Roscelin or Roscellinus in the late 11th cent., but very little is known of him and none of his works remains except for a single letter to Peter Abelard who was his pupil. Roscelin was born in France, accused twice of heresy but recanted and fled to England where he attacked the views of Anselm, according to whom Roscelin used the phrase that universals were a *flatus voci* or breath of the voice. The most important nominalist was the Englishman William of Occam in the 13th cent. who, once and for all, separated the two schools by saying in effect that science is about things (the nominalist view) whereas logic, philosophy, and religion are about terms or concepts (the Platonic tradition). Both are justified, but we must distinguish between them. The proposition "man is a species" is not a proposition of logic or philosophy but a scientific statement since we cannot say whether it is true or false without knowing about man. If we fail to realise that words are conventional signs and that it is important to decide whether or not they have a meaning and refer to something, then we shall fall into logical fallacies of the type: "Man is a species, Socrates is a man, therefore Socrates is a species." This, in effect, is the beginning of the modern philosophy of logical analysis which, to oversimplify, tells us that a statement is not just true or untrue, it may also be meaningless. Therefore, in all the philosophical problems we have discussed elsewhere there is the third possibility that the problem we are discussing has no meaning because the words refer to nothing and we must ask ourselves before going any further "what do we mean by God", and has the word "freewill" any definite meaning?

Nonconformism, the attitude of all those Christian bodies, which do not conform to the doctrines of the Church of England. Up to the passing of the Act of Uniformity in 1662 they were called "puritans" or "dissenters" and were often persecuted. The oldest bodies of nonconformists are the Baptists, Independents, and (in England) the Presbyterians; the Methodists, although dating from 1738, did not consider themselves nonconformists until some time later. The Presbyterians are, of course, the official Church of Scotland where it is the Anglicans (known as "Episcopalians") who are the nonconformists, although not generally described as such.

O

Occam's Razor, the philosophical maxim by which William of Occam, the 14th cent. Franciscan has become best-known. This states in the form which is most familiar: "Entities are not to be multiplied without necessity" and as such does not appear in his works. He did, however, say something much to the same effect: "It is vain to do with more what can be done with fewer." In other words, if everything in some science can be interpreted without assuming this or that hypothetical entity, there is no ground for assuming it. This is Bertrand Russell's version and he adds: "I have myself found this a most fruitful principle in logical analysis."

Occultism. *See* **Magic, Alchemy, Astrology,** and **Theosophy.**

Orangemen, members of an Irish society formed in Ulster in 1795 to uphold Protestantism. Their name is taken from King William III, Prince of Orange, who defeated James II at the Battle of the Boyne (1690), hence the enormous banners depicting "King Billy on the Boyne" carried in procession on 12 July each year. The Unionist Party of Northern Ireland (the ruling political party from 1921 to 1972) is largely maintained by the Orange Order. The Order has branches in many English-speaking countries but flourishes chiefly in Ulster.

Orgonomy, a pseudo-psychological theory advanced by the German psychiatrist Wilhelm Reich (1897–1957), a pupil of Freud, who was expelled from Germany for attacking the Nazis and who started life afresh in the U.S.A. like so many of his colleagues. Moving quickly away from orthodox psychoanalytic theories, Reich became increasingly obsessed with the view that all living things were permeated with a unique force or energy which he termed "orgone" and which he believed could be photographed and measured with a geiger counter. The key to the successful flow of orgone throughout the body was sexual intercourse and the resulting orgasm (hence "orgone"). Reich achieved a substantial following for his increasingly bizarre views and when he was sentenced to two-years' imprisonment in 1956 for alleged medical malpractice a "civil rights" controversy developed which has not died down to this date. His unfortunate and rather tragic death in prison has fanned the emotional issues and granted him the important role of martyr to his cause. There is presently a strong revival of interest in Reich and orgonomy, partly in tune with the general occult revival. A recent witty, but not totally unsympathetic film about his work "W R—Mysteries of the Organism" has drawn the attention of a large new audience to his teachings.

Orphism. The Greeks in general thought very little of their gods, regarding them as similar human beings with human failings and virtues although on a larger scale. But there was another aspect of Greek religion which was passsionate, ecstatic, and secret, dealing with the worship of various figures among whom were Bacchus or Dionysus, Orpheus, and Demeter and Persephone of the Eleusinian Mysteries. Dionysus (or Bacchus) was originally a god from Thrace where the people were primitive farmers naturally interested in fertility cults. Dionysus was the god of fertility who only later came to be associated with wine and the divine madness it produces. He assumed the form of a man or a bull and his worship by the time it arrived in Greece became associated with women (as was the case in most of the Mystery Religions) who spent nights on the hills dancing and possibly drinking wine in order to stimulate ecstasy; an unpleasant aspect of the cult was the tearing to pieces of wild animals whose flesh was eaten raw. Although the cult was disapproved of by the orthodox and, needless to say, by husbands, it existed for a long time.

This primitive and savage religion in time was modified by that attributed to Orpheus whose cult was more spiritualised, ascetic, and substituted mental for physical intoxication. Orpheus may have been a real person or a legendary hero and he, too, is supposed to have come from Thrace, but his name indicates that he, or the movement associated with him, came from Crete and originally from Egypt, which seems to have been the source of many of its doctrines. Crete, it must be remembered, was the island through which Egypt influenced Greece in other respects. Orpheus is said to have been a reformer who was torn to pieces by the Maenad worshippers of Dionysus. The Orphics believed in the transmigration of souls and that the soul after death might obtain either eternal bliss or temporary or permanent torment according to its way of life upon earth. They held ceremonies of purification and the more orthodox abstained from animal food except on special occasions when it was eaten ritually. Man is partly earthly, partly heavenly, and a good life increases the heavenly part so that, in the end, he may become one with Bacchus and be called a "Bacchus".

The religion had an elaborate theology. As the Bacchic rites were reformed by Orpheus, so the Orphic rites were reformed by Pythagoras (*c.* 582–*c.* 507 B.C.) who introduced the mystical element into Greek philosophy, which reached its heights in Plato. Other elements entered Greek life from Orphism. One of these was feminism which was notably lacking in Greek civilisation outside the Mystery Religions. The other was the drama which arose from the rites of Dionysus. The mysteries of Eleusis formed the most sacred part of the Athenian state religion, and it is clear that they had to do with fertility rites also, for they were in honour of Demeter and Persephone and all the myths speak of them as being associated with the supply of corn to the country. Without being provocative, it is accepted by most anthropologists and many theologians that Christianity, just as it accepted elements of Gnossticism and Mithraism, accepted elements from the Mystery Religions as they in turn must have done from earlier cults. The miraculous birth, the death and resurrection the sacramental feast of bread and wine, symbolising the eating of the flesh and drinking of the blood of the god, all these are common elements in early religions and not just in one. None of this means that what we are told about Jesus is not true, but it surely does mean: (a) that Christianity was not a sudden development; (b) that the early Church absorbed many of the elements of other religions; (c) that perhaps Jesus Himself made use of certain symbols which He knew had a timeless significance for man and invested them with new meaning.

Orthodox Eastern Church. There are two groups of Eastern churches: (1) those forming the Orthodox Church dealt with here which include the ancient Byzantine patriarchates of Constantinople, Alexandria, Antioch, and Jerusalem, and the national churches of Russia, Greece, Yugoslavia, Bulgaria, Rumania, etc. (although Orthodox communities exist all over the world and are no longer confined to geographical areas); (2) the churches which rejected Byzantine orthodoxy during various controversies from the 5th to the 7th cent., notably the Coptic church (q.v.) and the Armenian church. Although all Orthodox churches share the same doctrine and traditions they are arranged as national independent bodies each with its own hierarchy. They do not recognise the pope, and the primacy of the patriarch of Constantinople is largely an honorary one. Although claiming to be the One Holy, Catholic, and Apostolic Church its alleged infallibility rests on universal agreement rather than on any one individual, and agreement over the faith comes from the Scriptures interpreted in the light of the Tradition. The latter includes dogmas relating to the Trinity, Christology, Mariology, and Holy Icons; the testimony of the Fathers (St. Athanasius, St. Basil, St. John Chrysostom, St. Cyril of Alexandria, etc.); the canons or rules as formulated by the Councils and the Fathers. The Orthodox Church did not take part in the great Western controversies about the Bible, nor, of course, in the Reformation. Attempts have recently been made to improve relations bebetween Rome and Constantinople: the two Churches agreed in 1935 to retract the excommunications cast on each other in A.D. 1054, which formalised the Great Schism.

Ouspensky, a contemporary of Gurdjieff (q.v.), Peter Ouspensky was another obscure mystic of Eastern European origin who believed he had an occult philosophical message to bring to the West. This he embodied in a series of lengthy books which are both humourless and self-indulgent.

Oxford Group. See **Moral Re-Armament.**
Oxford Movement. See **Tractarianism.**

P

Pantheism. See **God and Man.**
Papal Infallibility. The basis of papal infallibility is (a) that every question of morals and faith is not dealt with in the Bible so it is necessary that there should be a sure court of appeal in case of doubt, and this was provided by Christ when he established the Church as His Teaching Authority upon earth; (b) ultimately this idea of the teaching function of the Church shapes the idea of papal infallibility which asserts that the Pope, when speaking officially on matters of faith or morals, is protected by God against the possibility of error. The doctrine was proclaimed in July 1870.

Infallibility is a strictly limited gift which does not mean that the Pope has extraordinary intelligence, that God helps him to find the answer to every conceivable question, or that Catholics have to accept the Pope's views on politics. He can make mistakes or fall into sin, his scientific or historical opinions may be quite wrong, he may write books that are full of errors. Only in two limited spheres is he infallible and in these only when he speaks officially as the supreme teacher and lawgiver of the Church, defining a doctrine that must be accepted by all its members. When, after studying a problem

of faith or morals as carefully as possible, and with all available help from expert consultants, he emerges with the Church's answer—on these occasions it is not strictly an answer, it is *the* answer.

Historically speaking, the Roman Catholic Church of the early 19th cent. was at its lowest ebb of power. Pope Pius IX, in fear of Italian nationalism, revealed his reactionary attitude by the feverish declaration of new dogmas, the canonisation of new saints, the denunciation of all modern ideals in the Syllabus of Errors, and the unqualified defence of his temporal power against the threat of Garibaldi. It is not too much to say that everything regarded as important by freedom-loving and democratic people was opposed by the papacy at that time. In 1870, after a long and sordid struggle, the Vatican Council, convened by Pius IX, pronounced the definition of his infallibility. Döllinger, a German priest and famous historian of the Church, was excommunicated because, like many others, he refused to accept the new dogma. It is difficult not to doubt that there was some connection between the pronouncement of the Pope's infallibility and his simultaneous loss of temporal power.

After the humanism of the Second Vatican Council (1962–5) Pope Paul's encyclical *Humanae Vitae* (1968), condemning birth control, came as a great disappointment to the many people (including theologians, priests, and laymen) who had expected there would be a change in the Church's teaching. The Church's moral guidance on this controversial issue, however, does not involve the doctrine of infallibility. (The Roman Catholic Church teaches that papal pronouncements are infallible only when they are specifically defined as such.) That there is unlikely to be any immediate softening of the Church's line on infallibility was made clear in July 1973 when the Vatican's Sacred Congregation for the Doctrine of the Faith published a document strongly reaffirming papal infallibility. The document also reminded Catholics of their obligation to accept the Catholic Church's unique claims to authenticity.

Parapsychology, the name given to the study of psychical research (q.v.) as an academic discipline, and chosen to denote the topic's supposed status as a branch of psychology. The impetus behind parapsychology came from the psychologist William MacDougall who persuaded Duke University in North Carolina, U.S.A., to found a department of parapsychology under J. B. Rhine. Throughout the 1930s and 40s the work of Rhine and his colleagues, who claimed to have produced scientific evidence for the existence of E.S.P., attracted world-wide attention. Increasing reservations about the interpretation of Rhine's results and an apparent lack of any readily repeatable experiments, however, gradually eroded scientific confidence in the topic. The academic status of parapsychology is at the present time exceedingly uncertain. Rhine retired from university life in 1965 and the world-famous parapsychology laboratory at Duke University was closed. On the other hand the American Association for the Advancement of Science recently admitted the Parapsychology Association (the leading organisation for professional parapsychologists) as an affiliated member society. An American government body, the National Institute of Mental Health, has also officially supported some medical research into alleged telepathic dreams, the first "official" grant support of this kind. In Britain a poll of readers in the weekly journal, *New Scientist*, revealed a very high interest in the subject matter of parapsychology, and active research is currently going on at the Dept. of Psychology at Cambridge. Stories of intensive parapsychological research in Soviet Russia are however without foundation and are not supported by Western parapsychologists who have visited Russia.

Parsees. See **Zoroastrianism.**
Pavlovian theory. See **Behaviourism.**
Pentecostalism, a religious movement within the Protestant churches, holding the belief that an essential feature of true Christianity is a vigorous and profound spiritual or mystical ex-

perience which occurs after, and seemingly reinforces the initial conversion. The origins of modern Pentecostalism appear to lie in the occasion on 1 January 1901 when a member of a Bible College in Topeka, Kansas, one Agnes N. Ozman, spontaneously began to speak in an apparently unknown language at one of the College's religious meetings. This "speaking in tongues" was assumed to be evidence of her conversion and "spirit baptism", and became a feature of most Pentecostal meetings in due course. The movement spread rapidly across America, particularly in rural communities, and also was a strong feature of Welsh religious life in the early part of the century. Pentecostal services are enthusiastic and rousing with a strong emphasis on music and participation on the part of the congregation. Pentecostalism is evangelistic in nature and seems to be gaining in strength at the present time, at the expense of more orthodox and staid versions of Christianity. The fiery character Aimee Semple McPherson was one of its most prominent evangelists.

Phrenology, a psychological "school" founded in 1800 by two Germans, Franz Josef Gall and Johann Gaspar Spurzheim. Gall was an anatomist who believed there to be some correspondence between mental faculties and the shape of the head. He tested these ideas in prisons and mental hospitals and began to lecture on his findings, arousing a great deal of interest throughout both Europe and America, where his doctrines were widely accepted. Phrenology became fashionable, and people would go to "have their bumps read" as later men and women of fashion have gone to be psychoanalysed. Roughly speaking, Gall divided the mind into thirty-seven faculties such as destructiveness, suavity, self-esteem, conscientiousness, and so on, and claimed that each of these was located in a definite area of the brain. He further claimed that the areas in the brain corresponded to "bumps" on the skull which could be read by the expert, thus giving a complete account of the character of the subject. In fact, (a) no such faculties are located in the brain anywhere, for this is simply not the way the brain works; (b) the faculties described by Gall are not pure traits which cannot be further analysed and are based on a long outdated psychology; (c) the shape of the brain bears no specific relationship to the shape of the skull. Phrenology is a pseudo-science; there is no truth in it whatever. But, even so, like astrology, it still has its practitioners.

Physiocrats. A French school of economic thought during the 18th cent., known at the time as *Les Economistes* but in later years named physiocrats by Du Pont de Nemours, a member of the School. Other members were Quesnay, Mirabeau, and the great financier Turgot. The physiocrats held the view, common to the 18th cent., and deriving ultimately from Rousseau, of the goodness and bounty of nature and the goodness of man "as he came from the bosom of nature". The aim of governments, therefore, should be to conform to nature; and so long as men do not interfere with each other's liberty and do not combine among themselves, governments should leave them free to find their own salvation. Criminals, madmen, and monopolists should be eliminated. Otherwise the duty of government is *laissez-faire, laissez passer*. From this follows the doctrine of free trade between nations on grounds of both justice and economy; for the greater the competition the more will each one strive to economise the cost of his labour to the general advantage. Adam Smith, although not sharing their confidence in human nature, learned much from the physiocrats, eliminated their errors, and greatly developed their teaching.

Physiognomy. *See* **Characterology.**

Pietism, a movement in the Lutheran Church at the end of the 17th cent.—the reaction, after the sufferings of the thirty years' war, of a pious and humiliated people against learning, pomp and ceremony, and stressing the importance of man's personal relationship with God. The writings of Johann Georg Hamann (1730–88) who came from a Pietist family of Königsberg influenced Kierkegaard. The Pietist move-

ment was the root of the great Romantic movement of the 18th cent.

Plymouth Brethren, a religious sect founded by John Nelson Darby, a minister of the Protestant Church of Ireland, and Edward Cronin a former Roman Catholic, in 1827. Both were dissatisfied with the lack of spirituality in their own and other churches and joined together in small meetings in Dublin every Sunday for "the breaking of bread". Soon the movement began to spread through Darby's travels and writings and he finally settled in Plymouth, giving the popular name to the "Brethren". Beginning as a movement open to all who felt the need to "keep the unity of the Spirit", it soon exercised the right to exclude all who had unorthodox views and split up into smaller groups. Among these the main ones were the "Exclusives", the Kellyites, the Newtonites, and "Bethesda" whose main differences were over problems of church government or prophetical powers. Some of these are further split among themselves. Readers of *Father and Son* by Sir Edmund Gosse, which describes life with his father, the eminent naturalist Philip Gosse, who belonged to the Brethren, will recall how this basically kind, honest, and learned man was led through their teachings to acts of unkindness (*e.g.*, in refusing to allow his son and other members of his household to celebrate Christmas and throwing out the small tokens they had secretly bought), and lack of scientific rigour (*e.g.*, in refusing for religious reasons alone to accept Darwinism when all his evidence pointed towards it).

Today, the majority of Brethren belong to the "Open Brethren" assemblies and, unlike the "Exclusives" hold that the Lord's Supper (a commemorative act of "breaking the bread" observed once a week) is for all Christians who care to join them. Baptism is required and Brethren believe in the personal premillennial second coming of Christ.

Poltergeist, allegedly a noisy type of spirit which specialises in throwing things about, making loud thumpings and bangings, and occasionally bringing in "apports", *i.e.*, objects from elsewhere. Most so-called poltergeist activities are plain frauds, but the others are almost invariably associated with the presence in the house of someone (often, but not always a child) who is suffering from an adolescent malaise or an epileptic condition. The inference is that those activities which are not simply fraudulent are either due to some unknown influence exuded by such mentally disturbed people, or that they are actually carried out by ordinary physical means by such people when in an hysterical state—*i.e.*, unconsciously. The second hypothesis is much the more probable. *See* **Psychic Research.**

Polytheism. *See* **God and Man.**

Positivism, also known as the **Religion of Humanity,** was founded by Auguste Comte (1798–1857), a famous mathematician and philosopher born in Montpellier, France. His views up to the end of the century attracted many and it would have been impossible throughout that time to read a book on philosophy or sociology that did not mention them, but today his significance is purely of historical interest. In his *Cours de Philosophie Positive* (1830) he put forward the thesis that mankind had seen three great stages in human thought: (1) the theological, during which man seeks for supernatural causes to explain nature and invents gods and devils; (2) the metaphysical, through which he thinks in terms of philosophical and metaphysical abstractions; (3) the last positive or scientific stage when he will proceed by experimental and objective observation to reach in time "positive truth".

Broadly speaking, there is little to complain of in this analysis; for there does seem to have been some sort of general direction along these lines. However, Comte was not satisfied with having reached this point and felt that his system demanded a religion and, of course, one that was "scientific". This religion was to be the worship of Humanity in place of the personal Deity of earlier times, and for it he supplied not only a Positive Catechism but a treatise on Sociology in which he declared himself the High Priest of the cult. Since, as it stood, the religion was likely to appear somewhat abstract to many, Comte drew up a list of historical characters whom he regarded as worthy of the same sort of adoration as Catholics accord to their saints. The new Church attracted few members, even among those who had a high regard for Comte's scientific work, and its only significant adherents were a small group of Oxford scholars and some in his own country. Frederic Harrison was the best-known English adherent and throughout his life continued to preach Comtist doctrines in London to diminishing audiences.

Pragmatism, a typically American school of philosophy which comes under the heading of what Bertrand Russell describes as a "practical" as opposed to a "theoretical" philosophy. Whereas the latter, to which most of the great philosophical systems belong, seeks disinterested knowledge for its own sake, the former (a) regards action as the supreme good, (b) considers happiness an effect and knowledge a mere instrument of successful activity.

The originator of pragmatism is usually considered to have been the psychologist William James (1842–1910) although he himself attributed its basic principles to his life-long friend, the American philosopher, Charles Sanders Peirce (1839–1914). The other famous pragmatist is John Dewey, best-known in Europe for his works on education (for although American text-books on philosophy express opinions to the contrary, few educated people in Europe have taken the slightest interest in pragmatism and generally regard it as an eccentricity peculiar to Americans). James in his book *The Will to Believe* (1896) points out that we are often compelled to take a decision where no adequate theoretical grounds for a decision exist; for even to do nothing is to decide. Thus in religion we have a right to adopt a believing attitude although not intellectually fully convinced. We should believe truth and shun error, but the failing of the sceptical philosopher is that he adheres only to the latter rule and thus fails to believe various truths which a less cautious man will accept. If believing truth and avoiding error are equally important, then it is a good idea when we are presented with an alternative to believe one of the possibilities at will, since we then have an even chance of being right, whereas we have none if we suspend judgment. The function of philosophy, according to James, is to find out what difference it makes to the individual if a particular philosophy or world-system is true: "An idea is 'true' so long as to believe it is profitable to our lives" and, he adds, the truth is only the expedient in our way of thinking ... in the long run and on the whole of course". Thus "if the hypothesis of God works satisfactorily in the widest sense of the word, it is true". Bertrand Russell's reply to this assertion is: "I have always found that the hypothesis of Santa Claus 'works satisfactorily in the widest sense of the word'; therefore 'Santa Claus exists' is true, although Santa Claus does not exist." Russell adds that James's concept of truth simply omits as unimportant the question whether God really *is* in His heaven; if He is a useful hypothesis that is enough. "God the Architect of the Cosmos is forgotten; all that is remembered is belief in God, and its effects upon the creatures inhabiting our petty planet. No wonder the Pope condemned the pragmatic defence of religion."

Predestination. *See* Calvinism.

Presbyterianism, a system of ecclesiastical government of the Protestant churches which look back to John Calvin as their Reformation leader. The ministry consists of presbyters who are all of equal rank. Its doctrinal standards are contained in the *Westminster Confession of Faith* (1647) which is, in general, accepted by English, Scottish, and American Presbyterians as the most thorough and logical statement in existence of the Calvinist creed. The Church of Scotland is the leading Presbyterian church in the British Isles.

The Reformation in Scotland was preceded by the same sort of awareness of the moral corruption of the Roman Church as had happened elsewhere, but for various political and emotional reasons, which need not be dis-

cussed here, the majority of the Scottish people (unlike the English who had been satisfied with the mere exchange of Crown for Pope) were determined on a fundamental change of doctrine, discipline, and worship, rather than a reform of manners. The church preachers had learned their Protestantism not from Luther but from Calvin and their leader John Knox had worked in Geneva with Calvin himself and was resolved to introduce the system into Scotland. In 1557 the "Lords of the Congregation" signed the Common Band (*i.e.*, a bond or covenant) to maintain "the blessed Word of God and his congregation" against their enemies, and demanded the right to worship as they had chosen. However, the real date of the Scottish Reformation is August 1500 when Mary of Guise (the regent for Mary Queen of Scots who was not yet of age) died and the Estates met to settle their affairs without foreign pressure; the *Scots Confession* was drawn up and signed by Knox and adopted by the Estates.

The ideas on which the Reformed Kirk was based are found in the *Scots Confession*, the *Book of Discipline*, and the *Book of Common Order*, the so-called Knox's liturgy. Knox's liturgy, the same as that used in Geneva but translated into English, was used until Laud's attempt to force an Anglican liturgy on the Kirk led to an abandonment of both in favour of "free prayers."

The Presbyterian tradition includes uncompromising stress upon the Word of God contained in the Scriptures of the Old and New Testaments as the supreme rule of faith and life, and upon the value of a highly trained ministry, which has given the Church of Scotland, a high reputation for scholarship and has in turn influenced the standard of education in Scotland. The unity of the Church is guaranteed by providing for democratic representation in a hierarchy of courts (unlike the Anglican Church, which is a hierarchy of persons). The local kirk-session consists of the minister and popularly elected elders (laymen). Ministers, elected by their flocks, are ordained by presbyters (ministers already ordained). Above the kirk-session is the court of the presbytery which has jurisdiction over a specified area; above that the court of synod which rules over many presbyteries; and finally the General Assembly which is the Supreme Court of the Church with both judicial and legislative powers, and over which the Moderator of the General Assembly presides. The function of the elders is to help the minister in the work and government of the kirk. The episcopacy set up by James VI and I, and maintained by Charles I was brought to an end by the Glasgow Assembly (1638), but General Assemblies were abolished by Oliver Cromwell and at the Restoration Charles II re-established episcopacy. The Covenanters who resisted were hunted down, imprisoned, transported, or executed over a period of nearly thirty years before William of Orange came to the throne and Presbyterianism was re-established (1690). Today Presbyterians no less than other Christian communities are looking at Christianity as a common world religion in the sense that the principles which unite them are greater than those which divide them. A small but significant step in the direction of international Christian unity was made in 1972 when the Presbyterian and Congregationalist Churches in England were merged to form the United Reformed Church. *See* **Church of Scotland, Calvinism.**

Protestant, the name first applied to those who favoured the cause of Martin Luther and who protested against the intolerant decisions of the Catholic majority at the second Diet of Speyer (1529), revoking earlier decisions of the first Diet of Speyer tolerating the Reformers in certain cases (1526). In general the name "Protestant" is applied to those Churches which severed connection with Rome at the time of the Reformation. The essence of Protestantism is the acceptance by the individual Christian of his direct responsibility to God rather than to the Church. *See* **Lutheranism, Presbyterianism, Calvinism.**

Psychedelism. For all his recorded history man

has relied upon drugs of one kind or another to make his life more tolerable. These have generally been central nervous system depressants—*i.e.*, alcohol, hashish, etc.—and their use in most societies has been brought under careful government control. Most societies have also at some stage experimented with the use of certain drugs of another class—the hallucinogens. These, far from having the mentally tranquillising characteristics of small doses of alcohol, provoke striking changes in mental alertness, frequently coupled with visionary or hallucinatory experiences. The confusion and disorientation which accompany such states has led to social disapproval of their use in Western countries, and the favoured "legal" drug for centuries has been alcohol. In the 1950s the novelist Aldous Huxley in his essay *The Doors of Perception* wrote of his experiences with the drug mescalin, a derivative of the South American peyotl and a powerful hallucinogen. Huxley put forward the hypothesis that mescalin had given him not only an entirely original psychological experience but had also significantly "heightened" his perceptual ability—a development of the greatest possible interest to artists, writers, and poets. Huxley's book had considerable impact, stimulating other creative individuals into similar experiments, not always with such euphoric results. In England the author Richard Ward reported some frightening moments under the drug LSD in his *A Drug-taker's Notebook* and Huxley amplified the unpredictable nature of the drug-experience in *Heaven and Hell*, published in 1956. Although such experiments were technically illegal, public interest had been considerably aroused and in the 1960s, when it became easy to synthesise the most effective of the h llucinogens, LSD, its use began to be common among certain sections of society. In 1964 a sensational scandal rocked the great American university of Harvard when senior members of the teaching staff, including the psychologist Timothy Leary, were dismissed for using LSD and encouraging students in its use. Unrepentant, Dr. Leary set up a community near New York from whence the cult of psychedelism was propagated.

Psychedelism—which is not really an organised system of belief, but rather an attitude of mind—preaches that through the controlled use of drugs, particularly of the hallucinogenic variety, an individual may be made aware for the first time of the rich fields of experience which lie latent in the unconscious mind. The exploration of these territories will have both a liberating and an enriching effect, the outcome being to "turn on" the individual to the total reality of mind. So convinced do many of the proponents of psychedelia become of the significance of the experience of the so-called LSD "trip," that they are inclined to urge non-trippers to experiment with the drug. Herein, of course, lies one obvious danger, for the drug LSD is potentially a toxic substance which needs to be administered in minute doses if it is not to cause madness or even death. There is also much uncertainty about the possible long-term effects of "tripping," many psychologists and scientists believing that it leads to a progressive disorientation and destruction of the personality, a disintegration of which the individual drug-taker is seldom aware. If there is a credit side to psychedelism it may lie in the clear, if limited, evolution in popular music, art, and design and to a lesser extent, literature which has been inspired by these excursions. The wave of interest in LSD and similar drugs is beginning to slacken off, possibly because of an increasing awareness of the possible grievous side-effects and of the largely illusory nature of the "insights" which the "trip" is supposed to provide. The controversial Dr. Leary, the movement's most literate and influential figure, later disavowed many of his original statements, and warned young people against the indiscriminate use of drugs as an aid to insight or self-awareness.

Psychic Research is a general term for the various approaches to the scientific investigation of the paranormal, in particular supposed extrasensory powers of the mind, but also manifestations such as ghosts, poltergeists, spiritualistic phenomena, etc. In recent years the word parapsychology has also come into use, particularly for the investigation of ESP in a laboratory setting, but it is really part of psychic research as the subject's fascinating history reveals.

For all recorded history, and no doubt very much earlier, man has been puzzled at his apparent ability to perceive features of the universe without the use of the normal senses—mind-to-mind contact, dreams about the future which come true, etc. He has also been intrigued by the notion that in addition to the natural world of people and things, there exists in parallel, a *supernatural* world of ghosts, spirits and other similar strange manifestations. Belief in such oddities has been tremendously widespread and still forms one of the major casual conversational topics raised when people see each other socially today. Of course, until the 19th cent. or thereabouts such phenomena, while bizarre, unpredictable and possibly frightening, were not at odds with man's view of himself and his world as revealed through basic religious beliefs. Man was supposed to be in essence a supernatural being with eternal life, and the world was seen as the happy hunting ground of dynamic evil forces which could intervene directly in the lives of humans. The rise of material science in the 19th cent. however began to shake the orthodox religious framework, and as a result in due course scientists began to question the basis of all supernatural powers and manifestations, putting forward the reasonable argument: "if such things *are* real then they should be demonstrable in scientific terms—just as all other aspects of the universe are."

Once having advanced this argument, the next step was to carry it to its conclusion and set about the systematic investigation of the phenomena to see whether they *did* conform in any way to the immensely successful framework of 19th cent. science, and from this step psychic research was born. In fact one can date its origins rather precisely—to 1882 when a group of scholars formed the Society for Psychical Research in London—an organisation which still exists today. The first experiments in this slightly eccentric field of science were haphazard and tended to be confined to spiritualistic phenomena such as table tapping, mediumistic messages, ectoplasmic manifestations, etc., which were having a great wave of popularity among the general public at the time. In fact what one might term as the first phase of psychic research—it has gone through three phases in its history—was really heavily tied up with Spiritualism. Before ridiculing it for this, it is only fair to point out that many of the most eminent figures of the time—the great physicists Sir Oliver Lodge and Sir William Crookes, Alfred Russell Wallace, co-discoverer with Darwin of the theory of evolution by natural selection, the brilliant author and creator of Sherlock Holmes, Sir Arthur Conan Doyle, and many others—became convinced Spiritualists as the result of their early experiments. Nevertheless, despite the ardent support of such intellectual giants, medium after medium was in due course detected in fraud—sometimes of the most blatant kind—and the majority of scientists gradually became more critical and less likely to be taken in by even the subtlest of trickery. As a result, interest slowly shifted from the séance room to a different realm, and as it did so the first phase of psychic research drew to a close.

The second phase was, broadly speaking, the era of the ghost hunter. With the idea of spirits materialising in laboratories seeming intrinsically less and less credible, scientists began to study what struck them at the time to be basically more "plausible" matters—haunted houses, poltergeist phenomena and so on. For some reason the idea of a house dominated by a psychic presence as the result of some tragic history seemed (at the turn of the century) *somehow* scientifically and philosophically more acceptable than did the old spiritualist notions about direct communication with the spirit world. The key figure in the "ghost hunting" era was Mr. Harry Price, an amateur magician who became the scourge of fraudulent mediums, but who staked his name and credibility on the authenticity of the alleged poltergeist phenomena at Borley Rectory in Suffolk, which became world famous through his book, *The Most Haunted House in England.* The ancient rectory's catalogue of ghosts and marvels allegedly witnessed by numerous "reliable witnesses" seemed irrefutable. Unfortunately investigations by the Society for Psychical Research some years after Price's death now make it seem certain that Price was responsible for faking some of the Borley phenomena himself, and with these disclosures scientifically "respectable" ghost hunting took a nasty tumble. Thus, with an increasingly critical attitude developing among scientists, haunted houses and poltergeists gradually began to shift out of favour to usher in the third phase of psychic research.

The date of the commencement of this phase can be identified as 1927 when the Parapsychology Laboratory at Duke University in North Carolina was formed by Dr. J. B. Rhine. Here the emphasis was on laboratory studies along the traditional lines of experimental psychology; spirit forms and poltergeists were ignored in favour of the routine testing of literally thousands of people for telepathy, precognition (the ability to see into the future), etc., almost always involving card tests which could be rigidly controlled and the results statistically analysed. By the 1940s Rhine was claiming irrefutable evidence of telepathy achieved by these means, but once again critical forces began to gather and it was pointed out that results obtained in Rhine's laboratory rarely seemed to be replicable in other scientists' laboratories in different parts of the world. In fact the failure of ESP experiments of this kind to be easily repeatable has turned out to be crucial and has led to a growing scepticism on the part of uncommitted scientists who now question whether psychic research and parapsychology have really advanced our understanding of the world of the paranormal in any way. At the present time the topic is in a highly controversial phase.

Although Rhine's university parapsychology laboratory closed with his retirement in 1965 research in the field has continued ever since, especially with the work of Dr. Helmut Schmidt who has made important contributions. In recent years a new Chair and research laboratory has been introduced at the University of Utrecht in the Netherlands.

To sum up the topic one could say that in a curious way, while the third phase of psychic research is now drawing to a close, the evidence suggests that a fourth phase is appearing, and that this may well feature a return to the study of the more sensational and dramatic phenomena reminiscent of the Victorian séance room. If this is so, a century after its foundation the wheel will have turned full circle and psychic research will be back where it started, without in the opinion of most scientists, having solved any of the basic questions which it had set out to answer. *See* **Parapsychology, Poltergeist, Telepathy, Spiritualism.**

Psychoanalysis, an approach to the study of human personality involving the rigorous probing, with the assistance of a specially trained practitioner, of an individual's personal problems, motives, goals and attitudes to life in general. Often, and quite understandably, confused with psychology (of which it is merely a part), psychoanalysis has an interesting historical background and has attracted the interest of philosophers, scientists and medical experts since it emerged as a radical and controversial form of mental therapy at the turn of the century. The traditionally accepted founder is the great Austrian Sigmund Freud, but he never failed to acknowledge the impetus that had been given to his own ideas by his talented friend, the physiologist Joseph Breuer, who for most of his working life had been interested in the curious phenomena associated with hypnosis. Breuer had successfully cured the hysterical paralysis of a young woman patient and had noticed that under hypnosis the girl seemed to be recalling emotional experiences, hitherto forgotten, which bore some relationship to the symptoms of her illness. Developing this with other patients Breuer then found that the mere recalling and discussing of the emotional events under hypnosis seemed to produce a dramatic alleviation of the symptoms—a phenomenon which came to be known as *catharsis.* Breuer also noticed another curious side-effect, that his women patients fell embarrassingly and violently in love with him, and he gradually dropped the practice of "mental catharsis", possibly feeling that it was a bit too dangerous to handle. This left the field clear for Freud, whose brilliant mind began to search beyond the therapeutic aspects of the topic to see what light might be thrown on the nature of human personality and psychological mechanisms in general. The most important question concerned the "forgotten" emotional material which turned up, apparently out of the blue, during the hypnotic session. Freud rightly saw that this posed problems for the current theories of memory, for how could something once forgotten (a) continue to have an effect on the individual without his being aware of it, and (b) ultimately be brought back to conscious memory again. It must be remembered that at this time memory was considered to be a fairly simple process—information was stored in the brain and was gradually eroded or destroyed with the passage of time and the decay of brain cells. Once lost, it was believed, memories were gone for ever, or at best only partially and inaccurately reproducible. Furthermore, human beings were supposed to be rational (if frequently wilful) creatures who never did anything without thinking about it (if only briefly) beforehand and without being well aware of their reasons for so doing. It was within this framework that Freud had his great insight, one which many people believe to be one of the most important ideas given to mankind. This was simply the realisation that the human mind was not a simple entity controlling the brain and body more or less at will, but a complex system made up of a number of integrated parts with at least two major subdivisions—the conscious and the unconscious. The former concerned itself with the normal round of human behaviour, including the larger part of rational thought, conversation, etc., and large areas of memory. The latter was principally devoted to the automatic control of bodily functions, such as respiration, cardiac activity, various types of emotional behaviour not subject to much conscious modification and a large storehouse of relevant "memories" again not normally accessible to the conscious mind. Occasionally, Freud proposed, an exceedingly unpleasant emotional or otherwise painful event might be so troublesome if held in the conscious mind's store, that it would get shoved down into the unconscious or "repressed" where it would cease to trouble the individual in his normal life. The advantages of this mechanism are obvious, but they also brought with them hazards. With certain kinds of memory, particularly those involving psychological rather than physical pain—as for example a severe sexual conflict or marital problem—repression might be used as a device to save the individual from facing his problem in the "real" world, where he might be able ultimately to solve it, by merely hiding it away in the unconscious and thus pretending it did not exist. Unfortunately, Freud believed, conflicts of this kind were not snuffed out when consigned to the basements of the mind, but rather tended to smoulder on, affecting the individual in various ways which he could not understand. Repressed marital conflicts might give rise to impotence, for example, or even to homosexual behaviour. Guilt at improper social actions similarly repressed might provoke nervous tics, local paralysis, etc, etc. Following this line of reasoning, Freud argued that if the unwisely repressed material could be dredged up and the individual forced to face the crisis instead of denying it, then dramatic alleviations of symptoms and full recovery should follow.

To the great psychologist and his growing band of followers the stage seemed to be set for a dramatic breakthrough not only in mental therapy but also in a general understanding of the nature of human personality. To his pleasure—for various reasons he was never too happy about hypnosis—Freud discovered that with due patience, skill and guidance an individual could be led to resurrect the material repressed in his unconscious mind in the normal, as opposed to the hypnotic, state. This technique, involving long sessions consisting of intimate discussions between patient and therapist became known as psychoanalysis, and it has steadily evolved from its experimental beginnings in the medical schools and universities of Vienna to being a major system of psychotherapy with a world-wide following and important theoretical connotations. Psychoanalysis, as practised today, consists of a number of meetings between doctor and patient in which the latter is slowly taught to approach and enter the *territory* of his subconscious mind, and examine the strange and "forgotten" material within. A successful analysis, it is claimed, gives the individual greater insight into his own personality and a fuller understanding of the potent unconscious forces which are at work within him and in part dictating his goals.

Freud's initial ideas were of course tentative, and meant to be so. He was however a didactic and forceful personality himself, unwilling to compromise on many points which became controversial as the technique and practice of psychoanalysis developed. The outcome was that some of his early followers, notably the equally brilliant Carl Jung and Alfred Adler, broke away to found their own "schools" or versions of psychoanalysis, with varying degrees of success. Today, psychoanalysis is coming under increasingly critical scrutiny, and its claims are being treated with a good deal of reservation. Notable antagonists include the English psychologist Professor H. J. Eysenck who points out that there is little if any solid experimental data indicating that psychoanalysis is a valid method of treating or curing mental illness. Analysists respond by saying that their system is closer to an art than a craft and not amenable to routine scientific experiment. The controversy will no doubt continue for some time to come, but whatever its validity as therapy, the basic ideas behind psychoanalysis—notably the reality and power of the unconscious mind—are beyond question and have given human beings definite and major insights into the greatest enigma of all—the workings of the human mind. *See also* **Section Q.**

Psychometry, the supposed talent or faculty of divining something about the history and previous owners of an object by holding it in the hand. A common feature of modern Spiritualistic practice, and to a certain extent synonymous with clairvoyance, psychometry is based on an ancient magical assumption that objects somehow take on traces or "memories" of their surroundings which are detectable by specially sensitive individuals. Controlled scientific tests on people claiming to have this power have however proved totally negative. *See also* **Psychic Research.**

Puritans were a separate sect before the accession of Edward VI, but did not become prominent till the reign of Elizabeth. Afterwards they split up into Independents and Presbyterians, and the influence of Oliver Cromwell made the former supreme. Since the Revolution the word has been replaced by 'Nonconformist' or 'Dissenter', but, of course, Romanists in England and Protestant Episcopalians in Scotland are just as much Nonconformists or Dissenters as Baptists or Methodists are.

Pyramidology, a curious belief that the dimensions of the Great Pyramid at Giza, if studied carefully, reveal principles of fundamental historical and religious significance. The perpetrator of this was a Victorian publisher, John Taylor, who discovered that if you divide the height of the pyramid into twice the side of its base you get a number very similar to *pi*—a number of considerable mathematical importance. Later discoveries in the same vein include the finding that the base of the pyramid (when divided by the width of a single casing stone) equals exactly 365—number of days in the year. Many books have been written on the interpretation of the dimensions of the pyramid, none of which has any scientific or archaeological validity. Pyramidology is simply a classic example of the well-known fact that hunting through even a random array of numbers will turn up sequences which appear to be "significant"—always provided that one carefully selects the numbers one wants and turns a blind eye to those that one doesn't! A peculiar variant of pyramidology has recently arisen through the publication of a claim that razor blades kept beneath a cardboard model of a pyramid never lose their cutting edge! Scientific tests have shown that this is not so, but the belief persists—implicit testimony to the mystical power of certain common emblems and symbols.

Pyrrhonism, a sceptical philosophy which doubts everything.

Q

Quakers, a religious body founded in England in the 17th cent. by George Fox (1624–91). The essence of their faith is that every individual who believes has the power of direct communication with God who will guide him into the ways of truth. This power comes from the "inner light" of his own heart, the light of Christ, Quakers meet for worship avoiding all ritual, without ordained ministers or prepared sermons; there is complete silence until someone is moved by the Holy Spirit to utter his message.

In the early days Quakers gave vent to violent outbursts and disturbed church services. Friends had the habit of preaching at anyone who happened to be nearby, their denunciation of "steeple-houses" and references to the "inner light," their addressing everyone as "thee" and "thou," their refusal to go beyond "yea" and "nay" in making an assertion and refusing to go further in taking an oath, must have played some part in bringing about the savage persecutions they were forced to endure. Many emigrated to Pennsylvania, founded by William Penn in 1682, and missionaries were sent to many parts of the world. The former violence gave way to gentleness. Friends not only refused to take part in war but even refused to resist personal violence. They took the lead in abolishing slavery, worked for prison reform and better education. As we know them today Quakers are quiet, sincere, undemonstrative people, given to a somewhat serious turn of mind. The former peculiarities of custom and dress have been dropped and interpretation of the Scriptures is more liberal. Although Quakers refuse to take part in warfare, they are always ready to help the victims of war, by organising relief, helping refugees in distress, or sending their ambulance units into the heat of battle.

Quietism, a doctrine of extreme asceticism and contemplative devotion, embodied in the works of Michael Molinos, a 17th cent. Spanish priest, and condemned by Rome. It taught that the chief duty of man is to be occupied in the continual contemplation of God, so as to become totally independent of outward circumstances and the influence of the senses. Quietists taught that when this stage of perfection is reached the soul has no further need for prayer and other external devotional practices. Similar doctrines have been taught in the Moslem and Hindu religions. *See* **Yoga.**

R

Racism, the doctrine that one race is inherently superior or inferior to others, one of the bases of racial prejudice. It has no connection whatever with the study of race as a concept, nor with the investigation of racial differences, which is a science practised by the physical anthropologist (who studies physical differences), or the social anthropologist (who studies cultural differences). Racism is simply a vulgar superstition believed in by the ignorant or mentally unbalanced, and it may be categorically stated as a scientific fact that racial superiority is a myth believed in by no scientist of repute. *See also* **Race, Section L.**

Radiesthesia, the detection, either by some "psychic" faculty or with special equipment, of radiations alleged to be given off by all living things and natural substances such as water, oil, metal, etc. The word radiesthesia is in fact a fancy modern name for the ancient practice of "dowsing," whereby an individual is supposed to be able to detect the presence of hidden underground water by following the movements of a hazel twig held in his hands. Dowsers, or water diviners, as they are sometimes called, claim also to be able to detect the presence of minerals and, hard though it may seem to believe, have actually been hired by major oil companies to prospect for desert wells—though without any notable success. The theory of dowsing is that all things give off a unique radiation signal which the trained individual (via his twig, pendulum, or whatever) can "tune in" to, a theory which, while not backed up by any data known to orthodox sciences, is at least not too fantastically far-fetched. It is when radiesthesists claim to be able to detect the presence of oil, water, or precious metals by holding their pendulum *over a map* of the territory and declare that it is not necessary for them to visit the area in person to find the required spot that the topic moves from the remotely possible to the absurdly improbable. Some practitioners of this art state that they are able to perform even more marvellous feats such as determining the sex of chickens while still in the egg, or diagnosing illness by studying the movements of a pendulum held over a blood sample from the sick individual. Such claims when put to simple scientific test have almost invariably turned out as fiascos. Yet belief in dowsing, water-divining, and the like is still very widespread.

There is an important link between radiesthesia and the pseudo-science of *radionics*, which holds that the twig or pendulum can be superseded by complicated equipment built vaguely according to electronic principles. A typical radionic device consists of a box covered with knobs, dials, etc., by which the practitioner "tunes in" to the "vibration" given off by an object, such as a blood spot, a piece of hair, or even a signature. By the proper interpretation of the readings from the equipment the illness, or even the mental state, of the individual whose blood, hair, or signature is being tested, may be ascertained. The originator of radionics seems to have been a Dr. Albert Abrams who engaged in medical practice using radionic devices in America in the 1920s and 30s. The principal exponent in this country was the late George de la Warr who manufactured radionic boxes for diagnosis and treatment of illnesses, and even a "camera" which he believed to be capable of photographing thought. In a sensational court case in 1960 a woman who had purchased one of the diagnostic devices sued de la Warr for fraud. After a long trial the case was dismissed, the Judge commenting that while he had no good evidence that the device worked as claimed, he felt that de la Warr seriously believed in its validity and thus was not guilty of fraud or misrepresentation.

Ranters, a fanatical antinomian (the doctrine that Christians are not bound to keep the law of God) and pantheistic sect in Commonwealth England. The name was also applied to the Primitive Methodists because of their noisy preaching.

Rastafarianism, a Caribbean religious cult which took root among West Indians after the waning of Black Power (*q.v.*) in the mid-1970s. Rastafarians look to Ethiopia as their spiritual and racial home since that country was the one part of Africa not to be colonised. **Reggae** (*see* **Section E,** Special Topic) is their music, prominent in the West Indian Notting Hill Festival held in London during the August Bank Holiday weekend.

Rationalism is defined as "the treating of reason as the ultimate authority in religion and the rejection of doctrines not consonant with reason." In practice, rationalism had a double significance: (1) the doctrine as defined above, and (2) a 19th cent. movement which was given to what was then known as "free-thought," "secularism," or agnosticism—*i.e.*, it was in the positive sense anti-religious and was represented by various bodies such as the Secular Society, the National Secular Society, and the Rationalist Press Association (founded in 1899).

In the first sense, which implies a particular philosophical attitude to the universe and life, rationalism is not easy to pin down although, at first sight, it would appear that nothing could be simpler. Does it mean the use of pure reason and logic or does it mean, on the other hand, the use of what is generally called the "scientific method" based on a critical attitude to existing beliefs? If we are thinking in terms of the use of pure reason and logic then the Roman Catholic Church throughout most of its history has maintained, not that the whole truth about religion can be discovered by reason, but as St. Thomas Aquinas held, the basis of religion—*e.g.* the existence of God—can be rationally demonstrated. Nobody could have made more use of logic than the schoolmen of the Middle Ages, yet not many people today would accept their conclusions, nor would many non-Catholics accept St. Thomas's proofs of the existence of God even when they themselves are religious. The arguments of a First Cause or Prime Mover or the argument from Design on the whole leave us unmoved, partly because they do not lead up to the idea of a *personal God*, partly because we rightly distrust logic and pure reason divorced from facts and know that, if we begin from the wrong assumptions or premises, we can arrive at some very strange answers. If the existence of a Deity can be proved by reason, then one can also by the use of reason come to the conclusions, or rather paradoxes, such as the following: God is by definition all good, all knowing, all powerful—yet evil exists (because it if does not exist then it cannot be wrong to say "there is no God"). But if evil exists, then it must do so either because of God (in which case He is not all good) or in spite of God (in which case He is not all powerful).

Arguments of this sort do not appeal to the modern mind for two historical reasons: (1) many of us have been brought up in the Protestant tradition which—at least in one of its aspects—insists that we must believe in God by faith rather than by logic and in its extreme form insists on God as revealed by the "inner light"; (2) our increasing trust in the scientific method of observation, experiment and argument. Thus, no matter what Aristotle or St. Thomas may say about a Prime Mover or a First Cause, we remain unconvinced since at least one scientific theory suggests that the universe did not have a beginning and if scientific investigation proved this to be so, then we should be entirely indifferent to what formal logic had to say.

The secularist and rationalist movements of the 19th cent. were anti-religious—and quite rightly so—because at that time there were serious disabilities imposed even in Britain by the Established Church on atheism or agnosticism and freedom of thought. They are of little significance now because very little is left, largely thanks to their efforts, of these disabilities.

Finally, although most people are likely to accept the scientific method as the main means of discovering truth, there are other factors which equally make us doubt the value of "pure" logic and reason unaided by observation. The first of these is the influence of Freud which shows that much of our reasoning is mere rationalising—*e.g.*, we are more likely to become atheists because we hated our father than because we can prove that there is no God. The second is the influence of a movement in philosophy which, in the form of logical positivism or logical analysis, makes us doubt whether metaphysical systems have any meaning at all. Today, instead of asking ourselves whether Plato was right or wrong, we are much more likely to ask whether he did anything but make for the most part meaningless noises. Religion is in a sense much safer today than it ever was in the 19th cent. when it made foolish statements over matters of science that could be *proved* wrong; now we tend to see it as an emotional attitude to the universe or God (a "feeling of being at home in the universe," as William James put it) which can no more be proved or disproved than being in love.

Realism is a word which has so many meanings, and such contradictory ones, in various spheres, that it is difficult to define. We shall limit ourselves to its significance in philosophy. In philosophy, "realism" has two different meanings, diametrically opposed. (1) The most usual meaning is the one we should least expect from the everyday sense of the word— *i.e.*, it refers to all those philosophies from Plato onwards which maintained that the world of appearance is illusory and that ideas, forms, or universals are the only true realities, belonging to the world beyond matter and appearance— the world of God or mind. In early mediaeval times St. Thomas Aquinas was the chief exponent of this doctrine which was held by the scholastics as opposed to the Nominalists (*q.v.*). (2) In its modern everyday meaning "realism" is the belief that the universe is real and not a creation of mind, that there is a reality that causes the appearance, the "thing-in-itself" as Kant described it. Material things may not really be what they appear to be (*e.g.* a noise is not the "bang" we experience but a series of shock-waves passing through the atmosphere), yet, for all that, we can be sure that matter exists and it is very possible (some might add) that mind does not.

Reformation, the great religious movement of the 16th cent., which resulted in the establishment of Protestantism. John Wyclif (d. 1384), John Hus (d. 1415) and others had sounded the warning note, and when later on Luther took up the cause in Germany, and Zwingli in Switzerland, adherents soon became numerous. The wholesale vending of indulgences by the papal agents had incensed the people, and when Luther denounced these things he spoke to willing ears. After much controversy, the reformers boldly propounded the principles of the new doctrine, and the struggle for religious supremacy grew bitter. They claimed justification (salvation) by faith, and the use as well as the authority of the Scriptures, rejecting the doctrine of transubstantiation, the adoration of the Virgin and Saints, and the headship of the Pope. Luther was excommunicated. But the Reformation principles spread and ultimately a great part of Germany, as well as Switzerland, the Low Countries, Scandinavia, England, and Scotland were won over to the new faith. In England Henry VIII readily espoused the cause of the Reformation, his own personal quarrel with the Pope acting as an incentive. Under Mary there was a brief and sanguinary reaction, but Elizabeth gave completeness to the work which her father had initiated. *See* **Lutheranism, Calvinism, Presbyterianism, Baptists, Methodism.**

Renaissance is defined in the *Oxford English Dictionary* as: "The revival of art and letters, under the influence of classical models, which began in Italy in the 14th century." It is a term which must be used with care for the following reasons: (1) Although it was first used in the form *rinascita* (re-birth) by Vasari in 1550 and people living at that time certainly were aware that something new was happening, the word had no wide currency until used by the Swiss historian Jacob Burchardt in his classic *The Civilization of the Renaissance in Italy* (1860). (2) The term as used today refers not only to art in its widest sense but to a total change in man's outlook on life which extended into philosophical, scientific, economic, and technical fields. (3) Spreading from Italy there were renaissance movements in France, Spain, Germany, and northern Europe, all widely different with varying delays in time. As the historian Edith Sichel says: "Out of the Italian Renaissance there issued a new-born art; out of the Northern Renaissance there came forth a new-born religion. There came forth also a great school of poetry, and a drama the greatest that the world had seen since the days of Greece. The religion was the offspring of Germany and the poetry that of England."

The real cause of the Renaissance was not the fall of Constantinople, the invention of printing, or the discovery of America, though these were phases in the process; it was, quite simply,

money. The birth of a new merchant class gave rise to individualist attitudes in economic affairs which prepared the way for individualism and humanism. The new wealthy class in time became patrons of the arts whereas previously the Church had been the sole patron and controller. Thus the artist became more free to express himself, more respected, and being more well-to-do could afford to ignore the Church and even, in time, the views of his patrons.

It is true that art continued to serve to a considerable extent the purposes of faith, but it was judged from the standpoint of art. Mediaeval art was meant to elevate and teach man: Renaissance art to delight his senses and enrich his life. From this free and questing spirit acquired from economic individualism came the rise of modern science and technology; here Italy learned much from the Arab scholars who had translated and commented upon the philosophical, medical, and mathematical texts of antiquity, while denying themselves any interest in Greek art and literature. Arabic-Latin versions of Aristotle were in use well into the 16th cent. The Byzantine culture, though it had preserved the Greek tradition and gave supremacy to Plato, had made no move forward. But the Greek scholars who fled to Italy after the fall of Constantinople brought with them an immense cargo of classical manuscripts. The recovery of these Greek masterpieces, their translation into the vernaculars, and the invention of printing, made possible a completer understanding of the Greek spirit. It was the bringing together of the two heritages, Greek science, and Greek literature, that gave birth to a new vision. But it was not only Aristotle and Plato who were being studied but Ovid, Catullus, Horace, Pliny and Lucretius. What interested Renaissance man was the humanism of the Latin writers, their attitude to science, their scepticism.

The period *c.* 1400-1500 is known as the **Early Renaissance.** During this time such painters as Masaccio, Uccello, Piero della Francesca, Botticelli, and Giovanni Bellini were laying the foundations of drawing and painting for all subsequent periods including our own. They concerned themselves with such problems as anatomy, composition, perspective, and representation of space, creating in effect a grammar or textbook of visual expression. The term **High Renaissance** is reserved for a very brief period when a pure, balanced, classical harmony was achieved and artists were in complete control of the techniques learned earlier. The High Renaissance lasted only from *c.* 1500 to 1527 (the date of the sack of Rome), yet that interval included the earlier works of Michelangelo, most of Leonardo's, and all the Roman works of Raphael.

Ritualism, a tendency which, during the 19th cent., developed in the High Church section of the Church of England to make use of those vestments, candles, incense, etc. which are usually regarded as features of the Church of Rome. Since some opposition was aroused, a Ritual Commission was appointed in 1904 to take evidence and try to find some common basis on which High and Low Church could agree with respect to ceremonial. The report of 1906 in effect recommended the giving of greater powers to bishops to suppress objectionable practices. Although they are often associated together, it is worth while pointing out that there was no special connection between the Oxford Movement or Tractarians (*q.v.*) and Ritualism because Pusey disliked ritual and even Newman, who eventually went over to Rome, held extremely simple services at his church of St. Mary's.

Roman Catholic Church, the Christian organisation which acknowledges the Pope as the lawful successor of St. Peter, the apostle appointed by Christ to be the head of His Church. The reforming impulse at the Second Vatican Council (1962-5), summoned by Pope John, set in train movements towards religious unity and the reform and modernisation of the Church. Pope Paul made changes in the government and liturgy of the Church but refused to allow birth control, the marriage of priests and a greater role for women in the Roman Catholic Church.

The 1970s have seen rapid changes in the Roman Catholic Church and the papacy has found a strong and charismatic leader in Pope John Paul II whose first encyclical *Redemptor Hominus* (1979) declared that the Christian missionary must always begin with "a deep esteem for man, for his intellect, his will, his conscience and his freedom". A historic meeting took place in 1982 between Rome and Canterbury when Pope John Paul II, making the first papal visit to Britain, joined Dr. Runcie in Canterbury Cathedral in the cause of Christian unity. *See also* **Cardinals, Section L.**

Romantic Movement or **Romanticism** is the name given not so much to an individual way of thinking but to the gradual but radical transformation of basic human values that occurred in the Western world round about the latter part of the 18th cent. It was a great breakthrough in European consciousness and arose through the writings of certain men living during the half-century or more following, say, 1760. It arose then because both time and place were propitious for the birth of these new ideas. There was a revolution in basic values—in art, morals, politics, religion, etc. The new view was of a world transcending the old one, infinitely larger and more varied.

To understand the Romantic movement it is necessary first to take note of the climate of thought preceding the great change; then to account for its beginning in Germany where it did (*see* **Pietism**) during the latter part of the 18th cent., and finally to appraise the writings of those men whose ideas fermented the new awakening. Briefly, the shift was away from French classicism and from belief in the all-pervasive power of human reason (the Enlightenment) towards the unfettered freedom that the new consciousness was able to engender. What mattered was to live a passionate and vigorous life, to dedicate oneself to an ideal, no matter what the cost (*e.g.*, Byron).

The ideas of the Englightenment (*e.g.*, Fontenelle, Voltaire, Montesquieu) had been attacked by the Germans Hamann and Herder and by the ideas of the English philosopher Hume, but Kant, Schiller, and Fichte, Goethe's novel *Wilhelm Meister*, and the French Revolution all had profound effects on the aesthetic, moral, social, and political thought of the time. Friedrich Schlegel (1772–1829) said: "There is in man a terrible unsatisfied desire to soar into infinity; a feverish longing to break through the narrow bonds of individuality." Romanticism undermined the notion that in matters of value there are objective criteria which operate between men. Henceforth there was to be a resurgence of the human spirit, deep and profound, that is still going on.

Rosicrucians, an ancient mystical society founded in the 16th cent. by Christian Rosenkreuz which attempted to forge a theoretical link between the great Egyptian religions and the Church of Rome, drawing rituals and philosophy from both camps. The Society did not long survive the death of its founder (he managed to reach the age of 106 incidentally) but has been revived in succeeding centuries by a series of rivalling factions. Perhaps the most famous of these is the Rosicrucian Order (A.M.O.R.C) which has become well-known in the Western world as a result of its heavy advertising in the popular press. Founded by the American H. Spencer Lewis, this offers a simple and good-natured doctrine preaching the Brotherhood of Man, the reincarnation of the soul and the immense latent potential of the human mind. As with many American-based organisations of this kind, the boundary between business and religion is hard to define. It is probably best summed up as a modern secret society which serves an important function in the lives of many people of mystical inclinations.

S

Salvation Army. The religious movement which in 1878 became known by this name arose from the Christian Mission meetings which the Rev. William Booth and his devoted wife had held in the East End of London for the previous thirteen years. Its primary aim was, and still is, to preach the gospel of Jesus Christ to men and women untouched by ordinary religious efforts. The founder devoted his life to the salvation of the submerged classes whose conditions at that time were unspeakably dreadful. Originally his aim had been to convert people and then send them on to the churches, but he soon found that few religious bodies would accept these "low-class" men and women. So it was that social work became part of their effort. Practical help like the provision of soup-kitchens, accompanied spiritual ministration. Soon, in the interests of more effective "warfare" against social evils, a military form of organisation, with uniforms, brass bands, and religious songs, was introduced. Its magazine *The War Cry* gave as its aim "to carry the Blood of Christ and the Fire of the Holy Ghost into every part of the world.'

General Booth saw with blinding clarity that conversion must be accompanied by an improvement of external conditions. Various books had earlier described the terrible conditions of the slums, but in 1890 he produced a monumental survey entitled *In Darkest England and the Way Out.* From that time forward the Army was accepted and its facilities made use of by the authorities. Today the Army's spiritual and social activities have spread to countries all over the world; every one, no matter what class, colour, or creed he belongs to is a "brother for whom Christ died."

Sandemanians or Glassites, an obscure religious sect whose sole claim to fame is that one of its members was the great Michael Faraday, founder of the science of electromagnetism, who never failed to attend its Sunday services.

Sceptics. From Thales of Miletus (*c.* 624–565 B.C.) to the Stoics in the 4th cent. B.C. philosophers had been trying to explain the nature of the universe; each one produced a different theory and each could, apparently, prove that he was right. This diversity of views convinced the Sceptic school founded by Pyrrho (*c.* 360–270 B.C.) that man is unable to know the real nature of the world or how it came into being. In place of a futile search for what must be for ever unknowable, the Sceptics recommended that men should be practical, follow custom, and accept the evidence of their senses.

Schoolmen. From the time of Augustine to the middle of the 9th cent. philosophy, like science, was dead or merely a repetition of what had gone before. But about that time there arose a new interest in the subject, although (since by then Western Europe was entirely under the authority of the Catholic Church) the main form it took was an attempt to justify Church teaching in the light of Greek philosophy. Those who made this attempt to reconcile Christian beliefs with the best in Plato and Aristotle were known as "schoolmen" and the philosophies which they developed were known as "scholasticism." Among the most famous schoolmen must be counted John Scotus Erigena (*c.* 800–*c.* 877), born in Ireland and probably the earliest; St. Anselm, archbishop of Canterbury (1033–1109); the great Peter Abelard whose school was in Paris (1079–1142); Bernard of Chartres, his contemporary; and the best-known of all, St. Thomas Aquinas of Naples (1225–74), who was given the name of the "Angelic Doctor."

The philosophies of these men are discussed under various headings (**God and Man, Determinism and Free-will**), but being severely limited by the Church their doctrines differed from each other much less than those of later philosophical schools. However, one of the great arguments was between the orthodox Realists (*q.v.*) and the Nominalists (*q.v.*) and a second was between the Thomists (or followers of St. Thomas Aquinas) and the Scotists (followers of John Duns Scotus—not to be confused with John Scotus Erigena). The two latter schools were known as the Ancients, whilst the followers of William of Occam, the Nominalist, were known as the Terminalists. All became reconciled in 1482 in face of the threat from humanism of which the great ex-

,ponent was Erasmus of Rotterdam (1466–1536).

Scientology, an unusual quasi-philosophical system started by the American science-fiction writer L. Ron Hubbard, which claims to be able to effect dramatic improvement in the mental and physical well-being of its adherents. Originally developed in the United States as "Dianetics, the modern science of mental health," it was hailed in Hubbard's first book to be "a milestone for Man comparable to his discovery of fire and superior to his inventions of the wheel and the arch." Such extravagant statements exemplify the literature of the movement, which in the late 1950s began to expand in England when its founder came to live in East Grinstead. Followers of Dianetics and Scientology advance within the cult through a series of levels or grades, most reached by undertaking courses of training and tuition, payment for which may amount to hundreds and, in total, even thousands of pounds. These courses consist largely of mental exercises known as "processing" and "auditing" (now called "pastoral counselling" since more emphasis has recently been laid on the religious aspect). One of the principal goals of a Scientologist is the attainment of the state known as "Clear" (roughly speaking, one "cleared" of certain mental and physical handicaps) when it is believed he (she) will be a literally superior being, equipped with a higher intelligence and a greater command over the pattern of his (her) own life. The Scientologists' claims that their movement is a genuine religion have generally been met with resistance from establishment bodies. In 1967 the Home Office announced that its centres would no longer be recognised as educational establishments and foreigners arriving for its courses would not be granted student status. In 1980 the Home Office lifted this ban. The international headquarters have been moved from East Grinstead to Los Angeles.

Shakers, members of a revivalist group, styled by themselves "The United Society of Believers in Christ's Second Appearing," who seceded from Quakerism in 1747 though adhering to many of the Quaker tenets. The community was joined in 1758 by Ann Lee, a young convert from Manchester, who had "revelations" that she was the female Christ; "Mother Ann" was accepted as their leader. Under the influence of her prophetic visions she set out with nine followers for "Immanuel's land" in America and the community settled near Albany, capital of New York state. They were known as the "Shakers" in ridicule because they were given to involuntary movements in moments of religious ecstasy. Central to their faith was the belief in the dual role of God through the male and female Christ: the male principle came to earth in Jesus; the female principle, in "Mother Ann." The sexes were equal and women preached as often as men at their meetings which sometimes included sacred dances—nevertheless the two sexes, even in dancing, kept apart. Their communistic way of living brought them economic prosperity, the Shakers becoming known as good agriculturists and craftsmen, noted for their furniture and textiles. After 1860, however, the movement began to decline and few, if any, are active today.

Shamans, the medicine men found in all primitive societies who used their magical arts to work cures, and protect the group from evil influences. The *shaman* was a man apart and wore special garments to show his authority. Shamanism with its magical practices, incantations, trances, exhausting dances, and self-torture is practised even today by primitive tribes.

Shiites or Shia, a heretical Moslem sect in Persia, opposed by the orthodox Sunnites. The dispute, which came almost immediately after the death of the Prophet and led to bitter feuding, had little to do with matters of doctrine as such but with the succession. After Mohammed's death, there were three possible claimants: Ali, the husband of his daughter Fatima, and two others, one of whom gave up his claim in favour of the other, Omar. The orthodox selected Omar, who was shortly assassinated, and the same happened to his successor as Ali was passed over again. The Shiites are those who maintain that Ali was the true vicar of the Prophet, and that the three orthodox predecessors were usurpers.

Shintoism, literally means "teaching of the Gods" and is the specifically Japanese splinter version of Buddhism with a strong bias towards ancestor worship and the divine powers of natural forces. Unusual in that it had no recognised founder nor written dogma, Shintoism permeated Japanese life in a most vigorous way until the defeat of the country at the hands of the Allied Powers in 1945. In the 1500 years of its existence the Shinto religion produced tens of thousands of unique and beautiful shrines throughout Japan. Vast numbers of these were destroyed by bombing in the war, but a tolerant decision by the American airforce spared the Shinto capital, Kyoto, from air-attack. Shintoism was disestablished by the American occupying forces in 1945 and the Emperor Hirohito "abdicated" his divine powers. Current dissatisfaction among many Japanese with the worldly extravagance of their heavily industrialised society has led to a recent revival of interest in their ancient and selfless religion.

Sikhism. The Sikh community of the Punjab, which has played a significant part in the history of modern India, came into being during a period of religious revival in India in the 15th and 16th cent. It was originally founded as a religious sect by Guru (teacher) Nanak (1469–1538) who emphasised the fundamental truth of all religions, and whose mission was to put an end to religious conflict. He condemned the formalism both of Hinduism and Islam, preaching the gospel of universal toleration, and the unity of the Godhead, whether He be called Allah, Vishnu, or God. His ideas were welcomed by the great Mogul Emperor Akbar (1542–1605). Thus a succession of Gurus were able to live in peace after Nanak's death; they established the great Sikh centre at Amritsar, compiled the sacred writings known as the *Adi Granth,* and improved their organisation as a sect. But the peace did not last long, for an emperor arose who was a fanatical Moslem, in face of whom the last Guru, Govind Singh (1666–1708), whose father was put to death for refusal to embrace Islam, had to make himself a warrior and instil into the Sikhs a more aggressive spirit. A number of ceremonies were instituted by Govind Singh; admission to the fraternity was by special rite; caste distinctions were abolished; hair was worn long; the word singh, meaning lion, was added to the original name. They were able to organise themselves into 12 *misls* or confederacies but divisions appeared with the disappearance of a common enemy and it was not until the rise of Ranjit Singh (1780–1839) that a single powerful Sikh kingdom was established, its influence only being checked by the English, with whom a treaty of friendship was made. After the death of Ranjit Singh two Anglo-Sikh wars followed, in 1845–46, and 1848–49, which resulted in British annexation of the Punjab and the end of Sikh independence. In the two world wars the Sikhs proved among the most loyal of Britain's Indian subjects. The partitioning of the continent of India in 1947 into two states, one predominantly Hindu and the other predominantly Moslem, presented a considerable problem in the Punjab, which was divided in such a way as to leave 2 million Sikhs in Pakistan, and a considerable number of Moslems in the Indian Punjab. Although numbering less than 2 per cent. of the population (c. 8 million) the Sikhs are a continuing factor in Indian political life. Demands for Sikh independence led to the storming by Indian troops of the Golden Temple at Amritsar on 6 June 1984. In October 1984, Mrs. Gandhi was assassinated by Sikh extremists.

Socialism, is a form of society in which men and women are not divided into opposing economic classes but live together under conditions of approximate social and economic equality, using in common the means that lie to their hands of promoting social welfare. The brotherhood of man inspires the aims of socialism in foreign, colonial, social, and economic policies alike. The word "socialism" first came into general use in England about 1834 in connection with Robert Owen's "village of co-operation" at New Lanark. About the middle of the 19th cent., Charles Kingsley and others established a form of Christian socialism, and William Morris, John Burns, and others founded a Socialist League in 1886. With the development of trade unions the socialist movement took a more practical trend. Fabianism (q.v.) associated in its early days with the names of Beatrice and Sidney Webb and George Bernard Shaw, aims at the gradual reorganisation of society by creating intelligent public opinion by education and legislation. The British Labour Party believes in peaceful and constitutional change to socialism by democratic methods based upon popular consent. The Labour Government of 1945–51 initiated a major period of social reform and public ownership. Though beset by economic difficulties, the 1964–70 Labour Government continued a policy of radical reform. The minority Labour Government (of February–October 1974) and the subsequent administration continued this process, particularly in the area of state intervention in industry. The election defeats of 1979 and 1983 have inevitably led to a questioning of the future direction the party should take particularly set against the background of the establishment and early electoral success of the Social Democratic Party See also Section C, Part I.

Southcottians, followers of Joanna Southcott, who died in 1814 shortly after announcing that (although over 50) she was about to give birth to a divine human being named Siloh. Miss Southcott certainly produced all the symptoms of pregnancy, and was even examined by the Royal physician who pronounced her unquestionably "with child." Although she even went "into labour," no child, divine or otherwise, appeared and she seems to have died of something rather close to a broken heart. Her interesting symptoms would today be classed as "hysterical pregnancy"—a not uncommon condition which may mimic real pregnancy in a remarkable way. Joanna's followers remained loyal to her memory, however, and a tiny sect still survives to this day. Shortly before her death, incidentally, she handed to followers a number of locked and sealed boxes which she indicated contained, among other things, the secret of the universe. These were only to be opened 100 years after her death and then in the presence of 12 bishops. In 1927 one of these boxes unexpectedly turned up and it was ceremoniously opened at the Caxton Hall before a public audience. The organisers had to make do with only one bishop as most of the country's senior clerics pronounced themselves to be too busy to attend. Perhaps it was just as well for Miss Southcott's marvellous box was found to contain only a few rare coins, a horse pistol, a woman's embroidered nightcap, and a slightly improper novel, The Surprises of Love. One of the most endearing qualities of Joanna Southcott must have been her sense of humour.

Spiritualism is a religion which requires to be distinguished from psychical research (q.v.) which is a scientific attempt carried on by both believers and non-believers to investigate psychic phenomena including those not necessarily connected with "spirits"—e.g., telepathy or clairvoyance and precognition. As a religion (although for that matter the whole of history is filled with attempts to get in touch with the "spirit world") Spiritualism begins with the American Andrew Jackson Davis who in 1847 published Nature's Divine Revelations, a book which is still widely read. In this Davis states that on the death of the physical body, the human spirit remains alive and moves on to one or another of a considerable range of worlds or "spheres" where it commences yet another stage of existence. Since the spirit has not died, but exists with full (and possibly even expanded) consciousness, there should be no reason, Davis argues, why it should not make its presence known to the beings it has temporarily left behind on earth. In 1847, the year of the publication of Davis's book, two young girls, Margaret and Kate Fox, living in a farmhouse at Hydesville, New York, began apparently to act as unwitting mediums for attempts at such between-worlds communication. The girls

were the focus for strange rappings and bangs which it was alleged defied normal explanation and which spelt out, in the form of a simple alphabetical code, messages from the spirits of "the dead." The Fox sisters were later to confess that they had produced the raps by trickery, but by that time the fashion had spread across the world and before long "mediums" in all lands were issuing spirit communications (often in much more spectacular form). In the late 19th cent. Spiritualism went into a phase of great expansion and for various reasons attracted the attention of many scientists. Among these were Sir William Crookes, Sir Oliver Lodge, Professor Charles Richet, Alfred Russell Wallace, to say nothing of the brilliant and shrewd creator of Sherlock Holmes, Sir Arthur Conan Doyle. Today many people find it astonishing that people of such brilliance should find the phenomena of the seance room of more than passing interest, but the commitment of the Victorian scientists is understandable if we realise that Spiritualists, after all, claim to do no more than demonstrate as fact what all Christians are called on to believe—that the human personality survives bodily death. Furthermore, at the time of the late 19th cent. peak of Spiritualism, much less was known about human psychology and about the great limitations of sensory perception in typical seance conditions, when lights are dimmed or extinguished and an emotionally charged atmosphere generated. Today the most striking phenomena of the seance room—the alleged materialisation of spirit people and the production of such half-spiritual, half-physical substances as ectoplasm—are rarely if ever produced at Spiritualist meetings. Some say that the most probable explanation for this is that too many fraudulent mediums have been caught out and publicly exposed for the profession to be worth the risks. The movement today, which still has a large and often articulate following, now concentrates on the less controversial areas of "mental mediumship," clairvoyance and the like, or on the very widespread practice of "spirit healing." Where people are not deliberately deluded by bogus mediums acting for monetary reward (a practice which largely died out with the "death" of ectoplasm) Spiritualism probably has an important role to play in the life of many people whose happiness has been removed by the death of a much loved relative or spouse. It does not deserve the violent attacks that are often made on it by orthodox clergy who allege that Spiritualists are communicating not with the souls of the departed but with the devil or his emissaries. See also **Greater World Spiritualists.**

State and Man. Most of the early civilisations such as those of Egypt and Babylonia were theocratic, that is to say, they were arranged in a hierarchy with, at the peak, a king who was also an incarnation of the god. Needless to say, in such circumstances there was no room for philosophising about the nature of the state and the relationship which ought to exist between state and citizens. As usual, we have to turn to ancient Greece for the beginnings of thought about this problem. We do so as briefly as possible since in general it is only the later philosophers whose work has much contemporary interest and, in any case, most people today realise that the political philosophy of a particular time is bound to reflect the actual conditions prevailing then and as such is of mainly theoretical interest today.

The Greek Approach. The early pre-Socratic philosophers Democritus and the Pythagorean school for example, held that the individual should subordinate himself to the whole; they had no doubt that the citizen's first duty was to the state. The Greeks until the time of Plato were not really thinking in terms of individual rights, nor had they given much thought to what form the state should take—they simply accepted it. The first great attempt to describe the ideal state is to be found in Plato's *The Republic* which is referred to elsewhere (see **Education**). His pupil Aristotle did not try to form a utopia but made many comments on the nature of government. Thus, while agreeing that the state was more important than any individual person, he distinguished between good and bad states, and pointed out that to the extent that the state does not enable its citizens to lead virtuous and useful lives it is evil. A good constitution must recognise the inequalities between human beings and confer on them rights according to their abilities: among these inequalities are those of personal ability, property, birth, and status, as freeman or slave. The best forms of rule were monarchy, aristocracy, and democracy; the worst forms—tyranny, oligarchy (or rule of a powerful few), and ochlocracy (or mob-rule). The later Greek thinkers of Hellenistic times held two opposed points of view. The Epicureans (*q.v.*) taught that all social life is based upon self-interest and we become members of a group for our own convenience; therefore there are no absolute rights and laws—what is good is what members decide at that time to be good, and when they change their minds the law must change too. Injustice is not an evil in any god-given sense; we behave justly simply because if injustice became the general rule, we ourselves should suffer. The Stoics (*q.v.*), on the other hand, held that the state must dominate the individual completely and everyone must carry out, first and foremost, his social duties and be willing to sacrifice everything for it; but the state of the Stoics was no narrowly national one, but one that strove to become a universal brotherhood.

The Christian Approach. The orthodox Christian view is expressed in St. Augustine's book *The City of God.* Here it is held that the church, as the worldly incarnation of the City of God, is to be supreme over the state, and the head of the church is to be supreme over secular rulers. In addition it must be recognised that, whilst the secular ruler can make mistakes, the church does not, since it is the representative of God's kingdom on earth.

The Secular State. During the Renaissance (*q.v.*) people began to think for themselves and the results of their cogitations were not always pleasant; for it was during this time that many rulers, petty and otherwise, were seeking absolute authority. Two notable thinkers at this stage were Niccolo Machiavelli (1469–1527) in Italy and Thomas Hobbes (1588–1679) in England, where, of course, the Renaissance arrived later in history. Both supported absolute monarchy against the former domination of the church. The name of Machiavelli has become a by-word for any behaviour that is cunning and unscrupulous, but he was not really as bad as he is usually painted. It is, indeed, true that in his book *The Prince* he showed in the greatest detail the methods by which a ruler could gain absolute control and destroy civic freedom, but this despotism was intended as merely a necessary intermediate stage towards his real idea which was a free, united Italian nation wholly independent of the church. Hobbes was a materialist whose thesis was that man is naturally a ferocious animal whose basic impulse is war and pillage and the destruction of whatever stands in his way to gain his desires. But if he allowed himself to behave in this way his life would be "nasty, brutish, and short" so he creates a society in which he voluntarily gives up many of his rights and hands them over to a powerful ruler in his own interest. But having done this he must obey; even when the ruler is unjust, as he has no right to complain because anything is better than a return to his natural state. The religion of the king must be the religion of the people and the only things no ruler has the right to do is to cause a man to commit suicide or murder or to make him confess to a crime.

Views of Locke: Live and Let Live. John Locke (1632–1704) disagreed with these views. Man is naturally peaceful and co-operative and therefore social life comes readily to him. He sets up an authority in order to preserve the group and that is why laws are made; but the function of the state is strictly limited to maintaining the public good and beyond this men are to be left free. Therefore absolute power and the doctrine of the Divine Right of Kings were wrong because power ultimately rests with the people who have the right to make and break governments. It is also wrong that those who make the laws should be able to execute them. This is the important British doctrine of the separation of powers between the legislature and the executive which, in Britain and America, is regarded as one of the bases of democracy.

Rousseau's Social Doctrine. The only other views we need consider here are those of Jean-Jacques Rousseau (1712–78) and Herbert Spencer (1820–1903), since the views of the two important intervening figures, Hegel and Karl Marx, are dealt with elsewhere (*see* **Dialectical Materialism**) and after Spencer we come to a stage where political philosophy begins to merge with sociology and the social sciences. Rousseau is a puzzling figure. On the one hand he has been hailed as the prophet of freedom and on the other as the father of modern totalitarianism. His book *Social Contract* (1762) begins with the words: "Man is born free, and everywhere he is in chains." He says that he is in favour, not merely of democracy, but of direct democracy in which everyone has to give his assent to all measures as in the Greek city-states and in Geneva, of which city he was a citizen. (This method is still in force in respect of some measures in the Swiss cantons.) Natural society is based on a "social contract" or mutual agreement and Rousseau speaks of a "return to nature" which would ensure the sovereignty of the people at all times. Thus far, he seems to agree with Locke but soon we find that he is more akin to Hobbes, since (as we are learning in our own day) nothing is more tyrannical than the absolute rule of all the people. (Public opinion is more Hitlerian than Hitler.) As it turns out, then, the "social contract" consists in "the total alienation of each associate, together with all his rights, to the whole community" and "each of us puts his person and all his power in common under the supreme direction of the general will." Rousseau admired direct democracy in the small city-state, but if his doctrine is applied to large states, then the "general will" becomes absolute. It is in this sense that he is regarded as the forerunner of totalitarianism. Herbert Spencer is quoted only as an example of the inappropriate application of a biological theory to social issues. Influenced by Darwin's thesis of natural selection, he saw in society a struggle in which the fittest survived and the less fit perished. Each individual had the right to preserve himself, but in the case of human beings this depended upon group life in which, to some extent, each individual is limited by the rights of others. But this should not go too far, and he condemned the socialism of J. S. Mill which (*a*) would give over-much protection to the unfit, and (*b*) would give the state powers which it has no right to since the best government is the least government. In accordance with Darwinism free competition was essential.

Stoics, the followers of Zeno, a Greek philosopher in the 4th cent. B.C., who received their name from the fact that they were taught in the Stoa Poikile or Painted Porch of Athens. They believed that since the world is the creation of divine wisdom and is governed by divine law, it is man's duty to accept his fate. Zeno conceived virtue to be the highest good and condemned the passions. (*See* **God and Man, State and Man, Determinism and Free-will** for a more detailed account of their beliefs.)

Subud, a cultish movement surrounding the Javanese mystic Pak Subuh which established its headquarters in England in 1958 and made newspaper headlines because of alleged "miracle" cures of both psychological and physical ills. The basis of Subud (which is a contraction of three Sanskrit words, Susila Budhi Dharma, meaning "the right living of the soul") is a single spiritual exercise, the *latihan*, in which the individual comes into contact with, or is overwhelmed by a metaphysical force of some kind which is supposed to produce great mental and physical changes. During the latihan people may make strange movements, some violent, and utter unusual cries or chants. Now better known in America than in Britain, Subud did not live up to the expectations of its early followers, many of whom were people of considerable intelligence and professional standing. It is of particular interest because it represents a unique incursion of a rather obscure Eastern cult into Western life, and suggests again that there is growing dissatisfaction in many quarters with orthodox religion and its contribution to the philosophy of the modern world.

Sunnites, the othodox sect of Islam as contrasted with the Shiites or Shia (*q.v.*).

Swedenborgianism. The Church of the New Jerusalem, based on the writings of Emanuel Swedenborg (1688–1772), was founded by his followers eleven years after his death. The New Church is regarded by its members not as a sect but as a new dispensation bearing the same relationship to Christianity as Christianity does to Judaism.

Synchronicity, an attempt by the psychologist, Carl Gustav Jung, to explain the apparently significant relationship between certain events in the physical universe which seem to have no obvious "causal" link. This rather involved concept is easily understood if one realises that almost all scientific and philosophical beliefs are based on the notion that the continuous process of change which is taking place in ourselves and in the universe around us is dependent upon a principle known as causality. We can express this another way by saying that an object moves because it has been pushed or pulled by another. We see because light strikes the retina and signals pass up the nervous system to the brain. A stone falls to the ground because the earth's gravity is pulling it towards its centre, etc., etc. For all practical purposes every event can be looked upon as being "caused" by some other prior event and this is obviously one of the most important principles of the operation of the universe. Jung, however, felt that there is a sufficiently large body of evidence to suggest that events may be linked in a significant (*i.e.*, non-chance) way without there being any true causal relationship between them. The classic example he held to be the supposed predictive power of astrology by which there appears to be a relationship between the stellar configurations and the personality and life-pattern of individuals on earth. Jung was scientist enough to realise that there could be no causal connection between the aspect of the stars and the lives of people billions of miles from them, yet felt the evidence for astrology was strong enough to demand an alternative non-causal explanation. The trouble with synchronicity, which has not made much impact on the world of physics or of psychology, is that it is not really an explanation at all but merely a convenient word to describe some puzzling correspondences. The real question, of course, is whether there really are events occurring which are significantly but not *causally* linked, and most scientists today would hold that there were probably not. Still it was typical of the bold and imaginative mind of Jung to tackle head-on one of the principal mysteries of existence and come up with a hypothesis to attempt to meet it.

Syndicalism, a form of socialist doctrine which aims at the ownership and control of all industries by the workers, contrasted with the more conventional type of socialism which advocates ownership and control by the state. Since syndicalists have preferred to improve the conditions of the workers by direct action, *e.g.*, strikes and working to rule, rather than through the usual parliamentary procedures, they have been closely related to anarchists (*q.v.*) and are sometimes described as anarcho-syndicalists. Under syndicalism there would be no state; for the state would be replaced by a federation of units based on functional economic organisation rather than on geographical representation. The movement had bodies in the United Kingdom, where guild socialism (*q.v.*) was strongly influenced by its doctrines, in France, Germany, Italy, Spain, Argentina, and Mexico, but these gradually declined after the first world war losing many members to the communists. Fascism (*q.v.*) was also strongly influenced by the revolutionary syndicalism of Georges Sorel in making use of his concept of the "myth of the general strike" as an emotional image or ideal goal to spur on the workers; with Mussolini the "myth" became that of the state. Mussolini was also influenced by Sorel's doctrine of violence and the justification of force. Syndicalism had a certain influence in the Labour Party in its early days, but was crushed by men like Ernest Bevin who began to fear that by involving the workers in direct responsibility for their industries, it would put them at a disadvantage when bargaining for wages.

T

Taoism, a religion which, although in a degenerate state, is still one of the great Eastern creeds. Its alleged founder, Lao-tze, is said to have been born in Honan about 604 B.C.; he is also said to have been the author of the bible of Taoism, the *Tao-te-ching,* or in English *The Way of Life,* and to have disapproved of Confucius. This, if true, would hardly be surprising; for Taoism is eminently a mystical religion recommending doing nothing and resisting nothing, whereas **Confucianism** (*q.v.*) is eminently a practical code of living and its founder insisted on intervening in everything to do with social life. But the truth as revealed by modern scholarship is rather different. We are told that the poems of the *Tao-te-ching* are anonymous and probably originated among recluses in lonely valleys long before the time of Confucius; they were collected and given form at some time late in the 3rd cent. B.C. and their authorship attributed to Lao-tze. It is entirely possible that no such peson ever existed (unlike Confucius, who certainly did), but if there were such a man he appears to have used a pseudonym since "Lao" is not a surname but an adjective meaning "old" and it was customary to attribute important works to old men on account of their supposed wisdom. Lao-tze simply means "the old philosopher", and although the *Tao-te-ching* is one of the most remarkable and instructive books ever written it is as anonymous as the Border Ballads.

It is apparent that the religion learned both from the ancient Chinese mystics and from Brahmanism: *Tao,* the Way, is impalpable, invisible, and incapable of being expressed in words. But it can be attained by virtue, by compassion, humility, and non-violence. Out of weakness comes true strength whereas violence is not only wrong but defeats its own ends. There is no personal God and such gods as men imagine are mere emanations of *Tao* which gives life to all things. *Tao* is Being. Works are worthless and internal renunciation is far better than anything that follows from the use of force because passive resistance convinces the other from within that he is in error, whereas violence only compels the external appearance of conviction whilst inwardly the individual is as before. "It is wealth to be content; it is wilful to force one's way on others."

Later Lao-tze became a divinity and indeed one of a Trinity each worshipped in the form of idols (which the founder had hated). Soon there was worship of the forces of nature: the stars, the tides, the sun and moon, and a thousand other deities among whom Confucius was one. The purest mysticism and wisdom had been utterly corrupted by contact with the world.

Telepathy and Clairvoyance. Telepathy is the alleged communication between one mind and another other than through the ordinary sense channels. Clairvoyance is the supposed faculty of "seeing" objects or events which, by reason of space and time or other causes, are not discernible through the ordinary sense of vision. Such claims have been made from time immemorial but it was not until this century that the phenomena were investigated scientifically. The first studies were undertaken by the Society for Psychical Research, which was founded in 1882 with Professor Henry Sidgwick as its first president. Since then it has carried out a scholarly programme of research without —in accordance with its constitution—coming to any corporate conclusions. In America the centre of this research was the Parapsychology Laboratory at Duke University (*see* **Para-**

psychology) where at one time it was claimed clear scientific evidence for extra-sensory perception (ESP) had been obtained. These claims have been treated with great reservation by the majority of scientists but despite the belief that the study of ESP was going into eclipse, there remains a small but measurable residue of interest in scientific research in this area. It would be odd if some scientists were not interested in ESP because of the enormous weight of anecdotal evidence which has built up over centuries to support it. The weakness of the scientific as opposed to the casual evidence is however exemplified by the failure of ESP researchers to produce a reliable "repeatable" experiment.

Theism. *See* **God and Man.**

Theosophy (Sanskrit *Brahma Vidya* = divine wisdom), a system of thought that draws on the mystical teachings of those who assert the spiritual nature of the universe, and the divine nature of man. It insists that man is capable of intuitive insight into the nature of God. The way to wisdom, or self-knowledge, is through the practice of **Yoga** (*q.v.*). Theosophy has close connections with Indian thought through Vedic, Buddhist, and Brahmanist literature. The modern Theosophical Society was founded by Mme H. P. Blavatsky and others in 1875, and popularised by Mrs. Annie Besant.

Tractarianism, a Catholic revival movement, also known as the **Oxford Movement** (not to be confused with the so-called Oxford Group), which had its beginnings at Oxford in 1833. The leaders included the Oxford high churchmen E. B. Pusey, J. Keble and J. H. Newman. Through the *Tracts for the Times* (1833–41), a series of pamphlets which were sent to every parsonage in England, they sought to expose the dangers which they considered to be threatening the church from secular authority. The immediate cause of the movement was the Reform Act (1832) which meant that the state was no longer in the safe keeping of Tories and Churchmen but that power was falling into the hands of Liberals and Dissenters. They advocated a higher degree of ceremonial in worship nearer the Roman communion. In *Tract 90* (the last) Newman showed how the Thirty-nine Articles themselves, which were regarded as the bulwark of Protestantism, could be made to square with Roman doctrine. It was obvious which direction the movement was taking and the romanizing tendency was widely resented. In 1845 Newman went over to Rome. Pusey and Keble persisted in their efforts to secure recognition of Catholic liturgy and doctrine in the Anglican Church. Catholicism of the Anglican type (*i.e.*, Catholic in ritual, ceremony, and everything save submission to the Pope) is termed Anglo-Catholicism (*q.v.*).

Transcendental Meditation, popularised in the West by the Maharishi Mahesh Yogi, who achieved sensational worldwide publicity by his "conversion" of the Beatles a few years ago. This is a simple meditational system which it is claimed is an aid to relaxation and the reduction of psychological and physical stress. It is a technique which can be taught in a relatively short, concentrated period of time, provided that someone trained by the Maharishi is the teacher. The pupil or would-be meditator is given a mantra—a meaningless word which acts as a focal point for the imagination—letting his thoughts flow freely while sitting in a comfortable position. Extraordinary claims are made on behalf of the system. As with most cults, religious and occult systems, there is an initial psychological benefit to anyone who becomes deeply involved. Nevertheless, apart from this simple "participation-effect", there is some evidence that the body's autonomic functions (heart rate, respiratory cycle, brain waves, etc.) can be modified by certain individuals including yogis. Whether it is ultimately beneficial to be able to modify these autonomic functions or not is another matter. The TM movement in Britain is based at Mentmore Towers in Buckinghamshire. *See also* **Feedback Cult.**

Transmigration of Souls. *See* **Immortality, Buddhism, Hinduism.**

Transubstantiation, the conversion in the Eucharist of the bread and wine into the body and blood of Christ—a doctrine of the Roman Catholic Church.

Trotskyism, a form of communism supporting the views of Leon Trotsky, the assumed name of Lev Bronstein (1879–1940) who, in 1924, was ousted from power by Stalin and later exiled and assassinated in Mexico. Trotsky held that excessive Russian nationalism was incompatible with genuine international communism and that Stalin was concentrating on the economic development of the Soviet Union to an extent which could only lead to a bureaucratic state with a purely nationalist outlook. After the Hungarian uprising in 1956, which was ruthlessly suppressed by the Soviet Armed Forces, a wave of resignations from Western Communist parties took place, many of the dissidents joining the Trotskyist movement.

U

Ufology, cultish interest in the study of strange and unexplained aerial phenomena (unidentified flying objects, hence UFOs). *See* **Flying Saucers.**

Underground, the name given to an increasingly well-organised group, mainly composed of young people, university students, etc., which propagates anti-establishment and often highly controversial views. Its history, and to some extent its aims, are obscure, but it is a force of increasing power in Western society and its evolution is worth watching with care. The 1960s were years of great metamorphosis in Europe and America with rapid changes taking place in our attitudes to war and peace, to sex and morals, to marriage and family, to church and state. For large sections of the population these changes have been too rapid and too radical by far, but for others they have been too slow. In particular, the liberalisation of the law on the so-called "soft drugs," notably marijuana, is advocated by a vocal and increasing minority of young people. The expression of their views has been finding outlet in magazines and newspapers, privately published and printed, which reach a wide circulation despite the disinclination of many newsagents to stock them. These publications, while frequently containing material of an obscene and, to many people, highly offensive nature, also contain articles, features, and poems by writers of repute, many of whom contribute regularly to more orthodox publications and yet are sympathetic to the "underground cause." The word underground here, incidentally, refers back to the "underground press" that published revolutionary material at great risk in Nazi-occupied territories during the last war. With the exception of the risqué magazine *Private Eye*, which is largely concerned with acid political satire, the first of the genuine underground newsheets was the *International Times* (IT) which was followed in due course by *Oz* and *Rolling Stone*. All three papers were strongly anarchistic in flavour, uneven in literary merit, openly in favour of legalising marijuana ("pot"), and generally quite scandalous to the middle-class and middle-aged. This is not the place to argue the pros and cons of the underground arguments, nor to decide whether our "permissive society" has gone too far or not yet far enough. The important message that the appearance of the whole underground movement implies is that young people, because of greater financial independence, wider opportunities for travel, better education, and easier access to communication channels, such as printing presses, radio transmitters, etc., are beginning to make their admittedly controversial views more widely publicised. Furthermore, this is a trend which will inevitably develop rather than diminish and in the absence of authoritarian repression, these forces will have an increasing impact on our lives. By 1973 however signs of the decline in the power of the underground seemed to be appearing. One of its leading publications *Oz* had folded and its "drop-out" arguments seemed to be appealing less and less to students and young people. The most likely reason for this is that the movement in its decade of vigorous life was successful in inducing a number of reforms ranging from the propagation of a more liberal attitude to what may be printed, spoken about or shown on stage and screen, and an acceptance by school and university authorities that students should have a greater voice in academic affairs. These reforms, whether welcome or not to the middle-aged and the middle-class, have nevertheless reached fruition in the "permissive" society which in turn appears to have taken much of the steam out of the underground itself. See also **Weathermen**.

Unitarianism has no special doctrines, although clearly, as the name indicates, belief is in the single personality of God, *i.e.*, anti-trinitarian. This general statement, however, can be interpreted with varying degrees of subtlety. Thus unitarian belief may range from a sort of Arianism which accepts that, although Christ was not of divine nature, divine powers had been delegated to him by the Father, to the simple belief that Christ was a man like anyone else, and his goodness was of the same nature as that of many other great and good men. Indeed, today many Unitarians deny belief in a personal God and interpret their religion in purely moral terms, putting their faith in the value of love and the brotherhood of man. The Toleration Act (1689) excluded Unitarians but from 1813 they were legally tolerated in England. Nevertheless attempts were made to turn them out of their chapels on the ground that the preachers did not hold the views of the original founders of the endowments. But this ended with the Dissenting Chapels Act of 1845. In America no such difficulties existed, and in the Boston of the 19th cent. many of the great literary figures were openly unitarian in both belief and name: *e.g.*, Emerson, Longfellow, Lowell, and Oliver Wendell Holmes.

Utilitarianism, a school of moral philosophy of which the main proponents were J. S. Mill (1806–73) and Jeremy Bentham (1748–1832). Bentham based his ethical theory upon the utilitarian principle that the greatest happiness of the greatest number is the criterion of morality. What is good is pleasure or happiness; what is bad is pain. If we act on this basis of self-interest (pursuing what we believe to be our own happiness), then what we do will automatically be for the general good. The serious failing of this thesis is (1) that it makes no distinction between the quality of one pleasure and another, and (2) that Bentham failed to see that the law might not be framed and administered by men as benevolent as himself. J. S. Mill accepted Bentham's position in general but seeing its failings emphasised (1) that self-interest was an inadequate basis for utilitarianism and suggested that we should take as the real criterion of good the social consequences of the act; (2) that some pleasures rank higher than others and held that those of the intellect are superior to those of the senses. Not only is the social factor emphasised, but emphasis is also placed on the nature of the act.

Utopias. The name "utopia" is taken from a Greek word meaning "nowhere" and was first used in 1516 by Sir Thomas More (1478–1535) as the title of his book referring to a mythical island in the south Pacific where he sited his ideal society. Since then it has been used of any ideal or fanciful society, and here a few will be mentioned. (The reader may recall that Samuel Butler's 19th cent. novel, describing an imaginary society in New Zealand where criminals were treated and the sick punished, was entitled *Erewhon* which is the word "nowhere" in reverse.) It should be noted that not all utopias were entirely fanciful—*e.g.*, Robert Owen's and François Fourier's beliefs, although found to be impractical, were, in fact, tried out.

Sir Thomas More. More wrote at a time when the rise of the wool-growing trade had resulted in farming land being turned over to pasture and there was a great wave of unemployment and a rise in crime among the dispossessed. More began to think in terms of the mediaeval ideal of small co-operative communities in which class interests and personal gain played

a decreasing part, a society which would have the welfare of the people at heart both from the physical and intellectual points of view. His utopia was one in which there was no private property, because the desire for acquisition and private possessions lay at the root of human misery. There was, therefore, only common ownership of land and resources. Each class of worker was equipped to carry out its proper function in the economic scheme and each was fairly rewarded for its share in production so that there was neither wealth nor poverty to inspire conflict. Nobody was allowed to idle, until the time came for him to retire when he became free to enjoy whatever cultural pleasures he wished, but since the system was devoid of the waste associated with competition, the working day would be only six hours. There was to be compulsory schooling and free medical care for everybody, full religious toleration, complete equality of the sexes, and a modern system of dealing with crime which was free from vindictiveness and cruelty. Government was to be simple and direct by democratically-elected officials whose powers would be strictly limited and the public expenditure kept under close scrutiny. It will be seen that More was far in advance of his age, and to most democratically-minded people in advance of an earlier utopia, Plato's *Republic*, which is described under the heading of Education.

James Harrington. James Harrington published his book *The Commonwealth of Oceana* in 1656 and offered it to Oliver Cromwell for his consideration but without tangible results. Better than any other man of his time Harrington understood the nature of the economic revolution which was then taking place, and, like More, saw the private ownership of land as the main cause of conflict. He put forward the theory that the control of property, particularly in the shape of land, determines the character of the political structure of the state; if property were universally distributed among the people the sentiment for its protection would naturally result in a republican form of government. The Commonwealth of Oceana was a society "of laws and not of men"—*i.e.*, it was to be legally based and structured so as to be independent of the good or ill-will of any individuals controlling it. Thus there must be a written constitution, a two-house legislature, frequent elections with a secret ballot, and separation of powers between legislature and executive—all today familiar features of parliamentary democracy, but unique in his time.

Saint-Simon. The utopias of the late 18th and 19th cent. come, of course, into the period of the industrial revolution and of laissez-faire capitalism. Individual enterprise and complete freedom of competition formed the outlook of the ruling class. Naturally the utopias of this period tended to have a strongly socialist tinge since such theories are obviously produced by those who are not satisfied with existing conditions. Saint-Simon's *New Christianity* (1825) is one such, and by many, Claude Henri, Comte de Saint-Simon (1760–1825) is regarded as the founder of French socialism. His book urged a dedication of society to the principle of human brotherhood and a community which would be led by men of science motivated by wholly spiritual aims. Production property was to be nationalised (or "socialised" as he describes the process) and employed to serve the public good rather than private gain; the worker was to produce according to his capacity and to be rewarded on the basis of individual merit; the principle of inheritance was to be abolished since it denied the principle of reward for accomplishment on which the society was to be founded. Saint-Simon's proposals were not directed towards the poorer classes alone, but to the conscience and intellect of all. He was deeply impressed with the productive power of the new machines and his scheme was, first and foremost, intended as a method of directing that power to the betterment of humanity as a whole.

Fourier. François Marie Charles Fourier (1772–1837), although by conviction a philosophical anarchist who held that human beings are naturally good if allowed to follow their natural desires, was the originator of what, on the face of it, one would suppose to be the most regimented of the utopias. It consisted of a system of "phalanxes" or co-operative communities each composed of a group of workers and technicians assured of a minimum income and sharing the surplus on an equitable basis. Agriculture was to be the chief occupation of each phalanx and industrial employment planned and so carefully assigned that work would become pleasant and creative rather than burdensome. One of his ideas was that necessary work should receive the highest pay, useful work the next, and pleasant work the least pay. The land was to be scientifically cultivated and natural resources carefully conserved. Most of the members' property was to be privately owned, but the ownership of each phalanx was to be widely diffused among members by the sale of shares. Such "parasitic and unproductive" occupations as stockbroker, soldier, economist, middle-man and philosopher would be eliminated and the education of children carried out along vocational lines to train them for their future employment.

The strange thing was that Fourier's suggestions appealed to many in both Europe and the U.S.A. and such men (admittedly no economic or technical experts) as Emerson, Thoreau, James Russell Lowell, and Nathaniel Hawthorne strongly supported them. An American Fourier colony known as Brook Farm was established and carried on for eight years when it was dissolved after a serious fire had destroyed most of its property.

Robert Owen. Robert Owen (1771–1858), a wealthy textile manufacturer and philanthropist, established communities founded on a kind of utopian socialism in Lanarkshire, Hampshire, and in America. Of his New Lanark community an American observer wrote: "There is not, I apprehend, to be found in any part of the world, a manufacturing community in which so much order, good government, tranquillity, and rational happiness prevail." The workers in Lanark were given better housing and education for their children, and it was administered as a co-operative self-supporting community in Scotland. Later in life Owen returned to sponsoring legislation that would remove some of the worst evils of industrial life in those days: reduction of the working day to twelve hours, prohibition of labour for children under the age of ten, public schools for elementary education, and so on. But he lived to see few of his reforms adopted. He also promoted the creation of co-operative societies, the formation of trades unions, labour banks and exchanges, the workers' educational movement, and even an Anglo-American federation. There can be no doubt that, if he saw little result himself, he left the imprint of his convictions to benefit future communities who may not even know his name.

V

Vitalism, the philosophical doctrine that the behaviour of the living organism is, at least in part, due to a vital principle which cannot possibly be explained wholly in terms of physics and chemistry. This belief was held by the rationalist thinker C. E. M. Joad (1891–1953) and is implicit in Henri Bergson's (1859–1941) theory of creative evolution. It was maintained by Bergson that evolution, like the work of an artist, is creative and therefore unpredictable; that a vague need exists beforehand within the animal or plant before the means of satisfying the need develops. Thus we might assume that sightless animals developed the need to become aware of objects before they were in physical contact with them and that this ultimately led to the origins of organs of sight. Earlier this century a form of vitalism described as "emergent evolution" was put forward. This theory maintains that when two or more simple entities come together there may arise a new property which none of them previously possessed. Today biologists would say that it is the *arrangement* of atoms that counts, different arrangements exhibiting different properties, and that biological organisation is an essentially dynamic affair, involving the lapse of time.

W

Wahabis, members of an Arabian sect of Islam which originated in the teaching of Muhammad Ibn 'Abd-al-Wahab, born at the end of the 17th cent. He was deeply resentful of the Turkish rule which, in addition to its tyranny, had brought about innovations in the religion which Muhammad regarded as a perversion of its original form. He proceeded to reform Islam to its primitive conditions and impressed his beliefs on Mohammed Ibn Saud, a sheikh who spread them with the aid of his sword. Under the successors of Ibn Saud the power of the Wahabis spread over much of Arabia where it is dominant today in Saudi Arabia. Its particular characteristic is that it refuses to accept symbolic or mystical interpretations of the words of the Prophet and accepts quite literally the teaching of Islam. It is, in fact, a sort of Moslem fundamentalism. Although crushed by the Turks in 1811–15, the movement remains an important element in Mohammedanism.

Waldenses, a movement also known as "The Poor Men of Lyons," founded by Peter Waldo of that city about the same time, and in the same part of southern France, as the Albigenses (*q.v.*) with whom, however, they had nothing in common. Their main belief was a return to Apostolic simplicity, based on reading the Bible in their own language; their doctrines were somewhat similar to those of the Mennonites and the Quakers. However, they did not wish to separate themselves from the Church and were originally protected by several Popes until the Lateran Council of 1215 excluded them mainly for the crime of preaching without ecclesiastical permission. From this time they were subjected to persecution, yet maintained some contact with the Church until the Reformation when they chose to take the side of the Protestants. Situated mainly on the sides of the Alps, half in Piedmont and half in France, they were persecuted or not according to the contemporary political convenience of the Dukes of Savoy, and the major attempt to destroy them called forth Oliver Cromwell's intervention and the famous sonnet of Milton. In spite of torture, murder, deportation, and even the kidnapping of their children, to have them brought up in the Roman Catholic faith, the sect survived, and still exists, having been granted full equality of rights with his Roman Catholic subjects by Charles Edward of Piedmont in 1848.

Weathermen, a radical offshoot of the Students for a Democratic Society formed in 1969, making up the so-called "underground" in the United States of America. It derives its name from a line in Dylan's song "You don't need a weatherman to know which way the wind blows." Unlike most of the loosely-structured organisations involved in the growing anti-establishment front, the Weathermen appear to have direct rather than anarchistic political goals, taking a stand far to the left of traditional politics. Their avowed aim is the total overthrow of the current American political structure, with specific and carefully planned acts of violence as the tools of their trade and the civil police force as one of their prime targets. This has led to a series of bomb explosions, often cunningly planned, and brutal murders of police patrolmen which have deeply shocked the average American citizen. A particularly sinister and ominous feature, to most people's eyes, is the fact that the Weathermen appear to be largely drawn from the highly intelligent and well-educated strata, many of them with well-to-do and/or academic backgrounds. Members of this group make no secret of their contempt for the intellect and political attitudes of the American middle-class, and claim to demonstrate the impotence of Society by their ability to commit flagrant acts of violence with such ease and the equal ease with which they subsequently escape detection and arrest. The elusive nature of the organisation and its uncertain background have led to a number of fantastic speculations about its true origins. One of the oddest of these is the notion, widely held in America, that the Weathermen are in reality financed and backed by the country's extreme *right*—as a means of discrediting in the public eye the slow but steady move towards socialism that seemed to be developing there. The Weathermen appear to have ceased activity in the early 1970s, but bomb outrages in early 1975 were once more perpetrated in their name.

Witchcraft. There are various interpretations and definitions of witchcraft from that of Pennethorne Hughes who states that "witchcraft, as it emerges into European history and literature, represents the old paleolithic fertility cult, plus the magical idea, plus various parodies of contemporary religions" to that of the fanatical Father Montague Summers who says that Spiritualism and witchcraft are the same thing. A leading authority on witchcraft, however, the late Dr. Margaret Murray, distinguishes between Operative Witchcraft (which is really Magic (*q.v.*)) and Ritual Witchcraft which, she says, "embraces the religious beliefs and ritual of the people known in late mediaeval times as 'witches.'" That there were such people we know from history and we know, too, that many of them—the great majority of them women—were tortured or executed or both. Many innocent people perished, especially after the promulgation of the bull *Summis desiderantes* by Pope Innocent VIII in 1484. Himself "a man of scandalous life," according to a Catholic historian, he wrote to "his dear sons," the German professors of theology, Johann Sprenger and Heinrich Kraemer, "witches are hindering men from performing the sexual act and women from conceiving . . ." and delegated them as Inquisitors "of these heretical pravities." In 1494 they codified in the *Malleus Maleficarum* (Hammer of Witches) the ecclesiastical rules for detecting acts of witchcraft. Dr. Murray points out that there have ordinarily been two theories about witchcraft: (1) that there were such things as witches, that they possessed supernatural powers and that the evidence given at their trials was substantially correct; (2) that the witches were simply poor silly creatures who either deluded themselves into believing that they had certain powers or, more frequently, were tortured into admitting things that they did not do. She herself accepts a third theory: that there were such beings as witches, that they really did what they admitted to doing, but that they did not possess supernatural powers. They were in fact believers in the old religion of pre-Christian times and the Church took centuries to root them out. That there existed "covens" of witches who carried out peculiar rites Dr. Murray has no doubt whatever. The first to show that witchcraft was a superstition and that the majority of so-called witches were people suffering from mental illness was the physician Johann Weyer of Cleves (1515–88). His views were denounced by the Catholic Church. Few people realise how deeply the notion of witchcraft is implanted in our minds and how seriously its power is still taken. For example, the Witchcraft Act was not repealed in this country until the 1950s. Furthermore, as recently as 1944, when the allied armies were invading Europe, the Spiritualist medium Mrs. Helen Duncan was charged with witchcraft and actually sent to prison—a prosecution which brought forth caustic comments from the then prime minister, Winston Churchill. *See also* **Demonism.**

Women's Liberation Movement, the name given to a loosely organised collection of women drawn from all ages and walks of life which appears to be emerging as a latter-day "super-suffragette" movement. Unlike the original suffragette movement, however, which advocated "Votes for Women," the current version seems to have less definite aims. The principal argument hinges on the fact that with the development of highly efficient methods of contraception (the "pill") women need no longer be "slaves" to their family commitments and the traditional dominant and decision-making role of the male in our society must go. At the same time there should be no more wage or job discrimination against women. The movement has been going from strength to strength in America and is acquiring definite power in local and state politics. In Europe it has made somewhat less dramatic inroads. To many spectators, the movement's bible is the witty if polemical book *The Female Eunuch* by the Australian author Germaine Greer. An equally amusing, if perhaps somewhat less serious counterblast *The Manipulated Man* by the German woman doctor, Esther Vilar, traitorously takes an anti-feminist line. A small victory for the feminist cause has been the slow advance of the unpronounceable abbreviation "Ms" as an acceptable alternative for Mrs or Miss. 1975 saw the passage, in the United Kingdom, of the "Equal Opportunities Act"—a development which would have delighted the suffragettes of half a century ago.

World Congress of Faiths, an inter-religious movement which aims to break down barriers between faiths. The first step was taken by the world's parliament of religions held in Chicago in 1893; similar gatherings were held subsequently at intervals in Europe; but the actual organisation was formed in 1936 by Sir Francis Younghusband; and now an annual conference is held and educational activity carried on.

World Council of Churches, a union of Christian Churches from all over the world (including the Churches of the Protestant, Anglican, and Orthodox traditions, but excluding the Roman Catholic Church), engaged in extending Christian mission and unity throughout the world. This modern ecumenical movement stems from the great World Missionary Conference held at Edinburgh in 1910. The World Council was founded in 1948 and meets for consultation from time to time. In the light of the 1975 assembly in Nairobi, the Churches have monitored the suppression of human rights throughout the world. The Salvation Army resigned in 1981 in protest at the movement's involvement in African liberation. The 1983 assembly was held in Vancouver.

Y

Yoga, a Hindu discipline which teaches a technique for freeing the mind from attachment to the senses, so that once freed the soul may become fused with the universal spirit (*atman* or Brahman), which is its natural goal. This is the sole function of the psychological and physical exercises which the Yogi undertakes, although few ever reach the final stage of *Samadhi* or union with Brahman which is said to take place in eight levels of attainment. These are: (1) *Yama*, which involves the extinction of desire and egotism and their replacement by charity and unselfishness; (2) *Niyama*, during which certain rules of conduct must be adopted, such as cleanliness, the pursuit of devotional studies, and the carrying out of rituals of purification; (3) *Asana*, or the attainment of correct posture and the reduction to a minimum of all bodily movement (the usual posture of the concentrating Yogi is the "lotus position" familiar from pictures; (4) *Pranayama*, the right control of the life-force or breath in which there are two stages at which the practitioner hopes to arrive, the first being complete absorption in the act of breathing which empties the mind of any other thought, the second being the ability almost to cease to breathe which allegedly enables him to achieve marvellous feats of endurance; (5) *Pratyahara* or abstraction which means the mind's complete withdrawal from the world of sense; (6) *Dharana* in which an attempt is made to think of one thing only which finally becomes a repetition of the sacred syllable OM; (7) *dhyana*, meditation, which finally leads to (8) *Samadhi* the trance state which is a sign of the complete unity of soul with reality.

Yoga is very old, and when the sage Patanjali (c. 300 B.C.) composed the book containing these instructions, the *Yoga Sutras*, he was probably collecting from many ancient traditions. Some of the claims made by Yogis seem, to the Western mind, frankly incredible; but in the West and especially in recent years Yoga methods have been used at the lower levels in order to gain improved self-control, better posture, and improved health. Whether it achieves these ends is another matter, but the genuine Yogi regards this as a perversion of the nature and purpose of the discipline.

Z

Zen Buddhism, a Buddhist sect which is believed to have arisen in 6th cent. China but has flourished chiefly in Japan; for some reason it has of recent years begun to attract attention in the West thanks to the voluminous writings of Dr. D. T. Suzuki and the less numerous but doubtless much-read books of Mr. Christmas Humphreys. But the fact that these writings exist does not explain their being read, nor why of all possible Eastern sects this particular one should be chosen in our times. What is Zen's attraction and why should anyone take the trouble to read about something (the word "something" is used for reasons that will become evident) that is not a religion, has no doctrine, knows no God and no after-life, no good and no evil, and possesses no scriptures but has to be taught by parables which seem to be purposely meaningless? One of the heroes of Zen is the fierce-looking Indian monk Boddhidharma (fl. *c.* 516–34) who brought Buddhism to China, of whom it is recounted that when the Emperor asked him how much merit he had acquired by supporting the new creed, the monk shouted at him: "None whatever!" The emperor then wished to know what was the sacred doctrine of the creed and again the monk shouted: "It is empty—there is nothing sacred!" Dr. Suzuki, having affirmed that there is no God in Zen, goes on to state that this does not mean that Zen denies the existence of God because "neither denial nor affirmation concerns Zen." The most concrete statement he is prepared to make is that the basic idea of Zen is to come in touch with the inner workings of our being, and to do this in the most direct way possible without resorting to anything external or superadded. Therefore anything that has the semblance of an external authority is rejected by Zen. Absolute faith is placed in a man's own inner being. Apparently the intention is that, so far from indulging in inward meditations or such practices as the Yogi uses, the student must learn to act spontaneously, without thinking, and without self-consciousness or hesitation. This is the main purpose of the *koan*, the logically insoluble riddle which the pupil must try to solve. One such is the question put by master to pupil: "A girl is walking down the street, is she the younger or the older sister?" The correct answer, it seems, is to say nothing but put on a mincing gait, to *become* the girl, thus showing that what matters is the experience of being and not its verbal description. Another *koan:* "What is the Buddha?" "Three pounds of flax" is attributed to T'ungshan in the 9th cent. and a later authority's comment is that "none can excel it as regards its irrationality which cuts off all passages to speculation." Zen, in effect, teaches the uselessness of trying to use words to discuss the Absolute.

Zen came to Japan in the 13th cent., more than five centuries after Confucianism or the orthodox forms of Buddhism, and immediately gained acceptance whilst becoming typically Japanese in the process. One of the reasons why it appealed must have been that its spontaneity and insistence on action without thought, its emphasis on the uselessness of mere words, and such categories as logical opposites, had an inevitable attraction for a people given to seriousness, formality, and logic to a degree which was almost stifling. Zen must have been to the Japanese what nonsense rhymes and nonsense books, like those of Edward Lear and Lewis Carroll, were to the English intellectuals. Lear's limericks, like some of the *koans*, end up with a line which, just at the time when one expects a point to be made, has no particular point at all, and *Alice in Wonderland* is the perfect example of a world, not without logic, but with a crazy logic of its own which has no relationship with that of everyday life. Therefore Zen began to impregnate every aspect of life in Japan, and one of the results of its emphasis on spontaneous action rather than reason was its acceptance by the Samurai, the ferocious warrior class, in such activities as swordsmanship, archery, Japanese wrestling, and later Judo and the Kamikaze dive-bombers. But much of Japanese art, especially landscape gardening and flower-arrangement, was influenced similarly, and Zen is even used in Japanese psychiatry. The very strict life of the Zen monks is based largely on doing things, learning through experience; the periods of meditation in the Zendo hall are punctuated by sharp slaps on the face administered by the abbot to those who are unsatisfactory pupils. Dr. Suzuki denies that Zen is nihilistic, but it is probably its appearance of nihilism and its appeal to the irrational and spontaneous which attracts the Western world at a time when to many the world seems without meaning and life over-regimented. However, it has influenced such various aspects of Western life as philosophy (Heidegger), psychiatry (Erich Fromm and Hubert Benoit), writing (Aldous Huxley), and painting (Die Zen Gruppe in Germany).

Zionism, a belief in the need to establish an autonomous Jewish home in Palestine which, in its modern form, began with Theodor Herzl (1860–1904), a Hungarian journalist working in Vienna. Although Herzl was a more or less assimilated Jew, he was forced by the Dreyfus case and the pogroms in Eastern Europe to conclude that there was no real safety for the Jewish people until they had a state of their own. The Jews, of course, had always in a religious sense thought of Palestine as a spiritual homeland and prayed "next year in Jerusalem," but the religious had thought of this in a philosophical way as affirming old loyalties, not as recommending the formation of an actual state. Therefore Herzl was opposed both by many of the religious Jews and, at the other extreme, by those who felt themselves to be assimilated and in many cases without religious faith. Even after the Balfour Declaration of 1917, there was not a considerable flow of Jews to Palestine, which at that time was populated mainly by Arabs. But the persecutions of Hitler changed all this and, after bitter struggles, the Jewish state was proclaimed in 1948. Today Zionism is supported by the vast majority of the Jewish communities everywhere (although strongly disapproved of in the Soviet Union as "Western imperialism") and Zionism is now an active international force concerned with protecting the welfare and extending the influence of Israel.

Zoroastrianism, at one time one of the great world religions, competing in the 2nd cent. A.D. on almost equal terms from its Persian home with Hellenism and the Roman Imperial Government. Under the Achaemenidae (*c.* 550–330 B.C.) Zoroastrianism was the state religion of Persia. Alexander's conquest in 331 B.C. brought disruption but the religion flourished again under the Sassanian dynasty (A.D. *c.* 226–640). With the advance of the Mohammedan Arabs in the 7th cent. Zoroastrianism finally gave way to Islam. A number of devotees fled to India there to become the Parsees. In Persia itself a few scattered societies remain.

The name Zoroaster is the Greek rendering of Zarathustra, the prophet who came to purify the ancient religion of Persia. It is thought that he lived at the beginning of the 6th cent. B.C. He never claimed for himself divine powers but was given them by his followers. The basis of Zoroastrianism is the age-long war between good and evil, Ahura Mazda heading the good spirits and Ahriman the evil ones. Morality is very important since by doing right the worshipper is supporting Ahura Mazda against Ahriman, and the evil-doers will be punished in the last days when Ahura Mazda wins his inevitable victory.

The sacred book of this religion is the *Avesta.* If Zoroastrianism has little authority today, it had a very considerable influence in the past. Its doctrines penetrated into Judaism (*q.v.*) and, through Gnosticism, Christianity. The worship of Mithra by the Romans was an impure version of Zoroastrianism. Manichaeism (*q.v.*) was a Zoroastrian heresy and the Albigensianism of mediaeval times was the last relic of a belief which had impressed itself deeply in the minds of men.

GAZETTEER
OF THE
WORLD

An index and guide to the maps
with up-to-date descriptive matter.
Each year the Gazetteer is amended
to include the latest available
population figures.

GAZETTEER OF THE WORLD

Measurement of Geographical Phenomena.

(1) Physical Features.

In using the gazetteer the reader should note that it is impossible to make absolutely correct measurements of geographical phenomena. For example, measurement of height of land above sea-level depends, in the first instance, upon the definition of the elusive concept of sea-level itself. This is constantly changing and so an arbitrary value of *mean sea-level* is normally used, but the value adopted varies from country to country. As a result, height above sea-level has inbuilt inconsistencies and inaccuracies. Similarly, the length of a river will depend upon the scale of the survey from which measurements are made. Large-scale maps and aerial photographs can show in great detail the sinuous course of rivers, whereas a map on a smaller scale must reduce the amount of information shown and thereby the apparent length. We hope to include in a later edition the results of a yet unpublished work by a commission of the United Nations which is attempting to define in precise terms the area of the world's seas and oceans.

The gazetteer now records the heights of mountains, lengths of rivers, and land and sea areas in metric units. English equivalents will be found on p. 1 of the **Atlas**.

(2) Definition of Urban Area.

An even more difficult problem of measurement relates to the definition of the urban area of a town or city. It is possible to define the extent of urban areas in three major ways, by using (1) the administrative area, (2) the physically built-up area, and (3) the socio-geographic, metropolitan area. This latter concept is in many ways the most meaningful for it relates to the notion that a city exerts a strong influence over the population resident beyond its administrative or built-up boundary. For example, the city may provide employment opportunities or shopping and entertainment facilities for a population resident some distance away from it. In order to define "city" in these terms some means of measuring the degree of connection between it and its surrounding hinterland (the city-region) must be found and, needless to say, there is considerable disagreement among workers in this field as to what are the most suitable criteria to use. Different criteria produce different definitions and even the most recent measurements are obsolete within a short space of time. However, the real significance of this less tangible concept of "city" may be illustrated by the fact that the reform of local government in England rests in part upon the concept of the city-region.

The population figures given in the gazetteer normally relate to the city's administrative area. In the case of some large cities two figures are given—(1) for the administrative city, and (2) for the more extensive metropolitan area which surrounds and includes the administrative city.

The census of the United Kingdom is now based on the reorganised local government areas. Up-to-date population figures perforce refer to these areas which are both fewer in number and larger in size than their predecessors. As a result much local detail is lost in the most recent (post-1971) figures.

Place Names.

Where there have been recent changes in place names, the old name is given in brackets and a cross reference directs the reader to the new name.

Chinese place names.

The romanisation of Chinese characters has long posed problems. The characters which represent sounds cannot easily be "translated" into letters. The first system adopted in Western countries was **Wade-Giles** but this is very European in its approach. In 1975 the Chinese government issued a directive to adopt an alternative system called **Pinyin** which is more Chinese in its approach. This system, which since 1977 has been more widely accepted, is the script used within the Gazetteer and its maps. Cross-references are made from the Wade-Giles to the now official Pinyin version of each place name.

Reorganisation of Local Government in the United Kingdom.

The gazetteer has been modified to incorporate the new system of local government in the United Kingdom.

Editor's Note to Readers.

As a result of the indeterminate and dynamic nature of geographical phenomena inconsistencies and inaccuracies are bound to occur in a gazetteer of this size. The editor welcomes comments and criticisms of the entries based upon local knowledge and will try to make the fullest possible use of information received from readers.

ABBREVIATIONS USED IN THE GAZETTEER

GEOGRAPHICAL NAMES

Ala. = Alabama
Ark. = Arkansas
ASSR = Autonomous Soviet Socialist Republic
Atl. Oc. = Atlantic Ocean
B.C. = British Columbia
Brit. = British
BEF = British Expeditionary Forces
Cal. = California
CERN = European Centre for Nuclear Research
Col. = Colorado
Conn. = Connecticut
ČSSR = Czechoslovak Socialist Republic
Del. = Delaware
Eng. = England
E.E.C. = European Economic Community
Fla. = Florida
Fr. = French
Ga. = Georgia
ICI = Imperial Chemical Industries
Ill. = Illinois
Ind. = Indiana
Kan. = Kansas
Ky. = Kentucky

La. = Louisiana
Land = prov. (W. Germany)
Mass. = Massachusetts
Md. = Maryland
Me. = Maine
Mich. = Michigan
Minn. = Minnesota
Miss. = Mississippi
Mo. = Missouri
Mont. = Montana
NATO = North Atlantic Treaty Organisation
N.B. = New Brunswick
N.C. = North Carolina
N.D. = North Dakota
Neth. = Netherlands
N.H. = New Hampshire
N.J. = New Jersey
N.M. = New Mexico
N.S.W. = New South Wales
N.T. = Northern Territory (Australia)
N.Y. = New York
N.Z. = New Zealand
Oblast = aut. prov. (USSR)
O.F.S. = Orange Free State
Okla. = Oklahoma
Okrug = aut. dist. (RSFSR)

OPEC = Organization of Petroleum Exporting Countries
Ore. = Oregon
Pac. Oc. = Pacific Ocean
Penns. = Pennsylvania
R.I. = Rhode Island
R.o.I. = Republic of Ireland
RSFSR = Russian Soviet Federal Socialist Republic
S.C. = South Carolina
Scot. = Scotland
SHAPE = Supreme Headquarters, Allied Powers, Europe
S.D. = South Dakota
SSR = Soviet Socialist Republic
Tenn. = Tennessee
U.K. = United Kingdom
U.N. = United Nations
USA = United States of America
USSR = Union of Soviet Socialist Republics
Va. = Virginia
Vt. = Vermont
Wash. = Washington
W.I. = West Indies
Wis. = Wisconsin
Wyo. = Wyoming

OTHER ABBREVIATIONS

a. = area
admin. = administrative
agr. = agriculture
alt. = altitude
anc. = ancient
arch. = archaeological
a.s.l. = above sea-level
ass. = associated
aut. rep. = autonomous republic
bdy. = boundary
bldg. = building
bor. = borough
bdr. = border
C. = cape
c. = city; circa, c. = about
can. = canton
cap. = capital
cas. = castle
cath. = cathedral
ch. = chief
cm = centimetres
co. = county
C.B. = county borough
col. = colony
colly. = colliery
comm. = commercial
conurb. = conurbation
cst. = coast
ctr. = centre
cty. = country
dep. = department
dist. = district
div. = division
E. = east or easterly
elec. = electrical
engin. = engineering
esp. = especially
est. = estimate
exp. = exports

F. = firth
fed. = federal
fish. pt. = fishing port
fortfd. = fortified
G. = Gulf
gen. = general
G.N.P. = gross national product
gr. = great, group
ha = hectares
gtr. = greater
hgst. = highest
I. = island
impt. = important
inc. = including
indep. = independent
inds. = industries
industl. = industrial
Is. = Islands
km = kilometres
km² = square kilometres
L. = lake
l. = length
lge. = large
l.gov.dist. = local government district
lgst. = largest
lt. = light
m = metres
machin. = machinery
met. a. = metropolitan area
met. co. = metropolitan county
mftg. = manufacturing
mkg. = making
mkt. = market
mm = millimetres
mnfs. = manufactures
mng. = mining
mtn. = mountain

mun. = municipality
N. = north or northerly
nat. = national
non-met. co = non-metropolitan county
nr. = near
p. = population
par. = parish
penin. = peninsula
pref. = prefecture
prin. = principal
prod. = products
prot. = protectorate
prov. = province
pt. = port
R. = river
rep. = republic
residtl. = residential
rly. = railway
S. = south or southerly
shipbldg. = shipbuilding
sm. = small
spt. = seaport
st. = state
sta. = station
sub. = suburb
t. = town
Tan-Zam = Tanzania-Zambia rly.
terr. = territory
tr. = trade
trib. = tributary
Turk-Sib = Turkestan-Siberia rly.
univ. = university
U.D. = urban district
v. = village
W. = west or westerly
wat. pl. = watering place
wks. = works
wkshps. = workshops

A

Aachen (Aix-la-Chapelle), t., N. Rhine-Westphalia, **W. Germany**; anc. spa t. in coal-field dist.; industl., route ctr.; contains tomb of Charlemagne; p. (est. 1983) 243,700.

Aalen, t., Baden-Württemberg, **W. Germany**; on R. Kocher; iron, textiles, lens mkg.; p. (est. 1983) 62,800.

Aalst (Alost), t., E. Flanders, **Belgium**, 24 km N.W. Brussels; industl., comm. ctr. at rly. junc.; agr. tr.; p. (1982) 78,707.

Aarau, t., cap. of Aargau can., **Switzerland**; precision tools and instruments, shoes, textiles; hydroelectric power; p. (est. 1978) 16,000.

Aare, R., **Switzerland**; flows through Brienz and Thun Ls., thence into Rhine; Aare gorges above Meiringen; lgst R. wholly in Switzerland, 290 km long.

Aargau, can., N. **Switzerland**; occupies lower Aare R. valley; agr. in valleys, wooded uplands; cap. Aarau; a. 1,404 km²; p. (1980) 453,442.

Aba, t., **Nigeria**; N.E. of Pt. Harcourt; mkt., palm oil processing; p. (est. 1975) 177,000.

Abaco, Gt., I., Bahamas, **W.I.**; sheltered harbours, yachting; exp. crayfish; p. (1970) 6,501.

Abādān, c., **Iran**; spt., major oil terminal and refining ctr. on A.I. in Persian G.; p. (1976) 296,081.

Abakan, t., **RSFSR**, on R. A.; recent rly.; sawmilling, food inds.; p. (est. 1980) 133,000.

Abashiri, t., N. cst. Hokkaido, **Japan**; impt. fishing base; p. (1970) 43,904.

Abbeville, t., N. **France**; on R. Somme; connected with Paris and Belgium by canals; sugarmilling, carpets, biscuits, beer; p. (1982) 25,988.

Abbots-Langley, v., Herts., **Eng.**; birthplace of Nicholas Breakspeare (Pope Adrian IV).

Abenrå, spt., S.E. Jutland, **Denmark**; at head of A. fjord and admin. ctr. of S. Jutland prov.; vehicles, clothing, food processing; p. (1970) 20,264.

Abeokuta, t., **Nigeria**; cap. Ogun st.; N. of Lagos; palm oil, textiles; p. (est. 1975) 253,000.

Aberaeron, t., Ceredigion, Dyfed, S. **Wales**; p. (1981) 1,446.

Abercarn, t., Islwyn, Gwent, **Wales**; tinplate, knitting pins; former colliery t.; p. (1981) 17,604.

Aberconwy, l. gov. dist., Gwynedd, **Wales**; lower Conwy valley inc. ts. Conwy, Betws-y-Coed, Llanwrst and Llandudno; p. (1981) 52,503.

Aberdare, t., Cynon Valley, Mid Glamorgan, **Wales**; on R. Cynon; wire cables; former coalmng; p. (1981) 36,621.

Aberdare Range, mtns., Nat. Park, **Kenya**; rise to 4,000 m; form a section of E. rim of Gr. Rift Valley; equable climate attractive to white settlers; camphor forests, fruit and pastoral agr. at higher alts.

Aberdeen, royal burgh, l. gov. dist., Grampian Reg., **Scot.**; between mouths of Rs. Dee and Don; impt. fishing pt. under competition from claims of rapidly growing N. Sea oil ind.; "granite-city"—much granite used in central bldgs.; univ., cath.; p. (1981) 203,612.

Aberdeen, t., S.D., **USA**; ctr. for wheat and livestock region; p. (1970) 26,476.

Aberdeenshire, former co., E. **Scot.** *See* **Grampian Region.**

Aberfeldy, burgh, Perth and Kinross, **Scot.**; in Strath Tay, 6 km below Loch Tay; mkt.; salmon and trout fishing resort; p. (1981) 1,627.

Abergavenny, t., Gwent, **Wales**; on R. Usk; scene of massacre of Welsh chiefs; light engin., concrete prods.; cattle mkt.; cas.; p. (1981) 9,390.

Aberlour, Charlestown of, burgh, Moray, **Scot.**; on R. Spey, 19 km S. of Elgin; p. (1981) 879.

Abernethy, burgh, Perth and Kinross, **Scot.**; on R. Tay, once cap. of Pictish Kings; p. (1981) 881.

Abersoch, t., Gwynedd, **Wales**; yachting resort.

Abertillery, t., Blaenau Gwent, Gwent, **Wales**; collieries, tinplate; p. (1981) 19,319.

Aberystwyth, t., Ceredigion, Dyfed, **Wales**; on Cardigan Bay at mouth of R. Ystwyth; resort; cas., univ. college; Nat. Library of Wales; p. (1981) 8,666.

Abidjan, c., former cap. of **Ivory Coast**; pt.; exp. palm oil, cocoa, copra, hardwood, rubber; oil refining at Vridi nearby; p. (est. 1982) 1,800,000 (met. a.). *See* **Yamoussoukro**.

Abilene, t., Texas, **USA**; univ.; agr. processing, oil refining; p. (1980) 98,315 (c.), 139,192 (met. a.).

Abilene, t., on Smoky Hill R., Kansas. **USA**;

childhood home of Eisenhower; p. (1980) 6,572.

Abingdon, Vale of White Horse, Oxon., **Eng.**; mkt. t. on R. Thames; cars, leather gds.; mediaeval and Georgian bldgs.; p. (1981) 22,686.

Abingdon, t., Va., **USA**; timber inds., agr. processing and tr., tobacco; tourist ctr.; p. (1970) 4,376.

Abinger Hammer, v., Surrey, **Eng.**; former centre of Weald iron industry.

Abkhazskaya, aut. rep., Georgian SSR, **USSR**; borders Black Sea; sub-tropical crops, tourism; cap. Sukhumi; a. 8,599 km²; p. (1970) 487,000.

Abo. *See* **Turku.**

Abomey, anc. cap., former Kingdom of Dahomey, now **Benin**; former slave mkt.; cotton; p. (est. 1975) 41,000.

Abovyan, t., Armenian SSR, **USSR**; 16 km from Yerevan; new model t. founded 1963; planned p. 50,000.

Aboyne and Glentanner, par., Kincardine and Deeside, **Scot.**; on R. Dee nr. Ballater; Highland games; resort; p. (1981) 1,515.

Abraham, Plains of, nr. Quebec, **Canada**; Wolfe's victory over French under Montcalm, 1759.

Abram, t., Gtr. Manchester, **Eng.**; engin.; p. (1981) 7,083.

Abrantes, t., **Portugal**, on Tagus R.; French won battle here in Napoleonic Wars, 1807, dist. of Santarém; p. (1981) 48,653.

Abruzzo, region, central **Italy**; high limestone plateaux, narrow cstl. plain bordering Adriatic; poor agr., livestock; methane; forms part of Mezzogiorno; a. 8,513 km²; p. (1981) 1,217,791.

Abu Dhabi, I., emirate, lgst of **United Arab Emirates**; S.E. Arabian pen.; rich oil reserves; a. 207,200 km²; p. (est. 1982) 516,000.

Abuja, new t., **Nigeria**; planned new cap. for Nigeria built from oil revenue; building slowing down with fall in oil prices.

Abu Qir, v. on A. Bay, **Egypt**; site of anc. Canopus; Battle of the Nile fought in the Bay 1798; p. 7,086.

Abu Simbel, Nile Valley, **Egypt**; anc. temples carved out of solid sandstone, one to Rameses II and the other to his Queen; saved from waters of Lake Nasser.

Abydos, anc. t. of Phrygia, Asia Minor, in present **Turkey**; resisted Philip of Macedon; famed for story of Leander and Hero.

Abydus, ruined c., Upper **Egypt**; celebrated for its temple of Osiris.

Acajutla, spt., **El Salvador**; exp. coffee; cement, oil refining, fertilisers; p. (1961) 3,662.

Acapulco de Juárez, spt., Pac. cst., **Mexico**; major modern resort in bay surrounded by steep mtns.; exp. agr. prods.; p. (1979) 462,144.

Accra, c., cap. of **Ghana**; spt.; univ.; airpt.; consumer gds.; p. (1984) 636,067 (c.) 738,498 (met. a. inc. Tema).

Accrington, t., Hyndburn, Lancs., **Eng.**; 32 km N. of Manchester; former cotton ctr.; textile machin., more diversified new inds.; p. (1981) 35,891.

Achill I., Mayo, **R.o.I.**; mtnous.; agr., fishing, tourism at Dugort and Keal; a. 148 km²; p. (1971) 3,129.

Acireale, spt., Sicily, **Italy**; cath.; sulphur springs, p. (1981) 47,888.

Aconcagua, mtn., Andes, **Argentina**; highest peak of Western Hemisphere, alt. 6,956 m.

Aconquija, Nevada de, mtn. range, in E. Andes, N. **Argentina**; rises steeply from Chaco lowland to 5,500 m.

Acre. *See* **'Akko.**

Acre, st. W. **Brazil**; isolated within Amazon basin; rubber estates; major producer of coagulated rubber; cap. Rio Branco; a. 153,170 km²; p. (1970) 215,299.

Acton. *See* **Ealing.**

Adamawa Highlands, Nigeria; rise to over 5,490 m; stock rearing.

Adam's Bridge, chain of sandbanks, 35 km long, in Palk Strait, between **India** and **Sri Lanka**; construction of rail causeway mooted.

Adana, t., **Turkey**; on Seijhan R.; ctr. for fruit and cotton, impt. exp. from Turkey; cas.; cap. of A. prov.; 4th. t. of Turkey; p. (1980) 574,515.

Adapazari, t., **Turkey**; rly. junction; agr. and tr. ctr., silk, linen; high-grade concentrate from low-grade iron ore deposits in Camdagi a.; p. (1980) 130,977.

Adda, R., N. **Italy**; flows through L. Como to R. Po.; agr. in wide valley above L. Como; 240 km long.

Addis Ababa, c., cap. of **Ethiopia**; at 2,440 m in

central highlands; terminus of Djibouti rly., ctr. of coffee tr., main concentration of inds. in Ethiopa; consumer gds., food processing; new cotton mill (1981); admin. ctr.; univ., palaces; p. (est. 1980) 1,277,159.

Adelaide, c., spt., cap. of S. **Australia;** on alluvial plain of R. Torrens with Mount Lofty Range to E. and Gulf St. Vincent to W.; growth based on wheat, wool and fruit but heavy inds. since war (nearby coal and iron); cars, electrical goods, textiles, chems., oil refining; p. (1976) 13,773 (c), 900,379 (met. a.).

Adélie Land (Terre Adélie), Antarctica; French terr. and dependency of Réunion.

Adelsberg, t., **Yugoslavia.** *See* **Postojna.**

Aden, spt., cap. of **Democratic Rep.** of **Yemen;** former Brit. col.; bay behind headlands of Aden t. and Little Aden, excellent anchorage; p. (est. 1977) 271,590 (met. a.),

Aden, G. of W. **Arabian Sea;** one of most impt. shipping lanes in world; pts. of Aden, Berbera, Djibouti; length 880 km, width 480 km at mouth.

Adige, R., N. Italy; upper course forms impt. routeway through Alps between Italy and N.; flows via Verona to Adriatic; 360 km long.

Adirondack, mtns., **USA;** hgst. peak Mt. Marcy (1,630 m), average height 1,200 m; scenically attractive, ski resorts, sanatoria, iron-ore deposits.

Adlington, t., Lancs., **Eng.;** nr. Chorley; former cotton spinning t.; p. (1981) 5,626.

Admiralty Is., 27 km of sm. coral Is., one lge. I., S.W. **Pac. Oc.;** N. of New Guinea; forms part of Bismarck Archipelago; Australian mandate; anc. civilisation; pearl fishing, coconuts; ch. t. Lorengau; a. 2,072 km²; p. (1970) 22,447.

Adour, R., S.W. **France;** rises in Pyrenees, enters Bay of Biscay below Bayonne; 331 km long.

Adria, mkt. t., Rovigo, **Italy;** formerly on cst., now 22 km inland, old Etruscan c.; p. (1981) 21,785.

Adrianople. *See* **Edirne.**

Adriatic Sea, branch of the Mediterranean, between Italy and Balkan Peninsula; forms G. of Venice on the N.; chief trading pts., Venice, Trieste, and Ancona on the N., Brindisi and Dürres on the S.; a. 134,680 km², 720 km long.

Adriatic Highway, Yugoslavia; cst. road (in need of repair) across Dinaric Alps motivated by tourist boom.

Adullam or Aidelma, Judean c. of Canaanite origin, S.W. Jerusalem, **Israel,** where David hid in cave from Saul.

Adur, l. gov. dist., West Sussex, **Eng.;** lower A. valley and ts. of Shoreham-by-Sea and South-wick; p. (1981) 58,032.

Adwick le Street, t., South Yorks, **Eng.;** coal; home of George Washington's family; p. (1981) 19,162.

Adygeyskaya (Adygei), aut. region, **RSFSR;** in foot-hills of Caucasus; mainly agr. and lumber-ing; cap. Maykop; a. 7,599 km²; p. (1970) 386,000.

Adzharskaya, aut. rep., Georgian SSR, **USSR;** borders Turkey; mtnous.; sub-tropical crops; cap. Batumi; a. 2,849 km²; p. (1970) 310,000.

Aegades, gr. of rocky Is. off W. cst. of Sicily, **Italy;** ch. t. Favignana on I. of that name.

Aegean Is., between **Greece** and **Turkey;** called the Grecian Archipelago, inc. Crete, Cyclades, Sporades, and Dodecanese; a. 3,901 km²; p. (1981) 428,533.

Aegean Sea, branch of the Mediterranean; studded with Is., between **Greece** and **Turkey;** connected through the Dardanelles with Sea of Marmara and thence through the Bosporus Strait with the Black Sea; rich cultural history; coral sponge fishing; recent oil finds contested between Greece and Turkey; length 640 km, width 320 km.

Afan, l. gov. dist., West Glamorgan, **Wales;** comprises Glyncorrwg and Port Talbot; p. (1981) 54,663.

Afars and Issas. *See* Djibouti.

Affric, Glen, Inverness, **Scot.;** 48 km S.W. of Inverness; hydroelectric power.

Afghanistan, rep. (1973), former kingdom, **Asia;** land locked, lies N. and W. of Pakistan; cap. Kabul; comm. ctrs. Kabul, Kandahar; mtnous.; ch. Rs., Kabul and Helm; intense summer heat, severe winter cold, scanty rainfall; races, Afghans, aboriginal hill-tribes; languages, official Persian, spoken Pushtu; religion, Islam; cereals, fruit,

sheep, horses, camels; inds. carpets, woollens, silks; coal mng. at Dara-i-Suf; natural gas at Shibarghan; rich copper, lead, iron-ore resources undeveloped; no rly.; refugees totalled 5,000,000 by 1985; hydro-electr. at Asadabad; a. 647,500 km²; p. (est. 1984) 14,292,000 (inc. 2,600,000 nomadic p.);. Invaded by Russian troops, Dec. 1979.

Africa, second lgst. continent contains 22 per cent of world's land a. but only 11 per cent of p.; diverse physical and cultural conditions; plateaux interrupted in N. and S. by steeply folded, sharply eroded mtn. ranges and by mtn. massifs of Sahara and E. Africa; climate and vegetation vary from hot desert to equatorial rain forest and from Mediterranean woodland to tropical savannah; sparse but ethnically varied p., concentrated mainly along N.W. Mediterranean cst., Nile valley, cst. of W. Africa and N.E. of L. Victoria; little urbanisation; economic development hindered by colonial legacy and neo-colonial international companies, poorly developed transport network, poor soils, inadequate rainfall and fluctuating prices of primary prods. on world mkt.; petroleum deposits providing revenue for devel. in few ctys.; those ctys. without oil severely handicapped by high cost of imports; schemes like Volta R. multipurpose development and the Cabora Bassa dam designed to alleviate this poverty; continent contains 40 per cent of world hydroelectric potential and is storehouse of non-energy producing minerals, but many are exported in unprocessed form; agr. predominant economic activity, except in industl. enclaves of Egypt, Zimbabwe and S. Africa; 60 per cent land devoted to subsistence crops; 50 ctys. had achieved independence by 1977 compared with 4 in 1945; a c. 30,259,000 km²; p. (est. 1984) 536,685,000.

Agadir, spt., S. cst. **Morocco;** wrecked by earthquake, 1960; new t. built S. of former c. in a. of greater geological stability; p. (est. 1973) 189,600.

Agana, cap. of **Guam;** reconstructed after second world war; p. (1970) 2,131 (exc. armed forces).

Agen, t., cap. of Lot-et-Garonne, **France;** mkt. t.; aqueduct and bridge over Garonne R.; fruit tr. and processing; p. (1982) 58,288 (met. a.).

Agincourt (Azincourt), v., Pas-de-Calais, **France;** famed for battle in 1415 between English, led by Henry V and French under d'Albert.

Agra, c., Uttar Pradesh, **India;** on Jumna R., 184 km S.S.E. of Delhi; formerly cap. of Mogul Empire; famous Taj Mahal mausoleum; univ.; p. (1981) 694,191 (c.), 747,318 (met. a.).

Agrigento, t., S. Sicily, **Italy;** spt., exp. sulphur, salt. Formerly Girgenti, founded Akragas, c. 580 B.C., famous for its temples; birthplace of Empedocles; p. (1981) 51,325.

Aguadilla, spt., **Puerto Rico;** exp. coffee and sugar; p. (1970) 21,087.

Aguascalientes, st., **Mexico;** on central plateau at 1,800 m; agr.; mineral springs; cap. A.; a. 6,472 km²; p. (1970) 338,142.

Aguascalientes, t., cap. of A. st. **Mexico;** alt. over 1,800 m; 416 km N.W. of Mexico City; wide range of local inds.; hot springs; p. (1979) 257,179.

Agulhas, C., rocky projection, 160 km E. of C. of Good Hope, most southerly point of **Africa.**

Ahlen, t., N. Rhine-Westphalia, **W. Germany;** on R. Werse; coal mng., metal and engin. wks.; p. (est. 1983) 53,200.

Ahmadabad, temporary cap. of Gujarat, **India;** Jain temple, mosques; univ.; impt. textile ctr.; oilfield at Nawagam nearby; p. (1981) 2,059,725 (c.), 2,548,037 (met. a.).

Ahmadnagar, c., Maharashtra, **India;** admin. ctr.; old Bahmani cap.; lge. tr. in cotton and silk gds.; p. (1981) 143,937 (c.), 181,210 (met. a.).

Ahvāz (Ahwāz), c., cap. of Khuzestan prov., **Iran;** airpt.; oil, aluminium, steel pipes; p. (1976) 329,006.

Aigues-Mortes, t., Gard dep., **France;** on Rhône delta; canal ctr., once spt., now 5 km from Mediterranean; salt works; much of mediaeval t. preserved; tourism; p. (1982) 4,475.

Aiguille d'Arves, mtn., Dauphiné Alps, S.E. **France;** 3 rock needles; hgst. alt. 3,511 m.

Aiguille du Midi, mtn., Mt. Blanc massif, S.E. **France;** rock needle, funicular rly.; alt. 3,845 m.

Aiguille Verte, mtn., Mt. Blanc massif, S.E. **France,** rock needle overlooking Chamonix; alt. 4,130 m.

Ailefroid, mtn., Dauphiné Alps, S.E. **France;** double summit; alt. 3,962 m.

Ailsa Craig, rocky I., Kyle and Carrick, **Scot.;** alt. 340 m; gannetry.

Ain, dep., **France;** in Jura; mainly agr., famous for pigs and poultry; a. 5,822 km²; p. (1982) 418,300.

Ain, R., France; trib. of R. Rhône, flows S.S.W. from Jura; hydroelectric power; 194 km long.

Airdrie, burgh, Strathclyde Reg., **Scot.;** 19 km E. of Glasgow; iron inds., brick and concrete wks., steel tubes, pharmaceutics; p. (1981) 45,643.

Aire, R., West Yorks., **Eng.;** trib. of Ouse; major valley for power production; produces 20 per cent of U.K. power; length 112 km.

Aireborough, t., West Yorks., **Eng.;** woollens; p. (1981) 31,414.

Aisne, dep., **France;** borders Ardennes; forested; mainly agr., sugar-beet; sm. textile ts.; cap. Laon; a. 7.423 km²; p. (1982) 534,200.

Aisne, R., N.E. **France;** navigation improved by regularisation; 240 km long.

Aitolia and Akarnania, Greece; mtnous. prov. on N. side G. of Patras; arable cultivation on cstl. plain; cap. Missolonghi; a. 5,390 km²; p. (1971) 228,719.

Aix-en-Provence, t., Bouches-du-Rhône, **France;** 29 km N. of Marseilles; old cap. of Provence; thermal springs; cultural and comm. ctr., agr., inds.; p. (1982) 124,550.

Aix-la-Chapelle. See **Aachen.**

Aix-les-Bains, health resort, Savoy, **France;** p. (1982) 23,534.

Aizuwakamatsu, t. N. Honshu, **Japan;** lacquer ware, candles; p. (1979) 112,931.

Ajaccio, spt., cap. Corse du Sud, Corcisa, **France;** timber, flour, olive oil, tobacco; tourism; birthplace of Napoleon; p. (1982) 55,279.

Ajman, emirate, one of **United Arab Emirates;** p. (1980) 42,000.

Ajmer, t., Rajasthan, **India;** salt extraction, vegetable oils; p. (1981) 375,593 (met. a.).

Akhaia, prov., **Greece;** impt. currant producing a.; livestock; inc. pt. of Patras; a. 3,134 km²; p. (1981) 275,193.

Akhisar, t., **Turkey;** anc. Thyatira; in fertile agr. basin, p. (1965) 47,422

Akita, pref., **Japan;** a. 11,663 km²; contains Japan's lgst. oilfield and copper mine; mtns. and fertile lowlands; p. (1970) 1,242,376.

Akita, c., **Japan;** cap. Akita pref.; old cas. t.; pt; oil refining ctr., fertilisers, wood pulp; p. (est. 1984) 284,863.

'Akko (Acre), c., spt., **Israel;** famous for sieges during Crusades; withstood Napoleon for 61 days in 1799; pt. functions now assumed by Haifa; p. (est. 1970) 33,900.

Akmolinsk. See **Tselinograd.**

Akola, t., Maharashtra, **India;** cotton; p. (1981) 225,412.

Akosombo, pt. **Ghana;** pt. and new t. S. of L. Volta; textile factory being built; planned p. 50,000.

Akranes, t., **Iceland;** N. of Reykjavik; lge. cement wks.; p. (1983) 5,351.

Akron, c., Ohio, **USA;** lge. rubber mftg. ctr.; maize, mills, woollens, machin., chemicals; univ.; p. (1980) 237,000 (c.), 660,000 (met. a.).

Aktyubinsk, t., N.W. Kazakh SSR, **USSR;** at S. end of Ural mtns.; ferro-alloys, engin., lignite, elec. power, chemicals, copper; p. (est. 1980) 197,000.

Akureyri, t., N. **Iceland;** herring fishery, textiles, food processing; 2nd. t. of Iceland; p. (1983) 13,742.

Akyab, See **Sittwe.**

Alabama, st., **USA;** cap. Montgomery, ch. pt. Mobile; "cotton st.", cattle-rearing; fertilisers, chemicals, mng.; lgst. c. Birmingham; settled 1702; admitted to union 1819; st. flower camelia, st. bird yellowhammer; a. 133,667 km²; p. (1980) 3,890,000.

Alagôas, st., N.E. **Brazil;** hot, dry cattle rearing a., poor st. with low literacy rate; cap. Maceió; a. 28,648 km²; p. (est. 1983) 2,154,000.

Alameda, spt. Cal., **USA;** on I. in San Francisco Bay; impt. naval and air base; pt. inds.; p. (1980) 63,852.

Aland Is. (Ahvenanmaa), group belonging to **Finland** at entrance of G. of Bothnia; a. 1,481 km²; p. (1968) 21,500.

Alaska, Arctic st., **USA;** separated from other sts.; bought from Russia (1868); mtnous.; furs, timber, salmon; major oil and natural gas discoveries on N. slope present difficult ecological problems for exploitation; pipeline from Prudhoe Bay to Valdez; lgst. c. Anchorage; admitted to union 1959; st. flower forget-me-not,

st. bird Willow Ptarmigan; cap. Juneau (planned cap. at Willow South never built); a. 1,518,776 km²; p. (1980) 400,000.

Alaska G. of, S. cst. A., **USA.;** semi-circular G. with precipitous csts.; oil in Cook Inlet and Controller B.; a. 5,000 km².

Alaska Highway, from Dawson Creek, B.C., **Canada,** to Fairbanks, Alaska, **USA;** 2,443 km long; built for second world war programme; main supply base and H.Q., Edmonton, Alberta.

Alaska Range, mtn. massif, S.A., **USA;** extends in arc of 640 km; separates S. cst. and N. tundra; S.E. flowing glaciers; many peaks over 3,000 m; Mt. McKinley, 6,182 m.

Alatau, mtns., bdy. of Kazakhstan, **USSR;** and Sinkiang, **China;** group of 5 ranges, outliers of Tien-Shan; alt. up to 4,600 m; highest peak Khan Tengri, 6,954 m.

Alava, Basque prov., N. **Spain;** ch. t. Vitoria; viticulture; a. 3,043 km²; p. (1981) 257,827.

Albacete, prov., S.E. **Spain;** stock-raising; a. 14,864 km²; p. (1981) 339,370.

Albacete, t., cap. of A. prov., **Spain;** agr, mkt., fruit, saffron; p. (1981) 117,126.

Alba-Iulia, t. **Romania;** on R. Mures, formerly Carlsburgh; union of Transylvania with Romania proclaimed here 1918; p. (est. 1972) 29,935.

Albania, rep., **S.E. Europe;** lying along Adriatic, adjacent to Yugoslavia and Greece; Chinese economic aid and co-operation ended in 1978; food ch. ind.; petroleum reserves and refining, hydroelectric power, coal, chrome ore, copper, iron ore; fastest growing p. in Europe; cap. Tirana; a. 27,529 km²; p. (est. 1984) 2,985,000.

Albano, crater L., **Italy;** tourist attraction 24 km S.E. of Rome; steep sides; a. 8 km².

Albany, mkt. t., Ga., **USA;** on Flint R.; agr. ctr.; cotton, food; p. (1970) 72,623.

Albany, c., cap. of N.Y. st., **USA;** R. pt. on Hudson R.; admin. and industl. ctr.; p. (1980) 102,000 (c.), 795,000 (met. a. with Schenectady-Troy).

Albany, t., **W. Australia;** pt. on King George Sound; founded (1826) as penal col.; first white settlement in W. Australia, established to counter Fr. settlement of W.; p. (1976) 13,969.

Albert, L. See **Mobutu Seso, L.**

Alberta, prov., W. **Canada;** part of prairies; Rockies in W.; wheat, livestock, feed crops; coal less impt. with development of rich oil and gas resources; chemicals, timber; cap. Edmonton; a. 661,188 km²; p. (1976) 1,838,037.

Albertville. See **Kalemi.**

Albi, t., cap. of Tarn dep., **France;** cath., industl. and comm. ctr.; p. (1982) 60,181 (met. a.).

Ålborg, c., cap. of N. Jutland prov., **Denmark;** spt. on S. side of Lim fjord; shipping., cement, textiles; airpt.; p. (1976) 154,605.

Albula Alps, mtn. range, Rhaetian Alps, E. **Switzerland;** summits intersected by low passes; inc. several impt. Dolomitic peaks.

Albuquerque, t., N.M., **USA;** on Rio Grande; alt. 1,525 m.; univ.; food prod., engin.; resort; p. (1980) 332,000 (c.), 454,000 (met. a.).

Albury-Wodonga, t., N.S.W., Vic., **Australia;** regional urban growth ctr. (1974) on Murray R.; p. (1976) 45,567.

Alcalá de Henares, t., **Spain;** nr. Madrid; univ.; birthplace of Cervantes; p. (1981) 142,862.

Alcamo, t., Sicily, **Italy;** nr. ruins of anc. Segesra; p. (1981) 42,059.

Alcatraz, I., Cal., **USA;** San Francisco Bay; former prison.

Alcoy, t., **Spain;** textiles, paper; p. (1970) 61,371.

Aldabra Is., Seychelles Rep.; 400 km N.W. of Madagascar; leased (1971-1985) to Royal Society for wildlife research (unique animal and plant species).

Aldan, R., E. Siberia, **USSR;** flows from Stanovoy Range to Lena R. via Tommot gold-mng. dist.; coal in lower course; 2,682 km long.

Aldeburgh, spt., Suffolk Coastal, Suffolk, **Eng.;** 48 km from Ipswich; famous for annual music festival; p. (1981) 2,911.

Aldermaston, Berkshire, **Eng.;** atomic weapons research ctr.

Alderney, I., Channel Is., **Eng.;** horticulture tourism; a. 794 ha; p. (est. 1973) 1,700.

Aldershot, t., Rushmoor, Hants., **Eng.;** bricks; lge. military camp; p. (1981) 32,654.

Aldridge, t., West Midlands, **Eng.;** plastics, packing cases; expanded t.; p. with Brownhills (1981) 87,219.

Alençon, t. cap of Orne dep., **France**; textiles; p. (1982) 32,526.

Aleppo, c., **Syria**; 2nd. c. of Syria; in limestone hills; univ.; mkt and textile ctr.; p. (est. 1982) 905,944.

Alès, t., Gard dep., **France**; sm. coalfield; chemicals; p. (1982) 70,180 (met. a.).

Alessandria, t., N. **Italy**; rly. ctr. on Tanaro R.; engin.; p. (1981) 100,523.

Alesund, spt. on Giske I., W. **Norway**, fishing, fish processing; airpt. on I. to N.; p. (est. 1970) 39,390.

Aletsch, glacier, **Switzerland**; in Bernese Alps; lgst. in Europe; length 24 km.

Aletschhorn, mtn., Bernese Alps, **Switzerland**; alt. 4,198 m.

Aleutian Is.; Bering Sea, Alaska, **USA**; chain of over 150 Is. formed from partially submerged peaks of volcanic A. mtn. range; on earthquake belt; U.S. air base.

Alexander Archipelago, S.E. Alaska, **USA**; dense I. system; fjord scenery; well populated; furs, lumbering, fishing; a. 33,670 km².

Alexandria, ch. pt., **Egypt**; founded by Alexander the Great, 332 B.C.; floating dock; exp. cotton, wheat, rice, gum; second lgst. c. in Africa; p. (1976) 2,317,705.

Alexandria, c., spt., Va., **USA**; on Chesapeake Bay; indust. t.; p. (1980) 103,000.

Alford, t., East Lindsey, Lincs., **Eng.**; mkt.; brewing, food processing; p. (1981) 2,596.

Alfreton, t., Amber Valley, Derbys., **Eng.**; mkt. t.; formerly coal mng.; hosiery, knitwear; p. (1981) 23,124.

Algarve, prov., anc. kingdom, **Portugal**; in extreme S. of cty; tourism, fishing, fruit; p. (est. 1970) 316,200.

Algeciras, spt., **Spain**; W. of Gibraltar on A. Bay; nearby Campo de Gibraltar scheme for social and economic development to break down Gibraltar's economic isolation; p. (1981) 86,042.

Algeria, indep. st. (1962), N. **Africa**; former French colony; fertile cstl. plain borders Mediterranean Sea where cereal, wine, fruit and olive production and incr. mkt. garden prods. for exp.; Land reform (1980) encouraging livestock; afforestation to prevent N. spread of Sahara; exp. of high grade iron ore, phosphates, petroleum and natural gas are financing ambitious industrialisation plans; incr. tourism; new roads link Saharan oilfields to cst.; cap. El Djezair; a. 2,373,994 km²; p. (est. 1984) 21,272,000.

Algiers. *See* El Djezair

Alicante, spt., cap of A. prov., **Spain**; wine, fruits; oil refinery; p. (1981) 245,961.

Alice Springs, t., N.T., **Australia**; ch. t., of desert a.; major cattle raising ctr.; natural gas nearby; growth of winter tourism; p. (1976) 14,149.

Aligarh, t., Uttar Pradesh, **India**; 128 km S.E. of Delhi; univ.; p. (1981) 320,861.

Alkmaar, t., **Netherlands**; impt. cheese mkt. on N. Holland canal; p. (1982) 77,761.

Allahabad, t., Uttar Pradesh, **India**; at confluence of Jumna and Ganges Rs.; univ.; Hindu pilgrimage ctr.; p. (1981) 616,051 (c.), 650,070 (met. a.).

Allegheny Mtns., USA; part of Appalachian system, inc. several parallel ranges; water-shed between Atlantic and Mississippi R. drainage; forested, tourism; average alt. 1,500 m.

Allegheny R., Penns., N.Y., **USA**; rises in A. mtns., flows to Ohio R.; Pittsburg met. a. on lower reaches where R. entrenched 120 m below plateau making urban development difficult; used for coal and oil transport; 520 km long.

Allen, Bog of, R.o.I.; peat bogs, peat cutting, cultivation; a. 958 km².

Allentown, t., Penns., **USA**; coal, textiles, cement; p. (1980) 104,000 (c.), 635,000 (met. a.).

Alleppey, spt., Kerala, S. **India**; on sand spit coconut prods, p. (1981) 169,940.

Allerdale, l. gov. dist., Cumbria, **Eng.**; cstl. dist inc. Workington, Maryport, Cockermouth and Keswick; p. (1981) 95,664.

Alliance, t., Ohio, **USA**; iron, steel, engin.; p. (1980) 24,315.

Allier, dep., **France**; N. of Massif Central; coal and iron mng.; mineral springs, wine, wheat; a. 4,786 km²; p. (1982) 369,000.

Alloa, sm. burgh, Clackmannan, **Scot.**; on N. bank of R. Forth; bricks, tiles, glass, distilling p. (1981) 26,300.

Alma-Ata, c., cap. of Kazakh SSR, **USSR**; in foothills of Tien-Shan mtns.; univ.; comm.

agr., and ind. ctr.; food processing, machin., printing; p. (est. 1980) 928,000.

Almada, t., **Portugal**; on R. Tagus estuary opposite Lisbon; Salazar bridge (opened 1966) links it with Lisbon; p. (1981) 147,690.

Almelo, t., Overijssel, **Neth.**; 40 km S.E. of Zwolle; cotton textile mnfs.; p. (1982) 63,313.

Almeria, spt. on G. of A., S.E. **Spain**; cath.; exp. grapes, oranges; p. (1981) 130,913.

Alnwick, t., l. gov. dist., Northumberland, **Eng.**; cas.; mkt. t.; p. (1981) 28,734 (dist.).

Alor Star, t., cap. of Kedah, **W. Malaysia**; on main W. cst. road and rly.; p. 32,424.

Alost. *See* Aalst.

Alpes-de-Haute-Provence (Basses-Alpes), dep., S.E. **France**; mtnous., infertile a. bordering Italy; olives, wines; cap. Digne; a. 6,988 km²; p. (1982) 118,200.

Alpes-Maritimes, dep., S.E. **France**; ceded by Italy in 1860; ch. t. Nice; olives, wines, fruit; a. 3,737 km²; p. (1982) 878,600.

Alphen, t., S. Holland, **Neth.**; on Old Rhine, 16 km S.E. of Leiden; mkt. for dairy produce; p. (1982) 53,182.

Alps, hgst. mtns. in **Europe**; 960 km long, inc. 1,200 glaciers; separates S. and central Europe, forming a climatic divide; major tourist a., winter sports; hydroelec. power; main peaks Mont Blanc (4,814 m), Mont Rosa (4,641 m), Matterhorn (4,509 m).

Als, I., S. **Denmark**; in the Little Belt, a. 337 km²; linked to Jutland by bridge; p. (1965) 48,676.

Alsace-Lorraine, region, E. **France**; bordered to E. by W. Germany and Rhine R; incorporated into Germany at time of unification (1871), returned to France by Treaty of Versailles (1919); impt. iron-ore and iron and steel inds. in Lorraine; regional aid for economic development; well wooded; p. (1982) 1,558,400 (Alsace) *See* **Lorraine.**

Alsdorf, t., N. Rhine-Westphalia, **W. Germany**; 16 km N. of Aachen; tar-distillation plant; p. (est. 1983) 46,300.

Alston, t., Eden, Cumbria, **Eng.**; in upper reaches of south Tyne in N. Pennines; limestone quarrying.

Altai Mtns., Mongolia, **USSR**; border China; steppes and glaciers; silver and mercury; multi-purpose R. project at Kamenna-Obi; ctr. of USSR atomic ind, at Ust Kamenogorsk; stock-rearing; average alt. 3,000 m, highst. alt. 4,656 m at Tabun Bogdo.

Alta, R., N. **Norway**; scene of major new h.e.p. sta. fiercely opposed by Lapp residents.

Altamura, caves, N. **Spain**; prehistoric shelters; paintings of animals (Magdalenian).

Altamura, t., Apulia, **Italy**; at foot of Apennines; wines, wool; cath.; p. (1981) 51,328.

Altdorf, t., cap. of Uri can., **Switzerland**; rubber gds., wood workings; statue of William Tell and Tell Theatre; p. (1970) 8,647.

Altenahr, t., N. Rhine-Westphalia, **W. Germany**; site of anc. cas. of Counts von der Marck; metals, wine; p. (est. 1983) 23,400.

Altenburg, t., Leipzig, **E. Germany**; lignite mng., engin., metallurgy, mnfs. playing cards, textiles; p. (est. 1973) 49,459.

Alton, t., East Hants., **Eng.**; breweries, lt. engin.; p. (1981) 14,646.

Alton, t., Ill., **USA**; on Mississippi R.; oil refining; p. (1980) 34,171.

Altona, pt. of Hamburg, **W. Germany**; on the Elbe; chemical and fishing inds.; trawler pt.

Altoona, c., Penns., **USA**; rly. t.; p. (1970) 62,385 (c.), 134,142 (met. a.).

Altrincham, mkt. t., Trafford, Gtr. Manchester, **Eng.**; engin.; residtl.; p. (1981) 39,641.

Alva, burgh, Clackmannan, **Scot.**; at S. foot of Ochil Hills, 5 km N. of Alloa; woollens, printing, fruit and fish canning; p. (1981) 4,876.

Alwar, c., Rajasthan, **India**; in hilly agr. region; former cap. of A. princely st.; fort, palace; p. (1971) 100,378.

Alyn and Deeside, l. gov. dist., Clwyd, **Wales**; inc. Connah's Quay, Buckley and Hawarden; p. (1981) 72,003.

Amagasaki, c., **Japan**; nr. Osaka; chemicals polyethylene; iron and steel; oil refining; p. (est. 1984) 523,650.

Amalfi, spt., **Italy**; on G. of Salerno; tourist resort; fisheries; p. (1981) 6,052.

Amapá, fed. terr., N. **Brazil**; on equator; tropical rain forest, sparse p.; a. 137,423 km²; p. (est. 1983) 200,000.

Amãrah, Al, pt., **Iraq**; on left bank of R. Tigris 400 km below Baghdad; Arab t. and agr. mkt. at R. crossing; p. (1970) 80,078.

Amãrapura, t., **Burma**; on R. Irrawaddy 10 km. S.W. of Mandalay; former cap.; craft inds.

Amarillo, t., Texas, **USA**; oil refining, creameries, meat packing; p. (1980) 149,000.

Amasya, t., **Turkey**; on Yesil-Cekerek R.; tr. ctr.; p. (1970) 36,646.

Amazon, gr. R., **S. America**; drains lgst. a. and carries more water than any other R. in world; main Andean headstreams Huarco Ucayali and Marañón from Peru unite to flow across Brazil to Atl. Oc., receiving waters of many Rs. inc. the Madeira; lgst. rain forest in world; ocean steamers penetrate to Iquitos, Peru, c. 3,680 km from mouth; a. drained c. 6 million km² of sparsely populated cty., mostly in Brazil; length 6,448 km; basin inc. 40% of S. America; ocean pt. Belém.

Amazonas, lgst. st. of **Brazil**; isolated; tropical rain forest; tree prods.; vast mineral reserves; cap. Manáus; a. 1,595,823 km²; p. (est. 1983) 1,621,000 (mainly Indian).

Amazonas, fed. terr., **Venezuela**; cap. Puerto Ayacucho on Orinoco R., isolated, tropical rain forest; a. 181,300 km²; p. (1981) 45,667.

Amazonia, Peru, Colombia, Brazil; a. covered by Amazon R. and its tribs. and the surrounding lowland; thickly forested; underdeveloped.

Ambala, c., Haryana, **India**; cotton, flour; p. (1981) 121,203.

Ambato, c., **Ecuador**; S. of Quito, on slope of Mt. Chimborazo; alt. 2,702 m; textiles, canned fruits, leather gds.; p. (1982) 221,392.

Amberg, t., Bavaria, **W. Germany**; mediaeval walled t. on R. Vils; specialist steels, textiles; p. (est. 1983) 43,700.

Amber Valley, l. gov. dist., Derbys., **Eng.**; S. of co., nr. Notts.; inc. Alfreton, Ripley, Heanor and Belper; p. (1981) 109,379.

Ambès, t., Gironde, **France**; nr. Bordeaux; oil refining; p. (1982) 2,715.

Ambleside, tourist ctr., Cumbria, **Eng.**; N. of L. Windermere.

Amboise, t., Indre-et-Loire dep., **France**; 24 km E. of Tours; famous cas. and prison; p. (1982) 11,415.

Ambon, I., Moluccas, **Indonesia**; spices, coconuts; a. 818 km²; p. 73,000.

America, the lands of the Western hemisphere, comprising the continents of North and South America, separated by narrow Isthmus of Panama; most N. point over 14,400 km from C. Horn, the extreme S. point; p. (est. 1967) 479,000,000. *See also* North, South, and Central America.

Amersfoort, c., Utrecht, **Neth.**; walled c. on R. Eem; rapid growth of light inds.; p. (1982) 88,024.

Amersham, t., Bucks., **Eng.**; Radio chemical Ctr., renamed Amersham International after privatisation (1982); lt. inds., 17th cent. mkt. hall.

Ames, t., Iowa, **USA**; Iowa State Univ. of Science and Technology and many fed. and st. institutes; p. (1980) 45,775.

Amiens, c., cap. of Somme dep; major textile ctr. of **France**, on R. Somme; cath.; p. (1982) 136,358.

Amirante Is., British group, **Indian Ocean**; S.W. of Seychelles.

Amlwch, t., Gwynedd, **Wales**; N. cst of Anglesey; resort; pt.; oil terminal; p. (1981) 3,690.

Amman, c., cap. of **Jordan**; N.E. of Dead Sea; site of biblical Raboth Ammon; textiles, cement, tobacco; airpt.; univ.; p. (est, 1983) 744,000.

Ammanford, t., Dinefwr, Dyfed, **Wales**; anthracite, brick mkg.; p. (1981) 5,711.

Amoy. *See* **Xiamen.**

Ampthill, Mid Beds., **Eng.**; mkt. t.; p. (1981) 5,766.

Amravati, c., Maharashtra, **India**; cotton ctr., univ.; p. (1981) 261,404.

Amritsar, c., Punjab, N.W. **India**; Golden Temple sacred to Sikhs; trade ctr. for shawls and carpets; soaps, paints, engin.; Massacre of Indian nationalists by troops under British control, 1919; p. (1981) 594,844 (met. a.).

Amroha, t., Uttar Pradesh, **India**; pilgrimage ctr.; p. (1981) 112,682.

Amsterdam, spt., cap. of **Netherlands**; at junction of R. Amstel and the IJ; built on 96 Is. joined

by 300 bridges, harbour at terminus of N. Sea canal can hold 1,000 ships; two univs., Royal Palace, Bourse; extensive tr.; exp. dairy prod., sugar, tobacco; shipbldg., diamond polishing, aeronautical, marine, elec. machin., oil refining; p. (1982) 700,759.

Amu-Dar'ya (Oxus), R., marks boundary between **USSR** and **Afghanistan**; flows from Pamir mtns. to Aral Sea; Kara- and Ksyl-Kum deserts on either bank; rich in fish; 1,395 km long.

Amur (Heilong Jiang), major R. of E. **Asia**; flows from Mongolia between N.E. China and E. Siberia into Pac. Oc. opposite Sakhalin I.; with tribs. Argun and Ussuri forms lgst. R. frontier in world; crossed by Trans-Siberian rly. at Khabarovsk; 2,827 km long.

Anaconda, t., Mont., **USA**; one of lgst. copper mines in world; p. (1980) 12,518 (co.).

Anaheim, t., Cal., **USA**; tourism; Disneyland; p. (1980) 219,000 (c.), 1,933,000 (met a. with Santa Ana and Garden Grove).

Ahahuac, plateau, **Mexico**; average alt. 2,000 m; surrounded by higher cty. inc. volcano Popocatapetl (5,456 m); contains Mexico City heartland of Aztec Mexico; a. c. 3,900 km².

Anambas Is., Indonesia; 240 km W. of W. Malaysia; little development; p. c. 12,000.

Anatolia (Asia Minor), penin. approx. coextensive with Turkey bounded by Black Sea (N.), Mediterranean (S.), Aegean (W.).

Anching. *See* **Anqing.**

Anchorage, t., Alaska, **USA**; timber, salmon fishing and canning; earthquake 28 Mar. 1964; spt.; airpt.; p. (1980) 174,000.

Ancona, spt., central **Italy**; on the Adriatic Sea; founded by Dorians, 1500 B.C.; sugar refineries, shipbldg.; p. (1981) 106,498.

Andalucia, region, covering southern **Spain**; Córdoba, Seville, Jaén and Granada, celebrated ctrs. in Moorish times; irrigation for wines, olives, fruits.

Andaman and Nicobar Is., Bay of Bengal; constituted a union terr., **India**, 1956; hilly remnants of drowned mtn. chain; primitive pygmy tribes; a. 8,327 km²; p. (1981) 188,741.

Anderlecht, t., residtl. and industl. sub. of Brussels, **Belgium**; p. (est. 1983) 94,715.

Andermatt, v., Uri, **Switzerland**; at foot of Mt. St. Gotthard; tourist ctr., winter health resort; p. (1970) 1,589.

Anderson, t., Ind., **USA**; car components; p. (1980) 64,695 (c.), 139,336 (met. a.).

Andes, gr. volcanic mtn. system, **S. America**; extends over 6,400 km from N.–S.; physical and climatic divide rising to over 6,000 m; densely populated; high tropical plateaux; rich in minerals; hgst. peak, Aconcagua (6,965 m).

Andhra Pradesh, st. S.E. **India**; cap. Hyderabad; inc. valleys of lower Godavari and Krishna Rs.; sugar, rice; a. 275,278 km²; p. (est. 1981) 53,549,673.

Andizhan, c. Uzbek SSR, **USSR**; once residence of Khans of Khokan; industl. ctr.; in irrigation a.; cotton, silk; oilfields; p. (est. 1980) 233,000.

Andorra, sm. mtn. st., E. Pyrenees; under joint suzerainty of French President and Bishop of Urgel (Spain); virtually indep.; livestock, wines, tobacco; tourism having fundamental social and economic consequences; alt. 900–3,000 m; a. 495 km²; p. (est. 1974) 24,807.

Andover, mkt. t., Test Valley, Hants., **Eng.**; prehistoric earthwks.; expanded t.; p. (1981) 31,006.

Andria, t., S. **Italy**; Roman remains, cath., palaces; p. (1981) 83,319.

Andros, lgst. I., **Bahamas**; sponges, sisal, hemp; p. (est. 1969) 75,000.

Andújar, t., **Spain**; on Guadalquivir R.; mineral springs, pottery, soap, textiles, uranium plant; p. (1981) 30,875.

Angara, R., Siberia, **USSR**; trib. of Yenisey; navigable almost its entire length., rises nr. and flows through L. Baykal; length 2,080 km; hydro-electric power.

Angarsk, t., E. Siberia, **USSR**; on R. Angaar 32 km N.W. Irkutsk; engin., saw milling; p. (est. 1980) 241,000.

Angel Falls (Salto del Angel), waterfall, **Venezuela**; nr. Ciudad Bolivar; 980 m drop.

Angerman, R., N. **Sweden** rises nr. Norwegian border, falls to G. of Bothnia; timber transport; 448 km long.

Angers, t., cap. of Maine-et-Loire dep., **France**; on R. Maine; mkt. t. for local produce, fruit, vegetables, Anjou wines, Cointreau; textiles; cath., cas.; p. (1982) 141,143.

Angkor, c., **Cambodia;** jungle-covered ruins of c. from Khmer civilisation; discovered 1860.

Anglesey (Ynys Môn), former co., l. gov. dist., Gwynedd, **Wales;** separated from mainland by Menai Straits; former stronghold of Druids, attacked by Romans A.D. 61; mainly agr. and tourism; p. (1981) 67,340.

Angola, People's Rep. of (Port. W. Africa), W. Africa; interior forms part of central African plateaux, bounded by transitional escarpments in W. which face on to narrow coastal plain; rainfall diminishes from N.–S. with consequent crop zoning; coffee, cotton, oil palm in N., corn, peanuts, sisal in drier interior, cattle in S., semi-desert in S.E.; economy dependent upon primary inds., especially agr.; coffee major exp., produced on plantations; newly discovered oil-fields; diamonds in remote N.E. Luanda dis.; iron-ore mng. impt. at Cassinga; little mftg.; hydroelectric scheme on Cuarza R.; pts. on natural harbours impt. transhipment points for land-locked central African ctys.; indep. 1975, followed by civil war between rival guerrilla groups; cap. Luanda; a. 1,246,375 km²; p. (est. 1983) 8,339,000 (inc. Cabinda).

Angoulême, mftg. t., Charente, **France;** on R. Charente; cognac, paper; cath.; suffered during Huguenot wars; p. (1982) 50,151.

Angra do Heroismo, t., cap. admin. dist. **Azores;** pt. on Terceira I.; p. (est. 1970) 105,800 (dist.).

Angren, t., Uzbek SSR, **USSR;** E. of Tashkent; lgst. ctr. of lignite mng. in central Asia; p. (est. 1980) 108,000.

Anguilla I., Leeward Is., **W.I.;** dry climate, thin limestone soil; exp. cotton, salt; a. 91 km²; reverted to Brit. Crown after secession from St. Kitts-Nevis ass. st. 1967; status of separate Brit. dependency and withdrawal from St. Kitts-Nevis ass. statehood 1980; p. (est. 1971) 6,000.

Angus, l. gov. dist., former co., **Scot.;** part of Tayside Reg.; a. 1,937 km²; p. (1981) 92,841.

Anhui (Anhwei), prov., E. central **China;** in delta region of Chang Jiang; a. 140,686 km²; cap. Hefei; soya-beans, rice, tea, coal and iron; p. (est. 1983) 50,560,000.

Aniakchak, volcano, S.W. Alaska, **USA;** rich variety of flora and fauna on crater floor; alt. 1,384 m.

Anjou, former prov. of **France;** mainly S. of lower R. Loire; ch. t. Angers.

Ankara, c., cap. of **Turkey** since 1923; alt. 1,037 m; univ., cultural and admin. ctr.; p. (1980) 1,877,755.

Anklesvar, t., Gujarat, **India;** natural gas, oil; gas pipelines to Ultaran and Barodi; p. (1961) 20,287.

'Annaba, spt., **Algeria;** on fertile plain; phosphates, iron and steel wks.; p. (1966) 152,006 (c.), 168,790 (met. a.).

Annaberg-Bucholz, t., Karl-Marx-Stadt, **E. Germany;** in Erz Mtns.; cobalt, tin, uranium mng.; p. (est. 1970) 27,892.

Annam, region, **Vietnam;** formerly within French Union; divided by 17th parallel bdy. (1957); a. 147,560 km²; ch. t. Hué.

Annamese Cordillera, cstl. mtn. range, **Laos, Vietnam;** N.–S. watershed between Mekong and S. China Sea; rising to 2,000 m in Ngoc Linh; forested; inhabited by hill tribes.

Annan, royal burgh, Annandale and Eskdale, **Scot.;** on R. Annan, 3 km from its mouth in Solway F.; Chapelcross reactor sta.; p. (1981) 8,285.

Annandale and Eskdale, l. gov. dist., Dumfries and Galloway, **Scot.;** close to Borders Reg. and Eng.; p. (1981) 35,338.

Annapolis, c., cap. of Maryland, **USA;** naval academy; p. (1970) 29,592.

Annapolis Valley, Nova Scotia, **Canada;** famous fruit growing a., especially for apples.

Annapurna, massif, **Nepal;** part of Himalayas; many glaciers in W. and N.W.; alt. 8,080 m.

Ann Arbor, c., Mich., **USA;** on the Huron; univ. of Michigan.; motor lorries, farm implements, scientific instruments; p. (1980) 64,695 (c.), 139,336 (met. a.).

Annecy, t., **France;** dep. of Haute-Savoie; at lower end of beautiful L. Annecy; textiles, paper, watches; resort; p. (1982) 51,593.

Anqing (Anching), c., Anhui prov., **China;** R. pt. on Chang Jiang; tr. in agr. prods.; p. (est. 1970) 160,000.

Ansbach, t., Bavaria, **W. Germany;** machin.,

metallurgy, furniture indus.; rly. ctr.; p. (est. 1983) 38,000.

An-shan, c., Liaoning, N. **China;** at foot of Qian Shan, 96 km S.W. of Shenyang; lgst. iron and steel complex in China (fully automated steel plant), elec. and locomotive ind.; p. (est. 1983) 1,240,000.

Antakya (Antioch), anc. c., S. **Turkey;** on R. Orontes; cap. of Hatay prov., major Roman cap. and early ctr. of Christian culture; p. (1965) 57,584.

Antalya, c., S.W. **Turkey;** spt. with shallow harbour from which Paul and Barnabas sailed to Antakya; tourism; p. (1980) 173,301.

Antananarivo (Tananarive), cap. of **Madagascar;** ctr. of commerce and communications; airpt.; lge meat preserving factories, plastics, radios, car assembly, shoes, knitted gds.; rice mills; univ.; p. (est. 1985) 662,585.

Antarctica, plateau continent within A. circle; snow-covered, extensive ice sheets and glaciers; volcanoes and Is.; alt. 2,000–3,000 m; dependencies of U.K., Australia, N.Z., France, Norway but a. S. of 60° S reserved for peaceful international scientific research; a. 16 million km².

Antarctic Ocean, parts of Pac., Atl. and Indian Oceans, S. of 60° S.; cold and dangerous; no mammalian life other than whales.

Antibes, t., Alpes-Maritimes, N. of Cap d. A., S.E. **France;** spt. on Fr. Riviera; exp. oranges; flowers for perfume mnfs.; resort; Roman remains; p. (1982) 63,248.

Anticosti, barren I. in G. of St. Lawrence, Quebec, **Canada;** well wooded game reverse, lumbering; 224 km by 45 km.

Antigua, anc. c., **Guatemala;** 32 km W. of Guatemala c.; former cap., destroyed by earthquake 1773; comm. ctr. in coffee dist.; notable colonial ruins; tourism; p. (1971) 17,809.

Antigua and Barbuda, Leeward gr., **W.I.;** aut. st. in ass. with Gt. Britain; indep. 1981; semi-arid limestone; 75 per cent p. in N.E.; sugar, cotton, tourism; cap. St. Johns; a. (inc. Barbuda and Redonda) 440 km²; p. (est. 1980) 100,000.

Antilles, Greater and **Lesser,** archipelago enclosing Caribbean Sea and G. of Mexico, **W.I.;** complex political structure, tropical climate and crops; a. c. 259,000 km².

Antioquia, mtnous. dep. **Colombia;** colonial mng.; agr. now more impt.; one of major p. clusters in Colombia inc. dep. cap. Medellin; a 65,791 km²; p. (est. 1979) 3,647,246.

Antisana, volcano, central **Ecuador;** alt. 5,708 m.

Antofagasta, spt., **Chile;** cap., comm. and industl. ctr. of A. prov; exps. copper from Chuquicamata; situated in desert, water supply 240 km by aqueduct from Andes; p. (est. 1984) 172,669.

Antony, t., Hauts-de-Seine, **France;** brick wks., toys; sub. of Paris; p. (1982) 54,668.

Antrim, former co.; l. gov. dist., **N. Ireland;** fertile lowland a., arable agr.; borders L. Neagh in S.W. and A. mtns. in N.E.; p. (1981) 44,804.

Antrim, mkt. t., **N. Ireland;** on Lough Neagh; linen, nylon; p. (1981) 22,342.

Antsiranana, (Diego Suarez), t., extreme N. of **Madagascar;** oxygen plant; Fr. naval base; p. (1975) 40,443.

An-tung. See Dandong.

Antwerp, (Anvers), low-lying prov., N. **Belgium:** grain, flax; a. 2,859 km²; p. (est. 1983) 799,909.

Antwerp, (Anvers), spt., **Belgium;** on Scheldt R., 88 km from sea; major transit pt. for EEC, competes with Rotterdam; oil pt., refineries; diamonds; Gothic cath.; of artistic and historic interest; p. (1981) 185,897.

Anuradhapura, anc. cap., **Sri Lanka;** ctr. of Buddhism; comm. ctr of irrigated rice-growing a. in dry zone; p. (1981) 36,248.

An-yang, c., Henan prov., **China;** coal, cotton ind.; former cap. of Shang dynasty; p. (1980) 253,541.

Anzhero-Sudzhensk, t., S.W. Siberia, **USSR;** nr. Tomsk; coal mng., mng. equipment pharmaceutics; p. (est. 1980) 107,000.

Aomori, spt., N. Honshu, **Japan;** on A. Bay; cstl. tr. of timber, fish with Hokkaido; S. outlet of Seikan Tunnel between Honshu and Hokkaido; cap. of apple-growing A. prov.; p. (est. 1984) 287,594.

Aosta, t., cap. of Val d'Aosta, N. **Italy;** in valley of Dora Baltea at node of trans-Alpine routes; iron inds.; Mont Blanc road tunnel links to Chamonix, Switzerland, opened 1964; cath., p. (1981) 37,682.

Apapa, spt., sub. of Lagos, **Nigeria;** on mainland opposite I. on which Lagos is situated; modern pt. terminus of W. Nigerian rly. system; exp. agr. prods.; imports industl. prods.

Apeldoorn, c., Gelderland, **Netherlands**; holiday resort; royal summer palace of Het Loo; p. (1982) 142,367.

Apennines, mtn. "backbone" of **Italy**; rich in minerals inc. Carrara marble; cultivation on lower slopes; earthquakes, in S.; barrier to E.–W. communications; hgst. alt. 2,916 m, (Grand Sasso d'Italia); length N.–S. 1,280 km; width 120 km.

Apia, spt., N. Upolu, cap. of **W. Samoa**; exp. agr. prods.; p. (1974) 32,616.

Apolda, t., Erfurt, **E. Germany**; ball-casting and museum; p. (est. 1970) 29,087.

Appalachian Mtns., parallel ranges between Atl. Oc. and Mississippi basin, stretching for 2,560 km from Me. to Ala., **USA**; afforestation, hydro-elec. power, coal in N., iron ore in S.; region of human poverty; average alt. 900 m; Mt. Mitchell 2,039 m.

Appenzell, can., N.E. **Switzerland**; divided into the half-cans. Appenzell Inner-Rhoden, a. 174 km², cap. Appenzell; and Appenzell Ausser-Rhoden; textiles, agr.; a. 243 km², cap. Herisau; p. (1980) 60,455.

Appenzell, picturesque t., cap. of A. can., **Switzerland**; on R. Sitter; lace, embroidery; p. (1970) 5,217.

Appian Way, anc. highway; runs from Rome to Campania and S. **Italy**.

Appleby, t., Eden, Cumbria, **Eng.**; mkt. t. on R. Eden; cas.; p. (1981) 2,384.

Appleton, c., Wis., **USA**; industl. c. in rich dairy dist.; p. (1980) 291,000 (with Oshkosh).

Apsheron, peninsula, E. Azerbaydzhan SSR, **USSR**; on W. side of the Caspian; petroleum wells (nr. Baku) and mud volcanoes.

Apulia, region, S.E. **Italy**; hilly, cstl., pastoral plain; grain, fruits, livestock; wine, olive oil; a, 19,347 km²; p. (1981) 3,871,617.

Aqaba, t., **Jordan**'s only spt. at head of G. of A., 88 km from Israeli Elat.; exp. phosphates, imports petroleum; p. (est. 1964) 10,000.

Aqaba G., Red Sea, between **Sinai Peninsula** and **Saudi Arabia**; impt. Biblical waterway; few natural harbours, Dahab, Elat, Aqaba main pts; Elat ctr. of mng. a., and airpt.; length 160 km, width 24 km.

Aquila (L'Aquila), t., cap. of Abruzzi prov., **Italy**; on R. terrace of R. Aterno; mkt. and sm. inds. ass. with local farming; holiday resort; cath.; p. (1981) 63,678.

Aquitaine, Basin of, geographical region, S.W. **France**; to W. and S.W. of Central Massif, to N. of Pyrenees, bordered on W. by Atl. Oc.; warm, wet, oceanic climate; rich agr. lowland; inc. Landes, reclaimed sandy area; cath. ts. Bordeaux, Toulouse; p. (1982) 2,646,800.

Arabia, peninsula, **S.W. Asia**; mainly desert plateau, lying between Red Sea and Persian Gulf; inc. Saudi Arabia, South Yemen, North Yemen, Oman, United Arab Emirates, Kuwait, Bahrain, Qatar; coffee, dates, gums, horses, camels; E. Arabia rich in oil reserves; a. 2,590,000 km²; p. 8,000,000.

Arabian Desert, E. **Egypt**; between R. Nile and Red Sea; alt. approx. 350–2,000 m; a. 207,200 km².

Arabian Mtns., ridge along W. and S.W. csts. of **Arabia**; volcanic, hgst. peaks in Yemen Arab Rep.; average alt. 1,500 m, rising to over 3,500 km.

Arabian Sea, N.W. part of Indian Oc., tr. in Arab dhows; width 2,880 km.

Aracaju, spt., cap. of Sergipe st., **Brazil**; sugar, soap, textiles, tanneries; p. (est. 1980) 273,100.

Arad, new t. (1962) **Israel**; in Negev desert, nr. Beersheba; inds. to be based on gasfields at Zohar and Kanaim; chemicals.

Arad, t., **Romania**; industl., route ctr. on R. Mures; p. (1980) 174,411.

Arafura Sea, N. of Australia, S.W. of Papua-New Guinea, and E. of Timor.

Aragua, sm. upland cstl. st., **Venezuela**; lies in densely populated industl., agr., urban and political region of cty.; tropical climate; good road network; cap. Maracay in fertile Aragua valley; a. 7,014 km²; p. (1981) 891,623.

Araguaia, R., **Brazil**; trib. of Tocatins R.; splits into 2 parts in middle course to form Banaral I.; rapids; length 1,800 km.

Arak, t., **Iran**; mkt. and agr. processing ctr. for surrounding region on Trans-Iranian rly.; carpets; p. (1976) 114,507.

Aral Sea (Aral'skoye More), inland sea with no outlet, **USSR**; fed by Amu-Dar'ya and Syr Dar'ya Rs.; sparse p. on shore but attempts to develop agr.; a. 63,805 km².

Aran Is.; Galway, **R.o.I.**; inc. anc. religious ctr. and I. of Inishmore; fishing; agr.; a. 47 km²; p. (1966) 1,612.

Arandelovac, t., **Yugoslavia**; industl. a. based on local sources of refractory clays; tourist resort.

Aranjuez, t., **Spain**; 18th cent. planned t. on R. Tagus; mkt. gardens; strawberries, asparagus; p. (1981) 35,484.

Ararat, volcanic mtn., **Turkey**; supposed resting-place of Noah's Ark.; 5.168 m.

Ararat, t., Victoria, **Australia**; former gold rush t. on W. Highway and ctr. for Grampians; p. (1976) 8,288.

Aras (Araxes) R., flows from Bingöl Daḡlari mtns. (**Turkey**) to Caspian Sea forming long sections of USSR–Iran frontier; valley in rich fruit growing a.; home of anc. civilisation; length 880 km.

Araucania, terr., **Chile**; concentration of A. Indians, especially in Rio Tolten valley; a. 31,761 km²; p. (est. 1984) 675,741.

Arbroath, royal burgh, Angus cst., **Scot.**; engin., textiles, fishing pt.; holiday resort; p. (1981) 24,093.

Arcachon, t., Gironde, S.W. **France**; on S. side of Bassin d'Arcachon, Bay of Biscay; fish. pt., oysters; resort; p. (1982) 13,664.

Arcadia, region of anc. **Greece** in Peloponnesus; tradition of pastoral agr. in dry a.; ch. c. was Megalopolis.

Arctic Ocean, almost landlocked sea extending from N. Pole to Atl. Oc.; flora and fauna of scientific interest; a. 14,089,600 km².

Ardabil, anc. c. in fertile agr. a., Azerbaijan, **Iran**; tr. and route ctr.; carpets; p. (1976) 147,846.

Ardal, t., **Norway**; on Sogne fiord; site of aluminium wks.

Ardèche, dep., S. **France**; Cevennes Mtns.; olives, wine, silk, minerals; cap. Privas; a. 55,530 km²; p. (1982) 268,400.

Ardennes, hilly wooded region, **Belgium**, N. **France**, **Luxembourg**, rising to over 600 m; infertile; heavy fighting in both world wars.

Ardennes, dep., N.E. **France**; farming, woollens, iron; cap. Mézières; a. 5,250 km²; p. (1982) 301,900.

Ardglass, sm. t., Down, **N. Ireland**; one of N.I.'s impt. fishing pts.

Ardnacrusha, Clare, **R.o.I.**; power sta. on R. Shannon, 5 km N. of Limerick.

Ardrishaig, sm. spt., Argyll and Bute, **Scot.**; on Loch Gilp, at entrance to Crinan canal; p. (1981) 1,322.

Ardrossan, burgh, Cunninghame, S.W. **Scot.**; resort and spt. on Firth of Clyde; oil storage, ship-bldg., road bitumen, engin.; p. (1981) 11,337.

Ards, l. gov. dist., **N. Ireland**; formerly part of Down; N. of Strangford L.; main t. New-townards; p. (1981) 57,502.

Arecibo, spt., N. cst. **Puerto Rico**; sited in rich agr. a.; local hydroelec. power; p. (1970) 72,283.

Arendal, spt. **Norway**; on Skagerrak; wood pulp, aluminium, shipping; p. (est. 1970) 11,831.

Arequipa, c., **Peru**; cap. of A. prov. and former Inca c.; impt. wool mkt.; alpaca wool inds.; growth point for prov. industl. development; copper mng. nearby; earthquakes frequent; p. (1981) 447,431.

Arezzo, c., cap. of Arezzo prov., Tuscany, **Italy**; hill site in basin within Apennines at junc. of valley routes; in mediaeval times ctr. of learning and the arts; birthplace of Petrarch and Vasari; Gothic cath.; mkt. for silk, wine, olives; p. (1981) 92,105.

Arfon, l. gov. dist., Gwynedd, **Wales**; borders Menai Straits and inc. Bangor and Caernarvon; p. (1981) 52,284.

Argenteuil, t., Val-d'Oise, **France**; N.W. sub. of Paris; industl., mkt. gardens; p. (1982) 96,045.

Argentina, fed. rep., **S. America**; 2nd. in a., 3rd. in p. of S. American sts.; p. predominantly of European origin and highly urbanised; varied relief and climate, inc. Andes, tropical N., Chaco, Pampas, Patagonia in S.; agr. less impt. internally than other S. American sts., yet provides most of exp., inc. meat, wool, wheat, maize, cotton; petroleum, natural gas; cap. Buenos Aires; new cap. to be built in Patagonia (planned 1986); a. 2,797,109 km² p. (est. 1984) 30,094,000.

Argonne, hill ridge, S.E. Paris basin, **France;** composed of greensand; wooded; fighting in 2nd world war; alt. 300 m; a. c. 650 km².

Argos, c. of anc. **Greece;** N.E. Peloponnesus; leading c. in 7th cent. B.C. under King Pheidon; p. (1981) 20,955.

Argostólion, cap. of Cephalonia I., **Greece;** shipbldg.; earthquake 1953; p. (1971) 7,521.

Argyll, former co., N.W. **Scot.;** now divided between Highland and Strathclyde Regs.

Argyll and Bute, l. gov. dist., Strathclyde Reg., **Scot.;** rural a. N.W. of Glasgow conurb.; a. 6,754 km²; p. (1981) 68,786.

Arhus, c., **Denmark;** prin. spt. on E. cst. Jutland; admin. ctr. of A. prov.; Gothic cath.; univ.; comm. and industl. ctr.; pt. processing inds., oil refining; p. (est. 1977) 245,866.

Arica, spt., N. **Chile,** free zone; exp. tin, copper, sulphur mainly from Bolivia; rly. to La Paz and oil pipeline connects to Sica-Sica in Bolivia; p. (est. 1984) 125,574.

Ariège, dep., S. **France;** Pyrenees in S., fertile lowland in N.; livestock, fruit, iron, copper; cap. Foix; a. 4,900 km²; p. (1982) 135,200.

Arizona, st., **USA;** home of Apache Indians; much desert, rainfall increasing to E.; many lge. irrigation schemes for cotton, grain, fruit, vegetables; inc. Col. Plateau and Grand Canyon to N.; copper, lead mng. and refining; prin. ts. Phoenix (cap.), Tucson; huge meteorite crater nr. Winslow; admitted to union 1912; st. flower Saguaro Cactus blossom; st. bird cactus wren; a. 295,024 km²; p. (1980) 2,718,000.

Arkansas, st., **USA;** highland in N.W., inc. Ozark, Ouachita mtns., lowland in S.E. where Arkansas R. and Mississippi alluvium; humid climate; cotton cultivation; bauxite, coal, petroleum; admitted to union 1836; st. flower Apple Blossom, st. bird Mockingbird; cap. Little Rock; a. 137,534 km²; p. (1980) 2,286,000.

Arkansas, R., **USA;** rises in Rockies, trib. of Mississippi; completion (1971) of 704 km waterway (17 dams and locks), opening Okla. and Ark. to sea; flows through impt. agr. as.; several major cs. on banks; length 2,334 km.

Arkhangel'sk, c., major spt., **USSR;** on E. side Dvina estuary, White Sea; lge. harbour kept open in winter by ice breakers; fishery headquarters; inds. from local softwood resources; engin.; hydroelec. power; p. (est. 1980) 387,000.

Arklow, U.D., spt., Wicklow, **R.o.I.;** fisheries, pottery; fertiliser plant under construction; resort; p. (1981) 8,646.

Arlberg, Alpine pass, 1,803 m; main western entry to Austria; rly. tunnel 10 km long; road tunnel (1979) 14 km long.

Arles, t., Provence, S. **France;** on Rhône delta; anc. Roman t.; historic bldgs and monuments; van Gogh and Gauguin painted here; p. (1982) 50,772.

Arlington, t., Texas, **USA;** aircraft, missiles; rapid expansion; p. (1980) 160,000.

Arlington, t., Va., **USA;** Arlington National Cemetery contains tombs of the Unknown Soldier and President Kennedy.

Arlon, t., cap. of Luxembourg prov., **Belgium;** p. (1982) 22,364.

Armadale, burgh, West Lothian, **Scot.;** 16 km S.W. Linlithgow; p. (1981) 9,530.

Armagh, former co.; l. gov. dist., **N. Ireland;** lowland in N. rising to over 450 m adjoins R.o.I. border; mainly rural; p. (1981) 48,105.

Armagh, t., **N. Ireland;** caths.; linen, whiskey; p. (1981) 12,700.

Armavir, c., Krasnodar Terr., **RSFSR;** on Kuban R.; rly. junc.; engin.; food processing; p. (est. 1980) 163,000.

Armenia, constituent rep., **USSR;** former a. divided between Turkey, Russia, Iran; rich mineral deposits, mineral inds.; sub-tropical agr.; hydroelec. stas. under constr.; cap. Yerevan; a. 30.821 km²; p. (1970) 2,493,000.

Armenia, t., **Colombia;** coffee; p. (1973) 147,635.

Armentières, mftg. t., Nord, **France;** base of British operations against Lille in first world war; textiles; p. (1982) 55,913 (French met. a.).

Armidale, t., N.S.W., **Australia;** ctr. of New England wool producing dist.; p. (1976) 19,711.

Arnhem, c., cap. of Gelderland prov., **Neth.;** on R. Neder-Rhine; lge. rin smelter; lt. inds. using rubber and rayon; p. (1982) 129,160.

Arnhem Land, N. part of N.T., **Australia;** an aboriginal reserve; bauxite worked, uranium finds.

Arno, R., central **Italy;** flows past Florence and Pisa into Mediterranean; Val d'Arno is the fruitful valley of the R.; length 120 km.

Arnold, t., Gedling, Notts., **Eng.;** almost continuous with Nottingham; hosiery, brick mkg.; p. (1981) 37,242.

Arnstadt, t., Erfurt, **E. Germany;** on R. Gera, 16 km S. of Erfurt; artificial silk, leather gds., engin.; p. (est. 1970) 28,762.

Aroostook, dist., New England, **USA;** produces 12 per cent of USA potatoes.

Arran, I., Cunninghame, **Scot.;** in Firth of Clyde; contains many summer resorts; a. 427 km²; p. (1971) 3,576.

Arras, t., cap. of Pas-de-Calais dep., **France;** historic cap. of Artois; renowned for tapestry; agr. mkt.; brewing, textiles, metal inds.; almost destroyed in first world war; p. (1982) 80,477 (met. a.).

Árta, t., cap. of Árta prov., Epirus, **Greece;** agr. tr. ctr.; Ambracia was its name in anc. Greece; p. (1981) 20,004.

Artemovsk, t., Ukrainian SSR, **USSR;** industl. ctr. in Donets Basin; salt, coal, iron, mercury; p. (est. 1969) 81,000.

Arthur's Seat, famous hill, Edinburgh, **Scot.;** 251 m.

Artois, former prov. of N. **France;** now mainly with dep. of Pas-de-Calais.

Aru Is., gr., **Indonesia;** S.W. of W. Irian; fertile; sago, rice, sugar, coconuts, tobacco; a. 8,402 km²; p. 18,139.

Aruba, I., Leeward Is., **Neth. Antilles;** closure of oil refinery (1985) which provided employment and one-third gov. receipts; shipping; guano; voted for indep. from gr. (1977) internal self-government granted 1986; a. 176 km²; p. (1968) 59,020.

Arun, l. gov. dist., West Sussex, **Eng.;** W. section of S. Downs and ts. of Arundel, Littlehampton and Bognor Regis; p. (1981) 119,206.

Arunachal Pradesh, new union terr. (1972), N.E. Assam, **India;** formerly N.E. Frontier Agency; in Himalayas bordering Tibet and Burma; tribal p.; cap. Itanagar; a. 81,424 km²; p. (1981) 631,839.

Arundel, t., Arun, West Sussex, **Eng.;** mkt. t. on Arun R.; Arundel Castle, seat of Duke of Norfolk; p. (1981) 2,235.

Arusha, t., **Tanzania;** S.W. of Mt. Meru; mkt. for coffee; H.Q. of E. African Common Market; airpt. at 1,388 m (W. of t.); p. (est. 1978) 88,155.

Aruwimi, R., **Zaïre;** trib. of R. Zaïre; route of Stanley's famous forest march in 1887; 992 km long.

Arvida, t., S. Quebec, **Canada;** aluminium plant; nearby Saguenay power development; p. (1971) 18,433.

Arvika, t., N. of L. Vänern, **Sweden;** agr. machin. and implements, pianos, organs; p. (est. 1970) 15,998.

Asahigawa, c., Hokkaido, **Japan;** on Ishikari R.; industl., comm. and rly. ctr. for gr. agr. region; p. (est. 1984) 352,619.

Asansol, t., W. Bengal, **India;** in Damodar valley; rly. junc.; coal mng., iron, steel; p. (1981) 187,039 (c.), 366,424 (met. a.).

Ascension I., part of Brit. col. **St. Helena,** 1,216 km to S.E.; volcanic; ch. settlement Georgetown; nesting place of sooty tern; Brit. earth satellite sta. (1966); airstrip known as Miracle Mile; some arable and pastoral agr.; a. 88 km²; p. (est. 1976) 1,154.

Aschaffenburg, t., Bavaria, **W. Germany;** pt. on R. Main and Trans-European waterway; cas.; synthetic fibres, scientific-based inds.; p. (est. 1983) 59,600.

Aschersleben, t., Halle, **E. Germany;** potash and lignite mng., chemicals, textiles, engin., horticulture; p. (est. 1973) 37,150.

Ascoli Piceno, cath. c., central **Italy;** cap. of A.P. prov.; lies in wooded hills; agr. inds.; (1981) 54,298.

Ascot, v., Berks., **Eng.;** famous racecourse at Ascot Heath.

Ashanti, admin. region, central **Ghana;** formerly powerful native st.; timber, cocoa; growing importance of gold mines (15% Ghana's exp.); new mines opened 1984; cap. Kumasi; a. 24,390 km²; p. (1984) 2,089,683.

Ashbourne, t., West Derbys., **Eng.;** nr. Dovedale; mkt. t.; quarrying, milk processing; p. (1981) 5,960.

Ashburton, t., Teignbridge, Devon, **Eng.;** old mkt. t., S. gateway to Dartmoor; anc. stannary t.; p. (1981) 3,564.

Ashburton, t., S. Island, **N.Z.**; ctr. of gr. wheat growing dist.; p. (1976) 14,225.

Ashby-de-la-Zouch, t., North West Leics., **Eng.**; local coal-mng., hosiery; p. (1981) 11,518.

Ashby Woulds, t., North West Leics., **Eng.**; clay mng., pottery; p. (1981) 3,015.

Ashdod, pt., **Israel**; new modern deepwater pt. on Med. cst., 32 km S. of Jaffa.

Ashdown Forest, East Sussex, **Eng.**; heath and woodland; site of former iron industry.

Asheville, c., N.C., **USA**; economic and cultural ctr. of mtnous. region; winter resort; glass; p. (1980) 53,583 (c.), 177,761 (met. a.).

Ashfield, l. gov. dist., Notts., **Eng.**; comprises Sutton-in-Ashfield, Hucknall and Kirkby A.; p. (1981) 106, 521.

Ashford, t., l. gov. dist., Kent, **Eng.**; mkt. t., rly. works closing down but may be kept open if channel tunnel started; p. (1981) 85,832 (dist.).

Ashikaga, c., Honshu, **Japan**; cultural ctr.; old silk-weaving ctr.; anc. school with library of Chinese classics; p. (1979) 166,502.

Ashington, t., Wansbeck, Northumberland, **Eng.**; coal mng., p. (1981) 23,658.

Ashkhabad, c., cap. of Turkmen SSR, **USSR**; in foothills of Kopet-Dag mtns.; textiles, clothing, food processing; univ.; p. (est. 1984) 347,000.

Ashland, t., Ky., **USA**; on R. Ohio; iron, steel, lumber, leather; p. (1980) 27,064.

Ashtabula, t., Ohio, **USA**; pt. on L. Erie handling iron ore, coal; many diversified inds.; p. (1980) 23,449.

Ashton-in-Makerfield, t. Gtr. Manchester, **Eng.**; nr. Wigan; former coal mng.; p. (1981) 29,341.

Ashton-under-Lyne, t., Tameside, Gtr. Manchester, **Eng.**; textiles, lt. engin., rubber, tobacco; p. (1981) 44,671.

Asia, largest continent, extends over nearly one-third of the land surface of the earth; chief mtn. ranges, Himalayas, Kunlun, Tien Shan, Altai, Tibetan plateau; ch. Rs., Ob, Yangtze, Yenisey, Lena, Amur, Hwang-ho, Mekong; deserts, Arabia, Thar, Takla Makan, Gobi; some very fertile valleys and plains; climate very varied, extreme in N., monsoonal in S. and E.; gold, coal, oil, iron, manganese, antimony, tin; principal countries in Asia: Turkey in Asia, Israel, Jordan, Iran, Iraq, Afghanistan, India, Pakistan, Sri Lanka, Burma, China, Vietnam, Indonesia, Thailand, Malaysia, Korea, Japan, Bangladesh, Kampuchea, Laos, Philippines, Korea, Syria, Lebanon, Taiwan, and Soviet Asia; industrialisation greatest in Japan, China, India, and Soviet Asia; a. c. 43,250,000 km²; p. (est. 1984) 2,777,385,000 (58 per cent of world total).

Asia Minor. *See* Anatolia.

Asir, dist., S.W. **Saudi Arabia**; desert cstl. plain with parallel A. mtns.

Askja, volcanic crater, L. and lava plain, E. **Iceland**; surrounded by Dyngju-fjöll Hills; alt. 1,450 m.

Asmara, c., **Ethiopia**; alt. 2,226 m; on rly.; textiles, matches, soap, brewing; p. (est. 1980) 443,060.

Asnières, t., sub. N.W. Paris, Hauts-de-Seine, **France**; regattas; p. (1982) 71,220.

Aspra Spitia, t. central **Greece**; new industl. t. close to Andikira Bay; aluminium wks.

Aspull, t., Gtr. Manchester, **Eng.**; nr. Wigan; former coal mng.; p. (1981) 6,816.

Assab, pt. on Red Sea, **Ethiopia**; oil refinery; p. (est. 1970) 14,900.

Assam, st., **India**; on Brahmaputra R.; valley enclosed by mtns.; forested; extensive tea plantations; rice, cotton, coal; oil development at Brudrasagar; former cap. Shillong; since 1956 4 new sts. carved out – Nagaland (1963), Meghalaya, Manipur, Tripura (1972), and union terrs. of Arunachal Pradesh and Mizoram (1972); a. (1972) 121,973 km²; p. (est. 1981) 19,896,843.

Assen, t., prov. cap. Drenthe, **Neth.**; route ctr.; food processing; p. (1982) 45,517.

Assiniboine, R., Manitoba, **Canada**; joins Red R. at Winnipeg; 720 km long.

Assisi, t., Umbria, central **Italy**; 24 km S.E. of Perugia; birthplace of St. Francis; cath. and old cas.; p. (1981) 24,440.

Assyria, gr. anc. empire, northern plain Mesopotamia (Iraq), cap. Nineveh; drained by R. Tigris; now mainly pastoral farming a.

Astara, pt., Azerbaydzhan, **USSR**; on Caspian Sea, at frontier with Iran; natural gas pipeline.

Asti, t., **Italy**; route, industl., comm. ctr.; cath.; sparkling wines; p. (1981) 77,681.

Astin Tagh, (Aerchin Shan), mtn. range, S., Sinkiang, **China**; N. branch of Kunlun mtn. system which separates Tibet from Turkestan; rises to 5,000 m.

Astrakhan', c., **RSFSR**; major air and sea pt. on delta of R. Volga, 80 km from Caspian Sea; handles petroleum, timber; lge. fishing fleet; caviar; food and pt. processing inds.; astrakhan fur; cap. A. oblast; univ.; p. (est. 1980) 465,000.

Asturias, region and former kingdom, N.W. **Spain**; S. of Bay of Biscay; now Oviedo prov.; isolated from rest of Spain by Cantabrian mtns.; coal mng.

Asunción, c., cap. of **Paraguay**; at confluence of Rs. Paraguay and Pilcomayo; 25 per cent of p. of Paraguay in and around A.; admin., industl., comm. ctr.; cath.; p. (1982) 455,517.

Aswan, t., Upper **Egypt**; on Nile at first cataract; anc. name Syene. Aswan dam built 1902, 5 km S. of t., to control Nile flood; lge. cement plant; univ. proposed; p. (1976) 144,654.

Aswan High Dam (107 m high) opened 1971, on R. Nile, **Egypt,** 6 km S. of old Aswan dam, has harnessed R. to bring electricity and irrigation to hundreds of vs. and prevent Nile's flood from being lost into Mediterranean. *See also* Nile.

Asyût, major c. of Upper **Egypt**; nr. A. dam on Nile R.; anc. Lycopolis; noted pottery, wood, ivory carving; caravan tr. ctr.; cap, of A. prov.; p. (1976) 213,751.

Atacama Desert, N. **Chile**; arid coastal tract rich in nitrates; one of world's driest deserts.

Ataléia, t., Minas Gerais, **Brazil**; W. of Sierra des Aimorés; p. (est. 1967) 118,112.

Atami, t., Honshu, **Japan**; on Sagami Bay; seaside hot-spring resort; p. (1970) 51,281.

Atbara, t., **Sudan**; at confluence of Atbara R. with Nile; heavy inds.; international airpt.; p. (1983) 73,000.

Atbara R., or Black Nile, Ethiopia and **Sudan**; trib. of Nile; provides irrigation water for Sudan; length 1,264 km.

Athelney, hill, formerly encircled by marsh nr. Taunton, Somerset, **Eng.**; between the Rs. Tone and Parret; King Alfred's hiding-place.

Athens (Athínai), c., cap of **Greece**; on plain of Attica; admin., economic and cultural ctr.; varied mnfs., notably textiles; anc. c. of Greek art and learning; Acropolis and many splendid temples; univ.; airpt; p. (1981) 885,737 (c.) 3,027,331 (met. a.).

Athens, t., Ga., **USA**; univ.; cotton gds., lumber; p. (1980) 42,549 (c.), 130,015 (met. a.).

Athens, t., Ohio, **USA**; univ.; coal, lt. inds.; p. (1980) 19,743.

Atherstone, t., North Warwicks., **Eng.**; N. of Coventry; mkt. t., coal mng, footwear, granite quarrying.

Athlone, U.D., Westmeath, **R.o.I.**; on R. Shannon; radio sta.; textiles; p. (1981) 9,444.

Atholl, dist., N. Perth and Kinross, **Scot.**; extensive deer forests and grouse moors; a. 1,166 km².

Athos, peninsula, Khalkidhiki, N.E. **Greece**; Mt. Athos (2,034 m) at S. tip, known as Holy Mountain, home of monastic community; ch. t. Karves.

Athy, U.D., Kildare, **R.o.I.**; on Grand Canal; agr. machin.; p. (1968) 4,055.

Atitlán L., S.W. **Guatemala**; volcanic; famed for beauty; dense p. on shore; maize, fishing; a. 137 km².

Atlanta, c., st. cap. Ga., **USA**; univ.; cotton, paper, farm implements, printing, clothing; p. (1980) 425,000 (c.), 2,030,000 (met. a.).

Atlantic City, c., N.J., **USA**; summer resort, convention c.; p. (1980) 40,199 (c.), 194,119 (met. a.).

Atlantic Ocean, 2nd lgst ocean; a. est. 82,440,000 km²; connected to Pac. Oc. by Panama Canal; central ridge of volcanic activity runs S. from Iceland to Antarctic, some peaks emerging as Is. mainly in N. (*e.g.* Azores, Ascension, Tristan da Cunha); S, mainly a barren waste of water; chief deeps: Milwaukee Deep (9,225 m) nr. Bahamas and Nares Deep (8,531 m) nr. Puerto Rico.

Atlas, mtn. range, N.W. **Africa**; extends 2,400 km through Morocco, Algeria, to Tunisia; formed

K13

of several chains; mineralised, roads across passes; long been home of Berber tribes; average height 2,500–3,000 m; hgst. peak Jebel Toubkal, 4,141 m.

Atlixco Valley, t., Mexico; 16 km S.W. of Puebla; fertile volcanic soils; wheat, fruit, vegetables.

Attica, (Attikí), dep., Greece; agr., serving cap. Athens; a. 3,761 km²; p. (1981) 342,093.

Attleboro, c., Mass., USA; founded (1669) by immigrants from English Attleborough (Norfolk); jewellery, silverware; p. (1980) 34,196.

Attock, t., Pakistan; on Indus R. between Peshawar and Islamabad; oil wells, oil refining; impt. crossing of R. Indus.

Aubagne, t., Bouches-du-Rhône, **France;** bricks, tiles, corks, meat processing; p. (1981) 38,571.

Aube, dep., N.E. France; arid, infertile chalk in ctr. and N.W.; wooded and fertile S.E.; drained by Seine and A. Rs.; cap. Troyes; a. 6,024 km²; p. (1982) 289,800.

Aubervilliers, t., Seine-St. Denis, **France;** sub. of Paris; industl.; p. (1982) 67,775.

Auburn, t., N.Y., USA; shoes, woollens, farm implements; st. prison; p. (1980) 32,548.

Aubusson, t., Creuse dep., **France;** sited on Creuse R.; fine tapestries and carpets; p. (1982) 6,153.

Auch, t., cap. of Gers dep., **France;** agr., mkt., tr. in Armagnac brandy; agr. processing; p. (1982) 25,543.

Auchterarder, burgh, Perth and Kinross, **Scot.;** 24 km S.W. of Perth; health resort on S. slopes of vale of Strathearn; woollen inds.; p. (1981) 2,895.

Auchtermuchty, burgh, North East Fife, **Scot.;** at S. foot of Lomond Hills, 40 km N.E. of Alloa; distilling; p. (1981) 1,643.

Auckland, spt., c., N.I., N.Z.; lgst. c. in N.Z.; seat of government 1845–64; univ.; extensive tr. and shipping; sawmills, sugar refinery, shipbldg., glass; steelwks. projected 40 km S. of A., in Waikato iron sand a.; p. (1979) 147,600 (c.), 750,600 (met. a.).

Auckland Is., uninhabited gr. of S. **Pac. Oc.;** 320 km off N.Z.; discovered by British (1806); fur seals; a. 606 km².

Aude, dep., S. France; mtnous.; fertile N., salt from S. cstl. lagoons; drained by A. R. to Mediterranean; cap. Carcassonne; a. 6,340 km² p. (1982) 281,100.

Audenshaw, t., Gtr. Manchester, **Eng.;** metals, leather, pharmaceuticals; p. (1981) 10,744.

Aue, t., Karl-Marx-Stadt, **E. Germany;** 32 km S.E. of Zwickau; uranium mng., metallurgy, textiles; p. (est. 1973) 32,989.

Aughrim, v., Galway, **R.o.I.;** battle (1691) between William III and James II.

Augsburg, c., Bavaria, **W. Germany;** at confluence of Rs. Lech and Wertach; cath.; theological institute; major industl. ctr., textiles, engin.; route ctr.; p. (est. 1983) 246,700.

Augusta, t., Sicily, **Italy;** on E. cst. peninsula; gd. harbour used as naval base; fishing; lubricants; p. (1981) 38,900.

Augusta, c., Georgia, **USA;** pt.; on Savannah R. and boundary with S.C.; cotton, cotton-seed oil, chemicals, foundries; p. (1970) 58,483 (c.), 249,842 (met. a.).

Aulnay-sous-Bois, t., Seine-St. Denis, **France;** residtl. sub. of Paris; p. (1982) 76,032.

Aurangabad, t., admin. ctr., Maharashtra, **India;** textiles, grain tr.; p. (1971) 150,483 (t.), 165,253 (met. a.).

Aurès, mtn. massif, **Algeria;** Berber stronghold.

Aurignac, v., Haute-Garonne, S. **France;** at foot of Pyrenees; caves, paleolithic remains.

Aurillac, t., cap., mkt. t. for dep. of Cantal, **France;** cheeses, umbrellas, leather goods; p. (1982) 33,197.

Aurora, t., Ill., **USA;** rly. wks., foundries, office equipment; p. (1980) 159,000.

Aussig. See **Usti Nad Labem.**

Austin, st. cap., Texas, **USA;** educational and artistic ctr., st. univ.; food processing; international airpt.; p. (1980) 345,000 (c.), 537,000 (met. a.).

Australasia, div. of **Oceania;** inc. Australia, Tasmania, N.Z., New Guinea and neighbouring archipelagos.

Australia, Commonwealth of, lgst. I., smallest continent in world; forms part of **Australasia;** Cook took possession for Britain 1770; Com-

monwealth proclaimed 1901; fed. of N.S.W., Victoria, Queensland, S.A., W. Australia, Tasmania; inc. also Cap. Terr. (Canberra) and N.T.; p. and inds. concentrated around cst. and in st. caps.; 41 per cent live in Gtr. Sydney and Melbourne; agr. economy (sheep, wheat, dairying) giving way to mineral inds. esp. in W.A. where lge. and diverse deposits abound; offshore petroleum deposits; N. cst. tropical, interior dry, S.E. cst. more moderate, Mediterranean climate in S.W.; mtns. in E. form Gr. Dividing Range separating E. cst. from interior, where plains drained by Murray-Darling and L. Eyre R. systems (used for hydroelec. power and irrigation); cap. Canberra; a. 7,682,300 km²; p. (est. 1984) 15,519,000.

Australian Alps, form S. part of Gr. Dividing Range, between E. cst. and interior, **Australia;** extend for 320 km.; contain hgst. mtns. in Australia; Mount Kosciusko (2,228 m.); snow melt vital for irrigation of S.E.; popular tourist and naturalist a.

Australian Antarctic Terr., part of **Antarctica;** between 145° E. and 160° E. and S. of 60° S. excluding Adélie Land; research stas. of Mawson, Davis and Casey.

Australian Bight, Gr.; gr. cstl. indentation S. of Nullarbor Plain, **Australia.**

Australian Capital Territory, fed. terr. surrounding Canberra, seat of Fed. Govt. of **Australia;** also inc. a. around Jervis Bay, originally planned to serve as pt. (1976) 197,622.

Austria, rep., Europe; after long and glamorous history under the Hapsburg (**L53**), instability between A. and Hungary a cause of first world war; forcibly incorporated in German Reich, 1938, liberated 1945, recovered indep. 1955; almost entirely within Alps; drained mainly by Danube; continental climate; magnificent scenery generates a major tourist ind. but much food must be imported; forests and timber inds.; mineralised, iron-ore of Styria; hydroelec.; inds. located in ts.; cap. Vienna; a. 83,898 km²; p. (est. 1984) 7,489,000, mainly Roman Catholic.

Austria, Lower, st., Austria; impt. agr. a.; cap. Vienna; a. (excluding Vienna) 18,384 km²; p. (excluding Vienna) (1971) 1,414,161.

Auvergne, old French prov. forming the present deps. of Puy-de-Dôme, Cantal and a small part of Haute-Loire; part of Massif Central; volcanic scenery; ch. t. Clermont-Ferrand; p. (1982) 1,332,200.

Auvergne Mtns., mtns., central **France;** in N.W. of Central Massif; highest peak Puy de Sancy in Mt. Dore, 1,887 m; volcanic landscape.

Auxerre, t., cap. of Yonne dep., **France;** comm. and industl. ctr.; wine; tr.; Gothic cath.; p. (1982) 41,164.

Ava, c., Burma; on the Irrawaddy R.; former cap.; many pagodas, now ruins; bridge over R.

Avebury, v., Wilts,. **Eng.;** mediaeval v. outside Neolithic circle and avenues, nr. Silbury Hill; lgst. prehistoric structure in England.

Aveiro, t., Portugal; on Vouga estuary, connected to sea by canal; fish. pt. salt from lagoons; p. (1981) 28,625.

Avellaneda, industl. sub. of Buenos Aires, **Argentina;** hides, wool; p. (1970) 337,538.

Avellino, t., cap. of A. prov., **Italy;** on motorway from Naples to W.; monastery; sulphur mng. and refining; hats; p. (1981) 56,892.

Aversa, t. Italy; in fertile plain of Campania; agr. and route ctr.; p. (1981) 50,525.

Avesta, t., Kopparberg, **Sweden;** on Dal R.; iron, aluminium and charcoal wks.; p. (est. 1970) 28,545.

Aveyron, dep., France; on S.W. rim of Central Massif, inc. Causses limestones; extensive forests; grain, dairying, sheep; coal; cap. Rodez; a. 8,767 km²; p. (1982) 277,800.

Aviemore, t., Badenoch and Strathspey, **Scot.;** on R. Spey, 19 km S.W. of Grantown; winter sports; p. (1981) 2,426.

Avignon, t., cap. of Vaucluse, dep., **France;** anc. Roman t. at crossing of R. Rhône; Provençal tourist ctr.; diversified inds. inc. wine tr.; p. (1982) 91,474.

Avila, t., cap. of A. prov., **Spain;** in Old Castile; univ., cath.; mediaeval architecture; birthplace of St. Teresa; p. (1970) 30,938.

Avon, non-met. co., S. **Eng.;** based on Lower

Avon valley and Severnside; major ctrs. of p. at Bristol and Bath; pt. at Avonmouth; cstl. resort of Weston-super-Mare; bordered by Mendips in S.; a. 1,336 km²; p. (1981) 909,408.

Avon, R., Avon/Wiltshire, Eng.; flows from Cotswolds to enter Bristol Channel at Avonmouth; spectacular limestone gorge between Bristol and the sea; length 128 km.

Avon, R., Warwicks, Eng.; flows past Stratford-on-A., to reach Severn R. at Tewkesbury; fertile agr. valley; string of ts. along course; length 152 km.

Avon, R., Wilts./Hants./Dorset, Eng.; flows past Salisbury into English Channel at Christchurch; length 112 km.

Avonmouth, outport of Bristol, at mouth of R. Avon, Eng.; docks; seed crushing, petrol refinery, non-ferrous metal and chemical plants.

Avranches, t., Manche, France; Normandy mkt. t.; cider and dairy produce; p. (1982) 10,419.

Awe, Loch, Argyll and Bute, Scot.; 13 km W. of Inveraray, bordered by Ben Cruachan; a. 41 km², length 40 km; salmon and trout fishing; hydroelec. sta. at Cruachan.

Axholme, Isle of, flat lowland a., Boothferry, N.W. Lincs., Eng.; W. of Trent R.; drained by Vermuyden in 17th cent.

Axminster, t., East Devon, Eng.; brushes; flour and sawmills; carpet and press tool mftg.

Ayacucho, t., Peru; cap. of A. dep.; founded by Pizarro in 1539; lies in equable fertile valley; p. (est. 1970) 24,374.

Aydin, t., Turkey; anc. Tralles; rly. and agr. tr. ctr. for surrounding a.; p. (1970) 50,566.

Ayers Rock, N.T., Australia; giant terra-cotta monolith rising abruptly to 335 m; sacred to Aborigines; major tourist attraction.

Aylesbury, co. t., Aylesbury Vale, Bucks., Eng.; mkt. t.; expanded t.; p. (1981) 48,159.

Aylesbury Vale, l. gov. dist., Bucks., Eng.; a. in N.W. of co. inc. Aylesbury and Buckingham; p. (1981) 132,709.

Aylesford, mkt. t., Kent, Eng.; N.W. Maidstone.

Ayr, royal burgh, Kyle and Carrick, Scot.; pt. on F. of Clyde, 48 km S.W. of Glasgow; Burns born nearby; p. (1981) 49,481.

Ayrshire, former co. Scot.; now part of Strathclyde Region.

Aysgarth, v. Richmondshire, North Yorks., Eng.; on R. Ure in Wensleydale; famous waterfalls.

Ayutthaya, t., Thailand; former cap. on Menam Chao Phraya R. delta; p. (est. 1969) 40,352.

Azerbaijan, E. and W., provs., N. Iran; border USSR (Azerbaydzhan SSR) and Turkey; cap. (E.A.) Tabriz; cap. (W.A.) Rezayeh; p. (est. 1978) 5,900,000.

Azerbaydzhan, Transcaucasia, constituent rep. USSR; Caucasus and Lesser Caucasus separated by hot dry irrigated steppe; impt. oil ind.; 86,661 km²; p. (1970) 5,111,000.

Azores, Portuguese gr. of physically and climatically attractive Is. in mid-Atlantic about 1,440 km W. of Lisbon; partial indep. by regional gov. (1977); volcanic; fruit, wine; ch. spts: Ponta Delgada, Horta (a major whaling ctr.), Angra do Heroismo; U.S. air bases on Terceira I.; a. 2,569 km²; p. (1981) 243,410.

Azov Sea (Azouskoye More), USSR; joins Black Sea by Kerch strait; receives Don R.; fisheries; a. 36,000 km².

Azpeitia, t., N. Spain; mineral springs; local quarrying; timber inds., agr. processing; p. (1981) 12,509.

Azraq Desert Nat. Park, Jordan; first Jordanian nat. park around oasis of Azraq, 96 km E. of Amman; a. 3,900 km².

B

Baalbek, c., Lebanon, S.W. Asia; old Heliopolis; ruins; tourism.

Bab-el-Mandeb, strait connecting Red Sea and Indian Oc.; dangerous but impt. shipping lane; length 32 km, width 27 km.

Babergh, l. gov. dist., S. Suffolk, Eng.; inc. Sudbury and Hadleigh; p. (1981) 73,697.

Babol, t., Iran, Mazandaran prov.; airport; p. (1966) 49,973.

Babylon, anc. cap. of Babylonian Empire, in Euphrates valley about 96 km S. of Baghdad, Iraq.

Bacau, t., E. Romania; on R. Bistrita; oil, saw-milling, textiles; p. (1978) 135,841.

Bacolod City, t., Negros, Philippines; sm. pt.; exp. sugar; p. (1980) 262,415.

Bacton, v., Norfolk, Eng.; terminal for S. gasfields in N. Sea.

Bacup, t., Rossendale, S.E. Lancs., Eng.; 32 km N. of Manchester; textiles, felts, footwear; p. (1981) 15,259.

Badagri, t., W. of Lagos, Nigeria; on the Bight of Benin; formerly a gr. slave pt.; coir sacks.

Badajoz, lgst. prov., Spain; gr. reclamation scheme in progress; a. 21,624 km²; p. (1981) 643,512.

Badajoz, c., cap. of B. prov., W. Spain, in Estremadura; anc. fortress c.; transit tr.; p. (1981) 99,343.

Baden, t., Switzerland; health resort, mineral springs; p. (est. 1974) 67,300.

Baden-Baden, t., Baden-Württemberg. W. Germany; fashionable spa; p. (est. 1983) 48,900.

Baden-bei-Wien, wat. pl., Austria; 22 km S.W. of Vienna; p. (1961) 22,484.

Badenoch and Strathspey, l. gov. dist., Highland Reg., Scot.; mtn. a. S. of Inverness inc. Aviemore and Kingussie; p. (1981) 12,355.

Baden-Württemberg, Land, S. W. Germany; created 1952; bounded by Rhine in W., drained by Neckar and Donau R. systems; mtnous., inc. Black Forest and Swabian Jura; received much immigrant ind. from E. Europe, so encouraging prosperous and diversified industl. structure; several impt. industl. regions centred on Mannheim, Karlsruhe, and cap. Stuttgart; a. 35,750 km²; p. (1982) 9,270,600.

Bad Lands, S.D., USA; stretches of infertile badly eroded soil.

Badrinath, mtn. and t., Uttar Pradesh, India; pilgrim shrine of Vishnu.

Badulla, t., Sri Lanka; tea; anc. t.; rly. terminus; ctr. of tea estates; p. (1981) 32,954.

Badwater, salt pool, Cal., USA; 85 m below sea-level, lowest point in N. America.

Baeza, t., S. Spain; anc. Moorish c.; olives, wine; p. (1981) 12,841.

Baffin B., between Greenland and Canada; joined to Atl. Oc. by Davis Strait, to Arctic Oc. by Nares Strait; open 4 months per year; B.I., in W., ctr. of Arctic research and communications; length 1,120 km, width 100–650 km.

Bagé, t., S. Brazil; ctr. of cattle tr.; p. (est. 1968) 90,593.

Baghdad, c., cap. of Iraq; anc. c. on R. Tigris; terminus Baghdad rly.; airport; univ.; textiles, gum, bricks, tiles, metal inds.; p. (1977) 3,236,000.

Baghdad, prov. or liwa, Iraq; between Iran and Syrian Desert; inc. some of the most fertile lands in the Tigris and Euphrates valleys; p. (est. 1982) 4,038,000.

Baghlan, t., Afghanistan; new industl. t. in ctr. of sugar producing a.; alt. 518 m; p. (est. 1982) 41,240.

Bagnolet, t., Seine-St. Denis, France; sub. of Paris; famous for "plaster of Paris" from local gypsum; textiles; p. (1982) 32,521.

Bagshot, t., Surrey Heath, Surrey, Eng.; heath of same name; historically old postal town, 42 km S.W. of London; residtl.

Baguio, Luzon, N.W. of Manila, summer cap. of Philippines, alt. 1,500 m; gold mines; p. (1975) 100,209.

Bahamas, indep. st. (1973) within Brit. Commonwealth, W.I.; more than 700 coral atolls; subtropical climate; infertile but valuable tourist tr.; exp. crayfish; cap. Nassau; a. 11,406 km²; p. (est. 1981) 300,000.

Bahawalpur, t., Pakistan; former cap. of B. princely st.; impt. bridging point over Sutlej R.; p. (1981) 133,956.

Bahia, st., Brazil; cap. Salvador; cattle, cacao, sugar, coffee, tobacco; oil, extensive mineral deposits; a. 560,139 km²; p. (est. 1983) 10,281,000.

Bahia Blanca, spt., Argentina; industl. ctr., oil refining; prin. shipping point of S.; exp. oil, grain, wool, hides; p. (1980) 233,126.

Bahrain Is., indep. st. (1971) in Persian G.; low sandy Is. linked by road causeway to Saudi Arabia (1985); springs allow cultivation of dates; oil wells, oil and aluminium refining; trading ctr., cap. Manamah; airpt. at Muharraq; a. 570 km²; p. (est. 1984) 414,000.

Baia, historic v., Campania, **Italy;** beautifully situated on Bay of Naples; celebrated Roman pleasure resort; p. (1981) 2,087.

Baia-Mare, t., N.W. **Romania;** on Somesul R., in region mining copper, lead, zinc, gold, silver; mtn. resort; p. (1978) 107,945.

Baikal L. *See* **Baykal L.**

Baildon, t., West Yorks., **Eng.;** nr. Bradford; moorland resort; p. (1981) 15,904.

Baja, t., **Hungary;** impt. bridging point of R. Danube in Gr. Plain; p. (1966) 33,800.

Baja California. *See* **Lower California.**

Bakar, pt., **Yugoslavia;** S. of Rijeka; new pt. and oil harbour.

Bakersfield, t., Cal., **USA;** ctr. of oil prod. and refining; aircraft assembly; p. (1980) 106,000 (c.), 403,000 (met. a.).

Bakewell, t., West Derbys., **Eng.;** tourist ctr. Peak District; agr., mng.; p. (1981) 3,946.

Bakhchisaray, t., Crimea, Ukrainian SSR, **USSR;** old cap. of Tartar Khans; copper, leather; p. 16,000.

Bakhuis Gebergte mtns., W. **Surinam;** major aluminium complex based on local power and bauxite.

Bakony Wald, mtns., **Hungary;** forested; vine-yards; bauxite, manganese.

Baku, cap. of Azerbaydzhan SSR, **USSR;** pt. on Caspian Sea; univ.; oil-wells; oil pipeline connects with Batumi; shipbldg.; p. (est. 1980) 1,550,000 (met. a.).

Bala, t., Meirionnydd, Gwynedd, N. **Wales;** nr. Denbigh, lt. engin., resort; p. (1981) 1,848.

Bala, L., Meirionnydd, Gwynedd, N. **Wales;** drained by the Dee.

Balaklava, pt., S. Crimea, **USSR;** scene of the charge of the Light Brigade (1854); p. 2,000.

Balashov, t., Saratov area, **RSFSR;** on Khoper R.; engin., aircraft plant; p. (est. 1969) 76,000.

Balaton, L., lgst. in **Hungary;** a. 596 km²; long history of settlement in a.; shores forested; vineyards; tourism.

Balboa, t., **Panama Canal Zone;** pt. on Pac.; p. (est. 1977) 3,000.

Balbriggan, spt., Dublin, **R.o.I.;** hosiery; p. (1971) 3,741.

Baldock, t., North Herts., **Eng.;** on N. edge of Chiltern Hills and Gr. N. Road; hosiery, malt-ing, lt. engin.; p. (1981) 6,679.

Baldwin, t., N.Y., **USA;** on S. Long I.; fisheries; p. (1980) 31,630.

Balearic Is., in Mediterranean Sea, **Spain;** inc. Majorca, Minorca, Ibiza, Formentera; limestone scenery and mild climate encourage tourism which has swamped Moorish influence; agr.; ch. t. Palma; a. 5,014 km²; p. (1981) 685,088.

Bali, I. off Java, **Indonesia,** in Lesser Sundas; equable climate, fertile soil, luxurious vegeta-tion; p. mainly engaged in agr.; noted native dancers; a. (inc. Lombok) 10,196 km²; p. (est. 1983) 2,593,900.

Balikesir, t., **Turkey;** rly. junc.; ctr. of fertile agr. region; p. (1979) 111,027.

Balikpapan, t., Kalimantan, **Indonesia;** new oil refinery; p. (1980) 280,875.

Baliuag, t., Luzon, **Philippines;** rice, bamboo hats, mkt.; p. (est. 1969) 51,400.

Balkan Mtns., Bulgaria; fine alpine meadows, forested; tourism based on Sofia; average alt. 900–1,200 m, lgst. point Botev Peak, 2,377 m.

Balkan Peninsula, the easternmost of the three gr. southern peninsulas of Europe, between the Adriatic and Ionian seas on the W., and the Black Sea, Sea of Marmara and the Aegean Sea on the E., with an area of, roughly, 500,000 km²; includes Turkey, Yugoslavia, Bulgaria, Albania, Greece; ch. mtns.: Rodopi, Pindhus, Balkan; ch. Rs.: Danube, Maritsa, Vardar; ch. Ls.: Scutari, Okhrida.

Balkh. *See* **Wazirabad.**

Balkhash, t., Kazakh SSR, **USSR;** on N. shore of L.B.; smelting, esp. local copper; vermiculite deposits nearby, salt; p. (est. 1969) 77,000.

Balkhash, L., Kazakh SSR, **USSR;** receives Ili R., but has no outlet; salt water; fishing, salt-panning; a. 17,301 km².

Ballachulish, v., Argyll and Bute, **Scot.;** on S. shore of Loch Leven, N.E. of Oban; tourism; ferry across Loch Linnhe, new road bridge.

Ballarat, t., Victoria, **Australia;** 117 km N.W. of Melbourne, former gold-field dist.; mkt. ctr.;

fine examples of 19th century architecture; 2 caths.; p. (1976) 60,737.

Ballater, burgh, Kincardine and Deeside, **Scot.;** on R. Dee, 59 km S.W. of Aberdeen; tourist resort, mineral wells; nr. the royal Highland residence of Balmoral; p. (1981) 1,238.

Ballina, U.D., spt., Mayo, **R.o.I.;** agr. machin. salmon fishing; p. (1981) 6,856.

Ballina, t., N.S.W., **Australia;** at mouth of Richmond R.; resort, fishing; p. (1976) 7,323.

Ballinasloe, U.D., Galway and Roscommon, **R.o.I.;** agr. ctr.; cattle mkt.; terminus of Grand Canal; p. (1981) 6,374.

Ballinrobe, R.D., Mayo, **R.o.I.;** E. of Lough Mask; trout fishing; p. (est. 1977) 1,586.

Ballybunion, resort, Kerry, **R.o.I.;** at mouth of R. Shannon; p. (1981) 1,364.

Ballycastle, spt., mkt. t., Moyle, **N. Ireland;** abbey and cas. ruins; seaside resort; p. (1971) 2,895.

Ballyclare, t., Newtownabbey, **N. Ireland;** paper, linen, dyeing, asbestos-cement prod.; p. (1981) 6,159.

Ballymena, mkt. t., l. gov. dist., **N. Ireland;** on R. Braid; linen and dyeing; p. (1981) 28,166 (t.), 54,459 (l. gov. dist.).

Ballymoney, mkt. t., l. gov. dist., **N. Ireland;** 64 km N.W. of Belfast; linen; p. (1981) 22,742 (dist.).

Ballynahinch, t., Down, **N. Ireland;** 19 km from Downpatrick.

Ballyshannon, spt., Donegal, **R.o.I.;** at mouth of R. Erne; salmon fishery; resort; hydro-electric power plant; p. (1971) 2,325.

Balmoral Cas., Kincardine and Deeside, **Scot.;** royal residence, on R. Dee, 13 km W. of Ballater.

Balsas, R., and lowland, **Mexico;** R. flows E. to Pacific through rich agr. valley of Morelos; length 800 km.

Baltic Sea, an arm of Atl. Oc., opens into N. Sea by narrow channels between Denmark and Sweden; joined to Arctic by White Sea Canal; low, dune-backed cst.; shallowness, tendency to freeze reduce its importance for shipping; a. 414,400 km².

Baltic White Canal. *See* **Volga Baltic Waterway.**

Baltimore, industl. c., spt., Md., **USA;** fine harbour nr. head of Chesapeake B.; pt. processing and diversified inds.; steel wks. at Sparrow's Point; educational, cultural ctr., seat of Johns Hopkins univ.; many fine public bldgs. despite disastrous fire of 1904; p. (1980) 787,000 (c.), 2,174,000 (met. a.).

Baltoro Glacier, Karakoram Mtns., **Pakistan;** drains into tribs. of Indus; alt. 3,532 m.

Baluchistan, prov. (revived 1970), **Pakistan;** S. of Afghanistan; largely desert and rugged barren mtns.; cap. Quetta; cereals, potatoes, fruits, dates; new oil and natural gas discoveries; a. 137,011 km²; p. (1981) 4,332,349.

Bamako, cap. of **Mali;** impressive site at foot of escarpment on R. Niger; admin. and agr. tr. ctr.; R. pt.; univ.; main industl. ctr. of Mali; p. (est. 1976) 419,239.

Bamberg, c., Bavaria, **W. Germany;** cath.; textiles, elec., leather and engin. inds.; impt. R. pt. on Trans-European waterway; p. (est. 1983) 70,600.

Bamburgh, t., Northumberland, **Eng.;** former cap. of Bernicia and Northumbria; cas.; birthplace of Grace Darling.

Banaba I. *See* **Ocean I.**

Banagher, v., Offaly, **R.o.I.;** impt. crossing of R. Shannon.

Banam, t., **Cambodia;** on Mekong R.; boat-bldg., rice milling; p. 28,000.

Banat, terr., Vojvodina, **Yugoslavia;** major source of petroleum, natural gas, vineyards, but eco-nomically backward.

Banbridge, t., l. gov. dist., **N. Ireland;** on Bann R.; linen; p. (1981) 29,768.

Banbury, mkt. t., Cherwell, Oxford, **Eng.;** 128 km from London; aluminium ind., furniture, printing, ladies' wear; expanded t.; p. (1981) 35,796.

Banchory, burgh, Kincardine and Deeside, **Scot.;** on R. Dee, 27 km S.W. of Aberdeen; p. (1981) 4,779.

Banda Is., volcanic gr. in Moluccas, in Banda Sea Indonesia; nutmegs and mace; a. 103 km².

Bandama, R., **Ivory Coast;** major power and irrigation scheme at Kossou Dam; length c. 320 km.

Bandar. *See* **Masulipatnam.**

Bandar 'Abbās, spt., S. **Iran;** airport; oil ex-ploration; new deepwater harbour; p. (1967) 163,133.

Bandar Anzali, spt., N. **Iran**; on Caspian Sea; p. (1967) 59,737.

Bandar-e-Būshehūr (Bushire), spt., S.W. **Iran**; on Persian G., Iran's major pt.; petrochem. complex project; p. (est. 1971) 40,000.

Bandar-e-Torkeman, spt., N. **Iran**; on Caspian Sea, on rly. from Tehran; p. (1966) 13,081.

Bandar Khomeynī, spt., **Iran**, on Persian G., terminus of rly. from Tehran; petrochemical plant; p. (1966) 6,013.

Bandjarmasin, c., cap. of Kalimantan, **Indonesia**; pt. on Martapura R., nr. confluence with Barito R.; tr. ctr.; oil, timber, rubber, printing plant; p. (1980) 381,286.

Bandon, t., Cork, **R.o.I.**; on B.R.; agr. processing; p. (1971) 2,257.

Bandung, c., W. Java, **Indonesia**; industl. and tourist ctr.; tech. institute; radio sta. at nearby Malabar; p. (est. 1983) 1,602,000.

Banff Nat. Park, Canada; first Canadian Nat. Park; in Rocky Mtns.; variegated scenery, many tourist facilities; a. 6,695 km².

Banff, royal burgh, Banff and Buchan, **Scot.**; on Moray Firth at mouth of R. Deveron; fisheries; tourism; p. (1981) 3,929.

Banffshire, former co., **Scot.**; lge. part now forms Banff and Buchan l. gov. dist., Grampian Reg.; a. of dist. 1,525 km²; p. of dist. (1981) 81,446.

Bangalore, c., Karnataka, **India**; well-planned c., former Brit. military sta. and admin. H.Q.; route ctr.; textiles, engin.; p. (1971) 1,540,741 (c.), 1,653,779 (met. a.).

Bangka (Banka), I., between Sumatra and Kalimantan, **Indonesia**; tin; a. 11,942 km²; p. 280,000.

Bangkok (Krung Thep), cap. c., **Thailand**; pt. on Menam Chao Phraya R., 32 km from sea; built originally round canals; major industl. ctr.; royal palace, univ.; p. (1977) 4,702,273.

Bangladesh (East Pakistan), indep. sov. st., S. **Asia**; within Commonwealth (1972); occupies former Indian prov. of E. Bengal and E. part of Ganges delta; dense rural p. engaged in intensive farming of rice and jute; illiteracy 80 per cent; poor internal communications hinder devel.; exp. textiles; susceptible to flooding and cyclones, cstl. embankment project; open warfare between India and Pakistan (Dec. 1971) resulted in creation of indep. st.; cap. Dacca; a. 142,776 km²; p. (est. 1984) 98,464,000 (+ 6 per cent since 1981).

Bangor, t., North Down, N. **Ireland**; spt. on S. shore of Belfast Lough, 16 km N.E. of Belfast; lt. inds.; carpets, hosiery; seaside resort; p. (1981) 46,585.

Bangor, t., S. Me., **USA**; pt. of entry on Penobscot R.; timber inds., shoes; p. (1980) 31,643.

Bangor, t., Arfon, Gwynedd, **Wales**; pt. on S. shore of Menai Strait; cath., univ. college; lt. engin.; tourist ctr.; p. (1981) 12,174.

Bangui, c., cap. of **Central African Rep.**; pt. on R. Ubangi; airpt.; p. (est. 1982) 350,000.

Bangweulu, L., **Zambia**; 240 km long, 128 km wide, contains 3 islands. Dr. Livingstone died at Illala, on S. shore of this L., in 1873.

Baniyas, spt., **Syria**; terminus of oil pipeline from Kirkuk, opened 1952.

Banja Luka, t., N. Bosnia, **Yugoslavia**; caths., mosques; recent industl. development; cellulose; rly. junc.; p. (1981) 183,618.

Banjul (Bathurst), t., cap. of Gambia, **Senegambia**; pt. at mouth of Gambia R., exp. groundnuts; airport; p. (est. 1980) 49,181.

Banks I., **Canada**, Arctic Oc.; separated by McClure Strait from Melville I.

Banks Is., gr. of sm. Is. in S. Pacific; N.E. of New Hebrides.

Banks Peninsula, on E. cst. of S.I., **N.Z.**; prominent feature of Canterbury cst.

Banks Strait, separating Furneaux Is. from Tasmania, **Australia**.

Bankura, t., W. Bengal, **India**; on Hooghly R.; shellac, silk; p. (1961) 62,833.

Bann, Upper and Lower R., N. **Ireland**; rises in Mtns. of Mourne, and flows through Lough Neagh to Atlantic nr. Coleraine; length 144 km.

Bannockburn, moor, nr. Stirling, **Scot.**; Bruce's victory over Edward II on June 23–24, 1314, established Scotland's independence.

Banovici, basin, **Yugoslavia**; in Bosnia; brown coal.

Banská Bystrica, region, Slovakia, **ČSSR**; copper and silver mng., metal wks.; a. 9,230 km²; p. (est. 1968) 38, 865 (commune).

Banstead, Surrey, **Eng.**; dormitory t.; p. (1981) 43,163. *See* **Reigate**.

Bantam, t. and dist., W. Java, **Indonesia**; suffered severely from fever and volcanic eruption; former pt. and sultanate; cattle rearing.

Bantry, t., Cork, **R.o.I.**; tweed; p. (1971) 2,579.

Bantry Bay, Cork, **R.o.I.**; Atlantic inlet; natural harbour utilised mainly by oil-storage depot.

Baoding (Paoting), c., Hebei prov., **China**; on main rly. to Beijing; p. (est. 1970) 350,000.

Baoji (Paoki), c., Shaanxi prov., **China**; ctr. of arable agr. a.; cotton weaving; nearby gorge on Huang-He used for multi-purpose dams; p. (est. 1970) 275,000.

Baotou (Paotow), c., Mongol Zizhiqu, **China**; on left bank of Huang-He, on road and rly. routes to E. China; terminus of caravan routes through Gobi Desert and Tarim basin to Turkestan; tr. in non-perishable livestock prods., cereals; modern steel ind.; p. (est. 1983) 1,051,000.

Bar, spt., Dalmatian cst., **Yugoslavia**; terminal of new Belgrade-Bar rly.; p. 5,500.

Baracaldo, pt., N.E. **Spain**; rapidly growing industl. t. on Bilbão estuary; p. (1981) 117,422.

Baracoa, spt., **Cuba**; exp. bananas, coconuts; p. (est. 1967) 105,090.

Baranovichi, c., Belorussiya, **USSR**; admin. ctr. of agr. dist.; impt. rly. ctr.; p. (est. 1980) 135,000.

Barataria Bay, S.E. Louisiana, **USA**; 56 km S. of New Orleans; ctr. of shrimp ind., petroleum extraction; picturesque stilt vs.; a. 466 km².

Barauni, t., N. Central Bihar, **India**; oil refining; oil pipelines to Gauhati, and Kanpur and from Haldia; p. (1961) 40,321.

Barbados, I., indep. sovereign st., within Brit. Commonwealth, **W.I.**; fertile soils; economy based on intensive agr. supporting dense p.; sugar, molasses, rum; fishing; tourism; cap. and spt. Bridgetown; a. 429 km²; p. (est. 1984) 262,000.

Barbary Coast, gen. name applied to Mediterranean cst. of N. Africa between Strait of Gibraltar and C. Bon.

Barberton, t., Ohio, **USA**; S.W. of Akron; tyre mftg.; p. (1980) 29,751.

Barberton, t., Transvaal, **S. Africa**; developed from 19th cent. gold rush; ctr. of rich agr. dist.; p. (est. 1967) 13,200.

Barbican, dist., City of London, **Eng.**; inc. major housing scheme to attract p. back into c.; cultural amenities.

Barbizon, v., nr. forest of Fontainebleau, **France**; haunt of painters, especially those ass. with the Barbizon school.

Barbuda and Redonda, Is., Leeward Is., **W.I.**; dependencies of Antigua and Barbuda; sea-island cotton; a. 163 km²; p. (est. 1972) 14,000, with Antigua.

Barcellona, t., N.E. cst., Sicily, **Italy**; mkt. t.; p. (1981) 36,869.

Barcelona, c., cap. of B. prov., major spt. of **Spain**; industl. and comm. ctr., "Manchester of Spain", textiles and varied inds.; exp. agr. prod. inc. cork; cath., univ.; p. (1981) 1,752,601.

Barcelona, t., N. **Venezuela**; cap. of Anzoátegui st.; agr. tr.; brewing; adjoins Puerto la Cruz on Caribbean cst.; joint p. (est. 1980) 267,000.

Barcoo Creak. *See* **Cooper's Creek**.

Bardsey, I., Irish Sea; off cst. of **Wales**, nr. N. point of Cardigan Bay; lighthouse.

Bareilly, c., Uttar Pradesh, **India**; mkt., sugar refining, cotton mills, bamboo furniture; p. (1981) 386,734.

Barents Sea, part of Arctic Oc., E. of Spitzbergen to N. Cape; impt. cod fisheries; oil potential; short Rs. to be diverted from Sea to Volga to carry water to Karakum Desert.

Bari, c., cap. of B. prov., Apulia, **Italy**; spt. on Adriatic handling agr. prods.; agr. processing inds., oil refinery; p. (1981) 371,022.

Barinas, t., cap. of B. st., **Venezuela**; cattle, oil in surrounding Llanos; p. (1971) 56,329.

Barisal, t., **Bangladesh**; nr. Tetulia at mouth of Ganges; river pt.; gr. damage and loss of life from cyclone 1965; p. (1981) 172,905.

Barito R., Borneo, **Indonesia**; a. of swampland in lower valley; proposals to develop valley for rice cultivation; length c. 440 km.

Barking and Dagenham, outer bor., E. London, **Eng.**; on Rs. Roding and Thames; diversified inds. inc. huge R.side Ford motor wks.; high proportion of council housing; p. (1981) 150,175.

Barlad, t., Moldavia, **Romania**; soap, textiles; p. (1966) 41,060.

Bar-le-Duc, t, cap. of Meuse dep., **France**; in picturesque Ornain valley; many fine old houses; varied inds.; p. (1982) 20,029.

Barletta, t., spt., **Italy**; diversified pt. processing inds.; wine tr.; p. (1981) 83,719.

Barmouth, t., Meirionnydd, Gwynedd, **Wales**; pt. on Cardigan Bay; chemicals; resort; p. (1981) 2,136.

Barnard Castle, Teesdale, Durham, **Eng.**; mkt. t., resort; woollens, penicillin; cas.; p. (1981) 5,016.

Barnaul, t., W. Siberia, **RSFSR**; route ctr. in cotton-growing dist. nr. industl. Kuznetsk Basin; varied inds.; p. (est. 1980) 542,000.

Barnet, former U.D., Herts., **Eng.**; now outer bor., Greater London; comprising Finchley, Hendon, Barnet, East Barnet and Friern Barnet; p. (1981) 292,331.

Barnsley, t., met. dist., South Yorks., **Eng.**; machin., plastics; carpets; coal-mng. ctr.; p. (1981) 224,906.

Barnstaple, North Devon, **Eng.**; mkt. t., pt. on R. Taw; seaside resort; p. (1981) 19,025.

Baroda, t., Gujarat, **India**; univ.; palaces, Hindu temples; natural gas pipeline from Ankleshwar; oil refining nearby at Jawaharnagar; heavy water plant; p. (1987) 734,473.

Barquisimeto, t., **Venezuela**; well built c.; comm. ctr. for fertile agr. a.; p. (est. 1980) 489,000.

Barra Is., Outer Hebrides, **Scot.**; a. 901 km²; lighthouse on Barra Head; p. (1971) 1,088.

Barrancabermeja, R. pt., **Colombia**; oilfield, oil refining, paper mkg., petrochemicals; p. (est. 1972) 94,000 (t.), 106,000 (met. a.).

Barranquilla, t., **Colombia**; major spt. nr. mouth of Magdalena R.; impt. industl. ctr.; international airpt.; p. (est. 1979) 855,195.

Barreiro, t., Setúbal, **Portugal**; on S. bank of Tagus estuary; agr. processing; p. (1981) 50,863.

Barrow-in-Furness, spt., l. gov. dist., Cumbria, **Eng.**; iron and steel ind. once based on local haematite ores; shipbldg., submarines; p. (1981) 72,635 (dist.).

Barrow I., W. **Australia**; since 1967 one of Australia's richest oilfields.

Barrow Point, most N. headland in Alaska, **USA**.

Barry, t., Vale of Glamorgan, South Glamorgan, **Wales**; rapid growth in 19th cent. as outport of Cardiff; modern light inds., replacing coal and tinplate inds.; p. (1981) 41,681.

Barth, spt., Rostock, **E. Germany**; shipyard engin., furniture, sugar; p. (1963) 12,406.

Bartlesville, t., Okla., **USA**; oil refining, metal inds.; p. (1980) 34,568.

Barton-on-Humber, mkt. t., Glanford, Humberside, **Eng.**; anc. Eng. pt.; S. site of new Humber Bridge; p. (1981) 8,498.

Basel, c., cap. of B. can., 2nd. t. of **Switzerland**; cath., univ.; burial place of Erasmus; comm., industl. rly. ctr. at head of barge navigation on R. Rhine; p. (1980) 364,813 (met. a.).

Basel, can., **Switzerland**; divided into 2 half cantons: (1) B.—Stadt; in immediate vicinity of B.c.; cap. B.; a. 36 km²; p. (1980) 203,915; (2) B.—Land; on N. Jura slopes; watchmaking; cap. Liestal; a. 427 km²; p. (1980) 219,822.

Basford, t., Gedling, Notts., **Eng.**; outskirts of Nottingham; hosiery.

Bashkir (Bashirskaya) ASSR, occupies Belaya R. basin in S.W. Urals, **RSFSR**; impt. mng. and metal inds., inc. major oilfield; arable agr.; cap. Ufa; a. 143,486 km²; p. (1970) 3,819,000.

Basildon, t., l. gov. dist., Essex, **Eng.**; in lower Thames valley; new t. 1949; light inds.; p. (1981) 152,301 (dist.), 94,277 (t.).

Basilicata, region, S. **Italy**; mtnous. in W., drains to G. of Taranto; arable agr.; a. 9,984 km²; p. (1981) 610,186.

Basingstoke and Deane, l. gov. dist., N. Hants., **Eng.**; 80 km W. of London; expanded t.; engin., light inds.; p. (1981) 129,899.

Basle. See Basel.

Basotho ba Borwa (S. Sotho), Bantu Terr. Authority, O.F.S., **S. Africa**; cap. Witziesnoek; a. 52,000 hectares; p. (est. 1969) 144,000.

Basque Provs., N. **Spain**; comprise 3 provs.: Alava, Guipuzcoa and Vizcaya where Basque language spoken; recent claims that French dep. of Pyrénées-Atlantiques should be inc. within an indep. Basque prov.; regional parliaments for provs. in Spain to help offset separatist moves (1980); lgst. c. Bilbao; p. (1981) 2,141,809.

Basra, t., **Iraq**; cap. of B. prov.; R. pt., 64 km from mouth of Tigris R., on main rly. from Baghdad; exp. agr. prods.; p. (1977) 1,540,000.

Bas-Rhin, dep., E. **France**; N. part of Alsace; extends to Rhine rift valley, inc. Vosges Mtns.; impt. agr. dist.; many industl. ts.; cap. Strasbourg; a. 4,791 km²; p. (1982) 912,000.

Bass Rock, lighthouse in Firth of Forth, opposite Tantallon Cas., E. Lothian, **Scot.**; gannetry.

Bass Strait, **Australia**; between Victoria and Tasmania; length 320 km; width 224 km.

Bassano del Grappa; cap. of Vicenza prov., on R. Brenta, **Italy**; light and craft inds.; cath.; p. (1981) 64,676.

Bassein, t., **Burma**; on mouth of Irrawaddy R., univ.; airfield; rice tr. and milling; p. (est. 1983) 335,000.

Bassenthwaite, L., L. Dist., Cumbria, **Eng.**; most N. of lge. Ls.; drained to Solway Firth by R. Derwent; length 6 km, width 1·6 km.

Basses-Alpes. See Alpes-de-Haute-Provence.

Basses-Pyrénées. See Pyrénées-Atlantique.

Basse-Terre, l., cap. of Guadeloupe, **Fr. W.I.**; pt.; p. (1975) 15,930.

Basseterre, t., St. Kitts I., **W.I.**; cap. St. Kitts-Nevis-Anguilla ass. st.; pt.; sugar refining; p. (est. 1970) 14,133.

Bassetlaw, l. gov. dist., N. Notts., **Eng.**; lge. a. based on Worksop and East Retford; p. (1981) 101,970.

Bastia, c. spt., cap. Haute Corse, N.E. Corsica, **France**; lgst. t. of Corsica; agr. exp. and inds.; tourism; p. (1982) 50,596 (met. a.).

Basutoland. See Lesotho.

Bata, t., ch. spt., **Equatorial Guinea**; cap. of Rio Muni prov.; airpt.; p. (1969) 27,024.

Bataan, peninsula and prov., W. Luzon, **Philippines**; mtnous.; inc. t. of Balanga; timber inds., oil refining; proposed nuclear power sta.

Batangas, prov. and spt., S.W. Luzon, **Philippines**; oil refining; agr. tr.; p. (1980) 143,570 (spt.).

Batavia. See Djakarta.

Bath, c., l. gov. dist., Avon, **Eng.**; Roman baths, hot springs, medicinal waters; fine Regency architecture; univ.; elec. engin., metal inds.; p. (1981) 79,965.

Bathgate, burgh, W. Lothian, **Scot.**; coal mng. automobile ind.; p. (1981) 14,388.

Bathurst, t., N.S.W., **Australia**; former gold t., reliant on wool and wheat; diversifying with secondary inds.; with Orange to form site of major inland c. of 200,000 as part of decentralisation plan; p. (1976) 18,589.

Bathurst, I., off cst. of N.T., **Australia**; separated from Melville I. by Apsley Str.; aboriginal reserve; cypress pine milling; (1976) 895.

Bathurst, t., N.B., **Canada**; pt. on Nipisiguit Bay; paper mill; salmon fishing; local mng.; p. (1971) 16,404.

Bathurst. See Banjul.

Bâtinah, Al, fertile coastal plain, **Oman**, Arabia; produces early-ripening dates famous for flavour.

Batley, t. West Yorks., **Eng.**; heavy woollens, shoddy; p. (1981) 42,572.

Baton Rouge, st. cap., La., **USA**; on Mississippi; major tr. ctr.; univ.; oil refining, chemical plants; p. (1980) 219,000 (c.), 494,000 (met. a.).

Battambang, t., **Kampuchea**; 288 km N.W. of Phnom-Penh; cotton mill; p. (1962) 38,846.

Battersea, dist., London, **Eng.**; S. of R. Thames; famous park; lge. power sta.; part of Wandsworth.

Batticaloa, t., cap. of E. Prov., **Sri Lanka**; on E. cst.; comm. ctr.; p. (est. 1968) 24,000.

Battle, t., Rother, East Sussex, **Eng.**; battle of Hastings 1066; abbey.

Battle Creek, t., Mich., **USA**; on Kalamazoo R.; engin., local cereal prod.; p. (1980) 35,724, (t.), 187,338 (met. a.).

Batu Arang, t., **Malaya**; ctr. of only worked coalfield in Malaya; 45 km from Kuala Lumpur.

Batumi, t., spt. on E. shore of Black Sea; Georgian SSR, **USSR**; oil, engin., citrus fruits, tea; oil pipeline connects with Baku; resort; airpt; p. (est. 1980) 124,000.

Bauchi, t., **Nigeria**; cap. Bauchi st.; ctr. of Jos plateau; tin-mng. ctr.

Bauld, C., northernmost part of Newfoundland, **Canada**.

Bauru, t., São Paulo st., **Brazil**; comm. ctr.; food inds.; p. (1980) 185,600.

Bautzen, t., Dresden, **E. Germany**; on R. Spree; textiles, engin., iron inds.; cath.; p. (est. 1970) 43,670.

Bavaria (Bayern), Land, W. **Germany**; mtnous., bounded in S. by Alps, inc. Böhmerwald, Fichtelgebirge, Franconian Forest; main Rs. Danube and Main; fertile agr. valleys; forestry and agr.; economic life concentrated in ts., esp. cap. Munich, now a focus of p. immigration; rural beauty attracts tourist tr.; celebrated beer; a. 70,220 km²; p. (1982) 10,966,700.

Bavarian Alps, mtn. range, W. **Germany**, along Austrian border; Zugspitze (2,969 m) highest mtn. in W. Germany.

Bavarian Forest. See **Böhmerwald.**

Bawdwin, t., **Burma;** in Shan plateau; impt. mng. ctr.; wolfram, lead, zinc, silver, rubies.

Bayamón, t., **Puerto Rico;** in fertile valley; oil refining; p. (est. 1976) 208,600.

Baybay, t., Leyte, **Philippines;** impt. comm. pt.; p. (est. 1969) 70,200.

Bay City, t., Mich., **USA;** comm. pt. nr. head of Saginaw B.; fishing; pt. processing inds.; p. (1980) 41,593 (c.), 119,881 (met. a.).

Bayeux, t., Calvados, **France;** mkt. t.; cath., museum, Bayeux tapestry; p. (1982) 15,237.

Baykal, L. (Ozero Baykal), Siberia, **RSFSR;** sixth largest fresh-water L. in world; basin forms deepest depression in world (1,616 m); many pts. around shores but frozen Nov.–May; skirted by Trans-Siberian rly.; sturgeon, salmon; tourism; a. 35,483 km².

Bayonne, spt., Pyrénées-Atlantique, S.W. **France;** cath.; noted for invention of bayonet; Basque Museum; p. (1982) 127,477 (met. a.).

Bayonne, t., N.J., **USA;** 10 km from New York; chemicals, oil refining; dry docks; p. (1980) 65,047.

Bayreuth, t., Bavaria, **W. Germany;** home of Wagner; famous for musical festivals in national theatre; p. (est. 1983) 71,100.

Baytown, pt., S.E. Texas, **USA;** industl. t., oil refining and exp.; p. (1980) 56,923.

Beachy Head, chalk headland, S.W. of Eastbourne, East Sussex, **Eng.;** 175 m high.

Beaconsfield, t., South Bucks., **Eng.;** residtl; home of Edmund Burke; p. (1981) 10,909.

Beardmore Glacier, Antarctica; one of world's lgst. valley glaciers; over 176 km in length.

Bear I. (Björnöya I.), **Norway;** in Arctic Oc., 208 km S. of Spitzbergen; cod fisheries.

Bearsden, burgh, l. gov. dist. with Milngavie, **Scot.;** residtl.; p. (1981) 39,322 (l. gov. dist.), 27,151 (burgh).

Beas (Bias), R., Punjab, **India;** trib. of Sutlej R.; part of irrigation scheme.; marked limit of Alexander's advance into India, 327 B.C.

Beattock, pass, S. Uplands, **Scot.;** gives access from valley of R. Clyde to R. Annan; used by main W. cst. rly. route from Carlisle to Glasgow and Edinburgh; alt. 309 m.

Beauce, region, central **France;** flat limestone plateau; arid, few surface streams; thin layer of loam (limon) permits agr.; impt. wheat growing a. ("the granary of France"); p. mainly grouped in vs.

Beaufort Sea, off N. Alaska, **USA;** part of Arctic Oc.

Beaujolais, France; in upper Rhône valley, N.E. Massif Central; wine-growing dist.

Beaulieu, v., Hants, **Eng.;** on Beaulieu R.; Cistercian abbey; car museum.

Beauly, t., Inverness, **Scot.;** on B. R.; ruined priory; p. (1981) 1,145.

Beaumaris, t., Anglesey, Gwynedd, N. **Wales;** pt. on Menai Strait; lt. engin.; resort; p. (1981) 2,088.

Beaumont, t.; 2nd. pt. of Texas, **USA;** ctr. of petrochemical inds.; p. (1980) 118,000 (c.), 375,000 (met. a. with Orange-Port Arthur).

Beaune, t., Cote d'Or, **France;** mediaeval walled t.; ctr. of wine tr.; p. (1982) 21,127.

Beauvais, agr. mkt. t., cap. of Oise dep., N. **France;** cath.; Gobelin tapestry removed to Paris; p. (1982) 54,147.

Bebington, Wirral, Merseyside, **Eng.;** part of pt. of Liverpool; soap, chemicals, engin.; p. (1981) 64,174.

Becancourt, t., Quebec, **Canada;** on S. bank of St. Lawrence; integrated steel mill projected.

Beccles, Waveney, Suffolk, **Eng.;** mkt. t. on R. Waveney S. of Broads; resort, agr. inds.; p. (1981) 8,903.

Béchar (Colom-Béchart) t., N.W. **Algeria;** airpt.; coal; p. (1966) 42,090.

Bechuanaland. See **Botswana.**

Beckum, t., N. Rhine-Westphalia, **W. Germany;** cement, chalk, engin. wks.; p. (est. 1983) 37,200.

Beddington and Wallington. See **Sutton.**

Bedford, co. t., North Beds., **Eng.;** on R. Ouse, 80 km N. of London; gen. engin., inc. marine and elec., bricks, aero research; Bunyan imprisoned here; p. (1981) 74,245.

Bedfordshire, non-met. co., **Eng.;** co. t., Bedford; crossed by Chilterns; agr., mkt. gardening, brickmkg., cement, vehicles, engin.; a. 1,232 km²; p. (1981) 464,277.

Bedfordshire, North, l. gov. dist., Beds., **Eng.;** a. inc. Bedford and surrounding rural a.; p. (1981) 89,829.

Bedfordshire, South, l. gov. dist., Beds., **Eng.;** close

to Luton and inc. Dunstable and Leighton-Linslade; p. (1981) 88,489.

Bedford Level, once over 162,000 ha. of peat marsh in S. Fenland, **Eng.;** first successful draining initiated by Earl of Bedford 1634.

Bedlington, t., Wansbeck, Northumberland, **Eng.;** nr. Blyth; coal mng.; electronics; p. (1981) 26,707.

Bedloe's I., or **Liberty I.,** N.Y. harbour, **USA;** on which the statue of Liberty stands.

Bedwas and Machen, t., Rhymney Valley, Mid Glamorgan, **Wales;** gas, coal and coke by-prods.; p. (1981) 13,152.

Bedwellty, t., Islwyn, Gwent, **Wales;** elec. gds., car upholstery; p. (1981) 24,670.

Bedworth, t., Warwicks., **Eng.;** nr. Coventry; coal mng., limestone quarrying, engin., textiles; p. (1981) 41,991. See **Nuneaton.**

Bedzin, t., S. **Poland;** coalmng. t. in Upper Silesia; p. (1970) 42,800.

Beerenberg, mtn., Jan Mayen I., **Norway,** Arctic Oc.; one of lgst. volcanic cones in world; glaciated; alt. 2,546 m.

Beersheba, t., **Israel;** ctr. for development of the Negev; p. (est. 1982) 112,600.

Beeston and Stapleford, Broxtowe, Notts., **Eng.;** sub. of Nottingham; engin., drugs, telephones; p. (1981) 64,599.

Bègles, t., Gironde, **France;** mftg.; p. (1982) 23,426.

Begovat, t., E. Uzbek SSR, **USSR;** on Syr Dar'ya R.; iron and steel wks.; hydroelectric power; p. (1967) 59,000.

Beijing (Peking), t. and mun., cap. of **China;** cultural ctr. and c. of gr. architectural beauty; for hundreds of years seat of Chinese emperors (Mongol, Ming, Manchu); formerly surrounded by walls; lge square; seat of govt.; univ.; many sm. factories; textiles, synthetic fibres, machin., precision instruments, printing, publishing; route ctr., rly. junc., airpt.; a. 8,770 km²; p. (est. 1983) 9,340,000.

Beira, spt., **Moçambique;** airpt; rly. runs inland to Harare (Zimbabwe) and Blantyre (Malawi); exp. sugar, maize, cotton; oil pipeline to Umtali; p. (1960) 64,600.

Beirut, c., cap. of **Lebanon;** pt. on Mediterranean; anc. Phoenician c., now busy shipping and mercantile ctr.; silk, wool, fruits; 4 univs.; p. (est. 1977) 950,000.

Beisan (Bet She'an), t., **Israel;** in Jordan valley, c. 90 m below sea-level; archaeological finds date from 1500 B.C.; rebuilt since 1948 by Israelis; p. (est. 1970) 11,900.

Bejaia (Bougie), spt., **Algeria;** impt. tr. ctr.; exp. wood, hides; oil pipeline connection to Hassi-Messoud; p. (1967) 63,000.

Belaya Tserkov, t., N. Ukrainian SSR, **USSR;** agr. and comm. ctr.; p. (est. 1980) 157,000.

Békéscsaba, t., **Hungary;** milling; rly. junc.; poultry processing plant; p. (est. 1978) 65,427.

Belau, Rep. of, formerly Western Carolines; group of Is. 300 km. E. of Philippines; renamed 1981; part of U.S. Trust Terr. of Pacific Is.; also known as Palau Is.

Belém, spt., cap. of Pará st., **Brazil;** comm. ctr., ch. pt. of Amazon basin, entrepôt for riverside settlements, exp. forest prod. inc. jute, cocoa and cotton; inds. dominated by food processing and textiles; new steel works; univ.; p. (est. 1980) 934,000.

Belfast, l. gov. dist., cap. of **N. Ireland;** pt. on Belfast Lough; Britain's lgst. single shipyard; freeport (1984) for air freight; linen mnf., rope, tobacco, distilling, aircraft, fertilisers, computers; oil refinery on E. side of harbour; univ.; Stormont Castle; p. (1981) 297,983.

Belfort, t., cap. of Belfort dep., E. **France,** in Alsace; fortress t. between Jura and Vosges; heavy inds., rly. wks., cotton ind.; elec. engin.; p. (1982) 52,739.

Belfort (Territoire de), dep., **France;** ch. t. Belfort; a. 608 km²; p. (1982) 131,900.

Belgaum, t., Karnataka, **India;** cotton; alt. 760 m; Jain temples; p. (1981) 274,430 (c.), 300,372 (met. a.).

Belgium, kingdom, W. **Europe,** comprises 9 admin. provs.; low-lying except in Ardennes in S.E.; very high density of p., intensive agr. and highly industl.; severe social and economic problems have resulted from decline of Sambre-Meuse coalfield and associated heavy engin. inds., similar difficulties in textile inds. in N.W.; industl. expansion on Kempenland coalfield in N.E. and around Brussels, Antwerp, and Ghent; heavily dependent upon foreign tr. for economic survival; member of EEC; major spt. of Antwerp competing with Rotter-

Atlas of the World

Contents

Symbols

——— Principal Railways   --------- Internal Boundaries

=== Motorways

——— Principal Roads   4125   Heights in Metres

▬▬▬ International Boundaries   ☼   Principal Airports

Height of Land

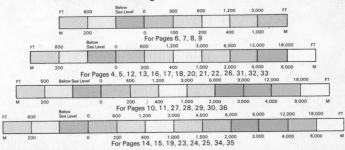

© 1986 and Printed in Great Britain by George Philip & Son, Ltd., London.

WORLD : Political

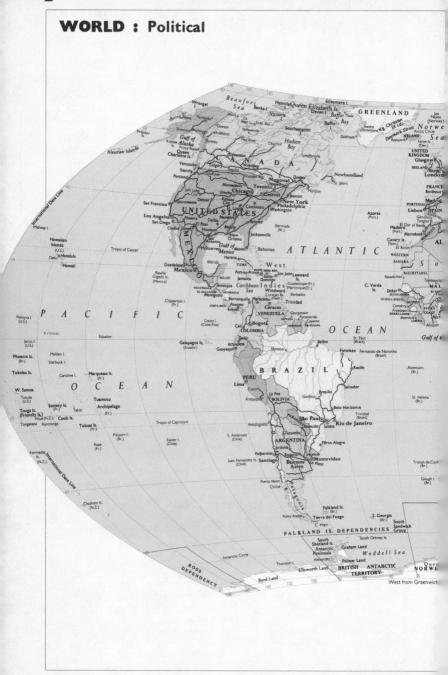

Beaufort Sea
Melville I. Queen Elizabeth Is.
Ellesmere I.
GREENLAND
Jan Mayen (Norway)
Bering Strait
Banks I.
Devon I.
Baffin Bay
Thule
Norwe
Sea
Victoria I.
Barrow
Fairbanks
Southampton
Baffin
Sondre
Stromfjord
K. Christian
IX Ld.
Arctic Circle
Dawson
Echo Bay
ICELAND
Faroe Is.
(Den.)
Yellowknife
Reykjavik
Seward
Gulf of
Alaska
Kodiak I.
Prince Rupert
Hudson
Bay
Churchill
Schefferville
UNITED
KINGDOM
Glasgow
IRELAND
London
Pribilov
Is.
Aleutian Islands
Queen
Charlotte Is.
Vancouver
Seattle
Portland
Edmonton
CANADA
Calgary
Regina
Thunder Bay
Montreal
Toronto
Quebec
Newfoundland
St. John's
Halifax
FRANCE
Bordeaux
International Date Line
San Francisco
Salt Lake
City
Denver
Minneapolis
Omaha
Chicago
Detroit
Boston
New York
Philadelphia
Washington
PORTUGAL
SPAIN
Lisbon
Madrid
Los Angeles
San Diego
Sacramento
UNITED STATES
Kansas
City
St. Louis
Cincinnati
Azores
(Port.)
Midway
Phoenix
El Paso
Dallas
Memphis
Atlanta
Bermuda
(Br.)
Madeira
(Port.)
El Dar el Beida
Marrakesh
Hawaiian
Islands
(U.S.)
Tropic of Cancer
Ciudad Juarez
MEXICO
Antonio
Houston
New
Orleans
Mobile
Jacksonville
Miami
Canary Is.
(Span.)
AL
Oahu
Honolulu
Monterrey
Gulf of
Mexico
Havana
Bahamas
WESTERN
SAHARA
El Aaiún
Hawaii
Guadalajara
Mexico
Mérida
CUBA
West
HAITI
DOM. REP.
MAURITANIA
Nouakchott
Revilla
Gigedo Is.
(Mexico)
BELIZE
Port-au-Prince
San Juan
Leeward
Is.
Guadeloupe (Fr.)
C. Verde
Is.
Tombouctou
GUATEMALA
HONDURAS
Jamaica
Santo
Domingo
MALI
SENEGAL
Dakar
PACIFIC
Palmyra I.
(U.S.)
Clipperton I.
(Fr.)
EL SALVADOR
NICARAGUA
Managua
Caribbean
Sea
Windward
Is.
Martinique (Fr.)
Curaçao Is.
(Neth.)
Barbados
GUINEA-BISSAU
GUINEA
Conakry
Freetown
IVORY
COAST
Kiritimati
COSTA RICA
Panama
PANAMA
Maracaibo
Trinidad
SIERRA LEONE
LIBERIA
Monrovia
Abidjan
Jarvis I.
(U.S.)
Equator
Cocos I.
(Costa Rica)
VENEZUELA
Caracas
GUYANA
Georgetown
Paramaribo
Cayenne
FR. GUIANA
OCEAN
Gulf of
Phoenix Is.
(Br.)
Malden I.
Galapagos Is.
(Ecuador)
Cali
COLOMBIA
Quito
Bogota
SURINAM
Tokelau Is.
(N.Z.)
Starbuck I.
ECUADOR
Guayaquil
Manaus
St. Paul
(Brazil)
Caroline I.
Belém
Ascension
(Br.)
W. Samoa
Marquesas Is.
(Fr.)
PERU
BRAZIL
Fortaleza
Fernando de Noronha
(Brazil)
Tutuila
(U.S.)
Tuamotu
Archipelago
(Fr.)
Lima
Cuzco
Recife
St. Helena
(Br.)
Tonga Is.
(Friendly Is.)
Society Is.
(Fr.)
Tahiti
La Paz
BOLIVIA
Goiânia
Brasília
Salvador
OCEAN
Niue (N.Z.)
Cook Is.
(N.Z.)
Tongatapu
Rarotonga
Tubuai Is.
(Fr.)
Tropic of Capricorn
Arequipa
Belo Horizonte
Trinidad
(Brazil)
Pitcairn I.
(Br.)
Antofagasta
PARAGUAY
São Paulo
Rio de Janeiro
Santos
Kermadec
Is.
(N.Z.)
Easter I.
(Chile)
S. Ambrosio
(Chile)
Tucumán
Asunción
Pôrto Alegre
International Date Line
Rapa
(Fr.)
ARGENTINA
Córdoba
URUGUAY
Montevideo
Chatham Is.
(N.Z.)
Juan Fernandez Is.
(Chile)
Valparaiso
Santiago
Rosario
Buenos
Aires
Rio de la Plata
Tristan da Cunha
(Br.)
Gough I.
(Br.)
Puerto Montt
Chiloé
PATAGONIA
Puerto Arenas
Falkland Is.
(Br.)
Tierra del Fuego
S. Georgia
(Br.)
South
Sandwich
Group
C. Horn
FALKLAND IS. DEPENDENCIES
Antarctic Circle
Thurston I.
South
Shetland Is.
Antarctic
Peninsula
Alexander I.
Graham Land
Palmer Land
Weddell Sea
Que
NORWE
ROSS
DEPENDENCY
Byrd Land
Ellsworth Land
BRITISH ANTARCTIC
TERRITORY
West from Greenwich

3

Scale 1:135,000,000

COPYRIGHT. GEORGE PHILIP & SON. LTD.

5

EUROPE

0	100	200	300	400 miles
0	200	400	600	km

E.E.C. members

E.F.T.A. members

COPYRIGHT. GEORGE PHILIP & SON, LTD.

ENGLAND AND WALES

0	20	40	60 miles
0	20	40	60	80	100 km

NORTH SEA

Dogger Bank

IRISH SEA

North Channel

SCOTLAND

TAYSIDE · FIFE · CENTRAL · STRATHCLYDE · LOTHIAN · BORDERS · DUMFRIES AND GALLOWAY

Dundee · Firth of Tay · St Andrews · Perth · Crieff · Stirling · Glasgow · Paisley · Motherwell · Hamilton · Kilmarnock · Ayr · Edinburgh · Leith · Dunbar · Berwick-upon-Tweed · Kelso · Selkirk · Hawick

Southern Uplands · Galloway · Dumfries · Annan · Carlisle

ISLE OF MAN · Douglas · Ramsey · Peel · Castletown

NORTHERN IRELAND · ULSTER

Belfast · Lisburn · Larne · Bangor · Newtownards · Newcastle · Mourne Mts. · Newry · Armagh · Dungannon · Coleraine · Ballymena · Antrim · Carrickfergus

IRELAND

Dublin (Baile Átha Cliath) · Dún Laoghaire · Bray · Drogheda · Dundalk · Navan

ENGLAND

NORTHUMBERLAND · TYNE AND WEAR · DURHAM · CUMBRIA

Newcastle · Tynemouth · South Shields · Sunderland · Gateshead · Hexham · Morpeth · Alnwick · Blyth · Hartlepool · Durham · Bishop Auckland · Barnard Castle · Darlington · Stockton · Middlesbrough · Billingham · Redcar

Cumbrian Mts. · Skiddaw · Keswick · Kendal · Ambleside · Windermere · Workington · Whitehaven · St Bee's Hd. · Maryport · Barrow · Walney

PENNINES

NORTH YORKSHIRE · HUMBERSIDE · WEST YORKSHIRE · SOUTH YORKSHIRE · LANCASHIRE · MERSEYSIDE · GREATER MANCHESTER · CHESHIRE

York · Harrogate · Ripon · Northallerton · Thirsk · Whitby · Scarborough · Bridlington · Flamborough Hd. · Hornsea · Withernsea · Spurn Hd. · Mablethorpe · Skegness · Beverley · Hull · Grimsby · Cleethorpes · Louth · Lincoln · Lincoln Wolds

Leeds · Bradford · Halifax · Huddersfield · Wakefield · Dewsbury · Barnsley · Sheffield · Rotherham · Doncaster · Worksop

Preston · Blackpool · Fleetwood · Lancaster · Morecambe · Blackburn · Burnley · Nelson · Colne · Bolton · Bury · Rochdale · Oldham · Manchester · Salford · Stockport · Macclesfield

Liverpool · Southport · Formby · Wallasey · Birkenhead · St Helens · Warrington · Widnes · Runcorn · Northwich · Crewe

Flint · Anglesey · Holyhead · Beaumaris · Holy I. · St Asaph

COPYRIGHT. GEORGE PHILIP & SON, LTD.

FRANCE

ENGLISH CHANNEL

St. George's Channel

Bristol Channel

Cardigan Bay

The Wash

Strait of Dover

NORFOLK
SUFFOLK
ESSEX
KENT
SURREY
SUSSEX
WEST SUSSEX
HANTS
DORSET
DEVON
CORNWALL
SOMERSET
WILTS
BERKS
OXFORD
BUCKS
BEDFORD
HERTFORD
NORTHAMPTON
CAMBRIDGE
LEICESTER
WARWICK
STAFFORD
SHROPSHIRE
HEREFORD AND WORCESTER
GLOUCESTER
GWENT
MID GLAMORGAN
WEST GLAMORGAN
POWYS
DYFED
GWYNEDD
CLWYD

LONDON
Birmingham
Coventry
Leicester
Nottingham
Derby
Stoke-on-Trent
Wolverhampton
Dudley
Worcester
Gloucester
Bristol
Cardiff
Swansea
Newport
Exeter
Plymouth
Bournemouth
Southampton
Portsmouth
Brighton
Worthing
Eastbourne
Hastings
Folkestone
Dover
Canterbury
Margate
Ramsgate
Maidstone
Chatham
Southend
Colchester
Ipswich
Norwich
Great Yarmouth
Lowestoft
King's Lynn
Peterborough
Northampton
Bedford
Luton
Oxford
Reading
Guildford
Southport

Cardiff
Aberystwyth
Lampeter
Fishguard
Milford Haven
Pembroke
Carmarthen

Land's End
Penzance
St. Ives
Truro
Falmouth
Newquay
Bideford
Barnstaple
Ilfracombe
Taunton
Weston-super-Mare
Bridgwater
Yeovil
Weymouth
Poole
Swanage
Newport
Isle of Wight

Calais
Boulogne-sur-Mer
Dieppe
Abbeville

SCOTLAND

0 20 40 60 miles
0 20 40 60 80 100 km

SHETLAND

Unst
Fetlar
Yell
Whalsay
Shetland Is.
Rona
Mainland
Bressay
Lerwick
Foula

On same scale   Sumburgh Hd.

Mainland
Sumburgh Hd.
Fair Isle

ATLANTIC

OCEAN

N. Ronaldsay
Westray
Rousay   Eday   Sanday
ORKNEY   Shapinsay Stronsay
Mainland   Orkney Is.
Kirkwall
Hoy   South
Ronaldsay

Pentland Firth

C. Wrath   Strathy Pt.   Dunnet Hd.   John O'Groats
Thurso   Duncansby
Noss Hd.
Ben Hope   Halladale   Wick

NORTH

SEA

Butt of Lewis

Stornoway   Broad Bay
LEWIS
WESTERN
Tarbert
Harris
ISLES

The Aird
North Uist
Monach Is.
Benbecula
Ben More
619
South Uist

Barra
Barra Hd.

Eddrachillis Bay
L. Laxford
Assynt
B. More
Assynt 998
Loch Shin   Lairg
Ullapool   Dornoch   Tarbat Ness
Golspie
Dornoch Firth
Tain

Little Minch
L. Broom   B. Dearg
1081
HIGHLAND
Invergordon
Ben Wyvis
1045   Dingwall   Cromarty
Beauly   Nairn   Forres   Elgin   Buckie
Inverness   Keith   Huntly   Turriff   Peterhead
GRAMPIAN
Don   Aberdeen
Girdle Ness

Ord of Caithness
Helmsdale
Bonar Br.

Moray Firth

Kinnairds Hd.
Fraserburgh
Buchan
Oldmeldrum

NORTH WEST HIGHLANDS

The Minch
L. Maree
L. Torridon
Gairloch
Glen Carron
Glen Affric   Glen Moriston
L. Mullardoch
Farrar
Glen Garry
Glen Spean
Ben Nevis 1343
Fort William
Grantown-on-Spey   Cairn Gorm   Braemar
Kingussie   Cairngorm Mts.   1245   Balmoral Castle
1311   Lochnagar   Banchory
Pass of Killiecrankie   Braes of Angus
Stonehaven

North Minch
Portree
Raasay
Kyle
Lochalsh
Cuillin Hills
Cuillin Sound
Canna
Rhum
Eigg
Muck
Ardnamurchan Point
Coll
Tiree
Staffa
Iona
Mull
B. More 966
Colonsay
Oban
Ben Cruachan 942

SCOTLAND

GRAMPIAN MOUNTAINS

L. Shiel
Mallaig
L. Morar
Arisaig
L. Arkaig
Loch Eil
Ardgour
Morvern
Loch Linnhe
Sound of Mull
Tobermory
L. Sunart
Sound of Jura
Jura
Islay
Gigha
Rathlin I.
Fair Hd.
Mull of Kintyre
Campbeltown

Ben Lawers 1214
Aberfeldy   Pitlochry   Tummel   Blairgowrie
Rannoch   Forfar
L. Tay   Ben More 1174   TAYSIDE   Brechin   Montrose
Breadalbane   Sidlaw Hills   Arbroath
Scone   N. Esk   S. Esk
Crieff   Perth   Dundee
Earn   Firth of Tay   Tayport
Ben Vorlich   Comrie   Cupar   St. Andrews
Ben More 983   FIFE   File Ness
Trossachs   Glenrothes   Anstruther
Ben Ledi   Callander   Leven   Buckhaven   Forth
Ben Lomond   Kinross   Kirkcaldy   Bass Rock
CENTRAL   Stirling   Dunfermline   Firth of Forth   Dunbar
Alloa   Bannockburn   Leith   Haddington   St. Abb's Hd.
L. Lomond   Grangemouth   EDINBURGH   Musselburgh
Helensburgh   Falkirk   LOTHIAN   Dalkeith   Lammermuir Hills
Dunoon   Dumbarton   Peebles   Berwick-upon-Tweed
Greenock   Clydebank   Glasgow   Moorfoot Hills   Coldstream   Holy I.
Port Glasgow   Paisley   Coatbridge   Carstairs   Galashiels   Kelso   Farne Is.
Rothesay   Motherwell   Lanark   Selkirk   Jedburgh   Cheviot   Alnwick
STRATHCLYDE   Hamilton   Wishaw   BORDERS   Hawicks   816   Coquet
Ardrossan   Saltcoats   Kilmarnock   Carts Fell   Tweed   Cheviot Hills   NORTHUMBERLAND
Irvine   Prestwick   SOUTHERN   Morpeth
Brodick   Ayr   Sanquhar   UPLANDS   Newcastle
Arran   Doon   Merrick 843   Gretna Green   Blaydon   Gateshead
Giants Causeway   Ballycastle   Girvan   DUMFRIES   Tyne   Hexham   DURHAM   Bishop Auckland
Moville   Portrush   AND   Dumfries   Annan   Carlisle   ENGLAND   Durham
Coleraine   Ballymoney   GALLOWAY   Castle Douglas   Cross Fell   Penrith
Spertin Mts.   Savel 683   Trostan 554   Kirkcudbright   CUMBRIA   893
NORTHERN   Ballymena   Wigtown   Wigtown Bay   Solway Firth   Skiddaw 931   PENNINE RANGE
IRELAND   Larne   Stranraer   Maryport   Workington   Keswick
Antrim   Belfast   Portpatrick   Luce Bay   Derwent
Carrickfergus   Bangor   Mull of Galloway

Firth of Clyde
North Channel
North Firth of Clyde
Loch Fyne
Lochgilphead
Inveraray
Ben Vorlich
Kilmarnock

West from Greenwich

COPYRIGHT. GEORGE PHILIP & SON LTD.

9

IRELAND

0   20   40   60 miles
0 20 40 60 80 100 km

ATLANTIC

OCEAN

SCOTLAND

Tiree
Staffa
B. More
996
Iona
Mull
Oban
Colonsay
Lochgilphead
STRATHCLYDE
Rudh a' Mhail
Islay
Bowmore
Gigha
Arran
Campbeltown
Mull of Kintyre

North Channel

Malin Hd.
Giant's Causeway
Ballycastle
Rathlin I.
Fair Hd.
Tory I.
Sheep Haven
Lough Swilly
Inishowen Pen.
Moville
Portrush
Horn Hd.
Bloody Foreland
Buncrana
Coleraine
Ballymoney
Trostan
Londonderry
Errigal
752
Letterkenny
Aran I.
Derryveagh Mts.
Ballymena
Larne
DONEGAL
Sperrin Mts.
Sewel
683
Strabane
Carrickfergus
Gweebarra B.
Glenties
Finn
Lifford
NORTHERN
Loughros More B.
676
Bluestack
IRELAND
Belfast
Rossan Pt.
Mts.
Lough
Bangor
Rathlin O'Birne I.
Killybegs
Donegal
ULSTER
Neagh
Newtownards
Omagh
Dungannon
Lisburn
Donegal Bay
Ballyshannon
Erne
Portadown
Lurgan
Broad Haven
Enniskillen
Banbridge
Ardglass
Erris Hd.
Sligo B.
Upper
L. Erne
ARMAGH
Downpatrick
Mullet
Sligo
MONAGHAN
Monaghan
Donard
Newcastle
Peninsula
SLIGO
Armagh
952
Dundrum
Achill
Ballina
LEITRIM
Newry
Bay
Head
CAVAN
St. Gullion
Warrenpoint
Achill I.
L. Conn
Cootehill
Castleblayney
Carlingford L.
Clare I.
Nephin
806
Castlebar
Cavan
Louth
Dundalk
Clew Bay
MAYO
Boyle
Carrick-on-Shannon
Ardee
Dundalk Bay
Westport
ROSCOMMON
L. Gowna
Croagh Patrick
Claremorris
Inishbofin
765
CONNACHT
L. Sheelin
Ceanannus Mor
Drogheda
Mweelrea
819
LONGFORD
(Kells)
Balbriggan
Killary Harbour
L. Mask
Longford
An Uaimh
Slyne Hd.
Tuam
Roscommon
(Navan)
Twelve Pins
L. Corrib
L. Ree
MEATH
Howth Hd.
Connemara
WESTMEATH
Boyne
GALWAY
Athlone
Mullingar
Maynooth
Dublin (Baile Atha
Galway
REPUBLIC
Cliath)
Kilkieran B.
Athenry
Tullamore
Celbridge
Dun
Galway Bay
Ballinasloe
Laoghaire
Inishmore
Gort
OF
OFFALY
Naas
Bray
Aran Is.
Slieve Aughty
Clara
KILDARE
754
Birr
St. Bloom
Kildare
Poulaphouca
Wicklow
Liscannor Bay
IRELAND
Mountmellick
Res.
Mal Bay
CLARE
L. Derg
Roscrea
Portlaoise
WICKLOW
Lugnaquilla
Ennis
LEINSTER
Athy
925
Kilkee
LAOIS
Carlow
Mizen Hd.
Keeper
694
Nenagh
Arklow
Loop Hd.
Kilrush
Thurles
CARLOW
Shannon
TIPPERARY
Kilkenny
Foynes
Muine Bheag
Rathkeale
Limerick
Golden
KILKENNY
Gorey
Brandon B.
Listowel
LIMERICK
Vale
St. Mullins
Cahore Pt.
Tralee
Feale
Rath Luirc
Tipperary
722
Enniscorthy
Dingle
St. Mish
(Charleville)
Galtymore
Carrick-
WEXFORD
Great
920
on-Suir
Blasket
Feale
Mitchelstown
Clonmel
New Ross
I.
KERRY
Knockmealdown
Waterford
Wexford
Dingle Bay
Killarney
Mallow
Mts.
Comeragh Mts.
Rosslare
Macgillycuddy's
Blackwater
Fermoy
Tramore
Wexford Harbour
Valentia
Reeks
Dungarvan
Greenore Pt.
Harbour
Carrantuohill
Boggeragh Mts.
Tuskar Rock
1040
CORK
Dungarvan Bay
Carnsore Pt.
Valentia
Lakes of
Killarney
Youghal
Ballinskelligs B.
Macroom
Cork
Saltee Is.
Castletown Berehaven
Caha Mts.
Lee
Midleton
Youghal Harbour
Bantry
Cobh
Crow Head
Bandon
Cork Harbour
Dunmanus Bay
Clonakilty
Mizen Hd.
Bantry Bay
Galley Hd.
Old Head of Kinsale
Fastnet Rock
Clear I.
Clear

St. George's Channel

West from Greenwich

COPYRIGHT. GEORGE PHILIP & SON. LTD.

FRANCE

0 20 40 60 80 100 miles
0 40 80 120 160 km

Swansea • Newport • LONDON • Southend
Cardiff • Bristol • Bath • Swindon • Margate
Taunton • E N G L A N D • Dover • Cala
Southampton • Chichester • Brighton • Folkestone • Hastings • C. Gris • C. Nez • Boulogne
Exeter • Exmouth • Portsmouth • Ryde • Newhaven • Montreuil
Torquay • Weymouth • Bournemouth • Somme
St. Ives • Truro • Dartmouth • Portland • Le Tréport • Dieppe
Land's End • Penzance • Falmouth • Plymouth • Eddystone
50

E N G L I S H   C H A N N E L
C. de la Hague • St. Valery • Fécamp • Caux • Yvetot • S. Me.
Alderney • Cherbourg • Pte. de Barfleur • Le Havre • Bolbec • Rouen
Guernsey • St. Peter Port • Sark • Valognes • Trouville • Honfleur • Elbeu • Vexin
Channel Is. • St. Helier • Bessin • Bayeux • Lisieux • Evreux
(Br.) • Jersey • St. Lô • Caen • Falaise • Mantes • Versai
Granville • Mt. St. Michel • Vire • Or. • Perche • Dreux • E. L.
Ushant • Pte. de St. Mathieu • Brest • Morlaix • Guingamp • St. Brieuc • Avranches • Alençon • Chartres
Mts. B d'Arrée • St. Brieuc • Dinard • Fougères • Mayenne • Beauc
Pte. du Raz • Mts. Noire • Dinan • Rennes • Laval • M A I N E • Le Mans • Orléan
Quimper • I. V. • May. • Orléan
Pte. de Penmarch • Lorient • Mo. • Vannes • Châteaubriant • Sarthe • Loir • Blois • S. O. L.
Quimperlé • Carnac • Angers • Tours • TOURAINE • Amboise • Vie
Quiberon • Belle I. • St. Nazaire • Nantes • Cholet • Chinon • I. L. • Loches
Ile de Noirmoutier • Ve. • Bocage • D. S. • Châtellerault • Châteauroux • I.
Ile de Yeu • La Roche • P O I T O U • Poitiers • Creuse
Les Sables d'Olonne • Fontenay • Catine • Vi.
46 • Ile de Ré • Niort • Vienne • M A R C
Rochefort • La Rochelle • AUNIS • Guer
B A Y • Ile d' Oléron • Saintes • ANGOUMOIS • H. V.
Royan • Cognac • Angoulême • Limoges
O F • Le Verdon • Médoc • Ch. • LIMO
B I S C A Y • Périgueux • Limoges
Pauillac • D • Perigord • Sarlat
Libourne • Dordogne • Bergerac
Bordeaux • Gi. • G U Y E • Lot
Arcachon • Garonne • L. G. • Cahors
44 • L • Agen • T. G.
Mont de Marsan • Monta
Gijón • Llanes • S. Vicente de la Barquera • Gulf of • G A S C O N Y • Armagnac • Auch
Oviedo • Torrelavega • Santander • Gascony • Téour • Ge. • Toulouse
Picos de Europa 2648 • Santoña • Biarritz • Bayonne • Orthez • G. H.
Sa. de Alba • Reinosa • Guecho • Fuenterrabia • Pau • B E A R N • P. A. • Tarbes
Léon • Durango • Sestao • Bilbao • San Sebastian • Lourdes • Ari.
Talosa • Roncesvalles • Pic du Midi 2889 • H. Pyrénées • Fo
Astorga • Saldaña • Vitoria • Pamplona • Canfranc Mt. Perdu 3355 • N
S • Sahagún • Burgos • Logroño • Tafalla • Jaca • Andorra • La Seu d'
P • R • Miranda • 1631 • La Teste 1609

West from Greenwich   East from Greenwich

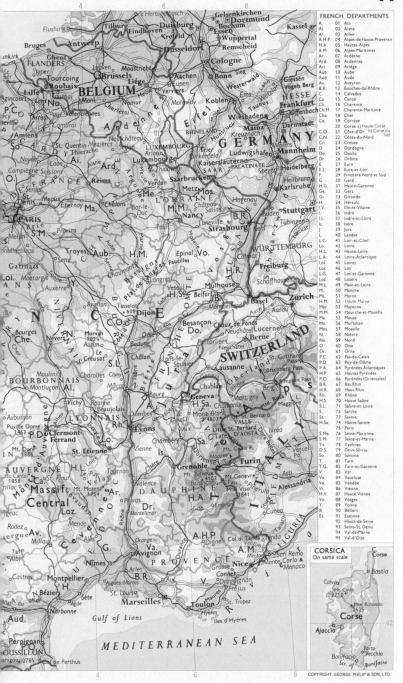

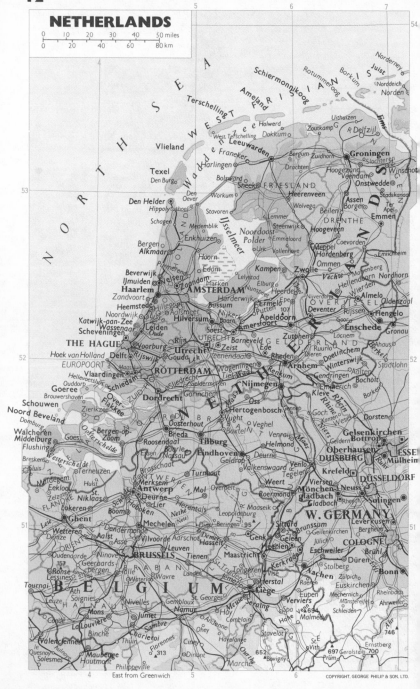

NETHERLANDS

12

0 10 20 30 40 50 miles
0   20   40   60   80 km

NORTH SEA

WEST FRISIAN ISLANDS

Norderney
Juist
Borkum
Norddeich
Norden
Rottumeroog
Rotummeroog
Schiermonnikoog
Ameland
Terschelling
West Terschelling
Vlieland
Holwerd
Dokkum
Zoutkamp
Uithuizen
R Delfzijl
Ems

Texel
Den Burg
Harlingen
Franeker
Leeuwarden
Bergum
Zuidhorn
Drachten
Groningen
Slochteren
Winschoten

Den Helder
Hippolytushoef
Schagen
Den Oever
Workum
Bolsward
Sneek
FRIESLAND
Heerenveen
Hoogezand
Veendam
Onstwedde
Stadskanaal
Wolvega
Beilen
Borger
Ter Apel
Emmen

Medemblik
Stavoren
Lemmer
Steenwijk
DRENTHE
Hoogeveen
Coevorden
Emmen

Bergen
Alkmaar
Enkhuizen
Noordoost-Polder
Urk
Emmeloord
Vollenhove
Meppel
Hardenberg
Emlichheim
Nordhorn

Hoorn
Kampen
Zwolle
Ommen
Vechte
Hellendoorn
Nordhorn

Edam
Marken
Lelystad
Elburg
Heerde
Wijhe
Raalte
OVERIJSEL
Almelo
Oldenzaal

Beverwijk
IJmuiden
Velsen
Zaandam
AMSTERDAM
Harderwijk
Nunspeet
Deventer
Rijssen
Hengelo

Haarlem
Zandvoort
Heemstede
Hillegom
Aalsmeer
Bussum
Hilversum
Ermelo
Nijkerk
Putten 107
Apeldoorn
Goor
Enschede
Gronau

Noordwijk
Katwijk-aan-Zee
Wassenaar
Leiden
Voorburg
Rijn
Soest
Baarn
Amersfoort
Zutphen
Ruurlo
Doetinchem
Ahaus
Berkel

THE HAGUE
Scheveningen
Oude
Delft
Rijswijk
Gouda
Utrecht
Zeist
Barneveld
GELDERLAND
Ede
Rhenen
Arnhem
Winterswijk
Stadtlohn

Hoek van Holland
EUROPOORT
Vlaardingen
Schiedam
ROTTERDAM
Lek
Veenendaal
Wageningen
Renkum
Gendringen
Aalten
Bocholt

Helvoetsluis
Maassluis
Maas
Gorinchem
Tiel
Waal
Nijmegen
Kleve
Rhein
Emmerich
Borken

Ouddorp
Goeree
Over Flakkee
Dordrecht
WAAL
Geldermalsen
Oss
Hertogenbosch
Genmep
Goch
Xanten
Wesel
Dorsten

Brouwershaven
Schouwen
Zierikzee
Oosterhout
Vught
Baxtel
Veghel
Venray
Gelsenkirchen
Bottrop

Noord Beveland
Domburg
Bergen-op-Zoom
Roosendaal
Breda
Tilburg
Helmond
Deurne
Venlo
Geldern
Oberhausen
DUISBURG
ESSEN
Mulheim

Walcheren
Middelburg
Flushing
Goes
Oosterschelde
Baarle Nassau
Eindhoven
Geldrop
Deurne
Tegelen
Krefeld
DÜSSELDORF

Breskens
Sluis
Terneuzen
Hulst
Eisen
Turnhout
Valkenswaard
Weert
Overpelt
Roermond
Viersen
Neuss
Mönchen-gladbach
Rheydt
Solingen

Maldegem
Eekloo
Zelzate
St Niklaas
Brasschaat
Merksem
ANTWERP
Deurne
Mol
Leopoldsburg
Maaseik
Sittard
Brunssum
Leverkusen
Bergheim
W. GERMANY

FLANDERS
Lokeren
Boom
Hoboken
Lier
Herentals
Nethe
Beringen 95
Geilenkirchen
Jülich
COLOGNE

Leie
Wetteren
Dendermonde
Mechelen
Diest
Hasselt
Genk
Geleen
Heerlen
Eschweiler
Brühl

Denze
Aalst
Asse
Vilvoorde
Aarschot
Demer
GENK
Sittard
Maastricht
Kerkrade
Aachen
Stolberg
Düren
Bonn

Oudenaarde
Ninove
Leuven
Tienen
Landen
St Truiden
Tongeren
Herstal
Eupen
Raeren
Zülpich
Euskirchen
Mechernich
Rheinbach
Ahrweiler

BRUSSELS
Geraards-bergen
Halle
Waterloo
Wavre
BRABANT
Namur
Liège
Verviers
Spa 694
Malmedy
Münstereifel
Schleiden

Tournai
Ronse 157
Lessines
Ath
Soignies
Nivelles
Gembloux
Huy
Hoei
Comblain
Hohe
Stavelot
St Vith
697
Gerolstein 700
Ernstberg

BELGIUM
Mons
Condé
La Louvière
Binche
Thuin
Charleroi
Florennes 313
Ciney
Dinant
Andenne
Ohey
Hamoir
Havelange
Marche
652
Bovigny
Prüm

Valenciennes
le Quesnoy
Solesmes
Maubeuge
Hautmont
Philippeville
Ahr 746

East from Greenwich

COPYRIGHT. GEORGE PHILIP & SON. LTD.

ICELAND
On same scale
as general map

SCANDINAVIA

	0	100	200 miles
0	100	200	300

COPYRIGHT. GEORGE PHILIP & SON. LTD.

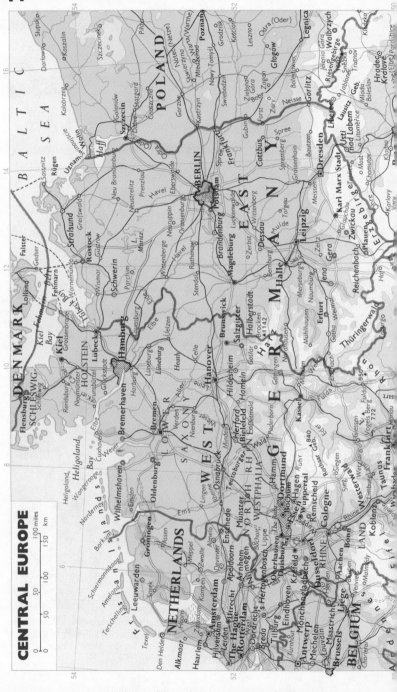

CENTRAL EUROPE

100 miles
km

0   50   100   150
0   50   100

BALTIC SEA

DENMARK
Flensburg
SCHLESWIG
Falster
Lolland
Gedser
Fehmarn
Fehmarn Bay
Kiel Bay
Kiel
Grossenbrode
Rendsburg
Neumünster
HOLSTEIN
Brunsbüttel
Glückstadt
Lübeck

Sassnitz
Rügen
Stralsund
Greifswald
Rostock
Güstrow
Wismar
Schwerin
Parchim

POLAND
Slupsko
Dartowo
Koszalin
Szczecinko
Slawno
Kolobrzeg
Stargard
Szczecin
Dobre
Gorzów
Kostrzyn
Odra (Oder)
Poznań
Grodzisk
Kościan
Leszno
Głogów

Swinoujście
Wolin
Haff
Uznam
Neu Brandenburg
Neustrelitz
Prenzlau
Eberswalde
BERLIN
Potsdam
Brandenburg
Luckenwalde
Wittenberg
Dessau
Torgau

Legnica
Wałbrzych
Jelenia Góra
Riesengebirge
Sněžka
Geb.
Trutnov
Hradec Králové

Görlitz
Bolesławiec
Zary
Zagan
Zielona Góra
Bóbr
Gubin
Forst
Cottbus
Spremberg
Sprenberg
Hoyerswerda
Bautzen
Görlitz

Gubin
Spree
Neisse
Frankfurt
EAST
Wittenberge
Neuruppin
Oranienburg
Havel
Rathenow
Genthin
Brandenburg
Magdeburg
Zerbst
Bernburg
Halle
Merseburg
Naumburg
Leipzig
Zeitz
Gera
Jena
Erfurt
Weimar
Gotha

GERMANY
Karl Marx Stadt
Zwickau
Plauen
Reichenbach
Hof
Dresden
Meissen
ERZGEBIRGE
Most
Chomutov
Karlovy Vary
Usti nad Labem
Litoměřice
Mladá Boleslav

Thüringerwald

LOWER SAXONY
Bremerhaven
Cuxhaven
Bremen
Verden
Nienburg
Celle
Lüneburg
Harburg
Uelzen
Salzgitter
Brunswick
Halberstadt
Brocken 1142
Harz
Nordhausen
Mühlhausen
Göttingen

Hamburg
Elbe
Lüneburg Heath
Hildesheim
Hanover
Hameln
Herford
Bielefeld
Minden

WEST
SAXONY
Oldenburg
Osnabrück
Lingen
Enschede
MÜNSTER
WESTPHALIA
Hamm
Dortmund
Bochum
Essen
Wuppertal
Hagen
Remscheid
Paderborn
Kassel
Fulda
Vogels Berg 772

NETHERLANDS
Groningen
Leeuwarden
Assen
Meppel
Zwolle
Deventer
Apeldoorn
Arnhem
Nijmegen
's Hertogenbosch
Eindhoven
Breda
Tilburg
Dordrecht
Rotterdam
The Hague
Leiden
Haarlem
Amsterdam
Utrecht
Hilversum
Alkmaar
Den Helder
Texel
Terschelling
Ameland
Schiermonnikoog
Borkum
Norderney
Juist
Emden
Wilhelmshaven
Wangerooge
Heligoland
Heligoland Bay

BELGIUM
Brussels
Mechelen
Antwerp
Louvain
Liège
Maastricht
Aachen
Cologne
Bonn
Düsseldorf
Krefeld
Mönchengladbach
RHINE
Rhine
Siegen
Koblenz
Frankfurt
Wiesbaden
Taunus
Westerwald
EIFEL
WESTERWALD
Thüringer

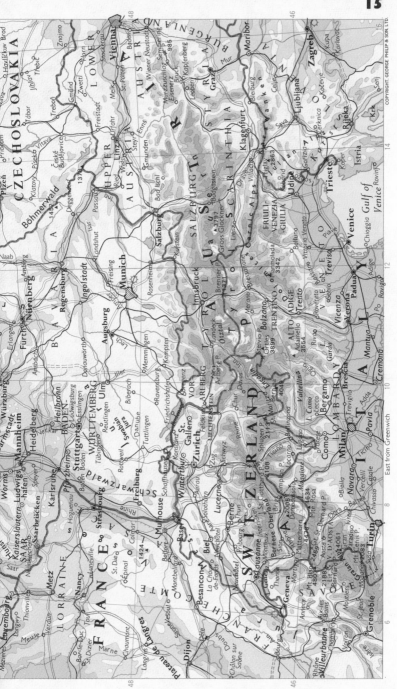

COPYRIGHT. GEORGE PHILIP & SON, LTD.

CZECHOSLOVAKIA

LOWER AUSTRIA

UPPER AUSTRIA

BAVARIA

WÜRTTEMBERG

BADEN

FRANCE

LORRAINE

FRANCHE COMTE

SWITZERLAND

TYROL

SALZBURG

STYRIA

CARINTHIA

SLOVENIA

BURGENLAND

FRIULI VENEZIA GIULIA

VENETO

LOMBARDY

ITALY

TRENTINO-ALTO ADIGE

Vienna
Wiener Neustadt
Baden
St. Pölten
Melk
Krems
Stockerau
Znojmo
Brno
Trebíč
Jihlava
Havlíčkův Brod
Příbram
Plzeň
Klatovy
Böhmerwald
Písek
České Budějovice
Tábor
Třeboň
Gmünd
Zwettl
Freistadt
Linz
Steyr
Enns
Amstetten
Wels
Gmunden
Bad Ischl
Salzburg
Kufstein
Innsbruck
Brenner P.
Rosenheim
Kempten
Passau
Deggendorf
Landshut
Freising
Munich
Augsburg
Donauwörth
Memmingen
Ingolstadt
Regensburg
Nürnberg
Fürth
Erlangen
Würzburg
Ansbach
Heilbronn
Ludwigsburg
Stuttgart
Esslingen
Reutlingen
Tübingen
Ulm
Biberach
Ravensburg
Friedrichshafen
Konstanz
St. Gallen
Feldkirch
LIECHTENSTEIN
Bregenz
VOR ARLBERG
Bludenz
Schwaz
Landeck
Ötztal
Meran
Bolzano
Trento
Rovereto
Treviso
Venice
Padua
Vicenza
Verona
Mantua
Cremona
Pavia
Milan
Bergamo
Brescia
Como
Lecco
L. Como
L. Garda
L. Maggiore
Lugano
Locarno
Bellinzona
Novara
Vercelli
Turin
Chivasso
Grenoble
Chambéry
Aix-les-Bains
Annecy
Geneva
Lausanne
Montreux
Neuchâtel
Bienne
Berne
Thun
Interlaken
Lucerne
Zug
Schwyz
Zürich
Winterthur
Schaffhausen
Aarau
Olten
Basel
Mulhouse
Colmar
Sélestat
Strasbourg
Saverne
Haguenau
Karlsruhe
Pforzheim
Baden Baden
Freiburg
Schwarzwald
Belfort
Montbéliard
Besançon
Pontarlier
Dijon
Dôle
Châlon sur Saône
Chaumont
St. Dizier
Bar-le-Duc
Verdun
Metz
Nancy
Lunéville
Épinal
St. Dié
Vesoul
Lons-le-Saunier
Bourg
Plateau de Langres
Thionville
Luxembourg
Diekirch
Longwy
Mézières
Kaiserslautern
Saarbrücken
Saarlouis
Worms
Mannheim
Heidelberg
Ludwigshafen
Speyer
Zagreb
Maribor
Ljubljana
Klagenfurt
Villach
Celje
Rijeka
Trieste
Gulf of Venice
Venezia
Udine
Pordenone
Belluno
Piave
Adige
Po
Rovigo
Chioggia
Velden
Leoben
Bruck
Graz
Mürzzuschlag
Semmering
Eisenerz
Mur
Drau
Sava
Kupa
Karlovac
Krk
Istria
Koper
Rovinj
Poreč
Pula
Crikvenica
Senj

Gross Glockner 3797
Ortles 3899
Adamello 3554
Bernina 4049
Monte Rosa 4634
Mt. Blanc 4807
Matterhorn 4505
St. Gotthard 3108
Grossglockner 3798
Gran Paradiso 4061

East from Greenwich

Rhine
Danube
Inn
Naab
Main
Lech
Isar
Iller
Rhône
Rhône
Saône
Doubs
Marne
Meuse
Saar
Ticino
Adda
Po
Dora

48
46
14
12
10
8
6

16

ITALY AND
S.E. EUROPE

| 0 | 50 | 100 | 150 | 200 miles |
| 0 | 100 | 200 | 300 | km |

GERMANY

Nuremberg • Plzeň • CZECHOS
Ostrava
Jablunk
Jihlava
Regensburg • Brno • Slavkov
Isar • Linz • Bratisl
Ulm • Augsburg • Inn • Danube
L. of Constance • Munich • Salzburg • Vienna
Belfort
Dijon • Besançon • Basel • Zürich • Innsbruck • Au • Sr • A • Bruck • Graz • H
Berne • Lausanne • TYROL • Brenner P. • Raab • Bulato
SWITZERLAND • Geneva • 1371 • Drava • Klagenfurt • Pécs
Lyons • Mt. Blanc • Simplon P. • Ortler • Trento • Piave • Mur
4807 • Mt. Cenis • 3899 • Ljubljana
Grenoble • Como • Bergamo • Brescia • Udine • Gorizia • Trieste • Zagreb
Turin • Milan • Novara • Gardo • Vicenza • Isonzo • Rijeka • YUGO
Po • Verona • Padua • Venice • Pula • Brod
Alessandria • Parma • Reggio • Ferrara • G. of • Una • Banja Luka
Avignon • Monaco • Genoa • Modena • Venice • BOSNI
Marseilles • Menton • La • Bologna • Ravenna
Cannes • Nice • Spezia • P. • Forlì • Zadar • Dinaric Alps
Toulon • Gulf of Genoa • Florence • Rimini • San Marino • Bosna
C. Corse • Leghorn • Arno • Arezzo • Anconal • Dalmati
Ligurian Sea • Siena • Perugia • Sibenik • Split
2710 • Elba • Gran Sasso • Vis
Mte. Cinto • Bastia • 2914 • Lastovo • Dubrovnik
Ajaccio • CORSICA • Civitavecchia • Sabine Mts. • ADRIATIC
Str. of Bonifacio • Caprera • ROME • Tiber • SEA
Sassari • Olbia • Gaeta • Mt. Gargano
Volturno • Foggia
Str. of Messina • Naples • Vesuvius • Barletta • Bari
Mti. del Gennargentu • ▼3719 • 1277 • Bri
1834 • Capri • Salerno • Otranto • G. of
Cagliari • Tyrrhenian Sea • Taranto • Tarant
Cosenza • La Sila • C.
1929 • Ma
SARDINIA • Catanzaro • di Le
Stromboli
MEDITER • Lipari Is. • Ion
Palermo • Messina • S
Skikda • Trapani • Egadi Is. • Mt. Etna • Reggio
Annaba • Marsala • 3340 • C. Spartivento
Bizerta • Agrigento • Catania • Str. of Messina
Constantine • C. Bon • Caltanissetta
Tunis • Pantelleria (It.) • Siracusa
ALGERIA • G. of Hammamet • C. Passero
Kairouan • Sousse • Gozo
Tébessa • Valletta
TUNISIA • Lampedusa • MALTA • R
(It.)
Sfax • Kerkennah • 4135 ▼ • A
Tozeur • Chott Djerid • Gabès
Djerba

East from Greenwich

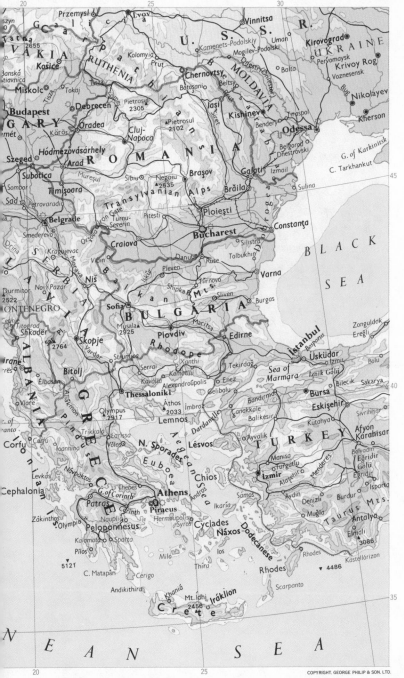

COPYRIGHT. GEORGE PHILIP & SON. LTD.

18

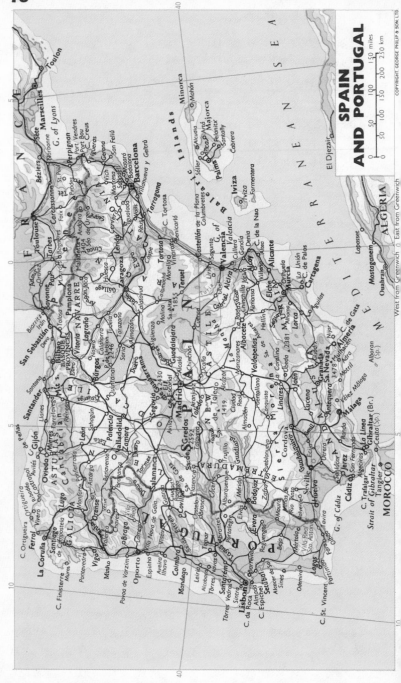

SPAIN
AND PORTUGAL

COPYRIGHT GEORGE PHILIP & SON, LTD

MIDDLE EAST

0 100 200 miles
0 100 200 300 km

- - - - - Division between Greeks and Turks
in Cyprus; Turks to the north.

East from Greenwich

COPYRIGHT. GEORGE PHILIP & SON, LTD.

Countries and regions: TURKEY, SYRIA, LEBANON, CYPRUS, ISRAEL, JORDAN, IRAQ, IRAN, SAUDI ARABIA, KUWAIT, EGYPT

MEDITERRANEAN SEA

AZERBAIJAN, KURDESTAN, BAKHTARAN, LORESTAN, KHUZESTAN

AN NAFUD, Sahrā al Hijārah, Ṣaḥrā' Al Ḥamād

SINAI, Gulf of Suez, Gulf of Aqaba, Red Sea, Dead Sea

Cities: Cairo, Baghdad, Damascus, Amman, Jerusalem, Tel Aviv-Jaffa, Beirut, Aleppo, Mosul, Kirkuk, Basra, Kuwait, Abadan, Hamadan, Tabrīz, Marāgheh, Zanjān, Suez, Port Said, Ismailîya, Tanta, Mansura, El Gîza, Beni Suef, El Minya, Nicosia, Famagusta, Limassol, Larnaca, Tripoli, Homs, Hama, Latakia, Tartûs, Tyre, Haifa, Tel Aviv, Ashdod, Gaza, Eilat, Al 'Aqabah, Tabūk, Al Jawf, Rafḥā, Ḥafar al Bāṭin, Al Qaysūmah, Az Zubayr, Khorramshahr, Dezful, Ahvāz, Al Amārah, An Nāṣirīyah, As Samāwah, An Najaf, Karbalā', Al Hillah, Ar Ramādī, Ar Ruṭbah, Sāmarrā', Tikrīt, Erbil

ICELAND

ATLANTIC OCEAN

Jan Mayen

ARCTIC

Franz Josef Land

Spitsbergen

BRITISH ISLES

North Sea

Bergen

Trondheim

Hammerfesto

North Cape

Barents Sea

Novaya Zemlya

Oslo

Stavanger

N O R W A Y

S W E D E N

Narvik

Kara Sea

Putih

Dickson

DENMARK

Hamburg

Esbjerg

Copenhagen

Göteborg

Gulf of Bothnia

F I N L A N D

Murmansk

Kolguyev

Pechora Gulf

Novaya Zemlya

Vaigach I.

Khabarovo

Kola Pen.

Kandalaksha

Berlin

Kaliningrad

Baltic Sea

Malmö

Szczecin

Stockholm

Helsinki

G. of Finland

Tallinn

ESTONIA

Riga

LATVIA

Petrozavodsk

L. Ladoga

L. Onega

White Sea

N. Dvina

Arkhangelsk

Pechora

Naryan Mar

Novy Port

Vorkuta

1894

Telpos Iz

1617

POLAND

Wrocław

Łódź

Warsaw

Gdynia

Vilnius

LITHUANIA

Minsk

Leningrad

Kalinin

Yaroslavl

Moscow

Vitebsk

Vologda

Kostroma

Katlas

Berezniki

R U S S I A N

Serov

U r a l s

West Siberian

S. S. R.

S O V I E T   F E D E

Plain

Brest

Lvov

Gomel

Smolensk

Orel

Tula

Ivanovo

Gorki

Kirov

Ustinov

Kama

Perm

Nizhniy Tagil

Sverdlovsk

Tyumen

Tobolsk

Irtysh

UKRAINE

Zhitomir

Kiev

Kharkov

Voronezh

Penza

Ulyanovsk

Kazan

Ufa

Chelyabinsk

Kurgan

Petropavlovsk

Omsk

Tomsk

Odessa

Dnepropetrovsk

Krivoy Rog

Zaporozhye

Donetsk

Saratov

Kuybyshev

Zlatoust

Magnitogorsk

Tatarsk

Novosibirsk

Barnaul

Chişinău

Nikolayev

Kherson

Rostov

Volgograd

Engels

Orenburg

Orsk

Aktyubinsk

Kokchetav

Pavlodar

Slavgorod

Sevastopol

Novorossiysk

Sea of Azov

Kerch

Krasnodar

Elbrus 5633

Stavropol

Astrakhan

Ural

Uralsk

Guryev

K A Z A K H S T A N

Tselinograd

Semipalatinsk

Leninogorsk

Ayaguz

Black Sea

TURKEY

Trabzon

Erzurum

GEORGIA

Tbilisi

Grozny

Caspian Sea

Ust Urt Plateau

Karaganda

Karsakpai

Balkhash

L. Balkhash

Kuldja

XIN

UY

Batumi

ARMENIA

Yerevan

Baku

Aral Sea

Syr Darya

Aralsk

Kzyl Orda

Dzhambul

Alma Ata

Przhevalsk

Pk. Pobedy 7439

Erzincan

Diyabakir

Tabriz

Krasnovodsk

Kara Kum

Khiva

UZBEKISTAN

Kyzyl Kum

Chimkent

Tashkent

KIRGHIZIA

Frunze

Namangan

Andizhan

Tarim

Tarim Pen

Mosul

I R A Q

Kirkuk

Hamadan

Rasht

Anzali

Ashkhabad

Bandar-e Torkeman

Chardzhou

Bukhara

Leninabad

Samarkand

Okand

Kashi

Kashgar

Shache

XIZANG

Baghdad

Tehran

TURKMENISTAN

Mary

TADZHIKISTAN

Dushanbe

Kommunism Pk 7495

Shache

(TIBET

Basra

Abadan

PERSIA (IRAN)

Esfahan

Yazd

Mashhad

Herat

Mazar-i-Sharif

Hindu Kush

Hotan

Kuwait

The Gulf

Bushire

Shiraz

Kerman

AFGHANISTAN

Kabul

Shghr-i-Kabul

PAKISTAN

Kashmir

ALASKA

Bering Strait

OCEAN

Komsomolets I.
October Revolution I.
Bolshevik I.

De Long Is.

New Siberian Is.

Lyakhov Is.

Wrangel I.

Chukot Sea

St. Lawrence I. (U.S.A.)

Gulf of Anadyr

Bering Sea

Anadyr

Chukot Range

East Siberian Sea

rrang Mts.
Taimyr Pen.
L. Taimyr

Nordvik
Khatanga

Laptev Sea

Tiksi

Buluno

Kotuy R.

Central

Zhigansk

Siberian

Lower Tunguska
Noginsk

Stony Tunguska

Plateau

Angara

Bratsk

Achinsk

Krasnoyarsk
Taishet
Nizhneudinsk
Kansk
Tulun
Kuznetsky
uznetsk
Cheremkhovo
Minusinsk
Munku-Sardyk
3491
Yenisei

Vilyuysk

Yakutsko

Olekminsk

Aldan

Lena

Kirensk
Bodaibo

Zhiganka

Verkhoyansk Range

Yana
Verkhoyansk

Srednе Kolymsk

Nizhne Kolymsk

Kolyma

Kolyma Ra.

Gizhigo

Shelikhov Gulf

Mogodan

Okhotsk

Sea of Okhotsk

Kamchatka

Ust Kamchatsk

Petropavlovsk-Kamchatskiy

Komandorskiye Is.

S. S. R.

SOVIET

SOCIALIST

REPUBLIC

Stanovoi Ra.

Dzhugdzhur Ra.

Shantar Is.

Okha

Nikolayevsk

Sakhalin

Aleksandrovsk

Kuril Is.

ka
ulsk
Lower Tunguska

Circle

Skovorodino

Belogorsk

Komsomolsk

Sovetskaya Govan

Yuzhno-Sakhalinsk
Korsakov

Gulf of Tartary

Sikhote Alin Range

Sapporo
Otori
Hakodate
JAPAN

Irkutsk
Petrovsk
Kyakhta
Selenga

Chita
Nerchinsk
Oloyovannaya
Khilok
Ulan-Ude
Angarsk

Sretensk
Blagoveshchensk

Amur

Birobidzhan

Khabarovsk

Ussuriysk

Vladivostok

Amur

Harbin

Songhua

Changchun

Shenyang

Sea of Japan

Wonsan

Seoul
KOREA

Pusan

Hiroshima

JAPAN

Nagasaki

Ulan Bator

Dzhibkhalantu

MONGOLIA

Gobi

NEI MONGGOL

Beijing (Peking)

Baotou
Datong

GREAT WALL

Hwang

Lanzhou

Xi'an

Zhengzhou

CHINESE REPUBLIC

Tianjin

Dallan

Pyongyang
Inchon
Kunsan

Qingdao

Mokpo

Jinan

Lianyungang

Lhasa

Munku-Sardyk

L. Baikal

Hailar

Manzhouli

U.S.S.R.

| 0 | 200 | 400 | 600 | 800 miles |

| 0 | 200 | 400 | 600 | 800 | 1000 | 1200 km |

COPYRIGHT. GEORGE PHILIP & SON. LTD.

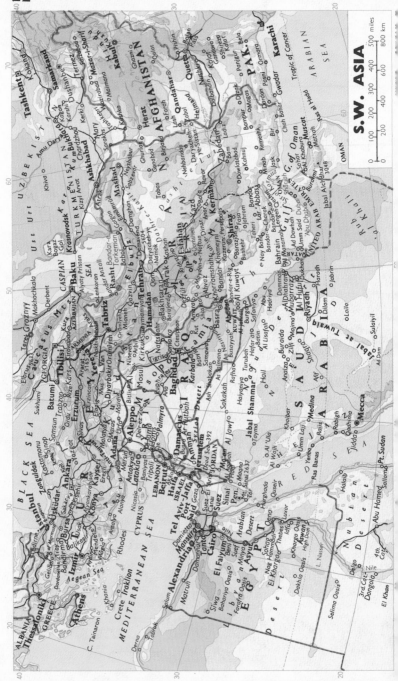

S.W. ASIA

0 100 200 300 400 500 miles
0 200 400 600 800 km

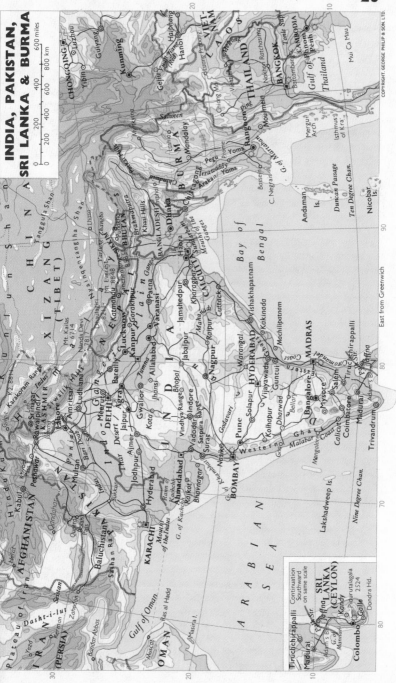

INDIA, PAKISTAN, SRI LANKA & BURMA

0   200   400   600 miles
0   200   400   600   800 km

East from Greenwich

COPYRIGHT GEORGE PHILIP & SON, LTD.

SRI LANKA (CEYLON)

Continuation Southward on same scale

24

CHINA

HAINAN
(Same scale as main map)

miles
0 100 200 300 400 500
0   200   400   600   800
km

JAPAN

REFERENCE TO PREFECTURES

HOKKAIDO DISTRICT	KANTO DISTRICT	CHUGOKU DISTRICT
1 Hokkaido	17 Gumma	31 Tottori
TOHOKU DISTRICT	18 Tochigi	32 Okayama
2 Aomori	19 Saitama	33 Shimane
3 Akita	20 Ibaraki	34 Hiroshima
4 Iwate	21 Tokyo	35 Yamaguchi
5 Yamagata	22 Chiba	SHIKOKU DISTRICT
6 Miyagi	23 Kanagawa	36 Kagawa
7 Fukushima	KINKI DISTRICT	37 Tokushima
CHUBU DISTRICT	24 Hyogo	38 Ehime
8 Niigata	25 Kyoto	39 Kochi
9 Ishikawa	26 Shiga	KYUSHU DISTRICT
10 Toyama	27 Osaka	40 Fukuoka
11 Fukui	28 Nara	41 Saga
12 Gifu	29 Mie	42 Nagasaki
13 Nagano	30 Wakayama	43 Kumamoto
14 Yamanashi		44 Oita
15 Aichi		45 Miyazaki
16 Shizuoka		46 Kagoshima

JAPAN

0   50   100   150   200 miles
0   50 100 150 200 250 300 km

East from Greenwich

COPYRIGHT. GEORGE PHILIP & SON. LTD.

SOUTH-EAST ASIA

Scale: 0 200 400 600 miles
0 200 400 600 800 km

COPYRIGHT GEORGE PHILIP & SON LTD.

East from Greenwich

PACIFIC OCEAN

Northern Marianas

Guam (U.S.A.)

Yap Is.

Caroline Islands

Trust Terr. of Pacific Is. (U.S.A.)

Rep. of Belau

Equator

PHILIPPINES

Luzon
Manila
Quezon City
Baguio
Vigan
Laoag
Batan Is.
C. Engaño
Bicol
Catanduanes
Legaspi
Samar
Tacloban
Catbalogan
Iloilo
Panay
Cebu
Negros
Bacolod
Mindoro
Palawan
Mindanao
Davao
Zamboanga
C.S. Augustin
Surigao
Cagayan
Cotabato
Basilan
Jolo
Sulu Sea
Celebes Sea

Batan Is.

SOUTH CHINA SEA

Hanoi
Haiphong
Vinh
Hué
Da Nang
Phan Rang
Ho Chi-minh City
VIETNAM
LAOS
CAMBODIA
Phnom Penh
THAILAND
Bangkok
Gulf of Thailand
Isthmus of Kra
MALAYSIA
Kuala Lumpur
Singapore
Penang
George Town
Medan
Palembang
INDONESIA
BORNEO
SARAWAK
Brunei
Bandar Seri Begawan
Kota Kinabalu
SABAH
Sandakan
Tarakan
Pontianak
Banjarmasin
Balikpapan
SULAWESI
Menado
Makassar
Ujung Pandang
Kendari
CELEBES
Celebes Sea
Molucca
Halmahera
Morotai
Ceram
Buru
Banda Sea
Ceram Sea
Molucca Sea
Flores Sea
Java Sea
JAVA
Jakarta
Bandung
Semarang
Surabaya
Bali
Lombok
Sumbawa
Flores
Sumba
Timor
Savu Sea
Java
INDIAN OCEAN
Sumatra
Mentawai Is.
Bangka
Belitung

IRIAN JAYA
PAPUA NEW GUINEA
Port Moresby
Owen Stanley Mts.
Torres Strait
Coral Sea
Arafura Sea
Banda Sea
New Britain
Bismarck Sea
Admiralty Is.
Aru Is.
Tanimbar Is.
Kai Is.
Timor Sea

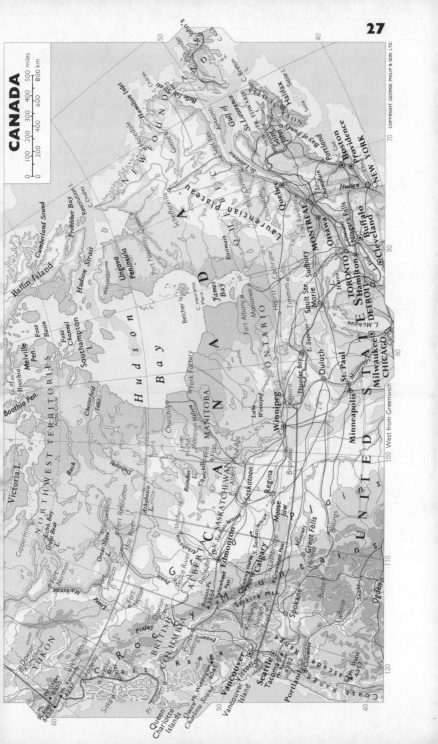

CANADA

0 100 200 300 400 500 miles
0 200 400 600 800 km

COPYRIGHT: GEORGE PHILIP & SON. LTD.

West from Greenwich

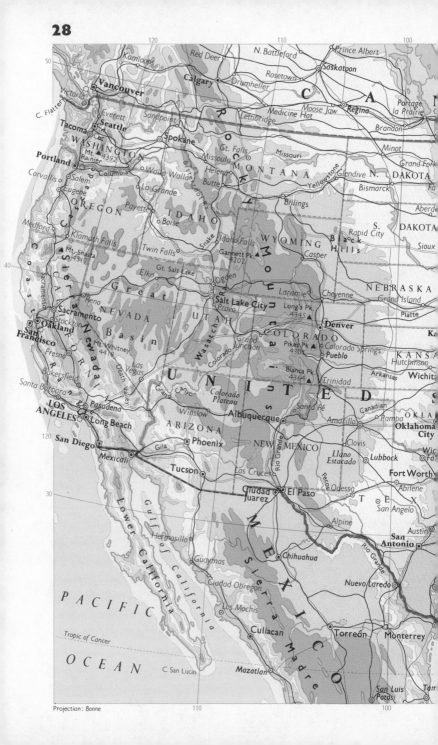

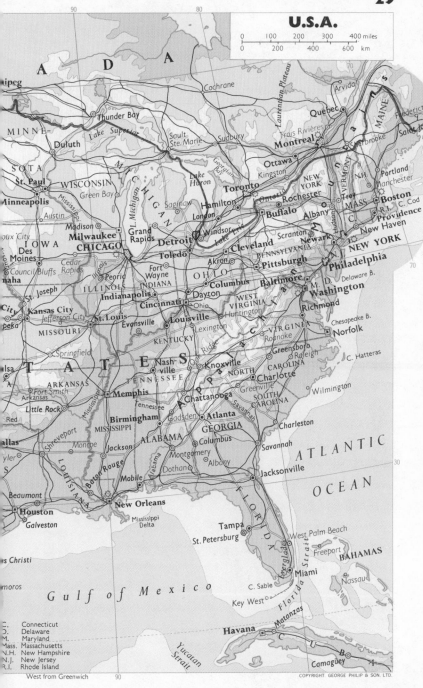

U.S.A.

| 0 | 100 | 200 | 300 | 400 miles |
| 0 | 200 | 400 | 600 | km |

ipeg

C A N A D A

Cochrane

Arvida

Laurentian Plateau

MINNE-

Thunder Bay

Sault Ste. Marie

Sudbury

Quebec

MAINE

Fredericton

Saint John

Duluth

Lake Superior

Trois Rivières

Montreal

Sherbrooke

SOTA

St. Paul

WISCONSIN

Green Bay

Lake Michigan

Saginaw

Georgian B.

Lake Huron

Ottawa

Kingston

VERMONT

N.H.

Portland

Manchester

Minneapolis

Austin

Mississippi

Madison

Milwaukee

Grand Rapids

Toronto

Hamilton

London

Windsor

Lake Erie

Rochester

Buffalo

Albany

NEW YORK

Troy

MASS.

Boston

R.I.

C. Cod

Providence

New Haven

oux City

Des Moines

IOWA

Cedar Rapids

Council Bluffs

naha

St. Joseph

ILLINOIS

Peoria

Fort Wayne

INDIANA

CHICAGO

Detroit

Toledo

Akron

Cleveland

Scranton

Newark

NEW YORK

40

PENNSYLVANIA

Pittsburgh

Philadelphia

70

City

Kansas City

Jefferson City

St. Louis

MISSOURI

Springfield

Indianapolis

Cincinnati

Columbus

OHIO

Dayton

WEST VIRGINIA

Ohio

Huntington

Baltimore

M.D.

Washington

Delaware B.

peka

Evansville

Louisville

KENTUCKY

Lexington

Richmond

VIRGINIA

Roanoke

Chesapeake B.

Norfolk

lsa

A

Fort Smith

Arkansas

ARKANSAS

Little Rock

Red

T A T E S

Nash-ville

TENNESSEE

Memphis

Tennessee

Knoxville

Ridge

APPALACHIAN

Greensboro

Raleigh

NORTH CAROLINA

Charlotte

C. Hatteras

llas

yler

S

Shreveport

Monroe

MISSISSIPPI

Jackson

Birmingham

Gadsden

ALABAMA

Chattanooga

Greenville

SOUTH CAROLINA

Savannah

Wilmington

Beaumont

Houston

Galveston

Baton Rouge

Montgomery

Albany

Dothan

Mobile

Columbus

GEORGIA

Atlanta

Alabama

Charleston

Savannah

New Orleans

Mississippi Delta

Jacksonville

ATLANTIC

OCEAN

30

s Christi

moros

Gulf of Mexico

Tampa

St. Petersburg

FLORIDA

Everglades

C. Sable

West Palm Beach

Freeport

BAHAMAS

Nassau

Miami

Key West

Florida Strait

Matonzas

C. | Connecticut
D. | Delaware
M. | Maryland
Mass. | Massachusetts
N.H. | New Hampshire
N.J. | New Jersey
R.I. | Rhode Island

West from Greenwich

90

Havana

C U B A

Yucatan Strait

Camagüey

COPYRIGHT. GEORGE PHILIP & SON. LTD.

MEXICO AND THE CARIBBEAN

0 100 200 300 400 500 miles
0 200 400 600 800 km

ATLANTIC OCEAN

PACIFIC OCEAN

Caribbean Sea

Gulf of Mexico

UNITED STATES

MEXICO

Tropic of Cancer

West from Greenwich

COPYRIGHT. GEORGE PHILIP & SON, LTD.

Charleston
Savannah
Jacksonville
Atlanta
Columbus
Montgomery
Birmingham
Jackson
Mobile
New Orleans
Baton Rouge
Houston
Dallas
Fort Worth
Austin
San Antonio
Corpus Christi
Matamoros
El Paso
Ciudad Juarez
Nogales
Mexicali
Hermosillo
Guaymas
Chihuahua
Piedras Negras
Nuevo Laredo
Monterrey
Saltillo
Torreón
Durango
Mazatlan
Aguascalientes
Guadalajara
León
San Luis Potosi
Rio Grande
Tampico
Veracruz
MEXICO CITY
Puebla
Oaxaca
Acapulco
Villahermosa
Coatzacoalcos
Tuxtla Gutierrez
Merida
Yucatan

Florida
Tampa
Miami
Havana
Sta. Clara
Camagüey
Holguin
Santiago de Cuba
Cuba
BAHAMAS
Turks & Caicos Is.
Hispaniola
HAITI
DOMINICAN REP.
Santiago
Santo Domingo
Port au Prince
PUERTO RICO
San Juan
Virgin Is.
Anguilla (Br.)
ANTIGUA
BARBUDA
ST. CHRISTOPHER-NEVIS
GUADELOUPE
DOMINICA
MARTINIQUE
ST. LUCIA
ST. VINCENT
BARBADOS
GRENADA
TRINIDAD & TOBAGO
Tobago
Port of Spain
JAMAICA
Kingston
Greater Antilles

BELIZE
Belmopan
GUATEMALA
Guatemala
EL SALVADOR
San Salvador
HONDURAS
Tegucigalpa
Gulf of Honduras
NICARAGUA
Managua
L. Nicaragua
Chinandega
COSTA RICA
San José
PANAMA
Panama
Colón
G. of Panama
Gulf of Darien

VENEZUELA
CARACAS
Barquisimeto
Maracaibo
L. Maracaibo
Orinoco
Ciudad Bolívar
Caroni
Caura
COLOMBIA
Barranquilla
Cartagena
Cúcuta
Bucaramanga
Medellín
Magdalena
Sa. Nevada de S. Marta

Gulf of California
Lower California
C. San Lucas
Revilla Gigedo Is. (Mexico)
C. Corrientes
Gulf of Campeche
G. of Tehuantepec
Yucatan Strait
Florida Strait
C. Sable
C. Catoche
C. Gracias á Dios

Eastern Sierra Madre
Western Sierra Madre
Southern Sierra Madre

20

70

80

90

100

110

30

20

10

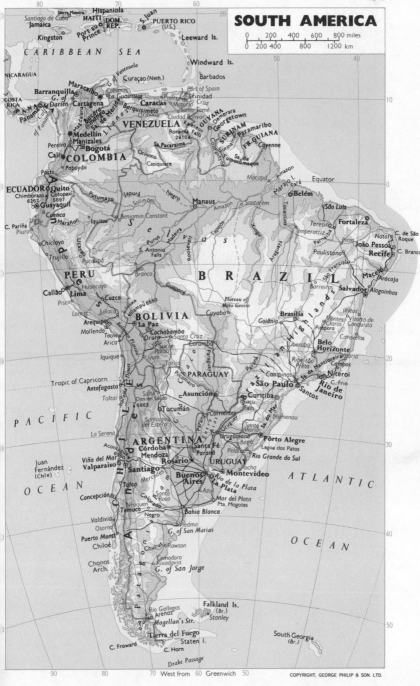

SOUTH AMERICA

0   200   400   600   800 miles
0   200 400   800   1200 km

COPYRIGHT, GEORGE PHILIP & SON. LTD.

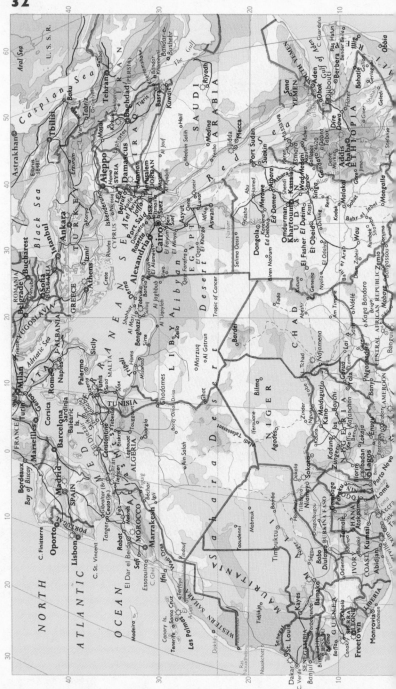

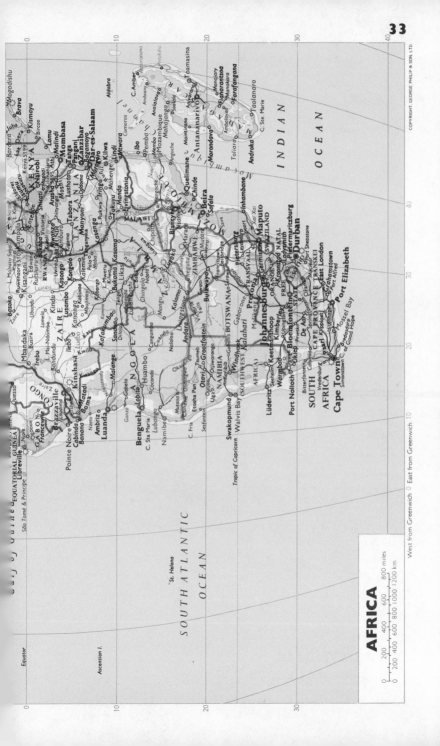

AFRICA

COPYRIGHT. GEORGE PHILIP & SON. LTD

West from Greenwich 0 East from Greenwich

| 0 | 200 | 400 | 600 | 800 miles |

| 0 | 200 400 | 600 800 | 1000 1200 km |

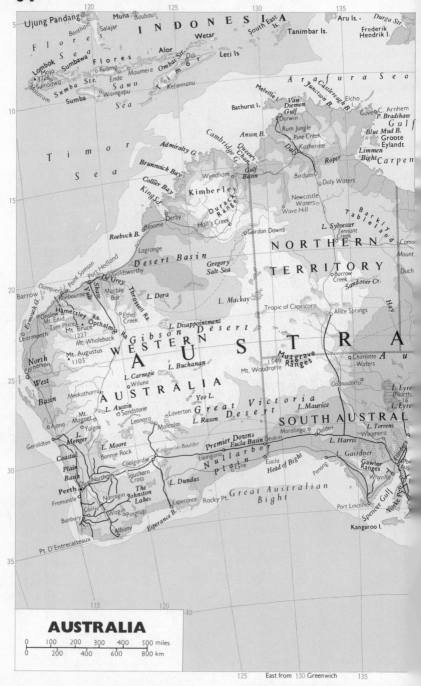

AUSTRALIA

0	100	200	300	400	500 miles
0	200	400	600	800 km	

East from 130 Greenwich

K20

W. Urals; salt, chemicals, paper; p. (est. 1980) 186,000.

Bergama, t., **Turkey;** anc. Pergamos, ruins; morocco leather inds.; agr. tr.; p. (1965) 24,113.

Bergamo, c., Lombardy, **Italy;** 54 km N.E. Milan; cath. and academy; silk industry; p. (1981) 122,142.

Bergen, spt., W. cst. **Norway;** univ.; most impt. comm. pt. in kingdom; shipping, fishing; mftg. inds.; birthplace of Grieg; p. (1979) 209,658.

Bergen op Zoom, t., N. Brabant, **Neth.;** sugar refining. engin.; p. (1982) 45,052.

Bergerac, t., Dordogne, S.W. **France;** impt. bridge over Dordogne R.; mkt. for wines and luxury foods; anc. Huguenot stronghold; p. (1982) 27,704.

Bergisches Land, terr., N. Rhine-Westphalia, **W. Germany;** specialised iron and steel prod.; chemicals, machin.; inc. ts. of Solingen, Remscheid, Velbert, Wuppertal.

Bergisch-Gladbach, t., N. Rhine-Westphalia, **W. Germany;** 11 km E. of Cologne, paper, metallurgy, textiles; p. (est. 1983) 100,900.

Berhampur, t., Orissa, **India;** admin. and educational ctr.; p. (1971) 117,662.

Bering Current (Okhotsk Current, or **Oyashio),** ocean current, N. **Pac. Oc.;** flows through Bering Strait from Arctic, along E. cst. of Kamchatka and Japanese Is. Hokkaido, Honshu; relatively cold; moderate summer temperatures along csts. causes fogs.

Bering Sea, part of N. **Pac. Oc.** between Aleutian Is. and B. Strait; fishing; a. 2,274,020 km².

Bering Strait, narrow sea which separates Asia from N. America, and connects Bering Sea with Arctic Oc.; 58 km wide at narrowest part.

Berkeley, v., Gloucs.. **Eng.;** nr. R. Severn, 24 km N. of Bristol; scene of murder of Edward II; civil nuclear power-sta.

Berkeley, c., Cal., **USA;** univ.; chemicals; now inc. in San Francisco; p. (1980) 103,328.

Berkhamsted, Dacorum, Herts., **Eng.;** mkt. t.; chemicals; cas. ruins, 17th cent. school; birth-place of William Cowper the poet; p. (1981) 15,461.

Berkshire, non-met. co., **Eng.;** chalk downland inc. Inkpen Beacon, White Horse Hills; drained by Thames and tribs.; residtl.; electronics, biscuits; dairying; Windsor Gr. Park; Ascot racecourse; a. 1,256 km²; p. (1981) 675,153.

Berlin, c., former cap. of **Germany,** Europe; on Spree R.; divided into 4 occupied zones 1945; Soviet (now E. Berlin), British, American, French (now W. Berlin); W. Berlin forms isolated enclave within E. Germany; focal point of escape attempts from E. to W. led to construction of "Berlin Wall"; W. Berlin major industl. ctr. aided by American and W. German capital; educational, cultural and tourist ctr.; E. Berlin, cap. of E. Germany, rebuilt as showpiece with high-rise housing, elect. manfs, machin., vehicles, chems. and clothing; p. (est. 1983) 1,860,500, (W. Berlin); 1,145,743 (E. Berlin).

Bermuda, Brit. gr. coral Is. (360 in no. of which 20 are inhabited) N. Atlantic; about 1,120 km E. of S.C.; Hamilton, on Long I. is the ch. t.; Brit. and US air and naval stas.; favourite winter resort for Americans; inds. attracted by tax incentives; no surface water; total a. 54 km²; p. (est. 1976) 57,000.

Bern, c., cap. of B. can. and fed. cap. **Switzerland;** on Aare R.; cath., univ.; textiles, musical instruments, chocolate; H.Q. of Postal Union; bear pit; p. (1980) 286,903 (met. a.).

Bern, can., **Switzerland;** fertile valleys, dairying; watches; hydroelectric power; plans for separate can. in Jura reg.; a. 6,881 km²; p. (1980) 912,022.

Bernard, Great St., one of the Alps in the S. of the Valais, **Switzerland;** highest point 3,390 m; height of mtn. pass between Italy (Aosta) and Switzerland (Martigny), 2,477 m; famous hospice for travellers in monastery on mtn.; road tunnel completed 1962.

Bernard, Little St., one of Graian Alps, Savoy, S. of Mt. Blanc, **France;** pass traversed by Hannibal 218 B.C.

Bernburg, t., Halle, **E. Germany;** cas.; chemicals, salt mng.; p. (est. 1970) 45,322.

Bernese Oberland (Berner Alpen), alpine region, **Switzerland;** 35 peaks over 3,000 m inc. Finsteraarhorn and Jungfrau; tourist a. inc. resorts of Interlaken and Grindelwald.

Bernina Alps, Switzerland; alt. 4,050 m.

Berri, t., S. **Australia;** ctr. of irrigated fruit growing a. on R. Murray; wines; p. (1966) 2,224.

Berri, oilfield, **Saudi Arabia;** 72 km N.W. of Ras Tannura; the field extends offshore.

Berwick, l. gov. dist., former co., Border Reg., S.E. Scot.; a. of sheep rearing and woollen inds. in S. Uplands; a. 875 km²; p. (1981) 18,092.

Berwick, t., Vic., **Australia;** satellite of Melbourne; to be expanded to planned p. of 100,000 by 1985; p. (1976) 25,328.

Berwick-upon-Tweed, l. gov. dist., Northumberland, **Eng.;** spt. on mouth of Tweed; border t., changed between Eng. and Scot. 15 times in history; fishing, lt. engin., tweeds, knitwear; cas. ruins; p. (1981) 26,230 (dist.).

Besançon, t., cap. of Doubs dep., **France;** cath., observatory, univ.; farm implements, textiles; watch- and clock-making; birthplace of Victor Hugo; p. (1982) 119,687.

Besche, t., Saarland, **W. Germany;** oil refining.

Beskids, W. and **E. (Beskidy Zachodnie),** mtn. range, **Poland, ČSSR,** E. Europe; northern range of Carpathian mtn. system, seldom exceeds alt. 1,200 m, many passes; forested; tourism; length 352 km.

Bessarabia, terr., ceded to **USSR** by Romania 1940, and now part of Moldavian SSR; agr. region.

Bessemer, t., Ala., **USA;** iron and steel; p. (1980) 31,729.

Bethany (El Azarieh), v., on Mt. of Olives 6 km W. of Jerusalem, **Jordan.**

Bethel, anc. c., the modern Beitin, Jordan; 16 km N. Jerusalem.

Bethesda, t., Arfon, Gwynedd, **Wales;** slate, lt. engin; p. (1981) 4,060.

Bethlehem, t., **Jordan;** 9 km S.W. Jerusalem; according to Matthew and Luke birthplace of Christ; p. (est. 1967) 16,313.

Bethlehem, t., Penns., **USA;** 80 km N. of Philadelphia; iron-wks.; univ.; p. (1980) 70,419.

Bethnal Green, dist., London, **Eng.;** in E. End of London; now in Tower Hamlets.

Béthune, t., Pas-de-Calais, **France;** rail and canal ctr. for coalfield; mkt. t.; p. (1982) 258,383 (met. a.).

Betteshanger, v., Kent, **Eng.;** on N. flank of N. Downs, 6 km W. of Deal; coal mng.

Bettws-y-Coed, t., Aberconwy, Gwynedd, **Wales;** waterfalls; tourism; p. (1981) 658.

Beuel, t., N. Rhine–Westphalia, **W. Germany;** on E. bank R. Rhine opposite Bonn; chemicals, furniture; p. (est. 1969) 38,668.

Beuthan. See **Bytom.**

Beverley, l. gov. dist., mkt. t., Humberside, **Eng.;** famous minster (13th cent.); agr. processing; p. (1981) 16,433 (t.).

Beverly, c., Mass., **USA;** footwear, machin.; p. (1980) 37,655.

Beverly Hills, t., Cal., **USA;** sub. of Los Angeles; home of many film celebrities; p. (1980) 32,367.

Beverwijk, t., nr. Haarlem, N. Holland, **Neth.;** agr. prods.; p. (1982) 35,534.

Bewdley, Wyre Forest, Hereford and Worcs., **Eng.;** mkt. t. on R. Severn; birthplace of Stanley Baldwin; residtl.; p. (1981) 8,742.

Bexhill-on-Sea, t., Rother, East Sussex, **Eng.;** resort; p. (1981) 35,529.

Bexley, former bor., W. Kent; now outer bor., Greater London, **Eng.;** inc. Chislehurst and Sidcup (N. of the A.20), Crayford and Erith; p. (1981) 214,818.

Béziers, t., Hérault, **France;** ctr. of wine, brandy tr. and inds.; chemicals; p. (1982) 78,477.

Bezwada. See **Vijayawada.**

Bhadravati, t., Karnataka, **India;** steel; p. (1981) 77,055 (t.), 130,606 (met. a.).

Bhagalpur, t., Bihar, **India;** agr. tr. ctr. on R. Ganges; p. (1981) 225,062.

Bhamo, t., Upper **Burma;** on Irrawaddy; inland limit of steam boats; mkt. ctr.; ruby mines; p. 10,000.

Bhandara, cap. of Bhandara dist., Maharashtra, **India;** 48 km E. of Nagpur; cotton cloth, brass mftg.; p. (1981) 56,025.

Bharuch, t., Gujerat, **India;** world's lgst. stream urea fertiliser plant; nearby oilfield.

Bhatpara, t., W. Bengal, **India;** on R. Hooghly; industl. t.; jute, engin.; p. (1981) 260,761.

Bhaunager, t., Gujarat, **India;** pt. on G. of Cambay; exp. cotton, oilseeds; p. (1981) 307,121.

Bhilai, t., Madhya Pradesh, **India;** steel plant; rails and rly. sleepers; p. (1961) of industl. t. (1981) 319,450.

Bhim-Gora, sacred pool, place of Hindu pilgrimage, Uttar Pradesh, **India.**

Bhopal, c., cap. of Madhya Pradesh, **India;** impt.

dam for hinterland of N. EEC; 2 language groups: Flemish (Dutch dialect) in N., French dialect in S. (Walloon a.); univs. at Brussels, Ghent, Liège, Louvain; cap. Brussels; a. 30,445 km²; p. (est. 1984) 9,877,000.

Belgorod, t., **RSFSR**; N.W. of Kharkov, on N. Donets R.; rly. junc. in agr. region; p. (est. 1980) 248,000.

Belgrade (**Beograd**), c., cap of **Yugoslavia**; inland pt. on Danube at mouth of Sava R.; industl., admin. and cultural ctr.; univ.; airport; p. (1981) 1,470,073.

Belitung or **Billiton**, I., between Sumatra and Kalimantan, Indonesia; tin; a. 4.832 km²; p. 102,375.

Belize, indep. rep. (1981), **Central America**; formerly Brit. Honduras; almost totally underdeveloped; heavy rainfall, hurricanes; tropical forest; only 15 percent of land is cultivated; 20 per cent unemployed; lowest p. density in Central America; S. dist. of Toledo claimed by Guatamala; new cap. Belmopen; a. 22,962 km²; p. (1980) 144,857.

Belize, c., former cap. of **Belize**; mahogany, dyewoods, bananas; almost devastated by hurricane 31 Oct. 1961; cap. moved to Belmopen 80 km further inland; spt.; p. (est. 1978) 49,749.

Bellary, c., Karnataka, **India**; fort; cotton processing and tr.; p. (1981) 201,579.

Bell Bay, pt., Tasmania, **Australia**; on bank of Tamar R.; modern pt. and aluminium refinery (1950s) for processing Queensland bauxite; ferry terminal; now part of Launceston.

Bell I., Newfoundland, E. **Canada**; in Conception Bay, 32 km N.W. of St. Johns; impt. Wabana iron-ore deposits outcrop on N.W. cst., smelted on Pictou coalfield, Nova Scotia; a. 31 km².

Belle Isle Strait, **Canada**; between Newfoundland and Labrador, on N. shipping route to Canada from Europe.

Belleville, pt., L. Ontario, **Canada**; agr. processing; white marble nearby, cement; light inds.; p. (1971) 34,498.

Belleville, t., Ill., **USA**; industl. ctr., domestic prod., coal; air force training school; p. (1980) 41,580.

Belleville, t., N.J., **USA**; machin., chemicals. p. (1980) 35,367.

Bellingham, t., spt., Wash., **USA**; agr. distribution ctr.; timber inds.; salmon canning; p. (1980) 45,794 (c.), 106,701 (met. a.).

Bellingshausen Sea, borders Antarctica; part of **S. Pac.**; ice floes obstruct passage.

Bellinzona, t., **Switzerland**; on R. Ticino; 22 km N. of Lugano; three castles built on hills dominating t.; rly. engin.; tourism; p. (est. 1978) 17,400.

Bell Rock (**Inchcape I.**), rock and lighthouse 19 km S.E. of Arbroath, Scot.

Belluno, t., cap. of B. prov., Venezia, N. **Italy**; route ctr. at S. foot of Dolomites; cath.; engin.; p. (1981) 36,634.

Belmopen, new cap., **Belize**; at geographic ctr. of cty.; replaces Belize.

Belo Horizonte, c., cap. of Minas Geraisst. **Brazil**; impt. inland c.; ctr. rich agr. and mng. region; steel mills, food inds., textiles, diamond cutting; oil pipeline from Guanabara; univ.; one of the fastest growing c. in Brazil, especially since building of Fiat factory; p. (1980) 1,937,200 (+72 per cent in 10 years).

Beloretsk, t., Bashkir ASSR, **RSFSR**; in Ural Mtns. on Belaya R.; iron, metal inds.; p. (est. 1969) 66,000.

Belorussiyan SSR, constituent rep., **USSR**; lowlying; timber; agr. on drained marshes; peat; 209,790 km²; p. (est. 1976) 9,371,000.

Belovo, t., W. Siberia, **RSFSR**; in Kuznetsk basin; coal mng., zinc, engin.; p. (est. 1980) 112,000.

Belper, mkt. t., Amber Valley, Derbys., **Eng.**; hosiery, textiles, oil wks., iron foundries; p. (1981) 16,453.

Belsen, v., 24 km N.W. of Celle, **W. Germany**; notorious second world war concentration camp.

Belterra, t., dist., Pará st., N.E. **Brazil**; nr. confluence of Tapajós and Amazon Rs; site of Fordlandia scheme.

Beltsy, t., Moldavian SSR, **USSR**; on trib. of Dniester R.; agr. ctr., food processing; p. (est. 1980) 128,000.

Belvoir (pronounced Beaver), **Vale of**, Melton Leics., **Eng.**; clay vale, cattle, sheep; Stilton cheese; recent discovery of valuable coal deposits (est. 500 m. tonnes).

Bembridge, v., E. cst., I. of Wight, **Eng.**; resort.

Benalla, t., dist., Victoria, **Australia**; pastoral and agr.; p. (1972) 8,235 (t.).

Benares. See Varanasi.

Benbecula I., Outer Hebrides, Western Isles, Scot.; between Is. of N. and S. Uist; airpt. in N.; fishing; a. 93 km²; p. 900.

Bendigo, c., Victoria, **Australia**; former gold mng. dist., gold rush 1851; mng. ceased 1955; primary prods.; impt. egg producing ctr.; p. (1976) 50,169.

Benevento, c., Campania, **Italy**; cap. of B. prov. which contains many Roman remains; cath.; agr. processing; p. (1981) 62,636.

Benfleet, t., Castle Point, Essex. **Eng.**; residtl.; p. (1981) 50,240.

Bengal, Bay of, part of **Indian Oc.** washing E. shores of India and W. shores of Burma, receives waters of Rs. Krishna, Ganges; Brahmaputra, Irrawaddy.

Bengbu (**Pengpu**), c., Anhui, **China**; on Kwo-Ho 168 km. N E of Nanjing; on Tianjin–Nanjing rly; p. (est. 1958) 330,000.

Benghazi, joint cap. (with Tripoli) of **Libya**; spt. and airpt. on G. of Sirte; univ.; former Greek Hesperides; p. (est. 1970) 170,000.

Benguela, t., Angola, S.W. Africa; rly. runs inland to Zaïre and Zambia; seaport now lost much tr. to Lobito; p. (est. 1975) 41,000.

Benha, t., Egypt; impt. mkt. t., rail and road ctr. in heart of cultivated a. of Nile delta 48 km N. of Cairo; airpt.; p. (est. 1970) 72,500.

Benin City, t., Nigeria; cap. of Benin st.; former notorious slave ctr.; p. (est. 1975) 136,000.

Benin, People's Republic of, (**Dahomey**), indep. st. (1960), **West Africa**; former French Colony; high standard of education reflected in heavy government sector and low level of productive activity in the economy; staple foods of groundnuts, palms, coffee, cocoa; intensive farming in fertile Terre de Barre; land held collectively; full potential of drier N. not yet exploited; concern about desert encroachment; oil found offshore from main pt. Cotonou; inds. process primary prods.; joint Benin-Nigerian rly; much tropical rain forest in S.; dependence on Nigeria; many joint industl. projects; cap. Porto Novo; a. 112,622 km²; p. (est. 1983) 3,720,000.

Beni Suef, t., Egypt; on Nile, 96 km S. of Cairo; ctr. of fertile agr. a.; carpets, cotton; p. (1976) 117,910.

Ben Lawers, mtn., Perth and Kinross, Scot.; by Loch Tay; arctic and alpine flora; alt. 1,215 m.

Ben Macdhui, mtn., Kincardine and Deeside, Scot.; Cairngorm gp.; second highest peak in Brit. Is.; alt. 1,310 m.

Ben Nevis, mtn., Lochaber, Scot.; volcanic; hgst. peak in Brit. Isles; alt. 1,344 m.

Benoni, t., Transvaal, **S. Africa**; gold mng. ctr.; p. (1970) 162,794.

Benrath, t., **W. Germany**; on Rhine R. nr. Düsseldorf; R. pt. and industl. t.; chemicals, machin.

Bensberg, t., N. Rhine–Westphalia, **W. Germany**; 16 km from Cologne; leather gds.; mainly residtl.; foundries; cas.; p. (est. 1971) 43,800.

Bensheim, t., Hesse, **W. Germany**; ctr. of fruit and wine dist. on E. edge Rhine valley; textiles, paper, metallurgy; p. (est. 1983) 33,000.

Bentley with **Arksey**, t., South Yorks., **Eng.**; p. (1981) 21,786.

Benton Harbor, t., Mich., **USA**; midway along E. cst. L. Michigan; p. (1980) 14,707 (t.), 171,276 (met. a.).

Benue R., **Nigeria–Cameroon**; rises in Adamawa mtns.; forms ch. trib. of Niger R.; R. pts. and agr. tr.; length 1,392 km.

Ben Vorlich. mtn., Perth and Kinross, Scot.; alt. 983 m.

Ben Wyvis, mtn., Ross and Cromarty, Scot.; nr. Dingwall; alt. 1,046 m.

Benxi (**Penki**), c., Liaoning prov., **China**; metallurgical ctr.; p. (est. 1983) 801,000.

Ben-y-Gloe, mtn., Glen Tilt, Perth and Kinross, Scot.; alt. 1,120 m.

Beograd. See Belgrade.

Beppu, c., Kyushu, **Japan**; hot spring resort: p. (1979) 134,306.

Berbera, pt., **Somalia**, on G. of Aden; exp. livestock from pastoral hinterland; new deep-sea pt. completed 1969; airport; p. (est. 1971) 14,400.

Berchtesgaden, v., **W. Germany**; mtn. resort 24 km S. of Salzburg; Hitler's mtn. retreat; tourism; potash.

Berck-Plage, resort, Pas-de-Calais, **France**, on Eng. Channel; p. (1982) 15,671.

Berdichev, t., Ukrainian SSR, **USSR**; ctr. of sugar a.; engin., lt. inds.; p. (est. 1969) 61,000.

Berdyansk, c., Ukrainian SSR, **USSR**; pt. on Sea of Azov; agr. ctr.; machin.; health resort; p. (est. 1980) 124,000.

Bere Regis, mkt. t., Dorset, **Eng.**; Saxon royal residence.

Berezina, R., **USSR**; trib. of Dnieper; forms part of Baltic-Black Sea waterway; 608 km long.

Berezniki, t., E. European **RSFSR**; pt. on Kolva R.,

145 **150** **155** **160**

PAPUA NEW GUINEA
Lae
Wau
G. of Papua
Mt. Victoria
4073
Port
Moresby
Rigo
Torres Strait
Cape York
ce of Wales I.

Bougainville
Choiseul
Solomon
Santa
Isabel
Independence Str.
Islands
Malaita
S. Cristóbal

D'Entrecasteaux Is.

Louisiade
Arch.

5

10

C   o   r   a   l

P A C I F I C

Weipa
Cape
York
Coleman
Peninsula
ria

Cooktown

S   e   a

O   C   E   A   N

Chesterfield Is.

15

Chillagoe
Mt. Bartle Frere 1611
Cairns
Innisfail
Normanton
Croydon
ketown

Townsville

Barrier

Norman
Flinders

lesley
ls.

Bird I.

Cato I.

20

*Charters
Towers*
Hughenden
Bowen
Mackay

Reef

QUEENSLAND
Longreach
arra *Winton*
Selwyn
Cluncurry

Great

Emerald
Mt. Morgan
Rockhampton
Gladstone

Diamantina

Dividing

Bundaberg

Windorah
dsville
B

Maryborough
Gympie
Fraser I.

Great
Divide

25

R
Grey
Range
L
A
U
S
T
R
A
L
I
A
N

Charleville
Cunnamulla
Dirranbandi

Darling
Toowoomba
Ipswich
Brisbane

Tibooburra
L. Callabonna

NEW
SOUTH
Warrego

Bourke
Walgett
Moree
Grafton
Coffs
Harbour

30

35

Broken
Hill
Menindee
Darling
borough
Wilcannia
Cobar
Nyngan
Dubbo
Rato

New England Range
Mts.

Newcastle

North C.
Doubtless B.

Murray
River
WALES
Mildura
aide
Basin

Bathurst
Cootamundra
SYDNEY
Wollongong

Kaipara Harb.
Auckland
Devonport
Great Barrier I.
Thames
Tauranga
B. of Plenty
East C.

Horsham
Stawell
VICTORIA
Wangaratta
Ararat
Ballarat
MELBOURNE
Colac
Geelong

Canberra
CAP.
TERR.
Queanbeyan
Goulburn
Snowy Mts.
Mt. Kosciusko 2230
Bombala

Jervis B.
Batemans
B.

NEW
ZEALAND

NORTH ISLAND
North Taranaki
Bight
New Plymouth

Hamilton
Rotorua
Gisborne
Hawke Bay

Wanganui
Patea

40

King I.
Bass Strait
Furneaux
Group

Karamea B.
Nelson
Cook
Strait
Wellington

SOUTH ISLAND
Westport
Blenheim
Campbell
Ross
Waiau

Chatham Is.
(N.Z.)

Burnie
Devonport
Scottsdale
Strahan
Launceston
Queenstown

Mt. Cook 3764
Mt. Aspiring
3035
Milford Sd.
Southern Alps
Canterbury
Plains
Christchurch
Lyttelton

Damaru

45

TASMANIA
P. Davey
Hobart
Tasman Penin.
P. Arthur
Storm B.
S.E. Cape

Kingston
Bluff
Stewart I.
Southwest I.

Invercargill
Bluff Harb.
Port Chalmers
Otago Harb.
Dunedin

180

NEW ZEALAND
on same scale

COPYRIGHT. GEORGE PHILIP & SON. LTD

145 **150** **170** **175**

PACIFIC OCEAN

Aleutian Islands

C. Lopatka

Kuril Islands

Petropavlovsk-Kamchatskiy

Sakhalin

Extreme limits of drift-ice

Bering Sea

Sea of Okhotsk

Kamchatka

Seas covered by pack-ice in Spring

Magadan

Okhotsk

Gulf of Alaska

Kodiak I.

Nunivak

St. Lawrence (U.S.A.)

Anadyr

Arctic Circle

Kolyma Ra.

Anchorage

Mt. McKinley 6194

Nome

Prince of Wales

East C.

Chukot Ra.

Kolyma

Cherskiy Ra.

Aldan

Yakutsk

ALASKA U.S.A.

Fairbanks

Bering Str.

Chukot Sea

Ust' Nera

Indigirka

Verkhoyansk Ra.

Mt. Logan 6050

Whitehorse

Dawson

Yukon

Brooks Ra.

Pt. Barrow

Wrangel I.

East Siberian Sea

Verkhoyansk

Mackenzie Mts.

Seas permanently covered by pack-ice

New Siberian Is.

Tiksi

Lena

Mackenzie

Inuvik

Beaufort Sea

ARCTIC OCEAN

Laptev Sea

Nordvik

Kotuy

Khatanga

Great Bear Lake

Echo Bay

Banks I.

Pr. Patrick I.

Severnaya Zemlya

Taimyr Pen.

Putorana Mts.

CANADA

Victoria I.

Melville I.

Magnetic Pole 1985

Sverdrup Is.

North Pole

Norilsk

Dikson

Yenisey

Igarka

Pr. of Wales I.

Somerset I.

Boothia Pen.

Axel Heiberg I.

Devon I.

Ellesmere I.

Franz Josef Land

Novy Port

Yamal Pen.

Melville Pen.

Thule

Novaya Zemlya

Kara Sea

Salekhard

Ob

Ural Mts.

Baffin Island

Baffin Bay

Disko

GREENLAND

Spitsbergen (Norway)

Barents Sea

Vorkuta

Pechora

Davis Str.

Godhavn

Naryan Mar

Godthåb

Greenland Sea

North C.

Murmansk

Kola Pen.

Syktyvkar

Mt. Forel 3360

Scoresbysund

Jan Mayen (Norway)

Hammerfest

White Sea

Arkhangelsk

Julianehåb

Angmagssalik

Narvik

N. Dvina

I. Onega

Denmark Strait

Akureyri

Norwegian Sea

FINLAND

Ladoga

Volga

Gorki

C. Farewell

ICELAND

Trondheim

NORWAY

SWEDEN

G. of Bothnia

Helsinki

Leningrad

Moscow

Reykjavik

ATLANTIC OCEAN

Faroe Is. (Den.)

Bergen

Oslo

Stockholm

Baltic Sea

W. Dvina

Dnieper

Kiev

Shetland Is.

North Sea

DENMARK

Copenhagen

Warsaw

Vistula

POLAND

Dniester

Black Sea

NORTHERN LANDS AND SEAS

UNITED KINGDOM

NETH.

WEST GERMANY

EAST

Berlin

CZECHOSLOVAKIA

London

0 200 400 600 800 miles

0 400 800 1200 km

West from 10 Greenwich   0   East from 10 Greenwich

COPYRIGHT. GEORGE PHILIP & SON. LTD

CIC

tr. ctr.; varied inds.; prehistoric cave paintings nearby; 2,000 killed in world's worst chem. accident (1984); p. (1981) 671,018.

Bhubaneswar, t., cap. of Orissa, **India**; 29 km from Cuttack; admin. ctr.; Hindu temples, pilgrimage ctr.; p. (1981) 219,211.

Bhutan, kingdom, indep. mtn. st., E. Himalayas; heavy monsoon rain, rich tropical vegetation. valuable forests; N.-S. ridges and valleys result in semi-closed communities; first motor link with India opened 1962; cap. Thimphu; a. c. 46,620 km²; alt. 7,558 m (Kula Kangri); p. scattered and nomadic (est. 1984) 1,388,000.

Biafra, Bight of. See **Bonny, Bight of.**

Biako, formerly Marcias Nguema (**Fernando Po**). I., **Equatorial Guinea**; in Bight of Bonny; mtnous.; coffee, cocoa, bananas, timber; p. (1968) 61,000.

Bialystok, t., **Poland**; cap. of B. prov., nr. Grodno; major industl. ctr.; rly. ctr.; p. (est. 1983) 240,300.

Biarritz, t., Pyrénées-Atlantique dep., **France**; on Bay of Biscay; seaside resort; p. (1982) 26,647.

Biberach, t., Baden-Württemberg, **W. Germany**; on R. Kinzig; spa; wood, metal and engin. inds.; p. (est. 1983) 28,100.

Bicester, Cherwell, Oxford, **Eng.**; anc. mkt. t., N.E. of Oxford; p. (1981) 14,436.

Biddulph, t., Staffs. Moorlands, Staffs., **Eng.**; coal mng., machin., textiles, furniture; residtl.; p. (1981) 19,160.

Bideford, Torridge, N. Devon, **Eng.**; pt. on estuary R. Torridge; mkt., boat-bldg.; resort; p. (1981) 12,211.

Biel (**Bienne**), t., Berne, **Switzerland**; nr. Lake B.; watches; impt. industl. ctr.; p. (est. 1977) 88,600.

Bielawa, t., Wroclaw prov., S.W. **Poland**; textiles; p. (1970) 31,000.

Bielefeld, t., Rhine-Westphalia, **W. Germany**; ch. ctr. of linen industry; machin., bicycles; p. (est. 1983) 307,900.

Biella, t., Vercelli, **Italy**; textiles; p. (1981) 53,572.

Bielsko-Biala, t., Katowice prov., **Poland**; woollens, linen, metal, chemicals; p. (est. 1983) 172,000.

Bien-hoa, t., nr. Ho Chi-minh City, S. **Vietnam**; sugar refining; cotton mills.

Bies-Bosch, reclaimed fenland area between N. Brabant and S.W. **Neth.**; sugar refining, dairying; a. 142 km².

Biggar, sm. burgh, Clydesdale, **Scot.**; 213 m in Southern Uplands; p. (1981) 1,931.

Biggin Hill, Greater London, **Eng.**; nr. Orpington; famous airfield of Battle of Britain.

Biggleswade, t., Mid Beds., **Eng.**; in valley of R. Ivel, 14 km S.E. of Bedford; ctr. of fruit-growing and mkt. gardening dist.; hydraulic machin. tools, hosiery, caravans; p. (1981) 10,928.

Big Horn Mtns., Wyo. and Mont., **USA**; Rockies; favourite film location; attractive agr. valleys; highest alt., 3,600 m.

Bihać, t., **Yugoslavia**; on R. Una; recent industl. development; timber processing.

Bihar, st., N.W. **India**; in Ganges basin; hilly; bulk of p. in agr. N.; irrigation; minerals in S.E.: coal, iron, mica; steelwks. at Jamshedpur, oil refining at Barauni; cap. Patna, admin. ctr. Ranchi; a. 173,882 km²; p. (1981) 69,914,734.

Bihar, t., Bihar, **India**; within middle Ganges valley nr. Patna; p. (1981) 151,343.

Biisk, c., Siberia, **USSR**; ctr. of rich agr. a.; meat packing, textiles; p. (est. 1980) 213,000.

Bijagós, Achipelago dos (**Bissagos Is.**), off W. cst. **Guinea-Bissau**; c. 14 Is.; coconuts, rice; ch. t. Bolama on Bolama I.; a. 1,554 km².

Bijapur, t., Karnataka, **India**; cotton tr. and inds.; ruins; former cap. of B. kingdom; p. (1981) 147,313.

Bikaner, t., Rajasthan, **India**; in Thar desert; on former caravan route; wool tr., bldg. stone, handicrafts; p. (1981) 253,174 (t.), 287,712 (met. a.).

Bikini, atoll, **Pac. Oc.**; atomic-bomb tests (1946).

Bilaspur, t., Madhya Pradesh, **India**; silks, cottons; p. (1981) 147,218 (t.), 179,791 (met. a.).

Bilbao, spt., N. **Spain**; cap. Basque prov. of Viscaya; formerly famous for rapier making; iron ore, smelting; pipeline from Ayoluengo oilfield; p. (1981) 433,026.

Billinge and Winstanley, t., Lancs., **Eng.**; former coal-mng. a.; p. (1981) 12,488.

Billingham, t. Cleveland, **Eng.**; on N. of Tees estuary; major petrochemical plant.

Billings, t., Mont., **USA**; agr. tr. ctr. in irrigated a.; sulphur plant; p. (1980) 66,842 (t.), 108,035 (met. a.).

Billingsgate, London, **Eng.**; old river-gate and wharf, now ch. fish mkt. of England; to be moved to Isle of Dogs.

Bilma (**Kawar**), oasis t., **Niger**; on caravan route from Tripoli to Agadès and L. Chad; p. c. 1,000.

Billiton I. See **Belitung.**

Biloxi, t., Miss., **USA**; fishing, tourist ctr.; US Coast Guard air base; p. (1980) 49,311 (c.) 191,918 (met. a.).

Bilston, t., West Midlands, **Eng.**; part of Wolverhampton; iron and steel.

Bingen, t., Rhineland Palatinate, **W. Germany**; at S. entrance to Rhine gorge; wine; beautiful scenery; tourism; p. (est. 1983) 22,900.

Bingerville, spt., **Ivory Coast**, W. Africa; rubber processing.

Bingham Canyon, t., N. Utah, **USA**; silver, gold, lead; major open pit copper mine; p. (1970) 31.

Binghampton, N.Y., **USA**; on Susquehanna R.; boot factories, aircraft components, cameras; p. (1980) 301,000 (met. a.).

Bingley, West Yorks., **Eng.**; mkt. t. on R. Aire 26 km N.W. of Leeds; textiles, engin., agr.; p. (1981) 28,070.

Bintan I., lgst. island of Riouw archipelago, **Indonesia**; bauxite, tin.

Bintenne, dist., **Sri Lanka**; remote a., sparse p.; lge. Gal Oya reservoir; tea and rubber estates.

Biratnagar, t., S.E. **Nepal**, in the Tarai; jute, sugar, cotton milling, stainless steel; p. (1971) 44,938.

Birbhum, dist., W. Bengal, **India**; cap. Suri; healthy climate; rice, sugar; mnfs. silk, cotton; a. 4,550 km²; p. (1961) 1,446,158.

Birkenhead, t., Wirral, Merseyside, **Eng.**; spt. on R. Mersey, opposite Liverpool; handles industl. goods; heavy and pt. processing inds.; shipbldg.; p. (1981) 123,907.

Birmingham, c., met. dist., West Midlands, **Eng.**; industl. cap. Midlands, second lgst. c. Gt. Britain; metal inds.; motor vehicles, components and accessories; major growth due to Industl. Revolution; univ., cath.; freeport (1984) for air freight; p. (1981) 1,006,908.

Birmingham, t., Ala., **USA**; coal, iron, limestone, steel, aircraft, chemicals, textiles; p. (1980) 284,000 (c.), 847,000 (met. a.).

Birnam, v., Perth and Kinross, **Scot.**; location of Birnam Wood in *Macbeth*; former royal forest; p. (1981) 990.

Birobidzhan, or Jewish aut. oblast, **RSFSR**; in Khabarovsk terr.; agr., timber and mng. inds.; a. 35,988 km²; cap. Birobidzhan City; p. (est. 1973) 60,000 (inc. 15,000 Jews).

Birr, U.D. Offaly, **R.o.I.**; mkt. t. on Brosna R.; observatory; p. (est. 1978) 4,000.

Bir Tlacsin, Libya; 192 km S.W. Tripoli; oilfields.

Bisbee, t., Arizona, **USA**; very rich copper deposits, gold, silver, lead; p. (1980) 7,154.

Biscarosse, Landes dep., **France**; 72 km S.W. Bordeaux; rocket and missile testing range projected; p. (1982) 8,979.

Biscay, Bay of, stormy a. of Atl. Oc., W. of France and N. of Spain, from Ushant to C. Ortegal; the Roman Sinus Aquitanicus; heavy seas.

Bisceglie, t., Apulia, **Italy**; spt. on E. cst. 35 km N.W. of Bari; tr. in wine and olives; light inds.; cath.; p. (1981) 45,899.

Bischofswerda, t., Dresden, **E. Germany**; quarrying, glass and iron inds.; rly. ctr.; p. (1963) 11,285.

Bishop Auckland, t., Wear Valley, Durham, **Eng.**; palace of Bishop of Durham; iron, lt. engin.; former coal mng.; p. (1981) 32,572.

Bishopbriggs, sm. burgh, Strathkelvin, **Scot.**; p. (1981) 23,367.

Bishop Rock, isolated rock, lighthouse, Scilly Is., **Eng.**; 58 km S.W. of Land's End, Cornwall; recognised internationally as E. end of trans-Atlantic ocean crossing.

Bishop's Stortford, East Herts., **Eng.**; mkt. t. on Stort R.; light inds.; Hatfield forest nearby; Norman cas.; p. (1981) 22,807.

Biskra, t., Algeria; admin. ctr., winter resort; oasis nearby; date mkt.; p. (1966) 59,052.

Bisley, v., Surrey, **Eng.**; ranges of Nat. Rifle Ass. on B. common.

Bismarck, t., st. cap. N.D., **USA**; on Missouri R.; agr. mkt. ctr.; p. (1980) 44,485.

Bismarck Archipelago, volcanic gr., S.W. Pac. Oc., off **New Guinea**, admin. by Australia; p. (est. 1962) 174,115.

Bisotún, t., **Iran**; in ruins; monuments to Darius I (the Great).

Bissagos Is. See **Bijagós, Achipelago dos.**

Bissau, t., cap of **Guinea-Bissau**; former ctr. of slave tr.; airpt.; plans to expand harbour; p. (1979) 109,214.

Bitola, t., Macedonia, **Yugoslavia**; varied mnfs., recent industl. development; mosques; p. (1971) 65,851.

Bitonto, t., Apulia, on E. cst. 11 km N.W. of Bari; **Italy**; cath.; p. (est. 1968) 41,749.

Bitterfeld, t. Halle, **E. Germany**; lignite mng., engin. chemicals; p. (est. 1970) 28,964.

Bitter Lakes, Isthmus of Suez, **Egypt**, utilised by Suez Canal.

Biwa-ko, lgst. lake in **Japan**, S. Honshu; 101 m a.s.l.; canal to Kyto provides hydroelectric power; superb scenery, historical associations; tourism; a. 675 km².

Biysk or **Bisk**, c., Altai terr., **RSFSR**; pt. on Biya R.; terminus of branch of Turk-Sib. rly.; p. (est. 1977) 212,000.

Bizerte, c., **N. Tunisia**; pt. and naval sta. on Med.; the anc. Hippo Zaritus; fishing, oil refining, steel wks., tyres; p. (est. 1975) 62,856.

Björnborg. See **Pori**.

Blaby, l. gov. dist. Leics., **Eng.**; sm. a. S.W. of Leicester; p. (1981) 77,210.

Black Belt, coastlands of Miss. and Ala., **USA**, where black soil prairie land is good for cotton.

Blackburn, t., l. gov. dist., Lancs., **Eng.**; once major cotton weaving ctr.; engin., lt. inds.; p. (1981) 141,758 (dist.).

Black Country, Midlands, **Eng.**; formerly impt. iron-working and coal-mng. dist. mainly in S. West Midlands; now a. of lt. engin.; c. 130 km².

Blackdown Hills, Devon and Somerset, **Eng.**; sandstone hills rising over 305 m.

Black Forest. See **Schwarzwald**.

Blackheath, open common, S.E. London, **Eng.**; mustering place of Wat Tyler's (1381) and Jack Cade's (1450) revolutionary peasants; now main attraction of expensive residtl. a.; a. 108 ha.

Black Hills, mtns. between S.D. and Wyo., **USA**; highest, Horney Peak, 2.208 m; form part of Nat. Park.

Black Isle, peninsula, between Cromarty and Beauly Firths, Ross and Cromarty, **Scot.**; agr., fisheries, quarrying; a. 280 km².

Black Mtns., Powys and Dyfed, S. **Wales**; rise to 802 m in Brecknock Van, sandstone plateau; moorland; valleys used for reservoirs; Nat. Park.

Black Mtns., Powys, S. **Wales**; rise to 811 m in Waun Fach.

Blackpool, t., l. gov. dist., Lancs., **Eng.**; on cst. of Fylde dist.; one of major Brit. resorts; p. (1981) 147,854 (dist.).

Black Prairie, region Texas, **USA**; extends 560 km S.W. from Ouachita Mtns. to Austin; contains very fertile Black Waxy and Grande Prairie sub-regions devoted almost entirely to cotton growing; ch. ts., Dallas, Fort Worth, Austin; a. 77,700 km².

Blackrod, t., Gtr. Manchester, **Eng.**; nr. Chorley; former cotton weaving; p. (1981) 5,628.

Black Sea, bordered by 4 sts., **USSR** (N. and E.), **Turkey** (S.), **Bulgaria**, **Romania** (W.); receives waters of Danube, Dniester, Dnieper, Don, Bug; stagnant and lifeless below 146 m; fisheries in N. and W.; oil exploration by Turkey; a. 424,760 km² (exc. Sea of Azov).

Blacksod Bay, cst. of Mayo, **R.o.I.**

Black Volta, R., rises in **Bourkina Fasso**, flows E. and S. into L. Volta, **Ghana**; length c. 1,200 km.

Blackwater, R., **N. Ireland**; rising in Dungannon, it forms border with **R.o.I.**; enters L. Neagh; 80 km long.

Blackwater, R., **R.o.I.**; flows from Knockanefune to enter Atl. Oc. at pt. and resort of Youghal; chain of sm. ts. along course; 144 km long.

Blaenau Gwent, l. gov. dist., Gwent. **Wales.**; inland valley a. inc. Ebbw Vale and Abertillery; p. (1981) 79,573.

Blaenavon, t., Torfaen, Gwent, **Wales**; former coal mng.; p. (1981) 6,363.

Blagoveshchensk, t., E. Siberia, **RSFSR**, on Chinese bdr. and R. Amur; wat. pl.; engin., sawmilling, flour milling; on Trans-Siberian rly.; p. (est. 1980) 175,000.

Blair Atholl, v., Perth and Kinross, **Scot.**; tourist resort; cas.; seat of Duke of Atholl.

Blairgowrie and Rattray, burgh, Perth and Kinross, **Scot.**; at foot of Scot. Highlands; mkt. t. in Strathmore fruit growing dist.; p. (1981) 7,049.

Blakeney, v., N. Norfolk, **Eng.**; nr. sand spit; yachting; wild fowl.

Blandford or **Blandford Forum**, North Dorset,

Eng.; on R. Stour; pastoral mkt. t. since 13th cent.; p. (1981) 3,915.

Blantyre, c., **Malawi**; in Shire Highlands; linked by rail to Beira (Moçambique); comm. ctr.; timber processing; p. (est. 1983) 313,600.

Blantyre, v., East Kilbride, **Scot.**; Lower B. birthplace of David Livingstone; p. (1981) 19,816.

Blarney, v., 6 km N.W. Cork, **R.o.I.**; cas. and Blarney stone; p. (1971) 1,128.

Blasket Is., Kerry. **R.o.I.**; rocky Is.; uninhabited since 1953.

Blaydon, t. Tyne and Wear. **Eng.**; former coal mng.; p. (1981) 30,563.

Bled, glacial L., Slovenia, **Yugoslavia**; tourism.

Blenheim, t., S.I., **N.Z.**; fruit; p. (1971) 14,760.

Blenheim, v., **W. Germany**; scene of battle (1704) when English and Austrians under Marlborough defeated the French and Bavarians; **Blenheim Palace**, Woodstock, Oxon. **Eng.**; named in honour of this victory.

Blessington, L., Wicklow. **R.o.I.**; glacial L., now serves as reservoir for Dublin.

Bletchley, Bucks., **Eng.**; expanded t.; p. (1981) 42,450.

Blida, t., Algeria; agr. tr., citrus fruits; p. (est. 1977) 90,000.

Bloemfontein, t. cap. O.F.S., **S. Africa**; on plateau, alt. 1,393 m; route and tr. ctr.; univ.; p. (1970) 180,179 (met. a.).

Blois, t., cap. of Loire-et-Cher dep., **France**; historic t. on Loire R.; Renaissance château; wines; p. (1982) 61,049 (met. a.).

Bloomfield, t., N.J., **USA**; pharmaceuticals, metal and elec. gds.; sub. N.J. c.; p. (1980) 47,792.

Bloomington, t., Ill., **USA**; comm. ctr. and industl. t. in rich agr. and coal-mng. a.; univ.; p. (1980) 44,189 (t.). 119,149 (met. a.).

Bloomington, t., Ind., **USA**; electronic equipment, furniture, structural glass; univ.; p. (1980) 52,044 (c.), 98,387 (met. a.).

Bloomsbury, dist., London, **Eng.**; fashionable dist. with many squares; famous for B. gr. of authors in first quarter of 20th cent.; inc. Brit. Museum, Univ. of London.

Bludenz, t., **W. Austria**; cotton, watches; p. (est. 1965) 11,400.

Blue Grass, dist., Ky., **USA**; area where blue grass abundant; horse breeding.

Blue Mountains, t., N.S.W., **Australia**; tourist ctr.; new t. (1947); p. (1976) 45,780.

Blue Mtns., **Jamaica**; famous for coffee; dense forest; tourism; average alt. 900–1,200 m, rising to 2,294 m in Blue Mtn. peak.

Blue Nile (Bahr-el-Azraq), R., rises in tablelands of Ethiopia, joins the White Nile at Khartoum; its seasonal flooding provides the bulk of water for irrigation in Sudan and Egypt.

Blue Ridge Mtns., S. Penn., Ga., **USA**; inc. Shenandoah valley; superb scenery, resorts; average alt. 600–1,200 m, rising to 1,737 m in Grandfather Mtn.

Bluff, bor., S.I., **N.Z.**; 29 km from Invercargill; spt. for Southland prov., major aluminium ctr.; p. (1976) 3,016.

Blumenau, mkt. t., Santa Catarina st., **Brazil**; butter, sugar; p. (est. 1980) 142,200.

Blyth., spt., Northumberland, **Eng.**; on coalfield; now as B. Valley forms l. gov. dist.; p. (1981) 76,787 (dist.).

Bo, t., **Sierra Leone**; gold; admin. H.Q.; p. (est. 1977) 27,000.

Boa Vista, t., R. pt., cap. Roraima st., **Brazil**; p. (est. 1977) 25,000.

Bobbio, t., Emilia-Romagna, **Italy**, in northern Apennines; ctr. European cultural life, 9th-12th cent.; St Columban founded monastery, 612; p. (1981) 4,215.

Bobo Dioulassa, t., **Bourkina Fasso**; agr. tr., gold mng.; p. (est. 1980) 148,962.

Bobigny, N.E. sub of Paris, cap. of Seine-St. Denis dep., **France**; varied inds.; p. (1968) 39,453.

Bobruysk, t., Belorussiyan SSR, **USSR**; pt. on R. Berezina; engin., sawmilling, paper, cellulose, grain; p. (est. 1980) 197,000.

Bocholt, t., N. Rhine-Westphalia, **W. Germany**; machin., textiles, elec. gds.; p. (est. 1983) 65,300.

Bochum, t., N. Rhine-Westphalia, **W. Germany**; heart of Ruhr iron and steel ind.; known since 9th cent.; new (1962) Univ. of Ruhr; p. (est. 1983) 391,300.

Bodensee (L. Constance), S.W. **West Germany** and

Switzerland; 72 km long, 14 km wide.; R. Rhine flows through; fruit and horticulture on warmer slopes of L.

Bodmin, co. t., North Cornwall, **Eng.**; on S.W. flank of Bodmin moor; china clay, lt. engin.; p. (1981) 12,148.

Bodmin Moor, upland, N.E. Cornwall, **Eng.**; lower slopes cultivated, higher slopes used for sheep pastures; average alt. 300 m, highest point, Brown Willy, alt, 419 m; major ctr. of china clay quarrying.

Bodö, t., **Norway**; nr. Lofoten Is.; spt., fish processing; N. rly, terminus; p. (est. 1973) 29,882.

Bodrum, t., on Aegean cst., **Turkey**; anc. Halicarnassus; 15th cent. Crusader castle; fishing.

Boeotia, region of anc. **Greece**; scene of many battles; Thebes was the ch. c.; home of Hesiod and Pindar; p. (1981) 117,175.

Bogda Ula, massif, Sinkiang, **China**; forms N. perimeter of Turfan depression; 240 km wide, average alt. 4,000 m, rising to 5,479 m in Turpanat Targh.

Bognor Regis, t., Arun, West Sussex. **Eng.**; residtl.; seaside resort; p. (1981) 39,536.

Bogor, t., Java, **Indonesia**; rubber factory, textiles, footwear; p. (est. 1983) 274,000.

Bogota, cap. and lgst. c. of **Colombia**; in E. Cordilleras, 2,745 m a.s.l.; univ., nat. observatory, colonial architecture; political, social and financial ctr. of rep.; p. (est. 1979) 4,055,909.

Bo Hai (Pohai), G. of, N. China; together with G. of Liaotung forms shallow expanse of water almost cut off from Yellow Sea by Liaotung and Shandong peninsulas; receives water and silt from Huang He; a. approx. 38,900 km².

Bohemia, historic region, former kingdom, W. **ČSSR**; plateau drained by R. Elbe; borders W. Germany; agr. dist.; minerals inc. lignite, graphite; textiles, sugar, pottery.

Böhmerwald (Bohemian Forest), forested range of mtns. between ČSSR and Bavaria, **W. Germany**; 240 km long; alt. 1,479 m at Aber; region of poor soils; sm. farms; some mng. and quarrying.

Bohol I., **Philippines**; maize, coconuts, rice; a. 3,864 km²; p. (1970) 674,806.

Boise, t., cap. of Idaho, **USA**; financial ctr.; timber mills; hot springs; p. (1980) 102,000.

Boksburg, t., Transvaal, **S. Africa**; industl., former coal-mng.; t. p. (1970) 104,745.

Bolan Pass, Baluchistan, **Pakistan**; pass from Pakistan to Afghanistan; summit 1,800 m.

Bolbec, t., Seine-Maritime, **France**; 19 km E. of Le Havre; textiles; elec. engin.; p. (1982) 12,578.

Boldon, t., Tyne and Wear, **Eng.**; coal mng.; p. (1981) 24,171.

Boleslawiec (Bunzlau), t., Lower Silesia, **Poland**; German before 1945; on the Bóbr R., pottery; p. (1970) 30,500.

Boliden, t., N. **Sweden**; impt. deposits of copper and arsenic.

Bolivia, inland rep., S. **America**; land-locked, 9 deps.; cap. nominally Sucre, actual admin. H.Q. La Paz; much US investment but discouraged by nationalism from late 1960s; p. dispersed over wide a.; relief makes transport difficult; moves towards gaining access to cst. via internat. corridor; forests; savannahs; agr. in backward conditions; embryonic industl. devel. suffered from social unrest and political instability; rubber, quinine, cattle, hides; ch. exp. tin; petroleum; mafia cocaine tr.; exp. illegal narcotics; language Spanish; a. 1,331,661 km²; p. (est. 1984) 6,200,000.

Bollington, t., Cheshire, **Eng.**; nr. Macclesfield; textile finishing; p. (1981) 6,930.

Bologna, c., N. **Italy**; cap. of B. prov. on N. flank of Apennines; impt. route ctr. commanding road and rly. across Apennines to Florence; preserved and restored in Arcadian style by Communist admin.; univ., service t.; p. (1981) 459,080.

Bolsa Island, Cal., **USA**; nuclear power and desalination project in progress.

Bolsena, L., Latium region, **Italy**; occupies lge. extinct volcanic crater in S. of Tuscan Hills 96 km N.W. of Rome; a. (approx.) 129 km²; p. (1981) 3,960.

Bolshoya Volga, t., **RSFSR**; 128 km N. of Moscow, at junct. of Volga and Moscow Volga Canal; Soviet Institute of Nuclear Studies.

Bolsover, t., l. gov. dist., Derbys., **Eng.**; limestone, coal, textiles; cas.; Hardwick Hall 6 km to S., p. (1981) 70,423 (dist.).

Bolton, t., met. dist., Gtr. Manchester, **Eng.**; cotton, textiles, engin.; p. (1981) 260,830.

Bolton Abbey, North Yorks. **Eng.**; ruined Augustinian Priory.

Bolzano, t., Trentino-Alto Adige **Italy**; on R. Isarco at S. approach to Brenner Pass; resort; p. (1981) 105,180.

Boma, t., **Zaïre**; pt. on estuary of R. Zaïre; exp. timber, cocoa, palm prods., bananas; p. (est. 1970) 61,054.

Bombay, spt., cap. of Maharashtra st., **India**; harbour, docks, rly. ctr.; univ.; greatest cotton ctr. in republic; pt. handles nearly half of India's foreign tr.; oil refinery; film industry; univ., fine public bldgs.; p. (1981) 8,243,405 (met. a.).

Bonaire I., Neth. **Antilles**; a. 287 km²; p. (1968) 7,537.

Bône. See Annaba.

Bo'ness, burgh, Falkirk, **Scot.**; spt. on Firth of Forth, 6 km E. of Grangemouth; foundries, timber yards; p. (1981) 14,669.

Bonifacio, spt., Corse du Sud, Corsica, **France**; opposite Sardinia, on Strait of Bonifacio; p. (1982) 2,736.

Bonin Is., Pac. Oc., **Japan**; 15 Is., volcanic; 960 km S. of Tokyo; a. 103 km²; p. (est. 1970) 300.

Bonn, c., fed. cap. of **W. Germany**; at confluence of Rs. Sieg and Rhine; univ.; seat of W. German parliament; birthplace of Beethoven; founded in Roman times; varied inds. inc. printing, publishing; p. (est. 1983) 292,900.

Bonnet a l'Eveque, mtn., **Haiti**; sheer sides, flat top; site of La Ferrière fortress, alt. 900 m.

Bonneville Dam, Ore., Wash., **USA**; across R. Columbia 64 km above Portland (Ore.), provides irrigation to valleys on Columbia-Snake Plateau; locks permit navigation and provide hydroelectric power.

Bonneville Salt Flats, Utah, **USA**; remains of anc. lake; world automobile speed test, 1937–47.

Bonny, t., S. **Nigeria**; at mouth of R. Bonny, Niger delta; oil terminal.

Bonny, Bight of (Bight of Biafra until 1975), **W. Africa**; bay lying E. of the G. of Guinea between the Niger and C. Lopez.

Bonnyrigg and Lasswade, burgh, Midlothian, **Scot.**, 11 km S.E. of Edinburgh, p. (1981) 14,301.

Boothferry, l. gov. dist., Humberside, **Eng.**; lowland a. of I. of Axholme and inc. Goole; p. (1981) 60,290.

Boothia, peninsula on Arctic cst., Franklin dist. **Canada**; separated from Baffin I., by G. of B.

Bootle, t., Sefton, Merseyside, **Eng.**; on E. side of entrance to Mersey estuary; shares line of docks with Liverpool; dockside inds. inc. tanning, ship-repairing; tin plant; p. (1981) 62,463.

Bophuthatswana, indep. Bantu Terr. (1977) not recognised by UN as designed to consolidate apartheid; some mineral wealth (asbestos, platinum) but land produces only 10 per cent of agricultural requirements; heavily dependent on S. Africa; home of Sun City, tourist centre for S. Africa; cap. under construction at Mmabatho; a. 40,330 km²; p. (1977) 1,178,000.

Bor, t., Serbia, **Yugoslavia**; copper mng. and processing; p. (est. 1965) 20,000.

Borås, t., S. **Sweden**; on R. Viske, nr. Göteborg; ctr. of textile and clothing inds.; p. (1983) 100,184.

Bordeaux, spt., cap. of Gironde, **France**; nr. mouth of R. Garonne; cath., univ.; exp. wines, liqueurs, sugar, potatoes, pit props; oil refining nearby; p. (1982) 211,197.

Borders Region, l. gov. reg., **Scot.**; occupies E. half of Southern Uplands; hilly cty. drained by R. Tweed and tribs.; rural a. interspersed by mkt. and mill ts., a 4,670 km²; p. (1981) 99,248.

Bordighera, t., **Italy**; Riviera winter resort; p. (est. 1968) 12,172.

Boreham Wood, t., Herts., **Eng.**; lt. engin., computers, film studios.

Borinage, dist. around Mons, **Belgium**; impt. but declining coalfield.

Borislav, t., Ukrainian SSR, **USSR**; formerly Polish (1919–39); oilfield, natural gas; richest ozocerite deposits in Europe; oil pipeline links to Drogobych and Dashava; p. (est. 1967) 32,000.

Borisoglebsk, t., **RSFSR**; food processing; p. (est. 1969) 65,000.

Borisov, t., Belorussiyan SSR, **USSR**; defeat of Napoleon, 1812; chemicals, sawmills, hardware; p. (est. 1980) 115,000.

Borkum, I., **W. Germany**; off Ems R. estuary; a. 36 km²; p. (est. 1971) 30,000.

Borlänge, t., **Sweden**; iron, paper, engin. and chemical wks.; p. (1983) 46,407.

Borneo, lgst. I. in Malay archipelago and 3rd lgst. in world; high mtn. range extends from ctr. to N. rising to 4,180 m; low-lying swamp in S.; politically divided into Kalimantan (Indonesian B.), Sabah and Sarawak (E. Malaysia) and Brunei; jungle-covered and underdeveloped; scattered tribes inc. Dyaks; few nodes of development around oilfields (Sarawak and Brunei), as, of forest exploitation (Sabah); new settlement in Barito valley (Kalimantan); a. 738,150 km²; p. (est. 1983) 7,350,000.

Bornholm, I. in Baltic Sea, **Denmark;** mostly granite with poor soils; cattle rearing; kaolin; tourism and fishing impt.; cap. Rønne; a. 543 km²; p. (1971) 47,241.

Bornu, region, **Nigeria;** S.W. of L. Chad; former Moslem st.; a. 132,090 km²; p. (est.) 5,000,000.

Borobudur, Java, **Indonesia;** gr. Buddhist temple; ruins now restored.

Borrowdale, valley, Cumbria, **Eng.;** tourist resort; former graphite mines.

Boscastle, spt., Cornwall, **Eng.;** resort; pilchard fishing; sm. harbour built for slate exp.

Bosnia and Hercegovina, rep., **Yugoslavia;** mtnous., forested, watered by R. Sava and tribs.; one-fourth cultivated; tobacco, cereals, fruit; cattle, sheep, pigs; mineral deposits in Bosnia; cap. Sarajevo; a. 51,199 km²; p. (1971) 3,742,842.

Bosporus or **Strait of Constantinople (Karadeniz Boğazi),** between Black Sea and Sea of Marmara; suspension bridge, first to link Europe and S.W. Asia, opened 1973; badly polluted by sewage from Istanbul and oil spillage from shipping.

Bossier City, t., La., **USA;** oil refineries, rly. wks., chemical and processing plants; p. (1980) 50,817.

Boston, t., l. gov. dist., Lincs., **Eng.;** sm. pt. on Witham R., agr. mkt., fruit and vegetable canning; p. (1981) 52,634 (dist.).

Boston, c., st. cap. Mass., **USA;** fine harbour and leading pt. at head of Boston Bay; cultural, comm. and financial ctr., impt. mkt. for fish and wool; 3 univs.; leading c. in 19th cent.; varied inds. inc. leather, rubber, textiles, shoes and elec. gds.; p. (1980) 563,000 (c.), 2,760,000 (met. a.).

Bosworth or **Market Bosworth,** t., Leics., **Eng.;** battle between Richard III and Henry VII, 1485; *see* Hinckley.

Botany Bay, N.S.W., **Australia;** inlet of Tasman Sea on E. cst., site of landing of James Cook, 1770; 8 km S. of Sydney; resort; first settled by Brit. in 1787; old penal colony; deep-water pt. (1961) for oil tankers supplementary to Pt. Jackson.

Botasani, t., N. Moldavia, **Romania;** in rich pastoral a.; p. (est. 1972) 29,727.

Bothnia, G. of, N. of Baltic; between Finland and Sweden; shallow sea, many Is.

Botswana, Rep. of, indep. sov. st. within Brit. Commonwealth (1966), **Southern Africa;** stretches from Orange R. to Zambesi R., and merges in W. with Kalahari desert; land locked; depends on rly. link to Zimbabwe and S. Africa; coal produced since 1980 to reduce dependence on S. Africa; minerals located but few mined; diamonds since 1971 (50 percent of exp.); copper, nickel; limited livestock agr.; potential arable land of Okavango chobe swamp; few inds. cap. Gaborone; a. 582,000 km²; p. (1981) 941,027.

Bottrop, t., N. Rhine-Westphalia, **W. Germany;** once a sm. t., now ctr. of Ruhr coal basin; p. (est. 1983) 113,400.

Bouches-du-Rhône, dep., S. **France;** covers Rhône delta and inc. the Camargue and Crau; lagoon cst.; mainly agr. but inc. industl. complex ass. with cap. of Marseilles; a. 5,270 km²; p. (1982) 1,715,900.

Bougainville, I. seceded from **New Guinea** to form Rep. of N. Solomons; secession ended 1977; major reserve of copper in Panguna valley; new mng. ts. of Anewa Bay and Panguna; forested; a. 10,619 km²; p. (1970) 77,880.

Bougie. See **Bejaia.**

Boulder, t., Col., **USA;** gold- and silver-mng. dist.; univ.; resort; *see* Denver.

Boulder City, t., Nevada, **USA;** nr. Gr. Boulder Dam. gr. engin. project; model t., ctr. for Nat. Park services; p. (1980) 9,590.

Boulogne-Billancourt, S.W. sub. of Paris, **France;** car, aircraft inds.; p. (1982) 102,595.

Boulogne-sur-Mer, t., Pas-de-Calais dep., **France;** on English Channel; comm. and fish. pt.; Channel ferry; pt. inds.; p. (1982) 98,566 (met. a.).

Bounty I., N.Z., S. Pac. Oc.; uninhabited guano covered I.

Bourg-en-Bresse, t., cap. of Ain dep., **France;** route ctr., varied inds.; p. (1975) 75,200.

Bourges, t., cap. of Cher dep., **France;** cath., univ.; industl. and transit ctr.; p. (1982) 79,408.

Bourget, L., Savoie, **France;** tourist a.

Bourkina Fasso, (Upper Volta), W. Africa; landlocked st. under Fr. rule until 1960; savana and low hills, hot and dry desert in N.; p. concentrated in S. and dependent on nomadism and subsistence agr.; many migrate to Ivory Coast and Ghana for work; soil erosion and desert encroachment reduce potential; poorest cty. in Africa; low life expectancies; dependent on aid; much emigration; cap. Ouagadougou; a. 274,123 km²; p. (est 1983) 6,637,205.

Bourne, t., South Kesteven, Lincs., **Eng.;** home of Hereward the Wake; agr. machin.; p. (1981) 8,142.

Bournemouth, t., l. gov. dist., Dorset, **Eng.;** on S. cst., E. of Poole Harbour; seaside resort; conference ctr.; p. (1981) 148,382 (t.), 327,807 (l.gov.dist.).

Bournville, garden sub. founded by George Cadbury (1897), 6 km S.W. of Birmingham **Eng.;** chocolate and cocoa wks.

Bourton-on-the-Water, v., Gloucs. **Eng.;** tourist ctr.

Bouvet I., uninhabited island in S. Atlantic belonging to **Norway;** a. about 56 km².

Bovey Tracey, v., Devon, **Eng.;** ball clay excavating.

Bow or **Stratford-de-Bow,** Tower Hamlets, E. London, **Eng.;** 5 km from St. Paul's.

Bow, R., Alberta, N.W. **Canada;** head of Saskatchewan R., flows through Banff Nat. Park; irrigation; 504 km long.

Bowdon, t., Gtr. Manchester, **Eng.;** p. (1981) 4,925.

Bow Fell, mtn., Cumbria, **Eng.;** at head of Borrowdale, 6 km N.W. of West Water alt. 903 m.

Bowland, Forest of, W. offshoot of Pennines, Lancs., **Eng.;** between Rs. Lune and Ribble; designated a. of outstanding natural beauty; reservoirs.

Bowling, v., Dunbarton, **Scot.;** on N. bank of R. Clyde, 16 km N.W. of Glasgow; lge. oil refinery; p. (1981) 450.

Bowling Green, t., Ky., **USA;** tr. ctr. for agr. a. producing tobacco, livestock, limestone and dairy prods.; univ.; p. (1980) 40,450.

Bowness, v., Cumbria, **Eng.;** W. end of Hadrian's Wall.

Bowness, t., Cumbria, **End.;** on L. Windermere; tourist ctr.

Box Hill, nr. Dorking, Surrey, **Eng.;** E. of R. Mole gap through N. Downs; chalk; wooded, fine views; alt. 233 m.

Boyle, mkt. t., Roscommon, **R.o.I.;** nr. R. Boyle; dairying; p. (1971) 1,727.

Boyne, R., R.o.I.; flows to Irish Sea; Battle of the Boyne (1690) fought at Oldbridge, 5 km W. of Drogheda; salmon fishing; 128 km long.

Boyoma Falls (Stanley Falls) on Upper Zaïre R., Zaïre; nr. equator; originally named after the explorer.

Bozrah, c. of anc. Edom, probably modern Buseira (Jordan), S.E. of Dead Sea.

Brabant, prov., **Belgium;** S. section of former Duchy; fertile and wooded; many breweries; mnfs. linen, cloth, paper, lace; cap. Brussels; a. 3,281 km²; p. (1981) 2,221,222.

Brabant, North, prov., **Neth.;** S. of Gelderland; N. half of former Duchy; cattle rearing; grain, hops, beetroot; cap. 's-Hertogenbosch; a. 4,972 km²; p. (1983) 2,093,969.

Brač, I., Adriatic Sea, **Yugoslavia;** lgst. of Dalmatian Is.; tourism, fishing; a. 393 km².

Brackley, t., South Northants., **Eng.;** flour milling, brewing; former prosperous wool tr.; Magdalen College School (1447); p. (1981) 6,527.

Bracknell, t., l. gov. dist., Berks., **Eng.;** on Thames Valley terrace, 16 km S. of Windsor; new t. designated 1949 to meet overspill needs from London; extends N. and W. of old v. of Bracknell; Meteorological Office H.Q., chosen (1983) as one of world's 2 forecasting stas.; engin., sealing compounds, plastics; p. (1981) 81,885 (dist.), 48,752 (t.).

Brackwede, t. N. Rhine-Westphalia, **W. Germany;** iron and machin.; p. (1969) 26,448.

Bradford, c., met. dist., West Yorks., **Eng.;** 14 km W. of Leeds; comm. ctr. of wool-textile inds.; impt. for worsted; engin. and chem. inds.; univ.; birthplace of Delius and J. B. Priestley; p. (1981) 457,677.

Bradford-on-Avon, t., West Wilts., **Eng.;** on E. flank of Cotswolds from which bldg. stone derived; former ctr. of wool ind.; p. (1981) 8,752.

Bradwell, v., Essex, **Eng.**; at mouth of R. Blackwater; civil nuclear power-sta.

Braemar, dist. in Grampians, Kincardine and Deeside, **Scot.**; containing Balmoral estate.

Braeriach, mtn., **Scot.**; borders Badenoch and Strathspey, alt. 1,296 m.

Braga, t., cap. of B. dist., N.W. **Portugal**; agr. tr. ctr.; religious ctr.; cath.; p. (1970) 101,877.

Bragança, t., cap. of B. dist., N.E. **Portugal**; agr. tr.; p. (1970) 33,928.

Brahmaputra, one of longer Rs. in **Asia**; flows for much of its length through Himalayas and Assam; called **Tsangpo** in Tibet; fertile agr. valley subject to flooding and silting; 2,880 km long.

Braich-y-Pwll, headland, Gwynedd, **Wales**.

Brăila, t., **Romania**; R. pt. on Danube, nr. Galati; grain tr., boatbldg., reed processing; p. (1978) 200,435.

Braintree, t., Mass., **USA**; elec. machin., rubber gds., glassware; p. (1980) 36,337.

Braintree, t., l. gov. dist., Essex, **Eng.**; on Blackwater; rayon mftg., metal windows, engin.; p. (1981) 111,818 (dist.).

Brakpan, t., Transvaal, **S. Africa**; gold mng.; p. (1970) 113,115.

Brampton, t., Ontario, **Canada**; noted for its greenhouses; p. (1971) 41,238.

Brandenburg, t., **E. Germany**; on R. Havel; former cap. of prov. of B.; tractors, textiles, machin.; p. (est. 1970) 93,660.

Brandenburg. See **Neubrandenburg**.

Brandon, t., Manitoba, **Canada**; on Assiniboine R., W. of Winnipeg; comm. ctr. wheat a.; agr. equipment oil refining; p. (1971) 30,832.

Brandon, t., Suffolk, **Eng.**; ctr. of Breckland; expanded t.

Brandon and Byshottles, ts., former U.D., Durham, **Eng.**; former coal-mng. a.; p. (1981) 17,905.

Brandywine Creek, R., Penns., **USA**; Americans defeated by British 1777; length 32 km.

Brantford, t., Ontario, **Canada**; on Grand R., S.W. of Hamilton; leading mnf. t.; farm implements, cycles, bus and truck parts; p. (1971) 62,853.

Brasilia, cap. of **Brazil**, Goiás st., 960 km N.W. of Rio de Janeiro; ch. of many cities designed to open up interior of rep.; modern architecture; inaugurated 1960; p. (1980) 1,176,908.

Brasov, t., **Romania**; at foot of Transylvanian Alps; aircraft, engin., lge. German and Hungarian p.; p. (1978) 268,226.

Bratislava, c., cap. of Slovakia, **ČSSR**; pt. on Danube 48 km below Vienna; univ.; industl. and comm. ctr.; textiles, chemicals; engin., oil refining; linked to Mozyr', USSR, by "friendship oil pipeline"; p. (1980) 381,476.

Bratsk, c., central Irkutsk oblast, **RSFSR**; on Angara R., ship-repair yards, lumber, iron-ore, wood processing, chemicals; lge. hydroelectric sta.; p. (est. 1980) 219,000.

Braunschweig. See **Brunswick.**

Brava, spt., **Somalia**; leather, shoes; p. (est. 1965) 7,665.

Bray, U.D., Wicklow, **R.o.I.**; on Irish Sea cst.; popular resort; p. (1981) 22,853.

Brazil, Federative Republic of, S. America; a. 8,512,035 km², 5th lgst. cty. in world, exceeded in size only by USSR, China, Canada and USA; covers variety of land and climate; in S., gr. Brazilian plateau, in N., Amazon R. basin (thickly forested); leading industl. nation of **Latin America**; agr.; coffee, cotton, sugar, cocoa, rubber, fruits, hardwoods; cattle-raising; vast mineral reserves inc. manganese, iron, gold, diamonds; admin. through 22 sts., 4 terrs., and Fed. Dist.; cap. Brasilia; lgst. industl. ctr. São Paulo and Belo Horizonte; many multinational companies, inc. car mftg., chems., construction materials; p. mainly White, Negro, Indian, Mestizo; Portuguese official language; p. concentrated in coastal belt, leaving vast a. of interior relatively underdeveloped; p. (est. 1984) 132,648,000.

Brazos, R., Texas, **USA**; flows through agr. and industl. Young Co. via Waco to industl. Brazosport; length 1,520 km.

Brazzaville, c., cap. of **Congo Rep.**; connected by rly. with the Atlantic at Pointe-Noire; R. pt. under construction; airport; p. (est. 1980) 422,400.

Brechin, royal burgh, Angus, **Scot.**; on S. Esk; cath.; linen, paper, whisky; p. (1981) 7,674.

Breckland, dist., S.W. Norfolk, N.W. Suffolk, **Eng.**; chalk overlain by glacial sands; heathland and coniferous plantations; a. 518 km²; lge. a. within Norfolk forms l. gov. dist., inc. Thetford, Swaffham and East Dereham; p. (1981) 96,444.

Brecknock (Breconshire), former co., **Wales**; now mostly inc. in Powys; sm. parts in Mid-Glamorgan and Gwent; now forms l. gov. dist., within Powys inc. Builth Wells, Hay on Wye and Brecon; p. (1981) 40,691.

Brecon (Brecknock), t., Powys, **Wales**; on R. Usk; agr. ctr.; p. (1981) 7,422.

Brecon Beacons, mtns., S. **Wales**; 8 km S. of Brecon; highest peak 888 m; sandstone moorland; Nat. Park.

Breda, c. N. Brabant prov., **Neth.**; mnf. ctr.; machin., foundries, canneries, refineries; historic t., 13th cent. cath.; p. (1982) 117,754.

Bredbury and Romiley, ts., Gtr. Manchester, **Eng.**; paper, engin., dyeing, textiles; p. (1981) 29,122.

Bregenz, t., cap. of Vorarlberg, **Austria**; on Bodensee; hydroelec. power; textiles; resort nr. Bregenz Forest; p. (1971) 21,839.

Breidha Fjord, lge. inlet, W. cst. **Iceland**.

Bremen, Land, **W. Germany**; a. 404 km²; cap. Bremen; p. (est. 1972) 734,330.

Bremen, c., cap. of Land B., **W. Germany**; old t. on right bank of Weser R., 64 km from N. Sea; new t., founded 17th cent., on left bank; leading pt., industl. and comm. ctr.; but hinterland divided by post-war division of Germany; former member of Hanseatic League; p. (est. 1983) 545,100.

Bremerhaven, c., Bremen, **W. Germany**; outport of Bremen at mouth of R. Weser; docks; impt. passenger and fish. pt.; shipbldg.; united with Wesermünde 1941; p. (est. 1983) 137,300.

Bremerton, t., Wash., **USA**; on Puget Sound; naval dockyard; elec. equipment, machin.; p. (1980) 36,208 (t.), 146,609 (met. a.).

Brendon Hills, Somerset, **Eng.**; extension of Exmoor, rising to over 400 m.

Brenner Pass, lowest Alpine pass from Bolzano **(Italy)** to Innsbruck **(Austria)**; used by road and rail; frequent meeting place of Mussolini and Hitler (1940–2).

Brent, outer bor., Greater London, **Eng.**; inc. Wembley and Willesden; p. (1981) 251,257.

Brenta, R., N. **Italy**; rises in picturesque Alpine valley; forestry, silk, tourism; flows to Adriatic Sea; navigable in lower course; length 180 km.

Brentford and Chiswick. See **Hounslow.**

Brentwood, t., l. gov. dist., Essex, **Eng.**; residentl.; p. (1981) 71,978 (dist.).

Brescia, c., cap. B. prov., Lombardy, N. **Italy**; industl. ctr.; iron, steel, engin., textiles; many historic bldgs.; p. (1981) 206,661.

Breslau. See **Wroclaw.**

Bressay I., Shetland Is., **Scot.**; p. (1971) 251.

Brest, naval pt., Finistère dep., N.W. **France**; base of French Atlantic fleet; used by Germans as fortfd. submarine base 1940–4; exp. agr. prods.; impt. industl. ctr.; p. (1982) 160,355.

Brest (Brest-Litovsk), c., Belorussiyan SSR, **USSR**; nr. Polish border; route ctr. and agr. mkt.; timber, food-processing, textiles. Captured by Germans in 1915. Treaty of Brest-Litovsk signed with Soviet Russia 1918; p. (est. 1980) 186,000.

Bretton Woods, resort, N.H., **USA**; site of US monetary and financial conference, 1944, leading to establishment of the International Monetary Fund and the World Bank.

Briançon, t., Hautes-Alpes, **France**; in upper Durance R. valley; winter sports; p. (1982) 11,851.

Bridgend, t., Ogwr, Mid-Glamorgan, S. **Wales**; industl. trading estate; iron, stone, paper; coal mng.; p. (1981) 15,699.

Bridge of Allen, burgh, Stirling, **Scot.**; 3 km N. of Stirling; p. (1981) 4,668.

Bridgeport, c., Conn., **USA**; on Long Island Sound; impt. industl. c., firearms, hardware, elec. equipment, metal products, plastics; p. (1980) 143,000 (c.), 395,000 (met. a.).

Bridgeton, t., N.J., **USA**; founded by Quakers; glasswks., fruit; p. (1980) 18,795.

Bridgetown, t., spt., cap. **Barbados**; deepwater harbour opened 1961; comm. ctr.; exp. sugar, molasses, rum; tourism; p. (1970) 8,789.

Bridgewater Canal, Worsley–Manchester–Runcorn, Gtr. Manchester and Cheshire, **Eng.**; crosses ship canal by means of Barton swing bridge; 61 km long.

Bridgnorth, t., l. gov. dist., Shrops., **Eng.**; cas.; carpets, radio equipment; p. (1981) 50,259.

Bridgwater, t., Sedgemoor, Somerset, **Eng.**;

on R. Parrett, 16 km from Bristol Channel; engin., wire rope, fibre fabrics, cellophane; p. (1981) 26,132.

Bridlington, t., East Yorks., Humberside, **Eng.**; on Bridlington Bay, S. of Flamborough Head; fishing; seaside resort; p. (1971) 26,729.

Bridport, West Dorset, **Eng.**; mkt. t.; seaside resort; p. (1981) 6,876.

Brie, region, Marne and Seine-et-Marne deps., **France;** low, level plateau of limestones and clays, S.E. of Paris; loam (limon) cover and plentiful water supply encourage agr.; grains, sugar-beet, fruit, dairy cattle; famous cheese; densely populated.

Brienz, t., **Switzerland;** resort on L. Brienz; wood carving; p. (1970) 2,796.

Brierley Hill, t., West Midlands, **Eng.**; on W. edge of Black Cty.; cut glass, castable metal gds., firebricks, roofing and tiling, iron and steel.

Brigg, mkt. t., Glanford, Humberside, **Eng.**; ctr. of agr. dist. between Lincoln Heights and Wolds; sugar-beet, jam, seed crushing, canning; p. (1981) 5,358.

Brighouse, t., Calderdale, West Yorks., **Eng.**; on R. Calder, 5 km S.E. of Halifax; textiles and engin.; p. (1981) 35,241.

Brightlingsea, t., Tendring, Essex, **Eng.**; on R. Colne; oysters, boatbldg., yachting; p. (1981) 7,245.

Brighton, t., l. gov. dist., East Sussex, **Eng.**; 80 km S. of London on S. cst.; seaside resort and residtl. t.; Royal Pavilion (1817), univ.; lt. inds.; birthplace of Aubrey Beardsley; p. (1981) 146,134, (t.) 431,197 (urban area of Brighton, Worthing and Littlehampton).

Brindisi, c., Apulia, S. **Italy;** spt. on Adriatic cst., sea and air connections to Middle E.; cath.; cas.; wine, olive oil, silk, petrochemicals; oil refining; p. (1981) 89,786.

Brisbane, t., cap. of Queensland, **Australia;** third c. of A., set on winding B. river, 20 km from attractive sandy cst.; caths., univ.; consumer goods, processing of primary prods.; severe flooding 1974; rapid growth in past 30 years; p. (1976) 696,719 (c.), 957,710 (met. a.).

Brisbane Water, t., N.S.W., **Australia;** N. of Broken Bay; rapid growth with electrification of commuting rly. to Sydney; p. (1976) 49,948.

Bristol, c., l. gov. dist., Avon, **Eng.**; pt. on R. Avon 14 km from Bristol Channel; outport at Avonmouth; cath., univ.; docks; aircraft engin., tobacco, paint, printing and lt. inds.; p. (1981) 387,977 (c.), 420,234 (met. a.).

Bristol, t., Conn., **USA;** foundries, ball bearings, clocks, bells; p. (1980) 57,370.

Bristol Channel, arm of Atl. Oc. between S. cst. of Wales and Somerset and Devon, **Eng.**; noted tidal bores.

British Antarctic Territory, Brit. col., created 1962; consists of all land and Is. S. of lat. 60° S. and between 20° and 80° W. longitude; comprising Graham Land peninsula, S. Shetlands, S. Orkneys and smaller Is., excluding S. Georgia and S. Sandwich Is.; a. 1,222,500 km².

British Columbia, W. prov. separated from rest of **Canada** by Rockies, borders Pac. Oc.; little lowland; parallel N.W.–S.E. ranges of Rockies crossed by Rs. Fraser, Columbia, Kootenay and Peace; vast coniferous forest and hydroelec. resources; salmon fishing on cst.; mng.; p. concentrated in S.W. around Vancouver; a. 948,600 km²; p. (1976) 2,466,608.

British Honduras. *See* **Belize.**

British Indian Ocean Terr., Brit. col., created 1965; consists of the Chagos Archipelago (of which Diego Garcia [Anglo-American naval communications ctr.] is lgst. I.) 1,920 km N.E. of Mauritius, and formerly Is. of Aldabra, Farquhar, and Desroches in the W. Indian Oc. now part of Seychelles Rep.; p. (est. 1982) 3,000.

British Is., archipelago, N.W. **Europe;** comprising 2 lge. Is.; Great Britain, Ireland; and 5,000 sm. Is.; a. 315,029 km².

British Solomon Is. *See* **Solomon Is.**

British West Africa, formerly comprised Gambia, Sierra Leone, Gold Coast (Ghana), Nigeria, and parts of Togoland and Cameroons. *See* under their separate headings.

Briton Ferry, t., West Glamorgan, S. **Wales;** pt. at mouth of R. Neath; steel wks., engin., shipbreaking.

Brittany, region, N.W. **France;** penin. between Eng. Channel and Bay of Biscay; contrast between productive cst. lands (fishing, early

vegetables, tourism) and barren moorland interior; economically depressed; oil refinery projected at St. Livy; p. (1982) 2,703,700.

Brive-la-Gaillarde, t., Corrèze dep., **France;** regional mkt. in fertile basin on edge of Central Massif; p. (1982) 54,032.

Brixham, S. Devon, **Eng.**; incorporated in Torbay; fishing; resort.

Brno (Brünn), c., **ČSSR;** cap. of Moravia; finely situated at confluence of Svratka and Svitava Rs., 109 km N. of Vienna; industl. and communications ctr. with mnfs. of machin., precision tools, textiles; annual tr. fair; p. (1980) 376,001.

Broad Haven, t., new t. planned on St. Brides Bay, Wales.

Broadstairs, Thanet, Kent, **Eng.**; seaside resort; 5 km N.E. of Ramsgate; p. (1981) 23,400.

Broads, The, Norfolk, **Eng.**; series of Ls. formed by mediaeval turf cutting in lower alluvial reaches of Rs. Bure, Waveney, and Yare; yachting, fishing, tourism; plans to create a Nat. Park to help relieve pollution; lge. part now forms Broadland, l. gov. dist., p. (1981) 98,323.

Brockton, c., Mass., **USA;** S. of Boston; lge. shoe and leather ind., machin.; annual tr. fair; p. (1980) 95,172 (c.), 169,374 (met. a.).

Brockville, t., Ontario, **Canada;** R. pt. on St. Lawrence R. below Thousand Is.; telephone equipment, wire cables, elec. tools; p. (1971) 19,707.

Broken Hill, t., N.S.W., **Australia;** major mng. (silver, lead, zinc) ctr. in arid W. of st.; p. (1976) 27,647.

Bromberg. *See* **Bydgoszcz.**

Bromley, outer bor. of London, **Eng.**; inc. Beckenham, Orpington, Penge, and part of Sidcup; p. (1981) 294,451.

Bromsgrove, l. gov. dist., Hereford and Worcs., **Eng.**; mkt. t., 21 km S.W. Birmingham; wrought ironwk., lt. engin.; p. (1981) 88,004.

Bromyard, Hereford and Worcs., **Eng.**; sm. mkt. t.

Bronx, The, one of the five bors. of New York City, **USA;** connected by bridges to bor. of Manhattan; residtl. with parks, zoological and botanical gardens, colleges and professional schools; p. (1980) 1,168,972.

Brooklyn, bor., N.Y. City. **USA;** linked with Manhattan bor. by Brooklyn, Manhattan, and Williamsburgh suspension bridges across East R.; and with Staten I. by Verrazano-Narrows bridge (longest in world); mainly residtl. with numerous mftg. and comm. interests; p. (1980) 2,230,936.

Brooks Range, mtns., N. Alaska, **USA;** forms N. section of Rocky Mtns.; Eskimo p.; Arctic climate, flora and fauna; alt. 2,000 m rising to 2,818 m (Mt. Michelson).

Broom, loch on N.W. cst. of Ross and Cromarty, **Scot.**

Brora, t., Sutherland, **Scot.**; on E. cst., 19 km N.E. of Dornoch Firth; ctr. of sm. coalfield; Harris Tweed ind.; tourism; p. (1981) 1,728.

Brownhills, t., West Midlands, **Eng.**; former mng. t.; expanded t.

Brownsville, t., Texas, **USA;** pt. on Rio Grande nr. Mexican border; livestock, sugar-cane, fruit processing, chemicals; p. (1980) 210,000 (met. a. with Harlingen-San Benito).

Broxbourne, t., l. gov. dist., Herts., **Eng.**; on gravel terrace to W. of R. Lea; ctr. of very intensively cultivated dist.; lt. inds.; "dormitory" t. linked with London; p. (1981) 79,562.

Broxtowe, l. gov. dist., Notts., **Eng.**; made up of Beeston and Stapleford and Eastwood; p. (1981) 102,801.

Bruay-en-Artois, t., Pas-de-Calais, **France;** coal mng.; p. (1982) 23,200.

Bruchsal, t., Baden-Württemberg, **W. Germany;** tobacco, paper, machin.; p. (est. 1983) 37,100.

Brugge (Bruges), c., cap. of W. Flanders prov., N. **Belgium;** mediaeval t. connected by canal to its outer pt. Zeebrugge; univ.; impt. mkt. for grain, cattle, horses; engin., ship-repairing, elec. gds., glass mkg., textiles, lace; p. (est. 1982) 118,048.

Brühl, t., N. Rhine-Westphalia, **W. Germany;** 13 km S. of Cologne; cas.; lignite; p. (est. 1983) 42,100.

Brunei, indep. st. (1984), N. **Borneo;** enclave of Sarawak; Brit. protectorate until 1888; thriving economy based on Seria and offshore oil and gas fields; oil and gas provide 95 per cent of exp.; need to diversify as reserves dwindle and prices fall; 80 percent of food is imported; cap. Bandar Seri Begawan; a. 5,765 km²; p. (est. 1981) 200,000.

Brünn. *See* Brno.

Brunsbüttelkoog, pt. at mouth of R. Elbe.

Brunswick (Braunschweig), c., Lower Saxony, **W. Germany;** on R. Oker; formerly cap. of st. of Brunswick, now a comm. and industl. ctr.; mnfs. inc. canning, tinplate, optics, pianos, lorries; p. (est. 1983) 257,100.

Brussels (Bruxelles), cap. of **Belgium** and of prov. of Brabant; impt. comm., industl. and cultural ctr.; varied mnfs., inc. pharmaceuticals, electronic equipment, machine tools; lge. oil refinery at Feluy; noted for carpets and lace; occupied by the Germans 1914–18, 1940–4; univ.; mediaeval and Renaissance monuments; H.Q. of EEC; p. (1982) 994,774.

Bryan, t., Texas, **USA;** mkt. ctr., agr. college; p. (1970) 33,719.

Bryansk, c., cap. of B. oblast, **RSFSR,** on Desna R.; rly. junc.; a fortress until 19th cent.; sawmilling, engin., textiles, chemicals, steel; oil pipeline from Kuybyshev; p. inc. Bezhitsa (est. 1980) 401,000.

Brynmawr, t., Gwent, **Wales;** former coal-mng. a.; industl. estate; p. (1981) 5,528.

Brzeg (Brieg), t. Silesia, **Poland;** on R. Oder; German until 1945; textiles, leather, chemicals; p. (1968) 29,900.

Bucaramanga, c., N. central **Colombia,** 900 m a.s.l. in E. highlands of Andes; ctr. of coffee-growing dist.; cigar and cigarette mkg.; p. (1973) 315,565.

Buchan Ness, C., nr. Peterhead, E. **Scot.**

Bucharest (Buckresti), cap. and lgst. c. of **Romania;** "Little Paris," on the Dambovita, trib. of Danube; cath., univ.; textiles, chemicals, pharmaceuticals, oil refining, engin.; 20 per cent industl. output of rep.; badly damaged by earthquake (1977); p. (1978) 1,858,418.

Buckfastleigh, t., S. Devon, **Eng.;** wool, quarrying; nearby Benedictine abbey on site of mediaeval Cistercian abbey; p. (1981) 2,889.

Buckhaven and Methil, burgh, Kirkcaldy, **Scot.;** on N. Side of Firth of Forth, 13 km N.E. of Kirkcaldy; coal; p. (1981) 18,236.

Buckie, burgh, Moray, **Scot.;** boat- and yacht-bldg.; fisheries; p. (1981) 7,763.

Buckingham, Aylesbury Vale, Bucks., **Eng.;** mkt. t. on R. Ouse, 24 km N.W. of Aylesbury; p. (1981) 6,627.

Buckinghamshire, non-met. co., **Eng.;** crossed by Chilterns and Vale of Aylesbury; rural and wooded, emphasis is on dairy farming; co. t. Aylesbury; mnfs. chiefly in High Wycombe; decline in traditional handicrafts (lace mkg. and furniture parts); a. 1,882 km²; p. (1981) 565,992.

Buckley, t., Alyn and Deeside, Clwyd, **Wales;** sm. castings; p. (1981) 13,836.

Budapest, cap. and lgst. c. of **Hungary;** stands on both banks of Danube (Buda on right, Pest on left); attractive townscape; univ.; varied mnfs., inc. steel, textiles, chemicals, engin., motorbuses, oil refining; employs 40 per cent industl. workers of Hungary; p. (est. 1979) 2,058,000.

Budaun, t., Uttar Pradesh, **India;** agr. processing; ruins; p. (1961) 58,770.

Bude. *See* Stratton and Bude.

Budel, t., N. Brabant, S. **Neth.;** 19 km S. of Eindhoven; major zinc smelter project.

Budge-Budge, t., W. Bengal, **India;** on lower Hooghly R.; hemp, rice; p. (1961) 39,824.

Budleigh Salterton, East Devon, **Eng.;** resort; birthplace of Raleigh nearby; p. (1981) 4,436.

Buena Park, t., Cal., **USA;** agr. processing mkt.; oilfields; p. (1970) 63,646.

Buenaventura, spt., **Colombia;** lumber yards, tanning, fish canning; p.(1973) 108,710.

Buenos Aires, c., cap. of **Argentina;** cap. to be rebuilt in Patagonia (planned 1986); ch. spt. at head of Rio de la Plata, on E. edge of Pampa; connected to Uruguay, Paraguay, and Brazil by gr. R. system; industl. and tr. ctr. for outlying regions; p. (1980) 2,908,001 (c.) 9,927,404 (met. a.).

Buffalo, c., N.Y., **USA;** pt. on L. Erie; focus of communications on Gr. Ls. has encouraged many heavy inds.; diversified lt. inds.; univ.; p. (1980) 358,000 (c.), 1,243,000 (met. a.).

Bug, R., Ukrainian SSR, **USSR;** known as S. or Ukrainian B.; flows from Volyno-Podolsh upland to Black Sea; navigable in lower course; 853 km long.

Bug, R., the western Bug rises in the Ukraine, **USSR,** not far from the southern Bug and flows N. to join the Vistula below Warsaw; forms bdy. between Poland and Ukrainian SSR; 774 km long.

Bugul'ma, t., Tatar ASSR, **RSFSR;** oil ctr.; p. (est. 1967) 74,000.

Buganda, prov., **Uganda,** E. Africa; located W. of L. Victoria largely at alt. between 1,300 and 1,800 m; intensive cultivation, cotton (ch. comm. crop), plantains, millets; cap. Kampala.

Builth Wells, t., Brecknock, Powys, **Wales;** on upper course of R. Wye; medicinal springs; p. (1981) 1,287.

Buitenzorg. *See* Bogor.

Bujumbura, t., cap. of **Burundi;** pt. on L. Tanganyika; varied inds.; airpt.; p. (1979) 172,201.

Bukavu, t., **Zaïre;** cement, quinine processing; p. (1982) 209,051.

Bukhara (Bokhara), t., Uzbek SSR, **USSR;** in Amu-Dar'ya valley at W. foot of Tien Shan; agr. mkt. at W. terminus of anc. caravan route from China; modern route ctr.; local natural gas, textiles; p. (est. 1980) 188,000.

Bukittinggi, t., Sumatra, **Indonesia;** in Padang Highlands at 1,068 m; p. 53,700.

Bukoba, t., **Tanzania;** pt. midway along W. shore of L. Victoria; exp. coffee, rice and other foodstuffs to L. pts. in Kenya and Uganda.

Bukovina, Northern; terr., formerly belonging to Romania, ceded to **USSR** in 1940; now part of Ukrainian SSR; a. 5,542 km²; ch. t. Chernovitsy; Carpathian Mtns., forested; farming, cereals; cattle.

Bulawayo, t., **Zimbabwe;** impt. rly. ctr.; major ctr. of commerce and heavy engin., airpt.; p. (1982) 413,800.

Bulgaria, People's Rep. of, S.E. Europe; in E. Balkans, bounded by Black Sea in E., and by Danube R. in N. which separates it from Romania; Rodopi range in S.W.; Maritsa R. basin forms central lowland a.; sharp climatic contrasts between winter and summer; fertile lowland areas organised into lge.-scale cooperative farms producing grain; impt. exp. tr. in agr. prods., inc. fruit, vegetables, tobacco; rapidly increasing industl. output; mineral and oil resources; popular tourist a. on Black Sea cst.; cap. Sofia; a. 110,911 km²; p. (est. 1981) 8,900,000.

Bunbury, t., spt., **W. Australia;** 3rd. t. of st., exp. hardwoods, coal, mineral sands; growth since 1970 with establishment of alumina refinery and expansion of pt.; p. (1976) 19,153.

Buncrana, U.D., mkt. t., Donegal, **R.o.I.;** salmon fishing; seaside resort; p. (1971) 2,955.

Bundaberg, t., Queensland, **Australia;** on Burnett R.; ctr. of sugar refining; p. (1976) 31,189.

Bundoran, v., Donegal, **R.o.I.;** fish, pt. and resort; p. (est. 1978) 1,437.

Bungay, Waveney, Suffolk, **Eng.;** mkt. t. on R. Waveney; printing, malting, leather gds.; p. (1981) 4,106.

Bungosuido Channel, Japan; E. entrance into Inland Sea.

Bunzlau. *See* Boleslawiec.

Buraimi, oases lying between **Oman** and United Arab Emirates; rich in oil.

Buraydah (Buraida), t. Nejd., **Saudi Arabia;** oasis; tr. ctr.; p. (est.) 70,000.

Burbank, c., Cal., **USA;** airpt.; aeroplanes, film studios; p. (1970) 88,871.

Burdwan, t., W. Bengal, **India;** agr. processing and tr. ctr. in Damodar valley close to Raniganj coalfield; p. (1971) 143,318.

Bure, R., Norfolk, **Eng.;** lower course forms part of Norfolk Broads; joins Yare at Yarmouth; 93 km.

Burg, t., Magdeburg, **E. Germany;** on Ihle Canal; p. (est. 1970) 29,994.

Burgas, c., **Bulgaria;** spt. and comm. ctr. on Black Sea; ch. exp. pt. for rep.; pt. for oil tankers under construction; p. (est. 1975) 144,000.

Burgenland, prov., **Austria;** bordered on E. by Hungary; low-lying in N., agr.; hilly in S.; cap. Eisenstadt; a. 3,962 km²; p. (1971) 272,119.

Burgess Hill, t., Mid Sussex, West Sussex, **Eng.**; bricks, tiles; p. (1981) 23,542.

Burghausen, t., **W. Germany**; chemicals, oil refining; pipeline to Munich.

Burghead, burgh, Moray, **Scot.**; fish pt., resort; p. (1981) 1,365.

Burgos, c., N. **Spain**; cap. of B. prov.; anc. cap. of Castile and cap. of Franco's regime 1936–9; cath; home of the Cid; tourism, varied inds.; p. (1981) 154,174.

Burgos, prov., Old Castile, **Spain**; cap. B.; a. 14,050 km²; p. (1981) 363,516.

Burgstädt, t., Karl-Marx-Stadt, **E. Germany**; textiles, machin.; p. (1963) 17,167.

Burgundy, former kingdom and prov., N.E. **France**; composed largely of upper valley of R. Saône; famous vineyards; strategic position on route leading between plateau of Vosges and Jura Mtns., from Rhône valley to Rhine valley.

Burhanpur, t., Madhya Pradesh, **India**; anc. walled Mogul c.; textiles, brocades; p. (1971) 105,246.

Burkina Faso. *See* Bourkina Fasso.

Burlington, t., S. Ontario, **Canada**; on L. Ontario, sub., N.E. of Hamilton; in fruit-growing a.; industl.; tourism; p. (1971) 86,125.

Burlington, t., Iowa, **USA**; on bluffs of Mississippi R.; machin., furniture; p. (1980) 29,529.

Burlington, t., Vt., **USA**; on L. Champlain; pt. of entry and ch. industl. and comm. t. in st.; numerous mnfs.; p. (1980) 37,712 (t.), 114,070 (met. a.).

Burma, Union of, rep., **S.E. Asia**; Irrawaddy R. basin, developed by British in 19th cent., forms major cluster of p., routeways and source of rice of which B. is one of few exporters; surrounding mtns. relatively underdeveloped, although they are a source of teak and hardwood exps.; almost self-sufficient in petroleum from deposits in N.; natural gas prod. increasingly impt.; monsoon climate; p. mainly Buddhist; secessionist moves in Moslem Arakan st., ch. ts., Mandalay, cap. Rangoon; a. 676,580 km²; p. (est. 1984) 38,513,000.

Burnham Beeches, Berks./Bucks., **Eng.**; part of anc. forest acquired 1879 for public use; a. 243 ha.

Burnham-on-Crouch, t., Essex, **Eng.**; pt., yachting, boat-bldg.; p. (1981) 6,291.

Burnham-on-Sea, t., Sedgemoor, Somerset, **Eng.**; on Bridgwater Bay; resort; p. (1981) 14,920.

Burnie, spt., Tasmania, **Australia**; pulp and paper mills; impt. mineral pt. (tin); p. (1976) 19,115.

Burnley, t., l. gov. dist., Lancs., **Eng.**; textiles, engin., car accessories; p. (1981) 93,779 (dist.).

Burntisland, royal burgh, Kirkcaldy, **Scot.**; on F. of Forth; p. (1981) 5,875.

Burray, one of the Orkney Is., **Scot.**; p. (est. 1969) 595.

Burrinjuck, t., N.S.W., **Australia**; on Murrumbidgee R., N. of Canberra; site of impt. dam providing irrigation in Riverina dist.

Burry Port, t., Dyfed, **Wales**; p. (1981) 5,951.

Bursa, c., N.W. **Turkey**; noted for its textiles; cap. of anc. Bithynia (3rd cent. B.C.) and later of Ottoman empire; mosques; p. (1980) 445,113.

Burslem. *See* Stoke-on-Trent.

Burton-on-Trent, t., East Staffs., **Eng.**; brewing, malting, rubber gds.; p. (1981) 47,930.

Burujird, t., **Iran**; textiles and mkt. ctr. at alt. 1,678 m; p. (1966) 71,486.

Burundi, rep., E. central **Africa**; high plateau on N.E. shore of L. Tanganyika; tropical climate, irregular rainfall; economy based on agr., inc. subsistence crops of manioc. sweet potatoes, and cash crops of cotton, coffee; coffee major exp.; (89 percent of export earnings in 1980); one of poorest states in world; sm. mftg. inds. developing, but no rlys.; home of ruling Tutsi and rebel Hutu; cap. Bujumbura; a. 27,834 km²; p. (est. 1983) 4,421,000.

Bury, t., met. dist., Gtr. Manchester, **Eng.**; on R. Irwell to S. of Rossendale Fells; cotton, textiles; birthplace of Robert Peel; p. (1981) 176,578.

Buryat (Buryatskaya), aut. rep. **RSFSR**; borders L. Baykal; mtnous., forested; lge. mineral deposits; cap. Ulan Ude; a. 350,945 km²; p. (est. 1973) 834,000.

Bury St. Edmunds, St. Edmundsbury, Suffolk, **Eng.**; old mkt. t., on R. Lark, abbey ruins; farm implements, sugar-beet processing; expanded t.; p. (1981) 28,914.

Bushey, t., Hertsmere, Herts., **Eng.**; residtl.; p. (1981) 23,240.

Bushir. *See* Bandar-e-Būshehr.

Busto Arsizio, t., Varese prov., N. **Italy**; 30 km. N.W. of Milan; cotton milling ctr., iron, steel, rayon, textile machin.; p. (1981) 79,769.

Bute, Kyles of, strait, 10 km between isles of Bute and Argyll, **Scot.**

Buteshire, former co., now part of Strathclyde Region, **Scot.**

Butte, t., Mont., **USA**; mng. t. (copper, zinc. silver, manganese, gold, lead, arsenic); also a farming ctr.; p. (1980) 37,205.

Buttermere, L., Cumberland, **Eng.**

Butt of Lewis, promontory with lighthouse; Lewis, Hebrides, **Scot.**

Buxton, t., High Peak, Derbys., **Eng.**; spa; lime-quarrying nearby; p. (1981) 20,797.

Buzau, t., **Romania**; rly. ctr.; cath.; wheat, timber, petroleum; p. (1978) 102,868.

Bydgoszez, prov., **Poland**; cap. B.; drained by Rs. Vistula, Brda, and Notec; formerly called Pomorze; salt and lime deposits aid chemical inds.; a. 20,800 km²; p. (est. 1983) 1,064,000.

Bydgoszez (Bromberg), c., N. central **Poland**; on R. Brda; R. pt., rly. ctr.; elec. equipment, machine tools, timber mnfs.; p. (est. 1983) 357,700.

Byelorussian SSR. *See* Belorussiyan SSR.

Byron C., most E. point of **Australia**, Pacific cst. of N.S.W.

Bytom, c., S.W. **Poland**; formerly in Prussian prov. of Upper Silesia; ctr. of Katowice mng. a.; p. (est. 1983) 238,000.

C

Cabinda, enclave, **Angola**; separated by Zaïre R. estuary from Angola; tropical climate encourages thick forest cover; tropical crops; offshore oil production; uranium; attempts at secession; a. 7,236 km²; p. (1970) 81,265.

Cabot Strait, entrance of G. of St. Lawrence between C. Breton I. and Newfoundland, **Canada**.

Cáceres, c., and cap. of C. prov., W. **Spain**; in Estremadura, above Tagus valley; mkt. t. lies below the old t. topping the hill; p. (1981) 421,444 (prov.).

Cachar, dist., Assam, **India**; tea-growing ctr.; a. 6,961 km²; p. (1961) 1,378,476.

Cachoeira, t., Bahia, **Brazil**; historic c.; p. (est. 1980) 125,800.

Cachoeira do Sul, t., Rio Grande do Sul, **Brazil**; p. (est. 1980) 112,500.

Cadarache, t., S. **France**; nr. Aix-en-Provence; nuclear research centre.

Cader Idris, mtn., Gwynedd, **Wales**; alt. 893 m.

Cádiz, maritime prov., S.W. **Spain**; cap. Cádiz; a. 7,321 km²; p. (1981) 988,378.

Cádiz, c., cap. of C. prov., S.W. **Spain**; in Andalusia; pt. on Bay of C.; fortress t., naval base; exp. sherry, cork, fruit, olive oil, tunny fish; univ., cath.; one of the most anc. ts. in Europe, built by Phoenicians, c. 1100 B.C.; p. (1981) 157,766.

Caen, c., cap. of Calvados dep., **France**; church and abbey, tomb of William the Conqueror; univ.; iron-ore mng. and processing; severely damaged in second world war; p. (1982) 117,119.

Caerleon, t., Gwent, **Wales**; on R. Usk, 5 km N.E. of Newport; Roman Isca Silurum; remains still present; agr. machin., tools, bricks; p. (1981) 6,711.

Caernarvon, t., Arfon, Gwynedd, N. **Wales**; pt. on S. shore of Menai strait; cas. where first Prince of Wales (Edward II) was christened; bricks, plastics; p. (1981) 9,506.

Caernarvonshire, former co., N. **Wales**. *See* Gwynedd.

Caerphilly, t., Rhymney Valley, Mid-Glamorgan, S. **Wales**; cas.; lt. inds.; former coal-mng. a.; p. (1981) 42,736.

Caesar Mazaca, anc. c., Asia Minor; residence of the Cappadocian Kings; the modern Kayeri, **Turkey**.

Caesarea Palestinae, old c., **Israel**, 32 km S. Mt. Carmel; cap. of Herod the Great.

Caeté, t., Minas Gerais st., **Brazil**; lge. iron and steel wks.; p. (est. 1968) 36,411.

Cagliari, cap. and ch. pt. of Sardinia, **Italy;** univ., cath.; p. (1981) 233,848.

Cahir, t., Tipperary, **R.o.I.;** on R. Suir; anc. cas. and abbey; salmon fishing; p. (1981) 2,082.

Cahors, t., cap. of Lot dep., **France;** comm. ctr.; many historic bldgs., inc. cath., palace; distilleries, shoe factory; p. (1982) 20,774.

Cairngorm, mtns., Moray, Badenoch and Strathspey, **Scot.;** rise to 1,310 m (Ben Macdhui); form part of Highlands; nat. nature reserve of arctic flora and fauna; winter sports.

Cairns, spt., Queensland, **Australia;** on Trinity Bay; bulk sugar terminal; resort for Barrier Reef; p. (1976) 39,305.

Cairntoul, mtn., Kincardine and Deeside, **Scot.;** alt. 1,294 m.

Cairo (El Qâhira), c., cap. of **Egypt;** on E. bank of Nile, at head of delta; lgst. c. in rep.; univ., mosques, palace; fortress of Babylon in old c.; p. (1976) 5,074,016.

Cairo, Ill., **USA;** at confluence of Mississippi and Ohio; busy traffic ctr.; p. (1970) 6,277.

Caistor, t., West Lyndsey, Lincs., **Eng.;** site of Roman camp in Lincs. Wolds.

Caithness, l. gov. dist., former co., **Scot.;** most N. part of mainland; flat, with much moorland; herring fishery; poor agr.; quarrying; ch. ts. Wick, Thurso; a. 3,152 km²; p. (1981) 27,383.

Cajamarca, t., cap. of C. dep., **Peru;** in mtn. valley, 2,745 m; impt. in Inca times; p. (est. 1977) 30,000.

Calabar, spt., S.E. **Nigeria;** cap. Cross River st.; exp. palm oil, kernels, rubber, ivory, cement; p. (est. 1975) 103,000.

Calabria, region, extreme S.W. **Italy;** mtnous. pen.; highest point Mt. Pollino 2,234 m; ch. R. Crati; socially and economically underdeveloped; cap. Catanzaro; p. (1981) 2,061,182.

Calais, spt., Pas-de-Calais, N.E. **France;** cross-channel ferry pt. opposite to and 33·6 km distant from Dover; nearby Sangatte to be exit of proposed Channel Tunnel (1993); p. (1982) 76,935.

Calama, oasis, Antofagasta prov., N. **Chile;** in Atacama desert at foot of Andean Cordillera; water from R. Loa supplies Antofagasta and used for irrigation locally.

Calatafimi, t., Sicily, **Italy;** Garibaldi defeated Neapolitans, May 1860; p. (1981) 8,159.

Calbayog, t., Samar, **Philippines;** hemp tr., fisheries; p. (1975) 101,748.

Calbe, t., Magdeburg, **E. Germany;** on R. Saale; p. (est. 1970) 16,296.

Calcutta, c., cap. of W. Bengal st., **India;** pt. on Hooghly R., lgst. c. in rep. and one of most densely populated areas of world; vast tr. from Ganges plain; univ.; jute-mills, textiles, chems., engin.; exp. jute, cotton, sugar-cane, rice, tea, coal; "black hole" (1756); p. (1981) 3,288,148 (c.), 9,194,018 (met. a. covering 1,036 km²).

Calder, R., West Yorks., **Eng.,** trib of Aire R.

Calderdale, met. dist., West Yorks., **Eng.;** chief t. Halifax; also inc. Todmorden, Brighouse, Hebden Royd, Ripponden and Sowerby Bridge; p. (1981) 191,292.

Calder Hall, Cumbria, **Eng.;** first full-scale nuclear power sta. in world (1956) owned and operated by AEA, produces electricity for nat. grid.

Caldy I., off Dyfed cst., **Wales;** lighthouse; Trappist monastery.

Caledonian Canal, from Moray Firth to Loch Linnhe, **Scot.,** connecting North Sea with Atl. Oc.; 100 km long; opened 1822.

Calf of Man, sm. I., S.W. I. of Man, **Eng.;** a. 250 ha.

Calgary, ch. t., Alberta, **Canada;** ctr. of ranching cty.; lumber mills, tanneries, oil refining, flour milling; p. (1979) 469,915.

Cali, c., cap. of Valle del Cauca dep., W. **Colombia;** 1,068 m on Cauca R.; comm. and transport ctr. for rich agr. a.; p. (est. 1979) 1,316,137.

Calicut (Kozhikade), t., Kerala, **India;** first pt. reached by Vasco da Gama (1498); gave its name to calico cloth; p. (1981) 394,447 (t.), 546,058 (met. a.).

California, st., W. **USA;** admitted to Union 1850; st. flower golden poppy, st. bird California Valley quail; mtnous., forested, fertile valleys; subject to earthquakes from San Andreas fault; rich in minerals, oil, natural gas, gold, silver, copper; fruits; film ind.; attractive climate and scenery; cap. Sacramento; ch. pt. San Francisco, lgst. c. Los Angeles; most populous st. in USA; a. 411,014 km²; p. (1980) 23,669,000.

California Current, E. Pac. Oc.; flows N. to S. along cst. of Ore. and Cal., USA; relatively cold water; reduces summer temp. and causes fog in cst. a. especially nr. San Francisco.

California, G. of, arm of Pac. Oc., N.W. **Mexico;** 1,120 km long; same rift as Imperial and Coachella valleys in S.E. Cal.

Callander, burgh, Stirling, **Scot.;** mkt. t. on R. Teith, 24 km N.W. of Stirling; "the gate of the Highlands," tourism; p. (1981) 2,519.

Callao, c., W. **Peru;** pt. of Lima; sheltered harbour; sacked by Drake in 16th cent.; p. (1981) 441,374.

Calne, North Wilts., **Eng.;** mkt. t. on Marden R.; lge. bacon factory closed (1982); p. (1981) 10,268.

Caltagirone, t., Catania, Sicily, **Italy;** cath.; majolica ware; p. (1981) 35,682.

Caltanissetta, t., cap. of C. prov., Sicily, **Italy;** cath.; agr., sulphur ctr.; p. (1981) 61,146.

Calvados, dep., N.E. **France;** low-lying cty. and damp climate aid dairying; butter and cheese prods.; apple orchards produce Calvados brandy; cap. Caen; a. 5,690 km²; p. (1982) 589,400.

Cam (Granta), R., Cambridge, **Eng.;** trib. of R. Ouse; flows through the "backs" at Cambridge; 64 km long.

Camagüey, c., **Cuba;** comm. ctr. in rich agr. region; cattle, sugar-cane; p. (1975) 221,826.

Camargue, delta dist., Bouches-du Rhône, **France;** at mouth of R. Rhône; famous col. of flamingoes; gypsies; bull-rearing; a. 777 km².

Camberley, t., Surrey, **Eng.;** Royal Military Staff College, Royal Military Academy.

Cambodia. See Kampuchea.

Camborne, t., Cornwall, **Eng.;** 18 km S.W. Truro; old tin and copper mines; engin., radio-television assembly; textiles, chemicals; p. (1981) 46,482 (inc. Redruth).

Cambrai, t., Nord dep., **France;** on R. Scheldt; textiles (gave its name to cambric), agr. processing; suffered in both world wars; p. (1982) 36,618.

Cambrian Mtns., Wales; collective name for mtns. of N. and Central Wales inc. Snowdonia and Cader Idris.

Cambridge, univ. c., co. t., l. gov. dist., Cambridgeshire, **Eng.;** on Cam R.; famous univ. with residtl. colleges; leading ctr. of research-based inds.; p. (1981) 90,440.

Cambridgeshire, non-met. co., **Eng.;** low-lying, sloping from E. Anglian Heights in S.E. to Fens in N.; crossed by Rs. flowing to Wash; rich soils aid intensive agr. and mkt. gardening; inc. former cos. of Huntingdon, Peterborough and Isle of Ely; ch. t. Cambridge; a. 3,408 km²; p. (1981) 575,177.

Cambridgeshire, East, l. gov. dist., Cambs., **Eng.;** a. N.E. of Cambridge inc. Ely; p. (1981) 53,629.

Cambridgeshire, South, l. gov. dist., Cambs., **Eng.;** rural a. surrounding Cambridge; p. (1981) 107,979.

Cambridge, c., Mass., **USA;** 5 km from Boston; seat of Harvard Univ. and MIT; mftg.; impt. research ctr.; now inc. in Boston met. a.; p. (1980) 95,322.

Camden, inner bor., N. London, **Eng.;** inc. Hampstead, Holborn, and St. Pancras; p. (1981) 171,563.

Camden, c., N.J., **USA;** pt. of entry on Delaware R., opposite Philadelphia; comm., mftg. and residtl.; iron foundries, chemicals, shipbldg.; p. (1980) 84,910; inc. in Philadelphia met. a.

Camerino, t., central **Italy;** in Apennines; univ. cath.; the anc. Camerium; p. (1981) 7,920.

Cameroon, United Rep. of, unitary st. (1972) W. **Africa;** on G. of Guinea; fed. cap. Yaoundé; dependence on primary exports of coffee and cocoa now reduced by rapid incr. in petroleum production since 1977; growing industrial sector; now graduated to middle income developing country; a. 475,500 km²; p. (est. 1984) 9,467,000.

Cameroon Mtn., volcano, massif, **Cameroon;** cstl-mtn., hgst. in W. Africa; last eruption 1959; alt. 4,072 m.

Campagna di Roma, Latium, **Italy;** malarial coastal plain around Rome; now reclaimed and used for pasture.

Campania, region, S. **Italy;** comprising provs. Avellino, Benevento, Caserta, Naples, Salerno; admin. and comm. ctr. Naples; high p. density; fertile; intensive agr.; p. (1981) 5,463,134.

Campbelltown, t., N.S.W., **Australia;** dairy and

poultry ctr. for Sydney; proposed growth ctr. for 340,000; p. (1976) 52,285.

Campbeltown, royal burgh, spt., Kintyre, Argyll and Bute, **Scot.**; distilling, fishing; planned ctr. for construction of off-shore oil platforms; p. (1981) 6,077.

Campeche, spt., S.E. **Mexico**; on G. of Campeche; gives its name to prov. (a. 56,099 km², p. (1970) 251,556); clothing; exp. timber, sisal hemp; p. (1979) 108,680.

Campina Grande, t., Paraiba, **Brazil**; inland mkt. t. benefitting from industl. devel. from recent SUDENE development plan; (est. 1980) 265,600.

Campinas, t., **Brazil**; 88 km N. of São Paulo; coffee; machin.; rubber gds.; p. (1980) 586,500.

Campine or **Kempenland,** region in Limburg and Antwerp provs., **Belgium**; concealed coalfield in heathland a.

Campobasso, t., cap. of C. prov., S. **Italy**; agr. ctr.; famed for cutlery; 15th cent. cas.; p. (1981) 48,291.

Campo Belo, t., Minas Gerais st., **Brazil**; impt. cattle ctr. nr. L. formed by Furnas Dam on Rio Grande; p. (est. 1968) 30,810.

Campo Duran, terr., **Argentina**; oilfield and refining.

Campos, c., Rio de Janeiro st., **Brazil**; ctr. for rich agr. region; sugar refining; p. (est. 1980) 356,600.

Campos do Jordão, t., **Brazil**; alt., 1,699 m; health resort, known as the Switzerland of Brazil; p. (est. 1968) 19,676.

Campsie Fells, range of hills, Stirling, **Scot.**; highest point, 578 m.

Campulung, t., **Romania**, in Walachia, at foot of Transylvanian Alps; summer resort; p. (est. 1970) 26,675.

Canada, indep. st., within Commonwealth; occupies N. part of **N. America**; enclave of Alaska (USA) in N.W.; second lgst. cty. in world, consisting of 10 provs., 2 terrs.; coastal mtns. and Rockies in W., interior plains in ctr., Hudson Bay lowlands in N., plateau a. of Quebec and Newfoundland in E.; many Is. off Arctic cst.; continental climate, severe in interior but moderated on csts.; less than 8 per cent of total land a. classified as cultivated land but agr. prods. (especially wheat) very valuable exp.; enormous forest resources but many economically inaccessible; fur trapping in N., impt. fishing inds. on both Pac. and Atl. csts.; considerable mineral resources; lgst. world producer of asbestos, silver, nickel, zinc.; major oil and gas resources in Alberta; one of most urbanised ctys. in world; p. concentrated along E.-W. axis in S. parts of W. provs. and along Gr. Ls. and St. Lawrence lowland; economy highly integrated with USA; 80 per cent of mftg. inds. based on US investment and 70 per cent of external tr. with USA; major cultural differences between English and French communities; strong separatist movements in Quebec; both nat. languages official (30 per cent p. speak French); cap. Ottawa; a. 9,976,185 km²; p. (est. 1984) 25,302,000.

Canada Dam, Bihar, **India**; on R. Mayurakshi, 256 km from Calcutta.

Canadian Coast Range, mtns., B.C., W. **Canada**; penetrated by deep inlets (fjords) with very little cst. plain; crossed only by R. Skeena in N., R. Fraser in S.

Canadian R., S.W. **USA**; trib. of Arkansas R., not navigable but impt. for irrigation; 1,440 km long.

Canadian Shield (Laurentian Shield), Canada; vast region of hard anc. rock surrounding Hudson Bay, deeply eroded by ice, and lake covered; mng. and forestry.

Canal du Centre, canal, **France**; links Rhône-Saône valley at Chalon-sur-Saône with R. Loire at Digoin; serves Le Creusot coalfield; length 96 km.

Canal Zone, Panama; strip of land leased to USA since 1903 for Panama Canal; p. (1970) 44,650.

Canaries Current, ocean current, flows S. along N.W. coast of Africa from El Dar-el-Beida to C. Verde; relatively cold and has very marked cooling effect on Saharan coastlands.

Canary Is., or **Canaries,** N. Atl. Oc.; gr. of 7 volcanic Is. belong to Spain, 96 km off cst. Africa; desires independence; inc. Tenerife (the lgst. I.), Gran Canaria, La Palma, Gomera, Hierro, Fuerteventura, Lanzarote; dry sunny climate and impressive volcanic landscape encourage tourism; intensive, irrigated agr. for bananas, tomatoes, oranges and vegetables; cap. Las Palmas, the "Fortunate Isles" of many myths and legends; a. 7,272 km²; p. (1981) 1,444,626.

Canberra, cap. **Australia;** midway between Melbourne and Sydney, lgst. inland c.; rapid growth since cap. established (1912); half work-force employed in government; spacious plan-ned c. centred around L. Burley Griffin, reliant on high car ownership; p. (1976) 196,640.

Candia. See **Iráklion.**

Canea. See **Khaniá.**

Canna, sm. I., Hebrides, **Scot.**; basaltic pillars.

Cannanore, t., Kerala, **India**; exp. timber, coconuts; p. (1981) 60,904 (t.), 157,797 (met. a.).

Cannes, spt., dep. Alpes-Maritimes, **France**; 32 km S.W. Nice; famous resort; perfumes; airpt.; annual spring international film festival; p. (1982) 72,787.

Cannock Chase, upland a., Staffs., **Eng.**; open a. close to Midlands conurb.; now forms l. gov. dist. based on Cannock t.; p. (1981) 84,526.

Canopus, c. of anc. **Egypt**; 19 km E. of Alexandria; here bdy. between Asia and Africa was drawn; Aboukir nr. ruins of temple of Serapis.

Cantabrians (Sierra de Cantabria), mtns., N. **Spain**; stretch from Pyrenees to C. Finisterre; form barrier between sea and central plateau; thick vegetation on lower slopes; coal, iron, hydroelec. power; hgst. peak Peña Vieja (2,673 m).

Cantal, dep., S.E. **France**; volcanic a., part of Massif Central; hgst. peak Plomb du Cantal (1,859 m); difficult agr., sparse p.; cap. Aurillac; a. 5,778 km²; p. (1982) 162,000.

Canterbury, c., l. gov. dist., Kent, **Eng**; at foot of N. Downs on R. Stour; univ.; cath. founded A.D. 597 by St. Augustine; shrine of Thomas Becket; for centuries a place of pilgrimage; p. (1981) 116,829 (dist.).

Canterbury, prov., S.I., **N.Z.**; cap. Christchurch; a. 36,104 km²; p. (1976) 428,586.

Canterbury Plains, rich grazing and wheat-growing dist., on merged alluvial fans; S.I., **N.Z.**; ch. t. Christchurch; ch. pt. Lyttelton.

Can-tho, t., **Vietnam**; on Mekong R. delta, tr. ctr.; rice, fish; p. (1973) 182,424.

Canton. See **Guangzhou.**

Canton R. See **Zhujiang.**

Canton, c., Ohio, **USA**; iron and steel, pulleys, hydraulic presses; p. (1980) 93,077 (c.), 404,421 (met. a.).

Canvey I., Castle Point, Essex, **Eng.**; fronting the Thames; expanded t.; resort; radio components, bookbinding, iron and wire wks., oil storage; oil refinery projected; liquid gas terminal; p. (1981) 35,293.

Cap de la Madeleine, t., S. Quebec, **Canada**; varied mnfs.; p. (1966) 29,433.

Cape Breton I., Nova Scotia, **Canada**; coalmng., steelwks.; farming, timber, fishing; ch. t. Sydney; discovered in 1497 by John Cabot; a. 9,324 km²; p. (1966) 166,943.

Cape Canaveral, E. Fla., **USA**; formerly Cape Kennedy; barrier I. separating Banana R. lagoon from Atl. Oc.; military base for testing missiles.

Cape Coast, t., **Ghana**; pt. of G. of Guinea, 96 km S.W. of Accra; cap. of Gold Coast until 1876; exp. cacao; cas.; p. (1984) 51,653.

Cape Cod, low sandy penin., Mass. Bay, **USA**; resort; fishing, boat bldg.; encloses C. C. Bay where Pilgrim Fathers first arrived in America 1620.

Cape Girardeau, t., Mo., **USA**; on Mississippi R.; footwear, clothing; p. (1980) 34,361.

Cape Kennedy. See **Cape Canaveral.**

Cape of Good Hope, S. Africa; famous headland, S. of Cape Town; 305 m high.

Cape Province, prov., Rep. of S. **Africa**; formerly Cape of Good Hope Colony; southernmost tip of Africa; cap. Cape Town; mostly plateau; inc. Transkeian terrs. in E.; sheep raising; wheat, citrus fruits, grapes, tobacco; fisheries; diamond and copper mng. in Namaqualand; automobile assembly, textiles, food canning; a. 721,224 km²; p. (1980) 5,091,360.

Capernaüm, in time of Christ impt. place in Palestine, on N. shore of L. Galilee; the modern Tell Hum (Israel).

Cape Town, c., cap. of Province, and legislative cap. of **Rep. of S. Africa**; spt. on Table Bay, 48 km N. of C. of Good Hope; communication by rail direct with Zimbabwe, Transvaal, O.F.S., and Natal; docks; cath.; univ.; exp. wool, gold, diamonds; oil refinery under construction at Milnerton 10 km N.E., p. (1970) 1,096,257 (met. a.).

Cape Verde Is., archipelago off W. cst. **Africa**; former Portuguese col.; 15 volcanic Is. and islets, divided into two grs.; windward and leeward; a. 4,040 km²; cap. Praia; agr. sugar, fruit-growing; São Vicente fuelling sta. for navigation to S. America; indep. achieved 1975; irrigation and reafforestation projects; p. (est. 1984) 317,000.

Cap-Haïtien, t., N. **Haiti**; spt., on N. cst.. exp. coffee, cacao, sugar; p. (1971) 44,123.

Capraia, I., 26 km E. of Corsica, belonging to **Italy**; volcanic; part of Genoa prov.

Caprera, I., off N.E. cst. Sardinia, **Italy**; Garibaldi buried here.

Capri, I. and tourist resort in Bay of Naples, **Italy**; famous Blue Grotto; celebrated in times of Augustus and Tiberius; wines; a. 10 km²; p. (1981) 7,489.

Capua, t., Campania, S. **Italy**; on Volturno R.; founded by Etruscans, impt. ctr. under Roman rule, sacked by Gaiseric; modern t. 5 km N. of site of anc. Capua; cath., Roman bridge; p. (1981) 18,053.

Caracas, c., cap. of **Venezuela**; in mtn. valley 921 m a.s.l.; 13 km inland from its pt. La Guaira; modern c.; contains 20 per cent of p. of rep.; cath., univs.; oil, textile mills, sugar refining; p. (est. 1980) 1,662,627 (c.), 2,849,191 (met.a.).

Caradon, l. gov. dist., Cornwall, **Eng.**; a. between Tamar and S. cst.; inc. Looe, Saltash and Liskeard; p. (1981) 67,894.

Carbon County, N. Utah, **USA**; contains immense reserves of gd. coking coal suitable for blast furnaces; not yet developed.

Carbonia, t., Sardinia, **Italy**; built 1937–8 nr. lignite and barytes a.; p. (1981) 32,130.

Carcassonne, c., cap. of Aude dep., S. **France**; historic citadel guarding impt. routeway from Aquitaine to Rhône valley; old c. divided from new by Aude R.; tourism; p. (1982) 42,450.

Cardamom Hills, Kerala, S. **India**; highland formed where W. and E. Ghats meet; rise to over 2,400 m; hgst. land of Indian penin.; rainfall less seasonal than most of India; "China" tea plantations on middle slopes.

Cárdenas, t., W. **Cuba**; pt. on Cárdenas Bay; processes and exp. sugar; p. (est. 1967) 67,400.

Cardiff, c., l. gov. dist., South Glamorgan, cap. of **Wales**; at mouth of R. Taff on Bristol Channel, one of world's gr. coal-shipping pts.; univ. colls., cath., cas.; docks at Barry; iron and steel wks., flour mills; freeport (1984) to help redevelopment of docks; p. (1981) 273,856.

Cardigan, t., Ceredigion, Dyfed, S. **Wales**; at mouth of Teifi R.; former pt., now mkt. ctr.; p. (1981) 4,184.

Cardiganshire, former c., **Wales**. See Dyfed.

Caribbean Sea, part of Atl. Oc., between W.I. and Central and S. America; warm sea, entirely within tropics; a. 19,425 km².

Cariboo Range, mtns., B.C., W. **Canada**; mass of anc. crystalline rocks inside the gr. bend of R. Fraser; widespread occurrence of lode and alluvial gold; mainly above 1,500 m; hgst. point Mt. Sir Wilfred Laurier (3,584 m).

Carinthia (Karnten), prov., **Austria**; cap. Klagenfurt; contains hgst. mtn. in Austria, Grossglockner, alt. 3,801 m; many Ls.; p. (1971) 525,728.

Carlisle, c., l. gov. dist., Cumbria, **Eng.**; on Eden R.; pt. and route ctr.; Norman cas.; cath.; textiles, plasterboard, flour, bacon, biscuits, metal boxes; p. (1981) 100,692 (dist.).

Carlow, co., S.E. Leinster, **R.o.I.**; arable agr. and livestock; co. t. Carlow; a. 896 km²; p. (1981) 17,977.

Carlow, co. t., Carlow co., **R.o.I.**; cath.; mkt., agr. processing; p. (1971) 9,588.

Carlsbad, t., N.M., **USA**; tourist resort; impt. potash deposits; p. (1980) 25,496.

Carlsbad Caverns National Park, N.M., **USA**; in foothills of Guadalupe mtns.; limestone caves; a. 18,600 ha.

Carlton, t., Gedling, Notts., **Eng.**; 3 km N.E. Nottingham; hosiery; p. (1981) 46,456.

Carmarthen, t., l. gov. dist., Dyfed, **Wales**; on Towy R.; impt. agr. ctr.; cas. ruins; p. (1981) 51,733 (dist.).

Carmarthenshire, former co., **Wales**. See Dyfed.

Carmiel, t., N. **Israel**; new t. built built between Acre and Safad, in the Galilean hills.

Carmona, t., **Spain**; Roman walls and necropolis; p. (1970) 24,378.

Carnac, sm. t., Brittany, N.W. **France**; famous for its megalithic monuments; p. (1982) 3,964.

Carnarvon, t., W. **Australia**; on R. Gascoyne; NASA tracking sta.; p. (1976) 5,341.

Carnoustie, burgh, Angus, **Scot.**; on N. Sea; 10 km S.W. of Arbroath; resort; p. (1981) 9,217.

Caroline Is., archipelago in W. Pac. Oc.; internal self-government (1978); 549 in no., lying between the Philippines and the Marshall gr., former Japanese mandate now part of US Pac. Trust Terr.; Western Carolines became **Rep. of Belau** (1981); ch. exp. copra; a. 1,193 km; p. (est. 1967) 66,900.

Caroni, R., **Venezuela**, hydroelec. complex at confluence Orinoco R.; steelwks.

Carpathian Mtns., range, E. **Europe**; arc of mtns. extending from CSSR into Ukrainian SSR and Romania; major European range; 1,288 km long; contains oilfields.

Carpentaria, G. of, N. **Australia**; between Arnhem Land and C. York.

Carpentras, t., Vaucluse, **France**; on R. Auzon; antiquities; sweetmeats; p. (1982) 25,886.

Carpi, t., central **Italy**; 16 km N. of Modena; cath.; food processing; p. (1981) 60,507.

Carrantuohill, mtn., Kerry, **R.o.I.**; 1,041 m, loftiest in all Ireland.

Carrara, t., Massa Carrara, central **Italy**; famed for white marble used by Michelangelo; p. (1981) 65,687.

Carrick, l. gov. dist., Cornwall, **Eng.**; stretches across penin. and surrounds Fal estuary; inc. Truro, Penryn and Falmouth; p. (1981) 76,188.

Carrickfergus, t., l. gov. dist., **N. Ireland**; pt. on N. shore of Belfast Lough; textiles, nylon fibres, tobacco inds.; p. (1981) 28,365 (dist.), 17,633 (t.).

Carrickmacross, mkt. t., U.D. Monaghan, **R.o.I.**; p. (1981) 1,768.

Carrick-on-Shannon, co. t., R. D., Leitrim, **R.o.I.**; on flat land in Upper Shannon valley; p. of t. (1981) 1,677.

Carrick-on-Suir, mkt. t., U.D., Tipperary, **R.o.I.**; leather prods.; N.W. of Waterford; p. (1981) 5,511.

Carron, v., Falkirk, **Scot.**; nr. Falkirk; site of first ironwks. in E. Lowlands of Scot.

Carron, Loch, inlet, W. cst., Ross and Cromarty, **Scot.**; followed by rly. from Dingwall to Kyle of Lochalsh.

Carse of Gowrie, Perth and Kinross, **Scot.**; fertile coastal dist. between Perth and Dundee, S. of Sidlaw Hills; soft fruits, especially raspberries.

Carson City, cap. Nevada, **USA**; smallest st. cap. at 1,427 m; tourist ctr.; p. (1980) 32,022.

Carstenz Mtns., Irian Jaya, **Indonesia**; major copper and base metal deposits and mng.; slurry pipeline to pts. on Tipoeka R.

Cartagena, spt., cap. dep. Bolivar. **Colombia**; shares with Barranquilla tr. from Magdalena R. valley; platinum, coffee, chemicals, textiles, fertilisers, oil refinery; p. (est. 1979) 435,361.

Cartagena, c., Murcia prov., S.E. **Spain**; on Mediterranean; spt. and naval base; cath.; shipbldg., metalwkg.; p. (1981) 172,751.

Cartago, t., **Colombia**; in Cauca valley, ctr. of rich agr. a.; p. (est. 1970) 64,830.

Cartago, c., **Costa Rica**; former cap.; 1,504 m at foot of volcanic Mt. Irazu; coffee, fruits; subject to earthquakes; p. (est. 1970) 22,000.

Cartago Basin, Meseta Central, **Costa Rica**; alt. 5,000 ft.; a. of early Spanish settlement.

Carter Fell, mtn., a summit of the Cheviot hills, on the **Eng./Scot.** border, 554 m.

Carthage, anc. c., N. **Africa**; on Bay of Tunis; destroyed by Romans 146 B.C.; site is sub. of Tunis.

Casablanca. See El Dar-el-Beida.

Casale Monferrato, t., Piedmont, **Italy**; on R. Po; cath.; cement; p. (est. 1968) 43,896.

Cascade Range, USA and **Canada**; extends N. and S. through B.C., Wash., and Ore. between Rocky Mtns. and Pac. cst.; timber resources, hydroelec. power; hgst. peak Mt. Rainier, 4,395 m.

Cascade Tunnel, longest rly. tunnel in N. America, Wash., **USA**; carries trunk rly. from Spokane to Seattle through Cascade Mtns.; length 12·5 km.

Caserta, t., Italy; on N.E. edge of plain of Campania; impt. route ctr. and agr. mkt.; cath.; palace; p. (1981) 66,318.

Cashel, mkt. t., UD. Tipperary, **R.o.I.**; anc. seat of kings of Munster; ruins of cath. on Rock of Cashel; p. (1981) 2,692.

Casiquiare, R., and canal, **Venezuela**; joins Orinoco to the Rio Negro, a trib. of the Amazon.

Casper, t., Wyo., **USA**; petroleum; airpt.; p. (1980) 51,016.

Caspian Sea, salt lake, **USSR** and **Iran**, between Europe and Asia; lgst. inland sea in world; a. 422,170 km² but shrinking; 28 m below sea level; maximum depth 975 m; fed by R. Volga; agr. and dense p. on S. shore; pts.; Astrakhan, at mouth of Volga, Baku (oil ctr.).

Casquets, dangerous rocks, 11 km W. of Alderney, Channel Is., **Eng.**; lighthouse.

Cassino, t., Frosinone, **Italy**; in Apennines, on Rapido R.; t. and nearby monastery (Montecassino) destroyed 1944, now rebuilt; p. (1981) 31,139.

Castel Gandolfo, t., central **Italy**; in Alban Hills; papal summer residence; tourist centre; p. (1981) 13,348.

Castellammare del Golfo, spt., N.W. Sicily, **Italy**; wat. pl., tuna fishing; p. (est. 1968) 15,498.

Castellammare di Stabia, t., Campania, **Italy**; on Bay of Naples, at foot of Vesuvius; historic arsenal and dockyards; mineral springs; cath.; resort; p. (1981) 70,317.

Castellón de la Plana, prov., **Spain**; on Mediterranean, part of anc. Valencia, mainly mtns. a. 6,679 km²; cap. Castellón; p. (1981) 431,886.

Castellón de la Plana, t., **Spain**; on plain inland from Mediterranean cst.; varied agr. inds.; oil refining; p. (1981) 126,464.

Castelnaudary, t., Aude dep., **France**; in strategic gap between Central Massif and Pyrenees; captured by Black Prince 1355; mkt. for cereals; pottery; p. (1982) 11,381.

Castelo Branco, t., **Portugal**, prov. cap. Beira Baixa; agr. mkt. t.; p. (1970) 21,730.

Castelvetrano, agr. t., W. Sicily, **Italy**; wine mkg.; p. (1981) 30,577.

Castile, region in the high plateaux of central **Spain**; former kingdom; divided into Old Castile in N. (Avila, Burgos, Logroño, Santander, Segovia, Soria) and New Castile in S. (Ciudad Real, Cuenca, Guadalajara, Madrid, Toledo). Its dialect became the standard language of Spain.

Castlebar, U.D., cap. Mayo, **R.o.I.**; mkt. t.; pursuit of Brit. by Fr. who captured t. 1798 known as the "Castlebar races"; p. (1981) 6,409.

Castleblayney, U.D., Monaghan, **R.o.I.**; nr. Dundalk; mkt. t.; shoes; p. (1981) 2,425.

Castlecary, v., Central Reg., **Scot.**; sta. on Roman wall; silica, fire clay deposits.

Castle Donington, t., North West Leics., **Eng.**; airpt; power sta.

Castle Douglas, burgh, Stewartry, **Scot.**; nr. R. Dee; nearby cas.; stock mkt.; p. (1981) 3,502.

Castleford, t., West Yorks., **Eng.**; 16 km S.E. of Leeds at confluence of Rs. Aire and Calder; coal mng., chemical, glass, and clothing mnfs, flour milling, brick mkg.; p. (1981) 36,032.

Castle Morpeth, l. gov. dist., Northumberland, **Eng.**; based on Morpeth; p. (1981) 50,570.

Castle Point, l. gov. dist., Essex, **Eng.**; comprises Canvey I. and Benfleet; p. (1981) 85,533.

Castlereagh, l. gov. dist., **N. Ireland**; inc. S.E. outskirts of Belfast; p. (1981) 61,113.

Castleton, v., Derbys., **Eng.**; on Hope R.; tourist ctr. for the Peak District; nearby fluorspar mines.

Castletown, t., Isle of Man, **Eng.**; former cap.; pt., cas. tower.

Castres, t., Tarn, **France**; on R. Agout; former Huguenot stronghold; cath.; textiles, soap, earthenware; p. (1982) 46,877.

Castries, t., cap. St. Lucia, Windward Is., **W.I.**; fine harbour; p. (est. 1970) 40,000.

Castrop-Rauxel or **Kastrop Rauxel,** t., N. Rhine-Westphalia, **W. Germany**; part of Ruhr conurb.; industl.; coal, cement, tar prod., tiles, brandy; p. (est. 1983) 77,400.

Catalonia, region, N.E. **Spain**; ch. industl. a.; comprises 4 provs.; Barcelona, Gerona, Lérida, Tarragona; cap. Barcelona; hilly, drained by Ebro R.; cereals, olive oil, wines; textiles, cars; hydroelec. power stas.; nuclear power sta. projected; a. 32,185 km²; p. (1981) 5,956,598.

Catamarca, t., cap. of Catamarca prov., N.W. **Argentina**; in Andean foothills 128 km S. of San Miguel de Tucumán; ctr. of irrigated oasis producing vines, apricots, cherries, cotton; thermal springs; p. (est. 1970) 29,000.

Catanduanes, I., off S. Luzon, **Philippines**; hilly, fertile; rice, corn, cotton, hemp, coconuts; a. 1,429 km²; p. (1970) 162,679.

Catania, c., Sicily, **Italy**; cap. of C. prov.; pt. on E. cst. at foot of Mt. Etna; rebuilt several times after earthquakes and volcanic eruption; cath., univ., cas.; p. (1981) 380,328.

Catanzaro, t., S. **Italy**; univ.; service ctr., regional cap. of Calabria; p. (1981) 100,832.

Catastrophe, C., S. extremity of Eyre Peninsula, **S. Australia.**

Catawba, R., S. and N.C., **USA**; rises in Blue Ridge Range, flows to Santee R.; extensively dammed; 480 km long.

Caterham and **Warlingham,** ts., former U.D. Tandridge, Surrey, **Eng.**; on N. Downs; residtl.; p. (1981) 33,083.

Cathay, anc. name for China and E. Tartary.

Catoche, C., N.E. point of Yucatan, **Mexico.**

Catskill Mtns., N.Y., **USA**; gr. in Appalachians, W. of Hudson R., well wooded; resort for p. of N.Y. c.; alt. c. 900 m.

Cauca, dep., Colombia; cap. Popayán; a. 30,191 km²; p. (est. 1979) 830,815.

Cauca, R., Colombia; trib. of Magdalena; 960 km long.

Caucasia, region between Black Sea and Caspian, **USSR**; divided by Caucasus Mtns. into N. or Cis-Caucasia and S. or Trans-Caucasia.

Caucasus (Bol'shoy Kavkaz), mtns., separate RSFSR from Georgian SSR and Azerbaydzhan SSR, **USSR**; run from Black Sea to Caspian Sea; divided into 3 ranges; hgst. summits Mt. Elbruz (5,631 m) and Kasbek (5,047 m); many lofty passes and glaciers; total l. c. 1,520 km.

Caucun, I., off Yucatan penin., **Mexico**; developing tourist ctr.; airpt.

Causses, Les, limestone plateau, Aveyron, Tarn deps., S. **France**; on S.W. flank of Central Massif; caverns, gorges of Rs. Lot and Tarn; sheep provide milk for Roquefort cheese; alt. 900–1,800 m.

Cauvery, R., S. **India**; rises in W. Ghats, flows into Bay of Bengal through Karnataka and and Tamil Nadu; length 640 km; lge. irrigation and hydroelec. power project.

Caux, region of Normandy, **France**; fertile loess-covered chalk plateau adjacent to English Channel; arable agr.

Cava de' Tirreni, t., Salerno, **Italy**; summer resort; textiles; p. (1981) 50,558.

Cavaillon, t., Vaucluse, **France**; cath.; ctr. of mkt. gardening dist.; p. (1982) 20,830.

Cavan, inland c., **R.o.I.**; agr. a. with many Ls.; depopulation; borders Ulster; a. 1,932 km²; p. (1981) 6,840.

Cavan, U.D., co. t., Cavan, **R.o.I.**; 115 km S.W. Belfast; mkt.; cath.; p. (1971) 3,273.

Cavite, spt., Luzon, **Philippines**; walled t.; oil refining nearby; p. (est. 1970) 77,100.

Cavour Canal, irrigation canal, Piedmont and Lombardy regions, N. **Italy**; links R. Po nr. Chivassa with R. Ticino 16 km N.E. of Novara; provides water for 101,000 ha of rice-fields and meadow-land; length 128 km.

Cawnpore. *See* Kanpur.

Caxias, t., Marahão, **Brazil**; on Itapicuru R. p. (1968) 124,403.

Caxias do Sul, t., Rio Grande do Sul, **Brazil**; wines; p. (est. 1980) 207,800.

Cayambe, volcanic mtn., Andes, **Ecuador**; alt. 5,958 m.

Cayenne, c., cap of **French Guiana**, at mouth of Cayenne R.; exp. gold; gave its name to Cayenne pepper; p. (1982) 38,135.

Cayman Is., W.I.; consists of Grand Cayman, cap. Georgetown; Little Cayman; and Cayman

Brac.; turtle and shark fishing; a. 259 km²; p. (est. 1976) 14,000.

Ceará, st., N. **Brazil**; stretches from Brazilian Plateau to Atl. cst.; poor cattle rearing a. with many droughts; cap. Fortaleza; a. 148,078 km²; p. (est. 1983) 5,680,000.

Cebu, one of Visayan Is., **Philippines**; mtnous.; forested; coal, oil, gold; coconuts, maize; 4,408 km²; p. (1970) 1,632,642 (prov.).

Cebu, t., Cebu I., **Philippines**; tr. ctr. of Visayan Is.; pt. for abaca and copra; p. (1980) 490,281.

Cedar Falls, t., N. Iowa, **USA**; on Cedar R.; p. (1980) 36,322.

Cedar Mountain, hill, Va., **USA**; here Stonewall Jackson defeated Banks in Civil War (second battle of Bull Run, 1862).

Cedar Rapids, c., Iowa, **USA**; distribution and rly. ctr. for agr. a.; p. (1980) 110,243 (c.), 169,775 (met. a.).

Cegléd, t., Hungary; on edge of Central Plain in fruit growing a.; vehicle repair shops; p. (1966) 37,200.

Celaya, mkt. t., Guanajuato, **Mexico**; rly. junc.; ctr. of rich farming a.; many inds.; sweet-meats; p. (1979) 118,665.

Celebes. See Sulawesi.

Celje, t., **Yugoslavia**; industl., agr. ctr., zinc refining, fertilisers; close to Austrian border; p. (est. 1965) 30,000.

Celle, t., Lower Saxony, **W. Germany**; on R. Aller; cas. was residence of dukes of Brunswick-Lüneburg until 1705; oil refining, machin., textiles; p. (est. 1983) 71,900.

Celtic Sea, a. bounded by S. Ireland, Wales, Cornwall and Brittany; rich natural gas deposits 48 km S.W. of Kinsale.

Central African Republic, indep. st., former empire until 1979; within Fr. Community, Equatorial Africa; formerly Fr. colony of Ubangi-Shari; land-locked natural plateau covered by savannah grassland; S.W. forest zone likely to develop with proposed rail link with Transcameroon rly.; cotton, diamonds; cap. Bangui; a. 622,984 km²; p. (est. 1982) 2,442,000.

Central America, stretch of land between Mexico and S. America, from the Isthmus of Tehuantepec to that of Panama; includes Guatemala, Honduras, Mexico, Nicaragua, Salvador, Costa Rica, Panama, Belize; tropical climate; forests, savannahs; p. (est. 1981) 93,000,000.

Central Asia, usually applied to regions between 30° and 40° N. lat. and 55° and 85° E. long.; Soviet C.A. is the land between China and Afghanistan and the Caspian, consisting of Kazakh SSR, Tadzhik SSR, Turkmen SSR, Uzbek SSR, and Kirghiz SSR.

Central Clydeside Conurbation, conurb., **Scot.**, based on Glasgow and includes other urban areas (Bearsden, Milngavie, Clydebank, Cumbernauld, Kilsyth, East Kilbride, Eastwood, Hamilton, Monklands, Motherwell, Renfrew and Strathkelvin); p. (1981) 1,713,287.

Central Lancashire, new t., Lancs., **Eng.**; site of 14,186 ha.; t. created from expansion of Chorley and Leyland; biggest new t. in Eng.; p. (1981) 247,224.

Central Region, l. gov. reg., **Scot.**; stretches from Grampian mtns. to Central Lowlands, inc. Forth valley; main ts. Falkirk and Stirling; a. 2,631 km²; p. (1981) 273,078.

Central Valley, Cal., **USA**; valleys of Rs. San Joaquin and Sacramento; main agr. a. of Cal.; vast scheme for irrigation, hydroelec. power, flood control and protection of wildlife.

Cephalonia (Kefalliniá), lgst. of Ionian Is., **Greece**; mtnous. with fertile valleys; impt. harbours of Argostólion and Lexourion; currant production; a. 751 km²; p. (1981) 31,297.

Ceram. See Seram.

Ceredigion, l. gov. dist., Dyfed, **Wales**; lge a. inc. Cardigan and Lampeter in S. and Aberystwyth in N.; p. (1981) 57,372.

Cérignola, t., Apulia, **Italy**; agr. ctr.; Spanish victory over French in Italian wars 1503; p. (1981) 50,682.

Cerigo (Kíthira) I., **Greece**; sm. I. between Crete and Peloponnesus.

Cernauti. See Chernovtsy.

Cerro de Pasco, t., Pasco dep., **Peru**; mng. ctr. at 4,403 m; univ.; copper, gold, lead, zinc; p. (est. 1970) 29,000.

Cerro Rico, mtn., **Bolivia**; in Andes, W. of Potosí; alt. 4,782 m; rich silver, tin tungsten ores.

Cesena, t., Emilia-Romagna, **Italy**; flourished in Renaissance times; cath., Malatesta library; agr. mkt. t.; p. (1981) 89,640.

České Budějovice (Budweis), t., **ČSSR**; on R. Vitava, 128 km S. of Prague; major industl. ctr.; pencils, porcelain, brewing, anthracite; p. (1970) 77,000.

Český Těšín, t., **ČSSR**; on Olše R., trib. of Oder; part of former t. of Teschen on Czech side of frontier with Poland; coal mng.

Cessnock-Bellbird, t., N.S.W., **Australia**; coal mng. declining since 1968; ctr. for Hunter Valley vineyards; p. (1976) 16,256.

Ceuta, spt., **Spanish N. Africa**, naval base; opposite to and 26 km from Gibraltar; cath.; the anc. Abyla, one of the Pillars of Hercules; p. (1981) 65,263.

Cevennes, mtns., S. **France**; separating basins of Rhône, Loire, and Tarn; highest point Mt. Mézenc, alt. 1,767 m.

Ceylon. See Sri Lanka.

Chaco, prov., N. **Argentina**; farming and prairie land; cap. Resistencia; a. 99,632 km²; p. (1980) 692,410.

Chad, indep. st. within Fr. Community, Equatorial Africa; landlocked, focus of trans Sahara and Equatorial tr. routes; N. frontier occupied by Libya; valuable uranium and oil reserves but no exploitation; severe droughts (1982–3) reduced cattle and restricted arable crops; cash crops of cotton and ground nuts; cap. Ndjamena; a. 1,282,050 km²; p. (est. 1984) 4,901,000.

Chad, L., lge. sheet of water bordering **Nigeria, Niger, Chad** and **Cameroon**; a. 129,500 km² when in flood; varies in extent with season, and is drying up; shallow, many Is., lies between the wooded region of the Sudan and the steppes leading to the Sahara desert; joint project for devel. by neighbouring ctys.

Chadderton, t., Gtr. Manchester, **Eng.**; engin., chemicals, textiles; p. (1981) 34,013.

Chagos Is., 5 coral Is., **Indian Oc.**; admin. by Seychelles since 1965; fine harbour in Diego Garcia (Anglo-American naval communications ctr.).

Chainat, t., **Thailand**; on Menam Chao Phraya; major barrage for hydroelec. power and flood control.

Chalcis, t., **Greece**; resort for Athens; joined to mainland by swing bridge; p. (1981) 44,867.

Chalfont St. Giles, v., Bucks., **Eng.**; in London commuter belt; home of Milton.

Châlons-sur-Marne, t., cap. of Marne dep., N.E. **France**; comm. and industl.; cath., churches; p. (1982) 54,359.

Châlon-sur-Saône, t., Saône-et-Loire dep., E. **France**; R. pt., comm. ctr. for Burgundy; historic t.; p. (1982) 57,967.

Chambal, R., trib. of R. Jumna, rising in Vindhya hills, Madhya Pradesh, **India**; major power, irrigation and industl. scheme; agr. in lower valley causing soil erosion, major soil conservation projection; 880 km long.

Chambéry, t., cap. of Savoie dep., S.E. **France**; leather gds.; tourism; p. (1982) 54,896.

Chambord, v., Loir-et-Cher dep., **France**; on R. Cosson, trib. of Loire; Renaissance château; p. (1981) 206.

Chamonix, t., Haute-Savoie, **France**; at foot of Mont Blanc, in valley of R. Arve; winter sports ctr., road tunnel links to Aosta; p. (1982) 9,255.

Champagne, region and former prov., **France**; covers deps. of Aube, Marne, Haute-Marne, Ardennes, and parts of Yonne Aisne, Seine-etMarne, and Meuse; famous for its champagne wine; wheat, sheep; impt. tr. fairs in Middle Ages., main ctr. Reims. See **Champagne Humide** and **Champagne Pouilleuse**.

Champagne Humide, region, **France**; clay vale, runs 160 km N.E. from Auxerre to Barle-Duc; drained by Seine, Aube, Marne, Aisne, and many tribs.; heavily wooded, marshy; where cleared and drained, grain cultivation.

Champagne Pouilleuse, region, **France**; barren chalk plateau, extends 128 km N.E. from Sens to Reims; drained by Aisne, Vesle, Seine, Aube, Marne; dusty chalk downland pastures; sheep; vine growing on S.-facing valley sides and S.E.-facing escarpment of Falaise de l'Ile de France favours production of Champagne wines; ch. producing ctrs.; Châlons-sur-Marne, Reims, Epernay.

Champaign, t., Ill., **USA**; close to Urbana; univ.; foundries; food processing; p. (1980) 59,133 (c.), 168,392 (met. a.).

Champigny-sur-Marne, t., Val-de-Marne dep., **France**; E. sub. of Paris; varied inds.; p. (1982) 76,260.

Champlain Canal, N.Y., **USA**; follows gap

between Adirondack Mtns. and Green Mtns. occupied by Hudson R.; links Albany with L. Champlain and allows through barge traffic between New York and St. Lawrence valley.

Champlain, L., USA; N. frontier of N.Y. st.; discharges by Richelieu R. into St. Lawrence; flanked by trunk route from New York to Montreal; forms link between Hudson R. and St. Lawrence waterway; a. 1,126 km².

Chañaral, spt., N. Atacama, **Chile;** lies in gold and copper-mng. a.; p. (1960) 21,098.

Chanda, t., Nagpur, Maharashtra, **India;** anc. temples; p. (1961) 51,484.

Chandausi, t., Uttar Pradesh, **India;** cotton, hemp; rly. ctr.; p. (1961) 48,557.

Chandernagore, t., W. Bengal, **India;** on Hooghly R., N. of Calcutta; founded by French 1686; p. (1961) 67,105.

Chandigarh, union terr. (1966) and former cap. of both Punjab and Haryana sts., **India;** new c. designed by Le Corbusier to replace former cap. Lahore, now in Pakistan; to be sole capital of Punjab (1986) on plateau at foot of Himalayas, S.W. of Simla; univ.; a. of terr. 114 km²; p. of c. (1981) 451,610.

Changchun, c., Jilin, **China;** rly. ctr.; univ.; China's biggest motor vehicle plant, machine tools; p. (est 1983) 1,770,000.

Changnacheri, t., Kerala, S. **India;** tea, cotton-spinning, silk; p. (1961) 42,376.

Changbai Shan, mtns.; form bdy. between **China** and **N. Korea;** drained by Rs. Yalu and Tumen; hgst. point Pai-t'ou-shan, 2,442 m.

Chang Jiang (Yangtse Kiang), R., **China;** rises in plateau at Xizang Zizhiou (Tibet) and flows E. to E. China Sea nr. Shanghai; one of China's major Rs.; crosses 'Red Basin' of Sichuan, a deep gorge above Yichang and finally a broad level plain; many lge. cs. on its banks inc. Yichang, Nanjing, Wuhan, Zhenjiang, Chongqing; major water control project; navigable by ocean-going vessels for 2,880 km. to Yichang; total length 5,600 km.

Changsha, c., cap. of Hunan prov., **China;** pt. on Xiang Jiang; univ.; tea, rice, antimony; p. (est. 1983) 1,098,000.

Changshu. _see_ **Yangzhou.**

Changzhou (Changchow), c., Jiangsu, **China;** in valley of Chang Jiang, on Grand Canal 112 km S.E. of Nanjing; mkt. for intensively cultivated dist.; silk; p. (1953) 297,000.

Channel Is., gr. of self-governing Is. belonging to the Brit. Crown off N.W. cst. France, of which the lgst. are Jersey, Guernsey, Alderney, and Sark; part of the old duchy of Normandy; vegetables, flowers, fruit, granite; two famous breeds of dairy cattle; tourist resort; impt. banking and insurance ctr. encouraged by low taxes; retirement ctr.; a. 194 km²; p. (est. 1976) 129,000.

Chantilly, t., Oise, **France;** famous racecourse; formerly famous for lace and porcelain; p. (1982) 10,208.

Chao Phraya. _See_ **Menam Chao Phraya.**

Chaozhou (Chaochow), c., Guandong, S. **China;** on Han R., 32 km N. of Shantou; ctr. of cultivated plain; rice, sugar, tea; linked to Shantou by rly.; p. (1953) 101,300.

Chapala, L., Mexico; chiefly in Jalisco st.; attractive site and climate encourage tourism; pastoral agr. on shores; a. 1,080 km².

Chapayevsk, t., Kuybyshev region, **RSFSR;** in Volga valley; chemicals; agr. machin.; p. (est. 1969) 87,000.

Chapelcross, nr. Annan, Annandale and Eskdale, **Scot.;** AEA nuclear power sta., producing electricity for nat. grid.

Chapel-en-le-Frith, mkt. t., High Peak, Derbys., **Eng.;** brake-linings.

Chapra, t., Bihar, **India;** on Ganges R.; ctr. of former saltpetre and indigo tr.; p. (1981) 111,564.

Chard, mkt. t., Somerset **Eng.;** lace, engin., shirt and cotton mftg.; p. (1981) 9,384.

Chardzhou, t., Turkmen SSR, **USSR;** inland pt. on Amu-Dar'ya R.; shipyards, textiles, chemicals; major oil refinery project; p. (est. 1980) 143,000.

Charente, dep., S.W. **France;** cap. Angoulême; ctr. of distilling tr., cognac; a. 5,970 km²; p. (1982) 340,300.

Charente, R., S.W. **France;** rises W. of Limoges and flows into Bay of Biscay below Rochefort; valley slopes beyond' Angoulême produce celebrated grapes from which brandy is made at Cognac and Jarnac.

Charente-Maritime, dep., S.W. **France;** cap. La Roch-

elle; borders Bay of Biscay; wine, wheat; oysters, pilchards; a. 7,229 km²; p. (1982) 512,800.

Charleroi, t., Hainaut, **Belgium;** on R. Sambre; coal mng.; glass; p. (1982) 219,579.

Charleston, c., spt., S.C., **USA;** industl. and comm. ctr. on Atl. cst. founded 1670; scene of onset of Civil War; p. (1980) 430,000 (met. a. with North Charlestown).

Charleston, t., cap. W. Va., **USA;** on Kanawha R.; in bituminous coal dist.; chemicals, glass, tools, oil, natural gas, lumber, coal processing; p. (1980) 270,000 (met. a.).

Charleville-Mézières, twin t., Ardennes dep., N.E. **France;** on Meuse R.; iron, bricks, nails, hardware; p. (1982) 61,588.

Charlotte, c., N.C., **USA;** key rly. junc.; machin., chemicals, textiles; p. (1980) 314,000 (c.), 637,000 (met. a. with Gastonia).

Charlotte Amalie, t., cap. of Virgin Is. of **USA;** on St. Thomas I.; excellent natural harbour; former coaling sta.; p. (1980) 11,842.

Charlottenburg, sub. of Berlin, **Germany** (in W. Berlin); on R. Spree.

Charlottesville, t., Va., **USA;** on Rivanna R.; in apple-growing region; univ.; Monticello nearby, home of Jefferson; textiles; p. (1980) 39,916 (t.), 113,568 (met. a.).

Charlottetown, t., ch. pt. Prince Edward I., **Canada;** originally named after Queen Charlotte, consort of George III; univ.; p. (1971) 18,631.

Charlton Kings, t., Cheltenham, Gloucs., **Eng.;** at foot of Cotswolds; p. (1981) 10,785.

Charnwood Forest, upland dist., Leics., **Eng.;** to W. of Soar valley, 19 km N.W. of Leicester; composed of anc. rocks; stone-crushing; largely forests; used for recreation by industl. ts. of E. Midlands; alt. 180–275 m; now forms l. gov. dist. of Charnwood and inc. Loughborough and Shepshed; p. (1981) 134,204.

Charters Towers, t., N. Queensland, **Australia;** fine bldgs. remain from 1872 gold rush; ctr. of agr. dist.; p. (1976) 7,914.

Chartres, t., cap. of Eure-et-Loir dep., **France;** mkt. for cereals from Beauce region; famous Gothic cath.; p. (1982) 77,795 (met. a.).

Châteauroux, t., cap. of Indre dep., **France;** 96 km S.E. of Tours, on R. Indre; agr. ctr., woollens, pottery; p. (1982) 53,967.

Chateau Thierry, t., Aisne, **France;** on R. Marne; mkt. t.; cas.; precision instruments; p. (1982) 14,920.

Châtellerault, t., Vienne, **France;** 64 km S. of Tours on R. Vienne; cutlery, metallurgical and aeronautical engin. Descartes lived here; p. (1982) 36,870.

Chatham, t., Rochester upon Medway, Kent, **Eng.;** on estuary of R. Medway; lt. inds.; famous naval dockyard established by Henry VIII, now closed; p. (1981) 61,909.

Chatham, t., spt., N.B., **Canada;** lumbering, fish exporting; p. (1971) 7,812.

Chatham, c., Ont., **Canada;** on extinct L. plain on R. Thames; agr. prods.; p. (1971) 34,601.

Chatham Is., N.Z. dependency, S. Pac. Oc.; volcanic Is.; sheep rearing and fishing; a. 963 km²; lgst. I. Wharekauri; p. (est. 1968) 500.

Chatsworth, par., Derbys., **Eng.;** on R. Derwent; seat of the dukes of Devonshire.

Chattanooga, c. Tenn., **USA;** on Tennessee R.; univ.; rly. ctr.; cottons; iron, steel, chemicals, paper, metals; p. (1980) 170,000 (c.), 427,000 (met. a.).

Chatteris, Fenland, Cambridge, **Eng.;** mkt. t.; p. (1981) 6,180.

Chaudière Falls, on Ottawa R., above Ottawa, **Canada;** hydroelec. sta.

Chauk, t., Burma; on R. Irrawaddy; ctr. of oilfield; oil refining; fertilisers.

Chaumont, t., cap. of Haute-Marne dep., **France;** on R. Marne; gloves, leather; p. (1982) 29,552.

Chautauqua, t., N.Y. st., **USA;** summer resort; vineyards.

Chaux-de-Fonds, La, t., can. Neuchâtel, **Switzerland;** ctr. of watchmkg. ind.; p. (1969) 43,200.

Cheadle, t., Staffs. Moorland, Staffs., **Eng.;** metal mnfs.; former coal-mng. a.; p. (1971) 4,070 (dist.).

Cheadle and Gatley, ts., Gtr. Manchester, **Eng.;** textile finishing and bleaching, engin.; residtl.; p. (1981) 58,683.

Cheb, t., ČSSR; nr. Bavarian frontier; comm. ctr.; machin.; p. (1967) 25,633.

Cheboksary, c., cap. of Chuvash ASSR, **RSFSR;** R. pt. on Volga; agr. ctr.; hydroelec. plant; p. (est. 1980) 323,000.

Checheno-Ingush ASSR, USSR; oilfield, petrochemicals; p. (1970) 1,065,000.

Cheddar, v., Somerset, **Eng.**; famous limestone caves and gorge in Mendips; cheese, strawberries.

Chefoo. See **Yentai.**

Cheju (Quelpart), I., off **S. Korea**, E. China Sea; extinct volcano Mt. Halla, 1,968 m.

Chekiang. See **Zhijiang.**

Che-ling Pass, on bdy. between Guandong and Hunan, S. **China**; historic route across Nanling mtns., now followed by Wuhan to Guangzhou trunk rly.; alt. 300 m.

Chelm, t., E. **Poland**; nr. Lublin; cath.; flour-milling; p. (1968) 37,100.

Chelmsford, co. t., l. gov. dist., Essex, **Eng.**; 48 km N.E. London; cath.; agr. mkt.; p. (1981) 138,318 (dist.).

Chelsea, dist., London, **Eng.**; fashionable residtl. dist. See **Kensington.**

Chelsea, t., Mass., **USA**; industl. sub. on Boston harbour; p. (1980) 25,431.

Cheltenham, t., l. gov. dist., Gloucs., **Eng.**; spa; educational ctr.; precision instruments; birthplace of Gustav Holst; p. (1981) 84,014 (dist).

Chelyabinsk, t., **RSFSR**; major industl. ctr. on Miass R., Siberian lowlands; steel wks.; metallurgy, machin.; on natural gas pipeline from Gazli gasfield; p. (est. 1980) 1,042,000.

Chelyuskin, Cape, most N. point in Asia, in Krasnoyarsk Terr., **RSFSR**; named after Russian navigator who discovered it in 1742.

Chemnitz. See **Karl-Marx-Stadt.**

Chemulpo. See **Inchon.**

Chenab, R., W. Punjab, **Pakistan**; one of "five rivers" of Punjab; rises in Himalayas, flows S.W. into R. Sutlej; dams at Marala and Khanki; c. 1,440 km long.

Chengchow. See **Zhengzhou.**

Chengdu (Chengtu), c., cap. of Sichuan prov., **China**; ctr. of tobacco and cotton-growing a.; oil refinery; chemicals, textiles, machin.; p. (est. 1983) 2,510,000.

Chepstow, mkt. t., Gwent, **Wales**; on R. Wye, 3 km above confluence with R. Severn; Severn Bridge links to Aust (Avon); ruined cas.; p. (1981), 9,309.

Chequers, official residence of Brit. prime ministers, 3 km S. of Wendover, Bucks., **Eng.**; gift of Lord Lee of Fareham.

Cher, dep., **France**; cap. Bourges; crossed by Cher R.; chiefly pastoral agr.; a. 7,301 km²; p. (1982) 319,000.

Cher, R., central **France**; rises in Central Massif, joins Loire below Tours; length 320 km.

Cherbourg, spt., Manche, **France**; N. cst. of Contentin peninsula; opposite to and 128 km dist. from Portsmouth; naval arsenal, shipbldg.; metals, ropes, fishing; p. (1982) 85,485 (met. a.).

Cheremkhovo, t., **RSFSR**; N.W. of Irkutsk; coal, engin., chemicals; on Trans-Siberian rly.; p. (est. 1970) 110,000.

Cherepovets, c., **RSFSR**; on Rybinskoye reservoir of R. Volga; steel, engin., sawmills, shipbldg.; p. (est. 1980) 274,000.

Cheribon. See **Tjirebon.**

Cheriton, dist. near Folkestone, Kent, **Eng.**; proposed site for emergence of Channel Tunnel, linked to Sangatte, Calais, France; proposed start 1987, to open 1993.

Cherkassy, t., Ukrainian SSR, **USSR**; nr. Kiev, on reservoir formed by Dnieper R.; sugar, engin., sawmilling; p. (est. 1980) 234,000.

Cherkessk, t., **RSFSR**; rly. terminus, industl. ctr.; p. (1970) 76,000.

Chernobyl, Ukraine, **USSR**; site of world's worst nuclear accident (1986).

Chernigov, t., Ukrainian SSR, **USSR**; on Desna R.; caths.; univ.; flour, textiles, chemicals; p. (est. 1980) 245,000.

Chernogorsk, t., **RSFSR**; 16 km N.W. of Abakan; ctr. of Minusinsk coal-mng. basin; p. (est. 1967) 63,000.

Chernovtsy, t., Ukrainian SSR, **USSR**; univ.; Greek cath.; wheat, dairy produce, textiles, engin., chemicals; p. (1980) 221,000.

Chernyakhovsk (Insterberg), t., Lithuanian SSR, **USSR**; chemicals, textiles; p. (est. 1967) 29,000.

Cherrapunji, t., Assam, **India**; in Khasi Hills; reputed wettest place in world, average annual rainfall 12,700 mm.

Chertsey, t., Runnymede, Surrey, **Eng.**; on S. bank of R. Thames, 6 km below Staines; residtl.; p. (1981) 43,265.

Cherwell, l. gov. dist., Oxon., **Eng.**; stretches from Banbury to Bicester; p. (1981) 106,947.

Cherwell, R., trib. of Thames, nr. Oxford, **Eng.**; length 48 km.

Chesapeake Bay, inlet on Atl. cst., **USA**; extending 320 km from mouth of Susquehanna R. to C. Charles; shellfish ind.; bridge-tunnel (opened 1964) spans entrance to Bay; p. of c. (1980) 114,000.

Chesham, t., Bucks., **Eng.**; in heart of Chiltern Hills; printing, textiles, lt. engin.; residtl. p. (1981) 20,655.

Cheshire, non-met. co., N.W. **Eng.**; lowland a. drained by Rs. Dee and Mersey, bounded by Pennines in E.; dairying and mkt. gardening; chemical ind. based on salt deposits around Northwich; heavy inds. in and around Warrington; attracting many high technology inds.; much of co. residtl. for Liverpool and Manchester; cap. Chester; a. 2,323 km²; p. (1981) 926,293.

Cheshunt, t., Herts., **Eng.**; in Lea valley, 11 km S. of Hertford; bricks, mkt. gardening, horticulture; p. (1980) 49,670.

Chesil Bank, Dorset, **Eng.**; shingle ridge enclosing the Fleet lagoon running from I. of Portland to Bridport.

Chester, c., l. gov. dist., Cheshire, **Eng.**; at head of estuary of R. Dee; cath.; anc. walls and old timbered houses; Roman c. of Deva site of legionary barracks; engin., metal gds.; p. (1981) 116,157 (dist.).

Chester, t., Penns., **USA**; on Delaware R. S.W. Philadelphia; called Uppland by Swedish settlers 1643, renamed by William Penn; pt. of entry; shipbldg.; p. (1980) 45,794.

Chesterfield, mkt. t., colly. dist., l. gov. dist., Derbys., **Eng.**; on Rother R.; 13 km S. of Sheffield; variety of heavy inds.; 14th-cent. church with crooked spire; p. (1981) 96,710 (dist.).

Chesterfield Inlet, arm of Hudson Bay, **Canada**; 400 km by 40 km.

Chester-le-Street, t., l. gov. dist., Durham. **Eng.**; clothing, confectionery, sand wkg.; p. (1981) 51,719 (dist.).

Cheviot Hills, range between **Scot.** and **Eng.**; hgst. summit, the Cheviot, 816 m.

Cheyenne, t., cap. of Wyo., **USA**; cattle-ranching dist.; rly. ctr.; p. (1980) 47,283.

Chiana, Val di, valley, central **Italy**; separates Tuscan hills from central Apennines; occupied by upper course of R. Arno, middle course of R. Tiber; followed by main route from Florence to Rome.

Chiang Mai, c., cap of C. prov., and 3rd c. of **Thailand**; rly. terminus on Ping R.; tr. ctr.; teak; p. (1980) 101,594.

Chiapa, R., flows N. from **Guatemala** through **Mexico** to G. of Campeche; impt. routeway in lower course; length 320 km.

Chiapas, Pac. st., **Mexico**; mtnous., forested; bananas, tobacco, sugar and cocoa; cattle; oil reserves; close associations with Guatemala; cap. Tuxtla-Gutierrez; a. 74,408 km²; p. (1970) 1,578,180.

Chiasso, frontier t., S. **Switzerland**; rly. sta. on Italian border; p. (1970) 8,868.

Chiatura, t., Georgian SSR, **USSR**; impt. manganese deposits; p. (est. 1967) 27,000.

Chiba, c., cap. of C. pref. **Japan**; part of Keihin conurb. on Tokyo B.; tr. ctr., giant shipyard, oil refining, aluminium, chemicals, iron and steel; airpt.; p. (est. 1984) 746,430.

Chicago, c., Ill., **USA**; on S. shore of L. Michigan; second lgst. US c.; economic heart of Mid-West; comm. ctr. called "The Loop"; immense tr. by rail and Gr. Ls.; univs.; grain mills, meat packing plants, iron and steel wks., major iron-ore mkt., electronic equipment, furniture; lgst. airport in world; p. (1980) 3,005,000 (c.), 7,104,000 (met.a.).

Chichester, t., l. gov. dist., West Sussex, **Eng.**; on S. cst. plain, 18 km W. of Arundel; cath.; yachting basin; p. (1981) 97,617 (dist.).

Chickamauga Creek, **USA**; branch of Tennessee R. above Chattanooga, forming part of Tenn. Valley Authority scheme; Civil War battles; site of Nat. Park.

Chickerell, t., Dorset, **Eng.**; 5 km N.W. of Weymouth; East Fleet, a sea-fed tidal estuary, lies to the west of the village.

Chiclayo, c., Lambayeque dep., **Peru**; mkt. ctr. for irrigated desert a. between Andes and Pac. Oc. producing mainly rice and sugar; p. (1981) 280,244.

Chicopee, t., Mass., **USA**; on Connecticut R. nr. Springfield; p. (1980) 55,112.

Chicoutimi, t., Quebec, **Canada**; pt. on Chicoutimi R.; lumber, pulp, paper; hydroelectric power; p. (1979) 130,000. (met. a. with Jonquière).

Chiemsee, L., lge. lake nr. Munich, **W. Germany**; c. 460 m a.s.l.

Chieti, t., cap. of C. prov., S. **Italy**; cath.; anc. Teate Marrucinorum; Europe's lgst. glass plant, using methane from Abruzzi field; p. (1981) 54,927.

Chigrik, t., Uzbek SSR, **USSR**; new t. (1963) 34 km S. of Tashkent.

Chigwell, t., Epping Forest, Essex, **Eng.**; on borders of Epping Forest; Hainault Estate now incorporated in Redbridge, Greater London; resdtl.; p. (1981) 51,290.

Chihli, Gulf of. See **Pohai.**

Chihuahua, lgst. st. in **Mexico**; dry climate impedes agr.; mng., cotton, cattle, Chihuahua dogs; a. 247,024 km²; p. (1970) 1,612,525.

Chihuahua, c., cap. Chihuahua st., **Mexico**; univ., cath.; ctr. silver-mng. ind.; p. (1979) 385,953.

Chikchi, peninsula, **RSFSR**; world's first Arctic nuclear power sta. being built.

Chikugo, t., N. Kyushu, **Japan**; lgst. coal mines in country.

Chilaw, t., **Sri Lanka**; ctr. of coconut plantations.

Chile, rep., **S. America**; extends between Andes and Pac. for 4,160 km to C. Horn, E. to W. 400 km; Atacama desert; Spanish language; Roman Catholic; similar climate to that of Argentina but lacks space for extensive agr., dairying, sheep, wool; ch. exp. nitrates, copper, iron-ore, coal, iodine, petroleum, paper; cap. Santiago; ch. pt. Valparaiso; earthquake 1960, hgst. recorded magnitude; a. 738,494 km²; world's lgst. producer of copper; p. (est. 1984) 11,878,000.

Chillán, t., cap. of Nuble prov., **Chile**; destroyed 1939 by one of world's worst recorded earthquakes; since rebuilt; agr. and comm. ctr.; p. (est. 1980) 115,811.

Chiloé, I. and S. prov., **Chile**; cap. San Carlos, earthquakes 1939 and 1960; ch. pt. Ancud destroyed 1960; heavy rainfall, tropical forest; a. 23,460 km²; p. (1970) 110,728.

Chilpancingo de los Bravos, t., cap. of Guerrero st., **Mexico**; ctr. of pre-Aztec culture; univ.; p. (1970) 56,904.

Chiltern, l. gov. dist., Bucks., **Eng.**; inc. part of C. Hills and Chesham and Amersham; p. (1981) 91,728.

Chiltern Hills, chalk escarpment, Oxon., Bucks., Beds., and Herts., **Eng.**; cut by no. of impt. gaps used by main communications; sheep and barley; hgst. point 276 m nr. Wendover.

Chimborazo, mtn., **Ecuador**; 6,286 m; Andes; extinct volcano, first explored by von Humboldt (1802), first scaled by Whymper (1880).

Chimbote, spt., **Peru**; steel, iron-ore, coal; tinned fish, fish-meal; p. (1981) 216,406.

Chimkent, t., Kazakh SSR, **USSR**; in W. foothills of Tien Shan; nearby oasis fed by Arys R.; major industl. ctr.; lead smelting; p. (est. 1980) 327,000.

China, People's Republic of, Asia; Third lgst. cty. of world; 22 provs.; anc. conservative civilisation overthrown by long civil war and establishment of communist régime (1949); lge. p. crowded on cultivable valleys of Hwang-ho (Yellow R.), Yangtze and Si-kiang in E.; rest of cty. either mtnous. (plateau of Tibet) or desert (Sinkiang); rapid economic growth following onset of communist régime; agr. organised on commune basis, becomes increasingly intensive in S. where climate is less extreme; vast mineral resources, many undeveloped; recent industl. growth; heavy inds. at Wuhan, Baotou and in N.E. (Manchuria); special economic zones to attract foreign investment; poor communications except in E.; increasingly self-sufficient in petroleum; nuclear power programme; cap. Beijing; 35 m. only children resulting resulting from one-child family birth control policy; a. 9,595,961 km²; p. (est. 1984) 1,051,551,000, lgst. p. of any cty.

China Sea, part of W. Pacific between Korea and Philippines; divided by the narrow Formosa Strait into two areas; E. China Sea, inc. Yellow Sea, and S. China Sea.

Chinandega, mkt. t., cap. of C. dep., **Nicaragua**; sugar refining; p. (est. 1970) 37,000.

Chincho. See **Jinzhou.**

Chindwin, R., **Burma**; ch. trib. of Irrawaddy; rises in Patkai Hills, navigable in rainy season; dense p. on lower reaches; 800 km long.

Chinghai. See **Qinghai.**

Chinkiang. See **Zhenjiang.**

Chingola, t., **Zambia**; copper mng.; metal prod., printing; p. (1980) 145,869.

Chinon, t., Indre-et-Loire, central **France**; on R. Vienne, industl.; ruined cas., once a royal residency; nuclear power sta.; p. (1982) 8,873 (t.), 78,131 (met. a.).

Chinqui, volcano, **Panama**; 3,480 m.

Chinwangtao. See **Qinhuangdao.**

Chioggia, spt., cath. t., N. **Italy**; on I. in G. of Venice; fishing; p. (1981) 53,566.

Chios (Khios) I., in Aegean Sea, **Greece**; mainly agr.; wines, fruits and figs; supposed birthplace of Homer; p. (1981) 49,865.

Chippenham, North Wilts., **Eng.**; mkt. t. on R. Avon; rly. signal and brake equipment, bacon curing, tanning; p. (1981) 19,290.

Chipping Campden, v., Gloucs., **Eng.**; in Cotswold Hills; formerly impt. for woollens; tourism.

Chipping Norton, mkt. t., Oxford, **Eng.**; nr. Banbury; formerly impt. for woollens; p. (1981) 5,035.

Chipping Sodbury, mkt. t., Avon. **Eng.**; 13 km N.E. of Bristol.

Chirchik, c., Uzbek SSR, **USSR**; 32 km N.E. Tashkent; engin., chemicals; hydroelec. power stas.; p. (est. 1980) 134,000.

Chiricahua Mtns., Arizona, **USA**; form part of Coronado Nat. Forest; long inhabited by Apache Indians; spectacular volcanic scenery; alt. 2,987 m.

Chirk, t. Clwyd, **Wales**; on R. Cleriog, S. of Wrexham; slate, formerly coal-mng. a.; cas.

Chislehurst. See **Bromley.**

Chistyakovo. See **Torez.**

Chita, c., rly. ctr., Siberia, **RSFSR**; on upper R. Ingoda, 640 km E. of L. Baykal; coal, engin., chemicals, sawmilling; p. (est. 1980) 308,000.

Chittagong, c., **Bangladesh**; main pt. on Karnafuli R., nr. Bay of Bengal; exp. jute, tea; oil refining; steel mill; hydroelec. power; p. (1974) 416,733.

Chittaranjan, t., West Bengal, **India**; new t. on Barakhar R., in steel ctr. of Damodar valley; rly. locomotive wks.; p. (1961) 28,957.

Chkalov. See **Orenburg.**

Choisy-le-Roi, t., Val-de-Marne dep., **France**, industl. sub. of Paris on R. Seine; p. (1982) 35,531.

Cholet, t., Maine-et-Loire, **France**; textile ctr. on R. Seine; p. (1982) 56,528.

Cholon (Cho Lon), t., S. **Vietnam**; 16 km S.W. of Ho Chi-minh City; ctr. of rice tr.; p. inc. Ho Chi-minh City (1968) 1,682,000.

Cholula, anc. c. of Puebla prov., **Mexico**; Aztec temple, pyramid of Cholula, and other remains.

Chomo Lhari, mtn., Tibet, China and Bhutan; sacred to Buddhists; part of Himalayas; alt. 7,319 m.

Chomutov, t., N. **ČSSR**; industl. ctr. of lignite mng. a.; coal, steel, glass; p. (1970) 40,000.

Chongqing (Chungking), c., S.E. Sichuan prov., **China**; on Chang Jiang; comm. ctr. of W. China; ctr. of rich agr. dist. of Red Basin of Sichuan; coal, iron and steel, heavy machin.; lorries, vans, chemical fertilisers; former treaty pt.; p. (est. 2,700,000.

Chooz, t., Ardennes, **France**; pressurised water reactor; nuclear power sta. linked with Belgian grid.

Cho Oyu, mtn., between **Nepal** and Tibet, **China**; sixth hgst. in world; alt. 8,225 m.

Chorley, t., l. gov. dist., N. Lancs., **Eng.**; on W. flank of Rossendale Fells, 11 km S.E. of Preston; cotton, engin.; expansion as new t. with Leyland p. (1981) 90,986. See **Central Lancashire.**

Chorleywood, t., Three Rivers, Herts., **Eng.**; nr. Watford; p. (1981) 8,415.

Chorrilos Pass, **Argentina**; in E. cordillera of Andes at alt. 4,470 m; used by rly. from San Miguel de Tucumán to Antofagasta.

Chorzów (Królewska Huta), t., Upper Silesia, **Poland**; coal, iron and steel, chemicals, engin.; p. (est. 1983) 145,100.

Chota Nagpur, plateau, Madhya Pradesh, **India**; produces lac; impt. mng. ctr.; bauxite, mica.

Chou Kou Tien, site nr. Beijing, **China**; discovery of fossil bones of Beijing (Peking) man (*Sinanthropus pekinensis*).

Christchurch, t., l. gov. dist., Dorset, **Eng.**; on S. cst. 8 km E. of Bournemouth; holiday resort, aircraft. lt. inds.; p. (1981) 37,708 (dist.).

Christchurch, c., Canterbury prov., S.I., **N.Z.**; lgst. c. of S.I.; comm. ctr. for lamb, wool, and grain; cath., univ.; airpt; p. (est. 1979) 171,300 (c.), 296,500 (met. a.).

Christianshab, Danish settlement on Disko Bay, **W. Greenland**; meteorological sta.

Christmas I., in Indian Oc., Australian terr. since 1958; a. 140 km², healthy climate, phosphate deposits; p. (est. 1975) 3,022.

Christmas I., lge. coral atoll in Pac. Oc., one of Line Is.; discovered by Cook 1777; a. 135 km²; nuclear test site, 1957–64.

Chu, R. Kazakh SSR, **USSR**; rises in Tien Shan flows N.W. for 800 km into inland drainage basin; Chumysh Dam provides hydroelectricity and water for intensive cultivation of cotton, sugar-beet, citrus fruits.

Chuanchow. See Quauzhu.

Chubut, R., **Argentina**; drains from Andes into Atl. Oc.; continual irrigation reducing soil fertility of valley; 640 km long.

Chuchow. See Zhuzhou.

Chudleigh, mkt. t., Devon, **Eng.**; on R. Teign; stone quarrying.

Chu-kiang. See Zhujiang.

Chukotskiy, peninsula, **USSR**; extreme N.E.; rich gold deposit; hunting.

Chukyo, industl. area, Honshu, **Japan**; centred on Nagoya; textiles, ceramics, chemicals.

Chula Vista, t., Cal., **USA**; agr., aircraft; p. (1980) 83,927.

Chungking See Chongqing.

Chuquibamba Mtns. (alt. c. 6,400 m), **Peru**.

Chuquicamata, t., N. **Chile**; 3,050 m in Andes; lgst copper mine in world; p. (est. 1970) 29,000.

Chur (Coire), t., cap. Graubünden, **Switzerland**; in valley of upper Rhine; historic bldgs.; fruit, wine, tourist ctr.; p. (est. 1977) 32,800.

Church, Hyndburn, sub. of Accrington, Lancs., **Eng.**; engin.; p. (1981) 4,332.

Churchill, R., formerly Hamilton R., flows into Hamilton inlet, cst. of Labrador, **Canada**; magnificent waterfall, Churchill Falls with lge. hydroelec. scheme.

Church Stretton, mkt. t., Shrops., **Eng.**; tourism.

Chusan I. See Zhoushan.

Chusovoy, t., **RSFSR**; in Urals; iron and steel; p. (est. 1969) 62,000.

Chuvash ASSR, aut. rep., **RSFSR**; in middle Volga valley; arable agr., lumbering, food processing; a. 18,407 km²; p. (est. 1973) 1,251,000.

Chysauster, Cornwall, **Eng.**; prehistoric v.

Cibao, lowland a., **Dominican Rep.**, Central America; extends along N. side of Cordillera de Cibao for 180 km; 16–56 km wide; early a. of Spanish settlement; E. part called Vega Real; richest agr. a. of Hispaniola; cacao, tobacco, maize; dense p.; ch. t. Santiago.

Cicero, t., Ill., **USA**; adjoins Chicago; electrical appliances, hardware; p. (1970) 67,058.

Ciechanów, t., **Poland**; 78 km N.W. of Warsaw; agr. inds.; p. (1970) 23,200.

Cienaga, spt., N. **Colombia**; p. (est. 1972) 69,100 (t.), 168,100 (met. a.).

Cienfuegos, t., **Cuba**; sugar, tobacco; picturesque; nuclear power sta. proposed, built with Soviet assistance; p. (est. 1967) 91,800.

Cieszyn, t., Katowice prov., **Poland**; part of former Teschen on Polish side of frontier with **ČSSR**; p. (1970) 25,200.

Cimpina, t., **Romania**; in Walachia; petroleum ctr.; oil pipeline links to Ploiesti and Constanta on Black Sea.

Cincinnati, c. Ohio, **USA**; route and comm. ctr. on terraces of Ohio R.; food processing and many varied inds.; univs.; p. (1980) 385,000 (c.), 1,401,000, (met. a.).

Cinderford, t., Gloucs., **Eng.**; former ctr. of coal-mng. a. of Forest of Dean; new lt. industl. estate.

Cinque Ports, confederation of anc. **Eng.** pts. on cst. of Kent and Sussex; original 5: Sandwich, Dover, Hythe, Romney, Hastings; Winchelsea, and Rye added later. See L23.

Cirencester, t., Cotswold, Gloucs., **Eng.**; the Roman Corineum; former woollen t.; p. (1981) 15,622.

Ciskei, Bantu Terr. Authority, **S. Africa**; established 1961 between Fish and Kei Rs. on S.E. cst.; indep. (1981) but only recognised by S. Africa; 40 per cent of males work outside Ciskei; new cap. Bisho (under contruction); cap. Zwelitsha; p. (1980) 677,820.

Citta di Castello, walled t., **Italy**; in upper Tiber valley; impt. in Roman times; Renaissance cath., palaces; p. (1981) 37,242.

Citta Vecchia (Mdina), c., central **Malta**; former cap.; Roman remains; cath.

Ciudad Bolivar, c., Bolivar st., **Venezuela**; pt. on Orinoco R.; formerly called Angostura; coffee, cattle; ctr. of new industl. development on lower Orinoco; p. (est. 1980) 147,000.

Ciudad Juarez, c., **Mexico**; comm. ctr. on USA border; agr. processing; tourism; p. (1979) 625,040.

Ciudad Madero, t., **Mexico**; styrene and detergent plants, oil refining; p. (1979) 141,571.

Cuidad Obregón, t., Sonora, **Mexico**; on Yaqui R.; ctr. of irrigated agr. a.; p. (1979) 181,733.

Ciudad Presidente Stroessner, t., **Paraguay**; rapidly growing t. close to Itaipú Dam on Parana R.; p. (1982) 60,000.

Ciudad Real, c., cap. of Cuidad Real prov., **Spain**; mkt. t. founded 1255; textiles; p. (1970) 41,708.

Ciudad Real, prov., central **Spain**; mostly at 600 m; covering la Mancha dist.; agr.; cap. C.R.; a. 19,741 km²; p. (1981) 475,124.

Ciudad Rodrigo, old fortress t., Salamanca prov., **Spain**; strategic position nr. Portuguese bdy.; in Peninsular War fell to Fr. (1810) and captured by Wellington (1812); p. (1970) 13,320.

Civitavecchia, t., Latium, **Italy**; pt. for Rome on Tyrrhenian cst., 48 km N. of mouth of R. Tiber; p. (1981) 45,836.

Clackmannan, former co., l. gov. dist., Central Reg., **Scot.**; a. 161 km²; p. (1981) 47,806.

Clacton-on-Sea, t., Tendring, Essex, **Eng.**; on E. cst. 19 km S.E. of Colchester; seaside resort; lt. inds.; residtl.; p. (1981) 43,571.

Clairvaux, v., Aube, **France**; famous Cistercian abbey.

Clamart, t., Hauts-de-Seine, **France**; sub. of S.W. Paris; p. (1982) 48,678.

Clare, co., Munster, **R.o.I.**; cstl. co. bounded in S. and E. by R. Shannon; mainly agr. and tourism; inc. cliffs of Moher; Shannon airpt. and tax-free industl. development scheme; co. t. Ennis; a. 3,351 km²; p. (1981) 27,701.

Clare I., Clew Bay, Mayo, **R.o.I.**

Clarence Strait, between Melville I. and Darwin, N.T., Australia.

Clarksburg, t., W. Va., **USA**; industl. ctr. for coal-mng. a., oil and natural gas fields; machin. glass, pottery; p. (1980) 22,371.

Clarksdale, t., Miss., **USA**; processing ctr. for rich farming a.; p. (1980) 21,137.

Clarksville, t., Tenn., **USA**; on Cumberland R.; tobacco mkt.; p. (1980) 54,777 (t.), 150,220 (met. a.).

Clausthal-Zellerfeld, t., Lower Saxony, **W. Germany**; in Harz mtns.; tourism.

Clay Cross, t., Derbys., **Eng.**; former ctr. coal mng. (first developed by George Stephenson 1838) iron, engin.; p. (1981) 9,725.

Clayton-le-Moors, t., Hyndburn, Lancs., **Eng.**; nr. Blackburn; textile machin., cotton and blanket weaving, bristles, soap; p. (1981) 6,309.

Clear C., southernmost point of Ireland, Clear I., **R.o.I.**; off S.W. cst. of Cork.

Cleare, c., Alaska, **USA**; site of ballistic missile early warning sta.

Clearwater, t., Fla., **USA**; citrus fruit, flowers, fish; resort; p. (1980) 85,528.

Cleator Moor, t. Cumbria, **Eng.**; former colly. t.

Cleckheaton t., West Yorks., **Eng.**; nr. Bradford; woollens, blankets, asbestos.

Clee Hills, Shrops., **Eng.**; between Rs. Severn and Teme; alt. 550 m.

Cleethorpes, t., l. gov. dist., Humberside, **Eng.**; 5 km S. of Grimsby; resort; p. (1981) 68,241 (dist.).

Clent Hills, Hereford and Worcs., **Eng.**; about 16 km S.W. of Birmingham, overlooking valley of R. Stour; recreation; maximum alt. 316 m.

Clerkenwell, industl. dist., London, **Eng.**; immediately N. of the City; noted for jewellry.

Clermont-Ferrand, c., cap. Puy-de-Dôme dep. central **France**; in Auvergne; rubber tyres, chemicals, food inds.; Gothic cath., Romanesque church; p. (1982) 151,092.

Clevedon, t., Woodspring, Avon, **Eng.**; at mouth of R. Severn; seaside resort; quarrying, bricks, footwear; p. (1981) 17,915.

Cleveland, c., Ohio, **USA**; impt. Gr. Ls. pt. handling iron ore and coal which support a major iron and steel ind.; oil refining, food processing, many varied inds.; univ.; p. (1980) 573,000 (c.), 1,896,000 (met. a.).

Cleveland, non-met. co., N.E. **Eng.;** heavy industl. region centred around ts. of Tees estuary; chems., iron and steel mftg.; inc. part of N. York Moors to S.; a. 583 km²; p. (1981) 565,775.

Cleveland Hills, North Yorks./Cleveland, **Eng.;** part of N. York Moors; once mined for iron ore, impt. potash deposit.

Clichy, t., Hauts-de-Seine, **France;** N.W. sub. of Paris; oil refining, aircraft, automobile components; p. (1982) 47,000.

Clifton, sub., Bristol, Avon, **Eng.;** on R. Avon; mineral springs; famous suspension bridge.

Clifton, t., N.J., **USA;** industl. t., nr. Passaic; p. (1980) 74,388.

Clinton, t., Iowa, **USA;** on Mississippi R.; iron and steel, machin.; p. (1980) 32,828.

Clitheroe, t., Ribble Valley, Lancs., **Eng.;** in Ribble valley; mkt. t. for rural a.; limestone quarrying nearby; p. (1981) 13,552.

Clonakilty, t., Cork, **R.o.I.;** nr. Bandon; sm. harbour; agr. prods.; p. (1966) 2,341.

Cloncurry, t., Queensland, **Australia;** rly junction and air terminal in ctr. of copper field; uranium nearby; p. (1976) 2,079.

Clones, mkt. t. on Ulster border, Monaghan, **R.o.I.;** rly. ctr.; p. (1981) 2,384.

Clonmacnoise, v., Offaly, **R.o.I;** ecclesiastical ruins.

Clonmel, t., Tipperary, **R.o.I.;** on R. Suir; agr. ctr.; fairs; cider, footwear; p. (1981) 12,407.

Clovelly, v., Devon, **Eng.;** seaside resort.

Clowne, t., Derbys., **Eng.;** coal mng.

Cluj, c., **Romania;** in Transylvania on Somesul R.; univs., historic bldgs.; industl. ctr.; p. (1978) 273,199.

Clutha R., R. of S.I., **N.Z.,** hydroelec. power; 320 km long.

Clwyd, co. N. **Wales;** inc. most of Denbigh and Flintshire; mtnous. to S.; N. cstl. resorts inc. Colwyn Bay, Prestatyn and Rhyl; sm. coalfield; lgst. t. Wrexham; a. 2,424 km²; p. (1981) 390,173.

Clwyd, R., Clwyd, N. **Wales;** flows into Irish Sea at Rhyl; length 48 km.

Clydach, t., West Glamorgan, **Wales;** on R. Tawe, 8 km N.E. Swansea; steel wks.; nickel refineries.

Clyde, R., Strathclyde Reg., S.W. **Scot.;** flows through industl. belt into Firth of C.; Glasgow, Greenock, Clydebank main pts.; hydroelec. stas.; twin-road tunnel under R. in Glasgow (Whiteinch-Linthouse) completed 1963; 170 km long.

Clydebank, t., l. gov. dist., Strathclyde Reg., **Scot.;** on Clyde adjoining Glasgow; tyres, biscuits; p. (1981) 51,825.

Clyde, Firth of, stretches from Dumbarton to Ailsa Craig, **Scot.;** Bute, Arran, Gr. and Little Cumbrae ch. Is.; 102 km long.

Clydesdale, l. gov. dist., Strathclyde Reg., **Scot.;** small dist. formerly known as Lanark; p. (1981) 57,361.

Coachella Valley, arid region, S.E. Cal., **USA;** part of G. of Cal.; dates and citrus fruits under irrigation from Imperial Valley irrigation system.

Coahuila, st., **Mexico;** 3rd st. of Mexico; lies S. of Texas, bordering Rio Grande valley; main coal deposits; mnfs. impt.; irrigated agr.; cap. Saltillo; a. 142,611 km²; p. (1970) 1,114,956.

Coalbrookdale, v., Salop, **Eng.;** old coal and iron mines; home of iron master Abraham Darby. See **Bridges, Section L.**

Coalville, t., North West Leics., **Eng.;** nr. Ashby-de-la-Zouch; coal mng., engin., elastic webbing; p. (1981) 30,832.

Coast Range, mtns., **USA;** along Pac. cst.; wooded ranges causing rain shadow to E. valleys; alt. up to 600 m.

Coatbridge, burgh, Strathclyde Reg., **Scot.,** 16 km E. of Glasgow; coal, iron and steel, prefabricated houses, tubes engin.; p. (1981) 50,866.

Coats I., S. of Southampton I. Hudson Bay, **Canada.**

Coatzacoalcos (Puerto Mexico), spt., **Mexico;** on G. of Campeche; oil refinery; chemicals, fertilisers; p. (1979) 128,115.

Cobalt, t., Ont., **Canada;** silver, cobalt, arsenic,

nickel; p. (1971) 2,191.

Cobán, t., **Guatemala,** mkt. t.; coffee and Peruvian bark tr.; p. (est. 1971) 13,117.

Cóbh (Queenstown), U.D., Cork, **R.o.I.;** spt. on Great I. in Cork Harbour; lge. docks; H.Q. of Royal Cork Yacht Club; seaside resort; p. (1981) 6,587.

Coburg, t., Bavaria, **W. Germany;** old cas.; wickerwork, furniture, metal, machines, toy inds.; p. (est. 1983) 44,700.

Cochabamba, dep., **Bolivia;** E. of Andes; lgst. p. concentration of Bolivia in C. basin; a. 65,496 km²; p. (est. 1982) 908,674.

Cochabamba, c., cap. of C. dep., **Bolivia;** second lgst. c. in rep.; alt. 2,559 m; univ., cath.; oil refining, shoes, rubber tyres, fruit-canning, modern milk plant; hydroelectric power; p. (est. 1982) 281,962.

Cochin, spt., Kerala, **India;** on Malabar cst.; exp. coconut oil, tea; oil refining; silting pt.; p. (1981) 513,249.

Cochin China, region, formerly part of Indo-China; now roughly coincides with S. Vietnam; comprises the Mekong delta. See **Vietnam.**

Cockenzie and Port Seton, small burgh, E. Lothian, **Scot.;** two fishing pts. on F. of Forth; p. (1981) 3,756.

Cockermouth, t., Allerdale, Cumbria, **Eng.;** slate, shoe mftg., plywood, concrete prods.; birthplace of Wordsworth; p. (1981) 7,149.

Cockpit Country, upland a., W. **Jamaica;** classic karst landscape forming rugged upland; some cultivation in hollows; a. 500 km²; alt. 300–800 m.

Coco, R., **Honduras** and **Nicaragua;** flows to Caribbean Sea through economically impt. valley; agr., forestry, mng.; potential as routeway; 480 km long.

Cocos or **Keeling Is.,** 27 coral atolls, **Indian Oc.;** since 1955 terr. of Australia purchased by Australia (1978) to ensure democracy; strategic position S.E. of Sri Lanka, radio and cable sta. German cruiser *Emden* destroyed by Australian cruiser *Sydney* on N. Keeling I. in 1914; uninhabited until 1826; developed by Clunies Ross family for coconut prod.; controlled emigration since 1948 to solve problem of overpopulation; voted to integrate with Northern Territory, Australia (1984); a. 13 km²; p. (est. 1975) 604.

Coesfeld, t., N. Rhine–Westphalia, **W. Germany;** textiles, machin.; p. (est. 1983) 31,200.

Cognac, t., Charente, **France;** cognac, bottles; p. (1982) 20,995.

Coiba I., S. cst. of **Panama.**

Coimbatore, t., Tamil Nadu, **India;** commands Palghat Gap; varied inds. benefit from local hydroelec. power; p. (1981) 704,514 (c.), 920.355 (met. a.).

Coimbra, t., **Portugal;** cath., oldest univ. in Portugal; wine-growing; earthenware mfns.; p. (1981) 74,616 (t.), 138,930 (met. a.).

Colchester, t., l. gov. dist., Essex, **Eng.;** pre-Roman t. of Camulodunum on R. Colne; univ.; lt. inds., engin., oyster fisheries; pt.; p. (1981) 133,681 (dist.).

Cold Fell, mtn., Northumberland, **Eng.;** 622 m.

Cold Harbour, v., Va., **USA;** battles between Grant and Lee 1864.

Coldstream, t., Berwick, **Scot.;** on Eng. border; agr. machin., knitwear; p. (1981) 1,649.

Coleraine, t., l. gov. dist., **N. Ireland;** pt. on R. Bann, 6 km from sea; univ.; linen, acrilan mftg., distilling; p. (1981) 46,668 (dist.), 15,967 (t.).

Coleshill, t., l. gov. dist., North Warwickshire, **Eng.;** lurgi gasification plant; new colly. 1965.

Colima, mkt. t., **Mexico;** on Colima R. in fertile valley; univ.; agr. processing; p. (est. 1969) 44,000.

Colima, st., **Mexico;** on Pac. cst.; cap. Colima; pt. Manzanillo; cotton, sugar, rice, coffee; a. 5,203 km²; p. (1970) 241,153.

Colima, volcano (48 km N.E. of c.), **Mexico,** alt. 3,869 m.

Coll, I. off cst. of Mull, Argyll and Bute, **Scot.;** agr. lobster fishing; p. (1981) 951.

Collie, t., W. **Australia;** impt. coal deposits supply power for much of W. Australia; p. (1976) 6,771.

Collingwood, t., Ont., **Canada;** on Georgian Bay, L. Huron; shipbldg., steel; p. (1971) 9,719.

Colmar, t., cap. Haut-Rhin dep., **France;** ctr.

of Alsace textile ind.; attractive mediaeval t.; mkt. for vineyards; p. (1982) 63,764.

Colne, t., Pendle, E. Lancs., **Eng.**; cotton mnfs., felts; p. (1981) 18,203.

Colne, R., Eng.; trib. of Thames rising in Chilterns.

Colne Valley, t., West Yorks., **Eng.**; woollens; p. (1981) 21,659.

Cologne (Köln), c., N. Rhine–Westphalia, **W. Germany**; on Rhine at N. end of Rhine gorge; cath., univ.; impt. R. pt., route and comm. ctr., eau-de-Cologne, electro-technical ind., machin., metallurgy, paper, chemicals, cars, oil refining, textiles; p. (est. 1983) 953,300.

Colombes, t., Hauts-de-Seine dep., **France**; mftg. sub. of Paris on R. Seine; p. (1982) 78,783.

Colombia, rep., N.W. **S. America**; cap. Bogotá; Andes contain most of p.; the savannahs (llanos) to S.E. are almost uninhabited; industl. employment growing; birth and death rates high in mainly tropical climate and many diseases endemic; agr. impt.; coffee, bananas; major oil reserves discovered (1985); eruption of Nevado del Ruiz (1985); a. 1,139,592 km²; p. (est. 1981) 27,800,000.

Colombo, c., cap. of **Sri Lanka**; on W. cst.; univ.; impt. pt. (artificial) built by British; exp. tea, rubber, coconuts; p. (est. 1983) 623,000.

Colón, t., **Panama**; at Atl. end of Panama Canal; free tr. zone; comm. and industl. ctr.; oil refining nearby; p. (1970) 95,308.

Colonsay, I., Inner Hebrides, Argyll and Bute, **Scot.**; 13 km long; ecclesiastical antiquities; p. (inc. Jura 1971) 349.

Colorado, st., **USA**; admitted to Union 1876; st. flower Rocky Mtn. Columbine, st. bird Lark Bunting; hgst. st. in USA; in the Rockies extending up to 4,401 m (Mt. Elbert), no land below 1,000 m; drained by headwaters of Rs. Arkansas and Colorado; major stockrearing a.; many valuable minerals esp. uranium, radium and molybdenum; cap. Denver; a. 270,000 km²; p. (1980) 2,889,000.

Colorado, plateau, Arizona, Utah, Col., N.M., **USA**; arid upland with spectacular scenery, inc. Grand Canyon; alt. 1,500–3,300 m.

Colorado, R., Argentina; flows from Andes to Atl. Oc.; limited irrigation in pastoral valley; length 848 km.

Colorado, major R. of W. **USA**; drains 8% of USA; formed by confluence of Green and Grand Rs.; spectacular canyons inc. Grand Canyon; hydroelec. power from many dams inc. Hoover Dam; irrigation supplies intensive horticultural a. in S. section and consequent rapid decrease in volume to a sm. stream in lower course; length 2,320 km.

Colorado, R., rises N.W. Texas, **USA**; flows to G. of Mexico; irrigation and power; 1,552 km long.

Colorado Desert, Cal., **USA**; inc. Imperial Valley, a fertile irrigated a.

Colorado Springs, t., Col., **USA**; 102 km S. Denver; resort; p. (1980) 215,000 (c.), 317,000 (met. a.).

Colton, t., S.E. Cal., **USA**; fruit- and vegetable-canning; mkt. gardening; p. (1980) 15,201.

Columbia, t., Mo., **USA**; W. of St. Louis; st. univ.; flour, lumber; p. (1980) 62,061 (t.), 100,376 (met. a.).

Columbia, t., st. cap. S.C., **USA**; in ctr. of rich farming a.; textiles, clothing; burned down in Civil War 1865; p. (1980) 101,000 (c.), 410,000 (met. a.).

Columbia, District of (D.C.); area on east bank of Potomac R., coterminus with c. of Washington, cap. of **USA**; a. 179 km²; p. (1980) 638,000.

Columbia, R., major R. of western N. **America**; rises in Rocky Mtns., B.C., flows though Washington, USA; power sources, inc. Grand Coulee Dam, Bonneville Dam; deepwater harbour at mouth; length 2,240 km.

Columbus, c., Ga., **USA**; at head of navigation on Chattahoochee R.; industl. and shipping ctr.; textile mills, food-processing; cotton-ginning machin.; p. (1980) 169,000 (c.), 239,000 (met. a.).

Columbus, t., Ind., **USA**; engin.; leather gds.; p. (1980) 30,614.

Columbus, t., Miss., **USA**; agr. prods.; p. (1980) 27,383.

Columbus, c., st. cap. Ohio, **USA**; rly. ctr.; st. univ.; machin., paper, aircraft machin., chemicals; p. (1980) 565,000 (c.), 1,093,000 (met. a.).

Colwyn Bay, t., Clwyd, N. **Wales**; on cst. 10 km E. of Llandudno; furniture; seaside resort; p. (1981) 26,278; as **Colwyn** forms basis of l. gov. dist. inc. Abergele; p. (1981) 48,639.

Comayagüela, c., former cap. of **Honduras**; twin c. of Tegucigalpa from which it is separated by Choluteca R.; both cs. administered together as Central Dist.

Combe Martin, v., Devon, **Eng.**; 8 km E. of Ilfracombe; seaside resort.

Comber, t., Ards, **N. Ireland**; linen; p. (1966) 3,925.

Como, c., N. **Italy**; at foot of Alps, on L. Como; oranges, olives; textiles; cath.; tourism; p. (1981) 95,571.

Como, L., N. **Italy**; beautiful mtn. scenery, tourism, villas; a. 145 km².

Comodoro Rivadavia, spt., Chubut prov., **Argentina**; on San Jorge G., 880 km S.W. of Bahía Blanca; military zone; univ.; ch. source of oil in Argentine; oil refining; p. (est. 1970) 70,000.

Comorin, C., most S. point of **India**.

Comoro Is., arch., **Indian Oc.**; in Moçambique channel, midway between African and Madagascar; cap. Moroni; total a. 2,170 km²; turtle fishing; vanilla, copra, sisal, timber, perfume plants; indep. from France declared 1975 but rejected by Mayotte Is. whose future is still undecided; p. (est. 1983) 421,000.

Compiègne, t., Oise, **France**; sugar mills, rope; Armistice signed between Allies and Germany 1918; Fr. surrendered to Hitler 1940; resort; p. (1982) 62,778 (met. a.).

Compton, t., Cal., **USA**; residtl. for Los Angeles; heavy engin., glass, oil refining; p. (1980) 81,286.

Conakry, c., cap. of **Rep. of Guinea**; impt. pt. on offshore islet; exp. iron-ore and alumina; experimental fruit gardens; p. (est. 1972) 525,671 (met. a.).

Concarneau, pt., Finistère, **France**; 19 km S.E. Quimper; fisheries; p. (1982) 18,225.

Concepción, c., prov. cap., **Chile**; shipping ctr. through its pt. Talcahuano; univ.; comm. and cultural t.; severe earthquakes 1939 and 1960; nr. to coalfield; p. (est. 1984) 213,818.

Concepción, prov., **Chile**; cap. C.; Lota-Coronel coalfield lgst. in Chile; a. 5,701 km²; p. (1970) 638,118.

Concepción, t., cap. of C. prov., **Paraguay**; main comm. ctr. for Chaco, pt. on R. Paraguay; p. (est. 1970) 34,000.

Conchos, R., Chihuahua prov., **Mexico**; flows N.E. from Madre Occidental to Rio Grande; cotton under irrigation in upper valley; hydroelec. power; length 560 km.

Concord, t., Cal., **USA**; residtl. and comm. ctr. in San Francisco met. a.; rapid p. growth; p. (1980) 103,000 (t.).

Concord, t., Mass., **USA**; literary ctr.; textiles; p. (1980) 16,293.

Concord, t., st. cap., N.H., **USA**; on Merrimack R.; granite, machin., textiles; p. (1980) 30,400.

Concordia, t., **Argentina**; pt. on Uruguay R.; exp. agr. prod.; p. (est. 1977) 56,000.

Condamine, R., Queensland, **Australia**; trib. of R. Darling; used for irrigation.

Coney I., t., N.Y., **USA**; on Long I., 8 km long, comprises Manhattan Beach, Brighton Beach, W. Brighton, and W. End; seaside resort.

Congleton, t., l. gov. dist., E. Cheshire, **Eng.**; on S.W. margin of Pennines; clothing, textiles; once impt. for silk; p. (1981) 79,028 (dist.).

Congo, People's Rep. of the, indep. st. within Fr. Community. Equatorial Africa; cap. Brazzaville; agr. and forestry; hardwoods; economy heavily dependent on petroleum; a. 342,000 km²; p. (est. 1981) 1,580,000.

Congolese Republic. See **Zaïre.**

Congo R. See **Zaïre R.**

Conisborough, t., South Yorks., **Eng.**; limestone, bricks, tiles; p. (1981) 16,114.

Coniston, t., Ont., **Canada**; on rly. 13 km E. of Sudbury; nickel smelting; t. built by and for nickel-mng. company.

Coniston Water, L., Cumbria, **Eng.**; focus of tourism in L. Dist.; 8·8 km long.

Conjeeveram. See **Kanchipuram.**

Connacht, prov., **R.o.I.**; inc. Galway, Mayo, Sligo, Leitrim, Roscommon; mtnous in W.; farming, fishing; a. 17,775 km²; p. (1981) 106,553.

Connah's Quay, t., Alyn and Deeside, Clwyd, **Wales**; p. (1981) 14,801.

Connaught Tunnel (Can. Pac. Rly.), B.C., **Canada**;

longest in N. America (8 km) 1,500 m under mt. Sir Donald (Selkirk Mtns.).

Connecticut, R., New Eng.; **USA**; middle course forms fine agr. land; investment in navigation, irrigation and flood control; 566 km long.

Connecticut, st., New England, **USA**; one of original 13 sts.; admitted to Union 1788; st. flower mountain Laurel, st. bird robin; humid climate; arable agr.; diversified inds.; many natural harbours on cst.; cap. Hartford; lgst. c. Bridgeport; a. 12,973 km²; p. (1980) 3,108,000.

Connemara, mtns., dist., **R.O.I.**; Co. Galway; many lakes and bogs; tourist resort.

Consett, t., Derwentside, Durham, **Eng.**; on edge of Pennines, 16 km S.W. Newcastle; iron, steel closed (1980), coal mng.; p. (1981) 33,433.

Constance (Konstanz), c., Baden-Württemberg, **W. Germany**; on Bodensee; cath.; textiles, machin., chemicals, elec. inds.; route ctr.; tourism; p. (est. 1983) 69,100.

Constance, L. *See* Bodensee.

Constanţa, ch. spt. S.E. **Romania**; on Black Sea; oil pipeline to Ploiesti and Cimpina; new Danube-Black Sea canal (1984) shortens route of Trans-European waterway to Black Sea; exp. petroleum, wheat; cement, chemicals, machin.; p. (1978) 267,612.

Constantine, c., N.E. **Algeria**; stands 650 m high on gorge of Rhumel R.; planned textile and engin. wks.; p. (1966) 243,558.

Constantinople. *See* Istanbul.

Conwy (Conway), Aberconwy, Gwynedd, spt., N. **Wales**; mediaeval walled t.; at mouth of R. Conway; sm. seaside resort; cas.; quarrying, lt. engin.; p. (1981) 12,969.

Cook, mtn., alt. 3,764 m; hgst. point in S. Alps. and **N.Z.**; 3 peaks.

Cook Inlet, S. cst. Alaska, **USA**; oil pipeline connects oilfields of Granite Point with marine terminal at Dritt R.

Cook Is., Brit. gr. (Rarotonga, lgst.) in **S. Pac.**; annexed to N.Z., 1901; internal self-govt. 1965; bananas, oranges, copra; a. 241 km²; p. (1976) 18,112.

Cookstown, mkt. t., l. gov. dist., **N. Ireland**; cement wks.; p. (1981) 26,402 (dist.), 7,649 (t.).

Cook Strait, channel between N. and S. Is. of **N.Z.**; 24–29 km wide; undersea cable completed 1965.

Cooma, t., N.S.W., **Australia**; mkt. t.; tourist ctr. for Kosciusko Nat. Park; H.Q. of Snowy Mts. Authority; p. (1976) 7,353.

Coonoor, t., Tamil Nadu, **India**; in Nilgiri Hills; sanatorium c. 1,800 m a.s.l.; p. (1981) 44,750.

Cooper Creek (Barcoo), intermittent R., central **Australia**; rises in Warrego Range, Gr. Dividing Range, flows S.W. into marshes of L. Eyre; provides water for livestock in semi-arid region; 1,408 km long.

Copeland, l. gov. dist., Cumbria, **Eng.**; cstl. a. N. of Barrow and inc. Whitehaven and Millom; p. (1981) 72,788.

Copenhagen (København), ch. spt., cap. of **Denmark**; on E. cst. of Sjaelland I.; royal palace, univ., library; naval sta.; freeport; steel, metal, textiles, clothing, breweries; airpt.; p. (1979) 502,416 (c.), 1,391,634 (met. a.).

Copiapó, t., cap. of Atacama prov., **Chile**; copper-and iron-mng. ctr.; p. (est. 1970) 47,122.

Coquet, R., Northumberland, **Eng.**; rises in the Cheviots and flows into North Sea.

Coquimbo, spt., **Chile**; exp. iron. copper, and manganese ores; p. (est. 1970) 65,000.

Coral Sea, Pac Oc., extends from the New Hebrides to Australia.

Coral Sea Islands Territory, Fed. terr., **Australia**; scattered Is., E. of Gr. Barrier Reef, off Queensland cst.; possibility of oil exploration.

Corbeil-Essonnes, t., Essonne, **France**; on R. Seine, 19 km S.E. of Paris; flour mills, printing, paper; p. (1982) 38,081.

Corbridge, t., Northumberland, **Eng.**; on R. Tyne, nr. Hexham; 17th cent. bridge; Roman t. nearby.

Corby, t., l. gov. dist., Northants., **Eng.**; 11 km N. of Kettering; new t.; steel wks.; now mostly closed down, shoes, clothing, lamps; p. (1981) 52,667 (dist.), 47,772 (t.).

Córdoba, c., central **Argentina**; univ.; cultural and comm. ctr.; exp. wheat, cattle, lumber; health resort; local hydroelec. power from La Vina; p. (1980) 990,007.

Córdoba, c., Veracruz, **Mexico**; mkt. t. in coffee-growing a.; p. (1979) 121,723.

Córdova, prov., Andalusia, **Spain**; cap. Córdova;

olives, vines, livestock; a. 13,724 km²; p. (1981) 720,815.

Córdova, c., Andalusia, **Spain**; cap. of C. prov., on Guadalquivir R.; cath. originally built as a mosque in 8th cent.; tourist ctr.; p. (1981) 279,383.

Corfu (Kérkira), most N. of Ionian Is., **Greece**; traversed by mtns. but largely lowland producing olive oil, figs, wine, oranges; a. 637 km²; p. (1981) 99,477 (prov.).

Corinth (Kórinthos), t., cap. Corinthia prov., **Greece**; at end of Isthmus of C.; occupies site 5 km from anc. classic c. destroyed by earthquake 1858; raisins, wine; p. (1981) 22,658.

Corinth Canal, ship canal, S. **Greece**; traverses Isthmus of Corinth, links G. of Corinth and Ionian Sea with Saronic G. and Aegean Sea; opened 1893; length 5·6 km, depth 8 m.

Corinth, Isthmus of, connects the Peloponnesus with the mainland of **Greece**; cut across by canal.

Corinto, ch. spt., N.W. **Nicaragua**; handles 50 per cent of cty's tr.; exp. hides, sugar, coffee; p. (est. 1970) 12,985.

Cork, co., **R.O.I.**; lgst. and most S.; mtns.; dairying, brewing, agr., fisheries; cap. Cork; a. 7,485 km²; p. (1981) 136,344.

Cork, spt., C.B., Cork, **R.O.I.**; at mouth of R. Lee; cath., univ.; woollens, butter, cattle, brewing, cars, fertilizers; p. (1981) 91,323.

Corner Brook, c., W. Newfoundland, **Canada**; gd. harbour; iron foundries, cement, gypsum; one of world's lgst. newsprint mills; p. (1971) 25,929.

Cornwall, t., Ont., **Canada**; on St. Lawrence R.; H.Q. of Seaway Authority; textiles, pulp, paper, flour; p. (1971) 46,429.

Cornwall and Isles of Scilly, non-met. co., S.W. **Eng.**; penin. bordering Atl. Oc. and Eng. Channel; granite moorlands supply kaolin; tin mines due to close (1986); mild maritime climate encourages tourism, dairying, and mkt. gardening; many small fishing vs.; co. t. Bodmin; a. 3,515 km²; p. (1981) 430,506.

Cornwall, North, l. gov. dist., **Eng.**; lge. a. on N. cst. stretching from Bodmin to Bude; p. (1981) 66,189.

Coro, c., Falcón, **Venezuela**; on Paraguaná penin.; agr. processing; nearby oil refineries; p. (1971) 68,701.

Corocoro, t., La Paz dep., **Bolivia**; at alt. c. 4,000 m in central Andes, 80 km S. of La Paz; impt. copper-mng. ctr.

Coromandel Coast (Carnatic region), cst. of Tamil Nadu, **India**; where earliest European settlements established; extensive a. of flat land built up by R. Cauvery.

Coronation Gulf, arm of Beaufort Sea; extreme point N. Canadian mainland; discovered by Franklin.

Coronel, spt., **Chile**; coal mng., pt. inds.; p. (est. 1966) 43,324.

Coronel Oviedo, t., **Paraguay**; comm. ctr.; p. (est. 1970) 59,307.

Corpus Christi, c., Texas, **USA**; cotton, oil refining, chemicals; resort; p. (1980) 232,000 (c.), 326,000 (met. a.).

Corréze, dep., S. central **France**; part of Massif Central, mostly over 600 m; sparse p. based on livestock agr. and forestry; cap. Tulle; a. 5,884 km²; p. (1982) 239,000.

Corrib, Lough, Galway and Mayo, **R.O.I.**; drained by Corrib R. into Galway Bay; impt. brown trout fishery; a. 176 km².

Corrientes, t., **Argentina**; agr. tr. ctr. on Paraná R.; univ.; cattle, sugar, rice, cotton; river navigation reduces isolation; p. (1980) 186,130.

Corryvreckan, strait and whirlpool between Jura and Scarba Is., Inner Hebrides, **Scot.**; whirlpool caused by tidal movement over variable sea bed.

Corse du Sud. *See* Corsica.

Corsica (Corse), I., **France**; in Mediterranean Sea; violent history in 16th and 17th cent.; high granite peaks (Monte Cinto), mtn. torrents, fertile plains; inland and sea fishing; rapid growth of tourism with little benefit to indigenous Corsicans; split into 2 deps. to help overcome autonomist agitation (1975); Haute Corse, cap. Bastia (1982) 127,200, Corse du Sud, cap. Ajaccio (1982) 102,800; a. 8,721 km²; p. (1982) 230,000.

Corsicana, t., Texas, **USA**; site of first oil drilling in USA; p. (1980) 21,712.

Cortona, t., Tuscany, **Italy**; nr. Perugia; Roman remains, cath.; p. (1981) 22,281.

Corumbá, pt., Mato Grosso, **Brazil**; on R. Paraguay; exp. agr. products; mkt. t.; p. (est. 1970) 39,000.

Corunna. *See* **La Coruña.**

Corvallis, t., Ore., **USA**; in fertile farming valley; lumbering; univ.; p. (1970) 35,056.

Coryton, t., Essex, **Eng.**; on Thames, oil refining; oil pipeline to Stanlow refinery.

Cos (Kos), I., Dodecanese, **Greece**; in Aegean Sea, second lgst. of gr.; gave name to Cos lettuce; birthplace of Hippocrates; p. (1981) 20,350.

Cosenza, c., S. **Italy**; ctr. for figs, oranges, olive oil, wine; cath., univ., cas.; p. (1981) 106,801.

Costa Brava, region, Catalonia, **Spain**; tourism.

Costa del Sol, region, Málaga cst., **Spain**; tourism.

Costa Rica, rep. **Central America**; over half p. in equable Meseta Central; forests, volcanic mtns.; agr. 40 per cent G.N.P.; coffee, bananas, cacao; high literacy and living standards; a. 50,909 km²; p. (est. 1984) 2,534,000.

Côte d'Azur, **France**; Mediterranean littoral E. of Rhône R.; inc. resorts of Nice, Cannes, Monte Carlo, and St. Tropez.

Côte d'Or, dep., E. **France**; heart of anc. Burgundy, traversed by R. Saône; cap. Dijon; wines, livestock, iron and steel; a. 8,783 km²; p. (1982) 473,200.

Cotentin, peninsula, N. **France**; 80 km long; Cherbourg, at its extremity, 128 km from Portsmouth.

Côtes-du-Nord, dep., N. Brittany, **France**; rugged cst. and Is. and mild climate encourage tourism; mkt. gardens along cst.; many fishing ts.; cap. St. Brieuc; a. 7,218 km²; p. (1982) 539,100.

Cotonou, pt., **Benin Rep.**; new artificial pt.; fishing; lt. inds.; offshore oilfields (drilling from 1982); p. (est. 1980) 253,900.

Cotopaxi, volcano, (alt. 5,982 m) in the Andes of Ecuador, nr. Quito; loftiest active volcano in the world; recent eruptions have caused great damage to Ecuador.

Cotswold, l. gov. dist., Gloucs., **Eng.**; lge a. covering C. Hills and inc. Cirencester and Northleach; p. (1981) 68,382.

Cotswold Hills, W. Eng.; limestone escarpment, Gloucs., Oxon.; once famous for woollens; source of Thames and tribs.; highest point Cleeve Cloud, 309 m; tourism.

Cottbus or **Kottbus, E. Germany**; on R. Spree; rly. ctr.; textile and metal mnfs.; p. (1983) 120,723.

Cottian Alps, mtn. range on border of **France** and **Italy** crossed by Hannibal; craggy; max. alt. 2,844 m (Monte Viso).

Coulsdon and Purley. *See* Croydon.

Council Bluffs, t., Iowa, **USA**; on Missouri R. nr. Omaha; rly. ctr.; farm implements, paper, machin.; p. (1980) 56,449.

Courantyne, R., **Guyana**; rises in Serra Acari; passes through bauxite mng. region to Atl. Oc.; navigation in lower course; 720 km long.

Courtrai. *See* Kortrijk.

Cove and Kilcreggan, burgh, Dumbarton, **Scot.**; at junc. of Loch Long and R. Clyde; p. (1981) 1,218.

Coventry, c., met. dist., West Midlands, **Eng.**; 29 km E.S.E. of Birmingham; ctr. of cycle, motorcycle, motor-car ind.; aircraft, tools; chemicals; projectiles, textiles; cath.; univ.; p. (1981) 314,124.

Covilhã, t., Portugal; cloth factories; p. (1981) 21,807 (c.), 60,945 (met. a.).

Covington, t., Ky., **USA**; on R. Ohio, opp. Cincinnati; machin., leather, furniture; p. (1980) 60,065.

Cowbridge, t., Vale of Glamorgan, South Glamorgan, S. **Wales**; nr. Cardiff; p. (1981) 1,224.

Cowdenbeath, burgh, Dunfermline, **Scot.**; 8 km N.E. of Dunfermline; coal; p. (1981) 12,235.

Cowes, resort and pt., Medina, I. of Wight, **Eng.**; on estuary of R. Medina; regattas and yacht bldg.; hovercraft; p. (1981) 19,663.

Cowra, t., N.S.W., **Australia**; famous wheat dist. and site of state experimental farm; p. (1976) 7,734.

Cozumel I., E. of Yucatan peninsula, **Mexico**.

Crac6w. *See* Kraków.

Cradle, Mt., mtn., Tasmania, **Australia**; alt. 1,546 m; Nat. Park.

Cradock, t., Cape Prov., **S. Africa**; wool tr.; p. (est. 1967) 21,300.

Craigavon, c., l. gov. dist., **N. Ireland**; new "city in a garden" under construction, 16 km long, merging Portadown and Lurgan, linked by motorway, to provide major base for ind.; p. (1981) 71,416 (dist.), 10,195 (c.).

Crail, royal burgh, North East Fife, **Scot.**; cstl. resort; p. (1981) 1,158.

Craiova, c., S. **Romania**, in Wallachia; tr. ctr.; agr. processing, textiles, engin., chemicals; p. (1978) 230,721.

Cramlington, t., Northumberland, **Eng.**; 13 km N. of Newcastle; new t., proposed; p. 60,000.

Cranborne Chase, Wilts., **Eng.**; chalk upland of over 275 m; extension of Salisbury Plain.

Cranbrook, mkt. t., Kent, **Eng.**; hops and grain; former weaving t.; p. (1971) 16,022 (dist.).

Cranston, t., R.I., **USA**; machin., chemicals, textiles; p. (1980) 71,992.

Crater L., Ore., **USA**; in Nat. Park, is a body of water 600 m deep and 10 m across, set in a crater of an extinct volcano, c. 2,400 m high; varied flora and fauna on shore.

Craters of the Moon, dist., Idaho, **USA**; Nat. Monument of volcanic craters and cones; a. 192 km².

Crato, t., Ceara st., **Brazil**; ctr. of irrigated area producing cotton, sugar, rice; p. (1960) 27,649.

Crau, La, region, Bouches-du-Rhône dep., S.E. **France**; dry, pebbly area E. of Rhône delta; winter pasture for sheep.

Craven, dist., central Pennines, **Eng.**; relatively low limestone plateau, alt. mainly below 240 m; drained by R. Ribble to S.W., R. Aire to S.E.; sheep rearing in valleys, cattle for fattening, root and fodder crops; now forms l. gov. dist. based on Skipton and Settle; p. (1981) 47,653.

Crawley, t., l. gov. dist., West Sussex, **Eng.**; on N.W. flank of Weald, 14 km S. of Reigate; new t. (1947); engin., pharmaceuticals, metal, leather, wooden gds.; p. (1981) 73,081 (dist.), 47,508 (t.).

Crayford. *See* Bexley.

Creag Meagaidh, mtn., Lochaber, **Scot.**; alt. 1,128 m.

Crediton, mkt. t., Devon, **Eng.**; p. (1981) 6,169.

Cree, R., Wigtown, **Scot.**; flows into Wigtown Bay.

Crema, industl. and agr. t., N. **Italy**; S.E. of Milan; cath.; p. (1981) 34,610.

Cremona, t., cap. of C. prov., Lombardy, N. **Italy**; famed as a ctr. of learning and later for mnf. of violins and violas; revived in last 20 years; birthplace of Stradivari; cath.; pt. on new Milan-Adriatic Waterway; p. (1981) 80,929.

Crete (Kriti), I., E. Mediterranean, lgst. I. of **Greece**; cradle of Minoan civilisation between 1600 and 1400 B.C.; mild climate; sm. a. of cultivable land; few minerals; part of Greece since Balkan Wars (1913); cap. Iraklion; birthplace of El Greco; a. 8,379 km²; p. (1981) 502,165 (admin. reg.).

Creus, c., juts out into Mediterranean Sea, **Spain**; nr. Fr. border.

Creuse, dep., in Massif Central, **France**; soil infertile, harsh climate, limited agr.; a. 5,605 km² p. (1982) 138,500.

Crewe, t., Cheshire, **Eng.**; 32 km S.E. of Chester; lge. rly. wks.; impt. rly. junc.; aircraft and refrigerator wks., clothing, engin., motor vehicles; expanded t.; with Nantwich forms l. gov. dist.; p. (1981) 98,217.

Crewkerne, mkt. t., Somerset, **Eng.**; 13 km S.W. of Yeovil; leather gds.; grammar school (1499); p. (1981) 5,330.

Criccieth, t., Dwyfor, Gwynedd, N. **Wales**; on N. shore of Cardigan Bay; seaside resort; p. (1981) 1,570.

Cricklade, t., N. Wilts., **Eng.**; on R. Thames, 13 km N.W. of Swindon; fortified township in Saxon times; p. (1971) 22,368 (dist.).

Crieff, t., Perth and Kinross, **Scot.**; on R. Earn; summer resort; p. (1981) 5,442.

Crimea (Krym) Peninsula, juts into Black Sea, Ukrainian SSR, **USSR**; wheat, tobacco, fruit; campaign 1854–55 between Russia and Allied Forces of Turkey, Britain, France, and Sardinia was chiefly fought out here (Alma, Balaclava, and Sevastopol); tourism.

Crimmitschau, t., Karl-Marx-Stadt, **E. Germany**; nr. Zwickau; impt. textile ind.; p. (est. 1970) 29,932.

Crinan Canal, across peninsula of Argyll and Bute, S.W. **Scot.;** connects Loch Gilp with Atl. Oc.; 14 km long.

Cristóbal, dist., **Panama Canal Zone;** adjoins Colon at N. entrance to Canal; p. (1970) 11,600.

Croaghpatrick, mtns., May, **R.o.I.;** 766 m.

Croatia, constituent rep., **Yugoslavia;** stretches from Istria on Adriatic cst. to Dinaric Alps; crossed by Drava and Sava Rs.; traditional agr. being replaced by new inds.; impt. aluminium wks. based on local bauxite; chemicals, shipbldg.; new oilfields supply 70 per cent of Yugoslavia's needs; cap. Zagreb; a. 56,524 km²; p. (1971) 4,422,564.

Crocodile R. See Limpopo.

Cromarty, burgh, Ross and Cromarty, **Scot.;** N.E. cst. of Black Isle; offshore oil platforms at Nigg, C.Firth; p. (1981) 685.

Cromer, t., North Norfolk, **Eng.;** on N. cst. of E. Anglia; seaside resort; p. (1981) 6,192.

Cromford, v., Derbys., **Eng.;** Richard Arkwright's first waterpowered mill (1771); cotton.

Crompton, t., Gtr. Manchester, **Eng.;** 3 km S. of Rochdale; cotton, engin., elec. lamps; p. (1981) 19,938.

Crook and Willington, ts., former U.D., Wear Valley, Durham, **Eng.;** varied inds. to replace coal mng.; p. (1981) 21,619.

Crosby, t., Sefton, Merseyside, **Eng.;** on Liverpool Bay 5 km N. of Bootle, Seaforth container pt.; residtl.; seaside resort; p. (1981) 53,660.

Cross, R., S.E. **Nigeria;** rises in Cameroon Highlands, flows W. and S. into G. of Guinea at Calabar; useful inland waterway; 640 km long.

Cross Fell, mtn., Cumbria, **Eng.;** on E. border of co.; alt. 894 m; highest point of the Pennines.

Crotone, t., S. **Italy;** pt. on E. cst. Calabria; electro-chemicals and metallurgical inds.; on site of anc. Crotona founded as Greek col.; home of Pythagoras; p. (1981) 58,281.

Crowland, t., Lincs., **Eng.;** mkt. t. in the Fens, on R. Welland; 8th-cent. abbey ruins.

Crows Nest Pass, B.C., Alberta, **Canada;** southernmost pass across Canadian Rocky Mtns.; used by rly. from Medicine Hat to Syokane (USA); summit 1,360 m.

Croydon, residtl. t., **Eng.;** now outer bor. Greater London; inc. Coulsdon and Purley; lt. inds.; major office ctr.; p. (1981) 316,557.

Crummock Water, L. Dist., Cumbria, **Eng.;** ribbon L.

Csepel, sub., Budapest, **Hungary;** iron and steel, oil refining, leather, paper; p. incorporated with Budapest 1950.

Csongrad, mkt. t., agr. dist., **Hungary;** at junc. of Rs. Tisza and Körös; p. (1970) 20,331.

Cuba, I., indep. rep., **W.I.;** cap. Havana; lies within tropics; highly fertile although half land a. is mtnous.; exp. sugar, nickel, tobacco, rum, citrus fruits; revolution (1959) reoriented economic and political connections away from USA towards USSR; 70 per cent of cultivated land in state farms or cooperatives; recent attempts to diversify economy but sugar still mainstay; a. 114,494 km²; p. (est. 1984) 9,966,000.

Cubatão, t., **Brazil;** N.E. of Santos; rapidly growing t. from industl. expansion; hydro-electric, oil refinery, petro-chems., new integrated steel wks. to aid vehicle ind. of São Paulo; p. (est. 1980) 66,000.

Cuckfield, mkt. t., Mid Sussex, West Sussex, **Eng.;** p. (1981) 28,254.

Cuckmere, R., Sussex, **Eng.;** passes through S. Downs in beautiful gap; length 37 km.

Cúcuta, t., cap. of Norte de Santander, **Colombia;** close to Venezuelan border; nr. oilfield; destroyed by earthquake, 1875; new planned t.; p. (est. 1979) 376,625.

Cuddalore, spt., Tamil Nadu, **India;** nr. Pondicherry; exp. oilseeds, cottons; p. (1981) 127,625.

Cuddapah, t., Andhra Pradesh, **India;** cotton, cloth factories, millet, rice; p. (1981) 103,125.

Cudworth, South Yorks., **Eng.;** p. (1981) 9,361.

Cuenca, t., cap. of Azuay prov., 3rd. c. of **Ecuador;** in fertile agr. basin of Andes; sugar, tyres, flour mills, Panama hats; p. (1982) 272,397.

Cuenca, agr. and mng. prov., central **Spain;** furniture, leather, paper; a. 17,063 km²; p. (1981) 215,973.

Cuenca, t., cap of C. prov., **Spain;** on gorge above R. Júcar; mkt. t.; famed in mediaeval times for silver and cloth mnfs.; p. (1981) 41,791.

Cuernavaca, t., cap. of Morelos st., central **Mexico;** anc. Indian t. captured by Cortes; tourist resort; univ.; p. (1979) 241,337.

Cuiabá, t., cap. of Mato Grosso st., **Brazil;** ctr.

pastoral a.; gold and diamonds produced; galena deposit nearby; p. (est. 1970) 99,000.

Cuillin Hills, mtns., I. of Skye, **Scot.;** attaining 992 m in Sgurr Alasdair.

Culiacán, c., of Sinaloa, N.W. **Mexico;** anc. c.; Pacific pt. Altata; p. (1979) 324,292.

Culloden Moor, 10 km E. of Inverness, **Scot.;** defeat of Prince Charles Edward Stuart's highlanders by duke of Cumberland's forces (1746).

Culross, royal burgh, Dunfermline, **Scot.;** belongs to Nat. Trust; abbey; p. (1971) 523.

Culver City, t., Cal., **USA;** sub. of Los Angeles; lge. motion-picture plant; electronic equipment, machin., chemicals, tools; p. (1980) 38,139.

Cumaná, c., N.E. **Venezuela;** pt. on Caribbean; European settlement since 1510; exp. coffee, cacao; sardine canning; airpt.; p. (est. 1980) 168,000.

Cumaná, G., N. cst., **Venezuela.**

Cumberland, former co., **Eng.;** now part of Cumbria non-met. co.

Cumberland, industl. t., Md., **USA;** on Potomac R.; iron and steel, tyres, glassware; p. (1980) 25,933 (t.), 107,782 (met. a.).

Cumberland Gap, Ky., **USA;** ch. break in high E. wall of Cumberland plateau; gives access from upper Tennessee valley to Cumberland and Ohio valleys; impt. routeway in colonisation of Ky.

Cumberland Is., off cst. of Queensland, **Australia.**

Cumberland Plateau, mtn. region, Ky., Tenn., Ala., **USA;** forms S.W. zone of Appalachian mtn. system terminating abruptly towards Tennessee valley to E., Cumberland valley to W.; drained W. by tribs. of Cumberland and Ohio Rs; composed of horizontal sandstones overlying coal; thinly populated by backward farming communities except where mng. ts. occur in valleys cut down to coal; mainly between 360–900 m.

Cumberland R., Tenn. and Ky., **USA;** trib. of Ohio R., rises in C. plateau; upper course forested; crosses coal-mng. a. and fertile agr. valley; part of Tenn. Valley Authority scheme; hydroelec. power; 1,104 km long.

Cumbernauld, new t. (1955), Strathclyde Reg., **Scot.;** to house 50,000 overspill from Glasgow; adding machines; p. (1981) 48,207; with Kilsyth forms larger l. gov. dist.; p. (1981) 61,707.

Cumbrae, Gt. and Little, Is., in F. of Clyde, off cst. of Cunninghame, **Scot.**

Cumbria, non-met. co., N.W. **Eng.;** centred on L. Dist. where rugged glaciated scenery encourages tourism, sheep-farming, forestry and water storage; Cumberland coalfield on W. cst. where declining heavy inds. being replaced by new lt. inds.; major ts. Carlisle and Barrow; a. 6,809 km²; p. (1981) 483,427.

Cumbrian Mtns., L. Dist., Cumbria, **Eng.**

Cumnock and Doone Valley, l. gov. dist., Strathclyde Reg., **Scot.,** hilly dist. S. of Glasgow; p. (1981) 45,509.

Cundinamarca, dep., **Colombia;** contains many Andean Ls. and the fed. cap Bogotá; a. 23,585 km²; p. (est. 1979) 1,226,521.

Cunene. See Kunene R.

Cuneo, prov., **Italy;** a. 7,433 km²; p. (1981) 548,452.

Cuneo, t., cap. of C. prov., Piedmont, **Italy;** mkt. for prod. of surrounding a.; withstood many sieges under the rule of house of Savoy; p. (1981) 55,875.

Cunninghame, l. gov. dist., Strathclyde Reg., **Scot.;** borders F. of Clyde and inc. I. of Arran; p. (1981) 138,265.

Cupar, royal burgh, North East Fife, **Scot.;** on R. Eden, W. of St. Andrews; linen; sugar-beet; p. (1981) 6,642.

Curaçao, I. (Neth. Antilles), off N. cst. **Venezuela;** major ctr. for refining and trans-shipping Venezuelan oil; picturesque Dutch architecture in cap. Willemstad; a. 544 km²; p. (est. 1972) 150,008.

Curepipe, t., central **Mauritius;** health resort; p. (1983) 57,613.

Curicó, t., **Chile;** agr. and comm. ctr.; earthquake 1928; p. (est. 1970) 96,418.

Curitiba, c., cap. of Paraná st., **Brazil;** univ.; industl. and comm. ctr. at c. 900 m; coffee, maté, chemicals, pharmaceutical and forest prods., foodstuffs; p. (est. 1980) 943,400.

Curragh, plain, Kildare, **R.o.I.;** turf; racecourse.

Curtis I., Queensland, Australia; low volcanic I.; wooded; cattle.

Curzola. See Korčula.

Cuttack, t., Orissa st., India; on Mahanadi R.; long famous for gold and silver filigree work; p. (1981) 269,950 (t.), 327,412 (met. a.).

Cuxhaven, spt., Lower Saxony, W. Germany; outport of Hamburg at the mouth of R. Elbe; fine harbour; p. (est. 1983) 57,800.

Cuyahoga Falls, t., Ohio, USA; industl. and residtl.; p. (1980) 43,890.

Cuzco, dep., Peru; inc. Central Cordilleras, reaching c. 5,800 m; tropical climate; agr. varies with alt.; minerals; cap. C.; a. 144,304 km²; p. (est. 1969) 742,100.

Cuzco, t., cap. of C. dep., S. Peru; in Andes at alt. 3,418 m in valley of Urubamba R.; once cap of Incas; sacked by Francisco Pizarro 1533; cath., ruins of Inca fortress; tr. ctr. for agr. prod.; p. (1981) 181,604.

Cwmmamman, t., Dinefwr, Dyfed, Wales; on R. Loughor; p. (1981) 3,721.

Cwmbran, t., Torfaen, Gwent, Wales; in valley of Avon-Lwyd, 8 km N. of Newport; new t. (1949); motor accessories, wire, elec. gds., bricks, tiles, pipes; p. (1981) 44,309.

Cwm Dyli, Gwynedd, Wales; hydroelec. sta.

Cyclades (Kirkádhes), gr. of about 220 Is., Greece; rugged and barren csts, conceal sheltered agr. valleys; ch. t. and pt. Hermoupolis; a. 2,650 km²; p. (1981) 88,458.

Cynon Valley, l. gov. dist., Mid Glamorgan, Wales; inland valley inc. Aberdare and Mountain Ash; p. (1981) 67,188.

Cyprus, Rep. of, I., indep. state, E. Mediterranean, 64 km S. of Turkey; N., most developed a., inc. main pt. of Famagusta, occupied by Turkey from 1974; indep. st. of Turkish Rep. of Cyprus declared (1983) but only recognised by Turkey; varied csts., limestone hills in N., forested mtns. in S., central plains of Messarois in which cap. Nicosia is situated; agr. employs 30 per cent of p.; many irrigation schemes also aid soil and water conservation; land reform programmes to reduce fragmentation of holdings; copper in Troodos mtns. but asbestos of increasing importance; lt. inds. and tourism helping to restructure economy but agr. provides over 50 per cent of exp., inc. wine, citrus fruit, vegetables; a. 9,251 km²; p. (est. 1984) 659,000.

Cyrenaica, prov., Libya; impt. region in anc. times; Greek col. 7th cent. B.C., Roman prov. 1st cent. B.C., captured by Arabs A.D. 642, part of Ottoman Empire 16th cent.; animal grazing, dates, oilwells; a. 854,700 km²; p. (est. 1963) 350,024.

Czechoslovak Socialist Republic (ČSSR), fed. two-rep. st. (Czech Socialist Rep. and Slovak Socialist Rep.); Central Europe; ch. ts. Prague (cap.) Brno, Bratislava, Ostrava, Plzen; Rs. Danube, Elbe, Vltava, Oder of gr. economic importance for landlocked cty.; inds. highly developed; high standard of living; coal, non-ferrous metals, little petroleum; hydroelec. power; a. 127,897 km²; p. (est. 1984) 15,558,000.

Czeladz, t., S. W. Poland; coal; p. (1970) 31,800.

Czernowitz. See Chernovtsy.

Czestochowa, c., Katowice prov., S. Poland; on Warta R.; rly. and industl. ctr.; iron and steel, textiles; celebrated religious ctr.; monastery; p. (est. 1983) 244,100.

D

Dacca, c., cap. of Bangladesh; on Buriganga R., old channel of Ganges; jute, muslin, paper mnfs.; medical radioisotope ctr.; univ.; p. (1981) 3,430,312.

Dabrowa Gornicza, t., Katowice, Poland; coal, zinc, iron ore; p. (est. 1983) 141,600.

Dachau, t., Bavaria, W. Germany; paper, elec. gds., brewing; concentration camp during last war; p. (est. 1983) 33,400.

Dachstein, mtn., Salzkammergut, Austria; alt. 2,998 m.

Dacorum, l. gov. dist., Herts., Eng.; a. of Chilterns inc. Tring, Berkhamsted and Hemel Hempstead; p. (1981) 128,801.

Dadra and Nagar Haveli, union terr., India;

admin. ctr. Silvassa; a. 490 km²; p. (est. 1971) 74,170.

Dagenham, dist. former M.B., Eng.; now forms part of Greater London bor. of Barking; on N. bank of R. Thames with riverside Ford motor works.

Dagestan, Caucasian aut rep., RSFSR; mtnous.; cap. Makhachkala; cotton, orchards and vineyards; machin., engin. oil; a. 50,246 km²; p. (1970) 1,429,000.

Dagupen, t., Pangasiman, Luzon, Philippines; on Lingayen Bay; comm. ctr.; p. (est. 1970) 89,000.

Daharki Mari, t., Pakistan; 560 km N.E. of Karachi; fertiliser plant.

Dahlak Archipelago, Ethiopia; in Red Sea; only 2 Is. inhabited; noted for pearl fishing.

Dahomey. See Benin, People's Rep. of.

Daimiel, mkt. t., Ciudad Real, Spain; cheeses, oil, wine; p. (1981) 16,260.

Dakar, spt., cap. of Senegal, Senegambia, W. Africa; S.E. of C. Verde behind Gorée I. on Atl. cst.; exp. groundnuts; some industl. development; free tr. zone, international airport; univ. and medical ctr.; p. (est. 1977) 581,000.

Dakhla, oasis, Libyan Desert, Egypt; 272 km S.W. of Asyût; dates, olives; stage on caravan route from Cyrenaica to Upper Egypt; site of New Valley Project for irrigation.

Dalälven, R., S. central Sweden; length 520 km, used for timber transport.

Da Lat (Dalat), t., Vietnam; 224 km N.E. Ho Chiminh City; in Annamite hills; nuclear reactor (1963); airport; p. (1973) 105,072.

Dalbeattie, burgh, Stewartry, Scot.; granite, dairy prod., gloves; p. (1981) 3,891.

Dalby, t., Queensland, Australia; 1961 oil strike of Moonie oilfield; rich volcanic soils aid grain and beef production; p. (1976) 8,997.

Dalgety, t., on Fife cst., Scot.; new t. proposed; p. 10,000.

Dalkeith, burgh, Midlothian, Scot.; 10 km S.E. of Edinburgh; mkt. t.; p. (1981) 11,077.

Dalkey, t., Dublin, R.o.I.; on E. cst.; 6 km N. of Wicklow border; resort; residtl.; p. 5,526.

Dallas, c., Texas, USA; in cotton- and grain-growing a.; machin., aircraft, petroleum prod.; univ.; scene of assassination of President Kennedy (1963); p. (1980) 904,000 (c.), 2,975,000 (met. a. with Fort Worth).

Dalmatia, region of Yugoslavia and prov. of Croatia, N.E. Adriatic cst.; high Karst plateaux; olive oil, wine; tourism; contains many resorts; a. 12,732 km²; p. 622,000.

Daltonganj, t., Bihar, India; on R. Koël; coal, cement; p. (1961) 25,270.

Dalton-in-Furness, t., Cumbria, Eng.; limestone quarrying, textiles; abbey ruins; p. (1981) 10,931.

Daman (Damão), spt., India; 160 km N. Bombay; fishing, ship-bldg., cotton; former Portuguese settlement; p. (est. 1971), 17,317.

Damanhûr, t., Egypt; on W. margin of Nile delta, 40 km S.E. of Alexandria; mkt. for local agr. produce; p. (1976) 170,633.

Damaraland, region, South-West Africa; high plateau; admin. by Rep. of S. Africa; pt., Walvis Bay; cattle rearing.

Damascus (Arabic Esh-Sham), cap. c., Syria; 91 km S.E. of its pt. Beirut; claims to be oldest continuously inhabited c. in world; metal-wk., glass, cement; univ.; p. (est. 1982) 1,036,000.

Dambovitta (Dimbovita), R., Romania; rises in Mt. Omul (Transylvanian Alps), flows S. through Bucharest to R. Danube, via impt. oilfields; 320 km long.

Damietta (Dumyât), t., Lower Egypt; on main distributary of R. Nile delta; cotton; p. (est. 1970) 98,000.

Dammam, spt. on Persian G., Saudi Arabia; oil pt.; planned industl. growth; p. (1974) 127,844.

Damodar, R., Bihar, India; flows through India's major coalfields; valley forms ch. industl. a. of India; multipurpose scheme for hydro-electric power, irrigation and flood control.

Dampier, spt., W. Australia; on Indian Oc.; new pt. (1965) for shipping iron ore from Mt. Tom Price and Mt. Wittenoom; pelletising plant; p. (est. 1976) 2,727.

Dampier Archipelago, gr. of sm. Is., off N.W. Australia, in Indian Oc.

Dampier Strait, Bismarck Archipelago, channel between W. New Britain and Umboi I.

Dampier Strait, channel between Irian Jaya and Waigeo I.

Danakil Land (Dankalia), coastal desert a., mainly in Ethiopia, but partly in Djibouti; includes D. depression; potash; sm. pt. and road projected.

Da-nang (Tourane), c., S. **Vietnam**; ch. pt. of Annam on S. China Sea; exp. agr. prod.; p. (1973) 492,194.

Danao, t., Cebu, **Philippines**; rice and sugar dist.; p. (est. 1970) 45,500.

Danapur, t., Bihar, **India**; on Ganges R., nr. Patna; p. (1961) 70,766.

Dandenong, t., Victoria, **Australia**; 30 km E. of Melbourne; growing industl. ctr.; p. (1976) 48,440.

Dandong (Antung), c., Liaoning, **China**; pt. on Yalu R., 24 km. from mouth; Chinese frontier sta. on main rly. from China into N. Korea; mkt. for agr. prod.; lumbering; p. (est. 1968) 450,000.

Dannemora, t., **Sweden**; 40 km N.E. of Uppsala; iron ore worked since 1579; p. (est. 1970) 4,147.

Danube (Donau), R., second longest R. in Europe; rises in Black Forest, Germany, and flows E. into Black Sea; forms comm. highway; Iron Gate hydro-electric and navigation project inaugurated by 1978; increased no. of dams causing concern with conservationists; linked by canals with Main, Rhine and Oder; completion of Rhine-Main-Danube canal and Danube-Black Sea canal (1984) now creates Trans-Europe Waterway of 3,500 km.; Vienna, Budapest, Belgrade, and other lge. cs. on its banks; 2,706 km long.

Danube-Tisa Canal, N. **Yugoslavia**; irrigation, flood control, navigable: 261 km long.

Danville, t., Ill., **USA**; coal; mftg. tr.; p. (1980) 38,985.

Danville, t., Va., **USA**; cotton, tobacco; p. (1980) 45,642 (t.), 111,789 (met. a.).

Danzig. See **Gdańsk**.

Dap Cau, t., **Vietnam**; bamboo pulp and paper factories.

Darbhanga, t., Bihar, **India**; rice, oil-seeds, grain, sugar tr.; univ.; p. (1981) 176,301.

Dardanelles, strait between European and Asian Turkey, connecting Aegean Sea with Sea of Marmara; (the anc. Hellespont), 64 km long.

Daresbury, v., Cheshire, **Eng.**; birthplace of C. L. Dodgson (Lewis Carroll).

Dar-es-Salaam, spt., cap. of **Tanzania**; univ.; textile mill projected; oil refining; pipeline to Ndola, Zambia; naval base and Tanzam rly. built with Chinese aid; p. (1978) 870,020.

Darien, region, **Panama**; tortoiseshell, pearls, gold, but agr. is basis of economy; cap. La Palma; a. 15,540 km²; p. (est. 1973) 25,000.

Darien, Gulf of, inlet of Caribbean Sea; separates Colombia and Panama.

Darjeeling, hill t., W. Bengal, **India**; tea, quinine; Himalayan resort; p. (1984) 63,600.

Darkhan, new t., **Mongolia**; on R. Hara; industl.

Darlaston, t., West Midlands, **Eng.**; nuts, bolts, fabricated steel mnfs., drop forgings, car components; pig iron plant closed after 100 years of production.

Darling Downs, plateau, S.E. **Queensland, Australia**; rich agr. region, fertile black soils aid wheat growing; ch. t. Toowoomba.

Darling R., N.S.W., **Australia**; longest trib. of the Murray, forming part of the Murray-Darling Rs. scheme for irrigation and flood control; 2,723 km long.

Darlington, t., l. gov. dist., Durham, **Eng.**; bridge bldg., woollen yarn mnf., engin., rly. wagons, steel wks.; p. (1981) 97,788 (dist.).

Darmstadt, c., Hesse, **W. Germany**; cas.; comm. ctr.; metallurgical prods., paper, machin., radio, chemicals, plastics; technical univ.; p. (est. 1983) 137,800.

Dart, R., Devon, **Eng.**; rises in Dartmoor, flows S. into English Channel at Dartmouth; picturesque estuary; 74 km long.

Dartford, t., l. gov. dist., Kent, **Eng.**; nr. S. cst. of Thames estuary; Dartford-Purfleet road tunnel (1963); engin., chemicals, quarrying, paper; mkt.; p. (1981) 78,236 (dist.).

Dartmoor, high granite plateau, S.W. Devon, **Eng.**; rough moorland; sheep, cattle, and wild ponies; granite tors; Nat. Park; tourism; granite quarries, reservoirs; prison at Princetown; china clay (Lee Moor) now extends into Nat. Park; recent discovery of tungsten, lgst. deposit in W. Europe but conflicts with conservation; a. 583 km²; hgst. point High Willays, 622 m.

Dartmouth, spt., S. Devon, **Eng.**; on W. of estuary of R. Dart; Royal Naval College; pottery; yachting, holiday resort; p. (1981) 6,298.

Dartmouth, industl. spt., sub. of Halifax, Nova

Scotia, **Canada**; oil refining, shipbldg.; p. (1971) 64,002.

Darvel, burgh, Strathclyde Reg., **Scot.**; on R. Irvine, 13 km E. Kilmarnock; birthplace of Sir Alexander Fleming, discoverer of penicillin; p. (1981) 3,455.

Darwen, t., N.E. Lancs., **Eng.**; on flank of Rossendale Fells, 5 km S. of Blackburn; tile and glaze bricks, paint, wallpaper, plastics; p. (1981) 30,048.

Darwin, c., cap. N.T., **Australia**; pt. and regional ctr., invigorated in the 1950s by nearby uranium mng. (Rum Jungle); devastated by cyclone 1974, rebuilding complete by 1979; international airpt.; p. (1976) 41,374.

Daryal Gorge, Caucasus, Georgian SSR, **USSR**; deep gorge (1,800 m) cut by Terek R.; identified as the classical Caspian or Iberian Gates from which distances were reckoned; forms part of Georgian military road.

Dashava, settlement on Lvov oblast, W. Ukraine, **USSR**; ctr. of rich natural gas field and starting point of gas pipeline to Kiev and Moscow, built after second world war.

Datia, t. Madhya-Pradesh, **India**; stone-walled, palaces; p. (1981) 60,991.

Datong (Tatung), c., Shanxi prov., **China**; impt. coalfield; steam and diesel locomotives; p. (est. 1983) 926,000.

Datteln, t., N. Rhine-Westphalia, **W. Germany**; coal, leather, iron; p. (est. 1983) 37,300.

Daugavpils, t., Latvian SSR, **USSR**; on Dvina R.; textiles, engin., rly. repair wks., food prods.; p. (est. 1980) 117,000.

Dauphiné Alps, mtn. range, S.E. **France**; 24 peaks over 3,050 m.

Daura, t., nr. Baghdad, **Iraq**; oil refining.

Davangere, t., Karnataka, S. **India**; on 600 m plateau in Indian Penin.; p. (1981) 196,621.

Davao, t., Mindanao, **Philippines**; pt. for sugar; p. (1980) 610,375.

Davenport, t., Iowa, **USA**; on Mississippi R. where it is spanned by bridges to Rock Island, Molise and East Molise; rly., comm. and industl. ctr.; p. (1980) 103,000 (c.), 384,000 (met. a.).

Daventry, t., l. gov. dist., Northampton, **Eng.**; 14 km S.E. of Rugby; boot-mkg., lt. engin.; wireless-transmission sta.; expanded t.; p. (1981) 57,656 (dist.).

David, t., cap. of Chiriqui prov., **Panama**; timber coffee, cacao, sugar; p. (1970) 58,827.

Davis Strait, channel between Greenland and Baffin I., N.W. Terr., **Canada**; connects Atl. Oc. with Baffin Bay; navigable.

Davos-Platz and Dörfli, ts., Grisons, **Switzerland**; Alpine winter resorts; alt. 1,478 m; p. (1970) 10,238.

Dawley, t., The Wrekin, Shrops., **Eng.**; on S.E. flank of the Wrekin: ironwks., pipe, cement, roadstone, asphalt and brick wks., engin.; new t. (1963); p. (1981) 49,137. See **Telford**.

Dawlish, t., Teignbridge, S. Devon, **Eng.**; on S. cst. between estuaries of Rs. Exe and Teign; seaside resort; flower tr.; p. (1981) 10,755.

Dawson, t., Yukon Terr., **Canada**; on Yukon R., nr. Klondike goldfields; asbestos mng. projected 1968; p. (1971) 500.

Dayton, c., Ohio, **USA**; on Great Miami R.; univ.; aircraft, elec. machin., rubber gds.; p. (1980) 203,000 (c.), 830,000 (met. a.).

Daytona Beach, t., Fla., **USA**; resort; shipping, ctr.; motor speed trials; p. (1980) 259,000 (met. a.).

De Aar, t., rly. junc., Cape Prov., **S. Africa**; 500 m. from Cape Town; rlys. from N.W. (Luderitz, Walvis Bay) and S.E. (Pt. Elizabeth, E. London) join Cape Town to Johannesburg trunk rly.; p. (est. 1967) 16,640.

Dead Sea, salt-water L. between **Israel** and **Jordan**; surface 392 m below level of Mediterranean; a. 881 km², length 76 km, greatest width 15 km, greatest depth 399 m; receives waters of Jordan; high mineral content, very saline; Israeli plans to link to Mediterranean Sea by underground canal to generate hydro-electric power with difference in height.

Deal, anc. pt., E. Kent, **Eng.**; on S.E. cst., 11 km N.E. Dover; opposite Goodwin Sands; seaside resort; lifeboat service; p. (1981) 25,989.

Dean, Forest of, Gloucs., **Eng.**; between Wye and Severn Rs.; former Royal Forest; Forestry Commission plantations; former coal-mng. a.; tourism; new lt. industl. estates; now forms l. gov. dist.; p. (1981) 72,651.

Dearborn, t., Mich., **USA**; birthplace of Henry Ford; p. (1980) 90,660.

Death Valley, depression, Cal., **USA**; N. of Mojave Desert, 240 km N.E. of Los Angeles; completely arid; floor covered with saline deposits; tourist attraction; depth of valley floor 84 m below sea-level.

Deauville, seaside resort, Calvados dep., N. **France**; on Eng. Channel; racecourse, casino; p. (1968) 5,370.

Debra Markos, t., cap. of Gojam prov., **Ethiopia**; vegetable oil extraction; p. (est. 1980) 40,686.

Debrecen, t., **Hungary**; 183 km E. of Budapest; univ.; ctr. of pastoral dist.; fairs; pharmaceutics, medical instruments, furniture; ctr. of Calvinism; p. (est. 1979) 191,000.

Decatur, t., Ala., **USA**; steel textiles; industl. development after establishment of Tenn. Valley Authority; p. (1980) 42,002.

Decatur, t., Ill., **USA**; on Sangamon R.; industl.; rly. engin., food processing; univ.; p. (1980) 94,081 (t.), 131,375 (met. a.).

Decazeville, t., Aveyron, S. **France**; ctr. of sm. coalfield (no longer worked), metallurgy; p. (1982) 9,204.

Deccan, The, upland of S. **India**, bounded by the Narbada and Kistna Rs.; coincides with Maharashtra st.; area of very fertile lava soils; impt. cotton-growing region.

Dee, R., N. **Wales** and Cheshire, **Eng.**; 144 km long; lge. silted estuary, use for water storage planned.

Dee, R., Kincardine and Deeside, **Scot.**; picturesque, tourism; 139 km long.

Dehiwala-Mt Lavina, t., **Sri Lanka**; on cst. S. of Colombo; p. (est. 1983) 181,000.

Dehra Dun, t., Uttar Pradesh, **India**; scientific research ctr.; sawmills; p. (1981) 211,416 (t.), 293,010 (met. a.).

Deir-ez-Zor, t., **Syria**; on Euphrates R.; on motor route between Baghdad and Baghdad; p. (1970) 66,143.

Dej, t., **Romania**; on Somesul R., distillery; p. (est. 1970) 30,869.

Delabole, v., Cornwall, **Eng.**; on N.W. flank of Bodmin Moor; slate quarries.

Delagoa Bay, natural harbour, **Moçambique**; ch. pt. Maputo.

Delaware, st., **USA**; admitted to Union 1787, popular name First State; st. flower Peach Blossom, st. bird Blue Hen Chicken; low-lying a. of Atl. cst. plain; agr., lumber; fertilisers, minerals, leather, chemicals, machin.; cap. Dover; ch. pt. Wilmington; a. 6,138 km²; p. (1980) 595,000.

Delaware Bay, inlet, Atl. cst., **USA**; drowned estuary of R. Delaware, extends 128 km inland from C. May into heart of highly industl. a. of Philadelphia.

Delaware, R., flows between N.Y. st., **USA** along the Penns. border, through N.J. to Delaware Bay; 504 km long.

Delft, c., pt., S. Holland, **Neth.**; on Schie R. (canalised), nr. Rotterdam; technical univ.; ceramics (delft-ware), tool mftg., precision instruments; 13th cent. Old church and 15th cent. New church; p. (1982) 85,268.

Delhi, c., cap. of **India**; on watershed between Rs. Indus and Ganges; made up of Old Delhi with walls, palace, and fort, and New Delhi with admin. ctr.; univ.; p. (1981) 273,036 (New Delhi), 4,884,234 (c.), 5,729,283 (met. a.).

Delhi, union terr., **India**; hot and arid region between Indus valley and alluvial plain of Ganges; irrigation to support agr.; New Delhi and Old Delhi ch. ctrs.; a. 1,497 km²; p. (1981) 6,220,406.

Delitzsch, t., Leipzig, **E. Germany**; 26 km E. of Halle; sugar, chemicals; p. (est. 1970) 24,270.

Delmarva, peninsula, Del., **USA**; between Chesapeake Bay and Del. Bay; horticulture, poultry, forestry, fishing.

Delmenhorst, t., Lower Saxony, **W. Germany**; nr. Bremen; jute, woollens, linoleum, foodstuffs; p. (est. 1983) 71,700.

Delphi, anc. Phocis, central **Greece**; N. of G. of Corinth; famous for Delphic oracle on Mt. Parnassus.

Del Rio, t., Texas, **USA**; pt. of entry on Rio Grande; mkt. for agr. a.; grapes; exp. wool; border t., bridge to Mexico; p. (1980) 30,034.

Delyn, l. gov. dist., Clwyd, **Wales**; W. of Dee estuary inc. Holywell, Flint and Mold; p. (1981) 65,140.

Demavend, dormant volcano, **Iran**; hgst. peak in Elburz range, c. 5,673 m.

Demerara, co., **Guyana**; between Essequibo and Demerara Rs.; exp. sugar, molasses, rum.

Demerara, R., **Guyana**; drains N. to Atl. Oc.; bauxite transport.

Denain, t., Nord dep., N. **France**; industl. ctr.; p. (1982) 21,872.

Denbigh, former co., N. **Wales**; now mostly in Clwyd; sm. part in Gwynedd.

Denbigh, t., Glyndŵr, Clwyd, **Wales**; in Vale of Clwyd, 16 km S. of Rhyl; cas.; tourism; dairy prods.; birthplace of Stanley the explorer; p. (1981) 9,040.

Denby Dale, t., West Yorks., **Eng.**; 13 km W. of Barnsley; woollen textiles; earthenware pipes; p. (1981) 13,476.

Den Haag. *See* **Hague, The.**

Den Helder. *See* **Helder.**

Denholme, t., West Yorks., **Eng.**; nr. Bradford; dairying, textiles; p. (1981) 2,676.

Denizli, t., **Turkey**; 75 km S.E. of Izmir; gardens —"the Damascus of Anatolia"; nr. site of Laodica; p. (1979) 127,661.

Denmark, kingdom, N.W. **Europe**; part of Scandinavia; member of E.E.C.; consists of Jutland peninsula, Is. of Sjaelland, Fyn, Falster, Lolland, and Bornholm, and 400 smaller Is., between N. Sea and Baltic; emphasis on dairy agr., producing butter, eggs, and bacon; increasing industrialisation; industl. prods. now account for 62 per cent of exp.; cap. Copenhagen; a. 42,932 km²; p. (est. 1984) 5,141,000.

Denny and Dunipace, burgh, Falkirk, **Scot.**; 10 km W. of Falkirk; steel castings, precast concrete, p. (1981) 23,172.

Dent du Midi, mtn. gr., Vaud can., S.W. **Switzerland**; rises to 10,694 ft. in Haut Cime.

Denton, t., Gtr. Manchester, **Eng.**; nr. Manchester; felt-hat mkg.; p. (1981) 37,729.

Denton, mkt. t., Texas, **USA**; univs.; food processing; p. (1980) 48,063.

D'Entrecasteaux Is., volcanic gr. off S.E. New Guinea, Pac. Oc., part of **Papua-New Guinea**.

Denver, c., cap. of Col., **USA**; on E. slope of Rockies, on South Platte R.; univs.; oil, electronic equipment, mng. machin., livestock, canning; tourism; p. (1980) 492,000 (c.), 1,621,000 (met. a. with Boulder).

Deogarh, t., Bihar, **India**; temples, place of pilgrimage; p. (1961) 30,813.

Deptford. *See* **Lewisham.**

Dera Ghazi Khan, t., **Pakistan**; on W. bank of Indus R.; silk, brass; p. (1961) 47,105.

Dera Ismail Khan, t., **Pakistan**; on Indus R.; admin. ctr., caravan ctr.; p. (1961) 46,100.

Derbent, c., S.E. Dagestan, **RSFSR**; on Caspian Sea; textiles, fish inds.; glass; oil and natural gas nearby; anc. c. founded by Persians; p. (est. 1970) 50,000.

Derby, c., l. gov. dist., Derbys., **Eng.**; on R. Derwent; general engin., aero-engines, man-made fibres; p. (1981) 215,736.

Derbyshire, non-met. co., **Eng.**; much of a. occupied by Pennines and Peak Dist. Nat. Park; coalfield and industl. a. in E.; forms part of Manchester met. a. in N.W.; co. t. Derby; a. 2,631 km²; p. (1981) 906,929.

Derbyshire, North East, l. gov. dist., Derbys., **Eng.**; industl. a. of Clay Cross and Dronfield; p. (1981) 96,547.

Derbyshire, South, l. gov. dist., Derbys., **Eng.**; a. S. of Derby and inc. Repton and Swadlincote; p. (1981) 67,669.

Derg, Lough, in basin of R. Shannon, **R.o.I.**; separating Galway and Clare from Tipperary.

Derg, L., Donegal, **R.o.I.**, with cave on I. visited by R.C. pilgrims and known as "St Patrick's Purgatory".

Derwent, lgst R. of Tasmania, **Australia**; flows to Storm Bay via Hobart; hydroelec. power; 190 km long.

Derwent, R., Derbys., **Eng.**; trib. of R. Trent; length 96 km.

Derwent, R., North Yorks, Humberside, **Eng.**; trib. of R. Ouse; length 91 km.

Derwentside, l. gov. dist., Durham, **Eng.**; inc. Consett, Stanley and surrounding a.; p. (1981) 88,132.

Derwentwater, L., Cumbria, **Eng.**; 5 km long.

Desaguadero, R., **Bolivia**; outlet of L. Titicaca; used for irrigation; 320 km long.

Desborough, t., Northants., **Eng.**; boot and shoe mnfs., iron mng.; p. (1981) 6,393.

Des Moines, c., cap. of Iowa st., **USA**; in heart of

corn belt; transport and industl. ctr.; univ.; p. (1980) 191,000 (c.), 338,000 (met. a.).

Des Moines, R., Iowa, **USA;** trib. of Mississippi rising in Minn.; 880 km long.

Desna, R., main trib. of Dnieper R., **USSR;** navigable below Bryansk; 1,184 km long.

Des Plaines, t., Ill., **USA;** sub. of Chicago on Des Plaines R.; p. (1980) 53,568.

Dessau, t., Halle, **E. Germany;** at confluence of Mulde and Elbe Rs.; cas.; machin., rly. carriages, paper, sugar, chemicals; route ctr.; p. (1983) 103,738.

Detmold, t., N. Rhine–Westphalia, **W. Germany;** cas.; paints, wood inds.; p. (est. 1983) 67,000.

Detroit, ch. c., pt., Mich., **USA;** busy comm. and industl. ctr.; univ.; gr. grain mart; and ctr. of the "Ford" motor-car wks., aeroplanes, military tanks, synthetic diamonds, pharmaceutics, tools, chemicals, steel; lgst exporting t. on Great Lakes; 850 murders per year; p. (1980) 1,203,000 (c.), 4,353,000 (met. a.).

Detroit, R., channel between L. St. Clair and L. Erie (40 km) separates st. of Mich., **USA,** from Ontario, **Canada;** carries more shipping than any other inland waterway in the world.

Deurne, t., **Belgium;** nr. Antwerp, airport; p. (est. 1972) 81,257.

Deux Sèvres, dept., Poitou-Charentes, **France;** mainly agr.; vineyards; cap. Niort; a. 6,053 km²; p. (1982) 342,500.

Deventer, t., Overijssel, **Neth.;** on IJssel R.; indstl. ctr., Hanse t. in Middle Ages; p. (est. 1982) 64,505.

Devil's Island (I. du Diable), I., Atl. Oc. off **Fr. Guiana;** former penal settlement where Dreyfus was confined in 1894.

Devils Tower, N.E. Wyo., **USA;** tower rock of volcanic origin with fluted columns of igneous rock; alt. 264 m.

Devizes, Kennet, Wilts., **Eng.;** mkt. t., on Kennet and Avon canal at foot of Marlborough Downs; bricks, tiles, bacon-curing; p. (1981) 10,629.

Devonport, spt., N. Tasmania, **Australia;** pt. for fruit dist. of R. Mersey; mnfs. primary prods.; nearby Mersey–Forth power project (1970) attracts growth; p. (1976) 19,399.

Devonport, bor., Auckland, **N.Z.;** naval base and dockyard; sub. of Auckland; p. (1971) 10,925.

Devon, non-met. co., S.W. **Eng.;** between English and Bristol Channels; attractive cstl. scenery, Nat. Parks of Dartmoor and Exmoor encourage tourism; mixed farming; modern lt. inds.; major ctrs. of p. at Plymouth, Torbay, Exeter; a. 6,713 km²; p. (1981) 952,000.

Devon, East, l. gov. dist., Devon, **Eng.;** Exmouth, Sidmouth and Seaton on cst. and inland to Honiton and Ottery St. Mary; p. (1981) 106,320.

Devon, North, l. gov. dist., **Eng.;** inc. Exmoor and ts. of Barnstaple, Ilfracombe and Lynton; p. (1981) 78,728.

Dewsbury, t., West Yorks., **Eng.;** on R. Calder, 13 km from Leeds; heavy woollens, shoddy, coalmng.; dyewks.; p. (1981) 48,339.

Dez Dam, over Dez R., Khurzistan prov., **Iran;** opened 1963.

Dezfûl, r., **Iran;** mkt. ctr.; oil fields nearby; p. (1976) 110,287.

Dhahran, spt., **Saudi-Arabia;** main oil pt. of S.A.; airpt.; College of Petroleum and Minerals; p. 12,001.

Dhanbad, t., Bihar, **India;** lead, zinc, tools, radio assembly, fertilisers; p. (1981) 120,221 (t.), 678,069 (met. a.).

Dhanushkodi, t., Tamil Nadu, **India;** on I. in Palk Strait; ferry pt. for passenger traffic from India to Sri Lanka.

Dhar, t., Madhya Pradesh, **India;** cultural and tr. ctr.; p. (1961) 28,325.

Dharmsala, hill sta., Himachal Pradesh, **India;** 160 km N.E. of Amritsar; sanatorium; c. 1,800 m; imposing mtn. scenery; p. (1981) 14,522.

Dharwar, t., Karnataka, **India;** 112 km E. of Goa; univ.; cotton mnf.; p. (1961) 77,163.

Dhaulagiri, mtn. peak, 8,172 m, **Nepal,** 4 summits in Himalayas.

Dhekélia, Cyprus; Brit. sovereign a. within Rep.; p. (1960) 3,602.

Dhufar, fertile prov., **Oman,** Arabia; sugar-cane, cattle; ch. t. Salâlah; ch. pt. Mirbat.

Dhulia, t., Khandesh dist., Maharashtra, **India;** cotton ind.; rly. ctr.; p. (1981) 210,759.

Diamante, R., Mendoza prov., **Argentina;** rises in Andes, flows E. to R. Salado; irrigates oasis of San Rafael; 320 km long.

Diamantina, t., Minas Gerais, **Brazil;** former diamond mng. ctr.; p. (est. 1970) 25,000.

Dibrugarh, t., Assam, **India;** former terminus of rail communications from Calcutta; since 1965 Indo-Pakistan war river communications disrupted; p. (1961) 58,480.

Didcot, sm. t., Oxon, **Eng.;** 16 km S. of Oxford; ordnance depots.

Diego Garcia, I., Brit. Indian Oc. Terr.; Anglo-American naval communications ctr.; c. 1,000 islanders evacuated to Mauritius 1966–71; major US military staging base projected 1975; part of Brit. Indian Oc. Terr.

Diego Suarez. See **Antsiranana.**

Dieppe, pt., Seine-Maritime, **France;** 56 km N. of Rouen; fisheries, shipbldg., machin.; cross-Channel ferry; p. (1975) 26,111.

Differdange, t., S.W. **Luxembourg;** iron ore; cattle; p. (1981) 16,700.

Digboi, N.E. Assam, **India;** oil fields and refinery; p. (1961) 35,028.

Digne, t., cap. of Alpes-de-Haute-Provence, **France;** nr. Aix; cath.; p. (1968) 14,661.

Dijôn, c., cap. Côte-d'Or, **E. France;** the Roman Divonense castrum; route ctr.; Seine-Saône watershed; wine tr.; industl. ctr.; univ., cath.; p. (1982) 145,569.

Dili, t., cap. of E. Timor, **Indonesia;** major spt.; exp. cotton, copra, coffee; p. (1970) 29,312.

Dimitrovgrad, t., **Bulgaria;** founded 1947; fertilisers, chemicals, superphosphate plant, iron, thermo-electric sta.; p. (est. 1968) 44,302.

Dimitrovo. See **Pernik.**

Dinajpur, t., **Bangladesh;** comm. ctr.; univ.; p. (1961) 37,711.

Dinan, t., Brittany, **France;** mediaeval t. above Rance R.; hosiery, brewing; holiday resort; p. (1982) 14,157.

Dinant, t., Namur, **Belgium;** on R. Meuse; mkt. t., tourist resort; exported copperware (*dinanderie*) in Middle Ages; cath., citadel (1040); p. (1968) 9,901.

Dinard, t., Brittany, **France;** resort, especially for English; p. (1982) 10,016.

Dinaric Alps, mtn. range, **Yugoslavia, Albania** and **Italy** (Trieste); extend 640 km along Adriatic; hgst. peak Durmitor, 2,515 m.

Dindigul, t., Tamil Nadu, **India;** 40 km S. of Tiruchirapalli; cigars; p. (1981) 164,103.

Dinefwr, l. gov. dist., Dyfed, **Wales;** inland a. inc. Llandovery, Llandeilo, Ammanford and Cwmamman; p. (1981) 36,717.

Dingle B., Kerry, **R.o.I.;** long inlet of sea on Atl. cst.

Dingwall, royal burgh, Ross and Cromarty, **Scot.;** at head of Cromarty F.; rly. junc.; cattle mkt.; admin. ctr.; distilling, handloom weaving; p. (1981) 4,815.

Dinslaken, t. N. Rhine-Westphalia, **W. Germany,** N. of Duisburg; coal, steel, iron, footwear, timber; oil pipeline from Wesseling under construction; p. (est. 1983) 60,400.

Diomede Is., two barren granitic islets in Bering Strait between Alaska and Siberia; accepted bdy. between Soviet and US terr.

Diredawa, t., **Ethiopia;** 40 km N. of Harar; rly. wks.; mkt and comm. ctr.; new cement wks.; p. (est. 1980) 82,024.

Dirk Hartog I., off Shark Bay, W. **Australia.**

Disko U., off W. cst. of **Greenland** in Baffin Bay; contains harbour of Godhavn, cap. N. Greenland; rendezvous for whalers; shrimp beds; a. 8,448 km².

Dismal Swamp, morass, S. Va. and N.C., **USA;** contains L. Drummond and extends 50–65 km S. from nr. Norfolk.

Diss, South Norfolk, **Eng.;** mkt. t. on R. Waveney, 45 km S.W. of Norwich; agr. implements; p. (1981) 5,423.

Distaghil, major peak, Gr. Karakoram, N. Kashmir, **Pakistan;** two summits connected by a ridge, max. alt. 7,890 m.

Distrito Federal, federal dist., **Brazil;** inc. cap. c. of Brasilia; a. 5,815 km²; p. (est. 1983) 1,434,000.

Ditchling Beacon, 10 km N. of Brighton, East Sussex, **Eng.;** hgst point of South Downs, 248 m.

Diu, spt., I., off S. cst. of Bombay, **India;** oil nearby at Kayakov; p. (1960) 14,271.

Dîwânîyah, Ad, t., **Iraq;** cap. D. prov.; on Baghdad-Basra rly.; p. (1965) 181,000 (met. a.).

Diyarbakir, c., cap. of D. prov., central **Turkey;** on Tigris R.; comm. and mnf. ctr.; flour and rice mills; the anc. Amida, old walls, gates, citadel; p. (1980) 235,617.

Djajapura (Sukarnapura), t., cap. of Irian Jaya, **Indonesia**; on Humboldt B., an inlet of Pac. Oc.

Djakarta (Batavia), c., cap. of **Indonesia**, N.W. Java; comm. ctr.; textiles; exps. rubber, tea; printing; airport; p. (est. 1983) 7,636,000.

Djambi, dist., and t., Sumatra, **Indonesia**; on E. cst. plain 160 km N.W. of Palembang; univ.; field; a. (dist.) 44,924 km²; p. (1971) 158,559 (t.).

Djerba, t. and I., **Tunisia**, at S. entrance to G. of Gabès, joined to mainland by causeway; olives, dates, textiles, pottery; a. 510 km²; p. (1975) 70,217.

Djibouti, c. cap. of **Djibouti**; rly. terminus; main pt. free pt. (1981), container terminal (1985); p. (est. 1976) 200,000.

Djibouti, Rep. of, indep. st. (1981) N.E. **Africa**; former French Somaliland, renamed Fr. Terr. of Afars and Issas 1967; extends inland from straits of Bab-el-Mandeb; economy based on trade through international p. of D.; plain, mainly below 180 m; hot, dry climate; shark and mother-of-pearl fisheries; little cultivable land; a. 23,051 km²; p. (est. 1984) 405,000 of whom 200,000 live in cap. Djibouti.

Dneprodzerzhinsk, t., Ukrainian SSR, **USSR**; W. of Dnepropetrovsk on Dnieper R.; iron and steel, engin., chemicals; hydroelec. sta. nearby; p. (est. 1980) 253,000.

Dneproges (abbrev. Dnieper hydroelectric sta.), Ukrainian SSR, **USSR**; nr. Zaporoz'ye, on Dnieper: lgst dam and power sta. in Europe; destroyed by Germans, rebuilt 1944–9.

Dnepropetrovsk, c., Ukrainian SSR, **USSR**; on R. Dnieper; univ.; impt. rly. and industl. ctr., using iron ore (from Krivoy Rog), coal (Dombas), manganese (Nikopol) and electric power from Dnieper dam; heavy machin., chemicals; p. (est. 1980) 1,083,000.

Dneprorudnyy, t., Ukrainian SSR, **USSR**; new t. on S. shore of Kakhvota reservoir; p. (1964) 6,000.

Dneprostroy. *See* **Zaporoz'ye.**

Dnieper (Dnepr), gr. R. of Ukrainian SSR, **USSR**; 3rd longest R. of Europe; rises in Valdai hills, flows into Black Sea, 2,240 km long; connected by canals to Baltic; tribs. inc. Berezina, Pripet, Desna, Orel, Samara; since erection of Dneproges dam navigable for almost entire length.

Dniester (Dnestr), R., Ukraine SSR, **USSR**; rises in Carpathians and flows into the Black Sea; 1,403 km long.

Döbeln, t., Leipzig, **E. Germany**; machin., metallurgy, wood, cigar and sugar inds.; p. (est. 1973) 27,471.

Dobrich. *See* **Tolbukhin.**

Dobruja, historic region, S.E. **Europe**; along Black Sea cst., S.E. Romania, and N.E. Bulgaria; mainly agr.; ch. pt. Constanta.

Dobšiná, t., **ČSSR**; cave containing ice-field of 0·8 ha; asbestos, iron ore; p. 5,300.

Dodecanese (S. Sporades), gr. of some 20 Greek Is. (originally 12) in S. Aegean Sea; most impt. are Rhodes, Cos, and Leros; Italian 1912–46; p. (1981) 145,071.

Dodoma, proposed new cap. of **Tanzania**; at geographical ctr. of T. in rural a.; transfer planned for 1983.

Dodworth, t., South Yorks., **Eng.**; nr. Barnsley; coal; p. (1981) 4,922.

Dogger Bank, sandbank in N. Sea, between England and Denmark; depth varies from 6 to 37 m; valuable fishing ground; action between British fleet under Beatty and German fleet under Hipper; *Blücher* sunk Jan. 1915.

Dogs, I. of, riverside dist., formed by bend in the R. Thames off Greenwich, London, **Eng.**; Millwall and India docks, shipbldg. yards.

Doha, t., cap. of **Qatar**; spt. on E. of Qatar peninsula, Persian Gulf; internat. airpt., deep sea pt.; contains 80 per cent of p.; p. (est. 1970) 80,000.

Dokai Bay, inlet, N. Kyushu, **Japan**; landlocked bay on S. side of Shimonoseki Straits; flanked by highly industl. zone inc. Yawata, Wakamatsu, Tobata cs.; requires constant dredging; length 6 km, width 0·8–2·4 km.

Dôle, t., Jura, **E. France**; on R. Doubs, nr. Dijon; industl. ctr.; anc. cap. of Franche-Comté, ceded to France in 1678; birthplace of Pasteur; p. (1982) 27,959.

Dolgarrog, sm. t., Meirionnydd, Gwynedd, **Wales**; site of hydroelectric sta.

Dolgellau, t., Gwynedd, N. **Wales**; agr., quarrying, timber; p. (1981) 2,321.

Dollar, burgh, Clackmannan, **Scot.**; at foot of Ochil hills; p. (1981) 2,480.

Dollar Law, mtn., nr. Peebles, **Scot.**; alt. 817 m.

Dolomites, gr. of limestone mtns., S. Tyrolese Alps, N.E. **Italy**; tourist dist.; peaks assume fantastic forms; principal peak Marmolada 3,355 m.

Dominica, Commonwealth of, W.I.; indep. st. (1978); most N. of Windward Is.; 25 per cent under cultivation; volcanic soils highly suitable for bananas; N.–S. mtn. range has spectacular volcanic scenery; cap. Roseau; a. 751 km²; p. (est. 1981) 100,000.

Dominican Rep., rep., **W.I.**; shares I. of Hispaniola with Haiti; comprises Nat. Dist. (inc. cap. Santo Domingo) and 25 admin. provs.; mtnous. with sub-tropical climate; in path of tropical cyclones; badly devastated by hurricane (1979); comm. economy mainly agr.; transport system geared to exp. of sugar; govt. investment in agr. and mng.; oil refining at Nigua; exp. bauxite; tourism growing and leading earner of foreign exchange; official language Spanish; a. 48,430 km²; p. (est. 1984) 6,101,000.

Domodossola, frontier t., Piedmont, N. **Italy**; nr. Alpine tourist resort in Toce valley, nr. Simplon; p. (1981) 20,069.

Don, R., South Yorks., **Eng.**; trib. of R. Ouse, 112 km long.

Don, R., Gordon, **Scot.**; flows into N. Sea nr. Aberdeen; salmon; 131 km long.

Don, major R. of southern **RSFSR**; falls into Sea of Azov below Rostov, its ch. pt.; navigable to Voronezh; ch. trib., Donets; access to Volga by Don-Volga canal; fisheries; 1,955 km long.

Donaghadee, t., Ards, **N. Ireland**; nearest point to Scot.; spt. and seaside resort; p. (1971) 3,687.

Donauwörth, t., W. Bavaria, **W. Germany**; bridge t. on N. bank of Danube at Wörnitz confluence; p. (est. 1968) 11,130.

Donbas, industl. region, Ukrainian SSR, **USSR**; in valleys of Rs. Donets and lower Dnieper; about 23,300 km²; produces 60 per cent of Russia's coal; adjoins Krivoy Rog ironfields; many lge. industl. ts.

Doncaster, t., met. dist., South Yorks., **Eng.**; on Don R., 27 km N.E. of Sheffield; coal mines, tractors, nylon mftg.; racecourse; p. (1981) 288,801.

Donegal, spt., Co. Donegal, **R.o.I.**; on W. cst. on Donegal Bay; homespun tweeds, carpets; p. (1971) 1,725.

Donegal (Tirconnail), co., N.W. **R.o.I.**; fishing poor agr.; cloth, hydroelectric power; co. t. Lifford; a. 4,830 km²; p. (1981) 24,626.

Donets, R., rises in uplands of central **RSFSR**; N.E. of Belgorod, flows S.E. to join R. Don; crosses Donets coalfield; length 1,040 km. *See* **Donbas.**

Donetsk (Stalino), t., Ukrainian SSR, **USSR**; industl. ctr. of Donets coal basin; iron, steel, engin., chemicals; p. (est. 1980) 1,032,000.

Donges, t., Loire Atlantique, **France**; nr. St. Nazaire; oil refinery; synthetic textiles, plastics; p. (1968) 6,458.

Dongola (Dunqulah), t., **Sudan**; on left bank of Nile above Third Cataract; Old D. was 120 km to S.; p. (est. 1965) 4,970.

Dong Ting (Tung Ting), lge. L., Hunan, **China**; receives water from Xi Jiang and Yuan Rs., drains N. to Chang Jiang; surrounded by flat intensively cultivated land; rice, sugar; size varies with season; max. (in late summer) 6,500 km².

Donner Pass, E. Cal., **USA**; highway pass through Sierra Nevada at 2,176 m.

Donzère-Mondragon, Vaucluse, **France**; site of Rhône barrage supplying hydroelectric power.

Dora Baltea, R., N. **Italy**; rises in Mt. Blanc, flows E. and S. through Val d'Aosta to R. Po at Chivasso; impt. routeway from N. Italy to Switzerland (through Gr. St. Bernard Pass) and France (through Little St. Bernard Pass); 152 km long.

Dorchester, co. t., West Dorset, **Eng.**; mkt. t. on R. Frome; lime, agr., engin.; Roman remains; nearby prehistoric Maiden Castle; linked with the name of Thomas Hardy; p. (1981) 14,049.

Dordogne, dep., S.W. **France**; cap. Périgueux; crossed by Dordogne R.; fertile valleys; p. (1982) 377,500.

Dordogne, R., S.W. **France**; rises in Central Massif, joins Garonne to form Gironde; vineyards; upper reaches used for hydroelectric power.

Dordrecht, c., nr. Rotterdam, **Neth.**; on R. Merwede; timber, shipbldg., seaplanes; p. (1982) 108,576.

Dorking, t., Mole Valley, Surrey, **Eng.**; on R. Mole to S. of gap through N. Downs; mkt., residtl.; lt. inds.; p. (1981) 21,654.

Dornbirn, t., Vorarlberg, **Austria**; textiles; p. (1971) 33,810.

Dornoch, burgh, Sutherland, **Scot.**; N. of Dornoch F.; resort; p. (1981) 1,006.

Dorset, non-met. co., S. **Eng.**; borders Eng. Channel along attractive cliffed cst. formed by E.-W. limestone ridges; Portland stone quarried; many tourist resorts inc. Bournemouth; mkt. ts. serve agr. interior; a. 2,655 km²; p. (1981) 591,990.

Dorset Heights, hills, extend E. to W. across central Dorset, **Eng.**; chalk; pastoral farming, sheep; some cultivation where soil is deep enough; rise to 250–275 m.

Dorset, North, l. gov. dist., Dorset, **Eng.**; mainly rural but inc. ts. of Shaftesbury, Sturminster Newton and Blandford Forum; p. (1981) 46,479.

Dorsten, t., N. Rhine-Westphalia, **W. Germany**; on R. Lippe; coal, iron, elec., chemical inds.; p. (est. 1983) 71,700.

Dortmund, c., N. Rhine-Westphalia, **W. Germany**; on Dortmund-Ems Canal; industl. ctr. and pt. of Ruhr; coal, iron, steel, machin.; p. (est. 1983) 595,200.

Dortmund-Ems Canal, N. Rhine-Westphalia, **W. Germany**; links Dortmund on Ruhr coalfield with R. Ems 8 km above Lingen; coal, iron-ore traffic; 144 km long.

Douai, t., Nord, **France**; nr. Lille on Scarpe R.; coal, iron and engin. wks.; bell founding, arsenal; p. (1982) 202,366 (met. a.).

Douala, spt., **Cameroon**; rly. to Yaoundé; exp. hardwoods; p. (est. 1984) 850,000.

Douarnenez, spt., Finistère, N.W. **France**; on D. Bay; sardine fisheries; p. (1982) 17,813.

Doubs, dep., E. **France**; traversed by Jura range and R. Doubs; mainly agr.; watchmkg., motor vehicles; cap. Besançon; a. 5,315 km²; p. (1982) 477,200.

Douglas, t., cap. of I. of Man; 120 km W. of Liverpool, **Eng.**; spt; resort; nearby freeport (1983) gaining from low tax rate; p. (1976) 19,897.

Douglas Point, on shore of L. Huron, Ont., **Canada**; nuclear power sta.

Dounreay, Caithness, **Scot.**; fast-breeder nuclear reactors.

Douro, R., **Portugal** and **Spain**; enters Atl. Oc. below Oporto; known as Duero R. in Spain; l. 776 km; famous port wine a.

Dove, R., Derbs. and Staffs., **Eng.**; trib. of Trent; flows through beautiful dales; 77 km long.

Dovedale, valley, Derbys., **Eng.**; steeply sloping limestone ravine of R. Dove; tourism.

Dover, packet pt., l. gov. dist., Kent, **Eng.**; one of old Cinque pts.; nearest spt. to France for Strait of D. being only 34 km wide; ch. pt. for passenger and mail traffic with Continent; cas.; p. (1981) 100,751.

Dovey, R., **Wales**; flows from Cambrian Mtns. and enters Cardigan Bay by a wide estuary.

Dowlais, dist., Merthyr Tydfil, Mid Glamorgan, S. **Wales**; coal mng., iron founding, engin.

Down, former co.; l. gov. dist., **N. Ireland**; borders Strangford Lough and Dundrum Bay; agr. and fisheries; p. (1981) 52,855 (dist.).

Downham Market, t., West Norfolk, **Eng.**; on R. Ouse; flour-milling, malting, sheet-metal wks.; p. (1981) 4,687.

Downpatrick, t., Down, **N. Ireland**; on R. Quoile; linen; p. (1981) 8,245.

Downs, natural harbour of refuge for shipping between Kent cst. and Goodwin Sands in the English Channel.

Drachenfels, mtn. peak of the Rhine, **W. Germany**; the steepest of the Siebengebirge range, nr. Königswinter; alt. 325 m; ascended by lt. rly.; famous cave of legendary dragon.

Draguignan, t., S.E. **France**; cap. of Var. dep. until 1974; mkt. t., service ctr.; p. (1982) 28,194.

Drakensberg, mtn. chain between Natal and Orange Free State, **S. Africa**, and **Lesotho**; extending 800 km from Gt. Fish R. to Olifants R.; hgst. peak Mont-aux-Sources 3,283 m; rly. crosses range by Van Reenen Pass.

Drammen, spt., **Norway**; nr. Oslo, on the Drammen R.; shipyard; exp. timber, wood-pulp, paper; p. (est. 1973) 50,138.

Drancy, t., Seine-St. Denis, **France**; N.E. sub. of Paris; p. (1982) 60,224.

Drava (Drau), R., trib. of Danube, **Austria** and **Yugoslavia**; flows from the Tyrol across Carinthia and Styria, joining Danube nr. Osijek; length 720 km; used for hydroelec. power.

Drax, West Yorks., **Eng.**; thermal elec. power sta. linked to new Selby coalfield; when complete will be Europe's lgst. coalfired sta.

Drenthe, prov., **Neth.**; on German frontier; cap. Assen; a. 2,663 km²; p. (1983) 424,720.

Dresden, c., **E. Germany**; R. pt. on Elbe, 80 km E. of Leipzig; impt. route ctr.; engin., chemicals, optical and photographic apparatus, porcelain, glass, brewing; fine art collections; scientific research; oil pipeline from Schwedt under construction; p. (1983) 522,532.

Driffield, t., East Yorks, Humberside, **Eng.**; on Yorks. Wolds 21 km N. of Beverley; oil-cake wks.; p. (1981) 9,090.

Drin, R., N. **Albania**; rises in Yugoslavia and flows through deep gorges into Adriatic; hydroelec. power; 288 km long.

Drina, R., trib. of Sava R., **Yugoslavia**; ch. source of hydroelec. power in rep.; 480 km long.

Dröbak, spt., S.E. **Norway**; winter pt. for Oslo; summer resort.

Drogheda, spt., Louth, **R.o.I.**; considerable tr. in agr. produce, salmon, etc.; stormed by Cromwell in 1649; p. (1981) 22,556.

Drogobych, t., Ukrainian SSR, **USSR**; 64 km S.W. of Lvov; ctr. of lge. oilfields, refineries; mftg.; p. (est. 1968) 56,000.

Droitwich, t., Wychavon, Hereford and Worcs., **Eng.**; brine baths; lt. inds.; expanded t.; p. (1981) 18,073.

Drôme, dep., S.E. **France**; traversed by Alps and watered by Rs. Rhône, Drôme, and Isère; cap. Valence; agr., forestry, sericulture, textile ind.; a. 6,560 km²; p. (1982) 389,200.

Dromore, mkt. t., Banbridge, **N. Ireland**; on Lagan R.; linen; p. (1971) 2,303.

Dronfield, t., North East Derbys., **Eng.**; between Chesterfield and Sheffield; edged tools, engin. and agr. implements; p. (1981) 23,304.

Droylsden, t., Gtr. Manchester, **Eng.**; sub. of Manchester; chemicals; textiles; p. (1981) 22,513.

Drumochter Pass, Grampian Mtns., **Scot.**; carries main Perth to Inverness rly. and main road from Glen Garry into valley of R. Spey; highest alt. reached by any main rly. in Gt. Britain, 453 m.

Dschang, t., **Cameroon**; quinine processing; bauxite mng.

Dubai (Dubayy), emirate, one of **United Arab Emirates**, Arabian Gulf; recently developed as free pt. (modelled on Singapore), major comm. ctr. of a.; offshore oil with vast underwater storage tanks; international airpt.; deepwater pt. (Port Rashid) under construction; p. (est. 1982) 296,000.

Dubbo, t., N.S.W., **Australia**; busy road, rail, air junction in rich agr. dist.; p. (1976) 20,149.

Dublin, co., **R.o.I.**; co. t. Dublin; a. (inc. c. of Dublin) 922 km²; p. (1981) 977,700.

Dublin (Irish *Baile Atha Cliath*), C.B., cap. of **R.o.I.**; co. t. Co. Dublin; at mouth of R. Liffey; ctr. of govt., commerce, ind., and culture; cath., univ., Abbey Theatre; brewing, distilling, food processing; Swift was buried here; p. (1981) 525,882 (c.), 915,115 (met. a.).

Dubrovnik (Ital. Ragusa), t., **Yugoslavia**; impt. pt. on Adriatic; retains much of its mediaeval architecture; tourism; airport; p. (est. 1976) 31,000.

Dubuque, t., Iowa, **USA**; pt. on Mississippi R.; varied inds. inc. meat-packing; p. (1980) 62,321.

Dudinka, Arctic spt. on R. Yenisey, **RSFSR**; nickel.

Dudley, t., met. dist., West Midlands, **Eng.**; cas.; engin.; cables, chains; p. (1981) 299,351.

Duisburg, c., N. Rhine-Westphalia, **W. Germany**; R. pt. on E. bank of Rhine at confluence with R. Ruhr, 16 km N. of Düsseldorf; iron and steel inds., machin., textiles, chemicals, pt. inds., route and R. tr. ctr.; p. (est. 1983) 541,800.

Dukeries, dist., Sherwood Forest, Notts., **Eng.**; so called from ducal mansions in dist.; tourism.

Dukinfield, t., Tameside, Gtr. Manchester, **Eng.**; 10 km S.E. of Manchester; textiles, engin., rope and twine; p. (1981) 18,063.

Dukla Pass, anc. and easy route across Carpathians, linking Poland, Hungary and Slovakia, 497 m a.s.l.

Duluth, t., Minn., **USA**; at W. end of L. Superior; gr. tr. in grain, timber and iron ore; natural gas pipeline into the Mesabi Iron Range; p. (1980) 267,000 (met. a.).

Dulwich, residtl. sub. in bor. of Southwark, Greater London, **Eng.**; village character with lge. park and public school.

Dumbarton, royal burgh, l. gov. dist., Strathclyde Reg., **Scot.**; on N. bank of R. Clyde, 19 km below Glasgow; shipbldg., valve and tube-mkg., iron and brassware; p. (1981) 78,041 (l. gov. dist.).

Dum-Dum, t., W. Bengal, **India**; ammunition; impt. airpt.; p. (est. 1970) 195,693.

Dumfries, royal burgh, Nithsdale, **Scot.**; on R. Nith, 16 km from Solway F.; p. (1981) 32,084.

Dumfries and Galloway Region, l. gov. reg., **Scot.**; occupies W. half of Southern Uplands; drained by S. flowing rivers to Solway F.; sparse rural p.; a. 6,369 km²; p. (1981) 145,078.

Dumfriesshire, former co., **Scot.**; now part of Dumfries and Galloway Reg.

Dumaujváros, t., **Hungary**; new t. built from v. of Dunapentele; iron and steel wks.; paper inds., engin.; p. (1966) 43,400.

Dunbar, royal burgh, E. Lothian, **Scot.**; sm. fishing pt.; Cromwell's victory 1650; p. (1981) 6,015.

Dunbartonshire, former co., **Scot.**; now part of Strathclyde Reg.

Dunblane, mkt. burgh, Stirling, **Scot.**; on Allan Water, 8 km from Stirling; Gothic cath. now used as par. church; p. (1981) 6,824.

Dundalk, U.D., cap. of Co. Louth, **R.o.I.**; harbour, rly. ctr.; engin., footwear, tobacco, brewing; p. (1981) 25,663.

Dundee, c., spt., royal burgh, l. gov. dist., Tayside Reg., **Scot.**; on F. of Tay, 80 km N. Edinburgh; jute mnf., engin., computers, refrigerators, clocks, watches, preserves, linoleum; publishing., univ.; p. (1981) 180,064.

Dunedin, c., Otago, S.I., **N.Z.**; univ.; wool and dairy produce; named after the old name of Edinburgh; p. (1976) 82,546 (c.), 120,426 (met. a.).

Dunfermline, royal burgh, l. gov. dist., Fife Reg., **Scot.**; 22 km E. of Alloa; linen, rubber gds., synthetic fibre; birthplace of Charles I and Andrew Carnegie; cap. of Scot. 1057–93; p. (1981) 122,232. (l. gov. dist.), 52,057 (burgh).

Dungannon, mkt. t., l. gov. dist., **N. Ireland**; linen, bricks; p. (1981) 8,295 (t.), 41,039 (dist.).

Dungarvan, U.D., Co. Waterford, **R.o.I.**; spt., mkt. t.; leather processing; p. (1981) 6,631.

Dungeness, headland of shingle, Kent, **Eng.**; 16 km S.E. of Rye; civil nuclear power stas.; linked by power cable to France 1961.

Dunkeld, t., Perth and Kinross, **Scot.**; on R. Tay at entrance to Strathmore; cath., ecclesiastical ctr. in 9th century; tourist resort.

Dunkirk, spt., Nord dep., **France**; strong fort; gd. harbour and tr.; fisheries, shipbld., oil refining; steel mill; scene of evacuation of B.E.F. 1940; p. (1982) 73,618.

Dun Laoghaire (Kingstown), C.B., Dublin, **R.o.I.**; spt., mail packet sta., fishing; ferry to Eng.; p. (1981) 54,496.

Dunmanway, t., Cork, **R.o.I.**; on R. Brandon; tweeds, blankets.

Dunmow, Great, mkt. t., Uttlesford, Essex, **Eng.**; on R. Chelmer; 16 km N.W. of Chelmsford.

Dunmow, Little, v., 3 km E. of Great Dunmow; Uttlesford, Essex, **Eng.**; historic Dunmow Flitch (side of bacon); bacon factory closed (1983).

Dunoon, burgh, Argyll and Bute, **Scot.**; on N. side of F. of Clyde, anc. cas.; holiday resort; p. (1981) 9,372.

Duns, burgh, Berwick, **Scot.**; agr. and allied inds.; mkt. t.; cas.; p. (1981) 2,249.

Dunsinane, hill, Sidlaws, **Scot.**; nr. Perth; alt. 309 m; referred to by Shakespeare in *Macbeth*.

Dunstable, t., South Beds., **Eng.**; on N. edge of Chiltern Hills, 6 km W. of Luton; motor vehicles, engin., cement, rubber, and plastic gds.; p. (1981) 30,912.

Duque de Caxias, t., **Brazil**; Brazil's largest oil refinery, petro-chemicals; Alfa-Romeo car plant; p. (est. 1980) 666,400.

Durance, R., S.E. **France**; trib. of Rhône; rapid current, 347 km long; provides irrigation and hydroelec. power.

Durango, c., cap. of D. st., **Mexico**; cath.; silver, gold, copper, iron-ore; p. (1979) 228,686.

Durango, st., N.W. **Mexico**; mng., agr., cotton, wheat; a. 109,484 km²; p. (1970) 939,208.

Durant, t., S. Okla, **USA**; cotton gins and compresses, cottonseed oil; p. (1980) 11,972.

Durban, c., **S. Africa**; on Durban Bay; ch. comm. c. of Natal; exp. coal, manganese, wool, hides; oil and sugar refining, chemicals, textiles, engin.; oil pipeline to Johannesburg; univ.; main pt. and seaside resort; p. (1970) 721,265 (met. a.).

Düren, t., N. Rhine–Westphalia, **W. Germany**; on R. Rur 37 km S.W. of Cologne; rly. ctr.; iron and steel wks., vehicles; p. (est. 1983) 85,600.

Durgapur, t., W. Bengal, **India**; site of barrage on Damodar R.; p. (1981) 311,798.

Durham, c., co. t., l. gov. dist., Durham, N.E. **Eng.**; sited within a meander of R. Wear; cath., cas., univ.; carpets, organ mftg., confectionery; p. (1981) 85,190.

Durham, non-met. co., N.E. **Eng.**; between Rs. Tyne and Tees; stretches from attractive Pennine moorland in W. to coalfield and industl. a. with many sm. ts. in E.; borders the N. Sea; a. 2,437 km²; p. (1981) 604,728.

Durham, t., N.C., **USA**; tobacco ind., textiles; univ.; p. (1980) 101,000.

Durrës (Durazzo), ch. spt., **Albania**; on Adriatic; pt. for Tirana; tobacco ind., plastics; tourism; p. (est. 1970) 53,000.

Dursley, t., Gloucs., **Eng.**; 21 km S.W. of Gloucester; engin., agr. machin.; 18th cent. mkt. house.

Dushanbe, c., cap. of Tadzhik SSR, **USSR**; univ.; industl. and agr. ctr.; rly. junc.; earlier called Stalinabad; p. (est. 1984) 539,000.

Düsseldorf, c., cap. of N. Rhine-Westphalia, **W. Germany**; on R. Rhine, 32 km N. of Cologne; admin. and cultural ctr., art and medical academies; iron, steel, machin., soap, cars, paper, chemical inds.; impt. trans-shipment pt.; p. (est. 1983) 579,800.

Dust Bowl, region, **USA**; name applied to great plains on E. flank of Rocky Mtns.; subject to severe soil erosion by wind, particularly in drought years (1933, 1936) due to destruction of natural vegetation by over-grazing or by excessive ploughing.

Dutch Harbour, t., Unalaska I., Aleutian gr., N. Pac. Oc.; strategic American naval base.

Dvina or Northern Dvina, R., **RSFSR**; flows to White Sea at Arkhangelsk, formed by the junction of Rs. Sukhona and Vychegda at Kotlas; connected by canal with Neva and Volga; used for timber transport; 744 km long.

Dvina or Western Dvina, R., Latvian SSR, RSFSR, **USSR**; rises in Valdai Hills nr. sources of Volga and Dnieper, flows through Latvia to G. of Riga; connected by canal to Berezina and Dnieper; c. 1,016 km long.

Dwyfor, l. gov. dist., Gwynedd, **Wales**; Lleyn penin. and ts. of Pwhelli, Criccieth and Porthmadog; p. (1981) 26,285.

Dyfed, co., S.W. **Wales**; inc. former cos. of Cardiganshire, Carmarthenshire and Pembroke; upland a. crossed by valleys of Teifi and Towy Rs.; stock rearing and fattening; tourism impt. around cst.; industl. in S.E.; a. 5,765 km²; p. (1981) 329,977.

Dzaudzhikau. See **Ordzhonikidze.**

Dzerzhinsk, c., **RSFSR**; R. pt. of Oka; chemicals (fertilisers, explosives); p. (est. 1980) 260,000.

Dzhalil, t., **RSFSR**; new t. 48 km N.E. of Almetyevsk to serve new oilfield there.

Dzhambul, c., Kazakh SSR, **USSR**; on Talas R. and on Turk-Sib rly.; chemicals, food-processing; p. (est. 1980) 270,000.

Dzhezkazgan, t., Kazakh SSR, **USSR**; 560 km W. of L. Balkhash; copper-mines; manganese ore nearby; p. (est. 1967) 58,000.

Dzierzoniow (Reichenbach), t., Wroclaw, S.W. **Poland**; mnf. ctr.; textiles, machin., elec. equipment; formerly in Germany; p. (1970) 32,900.

Dzungaria, inland basin, Xinjiang prov., N.W. **China**; lies between Tien-Shan highlands of Soviet–Chinese frontier and Altai mtns.; former historic kingdom of Zungaria.

E

Ealing, outer bor., Greater London, **Eng.**; comprising former bors. of Acton, Ealing, and Southall; p. (1981) 280,042.

Earl's Court, residtl. a., London, **Eng.**; Bor. of Kensington and Chelsea, contains E.C. exhibition hall.

Earn R., Perth. and Kinross, **Scot.**; issues from Loch Earn (10 km long) and flows into Tay R.; 74 km long.

Easington, l. gov. dist., Durham, **Eng.**; colly. v.; now part of Peterlee new t.; p. (1981) 100,717.

Easington, v., Humberside, **Eng.**; nr. Hull; natural gas terminal.

East Anglia, comprises Norfolk and Suffolk, **Eng.**; former Anglo-Saxon kingdom; one of Britain's most productive agr. regions.

East Anglian Heights, hills, extend S.W. to N.E. across N.E. Hertfordshire, N. Essex, and S.W. Suffolk, **Eng.**; chalk overlain by glacial clays and sands; smooth, rolling surface; region of lge. farms and lge. fields, mixed farms mainly grain; rarely exceed 180 m.

East Bergholt, v., Suffolk, **Eng.**; birthplace of Constable.

Eastbourne, t., l. gov. dist., East Sussex, **Eng.**; on S. cst. to E. of Beachy Head; seaside resort; p. (1981) 77,608.

East Cape, extreme N.E. point of Asia; on Chukchi peninsula, **RSFSR**; Russian name Cape Dezhnova.

East Cape, extreme E. point of **N.Z.**; named by Cook on his first voyage in 1769.

East Chicago, t., Ind., **USA**; L. Michigan; iron and steel wks., oil refining; p. (1980) 39,786.

East Cleveland, t., Ohio, **USA**; residtl.; p. (1980) 36,957.

East Coast Bays, bor., N.I., **N.Z.**; series of settlements on bays N. of Auckland; amalgamated 1954; p. (1976) 23,490.

East Dereham, t., Breckland, Norfolk, **Eng.**; 22 km W. of Norwich; agr. implements; p. (1981) 11,845.

Easter Island, S. Pac. Oc., 3,760 km W. of Chile; various theories to explain origin of gigantic statues; p. (est. 1970) 1,000.

East Grinstead, t., West Sussex, **Eng.**; in ctr. of Weald, 14 km W. of Tunbridge Wells; agr. mkt.; famous hospital for plastic surgery; p. (1981) 22,263.

East Ham. See **Newham.**

East Hartford, t., Conn., **USA**; industl.; p. (1980) 52,563.

East Indies, name commonly applied to Is. between S.E. Asia and N. Australia, variously known as Malay archipelago, Malaysia, Indonesia.

East Kilbride, t., l. gov. dist., Strathclyde Reg., **Scot.**; 11 km S.S.E. of Glasgow; new t. 1947; lge. agr. machin., aero engines, engin., elec. gds., seawater distillation plant; knitwear, clothing; p. (1981) 82,499.

East Lansing, t., Mich., **USA**; residtl.; univ.; p. (1980) 51,392.

Eastleigh, t., l. gov. dist., Hants., **Eng.**; rly. engin.; many new inds.; p. (1981) 92,491.

East London, spt., C. Prov., **S. Africa**; at mouth of Buffalo R.; holiday resort; trading ctr.; inds. inc. car assembly, textiles, engin.; titanium deposits nearby; p. (1970) 123,294 (met. a.).

East Lothian (Haddington), former co., l. gov. dist., **Scot.**; part of Lothian Reg.; p. (1981) 80,187.

East Main, R., Quebec, **Canada**; flows into James Bay; 432 km long.

Easton, t., Penns., **USA**; on Delaware R.; rly. ctr., coal, steel, machin., p. (1980) 26,027.

East Orange, t., N.J., **USA**; residtl. sub. of New York; p. (1980) 77,690.

East Pakistan. See **Bangladesh.**

East Point, t., Ga., **USA**; textiles, fertilisers; p. (1980) 37,486.

East Providence, t., Rhode I., **USA**; textiles, machin.; p. (1970) 48,207.

East Retford, t., Bassetlaw, Notts., **Eng.**; on R. Idle, 10 km E. of Worksop; rubber, wire ropes, engin.; p. (1981) 19,348.

East Riding, Yorkshire. See **Yorkshire.**

East River, tidal strait about 26 km long and from 180–1,200 m wide; separates the bors. of Manhattan and Bronx from the bors. of Queens and Brooklyn, N.Y., **USA.**

East St. Louis, t., R. pt., Ill., **USA**; on Mississippi R.; lge stockyards, meat-packing, aluminium, chemicals; p. (1980) 55,200.

East Sussex, non-met. co., S.E. **Eng.**; mainly rural, urban growth on cst., where resorts, retirement and dormitory ts. for London, inc. Brighton, Hastings and Eastbourne; crossed by S.

Downs in S. terminating at Beachy Head, Ashdown Forest in N.; a. 1,795 km²; p. (1981) 652,568.

East Timor, prov., **Indonesia**; Port. terr. until 1975; mtnous; underdeveloped; cap. Dili; a. 14,693 km²; p. (est. 1984) 638,000.

Eastwood, t., Broxtowe, Notts., **Eng.**; birthplace of D. H. Lawrence; coal; p. (1981) 11,700.

Eastwood, l. gov. dist., Strathclyde Reg.; **Scot.**; part of Central Clydeside conurb.; p. (1981) 53,547.

East Yorkshire (formerly **North Wolds**), l. gov. dist., Humberside, **Eng.**; lge. a. inc. Pocklington, Driffield and Bridlington; p. (1981) 74,997.

Eau Claire, t., Wis., **USA**; on Chippewa R.; agr. mkt.; univ. food processing, varied mnfs.; p. (1980) 51,509 (t.), 130,507 (met. a.).

Ebal, Mt., **Israel**; opposite Gerizim; alt. 911 m.

Ebbw Vale, t., Blaenau Gwent, Gwent, **Wales**; 27 km N.W. of Newport; coal, iron, tinplate, bricks, pipes, precast concrete; some steel wks. to close; p. (1981) 24,422.

Eberswalde, t., Frankfurt, **E. Germany**; N.E. of Berlin; iron, wood, and cardboard wks., chemicals; p. (est. 1970) 46,090.

Ebro, ch. R. of N.E. **Spain**; flows to Mediterranean from Cantabrian Mtns.; feeds hydroelectric plants, irrigation, esp. around Zaragoza; 928 km long.

Eccles, Gtr. Manchester, **Eng.**; 6 km W. of Manchester; chemicals, oil refining, engin.; p. (1981) 37,166.

Echo L., Tasmania, **Australia**; used to store water for hydroelectric power.

Echuca, t., Victoria, **Australia**; major inland pt. on Murray R. in mid 19th century; in 1970s original pt. and bldgs. restored; p. (1976) 9,075 (inc. Moama).

Écija, t., Seville, **Spain**; olive oil, wine, pottery; the Roman Astigi; p. (1981) 34,619.

Eckernförde, spt., Schleswig-Holstein, **W. Germany**; on Baltic, N.W. of Kiel; p. (est. 1983) 23,300.

Ecrins, mtn. peak, S.E. **France**; hgst. point of massif du Pelvoux and Dauphiné Alps; alt. 4,106 m.

Ecuador, rep., **S. America**; on equatorial Pac. cst., bounded by Colombia to N. and Peru to W. and S.; inc. Galapagos Is. in Pac. Oc.; lowland to E. and W. of central Andes; climate temperate in Andes and hot and humid in lowlands; comm. economy mainly agr. with impt. exp. of bananas, coffee, hemp, cocoa; petroleum increasingly impt.; pipeline across Andes to pt. of Esmeraldas; communications difficult but vital for economic development; major pts. Guayaquil and Manta; official language Spanish; cap. Quito; a. inc. Galapagos Is. 454,752 km²; p. (est. 1984) 9,090,000.

Edam, t., N. Holland, **Neth.**; on cst. IJsselmeer; cheese, tool mftg.; p. (1967) 16,558.

Eday, I., Orkney Is., **Scot.**; the Ocelli of Ptolemy; p. (1971) 179.

Eddystone, rock with lighthouse, Eng. Channel; S.W. of Plymouth.

Ede, t., Gelderland, **Neth.**; livestock; pianos; p. (1982) 85,025.

Edea, t., pt., **Cameroon**; aluminium smelting based on nearby hydroelectric power plant.

Eden, Vale of, fertile belt in Cumbria, **Eng.**; between barren hills of Pennines and L. Dist.; occupied by R. Eden; mkt. ts. Appleby and Penrith; now forms l. gov. dist. inc. Penrith, Alston and Appleby; p. (1981) 43,984.

Eder, R., **W. Germany**; joins Fulda R. S. of Kassel; Eder dam lgst. in Germany.

Edessa (Edhessa), t., N.E. **Greece**; agr. tr. ctr.; the anc. Ægae, burial place of Macedonian kings; p. (1981) 16,642.

Edgehill, ridge, 24 km S. of Warwick, **Eng.**; scene of first battle of civil war, 1642.

Edgewater, t., N.J., **USA**; sub., connected by ferry with New York; p. (1980) 4,628.

Edinburgh, c., cap. of **Scot.**, l. gov. dist., Lothian Reg.; royal burgh on F. of Forth; univ., cas.; palace (Holyrood); printing, publishing, brewing, electronics equipment, rubber gds.; Edinburgh Festival in August; Leith, with docks is joined to E.; p. (1981) 436,271.

Edirne, t., **Turkey**; in Thrace, on R. Maritsa; comm. ctr. with tr. in wine, tobacco, silk, perfume; the anc. Adrianople, named after the emperor Hadrian, later cap. of Ottoman sultans 1366–1453; p. (1970) 53,806.

Edmonton, c., cap. of Alberta, **Canada**; fast-growing c. (119 km²) on both sides of N. Saskatchewan R.; high-level bridge links

Strathcona; major military ctr.; univ.; international air ctr.; oilfields and farming; oil and chemical inds.; p. (1979) 461,365 (met. a.).

Edremit, t., Balikesir, N.W. **Turkey**; cereals, opium; silverwk.; p. (1965) 25,003.

Edward, L., on frontier of Uganda and Zaire, one of the sources of R. Nile; occupies Gr. Rift Valley; alt. c. 900 m, 70km long, breadth 51km; salt, fishing, wildlife.

Eger, t., N.E. **Hungary**; mkt. t. in wine producing region; mediaeval fortress t.; p. (est. 1978) 60,093.

Egersund, pt., S. cst. **Norway**; fishing; mentioned in Norwegian sagas; p. (est. 1970) 10,097.

Egham, t., Runnymede, Surrey, **Eng.**; on R. Thames, nr. Staines; contains field of Runnymede; residtl.; p. (1981) 27,817.

Egmont, mtn., N.I., **N.Z.**; extinct volcano; alt. 2,501 m.

Egremont, mkt. t., Cumbria, **Eng.**; 16 km S. of Whitehaven; limestone; former iron ore mng.

Egypt, Arab Republic of, indep. st., N.E. corner **Africa**; member of Federation of Arab Reps.; 96 per cent a. is desert except Nile valley and delta where 95 per cent of p. live; agr. depends on annual rise of Nile waters and irrigation; cereals, sugar-cane, vegetables, fruit; cotton main cash crop; phosphates; oilfield in Israeli-occupied Sinai and recent finds offshore in G. of Suez and in Western Desert; nat. gas since 1974; 6 oil refineries; major port development on Red Sea to handle mineral exp.; textiles account for ⅓ of manuf. output; cap. Cairo; Aswan High Dam has produced problems; (1) silting up of reservoir (L. Nasser) behind dam; (2) reduction in fertilising silt deposits in lower Nile valley; (3) erosion of Nile delta itself; (4) reduction of fish p. in E. Med.; a. 999,740 km²; p. (est. 1984) 45,657,000 (75 per cent illiterate).

Eider, R., **W. Germany**; separates Holstein from Schleswig; flows into N. Sea; 125 m. long.

Eifel, plateau of volcanic rocks, **W. Germany**; lies N. of R. Moselle, forming W. edge of Rhine gorge between Koblenz and Bonn; formerly cultivated, now largely woodland and moorland; farming in valleys; rises to just over 600 m.

Eiger, mtn., one of the hgst. peaks of the Bernese Oberland, **Switzerland**; famous for steep N. wall; alt. 3,978 m.

Eigg, I., Inner Hebrides, **Scot.**; 24 km S.W. of Mallaig; basaltic rocks on cst.; rises to 393 m.

Eilat, new spt., Negev, **Israel**; on G. of Aqaba; growing tourist tr.; copper at Timna; oil pipeline from Ashdod (1970).

Eildon Hills, Roxburgh, **Scot.**; S. of Melrose; hgst. point 422 m.

Eindhoven, c., N. Brabant, **Neth.**; electronic equipment, motor vehicles, tobacco and textile inds.; technical univ.; p. (1982) 195,599.

Eire. See Ireland, Republic of.

Eisenach, t., Erfurt, **E. Germany**; on R. Hörsel, at foot of Thuringian forest; ctr. of Werra potash field; cars, machin., textiles; birthplace of J. S. Bach; p. (est. 1973) 50,457.

Eisenerz Alps, mtn. range, **Austria**; most N. range of Alps, overlooking Danube valley between Linz and Vienna; impt. iron-ore deposits; alt. from 1,800–2,700 m.

Eisenhüttenstadt, t., Frankfurt, **E. Germany**; iron smelting; terminus of Oder–Spree canal; p. (est. 1970) 45,194.

Eisleben, t., Halle, **E. Germany**; machin., copper- and silver-mng. ctr.; birthplace of Luther; p. (est. 1970) 30,386.

Ekibastuz, t., Kazakh SSR, **USSR**; 120 km S.W. of Pavlodar; ctr. of rapidly developing mng. a. coal, gold, metals; coal-fed generating plant projected to supply power to European Russia; p. (est. 1967) 40,000.

El Aaiun, pt., **Western Sahara**; main pt. for exp. of phosphates; p. (est. 1974) 20,010.

El Alamein, v., **Egypt**; in Libyan Desert 96 km S.W. of Alexandria, scene of Allied victory, second world war; oilfield nearby; terminal nr. Sidi Abd el-Rahman.

Elan, R. Powys, **Wales**; rises on S.E. sides of Plynlimon, flows into R. Wye; lower valley contains series of 4 lge. reservoirs, capacity 45,460 million litres; ch. source of water for Birmingham.

Elâzig, t., E. **Turkey**; dam and hydroelec. project at Keban, 48 km to N.W. at confluence of E. and W. branches of Euphrates; p. (1979) 151,310.

Elba, I., off Tuscan cst., **Italy**; iron ore, wine,

marble, salt; ch. t. Portoferraio; Napoleon's first exile here; a. 363 km²; p. (1981) 10,755.

Elbe (Labe), R., in **CSSR** and **Germany**; rises in Riesengebirge and flows into N. Sea at Cuxhaven; navigable for 840 km of total l. of 1,160 km; connected with Rhine and Weser Rs. by Mittelland canal; forms part of border between E. and W. Germany.

Elbert, mtn., Col., **USA**; hgst. peak of Rocky Mtns. in USA, 4,401 m.

Elbiag or **Elbing**, spt., Gdansk, N. **Poland**; shipbldg., machin., vehicles; p. (est. 1983) 115,900.

Elbruz Mt., Caucasus, Georgian SSR, **USSR**; hgst. in Europe (5,636 m), over-topping Mont Blanc by 822 m; twin volcanic peaks.

Elburz, mtn. range, N. **Iran**; bordering on Caspian Sea; hgst. peak, Demavend, 5,642 m.

Elche, t., Alicante, **Spain**; palm groves; oil, soap, footwear; p. (1981) 143,000.

El Dar-el-Beida (Casablanca), c., **Morocco**; pt. on Atl. Oc.; artificial harbour; fish canning, textiles; exp. phosphate; p. (est. 1973) 1,371,300 (c.), 1,753,400 (met. a.).

Eldorado, radium mine, N.W. Terr., **Canada**; on E. shore of Gr. Bear Lake nr. Arctic Circle; produces 40 per cent of world's radium, sent to Pt. Hope, Ontario, for refining.

El Djezair (Algiers), pt., cap. c. of **Algeria**; old t. surmounted by 16th cent. Casbâh (fortress); univ.; exp. wine, citrus fruit, iron ore; oil refining at Maison Carrée; airpt. at Maison Blanche, 16 km E. of c.; p. (est. 1974), 1,503,720 (c.), 943,142 (met. a.).

Elektrenai, t., Lithuanian SSR, **USSR**; new township nr. Vievis, at site of thermal power sta.

Elektrostal, t., **RSFSR**; 56 km E. of Moscow; steel, engin.; p. (est. 1980) 141,000.

Elephanta I., Bombay Harbour, **India**; Brahmanic caves with monolithic carvings.

Elephant Butte Dam, N.M., **USA**; on Rio Grande; built to control flood water; lake, a. 115 km² supplies irrigation water to 2,020 km² in N.M. and Texas, water also supplied to Mexico.

El Ferrol del Caudillo, spt., **Spain**; on N.W. cst.; fortfd., fishing; p. (1981) 91,764.

Elgin, royal burgh, Moray, Scot.; pt. Lossiemouth; woollens, whisky; ruins anc. cath.; p. (1981) 18,905.

Elgin, t., Ill., **USA**; watches, electrical equipment; p. (1980) 63,981.

Elgon Mt., extinct volcano, bdy. of **Kenya** and **Uganda**; 4,300 m; cave dwellings on slopes.

Eli and Earlsferry, burgh, North East Fife, **Scot.**; summer resort; p. (1981) 888.

Elisabethville. See Lubumbashi.

Elizabeth, t. S. **Australia**; planned t. built 1950s, now merges with Adelaide met. a.; p. (1976) 33,721.

Elizabeth, c., N.J., **USA**; univ.; sewing machines, oil refining, cars, aircraft components; now inc. in Newark; p. (1980) 106,000.

Elk I., Nat. Park, **Canada**; animal reserve, tourism.

El Khârga, oasis, Libyan desert, **Egypt**, 136 km S.W. of Asyût; site of New Valley Project for irrigation.

Elkhart, t., Ind., **USA**; E. of Chicago; paper, machin.; elec. equipment, musical instruments; p. (1980) 41,305 (t.), 137,330 (met. a.).

Elk Mtns., W. Col., **USA**; highest point Castle Peak, 4,305 m.

Elland, t., West Yorks., **Eng.**; on R. Calder, 5 km S.E. of Halifax; textiles; p. (1981) 18,011.

Ellesmere, agr. dist., S.I., **N.Z.**; on Canterbury Plain nr. Christchurch.

Ellesmere, mkt. t., Shrops., **Eng.**; nearby lake; tourism.

Ellesmere I., extreme N. of Arctic **Canada**; barren uninhabited; a. 106,200 km².

Ellesmere Port, l. gov. dist., N.W. Cheshire, **Eng.**; on Manchester Ship Canal and 14 km S.S.E. of Liverpool; metal mftg., paper, engin., oil refineries; cars; expanded t.; with Neston forms l. gov. dist.; p. (1981) 81,549.

Elliot Lake, t., N. Ont., **Canada**; ctr. of uranium mines.

Ellice Is. See Tuvalu I.

Ellis I., N.Y. harbour, **USA**; served as ch. immigration ctr., 1892–1943.

Ellon, burgh, Gordon, **Scot.**; on R. Ythan; p. (1981) 6,293.

El Mahalla el Kubra, t., **Egypt**; N. of Cairo on Nile delta; textile ctr.; p. (1976) 292,114.

Elmbridge, l. gov. dist., Surrey, **Eng.**; close to Gtr. London; inc. Esher, Walton and Weybridge; p. (1981) 110,683.

Elmira, t., N.Y., **USA**; rly. gds., farm implements; famous as burial place of Mark Twain; p. (1970) 39,945.

El **Misti**, mtn., S. **Peru**; dormant volcano with snow cap; alt. 5,846 m.

Elmshorn, t., **W. Germany**; N.W. of Hamburg; shipbldg.; p. (est. 1983) 41,500.

El Paso, c., Texas, **USA**; on E. bank Rio Grande opposite Ciudad Juárez (Mexico); natural gas distribution, oil refining, metallurgy; tourism; p. (1980) 425,000 (c.), 480,000 (met. a.).

El Salvador. *See* **Salvador**.

El Segundo, t., Cal., **USA**; lge. oil refinery; assembly of aircraft components; p. (1980) 13,752.

Elsinore (Helsingör), t., spt., **Denmark**; shipbldg.; setting of Shakespeare's *Hamlet*; p. (1970) 3,530.

Elstow, v., Beds., **Eng.**; the birthplace of John Bunyan.

Elstree, t., Hertsmere, Herts., **Eng.**; 6 km W. of Barnet; residtl.; films, lt. engin., silk hosiery.

El Teniente, Andean t., central **Chile**; copper mng. and smelting; p. 11,761.

Eluru, t., Andhra Pradesh, **India**; cotton, carpets, hosiery, oil; p. (1981) 168,154.

Elvas, mkt. t., **Portugal**; on Guadiana R.; plums, olives, jams; cath.; once strongly fortfd.; p. (1981) 12,880.

Ely, t., Cambridge, **Eng.**; on S. fringe of Fens; mkt., cath.; agr. ctr.; p. (1981) 10,268.

Ely, I. of. *See* **Cambridgeshire**.

Elyria, t., Ohio, **USA**; mftg.; p. (1980) 57,538.

Emba, R., Kazakh SSR, **USSR**; rises in Urals, flows S.W. to Caspian Sea; crosses productive Ural–Emba oilfield; 608 km long.

Emden, t., Lower Saxony, **W. Germany**; impt. N. Sea pt. nr. mouth of R. Ems and on Dortmund-Ems and Ems-Jade canals; exp. coal and iron from Ruhr; shipyards, fisheries; p. (1983) 50,900.

Emene, t., **Nigeria**; nr. Enugu; steel plant; cement.

Emilia-Romagna, region, N. **Italy**; S. of Po R.; divided into 8 provs.; fertile agr. a.; a. 22,124 km²; p. (1981) 3,957,513.

Emmen, t., Drenthe, **Neth.**; 48 km S.E. of Groningen; elec. machin., ball bearings, tinplate, iron wks.; p. (1982) 90,662.

Emmental, dist., **Switzerland**; dairy produce, especially cheese.

Empoli, t., Tuscany, **Italy**; on R. Arno; textile mnfs., glass; p. (1981) 44,961.

Ems, R., N. **W. Germany**; rises in Teutoburger Wald, flows N. to N. Sea at Emden; 333 km long.

Emscher, R., **W. Germany**; rises in Sauerland, flows W. through heart of Ruhr coalfield to enter R. Rhine at Hamborn; canalised for most of its course; very highly polluted; 88 km long.

Encarnación, pt., cap. of Itapuá dep. S.E. **Paraguay**; on Paraná R.; exp. timber, maté, tobacco, cotton, hides; p. (est. 1970) 47,333.

Enderby Land, Australian terr., S. of C. of Good Hope, **Antarctica**.

Enfield, former M.B., Middlesex, **Eng.**; now outer bor. Greater London; comprising Edmonton, Enfield, and Southgate; p. (1981) 258,825.

Enfield, t., Conn., **USA**; mftg.; p. (1980) 42,695.

Engadine, **Switzerland**; upper valley of Inn R., health resort; ch. t. St. Moritz; Swiss Nat. Park.

Enggano, I., Sumatra, **Indonesia**; sparse primitive p.; hunting, fishing, shifting cultivation.

Engels, c., **RSFSR**; on Volga; R. pt., mftg. and food-processing ctr.; engin., petroleum refining, textiles; p. (est. 1980) 165,000.

England, southern and lgst political div. of U.K.; bounded by Wales on W., by Scot. on N. and separated from continent of Europe by English Channel and North Sea; highly industl., circa 80 per cent of p. live in urban areas; major trading nation through main pts. London, Liverpool, Southampton; increasing contrast between prosperous S. and depressed N. and W.; very varied geology and topography produce contrasts in landscape, matched by climatic variability; increasingly attractive as tourist area although urban and agr. pressures on rural countryside cause concern in such a densely populated cty.; excellent road and rail network improved by construction of motorways and rly. electrification between London and Glasgow (Scot.); rich and

varied cultural heritage and numerous historic bldgs.; cap. London; a. 130,368 km²; p. (1981) 46,220,955.

Englewood, t., Col., **USA**; sub. of Denver; glasshouses; p. (1980) 30,021.

Englewood, t., N.J., **USA**; elevators, leather gds.; p. (1980) 23,701.

English Channel (La Manche), narrow sea separating England from France; extends from Strait of Dover to Land's End in Cornwall; length 480 km, greatest width 248 km.; to be crossed by Channel Tunnel (1993); *See* **Cheriton**.

Enham-Alamein, Hants., **Eng.**; rehabilitation ctr. for disabled ex-service men; 4 km N. of Andover; lt. inds.

Enid, t., Okla., **USA**; univ.; ironwks., farm implements; wheat mkt.; p. (1980) 50,363.

Enkhuizen, t., R. pt., **Neth.**; on IJsselmeer; p. (1967) 11,231.

Enna (Castrogiovanni), t., Sicily, **Italy**; sulphurmines; famous for its connection with the Proserpine legend; p. (1981) 27,838.

Ennepetal, t., N. Rhine–Westphalia, **W. Germany**; t. created 1949 with merging of Milspe and Voerde; iron, machin.; p. (est. 1983) 34,300.

Ennerdale Water, L., Cumbria, **Eng.**

Enniscorthy, mkt. t., U.D., Wexford, **R.O.I.**; cath.; p. (est. 1978) 7,040.

Enniskillen, t., Fermanagh, **N. Ireland**; brewing, nylon mftg., meat processing; p. (1981) 10,429.

Enschede, c., Overijssel, **Neth.**; textile ctr.; technical univ.; p. (est. 1982) 144,590.

Ensenada, t., **Mexico**; spt., exp. cotton; fishing and fish processing; p. (1979) 139,317.

Entebbe, t., **Uganda**; on L. Victoria; univ.; cotton ginning; airport; p. (est. 1977) 22,000.

Entre Ríos, prov., **Argentina**; between Paraná and Uruguay Rs.; wheat, linseed, livestock; cap. Paraná; a. 76,216 km²; p. (1980) 902,241.

Enugu, cap. of E. prov., **Nigeria**; coal; cloth mill; p. (est. 1975) 187,000.

Epernay, t., on S. bank of Marne, **France**; champagne ctr.; p. (1982) 28,876.

Ephesus, anc. Ionian c., in what is now **Turkey**, S. of Izmir; sacked by Goths A.D. 262; excavations.

Epinal, t., cap. of Vosges dep., **France**; on Moselle R.; textiles, printing, liqueur; p. (1982) 51,495 (met. a.).

Epirus, dist., N.W. **Greece**; a. 9,552 km²; p. (1981) 324,541.

Epping Forest, Essex, **Eng.**; forest a. N.E. of London free to public (opened by Queen Victoria 1882); formerly part of royal hunting forest; also l. gov. dist., inc. Chigwell, Waltham Abbey and Ongar; p. (1981) 116,204.

Epsom and Ewell, ts., l. gov. dist., Surrey, **Eng.**; 29 km S.W. of London; residtl., racecourse; p. (1981) 69,230.

Epworth, v., Humberside, **Eng.**; birthplace of John Wesley.

Equatorial Guinea, unitary state, W. **Africa**; former Spanish col.; indep. 1968; comprises 2 provs.; Rio Muni (mainland and Is. of Corisco, Elobey Grande, Elobey Chico) and Biako (Is. of Biako and Pagalu); narrow coastal plain and dissected upland plateau (600 m); economy almost entirely based on agr. and timber; exploration for oil; cap. Malabo on Biako I.; a. 28,051 km²; p. (1983) 304,000.

Erbil, t., **Iraq**; comm. ctr.; rly. terminus; p. (1965) 134,000 (met. a.).

Erebus, mtn., active volcano, Victoria Land, **Antarctica**; alt. 4,027 m.

Erewash, l. gov. dist., Derbys., **Eng.**; a. close to Nottingham inc. Ilkeston and Long Eaton; p. (1971) 101,838.

Erfurt, admin. dist., **E. Germany**; a. 7,322 km²; p. (1983) 1,238,200.

Erfurt, c., **E. Germany**; on Gera R.; cath., ctr. of mkt. gardening and seed-growing dist., textiles, machin., foodstuffs, footwear, radios, heavy engin.; p. (1983) 214,231.

Ericht, loch, **Scot.**; in central Grampians; 25 km long; hydroelec. scheme.

Erie, c., N.W. Penns., **USA**; pt. on L. Erie; coal, iron, grain, petroleum; machin., domestic appliances; p. (1980) 119,000 (c.), 280,000 (met. a.).

Erie Canal. *See* **New York State Barge Canal**.

Erie, one of Great Lakes (the shallowest), **N. America**, separating Canada from USA; 386 km long, 48–91 km wide; polluted waters; petroleum resources.

Erith, former M.B., Kent, **Eng.**; on Thames estuary; plastics, paints, varnishes, timber, concrete; now inc. in London bor. of Bexley.

Eritrea, prov., **Ethiopia**; tobacco, cereals, pearl fishing; demands for autonomy; secessionist rebellion crushed (1978); severe drought 1982–3; cap. Asmara, a. 118,503 km²; p. (est. 1980) 2,426,200.

Erivan. See Yerevan.

Erlangen, t., Bavaria, **W. Germany**; univ.; textiles, elec. and precision engin., gloves; p. (est. 1983) 102,400.

Ermelo, t., **Neth.**; ctr. of agr. dist.; p. (1968) 35,434.

Ernakulam, t., Kerala, **India**; cotton, coffee, hides; p. (est. 1970) 213,811 (c.), 493,460 (met. a.).

Erne, R., **N. Ireland/R.o.I.**; links Ls. in Cavan and Fermanagh; 115 km long.

Erode, t., S. Tamil Nadu, **India**; on R. Cauvery; p. (1981) 142,252 (t.), 275,991 (met. a.).

Erzgebirge (Ore Mtns.), mtn. range along border of **ČSSR** and **Germany**; reaching highest peak in Mt. Klinovec (1,240 m) in ČSSR; uranium; tourism.

Erzurum, t., **Turkey**; agr. ctr. on fertile plateau c. 1,890 m a.s.l.; formerly of gr. strategic importance; univ.; earthquake (1983); p. (1980) 190,241.

Esbjorg, spt., **Denmark**; W. cst. of Jutland; export harbour on N. Sea cst.; exp. agr. prod.; fishing; airport; p. (est. 1977) 77,354.

Esch-sur-Alzette, t., **Luxembourg**; mng. ctr.; steel; p. (1981) 25,100.

Eschwege, t., Hesse, **W. Germany**; cas.; machin., textiles, leather, cigars, chemicals; p. (est. 1983) 23,400.

Eschweiler, t., N. Rhine–Westphalia, **W. Germany**; N.W. of Aachen; lignite mng., steel, iron metallurgy; p. (est. 1983) 53,200.

Esdraelon, plain, **Israel**; between Carmel and Gilboa Mtns.

Eṣfahān (Isfahan, anc. Aspadana), c., central **Iran**; prov. cap.; historic, picturesque c. noted for carpets and metal ware; tourism, airpt.; new steel mill; p. (1976) 671,825.

Esher, t., Elmbridge, Surrey, **Eng.**; on R. Mole, residtl.; Sandown Park racecourse; p. (1981) 61,446.

Eshowe, health resort, Natal, **S. Africa**; 64 km from Tugela R.; p. (est. 1967) 4,800.

Esk, R., Annandale and Eskdale, **Scot.**; Cumbria, **Eng.**; attractive agr. valley; flows into Solway F. from confluence of Black and White Esk Rs.; 37 km long.

Eskilstuna, t., **Sweden**; on R. of same name; iron, steel, machin., machin. tools; p. (1983) 88,987.

Eskisehir, t., **Turkey**; W. of Ankara, anc. Dorylaeum; rly. ctr.; meerschaum; p. (1980) 309,431.

Esmeraldas, prov., **Ecuador**; cap. E. on R. of same name; cacao, tobacco; a. 14,152 km²; p. (1982) 247,870.

Esmeraldas, pt., **Ecuador**; bananas, timber, tobacco, cacao, rubber; gold mines nearby; terminal of petroleum pipeline from Oriente; p. (1982) 141,030.

Esneh. See Isna.

Espirito Santo, I., **Brazil**; sugar, cotton, coffee, fruits, lumber, thorium; cap. Vitória; a. 40,883 km²; p. (est. 1983) 2,192,000.

Espiritu Santo, I., **New Hebrides**; volcanic I., lgst. of gr.; depopulation.

Essaouira (Mogador), spt., **Morocco**; cereals, almonds, gum-arabic, crude oil; p. (1960) 26,392.

Essen, c., N. Rhine–Westphalia, **W. Germany**; gr. industl. c., ctr. of Ruhr conurbation; coal, steel (Krupp), electric power, engin.; canal links with Dortmund–Ems and Mittelland canals and with Rhine; minster severely damaged in second world war; p. (est. 1983) 635,200.

Essequibo, R.; flows N. from Brazilian border draining half **Guyana**; lower course navigable, rapids; timber in upper valley; 960 km long.

Essex, non-met. co., **Eng.**; bounded on S. by Thames, on E. by N. Sea; co. t. Chelmsford; on London clay and chalk; agr.; wheat, barley, sugar-beet; mkt. gardens; S.W. of co. forms part of Greater London with mftg. subs.; oil refineries at Shell Haven; civil nuclear power sta. at Bradwell; univ. at Colchester; a. 2,637 km²; p. (1981) 1,469,065.

Esslingen, t., Baden-Württemberg, **W. Germany**; on R. Neckar; mach. and rly. shops; textiles,

chemicals, leather gds.; Liebfrauen church (1440); p. (est. 1983) 88,400.

Essonne, dep., **France**; S. of Paris; cap. Ivry; a. 1,810 km²; p. (1982) 988,400.

Esteli, cap., Esteli, **Nicaragua**; on Inter-American Highway; p. (est. 1972) 26,764.

Eston, t., Cleveland, **Eng.**; 5 km E. of Middlesbrough; shipbldg. and repairing.

Estonia (Estoniya), constituent rep. **USSR**; borders on Baltic, G. of Finland, G. of Riga; lowland with many Ls.; farming and dairying, fishing; oil deposits; hydroelec. power; mainly Lutheran; univ.; cap. Tallinn; a. 45,610 km²; p. (1970) 1,357,000.

Estoril, wat. pl. and thermal spa, **Portugal**; N. side of Tagus estuary; holiday resort; p. (1981) 24,312.

Estremadura, maritime prov., **Portugal**; agr., tourism; cap. Lisbon; a. 5,348 km²; p. (1981) 1,064,976.

Estremadura, region, S.W. **Spain**; on the border of Portugal; largely plateau, alt. 450–900 m.; heathy moorland; sheep; less arid conditions than in remainder of central Spain allow olives, vines, cereals; irrigation in valleys of Tagus, Guadiana; govt. project to develop a. in progress.

Esztergom, t., **Hungary**; R. pt. on Danube; iron foundries, machine tools; mineral springs; cath.; p. (est. 1966) 26,000.

Etang de Berre, lagoon, Bouches-du-Rhône, S.E. **France**; E. of Rhône delta; traversed by Rhône–Marseille canal; salt pans; oil refineries in a.; approx. a. 260 km².

Étaples, t., Pas-de-Calais, **France**; seaside resort; p. (1982) 11,310.

Etawah, t., Uttar Pradesh, **India**; textiles; p. (1981) 112,174.

Ethiopia (Abyssinia), indep. st. N.E. **Africa**; temperate climate as a result of high plateau terrain; coffee most impt. comm. crop, but poor communications inhibit economic development; low per capita income and rapid growth of p.; potential for hydro-electric power is lge., one sta. open on Awash R.; mftg. dominated by textiles; agr. improvements encouraged by Peasant's Association; severe drought began in 1970's and continued in 1980's, affects low-lying and Eastern regions; cap. Addis Ababa; monarchy abolished 1975; a. 1,221,900 km²; p. (1984) 42,000,000.

Ethiopian Highlands, mtns., **Ethiopia**; rise over 4,500 m; source of headwaters of tribs. of R. Nile.

Etna, volcano, N.E. Sicily, **Italy**; most recent eruptions 1971 and 1979; alt. 3,276 m.

Eton, t., Berks., **Eng.**; on N. bank of R. Thames opposite Windsor; public school, founded by Henry VI; p. (1981) 3,523.

Etruria, anc. dist., **Italy**; now forms Tuscany; home of the Etruscans and part of the Roman empire by 400 B.C.

Etruria, t., Staffs., **Eng.**; part of Stoke-on-Trent; seat of Josiah Wedgwood's potteries (1769).

Ettrick and Lauderdale, l. gov. dist., part of Borders Reg. in Tweed Valley, **Scot.**; p. (1981) 31,594.

Euboea (Evvoia), lgst. of Greek Is., Aegean Sea; mtnous. (Mt. Delphi 1,746 m); vines and olives in lowlands, sheep and goats in highlands; a. 3,864 km²; p. (1981) 188,410.

Euclid, t., Ohio, **USA**; electrical and agr. machin.; p. (1980) 59,999.

Eucumbene Dam and **L.,** N.S.W., **Australia**; major storage of Snowy Mtns. hydroelectric scheme; holds eight times as much water as Sydney harbour.

Eugene, c., Ore., **USA**; univ.; mkt. ctr. for rich agr. and lumbering region; fruit-canning, sawmilling; headquarters of Willamette National Forest; p. (1980) 106,000 (c.), 275,000 (met. a. with Springfield).

Euphrates, lgst. R. in S.W. **Asia**; rises in Armenian uplands and joined by the Tigris enters Persian G. as the Shatt-al Arab; anc. ctr. of civilisation; modern irrigation, navigation, high dam opened 1973 and Ataturk Dam (1981) part of multi-purpose project; 2,848 km long.

Eure, dep., Normandy, **France**; agr., fruit, livestock, textiles; cap. Evreux; a. 6,037 km²; p. (1982) 462,000.

Eure-et-Loire, dep., N. **France**; mainly agr.; cap. Chartres; a. 5,934 km²; p. (1982) 362,000.

Europe, continent; W. peninsula of Eurasian land mass; no well-defined bdy. with Asia but line normally accepted runs along Ural Mtns. to Caspian Sea and Caucasus to Black Sea,

Sea of Marmara and Dardanelles; after Australia, Europe is smallest continent in a., but contains 11 per cent of world's p. and even more of world's economic activity; climate varies from Arctic to Mediterranean and from temperate maritime to severe continental; major physical features inc. Alps, Pyrenees in S., Baltic Shield in N.; major political div. between E. and W. Europe along Iron Curtain; W. Europe also divided into economic grs. EEC and EFTA; major concentration of p. and economic activity within Golden Triangle (q.v.), total a. c. 10,360,000 km²; p. (est. 1984) 490,456,000 (excl. USSR).

Euro-port, name of the post-war expansion of the port of Rotterdam, **Neth.**; capable of handling 100,000 tonne oil-tankers; oil refining; European oil supply ctr.; joined to Rotterdam by the New Waterway.

Evanston, t., Ill., **USA**; on L. Michigan, sub. of Chicago; univ.; p. (1980) 73,706.

Evansville, c., Ind., **USA**; on Ohio R.; shipping and comm. ctr. for agr. region; coal mng.; p. (1980) 130,496 (c.), 309,408 (met. a.).

Eveneki National Area, Siberia, **RSFSR**; forest and tundra covered; home of Eveneki people; cap. Tura; a. 740,740 km²; p. (1970) 13,000.

Everest, Mt. (Chomolungma = Goddess Mother of the Earth), Himalaya, on frontier of Nepal and Tibet, **China**; alt. 8,854 m; hgst. mtn. in the world; Hillary and Tenzing first to reach summit in 1953; within Nepal Nat. Park.

Everett, mftg. t., Mass., **USA**; nr. Boston; iron and steel; p. (1980) 37,195.

Everett, t., Wash., **USA**; on Puget Sound; harbour; comm. ctr.; timber; tourism; p. (1980) 54,413.

Everglades, Fla., **USA**; subtropical a.; extensive marshes; home of Seminole Indians; lge. scale drainage since 1905; early vegetables.

Evesham, mkt. t., Wychavon, Hereford and Worcs., **Eng.**; on R. Avon, in Vale of Evesham, 24 km S.E. of Worcester; fruit ctr.; tourism; p. (1981) 15,271.

Évora, t., cap. of Upper Alentejo prov., S. **Portugal**; mkt. for agr. prod.; cath.; p. (1981) 34,851.

Évreux, t., cap. of Eure dep., **France**; mkt. ctr.; p. (1982) 54,645 (met. a.).

Evros, prov., **Greece**; borders Bulgaria and Turkey; a. 4,191 km²; p. (1981) 148,486.

Exe, R., Somerset and Devon, **Eng.**; rises on Exmoor, flows S. via Exeter to English Channel at Exmouth; 86 km long.

Exeter, l. gov. dist., cath. c., co. t., Devon, **Eng.**; former Roman Isca; E. of Dartmoor on R. Exe; mkt. t.; univ.; aircraft components; airport; p. (1981) 95,621.

Exmoor, Somerset and Devon, **Eng.**; sandstone moorland, deep wooded valleys; Nat. Park.

Exmouth, t., East Devon, **Eng.**; on estuary of R. Exe; holiday resort; p. (1981) 28,787.

Exploits, R., Newfoundland, **Canada**; length 240 km; used for hydroelectric power.

Eye, mkt. t., Mid Suffolk, **Eng.**; 29 km N. of Ipswich; anc. church; p. (1981) 1,786.

Eyemouth, burgh, Berwick, **Scot.**; on E. cst. 14 km N. of Berwick; fishing; p. (1981) 3,353.

Eyre Lake, shallow salt L., S. **Australia**; 16 m rapid incr. in a. in wet year of 1974 caused lge. incr. in pelican p.; a. 7,800 km².

Eyre Peninsula, S. **Australia**; between Gr. Australian Bight and Spencer G.; iron-ore deposits; a. 51,800 km².

F

Fabriano, t., Marches, **Italy**; in Apennines; cath.; paper mills; p. (1981) 28,708.

Faenza, t., Ravenna, **Italy**; at foot of Apennines; majolica, textiles; p. (1981) 55,003.

Fagersta, t., Västmanland, **Sweden**; iron, steel smelting; p. (est. 1970) 17,054.

Failsworth, t., Gtr. Manchester, **Eng.**; N.E. of Manchester; textiles, elec. gds.; p. (1981) 21,751.

Fairbanks, t., Alaska, **USA**; univ.; sawmilling; mng.; p. (1980) 22,645.

Fairfield, t., Conn., **USA**; chemicals, automobile parts; univ.; p. (1970) 56,487.

Fair I., midway between Shetland and Orkney,

Scot.; bird sanctuary; famous for brightly patterned, hand-knitted articles.

Fairmont, t., W. Va., **USA**; glass, machin., coal by-products; p. (1980) 23,863.

Faiyum (El Faiyûm), t. and region, N. **Egypt**; oasis nr. L. Karun (anc. L. Moeris), fertilised by Nile water and silt; cereals, sugar-cane, fruits, cotton; archaeological finds; p. of t. (1976) 166,910.

Faizabad, t., Uttar Pradesh, **India**; rly. junc.; sugar refining; p. (1981) 101,873 (t.), 143,167 (met. a.).

Falaise, t., Calvados, **France**; birthplace of William the Conqueror; p. (1982) 8,820.

Falaise de l'Ile de France, low S.E.-facing escarpment, 80 km S.E. and E. of Paris, **France**; overlooks Champagne Pouilleuse; ch. vine-growing dist. for champagne-wine ind. of Reims, Epernay.

Falcón, st., **Venezuela**; bordering Caribbean Sea; cap. Coro; p. (est. 1970) 408,051.

Falconara Marittima, t., **Italy**; nr. Ancona; spt.; oil refining, shipbldg.; p. (1981) 29,071.

Falkirk, burgh, l. gov. dist., Central Reg., **Scot.**; 16 km S.E. of Stirling; foundries, bricks, chemical, aluminium wks., concrete, timber yards; battles 1298 and 1746; p. (1981) 144,437 (l. gov. dist.) 36,875 (burgh).

Falkland, burgh, North East Fife, **Scot.**; 5 km S. of Auchtermuchty; mkt.; p. (1981) 960.

Falkland Is., Brit. Crown col., **S. Atl.,** comprises E. and W. Falkland and adjacent Is.; sheep rearing (for wool); cap. Port Stanley on E. Falkland I.; invasion by Argentina led to Falklands War (1982); airpt. opened (1985) capable of taking long range wide bodied aircraft; a. 12,173 km²; p. (est. 1980) 2,000.

Falkland Is. Dependencies, S. Atl.; inc. Is. of S. Georgia and S. Sandwich; a. 4,092 km²; p. (of S. Georgia) 11 males; now form part of Brit. Antarctic Terr.

Fall River, c., Mass., **USA**; on Mt. Hope Bay; pt. of entry; clothing, rubber gds., food prods., paper; p. (1980) 92,574 (c.), 176,831 (met. a.).

Falmouth, t., Carrick, Cornwall, **Eng.**; on W. side of estuary of R. Fal. 16 km S. of Truro; sheltered harbourage; offshore oil supply base; seaside resort; fisheries, ship repairing, mng., quarrying, lt. engin.; cas.; pt.; p. (1981) 18,525.

False Bay, inlet on E. side of C. of Good Hope peninsula, **S. Africa.**

Falster, I., Baltic, **Denmark**; cap. Nyköbing; p. (1965) 45,906.

Falun, t., Kopparberg, **Sweden**; paper; copper mines now exhausted; p. (1983) 51,192.

Famagusta, t., spt., **Cyprus**; on E. cst.; resort; anc. crusade pt.; p. (est. 1970) 42,500.

Famatina, t., La Rioja prov., **Argentina**; in foothills of Andes, 576 km N.W. of Córdoba; copper-mines.

Fano, t., **Italy**; sm. pt. on Adriatic cst., N. of Ancona; seaside resort; p. (est. 1971) 48,259.

Fareham, t., l. gov. dist., Hants., **Eng.**; at N.W. corner of Portsmouth Harbour; p. (1981) 88,274.

Farewell (Kap Farvel), C., southernmost tip of **Greenland.**

Farewell, C., most N. point S.I., **N.Z.**

Fargo, t., N.D., **USA**; rly. ctr. and R. pt.; grain, farm machin.; p. (1980) 61,383.

Faringdon, mkt. t., Vale of White Horse, Oxon., **Eng.**; Faringdon Folly.

Farnborough, t., Rushmoor, Hants., **Eng.**; 5 km N. of Aldershot military camp; Royal Aircraft Establishment; p. (1981) 45,453.

Farne Is., gr. of islets off Northumberland cst., **Eng.**; bird sanctuary; National Trust.

Farnham, t., Waverley, Surrey, **Eng.**; at N. foot of N. Downs, 16 km W. of Guildford; mkt.; p. (1981) 35,289.

Farnworth, t., Gtr. Manchester, **Eng.**; nr. Bolton; textiles, engin., paper; p. (1981) 24,589.

Faro, spt., cap. of Algarve prov., **Portugal**; cork, figs, oranges; p. (1981) 27,974.

Faroe Is., 320 km N.W. of the Shetlands, **Scot.**; cap. Thórshavn (Strömö I.); Danish possession but not member of EEC; impt. fisheries; a. 1,399 km²; p. (est. 1975) 41,000.

Farrukhabad, t., Uttar Pradesh, **India**; on Ganges R.; gold, lace, brass wk.; p. (1981) 145,793.

Fars, prov., S. **Iran**; agr.; cap. Shīrāz; p. (est. 1971) 1,500,000.

Fastnet, lighthouse in Atl. Oc., 7·2 km S.W. C. Clear, Irish cst.

Fatima, v., W. **Portugal**, nr. Leiria; R.C. pilgrimage.

Fatshan *See* **Foshan.**

Faversham, pt., Swale, N.E. Kent, **Eng.**; at head of F. creek; mkt.; fruit, hops, bricks, brushes, engin.; p. (1981) 16,098.

Fawley, t., Hants., **Eng.**; on W. shore Southampton Water; lge. oil refinery with pipeline to Staines and Heathrow Airpt.; synthetic rubber.

Fayetteville, t., N.C., **USA**; agr. processing; p. (1980) 247,000 (met. a.).

Feather, R., N. Cal., **USA**; R. project for water supply irrigation, and hydroelectric power.

Featherstone, t., West Yorks., **Eng.**; p. (1981) 14,043.

Fécamp, sm. spt. on cst. of Normandy, **France**; fishing, tourism, 12th cent. abbey; p. (1982) 21,696.

Fedchenko, glacier, lgst. in **USSR**; in Pamir-Altai mtns. of central Asia; 80 km long.

Federal German Republic. *See* **Germany, Fed. Rep. of.**

Feira de Santana, t., Bahia, **Brazil**, inland mkt. t.; recent industl. expansion results from SUDENE development plan; p. (est. 1980) 273,800.

Feldberg, highest peak in Black Forest, **W. Germany**; alt. 1,495 m.

Feldkirch, t., Vorarlberg, **Austria**; on Swiss frontier; p. (1961) 17,343.

Felixstowe, pt., Suffolk Coastal, Suffolk, **Eng.**; now one of country's best container pts.; seaside resort; p. (1981) 20,858.

Felling, Tyne and Wear, **Eng.**; Tyneside mftg. dist.; p. (1981) 36,431.

Feltham. *See* **Hounslow.**

Fenland, l. gov. dist., Cambs., **Eng.**; agr. a. in N. of co. inc. Wisbech, Chatteris, March, Whittlesey and North Witchford; p. (1981) 67,215.

Fens, The, low-lying dist. around the Wash, **Eng.**; artificial drainage begun in 17th cent.; impt. agr. dist.; root crops, wheat, fruit, bulbs; a. 3,367 km².

Feodosiya, t., Ukrainian SSR, **USSR**; in Crimea; major Black Sea pt., tobacco, hosiery; exp. wheat; resort and sanatoria; p. (est. 1968) 59,000.

Ferghana, region, Uzbek SSR, **USSR**; deep basin at W. end of Tien Shan Mtns.; drained W. by R. Syr Dar'ya; semi-arid but extensive irrigation system allows intensive cultivation of cotton, citrus fruits, silk, rice; ch. ts. Kokand, Namangan.

Ferghana, c., Uzbek SSR, **USSR**; hydroelectric power, petroleum refining, textiles; deposits of ozocerite nearby; p. (est. 1980) 177,000.

Fermanagh, former co.; l. gov. dist., **N. Ireland**; bisected by R. Erne and lakes; stock raising, dairying; p. (1981) 51,558 (dist.).

Fermoy, t., Cork, **R.o.I.**; on R. Blackwater; cath.; woollens; p. (1971) 3,237.

Fernando de Noronha, l., fed. terr., N.E. cst. Brazil; penal settlement and met. sta.; cap. Vila dos Remédios; a. 26 km²; p. (est. 1975) 1,300.

Fernando Po. *See* **Biako.**

Ferozepore, t., Punjab st., N.W. **India**; rly. t.; admin. ctr.; p. (1961) 97,932.

Ferrara, c., N. **Italy**; nr. head of Po delta; cath., univ., palaces; mkt. for fertile plain; silk, hemp, wine; oil refinery nearby; petrochemicals; birthplace of Savonarola; p. (1981) 149,453.

Ferro (Hierro), most S. of the **Canary Is.**; a. 275 km²; cap. Valverde; chosen by Ptolemy (A.D. 56) for his prime meridian and used by French scientists in 17th cent.; reckoned as exactly W. 20° of Paris.

Ferryhill, v., Durham, **Eng.**; 8 km S. of Durham, in gap through limestone ridge which separates Wear valley from Tees valley; commands main N. to S. route along lowland E. of Pennines.

Fertile Crescent, an arc of fertile land from the Mediterranean Sea, N. of the Arabian Desert, to Persian G.; home of some very early civilisations and migrations.

Fez (Fès), c., **Morocco**; lies inland 160 km E. of Rabat; one of the sacred cities of Islam; univ. attached to mosque (one of lgst. in Africa); comm. ctr.; p. (1973) 321,460 (c.), 426,000 (met. a.).

Fezzan, prov., S.W. **Libya**; desert plateau with numerous wells and inhabited oases; p. (1964) 78,326.

Ffestiniog (Festiniog), t., Meirionnydd, Gwynedd, N. **Wales**; at head of Vale of Ffestiniog, 14 km E. of Portmadoc; contains Ffestiniog and Blaenau Ffestiniog; slate quarries; pumped-storage hydroelec. sta. (1963); cement; narrow gauge rly.; p. (1981) 5,437.

Fianarantsoa, t., **Madagascar**; rice mills, meat preserves; p. (1975) 68,054.

Fichtelgebirge, mtn. range, N.E. Bavaria, **W. Germany**; extending into ČSSR, rising to 1,051 m in Schneeberg; forested slopes.

Fiesole, t., Tuscany, **Italy**; on summit of wooded hill overlooking Florence and the Arno; residtl.; 11th cent. cath.; p. (1981) 14,486.

Fife, l. gov. reg., former co., E. **Scot.**; occupies a. between Tay and Forth estuaries; industl. dist. based originally on coalfields; a. 1,305 km²; p. (1981) 326,480.

Fiji, S.W. Pac. Oc., former Brit. col., gained independence in 1970; comprises over 800 Is.; tropical climate; agr. basis of economy, especially sugar and coconut prods.; gold an impt. exp.; forestry and tourism developing; forms ctr. of communications in S.W. Pac. Oc.; international airport at Nadi; ch. pt. and cap. Suva; a. 18,272 km²; cosmopolitan p. (est. 1984) 674,000.

Filey, t., North Yorks., **Eng.**; 8 km S.E. of Scarborough; seaside resort; p. (1981) 5,702.

Filton, Bristol, Avon, **Eng.**; aircraft wks.

Fincmley. *See* **Barnet.**

Findhorn, v., Moray, **Scot.**; resort; 12th cent. abbey; fishing; p. (1981) 530.

Findlay, t., Ohio, **USA**; on Blanchard R.; agr. machin., tyres, beet sugar refining; p. (1980) 35,594.

Fingal's Cave, Staffa I., Inner Hebrides, W. **Scot.**; basaltic columns.

Finger Lakes, gr. of narrow glacial Ls., N.Y., **USA**; picturesque resorts and state parks.

Finistère (Lat. *finis terrae* = land's end), dep. N.W. **France**, in Brittany; cap. Quimper; fishing, tourism; a. 7,071 km²; p. (1982) 828,700.

Finland, rep., N. **Europe**; part of Scandinavia; low-lying plateau severely eroded by ice to form 60,000 Ls.; economy based on timber (forests cover 72 per cent of a.); world's leading exporter of pulp and paper; increasing importance of metal and engin. inds.; cap. Helsinki; a. 360,318 km²; p. concentrated in S.; p. (est. 1984) 4,859,000.

Finland, G. of, E. arm of Baltic Sea, between Finland and USSR.

Finnart, Dumbarton, **Scot.**; crude oil terminal situated in Loch Long. N.W. Glasgow; pipeline to Grangemouth.

Finnmark, most N. co., **Norway**; inhabited by Lapps; whale fisheries; lge. copper deposits discovered nr. Reppan fjord; a. 48,125 km²; p. (est. 1972) 77,060.

Finsbury. *See* **Islington.**

Finsteraarhorn, highest peak in Bernese Oberland, **Switzerland**; 4,277 m.

Finucane I., pt., W. **Australia**; deepwater pt. to ship ion ore and new t. projected.

Firenze. *See* **Florence.**

Firozabad, t., Uttar Pradesh, **India**; glassware; agr. tr.; p. (1961) 98,611.

Fishguard and Goodwick, spt., Preseli, Dyfed, **Wales**; on S. of Cardigan Bay; steamer connection to Cork and Rosslare (Ireland); p. (1981) 4,908.

Fitchburg, t., Mass., **USA**; paper, machin., textiles; p. (1980), 39,580 (t.), 99,957 (met. a.).

Fitzroy, R., W. **Australia**; flows into King Sound; dry in winter; irrigation; 560 km long.

Flamborough Head, promontory of Yorks. cst., **Eng.**; steep chalk cliffs; lighthouse; anc., Brit. earthwork (Danes' dyke).

Flanders, region between R. Scheldt and cst., crossed by Franco-Belgian frontier; Dunkirk, Lille ctrs. of French F.; Belgian F. divided into 2 provs., E. and W., p. (est. 1983) 676,398 and 549,525 respectively; caps. Bruges and Ghent.

Fleet, t., Hart, Hants., **Eng.**; 6 km N.W. of Aldershot; p. (1981) 26,004.

Fleetwood, spt., Wyre, Lancs., **Eng.**; at mouth of Wyre, Morecambe Bay; deep-sea fish. pt.; fish processing; lge. chemical plant nearby; p. (1981) 28,467.

Flensburg, spt., Schleswig-Holstein, **W. Germany**; on Baltic, close to Danish border; shipbld., machin., chemicals, rum distilleries, fishing; p. (est. 1983) 86,400.

Flevosted, t., **Neth.**; admin. ctr. of new S.E. Polder.

Flinders I., Australia; lgst I. in the Furneaux gr., Bass Strait; famous for mutton birds.

Flinders Range, chain of mtns., S. **Australia**; extending 400 km N.E. from head of Spencer G., reaching 1,190 m in St. Mary's Peak; named after Matthew Flinders; uranium ore at Mt. Painter.

Flint, t., Delyn, Clwyd, **Wales**; viscose textile yarn, cas. ruins; p. (1981) 16,454.

Flint, t., Mich., **USA**; motorcars, aircraft engines; p. (1980) 160,000 (c.), 522,000 (met. a.).

Flintshire, former co., N. **Wales**; now part of Clwyd.

Flodden, v. Northumberland, **Eng.**; on R. Till; battle between James IV of Scot. and the English under the Earl of Surrey 1513.

Flora, t., **Norway**; new t. 136 km N. of Bergen; p. (1965) 7,700.

Florence (Firenze), c., Tuscany, **Italy**; on R. Arno; univ.; leather-work; famous for art treasures, cath. and churches; ruled by Medici 1421–1737; birthplace of Dante and Machiavelli; severely affected by heavy floods Nov. 1966; EEC univ.; p. (1981) 448,331.

Florence, t., N.W. Ala., **USA**; on Tennessee R., nr. Wilson dam; textile, steel plants; p. (1980) 37,029 (t.), 135,023 (met. a.).

Flores, I., most northwesterly of Azores gr., Portuguese; cap. Santa Cruz; French to set up ballistic missiles tracking sta.; a. 142 km²; p. (1970) 5,630.

Flores, I., **Indonesia**; mtnous.; volcanic, densely forested; a. 22,973 km²; p. (1961) 803,000.

Flores Sea, between Sulawesi and Flores, **Indonesia.**

Florianópolis, spt., cap. of Santa Catarina st., **Brazil**; comm. ctr., fishing; p. (est. 1980) 197,900.

Florida, st., **USA**; Sunshine St.; admitted to Union 1845; st. flower Orange Blossom, st. bird Mockingbird; between Atl. Oc. and G. of Mexico; lowlying, swampy, inc. Everglades; sea resorts on Atl. cst.; citrus fruit and subtropical agr.; agr. processing; cap Tallahassee; a. 151,670 km²; p. (1980) 9,740,000.

Florida Keys, archipelago, **USA**; extends in an arc from S.E. cst. Florida W.S.W. to Key West in G. of Mexico; fishing resorts.

Florida Strait, between Florida and Bahama Is.; course of Gulf Stream from G. of Mexico.

Florina. See **Phlorina.**

Florissant (St. Ferdinand), t., Mo., **USA**; sub. of St. Louis on Missouri R.; p. (1980) 55,372.

Flushing. See **Vlissingen.**

Fly, lgst. R. of **Papua New Guinea**; flows S.E. from Victor Emmanuel Range to G. of Papua; 1,280 km long.

Fochabers, v., Moray, **Scot.**; nr. mouth of Spey; tourist resort; food canning; p. (1981) 1,496.

Focsani, t., **Romania**; at foot of Transylvanian Alps; wine and grain ctr.; p. (est. 1970) 39,629.

Foggia, cath. c., S. **Italy**; rly. ctr. and mkt. ctr. for plain of Apulia; site of cas. of Frederick II; p. (1981) 156,467.

Foix, t., cap. of Ariège dep., S. **France**; historic t.; p. (1982) 10,064.

Foligno, t., central **Italy**; in Apennines, on Topino R.; cath., textiles, paper; p. (1981) 52,484.

Folkestone, t., Shepway, Kent, **Eng.**; seaside resort; pt. for Folkestone–Boulogne ferry to France 46 km; p. (1981) 43,742. See **Cheriton.**

Fond du Lac, t., Winnebago L., Wis., **USA**; cath.; machine tools, domestic appliances; resort; p. (1980) 35,863.

Fonseca, Gulf of, Honduras; lgst. indentation along Pac. cst. of Central America; sm. pt. of Amapala, US naval base, and new deepwater pt.

Fontainebleau, t., Seine-et-Marne, **France**; on R. Seine, 56 km S.E. Paris; in former royal forest (a. 17,200 ha); magnificent palace; p. (1982) 18,753.

Fontenoy, v., **Belgium**; nr. Tournai; scene of battle (1745) when the French under Marshal Saxe defeated the English and their allies; p. (est. 1969) 655.

Foochow. See **Fuzhou.**

Fordlandia. See **Belterra.**

Foreland, N. and **S.,** two headlands on E. cst. Kent, **Eng.**; between which are the Goodwin Sands and Pegwell Bay; lighthouses; sea battle between de Ruyter and Monk (1666).

Forest Heath, l. gov. dist., Suffolk, **Eng.**; part of Breckland inc. Mildenhall and Newmarket; p. (1981) 51,907.

Forest Hills, residtl. a., central Queen's bor., N.Y., **USA**; national and international matches played at West Side Tennis Club.

Forest of Dean. See **Dean, Forest of.**

Forfar, royal burgh, Angus, **Scot.**; former cty. t.; jute, linen; p. (1981) 12,742.

Forli, c., Emilia-Romagna, central **Italy**; route ctr. in Appennine foothills; felt, textiles, footwear; p. (1981) 110,806.

Formby, t., Merseyside, **Eng.**; on W. cst., 10 km S.W. of Southport; residtl.; p. (1981) 25,798.

Formosa, prov., N. **Argentina**; bordering on Paraguay; timber; cap. Formosa; a. 72,067 km²; p. (1980) 292,479.

Formosa. See **Taiwan.**

Forres, royal burgh, Moray, **Scot.**; on Findhorn R. nr. Moray F.; agr., forestry, engin., distilleries; cas.; p. (1981) 8,346.

Forst, t., Cottbus, **E. Germany**; on R. Neisse; E. section of t. Polish since 1945; textiles; p. (est. 1970) 29,284.

Fortaleza, c., cap. of Ceará st., **Brazil**; in the dry Sertão reg. of the N.E.; terminus of cattle droving route; recent growth resulting from planned industl. devel. to revitalise reg.; p. (est. 1980) 1,306,800.

Fort Collins, t., Col., **USA**; ctr. of rich farming a.; grain, sugarbeet, livestock; univ.; p. (1980) 65,092 (t.), 149,184 (met. a.).

Fort de France, cap. of **Martinique,** Fr. W.I.; landlocked harbour; exp. sugar, rum; comm. ctr.; Fr. naval base; p. (est. 1972) 99,051.

Fort Dodge, t., Iowa, **USA**; on Des Moines R., in rich agr. a.; grain, gypsum, coal; p. (1980) 29,423.

Fort George, R., W. Quebec, **Canada**; rises in Labrador and flows into Hudson Bay; 880 km long.

Fort Gouraud, t., **Mauritania**; modern iron-ore mines.

Forth, R., **Scot.**; formed by two headstreams rising to N. of Ben Lomond which meet nr. Aberfoyle; takes meandering course to Alloa, whence it expands into Firth of Forth (q.v.); 165 km long.

Forth, Firth of, lge. inlet, E. cst. of **Scot.**; submerged estuary of R. Forth; navigable by lge. vessels for 64 km inland to Grangemouth; other pts., Leith, Rosyth (naval), Bo'ness; l. (to Alloa) 80 km; the Forth rly. bridge (1890) spans the F. at Queensferry; the road bridge (1964) is the longest suspension bridge in Europe.

Forth and Clyde Canal, Scot.; links F. of Forth at Grangemouth and F. of Clyde at Glasgow; not completely navigable; 61 km long.

Fort Johnston, t., S. **Malawi**, on L. Malombe; new t., 1966; tobacco; airpt.

Fort Knox, Ky., **USA**; nation's gold bullion depository; military air-base.

Fort Lamy. See **Ndjamene.**

Fort Lauderdale, c., Fla., **USA**; on Atl. cst. N. of Miami; lge. marina; citrus fruits, mkt. garden prod.; holiday resort; p. (1980) 153,000 (c.), 1,018,000 (met. a. inc. Hollywood and military personnel and families).

Fort Myers, t., Fla., **USA**; on G. of Mexico; resort; Eddison experimented here; p. (1980) 168,000 (met. a. inc. Cape Coral).

Fortrose, t., royal burgh, Ross and Cromarty, **Scot.**; on S. cst. of Black Isle, on Moray F.; p. (1981) 1,319.

Fort Smith, c., Ark., **USA**; on Arkansas R.; mkt. ctr. for agr. a.; varied mnfs., inc. furniture, glass; coal and zinc mined nearby; p. (1980) 204,000 (met. a.).

Fort Victoria, (Masvingo), t., **Zimbabwe**, agr. and mng. ctr.; cattle, historic ruins in Zimbabwe Nat. Park; p. (1982) 30,600.

Fort Wayne, c., Ind., **USA**; at confluence of 2 headstreams of Maumee R.; rly. repair shops; elec. machin. and domestic appliances, originally a Fr. fort; p. (1980) 172,000 (c.), 383,000 (met. a.).

Fort William. See **Thunder Bay.**

Fort William, burgh, Lochaber, **Scot.**; nr. head of Loch Linnhe, at base of Ben Nevis; aluminium factory; pulp- and paper-mill at Corpach; p. (1981) 11,079.

Fort Worth, c., Texas, **USA**; rly. and comm. ctr. on Trinity R.; livestock and grain mkt.; oil refining, meat packing, oilfield equipment; p. (1980) 1,284,000 (c.), 2,964,000 (met. a.) with Dallas.

Fort Yukon, trading sta. on Yukon R., N.E. Alaska, **USA.**

Foshan (Fatshan), c., Guandong, **China;** S.W. of Guangzhou; iron and steel, textiles; p. (1953) 123,000.

Fos-sur-Mer, t., Bouches-du-Rhône, S. **France;** nr. Marseilles; new deepwater pt. and oil refinery; bauxite terminal; iron and steel plant; p. (1982) 9,446.

Fotheringhay, v., Northampton, **Eng.;** on R. Nene; Mary Queen of Scots beheaded (1587) in F. Castle.

Fougères, t., Ille-et-Vilaine, **France;** cas.; footwear, clothing; p. (1982) 25,131.

Foulness I., S. Essex, **Eng.;** at mouth of R. Crouch; owned by Min. of Defence; site of projected third London airport of Maplin, now abandoned; projected container and oil pt.

Fountains Abbey, ruined 12th cent. Cistercian abbey, North Yorks., **Eng.;** nr. Ripon.

Fowey, sm. spt., Cornwall, **Eng.;** nr. mouth of R. Fowey; exp. kaolin; resort; fishing; p. with St. Austell (1981) 36,639.

Foxe Basin and Channel, to N. of Hudson Bay, between Baffin I. and Southampton I., **Canada.**

Foyers, Falls of, Inverness, **Scot.;** E. of Loch Ness, nr. Fort Augustus; aluminium wks., the first hydroelectric plant erected in Britain (1896).

Foyle, Lough, inlet, **N. Ireland;** between Donegal (R.o.I.) and Londonderry; outlet of R. F.; Londonderry t. at head of inlet.

Foynes Is., R.o.I.; oil terminal on N. side, E. of Battery Point.

Foz do Iguacú, t., Paraná, **Brazil;** highway (coffee road) from Paranaguá; rapid growth with opening of Itaipú Dam; p. (1982) 150,000.

Framingham, t., Mass., **USA;** 32 km W. of Boston; lt. inds.; p. (1980) 65,113.

Framlingham, mkt. t., Suffolk, **Eng.;** N.E. of Ipswich; cas. remains.

Francavilla Fontana, t., Apulia, **Italy;** rly. junc.; agr. tr.; p. (1981) 32,588.

France, rep., W. **Europe;** bounded by 3 seas; Eng. Channel, Atl. Oc., Mediterranean; variety of climate and relief; leading agr. cty. of Europe; 75 per cent under cultivation; exps. grain, fruit, vegetables, wine; industl. expansion since second world war; lgst. inds. inc. iron and steel, motor vehicles, aircraft, engin., textiles, chemicals; tourism impt.; EEC member; cap. Paris; 96 deps.; excessive social, economic, and political concentration around Paris promotes description of France as "Paris and the French Desert"; recent attempts to break this down using framework of 21 economic planning regions; a. 550,634 km²; p. (est. 1984) 54,449,000.

Franceville, t., Gabon, Equatorial Africa; on R. Ogooué; lined to Libreville as part of the Trans-Gabon rly. project; manganese mines opened 1962; founded by De Brazza.

Francistown, t., Botswana, **Southern Africa;** airpt.; butter, coppermng.; p. (1981) 31,065.

Frankenthal, t., Rhineland-Palatinate, **W. Germany;** in industl. dist. of Mannheim-Ludwigshafen, engin., machin.; p. (est. 1983) 43,600.

Frankfurt-on-Main, c., Hesse, **W. Germany;** local point in Rhine-Main urban region; rly. ctr., transit pt.; machin., cars, chemicals, elec. engin., publishing; airport; cath., univ.; birthplace of Goethe; p. (est. 1983) 614,700.

Frankfurt-on-Oder, c., Brandenburg, **E. Germany;** agr. ctr., R. pt., rail junc.; machin., chemicals; E. part of t. (Slubice) Polish since 1945; p. (est. 1973) 65,644.

Frankischer (Franconian) Jura, plateau with steep N.-facing edge, S.E. of **W. Germany;** runs 128 km S.W. from Fichtelgebirge; drained by Regnitz and Altmühl Rs.

Franklin, dist., N.W. Terr., **Canada;** comprising the Is. of Arctic Canada from Banks I. to Baffin I., including Boothia Peninsula and Melville Peninsula; sparsely populated; furs; a. 1,434,943 km².

Františkovy Lázne (Franzensbad), famous spa, W. Bohemia, **ČSSR;** 445 m a.s.l., between the Erzgebirge and the Fichtelgebirge.

Franz Josef Land (Zemlya Frantsalosifa), RSFSR; archipelago in Arctic Oc. N. of Novaya Zemlya; a. 20,720 km²; mainly ice-covered.

Frascati, t., **Italy;** 19 km S.E. of Rome; summer resort; famous villas and arch. remains; nuclear research ctr.; p. (1981) 18,728.

Fraser I. (Great Sandy I.), Queensland, **Australia;** low sandy I., timber reserve and Nat. Park; concern over ecology caused discontinuation of mineral sand exp. (1977).

Fraser, R., B.C., **Canada;** rises at c. 1,800 m on W. slopes Rocky Mtns.; famous salmon fisheries; routeway; Vancouver nr. delta; 1,360 km long.

Fraserburgh, spt., burgh, Banff and Buchan, **Scot.;** one of the main E. cst. herring pts.; p. (1981) 12,479.

Frauenfeld, t., cap. of Thurgau can., **Switzerland;** 11th cent. cas.; textiles; p. (1970) 17,576.

Fray Bentos, t., cap. of Rio Negro dep., **Uruguay;** pt. on R. Uruguay 80 km from mouth; meatprocessing; p. (est. 1970) 14,000.

Fredericia, t., pt., E. Jutland, **Denmark;** major rly. junc.; textiles, silver and electroplated gds., fertilisers; oil refinery; p. (est. 1970) 43,513.

Fredericton, c., cap. of N.B., **Canada;** on St. John R.; univ., cath.; timber, shoes, plastics; p. (1971) 23,612.

Frederiksberg, sub. of Copenhagen, **Denmark,** with indep. municipal status; p. (est. 1974) 95,870.

Frederikshaab, sm. spt. on W. cst. of **Greenland;** fish processing.

Frederikshavn, fish. pt., N. Jutland, **Denmark,** on Kattegat; p. (est. 1970) 32,826.

Frederikstad, t., **Norway;** at mouth of Glomma R.; ctr. of pulp and paper-producing ind.; electrotechnical inds., shipbldg., fish canning; p. (est. 1971) 29,671.

Frederiksvaerk, t., Sjaelland, **Denmark;** impt. iron and steel wks.

Freetown, c., cap. of **Sierra Leone;** pt. on Atl. Oc.; one of lgst. natural harbours in world; humid, oppressive climate; exp. diamonds, palm oil; engin., food processing, oil refining; fishing; p. (est. 1974) 214,443.

Freiberg, t., **E. Germany;** S.W. of Dresden, at foot of Erzgebirge; mng. academy (silver discovered 12th cent.); metallurgy, textiles, glass, porcelain; p. (est. 1973) 50,750.

Freiburg im Breisgau, c., Baden-Württemberg, **W. Germany;** in Black Forest; cath., univ.; cultural ctr.; tourism; p. (est. 1983) 178,400.

Freising, t., Bavaria, **W. Germany;** N.E. of Munich; cath.; agr. machin., textiles, chemicals; p. (est. 1983) 35,500.

Freital, t., **E. Germany;** S.W. Dresden; glass, uranium ore processing; coalmines nearby; p. (est. 1970) 42,159.

Fréjus, t., Var dep., S.W. **France;** cath., Roman ruins; resort on Fr. Riviera; p. (1982) 32,698.

Fréjus, Col de, Alpine pass, **France** and **Italy,** 2,083 m, under which runs the Mont Cenis tunnel (13·6 km).

Fremantle, spt., W. **Australia;** at mouth of Swan R., 19 km S.W. from Perth, principal pt. in W. Australia and first Australian pt. of call for mail steamers; part of Perth met. a.; giant industl. complex at Kwinana; p. (1976) 29,940.

French Equatorial Africa, formerly included Gabon, Congo (Brazzaville), Ubangi-Shari and Chad, sts. which are now independent.

French Guiana, Fr. Overseas dep., on N. cst. of **S. America,** between Surinam to W. and Brazil to S. and E.; tropical climate; little developed and thinly populated; ch. ctr. of p. and spt. at cap. of Cayenne; economy based on agr. especially sugar and forestry; some gold and bauxite mng.; a. 90,650 km²; p. (1982) 73,022.

French Polynesia, Fr. overseas terr., in **S. Pac. Oc.,** comprising several archipelagos; Society Is., Marquesas Is., Tubuai Is., Tuamotu Is., and Gambier Is.; increased autonomy from 1977; cap. Papeete; a. 4,002 km²; p. (1977) 137,400.

French Somaliland. See **Djibouti.**

French S. and Antarctic Terrs., Fr. overseas terr., comprising several grs. of Is. and Antarctic terr. of Adélie Land; a. 409,220 km²; p. 132 (mainly scientists).

French West Africa, comprised former Fr. cols. of Dahomey (Benin), Ivory Coast, Mauritania, Niger, Fr. Guinea, Upper Volta, Senegal, Fr. Soudan (Mali).

Freshwater, sm. t., I. of Wight, **Eng.;** at W. end of I., 13 km W. of Newport; resort.

Fresnillo de Gonzalez Echeverria, t., Zacatecas, **Mexico;** alt. 2,227 m; mkt. t., silver mng.; p. (1970) 101,316.

Fresno, c., Cal., **USA;** ctr. of vast irrigated fruitgrowing dist.; p. (1980) 218,000 (c.), 515,000 (met. a.).

Fribourg (Freiburg), c., cap. of F. can., **Switzerland**; between Berne and Lausanne; viaduct and bridges; cath., univ.; p. (est. 1978) 39,300.

Fribourg (Freiburg), can., **Switzerland**; mainly dairy farming; cereals, sugarbeet, cheese; a. 1,671 km²; p. (1980) 185,246.

Friedrichshafen, t., **W. Germany**; on Bodensee; machin., boat bldg., motors; resort; p. (est. 1983) 51,800.

Friendly Is. *See* **Tonga.**

Friern Barnet. *See* **Barnet.**

Friesland, prov., N. **Neth.**; cap. Leeuwarden; dairying, horses, cattle; natural gas on Ameland I.; a. 3,432 km²; p. (1983) 595,248.

Frimley and Camberley, ts., Surrey Heath, former U.D., Surrey, **Eng.**; 5 km N. of Farnborough; lt. engin., plastics; military training ctr.; p. (1981) 52,017.

Frinton and Walton, Tendring, Essex, **Eng.**; on E. cst., 8 km N.E. of Clacton; seaside resort; p. (1981) 14,651.

Frisches Haff, shallow freshwater lagoon, Baltic cst. of **Poland**; 85 km long, 6–18 km broad.

Frisian Is., chain of Is. stretching from Den Helder to Jutland, along csts. of Neth., Germany, and Denmark; ch. Is. are Texel, Vlieland, Terschelling, Ameland (West F. Is.), Nordeney, Borkum (East F. Is.), Sylt, Föhr, Rømø (North F. Is.); severe erosion; Sylt now half size it was 500 years ago.

Friuli-Venezia Giulia, aut. reg. (created 1963), N.E. **Italy**; comprising 3 provs. Udine, Gorozia, Trieste; p. (1981) 1,233,984.

Frobisher Bay, inlet in S. Baffin I., N. **Canada**, extending 320 km between Cumberland Sound and Hudson Strait.

Frodingham, t., Humberside, **Eng.**; on W. flank of limestone ridge, Lincoln Edge; impt. iron-ore open-cast mines; mnfs. iron and steel.

Frome, mkt. t., Mendip, Somerset, **Eng.**; on R. Frome, 18 km S. of Bath; p. (1981) 14,527.

Frome, R., Dorset, **Eng.**; flows from N. Dorset Downs into Poole Harbour.

Frontignan, t., Hérault, S. **France**; oil refining; pipeline under sea from Sète; produces muscat; p. (1982) 14,961.

Frunze, c., cap. of Kirghiz SSR, **USSR**; univ.; engin., textiles, meat-packing; p. (est. 1984) 590,000.

Fuerteventura, I., **Canary** gr.; a. 1,717 km²; p. (1970) 18,192.

Fujayrah, emirate, one of **United Arab Emirates,** Persian G.; p. (est. 1982) 38,000.

Fujian (Fukien), prov., **China**; cap. Fuzhou; intensive agr., rice and sugar-cane; shellfish raised along cst.; a. 123,103 km²; p. (est. 1983) 26,400,000.

Fujisawa, t., Honshu, **Japan**; bearings, machin.; p. (est. 1984) 300,248.

Fujiyama, extinct volcano, **Japan**; 96 km S.W. of Tokyo; pilgrim resort; hgst. peak of Japan; alt. 3,780 m.

Fukui, c., cap. of F. pref., central Honshu, **Japan**; synthetic fibres, paper; old silk-weaving ctr.; p. (1979) 237,080.

Fukuoka, c., N. Kyushu, **Japan**; pt. on Hakata Bay; univ. ctr., old cas. t.; textiles, dolls, shipbldg.; p. (est. 1984) 262,837.

Fukushima, c., N. Honshu, **Japan**; ceramics, foods, steel; publishing; p. (est. 1984) 346,030.

Fukuyama, c., S. Hokkaido, **Japan**; p. (1979) 344,484.

Fulda, t., Hesse, **W. Germany**; nr. Kassel; on R. Fulda; palace, abbey; textiles, metallurgy, rubber; route ctr.; p. (est. 1983) 56,400.

Fulham. *See* **Hammersmith.**

Fulwood, t., Lancs., **Eng.**; 3 km N.E. of Preston; part of Central Lancashire New Town.

Funchal, cap. of **Madeira Is.**; pt., winter resort; cath.; p. (1970) 105,791.

Fundy, Bay of, inlet between Nova Scotia and New Brunswick, **Canada**; lge. tidal range of 21 m.

Furka Pass, Switzerland; between Valais and Uri cans.; 2,433 m.

Furneaux Is., S.E. **Australia**; in Bass Strait, belonging to Tasmania; lgst. is Flinders I.; p. (1966) 1,220.

Furness, dist., Cumbria, **Eng.**; between Morecambe Bay and the Irish Sea.

Fürstenwalde, t., Frankfurt, **E. Germany**; on R. Spree; metallurgy, leather, tyres; p. (est. 1970) 30,830.

Fürth, t., Bavaria, **W. Germany**; nr. Nürnberg; toy and glass inds.; p. (est. 1983) 99,000.

Fusan. *See* **Pusan.**

Fuse, t., Honshu, **Japan**; machin., textiles, chemicals; now part of Higashiosaka; p. (1970) 500,173.

Fushimi, c., Honshu, **Japan**; sub. of Kyoto.

Fushun, c., Liaoning, N. **China**; at foot of Changbai Shan, 35 km N.E. of Shenyang; major industl. ctr.; possesses world's thickest bituminous coal seam (127 m) worked by deep and opencast mines; oil refinery based on local oil shales; steelwks., chemicals; p. (est. 1983) 1,210,000.

Fuskiki, spt., Honshu, **Japan**; serves Toyama c. with metals, coal.

Futa, La, pass, Tusco-Emilian Apennines, N. **Italy**; used by main road from Bologna to Florence; alt. 903 m.

Futa Jalon (Fouta Djalon), upland dist., mostly in **Guinea**, W. Africa with outliers in Liberia and Sierra Leone.

Fuxin (Fuzin), c., Liaoning, N. **China**; ctr. of lge. coalfield; p. (est. 1983) 646,000.

Fuzhou (Foochow), c., cap. of Fujian prov., **China**; at mouth of Min R., major comm. and industl. ctr.; became impt. with tea exp.; former treaty pt.; p. (est. 1983) 1,142,000.

Fylde, W. Lancs., **Eng.**; low plain behind coastal sand dunes; pig- and poultry-rearing dist.; ch. t. Blackpool; as l. gov. dist. excluding Blackpool p. (1981) 68,440.

Fylingdales, ballistic missile early warning sta. on N. Yorks. moors, **Eng.**

Fyn, I., **Denmark**; in Baltic Sea; a. 3,419 km²; cap. Odense; dairying, sugarbeet; p. (1971) 433,765.

Fyne, loch on Argyll and Bute cst., W. **Scot.**; an arm of F. of Clyde; offshore oil platform construction: 64 km long.

Fyzabad, t., Uttar Pradesh, **India**; mkt. t.; sugar refineries; p. (1961) 88,296.

G

Gabès, spt., **Tunisia**; on G. of Gabès, 320 km S. of Tunis; dates, henna, wool; p. (1975) 40,585.

Gabon, rep., W. **Africa**; Cameroon to N., Zaïre to S. and E.; tropical climate, hot, humid; much tropical rain forest; forestry main ind. but mng. increasingly impt.; petroleum exp. creating increasing prosperity; manganese at Moanda (S.), iron-ore at Mekambo (N.E.); communications geared mainly to mng. areas; major pts. Libreville (cap.), Port Gentil; Trans-Gabon rly. project to promote exploitation of timber; first part opened 1979; intense forest cover makes internal air services very impt.; airport at Libreville; agr. development limited by small size of p.; a. 266,770 km²; p. (est. 1983) 1,127,000.

Gaborone (Gaberones), cap. **Botswana**; formerly sm. v.; chosen as cap. for new rep., bldg. began 1964; p. (1981) 59,657.

Gadag-Betgeri, t., Karnataka, **India**; cotton and silk weaving; p. (1981) 117,368.

Gaeta, t., naval pt., **Italy**; on promontory on shore of G. of Gaeta; the anc. Caietae Portus; cath.; p. (1981) 22,605.

Gafsa, t., **Tunisia**; phosphate mng. ctr.; p. (1975) 42,225.

Gaillard Cut, excavated channel, **Panama Canal Zone**; carries Panama Canal through Culebra Mtn. from L. Gatun to Pac. Oc.; 11 km long.

Gainesville, t., Fla., **USA**; univ.; mkt. gardening; electronics, wood prod.; p. (1980) 81,371 (c.), 151,348 (met. a.).

Gainsborough, t., West Lindsey, Lincs., **Eng.**; on R. Trent; agr. implements, milling, packing and wrapping machin.; some R. traffic; mkt.; George Eliot's St. Ogg's in *Mill on the Floss*; p. (1981) 18,691.

Gairdner, salt L., S. **Australia**; a. 4,766 km².

Gairloch, sea loch and v., W. Ross and Cromarty, **Scot.**; resort, fishing.

Galapagos, volcanic Is., Pac. Oc.; 960 km W. of **Ecuador** (to whom they belong) on equator; flora and fauna peculiar to each I.; visited by Darwin 1835; now a wildlife sanctuary; a. 7,428 km²; p. (est. 1970) 3,550.

Galashiels, burgh, Ettrick and Lauderdale, **Scot.**; on Gala Water, 3 km above confluence with R. Tweed; tweeds, woollens; p. (1981) 12,294.

Galati or **Galatz**, c., E. **Romania**; major inland pt. on lower Danube; cath.; p. (1978) 252,592.

Galesburg, t., Ill., **USA**; engin., coal mng.; p. (1970) 36,290.

Galicia, historic region, S.E. **Poland** and W. Ukraine, **USSR**.

Galicia, region, N.W. **Spain**; comprising provs. La Coruña, Lugo, Orense, and Pontevedra; p. (1981) 2,811,942.

Galilee, northern div. of Palestine in Roman times, containing the ts. Cana, Capernaum, Tiberias, Nazareth; the ch. scene of Christ's ministry.

Galilee, Sea of (Lake Tiberias), also known as L. Gennesaret; Biblical associations; 207 m below level of Med.; Israel plans to draw water from L. to irrigate Negev; a. 166 km².

Gallarate, t., **Italy**; textiles; p. (1981) 46,915.

Galle, c., pt. on S.W. cst. of **Sri Lanka**; exp. tea, rubber, coconut oil; suffered from competition with Colombo after construction of modern harbour there; p. (est. 1983) 88,000.

Gallego, R., N.E. **Spain**; rises in Pyrenees, flows S. to R. Ebro at Zaragoza; provides irrigation around Zaragoza; valley used by main rly. across Pyrenees from Pau (France) to Zaragoza; 176 km long.

Gallipoli. *See* **Gelibolu.**

Gällivare, dist., N. **Sweden**, in Norrbotton prov.; rich iron-ore deposits; p. (1976) 25,276.

Galloway, anc. dist. S.W. **Scot.**; inc. l. gov. dists. of Stewartry and Wigtown; dairying.

Galloway, Mull of, the extremity of the Rinns of G., the most southern pt. of **Scot.**

Galston, burgh, Kilmarnock and Loudoun, **Scot.**; on R. Irvine, nr. Kilmarnock; p. (1981) 5,295.

Galt., t., Ont., **Canada**; textiles, shoes; p. (1971) 38,134.

Galveston, c., spt., Texas, **USA**; on I. in Bay at entrance to G. of Mexico; gr. cotton and sulphur pt. with lge. exp. of agr. prod.; mills, foundries, food-processing, chemicals; univ., resort; p. (1980) 61,902 (c.), 195,940 (met. a.).

Galway, co., Galway Bay, Connacht, **R.o.I.**; fishery, cattle, marble quarrying; a. 6,351 km²; p. (1981) 57,725.

Galway, co. t., Galway, **R.o.I.**; univ.; spt., fishing; sawmills, textiles, printing; p. (1981) 37,835.

Gambia, The, member st. of **Senegambia**, W. **Africa**, on Atl. Oc.; comprises St. Mary's I. (on which is Banjul, the cap.) and narrow mainland enclave (average width 32 km) extending 320 km inland astride R. Gambia, hot all year, summer rain, but savannah inland; agr. is basis of economy, esp. groundnuts; economic aid from Taiwan; communications developed around Banjul (spt. and airpt.); union with Senegal, 1982; one of Africa's smallest sts.; a. 11,295 km²; p. (1983) 695,886.

Gambia, R., Senegambia, rises in Futa Jalon Plateau, flows N. and W. into Atl. Oc. at Banjul; forms main channels of communication through Gambia, 1,120 km long.

Gambier Is., Fr. Polynesia, **S. Pac. Oc.**, 4 coral Is.; a. 31 km².

Gand. *See* **Ghent.**

Gandhinagar, new cap. of Gujarat, **India**; on Sabarmati R., 21 km N. of Ahmadabad; under construction; planned initial p. 75,000 rising to 200,000.

Ganges (Ganga), sacred R. of **India**; rises in Himalayas and flows to Bay of Bengal via alluvial cones at foot of Himalayas and by several delta mouths, on one of which stands Calcutta; navigable for lge. ships from Allahabad; delta alone larger than Eng. and Wales; flood plain and delta very fertile and densely populated; removal of irrig. water by India causes friction with Bangladesh; agreement over division of water at Farraka barrage reached (1978); 2,400 km long.

Gangtok, t., cap. of **Sikkim**, E. Himalayas; agr. tr. ctr.; carpets; p. (est. 1971) 15,000.

Gan Jiang (Kan R.), S. **China**; flows N. to L. Poyang; valley provides road route from Guandong to Jianxi prov.; c. 880 km. long.

Gansu (Kansu), prov., N.W. **China**; borders Inner Mongolia; cap. Lanzhou; pastoral agr., wheat, cotton, tobacco; coal reserves; rich iron ore deposits; attemps to break down isolation by attracting foreign investment; a. 391,507 km²; p. (est. 1982) 60,500,000.

Gap, t., Hautes Alpes, S.E. **France**; textiles; p. (1982) 32,097.

Gard, dep., S. **France**; in Languedoc, on Mediterranean; cap. Nimes; vines, olives, sericulture; a. 5,879 km²; p. (1982) 532,000.

Garda, L., between Lombardy and Venezia, **Italy**; variety of scenery, winter resort; a. 370 km²; greatest depth, 346 m.

Gardéz, t., **Afghanistan**; alt. 2,287 m; ctr. of comm. and transport; p. (est. 1969) 39,142.

Garforth, t., West Yorks., **Eng.**; coalmng., lt. inds.; p. (1981) 28,405.

Garigliano, R. and dist., S. central **Italy**; where Liri R. joins Gari R. below Cassino; nuclear power plant.

Garmisch-Partenkirchen, t., Bavaria, **W. Germany**; winter sports; p. (est. 1983) 27,900.

Garo Hills, mtnous. dist., Assam, **India**; a. 8,078 km²; dense forests; p. (1961) 307,228.

Garonne, R., S.W. **France**; rises at foot of Mt. Maladetta (Pyrenees), flows via Toulouse and agr. valley, and enters Gironde estuary 32 km below Bordeaux; 720 km long.

Garrigue, region, Languedoc, S. **France**; low limestone hills, run N.E. to S.W., W. of Rhône delta; semi-arid; Mediterranean vegetation to which region gives name; winter pasture for sheep; olives; Montpellier, Nimes located on S. flank.

Garut, t., W. Java, **Indonesia**, mtn. resort, lge. spinning mill; p. 24,219.

Gary, c., Ind., **USA**; on S. shore of L. Michigan; leading producer of steel, tinplate, cement; p. (1980) 139,000 (c.), 643,000 (met. a. inc. Hammond NE. Chicago).

Gascony, anc. prov., S.W. **France**; now comprises deps. along Atl. cst. and Pyrenees; Landes, Gers, Hautes-Pyrenees, and parts of Lot-et-Garonne, Tarn-et-Garonne, Haute Garonne, Gironde, and Ariège. Battleground in Hundred Years War.

Gastonia, t., N.C., **USA**; impt. textile ctr.; p. (1980) 47,333.

Gateshead, t., met. dist., Tyne and Wear, **Eng.**; on R. Tyne opposite Newcastle; engin., food-processing, pumps, paper; pt.; p. (1981) 211,658.

Gatineau, R., **Canada**; trib. of Ottawa R., which it joins nr. Ottawa; length 480 km; hydroelec. power; forested valley.

Gatwick, West Sussex, **Eng.**; 40 km S. London; first airport in world where trunk road, main rly. line and air facilities combined in one unit.

Gauhati, t., **India**; temporary cap. of Assam being developed in E. suburb of Dispur; univ.; silk, cotton, lace, oil refinery; pipeline from Barauni; p. (1971) 123,783 (t.), 200,377 (met. a.).

Gaul (Lat. *Gallia*), embraced in the lands inhabited by Celtic peoples in Roman times, covering what is now modern France (Gaul proper), Belgium, N. Italy, and parts of Germany, Neth., and Switzerland. South of the Alps was known as Cisalpine Gaul, north of the Alps as Transalpine Gaul.

Gauri-Sankar, mtn. in Himalayas, Nepal and Tibet, **China**; 56 km W. of Mt. Everest; alt. 7,149 m.

Gävle, spt., **Sweden**; timber, textiles, steel, porcelain; p. (1983) 87,671.

Gävleborg, co., **Sweden**; ch. t., Gävle; a. 18,544 km²; p. (est. 1983) 291,497.

Gaya, t., Bihar, **India**; Buddhist pilgrim ctr.; cottons, silks; p. (1981) 247,075.

Gaza, t., N.E. **Egypt**; ch. t. of Gaza Strip (q.v.); anciently the t. where Samson brought down the temple.

Gazankulu (Machangana), Bantu Terr. Authority (1969), **S. Africa**; home of Shangana and Tsonga p.; cap. Giyana; p. (1980) 514,280.

Gaza Strip, coastal a. under Egyptian admin. since 1949; occupied by Israeli troops, Nov. 1956–March 1957, and since June 1967.

Gaziantep, t., **Turkey**; S.W. of Malatya; mkt. t.; p. (1980) 374,290.

Gazli, Uzbek SSR, **USSR**; 96 km N.W. of Gukhara; natural gas field; pipeline to Chelyabinsk opened 1963; destroyed by earthquake (1976).

Gdańsk (Danzig), c., spt., N. **Poland**; Baltic pt.; on branch of Vistula; annexed to Germany 1939, restored to Poland 1945; shipbldg., machin., chemicals, metals; Gdańsk, Gdynia and Sopot admin. as single c. (Trójmiasto = tricity); p. (est. 1983) 464,600.

Gdynia, spt., Gdańsk, N. **Poland**; competes with spt. of Gdańsk for Polish hinterland; impt. comm., rly. and industl. ctr.; part of the Trójmiasto; p. (est. 1983) 240,200.

Gedling, l. gov. dist., Notts., **Eng.**; Basford, Carlton and Arnold and N.E. outskirts of Nottingham; p. (1981) 104,184.

Geelong, c., Victoria, **Australia**; spt. on Corio Bay (part of Pt. Phillip Bay); expanding comm. and industl. ctr.; improved pt. facilities in 1960s, bulk grain terminal; p. (1976) 122,080 (c.).

Gejiu (Kokiu), t., Yunnan prov., **China**; leading tin-mng. ctr. of China; p. (1953) 159,700.

Gela, t., S. Sicily, **Italy**; in cotton-growing a.; petrochemicals; p. (1981) 74,789.

Gelderland, prov., **Neth.**; E. and S. of Utrecht prov., a. 5,022 km²; cap. Arnhem; cereals, tobacco; cattle rearing; p. (1982) 1,727,487.

Gelibolu (Gallipoli), pt. and penin. on the Dardanelles, **Turkey**; scene of unsuccessful landing by British and Anzac troops 1915; 176 km long.

Gelligaer, t., Rhymney Valley, Mid Glamorgan, **Wales**; 6 km N.E. of Pontypridd; coal mng.; p. (1981) 34,118.

Gelsenkirchen, t., N. Rhine–Westphalia, **W. Germany**; in Ruhr conurb. on Rhine–Herne canal; collys., ironwks., glass, chemicals, oil refining; p. (est. 1983) 295,400.

Geneva, c., cap of G. can., **Switzerland**; at exit of Rhône from L. Geneva; cath., univ.; former H.Q. of League of Nations; H.Q. of ILO, WHO, and Red Cross; watchmkg., jewellery, elec. gds., optical instruments; tourist resort; birthplace of Rousseau; p. (1980) 335,401 (met. a.), 349,040 (Canton).

Geneva (L. Léman), L., S.W. corner of **Switzerland**; forms a gr. crescent of water, source of poetic inspiration; 371 m a.s.l.; a. 578 km².

Génissiat, **France**; site of gr. barrage and hydro-elec. power sta. on Rhône below Geneva.

Genk, t., Limburg, **Belgium**; stainless steel wks., petrochemicals; p. (1981) 61,502.

Gennevilliers, t., Hauts-de-Seine, **France**; N.W. sub. of Paris; R. pt.; p. (1982) 45,445.

Genoa (Genova), c., ch. pt. **Italy**; cath., univ., palaces; handles one-third of Italy's foreign tr.; pt. and airpt. expansion, shipyards, steel-wks., engin., textiles, tanning; p. (1981) 762,595.

George L., N.Y., **USA**; Adirondack mtns.; picturesque resort.

Georgetown, cap., **Cayman Is.**; pt.; p. (1970) 3,975.

Georgetown (Demerara), c., cap. of **Guyana**; on Demerara R.; exp. sugar, cocoa, coffee, timber, gold, diamonds, bauxite; airpt. nearby; botanical gardens; p. (est. 1976) 72,049 (c.), 187,056 (met. a.) (25 per cent of cty's p.).

Georgetown. *See* **Penang.**

Georgia, st., S.E. **USA**; one of 13 original sts., admitted to Union 1788; st. flower Cherokee Rose, st. bird Brown Thrasher; on Atl. cst.; rising to Appalachians; impt. arable agr.; cotton and lumber inds.; major source of kaolin; ch. ts., Atlanta (cap.), Savannah; a. 152,489 km²; p. (1980) 5,464,000.

Georgia (Gruziya), constituent rep., **USSR**; rich agr., fruit, tobacco, grain; mng. inc. manganese, gold, oil; several hydroelectric power plants; coastal and mtn. resorts; active Jewish community; cap. Tbilisi; a. 69,671 km²; p. (1970) 4,688,000.

Georgian Bay, arm of L. Huron, S. Ont., **Canada**; separated from L. by Manitoulin I. and Saugeen peninsula; c. 160 km long, c. 80 km wide; L. pts., Owen Sound, Midland, Parry Sound; Georgian Bay Is., Nat. Park.

Gera, c., cap. of G. admin. dist., **E. Germany**; on White Elster R.; woollens, printing; lignite mined nearby; p. (1983) 129,891.

Geraldton, spt., W. **Australia**; N. outlet for wheat belt; also exps. wool and manganese; early tomatoes; super phosphate; p. (1976) 18,773.

Germany, Democratic Rep. of, and **E. Berlin** (**E. Germany**), rep., Central Europe; partition from W. Germany complete by 1948; part of N. European Plain; 7th industl. nation of world; lignite field supplies 70 per cent of energy; main inds., optics, electronics and precision machin., chemicals, heavy engin.; member of Comecon; 15 admin. dists. (Bezirke); cap. E. Berlin; a. 108,267 km²; p. (est. 1984) 16,658,000.

Germany, Fed. Rep. of (**W. Germany**), **W. Europe**; partition complete by 1948; N. half part of N. European Plain; rises in S. to Bavarian Alps; 2nd lgst. trading nation of world; mainly industl. with core in Ruhr conurb.; motor vehicles, chemicals, precision engin.; member of EEC; tourism; 10 admin. dists. (*Länder*); W. Berlin, former cap. now isolated in E.

Germany; cap. Bonn; a. (inc. W. Berlin) 248,459 km²; p. (est. 1984) 61,214,000.

Germiston, t., Transvaal, **S. Africa**; nr. Johannesburg; gold-mng.; rly. wkshps., engin., machin., chemicals; gas pipeline from Sasolburg, p. (1970) 281,494 (met. a.).

Gerona, c., cap. of G. prov., **Spain**; cath.; textiles, chemicals; p. (1981) 466,997 (prov.).

Gerrards Cross, t., S.E. Bucks., **Eng.**; 14 km E. of High Wycombe; residtl.

Gers, dep. S.W. **France**; cap. Auch; grain, vines, brandy; a. 6,291 km²; p. (1982) 174,154.

Gersoppa Falls, Sharavati R., Karnataka, **India**; hgst. cascade 253 m; hydroelec. power.

Gezira, dist., **Sudan**, N.E. Africa; between Blue and White Niles; c. 12,173 km² capable of irrigation provided by Blue Nile at Sennar Dam; lge-scale growing of high-quality cotton; total a. c. 20,200 km².

Ghadames (Ghudamis), oasis, Sahara Desert, **Libya**; at point where Tunis, Algeria, Libya converge 480 km S.W. of Tripoli.

Ghaghara (Gogra), sacred R., **India**; trib. of Ganges, rises in Tibet, flows through Uttar Pradesh; lge. catchment a. but poorly developed floodplain; 960 km long.

Ghana, rep., W. **Africa**; indep. st., member of Brit. Commonwealth; tropical monsoon climate, but rainfall decreases inland; badly affected by Sahelian drought; S. Ghana more developed than N.; agr. basis of comm. economy and cocoa (of which Ghana is world's lgst producer) major exp.; Volta R. scheme produces power from main dam at Akosombo and an aluminium smelter plant began production in 1967; oil refining and production; communications network based on Accra and Takoradi on cst., and inland ctr. of Kumasi; development of road network vital for expansion of comm. agr.; 3 univs.; pts. at Takoradi and Tema closely linked with internal economic growth; cap. Accra; a. 238,539 km²; p. (est. 1984) 12,205,574.

Ghardaia, t., **Algeria**; N. of Sahara; ch. t. of Mzab valley; p. (1966) 30,167.

Ghats, mtn. ranges which border the Deccan plateau in S. **India**. The **Eastern Ghats** are broken by many Rs. and rise only to 1,362 m in Northern Circars. The **Western Ghats** form an almost unbroken range, reaching 2,672 m in Dodabetta in Nilgiri hills; rainfall extremely heavy; forests; hydroelectric power.

Ghaziabad, t., Uttar Pradesh, **India**; on R. Jumna opposite Delhi; p. (1981) 271,730.

Ghazipur, t., Uttar Pradesh, N. **India**; on Ganges, E. of Varanasi; p. (1961) 37,147.

Ghazni, mtn. t., E. **Afghanistan**; once cap. of empire of Mahmud, c. A.D. 1000; now mkt. t.; p. (est. 1982) 31,985.

Ghent, c., cap. of E. Flanders prov., **Belgium**; pt. at confluence of Rs. Scheldt and Lys; cath., univ.; textiles, steel, plastics, chemicals; oil refinery; p. (1982) 237,687.

Ghor, El, depression, **Jordan** and **Israel**, between Sea of Galilee and Dead Sea 3–24 km wide; agr. resettlement scheme.

Giant's Causeway, basaltic columns on promontory of N. cst. of Moyle, **N. Ireland**.

Gibraltar, City of, Brit. terr. at W. entrance to Mediterranean; rocky I., 426 m, joined to Spain by sandy isthmus; few natural resources; economy depends on tourism, Admiralty dockyard, services to shipping, and entrepôt tr., to close 1983; Spanish govt. lays claim to terr.; frontier with Spain opened (1985); a. 6·5 km²; p. (1981) 28,7219

Gibraltar, Strait of, connects Mediterranean with Atl., 13·6 km wide; of strategic importance.

Gidgelpha-Moomba, dist., S. **Australia**; lge. natural gas field; pipeline to Adelaide.

Giessen, t., Hesse, **W. Germany**; on R. Lahn; univ.; various mnfs.; p. (est. 1983) 73,200.

Gifu, t., Central Honshu, **Japan**; cas.; fans, lanterns, textiles; tourism for cormorant fishing; p. (est. 1984) 410,357.

Gigha, I, Argyll and Bute, **Scot.**; off W. cst. of Kintyre; 10 km by 3 km.

Gijón, spt., Oviedo, **Spain**; on Bay of Biscay; gd. harbour; tobacco, petroleum, coal, earthenware; steel wks. nearby; p. (1981) 256,432.

Gila, R., N.M. and Arizona, **USA**; trib. of R. Colorado; used for irrigation in Imperial valley; 1,040 km long.

Gilan, prov., N.W. **Iran**; on Caspian Sea, bounded by USSR; sub-tropical climate; agr., inc. cotton and rice; cap. Rasht; p. (1976) 1,579,317.

Gilbert Is. *See* **Kiribati.**

Gilgit, dist., Kashmir, **India;** mtnous., exceeding 6,000 m on N. and W.; with Ladakh links India with Tibet; p. 77,000.

Gillingham, t., l. gov. dist., Kent, **Eng.;** 3 km E. of Chatham; on R. Medway; naval and military establishments; cement, lt. inds.; p. (1981) 93,741.

Gippsland, dist., S.E. Victoria, **Australia;** between Dividing Range and cst.; main brown coal field supplying local power plants; intensive dairying and mkt. gardens for Melbourne.

Girardot, t., **Colombia;** R. pt. and airport on upper course of Magdalena R.; linked by rly. to Bogotá; coffee, hides, ceramics; p. (est. 1970) 50,000.

Girgenti. *See* **Agrigento.**

Gironde, dep., S.W. **France;** vineyards, grain, fruit, wines; cap. Bordeaux; a. 10,723 km²; p. (1982) 1,122,400.

Gironde, estuary, S.W. **France;** formed by junc. of Rs. Garonne and Dordogne; navigable to Pauillac and Bordeaux.

Girvan, burgh, Kyle and Carrick, **Scot.;** on F. of Clyde, 29 km S.W. of Ayr; summer resort; p. (1981) 7,878.

Gisborne, c., spt., N.I., **N.Z.;** on Poverty Bay, 96 km N.E. of Napier; freezing-wks.; fishing; p. (1976) 31,790.

Giuba, R. *See* **Juba** R.

Giurgiu, t., **Romania;** pt. on Danube; opposite Ruse, Bulgaria; linked by oil pipelines with Ploiesti; p. (1966) 32,300.

Givors, t., Rhône dep., **France;** on Rhône R. 16 km S. of Lyons; mnfs. inc. glass; oil refining near by at Feyzin; p. (1982) 20,554.

Giza, El, t., **Egypt;** on Nile, sub. of Cairo; nr. pyramids of Khufu (Cheops), Khafra (Chephren), and the Sphinx; film ind.; p. (1976) 1,230,446.

Gjövik, t., S. **Norway;** on L. Mjösa; furniture, footwear, lt. inds.; p. (est. 1970) 25,164.

Glace Bay, t., Cape Breton I., Nova Scotia, **Canada;** coal; harbour; p. (1971) 22,276.

Glacier National Park, B.C., **Canada;** mtn. scenery, resorts; a. 1,349 km².

Glacier National Park, Mon., **USA;** Rocky mtns., picturesque; a. 4,040 km².

Gladbeck, t., N. Rhine–Westphalia, **W. Germany;** N. of Essen; coalmng; p. (est. 1983) 78,400.

Gladstone, t., Queensland, **Australia;** pt. exports coal to Japan; alumina plant (1973), oil storage; p. (1976) 18,591.

Glamis, v., Angus, **Scot.;** G. cas. childhood home of Queen Elizabeth the Queen Mother, and featured in Shakespeare's *Macbeth.*

Glamorgan, former co., S. **Wales;** now divided into 3 cos., **South, West** and **Mid-Glamorgan.**

Glamorgan, Vale of. *See* **Gwent, Plain of.**

Glanford, l. gov. dist., Humberside, **Eng.;** a. S. of Humber and inc. Brigg and Barton; p. (1981) 65,761.

Glarus, can., **Switzerland;** E. of Schwyz; a. 684 km²; sheep, cheese, cottons; p. (1980) 36,718.

Glarus, t., cap. of can. G., **Switzerland;** on R. Linth, nr. Wessen; p. (1970), 6,189.

Glasgow, c., burgh, l. gov. dist., Strathclyde Reg., **Scot.;** on R. Clyde; leading spt. and 3rd lgst. c. in Gt. Britain; major problems of urban renewal; ctr. of industl. belt; shipbldg., iron and steel, heavy and lt. engin., electronics equipment, printing; univ., cath.; p. (1981) 763,162; Central Clydeside conurb. 1,713,287.

Glas Maol, mtn., Angus, Kincardine and Deeside, **Scot.;** part of the Braes of Angus; 1,068 m.

Glastonbury, t., Somerset, **Eng.;** on R. Brue, ruins of 10th century abbey; nearby prehistoric lake villages; p. (1981) 6,773.

Glatz. *See* **Kłodzko.**

Glauchau, t., Karl-Marx-Stadt, **E. Germany;** on R. Mulde; woollens, calicoes, dyes, machin.; p. (est. 1970) 32,127.

Gleiwitz. *See* **Gliwice.**

Glen Affric, Inverness, **Scot.;** drained E. to Moray F.; hydroelectric scheme.

Glencoe, valley, **Scot.;** S.E. of Ballachulish; scene of massacre of MacDonalds 1692.

Glendalough, Wicklow, **R.o.I.;** scenic valley with Ls. and monastic ruins; tourism.

Glenelg, t., S. **Australia;** on St. Vincent G.; sub. of Adelaide; first free settlement in Australia; p. (1976) 14,413.

Glen Garry, Perth and Kinross, **Scot.;** used by Perth to Inverness rly. on S. approach to Drumochter Pass.

Glen More, Scottish valley traversed by Caledonian canal, from Fort William to Inverness.

Glenrothes, t., Kirkaldy, **Scot.;** new t. (1948); coal, transistors, mng. machin., photoprecision ind.; p. (1981) 32,700.

Glen Roy, Lochaber, **Scot.;** 24 km N.E. of Fort William; remarkable terraces, remains of series of glacial lakes.

Glen Spean, Lochaber, **Scot.;** used by Glasgow to Fort William rly.

Glittertind, mtn., Opland co., S. **Norway;** highest peak in Scandinavia; alt. 2,483 m.

Gliwice (Gleiwitz), c., S.W. **Poland** (since 1945); coal mng. and steel ctr. of Katowice region; machin., chemicals; p. (est. 1983) 211,200.

Glomma (Glommen), R., S. **Norway;** lgst. R. in Scandinavia; flows to Skaggerak; timber inds.; hydroelec. power; 400 km long.

Glossop, t., High Peak, Derbys., **Eng.;** at foot of Pennines; paper, food-canning, textile finishing; mkt.; p. (1981) 25,339.

Gloucester, cath. c., l. gov. dist., **Eng.;** on R. Severn; the Roman Glevum; cath., on site of Benedictine abbey; aircraft mftg. and repair; engin., nylon; p. (1981) 92,133.

Gloucester, t., Mass., **USA;** pt. at head of G. Harbour; resort, fish-processing; p. (1980) 27,768.

Gloucestershire, non-met. co., W. **Eng.;** situated around lower Severn basin, Cotswolds, Forest of Dean; sheep, dairy and fruit farming; major ctrs. of p. at Gloucester and Cheltenham; a. 2,639 km²; p. (1981) 499,351.

Glyncorrwg, t., Afan, West Glamorgan, **Wales;** 6 km N. of Maesteg; coal-mng. dist.; p. (1981) 8,647.

Glynde, v., Sussex, **Eng.;** nearby Tudor manor and opera house of Glyndebourne.

Glyndŵr, l. gov. dist., Clwyd, **Wales;** lge inland a. inc. Denbigh, Ruthin and Llangollen; p. (1981) 40,329.

Gmünd. *See* **Schwäbish-Gmünd.**

Gniezno (Gnesen), c., W. **Poland;** E. of Poznan; first cap. of Poland (11th cent.); cath.; p. (1970) 50,600.

Goa, Daman and Diu, terr., **India;** former Portuguese enclaves; iron pyrites, manganese, coconuts, fish, spices, cashew nuts, salt, copra; a. 3,693 km²; p. (1981) 1,086,730.

Goat Fell, mtn., I. of Arran, Cunninghame, **Scot.;** alt. 874 m.

Gobi, steppes and stony or sandy desert, **China** and **Mongolia;** divided into two principal divs.; Shamo in Central Mongolia, and the basins of the Tarim, E. Turkestan; l. about 2,400 km (E. to W.), breadth 800–1,120 km; average elevation 1,200 m; crossed by Kalgan–Ulan Bator highway.

Godalming, t., Waverley, Surrey, **Eng.;** 6 km S.W. of Guildford; first public supply of elec. 1881; Charterhouse School; p. (1981) 18,209.

Godavari, sacred R., **India;** rises in W. Ghats, flows E. across Deccan through gap in E. Ghats to Bay of Bengal; forms lge. delta; used for irrigation and hydroelec. powers; *c.* 1,440 km long.

Godesberg, Bad, t., N. Rhine–Westphalia, **W. Germany;** nr. Bonn; spa; meeting place of Chamberlain and Hitler 1938; p. (est. 1969) 73,512.

Godhavn, Danish settlement, Disco I., W. of **Greenland;** arctic research sta.; fish processing.

Godthåb, t., admin. ctr., **Greenland;** first Danish col. 1721; sm. pt.; fish processing; p. (est. 1968) 6,104.

Godwin Austen Mt. or **K2,** peak (8,616 m) in Karakoram between Tibet and Sinkiang, **China,** after Everest highest in world; summit reached by Prof. Desio 1954; also named Chobrum.

Gogmagog Hills, Cambs., **Eng.;** low chalk upland, S. of Breckland; traces of Roman entrenchment.

Gora. *See* **Ghaghara** R.

Goiânia, t., cap of Goiás st., **Brazil;** comm. and industl. ctr.; p. (est. 1980) 680,300.

Goiás, st., central **Brazil;** mtnous., forested; stock-raising, tobacco; gold, diamonds; cap. Goiânia, on Vermelho R.; a. 642,061 km²; p. (est. 1983) 4,243,000.

Gökçeada I. (Imbroz I.), off W. Turkey, in Aegean Sea at entrance to Dardanelles; a. 280 km²; p. (est. 1970) 1,856.

Golconda, fort and ruined c., nr. Hyderabad, S. **India;** famous for its legendary diamond troves.

Gold Coast, City of, Queensland, **Australia;** 40 km cstl. a. inc. 18 townships, named 1959; rapid tourist devel. inc. Surfer's Paradise; p. (1976) 105,777.

Golden Gate, strait between San Francisco Bay and Pac. Oc., Cal., **USA**; spanned by Golden Gate Bridge, opened 1937.

Golden Horn, peninsular on the Bosporus, forming the harbour of Istanbul, **Turkey**.

Golden Triangle, a. of Britain and Europe roughly bounded by Birmingham, Frankfurt, and Paris; economic core a. of **W. Europe**.

Golden Vale, dist., Limerick, Tipperary, **R.o.I.**; drained W. to Shannon and E. to Suir; rich farming a., beef and dairy cattle, pigs.

Gold River, t., B.C., **Canada**; on W. cst. of Vancouver I. at junc. of Heber and Gold Rs.; new t. 1967.

Golspie, co. t., Sutherland, **Scot.**; p. (1981) 1,491.

Gomal Pass, a pass in Sulaiman ranges, **Pakistan**, leading from Indus valley to Afghanistan.

Gomel', c., S.E. Belorussiyan SSR, **USSR**; on R. Sozh, trib. of Dnieper; R. pt., agr. ctr.; engin., chemicals, clothing inds.; p. (est. 1980) 393,000.

Gomera, I., Canaries; 21 km S.W. Tenerife; cap. San Sebastian; p. (1970) 19,389.

Gondar, t. N.W. **Ethiopia**; N. of L. Tana; airport; p. (est. 1980) 76,932.

Goodwin Sands, dangerous sandbanks off E. cst. of Kent, **Eng.**; shielding the Down roadstead.

Goodwood, v., West Sussex, **Eng.**; racecourse and motor racing; home of Dukes of Richmond.

Goole, t., Boothferry, Humberside, **Eng.**; seaport pt. of Hull on Humber; shipbldg., flour milling, fertilisers, alum and dextrine mftg.; p. (1981) 17,127.

Goonhilly Downs, Cornwall, **Eng.**; satellite communications sta. of Post Office.

Goose Bay, t., Labrador, **Canada**; on Churchill R., international airpt.

Göppingen, t., Baden-Württemberg, **W. Germany**; between Ulm and Stuttgart; machin., iron, wood, chemicals; p. (est. 1983) 52,400.

Gorakhpur, t., Uttar Pradesh, **India**; on Rapti R., N. of Varanasi; grain, timber; fertilisers; univ.; p. (1981) 290,814 (t.), 307,501 (met. a.).

Gordon, l. gov. dist., Grampian Reg., **Scot.**; formerly part of Aberdeenshire; p. (1981) 62,157.

Gorgān, c. **Iran**, Mazandaran prov.; nr. Caspian Sea; p. (1967) 300,878 (met. a.).

Gori, t., central Georgian SSR, **USSR**; at confluence of Bolshoy, Liakhvi, and Kura Rs.; birthplace of Stalin; p. (1968) 33,100.

Gorinchem, t., S. Holland, **Neth.**; on R. Merwede; p. (1982) 28,484.

Goring Gap, Berks./Oxon., **Eng.**; where R. Thames cuts through Chilterns and Berkshire Downs.

Gorizia (Görz), c., cap. of Gorizia prov., N.E. **Italy**; on Yugoslav border; cas.; agr. mkt., fruit, wine; textile machin.; p. (1981) 41,557.

Gorki or Gorky (formerly Nizhni-Novgorod), c., **RSFSR**; cap. of forested G. region, on Rs. Oka and Volga; univ., churches, 13th cent. kremlin; gr. industl. ctr. with heavy engin., steel, textiles, chemicals, oil refining, cars, glass, timber inds.; birthplace of Maxim Gorky; p. (est. 1980) 1,358,000.

Görlitz, t. E. **Germany**; on W. Neisse on Polish border; lignite mines; textile mills; religious mystic Jacob Boehme lived here; p. (est. 1973) 86,034.

Gorlovka, t., Ukrainian SSR, **USSR**; in Donets Basin; coal, chemicals, engin.; oil pipeline connects with Grozny oilfields; p. (est. 1980) 337,000.

Gorno-Altai, aut. region, S.E. Altai terr., **RSFSR**; in Altai mtns. on Mongolian border; cap. Gorno-Altaisk; forested, pastoral agr., mng. (gold, manganese, mercury); a. 92,567 km; p. (1970) 168,000.

Gorno-Altaisk, t., **RSFSR**; cap. of Gorno-Altai aut. region; nr. Chuya highway to Mongolia; food-processing of agr. prod. from region; p. (1970) 34,000.

Gorno Badakhshan, aut. region, S.E. Tadzhik SSR, **USSR**; in Pamirs, bordered by China and Afghanistan; mng. (gold, mica, salt, limestone); livestock; cap. Khorog; a. 63,688 km²; p. (1970) 98,000.

Gornyy Snezhnogorsk, t., **RSFSR**; new t. in Siberia Arctic on R. Hantaiki, 56 km W.N.W. Komsomolsk; tin-mng.

Gorseinon, v., West Glamorgan, S. **Wales**; nr. Loughour estuary, 6 km N.W. of Swansea; steel-wks., zinc refineries.

Gorzów Wielkopolski (Landesberg an der Warthe), c., W. **Poland** (since 1945); industl. ctr.; lignite mines; p. (est. 1983) 113,000.

Gosainthan (Xixabangma Feng), mtn. massif, **Nepal–Tibet (China)** border; part of Himalayas; rises to 8,091 m.

Gosford-Woy Woy, t., N.S.W., **Australia**; electric rly. connecting Sydney (80 km to S.) led to growth of commuting, dairying, mkt. gardening and tourism; p. (1976) 38,205.

Gosforth, t., sub. to Newcastle upon Tyne, Tyne and Wear, **Eng.**; coal; p. (1981) 23,835.

Goslar, t., Lower Saxony, **W. Germany**; mng. ctr. at foot of Harz mtns.; lt. inds., tourism; p. (est. 1983) 52,000.

Gosport, t., l. gov. dist., Hants., **Eng.**; naval depot W. of Portsmouth to which it is linked by ferry; marine engin.; p. (1981) 77,276.

Göta, R., **Sweden**; flows from L. Vänern to the Kattegat; also canal connecting L. Vänern with the Baltic; the G. Canal provides a popular tourist trip from Stockholm to Göteborg.

Götaland, southernmost of 3 old provs. of **Sweden**; a. 87,262 km²; p. (1983) 3,984,336.

Göteborg or Gothenburg, c., cap. of Göteborg and Bohus, S.W. **Sweden**; at mouth of R. Göta on Kattegat; second c. in Sweden for commerce and ind.; univ.; shipbldg., oil refining; deepwater tanker terminal; p. (1983) 424,186 (c.), 695,535 (met. a.).

Gotha, t., Erfurt, E. **Germany**; iron, machin., engin., musical instruments, textiles, porcelain, printing, cartography; p. (est. 1973) 57,098.

Gotham, v., Notts., **Eng.**; gypsum mng. and plaster wks.

Gotland, I. in the Baltic, **Sweden**; many historic bldgs.; cap. Visby; tourism; a. 3,173 km²; p. (est. 1983) 55,987.

Göttingen, t., Lower Saxony, **W. Germany**; univ.; scientific instruments, pharmaceutics, film studios; p. (est. 1983) 132,700.

Gottwaldov (Zlín), t., **ČSSR**; 64 km E. of Brno; footwear, leather and domestic woodware inds.; home of Bata footwear; p. (1970) 65,000.

Gouda, t., S. Holland, **Neth.**; on R. IJssel, 18 km from Rotterdam; cheese, candles, ceramics, pipes; p. (1982) 59,212.

Gough I., Atl. Oc. dependency of St. Helena; breeding ground of the great shearwater; guano.

Goulburn, t., N.S.W., **Australia**; commands route across Gr. Dividing Range; in agr. dist. W. of Sydney; cath.; wool, shoes; p. (1976) 21,073.

Goulburn Is., N.T., **Australia**; 2 sm. Is. off N. cst. of Arnhem Land; Methodist Mission sta.

Goulburn, R., Victoria, **Australia**; irrigation.

Gourock, burgh, Inverclyde, **Scot.**; on F. of Clyde, 3 km W. of Greenock; ferry to Dunoon; resort; p. (1981) 11,158.

Gove Peninsula, N.T., **Australia**; N.E. extremity of Arnhem Land; giant bauxite and alumina production complex (1968); model t. of Nhulunbuy.

Gower, peninsula, W. Glamorgan, **Wales**; tourism.

Gowrie, Carse of, fertile tract N. side F. of Tay, **Scot.**; includes Dundee, Kinnoul, Perth.

Gozo, I. in Mediterranean, belonging to **Malta**; the anc. Gaulos; surrounded by perpendicular cliffs; a. 67 km²; p. (est. 1975) 24,000.

Grado-Aquileia, t., Friuli-Venezia Giulia, N.E. **Italy**; pleasure resort and former Roman spt.; rich in early Christian mosaics and antiquities; Grado joined to mainland by bridge; p. (est. 1968) 10,065.

Graengesberg, dist., Kopparberg co., **Sweden**; on S. fringe of Scandinavian mtns.; iron ore.

Grafton, t., N.S.W., **Australia**; on Clarence R.; dairy prod., timber; annual jacaranda festival; p. (1976) 16,516.

Graham Land, Falkland Is. Dependencies, **Antarctica**; mtnous., icebound; discovered 1832.

Grahamstown, t., C. Prov., S. **Africa**; univ. cath.; p. (1970) 41,086.

Graian Alps, mtns. between Savoie, **France**, and Piedmont, **Italy**; hgst. point Gran Paradiso, 4,063 m.

Grain Coast, name formerly applied to cst. of Liberia, **W. Africa**; "grain" refers to spices.

Grammichele, t., E. Sicily, **Italy**; 37 km S.W. of Catania; planned settlement after 1968 earthquake; p. (1981) 13,607.

Grampian Region, l. gov. reg., N.E. **Scot.**; inc. former cos. of Aberdeenshire, Banff, Kincardine and Moray; highland a.; rapid devel. of cst. with N. Sea oil discoveries; a. 8,702 km²; p. (1981) 470,596.

Grampians, mtns. of Scot.; forming natural bdy. between Highlands and Lowlands; inc. Ben Nevis, the hgst. peak (1,344 m), the Cairngorms and Schiehallion.

Granada, t., W. **Nicaragua**; on L. Nicaragua; in rich agr. region; distilling, soap, furniture; p. (est. 1970) 41,000.

Granada, c., cap. of G. prov., S. **Spain**; in Andalusia, at foot of Sierra Nevada; formerly cap. of Moorish kingdom of G.; univ., cath., famous 14th cent. Alhambra; tourism; p. (1981) 246,639.

Granada, prov., S. **Spain**; traversed by Sierra Nevada; wheat, olives, textiles, liqueurs, paper; a. 12,530 km²; p. (1981) 758,612.

Granby, t., Quebec, **Canada**; on Yamaska R.; sawmills, leather, textiles, rubber, plastics; p. (1966) 34,349.

Gran Chaco, extensive lowland plain, **Argentina**, **Paraguay**, and **Bolivia**, between Andes and Paraguay–Paraná Rs.; hot, wet, swampy region with forests containing quebracho trees, a source of tannin; potential for petroleum.

Grand Banks, submarine plateau, extending S.E. from Newfoundland, **Canada**; a. 1,295,000 km²; impt. cod fisheries.

Grand Bassam, t., spt., **Ivory Coast**; exp. bananas, palm-kernels; mnf. prefabricated houses; p. (est. 1963) 22,994.

Grand Canal, canal, N. **China**; c. 1,600 km long from Tianjing to Hangzhou; built between A.D. 605–18 and 1282–92; rebuilt for navigation and flood control.

Grand Canary, I., Canaries; cap. Las Palmas; tomatoes, bananas, potatoes; tourism; extinct volcanoes; p. (1970) 519,606.

Grand Cayman I., W.I.; a. 220 km²; coconuts; cap. Georgetown; p. (est. 1970) 8,932.

Grand Combin, mtn., **Switzerland**; part of Pennine Alps nr. Italian border; alt. 4,320 m.

Grand Coulee Dam, Wash., **USA**; on Columbia R., 176 km below Spokane; one of lgst. concrete dams in world (1,924,000 kW); reservoir (Franklin D. Roosevelt Lake) recreational a.; supplies irrigation water to 4,900 km² between Rs. Columbia and Snake.

Grande Chartreuse, limestone massif, Isère, **France**; brandy from monastery of La Grande Chartreuse.

Grand Falls, t., Newfoundland, **Canada**; newsprint; falls provide hydroelectric power; p. (1971) 7,677.

Grand Island, t., Nebraska, **USA**; cattle and grain t.; p. (1980) 33,180.

Grand' Mère, t., Quebec, **Canada**; pulp and paper mills; p. (1971) 17,144.

Grand Prairie. See Black Prairie.

Grand Rapids, c., Mich., **USA**; on Grand R.; furniture mkg., car and aircraft parts, chemicals, paper; p. (1980) 182,000 (c.), 602,000 (met. a.).

Grand R., Mich., **USA**; enters L. Mich. at Grand Haven, navigable to Grand Rapids; hydroelec. power; 400 km long.

Grand Turk, I., cap. of **Turks and Caicos Is.**; p. (1970) 2,300.

Grange, t., South Lakeland, Cumbria, **Eng.**; on N. cst. of Morecambe Bay; summer resort; p. (1981) 3,646.

Grangemouth, burgh, Falkirk, **Scot.**; on F. of Forth; shipbldg. and repair, marine engin., oil refining, projected oil tanker terminal; petroleum prods., chemicals, pharmaceutics; electronics and elec. ind.; oil pipeline to Finnart; p. (1981) 21,666.

Granite City, Ill., **USA**; iron and steel, tinplate, rly. engin., chemicals; p. (1980) 36,185.

Gran Sasso d'Italia, rugged limestone highlands, Abruzzi e Molise, central **Italy**, in highest part of Apennines, rising to 2,923 m in Monte Corno; Mussolini was rescued from here by German paratroopers 1943; Aquila at foot of Gran Sasso winter sports ctr.

Grantham, t., S. Kesteven, Lincs., **Eng.**; on Witham R.; tanning, agr. machin., engin., brewing, malting, basket mkg.; expanded t.; p. (1981) 30,084.

Grantown-on-Spey, burgh, Badenoch and Strathspey, **Scot.**; on R. Spey; resort; p. (1981) 2,037.

Granville, spt., Manche dep., **France**; on Golfe de St. Malo; fisheries, food-processing; p. (1982) 15,015.

Grasmere, v., Cumbria, **Eng.**; at head of Grasmere L.; home of Wordsworth.

Grasse, t., Alpes-Maritimes dep., S.E. **France**, in Provence in hills above Cannes; perfumers; birthplace of Fragonard; p. (1975) 35,330.

Graubünden. See Grisons.

Graudenz. See Grudziadz.

's-Gravenhage. See Hague.

Graves, Pointe de, N. point of Médoc peninsula, **France**; in famous wine dist.

Gravesend, spt., Gravesham, Kent, **Eng.**; S. bank R. Thames facing Tilbury; pilot sta. for Port of London; paper, cement; oil refinery projected; p. (1981) 52,963.

Gravesham, l. gov. dist., Kent, **Eng.**; based on Gravesend and surrounding dist.; p. (1981) 95,841.

Graz, c., cap. of Styria, **Austria**; on R. Mur at foothills of Alps; second lgst. c.; univ., cath.; machin., iron and steel, rly. wks.; p. (1978) 247,150.

Great Altai, range of mtns., lying mainly in **Outer Mongolia** but also in Western Siberia, **USSR**; rising to 4,200 m.

Great Atlas (Haut Atlas), mtn., N.W. **Africa**; alt. c. 2,000 m; part of the Atlas mtns.

Great Artesian Basin, Central **Australia**; underlies plains of Queensland, N.S.W., S. **Australia**; supplies water for cattle and sheep stations; too saline for use in some a. and too hot in others (cooling towers necessary); a. 2 million km².

Great Australian Bight, wide inlet of **Indian Oc.**, S. cst. of **Australia**.

Great Barrier Reef, coral reef barrier off N.E. cst. of **Australia**; 1,600 km long, 120–160 km from cst.; currently being eaten away by the star fish, *Acanthaster planci*; many reef Is. form Nat. parks.

Great Basin, high plateau region between the Wasatch and Sierra Nevada mtns., **USA**; inc. most of Nevada, parts of Utah, Cal., Idaho, Ore., Wyo.; drainage ctr. Great Salt Lake; a. 543,900 km²; much desert; sparse p.

Great Bear Lake, lge. L., N.W. Terr., **Canada**; c. 280 km long; a. 36,260 km²; outlet through Great Bear R. to Mackenzie R.

Great Belt (Store Bælt), strait **Denmark**; separates Fyn I. from Sjaelland I.; sinuous shape makes navigation difficult; rly. ferry at narrowest point (18 km) between Nyborg and Korsør; 64 km long; proposed bridge.

Great Britain. See England, Scotland, Wales, British Isles.

Great Dividing Rrange, mtn. system, E. **Australia**; extends, under different local names, from Queensland to Victoria and separates E. cst. plains from interior; reaches max. alt. in Mt. Koskiusko (2,228 m), in Australian Alps, on bdy. between Victoria and N.S.W.

Greater Manchester, former met. co., pt., N.W. **Eng.**; lge. urban a. centred on major comm. ctr. of M., with former cotton spinning ts. to N., inc. Bolton, Bury and Rochdale; dormitory ts. to S.; former concentration on textile mftg. now reduced and inds. diversified; major industl. estate at Trafford Park; p. (1981) 2,338,725.

Great Falls, c., Mont., **USA**; on Missouri R.; lgst. c. in st.; mkt. for irrigated farming a.; ctr. of hydroelectric power, called the "electric city"; copper- and oil-refining, flour mills; p. (1980) 56,725 (c.), 80,696 (met. a.).

Great Fisher Bank, submarine sandbank in N. Sea; 320 km E. of Aberdeen, 160 km S.W. of Stavanger; valuable fishing-ground; depth of water, from 45–75 m.

Great Gable, mtn., Cumbria, **Eng.**; alt. 899 m.

Great Harwood, t., Hyndburn, Lancs., **Eng.**; 8 km N.E. of Blackburn; textiles, aero-engin.; p. (1981) 10,921.

Great Lake, Tasmania, **Australia**; lgst. freshwater L. in Australia.

Great Lakes, N. America; 5 freshwater Ls.: Superior, Michigan, Huron, Erie, Ontario; glacial genesis; frozen 4 to 5 months in winter; traffic in cereals, iron, coal, etc.; major ctr. of heavy inds.; resorts; serious pollution; a. 248,640 km².

Great Plains, lowland a. of central **N. America**; extending E. from Rocky mtns., and S. from Mackenzie to S. Texas.

Great Rift Valley, geological fault system extending from S.W. Asia to E. Africa, 4,800 km in l.; inc. L. Tiberias (Sea of Galilee), Jordan valley, Dead Sea, G. of Aqaba, Red Sea, and chain of Ls., notably L. Rudolf and L. Malawi; a branch runs through Ls. Tanganyika, Mobutu and Edward; used increasingly for geothermal power.

Great Salt Lake, shallow salty L., N. Utah, **USA**; in Great Basin plateau of N. America; remnant of L. Bonneville; alt. 1,286 m; varies in size and depth; receives Bear, Jordan and Beaver Rs.; many ls., no outlet.

Great Sandy Desert, W. **Australia**; mostly sandhills, stony in ctr.; one of A. 3 great deserts.

Great Slave Lake, N.W. Terr., **Canada**; a. 28,490 km²; 496 km long; drained by Mackenzie R.; navigable.

Great Smoky Mtns., Tenn., **USA**; with Blue Ridge mtns. form E. zone of Appalachian mtn. system; hgst peak Clingmans Dome 2,026 m; largely preserved as Nat Park.

Great Torrington, t., Torridge, Devon, **Eng.**; on R. Torridge; mkt., processing of agr. prod.; p. (1981) 4,107.

Great Wall of China, wall built in N. **China** along S. edge of Mongolian plateau to keep out invading Mongols; length 2,400 km; begun in Ch'in dynasty by Shih Huang Ti, c. 220 B.C.; present form dates from Ming dynasty (1368–1644).

Great Whale R. (R. de la Baleine), Quebec, **Canada**; rises in L. Bienville, flows to Hudson Bay; difficult transport; 400 km long.

Great Yarmouth. *See* Yarmouth.

Greece, rep., S.E. **Europe**; mtnous. peninsula, between Mediterranean and Ægean Sea, inc. many sm. ls. to S., lgst Crete; inds. increasingly impt. but agr. prods. still ch. exp. (tobacco, olive oil, cotton, citrus fruit, wine); only 25 per cent a. cultivable; economy also helped by lge. merchant fleet and tourism; deposed king in exile; executive power held by military junta 1967–74; 10th member of E.E.C. (1981); cap. Athens; a. 132,561 km²; p. (est. 1984) 9,884,000.

Greenland, I., between Arctic Oc. and Baffin Bay; lofty ice-capped plateau; peopled by coastal settlements of Eskimos; fisheries; whale oil, seal skins; lge. uranium deposits, potential for petroleum; first onshore drilling (1984) in Scoresby Land; some coal, lead, zinc; US base at Thule; part of Danish kingdom; internal autonomy (1979) but leaving E.E.C. (1985) after results of referendum; cap. Godthåb; a. 2,175,600 km² of which 1,833,720 km² are under a permanent ice-cap; p. (est. 1976) 50,000.

Greenland Sea, Arctic Oc., between Greenland and Spitzbergen; ice-covered.

Green Mtns., Vt., **USA**; part of Appalachians reaching 1,340 m (Mt. Mansfield); Nat. Forest, tourism.

Greenock, spt., burgh, Inverclyde, **Scot.**; on S. shore of F. of Clyde, 40 km W. of Glasgow; container facilities; shipbldg., sugar refining, woollens, chemicals, aluminium casting, tinplate inds.; birthplace of James Watt; p. (1981) 57,324.

Green River, Wyo., Utah, **USA**; rises in Wind R. Range (major watershed in Rockies); flows via spectacular scenery to Colorado R.; impt. routeway; 1,168 km long.

Greensboro', c., N.C., **USA**; cotton, tobacco, chemicals; regional financial ctr.; educational institutes; p. (1980) 156,000 (c.), 827,000 (met. a. inc. Winston-Salem-High Point).

Greenville, t., Miss., **USA**; on Mississippi R.; deep-water harbour; tr. ctr. for cotton, agr. prod.; chemicals, metal gds.; p. (1980) 40,613.

Greenville, t., S.C., **USA**; univ.; industl. and comm. ctr.; textile mills, farm prod. processing; p. (1980) 569,000, (met. a. with Spartanburg).

Greenwich, outer bor., London, **Eng.**; inc. most of former bor. of Woolwich on S. bank of R. Thames; famous for its hospital, observatory (now moved to Herstmonceux) and R.N. College; longitudes conventionally calculated from Greenwich meridian; p. (1981) 211,806.

Greenwich Village, lower Manhattan, N.Y. city, **USA**; bohemian quarter.

Greifswald, spt., Rostock, **E. Germany**; on Baltic inlet; shipbldg., textiles, wood inds.; p. (est. 1973) 50,949.

Greiz, t., Gera, **E. Germany**; paper, textiles, chemicals; p. (est. 1970) 39,058.

Grenada, W.I., most S. of Windward Is.; inc. archipelago of Grenadines; known as the "spice islands" as major exp. is nutmeg; cloves and vanilla also grown; sugar and sugar

prods.; cotton-ginning; cap. St. George's; former Brit. col.; achieved indep. 1974; Pt. Salinas airport opened (1984) to encourage tourism; a. 344 km²; p. (est. 1981) 100,000.

Grenadines, dependency of Grenada I., **W.I.**; gr. of over 100 sm. Is., between Grenada and St. Vincent, Windward Is.; sea-island cotton.

Grenoble, c., cap of Isère dep., S.E. **France**; on Isère R. at foot of Alps; univ.; thriving cultural and scientific ctr.; impt. hydroelectric ctr.; science-based inds., joint Franco-German nuclear research reactor; gloves, paper, cement, liqueurs; tourism based on skiing; p. (1982) 159,503.

Gretna Green, v., Annandale and Eskdale, **Scot.**; on Eng. border; famous as place of runaway marriages 1754–1856; p. (1981) 2,809.

Greymouth, spt., S.I., **N.Z.**; on W. cst. at mouth of Grey R.; ch. t. prov. of Westland; grew with gold mng., now replaced by coal and timber; p. (1976) 8,282.

Grimaldi, caves, N.W. **Italy**; remains of prehistoric man, late Paleolithic, found there.

Grimsby, Great, spt., l. gov. dist., Humberside, **Eng.**; on S. bank of R. Humber; major distant waters fish. pt.; food-processing; chemical ind. at nearby Immingham; p. (1981) 92,147.

Grindelwald, v., Bernese Oberland, **Switzerland**; tourist ctr.; p. (1970) 3,511.

Gris-Nez, C., N.E. **France**; nearest point on Fr. cst. to Dover.

Grisons (Graubünden), can., E. **Switzerland**; region of glaciers and magnificent peaks; ch. resorts Davos, Arosa, St. Moritz; Swiss Nat. Park; lgst. can.; sparse p.; ctr. Romansch language; a. 7,112 km²; p. (1980) 391,995.

Grodno, c., W. Belorussiyan SSR, **USSR**; pt. on Neman R.; a Polish t. until 1939; machine parts, cloth; historic bldgs.; p. (est. 1980) 202,000.

Groningen, c., cap. of G. prov., **Neth.**; univ.; impt. trading ctr.; p. (1982) 165,146.

Groningen, prov., N.E. **Neth.**; agr. and dairying; major natural gas deposits at Slochteren; a. 2,157 km²; p. (1982) 560,708.

Groote Eylandt, I., G. of Carpentaria; off cst. of N.T., **Australia**; aboriginal reserve; manganese ore-mng.

Grosseto, t., cap. of G. prov., Tuscany, **Italy**; cath.; agr. mkt.; severely affected by floods 1966; p. (1981) 69,523.

Gross Glockner, mtn. (3,801 m) and pass (2,370 m), **Austria**, part of Hohe Tauern range; hgst. peak in Austria.

Groznyy, t., N. Caucasia, **RSFSR**; on R. Terek; naphtha wells, refinery, engin.; starting point of oil pipelines to Makhachkala, Tuapse and Gorlovka; p. (est. 1980) 377,000.

Grudziadz (Graudenz), t., on R. Vistula, Bydgoszcz, **Poland**; mftg.; p. (1970) 75,500.

Grünberg. *See* Zielona Góra.

Gruyères, dist., can. Fribourg, **Switzerland**; cattle; cheese.

Guadalajara, c., cap. of Jalisco st., W. **Mexico**; c. 1,500 m high; impt. industl. and comm. ctr.; textiles, agr. processing, traditional pottery and glassware; cath.; gas pipeline from Salamanca; health resort; p. (1979) 1,906,145 (c.), 2,467,657 (met. a.).

Guadalajara, c., cap. of G. prov., **Spain**; on Henares R., N. of Madrid; palace of Mendoza family; battle of Spanish Civil War, March 1937, fought nearby; p. (1981) 143,472 (prov.).

Guadalaviar, R., E. **Spain**; flows into Mediterranean, below Valencia; 208 km long.

Guadalcanal, volcanic I., **Pac. Oc.**; lgst. of Solomon Is.; jungle and mtns.; exp. copra; ch. t. Honiara.

Guadalquivir, R., S. **Spain**; flows through Andalusia via Seville to Atl.; c. 560 km long; hydroelec. plants; agr.

Guadalupe Hidalgo, place of pilgrimage, N.W. Mexico City, **Mexico**; basilica and shrine; treaty ending Mexican–U.S. war signed here 1848.

Guadarrama, Sierra de, mtn. range, central **Spain**; rugged, forest covered; affects Madrid's climate; reaches 2,431 m.

Guadeloupe, overseas dep. France, **W.I.**; comprises most S. of Leeward gr., Basse-Terre, Grande-Terre, Marie-Galante and other Is.; economy based on sugar exports to France; rapidly rising p. aggravates process of econ. development; attempts to develop tourism and food-processing inds.; ch. comm. ctr. and pt. Pointe à Pitre (Grande Terre); cap. Basse-Terre; a. 1,748 km²; p. (est. 1984) 319,000.

Guadiana, R., forms part of Spanish and Portuguese

frontier; flows into G. of Cádiz; Estremadura valley reclamation scheme in progress; 816 km long.

Guam, I., U.S. air and naval base in W. Pac.; developing tourist ind.; free-port and tax incentives aid investment; ch. t. Agaña; a. 541 km²; p. (est. 1975) 104,000.

Guanabara, st., S.E. **Brazil**; cap. Rio de Janeiro; formerly the Fed. Dist., before Brasilia became the cap.; a. 1,357 km²; p. (1970) 4,315,746.

Guanajuato, st., central **Mexico**; average elevation 1,800 m; mng. (silver, gold, tin, copper, iron, lead, opals); a. 30,572 km²; p. (1970) 2,270,370.

Guanajuato, cap. of G. st., **Mexico**; 1,990 m high in gorge; resort; p. (1970) 65,258.

Guangdong (Kwantung), prov., S. **China**; on S. China Sea; cap. Guangzhou; occupied by delta of Xijiang and its confluents; Hong Kong in estuary; tropical monsoon climate; densely p. on R. plains and valley slopes; intensive farming of rice, sugar, fruits; 2 Special Economic Zones to encourage foreign investment; a. 221,308 km²; p. (est 1983) 60,750,000.

Guangzhou (Canton), c., cap. Guangdong prov., S. **China**; industl. and educational ctr.; mnfs. inc. silk, paper, cement; univ.; former treaty pt. and major spt. of S. China but site on Zhujiang R. delta results in silting and expensive harbour wks., hence Chinese interest in Hong Kong; ctr. of revolutionary movement from days of Sun Yat-Sen; p. (est. 1983) 3,170,000.

Guang Zhuang (Kwangsi Chuang), aut. region, S. **China**; borders on Vietnam; cap. Nanning; drained by Xijiang and tribs.; rice most impt. crop; timber from sub-tropical forests; home of the Zhuang people (over 7 million); a. 221,321 km²; p. (est. 1983) 37,330,000.

Guantánamo, c., S.E. **Cuba**; sugar, coffee, bananas, cacao; pt. at Caimanera on G. Bay; p. (1975) 148,833.

Guaporé, R., **Brazil**; rises in Mato Grosso st., forms Brazil-Bolivia bdy. before joining the Mamoré; length 1,440 km.

Guarulhos, c., **Brazil**; N.E. of São Paulo; mechanical and electrical engin.; metals; benefits from rapid industl. growth of São Paulo; p. (est. 1980) 403,600.

Guatemala, rep., **Central America**; straddles Central American isthmus; interior mtnous. with temperate climate; coastal lowlands hot and humid; economy based on agr., coffee accounting for half exp.; timber exploitation, food processing; two oil refineries; trades mainly with USA, ch. pts. Puerto Barrios, San José, Santo Tomas de Castilla; 4 univs.; cap. Guatemala City; a. 108,889 km²; p. (est. 1984) 8,165,000.

Guatemala City, c., cap. of G. rep.; cath., univ.; fruit and vegetable mkts.; coffee tr.; remains Mayan civilisation; partially destroyed by earthquake (1976); p. (est. 1979) 793,336.

Guayama, t., **Puerto Rico**; ctr. of agr. region; sugar-milling and food-processing; p. (1970) 36,159.

Guayaquil, ch. pt., **Ecuador**; cap. of Guayas prov. on Guayas R., nr. Bay of G.; recent new pt. nearby and improvement to transport in hinterland; univ., cath.; sawmills, foundries, machin., brewing, oil refinery; p. (1982) 1,300,868.

Guayas, prov., **Ecuador**; cst. lowlands; plantations for coffee, cocoa, bananas, rice; cap. Guayaquil; p. (1982) 2,016,819.

Gubin (Polish **Guben**), border t., **E. Germany/ Poland**; on R. Neisse; comm. ctr.; textiles, machin., leather, synthetic fibre.

Gudbrandsdal, valley, S. **Norway**; leads S.E. from Dovrefjell towards Oslo; drained by R. Logan; used by main road Oslo to Trondheim; provides relatively lge. a. of cultivable land; hay, oats, barley, dairy cattle; 368 km long.

Guelph, t., Ont., **Canada**; on Speed R.; univ.; mkt. ctr. in rich farming a.; cloth, elec. equipment; p. (1971) 58,364.

Guernsey, I., Channel Is., between cst. of France and Eng.; tomatoes, grapes (under glass), flowers, cattle, tourist resort, t. and ch. spt. St. Peter Port; banking; a. 6,335 ha; p. (1981) 56,000 (with ass. Is.).

Guerrero, st., S. **Mexico**; on Pac. cst.; mtnous.; cereals, cotton, coffee, tobacco; cap. Chilpancingo; ch. pt. Acapulco; a. 64,452 km²; p. (1970) 1,597,360.

Guiana Highlands, plateau, S. **America**; extend c. 1,440 km from E. to W. across S. parts of Venezuela, Guyana, Surinam, Fr. Guiana; steep sides, rounded tops c. 900 m but rise to 2,852 m in Mt. Roraima; chiefly composed of crystalline rocks rich in minerals.

Guienne, former prov., **France**, partly coincides with the Aquitaine basin (q.v.); controlled by England 1154–1451.

Guildford, co. t., l. gov. dist., Surrey, **Eng.**; 48 km S.W. London; on gap cut by R. Wey through N. Downs, cath., univ.; vehicles, agr. implements, lt. inds.; residtl., cas.; p. (1981) 120,072 (dist.).

Guilin (Kweilin), c., Guang Zhuang, **China**; on R. Gui; univ.; textiles, sugar refining, timber; noted for its beautiful setting; p. (est. 1970) 235,000.

Guinea, People's Revolutionary Rep. of, rep., **W. Africa**; climate hot and humid on cst. but temperate in higher interior; 95 per cent p. engaged in agr., but bauxite dominates exp. from deposits at Boké; hydroelectric dam and aluminium smelter at Konkouré; all foreigners barred from business in G. (1968); poorly developed transport system, new rly. and pt. at Kamsar for mineral exp.; major spt. at cap. Conakry; socialist economic policies have been adopted since independence from France (1958); a. 245,861 km²; p. (est. 1983) 5,177,000.

Guinea, gen. name for W. African coastlands from Senegal to Angola.

Guinea-Bissau, formerly Portuguese Guinea, **W. Africa**; indep. 1974; poor econ. infrastructure; no manf. inds.; depends on agr. of rice, groundnuts and stock raising; cst. edged by mangroves; offshore oil potential; a. 36,125 km² p. (est. 1984) 875,000.

Guinea, Spanish. See **Equatorial Guinea.**

Guinea Current, ocean current, flows W. to E. along Guinea cst., diverted away from cst. in Bight of Benin by C. Three Points.

Guinea, Gulf of, arm of Atl. Oc. formed by gr. bend of cst. of W. **Africa** between Ivory Coast and Gabon; Bight of Benin and Bight of Bonny are inner bays.

Guisborough, t., Langbaurgh, Cleveland, **Eng.**; at foot of Cleveland hills; former ctr. of iron-mng.; 12 cent. abbey ruins; p. (1981) 19,903.

Guiyang (Kweiyang), c., Guizhou prov., **China**; univ.; comm. and industl.; coal; iron and steel, textiles, chemicals; p. (est. 1983) 1,330,000.

Guizhou (Kweichow), inland prov., S.W. **China**; upland a. with p. concentrated in valley urban areas; cap. Guiyang; cereals, tung oil; forestry; coal, mercury; a. 176,480 km²; p. (est. 1983) 29,010,000.

Gujarat, st., **India**; formerly part of Bombay st.; cap. temporarily Ahmedabad; new cap. Gandhinager, 21 km N. of A. under construction; oil development in Cambay area; fertiliser plant projected; a. 187,115 km²; p. (1981) 34,085,799.

Gujranwala, c. **Pakistan**; N. of Lahore; power plant, engin.; p. (1981) 597,000.

Gujrat, t., Rawalpindi, **Pakistan**; agr. ctr., handicraft inds.; p. (1972) 100,581.

Gulbarga, t., Karnataka, **India**; cotton, flour, paint; (1981) 221,325.

Gulfport, t., Miss., **USA**; pt. of entry; exp. wood, cottonseed; mnfs., textiles, fertilisers; resort; p. (1980) 39,676.

Gulf Stream, warm current of the Atl. Oc., issuing from G. of Mexico by Fla. Strait. See **L50.**

Guntur, c., Andhra Pradesh, **India**; on E. cst. N. of Madras; cotton mkt.; p. (1981) 367,699.

Gur'yev, c., Kazakh SSR, **USSR**; pt. on R. Ural at entrance to Caspian Sea; oil refining; pipeline to Orsk; p. (est. 1980) 134,000.

Gus-Khrustalnyy, t., **RSFSR**; 64 km S. of Vladimir; impt. ctr. of glass ind.; p. (est. 1969) 65,000.

Güstrow, t., Schwerin, **E. Germany**; S. of Rostock; cas., cath.; mkt. t.; p. (est. 1970) 37,213.

Gütersloh, t., N. Rhine–Westphalia, **W. Germany**; nr. Bielefeld; silk and cotton inds.; famous for its Pumpernickel (Westphalian rye bread); machin., furniture, publishing, metallurgy; p. (est. 1983) 78,200.

Guyana, rep., N. cst. S. **America**; former Brit. col.; largely covered by dense jungle, p. concentrated on narrow coastal belt; economy based on agr., especially sugar and rice; forestry inds. limited by lack of transport; impt. bauxite deposits; high birth-rate creates social and economic problems, especially on overpopulated coastal belt; airport at Timehri; univ. at Turkeyen; cap. Georgetown; a. 214,970 km²; p. (est. 1984) 936,000.

Gwalior, t., Madhya Pradesh, **India**; adjoins Lashkar (q.v.); dominated by rock of Gwalior with Jain sculptures; p. (1981) 539,015 (t.), 555,862 (met. a.).

Gwent, co., S.E. **Wales**; inc. most of Monmouth and sm. part of Brecon; upland in N. where coalfield and former mng. ts., lowland a. bordering Severn estuary to S. where lge. industl. ts. inc. Newport; a. 1,375 km²; p. (1981) 439,684.

Gwent, Plain of (Vale of Glamorgan), lowland dist., South and Mid Glamorgan, S. **Wales**; lies S. of moorland of S. Wales coalfield, extends E. into Monmouth; fertile soils; mixed farming except in industl. areas of Cardiff, Barry.

Gweru, t. **Zimbabwe;** ctr. of farming dist.; shoes, glass, containers; p. (1982) 78,900.

Gwynedd, co., N.W. **Wales;** comprises former cos. of Anglesey, Caernarvon, most of Merioneth and a sm. part of Denbigh; mtnous. a. except est. and Anglesey; inc. Snowdonia Nat. Park; sparse p. inland where hill farming; cstl. resorts inc. Llandudno; a. 3,867 km²; p. (1981) 230,468.

Gymple, t., Queensland, **Australia;** on Mary R., 106 m. from Brisbane; former goldfield; now dairying and pastoral dist., tropical fruits, especially pineapples; p. (1976) 11,205.

Györ, t., **Hungary;** at confluence of Rs. Raba and Danube; cath.; textile ctr., rolling stock, chemicals, machine tools; p. (1978) 124,454.

H

Haarlem, c., cap. of N. Holland prov., **Neth.;** nr. N. Sea cst.; tulip-growing, textiles, printing; 15th cent. church; p. (1982) 156,025.

Hachinohe, c., Honshu, **Japan;** cas.; fishing, fish-processing, metal-refining; p. (1979) 236,909.

Hackney, inner bor., N.E. London, **Eng.;** incorporates former bors. of Shoreditch and Stoke Newington; furniture, clothing, p. (1981) 180,237.

Haddington, burgh, E. Lothian, **Scot.;** on R. Tyne, 26 km E. of Edinburgh; woollen mnf.; grain mkt., corn mills, lt. engin., hosiery; p. (1981) 8,117.

Haderslev, t., **Denmark;** tobacco, clothing, knitted gds.; p. (est. 1970) 29,647.

Hadhramaut, dist., **S. Yemen;** ch. pt. and c. Al Mukallá; fertile coastal valley; frankincense, aloes, tobacco, shawls, carpets; p. (1961) 240,000.

Hadleigh, t., Babergh, Suffolk, **Eng.;** mkt.; flourmilling; p. (1981) 5,876.

Hadrian's Wall, part of frontier barrier, N. **Eng.;** stretching across Tyne–Solway isthmus, 118 km long. *See* **Roman Walls, Section L.**

Hafnarijördur, t., S. of Reykjavik, **Iceland;** p. (1983) 12,700.

Hagen, t., N. Rhine–Westphalia, **W. Germany;** N.E. of Wuppertal; iron, steel, chemicals, textiles, paper; p. (est. 1983) 212,500.

Hagerstown, t., Md., **USA;** machin., furniture, chemicals, aircraft; p. (1980) 34,132 (t.), 113,086 (met. a.).

Hagersville, t., Ont., **Canada;** main producer of gypsum in Canada.

Hagfors, t., Värmland, **Sweden;** site of lge. iron and steel wks. since 1878.

Hague, The, or **'s-Gravenhage** or **Den Haag,** c., S. Holland, **Neth.;** seat of government; permanent court of international justice; admin. ctr.; urban inds.; machin. and metal wares; engin., printing; p. (1982) 454,300.

Haifa, c., ch. spt., **Israel;** on Bay of Acre at foot of Mt. Carmel; terminus of Iraq oil pipeline; oil refining and heavy inds.; p. (est. 1982) 226,100.

Hail, t., and oasis, Neid, **Saudi Arabia;** p. 30,000.

Hailsham, mkt. t., Wealden, East Sussex, **Eng.;** 8 km N. of Eastbourne; mats, rope, and twine.

Haikou (Hoihow), c., ch. pt. of Hainan I., Guangdong prov., **China;** p. (est. 1970) 500,000.

Hainan, I., S. cst. of **China;** densely wooded; camphor, mahogany, rosewood, sugar; new rubber plantations; ch. t. Haikou; a. 36,193 km².

Hainaut, prov., **Belgium,** adjoining N.E. border of **France;** industl. and agr.; coal- and iron-mines; a. 3,719 km²; p. (1983) 668,618.

Haiphong, c., ch. pt., **Vietnam;** on Red R. delta; comm. and trading ctr.; cotton, thread, soap, glass, enamel ware, fish-canning; former naval base of Fr. Indo-China; p. (1979) 1,279,067.

Haiti, rep., **W.I.,** W. third of I. of Hispaniola; tropical climate modified by alt.; agr. basis of economy; coffee accounts for 45 per cent exp.; irrigation scheme in Artibonite valley; unexploited mineral resources, some bauxite mng. and exp.; sm.-scale inds.; well-developed road network and international shipping services; cap. Port-au-Prince; corrupt Duvalier dictatorship ousted in 1986. a. 27,713 km²; p. (est. 1984) 6,419,000 (predominantly Negro).

Hakodate, c., S. Hokkaido, **Japan;** Seikan tun-

nel to Honshu (Aomori) under construction; fishing pt.; fish food processing; p. (1979) 318,029.

Halberstadt, t., Magdeburg, **E. Germany;** cath.; metallurgy, rubber inds., engin., sugar refining; rly. junc.; p. (est. 1970) 46,774.

Halden, t., S.E. **Norway;** wood-pulp, paper, footwear, cotton spinning; nuclear research reactor; p. (est. 1970) 26,271.

Haldia, pt., W. Bengal, **India;** nr. mouth of R. Hooghly; satellite pt. for Calcutta to handle coal, ore, grain; oil pipeline to Barauni; refinery.

Hale, t., Trafford, Gtr. Manchester, **Eng.;** residtl.; p. (1981) 16,247.

Halesowen, t., S.W. of Birmingham, West Midlands, **Eng.;** weldless tubes, elec. gds., stainless steel forgings, engin.; p. (1981) 57,453.

Halesworth, t., Suffolk, **Eng.;** on R. Blyth, 14 km S.W. of Beccles; p. (1981) 3,927.

Halifax, spt., cap. of Nova Scotia, **Canada;** univ.; naval sta. and dockyard, open in winter; machin., iron foundries, footwear, oil refining, food-processing; scene of explosion of munitions ship (1917); p. (1979) 117,880.

Halifax, t., Calderdale, West Yorks., **Eng.;** on E. flanks of Pennines; carpets, textiles, machine tools; cast iron wks.; p. (1981) 87,488.

Halle, c., cap. of H. admin. dist., **E. Germany;** on R. Saale; univ.; lignite and potash mined nearby; engin., chemicals, food-processing; p. (1983) 236,139.

Hallstatt, v., Upper **Austria;** in the Salzkammergut; early Iron Age culture type site.

Halmahera, I., **Indonesia;** mtnous., active volcanoes, tropical forests; spices, pearl fisheries, sago, rice; a. 17,218 km².

Halmstad, spt., Kattegat, **Sweden;** iron and steel wks., machin. engin., cycles, textiles, leather, jute, wood-pulp; p. (1983) 76,572.

Hälsingborg. *See* **Helsingborg.**

Halstead, t., Essex, **Eng.;** on R. Colne, N.W. of Colchester; rayon weaving; p. (1981) 9,276.

Haltemprice, t., Humberside, **Eng.;** p. (1981) 53,633.

Halton, l. gov. dist., **Cheshire, Eng.;** surrounds Mersey R. and inc. Runcorn and Widnes; p. (1981) 121,972.

Haltwhistle, mkt. t., Tynedale, Northumberland, **Eng.;** on R. South Tyne; former coal-mng. dist.

Hama, c., N. **Syria,** on R. Orontes; the anc. Hamath, ctr. of Hittite culture; food tr., rural inds.; p. (est. 1979) 197,804.

Hamadän, t., W. **Iran;** alt. c. 1,800 m; the anc. Ecbatana, cap. of Media; carpets, pottery; airport.; tomb of Avicenna; p. (1976) 155,846.

Hamamatsu, c., S. Honshu, **Japan;** on cst. plain 96 km S.E. of Nagoya; ctr. of impt. cotton-mftg. region; textiles, dyeing, musical instruments, motor cycles; p. (est. 1984) 490,824.

Hamar, t., **Norway;** on L. Mjösa; ctr. of rich agr. dist.; tr. and mftg. inds.; p. (est. 1970) 15,189.

Hamble, Hants, **Eng.;** popular yachting ctr.

Hambleton, l. gov. dist., North Yorks., **Eng.;** inc. Northallerton, Bedale and Thirsk; p. (1981) 74,153.

Hamburg, c., *Land* H., **W. Germany;** astride R. Elbe, nr. N. Sea; 2nd. lgst. German c. and ch. pt.; freeport since 1189; pt. to be extended by reclaiming Is. of Neuwerk and Scharhörn; diversified tr. inc. liner traffic, barge traffic down Elbe, entrepôt goods; major pt. processing inds., airpt., univ.; cultural and musical ctr.; heavily bombed in second world war; p. (est. 1983) 1,617,800.

Hämeenlinna (Tavastehus), c., cap. of Häme co., S.W. **Finland;** L. pt.; tourist ctr.; birthplace of Sibelius; p. (1970) 37,584.

Hameln (Hamelin), t., Lower Saxony, **W. Germany;** pt. on R. Weser; iron, textiles; scene of legend of the Pied Piper; p. (est. 1983) 57,000.

Hamhung, c., **N. Korea;** industl. and comm. ctr., oil refinery, petrochemicals; coal nearby; p. (est. 1962) 125,000.

Hamilton, spt., cap. of **Bermuda;** tourism. comm. and service ctr.; p. (est. 1970) 3,000.

Hamilton, c., and L. pt., S.E. Ont., **Canada;** at W. end of L. Ont.; univ.; varied metallurgical mnfs., fruit ctr.; p. (1979) 312,000.

Hamilton, ctr. of major pastoral region; N.I., **N.Z.;** on Waikato R.; univ.; p. (1976) 87,986 (c.), 154,606 (met. a.).

Hamilton, burgh, l. gov. dist., Strathclyde Reg., **Scot.;** in Clyde valley, 16 km S.E. of Glasgow; admin. ctr.; elec. gds., carpet mftg., cottons, woollens, knitwear; Rudolf Hess landed near Duke of Hamilton's estate 1941; p. (1981) 107,987.

Hamilton, t., Ohio, **USA;** on Great Miami R.;

industl. ctr.; mnfs. metal prods., paper, machin.; p. (1980) 259,000 (inc. Middletown).

Hamilton, R. *See* **Churchill R.**

Hamm, t., N. Rhine–Westphalia, **W. Germany**; on R. Lippe, in Ruhr conurb.; rly. marshalling yards, iron and steel foundries; p. (est. 1983) 170,000.

Hammerfest, spt., **Norway**; world's most N. t., on Kvalöya I.; fishing; p. (est. 1973) 7,418.

Hammersmith and Fulham, Thames-side inner bor., London, **Eng.**; inc. former bor. of Fulham; industl., residtl.; p. (1981) 148,054.

Hammond, c., N.W. Ind., **USA**; on Grand Calumet R., nr. Chicago; originally slaughtering and meat-pkg. ctr., now ch. mnfs., petroleum and steel prods., soap; p. (1980) 93,714.

Hampshire, non-met. co., S. **Eng.**; inc. Hampshire basin of chalk covered in clay and sand; inc. infertile heath and New Forest; leading pts. Southampton, Portsmouth; lt. inds.; tourism, seaside resorts; co. t. Winchester; a. 3,771 km²; p. (1981) 1,456,367.

Hampshire, East, l. gov. dist., Hants., **Eng.**; stretches from Alton to Petersfield; p. (1981) 89,831.

Hampstead, inc. in Greater London, **Eng.**; hilltop v. with nearby heathland. *See* **Camden.**

Hampton, Thames-side t., Richmond upon Thames, London, **Eng.**; Hampton Court Palace; Hampton Wick E. of H. Court.

Hampton, t., S.E. Va., **USA**; oldest English community in US; fishing, oyster and crab packing; p. (1980) 123,000.

Han, R., Hubei, **China**; rises in S.W. Shaanxi prov., flows E. to join Chang Jiang at Wuhan; ch. trib. of Chang Jiang; 1,280 km long.

Han, R., S. **China**; forms rich agr. delta nr. Shantou; *c.* 400 km long.

Hanau, t., Hesse, **W. Germany**; on Rs. Mein and Kinzig; jewellery ctr., rubber and non ferrous metals inds.; birthplace of Jakob and Wilhelm Grimm, Paul Hindemith; p. (est. 1983) 86,000.

Hanchung. *See* **Hanzhong.**

Hangzhou (Hangchow), c., cap. of Zhejiang prov., E. **China**; picturesque setting at head of H. Bay; former treaty pt., now silted up; silk weaving, chemicals, jute cloth; tourism; p. (est. 1983) 1,201,000.

Hankou, c., Hubei, **China**; at junc. of Han and Chang Jiang, 960 km from mouth of Yangtze but accessible to ocean-going ships; ch. comm. and mnf. ctr. of central China; former treaty pt., now part of Wuhan conurb.; machin., chemicals, cigarettes, silk. *See* **Wuhan.**

Hannibal, t., Mo., **USA**; on Mississippi R.; shoes, cement, metal gds.; boyhood home of Mark Twain; p. (1980) 18,811.

Hanoi, c., cap. of **Vietnam**; on Red R.; old Annamese fort, now modern comm. ctr.; univ.; cotton, silks, tobacco, pottery; superphosphate and magnesium phosphate nearby; bricks, concrete, rubber; p. (est. 1983) 2,674,400.

Hanover (Hannover), c., cap. of Lower Saxony, **W. Germany**; route ctr.; iron, textiles, machin., paper, biscuits, cigarettes, cars, rubberprocessing, chemicals; p. (est. 1983) 524,300.

Hanyang. *See* **Wuhan.**

Hanzhong (Hanchung), c., S.W. Shaanxi, **China**; on Han R.; nr. Sichuan border; agr. and tr. ctr.; former Nancheng; p. (est. 1970) 120,000.

Haparanda, spt., N. **Sweden**; salmon fishing; exp. timber, and prod. of the Lapps; p. (1970) 8,963.

Hapur, t., W. Uttar Pradesh, **India**; tr. in sugar, timber, cotton, brassware; p. (1981) 102,837.

Harar, (Harer), t., cap. H. prov., **Ethiopia**; unique African hilltop t. with medieval walls, towers and gates; anc. c. of Islamic learning; overlooks Rift Valley; brewery (1984'); p. (est. 1980) 62,921.

Harare (Salisbury), c., cap. of **Zimbabwe**; admin. and industl. ctr. in agr. region with gold and chrome mines nearby; tr. in agr. prods., inc. tobacco; clothing, furniture, fertilisers; univ.; airpt.; p. (est. 1982) 656,000 (met. a.).

Harbin (Haerhpin), c., cap. of Heilongjiang prov., **China**; pt. on Songhu Jiang; tr. and comm. ctr. of N.E. China; exp. soyabeans; food-processing, machin., paper-mills, oil refining, hydro-turbines, textiles; former treaty pt.; p. (est. 1970) 2,750,000.

Harborough, l. gov. dist., S. Leics., **Eng.**; based on Market Harborough and Lutterworth; p. (1981) 60,766.

Harburg-Wilhelmsburg, industl. pt. of Hamburg, **W. Germany**; oil refining.

Hardanger Fjord, W. cst. **Norway**; 120 km long; magnificent scenery; tourism.

Hardt Mtns., W. Germany; northward continuation of Vosges on W. of Rhine rift valley; formerly forested, now largely cleared for pasture; hgst. points reach just over 600 m.

Hardwar, t., Uttar Pradesh, **India**; on R. Ganges; gr. annual fair and pilgrimage; nearby dam; p. (1961) 58,513.

Hargeisa, t., **Somalia**; comm. ctr. of livestockraising region; airport; p. (est. 1972) 50,000.

Haringey, inner bor., Greater London, **Eng.**; comprising former bors. of Hornsey, Tottenham, and Wood Green; p. (1981) 203,175.

Hari-Rud, R., N. **Afghanistan** and **Iran**; the anc. "Arius''; length 1,040 km; (*Rud* = river).

Harlech, t., Gwynedd, **Wales**; on Cardigan Bay 16 km N. of Barmouth; farming; cas.; seaside resort.

Harlem, upper Manhattan, N.Y. city, **USA**; residtl. and business section of c. with lge. Negro p.; depressed economic a. with much poverty.

Harlem, R., N.Y., **USA**; separates Manhattan I. from bor. of Bronx; with Spuyten Duyvi Creek forms waterway 13 km long from East R. to Hudson R.

Harlingen, spt., Friesland, **Neth.**; natural gas; p. (1980) 43,543.

Harlingen, spt., S. Texas, **USA**; ctr. of productive agr. a.; p. (1970) 33,503.

Harlow, t., l. gov. dist., Essex, **Eng.**; in valley of R. Stort, 35 km N.E. of London; new t. (1947); spreads S.W. from nucleus of old mkt. t. of H.; engin., glass, furniture mkg., metallurgy; p. (1981) 79,253.

Harpenden, t., Herts., **Eng.**; in Chiltern Hills, 8 km N. of St. Albans; Rothamsted agr. experimental sta.; residtl.; p. (1981) 27,896.

Harris, S. part of Lewis I., Outer Hebrides, **Scot.**; and several sm. Is.; p. (1971) 2,879.

Harrisburg, c., cap. of Penns., **USA**; on Susquehanna R.; iron and steel ind.; machin., cigarettes, cotton gds.; p. (1980) 447,000 (met. a.).

Harrogate, t., l. gov. dist., North Yorks, **Eng.**; in valley of R. Nidd, 22 km N. of Leeds; spa; favoured a. for retirement; p. (1981) 139,736 (l. gov. dist.).

Harrow, outer bor., Greater London, **Eng.**; public school; camera mftg.; p. (1981) 195,999.

Harspränget, t., Norrbotten, **Sweden**; lge. hydroelectric plant.

Harstad, ch. t., Lofoten Is., N.W. **Norway**; herring ind., woollen gds.; p. (1960) 4,028.

Hart, l. gov. dist., N.E. Hants, **Eng.**; comprises Fleet and Hartley Wintney; p. (1981) 75,654.

Hartebeestpoort, Dam, Transvaal, **S. Africa**; on R. Crocodile (Limpopo), 40 km W. of Pretoria; supplies water for cultivation, under irrigation, of cotton, maize, tobacco.

Hartford, c., cap. of Conn., **USA**; comm. and insurance ctr.; univ.; sm. arms, typewriters, elec. machin., aircraft engin., ceramics, plastics; Mark Twain lived here; p. (1980) 136,000 (c.), 726,000 (met. a.).

Hartland Point, Barnstaple Bay, N. Devon, **Eng.**

Hartlepool, spt., l. gov. dist., Cleveland, **Eng.**; on E. cst., 5 km N. of Tees estuary; shipbldg., lt. inds., timber, iron and steel inds., pipe making; gd. sands for holiday-makers to the S.; p. (1981) 94,359.

Harvey, t., N.E. Ill., **USA**; nr. Chicago; rolling stock, diesel engines, heavy machin.; p. (1980) 35,810.

Harwell, v. Oxon., **Eng.**; 19 km S. of Oxford; AEA nuclear power research establishment.

Harwich, spt., Tendring, Essex, **Eng.**; on S. cst. of estuary of R. Stour; packet sta. for Belgium, Neth., Denmark; docks, container facilities, naval base; p. (1981) 15,076.

Haryana, st. **India**; formed 1966 from Hindispeaking areas of Punjab; former cap. Chandigarh; Hindu speaking a. transferred from Chandigarh (1986); a. 45,584 km²; p. (1981) 12,922,618.

Harz Mtns., range, E. and **W. Germany**; between the Weser and the Elbe; highest peak the Brocken; ch. t. Goslar (W. Germany); forested slopes; rich in minerals; tourism.

Haslemere, t., Waverley, Surrey, **Eng.**; nr. Hindhead; mkt., residtl., lt. inds.; p. (1981) 13,900.

Haslingden, t., Rossendale, Lancs., **Eng.**; on Rossendale Fells, 5 km S. of Accrington; heavy industl. textiles, waste-spinning; textilefinishing; p. (1981) 15,900.

Hasselt, t., prov., Limburg, **Belgium**; mkt. t.; gin distilleries; p. (1982) 65,100.

Hassi Messacued, t., **Algeria**; lge. oilfield; pipeline to Bejaia.

Hassi R'Mel, t., **Algeria**; lge. natural gasfield.

Hastings, t., l. gov. dist., East Sussex, **Eng.**; on S. cst., midway between Beachy Head and Dungeness; seaside resort; one of the Cinque Ports; cas.; p. (1981) 74,803.

Hastings, c., N.I., **N.Z.**; on Hawke's Bay, nr. Napier; ctr. for fruit growing dist.; fruit-canning; p. (1976) 50,814.

Hatay (Sanjak of Alexandretta), dist., S. **Turkey**; comprising Antioch (now Antakya) and its pt. Alexandretta (now Iskenderun), ceded to Turkey by France 1939; p. (1980) 856,271.

Hatfield, t., Welwyn and Hatfield, Herts., **Eng.**; 30 km N. of London; new t. (1948) which grew around old t. of Bishops Hatfield; lt. engin., aircraft; p. (1981) 25,160.

Hathras, t., Aligarh dist., Uttar Pradesh, **India**; sugar, cotton, carved work; p. (1961) 64,045.

Hatteras, Cape, promontory on I. and cays off N.C., **USA**; stormy region, marked by lighthouse.

Hattiesburg, t., Miss., **USA**; sawmilling, clothing, fertilisers; p. (1980) 40,829.

Haugesund, spt., S. **Norway**; on S.W. cst., 35 m. N. of Stavanger; ctr. of herring fishery; canning inds.; p. (est. 1971) 27,300.

Hauraki Gulf, arm of Pac. Oc.; E. cst. N.I., **N.Z.**; forming entrance to harbour of Auckland; Nat. Park.

Haute Corse. See **Corsica**.

Haute Garonne, dep., S. **France**; in Languedoc; cap. Toulouse; a. 6,366 km²; p. (1982) 815,000.

Haute-Loire, dep., **France**; mainly in Massif Central; cap. Le Puy; cattle, fruit, vineyards; a. 4,999 km²; p. (1982) 206,500.

Haute-Marne, dep., **France**; mainly in Champagne; metallurgical inds.; a. 6,268 km²; p. (1982) 210,500.

Hautes-Alpes, dep., **France**; mtnous.; on Italian border; sheep; cap. Gap; a. 5,641 km²; p. (1982) 104,500.

Haute-Saône, dep., **France**; inc. part of Vosges mtns.; mainly agr.; cap. Vesoul; a. 5,372 km²; p. (1982) 232,100.

Haute-Savoie, dep., **France**; borders on Italy and Switzerland; reaches highest alt. in Mont Blanc; cap. Annecy; winter sports; a. 4,595 km.; p. (1982) 494,700.

Haute-Pyrénées, dep., S. **France**; rises in S. to steep peaks of Pyrenees, forming bdy. with Spain; Basques live on both sides of border; cap. Tarbes; Lourdes place of pilgrimage; a. 4,533 km²; p. (1982) 228,800.

Haute-Vienne, dep., **France**; entirely in Massif Central; cap. Limoges; cattle-raising; a. 5,488 km²; p. (1982) 355,000.

Haut-Rhin, dep., E. **France**; in lower Alsace; cap. Colmar; ch. industl. t. Mulhouse; a. 3,507 km²; p. (1982) 646,400.

Hauts-de-Seine, new dep., **France**; W. of Paris; cap. Nanterre; a. 176 km²; p. (1982) 1,386,700.

Havana (La Habana), c., cap. of **Cuba**; ch. pt. of W.I., with lge. harbour; cigars, tobacco, sugar, rum, coffee, woollens, straw hats, iron-ore; oil refining on outskirts of c.; p. (1975) 1,008,500 (c.), 1,861,441 (met. a.).

Havant, t., l. gov. dist., **Eng.**; at foot Portsdowns Hill, 10 km N.E. of Portsmouth; p. (1981) 116,649.

Havel, R., E. **Germany**; rises in Neubrandenburg L. region; flows to Elbe R.; partially canalised nr. Berlin; 354 km long.

Haverfordwest, t., Preseli, Dyfed, **Wales**; 10 km N.E. of Milford Haven; agr. mkt.; Norman cas.; p. (1981) 9,936.

Haverhill, t., St. Edmundsbury, Suffolk, **Eng.**; expanded t.; textiles; p. (1981) 17,146.

Haverhill, t., Mass., **USA**; industl.; shipping containers; p. (1980) 46,865.

Havering, outer bor., E. London, **Eng.**; inc. Hornchurch and Romford; p. (1981) 240,318.

Hawaii, I., N. central Pac. Oc.; lgst. of Hawaiian gr.; three gr. volcanic mtns., Mauna Kea (4,208 m), Mauna Loa (4,172 m), Hualalai (last erupted, 1801); ch. pt. Hilo (devastated by tidal wave, 1946); lava deserts, bamboo forests; sugar-cane, cattle, coffee; tourism; deep-sea fishing; admitted to Union 1959; st. flower Hibiscus, st. bird Nene; p. (1970) 61,332.

Hawaiian Is. (Sandwich Is.), st., Pac. Oc., admitted 1959 as 50th st. of **USA**; chain of coral and volcanic Is.; cap. Honolulu on S.E. cst. of Oahu I.; tourism; ctr. of international shipping routes; sugar, pineapples; a. 16,638 km²; p. (1980) 965,000.

Hawarden, t., Alyn and Deeside, Clwyd, N. **Wales**; steel plant; home of Gladstone.

Hawes Water, L., Cumbria, **Eng.**; 4 km long.

Hawick, burgh, Roxburgh, **Scot.**; on R. Teviot, 28 km S.W. of Kelso; hosiery, tweed, and woollens; p. (1981) 16,333.

Hawke Bay, prov. dist., N.I., **N.Z.**; on E. cst.; cap. Napier; a. 11,033 km²; p. (1976) 145,061.

Hawkesbury, R., N.S.W., **Australia**; impt. waterway flowing into Broken Bay; spectacular gorges.

Haworth, t., West Yorks., **Eng.**; nr. Keighley; home of the Brontës.

Hawthorne, t., S.W. Cal., **USA**; residtl.; in gasand oil-producing a.; aircraft and electronics; p. (1980) 56,447.

Hay, t., Brecknock, Powys, **Wales**; on R. Wye; cas.; mkt.; p. (1981) 1,293.

Hay, R., Alberta, **Canada**; flows into G. Slave Lake; 560 km long.

Haydock, t., Merseyside, **Eng.**; coal mng.; inc. H. Park racecourse; p. (1981) 16,584.

Hayes and Harlington. See **Hillingdon**.

Hayling Island, resort, Hants., **Eng.**; E. of Portsmouth.

Hayward, t., Cal., **USA**; fruit-canning, poultry; p. (1980) 94,342.

Haywards Heath, residtl. t. West Sussex, **Eng.**

Hazel Grove and **Bramhall**, sub. of Stockport, Gtr. Manchester, **Eng.**; p. (1981) 41,529.

Hazleton, t., Penns., **USA**; anthracite region; textiles, iron and steel mnfs.; p. (1970) 30,246.

Headingley, sub., Leeds, West Yorks., **Eng.** mainly residtl.; county cricket ground.

Heanor, t., Amber Valley, Derbys., **Eng.**; 11 km N.E. of Derby; hosiery, pottery, prefabricated timber bldgs. mftg.; p. (1981) 24,655.

Heard, I., S. **Indian Oc.**; 448 km S.E. of Kerguelen I.; Australian possession; volcanic.

Heathrow, site of London airport, **Eng.**; 24 km W. of central London, S. of M4 motorway; on Piccadilly tube line; handles 75 per cent of all U.K. air cargo and 26.7 million passengers in 1982; more imports (by value) than any U.K. port; resdtl. a.

Hebburn, t., Tyne and Wear, **Eng.**; on R. Tyne 6 km below Gateshead; shipbldg., engin.; p. (1981) 22,103.

Hebden Royd, t., Calderdale, West Yorks., **Eng.**; cotton factories, dyewks., heavy engin., woollens and worsteds; p. (1981) 8,975.

Hebei (Hopeh), prov., N.E. **China**; part of N. China plain; bounded on N. by Great Wall; cap. Tianjin; wheat, kaoling, cotton, coal mng., a. 194,250 km²; p. (est. 1983) 54,200,000.

Hebrides or **Western Is.**, **Scot.**; grouped as Outer and Inner Hebrides; ch. t. Stornoway, Lewis; a. 7,382 km².

Hebron, t., **Jordan**; 26 km. S.W. of Jerusalem; p. (1967) 43,000.

Heckmondwike, t., West Yorks., **Eng.**; wool textiles; p. (1981) 9,738.

Hedon, t., Humberside, **Eng.**; former spt.; p. (1981) 4,525.

Heerenveen, t., Friesland prov., N. **Neth.**; bicycles; p. (1982) 37,353.

Heerlen, t., Limburg, **Neth.**; 22 km E. of Maastricht; coal mng.; p. (1982) 91,291.

Heide, t., Schleswig-Holstein, **W. Germany**; ctr. of Ditmarschen oilfields; p. (est. 1983) 21,200.

Heidelberg, c., Baden–Württemberg, **W. Germany**; on R. Neckar, nr. Mannheim; celebrated univ., cas.; tobacco, wood, leather, rly. carriages; nylon plant projected; p. (est. 1983) 133,600.

Heidenheim, t. Baden–Württemberg, **W. Germany**; N.E. of Ulm; textiles, machin., metallurgy, furniture; p. (est. 1983) 47,700.

Heilbronn, t., R. pt., Baden–Württemberg, **W. Germany**; engin., vehicles, foodstuffs; p. (est.1983) 110,000.

Heilongjiang (Heilungkiang), prov., N.E. **China**; separated from USSR by Amur and Ussuri Rs.; mtnous.; crossed by Songua R. in central plain; maize, soyabeans, millets; opencast coalmines; gold; cap. Harbin; a. 466,200 km²; p. (est. 1983) 33,060,000.

Hejaz, region, **Saudi Arabia**; mainly desert; very poor communications; ch. t. Mecca; a. 388,500 km²; p. (est. 1973) 2,000,000, mainly Bedouin.

Hekla, volcano, **Iceland**; erupted in 1970; alt. 1,554 m.

Helder (Den Helder), t., N. Holland, **Neth.**; on strait between peninsula and I. of Texel; naval base; p. (1982) 63,364.

Helena, st. cap., Mont., **USA**; grew up as gold-

and silver-mng. t.; bricks, pottery; resort; p. (1970) 22,730.

Helensburgh, t., Dumbarton, W. **Scot.**; on the Clyde; resort; p. (1981) 16,478.

Helford, R., Cornwall, **Eng.**; oysters, tourism.

Helicon, mtn. gr., **Greece**; abode of classical muses.

Heligoland (Helgoländ), sm. I., N. Sea; off mouth of Elbe; ceded by Britain to Germany 1890 in return for Zanzibar.

Hellespont. See **Dardanelles.**

Helmand or **Helmund,** R., **Afghanistan;** flows *c.* 1,360 km from mtns. of Kabul to Hamun-i-Helmand swamp on Iranian border; cultivation in valley; major irrigation project.

Helmond, t., N. Brabant, **Neth.**; on Zuid-Willemsvaart (canal); textiles; p. (1982) 58,787.

Helmsley, mkt. t., Ryedale, North Yorks., **Eng.**; cas.

Helmstedt, t., Lower Saxony, W. **Germany;** E. of Brunswick; on E. German border; textiles, machin.; p. (est. 1983) 26,300.

Helsingborg (Hälsingborg), spt., Malmöhus, **Sweden**; industl. ctr.; train ferry to Elsinore, Denmark; p. (1983) 103,870.

Helsingör. See **Elsinore.**

Helsinki or **Helsingfors,** c., cap. of **Finland**; spt. on G. of Finland; harbour ice-bound Jan. to Apr., channel opened by ice-breakers; cultural ctr., univ.; timber, textiles, carpets; exp. mainly timber prods.; p. (1979) 484,311 (c.), 888,970 (met. a.).

Helston, mkt. t., Kerrier, Cornwall, **Eng.**; on R. Cober, 13 km W. of Falmouth; tourist ctr.; famous for festival of floral dance (8 May); fishing, soupcanning; p. (1981) inc. Porthleven, 10,741.

Helvellyn, mtn., L. Dist., Cumbria, **Eng.**; severely eroded by ice; alt. 951 m; sharp ridge of Striding Edge.

Helwan, t., **Egypt**; 24 km S. of Cairo; sulphur springs; iron and steel complex, fertilisers, cement; car assembly; p. 51,000.

Hemel Hempstead, t., Dacorum, Herts., **Eng.**; new t. (1947), on S. slopes of Chilterns; scientific glass, elec. engin., cars; p. (1981) 76,257.

Henan (Honan), prov., N.E. **China**; traversed by Huang He; cap. Zhengzhou; densely p. in fertile E.; mainly agr.; wheat, cotton, kaolin, anthracite; a. 167,172 km²; p. (est. 1983) 75,910,000.

Hengelo, t., Overijssel, **Neth.**; industl. ctr.; cattle mkt.; metals, textiles; p. (est. 1983) 76,399.

Hengyang, c., Hunan, **China**; on Xiang Jiang in foothills to S. Chang Jiang plain; on main Guangzhau-Beijing rly.; lead and zinc mines nearby; p. (est. 1970) 240,000.

Hénin-Beaumont, t., Pas-de-Calais, **France**; on coalfield; p. (1982) 26,212.

Henley-on-Thames, t., South Oxfordshire, Oxon., **Eng.**; 8 km N.E. of Reading; mkt. gardening, brewing; annual regatta; p. (1981) 10,976.

Hensbarrow, upland a., Cornwall, **Eng.**; granite; kaolin-mng. dist., kaolin exp. by sea from Fowey; rises to over 300 m; a. 70 km².

Henzada, t., **Burma,** on Irrawaddy delta; in tobacco and rice-growing dist.; p. (est. 1962) 896,863.

Herakleion. See **Iráklion.**

Herāt, c., cap. of H. prov., N.W. **Afghanistan**; on Hari Rud R.; of historic and strategic importance, has been called "the key of India''; crude petroleum and chrome-ore nearby; tr. ctr.; textiles; p. (est. 1982) 150,497.

Hérault, dep. S.W. **France**; in Languedoc; agr.; cap. Montpellier; govt.-sponsored tourist developments along shores of Mediterranean; a. 6,221 km²; p. (1982) 715,500.

Herculaneum, anc. c., S. **Italy**; 6 km E. of Naples; buried along with Pompeii by eruption from Vesuvius A.D. 79; rediscovered 1709; site of modern Resina and Portici.

Hereford and **Worcestershire,** non-met. co., **Eng.**; crossed by Wye and Severn valleys, separated by Malvern Hills; mainly agr.; beef, dairy and fruit farming; major ts. Hereford and Worcester; a. 3,906 km²; p. (1981) 630,218.

Hereford, c., l. gov. dist., Hereford and Worcs., **Eng.**; on R. Wye; cath.; mkt.; tiles, engin.; timber, cider and preserves; furniture, brassware; p. (1981) 47,652.

Herefordshire, South, l. gov. dist., H. and Worcs., **Eng.**; lge rural a. inc. Ross-on-Wye; p. (1981) 47,511.

Herford, t., N. Rhine-Westphalia, W. **Germany**; on R. Werra; cotton, flax, furniture, cigars, confectionery, metallurgy; p. (est. 1983) 61,300.

Herisau, t., cap. of Appenzell Ausser-Rhoden half-can., N.E. **Switzerland**; muslin, embroideries; p. (1970) 14,597.

Herm, sm. I. of **Channel Is.**, English Channel; 6 km N.W. Sark and N.E. of Guernsey; remarkable shell-beach; a. 130 ha; p. (1971) 96.

Hermon, Mount (Jebel esh Sheikh), mtn., in Anti-Lebanon range, on **Syria–Lebanon** bdy., nr. Israel; alt. 2,862 m.

Hermosillo, c., cap. of Sonora st., N.W. **Mexico;** on San Miguel R.; oranges; agr. and mng. ctr.; p. (1979) 319,257.

Hermoupolis or **Hermopolis,** t., Syros I., **Greece**; cap. of Cyclades; Aegean pt. and comm. ctr.; p. (1971) 13,460.

Herne, t., N. Rhine-Westphalia, W. **Germany**; pt. on Rhine-Herne canal; industl. t. of Ruhr conurb.; p. (est. 1983) 177,700.

Herne Bay, t., Kent, **Eng.**; on cst., 19 km W. of Margate; p. (1981) 27,528.

Herning, t., Jutland, **Denmark**; knitting ind.; p. (est. 1970) 32,512.

Herøya, S. **Norway**; nuclear power plant; chemicals, fertilisers.

Herstal, t., **Belgium**; nr. Liège; armaments, aero-engines; p. (1982) 38,189.

Herstmonceux, v. nr. Hastings, Sussex, **Eng.**; cas.; site of Royal Greenwich Observatory.

Hertford, co. t., East Herts., **Eng.**; on R. Lea, 32 km N. of London; pharmaceutics, flour milling, rolling stock, diesels, brewing; p. (1981) 21,412.

Hertfordshire, non-met. co., **Eng.**; borders Greater London on S.; co. t., Hertford, ch. ctr. St. Albans; drained by Rs. Thames and Lea; intensive agr.; lt. inds.; new ts. Welwyn, Stevenage, Hatfield, Hemel Hempstead; a. 1,637 km²; p. (1981) 954,535.

Hertfordshire, East, l. gov. dist., Herts., **Eng.**; lge a. inc. Ware, Bishop's Stortford, Hertford and Sawbridgeworth; p. (1981) 106,994.

Hertfordshire, North, l. gov. dist., Herts., **Eng.**; stretches from Baldock, Letchworth and Hitchin to Royston; p. (1981) 106,986.

's-Hertogenbosch, t., **Neth.**; on Rs. Dommel and Aa; cap. of N. Brabant prov.; cath.; cattle mkt.; industl. development; p. (1982) 89,601.

Hertsmere, l. gov. dist., Herts., **Eng.**; a. close to London, inc. Bushey, Elstree and Potters Bar; p. (1981) 87,752.

Hesse, Land, W. **Germany**; part of former Prussian prov. Hesse-Nassau; mainly upland; inds. at Frankfurt, Kassel, Darmstadt; wine produced along Rhine valley; cap. Wiesbaden; tourism; a. 21,103 km²; p. (1982) 5,599,800.

Hetch Hetchy Dam, Cal., **USA**; on R. Toulumne upstream from San Joaquin R.; ch. source of irrigation for middle San Joaquin valley; supplies water and generating power to San Francisco.

Hetton, t., Tyne and Wear, **Eng.**; 8 km N.E. of Durham; coal-mng. dist.; p. (1981) 15,903.

Hexham, mkt. t., Tynedale, Northumberland, **Eng.**; on R. Tyne, 32 km W. of Newcastle; priory; p. (1981) 9,630.

Heywood, t., Gtr. Manchester, **Eng.**; 5 km E. of Bury; chemicals, engin.; p. (1981) 30,672.

Hialeah, t., Fla., **USA**; sub. of Miami; racecourse; p. (1980) 145,000.

Hidalgo, st., central **Mexico**; mtnous. with fertile valleys in S. and W.; cap. Pachuca; mng. (silver, gold, copper, lead, iron, sulphur); maguey (type of lily), tobacco, cotton, coffee; a. 20,868 km²; p. (1970) 1,193,845.

Higashiosaka, c., **Japan**; E. of Osaka; formed from amalgamation of Fuse, Kawachi, Hiraoka and many sm. ts.; p. (est. 1984) 521,558.

Higham Ferrers, mkt. t., East Northants, **Eng.**; 5 km E. of Wellingborough; footwear and leather dressing; p. (1981) 5,189.

Highgate, residtl. dist., N. London, **Eng.**; hilltop v. in bor. of Camden.

Highland Park, t., Mich., **USA**; sub. of Detroit; grew up with expansion of motor-car ind.; p. (1980) 27,909.

Highland Region, l. gov. reg., N. **Scot.**; rugged mtns. inland; p. concentrated around cst.; offshore oil development; stock raising, forestry, tourism; a. 25,128 km²; p. (1981) 200,030.

High Peak, l. gov. dist., Derbys., **Eng.**; a. of Pennines inc. New Mills, Glossop, Whaley Bridge and Buxton; p. (1981) 82,142.

High Point, t., N.C., **USA**; furniture ctr., hosiery; p. (1980) 63,808.

High Willhays, hgst. summit, Dartmoor, Devon, **Eng.**; 621 m.

High Wycombe, t., Bucks., **Eng.**; 13 km N. of Maidenhead; furniture, paper-mkg., egg processing; in London commuter belt; p. (1981) 60,516.

Hildesheim, t., Lower Saxony, **W. Germany**; at foot of Harz mtns.; cath.; machin., farm implements, textiles, ceramics; p. (est. 1983) 101,900.

Hillah, Al, mkt. t., **Iraq**; on R. Euphrates; nr. anc. Babylon; food tr. rugs, leather; p. (1970) 128,811.

Hilleröd, t., **Denmark**; admin. ctr. of Frederiksborg prov.; p. (est. 1970) 23,500.

Hillingdon, outer bor. Greater London, **Eng.**; comprising former U.D.s of Hayes and Harlington, Ruislip and Northwood Yiewsley, W. Drayton, and former M.B. of Uxbridge; p. (1981) 229,183.

Hilo, t., Hawaii; pt. of entry and main tr. and shipping ctr. of I.; tourism; Mauna Loa volcano nearby; p. (1970) 26,353.

Hilversum, t., **Neth.**; nr. Utrecht; radio broadcasting ctr.; noteworthy modern architecture; p. (1982) 90,883.

Himachal Pradesh, st., N.W. **India**; bounded by Tibet on E.; forested mtns., cultivated valleys; cap. Simla; a. 56,019 km²; p. (1981) 4,280,818

Himalayas, vast chain of mtns. along N. border of India, between the Indus and Brahamaputra Rs., and lying in Pakistan, India, Nepal, Sikkim, Bhutan, and China; made up of several parallel ranges inc. the Siwaliks, the Hindu Kush, and the Karakorams; crossed by passes, mainly in W.; 2,560 km long; hgst. peak Mt. Everest, 8,854 m.

Himeji, c., S. Honshu, **Japan**; mkt. ctr. on shore of Inland Sea, 48 km W. of Kobe; iron and steel ind., heavy engin.; oil refining; p. (est.1984) 446,256.

Hinckley, mkt. t., Leics., **Eng.**; hosiery, cardboard boxes, dye-wks., engin.; nr. Watling Street; with Market Bosworth forms l. gov. dist. of Hinckley and Bosworth; p. (1981) 87,518 (dist.).

Hindenburg. See **Zabrze.**

Hindhead, hill common, Surrey, nr. Haslemere, **Eng.**

Hindiya Barrage, dam, **Iraq**; across R. Euphrates, 48 km above Al Hillah; provides flood control and irrigation in a. between Shatt al Hillah and R. Euphrates.

Hindley, t., Gtr. Manchester, **Eng.**; 3 km S.E. of Wigan; paint, knitwear, rubber, asbestos; p. (1981) 25,537.

Hindu Kush, mtn. range, mainly in N.E. **Afghanistan**; hgst peak Tirich Mir (7,755 m) in Chitral dist., **Pakistan**; Salang tunnel (opened 1964) with 2-lane motor highway cuts H.K. at height of 3,300 m, runs 240 m below mtn. top, 3·2 km.

Hindustan, former name of part of N. **India** between Himalayas and Vindhya ranges.

Hinkley Point, Somerset, **Eng.**; civil nuclear power-sta.; second sta. now being built.

Hirfanli Dam, project on R. Kizilirmak, 144 km S.E. Ankara, **Turkey,** 1961.

Hirosaki, c., Honshu, **Japan**; mkt., lacquer-ware; cas.; p. (1979) 175,157.

Hiroshima, c., S.W. Honshu, **Japan**; on delta of Ota R.; first c. to be destroyed by atomic bomb (6 Aug. 1945); since rebuilt; motor vehicles, shipbldg.; p. (est. 1984) 899,399.

Hirschberg. See **Jelenia Góra.**

Hispaniola, second lgst. I. of **W.I.**; lies between Cuba and Puerto Rico; divided between Haiti (Fr.-speaking) and Dominican Rep. (Spanish-speaking); complex relief, climate, and vegetation, but strong cultural differences make international bdy. a sharp divide; a. 76,498 km².

Hitchin, t., North Herts., **Eng.**; in gap through Chiltern Hills, 56 km N. of London; lt. engin., tanning, chemicals, distilling; mkt.; p. (1981) 30,317.

Hjälmaren Lake, central **Sweden**; drained into L. Malaren by Esk R.; linked by canal to Arboga; a. 474 km².

Hjörring, t., Jutland, N. **Denmark**; biscuit and clothing wks.; p. (est. 1970) 15,699.

Hobart, cap. and ch. pt. of Tasmania, **Australia**; on R. Derwent; univ.; fruit exp.; mostly light inds.; zinc; cadmium, superphosphates, textiles; p. (1976) 50,381 (c.), 162,059 (met. a.).

Hoboken, t., Antwerp, **Belgium**; shipbldg.; refractory metals; p. (1981) 34,563.

Hoboken, t., N.J., **USA**; on Hudson R. above Jersey City, opp. N.Y. to which it is linked by subway and ferry; pt. for ocean commerce; industl. ctr.; p. (1980) 42,460.

Ho Chi-minh City (Saigon), c., spt., **Vietnam**; former cap. of S. Vietnam; on Saigon R. to E.

of Mekong Delta; tree-lined boulevards; cath., univ., modern airport; comm. ctr.; exp. rice, rubber; food processing; p. declining rapidly since reunification of Vietnam; p. (1979) 3,419,978 (inc. Cholon).

Höchst, t., Hesse, **W. Germany**; industl. sub. of Frankfurt-on-Main; site of German chemical ind.

Hochstetter, mtn., S.I., **N.Z.**; in Southern Alps; alt. 3,416 m.

Hoddesdon, t., Herts., **Eng.**; in Lea valley, 6 km S. of Ware; nursery tr., tomatoes, etc.; p. (1981) 29,892.

Hodeida (Al Hudaydah), t., **Yemen Arab Rep.,** on Red Sea; pt. and naval base; exp. dates, hides, coffee; p. (1981) 126,386.

Hódmezővásárhely, t., S.E. **Hungary**; wheat, fruit, tobacco, cattle; natural gas pipeline from Szeged; p. (est. 1978) 54,444.

Hof, t., Bavaria, **W. Germany**; on R. Saale; textiles, iron, machin., porcelain, glass, brewing; p. (est. 1983) 52,500.

Hofei or **Hefei,** c., cap. of Anhui prov., **China**; rice-growing a.; cotton and silk, iron and steel; p. (est. 1983) 830,000.

Hoffman, mtn. peak of the Sierra Nevada, Cal., **USA**; alt. 2,473 m.

Hofuf (Al Hufuf), t., El Hasa, **Saudi Arabia**; dates, wheat, fruit; textiles, brass- and copper-ware; oil-fields nearby; p. (est. 1977) 102,000.

Hog's Back, Surrey, **Eng.**; steep chalk ridge; alt. 154 m.

Hohenlimburg, t., N. Rhine–Westphalia, **W. Germany**; nr. Dortmund; cas.; textiles, iron, steel; p. (est. 1971) 26,500.

Hohenstein-Ernstal, t., Karl-Marx-Stadt, **E. Germany**; textiles, metal gds.; p. (est. 1970) 16,800.

Hohe Tauern, Alpine range, Tyrol, **Austria**; rugged crystalline rocks; highest point Gross Glockner, 3,801 m; traversed by rly. tunnel 8 km long.

Hohhot (Huhehot), c., Mongol Zizhiqu, **China**; diesel engines; new woollen mill; p. (est. 1983) 754,000.

Hoihow. See **Haikou.**

Hokkaido, lge. I., **Japan**, N. of Honshu; colder than other Is.; less dense p.; temperate agr.; skiing; tunnel link (1983) with Honshu to aid economic development; a. 88,775 km²; p. of pref. (1970) 5,184,287.

Holbaek, t., Sjaelland, **Denmark**; W. of Copenhagen; engin. and motor wks.; p. (est. 1970) 17,892.

Holbeach, mkt. t., S. Lincs., **Eng.**; in Fens, 11 km E. of Spalding; brewing; ctr. of bulb-growing dist.

Holborn. See **Camden.**

Holderness, peninsula, l. gov. dist., Humberside, **Eng.**; between R. Humber and N. Sea; agr.; p. (1981) 45,877.

Holguin, t., N.E. **Cuba**; comm. ctr.; sugar, tobacco, coffee, cattle; exps. handled by pt. Gibara; p. (1975) 151,938.

Holland. See **Netherlands.**

Holland, N., prov., **Neth.**; inc. Texel Is.; dairying; a. 2,629 km²; p. (1983) 2,308,047.

Holland, Parts of. See **Lincolnshire.**

Holland, South, l. gov. dist., Lincs., **Eng.**; fenland a. around Spalding; p. (1981) 61,734.

Holland, S., prov., **Neth.**; crossed by R. Rhine; mkt. gardening; a. 2,927 km²; p. (1983) 3,129,913.

Hollandia, former name of cap. W. Irian, **Indonesia**; renamed Kota Baru by Indonesia, then Sukarnapura, now Djajapura.

Holloman, t., N.M., **USA**; atomic and space research ctr.; site of 1st. man-made atomic explosion.

Hollywood, t., Fla., **USA**; seaside resort on Atl. cst.; cement, furniture; p. (1980) 121,000; part of Fort Lauderdale met. a.

Hollywood, sub. of Los Angeles, Cal., **USA**; ctr. of film industry.

Holmesdale, Vale of, Kent, E. Surrey, **Eng.**; extends along foot of N. Downs escarpment; drained by Rs. Mole, Darent, Medway, Len, Stour; heavy clay soils; ch. ts. Dorking, Reigate, Sevenoaks, Maidstone, Ashford, which have grown up in gaps through hills to N. and S. of Vale; length 96 km, average width 2 km.

Holmfirth, t., West Yorks., **Eng.**; 8 km S. of Huddersfield, textiles, engin.; p. (1981) 21,839.

Holt, mkt. t., N. Norfolk, **Eng.**; 8 km S.W. of Sheringham; 16th-cent. school.

Holt, t., Clwyd, **Wales**; on R. Dee, 11 km S. of Chester; cas. ruins.

Holyhead, spt., Anglesey, Gwynedd, **Wales**; on Holyhead I.; mail packet sta. for Ireland;

lt. engin., woodwkg., clocks; site for aluminium smelter; pt. traffic reduced as result of damage to Menai Bridge; p. (1981) 10,467.

Holy I. (Lindisfarne), off cst. of Northumberland, Eng.

Holy I., Scot., in F. of Clyde, nr. I. of Arran; submarine base.

Holy I., off cst. of Anglesey, Gwynedd, Wales.

Holyoke, t., Mass., USA; on Connecticut R., above Springfield; paper, machin.; p. (1980) 44,678.

Holywell, mkt. t., Delyn, Clwyd, N. Wales; woollen, rayon and paper inds.; p. (1981) 8,905.

Holywood, spt., North Down, N. Ireland; on S. shore of Belfast Lough; seaside resort; p. (1981) 9,462.

Homburg (Bad Homburg), c., Hesse, W. Germany; famous spa; p. (est. 1983) 50,600.

Home Counties, term applied to the geographical counties adjoining London, i.e., Middlesex, Surrey, Essex, and Kent; sometimes Hertfordshire, Buckinghamshire, and Berkshire are included, and occasionally Sussex; (Middlesex and parts of Essex, Surrey, Kent, and Hertfordshire incorporated in Greater London 1965).

Homs, t., W. Syria; on R. Orontes in fertile plain; anc. Emesa; steel plants, fertilisers, lt. inds.; pipeline from Kirkūk oil fields; p. (1979) 325,724.

Honan. See Henan.

Honda, old Spanish t., Colombia; on Magdalena R., at rapids; former comm. ctr.; p. (est. 1968) 22,315.

Honduras, rep., straddles Central American isthmus with longest cst. on Caribbean; comprises 18 deps. inc. offshore Bay Is.; coastal lowlands hot and humid, more temperate in interior highlands which rise to over 2,000 m; agr. basis of economy, especially American-owned banana plantations; bananas almost half exp.; some mng.; rlys. oriented to banana-producing areas to facilitate exp.; nationalised forests; land reform; cap. Tegucigalpa; 5 airports.; a. 111,958 km², p. (est. 1984) 5,498,000.

Honduras, British. See Belize.

Hong Kong, Brit. Crown Col., S.E. cst. China, comprises Hong Kong I., Kowloon peninsula and New Territories (on lease from China until 1997); tunnel (1972) links H.K. with Kowloon; deepwater harbour of Victoria has lost much tr. from China; industl. development rapid since second world war yet few natural resources; dense p. aggravated by immigration from China; to return to Chinese sovereignty (1997) with status of special admin. reg.; present capitalist system to remain for 50 years; a. 1,031 km², p. (est. 1984) 5,364,000.

Honiara, t., cap. of Solomon Is.; on Guadalcanal I.; p. (1976) 14,942.

Honiton, t., East Devon, Eng.; on R. Otter, 26 km E. of Exeter; mkt.; trout-fishing; once produced lace, an ind. introduced by Flemish refugees; p. (1981) 6,567.

Honolulu, c., cap. of Hawaii; on Oahu I.; social and comm. ctr. and ch. pt. of archipelago; gd. harbour; univ.; airport; fruit-canning, sugar-processing; tourism; p. (1980) 365,000 (c.), 763,000 (met. a.).

Honshu, lgst. I. of Japan; contains most of p. along E. cst in 320 km industl. belt; new Seikan tunnel links I. to Hokkaido; a. 230,300 km²; p. (1970) 82,569,581.

Hoogeveen, t., Drenthe, Neth.; fruit- and vegetable-canning; p. (1982) 44,389.

Hooghly, R., arm of Ganges R., India; flows into Bay of Bengal; used in jute-milling and navigable as far as Calcutta; 256 km long.

Hooghly Chinsura, t., W. Bengal, India; on Hooghly R.; rice-milling; p. (1981) 125,193 (part of Calcutta met. a.).

Hook of Holland (Hoek van Holland), spt., Neth.; packet sta. with steamer connections to Harwich, Eng.

Hoorn, old fishing t., N. Holland, Neth.; on IJsselmeer, 39 km N. of Amsterdam; cattle mkts.; birthplace of Jan P. Coen, founder of Batavia; p. (1982) 44,003.

Hoover Dam, USA; on Colorado R.; used for irrigation (parts of Cal., Arizona, and Mexico), flood control and hydroelectric power; Lake Mead, 184 km long, 2–13 km wide, one of world's lgst. man-made Ls.

Hopeh. See Hebei.

Hor, unlocated biblical mtn. between Dead Sea and G. of Aqaba, the place of Aaron's death.

Horbury, t., West Yorks., Eng.; nr. Wakefield; p. (1981) 9,136.

Horeb. See Sinai.

Hormuz, Strait of, between Persian G. and G. of Oman.

Horn, C., S. Chile, most S. point of S. America.

Horncastle, mkt. t., E. Lindsey, Lincs., Eng.; at confluence of Rs. Bain and Waring at foot of Lincoln Wolds; mkt.; vegetable-processing; p. (1981) 4,207.

Hornsea, t., Humberside, Eng.; on E. cst., N.E. of Hull; seaside resort; p. (1981) 7,204.

Hornsey. See Haringey.

Horsens, t., Denmark, E. Jutland; on inlet of Kattegat; industl. and comm. ctr.; p. (est.1970) 35,621.

Horsforth, t., West Yorks., Eng.; in Aire valley N.W. of Leeds; cloth, tanning, lt. engin.; p. (1981) 19,290.

Horsham, t., Victoria, Australia; on R. Wimmera; pastoral, dairying and agr. dist.; p. (1976) 11,647.

Horsham, t., l. gov. dist., West Sussex, Eng.; on R. Arun at W. end of forested dist. of the High Weald; agr., timber, engin., chemicals; Horsham stone once quarried here; Shelley's birthplace; p. (1981) 100,647 (dist.).

Horta, t., cap. of H. dist., Azores; on Fayal I.; excellent harbour and base for transatlantic flights; p. (1970) 6,145.

Horten, spt., Norway; nr. Oslo; naval base; shipbldg., mftg. inds.; p. (est. 1970) 14,050.

Horton, R., N.W. Terr., Canada; flows into Beaufort Sea, Arctic Oc.; reindeer reserve along cst.

Horwich, t., Gtr. Manchester, Eng.; on W. edge of Rossendale Fells, N.W. of Bolton; rly. t.; engin.; rly. workshops closed (1983); p. (1981) 17,970.

Hospitalet de Llobregat, t., Spain; sub. of Barcelona, in Llobregat valley; p. (1981) 294,033.

Hotan (Khotan), c., S.W. Xinjiang, China; in fertile H. oasis at base of Kunlun Shan; silk, carpets, jade-ware; on anc. Silk Road; early ctr. of Buddhism; visited by Marco Polo 1274; p. (est. 1970) 50,000.

Hot Springs, c., Ark., USA; in Ouachita mtns. S.W. of Little Rock; Nat. Park since 1832; health resort; p. (1980) 35,781.

Houghton-le-Spring, t., Tyne and Wear, Eng.; S.W. of Sunderland; former colly. t.; coal-mng. dist.; p. (1981) 31,036.

Hounslow, outer bor., Greater London, Eng.; inc. former bors. of Brentford and Chiswick, Heston and Isleworth, Feltham and Hounslow; rubber goods; p. (1981) 199,782.

Housatonic, R., W. Mass., Conn., USA; falls attracted early Puritan settlement and industrialisation; dairy farming; 240 km long.

Houston, c., spt., S. Texas, USA; on Galveston Bay; gr. pt., lgst. c. of S.; univ.; oil refineries, oilfield machin., steel, chemicals, paper, processing, milling and assembling plants; NASA's manned space flight ctr. and lunar science institute; p. (1980) 1,574,000 (c.), 2,891,000 (met. a.).

Houston Ship Canal, Texas, USA; links Houston to head of shallow Galveston Bay and continues through bay to deep water; provides site for heavy inds.; opened 1915; total length 72 km.

Hove, t., l. gov. dist., East Sussex, Eng.; on S. cst., contiguous with Brighton; residtl.; holiday resort; p. (1981) 84,740.

Howrah, c., W. Bengal, India; on W. bank of Hooghly R., in met. a. of Calcutta; p. (1981) 744,429.

Hoy, I., Orkneys, Scot.; lofty cliffs along W. cst.; separated from Mainland I. by Sound of Hoy; Old Man of Hoy rock 137 m high; p. (1971) 531 (inc. Walls).

Hoylake, t., Wirral, Merseyside, Eng.; on N. cst. of Wirral peninsula; residtl.; golf course; p. (1981) 32,914.

Hradec Králové, t., ČSSR; at confluence of Elbe (Labe) and Orlice Rs.; industl. ctr.; mnfs. machin., precision instruments; 14th-cent. cath. and town hall; p. (est. 1970) 68,000.

Huainan (Hwainan), c., Anhui prov., central China; ctr. of China's ch. coal mng. region; p. (est. 1983) 1,071,000.

Huai He (Hwai-ho), R., China; flows E. between N. China plain and lower Chang Jiang; subject to disastrous floods and changes of course; since 1950 flood control and irrigation canal to sea; 1,224 km long.

Huambo. See Nova Lisboa.

Huancayo, t., cap. of Junin dep., Peru; in high valley of Andes, c. 3,300 m; textiles; p. (est. 1981) 165,132.

Huang Hai (Hwang-hai or Yellow Sea), arm of **Pac. Oc.** between Korea and China; branches into Gs. of Bo Hai and Liaotung; shallow sea rapidly infilling; named after yellow silt from Huang He; length 960 km, greatest width 640 km.

Huang He (Hwang Ho), R., **China;** the Yellow R., rises in Kunlun Shan; flows c. 4,800 km. into G. of Bo Hai; cuts through Shaanxi in a deep gorge; filled with yellow silt (loess) from this a.; floods frequently and changes course (once entered sea S. of Shandong); in lower part forms fertile plain; now part of multipurpose scheme for hydro-electric power, irrigation and flood control; lgst. dam in China opened at Liuchia in 1975; 4,640 km long.

Huangshi (Hwangshih), c., Hubei prov., China; main iron and steel ctr. of central China, built since 1950; p. (est. 1970) 200,000.

Hua Shan (Tsinling Shan), mtn. range, central China; rises to over 1,830 m; watershed between Huang He and Chang Jiang basins; impt. climatic divide between temperate N. China and tropical S. China.

Huarás or **Huaráz,** cap. of Ancash dep., **Peru;** on Santa R., c. 3,000 m; mainly agr., some mng.; avalanche 1941 killed 6,000 inhabitants; p. (est. 1972) 30,000 (predominantly Indian).

Huascarán, extinct volcano, Peruvian Andes, nr. Huarás, 6,773 m high; avalanche 1970 killed 20,000 people.

Hubei (Hupeh), prov., central China; N. of the Chang Jiang; many Ls. and Rs.; rice, wheat, cotton; iron ores; Wuhan is major industl. ctr. of prov. and central China; cap. Zhifang; a. 186,363 km²; p. (est. 1983) 48,350,000.

Hubli, c., Karnataka, **India;** E. of Goa; textiles, rly. engin.; p. (1981) 527,108.

Hucknall, t., Ashfield, Nottingham, **Eng.;** hosiery, coal; p. (1981) 28,142.

Huddersfield, t., West Yorks., **Eng.;** on edge of Pennines, 16 km S. of Bradford; wool, textiles, chemicals, engin.; p. (1981) 123,888.

Hudson, R., N.Y., **USA;** flows from Adirondacks to N.Y. harbour; with valley of Mohawk R. makes gr. highway of tr. between Great Ls. and N.Y.; scenic beauty; hydroelec. power; 560 km long.

Hudson Bay, gr. inland sea, **Canada;** communicates by Hudson Strait with Davis Strait (Atl. Oc.); ice-free mid-July to Oct.; salmon, cod; a. 1,398,600 km².

Hué, c., **Vietnam;** on Hué R., 16 km from S. China Sea; pt. and tr. ctr.; former cap. of Annam; royal palace; p. (1973) 209,043.

Huelva, coastal prov., S.W. **Spain;** copper mng., vine-and olive-growing, stock-raising, fisheries, brandy distilling; a. 10,117 km²; p. (1981) 418,579.

Huelva, c., cap. of Huelva prov., **Spain;** pt. on G. of Cadiz; oil refining, chemicals, food processing; exp. of minerals from nearby Rio Tinto; p. (1981) 127,806.

Huesca, c., cap. of H. prov., N.E. **Spain;** at foot of Pyrenees on R. Isuela; cath.; agr. ctr.; wine and timber tr. with France; p. (1981) 214,905 (prov.).

Huhehot. See Hohhot.

Hula L. See **Waters of Merom.**

Hull, t., S.W. Quebec, **Canada;** within met. a. of Ottawa; sawmills, paper; p. (1971) 62,842 (c.), 137,759 (met. a.).

Hull or **Kingston-upon-Hull,** c., l. gov. dist., Humberside, **Eng.;** major spt. of U.K.; at influx of R. Hull in estuary of Humber; originally laid out by Edward I; lge. docks; premier distant water fishing pt.; inds. inc. oil-extracting, flour milling, sawmilling, chemicals, engin., univ.; p. (1981) 268,302.

Humber, estuary of Rs. Ouse and Trent, **Eng.;** fine waterway; 2–13 km wide, 61 km long; Humber bridge opened (1981), longest single span suspension bridge in world; oil recently found (1981).

Humberside, non-met. co., **Eng.;** inc. most of E. Riding of Yorks., and Humber estuary where growth of pt. processing and chem. inds. and impt. pts. of Hull and Grimsby; iron and steel at Scunthorpe; cstl. resort of Bridlington in N.E.; a. 3,512 km²; p. (1981) 847,666.

Humboldt, R., N. Nevada, **USA;** rises in Ruby Mtns., flows for 480 km before disappearing by evaporation and percolation; impt. 19th cent. routeway.

Humboldt Bay, inlet, Cal., **USA;** nuclear experimental breeder reactor.

Humboldt Current. See **Peru Current.**

Hume Lake, reservoir, N.S.W., **Australia;** formed by dam where R. Murray leaves Gr. Dividing

Range; supplies water for irrigation in upper Riverina dist.; capacity c. 113 million m³.

Hugh Town, cap. of the Scilly Isles, **Eng.;** on St. Mary's I.

Hunan, prov., central **China;** S. of the Chang Jiang; hilly in S. and W.; rice, wheat, beans; rich mineral resources, inc. mercury, tin, tungsten; cap. Changsha; Mao Tse-tung came from Hunan peasant stock; a. 205,589 km²; p. (est. 1983) 55,090,000.

Hunedoara, t., H. dist., **Romania;** iron and steel; p. (1966) 68,300.

Hungary, rep., **E. Europe;** bounded by USSR, ČSSR, Romania, Yugoslavia, and Austria; lies in basin of middle Danube (Duna), with plain in E. and Carpathian mtns. in W.; mainly agr.; exp. meat, fruit, vegetables to W. Europe; inds. increasingly impt. and now account for over 50 per cent of income; plans to make H. leading exporter of buses in Europe; 19 cos., cap. Budapest; a. 93,012 km²; p. (est. 1984) 10,786,000.

Hunsrück (= dog's back), forested highlands, Rhineland–Palatinate, **W. Germany;** between Mosel and Nahe Rs.; vineyards on S. slopes; hgst. point 816 m.

Hunstanton, t., West Norfolk, **Eng.;** S.E. shore of Wash; seaside resort; p. (1981) 4,089.

Hunter, R., N.S.W., **Australia;** rises in Liverpool range of Gr. Dividing Range, flows S. and E. into Tasman Sea at Newcastle; world famous grape growing and wine producing reg.; coal exp.; c. 400 km long.

Hunterston, Cunninghame, **Scot.;** civil nuclear power sta.; integrated iron and steel wks., engin. of oil platforms and oil terminal planned.

Huntingdon, t., l. gov. dist., Cambs., **Eng.;** on R. Ouse; expanded t.; canning, engin., processed rubber, confectionery; birthplace of Cromwell and home of the poet Cowper; p. (1981) 123,450.

Huntingdon and Peterborough, former co., **Eng.;** now part of Cambridgeshire non-met. co.

Huntington, c., W. Va., **USA;** on Ohio R.; R. pt. comm. ctr.; rly. wks., steel; p. (1980) 311,000. (met. a. with Ashland).

Huntly, burgh, Gordon, **Scot.;** at confluence of Rs. Bogie and Deveron; agr. mkt.; angling resort; p. (1981) 3,957.

Huntsville, c., Ala., **USA;** textiles; rocket research ctr.; p. (1980) 143,000 (c.), 309,000 (met. a.).

Hupeh. See **Hubei.**

Huron, L., between **Canada** and **USA;** one of the Gr. Ls. of the St. Lawrence basin; a. 59,596 km²; 330 km long.

Husum, spt., Schleswig-Holstein, **W. Germany;** on N. Sea cst.; cattle mkt.; p. (est. 1983) 24,100.

Hutchinson, t., Kan., **USA;** salt-mng., meat-packing, flour milling, oil refining; p. (1980) 40,284.

Huyton with Roby, Knowsley, Merseyside, **Eng.;** sub. of Liverpool; p. (1981) 57,671.

Hwai-ho. See **Huai He.**

Hwainan. See **Huainan.**

Hwang-hai. See **Huang Hai.**

Hwang-ho. See **Huang He.**

Hwangshih. See **Huangshi.**

Hyde, t., Tameside, Gtr. Manchester, **Eng.;** on R. Tame, 8 km S.E. of Manchester; paints, chemicals, food-processing, tobacco, rubber; p. (1981) 35,600.

Hyderabad, ch. c., Andhra Pradesh, **India;** on R. Musi; walled t. and impt. comm. ctr.; univ., nuclear fuel fabrication plant; p. (1981) 2,187,262 (c.).

Hyderabad, c., **Pakistan;** 5 km W. of Indus; 144 km N.E. of Karachi; old cap. of Sind; univ.; noted for silk, gold and silver embroidery; now varied mnfs.; dam at nearby Kotri; p. (1981) 795,000.

Hyndburn, l. gov. dist., Lancs., **Eng.;** inc. Colne Valley ts. of Accrington, Great Harwood, Rishton, Clayton-le-Moors, Church and Oswaldtwistle; p. (1981) 78,860.

Hythe, t., Shepway, Kent, **Eng.;** on S. cst., 5 km W. of Folkestone; one of the Cinque pts.; military canal passing through t., used for boating; p. (1981) 12,723.

I

Iasi (Jassy), c., **Romania;** former cap. of Moldavia; in fertile agr. region; univ., cath.; cultural ctr.; textiles, plastics, chems.; p. (1978) 278,545.

Ibadan, c., cap. Oyo st.; S.W. **Nigeria**; univ.; ctr. of rich agr. a., between the savannah and forest regions; p. mainly Yoruba; crafts, small inds.; p. (est. 1975) 847,000.

Ibagué, c., cap. of Tolima dep., **Colombia**; transport ctr.; cotton, tobacco, sugar, leather gds.; p. (1973) 193,879.

Ibarra, t., **Ecuador**; alt. 2,226 m at foot of Imbabura volcano; on Pan-American highway; p. (est. 1970) 37,100.

Iberian Peninsula, S.W. peninsula of **Europe**; containing sts. of Spain and Portugal; lge. a. of high tableland; interior isolation and regionalism; historical and contemporary importance for minerals; a. 593,250 km²; p. (1968) 41,500,000.

Ibiza. See **Iviza.**

Iceland, rep., N. **Alt. Oc.**; volcanic I. with ice-covered plateaux; glacier fields cover 13,000 km²; only 1 per cent of a. cultivated; cold climate; hot house cultivation using thermal springs; economy dependent on fishing and fish-processing inds.; high standard of living; tourism increasingly impt.; 7 admin. dists.; cap. Reykjavik; a. 102,846 km²; p. (est. 1984) 239,000.

Ichang. See **Yichang.**

Ichinomiya, c., S.E. Honshu, **Japan**; anc. Shinto shrine; textiles, pottery; p. (1984) 253,139.

Ichow. See **Lin-i.**

Icknield Way, prehistoric route running from near Avebury, Wilts., **Eng.**; along the Berkshire Downs, Chilterns and East Anglian Heights into Norfolk, crossing the Thames at Streatley.

Idaho, st., **USA**; Gem State; admitted to Union 1890; St. flower Syringa, St. bird Mountain Bluebird; one of the Rocky Mtn. sts.; rich in minerals; agr. mainly in irrigated Snake R. valley; cap. Boise; a. 216,413 km²; p. (1980) 944,000.

Idaho Falls, c., Idaho, **USA**; on Snake R.; food-processing, lumbering; silver, lead, and gold mines nearby; nuclear experimental breeder reactor; p. (1980) 39,590.

Ida Mountains, range, N.W. **Turkey**; volcanic, hot springs; max. alt. Mount Gargarus, 1,768 m.

Idle, t., West Yorks., **Eng.**; in Aire valley, 5 km N. of Bradford; woollens.

Ife, t., **Nigeria**; ctr. of the cacao tr.; univ.; p. (est. 1975) 176,000.

Ifni, enclave, S. **Morocco**; ceded by Spain to Morocco (1969); cap. Sidi Ifni; a. 1,500 km²; p. (est. 1971) 46,000.

Igarka, sm. t., Siberia, **RSFSR**; on R. Yenisey, 640 km from its mouth; graphite plant, nickel-mines, lumber mills; p. (est. 1970) 16,000.

Iglesias, t., Sardinia, **Italy**; N.W. of Cagliari; mng. for lead, pyrites, zinc; p. (1981) 30,117.

Iguaçu, R., trib. of Paraná; mostly in Brazil; famous falls where Argentina, Brazil, and Paraguay meet, excelling Niagara, height 64 m; hydroelec. power potential.

IJmuiden, c., N. Holland, **Neth.**; on cst. at mouth of N. Sea canal; fishing; gasification plant, major iron and steel plant.

IJsselmeer (Lake IJssel), freshwater reservoir, **Neth.**; formerly Zuider Zee; separated from N. Sea by Wieringen–Friesland Barrage; active land reclamation in progress; Wieringermeer drained 1930, N.E. Polder 1942, E. Flevoland 1957, S. Flevoland 1968, Markerwaard still to be drained; when reclamation complete by end of cent. a. of Neth. will have increased by some 6 per cent.; ch. c. on inlet (IJ) Amsterdam; p. (1982) 101,253.

Ilchester, t., Somerset, **Eng.**; on R. Yeo; N.W. of Yeovil; birthplace of Roger Bacon.

Îles d'Hyères, I. gr., **France**; in Mediterranean off Toulon; tourism.

Ilesha, t., **Nigeria**; tr. ctr., cotton weaving; p. (est. 1975) 224,000.

Ilford. See **Redbridge.**

Ilfracombe, t., North Devon, **Eng.**; sm. pt. on cst. of Bristol Channel; seaside resort; p. (1981) 10,133.

Ilhéus, spt., Bahia, **Brazil**; exp. cacao, timber; losing tr. to lge. pts.; p. (est. 1980) 132,600.

Ili, R., **Central Asia**; rises in Tienshan, China, and flows into L. Balkhash in Soviet terr.; new t. of I. at site of hydroelec. sta.; c. 1,200 km long.

Iligan, t., Mindanao, **Philippines**; integrated steel mill; cement; p. (1980) 167,358.

Ilkeston, t., Erewash, Derbys., **Eng.**; W. of Not-

tingham, iron, engin., locknit fabrics, needles, plastics; p. (1981) 33,031.

Ilkley, t., spa, West Yorks., **Eng.**; on R. Wharfe, N.W. of Leeds; local mkt.; p. (1981) 24,082.

Illawara, dist., N.S.W., **Australia**; forming belt of land between S. tableland and cst.; very fertile; dairy farming; coal seams; ch. ts., Kiama, Wollongong, Bulli, Gerringong.

Ille-et-Vilaine, dep., N.W. **France**; on English Channel; a. 6,990 km²; agr.; cap. Rennes; p. (1982) 745,000.

Illimani, one of the high peaks of the Cordillera Real, Andes, **Bolivia**, 6,461 m, E. of La Paz.

Illinois, st., **USA**; Prairie State; admitted to Union 1818; St. flower Native Violet; St. bird Cardinal; in Middle West; named after its principal R., a lge. trib. of Mississippi; many Rs.; cap. Springfield, metropolis Chicago; rich agr.; fuel and mineral resources; major coal-mng. st.; inds. inc. meat-processing, farm implements; a. 146,076 km²; p. (1980) 11,418,000.

Illinois, R., Ill., **USA**; glacial valley; long history of settlement; impt. routeway; 437 km long.

Illyria, region, mainly in **Yugoslavia**, stretching along Adriatic Sea from Trieste in N. to **Albania** in S. and inland as far as Rs. Danube and Morava.

Ilmen, L., **RSFSR**, nr. Novgorod; drained by Volkhov R. into L. Ladoga; a. 932 km²; fisheries.

Ilminster, t., Somerset, **Eng.**; 16 km S.E. of Taunton; cutstone, concrete, collars, radio valves; p. (1981) 3,716.

Iloilo, c., cap. of I. prov., Panay, **Philippines**; ctr. of rly. network; impt. pt. exp. sugar, rice, copra, hemp; p. (1980) 244.827.

Ilorin, t., N. **Nigeria**; on Lagos–Kano rly.; agr. and caravan ctr.; govt. sugar-growing scheme at Bacita; p. (est. 1975) 282,000.

Imabari, t., spt., N.W. Shikoku, **Japan**; on shore of Indian Sea; mnfs. cotton textiles, paper, canned fruits; p. (1979) 123,934.

Imatra, t., Kymi, **Finland**; hydroelec. power sta. supplies S. Finland; electro-metallurgy; p. (1970) 34,410.

Imbroz. See **Gökçeada I.**

Immingham, pt., Humberside, **Eng.**; on the Humber, N.W. of Grimsby; lge. docks; new deep-sea oil and coal terminals; chemicals engin., refinery nearby at Killingholme.

Imola, t., **Italy**; S.E. of Bologna; cath.; glass, pottery; p. (1981) 60,010.

Imperia, t., **Italy**; on G. of Genoa; sm. pt. olive-growing ctr.; resort; p. (1981) 41,609.

Imperial Valley, S. Cal., **USA**; extends 48 km S.E. from Salton Sea to Mexican bdy.; mainly below sea-level; hot, arid climate; irrigation from Colorado R. chiefly by All-American Canal nr. Yuma; total irrigated a. 405,000 ha; principal crops, fruit, dates, tomatoes, cotton, and dairy prod.

Imphal, cap. of Manipur, **India**; in rice-growing basin in hills of Assam nr. Burma bdy.; p. (1971) 100,366.

Inari L., extensive L., Lappi, **Finland**; outlet into Barents Sea; hydroelec. power; a. 1,774 km².

Ince-in-Makerfield, t., Gtr. Manchester, **Eng.**; nr. Wigan; engin.; p. (1981) 14,498.

Inchon, c., S. **Korea**; on Yellow Sea; pt. for Seoul; exp. soyabeans, rice; textile ctr., steel mill, glass, diesel engines; p. (1980) 1,084,730.

Independence, c., Mo., **USA**; E. of Kansas; oil refining; agr. machin.; p. (1980) 112,000.

India, rep., indep. st. (since 1947), S. **Asia**; second cty. of world by p.; 22 sts. and 9 union terrs.; peninsula bounded by Himalayas in N. extends in wide plateau to Indian Oc. in S.; most of p. concentrated in Indo-Gangetic Plain; unpredictable monsoon climate; heavy dependence on agr.; 70 per cent of p. farmers; few cash crops except cotton (the Deccan), tea (Himalayas), and jute (W. Bengal); 854 languages and dialects impede economic development; strong caste system; 36 per cent literate (compared with 15 per cent in 1961); new inds. expanding rapidly; chems., engin. electronics; cap. New Delhi; main pts. Bombay, Calcutta; a. 3,268,580 km²; p. (est. 1984) 746,742,000 (25 per cent growth in 10 years and 2nd most populated cty. of world).

Indiana, st., **USA**; Hoosier State; admitted to Union 1816; St. flower peony; St. bird Cardinal; in Middle

West, bounded by Mich., Ohio, Ill. and sep. from Ky. by Ohio R.; agr.; coal, limestone, petroleum; steel, metal prods., machin., food prod.; cap. Indianapolis; a. 93,994 km²; p. (1980) 5,490,000.

Indianapolis, c., cap. of Ind., **USA**; on White R.; univ.; rly. ctr.; meat-packing, jet engines, aircraft parts, chemicals, pharmaceutics; p. (1980) 701,000 (c.), 1,167,000 (met. a.).

Indian Ocean extends from S. of Asia and E. of Africa to the C. of Good Hope and C. Leeuwin in Australia, separated from the Pacific by the Malay Archipelago and Australia; a. 75,990,600 km².

Indigirka, R., Yakut ASSR, **RSFSR**; flows into Arctic Oc.; hydroelec. power; 1,760 km long.

Indo-China, S.E. Asia; federation in Fr. Union until end of hostilities July 1954; consisted of the three sts. of Vietnam, Cambodia, and Laos.

Indo-Gangetic Plain, India, Bangladesh and **Pakis-tan;** name applied to flat land created by the Indus and Ganges basins; densely populated a.

Indonesia, rep., S.E. **Asia**; former Neth. E. Indies; made up of many sm. Is. straddling equator for over 4,800 km; many Is. in W. volcanic and E. coral; lgst. Is. inc. Java, Sumatra, Kalimantan (S. Borneo), Sulawesi, and Irian (W. New Guinea); mostly underdeveloped except Java; rapidly developing oil industry; 64 per cent p. on Java, planned decentralisation to other Is.; cap. Djakarta; a. 1,907,566 km²; p. (est. 1984) 162,167,000.

Indore, c., Madhya Pradesh, **India**; nr. valley of Narbada R.; comm. ctr.; cotton-mills; p. (1981) 829,327.

Indre, dep., central **France**; agr. and industl.; cap. Châteauroux; a. 6,905 km²; p. (1982) 242,000.

Indre-et-Loire, dep., central **France**; drained by Indre and Loire Rs.; vineyards, orchards; cap. Tours; a. 6,156 km²; p. (1982) 506,000.

Indus, R., **Pakistan**, rises in Tibet, flows through Kashmir, Punjab, Sind, to Arabian Sea; 5 tribs. Jhelum, Chenab, Ravi, Beas, Sutlej, now one of world's major R. systems, now used extensively to irrigate the Punjab and the Sind; impt. cotton, wheat, and sugar dist.; hydroelec. power; supported Indus valley civilisation 3000–1500 B.C.; 2,880 km long.

Ingleborough, mtn., near Settle, North Yorks., **Eng.**; underground caves, stalactites; made of limestone and millstone grit; alt. 724 m.

Inglewood, t., S. Cal., **USA**; sub. of Los Angeles; chinchilla farms; furniture, lt. engin., aircraft parts; p. (1980) 94,245.

Ingolstadt, t., Bavaria, **W. Germany**; on Danube, nr. Munich; cas.; machin., cars, tobacco, oil refining; pipeline from Genoa; transalpine oil pipeline from Trieste, through N.E. Italy and Austria to I.; p. (est. 1983) 90,500.

Inhambane, spt., **Moçambique**; sugar, copra, oil-seeds, bricks, soap, tiles; p. (1970) 745,911.

Inishboffin, I., Galway, **R.o.I.**, sm. I. off Connemara; farming, fishing.

Inishmore, lgst. of Aran gr., Galway, **R.o.I.**; fishing.

Inkpen Beacon, hill, Berks., **Eng.**; highest point reached by chalk hills in Eng.; alt. 297 m.

Inland Sea, Japan; between Honshu on N. and Shikoku and Kyushu on S.; sheltered sea with many Is.; ch. spts. Osaka, Amagaski, Kōbe, Okayama, Hiroshima, Kure; Nat. Park; a. c. 9,500 km².

Inn, R., traversing **Switzerland**, the Tyrol, **Austria** and Bavaria; enters R. Danube at Passau; hydroelec. plants; 512 km long.

Innerleithen, burgh, Tweeddale, **Scot.**; on R. Tweed, 8 km S.E. of Peebles; woollen cloth and knitwear; mineral springs; p. (1981) 2,397.

Inner Mongolia (Mongol Zizhiqu), Chinese aut. region, N.E. **China**; stretches along S. border of Mongolian People's Rep.; vast steppelands, sparse p.; st. farms for animal husbandry; cap Hohhot; a. 1,177,518 km²; p. (est. 1983) 19,550,000.

Innisfail, t., Queensland, **Australia**; ch. sugar-producing ctr. of Australia; p. (1976) 7,933.

Innsbruck, c., cap. of the Tyrol, W. **Austria**; on R. Inn; commands N. approach to Brenner Pass; univ.; tourism; fortfd. 12th cent.; p. (1978) 123,100.

Inowroclaw, t., N. **Poland**; nr. Bydgoszcz; rock-salt. iron pyrites; agr. prod.; p. (1970) 54,800.

Insterburg. See **Chernyakhovsk.**

Inter-American Highway, section of Pan-American Highway system, from Mexico to Panama.

Interlaken, t., Bernese Oberland, Berne, **Switzerland**; on R. Aare between Ls. Thun and Brienz; tourist resort; p. (1970) 4,735.

Intracoastal Waterway, USA; toll-free waterway along Atl. and Gulf of Mexico csts.; completed 1949 using bays, rivers and canals; 4,960 km long.

Inuvik, t., Arctic, **Canada**; above the permafrost.

Inveraray, burgh, Argyll and Bute, **Scot.**; nr. head of Loch Fyne; herring fishing.

Inverbervie, burgh, Kincardine and Deeside, **Scot.**; on E. cst., 13 km S.. of Stonehaven; linen, rayon inds.; p. (1981) 1,826.

Invercargill, c., S.I., **N.Z.**; on S.E. cst.; sawmills, freezing wks.; aluminium smelter; served by Bluff Harbour; p. (1976) 53,762.

Inverclyde, l. gov. dist., Strathclyde Reg., **Scot.**; on F. of Clyde, inc. Gourock and Greenock; p. (1981) 99,966.

Inverell, t., N.S.W., **Australia**; 655 km N. of Sydney; wheat and lamb cty.; tin; p. (1976) 9,432.

Invergordon, burgh, spt., Ross and Cromarty, **Scot.**; on N. side of Cromarty F., 19 km N.E. of Dingwall; former naval pt.; whisky distillery; large aluminium plant was threatened with closure, (1981); p. (1981) 4,050.

Inverkeithing, royal burgh, Dunfermline, **Scot.**; on F. of Forth, nr. Dunfermline; shipbreaking, papermkg., quarrying; p. (1981) 5,751.

Inverkip, par., v., Inverclyde, **Scot.**; 10 km S.W. of Greenock; par. contains Gourock; resort; p. (1981) 896.

Inverness, royal burgh, Inverness, N.E. **Scot.**; on Moray F.; distilling, lt. engin., tweeds; sm. pt. for general cargo; tourism; p. (1981) 39,736.

Inverness-shire, former co., l. gov. dist., N.E. **Scot.**; part of Highland Reg.; a. 11,269 km²; p. (1981) 56,557.

Inverurie, royal burgh, Gordon, **Scot.**; on R. Don, 22 km N.W. of Aberdeen; rly. ctr., mkt. t.; tourism; p. (1981) 7,701.

Inyokern, t., E. Cal., **USA**; naval ordnance research sta.

Ioánnina (Janina), t., Epirus, **Greece**; nr. Albanian frontier; agr. tr.; embroidery; univ.; p. (1981) 44,829.

Iona, I., off cst. of Mull, Argyll, **Scot.**; early Scottish Christian ctr.; restored abbey; St. Columba's burial place; anc. burial place of Scottish kings.

Ionian Is., gr. in Mediterranean, belonging to **Greece**; comprising Corfu, Paxos, Levkas, Cephalonia, Zakinthos, Ithake; severe earthquake 1953; total a. 1,948 km²; p. (1981) 182,651.

Ionian Sea. Mediterranean; between Greece on E.; Italy and Sicily on W.

Iowa, st., **USA**; Hawkeye St.; admitted to Union 1846; St, flower Wild Rose, St. bird Eastern Goldfinch; in Middle West; prairie cty.; watered by Mississippi and Missouri; rich farm land; maize, oats, and other grains; hogs, pigs; processing of farm prod.; flood control, reforestation; diverse inds.; cap. Des Moines; a. 145,791 km²; p. (1980) 2,913,000.

Iowa City, c., S.E. Iowa, **USA**; former st. cap. (1839–56); univ.; p. (1980) 50,508 (c.), 81,717 (met. a.).

Ipin. See **Yibin.**

Ipoh, c., cap. of Perak st., N.W. **Malaya**; tin-mng. ctr.; Chinese rock temples; p. (1980) 300,727.

Ipswich, t., S.E. Queensland, **Australia**; nr. Brisbane; coalmng. ctr.; woollens; p. (1976) 69,242.

Ipswich, co. t., l. gov. dist., Suffolk, **Eng.**; pt. on estuary of R. Orwell; incr. impt. container pt.; exp. timber, grain and malt; birthplace of Cardinal Wolsey; diesel engines, gen. engin.; p. (1981) 120,447.

Iquique, t., N. **Chile**; pt. on Pac. Oc.; exp. nitrates and iodine from Atacama desert; fish-canning; p. (est. 1984) 116,772.

Iquitos, t., N.E. **Peru**; on Amazon, 3,680 km from mouth; comm. ctr.; exp. timber, cotton; sawmills, oil refining; p. (1981) 173,629.

Iráklion (Candia or Herakleion), t., cap. of Crete, **Greece**; impt. spt. on G. of I., arm of Aegean Sea; at foot of terraced hill slopes; wine, olive oil, fruit, fishing; tourism; p. (1981) 102,398.

Iran, former kingdom, Islamic st. (1979), S.W.

Asia; known as Persia until 1935; interior plateau at c. 900 km, ringed by mtn. ranges of up to c. 5,500 m; much of a. is desert; settled agr. limited to Caspian plain; heavy dependence on oil; oil-fields centred on Abādān; high quality carpets exported, esp. to USA; cap. Tehran; a. 1,626,520 km²; p. (est. 1984) 43,799,000.

Irapuato, c., central **Mexico**; agr. tr. and processing; iron-founding; p. (1979) 161,047.

Iraq, rep., S.W. **Asia**; the anc. Mesopotamia; dominated by 2 Rs., Tigris and Euphrates; much of a. desert and semi-desert but irrigation in S. and centre enables settled agr. for barley, wheat, dates, and tobacco; only outlet to sea at N.W. end of Persian G.; oil principal source of wealth; main oilfield at Kirkūk; main oil pt. at Basra; pipelines to Lebanon and Syria; new inds. based on oil; 14 provs.; cap. Baghdad; a. 435,120 km²; p. (est. 1984) 15,158,000.

Irazu, active volcano, 3,437 m high, **Costa Rica.**

Irbid, t., **Jordan**; comm. and agr. tr. ctr.; p. (est. 1983) 131,200.

Ireland, I., W. of Gt. Britain, separated by Irish Sea; divided politically into R.o.I. (Eire) and N. Ireland (Ulster, part of U.K.); ch. physical features, L. Neagh in N.E., Ls. of Killarney in S.W.; Rs. Shannon, Boyne, Blackwater; mtns. of Mourne, Wicklow, and Kerry; mild moist climate; called "emerald isle" because of grasslands; pastoral agr., especially dairying; tourism; a. 83,937 km²; p. (1981) 4,888,077.

Ireland, Republic of, ind. st., W. **Europe**; comprises 26 of 32 cos. making up I. of Ireland; remaining 6 cos. belong to U.K.; ring of highlands surround central lowland basin, much of which is peat-covered; economy based on agr., especially dairying; exps. butter, cheese, bacon; new govt.-encouraged inds.; mineral resources; tourism; cap. Dublin; a. 68,894 km²; p. (est. 1984) 3,555,000.

Irian Jaya (formerly Dutch New Guinea, later W. Irian), prov., **Indonesia**; formerly W. New Guinea and Dutch col.; part of Indonesia, 1963; inaugurated as prov., 1969; primitive agr. of rice, poultry, cocoa; few oil deposits; cap. Djajapura; a. (inc. Ternate) 412,784 km²; p. (est. 1983) 1,268,600.

Irish Sea, Brit. Is.; between Gt. Britain and Ireland, connecting N. and S. with Atl. Oc.; 320 km long; 80–224 km wide; greatest depth 840 m; a. 18,130 km².

Irkutsk, c., cap. of I. oblast, **RSFSR**; on Angara R. in E. Siberia; on Trans-Siberian rly., 64 km W. of L. Baykal; univ.; engin., sawmilling, petroleum refining, chemicals, hydroelec. power sta.; p. (est. 1980) 561,000.

Irlam, t., Gtr. Manchester, **Eng.**; engin., tar, soap, glycerine, margarine; steel wks. to close; overspill p.; p. (1981) 19,900.

Ironbridge, t., Shrops., **Eng.**; scene of Darby's iron ind.; derives name from first cast-iron bridge (1779) which here crosses Severn; now inc. in Dawley new t.

Iron Country, Utah, **USA**; vast reserves of iron ore; undeveloped due to inaccessibility.

Iron Gate (Portile de Fier), **Romania**; famous rapids in R. Danube; Romanian–Yugoslavian hydroelectric and navigation project, 1964–71.

Irrawaddy, R., **Burma**; flows S. to Bay of Bengal; navigable for lge. steamers 1,440 km; irrigation wks.; major Asian rice bowl; 2,000 km long.

Irtysh, R., W. Siberia, **USSR**; ch. trib. of R. Ob'; crossed by Turk–Sib rly. at Semipalatinsk and by Trans-Siberian rly. at Omsk; hydroelectric power stas.; 2,960 km long.

Irvine, royal burgh, Cunninghame, **Scot.**; nr. mouth of R. Irvine; new t. (1966); cas.; hosiery, lt. engin., bottle wks., chemicals; p. (1981) 32,852.

Irvington, t., N.J., **USA**; industl. sub. of Newark; machin.; p. (1980) 61,493.

Irwell, R., Gtr. Manchester, **Eng.**; flows through Manchester to the Mersey via Manchester Ship Canal; 48 km long.

Isar, R., **Austria** and **W. Germany**; rises in Austrian Tyrol, flows N.E. to Danube; hydroelectric power stas. below Munich; 261 km long.

Isarco, R., N. **Italy**; rises nr. Brenner Pass, flows S. into R. Adige at Bolzano; 80 km long.

Isdud, anc. c. of the Philistines. *See* **Ashdod.**

Ise (Ujiyamada), t., Honshu, **Japan**; sacred c. of Shintoism; p. (1979) 106,805.

Ise Bay, inlet, S. Honshu, **Japan**; flanked by ch.

textile mftg. a. of cty. with 5 million people centred on Nagoya; 64 km long, 24–32 km wide.

Iseo, L., N. **Italy**; E. of Bergamo; 124 km².

Isère, dep., S.E. **France**; drained by Rs. Isère and Rhône; cap. Grenoble; mtnous.; cereals; wine, butter, cheese; iron, coal, lead, silver, copper; gloves, silks; a. 8,231 km²; p. (1982) 935,500.

Isère, R., S.E. **France**; rises in Graian Alps, flows W. into R. Rhône nr. Valence; used to generate hydroelec. power; used, with trib. R. Arc, by main rly. from France to N. Italy through Mt. Cenis (Fréjus) tunnel.

Iserlohn, t., N. Rhine–Westphalia, **W. Germany**; S.E. of Dortmund; metal gds.; p. (est. 1983) 91,800.

Isfahan. *See* **Esfahān.**

Ishikari, t., Hokkaido, **Japan**; on cst. of Otaru Bay, 16 km N. of Sapporo; ctr. of second lgst. coalfield in Japan; sm. petroleum production.

Ishimbay, c., Bashkir ASSR, **RSFSR**; on R. Belaya; ctr. of Ishimbay oilfields; pipelines to Ufa, Orsk, and Shkaparo; p. (est. 1967) 53,000.

Isiro (Paulis), t., N.E. **Zaïre**; admin. offices; cotton ginneries; rly. repair shops.

Isis, R., headstream of R. Thames, **Eng.**; so named around and above Oxford.

Iskenderun (Alexandretta), spt., S. **Turkey**; recent modernisation for new Iran/Turkey rly.; new steel wks.; p. (1980) 124,824.

Islamabad, new cap. of **Pakistan**, to N. of Rawalpindi below Himalayas; nuclear power sta.; p. (1981) 201,000.

Islay, I. Inner Hebrides, Argyll and Bute, **Scot.**; a. 609 km²; farming, dairying distilleries; p. (1971) 3,827.

Isle of Grain, Kent, **Eng.**; flat promontory at confluence of Thames and Medway, once separated from mainland by a tidal estuary; lge oil refinery; pipelines to Walton-on-Thames and Heathrow Airport.

Isle of Man, Irish Sea; 43 km from **Eng.** (Cumbria) and N. Ireland (Down); high plateau N.E. to S.W.; ch. t. Douglas; old cap. Castletown; admin. according to own laws; tourism; freeport (1983) to take advantage of low tax rate; a. 572 km²; p. (est. 1976) 61,000.

Isle of Wight. *See* **Wight, I. of.**

Islington, inner bor., London, **Eng.**; N. of City; incorporates Finsbury; univ.; residtl.; clocks, precision engin.; p. (1981) 159,754.

Islwyn, l. gov. dist., Gwent, **Wales**; inland ts. of Risca, Abercarn, Bedwellty and Mynyddislwyn; p. (1981) 64,769.

Ismailia (Ismā'īlīya), t., **Egypt**; at mid-point of Suez Canal on L. Timsah; rail connections with Cairo, Suez, Port Said; declined during canal closure; p. (1976) 145,930.

Isna (Esneh), t., Upper **Egypt**; on Nile; agr. ctr.; cottons, pottery; p. (1966) 27,400.

Ispra, t., Varese, **Italy**; nr. L. Maggiore; nuclear research ctr.; p. (1981) 4,629.

Israel, rep., S.W. **Asia**; occupies narrow corridor between Jordan valley and Mediterranean Sea; extends S. into the Negev desert (half a. of rep.); Mediterranean climate enables cultivation of early fruits and vegetables, especially citrus fruits; special feature of agr. is cooperative settlements (Kibbutz); main factor limiting agr. development is availability of water; diamonds hgst. exp. earner; most highly industrialised cty. of S.W. Asia, especially for textiles and clothing; petroleum of increasing impt.; tourism; Jewish rep. since 1948; until then part of the mandate Palestine; surrounded by hostile Arab sts.; difficulties of increasing Jewish immigration; cap. Jerusalem; a. 20,850 km²; nat. a. in dispute, particularly since Arab-Israeli wars of 1967 and 1973; p. (est. 1984) 4,216,000. (75 per cent Jewish).

Issyk Kul, mtn. L., Kirghiz SSR, **USSR**; in Tien-Shan mtns., alt. 1,568 m; a. 6,216 km²; ice-free in winter.

Issy-les-Moulineaux, sub. S.W. Paris, Hauts-de-Seine, **France**; engin.; p. (1975) 48,380.

Istanbul (Constantinople), ch. spt., former cap., **Turkey**; on Golden Horn peninsula on European cst. at entry of Bosporus into Sea of Marmara; divided into old "Stamboul" on S. side, and dists. of Galata and Beyoglu (Pera) on N.; the anc. Byzantium; magnificent mosque of Sta. Sophia; univ.; industl. and comm. ctr.; tourism; p. (1980) 2,772,708.

Istria, peninsula, N. Adriatic, **Yugoslavia**; ch. c. Pula; agr., olives, vines, oranges, maize; p. Yugoslav and Italian; a. c. 5,200 km².

Itabira, t., Minas Gerais st., **Brazil**; on Brazilian Plateau, 96 km N.E. of Belo Horizonte; lgst. deposits of iron ore in Brazil; p. (est. 1968) 42,836.

Itabuna, t., Bahia, E. **Brazil**; cocoa, livestock; p. (est. 1980) 159,400.

Itajai, spt., Santa Catarina, S. **Brazil**; exp. lumber, cement, agr. prods.; (est. 1968) 59,423.

Italy, rep., S. **Europe**; peninsula extending into Mediterranean; inc. 2 main Is. of Sicily and Sardinia; bounded by Alps to N.; central spine of Apennines; Mediterranean climate; contrast between industrialised N. and less developed agr. S. (Mezzogiorno); agr. impt., especially in Po basin; tourism attracted by Roman and Renaissance architecture and by climate; inds. based on hydroelectric power in N., inc. elec. engin., motor vehicles and textiles, centred at Milan and Turin; 19 admin. regions; cap. Rome; a. 301,049 km²; p. (est. 1984) 56,724,000.

Ithaca, t., N.Y., **USA**; on Cayuga L.; seat of Cornell Univ.; elec. clocks; machin.; p. (1980) 28,732.

Ithake, one of the Ionian Is., **Greece**; a. 96 km²; ch. t. Ithake; severe earthquake, 1953.

Itzehoe, t., Schleswig-Holstein, **W. Germany**; founded by Charlemagne; wood, cement, machin.; p. (est. 1983) 32,800.

Ivano-Frankovsk (**Stanislav**), c., Ukrainian SSR, **USSR**; in Carpathian foothills; industl. ctr.; oilfields nearby; oil refineries, engin.; p. (est. 1980) 159,000.

Ivanovo, t., **RSFSR**; N.E. of Moscow; textiles, iron and chemical wks.; peat-fed power stas.; p. (est. 1980) 466,000.

Iviza (**Ibiza**), I., Balearic gr. in the W. **Mediterranean**; Spanish; cath.; tourism.

Ivory Coast, rep., on G. of Guinea, **W. Africa**; formerly a Fr. overseas terr.; hot, humid climate; coastal lagoons, interior plateau (300–1,200 m); economy based on subsistence agr. although an impt. coffee and timber producer; world's third lgst. coffee producer; half p. relies on coffee as principle source of income; underdeveloped mineral resources; poorly developed rail network but extensive road system; new pt. at San Pedro; Pt. Bouet outport of former cap. Abidjan; new cap. Yamoussoukro (1983); a. 322,481 km²; p. (est. 1984) 9,474,000.

Iwaki, t., Honshu, **Japan**; ctr. of apple producing dist., p. (est. 1984) 342,074.

Iwakuni, t., Honshu, **Japan**; on Inland Sea; p. (1979) 112,628.

Iwo, t., **Nigeria**; nr. Ibadan; tr. ctr.; p. (est. 1975) 214,000.

Izhevsk, c., cap. of Udmurt ASSR, **RSFSR**; steel ctr., engin.; p. (est. 1980) 562,000.

Izmail, c., Ukrainian SSR, **USSR**; in Bessarabia, on Danube delta, nr. Romanian border; naval base of Soviet Danube flotilla; former Turkish fortress; p. (est. 1970) 48,000.

Izmir (**Smyrna**), c., **Turkey**; at head of G. of I., Anatolia; exp. figs, raisins, tobacco, carpets, rugs; anc. and historic c.; ch. comm. ctr. of the Levant; ambitous industl. project, refinery and chem. complex (1972–86); univ.; p. (1980) 757,854.

Izmit, c., **Turkey**; E. end of Sea of Marmara; cereals, tobacco, oil refinery and polythene plant under construction; p. (1980) 190,423.

J

Jabalpur (**Jubbulpore**), c., Madhya Pradesh, **India**; rly. ctr.; ordnance wks.; p. (1981) 614,162 (c.), 757,303 (met. a.).

Jablonec nad Nisou, t., **ČSSR**; on R. Neisse; glassware ctr., inc. glass jewellery and imitation stones; p. (est. 1968) 33,722.

Jáchymov, t., **ČSSR**; spa; uranium mines, pitchblende, lead, silver, nickel, cobalt.

Jackson, t., Mich., **USA**; on Grand R.; locomotives, motorcar accessories, electronic equipment, metal gds.; p. (1980) 39,739 (t.), 151,495 (met. a.).

Jackson, t., cap. of Miss., **USA**; comm. and industl. ctr.; p. (1980) 203,000 (c.), 320,000 (met. a.).

Jacksonville, c., Fla., **USA**; pt. on St. John's R.; impt. ctr. on Atl. cst.; chemicals, shipbldg. and repair, printing, lumber, cigar mftg.; tourism; p. (1980) 541,000 (c.), 738,000 (met. a.).

Jacobabad, t., Sind, **Pakistan**; driest and hottest place in Indian sub-continent; p. (1961) 35,200.

Jacui, R., S. **Brazil**; rises in S. edge of Brazilian Plateau, enters Atl. Oc., through lagoon, Lagoa dos Patos; 560 km long.

Jadotville. See Likasi

Jaduguda, Bihar, **India**; uranium mine and mill to supply India's growing nuclear power production.

Jaén, c., cap. of prov. of Jaén, S. **Spain**; in foothills of Andalusian mtns.; cath.; olive oil, wine, chemicals; p. (1981) 639,810 (prov.).

Jaffna, spt., N. **Sri Lanka**; on J. peninsula; second t. of rep.; p. (est. 1983) 128,000.

Jaipur, c., cap. of Rajasthan, **India**; univ.; fine fabrics, jewellery; tourism; old cap. Amber is 8 km away; p. (1981) 977,165 (c.), 1,015,160 (met. a.).

Jajce, t., **Yugoslavia**; in Bosnia, at junc. of Rs. Vrbas and Pliva (hydroelectric power); Fed. People's Rep. of Yugoslavia declared here by Tito (1943).

Jakarta. See Djakarta.

Jalalabad, c., E. **Afghanistan**; on Kābul R., nr. Khyber Pass; univ.; agr. tr. ctr.; p. (est. 1982) 57,824.

Jalapa, c., cap. of Veracruz st., **Mexico**; c. 1,370 m; a.s.l.; luxuriant vegetation; agr. ctr.; tourism; p. (1979) 201,473.

Jalgaon, t., Maharashtra, **India**; in Tapti R. valley nr. Bhusawal; p. (1981) 145,335.

Jalisco, st., **Mexico**; on Pac. Oc.; traversed by Sierra Madre; well timbered, agr.; minerals; tourism; a. 80,876 km²; p. (1970) 3,296,586.

Jalón, R., **Spain**; rises in Iberian Mtns., flows N.E. into R. Ebro nr. Zaragoza; valley forms main rly., road route from Madrid to Ebro valley.

Jalpaiguri, t., W. Bengal, **India**; frontier t.; rly. ctr.; p. (1961) 48,738.

Jamaica, rep., **W.I.**; member of Brit. Commonwealth; mtnous.; Blue Mtn. range runs E. to W. and rises to 2,258 m; tropical climate modified by alt.; economy based on agr. and mng.; major exp. crops sugar and bananas; major world producer of bauxite (recent contraction) and alumina; tourist ind. expanding; member of Caribbean Free Trade Association; 25 per cent unemployment; major pts. Kingston, Montego Bay, Pt. Antonio; international airpt.; univ. at cap. Kingston; a. 11,424 km²; p. (est. 1984) 2,290,000, of which 22 per cent are in Kingston.

James, R. Va., **USA**; hydroelec. power in upper reaches, wide estuary in lower course; outlet to Chesapeake Bay; 544 km long.

James Bay, S. arm of Hudson Bay, **Canada**; c. 480 km long, 224 km wide.

Jamestown, spt., cap. of St. Helena I.; flax; p. (1976) 1,516.

Jamestown, t., dist., Va., **USA**; nr. mouth of James R., where first English permanent settlement was founded 1607.

Jammu, t., J. and Kashmir, **India**; winter cap. of st.; univ.; fort, palace; p. (1981) 206,135.

Jammu and Kashmir, st., N.W. **India**; traversed by ranges of Himalayas; in Jhelum valley is celebrated vale of Kashmir, producing abundant crops of wheat and rice; cap. Srinagar; Muzaffarabad ch. c. of a. occupied by Pakistan (Azad Kashmir); total a. 222,823 km²; p. (1981) 5,987,389.

Jamnagar, t., Gujarat, **India**; on G. of Kutch; p. (1981) 277,615 (t.), 317,362 (met. a.).

Jamshedpur, c., Bihar, **India**; W. of Calcutta; major industl. ctr. of rep.; Tata iron and steel wks.; engin.; p. (1981) 438,385 (c.), 669,580 (met. a.).

Janina. See Ioánnina.

Jan Mayen I., volcanic I. between Spitzbergen and Iceland, Arctic Oc.; annexed by **Norway** 1929; meteorological sta.; a. 373 km²; p. (1967) 36.

Japan, monarchy, E. **Asia**; 4 main Is., Honshu (lgst.), Hokkaido, Shikoku, Kyushu; mtnous.; 18 active volcanoes; subject to earthquakes; only 17 per cent of land cultivable; intensive and mechanised agr.; rice, fruits, vegetables; few animals; inds. highly developed and based on imports of raw material and export of finished prods.; rapid industrialisation since second world war; economic growth likely to continue; rapid technological innovation; stable labour management relationships; inds. inc. shipbldg., motor vehicles, textiles, steel, electronics, chemicals, cheap consumer gds.; cap. Tokyo; a. 370,370 km²; p. (est. 1984) 119,492,000 (inc. Okinawa and Ryuku Is.).

Japan Current. See Kuroshio.

Japan, Sea of, portion of **Pac. Oc.** between Korea, USSR, and Japan.

Japurá, R., Colombia, **Brazil**; rises as Caquetá in Colombian Andes, flows S.E. through Brazil to Amazon; 2,080 km long.

Jari, new t., Amazonia, **Brazil;** ambitious project of timber and pulp plant in the rain forest; not as successful as hoped.

Jaroslaw, t., Rzeszow prov., S.E. **Poland;** on R. San; food-processing; found 11th cent.; impt. tr. ctr. 16th cent.; p. (1970) 29,100.

Jarrow, t., South Tyneside, Tyne and Wear, **Eng.;** on S. bank of Tyne, 11 km below Gateshead; grew up as shipbldg. ctr.; hit by depression of 1930s; hunger march to London 1936; new enterprises introduced; steel and tube wks., oil storage; die-castings, knitting-wool-mkg. at Bede trading estate; the Venerable Bede lived and died here; p. (1981) 27,074.

Jasper National Park, Alberta, **Canada;** Rocky mtns., tourism.

Jaunpur, t., Uttar Pradesh, **India;** mkt. t.; ctr. of Moslem learning and architecture in 15th cent.; p. (1981) 105,140.

Java, I., **Indonesia;** most developed of Indonesian Is.; traversed E. to W. by forested volcanic mtns.; fertile volcanic soils aid intensive rice cultivation; over-populated; contains 70 per cent of cty.'s p. yet only 8 per cent of land a.; exps. inc. coffee, rubber, sugar, copra, teak; noted for silver craft and batik work (anc. craft of fabric decoration); a. 130,510 km²; p. (est. 1983) 96,892,900.

Javari, R., forms bdy. between Peru and Brazil; trib. of R. Amazon.

Java Sea, part of the Pac. Oc. between N. cst. Java, Borneo, and Sumatra.

Jebba, t., **Nigeria;** on R. Niger; dam proposed for 1982.

Jebel Aulia, v., **Sudan;** S. of Khartoum; dam across White Nile R.

Jebel-Hauran, high tableland of **Syria,** alt. c. 1,800 m.

Jedburgh, royal burgh, Roxburgh, **Scot.;** on Jed Water, S.W. of Kelso; tweeds, woollens, rayon; abbey ruins; ctr. of Border warfare in Middle Ages; p. (1981) 4,053.

Jeddah. See Jiddah.

Jefferson City, st. cap. Mo., **USA;** on Missouri R.; univ.; comm. and processing ctr. of agr. a.; shoes, tiles, farm implements; p. (1980) 36,619.

Jelenia Góra (Hirschberg), t., S.W. **Poland** (since 1945), formerly in Lower Silesia; mftg.; spa; p. (1970) 55,700.

Jelgava (Mitau), t., Latvian SSR, **USSR;** on Lielupe R.; textiles, foodstuffs, refractory materials; p. (est. 1972) 58,000.

Jemappes, t., **Belgium;** 5 km W. of Mons; industl.; Fr. victory over Austria 1792; battle of Mons 1914; p. (est. 1969) 12,548.

Jena, c., **E. Germany;** on R. Saale, 72 km S.W. of Leipzig; univ., observatory; optical glass-ware, precision instruments; leading cultural ctr. late 18th and early 19th cent., defeat of Prussians by Fr. 1806; p. (1983) 106,555.

Jensen, t., Utah, **USA;** oil refinery; on R. Green.

Jerez de la Frontera, t., **Spain;** in Andalusia, 22 km N.E. of Cádiz; in fertile agr. a.; sherry; p. (1981) 150,481.

Jericho, v., Jordan Valley, **Jordan;** est. through recent excavations as one of oldest towns in the world (6000 B.C.); p. (1961) 10,284.

Jersey, I., lgst. of **Channel Is.,** 21 km W. of Fr. cst.; potatoes, tomatoes, cauliflowers, flowers, fruit. cattle; tourist resort; banking; ch. t. St. Helier; a. 117 km²; p. (1981) 77,000.

Jersey City, c., N.J., **USA;** E. of Newark, on Hudson R.; comm. and industl. ctr.; diverse inds.; p. (1980) 224,000 (c.), 557,000 (met. a.).

Jerusalem, c., **Israel** and **Jordan;** 811 m a.s.l.; between Dead Sea and Mediterranean; the "Holy City" of the Jews and the sacred c. of the Christians and Moslems; Israeli western sector and Arab eastern sector declared by Israeli parliament (1980) united c. and cap.; modern mftg.; p. (est. 1982) 424,400 inc. E. Jerusalem.

Jervis Bay, inlet of Pac. Oc., Australian Capital Territory, **Australia;** acquired by Fed Govt. as site for establishment of pt. for Canberra 1909; plans to develop pt. and steelworks (1970s); a. 73 km².

Jesenice, t., **Yugoslavia;** integrated iron and steel wks.; terminal of Brotherhood and Unity Highway.

Jesselton. See Kota Kinabalu.

Jhang Maghiana, t., **Pakistan;** textiles; mkt.; on R. Chenab; p. (1972) 135,722.

Jhansi, c., Uttar Pradesh, **India;** ctr. rly. ctr., mkt.; formerly of strategic importance; p. (1981) 246,172 (c.), 284,141 (met. a.).

Jharia, t., Bihar, **India;** ctr. of most impt. coal-field in India; p. (1961) 33,683.

Jhelum, R., W. Punjab, **Pakistan;** most W. of the five Rs. of the Punjab; forms Vale of Kashmir in upper course; Mangla Dam under Indus Waters Treaty, completed 1967.

Jhelum, t., **Pakistan;** on Jhelum R.; p. (est. 1975) 68,000.

Jiamusi (Kiamusze), c., Heilongjiang, **China;** ch. pt. on Songhua R; p. (est. 1970) 275,000.

Jiangsu (Kiangsu), coastal prov., **China;** on Yellow Sea; low lying a. N. of Chang Jiang delta; rich agr., dense p.; cotton, sericulture, tea, sugar, fish (many Ls.); cap. Nanjing; a. 109,000 km²; p. (est. 1983) 61,350,000.

Jiangxi (Kiangsi), prov., S.E. **China;** in basin of navigable Gan R. which drains through L. Poyang to Chang Jiang; ch. cs. Shanghai, Zhenjiang, Wuxi, Nanchong (cap.); rice, wheat, tea, cotton; tungsten, coking coal, kaolin; a. 172,494 km²; p. (est. 1983) 33,840,000.

Jiddah or **Jeddah,** c., admin. cap., Hejaz, **Saudi Arabia;** on Red Sea, pt. of Mecca; pilgrims; steel mill projected; new King Faisal Port nearby; univ. (with Mecca); p. (1974) 561,104.

Jihlava, t., Moravia, **ČSSR;** on Jihlava R.; 519 m a.s.l.; timber, grain, textiles; Prague Compactata signed here 1436; p. (est. 1970) 40,000.

Jilin (Kirin), prov., N.E. **China;** N. of Korea and Liaotung peninsula; crossed by Songhua R.; in fertile Manchurian plain; impt. industl. a.; soya beans, grain, lumber, coal, gold, lead; cap. Changchun; a. 186,998 km²; p. (est. 1983) 22,700,000.

Jilin (Kirin), c., Jilin, N.E. **China;** former prov. cap.; on Songhua R., at outlet of Songhua reservoir; impt. position on rly. from Changchun to coastal pts.; chemical fertilisers, steel, oil refinery; p. (est. 1983) 1,099,000.

Jimma, t., **Ethiopia;** ch. prod. Jimma coffee; connected by road with Addis Ababa; Agricultural Technical School; p. (est. 1980) 63,837.

Jinan (Tsinan), c., cap of Shandong prov., **China;** on S. bank of Huang He, 160 km. from G. of Bo Hai; agr. ctr.; glass, textiles, precious stones, trucks; p. (est. 1983) 1,360,000.

Jinja, t., **Uganda;** on N. shore of L. Victoria where Nile drains from L. over Ripon Falls; (now inundated by Owen Falls dam 2·4 km upstream); cotton mnfs., copper smelting, flour and maize milling; rly. to Kampala; p. (1980) 45,060.

Jinzhou (Chincho), c., Liaoning prov., **China;** cement, glass, bricks, tiles, paper, wood and pulp, oil; p. (est. 1983) 735,000.

Jiujiang (Kiukiang), c., Jianxi prov., **China;** pt. of Chang Jiang at foot of forested mtn.; entrepôt tr.; former treaty pt.; p. (est. 1970) 120,000.

João Pessoa, t., cap. of Paraíba st., **Brazil;** through its pt. Cabedelo expts. cotton, sugar, minerals; recent industl. expansion results from SUDENE development plan; p. (est. 1980) 332,100.

Joban, dist., N.E. Honshu, **Japan;** third lgst. coalfield in Japan; ch. t. Fukushima.

Jodhpur, t., Rajasthan, **India;** ctr. of Thar desert; old fortress t.; p. (1981) 506,345.

Jogjakarta, c., Java, **Indonesia;** univ., cultural ctr.; handicrafts; citadel with palace; p. (1971) 342,367.

Johannesburg, c., Transvaal, S. **Africa;** univ.; gold-mng. ctr. of Witwatersrand; diamond cutting, engin., textiles, chemicals; oil pipeline from Durban; p. (1970) 1,432,643 (met. a.).

John o' Groat's House, place nr. Duncansby Head, Caithness, **Scot.**

Johnstone, burgh, Renfrew, **Scot.;** on R. Black Cart, nr. Paisley; machine tools, textiles, iron and brass foundry; p. (1981) 42,707.

Johnstown, industl. t., Penns., **USA;** on Conemaugh R.; coal-mng. and steel ctr.; machin.; p. (1980) 265,000 (met. a.).

Johore, st., **Malaysia;** at S. end of Malaya; forested; cap. Johor Baharo; rubber, rice, copra, pineapples; tin, iron, bauxite; a. 18,985 km²; p. (1980) 1,638,229.

Joina Falls, Mali; dam projected for hydroelectric power and irrigation under auspices of Organisation of Riparian States of R. Senegal (Guinea, Mali, Mauritania, Senegal).

Joinville, t., Santa Catarina, **Brazil;** exp. timber, maté tea; textiles, machin., car parts, plastics; p. (est. 1980) 194,300.

Joliet, c., Ill., **USA;** on Des Plaines R., S.W. of Chicago; R. pt.; coal and limestone nearby; rly. engin., oil refining; p. (1980) 77,956.

Joliette, t., Quebec, **Canada;** textile mills, paper, tobacco-processing; p. (1970) 78,887.

Jönköping, t., cap. of J. co., **Sweden**; safety-matches, textiles, footwear; p. (1983) 106,899.

Jonquière, t., S. Quebec, **Canada**; paper and pulp mills. *See* **Chicoutimi**.

Joplin, t., Mo., **USA**; in dairy and livestock region; lead and zinc mng.; mnfs. metal and leather gds.; p. (1980) 39,023 (t.) 127,513 (met. a.).

Jordan, kingdom, S.W. **Asia**; bounded by Israel, Syria, Saudi Arabia, and Iraq; consists of high plateau (600 m), Jordan valley, and hill cty. to W. of R. Jordan; only 25 per cent of a. sufficiently humid for agr., much is migratory herding of animals and subsistence agr.; sm. mineral wealth; only outlet to sea Aqaba, pt. on G. of Aqaba; only one single-track rly.; new rail link built to Al-Hara phosphate mines, now major exp.; dependant on oil imports; cap. Amman; W. Bank of R. Jordan occupied by Israeli forces since June 1967; plan mooted (1972) to unify J. and W. Bank to form United Arab Kingdom; a. 101,140 km²; p. (est. 1984) 3,375,000 (80 per cent Moslem and 70 per cent under 24).

Jordan, R., Israel and Jordan; flows S. from Anti-Lebanon along sinuous course, mostly below sea-level to Dead Sea; its rapidly and variant depth render it unnavigable, and no t. of any importance has ever been built on its banks; Jesus was baptised in its waters; contemporary strife over use for irrigation; 368 km long.

Jos, t., central **Nigeria**; on Bauchi Plateau, 96 km S.W. of Bauchi; impt. tin mines; new steel rolling mill; p. (est. 1969) 104,838.

Jostedalsbre, icefield, W. **Norway**, lgst. icefield of European mainland; a. 881 km²; rises to 2,043 m.

Jotunheimen, mtn. region, central **Norway** hgst. in Scandinavia; Galdhopiggen 2,470 m, Glittertind 2,482 m.

Juan Fernández, two rocky volcanic Is., S. **Pac. Oc.**, belonging to Chile; a. 98 km²; the buccaneer Alexander Selkirk marooned here 1704–9 gave idea for Defoe's *Robinson Crusoe*.

Juan les Pins, resort, Alpes-Maritimes dep., S.E. **France**.

Juba (Giuba), R., **Somalia**; narrow fertile valley, imp. agr. a.; 872 km long.

Jubbulpore. *See* **Jabalpur**.

Jucar, R., E. **Spain**; rises in Montes Universales, and flows to Mediterranean; irrigation and hydroelec. power; 400 km long.

Judaea, div. of Palestine in the Roman period.

Juggernaut. *See* **Puri**.

Juiz de Fora, t., Minas Gerais, **Brazil**; textile ctr.; p. (est. 1980) 334,400.

Julfa (Jolfa), c., N. **Iran**; on frontier with USSR, customs and transit ctr. on overland route from Europe.

Julian Alps, mtn. range, **Yugoslavia** and **Italy**; hgst. peak 2,865 m.

Julianehåb, t., S.W. **Greenland**; N.W. of C. Farewell; tr. ctr., fish. pt.

Jülich, t., N. Rhine–Westphalia, **W. Germany**; nuclear reactor; p. (est. 1983) 30,400.

Jullundur, c., Punjab, **India**; rly. ctr.; st. cap. until Chandigarh was built; p. (1981) 408,196.

Jumna, R., N. India; ch. trib. of R. Ganges; rises in the Himalayas and flows past Delhi and Agra to Allahabad; 1,376 km long.

Junagadh, t., Gujarat, **India**; agr. tr. and food-processing; industl. ctr.; formerly cap. of principality of J.; p. (1981) 118,646.

Jundiai, t., São Paulo st., **Brazil**; industl. ctr.; nr. São Paulo; p. (1980) 249,300.

Juneau, c., cap. of Alaska, **USA**; at foot of Chilkoot mtns., lumbering; fisheries; gold settlement (1881); p. (1980) 19,528. *See* **Willow South**.

Jungfrau, peak, Bernese Oberland, **Switzerland**; height 4,161 m; electric rly. from Kleine Scheidegg to Jungfraujoch.

Junin, t., **Argentina**; agr. tr., rly. engin., pottery, furniture; p. (1960) 53,489.

Jura, dep., E. **France**; named from mtn. range on Franco-Swiss border; agr. and pastoral; cap. Lons-le-Saunier; a. 5,053 km²; p. (1982) 243,000.

Jura, I., Argyll and Bute, Scot.; off W. cst.; a. 378 km²; p. (1971) 349 inc. Colonsay.

Jura, mtn. range, **Switzerland** and **France**; folded parallel ranges separated by deep R. valleys; hgst. peak Crêt de la Neige, 1,724 m; 240 km long, breadth 48–64 km.

Jura, new canton (1979), **Switzerland**; between Berne and Basle in a strong French speaking dist. in Jura Mtns; p. (1980) 64,986.

Juruá R., lge. trib. of Amazon; rises in E. Peru and flows through Acre and Amazonas sts., **Brazil**; over 3,200 km long.

Jutland (Jylland), peninsula, **Denmark**; intensive agr. and poultry farming; sandy heath in W.; more fertile clay in E. used for dairying; a. 29,554 km²; p. (1971) 2,193,070.

Jyväskylä, t., central **Finland**; pt. on L. Päijänne; pulp. paper, plywood; univ.; p. (1970) 57,025.

K

K2. *See* **Godwin-Austin, Mt.**

Kabardin-Balkar ASSR, aut. rep., Transcaucasia, **RSFSR**; cap. Nalchik; livestock, lumber, wheat, fruit; non-ferrous metals; hydro-metallurgy plant; a. 12,432 km²; p. (1970) 589,000.

Kabelega Falls (Murchison Falls), on Victoria Nile, **Uganda**; falls between L. Kioga and L. Mobutu Seso.

Kabinda. *See* **Cabinda**.

Kâbul, c., cap. of **Afghanistan**; on Kâbul R. S. of Hindu Kush; 2,104 m a.s.l.; excellent climate; univ.; comm. and cultural ctr.; textiles, leather, timber inds.; p. (est. 1979) 892,194 (met. a.).

Kâbul, R., flows from Hindu Kush through gorges in Khyber Pass to Indus; site of dam for hydroelec. power and irrigation; length c. 480 km.

Kabwe (Broken Hill), **Zambia**; comm. and mng. ctr.; lead, zinc, cadmium, silver; p. (1979) 139,000.

Kachin State, semi-aut. st., **Burma**; comprising former Myitkyina and Bhamo dists.; home of Kachins; a. 89,042 km².

Kadiyevka, t., Ukrainian SSR, **USSR**; coal, iron and steel, synthetic rubber; p. (est. 1977) 141,000.

Kaduna, t., N. **Nigeria**; cap of Kaduna st.; rly. junc.; aluminium wks.; spinning and weaving; new oil refinery; p. (est. 1982) 1,036,407.

Kaffa, region, **Ethiopia**; mtnous., forested; natural habitat of coffee plant; p. (est. 1980) 1,615,400.

Kagoshima, c., at S. end of Kyushu I., **Japan**; pt. on K. Bay; univs., cas.; porcelain, silk and cotton clothing, food-processing, publishing; rocket launching site nearby at Uchinoura; p. (est. 1984) 505,360.

Kahoolawe, I., **Hawaiian Is.**; a. 117 km²; uninhabited.

Kaieteur Falls, waterfall, **Guyana**; where R. Potaro leaves Guiana Highlands; among world's hgst. falls (226 m).

K'ai-feng, c., Honan, **China**; nr. S. bank of Huang He; one of the most anc. cities in China; cottons, chemicals; p. (est. 1970) 330,000.

Kai Islands, Is., **Indonesia**; between New Guinea and Timor; timber; a. 1,761 km²; p. 51,000.

Kaikoura, t., S.I., N.Z.; on E. cst., 128 km N.E. of Christchurch; in this region are the Kaikoura ranges, in which the hgst. peaks are Tapuaenuku (2,887 m) and Alarm (2,867 m); p. (1971) 1,607.

Kailas (Kang-ti-ssu Shan), range and peak, S.W. Tibet, **China**; unclimbed sacred mtn.; source of Indus, Ganges, Sutlej and Zangbo (headstream of Brahmaputra).

Kainji Dam, **Nigeria**; power sta. transmission system and river transportation on R. Niger.

K'ai-ping, t., Hebei, N. **China**; second lgst. coal-mng. a. (Kailan mines) in China; coal exported through Qinhuangdao.

Kairouan, holy c. of Moslems, **Tunisia**; 128 km S.S.E. of Tunis; founded A.D. 670; mosque; p. (1975) 54,546.

Kaiserslautern, c., Rhineland–Palatinate, **W. Germany**; nr. Mannheim; iron, textiles, machin., tobacco, wood; p. (est. 1983) 98,700.

Kaiser Wilhelm's Land, Australian dependency, **Antarctica**.

Kakamega, t., **Kenya**; E. Africa; 48 km N. of Kisumu; ctr. of gold-mng. dist.

Kakinada, t., spt., Andhra Pradesh, **India**; cotton, oilseeds; p. (1981) 226,409.

Kalahari Desert, region of semi-desert, southern **Africa**; between Orange and Zambesi Rs.; mainly in **Botswana**; alt. 1,128 m; a. 51,800 km²; inhabited chiefly by Bushmen.

Kalamata, t., Peloponnesus, **Greece**; nr. Sparta; figs, currants, flour-milling, cigarette mftg.; p. (1981) 43,235.

Kalamazoo, c., Mich., **USA**; industl. and comm. ctr. in farming a.; paper, pharmaceuticals; fish hatchery nearby; p. (1980) 279,000 (met. a.).

Kalemie (Albertville), t., **Zaïre**; on L. Tanganyika; rail-steamer transfer point; p. (est. 1967) 86,687.

Kalewa, t., **Burma**; at confluence of Irrawaddy and Chindwin Rs.; coal deposits.

Kalgan See **Zhangjiakou**.

Kalgoorlie, t., W. **Australia**; gold mng. ctr. in arid region adjacent to "Golden Mile" auriferous reef; nickel mng. more impt.; nickel smelter (1971); p. (1976) 19,041 (inc. Boulder).

Kalimantan (Indonesian Borneo); straddles equator; sparse p.; poor soils; lge. areas of swamp; plans for reclamation; coal, oil, diamonds, gold in sm. quantities; rice, pepper, copra; a. 539,461 km²; p. est. (1970) 626,000.

Kalinin (Tver), c., **RSFSR**; on upper Volga; diversified inds.; 17th cent. cath. and cas.; p. (est. 1980) 416,000.

Kaliningrad (Königsberg), c., **RSFSR**, former cap. of E. Prussia; on R. Pregel, linked by canal to outer pt. Pillau; univ., cath.; shipbldg., machin., wood-pulp, chemicals, exp. agr. prods.; Kant lived here all his life; p. (est. 1980) 361,000.

Kalisz, t., Poznan, **Poland**; on R. Prosna; industl. ctr., textiles; oldest Polish t. mentioned in 2nd cent. A.D. by Ptolemy; p. (est. 1983) 102,900.

Kalmar, t., spt., S. **Sweden**; on I. in Kalmar Sound; cath., cas.; matches, food inds., shipbldg.; p. (1983) 53,516.

Kalmuk (Kalmytskaya) ASSR, aut. rep., **RSFSR**; on Caspian Sea; harsh and infertile steppe; pastoral agr.; cap. Elista; a. 75,887 km²; p. (1970) 268,000.

Kalna, v., on Mt. Stara Planina, **Yugoslavia**; uranium mine and plant; nuclear power sta.

Kaluga, c., **RSFSR**; pt. on Oka R.; chemicals, engin., hydroelec. power plant; p. (est. 1980) 270,000.

Kalyan, spt., Maharashtra, **India**; nr. Bombay; bricks, tiles; p. (1981) 136,052.

Kalymnos, I., Dodecanese, **Greece**; mtnous.; a. 106 km²; p. 13,600.

Kama, R., **RSFSR**; ch. trib. of Volga which it joins below Kazan; rises in foothills of Urals; lge. hydroelectric sta. at Perm; navigable; 2,016 km long.

Kamaishi, t., spt., N.E. Honshu, **Japan**; serves Kamaishi-Sennin iron-ore field, lgst. worked deposits and reserves in Japan; impt. iron and steel ind.; p. (1970) 72,923.

Kamakura, t., Honshu, **Japan**; on shore of Sagami Bay; tourism; p. (1979) 173,652.

Kamaran I., Red Sea, **Democratic Rep. of Yemen**; formerly under Brit. occupation, 1915–67; a. 57 km²; p. 2,200.

Kamchatka, peninsula, E. Siberia, **USSR**; volcanic ranges; geothermal power sta.; mineral wealth, fisheries on cst., climate cold, wet and foggy; contains part of Koryak nat. okrug; cap. Petropavlovsk.

Kamenets-Podolskiy, t., Ukrainian SSR, **USSR**; on Smotrich R.; lt. inds.; mediaeval fortress t.; p. (est. 1970) 113,000.

Kamensk-Shakhtinskiy, c., **RSFSR**; on Donets R.; coal-mng. ctr., engin., food processing, artificial fibres; p. (est. 1967) 71,000.

Kamensk-Uralsk, c., **RSFSR**; aluminium, iron, steel, engin.; p. (est. 1980) 189,000.

Kamet, Himalayan peak, on border of **India** and Tibet, **China**; 7,761 m; highest mtn. climbed (Smythe, 1931) until 1953 (Everest).

Kamloops, t., B.C., **Canada**; on Thompson R.; formerly Fort Thompson; on transcontinental rlys.; suppl ctr. for mng. and grazing dist.; fruit and livestock mkts.; p. (1971) 25,599.

Kampala, c., cap. of **Uganda**; univ., ch. comm. ctr.; lt. inds., coffee-processing; p. (1980) 458,423.

Kampen, t., Overijssel, **Neth.**; on R. IJssel; cigar-mkg.; p. (1982) 30,989.

Kampot, t., **Cambodia**; spt. on G. of Siam; ctr. of pepper ind.; p. (est. 1973) 337,879.

Kampuchea, Democratic (Cambodia), S.E. **Asia**; between Thailand and Vietnam; former ass. st. of Fr. Union; cap. Phnom-Penh on Mekong R.; mainly agr., rice, rubber, maize, pepper, kapok, livestock; Tonle Sap impt. for fishing; car assembly, cigarette mkg., textiles, plywood, paper, tyres, cement; oil refinery nr. Kompong Som; new constitution established after civil war 1970–5; invaded by Vietnam (1979) and Khmer Rouge overthrown; a. 181,300 km²; p. (est. 1984) 7,149,000 (lge decrease since 1975 from war, famine and migration).

Kamyshin, t., **RSFSR**; pt. on Volga; textiles, mkt. gardening, grain; p. (est. 1980) 112,000.

Kan, R. See **Gan Jiang**.

Kananga (Luluabourg), c., cap. of Kasai Occidental prov., **Zaïre**; on Lulua R.; comm. and communications ctr. in cotton-growing a.; p. (1982) 704,211 (met. a.).

Kanawha, R., W. Va., **USA**; rises in Allegheny mtns., flows into R. Ohio; runs through ch. mng. a. of W. Va. coalfield nr. Charleston.

Kanazawa, c., Honshu, **Japan**; in Kana plain, on Sea of Japan; machin., silk and cotton textiles; landscape gardens. No theatre; p. (est. 1984) 417,684.

Kanchenjunga, mtn., on Nepal–Sikkim bdy., N.E. **India**; third hgst. mtn. in world, 8,585 m.

Kanchipuram (Conjeeveram), t., Tamil Nadu, S. **India**; on plain S.W. of Madras; pilgrimage ctr.; textiles; p. (1971) 110,657 (t.). 119,693 (met. a.).

Kandahar, c., former cap. of **Afghanistan**; alt. 1,037 m; 592 km from Herat; linked by road to Kushka (Turkmen SSR) via Herat; fruit preserving and canning; textiles; p. (est. 1979) 243,103.

Kandy, c., **Sri Lanka**; in mtns. in ctr. of I.; 120 km from Colombo; univ. at sub. of Peradeniya; resort in hot season; tea, cocoa; p. (est. 1977) 103,000.

Kangaroo I., lgst. I. off S. **Australia** cst.; tourists attracted by spectacular granite scenery and varied flora and fauna; p. (1976) 3,262.

Kano, c., N. **Nigeria**; emporium for whole of Sudan region; impt. airport and rly. terminus; groundnut ctr.; p. (est. 1975) 399,000.

Kanpur (Cawnpore), c., Uttar Pradesh, N. **India**; on R. Ganges; impt. mftg. ctr.; textiles, chemicals, leather goods, foodstuffs; p. (1981) 1,481,789 (c.), 1,639,064 (met. a.).

Kansas, st., **USA**; called the "sunflower state"; prairie; farming, maize, wheat; cattle, dairying, pigs; coal, petroleum, natural gas, lead, meat packing, flour milling, aircraft, chemicals, machin.; admitted to Union 1861; st. flower sunflower, st. bird Western Meadowlark; cap. Topeka; a. 213,095 km²; p. (1980) 2,363,000.

Kansas, R., Kan., **USA**; trib. of Missouri R., confluence at Kansas City; vegetable growing in valley; periodic flooding; 272 km long.

Kansas City, Kansas and Mo., **USA**; at confluence of Kansas and Missouri Rs.; univ.; gr. livestock mart, car and aircraft assembly, steel prods., meat-packing, food processing; p. (1980) 161,000 (Kansas) 448,000 (Mo.); 1,327,000 (joint met. a.).

Kansu. See **Gansu**.

Kant, t., Kirghiz SSR, **USSR**; 19 km E. of Frunze; to be expanded to industl. c.; proposed p. 100,000.

Kanye, t., **Botswana**, S. Africa; lgst. t. in rep.; p. (1971) 39,200.

Kaohsiung, spt., **Taiwan**; on S.W. cst.; industl. ctr., road and rly. terminus; oil refining, aluminium wks.; p. (est. 1984) 1,285,132.

Kaolack, inland pt., **Senegambia**; 112 km up Saloum R.; groundnut ctr., integrated textile complex; p. (1976) 106,899.

Kaposvár, t., S.W. **Hungary**; on Kapos R.; comm. ctr.; textiles, foodstuffs; p. (est. 1978) 72,458.

Kara-Bogaz-Gol, lge. shallow bay, Turkmen SSR, **USSR**; an arm of Caspian Sea; rapid evaporation allows huge quantities of salt from Caspian to be deposited along its shores (world's lgst. source of Glauber's salt); a. 18,130 km².

Karabuk, t., **Turkey**; N. of Ankara; steel wks.; p. (1965) 47,660.

Karacheyevo-Cherkesskaya, aut. region, **RSFSR**; in Greater Caucasus; cap. Cherkessk; livestock, grain; coal, lead, zinc; a. 14,095 km²; p. (1970) 345,000.

Karachi, c., **Pakistan**; on Arabian Sea, nr. Indus delta; former cap. of Pakistan; univ.; spt., air ctr.; oil refining, industl. gases, steel mill, natural gas from Sui; nuclear power sta.; p. (1981) 5,103,000.

Karaganda, c., Kazakh SSR, **USSR**; on impt. coalfield developed since 1926; supplies industl. ctrs. of Urals; iron and steel wks., power sta.; p. (est. 1980) 577,000.

Kara-Kalpak ASSR, aut. rep., N.W. Uzbek SSR, **USSR**; inc. Ust-Urt plateau, Kyzyl-Kum desert; irrigated agr.; cap. Nukus; a. 165,553 km²; p. (1970) 702,000.

Karakorum Range, part of Himalayas between **Kashmir** and **China**; many lofty peaks, inc. Mt. Godwin-Austen; Karakorum highway linking Pakistan with Xinjiang prov. of China, opened 1971.

Kara-Kum, sand desert, Turkmen SSR, **USSR**; E. of S.E. shore of Caspian Sea; to be irrigated with water diverted from Rs. which flow to Barents Sea. a. 349,650 km²; canal 1,440 km long across desert.

Karamay (K'o-la-ma-i), t. Xianjiang, **China**; ctr. of lge. oilfield; pipeline to Fushantzu refinery.

Kara Sea, Arctic Oc.; E. of Novaya Zemlya; navigation to and from Siberian pts. July–Sept.

Karbala, c., **Iraq**; N.W. of Al Hillah; ctr. of pilgrimage; sacred c. of Moslem Shiite sect; p. (1970) 107,496.

Karelian ASSR, aut. rep., **RSFSR**; between Kola peninsula and Finland; lake-covered, coniferous forests; cap. Petrozavodsk; rich in timber, minerals, precious metals; granite and mica quarried; paper and pulp milling; a. 179,408 km²; p. (1970) 714,000.

Karelian Isthmus, **RSFSR**; strategic route between Finland and USSR impt. for defence of Leningrad.

Kariba Dam, in Kariba gorge of Zambesi R., on **Zimbabwe–Zambia** border; operated jointly by the two govts.; one of lgst. dams in world with vast artificial lake supplying hydroelectric power to Zimbabwe and the copperbelt of Zambia; badly polluted with use of D.D.T. in tsetse and malaria control; involved resettlement of Batonka peoples; completed 1960; following Rhodesian U.D.I., construction began on a second generating sta. on the Zambian side.

Karikal, former Fr. settlement on E. cst. of **India**.

Karkonosze. *See* **Riesengebirge**.

Karl-Marx-Stadt (Chemnitz), c., Karl-Marx-Stadt dist., **E. Germany**; leading industl. ctr.; cotton, woollens, machin., cars, furniture, chemicals, engin.; nr. lignite mines; p. (1983) 318,917.

Karlovac, t., Croatia, **Yugoslavia**; S.W. of Zagreb; chemicals, textiles, food processing; p. (1971) 47,532.

Karlový Vary (Carlsbad), t., Bohemia, **ČSSR**; on R. Ohře; hot mineral springs; health resort; porcelain; p. (1970) 45,000.

Karlskoga, t., **Sweden**; E. of L. Vänern; seat of Bofors armament wks.; iron and steel, explosives, chemicals; p. (1983) 35,539.

Karlskrona, spt., S. **Sweden**; on Baltic Sea; main naval sta.; lighting fixtures, china; p. (1983) 59,696.

Karlsruhe, c., Baden-Württemberg, **W. Germany**; road and rly. ctr.; outport on Rhine; chemicals, engin., elec., tobacco inds.; oil refining; nuclear reactor; oil pipeline to Lavera, nr. Marseilles; p. (est. 1983) 270,300.

Karlstad, t., **Sweden**; on N. shore L. Väner; ironwks., engin., machin.; p. (1983) 73,939.

Karnak, t., **Egypt**; on Nile, E. of Luxor; site of the anc. Thebes; ruined temples; p. *c.* 11,000.

Karnal, t., Haryana, **India**; clothing inds.; p. (1981) 132,107.

Karnataka (Mysore), st., S.W. **India**; borders Arabian Oc.; inc. W. Ghats where high rainfall and hydroelec. power; rainfall decreases to E.; cap. Bangalore; a. 192,203 km²; p. (1981) 37,135,174.

Karpathos, I., Dodecanese, **Greece**; Aegean Sea; between Rhodes and Crete; p. 8,747.

Karroo, W. Cape Prov., **S. Africa**; high plateau, scrub-covered; irrigated by Verwoerd dam on Orange R.

Kars, t., N.E. **Turkey**; in Armenia, alt. *c.* 1,800 m, in strategic position nr. Soviet border; p. (1970) 53,338.

Karst, dist., **Yugoslavia**; in Dinaric Alps; gives name to limestone landforms which are well developed here.

Karun, R., S.W. **Iran**; mainly mtn. torrent; difficult access, sparse p.; 752 km long.

Karvina, t., **ČSSR**; on Polish border; ctr. of Ostrava-Karvina coalfield; p. (1970) 77,000.

Kasai, R., Angola and **Zaïre**, Central Africa; rises in Bihé Plateau (Angola) and flows over 1,920 km into R. Zaïre 192 km above Kinshasa; alluvial diamond mng. at Chicopa.

Kasai, former prov., **Zaïre**; agr.; impt. source of industl. diamonds; attempted secession 1960; now divided into E. Kasai (cap. Mbuji-Mayi), and W. Kasai (cap. Luluabourg).

Kāshān, c., central **Iran**; in agr. oasis; carpets, velvet; p. (est. 1975) 80,000 (c.), 153,980 (dist.).

Kashi (Kashgar) c., Xinjiang, prov., **China**; on anc. imperial silk route through central Asia; growth rapid with irrigation; visited by Marco Polo 1275; p.(est. 1970) 175,000.

Kashmir. *See* **Jammu and Kashmir**.

Kassala, t., N.E. **Sudan**; ctr. of cotton-growing dist.; p. (est. 1972) 106,000.

Kassel, c., Hesse, **W. Germany**; on R. Fulda; cas.; machin., vehicles, science-based inds.; route ctr.; p. (est. 1983) 190,400.

Kastamonu, t., N. **Turkey**; cap. of K. prov.; ctr. of dist. rich in minerals; textiles, copper gds.; p. (1970) 29,338.

Katanga. *See* **Shaba**.

Kathiawar, peninsula, Gujarat, **India**; between G. of Kutch and G. of Cambay; ch. pt. Bhaunagar; very dry a.

Katmai, Mount, S. Alaska, **USA**; active volcano with crater L.; alt. 2,135 m.

Katmandu (Kathmandu), cap. of **Nepal**; on Vishnumati R., 120 km from Indian frontier; highway to Kodari; hydroelec. sta.; brick and tile wks.; many palaces and temples; p. (1981) 393,494.

Katoomba, t., N.S.W., **Australia**; holiday resort at 1,017 m in the Blue Mountains; since 1947 part of City of Blue Mtns.; p. (1976) 12,301 (inc. Wentworth Falls).

Katowice, prov., S. **Poland**; in Upper Silesia; cap. K.; mng. and industl. a. drained by Warta R.; a. 9,516 km²; p. (1970) 3,691,000.

Katowice, c., S. **Poland**; cap. of K. prov.; impt. iron-mng. and industl. ctr.; heavy machin. chemicals; p. (est. 1983) 361,306.

Katrine, Loch, S.W. Stirling, **Scot.**; beautiful woodland and moorland scenery; source of Glasgow water supply; scene of Scott's *Lady of the Lake*; 13 km long, *c.* 1·6 km wide.

Katsina, t., **Nigeria**; nr. Niger border; agr. tr. ctr., groundnuts, cotton; rural craft inds.; new steel rolling mill; Hausa cultural ctr.; p. (est. 1971) 109,424.

Kattegat, arm of N. Sea linked with Baltic; separates **Denmark** (Jutland) from **Sweden**; 64–112 km wide.

Katwijk, t., S. Holland, **Neth.**; on N. Sea 24 km from the Hague; resort; synthetic resins; p. (1982) 38,494.

Kaufbeuren, t., Bavaria, **W. Germany**; on R. Wertach; textile mnfs.; p. (est. 1983) 41,700.

Kaunas (Kovno), c., Lithuanian SSR, **USSR**; on R. Nemen; R. pt. and comm. ctr.; univ.; 11th cent. c.; metal gds., chemicals, textiles, hydroelec. power; Jewish p. (circa 30 per cent) exterminated during German occupation 1941–4; p. (est. 1980) 377,000.

Kavalla, c., E. Macedonia, **Greece**; on Bay of Kavalla; processes and exp. tobacco; the anc. Neapolis; p. (1981) 56,705.

Kawagoe, c., Honshu, **Japan**; in Kanto plain; silk textiles; p. (est. 1984) 259,314.

Kawasaki, S. sub. Tokyo, Honshu, **Japan**; pt. for import of industl. raw materials; heavy inds.; p. (est. 1984) 1,040,802.

Kawthoolei State, st., **Burma**; former Karen st., extended to inc. areas in Tenasserim and Irrawaddy; a. 30,383 km².

Kayah State, semi-aut. st., **Burma**; on Thai border; forested plateau; tungsten mines; teak; a. 11,730 km².

Kayseri, c., **Turkey**; S.E. of Ankara; textiles, carpets, food tr.; anc. Hittite c.; p. (1980) 281,320.

Kazakh SSR (Kazakhstan), constituent rep., **USSR**; in central Asia; cap. Alma-Ata; steppe with stock-raising; lge. desert areas being made fertile by irrigation; plans to divert Ob R.; grain in N.; coal at Karaganda; asbestos at Dzhetygara; minerals inc. metaborite (richest boron mineral); oil; atomic power sta. to W. of Caspian Sea; cosmodrome at Leninsk, E. of Aral Sea; a. 2,778,544 km²; p. (est. 1985) 15,842,000.

Kazan', c., **RSFSR**; cap. of Tatar ASSR; pt. on Volga; impt. tr. ctr. for E. USSR, Turkestan Bokhara and Iran; cath., univ. (where Tolstoy and Lenin were educated); engin., chemicals, synthetic rubber, textiles, paper, oil refining; natural gas pipeline to Minnibayevo; p. (est. 1980) 1,002,000.

Kazanluk, t., central **Bulgaria**; in region famous for attar of roses; p. (est. 1968) 48,816.

Kazan-retto or **Volcanic Is.**; gr. of Is., W. Pac. Oc. S. of Tokyo; sugar plantations, sulphur; returned to **Japan** by USA 1968.

Kazbek, extinct volcano, N. Georgian SSR, **USSR**; second hgst. peak of Caucasus; alt. 5,045 m.

Kāzerūn, t., S.W. **Iran**; ctr. of agr. dist. where fruit, tobacco, opium, cotton grown; p. (1966) 39,758.

Kazvin or **Qazvin**, c., N.W. **Iran**; transit tr.; carpets, textiles; p. (1976) 138,257.

Kearsley, t., Gtr. Manchester, **Eng.**; chemicals, paper; p. (1981) 11,352.

Keban Dam, S.E. **Turkey**; at confluence of the E. and W. branches of Euphrates.

Kecskemet, c., central **Hungary**; fruit-canning and wine-distilling from locally grown prods.; 4th cent. c.; p. (1970) 77,000.

Kedah, st., **Malaysia**; on Strait of Malacca, N.W. Malaya; rice, rubber, coconuts, tungsten; cap. Alor Star; a. 9,479 km²; p. (1980) 1,116,140.

Kediri, t., E. Java, **Indonesia**; food processing; p. (1980) 221,830.

Keeling Is. *See* **Cocos Is.**

Keelung (Chi-lung), c., N. **Taiwan**; on E. China Sea; naval base and ch. pt.; exp. agr. prods.; chemicals; gold, sulphur, copper mined nearby; p. (est. 1984) 352,666.

Keewatin, dist., N.W. Terr., **Canada**; barren grounds; fur-trapping; a. 590,934 km².

Keighley, t., West Yorks., **Eng.**; in Aire valley, 24 km N.W. of Leeds; engin., woollen and worsteds; p. (1981) 57,451.

Keihin, vast conurb. of Tokyo, Yokohama and Kawasaki, **Japan**; p. (1971) 14,650,000.

Keith, burgh, Moray, **Scot.**; mkt. t. in agr. dist.; p. (1981) 4,315.

Kelantan, st., **Malaysia**; one of most fertile areas on E. cst. Malaya; cap. Kota Bharu; rice, coconuts, rubber; a. 14,815 km²; p. (1980) 893,753.

Kells or **Ceannanus Mor**, mkt. t., Co. Meath, **R.o.I.**; notable for monastic remains and illuminated Book of Kells, now in library of Trinity College, Dublin; p. (1971) 2,391.

Kelso, burgh, Roxburgh, **Scot.**; at confluence of Rs. Teviot and Tweed; p. (1981) 5,609.

Kemerovo, c., **RSFSR**; S.E. of Tomsk; coalmng. ctr.; chemicals, textiles, plastics; p. (est. 1980) 478,000.

Kemi, t., N.E. **Finland**; spt. on G. of Bothnia; sawmills; p. (1972) 27,834.

Kemi, R., N.E. **Finland**; used for hydroelectric power and timber transport; 480 km long.

Kempten, t., Bavaria, **W. Germany**; nr. Bodensee; Benedictine abbey; p. (est. 1983) 57,300.

Kendal, l. gov. dist., Cumbria, **Eng.**; mkt. ctr.; tourism; p. (1981) 23,411.

Kenilworth, t., Warwicks., **Eng.**; 6 km S.W. of Coventry; mkt.; ruined cas.; p. (1981) 19,315.

Kenitra. *See* **Mina Hassan Tani**.

Kennet, l. gov. dist., Wiltshire, **Eng.**; stretches from Marlborough to Devizes; p. (1981) 63,333.

Kennet, R., Wilts. and Berks., **Eng.**; trib. of R. Thames; followed by main rly. London to W. of Eng.; 70 km long.

Kennington, dist., in London bor. of Lambeth, **Eng.**; inc. the Oval cricket ground, home of Surrey C.C.

Kenosha, t., Wis., **USA**; on W. shore of L. Mich.; p. (1980) 77,685 (t.), 123,137 (met. a.).

Kensington and Chelsea, Royal Borough of, inner bor., W. London, **Eng.**; mainly residtl.; contains Kensington Palace and Gardens; p. (1981) 138,759.

Kent, non-met. co., **Eng.**; intensive agr., mkt. gardening, orchards, hops; "Garden of England"; crossed by N. Downs and Weald; industl. zone bordering Thames and Medway estuaries; tourist resorts and cross-channel ferry pts. on cst. proposed Channel Tunnel link (1993) liable to make lge impact on co.; London commuter hinterland; co. t. Maidstone; a. 3,730 km²; p. (1981) 1,463,055.

Kentucky, E. central st., **USA**; in W. foothills of Appalachians and crossed by tribs. of Mississippi; "Bluegrass" st.; mainly agr.; some coal; cap. Frankfort; lgst. c. Louisville, at falls of Ohio R.; hydroelec. power; tourism; admitted to Union 1792; st. flower Goldenrod, st. bird Cardinal; a. 104,623 km²; p. (1980) 3,661,000.

Kentucky, R., Ky., **USA**; flows from Cumberland plateau to Ohio R.; length 400 km.

Kenya, rep., E. **Africa**; member of Brit. Commonwealth; comprises 7 provs.; straddles equator but climate modified by alt.; marked contrast between sparsely populated and arid N. and well-developed S. where upland climate has attracted the European p.; economy based on prod. and processing of arable and pastoral prods., inc. dairy prod.; relatively well developed cooperative African farming; 80 per cent of p. earn living on the land; most industl. of E. African cty., mostly exp. orientated; growth in exp. of cement and fluorspar; tourism incr. impt; ch. spt. Mombasa, airports at Nairobi and Mombasa; famous for big game; univ.; cap. Nairobi; a. 582,646 km²; p. (est. 1983) 18,784,000.

Kenya, Mt., volcano, **Kenya**; just S. of equator; snow-covered; alt. 5,197 m; 2nd hgst. peak in Africa; Nat. Park.

Kephallenia. *See* **Cephalonia**.

Kerala, st., **India**; cap. Trivandrum; plantations producing rubber, tea, pepper; higher proportion of literacy than in any other st.; a. 38,855

km²; p. (1981) 25,453,680.

Kerch, c., Ukrainian SSR, **USSR**; in Crimea, commanding K. strait connecting Black Sea and Azov Sea; spt. and industl. ctr.; metallurgical plant, iron and steel mills, shipbldg., fisheries; iron-ore, vanadium, natural gas nearby; p. (est. 1980) 159,000.

Kerguelen, archipelago, S. **Indian Oc.**; part of Fr. Antarctic terr.; whaling, fishing; famous for K. cabbage (*Pringlea antiscorbutica*) discovered by Cook.

Kerkrade, t., Limburg prov., **Neth.**; coal mng.; anc. abbey; p. (1982) 53,177.

Kérkira. *See* **Corfu**.

Kermadec Is., volcanic gr. **Pac. Oc.**; 960 km N.E. of N.Z.; a. 34 km²; met. sta. on Sunday I. (lgst. of gr.); annexed to N.Z. 1887; p. (1961) 10.

Kerman, region, S.E. **Iran**; mtnous., much desert land; agr.; carpet-weaving; coal and iron-ore mng. being developed; recent copper find; irrigation scheme projected; p. (1967) 243,770.

Kermān, c., S.E. **Iran**; prov. cap.; carpet-weaving ctr.; textile mftg.; airpt.; mediaeval mosques; p. (1976) 140,309.

Kermānshāh, (Qahremānshahr) t., N.W. **Iran**; cap. of Kermānshāhān prov.; agr., comm. and route ctr.; airpt.; oil refinery; p. (1976) 290,861.

Kern, R., E. Cal., **USA**; one of most impt. power-generating Rs. in st.

Kerrier, l. gov. dist., Cornwall, **Eng.**; a. inc. Lizard penin. and Helston; p. (1981) 83,009.

Kerry, coastal co., Munster, **R.o.I.**; deeply indented cst.; cap. Tralee; tourism; a. 4,703 km²; p. (1981) 31,993.

Kerulen, R., N.E. **Mongolia** and **China**; flows parallel to edge of Gobi Desert; a. designated for economic development; 1,256 km long.

Kesteven, North, l. gov. dist., Lincs., **Eng.**; rural a. based on Sleaford; p. (1981) 78,527.

Kesteven, South, l. gov. dist., Lincs., **Eng.**; rural a. and ts. of Grantham and Bourne; p. (1981) 97,600.

Keswick, Allerdale, Cumbria, **Eng.**; on Greta R.; at N. end of L. Derwentwater; tourist ctr.; mkt.; pencils; p. (1971) 5,169.

Kettering, l. gov. dist., mkt. t., Northants., **Eng.**; nr. Wellingborough; footwear; iron mng.; p. (1981) 71,314 (dist.).

Kew, dist., London bor. of Richmond-upon-Thames, **Eng.**; contains Kew botanical gardens.

Keweenaw, peninsula, L. Superior, **USA**; former impt. copper deposits.

Keynsham, t., Wansdyke, Avon, **Eng.**; expanded t.; p. (1981) 20,443.

Key West, c., Fla., **USA**; on I. c. 240 km from mainland; naval sta., coastguard base; cigar-mftg.; nearest US pt. to Panama canal; tourism; p. (1980) 24,382.

Khabarovsk, c., **RSFSR**; cap. of K. terr., E. Siberia, on Amur R.; cath.; oil refining, aircraft engin., wood and paper inds.; pipeline links with oilfields in N. Sakhalin; transport ctr. of Far East; p. (est. 1980) 538,000.

Khairpur, t., **Pakistan**; nr. Sukkur barrage; textiles; p. (est. 1975) 56,500.

Khakass Autonomous Oblast, admin. div. of Krasnoyarsk region, **RSFSR**; pastoral agr., timber and mng. inds.; a. 61,784 km²; p. (1970) 446,000.

Khandwa, t., Madhya Pradesh, **India**; S. of Indore; cotton, oil-pressing; p. (1981) 114,725.

Khaniá, or **Canea**, c., Crete, **Greece**; in sheltered bay on W. cst.; historic sites; p. (1981) 47,451.

Khanka, L., **China–USSR** border; dairy farming, fishing; branch of Trans-Siberian rly. to W. shore; a. 4,403 km².

Khanty-Mansi, admin. div., **RSFSR**; in W. Siberian lowland; sparse p.; cap. Khanty-Mansiisk (at confluence of Ob' and Irtysh Rs.); natural gas; a. 556,850 km²; p. (1970) 272,000.

Kharagpur, c., W. Bengal, **India**; industl., scientific research ctr.; rly. junc.; p. (1981) 150,475 (c.) 232,575 (met. a.).

Khārk, I., Persian Gulf, **Iran**; oil terminal for super-tankers, 48 km from mainland.

Khar'kov, c., Ukrainian SSR, **USSR**; impt. industl. ctr. in Donets coal region; cap. of K. region; univ., cath.; rly. ctr.; extensively rebuilt after second world war; p. (est. 1980) 1,484,000.

Khartoum, c., cap. of the **Sudan**; at confluence of

Blue and White Niles; univ.; famous siege under Gordon 1884–5; p. (1983) 476,218.

Khashm el Girba, t., **Sudan;** new t. on Atbara R., between Khartoum and Ethiopian border; for p. of Wadi Halfa inundated by Aswan L.; sugar refinery.

Khasi Hills, Meghalaya, N.E. **India;** form abrupt S. edge to middle Brahmaputra valley; very heavy monsoon rains on S.-facing slopes; lower slopes forested; middle slopes impt. tea-growing region; rise to over 1,800 m.

Khaskovo, t., **Bulgaria;** woollens, carpets, tobacco; p. (est. 1971) 63,670.

Kherson, c., Ukrainian SSR, **USSR;** 24 km up R. Dnieper from Black Sea; sea and R. pt., rly. junc.; grain, oil refining, engin., textiles, shipbldg; founded by Catherine the Great as fortress t.; p. (est. 1980) 324,000.

Khingan, Gr. and **Little,** mtn. ranges, Inner Mongolia and Heilongjiang prov., N.E. **China;** rich timber resources; rise to over 1,800 m.

Khios or **Chios,** I., **Greece;** in Aegean Sea; wines, figs, fruits; marble; cap. Khios; supposed birthplace of Homer; p. (1972) 53,942.

Khiva, former vassal st. of Russia; now part of Uzbek SSR and Turkmen SSR, **USSR.**

Khiva, c., N.W. Uzbek SSR, **USSR;** in oasis nr. Kara-Kum desert; cottons, carpets; anc. c.; p. (est. 1970) 25,000.

Khmel'nitskiy (Proskurov), c., Ukrainian SSR, **USSR;** on R. Bug; machin. tools, textiles, food inds.; p. (est. 1980) 179,000.

Khmer Republic. See **Kampuchea, Democratic.**

Khor Abdulla, Iraq; in Persian G. nr. Basra; deepwater oil-loading island terminal (1963).

Khorāsan or **Khurasan,** prov., N.E. **Iran;** bounded by USSR and Afghanistan; sparsely p.; agr.; wool; turquoises; cap. Mashhad; p. (1972) 3,250,085.

Khorramshahr, spt., S.W. **Iran,** leading pt. on Persian G.; increased in importance in second world war when harbour facilities expanded; handles major part of foreign trade; main exp. dates; linked by pipeline to oilfields and by road and rail to Ahvāz and Tehran; p. (1976) 146,709.

Khotan. See **Hotan.**

Khovu-Aksy, t., Tuva ASSR, **RSFSR;** on R. Elegest, 80 km S.W. of Kyzyl; new t. 1956; cobalt deposit being developed.

Khulna, c., **Bangladesh;** in low-lying a. in W. Ganges delta; p. (1981) 646,359.

Khunjerab Pass, Kashmir, **India;** 5,000 m. pass in Karakoram Range; links Sinkiang (China) with Pakistan and Middle East; new metal route opened (1982) making shorter route to W. for China and took 20 years to build.

Khuzestan, prov., W. **Iran;** frontier Iraq; leading petroleum ctr.; lge. dams; cap. Ahvāz; p. (1976) 2,187,198.

Khyber Pass, pass in Hindu Kush mtns., between **Pakistan** and **Afghanistan;** followed by route from Peshawar to Kabul; historically most famous route into India, used by many invaders, inc. Alexander the Great.

Kiamusze. See **Jiamusi.**

Kianga-Moura, dist., Queensland, **Australia;** lge. coalfield; coking coal exp. to Japan via Gladstone.

Kiangsi. See **Jiangxi.**

Kiangsu. See **Jiangsu.**

Kicking Horse Pass, mtn. pass (1,628 m), over Rocky Mtns., B.C., **Canada;** used by Canadian Pac. rly.

Kidderminster, t., Wyre Forest, Hereford and Worcs., **Eng.;** on R. Stour 6 km above its confluence with R. Severn; carpets, engin., sugarbeet refining, textile machin., elec. vehicles, drop forgings; p. (1981) 51,261.

Kidsgrove, t., "Potteries," Staff., **Eng.;** 5 km N.W. of Stoke-on-Trent; chemicals, metal wks., rayon, silk and nylon spinning, precast concrete, ceramics; p. (1981) 24,227.

Kidwelly, Dyfed, **Wales;** mkt. t.; sm. harbour; cas.; p. (1981) 3,152.

Kiel, spt., cap. of Schleswig-Holstein, **W. Germany;** univ.; Baltic naval pt.; shipbldg. and allied inds., elec. gds., textiles, fishing; p. (est. 1983) 248,400.

Kiel Canal (North Sea-Baltic Canal or **Kaiser-Wilhelm-Kanal) W. Germany;** connects Elbe estuary on North Sea with Baltic; 98 km long; opened 1895, reconstructed 1914; inter-

nationalised 1919 by Treaty of Versailles, but repudiated by Hitler 1936.

Kielce, c., central **Poland;** cap. of K. prov.; in Swietokrzyskie mtns.; cath., route ctr.; agr. machin., chemicals; minerals quarried in prov.; founded 12th cent.; p. (est. 1983) 197,000.

Kiev (Kiyev), c., cap. of Ukrainian SSR, **USSR;** on R. Dnieper; leading cultural, industl. and comm. ctr.; cath., univ.; machin., textiles; in a. of rich mineral deposits; natural gas pipeline runs from Dashava; historic c., once cap. of Muscovite empire; p. (est. 1980) 2,192,000.

Kigali, cap. of **Rwanda;** comm. ctr.; airport; new tungsten and iron foundries; p. (1978) 117,749.

Kigoma, t., W. **Tanzania;** pt. on E. shore of L. Tanganyika; W. terminus of Central rly. to Dar-es-Salaam; p. (est. 1967) 21,639.

Kii, peninsula, **Japan;** highland area and inlet of same name, S. Honshu.

Kikinda, t., Vojvodina, **Yugoslavia;** agr. tr.; rly. junc.; p. (1971) 50,503.

Kilauea, crater, 1,112 m high, on S.E. slope of Mauna Loa, **Hawaii,** one of lgst. active craters in world; over 3 km in diameter.

Kildare, inland co., Leinster, **R.o.I.;** dairying, cereals; co. t. Naas; a. 1,694 km²; p. (1981) 51,320.

Kildare, mkt. t., cap. of Kildare, **R.o.I.;** cath.; close by is the famous racecourse, the Curragh of Kildare; p. (1971) 3,137.

Kilimanjaro, volcanic mtn., N. **Tanzania;** hgst. peak in Africa, 5,895 m; international airpt. at 894 m on Sanya Plain; Nat. Park.

Kilindini, spt., **Kenya;** adjoins Mombasa; the finest harbour on E. cst. of Africa.

Kilkenny, inland co., Leinster, **R.o.I.;** cap. Kilkenny; pastoral farming, black marble; a. 2,062 km²; p. (1981) 20,883.

Kilkenny, t., cap. of Kilkenny, **R.o.I.;** on R. Nore; local mkt., caths., cas.; p. (1971) 9,838.

Killala Bay, Mayo and Sligo, **R.o.I.;** wide bay fed by R. Hoy.

Killaloe, v., Co. Clare, **R.o.I.;** crossing point for R. Shannon; cath.; p. 500.

Killarney, t., U.D., Kerry, **R.o.I.;** local mkt.; tourist ctr. for the Ls. of K.; p. (1981) 7,693.

Killarney, Lakes of, Kerry, **R.o.I.;** Lower, Middle, and Upper, celebrated for their beauty; tourist resorts; Muckross on Middle L. site of anc. abbey.

Killiecrankie, Pass of, Scot.; on R. Garry; at S. approach to Drumochter Pass; used by main rly. Perth to Inverness; scene of battle 1691.

Killingworth, t., Tyne and Wear, **Eng.;** 6 km N.E. of Newcastle; new t.; proposed p. 20,000.

Kilmarnock, burgh, Strathclyde Reg., **Scot.;** forms l. gov. dist., with Loudoun; on R. Irvine, 17 km N.E. of Ayr.; carpet factory closed increasing unemployment to 27 per cent; p. (1981) 82,149 (l. gov. dist.), 52,080 (t.).

Kilo-Moto, goldfield, **Zaïre;** in N.E. of st., 80 km W. of L. Mobutu Seso; linked by motor road to R. Zaïre (Kisangani) and L. Mobutu Seso (Kasenyi).

Kilrenny and Anstruther, t., North East Fife, **Scot.,** at entrance to F. of Forth; fishing, hosiery, oilskin mnfs.; p. (1971) 3,037.

Kilrush, sm. spt., U.D., Co. Clare, **R.o.I.;** on R. Shannon; p. (1971) 2,671.

Kilsyth, burgh, Stirling, **Scot.;** at S. foot of Campsie Fells, 16 km W. of Falkirk; See **Cumbernauld.**

Kilwinning, burgh, Cunninghame, **Scot.;** 8 km E. of Ardrossan; to be incorporated in new t. Irvine; p. (1981) 16,193.

Kimberley, former goldfield dist., W. **Australia;** sparsely populated beef producing a., bauxite and iron mng.

Kimberley, t., B.C., **Canada;** on R. Kootenay; site of Sullivan mine, silver, lead, zinc; ores smelted at Trail; p. (1971) 7,441.

Kimberley, t., C. Prov., **S. Africa;** diamondmng. dist.; asbestos, manganese, iron, cement, engin.; founded 1871; p. (1971) 103,789.

Kinabalu, Mount, Sabah, **Malaysia;** in Crocker mtns.; hgst. peak in Borneo, alt. 4,104 m.

Kincardine, former co., **Scot.;** with Deeside forms l. gov. dist. in Grampian Reg.; a. 2,546 km²; p. (1981) 42,112.

Kinder Scout, mtn., N. Derbys., **Eng.;** hgst. point of the Peak dist.; alt. 637 m.

Kindia, t., **Guinea;** rich bauxite deposits worked since 1974 but output restricted by poor rail links.

Kineshma, c., **RSFSR;** on Volga, N.W. of Gorki; pt. for Ivanovo industl. a.; textiles; dates from early 15th cent.; p. (est. 1980) 102,000.

King George's Sound, W. **Australia**; nr. Albany; fine harbour and bay.

Kinghorn, t., Kircaldy, **Scot.**; on F. of Forth, 5 km S. of Kirkcaldy; p. (1981) 2,681.

Kingsbridge, t., South Hams, S. Devon, **Eng.**; at head of Kingsbridge estuary, 16 km S.W. of Dartmouth; mkt.; p. (1981) 4,142.

King's Lynn, spt., West Norfolk, **Eng.**; at mouth of Gr. Ouse; docks; fishing base; agr. machin., canning, chemical fertilisers, shoes; expanded t.; p. (1981) 33,340.

Kingston, t., Ont., **Canada**; E. end of L. Ontario; univ., military college; p. (1976) 54,804.

Kingston, spt., cap. of **Jamaica**; ch. comm. ctr. for J.; landlocked harbour; agr.-processing; univ.; p. (1970) 117,400 (c.), 475,548 (met. a.).

Kingston-upon-Hull. See Hull.

Kingston-upon-Thames, former M.B., Surrey, **Eng.**; now **The Royal Borough of Kingston-upon-Thames**, outer bor. of Greater London; inc. bors. of Malden and Coombe and Surbiton; residtl. with Richmond Park, Hampton Court, Bushey Park nearby; aircraft parts; p. (1981) 132,411.

Kingstown, spt., cap. of St. Vincent, **W.I.**; cath. botanic gardens; p. (1972) 22,000.

Kingswood, t., l. gov. dist., Avon, **Eng.**; nr. Bristol; elec. vehicles, motor cycles, boots, brushes, tools; school founded by John Wesley; p. (1981) 84,045 (dist.).

Kington, mkt. t., Hereford and Worcs., **Eng.**; 19 km W. of Leominster; p. (1981) 1,951.

Kinki, dist., S.W. Honshu, **Japan**; agr., industl. and comm. complex centred on Osaka, Kyoto, and Kōbe.

Kinlochleven, v., Lochaber, **Scot.**; at head of Loch Leven; hydroelec. power sta.; aluminium smelting; p. (1981) 1,041.

Kinnairds Head, promontory, nr. Fraserburgh, on N.E. cst., **Scot.**

Kinross, burgh, Perth and Kinross, **Scot.**; on Loch Leven, 26 km N.E. of Alloa; textiles; resort; p. (1981) 3,495.

Kinross-shire, former co., **Scot.**; now part of Perth and Kinross l. gov. dist., Tayside Reg.

Kinsale, U.D., Cork, **R.o.I.**; sm. fish pt. on K. harbour; tourism; natural gas field, gas to be piped to N. Ireland; p. (1971) 1,628.

Kinshasa (Leopoldville), c., cap. of **Zaïre**; above the cataracts on R. Zaïre; univ.; textiles, shoes; founded by Stanley 1887; p. (est. 1976) 2,443,876.

Kinta Valley, S.E. Perak, **W. Malaysia**; tin mng., rubber plantations.

Kintyre, peninsula, Argyll and Bute, **Scot.**; terminates in Mull of Kintyre; 67 km long, 16 km wide.

Kioga (Kyoga), L., **Uganda**; on R. Nile midway between L. Victoria and L. Mobuto Seso.

Kjölen or **Kjölen**, mtn. range, **Norway** and **Sweden**; hgst. point Mt. Sulitjelma, 1,876 m.

Kirghiz SSR (Khirghizia), constituent rep., **USSR**; S.W. of Siberia; mtnous. cty., in Tienshan and Pamir systems; livestock breeding; mineral resources, food processing; cap. Frunze; a 196,581 km²; p. (est. 1985) 3,976,000.

Kiribati (Gilbert Is), indep. st. (1979), former Brit. col., central Pac. Oc.; chain of coral Is. across equator; economy based on phosphate mng. and copra; cap. Tarawa; Ellice Is. separated 1976 and renamed Tuvalu; a. 956 km²; p. (est. 1980) 59,000.

Kirin. See Jilin.

Kirkburton, t., West Yorks., **Eng.**; S.E. of Huddersfield; woollens; p. (1981) 21,387.

Kirkby, t., Knowsley, Merseyside, **Eng.**; p. (1981) 50,898.

Kirkby in Ashfield, t., Ashfield, Notts., **Eng.**; 16 km N.W. of Nottingham; coal mng.; p. (1981) 24,467.

Kirkby Moorside, t., Ryedale, North Yorks., **Eng.**; nr. Vale of Pickering; mkt.-place; sailplanes, gliders.

Kirkcaldy, royal burgh, l. gov. dist., Fife Reg., **Scot.**; spt. on N. side of F. of Forth; submarine coal mng.; linoleum, potteries, engin.; birthplace of Adam Smith; p. (1981) 141,861.

Kirkcudbright, royal burgh, Stewartry, **Scot.**; on R. Dee at influx into K. Bay, S.W. of Dumfries; agr. ctr., hosiery; cas., abbey; p. (1981) 3,406.

Kircudbrightshire, former co., **Scot.**; now part of

Stewartry l. gov. dist., Dumfries and Galloway Reg.

Kirkenes, t., Finnmark prov., N.E. **Norway**; on S. arm of Varanger fjord, nr. Soviet border; pt. for iron-mng. dist.

Kirkham, t., Kirklees, Lancs., **Eng.**; textiles; p. (1981) 6,289.

Kirkintilloch, burgh, Strathkelvin, **Scot.**; on Forth and Clyde canal; engin.; p. (1981) 32,992.

Kirklees, met. dist., West Yorks., **Eng.**; comprises Huddersfield, Dewsbury, Batley, Spenborough, Colne Valley, Meltham, Holmfirth, Denby Dale, Kirkburton, Heckmondwike, and Mirfield; p. (1981) 371,780.

Kirkstone Pass, mtn. pass, Cumbria, **Eng.**; used by main road between Ullswater and Windermere Ls.

Kirkūk, t., **Iraq**; most imp. centre of Iraqi oil industry; p. (est. 1972) 559,000.

Kirkwall, royal burgh, Mainland I., Orkneys, **Scot.**; cath.; p. (1981) 5,947.

Kirov, c., **RSFSR**; pt. on Vyatka R.; rly. junc.; engin., saw milling, chemicals, leather inds.; cath.; p. (est. 1980) 392,000.

Kirovabad, c., W. Azerbaydzhan SSR, **USSR**; on Gandzha R.; industl. ctr.; textiles, agr. implements, wine; copper and manganese mines; aluminium plant; p. (est. 1980) 237,000.

Kirovograd, c., Ukrainian SSR, **USSR**; on Ingul R.; cap. of K. oblast; agr. ctr.; engin.; p. (est. 1980) 242,000.

Kirovsk, c., **RSFSR**; on Kola peninsula; apatite and nephelite mng.; chemicals; p. (est. 1967) 50,000.

Kirriemuir, burgh, Angus, **Scot.**; on N. margin of Strathmore, 8 km W. of **Forfar**; jute-weaving; birthplace of J. M. Barrie; p. (1981) 5,308.

Kirtland, t., N.M., **USA**; atomic and space research sta.

Kiruna, t., N. **Sweden**; inside Arctic Circle, N.W. of Luleå; linked by rly. to Narvik (Norway); impt. deposits of iron ore; p. (1976) 31,222.

Kiryu, c., Honshu, **Japan**; major textile ctr.; p. (1979) 134,505.

Kisangani (Stanleyville), t., **Zaïre**; on R. Zaïre nr. Boyoma Falls; airpt.; univ.; p. (1982) 339,210.

Kiselevsk, c., S.W. Siberia, **RSFSR**; coal-mng. ctr. in Kuznetsk basin; p. (est. 1980) 122,000.

Kishinev, c., cap. of Moldavian SSR, **USSR**; on Byk R., trib. of Dniester; cath., univ.; industl., comm. ctr. in rich farming a.; tourism; p. (est. 1980) 519,000.

Kislovodsk, c., **RSFSR**; in N. Caucasus; famous spa; p. (est. 1980) 102,000.

Kismayu, pt., **Somalia**; new deep-water harbour; airpt.

Kisumu, spt., cap. of Nyanza prov., **Kenya**; at head of Kavirondo G. on L. Victoria; handles bulk of cotton from Buganda and coffee from N. Tanzania for transhipment E. by rail; lge. brewery; p. (1979) 152,643.

Kitakyūshū, c., N. Kyushu, **Japan**; one of Japan's lgst. muns. on merging (1963) of ts. Moji, Kokura, Tobata, Yawata, and Wakamatsu; sixth c. to enjoy special aut. rights; p. (est. 1984) 1,065,078.

Kitami, c., Hokkaido, **Japan**; mkt.; food-processing; p. (1979) 100,959.

Kitchener, c., Ont., **Canada**; agr. machin., tyres, hardware, agr. processing; p. (1979) 131,870.

Kithira. See Cerigo.

Kitimat, t., B.C., **Canada**; lge. aluminium smelter powered by hydroelectricity from diversion of R. Fraser trib. through the Rockies.

Kitwe, t., **Zambia**; contiguous to mng. township of Nkana, ctr. of copperbelt; p. (1980) 314,794.

Kiukiang. See Jiujiang.

Kivu, L., on border of **Zaïre** and **Rwanda**; in highlands of Gr. Rift Valley; natural gas discoveries; 1,473 m high, 96 km long.

Kizel, c., **RSFSR**; on Kizel R., on W. slopes of Urals; coal-mng. ctr.; mng. equipment; p. (est. 1967) 55,000.

Kizil, lgst. R. of **Turkey**; rises in Kisil Dagh, flows to Black Sea via Sivas; 1,120 km long.

Kladno, t., **ČSSR**; 16 km N.W. of Prague; coal-mng. ctr.; iron and steel wks., machin.; p. (est. 1970) 57,000.

Klagenfurt, t., cap. of Carinthia, **Austria**; winter sports ctr.; varied mnfs.; p. (1971) 74,326.

Klaipeda (Memel), c. Lithuanian SSR, **USSR**; ice-free spt. on Baltic Sea; exp. timber, textiles, chemicals, paper; p. (est. 1980) 178,000.

Klamath, mtns., N. Cal., S.W. Ore., **USA**; beautiful ranges containing Nat. Park and Indian reserve; hgst. alt. Mt. Eddy, 2,757 m.

Klamono, t., W. Irian, **Indonesia**; ctr. of oilfield; pipeline to Sorong harbour.

Klerksdorp, t., S. Transvaal, **S. Africa**; gold, diamonds; p. (1970) 75,686.

Klodzko (Glatz), t., S.W. **Poland**; formerly in Prussian Silesia; rly. junc.; on R. Neisse; comm. and mftg.; p. (1970) 26,100.

Klondike, R., Yukon, **Canada**; sm. trib. of Yukon in gold-mng. region; gold rush 1896; 160 km long.

Klyuchevskaya Sopka, one of 18 active volcanoes, **RSFSR**; in N.E. Siberia, on Kamchatka peninsula; alt. 4,748 m.

Knaresborough, t., North Yorks., **Eng.**; 5 km N.E. of Harrogate; mkt.; cas. ruins; p. (1981) 13,375.

Knighton, t., Radnor, Powys, **Wales**; on R. Teme; mkt.; p. (1981) 2,682.

Knockmealdown Mtns., Waterford and Tipperary, **R.o.I.**; highest point 796 m; tourism.

Knob Lake. See **Schefferville**.

Knossos, ruined c., cap. of anc. Crete, **Greece**; S.E. of Iráklion; ctr. of Cretan bronze age culture, 1800 B.C.; archaeological source of knowledge about the Minoans.

Knottingley, t., West Yorks., **Eng.**; on R. Aire, 19 km S.E. of Leeds; engin., glass, tar distilling, chemicals; coal mng; p. (1981) 15,953.

Knowsley, met. dist., Merseyside, **Eng.**; comprises Kirkby, Prescot and Huyton with Roby; p. (1981) 173,356.

Knoxville, c., Tenn., **USA**; univ.; livestock and tobacco mkt.; textiles, marble, plastics, chemicals, aluminium; p. (1980) 175,000 (c.), 477,000 (met. a.).

Knutsford, t., N.E. Cheshire, **Eng.**; mkt.; home of Mrs. Gaskell, author of *Cranford*; p. (1981) 13,675.

Kōbe, c., spt., Honshu, **Japan**; at E. end of Inland Sea; 5th c. of Japan; developed as pt. for Osaka and Kinki plain; iron and steel, shipbldg., rubber; p. (est. 1984) 1,367,390.

Koblenz (Coblenz), t. Rhineland-Palatinate, **W. Germany**; at confluence of Rs. Rhine and Moselle; fine buildings; wine, paper, machin., leather, ceramics; p. (est. 1983) 112,200.

Kōchi, plain and c., Shikoku, **Japan**; early vegetables, double rice cropping; p. (est. 1984) 300,822.

Kodiak I., lgst. of Is. of Alaska, **USA**; 144 km long; forested mtns.; fur-trading, salmon-fishing, canning; earthquake 1964; p. (1980) 4,756.

Kōfu, basin and c., Honshu, **Japan**; rice, vine-yards, orchards, silk, wine; p. (1979) 199,235.

Kohat, t., **Pakistan**; on trib. of Indus; military t.; cement wks.; p. (est. 1970) 36,000.

Koh-I-Baba Mtns., **Afghanistan**; spur of the Hindu Kush; highest point 5,380 m.

Kokand, c., Uzbek SSR, **USSR**; in the Ferghana Valley; mftg. ctr., textiles, chemicals, engin.; p. (est. 1980) 154,000.

Kokiu. See **Gejiu**.

Kokkoka (Gamla Karleby), t. **Finland**; on cst. of G. of Bothnia; sulphur plant; p. (est. 1970) 20,748.

Kokomo, c., Ind., **USA**; on Wild Cat R.; ctr. of agr. region; car components; p. (1980) 47,808 (c.) 103,715 (met. a.).

Koko-Nor. See **Qinghai Hu.**

Kokura. See **Kitakyūshū.**

Kola Peninsula, peninsula, **RSFSR**; extension of Lapland; rich mineral deposits; hydro-electric plants and missile base.

Kolar, c., Karnataka, **India**; p. (1981) 144,385 (met. a.).

Kolarovgrad (Shumen), c., cap. of K. prov., N.E. **Bulgaria**; agr. tr., leather, cloth, metal gds.; Moslem architecture; p. (est. 1972) 79,134.

Kolding, c., at head of Kolding fjord, Jutland, **Denmark**; spt. and fishing base; lt. inds.; p. (est. 1977) 54,617.

Kolhapur, c., Maharashtra, S.W. **India**; cap. of

Klagenfurt, t., cap. of Carinthia, **Austria**; winter

former princely st. of K.; bauxite; anc. Buddhist ctr.; p. (1971) 259,050 (c.), 267,513 (met. a.).

Köln. See **Cologne.**

Kolobrzeg (Kolberg), t., N.W. **Poland**; spt. on Baltic cst.; comm. and fishing harbour; resort and spa; p. (1970) 25,400.

Kolomna, c., **RSFSR**; on Moskva R., nr. confluence with Oka R.; industl. ctr.; engin., locomotives, machin., synthetic rubber; p. (est. 1980) 149,000.

Kolomyya, c., Ukrainian SSR, **USSR**; on Pruth R.; in Carpathian foothills; agr. tr., metal gds., oil refining, textiles; p. (est. 1974) 141,000.

Kolwezi, c., S. Shaba, **Zaïre**; comm. ctr. for mng. dist. (cobalt and copper); p. (est. 1968) 70,558.

Kolyma, R., N.E. Siberia, **RSFSR**; flows into Arctic Oc., via Kolyma goldfields; navigable in summer; basin largely covered with tundra, sparsely p.; 2,560 km long.

Komárno, c., **ČSSR**; on left bank, of Danube, opposite Hungarian Komárom, on right bank; R. pt., shipbldg., oil refining.

Komi ASSR, aut. rep., **RSFSR**; wooded lowland, pastoral agr.; coal from Pechora basin, oil at Ukhta and Troitsko-Pechorsk; mng. now ch. economic activity; cap. Syktyvkar, lumber ctr.; a. 415,799 km²; p. (est. 1972) 984,000.

Komló, t., **Hungary**; new mng. t.; coking coal; p. (1965) 27,800.

Kompong Som (Sihanoukville) c., **Kampuchea**; deepwater pt. on G. of Thailand; linked to Phnom Penh by modern highway; textile mills, tractors, oil refining; p. (1962) 6,578.

Kommunarsk (Voroshilovsk), t., Ukrainian SSR, **USSR**; 40 km S.W. of Lugansk; ctr. of iron, steel and coking inds.; p. (est. 1980) 120,000.

Komsomolsk, c., **RSFSR**; built by volunteer youth labour, after 1932; heavy industl. development; oil refining; pipeline connects with oilfield in N. Sakhalin; p. (est. 1980) 269,000.

Komi-Permyak, admin. div. **RSFSR**; forestry, cellulose, paper; cap. Kudymbar; a. 31,080 km²; p. (1970) 212,000.

Konstantinovka, industl. t., Ukrainian SSR, **USSR**; in heart of Donbas industl. region, 61 km N. of Donetsk; heavy engin., iron and steel, zinc smelting; p. (est. 1980) 113,000.

Konya, c., **Turkey**; cap. of K. prov.; agr. tr. ctr.; mnfs. textiles, carpets, leather gds.; the anc. Iconium, fortress of the Hittite empire; p. (1980) 329,139.

Kooland I., W. **Australia**; rugged I. with iron-ore deposits worked since 1960 and exp. to **Japan**.

Koolyanobbing, mng. t., W. **Australia**; high-grade haematite and limonite ores mined since 1961 and t. constructed as residential and service ctr.; p. (1976) 296.

Kootenay or **Kootenai**, R., flows from B.C., **Canada**; through Montana and Idaho, **USA**, into K. L., draining it by narrow channel into Colombia R.; beautiful scenery; 720 km long.

Kopeysk, t., **RSFSR**; in Urals; lignite mng., agr. and mng. machin.; p. (est. 1980) 146,000.

Korat Plateau, E. **Thailand**; headwaters of Mekong tribs.; cattle-rearing; tr. ctr. Korat.

Korçe (Koritsa), t., S.E. **Albania**; in infertile basin at 854 m nr. Greek border; mkt.; cultural ctr.; p. (est. 1970) 47,000.

Korcula (Curzola), I., **Yugoslavia**; sm. I. in Adriatic Sea; ch. pt. K. a. 277 km²; p. (1961) 10,223.

Korea, Democratic People's Republic of, (N. Korea); occupies N. part of Korean peninsula (N. of 38th parallel), **E. Asia**; bounded on N. by China and USSR; continental climate; cold dry winters, hot humid summers; predominantly mtnous. with many uninhabited offshire Is.; all inds. nationalised and collective agr.; rapid mechanisation, agr. employs 43 per cent working p.; development emphasis on mng. resources of coal, iron-ore and on growth of heavy inds.; most industl. resources located in N. Korea; rapid incr. in industrialisation; transport network under reconstruction after devastation of Korean war; some R. transport, international airport at cap. of Pyongyang; a. 121,248 km²; p. (est. 1984) 19,630,000.

Korea, Rep. of (S. Korea), occupies S. part of Korea peninsula (S. of 38th parallel); climate and topography resemble N. Korea's; massive US aid revitalised economy after Korean war; 33 per cent work-force engaged in agr.; yet most rapidly growing industl. country in world; textiles, electronics, shipbldg., vehicles; iron and steel ind. at Pusan; fishing is both source of subsistence and exp.; irrigation and power project (1971–81) for 4 Rs.—Hangang, Naktangang, Kum-Gang, and Yongsan-Gang; cap. Seoul; a. 99,591 km²; p. (est. 1984) 40,309,000, (36 per cent in cap.).

Korea Bay, Yellow Sea; between N. Korea and North-East China (Manchuria).

Koriyama, Honshu, **Japan**; textiles, chemicals; p. (est. 1984) 286,451.

Korsör, spt., Sjaelland I., **Denmark**; fine harbour; glass wks.; p. (est. 1970) 13,674.

Kortrijk (Courtrai), t., W. Flanders prov., N.W. **Belgium**; textiles; 13th cent. Notre Dame church; battle of the Spurs 1302; p. (1982) 75,731.

Koryak, admin. div., N.E. Siberia, **RSFSR**; sparse p.; a. 393,680 km²; p. (1970) 31,000.

Kos, I. See Cos, I.

Kosciusko, Mount, N.S.W., in Australian Alps; highest peak in **Australia**; 2,228 m; Nat. Park popular for skiing.

Kosi, R., **India**; flows from Himalayas to Ganges; site of barrage for hydroelectric power and irrigation.

Košice, c., S.E. Slovakia, **ČSSR**; lies in fertile basin; major industl. ctr.; heavy inds., iron and steel plant; agr.-processing; univ., Gothic cath.; mediaeval fortress t.; p. (1980) 204,710.

Kosovo-Metohija, aut. region, S.W. Serbia, **Yugoslavia**; mtnous., fertile valleys; stock raising, forestry; ch. t. Priština; a. 10,352 km²; p. (1971) 1,244,755.

Kostroma, c., cap. of K. oblast, **RSFSR**; at confluence of Volga and Kostroma; in flax growing a.; textiles, engin.; cath.; p. (est. 1980) 255,000.

Koszalin (Köslin), c., cap. of K. prov., N.W. **Poland**; nr. Baltic cst.; paper mills, textiles, building materials; p. (1970) 64,400.

Kota, t., Rajasthan, **India**; on R. Chambal; textiles; two nuclear reactors and heavy water plant; p. (1981) 358,241.

Kota Kinabalu (Jesselton), t., cap of Sabah, **Malaysia**; on W. cst.; main rubber pt.; rly. terminal; p. (1980) 59,500.

Köthen, t., Halle, **E. Germany**; in former st. of Saxony-Anhalt; lignite mines, sugar-refining, machin., chemicals; p. (est. 1973) 35,798.

Kotka, spt., S.E. **Finland**; on G. of Finland, at mouth of Kymi R.; major exp. pt. for timber, paper, pulp; p. (1970) 33,463.

Kotor, spt., S. Montenegro, **Yugoslavia**; on Bay of K., inlet of Adriatic; cath.; tourism.

Kotri, t., **Pakistan**; on R. Indus, opposite Hyderabad; barrage N. of the t., to help irrigate Sind; p. (1961) 52,685.

Kottbus. See Cottbus.

Koulikoro, t., **Mali**, W. Africa; on upper course of R. Niger; mkt. for groundnuts, gumarabic, sisal; linked by R. to Timbuktu and Gao; rly. terminus, 1,216 km from Dakar.

Kovrov, c., **RSFSR**; on Gorki rly. line and R. Klyazma; impt. agr. exp. ctr.; engin., textiles; p. (est. 1980) 144,000.

Kowloon, peninsula, S.E. **China**; on mainland opposite Hong Kong I.; pt. installations; major industl. and tr. ctr.; held by Britain on lease expiring 1998; p. (1961) 726,976.

Kozáni, dep., Macedonia, **Greece**; cap. K.; mainly agr.; a. 6,143 km²; p. (1971) 135,619.

Kozhikode. See Calicut.

Kra Isthmus, neck of land between B. of Bengal and G. of Thailand, linking Malay peninsula with continent of Asia.

Kragujevac, t., central Serbia, **Yugoslavia**; on both banks of Lepenica R.; cath.; arsenal and garrison; route ctr., developing agr. and industl. ctr.; p. (1981) 164,823.

Krakatoa (Rakata), volcanic I., Sunda strait, **Indonesia**; between Java and Sumatra; greater part disappeared in violent eruption 1883.

Kraków (Cracow), c., cap. of K. prov., S. **Poland**; pt. on Vistula; cultural ctr., univ. (Copernicus

matriculated here); many historic monuments; inc. c. of Nowa Huta lgst. iron and steel ctr. of rep.; machin., chemicals, farm implements; p. (est. 1983) 735,100.

Kramatorsk, c., Ukrainian SSR, **USSR**; in Donets basin; heavy engin., metallurgy; p. (est. 1980) 180,000.

Kramfors, t., **Sweden**; on G. of Bothnia; papermill and sulphite pulp wks.

Krasnodar Territory, region, **RSFSR**; extends from Sea of Azov and Black Sea to N.W. end of Caucasus; contains Kuban steppe and Maikop oilfields; fertile black soil; main pt. Tuapse; many health resorts.

Krasnodar, c., cap. of K. region, **RSFSR**; R. pt. Kuban R.; ctr. of industl. and agr. region; p. (est. 1980) 572,000.

Krasnoturinsk, t., **RSFSR**; in Urals, 9 km N.W. of Serov; aluminium, coal; p. (est. 1969) 61,000.

Krasnovodsk, c., Turkmen SSR, **USSR**; pt. on Caspian Sea; oil-refining ctr.; handles agr. and oil prods.; p. (est. 1970) 45,000.

Krasnoyarsk Territory, extensive region, **RSFSR**; extends across Siberia to Arctic Oc.; traversed by Yenisey and tribs.; minerals, grain from Minusinska basin and timber from coniferous forests; cap. K.; a. of labour camps in Stalin era.

Krasnoyarsk, c., cap. of K. terr., E. Siberia, **RSFSR**; on Trans-Siberian rly. at crossing of Yenesey R.; hydroelectric sta.; industl. ctr.; local copper and iron-ore deposits; ctr. for grain and timber; p. (est. 1980) 807,000.

Krefeld, t., N. Rhine–Westphalia, **W. Germany**; chemicals, steel, machin., textiles, soap; former ctr. of silk inds.; p. (est. 1983) 222,100.

Kremenchug, c., Ukrainian SSR, **USSR**; on R. Dnieper; timber, engin., textiles; hydroelectric sta.; oil refining; p. (est. 1980) 212,000.

Krems, mkt. t., **Austria**; on R. Danube; fruit processing; founded in 10th cent. as imperial fortress; p. (1971) 22,399.

Kreuznach, Bad, c., Rhineland Palatinate, **W. Germany**; on R. Nahe; metallurgy, leather, optical and chemical inds.; viticulture, mineral baths; p. (est. 1983) 40,400.

Krishna (Kistna), R., S. India; rises in W. Ghats, flows E. across Deccan plateau into Bay of Bengal; lower valley and delta under intensive rice cultivation; densely populated; 1,360 km long.

Kristiansand, spt., S. **Norway**; on Skagerrak; shipbldg., ships, timber, paper, pulp, fish; electro-metallurgy; p. (est. 1971) 57,748.

Kristianstad, c., cap. of K. prov., **Sweden**; on Helge R.; its pt. Ahus is on Baltic; foodprocessing, clothing, machin.; founded 1614 as fortress; p. (1983) 69,354.

Kristiansund, spt., W. cst. **Norway**; built on 3 Is.; trawler fleet base; exp. dried fish; heavily damaged in second world war; since rebuilt; p. (est. 1973) 18,784.

Kristinehamn, L. pt. on L. Vänern, central **Sweden**; p. (est. 1970) 22,018.

Krivoy Rog., c., Ukrainian SSR, **USSR**; on R. Ingulets; ctr. of ch. iron-mng. a. of USSR; p. (est. 1980) 657,000.

Krk, I., N. Adriatic Sea, **Yugoslavia**; S. of Rijeke; agr.; tourism; ch. t., K.; p. 14,500.

Krkonose. See Riesengebirge.

Kronshlot (Kronstadt), spt., on I. of Kotlin, **RSFSR**; at head of G. of Finland, nr. Leningrad; Baltic pt. and naval base; scene of naval mutiny which precipitated the Russian revolution; founded by Peter the Great 1710; p. (est. 1970) 50,000.

Kroonstad, t., O.F.S., **S. Africa**; on R. Vals; rly. junc.; agr. mkt.; engin., milling; p. (1970) 50,898.

Kropotkin, c., E. Krasnodar Terr., **RSFSR**; foodprocessing, engin.; p. (est. 1970) 55,000.

Kruger Nat. Park, N.E. Transvaal, **S. Africa**; game reserve; a. 20,720 km².

Krugersdorp, t. Transvaal, **S. Africa**; gold mng., uranium, manganese; p. (1970) 91,202.

Kuala Lumpur, c., fed. terr., **W. Malaysia**; cap. of Fed. of Malaysia and of Selangor st.; univ.; ctr. of rubber and tin dist.; outport Port Kelang; p. (1980) 937,875.

Kuangchow. *See* **Guangzhou.**

Kuantan, main t. on E. cst. **W. Malaysia;** linked to Kuala Lumpur; tin mng; p. (1980) 136,625.

Kuching, c., cap. of Sarawak, **Malaysia;** pt. on Sarawak R.; gold discovered nearby at Bau; p. (1980) 74,229.

Kucovë (Qyteti Stalin), Albania; nr. Berat; oil prod. and refining; pipeline connects to Vlore.

Kufra, oasis, **Libya;** dates, barley; on caravan route.

Kuldja. *See* **Yining.**

Kumakoto, c., W. Kyushu, **Japan;** 3rd c. of K.; cas., univs.; food inds.; business ctr.; p. (est. 1984) 525,662.

Kumasi, c., cap. of Ashanti region, **Ghana;** univ., aerodrome; road and rly. junc.; ctr. of cocoa-producing a.; bauxite nearby; jute bags; p. (1984) 260,286 (c.), 345,117 (met. a.).

Kumba Konam, t., Tamil Nadu, **India;** on Cauvery delta; silks, cotton; sacred Hindu c.; p. (1971) 113,130.

Kunene (Cunene), R., **Angola;** scheme to channel water from Angola to S.W. Africa; 1,200 km long.

Kungur, t., **RSFSR;** S.E. of Perm; oil ind. equipment; p. (est. 1970) 65,000.

Kun Lun (Kwen Lun), mtn. ranges, Xizang Zizhiou (Tibet), **China;** extend 2,900 km E. from Pamirs along N. edge of high plateau of Xizang Zizhiou; drained N. into inland drainage basin of Lop Nor; alt. frequently exceeds 5,400 m; rising to 7,729 m.

Kunming, c., cap. of Yunnan prov., S.W. **China;** univ.; comm. and cultural ctr., noted for its scenic beauty; iron and steel, milling and boring machin., textiles, chemicals; p. (est. 1983) 1,450,000.

Kunsan, spt., S.W. **S. Korea;** on Yellow Sea, on estuary of R. Kum; p. (1966) 102,800.

Kununurra Dam, Ord R., **W. Australia;** opened 1963; to irrigate 81,000 ha of semi-arid land for cotton, rice, and cattle.

Kuopio, t., **Finland;** on L. Kalki; timber inds.; tourism; p. (1970) 63,766.

Kura, R., rises in **Turkey,** chief R. of Trans-caucasia, **USSR;** flows into Caspian Sea; agr., fishing, hydroelec. power; 1,504 km long.

Kurdistan (Country of the Kurds), includes parts of E. Turkey, Soviet Armenia, N.E. Iraq, and N.W. Iran; attempts at autonomy.

Kure, c., S.W. Honshu, **Japan;** spt. and naval base; engin.; shipbldg.; p. (1979) 236,600.

Kurgan, c., **RSFSR;** on Tobol R.; impt. junc. on Trans-Siberian rly.; tr. in cattle and foodstuffs; agr. engin.; p. (est. 1980) 316,000.

Kuria Muria Is., 5 barren Is. in Arabian Sea off cst. of Oman; admin. by U.K. until 1967.

Kurile Is., chain of volcanic Is., N. Pac., **RSFSR;** extend from Kamchatka to Hokkaido; mainly mtnous.; sulphur, hunting, fishing; Japan claims sovereignty over 4 Is.; a. 15,592 km²; p. 18,000.

Kurisches Haff (Kurštu Martos), shallow lagoon, Baltic cst. of Lithuanian SSR, **USSR;** receives water of R. Niemen; narrow entrance to Baltic Sea at N. end of lagoon commanded by pt. of Klaipeda (Memel); length 92 km, maximum width 32 km.

Kurische Nehrung, sandspit, Baltic Sea; almost cuts off Kurisches Haff from Baltic Sea; 88 km long.

Kurnool, t., Andhra Pradesh, **India;** agr. comm. ctr.; p. (1971) 136,710.

Kuroshio (Japan Current), ocean current, flows N.E. along Pac. cst. of Kyushu, Shikoku and S. Honshu, relatively warm water, exerts slight warming influence on this cst. in winter.

Kursk, c., cap. of K. oblast, **RSFSR;** on Tuskor R.; rly. junc.; in fertile fruit-growing a.; engin., textiles, synthetic rubber; p. (est. 1980) 383,000.

Kurume, t., W. Kyushu, **Japan;** on Chikugo plain; comm. ctr.; p. (1979) 212,865.

Kushiro, spt., S.E. Hokkaido, **Japan;** exp. lumber; local coal; fishing; p. (1979) 216,012.

Kustanay, c., Kazakh SSR, **USSR;** on Tobol R.; agr.-processing, lt. inds.; p. (est. 1980) 169,000.

Kütahya, t., cap. of K. prov., central **Turkey;** agr. mkt. ctr.; ceramics; chemical complex; p. (1970) 62,222.

Kutaisi, c., Georgian SSR, **USSR;** on R. Rion (hydroelectric plant); chemicals, textiles, mng. equipment; big coal deposits being mined; mkt. gardening a.; p. (est. 1980) 197,000.

Kut-al-Amara, t., cap. of K. prov., **Iraq;** on R. Tigris; agr. tr. ctr.; p. (1970) 58,647.

Kutch, peninsula, Gujarat st., N.W. **India;** bounded on N. by Pakistan; largely barren except for fertile strip along Arabian Sea; p. (1961) 696,440.

Kutch, Rann of, desert region covered with salt, but flooded during monsoons; nine-tenths belongs to **India;** one-tenth to **Pakistan.**

Kutchan, t., S.W. Hokkaido, **Japan;** ctr. of lge. iron-ore field; ore smelted at Muroran.

Kutno, t. Lodz, **Poland;** route ctr.; sm. textile ind.; p. (1970) 30,300.

Kuwait, indep. Arab st., **S.W. Asia;** under Brit. protection until 1961; lies at head of Persian G.; inc. mainland and 9 sm Is.; mainly desert with a few oases; imports most of food requirements; possesses 17 per cent of the proved world reserves of oil; heavily dependent on oil and natural gas exports; industl. complex of petrochemical inds. at Shuaiba projected, 48 km S. of Kuwait (cap.) which contains nearly half of p.; freshwater scarce; one of hgst. incomes per capita in world, but most of p. remains poor; a. 24,235 km²; p. (est. 1984) 1,703,000.

Kuwait, c., cap. of **Kuwait;** pt. with natural harbour on Persian G.; univ.; p. (1980) 60,525.

Kuybyshev, c., cap. of K. oblast, **RSFSR;** on R. Volga; major R. pt., rly. junc. on Moscow-Siberian line, airport; hydroelectric power sta.; comm. ctr. with varied mnfs., inc. cars, aircraft, textiles, synthetic rubber; oil refining; grain and livestock exp.; p. (est. 1980) 1,226,000.

Kuzbas (Kuznetsk Basin), industl. region, Siberia, **USSR;** lies S. of Trans-Siberian rly. in upper valleys of Rs. Ob and Tom; second lgst. coal output in USSR, iron and steel mftg., heavy metallurgical ind.; ch. ts., Novosibirsk, Novokuznetsk, Kemerovo, Leninsk-Kuznetsky.

Kwangsi Chuang. *See* **Guang Zhuang.**

Kwantung. *See* **Guangdong.**

Kwanto Plain, S.E. Honshu, **Japan;** lgst. a. of continuous lowland in Japan, extends 128 km inland from Tokyo; plain devoted to intensive rice cultivation; higher, drier terraces under mulberry, vegetables, tea, tobacco; very dense rural p.; lge. number of urban ctrs., inc. Tokyo, Yokohama; a. 13,000 km²; p. (1960) 27,000,000.

Kwazulu, Bantu Terr. Authority (1970), E. S. **Africa;** runs 480 km from Moçambique to Cape Prov. but in 29 separate as. interspersed by white as.; cap. Nongoma in N. highland; p. (1980) 3,442,140.

Kweichow. *See* **Guizhou.**

Kweilin. *See* **Guilin.**

Kweiyang. *See* **Guiyang.**

Kwidzyn (Marienwerder), c., Gdansk, N. **Poland** (since 1945); cath., cas.; industl. ctr. nr. Vistula R.; p. (1970) 23,100.

Kwinana, new t. (1952), pt., W. **Australia;** oil refinery and steel plant, alumina reduction, integrated steelwks.; p. (1976) 10,981.

Kyle and Carrick, l. gov. dist., Strathclyde Reg., **Scot.;** lge. dist. inc. t. of Ayr; p. (1981) 114,463.

Kyle of Lochalsh, v., Skye and Lochalsh, **Scot.;** at entrance to Loch Alsh, facing S. end of I. of Skye; terminus of rly. across Highlands from Dingwall; ch. pt. for steamers to N.W. cst.; I. of Skye, Outer Hebrides; p. (1981) 803.

Kymi, R., **Finland;** rises in L. Päijänne, flows to G. of Finland; many Ls., timber transport, hydroelec. power; 144 km long.

Kyoto, c., Honshu, **Japan;** cultural and religious ctr., without lge.-scale inds.; former cap. 794–1868; univ.; shrines, old Imperial palace; p. (est. 1984) 1,473,065.

Kyushu, most S. of 4 major Is. of **Japan;** mtnous.; coal mng. in Chikugo basin; heavy inds.;

agr. on coastal lowlands; joined to Honshu by bridge and rly.; a. 42,007 km²; p. (1960) 12,903,515.

Kyustendil, t., **Bulgaria;** in foothills of Osogovo mtns.; lge. lead and zinc deposits; combined plant for mng. and ore dressing projected.

Kzyl Orda, R. and t., Kazakh SSR, **USSR;** lge. dam to irrigate rice plantations; p. of t. (est. 1980) 159,000.

L

Laaland I. *See* Lolland I.

Labrador, mainland a. of prov. Newfoundland, **Canada;** separated from I. by Strait of Belle I.; barren, severe climate; impt. cod fisheries; rich iron ore reserves nr. Quebec bdy.; Churchill R. power project; cap. Battle Harbour; a. 292,219 km²; p. (est. 1971) 28,200.

Labrador City, t., Newfoundland, **Canada;** new t. built 1965, nr. Wabush L. to house workers of iron-ore mines.

Labuan, I., Sabah, **Malaysia;** rubber, rice, coconuts; cap. Victoria; a. 81 km²; p. (est. 1970) 7,250.

Laccadive Is., coral Is., Arabian Sea; about 320 km off Malabar cst. joined with Minicoy and Amindivi Is. to form union terr., **India;** renamed Lakshadweep Is. (1974); coir, coconuts; cap. Kavaratti; a. 28 km²; p. of terr. (1971) 31,798.

Lachine, c., Quebec, **Canada;** on Montreal I. where St. Lawrence R. leaves St. Louis L.; iron and steel, wire, rope; Lachine canal by-passes rapids; summer resort; p. (est. 1971) 44,500.

Lachlan, R. N.S.W., **Australia;** main trib. of R. Murrumbidgee; irrigation; 1,472 km long.

La Coruña, spt., cap. of La Coruña prov., N.W. **Spain;** fishing; p. (1981) 231,730.

Ladakh, dist., of the Upper Indus, **India,** bordering Tibet; ch. t. Leh; isolated and remote; alt. 3,600 m; p. (1961) 88,651.

Ladoga (Ladozhskoye), L., Leningrad, **USSR;** a. 18,389 km²; (lgst. in Europe); drained to G. of Finland by R. Neva; fishing; link in new deepwater canal between White and Baltic Seas.

Ladybank, burgh, North East Fife, **Scot.;** 8 km S.W. of Cupar; p. (1981) 1,353.

Ladysmith, t. Natal, **S. Africa;** cotton mills; besieged by Boers 1899–1900; p. (est. 1970) 28,500.

Lae, t., **Papua New Guinea;** pt. on Huon Gulf serving goldmng. dist.; outlet for Morobe; plywood; air ctr.; p. (1971) 38,707.

Lagan (Laggan), R., N. **Ireland;** flows into Belfast Lough; canal link to Lough Neagh; 56 km long.

Lagôa dos Patos, L., **Brazil;** drained by Rio Grande do Sul; 224 km long.

Lagôa Mirim, L., on bdy. between **Brazil** and **Uruguay;** drains N.; 176 km long.

Lagos, spt., cap. of **Nigeria;** unhealthy and congested; cap. to be moved to Abuja by 1986; on G. of Guinea; gd. natural harbour; exp. cocoa, groundnuts, palm oil and kernels, timber, hides and skins, cotton, rubber, crude oil; mnfs. textiles, confectionery, chemicals, car assembly; univ.; p. (est. 1975) 1,060,848 (c.), 1,476,837 (met a.).

La Grande Chartreuse, limestone region between Chambéry and Grenoble, **France;** famous monastery and liqueur.

La Grande Rivière, N. Quebec, **Canada;** major hydroelec. scheme; mineral and timber inds.

Laguna, dist., Durango st., **Mexico;** former L. bed irrigated by Rs. Nazas and Aguanaval; ch. cotton-growing region in Mexico; ch. t., Torréon; a. 259,000 km².

Lahore, ch. c., **Pakistan;** univ., cath., temples, mosques; textiles, pottery, carpets, industl. gases; atomic research ctr.; second c. of Pakistan; p. (1981) 2,922,000.

Lahti, t., S. **Finland;** wood, plywood, brewing, textiles; p. (1970) 88,393.

Lake Champlain, N.Y., **USA;** forms lowland a. for main routes between Montreal and N.Y.

Lake Charles, c., La., **USA;** spt. at mouth of Calcasieu R.; connected to G. of Mexico by channel; exp. oil, chemicals, rice, cotton; p. (1980) 75,226 (c.), 167,048 (met. a.).

Lake District, almost circular mtnous. a., Cumbria, **Eng.;** 17 major and many smaller Ls. formed by glacial erosion and deposition; increasing tourist pressure on Nat. Park as motorways improve accessibility.

Lakeland, c., Fla., **USA;** citrus fruit ctr.; holiday resort; p. (1980) 322,000 (met. a. inc. Winter Haven).

Lakeland, South, l. gov. dist., Cumbria, **Eng.;** lge. a. surrounding Morecambe Bay and inc. Ulverston, Grange, Kendal and Sedbergh; p. (1981) 97,664.

Lake of the Woods, L., Ont., S.E. of Winnipeg, on bdy. between **Canada** and **USA;** in pine forest; tourism.

Lakeview, t., Ont., **Canada;** thermal elec. power plant projected; to be lgst. in world.

Lakshadweep, union terr., **India;** made up of Laccadive, Minicoy and Aminidivi Is; a. 32 km²; p. (1981) 40,249.

La Linea, t., **Spain;** on isthmus connecting Gibraltar with mainland; p. (1981) 55,590.

La Mancha, plain, Cuidad-Real prov., S. **Spain;** in shallow depression on central plateau, alt. between 450–900 m, drained by headstreams of R. Guadiana; semi-arid climate with hot summers, cold winters; widespread salt deposits; Merino sheep, esparto grass; Spain's lgst. grape-growing region.

Lambaréné, t., **Gabon;** site of Schweitzer's hospital on Ogooué R.; p. (1975) 22,682

Lambayeque, prov., N.W. **Peru;** ctr. of irrigated dists.; sugar, cotton, tobacco; cap. Chiclayo, ch. pt. Pimental; a. 11,948 km²; p. (1972) 515,363.

Lambeth, inner bor., London, **Eng.;** L. palace, residence of Archbishop of Canterbury; p. (1981) 245,739.

Lammermuir Hills, E. Lothian, **Scot.;** highest peak Lammer Law, 529 m.

Lampang, t., **Thailand;** modern sugar plant; p. (est. 1969) 39,400.

Lampedusa, lgst. of Pelagi Is., between Malta and Tunisian cst., belonging to **Italy;** barren limestone; a. 21 km²; p. (1981) 4,792.

Lampeter, t., Ceredigion, Dyfed, S. **Wales;** on R. Teifi; mkt.; univ. college of Wales; p. (1981) 1,972.

Lamu, t., **Kenya;** impt. historical and tourist ctr. on Indian Ocean.

Lanark, former co., central **Scot.;** now forms several sm. l. gov. dists. known as Clydesdale within Strathclyde Reg.

Lanark, royal burgh, Clydesdale, **Scot.;** in Clyde valley 35 km S.E. of Glasgow; hosiery; ctr. of mkt. gardening a.; nr. New Lanark model t. built by Robert Owen; p. (1981) 9,778.

Lancashire, non-met. co., N.W. **Eng.;** major growth of p. in 19th cent. based on prod. of cotton and coal; main industl. ctrs. now outside co. in Merseyside and Gtr. Manchester met. cos.; Pennines in E.; extensive lowland in W.; admin. ctr. Preston, co. t. Lancaster; a. 2,738 km²; p. (1981) 1,372,118.

Lancaster, c., co. t., l. gov. dist., Lancs., **Eng.;** 10 km up R. Lune; mediaeval cas., univ.; linoleum, vinyl, clothing; p. (1981) 120,914 (dist.).

Lancaster, c., Penns., **USA;** agr. ctr., tobacco mkt.; stockyards; mnfs. linoleum, watches; birthplace of Robert Fulton; p. (1980) 362,000 (met. a.).

Lanchow. *See* Lanzhou.

Lancing, v., West Sussex, **Eng.;** on S. cst., 3 km E. of Worthing; seaside resort; lt. inds.; public school.

Landau, t., Rhineland-Palatinate, **W. Germany;** on R. Queich; cigar mftg., wine, iron ind.; here the carriages called Landaus were first made; p. (1983) 35,800.

Landes, dep., S.W. **France;** on Atl. cst.; agr., vineyards, resin; cap. Mont-de-Marsan; a. 9,334 km²; p. (1982) 297,100.

Landes, Les, region, Aquitaine, S.W. **France;** fringes Bay of Biscay from Pointe de Grave to Biarritz; coastal sand dunes and lagoons backed by low, flat plain of alternate sandy tracts and marsh; reclaimed by drainage and afforestation, now over half a. covered by pine forests; turpentine, timber; oilfield.

Land's End, extreme S.W. point of **Eng.** on Cornish cst.

Landshut, t., Bavaria, **W. Germany;** on R. Isar; cas.; elec. inds., glass, metallurgy, textiles, coal; rly. junc.; p. (1983) 56,400.

Landskrona, spt., **Sweden;** on the Sound; shipping and tr. ctr.; agr.-processing; on nearby I. of Ven; Tycho Brahe built his observatory; p. (1983) 35,656.

Langbaurgh, l. gov. dist. Cleveland, **Eng.**; a. of N. York Moors inc. Loftus, Skelton, Gainsborough and Saltburn; p. (1981) 149,508.

Langdale Pikes, L. Dist., **Eng.**; 2 peaks Harrison Stickle (733 m), Pike o'-Stickel (709 m); popular rambling and climbing a.; 5 km W. of Grasmere.

Langebergen, mtns., Cape Prov., **S. Africa**; 240 km E. to W. parallel to S. cst. of Africa; form barrier to access from cst. plain to Little Karroo, broken across by valley of R. Gouritz; max. alt. exceeds 1,370 m.

Langreo, t., N. **Spain**; in Asturias, 19 km S.E. of Oviedo; coal and iron mines; p. (1981) 55,758.

Langres, t., Haute-Marne, **France**; cath., medieval fortifications; famous for its cutlery; birthplace of Diderot; p. (1982) 11,359.

Languedoc, region, former prov., S. **France**; inc. deps. Gard, Aude, Hérault, Lozère, Ardèche, Tarn, and parts of Haute Garonne, Tarn-et-Garonne, and Haute Loire; major govt. sponsored investment in tourist inds., along Mediterranean cst.; mono-cultural vine prod., irrigation scheme to aid agr. diversification.

Lannemezan, region, Aquitaine, S.W. **France**; belt 80 km wide stretches over 160 km along foot of Pyrenees W. of Toulouse; consists of immense deltas of glacial gravel deeply cut by tribs. of Rs. Garonne and Adour; valleys liable to severe floods in summer, intervening plateau dry, bare; scantily populated.

Lansing, c., cap of Mich., **USA**; on Grand R. at confluence with Cedar R.; automobiles, chemicals; p. (1980) 130,000 (c.), 472,000 (met. a.).

Lanzarote, I., Canary **Is.**; volcanic mtns.; developing tourist ind.; cochineal; cap. Arrecife; p. (1970) 41,912.

Lanzhou (Lanchow), c., cap. of Gansu prov., **China**; on Huang He; tr. ctr.; oil refining, gaseous diffusion plant, woollen mills, coal mng. nearby; p. (est. 1983) 1,430,000.

Laoag, t., N. Luzon I., **Philippines**; agr.-processing; p. (1970) 69,300.

Laoighis or Leix Co., Leinster, **R.o.I.**; mtns. and bog; inland pasture and tillage; cap. Port Laoighise (Maryborough); a. 1,720 km²; p. (1981) 13,837.

Laon, t., cap. of Aisne dep., **France**; on rocky height above plain; historic fortress t.; cath.; p. (1982) 29,074.

Laois. *See* Laoighis.

Laos, People's Dem. Rep. of, S.E. **Asia**; kingdom until 1975; bordered by China, Vietnam, Kampuchea, Thailand and Burma; formerly part of Fr. Indo-China; under-developed and isolated cty.; considerable mineral resources but only tin exploited; disrupted by civil war, drought, crop pests; economic ctr. is Mekong valley, scene of recent Mekong R. Development Project; elsewhere thickly forested mtns.; 90 per cent of p. engaged in subsistence agr. for dry rice; lge. food imports necessary; main exp., hardwoods; no rlys.; royal cap. Luang Prabang, admin. cap. Vientiane; a. 231,399 km²; p. (est. 1984) 4,315,000.

La Paz, dep., **Bolivia**; traversed by Andes; de facto cap. La Paz, legal cap. Sucre; cocoa, coffee, rubber, tin-mng. at Catari; a. 105,377 km²; p. (est. 1982) 1,913,184.

La Paz, c., **Bolivia**; seat of govt.; comm. ctr.; copper, alpaca wool, cinchona, textiles; highest cap. c. in world; p. (est. 1982) 881,404.

Lapland, terr., N. **Europe**, in Norway, Sweden, Finland, and USSR, extending from Norwegian cst. to White Sea; mainly mtn. and moorland, with many lakes; Lapps are nomadic pastoralists with reindeer herds; iron-ore at Kiruna and Gällivare; a. 336,700 km²; p. of Swedish Co. of L. (1983) 118,819.

La Plata, c., spt., **Argentina**; cap. of Buenos Aires prov., univ.; mftg. ctr.; iron and steel, oil refining, refrigerated meat prods.; p. (1980) 473,233.

La Plata, Rio de. *See* Plata, Rio de la.

Laptev Sea (Nordenskjöld Sea), inlet of Arctic Oc.; between Severnaya Zemlya and New Siberian Is., **RSFSR**.

Larache, spt., **Morocco**; on Atl. cst. 64 km S. of Tangier; exp. cork, wool; p. (1971) 47,710.

Laramie, t., Wyo., **USA**; univ.; industl. ctr. for cattle and timber region; rly. engin.; p. (1980) 24,410.

Laredo, t., Texas, **USA**; frontier t. on Rio Grande; smuggling; ctr. of Chicanos; p. (1980) 91,449 (t.), 99,258 (met. a.).

Largo, v., North East Fife, **Scot.**; fishing, holiday resort; birthplace of Alexander Selkirk.

Largs, burgh, Cunninghame, **Scot.**; on F. of Clyde opposite Is. of Bute and Cumbrae; seaside resort, fishing; battle 1263 defeating last attempt by Norsemen to conquer Scot.; p. (1981) 9,763.

Larissa, dep., Thessaly, **Greece**; inc. infertile basin of R. Pinios; cap. Larissa; ch. pt. Volos; p. (1981) 102,426.

Larnaca, spt., **Cyprus**; the anc. Citium; grain, cotton, fruit; oil refinery; growing tourist ctr.; p. (est. 1970) 21,400.

Larne, spt., l. gov. dist., **N. Ireland**; at entrance to Larne Lough; cross channel service to Stranraer; tourism; p. (1981) 29,351 (dist.), 18,224 (t.).

La Rochelle, spt., cap. of Charente-Maritime dep., **France**; on Atl. cst.; its deepwater pt. is La Pallice; cath.; fishing pt.; chemicals, food-processing; tourism; p. (1982) 78,231.

Larut Hills, W. **Malaysia**; rise to over 1,500 m; lge. tin-field.

Larvik, spt., **Norway**; S.W. of Oslo; seaside resort; engin., pulp, stone; former whaling pt.; p. (est. 1970) 10,376.

Las Cruces, t., N.M., **USA**; on Rio Grande R.; irrigated agr.; univ.; p. (1980) 45,086.

La Serena, c., cap. of Coquimbo prov., **Chile**; 14 km inland from its pt. Coquimbo; cath.; resort; p. (est. 1966) 48,647.

Lashio, t., **Burma**; on R. Salween; rly. terminus; Burma road links with China; ctr. of silver-lead mines; p. 4,638.

Lashkar, c., Madhya Pradesh, central **India**; modern industl. t., adjoining Gwalior.

La Skhirra, pt. on G. of Gabès, **Tunisia**; oil; pipeline to Edjelé.

Las Palmas, prov., Canary Is., **Spain**; inc. Gran Canaria, Lanzarote, Fuerteventura and smaller Is.; intensive irrigated agr. of bananas, tomatoes, potatoes; tourism encouraged by climate and volcanic landscape; a. 4,053 km²; p. (1981) 708,754.

Las Palmas, c., N.E. Gran Canaria, ch. pt. of Canary **Is.**; exp. agr. prods.; cath.; p. (1981) 360,094.

La Spezia, spt., Liguria, N.W. **Italy**; on Bay of Spezia; ch. Italian naval sta., arsenal and docks; maritime inds., elec. machin., olive oil, oil refining; p. (1981) 115,392.

Lassen Peak, Nat. Park, Cascade Range, Cal.; only active volcano in **USA**.

Lasswade. *See* Bonnyrigg and Lasswade.

Las Vegas, c., Nevada, **USA**; noted for its gambling casinos; ranching and mng. a.; p. (1980) 165,000 (c.), 463,000 (met. a.).

Latacunga, t., **Ecuador**; at c. 2,740 m in Andean basin, not far from Cotopaxi volcano; anc. Inca t.; ctr.; p. (est. 1970) 17,300.

Latakia, spt., **Syria**; exp. tobacco, olive oil, sponges; p. (1970) 126,000.

Latina (Littoria), c., cap. of Latina prov., in Latium central **Italy**; in ctr. of reclaimed a. of Pontine marshes; mkt. ctr., on which planned road system converges; built since 1932; nuclear power sta. nearby; p. (1981) 93,738.

Latin America, the Spanish-, Portuguese- and Fr.-speaking countries of N. America, S. America, Central America, and the W.I. inc. the reps. of Argentina, Bolivia, Brazil, Chile, Colombia, Costa Rica, Cuba, Dominican Republic, Ecuador, Salvador, Guatemala, Haiti, Honduras, Mexico, Nicaragua, Panama, Paraguay, Peru, Uruguay, and Venezuela; sometimes Puerto Rico, Fr. W.I., and other Is. of the W.I. are included, and occasionally Belize, Guyana, Fr. Guiana, and Surinam; p. (est. 1984) 397,138,000.

Latium (Lazio), region, central **Italy**; between Apennines and Tyrrhenian Sea, comprising provs. of Rome, Frosinone, Latina, Rieti, Viterbo; a. 17,182 km²; p. (1981) 5,001,684.

Latrobe Valley, one of most impt. economic a. in Victoria, **Australia**; major brown coal and electric power production; secondary inds. attracted by cheap power.

Latvia, constituent rep., **USSR**; borders on Baltic Sea; dairying, stock-raising, forestry; cap. Riga; spts. Ventspils, Liepaya; a. 66,278 km²; p. (est. 1977) 2,500,000.

Launceston, t., Tasmania, **Australia**; at head of Tamar estuary, inc. Bell Bay where many heavy inds.; p. (1976) 63,386.

Launceston, t., North Cornwall, **Eng.**; agr. mkt.; quarrying, lt. engin.; p. (1981) 6,199.

Laurencekirk, burgh, Kincardine and Deeside, **Scot.;** agr. ctr. in the Howe of Mearns; p. (1981) 1,296.

Laurion or **Laurium,** pt. on Attic peninsula, **Greece;** lead, manganese, zinc, and silver mines; silver mined 5th cent. B.C.

Lausanne, c., cap. of Vaud can., **Switzerland;** nr. L. Geneva; cath., univ.; impt. rly. junc.; seat of Swiss high courts of justice; tourism; p. (1980) 221,237.

Lauterbrunnen, Alpine valley, Bern can., **Switzerland;** famous for its waterfalls, the highest of which is Staubbach 299 m; tourist and winter sports ctr.

Laval, t., cap. of Mayenne dep., **France;** Mayenne R. divides old and modern parts; cotton, paper, machin., marble; cas., church; p. (1982) 53,766.

Lavenham, t., Suffolk, **Eng.;** a ctr. of the wool tr. in 15th cent., still preserves its mediaeval character.

Lavera, pt., nr. Marseilles, S.E. **France** commencement of 752 km oil pipeline to Karlsruhe, W. Germany; oil refining.

Lawrence, t., Mass., **USA;** on Merrimac R., N.W. of Boston; textiles, paper, footwear, engin.; p. (1980) 282,000 (met. a. inc. Haverhill).

Lawton, t., Okla., **USA;** mnfs. cottonseed oil; p. (1980) 80,054 (t.), 112,456 (met. a.).

Laxey, v., I. of Man, **Eng.;** flour milling, woollen mills, meerschaum pipes.

Lazio. *See* Latium.

Lea or **Lee,** R., **Eng.;** rises in Chiltern Hills nr. Luton, flows S. and E. into R. Thames through industl. zone of N.E. London; valley to become a regional park; mkt. gardening a.; 74 km long.

Leamington (Royal Leamington Spa), t., Warwicks., **Eng.;** on R. Leam, trib. of Avon, 3 km N.E. of Warwick; fashionable spa; engin. inds.; p. (1981) 42,953.

Leatherhead, t., Mole Valley, Surrey, **Eng.;** on R. Mole to N. of gap through N. Downs; residtl.; p. (1981) 40,473.

Lebanon, mtn. range, **Lebanon,** extending to cst. of Syria; snow-capped most of year; highest peak Timarum, 3,214 m; famous in anc. times for cedar forests.

Lebanon, rep., S.W. **Asia;** at E. end of Mediterranean Sea; bordered by Syria to N. and Israel to S.; narrow coastal strip backed by mtnous. interior; free mkt. a., with economy based on transit tr.; most of p. involved in tourism, finance and commerce; oil refining based on imports; cap. Beirut; strife-torn by civil war and Israeli invasions; a. 8,806 km²; p. (est. 1984) 2,644,000.

Le Bourget, t., N.E. of Paris, **France;** airpt.; p. (1982) 11,021.

Lebórk (Lauenburg), t. Gdansk, **Poland** (since 1945); in agr. dist.; timber and food inds.; p. (1970) 25,000.

Lebowa Territory, Bantu Terr., **S. Africa;** home of N. Sotho and Ndebele peoples; self-gov. Oct. 1972; cap. Seshego; p. (1980) 1,746,500.

Lecce, c., Apulia, S. **Italy;** agr. and route ctr. with ceramic and glass inds.; anc. Greek col.; baroque churches and palaces; p. (1981) 91,289.

Lecco, t., **Italy;** in Lombardy, on L. Como; iron and copper wks.; agr.-processing, cheese; one of first ts. in Europe to be run by elec.; p. (est. 1970) 53,600.

Lech, R., rises in Austria and flows past Augsburg in Bavaria, **W. Germany,** to join Danube; 283 km long.

Le Creusot, t., Saône-et-Loire, **France;** ctr. of one of sm. coalfields bordering the Massif Central; steel, engin.; p. (1982) 32,309.

Ledbury, t., Hereford and Worcs., **Eng.;** at W. foot of Malvern hills; fruit preserving, tanning; 17th cent. mkt. hall; birthplace of John Masefield.

Leeds, c., met. dist., West Yorks., **Eng.;** on R. Aire; at E. margin of Pennines; univ.; lge. clothing ind., varied engin. mnfs., paper and printing; with Bradford forms conurb. of W. Yorks., p. (1981) 704,974.

Leek, mkt. t., Moorland, Staffs., **Eng.;** 18 km N.E. of Stoke-on-Trent; silk mnfs., butter; expanded t.; p. (1981) 19,739.

Lee-on-Solent, t., Hants., **Eng.;** on Southampton Water.

Lees, t., Gtr. Manchester, **Eng.;** textiles; p. (1981) 4,838.

Leeuwarden, c., cap. of Friesland prov., **Neth.;** noted cattle mkt.; rly. junc.; p. (1982) 84,689.

Leeuwin, C., S.W. point of **Australia;** notorious storms; Nat. Park (1971).

Leeward Is., W.I., northern gr. of Lesser Antilles archipelago; so-called because winds in this a. generally blow from E.; inc. Virgin Is. of US; Fr. I. of Guadaloupe, Dutch Is. of St. Eustatius and Saba, and Brit. Leeward Is. (Montserrat, Virgin Is., and former cols. of Antigua, St. Kitt-Nevis, Anguilla).

Legaspi, t., cap. of Albay prov., **Philippines;** spt. in S.E. Luzon; linked by rly. with Manila; p. (est. 1970) 84,700.

Leghorn. *See* Livorno.

Legionowa, t., **Poland;** new t. (1951) on outskirts of Warsaw; nr. artificial L. in R. Bug valley; p. (1970) 20,800.

Legnano, t., Lombardy, **Italy;** N.W. of Milan; textiles, machin.; p. (1981) 49,308.

Legnica (Liegnitz), c., Wroclaw, S.W. **Poland** (since 1945); on Katzbach R., in rich agr. region; p. (1970) 75,800.

Leh, cap. of Ladakh, Kashmir, **India;** isolated t. in Himalayas on caravan route to Tibet; p. (1981) 8,000.

Le Havre, spt., Seine-Maritime dep., N. **France;** at mouth of Seine on English Channel; shipbldg., engin., chemicals, ropes, cottons, oil refining; pipeline to Grandpuits; p. (1982) 200,411.

Leicester, c., co. t., l. gov. dist., Leics., **Eng.;** on R. Soar; univ.; footwear, hosiery, knitwear, textile machin.; Roman remains; p. (1981) 279,791.

Leicestershire, non-met. co., **Eng.;** mainly rural, low-lying Midland co., but inc. Charnwood Forest; mixed agr., sm. coalfield; hosiery and footwear inds.; now inc. Rutland; ch. t. Leicester; a. 2,554 km²; p. (1981) 842,577.

Leicestershire, North West, l. gov. dist., Leics., **Eng.;** inc. Ashby de la Zouch, Ashby Woulds, Coalville and Castle Donington; p. (1981) 78,589.

Leiden or **Leyden,** c., S. Holland prov., **Neth.;** on Oude Rijn; famous univ.; printing, textiles, medical equipment; gr. weaving ctr. in Middle Ages; revolt against Spanish rule 1573–4; birthplace of Rembrandt; p. (1982) 103,457.

Leigh, t., Gtr. Manchester, **Eng.;** 8 km S.E. of Wigan; mkt.; coal mng.; textiles; p. (1981) 45,341.

Leigh-on-Sea, t., Essex, **Eng.;** on N. cst. of Thames estuary, 3 km W. of Southend; holiday resort, fishing.

Leighton Buzzard, t., South Beds., **Eng.;** at N.E. end of Vale of Aylesbury; tiles, engin., sand quarrying; p. (1981) 29,772 (inc. Linslade).

Leinster, S.E. prov., **R.o.I.;** bulk of recent Irish p. increase; a. 19,637 km²; p. (1981) 1,294,039.

Leipzig, c., E. **Germany;** comm., industl., and cultural ctr. at junc. of Rs. Pleisse, Elster, and Parthe; famous univ.; inds. inc. publishing, steel, textiles, chemicals, machin., cars; tr. fairs; Bach was organist at Thomaskirche; birthplace of Leibnitz and Wagner; p. (1983) 558,994.

Leiston-cum-Sizewell, t., Suffolk Coastal, Suffolk, **Eng.;** on cst. 6 km E. of Saxmundham; agr. implements; nuclear power sta.; p. (1981) 5,133.

Leith, t., Edinburgh City, **Scot.;** shipbldg., timber, whisky; outport for Edinburgh.

Leith Hill, Surrey, **Eng.;** nr. Dorking; alt. 294 m; Lower Greensand crest.

Leitmeritz. *See* Litoměřice.

Leitrim, co., Connacht, **R.o.I.;** agr.; cap. Carrick-on-Shannon; a. 1,588 km²; p. (1981) 1,677.

Leix. *See* Laoighis.

Leixões, the modern harbour of Oporto, **Portugal;** oil refinery.

Lek, R., **Neth.;** one of the branches of the Neder Rijn; from Wijk-bij-Duurstede to Krimpen nr. Rotterdam; 64 km long.

Le Locle, t., Neuchâtel, **Switzerland;** ctr. of watch-mkg. ind.; p. (1969) 15,200.

Léman L. *See* Geneva, L.

Le Mans, t., cap. of Sarthe dep., N.W. **France;** cath., linen, ironmongery, chemicals, motor cars, aeroplanes; motor-racing; p. (1982) 150,331.

Lemnos, Greek I., Aegean Sea, **Greece;** 64 km S.W. of Dardanelles; ch. t. Kastro (the anc. Myrina); tobacco, wine; a. 466 km²; part of Lesvos dep.

Lena, one of gr. Siberian Rs., **RSFSR**; rises in Oc.; navigable; 4,480 km long.

Leninabad, c., Tadzhik SSR, **USSR**; on Syr Dar'ya R., S. of Tashkent; silks, cottons, fruit-preserving; hydroelectric power sta.; p. (est. 1980) 132,000.

Leninakan, c., Armenian SSR, **RSFSR**; nr. Turkish border; textiles, engin., rug-mkg.; p. (est. 1980) 210,000.

Lenin Dam (Dnieper Dam). See **Zaporozh'ye.**

Leningrad, c., cap. of Leningrad oblast, **RSFSR**; at mouth of Neva R.; cultural ctr. with many fine bldgs., inc. winter palace, Hermitage museum, cath., admiralty bldg.; former cap. of Russia; major pt. and industl. ctr.; exp. timber, furs, and raw materials; ice-bound December–March; founded (1703) by Peter the Great as St. Petersburg; p. (est. 1980) 4,638,000.

Leninogorsk, c., Kazakh SSR, **USSR**; in Altai mtns.; lead, zinc, and silver mines; metallurgical plants; p. (est. 1967) 70,000.

Lenin Peak (Mt. Kaufmann), Trans-Altai Range, Kirghiz-Tadzhik SSR border, 2nd. hgst. mtn. of **USSR**; adjoining glacier; salt. 7,132 m.

Leninsk-Kuznetski, t., **RSFSR**; in W. Siberia on Inya R.; coalfield in Kuznetsk basin; heavy engin., power sta.; p. (est. 1980) 133,000.

Lenkoran, c., pt. Azerbaydzhan SSR, **USSR**; on Caspian Sea, nr. Iranian border; rice, citrus fruits, tea, fisheries, food-processing; p. (est. 1967) 31,000.

Lennoxtown, t., Stirling, **Scot.**; alum. wks.; p. (1981) 4,825.

Lens, t., Pas-de-Calais dep., N. **France**; industl. ctr. in coal a.; p. (1982) 327,383 (met. a.).

Leoben, t., Styria, **Austria**; lignite mng. ctr.; p. (1971) 35,153.

Leominster, mkt. t., l. gov. dist., Hereford and Worcs., **Eng.**; 19 km N. of Hereford; once famed for woollen ind.; p. (1981) 37,196.

León, c., central **Mexico**; at c. 1,700 m; comm., agr. and mng. ctr. (gold, copper, silver, lead, tin); textiles, leather; p. (1979) 624,816.

León, c., cap. of León dep., N.W. **Nicaragua**; cath., univ.; ctr. for agr. and industl. prods.; footwear, textiles; p. (1981) 131,134.

León, cap. of L. prov., N.W. **Spain**; gothic cath.; craft inds.; p. (1978) 119,262.

Léopoldville. See **Kinshasa.**

Lepontine Alps, major gr., **Switzerland–Italy**; alt. over 3,300 m.

Le Puy, t., cap. of Haute Loire dep., **France**; lace, liqueurs; cath. sited on old volcanic plug; tourism; p. (1982) 25,968.

Lérida, t., cap. of L. prov., **Spain**; on R. Segre; 2 caths.; textiles, leather, glass; p. (1981) 109,573.

Lerwick, t., Shetland Is., **Scot.**; on Mainland; fishing; p. (1981) 7,223.

Lesbos. See **Lesvos.**

Les Causses. See **Causses, Les.**

Leskovac, t., Serbia, **Yugoslavia**; on Morava R.; in economically backward a.; textiles, soap, furniture, tobacco-processing; p. (1971) 44,255.

Les Landes. See **Landes, Les.**

Leslie, burgh, Kirkcaldy, **Scot.**; 11 km N. of Kirkcaldy; paper, bleaching; p. (1981) 3,472.

Lesotho (Basutoland), kingdom, southern **Africa**; surrounded by Rep. of S. Africa; at head of Orange R. and enclosed by Drakensberg mtns.; economy mainly agr., especially pastoral farming; exp. livestock, wool, mohair, diamonds; 50 per cent revenue from U.K. grants; poor communications; many workers migrate to S. Africa (23 per cent in 1981); inds. encouraged by tax concessions becoming increasingly impt.; cap. Maseru; a. 30,344 km²; p. (est. 1981) 1,365,900.

Lesser Antilles. See **Antilles.**

Lesvos (Lesbos, Mytilene), I., off Turkey, Aegean Sea, belonging to **Greece**; highest point 939 m; agr., antimony, marbles; cap. Mytilene; a. 1,601 km²; p. (1981) 104,620 (dep.).

Leszno, t., Poznan, W. **Poland**; engin., distilling, tobacco; p. (1970) 33,900.

Letchworth (Garden City), t., North Herts., **Eng.**; at foot of Chiltern Hills, 3 km N.E. of Hitchin; first garden c., founded by Sir Ebenezer Howard 1903; engin., office equipment; expanded t.; p. (1981) 31,835.

Lethbridge, c., Alberta, **Canada**; in foothills of Rockies; ctr. of lge. coal-mng. dist. and of irrigated wheat-growing a.; p. (1978) 49,638.

Le Touquet-Paris Plage, fashionable resort, W. cst. **France**; S. of Canche estuary.

Letterkenny, t., Co. Donegal, **R.o.I.**; on Lough Swilly; tourist ctr.; p. (1981) 6,444.

Leuna, t., Halle, **E. Germany**; 5 km S. of Merseburg; synthetic chemical ind.; oil pipeline from Schwedt; p. (est. 1971) 11,000.

Levant, French and Italian name for E. cst. of Mediterranean.

Leven, burgh, Kirkcaldy, **Scot.**; on N. side of F. of Forth; resort; p. (1971) 9,472.

Leven, L., Perth and Kinross, **Scot.**; ass. with escape of Mary Queen of Scots from Castle I. 1568.

Leverkusen, t., N. Rhine–Westphalia, **W. Germany**; on R. Rhine, N. of Cologne; iron, machin., textiles, chemicals; p. (1983) 157,400.

Levkás or **Santa Maura,** one of Ionian Is., off W. **Greece**; wine, olive oil, currants; p. (1981) 21,863.

Lewes, t., l. gov. dist., East Sussex, **Eng.**; on R. Ouse at N. entrance to gap through S. Downs; mkt., cas., printing, light inds.; p. (1981) 77,507 (l. gov. dist.), 14,971 (t.).

Lewis, I., Outer Hebrides, **Scot.**; fishing, tweeds; ch. t. Stornoway; a. 1,994 km²; p. (1971) 15,174.

Lewisham, inner bor., London, **Eng.**; inc. Deptford; residtl.; industl.; p. (1981) 233,225.

Lewiston, t., Maine, **USA**; power for textile mill supplied by waterfall since early 19th cent.; p. (1980) 40,481.

Lexington, c., Ky., **USA**; in heart of Blue Grass region; univ.; ch. tobacco mkt. and horse-breeding ctr. of USA; p. (1980) 204,000 (c.), 318,000 (met. a.) inc. Fayette.

Lexington, t., Mass., **USA**; nr. Boston; residtl.; first battle in war of independence 19 Apr. 1775; p. (1980) 29,479.

Leyburn, t., Richmondshire, North Yorks., **Eng.**; in lower Wensleydale; mkt.

Leyden. See **Leiden.**

Leyland, t., Lancs., **Eng.**; 8 km S. of Preston; motor vehicles, rubber; p. (1981) 26,567. See **Central Lancashire.**

Leyte, one of Visayan Is., central **Philippines**; maize, abaca, rice; Japanese fleet defeated by US in battle of Leyte Gulf 1944; a. 7,213 km²; p. (1970) 1,340,015.

Leyton. See **Waltham Forest.**

Lhasa (Lasa), c., cap. of Tibet, **China**; "forbidden" c.; Buddhist ctr., temple, monasteries, shrines; caravan tr. in carpets, silks, lace, gold, tea; pharmaceutical factory, turbine pumps, fertilisers; p. (est. 1982) 105,000.

Lhotse, mtn., Tibet, **China–Nepal**; 4th hgst. mtn. in world; alt. 8,506 m.

Lianyungang, c., Jiangsu, **China**; formed by merger of 3 cities; agr. comm. ctr., tr. in cereals, cotton; p. (1953) 207,600.

Liao-ho, R., Liaoning, N.E. **China**; flows into G. of Liaotung, Yellow Sea; navigable for last 640 km of course; c. 1,600 km long.

Liaoning, prov., N.E. **China**; inc. lower course and delta of Liao-ho; part of N.E. China (formerly called Manchuria); maize, millets, soyabeans; lge. mineral reserves of coal and iron ore; cap. Shenyang; a. 150,220 km²; p. (est. 1983) 36,290,000.

Liaotung, peninsula, N.E. **China**; nr. G. of same name.

Liaoyang, c., E. Liaoning prov., N.E. **China**; in fertile valley of Liao-ho; cotton-growing; textile mills; p. (est. 1970) 250,000.

Liao-yuang, c., S.W. Jilin, **China**; lge. coal-mng. ctr.; p. (1953) 120,100.

Liberec, t., **ČSSR**; on R. Neisse; univ.; textiles, chemicals, tr. ctr.; p. (est. 1975) 75,500.

Liberia, rep., **W. Africa**; founded (1847) by free slaves from USA; tropical climate; 72 per cent of p. involved in agr.; few cash crops, inc. rubber and cocoa; rich iron deposits provide main exp.; world's lgst. merchant fleet as result of "flag of convenience"; cap. and ch. pt. Monrovia; a. 99,068 km²; p. (est. 1981) 1,911,094.

Libourne, t., Gironde, **France**; on R. Dordogne, 35 km N.E. of Bordeaux; wine tr.; p. (1982) 23,312.

Libreville, c., cap. of Gabon; pt. on G. of Guinea; exp. tropical hardwoods, rubber, cacao; Trans-Gabon rly. project to link L. to Booué to promote timber exploitation; p. (1975) 251,400.

Libya, or **Popular Socialist Libyan Arab Jamahiriyah** (since 1977), rep., N. **Africa**; on Mediterranean cst.; desert conditions prevail; radical attitude towards oil companies as oil accounts for 99 per cent of exp. earnings and forms basis of new-found wealth; petro-chemical inds.; over half working p. are foreigners; most of p. engaged in subsistence agr. (nomadic pastoralism); most food and mnfs. imported; plans for unity with Chad; joint caps. Tripoli (site of government deps.), Benghazi; a. 1,759,537 km²; p. (est. 1984) 3,471,000.

Libyan Desert, part of the Sahara, **Africa**.

Licata, t., Sicily, **Italy**; spt.; sulphur-processing; p. (1981) 40,050.

Lichfield, c., l. gov. dist., Staffs., **Eng.**; cath.; agr. and lt. inds.; expanded t.; birthplace of Dr. Samuel Johnson; p. (1981) 88,454 (dist.).

Lickey Hills, gr. of hills, Hereford and Worcs., **Eng.**; 6 km S.W. of Birmingham; reveal anc. rocks underlying younger sediments; rise to 292 m, largely wooded.

Liechtenstein, principality, between Austria and Switzerland; official language German; economy based on sm.-scale inds. and tourism in picturesque Alpine scenery aided by mild climate; wine; cap. Vaduz; a. 161 km²; p. (1983) 26,512, one-third foreign born.

Liège (Luik), industl. c., E. **Belgium**; on R. Meuse nr. confluence of Ourthe; cath., univ.; conurb. inc. Herstal, Bressoux, Ougrée, Angleur, Grivegnée; metallurgy, armaments, vehicles, chemicals, textiles, glassware, tyres; p. (1982) 211,528.

Liepaja (Libau), c., Latvian SSR, **USSR**; ice-free pt. on Baltic Sea, second to Riga; shipyards, steel-wks., paper mills, chemicals; exp. timber, grain; p. (est. 1980) 108,000.

Liestal, t., cap. of the half-can. Baselland, **Switzerland**; p. (1970) 12,500.

Liffey, R., **R.o.I.**; rises in Wicklow Mtns. and enters Irish Sea at Dublin; water supply for Dublin; inds. along estuary.

Liguria, region, N.W. **Italy**; inc. provs. of Genoa and Porto Maurizio; a. 5,411 km²; p. (1981) 1,807,893.

Ligurian Sea, Mediterranean; N. of Corsica.

Likasi (Jadotville), t., **Zaïre**; ctr. for copper mng. and refining; p. (1982) 146,394.

Lille, c., cap. of Nord dep., N. **France**; on R. Deûle; mftg., comm. and cultural ctr.; former cap. of Fr. Flanders (1668); textiles (the term lisle derived from earlier spelling of city's name); metallurgy, engin.; univ., art museums; p. (1982) 174,039.

Lilongwe, c., main ctr. of Central Region, **Malawi**; replaced Zomba as cap. 1975; p. (est. 1983) 158,500.

Lima, c., cap. of **Peru**; 13 km from its pt. Callao; dominates comm., industl. and social life of cty.; cath., univ., imposing architecture; seaside subs. Miraflores, Barranco, Chorillos; shanty ts. on outskirts; p. (1981) 3,968,972 (10 times bigger than next c., Arequipa).

Lima, t., Ohio, **USA**; on Ottawa R.; rly. wks., oil, car bodies, refrigerators; p. (1980) 218,000 (met. a.).

Limassol, t., S. **Cyprus**; spt. on Akrotiri Bay; new artificial harbour; ctr. of admin. dist.; wine, agr.-processing; exp. foodstuffs; tourism; p. (est. 1970) 51,500.

Limavady, t., l. gov. dist., **N. Ireland**; mkt.; linen; p. (1981) 26,353 (dist.), 8,015 (t.).

Limbach, t., Karl-Marx-Stadt, **E. Germany**; hosiery, textiles, machines; p. (est. 1970) 25,460.

Limbe. See Blantyre-Limbe.

Limburg, prov., N.E. **Belgium**; bordering Neth.; mainly agr.; coal-mng. in Campine region; cap. Hasselt; a. 2,409 km²; p. (1983) 359,005.

Limburg, prov., S.E. **Neth.**; bordering on Belgium and W. Germany; drained by R. Maas; former coalmng.; new inds. to relieve unemployment; p. 2,191 km²; p. (1983) 1,080,516.

Limeira, t., São Paulo, **Brazil**; ctr. of orange cultivation; hats, matches; p. (est. 1980) 129,600.

Limerick, co., Munster, **R.o.I.**; agr., livestock, fishing; a. 3,385 km²; p. (1981) 60,736.

Limerick, C.B., cap. of Limerick, **R.o.I.**; spt. at head of Shannon estuary; bacon, tanning, shipbldg.; p. (1981) 18,002 (c.).

Limmat, R., **Switzerland**; trib. of R. Aare; flows through c. of Zürich; 128 km long.

Lim Fjord, shallow strait, Jutland, **Denmark**; connects N. Sea with Kattegat; contains I. of Mors.

Limoges, c., cap. of Haute-Vienne dep., **France**; to N.W. of Central Massif; anc. t., celebrated in middle ages for goldsmith's work, later for enamel ware and porcelain; cath.; p. (1982) 144,082.

Limón, spt., **Costa Rica**; on Caribbean; oil refining nearby; p. (est. 1970) 35,846.

Limousin, region and former prov., central **France**; to W. of Auvergne; now divided into deps. Haute-Vienne, Corrèze, Dordogne; plateau, average alt. 300 m, composed of old crystalline rocks; exposed damp climate; infertile, some pastoral agr.; kaolin; ch. t. Limoges; p. (1982) 732,500.

Limpopo or **Crocodile R.**, **S. Africa, Moçambique**, and **Zimbabwe**; lower R. forms a fertile valley 1,600 km long.

Linares, prov., central **Chile**; thermal springs in Andes; cereals and vineyards in valleys; cap. Linares; a. 9,816 km²; p. (1970) 189,010.

Linares, t., Jaén prov., **Spain**; silver-lead mines; metallurgical inds.; p. (1981) 51,278.

Lincoln, c., co. t., l. gov. dist., Lincs., **Eng.**; on R. Witham in gap through Lincoln Edge; impt. Roman t.; cath., cas.; heavy engin., iron foundries, bricks, lime, seed milling, malting; p. (1981) 76,660.

Lincoln, c., cap. of Nebraska, **USA**; univ.; educational ctr.; grain and cattle mkt.; flour mills, agr. machin., cars, chemicals, rubber gds.; p. (1980) 172,000.

Lincoln Edge, limestone ridge, Lincs. and Humberside, **Eng.**; runs N. from Ancaster through Lincoln to Humber; narrow ridge with steep scarp slope to W., broken by R. Witham at Lincoln; iron-ore deposits worked in N. nr. Scunthorpe; sheep, barley; rarely exceeds 90 m alt.

Lincolnshire, non-met. co., **Eng.**; between Humberside non-met. co. and the Wash; fertile soil on low-lying fenland; intensive agr., arable crops, bulbs, market gardening; food-processing; formerly divided into 3 admin. parts: Holland, Kesteven, and Lindsey; a. 5,884 km²; p. (1981) 547,560.

Lincoln Wolds, low plateau, Lincs. and Humberside, **Eng.**; runs N. 72 km from Wash to Humber; chalk covered with glacial deposits; mixed farming, grains, roots, sheep; lge. farm units; scantily populated; rise to approx. 135 m.

Lindau, t. Baden-Württemberg, **W. Germany**; on I. in Bodensee; tourist resort; p. (1983) 23,800.

Lindisfarne or **Holy I.**, off cst. of Northumberland, **Eng.**; connected to mainland by stretch of sand and causeway at low tide; abbey founded 635 A.D. as first establishment of Celtic Christianity in Eng.

Lindsey. See Lincolnshire.

Lindsey, East, l. gov. dist., Lincs., **Eng.**; lge. a. on E. cst. inc. Louth, Mablethorpe, Horncastle, Woodhall Spa, Skegness and Alford; p. (1981) 104,546.

Line Is., Pac. Oc., coral gr. admin. by U.K., except Palmyra, Kingman and Jarvis, which belong to USA; coconuts; airfields, meteorological stas.

Lin-i (formerly **Ichow**), t., Shandong, **China**; at foot of Shandong Highlands.

Linköping, t., S.E. **Sweden**; aero-engin., pianos, furniture; cath.; p. (1983) 114,681.

Linlithgow, burgh, W. Lothian, **Scot.**; distilling, brewing, paper, shoes; birthplace of Mary Queen of Scots; p. (1981) 9,524.

Linnhe, Loch, Lochaber, Argyll and Bute, Scot.; 21 m. long; entrance to Caledonian canal.

Linslade. See Leighton Buzzard.

Linz, c., cap. of Upper **Austria**; pt. on Danube; comm. and industl. ctr. with iron and steel wks.; cath.; p. (1978) 208,700.

Lipa, t., Luzon, **Philippines**; sugar, tobacco, cocoa, maize; processing; p. (1975) 112,006.

Lipari Is. or **Aeolian Is.**, volcanic gr. between Sicily and toe of Italy; inc. Stromboli (927 m), Lipari, Vulcano, Salina; olives, grapes, currants, pumice; p. (1981) 10,208.

Lipetsk, c., **RSFSR**; on Voronezh R.; ctr. of iron-ore mng. a.; engin., steel, ferro-alloys; health resort; p. (est. 1980) 405,000.

Lippe, R., **W. Germany**; trib. of Rhine; paralleled by L. canal; forms N. bdy. of Ruhr industl. dist.; 176 km long.

Lippstadt, t., N. Rhine–Westphalia, **W. Germany**; on R. Lippe; metallurgy, textiles rly. ctr.; p. (1983) 60,700.

Liri, R., central **Italy**; rises in Alban Hills, flows S.E. to Cassino and then S.W. to G. of Gaeta; valley followed by main road from Rome to Naples; length 168 km.

Lisbon (Lisboa), c., cap. of **Portugal**; on R. Tagus, 14 km from mouth; spt. with fine natural harbour; cas., cath., univ.; admin., comm., and

industl. ctr.; expanding inds., airpt.; attracts p. from rural areas; p. (1981) 807,167 (c.), 1,469,484 (met. a.).

Lisburn, t., l. gov. dist., **N. Ireland**; on R. Lagan, 10 km S.W. of Belfast; p. (1981) 82,973 (dist.), 40,391 (t.).

Lisieux, t., Calvados dep., N. **France**; historic t., severely damaged in second world war; cath.; Camembert cheese; p. (1982) 25,823.

Liskeard, mkt. t., Caradon, Cornwall, **Eng.**; on R. Looe at S. edge of Bodmin Moor; p. (1981) 6,316.

Lismore, t., N.S.W., **Australia**; within met. a. of Sydney; pt. on Richmond R.; dairying, sugar refining, maize, potatoes, textiles, engin., bacon; p. (1976) 22,082.

Lismore, mkt. t., R.D., Waterford, **R.o.I.**; on Blackwater R.; cas.; p. (1975) 900.

Listowel, U.D., Kerry, **R.o.I.**; on R. Feale; cas. ruins; p. (1981) 3,542.

Litherland, t., Sefton, Merseyside, **Eng.**; N. sub. of Liverpool; p. (1981) 21,946.

Lithuania (Litva SSR), constituent rep., **USSR**; borders Baltic Sea; agr. development on reclaimed marshland; dairy farming, stock-raising, fishing, timber inds., food-processing, ship bldg., textiles, machin.; cap. Vilna; a. 65,201 km²; p. (1970) 3,129,000.

Litoměřice, t., **ČSSR**; in Bohemia on R. Elbe (Labe); cath.; brewing, agr. ctr.; p. (est. 1968) 18,894.

Little Belt (Lille Bælt), strait, **Denmark**; separates Fyn I. from Jutland; too shallow for lge. ships; road/rly., motorway bridges cross narrow N. section nr. Frederidicia; 48 km long.

Little Bighorn, R., Wyo, Mont., **USA**; Custer's last battle on ridge overlooking R. (1876); 144 km long.

Littleborough, t., Gtr. Manchester, **Eng.**; textiles and textile finishing; p. (1981) 13,861.

Littlehampton, t., Arun, West Sussex, **Eng.**; on S. cst. at mouth of R. Arun; holiday resort, sm. spt.; p. (1981) 22,181.

Little Lever, t., Gtr. Manchester, **Eng.**; 5 km S.E. of Bolton; residtl. and industl.; p. (1981) 11,439.

Little Rock, t., cap. of Ark., **USA**; N.E. of Hot Springs, on Ark. R. opposite N. Little Rock; comm. and mnf. ctr. in rich cotton and dairy farming a.; bauxite nearby; p. (1980) 158,000 (c.), 394,000 (met. a.).

Littoria. See **Latina.**

Liuchow. See **Liuzhou.**

Liuzhou (Liuchow), c., Guang Zhuang, S. **China**; on trib. of Xijiang; route ctr. and R. pt.; p. (1958) 190,000.

Liverpool, c., spt., met. dist., Merseyside, **Eng.**; second pt. in Gr. Britain, on N. bank at entrance to Mersey estuary; deep-sea container berths at Seaforth; shipping and ship-repairing; elec. mnfs. and engin., flour milling, sugar refining, seed and rubber processing, cars; cath., univ.; second Mersey tunnel opened 1971; freeport (1984) to help revive docks; p. (1981) 544,861 (c.), 1,368,630 (Gtr. Liverpool).

Liverpool, t., N.S.W., **Australia**; within met. a. of Sydney; major source of poultry, vegetables and dairy prod. for Sydney; p. (1976) 89,656.

Livingston, new t. (1962), W. Lothian, **Scot.**; p. (1981) 38,594.

Livingstone, t., **Zambia**; on Zambesi R. where rly. bridges R.; stands at *c.* 900 m; former cap.; sawmilling ctr.; p. (1980) 71,987.

Livorno (Leghorn), spt., cap. of L. prov., **Italy**; on Ligurian Sea; shipbldg., machin., chemicals, iron and steel wks., oil refining; exp. wine, olive oil, textiles, marble; p. (1981) 175,741.

Lizard, The, c., Cornwall, **Eng.**; S. point of Eng.

Ljubljana, c., cap. of Slovenia, N.W. **Yugoslavia**; on trib. of Sava R.; industl. ctr., local coal, hydroelectric power; route ctr.; airport; univ.; mediaeval fortress; ctr. of Slovene nat. movement in 19th cent.; p. (1981) 305,211.

Llanberis, pass, Gwynedd, N. **Wales**; between Snowdon and Clyder Fawr; road carries heavy tourist traffic; summit 356 m; nearby tourist resort of Llanberis.

Llandarcy, v., West Glamorgan, S. **Wales**; on cst. Swansea Bay, Bristol Channel; lge. oil refinery; pipeline to Angle Bay, Pembroke.

Llandeilo, mkt. t., Dinefwr, Dyfed, **Wales**; in vale of Towy, E. of Carmarthen; cas.; p. (1981) 1,614.

Llandovery, t., Dinefwr, Dyfed, **Wales**; on R. Bran, nr. confluence with Towy; mkt. ctr. for rural a.; p. (1981) 1,691.

Llandrindod Wells, t., Radnor, Powys, **Wales**; medicinal waters; p. (1981) 4,186.

Llandudno, t., Aberconwy, Gwynedd, **Wales**; between Gr. Ormes and Little Ormes headlands; resort; p. (1981) 18,991.

Llanelli, l. gov. dist., Dyfed, **Wales**; pt. on Burry inlet, 18 km N.W. of Swansea; industl. and comm. ctr.; coal mng., steel, and tin-plate wks., mng. machin.; cas.; p. (1981) 75,422 (dist.).

Llanfairfechan, t., Aberconwy, Gwynedd, **Wales**; at foot of Penmaenmawr mtn.; seaside resort; granite quarrying; p. (1981) 3,780.

Llanfyllin, t., Powys, **Wales**; anc. mkt. t.; p. (1981) 1,207.

Llangefni, t., Anglesey, Gwynedd, **Wales**; in ctr. of the I.; mkt. and agr. t.; p. (1981) 4,265.

Llangollen, t., Glyndwr, Clwyd, **Wales**; on R. Dee; vale of L., tourist ctr.; annual Eisteddfod; p. (1981) 3,058.

Llanidloes, t., Powys, **Wales**; on R. Severn; surrounded by hills; anc. mkt. house; p. (1981) 2,416.

Llanos, lowland region, **Venezuela** and **Colombia**, S. America; drained by R. Orinoco and tribs.; high temperatures throughout year, but rain chiefly in summer; ch. vegetation, coarse grass which withers during dry season (Dec. to May); little developed, some cattle-rearing.

Llanos de Urgel, upland region, Lérida, N.E. **Spain**; semi-arid; formerly steppe-land, now irrigated by R. Segre; vine, olive, maize, tobacco.

Llanrwst, mkt. t., Aberconwy, Gwynedd, **Wales**; on R. Conway; tourist ctr.; p. (1981) 2,931.

Llanstephan, v., Dyfed, **Wales**; at mouth of R. Towy; ruins of Norman cas.

Llantrisant, new t., Taff-Ely, Mid Glamorgan, S. **Wales**; iron-ore quarrying; Royal Mint.

Llanwrtyd Wells, t., Brecknock, Powys, **Wales**; once a spa; resort; p. (1981) 488.

Lleyn, peninsula, Gwynedd, N. **Wales**; from Snowdonia to Bardsey I.; crystalline rocks form hills in E., otherwise low, undulating; pastoral farming, sheep, cattle; sm. seaside resorts; ch. t. Pwllheli; a. 466 km².

Lliw Valley, l. gov. dist., West Glamorgan, **Wales**; comprises Pontardawe and Llwchwr; p. (1981) 59,745.

Llwchwr, t., Lliw Valley, West Glamorgan, S. **Wales**; p. (1981) 26,864.

Llwchwr or **Loughor,** R., S. **Wales**; in lower course forms bdy. between Dyfed and West Glamorgan, empties into Burry inlet.

Loanhead, burgh, Midlothian, **Scot.**; 8 km S.E. of Edinburgh; coal, engin.; p. (1981) 6,135.

Lobito, spt., **Angola**; on Atl. Oc.; 29 km N. of Benguela; fine natural deepwater harbour; rly. terminus; varied exps.; oil-refinery under construction; p. (est. 1976) 70,000.

Locarno, t., **Switzerland**; on L. Maggiore; tourist ctr.; L. treaty 1925; p. (est. 1978) 15,300.

Lochaber, mtnous. l. gov. dist., Highland Reg., **Scot.**; bounded by Loch Linnhe and Loch Leven; inc. Ben Nevis; hydroelec. power; a. 4,465 km²; p. (1981) 20,539.

Lochalsh. See **Kyle of Lochalsh.**

Lochgelly, burgh, Dunfermline, l. gov. dist., **Scot.**; nr. Dunfermline; p. (1981) 7,308.

Lochgilphead, co. t., Argyll and Bute, **Scot.**; at head of Loch Gilp, 3 km N. of Ardrishaig; tourist ctr.; p. (1981) 2,459.

Lochmaben, burgh, Annandale and Eskdale, **Scot.**; in Annandale, 11 km N.E. of Dumfries; p. (1981) 1,710.

Lockerbie, burgh, Annandale and Eskdale, **Scot.**; in Annandale, 16 km E. of Dumfries; sheep mkt.; p. (1981) 3,530.

Lockport, t., N.Y., **USA**; on N.Y. st. barge canal, 38 km N.E. of Buffalo; power from Niagara falls supplies paper, metal, and other inds.; p. (1980) 24,844.

Lodi, t., **Italy**; on R. Adda, S.E. of Milan; cath.; scene of Napoleon's victory over Austrians 1796; p. (1981) 42,873.

Lodore Falls, waterfalls, Cumbria, **Eng.**; in Watendlath beck at foot of Derwentwater.

Łódź, c., cap. of L. prov., central **Poland**; second c. of rep. and ctr. of textile ind.; machin., elec. equipment, chemicals, metals; univ.; cultural ctr.; problems of water-supply; p. (est. 1983) 848,500.

Lofoten Is., storm-swept chain of Is. off N.W. cst.

Norway within Arctic Oc., stretching 240 km; cod and herring fisheries among richest in world.

Loftus, t. Langbaurgh, Cleveland, **Eng.**; on N.E. flank of Cleveland Hills; p. (1981) 8,477.

Logan, Mount, S.E. Yukon, **Canada,** E. of Alaska; alt. 6,054 m; highest mtn. in Canada and second highest in N. America.

Logroño, t., N. **Spain**; on Ebro R.; in wine growing a.; industl. and agr. ctr.; p. (1981) 109,889.

Loire, R., France; longest in cty., flows from Cevennes mtns. to Atl. Oc. at St. Nazaire; vineyards and many castles in attractive valley; 1,000 km long.

Loire, dep., E. central **France;** in part of the former provs. of Beaujolais and Lyonnais; agr.; coal mng., cattle raising; cap. St. Etienne; a. 4,799 km²; p. (1982) 737,400.

Loire-Atlantique, dep., W. **France;** mainly agr., salt-marsh on cst.; inds. at cap. Nantes; a. 6,980 km²; p. (1982) 994,700.

Loiret, dep., N. central **France;** agr., vineyards, distilling, mftg.; cap. Orléans; a. 6,812 km²; p. (1982) 537,000.

Loir-et-Cher, dep., central **France;** contains fertile a. of Beauce; cap. Blois; a. 6,421 km²; p. (1982) 296,000.

Lokoren, industl. t., **Belgium**; between Ghent and Antwerp; textiles, chemicals, tobacco; p. (1981) 33,369.

Lokoja, t. **Nigeria**; at confluence of Rs. Niger and Benue; R. pt.; iron-ore nearby.

Lolland or **Laaland,** Danish I. in Baltic Sea; a. 1,241 km²; agr. forests; ch. ts. Maribo, Nakshov; p. (1965) 81,760.

Lomami, R., central **Zaïre;** trib. of Zaïre R., rich coal-bearing strata at confluence; 1,812 km long.

Lombardy, Plain of, N. **Italy;** extensive lowland flanked by Alps, Apennines, Adriatic Sea; built up by alluvium from R. Po, its tribs. and R. Adige; intensively cultivated; rice, maize, flax, clover, lucerne, wheat, apples, dairy cattle; densely populated; many industl. ts., Milan, Novara, Pavia, etc.; p. of region (1981) 8,891,652.

Lombok, one of the lesser Sunda Is., **Indonesia**; mtnous. volcanic terrain; Wallace's Line passes between Lombok and Bali; ch. t. Mataram; p. 1,300,000.

Lomé, spt., cap. of **Togo,** W. Africa; on G. of Guinea; deepwater pt.; exp. cacao, cotton, palm prods.; phosphates; p. (est. 1977) 229,400.

Lomond, Loch, Stirling, lgst. loch in **Scot.**, studded with Is., surrounded by hills with Ben Lomond on E. side; a. 70 km².

Lomża, t. Bialystok, **Poland**; on Narew R., metal inds., foodstuffs; p. (1970) 25,500.

London, cap. of UK, **Eng.**; at head of Thames estuary; seat of govt.; world ctr. of finance and communication; cultural and artistic ctr.; comprises the City, 12 inner and 20 outer bors.; Port of London; upstream docks now closed; main pt. downstream at Tilbury; currently losing p. and inds. to outer met. a.; univs. (London, Brunel, City), caths., many historic bldgs., theatres, museums, galleries, libraries, and parks; p. (1981) 5,893 (City of London), 2,496,756 (Inner London), 7,677,719 (Greater London).

London, t., Ont., **Canada**; on R. Thames, 104 km W. of Hamilton; industl. ctr.; univ.; p. (1979) 240,390.

Londonderry, formerly co.; l. gov. dist., **N. Ireland;** borders R.o.I. and L. Foyle; Sperrin Mtns. in S.; p. (1981) 83,494 (dist.).

Londonderry (or **Derry**), c., l. gov. dist., **N. Ireland;** on left bank of R. Foyle, 6 km upstream from Lough Foyle; shirt mftg.; textiles; acetylene from naphtha; training ctr. for ind.; p. (1981) 62,697 (t.).

Londrina, c., Paraná, **Brazil**; industl. and agr. ctr., coffee, maize, cotton, livestock; p. (est. 1980) 349,200.

Long Beach, c., Cal., **USA**; Pac. cst. resort and industl. suburb of Los Angeles met. a.; (1980) 361,000 (c.). *See* Los Angeles.

Longbenton, t., Tyne and Wear, **Eng.**; 5 km N.E. of Newcastle; former coal mng.; expanded t.; p. (1981) 50,646.

Long Eaton, t. Erewash, Derbys., **Eng.**; on R. Trent, 8 km S.W. of Nottingham; rly. wks., lace mftg., elec. cables, flexible tubing, hosiery; p. (1981) 32,895.

Longford, co., Leinster, **R.o.I.**; peat bogs; dairy

farming; co. t. Longford; a. 1,090 km²; p. (1981) 6,548.

Longford, co. t., Longford, **R.o.I.**; cas., cath.; mkt. t.; p. (1971) 3,876.

Long Forties Bank, submarine sandbank, N. Sea; 128 km E. of Aberdeen; valuable fishing-grounds; depth of water, from 45–75 m.

Long I., part of N.Y., **USA**; separated from mainland by East R.; contains Queens and Brooklyn bors. of N.Y. City; mkt. gardening, fisheries, oysters, holiday resorts; a. 4,356 km².

Longreach, t. Queensland, **Australia**; in ctr. of Gr. Australian (artesian) basin; collecting ctr. for cattle and wool; p. (1976) 3,354.

Longridge, t., Ribble Valley, Lancs., **Eng.**; 10 km N.E. of Preston; p. (1981) 7,161.

Longview, t. Texas, **USA**; oil, chemicals, plastics; p. (1980) 62,762 (t.), 151,752 (met. a.).

Longwy, t., Meurthe-et-Moselle dep., N.E. **France**; on Belgian–Luxembourg frontier; upper part fortfd.; lower part industl. with iron and steel ind.; p. (1968) 21,087.

Lons-le-Saunier, cap. of Jura dep., E. **France**; saline springs; agr. ctr.; p. (1982) 21,886.

Looe, t. Caradon, Cornwall, **Eng.**; on Looe estuary; holiday resort; p. (1981) 4,499.

Lopburi, t., **Thailand**; ctr. of haematite iron deposits; former cap.

Lop Nor, marsh, Xinjiang, W. **China**; in Tarim Basin at foot of Altun Shan; ctr. of inland drainage, receives water from R. Tarim; atomic testing grounds.

Lorain, t., Ohio, **USA**; on L. Erie; shipbldg., steelwks., fisheries; p. (1980) 275,000 (met. a.).

Lorca, t., Murcia, **Spain**; agr. prod., woollens, chemicals; bishop's palace; p. (1981) 60,627.

Lord Howe I., forested volcanic I., S. Pac. Oc., 698 km N.E. of Sydney; palm seed ind.; admin. by N.S.W.; p. (1976) 244.

Lorient, spt., Morbihan dep., N.W. **France**; on Atl.; naval shipyard, fishing harbour; p. (1982) 64,675.

Lorraine, region and former prov., N.E. **France**; inc. deps. Moselle, Meurthe-et-Moselle, Meuse, and Vosges; ch. t. Nancy; rich iron-ore deposits; impt. but declining industl. a.; mkt. gardening, vineyards; with Alsace long disputed between Germany and France; p. (1982) 2,318,000.

Los Alamos, t., N.M., **USA**; site of research for first atomic bomb; p. (1980) 11,039.

Los Angeles, c., S. Cal., **USA**; booming modern c. ("the city of angels"), busiest pt. in Cal.; fine harbour; one of world's lgst. urban areas; miles of freeway (2,400 km planned by 1980); many prosperous inds., inc. aircraft, missiles, chemicals, machin., electronic equipment, food-processing, oil refining; film ctr.; p. (1980) 3,309,000 (c.), 7,446,000 (met. a.) with Long Beach.

Lossiemouth, burgh, Moray, **Scot.**; on Moray F., 8 km N. of Elgin; birthplace of Ramsay Macdonald; fishing; p. (1981) 6,801.

Lostwithiel, mkt. t. Cornwall, **Eng.**; on R. Fowey S.E. of Bodmin; anc. Stannary t.

Lot, dep., S.W. **France**; livestock, wine, cereals, coals, iron; a. 5,227 km²; cap. Cahors; p. (1982) 154,500.

Lot, R., S. **France**; trib. of Garonne R., 435 km long.

Lota, pt., **Chile**; coal-mng. ctr.; ceramics, copper smelting; p. (est. 1970) 47,725.

Lot-et-Garonne, dep., S.W. **France**; agr. (cereals, vines, fruit); cap. Agen; a. 5,385 km²; p. (1982) 298,700.

Lothian Region, l. gov. reg., central **Scot.**; borders F. of Forth, and inc. a. around Edinburgh; mainly in-dustl.; a. 1,753 km²; p. (1981) 735,892.

Lötschental, picturesque valley, Valais, **Switzerland**; ch. v. Kippel.

Loughborough, t., Charnwood, Leics., **Eng.**; on R. Soar 16 km N. of Leicester; engin., elec. gds., chemicals, textiles; univ.; former hosiery t.; bell foundry; p. (1981) 47,647.

Loughrea, mkt. t., Galway, **R.o.I.**; cotton mill; p. (1981) 3,377.

Louisiana, southern st., **USA**; Pelican St.; admitted to Union 1812; st. flower Magnolia, st. bird Eastern Brown Pelican; leading producer of rice, sugarcane, sweet potatoes, also cotton, maize, tobacco, oil, natural gas, lumber; cap. Baton Rouge; New Orleans major pt.; a. 125,675 km²; p. (1980) 4,204,000.

Louisville, c., Ky., **USA**; on Ohio R.; univ.; lgst. tobacco mkt. in world; chemicals, paints, cars, machin., elec. gds., synthetic rubber; p. (1980) 298,000 (c.), 906,000 (met. a.).

Lourdes, t., **France**; on R. Pau; Catholic pilgrim centre.; slate, marble; p. (1982) 17,619.

Lourenço Marques. *See* **Maputo.**

Louth, t., East Lindsey, Lincs., **Eng.**; on E. edge of Lincoln Wolds; abbey ruins; cattle mkt., farm implements, rope mkg., lime, malting, canning; p. (1981) 13,296.

Louth, maritime co., Leinster, **R.o.I.**; mtns., bog and barren land; salmon fishing; cap. Dundalk; a. 818 km²; p. (1981) 55,734.

Louvain (Leuven), c., Brabant prov., **Belgium**; on R. Dyle; univ. (Erasmus taught here); brewing ctr., bell foundries; p. (1982) 84,914.

Low Archipelago. *See* **Tuamotu Is.**

Low Countries, name applied to Belgium and the Neth.

Lowell, c., Mass., **USA**; at junc. of Merrimac and Concord Rs.; 48 km N. of Boston; textiles, machin., chemicals, carpets; birthplace of Whistler; p. (1980) 233,000 (met. a.).

Lower California (Baja California), peninsula, N.W. **Mexico**; separating G. of Cal. and Pac. Oc.; isolated, arid; divided into 2 sts., Baja California (cap. Tijuana), and Baja California, Territorio Sur (cap. La Paz); a. 143,963 km²; p. (1969) 1,150,000.

Lower Hutt, c., N.I., **N.Z.**; rapid industl. devel. in last 45 years; engin., plastics, textiles, vehicle assembly; p. (1976) 64,553.

Lower Saxony (Nieder Sachsen), *Land*, **W. Germany**; inc. Lüneburg heath and Harz mtns.; cap. Hanover; a. 47,205 km²; p. (est. 1988) 7,256,800.

Lowestoft, fish pt., Waveney, Suffolk, **Eng.**; on E. Anglian cst. 14 km S. of Gr. Yarmouth; holiday resort, nr. Broads; food and fish processing plants; base for N. Sea gas; p. (1981) 55,231.

Lowther Hills, mtns., between Strathclyde and Dumfries and Galloway Regs., **Scot.**; hgst. point 733 m.

Loyalty Is., S. **Pac. Oc.**; included in Fr. administration of New Caledonia; copra; lgst. Is. Maré, Lifou, Uvéa; a. *c.* 2,100 km².

Lozère, dep., S.E. **France**; traversed by Cevennes mtns.; cap. Mende; a. 5,170 km²; p. (1982) 74,200.

Lualaba, R., **Zaïre**, central **Africa**; rises nr. Lubumbashi in Shaba prov., flows N. circa 800 km to Kikondja, where joined by R. Lufira to form R. Zaïre; name also applied to main stream of R. Zaïre as far downstream as Ponthierville.

Luanda, c. cap. of **Angola**; pt. on Atl. Oc.; exp. coffee, cotton, palm prod.; industl. ctr.; foodstuffs, tobacco, clothing, plastics; oil refining; hydroelectric power; p. (est. 1982) 1,200,000.

Luang Prabang, c., N.W. **Laos**; at confluence of Mekong and Kahn Rs.; rubber, rice, teak; former royal cap.; p. (est. 1970) 25,000.

Lubbock, c., N.W. Texas, **USA**; on Double Mountain fork of Brazos R.; ctr. of cotton-growing a.; p. (1980) 174,000 (c.), 212,000 (met. a.).

Lübeck, c., pt. of Schleswig-Holstein, **W. Germany**; on Baltic Sea at mouth of Trave R.; cath.; shipbldg., machin., chemicals, textiles, iron, foodstuffs; birthplace of Thomas Mann; p. (1983) 216,100.

Lublin, c., cap. of L. prov., E. **Poland**; motor vehicle and elec. engin.; agr. tr. and processing; cultural ctr., univ.; cas.; p. (est. 1983) 320,000.

Lubumbashi (Elizabethville), t., Shaba, **Zaïre**; copper-mng. ctr.; p. (1982) 451,332.

Lucca, c., cap. of L. prov., Tuscany, **Italy**; cath., churches, palaces; noted for olive oil, pasta, wine; silk, cotton, jute, tobacco inds.; p. (1981) 91,246.

Lucena, t., Córdoba, **Spain**; olive oil, ceramics, gilt metals, wine; p. (1970) 27,920.

Lucenec, t., **ČSSR**; on Hungarian border; magnesite, textiles, sawmilling; p. (est. 1968) 20,156.

Lucerne (Luzern), can., **Switzerland**; agr., pastoral, vineyards; oil refinery projected at Schötz/Ettiswil; cap. Lucerne; a. 1,492 km²; p. (1980) 296,159.

Lucerne (Luzern), c., cap. of L. can., **Switzerland**; at N.W. end of L. Lucerne; aluminium gds., sewing machin.; tourist ctr.; p. (1979) 63,200.

Lucerne, L., **Switzerland**; also known as L. of the Four Cantons; length 37 km; a. 70 km².

Luchon or **Bagnères-de-Luchon**, resort in Fr. Pyrenees, Haute-Garonne dep., S. **France**; warm sulphur springs; winter sports ctr.

Luchow. *See* **Zuzhou.**

Luckenwalde, t., **E. Germany**; on R. Nuthe; textiles, footwear, machin., wood and metals, chemicals; p. (est. 1970) 28,984.

Lucknow, c., cap. of Uttar Pradesh st., N. **India**; on R. Gumti (trib. of Ganges); educational and cultural ctr. with textile inds.; rly. ctr.; scene of 1857 mutiny; p. (1981) 895,721 (c.), 1,007,604 (met. a.).

Lüda, special mun., S. Liaoning prov., **China**; comprising Port Arthur Naval Base District and the pts. of Port Arthur and Talien (Dairen); chemicals, machin., shipbldg., textiles; p. (est. 1970) 4,000,000.

Lüdenscheid, t., N. Rhine–Westphalia, **W. Germany**; metal mngs., domestic hardware; supplied structures for first Zeppelins; p. (1983) 73,800.

Lüderitz, t., **Namibia**; rly. pt. on desert cst.; diamonds, fishing; p. (est. 1970) 6,642.

Ludhiana, t., Punjab st., N.W. **India**; S. of Sutlej R.; industl. ctr.; hosiery, knitwear; p. (1981) 607,052.

Ludlow, t., South Shrops., **Eng.**; agr. mkt.; agr. engin.; cas.

Ludwigsburg, t. Baden-Württemberg, **W. Germany**; N. of Stuttgart; cas.; textiles, foodstuffs, machin., toys; p. (1983) 79,000.

Ludwigshafen, t., Rhine-Palatinate, **W. Germany**; on R. Rhine, opposite Mannheim; chemicals, marine diesel engines, metallurgy, glass; R. pt. and rly. junc.; oil pipeline from Rotterdam under construction; p. (1983) 157,400.

Lugano, t., Ticino can., **Switzerland**; on L. Lugano; tourist resort; p. (est. 1978) 28,600.

Lugano, L., lies at S. foot of Alps between **Switzerland** and **Italy**; attractive scenery, tourism; a. 49 km².

Lugansk (Voroshilovgrad), industl. t., Ukrainian SSR, **USSR**; S. of R. Donets in Donbas region; impt. rly. engin. factories; textiles; p. (est. 1980) 469,000.

Lugnaquilla, mtn., loftiest summit in Wicklow, **R.o.I.**; 927 m.

Lugo, c., cap. of L. prov., N.W. **Spain**; in Galicia, on Miño R.; in fertile agr. a.; cath.; p. (1981) 405,361 (prov.).

Lukuga, intermittent outlet of L. Tanganyika, **Zaïre**, linking with R. Zaïre.

Luleå, spt., N. **Sweden**, cap. of Norrbotten co.; on Lule R. at head of G. of Bothnia; iron ore; smelting plant, engin.; p. (1983) 66,512.

Luluabourg. *See* **Kananga.**

Lulworth Cove, sm. inlet, Dorset, **Eng.**; formed by sea breaching limestone cliffs and eroding clay behind; tourism.

Lund, t., S. **Sweden**; 16 km N.E. of Malmö; 11th cent. Romanesque cath.; univ.; publishing ctr.; p. (1983) 80,458.

Lundy I., Bristol Channel, N. Devon, **Eng.**; 19 km N.W. of Hartland Point; wildlife sanctuary; about 5 km long and 1 km wide.

Lune, R., Cumbria, **Eng.**; flows 72 km to Irish Sea; attractive valley.

Lüneburg, t., Lower Saxony, **W. Germany**; on Ilmenau R., S.E. of Hamburg; rly. junc., R. pt.; iron wks., chemicals; dates from 8th cent.; p. (1983) 61,100.

Lüneburg Heath, Lower Saxony, **W. Germany**; lies to S. of Lüneburg; glacial outwash plain of sands and gravels; heather, scrub; some agr. but infertile acid soils.

Lünen, t., N. Rhine–Westphalia, **W. Germany**; in Ruhr conurb.; coal, metallurgy, glass, wood; R. pt. and rly. ctr.; p. (1983) 85,300.

Lunéville, t., Meurthe-et-Moselle dep., N.E. **France**; in Lorraine, on R. Meurthe; 18th cent. château; p. (1975) 24,700.

Lungi, t., Sierra Leone, W. **Africa**; nr. Freetown; only civil airport in st.

Luoyang (Loyang), c., Henan prov., **China**; industl.; ball bearing and mng. machin.; lge. car and tractor plant, oil refinery, textiles; p. (est. 1983) 999,000.

Lupata Gorge, **Moçambique**, E. **Africa**; narrow pass occupied by R. Zambezi.

Lurgan, t., Craigavon, **N. Ireland**; textiles, tobacco mftg.; merging with Portadown to form new c. of Craigavon; p. (1981) 20,991.

Lusaka, c., cap. of **Zambia**; comm. and admin. ctr.; at junc. of routes to Tanzania and Malawi; motor assembly, footwear, metal prods., clothing; p. (1980) 538,469.

Lushun. See **Lüda**.

Luton, t., l. gov. dist., Beds., **Eng.**; in Chiltern Hills nr. source of R. Lea; motor vehicles, engin., hat mkg., aircraft, gear instruments, chemicals; expanded t.; p. (1981) 164,049.

Lutong, main oil pt. of Sarawak, E. **Malaysia**; oil refining.

Lutsk, c., Ukrainian SSR, **USSR**; pt. on Styr R.; one of oldest ts. in Volhynia; coal mng., machin.; architectural monuments; p. (est. 1980) 146,000.

Luxembourg, prov., S.E. **Belgium**; on Fr. border; wooded and hilly; a. 2,784 km²; cap. Arlon; p. (1981) 221,926.

Luxembourg, grand duchy, W. **Europe**; lies between Belgium, W. Germany, and France; divided into 12 admin. cans.; official language French though German frequently used; well wooded, most of a. over 300 m; economic prosperity based upon iron and steel inds. and lge. deposits of iron-ore; agr. and cattle raising impt.; sm. size of home market makes L. keen protagonist of European economic unity and cap. of L. contains many European organisations; tourist ind. based upon scenery and cas. ts.; a. 2,587 km²; p. (est. 1984) 363,000.

Luxembourg, c., cap. of grand duchy of **Luxembourg**; historic t., perched above valleys of Alzette and Petrusse Rs.; cath.; seat of European Court of Justice; p. (1981) 78,900.

Luxor, v., Upper **Egypt**; on E. bank of Nile; site of Thebes; tomb of Tutankhamun; p. (est. 1970) 84,600.

Luxulyan, St. Austell, Cornwall, **Eng.**; proposed site for nuclear power sta., fiercely opposed.

Luzon, I., lgst. and most N. of **Philippines**; mtn. ranges; fertile Cagayan valley; rice, sugar cane, cotton, coffee, hemp, tobacco; mineral deposits; cap. Manila; a. 104,688 km²; p. (1970) 16,669,724.

L'vov, c., Ukrainian SSR, **USSR**; founded 13th cent.; univ., caths.; major industl. ctr.; petroleum refining; natural gas nearby; p. (est. 1980) 676,000.

Lyalpur, t., W. Punjab, **Pakistan**; univ.; cotton, chemicals, fertilisers; p. (est. 1969) 854,000.

Lydd, Shepway, Kent, **Eng.**; anc. t. on Romney marsh, at edge of Dungeness shingle; name given to explosive lyddite mnf. here; airport; p. (1981) 4,721.

Lydda, c., Israel, S.E. of Tel-Aviv; major airport; mentioned in the Bible and reputed birthplace of St. George; p. (est. 1971) 31,200.

Lydney, t., Gloucs., **Eng.**; in Forest of Dean; spt. on Severn estuary; timber imports; new lt. inds.

Lyme Regis, spt., West Dorset, **Eng.**; on bdy. between Devon and Dorset; holiday resort; p. (1981) 3,447.

Lymington, t., Hants, **Eng.**; on the Solent; ferry to I. of Wight; abbey; p. (1981) 38,698.

Lymm, t., Cheshire, **Eng.**; 8 km W. of Altrincham; mainly residtl.; p. (1981) 10,364.

Lynchburg, c., Va., **USA**; on James R. in foothills of Appalachians; tobacco ctr.; p. (1980) 66,743 (c.), 153,260 (met. a.).

Lyndhurst, v., Hants, **Eng.**; recognised as cap. of New Forest; tourism.

Lynemouth, nr. Blyth, Northumberland, **Eng.**; aluminium smelter.

Lynn, industl. c., Mass., **USA**; on Mass. Bay; footwear, elec. appliances; Mary Baker Eddy lived here; p. (1980) 78,471.

Lynton, t., North Devon, **Eng.**; 27 km W. of Minehead on Bristol Channel; tourist ctr. for Exmoor; sm. harbour of Lynmouth 130 m below; devastating flood of R. Lyn 1952; p. (1981) 2,037.

Lyons, c., cap. of Rhône dep., **France**; at confluence of Rs. Saône and Rhône; silk, rayon, chemicals, engin., heavy lorries; oil refinery nearby; univ.; world ctr. for cancer research; p. (1982) 418,476 (c.), 1,220,844 (met. a.).

Lytham St. Annes, t., N. Lancs., **Eng.**; on N. cst. of Ribble estuary, 6 km S. of Blackpool holiday ctr.; p. (1981) 39,707.

Lyttleton, spt., S.I., **N.Z.**; on N. cst. of Banks peninsula; imp. pt.; p. (1976) 3,327.

M

Ma'an, t., S. **Jordan**, terminus of rly. through Amman to Beirut; Hijaz rail line to Medina; p. (est. 1971) 12,000.

Maas, R., Dutch name for the R. Meuse after it has entered the Neth.

Maastricht, t., cap. of Limburg prov., **Neth.**; on R. Maas; pottery, glass, textiles, brewing; p. (1982) 111,487.

Mablethorpe, t., East Lindsey, Lincs., **Eng.**; holiday resort; p. (1981) 7,456.

Macao, Portuguese col., S.E. **China**; increased indep. since 1975; gambling, tourism, recreation for Hong Kong; new deep water port; rapid recent industl. growth (toys, textiles and transistors) with influx of capital resulting from uncertainty over the future of Hong Kong; oldest European col. in Far East (1557); a. 16 km²; p. (est. 1984) 350,000.

Macapá, c., cap. of Amapá st., **Brazil**; at mouth of R. Amazon; rubber, cattle tr.; p. (est. 1980) 135,100.

MacArthur (**Ormoc**), t., W. Leyte, **Philippines**; pt. and agr. ctr., exp. hemp, rice; p. (est. 1970) 85,900.

Macclesfield, t., l. gov. dist., Cheshire, **Eng.**; at foot of Pennines, 16 km S. of Stockport; on R. Bollin; mkt., textiles, clothing, paper prods., engin.; expanded t.; p. (1981) 149,003 (dist.).

Macdonald Is., terr. of Australia, **Antarctica**.

Macdonnell Range, mtns., N.T., **Australia**; highest part of desert tableland, centrally situated within the continent; some gold and mica mines, but development hampered by aridity and isolation; highest alt. 1,500 m.

Macduff, spt., burgh, Banff and Buchan, **Scot.**; 3 km E. of Banff; fishing; p. (1981) 3,894.

Macedonia, region of Balkan peninsula, covering parts of Greece, Yugoslavia, and Bulgaria.

Macedonia, dist., **Greece**; mtnous.; cereals, tobacco; chromium; cap. and pt. Salonika; a. 33,945 km²; p. (1981) 2,121,953.

Macedonia, constituent rep., **Yugoslavia**; agr.; chromium; cap. Skopje; a. 27,436 km²; p. (1971) 1,647,104.

Maceio, spt. cap. of Alagôas st., **Brazil**; cotton, sugar, tobacco, soap, sawmills, distilleries; p. (est. 1980) 389,800.

Macerata, t., cap. of M. prov., **Italy**; cath. univ.; terracotta, glass, chemicals; p. (1981) 43,782.

Macgillicuddy's Reeks, mtns., Kerry, **R.o.I.**; highest peak, Carrantuohil, 1,041 m.

Machala, t., Tibet, **China**; hgst. coalmine in world.

Machilipatnam (**Bandar, Masulipatnam**), spt., Andhra Pradesh, **India**; on Coromandel cst.; cotton mftg., rice; p. (1981) 138,530.

Machynlleth, t., Powys, **Wales**; on R. Dovey; clothing; tourism; p. (1981) 1,768.

Macintyre, R., N.S.W., **Australia**; forms border between Queensland and N.S.W.; trib. of R. Darling; 645 km. long.

Mackay, spt., Queensland, **Australia**; "Sugar Cap. of Australia"; artificial deep-water pt. for sugar exp.; p. (1976) 31,522.

Mackenzie, R., N.W. Terr., **Canada**; lgst. in N. America; rises in Rocky mtns. as Athabaska, flows into Athabaska L., leaves as Slave R., thence into Gr. Slave L., below which it is known as Mackenzie R., across arctic plains to Beaufort Sea; 4,000 km. long.

Mackenzie Mtns., N.W. Terr., **Canada**; range of Rockies, still much unexplored; game preserve; max. alt. 2,760 m.

Mâcon, t., cap. of Saône-et-Loire dep., **France**; on R. Saône; Burgundy wines; p. (1982) 39,866.

Macon, c., Ga., **USA**; on Ocmulgee R.; industl. and shipping ctr. for agr. a., cotton, livestock; cotton mftg.; p. (1980) 117,000 (c.), 254,000 (met. a.).

Macquarie, I., Australian I., **S. Pac.**; 1,440 km S.E. of Tasmania; rich in wildlife, Tasmanian st. reserve (1972).

Macquarie, R., N.S.W., **Australia**; trib. of R. Darling; 960 km long.

Macroom, t., Cork, **R.o.I.**; on R. Sullane; agr.; fishing; p. (1971) 2,256.

Madagascar (formerly **Malagasy Rep.**), I. off Moçambique; former Fr. col.; distinctive evolution of flora and fauna; p. engaged in agr.; rice staple food, coffee and cloves main exp.; inds. based on processing; offshore petroleum deposits; new refinery at ch. pt. of Toamasina; cap. Antananarivo; a. 587,041 km.²; p. (est. 1983) 9,400,000.

Madang, t., **Papua New Guinea;** entrepôt pt. on N. cst.; international airpt.; p. (1971) 16,865.

Madeira, R., **Brazil;** trib. of Amazon; with Mamoré R., c. 3,200 km long.

Madeira Is., volcanic archipelago, Atl. Oc., part of met. **Portugal;** partial autonomy by regional gov. (1977); wine, sugar, fruits; tourism; cap. Funchal on Madeira I., lgst. of gr.; a. 790 km²; p. (1981) 252,844.

Madhya Pradesh, st., **India;** absorbed sts. Bhopal, Vindhya Pradesh, Madhya Bharat, 1956; rice, jute, pulses, oilseeds, cotton; forests; manganese, coal, marble, limestone; cotton textile mftg.; cap. Bhopai; a. 443,452 km²; p. (1981) 52,178,844.

Madinat ash Sha'b (Al Ittihad), cap. of **Democratic Rep. of Yemen;** N.W. of Aden.

Madison, c., cap. of Wis., **USA;** educational and admin. ctr.; univ.; mnfs. agr. tools, footwear; p. (1980) 171,000 (c.), 324,000 (met. a.).

Madiun, t., Java, **Indonesia;** agr. and comm. ctr.; engin.; p. (1980) 150,502.

Madras, c., cap. of Tamil Nadu st., **India;** spt. on Bay of Bengal, on Coromandel cst.; cath., univ.; comm. and mftg. ctr.; textile mills, tanneries, potteries, chemical plants; oil refinery projected; p. (1981) 3,276,622.

Madras. See Tamil Nadu.

Madre de Dios, R., **Bolivia;** trib. of R. Madeira; rises in Peru; 960 km long.

Madrid, c., cap. of **Spain;** and of M. prov. on Manzanares R.; stands at 665 m (highest cap. in Europe) in vast open plains; although remote with relatively few inds. is ctr. of Spanish admin. and communications; univ., cath., Prado gallery; printing, publishing; p. (1981) 3,158,794.

Madura, I., **Indonesia;** off N.E. Java; dry climate, limestone soils; arable and pastoral agr.; salt; a. 4,584 km²; p. c. 2,000,000.

Madurai, t., Tamil Nadu, **India;** univ., impt. textile ctr.; p. (1981) 820,891 (c.), 907,732 (met. a.).

Maebashi, c., central Honshu, **Japan;** N.W. Kanto plain; silk textile ctr.; p. (est. 1984) 265,169.

Maelstrom, tidewater whirlpool, in Lofoten Is., **Norway.**

Maentwrog, v., Gwynedd, N. **Wales;** in Vale of Ffestiniog, 3 km E. of Ffestiniog; ch. hydro-electric power sta. in N. Wales.

Maesteg, t., Ogwr, Mid Glamorgan, **Wales;** dormitory t. for steel wks. at Pt. Talbot; coal mng., cosmetics; p. (1981) 20,888.

Mafeking, (Mafikeng) t., N.E. Cape Prov., **Bophuthaswana S. Africa;** famous siege at outbreak of Boer War 1899-1900; p. (est. 1971) 6,493.

Magadan, spt., **RSFSR;** on N. side of Sea of Okhotsk; marine engin.; fishing; p. (est. 1980) 124,000.

Magadi, L., Kenya; in Gr. Rift valley; carbonate of soda extracted.

Magdalena, R., **Colombia;** forms basis of inland navigation system, opening up interior; 1,600 km long.

Magdeburg, c., Magdeburg, **E. Germany;** on R. Elbe; cath.; beet-sugar ctr., sugar-refineries; chemicals, steel, mng. machin., heavy engin.; route ctr. and lge. inland pt.; p. (1983) 289,075.

Magelang, t., Java, **Indonesia;** tr. ctr.; tannery; p. (1971) 110,308.

Magellan, strait, between Tierra del Fuego and Chile, separates Atl. and Pac. Ocs.

Maggiore, L., N. **Italy-Switzerland;** a. 212 km²; contains Borromean Is.; tourist resort.

Magherafelt, l. gov. dist., centred on t. of M., N. **Ireland;** agr. a. bordering L. Neagh; (1981) 30,656 (dist.), 5,044 (t.).

Maghreb, collective name given to Arabic-speaking countries bordering Mediterranean in N. Africa, inc. Algeria, Morocco and Tunisia.

Magnet Mtn., S. Urals, **RSFSR;** very rich deposit of magnetite iron ore; smelted at Magnitogorsk, and in Kuzbas region.

Magnitogorsk, c., **RSFSR;** in S. Urals, on R. Ural; sited on magnetite deposits; metallurgical ctr.; oil pipeline from Shkapovo in Bashkira; p. (est. 1980) 410,000.

Mahajanga (Majunga) t., **Madagascar;** second t. and pt.; meat conserves, sacks, cement; p. (1975) 65,864.

Mahalla El Kubra. See El Mahalla el Kubra.

Mahanadi, R., **India;** flows from Orissa to Bay of Bengal; forms extensive delta; sugar and rice growing; 832 km long.

Maharashtra, st., **W. India;** on Arabian Sea; ch. ts. Bombay (cap.), Poona, Nagpur; fertile lava soils; impt. cotton-growing dist. of Deccan; a. 307,477 km²; p. (1981) 62,784,171.

Mahé, former Fr. prov., S. **India;** united with India 1954; cap. Mahé.

Mahon, spt., cap. of Minorca, Balearic Is., **Spain;** p. (1981) 21,624.

Maidenhead, t., Windsor and Maidenhead, Berks., **Eng.;** on R. Thames, 14 km above Windsor; residtl.; p. (1981) 49,038; See Windsor.

Maidens, The, gr. of dangerous rocks off Larne cst., N. Ireland.

Maidstone, co. t., l. gov. dist., Kent, **Eng.;** on R. Medway; regional ctr.; brewing, paper, agr. tools, confectionery, timber inds.; p. (1981) 130,053 (dist.).

Maiduguri, t., **Nigeria;** cap. Bornu st.; on rly. from Bornu; mkt.; p. (est. 1975) 189,000.

Maikop, c. cap. of Adygei aut. oblast, Krasnodar terr., **RSFSR;** oilfields nearby; oil-refineries, woodwkg., food-processing; p. (est. 1980) 130,000.

Main, R., **W. Germany;** joins Rhine opposite Mainz; linked with Danube via Ludwig canal; and newer Rhine-Main-Danube canal creating waterway from N. Sea to Black Sea of 3,500 km; 448 km long.

Main Range, central mtns. of **W. Malaysia;** rise to over 2,100 m.

Maine, st., New England, **USA;** Pine tree St.; admitted to Union 1820; st. flower White Pine Tassel, st. bird Chickadee; mtnous., with much forest; potatoes, paper, pulp, metals, woollens, shoes, processed foods; cap. Augusta; ch. spt. Portland; a. 86,027 km²; p. (1980) 1,125,000.

Maine-et-Loire, dep., **France;** agr. vineyards; cap. Angers; a. 7,280 km²; p. (1982) 676,100.

Mainland. (1) I., lgst. of Shetlands, **Scot.** (2) I., lgst. of Orkneys, see Pomona.

Mainz, c., cap of Rhineland-Palatinate, **W. Germany;** at confluence of Rs. Rhine and Main; R. pt.; cath., univ., cas.; cement, engin., optical glass, food-processing; p. (1983) 186,400.

Maisons-Alfort, t., **France;** S.E. sub. of Paris; p. (1982) 51,591.

Maitland, t., N.S.W., **Australia;** on R. Hunter, nr. Newcastle; ctr. for fertile Hunter Valley; coal mng. decreasing; p. (1976) 36,030.

Majes, R., S. **Peru;** valley a. site of projected irrigation scheme; 240 km. long.

Majorca (Mallorca), lgst of Balearic Is., **Spain;** major tourist ctr.; ch. t. and pt. Palma; a. 3,639 km²; p. (1970) 460,030.

Majunga. See Mahajanga.

Makalu, mtn., Nepal and Tibet, **China;** fifth hgst. mtn. in world; part of Himalayas; alt. 8,486 m.

Makasar. See Ujung Pandang.

Makasar, strait, **Indonesia;** separates Kalimantan from Sulawesi; 384 km wide.

Makeyevka, c., Ukrainian SSR, **USSR;** in Donets basin; metallurgical and coal-mng. ctr.; p. (est. 1980) 439,000.

Makhachkala, c., cap. of Dagestan ASSR, **RSFSR;** pt. on Caspian Sea; comm. and industl. ctr.; oil refineries linked by pipeline to Grozny fields; p. (est. 1980) 261,000.

Makó, t., **Hungary;** on Maros R., nr. Romanian bdy.; comm. and agr. ctr.; p. (1966) 29,600.

Makran, dist., **Pakistan** and **Iran;** coastal dist.; lowland route between India and Middle E.

Makurdi, t. **Nigeria,** W. Africa; on R. Benue; mkt. for palm prod., groundnuts; rly. bridge across R. Benue.

Makwar, v., **Sudan,** N.E. Africa; on Blue Nile; site of Sennar Dam.

Malabar Coast, India; name applied to W. cst. of India from Goa to southern tip of peninsula at C. Comorin; sand dunes backed by lagoons; coastlands intensively cultivated, rice, spices, rubber, coconuts; ch. pt. Cochin.

Malabo (Santa Isabel), cap of **Equatorial Guinea;** on Marcias Nguema I.; ch. pt. for I., exp. cacao; comm. and financial ctr.; p. (1970) 19,500.

Malacca, st., S.W. **W. Malaysia;** originally part of Brit. Straits Settlements (q.v.); cap. M.; a. 1,658 km²; p. (1980) 464,754.

Malacca, strait, separates Sumatra, **Indonesia,** from **W. Malaysia;** 38 km wide at narrowest point; international routeway but attempts by Malaysia and Indonesia to claim it as territorial water.

Maladetta, with **Pic d'Anéto,** hgst. point in Pyrenees, **Spain;** alt. 3,408 m.

Malaga, c. cap. of Malaga prov., **Spain**; in Andalusia on Bay of M.; impt. spt.; olive oil, wine, fruit; oil pipeline from Puertollano refinery; winter resort; cath., citadel; birthplace of Picasso; p. (1981) 502,228.

Malagassy Rep. *See* **Madagascar.**

Malakoff, t. S.W. sub. of Paris, Hauts-de-Seine, **France**; residtl. and also industl.; p. (1975) 34,215.

Malang, t., Java, **Indonesia**; ctr. of fertile agr. basin; p. (1971) 422,428.

Mälar, L., S.E. **Sweden**; connected with Baltic by Södertelge canal; 1,260 Is.; length 128 km; a. 1,235 km².

Malatya, c., cap. of M. prov., central **Turkey**; at foot of Taurus mtns.; ctr. of rich agr. a.; fruit, opium; p. (1979) 175,460.

Malawi, land locked rep., Central **Africa**; L. Malawi to S. and E.; tropical climate modified by alt.; few natural resources; economy based on agr.; one of most fertile soils in Africa but only 50 per cent cultivated; exp. tobacco and tea; new cap at Lilongwe (old cap. Zomba); a. 117,614 km²; p. (est. 1983) 6,618,400.

Malawi, L., central **Africa**; southward extension of the Gr. Rift valley; c. 450 m a.s.l.; 560 km by 64 km; drains by R. Shire into R. Zambezi; petroleum under L. bed.

Malaya. *See* **Malaysia, West.**

Malay Archipelago, lge. gr. of Is. extending 7,680 km from Nicobar Is. in Bay of Bengal to Solomon Is. in Pac.; inc. Sumatra, Java, Kalimantan, Sulawesi, Philippines, New Guinea, Bismarck archipelago.

Malaysia, East, part of **Fed. of Malaysia**; inc. Sarawak and Sabah (formerly Brit. N. Borneo); less developed than W. Malaysia; p. concentrated on cst; hill tribes engaged in hunting in interior; oil major exp., exploration off cst.; separated from W. Malaysia by S. China Sea; a. 200,971 km²; p. (1968) 1,582,000.

Malaysia, Federation of, indep. federation (1963), S.E. **Asia**; member of Brit. Commonwealth; inc. W. Malaysia (Malaya) and E. Malaysia (Borneo sts. of Sarawak and Sabah); cap. Kuala Lumpur; a. 334,110 km²; p. (est. 1984) 15,204,000.

Malaysia, West (Malaya), part of **Federation of Malaysia**; consists of wide peninsula S. of Thailand; most developed in W.; world's leading producer of natural rubber, grown in plantations; oil palm and pineapples also grown; world's leading exporter of tin; 35 per cent of p. Chinese; a. 131,588 km²; p. (1968) 8,899,000.

Malbork (Marienburg), t., Gdansk, **Poland**; R. pt. on Nogat R.; cas.; p. (1970) 30,900.

Malden, t., Mass., **USA**; mftg. sub. of Boston; rubber gds., hosiery, furniture; p. (1980) 53,386.

Maldive Is., indep. rep. (1968) former Brit., prot., **Indian Oc.**; chain of coral atolls c. 640 km S.W. of Sri Lanka; 1,067 Is., 193 inhabited; economy based on fishing (bonito and tuna); dried fish main exp.; modernisation of fishing with Japanese aid; coconuts, copra, coconut oil, coir, cowrie shells; cap. Male; former Brit. air base on Gan. I. (until 1976); a. 298 km²; p. (est. 1981) 200,000.

Maldon, t., l. gov. dist., Essex, **Eng.**; sm. pt. at head of Blackwater estuary; agr. machin., steel window-frames, flour-milling; p. (1981) 47,726 (dist.).

Malegaon, t., Maharashtra, **India**; in Satmala Hills N.E. of Bombay; p. (1971) 191,847.

Malham Cove, North Yorks., **Eng.**; in Craven dist. of N. Pennines, 16 km N.W. of Skipton; semicircular amphitheatre limestone cliffs from base of which emerges R. Aire.

Mali, Rep. of, W. Africa; landlocked st.; former Fr. col. of Soudan; dry semi-desert climate in S.; extends into Sahara desert in N.; badly affected by Sahelian drought since 1971; few natural resources; nomadic pastoralist p. in N.; only 20 per cent of a. cultivable; livestock basis of inds. (hides, wool, etc.) and exps.; many minerals but not exploited; cap. Bamako; a. 1,204,350 km²; p. (est. 1983) 7,528,000.

Malinda, t., **Kenya**; growing tourist resort on Indian Ocean cst.

Malin Head, Donegal, **R.o.I.**; most N. point.

Malines (Mechelen), t., **Belgium**; on R. Dyle; cath.; rly. ctr.; textiles, furniture; once famous for lace; p. (1981) 77,269.

Malling, t., Kent, **Eng.**; 5 km W. of Maidstone; fruit, chemicals. *See* **Tonbridge.**

Mallow, mkt. t., Cork, **R.o.I.**; on R. Blackwater; agr. fishing, flour mills, tanneries, condensed

milk, dehydrated foods; p. (1981) 6,572.

Malmesbury, t., North Wilts., **Eng.**; anc. hilltop t. in Cotswolds; mkt.; abbey; elec. engin.; birthplace of Thomas Hobbes; p. (1981) 2,552.

Malmö, c., spt., S. **Sweden**; on the Sound opposite Copenhagen; third lgst. c. in cty.; naval and comm. pt.; shipbldg., textiles, machin.; founded in 12th cent.; proposed terminus of tunnel to Denmark; p. (1983) 229,380 (c.), 454,131 (met. a.).

Malta, indep. st. within Br. C. (1964), rep. (1974); I. in Mediterranean, 93 km S. of Sicily; strategic location; former British naval and military base; agr. ch. occupation with ship-repairing at dry-docks of Valletta; sm.-scale inds. growing; tourism exploits Mediterranean climate; major airport at Luqa; awarded George Cross for bravery in second world war; cap. Valletta; a. 316 km²; p. (est. 1984) 380,000. (inc. Gozo and Comino).

Maltby, t., Ryedale, South Yorks., **Eng.**; p. (1981) 16,749.

Malton, mkt. t., North Yorks., **Eng.**; on R. Derwent, in S.W. of Vale of Pickering; brewing; p. (1981) 4,143.

Malvern, t., Hereford and Worcs., **Eng.**; at E. foot of Malvern hills; spa; annual dramatic festival; Elgar lived here; p. (1981) 30,187.

Malvern Hills, narrow ridge forming bdy. between Worcs. and Hereford, **Eng.**; rises very abruptly from Severn valley to cover 300 m between Malvern and Bromsberrow; moorland, woodland on lower slopes; now forms l. gov. dist.; p. (1981) 81,875.

Mammoth Cave, Ky., **USA**; to S. of Green R. in hilly forested parkland; spectacular limestone formations (stalactites, stalagmites), lakes and rivers (e.g. Echo R., 110 m below surface) in avenues aggregating 240 km long; included in Nat. Park. [1,920 km long.

Mamoré, R., N. **Bolivia** and **Brazil**; rises in Andes;

Mam Soul, mtn., Kyle of Lochalsh and Inverness, **Scot.**; alt. 1,178 m.

Manacle Rocks, dangerous reef off cst. of Cornwall, **Eng.**; 12 km S. of Falmouth.

Manacor, t., Majorca, **Spain**; artificial pearls, wine, stalactite caves of Drach and Hams; p. (1981) 24,153.

Managua, c., cap. of **Nicaragua**; on S. shore of L. Managua; industl. and comm. ctr.; oil refining, agr. processing, textiles, steel; univ.; 48 km from pt. Puerto Somoza; violent earthquake Dec. 1972; p. (1979) 608,020.

Managua, L., **Nicaragua**; second lgst. L. in Central America.

Manāmah, Al, cap. and ch. pt. **Bahrain,** Persian G.; free pt., comm. ctr.; declining pearl-fishing ind.; linked by causeway to internat. airpt.; p. (1971) 89,728.

Manáus (Manaos), c., cap. of Amazonas st., N.W. **Brazil**; on Río Negro nr. confluence with Amazon; impt. R. pt., airport.; oil refinery; former rubber ctr.; in free zone (10,360 km²) recently set up to encourage development in Amazonas; new inds. include steel wks., oil refinery; boom now far exceeds 19th century rubber boom; tourism; internat. airpt.; p. (est. 1980) 482,600.

Manche, dep., N.W. **France**; on English Channel; agr. and dairying; cap. Saint Lô; ch. pt. Cherbourg; a. 6,410 km²; p. (1982) 482,600.

Manchester, c., Gtr. Manchester, **Eng.**; on R. Irwell; terminus of Manchester Ship Canal; but only 1 dock out of 8 left open; ctr. of cotton and manmade fibre textile inds.; heavy, lt., and elec. engin., machine tools, petro-chemicals, dyestuffs, pharmaceutical gds.; univ.; comm., cultural and recreational cap. of N.W. Eng.; p. (1981) 449,168 (met. dist.), 2,594,778 (Greater Manchester).

Manchester, t., Conn., **USA**; textiles (silk); p. (1980) 49,761.

Manchester, c., N.H., **USA**; at Amoskeag falls, on the Merrimac R.; textiles, footwear, machin.; p. (1980) 90,336 (c.), 160,767 (met. a.).

Manchester Ship Canal, ship canal, Cheshire/ Merseyside/Gtr. Manchester, **Eng.**; joins Manchester to Mersey estuary at Eastham; can be used by ocean steamers; 57 km long.

Manchuria. *See* **North-East China.**

Mandalay, c., **Burma**; on R. Irrawaddy, 640 km N. of Rangoon; former cap.; lost importance with rise of Irrawaddy delta; many temples, palaces; p. (est. 1977) 458,000.

Manfredonia, mkt. t., Foggia, **Italy**; fish. pt.; cath.; p. (1981) 52,674.

Mangalore, spt., Karnataka, **India**; exp. coffee, coconuts, rice, spices, fertiliser; p. (1971) 165,174 (c), 215,122 (met. a.).

Mangere, N.I., **N.Z.**; 21 km S. of Auckland; international airport (opened 1965).

Mangla Dam, Pakistan; world's lgst. earth-filled dam, on Jhelum R., part of Indus Basin irrigation scheme.

Manhattan, I., N.Y., **U.S.A.**; at mouth of Hudson R.; a. 57 km²; forms major part of bor. of Manhattan of N.Y. City.

Manila, c., S.W. Luzon, **Philippines**; leading c. and ch. pt. of Is.; entrepôt tr.; modern skyscrapers; univ., cath.; major airpt.; p. (1975) 1,438,252.

Manipur, new st. (1972), E. **India**; borders Burma; former princely st.; cap. Imphal; a. 22,274 km²; p. (est. 1972) 1,070,000.

Manisa, c., cap. of M. prov., W. **Turkey**; agr. ctr.; mineral deposits nearby; p. (1970) 70,022.

Manitoba, prov., **Canada**; wheat, rich mineral deposits, fisheries; diverse inds.; cap. Winnipeg; a. 650,090 km²; p. (1976) 1,021,506.

Manitowac, c., Wis., **USA**; on L. Mich.; shipbldg., aluminium wks., flour mills; p. (1980) 32,547.

Manizales, c., cap. of Caldas, **Colombia**; at 2,155 m in the Central Cordillera; in rich coffee a.; route ctr.; p. (1973) 205,780.

Mannar, G., with Palk Strait separates **India** from **Sri Lanka.**

Mannheim, c., Baden-Württemberg, **W. Germany**; major R. pt. at confluence of Rs. Neckar and Rhine, opposite Ludwigshafen; heavy and lt. inds., notably precision instruments, machin., vehicles; p. (1983) 299,700.

Manono, t. **Zaïre**; ctr. for tin-mng.; foundries.

Manresa, industl. t., N.E. **Spain**; in Catalonia; textiles; associated with Ignatius of Loyola; place of pilgrimage; p. (1981) 64,745.

Mansfield, t., l. gov. dist., Notts., **Eng.**; on E. flank of Pennines, 19 km N. of Nottingham; coal mng., sand-quarrying, textiles, footwear, metal boxes, machin.; p. (1981) 99,349 (l. gov. dist.).

Mansfield, t., Ohio, **USA**; machin. farm tools, paper, rubber gds.; p. (1980) 53,927 (t.), 131,205 (met. a.).

Mansfield Woodhouse, t., Notts., **Eng.**; 3 km N. of Mansfield; stone quarries; Roman remains; p. (1981) 26,725.

Mansûra, c., Lower **Egypt**; pt. on Nile; cotton mftg.; univ. proposed; p. (1976) 259,387.

Mantua, c., cap. of M. prov., N. **Italy**; on R. Mincio; comm. and agr. ctr.; old fortfd. c.; p. (1981) 60,866.

Manukau, c., N.I., **N.Z.**; new c. (1965) formed from amalgamation of suburban communities around Auckland; p. (est. 1979) 143,500, now lgst. c. of N.Z.

Manukau Harbour, N.I., **N.Z.**; lge. shallow inlet on W. cst. of Auckland peninsula; provides additional harbour facilities for spt. of Auckland; recreational sailing; fishing.

Manych, R., **RSFSR**; trib. of R. Don; 480 km long; canal being built through R. to Caspian to provide through connection with Black Sea.

Manzala (Menzala), lagoon, Mediterranean cst., **Egypt**; extends E. from Damietta mouth of Nile to Pt. Said; fringed by salt marsh; a. 2,072 km².

Manzanillo, spt., S.E. **Cuba**; exp. sugar, rice, tobacco; p. (1966) 87,000.

Manzanillo, c. Colima, W. **Mexico**; ch. pt. on Pac. Oc.; exp. coffee, timber, minerals; p. (est. 1970) 21,000.

Maputo (Lourenço Marques), spt., cap. of **Moçambique**; at head of Delagoa Bay; rly. terminus; oil refining, deposits of bentonite worked nearby; ore terminal, much transit tr.; second lgst. pt. in Africa; p. (est. 1981) 785,512.

Maracaibo, spt., cap. of Zulia st., **Venezuela**; deepwater harbour; on W. of narrow entrance on L. Maracaibo; univ.; oilfields and refineries; exp. coffee, cocoa, hardwoods; p. (est. 1979) 874,000.

Maracaibo, G., and L., Zulia st., **Venezuela**; brackish lake, 192 km long, 96 km wide; oilwells on fringes and drilled into lake floor.

Maracay, c., N. **Venezuela**; on L. Valencia, 112 km from Carácas; p. (est. 1979) 333,000.

Maragheh, t., **Iran**; on N. end of L. Urmia; comm. and fruit ctr.; p. (est. 1970) 60,000.

Marajó, I., at mouth of the Rs. Amazon and Pará, **Brazil**; a. 38,850 km².

Maralinga, S. **Australia**; 320 km N.E. Eucla; joint U.K.–Australian atomic testing ground, first weapon exploded here 27 Sept. 1956.

Maranhão, st., N.E. **Brazil**; rice, cotton, sugar, tobacco, coffee, cattle, gold, copper; oil in the Barrierinhas a.; cap. São Luiz; a. 334,812 km²; p. (est. 1970) 3,037,135.

Marañon, R. See **Amazon, R.**

Maras, t., S. central **Turkey**; tr. in Kurdish carpets; p. (1975) 128,891.

Marathon, v. and plain, **Greece**; 32 km N.E. of Athens; here the Athenians defeated the Persians 490 B.C.

Marazion, mkt. t., Cornwall, **Eng.**; on Mount's Bay, nr. St. Michael's Mount; pilchard fisheries.

Marble Bar, t., W. **Australia**; 136 km inland by rail from Pt. Hedland; ctr. of Pilbara goldfields; p. (1976) 262.

Marburg on Lahn, t., Hesse, **W. Germany**; univ., cas.; noted for optical instruments; p. (1983) 79,100.

March, mkt. t., Fenland, Cambs., **Eng.**; on R. Nene in Fens; rly. junc.; farm tools; p. (1981) 14,475.

Marches, The, region, central **Italy**; extending from eastern slopes of Apennines to Adriatic cst.; embracing provs. of Macerata, Ascoli-Piceno, Ancona, and Pesaro e Urbino; a. 9,697 km²; p. (1981) 294,990.

Marchfeld, plain, Lower **Austria**; between Rs. Danube and Morava which here forms bdy. between Austria and ČSSR.

Marcias Nguema. See Biako.

Mar del Plata, c., **Argentina**; on C. Corrientes; Atl. cst. resort; p. (1975) 302,282.

Maree, L., Ross and Cromarty, **Scot.**; 21 km long, c. 3 km wide; rocky shores; studded with wooded islets.

Maremma, coastal region along Tyrrhenean Sea, S. Tuscany, **Italy**; once malarial, now drained with wide fertile areas.

Mareotis or **Birket-et-Mariut,** L., Lower **Egypt**; separated from Mediterranean by ridge of sand on which stands Alexandria; 80 km long, 32 km wide.

Margam, t., in Pt. Talbot, West Glamorgan, S. **Wales**; on cst. of Swansea Bay; lge. new steel-wks., lgst. steel-rolling mill in Europe.

Margarita, I., in Caribbean off N. **Venezuela**; tourism; formerly pearl-fishing ctr.; cap. Asunción; a. 1,166 km²; p. (est. 1970) 26,000.

Margate, t., Kent, **Eng.**; W. of N. Foreland, in the Isle of Thanet; seaside resort; p. (1981) 53,280.

Margolan, t., E. Uzbek SSR, **USSR**; in Ferghana Valley; noted for silk ind.; p. (est. 1980) 112,000.

Mari, aut. rep., **RSFSR**; timber, paper inds.; p. (1970) 685,000.

Mariana Is. (Marianas), chain of Is., **W. Pac.**; US Trust Terr.; most impt. are Guam, Saipan, and Tinian; US Commonwealth status planned for N. Mariana Is.; a. 479 km²; p. (est. 1974) 14,335.

Maribor, t., Slovenia, **Yugoslavia**; on Drava R., nr. Austrian border; metallurgical inds.; ctr. of agr. a.; p. (1981) 185,699.

Marilia, t., São Paulo st., **Brazil**; coffee, cotton, oil peanuts; p. (est. 1980) 111,500.

Mariinsk Canal. See **Volga Baltic Waterway.**

Marion, c., Ind., **USA**; mkt. ctr. within corn belt; varied inds.; p. (1980) 35,874.

Marion, t., Ohio, **USA**; agr. ctr., with varied agr. mnfs.; p. (1980) 37,040.

Maritime Provinces, include Canadian provs. of Nova Scotia, New Brunswick, Prince Edward I.

Maritsa, R., **Bulgaria** and **Greece**; used for irrigation and hydroelectric power; 416 km long.

Market Drayton, t., North Shrops., **Eng.**; on R. Tern, 21 km S.W. of Newcastle-under-Lyme; agr. implements, nylon mftg.

Market Harborough, t., Harborough, Leics., **Eng.**; on R. Welland, 13 km N.W. of Kettering; elec. engin., foodstuffs, corsetry; p. (1981) 15,934.

Market Rasen, t., West Lindsey, Lincs., **Eng.**; agr. ctr.; racecourse; p. (1981) 2,689.

Markinch, burgh, Kirkcaldy, **Scot.**; 13 km N. of Kirkcaldy; paper mftg., whisky blending and bottling factory closed 1983; p. (1981) 2,044.

Marl, t., N. Rhine–Westphalia, **W. Germany;** in Ruhr; coal mng.; chemicals; p. (1983) 88,000.

Marlborough, t., Wycombe, Wilts., **Eng.;** on R. Kennet in heart of Marlborough Downs; public school; p. (1981) 5,771.

Marlborough, prov., S.I., **N.Z.;** pastoral; a. 10,930 km²; cap. Blenheim; p. (1976) 35,030.

Marlborough Downs, hills, Wilts., **Eng.;** chalk; highest point, Milk Hill, 298 m.

Marlow, t., Bucks., **Eng.;** on R. Thames; mkt., tourist ctr.; home of Shelley; p. (1981) 14,132.

Marmara, Sea of, separates Europe from Asia; connected with Black Sea through the Bosporus, with Aegean Sea through Dardanelles; shores belong to Turkey.

Marne, dep., N.E. **France;** in Champagne; ctr. of champagne ind.; cap. Châlons-sur-Marne; a. 8,205 km²; p. (1982) 544,800.

Marne, R., central **France;** rises in Plateau de Langres, flows across Champagne Humide, Champagne Pouilleuse, and Beauce, joins R. Seine just above Paris; with Marne–Rhine and Marne-Saône canals forms impt. inland waterway linking Seine with Rhine and Rhône valleys; *c.* 520 km. long.

Marple, t., Gtr. Manchester, **Eng.;** 5 km. E. of Stockport; engin., residtl.; p. (1981) 23,899.

Marquesas Is., volcanic gr. in central **Pac. Oc.,** part of Fr. Polynesia; lgst. Nukuhiva and Hivaoa; mtnous., fertile; exp. copra, vanilla, tobacco, cotton; a. 1,274 km²; p. (est. 1972) 5,593.

Marrakesh, c., **Morocco;** tourist ctr.; leather gds., carpets; p. (est. 1973) 330,400 (c.), 436,300 (met. a.).

Marsa el-Brega, new pt., G. of Sirte, **Libya;** oil pipeline from Zelten; gas liquefaction plant opened 1970; airport.

Marsala, pt., Sicily, **Italy;** on site of anc. Carthaginian settlement; wine ctr.; p. (1981) 79,093.

Marseilles, c., spt., cap. of Bouche-du-Rhône dep., S. **France;** on Provence cst.; passenger and gds. traffic; pt. inds., marine engin., oil refining; oil pipeline to Karlsruhe; industl. expansion at G. of Fos; cath., univ., palace; founded as Massilia by Phocaean Greeks of Asia Minor 600 B.C.; p. (1982) 878,689 (c.), 1,110,511 (met. a.).

Marshall Is., gr. of coral Is., central **Pac. Oc.;** internal self-government (1978), comprising 34 atolls; exp. copra, sugar, coffee; admin. ctr. Jaluit I.; US Pac. Trust Terr.; a. 181 km²; nuclear bomb tests; p. (est. 1974) 25,044.

Martha's Vineyard, I., S.E. Mass., **USA;** state forest; summer resort; ch. ts., Vineyard Haven, Oak Bluffs, Edgartown; summer resort.

Martigny, t., Valais, **Switzerland;** linked by road tunnel to Aosta, Italy; p. 6,572.

Martina Franca, t., S. **Italy;** in Apulia; wine, olive oil; summer resort; p. (est. 1968) 38,771.

Martinique, I., Fr. overseas dep., Windward Is., **W.I.;** dominated by volcanic peak Mt. Pelée which erupted 1902 destroying t. of St. Pierre; hurricanes, earthquakes; economy based on sugar-cane and fruit prod.; much emigration to France; cap. Fort de France; a. 1,088 km²; p. (est. 1984) 312,000.

Martos, t., Jaen prov., Andalusia, **Spain;** castled hilltop t.; wines, sulphur springs; mftg.; p. (1981) 21,672.

Mary (Merv), c., Turkmen SSR, **USSR;** in oasis in Kara-Kum desert; anc. c. founded 3rd cent. B.C.; textile ctr.; p. (1969) 61,000.

Maryborough, t., Queensland, **Australia;** pt. on Mary R.; exp. fruit, sugar, timber, coal; p. (1976) 20,670.

Maryborough. *See* Port Laoighise, Ireland.

Mary Kathleen, t., Queensland, **Australia;** new t., nr. uranium field in Cloncurry a.

Maryland, one of original 13 sts. of **USA;** Old Line St.; admitted to Union 1788; st. flower Black eyed Susan, st. bird Baltimore Oriel; on shores of Chesapeake Bay; humid continental climate; arable agr. and mkt. gardening; sea-fishing; cap. Annapolis; lgst. c. Baltimore; a. 27,394 km²; p. (1980) 4,217,000.

Maryport, t., Allerdale, Cumbria, **Eng.;** former pt.; modern lt. inds. in industl. estate to S. of t.; p. (1981) 11,598.

Masaya, t., W. **Nicaragua;** comm. ctr. in rich agr. a.; p. (est. 1970) 49,691.

Masbate, I., **Philippines;** gold mng.; a. 3,269 km²; p. (1970) 492,868.

Mascarene Is., collective name of **Mauritius,** Rodriguez and Réunion, in Indian Oc.

Maseru, t., cap. **Lesotho;** nr. border with S. Africa on Caledon R.; two new industl. estates to encourage light inds.; tourists from S. Africa; p. (est. 1981) 292,200 (met. a.), 45,000 (c.).

Masham, t., North Yorks., **Eng.;** on R. Ure; 14 km N.W. of Ripon; mkt.

Mashhad, c., N.E. **Iran;** cap. of Khorassan prov.; p. (1976) 670,180.

Mashonaland, dist., **Zimbabwe;** a. inhabited by the Mashona tribe; ch. t. Salisbury.

Masjid-i-Sulamain, t., **Iran;** impt. oilfield and refinery.

Mask, L., Mayo and Galway, **R.o.I.;** 19 km long 3–6 km wide.

Mason City, t., Iowa, **USA;** on Sheel Rock R.; tr. ctr. of lge. agr. a.; p. (1980) 30,144.

Mason–Dixon Line. *See* Section L.

Massachusetts, st., New England, **USA;** Bay St.; admitted to Union 1788; st. flower Mayflower, st. bird Chickadee; on Atl. cst.; humid continental climate; hilly interior severed by N.–S. Connecticut valley; major fishing ind.; replacement of traditional textile inds. by modern science-based inds., especially around M. Institute of Technology; impt. arable gr. a.; cap. Boston; a. 21,386 km²; p. (1980) 5,737,000.

Massa di Carrara. *See* Carrara.

Massawa, spt., **Ethiopia;** on Red Sea; fine harbour; fishing; fish meal; p. (est. 1980) 32,977.

Massif Central, upland a., **France;** variable geology and scenery inc. volcanic Auvergne and limestone Causses; much rural depopulation, pastoral agr.; industl. ts. inc. St. Etienne based on sm. coalfields in N.E.; others ts. inc. Limoges and Clermont-Ferrand.

Masterton, bor., N.I., **N.Z.;** meat-packing; dairy prods., woollen mills; p. (1976) 21,001.

Masulipatnam. *See* Machilipatnam.

Masvingo. *See* Fort Victoria.

Matabeleland, dist., **Zimbabwe;** a. inhabited by Matabele tribe; ch. t. Bulawayo.

Matadi, spt., **Zaire;** on R. Zaïre; main pt.; exp. forest prod.; proposed Inga power project nearby; p. (1982) 162,396.

Matagalpa, t., **Nicaragua;** ctr. of agr. a., food processing; second lgst. t. of Nicaragua; p. (est. 1970) 61,383.

Matamoros, irrigated region, **Mexico;** around t. of M. on Rio Grande delta; Mexico's leading producer of cotton.

Matamoros, t., **Mexico;** on Rio Grande; livestock tr. ctr.; p. (1979) 193,305.

Matanzas, spt., cap. of M. prov., **Cuba;** exp. sugar, cigars; rayon plant; p. (est. 1967) 84,100.

Matarani, new spt., S. **Peru;** oil refinery.

Mataró, spt., **Spain;** nr. Barcelona; fisheries, textiles, chemicals, paper; p. (1981) 96,467.

Matera, t., cap. of M. prov., S. **Italy;** stands on limestone ridge cleft by canyon; agr. ctr.; cave dwellings; 13th cent. cath. and cas.; p. (1981) 50,712.

Mathura (Muttra), t., Uttar Pradesh, **India;** sacred t. on R. Jumna; Hindu pilgrimage ctr.; textiles; p. (1971) 132,028 (t.), 140,150 (met. a.).

Matlock, t., West Derbys., **Eng.;** on R. Derwent; 24 km N. of Derby; tourist ctr., limestone quarrying, lt. inds.; p. (1981) 20,610.

Mato Grosso, st., **Brazil;** cap. Cuiabá; a. 1,232,081 km²; p. (est. 1968) 1,363,980.

Mato Grosso, plateau, Mato Grosso st., **Brazil;** average alt. 900 m, acts as divide between Amazon and Paraná–Paraguay R. systems; reserves of gold, diamonds, manganese but largely undeveloped; lge. areas of tropical rain forest.

Matosinhos, t., **Portugal;** fish. pt. at mouth of Leca R.; seaside resort; p. (1981) 43,488.

Matrah, t., **Oman;** ch. comm. ctr.; agr. tr.; site of Port Qaboos, new deep water pt.; p. 14,119.

Matsue, c., S.W. Honshu, **Japan;** on L. Shinji; old cas.; p. (1979) 132,092.

Matsumoto, c., central Honshu, **Japan;** machin., food-processing, paper; once impt. for silk; remains of 16th cent. cas.; p. (1979) 189,482.

Matsuyama, c., **Japan;** pt. based inds. of oil refining and petrochemicals; univ., feudal cas.; p. (1979) 396,237.

Matterhorn (Fr. Mt. Corvin. It. Monte Cervino); alt. 4,477 m; Pennine Alps, **Switzerland.**

Mauchline, mkt. t., Strathclyde Reg., **Scot.;** associated with Robert Burns; p. (1981) 3,776.

Mauna Kea, volcano, Hawaii; alt. 4,208 m; now dormant.

Mauna Loa, volcano, **Hawaii**; alt. 4,172 m; one of the world's lgst. volcanoes.

Mauritania, Islamic Rep. of, W. Africa; desert in N., S. more fertile; Senegal R. forms main artery of transport; mainly pastoral agr. (nomadic); severe effects of Sahelian drought since 1971 caused p. to become settled and move to ts.; urban p. 35% (1984); deposits of iron ore (Fort Gouraud) and copper (Bakel Akjoujt); fishing being developed; new pt. development at Nouadhibou; cap. Nouakchott; a. 1,085,210 km²; p. (est. 1983) 1,780,000.

Mauritius, I., indep. st. within Brit. Commonwealth; **Indian Oc.**; volcanic I., surrounded by coral reefs, 800 km E. of Madagascar; subtropical climate, prone to cyclone; racially mixed; dependent on sugar for 95 per cent of exps.; dense p. and unemployment cause social tension; former residents of Chagos Arch. resettled on 2 of Agalega Is.; tourism incr. impt.; cap. Port Louis; a. (inc. Rodriguez and Agalega) 2,038 km²; p. (1983) 966,863.

Mawson, Australian national research base, **Antarctica**.

Mayagüez, c., spt., **Puerto Rico**; ctr. of fertile region producing sugar, coffee, tobacco; cultural and educational ctr.; p. (est. 1976) 102,500.

Maybole, burgh, Kyle and Carrick, **Scot.**; 13 km S. of Ayr; footwear, agr. implements; cas.; p. (1981) 4,769.

Mayenne, dep., N.W. **France**; pastoral and agr.; cap. Laval; a. 5,146 km²; p. (1982) 271,500.

Mayfair, dist., City of Westminster, London, **Eng.**; fashionable residtl. and comm. a., to E. of Hyde Park; clubs and hotels.

Mayo, maritime co., Connacht, **R.o.I.**; broken cst., much barren mtn. land, many lge. lakes; agr., fishery; co. t. Castlebar, a. 5,506 km²; p. (1981) 20,695.

Ma‚ otte, ch. I., **Fr.** terr., Comoro Archipelago, Moçambique Channel; rejected indep. to remain Fr. dep. (1975); sugar-cane, vanilla, cacao; a. 363 km²; p. (1980) 52,000.

Mazandaran, prov., N.E. **Iran**; Caspian Sea, borders USSR; subtropical climate; agr.; cap. Sari; p. (1967) 1,843,388.

Mazar-i-Sharif, c., **Afghanistan**; chemical fertilisers from natural gas; textiles, bricks, flour-milling; noted mosque; p. (est. 1969) 43,197.

Mazatlán, c., N.W. **Mexico**; major spt. on Pac. cst.; comm. and industl. ctr.; exp. metals, hides, fish prods., woods; oil refinery; fishing, tourism; p. (1979) 186,290.

M'babane, cap. of **Swaziland**; stands at c. 1,160 m; admin. ctr.; tin mng.; p. (1982) 38,636.

M'Bao, Senegal, W. Africa; oil refinery.

McMurdo Sound, ice-locked channel, Antarctica; base for many expeditions.

Mead, L., Cal., **USA**; on R. Colorado behind Boulder (Hoover) Dam; world's lgst. reservoir; stores water for irrigation in Imperial Valley and Yuma dist.; tourist attraction; 184 km long.

Meath, maritime co., Leinster, **R.o.I.**; pastoral; co. t., Trim; a. 2,347 km²; p. (1981) 24,015.

Meaux, t., Seine-et-Marne dep., **France**; on R. Marne; cath.; comm. and industl. ctr.; p. (1982) 55,797 (met. a.).

Mecca, holy c. of Islam, cap. of **Saudi Arabia**; birthplace of Mohammed; pilgrimage ctr.; Gr. Mosque enclosing the Kaaba; univ. (with Jidda); p. (1974) 366,801.

Mechelen. *See* Malines.

Mecklenburg, region, E. **Germany**; part of N. European plain, bordering Baltic Sea; Schwerin was cap. of former st.; a. 22,947 km².

Medan, c., cap. of N. Sumatra prov., **Indonesia**; ctr. for rubber, tobacco, tea; printing; univ.; pt. is Belawan; p. (1971) 635,562.

Médéa, t., 80 km S. of El Djezair, **Algeria**; projected industl. complex; p. (est. 1975) 37,000.

Medellín, c., cap. of Antiquia prov., **Colombia**; at 1,533 m in Central Cordillera; second c. of rep.; univ.; cultural ctr.; coffee; textiles, steel, sugar refining, glass; coal, gold, silver mined nearby; hydroelec. power; p. (1973) 1,112,390 (c.), 1,159,194 (met. a).

Medicine Hat, t., Alberta, **Canada**; on S. Saskatchewan R.; rly. junc.; coal, natural gas, flour mills; p. (1971) 26,058.

Medina, c., Hejaz, **Saudi Arabia**; 352 km N. of Mecca; tomb of Mohammed; place of Moslem pilgrimage; univ.; harbour at Yanbu' on Red Sea; p. (1974) 198,186.

Medina, l. gov. dist., I. of Wight, **Eng.**; N.E. part of I. inc. Ryde, Newport and Cowes; p. (1981) 67,569.

Mediterranean, gr. inland sea, almost tideless, dividing Europe from Africa; communicating with Atl. by Strait of Gibraltar and Black Sea by Dardanelles, Sea of Marmara and Bosporus, E. part touches Asia in the Levant; total length W. to E. 3,520 km; greatest width of sea proper c. 1,120 km; water a. 2,331,000 km²; greatest depth 4,482 m; ch. Is.; Corsica, Sardinia, Sicily, Crete, Cyprus, and the Balearic, Lipari, Maltese, Ionian grs., also Greek arch.

Médoc, region, Gironde, **France**; extending for about 77 km along Garonne R.; noted for wines.

Medway, R., Kent, **Eng.**; flows N.E. past Tonbridge, Maidstone and Rochester (where it becomes estuarial) to mouth of Thames; 112 km long; Medway Bridge (part of London–Dover motorway) completed 1962.

Medway, former l. gov. dist., Kent, **Eng.**; now Rochester upon Medway.

Meekatharra, t., W. **Australia**; Flying Doctor and School of the Air ctr.; p. (1976) 829.

Meerut, c., Uttar Pradesh, **India**; scene of outbreak of Indian mutiny 1857; p. (1971) 270,993 (c.), 367,754 (met. a.).

Meghalaya ("Home of the Clouds"), new st. (1972), **India**; former Khasi-Jaintia Hills and Garo Hills dists. of Assam; cap. Shillong; a. 22,549 km²; p. (est. 1972) 1,000,000.

Meiling Pass, on bdy. between Guandong, Jianxi, S. **China**; provides historic routeway across Nanling mtns., followed by old imperial highway from Nanjing to Guangzhou; alt. c. 300 m.

Meiningen, t., **E. Germany**; on R. Werra; cas.; machin., chemicals, timber inds.; drama ctr. in second half 19th cent.; p. (est. 1970) 25,357.

Merionnydd, l. gov. dist., Gwynedd, **Wales**; based on former co. of Merioneth; stretches from Ffestiniog and Bala to Tywyn and Dolgellau; p. (1981) 32,056.

Meissen, t., Dresden, **E. Germany**; on R. Elbe; cath.; famous porcelain popularly known as Dresden china; p. (est. 1970) 45,571.

Meknès, t., **Morocco**; one of the caps. of M.; agr. ctr., olives; p. (est. 1973) 244,520 (t.), 403,000 (met. a.).

Mekong, R., S.E. **Asia**; rises in Tibet, flows through China, Laos, Kampuchea, and S. Vietnam, entering China Sea in extensive swampy delta; used for sm. boats but many rapids; longest R. in Asia; 4,000 km long; new R. project for flood control, irrigation and hydroelectric power.

Melanesia, archipelago, S.W. **Pac. Oc.**; inc. Admiralty, Solomon, Santa Cruz, New Hebrides, Loyalty, New Caledonian, and Fiji Is.; New Guinea is sometimes included; ethnic region; arable subsistence agr.

Melbourne, c., cap. of Victoria, **Australia**; at mouth of Yarra R. and N. head of Port Phillip Bay; focal point of trade, transport and inds.; produces 30 per cent of total factory output in Australia; varied inds. inc. car and aircraft assembly, petrochemicals, foodstuffs; internat. airport; 2 univs., 2 caths.; p. (1976) 65,065 (c.), 2,603,578 (met. a.).

Melilla, spt. and enclave in **Morocco**, on Mediterranean cst., belonging to Spain; exp. iron ore; p. (1981) 53,593.

Melitopol, c., Ukrainian SSR, **USSR**; on Molochnoy R.; ctr. of rich fruit-growing a.; heavy machin., food-processing; p. (est. 1980) 163,000.

Melksham, t., West Wilts., **Eng.**; on R. Avon, 8 km N.E. of Bradford-on-Avon; rubber wks., engin., flour mills, creameries, rope and matting; p. (1981) 9,621.

Melrose, burgh, Ettrick and Lauderdale, **Scot.**; on R. Tweed; 6 km E. of Galashiels; ruined abbey; p. (1981) 2,221.

Melton Mowbray, t., Leics., **Eng.**; on Lincoln Heights, 24 km N.E. of Leicester; mkt., hunting dist.; famous pork pies; footwear, pet foods, Stilton cheese; with surrounding a. forms l. gov. dist. of **Melton**; p. (1981) 43,260 (dist.).

Melun, t., cap. of Seine-et-Marne dep., N. **France**; on R. Seine; agr. tools and prod.; Romanesque church; p. (1982) 82,479 (met. a.).

Melville I., off N. cst., Arnhem Land, **Australia**; Aboriginal settlement; a. 4,350 km²; p. (1976) 542.

Melville I., N.W. Terr., Arctic **Canada**; natural gas; a. 41,958 km².

Memaliaj, t., **Albania;** new mng. t. on banks of R. Vjosa.

Memel. *See* **Klaipeda.**

Memmingen, t., Bavaria, **W. Germany;** rly. junc.; machin., textiles; p. (1983) 37,700.

Memphis, anc. c., **Egypt;** on R. Nile; 19 km S. of Cairo; nearby are Sakkara ruins.

Memphis, c., Tenn., **USA;** on R. Mississippi; rly. ctr., pt. of entry, lgst. c. in st., mkt. ctr. for cotton and hardwoods; cottonseed oil, textiles, farm machin.; natural gas and hydroelectric power; univ.; Martin Luther King assassinated here (1968); p. (1980) 646,000 (c.), 913,000 (met. a.).

Menado, t., Sulawesi, **Indonesia;** second t. of I.; pt. for transit tr.; p. (1971) 169,684.

Menai Strait, separates Isle of Anglesey from mainland, **Wales;** crossed by Telford's suspension bridge (1825) and Britannia rly. bridge (1850).

Menam Chao Phraya, R., **Thailand;** main R. of cty.; dense p. in valley; lge. multi-purpose scheme for hydroelectric power and irrigation; 1,120 km long.

Mendip Hills, Avon/Somerset, **Eng.;** limestone range containing many karst features inc. Cheddar gorge and Wookey Hole; a. of outstanding natural beauty; quarrying; motorway; hgst. point. 325 m; now forms l. gov. dist. within Somerset, inc. Frome, Wells, Shepton Mallet, Glastonbury and Street; p. (1981) 87,030.

Mendoza, prov., W. **Argentina,** on Chilean border; Andean peaks Aconcagua and Tupungato; oilfields; alfalfa, vines, olives, fruit, peppermint; cap. M.; a. 148,783 km²; p. (1970) 973,075.

Mendoza, c., cap. of M. prov., W. **Argentina;** stands at c. 730 m in oasis known as "garden of the Andes"; starting point of Transandine rly.; univ.; wine, fruit; petroleum, agr. processing; p. (1975) 118,568.

Mendoza, R., **Argentina;** enters L. Guanacache; used for hydroelectric power; 320 km long.

Menin (Meenen), t., **Belgium;** on R. Lys on Fr. border; mediaeval cloth ctr.; tobacco tr., textiles, rubber gds., soap; scene of fierce fighting in first world war; p. (1981) 33,542.

Mentawei Is., S.W. Sumatra, **Indonesia;** hilly and forested; primitive p.; fishing, shifting cultivation.

Menteith, Lake of, Stirling, **Scot.;** contains 3 Is.; 2·4 km by 1·6 km.

Menton, t., Alpes-Maritimes dep. S. **France;** Riviera resort; p. (1982) 25,449.

Meppel, t., Drenthe, **Neth.,** 21 km N. of Zwolle; shipbldg.; p. (1967) 19,192.

Merauke, t. W. Irian, **Indonesia;** pt. on S. cst.; ctr. of livestock raising region.

Mercedes, t., S.W. **Uruguay;** livestock ctr., E. of its pt. Fray Bentos; p. (est. 1970) 34,000.

Mergui, archipelago, Tenasserim cst., S. **Burma;** teak, rice, pearl fishing.

Mérida, c., cap. of Yucatan st., S.E. **Mexico;** sisal-hemp; Spanish colonial architecture; tourism; Mayan ruins; p. (1979) 269,582.

Mérida, c. Badajoz prov., S.W. **Spain;** on Guadiana R.; comm. ctr. of Estremadura; impt. Roman remains; p. (1981) 41,783.

Mérida, t. cap. of M. st., **Venezuela;** in Andes; univ., cath.; tourist ctr.; world's highest cable rly. to Espejo peak (4,690 m); p. (est. 1970) 75,634.

Meriden, t., Conn., **USA;** hardware mftg.; p. (1980) 57,118.

Meridian, t., Miss., **USA;** mkt. ctr. in cotton, livestock, lumber a.; rly. and route ctr.; textiles, clothing; p. (1980) 46,577.

Merioneth, former co., **Wales.** *See* **Meirionnydd.**

Merksem, industl. t., Antwerp, **Belgium;** p. (est. 1972) 40,440.

Merrick, mtn., Wigtown, **Scot.;** hgst. peak in S. Uplands of Scot.; alt. 843 m.

Mersea, I., at mouth of R. Colne, Essex, **Eng.;** oysters; holiday resort; 8 km long, 3 km wide.

Merseburg, c., Halle, **E. Germany;** on R. Saale; ctr. of gr. lignite field; paper mills, chemical wks.; historic c.; p. (est. 1970) 55,986.

Merse of Berwick, region, S.E. **Scot.;** lower valleys of Rs. Tweed and Teviot; glacial clays; arable agr. for barley, wheat; dairy cattle; ch. t. Berwick-on-Tweed; a. 570 km².

Mersey, R., Cheshire/Gtr. Manchester/Merseyside,

Eng.; enters Irish Sea by fine estuary at Liverpool; 109 km long.

Merseyside, former met. co., N.W. **Eng.;** a. around lower Mersey estuary inc. N. Wirral penin., pts. of Liverpool, Birkenhead and Bootle; many chem. and pt. processing inds.; p. (1981) 1,513,070.

Mersin, c., S. **Turkey;** spt. on Mediterranean cst.; oil refinery; dates from c. 3,600 B.C.; p. (1979) 152,186.

Merthyr Tydfil, t., l. gov. dist., Mid Glamorgan, S. **Wales;** in narrow valley of R. Taff, 35 km N.W. of Cardiff; coal-mng. ctr.; hosiery, aircraft, bricks, elec. domestic gds.; p. (1981) 60,528 (dist.).

Merton, outer bor., Greater London, **Eng.;** inc. former bors. of Mitcham, Wimbledon, and Merton and Morden; p. (1981) 164,912.

Meru, mtn., **Tanzania,** E. Africa; extinct volcano overlooking E. arm of Gt. Rift valley; coffee plantations at alt. 1,500–1,800 m, some rubber below 1,200 m; alt. summit 4,560 m.

Merv. *See* **Mary.**

Mesa, t., Arizona, **USA;** in Salt River Valley, founded by Mormons 1878; agr. ctr., helicopter mftg.; p. (1980) 152,000.

Mesa Central, plateau, **Mexico;** part of Mexican plateau, major a. of comm. agr. (maize, wheat, agave); contains cap. Mexico City; dense p. and industl. comm. ctrs.

Mesa del Norte, plateau, **Mexico;** northern part of Mexican plateau.

Mesabi Range, hills, N.E. Minn., **USA;** vast iron ore deposits, now running out.

Mesa Verde National Park, S.W. Col., **USA;** Indian cliff dwellings.

Mesopotamia, anc. region, S.W. **Asia;** between Tigris and Euphrates Rs.; a. of early civilisation.

Messenia, anc. region, Peloponnesus, **Greece;** corresponding to present Messinia, densely p. agr. dep., cap. Kalamata; a. 3,406 km²; p. (1971) 172,850.

Messina, c., spt., Sicily, **Italy;** opposite Reggio; univ.; exp. fruit, wine, oil; p. (1981) 260,233.

Messina, strait, between Sicily and Italian mainland; length 35 km, minimum width 5 km.

Mesta, R., **Bulgaria, Greece;** rises in Rodopi mtns., flows S.E. into Aegean Sea 24 km E of Kavalla; valley famous for tobacco; known in Greece as Nestos; c. 280 km long.

Mestre, t., **Italy;** on lagoon at landward end of causeway linking Venice to mainland.

Meta, R., **Colombia** and **Venezuela;** navigable for 640 km; trib. of R. Orinoco; 1,200 km long.

Metz, c., cap of Moselle dep., N.E. **France;** on R. Moselle 40 km N. of Nancy; cultural and comm. ctr. of Lorraine; impt. iron mines; wines, preserved fruits; mediaeval bldgs.; birthplace of Verlaine; p. (1982) 118,502.

Meudon, t., Hauts-de-Seine, **France;** S.W. sub. of Paris; observatory; glass, linen, ammunition; p. (1982) 49,004.

Meurthe, R., N.E. **France;** rises in Vosges and joins Moselle N. of Nancy.

Meurthe-et-Moselle, dep., N.E. **France;** borders on Belgium and Luxembourg; cap. Nancy; a. 5,276 km²; p. (1982) 715,800.

Meuse, dep., N.E. **France;** borders on Belgium; cap. Bar-le-Duc; a. 6,237 km²; p. (1982) 200,200.

Meuse (Maas), R., **France;** rises in Haute-Marne, flows past Verdun into Belgium past Namur, and Liège into the Neth. and joins the Waal, left arm of the Rhine; impt. routeway; 912 km long.

Mexborough, t., South Yorks., **Eng.;** on R. Don, 16 km above Doncaster; potteries; p. (1981) 15,683.

Mexicali, c., Baja Cal., **Mexico;** border resort; p. (1979) 348,528.

Mexican Plateau, central plateau, **Mexico;** between the branches of the Sierra Madre; highest point over 2,400 m; impt. landform and a. of human settlement.

Mexico, fed. rep., Central America; inc. 31 sts., and fed. dist. of Mexico City: mtnous.; Sierra Madre covers most of rep.; variety of climate according to alt.; W. mostly desert; agr. requires irrigation; major world exporter of cotton, sisal, sulphur, silver; oil impt.; 14 oil refineries, new petrochemical complex at Cosoleacaque; rapid industl. expansion for consumer gds.; decentralisation of inds. from Mexico City; tourism for Americans; cap.

Mexico City; a. 1,972,360 km²; p. (est. 1984) 77,040,000.

Mexico, st., Mexico; encircles fed. dist. of Mexico City; cap. Toluca; a. 21,412 km²; p. (1970) 3,833,185.

Mexico City, c., cap. of **Mexico;** lgst. c. in Latin America; on plain at 2,275 m; altitude and basin site trap pollutants; many note-worthy bldgs., cath., univ.; admin., comm. and industl. ctr.; nuclear reactor nearby; lge. earthquake (1985) destroyed many parts of c.; surrounded by shanty ts., growing by 1,000 people per day; p. (1979) 9,191,295 (c.), 14,750,182 (met. a.); p. (est. 2000) 32,000,000 (lgst. met. a. in world).

Mexico, Gulf of, lge. inlet of Atl. Oc. (1,600 km E. to W. by 1,280 km N. to S.) lying S. of USA and E. of Mexico; communicates by Florida strait with Atl. and by Yucatan strait with Caribbean Sea; submarine oil drilling.

Mexico, Valley of, Meseta Central, **Mexico;** major industl. zone; over 60 per cent by value of Mexican mngs. produced; wide range of inds.; major ctr. Mexico City; attempts to decentralise p. and economic activity throughout Mexico; once ctr. of Aztec p.

Meyrin, t., **Switzerland;** H.Q. of CERN, nr. Geneva.

Mezhdurechensk, t., RSFSR; W. Siberia, on R. Rom'; new coal-mng. ctr.; p. (est. 1969) 81,000.

Mezzogiorno, lge. underdeveloped region, southern **Italy;** comprising Abruzzo and Molise, Campania, Basilicata, Apulia, Calabria and the Is. of Sicily and Sardinia; major govt. attempts to develop a.; agr. reforms and industl. growth, oil refining, iron and steel, petrochemicals; contains 35 per cent of p. of Italy, much emigration; much devastated by earthquake (1980); p. (1981) 20,053,334.

Miami, c., **Fla., USA;** on Biscayne Bay, at mouth of Miami R.; famous resort and recreational ctr.; varied inds.; international airport; world's fifth lgst. cargo airpt.; 3rd container pt. on U.S. East cst.; lge. freeport; M. beach across Biscayne Bay; p. (1980) 347,000 (c.), 1,626,000 (met. a.).

Miass, c., **RSFSR;** in Urals, 90 km S.W. of Chelyabinsk; gold-mng. ctr.; cars; p. (est. 1980) 152,000.

Michigan, st., USA; Wolverine St.; admitted to Union 1837; st. flower Apple Blossom, st. bird Robin; in valley of Gr. Ls.; industl.; cars, iron and steel gds., petroleum, minerals; some agr.; cap. Lansing; a. 150,779 km²; p. (1980) 9,258,000.

Michigan Lake, 3rd lgst of Gr. Ls. and the only one wholly in **USA;** in basin of St. Lawrence R., enclosed by two peninsulas of the st. of Mich. and by Wis., Ill., and Ind.; a. 61,901 km²; discharges by Straits of Mackinac to L. Huron.

Michipicoten, R., Ont., **Canada;** flows 200 km to L. Superior; iron ore deposits in valley.

Michoacan, st., Mexico; on Pac. Oc.; mtnous., rich in minerals; cap. Morelia; a. 60,088 km²; p. (1970) 2,324,226.

Michurinsk, t., RSFSR; N.W. of Tambov; engin., textiles, food inds.; agr. exp. ctr.; p. (est. 1980) 102,000.

Micronesia, Federated States of, Is., **S. Pac.;** Internal self-government (1978); Carolines, Marshalls; most are coral atolls; p. (est. 1984) 348,000.

Mid Bedfordshire, l. gov. dist., Beds., **Eng.;** a. N. of Luton and inc. Biggleswade, Sandy and Ampthill; p. (1981) 102,063.

Mid Devon, l. gov. dist., Devon, **Eng.;** based on Tiverton; p. (1981) 58,057.

Middleburg, t. cap. of Zeeland prov., **Neth.;** on Walcheren I. nr. Flushing; margarine, timber, optical instruments; cloth ctr. in mediaeval times; p. (1982) 38,655.

Middlesbrough, t., l. gov. dist., Cleveland, **Eng.;** expanded t.; pt. on S. side of Tees estuary; impt. iron and steel ind., heavy engin., chemicals; p. (1981) 149,770.

Middlesex, former co., S.E. **Eng.;** N. of R. Thames; largely absorbed in Greater London 1964.

Middleton, t., Gtr. Manchester, **Eng.;** in valley of R. Irk; textiles, engin., chemicals, foam rubber; p. (1981) 51,696.

Middleton, t., Ohio, **USA;** on Miami R. and canal; steel, paper; p. (1980) 43,719.

Middlewich, t., Cheshire, **Eng.;** on Rs. Dane, Wheelock and Croco, 8 km N. of Crewe; salt, chemicals, clothing; p. (1981) 8,170.

Mid Glamorgan, co., S. Wales; upland in N. dissected by deep R. valleys containing former coal-mng. settlements; lowland to S. borders Bristol Channel; a. 1,018 km²; p. (1981) 537,866.

Midhurst, t., West Sussex, **Eng.;** on R. Rother; famous polo grounds; birthplace of Richard Cobden; p. (1971) 18,983 (dist.).

Midland, t., Texas, **USA;** oilfield ctr., cotton ginning, natural gas; p. (1980) 70,525.

Midlands, region, **Eng.;** comprises non-met. cos. of Staffs, Derbys., Notts., Leics., Warwicks., Northants., and met. co. of West Midlands; impt. a. for lt. engin.

Midlothian, former co., l. gov. dist., Lothian Reg., **Scot.;** adjoins Edinburgh; a. 357 km²; p. (1981) 81,661.

Midnapore, t., W. Bengal, **India;** mkt. for agr. prods.; p. (est. 1971) 71,000.

Mid Suffolk, l. gov. dist., Suffolk, **Eng.;** rural a. inc. Eye and Stowmarket; p. (1981) 69,787.

Mid Sussex, l. gov. dist., West Sussex, **Eng.;** a. inc. Cuckfield and Burgess Hill; p. (1981) 118,311.

Midway Island, I., **Pac. Oc.;** calling-place on air-routes betweeen San Francisco and Asia, mid-way between Asia and USA (to which it belongs); p. (1970) 2,220.

Mieres, t., Oviedo prov., N. **Spain;** in Asturias; coal-mng. ctr., iron and steel inds.; p. (1981) 58,098.

Mihoro, Gifu, **Japan;** power plant under construction.

Mikkeli, c., cap. of M. prov., **Finland;** L. pt. in Saimaa L. region; p. (est. 1970) 25,188.

Milan, c., cap. of M. prov., N. **Italy;** route ctr. in Lombard plain; second lgst. c. in rep.; ctr. of commerce and ind.; textiles, chemicals, printing, publishing, machin., cars, aircraft, porcelain; cath., univ.; p. (1981) 1,604,773.

Mildenhall, t., Forest Heath, Suffolk, **Eng.;** on R. Lark; 13th cent. church; R.A.F. sta. nearby; expanded t.

Mildura, t., Victoria, **Australia;** on R. Murray; irrigation ctr.; wine, citrus fruits, tomatoes; ctr. for dried fruit; p. (1976) 14,417.

Milford Haven, spt., Preseli, Dyfed, **Wales;** magnificent deepwater harbour recently developed; major tanker terminal (250,000 tonnes); 2 refineries; pipeline from Angle Bay to Llandarcy (nr. Swansea); major white fish pt.; trawlers built and repaired; net mkg.; p. (1981) 13,934.

Milford Sound, inlet, at S. of S.I., **N.Z.;** tourist resort; noted for scenery and rare birds.

Millau, t., Aveyron, **France;** on R. Tarn; glove mnfs.; p. (1982) 22,256.

Millom, t., Copeland, Cumbria, **Eng.;** on N.W. cst. of Duddon estuary; ironwks. (closed 1968 after 100 years); hosiery; declining p.

Millport, burgh, Cunninghame, **Scot.;** on Gr. Cumbrae I., in F. of Clyde; resort; cath.; quarries; p. (1981) 1,489.

Milngavie, burgh, Bearsden and M., Strathclyde Reg., **Scot.;** 8 km N.W. of Glasgow, textiles; p. (1981) 8,654.

Milnrow, t., Gtr. Manchester, **Eng.;** sub. of Rochdale; cotton and waste spinning engin., brick mkg., paper and tub mftg.; p. (1981) 11,759.

Milo or **Melos,** I., Cyclades, **Greece;** cap. Plaka, nr. site of anc. c.; famous statue of Venus of Milo (now in Louvre) found here in 1820.

Milton Keynes, t., l. gov. dist., Bucks., **Eng.;** a. 9,000 ha; site and name of new c. for London overspill to comprise Bletchley, Wolverton and Stony Stratford; Open University; p. (1981) 123,782 (fastest growing t. in Eng.).

Milwaukee, c., Wis., **USA;** lgst. c. and ch. pt. of st.; on L. Mich.; 112 km N. of Chicago; univ.; major mftg. ctr. with numerous inds., notably machin. and transport equipment, meat-canning, beer; p. (1980) 636,000 (c.), 1,397,000 (met. a.).

Min, R., Fujian, S. **China;** descends steeply on S.E. course to enter S. China Sea nr. Fuzhou, length 480 km, navigable.

Min, R., Sichuan, W. **China;** flows S., diverted into irrigation channels; joins Chang Jiang at Yibin; length 800 km, navigable.

Mina Hassan Tani (Kenitra), spt., **Morocco;** exp. grain; p. (est. 1973) 135,960 (c.), 341,600 (met. a.).

Minas Gerais, st., Brazil; vast iron ore reserves; gold, diamonds, manganese, uranium, aluminium; cotton, coffee; hydroelec. power sta.; cap. Belo Horizonte; plans for development of heavy inds.; a. 585,472 km²; p. (1970) 11,645,095.

Minas Novas, t., Minas Gerais, **Brazil;** p. (est. 1968) 24,003.

Mina Sulman, free transit pt., **Bahrain**; deepwater pt., dry dock for OPEC super-tankers, entrepôt.

Minatitlán, t., E. **Mexico**; petroleum refineries; petrochemicals; p. (1979) 119,432.

Minch, The, channel between the mainland of **Scot.** and the N. portion of Outer Hebrides, 38–64 km wide; very rapid current.

Minch, The Little, channel between l. of Skye, **Scot.**, and the middle portion of Outer Hebrides, 22–32 km wide.

Minchinhampton, t., Gloucs., **Eng.**; in Cotswolds, 6 km S.E. of Stroud.

Mindanao, second lgst. I. of **Philippines**; forested mtns., volcano Mt. Apo; exp. pineapples, hemp, coconuts, coffee; iron, gold, copper mined; ply-woods and veneer, paper, pulp; ch. ts. Zamboanga, Davao; a. of govt. sponsored immigration; lge. Moslem p. seeking indep. for I.; greatest ocean depth Mindanao Deep, off Philippines, 11,524 m; a. 94,628 km²; p. (1970) 7,292,691.

Minden, c., N. Rhine-Westphalia, **W. Germany**; on R. Weser at crossing of Mittelland canal; pt., rly. junc.; cath. (12th–14th cent.) destroyed in second world war; p. (1983) 76,400.

Mindoro, I., **Philippines**, S. of Luzon; mtnous., thickly forested; rice, coconuts grown on cst., a. 9,376 km²; p. (1970) 473,940.

Minehead, t., West Somerset, **Eng.**; at N. foot of Exmoor, on Bristol Channel cst.; mkt., holiday resort; shoe factory closed 1981; p. (1981) 11,176.

Minho, R., separates Portugal from Spain in N.W.; length 272 km.

Minicoy Is., Arabian Sea; joined with Laccadive and Amindivi Is. to form union terr. of India.

Minneapolis, c., Minn., **USA**; on Mississippi R., at falls of St. Anthony; lgst. c. of st., pt. of entry, rly. terminus; wheat mkt., comm. and industl. ctr.; wide range of inds.; univ.; p. (1980) 371,000 (c.), 2,114,000 (met. a.) inc. St. Paul which it faces.

Minnesota, st., **USA**; North Star St.; admitted to Union 1858; st. flower Lady's Slipper, st. bird Common Loon; W. of L. Superior; studded with Ls., many Rs.; iron ore; maize, wheat, livestock, dairying; cap. St. Paul; a. 217,736 km²; p. (1980) 4,077,000.

Minorca (Menorca), I. off **Spain**; 2nd lgst. of Balearic Is.; Mediterranean agr.; developing tour-ism; cap. Mahón; a. 733 km²; p. (1970) 50,217.

Minsk, c., cap. of Belorussiyan SSR, **USSR**; lge. rly. junc.; cultural and industl. ctr.; univ.; engin., computers; rebuilt since second world war; p. (est. 1980) 1,295,000.

Minya, c., central **Egypt**; on Nile; cotton tr. ctr.; p. (1976) 146,366.

Minya Konka, mtn., S.W. Sichuan prov., **China**; in Himalayas; highest peak in China; 7,570 m.

Mirfield, t., West Yorks., **Eng.**; on R. Calder, 5 km S.W. of Dewsbury; woollens; p. (1981) 18,686.

Miri, t., Sarawak, E. **Malaysia**; impt. oil ctr.; p. (1960) 13,350.

Mirzapur, t. Uttar Pradesh, **India**; on R. Ganges; carpets, brassware; p. (1971) 105,939.

Miskolc, c., N.E. **Hungary**; impt. industl. ctr.; iron ore, lignite nearby; varied inds., inc. textiles, porcelain, engin., bricks, refrigeration plants; p. (est. 1978) 207,828.

Mississippi, st., S. **USA**; Magnolia St.; admitted to Union 1817; st. flower Magnolia, st. bird Mock-ingbird; in lower M. valley; bounded on S. by G. of Mexico; cotton, sweet potatoes, pecan nuts, rice, sugar-cane, sorghum-cane, fruit, livestock raising; petroleum, natural gas; cotton textiles, chemicals, fish-processing; cap. Jackson; a. 123,584 km²; p. (1980) 2,521,000.

Mississippi, principal R. of **USA**; rises in N. Minn. nr. L. Itasca; drains c. 3,170,000 km²; enters G. of Mexico in lge. delta nr. New Orleans; navigable, flood control problems; length 3,760 km (Mississippi–Missouri–Red Rock 6,176 km).

Missolonghi, t., **Greece**; pt. on inlet of G. of Patras; fish, tobacco; Byron died here 1824; p. (1981) 11,375.

Missoula, t., Mont., **USA**; on Klark R.; univ.; rly. wks., agr., fruit, oil refinery; tourism; p. (1980) 33,388.

Missouri, st., central **USA**; Show-me St.; admitted to Union 1821; st. flower Hawthorn, st. bird Blue-bird; dominated by Mississippi and Missouri Rs.; predominantly agr.; livestock, maize; coal, iron; transport equipment; cap. Jefferson City; ch. t. St. Louis; a. 180,456 km²; p. (1980) 4,917,000.

Missouri, longest R. of **USA**; 3,942 km; trib. of Mississippi R.; main headstream Jackson R.; flood, power and irrigation schemes.

Missouri Coteau, hill ridge, N. **America**; runs N.W. to S.E. across prairies of Saskatchewan (Canada), N. and S. Dakota (USA); rises abruptly from 480–600 m.

Mistassini, L., Quebec, **Canada**; 160 km long.

Misurata, t., Tripolitania, **Libya**; on cst. of Medi-terranean, 176 km E. of Tripoli; mkt. for local agr. produce; p. (1964) 37,000.

Mitau. See Jelgava.

Mitchelstown, t., Cork, **R.o.I.**; nr. Fermoy; dairy prods.; p. (1966) 2,617.

Mitidja, plain, **Algeria**, N. Africa; borders Mediterranean; intensive cultivation of vine; ch. ts. Algiers, Blida.

Mito, c. Honshu, **Japan**; cas., comm. ctr.; famous for lime trees; p. (1979) 211,923.

Mittelland Canal, inland waterway system, **W. Germany**; system of canals and canalised Rs.; links Dortmund-Ems canal nr. Rheine through Minden, Hanover, Magdeburg, Berlin to R. Oder at Frankfurt-on-Oder; makes use of nat-ural E.–W. troughs across the N. German plain.

Mittweida, t., Karl-Marx-Stadt, E. **Germany**; metallurgy, textiles; p. (est. 1970) 19,600.

Miyazaki, c., Kyushu, **Japan**; famous shrine; ctr. of sandy plain with lagoons; p. (1979) 258,710.

Mizoram ("Land of Highlanders"), new union terr. (1972), Assam, N.E. **India**; former Mizo Hills dist. of Assam; 80 per cent p. Christian; 44 per cent literate, higher proportion than any other a. except **Kerala**; new cap. Aizawl; a. 21,238 km²; p. (est. 1971) 400,000.

Mjosa, lgst. L., **Norway**; 88 km long.

Mladá Boleslav (Jungbunziau), t., Bohemia, **ČSSR**; vehicles, agr. machin., textiles; once ctr. of Bohemian Brethren (followers of John Hus); p. (est. 1968) 28,790.

Moanda, spt. at mouth of Zaïre R., **Zaïre**; oil refinery, aluminium smelter.

Mobutu Seso, L., **(L. Albert)**, **Zaïre, Uganda**; on floor of Gt. Rift Valley; crocodile farming; tourism; main pt. Kasenyi; 160 km long, 32 km wide; alt. 640 m; a. 5,346 km².

Mobile, c., spt., Ala., **USA**; on R. M.; shipbldg. pt. inds.; exp. cotton; p. (1980) 200,000 (c.), 444,000 (met. a.).

Moçambique, former Portuguese prov., indep. st. (1975), **E. Africa**; wide cstl. plain rising inland to 2,100 m; crossed by Zambesi R.; few exp. inc. cashew nuts, cotton, sugar, tea; deposits of coal and bauxite; Beira and Maputo (cap.) serve as import pts. for transit tr.; 40% GNP from tourism and transport; Cabora Bassa Dam project in Tete dist.; border with Zimbabwe closed March 1976 now reopened; a. 771,820 km²; p. (1981) 12,615,200.

Moçambique Channel, strait, **Indian Oc.**; separ-ates Madagascar from mainland of Africa; 1,600 km long, 400–960 km wide.

Moçambique Current, ocean current, flows N. to S. along E. cst. of Moçambique and Natal, E. Africa; relatively warm water.

Moçâmedes, pt., **Angola**, W. Africa; ore pier; linked by rail to Cassinga mines; fishing; p. 8,000.

Mocha or **Al-Mukha**, t., **N. Yemen**; S.W. Arabia; on Red Sea; formerly noted for exp. of coffee; p. 5,000.

Modane, t., S.E. Savoie, **France**; commands routes via Mont Cenis Pass and tunnel; electro-metallurgy; p. (1982) 4,877.

Modena, t., cap. of M. prov. **Italy**; cath.; univ.; textiles, leather, engin.; p. (1981) 180,132.

Modesto, t., Cal., **USA**; fruit (especially peaches), vegetable-processing; p. (1980) 107,000 (c.), 266,000 (met. a.).

Modica, t., S.E. Sicily, **Italy**; agr. ctr.; limestone grottoes, cave dwellings; Cava d'Ispica; p. (1981) 45,769.

Moe. See Yallourn.

Moffat, burgh, Annandale and Eskdale, **Scot.**; 24 km N.W. of Lockerbie; resort; p. (1981) 2,034.

Moffat Tunnel, Col., **USA**; carries trunk rly. from Chicago to San Francisco under Rocky mtns. between Denver and Salt Lake City; 10 km long; alt. 2,774 m.

Mogadishu, c., cap. of **Rep. of Somalia**; on Indian Oc.; modernised deep-sea pt., airpt.; p. (est. 1973) 350,000.

Mogador. See **Essaouira.**

Mogi das Cruzes, t., São Paulo, **Brazil**; agr.; bauxite mng.; p. (est. 1980) 104,500.

Mogilev, c., Belorussiyan SSR, **USSR**; on R. Dnieper; industl.; rly. and route junc.; p. (est. 1980) 300,000.

Mohács, t., S. **Hungary**; on Danube; impt. R. pt.; strategic site; battle 1526; p. (est. 1967) 15,900.

Mohammedia, t., Morocco, N. **Africa**; oil refining; p. (1960) 35,010.

Mohawk, R., N.Y., **USA**; trib. of Hudson R.; followed by impt. road, rly. and canal routes across Appalachian mtns.; 280 km long.

Mojave or **Mohave,** S. Cal., **USA**; desert region of mtns. and valleys; a. 38,850 km².

Moji, spt., Kyushu, **Japan**; exp. coal, cement, timber; linked by bridge to Honshu. See **Kitakyushu.**

Mokpo, spt., W. cst. **S. Korea**; ctr. of food-processing and cotton-ginning; p. (est. 1970) 178,000.

Mol, t., N.E. **Belgium**; nuclear energy research ctr.; p. (est. 1983) 29,970.

Mold, t., Delyn, Clwyd, N. **Wales**; on R. Alyn; chemicals, roadstone; p. (1981) 8,589.

Moldau. See **Vltava.**

Moldavian SSR, constituent rep., **USSR**; fertile fruit growing a. especially for vines; inds. based on fruit; cap. Kishinev; a. 34,188 km²; p. (est. 1978) 3,900,000.

Mole Valley, l. gov. dist., Surrey, **Eng.**; based on Mole R. ts. of Leatherhead and Dorking; p. (1981) 76,614.

Mole R., Surrey, **Eng.**; rises in central Weald, flows N. into R. Thames nr. Molesey; cuts impt. gap through N. Downs between Dorking and Leatherhead; 80 km long.

Molenbeek-Saint-Joan, t., **Belgium**; nr. Brussels; lge mftg. ctr.; p. (est. 1983) 71,181.

Molfetta, spt., Apulia, **Italy**; olive oil, macaroni, wine, caths.; p. (1981) 65,951.

Moline, t., Ill., **USA**; on Mississippi R.; agr. implements, ironwks., flour; p. (1980) 46,278.

Mollendo, t., S.W. **Peru**; pt. on Pac. Oc.; former outlet for Arequipa; replaced by Matarani; wool textiles, fishing; p. (est. 1970) 14,251.

Mölndal, t., S.W. **Sweden**; paper, textiles; margarine; p. (1983) 48,327.

Moluccas or **Spice Is.,** prov. **Indonesia**; gr. of Is. between Sulawesi and W. Irian; mtnous., fertile; spices, sago, timber, pearls, rice, copra, ch. t. Ternate; attempts at secession by S. Moluccans; a. 496,454 km²; p. (est. 1970) 995,000.

Mombasa, spt., **Kenya**; ch. harbour, Kilindini; rly. terminus; oil refinery; exp. tropical produce (ivory, hides, rubber, etc.); fertiliser plant, sheet glass, steel rolling mill; p. (est. 1983) 409, 616.

Mon, I., off cst. of Sjaelland, **Denmark**; a. 233 km²; cap. Stege; p. (1965) 12,318.

Monaco, principality on Mediterranean cst. between France and Italy, W. **Europe**; economy based on tourism; benefits from climate and amenities, inc. famous casino; tax laws attract p. and shortage of land causes M. to build out into sea; much revenue derived from transactional laws, sales of tobacco and postage stamps; cap. Monte Carlo; a. 146 ha; p. (1982) 27,063.

Monadhliath Mtns., Badenoch and Strathspey, **Scot.**; between Spey R. and Loch Ness; hgst. peak Carn Mairg 1,216 m.

Monadnock Mt., peak, 965 m high, N.H., **USA**; name used as a term for the geomorphological feature of an isolated hill which has successfully resisted erosion.

Monaghan, co., **R.o.I.**; mainly pastoral and agr.; a. 1,295 km²; p. (1981) 15,196.

Monaghan, co. t., Monaghan, **R.o.I.**; on the Ulster canal; cath.; p. (1981) 6,172.

Mona Passage, strait, Caribbean Sea; separates Hispaniola from Puerto Rico.

Monastir. See **Bitola.**

Mönch, peak, Bernese Alps, **Switzerland**; 4,101 m.

Monchegorsk, t., RSFSR; on L. Imandra; copper and nickel smelting; p. (est. 1969) 53,000.

Mönchengladbach, t., N. Rhine–Westphalia, **W. Germany**; 26 km W. of Düsseldorf; rly. ctr. textiles; p. (1983) 258,200.

Monchique, t., Algarve, **Portugal**; spa; wine, oil, chestnuts; p. (1981) 9,609.

Moncton, t., N.B., **Canada**; rly. ctr., textiles; oil nearby; p. (1971) 47,781.

Mondego, R., Portugal; 208 km long.

Monfalcone, t., N.E. **Italy**; on Adriatic; modern industl. t.; shipbldg., oil refining; p. (1981) 30,277.

Monferrato, low hills, Piedmont, N. **Italy**; S. and S.E. of Turin between valleys of Po and Tanaro; celebrated vineyards, produce Asti Spumante wines; alt. never exceeds 460 m.

Monghyr, t., Bihar, **India**; on R. Ganges; mkt. ctr.; p. (1971) 102,474.

Mongla, pt., **Bangladesh**; on Pussur R.; shipping pt. under construction.

Mongolia, vast elevated plateau in heart of Asia between China and USSR. See **Mongolian People's Rep.** and **Inner Mongolia.**

Mongolia, Inner. See **Inner Mongolia.**

Mongolia, People's Rep. of (Outer Mongolia), central **Asia**; extensive plateau at 1,200 m bordering Gobi desert in S.; dry continental climate with extremely cold winters; pastoral agr. collectively organised for horses, sheep, camels, oxen, and goats; extensive state farms for cereals; 60 per cent of tr. with USSR; cap. Ulan Bator; a. 1,564,360 km²; p. (est. 1984) 1,851,000 (dist.).

Monklands, l. gov. dist., Strathclyde Reg., **Scot.**; part of Central Clydeside conurb. inc. Airdrie and Coatbridge; p. (1981) 110,455.

Monmouth, t., l. gov. dist., Gwent, **Wales**; at confluence of Rs. Wye and Monnow; mkt. ctr.; timber, crushed limestone, wrought ironwk.; p. (1981) 71,511 (dist.).

Monmouthshire, former co., S. **Wales**; mostly inc. in Gwent; parts in South and Mid Glamorgan.

Monongahela, R., W. Va., **USA**; joins Allegheny R. at Pittsburgh to form Ohio R.; impt. waterway.

Monopoli, spt., Apulia, **Italy**; oil, wine, fruit, flour tr.; p. (1981) 43,424.

Monroe, t., La., **USA**; cotton ctr., natural gas, paper, printing ink; p. (1980) 57,597 (t.), 139,241 (met. a.).

Monrovia, c., cap. of **Liberia**; W. Africa; free port and industl. free zone on Atl. at mouth of St. Paul R.; exp. rubber, palm oil; ship registration; p. (est. 1978) 208,629.

Mons, c., cap. of Hainaut prov., W. **Belgium**; nr. Fr. border; cath.; inds. linked with Borinage coal-mng. dist.; varied mnfs.; scene of many battles; NATO (SHAFE) H.Q. nearby at Casteau; p. (1982) 93,377.

Montana, st., N.W. **USA**; Treasure St.; admitted to Union 1889; st. flower Bitterroot, st. bird Western Meadowlark; in Rocky mtns. region; cap. Helena; lgst. c. Great Falls; copper, silver, gold, zinc, lead, manganese; coal, petroleum, natural gas; pastoral agr.; Glacier Nat. Park, tourism; a. 377,456 km²; p. (1980) 787,000.

Montauban, t., Tarn-et-Garonne dep., **France**; on R. Tarn; cath., agr. prod., wines; p. (1982) 53,147.

Montbéliard, t., Doubs dep., **France**; S. of Belfort; textiles, watches, typewriters, vehicles; p. (1982) 128,194 (met. a.).

Mont Blanc, mtn., Alps; on confines of Italy and **France**; alt. 4,814 m; longest road tunnel in world (opened to traffic 1965) linking Courmayeur (Italy) and Chamonix (France), length 12 km.

Montceau-les-Mines, t., Saône-et-Loire dep., **France**; coal, textiles, metal-working; p. (1982) 51,290 (met. a.).

Mont Cenis Pass, W. Alps; on bdy. between **France and Italy**; approached from W. by Isère–Arc valleys, from E. by Dora Riparia; alt. 2,097 m.

Mont Cenis Tunnel, W. Alps; on bdy. between **France and Italy**; carries main rly. between Lyons to Turin under Col de Fréjus; approached from W. by Isère–Arc valleys, from E. by Dora Riparia; opened 1871; 12 km long.

Montclair, t., N.J., **USA**; residtl. sub. of N.Y.; paper gds. manfs.; p. (1980) 38,321.

Mont-de-Marsan, t., Landes dep., **France**; mkt. ctr.; p. (1982) 30,894.

Mont-Dore, spa, Puy-de-Dôme dep., **France**; 48 km S.W. of Clermont-Ferrand; Puy de Sancy (1,887 m) hgst. peak of Mont-Dore mtn. gr.; p. (1982) 2,394.

Monte Bello Is., gr. off N.W. cst., **Australia**; about 136 km N. of pt. of Onslow; first Brit. atomic weapon exploded here 3 Oct. 1952.

Monte Carlo, t., **Monaco**; tourist resort, casino; p. (est. 1975) 10,000.

Monte Corno, mtn., **Italy**; in Central Apennines; alt. 2,923 m.

Monte Cristo, Italian I., 42 km S. of Elba, in Tyrrhenian Sea; famed by novel by Dumas.

Monte Gargano, peninsula, S. **Italy**; projects into Adriatic Sea nr. plain of Foggia; formed by limestone plateau, alt. over 900 m; pasture on upper slopes, woodland on lower slopes; a. 1,030 km².

Montego Bay, spt., **Jamaica**; main ctr. for tourism; p. (est. 1970) 42,800.

Montélimar, t., Drôme dep., **France**; bricks, tiles, nougat; hydroelectric barrage on R. Rhône; p. (1982) 30,213.

Montenegro, constituent rep., S.W. **Yugoslavia**; agr., pastoral; cap. Titograd; a. 13,812 km²; p. (1971) 530,361.

Monterey, t., Cal., **USA**; S. of San Francisco, resort of artists and writers; sardine ind., fruit and vegetable canneries; p. (1980) 27,558.

Monteria, c., cap. of Cordoba prov., **Colombia**; tobacco, cacao, cotton, sugar; p. (1973) 98,897.

Monte Rosa, hgst. peak, 4,637 m, Pennine Alps, on border of **Italy** and **Switzerland**.

Monte Rotondo, hgst. mtn., Corsica, **France**; 2,767 m.

Monterrey, t., cap. of Nuevo León prov., **Mexico**; third lgst. c.; cath.; textiles, brewing, ironwks., minerals; thermoelec. plant; sheet metal; p. (1979) 1,064,629 (c.), 2,018,625 (met. a.).

Monte Sant'Angelo, hilltop t., **Italy**; on Gargano promontory; notable ctr. of pilgrimage; p. (est. 1981) 16,500.

Montevideo, c., cap. **Uruguay**; major pt. on Rio de la Plata; dominates life of rep. as financial, comm. and industl. ctr.; fisheries, oil-refining, food-processing, tourism; cath., univ.; p. (est. 1975) 1,229,748.

Montgomery, t., l. gov. dist., Powys, central **Wales**; in upper Severn valley, 13 km N.E. of Newtown; agr. mkt.; cas.; p. (1981) 48,201 (dist.).

Montgomery, t., W. Punjab, **Pakistan**; livestock; leather, cotton; p. (1961) 25,100.

Montgomery, c., cap. of Ala., **USA**; at head of Alabama R.; cotton, livestock, timber, dairying, fertilisers; hydroelec. power; p. (1980) 178,000 (c.), 273,000 (met. a.).

Montgomeryshire, former co., Central **Wales**. See Powys.

Montluçon, t., Allier dep., **France**; on R. Cher; terminus of Berry canal, linking Commentry coalfields with Loire; iron foundries, glassmaking; cas.; p. (1982) 51,765.

Montmartre, dist., N. Paris, **France**; on Butte de M. (101 m), commands superb view S. over Paris; picturesque square, frequented by artists; basilica of Sacré Coeur.

Montparnasse, dist., Paris, **France**; on left bank of Seine R.; haunt of artists and writers.

Montpelier, st. cap., Vermont, **U.S.A.**; sm. t. in Green Mtns. and on Winooski R.

Montpellier, t., cap. of Hérault dep., **France**; 8 km N. of Mediterranean cst. on coastal lowland route to S.W. France; comm. and cultural ctr.; univ.; wines, fruit tr.; silk, chemicals; many anc. bldgs. inc. cath.; p. (1982) 201,067.

Montreal, c., spt., Quebec, **Canada**; at confluence of Ottawa and St. Lawrence Rs.; caths., univs.; major industl., comm. and financial ctr.; extensive harbour installations, lge. grain exp.; diverse mnfs.; lgst. c. and spt. in Canada; p. mainly French-speaking; p. (1979) 1,080,545 (c.); 2,813,300 (met. a.).

Montreuil-sous-Bois, E. sub. Paris, **France**; hothouse flowers and fruit for Paris mkt.; peach growing; mnfs.; p. (1982) 93,394.

Montreux, t., **Switzerland**; on L. Geneva; tourist ctr.; Chillon cas.; p. (est. 1978) 20,300.

Montrose, spt., burgh, Angus, **Scot.**; on E. cst. at mouth of S. Esk R.; chemicals, rope wks., vegetable-canning, boat-bldg., fishing; supply base for N. Sea oil; p. (1981) 12,286.

Mont-Saint-Michel, rocky granite I., in English Channel, off Normandy cst., **France**; tourist ctr. with Benedictine abbey; connected to mainland by causeway; surrounding marshland reclaimed for agr.; alt. 79 m; p. (1982) 80.

Montserrat, volcanic I., Leeward Is., **W.I.**; chiefly agr.; exp. sea-island cotton, limes, sugar-cane and tomatoes; cap. Plymouth; a. 101 km²; p. (est. 1974) 13,000.

Montserrat, mtn., Catalonia, **Spain**; Benedictine monastery, alt. 1,236 m.

Monument Valley, Utah and Arizona, **USA**; home of Navajo Indians.

Monza, c., Lombardy, N. **Italy**; 14 km from Milan; cath.; textiles, leather, hats; former royal residence; motor-racing circuit; p. (1977) 122,017.

Moonie, t., Queensland, **Australia**; 320 km W. of Brisbane; oilfields; pipeline to Lytton, at mouth of Brisbane R.; expected to be economically depleted by 1980.

Moose Jaw, c., Saskatchewan, **Canada**; rly. junc.; agr. ctr.; agr. implements, oil refining, p. (1976) 31,884.

Moradabad, c., Uttar Pradesh, N. **India**; rly. junc.; cotton mills, brassware; mosque; p. (1971) 258,590 (c.), 272,652 (met. a.).

Morava, R., ČSSR and Austria; trib. of R. Danube; navigable in lower course; 339 km long.

Morava, R., **Yugoslavia**; formed from W. Morava and S. Morava, flows N. into Danube 80 km below Belgrade to Istanbul; 560 km long.

Moravia, region, **ČSSR**; part of Bohemian plateau, drained by Morava R.; inc. fertile agr. a.; mineral resources and industl. ts.

Moray, former co., l. gov. dist., Grampian Reg., **Scot.**; borders M. Firth; arable agr. benefiting from glacial soils; a. 2,230 km²; p. (1981) 81,269.

Moray Firth, arm of N. Sea; on Scottish E. cst., between Highland and Grampian Regs.; plans for lge.-scale industl. expansion; offshore oil platforms at Arderseir; valuable inshore oilfield.

Morbihan, dep., N.W. **France**; on Bay of Biscay; agr., fishing; cap. Vannes; a. 7,094 km²; p. (1982) 590,900.

Mordovian ASSR, RSFSR; forested steppe between Rs. Oka and Volga; pastoral agr., lumbering; food processing; a. 25,493 km²; p. (1970) 1,030,000.

Morea. See Peloponnesus.

Morecambe and Heysham, t., N. Lancs., **Eng.**; on S. shore of M. Bay; M. holiday resort; H., pt. for N. Ireland and oil refinery; nuclear power sta. being built on cst. S. of M.; p. (1981) 41,187.

Morecambe Bay, between Lancs. and Cumbria, **Eng.**; isolates Furness dist. of Lancs.; many proposed barrages across Bay, now project increasingly probable as water shortage in N.W. Eng. grows; discoveries of nat. gas could be comm. impt.

Morelia, c., cap. of Michoacán st., W. **Mexico**; on rocky hill, 1,891 m in fertile valley; cath.; textiles, pottery; p. (1979) 251,011.

Morelos, inland st., **Mexico**; mtns., forested; arable agr.; cap. Cuernavaca; a. 4,962 km²; p. (1970) 616,119.

Morez, t., Jura dep., **France**; precision instruments, optical equipment; winter sports.

Morgan, t., R. pt., S. **Australia**; transhipment ctr.; from here water pumped from R. Murray and sent by pipeline to Whyalla; p. (1976) 340.

Morgantown, c., W. Va., **USA**; univ.; coal, oil, gas fields; chemicals, heavy ind.; p. (1980) 27,605.

Morioka, c., N. Honshu, **Japan**; textiles, ironwks.; p. (1979) 227,658.

Morlaix, spt., Finistère, **France**; tobacco, paper, brewing, agr.; p. (1982) 19,541.

Morley, t., West Yorks., **Eng.**; 5 km S.W. of Leeds; woollens, stone quarrying; p. (1981) 44,134.

Morocco, kingdom, N.W. **Africa**; csts. on Atl. Oc. and Mediterranean Sea; rises to Atlas mtns. inland; leading world producer of phosphates; other minerals inc. iron-ore, lead and manganese; agr. main occupation, provides 30 per cent of exp.; fishing and tourism well developed; cap. Rabat; a. 466,200 km²; p. (est. 1984) 22,848,000.

Morogoro, t., **Tanzania**, E. Africa; on E. edge of Central African plateau, alt. c. 900 m, 176 km by rail W. of Dar-es-Salaam; ctr. of sisal- and cotton-growing a.

Moron, t., **Venezuela**; on cst. nr. Puerto Cabello; industl.; natural gas, oil refining.

Morón de la Frontera, t., S.W. **Spain**; agr. tr. ctr.; ruined Moorish cas.; p. (1981) 27,311.

Morpeth, t., Castle Morpeth, Northumberland, **Eng.**; finely situated in valley of Wansbeck; coal mng., iron-founding; mkt.; Norman cas. remains; p. (1981) 14,545.

Morro Velho, gold mng. dist., Minas Gerais, **Brazil**; in Serra do Espinhaco; ch. t. Nova Lima.

Mors, I., N. Jutland, **Denmark**; in Lim fjord; a. 357 km²; p. (1965) 25,739.

Morwell, t., Victoria, **Australia**; ctr., for brown coal extraction and briquettes; inds. attracted by cheap power; (1976) 16,094.

Moscow, c., cap. of USSR, and of RSFSR; leading cultural, political, comm., industl. and route ctr. of USSR; on Moskva R.; served by several airpts., R. and canal pts.; contains Kremlin in c. ctr. with Red Square; caths., univs., palaces, many famous theatres and art galleries; p. (est. 1980) 8,099,000 (c.), 8,011,000 (met. a.).

Moscow Sea (**Ucha Reservoir**), artificial l., RSFSR; created behind dam on R. Volga at Ivankovo; supplies water to Moscow, maintains level on Moscow–Volga canal, and supplies water to 8 hydroelec. power-stas.; a. 329 km².

Moscow–Volga Canal, RSFSR; links R. Volga at Ivankovo with Khimki sub. of Moscow; forms part of Leningrad–Moscow inland waterway; opened 1937; 128 km long.

Moselle, dep., N.E. **France**; iron-ore, coal mng.; metal inds.; cap. Metz; a. 6,224 km²; p. (1982) 1,006,600.

Moselle, R., **France** and **Germany**; trib. of R. Rhine; canalised between Thionville and Koblenz (269 km); lower valley forms famous wine dist.; 525 km long.

Moshi, t., N. **Tanzania**; on southern slope of Mt. Kilimanjaro; ctr. of coffee-growing dist., airpt. at 854 m (S.W. of t.); p. (est. 1976) 52,223.

Mosi-oa-Toenja. See **Victoria Falls**. The local name means "Smoke of the Thunders."

Mosjoen, t., N. **Norway**; recent aluminium wks.

Moskva, R., central RSFSR; trib. of R. Oka; Moscow stands on its banks; linked with upper Volga by Moscow–Volga canal (128 km long); 400 km long.

Mosonmagyaróvár, t., **Hungary**; aluminium wks.; agr. machin.; p. (1966) 24,100.

Mosquito Cst., lowland, E. cst. **Nicaragua**; 400 km N.-S., 192 km E.-W.; lumbering, bananas; ch. t. Bluefields; sparse p.

Moss, spt., **Norway**; pulp, paper, machin., textile inds.; p. (est. 1970) 24,580.

Mossamedes. See **Moçâmedes**.

Mossel Bay, pt. and seaside resort, Cape Prov., **S. Africa**; between Cape Town and Port Elizabeth; p. (est. 1967) 15,600.

Mossley, t., Tameside, Gtr. Manchester, **Eng.**; 5 km E. of Oldham; mkt. t., textiles; p. (1981) 10,224.

Most, t., ČSSR; lignite, chemicals; Druzhba crude oil pipeline extended to chemical wks.; p. (est. 1970) 55,000.

Mostaganem, t., **Algeria**; spt. on Mediterranean cst., E. of Oran; exp. wine and fruits; gas pipeline from Hassi Messoud; p. (est. 1970) 65,000.

Mostar, t., Herzegovina, **Yugoslavia**; on R. Naretva; bauxite, lignite; developing inds., wine, food processing, aluminium plant; p. (1971) 47,606.

Mosul, t., N. **Iraq**; on R. Tigris; in region producing cereals, citrus fruit, cattle; impt. oilfields nearby; metal works; impt. during crusades; p. (1970) 293,560.

Motala, t., on L. Vättern, **Sweden**; radio sta.; engin., woollen gds.; p. (1983) 41,432.

Motherwell, burgh, l. gov. dist., Strathclyde Reg., **Scot.**; in Clyde valley, 24 km S.E. of Glasgow; iron, steel, machin., engin., textiles; p. (1981) 150,015.

Moulins, c., cap. of Allier dep., **France**; on Allier R.; leather gds., clothing; cath., ruined château, art treasures; p. (1982) 25,548.

Moulmein, spt., **Burma**, on R. Salween; exp. teak, rice; p. (est. 1977) 188,000.

Mountain Ash, t., Cynon Valley, Mid Glamorgan, **Wales**; in narrow valley 5 km S.E. of Aberdare; coal-mng. a.; p. (1981) 26,231.

Mount Adams, mtn., S. Wash. **USA**; beautiful volcanic scenery in Cascade Range; pine forests; alt. 3,803 m.

Mount Alberta, mtn., W. Alberta, **Canada**; in Canadian Rockies and Jasper Nat. Park; alt. 3,622 m.

Mount Assiniboine, mtn., Alberta, B.C., **Canada**; "Matterhorn" of Canadian Rockies; alt. 3,620 m.

Mount Carmel, mtn., N.W. **Israel**; rises to 554 m and extends 10 km as penin. into Mediterranean Sea, forming S. limit to Bay of Acre; ass. with prophets Elijah and Elisha.

Mount Gambier, t., S. **Australia**; at foot of extinct

volcano; forestry, sawmilling of radiata pine; p. (1976) 19,292.

Mount Goldsworthy, t., W. **Australia**; new t. being developed in iron ore mng. a.

Mount Isa, t., W. Queensland, **Australia**; in Selwyn Range 128 km W. of Cloncurry; copper, silver, lead mng.; p. (1976) 25,377.

Mount Lofty Range, mtn. range, S. **Australia**; forms barrier to routes leaving Adelaide; lower slopes support vineyards and outer suburbs of Adelaide; rises to over 700 m.

Mount Lyell, Tasmania, **Australia**; impt. copper mines, and refinery.

Mount McKinley, Alaska, **USA**; in Alaska Range and Nat. Park; highest point in N. America, c. 6,191 m.

Mountmellick, t., R.D., Laoighis, **R.o.I.**; p. (1961) 22,596 (R.D.).

Mount Newman, W. **Australia**; new t. built 1967 to exploit nearby iron ore.

Mount of Olives, Jordan; ridge (817 m), E. of Jerusalem; Garden of Gethsemane on lower slopes.

Mount's Bay, inlet, S. cst., Cornwall, **Eng.**; 32 km wide; fishery grounds.

Mount Tom Price, t., W. **Australia**; new t., being developed in iron ore mng. a.

Mount Vernon, c., N.Y., **USA**; on Bronx R.; sub. of N.Y.; residtl.; takes name from George Washington's house on Potomac, Va., 24 km S. of Washington D.C.; varied inds., notably electronic equipment; p. (1980) 66,713.

Mourenx, t., Pyrénées-Atlantique, **France**; nr. Lacq; new t., in oil dist.; p. (1982) 9,036.

Mourne Mtns., Newry and Mourne, **N. Ireland**; hgst. peak, 853 m.

Mouscron, t., **Belgium**; textile ctr. nr. Fr. border; p. (1982) 54,562.

Moyle, l. gov. dist., **N. Ireland**; borders N.E. cst.; inc. Rathlin I., Giants Causeway; main t. Ballycastle; p. (1981) 14,251.

Mozambique. See **Moçambique**.

Mudanjiang (**Mutankiang**), c., Heilongjiang prov., **China**; pulp (paper, machin., flour milling; site of dam on Mudan R.; oil shale found locally; p. (est. 1970) 400,000.

Mühlhausen, t., Erfurt, **E. Germany**; on R. Unstrut; textiles, machin., tobacco; p. (est. 1970) 45,385.

Mukden. See **Shenyang**.

Mulhacén, mtn., Sierra Nevada range, **Spain**; 3,483 m (hgst. peak Europe, outside Alps).

Mülheim-an-der-Ruhr, t., N. Rhine-Westphalia, **W. Germany**; on R. Ruhr; cas.; coal mng., iron, steel, tobacco, engin., elec., oil refining; airpt.; p. (1983) 177,200.

Mulhouse, t., Haut-Rhin dep., **France**; impt. textile ctr.; potash deposits to N. supply chemical inds.; p. (1982) 113,794.

Mull, I., Argyll and Bute, **Scot.**; included in Hebrides; a. 925 km²; pastoral farming, fishing, tourism; ch. t. Tobermory; p. (1971) 1569.

Mullet, The, peninsula, W. cst. Mayo, **R.o.I.**

Mullingar, c. t., Westmeath, **R.o.I.**; on Brosna R.; mkt., agr. ctr.; cath.; p. (1981) 7,854.

Mull of Galloway, S. point of Wigtown, **Scot.**

Multan, t., W. Punjab, **Pakistan**; on R. Chenab; carpets, silks, pottery, steel, thermal sta.; import gas pipeline to Lyallpur; nuclear fuel enrichment plant based on Pakistan's main uranium deposits nearby; p. (1979) 542,195.

Muncie, t., Ind. **USA**; on White R.; iron, steel, glass and paper; p. (1980) 77,216.

Munich or **München**, c., cap. Bavaria, **W. Germany**; on R. Isar; cultural ctr. with univ., cath., many old bldgs.; inds. varied, notably scientific instruments, brewing, elec. engin., chemicals; famous film studios; p. (1983) 1,284,300.

Münster, c., N. Rhine-Westphalia, **W. Germany**; pt. on Dortmund-Ems canal; heavy machin., with varied mnfs.; cath., univ. and mediæval bldgs. damaged or destroyed in second world war; p. (1983) 273,500.

Munster, prov., S.W. **R.o.I.**; includes cos. Waterford, Kerry, Cork, Limerick, Clare, Tipperary; a. 24,540 km²; p. (1981) 467,531.

Muonio, R., part of bdy. between **Finland** and **Sweden**; flows into G. of Bothnia.

Murano, t., Venice, **Italy**; famous since Middle Ages for glass ind.

Murchison Falls. See **Kabelega Falls.**

Murchison, R., W. **Australia**; flows to Indian Oc., spectacular gorge, Nat. Park; length 1,280 km.

Murcia, prov. and former Moorish kingdom, S.E. **Spain**, on Mediterranean ("Almonds and Raisins Coast"); irrigated agr., cereals and fruit; cap. Murcia; a. 8.467 km²; p. (1981) 955,473.

Murcia, c., cap. of Murcia prov., S.E. **Spain**; on R. Segura; cath., univ.; textiles and food inds.; p. (1981) 284,582.

Murgab or **Murghab,** R., **Afghanistan**; flows 400 km to desert swamps.

Murmansk, spt., **RSFSR**; on Kola peninsula; ice-free throughout year; engin., elec. power; fishing, shipbldg.; submarine base; marine power sta. utilising tidal energy projected; p. (est. 1980) 388,000.

Murom, t., **RSFSR**; pt. on Oka R.; anc. t.; textiles, engin.; p. (est. 1980) 116,000.

Muroran, spt., Hokkaido, **Japan**; on W. cst.; impt. iron and steel ctr.; p. (1979) 161,527.

Murray, R., separates N.S.W. and Victoria, **Australia**; major irrigation schemes support intensive agr.; hydro-electric power; 2,560 km long; length Murray-Darling system 3,696 km.

Murrumbidgee, R., N.S.W., **Australia**; trib. of R. Murray; used extensively for irrigation; 2,160 km long.

Mururoa, coral Is., S. **Pac. Oc.**; Fr. nuclear testing site; See **Tuamotu.**

Musa Jebel, mtn., **Egypt**; 2,249 m; identified with the biblical Sinai.

Muscat, t., cap. of **Oman,** Arabia; on S. cst. of G. of Oman; gd. harbour; dates, mother-of-pearl; terminal of oil pipeline; p. (est. 1969) 9,973.

Muscat and Oman. See **Oman.**

Musgrave Range, mtns., on bdy. between S. Australia and N.T., **Australia**; isolated highland in ctr. of continent; arid; rise to 1,520 m.

Muskingum, R., Ohio, **USA**; trib. of Ohio R.; canalised for navigation; 384 km long.

Musselburgh, burgh, East Lothian, **Scot.**; on F. of Forth at mouth of R. Esk; wire, cables, nets, twine; paper mkg.; golf course; p. (1981) 18,805.

Mutankiang. See **Mudanjiang.**

Mutari. See **Umtali.**

Muttra. See **Mathura.**

Muzaffarnagar, t., Uttar Pradesh, **India**; N.E. of Delhi; p. (1971) 114,783.

Muzaffarpur, t., Bihar, **India**; in middle Ganges valley N. of Patna; p. (1971) 126,379.

Mwanza, t., N. **Tanzania**; pt. on L. Victoria; rly. term.; gold and diamonds mined; p. (1976) 110,611.

Mweelrea, mtn., Mayo, **R.o.I.**; 820 m.

Mweru, L., between **Zaïre** and **Zambia**; a. 6,993 km² at c. 900 m.

Mycenae, anc. c., N.E. Peloponnesus, **Greece**; excavations by Schliemann.

Myingyan, t., **Burma**; on R. Irrawaddy, S.W. of Mandalay; cotton spinning mill, zinc smelting, chemicals, fertilisers.

Myitkyina, t., **Burma**; on R. Irrawaddy; terminus of caravan route to China.

Mymensingh, t., **Bangladesh**; rice, jute; p. (est. 1975) 64,000.

Mynyddislwyn, t., Islwyn, Gwent, **Wales**; in narrow valley of W. Ebbw R., 11 km N.W. of port; elec. gds., kerb- and flagstones; p. (1981) 15,547.

Mystowice, t., Katowice, **Poland**; ctr. of coal-mng. dist.; technical porcelain; p. (1970) 44,700.

Mysore. See **Karnataka.**

Mysore, t., Karnataka, **India**; univ.; new inds. based on hydroelec. power; p. (1971) 355,685.

Mytilene, pt. Aegean Sea, **Greece**; ch. c. of I. of Lesvos (sometimes called Mytilene); p. (1981) 24,991.

N

Naantali, t., S.W. **Finland**; pt. for Turku, on Baltic Sea; oil-refining, chemicals; founded 15th cent.; p. (est.) 2,778.

Naas, co. t., Co. Kildare, **R.o.I.**; former cap. of Leinster prov.; p. (1971) 5,078.

Nabeul, t., **Tunisia,** N. Africa; winter resort; p. (est. 1975) 34,100.

Nablus, t., **Jordan,** N. of Jerusalem; nr. site of anc. Schechem and Jacob's Well; p. (est. 1971) 44,200.

Nadiad, t., Gujarat, **India**; S. of Ahmadabad; p. (1971) 108,269.

Nagaland, st., **India** (1963); incorporates Naga Hills and Tuengsang; tribal a., formerly parts of Assam; cap. Kohima; a. 16,488 km²; p. (1971) 515,561.

Nagano, c., central Honshu, **Japan**; on R. Sinanogawa, 160 km S.W. of Nigata; cultural ctr.; publishing, machin., food-processing; textiles; p. (1979) 320,614.

Nagaoka, t., N.W. Honshu, **Japan**; lge. oil production ctr.; p. (1979) 177,253.

Nagapattinam, t., Tamil Nadu, **India**; spt. at mouth of R. Vettar; exp. cotton, tobacco, groundnuts; rly. terminus; p. (est. 1971) 68,015.

Nagasaki, c., spt., Kyushu, **Japan**; on narrow peninsula; second c. destroyed by atomic bomb in second world war; impt. shipbldg. ctr. and associated engin.; p. (1979) 444,815.

Nagercoil, t., Tamil Nadu, **India**; extreme S. of Indian peninsula; coconut-processing; p. (1971) 141,288.

Nagh Hamadi (Nag' Hammâdi), t., Upper **Egypt**; on R. Nile 256 km above Asyût; site of barrage (opened 1930) to regulate Nile flood and ensure irrigation of Girga prov.; barrage carries Cairo–Shellal rly. across Nile.

Nagorno-Karabakh, aut. oblast, S.W. Azerbaydzhan SSR, **USSR**; on E. of Lesser Caucasus; forested mtns.; cap. Stepanakert; a. 4,403 km²; p. (1970) 149,000.

Nagoya, third c. of **Japan**; on Ise Bay, central Honshu; major pt. and industl. ctr.; univ.; textile mills, ceramic ctr., oil-refining; 16th cent. fortress t.; p. (1979) 2,089,332.

Nagpur, c., Maharashtra st., **India**; univ.; admin. ctr.; textiles; Hindu temples; p. (1971) 866,076 (c.), 930,459 (met. a.).

Nagy Banya. See **Baia-Mare.**

Nagykanizsa, t., S.W. **Hungary**; industl. ctr.; heavy equipment, glasswks., beer; p. (est. 1970) 39,500.

Nagykörös, mkt. t., S.W. **Hungary**; in fruit-growing region; wine, food-processing; p. (1966) 25,400.

Nagymáros, t., **Hungary**; on Danube R. between Budapest and Austrian border; site of hydroelectr. dam built jointly with Austria.

Naha, spt., cap. of Okinawa I., **Ryuku Is.**; (under 1971 treaty U.S. returns Is. to Japan); p. (1979) 299,105.

Nailsworth, t., Gloucs., **Eng.**; in Cotswold Hills 6 km S. of Stroud; p. (1981) 5,086.

Nain, t., **Iran**; noted for very fine carpets; p. (1967) 40,289.

Nairn, former co., l. gov. dist., Highland Reg. **Scot.**; on Moray F., agr. a.; a. 420 km²; p. (1981) 10,139.

Nairn, royal burgh, Nairn, N.E. **Scot.**; fishing ctr.; cas.; p. (1981) 7,721.

Nairobi, c., cap. of **Kenya**; stands at c. 1,500 m on edge of Kenya highlands; modern c., 528 km from Mombasa; univ.; tourist ctr.; lt. inds.; steel rolling mill; inland ctr. for containers; wildlife game reserve; p. (est. 1983) 1,407,951.

Naivasha, L., **Kenya**; on floor of Gt. African Rift Valley; alt. 1,800 m.

Najaf or **Nejef,** c., **Iraq**; in Euphrates valley; Shiite Moslem pilgrimage ctr.; p. (1965) 134,027.

Nakhichevan, c. Azerbaydzhan SSR, **USSR**; food and wine inds.; ctr. of Nakhichevan aut. region; p. (1970) 33,000.

Nakhichevan ASSR, aut. rep. Azerbaydzhan SSR, **USSR**; borders Iran and Turkey; cotton, tobacco, rice, wheat in irrigated lowlands; salt and mineral deposits; a. 5,439 km².

Nakhodka, t., **RSFSR**; outpt. for Vladivostok on Sea of Japan; new t. 1950; p. (est. 1980) 136,000.

Nakhon Pathom, t., **Thailand**; in central plain, S.W. of Bangkok; mkt. t.; p. (est. 1970) 34,000.

Nakhon Ratchasima, t., **Thailand**; on Mun R., in Korat plateau; rly. junc.; copper deposits nearby; p. (est. 1970) 103,000.

Nakhon si Thammarat, t., **Thailand**; in S. of Isthmus of Kra, on G. of Siam; anc. t.; mkt.; p. (est. 1970) 41,000.

Nakshov, spt., Lolland I., **Denmark**; sugar-refining; p. (est. 1970) 15,994.

Nakuru, t., **Kenya** rift valley (1,837 m), E. Africa; protected bird sanctuary (flamingoes) on L. Nakuru; wool-processing, fertilisers; p. (est. 1972) 47,800.

Nalchik, c., cap. of Kabardino-Balkar ASSR, **RSFSR**; in foothills of N. Caucasus; food-processing; tourist resort; p. (est. 1980) 211,000.

Namangan, c., Uzbek SSR, **USSR**; on Syr Dar'ya R., in Ferghana Valley; textiles, leather; p. (est. 1980) 234,000.

Namaqualand, region, S.W. cst. of **Africa**; divided by Orange R. into Gr. N. in S.W. Africa, and Little N. in Cape Prov., Rep. of S. Africa; semi-arid; a. 259,000 km²; copper, diamonds.

Nam Co (**Nam Tso**), L., Tibet, **China**.

Nam Dinh, t., **Vietnam**, p. 25,000.

Namhol. *See* **Foshan**.

Namib Desert, desert a. along coastal strip of S.W. Africa for 1,200 km; very dry a., and almost unused.

Namibia (**South West Africa**); mandated terr. under U.N. responsibility admin. by South Africa; planned indep. disputed by S. Africa as it wishes to keep Walvis Bay; desert, scanty rainfall; stock rearing; alluvial diamonds from Lüderitz on Orange R.; copper, lead, zinc mng. in Grootfontein dist.; coal and offshore natural gas discovered; minerals provide 60 per cent exp. earnings; ch. pt. Walvis Bay; cap. Windhoek; summer cap. Swakopmund; a. 824,296 km²; p. (est. 1985) 1,500,000.

Namsos, spt., central **Norway**; on Folda fjord; lumber, fish canning; textiles; copper; p. (est. 1970) 11,223.

Namur, c., cap. of N. prov., **Belgium**; at confluence of Meuse and Sambre Rs.; agr. processing, cutlery, glass; p. (1982) 102,075.

Nanaimo, t., B.C., **Canada**; pt. on Vancouver I.; timber and allied inds.; fisheries; boating and yachting; tourism; p. (1971) 14,762.

Nanchong, c., Jiangsu, **China**; on Kan R.; major transportation and industl. ctr.; textiles, machin., chemicals, paper; tractor wks.; dates from Sung dynasty (12th cent.); p. (est. 1970) 900,000.

Nancheng. *See* **Hanzhong**.

Nancy, c., Meurthe-et-Moselle dep., **France**; industl. and admin. ctr.; univ., cath.; chemical ind. (based on local salt); anc. cap. of duchy of Lorraine; p. (1982) 99,307.

Nanda Devi, mtn., Uttar Pradesh, **India**; in Himalayas, 7,822 m; first scaled, 1936.

Nanded, t., Maharashtra, **India**; p. (est. 1971) 126,538.

Nanga Parbat, mtn., N.W. Kashmir, **India**, in W. Himalayas; alt. 8,131 m.

Nanjing (**Nanking**), c., Jiangsu, **China**; on Chang Jiang; cap. of China during Kuomintang régime 1928–49; famous seat of learning; tombs of founders of Ming dynasty; lge. motor vehicle plant, precision instruments, insecticides, cotton cloth, oil-refining; road-rail bridge over lowest reaches of Chang Jiang opened 1969; p. (est. 1970) 2,000,000.

Nanling, mtns., S. **China**; form divide between Rs. flowing N. to Chang Jiang and S. to Xi R.; crossed by historic Cheling and Meiling Passes; alt. mainly below 1,800 m.

Nanning, c., cap. of Guang Zhuang prov., **China**; on Yu R.; ch. mkt. on S. frontier; rice transplanter factory; p. (est. 1970) 375,000.

Nan Shan, mtns., central **China**; branch range of Kunlun; rise to over 3,600 m.

Nanterre, N.W. sub. of Paris, **France**; cap. of Hauts-de-Seine dep.; aluminium mftg.; p. (1982) 90,371.

Nantes, spt., cap. of Loire-Atlantique dep., W. **France**; on R. Loire; ocean pt. St. Nazaire; impt. industl. and shipping ctr.; univ., cath., cas.; p. (1982) 247,227.

Nantong (**Nantung**) c., Jiangsu, **China**; on N. bank of Chang Jiang estuary; cotton; p. (est. 1970) 300,000.

Nantucket, I., Mass., **USA**; official W. of trans-Atlantic sea-crossing; summer resort; fishing; p. (1980) 3,229.

Nantung. *See* **Nantong**.

Nantwich, mkt. t., Crewe and N. Cheshire, **Eng.**; on R. Weaver, 5 km S.W. of Crewe; brine baths; clothing, food prods.; p. (1981) 11,958; *see* **Crewe**.

Natyglo and Blaina, t., Blaenau Gwent, Gwent, **Wales**; in narrow valley 3 km N. of Abertillery; footwear, rubber prods.; p. (1981) 9,862.

Napier, c., N.I., **N.Z.**; pt. and ch. c. of Hawke Bay prov. dist.; exp. frozen meat; timber processing, fishing; p. (1976) 50,164.

Naples (**Napoli**), c., Campania, S. **Italy**; spt. on Bay of N., at foot of Vesuvius, opposite anc. Pompeii; exp. food prods.; impt. industl. ctr.; shipbldg., oil refining, food-processing; cultural and artistic ctr.; univ., cath.; tourism; earthquake, 1980; p. (1981) 1,212,387.

Napo, R., rises in Ecuador; 880 km long.

Nara, c., S. Honshu, **Japan**; anc. religious ctr. and place of pilgrimage; colossal image of Buddha (16·3 m high); cap. of Japan A.D. 710–84; tourism; p. (1979) 267,058.

Nara Basin, Honshu, **Japan**; agr. dist. serving the Kinki plain; intensive rice and vegetable cultivation.

Narayanganj, c., **Bangladesh**; S. of Dacca in middle Ganges delta; p. (1974) 212,844.

Narbeth, mkt. t., South Pembrokeshire, Dyfed, **Wales**; nr. head of Milford Haven; p. (1981) 1,072.

Narbonne, t., Aude dep., S. **France**; in Languedoc; nr. Mediterranean cst.; in wine-growing a.; impt. in Roman times; cath., palace (now town hall); p. (1982) 42,657.

Narew, R., **Poland** and **USSR**; flows to R. Vistula nr. Warsaw, c. 432 km long; ch. trib. W. Bug.

Narmada, R., central **India**; flows W. through Madhya Pradesh and Gujarat to G. of Cambay; 1,280 km long.

Narrabri, t., N.S.W., **Australia**; 570 km N.W. Sydney; observatory with stellar interferometer (1964); p. (1976) 6,951.

Narrandera, t., N.S.W., **Australia**; on R. Murrumbidgee; collecting ctr. for wool, mutton, wheat, fruits produced in irrigated a.; p. (1976) 4,984.

Narrogin, t., W. **Australia**; major ctr. of wheat belt; p. (1976) 4,812.

Narva, t., N.E. Estonia, **USSR**; textiles, machin., sawmills; hydroelectric power; founded by Danes 1223; p. (est. 1973) 66,000.

Narvik, pt., N.W. **Norway**; sheltered by Lofoten Is.; ice-free; linked by rly. to iron-ore fields in N. Sweden; scene of fierce sea-battles between British and Germans 1940; p. (est. 1973) 12,839.

Naseby, v., Northants., **Eng.**; battle where parliamentarians under Fairfax and Cromwell beat royalists under Charles I and Prince Rupert 1645.

Nashville, c., st. cap. Tenn., **USA**; pt. on Cumberland R.; rly. ctr.; impt. shipping, industl. and educational ctr.; food and tobacco prods., cellophane, rayon; univs. and colleges; p. (1980) 456,000. (c.), 851,000 (met. a.).

Nasik, t., Maharashtra, **India**; on R. Godavari; Hindu pilgrimage ctr.; metal work; p. (1971) 176,091 (t.), 271,681 (met. a.).

Nassau, spt., cap. Bahamas, **W.I.**; exp. forest, sea and agr. prods.; resort; p. (1970) 3,233 (t.), 101,503 (met. a.).

Nassau, I., Cook Is., S. **Pac. Oc.**; **N.Z.** terr.; uninhabited; radio telegraph sta.

Nasser City, t., **Egypt**; rural development at Kom Ombo, N. of Aswan, for resettlement of 50,000 Nubians before formation of Lake Nasser behind the High Dam.

Natal, spt., cap. of Rio Grande do Norte st., **Brazil**; above mouth of Potengi R.; exp. sugar, cotton, salt, carnauba wax, hides; recent industl. expansion results from SUDENE development plan; new textile mills; airport on main routes from Africa to S. America; p. (est. 1980) 400,600.

Natal, prov., S. **Africa**; subtropical coastal climate; sugar-cane, tea, cereals; coal; cap. Pietermaritzburg; a. 91,385 km²; p. (1980) 2,676,340.

Natanya or **Nathania**, t., **Israel**; resort on Mediterranean cst.; food-processing; p. (est. 1971) 62,500.

Natuna Is., Indonesia; I. gr. in S. China Sea, N.W. of Borneo; little developed; a. 2,113 km²; p. 27,000.

Naucratis, anc. c., **Egypt**; between Cairo and Alexandria; excavated by Flinders Petrie and Gardiner.

Naumburg, t., Halle, **E. Germany**; on R. Saale; cath.; textiles, leather, toys, chemicals; p. (est. 1973) 37,106.

Nauplia (Gr. **Nauplion**), pt. and comm. ctr., on E. cst. Peloponnesus, **Greece**; the anc. Argos; first cap. of indep. Greece 1830–4, when it was superseded by Athens; p. (1981) 10,611.

Nauru, I., indep. rep. (1968), central **Pac. Oc.**; formerly admin. by Australia; coral I., heavily dependent on phosphate-mng.; deposits will be exhausted by 1993 and plans to ship out new soil by UN; a. 21 km²; p. (est. 1980) 8,000.

Navan (**An Uamh**), U.D., Meath, **R.o.I.**; carpets; lead and zinc ores; p. (1971) 4,607.

Navarre, prov., N. **Spain**; bounded by Pyrenees; thickly wooded; cap. Pamplona; sugar-beet, cereals, cattle, hardwoods, vineyards; former kingdom; p. Basque; p. (1981) 508,722.

Naver, R., Sutherland, **Scot.**; flows N. to Pentland Firth; valley once densely p., cleared early 19th cent. to make room for sheep.

Naxos, I., **Greece**; in Aegean Sea, lgst. of the Cyclades; famous for wine and fruit; a. 425 km²; p. 19,000.

Nazareth, t., **Israel**; 34 km S.E. Acre; home of Jesus Christ; p. (est. 1970) 34,000.

Naze, The, C., S. point of **Norway**.

Nazilli, t., S.W. **Turkey**; on R. Menderes; agr., especially olives; p. (1965) 41,121.

Ndjamena (Fort Lamy), c., cap. of **Chad Rep.**; at confluence of Shari and Logone Rs.; isolated but ctr. of caravan tr.; airpt.; p. (est. 1979) 303,000.

Ndola, t., **Zambia**; nr. bdy. with Zaïre, 176 km by rail N. of Kabwe; ctr. of rich copper-mng. a., less impt. lead- and zinc-mng.; minerals despatched by rail E. to Beira and W. to Lobito Bay; oil refining nearby; international airpt. being built; p. (1980) 282,439.

Neagh, Lough, L., **N. Ireland**; lgst. freshwater L. in Brit. Is.; a. 396 km²; drained by R. Bann.

Neath, t., l. gov. dist., West Glamorgan, **Wales**; 10 km up R. Neath from Swansea Bay; coal, aluminium inds., oil refining; cas., abbey; p. (1981) 66,587 (dist.).

Nebraska, st., **USA**; Cornhusker St.; admitted to Union 1867; st. flower Golden rod, st. bird Western Meadowlark; mainly prairie; cap. Lincoln; farming, meat-packing, wheat, maize, hay, potatoes, sugar-beet, apples, wool, livestock, petroleum, cement; a. 200,147 km²; p. (1980) 1,570,000.

Neckar, R., **W. Germany**; rises between Swabian Jura and Black Forest; flows through Baden-Württemberg to Rhine at Mannheim; 384 km long.

Needles, chalk stacks in English Channel, off W. cst. of I. of Wight, **Eng.**

Neftyne Kamni, t., **USSR**; built on piles over Caspian Sea for Russian oil workers.

Negev, desert, region, S. **Israel**; new a. of irrigated agr.; oil and natural gas; p. (1962) c. 33,000.

Negombo, t., S.W. **Sri Lanka**; at mouth of Negombo lagoon; ctr. of coconut belt; metalware, ceramics; p. (est. 1970) 52,000.

Negril Beach, Jamaica; 40 km W. of Montego Bay; new resort to further Jamaica's tourist tr.

Negri Sembilan, st., W. **Malaysia**; on Strait of Malacca; tin and rubber; cap. Seremban; a. 6,682 km²; p. (1970) 479,312.

Negro Rio, R., **Argentina**; flows into G. of St. Mathias, Atl. Oc.; used for irrigation, partly navigable.

Negro Rio, R., **Brazil**; one of ch. tribs. of R. Amazon; rises in Colombia, joins Amazon nr. Manaus; c. 1,520 km long.

Negro Rio, R., **Uruguay**; flows from Brazil border to Uruguay R.; major multi-purpose project at Rincon del Bonete; 800 km long.

Negros, I., **Philippines**; S. of Mindanao; impt. sugar producing I.; copper deposits; a. 12,704 km²; p. (1970) 2,307,493.

Neheim-Hüsten, t., N. Rhine–Westphalia, **W. Germany**; at confluence of Rs. Möhne and Ruhr; chemicals; p. (est. 1971) 36,300.

Neijiang (Neikiang), c., Sichuan prov., **China**; on To R.; agr. ctr.; p. (est. 1970) 240,000.

Neisse or Nisa, two tribs. of R. Oder, (1) Western or Glatzer Neisse, frontier between Poland and E. Germany, 224 km long; (2) Eastern or Lausitzer Neisse, E. Silesia, Poland, 192 km long.

Neiva, t., **Colombia**; at head of navigation of R. Magdalena; tr. in cattle and coffee; panama hats; p. (1973) 112,479.

Nejd, dist., central **Arabia**; with Hejaz, forms kingdom of Saudi Arabia; mainly desert; impt. oil wells, horses, camels, dates, various fruits; cap. Riyadh; a. 1,087,800 km²; p. (est.) 4,000,000.

Nellore, t., Andhra Pradesh, **India**; admin. ctr.; p. (1971) 133,590.

Nelson, t., **Canada**; drains L. Winnipeg to Hudson Bay; length (with its gr. trib. the Saskatchewan) 2,320 km.

Nelson, t., Pendle, Lancs., **Eng.**; on N. flank of Rossendale 5 km N.E. of Burnley; cotton, iron and brick wks., lt. engin., paper; p. (1981) 30,435.

Nelson, c., S.I., **N.Z.**; pt. nr. head of Tasman Bay; fishing, fruit-packing, timber; coalfield; cath.; p. (1976) 42,433.

Neman (Pol. **Nieman**, Ger. **Memel**), R., Lithua-

nian SSR and Belorussiyan SSR, **USSR**; rises S.W. of Minsk and flows c. 920 km into Kurisches Haff (Courland Lagoon), Baltic Sea, forming sm. delta.

Nene, R., Northants., **Eng.**; rises nr. Naseby and flows 144 km to the Wash.

Nepal, indep. kingdom, S.E. **Asia**; on S. slopes of Himalayas and inc. Mt. Everest; isolated from India by malarial forested zone of Terai; N. mostly tropical forest and jungle; home of Gurkhas; poor transport; only 1,600 km of road; agr. in fertile valleys, rice, wheat, maize; cap. Katmandu; a. 141,414 km²; p. (est. 1984) 16,107,000.

Nerbudda. See **Narmada**.

Ness, Loch, L., Inverness, **Scot.**; occupies N.E. end of Glenmore; forms link in Caledonian Canal; very deep; 36·4 km long.

Neston, t., Cheshire, **Eng.**; on N. side of Dee estuary; residtl.; sea bed engin.; p. (1981) 18,415; See **Ellesmere Port.**

Nestos, R. See **Mesta**.

Netherlands, kingdom, N.W. **Europe**; bounded by N. Sea, Belgium and W. Germany; comprises 11 provs.; since second world war has taken advantage of location at mouth of Rhine, opposite Thames estuary, to develop lge.-scale coastal inds., inc. iron and steel at IJmuiden, oil refining, petrochemicals at major European pt. complex of Rotterdam–Europort; similarly major industl. growth in conurbation of Randstad Holland in steering economy far away from formerly predominant agr. basis; agr. still impt. and major sea-flood control schemes around IJsselmeer and Rhine estuary are creating valuable land for intensive agr. in a densely populated cty.; recent discoveries of natural gas in Groningen have also turned cty. into major supplier of energy for European mkts.; practises advanced policy of social welfare; cap. Amsterdam; seat of govt. at The Hague; a. 36,175 km²; p. (est. 1984) 14,456,000.

Netherlands Antilles (Curaçao), 2 gr. of Is. in Caribbean Sea, part of Lesser Antilles; main gr. off Venezuela inc. Curaçao, Bonaire and formerly Aruba; 2nd gr. inc. volcanic Is. of St. Eustatius, Saba, and St. Maarten (S. part only); agr. of sm. importance as a result of low rainfall; benefits from Venezuelan oil ind.; oil refineries in Curaçao; petrochemical inds.; indep. planned; Aruba separated (1986) with full internal self-government; cap. Willemstad; a. 1,020 km²; p. (est. 1981) 300,000.

Netze. See **Notec**.

Neubrandenburg, c., cap. of N. admin. dist., **E. Germany**; fibreglass, machin., chemicals; p. (est. 1982) 620,600 (dist.).

Neuchâtel, can., **Switzerland**; in Jura mtns.; forested with some pastures; cattle, cheese, wine; watches, cutlery, cottons, hosiery; asphalt from Val de Travers; a. 800 km²; p. (1980) 158,368.

Neuchâtel, cap. of Neuchâtel can., **Switzerland**; on N. slope of Lake Neuchâtel; cas.; univ.; watches, jewellery, condensed milk; p. (est. 1978) 35,400.

Neuchâtel, L., Switzerland; at S.E. foot of Jura mtns.; drains N.E. to R. Aare; vineyards on S. facing slopes; remains of lake dwellings, anc. Celtic site of La Tène culture.

Neuilly-sur-Seine, sub., W. of Paris, Hauts-de-Seine, **France**; fine bridge and cas.; engin.; p. (1982) 64,450.

Neumünster, t., Schleswig-Holstein, **W. Germany**; rly. ctr.; leather, paper and textile inds.; p. (1983) 79,600.

Neunkirchen, t., Saarland, **W. Germany**; iron and steel mngs.; coal mng.; p. (1983) 50,800.

Neuquén, t., cap. of N. prov., **Argentina**; at confluence of Rs. Limay and Neuquén, in ctr. of fruit-farming dist.; p. (1960) 17,500.

Neusalz. See **Nowa Sól**.

Neusandetz. See **Nowy Sacz**.

Neuss, c., N. Rhine–Westphalia, **W. Germany**; rly. junc., canal pt.; nr. Rhine, opposite Düsseldorf; metal gds., food-processing; p. (1983) 146,800.

Neustadt, t., Rhineland-Palatinate, **W. Germany**; on R. Haardt; agr. machinery; impt. wine tr.; p. (1983) 49,800.

Neustadt. See **Wiener-Neustadt**.

Neutitschein. See **Nový Jičín**.

Neva, R., **RSFSR**, on which Leningrad stands;

drains L. Ladoga to G. of Finland; navigable but liable to flooding; 74 km long.

Nevada, st., **USA**; Silver St.; admitted to Union 1864; st. flower Sagebrush, st. bird Mountain Bluebird; in Rocky mtns., continental climate; mng. basis of economy gold, silver, copper, tungsten, gypsum, iron, lead; livestock agr., timber; tourism; ts. inc. Las Vegas and cap. Carson City; a. 286,299 km²; p. (1980) 799,000, grew rapidly during 1960s.

Nevers, c., cap. of Nièvre dep., **France**; on R. Loire; anc. iron and steel ind.; porcelain and faience; cath., historic bldgs.; p. (1982) 59,274 (met. a.).

Neves, t., Rio de Janeiro st., S.E. **Brazil**; sugar, coffee; p. (1960) 85,741.

Nevis, I., Leeward Is., **W.I.**; cotton, sugar; ch. t. Charlestown; desire for indep. from St. Kitts; a. 130 km²; p. (1970) 11,230.

New Albany, c., Ind., **USA**; on R. Ohio; domestic glassware, furniture, leather, iron and steel, car bodies; p. (est. 1980) 37,103.

New Amsterdam, spt., **Guyana**; on Berbice R.; processes agr. prods. from surrounding lowland; p. (1970) 18,199.

New Amsterdam, Dutch settlement, Manhattan I., **USA**; taken by English 1664, and renamed New York.

Newark, mkt. t., l. gov. dist., Notts., **Eng.**; on R. Trent 27 km N.E. of Nottingham; ball bearings, brewing and malting; cas.; p. (1981) 104,139 (l. gov. dist.).

Newark, c., N.J., **USA**; meat-packing, printing, elec. gds., paints, chemicals, cars, aircraft, leather; route ctr.; p. (1980) 329,000 (c.), 1,966,000 (met. a.).

New Bedford, c., spt., Mass., **USA**; on estuary of R. Acushnet; whale-fishery ctr.; mnfs. cottons, cordage, glass, shoes; resort; p. (1980) 98,478 (c.), 169,425 (met. a.).

Newbiggin-by-the-Sea, t., Wansbeck, Northumberland, **Eng.**; sm. seaside resort; coal mng.; p. (1981) 12,132.

New Brighton, t., Merseyside, **Eng.**; at entrance to Mersey estuary; residtl. dist. of Wallasey, resort.

New Britain, lgst. I., Bismarck Archipelago, **Papua New Guinea**; volcanic mtns.; exp. copra, cacao; a. (with adjacent Is.) 37,814 km²; p. (est. 1970) 154,000.

New Britain, t., Conn., **USA**; iron and brass mnfs.; p. (1980) 73,840 (t.), 142,241 (met. a.).

New Brunswick, maritime prov., **Canada**; forest-clad mtns., impt. timber inds.; fishing and fish-processing; many minerals; road and rail link with Prince Edward I.; cap. Fredericton; a. 72,481 km²; p. (1976) 677,250.

New Brunswick, t., N.J., **USA**; on Raritan R.; chemicals, motor lorries, leather, hosiery and hardware; univ.; p. (1980) 596,000 (met. a.).

Newburgh, burgh, North East Fife, **Scot.**; on S. side of F. of Tay, 13 km E. of Perth; fish. pt.; linoleum; p. (1981) 2,008.

Newburn, t., Tyne and Wear, **Eng.**; on R. Tyne. 5 km W. of Newcastle; pure graphite for nuclear reactors; p. (1981) 43,700.

Newbury, t., l. gov. dist., Berks., **Eng.**; on R. Kennet, 27 km S.W. of Reading; engin., furniture, paper, cardboard boxmaking; mkt.; racecourse; p. (1981) 120,231.

New Caledonia, overseas terr. of **France**; volcanic I. in S. Pac. Oc.; nickel and chrome deposits; nickel processing; cap. Nouméa; independence movements to establish separate Melanesian reg. in S. Pacific and much unrest since 1984; to be decided by referendum (1989); a. 22,139 km² p. (est. 1976) 135,000.

Newcastle, c., N.S.W., **Australia**; spt. at mouth of R. Hunter; second c. of st.; lgst. exporter of coal in Australia; iron and steel based on coal resources; new inds. on reclaimed land; mineral sand mng. (rutile, zircon); p. (1976) 251,132.

Newcastle, spt., on Dundrum Bay, Down, **N. Ireland**; resort; p. (1971) 4,621.

New Castle, t., Penns., **USA**; tinplate, glass, steel wire, iron, coal, limestone; p. (1980) 33,621.

Newcastle Emlyn, t., Dyfed, **Wales**; on R. Teifi; p. (1981) 664.

Newcastle-under-Lyme, t., l. gov. dist., Staffs., **Eng.**; 3 km W. of Stoke-on-Trent, on Lyme Brook; coal mng.; brick and tile mnfs.; p. (1981) 72,853.

Newcastle upon Tyne, c., met. dist., Tyne and Wear, **Eng.**; spt. on N. bank of Tyne R., 16 km from N. Sea; shipbldg., heavy engin., chemicals; connected by bridges across Tyne to Gateshead;

univ., cath., many fine public bldgs., partially preserved in redevelopment of c. ctr.; airport; new metro system; p. (1981) 277,674.

New Delhi. *See* Delhi.

New England, N.S.W., **Australia**; dist. of N. Tablelands; pastoral cty. for sheep and beef; ch. ts. Armidale, Glen Innes, and Tenterfield.

New England, the six N.E. Atl. sts. of **USA**; Me., N.H., Vt., Mass., R.I., Conn.; humid-continental climate, infertile soils, poor agr. conditions; fishing; recent industl. metamorphosis as traditional inds. are replaced by modern science-based, high-value inds.; tourism; ch. t. Boston; p. (1980) 12,349,000.

Newent, mkt. t., Gloucs., **Eng.**; 13 km S. of Ledbury.

New Forest, forest and heathland, Hants., **Eng.**; relic of Royal Forest; now partly owned by Forestry Commission; pasture, ponies, tourism, residtl.; oil reserves but no drilling yet as conflicts with conservation; ch. t. Lyndhurst; rapid growth of p. since 1951; now forms l. gov. dist.; p. (1981) 145,123.

Newfoundland, I., with Labrador, prov., of **Canada**; E. of the G. of St. Lawrence; in E. low; in W. rugged mtns., many Ls.; coniferous forest; fishing, cod, salmon, halibut, lobster, seal; lumber, wood-pulp, paper; iron ore, lead, zinc, copper, asbestos; hydroelec. power; climate is severe; cap. St. John's; a. prov. 404,519 km² (I. 112,300 km², Labrador 292,219 km²); p. (1976) 557,725.

New Galloway, burgh, Stewartry, **Scot.**; on R. Dee; nearby Clatteringshaws hydroelec. sta..

New Guinea, I., S.W. Pac. Oc.; N. of Australia; equatorial climate; dense forest; central mtn. chain; lge. a. of lowland in S.; divided politically between Irian Jaya in W. (Indonesia) and Papua New Guinea in E.; economically under-developed; a. 831,390 km². *See* Papua New Guinea, Irian Jaya.

Newham, inner bor. Greater London, **Eng.**; W. of R. Lea; contained Royal group of London docks (now all closed); p. and industl. decentralisation from a.; p. (1981) 209,290.

New Hampshire, st., New England, **USA**; borders on **Canada**; Granite St.; admitted to Union 1788; st. flower Purple Lilac, st. bird Purple Finch; forested mtns.; agr., fruit-growing; paper and forest prods.; textiles, shoes; granite; cap. Concord; ch. spt. Portsmouth; ch. mftg. ctr. Manchester; a. 24,097 km²; p. (1980) 921,000.

Newhaven, t., East Sussex, **Eng.**; on S. cst. at mouth of R. Ouse, 14 km E. of Brighton; passenger pt. for Dieppe; boat-bldg. and lt. indus.; p. (1981) 9,857.

New Haven, c., pt., Conn., **USA**; on inlet of Long I. Sound; Yale Univ.; firearms, clocks, hardware, radiators, rubber gds.; p. (1980) 126,000 (c.), 418,000. (met. a.).

New Hebrides. *See* Vanuatu.

New Holland, v., rly. terminus, ferry pt. for crossing to Hull, Humberside, **Eng.**

New Ireland, volcanic I., **Papua-New Guinea**, in Bismarck archipelago; mtnous.; ch. pt. Kavieng; exp. copra; a. (with adjacent Is.) 9,842 km²; p. (est. 1973) 50,522.

New Jersey, st., **USA**; admitted to Union 1787; st. flower Purple Violet. st. bird Eastern Gold Finch; on Atl. cst. plain, adjacent to N.Y. c.; intensive agr., mkt. gardening; heavily industrialised; oil refining, glass sand, zinc, iron ore, clay, chemicals, motor vehicles; cap. Trenton; ch. cs. Newark, Jersey City; a. 20,295 km²; p. (1980) 7,364,000.

Newmarket, t., Forest Heath, Suffolk, **Eng.**; at foot of E. Anglian Heights; the "racing capital of England"; p. (1981) 16,235.

New Mexico, st., **USA**; popular name 'Land of Enchantment'; admitted to Union 1912; st. flower Yucca, st. bird Road Runner; N. of Mexico, S. of Col. st.; traversed by Rocky mtns.; dry climate; agr. dependent upon irrigation; dry farming, arable crops, livestock; uranium, potash salts, pumice, beryllium, copper, petroleum; ch. ts., Albuquerque and cap. Santa Fé; a. 315,115 km²; p. (1970) 1,300,000.

New Mills, industl. t., High Peak, Derbys., **Eng.**; at W. foot of Pennines; textile printing, bleaching and dyeing; rayon, paper; confectionery; p. (1981) 9,084.

Newmilns and Greenholm, burgh, Kilmarnock and Loudoun, **Scot.**; on R. Irvine, 19 km E. of Kilmarnock; muslin and lace curtain mnf.; p. (1981) 3,230.

New Mirpir, t., Pakistan; new t. 3 km. from old Mirpur submerged by Mangla L. 1967; planned p. 40,000.

New Orleans, c., spt., La., USA; on delta of Mississippi R.; the gr. cotton mart of America, busy comm., mftg. and cultural ctr., home of jazz; sugar refining, oil refining; p. (1980) 558,000 (c.), 1,187,000 (met. a.).

New Plymouth, c., spt., N.I., N.Z.; on W. cst. at N. foot of Mt. Egmont; oil and natural gas deposits; ctr. of dairy-farming dist.; p. (1976) 43,914.

Newport-on-Tay, burgh, North East Fife, Scot.; on S. side of F. of Tay, opposite Dundee; p. (1981) 3,681.

Newport, Medina, cap. I. of Wight, Eng.; on R. Medina, in gap through central chalk ridge; mkt.; brewing, joinery, bait mnfs.; prison; p. (1981) 23,570.

Newport, mkt. t., The Wrekin, Shrops., Eng.; 13 km N.E. of Wellington; p. (1981) 8,983.

Newport, spt., Vietnam; on N. outskirts of Ho Chi-minh City; lge. pt. inaugurated 1967.

Newport, t., R.I., USA; on Narragansett Bay; fashionable seaside resort; precision instruments; p. (1980) 29,259.

Newport, t., l. gov. dist., Gwent, Wales; on R. Usk, 8 km from its mouth; timber terminal and deep-water berth; engin., iron and steel, aluminium, paperboard, confectionery, chemicals, plastics; p. (1981) 133,698 (dist.).

Newport News, c., spt., Va., USA; on N. shore of estuary of James R. on Hampton Roads; lge. harbour; shipbldg.; outlet for Virginian tobacco and Appalachian coal; p. (1980) 145,000 (c.), 364,000 (met. a.).

Newport Pagnell, mkt. t., Bucks., Eng.; on R. Ouse; mnfs. Aston Martin cars; p. (1981) 10,810.

Newquay, t., Restormel, Cornwall, Eng.; on N. Cornish cst.; seaside resort; p. (1981) 16,050.

New Quay, t., Ceredigion, Dyfed, Wales; on cst. of Cardigan Bay; fishing; resort; p. (1981) 766.

New Radnor, t., Powys, Wales; on slope of Radnor Forest, 10 km S.W. of Presteign.

New Rochelle, t., N.Y., USA; on Long I. Sound; residtl.; p. (1980) 70,794.

New Romney, t., Shepway, Kent, Eng.; nr. S. cst. to E. of Dungeness; in rich agr. dist. of Romney Marsh; Cinque pt.; old harbour silted up by shingle, now a mile from sea; p. (1981) 4,563.

New Ross, mkt. t. U.D., Wexford, R.o.I.; brewing and malting; p. (est. 1978) 5,500.

Newry, t., Newry and Mourne, N. Ireland; pt. at head of Carlingford Lough; machin., rope, brewing, granite; p. (1981) 19,426.

Newry and Mourne, l. gov. dist., N. Ireland; surrounds t. of N., borders R.o.I., Irish Sea; inc. Mtns. of Mourne; p. (1981) 72,748.

New South Wales, st., S.E. Australia; first col. established by Brit. in A.; much mineral wealth in tablelands and mtns.; climate equable and well suited to both arable and pastoral agr.; leading agr. st. in Australia; major irrigation schemes in drier E. plains of Murray, Murrumbidgee, and Lachlan Rs.; coal mng. and heavy inds. at Newcastle, Port Kembla, Wollongong; hydroelectric power from Snowy mtns. scheme; lge. concentration of p. in cap. c. of Sydney; a. 801,431 km² (excluding Cap. Terr. of Canberra); p. (1976) 4,777,103.

Newton, t., Mass., USA; on R. Charles; in met. a. of Boston; lt. inds.; p. (1980) 83,622.

Newtonabbey, t., l. gov. dist., N. Ireland; sub. of Belfast, textiles, lt. inds.; p. (1981) 71,825 (dist.), 56,149 (t.).

Newton Abbot, mk. t., Teignbridge, Devon, Eng.; at head of Teign estuary; rly. junc.; pottery, lt. engin.; agr. processing; p. (1981) 20,927.

Newton Aycliffe, t., Durham, Eng.; 10 km N.W. of Darlington; new t. (1947); engin., textiles, plastics, paint; p. (1981) 24,720.

Newton-le-Willows, t., Merseyside, Eng.; engin., printing, sugar-refining; p. (1981) 19,723.

Newton-Stewart, burgh, Wigtown, Scot.; on R. Cree, 8 km N. of Wigtown; mkt.; wool, creameries and agr. inds.; p. (1981) 3,220.

Newtown and Llanllwchaiarn, mkt. t., Powys, Wales; on R. Severn 13 km S.W. of Montgomery; precision instruments, machine tools; plan for expansion as growth-pole for central Wales; p. (1981) 8,660.

Newtownards, spt., mkt., Ards, N. Ireland; 11 km E. of Belfast; textile and engin. inds.; p. (1981) 20,531.

New Waterway. *See* **Nieuwe Waterweg.**

New Westminster, t., B.C., Canada; spt. on estuary of R. Fraser; exp. timber; agr. ctr., food-processing and canning; fishing; oil refining; forms part of Vancouver met. a.; p. (1971) 42,083.

New York, st., N.E. USA; popular name 'Empire St.'; admitted to Union 1788; st. flower Rose, st. bird Bluebird; one of 13 original sts., borders Canada on N., faces Atl. Oc. in S.; Adirondack mtns. in N., with lowland in E. alongside L. Ontario; Hudson valley impt. routeway; humid-continental climate; second lgst. st. in p. size and despite p. movement to W., remains major a. of urbanisation (megalopolis) with comm. and industl. activity; ch. ts. inc. Buffalo, Rochester, Syracuse; st. cap. Albany, metropolis New York city; decline of N. ts. offset by inds. from Quebec, leaving because of separatist moves; dairy farming and intensive agr. serve urban mkts.; a. 128,402 km²; p. (1980) 17,557,000.

New York, c., spt., N.Y., USA; on N.Y. Bay at mouth of Hudson R.; lgst. c. in USA and one of lgst. in world; comprises 5 bors., Manhattan, Bronx, Queens, Brooklyn, Richmond; originally founded by Dutch settlers as New Amsterdam on Manhattan I.; gr. comm. ctr. and cultural cap.; univ.; fine parks, bridges, skyscrapers, and deepwater harbour; varied inds., inc. clothing, food-processing, printing and publishing, shipbldg.; despite p. and industl. decentralisation concentration of socially needy in c. causing financial difficulties to c. govt.; 2 intern. airports; p. (1980) 7,035,000 (c) 9,081,000 (met. a.).

New York State Barge Canal (Erie Canal), N.Y. st., USA; links Tonawanda on Niagara R. with Hudson R. via the Mohawk gap through Appalachian mtns.; provides through water route from N.Y. to Gr. Ls.; opened as Erie Canal 1825, improved 1918; length 542 km (with branches 840 km), depth 4 m.

New Zealand, indep. sov. st. within Brit. Commonwealth, S. Pac. Oc.; 1,920 km E. of Sydney, Australia; consists of two major Is., N.I. and S.I., separated by Cook Strait, and several smaller Is., inc. Stewart I. to S.; mtnous., glaciated, volcanic; landscapes with superb scenery; dependent upon pastoral prods., taking advantage of equable climate and excellent grass growing conditions, but mainly reliant on Brit. mkts.; economic diversification; expansion of lt. indus., inc. car assembly, pulp and paper, textiles; hydroelec. potential being developed; oil and natural gas recently discovered; advanced social services; cap. Wellington; ch. pt. Auckland; a. 268,676 km²; p. (est. 1984) 3,264,000.

Neyland, t., Preseli, Dyfed, Wales; on Milford Haven; rly. terminus and sm. pt.; p. (1981) 3,097.

Ngami, L., Botswana, S.W. Africa; swamp, the remnant of a much larger L.

Ngauruhoe, mtn., N.I., N.Z.; an active volcano; 2,292 m.

Niagara, R., forms part of boundary between Canada and USA; flows from L. Erie to L. Ontario; rapids and famous falls utilised by gr. hydroelec. power sta. heavily polluted with toxic waste; 56 km long.

Niagara Falls, waterfall, Niagara R., on bdy. of USA and Canada; in two sections, American (51 m high) and Canadian (48 m high), separated by Goat I.; major tourist attraction and hydroelec. power sta.

Niagara Falls, t., Ontario, Canada; opposite the falls; hydroelectric power sta.; timber and agr., inds., tourism; p. (1971) 65,271.

Niagara Falls, c., N.Y., USA; extends along summit of cliff for 5 km; paper, flour, aluminium, chemicals, hydroelectric power stas.; univ.; p. (1980) 71,384; inc. in Buffalo met. a.

Niamey, t., cap of Rep. of Niger, W. Africa; one of the termini (the other is Zinder) of the trans-Sahara motor routes; agr. tr. ctr.; p. (est. 1981) 360,000.

Nicaragua, rep., Central America; civil war (1970), lies across isthmus with Pac. Oc. to W., Caribbean Sea to E.; sparsely populated; central mtn. range, marshy E. cst.; tropical rain forest and climate; limited a. of fertile soils but 70 per cent. p. farmers; main exps. coffee, cotton;

industl. growth based on US investment, gold and silver mng.; politically unstable; cap. Managua; a. 148,006 km²; p. (est. 1984) 3,162,000.

Nicaragua, Lake, S.W. **Nicaragua**; lgst. L. in Central America; 24 km from Pac. Oc., but discharges into Caribbean via San Juan R.; fisheries; 160 km N.W. to S.E., 67 km S.W. to N.E.

Nicaraguan Depression, lowland, **Nicaragua**; contains Ls. Maragua and Nicaragua.

Nice, c., spt., cap. of Alpes Maritimes dep., **France**; on Mediterranean cst., at foot of Alps; pleasant climate and surroundings; adjoins anc. t. of Cimiez; ceded to France 1860 by Sardinia; resort; fruit and flower exp., perfume mftg.; attracting science-based inds.; major airport; p. (1982) 338,486.

Nicobar Is. *See* **Andaman and Nicobar Is.**

Nicosia, c., cap. of **Cyprus**; agr. tr. ctr.; textiles, cigarettes, leather, pottery mnfs.; remains of Venetian fortifications; mosques; new airport; cap. of admin. dist. of Nicosia; tourism; p. (est. 1973) 115,718.

Nidd, R., trib. of R. Ouse, North Yorks., **Eng.**; 80 km long.

Nidwalden. *See* **Unterwalden.**

Nieder Sachsen. *See* **Lower Saxony.**

Niemen R. *See* **Neman.**

Nieuwe Waterweg, ship canal, S. Holland, **Neth.**; connects R. Lek 11 km below Rotterdam with N. Sea cst. at Hook of Holland.

Nieuwveld Range, mtns., Cap Prov., **S. Africa**; part of S. terminal escarpment of African tableland; overlooks Gr. Karroo to its S.; forms impenetrable barrier to routes; mainly over 1,500 m. max. alt. 1,914 m.

Nièvre, dep., central **France**; traversed by Morvan mtns., forests, arable agr.; cap. Nevers; a. 6,887 km²; p. (1982) 239,500.

Nigel, t., Transvaal, **S. Africa**; gold mng.; industl.; p. (est. 1967) 38,400.

Niger, landlocked rep., W. **Africa**; 90 per cent p. dependent upon agr. but only 3 per cent of land cultivated; livestock (cattle, sheep, goats), cotton; exp. of groundnuts main source of wealth; rainfall diminishes to N. giving way to Sahara Desert; discovery and exploitation of uranium (1967), 75 per cent of exp. earnings in 1980 but now declining; fishing in L. Chad; game hunting; close economic ties with France; cap. Niamey; a. 1,253,560 km²; p. (est. 1984) 5,940,000.

Niger, R., W. **Africa**; rises nr. sea in outer mtn. zone of W. Africa as R. Tembi, sweeps round by Timbuktu to delta in G. of Guinea, on circuitous course of 4,160 km, receiving its gr. trib., the R. Benue, about 400 km from the mouth; navigable for 1,600 km; Kainji (Nigeria) hydroelec. plant and dam opened 1969; now organised by international Niger Basin Authority.

Nigeria, fed rep., W. **Africa**; within Brit. Commonwealth; federation of 19 sts.; climate, wet, tropical in S., increasingly dry to N.; main economic development in S.; exp. agr. prods., especially cocoa; exp. hardwoods; economic growth based on cstal. oil deposits (sulphur free); fall in oil prices causing decline in production and exp.; 2nd oil producer in Africa; 6th in world; cap. Lagos, lgst. c. Ibadan; cap. Abuja (1986); a. 923,773 km²; p. (est. 1983) 89,022,000.

Niigata, c., Honshu, **Japan**; pt. on W. cst. exp. locally produced petroleum; chemical inds.; p. (1979) 444,610.

Niihama, c., N. Shikoku, **Japan**; on cst. of Inland Sea, 32 km S.E. of Imabari; refines copper obtained from Besshi mines 19 km to the S.; petrochemicals; p. (1979) 135,814.

Nijmegen, c., E. **Neth.**; on R. Waal, nr. German bdr., 18 km S. of Arnhem; Hanse t. in Middle Ages; historic bldgs., univ.; p. (1982) 147,172.

Nijni-Novgorod. *See* **Gorki.**

Nikko, t., Honshu, **Japan**; famous temples and shrines; tourist resort; p. (1966) 32,031.

Nikolayev, c., cap. of N. oblast, Ukrainian SSR, **USSR**; major spt. at head of Dnieper–Bug estuary on Black Sea; shipbldg., ctr.; exp. minerals, grains; founded 1784 as fortress; p. (1980) 449,000.

Nikolayevsk, lge. R. pt., Khabarovsk terr., **RSFSR**; on R. Amur; shipyards; fishing, canning, lumbering, oil refining; p. (est. 1967) 32,000.

Nikopol, c., Ukrainian SSR, **USSR**; on Dnieper; manganese mng. ctr.; steel, machin.; p. (est. 1980) 149,000.

Nikšić, t., Montenegro, **Yugoslavia**; N. of Cetinje; bauxite mng., growing industl. ctr.; p. (est. 1965) 27,000.

Nile, longest R. in Africa (*see* **White Nile** (Bahr-el-Abiad) and **Blue Nile** (Bahr-el-Azrek)); flows through a longer stretch of basin (over 3,920 km in a direct line) than any other R., and along all its windings measures 6,670 km; on Upper Nile navigation is hindered by sudd (floating vegetation); R. rises April, overflows Sept.; formerly cultivation entirely dependent on annual floods, but now assisted by dams, at Asyût, Aswan, Sennar, for regulating flow and navigation; Aswan High Dam completed 1970, but complex problems of delta erosion and dam-lake silting. *See also* **Egypt.**

Nilgiri Hills, Tamil Nadu, S. **India**; tea-growing dist.; resort a.

Nîmes, c., cap. of Gard dep., S. **France**; in Cevennes; Roman antiquities, notably Maison Carrée; silk, cotton, carpets, wines; tourism; p. (1982) 129,924.

Nineveh, celebrated anc. c., **Iraq**; stood on E. bank of upper R. Tigris, opposite modern Mosul.

Ningbo (**Ningpo**), c., spt., Zhejiang, **China**; 160 km from Shanghai; leading fish, pt., comm. and mnf. ctr.; exp. agr. and fish prods.; p. (est. 1970) 350,000.

Ningxia Hui, aut. region, N.W. **China**; bounded on N. by Inner Mongolia; dry a. but modern irrigation projects allow growth of spring wheat and rice; coal reserves, salt; cap. Yingchuan; a. 66,408 km²; p. (est. 1968) 2,000,000.

Niobrara, R., **USA**; trib. of Missouri R.; flows from Wyoming to Nebraska; 960 km long.

Niort, c., cap. of Deux-Sèvres dep., W. **France**; noted for mkt. gardens and leather gds. (gloves); birthplace of Mme de Maintenon; p. (1982) 60,230.

Nipigon, Lake, in Thunder Bay dist., Ont. **Canada**; 106 km long, 74 km wide; studded with Is.; discharges by Nipigon R. to L. Superior.

Nipissing, Lake, S. Ont., **Canada**; 855 km²; drained by French R. to Georgian Bay.

Niš, t., **Yugoslavia**; on R. Nishava; route ctr.; rly. engin., developing mftg.; univ.; p. (1981) 643,470.

Nišava, R., **Yugoslavia**; flows N.W. into R. Morava nr. Niš; valley used by trunk rly. from Belgrade to Istanbul; length over 160 km.

Nishapur, mkt. t., N.E. **Iran**; S.W. of Mashhad; in fertile a.; cotton, fruits; famous turquoise mines nearby; birthplace of Omar Khayyám; impt. archaeological finds dating 9th and 10th cent.; p. (1966) 33,482.

Nishinomiya, c., S. Honshu, **Japan**; produces famous liquor called saké; machin., chemicals; p. (1979) 398,653.

Niterói, t., cap. of Rio de Janeiro st., **Brazil**; shipbldg.; residtl. sub. of Rio de Janeiro c. to which it is linked by bridge; p. (est. 1980) 433,400.

Nith, R., S.W. **Scot.**; flows to Solway F., S. of Dumfries; followed by main rly. from Carlisle to Kilmarnock and Glasgow; 114 km long.

Nithsdale, l. gov. dist., Dumfries and Galloway, **Scot.**; a. based on Dumfries; p. (1981) 56,493.

Niue or **Savage I., Pac. Oc.**; one of Cook Is., formerly part of N.Z., self government 1974; ch. pt. Alofi; copra, plaited basketware, sweet potatoes; a. 259 km²; p. (est. 1976) 4,000.

Nivernais, former prov. of **France**, now forming Nièvre prov. and part of Cher.

Nizamabad, t., Andhra Pradesh, **India**; road and rly. ctr. N. of Hyderabad; p. (1971) 115,640.

Nizhneudinsk, t., W. Irkutsk, **RSFSR**; new mftg. t.; p. (est. 1967) 38,000.

Nizhni Novgorod. *See* **Gorki.**

Nizhniy Tagil, t., **RSFSR**; in Ural mtns.; metallurgical ctr. using ore from Mt. Visokaya; rly. cars, iron, and steel plants, chemicals; p. (est. 1980) 400,000.

No, Lake, Bahr-el-Ghazal prov., **Sudan**; N.E. Africa; vast swamp a., 906 km S.W. of Khartoum; flow of water blocked by papyrus reed and floating weed (sudd).

Nobeoka, t., Kyushu, **Japan**; on E. cst.; p. (1979) 140,822.

Nobi Plain, S. Honshu, **Japan**; at head of Ise Bay; composed of: (1) low, badly drained alluvial plain on W. under intensive rice cultivation, (2) higher, drier, terraces on E. under mulberry, vegetables, pine-woods; very dense urban and rural p.; ch. textile and pottery mftg. a. in Japan; inc. cs. Nagoya, Gifu, Yokkaichi; a. 1,865 km²; p. (1960) 5,400,000.

Nocera Inferiore, t., Italy; nr. Naples; vegetable-canning, textile mnfs.; p. (1981) 47,698.

Nogales, twin ts., Sonora, **Mexico** and Arizona, **USA;** mng. and agr. ctr.; total p. (1980) 15,683.

Noginsk, t., **RSFSR;** nr. Moscow; textiles, metals; natural gas pipeline from Central Asia projected; p. (est. 1980) 120,000.

Nola, c., Italy; at foot of Vesuvius, 19 km N.E. of Naples; ctr. of fertile arable agr. a. in Campania plain; anc. c., home of Giordano Bruno; p. (1981) 30,979.

Nome, c., W. Alaska, **USA;** on Seward peninsula; gold rush (1900); now admin. and route ctr.; airport; tourism; p. (1980) 2,301.

Noord Brabant, prov., Neth.; cap. 's-Hertogen-bosch; a. 4,973 km²; p. (est. 1972) 1,879,848.

Noord Holland, prov., **Neth.;** a. 2,722 km²; cap. Haarlem; natural gas in Schermer Polder nr. Alkmaar; p. (est. 1972) 2,283,414.

Noordoostpolder, Overijssel, **Neth.;** land reclaimed from Zuider Zee, 1942; now used for intensive agr.; a. 479 km²; p. (1982) 37,545.

Nord, dep., N. **France;** borders on Belgium and N. Sea; flourishing agr., mng. iron and coal, textile and chemical mnfs.; cap. Lille; a. 5,773 km²; p. (1982) 2,526,300.

Nordenham, pt. on Lower Weser R., Lower Saxony, **W. Germany;** lead and zinc smelting; fishing; p. (1983) 29,700.

Norderney, one of the E. Frisian Is., **W. Germany;** low-lying sand-dunes; resort and fish. pt. at Nordseebad.

Nordhorn, t., Lower Saxony, **W. Germany;** nr. Neth. frontier; textiles; p. (1983) 48,000.

Nordkyn, Cape, northernmost pt. of European mainland, Finnmark prov., N. Norway.

Nordland, co., N. **Norway;** fjord cst.; p. on cst. lowlands; fishing, livestock; iron-ore, electro-chemical and metallurgical inds. based on local hydroelec. power; spt. Narvik; a. 38,146 km²; **p.** (est. 1972) 241,142.

Norfolk, non-met. co., E. **Eng.;** low-lying fens in W.; low sandy cst. suffers from erosion; intensive arable agr. on lge. farms; wheat, barley, root crops; inds. based on agr. process-ing and provision of agr. requisites; tourism intensively developed on Norfolk Broads; cap. Norwich; a. 5,354 km²; p. (1981) 693,490.

Norfolk, c., Va., **USA;** naval base on Hampton Roads; fine deepwater harbour; exp. coal, industl. prods.; shipbldg., car assembly, food-processing, timber inds., fertilisers; p. (1980) 267,000 (c.), 807,000 (met. a.).

Norfolk I., remote dependency of Australia; **Pac. Oc.;** volcanic I., 1,676 km N.E. of Sydney; unique ecology; fertile agr.; discovered by Cook 1774; penal settlement 1788–1853; tourism; a. 34 km²; p. (est. 1975) 1,900.

Norfolk, North, l. gov. dist., Norfolk, **Eng.;** cstl. a. inc. Wells-next-the-Sea, Cromer, Shering-ham, Walsingham and North Walsham; p. (1981) 82,037.

Norfolk, South, l. gov. dist., Norfolk, **Eng.;** lge. a. inc. Diss and Wymondham; p. (1981) 92,842.

Norilsk, t., Krasnoyarsk terr., **RSFSR;** in N. Siberia; northernmost t. in Russia; mng. of coal, uranium, nickel, copper; natural gas pipeline from W. Siberia; p. (est. 1980) 182,000.

Normandy, historic prov. of **France;** on English Channel; now divided into deps. Manche, Calvados, Eure, Seine-Maritime and part of Orne; Rouen was cap.; Channel Is. were part of the old duchy; conquered England 1066; allied invasion of Europe 1944.

Normanton, t., West Yorks., **Eng.;** 5 km N.E. of Wakefield; coal mng.; p. (1981) 17,256.

Norman Wells, t., N.W. Terr., **Canada;** at con-fluence of R. Mackenzie and Gr. Bear R., 112 km W. of Gr. Bear L.; ctr. of rich oil-field.

Norrbotten, prov., N. **Sweden;** rich iron deposits at Kiruna; ore exp. via ice-free Narvik on Norwegian cst.; many Ls. and Rs., highest peak in Sweden, Kebnekaise; cap. Pitea; a. 105,553 km²; p. (est. 1983) 264,457.

Norris Dam, Tenn., **USA;** across R. Clinch at confluence with R. Tennessee, N.W. of Knox-ville; lgst. dam Tenn. Valley Authority (TVA); built for flood control and hydroelectric power.

Norrköping, c., S.E. **Sweden;** nr. inlet of Baltic

Sea; industl. and shipping ctr.; ocean-going shipping through Lindö canal; p. (1983) 118,064.

Northallerton, mkt. t., Hambleton, North Yorks., admin. ctr., **Eng.;** in broad gap between Cleve-land hills and Pennines; in dairy farming and agr. dist.; p. (1981) 9,622.

North America, northern continent of W. hemi-sphere; comprises Greenland (on N. American continental shelf), Canada, USA, Mexico; high W. Cordilleras, inc. Rocky mtns., run N. to S. from Alaska to Mexico; lower range of Ap-palachian mtns. in E. with vast interior basin, inc. Gr. Ls., Saskatchewan, St. Lawrence, and Miss.-Mo. R. systems; gr. variation in climate and vegetation from subtropical in S. and Mediterranean in W. to Arctic in N. and continental in interior; enormous endowment of natural resources provide basis for vast economies of USA and Canada, but contem-porary public concern for natural environment of continent; formerly inhabited by Indians, now mainly occupied by a white p. with lge. Euro-pean minorities, and an African-based, black p.; p. (est. 1984) 261,120,000 (inc. Hawaii).

Northampton, t., l. gov. dist., Northampton, **Eng.;** on R. Nene; footwear, engin., leather gds.; new t. designation; p. (1981) 156,848.

Northamptonshire, non-met. co., **Eng.;** E. Mid-lands; chiefly agr.; iron mng. and mftg.; foot-wear, engin., leather; co. t. Northampton; a. 2,367 km²; p. (1981) 527,582.

Northamptonshire, East, l. gov. dist., Northants., **Eng.;** stretches from Oundle to Irthlingborough, Rushden, Raunds and Higham Ferrers; p. (1981) 60,843.

Northamptonshire, South, l. gov. dist., Northants., **Eng.;** inc. Brackley and Towcester; p. (1981) 64,057.

North Atlantic Drift, drift of surface waters of Atl. Oc. N.E. from Gulf Stream towards Europe; relatively warm; supplies prevailing S.W. winds with warmth and moisture to modify climate of Brit. Is. and N.W. Europe.

Northavon, l. gov. dist., Avon, **Eng.;** a. N. of Bristol, inc. Sodbury; p. (1981) 118,804.

North Bay, t., Ont., **Canada;** on L. Nipissing; air base; tourism, route ctr.; p. (1971) 49,063.

North Berwick, royal burgh, E. Lothian, **Scot.;** on S. of F. of Forth, 32 km E. of Edinburgh; seaside resort; golf course; fishing pt.; p. (1981) 5,388.

North Beveland, I., **Neth.;** in Scheldt estuary; arable agr.; a. 91 km².

North Carolina, st., S.E. **USA;** Tarheel St.; admitted to Union 1789; st. flower Flowering Dogwood., st. bird Cardinal; bounded on E. by Atl. Oc.; one of 13 original sts.; sandy, indented cst., rising in W. to Appalachian mtns.; humid subtropical climate, modified by alt.; agr. impt.; maize, cotton, tobacco; mica; textiles; ch. pt. Wilmington; cap. Raleigh; a. 136,524 km²; p. (1980) 5,874,000.

North Channel, Brit. Is.; gives access from Atl. Oc. to Irish Sea between S.W. Scotland (Gallo-way) and N.E. Ireland (Larne); length 96 km; narrowest width 24 km.

North China Plain, China; alluvial lowland of Huang-He basin; notorious floods but R. now controlled; wheat and millets; very dense p.

North Crimean Canal, USSR; links R. Dnieper with Black Sea and Sea of Azov, crossing steppes of S. Ukraine and Crimea, terminating at Kerch; first section (123 km long) opened 1963; when completed will be 352 km long, 200 km of which will be navigable.

North Dakota, st., N.W. **USA;** Flickerhill St.; admitted to Union 1889; st. flower Wild Prairie Rose, st. bird Western Meadowlark; rolling prairie, rising from E.-W.; drained by Missouri R., controlled by multi-purpose Garrison Reservoir; arable agr., mainly grains, but eroded "Badlands" in S.; coal mng., petroleum; a. 183,022 km²; p. (1980) 653,000.

North Down, l. gov. dist., **N. Ireland;** borders Belfast Lough; main ts. Bangor, Holywood; p. (1981) 65,666.

North Downs, Surrey/Kent, **Eng.;** chalk escarp-ment running E. to W. across S.E. Eng., flanking the Weald to N.; form "white cliffs of Dover"; followed in part by Pilgrim's Way; Box Hill 233 m.

North-East China, formerly known as Manchuria, comprising provs.—Liaoning, Jilin, Heilong-jiang; mtnous., N.W. and E.; drained to N. by Songhua Jiang and S. by Liao Rs.;

K114

forested; soya-beans, wheat, coal, iron; impt. a. for iron and steel; occupied by Japanese in second world war; p. (est. 1968) 66,000,000.

North East Fife, l. gov. dist., Fife Reg., **Scot.**; a. between F. of Forth and F. of Tay; impt. ts. St. Andrews and Cupar; p. (1981) 62,387.

North-East Frontier Agency. *See* **Arunachal Pradesh.**

North East Passage, along N. cst. Europe and Asia between Atl. and Pac. *See* **Section L.**

Northern Ireland, part of **U.K.**; occupies N.E. a. of Ireland, consisting of 26 l. gov. dists.; mild, temperate climate, exploited by dairy farming using excellent grass; arable agr. inc. barley, potatoes; traditional inds. inc. linen, shipbldg., food-processing, tobacco; modern inds. encouraged by extensive government aid inc. artificial fibres, carpets, elec. and aero-engin.; heavily dependent upon Brit. mkt.; serious social disturbance since 1969, based upon long-standing religious differences between Roman Catholic and Protestant as a result of discrimination against minority; Stormont Parliament replaced by Assembly (suspended 29 May 1974 and direct rule resumed); returns 12 members to Westminster; a. 14,121 km²; p. (1981) 1,488,077.

Northern Territory, self governing st. (1978) N. **Australia;** variable rainfall decreasing inland from N. to S.; land rises generally N. to S. and reaches over 1,800 m in Macdonnell ranges; lge. semi-nomadic Aboriginal p.; livestock agr. dependent upon rail, road access to mkt.; mng.; newly opened uranium mines abuse aborigine terr.; ch. ts. Darwin on N. cst., Alice Springs; a. 1,356,176 km²; p. (1976) 97,090.

Northfleet, t., Kent, **Eng.**; on S. bank of R. Thames, adjoining Gravesend; cement, paper, rubber, tyres, cables; p. (1981) 26,250.

North Foreland, E. Kent, **Eng.**; chalk headland.

North Island, I., **N.Z.**; one of the two major Is. of N.Z., separated from S.I. by Cook Strait, volcanic mtns., Waikato R. drains L. Taupo, cap. Wellington, spt. Auckland, oil deposits on E. and W. csts.; a. 114,688 km²; p. (1976) 2,268,393.

Northleach, t., Cotswold, Gloucs., **Eng.**; once impt. woollen tr.

North Little Rock, t., Ark., **USA**; agr. processing, engin.; p. (1980) 64,288.

North Ossetian ASSR, RSFSR; on N. slope of Gr. Caucasus; cap. Ordzhonikidze; agr. in valleys; lead, silver, zinc, and oil deposits with metallurgical and food-processing inds.; a. 8,029 km²; p. (1970) 553,000.

North Platte, t., Nebraska, **USA**; on N. Platte R.; p. (1980) 24,509.

North Platte, R., **USA**; rises N. Col., flows 1,088 km through Wyo., across W. Nebraska to join S. Platte at c. of North Platte; extensive power and irrigation developments.

North Rhine–Westphalia, *Land*, **W. Germany**; highly industrialised, coal mng., iron and steel, textiles; a. 34,066 km²; p. (1982) 16,961,200.

North River (Beijiang), Guandong, **S. China**; rises in Nanling mtns., flows S. into Xi Jiang delta; 480 km long.

North Sea, arm of the Atl., E. of Gr. Brit., W. of Norway, Sweden, and N. Germany, and N. of Holland, Belgium, and France; length 960 km, width 640 km; gd. fisheries; major natural gas, coal and oil deposits.

North Sea Canal, ship canal, N. Holland, **Neth.**; connects Amsterdam to N. Sea at Ijmuiden; depth 14 m, length 26 k.

North Shields, t., Tyne and Wear, **Eng.**; Tyne pt.; major new fishing pt. planned; marine engines, chain cables, anchors, rope; mkt.

North Solomons, Rep. of, formed 1975 when Bougainville I. seceded from Papua New Guinea.

North Tonawanda, t., N.Y., **USA**; on Niagara R.; timber tr., paper mnfs.; p. (1980) 35,760.

Northumberland, non-met. co., N **Eng.**; on border of Scot. along Cheviots and R. Tweed; drained by Tyne, Blyth, Coquet Rs.; pastoral agr., especially sheep; coal mng., with former impt. exp. to London and S.E. Eng.; industl. a. now inc. in Tyne and Wear met. co.; isolation and wild landscape attractive as tourist resort; a. 5,032 km²; p. (1981) 299,905.

Northumberland Straits, separate Prince Edward I. from Nova Scotia and New Brunswick; 14 km combined road and rail tunnel, bridge and causeway to link provs. projected.

Northumbria, Anglo-Saxon kingdom stretching from the Humber to the Forth; conquered by the Danes 9th cent.

North Walsham, mkt. t., North Norfolk, **Eng.**; 22 km N. of Norwich; former wool-weaving ctr.; p. (1981) 7,944.

North-West Passage, between Atl. and Pac. along Arctic cst. of **Canada**; potentially of gr. importance as a W. outlet for Alaskan oil; sovereignty claimed by Canada but disputed by U.S.A. who claims it is an internat. strait. *See* **Section L.**

Northwest Territories, N.W. region and terr. of **Canada**; N. of 60° Lat. N., between Yukon (W.) and Hudson Bay (E.); comprises 3 dists., Franklin, Mackenzie, Keewatin; varied physical geography, inc. vast areas of lowland with some of highest peaks in E.N. America; tree-line marks physical bdy. between N. and S.; drained in W. by Mackenzie R.; major inds. gold and silver mng. around cap. Yellowknife; petroleum, fur-trapping fisheries; incr. indep. since 1983; a. 3,379,711 km²; p. (1976) 42,609 (two-thirds Eskimos and Indians).

Northwich, t., Cheshire, **Eng.**; on R. Weaver; impt. chemical inds. based originally upon local salt deposits, now much subsidence in a. due to salt extraction; p. (1981) 17,126.

North Wolds. *See* **East Yorkshire.**

North York Moors, limestone plateau, North Yorks./Cleveland, **Eng.**; lies S. of estuary of R. Tees, heather moorland; some pastoral farming on lower slopes; alt. varies from 300–450 m; formerly impt. iron-ore quarrying along N. edge in Cleveland dist.; now potential for potash mng. threatening N.Y.M. Nat. Park.

North Yorkshire, non-met. co., N. **Eng.**; inc. much of former N. Riding; stretches from Pennines (W.) to Vale of York (central), N. York Moors and Yorks. Wolds (E.); crossed by R. Ouse and tribs.; mainly rural, mixed agr.; major ctrs. of p. at York, cstl. resort of Scarborough and spa of Harrogate; a. 8,316 km²; p. (1981) 666,610.

Norton-Radstock, t., Avon, **Eng.**; footwear, sm. coalfield; p. (1981) 18,338.

Norwalk, t., Cal., **USA**; oil refining; p. (1980) 85,286.

Norwalk, t., Conn., **USA**; gd. harbour on Long I. Sound; lt. inds., clothing; formerly impt. oyster ind. diminished by industl. pollution; p. (1980) 77,767.

Norway, kingdom, W. Scandinavia, N. **Europe**; long fjord cst. stretches from Arctic to N. Sea; mtnous.; cool damp climate, influenced by prevailing W. winds; excellent conditions for hydroelectric power and electro-inds.; sm. p. makes N. heavily dependent upon foreign tr., especially exp. of aluminium, wood-pulp, paper, fish; now possesses lge. deposits of petroleum in N. Sea; arable agr. limited to fjord lowlands and a. around cap. Oslo; pastoral transhumance in mtnous. interior; a. 322,600 km², p. (est. 1984) 4,140,000.

Norwich, c., co. t., l. gov. dist., Norfolk, **Eng.**; on R. Wensum just above confluence with R. Yare; univ.; cath., cas.; cult. and agr. ctr.; food mnfs., footwear, printing; decentralization of office employment from London; p. (1981) 122,270.

Norwich, t., Conn., **USA**; sm. pt. on Thames R.; machin., textiles; p. (1980) 38,074.

Nossi-Bé, lgst. of sm. Is., off W. cst. **Malagasy**; sugar, perfumery oils; ch. t. Hellville, resort and ctr. of cst. tr.; a. 337 km²; p. c. 26,000.

Notec (Netze), R., **Poland**; trib. R. Warta; partially navigable; 224 km long.

Notodden, t., S. **Norway**; nr. Tinnfoss falls which provide hydroelectric power; iron smelting, nitrates; p. (est. 1970) 13,422.

Nottingham, c., co. t., l. gov. dist., Nottinghamshire, **Eng.**; a bridging pt. over Trent R.; lace, hosiery, tobacco, pharmaceutical and cycle inds., all based upon local capital; univ., cas., p. (1981) 271,080.

Nottinghamshire, non-met. co., Midlands, **Eng.**; contains part of productive E. Midlands coalfield serving many power stas. along Trent R.; urban growth concentrated mainly on coalfield; ch. and co. t. Nottingham; engin., hosiery; wheat, barley, cattle, roses; brilliantly characterised in writings of D. H. Lawrence; a. 2,165 km²; p. (1981) 982,631.

Nouadhibou, pt., **Mauritania;** new pt. for bulk carriers to exp. iron ore; fish processing plants; pelletizing plant; p. (1976) 21,961.

Nouakchott, t., cap. of **Mauritania**, W. Africa; comm. ctr. on caravan route; tr. in agr. prods.; planned industl. zone; rapid growth with mass migration of nomadic p. to shanty ts. as response to Sahelian drought; p. (est. 1984) 500,000, (1976) 135,000.

Nouméa (**Port de France**), t., cap. of Fr. **New Caledonia**; ch. pt. of Is.; exp. nickel, chrome; p. (est. 1976) 74,335.

Nouvelle Amsterdam, I., **Indian Oc.**; part of Fr. Southern and Antarctic Terrs.; volcanic; ctr. of meteorological research; a. 65 km².

Nova Frilburgo, t., Rio de Janeiro, **Brazil**; health resort; p. (est. 1980) 121,200.

Nova Iguaçú, t., Rio de Janeiro, **Brazil**; steel, tyres, chemicals; p. (est. 1980) 1,183,600.

Nova Lima, t., Minas Gerais st., **Brazil**; in Serra do Espinhaço, 16 km S. of Belo Horizonte; adjacent to impt. gold-mines of Morro Velho; p. (est. 1968) 32,336.

Nova Lisboa (**Huambo**), central **Angola**, Africa; E. of Benguela; rly. repair shops; agr. comm. ctr.; p. (est. 1970) 61,885.

Novara, c., cap. of N. prov., N. **Italy**; agr. and mnf. ctr., textiles, chemicals, cheese; Romanesque church; p. (1981) 102,086.

Nova Scotia, maritime prov., **Canada**; mainly fertile upland and rich valleys with agr. aided by temperate maritime climate; fruit, livestock, dairying; forested uplands along cst. nr Bay of Fundy give rise to impt. timber inds. with many pts. along indented cst.; fishing and fish-processing; local coal supplies, iron and steel ind.; cap. Halifax; a. 54,556 km²; p. (1976) 828,571.

Novaya Kakhovka, c., Ukrainian SSR, **USSR**; built (1951) on K. Sea nr. hydroelec. power sta. on Dnieper R.; tourism.

Novaya Zemlya, archipelago, Arctic Oc., **USSR**; 2 main Is.; lofty and rugged, severe climate; nuclear testing a.; a. 90,750 km².

Novgorod, c., **RSFSR**; on Volkhov R. nr. exit from L. Ilmen; food and timber inds., engin.; in mediaeval times gr. comm. and cultural ctr., cap. of an indep. rep.; architectural monuments; damaged by Germans in second world war; p. (est. 1980) 192,000.

Novi Sad, c., **Yugoslavia**; R. pt. on Danube R., formerly royal free c.; almost destroyed by Austrians 1849; tr. in fruit, wine, vegetables, corn; p. (1981) 257,685.

Novokuybyshevsk, t., **RSFSR**; S.W. of Kuybyshev; lge. oil processing plant; p. (est. 1980) 110,000.

Novo Kuznetsk (**Stalinsk**), c. **RSFSR**; grew up as iron and steel ctr. of Kuznetsk Basin; engin., chemicals, aluminium, ferro-alloys; p. (est. 1980) 545,000.

Novomoskovsk (**Stalinogorsk**), c., **RSFSR**; on R. Don; lignite, fertilisers, p. (est. 1980) 147,000.

Novorossiisk, spt., **RSFSR**; on N.E. cst. of Black Sea; engin., textiles; lgst. cement producer in USSR; exp. industl. prods.; p. (est. 1980) 162,000.

Novoshakhtinsk, c., **RSFSR**; on Rostov–Kharkov highway; coal mng., chemicals; p. (est. 1980) 106,000.

Novosibirsk, c., **RSFSR**; on Ob R. and Trans-Siberian rly.; lgst. industl. ctr. of Siberia, nr. Kuznetz Basin; hydroelec. power; varied inds., uranium nearby; univ.; p. (est. 1980) 1,328,000.

Novo Troitsk, t., **RSFSR**; in Urals, 18 km S.W. of Orsk; cement, special steels; p. (est. 1973) 88,000.

Novovoronezh, **USSR**; on R. Don, S. of Voronezh; nuclear power sta.

Noý Jičín (**Neutitschein**), t., Moravia, **ČSSR**; farm machin., and eng.; p. (est. 1968) 19,000.

Nowa Huta, t., **Poland**; 10 km S.E. Kraców on Vistula R.; newly developed Lenin metallurgical combine and modern residtl. a. within c. of Kraców; p. (est. 1970) 160,000.

Nowa Sól (**Neusalz**), t., Lower Silesia, **Poland**; pt. on R. Oder; metal-working, food and timber inds.; p. (1970) 33,300.

Nowgong, t., Assam, **India**; agr. and comm. ctr.; rice, tea; p. (est. 1971) 11,500.

Nowra–Bomaderry, t., N.S.W., **Australia**; on E. cst. at mouth of Shoalhaven R.; now expanded (1979) into c. of Shoalhaven; collecting ctr. for coastal agr. prod.; powdered milk, paper mill; p. (1976) 15,496.

Nowy Sącz, t., Kraków prov., S. **Poland**; on Dunajec R.; lignite nearby; rly. engin., mftg.; ctr. of a. renowned for beauty and tourist attractions; p. (est. 1970) 46,000.

Nubia, anc. region, N.E. **Africa**, extending on both sides of Nile from first cataract at Aswan to Khartoum, Sudan; largely desert, some irrigation alongside Nile.

Nuble, prov., **Chile**; borders on Argentina; comprehensive attempt to develop agr.; most industl. development and agr. mkt. at cap. Chillán; a. 14,204 km²; p. (1970) 314,738.

Nueva Esparta, st., **Venezuela**; consists of over 70 Is.; impt. fisheries; cap. La Asunción; a. 1,150 km²; p. (est. 1970) 112,611.

Neuva San Salvador, t., **El Salvador**; agr. comm. ctr. in coffee-growing and livestock region; p. (est. 1970) 38,063.

Nuevo Laredo, c., N.E. **Mexico**; entry point for American tourists driving to Mexico; tr. ctr. in pastoral and arable agr. a.; p. (1979) 223,606.

Nuevo Léon, st., N.E. **Mexico**; arable agr. needs irrigation in arid climate; impt. iron and steel inds.; cap. Monterrey; a. 65,097 km²; p. (est. 1969) 1,678,000.

Nukualofa, cap. of Polynesian kingdom of **Tonga**; p. (1976) 18,396.

Nukus, c., cap. of Karakalpak ASSR, Uzbek SSR, **USSR**; on Amu Dar'ya R. in Khorezm oasis; clothing inds.; p. (est. 1980) 113,000.

Nullarbor Plain, S. **Australia**; low, level, limestone plateau fringing Gr. Australian Bight; arid; treeless, salt-bush scrub; crossed by Trans-continental rly. between Naretha (W. Australia) and Ooldea; rly. is dead straight, dead level for 477 km.

Numazu, t., Honshu, **Japan**; nr. Tokyo; ctr. of industl. dist. with varied mnfs. inc. machin.; p. (1979) 206,412.

Nuneaton, t., with Bedworth forms l. gov. dist., Warwicks., **Eng.**; on Anker R.; coal mng., textiles, lt. inds.; mkt.; birthplace of George Eliot; p. (1981) 113,521 (dist.).

Nunivak, I., Alaska, **USA**; lge. reindeer herds.

Nunjiang, former prov., N.E. **China**; crossed by Nen Jiang, trib. of Songhua Jiang; now part of Heilung-kiang prov.

Nürnberg (**Nuremberg**), c., Bavaria, **W. Germany**; historic c. of architectural beauty; indust.. ctr. with elec. mnfs., machin., heavy vehicles, precision instruments, chemicals, toys, pencils and crayons; rly. junc.; inland pt. on Rhine–Danube waterway; p. (1983) 476,400.

Nusa Tenggara, Is., **Indonesia**; part of Lesser Sunda Is.; p. (est. 1970) 4,752,000.

Nuwara Eliya, hill t., (c. 1,800 m), **Sri Lanka**; health resort; p. (est. 1968) 16,000.

Nyasa, L. See **Malawi L.**

Nyasaland. See **Malawi.**

Nyíregyháza, t., N.E. **Hungary**; ctr. of reclaimed agr. a.; mkt. for tobacco, wine, fruits; domestic ware; p. (est. 1978) 100,144.

Nyborg, pt., **Denmark**; on Fyn I.; terminal of train-ferry across Gr. Belt; shipyards; textile ind.; p. (est. 1970) 11,698.

Nyköbing, spt., Falster I., **Denmark**; varied inds.; admin. ctr. of Storstrøms prov.; p. (est. 1970) 17,364.

Nyköping, spt., **Sweden**; at head of inlet on Baltic cst.; comm. and industl. ctr.; p. (1983) 64,756.

Nystad. See **Uusikaupunki.**

O

Oadby, t., Leics., **Eng.**; 5 km S.E. of Leicester; footwear; with Wigston forms small l. gov. dist., S. of Leicester; p. (1981) 50,569 (dist.).

Oahu, I., **Hawaiian Is.**, Pac. Oc.; sugar, pineapples; tourist tr.; cap. Honolulu; a. 1,564 km²; p. (1970) 630,528.

Oakengates, t., The Wrekin, Shrops., **Eng.**; 24 km N.W. of Wolverhampton; iron and steel, precast concrete, engin.; now part of new t. of Telford; p. (1981) 17,663.

Oakham, t., Rutland, Leics., **Eng.**; mkt.; hosiery, footwear; p. (1981) 7,996.

Oakland, c., Cal., **USA**; on San Francisco Bay; residtl. sub.; cars, shipbldg., fruit canning, elec. machin., clothing, tanneries, chemicals; p. (1980) 339,000 (c.) See **San Francisco.**

Oak Park Village, t., Ill., **USA**; now included in Chicago; birthplace of Ernest Hemingway; p. (1980) 54,887.

Oak Ridge, t., Tenn., **USA**; Atomic Energy Commission's major research ctr.

Oamaru, bor., spt., S.I., **N.Z.**; wool, frozen meat; exp. agr. prods.; p. (1976) 13,480.

Oaxaca, st., Pac. cst., S. **Mexico**; mtnous., subsistence agr. in fertile valleys; comm. prod. of coffee, cotton, tobacco; stock-raising; mng. in mtns.; cap. Oaxaca; a. 94,201 km²; p. (1970) 2,015,424.

Oaxaca, c., cap. of O. st., S. **Mexico**; stands at c. 1,500 m; coffee; gold and silver mines; handi-craft mkt.; table linen weaving, wool zarapes; tourist ctr.; p. (1979) 135,601.

Ob', R., W. Siberia, **RSFSR**; one of the world's lgst. Rs., flows from Altai mtns. to G. of Ob'; crossed by Turk-Sib. rly. at Barnaul and by Trans-Siberian rly. at Novosibirsk; ch. trib. Irtysh; hydroelec. power; navigable; oilfields in middle section; outlet of Ob basin Novy-Port (Gdansk); plans to divert waters to irrigate Kazakhstan by 2,500 km canal; 4,160 km long.

Oban, spt., burgh, Argyll and Bute, **Scot.**; on F. of Lorne; resort; ctr. for local shipping; woollens, tartans; p. (1981) 8,134.

Obed, Alberta, **Canada**; 240 km W. of Edmonton; major natural gas a.

Obeid, El, t., Kordofan, **Sudan**; economically dependent upon rly. link to Khartoum; agr. tr. ctr.; p. (1983) 140,024.

Oberammergau, v., Upper Bavaria, **W. Germany**; scene of decennial Passion Play; winter sports; p. (est. 1976) 5,000.

Oberhausen, t., N. Rhine–Westphalia, **W. Ger-many**; industl. ctr. of Ruhr conurb.; rly. junc., canal pt.; p. (1983) 226,200.

Obidos, t., R. p., **Brazil**; 800 km up R. Amazon; cacao, cotton; p. (est. 1968) 25,021.

Obihiro, t., Hokkaido, **Japan**; mkt; sugar-beet re-fining, flax, dairy prods.; p. (1979) 152,144.

Obuasi, t. **Ghana**, E. Africa; ctr. of gold mng.; lge. deep-level mine, modernised 1984; p. (1970) 31,018.

Obwalden, demi-canton, **Switzerland**; a. 492 km²; p. (1980) 25,865.

Ocaña, t., Magdalena st., **Colombia**; coffee, hides; isolated by difficult transport conditions; p. (est. 1968) 43,481.

Ocean City, t., N.J., **USA**; seaside resort founded by the Methodists; p. (1980) 13,949.

Ocean I. (Banaba), Gilbert Is., Pac. Oc.; high grade phosphate (guano) worked by Brit., need for compensation and restoration of land sub-ject of legal action 1971–76; many Banabans evacuated to Rabi I. (Fiji) 1945; future still unsettled; p. (est. 1975) 2,500.

Oceania, name given to the Is. of the Pacific; comprising Australasia, Polynesia, Melanesia, Micronesia; p. (est. 1984) 24,460,000.

Ochil Hills, volcanic hill-range, **Scot.**; stretching 40 km N.E. to S.W. from F. of Tay to nr. Stirling; loftiest Ben Cleugh 721 m; beautiful glens and valleys.

Odawara, t., **Japan**; pt. with rail connections to Tokyo, 48 km to N.E.; p. (1979) 177,047.

Odemis, t., Asiatic **Turkey**; N.E. of Aydin; to-bacco, cereals, silk, cotton, flax, olives, raisins, figs; minerals; p. (1965) 30,621.

Odense, spt., **Denmark**; admin. ctr. of Fyn prov.; varied inds.; exp. dairy prod.; birthplace of Hans Andersen; p. (1984) 170,961.

Odenwald, forested hills, Hesse and Baden-Württemberg, **W. Germany**; highest point Katzenbuckel 626 m.

Oder (Pol. Odra), R., central **Europe**; flows from Moravia to Baltic through Silesia and Pomer-ania, forming from junc. with Neisse R. fron-tier between Poland and E. Germany; ch. trib. Warta R.; impt. comm. waterway below Wrocław; 896 km long.

Odessa, t., Texas, **USA**; impt. oil ctr., chemicals, foundry prod., livestock tr.; p. (1980) 90,027 (t.), 115,374 (met. a.).

Odessa, spt., Ukrainian SSR, **USSR**; on Black Sea; cultural, industl. ctr.; cath., univ.; gr. grain exp.; engin., oil refining, chemicals; ice-bound for a few weeks in winter; p. (est. 1980) 1,057,000.

Offaly, co., Leinster, **R.o.I.**; much marshy land (inc. Bog of Allen), barren uplands (inc. Slieve Bloom); pastoral agr., wheat; p. mainly rural; sm.-scale domestic prods. and agr.-processing inds. in ts.; co. t. Tullamore; a. 1,999 km²; p. (1981) 20,336.

Offa's Dyke, earthwork constructed by Offa, king of Mercia (757–96) as bdy. between the English and the Welsh; still forms part of

border between the two countries; long-distance footpath along the Welsh marches, 269 km.

Offenbach, t., Hesse, **W. Germany**; on R. Main; cas., leather museum; machin., chemicals, leather gds., metals; p. (1983) 108,600.

Offenburg, t., Baden–Württemberg, **W. Germany**; on R. Kinzig; textiles, glass, rly. junc.; cas.; p. (1983) 50,200.

Ogaden, arid region, S.W. **Ethiopia**; on border of Rep. of Somalia; oil exploration with Soviet assistance.

Ogaki, t., Honshu, **Japan**; route ctr. in lowland em-bayment, 40 km N.W. of Nagoya; p. (1979) 142,007.

Ogbomosho, t., S.W. **Nigeria**; ctr. of agr. dist.; cotton weaving; p. (est. 1975) 432,000.

Ogden, c., Utah, **USA**; stands at 1,324 m., nr. Gr. Salt L.; rly. ctr.; beet-sugar, meat-packing, flour-milling, clothing, cement; p. (1980) 64,407.

Ogdensburg, c., pt., N.Y., **USA**; on St. Lawrence R., opposite Prescott; impt. R. pt.; p. (1980) 12,375.

Ogmore and Garw, t., Ogwr, Mid Glamorgan, **Wales**; in narrow valley, 10 km N. of Bridgend; industl.; cas.; p. (1981) 18,220.

Ogooué, R., **Gabon, Congo**; site of Schweitzer's hospital at Lambaréné; 800 km long.

Ogwr, l. gov. dist., Mid Glamorgan, **Wales**; inc. Ogmore, Maesteg and Bridgend inland and Porthcawl on cst.; p. (1981) 129,773.

Ohau, Lake, S.I., **N.Z.**; in Mt. Cook dist.; fed by glaciers; 19 km by 35 km; hydroelectric power potential.

Ohio, R., trib. of Mississippi R., **USA**; formed in Penns., by junc. of Monongahela and Alleg-heny Rs. at Pittsburgh, thence navigable for 1,560 km to Cairo in Ky.; an impt. comm. waterway for industl. raw materials; flood pro-tection schemes.

Ohio, st., N. **USA**; Buckeye St.; admitted to Union 1803; st. flower Scarlet Carnation, st. bird Cardinal; gr. agr. and industl. region; maize, wheat, cattle; major deposits of coal form basis of heavy inds., especially in major ts. of Cleveland, Cincinnati, Toledo, Akron, Dayton, Youngstown; petroleum; timber inds.; cap. Columbus; a. 106,508 km²; p. (1980) 10,797,000.

Ohre (Eger), R., Bohemia, **ČSSR**; rises in Fichtel-gebirge, flows N.E. into Labe (Elbe) and through Karlovy Vary; 224 km long.

Ohrid or Ochrida, L., forms part of bdy. between **Albania and Yugoslavia**; alt. c. 850 m; deepest L. in Balkans; scenic tourist a.; monasteries on shores.

Ohrid or Ochrida, t., Macedonia, **Yugoslavia**; on N.E. shore of L.; airport and tourist ctr.; p. (est. 1965) 19,000.

Oich, Loch, L., Gr. Glen, Inverness, **Scot.**; forms part of Caledonian Canal.

Oise, dep., N. **France**; traversed by R. Oise; fertile, forested; cap. Beauvais; a. 5,884 km²; p. (1982) 662,200.

Oise, R., trib. of R. Seine, **France**; canalised navigable to Chauny; 298 km long.

Oita, c., spt., N.E. Kyushu, **Japan**; on Beppu Bay; wire, carbon, iron, and steel; oil refinery; p. (1979) 347,623.

Ojos del Salado, mtn., N.W. **Argentina**; alt. 6,884 m.

Oka, R., Kursk, **RSFSR**; rises S. of Orel, flows past Kaluga, Serpukhov, Kolomna, Ryazan, Murom, to become trib. of Volga at Gorki; navig-able, carrying grain and timber; 1,520 km long.

Oka, R., Irkutsk, Siberia, **USSR**; joins Angara R. below Bratsk; 800 km long.

Okayama, c., Honshu, **Japan**; textiles; lt. inds.; p. (1979) 543,079.

Okazaki, t., Honshu, **Japan**; nr. G. of Ovari; industl. ctr.; textiles, chemicals, machin.; p. (1979) 253,973.

Okeechobee, L., S. Fla., **USA**; drains to Atl. Oc. via Everglades; tourist attraction especially for fishing; also comm. fisheries.

Okefenokee, swamp, Ga./Fla., **USA**; forms O. Nat. Wildlife Refuge.

Okehampton, mkt. t., West Devon, **Eng.**; on N. flank of Dartmoor; granite quarries; p. (1981) 4,181.

Okha, spt., E. cst. Sakhalin I., **RSFSR**; exp. petroleum; lge. refinery; p. 50,000.

Okhotsk, Sea of, N.E. **Asia**; 1,600 km by 800 km; enclosed by the Siberian mainland, Kamchatka, the Kurils and Sakhalin I.

Oki Is., off cst. of Honshu, **Japan**; a. 350 km².

Okinawa, I., Japan, under U.S. control until 1972; lgst. and most impt. of Ryuku Is.

US air bases at Kadena and cap. Naha; a. 1,500 km²; p. (est. 1971) 797,615.

Oklahoma, st., USA; Sooner St.; admitted to Union 1907; st. flower Mistletoe, st. bird Scissor tailed Fly-catcher; prairie, plains and mtns.; continental climate; cereals, cotton, stock-raising; petroleum, gas, zinc, coal, gypsum, lead; ch. ind. petroleum refining; cap. Oklahoma City; a. 181,090 km²; p. (1980) 3,025,000.

Oklahoma City, c., cap. of Okla. st., **USA;** univ.; livestock mkt.; tr. and processing ctr.; oil and by-prods., field machin., flour mills, meat-packing; p. (1980) 403,000 (c.), 834,000 (met. a.).

Okovango, R.; rises in **Angola,** flows to Ngami depression, **Botswana,** where it forms swampy delta; 1,600 km long.

Obtyabrsky, t., Bashkir ASSR, **USSR;** on R. Ik; in new oil-mng. dist., the "New Baku"; p. (est. 1970) 77,000.

Öland, I., Baltic Sea; off E. cst. **Sweden;** connected by Europe's longest bridge to mainland; agr., limestone quarries; ch. t. Borgholm; seaside resorts; a. 1,341 km²; p. (1983) 23,874.

Oldbury, t., West Midlands, **Eng.;** N.W. of Birmingham; chemicals, bricks, glass.

Oldbury-on-Severn, Avon, **Eng.;** nuclear power sta.

Old Castile, historical div., **Spain;** now divided into Santander, Soria, Segovia, Logrono, Avila, Valladolid, Palencia, and Burgos provs.

Oldenburg, c., Lower Saxony, **W. Germany;** on R. Hunte nr. Hunte–Ems canal; rly. junc.; mkt. for horses and cattle; lt. inds.; natural gas nr. to cst.; p. (1983) 138,800.

Old Fletton, Cambs., **Eng.;** on R. Nene opposite Peterborough; bricks, gen. and elec. engin., beet sugar, fruit and vegetable canning; p. (1981) 13,657.

Oldham, c., met. dist., Gtr. Manchester, **Eng.;** on R. Medlock, 6 km N.E. of Manchester; manmade fibre and cotton textiles, machin.; recent industl. diversification inc. electro- and aero-engin., leather, paints; p. (1981) 219,817.

Oldmeldrum, burgh, Gordon, **Scot.;** 6 km N.E. of Inverurie; p. (1981) 1,358.

Olenek, R., **RSFSR;** N. Siberia; flows W. of Lena R. into Laptev Sea, Arctic Oc.; abounds in fish; 2,160 km long, 960 km navigable.

Oléron, Ile d', I., Charente-Maritime dep., **France;** lies off estuary of Charente, Bay of Biscay; oysters, early vegetables; a. 176 km².

Olifant, R., Transvaal, **S. Africa;** trib. of Limpopo; irrigation scheme for intensive agr. in valley.

Olinda, c., Pernambuco st., **Brazil;** seaside resort; phosphates; p. (est. 1980) 307,700.

Oliva, t., Valencia, **Spain;** nr. Alicante; wine dist., ducal palace; p. (1981) 19,232.

Olivos, sub., Buenos Aires, **Argentina.**

Olmütz. See Olomouc.

Olney, t., Bucks., **Eng.;** mkt., dairy produce; annual Shrove Tuesday pancake race.

Oloibiri, S. **Nigeria;** oilfields; pipeline to Pt. Harcourt, 128 km W.

Olomouc (Olmütz), ČSSR; industl. ctr., steel wks., elec. equipment, textiles, food prod.; cath., univ.; formerly one of ch. fortresses of Austria; p. (1980) 103,787.

Oloron-Sainte-Marie, t., Pyrénées-Atlantique, **France;** in Pyrenean foothills; caths.; p. (1982) 12,237.

Olsztyn (Allenstein), t., N.W. Poland; cap. of Olsztyn prov.; on R. Alle, 160 km N. of Warsaw; cas.; machin., wood inds.; p. (est. 1983) 144,400.

Olten, t., N. **Switzerland;** rly. junc., on R. Aare; p. (1970) 21,209.

Olympia, anc. c., Peloponnesus, S. **Greece;** at confluence of Alphaeus and Cladeus Rs.; site of gr. temple of Zeus and scene of Olympic games; modern v. of O. nearby; museum.

Olympia, cap. of Washington st., **USA;** spt. on Puget Sound; exp. timber; machin., agr.-processing inds.; p. (1980) 27,447 (t.), 124,264 (met. a.).

Olympus, Mt., highest mtn. in **Greece;** on border of Thessaly and Macedonia, nr. Aegean cst.; alt. 2,975 m; regarded by anc. Greeks as home of the Olympian gods.

Omagh, t., l. gov. dist., **N. Ireland;** on R. Stule agr. mkt.; tourist ctr.; p. (1981) 41,110 (dist.), 14,627 (t.).

Omaha, c., Nebraska, **USA;** on Missouri R.;

one of lgst. livestock and meat-packing ctrs. in US, gold and silver smelting and refining, steel fabrication, industl. alcohol prod.; univ.; p. (1980) 314,000 (c.), 570,000 (met. a.).

Oman (Muscat and Oman until 1970), sultanate, S.W. **Asia;** fertile coastal plain, interior desert plateau; irrigated agr., especially impt. for dates; recent oil discoveries (1964); oil now main exp.; a. 212,380 km²; p. (est. 1984) 1,181,000.

Oman, G. of, Arabian Sea; connected through strait of Kormuz to Persian G.; length 480 km, width 208 km.

Omaruru, t., **S.W. Africa;** creamery; aerodrome; p. (1960) 2,689.

Omdurman, c., central **Sudan,** on Nile, opposite Khartoum; site of Mahdi's tomb; here Kitchener defeated the dervishes 1898; native mkts.; p. (1983) 526,287.

Ometepe, I., L. Nicaragua, **Nicaragua;** volcanic; alt. 1,753 m.

Omsk, c., W. Siberia, **RSFSR;** at confluence of Irtysh and Om Rs.; major R. pt. on Trans-Siberian rly.; in agr. region; engin., chemicals, textiles, oil refining, food processing; cath.; founded as fortress 1716; p. (est. 1980) 1,028,000.

Omuta, t., W. Kyushu, **Japan;** on Amakusa Sea; local coal at Miike giving rise to chemical inds.; pt. exp. coal; p. (1979) 166,535.

Onega, Lake, RSFSR; between L. Ladoga and White Sea; second lgst. L. in Europe (L. Ladoga is lgst.); a. 9,751 km²; ch. c. Petrozavodsk; Onega canal forms part of Volga-Baltic waterway.

Onega, R., **RSFSR;** flows to G. of Onega; 640 km long.

Onitsha, t., **Nigeria;** on R. Niger; agr. tr. ctr.; p. (est. 1975) 220,000.

Onstwedde, t., Groningen, **Neth.;** mnfs.; p. (1967) 27,666.

Ontario, prov., **Canada;** bounded on N. by Hudson Bay, on S. by Gr. Ls.; extreme continental climate in N., milder in S. peninsula; extensive coniferous forest in N.; temperate agr. in S.; leading mineral producer, nickel, uranium, copper, gold; well-developed inds. using plentiful hydroelectric power; agr.-processing, machin., engin.; cap. Toronto; contains fed. cap. of Ottawa; a. 1,068,587 km²; p. (1976) 8,264,465, concentrated in S.E.

Ontario, L., **N. America;** smallest of the Gr. Ls. of the St. Lawrence basin, separating the Canadian prov. of Ont. from N.Y., **USA;** navigable, carries industl. raw materials; polluted waters; a. 19,425 km²; depth 226 m.

Ontario, t., Cal., **USA;** aircraft components; fruit comm. ctr.; p. (1980) 88,820.

Onteniente, t., Valencia, **Spain;** on R. Clariano; woollen gds., paper mills; p. (1981) 28,123.

Oosterhout, t., N. Brabant, **Neth.;** nr. Breda; footwear, tobacco; p. (1982) 44,994.

Ootacamund, t., Tamil Nadu, **India;** in Nilgiri hills, c. 2,100 m; summer H.Q. of st. govt.; sanatorium; p. (1961) 50,140.

Opatija (It. Abbazia), t., **Yugoslavia;** tourist resort, known as the Nice of the Adriatic; p. (est. 1971) 27,000.

Opava (Troppau), t., N. Moravia, **ČSSR;** nr. Polish border; industl. ctr. in agr. a.; p. (1970) 48,000.

Opladen, t., N. Rhine–Westphalia, **W. Germany;** on R. Wupper; metals, textiles, chemicals; p. (est. 1967) 44,700.

Opland or **Oppland,** co., central **Norway;** mtnous. N. inc. alpine region of Jotunheimen; forestry prods.; a. 24,885 km²; p. (est. 1972) 174,174.

Opole (Oppeln), c., S. **Poland;** on R. Oder; R. pt., rly. junc.; cement, metals, furniture; 3 univ. schools; cap. Prussian prov. of Upper Silesia 1919–45; p. (est 1983) 121,900.

Oporto (Porto), c., spt., **Portugal;** second c. of rep., built high above Douro R.; ctr. of port wine tr.; cath., univ., historic bldgs.; sardine fisheries, cotton and wool textiles, sugar refining, dis-tilling, oil refining; outer harbour at Leixões; p. (1981) 327,368 (c.), 1,562,287 (met. a.).

Oradea (Hung. Nagy Varad), t., W. **Romania;** on Crisul Repede R., nr. Hungarian border; p.; ctr.; baroque architecture; lge. Hungarian rly. p. (1978) 179,780.

Öraefa Jokull, hgst mtn., **Iceland;** alt. 1,955 m.

Oran. *See* **Ouahran.**

Orange, t., N.S.W., **Australia;** in fertile fruit growing a., agr. processing; tourism; with Bathurst is planned growth ctr.; p. (1976) 26,254.

Orange, historic t., Vaucluse, **France;** title founded by Charlemagne passed to William the Silent of the house of Nassau; Roman amphitheatre; tourism; p. (1982) 27,502.

Orange, R., Cape Prov., **S. Africa;** flows from Lesotho to Atl.; part forms S. bdy. between Cape Prov. and Orange Free State; Verwoerd dam (1972) for power, irrigation, flood control; 2,080 km long.

Orange Free State, prov., **Rep. of S. Africa;** plateau land, Drakensberg to N.E., Rs. Orange, Vaal and Caledon; sheep, cattle, horses, wheat, maize, fruit, tobacco, coal, diamonds; cap. Bloemfontein; a. 128,586 km²; p. (1980) 1,931,860.

Oranienburg, t., Potsdam, **E. Germany;** on R. Havel; industl.; chemicals, metals, machin.; p. (est. 1970) 20,442.

Ord of Caithness, hill, headland, nr. Helmsdale, Scot.; alt. 366 m.

Ordos, desert region, Inner Mongolia, **China;** lies S. of Huang He; mean alt. 1,000 m; dry cropping, especially millets; pastoral farming.

Ord, R., W. **Australia;** in Kimberley dist.; since 1972 Ord Irrigation Project; hydroelectric power.

Ordu, spt., **Turkey;** on Black Sea; exp. manganese; p. (1970) 38,483.

Ordzhonikidze, c., cap. of N. Ossetian ASSR, **RSFSR;** on R. Terek at foot of Caucasus, ind. ctr., metallurgical inds.; natural gas pipeline to Tbilisi; hydroelec. power sta.; p. (est. 1980) 283,000.

Örebro, c., cap. of Örebro prov., **Sweden;** on R. Svartå at entrance to Hjälmar l.; anc. t., cas.; footwear, biscuits; p. (1983) 117,473.

Oregon, st., N.W. **USA;** Beaver St.; admitted to Union 1859; st. flower Oregon Grape, st. bird Western Meadowlark; borders Pac. Oc.; ch. physical features, Coast ranges, Cascade mtn. region, Blue mtns., Columbia R. and tribs., Willamette valley; rainy ctr., drier interior (agr. with irrigation); cereals, sugar-beet, fruit, cattle; gold, silver, copper, coal, uranium; fisheries, canning, meat-packing, timber, military; cap. Salem; a. 250,948 km²; p. (1980) 2,633,000.

Orekhovo-Zuyevo, t., **RSFSR;** E. of Moscow, on R. Klyazma; textile inds.; p. (est. 1980) 133,000.

Orel, c., **RSFSR;** on R. Oka; univ.; rly. junc.; engin., textile mills, food prods.; birthplace of Turgenev; p. (est. 1980) 309,000.

Orenburg (Chkalov), c., cap. of Orenburg oblast, **RSFSR;** on Ural R.; rly. junc.; food processing, agr. machin.; oil and natural gas in region; p. (est. 1980) 471,000.

Orense, t., cap. of Orense prov., **Spain;** on R. Minho; flour, leather, iron; p. (1981) 430,151 (prov.).

Ore Sound, strait, between Sjaelland, Denmark, and S. Sweden; protected by agreement of adjacent countries; freezes occasionally.

Orford Ness, coastal sandspit, Suffolk, **Eng.;** cas. keep at Orford.

Oriente, prov., **Cuba;** contains mtns. of Sierra Maestra; sugar cane grown in lowlands; manganese mng.; a. 36,592 km²; p. (est. 1970) 2,998,972.

Oriente, terr., **Peru/Ecuador;** for long in dispute between the two ctys., partially settled by treaty (1942); lies E. of Andes, between Putumayo and Marañon Rs.; mainly dense forest, reputedly rich in minerals.

Orihuela, t., Alicante, **Spain;** on R. Segura; leather, textiles, wine; univ., cath.; p. (1981) 49,851.

Orinoco, R., **Venezuela;** rises in Parima mtns., flows to Atl., connected to Rio Negro and Amazon; impt. industl. development on lower O., based on hydroelec. power and iron ore; experimental scheme to reclaim delta for agr.; 2,368 km long.

Orissa, st., **India;** agr. with few ts.; Hirakud dam across Mahanadi R.; Paradeep being developed as pt.; rice; cap. Bhuvaneshwar; a. 155,825 km²; p. (1971) 21,934,827.

Orizaba, t., Veracruz, **Mexico;** textiles, paper mills, breweries; resort; p. (1979) 121,053.

Orizaba, mtn., Veracruz, **Mexico;** volcanic; called Citlatepetl in Aztec times; alt. 5,704 m.

Orkney, l. gov. reg., **Scot.;** gr. of 68 Is. in N. Sea,

inc. Pomona, Sanday, Westray; 29 inhabited; antiquarian remains, stone circles; farming, fishing; North Sea oil finds; cap. Kirkwall; total a. c. 932 km²; p. (1981) 18,906.

Orlando, c., Fla., **USA;** winter resort; inds. based on citrus fruit and mkt. garden prods.; p. (1980) 128,000 (c.), 700,000 (met. a.).

Orléannais, region and former prov., **France;** inc. deps. of Loire-et-Cher, Loiret, and parts of Eure-et-Loire and Yonne.

Orléans, c., cap. of Loiret dep., **France;** on R. Loire; cath., univ.; regional tr. ctr.; wine, textiles, chemicals, farm implements; statue of Joan of Arc; p. (1982) 105,589.

Ormoc. *See* **MacArthur.**

Ormskirk, t., West Lancs., **Eng.;** 22 km N.E. of Liverpool; in mkt. gardening a.; lt. engin., clothing; p. (1981) 27,753.

Orne, dep., N. **France;** agr., dairying, stock-keeping, fruit-growing. Camembert cheese; cap. Alençon; a. 6,143 km²; p. (1982) 295,300.

Orontes, R., rises in **Lebanon,** flows through **Syria** past Hama into **Turkey** past Antioch to Mediterranean; unnavigable but used for irrigation; part of valley followed by rly.; irrigated areas intensively cultivated; c. 400 km long.

Oroya, t., **Peru;** impt. mng. and refining ctr.; p. (est. 1970) 35,000.

Orpington. *See* **Bromley.**

Orsha, c., Belorussiyan SSR, **USSR;** impt. industl. and transport ctr. on R. Dnieper; textiles, metal wks., food-processing; once a frontier fortress; p. (est. 1980) 113,000.

Orsk, c., Bashkir ASSR, **RSFSR;** in Ural mtns. on Ural R.; inds. based on surrounding mng. a.; oil pipeline terminus; oil refining; hydroelectric power sta. nearby; p. (est. 1980) 252,000.

Orta, L., **Italy;** W. of Lago Maggiore; a. 18 km².

Orthez, t., Pyrénées-Atlantique, **France;** scene of Wellington's victory over Soult (1814); Bayonne hams; p. (1982) 11,542.

Orumiyeh. *See* **Rezaiyeh.**

Oruro, t., **Bolivia;** cap. of O. prov. at alt. 3,709 m; once impt. ctr. for silver mng.; now other minerals impt.; p. (1976) 124,091.

Oruwala, t., **Sri Lanka;** steel rolling mill.

Orvieto, t., Umbria, **Italy;** on R. Paglia; cath., Etruscan antiquities; wines, olive oil, cereals; pottery; p. (est. 1971) 25,200.

Osaka, c., Honshu, **Japan;** ctr. of Kinki plain; built on delta in shallow O. Bay; comm. ctr.; banking, heavy industry, metals, machin., clothing; p. (1979) 2,682,221.

Osasco, t., São Paulo st., **Brazil;** industl. satellite of São Paulo with traditional and new inds.; p. (est. 1980) 491,800.

Osh, t., S.W. Kirghiz SSR, **USSR;** textiles, food-processing; one of oldest ts. in central Asia; p. (est. 1980) 173,000.

Oshawa, t., Ont., **Canada;** pt. on L. Ont.; motor vehicles; p. (1979) 107,020.

Oshima, i., Tokyo Bay, **Japan;** lgst. and most N. of Izu-shichito gr.; site of volcanic Mt. Mihara (755 m).

Oshkosh, t., Wis., **USA;** on Fox R.; meat packing, flour, motors. *See* **Appleton.**

Oshogbo, t., **Nigeria;** comm. and educational ctr.; serves agr. dist.; cotton-ginning; new steel rolling mill; p. (est. 1975) 282,000.

Osijek, t., Croatia, **Yugoslavia;** on Drava R.; growing industl. ctr. for textiles and leather; p. (1981) 867,646.

Osinniki, t., **RSFSR;** W. Siberia; new ctr. of coal mng.; thermal power sta.; p. (est. 1969) 67,000.

Osipenko. *See* **Berdyansk.**

Oslo (Christiania), c., cap. of **Norway;** at head of Oslo Fjord; ch. spt., comm., industl., and cultural ctr.; ice-free harbour, cath., univ.; exp. timber, fish, matches; wood pulp, paper; occupied by Germans 1940–5; p. (1979) 456,132.

Osnabrück, c., Lower Saxony, **W. Germany;** on R. Hase; stands on a branch of the Mittelland canal; inland pt. and industl. ctr.; iron and steel mills; mach., textile and paper mnfs.; p. (1983) 156,100.

Osorno, t., **Chile;** agr. ctr.; in beautiful forested cty.; Germanic influence; food-processing; tourism; p. (est. 1970) 160,125.

Ossett, t., West Yorks., **Eng.;** 5 km W. of Wakefield; woollens, shoddy-processing, engin.; p. (1981) 20,416.

Ostend, spt., **Belgium**; passenger route between Britain and continent of Europe; popular resort; casino, fisheries, shipbldg., textiles, tobacco; p. (1984) 69,039.

Östergötland, co., **Sweden**; on Baltic cst.; rises to uplands of Småland in S. where p. declining; lowland, a. crossed by Gota canal; cap. Linköping; a. 11,050 km²; p. (est. 1983) 392,310.

Östersund, t., Jämtland, **Sweden**; on Storsjön L.; p. (1983) 56,305.

Östfold, co., S.E. **Norway**; hilly a. crossed by R. Glomma; dairy prods. for Oslo; a. 4,178 km²; p. (est. 1972) 224,041.

Ostia, anc. c., **Italy**; once pt. of Rome, at mouth of R. Tiber, founded 4th cent. B.C.; layout revealed by excavations; modern v. of O. nearby on plain reclaimed from salt marsh.

Ostrava, c., **ČSSR**; at junc. of Oder and Ostravice Rs.; industl. ctr. of Ostrava-Karvinna coalmng. region; iron and steel, machin., chemicals, oil refining; p. (1980) 326,716.

Ostrow Wielkopolski, t., Poznan, **Poland**; agr. machin., clothing; p. (1970) 49,500.

Ostrowiec Swietokrzyski (Ostrovets), t., Kielce, **Poland**; on R. Kamienna; ceramic and metallurgical inds.; p. (1970) 50,000.

Oswaldtwistle, t., Hyndburn, Lancs., **Eng.**; at N. foot of Rossendale Fells; chemicals, textiles; p. (1981) 14,519.

Oswego, t., N.Y., **USA**; pt. on L. Ontario; mnfs. hosiery, matches, textiles, boiler engines, paper; p. (1980) 19,793.

Oswestry, t., l. gov. dist., Shrops., **Eng.**; at foot of Welsh mtns., cas.; engin.; p. (1981) 30,679.

Oświecim (Ger. **Auschwitz**), t., Kraków, **Poland**; at confluence of Rs. Iola and Vistula; lge. chemical wks.; German concentration camp (1940–44); p. (1970) 39,600.

Otago, prov., S.I., **N.Z.**; forested mtns.; gold; farming, sheep, fruit; lge. deposit of jade found at head of L. Wakatipu; coalfields; cap. Dunedin; a. 65,320 km²; p. (1976) 188,903.

Otago Harbour, Otago dist., S.I., **N.Z.**; Dunedin and Port Chalmers are ports on this harbour.

Otanmäki, Finland; rich deposit of magnetite-ilmenite ore.

Otaru, spt., Hokkaido, **Japan**; herring fisheries; coal mng., lumbering; p. (1979) 185,301.

Otley, t., West Yorks., **Eng.**; on R. Wharfe; printing, machin., wool, paper mkg., leather, furnishings; birthplace of Thomas Chippendale; p. (1981) 13,806.

Otranto, t. S. **Italy**; on Strait O.; once a flourishing c., fine mosaic pavement, cath., cas.; submarine cable sta.; bauxite exp., fishing; p. (est. 1981) 4,811.

Otsu, t., Honshu, **Japan**; on L. Biwa; p. (1979) 206,674.

Ottawa, c. Ont. cap. of **Canada**; on R. Ottawa; univ., caths., parliament bldgs.; hydroelec, power, lumbering, sawmills, paper, flour, leather, matches, machin., ironware; p. (1979) 304,460 (c.), 738,600 (met. a.).

Ottawa, R., **Canada**; trib. of St. Lawrence, forming bdy. between Ont. and Quebec; timber transport, hydroelec. power; 1,000 km long.

Ottery St. Mary, mkt. t., East Devon, **Eng.**; 16 km E. of Exeter; birthplace of Coleridge; p. (1981) 7,069.

Ottumwa, t., Iowa, **USA**; on Des Moines R.; in coalfield and agr. dist.; iron and steel, meat-packing; p. (1980) 27,381.

Ötzal, valley, **Austria**; longest side valley of R. Inn; tourist dist.

Ouachita or **Washita,** R., Ark., **USA**; trib. of Red R.; 880 km long.

Ouachita National Forest, Ark., Okla., **USA**; part of forested O. highlands.

Ouagadougou, cap. of **Bourkina Fasso**; and comm. ctr.; p. (est. 1980) 247,877.

Ouahran (Oran), spt., N. **Algeria**; founded by Moors 10th cent.; occupied by French 1831–1962; handles wines, wool, cereals, meat, skins; fine roadstead at Mers-el-Kebir; former French naval and military sta.; p. (est. 1975) 330,000.

Oudenaarde (Audenarde), t., **Belgium**, on R. Scheldt; textile ctr.; scene of Marlborough's victory over French 1708; p. (1981) 27,318.

Ouenza, c., **Algeria**; 75 per cent of Algerian iron-ore produced in dist.

Oujda, t., N.E. **Morocco**; comm. ctr.; phosphate, lead and zinc-mng. dist.; p. (est. 1973) 155,800 (t.), 394,400 (met. a.).

Oulton Broad, L., Suffolk, **Eng.**; nr. Lowestoft. See **Broads.**

Oulu, spt., cap. of Oulu prov., N.W. **Finland**; on G. of Bothnia at mouth of R. Oulu; univ.; p. (1970) 86,964.

Oundle, mkt. t., East Northants., **Eng.**; on R. Nene; public school; p. (1981) 3,290.

Ouro Prêto, old colonial t., **Brazil**; former cap. of Minas Gerais st.; grew as gold mng. ctr.; since p. has declined; now other minerals; school of mines; p. (est. 1968) 38,372.

Ouse or Great Ouse, R., **Eng.**; rises in S. Northamptonshire and flows N.E. via the Fens to the Wash; 250 km long.

Ouse, R., East Sussex, **Eng.**; flows to English Channel at Newhaven; 48 km long.

Ouse, R., North Yorks./Humberside, **Eng.**; formed by Rs. Swale and Ure, flows to Humber estuary; 208 km long.

Ovalle, t., Coquimbo prov., **Chile**; ctr. of fruit and pastoral dist.; p. (est. 1970) 61,605.

Overijssel, prov., **Neth.**; dairying, fishing; ch. ind. textiles; a. 3,364 km²; p. (1982) 1,038,369.

Oviedo, coastal. prov., N. **Spain**; agr., fruit, sardine, and other fisheries; cap. O.; a. 10,888 km²; p. (1981) 1,129,545.

Oviedo, c., cap. of O. prov., **Spain**; on R. Nalón; cath., univ.; industl. and comm. ctr. for agr. and mng. dists. of Asturia; p. (1981) 168,951.

Owenus, pt., **Liberia**, deepwater pt. built to serve iron ore mines at Belinga.

Owen Falls, Uganda; dam inaugurated 1954; converts L. Victoria into reservior for irrigation of Egypt and Sudan; also to supply Uganda with hydroelectric power.

Owensboro', t., Ky., **USA**; petroleum; ctr. for stock raising and tobacco growing a.; p. (1980) 54,450 (t.), 85,949 (met. a.).

Owens, L., S. Cal., **USA**; on E. flank of Sierra Nevada, 32 km S.E. of Mt. Whitney; water taken by 360 km-long aqueduct to Los Angeles; a. 311 km².

Owen Sound, t., L. pt., Ont., **Canada**; on S.W. cst. of Georgian Bay, L. Huron; E. terminus of lgst. wheat-carrying L. steamers; linked by rly. to Toronto (200 km) and Montreal; p. (1971) 18,281.

Oxelösund, spt., E. **Sweden**; on Baltic cst., S. of Stockholm; steelwks., glass; p. (1961) 10,007.

Oxford, c., l. gov. dist., Oxon., **Eng.**; between R. Thames and R. Cherwell; 13th cent. univ. and residtl. colleges; printing, cars, elec. engin.; p. (1981) 98,521.

Oxfordshire, non-met. co., **Eng.**; formed by Chilterns and Cotswolds, drained by R. Thames and tribs.; mainly agr. with lge. arable farms; being prospected for new coalfield; ch. t. Oxford; a. 2,611 km²; p. (1981) 515,079.

Oxfordshire, South, l. gov. dist., Oxon., **Eng.**; Wallingford, Thame and Henley-on-Thames; p. (1981) 128,596.

Oxnard, t., Cal., **USA**; citrus fruits, sugar beet, oil refining; (p. 1980) 108,000 (c.), 448,000 (met. a.).

Oxus, R. See Amu Dar'ya.

Oyashio. See Bering Current.

Oyo, t., **Nigeria**; cotton weaving; mkt.; p. (est. 1975) 152,000.

Ozark Mtns., Okla. and Ark., **USA**; lead, zinc; ch. t. Joplin; forested.

Ozd, t., **Hungary**; iron and steel; p. (1966) 39,900.

P

Paarl, t., Cape Prov., **S. Africa**; summer resort extending along Gt. Berg R.; wines, fruit, tobacco; flour, saw and textile mills; p. (1970) 48,597.

Pabianice, t., **Poland**; nr. Lodz; textiles, farming implements, paper; cas.; p. (1969) 62,000.

Pabna, t., and dist., Bengal, **Bangladesh**; dist. is a fertile alluvial plain; t. serves as trading, industl. and admin. ctr. for a.; hosiery, carpets; p. (est. 1971) 41,000 (t.).

Pacasmayo, spt., **Peru**; exp. rice, sugar, cotton, cacao, hides, copper, lead, zinc, silver; p. (1961) 6,000.

Pachitea, R., **Peru**; rises in Andes, flows N. to R. Ucayali; sm. German immigrant colonies in upper valley; 512 km long.

Pachmarhi, Madhya Pradesh, **India**; summer cap., tourist ctr.; p. (1961) 6,142.

Pachuca, cap., Hidalgo st., **Mexico**; silver mnfs. and mng.; woollen and leather gds.; p. (1979) 108,119.

Pacific Islands, Trust Terr. of, external terr. of USA held under U.N. trusteeship; consists of Mariana Is. (except Guam), Caroline and Marshall Is., W. Pac. Oc.; inc. 2,141 Is., grouped into 6 admin. dists.; cap. (provisional) Saipan, **Mariana Is.**; total land a. c. 1,800 km²; p. (1970) 250,250.

Pacific Ocean, a. 176,120,000 km²; lgst. ocean in the world; extends from W. cst of America to E. cst of Asia and Australia and the S. Ocean in the S.; enters Arctic Oc. via Bering Strait; greatest length N. to S. 1,280 km; breadth, 16,000 km; mean depth 3,830 m, 11,524 m in the Mindanao trench; many coral and volcanic Is. in S.W.

Padang, spt., W. cst. Sumatra, **Indonesia**; exp. agr. prods., coffee, copra, rubber and coal; cement mnfs.; univ.; p. (1971) 196,339.

Paddington. See **Westminster, City of**.

Paderborn, c., N. Rhine-Westphalia, **W. Germany**; cath. and other historic bldgs. severely damaged in second world war; foodstuffs, textiles, metals; p. (1983) 110,300.

Padiham, t., Lancs., **Eng.**; at N. foot of Rossendale Fells, textiles, engin., gas appliances; p. (1981) 9,246.

Padstow, mkt. t., Cornwall, **Eng.**; on W. side of Camel estuary in which silting has caused pt. of P. to decline; lt. inds.; seaside resort.

Padua (Padova), c., cap. of P. prov., N.E. **Italy**; cath., arcades, anc. bridges; univ. founded 1222 (Galileo taught here); flourished as artistic ctr.; birthplace of Livy; machin., chemicals, cloth, distilling; agr. ctr.; p. (1981) 234,678.

Paducah, c., Ky., **USA**; pt. on Ohio R.; saw-mills, tobacco, railway wks.; atomic energy plant; p. (1980) 29,315.

Paestum, anc. c., S. **Italy**; S.E. of Salerno; founded by the Greeks 600 B.C.; ruins of temples, Roman forum and amphitheatre.

Pagan, ruined c., central **Burma**; on Irrawaddy R.; founded circa 849, sacked 1299; in ctr. of a. covered with pagodas, place of Burmese pilgrimage; lacquer work.

Pago Pago, spt., cap. of American **Samoa**, S. Pac.; on Tutuila I., magnificent harbour; US naval and radio sta.; airport; p. (1970) 2,491.

Pahang, st., **Malaysia**, central Malaya; isolated from rest of Malaya, less economically developed; largely covered with forest; some rubber production, gold, tin mng.; cap. Kuala Lipis; a. 34,395 km²; p. (1970) 504,945.

Pahlevi. See **Bandar-e-Pahlevi**.

Paignton, t., S. Devon, **Eng.**; incorporated in Torbay; resort.

Painted Desert, Arizona, **USA**; a. of bare multicoloured shale and sandstones; arid; a. c. 19,400 km².

Paisley, burgh, Renfrew, **Scot.**; 8 km W. of Glasgow; anc. abbey; shipbldg., chemicals, engin., preserves, car bodies, cotton thread; p. (1981) 84,789.

Paita, pt., **Peru**; exp. cotton, wool, flax, panama hats; lge. whaling sta. to S.; p. 37,000.

Pakistan, Islamic Rep. of, forms part of Indian subcontinent, **S. Asia**; formerly split into two separate units, E. Pakistan (cap. Dacca) and W. Pakistan (cap. Lahore), 1,600 km apart; politically separate since 1972; W. part now forms Pakistan, E. part indep. st. of Bangladesh; dry semi-desert, irrigated by Indus R. and tribs.; cash crops, sugar, wheat, cotton; natural gas fields; new cap. Islamabad; main spt. Karachi; a. 803,944 km²; p. (est. 1981) 88,900,000 (+ 27 per cent. in 6 years).

Paknampoh, t., **Thailand**; on R. Menam, at upper limit of navigation; terminus of private rly.; fish breeding in L. created from swamp.

Pakokku, t., Upper **Burma**; pt. on Irrawaddy R.; shipping ctr. for a. producing sugar, tobacco, peanuts, teak, petroleum; Yenangyaung oilfields nearby; p. (est. 1962) 156,960.

Paktia, prov., **Afghanistan**; mtnous., forested; difficult to govern, inhabited by sm. and indep.

tribes, but sparse p.; livestock basis of agr.; timber exp; a. c. 12,950 km²; p. (est. 1970) 732,779.

Palau Is., archipelago, **Pac. Oc.**; volcanic and coral Is.; exp. agr. prods., dried fish; p. (1974) 12,674. Rep. of Belau, 1 Jan. 1981.

Palawan I., **Philippines**; elongated I., rising to 1,731 m; coffee, resin, timber; sparse p.; a. 11,784 km²; p. (1970) 232,322.

Palembang, cap. of S. Sumatra prov., **Indonesia**; R. pt. of Musi R., 80 km from sea; terminus of S. Sumatran rly. systems; exp. coffee and petroleum prods. from nearby oilfields; inds. based on agr. processing and oil refining; p. (1971) 582,961.

Palencia, t., cap. of P. prov., N.W. **Spain**; industl. ctr.; rly. engin.; cath.; p. (1981) 188,477 (prov.).

Palermo, spt., Sicily, **Italy**; cath., univ.; shiprepairing; processes agr. prod. from surrounding fertile Conca d'Oro; p. (1981) 701,782.

Palestine or **The Holy Land**, historic region, bounded by Syria and Lebanon on the N., Jordan on the E., the Egyptian prov. of Sinai on the S., and the Mediterranean on the W.; a. when under Brit. mandate 2,701 km²; p. (est. 1948) 782,000. See **Israel**.

Palghat, t., Kerala, **India**; commands Palghat gap through W. Ghats; p. (1961) 77,620.

Palitana, t., Gujarat, **India**; t. of Jain temples inhabited by priests and their servants; p. (1961) 24,581.

Palk Strait, India; separates India from Sri Lanka.

Palma de Mallorca, spt., Mallorca I, **Spain**; cath., palaces, varied inds.; agr. exp.; well-known tourist resort; p. (1981) 290,370.

Palm Beach, t., Fla., **USA**; Atl. coastal resort; permanent p. (1980) 9,729.

Palmerston North, c., N.I., **N.Z.**; rly. junc. at ctr. of Manawatu R. lowlands; sheep and dairy prod.; univ.; p. (1976) 63,873.

Palmira, t., W. **Colombia**; agr. ctr. in Cauca valley; p. (1973) 140,338.

Palm Springs, Cal., **USA**; resort; p. (1980) 32,366.

Palmyra, anc. c. in Syrian desert, 192 km. N.E. of Damascus; Bible name Tadmor = city of palms; extensive ruins.

Palmyra Is. See **Line Is.**

Palo Alto, t., sub. development 48 km S.E. San Francisco, **USA**; attractive wooded site of variable relief; on shore of San Francisco Bay peninsula; Stanford Univ.; science-based inds.; p. (1980) 55,225.

Palomar, Mount, peak, 1,868 m high, S. Cal., **USA**; observatory with 5,080 mm reflecting telescope.

Palos de la Frontera, t., Huelva, S.W. **Spain**; on Rio Tinto; starting point for Columbus in 1492; pt. now silted up; p. (1981) 4,014.

Palua, pt., **Venezuela**; pt. of shipment for iron mines at El Pao; nearby Caroni hydroelec. plant built to serve steel wks. and aluminium plant.

Pamir Mtns., high mtn. plateau ("roof of the world"), Tadzik SSR, **Central Asia**; Mt. Communism (7,400 m) climbed by Russo-British team 1962; name derives from high mtn. valleys known as "Pamirs."

Pampas, Argentina; vast plains stretching from the Rio Negro on the S. to the Gran Chaco in the N., and E. from the Andes to the Atl.; woodless, level country; rich pastures in E., supporting countless numbers of sheep and cattle, a major influence upon the Argentinian economy, source of livestock exps.; W. mostly barren.

Pamplona, t., Norte de Santander, **Colombia**; agr., comm. and tr. ctr.; inds. based on agr. processing; p. (1970) 22,800.

Pamplona, c., cap. of Navarre, N. **Spain**; at foot of Pyrenees, anc. Baxque c.; cath., fortress, univ.; industl. ctr. with varied mnfs.; p. (1981) 178,504.

Panama, rep., **Central America**; narrow strip of terr. at S. end of isthmus separating N. and S. America; mtnous. and tropical, thickly forested; split by Canal Zone from which rep. earns 25 per cent of revenue; to have control over zone by 2000; shipping registration impt.; subsistence agr.; exp. bananas, rice, maize; sea fisheries; rich copper deposits found 1975; poor communications; cap. Panama City; a. 74,009 km²; p. (est. 1984) 2,134,000.

Panama Canal Zone, Panama; strip of land 82 km long 16 km wide on either side of Canal, leased to USA for military base; control to Panama by 2000; a. 1,675 km²; p. (est. 1976) 44,000.

Panama, c. spt., cap. of **Panama**; free pt. at S. entrance to Canal; cath.; oil refining, steel rolling mill, cement plant, lt. inds.; contains 25 per cent p. Panama rep.; p. (1979) 452,360.

Panama City, t., Fla., **USA**; pulp and paper mill; resort; p. (1980) 33,346 (t.), 97,740 (met. a.).

Pan American Highway, international road project, not yet fully complete, from Alaska to Chile, down W. csts. of continents; section between USA and Mexico is called Central American Inter-American Highway.

Panay, I., Philippines; between Negros I. and Mindoro I.; coconuts, maize grown in E., fertile lowland; ch. t. Iloilo; a. 11,515 km²; p. (1970) 2,116,545.

Pančevo, t., N.E. Serbia, **Yugoslavia**; agr. ctr. for grain growing a., flour-milling; developing industl. ctr., fertilizers, oil refining; p. (1971) 24,269.

Pangalanes Canal (Canal Des Pangalanes), Malagasy Rep.; follows E. cst from Farafangana to Tamatave, through series of lagoons; 480 km long.

Panipat, t., Haryana, N.W. **India**; on Jumna R.; on route from Afghanistan to central India; scene of battles; p. (1961) 67,026.

Panjim, cap. of Goa, **India**; pt.; old cap. (Velha Goa) in ruins; p. (est. 1971) 35,000.

Panjsher Valley, Afghanistan; silver and mica mines.

Pantelleria, volcanic I., Mediterranean, **Italy**; midway between W. Sicily and Tunisia; figs, raisins, vines, capers, cereals; fishing; a. 150 km²; ch. t. P.; p. (1981) 7,917.

Pantin, N.E. sub., Paris, Seine-St. Denis, **France**; glasswks., sugar refining, tobacco factories, chemicals, leather, tallow; p. (1982) 43,553.

Paoki. *See* **Baoji.**

Paoting. *See* **Baoding.**

Paotow. *See* **Baotou.**

Papakura, c., N.I., **N.Z.**; residtl. a. for Auckland; p. (1976) 21,542.

Papoloa, R., **Mexico**; agr. and industl. development; Papaloan project for flood control and electricity generation.

Papal States, Italy, areas ruled by the Pope until 1870; comprised Latium, Umbria, the Marches, and Emilia-Romagna.

Papatoetoe, c., N.I., **N.Z.**; residtl. ctr. close to Auckland; p. (1976) 22,864.

Papeete, t., pt., **Tahiti I.**, Pac. Oc.; cap. Tahiti and of Fr. Settlements in Oceania; exp. copra, vanilla, phosphates and mother-of-pearl; p. (1971) 25,432.

Paphos, admin. dist., W. cst. **Cyprus**; anc. c.; Old P. dates from 3000 B.C., New P. impt. spt.; rich deposits of copper and iron pyrites, sulphur in Vretsia a.; p. (est. 1970) 11,800 (t.).

Papua New Guinea, E. New Guinea, S.E. Asia; indep. st. (1975); mtnous., thickly forested; under-developed; copra, rubber and timber prods.; cap. Pt. Moresby; a. 461,693 km²; p. (est. 1984) 3,601,000.

Pará, st., **Brazil**; densely forested; rubber, fruits, cacao, Brazil nuts; cap. Belem; a. 1,228,061 km²; p. (1970) 2,167,018.

Paracel Is., S. China Sea; claimed by China, Taiwan and Vietnam.

Paraguay, landlocked rep., **S. America**; undulating cty.; swamps, forest; hot summers, warm winters, high but seasonal rainfall; sm. densely populated areas, lge. areas with no p.; most economically developed in E.; in and around cap. Asunción 25 per cent p.; economy based on agr., cereals, livestock, fruit, cotton, oil-seeds, but food imported; aid from USA for rural development; few fuel resources (a few oilfields in the Chaco Borea) and low energy consumption; hydroelectric plant on Paraná (Itaipu dam), Paraguay Rs. and at Guaira Falls; electricity exp. to Brazil; new inds. with cheap power; first steel mill (1982); some agr. based inds.; a. 406,630 km²; p. (est. 1984) 3,576,000.

Paraguay, R., **S. America**; rises in plateau of Mato Grosso, flows S. and joins R. Paraná nr. Corrientes; forms bdy. between Brazil and Bolivia, Brazil and Paraguay; impt. navigable waterway to Cáceres (Brazil); 1,920 km long.

Paraíba, st., N.E. **Brazil**; livestock, cotton, sugar cane; tin, scheelite; cap. João Pessoa; a. 56,462 km²; p. (1970) 2,382,617.

Paraíba do Sul, R., S. **Brazil**; rises in São Paulo st., and flows between Rio de Janeiro and Minas Gerais to Atl. N.E. of Rio de Janeiro; forms routeway between São Paulo and Rio de Janeiro; 1,040 km long.

Paramaribo, spt., cap. of **Surinam**; on Surinam R.; exp. bauxite, timber, rubber, rice, fruit; t. built on grid pattern with canals and tree-lined streets; p. (est. 1970) 102,300.

Paraná, c., cap. of Entre Ríos prov., N.E. **Argentina**; pt. of P. R. for grain, cattle, sheep; road tunnel to Santa Fé; p. (1975) 127,635.

Paraná, R., S.W. **Brazil**; formed by junc. of Rs. Rio Grande and Paranaíba; flows W. between Paraguay and Argentina; flows into Rio de la Plata; navigable to Brazil frontier nr. Iguaçu Falls; forms part of international inland waterway system; hydroelec. power, Itaipú lgst. sta. in world; joint hydroelec. scheme between Paraguay, Brazil and Argentina; 3,280 km long; rapid rise in p. with indust. expansion from electricity.

Paraná, st., S. **Brazil**; between Paraná R. and Atl. Oc.; extensively forested; maté, timber, coffee; cap. Curitiba; a. 201,287 km²; p. (1970) 6,929,868.

Paranaguá, spt., Paraná st., **Brazil**; ch. pt. for Paraná; in lagoon harbour; modern highway links with Asunción (Paraguay); p. (est. 1970) 39,500.

Paraduboix, t., **CSSR**; univ., cath.; rly. junc., industl. ctr.; distilling, oil refining; p. (1967) 66,000.

Paricutin, Mt. Michoacán, **Mexico**; volcano formed between 1943 and 1952, 2,501 m high; of great interest to scientists.

Paris, c., cap. of **France**; dominates rep. politically, economically, and socially, partly as result of extreme centralisation of political power in cap.; on R. Seine, 176 km from mouth, in ctr. of Paris Basin; forms major ctr. of communications; planning of Haussmann gives spacious appearance, 12 boulevards radiate from Arc de Triomphe; many historic bldgs., especially on and around Ile de la Cité, an I. on R. Seine, site of cath. of Notre Dame; major cultural and tourist ctr.; univs.; comprises 20 admin. arrondissements; major ctr. of inds. with concentration of modern science-based inds. hindering planned attempts at decentralisation; p. (1982) 2,188,918 (c.), 8,706,963 (met. a.).

Paris Basin, concentric limestone escarpments form saucer-shaped depression with Paris at ctr.; impt. agr. dist., wheat, dairy prod. and wines.

Parkersburg, t., W. Va., **USA**; on Ohio R.; iron- and steel-wks., oil and natural gas, coal, glassware, rayon, porcelain; p. (1980) 39,967 (t.), 162,836 (met. a.).

Parkes, t., N.S.W., **Australia**; mkt.; rly. junc.; radio telescope; p. (1976) 8,905.

Parma, c., cap. of P. prov., **Italy**; between Apennines and Po R.; tr. ctr. rly. junc.; food-processing, wine, Parmesan cheese, precision instruments, agr. machin.; Roman remains, many historic bldgs., univ., cath.; p. (1981) 179,019.

Parma, t., Ohio, **USA**; motor vehicle parts; residtl.; p. (1980) 92,548.

Parnaiba, spt., Piauí, **Brazil**; agr. comm. ctr., cotton, cattle; exp. agr. prods.; p. (est. 1970) 40,000.

Parnaíba, R., rises in Brazil; flows into N. Atl. Oc., forms bdy. between Maranhão and Piauí; 1,200 km long.

Parnassus, mtn. ridge, **Greece**; 133 km N.W. of Athens, nr. the anc. Delphi, the modern Liakhura; hgst. peak Licoreia 2,461 m.

Parnu or **Pyarnu**, spt., S.W. Estonian SSR, **USSR**; of G. of Riga; exp. timber flax; health resort; p. (est. 1970) 46,000.

Páros, I., Grecian Archipelago; W. of Naxos; source of Parian marble; cap. P.; a. 163 km²; p. (1961) 7,800.

Parramatta, c., N.S.W., **Australia**; pt. nr. head of Parramatta R. in met. a. of Sydney; 2nd Brit. settlement in Australia; p. (1978) 131,655.

Parrett, R., Somerset, **Eng.**; flows to Bristol Channel, nr. Bridgwater; 56 km long.

Pasadena, c., Cal., **USA**; N. of Los Angeles; in fruit-growing region, base of San Gabriel mtns.; 5,080 mm telescope on Mt. Palomar;

famous for its carnival; p. (1980) 119,000; inc. in met. a. of Los Angeles.

Pasco, t., Wash., **USA**; on Snake R.; atomic energy plant; p. (1980) 18,425.

Pasco. *See* **Cerro de Pasco.**

Pas-de-Calais, dep., N. **France**; impt. heavy industl. a. based upon local extensive coal deposits; heavy inds. inc. iron and steel, but many ts. in decline as importance of coal diminishes; prosperous agr. based on arable farming; N. cst. faces English Channel and inc. pts. of Calais and Boulogne; severe devastation in both world wars; cap. Arras; a. 6,750 km²; p. (1982) 1,412,200.

Passage West, U.D., Cork, **R.o.I.**; declining pt., fishing; p. (1961) 2,000.

Passaic, c., N.J., **USA**; rubber gds., springs, steel cabinets, tin cans; p. (1980) 52,463.

Passau, c., **W. Germany**; at confluence of Rs. Danube, Inn and Ilz, nr. Austrian frontier; trans-shipment base, inds. inc. leather, porcelain, tobacco and brewing; cath., picturesque tourist ctr.; p. (1983) 51,800.

Passchendaele, t., **Belgium**; strategic point in first world war; battle 31 July-6 Nov. 1917; p. (est. 1969) 3,112.

Passero I., Mediterranean Sea; off S.E. cst. of Sicily, **Italy.**

Passy, residtl. part of W. Paris, **France**; between Bois de Boulogne and right bank of Seine; residence of Balzac.

Pasto, t., cap. of Narino dep., **Colombia**; on flank of Pasto volcano; univ.; agr. comm. ctr.; gold nearby; p. (1973) 127,811.

Patagonia, extensive region, E. of Andes, **Argentina/Chile**; elevated plateau, arid, sterile; prin. Rs. Colorado, Rio Negro, and Chubut; impt. source of oil at Commodoro Rivadavia; lge. tracts of grazing for livestock; much of p. Welsh descendants.

Patan, Gujarat, **India**; impt. ctr. of Buddhism; gold and silver gds.; p. (1961) 50,264.

Patani or **Pattani,** pt., S. **Thailand**; on E. cst. of Malay peninsula; spices, rubber, coconuts; tin mng.; former Malay sultanate; p. of t. (est. 1964) 19,902.

Paterno, t., Sicily, **Italy**; N.W. of Catania; cath., cas.; mineral springs, wines; p. (1981) 45,144.

Paterson, c., N.J., **USA**; on Passaic R. whose falls provide hydroelectric power for gr. silk mnf. ind.; now inds. diversified; in addition to textiles and textile machin., aeroplane engines, metallurgical inds., electronic equipment; p. (1980) 138,000 (c.), 448,000 (met. a.).

Patiala, t., Punjab, **India**; metal gds., flour; cement; p. (1970) 142,891 (c.), 1,369,374 (met. a.).

Patino Mines. *See* **Unicia.**

Pátmos, I., one of the Dodecanese, **Greece**; in Aegean Sea; a. 34 km²; p. (est.) 3,000. (According to Rev. 1. 9. the exiled St. John wrote the Revelation here.)

Patna, c., cap. of Bihar, **India**; univ.; rly. junc.; agr. tr., rice, oilseeds, cotton; handicraft inds.; p. (1971) 473,001 (c.), 491,217 (met. a.).

Patras (Pátrai), spt., cap. of Akhaia, **Greece**; citadel and cas.; exp. currants, raisins, figs, olive oil; inds. based on agr. processing; p. (1981) 142,163.

Pau, c., cap. of Pyrénées-Atlantique dep., **France**; on Gave-de-Pau; impt. mkt. and regional ctr.; summer and winter resort; linen, chocolate, hams, wine; natural gas nearby; p. (1982) 85,766.

Pauillac, t., Gironde dep., **France**; pt. on Gironde estuary; ships, wines, timber; oil refinery, natural gas; p. (1982) 6,359.

Paulo Affonso, falls, São Francisco R., **Brazil**; 79 m; Tres Marías dam and power sta. opened 1960; in Nat. Park.

Pavia, c., prov. cap., N. **Italy**; on R. Ticino; route ctr. and agr. mkt. in Po valley; olives, wine, Parmesan cheese; oil refining at Spinetta; walled c.; battle 1525; birthplace of Lanfranc; p. (1981) 85,029.

Pavlodar, pt., Kazakh SSR, **USSR**; on R. Irtysh; chemicals, sulphates, agr. machin., locomotives, aluminium, oil processing; food prod.; p. (est. 1980) 281,000.

Pawtucket, c., R.I., **USA**; on Pawtucket R. at

head of navigation; first water-power cotton spinning factory in USA 1790; textiles remain most impt. ind.; p. (1980) 71,204.

Paysandú, dep., W. **Uruguay**; rich pastoral a.; ranching, cattle, sheep; arable agr., cereals, mkt. gardening around c. of P.; a. 13,406 km²; p. (est. 1969) 90,800.

Paysandú, cap. of P. dep., W. **Uruguay**; pt. on Uruguay R. with meat-packing, soap and footwear inds.; p. (1970) 60,000.

Pazardzhik, t., **Bulgaria**; on main rly. line to Istanbul; industl., hemp spinning and weaving; p. (1972) 66,251.

Paz de Rio, t., Boyacá, **Colombia**; iron and steel wks.; iron ore, coal, limestone nearby; hydroelec. sta. projected.

Peace, R., **Canada**; one of ch. headstreams of Mackenzie R.; rises in Rocky mtns., and flows generally N. to Gr. Slave R. nr. L. Athabaska; a. of very mild climate in lower course, fertile agr. valley; 1,680 km long.

Peak Dist., Pennine hill dist., mid-**Eng.**; extends from Chesterfield to Buxton, and Ashbourne to Glossop; composed of limestone with typical karst features; within P.D. Nat. Park, tourist and recreation a. for cities to E. (Sheffield) and W. (Manchester); limestone quarrying for cement; Kinder Scout 634 m.

Pearl Harbor, landlocked harbour, Oahu I., **Hawaiian Is.,** one of finest natural harbours in E. Pac.; US naval base; attacked by Japanese without warning 7 Dec. 1941. (7.55 a.m., local time).

Pearl Is., archipelago, G. of Panama; sea fishing, pearls.

Pearl R. *See* **Chu-kiang.**

Pechenga (Petsamo), spt., **RSFSR**; on inlet of Barents Sea; formerly Finnish, ceded to USSR Sept. 1944; ice-free throughout year; exp. nickel, timber, cobalt.

Pechora, dist., **RSFSR**; E. of Urals; one of 4 main coalfields of USSR; coking coal; ch. ts., Vorkuta and Inta.

Pechora, R., **RSFSR**; rises in Urals and flows N. into Arctic Oc.; 1,120 km navigable between June and Sept. for transport of timber from its basin; fishing; 1,792 km long.

Pecos, R., N.M. and Texas, **USA**; trib. of Rio Grande; water control schemes provide irrigation for lge. a.; 1,482 km long.

Pécs, c., S.W. **Hungary**; on Yugoslav border; one of oldest and most pleasantly situated ts. of Hungary; cath., univ., airport; in coal-mng. a.; coke, chemicals, majolica, leather gds., engin., brewing; p. (est. 1978) 168,767.

Peebles, royal burgh, Tweeddale, **Scot.**; on upper course of R. Tweed; woollen cloth, knitwear; mkt., tourist ctr.; p. (1981) 6,705.

Peeblesshire, former co., S. **Scot.**; now part of Borders Reg.

Peel, t., I. of Man, **Eng.**; resort, fishing pt. midway along W. cst.; cas., cath.; p. (1971) 3,081.

Peel Fell, mtn. Northumberland, Eng.; 1,964 ft.

Pegu, c., Pegu prov., S. **Burma**; R. pt., rly. junc.; many temples, notably Shwe May Daw Pagoda; once cap. of Burmese kingdom; came under Brit. rule 1852; p. (est. 1977) 135,000.

Pegu Yoma, mtns., **Burma**; between valleys of Rs. Irrawaddy and Sittang; thickly forested with teak which is comm. exploited and forms impt. exp.

Peine, t., Lower Saxony, **W. Germany**; N.W. of Brunswick; iron, furniture, textiles; p. (1983) 47,000.

Peipus, Lake, Estonian SSR, **RSFSR**; drained by Narva R. into G. of Finland; Pskov lies to S.; scene of Alexander Nevsky's victory over the Germans 1242; a. 3,626 km².

Pekalongan, t., N. cst. Java, **Indonesia**; exp. sugar, rubber; p. (est. 1975) 97,000.

Peking. *See* **Beijing.**

Pelagi, gr. of Italian Is., inc. Lampedusa and Linosa, between Malta and Tunisian cst.

Pelée, mtn., **Martinique**; active volcano, devastated town of St. Pierre 1902; alt. 1,342 m.

Pella, dep. of Macedonia, **Greece**; mtnous.; cotton, wheat, tobacco; cap. Edessa; a. 2,802 km²; p. (1971) 126,201.

Peloponnesus (Peloponnisos), peninsula, S. **Greece**; separated from mainland by G. of Corinth, but joined in N.E. by Isthmus of Corinth; mtnous.; livestock agr., drought-resistant sheep and goats; ch. ts., Kalamata, Tripolis; a. 21,642 km²; p. (1981) 1,012,528.

Pelotas, t., Rio Grande do Sul, **Brazil;** pt. on lagoon S.S.W. Pôrto Alegre; meat-packing and industl. ctr.; p. (est. 1980) 255,500.

Pemba, I., part of **Tanzania;** cloves, copra, coconuts; exp. mangrove bark for tannin; a. 984 km²; p. (1967) 164,243.

Pemba (Port Amelia), spt., **Moçambique;** sisal, coconuts, cotton, maize, groundnuts; p. (1960) 55,902.

Pembroke, mkt. t., South Pembs., Dyfed, **Wales;** on S. side of Milford Haven; sm. pt.; dock facilities; cas., ruins of Monkton priory; birthplace of Henry VII; p. (1981) 15,618.

Pembroke Dock, Dyfed, **Wales;** site of government dockyard (1814) with consequent growth of a new t.

Pembrokeshire, former co., **Wales.** *See* **Dyfed.**

Pembrokeshire, South, l. gov. dist., Dyfed, **Wales;** from Pembroke and Tenby on cst. to Narbeth inland; p. (1981) 39,410.

Penang, I., st. W. **Malaysia;** cap. Georgetown, pt. for N. Malaya handling rubber and tin; paper mill; the first Brit. Straits Settlement (*q.v.*); a. 1,036 km²; p. (1970) 776,124.

Penarth, t., Vale of Glamorgan, South Glamorgan, **Wales;** former sm. pt. on Severn estuary, 3 km S. of Cardiff; seaside resort; p. (1981) 24,000.

Pendle, l. gov. dist., Lancs., **Eng.;** ts. of Barrowford, Colne and Nelson; p. (1981) 85,573.

Pengpu. *See* **Bengbu.**

Penicuik, burgh, Midlothian, **Scot.;** on R. Esk; paper; p. (1981) 17,430.

Penistone, t., South Yorks., **Eng.;** on R. Don; steel; mkt.; p. (1981) 8,990.

Penki. *See* **Benxi.**

Penmaenmawr, t., Aberconwy, Gwynedd, **Wales;** 6 km. S.W. of Conway; resort; p. (1981) 3,903.

Pennine Alps, Switzerland; div. of Alpine system; ch. peaks; Mont Blanc (4,814 m) Monte Rosa (4,637 m), Matterhorn (4,477 m); winter sports.

Pennine Range, mtn. range, "backbone of England," extends 224 km southwards from Cheviot hills to Derbyshire; limestone, millstone grit; moorland sheep, dairying in valleys, quarrying, tourism; inc. Peak Dist. Nat. Park and Pennine Way long distance route; water supply, forestry; Cross Fell, 895 m.

Pennsylvania, st., **USA;** 'Keystone St.'; admitted to Union 1787; st. flower Mountain Laurel, st. bird Ruffed Grouse; originally proprietary colony of Penn family, later one of the 13 original sts. in the Union; traversed N.E. to S.W. by Appalachians; ch. Rs.: Delaware, Susquehanna, Allegheny, and Monogahela; major industl. st.; iron and steel, coal (bituminous and anthracite), natural gas, petroleum; maize, wheat, oats, rye; textiles, machin., motor cars, tobacco; cap. Harrisburg; ch. ts.; Pittsburgh, Philadelphia; a. 117,412 km²; p. (1980) 11,867,000.

Penrith, t., N.S.W., **Australia;** in Sydney met. a.; ctr. for mkt. gardening; p. (1976) 79,038.

Penrith, mkt. t., Eden, Cumbria, **Eng.;** at N. foot of Shap Fell, 29 km S.E. of Carlisle; agr. mkt.; tourist ctr.; p. (1981) 12,205.

Penryn, t., Carrick, Cornwall, **Eng.;** on R. Fal estuary; sm. pt., boat repairs; once ctr. of granite quarrying; p. (1981) 5,090.

Pensacola, t., Fla., **USA;** on N. shore of P. Bay; originally a Spanish settlement, retaining much Spanish influence in squares, bldgs., street names; fishing, sea food inds.; univ.; naval air training school; p. (1980) 290,000 (met. a.).

Penticton, B.C., **Canada;** comm. fruit ctr.; p. (1971) 17,702.

Pentonville, dist., London, **Eng.;** prison; birthplace of John Stuart Mill.

Pentland Firth, strait, between Orkney Is. and Caithness, **Scot.,** connecting N. Sea and Atl. Oc.; dangerous tidal currents.

Pentland Hills, range, **Scot.;** extend from Lanark to Edinburgh; Scald Law, 878 m.

Penwith, l. gov. dist., Cornwall, **Eng.;** S.W. tip of Cornwall inc. Penzance, St. Just and St. Ives; p. (1981) 55,431.

Pen-y-Ghent, peak, Pennines, North Yorks., **Eng.;** alt. 680 m.

Penza, c., cap. of P. oblast, **RSFSR;** on Sura R.;

rly. junc.; agr. ctr., especially for grain tr. to Moscow; food-processing and wide range of mnfs.; oil pipeline from Mozyr'; p. (1980) 490,000.

Penzance, t., Penwith, Cornwall, **Eng.;** on Mount's Bay; tourist ctr.; ferry to Scilly Isles; engin.; birthplace of Sir Humphrey Davy; p. (1981) 19,521.

Peoria, t., Ill., **USA;** machin., domestic gds.; grain tr.; univ.; p. (1980) 124,000 (c.), 366,000 (met. a.).

Perak, st., **W. Malaysia;** ch. tin-dredging a., in basin of Perak R.; rubber; cap. Taiping; a. 20,668 km²; p. (1970) 1,569,139.

Pereira, t., Caldas, **Colombia;** cath.; comm. ctr. for coffee; p. (1973) 186,615.

Perekop, Isthmus of, connects Crimea with Ukraine, **USSR.**

Pergamino, t., Buenos Aires, **Argentina;** road and rail focus in maize-growing dist.

Périgord, dist., S.W. **France;** limestone plateau crossed by Dordogne R.; famous for truffles.

Périgueux, t., cap. Dordogne, **France;** on R. Isle; cath.; famous for pâté de foie gras; engin., china; p. (1982) 59,716 (met. a.).

Perim, I. in strait of Bab-el-Mandeb at S. entrance to Red Sea; part of **Democratic Rep. of Yemen;** former coaling sta.; a. 13 km²; p. 1,700.

Perlis, st., **W. Malaysia;** agr. dist. for rice and coconuts; tin; a. 803 km²; p. (1967) 117,606.

Perm, oblast, RSFSR; major mng., timber, and paper dist.; produces oil (Krasnokamsk), coal (Kizel), hydroelectricity, and potash (Solikamsh); cap. Perm.

Perm (Molotov), c., cap. of P. oblast, **RSFSR;** on Kama R.; machin., chemicals, oil refineries; univ.; p. (1980) 1,008,000.

Pernambuco, st., N.E. **Brazil;** mtnous. interior, cst. fertile; cap. Recife; sugar, cotton, manioc, tobacco, fruits; a. 98,322 km²; p. (1970) 5,160,640.

Pernik (Dimitrovo), c., **Bulgaria;** iron and steel inds.; p. (est. 1972) 81,893.

Pernis, t., opposite Rotterdam, **Neth.;** lge. oil refinery; pipeline to Wesserling (nr. Cologne). *See also* **Terneuzen.**

Perovo, t., **RSFSR;** nr. Moscow; engin., chemicals; agr. research institute; p. inc. in Moscow.

Perpignan, c., cap. of Pyrénées-Orientales dep., **France;** nr. Spanish border and Mediterranean; on Paris-Barcelona rly.; mkt. and comm. ctr. for wines and fruits; cath.; tourism; p. (1982) 113,646.

Persepolis, anc. c., **Iran;** former cap. of Persian empire, now in ruins; tourism.

Pershore, t., Wychavon, Hereford and Worcs., **Eng.;** on R. Avon; ctr. of fruit-growing a.

Persia. *See* **Iran.**

Persian Gulf, inlet from Indian Oc. through G. of Oman and Strait of Kormuz, between Iran and Arabia; oilfields in surrounding land and now in G. itself; ch. pts. Bandar-e-Bushehr, Abadan, Kuwait, Dubai; Bahrain, lgst. I.

Perth, c., cap. of W. **Australia;** on R. Swan; well planned garden c.; univ., cath., airport; many employed in services; inds. moving to Fremantle (pt.) or to Kwinana; p. (1976) 87,576 (c.), 805,439 (met. a.).

Perth, c., royal burgh, Perth and Kinross, **Scot.;** on R. Tay; rly. junc.; cap. of Scot. until assassination of James I, 1437; dyeing, textiles, whisky distilling; cath., historical associations; p. (1981) 41,998.

Perthshire, former co., **Scot.;** now part of Perth and Kinross, l. gov. dist., Tayside Reg.; p. (1981) 118,624.

Peru, Andean rep., **S. America;** consists of 3 N.W.-S.E. regions; Costa (cst.) Sierra (Andes, rising to over 6,100 m) and Selva (interior *montaña* and R. basins); 40 per cent p. in Costa, 60 per cent in Sierra, yet Selva covers 70 per cent total a.; ch. Rs. Ucayali, Marañon; L. Titicaca shared with Bolivia; El Misti volcano in S.; cap. Lima on Pac. cst. with 20 per cent p.; agr. diversified and being extended by irrigation schemes; fishing main single ind.; mng. impt. in Andes; major world producer of silver, phosphates, potash, copper, petroleum; a. 1,249,048 km²; p. (est. 1984) 19,197,000 (of whom 3,320,000 live in Lima-Callao met. a.).

Peru Current (Humboldt), ocean current, S. Pac.

Oc.; flows N. along cst. of N. Chile and Peru; causes clouds and fog.

Perugia, t., Umbria, **Italy;** on R. Tiber; univ., observatory; woollens, silks, lace; foodstuffs, furniture, pottery, chemicals, agr. machin.; p. (1981) 142,348.

Pervouralsk, t., **RSFSR;** in Urals; metallurgical ctr.; p. (est. 1980) 130,000.

Pesaro, c., central **Italy;** on Adriatic cst.; agr. ctr., seaside resort; birthplace of Rossini; p. (1981) 90,412 (inc. Urbino).

Pescadores Is. (P'eng-hu Lieh-tao), archipelago, between Taiwan and mainland **China;** fishing, fish-processing; a. 132 km²; p. 86,000.

Pescara, c., cap. of P. prov., S. **Italy;** on estuary of R. Aterno; fish. pt., olive oil, soap, pasta, pottery; resort; birthplace of D'Annunzio; p. (1981) 131,330.

Peshawar, c., cap. of North-West Frontier Prov., **Pakistan;** 18 km E. of Khyber pass, commanding route to Afghanistan; military sta.; univ.; handicrafts, textiles, furniture; p. (1972) 268,366.

Petah Tikva, oldest modern Jewish settlement in **Israel** (1878); ctr. for oranges; mnfs. inc. textiles; p. (est. 1979) 117,000.

Petaling Jaya, t., **W. Malaysia;** industl. estate nr. Kuala Lumpur; tyres, aluminium rolling mill.

Peter I., uninhabited I., **Antarctic Oc.,** belonging to Norway; a. c. 243 km².

Peterborough, t., Ont., **Canada;** flour-milling, elec. machin., trailers, agr. equipment, plastics, textiles, paper; p. (1971) 57,498.

Peterborough, c., l. gov. dist., Cambs., **Eng.;** on R. Nene on margin of Fens; cath.; rly ctr.; ctr. of brick ind. (Oxford clay around Fletton); diesel engines, agr. machin., gen. engin.; major planned expansion as new t.; p. (1981) 132,464, (53,471 in 1951).

Peterborough, Soke of. See **Cambridgeshire.**

Peterhead, spt., burgh, Banff and Buchan, Scot.; on E. cst., 43 km N.E. of Aberdeen; herring fisheries, leading U.K. fish. pt. by value of fish landed (1982); fish-processing, granite quarrying; supply base for N. Sea oil; p. (1981) 17,015.

Peterlee, new t. (1948), Durham, **Eng.;** coal-mng. dist.; textiles, science-based inds.; p. (1981) 22,756.

Petersfield, t., East Hants., **Eng.;** on R. Rother, N.W. of Chichester; mkt.; p. (1981) 10,001.

Petra, anc. c., **Jordan;** temples, rock tombs and Roman ruins; called Sela in Bible (2 Kings 14. 7); rediscovered by Burckhardt 1812.

Petropavlovsk, t., Kazakh SSR, **USSR;** on Ishim R.; rly. junc.; flour, leather, meat canneries, furs, engin.; p. (est. 1980) 209,000.

Petropavlovsk-Kamchatsky, t., **RSFSR;** spt. on Pac. cst.; shipyard, timber mills, engin.; fishing and whaling fleet; p. (est. 1980) 219,000.

Petrópolis, t., Rio de Janeiro, **Brazil;** health resort, c. 700 m a.s.l.; cath.; p. (est. 1980) 245,700.

Petsamo. See **Pechenga.**

Petten, t., **Neth.;** 48 km N.W. of Amsterdam, on cst.; atomic research ctr.

Petworth, mkt. t., West Sussex, **Eng.;** in Rother valley, 19 km N.E. of Chichester; associated with Turner.

Pevensey Levels, marshy a., East Sussex, **Eng.;** lie behind coastal sand-bars between Eastbourne and Bexhill, extend 8 km inland to Hailsham; now largely drained, cattle pastures; a. 62 km².

Pforzheim, t., Baden-Württemberg, **W. Germany;** S.E. of Karlsruhe; gold, silver, metal wks., jewellery; p. (1983) 105,200.

Phan Thiet, spt., **Vietnam;** exp. dried and salt fish; p. 5,000.

Phetburi, t. and prov., **Thailand;** on Isthmus of Kra crossed by Phetburi R.; p. (1960) 24,654 (t.), 237,835 (prov.).

Philadelphia, c., pt., Penns., **USA;** on Delaware R.; comm., industl. and cultural ctr.; univ., R.C. cath.; masonic temple, mint, academy of fine arts; shipbldg., locomotives, machin., surgical instruments, carpets, woollens, cottons, worsteds; sugar, and petroleum refining; ctr. of War of Independence 1775–1783; founded as Quaker col. by William Penn 1682; p. (1980) 1,681,000 (c.), 4,701,000 (met. a.).

Philae, I. in Nile R., **Egypt;** flooded by waters of Aswan Dam; contains anc. ruined temples which have been removed to a safer site.

Philippeville. See **Skikda.**

Philippines, Rep. of, S.E. **Asia;** island chain in Pac. Oc., stretching over 1,760 km; ch. Is. Luzon, Mindanao, Negros, Cebu, Mindoro, and Palawar; lie in track of cyclones; tropical climate; mtnous., agr. aided by intricate terracing system; most Is. underdeveloped except Luzon where p. concentrated; subsistence agr. rice and maize; cash crops sugar, coconuts, hemp, tobacco; close connections with USA; cap. Quezon City (admin. functions at Manila); a. 299,681 km²; p. (est. 1984) 53,395,000.

Phlorina (Florina), t., Macedonia, **Greece;** in basin at 900 m, 16 km from Yugoslav border; agr. ctr.; p. (1981) 12,573.

Phnom-Penh, c., cap. of **Kampuchea,** S.E. Asia; pt. on Mekong R.; handles ships up to 2,500 tonnes; linked to Kompong Som by modern highway; multi-purpose dam to W.; univ., royal palace; airport; p. (1971) 1,500,000; p. est. 400,000 since Communist takeover but many not permanently settled there.

Phoenix, c., Arizona, **USA;** on Salt R., ctr. of Salt River Valley irrigated region; electronics research, steel, aircraft, clothing; p. (1980) 790,000 (c.), 1,509,000 (met. a.).

Phoenix Group, Is., **Pac. Oc.;** part of Gilbert I. col.; a. 41 km²; US have some rights over Canton and Enderbury; Canton used as international airport; p. (1963) 1,014.

Phuket I., Thailand; off Kra Isthmus; main alluvial tin-working region of Thailand; ch. t. Phuket where a tin-smelting plant is to be established; a. 534 km².

Piacenza, c., cap. of P. prov., **Italy;** in Emilia-Romagna, on R. Po; agr. and comm. ctr.; cath., palaces, arsenal; cars, chemicals, cement; p. (1981) 109,039.

Piatra-Neamt, t., Moldavia, **Romania;** timber, pharmaceuticals, soap; oil refineries; p. (est. 1972) 61,226.

Piauí, st., **Brazil;** semi-arid, underdeveloped dist.; thorn scrub; livestock rearing; cap. Teresina; a. 249,319 km²; p. (1970) 1,680,573.

Piave, R., N.E. **Italy;** flows to Adriatic, 200 km long.

Picardy, former prov., **France;** included the Somme dep. and parts of Pas-de-Calais, Aisne and Oise; old battle sites, Agincourt and Crécy; rich agr. a.; textiles; p. (1982) 1,740,000.

Pichincha, prov., **Ecuador;** p. concentrated in Andes; many natural resources inc. lime, gypsum, silver; tropical hardwoods; cattle raising; cap. Quito; a. 16,105 km²; p. (est. 1970) 843,000.

Pickering, mkt. t., Ryedale, North Yorks., **Eng.;** on N. margin of Vale of P.; church with murals; cas.; gas terminal; p. (1981) 5,942.

Pickering, Vale of, North Yorks., **Eng.;** wide, flat-floored vale, once occupied by glacial lake; bounded to N. by N. York Moors, to S. by York Wolds; drained W. by R. Derwent, alluvial soils, marshy in ctr.; crop farming along margins, cattle grazing in damper meadows in ctr., ch. ts. Pickering, Malton, Helmsley.

Picos de Europa, mtn. massif, N. **Spain;** hgst. massif in Cantabrian mtns., rising to 2,650 m; partially inc. in Nat. Park.

Picton, t., S.I., **N.Z.;** freezing wks.; tourist and fishing ctr.; pt.; p. (1976) 3,276.

Pictou, t., Nova Scotia, **Canada;** on Northumberland Strait; founded by Scottish settlers.

Pidurutalagala, mtn., **Sri Lanka;** alt. 2,530 m; hgst. peak in rep.

Piedmont, region, N. **Italy;** rice, wheat, vines, fruits; cottons, woollens; a. 25,416 km²; p. (1981) 4,479,031.

Pietermaritzburg, c., cap. of Natal, **S. Africa;** named after Piet Retief and Gerhardus Maritz, two Boer leaders; lt. inds.; tanning; iron-ore mng. in a.; part of univ. of Natal; 2 caths.; p. (1970) 158,921 (met. a.).

Pietersburg, t., Transvaal, **S. Africa;** gold, asbestos, tin; comm. ctr. for cereals, tobacco, cotton, citrus fruits; p. (est. 1975) 27,000.

Pila (Schneidemühl), t., N.W. **Poland** (since 1945);

formerly in Prussian prov. of Pomerania; tr. ctr., lignite mines nearby; p. (1970) 43,800.

Pilar, t., **Paraguay**; impt. R. pt.; sawmills; textiles; p. (est. 1970) 15,324.

Pilbara, dist., W. **Australia**; extensive iron mng.; other minerals inc. salt, oil, nat. gas; rapid growth of p.; p. (est. 1975); 35,000 (1960) 2,250.

Pilcomayo, R., northernmost R. of **Argentina**; rises in Bolivian Andes, flows across the Gran Chaco, to enter Paraguay, joining the Paraguay R. nr. Asunción; hydroelec. power; 1,120 km long.

Pilibhit, t., Uttar Pradesh, N. **India**; admin. ctr.; sugar-refining; p. (1961) 57,527.

Pilsen. See Plzeň.

Pinar del Rio, c., prov. cap., **Cuba**; tobacco; p. (est. 1970) 542,432.

Pinawa, t., Manitoba, **Canada**; 88 km N.E. of Winnipeg; nuclear research; p. (1965) 8,000.

Pindus, mtn. chain, between Thessaly and Albania, **Greece**; hgst. peak 2,455 m.

Pingxiang, t., Jianxi, **China**; supplies coking coal to Wuhan.

Pinneberg, t., Schleswig-Holstein, **W. Germany**; N.W. of Hamburg; rose cultivation, metals, leather; p. (1983) 36,200.

Pinsk, c., Belorussiyan SSR, **USSR**; in Pripet Marshes, pt. on Pina R.; paper, wood-working inds., matches; Jewish residents exterminated during German occupation second world war; p. (est. 1973) 73,000.

Piombino, t., **Italy**; mainland pt. for island of Elba; steel wks.; p. (1981) 39,389.

Piotrkow Trybunalski, t., **Poland**; cas.; timber and glass inds.; new textile combine; p. (1970) 59,700.

Piqua, t., Ohio, **USA**; N. of Dayton; ironwks., woollens; nuclear reactor; p. (1980) 20,480.

Piracicaba, t., São Paulo, **Brazil**; ctr. of agr. dist.; sugar-refining, brandy, flour; p. (est. 1980) 201,800.

Piraeus, c., **Greece**; pt. of Athens and prin. pt. of Greece; major industl. and comm. ctr.; p. (1981) 196,389.

Pirmasens, t., Rhineland-Palatinate, **W. Germany**; S.W. of Mannheim; footwear, leather gds.; p. (1983) 47,600.

Pirna, t., Dresden, **E. Germany**; on R. Elbe; textiles, paper, glass; p. (est. 1973) 49,946.

Pirot, t., **Yugoslavia**; nr. Bulgarian border; in economic development a.; p. (est. 1965) 21,000.

Pisa, c., **Italy**; at head of Arno delta, 19 km N.E. of Livorno; famous leaning tower, cath., univ.; textiles, chemicals, engin.; airport; tourism; p. (1981) 104,509.

Pisco, spt., **Peru**; famous for P. brandy; p. (est. 1970) 28,519.

Pistoia, t., Tuscany, **Italy**; on Arno plain, N.W. of Florence; iron and steel gds.; macaroni; p. (1981) 92,274.

Pit, R., Cal., **USA**; rises in Goose L.; cuts spectacular gorges in the Cascades; used for hydroelectric power.

Pitcairn I., E. Pac. Oc., Brit. col.; inc. atolls of Ducie and Oeno and I. of Henderson; sweet potatoes, bananas, oranges, coconuts; a. 5 km²; p. mostly descendants of mutineers of the *Bounty*; p. (1971) 92.

Pitch Lake, Trinidad, **W.I.**; S. of I., 16 km S.W. of San Fernando; natural deposit of asphalt; tourism; a. 86 ha.

Pitea, spt., N. **Sweden**; on G. of Bothnia; sawmills; p. (1983) 38,700.

Pitesti, t., **Romania**; on Arges R.; petroleum, fruit, grain; lge. automobile plant; oil refinery under construction; p. (1978) 133,081.

Pitlochry, burgh, Perth and Kinross, **Scot.**; on R. Tummel, 6 km S. of Pass of Killiecrankie; summer resort; distilleries, hydros; p. (1981) 2,610.

Pittenweem, burgh, North East Fife, **Scot.**; at entrance to F. of Forth; fisheries; p. (1981) 1,537.

Pittsburgh, c., Penns., **USA**; univ.; R.C. cath.; pt. on Ohio R.; ctr. of richest American coalfield; natural gas, petroleum, iron and steel, machin., metal gds., meat-packing, glass, aluminium, chemicals, p. (1980) 424,000 (c.), 2,261,000 (met. a.).

Pittsfield, c., Mass., **USA**; textiles, paper, plastics, elec. machin.; resort; p. (1980) 51,974.

Piura, t., N. **Peru**; on Piura R.; oldest Spanish t. in Peru; cotton mkt. and processing, p. (est. 1980) 179,300.

Pladju, t., S. Sumatra, **Indonesia**; oil refining; linked by pipeline with Tempino and Bejubang.

Plata, Rio de la (Plate R.), estuary between **Argentina** and **Uruguay**; receives waters of Rs. Paraná and Uruguay; cst. provides sites for lge. spts., Buenos Aires, La Plata, Montevideo.

Platte, R., Nebraska, **USA**; formed by union of N. Platte and S. Platte Rs.; total length 2,240 km; irrigation, hydroelec. power.

Plauen, t., Karl-Marx-Stadt, **E. Germany**; textiles, machin., cable, leather, paper, radios; rly. junc; p. (est. 1970) 81,907.

Plenty, Bay of, prov. and bay, N.I., **N.Z.**; on E. cst.; 208 km wide; p. (1976) 472,083.

Plettenberg, t., N. Rhine-Westphalia, **W. Germany**; on R. Lenne; iron wks.; p. (1983) 27,900.

Pleven, mkt. t., **Bulgaria**; many mosques; famous siege 1877; textiles, wines; p. (1978) 116,368.

Plitvička Jezera, lakes, **Yugoslavia**; beautiful scenery; tourism; fishing.

Ploče, new spt., **Yugoslavia**; on Dalmatian cst.; industl. and rly. ctr.

Plock, t., **Poland**; on R. Vistula, nr. Warsaw; agr.; oil refinery and petrochemical plant; food processing; agr. machin.; p. (est. 1983) 112,400.

Ploiești, t., Prahova dist., **Romania**; petroleum, engin.; p. (1978) 206,138.

Plovdiv (Philippopolis), c., **Bulgaria**; on R. Maritsa; univ., Greek cath.; second c. of rep.; agr. processing, clothing, metals, engin.; p. (1978) 328,031.

Plymouth, c., spt., l. gov. dist., S. Devon, **Eng.**; on Plymouth Sound; comprises the "three towns" of Plymouth, Devonport, and Stonehouse; Brit. fleet faced Armada 1588; R.C. cath., guildhall, museum; shipbldg.; seaside resort; fishing and fish-canning, lt. inds.; recently discovered deposit of tungsten, thought to be lgst. in W. Europe but lies within Dartmoor Nat. Park; p. (1981) 243,895.

Plymouth, ch. t., Montserrat I., **W.I.**; p. (1970) 3,500.

Plymouth, spt., Mass., **USA**; on Plymouth Bay, S.E. of Boston; here Pilgrim Fathers landed 1620 from *Mayflower* to form first English col.; Pilgrim Hall, Pilgrim Rock; textiles, cordage, machin.; tourism; p. (1980) 7,232.

Plynlimmon, mtn., Powys and Dyfed, **Wales**; alt. 753 m; source of R. Severn.

Plzeň (Pilsen), c., W. Bohemia, **ČSSR**; ctr. of coal-mng. region; famous for beer and Lenin (former Skoda) armament wks.; p. (1980) 171,275.

Po, R., **Italy**; flows from Monte Viso, through Piedmont and Lombardy to the Adriatic; valley forms a major component of N. Italian lowland; natural gas deposits in valley; liable to flooding; 648 km long.

Pocklington, mkt. t., East Yorks., Humberside, **Eng.**; foot of York wolds, 19 km E. of York; ctr. of agr. dist.; 16th cent. grammar school.

Podolsk, c., RSFSR; on main rly. from Moscow to S.; engin., tin-smelting, food-processing; p. (est. 1980) 203,000.

Pohai. See Bo Hai.

Point-à-Pierre, Trinidad; oil refinery; natural gas pipeline from Forest Reserve field.

Point-à-Pitre, ch. t. and pt. Guadeloupe, **Fr. W.I.**; on Grande Terre I.; exp. agr. prods., bananas, sugar; p. (1970) 29,538.

Pointe-des-Galets or Le Port, ch. pt., La Réunion (Fr.), Indian Oc.

Pointe-Noire, spt., **Congo Rep.**; airport, rly. to Brazzaville; agr. exp.; potash deposits nearby; linked to deepwater terminal for bulk carriers but mine closed due to flooding; petroleum refinery (1982); gas reserves; p. (est. 1980) 185,110.

Point Fortin, t., Trinidad; oilfield and refinery.

Poitiers, c., cap. of Vienne dep., **France**; many attractive bldgs., cath.; agr. tr.; mnfs. chemicals, hosiery; Black Prince defeated Fr. 1356; p. (1982) 82,884.

Poland, People's Republic, E. **Europe**; history dominated by constantly changing sovereignty between E. and W. powers; mainly lowland; continental climate; economy retarded by history of political fluctuation but growth of inds. and urbanisation are both proceeding rapidly; major ctr. of mng. and heavy inds. in conurb. of Upper Silesia, agr. land remains largely in private ownership, but govt. attempts to rationalise farm structure, major pts. at Gdynia, Gdansk, and Szczecin, international airport at cap. Warsaw, 17 historic provs. to be replaced by 49 large dists., a. 311,700 km²; p. (est. 1984) 37,228,000.

Polotsk, c., Belorussiyan SSR, **USSR**; cath.; gasoline prod., oil refining; pipeline to Latvian pt. of Ventspils; food processing; p. (est. 1970) 64,000.

Polotskiy, t. Belorussiyan SSR, **USSR**; 13 km W. of Polotsk; new oil workers' t. 1963.

Poltava, c., Ukrainian SSR, **USSR**; industl. and food-processing ctr. in rich agr. dist.; countryside described in Gogol's work; textiles, synthetic diamond plant; battle 1709 between Swedish and Russian armies; p. (est. 1980) 282,000.

Polynesia, ethnic region, **Oceania**; I. grs. in Pac. Oc. within 30° N. and S. of equator; between longitude 135° E. and W.; p. (est. 1984) 498,000.

Pomerania, former prov., N. Germany; in post-war redivision part E. of R. Oder to **Poland**; part W. of R. Oder incorporated in Mecklenburg, **E. Germany**; farming, shipbldg., fishing.

Pomona or **Mainland,** lgst of the Orkney Is., **Scot.**; Kirkwall (cap.) and Stromness on I.; p. (1970) 87,384.

Pomorze. See **Bydgoszcz.**

Pompeii, ruined c., **Italy**; stood 21 km S.E. of Naples, at foot of Vesuvius; destroyed A.D. 79 by volcanic eruption, site re-discovered 1748; many interesting excavations; also modern c. nearby; fine church with famous collection of silver and gold plate; p. (1981) 22,886.

Ponape, volcanic I., Caroline Is., W. Pac. Oc.; copra, ivory, nuts, starch, bauxite; a. 334 km².

Ponce, c., **Puerto Rico**; recently improved harbour on S. cst.; well connected with other ts. in rep.; ctr. of fertile, irrigated sugar-cane a.; industl. ctr.; p. (1980) 253,000.

Pondicherry, spt., Tamil Nadu st., **India**; on Coromandel cst.; cap. of P. terr.; tr. ctr. for local prod.; p. (1971) 90,637.

Ponta Delgada, ch. t., spt., San Miguel I., **Azores**; attractive scenery, mild climate attract tourists; p. (1970) 69,930.

Ponta Grossa, t., Paraná, **Brazil**; rly. junc.; comm. ctr.; maté, rice, timber, tobacco, bananas, cattle, jerked beef; p. (est. 1980) 175,700.

Pontardawe, t., Lliw Valley, West Glamorgan, S. **Wales**; on R. Tawe, N.E. of Swansea; zinc smelting and refining; p. (1971) 29,431 (dist.).

Pontchartrain, Lake, shallow L., lower Mississippi flood plain, **USA**; connected by canal to New Orleans 10 km to S., and by deltaic channels to G. of Mexico.

Pontefract, mkt. t., West Yorks., **Eng.**; 11 km E. of Wakefield; coal, furniture, confectionery, mkt. gardening; cas. ruins; p. (1981) 31,971.

Pontevedra, prov., **Spain**; on deeply indented Atl. cst.; transatlantic pt. Vigo; scenery and fiesta attractions for tourists; agr., livestock, timber, fisheries; cap. P.; a. 4,390 km²; p. (1981) 883,258.

Pontevedra, c., cap. of P. prov., N.W. **Spain**; fish. pt., handicrafts, agr. tr.; p. (1981) 65,137.

Pontiac, t., Mich., **USA**; on Clinton R.; fishing and shooting, motor cars, rubber gds., machin., varnish; p. (1980) 76,715.

Pontianak, t., cap. of Kalimantan, **Indonesia**; exp. rubber, copra; rubber processing; p. (1971) 217,555.

Pontine Is., off W. cst. of **Italy**; in Tyrrhenian Sea; a. 11·6 km²; p. 6,000.

Pontine Marshes, region, Latium, S. **Italy**; coastal zone S.E. of Rome extending from Velletri to Terracina; formerly highly malarial fens, largely drained and colonised 1930–35; 3,200 new farms, 4 new ts.; ch. t. Littoria; a. 647 km².

Pontresina, t., Grisons, **Switzerland**; E. of St. Moritz; tourist resort; p. (est. 1970) 1,250.

Pontypool, t., Torfaen, Gwent, **Wales**; coal, steel, glass, bricks, tin galvanising, nylon at Manhilad; p. (1981) 36,761.

Pontypridd, t., Taff-Ely, Mid Glamorgan, **Wales**; on R. Taff, 19 km N.W. of Cardiff; coal, iron-founding; p. (1981) 32,992.

Pool Malebo (Stanley Pool), Congo and **Zaïre**; lake formed by expansion of R. Zaïre; length 40 km.; width 26 km.

Poole, t., l. gov. dist., Dorset, **Eng.**; spt. on Poole Harbour, 6 km W. of Bournemouth; imports clay for local pottery inds. petroleum production began 1979; tourism, yachting, marine engin., chemicals; p. (1981) 118,992.

Poona. See **Pune.**

Poopó, salt L., Oruro dep., **Bolivia**; fed from L. Titicaca by R. Desaguadero, which flows over saline beds; no outlet; c. 3,600 m a.s.l.; a. 2,600 km².

Popayan, c., S.W. **Columbia**; 1,677 m above Cauca R.; cath., univ.; food processing, coffee, flour; mng. nearby; p. (est. 1972) 82,100 (c.) 103,900 (met. a.).

Poplar. See **Tower Hamlets.**

Popocatepetl, volcano, nr. Puebla, **Mexico**; alt. 5,456 m; dormant since 1702.

Porbander, spt., Gujarat, **India**; exp. silk, cotton; imports coal, dates, timber, machin., petroleum; birthplace of Mahatma Gandhi; p. (1971) 96,881.

Pori (Björneborg), spt., S. **Finland**; at mouth of R. Kokemäen; copper refinery, rolling mills, match, paper and pulp wks.; p. (1972) 78,076.

Porirua, c., Wellington, N.I., **N.Z.**; dormitory for Wellington; p. (1976) 55,698.

Porjus, t., Norrbotten, N. **Sweden**; on R. Lulea, hydroelectric plant supplies power to iron-ore mng. dists. of Gallivare and Kiruna, also to Narvik rly.

Porsgrunn, spt., **Norway**; timber, shipping, engin., porcelain, explosives; p. (est. 1973) 31,648.

Port Adelaide, main pt., S. **Australia**; serves Adelaide; exp. agr. prods. from hinterland; imports bulk cargoes (petroleum, phosphate, limestone); p. (1976) 36,020.

Portadown, t., Craigavon, **N. Ireland**; on R. Bann, 40 km S.W. of Belfast; linen, food processing; merged with Lurgan to form new c. of Craigavon; p. (1981) 21,333.

Portaferry, spt., Ards, **N. Ireland**; shipping fisheries; p. (1966) 1,426.

Portage la Prairie, t., Manitoba, **Canada**; sm. pt. on Assiniboine R.; grain and potato tr.; p. (1976) 11,719.

Port Alberni, spt., Vancouver I., B.C., **Canada**; exp. timber; fisheries; timber inds.; p. (1971) 19,749.

Port Alfred, pt., **Canada**; upper St. Lawrence R.; imports bauxite for smelting at Arvida.

Port Amelia. See **Pemba.**

Portarlington, mkt. t., Offaly, **R.o.I.**; farming; first place to have elec. power-sta. using local peat fuel; p. (1966) 2,804.

Port Arthur. See **Thunder Bay.**

Port Arthur (China). See **Lushun.**

Port Arthur, t., Texas, **USA**; pt. on L. Sabine; exp. petroleum, chemicals, grain; p. (1980) 61,251.

Port Arzew, pt., **Algeria**; world's first plant to liquefy natural gas (1964); oil pipeline from Haoud el Hamra; oil refinery.

Port Augusta, t., spt., S. **Australia**; at head of Spencer G.; fine harbour; salt field; exp. wheat, fruit; impt. rly. junction; p. (1976) 13,092.

Port-au-Prince, c., cap. of **Haiti**; spt. on bay in G. of La Gonave; cultural and political ctr.; univ., cath.; food processing and exp.; oil refinery; p. (est. 1980) 862,900.

Port Blair, spt., cap. of Andaman and Nicobar Is. p. (est.) 16,000.

Port Chalmers, t., bor., S.I. **N.Z.**; container pt.; timber exp.; p. (1976) 3,123.

Port Colborne, t., Ont., **Canada**; pt. on L. Erie; iron smelting; nickel and copper refining; power from Niagara falls; p. (1971) 21,388.

Port Elizabeth, spt., Cape Prov., S. **Africa**; on Algoa Bay; bilingual univ.; exp. skins, wool, ostrich feathers, mohair; foundries, soap, chemicals, car assembly, food preservation, sawmills; p. (1970) 468,577 (met. a.).

Port Erin, v., I. of Man, **Eng.**; on S.E. cst.; seaside resort, fisheries.

Port Essington, N. point, of Coburg peninsula, N.T., **Australia**; pearl culture experiments.

Port Etienne, See **Nouadhibou.**

Port Franequi, t., **Zaïre;** present terminus of Zaïre rly. on Kasai R.; p. (est. 1970) 48,190.

Port Fuad, t., **Egypt;** N. entrance to Suez Canal.

Port Gentil, spt., **Gabon,** Eq. Africa; exp. palm-oil, mahogany, ebony; sawmills, fishing, centre of Gabon's main oil reserves, oil refining; p. (1975) 77,611.

Port Glasgow, burgh, spt., Inverclyde, **Scot.;** on S. bank of R. Clyde, 27 km below Glasgow; ship-bldg. and repairing, textiles, rope, canvas mftg.; p. (1981) 21,554.

Port Harcourt, spt., **Nigeria;** 48 km from sea on E. branch of Niger delta; terminus of E. Nigerian rly. system; tin, palm oil, groundnuts; bitumen plant, tyres; oil refining; p. (est. 1975) 242,000.

Porthcawl, t., Ogwr, Mid Glamorgan, **Wales;** on cst. 16 km S.E. of Pt. Talbot; resort; p. (1981) 15,566.

Port Hedland, sm. spt., **W. Australia;** new t. being built 8 km inland to absorb impact of Mt. Newman ore project; twin ts. to be linked by industl. belt; exp. iron ore to Japan; p. (1976) 11,144.

Porthmadog (Portmadoc), t. Dwyfor, Gwynedd, **Wales;** pt. on Tremadoc Bay; terminus of Ffestiniog lt. rly.; p. (1981) 3,927.

Port Hope, t., Ont., **Canada;** midway along N. shore of L. Ont., fruit, dairying, radium refining; p. (1971) 8,747.

Port Huron, t., Mich., **USA;** on L. Huron; summer resort, dry docks, grain elevators; motor-car parts; p. (1980) 33,981.

Portici, spt., Campania, **S. Italy;** on Bay of Naples; dockland sub. of Naples; p. (1981) 79,259.

Portile de Fier. See **Iron Gate.**

Portishead, pt., Woodspring, Avon, **Eng.;** on Severn estuary 5 km S.W. of Avonmouth; shipping; p. (1981) 11,331.

Port Jackson, N.S.W., **Australia;** deep natural harbour used by Sydney and crossed by Sydney bridge.

Port Kelang (Port Swettenham), major spt. of **Malaysia;** 48 km W. of Kuala Lumpur; exp. primary prods. inc. tin, rubber, fruit; imports mnfs.; p. 11,300.

Port Kembla, spt., N.S.W., **Australia;** part of Wollongong; artificial pt. built to exp. coal; many expansion programmes; integrated steel-works; p. (1976) 197,127 (inc. Wollongong).

Portknockie, burgh, Grampian Reg., **Scot.;** on N. Buchan cst., 8 km E. of Buckie; sm. fish. pt.; p. (1981) 1,237.

Portland, t., Weymouth and P., Dorset, **Eng.;** 6 km S. of Weymouth on sheltered N.E. side of I. of Portland; lge artificial harbour; naval base, prison; p. (1981) 10,915.

Portland, t., spt., Me., **USA;** comm. cap. of Me.; lge fisheries; paper, pulp, lumber, processed food, clothing; p. (1980) 61,572 (t.), 183,626 (met. a.).

Portland, c., Ore., **USA;** gr. wheat and wool tr.; flour milling, shipbldg., fishing and canning, aluminium, lumber; p. (1980) 366,000 (c.), 1,243,000 (met. a.).

Portland Canal, fjord, N.W. cst of America, forming bdy. between Alaska and B.C.

Portland, I. of, Dorset, **Eng.;** limestone mass, linked to mainland by shingle spit, Chesil Bank, terminates S. in Portland Bill; naval base, Borstal institution; limestone quarrying; masonry wks.

Portlaoighise, mkt., t., Laoighis, **R.o.I.;** flour, malting; p. (1971) 3,902.

Port Louis, c., cap., of **Mauritius;** pt. on Indian Oc.; exp. sugar; contains 42% of Mauritius p. in met.a.; port extension and bulk sugar terminal; p. (1983) 148,040.

Port Macquarie, t., N.S.W., **Australia;** former penal settlement on Hastings R.; resort; p. (1976) 13,362.

Port Moresby, t., cap. of **Papua New Guinea,** 2,880 km from Sydney; spt., airpt.; univ.; p. (1980) 122,761.

Port Nelson, spt., Manitoba, **Canada;** on cst. of Hudson Bay at mouth of R. Nelson; linked by rly. to trans-continental systems; exp. wheat, minerals; closed by ice for 7 months each year.

Port Nolloth, spt., Cape Prov., **S. Africa;** serves copper- and diamond-mng. dists.; declining crayfish pt.

Pôrto Alegre, c., cap. of Rio Grande do Sul st., **Brazil;** exp. lard, preserved meats, rice, timber, tobacco; textiles, chemicals, furniture, brewing, metallurgy; oil refinery under con-struction; pipeline connects with Rio Grande; 2 univs.; p. (est. 1980) 1,221,000.

Portobello, resort, Midlothian, **Scot.;** on F. of Forth, 5 km E. of Edinburgh; bricks, pottery, paper.

Port of Spain, c., cap. of **Trinidad;** attractive c. with squares; 2 caths., mosque; spt. exp. cocoa, sugar, asphalt, oil; natural gas pipeline from Penal; food processing; p. (1970) 11,032 (c.), 67,867 (met. a.).

Porto Marghera, spt., Venezia, **N. Italy;** the modern pt. of Venice, reached by ship canal dredged through shallow lagoon; oil refineries; chemicals, metal refining.

Porto Novo, t., cap. of **Benin Rep.;** on coastal lagoon; spt.; fishing; many old colonial bldgs.; p. (est. 1980) 132,000.

Pôrto Velho, c., cap of Rondônia st., **Brazil;** in a. producing maize, rice, rubber, tin; p. (est. 1980) 131,200.

Portoviejo, c., **Ecuador;** mkt. and comm. ctr. for agr. dist.; p. (est. 1970) 31,835.

Port Phillip, lge. inlet., Victoria, **Australia,** landlocked bay, Melbourne on N., Geelong on W.

Port Pirie, t., spt., **S. Australia;** major pt. on Spencer Gulf; refines zinc and lead from Broken Hill; exp. wheat; p. (1976) 15,005.

Port Radium, t., N.W. Terr., **Canada;** on Gr. Bear L.; pitchblende deposits; p. 300.

Portree, spt., v., I. of Skye, **Scot.;** landlocked harbour on P. Bay, Sound of Raasay; fishing; tweed mill; p. (1981) 1,533.

Portrush, spt., Coleraine, **N. Ireland;** 8 km N. of Coleraine; tourism; p. (1971) 4,749.

Port Said, spt., **Egypt;** at N. end of Suez Canal; free tr. a.; impt. fuelling sta.; entrepôt tr.; p. (1976) 262,760.

Port St. Mary, v., I. of Man, **Eng.;** on S.E. cst.; resort; fisheries, boat-bldg.

Portsdown Hill, chalk ridge, Hants., **Eng.;** extends E. to W. behind Portsmouth from Havant to Fareham.

Portsea I., fortfd. I., between Portsmouth and Langston harbours, Hants., Eng.

Portslade-by-Sea, t. East Sussex, **Eng.;** W. of Hove; p. (1981) 18,128.

Portsmouth, c., naval pt., l. gov. dist., Hants., **Eng.;** opposite I. of Wight; naval establishment; Portsmouth is the garrison t.; Portsea has the naval dockyards, Landport is residtl., and Southsea is a popular resort; navai dock yard closed (1984) fleet maintenance and repair; across the harbour is Gosport; shipbldg.; gen. mnfs.; birthplace of Dickens and I. K. Brunel; p. (1981) 179,419.

Portsmouth, t., N.H., **USA;** summer resort, naval dockyard, cotton; the 1905 Peace Treaty between Japan and Russia was negotiated here; p. (1980) 26,254.

Portsmouth, t., Ohio, **USA;** iron and steel gds., air-craft, boots, shoes, bricks; p. (1980) 25,943.

Portsmouth, spt., Va., **USA;** naval dockyard; farm produce, cotton, rly. wks.; p. (1980) 105,000; inc. in Norfolk met. a.

Portsoy, burgh, Banff and Buchan, **Scot.;** spt. 8 km W. of Banff; fisheries and meal milling; p. (1981) 1,784.

Port Stanvac, S. Australia; 24 km S. of Adelaide; oil refining.

Port Sudan, spt., **Sudan;** 48 km N. of Suakin; linked by rail to Atbara and Khartoum; oil refining; p. (1983) 206,727.

Port Sunlight, Merseyside, **Eng.;** garden v. founded 1888 by Lord Leverhulme for the employees of the Port Sunlight factories.

Port Swettenham. See **Port Kelang.**

Port Talbot, t., Afan, West Glamorgan, **S. Wales;** on E. side of Swansea Bay; impt. iron and steel ind., copper, coal; new deep-water harbour serves as ore terminal; p. (1981) 50,729.

Port Taufiq, spt., **Egypt;** S. end of the Suez canal.

Portugal, rep., Iberia, **W. Europe;** member of E.E.C. (1986); mild temperate climate on cst., drier and hotter in interior; economy based on an inefficient agr. sector, located in wide fertile valleys, and associated processing inds.; major exp. of cork, but few industl. raw materials; textiles; post-war growth of tourist inds.; cap. and airport Lisbon; a. 91,945 km²; p. (est. 1984) 10,008,000.

Portuguesa, st., **Venezuela;** inc. llanos plains; livestock raising; cap. Guanare; a. 15,200 km²; p. (est. 1970) 284,523.

Portuguese Guinea. See **Guinea-Bissau.**

Portuguese Timor. See **East Timor.**

Porvoo, spt., S. **Finland;** on G. of Finland; exp. ctr. for forest prods.; p. (1966) 13,687.

Porz, t., N. Rhine–Westphalia, **W. Germany;** on R. Rhine, S.E. of Cologne; glass, metals, paper; p. (est. 1967) 71,800.

Posadas, c., cap. of Misiones prov., N.E. **Argentina;** on upper Paraná R.; on border of Paraguay; yerba-maté, tobacco, cereals; connection for Iguaça falls; p. (1970) 97,514.

Posen. See Poznań.

Pössneck, t., Gera, **E. Germany;** S.E. of Weimar; porcelain, textiles, leather; p. (est. 1970) 19,074.

Postillon Is., Lesser Sunda Is., **Indonesia;** coconuts.

Postojna (Adelsberg,) t., **Yugoslavia;** 32 km N.E. of Trieste; extensive grotto and stalactite cavern.

Potchefstroom, t., Transvaal, **S. Africa;** on Mooi R.; univ.; agr.; malt, timber, engin.; p. (1970) 68,207.

Potenza, t., cap. of P. prov., **Italy;** on hill 220 m above Basento R.; agr. and industl. ctr.; p. (1981) 64,358.

Poti, spt., Georgian SSR, **USSR;** exp. manganese; fish processing, timber-milling, engin.; p. (est. 1973) 42,500.

Potomac, R., **USA;** divides Va. from Md.; flows past Wash., to Chesapeake Bay; 464 km long.

Potosí, dep., **Bolivia;** famous for silver- and tin-mines; zinc ore; cap. Potosí; a. 116,630 km²; p. (est. 1969) 850,400.

Potosí, c., **Bolivia;** on slope of Cerro Gordo de Potosí, 4,072 m a.s.l.; tin, silver, copper, lead mng.; p. (est. 1970) 97,000.

Potsdam, c., cap. of admin. dist., **E. Germany;** on R. Havel, 29 km S.E. of Berlin; beautiful parks and gardens, many palaces; scene of conference between Allies on bdy. questions, 1945; motor and locomotive wks., engin.; precision instruments; p. (1983) 135,922.

Potteries, The, dist., N. Staffs., **Eng.;** ctr. of earthenware ind., comprising ts. Burslem, Hanley, Fenton, Tunstall, Stoke and Longton.

Potters Bar, t., Hertsmere, Herts., **Eng.;** residtl.; in London commuter belt; p. (1981) 23,159.

Poulton-le-Fylde, t., Lancs., **Eng.;** ctr. of mkt. gardening, poultry rearing dist.; p. (1981) 17,608.

Powys, co., central **Wales;** mtnous. a. made up of former cos. of Radnorshire, Montgomery and most of Brecon and bordering Eng.; forestry, stockraising and water catchment for Eng.; crossed by Rs. Wye and Severn; sparse p.; a. 5,076 km²; p. (1981) 110,467.

Powys, Vale of, Powys, **Wales;** drained by R. Severn; cattle-rearing; ch. t. Welshpool.

Poyang Hu, lge. L., Jiangxi, **China;** on S. margin of Chang Jiang plain; surrounded by flat, intensively cultivated land, rice, sugar, mulberry; size varies greatly with season, max. a. (in late summer) 4,662 km².

Poznań, prov., W. **Poland;** drained by Warta and Notec Rs.; mainly agr.; stock-raising; mnfs. inc. locomotives; a. 26,705 km²; p. (est. 1983) 1,278,000.

Poznań, c., cap. of P. prov., **Poland;** on Warta R.; route ctr., industl. and educational ctr.; cath. univ.; engin., iron-founding, chemicals; anc. c., once cap. of Poland; p. (est. 1983) 570,900.

Pozzuoli, t., **Italy;** 3 km W. of Naples; anc. Puteoli; mineral baths, ordnance wks.; Roman ruins; p. (1981) 70,350.

Prague (Praha), c., cap. of **ČSSR;** picturesque, anc. c. on R. Vltava; comm. and cultural ctr.; univ. (founded 1348); outstanding architecture; extensive mnfs., machin., sugar, leather, milling, chemicals; p. (1980) 1,193,135.

Prahova, R., Walachia, **Romania;** rises in Transylvanian Alps, flows S. into R. Ialomita; c. 176 km long.

Prato, t., **Italy;** 13 km N.W. of Florence; cath., mediaeval cas. and fortifications; cottons, woollens, machin.; p. (1977) 155,791.

Predeal Pass, Romania; carries main road and rly. across Transylvanian Alps from Bucharest to Brasov; alt. over 1,200 m.

Pregel, R., **Poland;** flows to Frisches Haff, nr. Kaliningrad; 200 km long.

Prek Ihnot, Khmer Rep.; power and irrigation development project on lower Mekong R.

Prerov, t., **ČSSR;** S.E. of Olomouc; hardware, textiles; p. (est. 1970) 39,000.

Presall, t., Wyre-Lancs., **Eng.;** N. of Blackpool; p. (1981) 4,608.

Prescot, mftg. t., Knowsley, Merseyside, **Eng.;** 6 km. S.W. of St. Helens; mkt., elec. cable ind.; p. (1981) 10,992.

Preseli, l. gov. dist., Dyfed, **Wales;** W. penin. with ts. of Fishguard, Haverfordwest and Milford Haven; p. (1981) 69,323.

Prešov, mkt. t., **ČSSR;** linen mnfs.; p. (est. 1970) 41,000.

Prestatyn, t., Rhuddlan, Clwyd, **Wales;** on N. cst., 5 km E. of Rhyl; seaside resort; p. (1981) 16,439.

Presteign, mkt. t., Radnor, Powys, **Wales;** on R. Lugg, 16 km N.W. of Leominster; p. (1981) 1,213.

Preston, t., l. gov. dist., Lancs., **Eng.;** pt. on R. Ribble; textiles, engin., aircraft wks.; p. (1981) 125,886 (dist.).

Prestonpans, burgh, E. Lothian, S.E. **Scot.;** on F. of Forth, 14 km E. of Edinburgh; scene of Jacobite victory 1745; p. (1981) 7,620.

Prestwich, t., Gtr. Manchester, **Eng.;** in valley of R. Irwell, 5 km N.W. of Manchester; cotton bleaching and dyeing, soap, furnishings; p. (1981) 31,198.

Prestwick, burgh, Kyle and Carrick, **Scot.;** on F. of Clyde, 5 km N. of Ayr; golfing ctr. and transatlantic airpt. and freeport (1984); resort; p. (1981) 13,532.

Pretoria, c., Transvaal, admin. cap. of **Rep. of S. Africa;** univ., tr. ctr.; inds. inc. engin., chemicals, iron, and steel; p. (1970) 516,703 (met.a.).

Preveza, ch. pt. and t. of P. dep. of Epirus, N.W. **Greece;** guards G. of Arta; p. (1981) 13,624.

Pribilof Is., off S.W. Alaska, **USA;** seal fur; a. 168 km²; p. (est.) 550.

Pribram, t., Bohemia, **ČSSR;** impt. lead and silver mines, zinc, barium and antimony; p. (est. 1968) 29,689.

Prijedor, t., Bosnia and Hercegovina, **Yugoslavia;** on E. flank of Dinaric Alps, 104 km S.E. of Zagreb; rly. junc.; iron-ore mines.

Prilep, t., Macedonia, **Yugoslavia;** mkt., refractory materials, tobacco processing; p. (1971) 48,242.

Primorskiy Kray, terr., **RSFSR;** S.E. Siberia, on Sea of Japan; coal, iron ore, and various metals in vicinity; fisheries; millet and rice; slow economic development results from isolation; wants economic links with China; ch. cs., Vladivostok (cap.), Ussuriysk; a. 168,350 km²; p. (1970) 1,722,000.

Prince Albert, t., Saskatchewan, **Canada;** lumbering, furs; p. (1976) 28,240.

Prince Edward I., prov., **Canada;** sm. I. in G. of St. Lawrence; physically poorly endowed; rocky, with thin soils; pastoral agr., furfarming, fishing; cap. Charlottetown; a. 5,657 km²; p. (1976) 118,229.

Prince George, t., B.C., **Canada;** oil refining; lumbering, mng., fur tr.; p. (1971) 32,755.

Prince Rupert, t., B.C., **Canada;** Pac. pt. of Canadian National rly.; service ctr., fishing and fish-processing; p. (1971) 15,355.

Princeton, bor., N.J., **USA;** seat of Princeton Univ.; p. (1980) 12,035.

Principe. See São Tomé.

Pripet Marshes, Belorussiyan SSR, **USSR;** forested swampy region crossed by Pripet R. and its streams; greater part reclaimed; coal and petroleum; a. 46,620 km².

Pripet (Pripyat), R., Belorussiyan SSR, **USSR;** trib. of R. Dnieper; 560 km long.

Pristina, c., cap. of Kossovo aut. region, S.W. Serbia, **Yugoslavia;** on Sitnic R.; admin. ctr.; many mosques; p. (1981) 210,040.

Prokopyevsk, t., S.W. Siberia, **RSFSR;** in Novosibirsk dist.; one of the main coalfields of Kuznetsk Basin; mng. machin., metallurgy; p. (est. 1980) 266,000.

Prome, c. **Burma;** pt. on R. Irrawaddy; connected by rail and road to Rangoon; tr. in rice, cotton, tobacco; one of oldest cs. in Burma, founded 8th cent.; p. (est. 1970) 65,392.

Proskurov. See Khmel'nitskiy.

Prostejov, t., N. Moravia, **ČSSR;** rly. junc.; agr. machin., textiles; historic bldgs.; p. (est. 1970) 37,000.

Provence, region and former prov., S.E. **France;** along Mediterranean; now embraces deps. of Var, Bouches-du-Rhône, Vaucluse and parts of Alpes-de-Haute-Provence and Alpes-Maritimes; tourism; fastest growing p. of France; mkt. gardening; intensive investment along cst.

Providence, c., R.I. **USA**; at head of Narragansett Bay; univ.; jewellery, textiles, silverware, rubber gds., machin., oil, coal; p. (1980) 157,000 (c.), 919,000 (met. a.).

Provo, t., Utah, **USA**; at base of Wasatch mtns., nr. shore of Utah L.; univ.; flour, bricks, blast furnaces; p. (1980) 218,000 (met. a.).

Prudhoe, Tynedale, Northumberland, **Eng.**; former coal mng. t.; chemicals, paper; p. (1981) 11,820.

Prudhoe Bay, N.E. Alaska, **USA**; ctr. of recent extensive oil finds; arctic conditions make extraction and transport of oil difficult and ecologically dangerous but despite opposition from environmentalist groups 1,262 km pipeline to ice-free pt. of Valdez approved (1973).

Prussia, former kingdom (1701–1806); former st. (1806–1945), **Germany**; consisted of 13 provs., cap. Berlin; formally abolished 1947; E. Prussia partitioned between USSR and Poland.

Pruszkow, t., **Poland**; nr. Warsaw; elec. plant; engin.; p. (1970) 43,000.

Prut, R., flows between **Romania** and **USSR**; from the Carpathian mtns. to the Danube R.; 576 km long.

Przemysl, c., S.E. **Poland**; on San R. (trib. of Vistula) nr. bdy. between Poland and Ukrainian SSR; anc. fortress t.; sewing machin.; p. (1970) 53,200.

Pskov, c., **RSFSR**; on R. Velikaya, nr. entry to L. Peipus; rly. junc.; flax tr.; historic bldgs.; scene of abdication of Nicholas II, March 1917; p. (est. 1980) 177,000.

Pudsey, t., West Yorks., **Eng.**; between Leeds and Bradford; woollens; p. (1981) 38,977.

Peubla de Zaragoza, c., cap. of P. st., **Mexico**; one of oldest and most impt. cs. of rep.; fine cath., theatre, univ.; cotton mills, onyx quarries, glazed tiles; p. (1979) 710,833.

Puebla, st., **Mexico**; on interior plateau at 2,400 m; fertile valleys for coffee and sugar; mng. impt.; dense p.; a. 33,991 km²; p. (1970) 2,258,226.

Pueblo, c., Col., **USA**; on R. Arkansas, in foothills of Rockies; iron and steel ctr.; coal and various metals nearby; p. (1980) 102,000.

Puente-Genil, t., Córdoba, **Spain**; olive oil, quince pulp; p. (1981) 25,615.

Puerto Barrios, pt., **Guatemala**; rly. terminus; oil refining; p. (est. 1971) 29,425.

Puerto Cabello, spt., N. **Venezuela**; on Caribbean nr. Valencia; excellent harbour; linked by rail and highway to Carácas; asbestos, vegetable oils, soap, candles, meat-packing; p. (est. 1970) 70,598.

Puerto Cortés, spt., N.W. **Honduras**; on Caribbean; exp. bananas, hardwoods; p. (1961) 17,412.

Puerto de Santa Maria, El, spt., S.W. **Spain**; on Bay of Cadiz; exp. mainly sherry; p. (1981) 45,933.

Puerto la Cruz, t., **Venezuela**; 16 km from Barcelona; oil refining; p. with Barcelona (est. 1980) 267,000.

Puerto Limón. *See* **Limón.**

Puerto Montt, spt., **Chile**; in sheep-farming dist.; S. terminus of rlys.; devastated by earthquake 1960; p. (est. 1970) 80,298.

Puerto Ordaz. *See* **Santo Tomé de la Guayana.**

Puerto Rico, I., terr. of USA, **W.I.**; since 1952 free commonwealth ass. with USA; democratic economic growth aided recently by falling birth-rate; mtnous., eroded soils, alt. modifies tropical climate; exp. minfs., but agr. impt. internally; 80 per cent land under cultivation, sugar, tobacco, coffee; tourism; cap. San Juan; a. 8,866 km²; p. (est. 1984) 3,404,000.

Puerto Saurez, R. pt., **Bolivia**; on R. Paraguay; collecting ctr. for rubber, coffee, Brazil nuts.

Puerto Varas, t., **Chile**; tourist ctr. in Chilean "Switzerland"; p. (est. 1970) 33,000.

Puget Sound, Wash., **USA**; inlet of Pac. Oc.

Puket. *See* **Phuket.**

Pula, spt., Croatia, **Yugoslavia**; on Adriatic; industl. ctr. with shipyards, docks, and various inds.; ch. naval base of Hapsburg empire; tourism; Roman remains; p. (1971) 47,414.

Pulia. *See* **Apulia.**

Puna, cold, bleak, and barren plateau of Andes in **Peru** and **Bolivia,** 3,600–5,500 m.

Pune (Poona), c., Maharashtra, **India**; in W. Ghats; temperate pleasant climate; cultural, educational (univ.) and political ctr.; military base; agr. tr. ctr.; cotton gds., paper; p. (1971) 856,105 (c.), 1,135,900 (met. a.).

Punjab, region N.W. Indus plains, Indian subcontinent; extensive irrigation from the "five rivers"—Jhelum, Chenab, Ravi, Bias, Sutlej; now divided politically between **India**

and **Pakistan**; impt. cotton, wheat, and sugar dist.; coal deposits.

Punjab (East), former st., **India**; partitioned on linguistic basis 1966; Punjab-speaking Punjab st. (a. 50,375 km²; p. (1981) 16,788,915 inc. 55 per cent Sikh); and Hindi-speaking Haryana st. (a. 44,056 km²; p. (1981) 12,922,618; joint cap. Chandigarh until 1986.

Punjab (West), prov., **Pakistan**; old prov. revived 1970; p. (1972) 37,374,000.

Punta Arenas, c., cap. of Magallanes prov., S. **Chile**; most S. c. in world; mutton, wool; coal nearby; natural gas pipeline from Kimiri-Aike; p. (est. 1970) 50,000.

Puntarenas, spt., **Costa Rica,** on G. of Nicoya; fishing; fish-processing; resort; p. (1970) 31,162.

Purbeck, I. of, sm. peninsula, Dorset cst., **Eng.**; anc. v. of Corfe Castle in ctr.; limestone ("Purbeck marble") quarries; site of Britain's lgst. onshore oilfield; once a royal deer forest; now forms l. gov. dist. inc. Wareham and Swanage; p. (1981) 40,414.

Puri, dist., Orissa, **India**; cap. P. famous for its temple and festival of the god Vishnu and his monster car, Juggernaut; p. (1961) 1,865,439.

Purley. *See* **Croydon.**

Purus, R., **Peru** and **Brazil**; rises in Andes, flows to Amazon R. through underdeveloped a.; 3,360 km long.

Pusan, main pt. of **S. Korea**; on Korean Strait at head of Naktong R. basin; textiles; steel mill at Pohang nearby; Korea's first nuclear power sta.; p. (1980) 3,160,276.

Pushkin, c., **RSFSR**; nr. Leningrad; summer palaces of Tsars; Pushkin museum; Pulkovo observatory nearby; p. (est. 1966) 66,000.

Puteaux, sub. Paris, **France**; woollens, dyes, engin., printing; p. (1982) 36,143.

Putney, sub. of London, **Eng.**; residtl.; Thames-side dist.

Putrid Sea. *See* **Sivash.**

Putumayo, R., trib. of R. Amazon; rises in Colombia, forming bdy. with Ecuador and Peru; here in wild-rubber region, Roger Casement exposed cruel exploitation of native labour; 1,600 km long.

Puy-de-Dôme, extinct volcano, Massif Central, **France**; hgst peak of Auvergne mtns., 1,466 m.

Puy-de-Dôme, dep., **France**; in Auvergne; cap. Clermont-Ferrand, industl. ctr. Thiers; a. 8,003 km². p. (1982) 954,700.

Puymorens Tunnel, Pyrenees, on bdy. between **France** and **Spain**; carries main rly. between Toulouse and Barcelona.

Pwllheli, t., Dwyfor, Gwynedd, N. **Wales**; sm. pt. on S. cst. Lleyn peninsula; seaside resort; inshore fishing, boat-bldg.; p. (1981) 3,989.

Pyatigorsk, c., N. Caucasus, **RSFSR**; ctr. of Caucasian mineral water springs; Lermontov shot here in duel 1841; p. (est. 1980) 112,000.

Pylos, pt., S.W. Peloponnesus, **Greece**; shipbldg. and repair yard, heavy metal wks. projected; sea-battles 1827 (Navarino), 425 B.C.

Pyongyang, c., cap. of N. **Korea**; stands high above Taedong R.; major industl. ctr. with coal and iron ore deposits nearby; univ.; many historic relics; p. (est. 1978) 1,500,000.

Pyrenees, range of mtns., S.W. **Europe**; dividing France from Iberian Peninsula; 432 km long; hgst peak Pic d'Anéto (Maladetta) 3,408 m.

Pyrénées-Atlantique, dep., S.W. **France**; mainly agr., sheep and cattle raising; ch. ts. Pau (cap.), Bayonne, Biarritz; a. 7,713 km²; p. (1982) 551,000.

Pyrénées-Orientales, dep., S. **France**; on Mediterranean; wine, fruit, olives; cap. Perpignan; a. 4,141 km²; p. (1982) 339,700.

Pyrgos, t., Elis, S.W. **Greece**; has suffered from earthquakes; p. (1981) 21,958.

Q

Qaidam (Tsaidam), depression, Qinghai prov., **China**; a. of salt marsh and Ls.; rich deposits of oil; state farms for intensive animals husbandary.

Qarun (Birker el Qarum). *See* **Karun.**

Qatar, emirate, indep. st. (1971), **Arabia**; crown prince appointed (1979); peninsula on Persian G.; economy based on oil; inland production declining, but increasing offshore drilling; political stability less certain after withdrawal of Brit. military protection (1971); cap. Doha; a.

10,360 km²; p. (est. 1984) 291,000.

Qattara Depression, N. **Egypt**; 134 m below sea level, salt marsh produced by seepage and evaporation of artesian water; marshes; few inhabitants.

Qena or **Kene**, t., central **Egypt**; on R. Nile; water jars and bottles; agr. tr., cereals, dates; p. (est. 1970) 77,600.

Qingdao (Tsingtao), c., Shandong prov., **China**; spt. with excellent harbour at head of bay; exp. soya beans, ground nuts, mnfs. locomotives, cement, textiles, machin., chemicals; special development zone to attract high technology inds.; oil jetty for Shengli oil field; p. (est. 1970) 1,900,000.

Qinghai (Tsinghai), prov., W. **China**; between Xinjiang and Xizang Zizhou (Tibet), inc. c. plateau; local coal and iron ore but exploitation hindered by isolation; two new iron and steel plants; new rly.; massive hydro-electricity plant; international airpt. link with Hong Kong; attempts to increase economic development; oil exploration; a. 721,004 km²; p. (est. 1970) 2,000,000.

Qinghai Hu (Koko Nor), salt L., Qinghai prov., **China**; at over 3,000 m. in Tibetan highlands; a. 5,957 km²; no outlet.

Qinhuangdao (Chinwangtao), c., spt., former treaty pt., Hebei, N. **China**; on Yellow Sea cst. 240 km N.E. of Tianjin; only good natural harbour on N. China cst.; exp. coal from Gailan mines; p. (1953) 186,800.

Qiqihar (Tsitsihar), c., Heilongjiang prov., N. **China**; on Vladivostok portion of Trans-Siberian rly.; food processing and tr., chemicals; potential oilfield; p. (est. 1970) 1,500,000.

Qisil-Qum, desert region, **Central Asia**; covering dried-up a. of extended Pleistocene Aral Sea.

Qizan, spt., **Saudi Arabia**; cereals, pearl-fishing, salt.

Qom (Qum), c., **Iran**; pilgrimage ctr., shrine of Fatima; rly. junction; p. (1976) 246,831.

Qornet es Sauda, mtn., Lebanon range, Levant, **Lebanon**; max. alt. 3,050 m.

Quantock Hills, Somerset, **Eng.**; S. of Bridgwater Bay; hgst. pt. 385 m; a Nat. Park.

Quauzhu, (Chengchow), c., cap. Henan prov., **China**; 24 km. S. of Huang He where it emerges on to N. China Plain; impt. route ctr. and rly. junc. where Beijing to Wuhan rly. crosses Xi'an to Zuzhou rly.; p. (est. 1970) 1,500,000.

Queanbeyan, t., N.S.W., **Australia**; rapid growth as commuter tr. as only 13 km from Canberra; pastoral, dairying dist.; mkt. and service ctr.; p. (1976) 18,920.

Quebec, c., cap. of Q. prov., **Canada**; spt. with fine harbour on St. Lawrence R. at mouth of St. Charles; cultural cap. of French Canada; inds. based on local raw materials of timber, agr. prods.; oil refining at St. Romuald; historic c. with many fine bldgs., univ., tourism; p. (1979) 177,080 (c.), 559,100 (met. a.).

Quebec, prov., **Canada**; mainly within Canadian Shield; continental climate; forests and timber inds.; agr. in S.; hydroelectric power and abundant minerals; p. mainly Frenchspeaking; ch. cs., Quebec (cap.), Montreal; strong separatist movements causing decline in investment and movement of some inds. to USA; a. 1,540,687 km²; p. (1976) 6,234,445.

Quebec-Labrador Trough, **Canada**; geological formation extending through central Quebec prov. to Ungava Bay, Hudson Strait; immense reserves of iron-ore (locally "red-gold").

Quedlinburg, t., Halle, **E. Germany**; at foot of Harz mtns.; cas., cath.; aniline dyes, metals, engin., horticultural mkt. t.; p. (est. 1970) 30,823.

Queen Charlotte's Is., archipelago, N. of Vancouver I., off cst. B.C., **Canada**; halibut fishing, lumbering; p. (est. 1971) 3,000.

Queen Charlotte Sound, strait, separating Vancouver I. from B.C. mainland, a continuation of Johnstone Strait.

Queen Elizabeth Is., **Canada**; I. gr. in Canadian Arctic; most N. land of N. America; a. 349,443 km²; p. (1961) 310.

Queen Mary Land, Norwegian sector of **Antarctica**; ice crystal mtns., 3,050 m high for 160 km along cst.

Queens, bor., N.Y. City, **USA**; residtl. dist.; lgst. bor. of N.Y. c.; p. (1980) 1,891,325.

Queensbury and Shelf, t., West Yorks., **Eng.**; textiles; p. (1981) 11,658.

Queensferry, royal burgh, Edinburgh City, **Scot.**; at S. end of Forth road and rail bridges; p. (1981) 7,529.

Queensland, st., N.E. **Australia**; sub-tropical a. rising from cst. to Gt. Dividing Range and Western Plains (inc. Gt. Artesian Basin); Barrier Reef off cst.; p. concentrated on cst. where sugar cane and tropical fruits grown, popular all year tourist resorts and retirement ctrs. (no death duties); all year mkt. gardening replaced by extensive cattle and sheep ranching in W.; mng. boom since 1960; coal, copper, uranium, bauxite; oil at Moonie; since 1970 rapid increase in mftg.; cap. Brisbane; a. 1,727,200 km²; p. (1976) 2,037,197.

Queenstown. See Cobh.

Queenstown, t., Tasmania, **Australia**; copper mng. t.; prosperity depends on continuation of mng. at Mount Lyell; p. (1976) 4,520.

Queenstown, t., Cape Prov., **S. Africa**; in agr. region producing wool and wheat; p. (est. 1970) 40,000.

Quelimane, pt., **Moçambique**; at head of estuary; rly. terminus; exp. copra, sisal, tea; notorious in 18th and 19th cent. as slave mkt.; p. c. 10,000.

Quelpart. See Cheju.

Quemoy, gr. of Is. off Chinese mainland nr. Amoy, held by Nationalist forces; p. (est.) 50,000 (plus garrison of 40,000).

QueQue, t., **Zimbabwe**; major new steel works has attracted many ancillary inds.; p. (1982) 47,600.

Querétaro, t., cap. of Q. st., **Mexico**; site of pre-Aztec settlement at 1,881 m; cath., many colonial bldgs.; old cotton ind.; p. (1979) 185,812.

Querétaro, st., **Mexico**; in Central Plateau; arid with fertile valleys; variety of crops; mng. impt.; famous for opals; cap. Q.; a. 11,479 km²; p. (1970) 485,523.

Quetta, t., cap. of Baluchistan, **Pakistan**; at 5,000 ft., commands routes to Bolan Pass; ctr. of irrigated agr. a.; military ctr.; coal mng. nearby; damaged by severe earthquake (1935); p. (1972) 140,000.

Quezaltenango, t., S.W. **Guatemala**; second c. of rep.; at 2,333 m at foot of Santa Maria volcano; univ.; comm. ctr. for rich agr. region; textiles, handicrafts; p. (est. 1971) 54,475.

Quezon City, cap. **Philippines**; new sub. 16 km N.E. of Manila; cap. since 1948; univ.; p. (1975) 994,679.

Quibdó, t., **Colombia**; in forested a. on R. Atrato; platinum, gold mng.; p. (est. 1974) 179,600.

Quillon, t., Kerala, **India**; on Malabar cst., ctr. of coconut tr. and processing; p. (1971) 124,208.

Quimes, t., Buenos Aires, **Argentina**; on Rio de la Plata estuary; English public school; resort; oil refining, textiles, chemicals, glass; p. (1970) 245,165.

Quimper, ch. t., Finistère, **France**; tourist ctr. for S. Brittany; Breton pottery; Gothic cath.; p. (1982) 60,162.

Quincy, t., Ill., **USA**; at bridging point of R. Mississippi; agr. machin., clothing, footwear, food inds.; p. (1980) 42,554.

Quincy, t., Mass., **USA**; in Mass. B., 13 km S.E. of Boston; shipbldg. ctr.; p. (1980) 84,743.

Quindio, pass, **Colombia**; provides impt. routeway through Cordillera Central; 11,099 ft.

Qui Nhon, t., S. **Vietnam**; on E. cst.; tr. in coconut prods.; fishing; p. (1973) 213,757.

Quintana Roo, st., S.E. **Mexico**; on Caribbean; low-lying swamp, underdeveloped; cap. Chetumal; a. 50,344 km²; p. (1970) 600,000.

Quito, c., cap. of **Ecuador**; in Andes at 2,852 m, 24 km S. of equator; anc. Inca c., cath., univ., slower growth than coastal ts.; impt. textile ctr.; p. (est. 1980) 807,665.

Quorndon or **Quorn**, sm. t., Leics., **Eng.**; on R. Soar, 5 km S. of Loughborough; ctr. of fox-hunting dist.

R

Raake, t., N. **Finland**; spt.; iron wks.

Raasay, I., E. of Skye, Skye and Lochalsh, **Scot.**; 21 km long, 5·6 km wide.

Rab I., at head of Adriatic, **Yugoslavia**; tourism; a. 192 km³; p. (1961) 8,369.

Rabat, c., cap. of **Morocco**; spt. at mouth of Bu Regreg R. on Atl. cst.; cath., univ.; textiles, carpets, rugs; p. (est. 1973) 435,510 (c.), 596,600 (met. a.).

Rabaul, spt., New Britain, **Papua New Guinea**; ch.pt., exp. copra; damaged by volcanic eruption (1937) former cap. of New Guinea; p. (1971) 26,619.

Raciborz (Ratibor), t., Upper Silesia, **Poland** (since 1945); on R. Oder; textiles, metals, wood engin.; p. (1970) 40,400.

Racine, c., Wis., **USA**; sm. pt. on L. Mich., 16 km S. of Milwaukee; agr. machin., tractors, car parts; p. (1980) 85,725 (c.), 173,132 (met. a.).

Radcliffe, t., Gtr. Manchester, **Eng.**; N.W. of Manchester; paper, rubber, paint, engin.; p. (1981) 30,501.

Radebeul, t., Dresden, **E. Germany**; on R. Elbe; satellite of Dresden; p. (est. 1970) 39,626.

Radium Hill, v., S. **Australia**; ctr. for radium mng. 1920–30 and uranium later; mines now closed (since 1961).

Radnorshire, former co., Central **Wales**. See **Powys**. Now as Radnor l. gov. dist. inc. Knighton, Presteigne and Llandrindodd Wells; p. (1981) 21,575.

Radom, t., **Poland**; in Radomska Plain; route ctr.; metal and chemical inds.; lge. tobacco factory; p. (est. 1983) 201,000.

Radomosko, t., **Poland**; on edge of Lodz Upland; metallurgical wks., food inds.; bentwood chairs for exp.; p. (1970) 31,200.

Radzionkow, t., Katowice, **Poland**; new t. (1951); p. (1970) 27,800.

Ragaz, Bad, spa, St. Gall can., **Switzerland**; at mouth of Tamina R.; hot springs from nearby v. of Pfäfers; p. (1960) 2,699.

Ragusa. See **Dubrovnik**.

Ragusa, t., Sicily, **Italy**; oil and asphalt production; p. (1981) 64,492.

Rahway, t., N.J., **USA**; on R. Rahway; residtl. for N.Y. business men; p. (1980) 26,723.

Raichur, t., Karnataka, **India**; comm. ctr.; agr. processing; p. (est. 1971) 80,000.

Rainford, t., Merseyside, **Eng.**; nr. St. Helens; former coal-mng. a.; p. (1981) 8,941.

Rainier, mtn., Wash., **USA**; 4,432 m; forms Nat. Park.

Rainy, L., on border of Canada and Minn., **USA**; drained by Rainy R. to L. of the Woods.

Raipur, t., Madhya Pradesh, **India**; ctr. of fertile rice growing a.; p. (1971) 174,518 (t.), 205,986 (met. a.).

Rajahmundry, t., Andhra Pradesh, **India**; on delta of Godivari R.; agr. tr.; p. (1971) 165,912 (t.), 188,805 (met. a.).

Rajasthan, st., **India**; dry a. inc. Thar desert; sparse p. where artificial irrigation; agr., millets, pulses, cotton; impt. gypsum deposits; cap. Jaipur; a. 342,274 km²; p. (1971) 25,742,142.

Rajkot, t., Gujarat, **India**; p. (1971) 300,612.

Rajshahi, t., Rajshahi dist., **Bangladesh**; on R. Ganges; univ.; silk inds.; p. (1974) 104,273.

Raki-Ura I. See **Stewart I.**

Raleigh, c., cap. of N.C., **USA**; educational ctr. univ.; printing, cotton tr. and processing; p. (1980) 150,000 (c.), 531,000 (met. a.).

Ralik, W. chain of Is., Marshall gr., **Pac. Oc.**; lgst. atoll Kwajalein; parallel with Ratak chain.

Ramat Gan, t., **Israel**; in plain of Sharon; univ.; lt. inds.; p. (est. 1979) 120,400.

Rambouillet, t., Yvelines, **France**; nr. Versailles; anc. château; p. (1982) 22,487.

Rameswaram, t., S. **India**; on Rameswaram I., Palk Strait; contains Dravidian temple, Hindu holy place of pilgrimage; p. (1961) 6,801.

Ramla, t., **Israel**; S. of Lydda; former cap. of Palestine; ass. with crusaders; p. (est. 1970) 30,800.

Rampur, t., Uttar Pradesh, **India**; N.W. of Bareilly; agr. tr.; sugar refining; chemicals; cap. of former princely st. of R.; p. (1971) 161,417.

Ramree I., Burma; in Bay of Bengal, off Arakan cst.; 80 km long.

Ramsbottom, t., Lancs., **Eng.**; on R. Irwell, 6 km N. of Bury; engin., paper, textiles; p. (1981) 17,799.

Ramsey, mkt. t., Cambs., **Eng.**; on edge of Fens, 11 km N. of St. Ives; engin.; abbey ruins; p. (1981) 5,828.

Ramsey, t., spt., I. of Man, **Eng.**; on N.E. cst.; holiday resort; p. (1971) 5,048.

Ramsgate, t., Kent, **Eng.**; on S. cst. of I. of Thanet; seaside resort; p. (1981) 39,642.

Rancagua, t., Colchagua prov., **Chile**; ctr. of fertile valley in Andean foothills; tractors, agr. processing; p. (est. 1980) 128,733.

Rance, R., Brittany, **France**; world's first major tidal hydroelectric power sta. (opened 1966).

Ranchi, t., Bihar, **India**; hot season seat of govt. in Chota Nagpur plateau; univ.; heavy engin.; p. (1971) 175,943 (c.), 255,551 (met. a.).

Rand. See **Witwatersrand.**

Randers, pt., **Denmark**; on Randers Fjord, inlet of Kattegat; machin., foundries; exp. dairy prod.; mediaeval monastery; p. (est. 1970) 41,253.

Randfontein, t., Transvaal, **S. Africa**; gold-mng. ctr.; uranium plant; p. (est. 1970) 2,951.

Randstad, conurb., **Neth.**; Dutch "urban ring." inc. Rotterdam, The Hague, Leiden, Amsterdam and Utrecht, contained within radius of 16 km; a. of rapid industrialisation.

Rangitaiki, R., N.I., **N.Z.**; flows into Bay of Plenty; 192 km long.

Rangoon, c., cap. of **Burma**; on E. arm of Irrawaddy delta; 2 caths., many mosques, temples and pagodas; replaced Mandalay as cap. with the increasing importance of delta under the Brit. as ctr. of rice tr. and exp.; oil refining; teak collecting ctr.; p. (est. 1970) 2,276,000.

Rangpur, t., **Bangladesh**; on R. Ghaghat; jute; p. (1961) 40,600.

Raniganj, t., W. Bengal, **India**; coalfield in Damodar basin; engin.; p. (1961) 30,113.

Rannoch, Loch, Perth and Kinross, **Scot.**; 14 km long, 1·6 km wide; drained to R. Tay.

Rapallo, t., Liguria, N.W. **Italy**; on G. of Genoa, 35 km E. of Genoa; most celebrated resort on Italian Riviera di Levante; p. (1981) 28,318.

Rapanui. See **Easter I.**

Rapid City, t., S.D., **USA**; second t. of st.; comm. ctr. for agr. and mng. a.; p. (1980) 46,492.

Rarotonga, volcanic I., **Pac. Oc.**; cap. of Cook Is.; fruit canning; ch. t. and pt. Avarua; p. (est. 1968) 10,853.

Ra's al Khaymah. See **United Arab Emirates.**

Rasht (Resht), c., Iran; cap. of Gilan prov., in a. producing rice, cotton, silk; carpets; nearby Pahlevi serves as pt.; p. (1976) 187,203.

Ras Lanug, oil terminal, on G. of Sidra, **Libya**; pipeline from Hofra oilfield.

Ras Tannura, spt., Nejd, **Saudi Arabia**; lge. oil refinery; oil exp.

Ratak, E., chain of Is., Marshall gr., **Pac. Oc.**; ch. I. Majuro; parallel with Ralik chain.

Rathenow, t., Potsdam, **E. Germany**; on R. Havel; optical and precision instruments; p. (est. 1970) 29,823.

Rathlin, I., off Fair Head, Moyle, **N. Ireland**; 8 km by 1·6 km.

Ratibor. See **Raciborz.**

Ratingen, t., N. Rhine–Westphalia, **W. Germany**; N.E. of Düsseldorf; textiles, machin., glass; famous for Blue L.; p. (1983) 88,300.

Ratisbon. See **Regensburg.**

Ratlam, t., Madhya Pradesh, **India**; rly. junc. in Malwa Plateau; p. (1971) 106,666.

Ratnapura, t., **Sri Lanka**; former ctr. of gem mng.; p. (est. 1968) 24,000.

Rauma, spt., S.W. **Finland**; on Baltic Sea; p. (1972) 27,445.

Raunds, t., East Northants., **Eng.**; 8 km N.E. of Wellingborough; p. (1981) 7,401.

Raurkela, t., Orissa, **India**; steel, tinplate, iron, fertilisers; p. (1961) 90,287.

Ravenglass, t., Cumbria, **Eng.**; nr. mouth of R. Esk; old pt.; Roman remains.

Ravenna, c., cap. of Ravenna prov., Emilia-Romagna, **Italy**; on reclaimed plain nr. Po delta; connected to Adriatic by canal; ctr. of fertile agr. dist., agr. processing; new inds. aided by discovery of methane N. of c.; oil refineries, chemicals, fertilisers; cath., mausoleum, famous mosaics; p. (1981) 138,034.

Ravenna, prov., Emilia-Romagna, **Italy**; N. Italian plain rising to Apennines; fertile agr. a.; cap. R.; a. 1,852 km²; p. (1981) 358,654.

Ravensburg, t., Baden-Württemberg, **W. Germany**; nr. Konstanz; engin., textiles; p. (1983) 42,300.

Ravenscraig, t., nr. Motherwell, Strathclyde Reg., **Scot.**; hot strip steelmill; cold reduction mill at Gartcosh 13 km away; planned closure of steel wks.

Ravi, R., Punjab, **India**; trib. of Chenab; used for irrigation; 720 km long.

Rawalpindi, c., **Pakistan**; seat of govt. until completion of Islamabad; admin., comm. and rly. ctr.; foundries, oil refining, industl. gases; p. (1972) 615,392.

Rawmarsh, t., South Yorks., **Eng.**; 3 km N.E. of Rotherham; engin.; p. (1981) 18,985.

Rawtenstall, t., Rossendale, Lancs., **Eng.**; on R. Irwell in ctr. of Rossendale Fells; felts; footwear, textiles; p. (1981) 22,231.

Rayleigh, t., Rochford, Essex, **Eng.**; 8 km N.W.

of Southend; lt. inds.; dormitory for London; p. (1981) 29,146.

Ré, Ile de, I., W. cst. of Charente-Maritime dep. **France**; off La Rochelle; citadel (built 1681) at St. Martin de Ré is now a prison.

Reading, t., l. gov. dist., Berks., **Eng.**; at confluence of Rs. Thames and Kennet; univ.; biscuits, engin., electronics, mkt. gardening, tin-box mftg. printing; p. (1981) 132,037.

Reading, c., Penns., **USA**; on Schuylkill R.; steelwks. using local coal, optical gds.; p. (1980) 78,686 (c.), 312,509 (met. a.).

Recife, spt., cap. of Pernambuco st., N.E. **Brazil**; fine natural harbour; univ.; processing and exp. of sugar from surrounding a.; "Venice of Brazil" because of I. and peninsula site; lge. petrochemical wks. nearby; recent industl. expansion and diversification; engin., chem., electrical and telecommunications equipment; integrated steel wks.; p. (est. 1980) 1,432,800.

Recklinghausen, t., N. Rhine–Westphalia, **W. Germany**; nr. Dortmund; collieries, iron, machin., textiles, chemicals; p. (1983) 119,100.

Recôncavo, dist., Bahia st., N.E. **Brazil**; surrounds bay at mouth of R. Paraguassu; intensive cultivation of sugar-cane, cotton, tobacco, rice, by Negro farmers; oil production; ch. ts. São Salvador, Cachoeira.

Redbridge, outer bor., E. London, **Eng.**; incorporates Ilford, Wanstead and Woodford, Chigwell (Hainault Estate), Dagenham (N. Chadwell Heath ward); mainly residtl.; p. (1981) 225,019.

Redcar, t., Cleveland, **Eng.**; lge. iron and steel wks.; p. (1981) 84,931.

Redcliff, t., **Zimbabwe**; iron-mng.; iron and steel wks.; fertilisers.

Red Deer, t., Alberta, **Canada**; on Red Deer R.; mkt. t. in farming a.; lge. natural gas processing plant nearby; p. (1971) 27,428.

Redditch, t., l. gov. dist., Hereford and Worcs., **Eng.**; 19 km S. of Birmingham; needles, fishing tackle, cycles, springs, aluminium alloys; new t. (1964); p. (1981) 66,593 (dist.), 63,675 (t.).

Redlands, t., Cal., **USA**; univ.; citrus fruit packing and canning; p. (1980) 43,619.

Redonda, I., Leeward gr., **Antigua and Barbuda**; between Montserrat and Nevis; uninhabited.

Redondo Beach, t., Cal., **USA**; residtl.; tourism; p. (1980) 57,102.

Red R. (China and Vietnam). See Song-koi.

Red R., southernmost of lge. tribs. of Mississippi R.; derives name and colour from red clay in upper course; dammed for flood control and hydroelec. power; 2,560 km long.

Red R. of the North, USA; rises in Minn., flows N. into Canada to empty into L. Winnipeg; 1,040 km long.

Redruth, t., Cornwall, **Eng.**; once major ctr. of tin mng.; most mines now closed, although recent revival of some; p. (1981) 46,482 (inc. Camborne).

Red Sea, arm of sea separating Arabia from Africa; connects with Indian Oc. by Straits of Bab-el-Mandeb; extension of Great African Rift Valley which further N. encloses the Dead Sea; 2,240 km long.

Redwood City, t., W. Cal., **USA**; timber tr.; electronics; p. (1980) 54,951.

Ree, Lough, L., **R.o.I.**; between Roscommon, Longford and Westmeath, an extension of R. Shannon; 27 km long.

Regensburg (Ratisbon), c., R. pt., Bavaria, **W. Germany**; N.E. of Munich on R. Danube; timber processing, chemicals; p. (1983) 132,000.

Reggio di Calabria, spt., Calabria, **Italy**; on Strait of Messina; cath.; fishing, ferry to Sicily; mkt. for citrus fruit; tourism; agr. processing; rebuilt after 1908 earthquake; p. (1981) 173,486.

Reggio nell' Emilia, c., cap. of prov. of same name, in Emilia-Romagna, N. **Italy**; at foot of Apennines; Renaissance church of the Madonna della Ghiara; locomotives, aircraft, agr. engin.; birthplace of Ariosto; p. (1981) 130,376.

Regina, t., cap. of Saskatchewan, **Canada**; ctr. of wheat growing dist. of Prairies; connected by pipeline to Alberta oilfields; oil refining, chemicals, agr. machin.; p. (1979) 149,595.

Rehovoth, Israel; t., in citrus fruit dist.; Weizmann Institute of Science; p. (est. 1970) 36,600.

Reichenbach, t., Karl-Marx-Stadt, **E. Germany**; at foot of Erzgebirge; textile ctr.; p. (est. 1970) 28,818.

Reichenberg. See Liberec.

Reigate, t., Surrey, **Eng.**; at foot of N. Downs,

8 km E. of Dorking; dormitory for London; with Banstead forms l. gov. dist.; p. (1981) 116,191 (dist.).

Reims, c., Marne dep., N.E. **France**; on R. Vesle; famous Gothic cath.; univ.; champagne ctr., textiles; p. (1982) 181,985.

Reindeer L., Saskatchewan, Manitoba, **Canada**; Indian settlement on shore; a. 6,475 km².

Rejang R., Sarawak; navigable for 72 km by ocean boats; main R. of Sarawak.

Rembang, pt., N. cst. Java, **Indonesia**; in dry limestone R. plateau; proposed nuclear power plant; p. (est. 1960) 75,000.

Remscheid, t., N. Rhine–Westphalia, **W. Germany**; nr. Düsseldorf; iron and steel ctr.; machin. tools; p. (1983) 125,500.

Renaix. See Ronse.

Rendsburg, t., Schleswig-Holstein, **W. Germany**; on Kiel Canal; shipbldg., elec. gds.; p. (1983) 31,500.

Renfrew, royal burgh, Renfrew, **Scot.**; nr. R. Clyde, 8 km W. of Glasgow; p. (1981) 21,396.

Renfrewshire, former co., central **Scot.**; now reduced in size and forms l. gov. dist. within Strathclyde Reg.; a. of l. gov. dist. 308 km²; p. (1981) 205,884.

Renkum, t., Gelderland. **Neth.**; 13 km W. of Arnhem; paper mnfs.; p. (1982) 34,009.

Rennes, c., cap of Ille-et-Vilaine dep., **France**; only major inland t. of Brittany, in fertile agr. basin; univ., comm. ctr.; cars, engin.; p. (1982) 200,390.

Reno, lgst. t. of Nevada, **USA**; univ.; st. agr. college; famous for easy divorce procedure and gambling; p. (1980) 101,000.

Repton, t., South Derbyshire, **Eng.**; famous public school in priory; former Saxon cap. of Mercia.

Resende, t., Rio de Janeiro st., **Brazil**; chemicals, rly. junc.; univ.; p. (est. 1968) 64,950.

Resht. See Rasht.

Resina, t., S. **Italy**; on Bay of Naples at W. foot of Vesuvius; nr. site of anc. Herculaneum; resort; p. (est. 1970) 52,451.

Resistencia, t., cap. of Chaco terr., **Argentina**; served by R. pt. of Barranqueras on R. Paraná; tr. in cattle, timber, cotton; agr. processing; p. (1975) 142,848 (met. a.).

Resita, t., Banat region, **Romania**; developing steel inds. based on local iron ore; heavy engin.; p. (1968) 58,679.

Restormel, l. gov. dist., Cornwall, **Eng.**; inc. N. and S. cst. and ts. of Newquay and St. Austell; p. (1981) 79,167.

Retalhuleu, t., cap. of R. dep., **Guatemala**; comm. ctr. for coffee, sugar; p. (est. 1970) 42,000.

Réunion (Ile de Bourbon), I., overseas terr. of France; in **Indian Oc.**, between Mauritius and Madagascar; volcanic I.; impt. sugar producer; cap. St. Denis; a. 2,512 km²; p. (est. 1984) 555,000.

Reus, t., Tarragona, prov., **Spain**; textiles; agr. tr.; p. (1981) 75,987.

Reuss, R., **Switzerland**; flows N. from the St. Gotthard Pass through L. Lucerne, joining Aare R. nr. Brugg; 157 km long.

Reutlingen, t., Baden–Württemberg, **W. Germany**; S. of Stuttgart; textiles, metals, machin., leather; p. (1983) 31,500.

Reval. See Tallin.

Revelstoke, t., B.C., **Canada**; rly. junc.; in timber producing a.; ctr. for R. Nat. Park; p. (1966) 4,791.

Revillagigedo Islands, archipelago, Pac. Oc., off S.W. **Mexico**; ch. is., Socorro, San Benedicto (volcano suddenly arose on I. 1952).

Reykjavik, c., cap. of **Iceland**; on S.W. cst.; impt. fish. pt.; fish exp. and processing; water piped from geysers; airport; univ.; 2 caths.; p. (est. 1978) 118,570.

Rezayeh, (Orūmīyeh) c., **Iran**; cap. of W. Azerbaijan prov.; comm. ctr. of agr. region; p. (1976) 163,991.

Rheidol, R., Dyfed, **Wales**; flows from Plynlimmon in deeply incised valley (Devil's Bridge) to Aberystwyth; hydroelec. power; 38 km long.

Rheine, t., N. Rhine–Westphalia, **W. Germany**; on R. Ems; textiles, machin.; p. (1983) 71,200.

Rheingau, dist., **W. Germany**; famous wine a. on right bank of Rhine from Biebrich to Assmannshausen.

Rheinhausen, t., Rhine–Westphalia, **W. Germany**; on left bank of Rhine opposite Duisburg; coal mng., iron, textiles.

Rheydt, t., N. Rhine–Westphalia, **W. Germany**;

twin c. of adjacent Mönchengladbach; textiles, machin.

Rhin (Bas). *See* Bas Rhin.

Rhine, R., rises in Switzerland, can. Grisons, passes through L. Constance, skirts Baden, traverses Hesse, Rhineland, and the Neth., flowing to N. Sea by two arms, Oude Rijn and the Waal (the latter discharging finally by the Maas); famous for its beauty, especially between Bonn and Bingen; ch. falls at Schaffhausen; once a natural barrier between E. and W. Europe spanned by 30 rly. bridges; linked to Rhône by 1985 and Rhine-Main-Danube canal allows navigation from N. Sea to Black Sea for 3,500 km. (Trans European waterway); very polluted; 1,280 km long.

Rhine-Hern, canal, **W. Germany;** impt. Ruhr waterway, part of Mitelland Canal; 38 km long.

Rhineland Palatinate (Rheinland-Pfalz), *Land,* **W. Germany;** borders France, Luxembourg and Belgium; drained by Rhine and Moselle, inc. Hunsrück and Eifel mtns.; arable agr. in Rhine valley; vineyards; cap. Mainz; a. 19,852 km; p. (1982) 3,636,500.

Rhode Island, st., New England, **USA;** 'Little Rhody' admitted to Union 1790; st. flower violet, st. bird R.I. Red; washed by Atl. Oc., surrounded by Mass. and Conn.; divided by Narragansett Bay, with many Is. lgst. being that from which the st. takes its name; smallest and most densely populated st.; famous for poultry; major ind. textiles; cap. Providence; a. 3,144 km²; p. (1980) 947,000.

Rhodes (Rhodos), I., Dodecanese Is.; off S.W. cst., Anatolia, belonging to **Greece;** cap. R.; p. (1981) 87,831.

Rhodes, cap. of I. of Rhodes, **Greece;** on N.E. cst.; picturesque; p. (1981) 41,425.

Rhodesia. *See* Zimbabwe.

Rhodope Mtns. *See* Rodopi Mtns.

Rhondda, t., l. gov. dist., Mid Glamorgan, **Wales;** in narrow R. valley; coal-mng. ctr.; lt. inds. introduced since 1930s depression; picturesque a. in upper R. valley; p. (1981) 81,725.

Rhône, dep., S.E. **France;** drained by R. Rhône, and its trib. R. Saône, which unite at Lyons; agr. grain, potatoes, wine; vine-growing, many mnfs., silks, textiles; cap. Lyons; a. 2,859 km²; p. (1982) 1,440,900.

Rhône, R., **Switzerland** and **France;** rises in Rhône glacier of St. Gotthard mtn. gr., and flows through L. of Geneva and E. France to G. of Lyons in Mediterranean; power stas. at Sion and Geneva; canals, dams, locks and power stas. form part of Fr. Rhône Valley project (1937–72); linked to Rhine by 1985; 811 km long.

Rhône-Saône Corridor, routeway, **France;** impt. transport artery using Rhône, Saône R. valleys as a means for linking Paris, Lorraine and Rhine rift valley with Mediterranean cst.; rlys., roads, with major pt. of Marseilles serving the S. terminus.

Rhuddlan, l. gov. dist., Clwyd, **Wales;** cstl. a. of Rhyl, Prestatyn and St. Asaph; p. (1981) 52,338.

Rhyl, t., Rhuddlan, Clwyd, N. **Wales;** at entrance Vale of Clwyd; resort developed from sm. fishing v.; serves Lancs. conurbs.; p. (1981) 22,714.

Rhymney, t., Mid Glamorgan, **Wales;** on R. Rhymney, E. of Merthyr Tydfil; former colly. and iron founding ctr.; engin.; p. (1981) 7,360.

Rhymney Valley, l. gov. dist., Mid Glamorgan, **Wales;** based on Rhymney and inc. Caerphilly, Bedwas and Gelligaer; p. (1981) 105,525.

Ribble, R., North Yorks., Lancs., **Eng.;** rises in Pennines, flows W. to Irish Sea nr. pt. of Preston; 120 km long.

Ribble Valley, l. gov. dist., N. Lancs., **Eng.;** inc. Forest of Bowland and ts. of Clitheroe and Longridge; p. (1981) 51,968.

Ribe, mkt. t., Jutland, S. **Denmark;** admin. ctr. of R. prov.; impt. mediaeval c.; Romanesque cath.; many fine bldgs.; p. (est. 1970) 8,224.

Ribeirão Prêto, t., São Paulo st., **Brazil;** mkt. in rich agr. a., coffee, cotton, sugar; p. (est. 1980) 309,200.

Richard's Bay, Natal, **S. Africa;** new pt. to supplement congested Durban; on natural harbour; silting problem but designed for bulk carriers; plans to attract ass. industl. development.

Richborough, pt., Kent, **Eng.;** at mouth of R. Stour; Caesar's ch. pt., Roman remains; pt. has been privately redeveloped; chemicals.

Richmond, t., North Yorks., **Eng.;** at E. foot of

Pennines on R. Swale; mkt. t., agr. tr.; 14th cent. grammar school; Norman cas.; now as Richmondshire forms l. gov. dist. with surrounding a. of Aysgarth and Leyburn; p. (1981) 42,531 (l. gov. dist.).

Richmond, c., Cal., **USA;** deepwater pt.; oil refining; car assembly, chemicals, electronics; p. (1980) 74,676.

Richmond, c., cap. of Va., **USA;** on falls on R. James; pt. at head of navigation; financial and tr. ctr.; tobacco inds., and mkt.; chemicals, iron and steel; p. (1980) 219,000 (c.), 632,000 (met. a.).

Richmond-upon-Thames, outer bor., Greater London, **Eng.;** inc. Barnes, Richmond and Twickenham; industl. and residtl.; beautiful park and riverside scenery; p. (1981) 157,867. *See also* Kew.

Rickmansworth, t., Three Rivers, Herts., **Eng.;** residtl. sub of London; p. (1981) 29,408.

Rideau Canal, Ont., **Canada;** from Ottawa R. at Ottawa to Kingston on L. Ontario; 211 km long.

Riesa, t., Dresden, **E. Germany;** R. pt. on Elbe R. nr. Meissen; p. (est. 1970) 49,746.

Riesengebirge, mtn. range, between Silesia (**Poland**) and Bohemia (**ČSSR**); highest peak Schneekoppe (Czech Snežka, Polish Sniezka), 1,604 m.

Rieti, Latium, **Italy;** an anc. Sabine c. with mediaeval townscape, in fertile Apennine basin; route ctr. and cap. of R. prov.; chemicals, sugar refinery, textiles; p. (1981) 43,079.

Riff or **Rif,** mtns., **Morocco,** N.W. Africa; extend along N. African cst. for 320 km from Straits of Gibraltar; inaccessible and economically unattractive, terr. of semi-nomadic tribes; rise to over 2,100 m in many places.

Riga, cap. of Latvian SSR, **USSR;** Baltic pt.; exp. wheat, flax, hemp, dairy produce; industl. ctr., diesel rly. engin., furniture; univ.; local bathing beaches; p. (est. 1980) 843,000.

Rigi, mtn., nr. L. Lucerne, **Switzerland;** viewpoint reached by rack and pinion rly.; 1,801 m.

Rijeka-Susak, c., Croatia, **Yugoslavia;** formerly Fiume, ceded to Yugoslavia by Italy after second world war; rival pt. to Trieste on Adriatic Sea; oil refining, shipbldg., tobacco, chemicals; hydroelectric power; p. (1981) 193,044.

Rimac, R., Lima dep., **Peru;** rises in W. cordillera of Andes and flows W. to Pac. Oc.; provides water for irrigation and for c. of Lima; 120 km long.

Rimini, c., Emilia-Romagna, **Italy;** on Adriatic cst. at junc. of Via Emilia and Via Flaminia; mkt. for fertile agr. a.; sm. inds.; bathing resort; p. (1981) 126,949.

Ringerike, t., Buskerud, **Norway;** new t., 40 km N.W. of Oslo and inc. former t. of Hönefoss; p. (est. 1970) 28,828.

Riobamba, t., Chimborazo, **Ecuador;** on R. St. Juan; woollens, cotton gds., cement, ceramics; Inca palace ruins; p. (1966) 61,393.

Rio Branco, R., flows *c.* 560 km from Guiana Highlands through **Brazil** to join Rio Negro.

Rio Branco, t., cap. of Acre st., **Brazil;** p. (est. 1968) 70,730.

Rio Cuarto, t., Cordoba prov., **Argentina;** agr. ctr.; p. (est. 1970) 88,852.

Rio de Janeiro, c., spt., S.E. **Brazil;** cap. of Guanabara st., on G. Bay, Alt. Oc.; former fed. cap.; beautiful natural harbour, many fine bldgs., Sugar Loaf mtn., Copacabana beach; flourishing tr. and inds.; mnfs. inc. textiles, foodstuffs, pharmaceutics, china, sheet glass; oil refining; p. (est. 1980) 5,539,100.

Rio de Janeiro, st., S.E. **Brazil;** on Atl. Oc.; consists of cst. plain, central Sero do Mar escarpment, fertile Paraíba R. basin in W.; coffee, sugar, fruit; ctr. of heavy ind.; cement, textiles, sugar refineries at Campos, steel wks. at Volta Redonda; cap. Niterói; a. 42,735 km²; p. (1970) 4,742,884.

Rio Grande, headstream of R. Paraná, **Brazil;** Furnas dam, Estreito dam for hydroelec. power; 1,040 km long.

Rio Grande, R., flows from st. of Col. through N.M. to G. of Mexico; forms bdy. between Texas, **USA** and **Mexico;** Elephant Butte, Caballo, and Falcon multi-purpose dams; known also as Rio Grande do Norte and Rio Bravo; *c.* 3,016 km long.

Rio Grande do Norte, st., N.E. Brazil; cst. plain rising to S. plateau; climate semi-arid; cotton, sugar, salt, scheelite; cap. Natal; a. 53,038 km²; p. (1970) 1,550,244.

Rio Grande do Sul, st., S. Brazil; grassy plains, rolling plateaux; cool climate; stock-raising, meat-processing, wheat, wine, wool; lge. coal deposits at São Jeronimo; cap. Pôrto Alegre; a. 267,684 km²; p. (1970) 6,664,891.

Rioja, region and prov., N. Spain; upper Ebro valley; famous for wines and orange groves; ch. ctr. Logroño; p. (1981) 254,346.

Riom, t., Puy-de-Dôme dep., France; former cap. of Auvergne; old bldgs. built of lava; p. (1982) 18,901.

Rio Muni, terr., Equatorial Guinea; former Spanish terr., on cst. between Cameroon and Gabon, inc. offshore Is. of Corisco, Elobey Grande, Elobey Chico; with Biako forms Equatorial Guinea; equatorial forest; exp. tree prods. of cacao, coffee, hardwood; ch. t. Bata; a. 26,003 km²; p. (1968) 183,000.

Rion, R., Georgian SSR, USSR; flows from Caucasus to Black Sea; lower half navigable; hydroelec. sta. at Kutaisi. (In Greek mythology the R. Phasis of the Argonauts.)

Rio Negro, prov., Argentina; in N. Patagonia; irrigated agr. in R. valley, fruits, grain crops; elsewhere stock-raising; cap. Viedma; a. 201,010 km²; p. (1970) 193,848.

Rio Negro, dep., Uruguay; livestock fattening from N. Uruguay; grain crops; ch. t. and cap. Fray Bentos; a. 8,466 km²; p. (est. 1969) 48,700.

Rio Tinto, t., Spain; at W. end of Sierra Morena 64 km N.E. of Huelva; major world ctr. of copper production.

Riouw-Lingga Archipelago, I. gr., Indonesia; S. of Malaya; Bintan lgst. I. where bauxite mng.; pepper and rubber cultivation; a. 5,905 km²; p. (1961) 278,966.

Ripley, mkt. t., Amber Valley, Derbys., Eng.; 11 km N.E. of Derby; coal, iron, heavy engin., bricks, agr. implements; p. (1981) 18,691.

Ripon, c., North Yorks., Eng.; on R. Ure; cath.; old mkt. square; old custom of wakeman; tourism; p. (1981) 11,952.

Risca, t., Gwent, Wales; on R. Ebbw; former coal-mng. dist.; limestone quarrying; bricks, plastics; p. (1981) 14,860.

Risdon, t., Tasmania, Australia; first white settlement in Tasmania, opposite Hobart; electrometallurgy.

Rishton, t., Hyndburn, Lancs., Eng.; at N. foot of Rossendale Fells, 6 km N.E. of Blackburn; p. (1981) 6,212.

Rive-de-Gier, t., Loire dep., France; on R. Gier, nr. Lyons; coal mng., iron and steel, glass; p. (1982) 15,850.

Rivera, dep., Uruguay; on Brazilian border; noted for cattle and sheep ranches; cap. R.; a. 9,824 km²; p. (est. 1969) 80,700.

Rivera, t., cap. of R. dep., Uruguay; on Brazilian frontier opposite Santa Ana; agr. mkt.; p. (1964) 40,000.

Riverina, pastoral cty., N.S.W., Australia; between Lachlan-Murrumbidgee and Murray Rs.; merino sheep in W.; good wheat yields in E.; gtr. crop variety with irrigation; a. 68,894 km².

River Rouge, t., Mich., USA; ctr. of Ford car mnf.; many heavy inds.; rapidly growing t. p. (1980) 12,912.

Riverside, t., Cal., USA; ctr. for citrus fruit packing and tr.; resort; p. (1980) 171,000 (c.), 1,558,000 (met. a. inc. San Bernadino-Ontario).

Riviera, the belt of cst. between the Alps and the Mediterranean from Spezia to Hyères, France and Italy; picturesque scenery, sheltered, mild climate; fashionable health resorts.

Riyadh, t., cap. of Saudi Arabia; 368 km inland from Persian G.; palace; univ.; route and tr. ctr., linked by rail with pt. of Zahran; p. (1974) 666,840.

Rizaiyeh (Urmia), c., cap. of Azerbaijan prov., Iran; nr. L. Urmia; comm. ctr.; birthplace of Zoroaster; p. (1966) 110,749.

Rizal, prov., central Luzon, Philippines; rapidly growing prov. in fertile Central Plain; new inds. developing; cap. Pasig; a. 2,049 km²; p. (1970) 2,781,081.

Rize, t., Turkey; nr. Trabzon, on Black Sea; ctr. of Turkish tea inds.; p. (1970) 30,532.

Road Town, spt., Tortola; cap. of the Brit. Virgin Is.; tr. in fish, poultry; p. (1960) 900.

Roanne, t., Loire dep., France; on R. Loire; château ruins; textiles; p. (1982) 81,786 (met. a.).

Roanoke, R., Va., and N.C., USA; flows into Albemarle Sound; hydroelec. power; 656 km long.

Roanoke, c., S.W. Va., USA; between Blue Ridge and Allegheny mtns.; rly. junc.; engin. p. (1980) 100,000 (c.), 224,000 (met. a.).

Roanoke I., off cst. N.C., USA; attempted settlement of colony by Raleigh.

Roaring Creek, Belize, Central America; site of new cap. 80 km inland, at junc. of W. highway with Hummingbird highway.

Robben I., at entrance of Table Bay, Cape Prov., S. Africa; penal settlement and former leper colony.

Robin Hood's Bay, v., North Yorks., Eng.; picturesque site in inlet; tourism, fishing.

Robson, Mt., Canada; on B.C. and Alberta border; alt. 3,956 m; in Nat. Park.

Rocha, dep., Uruguay; borders Atl. Oc.; a. of cattle and sheep rearing; cap. R.; a. 11,850 km²; p. (est. 1972) 57,900.

Rochdale, t., met. dist., Gtr. Manchester, Eng.; at S. foot of Rossendale Fells, on R. Roch; textiles, engin., asbestos; co-operative movement started here 1844; p. (1981) 207,255.

Rochefort, t., Charente-Maritime dep., France; fishing pt.; former impt. naval base; p. (1982) 27,716.

Rochelle, La, t., cap. of Charente-Maritime dep. France; on Bay of Biscay; fishing pt.; shipbldg.; pt. tr. declining; p. (1982) 78,231.

Rochester upon Medway, t., l. gov. dist., Kent, Eng.; on R. Medway, adjoining Chatham; cath., cas.; many associations with Dickens; aeronautical, elec. and mechanical engin., paint, varnish, cement; p. (1981) 143,384 (dist.).

Rochester, t., Minn., USA; famous for Mayo clinic, and Mayo medical research ctr.; p. (1980) 57,890.

Rochester, c., N.Y., USA; on Genesee R.; univ.; cameras, films, optical instruments, thermocameras, electronic equipment; hydroelectric power; p. (1980) 242,000 (c.), 971,000 (met. a.).

Roche-sur-Yon, La, t., cap. of Vendée dep., France; on R. Yon; built by Napoleon I; p. (1975) 48,053.

Rochford, l. gov. dist., Essex, Eng.; cstl. a. inc. Rochford and Rayleigh; p. (1981) 73,540.

Rock, R., Wis., Ill., USA; formerly home of native Indians; focus of white settlement since 1830; 456 km long.

Rockall, sm. I., Atl. Oc.; lies 320 km W. of Outer Hebrides; forms hgst. part of submarine bank which forms gd. fishing-ground; uninhabited; annexed by Britain 1955; formally incorporated into Inverness-shire (1972) to ensure control of suspected oil and natural gas deposits; claimed also by Ireland and Iceland; rock samples aged 1,000 million years place it with some Canadian rocks.

Rockall Deep, submarine trench, N. Atl. Oc.; between N.W. Ireland and Rockall I.; suspected oil and natural gas reserves.

Rockford, c., Ill., USA; serves agr. dist.; agr. machin., machin. tools; p. (1980) 140,000 (c.), 280,000 (met. a.).

Rockhampton, t., pt., Queensland, Australia; on Tropic of Capricorn; outlet for vast pastoral and mng. a.; comm. cap. of central Queensland; meat-preserving; p. (1976) 50,132.

Rockingham, t., W. Australia; satellite of Perth; major pt. planned to serve Kwinana; p. (1976) 17,693.

Rock Island, c., Ill., USA; on R. Mississippi; former site of US arsenal; agr. machin., timber and agr. processing; p. (1980) 46,928.

Rocky Mtns., vast mtn. chain, N. America; extend from Alaska, through Canada, USA to Mexico; made up of several parallel ranges separated by intermontane basins and plateaus; barrier to spread of settlers to W. cst. in 19th cent.; climatic barrier; extensive snow and glacier fields in N.; dry desert landscapes in S.; many Nat. Parks; sparse p.; hydroelectric power; hgst. peak Mt. Logan (6,054 m); length 5,120 km.

Rodez, t., cap. of Aveyron dep., France; on R. Aveyron; cath.; woollens; p. (1982) 26,346.

Rodopi (Rhodope) Mtns., range S. Bulgaria; rise to 3,100 m.

Rodosto. See Tekirdag.

Rodriguez, I., Brit. dependency of Mauritius,

Indian Oc.; 560 km N.E. of Mauritius; mainly agr. and fishing; cap. Port Mathurin; a. 109 km²; p. (1983) 33,082.

Roermond, t., Limburg prov., Neth.; on R. Maas; minster; textiles; p. (1982) 38,192.

Roeselare, (Roulers) t., W. Flanders, Belgium; on R. Lys, nr. Kortrijk, textile ctr.; p. (1981) 51,984.

Rogerstone, t., Gwent, Wales; on R. Ebbw; lge. aluminium wks.

Rohtak, t., Haryana, India; N.W. of Delhi; p. (1971) 124,755.

Roissy-en-France; 26 km N.E. of Paris, France; site of Charles de Gaulle airport; p. (1982) 1,411.

Roman, t., Romania; on R. Moldava; cath.; agr. processing; p. (est. 1970) 43,188.

Romania (Rumania), Socialist Rep. of, S.E. Europe; bounded by USSR, Hungary, Yugoslavia, Bulgaria, and Black Sea; Carpathian mtns., Transylvanian Alps, wide Walachian plain, Moldavian plateau; drained by Danube and its tribs.; climate predominantly continental with cold winters and hot summers; since second world war transformation of economy from agr. to industl. basis, although agr. still impt., contributing many exps., especially timber, wine, fruit; major pt. Constanta on Black Sea; oilfields at Ploiesti; cap. Bucharest; ch. tr. partners USSR and E. Europe; Danube used for navigation; Iron Gates power and navigation system being constructed in co-operation with Yugoslavia; tourism from W. Europe and N. America encouraged; a. 237,428 km²; p. (est. 1984) 22,897,000.

Rome (Roma), cap. of Italy, and of Latium and Rome prov.; on R. Tiber, 24 km from sea; in Roman legend founded by Romulus 753 B.C.; once cap. of anc. Roman empire; inc. Vatican c., ctr. of Roman Catholic Church; situated on original "seven hills," and along the R.; leading cultural ctr.; St. Peter's church, Colosseum, Pantheon; univ.; admin. ctr.; tourism; created cap. of United Italy 1871; p. (1981) 2,840,259.

Romford. See Havering.

Romney Marsh, coastal marsh, Shepway, Kent, Eng.; formed by blocking of R. Rother by shingle spit of Dungeness which extends from Rye to Hythe; largely drained; pastures for special Romney Marsh breed of sheep; a. 129 km².

Romsey, t., Test Valley, Hants., Eng.; on R. Test, 14 km N.W. of Southampton; mkt. ctr.; Norman abbey; p. (1981) 12,941.

Ronaldshay, North, most N. of Orkney Is., Scot.; p. (1971) 134.

Ronaldshay, South, most S. of Orkney Is. Scot.; p. (1971) 991.

Roncesvalles, mtn. pass in Pyrenees, Navarre, Spain; 32 km N.E. of Pamplona; defeat and death of Roland 778.

Ronda, t., Málaga, Spain; in Andalusia; anc. Moorish t., divided by deep gorge crossed by bridge; p. (1981) 31,383.

Rondônia, fed. terr., Brazil; on Bolivian border; forest covered; forest prods.; nomadic Indian tribes; cap. Pôrto Velho; a. 243,071 km²; p. (1970) 111,064.

Rønne, t., Denmark; cap. of Bornholm I.; fish. pt.; shipyards, ceramics; p. (est. 1970) 12,440.

Ronse (Renaix), t., Belgium; nr. Ghent; textile ctr.; p. (1982) 24,287.

Roodepoort-Maraisburg, t., Transvaal, S. Africa; ctr. Witwatersrand goldfields; p. (1970) 114,191.

Roosendaal, t., S.W. of N. Brabant, Neth., sugar-refining; p. (1982) 55,754.

Roosevelt Dam (1903–11), Arizona, USA; on R. Salt in canyon E. of Phoenix on edge of Col. plateau; used for irrigation and hydroelectric power; part of Salt river project.

Roquefort-sur-Soulzon, t., S.E. Aveyron, France; caves in limestone cliffs used for ripening cheese; p. (1982) 880.

Roraima, mtn., at junc. of boundaries of Brazil, Guyana, and Venezuela; 2,852 m, hgst. point of Guiana Highlands.

Roraima (Rio Branco), fed. terr., Brazil; under-developed rain forest; cap. Boa Vista; a. 214,320 km²; p. (est. 1976) 49,700.

Rosa Monte, Pennine Alps, Swiss-Italian border; alt. 4,637 m.

Rosario, t., Santa Fé, Argentina; second t. of rep.; R. pt. on Paraná R.; agr.-processing, iron and steel, lt. inds.; univ., cath.; p. (1975) 750,455.

Roscommon, co. t., Roscommon, R.O.I.; mkt.; cas., priory; p. (est. 1978) 3,200.

Roscommon, inland co., Connaught, R.O.I.; extensive peat bog and ls.; pastoral agr., cap. R.; a. 2,458 km²; p. (1981) 8,454.

Rosetta (Rashid), t., Lower Egypt; nr. Rosetta mouth of Nile; Rosetta stone found nearby gave key to Egyptian hieroglyphics; p. (1966) 36,700.

Roskilde, t., spt., Sjaelland, Denmark; former cap.; cath. contains tombs of kings; admin. ctr. of R. prov.; p. (est. 1970) 39,984.

Ross and Cromarty, former co., l. gov. dist., Highland Reg.; Scot.; extends from N. Sea to Atl. Oc.; most of a. over 300 m, lake-covered; cattle breeding, fishing, tourism; a. 4,999 km²; p. (1983) 241,146.

Rossendale Fells (or Forest), upland, S.E. Lancs./ Gtr. Manchester, Eng.; extension of Pennines between Rs. Mersey and Ribble; millstone grit moorland used for reservoirs; alt. mainly above 360 m; now forms l. gov. dist. in Lancs. inc. ts. of Haslingden, Rawtenstall, Bacup and Whit-worth; p. (1981) 64,480

Ross Dependency, Antarctica; N.Z. sector; inlet of Ross Sea; a. 414,400 km; p. (1966) 262.

Rosslare, spt., Wexford, R.O.I.; on extreme S.E. of Ireland; steamer connections to Fishguard.

Ross-on-Wye, t., South Herefordshire, Hereford and Worcs., Eng.; mkt., tourism; p. (1981) 7,182.

Ross Sea, sea extending to 85° S. in Antarctic.

Rostock, c., cap. of R. dist., E. Germany; pt. nr. Baltic cst., outport of Warnemünde; shipbldg., fish-processing, chemicals; univ.; mediaeval t.; p. (1983) 241,146.

Rostov, c., RSFSR; pt. on R. Don, nr. Azov Sea (Black Sea); one of Russia's finest and oldest cs.; ctr. of agr. dist.; grain mkt.; agr.-processing; univ.; p. (est. 1980) 946,000.

Rosyth, t., Dunfermline, Scot.; naval dockyard.

Rothamsted, v., Herts., Eng.; in Chiltern Hills, S. of Harpenden; famous agr. research sta.

Rother, l. gov. dist., East Sussex, Eng.; rural a. inc. Rye, Bexhill and Battle; p. (1981) 75,278.

Rother, R., Derbys. and South Yorks., Eng.; flows to R. Don at Rotherham; 34 km long.

Rother, R., East Sussex and Kent, Eng.; rises in the Weald, flows S.E. into English Channel at Rye; 50 km long.

Rotherham, t., met. dist., South Yorks., Eng.; on R. Don, 6 km N.E. of Sheffield; iron, steel, wire, springs, glass; p. (1981) 251,336.

Rothes, burgh, Moray, Scot.; on R. Spey 19 km S.E. of Elgin; p. (1981) 1,429.

Rothesay, royal burgh, Argyll and Bute., Scot.; on E. cst. of I. of Bute in F. of Clyde; tourism; p. (1981) 5,408.

Rothwell, t., West Yorks., Eng.; on R. Aire, 5 km S.E. of Leeds; coal-mng. ctr., engin.; p. (1981) 29,142.

Rotorua, c., leading spa of N.Z.; on volcanic plateau, Auckland, N.I.; hot springs; p. (1976) 46,650.

Rotterdam, c., spt. Neth.; Europe's lgst. spt., on Nieuwe Maas, part of Rhine-Maas-Scheldt delta; linked to outport Europoort (q.v.) by New Waterway; serves hinterland of Rhine valley and central Europe; freeport; processing of imports, especially oil refining and petrochemical inds.; badly damaged in second world war; p. (1982) 568,167.

Roubaix, t., Nord dep., France; nr. Lille; on Roubaix canal close to Belgian frontier; major textile ctr., especially for woollens; p. (1982) 101,886.

Rouen, c., Seine-Maritime dep., France; gr. R. pt., 125 km up R. Seine; oil refining, textiles, chemicals; cath.; Joan of Arc burned here; birthplace of Corneille and Flaubert; badly damaged in second world war; p. (1982) 105,083.

Rourkela, t., Orissa, India; W. of Jamshedpur; p. (1971) 125,426 (c.), 172,502 (met. a.).

Rousay, Orkney Is., Scot.; p. (1971) 256.

Roussillon, former prov., S. France; now dep. of Pyrénées-Orientales; irrigated by many sm. streams; olives, wine, fruit; historical cap. Perpignan.

Rovaniemi, t., Finland; on Kemi R.; timber and saw mills; p. (1970) 26,667.

Rovigo, prov., Venetia, Italy; part of N. Italian plain extending to Adriatic; impt. agr. dist.;

cap. R.; a. 218 km²; p. (1981) 253,508.

Rovigo, t., cap. of R. prov., **Italy**; on R. Adige, cath., cas. ruins, palace; p. (1981) 52,218.

Rovno, c., cap. of R., oblast, Ukrainian SSR, **USSR**; rly. junct.; industl. ctr.; ruins of mediaeval palace; p. (est. 1980) 185,000.

Roxburgh, former co., S. **Scot.**; sheeprearing hilly cty. with wool-based inds.; new forms l. gov. dist. in Borders Reg.; a. 1,538 km²; p. (1981) 35,180.

Royal Oak, t., Mich., **USA**; residtl.; Detroit zoological park here; p. (1980) 70,893.

Royston, mkt. t., North Herts., **Eng.**; at N. foot of E. Anglian Heights, 11 km N.E. of Baldock; p. (1981) 11,799.

Royton, t., Gtr. Manchester, **Eng.**; 6 km N.E. of Manchester; textiles; p. (1981) 21,233.

Ruanda-Urundi. *See* **Rwanda** and **Burundi**.

Ruapehu, highest mtn., N.I., **N.Z.**; volcanic peak at S. extremity of central volcanic dist.; crater L. at summit; alt. 2,798 m.

Rubicon, R., central **Italy**; flows to Adriatic; crossed by Julius Caesar and his armies 49 B.C.; has been identified with the Fiumicino or the Uso.

Rubtsovsk, t., W. Siberia, **RSFSR**; agr. engin.; p. (est. 1980) 158,000.

Ruby Mines, dist., Mandalay, Upper **Burma**; hilly region of Shan plateau, once famous for rubies.

Ruda Slaska, t., Katowice, **Poland**; coal-mng. ctr.; iron and steel wks.; p. (est. 1983) 162,800.

Rudnyy, t., Kazakh SSR, **USSR**; new t. 48 km S.W. of Kustanay; iron-ore mng. and dressing plant supplying Magnitogorsk; p. (est. 1980) 111,000.

Rudolf, L., N.W. **Kenya**; in Great Rift Valley; a. 9,065 km²; ctr. of semi-arid region; renamed **Turkana**.

Rudolph I., N. of Franz Josef Land Arctic Oc.; Russian naval base; met. sta.

Rudolstadt, t., **E. Germany**; on R. Saale, in former st. of Thuringia; seat of counts of Schwarzburg-Rudolstadt (1584–1918); tourism; porcelain; p. (est. 1970) 31,539.

Rueil-Malmaison, sub. of Paris, **France**; château; tomb of the empress Josephine; p. (1982) 64,545.

Rufiji, R., **Tanzania**; E. Africa; flows to Indian Oc.; 720 km long.

Rufisque, t., **Senegambia**; sm. spt. nr. Dakar; growing industl. ctr. for consumer gds.; p. (est. 1967) 60,000.

Rugby, mkt. t., l. gov. dist., Warwicks, **Eng.**; on R. Avon, 18 km E. of Coventry; famous public school; elec. and gen. engin.; motor and aircraft patterns; p. (1981) 86,120 (dist.).

Rugeley, mkt. t., Staffs, **Eng.**; on R. Trent, 14 km S.E. of Stafford; coal, iron, tanning; expanded t.; p. (1981) 24,340.

Rügen, I., **E. Germany**; in Baltic Sea, off Stralsund; ch. t. Bergen; pt. Sassnitz, terminus of train ferry; steamer services to Trelleborg, Sweden.

Ruhr, industl. dist., **W. Germany**; lies to E. of R. Rhine, on either side of R. Ruhr; rich coalfield; impt. iron and steel, heavy engin. inds. based on local coal and iron ore from Luxembourg, Spain, Sweden; water communications to N. Sea along R. Rhine and Dortmund–Ems Canal; ch. ts. Essen, Duisburg, Düsseldorf, Dortmund, Bochum.

Ruhr, R., **W. Germany**; trib. of Rhine; flows S. of Ruhr conurb.; 232 km long.

Rukwa, L. **E. Africa**; between L. Tanganyika and L. Malawi in the rift valley; 48 km by 19 im, a. increasing.

Rum, I., Inner Hebrides, Lochaber, **Scot.**; nature reserve, highland ecology; a. 168 km².

Rumaila, **Iraq**; oilfield; pipeline links to the Zubair–Fao system.

Rum Jungle, N.T., **Australia**; 64 km S.E. of Darwin; site of Australia's first major uranium project; ceased operation in 1970.

Runcorn, t., Halton, Cheshire, **Eng.**; on S. side of Mersey estuary; new t. (1964); chemicals; pipeline carrying petrochemical feedstock from Teeside; new Runcorn–Widnes bridge over Mersey and Manchester Ship Canal opened 1961 (lgst. span arch in Europe); p. of new t. (1981) 63,813.

Rungis, Paris, **France**; site of major new mkt. to replace Les Halles; nr. Orly airpt., Val de Marne dep.; p. (1982) 2,650.

Runnymede, l. gov. dist., Surrey, **Eng.**; comprises Egham and Chertsey; p. (1981) 71,082.

Ruse, t., **Bulgaria**; on R. Danube, opposite Giurgiu in Romania; univ.; Roman t.; agr. processing; p. (est. 1972) 163,012.

Rushcliffe, l. gov. dist., Notts., **Eng.**; a. S.E. of Nottingham inc. West Bridgeford; p. (1981) 92,587.

Rushden, t., East Northants., **Eng.**; 5 km E. of Wellingborough; shoes; p. (1981) 22,253.

Rushmoor, l. gov. dist., Hants., **Eng.**; small a. of Farnborough and Aldershot; p. (1981) 78,107.

Rüsselsheim, t., **W. Germany**; impt. car factory; p. (1983) 59,300.

Russian Soviet Federated Socialist Republic (RSFSR), constituent rep., **USSR**; lgst. rep. by a. and p.; economic development; inds. centred on Leningrad and Moscow with new inds. being developed in Urals and Kuznetz basin; extends from Baltic to Pac. Oc. (8,000 km), from Arctic to Caspian Sea (4,000 km); part of N. European plain in W. and Siberian plain in E., separated by Ural mtns.; major Rs. Volga, Don, Ob, Yenisey, Lena, Amur; gr. variety in climate and p. density; major agr. region for wheat, sugar-beet, livestock; vast mineral deposits have aided economic growth; oil around Volga valley; metallic ores from Ural and Black Sea; hydroelectric power from Volga, Yenesey and Ob Rs.; cap. Moscow; a. 16,838,885 km²; p. (1970) 130,090,000.

Rustavi, t., Georgian SSR, **USSR**; new t., 32 km S.E. Tbilisi; iron and steel; lge. metallurgical plant; p. (est. 1980) 132,000.

Rustenburg, t., Transvaal, **Africa**; on N.W. edge of High Veld, 96 km W. of Pretoria; local mkt. for agr. produce; agr.-processing; p. (1970) 52,657.

Rutbah, t., **Iraq**; on oil pipeline from Iraq to Haifa; impt. ctr. on trans-desert routes.

Rutherglen, royal burgh, Strathclyde Reg., **Scot.**; on R. Clyde, S.E. of Glasgow; chemicals, tubes, paper, wire ropes, bolts.

Ruthin, t., Glyndwr, Clwyd, **Wales**; Vale of Clwyd, 13 km S.E. of Denbigh; p. (1981) 4,430.

Rutland, former Midland co., **Eng.**; sm. co. of 394 km², now part of Leics. and l. gov. dist. based on Oakham; p. (1981) 30,670.

Ruwenzori mtn. range, on **Uganda–Zaïre** border; overlooking W. arm of Gt. Rift Valley, midway between L. Mobutu Seso and L. Edward; hgst. peaks, Mt. Margherita (5,123 m), Mt. Alexandra (5,109 m); lower slopes covered in equatorial rain forest, coffee plantations on middle slopes above 1,500 m.

Rwanda, indep. rep., **Central Africa**; former kingdom of Ruanda, part of UN trust terr. of Ruanda-Urundi under Belgian admin. (until 1962); sm., landlocked st., S. of equator, consisting of upland plateau at 1,200 m; mainly subsistence agr. under gt. strain with rapid p. growth; coffee (ch. exp.), cotton, pyrethrum (3rd lgst. world producer), cattle; tin, tungsten and natural gas discoveries; little ind.; cap. Kigali; a. 26,338 km²; p. (est. 1984) 5,903,000.

Ryazan, c., cap. of R. oblast, **RSFSR**; on Oka R.; food inds., agr. machin., footwear, chemicals; mediaeval architecture; p. (est. 1980) 462,000.

Rybinsk, c., major R. pt., **RSFSR**; on upper Volga; tr. and shipping ctr. since 16th cent.; site of hydroelectric power sta.; shipbldg., engin.; p. (est. 1980) 241,000.

Rybinsk Sea (Rybinsk Reservoir), **RSFSR**; artificial L.; created behind dams on R. Volga and R. Sheksna at Rybinsk; part of scheme to regulate flow of R. Volga and to incorporate it in a vast inland waterway system; opened 1945; a. 3,885 km.

Rybnik, t., Katowice prov., S.W. **Poland**; ctr. of coal-mng. dist.; p. (est. 1983) 133,000.

Rydal Water, L., nr. Ambleside, Cumbria, **Eng.**; adjacent v. contains Rydal Mount, home of Wordsworth.

Ryde, t., Medina, I. of Wight, **Eng.**; on N.E. cst.; yachting ctr. and seaside resort; boat and yacht bldg.; steamer connection across Spithead to Portsmouth; p. (1981) 24,346.

Rye, t., Rother, East Sussex, **Eng.**; at mouth of R. Rother to W. of Dungeness; one of the Cinque pts.; Ypres cas.; tourist ctr.; p. (1981) 4,293.

Ryedale, l. gov. dist., North Yorks., **Eng.**; lge. a.

inc. Malton, Pickering, Norton, Kirby Moorside and Helmsley; p. (1981) 84,113.

Ryton, t., Tyne and Wear, **Eng.**; on R. Tyne, W. of Newcastle; p. (1981) 15,023.

Ryukyu Is., archipelago, between Kyushu I., **Japan,** and Taiwan; ch. t. Naha on Okinawa I.; following second world war Is. S. of Lat. 30° N. occupied by USA; Amami and Tokara grs. returned to Japan 1953; American military installations on Okinawa withdrawn 1972; lge. Is. mtnous., volcanic; sweet potatoes, sugarcane, pineapples; 3 lge. oil refineries; a. 2,196 km²; p. (est. 1970) 945,111.

Rzeszów, c., cap. of R. prov., S.E. **Poland;** at foot of Carpathian highlands; route ctr.; growing industl. t.; p. (est. 1983) 134,400.

Rzhev, c., **RSFSR**; on Volga R.; rly. ctr. on main line to Moscow; agr. processing; p. (est. 1970) 49,000.

S

Saale, R., **E. Germany**; rises in Fichtelgebirge flows N. through Thuringia to Elbe; attractive, well wooded valley; irrigation; hydroelec. power; 360 km long.

Saalfeld, t., Gera, **E. Germany**; on R. Saale; famous cas., iron-mng.; machin., chocolate; p. (est. 1970) 33,405.

Saarland, Land, **W. Germany**; heavy inds. based on lge. coalfields; drained by R. Saar; cap. Saarbrücken; admin. by League of Nations 1919–35. returned to Germany after plebiscite; economic attachment to France after second world war; reunited politically with W. Germany 1957; a. 2,567 km²; p. (1982) 1,057,500.

Saarbrücken, c., cap. of Saarland, **W. Germany**; on R. Saar, nr. Fr. border; cas.; rich coalfield; iron and steel wks., textiles, leather, paper, oil refining at Klarenthal nearby; p. (1983) 190,100.

Saaremaa (Osel), I., Baltic Sea; at entrance to G. of Riga, Estonian **SSR**; low plateau, bleak and barren; ch. t. Kingisepp (Kuressaare); a. 2,720 km².

Saariouis (Saarlautern), Saarland, **W. Germany**; on R. Saar; coal mng.; wood and metal inds.; founded by Louis XIV; birthplace of Marshal Ney; p. (1983) 37,900.

Sabadell, t., Spain; N.W. of Barcelona; textiles, fertilisers, paper; p. (1981) 176,554.

Sabah, E. Malaysia; attempted secession 1975; formerly N. Borneo; underdeveloped; tropical forest; forest prods., inc. rubber, the major exp.; main pt. Sandakan; cap. Kota Kinabalu; a. 76,112 km²; p. (est. 1970) 656,00.

Sabahiyah, t., **Kuwait**; new t. being built between Ahmadi and Fahahil.

Sabara, t., Minas Gerais, **Brazil**; historic c.; museum of gold; p. (est. 1968) 26,464.

Sabine, R., Texas and La., **USA**; flows through S. Lake (an expansion of the R. 29 km long) to G. of Mexico; 936 km long.

Sable I., off S.E. cst. Nova Scotia, **Canada**; sandy I., scene of many shipwrecks.

Sacramento, c., st. cap. Cal., **USA**; on R. Sacramento; shipping and industl. ctr.; rly. wk.-shps., smelting, meat and fruit packing, flour, lumber, metal prods., rocket and missiles ind.; p. (1980) 276,000 (c.), 1,014,000 (met. a.).

Sacramento, R., Cal., **USA**; forms N. section of Central Valley projected for irrigation, hydroelectric power and flood control; 624 km long.

Saddleback (Blencathara), mtn., Cumbria, **Eng.**; nr. Keswick; alt. 868 m.

Saddleworth, t., Gtr. Manchester, **Eng.**; in Pennines, 8 km N.E. of Oldham; woollens, paper mkg., engin.; p. (1981) 21,851.

Saffron Walden, mkt. t., Uttlesford, Essex, **Eng.**; on E. Anglian heights; cas., abbey ruins; saffron crocus once cultivated here; p. (1981) 12,515.

Safi, spt., **Morocco**; on Atl. Oc.; linked by rail

to phosphate deposits at Youssoufia; pottery, fish-processing; resort; p. (est. 1973) 129,100 (t.), 214,600 (met. a.).

Saga, c., cap. of S. pref., Kyushu, **Japan**; coalmng. ctr., textiles, ceramics; p. (1979) 163,793.

Saganoseki, t., N.E. Kyushu, **Japan**; on Bungo strait; impt. gold, copper, and silver mines; smelting.

Sagar, t., Karnataka, **India**; nr. Krishna R. valley; p. (1971) 118,574 (t.), 154,785 (met. a.).

Saginaw, c., Mich., **USA**; on R. Saginaw; former fur and lumbering region; coal; beans, sugarbeet; various mnfs.; p. (1980) 228,000 (met. a.).

Saguenay, R., Quebec, **Canada**; trib. of St. Lawrence R.; outlet of L. St. John; used for hydroelec. power; tourism; length c. 176 km.

Sagunto, t., **Spain**; nr. Valencia; integrated steelwks. projected; anc. t., sieged by Hannibal; p. (1981) 54,759 (met. a.).

Sahara, the gr. N. African desert between the Sudan and the Barbary sts., extending from the Atl. to the Nile, inc. Tripoli and Fezzan; a. 16,835,000 km²; numerous oases with ts. and tr. ctrs.; oil pipelines to Algerian and Tunisian csts.; p. (est. 2,500,000), nomadic Arab and Berber tribes.

Saharan Arab Democratic Rep. See **Western Sahara.**

Saharan Atlas, S. range of Atlas mtns. in Algeria; ch. peaks., Jebel Aurès, 2,331 m. J. Aissa, 2,242 m, J. Ksel, 2,011 m.

Saharanpur, c., Uttar Pradesh, N.W. **India**; woodcarving, furniture, agr.-processing inds.; p. (1971) 225,396.

Sahel, region of **W. Africa,** inc. Chad, Mali, Mauritania, Niger, Senegal and Bourkina Fasso, which suffered severe famine and drought 1972–4 and 1984–5 caused by desertification of an area marginal to Sahara Desert.

Saïda (Sidon), t., **Lebanon**; on Mediterranean, S. of Beirut; terminus of oil pipeline from Saudi Arabia; refinery; p. (est. 1975) 33,500.

Saigon. See **Ho Chi-minh City.**

Saimaa, L. system, **Finland**; a. of water which forms basin of R. Vuoksi; canal connects with C. of Finland and runs partly through Soviet terr.; a. 1,699 km².

Saingdin Falls, Burma; on Kaladan R.; site of new hydroelec. power sta.

St. Abb's Head, rocky promontory, lighthouse, Berwick, **Scot.**

St. Albans, c., l. gov. dist., Herts., **Eng.**; on N. margin of Vale of St. Albans, 32 km N.W. of London; faces remains of Roman Verulamium across R. Ver; lt. inds., electronics, instrument mkg.; cath.; residtl.; p. (1981) 124,867.

St. Amand, t., Cher dep., **France**; on R. Cher; Roman remains; new recreational park; p. (1982) 12,801.

St. Andrews, royal burgh, North East Fife, **Scot.**; seaside resort; univ.; famous golf course; p. (1981) 11,302.

St. Anthony, waterfalls, on R. Mississippi; **USA**; predominant factor in site of Minneapolis.

St. Asaph, t., Rhuddlan, Clwyd, N. **Wales**; on R. Clwyd; p. (1971) 11,755 (dist.).

St. Austell with Fowey, mkt. ts., Restormel, Cornwall, **Eng.**; on S. flank of Hensbarrow; ctr. of Cornwall's china clay ind.; p. (1981) 36,639.

St. Barthélemy, Fr. I., **W.I.**; dependency of Guadeloupe; cash crops of sugar, bananas, cacao; cap. Gustavia; p. (est. 1975) 2,500.

St. Bees Head, promontory, 4 km N.W. of St. Bees, Cumbria, **Eng.**; freestone quarries, anhydrite.

St. Bernard Pass, Great, on Italian–Swiss bdy., W. Alps; carries main road from W. Switzerland to Plain of Lombardy; 2,477 m a.s.l.; road tunnel (5·6 km) constr. 1958–62 links Cantine de Proz (Valais can., Switzerland) and St. Rhémy (Italy); under tunnel will run projected 416 km pipeline from Genoa to Aigle.

St. Bernard Pass, Little, on French–Italian bdy. W. Alps; links Isère valley with Val d'Aosta; alt. 2,190 m.

St. Boniface, t., Manitoba, **Canada**; sub. of Winnipeg; meat-packing, petroleum prods.; p. (1971) 46,661.

St. Bride's Bay, Dyfed, **Wales.**

St. Brieuc, t., cap. of Côtes-du-Nord dep., N.W. **France**; sm. fish. pt.; iron and steel wks.; cath.; p. (1982) 51,399.

St. Catharines, c., Ont., **Canada**; on Welland Ship Canal; mkt. for Niagara fruit-growing region; agr. implements, textile, paper and flour mills, vehicle components; resort; p. (1979) 123,350.

St. Chamond, t., Loire, **France**; nr. St. Etienne; ribbons, rayon; rly. wks.; coal mng.; p. (1982) 82,059 (met. a.).

St. Clair, L., **Canada–USA**; part of link between L. Huron and L. Erie; a. 1,191 km².

St. Clair, R., **N. America**; flows from L. Huron through L. of St. Clair into L. Erie; forms bdy. between Mich. (USA) and Ont. (Canada); impt. link in Gr. Ls. waterway; length 136 km, depth dredged to 6 m.

St. Clair Shores, t., Mich., **USA**; residtl. sub. of Detroit; p. (1980) 76,210.

St. Cloud, W. sub. of Paris, **France**; fine park; porcelain; p. (1982) 28,760.

St. Cloud, t., Minn., **USA**; on R. Mississippi; granite quarries; st. college; p. (1980) 42,566 (t.), 163,256 (met. a.).

St.-Cyr-l'Ecole, t., Yvelines, **France**; once famous for military school founded by Napoleon; bldgs. destroyed second world war; p. (1982) 16,380.

St. Davids, t., Dyfed, **Wales**; 24 km S.W. of Fishguard; on site of anc. Minevia; cath., ruins of Bishop Gower's palace (1342); p. 1,595.

St. David's Head, promontory, Dyfed, **Wales**.

St. Denis, t., N. sub., Paris, **France**; on R. Seine; abbey, burial place of Fr. kings; chemicals., machin.; p. (1982) 91,275.

St. Denis, spt., cap. of Ile de la Réunion (Fr.), Indian Oc.; p. (1982) 109,072.

St. Dié, t., Vosges, **France**; on R. Meurthe; cath.; textile ctr., hosiery; p. (1982) 24,816.

St. Dizier, t., Haute-Marne, dep. **France**; on R. Marne; metallurgy; p. (1982) 37,445.

St. Edmundsbury, l. gov. dist., Suffolk, **Eng.**; based on Bury St. Edmunds and inc. Haverhill; p. (1981) 86,054.

St. Elias, mtns., Alaska, **USA**; and Yukon, **Canada**; inc. Mt. McKinley (5,780 m); source of world's lgst. icefield outside polar regions.

Saintes, t., Charente-Maritime dep., **France**; cath.; Roman antiquities; suffered in Huguenot wars; agr. implements; earthenware; p. (1982) 27,486.

St. Etienne, t., cap. of Loire dep., **France**; nr. Lyons; in sm. coal basin on edge of Central Massif; famous for firearms; modern inds. inc. engin., dyes, chemicals, textiles, glass; p. (1982) 206,688.

St. Gall (St. Gallen), t., cap. of can. St. G., **Switzerland**; founded around Benedictine monastery (7th–8th cent.); embroidered cottons; p. (1978) 75,400.

St. Gall (St. Gallen), can., **Switzerland**; borders L. Constance, rising to S.; mainly industl.; ch. ind. textiles; cap. St. G.; a. 2,012 km²; p. (1980) 391,995.

St. George's Channel, Brit. Isles, part of Irish Sea, separating Wales from Ireland.

St. George's, t., cap. of Grenada, **W.I.**; ch. spt.; built around submerged volcanic crater forming St. G. Bay; p. (1970) 7,303.

St. Germain-en-Laye, t., Yvelines, **France**; on R. Seine; outer sub. of Paris; residtl.; popular resort; birthplace of Debussy; p. (1982) 40,829.

Saint Gotthard, mtn. gr., Alps, S. central **Switzerland**; crossed by St. G. pass (2,115 m); rly. passes through St. G. tunnel (14·8 km, max. alt. 1,155 m); road tunnel (16·3 km) opened 1980, longest in world; motorways linking pass with Zürich, Basle, and Lugano being built.

St. Gowan's Head, promontory, Dyfed, **Wales**.

St. Helena, I., Brit., col., **Atl. Oc.**; 1,920 km from W. cst. Africa; spt. and only t. Jamestown; Napoleon imprisoned 1815–21, and Boer captives 1900; famous for its wirebird, species of plover peculiar to I.; a. 122 km²; p. (1981) 5,268.

St. Helens, t., met. dist., Merseyside, **Eng.**; 19 km E. of Liverpool; connected by canal with R. Mersey; coal, iron, alkali; copper smelting, glass, fibreglass, plastics; p. (1981) 189,909.

St. Helier, spt., Jersey, Channel Is., **Eng.**; resort; cas.; tr. in early vegetables; p. (1976) 26,343.

St. Hyancinthe, t., spt., Quebec, **Canada**; on Yamaska R.; cath.; famous for organs; lt. inds.; p. (1971) 24,562.

St. Ives, t., Penwith, Cornwall, **Eng.**; at entrance to St. Ives Bay; fishing, holiday resort; p. (1981) 10,985.

St. Ives, t., Camb., **Eng.**; on R. Ouse, 6 km E. of Huntingdon; borders the Fens; R. Ouse crossed by 16th cent. bridge containing a chapel; p. (1981) 12,278.

St. Jean, t., Quebec, **Canada**; on Richelieu R.; timber, grain exps.; textiles, sewing machines, p. (est. 1971) 32,863.

St. John, c., spt., N.B., **Canada**; lgst. c. of N.B.; ice-free pt.; lge. dry docks; rly. terminus; impt. inds. inc. sugar- and oil-refining, paper, textiles; p. (1979) 147,900 (met. a.).

St. John, L., Quebec, **Canada**; on Saguenay R.; tourism; a. 971 km².

St. John, R., Maine, N.B., **Canada, USA**; flows to B. of Fundy forming section of international boundary; 720 km long.

St. John's, t., cap. of Antigua, **W.I.**; pt.; airpt.; cath.; ch. comm. ctr. of I.; p. (est. 1973) 14,000.

St. John's, c. spt., cap. of Newfoundland, **Canada**; on E. cst.; first English settlement in America early 16th cent.; gr. tr. in fish with allied inds.; univ., 2 caths.; p. (1979) 118,700.

St. Johns, R., **USA**; drains swamps of central Fla., 21 km from Atl. Oc.; 560 km long.

St. John's Wood, residtl. dist., Westminster London, **Eng.**; contains Lord's Cricket Ground.

St. Joseph, t., Mich., **USA**; pt. on L. Mich.; ctr. of fruit-growing a.; resort; p. (1980) 9,622.

St. Joseph, t., Mo., **USA**; declining pt. on R. Mississippi; agr. tr. and processing; p. (1980) 76,691 (t.), 101,868 (met. a.).

St. Just, t., Penwith, Cornwall, **Eng.**; nr. Lands End, 10 km W. of Penzance; former tin-mng. ctr.; p. (1981) 4,047.

St. Kilda, rocky I., most W. of the Hebrides, **Scot.**; 5 km long; bird sanctuary, famous for its wren, a sub-species.

St. Kitts-Nevis, Leeward gr. of Is., **W.I.**; aut. st. in association with Gt. Britain; indep. (1983); sugar, sea island cotton, molasses; a. 262 km²; cap. Basse-Terre; p. (est. 1980) 50,000.

St. Laurent, t., Quebec, **Canada**; industl. t. on Montreal I., W. of Montreal; p. (1976) 62,826.

St. Lawrence, G. of, Canada; arm of Atl. Oc., partly enclosed by Newfoundland and Nova Scotia; impt. fisheries.

St. Lawrence I., Alaska, **USA**; in Bering Sea; 160 km long.

St. Lawrence, R., Canada; major outlet from Gr. Lakes; forms bdy. between USA and Canada; ch. tribs. Ottawa, Richelieu, St. Maurice, Saguenay Rs.; with St. L. Seaway forms a major waterway facing Europe; grain, timber, oil, iron-ore traffic; used for hydroelectric power; total length from source (St. Louis) 3,360 km.

St. Lawrence Seaway, N. America; joint Canada–USA project links head of the Gr. Lakes with Atl. Oc., providing channel for lge. ocean-going vessels to reach American continent; provides major source of hydroelectric power to industl. a.; opened 1959.

St. Lô, t. cap. of Manche dep., N.W. **France**; built on rocky hill overlooking R. Vire; cath.; p. (1982) 24,792.

St. Louis, t., Ile de la Réunion, **Indian Oc.**; p. (1962) 7,753.

St. Louis, t., **Senegambia**, W. Africa; at mouth of R. Senegal; cath.; former cap.; comm. ctr.; impt. fish. pt.; p. (1976) 88,000.

St. Louis, c., Mo., **USA**; on R. Mississippi 16 km below confluence of Rs. Mississippi and Missouri; two univs., impt. rly. and river junc.; mkt. for furs, livestock, grain, farm prod.; banking and fin. ctr.; varied mnfs.; machin., cars, aircraft, leather gds., beer, chemicals; p. (1980) 451,000 (c.), 2,345,000 (met. a.).

St. Lucia I., fully indep. st. (1979); Windward Is., **W.I.**; volcanic, forested, fertile valleys; exp. bananas and other tropical agr. prod.; airpt.; cap. Castries; a. 616 km²; hurricane disaster 1980; p. (est. 1980) 124,000.

St. Malo, spt., Ile-et-Vilaine dep., N.W. **France**; on Normandy cst.; cath.; once fortfd.; shipping, fishing, and tourist inds.; p. (1982) 47,324.

St. Martin, I., Leeward Is., **W.I.**; N. part Fr. dependency of Guadeloupe, S. part belongs to Neth. Antilles; divided since 1648; ch. exp. salt; total p. (est. 1970) 5,061.

St. Marylebone. *See* **Westminster, City of.**

St. Mary's I., Scilly Is., Brit. Isles.

St. Maur-des-Fossés, residtl. garden sub. of Paris, Val-de-Marne dep., France; p. (1982) 80,954.

St. Maurice, v., Valais, Switzerland; nr. Martigny; 6th-cent. abbey; once a leading Burgundian t.; p. c. 10,000.

St. Maurice, R., Quebec, Canada; trib. of St. Lawrence R.; used for timber transport and hydroelec. power; 520 km long.

St. Mawes, v., Cornwall, Eng.; on E. cst. of estuary of R. Fal; cas.; holiday resort, fishing.

St. Michael's Mt., castled rock, Cornwall, Eng.; the anc. Ictis; alt. 70 m.

St. Monance, burgh, North East Fife, Scot.; resort; p. (1981) 1,248.

St. Moritz, resort and winter sports ctr., Switzerland; in the Upper Engadine; alt. 1,857 m; p. (1970) 5,699.

St. Nazaire, t., Loire-Atlantique dep., W. France; spt. at mouth of R. Loire, outport for Nantes; growing pt. and industl. ctr.; shipyds., iron and steel, fertilisers, aircraft, oil refining; p. (1982) 68,947.

St. Neots, mkt. t., Cambs. Eng.; on R. Ouse, 16 km N.E. of Bedford; brewing, milling, paper-mkg.; expanded t.; p. (1981) 21,185.

St. Nikilaas, mftg. t., E. Flanders, Belgium; nr. Antwerp; textile ctr., carpets; p. (1982) 25,432.

St. Omer, t., Pas-de-Calais dep., N. France; ctr. of mkt.-gardening a.; textiles, food inds.; cath., abbey ruins; p. (1982) 53,748 (met. a.).

St. Ouen, N. sub. of Paris, Seine-St. Denis dep., France; on R. Seine at base of Butte de Montmartre; metals, chemicals, glues, tanning; p. (1982) 43,743.

St. Pancras. See Camden.

St. Paul, spt., Ile de la Réunion, Indian Oc.; p. (1968) 43,129.

St. Paul, c., cap. of Minn., USA; faces Minneapolis across Mississippi; cath.; univ.; ctr. of agr. dist.; agr. mkt. and processing; car assembly, oil refining, electronics; p. (1980) 639,000 (c.), 2,109,000 (met. a.) with Minneapolis.

St. Paul, I., Indian Oc.; bare volcanic islet rising to 493 m; part of Fr. Southern and Antarctic Terr.; uninhabited.

St. Peter Port, spt., cap. of Guernsey, Channel Is.; exp. fruit, flowers, vegetables; resort; p. (1971) 16,303.

St. Petersburg, c., Fla., USA; resort on Tampa Bay; p. (1980) 239,000 (part of Tampa met. a.).

St. Pierre, t., Martinique I., Fr. W.I.; utterly destroyed and all inhabitants save one by eruption of Mt. Pelée 1902; tourism.

St. Pierre, t., Réunion, Indian Oc.; sm. artificial harbour; p. (est. 1971) 43,808.

St. Pierre and Miquelon, Fr. dep., consisting of 8 sm. Is. off S. cst. of Newfoundland; a. of St. Pierre gr. 26 km²; a. of Miquelon gr. 215 km²; ch. t. St. Pierre, fisheries; p. of St. P. and M. (1982) 6,000.

St. Pölten, t., Lower Austria; nr. Vienna; founded round an abbey; textiles, machin.; p. (1971) 50,144.

St. Quentin, t., Aisne dep., France; on R. Somme; impt. textile ctr.; p. (1982) 65,067.

St. Raphaël, t., Var dep., S.E. France; resort on Fr. Riviera, S.W. of Cannes; marina; p. (1982) 24,310.

St. Rémy, t., Bouches-du-Rhône dep., France; Roman antiquities; p. (1982) 8,439.

St. Thomas, t., Ont., Canada; ctr. of agr. dist.; rly. ctr.; lt. inds.; p. (1971) 25,062.

St. Thomas, I., Atl. Oc.; main economic ctr. of USA Virgin Is.; 80 per cent of p. live in pt. of Charlotte Amalie; tourism; p. (est. 1968) 31,867.

St. Thomas I. See São Tomé.

St. Trond, t., Limburg, Belgium; impt. fruit mkt.; p. (1982) 36,591.

St. Tropez, t., Var dep., S.E. France; on Fr. Riviera; popular, expanding tourist resort; marina; p. (1982) 6,248.

St. Vincent, C., S.W. Portugal; Spanish fleet defeated by British 1797.

St. Vincent, Gulf of, lge. inlet, S. Australia; penetrates 160 km inland, max. width 65 km; pt. Adelaide is on E. side.

St. Vincent, I., fully ind. st. (1979); one of Windward gr., W.I.; volcanic; exp. bananas, arrowroot from alluvial soils in S.W. which has majority of p.; subsistence agr. on hill slopes; cap. Kingstown; inc. 5 Is. in Grena-

dines; a. 389 km²; p. (est. 1980) 107,000.

Sakai, sub. of Osaka, Honshu, Japan; industl. ctr., engin., chemicals, textiles, electricity generation; p. (1979) 794,680.

Sakhalin, I., off cst. of Siberia; with Kuriles forms Sakhalin oblast of RSFSR; herring fisheries, coal, naphtha, alluvial gold, oil, timber, natural gas; oil pipelines connected to Komsomolsk and Khabarovsk refineries; a. c. 63,610 km²; p. (1970) 616,000.

Sakashima Is. See Ryuku.

Sakura-jima, peninsula, S. Kyushu, Japan; former I. joined to mainland by lava flows; famed for fruit and vegetables.

Sala, t., Västmanland, Sweden; silver mine worked for over 400 years, now to limited extent; lime, bricks; p. (1961) 11,015.

Salado, R., N.W. Argentina; impt. Andean trib. of Paraná R.; 800 km long.

Salamanca, t., Guanajuato st., Mexico; oil refining; ammonia plant; natural gas pipeline to Guadalajara; p. (1979) 105,543.

Salamanca, t., cap. of S. prov., Spain; on R. Tormes; old univ., 2 caths., many convents; p. (1981) 167,131.

Salamis, I., Greece; opposite harbour of Athens; spt. and ch. t. S.; famous naval battle 480 B.C.; p. (1981) 20,807.

Salar de Uyumi, windswept, dry, salt flat, S.W. Bolivia.

Salavat, t., RSFSR; in Bashkiria, 144 km S. of Ufa; ctr. of oilfield; glass factory; became t. in 1954; p. (est. 1980) 140,000.

Sala-y-Gomez, barren, uninhabited volcanic I., Pac. Oc.; belonging to Chile, 328 km E.N.E. of Easter I.

Salazar, Mexico; nr. Mexico City; alt. 2,897 m; nuclear reactor for radioisotopes for medical, industl. and agr. purposes.

Salcombe, t., South Hams, S. Devon, Eng.; mkt.; fishing; resort; p. (1981) 2,374.

Saldanha Bay, inlet on W. cst. C. of Good Hope, S. Africa; whaling, fishing; fish-canning at t. of S.B.; p. (1960) 2,195 (t.).

Sale, t., Victoria, Australia; tr. of lge. irrigated agr. a.; gas processing and crude oil stabilisation plant (1969) ; p. (1976) 12,111.

Sale, t., Trafford, Gtr. Manchester, Eng.; residtl. sub. of Manchester; p. (1981) 57,824.

Sale or Salch, spt., Fez, Morocco; former pirate headquarters; fishing, fish-processing, carpets; p. (est. 1971) 155,557.

Salekhard, t., R. pt., N.W. Siberia, RSFSR; on R. Ob; fisheries, collecting ctr. for furs; exp. timber; p. c. 22,000.

Salem, t., Tamil Nadu, India; industl. ctr., rly. junc. in picturesque valley; local iron ore, manganese mng.; mineral processing, textiles; p. (1971) 308,716 (t.), 416,440 (met. a.).

Salem, t., Mass., USA; 24 km from Boston; one of oldest New England ts.; many fine bldgs.; textiles, leather prods., machin., electronics; p. (1980) 38,220.

Salem, t., st. cap. Ore., USA; on Willamette R.; univ.; fruit packing, flour milling and canning; p. (1980) 250,000 (met. a.).

Salemi, t., Sicily, Italy; the anc. Halicyæ; famous Norman cas., terracotta vases; p. (1981) 12,289.

Salerno, c., cap. of Salerno prov., in Campania, S. Italy; on G. of S.; fishing pt. and comm. ctr.; machin., textiles, food processing; univ.; famous for Allied landing 1943; p. (1981) 157,385.

Salford, c., met. dist., Gtr. Manchester, Eng.; on R. Irwell, adjoining Manchester; inc. terminal docks of Manchester Ship Canal; univ.; varied inds.; p. and industl. decentralization; p. (1981) 24,736.

Salgótarján, t., N. Hungary; coal mng., agr. machin., tools, glass; p. (1970) 37,000.

Salina, t., Kan., USA; on Smoky Hill R.; univ.; flour milling, cattle mkt., farm implements; p. (1980) 41,843.

Salinas, t., Cal., USA; comm., tr. and processing ctr. for fertile Salinas valley; birthplace of John Steinbeck; p. (1980) 290,000 (met. a.).

Salinas, R., Cal., USA; rises in US Coast Range, flows N.W. into Bay of Monterey, Pac. Oc.; fertile valley floor irrigated to produce hard and stone fruits, mkt. garden produce (especially lettuce), alfalfa; 166 km long.

Salinas-Grandes, Las, gr. salt marsh region, Argentina; provs. Santiago del Estero and Cordoba; dry, no Rs.

Salisbury, t., South **Australia;** part of Adelaide; research ctr. for long-range weapons; p. (1976) 77,476.

Salisbury (New Sarum), cath. c., l. gov. dist., Wilts., **Eng.;** on S. edge of Salisbury Plain at confluence of Rs. Avon and Wily; Old Sarum to N. was the Roman Sorbiodunum and present site represents a move (1220) to a more sheltered and better watered a. in valley; cath. pure Early English with tallest spire in Eng. (123 m); ctr. mediaeval woollen ind.; regional ctr. with engin. and food-processing inds.; p. (1981) 100,929 (dist.).

Salisbury. *See* Harare.

Salisbury Plain, Wilts., **Eng.;** chalk upland, N. of Salisbury; Stonehenge; army training a.; a. 777 km².

Salonika. *See* Thessaloniki.

Salmon, R., Idaho, **USA;** canyon *c.* 1·6 km deep and 16 km wide in places; rapids navigable downstream only, thus its name of River of No Return; l. *c.* 680 km.

Salop. *See* Shropshire.

Salpau Selka, Finland; most S. gravel ridge.

Salsette, I., **India;** connected by bridge and causeway with Bombay; popular seaside resort at Juhu; a. 624 km².

Salt, R., Arizona, **USA;** rises in Colorado plateau, flows into Gila R. below Phoenix; rich, irrigated fruit growing valley in lower course; many multipurpose schemes in Salt River Valley project; length 384 km. *See also* Roosevelt Dam.

Salta, c., cap. of Salta prov., **Argentina;** on R. Salta; picturesque c. with colonial atmosphere, cath.; comm. ctr. for rich agr. a.; p. (1975) 176,216.

Saltash, mkt. t., Caradon, Cornwall, **Eng.;** on W. side of Tamar estuary; lowest bridging point of Tamar by Brunel's rly. bridge (1859) and toll road bridge; p. (1981) 12,659.

Saltburn and Markse-by-the-Sea, t., Langbaurgh, Cleveland, **Eng.;** seaside resort; 16 km E. of Middlesborough; p. (1981) 19,989.

Saltcoats, burgh, Cunninghame, **Scot.;** on Firth of Clyde 3 km S. of Ardrossan; sm. harbour; hosiery; mainly residtl.; p. (1981) 12,807.

Saltillo, c., cap. of Coahuila st., **Mexico;** comm., industl., and mng. ctr.; p. (1979) 258,492.

Salt Lake City, c., cap. of Utah, **USA;** nr. Gr. Salt L., H.Q. of Mormonism; temple and univ.; agr. comm. ctr. for irrigated a.; meat packing; p. (1980) 163,000 (c.), 963,000 (met. a.).

Salto, c., cap. of S. dep., **Uruguay;** on Uruguay R., nr. Concordia (Argentina); rly. and tr. ctr. for agr. a.; citrus fruit, grapes, wine; p. (est. 1970) 176,250.

Salton Sea, L., S. Cal., **USA;** 80 m below sealevel in depression which extends N.W. from head of G. of Cal.; ctr. of inland drainage; a. 699 km². *See also* Imperial Valley.

Salvador, spt., cap. of Bahia, **Brazil;** Brazil's first cap.; many years of economic stagnation now replaced by rapid growth; Brazil's first oil strike here in 1939; refining less impt. than petrochemicals at Camaçari complex (started 1972); new pt., naval base; hydro-elect. from Paulo Afonso encouraging many new light inds.; cement, aluminium, laminated timber, special alloys; p. (est. 1980) 1,501,700.

Salvador, El, rep., on Pac. cst. of **Central America;** bounded by Guatemala to W. and Honduras to N. and E.; comprises 14 administrative departments; serious internal unrest (1983); temperate volcanic uplands, hot humid coastal lowlands; comm. economy mainly agr., especially coffee, also developing comm. fisheries and iron and steel ind.; electric power from dam across Lempa R.; well-developed transport system, inc. Pan-American Highway; pt. at Acajutla and airport at Ilopango; member of Central American Common Market; cap. San Salvador; a. 21,331 km²; p. (est. 1984) 5,388,000.

Salween, R., S.E. **Asia;** rises in E. Tibet, crosses Yunnan, descending into Burma to empty in G. of Martaban; many rapids; navigable to Moulmein; hydroelec. scheme; 2,880 km long.

Salzburg, c., cap. of Salzburg prov., **Austria;** on R. Salzach; cath.; cas.; birthplace of Mozart; tourist resort; annual music festival; p. (1978) 140,000.

Salzburg, prov., **Austria;** adjoins Bavaria and the Tyrol, on N. slope of E. Alps; pastoral agr.; timber and some mineral wealth; hydroelectric power; cap. Salzburg; a. 7,154 km²; p. (1971) 399,000.

Salzgitter, t., Lower Saxony, **W. Germany;** S.W. of Brunswick; steel, engin., wagon bldg., fertilisers; p. (1983) 111,100.

Salzkammergut, lake dist., Upper **Austria;** saline baths at Aussee and Ischl; tourist region; stock-raising forestry.

Samar, I., **Philippines;** separated from Leyte by narrow strait; mainly forested mtns.; hemp, rice in lowlands; cap. Catbalogan; typhoons; a. 13,080 km²; p. (1970) 997,336.

Samarkand, c., Uzbek SSR, **USSR;** one of oldest cs. in world, sited in productive oasis on Zeravshan R.; many historical associations and anc. bldgs; agr. tr. ctr.; food processing; cotton, silk; univ.; p. (est. 1980) 481,000.

Samarra, t., Iraq; on Tigris R., N. of Baghdad; holy c. of Shiite sect; p. c. 10,000.

Sambalpur, t., Orissa, **India;** on Hirakud reservoir of Mahandi R.; p. (1971) 64,675.

Sambhar, salt lake, Rajasthan, **India;** exploited on lge. scale; a. 233 km².

Sambre, R., trib. of R. Meuse at Namur; crosses Franco-Belgian coal basin; part of N. Fr.–S. Belgian waterway system; 176 km long.

Samnan, t., N. **Iran;** in foothills of Elburz mtns.; iron, sulphur ores, petroleum.

Samoa, archipelago, S. Pac. Oc.; volcanic mtns., tropical climate; agr., fishing; comprises (1) American Samoa, a. 197 km²; p. (est. 1976) 31,000; (2) Western Samoa, indep. st., cap. and ch. spt. Apia; a. 2,841 km²; p. (est. 1981) 200,000. *See* Western Samoa.

Sámos, I., Aegean Sea, off W. cst. Anatolia. belonging to **Greece;** mtnous., fine climate, fertile soils; wine, tobacco, Med. crops; ch. t. Vathy; a. 466 km²; p. (1981) 40,519.

Samothrace, I., Aegean Sea, **Greece;** barren, mtnous.; sparse p.; goats, grain, olives, sponge fishing; a. 184 km²; p. c. 4,000.

Samsö, I., Kattegat, **Denmark;** a. 109 km²; p. (est. 1965) 5,852.

Samsun, spt., Trabzon, **Turkey;** on Black Sea cst.; exp. tobacco, grain, timber, wax, wool, skins, copper gds., antimony, chemical complex; p. (1979) 197,090.

San, R., S.E. **Poland;** trib. of R. Vistula; bdy. between Poland and Ukraine; navigable in lower course; 442 km long.

Sana'a, c., cap. of **Yemen Arab Rep.;** walled c. at 2,217 m; tr. in silk, cottons, hides, grapes; handicraft inds.; Islamic cultural and educational ctr.; p. (1975) 134,588.

San Andreas Fault, Cal., **USA;** shearing plate bdy. which extends from G. of Cal. to San Francisco; stress liable to cause sudden sharp earthquake as it did in 1906. *See* **F9**.

San Angelo, t., Texas, **USA;** on R. Concho; cattle, wool, mohair mkt.; dairy produce, petroleum, machine-shop prod.; p. (1980) 73,240.

San Antonio, sm. coastal t., **Angola,** Africa; at mouth of R. Zaïre; serves as occasional pt. of embarkation for travellers from lower regions of Zaïre.

San Antonio, spt., **Chile;** nearest pt. for Santiago; holiday resort; agr. prods.; exp. copper; p. (1970) 60,826.

San Antonio, C., most W. point of **Cuba.**

San Antonio, c., cap. of Bexar co., Texas, **USA;** in fertile San Antonio valley; serves farming and livestock a.; oil refining, food processing, meat packing; military installations in a.; warm climate attracts winter tourist tr.; Mexican atmosphere; siege of Alamo (1836); p. (1980) 786,000 (c.), 1,072,000 (met. a.).

San Bernardino, c., Cal., **USA;** founded and planned by Mormons (1852) rly. ctr.; citrus fruit packing and tr.; p. (1980) 876,000; part of Riverside met. a.

San Bruno, t., Cal., **USA;** 16 km S. of San Francisco; site of international airpt.; printing, mainly residtl.; p. (1980) 35,417.

San Carlos, t., Luzon, **Philippines;** p. (est. 1970) 90,000.

San Cristóbal, c., cap. of Táchira st., **Venezuela;** at 830 m nr. Colombian bdy.; mng. and comm. ctr.; coffee, cacao, sugar; food-processing, cement; cath.; p. (est. 1979) 264,000.

Sancti Spiritus, t., Las Villas, **Cuba;** comm. ctr.

in grazing dist.; tr. in sugar tobacco; agr. processing; p. (1970) 57,703.

Sandakan, t., Sabah, **Malaysia**; fine natural harbour on N.E. cst.; exp. agr. prods., timber, rubber; sawmilling, fishing; p. (1970) 42,000.

Sanday, I., Barra Is., Orkney, **Scot.**; flat, many shipwrecks; agr., fishing; p. (1971) 592.

Sandbach, mkt. t., Cheshire, **Eng.**; 8 km N.E. of Crewe; salt, chemicals, comm. vehicles; p. (1981) 14,747.

Sandefjord, t., Vestfold prov., S.E. **Norway**; whaling pt. nr. mouth of Oslo Fjord; shipyds., whale-processing; chemicals; p. (est. 1970) 31,723.

Sandhurst, v., Berkshire, **Eng.**; 16 km S.E. of Reading; Royal Military Academy, National Army Museum.

Sandia, t., N.M., **USA**; atomic research ctr.

San Diego, c., Cal., **USA**; first Spanish settlement in Cal. 1542; on Pac. cst., 16 km N. of Mexican border; fine natural harbour, naval base; fish-canning, aircraft; comm. ctr. for fruit-and vegetable-growing dist.; p. (1980) 875,000 (c.) 1,860,000 (met. a.).

Sandlings, The, S.E. Suffolk, **Eng.**; a. of glacial sands, forming heathland; difficult agr. conditions.

Sandown-Shanklin, t., South Wight, I. of Wight, **Eng.**; on Sandown Bay; resort; p. (1981) 16,852.

Sandringham, v., Norfolk, **Eng.**; Royal residence since 1861.

Sandusky, c., Ohio, **USA**; on S. cst. L. Erie; tr. in coal, fruit, foodstuffs; paper, farm implements, chemicals; summer resort of Cedar Point nearby; p. (1980) 31,360.

Sandviken, t., Gävleborg, **Sweden**; impt. steel inds.; p. (1983) 41,319.

Sandwell, met. dist., West Midlands, **Eng.**; comprises Warley and West Bromwich; p. (1981) 307,389.

Sandwich, t., Kent, **Eng.**; Cinque pt. at mouth of Stour R.; harbour silted up 16th cent.; mkt. lt. inds.; p. (1981) 4,227.

Sandwich Is., dependency of Falkland Is., Brit. Crown col. S. **Atlantic**.

Sandy, t., Mid Beds., **Eng.**; 5 km N.W. of Biggleswade; mkt. gardening; p. (1981) 8,048.

Sandy Hook, peninsula, N.J., **USA**; projects into lower bay of N.Y.; government reservation.

San Felipe, cap. of Aconcagua prov., **Chile**; 72 km N. of Santiago; agr., copper and gold-mng. ctr.; p. (est. 1970) 30,047.

San Felipe, cap. of Yaracuy st., **Venezuela**; ctr. of agr. dist. producing coffee, sugar and other tropical prods.; p. (est. 1970) 43,402.

San Fernando, N.W. sub. of Buenos Aires, **Argentina**; spt. on Rio de la Plata; industl. ctr., footwear, furniture, fish canning.

San Fernando, cap. of Colchagua prov., **Chile**; agr. mkt. ctr.; p. (1970) 42,324.

San Fernando, t., Bay of Cadiz, S. **Spain**; pt. has naval arsenal; salt mftg.; much of surrounding marshland now reclaimed; p. (1981) 78,048.

San Fernando, spt., Trinidad, **W.I.**; on W. cst. 40 km S. of Port of Spain; exp. sugar, asphalt, petrol; p. (1970) 37,313.

San Fernando, t., **Venezuela**; ctr. cattle ranching region of upper Llanos; oil; p. (est. 1970) 44,358.

San Francisco, c., Cal., **USA**; spt. on S. F. Bay; entrance spanned by Golden Gate Bridge; attractive hilly site; cosmopolitan c. with several immigrant quarters; comm. and financial ctr. with many varied inds.; univ.; sudden earthquake (1906) destroyed much of c. (*see* **F9**); p. (1980) 1,013,000 (c.), 3,227,000 (met. a.) with Oakland.

Sangihe Is., **Indonesia**; volcanic archipelago between Kalimantan and Philippines; sago, nutmeg, copra; ch. t. and spt. Tahuna; a. 813 km²; p. c. 90,000.

San Gimignano, hill t., Tuscany, **Italy**; overlooks Val d'Elsa; 13th cent. mediaeval t., preserved as national monument; tourist ctr.; p. (1981) 7,377.

San Giovanni in Fiore, t., Calabria, **Italy**; agr. ctr. at 1,006 m nr. confluence of Neto and Arvo Rs.; p. (1981) 20,154.

Sangli, t., Maharastra, **India**; nr. Miraj on Karna-

taka border; p. (1971) 115,138 (t.), 201,597 (met. a.).

Sangre de Cristo Mtns., part of Rocky mtns. **USA**; name (Span.—Blood of Christ) derives from reddish hue seen at sunset; highest summit Blanca Peak 4,367 m.

San Joaquin, R., Cal., **USA**; forms part of Central Valley project for irrigation of farmlands of R. valley; 512 km long.

San José, prov., **Costa Rica**; bauxite mng. nr. San Isidro del General projected with road to Punta Uvita where sm. pt. will be built; cap. San José.

San José, c., cap. of **Costa Rica**; sited at c. 1,160 m in S. J. basin; cath., univ., observatory, theatre, park; ch. industl. and comm. ctr. of rep.; oil refining, agr. processing; major route ctr., international airport; p. (1977) 236,474 (c.), 395,401 (met. a.).

San José, t., cap. of San José prov., **Uruguay**; impt. mkt.; flour-milling; p. (est. 1971) 27,500.

San José, c., Cal, **USA**; in fertile Santa Clara valley; fruit and vegetable canning and processing, chemicals, paper, electronics; p. (1980) 629,000 (c.), 1,295,000 (met. a.).

San Juan, prov., **Argentina**; at foot of Andes; gold, copper mng.; cap. S. J.; a. 89,179 km²; p. (1960) 352,000.

San Juan, c., cap. of San Juan prov., **Argentina**; comm. ctr. of agr. a., tr. in wine, fruit, cattle; p. (1975) 112,582 (met. a.).

San Juan, c., cap of **Puerto Rico**; built in part on I.; major spt. on N.E. cst.; exp. agr. prod. to USA; agr. processing; modern inds. inc. oil refining, cement, metallurgy, pharmaceuticals; cath., univ.; p. (1980) 1,086,000 (met. a.).

San Juan, R., **Central America**; divides Nicaragua and Costa Rica; plans made for its canalisation, which would give both countries a clear waterway from Caribbean to Pac.; 144 km long.

San Juan, R., Col., N.M., and Utah., **USA**; flows in goose-neck incised meanders; Navajo Dam part of Colorado River storage project, bringing irrigation to Navajo Indian reservation; 640 km long.

San Juan del Norte (Greytown), pt. on Caribbean cst. of **Nicaragua**; silting; sm. exp. of bananas, hardwoods; p. (1963) 599.

San Juan del Sur, spt., on Pac. cst., **Nicaragua**; exp. ctr. for coffee, sugar, cocoa, balsam; p. (est. 1970) 4,223.

Sankt Ingbert, t., Saarland, **W. Germany**; N.E. of Saarbrücken; coal mng.; iron, glass, machin., textiles, leather; p. (1983) 50,300.

Sankt Pölten, t., Lower Austria; rly. and industl. ctr.; hydroelectric power sta.; p. c. 41,000.

San Leandro, t., Cal., **USA**; food processing; Portuguese residents have annual religious festival; p. (1980) 63,952.

San Lorenzo, t., **Argentina**; 22 km N. Rosario; lge. chemical wks., oil refining.

Sanlúcar de Barrameda, pt., Cadiz prov., **Spain**; nr. mouth of R. Guadalquivir; wines and agr. prod.; mediaeval cas.; bathing resort; p. (1981) 48,496.

San Luis, c., cap. of S. L. prov., **Argentina**; ctr. of cattle, grain, wine producing dist.; rich mineral deposits in surrounding a.; hydroelectric power sta. and irrigation dam nearby; p. (1970) 50,771.

San Luis Potosí, st., **Mexico**; leading mng. st.; metals melting, food-processing; cap. San Luis Potosi; a. 63,235 km²; p. (1970) 1,281,996.

San Luis Potosí, t., cap. of San Luis Potosí st., **Mexico**; industl. and comm. ctr.; metallurgy textiles; cath.; palace; p. (1979) 327,333.

San Marino, sm. indep. rep., **Italy**; in Apennines nr. Rimini; has kept its independence since 4th cent. A.D.; exp. wine, textiles, building stone; cap. San Marino; a. 62 km²; p. (1983) 22,206 resident citizens.

San Marino, t., cap. of **San Marino rep.**; on slope of Mt. Titano, 19 km S.W. of Rimini; tourism; p. (1978) 4,695.

San Miguel, c., El Salvador, at foot of San Miguel volcano; sisal-fibre, coffee, cattle, cotton, indigo; cath.; p. (est. 1971) 110,966.

San Miguel de Allende, t., Guanajuato st., **Mexico**; picturesque hilly site; famous art institute.

San Miguel de Tucumán, c., cap. Tucumán prov., Argentina; on R. Sali; univ.; breweries, sawmills, flour, sugar; p. (1975) 321,567.

San Millán de la Cogolla, Spain; oldest (6th cent.) monastic foundation in Spain; in Cárdenas valley (Logrono prov.); p. (1981) 298.

San Nicolas, R. pt., Argentina; on Paraná R.; cattle, flour, agr. prod., distillery, steel plant; p. (1970) 64,730.

Sanniya Hor, shallow L., Iraq; linked to R. Tigris; acts as flood control reservoir.

Sanok, t., Rzeszow prov., S.E. Poland; picturesque site on steep banks of San R.; industl. ctr., comm. vehicles, rubber gds.; p. (1970) 21,600.

San-Pedro, spt., Ivory Coast; new pt. (1970) linked with development of timber production in hinterland and to Bangolo iron ore deposits; iron pelletizing plant; p. (planned for 1980) 50,000.

San Pedro, spt., a. of Los Angeles, Cal., USA; shipyds., oil refining, fruit canning.

San Pedro de Macoris, spt., Dominican Rep.; on Caribbean; exp. sugar, sugar prods.; clothing, soap; p. (1970) 70,092.

San Pedro Sula, t., Honduras; ctr. for banana and sugar inds.; food processing; p. (1974) 150,991.

Sanquhar, burgh, Nithsdale, Scot.; coal mng., brick mkg.; p. (1981) 2,169.

San Rafael, t., W. Argentina; comm. ctr. for agr. a.; food processing, meat, wine, fruit; p. c. 46,000.

San Remo, sm. pt., Italy; winter resort on Italian Riviera; flower mkt., olive oil, lemons, wine; 12th cent. church; p. (1981) 60,787.

San Salvador (Watling's I.), Bahama Is., W.I.; discovered by Columbus 1492, his first sight of the New World; a. 155 km²; p. (1970) 776.

San Salvador, c., cap. of El Salvador; stands c. 600 m a.s.l.; ch. comm. and industl. ctr.; food processing, textile and tobacco inds.; univ., observatory; oil refining; liable to earthquakes; p. (1971) 337,171.

Sansanding, t., Mali, W. Africa; lge. barrage across R. Niger.

San Sebastian, c., cap. of Guipúzcoa prov., N. Spain; spt. on Bay of Biscay, at foot of Mt. Urgull; seaside resort; fishing, textiles, paper, glass; captured by Wellington 1813; p. (1978) 169,985.

San Severo, mkt. t., S. Italy; hilltop site, 24 km N.W. of Foggia, Apulia; cath.; wine ctr., cream of tartar, bricks; p. (1981) 54,273.

Santa Ana, c., W. El Salvador; second lgst. c. of rep.; coffee, sugar, cattle; Santa Ana volcano nearby; p. (est. 1970) 162,937.

Santa Ana, c., Cal., USA; S.E. of Los Angeles; in fruit farming a.; fruit pkg., walnuts, oranges; p. (1980) 204,000 inc. in Anaheim met. a.

Santa Barbara, a., Cal., USA; resort on Pac. cst., picturesque setting, mild climate; p. (1980) 74,414 (c.), 299,827 (met. a.).

Santa Barbara Is., USA; along S. cst. of Cal.; inc. Santa Catalina I., a favourite resort.

Santa Catarina, st., Brazil; between Atl. and Argentina; tobacco, manioc, fruit, hogs; impt. coal producer; cap. Florianópolis; a. 95,830 km²; p. (1970) 2,930,411.

Santa Clara, c., Cuba; attractive site at over 360 m; agr. and comm. ctr. for sugar and tobacco; decisive victory for guerrilla army of Fidel Castro 1959; p. (1975) 146,651.

Santa Clara, c., W. Cal., USA; citrus fruit pkg.; electronics, plastics, chemicals; univ.; p. (1980) 87,700.

Santa Clara Valley, Cal., USA; extends S. from San Francisco Bay; intensive fruit-growing under irrigation, prunes; ch. t. San José.

Santa Cruz, c., cap. of S.C. dep., Bolivia; alt. 457 m; agr. mkt. for sugar, coffee, rice, cattle; oil refining; international airport; impt. reserves iron ore; univ.; p. (1976) 237,128.

Santa Cruz de la Sierra, t., Bolivia; on R. Piray; sugar, flour; distilling; p. (1967) 96,000.

Santa Cruz de Tenerife, pt. on Tenerife I., Canary Is.; cap. of S.C. de T. prov., Spain; gd. harbour, oil refinery; exp. agr. prods.; developing resort in attractive a. with mild climate; p. (1978) 205,458.

Santa Cruz Is., volcanic gr., S. Pac. Oc.; part of Solomon Is.; exp. copra.

Santa Fé, c., cap. of S.F. prov., Argentina; impt. R. pt. on I. in Salado R.; comm. ctr. for surrounding grain and livestock a.; food processing; univ., cath.; p. (1975) 244,655.

Santa Fé, t., N.M., USA; at base of Sangre de Cristo range; oldest capital in US founded by Spaniards 1610; tourist and comm. ctr.; p. (1980) 48,953.

Santa Isabel. See Malabo.

Santa Maria, t., Rio Grande do Sul, Brazil; rly. junc., rly. engin., agr. tr. and processing; p. (est. 1980) 211,100.

Santa Maria de Garoña, Spain; nr. Burgos; nuclear power plant being built.

Santa Marta, spt., cap of Magdalena dep., Colombia; banana pt. on deep bay at mouth of Manzanares R., serving local plantations; p. (1973) 108,007.

Santa Monica, c., Cal., USA; W. of Los Angeles; attractive site on Santa Monica Bay; aircraft, plastics, cosmetics; p. (1980) 88,314.

Santander, c., cap. of Santander prov., N. Spain; spt. and seaside resort on Bay of Biscay; exp. iron and zinc ore, agr. prods.; heavy inds., shipbldg., oil refining, chemicals; former summer resort of Spanish court; cath.; p. (1981) 180,328.

Santarém, t., Pará, Brazil; rubber, cacao, Brazil nuts, sugar; p. (est. 1980) 194,300

Santarém, t., cap. of Ribatejo prov., Portugal; on slope of hill overlooking Tagus R.; Moorish cas.; mkt. for agr. prod.; p. (1981) 52,138.

Santa Rosa, t., cap. of La Pampa terr., Argentina; p. (1970) 33,649.

Santa Rosa, t., Cal., USA; tr. and industl. ctr. for Somona Valley fruit-growing a.; p. (1980) 300,000 (met. a.).

Santiago, c., cap of Chile and S. prov.; planned t. ctr. in broad valley of Mapoche R., one of lgst. and most attractive cs. in S. America; cultural, comm., political and financial ctr., focus of routes; univ.; textiles, chemicals, paper, iron and steel; rapidly growing p.; p. (est. 1980) 3,853,275.

Santiago de Compostela, c., La Coruña, Spain; on R. Sar, surrounded by hills; univ., palace, cath. (with tomb of St. James); famous place of pilgrimage; agr. tr., food processing, tourism; p. (1981) 72,993.

Santiago de Cuba, c., Cuba; spt. on S. cst., exp. minerals, agr. prods., sugar, tobacco; oil refining, cigars, soap; cath., univ.; p. (1975) 315,801.

Santiago del Estero, c., cap. of S. del E. prov., Argentina; transportation ctr. of Argentine Chaco; agr. tr. ctr., cattle, food processing; p. (1975) 105,127.

Santiago de los Caballeros, t., Dominican Rep.; comm. agr. ctr. in fertile a.; food processing, coffee, rice, tobacco; cigars, cigarettes; p. (1970) 155,151.

Santis, mtn., on border cans. St. Gallen and Appenzell, Switzerland; alt. 2,506 m. Europe's hgst. television transmitter on summit.

Santo Andre, c., Brazil; part of industl. complex built to S.E. of São Paulo to relieve congestion; specialises in metalware and chems., p. (est. 1980) 633,900.

Santo Domingo, cap. Dominican Rep.; pt. on S. cst. exp. agr. prods.; reputed burial place of Columbus; univ.; p. (1970) 673,470 (c.), 817,641 (met. a.).

Santo Tomé de la Guayana (Puerto Ordaz) c., S.E. Venezuela; new industl. c. nr. confluence of Orinoco and Caroni Rs.; iron mines, steel, hydroelec. power and aluminium plants in a.; vast industl. complex projected.

Santorine. See Thira.

Santos, c., spt., São Paulo, Brazil; world's ch. coffee pt.; also exp. oranges, bananas, cotton, and industl. prod. from modern harbour; p. (est. 1980) 452,800.

San Vicente, t., cap. of S.V. dep., El Salvador; ctr. for coffee, sugar, tobacco; mnfs. leather gds., shawls, hats; p. (est. 1970) 44,204.

São Bernardo, c., Brazil; part of industl. complex built to relieve congestion in São Paulo which lies to N.W.; p. (est. 1980) 348,200.

São Caetono, c., Brazil; ctr. for metalwk. built to S.E. of São Paulo to relieve congestion; p. (est. 1980) 195,400.

São Carlos, t., São Paulo st., Brazil; 192 km N.W. of São Paulo; ctr. of coffee-growing a.; textiles, refrigerators, furniture; p. (est. 1968) 73,256.

São Francisco, R., Brazil; flows from Minas Gerais prov. to Alt.; navigable for 1,440 km of middle course; used for hydroelectric power at Paulo Afonso falls and Três Marias dam; 2,560 km long.

São Goncalo, t., Rio de Janeiro, Brazil; fastgrowing t.; p. (1970) 161,392.

São Jeronimo, t., Rio Grande do Sul, Brazil; lowgrade coal; p. (1970) 36,531.

São João do Meriti, t., Rio de Janeiro, **Brazil**; industl. and comm. ctr.; p. (1970) 163,934.

São José dos Campos, t., São Paulo, **Brazil**; ctr. of Brazil's aircraft ind.; synthetic fibres, telecommunication equipment, chems., motor vehicle components; p. (est. 1980) 239,900.

São Leopoldo, t., Rio Grande do Sul, S. **Brazil**; 32 km N. of Porto Alegre; mkt. t.; p. (est. 1968) 53,398.

São Luis, pt., cap. of Maranhão st., **Brazil**; on São Luis I.; noted cultural ctr. in 19th cent.; p. (1980) 405,300.

São Miguel, I., **Azores**; lgst. and most productive I. of archipelago; ch. t. and spt. Ponta Delgada, exp. agr. prods., pineapples; volcanic landscape a tourist attraction; p. (1981) 131,908.

Saône, R., **France**; rises in Vosges and flows to R. Rhône at Lyons; navigable, canalised; 451 km long.

Saone-et-Loire, dep., **France**; mtnous.; noted vineyards; cap. Mâcon; a. 8,627 km²; p. (1982) 571,500.

São Paulo, st., **Brazil**; on Atl. cst.; major industl. a. of S. America; coffee, cotton, sugar, rice, maize; vehicles, elec. gds., chemicals, textiles, telecomm. equipment, metal-wkg. plants; cap. São Paulo; Santos lgst pt. in Brazil; a. 247,226 km²; p. (1970) 17,958,693.

São Paulo, c., cap. of São Paulo st., **Brazil**; fast-growing c., comm. and industl. ctr. of rep. and leading c. of S. America; vehicles, machin., elec. gds., textiles, pharmaceuticals; aluminium refinery; nearby pt. Santos ships rich agr. prod. from hinterland; 2 univs., cath.; p. (est. 1980) 8,732,000.

São Roque, Cape of, Rio Grande do Norte, N.E. **Brazil**; most N.E. point of S. America.

São Tomé, cap. **São Tomé and Principe**; p. (est. 1985) 30,000.

São Tomé and Principe, former Port. col.; **W. Africa**; volcanic Is. in G. of Guinea; cocoa, coffee; cap. São Tomé; a. 963 km²; airpt. extended to encourage tourism; indep. achieved as democratic rep. 1975; p. (1981) 96,611.

São Vicente, c., S.E. São Paulo, **Brazil**; first Portuguese settlement in Brazil (1532), on I. off mainland; sub. of Santos; fashionable beach resort; p. (1980) 176,400.

Sapele, t., Benin st., **Nigeria**; S. of Benin; lge. lumber mill and plywood plant.

Sapporo, c., Hokkaido, **Japan**; main t. of Hokkaido; planned t.; univ.; brewing, dairy processing, sawmills; p. (1979) 1,371,108.

Saqqara, v., **Egypt**; necropolis of anc. Memphis; step pyramids; p. (1966) 12,700.

Sarajevo, c., cap. of Bosnia and Hercegovina, **Yugoslavia**; major route ctr., airport; ctr. of Yugoslav Moslems; mosques, caths.; diversified mnfs., metallurgy, elec. prods., textiles, tobacco, pottery; assassination 28 June 1914 of Archduke Francis Ferdinand precipitated First World War; p. (1981) 448,500.

Saransk, c., Mordovian ASSR, **RSFSR**; 232 km S.E. of Gorki; univ.; elec. equipment, engin., agr. processing; p. (est. 1980) 271,000.

Sarapul, c., **RSFSR**; pt. on R. Kama; radio equipment, machin., footwear, gloves; p. (est. 1980) 107,000.

Sarasota, Fla., **USA**; exp. fruit, veg.; resort; p. (1980) 202,000 (met. a.).

Saratoga Springs, N.Y., **USA**; summer resort at foot of Adirondack mtns., mineral springs; horse-racing; casino; p. (1980) 23,906.

Saratov, c., **RSFSR**; pt. on R. Volga; regional ctr. for agr. prod. of lower Volga valley and oil from Baku; univ.; engin., ball-bearings, textiles, oil refining, sawmilling; p. (est. 1980) 884,000.

Sarawak, st., **E. Malaysia**; mtnous. inland with sparse p.; rubber, sago, pepper grown along coast.; oil; cap. Kuching; a. 121,914 km²; p. (1970) 975,918.

Sardinia, I., aut. region, **Italy**; mtnous., dry climate; fertile Campidano plain with fruit, wines, sheep; zinc and lead mng.; tourism; fishing; major petrochemical complex at Ottana; part of former kingdom of Sardinia belonging to house of Savoy; a. 24,002 km²; p. (1981) 1,594,175.

Sargasso Sea, zone S.W. of N. Atl. Oc.; relatively still sea within swirl of warm ocean currents; noted for abundance of gulf-weed on its surface, rich in marine life; named by Columbus.

Sari, c., cap. of Mazandaran prov., **Iran**; p. (1967) 206,463.

Sark, I., **Channel Is.**; 10 km E. of Guernsey; picturesque scenery; tourist ctr.; farming; a. 516 ha; p. (est. 1973) 580.

Sark, R., forms extreme W. bdy. between **Scot.** and **Eng.**

Sarnia, c., and pt., Ont., **Canada**; on St. Clair R.; connected to Port Huron by rly. tunnel; oil refineries, petrochemical inds., agr. tr.; p. (1971) 56,727.

Sarno, t., Campania, **Italy**; spa at foot of mtns. on E. edge of fertile Sarno plain; agr. mkt., textile ctr.; cas.; p. (1981) 30,583.

Šar-Planina, **Yugoslavia**; nr. Skopje; impt. chrome deposits; attractive site, ctr. of mtn. tourism.

Sarpsborg, t., **Norway**; on R. Glommen; lgst. pulp and paper concern in kingdom; hydroelectric power sta.; p. (est. 1970) 13,165.

Sarreguemines, t., Moselle dep., **France**; in Lorraine; potteries based on local clay; coal mng.; p. (1982) 25,178.

Sarthe, dep., N.W. **France**; undulating surface; farming, apples, livestock; coal, linen, potteries; cap. Le Mans; a. 6,247 km²; p. (1982) 500,600.

Sarthe, R., **France**; trib. of R. Loire; 265 km long.

Sasebo, spt., Kyushu, **Japan**; ctr. of coalfield; engin., shipbldg.; p. (1979) 253,694.

Saskatchewan, prov., **Canada**; coniferous forests and plains; Rs. Saskatchewan and Churchill; many lge. Ls.; extreme climate; hydroelec. power; gr. wheat prov.; livestock, dairying; oil, copper, uranium, helium plants, furs, fisheries; cap. Regina; a. 651,903 km²; p. (1976) 921,323.

Saskatchewan, R., **Canada**; flows from Rocky mtns. through L. Winnipeg and thence by R. Nelson to Hudson Bay; 2,320 km long.

Saskatoon, c., Saskatchewan, **Canada**; grew rapidly after arrival of rly. (1890); comm. ctr. for grain producing a.; meat packing and tr.; varied inds., cement, oil refining; univ.; p. (1979) 133,750.

Sasolburg, t., O.F.S., **S. Africa**; oil from coal production; gas pipeline to Germiston a. p. (1960) 12,557.

Sassari, t., Sardinia, **Italy**; nr. G. of Asinara; cath., univ., palaces; tobacco and macaroni wks., cheese; p. (1981) 119,596.

Sattahip, pt., **Thailand**; new pt. inaugurated 1967.

Satu-Mare, t., N.W. **Romania**; agr. machin., handicraft inds. based on local prods., food-processing; cath.; p. (1978) 107,852.

Saudi Arabia, kingdom, Arabian peninsula, S.W. **Asia**; mainly desert, agr. in oases and S.W. upland region of Asir; lgst. producer of oil in Middle East; oil sales account for 85 per cent govt. revenue; steel inds. and oil refinery at Jidda, petrochemicals developing at Dammam; Moslem holy cs. Mecca and Medina; cap. Riyadh (royal), Mecca (religious); main pt. King Faisal Port.; a. 2,400,930 km²; p. (est. 1984) 10,824,000.

Sauerland, dist., N. Rhine–Westphalia, **W. Germany**; plateau, alt. from 150–450 m E. of Rhine; agriculturally poor, largely forested; crossed by R. Wupper, with which are associated industl. ts. Wuppertal (textiles), Solingen and Remscheid (cutlery and special steel); supplies hydroelectric power to Ruhr.

Sault Ste. Marie, t., Ont., **Canada**; pt. on St. Mary's R., opposite Sault Ste. Marie, Mich., to which it is connected by bridge; pulp, paper, iron and steel; tourist ctr. for L. and forest region; p. (1971) 78,175.

Sault Ste. Marie, t., Mich., **USA**; pt. on St. Mary's R.; opposite Sault Ste. Marie, Ont.; calcium carbide; tourist ctr. for fishing, hunting a.; p. (1980) 14,448.

Sault Ste. Marie Canals ("Soo"), **Canada** and **USA**; twin canals on Canadian and American side of shallow channel linking L. Superior and L. Huron; traversed by all wheat and iron-ore traffic from L. Superior pts.; length (Canadian) 2 km; depth 5 m.

Saumur, t., Maine-et-Loire dep., **France**; on R. Loire, 48 km S.W. of Tours; sparkling wines, brandy; flower, vegetable mkt.; cas.; p. (1982) 33,953.

Sauternes, v., Gironde, **France**; name applied to white wines of dist.

Sava, R., Slovenia, **Yugoslavia**; joins Danube at Belgrade; used for hydroelectric power; agr. in valleys; transport axis; 928 km long.

Savage or **Niue**, Cook Is., **Pac. Oc.**; under **N.Z.**; ch. exp. native plaited ware, bananas, copra, and sweet potatoes; ch. pt. Alofi; a. 259 km²; p. (1968) 5,240.

Savaii I., lgst. of Samoan gr., **Pac. Oc.**; volcanic, mtnous., fertile; exp. bananas, copra, cocoa; a. 1,821 km²; p. c. 30,000.

Savannah, c., Ga., **USA**; spt. nr. mouth of Savannah R.; rly., fishing and comm. ctr. for Sea Is., Savannah valley and surrounding plantations; mkt. for naval stores; sugar refining, paper, oil refining, diverse mnfs.; tourist ind. stimulated by mild climate; p. (1980) 141,000 (c.), 231,000 (met. a.).

Savannah, R., **USA**; flows between Ga. and S.C., to Atl. Oc.; used for hydroelectric power; 720 km long.

Saverne, Col de, low pass, N.E. **France**; carries trunk rly. from Paris to Strasbourg and the East between Vosges and Hardt mtns.; gradual approach from W., steep descent to E. into Rhine valley.

Savoie (Savoy), dep., **France**; borders Italy in Savoy Alps; part of former duchy; dairying and vineyards; hydroelectricity forms basis of metallurgical inds.; first Fr. National Park (Vanoise Park); cap. Chambéry; a. 6,188 km²; p. (1982) 320,600.

Savona, spt., Genoa, **Italy**; cath.; iron, shipbldg., glass and tinplate wks.; exp. preserved fruits and tomatoes; imports coal, oil, iron-ore; p. (1981) 75,353.

Savonlinna, t., Mikkeli, E. **Finland**; in Saimaa L. region; route ctr.; timber inds.; p. (est. 1970) 17,942.

Sawankalok, t., **Thailand**; impt. teak collecting ctr.

Sawbridgeworth, t., East Herts., **Eng.**; on R. Stort, 6 km S. of Bishops Stortford; malting, fruit preserving; p. (1981) 7,777.

Saxham, t., Suffolk, **Eng.**; agr. machin.

Saxmundham, mkt. t., Suffolk Coastal, Suffolk, **Eng.**; 29 km N.E. of Ipswich; p. (1981) 16,235.

Saxony, region, **E. Germany**; turbulent political and territorial history, now comprises admin. dists. of Leipzig, Dresden, Karl-Marx-Stadt. Halle and Magdeburg; inc. Erzgebirge in S., Vogtland in W. and N. European plain; drained by N. flowing Rs. Elster, Pleisse, Mulde, Elle, Neisse, Spree; kaolin deposits basis for porcelain ind. at Meissen; industrialised in 19th and 20th cent. with notable textile ind.; coal mng. nr. Zwickau; inds. concentrated around Karl-Marx-Stadt; cap. Dresden; comm. ctr. at Leipzig; a. 16,996 km².

Sayan Mtns., range of mtns.; between Rs. Yenisey and Angra, **RSFSR**; form part of Sino-Soviet border; mineral resources.

Scafell Pike, mtn., Cumbria, **Eng.**; in Cumbrian Mtns, Lake Dist.; highest in Eng.; alt. 979 m.

Scalby, t., North Yorks., **Eng.**; 5 km N.W. of Scarborough; p. (1981) 9,228.

Scalloway, Shetlands, **Scot.**; on W. cst. of Mainland; the anc. cap.; ruined cas.; fish. pt.; p. (1981) 1,018.

Scalpay, I., off E. cst. of Skye, **Scot.**

Scalpay, I., Harris, Outer Hebrides, **Scot.**; p. (1981) 466.

Scandinavia, name given to lge. peninsula in N.W. **Europe**; comprises kingdoms of Sweden and Norway; sometimes inc. Denmark, Finland and Iceland; rugged a. of anc. peneplained rocks; climate varies from arctic (N.) to humid maritime (S.W.); rich in timber and mineral ores. esp. iron and copper; W. cst. waters valuable fishing grounds.

Scapa Flow, strait, N. **Scot.**; between Pomona and Hoy, Orkney Is.; surrendered German fleet scuttled 1919; Brit. battleship *Royal Oak* sunk at anchor 1939.

Scarba, I., Argyll and Bute, **Scot.**; off N. end of Jura, red deer in woods and moorlands.

Scarborough, t., l. gov. dist., North Yorks., **Eng.**; on E. cst.; seaside resort; cas.; former spa; p. (1981) 101,425 (dist.).

Scarpanto. *See* **Karpathos.**

Schaffhausen, most. N. can., **Switzerland**; on R. Rhine; pastoral, forested; cereals, fruit, vegetables, wine; hydroelectric power from S. falls on Rhine; cap. S.; a. 298 km²; p. (1980) 69,413.

Schaffhausen, c., cap. of S. can., **Switzerland**; on Rhine below L. Constance; falls to S.W. of

c.; hydroelectricity supplies power for electro-chemical ind. and aluminium wks.; p. (est. 1978) 32,400.

Schaumburg-Lippe, former st., between provs. of Hanover and Westphalia, Germany, now part of Lower Saxony, **W. Germany**; farming, coal mng.

Schefferville, t., **Canada**; 576 km N. of St. Lawrence estuary and connected to it (at Seven Islands) by rly.; ctr. of iron-ore mines in Quebec-Labrador trough; p. (1971) 3,300.

Scheldt (Dutch **Schelde**, French **Escaut**), R., **France, Belgium, Neth.**; rises in Aisne, France, flows to N. Sea forming extensive delta with Rhine (Rijn) and Meuss (Maas) in Netherlands; navigable; 432 km long; network of canals.

Schenectady, c., N.Y., **USA**; on Mohawk R., N.W. of Albany; electrical plants, locomotive wks.; p. (1980) 67,972.

Scheveningen, seaside resort, **Neth.**; 3 km N.W. of The Hague; fish. pt.

Schiedam, t., **Neth.**, on Nieuwe Maas, 4 km downstream from Rotterdam; forms part of Rotterdam–Europort; diverse pt.-based inds.; gin; p. (1982) 72,903.

Schiehallion, mtn., Perth and Kinross, **Scot.**; alt. 1,082 m.

Schio, t., Veneto, **Italy**; at foot of Alps on Leogra R.; woollens, textiles, machin.; p. (1981) 35,596.

Schlei, narrow inlet of Baltic, Schleswig-Holstein, **W. Germany**; 40 km long.

Schleswig, t., Schleswig-Holstein, **W. Germany**; fish. pt. on Schlei inlet; lt. inds.; p. (1983) 29,400.

Schleswig-Holstein, Land, **W. Germany**; occupies S. part of Jutland peninsula; a. disputed between Denmark and Prussia in 19th cent.; mainly agr.; many sm. pts.; crossed by Kiel Canal; cap. Kiel; a. 15,664 km²; p. (est. 1983) 2,618,200.

Schneidemühtl. *See* **Pila.**

Schönebeck, t., Magdeburg, **E. Germany**; pt. on R. Elbe; metals, chemicals, machin.; p. (est. 1970) 46,146.

Schoonebeek, v., Drenthe, **Neth.**; S. of Emmen; lge. oilfield.

Schouten I., W. Irian, **Indonesia**; in Geelvink Bay; p. 25,487.

Schouwen-Duiveland, I., Zeeland prov., **Neth.**; cap. Zierikee; formerly 2 separate Is.,

Schuylkill, R., Penns., **USA**; flows into Delaware R.; navigable; length 208 km.

Schwäbisch-Gmünd, t., Baden–Württemberg, **W. Germany**; at foot of Swabian Jura, E. of Stuttgart; clocks, glass, optical, precious metal and jewellery inds.; mediaeval and baroque bldgs.; p. (1983) 56,400.

Schwarzwald (Black Forest), forested mtn. range, Baden–Württemberg, **W. Germany**; highest peak Feldberg 1,496 m; tourism; famous for clock and toy inds.

Schwechat, t., **Austria**; nr. Vienna; oil refining; pipeline to Trieste; p. (1961) 13,403.

Schwedt, t., Frankfurt, **E. Germany**; on R. Oder; lge. oil refinery; pipeline from Mozyr' (USSR); paper, fertilisers; p. (est. 1970) 34,134.

Schweinfurt, t., Bavaria, **W. Germany**; on R. Main, N.E. of Würzburg; metals, machin., ball bearings, dyes, brewing; p. (1983) 26,400.

Schwelm, t., N. Rhine-Westphalia, **W. Germany**; E. of Wuppertal; metals machin., textiles; p. (1983) 30,400.

Schwenningen, t., Baden–Württemberg, **W. Germany**; clocks, precision instruments, optical apparatus; p. with Villingen (1983) 77,300.

Schwerin, c., cap. of Schwerin, **E. Germany**; on Schwerin L., surrounded by smaller Ls.; comm. and industl. ctr. of agr. dist.; food processing, engin., furniture; cath., cas.; p. (1983) 124,975.

Schwyz, can., **Switzerland**; mtnous. in S.; forested; dairying impt.; original member of confederation; cap. S.; a. 907 km²; p. (1980) 97,354.

Schwyz, c., of Schwyz can., **Switzerland**; tourist ctr. nr. Lucerne; p. (est. 1978) 12,100.

Sciacca, sm. pt., Sicily, **Italy**; nr. Agrigento; mineral springs; p. (1981) 34,294.

Scilly Is., archipelago, l. gov. dist., 45 km. S.W. of Land's End, Cornwall, **Eng.**; early flowers and vegetables benefit from mild winter climate; tourism; p. (1981) 2,628.

Scioto, R., Ohio, **USA**; joins Ohio at Portsmouth; 400 km long.

Scone, par., Perth and Kinross, **Scot.**; place of residence and coronation of early Scottish kings; from here Edward I removed Stone of Destiny to Westminster Abbey 1297; tourist ctr.; civil aerodrome.

Scoresby Sound, E. **Greenland**; lgst. fjord system in the world; length 304 m; fishing and hunting; onshore oil drilling (1984).

Scotland, Brit. Is., N. part of **Gt. Britain**; 12 Gov. Regs.; home affairs admin. by Dept. of Sec. of State for Scot.; physically divided into 3 parts; (1) the Highlands and Is., an upland a. suffering from depopulation, economically reliant on stock-rearing, tourism, hydroelec. power, whisky and fishing; intrusive impact of N. Sea oil on N.E. cst.; (2) the Central Lowlands, containing most p., based in industl. ts. on sm. coalfields, inc. lgst. c. Glasgow and cap. Edinburgh; (3) the S. Uplands, a stock-rearing a. bordering Eng.; a. 78,772 km²; p. (1981) 5,116,000.

Scrabster, pt. nr. Thurso, **Scotland**; main ferry terminal for Orkneys.

Scranton, c., Penns., **USA**; on Lackawanna R.; anthracite ctr.; chemicals, shoes, textiles; univ.; p. (1980) 88,117 (c.), 640,396 (Scranton N.E. met. a.).

Scunthorpe, t., l. gov. dist., Humberside, **Eng.**; on Lincoln Edge, 10 km S. of Humber; iron, limestone mng. and major iron and steel ind.; p. (1981) 66,353.

Scutari (Albania). *See* **Shkodër.**

Scutari (Turkey). *See* **Usküdar.**

Seaford, t., East Sussex, **Eng.**; 5 km E. of Newhaven; seaside resort; declined as a pt. with shift of Ouse R. channel to Newhaven; p. (1981) 17,785.

Seaforth, Loch, Lewis, Outer Hebrides, **Scot.**; 22 km long.

Seaham, spt., Durham, **Eng.**; Seaham Harbour on E. cst. 6 km S. of Sunderland; modern colly. workings extend under sea; p. (1981) 21,130.

Sea Islands, USA; chain of Is. off Atl. cst. of S.C., Ga. and Fla.; formerly impt. for sea-island cotton but since 1919 infested with boll weevil.

Seathwaite, v., Cumbria, **Eng.**; 11 km from Keswick, close to Styhead (436 m); exceptionally heavy annual rainfall (above 3,800 mm).

Seaton, t., East Devon, **Eng.**; on Lyme Bay at mouth of R. Axe, seaside resort; freestone quarries; p. (1981) 4,974.

Seaton Carew, t., Cleveland, **Eng.**; site for nuclear power sta. nr. mouth of R. Tees; seaside resort.

Seaton Valley, t., Blyth Valley, Northumberland, **Eng.**; coal mng.; expanded t.; p. (1981) 46,141.

Seattle, c., Wash., **USA**; spt. between Puget Sound and L. Wash.; S.E. is Mt. Rainier, N.E. Mt. Baker; tr. with Far East and Alaska from wooded, agr. hinterland; fishing and fish exp.; lgst. c. of Wash., a major industl. and comm. ctr.; aircraft (home of Boeing), shipbld., food processing; univs., cath.; p. (1980) 494,000 (c.), 1,231,000 (met. a.).

Secunderabad, t., Andhra Pradesh, **India**; now incorporated within Hyderabad; comm. ctr., rly. junc.; p. (est. 1971) 94,500.

Sedan, t., Ardennes dep., **France**; on R. Meuse; machin., metal ware, woollens, flour; Napoleon III surrendered to Prussians 1870; p. (1982) 24,535.

Sedbergh, mkt. t., South Lakeland, Cumbria, **Eng.**; woollen ind.; public school.

Sedgefield, t., l. gov. dist., S.E. Durham, **Eng.**; in fertile agr. a.; cattle mkt.; racecourse; p. (1981) 92,887.

Sedgemoor, l. gov. dist., Somerset, **Eng.**; based on Bridgwater, Burnham and surrounding a.; p. (1981) 89,051.

Sedgley. *See* **Wolverhampton.**

Sefton, met. dist., Merseyside, **Eng.**; comprises Crosby, Bootle and Litherland; p. (1981) 300,011.

Ségou, t., R. pt., **Mali**; W. Africa; on R. Niger; ctr. of irrigation scheme; cotton, hides, cattle; once cap. of former kingdom; p. (est. 1976) 65,000.

Ségou Canal, Mali, W. Africa; leaves R. Niger 6 km below Bamako, extends 208 km N.E. to Segou; irrigates 7,770 km² on right bank of Niger and assists navigation.

Segovia, c., cap. of S. prov., Old Castile, **Spain**; on rocky hill above Eresma R.; Roman aqueduct, cath.; p. (1981) 149,360 (prov.).

Segovia, R., rises in N.W. Nicaragua, flows N.E. to Caribbean; forms part of S. limit of Mosquito cst., and bdy. between **Honduras** and **Nicaragua**; 480 km long.

Segre, R., Lérida, N.E. **Spain**; rises in E. Pyrenees flows S.W. into R. Ebro; water irrigates the a. around Lérida, the lgst. block of irrigated land in Spain; c. 272 km long.

Segura, R., **Spain**; flows to Mediterranean at Guardamar; 288 km long.

Seibersdorf, Austria; ENEA experimental food irradiation project.

Seikan Tunnel, Japan; links Honshu with Hokkaido under Tsugaru strait; 37 km long.

Seine, R., **France**; rises in Côte d'Or dep. and flows past Paris and Rouen to English Channel at Havre; navigable, part of French waterway network; 757 km long.

Seine-et-Marne, dep., N. **France**; agr., stock-raising, dairying; impt. source of food for Paris mkts.; Brie cheese; cap. Melun; a. 5,892 km²; p. (1982) 887,100.

Seine-Maritime, dep., N. **France**; undulating and fertile; grain, dairying; heavy inds. at cap. Rouen; oil refineries; beach resorts; p. (1982) 1,191,000.

Seine-Saint Denis, dep., N.E. Paris, **France**; mkt. gardens; cap. Bobigny; p. (1982) 1,321,000.

Seistan and Baluchistan, twin prov., **Iran**; co. ts. Zabol, Zahedan (rly. terminus Pakistan rly. from Quetta through Mirjaveh, the customs post on Iranian frontier).

Sekondi-Takoradi, t., S.W. **Ghana**; spt. on G. of Guinea; developed after construction of rly. (1903) to tap mineral, agr. and forest wealth of hinterland; deepwater harbour at Takoradi constructed 1928; fisheries, saw milling; p. (1984) 91,874 (c.), 160,868 (met. a.).

Selangor, st., central Malaya, **W. Malaysia**; former sultanate; economically well developed; chemicals, rubber, tin, coal, pineapples; ch. pt., Pt. Swettenham; fisheries; new st. cap. designated at Klang to relieve congestion of Kuala Lumpur; p. (1970) 1,630,366.

Selby, mkt. t., l. gov. dist., North Yorks., **Eng.**; on R. Ouse, 20 km. S. of York; anc. abbey church; flour milling, flax, oil-cake; development of major coalfield since 1983 linked to bldg. of power sta. in Aire Valley; p. (1981) 77,212 (l. gov. dist.).

Sele, R., S. **Italy**; rises in S. Apennines, flows W. into G. of Salerno; headwater carried E. through gr. Apennine tunnel (11 km) to irrigate plateau of Apulia in S.E. Italy.

Selenga, Asiatic R., rises in **Mongolia**, enters **USSR** nr. Kiachta from where it is navigable to its delta in L. Baykal; c. 1,100 km long.

Selkirk, royal burgh, Etterick and Lauderdale, **Scot.**; on Etterick Water; 6 km S. of Galashiels; mkt. t.; tartans, tweeds; p. (1981) 5,417.

Selkirk Mtns., B.C. **Canada**; run N.W. to S.E. parallel with Rocky mtns.; anc. rocks, highly mineralised; rise to over 2,700 m.

Selkirkshire, former co., S. **Scot.**; now part of Borders Reg.

Sellafield, nuclear power plant, Cumbria, **Eng.**; formerly Windscale; reprocesses nuclear waste.

Selma, t., Ala., **USA**; on Alabama R., in cotton, dairying, lumbering region; food processing, fertilisers; p. (1980) 26,684.

Selsey Bill, peninsula between Bognor Regis and Portsmouth, West Sussex, **Eng.**

Selukwe, t., **Rhodesia**; alt. 1,444 m; gold mng., chrome ore, molybdenum; ranching.

Selwyn Range, mtns., Queensland, **Australia**; extend 560 km W. from Gr. Dividing Range.

Semarang, spt., Java, **Indonesia**; exp. sugar, tobacco, tapioca, kapok; shipbldg., rly. repairs, cement, sawmills, tyres, elec. equipment; univ.; p. (est. 1971) 560,000.

Semipalatinsk, t., Kazakh SSR, **USSR**; on R. Irtysh; lge. meat-packing plant; textiles, engin.; rich gold deposit found in a. 1965; p. (est. 1980) 283,000.

Semmering Pass, low pass, **Austria**; provides route across E. Alps for rly. from Vienna to Venice; scenic resort; alt. below 915 m.

Semnan, t., Central Prov., **Iran**; comm. ctr. for tobacco growing region; p. (1966) 31,058.

Sena, t., Moçambique; on R. Zambesi; iron-ore mng.

Sendai, t., Honshu, **Japan**; cas.; univ.; metallurgy, food processing, lacquer ware; p. (est. 1979) 637,552.

Senegal, member st., **Senegambia**, W. cst. Africa; flat savannah; tropical climate with long dry season; agr. main occupation, groundnuts accounting for 72 per cent exp.; production hit by severe drought (1982–3); groundnut and agr. processing provide industl. basis; bauxite, phosphate, titanium, zirconium mng.; oil refinery at cap. Dakar; a. 197,109 km²; p. (est. 1984) 6,352,000; see Senegambia.

Senegal, R., W. Africa; flows from Kong mtns. W. and N.W. to Atl. at St. Louis, above Cape Verde; lower valley forms fertile agr. land; partially navigable; plans for economic development of valley; joint water scheme with 3 dams to relieve water shortages, improve navigation and provide hydro-electric power for Mali, Senegambia and Mauritania; 1,600 km long.

Senegambia, rep., W. Cst Africa; formed (1982) from unification of Senegal and Gambia following attempted coup (1981); secessionist attempts (1982). See Senegal and Gambia.

Senftenberg, t., Cottbus, **E. Germany;** inds. based on local lignite deposits; glassware, tiles; p. (est. 1970) 24,301.

Senigallia, t., Italy; resort and spt. on Adriatic; fishing and agr. ctr., food processing, agr. machin.; p. (1981) 40,108.

Senlis, t., Oise dep., **France;** Gallo-Roman wall; tourist ctr. in forested region, 43 km N.E. of Paris; mkt. t., furniture, rubber gds.; p. (1982) 15,280.

Sennar, t., **Sudan;** on Blue Nile, on rly. route to Khartoum, Suakin, Pt. Sudan; dam for irrigation, flood control and hydroelectric power; p. c. 8,000.

Sens, t., Yonne dep., **France;** on R. Yonne; known to Romans as Agedincum; Gothic cath.; agr. tr., food processing, farm implements, boots, chemicals, cutlery; p. (1982) 27,501.

Sensuntepeque, t., **El Salvador;** pottery, distilling; p. (1968) 6,006.

Senta, t., **Yugoslavia;** pt. on Tisa R.; agr. ctr.; food processing, agr. machin., chemicals; p. (1971) 24,714.

Seoul, c., cap. of **S. Korea;** in Han R. valley; food processing, textiles, rly. engin.; univs., anc. walls; international airport, connected by rly. to outport of Inchon; host of 1988 Olympic games; p. (1980) 8,366,756.

Sepik, R., N. **New Guinea;** flows E. to Bismarck Sea; drains vast mtn. a.; very fast flow; navigable by shallow craft; 800 km long.

Sept Isles (Seven Islands), pt., on St. Lawrence, Quebec, **Canada;** iron brought by rail from Schefferville; airline service but no highway.

Sequoia National Park, Cal., **USA;** sequoia trees.

Seraing, t., Liège, **Belgium;** on R. Meuse; coal mng.; iron and steel heavy inds.; seat of famous Cockerill iron wks. (1817) and glass wks. (1825); p. (1982) 63,749.

Seram (Ceram), I., Moluccas, **Indonesia;** W.-E. mtn. range rising to 3,357 m; tobacco; sago; a. 17,143 km²; p. (1961) 73,453.

Serampore, t., W. Bengal, **India;** former Danish settlement; cotton and silk weaving, pottery, jute and paper mills; p. (1971) 102,023.

Serbia, constituent rep., N.E. **Yugoslavia;** most impt. rep., "bread basket" of Yugoslavia; grain, fruit; mng. copper and antimony; cap. Belgrade; a. 87,879 km²; p. (1971) 8,436,574.

Seremban, t., cap. of Negri Sembilan st., **W. Malaysia;** on Linggi R.; linked by rly. to Pt. Dickson; comm. ctr. for rubber and tin a.; p. (1970) 79,915.

Sereth, R., rises in Carpathians, W. Ukrainian SSR, **USSR,** and enters **Romania** to join Danube above Galati; 720 km long.

Sergipe, cst. st., **Brazil;** sandy cst. rising to undulating plateau in interior; well wooded and cropped for sugar, cotton; drier interior devoted mainly to stock-raising; oil deposits; a. 21,054 km²; p. (1970) 911,251.

Sergo. See Kadiyevka.

Seria, t., Brunei; coastal t., protected from sea by 8 km dyke; oil ctr., linked by pipeline with Lutong; p. (1971) 20,801.

Serov, t., RSFSR; in Urals; iron and steel; natural gas pipeline from Ingrim; p. (est. 1980) 101,000.

Serowe, t., Botswana, Southern Africa; seat of Bamanguato tribe; mkt. ctr.; lge coal reserves widening economic base of Botswana and reducing dependence on S. Africa; p. (1981) 23,661.

Serpukhov, t., R. pt., RSFSR; on R. Oka, planned canal link to Moscow; p. (est. 1980) 141,000.

Serra da Mantiqueira, mtn. range, hgst. in Brazil.

Serra do Espinhaco, mtns., Brazil; highest peak, Itambe, 2,045 m; iron-ore deposits.

Serra do Mar, mtns., Brazil; form steep E. edge of Brazilian Plateau S. from Rio de Janeiro.

Serrai (Seres), dep., Macedonia, N. **Greece;** N. mtns. form frontier with Bulgaria in gorge of Struma R. valley; lower Struma R. basin fertile agr. a., producing cotton, tobacco; mkt. ctr. at cap. Serrai; a. 4,053 km²; p. (1981) 46,317 (t.).

Sertão, semi-arid hinterland. N.E. **Brazil;** stock-raising, but drought causes migration to Amazon basin; hydroelectric power and irrigation schemes; focus of social unrest documented in Brazilian novels.

Sesto San Giovanni, sub., Milan, **Italy;** machin., glass, chemicals, plastics; p. (1981) 94,738.

Sète, spt., Hérault dep., **France;** on Med. cst.; chemicals, fisheries; exp. oysters, brandy, wine; oil pipeline under sea to Frontignan; importance originally based upon canal network, now supplanted by rlys.; tourism of growing importance; p. (1982) 58,865 (met. a.).

Setesdal (Saetersdal), Aust-Agder, S. **Norway;** remote valley retaining traditional social customs; arable pastoral agr.

Sétif, cap. of Sétif dep., N.E. **Algeria;** agr. ctr. for surrounding plateaux; grain, livestock; phosphates in a.; p. (est. 1975) 88,000.

Seto, t., central Honshu, **Japan;** porcelain ctr. (since 13th cent.); based on local deposits of kaolin; p. (1979)117,627.

Setouchi, dist., S.W. Honshu, **Japan;** rice, mandarin oranges, reeds, salt, textiles; part of Japan's industl. belt.

Setté Cama, spt., **Gabon,** Equatorial Africa; open roadstead, landing difficult owing to swell; exp. timber; oil nearby.

Settle, mkt. t., Craven, North Yorks., **Eng.;** on R. Ribble in heart of Craven dist.; tourist ctr. for limestone cty. of N. Pennines; textiles.

Settsu Plain, S. Honshu, **Japan;** at head of Osaka Bay at E. end of Inland Sea; intensively cultivated alluvial lowlands, ch. crops, rice, vegetables, oranges; gr. industl. belt extends along cst. through Kobe, Osaka, Kishiwada; engin., chemicals, textiles; a. 1,295 km².

Setubal, t., Estremadura, S. **Portugal;** impt. pt. on Sado R., estuary; exp. cork, wine, oranges; fishing, fish processing, shipyds.; p. (1981) 78,274.

Sevan (Gokcha), lge. L., Armenian SSR, **USSR;** alt. 1,934 m; never freezes; surrounded by high barren mtns.; drained by Razdan R.; several hydroelectric power stas.

Sevastopol, spt., Ukrainian SSR, **USSR;** built on ruins left after famous siege 1855; Black Sea resort; rebuilt after second world war; one of most beautiful Crimean cs.; p. (est. 1980) 308,000.

Sevenoaks, mkt. t., l. gov. dist., Kent, **Eng.;** in Vale of Holmesdale; residtl.; agr., lt. inds.; Knole Park; public school founded in 1432; p. (1981) 109,402 (dist.).

Severn, R., Ont., **Canada;** flows to Hudson Bay; tr. post at mouth; 560 km long.

Severn, R., W. of **Eng.** and N. **Wales;** rises in Powys and flows to Bristol Channel; suspension bridge at estuary opened 1966; several proposals for major economic development around shores of estuary; 344 km long.

Severn Tunnel, Eng.; under estuary of R. Severn between Pilning (Avon) and Severn Tunnel Junction (Gwent); carries main rly. from London to S. **Wales;** longest main-line rly. tunnel in Brit. Is.; 7 km long.

Severodvinsk, t., RSFSR; on Dvina Bay, White Sea; metals, bldg. materials; p. (est. 1980) 203,000.

Seville, c., cap. of Seville prov. and of Andalusia, **Spain;** spt. on Guadalquivir R., canal link with Atl. Oc.; exp. agr. prod., imports industl. raw materials; major industl., comm. and cultural ctr.; diverse mnfs.; beautiful c. with Moorish influence, prominent in narrow streets of ctr. a.; Alcázar palace; Gothic cath.; bullfighting, tourist ctr.; p. (1981) 645,811.

Sèvres, t., Hauts-de-Seine, dep., N. **France;** S.W. sub. of Paris on Seine R.; celebrated porcelain mnfs.; headquarters of International Bureau of Weights and Measures; p. (1982) 20,225.

Seward, t., S. Alaska, **USA;** rly. terminal, airfield and ice-free harbour make it an impt. supply ctr. for interior Alaska; p. (1980) 1,843.

Seychelles Is., indep. rep. (1976), **Indian Oc.;** consists of 86 Is. (37 granitic, 49 coralline), among most beautiful in world; lgst. I. Mahé; cap. Victoria; fishing, heavy dependence on tourism pays for dependence on imported food; petroleum exploration; exp. copra, cinnamon bark; famous for species of nut; total a. 404 km²; p. (est. 1984) 64,718.

Seyne, or La Seyne-sur-Mer, t., Var dep., **France;** nr. Toulon; shipbld.; p. (1982) 58,146.

Sfax, spt., **Tunisia;** admin. ctr.; exp. phosphate, olive oil, salt, esparto grass, cereals, dates, hides; imports food, coal, textiles, soap; sponges; fishing; natural gas found in a.; surrounded by irrigated gardens and olive groves; p. (1975) 171,297.

Sgurr Mor, mtn., Ross and Cromarty, **Scot.;** alt. 1,109 m.

Shaanxi (Shensi), prov., N. **China;** Great Wall runs nr. N. border with Inner Mongolia; from N.–S. four main regions: (1) dry, fertile loess plateau, notorious famine region, but increasingly irrigated; (2) fertile Wei R. valley, ctr. of p. and agr.; (3) Hua Shan (4) agr. a. of upper Han R.; grain, livestock; coal, petroleum; developing transportation network aiding economic development; cap. Xi'an; a. 188,860 km²; p. (est. 1968) 21,000,000.

Shaba (Katanga), prov., **Zaïre;** many varied mineral deposits inc. copper, tin, iron-ore, cobalt, radium; cap. Lubumbashi; a. 466,200 km²; (1970) 2,700,000.

Shache (Yarkand), c., Xinjiang prov., **China;** tr. ctr. in S. oasis; tr. in wheat, rice, beans, fruit, carpets, textiles; p. (est.) 60,000

Shache (Yarkand), R., Xinjiang prov., **China;** trib. of Gan R.; 800 km long.

Shaftesbury, mkt. t, North Dorset, **Eng.;** Saxon hilltop t., abbey ruins; ctr. for agr. a.; p. (1981) 4,942.

Shahjahanpur, t., Uttar Pradesh, **India;** on Deoha R.; agr. mkt. t. and rly junc.; grain, sugar tr. and processing; p. (1971) 135,604 (t.), 144,065 (met. a.).

Shakhty (Alexandrovsk Grushevski), t., **RSFSR;** anthracite mng. in Donets Basin; leather, textiles, metal wkg., food inds.; p. (est. 1980) 212,000.

Shamaldy-Say, t., Kirghiz SSR, **USSR;** new t. on site of Uch-Kurgan hydroelectric power sta.

Shandakan Tunnel, N.Y. st., **USA;** carries water under Catskill mtns. to augment water supply of c. of N.Y.; 29 km long.

Shandong (Shantung), coastal prov., N. **China;** S. of fertile plain of Huang He; dense p. but agr. potential limited by dry climate; wheat, millet, maize, soyabeans, cotton, hemp, fruits; E. mtns. contain coal, iron, bauxite, kaolin; iron and steel inds. and cotton mills at main industl. ts. of Jinan and Qingdao; special economic zones to encourage foreign investment; birthplace of Confucius at foot of sacred peak Tai; cap. Jinan; a. 146,198 km²; p. (est. 1982) 74,400,000.

Shanghai, c. and mun., Jiangsu, **China;** major spt. on left bank of Huangpu (main waterway of Chang Jiang delta); despite marshy site its strategic location developed, largely by Brit. business-men (1843); handles major share of Chinese shipping, but much dredging required; in part a modern W. style c., but distinctively Chinese in original Chinese site; inds. developed in response to location at transit point for major economic region of China in Chang Jiang basin; major educational ctr.; 3rd most populous c. of world; a. 5,799 km²; p. (est. 1982) 11,860,000.

Shannon Airport, Clare, **R.o.I.;** N.W. of Limerick; on main transatlantic air route; ctr. of customs-free industl. estate built (1958) to compensate for decline in air traffic with larger planes; p. (1981) 7,998 (t.).

Shannon, R., Ireland; separates Connaught from provs. of Leinster and Munster, flows to Atl. at Loop Head; hydroelectric power sta. at Ardnacrusha; 358 km long.

Shan State, div., **Burma;** elevated plateau through which flows Salween R.; impt. mng. dist., lead, zinc, silver at Bawdwin, smelters at Namtu; also tungsten, tin, antimony, manganese; home of Shan people; former Shan and Wa sts.; cap. Taunggyi; a. 155,801 km².

Shantou (Swatow), c., spt., S.E. Guandong, **China;** at mouth of Han R.; mftg. and exp. tr., sugar refineries; special economic zone to attract foreign inds.; p. (est. 1970) 400,000.

Shanxi (Shansi), prov., N. **China;** bounded W. and S. by Huang He; mainly high plateaux; fertile loess deposits, but drought conditions limit agr. potential; dry crops and livestock; coal, iron-ore, petroleum; cap. Taiyuan; a. 156,420 km²; p. (est. 1967) 18,000,000.

Shaohing. See **Shaoxing.**

Shaoxing (Shaohing), c., N. Zhejiang prov., S.E. **China;** agr. ctr. on Hangzhou Bay; rice, wheat, cotton; p. (est. 1970) 225,000.

Shaoyang, c., Hunan prov., **China;** coal and iron mng.; timber; p. (est. 1970) 275,000.

Shap, mkt. t., Cumbria, **Eng.;** nearby in Shap Fell 279 m, an impt. pass traversed by rly. and by a main road; granite quarries.

Shapinsay, Orkney Is., **Scot.;** p. (1971) 346.

Shari, R., central **Africa;** formed by several head-streams in Central African Rep., flows across Chad Rep. into L. Chad in wide delta; navigable.

Sharjah, emirate, member of the **United Arab Emirates** (1971), Persian Gulf; international airport at cap. Shārjah (p. 25,000); natural harbour at Khawr Fakhan; oil exploration, fishing; p. (est. 1970) 40,000.

Sharon, plain, **Israel;** citrus fruits, vines, poultry.

Shashi, t., S. Hubei prov., **China;** agr. mkt. ctr. and canalised R. pt.; tr. in cotton, grain; flour milling, textiles; p. (est. 1970) 125,000.

Shasta Dam, Cal., **USA;** dams water of Rs. Pit, McCloud, Sacramento for hydroelectric power; irrigation, flood control and reclamation of lower Sacramento valley.

Shatt-al-Arab, R., **Iraq;** formed by union of Tigris and Euphrates, flows thence to head of Persian G.; swampy delta in rich agr. a.; deepest-water line of R.'s estuary defined (1975) as new Iraq/Iran bdy.; 192 km long.

Shawinigan Falls, c., Quebec, **Canada;** pulp and paper, chemicals, aluminium inds., powered by hydroelectric power from falls on St. Maurice R.; p. (1971) 28,000.

Shawnee, c., Okla., **USA;** rly. and tr. ctr. for rich agr. a.; electronics, aircraft components; p. (1980) 26,506.

Sheaf, R., South Yorks., **Eng.;** rises in S.E. Pennines, flows N.E. to join R. Don at Sheffield; 18 km long.

Shebelinka, natural gas fields nr. Kharkov, Ukrainian SSR, **USSR;** pipelines to Kharkov-Bryansk and Dnepropetrovsk-Odessa.

Sheboygan, t., Wis., **USA;** on L. Michigan; ctr. for dairy farming and resort a.; cheese, leather gds., hardware; p. (1980) 48,085 (t., 100,935 (met. a.).

Sheerness, Kent, **Eng.;** on I. of Sheppey at entrance to estuary of R. Medway; former royal dockyard and garrison; deepwater comm. pt.; electronics, furniture, coach bldg.

Sheffield, c., met. dist., South Yorks., **Eng.;** on cramped site at confluence of Rs. Sheaf and Don; univ.; heavy engin. ctr., famous for high quality steels, cutlery, tools; major post-war redevelopment of c. ctr. with ambitious and imaginative housebldg. programme by a socially conscious local council, taking advantage of hilly site has turned S. into a very attractive modern c.; p. (1981) 536,770.

Sheksna, R., **RSFSR;** rises in L. Beloye and flows S. to Rybinsk Reservoir; forms part of Volga–Baltic waterway; 160 km long.

Shellhaven, oil refineries, Essex, **Eng.;** on N. side of Thames estuary, nr. Standord-le-Hope.

Shenandoah National Park, Va., **USA;** extends along forested Blue Ridge mtns.; views of Shenandoah valley and Allegheny mtns.

Shenandoah, R., Va., **USA;** trib. of Potomac R.; picturesque valley noted for rich apple orchards and pastures; scene of several campaigns in Civil War; 272 km long.

Shensi. See **Shaanxi.**

Shen-yang (Mukden), c., cap. of Liaoning prov., N.E. **China;** on Hun R. in narrowest part of lowland with hilly country on both sides; impt. rly. junc. with main routes N. to Harbin and Trans-Siberian rly., S. to Beijing, Luta and into Korea; comm. and educational ctr.; impt. textile ctr., heavy inds., cement, chemicals, machin.; agr. tr.; p. (est. 1970) 3,750,000.

Shenzhen, special economic zone, Guandong, **China;** a. selected (1983) to encourage foreign investment; close to Hong Kong; soft drinks, cement, electronic equipment, petrochems. relocated from Hong Kong; planned nuclear power plant to supply Hong Kong.

Shepperton, t., Victoria, **Australia;** ctr. of vegetable and orchard a. of Goulburn valley irrigation; p. (1976) 25,848.

Sheppey, I. of, Kent, Swale, **Eng.;** in Thames estuary E. of mouth of R. Medway; cereals, sheep-raising; new steel wks.; ch. t., Sheerness; a. 117 km².

Shepshed, t., Charnwood, Leics., **Eng.**; 5 km W. of Loughborough; hosiery; p. (1981) 11,151.

Shepton Mallet, mkt. t., Mendip, Somerset, **Eng.**; at foot of Mendip Hills, 8 km S.E of Wells; old woollen ctr.; bacon curing, brewing; p. (1981) 6,303.

Shepway, l. gov. dist., S.E. Kent, **Eng.**; cstl. a. of Folkestone, Hythe, New Romney and Lydd; p. (1981) 86,074.

Sherborne, mkt. t., West Dorset, **Eng.**; 6 km E. of Yeovil; famous abbey and school; Norman cas. ruins; glass fibre; p. (1981) 7,572.

Sherbrook, t., S.E. Quebec, **Canada**; comm. and mkt. ctr. for surrounding agr. region; inds. based on local sources of hydroelectric power from Magog R.; textiles, paper mills, machin., flour milling; deposits of asbestos nearby; p. (1976) 75,137.

Sheringham, t., North Norfolk, **Eng.**; on cst. 6 km W. of Cromer; resort; fishing; p. (1981) 5,515.

Sherwood Forest, anc. royal woodland, Notts., **Eng.**; now restricted to infertile Bunter Sandstone cty.; inc. several estates and parks, notably the Dukeries.

Shetland Is., Scot.; 80 km N.E. of the Orkneys; about 100 in gr., ch. I., Mainland; lge. number of rainy days, but climate mild and tourism attracted by isolation, scenery and wildlife; Fair Isle famous for knitted clothes; fishing, livestock, agr., potatoes; rapid growth with oil drilling in N. Sea: lge oil terminal of Sullum Voe; lge. elderly p. due to attractions as a retirement a.; ch. t. Lerwick; a. 1,427 km²; p. (1981) 26,716 (1971 – 17,080).

Shibin el Kôm, Menûfiya, **Egypt**; rly. and mkt. ctr. in agr. a. of Nile delta; tobacco, textiles; p. (1976) 102,805.

Shigatze. *See* **Zigaze.**

Shijiazhuang (Shihkiachwang) c., Hebei prov., **China**; cotton milling, glass mftg.; grew rapidly with coming of rly.; p. (est. 1970) 1,500,000.

Shikarpur, t., N. Sind, **Pakistan**; tr. ctr. for grain, precious stones; engin., food processing; p. (est. 1971) 66,000.

Shikoku, I., **Japan**; S. of Honshu, smallest of Japan's 4 main Is.; sparsely populated, mtnous. interior, heavily forested; arable agr. in lowlands; ch. cs., Matsuyama, Kochi, Tokushima; a. 18,772 km²; p. (1970) 3,904,014.

Shilka, R., E. Siberia, **RSFSR**; trib. of R. Amur; 552 km long.

Shillelagh, v., R.D., Wicklow, **R.o.I.**; oak forest, gave its name to oak or blackthorn cudgel.

Shillong, c., cap. Meghalaya, former cap. of Assam, **India**; at alt. 1,372 m in Khasi hills; ctr. of impt. tea-growing dist.; admin. technical education; pleasant climate attracts summer tourists; p. (1971) 87,659 (c), 122,752 (met. a).

Shimizu, spt., **Japan**; exp. tea, oranges; fishing; p. (1979) 242,797.

Shimoda, spt., Honshu, **Japan**; between Nagoya and Yokohama; fishing; p. (1970) 30,318.

Shimoga, t., Karnataka, **India**; on Tunga R.; cotton-ginning, rice-milling; p. (1971) 102,709.

Shimonoseki, spt., Honshu I., **Japan**; at extreme S.W. of I.; tunnel and bridge links island of Kyushu; rly. ctr.; engin., chemicals based on local coal; fishing; p. (1979) 283,166.

Shin, Loch, Sutherland, **Scot.**; 26 km long; drained by R. Shin to R. Oykell.

Shipka Pass, **Bulgaria**; over the Balkan mtns., 75 km N.E. of Plovdiv.

Shipley, t., West Yorks., **Eng.**; on R. Aire, 13 km N.W. of Leeds; worsted mnfs.; inc. model v. of Saltaire, built by Titus Salt (1851) to house his alpaca mill workers; p. (1981) 27,894.

Shiraz, c., cap. of Fars prov., **Iran**; beautifully sited in vine-growing dist.; textiles, rugs, metal wks., lt. elec ind., tourist ctr.; tombs of mediaeval poets Saadi and Hafez; known as "city of roses and nightingales"; pleasant winter climate; univ., airpt.; oil refinery projected; p. (1976) 416,408.

Shire, R., flows out of L. Malawi south through **Malawi** and **Moçambique** to Zambesi; lge. hydro-elect. potential; 592 km long.

Shirwa or **Chilwah,** shallow L., **Malawi**; 64 km long, 22 km wide; has 4 Is.

Shizuoka, c., cap. of S. pref., Honshu, **Japan**; pt. on Suruga Bay; impt. ctr. for tea and oranges; lacquer-ware, textiles; p. (1979) 457,887.

Shkodër (Scutari) c., N. **Albania**; stands at foot of L. Scutari, 26 km from Adriatic; mkt. ctr., tobacco, cement, textiles; enjoyed greatest comm. prosperity after Ottoman conquest; several mosques; p. (1967) 50,000.

Shkodër (Scutari), L., on borders of Montenegro **(Yugoslavia)** and **Albania**; outlet via R. Boyana into Adriatic, 46 km long.

Sholapur, c., Maharashtra, **India**; between Hyderabad and Poona; rly. junc., impt. textile ctr.; p. (1971) 398,361.

Shoreham-by-Sea, t., Adur, West Sussex, **Eng.**; at mouth of R. Adur, 6 km E. of Worthing; spt. and mkt. t.; oil jetty; boat bldg., chemicals, soap, preserves; p. (1981) 20,827.

Shoshone Falls, on Snake R., Idaho, **USA**; height 61 m, used for irrigation projects.

Shott el Jerid, Algeria and **Tunisia**; deep depression in the desert.

Shotts, plateau, N. **Africa**; upland region with salt Ls., within Atlas mtns.

Shreveport, c., La., **USA**; industl. ctr. in cotton-growing dist.; petroleum; p. (1980) 206,000 (c.), 377,000 (met. a.).

Shrewsbury, co. t., Shrops., **Eng.**; on R. Severn 19 km above Ironbridge gorge between the Wrekin and Wenlock Edge; agr. and dairy equipment, machin., elec. gds.; cattle and sheep mkt.; public school; with Atcham forms l. gov. dist.; p. (1981) 87,218.

Shropshire, non-met co., **Eng.**; on Welsh border, crossed by R. Severn; fine pastoral cty.; with hills and woodland, agr. and dairying; industl. activity at co. t. Shrewsbury; a. 3,489 km²; p. (1981) 375,610.

Shropshire, North, l. gov. dist., Shrops., **Eng.**; a. N. of Shrewsbury and inc. Market Drayton; p. (1981) 50,114.

Shropshire, South, l. gov. dist., Shrops., **Eng.**; S. of Shrewsbury and inc. Ludlow; p. (1981) 33,815.

Shusha, t., Azerbaydzhan SSR, **USSR**; health resort; silk spinning, rug making; Armenian p. massacred by Tartars 1926; p. c. 6,000.

Shustar, t., **Iran**; carpets, woollens, pottery; shallow-draught boats can reach Shallili, nr. S. by R. Karun; p. (1966) 21,999.

Sialkot, t., **Pakistan**; N.E. of Lahore; sports gds., musical and surgical instruments, paper; agr. tr. and processing ctr.; p. (est. 1972) 204,000.

Siam. *See* **Thailand.**

Siam, G. of, lge. inlet, S. China Sea; sheltered with shallow water; length 616 km N.W. to S.E.

Sian. *See* **Xi'an.**

Siangtan. *See* **Xiangtan.**

Siauliai, t., Lithuanian SSR, **USSR**; 184 km N.W. of Vilna; impt. rly. junc.; food and leather inds.; p. (est. 1969) 88,000.

Sibenik, t., Croatia, **Yugoslavia**; Adriatic spt.; exp. timber, bauxite; aluminium, chemical and textile inds.; p. (est. 1971) 30,100.

Siberia, terr., **USSR**; extends from Urals to Sea of Okhotsk and Bering Strait, bounded by Arctic on N. and by Mongolia and Turkestan on S.; climate mostly severe; ch. ts., Novosibirsk (cap. W. S.) and Irkutsk (cap. E. S.); rich in coal, iron, minerals; oil and gas in W. Siberian lowland; resources not yet fully known but Soviet economic policy is to develop its natural resources to the full; liquified coal pipeline under construction to Moscow; p. and economic activity clustered around rlys., esp. Trans-Siberian rly.; a. c. 12,950,000 km².

Sibiu, t., central **Romania**; picturesque site at foot of Transylvanian Alps; retains mediaeval character despite being an impt. industl. ctr.; lge. German minority p.; caths.; p. (1978) 157,519.

Sibu, t., Sarawak, E. **Malaysia**; 128 km up R. Rejang; comm. ctr. at head of ocean navigation; airport; p. (est. 1970) 50,635.

Sichuan (Szechwan), prov., S.W. **China**; mostly occupied by Chang Jiang; known as Red Basin because of colour of its sandstone; fertile a. with mild climate; rice, tea, citrus fruits, tobacco, sugar-cane; lge coal reserves; exp. tung oil; silk producing a.; most populous prov.; cap. Chengdu; a. 568,977 km²; p. (est. 1982) 99,700,000.

Sicily, lgst. I., Mediterranean Sea; former kingdom and now aut. region of **Italy**; pleasant climate, mtnous.; fertile lowlands, especially plain of Catania, but gr. hampered by primitive methods, absentee landlords and need for irrigation; lge. range of Mediterranean crops; fishing; sulphur; petroleum reserves, refining and petrochemical inds.; volcanic Mt. Etna erupted in 1971; a. 25,708 km²; p. (1981) 4,906,878.

Sidi-bel-Abbès, t., W. **Algeria**; old fortress t., become H.Q. of Fr. Foreign Legion; agr. mkt. ctr. for region producing grain, grapes, olives, livestock; p. (est. 1975) 105,000.

Sidlaw Hills, low mtn. range, Tayside Reg., **Scot.**; max. alt. 455 m.

Sidmouth, mkt. t., East Devon, **Eng.**; on S. cst., 24 km S.E. of Exeter; seaside resort; retirement ctr.; p. (1981) 12,446.

Sidon. See **Saïda.**

Siebengebirge, sm. wooded range of seven hills, **W. Germany**; of volcanic origin rising to 457 m on right bank of Rhine; famous for Drachenfels association with the Siegfried saga.

Siedlce, t., **Poland**; 88 km E. of Warsaw; rly. junc.; agr. inds.; p. (1970) 39,000.

Siegburg, t., N. Rhine–Westphalia, **W. Germany**; on R. Sieg; Benedictine abbey; dyes, iron, ceramics; p. (1983) 34,600.

Siegen, t., N. Rhine–Westphalia, **W. Germany**; on R. Sieg; 2 cas.; iron mng. and smelting, machin., leather; p. (1983) 109,800.

Siemianowice Slaskie, t., **Poland**; nr. Katowice; ctr. of mng., industl. region; iron and steel, machin.; cas.; p. (1970) 67,300.

Siena, hill-town, Tuscany, **Italy**; 51 km S. of Florence; spreads over three hilltops with Piazza del Campo in between where celebrated Palio festival (horse-races) are held; 13th- and 14th-cent. arch., cath.; agr. mkt., tanning, glass, textiles, bricks; *panforte* confectionery; tourist ctr.; p. (1981) 61,989.

Sierra Leone, rep., W. cst. **Africa**; mangrove swamps on cst., high plateau, with peaks over 1,800 m in interior; climate hot, humid; economy based on subsistence agr. with rice, coffee and cocoa for exp.; iron ore mng. restarted (1983) at Marampa; main exp. diamonds, notorious smuggling problem; fishing along cst.; cap. Freetown; a. 72,326 km²; p. (est. 1984) 3,536,000.

Sierra Madre Occidental, mtn. range, **Mexico**; volcanic, forms W. edge of Mexican plateau; average alt. 2,100 m.

Sierra Madre Oriental, mtn. range, **Mexico**; limestone, forms E. edge of Mexican plateau; average alt. 2,400 m.

Sierra Maestra, mtn. range, Oriente prov., S.E. **Cuba**; rises abruptly from cst.; rich in minerals.

Sierra Morena, mtn. range, **Spain**; between Guadalquivir and Guadiana basins, highest point 1,677 m; rich in minerals.

Sierra Nevada, mtn. range, Granada, **Spain**; highest summit Mulhacén 3,483 m.

Sierra Nevada, mtn. chain, Cal., **USA**; highest peak Mt. Whitney 4,544 m; nat. parks.

Sierra Nevada de Mérida, mtn. range, W. **Venezuela**; extends N.E. from San Cristóbal to Barquisimeto; extension of E. range of Andes, alt. over 4,880 m; impt. coffee plantations from 900–1,800 m on slopes.

Sierra Pacaraima, mtn. range, Brazil, **Venezuela**; forms part of international bdy. and watershed between Amazon and Orinoco basins.

Sighet, frontier t., N. **Romania**; on R. Tisa, on border with USSR; extreme, continental climate; timber, agr. and livestock tr.; cotton textiles; p. (est. 1971) 33,361.

Siglufjörd, spt., N. **Iceland**; impt. herring fisheries; p. (1970) 2,161.

Sigtuna, t., Stockholm, **Sweden**; on Mälaren L.; first cap. of Sweden; educational ctr., tourist resort; p. (1983) 28,681.

Sihanoukville. See **Kompong Som.**

Sikhote-Alin, mtn. range, S.E. Asiatic **RSFSR**; rises to 1,800 m and extends for 1,200 km parallel to Pac. cst.; hinders access to W. basins; forestry, minerals.

Si-Kiang. See **Xi Jiang.**

Sikkim, st., **India**; on S. slopes of Himalayas; incorporated as 22nd st. 1975; forest covered; economically underdeveloped; scene of rivalry between India and China; cap. Gangtok; a. 7,110 km²; p. (1971) 208,609.

Sila, La, massif, Calabria, S. **Italy**; granite mass occupying full width of peninsula; alt. over 1,060 m, max. 1,930 m.

Silchester, par., Hants., **Eng.**; ruins of Roman t., Calleva Atrebatum; impt. ctr. of Roman communications network.

Silesia (Polish Slask, Czech Slezsko, German Schlesien), geographical region, Central Europe; since 1945 divided between Poland, ČSSR and E. Germany; extends along both banks of Oder R.; bounded in S. by Sudeten mtns.; forested mtns., fertile arable agr. in lowlands; major

concentration of economic activity based on coalfield of Upper Silesia (ceded to Poland 1922); complex territorial history; now forms highly urbanised industl. conurb. mainly in Poland, admin. by Katowice, Opole, Wroclaw, Wroclaw (c.), and part of Zielona Gora; ČSSR portion forms part of N. Moravia; E. Germany retains sm. part of Lower Silesia W. of Neisse R.; total a. 46,600 km².

Silistria, t., **Bulgaria**; on Danube opposite Romanian t. of Calarasi; cereals and timber tr.; mnfs. foodstuffs, ceramics, furniture; mosques; p. (est. 1970) 38,500.

Silkeborg, t., Jutland, **Denmark**; tourist resort in beautiful forest and lake region; p. (est. 1970) 26,129.

Silsden, t., West Yorks., **Eng.**; wool textiles; p. (1981) 6,742.

Silver Spring, t., Md., **USA**; sub. N. of Washington, D.C.; science-based inds. and research laboratories; p. (1980) 72,893.

Simcoe, L., S. Ont., **Canada**; several resorts; boating, fishing; 48 km by 42 km.

Simeulue, I., S.W. of Sumatra, **Indonesia**; primitive islanders; fishing and shifting cultivation.

Simferopol, t., Ukrainian SSR, **USSR**; on R. Salghir nr. Sevastopol; industl. ctr. in rich agr. a., fruit-canning, tobacco, machin.; p. (est. 1980) 307,000.

Simla, t., Himachal Pradesh, **India**; famous hill-station c. 2,158 m high on forested ridge of Himalayas, 280 km N. of Delhi.

Simonstown, W. Cape Prov., **S. Africa**; naval sta, docks; p. (est. 1970) 12,091.

Simplon, mtn., **Switzerland**; alt. 3,567 m; the pass over the Simplon (alt. 2,011 m) from Domodossola, Italy, to Brig in the Rhône valley, Switzerland, was originally made by Napoleon I. The Simplon rly. tunnel leads from Brig on the Swiss side to Iselle in the Val di Vedro on the Italian and is the longest in the world, 19.7 km.

Simpson Desert, Central **Australia**; uninhabited arid a. covered in ridge dunes and spinifex; a. 77,000 km².

Sinai, peninsula, easternmost part of **Egypt**; between Gs. of Aqaba and Suez, at head of Red Sea; mainly desert in N., granitic ridges in S. rising to 2,592 m at Jebel Katrun; Jebel Musa or Mt. Sinai (2,244 m) is one of numerous peaks; mineral resources; coal mine at Maghára; occupied by Israeli troops, Nov. 1956–March 1957, and since June 1967; phased Israeli withdrawal began 1979 after the Israeli–Egypt settlement; a. 28,632 km².

Sinaia, t., S. **Romania**; health and winter sports resort in Transylvanian Alps; until 1947 summer residence of Romanian kings; palaces; p. (est. 1971) 12,000.

Sinaloa, st., **Mexico**; on G. of Cal.; agr. and mng., rich in gold, silver, copper, iron and lead; cereals on uplands; sugar, cotton on lowlands; cap. Culiacán; a. 48,482 km²; p. (1970) 1,266,528.

Sind, prov. (revived 1970), **Pakistan**; lower Indus valley; dry climate; E. part reaches edge of Thar desert; agr. depends on irrigation; irrigated by Sukkur and Kotri systems; wheat, rice, cotton, oilseeds, sugar-cane, fruits; handicraft inds. in ts.; ch. ts., Karachi, Hyderabad, Sukkur, Shikarpur; a. 129,500 km²; p. (1972) 13,965,000.

Singapore, rep., S.E. **Asia**; I. separated from Malaysian mainland by Johore Strait and linked by causeway; equatorial climate; cap. Singapore on S. cst. has fine natural harbour; major entrepôt tr. for Malaysia and S.E. Asia; world ctr. of rubber and tin mkts.; tr. in rubber, tin, petroleum, imported foodstuffs; growing industl. estates; oil refining, shipbldg.; only 20 per cent land cultivated; fruit, mkt. gardening; offshore fishing; reduction in Brit. military presence from base on N. cst. of I.; a. 580 km²; p. (est. 1984) 2,540,000 (rep.).

Singhbhum, dist., Bihar, **India**; iron and steel wks. based on local iron mng.; a. 13,445 km²; p. (1961) 2,049,911.

Sinhailion. See **Lianyungang.**

Sining. See **Xining.**

Sinkiang-Uighur. See **Xinjiang Uygur.**

Sinop, cap. of S. prov., **Turkey**; sm. pt. with gd. harbour on Black Sea but poor communications with hinterland; p. (1970) 15,096.

Sintra (Cintra), t., **Portugal**; summer resort, 29 km from Lisbon; Moorish castle, royal palace; p. (1981) 126,010 (met. a.).

Sinuiju, c., W. N. **Korea**; spt. at mouth of Yalu R. on Yellow Sea; linked by bridge to Antung (China); industl. ctr.; chemicals, aluminium inds., using power from Supung Dam; p. (est. 1970) 125,000.

Sinyang. See **Xinyang**.

Sion, t., cap. of Valais can., **Switzerland**; on R. Rhône; built on two castled hills; cath.; horticultural mkt. ctr.; hydroelectric power stas. and coal mines nearby; p. (est. 1978) 23,400.

Sioux City, Iowa, **USA**; on R. Missouri; meat-packing, foundries, elec. gds., cement; p. (1980) 82,003 (c.), 117,457 (met. a.).

Sioux Falls, t., S.D., **USA**; on Big Sioux R.; in rich wheat region; machin., cars, farming implements; nuclear reactor; p. (1980) 81,343 (t.) 109, 435 (met. a.).

Siping (Szeping), c., Jilin prov., **China**; agr. distributing ctr.; cement; p. (est. 1970) 180,000.

Siret, R., Romania, **USSR**; flows E. from Carpathians to Danube; steep forested left bank, fertile terraced right bank; hydroelectric power and irrigation schemes; 448 km long.

Sisak, t., Croatia, **Yugoslavia**; developing indust. ctr. and R. pt.; iron and steel, oil refining.

Sistan and Baluchistan, twin prov., **Iran**; bounded by Afghanistan and Pakistan; cap. Zahedan; much desert land; arid, very hot; p. (1967) 456,435.

Sitapur, t., Uttar Pradesh, **India**; rly. junc.; agr. tr. ctr.; eye hospital; p. (est. 1971) 67,000.

Sitra, I., Persian G.; forms part of st. of Bahrain, 5 km long and 1·6 km wide; oil pipeline and causeway carrying road extends out to sea for 5 km to deep-water anchorage.

Sittang, R., **Burma**; rises in Pegu Yoma, flows S. to G. of Martaban through delta; valley intensively cultivated, delta forested; irrigation project; 976 km long.

Sittard, mkt. t., Limburg, **Neth.**; tanning; p. (1982) 43,856.

Sittingbourne and Milton, mkt. t., Swale, Kent, **Eng.**; on Milton Creek, 14 km E. of Chatham; paper mills, brick wks.; cement; insecticides; ctr. of fruit-growing dist.; p. (1981) 33,645.

Sittwe (Akyab), spt., **Burma**; at mouth of Kaladan R.; exp. rice; pt. suffered during war; p. (est. 1962) 86,451.

Sivas, c., cap. of S. prov., **Turkey**; impt. tr. and agr. ctr. in Kizil Irmak valley; cement, rugs; copper mng. nearby; foundations of modern Turkey laid here by Atatürk 1919; p. (1979) 161,210.

Sivash Sea or **Putrid Sea**, lagoon on N.E. cst. of Crimea, **USSR**; 20 per cent salt; a. 2,590 km².

Siwa, oasis, **Egypt**; in Libyan Desert, c. 480 km S.W. of Alexandria; dates, olives; remains of temple of Zeus Ammon (visited by Alexander the Great); 32 km long, 1·6 km wide; p. (1966) 3,600.

Sizewell, Suffolk, **Eng.**; nuclear power sta.; plans to build Britain's 1st pressurised water nuclear reactor here.

Sjaelland, I., **Denmark**; lgst. I., separated from Fyn I. by the Gr. Belt; fertile glacial clays but rapidly spreading ts.; ch. c. Copenhagen; a. 7,356 km²; p. (1965) 2,055,040.

Skagerrak, arm of N. Sea, giving access to the Kattegat, between Norway and Denmark, 112–144 km wide.

Skagway, sm. spt., Alaska, **USA**; at head of Lynn Canal inlet, 640 km N.W. of Prince Rupert; linked by rly. to Whitehorse on upper R. Yukon; boomed in gold rush (1898), p. 15,000, subsequently declined; p. (1980) 768.

Skåne (Scania), prov. and peninsula, extreme S. of **Sweden**; corresponds approx. to cos. Malmöhus, Kristianstad; most favoured part of Sweden in relief, soil, climate; intensive farming, wheat, barley, sugar-beet, fodder crops, dairy cattle; ch. ts. Malmö, Lund, Hälsingborg; a. 10,939 km², p. (1983) 1,024,152.

Skaraborg, co., **Sweden**; between Ls. Vänern and Vättern; dairy agr.; a. 8,467 km²; p. (est. 1983) 270,423.

Skara Brae, prehistoric v., Mainland, Orkneys, **Scot.**; v. excavated from under sand dunes.

Skarzysko-Kamienna, t., Kielce, **Poland**; ctr. of developing metallurgical ind.; p. (1970) 39,200.

Skaw The (Grenen), C., at extreme N. of **Denmark**.

Skeena, R., B.C., **Canada**; rises in N. Rocky mtns., flows S.W. to Pac. Oc. at Prince Rupert;

lower valley used by Canadian National Rly.; 640 km long.

Skegness, t., East Lindsey, Lincs., **Eng.**; on E. cst.; resort; lt. engin.; p. (1981) 14,425.

Skellefteå, t., N. **Sweden**; on Bothnia G.; growing since discovery of Boliden ores nearby; iron and copper ore smelting; p. (1983) 74,247.

Skelmersdale, t., West Lancs., **Eng.**; coal, bricks, drainpipes; new t. (1961); p. (1981) 39,144.

Skelton and Brotton, t., Langbaurgh, Cleveland, **Eng.**; at N. foot of Cleveland hills, 16 km E. of Middlesbrough; steel flooring; p. (1981) 16,208.

Skiddaw, mtn., Cumbria, **Eng.**; E. of Bassenthwaite L.; alt. 931 m.

Skien, spt., Bratsberg, **Norway**; on R. Skien; saw-mills, timber tr.; birthplace of Ibsen; p. (est. 1973) 46,037.

Skikda (Philippeville), t., spt., **Algeria**; exp. prods. from Saharan oases; oil pipeline to Mesdar; p. (est. 1970) 61,000.

Skipton, t., Craven, North Yorks., **Eng.**; on R. Aire; cotton and rayon inds.; cas.; p. (1981) 13,246.

Skopje, t., cap. of Macedonia, **Yugoslavia**; anc. Scupi, one of oldest ts. in Balkans; oriental appearance; destroyed by earthquake (1963); food processing, iron and steel wks.; new oil refinery; airpt., route ctr.; p. (1981) 506,547.

Skövde, t., **Sweden**; between Ls. Vänern and Vättern; garrison t., chemicals, cement; p. (1983) 46,009.

Skye, I., lgst. of Inner Hebrides, Skye and Lochalsh, **Scot.**; mtnous.; sheep-farming and fisheries; tourism; only t. Portree; a. 1,417 km²; p. (1981) 11,327 (Skye and Lochalsh l. gov. dist.).

Skyros, I., Sporades, **Greece**; in Aegean Sea; mainly agr.; a. 199 km²; p. (1961) 2,882.

Slagelse, t., Sjaelland, **Denmark**; food inds.; iron wks.; 11th cent. church; p. (est. 1970) 23,169.

Slave Coast, name given to the Guinea cst. of W. **Africa** between the Volta and Niger deltas where slaves were shipped from 16th to 19th cent.

Slave, R., N.W. Terr., **Canada**; flows into Gr. Slave L.; length 416 km.

Slavonia, historic region, **Yugoslavia**; between Drava R. (N.) and Sava R. (S.); now part of rep. of Croatia; ch. t. Osijek.

Slavyansk, t., Ukrainian SSR, **USSR**; in Donets basin; chemicals, engin.; p. (est. 1980) 141,000.

Sleaford, mkt. t., North Kesteven, Lincs., **Eng.**; 19 km N.E. of Grantham; agr. and agr. implements; p. (1981) 8,523.

Sleat, Sound of, Lochaber, Skye and Lochalsh, **Scot.**; separates I. of Skye from the mainland; 11 km wide.

Slezsko. See **Silesia**.

Sliema, t., **Malta**; E. of Valletta; resort; p. (est. 1983) 20,123.

Slieve Bloom, hill range, Offaly and Laoghis cos., **R.o.I.**; highest point 529 m.

Slieve Donard, mtn., N. **Ireland**; highest of the Mourne mtns.; alt. 835 m.

Sligo, co., Connacht, **R.o.I.**; borders Atl. Oc.; rises to Ox Mtns. over 600 m; pastoral agr.; fishing; co. t. S.; a. 1,909 km²; p. (1981) 18,002.

Sligo, co. t., Sligo, **R.o.I.**; on S. Bay; pt., exp. agr. prods.; abbey ruins; cath.; p. (1981) 17,232.

Sliven, t., **Bulgaria**; in Balkan mtns.; impt. woollen mnf. ctr.; carpets; p. (est. 1972) 88,260.

Slough, t., l. gov. dist., Berks., **Eng.**; on river terrace N. of R. Thames, 37 km W. of London; many lt. inds.; p. (1981) 97,088.

Slovakia (Slovak Socialist Rep.), ČSSR; extends from Carpathians to Danube valley; prosperous agr.; cap. Bratislava; with Czech Socialist Rep. forms Fed. Rep. of Czechoslovakia; a. 48,956 km²; p. (est. 1970) 4,563,460.

Slovenia, constituent rep., **Yugoslavia**; mtnous., but many minerals inc. coal; highly developed region; cap. Ljubljana; a. 16,229 km²; p. (1971) 1,725,088.

Slupsk (Stolp), t., N.W. **Poland** (since 1945); formerly in Pomerania; on R. Stupia, nr. Baltic Sea; cas.; wood, metal, food processing; p. (1970) 68,300.

Småland, historic prov., S. **Sweden**; barren upland a. S. of L. Vättern; moorland, deciduous forest; contrasts greatly with remainder of S. Sweden; a. 29,322 km²; p. (1983) 701,525.

Smederevo, t., Serbia, **Yugoslavia**; nr. Belgrade; pt. on R. Danube; walled t.; steel wks.; p. (1971) 27,182.

Smethwick. *See* **Warley.**

Smolensk, c., cap. of S. oblast, **RSFSR**; on upper Dnieper; anc. c. damaged in many wars; route ctr.; vehicles, machin., food processing; p. (est. 1980) 305,000.

Smyrna. *See* **Izmir.**

Snaefell, highest mtn., **I. of Man**; alt. 620 m.

Snake R., or **Lewis Fork**, trib. of Columbia R., flows from Wyo. to Wash., **USA**; gorges; hydroelectric power; 1,680 km long.

Sneek, t., Friesland, **Neth.**; butter, cheese mkt.; yachting ctr.; p. (1982) 28,431.

Sneeuwbergen, mtn. range, Cape Prov., **S. Africa.**

Snowdon, mtn., Gwynedd, **Wales**; highest in Eng. and Wales, alt. 1,086 m; forms part of Snowdonia Nat. Park.

Snowy Mtns., N.S.W., **Australia**; part of Australian Alps inc. Australia's hgst. peak (Mount Kosciusko); rise to over 2,000 m; S.M. scheme (1950) diverts water from headstreams in tunnels through mtns. to provide water for irrigation and hydroelectric power; completed 1972.

Snowy, R., N.S.W. and Victoria, **Australia**; rises in Mt. Kosciusko, flows S. into Bass strait 128 km W. of C. Howe; part of Snowy Mtn. scheme; 432 km long.

Soar, R., Leics., Notts., **Eng.**; rises S. of Leics., flows N.W. to join R. Trent; 69 km long.

Sobat, R., Sudan and Ethiopia; made up of several sm. Rs.; trib. of White Nile; 800 km long.

Soche. *See* **Yarkand.**

Sochi, t., **RSFSR**; on Black Sea at foot of main Caucasian range; health resort with subtropical climate and sulphur springs; developed since 1933; p. (est. 1980) 291,000.

Society Is., Fr. Polynesia, S. Pac. Oc.; comprise Windward Is. (Tahiti, Moorea, Mehetia, etc.) and Leeward Is. (Huahune, Raiatea, etc.); visited by Captain Cook; main prods. phosphate and copper; cap. Papeete; a. 1,647 km²; p. (1967) 61,519.

Socotra, I., G. of Aden, Indian Oc.; since 1967 part of **Democratic Rep. of Yemen**; under Brit. protection 1886–1967; lofty tableland; myrrh, frankincense, aloes; cap. Tamrida; a. 3,626 km²; p. (est.) 12,000.

Sodbury, t., Northavon, Avon. **Eng.**; former coalmng. ctr.; expanded t.

Söderhamn, spt., **Sweden**; on G. of Bothnia, N. of Gavle; timber, wood-pulp; p. (est. 1983) 30,736.

Södermanland, co., **Sweden**; between Baltic cst. and L. Mälar; cattle-rearing; mng.; a. 6,822 km²; p. (est. 1983) 965,182.

Södertälje, t., **Sweden**; on S. canal linking L. Mälar with Baltic cst.; vehicles, chemicals, tobacco; p. (1983) 79,553.

Soest, c., N. Rhine–Westphalia, **W. Germany**; one of oldest ts., member of Hanseatic league; suffered heavily in second world war; soap, textile machin., engin.; p. (1983) 41,100.

Soest, t., Utrecht, **Neth.**; residtl., agr. ctr.; p. (1982) 40,670.

Sofia, c., cap. of **Bulgaria**; Roman Serdica, and Triaditsa of Byzantine Greeks; nr. Yugoslav border; impt. route ctr. and ch. industl. ctr. of rep.; machin., textiles, chemicals, elec. engin.; cath., univ., and many historic bldgs.; p. (est. 1978) 1,014,059.

Sogne Fjord, Norway; longest fjord in Norway; length 176 km; tourism.

Sogn og Fjordane, co., W. **Norway**; borders Atl. Oc., indented by Sogne Fjord; lge. hydroelectric power resources; tourism; a. 18,480 km²; p. (est. 1972) 101,740.

Sohag, t., **Egypt**; on R. Nile; cotton processing; p. (1976) 102,914.

Soho, dist., London, **Eng.**; settled by Fr. Huguenots 16th cent.; high proportion of foreign residents, sometimes known as London's "Latin quarter"; night-clubs, theatres, restaurants, film-company offices.

Soissons, t., Aisne dep., **France**; anc. Augusta Suessionum; commands N.E. approaches to Paris; cath.; agr. tr.; p. (1982) 32,236.

Sokoto, t., **Nigeria**, W. Africa; founded 1809 as

cap. of native st. of S., p. mainly Hausa and Fulani; tr. ctr.; p. (est. 1971) 109,000.

Solent, The, strait separating I. of Wight from Hampshire mainland, **Eng.**;

Solihull, t., met dist., West Midlands, **Eng.**; 8 km S.W. of Birmingham; residtl.; motor vehicles chemicals; p. (1981) 198,287.

Solikamsk, t., **RSFSR**; on R. Kama; chemicals from local potash; rapidly growing t.; p. (est. 1980) 102,000.

Solingen, t., N. Rhine–Westphalia, **W. Germany**; 24 km E. of Düsseldorf; cutlery ctr.; p. (1983) 161,100.

Solnechnyy. *See* **Gornyy Snezhnogorsk.**

Solomon Is., S. Pac. Oc.; internal self-gov. (1976); full independence (July 1978); archipelago of volcanic Is.; N. Is. form part of Papua New Guinea; remainder Brit.; dependent on exp. of copra, timber, fish; threatened by insect pests; a. 29,785 km²; p. (est. 1981) 200,000 (mostly Melanesian).

Solothurn (Soleure), can., N.W. **Switzerland**, crossed by Jura mtns., and R. Aare; 97 per cent cultivated; dairying; many industl. ts.; cap. S.; a. 793 km²; p. (1980) 218,102.

Solothurn (Soleure), t., cap. of S. can., **Switzerland**; on R. Aare; anc. t.; cath.; watches, motor mnf.; p. (est. 1978) 15,800.

Solway Firth, arm of **Irish Sea**, Dumfries and Galloway Reg., Scot., and Cumbria, Eng.; 6 km long.

Somalia (Somali Democratic Rep.), E. cst. **Africa**; narrow cst. plain in N., widens in S., interior plateau reaching *c.* 2,400 m; dry, hot climate; 75 per cent. p. nomadic; livestock herding; permanent agr. in irrigated R. valleys; sugar, banana plantations in Webi Shebeli and Juba Rs. in S.; potential for mineral exploitation; cap. Mogadishu; recent conflict with Ethiopia; recent influx of immigrants from Ethiopia; a. 637,658 km²; p. (est. 1984) 5,423,000.

Somaliland, French. *See* **Djibouti.**

Sombor, t., Serbia, **Yugoslavia**; cattle, grain tr.; textiles; p. (1971) 43,971.

Somersby, v., Lincs., **Eng.**; the birthplace of Tennyson.

Somerset, non-met. co., S.W. **Eng.**; inc. part of Exmoor, Mendips, Quantocks and Blackdown hills; to N. is drained marshland of Somerset levels; dairying; coastal resorts; co. t. Taunton; a. 3,458 km²; p. (1981) 424,988.

Somme, dep., N. **France**; borders Eng. Channel; crossed by R. Somme; low-lying agr. a.; textile inds.; cap. Amiens; a. 6,327 km²; p. (1982) 543,600.

Somme, R., **France**; flows in deps. Aisne and Somme to English Channel; scene of battles 1916; linked to Rs. Oise and Scheldt by canal 186 km long.

Somport Tunnel, on bdy. **France–Spain**; carries main rly. from Pau to Zaragoza under Pyrénées; 8 km long.

Sönderborg, spt., S. Jutland, **Denmark**; older part of c. on Als I.; palace; textiles; p. (est. 1970) 23,069.

Sondrio, t., cap. of S. prov., **Italy**; commands the Adda valley, impt. routeway through Alps; agr. mkt.; textiles; p. (1981) 22,747.

Songhua R., (**Sungari R.**), N.E. **China**; trib. of R. Amur; length 1,840 km.; hydroelectric power.

Songkhla, t., **Thailand**; most S. t.; ctr. of rubber growing dist.; third t. of cty.; p. (est. 1975) 42,500.

Song-koi (Red R.), R., rises in Yunnan plateau, S.W. **China**, flows S.E. through N. **Vietnam**, enters G. of Tongking; Hanoi is nr. head of delta; Haiphong nr. one of R. mouths; lower valley densely populated and intensively cultivated; *c.* 1,280 km long.

Sonora, st., **Mexico**; on G. of Cal.; crossed by Sierra Madre Occidental; irrigated agr.; ch. producer of wheat, cattle; fish exp.; cap. Hermosillo; a. 182,535 km²; p. (1970) 1,098,720.

Sonoran Desert, Arizona, **USA**; alt. 900 m; enclosed basins and salt marshes.

Sonsonate, t., **El Salvador**; old t. with cath.; comm. ctr. of richest agr. region of rep., famed for coffee and dairy prod.; nr. Isalco volcano; p. (est. 1970) 45,634.

"Soo" Canals. *See* **Sault Ste. Marie Canals.**

Soochow. *See* **Suzhou.**

Sopot, spt., **Poland**; on Gdansk Bay; resort; spa; part of Trójmiasto; p. (1970) 47,600.

Sopron, t., N.W. **Hungary**; on R. Hunte; nr. Austrian border; textiles, chemicals; p. (est. 1978) 54,565.

Sorau. *See* Zary.

Soria, t., cap. of prov. of Soria, **Spain**; on R. Duero at *c.* 900 m; agr.-processing; retains mediaeval appearance; p. (1981) 100,718 (prov.).

Sorocaba, t., São Paulo st., **Brazil**; linked to São Paulo by 3 major highways yet has not attracted many new inds. unlike rest of reg.; textiles and food processing dominate; p. (est. 1980) 246,700.

Sorrento, cst. t., S. **Italy**; nr. S. extremity G. of Naples; popular resort, celebrated for its wines in anc. times; p. (1981) 17,301.

Sosnowiec, t., Katowice prov., **Poland**; coal-mng. ctr., iron wks.; metal and textile inds.; cas.; p. (est. 1983) 252,000.

Soufrière, volcano, St. Vincent, **W.I.**; alt. 1,235 m.

Sound, The, channel between Kattegat and Baltic, 5 km across at narrowest part; proposed tunnel between Denmark and Sweden.

Sousse (Susa), spt., **Tunisia**; exp. olive oil, phosphates; resort; p. (1975) 69,530.

South Africa, Republic of, lies in most S. part of **Africa** between Atl. and Indian Ocs.; comprises 4 provs., Cape Prov., Natal, O.F.S., Transvaal; narrow cst. plain, several interior plateaux (600–1,800 m) with upland grasslands (Veld) and fringed by escarpments; climate warm and sunny; most highly developed cty. in Africa, based on mineral resources of gold and diamonds, and more recent successful economic diversification; coal in Witbank and Vryheid dists. serves iron and steel ind. at Pretoria; growing textile, food-processing inds. at pts. Cape Town, Durban and rubber at Pt. Elizabeth; agr. dependent upon water supply; rich fruit growing a. around Cape Town, extensive grain growing and pastoral areas extended by irrigation; enforces practice of apartheid; caps. Pretoria (admin.), Cape Town (legislative), Bloemfontein (judicial); a. 1,224,254 km²; p. (1985) 23,438,590 5,500,000 (Bantu Homelands); whites only 17%.

South America, S. continent of Western Hemisphere; inc. all ctys. S. of Panama. *See* **Latin America.**

Southampton, c. spt., l. gov. dist., Hants., **Eng.**; at head of Southampton Water on peninsula between estuaries of Rs. Test and Itchen; univ.; decline of passenger liners, now one of Britain's biggest container pts.; ship repairing, oil refining, cable mkg., electronics, synthetic rubber; freeport (1984); p. (1981) 204,406.

Southampton Water, inlet, Hants., **Eng.**; comprises drowned estuaries of Rs. Itchen and Test; gives access from Solent and Spithead to spt. of Southampton; 14 km by 1·6–2·4 km.

South Australia, st. of the **Australian Commonwealth**; the "desert state"; barren undulating interior forms part of central plateau of continent but inc. mtns. in S. and S.E. and L. Eyre basin 12 m below sea level; Nullarbor Plain in S.W.; sheep in S.E., intensive agr. in Murray R. valley; some interior mng. inds. but st. cap. of Adelaide contains most inds. and 69 per cent of p.; a. 984,381 km²; p. (1976) 1,244,756.

South Bend, c., Ind., **USA**; on St. Joseph R.; ctr. of fruit and dairy region; motorcars, aircraft, agr. machin.; p. (1980) 110,000 (c.), 281,000 (met. a.).

South Bucks, l. gov. dist., Bucks., **Eng.**; based on Beaconsfield; p. (1981) 62,182.

South Carolina, st., **USA**; 'Palmetto St.'; admitted to Union 1788; st. flower Carolina Jessamine, st. bird Carolina Wren; level in E., mtns. in W.; subtropical climate; part of cotton belt; pigs and maize also impt.; cotton textiles; cap. Columbia; a. 80,432 km²; p. (1980) 3,119,000.

South Dakota, st., **USA**; 'Cayote St.'; admitted to Union 1889; st. flower Pasque flower, st. bird Ring Necked Pheasant; lies in Gt. Plains; crossed by R. Missouri; irrigated agr.; part of spring wheat belt, but now more diversified crops; agr. processing; cap. Pierre; a. 199,552 km²; p. (1980) 690,000 (inc. 25,000 Indians).

South Downs, chalk escarpment, East and West Sussex and Hants., **Eng.**; stretch from Chichester to Eastbourne; rise to over 240 m.

Southend-on-Sea, t., l. gov. dist., Essex, **Eng.**; on N. side of Thames estuary; varied lt. inds.; air

Southern Alps, mtns., S.I., **N.Z.**; alt. 3,000 m.

Southern Ocean, surrounds **Antarctica**; pack ice.

Southern Uplands, region, S. **Scot.**; broad belt of hilly cty., N. part bleak moorland, S. part deeply cut by glens; sheep-rearing; dairying in valleys.

South Georgia, Brit. I., S. Atl. Oc.; dependency of **Falkland Is.**; former whaling ctr.; a. 4,144 km²; p. (1967) 22.

South Glamorgan, co., S. **Wales**; mostly lowland borders Bristol Channel; inc. lge. industl. ts. and pts. of Cardiff and Barry; a. 417 km²; p. (1981) 384,633.

South Hams, l. gov. dist., S. Devon, **Eng.**; a. between Torquay and Plymouth inc. Totnes, Kingsbridge and Salcombe; p. (1981) 67,861.

South I., lge. I., **N.Z.**; inc. S. Alps (highest Mt. Cook, 3,764 m), Canterbury Plains, impt. sheep-rearing dist.; cool climate; considerable hydroelectric power resources; tourism; a. 150,461 km²; p. (1976) 860,990.

South Kensington, dist., W. London, **Eng.**; contains Victoria and Albert Museum, Geological and Science Museums, British Museum of Natural History, Commonwealth Institute, Albert Hall.

South Orkney Is., Antarctica; S.W. of S. Georgia; part of **Brit. Antarctic Terr.** (1962); meteorological sta.

South Ossetian, aut. oblast, Georgian SSR, **USSR**; in Caucasus mtns.; goat and sheep rearing dist.; a. 3,898 km²; p. (1971) 100,000.

Southport, t., Sefton, Merseyside, **Eng.**; on S. side of Ribble estuary; 29 km N. of Liverpool; leisure centre; residtl.; p. (1981) 89,745.

South Ribble, l. gov. dist., Lancs., **Eng.**; a. S. of Preston and inc. Walton-le-Dale; p. (1981) 97,164.

South Sandwich Is., Antarctica; dependency of **Falkland Is.**; sm. volcanic Is.; a. 337 km².

South Shetland, archipelago, S. Atl. Oc.; 640 km S. of C. Horn; part of **Brit. Antarctic Terr.** (1962).

South Shields, t., Tyne and Wear, **Eng.**; pt. on S. bank at mouth of R. Tyne; becoming holiday resort; marine engin., new lt. inds.; p. (1981) 87,203.

Southwark, inner bor., London, **Eng.**; S. of R. Thames, incorporating former bors. of Bermondsey and Camberwell; cath.; site of former Globe theatre; p. (1981) 211,708.

South West Africa. *See* **Namibia.**

Southwick, t., Adur, West Sussex, **Eng.**; on S. cst. 6 km W. of Brighton; p. (1981) 11,388.

South Wight, l. gov. dist., I. of Wight, **Eng.**; inc. Ventnor and Sandown-Shanklin; p. (1981) 50,623.

Southwold, spt., Waveney, Suffolk, **Eng.**; on E. cst. 13 km S. of Lowestoft; fishing; resort; p. (1981) 1,795.

South Yorkshire, former met. co., **Eng.**; mainly industl. a. E. of Pennines; inc. productive coalfield nr. Barnsley and Doncaster and steel producing ts. of Sheffield and Rotherham; p. (1981) 1,301,813.

Sovetsk (Tilsit), t., **RSFSR** (since 1945); on R. Niemen, formerly in E. Prussia; timber and paper inds.; famous for Treaty of Tilsit between Napoleon and Russia 1807; p. (est. 1970) 65,000.

Sowerby Bridge, t., Calderdale, West Yorks., **Eng.**; on R. Calder, 5 km W. of Halifax; woollens; p. (1981) 15,546.

Spa, t., Liège, **Belgium**; mineral springs, resort; gave name to "spas"; p. (1981) 9,619.

Spain, indep. sov. st., Iberia, S.W. **Europe**; member of E.E.C. (1986); lge. land a. takes up 80 per cent of Iberian peninsula and helps to make climate continental; mtnous. interior and narrow coastal strip encourages regional isolation and development of regional culture; civil war 1936–9 hindered modern economic growth; economy based on agr., but much of land is arid and although industl. raw materials in N. Spain and an oil refinery under construction at Bilbao, economic development has depended largely upon the spectacular growth of tourism; 42 million visitors each year; Europe's biggest car exporter; inds. attracted by cheap labour; monarchy revived 1975; cap. Madrid; a. 504,747 km²; p. (est. 1984) 38,717,000.

Spalding, mkt. t., South Holland, Lincs., **Eng.**; in Fens, 16 km up R. Welland from Wash; agr.,

K153

bulb mkt.; agr. machin.; sugar-beet, fruit canning; p. (1981) 18,223.

Spandau, t., Potsdam, **E. Germany**; previously gr. military ctr.; at confluence of Rs. Havel and Spree; now part of Berlin.

Spanish Guinea. See **Equatorial Guinea.**

Spanish Sahara (Spanish West Africa). See **Western Sahara.**

Sparrows Point, t., Md., **USA**; situated on Chesapeake Bay; impt. iron and steel inds.

Sparta (Spárti), t., famous anc. c., **Greece**; on R. Eurotas, in Peloponnesus; passed under Roman rule 146 B.C.; modern c. dates from 1834; p. (1981) 14,388.

Spelthorne, l. gov. dist., Surrey, **Eng.**; close to Gtr. London; inc. Staines and Sunbury-on-Thames; p. (1981) 92,898.

Spencer Gulf, lge. inlet, S. **Australia**; penetrates 384 km inland, many impt. pts. along cst. (Whyalla, Pt. Pirie, Pt. Augusta).

Spennymoor, t., Durham, **Eng.**; growing industl. t. S. of Durham; p. (1981) 20,630.

Sperrin Mtns., Strabane, **N. Ireland**; peat-covered schists; Sawell, 683 m.

Spey, R., Moray, Badenoch and Strathspey, the most rapid in **Scot.**; flows N.E. to Moray Firth; used for hydroelec. power; 171·2 km long.

Speyer, t., Rhineland–Palatinate, **W. Germany**; tobacco, footwear, paper, sugar, brewing, oil refining; cas., cath.; famous Diet 1529 condemning Reformation gave rise to term "Protestant"; p. (1983) 43,800.

Spitalfields, par., E. London, **Eng.**; formerly noted for silk weaving, introduced by Huguenots 17th cent.; name derives from spital or hospital of St. Mary, founded 12th cent.

Spithead, roadstead, between Portsmouth and I. of Wight, **Eng.**; used by ships of Royal Navy.

Spitsbergen (Svalbard), I. gr. belonging to **Norway**; within Arctic; mtnous.; sealing and whaling; coal mng.; asbestos, copper, gypsum; a. 62,921 km²; p. (1968) 2,808.

Split (Spalato), t., **Yugoslavia**; spt. on Adriatic; second spt. of rep.; airport; food processing; p. (1981) 235,922.

Spokane, c., Wash., **USA**; on R. Spokane at falls used for hydroelec. power; timber tr. impt.; flour and saw mills, elec. gds.; lge. aluminium wks.; p. (1980) 171,000 (c.), 342,000 (met. a.).

Spoleto, c., Umbria, central **Italy**; cath., many Roman remains; textiles; p. (est. 1981) 36,839.

Sporades, scattered Is. belonging to **Greece** in Aegean Sea, inc. Skyros, Skiathos and Skopelos.

Spratley Is., **S. China Sea**; cluster of about 50 reefs and sand bars, thought to contain petroleum; ownership disputed by China, Taiwan, Philippines, and Vietnam.

Spree, R., **E. Germany**; flows W. past Berlin to the Havel at Spandau; 363 km long.

Spremberg, t., Cottbus, **E. Germany**; on R. Spree; cas., older part of t. on I.; glass, textiles; p. (est. 1970) 22,629.

Springfield, c., cap. of Ill., **USA**; in rich agr. and coal mng. a.; farming and elec. machin., food processing; home of Abraham Lincoln; p. (1980) 100,054 (c.), 187,789 (met. a.).

Springfield, c., Mass., **USA**; varied mnfs.; US armoury establ. 1794; p. (1980) 152,000 (c.), 531,000 (met. a.).

Springfield, c., Mo., **USA**; agr. ctr.; flour milling, engin.; p. (1980) 133,000 (c.), 208,000 (met. a.).

Springfield, t., Ohio, **USA**; agr. mach., motor lorries; p. (1980) 72,563 (c.), 183,885 (met. a.).

Springs, t., Transvaal, **S. Africa**; E. of Johannesburg; gold mng., engin., cars, elec. gds.; uranium plant; p. (1970) 104,090 (met. a.).

Spurn Head, Humberside, **Eng.**; sand spit at mouth of Humber estuary.

Sri Lanka (Ceylon), indep. rep. (1972) within Brit. Commonwealth (1948); in **Indian Oc.**; S.E. of India; fertile plains with cash crops of coconuts and rubber (S.W.) but dry in N.; mtnous. interior ameliorates climate where tea cultivation; varied p. composition inc. Sinhalese (70 per cent of p.), Tamils, Burghers (Portuguese and Dutch); agitation for Tamil independence; dependent on exp. of primary produce; inds. growing; cap. and ch. spt. Colombo; a. 65,610 km²; p. (est. 1984) 16,076,000.

Srinagar, t., cap. of Kashmir, **India**; in vale at c. 1,600 m. on Jhelum R. in W. Himalayas;

beautiful surrounding cty.; summer resorts; mnfs. silks, woollens, carpets; tourism; p. (1967) 325,000.

Srirangam, t., Tamil Nadu, **India**; on R. Cauvery; temple dedicated to Vishnu; pilgrimage ctr.; p. (1961) 41,949.

Stade, t., Lower Saxony, **W. Germany**; nr. Hamburg; pt. on R. Schwinge; leather, wood, textiles; p. (1983) 43,000.

Staffa, I. on Inner Hebrides, W. **Scot.**; 10 km N. of Iona, off W. cst. Mull; grand basaltic caverns, inc. Fingal's Cave, 69 m long, 13 m wide, 20 m high.

Stafford, co. t., l. gov. dist., Staffs., **Eng.**; on R. Sow, 24 km N. of Wolverhampton; heavy elec. and other engin.; expanded t.; p. (1981) 117,555 (dist.).

Staffordshire, non-met. co., W. Midlands, **Eng.**; plain drained by R. Trent and tribs.; N. Staffs. coalfield inc. a. of "Potteries"; S. Staffs. coalfield now inc. in W. Midlands met. co.; a. 2,717 km²; p. (1981) 1,012,320.

Staffordshire, East, l. gov. dist., Staffs., **Eng.**; stretches from Uttoxeter to Burton-on-Trent; p. (1981) 94,862.

Staffordshire Moorlands, l. gov. dist., Staffs., **Eng.**; borders S. Pennines and inc. Leek, Biddulph and Cheadle; p. (1981) 95,842.

Staffordshire, South, l. gov. dist., Staffs., **Eng.**; a. bordering W. Midlands conurb.; p. (1981) 96,493.

Staines, mkt. t., Spelthorne, Surrey, **Eng.**; on R. Thames, 6 km S.E. of Windsor; linoleum, machin.; nr. birthplace of Matthew Arnold; p. (1981) 53,823.

Stainmore, pass, North Yorks./Durham, **Eng.**; crosses N. Pennines from Greta valley into upper Eden valley; used by main road; alt. 418 m.

Staithes, v., North Yorks., **Eng.**; potash mng.

Stalin. See **Brasov.**

Stalinabad. See **Dushanbe.**

Stalingrad. See **Volgograd.**

Stalino. See **Donetsk.**

Stalino. See **Varna.**

Stalinogorsk. See **Novomoskovsk.**

Stalinsk. See **Novo Kuznetsk.**

Stalybridge, t., Gtr. Manchester, **Eng.**; on R. Tame, 8 km E. of Manchester; cotton and wool engin., plastics, rubber, gds., elec. cables; p. (1981) 26,396.

Stamboul. See **Istanbul.**

Stamford, mkt. t., Lincs., **Eng.**; old bldgs., one of 5 Danelaw ts.; agr. inds., elec. gds., plastics; p. (1981) 16,153.

Stamford, c., Conn., **USA**; on shore of Long I. Sound; chemicals, engin.; p. (1980) 102,000.

Stanislav. See **Ivano-Frankovsk.**

Stanley, t., Derwentside, Durham, **Eng.**; former colly. dist.; p. (1981) 41,210.

Stanley, spt., cap of Falkland Is.; former whaling port., contains over half p. of Falklands; p. (est. 1972) 1,079.

Stanley Falls. See **Boyoma Falls.**

Stanley Pool. See **Pool Malebo.**

Stanleyville. See **Kisangani.**

Stanlow, Ches., **Eng.**; petrol refinery, oil storage, docks, chemicals, linked to Anglesey by pipeline.

Stanovoi Mtns., range of mtns., **USSR**; extending from N. of R. Amur to nr. Sea of Okhotsk.

Stara Zagora, t., central **Bulgaria**; textiles, agr. processing; educational ctr.; p. (1979) 129,347.

Stargard Szczecinski, t., N.W. **Poland** (since 1945); formerly in Pomerania; rly. junc.; metal chemical, and food inds.; devastated in second world war; p. (1970) 44,500.

Start Point, C., nr. Dartmouth, Devon, **Eng.**

Stassfurt, t., Magdeburg, **E. Germany**; in gr. potash mng. region; chemicals, machin., metals; p. (est. 1973) 26,270.

Staten I., the most S. point N.Y. st. **USA**; shipyds.; linked with Brooklyn by Verrazano-Narrows bridge (opened 1964); residtl.

Staten I., off Tierra del Fuego, **S. America.**

Stavanger, spt., cap. of Rogaland prov., S.W. **Norway**; comm. and industl. ctr.; fish curing and canning; oil refinery at Sola; cath.; airport; p. (est. 1973) 83,292.

Staveley, t., Derbys., **Eng.**; 5 km N.E. of Chesterfield; coal, iron, chemicals, concrete and iron pipes; p. (1981) 17,828.

Stellenbosch, t., Cape Prov., **S. Africa**; 40 km E.

of Cape Town; univ.; wines, saw milling, brick and tile mkg.; p. (est. 1975) 30,000.

Stelvio Pass, between **Italy** and **Switzerland**; road pass, alt. 2,762 m.

Stendal, c., Magdeburg, **E. Germany**; impt. rly. junct.; sugar, metal and food inds.; cath.; Stendhal (Henri Beyle) took his name from the c.; p. (est. 1973) 37,925.

Stepney. See **Tower Hamlets**.

Sterlitamak, t., Bashkir ASSR, **RSFSR**; on S.W. flank of Ural mtns.; impt. oil refineries on "second Baku" oilfield; linked by pipeline to Togliatti; p. (1980) 224,000.

Stettin. See **Szczecin**.

Stettiner Haff, lagoon, **E. Germany** and **Poland**; separated from Baltic Sea by Is. Usedom and Wollin; receives R. Oder; 56 km long.

Stevenage, t., l. gov. dist., Herts., **Eng.**; 6 km S.E. of Hitchin; first new t. to be designated under the New Towns Act 1946; old t. known in Domesday as Stevenach; agr., lt. engin., school furniture, elec. goods., chemicals, aircraft parts; p. (1981) 74,381.

Stevenston, burgh, Cunninghame, **Scot.**; explosives factory; p. (1981) 11,328.

Steventon, v., Hants., **Eng.**; birthplace of Jane Austen.

Stewart I., S. of S.I., **N.Z.**; a. 1,735 km²; rises to over 900 m; famous for oysters.

Stewarton, burgh, Kilmarnock and Loudoun, **Scot.**; woollens, carpets; p. (1981) 6,383.

Stewartry, l. gov. dist., Dumfries and Galloway, **Scot.**; replaces old co. of Kirkcudbright; p. (1981) 23,138.

Steyning, v., West Sussex, **Eng.**; on R. Adur, 6 km N. of Shoreham at entrance to gap through S. Downs; residtl.

Steyr, t., **Austria**; at confluence of Rs. Enns and Steyr; industl. ctr.; historic bldgs.; p. (1971) 40,578.

Stilton, v., Cambs., **Eng.**; 10 km S.W. of Peterborough; famous for cheese.

Stirling, royal burgh, Stirling, **Scot.**; on R. Forth in gap between Campsie Fells and Ochil hills; cas., univ.; coal mng., engin., concrete, wool, rubber gds.; p. (1981) 38,638.

Stirlingshire, former co., central **Scot.**; on S. edge of Grampians; now forms l. gov. dist. within the Central Reg.; a. of l. gov. dist. 2,168 km²; p. (1981) 80,835.

Stockholm, c., cap. of **Sweden**; freeport; on I. at outlet of L. Malar; called the "Queen of the Baltic" for the beauty of its surroundings; comm. ctr., machin., textiles, leather, sugar, chemicals; univ. and many academic institutions; p. (1983) 650,952 (c.), 1,409,048 (met. a.).

Stockport, t., met. dist., Gtr. Manchester, **Eng.**; on R. Mersey, S.E. of Manchester; cotton manmade fibres, engin.; p. (1981) 289,730.

Stocksbridge, t., South Yorks., **Eng.**; iron and steel; p. (1981) 14,015.

Stockton, t., Cal., **USA**; R. pt. on San Joaquin R.; agr. processing, farm implements; p. (1980) 150,000 (c.), 347,000 (met. a.).

Stockton-on-Tees, mkt. t., l. gov. dist., Cleveland, **Eng.**; 6 km W. of Middlesbrough; impt. iron and steel inds., plywood; first rly. for passenger traffic opened 1825 between Stockton and Darlington; 18th cent. town hall; racecourse; p. (1981) 172,138.

Stoke Newington. See **Hackney**.

Stoke-on-Trent, c., l. gov. dist., Staffs., **Eng.**; at S.W. foot of the Pennines; formed in 1910 by union of the "five towns" of Arnold Bennett's novels, Hanley, Burslem, Tunstall, Longton, and Fenton (with Stoke-upon-Trent); ceramics, coal, iron and steel, engin., brick and tile works, precast concrete, rubber gds.; p. (1981) 252,351.

Stolberg, t., N. Rhine-Westphalia, **W. Germany**; E. of Aachen; metals, glass, wood, chemicals; p. (1983) 56,900.

Stolp. See **Slupsk**.

Stone, mkt. t., Staffs., **Eng.**; on R. Trent, 11 km S. of Stoke-on-Trent; footwear, tiles, porcelain, scientific glassware; p. (1981) 12,115.

Stonehaven, t., burgh, Kincardine and Deeside, **Scot.**; fish. pt. on E. cst., 22 km S. of Aberdeen, distilling, net mftg.; p. (1981) 7,885.

Stonehenge, prehistoric gr. of monumental stones, on Salisbury Plain, Wilts., **Eng.**; date of erection est. between 2100–1600 B.C.

Stornoway, spt., burgh, **Scot.**; on E. cst. of I. of Lewis, Outer Hebrides; ctr. Harris Tweed ind.; fishing ctr.; p. (1981) 8,660.

Stour, R., Kent, **Eng.**; flows past Canterbury to Pegwell Bay; 64 km long.

Stour, R., Somerset, Dorset, **Eng.**; trib. of R. Avon; 88 km long.

Stour, R., Suffolk and Essex, **Eng.**; flows E. to sea at Harwich; 67 km long.

Stour, R., Hereford and Worcs./West Midlands, **Eng.**; trib. of R. Severn; 32 km long.

Stourbridge, t., West Midlands, **Eng.**; on R. Stour; 14 km W. of Birmingham; brick and glass wks.; p. (1981) 54,661.

Stourport-on-Severn, mkt. t., Wyre Forest, Hereford and Worcs., **Eng.**; at confluence of Rs. Stour and Severn; carpets, iron and steel gds., porcelain, ceramics; old canal and R. pt.; p. (1981) 19,092.

Stowmarket, t., Mid Suffolk, **Eng.**; on R. Gipping, 18 km N.W. of Ipswich; I.C.I. paint factory; p. (1981) 10,910.

Strabane, t., l. gov. dist., **N. Ireland**; agr. ctr., shirt mkg.; p. (1981) 34,871 (dist.), 10,340 (t.).

Straits Settlements, former Brit. crown col., Malay Peninsula; comprised Penang, Malacca, and Singapore, established 1867, dissolved 1946. See **Malaysia, West**.

Stralsund, spt., Rostock, **E. Germany**; opposite Rügen I.; grain tr., machin., metals, fish smoking, shipbldg.; p. (est. 1973) 72,236.

Strangford Lough, arm of sea, Down and Ards, **N. Ireland**; 29 km long, 10 km wide at entrance.

Stranraer, royal burgh, Wigtown, **Scot.**; at head of Loch Ryan; steamer service to Larne, N. Ireland; creameries, brewing, knitwear; cas.; mkt.; p. (1981) 10,837.

Strasbourg, c., cap. of Bas-Rhin dep., **E. France**; impt. pt. in Rhine valley on Ill R., 16 km S. of confluence with Rhine; terminus of Marne-Rhine and Rhône-Rhine canals; industl., comm. and cultural ctr. of economically impt. Alsace region; food processing and varied mnfs.; historic c., with many fine bldgs., inc. cath., univ., imperial palace; surrendered to Germany 1871, recovered 1919; meeting-place of European Parliament; p. (1982) 252,264.

Stratford. See **Newham**.

Stratford-on-Avon, t., l. gov. dist., Warwicks., **Eng.**; on R. Avon; birthplace of Shakespeare; memorial theatre, library; many bldgs. ass. with Shakespeare; tourist ctr. in attractive setting; lt. inds.; p. (1981) 100,431 (dist.).

Strathclyde Region, l. gov. reg., Central **Scot.**; indust. dist. formed around Glasgow, inc. ts. on Ayr and Lanarkshire coalfields; borders the F. of Clyde; a. 13,794 km²; p. (1981) 2,397,827.

Strathkelvin, l. gov. dist., Strathclyde Reg., **Scot.**; part of Central Clydeside conurb.; p. (1981) 86,884.

Strathmore, lowland belt, central **Scot.**; flanked to N. by Grampians, to S. by Sidlaw and Ochil hills; drained by Rs. Earn, Tay, Isla, S. Esk; famous for cereals and small fruits; length 96 km, width 11–16 km.

Strathspey, valley of the Spey, **Scot.**; 112 km long.

Stratton and Bude, North Cornwall, **Eng.**; 19 km S. of Hartland Point; resort; p. (1981) 6,783.

Straubing, t., Lower Bavaria, **W. Germany**; agr. mkt. ctr.; machin.; p. (1983) 42,400.

Strawberry, R., Utah, **USA**; on E. slopes of Wasatch mtns. 128 km S.E. of Salt Lake City; dammed to supply irrigation water led through tunnel under Wasatch mtns. to 259 km² cultivable land round L. Utah.

Street, t., Mendip, Somerset, **Eng.**; at foot of Polden Hills, 11 km S.W. of Wells; footwear, leather; p. (1981) 8,803.

Stretford, t., Gtr. Manchester, **Eng.**; borders Manchester Ship Canal; inc. Trafford Park industl. estate; residtl.; Lancashire co. cricket ground, Manchester United football ground at Old Trafford; p. (1981) 47,600.

Stromboli, I., Lipari Is., Tyrrhenian Sea, N. of Sicily, **Italy**; active volcano, alt. 927 m.

Stromness, burgh, Mainland, Orkney Is., **Scot.**; 21 km W. of Kirkwall; mkt., fish. pt.; p. (1981) 1,816.

Stronsay, Orkney Is., **Scot.**; p. (1971) 439.

Stroud, mkt. t., l. gov. dist., Gloucs., **Eng.**; on R. Frome, in Cotswolds; former ctr. of impt. cloth ind. in W. Eng.; woollens, dyes, plastics, engin.; p. (1981) 101,356.

Sturminster Newton, t., North Dorset, **Eng.**; impt.

cattle mkt. on Stour R.; creameries.

Sturts Stony Desert, a. N.W. of S. **Australia**; named after Charles Sturt, explorer.

Stuttgart, c., cap. of Baden–Württemberg, **W. Germany**; on Neckar R.; cas., cath., rly. junc.; industl. and comm. ctr.; publishing, science-based inds.; oil refinery nearby; p. (1983) 571,100.

Styria, prov., **Austria**; borders Yugoslavia on S.; mtnous. with forests and pastures; lignite and iron mng., inds. around cap. Graz; grain, wine, fruit, stock-rearing; tourism; p. (1971) 1,191,000.

Suakin, former pt., **Sudan**, N.E. Africa; on Red Sea; now used only for pilgrim traffic to Jeddah; replaced by Pt. Sudan; plans for new pt.

Suanhwa. *See* **Xuanhua.**

Subotica, t., Serbia, **Yugoslavia**; univ.; agr. ctr. with Hungarian culture; agr. processing; expanding industl. ctr.; p. (1981) 154,611.

Suceava, t., S. Bukovina, N.E. **Romania**; mkt. t. on Suceava R.; once the residence of Moldavian princes; p. (1968) 40,441.

Suchow. *See* **Zuzhou.**

Sucre, c., cap. of Chuquisaca dep. and *de jura* cap. of **Bolivia** (La Paz is *de facto* cap.); in valley of Andes at 2,600 m; agr. ctr., oil refining; p. (1973) 106,590.

Sucre, st., **Venezuela**; on Caribbean cst.; coffee and cacao; fishing impt.; fish canning at cap. Cumaná; a. 11,800 km²; p (est. 1970) 493,840.

Sudan, The, rep., N.E. **Africa**; climatic transition from N. desert to rainy equatorial S.; mainly plateaux, dissected by Nile R. system; sporadic conflict between N. and S. (1955–1972); 3 southern provs. now form an autonomous reg.; long staple cotton, grown in irrigated areas, provides most valuable exp.; gum arabic from lge. forest areas; food processing; dams constructed on Atbara and Blue Nile Rs.; cap. Khartoum; a. 2,530,430 km²; p. (est. 1984) 20,945,000.

Sudbury, t., Ont., **Canada**; nickel, copper mng.; refining; univ.; p. (1979) 153,400 (met. a.).

Sudbury, t., Babergh, Suffolk, **Eng.**; on R. Stour, 19 km N.W. of Colchester; p. (1981) 15,524.

Sudene, terr., N.E. **Brazil**; government sponsored economic development.

Sudetenland, region of ČSSR bordering Germany, until 1945 German-speaking; annexed by Hitler 1938, recovered by ČSSR 1945; named after Sudeten mtns.; contains 20 per cent of p. of ČSSR.

Sudeten Mtns. or **Sudetes**, mtn. range along borders of ČSSR and Poland; separating Bohemia and Moravia from Silesia; mineral resources.

Suez, spt., **Egypt**; the anc. Arsinoë; at head of G. of Suez (arm of Red Sea) and S. entrance of Suez canal, which crosses the isthmus of Suez to the Mediterranean at Port Said; Port Tewfiq adjoining has quay and docks; declined during closure of canal 1967–75; oil refining, fertilisers; p. (1976) 193,965.

Suez Canal, ship canal, **Egypt**; connects Mediterranean Sea (Pt. Said) with Red Sea (Suez) through Ls. Manzala, Timsah, and Bitter; length 162 km; closed after Arab-Israeli war of June 1967; reopened 1975; tunnel links Egypt and Israel (1980).

Suez, G., Red Sea; N.W. arm of Red Sea between Arabian desert and Sinai peninsula, **Egypt**; southern approach to Suez canal; length 304 km., width varies from 19–40 km.

Suffolk, non-met. co., E. Anglia, **Eng.**; bounded on E. by N. Sea, drowned coastline; rises to 90 m in E. Anglian Heights in W.; impt. agr. a., lge. farms, mixed farming; inds. based on agr.; many expanded ts. in S.; formerly divided into 2 admin. parts; co. t. Ipswich; a. 3,800 km²; p. (1981) 596,354.

Suffolk Coastal, l. gov. dist., E. Suffolk, **Eng.**; lge. rural a. inc. ts. of Leiston-cum-Sizewell, Saxmundham, Aldeburgh, Woodbridge and Felixstowe; p. (1981) 95,223.

Suhl, admin. dist., **E. Germany**; inc. Thuringian Forest; expanding inds. based on local potash and iron ore; a. 3,877 km²; p. (1982) 549,500.

Suhl, t., Suhl, **E. Germany**; once famous for

armaments; motor-cycles; p. (est. 1973) 35,274.

Sui, Baluchistan, **Pakistan**; natural gas; pipeline to Karachi.

Sukhumi, spt., Georgian SSR, **USSR**; agr. processing; resort; p. (1980) 116,000.

Sukkur, t., **Pakistan**; major bridging point of R. Indus; 368 km N.E. of Karachi; dam for irrigation; thermal sta.; p. (est. 1972) 159,000.

Sulaimaniya, t., **Iraq**; in hill dist. nr. Iran border; p. (1965) 131,000 (met. a.).

Sula Is., I. gr. in Molucca Sea, E. of Sulawesi, **Indonesia**; little developed.

Sulawesi (Celebes), I., **Indonesia**; mtnous., lge. forests; copra, coffee, gold, nickel, copper, asphalt; ch. pts. Menado, Makasar; a. 189,484 km²; p. (est. 1970) 8,925,000.

Sullum Voe, Shetland Is., **Scot.**; oil terminal and receiving ctr. for N. Sea oil.

Sultanabad. *See* **Arak.**

Sulu Is., **Philippines**; archipelago between Borneo and the Philippines; inc. over 400 volcanic Is. and coral islets; a. 2,461 km²; under US control 1899–1940.

Sumatra, I., **Indonesia**; relatively underdeveloped; sparse p.; main development in Cultuurgebied, rubber, oil palm, sisal, tobacco; impt. oil deposits and new oil refineries; a. 473,607 km²; p. (1971) 20,813,682.

Sumba or **Sandalwood I.**, S. of Flores, **Indonesia**; horse-breeding; rice, maize, tobacco, timber, cinnamon; cap. Waingapu; a. 11,150 km²; p. (1971) 251,126.

Sumbawa, I., **Indonesia**; between Flores and Lombok; wet climate, sparse p.; a. (inc. nearby Is.) 13,572 km²; p. (1971) 195,554.

Sumgait, t., Azerbaydzhan SSR, **USSR**; on Caspian Sea; 40 km N.W. of Baku; metallurgical ind.; chemicals; p. (1980) 196,000.

Sumy, t., Ukrainian SSR, **USSR**; engin., chemicals, textiles, agr. processing; p. (1980) 233,000.

Sunbury-on-Thames, t., Spelthorne, Surrey, **Eng.**; W of London; residtl., water wks., gravel pits; petrol research establishment; p. (1981) 39,075.

Sunda Is., **Indonesia**; between S. China Sea and Indian Oc.; form two grs., Greater Sunda Is., inc. Java, Sumatra, Borneo, Sulawesi, Banka, and the Lesser Sunda Is. (renamed Nusa Tenggara 1954) inc. Bali, Lombok, Sumbawa, Timor.

Sundarbans, The, tract of forest and swamps, fringing the delta of the Ganges, **India/Bangladesh**; 130 km wide; rice grown in N.; tigers and crocodiles found in S.

Sunda Strait, between Java and Sumatra, **Indonesia**; 21 km wide, contains the volcanic I. of Krakatao.

Sunday I., lgst. of Kermadec Is., **N.Z.**; 32 km in circuit and with a p. of 10 is the only one of the Kermadec Is. that is inhabited; meteorological and radio sta. established on I.

Sundyberg, t., **Sweden**; adjoins Stockholm; chemicals, paper; p. (1983) 26,985.

Sunderland, spt., met. dis., Tyne and Wear, **Eng.**; at mouth of R. Wear; precision and aero-engin., clothing, glass, shipbldg.; car plant; p. (1981) 295,096.

Sundsvall, spt., Västernorrland, **Sweden**; on a wide bay of the Baltic nr. Hernösand; timber and wood-pulp inds.; p. (1983) 93,947.

Sungari. *See* **Songhua R.**

Sunnyvale, t., Cal., **USA**; ctr. of fruit-growing a.; lt. inds.; p. (1980) 107,000.

Superior, t., Wis., **USA**; at head of L. Superior; tr. in grain, timber, coal; shipbldg. and flour mills; oil refining; p. (1980) 29,571.

Superior, L., **N. America**; lgst. sheet of fresh water in the world; lies between **Canada** and **USA**; one of chain of gr. Ls. in St. Lawrence system; outlet to L. Huron by St. Mary's R.; receives waters of St. Louis, Pigeon and Nipigon; impt. waterway; a. 82,880 km².

Surabaya, spt., Java, **Indonesia**; ch. naval base; handles nearly half Indonesia's tr.; shipbldg., oil refining, food processing; p. (1971) 1,556,255.

Surakarta (Solo), Java, **Indonesia**; on Solo R.; tr. ctr. for agr. region; former sultan's palace; p. (1971) 414,285.

Surat, c., Gujarat, **India**; on R. Tapti; textile ctr.; notable as first English trading post 1612; p. (1971) 471,656 (c.), 493,001 (met. a.).

Surbiton, Gtr. London, **Eng.**; on R. Thames, inc.

in Royal Borough of Kingston-upon-Thames; residtl.; lt. engin., bricks, tiles, elec. components.

Suresnes, t., Hauts-de-Seine dep., **France**; sub. of Paris; cars, chemicals; p. (1982) 35,744.

Surinam (**Dutch Guiana**), former self-gov. terr. of Neth.; indep. 1975; **S. America**; sub-tropical climate; p. concentrated on cst. where rice, sugar, and citrus fruits grown; main exp. bauxite (86 per cent of total exp.); cap. Paramaribo; a. 161,875 km²; p. (est. 1984) 352,000.

Surinumu Dam, 48 km from Port Moresby, **Papua New Guinea**; part of hydroelectric scheme; opened 1963.

Surrey, non-met. co., S. **Eng.**; S. of R. Thames inc. part of N. Downs; serves as dormitory a. and recreational dist. for London; mkt. gardening, dairying; co. t. Guildford; a. 1,655 km²; p. (1981) 999,393.

Surrey Heath, l. gov. dist., Surrey, **Eng.**; based on Bagshot, Frimley and Camberley; p. (1981) 76,519.

Susa. See Sousse.

Susquehanna, R., N.Y., Penns., and Md., **USA**; flows to Chesapeake Bay through highly industl. a.; routeway W. from Philadelphia and Baltimore across Appalachian mtns.; not navigable; hydroelectric power; 675 km long.

Sussex. See **East Sussex**, and **West Sussex**.

Susten Pass, alpine road, alt. 2,225 m between Hasli Tal and Reuss valley, links Bernese Oberland with Gotthard road, Switzerland.

Sutherland, l. gov. dist., former co., Highland Reg., **Scot.**; stretches from Atl. Oc. to Moray F.; sparsely p. reg.; a. 3,152 km²; p. (1981) 14,425.

Sutlej, R., **Pakistan**; rises in the Himalayas and flows to the R. Indus; used for lge. scale irrigation; 1,600 km long.

Sutton, outer bor., Greater London, **Eng.**; inc. former bors. of Beddington and Wallington, Sutton and Cheam, and Carshalton; residtl.; p. (1981) 168,407.

Sutton Coldfield, t., West Midlands, **Eng.**; 10 km N.E. of Birmingham; residtl.; hardware, plastics; p. (1981) 86,494.

Sutton-in-Ashfield, t., Ashfield, Notts., **Eng.**; 5 km S.W. of Mansfield; lt. engin.; hosiery; coal-mng. dist.; p. (1981) 41,270.

Suva, c., cap. of Fiji Is.; on Viti Levu I.; fine harbour; exp. coconut prods., sugar; international airport; p. (est. 1977) 63,628.

Suwalki, t., N.E. **Poland**; nr. Lithuanian bdy.; timber, grain, woollens; p. (1970) 25,400.

Suwannee, R., Fla., and Ga., **USA**; flows to G. of Mexico; known as "Swanee River", 400 km long.

Suzhou (**Soochow**), c., Jiangsu, **China**; nr. Shanghai; former treaty pt.; textile ctr.; p. (est. 1970) 1,300,000.

Svendborg, spt., Fyn, **Denmark**; exp. dairy prods.; textiles, machin.; p. (est. 1974) 36,615.

Sverdlovsk (**Ekaterinburg**), c., cap. of S. oblast, **RSFSR**; on R. Iset in E. foothills of Ural mtns.; on Trans-Siberian rly.; industl. expansion during second world war; heavy machin., metallurgical and chemical plants; univ.; p. (1980) 1,225,000.

Svir, R., **USSR**; flows between L. Onega and L. Ladoga; hydroelectric power; navigable; 200 km long.

Svishtov (**Sistova**), t., N. **Bulgaria**; R. pt. on Danube in vine-growing dist., nr. Romanian bdr.; cath., univ.; p. (est. 1968) 22,456.

Swabia, historic region, mediaeval duchy, **Germany**; now forms part of Baden-Württemberg and Bavaria; contains Black Forest.

Swabian Alps, mtns., Baden-Württemberg, **W. Germany**; inc. the Swabian Jura range between valleys of Neckar and Danube.

Swadlincote, t., South Derbys., **Eng.**; 5 km E. of Burton-on-Trent; potteries, engin., clothing, coal-mng. ctr.; p. (1981) 23,388.

Swaffham, mkt. t., Breckland, Norfolk, **Eng.**; fruit canning; p. (1981) 4,776.

Swale, R., North Yorks., **Eng.**; joins R. Ure to form R. Ouse, 96 km long.

Swale, l. gov. dist., mid Kent, **Eng.**; nr. Thames estuary inc. Sittingbourne, Faversham and I. of Sheppey; p. (1981) 109,506.

Swanage, mkt. t., Dorset, **Eng.**; on bay, E. cst. I. of Purbeck; seaside resort; p. (1981) 8,647.

Swansea, c., spt., l. gov. dist., West Glamorgan, **Wales**; on Swansea Bay; univ.; grew with exp.

of coal; now imports minerals; copper and zinc refining; steel, aluminium, wire, plastics; p. (1981) 186,199 (dist.).

Swatow. See Shantou.

Swaziland, indep. kingdom, S. **Africa**; within Brit. Commonwealth (1968), govt. based on tribal communities; bordered by S. Africa on S., W., and N. and by Moçambique on E.; four north-south regions; high, middle, low veld and Lebombo escarpment; rainfall increases with alt.; agr. basis of economy and sugar impt. exp., but iron-ore major exp.; asbestos mng., food processing inds.; cattle raising main internal activity; cap. Mbabane; a. 17,363 km²; p. (est. 1984) 630,000.

Sweden, kingdom, Scandinavia, N.W. **Europe**; divided for admin. purposes into 24 cos.; cap. c. Stockholm; mtnous. in N. and S. with central lowland belt containing major agr. a. and lge. proportion of p.; sm. home mkt. makes for dependency on exps., especially of minerals; inc. high-grade iron-ore from Kiruna and Malmberget, N. of Arctic circle; development of high-value science-based inds.; furniture, porcelain and glass mnfs. have international reputation; social democratic st. since 1932; remained neutral in second world war; highly advanced system of social security; a. 449,792 km²; p. (est. 1984) 8,284,000.

Swidnica (**Schweidnitz**), t., **Poland** (since 1945); formerly in Lower Silesia; metals, elec. machin., leather, textiles; p. (1970) 47,500.

Swilly, Lough, N.E. Donegal, **R.o.I.**; arm of Atl. Oc. between Fanad Point and Dunaff Head; extends 40 km inland.

Swindon, t., Thamesdown, Wilts., **Eng.**; in upper Thames Valley (Vale of White Horse), 43 km S.W. of Oxford; impt. rly. junc.; rly. workshops to close (1986); mkt. for local dist.; heavy engin., textiles, tobacco; expanded t.; p. (1981) 91,136.

Swinoujście (**Swinemünde**), spt., N.W. **Poland** (since 1945); formerly in Pomerania; on I. of Usedom (Uznam), Baltic Sea; spt. for Szczecin; spa and summer resort; fishing; p. (1971) 27,900.

Swinton and Pendlebury, ts., Gtr. Manchester, **Eng.**; 8 km W. of Manchester; cotton spinning, coal, engin.; p. (1981) 39,621.

Switzerland, confederation, central **Europe**; landlocked mtnous. st. with major physical features dominated by Alpine mtn. system; divided into 26 cantons and half-cantons for purposes of govt.; 3 official languages; German (72 per cent), French (20 per cent), Italian (6 per cent) in addition to Romansch; like Norway, major natural resource is water power; industl. specialisation on precision engin., especially watch and clock mnfs.; agr. in valleys with impt. output of dairy prod., transhumance between mtn. pastures and valley bottoms; tourism provides valuable source of income; neutral; voted to remain non-member of U.N. (1986) cap. Berne; a. 41,310 km²; p. (est. 1984) 6,309,000.

Sydney, c., cap. of N.S.W., **Australia**; pt. and c. built around natural harbour of Pt. Jackson, crossed by S. Harbour Bridge and bordered by many impt. bldgs. and parks (Opera House, Government bldgs.); one of best harbours on E. cst., pt. developed with improved transport; site of first European settlement; contains 61 per cent of state p., 22 per cent of Australia's p.; covers vast a. as suburbs grow rapidly; caths., 3 univs., airpt. on Botany Bay where heavy inds. developing; services most impt. employment, vast range of inds.; p. (1976) 52,152 (c.), 3,021,299 (met. a.).

Sydney, spt., Cape Breton I., Nova Scotia, **Canada**; coal mng. and exp.; steel, chemicals; p. (1971) 32,459.

Syktyvkar, c., Komi ASSR, **RSFSR**; R. pt. on Vychegda R.; shipyds., sawmilling, engin.; cultural ctr. of Komi people; p. (1980) 175,000.

Sylhet, t., **Bangladesh**; on Surma R. in tea growing dist.; fertilisers; p. (est. 1971) 38,000.

Syracuse, c., S.E. Sicily, **Italy**; old t. on Ortygia I., off E. cst., modern t. on mainland, connected by bridge; founded c. 734 B.C.; ctr. of anc. Greek culture; exp. olive oil, oranges, lemons, wine; chemicals at Priolo; many Greek and Roman remains; p. (1981) 117,615.

Syracuse, c., N.Y., **USA**; on Erie Barge canal; impt. industl. ctr. for chemicals, electronics, machin.; formerly salt-producing ctr.; univ.; p. (1980) 170,000 (c.), 643,000 (met. a.).

Syr Dar'ya, one of main Rs. of central Asia; formed in Ferghana Valley in Uzbek SSR, **USSR**; flows through Tadzhik SSR and Kazakh SSR to Aral Sea; not navigable but used for irrigation and hydroelectric power; 2,400 km long.

Syria (Syrian Arab Rep.), S.W. **Asia**; on E. cst. Mediterranean; much of a. mtnous. and semi-desert; climate hot, but cold winters in high-land interior; c. 70 per cent p. engaged in agr. which provides 30 per cent nat. income; mainly pastoral, but grains, fruit and cotton grown in well watered Euphrates R. valley and along cst.; oil exp. since 1968; textiles, food processing in Aleppo and cap. Damascus; a. 184,434 km²; p. (est. 1984) 10,189,000 (inc. Palestinian refugees).

Syriam, t., **Burma**; nr. Rangoon; main oil refining ctr. of cty.

Syros or **Syra,** I., one of Cyclades, Aegean Sea, S. **Greece**; heath-covered; most populous of Cyclades; ch. t. Hermoupolis; p. (est. 1971) 19,000.

Syzran, c., **RSFSR**; impt. R. pt. on Volga nr. confluence with Syzran R.; rly. ctr.; engin., oil refining; p. (1980) 168,000.

Szazhalombatta, t., **Hungary**; on Danube, 24 km S. of Budapest; lgst. oil refinery in rep.; oil supplied through Druzhba pipeline.

Szczecin (Stettin), c., N.W. **Poland** (since 1945); formerly cap. of Prussian prov. of Pomerania; impt. spt. at mouth of R. Oder; deep-sea fishing base; shipbldg., chemicals, technical univ.; p. (est. 1983) 389,200.

Szczecin, prov., **Poland**; borders Baltic Sea; drained by R. Oder; mainly agr.; a. 31,339 km²; p. (est. 1983) 924,000.

Szechwan. See **Sichuan.**

Szeged, t., **Hungary**; nr. confluence of Rs. Tisza and Maros; anc. R. pt. destroyed by floods 1879, since rebuilt; univ.; tr. in cereals, paprika; textiles; p. (est. 1978) 175,741.

Székesfehérvár, t., **Hungary**; nr. Budapest; mkt. t., with aluminium and metal inds., food processing; known since Roman times; once cap. of Hungarian kings; p. (1978) 102,048.

Szeping. See **Siping.**

Szolnok, t., **Hungary**; pt. on R. Tisa, E. of Budapest; route ctr.; machin., paper, cellulose, chemicals; p. (est. 1978) 75,658.

Szombathely, t., W. **Hungary**; rly. ctr.; agr. machin., textiles, shoes; birthplace of St. Martin of Tours (c. A.D. 316); p. (est. 1978) 81,363.

T

Tabasco, coastal st., **Mexico**; on Bay of Campeche; low-lying; rapid development with drainage of swamps; cash crops of cacao, coffee, sugar, tobacco; major petroleum deposits aiding industl. development; cap. Villa Hermosa; a. 25,335 km²; p. (1970) 768,387.

Table Bay, inlet of Atl., cst. of C. of Good Hope, **S. Africa**; site of Cape Town.

Table Mountain, Cape Prov., **S. Africa**; nr. Cape Town; alt. 1,082 m.

Tabor, t., **ČSSR**; S. of Prague, on R. Luznice; rly. junc.; textiles, tobacco; p. (1961) 20,142.

Tabora, t., central **Tanzania**, E. Africa; at junc. of rlys. from Dar es Salaam and L. Victoria; p. (est. 1972) 24,500.

Tabriz, c., **Iran**; cap. of Azerbaijan; metal inds., carpets, leather, soap; famous blue mosque; univ.; p. (1976) 598,576.

Tachira, st., **Venezuela**; mtnous. inland st. bordering Colombia; coffee; cap. San Cristobal; a. 11,100 km²; p. (est. 1970) 525,840.

Tacna, t., cap. of Tacna prov., **Peru**; in fertile valley of mtnous. region; agr. t.; p. (est. 1970) 33,821.

Tacna, prov., **Peru**; mtnous. and arid, some irrigated valleys; transferred from Chile by treaty 1929; cap. T.; subject to earthquakes; a. 12,769 km²; p. (est. 1969) 90,600.

Tacoma, spt., Wash., **USA**; on Puget Sound; shipping, fishing; grew with Alaskan and Pac. tr.; port inds. and agr. processing; p. (1980) 159,000 (c.), 486,000 (met. a.).

Tacuarembo, dep., **Uruguay**; N. of Rio Negro R., which provides hydroelectricity; mainly agr.; cap. T.; a. 15,812 km²; p. (est. 1975) 84,829.

Tadoussac, t., Quebec, **Canada**; on R. Saguenay, where it enters St. Lawrence R.; tourist ctr.; oldest settlement in Canada 1599; p. (1966) 1,059.

Tadzhik (Tadzhikistan) SSR, constituent rep., **USSR**; borders China and Afghanistan; mainly mtnous., inc. Pamirs and Turkestan and part of highly cultivated Ferghana Valley; cattle breeding; cotton main cash crop; impt. oil and hydroelec. power resources; cap. Dushanbe; a. 144,263 km²; p. (1970) 2,900,000.

Taegu, c., **S. Korea**; textiles, agr. processing; p. (1980) 1,607,458.

Taejon, t., **S. Korea**; S. of Seoul; fish, petroleum; p. (1980) 851,642.

Taff, R., Powys, South and Mid Glamorgan, **Wales**; rises in Brecon Beacons, flows S.E. across coalfield to Bristol Channel at Cardiff; 64 km long.

Taff-Ely, l. gov. dist., Mid Glamorgan, **Wales**; inland ts. of Pontypridd and Llantrisant; p. (1981) 93,127.

Tafilalet, Morocco, N. Africa; oasis of the Sahara, E. of Atlas; dates.

Tagab, c., **Afghanistan**; in Panjshir R. valley N.W. of Kābul; p. (est. 1979) 106,777.

Taganrog, c., **RSFSR**; spt. on Sea of Azov; iron and steel, engin.; site of fortress founded by Peter the Great 1698; birthplace of Chekhov; p. (1980) 278,000.

Tagliamento, R., N.E. **Italy**; rises in Carnic Alps, flows W. into Adriatic; 160 km long.

Tagus, R., **Spain** and **Portugal**; rises in E. Spain and flows across the Meseta to Atl. Oc. at Lisbon where there is a magnificent new bridge; its estuary forms one of the finest harbours in Europe.

Tahiti, ch. I., Society Is., **Fr. Polynesia**; contains Papeete, main admin. ctr. of Fr. Oceania; fertile alluvial belt; exp. copra, phosphates, vanilla; tourism; a. 1,041 km²; p. (1970) 84,552.

Taichow. See **Taizhou.**

Taichung, t., **Taiwan**; agr. mkt.; food processing; p. (est. 1970) 448,140.

Taif, t., Hejaz, **Saudi Arabia**; 80 km E. of Mecca; 1,800 m a.s.l.; summer resort; p. (1974) 204,857.

Tai Hu, L., Jiangsu, **China**; focus of intensive system of small canals and waterways, 96 km N. of Shanghai; a. c. 260 km².

Taimyr Peninsula, N. cst., Siberia, **USSR**; terminates with C. Chelyuskin; occupies most of Taimyr National Area, inhabited by nomadic Samoyeds; p. (1970) 38,000.

Tainan, t., S.W. cst. of **Taiwan**; former cap.; univ.; p. (est. 1970) 474,835.

Taipei, c., cap. of **Taiwan**; on cst. plain in N. Taiwan; nucleus of major industl. a.; major transport ctr., international airpt.; 2 univs.; p. (est. 1970) 1,769,568.

Taiwan (Formosa), I., off cst. of S.E. **China**; beautiful I. with intensive agr.; most densely populated cty. in the world; part of Japan 1895–1945; returned to China 1945; occupied by Nationalist government (Chiang Kia-Shek) since 1949; growing political isolation; cap. Taipei; a. 35,975 km²; p. (est. 1981) 18,200,000.

Taiyüan, c., cap. of Shanxi prov., N. **China**; on Fen R.; walled c.; univ.; ctr. of rapid industl. development; integrated iron and steel plant; chemicals, textiles; p. (est. 1970) 2,725,000.

Taiz, t., **Yemen Arab Rep.**; in fertile valley; former cap.; p. (est. 1979) 48,000.

Taizhou (Taichow), c., Jiangsu prov., **China**; rice ctr.; p. (est. 1970) 275,000.

Takamatsu, t., **Japan**; N. cst. Shikiku; ferry terminal; univ.; tourism; p. (1979) 312,052.

Takaoka, t., Honshu, **Japan**; ctr. of rice tr.; lacquer wk.; cars; p. (1979) 175,381.

Takapuna, c., N.I., **N.Z.**; connected by motorway to Auckland; residtl. ctr.; p. (1976) 62,220.

Takasaki, t., Honshu, **Japan**; radiation chemistry research ctr.; textiles; p. (1979) 221,200.

Taklimakan Shamo, desert, W. **China**; basin of inland drainage; home of the Turko people; surrounded by a ring of oases.

Takoradi. See **Sekondi-Takoradi.**

Talara, t., N. **Peru**; on C. Pariñas; spt.; ctr. of petroleum refining; p. (est. 1972) 30,000.

Talaud I., Indonesia; N.E. of Sulawesi; copra; underdeveloped; a. 1,279 km².

Talavera de la Reina, t., Toledo prov., central **Spain**; on Tagus R.; ceramics; scene of battle 1809; p. (1981) 69,307.

Talca, prov., **Chile**; predominantly agr.; various irrigated crops; livestock; cap. T.; a. 9,637 km²; p. (1961) 226,052.

Talca, t., cap. of Talca prov., **Chile**; S. of Santiago; lge. mftg. ctr.; matches, footwear, paper, and flour mills, foundries; p. (est. 1980) 128,363.

Talcahuano, spt., **Chile,** nr. Concepción; naval sta.; steel plant at Huachipato; fish processing, oil refining; p. (est. 1980) 185,744.

Talien. See **Lushun.**

Tallahassee, t., Fla., **USA**; univ.; timber-based inds.; p. (1980) 81,548 (t.), 159,542 (met. a.).

Tallinn, spt., cap. of Estonian SSR, **USSR**; on G. of Finland; diverse inds. inc. radio equipment; mediaeval architecture; p. (1980) 436,000.

Tamale, t., cap. of Kaduna st., **Ghana,** W. Africa; admin. ctr.; cotton milling, peanut processing; p. (1984) 83,653.

Tamar, R., Tasmania, **Australia**; formed at confluence of N. Esk and S. Esk at Launceston, flows into Bass Strait nr. George Town.

Tamar, R., Devon and Cornwall, **Eng.**; flows S. to Plymouth Sound; 72 km long.

Tamatave. See **Toamasina.**

Tamaulipas, st., **Mexico**; on G. of Mexico, S. of Texas; petroleum is main resource; fishing along lagoon cst.; cotton, livestock; cap. Ciudad Victoria; a. 79,593 km²; p. (1970) 1,456,858.

Tambao, t., **Bourkina Fasso**; rich deposits of manganese could diversify economy and provide valuable exports; development depends on railway extension.

Tambov, c., cap. of Tambov oblast, **RSFSR**; on Tsna R.; regional ctr. serving agr. dist.; engin.; p. (1980) 273,000.

Tameside, met. dist., Gtr. Manchester, **Eng.**; comprises Dukinfield, Ashton-under-Lyne, Hyde and Mossley; p. (1981) 217,341.

Tamil Nadu (formerly **Madras**), st., **India**; on S.E. cst. of peninsula; home of Tamils; crossed by R. Cauvery; dry crops; acute water shortages relieved by water and sewerage development plan; ch. ts. Madras, Madura; a. 130,357 km²; p. (1971) 41,103,125.

Tampa, c., Fla., **USA**; popular winter resort, cigar factories, phosphates, electronics; fruit growing and canning; p. (1980) 272,000 (c.), 1,569,000 (met. a.).

Tampere (Tammerfors), t., S. **Finland**; on rly. between Helsinki and Vaasa; textiles, leather, paper, based on local hydroelec. power; cath.; p. (1979) 164,245.

Tampico, spt., **Mexico**; on R. Panuco, 14 km from G. of Mexico; exp. petroleum; oil refining, fish processing, chemicals; tourism; p. (1979) 248,369 (c.), 389,940 (met. a.).

Tamworth, t., N.S.W., **Australia**; impt. service and shopping ctr. for N. Tablelands; p. (1976) 27,887.

Tamworth, t., l. gov. dist., Staffs., **Eng.**; on R. Tame, 8 km S.E. of Lichfield; anc. cas.; lt. engin.; expanded t.; p. (1981) 64,315 (dist.).

Tana, lge. freshwater L., N.W. **Ethiopia,** nr. Gondar; source of Blue Nile, surrounded by marsh, papyrus swamp.

Tana, R., **Kenya**; rises nr. Mt. Kenya and flows to Indian Oc.; impt. elephant habitat in valley; 4 major hydro-elect. sta.; 5th opening 1987; 800 km long.

Tananarive. See **Antananarivo.**

Tandridge, l. gov. dist., Surrey, **Eng.**; S. of Gtr. London, inc. Caterham and Godstone; p. (1981) 75,845

Tanga, spt., **Tanzania,** E. Africa; on plateau overlooking Tanga Bay; rly. terminus; new plywood plant; p. (1978) 143,878.

Tanganyika, gr. L., E. **Central Africa**; lies in Gt. Rift Valley; c. 672 km long, 24-32 km wide; lgst. L. in Africa and except for L.

Baykal deepest L. in world; c. 823 m a.s.l.; discovered by Burton and Speke 1858, explored by Livingstone and Stanley 1871.

Tangier, free pt., **Morocco,** N. Africa; on Strait of Gibraltar; no longer internationalised zone but integral part of kingdom of Morocco; summer cap.; shipyard; cigarettes, fishing; p. (est. 1973) 185,500 (c.), 208,000 (met. a.).

Tangshan, c., Hebei prov., **China**; impt. industl. ctr.; steel, machin.; textiles, cement, oil refining; devastated by a series of earthquakes (1976); p. (est. 1970) 1,200,000.

Tanimbar Is., Indonesia; gr. of Is. in Banda Sea, S. Moluccas; forests, swamps; maize, rice, coconuts, sago; p. (est. 1975) 50,000.

Tanta, t., Lower **Egypt**; 88 km N. of Cairo; impt. rly. junc.; religious fairs; cotton processing; univ. proposed; p. (1976) 280,324.

Tanzania, rep., E. cst. **Africa**; inc. Is. of Zanzibar and Pemba, united since 1964; narrow coastal plain rises to inland plateau (Mt. Kilimanjaro, 5,895 m, hgst. peak in Africa); climate varies with alt., tropical in Zanzibar, temperate inland; predominantly subsistence agr., maize, millet, groundnuts, livestock; comm. crops inc. sisal, sugar, cotton, coffee; cloves on Is., especially Pemba; food processing, textile inds.; 5-year planning system to assist economic development especially in rural a.; cap. Dar es Salaam; new cap. planned at Dodoma; a. 939,706 km²; p. (est. 1984) 21,710,000.

Taormino, resort, E. Sicily, **Italy**; 230 m above sea at foot of Mt. Etna; magnificent scenery and anc. ruins.

Tapachula, c., Chiapas st., S. **Mexico**; on Pac. cst. lowlands; comm. ctr. for agr. dist.; p. (1970) 108,464.

Tapti, R., W. **India**; flows W. to G. of Cambay from Betul dist., Madhya Pradesh; 702 km.

Tarai, marshy, jungle tract at foot of Himalayas, **India, Nepal**; barrier to economic development of Nepal, now much modified and reduced in area by human occupation.

Taranaki, prov., N.I., **N.Z.**; impt. stock rearing and dairying a.; offshore oil and gas fields; a. 9,713 km²; p. (1976) 107,071.

Taranto, t., Lecce, **Italy**; on G. of Taranto, inlet of Ionian Sea; maritime arsenal with gr. comm. and industl. interests; strong cas.; steel wks.; cement; oil refinery; famous for its oyster and mussel fisheries; p. (1981) 244,101.

Tarapacá, prov., N. **Chile**; hot, arid desert; nitrate deposits; a. 55,270 km²; p. (1970) 174,730.

Tarascon, t., Bouches-du-Rhône dep., **France**; connected by bridges with Beaucaire on opposite bank of R. Rhône; old cas., famous festival; p. (1982) 11,024.

Tarawera Mtn., volcanic peak, N.I., **N.Z.**; 305 m; in Hot Springs dist.; eruption 1886 destroyed L. Rotomahana (water later returned to form bigger and deeper L.).

Tarbes, t., cap. of Hautes-Pyrénées dep., **France**; on R. Adour; cath.; p. (1982) 54,055.

Targul-Mures, c., **Romania**; on R. Mures; ch. t. of Magyar aut. region in Transylvania; old fort, Gothic Calvinist cath.; agr. tr. and processing; p. (est. 1972) 106,159.

Tarifa, t., **Spain**; on Gibraltar Strait; most S. point of mainland of Europe; fish tr., cereals, oranges, wines; p. (1981) 15,220.

Tarija, prov., **Bolivia**; part of Gran Chaco rising to W.; extensive agr. and forests; cap. T.; a. 64,196 km²; p. (est. 1969) 201,800.

Tarija, t., cap. of T. prov., **Bolivia**; alt. 1,906 m; cath., univ.; mkt. t.; p. (1967) 26,787.

Tarim Basin, depression, Xinjiang, **China**; desert with oases; crossed by Silk Road; anc. civilisation; state farms for wheat, millet, maize, cotton.

Tarn, dep., S. **France**; watered by Tarn and its tribs.; between Central Massif and basin of Aquitaine; mainly agr.; cap. Albi; a. 5,781 km²; p. (1982) 340,400.

Tarn, R., **France**; trib. of R. Garonne; rocky gorge 50 km long in its upper course; 376 km long.

Tarn-et-Garonne, dep., W. **France**; alluvial plain formed by Rs. Tarn, Garonne and Aveyron; mainly agr.; cap. Montauban; a. 3,730 km²; p. (1982) 190,300.

Tarnow, t., **Poland**; E. of Kraków; industl. ctr.; lge. nitrogen factory; synthetic fibres, metallurgy; cath.; p. (1983) 111,000.

Tarpon Springs, t., Fla., **USA**; pt.; main source of sponges in USA.

Tarragona, prov., **Spain**; on Mediterranean; vineyards and agr.; cap. Tarragona; a. 6,283 km²; p. (1981) 513,048.

Tarragona, spt., cap. of T. prov., **Spain**; at mouth of R. Francoli; exp. agr. prod. of Ebro valley; cath.; many Roman remains, inc. aqueduct; liqueur; p. (1981) 111,689.

Tarsus, anc. c., S. **Turkey**; nr. Adana; orange and citrus grows; ruined Roman temple; birthplace of St. Paul; p. (1970) 78,033.

Tartary or **Tatary**, region, **Central Asia**; now divided into Chinese or E. Turkestan, and W. Turkestan, USSR.

Tartu, c., Estonian SSR, **USSR**; pt. on Emayygi R.; rly. junc.; famous univ. founded 1632; agr. machin., tobacco ind.; p. (1980) 106,000.

Tashkent, c., cap. of Uzbek SSR, **USSR**; cultural, industl. and scientific ctr. of central Asia; on Trans-Caspian rly. in fertile Ferghana valley; univ.; diverse inds.; terminus of gas pipeline; p. (1980) 1,816,000.

Tasman Bay, lge inlet, S.I., **N.Z.**; penetrates N. cst., between Separation Point and D'Urville I.; enclosed by mtns., sheltered, fertile, coastal fringe; ch. ts. Nelson, Motueka.

Tasman Glacier, S.I., **N.Z.**; one of the lgst. in the world.

Tasmania (formerly **Van Diemen's Land**), I., st., **Australia**; smallest and least populous st. of Australia, second to be colonised (in 1803); mountainous with rugged cst.; temperate climate aids hydro-electric development and consequent rapid industl. expansion; plans for hydro-electric sta. on Franklin R. to help relieve high unemployment but fiercely opposed because of region's rare and striking natural beauty; 9 Nat. Parks; mng.; pastoral agr.; forestry; cap. Hobart; a. 67,897 km²; p. (1976) 402,866.

Tasman Sea, Australia; part of Pac. Oc. between Australia and New Zealand.

Tatabánya, t., N. **Hungary**; lignite mng. ctr.; aluminium refining, chemicals; p. (1978) 74,349.

Tatar ASSR, **USSR**; in middle Volga valley; wooded steppeland; extensive oil deposits and natural gas fields; cap. Kazan; a. 67,988 km²; p. (1970) 3,131,000.

Tatra Mtns., highest mtn. gr. of W. Carpathians, on border of **CSSR** and **Poland**; highest peak Gerlach in Slovakia, 2,664 m; mountaineering and winter sports.

Tatung. See **Datong**.

Taubaté, t., São Paulo st., **Brazil**; industl. ctr.; p. (est. 1980) 153,600.

Taunton, co. t., Somerset, **Eng.**; on R. Tone at W. end of Vale of Taunton; old cas.; with Wellington forms l. gov. dist. of **Taunton Dean**; p. (1981) 86,025 (dist.).

Taunton, t., Mass., **USA**; cotton, iron foundries, machin., plastics; p. (1980) 45,001.

Taunus, mtn. range, Hesse, **W. Germany**; between Rs. Lahn and Rhine and Main; forests, vineyards and spas.

Taupo, L., N.I., **N.Z.**; lgst. L. in N.Z.; geysers, hot springs in vicinity; 40 km by 27 km.

Tauranga, t., N.I., **N.Z.**; spt. on Bay of Plenty; tourism; fishing; p. (1976) 48,153.

Taurus Mtns., range, S. **Turkey**; rise to over 3,660 m.

Tavastehus. See **Hämeenlinna**.

Tavistock, mkt. t., West Devon, **Eng.**; on R. Tavy; anc, stannary t.; Drake born nearby.

Taw, R., Devon, **Eng.**; flows from Dartmoor to Barnstaple Bay; 80 km long.

Taxco, t., **Mexico**; alt. 1,700 m; gold- and silver-mng.; tourist ctr.; anc. Aztec t.; p. (1970) 64,368.

Taxila, ruined c., **Pakistan**; nr. Rawalpindi; anc. seat of learning; ruins of Buddhist univ.

Tay, R., **Scot.**; flows S.E. from Loch Tay in Perth and Kinross, to Firth of Tay; longest R. in Scot., 188 km; salmon fisheries.

Tay, Firth of, lge. inlet, E. cst. **Scot.**; extends inland almost to Perth.

Tayeh, t., Hupeh, **China**; lies to S. of Yangtze R., 67 km S.E. of Wuhan; impt. iron-ore deposits; supplies Hwangshih; iron and steel inds., heavy engin.

Tayport, burgh, North East Fife, **Scot.**; at entrance to Firth of Tay; opposite Broughty Ferry; linen, jute; p. (1981) 3,014.

Tayside, l. gov. reg., **Scot.**; inc. former cos. of Perth and Angus bordering the Highlands; a. 7,500 km²; p. (1981) 391,529.

Tbilisi (**Tiflis**), c., Georgian SSR, **USSR**; route ctr. on Kura R.; major admin., economic and cultural ctr. of Transcaucasia; machin., textiles, tanneries, furniture, food processing; power from hydroelectric power stas.; anc. tr. ctr.; some mediaeval fragments in c. ctr.; p. (1980) 1,080,000.

Tczew (**Dirschau**), t., Gdansk prov., N. **Poland**; pt. on Vistula; rly. junc.; agr. implements; p. (1970) 40,800.

Team Valley, Tyne and Wear, **Eng.**; impt. trading estate has been developed here.

Tebessa, t., N.E. **Algeria**; in Atlas mtns., at 851 m; mkt.; carpets; phosphate deposits nearby; p. (est. 1975) 41,000.

Tees, R., N. **Eng.**; rises on Cross Fell, Cumbria, flows E. to N. Sea between Hartlepool and Redcar; heavy inds. in lower section; 112 km long.

Teesdale, l. gov. dist., Durham, **Eng.**; Pennine a. inc. Barnard Castle; p. (1981) 24,425.

Teesport, oil refinery, between Redcar and Middlesbrough, Cleveland, **Eng.**

Teesside, former admin. dist., Cleveland, **Eng.**; inc. Middlesbrough, Redcar, Thornaby-on-Tees, Stockton-on-Tees, Billingham, and Eston; p.(1981) 382,689.

Tegal, spt., Java, **Indonesia**; textiles, sugar refining; lge. dam nearby; p. (1971) 105,752.

Tegucigalpa, c., cap. of **Honduras**; on R. Choluteca at 976 m; inter-ocean highway connects with Caribbean and Pac. Oc.; former ctr. of silver mng.; inc. Comayagüela, the modern part of c., where the nat. univ. is situated; p. (1974) 273,894.

Tehran (**Teheran**), c., cap. of **Iran**, 112 km S. of Caspian Sea; mftg. and comm. ctr.; modern bldgs.; gas pipeline to USSR; international airpt.; univ.; car assembly, textiles, chemicals, glass; new oil refinery; p. (1976) 4,496,159.

Tehuantepec, Isthmus of, separates G. of Mexico from Pac. Oc. at narrowest point of **Mexico**; width 200 km.

Teifi, R., S. **Wales**; rises in Cambrian mtns., flows S.W. to Cardigan Bay; 150 km long.

Teign, R., Devon, **Eng.**; flows to sea at pt. of Teignmouth from Dartmoor; picturesque estuary; 48 km long.

Teignbridge, l. gov. dist., S. Devon, **Eng.**; lower T. valley and ts. of Dawlish, Teignmouth, Newton Abbot and Ashburton; p. (1981) 95,665.

Teignmouth, t., Teignbridge, Devon, **Eng.**; at mouth of R. Teign, 21 km S. of Exeter; resort; revival of pt. with ball clay exp.; p. (1981) 13,264.

Tekirdag, t., **Turkey**; on Sea of Marmara, W. of Istanbul; former Greek settlement; p. (1970) 35,387.

Tel Aviv-Jaffa, c., **Israel**; on Mediterranean; lgst. c. of cty.; financial and cultural ctr.; univ.; founded by Zionists 1909; p. (est. 1979) 338,300.

Telemark, co., **Norway**; borders Skagerrak; mtnous., lake-covered, much forested; hydro-electric power forms basis for electrochemical inds.; a. 15,118 km²; p. (est. 1972) 157,553.

Telford, new t. (1963), Shropshire, **Eng.**; 32 km W. of Wolverhampton; p. (1981) 103,411.

Tellicherry, t., spt., Kerala, **India**; exp. pepper; lge. college; furniture; p. (1961) 44,763.

Telok Betong, spt., Sumatra, **Indonesia**; exp. pepper, agr. products; p. (1971) 198,986.

Tema, pt. (opened 1962), nr. Accra, **Ghana**; deepwater harbour, oil refinery, aluminium smelter; impt. industl. development; p. (1984) 60,767.

Teme, R., on border of Wales and Hereford and Worcs., **Eng.**; trib. of R. Severn; 112 km long.

Temir-Tau, c., Kazakh SSR, **USSR**; on Nura R.; industl. ctr.; iron, steel, synthetic rubber, soda; lge. thermal power sta.; p. (1980) 215,000.

Temuco, c., cap. of Cautin prov., **Chile**; cath.; tr. in cereals, apples, timber; Araucanian Indian mkt.; p. (est. 1980) 155,683.

Tenali, t., Andhra Pradesh, **India**; nr. Guntur in Krishna delta; p. (1971) 102,937.

Tenasserim, div., lower **Burma**; on Thailand border; extends along Isthmus of Kra; tin and rubber; a. 92,945 km². p. (est. 1969) 1,856,000.

Tenby, mkt. t., S. Pembs., Dyfed, **Wales**; on W. side of Carmarthen Bay, Bristol Channel; seaside resort; walled cas. t.; p. (1981) 4,814.

Tendring, l. gov. dist., E. Essex, **Eng.**; inc. cstl. ts. of Harwich, Frinton, Clacton and Brightlingsea; p. (1981) 113,819.

Tenerife, I., **Canary Is.**; volcanic landscapes and mild climate attracts tourists; cap. Santa Cruz; a. 2,025 km²; p. (1970) 500,381.

Tennessee, R., Tenn., Ky., **USA**; lgst. and most impt. branch of Ohio R.; valley once liable to flooding, now controlled by dams, and improved by the Tenn. Valley Authority; 1,251 km long.

Tennessee, st., **USA**; 'Volunteer St.'; admitted to Union 1796; st. flower Iris, st. bird Mockingbird; rises to Appalachians in E., crossed by Tennessee R. and tribs.; a. of heavy rainfall and severe soil erosion necessitated the Tenn. Valley Authority scheme of conservation, dam bldg., and afforestation; cheap hydroelectric power and attracting new inds., many reservoirs attract tourists; cap. Nashville; a. 109,412 km²; p. (1980) 4,591,000.

Tenterden, mkt. t., Kent, **Eng.**; 13 km N. of Rye; grew with wool tr., church with famous tower; p. (1981) 6,209.

Teófilo Otoni, t., Minas Gerais, **Brazil**; semi-precious stone polishing; p. (est. 1980) 155,800.

Tepic, c., cap. of Nayarit st., **Mexico**, comm. ctr. for agr. dist.; nr. Sanguaney volcano; p. (1979) 139,881.

Teplice, wat. pl., **ČSSR**; N.W. of Prague; textile and hardware inds.; mineral springs; p. (1970) 53,000.

Teramo, c., cap. of T. prov., **Italy**; 24 km from Adriatic; route and agr. ctr.; cath.; textiles; the anc. Interamnium; p. (1981) 51,092.

Terek, R., N. Caucasia, **RSFSR**; flows to Caspian Sea; used for irrigation and hydroelectric power in lower course; 592 km long.

Teresina, t., cap. of Piauí st., **Brazil**; comm. ctr.; lt. inds.; p. (est. 1980) 348,900.

Terezópolis, t., Rio de Janeiro, **Brazil**; health resort; textiles; p. (est. 1968) 69,636.

Terneuzen, t., **Neth.**; on W. Schelde R.; pipeline to be constructed to carry ethylene from Pernis; p. (1982) 35,606.

Terni, t., Perugia, **Italy**; among the Apennines; iron and steel wks., arms factory; cath.; p. (1981) 253,912.

Ternopol (Tarnopol), t., Ukrainian SSR, **USSR**; E. of Lvov; rly. junc.; mkt.; agr. machin., food inds.; p. (1980) 149,000.

Terrassa, t., Barcelona, **Spain**; textile ctr.; p. (1981) 147,780.

Terre Adélie, name given to Fr. terr. and I. in Antarctic; est. a. 424,400 km².

Terre Haute, t., Ind., **USA**; coal, natural gas, flour, paper, glass, foundries; p. (1980) 61,125 (t.), 176,583 (met. a.).

Terreón, t., Coahuila, **Mexico**; ctr. of comm. agr.; oil pipeline connects to Chihuahua; thermoelec. plant; p. (1969) 243,234.

Teruel, t., cap. of Teruel prov., **Spain**; on R. Turia; walled t., cath.; p. (1981) 153,456 (prov.).

Test Valley, l. gov. dist., W. Hants., **Eng.**; stretches from Andover to Romsey; p. (1981) 90,853.

Tete, t., central **Moçambique**; on R. Zambesi; ctr. of coalfield; iron-ore, graphite, radioactive materials.

Tetovo, t., Macedonia, **Yugoslavia**; chemicals, electro-metallurgy, textiles.

Tetuan, ch. spt., **Morocco**, N. Africa; walled t. p. (1973) 137,080 (t.), 308,700 (met. a.).

Teviot, R., Roxburgh, **Scot.**; trib. of R. Tweed; 59 km long.

Tewkesbury, mkt. t., l. gov. dist., Gloucs., **Eng.**; on R. Avon, close to confluence with R. Severn; Norman abbey; p. (1981) 80,815.

Texarkana, t., Texas and Ark., **USA**; bdy. passes down middle of main street; timber and cotton region; total p. (1980) 31,271.

Texas, st., S.W. **USA**; 'Lone Star St.'; admitted to Union 1845; st. flower Bluebonnet, st. bird Mocking bird; second lgst. st. by a.; borders Mexico; dry plains in W., humid cst. in E.; problems of soil erosion yet leading agr. st.; leading producer of petroleum and natural gas; cap. Austin; a. 692,408 km²; p. (1980) 14,228,000.

Texel, one of the W. Frisian Is., **Neth.**; scene of several naval battles; p. (1967) 11,003.

Thailand (Siam), kingdom, **S.E. Asia**; 4 main regions; parallel N.–S. hill ranges (2,400 m) and valleys in N. producing teak; rice growing, fertile plain of Chao Phraya R. in ctr.; thinly populated E. plateau, drained by Mekong; S. coastal strip on G. of Siam; monsoon climate; predominantly agr., accounting for over 80 per cent p. and 30 per cent nat. income; lgst. world exporter of rice; forestry, fisheries, mng.; especially tin, wolfram; oil exploration; industl. development based on processing of Thai raw materials; cap. Bangkok; a. 519,083 km²; p. (est. 1984) 50,584,000.

Thal Desert, Pakistan; W. of Punjab; now irrigated for wheat and cotton.

Thame, mkt. t., South Oxford, **Eng.**; on R. Thame, 11 km S.W. of Aylesbury; p. (1981) 8,533.

Thames, R., **Eng.**; rises in Cotswold hills and flows past Oxford, Reading, Windsor, and London to the N. Sea; tribs. inc. Windrush, Cherwell, Thame, Kennet, Colne, Lea, and Roding; estuary impt. industl. a. with many oil refineries; flood barrier at Silvertown in Woolwich (to be opened 1983), 336 km long.

Thamesdown, l. gov. dist., N.E. Wilts., **Eng.**; based on Swindon; p. (1981) 152,112.

Thameshaven, lge. oil refinery, Essex, **Eng.**; on N. cst. of Thames estuary 13 km below Tilbury.

Thana, t., Maharashtra, **India**; textiles, chemicals; p. (1971) 170,675 (t.), 207,352 (met. a.).

Thanet, I. of, lge. promontory, N.E. extremity of Kent, **Eng.**; formed by bifurcation of R. Stour; now also l. gov. dist. which contains Margate, Ramsgate, and Broadstairs; p. (1981) 121,150.

Thanjavur, t., Tamil Nadu, **India**; silks, carpets, jewellery, inlaid metals; impt. Brahman ctr.; p. (1971) 140,547.

Thar Desert, on bdy. of **India** and **Pakistan**; covers slopes between N.W. Deccan and R. Indus; barren; lack of Rs. or level land prevents irrigation; crossed by caravan routes.

Thebes, c., of Boeotia, in anc. **Greece**; Mycenaean site; destroyed by Alexander the Great 335 B.C.; modern c. of Thivai occupies site; p. (1981) 18,712.

Thebes, c. of anc. **Egypt**; on banks of Nile; site now partly occupied by vs. Karnak and Luxor; archeological discoveries in Valley of the Kings 1922, inc. tomb of Tutankhamun.

The Entrance, t., N.S.W., **Australia**; tourist resort on waterway from L. Tuggerah to Tasman Sea; fishing; p. (1976) 20,107.

Thermopylae, celebrated pass between Mt. Oeta and the sea, N.E. **Greece**; heroic battle between Spartans and Persians 480 B.C.

Thessaloniki, c., **Greece**; spt. at head of G. of T.; with fiscal free zone; second c. of Greece; impt. route and industl. ctr.; univ.; p. (1981) 406,413.

Thessaly, prov., central **Greece**; fertile plain drained by R. Piniós; mainly agr.; a. 13,489 km²; p. (1981) 695,654.

Thetford, t., Breckland, Norfolk, **Eng.**; on Little Ouse; industl. estate for London overspill; fruit and vegetable canning, pulp mfg., engin.; p. (1981) 19,591.

Thetford Mines, t., Quebec, **Canada**; asbestos mng. ctr.; p. (1971) 22,000.

Thienen (Tirlemont), t., Brabant prov., **Belgium**; ctr. of Belgian beet-sugar refining; captured by Marlborough 1705; p. (est. 1981) 32,620.

Thiès, t., **Senegambia**; rly. ctr. and wkshps.; aluminium, phosphate quarrying; p. (1976) 117,333.

Thimphu, t., cap. **Bhutan**; hydroelectric plant; 176 km road link to Phuntsholing (Sikkim) 1968; p. (1977) 8,922.

Thionville, t., Moselle dep., N. **France**; in Lorraine ironfield conurb.; metallurgical and chemical inds.; p. (1982) 138,034 (met. a.).

Thira (Santorine), volcanic I., Cyclades, **Greece**; wine prods.; max. alt. 567 m; a. 75 km²; p. c. 10,000.

Thirlmere, L., Cumbria, **Eng.**; 5 km long; furnishes part of water supply of Manchester.

Thirsk, mkt. t., Hambleton, North Yorks., **Eng.**; in wide gap between Pennines and Cleveland hills, 11 km S.E. of Northallerton; racecourse.

Thompson, R., B.C., **Canada**; trib. of R. Fraser; forms impt. routeway through Rocky mtns.; 448 km long.

Thornburi, c., Thailand; on R. Menam opposite Bangkok; second c. of T.; former cap., "Temple of Dawn"; lt. inds.; p. (1970) 627,989.

Thorez (Chistyakovo), Ukrainian SSR, USSR; coal mng.; p. (est. 1967) 95,000 (c.), 300,000 (met. a.).

Thornaby-on-Tees. See Teesside.

Thornbury, mkt. t., Avon, Eng.; 16 km N. of Bristol; aircraft mftg.; expanded t.

Thornton Cleveleys, t., Wyre, Lancs., Eng.; 6 km N.E. of Blackpool; resort; p. (1981) 26,139.

Thörshavn, c., cap. of Faroe Is.; on Stromo I.; fish. pt.; anc. fortress; lighthouse; p. (1970) 10,726.

Thousand Isles, gr. of over 1,500 Is. in St. Lawrence R. which extend up-river for c. 48 km from Brockville to Gananoque, at junc. of L. Ont. and St. Lawrence R.; partly in N.Y. st. and partly in Canada.

Thrace, anc. name of terr. in S.E. Europe, part of which has been added to Greece; successively under Macedonian, Roman, Byzantine, and Turkish rule, before passing to Greece; tobacco; a. 8,586 km²; p. of dep. (1981) 345,220.

Three Rivers, l. gov. dist., S.W. Herts., Eng.; close to London and inc. Rickmansworth and Chorleywood; p. (1981) 77,836.

Thule, N.W. Greenland; 1,600 km from N. Pole; American air base and site of ballistic missile early warning sta.; spt. open 2-3 months per annum.

Thumba, Kerala, India; space science and technological ctr.

Thun, L., Berne can., Switzerland; occupies valleys of R. Aare where it leaves Alpine region; separated from L. Brienz by deltaic neck of land on which is Interlaken; a. 98 km².

Thun, t., Berne, Switzerland; on N.W. end of L. Thun; cas. on hill above t.; tourism; p. (est. 1978) 37,000.

Thunder Bay, t., Canada; formed from Port Arthur and Port William; pt. on N.W. cst. of L. Superior; grain exp. ctr.; p. (1979) 111,475.

Thurgau, can., N.E. Switzerland; on L. Constance, bordered by R. Rhine; prosperous agr. a.; inds. ass, with textiles; cap. Frauenfeld; a. 1,005 km²; p. (1980) 183,795.

Thuringia, former st., E. Germany; bordered by Bavaria, Saxony-Anhalt, Lower Saxony, and Hesse; drained by Rs. Saale and Werra; crossed by Thüringer Wald and extending to Harz mtns.; fertile arable agr. a.; now comprises dists. of Erfurt Suhl and Bera.

Thuringian Forest or Thüringer Wald, forested range of hills E. Germany; rising to 982 m in Beerberg; famous for romantic scenery and legends; resorts.

Thurles, mkt. t., Tipperary, R.o.I.; on R. Suir; agr. processing; cath., cas.; p. (1981) 7,352.

Thurrock, t., l. gov. dist. Essex, Eng.; on Thames. nr. Tilbury; oil refining, metal refining, cement, paper board; p. (1981) 126,870.

Thurso, burgh, Caithness, Scot.; nr. Dounreay; anc. stronghold of Vikings; p. (1981) 9,038.

Tianjin (Tientsin) c., Hebei prov., China 112 km S.E. of Beijing; impt. pt. using poor harbour on Hai R.; industl. ctr., textiles, elec. instruments, steel rolling mills, machine tools, chemicals, tobacco, food processing; p. (est. 1982) 7,760,000.

Tiaret, t., W. Algeria; N. Africa; in strategic pass; walled; agr. mkt.; cereals, wool, cattle; p. (1966) 37,059.

Tiber, R., Italy; flows from Apennines to Mediterranean, passing through Rome; 352 km long.

Tiberias, t., Israel; on Sea of Galilee (L. Tiberias); agr. ctr.; health resort with medicinal springs; p. (est. 1970) 23,900.

Tibesti, mtns., on bdy. between Libya and Chad. Equatorial Africa; barren in spite of slight rainfall; mainly above 1,800 m max. alt. 3,401 m.

Tibet (Xizang Zizhiou), aut. region, China; lofty plateau called "the roof of the world" its lowest plains being 3,660 m a.s.l.; semi-desert; network of roads being built inc. one across Himalayas to Katmandu; pastoral agr. sheep; arable agr. in R. valleys, especially Zangbo valley, wheat, barley, fruit, vegetables; tr. of wool, musk, gold, skins, drugs traditionally carried by yaks which can stand intense cold; salt, alluvial gold, radioactive ores; cap. Lhasa; a. 1,217,308 km²; p. (est 1968) 1,400,000.

Ticino, R. Switzerland and Italy; trib. of Po; forms S. approach to St. Gotthard Pass; irrigation in lower course; length 240 km.

Ticino, can., Switzerland; on S. slopes of central Alps, bordering Italy; contains parts of Ls. Maggiore and Lugano; mainly pastoral agr., but wine, corn, tobacco in valleys; industl. a., in S. based on hydroelectric power, chemicals, metallurgy; many tourist resorts inc. Locarno, Lugano; cap. Bellinzona; a. 2,813 km²; p. (1980) 265,899.

Ticonderoga, V., N.E., N.Y., USA; resort between Ls. George and Champlain; L. George falls provide hydroelectric power for paper mill; local graphite used in pencil ind.; p. (1980) 2,938.

Tideswell, t., Derbys., Eng.; tourist ctr.; limestone quarrying in a.; lge. 14th cent. church known as "cath. of the Peak." p. c. 1,500.

Tidore I., Moluccas, Indonesia; volcanic; densely populated; coffee, tobacco, spices, fruit; a. 78 km²; p. (est. 1969) 70,000.

Tien Shan (= Celestial Mtns.) mtn. chain, central Asia, along China-USSR border; highest peak 7,320 m; source of Syr-Dar'ya, Chu, Ili and many other Rs.

Tierra del Fuego, archipelago, southernmost part of S. America; separated from Patagonia by Strait of Magellan; divided politically between Chile and Argentina; timber, pastoral agr. sheep; oilfield at Rio Grande; mng.; a. c. 47,900 km².

Tigre, st., Ethiopia; formerly an independent kingdom; cap. Adua; severe drought 1982-3.

Tigris, R., S.W. Asia; rises in Taurus mtns. S. Turkey, flows through Iraq where it is joined by the Euphrates and proceeds to Persian G.; comm. routeway; dam projected 56 km N. of Mosul; many of the earliest cs. located in valley; 1,840 km long.

Tijuana, t., Baja Cal. st., Mexico; resort catering for Americans; casinos, race-tracks, bull-fights; p. (1979) 566,344.

Tiksi, t., USSR; Arctic spt., at mouth of Lena R.; local coal deposits; linked by air and R; to Yakutsk.

Tilburg, c., N. Brabant, Neth.; nr. Breda; woollens, textiles, tobacco, leather; p. (1982) 153,957.

Tilbury, pt., Essex, Eng.; on N. Bank of R. Thames 32 km E. of London; within Port of London; major container terminal.

Tillicoultry, burgh, Clackmannan, Scot.; on Devon R.; woollen and worsted fabrics, paper; p. (1981) 6,154.

Tilsit. See Sovetsk.

Timaru, c., S.I., N.Z.; E. cst. spt., exp. frozen foods; fishing; regional ctr. for S. Canterbury; p. (1976) 29,958.

Timbuktu, Mali, W. Africa; nr. Niger R. on border of Sahara; salt tr., handicraft inds.; flourished as comm. mart and Moslem ctr. 14th-16th cent.; p. (1975) 10,500.

Timisoara, c., W. Romania; comm., industl. and educational ctr.; univ., 2 caths., cas.; once a frontier fortress; p. (1982) 277,779.

Timmins, t., Ont., Canada; gold mng. declining; vast deposits of copper, zinc, silver, discovered 1964; timber inds., brewing; p. (est. 1971) 29,000.

Timok Basin, Serbia, Yugoslavia; industl. region; coal mng., copper smelting, chemicals, glass, food processing; arable agr., vines.

Timor, lgst. of Lesser Sunda Is., E. Indies; divided politically until 1975 into W. Timor part of Indonesia and Port Timor; now both part of Indonesia; a. 33,748 km²; p. (est. 1970) 3,085,541.

Timor Sea, that part of the Indian Oc. N.W. of W. Australia, and S. of Timor I.

Timsah, L., Egypt; sm. L. midway along Suez Canal; formerly used for recreational purposes by Brit. garrison in Canal zone.

Tinogasta, t., Catamarca prov., Argentina; in E. foothills of Andes, 192 km N.W. of Catamarca; impt. copper mines.

Tintagel, v., Cornwall, Eng.; ruined Norman cas.; reputed birthplace of King Arthur; tourism.

Tintern, v., Gwent, Wales; Cistercian abbey.

Tinto, R., Huelva prov., S.W. Spain; in Andalusia; flows W. to Alt. Oc.; gives its name to Rio Tinto copper mng. region which it crosses; 104 km long.

Tipperary, inland co., Munster, **R.o.I.**; drained by Rs. Suir and Shannon; mtnous., Knockmealdown and Galty mtns.; fertile Golden Vale in S.W.; dairying, sugar-beet; divided into N. and S. Ridings; co. t. Clonmel; p. (1981) 20,276 (N.R.), 30,018 (S.R.).

Tipperary, t., Tipperary, **R.o.I.**; 46 km S.E. Limerick; dairy processing; p. (1981) 4,929.

Tipton. *See* Dudley.

Tiranë, t., cap. of **Albania**; rapid growth since becoming cap. 1920; many new inds.; agr. processing, engin., clothing, glass; univ.; airport; p. (1967) 169,300.

Tiraspol, c., S.E. Moldavian SSR, **USSR**; on R. Dniester; agr. processing ctr.; heat and power sta. recently constructed; p. (1980) 142,000.

Tiree, I., Inner Hebrides, **Scot.**; off cst. of Mull; 22 km long, up to 10 km wide; sm. freshwater lochs and prehistoric forts; p. (1971) 1,019 (inc. Coll).

Tiruchirapalli (**Trichinopoly**), c., Tamil Nadu, S.E. **India**; on R. Cauvery; rly. ctr.; textiles, cigars, goldsmithery; p. (1971) 307,400 (c.), 464,624 (met. a.).

Tirunelveli (**Tinnevelly**), c., Tamil Nadu, S.E. **India**; agr. tr. ctr. with sugar refinery; p. (1971) 108,498 (c.), 266,688 (met. a.).

Tiruppur, t., Tamil Nadu, **India**; nr. Coimbatore; p. (1971) 113,302 (t.), 151,127 (met. a.).

Tisa (**Tisza**), R., **E. Europe**; rises in E. Carpathians, W. Ukraine, flows across Hungary into Yugoslavia where it joins the Danube 72 km below Novi Sad; ch. tribs. Koros and Mures; length *c.* 960 km; navigable in part.

Titicaca, L., **S. America**; between two ranges of Andes, on borders of Bolivia and Peru; 3,812 m a.s.l.; highest lge. L. in world; max. depth 300 m; crossed by steamers; fishing; a. c. 8,300 km².

Titograd (**Podgorica**), t., cap. of Montenegro, S. **Yugoslavia**; nr. Albanian frontier; anc. t. but now mainly modern with growing industl. activity; agr. processing, aluminium smelting; airport; p. (1971) 54,509.

Titov Veles, t., central Macedonia, **Yugoslavia**; on R. Vardar, and main rly. to Belgrade; recent industl. growth; textiles; p. (est. 1965) 31,000.

Tiverton, mkt. t., Mid Devon, **Eng.**; 22 km N. Exeter; once famous for lace; textiles, engin.; p. (1981) 16,539.

Tivoli, the anc. Tibur, nr. Rome, **Italy**; on Aniene R., magnificent situations; hydroelec. power; resort; remains of Hadrian's villa; p. (1981) 50,969.

Tjirebon (**Cheribon**), spt., Java, Indonesia; on N. cst. 192 km E. of Djakarta; rice, tea, coffee tr.; ctr. of irrigation scheme; oil refining; p. (1971) 178,529.

Tlaxcala, smallest st., **Mexico**; on Mesa Central; dense p.; mainly agr.; cap. T.; a. 4,027 km²; p. (1969) 454,000.

Tlemcen, t., cap. of T. dep., N.W. **Algeria**; picturesque mediaeval t.; agr. ctr. in fertile region; textiles, furniture, handicrafts; p. (1967) 80,000.

Toamasina (**Tamatave**), t., **Madagascar**; lge seapt. on Indian Oc., handles 70 per cent of M. tr.; industl. complex, car assembly, oil refinery; p. (1975) 77,395.

Tobago, southernmost I., Windward Is., **W.I.**; volcanic, forested, picturesque, irregular topography; resorts utilising pleasant climate; exp. coconuts, copra, cacao, limes; ch. t. Scarborough; seeks internal self-gov.; a. 300 km²; p. (1970) 39,280. *See* Trinidad and Tobago.

Tobata. *See* Kitakyushu.

Tobermory, burgh, Argyll and Bute, **Scot.**; on I. of Mull at N. entrance to Sound of Mull; fish. pt., resort; p. (1981) 843.

Tobol, R., W. Siberia, **RSFSR**; trib. of R. Irtysh; navigable in lower course; 800 km long.

Tobolsk, t., W. Siberia, **RSFSR**; R. pt. on Irtysh R.; shipbldg., sawmilling, fishing; p. (est. 1967) 47,000.

Tobruk, spt., **Libya**, N. Africa; on cst. 352 km E. of Benghazi; exp. oil, served by pipeline from Libyan oilfields; p. (est. 1970) 28,000.

Tocantins, R., central **Brazil**; rises in Goias prov., flows N. across plateau of Brazil through Pará estuary to Atl. Oc.; navigation interrupted by rapids 320 km above Pará; ch. trib. Araguaya R.; 2,560 km long.

Toce, R., N. **Italy**; rises in Lepontine Alps, flows

S. and S.E. into L. Maggiore; valley used by trunk rly. from Milan to Berne as S. approach to Simplon Tunnel; 86 km long.

Tocopilla, spt., **Chile**; exp. nitrate, copper ore, sulphates, iodine; p. (est. 1966) 23,140

Todmorden, mkt. t., Calderdale, West Yorks., **Eng.**; nr. source of R. Calder, 10 km N.E. of Rochdale; cottons, machin.; p. (1981) 14,665.

Togliatti (**Tol'yatti**), c., **RSFSR**; on R. Volga 56 km W.N.W. of Kuybyshev; engin., motor wks., natural gas pipeline to Moscow; chemicals; p. (1970) 251,000.

Togo, Rep. of, W. Africa; narrow strip between Ghana (W.) and Benin (E.); N. and S. lowlands separated by mtns. (1,000 m); climate hot and humid, but drier savannah conditions in N.; coffee on slopes of central mtns., cacao, copra in S., maize in N.; phosphate mng.; major iron ore deposits in N. now form ch. exp.; developing food-processing inds.; cap. Lomé; a. 54,960 km²; p. (est. 1984) 2,838,000.

Tokaido, Japan, one of gr. feudal highways, along S. cst. Honshu, now forms main line of modern communications network.

Tokaimura, v., Ibaraki, **Japan**; nuclear reactor and lge. nuclear power sta.

Tokaj, t., **Hungary**; at confluence of Bodrog and Tisa Rs.; nearby slopes of Hegyalia produce Tokay wine; p. (1960) 5,031.

Tokat, t., cap. of T. prov., **Turkey**; copper refining, leather mnfs.; p. (1965) 38,006.

Tokelau or **Union Isles**, gr. of 3 coral atolls, S. Pac., N. of W. Samoa, belonging to N.Z.; Fakaofo, Nukunono and Atafu; natives are Polynesians; subsistence economy; copra; a. 10 km²; p. (1972) 1,599.

Tokoroa, co. t., N.I., **N.Z.**; kraft paper, pulp, and sawn timber; p. (1971) 15,174.

Tokushima, t., Shikoku, **Japan**; spt. on E. cst.; mkt. ctr., cotton mnfs.; p. (1979) 246,189.

Tokyo, c., cap. of **Japan**; spt. with deepened harbour handling mainly S. coastal tr.; major industl. ctr. with diverse mnfs. and major problems of pollution; built on marshy site with much expensive reclamation from sea; planned decentralisation of p. and economic activity in progress; with Osaka–Kobe–Kyoto conurbs. (480 km long ribbon development) spoken of as Tokaido (*q.v.*) megalopolis; major educational ctr. with many univs.; p. (1979) 8,448,382 (c.); 11,667,222 (met. a.).

Tolbukhin, t., N.E. **Bulgaria**; comm. and agr. ctr. of Dobruja; food-processing, textiles, furniture, agr. machin.; formerly Dobrich, renamed in honour of Russian soldier who took it from Germans 1944; p. (est. 1968) 61,440.

Toledo, prov., **Spain**; mtnous.; agr., vineyards, stock-raising; a. 15,346 km²; p. (1981) 474,630.

Toledo, anc. c., cap. of T. prov., **Spain**; in New Castile; on hill above Tagus R.; Gothic, Moorish, and Castillian architecture; picturesque narrow streets; Alcázar citadel; associated with El Greco; sword mkg. still flourishes; sm. arms; tourism; p. (1981) 57,769.

Toledo, c., Ohio, **USA**; rly. ctr. and L. pt. with natural harbour on Maumee R.; exp. mnfs., oil, coal, agr. prod.; imports iron-ore; glass mkg., shipbldg., car components and many varied mnfs.; p. (1980) 355,000 (c.), 792,000 (met. a.).

Tolentino, t., in the Marches, central **Italy**; on R. Chienti; mediaeval walls and houses; cath.; sm. handicraft inds.; spa and tourist ctr.; p. (est. 1981) 17,984.

Tolosa, t., Guipúzcoa prov., **Spain**; in the Basque cty.; mediaeval bldgs., and armour; paper mills; (p. (1981) 18,894.

Tolpuddle, v., Dorset, **Eng.**; 11 km N.E. of Dorchester; famous for "Tolpuddle martyrs," agr. labourers condemned to transportation for trying to form a trade union (1834).

Toluca, c., cap. of Mexico st., central **Mexico**; stands at 2,672 m; brewing, flour, cottons, pottery; especially noted for basket weaving; p. (1979) 241,920.

Tom, R., Siberia, **RSFSR**; flows through Kuznetsk Basin and joins R. Ob; 704 km long.

Tomaszow Mazowiecki, t., Lodz prov., central **Poland**; industl. t. on Pilica R., surrounded by forests; textile ind., artificial silk; p. (1970) 54,900.

Tombigbee, R., Miss., **USA**; flows S. to join

Alabama R. to form Mobile and Tensaw Rs.; navigable, partially canalised; length 654 km.

Tomsk, c., cap. of marshy T. oblast, **RSFSR;** one of few lge. ts. in N. Siberia; major pt. on R. Tom; rly. junc. on Trans-Siberian rly.; educational ctr.; univ., cath.; engin., chemicals; p. (1980) 431,000.

Tonawanda, t., N.Y. st., **USA;** on Niagara R. at terminus of Erie Barge Canal; steel, plastics, chemicals; power from Niagara Falls, adjacent to N. Tonawanda; p. (1980) 18,693.

Tonbridge, t., Kent, **Eng.;** on R. Medway; food processing; lt. inds., inc. cricket balls; Norman cas. gatehouse; public school; with Malling forms l. gov. dist.; p. (1981) 96,205 (dist.).

Tone, R., Honshu, **Japan;** flows E. across Kanto Plain to Pac. Oc., N. of Tokyo; longest R. in Japan.

Tonga, I. gr., S. Pac. Oc.; Polynesian kingdom, gained independence 1970; 158 coral and volcanic Is.; 50 per cent. p. on Tongatabu I.; exp. copra, bananas; fishing; oil discovered 1969; airport; cap. Nuku'alofa; a. 699 km²; p. (est. 1980) 97,000.

Tongariro, volcanic peak, N.I., **N.Z.;** nat. park in ctr. of volcanic dist.; alt. 1,970 m.

Tongeren (Tongres), t., Limburg prov., N.E. **Belgium;** mkt. ctr. for fertile Hesbaye region; historic bldgs.; p. (1982) 29,765.

Tonghua (Tunghwa), c., S.W. Jilin, **China;** rly junc.; soya bean processing; local iron and coal reserves; p. (est. 1970) 275,000.

Tonkin, region, N. **Vietnam;** mtns. in N. and W., alluvial plain in E. around delta of Red R., containing most p. and lge. cs.; fertile agr.; ch. t. Hanoi; ch. pt. Haiphong; a. 104,973 km².

Tonle Sap, L., **Kampuchea;** major comm. fishing a.; L. acts as natural reservoir to control floods of Mekong R.

Tönsberg, c., Vestfold prov., S.E. **Norway;** one of oldest Norwegian cs., on Skagerrak at entrance to Oslo fjord; ctr. of whaling fleet; oil mills; p. (est. 1970) 11,260.

Toowoomba, t., S.E. Queensland, **Australia;** regional ctr. for Darling Downs, a rich wool and beef a; planned with parks and gardens: agr. based inds., engin.: p. (1976) 63,956.

Topeka, c., cap. of Kansas st., **USA;** on Kansas R.; impt. tr. ctr. in rich agr. region; food processing, rly. ctr. and engin.; p. (1980) 115,000.

Torbay, l. gov. dist., S. Devon, **Eng.;** formed by amalgamation of Torquay, Paignton and Brixham; located around Tor Bay; tourism; p. (1981) 115,582.

Torcello, I., with anc. Byzantine cath., on lagoon nr. Venice, **Italy.**

Torfaen, l. gov. dist., Gwent, **Wales;** based on Pontypool, Cwmbran and Blaenavon; p. (1981) 90,133.

Torgau, t., E. **Germany;** R. pt. on Elbe; industl. ctr.; American and Soviet armies met here 1945; p. (est. 1970) 21,688.

Torne, R., N. **Europe;** rises in Sweden, drains L. Tornetrask and flows S.W. to G. of Bothnia, forming Finno-Swedish bdy.; rich in salmon; 512 km long.

Torness, East Lothian, **Scot.;** site of advanced gas cooled nuclear power sta.

Toronto, c., cap. of Ont. prov., **Canada;** major Gt. Ls. pt., on L. Ont.; spacious harbour; exp. lge. quantities of wheat; comm., financial, industl. and educational ctr.; many varied mnfs., univ.; notable bldgs., parks; a. 622 km²; p. (1979) 633,320 (c.), 2,864,700 (met. a.).

Torpoint, t., Cornwall, **Eng.;** on Plymouth Sound; p. (1981) 8,423.

Torquay, t., S. Devon, **Eng.;** incorporated in Torbay; on N. side of Tor Bay; seaside resort with all-year season.

Torre Annunziata, Campania, **Italy;** at foot of Vesuvius; spt., spa, bathing resort on Bay of Naples; arms factory, pasta mnf.; p. (est. 1981) 57,097.

Torre del Greco, t., Campania, **Italy;** spt. and resort on Bay of Naples at foot of Vesuvius; coral fishing; pasta mnf.; p. (1981) 102,890.

Torremolinos, cst. resort, **Spain;** S. of Malaga; p. (1981) 22,535.

Torrens, L., S. **Australia;** 2nd lgst. salt L. in A.; varies from brackish lake to salt marsh.

Torreon, c., Coahuila, N. **Mexico;** developed rapidly after growth of cotton in surrounding Laguna dist.; cotton mills, rubber, smelting, food processing; rly. connection with ts. in S. Mexico; p. (1979) 274,717 (c.), 407,271 (met. a.).

Torres Strait, between C. York, Queensland, **Australia,** and **New Guinea;** 144 km wide, strong tidal currents endanger navigation; contains volcanic and coral Torres Strait Is., 20 of which are inhabited by Australian Melanesians.

Torridge, R., Devon, **Eng.;** flows from Hartland dist. to a confluence with the Taw at Bideford Bay; 85 km long.

Torridge, l. gov. dist., N.W. Devon, **Eng.;** inc. N. cst. ts. of Northam and Bideford and stretches inland to Great Torrington; p. (1981) 47,275.

Tortona, t., Piedmont, N. **Italy;** on Scrivia R.; textiles, metallurgy, engin., wines; cath.; the Roman Dertona; p. (1981) 28,806.

Tortosa, c., Tarragona prov., N.E. **Spain;** pt. on Ebro R., 35 km from mouth; food processing, soap, pottery; cath.; impt. Moorish t.; p. (1981) 31,445.

Tororo, t., **Uganda;** lge. chemical wks., cement, fertilisers.

Tortuga or Ile de la Tortue, I., Caribbean Sea; off N. cst. **Haiti;** provides shelter from N.E. tr. winds for Port-de-Paix; private development to convert I. into free pt. with tax incentives for inds.; scenic attractions being tapped to develop tourist tr.; airport under construction; subsistence agr. fishing; a. c. 65 km².

Torun (Ger. **Thorn**), c., Bydgoszcz prov., **Poland;** rly. junc., pt. on Vistula; industl. ctr.; chemicals, elec. gds., clothing, metallurgy, engin., food processing; univ. bears name of Copernicus who was born here; p. (est. 1983) 182,400.

Tory I., off N.W. cst., Donegal, **R.o.I.;** lighthouse; fishing; p. c. 200.

Totnes, t., South Hams, Devon, **Eng.;** on R. Dart 10 km N.W. of Dartmouth; mediaeval t.; agr. mkt., food processing; p. (1981) 5,627.

Tottenham. See Haringey.

Tottori, c., Honshu, **Japan;** spt. on Sea of Japan, exp. lumber, raw silk, fruit; industl. ctr.; p. (1979) 127,598.

Touggourt or Tuggurt, t., S. **Algeria;** on edge of Sahara; rly. terminus; dates; p. (1961) 26,000.

Toulon, c., Var dep., S.W. **France;** reinstated as cap. of Var dep. (1974); on Mediterranean cst.; base of Fr. navy; fine natural harbour; comm. pt. and industl. ctr.; many fine bldgs.; Port-Cros Nat. Park nearby; p. (1982) 181,405.

Toulouse, c., cap. of Haute-Garonne dep., S. **France;** in Languedoc on Garonne R. and Canal du Midi, commanding route through Gate of Carcassonne; industl. and agr. tr. ctr.; food processing, varied mnfs.; many fine bldgs., notably mediaeval univ., basilica, Gothic cath.; p. (1982) 354,289.

Touraine, region and former prov. of **France,** of which Tours was the cap.; now occupied by Indre-et-Loire dep. and part of Vienne dep.; known as the "garden of France."

Tourcoing, c., Nord dep., N. **France;** 16 km N.E. of Lille; with twin t. of Roubaix forms major wool textile ctr.; p. (1982) 97,121.

Tournai, c., Hainaut prov., W. **Belgium;** on R. Scheldt, nr. Mons; historic c.; famous cath.; textiles, carpet mftg., ctr. of cement ind.; p. (1982) 67,576.

Tours, c., cap. of Indre-et-Loire dep., **France;** in Touraine, on R. Loire; tourist ctr. for the châteaux of the Loire; route ctr.; agr. inds.; printing, engin.; Gothic cath.; p. (1982) 136,483.

Towcester, mkt. t., South Northants., **Eng.;** 14 km S.W. of Northampton; "Eatanswill" of *Pickwick Papers.*

Tower Hamlets, inner bor., E. London, **Eng.;** inc. former bors. of Bethnal Green, Stepney and Poplar; undergoing rapid economic and social change as p. and inds. are decentralised; site of lge. a. of London Docks (now all closed) with allied dockland inds.; clothing, brewing; p. (1981) 142,975.

Townsville, spt., Queensland, **Australia;** coastal outlet for rich dairying, pastoral and mng. a. along Great Northern Rly; artificial harbour; univ.; copper refining; p. (1976) 78,653.

Towton, v., North Yorks., **Eng.;** nearby Towton field, scene of bloodiest battle of Wars of the Roses 1461: Lancastrians under Henry VI defeated by Yorkists under Edward IV.

Towy, R., S. **Wales;** flows S.W. of Carmarthen Bay; 104 km long.

Toyama, c., Honshu, **Japan;** on Etchu plain to E. of Noto peninsula; regional admin. and comm. ctr.; patent medicines, aluminium smelting, machin.; p. (1979) 229,251.

Toyohashi, t., Honshu, **Japan;** food processing, textiles; p. (1979) 299,160.

Trabzon or **Trebizond,** spt., **Turkey;** on Black Sea; exp. tobacco, food prods., carpets; once a gr. tr. ctr. on caravan route between Persia and Europe; founded 8th cent. B.C. by Greek colonists; p. (1979) 110,680.

Trafalgar, C., S.W. cst., Cadiz, **Spain;** Nelson's famous victory 1805.

Trafford, met. dist. Gtr. Manchester **Eng.;** comprises Sale, Hale, Altrincham, Urmston and Stretford; p. (1981) 221,406.

Trail, t., B.C., **Canada;** lgst. metallurgical smelter in Commonwealth using local non-ferrous metals; chemicals; p. (1971) 10,843.

Tralee, mkt. t., spt., Kerry, **R.o.I.;** on R. Lee; exp. grain, butter; p. (1981) 16,495.

Trani, spt., N. Apulia, **Italy;** on Adriatic; mkt. t. for fertile coastal a.; fishing, food processing; cath., cas.; p. (est. 1981) 44,235.

Transbaykal, region, Siberia, **RSFSR;** E. of L. Baykal; mineral wealth; ch. t., Chita.

Transcaucasia, region between the Black Sea and the Caspian Sea, **USSR;** comprising the constituent reps. of Georgia, Armenia, and Azerbaydzhan; ch. t. Tbilisi.

Transkei, indep. Bantu Terr. (1976), **S. Africa;** not recognised by UN as designed to consolidate apartheid; mainly agr., maize and livestock; heavily dependent on S. Africa; p. mainly employed in mines in Transvaal and Orange Free State; cap. Umtata; a. 42,849 km²; p. (1976) 2,186,000.

Transvaal, prov., **Rep. of S. Africa;** high veld plateau (900–1,200 m) with Kruger Nat. Park in N.E.; hot summers, temperate winters; livestock on grasslands, grains, citrus fruits and temperate crops on irrigated land; lge. mineral wealth, especially gold in Witwatersrand; diamonds, uranium, platinum; inds. in ch. cs., Johannesburg and cap. Pretoria; a. 286,066 km²; p. (1980) 8,350,500.

Transylvania, historic region and prov., central **Romania;** high plateau surrounded by Carpathians; forested; mineral wealth not yet fully realised; arable agr. in valleys; ch. ts. Cluj, Brasov.

Transylvanian Alps, range of mtns., **Romania**.

Trapani, t., cap. of T. prov. W. Sicily, **Italy;** spt. on promontory, sheltering natural harbour; exp. wine, pasta, tuna fish caught locally; p. (1981) 71,927.

Traralgon, t., Victoria, **Australia;** industl. growth based on Yallourn brown coal; tourism; p. (1976) 15,089.

Trasimeno, L., Umbria, central **Italy;** occupies lge. extinct volcanic crater; drained S. to R. Tiber; a. c. 155 km².

Tras-os-Montes e Alto-Douro, prov., N. **Portugal;** high, bleak plateau, cultivated valleys; climate cold except in S.; port wine cty. of Douro R.; remote, sparsely populated; a. 11,834 km²; p. (1960) 667,054.

Trawsfynydd, Gwynedd, **Wales;** within N. Wales Nat. Park; nuclear power sta.

Trebizond. *See* Trabzon.

Tredegar, t., Blaenau Gwent, Gwent, **Wales;** in narrow valley 5 km W. of Ebbw Vale; engin.; home of Aneurin Bevan; p. (1981) 16,446.

Treforest, t., Mid Glamorgan, **Wales;** on R. Taff; lge. trading estate established in 1930s to alleviate unemployment in primary inds. of S. Wales; aircraft accessories, electronics, chemical, pharmaceutical, rayon, metal wks.

Trelleborg, spt., S. **Sweden;** on Baltic Sea; most impt. rubber factory in cty.; p. (1983) 34,146.

Trengganu, st., **Malaysia;** N.E. Malaya; rice, rubber, coconuts; tin, iron; cap. Kuala Trengganu; a. 13,080 km²; p. (1967) 378,738.

Trent, R., **Eng.;** rises in N. Staffs, flows round S. Pennines and joins the Ouse to form estuary of the Humber; many power stas. along its banks; polluted waterway, especially between Humber and Nottingham; 240 km long.

Trentino-Alto Adige, aut. region, N.E. **Italy,** between Austrian and Swiss Frontiers and L. Garda; embraces provs. Trento and Bolzano; cap. Trento; formerly called Venetia Tridentina; a. 13,598 km²; p. (1981) 873,413.

Trento, t., cap. of Trento prov. and ch. t. of Trentino-Alto Adige, N. **Italy;** on R. Adige and route to Brenner Pass; chemicals, cement, elec. engin.; picturesque t.; cath.; p. (1981) 99,179.

Trenton, c., cap. N.J. st., **USA;** on Delaware R.; transport and industl. ctr.; noted for its wire-rope and pottery inds., established mid-19th cent.; crockery, machin., metal and rubber gds.; p. (1980) 92,124 (c.), 307,863 (met. a.).

Tres Arroyos, t., E. **Argentina;** agr. and livestock ctr.; p. (1960) 40,000.

Trèves. *See* **Trier**.

Treviso, c., cap. of T. prov., Venetia, N.E. **Italy;** on R. Sile; agr. ctr. on fertile Venetian plain; silk mills, paper, furniture, fertilisers, pottery; p. (1981) 87,696.

Trichinopoly. *See* **Tiruchirapalli**.

Trichur, t., Kerala, **India;** comm. and educational ctr.; p. (1981) 73,038.

Trier (Trèves), c., Rhineland-Palatinate, **W. Germany;** on R. Moselle; Roman origin. (Augusta Trevorum, the Rome of the North), cath., Porta Nigra; ctr. of Moselle wine reg.; textiles, leather goods; birthplace of Marx; p. (1983) 94,700.

Trieste, spt., cap. of T. prov., Friuli-Venezia Giulia, N.E. **Italy;** shipbldg., fishing, oil refining; pipeline to Schwechat, nr. Vienna; cath., cas., Roman antiquities; univ.; p. (1981) 252,369.

Trieste Free Territory, former free st. on the Adriatic; constituted by Peace Treaty with Italy, 1947, as compromise between conflicting Yugoslav and Italian claims; a. 743 km²; Zone A handed over to Italy, Zone B to Yugoslavia 1954. Yugoslav/Italian agreement 1975 settled border dispute and established free industl. zone on both sides of border in region of Sezana-Fernetti.

Trikkala, t., cap. of T. dep., W. Thessaly, N. **Greece;** mkt. t. for pastoral prods.; damaged by earthquake 1954; p. (1981) 45,160.

Trim, co. t., U.D., Meath, **R.o.I.;** mkt. t. on R. Boyne; anc. seat of Irish Parliament; p. (1966) 1,467.

Trincomalee, t., N.E. cst. **Sri Lanka;** excellent natural harbour; formerly a British naval base; p. (est. 1968) 39,000.

Tring, mkt. t., Dacorum, Herts., **Eng.;** in gap through Chiltern hills, 14 km N.W. of Hemel Hempstead; p. (1981) 10,683.

Trinidad, t., cap. of Beni dep., **Bolivia;** exp. beef by air, but development hampered by isolation; p. (est. 1969) 17,360.

Trinidad, I., **W.I.;** N. of Venezuela; climate warm and humid; oil, natural gas, asphalt, sugar, rum, coconut oil, molasses, citrus fruits; tourism; cap. Port of Spain; a. 4,828 km²; p. (est. 1970) 1,010,000. *See* **Trinidad and Tobago.**

Trinidad, t., central **Cuba;** picturesque old t. of colonial period declared a national monument; p. (est. 1967) 57,840.

Trinidad and Tobago, indep. st. within Commonwealth (1962), rep. (1976), **W.I.;** main exps. crude oil and petroleum prods. which with natural asphalt represent over 20 per cent national income; lge. offshore gas reserves; oil refining; tropical crops and food processing; sugar, molasses, rum, fruits, textiles; cap. and major spt. Port of Spain; internal self-gov. sought by Tobago; a. 5,128 km²; p. (est. 1984) 1,105,000.

Trinity, R., Texas, **USA;** flows S.E. to Galveston Bay; used for reservoirs; valley contains lge. p. and much economic activity; 800 km long.

Trino, Piedmont, N. **Italy;** 18 km S.S.W. of Vercelli; nuclear power sta.; p. (1981) 9,067.

Tripoli, c., **Lebanon;** spt. on Mediterranean; admin. ctr. for N. Lebanon; terminus of oil pipeline from Iraq; oil refining; exp. agr. prods.; p. (est. 1964) 127,611.

Tripoli, c., joint cap. of **Libya** (with Benghazi), on Mediterranean; stands on edge of palm-oasis, site of anc. Oea; tourist, comm. and mnf. ctr.; gd. harbour; p. (est. 1968) 247,365.

Tripura, new st. (1972) **India;** N.E. Ganges delta, bordering Assam and Bangladesh; cap. Agartala; rice, jute, cotton, sugar-cane; a. 10,360 km²; p. (est. 1971) 1,556,822.

Tristan da Cunha, sm. gr. S. Is., **S. Atl. Oc.;** dependency of Brit. col. (t. Helena; ch. I. Tristan; evacuated 1961 volcanic eruption) but resettled 1963; weather sta. (Gough I.); a. 117 km²; p. (1984) 315.

Trivandrum, c., cap. of Kerala st., S.W. **India;** pt. on Arabian Sea; textiles coconut processing; univ.; p. (1971) 409,672.

Trnava, c., W. Slovakia, **ČSSR**; mkt. t. in fertile agr. region on Váh R.; food processing, steel wks.; cath., monasteries, called "little Rome"; p. (1967) 36,000.

Trnovo or **Tirnovo,** c., **Bulgaria**; on Jantra R.; food processing, textiles, leather; anc. cap. of Bulgaria; p. (est. 1970) 42,344.

Trogir, t., S. Croatia, **Yugoslavia**; sm. pt. and seaside resort, partly sited on I. of Čiovo; mediaeval bldgs., inc. cath., palaces; p. c. 20,000.

Trois Rivières, t., Quebec, **Canada**; industl. ctr. on St. Lawrence R.; noted for newsprint; hydroelectric power from St. Maurice R.; p. (1966) 57,540.

Trojmiasto (Tri-City), Poland; name given to the three municipalities of Gdansk, Gdynia, and Sopot, a loosely-knit conurb.

Trollhättan, t., S.W. **Sweden**; on Göta R., nr. T. falls which generate power for metallurgical and chemical inds.; car and aircraft components; p. (1983) 48,592.

Trombay, I., off Bombay, **India**; oil refining, atomic reactor; uranium processing and nuclear waste reprocessing plant; zirconium metal produced; fertilisers.

Troms, co., N. **Norway**; deep fjords, offshore Is.; fishing, livestock, boat-bldg.; cap. Tromsö; a. 25,916 km²; p. (est. 1972) 138,085.

Tromsö, t., cap. of Troms prov., N. **Norway**; spt. on sm. I. of T. in Norwegian Sea; arctic fishing, sealing; fish processing; p. (1968) 36,340.

Trondheim, c., spt., **Norway**; on W. cst. on S. side of T. fjord; shipbldg., engin.; exp. timber and wood-pulp, butter, fish, copper; anc. cath., burial place of early Norwegian kings and place of coronation of recent sovereigns; p. (est. 1977) 134,705.

Troon, burgh, Kyle and Carrick, **Scot.**; on F. of Clyde, 10 km N. of Ayr; gd. harbour and graving docks; shipbldg.; hosiery; seawater distillation research ctr. project; resort; p. (1981) 14,254.

Troppau. See **Opava.**

Trossachs, Stirling, **Scot.**; picturesque wooded glen; tourist resort.

Troste, nr. Llanelly, **Wales**; steel strip mill, tin plate.

Trouville, t., Calvados dep., N. **France**; popular seaside resort and fishing pt. on Normandy cst.; p. (1982) 6,012.

Trowbridge, mkt. t., West Wilts., **Eng.**; cloth wks., bacon curing, dairying, engin.; p. (1981) 22,984.

Troy, c., N.Y., **USA**; at confluence of Rs. Hudson and Mohawk; gr. shirt-mftg. ctr.; p. (1970) 62,918.

Troyes, c., cap. of Aube dep., N.E. **France**; on R. Seine; once cap. of Champagne; hosiery, textile machin., food processing; magnificent cath.; site of mediaeval fairs which standardised Troy weight; p. (1982) 64,769.

Trucial States. See **United Arab Emirates.**

Trujillo, c., N.W. **Peru**; comm. and mkt. ctr. for irrigated agr. region, on Moche R., in foothills of Andes; sugar, cocaine; univ., cath.; p. (est. 1980) 386,900.

Trujillo, t., cap. of T. st., W. **Venezuela**; on Transandean highway at 805 m; agr. mkt. for region producing coffee, cacao, tobacco, maize; p. (est. 1970) 27,107.

Truro, t., Nova Scotia, **Canada**; on Salmon R.; hosiery, lumber mills, printing, metallurgy, machin.; p. (1971) 12,968.

Truro, c., Carrick, Cornwall, **Eng.**; at confluence of Rs. Kenwyn and Allen; mkt. t. and former sm. pt.; admin. ctr. of Cornwall; cath.; p. (1981) 16,277.

Tsaidam. See **Qaidam.**

Tsamkong. See **Zhanjiang.**

Tsangpo. See **Zangbo.**

Tschenstokov. See **Czestochowa.**

Tselinograd, c., Kazakh SSR, **USSR**; cap. Virgin Lands terr.; on Ishim R., nr. Karaganda coalfield; chemicals, agr. machin.; p. (1980) 237,000.

Tsinan. See **Jinan.**

Tsinghai. See **Qinghai.**

Tsinling Shan. See **Hua Shan.**

Tsingtao. See **Qingdao.**

Tsitsihar. see **Qiqihar.**

Tskhinvali, c., N. Georgian SSR, **USSR**; elec. prods., lumber mills, fruit canning; p. (1970) 30,000.

Tsu, t., Honshu, **Japan**; textiles; p. (1979) 143,678.

Tsugaru Strait, Japan; separates Is. Hokkaido and Honshu; links Sea of Japan with Pac. Oc.; 72 km long, 24–32 km wide.

Tsuruga, spt., **Japan**; on W. cst. Honshu; rayon textiles, cotton, atomic power plant; p. (1970) 56,445.

Tuam, mkt. t., R.D., Galway, **R.o.I.**; sugar refining; p. (1981) 4,366 (t.).

Tuamotu, coral archipelago, Fr. Polynesia, S. **Pac. Oc.**; pearl fisheries; p. of gr. (est. 1967) 6,148.

Tuapse, c., S. Krasnodar terr., **RSFSR**; at foot of Caucasus on Black Sea; major petroleum pt. at W. end of pipeline from Baku and Makhachkala; oil refineries; p. (est. 1967) 49,000.

Tubarao, t., Santa Catarina st., S. **Brazil**; on E. cst., 280 km N.W. of Pôrto Alegre; coal mines; p. (est. 1968) 59,210.

Tübingen, t., Baden-Württemberg, **W. Germany**; on R. Neckar; 15th cent. univ., cas.; mediaeval c. ctr.; birthplace of Hölderlin, p. (1983) 74,700.

Tubuai, archipelago, Fr. Polynesia, S. **Pac. Oc.**; a. 163 km²; p. (est. 1967) 5,053.

Tucson, c., S.E. Arizona, **USA**; mkt. and distribution ctr. on Santa Cruz R.; cultural ctr. and winter resort based on Spanish heritage and warm dry climate; food processing, missile components; p. (1980) 331,000 (c.), 531,000 (met. a.).

Tucumán. See **San Miguel de Tucumán.**

Tudela, t., Navarre, N. **Spain**; mkt. ctr. for fertile fruit-growing dist. and I. of La Majana in Ebro R.; fine cath., Roman bridge; p. (1981) 24,629.

Tula, c., cap. of T. oblast, **RSFSR**; mnf. ctr. in Moscow industl. region; local iron and lighting mng.; Yasnaya Polyana, home of Tolstoy, nearby; p. (1981) 518,000.

Tulare, L., S. Cal., **USA**; ctr. of inland drainage 64 km S. of Fresno; streams feeding it used for irrigation; in drought years L. dries up completely; a. 233 km².

Tullamore, mkt. t., U.D., Offaly, **R.o.I.**; on Grand Canal; farming, distilling, brewing; p. (1981) 7,901.

Tulle-sur-Mer, t., cap. of Corrèze dep., **France**; firearms, textiles; p. (1982) 20,642.

Tulsa, c., Okla., **USA**; impt. oil ctr., based on lge. local deposits; machin., aeroplanes; well laid out with many parks; p. (1980) 361,000 (c.), 689,000 (met. a.).

Tumaco, t., S.W. **Colombia**; spt. on Pac. Oc., on sm. I. off cst.; exp. agr. prods.; climate hot and humid; p. (est. 1968) 80,279.

Tummel, R., Perth and Kinross, **Scot.**; trib. of R. Tay; used by Perth to Inverness rly. as S. approach to Drumochter Pass; hydroelec. scheme nr. Pitlochry; 88 km long.

Tunbridge Wells (officially **Royal Tunbridge Wells**), t., l. gov. dist., Kent, **Eng.**; on border of East Sussex; chalybeate waters; attractive 17th cent. promenade known as "The Pantiles"; p. (1981) 96,051 (dist.).

Tunghwa. See **Tonghua.**

Tung Ting Hu. See **Dong Ting.**

Tunguska, Upper, Stony and Lower, Rs., Siberia, **USSR**; all rise in Sayan mtns. nr. L. Baykal and flow N.W. through forested cty. into R. Yenisey.

Tunguska Basin, coalfield between Yenisey and Lena Rs., **RSFSR**; main ts., Norilsk, Igarka, Yeniseysk.

Tunis, c., cap. of **Tunisia**, N. Africa; spt. on inlet of Mediterranean; exp. raw materials; base for fishing fleets; univ., notable mosques; tourist ctr.; ruins of anc. Carthage to N.E.; p. (1966) 468,997 (c.), 647,640 (met. a.).

Tunisia, indep. st., N. **Africa**; bounded by Algeria on W., by Libya on E., indented Mediterranean cst.; Atlas mtns. penetrate into N.; temperate cst. climate, hot and dry in S. desert; agr. and mng. basis of economy; wheat, olive oil, wine, fruits, limited to wetter coastal areas and irrigated valleys; phosphates around Ghafsa; iron ore and lead in N.W.; steelwks. at Menzel Bourguiba; chemical and paper inds. based on local phosphates; cap. Tunis; a. 164,108 km²; p. (est. 1984) 7,042,000.

Tunja, c., cap. of Boyacá dep., **Colombia**; route and agr. tr. ctr.; p. (est. 1972) 55,600.

Turda, t., Transylvania, **Romania**; local salt mines and quarrying aid chemical and ceramic inds.; p. (est. 1970) 50,113.

Turfan, depression, E. Xinjiang prov., **China**; on S. slopes of Tien Shan mtns.; desert a. irrigated by wells and canals for animal husbandry, fruit, cotton, grain; 275 m below sea level; ch. t. Turfan; archaeological finds.

Turgutlu (Kassaba), t., Manisa prov., **Turkey**; 48 km E.N.E. of Izmir; lignite, cotton, melons; p. (1965) 35,079.

Turin or **Torino**, c., cap. of T. prov., N. **Italy**; on R. Po at confluence with the Dora Riparia; former cap. of Piedmont and kingdom of Sardinia; univ., cath., many historic monuments; headquarters of Italian motor ind.; clothing, machin., furniture, chemicals; oil refinery nearby; p. (1981) 1,117,154.

Turkana, L. *See* **Rudolf, L.**

Turkestan E., terr. included in Xinjiang, **China**; separated from W. or former Russian Turkestan by Pamir plateau; mainly desert.

Turkestan W., terr. of **USSR**; inc. Turkmen SSR, Uzbek SSR, Tadzhik SSR, Kirghiz SSR, and part of Kazakh SSR.

Turkey, rep., S.W. **Asia**; occupies mtnous. Anatolian penin.; equable climate on coastal margins, continental severity in interior; economy predominantly agr. but hampered by poor land resources; grain grown on Anatolian plateau and a Mediterranean variety of crops around cst.; noted for tobacco; industl. development based on mng. resources and oil in S.E.; lge cities in W. act as magnet for the poorer areas of E.; 30 percent of p. in 5 cities; many migrate to Europe & Middle East as migrant workers; cap. Ankara; a. 780,579 km²; p. (est. 1984) 48,811,000.

Turkmen (Turkmenistan), SSR, constituent rep., **USSR**; borders on Afghanistan, Iran, and the Caspian Sea; much of a. in Kara-Kum desert; agr. based on irrigation; fruit, cotton, wool; sulphates, petroleum; p. concentrated in oases and industl. ctrs. of cap. Ashkhabad, Mary-Chadzhou, along Trans-Caspian rly.; a. 491,072 km²; p. (1970) 2,158,000.

Turks and Caicos, Is., Caribbean Sea, **W.I.**; about 30 sm. Is., geographically S.E. continuation of Bahamas; dry climate, poor limestone soil; exp. salt, crawfish; cap. Gran Turk; a. 430 km²; p. (est. 1975) 6,000.

Turku (Abo), spt., S.W. **Finland**; on Baltic Sea; ctr. of fertile agr. a.; exp. agr. prods.; industl. ctr.; shipbldg., steel, machin., textiles; Finnish and Swedish univs.; p. (1979) 164,245.

Turnhout, t., N.E. **Belgium**, nr. Antwerp, on Campine canal; textiles, lace, printing; p. (est. 1983) 37,567.

Turnu Severin, c., S.W. **Romania**; R. pt. on Danube below Iron Gate cataracts; grain, salt, petroleum tr., shipbldg.; p. (1968) 46,010.

Tuscaloosa, c., Ala., **USA**; on Black Warrior R.; rly. and industl. ctr. based on local coal, iron, cotton, timber; univ.; p. (1980) 75,211 (c.), 137,473 (met. a.).

Tuscany, region, central **Italy**; inc. provs. Arezzo, Firenze, Livorno, Siena, Grosseto, Lucca, Pisa, Massa and Carrara, Pistoia; mainly mtnous., drained by Arno R. system; wines, olive oil, cereals; iron ore from Elba, marble from Apuan Alps around Carrara; pt. at Livorno (Leghorn); cap. Firenze (Florence); a. 22,989 km²; p. (1981) 3,581,051.

Tuticorin, t., Tamil Nadu, S.E. **India**; on G. of Manaar; fertiliser plant; declining cotton and tea pt.; heavy water plant; p. (1971) 153,310 (t.), 181,913 (met. a.).

Tuttlingen, t., Baden-Württemberg, **W. Germany**; on R. Danube; surgical instruments; footwear; p. (1983) 31,000.

Tuva ASSR, RSFSR; bounded by Siberia and Mongolia; mtn. basin, forested; timber inds., coal mng., asbestos, pastoral agr.; cap. Kyzyl; a. c. 165,800 km²; p. (1970) 231,000.

Tuvalu Is., formerly Ellice Is., until 1975 part of Gilbert and Ellice Is., W. Pac. Oc.; indep. (1979); p. mainly Polynesian; cap. Funafuti; coconut cultivation in high temps on poor coral soils; exp. copra; a. 25 km²; p. (est. 1980) 8,000.

Tuxtla Gutiérrez, c., cap. of Chiapas st., **Mexico**; in fertile valley at 450 m; ctr. for sisal, tobacco, coffee, cattle; on Inter-American Highway; Mayan ruins nearby; p. (1979) 106,894.

Tuz, L., **Turkey**; salt L.; a. 1,619 km² in winter much reduced in summer.

Tuzla, t., Bosnia-Hercegovina, **Yugoslavia**; salt,

lignite, coal; hydroelectric power in a.; agr. mkt. ctr.; textiles; p. (1971) 53,825.

Tweed, R., S.E. **Scot.**; rises in Tweeddale, and reaches sea at Berwick; salmon fisheries; length 155 km.

Tweeddale, l. gov. dist., Borders reg., **Scot.**; based on upper Tweed valley around Peebles; p. (1981) 14,382.

Twelve Pins, star-shaped mtn. range, Galway, **R.o.I.**; Benbaum, 730 m.

Twickenham. *See* **Richmond-upon-Thames.**

Tychy, t., Katowice prov., **Poland**; on edge of Upper Silesian industl. a.; surrounded by forest; brewing; p. (est. 1983) 178,100.

Tyler, c., Texas, **USA**; oil ctr. on E. Texan field; agr. ctr. for local mkt. gardening; famous for rose growing; p. (1980) 70,508 (c.), 128,336 (met.a.).

Tyne, R., Tyne and Wear, Durham and Northumberland, **Eng.**; formed by confluence of N. Tyne and S. Tyne at Hexham; flows E. to sea at Tynemouth and S. Shields; valley gives easy route across mtns. from Newcastle to Carlisle; lower course forms harbour (with shipbldg. and other wks.) from Newcastle to Tynemouth; road tunnel between Wallsend and Jarrow; 128 km long.

Tynedale, l. gov. dist., W. Northumberland, **Eng.**; lge. inland a. inc. Haltwistle, Hexham and Prudoe; p. (1981) 55,087.

Tynemouth, t., North Tyneside, Tyne and Wear, **Eng.**; pt. on N. bank of Tyne R.; ruined priory and cas.; residtl., resort; p. (1981) 60,022.

Tyne and Wear,former met. co., N.E. **Eng.**; mainly industl. a. around lower T. and W. Rs.; inc. Newcastle-upon-Tyne, Tynemouth, Gateshead, South Shields and Sunderland; traditionally ass. with shipbldg. and coal mng., but inds. incr. diversified; p. (1981) 1,143,245.

Tyneside, North, met. dist., Tyne and Wear, **Eng.**; comprises Tynemouth, Whitley Bay and Wallsend; p. (1981) 198,266.

Tyneside, South, met. dist., Tyne and Wear, **Eng.**; comprises Jarrow, Hebburn and South Shields; p. (1981) 160,551.

Tyre (Sur), Lebanon; anc. Phoenician c. and spt., founded c. 15th cent. B.C.; now sm. comm. t., tr. in cotton, tobacco; p. 12,000.

Tyrol, Alpine region, **Europe**; falls within Austria and Italy, linked by Brenner Pass; embraces highest peaks of Austrian Alps, culminating in Ortler Spitz; two-fifths forest, timber inds.; mtn. pasture; tourism; Austrian prov. of Tyrol; cap. Innsbruck; a. 12,650 km²; p. (1971) 539,000.

Tyrone, former co., **N. Ireland**; now replaced by Strabane, Omagh, Dungannon and Cookstown l. gov. dists.

Tyrrhenian Sea, part of Mediterranean between Italy and Corsica, Sardinia and Sicily.

Tyumen, c., **RSFSR**; one of oldest Siberian ts., rly. ctr. on Trans-Siberian rly., R. pt. on Tura R.; many heavy inds.; ctr. of oil and natural gas region; p. (1980) 369,000.

Tywyn, mkt. t., Meirionnydd, Gwynedd, **Wales**; on cst. of Cardigan Bay, 5 km N.W. of Aberdovey; p. (1981) 4,551.

Tzekung. *See* **Zigong.**

Tzepo. *See* **Zibo.**

U

Ubangi, major R., **Central Africa**; trib. of R. Zaïre, rises on bdr. of Central Africa Emp. and Zaïre flows W. and S. to join Zaïre R. at Irebu; partially navigable; 2,240 km long.

Ube, spt., S. Honshu, **Japan**; coal mng. and industl. ctr.; machin., synthetic petroleum; p. (1979) 165,841.

Ubeda, t., Jaén prov., **Spain**; on plateau between Guadalquivir and Guadalimar; food processing, olive oil, soap; p. (1981) 27,441.

Uberaba, t., Minas Gerais, **Brazil**; ctr. of cattle rearing and arable agr. region; sugar milling, mnfs. lime; p. (est. 1980) 174,000.

Ucayali, R., **Peru**; headstream of R. Amazon; over 2,240 km long, navigable for 1,600 km.

Uckfield, mkt. t., East Sussex, **Eng.**; 13 km N.E. of Lewes; a. ctr. of former Sussex iron ind.

Udaipur, c., Rajasthan, N.W. **India**; in picturesque valley at 760 m a.s.l.; cap. of former princely st. of U.; maharajah's palace; p. (1971) 161,278.

Uddevalla, spt., S. **Sweden**; N. Göteborg; former shipyds., prefab. houses, timber, granite quarrying, textiles; p. (1983) 45,827.

Udi, t., S. **Nigeria,** W. Africa; 160 km N. of Pt. Harcourt; impt. mng. ctr. on Enugu coalfield; linked by rail to Kaduna and Pt. Harcourt.

Udine, c., cap. of U. prov., Friuli-Venezia Giulia, N.E. **Italy**; between Alps and G. of Venice; route and industl. ctr. in agr. region; textiles, chemicals, engin., leather, woodwork; cath.; many attractive bldgs., piazzas; severe earthquakes (1976); p. (1981) 102,021.

Udmurt ASSR, RSFSR; part of Urals industl. a.; two-fifths forested, timber inds.; arable agr., flax; steel inds. at cap. Izhevsk, Votkinsk, Sarapul; p. (1970) 1,417,000.

Udokan Khrebet, mtns., **RSFSR;** world's lgst. reserve of copper.

Ufa, c., cap. of Bashkir ASSR, **RSFSR;** in Urals industl. a., at confluence of Rs. Belaya and Ufa; p. (1980) 986,000.

Uganda, rep., E. **Africa**; dictatorship overthrown (1979); 4 regs. established for economic devel.; equatorial cty., climate modified by alt.; forms part of E. African plateau (1,200 m); well-developed economy; coffee, tea, tobacco, cotton for exp.; developing pastoral economy, fishing on L. Victoria; copper at Kilembe, tin; hydroelectric power from Owen Falls, second project at Kabelega Falls; electricity exp. to Kenya; savannah areas contain abundant wildlife in Nat. Parks and Game Reserves; cap. Kampala; a. 235,887 km²; p. (est. 1984) 15,150,000.

Uist, N. and **S.,** Is., Outer Hebrides, N.W. **Scot.**; indented csts.; N. Uist boggy in E., hilly in W.; S. Uist smaller but mtnous.; crofting, fishing; p. (1971) 1,726 (N.), 3,872 (S.).

Uitenhage, t., Cape prov., **S. Africa**; fruit, wool, rly. wks., tyres, car assembly, textiles; summer resort; p. (1970) 69,048.

Ujiji, t., in sm. terr. same name (a. 2,383 km²) on E. shore L. Tanganyika, **Tanzania**; where Stanley found Livingstone 1871; p. c. 14,000.

Ujiyamada. See Ise.

Ujjain, t., Madhya Pradesh, **India**; sacred c. and formerly cap. of Malwa; univ.; p. (1971) 203,278 (t.), 208,561 (met. a.).

Ujpest, industl. sub., Budapest, **Hungary**; elec. engin., leather, shoes, textiles, furniture, pharmaceuticals; p. 76,000.

Ujung Pandang (Makasar), c., Sulawesi, **Indonesia**; in dist. of rich volcanic soils; major spt. and airpt., entrepot tr.; p. (1971) 434,766.

Ukhta t., **RSFSR**; ctr. of natural gas field in Pechora Basin; p. (est. 1969) 57,000.

Ukrainian SSR, constituent rep., **USSR**; in Eastern Europe; of dominating importance in Soviet economy; drained by Rs. Dnieper Dniester, S. Bug, Donets; Pripet Marshes in N., wooded steppes in ctr., fertile black-earth a. in S.; major wheat-growing a. of Europe; highly mineralised, many industl. raw materials and ctrs. of metallurgical and heavy inds.; cap. Kiev; a. 582,750 km²; p. (est. 1976) 49,100,000.

Ulan Bator, c., cap. of **Mongolian People's Rep.**; in stock-raising region; industl. ctr. of cty.; woollen gds., saddles, knitwear; new indust. ctr. at Darkhan nearby; rly. link to China and USSR; contains one-quarter of p. of rep.; p. (1980) 418,700.

Ulan-Ude (Verkhneudinsk), t., Siberia, **RSFSR**; major route and mnf. ctr.; pt. on R. Ude, junc. on Trans-Siberian rly., linked by rail to Peking; engin., textiles, glass, leather; p. (1980) 305,000.

Ullapool, v., Ross and Cromarty, **Scot.**; fish. pt. (herring landings), on L. Broom, 72 km N.W. of Inverness; landed more fish in 1981 than any other British pt.; attractive mtn. and cst. scenery in a.; p. (1981) 1,142.

Ullswater, L., Cumbria, **Eng.**; 13 km long; supplies water to Manchester; attractive tourist a.

Ulm, c., Baden-Württemberg, **W. Germany**; route ctr. at limit of barge navigation on Danube, although navigable limits being extended by canalisation; food-processing, metal gds., textiles, cement; p. (1983) 99,400.

Ulsan, t., **South Korea**; oil refining, fertilisers; nuclear power sta. (1983) built to reduce oil imports; p. (1980) 418,415.

Ulster. See **Northern Ireland.**

Ulúa-Chamelhcón, R. basin, N. cst. **Honduras**; major banana region of Central American cst.

Ulva, I., Argyll and Bute, **Scot.**; off W. cst. of Mull; 8 km long.

Ulverston, mkt. t., South Lakeland, Cumbria, **Eng.**; nr. Morecambe Bay; antibiotics, elec. gds., tanning; p. (1981) 11,963.

Ul'yanovsk (Simbirsk), c., cap. of U. oblast, **RSFSR**; industl. ctr. of middle Volga region; birthplace of Lenin whose real name was **Ulyanov**; p. (1980) 473,000.

Uman, c., Ukrainian SSR, **USSR**; at confluence of Kamenka and Umanka Rs.; rly. junc.; agr.-processing; p. (est. 1969) 64,000.

Umanak, t., W. **Greenland**; hunting and fishing base on arm of Baffin Sea; marble mng.; p. (est. 1968) 2,348.

Umbria, region, central **Italy**; comprising provs. of Perugia and Terni, crossed by Apennines and upper Tiber; agr. mainstay of economy; inds. based on hydroelectric power at Terni; chemicals; developing tourist tr.; cap. Perugia; a. 8,472 km²; p. (1981) 807,552.

Ume, R., **Sweden**; flows S.E. to the G. of Bothnia; length 400 km.

Umeå, c., cap. of Västerbotten prov., N.E. **Sweden**; on G. of Bothnia at mouth of Ume R.; cultural ctr.; woodpulp; p. (1983) 83,717.

Umm-al-Quaywayn, emirate, member of **United Arab Emirates**; p. (est. 1968) 8,000.

Umm Qasr, t., **Kuwait**; on Iraq border; new deepwater port planned.

Umtali (Mutare), t., **Zimbabwe**; comm. ctr. for rich agr. a.; oil refinery at Feruka; pipeline to Beira; paper milling, food processing, vehicle assembly; p. (1982) 69,600.

Umtata, t., Cape Prov., **S. Africa**; admin. ctr. for Transkei terrs.; cath.; p. (est. 1967) 17,200.

Uncia, t., Oruro dep., **Bolivia**; alt. 3,900 m in E. Cordillera of Andes, 96 km S.E. of Oruro; site of impt. Patino tin mines.

Ungava Bay, arm of Hudson Strait, projecting into Labrador, N.E. **Canada**; minerals abundant, recent exploitation of impt. medium and low-grade iron deposits.

Union of South Africa. See **South Africa, Rep. of.**

Union of Soviet Socialist Republics (USSR), E. **Europe, N. Asia**; major world economic and political power; ctr. of European communist bloc; extends over 9,600 km W.-E., 4,800 km N.-S.; continental climate with marked regional variations; comprises 1 fed. rep. and 14 constituent reps.; centrally planned economy emphasising development of heavy inds. at major sources of natural resources, and development of new resources in E.; timber inds. and textiles impt. with more recent developments in consumer inds.; lge.-scale, mechanised agr. with planned prod. reflecting regional variations in physical conditions; transport emphasis on rlys. to open up remote E. regions, but more recent road bldg. programme; 27 major pts. inc. Leningrad, Arkhangelsk, Riga, Murmansk, Odessa, Baku, Vladivostok; cap. Moscow; a. 22,272,290 km²; p. (est. 1984) 275,761,000 (3rd. lgst. p. of any cty.).

United Arab Emirates (Trucial Sts.), indep. sov. st. on Persian G., S.W. **Asia**; formed (1971) from Trucial Sts. (Abū Dhabi, Ajmān, Dubai, Al Fujayrah, Ra's al Khaymah, Shārjah, Umm-al-Quaywayn) after withdrawal of Brit. forces and termination of special defence treaty (1820-1971); p. immigration from Middle and Far East as oil-based economic growth proceeds, esp. in Abu Dhabi; a. 82,880 km²; p. (est. 1985) 1,556,000 (mainly nomadic).

United Kingdom, cty., N.W. **Europe**; separated from continent of Europe by English Channel; consists of Gr. Britain (Eng., Wales, Scot.) and N. Ireland; a. 244,022 km²; p. (1981) 55,865,000.

United States of America, fed. rep., N. **America**; world's major economic power and one of the 3 political "super powers"; variety of climatic and physical conditions (see **N. America**); economically self-supporting, but imports petroleum, coffee, machin., textiles; extremely diversified mnfs.; consists of 50 sts. and Dist. of Columbia, co-extensive with cap. of Washington; outlying dependencies inc.

Puerto Rico, U.S. Virgin Is., Panama Canal Zone, Guam, American Samoa, Trust Terr. of the Pac. Is.; a. 9,363,169 km²; p. (est. 1984) 235,681,000.

Unst, I., Shetlands, **Scot.**; most N. of gr.; length 20 km; p. (1971) 1,127.

Unterwalden, can., **Switzerland**; divided into Obwalden and Nidwalden; dairying, fruit and livestock; cap. Stans; a. 767 km²; p. (1980) 54,482.

Upernavik, t., W. **Greenland**; on sm. I. in Baffin Bay; sealing and whaling base; meteorological sta.; p. (est. 1968) 1,930.

Upper Austria, prov., **Austria**; borders on W. Germany and ČSSR; hilly and forested; drained by Danube R. system; inc. Salzkammergut resort a.; agr., forestry; inds. centred on Linz (cap.), Steyr and Wels; a. 11,979 km²; p. (est. 1968) 1,201,600.

Upper Hutt, c., N.I., **N.Z.**; shares rapid industl. growth of Hutt Valley; p. (1976) 35,584.

Upper Volta. See **Bourkina Fasso.**

Uppingham, mkt. t., Leics., **Eng.**; 16th cent. school.

Uppsala, c., cap. of U. prov., **Sweden**; on R. Sala, 72 km from Stockholm; historic ctr. of anc. Sweden; cultural ctr.; famous univ. (Linnaeus taught there); cath.; lt. inds.; p. (1983) 150,579.

Ur, anc. Chaldean c., **Iraq**; 208 km W.N.W. of Basra; ruins; flourished about 3,000 B.C.

Ural, R., **RSFSR**; flows S.W. and S. to Caspian Sea; used for domestic and industl. water supply; navigable; 2,400 km long.

Ural Mts., **USSR**; mtn. system, forms bdy. between Europe and Asia and separates Russian plain from W. Siberian lowlands; extends N.-S. for 2,400 km; highest peaks Narodnaya and Telpos-Iz; rich mineral resources have given rise to huge ctrs. of heavy ind., inc. Sverdlovsk, Chelyabinsk, Magnitogorsk.

Uralsk, W., Kazakh SSR; **USSR**; on R. Ural; grain-trading and cattle-mart ctr.; flour, leather, woollens, iron-ware; p. (1980) 173,000.

Uranium City, N. Saskatchewan, **Canada**; nr. N. shore of L. Athabasca, ctr. of Beaverlodge uranium-mng. a.; founded 1951; p. (1960) 3,349.

Urawa, t., Honshu, **Japan**; sub. of Tokyo; p. (1979) 353,880.

Urbino, t., in the Marches, central **Italy**; agr. mkt. and route ctr.; picturesque tourist ctr.; cath., univ., palace; p. with Pesaro (1981) 15,918.

Ure, R., North Yorks., **Eng.**; flows E. and S.E. to the Swale to form the Ouse; upper part of valley known as Wensleydale; 80 km long.

Urengoy, dist., Siberia, **USSR**; lge. natural gas field with 5,400 km. pipeline to W. Europe.

Urfa, t., **Turkey**; nr. Syrian bdr.; handicrafts, local agr. tr.; p. (1979) 160,561.

Urgench, t., cap. of Khorezm oblast, W. Uzbek SSR, **USSR**; pt. on Amu Dar'ya R. in Khiva oasis; cotton, food-processing; p. (1980) 103,000.

Uri, can., **Switzerland**; S. of L. of Lucerne; forest and mtns.; traversed by St. Gotthard rly. and R. Reuss; sparse p., German speaking; cap. Altdorf; a. 1,075 km²; p. (1980) 33,883.

Urmia, L., nr. Tabriz, N.W. **Iran**; 136 km by 48 km; salt and shallow; no outlet.

Urmston, Trafford, Gtr. Manchester, **Eng.**; residtl. sub. of Manchester; inc. part of Trafford Park industl. estate; p. (1981) 44,009.

Uruapan, t., Michoacán, W. **Mexico**; mkt. ctr. for semi-tropical mtnous. a.; famous handicrafts; parks, gardens; p. (1979) 147,030.

Urubamba, R., **Peru**; rises in E. Cordillera of Andes; forms one of headstreams of R. Amazon; length 560 km.

Urubupunga, t., **Brazil**; new. t. for 10,000, at site of hydroelectric power sta.

Uruguaiana, t., **Brazil**; on R. Uruguay; cattle ctr.; jerked beef, soap, candles; p. (est. 1968) 74,581.

Uruguay, rep., **S. America**; smallest of S. American reps.; situated on N. bank of Rio de la Plata estuary; low hills in N.; temperate climate; 60 per cent land a. devoted to livestock rearing, especially cattle, sheep, based on extensive natural grasslands; arable land in S., grains; ch. t. Montevideo, cap. and main ctr. of inds.; food processing, leather, metallurgy, textiles, rubber; a. 186,925 km²; p. (est. 1984) 2,990,000.

Uruguay, R., **S. America**; rises in S. Brazil,

flows 1,360 km to Rio de la Plata; forms bdy. between Argentina and Uruguay and part of bdy. between Argentina and Brazil.

Ürümqi (**Wulumuchi**), c., cap. of Xinjiang prov., N.W. **China**; admin., comm. and industl. ctr.; iron and steel, cement, textiles, nitrogenous fertilisers, agr. machin.; local coal, tin, silver mng.; p. (est. 1970) 500,000.

Usak, t., **Turkey**; connected by rail with Izmir; noted for pile carpet-weaving; p. (1965) 38,815.

Usambara, mtns., N.E. **Tanzania**; scene of early European settlement (1902); lumber, tea, coffee produced on slopes; max. alt. 2,560 m.

Usedom (**Uznam**), I., Baltic Sea; off mouth of R. Oder; since 1945 E. part belongs to **Poland**, W. (the larger part) to **E. Germany**; a. 445 km²; p. 45,000.

Ushant, I., off cst. of Finistère, **France**; at entrance to English Channel; it was off Ushant that Lord Howe gained his gr. naval victory on the "glorious first of June" 1794; lighthouse, fishing; p. 2,000.

Ushuaia, t., **Argentina**; most S. t. in world; sheep farming, timber, furs; freezing plant; p. 6,000.

Usk, mkt. t., Gwent, **Wales**; 13th cent. cas.; p. (1981) 1,907.

Usk, R., Gwent, S. **Wales**; flows S. past Newport to Bristol Channel; picturesque, gd. fishing; 91 km long.

Üsküdar (**Scutari**), t., **Turkey**; on Bosporus, opposite Istanbul; mkt. ctr.; new bridge to European side of Bosporus; Crimean memorial cemetery for Brit. troops; Muslim cemeteries; p. (1965) 133,883.

Uspallata Pass, 3,800 m high over Andes between Mendoza, **Argentina**, and Santiago, **Chile**; monument "Christ of the Andes" marks international bdy. settlement; used by Mendoza–Valparaiso rly.

Ussuri, R., rises in Maritime prov. of **RSFSR**; flows c. 800 km to R. Amur; final 480 km forms Sino-Soviet bdy.

Ussuriysk (**Voroshilov**), t., **RSFSR**; 112 km N. of Vladivostok; rly. junc. of Trans-Siberian and Chinese Eastern rlys.; engin., agr. prod.; p. (1980) 148,000.

Ustica, I., Palermo, **Italy**; basalt; agr., fishing, handicrafts; a. 8.6 km²; p. (1981) 1,157.

Usti-nad-Labem (**Aussig**), c., Bohemia, **ČSSR**; R. pt. on Elbe; route and industl. ctr.; chemicals, textiles, machin.; p. (1967) 73,000.

Ust Kamenogorsk, c., Kazakh SSR, **USSR**; on Irtysh R.; mng. ctr.; food processing, clothing, furniture; hydroelectric power sta. nearby; p. (1980) 280,000.

Usumbura. See **Bujumbura.**

Utah, st., **USA**; 'Beehive St.'; admitted to Union 1896; st. flower Sego Lily, st. bird Sea Gull; Rocky mtns. in E.; forms part of Gr. Basin in W.; Gr. Salt L. in N.W.; dry continental climate; poor agr. conditions, soil erosion; copper, gold; tourism; Nat. Parks; cap. Salt L. City; a. 219,932 km²; p. (1980) 1,461,000.

Utica, c., N.Y., **USA**; on Mohawk R. and Barge Canal; in rich dairying region; textiles, electronics, tools, firearms; p. (1980) 320,000 (met. a. inc. Rome).

Utrecht, c., **Neth.**; on Old Rhine (Oude Rijn); univ., cath.; chemical and cigar factories; printing, machin., woollens, silks, velvets; major transport and financial ctr.; picturesque; p. (1982) 234,543.

Utrecht, prov., **Neth.**; between Gelderland and N. and S. Holland; fertile agr., cattle rearing, horticulture; a. 1,362 km²; p. (1983) 923,182.

Utsunomiya, t., Honshu, **Japan**; ctr. for Nikko Nat. Park; p. (1979) 370,423.

Uttar Pradesh, st., **India**; Himalayas on N. bdy., drained by Ganges and Jumna; irrigation; wheat, rice, millet, barley, maize, cotton, sugar, oil-seeds; ch. ts. Allahabad, Lucknow (cap.), Varanasi, Kanpur, Agra, Meerut; a. 293,732 km²; p. (1981) 111,000,000; (p. increasing by 2 million a year).

Uttlesford, l. gov. dist., Essex, **Eng.**; inc. Saffron Walden and Dunmow; p. (1981) 61,341.

Uttoxeter, t., East Staffs., **Eng.**; on R. Dove; machin., biscuit mftg.; expanded t.; p. (1981) 10,012.

Uusikaupunki (Swed. **Nystad**), spt., Abo-Bjorneborg, S.W. **Finland**; on G. of Bothnia; p. (1966) 5,074.

Uzbek (Uzbekistan) SSR, constituent rep., **USSR**; crossed by Rs. Amu Dar'ya and Syr Dar'ya; contains part of fertile Ferghana Valley; intensive farming based on irrigation; rice, cotton, fruits, silk, cattle, sheep; ch. cs. Tashkent (cap.), Samarkand; alluvial gold deposits and bauxite in Kizil-Kum desert; a. 412,250 km²; p. (1970) 11,963,000.

Uzhgorod, c., Ukrainian SSR, **USSR**; economic and cultural ctr.; friendship pipeline from Kuybyshev; univ.; p. (est. 1967) 61,000.

V

Vaal, R., **S. Africa**; rises in Drakensberg mtns., flows between the Transvaal and Orange Free State to join the Orange R. nr. Kimberley. V. dam irrigates lge. a. of Witwatersrand; 896 km long.

Vaasa, c., cap. of Vaasa prov., W. **Finland**; pt. on G. of Bothnia; exp. timber and timber prods.; agr. ctr.; food processing, textiles, timber inds.; p. (1968) 48,679.

Vác, t., **Hungary**; on R. Danube; comm. ctr.; summer resort for Budapest; cath.; p. (1966) 28,700.

Vadso, cap. of Finnmark prov., N.E. **Norway**; ice-free Arctic pt. on N. side of Varangar fjord; whaling and fishing base; p. (est. 1970) 5,625.

Vaduz, mkt. t., cap. of **Liechtenstein**; nr. Rhine; sm. tourist resort; p. (1970) 3,921.

Vaigach, sm. I., between Novaya Zemlya and mainland of **USSR**; geological extension of Urals; low-lying reindeer pasture; seal fishing.

Valais, can., **Switzerland**; in upper valley of R. Rhône; surrounded by mtns., forested on slopes; vines and cereals in valleys; ch. resort Zermatt, cap. Sion; a. 5,234 km²; p. (1980) 218,707.

Valdai Hills, morainic ridges between Leningrad and Moscow, **RSFSR**; rise to c. 348 m and form ch. watershed of E. European Rs., Volga, Dvina and Dniester.

Val d'Aosta, aut. region, N.W. **Italy**; high Alpine cty., borders France and Switzerland; cap. Aosta; agr.; hydroelectric power; winter resorts; a. 3,263 km²; p. (1981) 112,353.

Val-de-Marne, dep., S.E. of Paris, **France**; cap. Créteil; a. 243 km²; p. (1982) 1,191,500.

Valdez, t., Alaska, **USA**; ice-free pt., fishing; terminal of oil pipeline from North Slope; p. (1980) 3,079.

Valdivia, c., cap. of V. prov., S. **Chile**; on R. Callecalle nr. the sea (pt. Corral); damaged by earthquake and tidal wave 1960; univ.; metal, wood and leather gds.; paper, flour, brewing; p. (est. 1980) 109,484.

Val d'Oise, dep., N.W. of Paris, **France**; cap. Pontoise; a. 1,248 km²; p. (1982) 920,500.

Valdosta, t., Ga., **USA**; rly. and tr. ctr. for region producing tobacco, cotton, timber; p. (1980) 37,596.

Valence, t., cap. of Drôme dep., S.E. **France**; on R. Rhône; silks., hosiery, vineyards; agr. mkt.; p. (1982) 68,157.

Valencia, region, E. **Spain**; on Mediterranean; comprises provs. of Alicante, Castellón de la Plana and Valencia; mtnous., with densely populated, fertile coastal plain; irrigation makes a. a major producer of Mediterranean fruit and crops; a. 23,305 km²; p. (1981) 2,065,680.

Valencia, c., cap. of V. prov., E. **Spain**; pt. on Mediterranean at mouth of R. Turia; one of most impt. agr. ts. of cty., and active industl. and comm. ctr.; univ., cath.; resort; p. (1981) 744,740.

Valencia, c., N. **Venezuela**; nr. L. Valencia; ctr. of agr. a., sugar-cane, cotton; leading industl. t.; cattle mart; cotton mills, meat packing; cath.; p. (est. 1979) 488,000.

Valenciennes, c., Nord dep., N. **France**; in Hainaut cty. on R. Escaut (Scheldt); metallurgical and chemical inds.; once famous for hand-made lace; birthplace of Froissart and Watteau; p. (1982) 349,505 (French met. a.).

Valentia, I., S.W. Kerry, **R.o.I.**; in Dingle Bay; agr., fishing; 10 km by 3 km.

Vale of Glamorgan, l. gov. dist., South Glamorgan, **Wales**; inc. cstl. ts. of Penarth, Barry and Cowbridge; p. (1981) 110,777.

Vale of White Horse, l. gov. dist., Oxon., **Eng.**; based on Abingdon, Faringdon and Wantage; p. (1981) 100,749.

Vale Royal, l. gov. dist., Ches., **Eng.**; a. in ctr. of co. and inc. saltfield ts. of Northwich and Winsford; p. (1981) 111,521.

Valladolid, c., cap. of V. prov., **Spain**; on R. Pisuerga (trib. of Douro); grain tr.; route, industl. and comm. ctr.; food processing, textiles; cath., univ.; p. (1981) 320,289.

Valle del General, upland, S.W. **Costa Rica**; pioneer subsistence agr., maize, tropical fruit, cattle; improving transport.

Vallejo, t., Cal., **USA**; at mouth of Napa R. on San Pablo Bay; pt. and processing ctr. for farm prod.; naval shipyard; p. (1980) 334,000 (met. a.).

Vallenar, t., Atacama prov., **Chile**; agr. ctr.; dried fruit, wines; iron ore nearby; p. (1960) 30,793.

Valletta, c., cap. of **Malta**; ch. spt. on rocky penin. of Mt. Scebarras, E. cst.; formerly naval base; cath., univ.; p. (est. 1983) 14,096.

Valli di Comacchio, lagoon a., N.E. **Italy**; ctr. of an impt. eel industry; a. 259 km².

Valparaiso, c., central **Chile**; leading pt. on Pac. cst. of S. America; attractive c. with backdrop of steep hills; mftg., comm. and industl. ctr. of rep. with textile mills, sugar refineries, paint, shoe and chemical factories; univ.; p. (est. 1980) 266,280.

Valtellina, fertile valley, **Italy**; in Lombard Alps above L. Como; impt. for vine cultivation; hydroelectric power resources; tourism.

Van, c., cap. of Van prov., S.E. **Turkey**; stands at 1,726 m on shore of salty L. Van; tr. ctr. of wheat-growing a.; new Turkish–Iranian rail link; p. (1965) 31,010.

Vancouver, c., B.C., **Canada**; Pac. cst. spt. with excellent natural harbour; international airport and terminus of transcontinental rly.; timber inds., shipbldg., fishing, oil and sugar refining; exp. prod. from these inds.; attractive hilly location and mild climate make c. a major tourist ctr.; univ.; p. (1979) 410,190 (c.), 1,175,200 (met. a.).

Vancouver, I., B.C., **Canada**; off W. cst.; mtnous., forested; woodpulp, paper; indented cst. provides many natural harbours; fishing; cap. Victoria; a. 33,797 km²; p. (1961) 290,835.

Vancouver, t., Wash., **USA**; spt. on Columbia R. opposite Portland (Ore.); exp. grain, timber; food processing; p. (1980) 42,834.

Vandellos, Tarragona, **Spain**; nuclear power sta.; p. (1981) 3,838.

Vanderbijlpark, t., Transvaal, **S. Africa**; on Vaal R.; ctr. for steel wks.; p. (1970) 78,745.

Vänern, lge. L., **Sweden**; W.N.W. of L. Vättern, with which it is connected by canal (and thence with the Baltic); a. 5,566 km².

Vänersborg, L. pt., **Sweden**; on tongue of land between R. Göta and the Vasobotten (southernmost bay of L. Väner); footwear, wood and sulphite pulp; p. (est. 1970) 20,280.

Vannes, t., cap. of Morbihan dep., N.W. **France**; sm. pt. on S. cst. Brittany; cath.; dates from Roman times; p. (1982) 45,397.

Vanuatu, **(New Hebrides)**, former Anglo-French condominion, S. **Pac. Oc.**; between New Caledonia and Fiji Is.; indep. st. 1980; strong separist moves in Santo I.; mostly subsistence agr.; few cash crops; ch. crop coconuts; no worked minerals; thickly forested; cap. Vila; a. 14,763 km²; p. (est. 1980) 117,000.

Var, dep., S.E. **France**; in Provence, on Mediterranean; mainly agr. with some inds. at Draguignan and Toulon (cap. since 1974); bauxite at Brignoles; rapid growth of p.; inc. many coastal resorts; a. 6,042 km²; p. (1982) 705,500.

Varanasi (Benares), c., Uttar Pradesh, **India**; famous holy c. on Ganges, 640 km N.W. of Calcutta; place of annual pilgrimage; univ.; handicrafts, brasses, brocades, embroideries, now debased; p. (1971) 466,696 (c.), 467,487 (met. a.).

Varanger Fjord, inlet of Arctic Oc. into Finnmark, **Norway**; iron mng. on S. shore.

Vardar, R., flows through Yugoslav and Greek Macedonia into Aegean Sea nr. Salonika; inc. V. agr. region; hydroelectric power; routeway; 448 km long.

Varde, t., W. Jutland, **Denmark**; agr. and route ctr.; food processing; steelwks.

Vardö, t., Finnmark prov., N.E. **Norway**; sm.

ice-free pt. on Vardoy I. with fish and oil interests; p. c. 3,500.

Vares, t., Bosnia, **Yugoslavia**; iron mng.; developing mnfs.

Varese, t., Lombardy, **Italy**; in Alpine foothills; resort and industl. ctr.; engin., furniture, paper, textiles, wines; p. (1981) 90,527.

Värmland, prov., **Sweden**; agr., iron mng. and processing, timber inds.; cap. Karlstad; a. 19,236 km²; p. (1983) 281,205.

Varna, t., **Bulgaria**; spt. on Black Sea; industl. ctr. of heavy inds.; summer resorts on cst. nearby; p. (1979) 275,375.

Varnsdorf, t., **CSSR**; rly. junc. on German bdr.; impt. textile ctr.; p. (est. 1968) 13,912.

Västerås, c., cap. of Västmanland prov., **Sweden**; on L. Mälar; impt. elec. and metallurgical inds.; power sta.; impt. mediaeval c., cath., cas.; p. (1983) 117,954.

Västerbotten, prov., **Sweden**; forested; timber inds.; cap. Umeå; a. 59,153 km²; p. (1983) 242,252.

Västernorrland, prov., **Sweden**; forests and timber inds.; cap. Harnosand; a. 25,706 km²; p. (1983) 266,038.

Vastervik, t., Kalmar prov., **Sweden**; on Baltic cst. engin., chemicals, paper; p. (1983) 40,671.

Västmanland, prov., **Sweden**; N. of L. Mälar; mkt. gardening in S.; iron and silver mng. in N.; iron and steel inds.; cap. Västerås; a. 8,363 km²; p. (1983) 287,514.

Vasto, t., Abruzzi e Molise, **Italy**; agr. ctr. on steep-sided, vine-producing plateau; sm. Adriatic fishing pt.; p. (1981) 30,036.

Vatican City, indep. sov. Papal st., **Italy**; forms an enclave in Rome; inc. Papal residence, St. Peter's cath.; a. 44 ha; p. (est. 1978) 728.

Vatna Jökull, mtn., **Iceland**; elevated snowfield; active volcano; alt. 2,120 m.

Vättern, L., **Sweden**; 40 km S.E. L. Vänern; a. 1,898 km².

Vaucluse, dep. S.E. **France**; in Provence; cap. Avignon; a. 3,577 km²; p. (1982) 428,900.

Vaud, can., W. **Switzerland**; N. of L. Geneva; forests and vineyards; cap. Lausanne; a. 3,209 km²; p. (1980) 528,747.

Växjö, t., S. **Sweden**; engin., timber wks., hosiery; p. (1983) 65,859.

Vejle, spt., Jutland, **Denmark**; admin. ctr. V. prov.; industl.; p. (est. 1970) 31,763.

Velbert, t., N. Rhine–Westphalia, **W. Germany**; N.W. of Wuppertal; metal ind., locks and keys; p. (1983) 91,300.

Vélez-Málaga, t., Málaga prov., S. **Spain**; famous for wine, raisins, sugar, olive oil; Moorish cas.; p. (1981) 41,776.

Veliki Ustyug, t., **RSFSR**; R. pt. on Sukhona R.; shipyards, mftg.; p. (est. 1967) 35,000.

Velletri, t., central **Italy**; at foot of Alban hills overlooking Pontine marshes; noted for its wine; Garibaldi routed Neapolitans here 1849; p. (1981) 41,114.

Vellore, t., Tamil Nadu, **India**; agr. mkt. t.; scene of Sepoy mutiny 1806; p. (1971) 139,082 (t.), 178,554 (met. a.).

Velsen, t., N. Holland prov., **Neth.**; nr. entrance to N. Sea Canal, inc. IJmuiden iron and steel wks.; lge. paper mill; p. (1982) 59,779.

Veluwe, dist., Gelderland, **Neth.**; between Arnhem and IJsselmeer; low hills of glacial sands and sand-dunes; heathland and pinewoods; relatively low p. density.

Venda, Bantu homeland, Transvaal, **S. Africa**; 3rd homeland granted "independence" (1979); nr. Zimbabwe border; p. (1979) 309,000.

Vendée, dep., W. **France**; on Bay of Biscay; fish. pts., beach resorts, agr. pasturage, vineyards; cap. La Roche-sur-Yon; a. 6,972 km²; p. (1982) 483,400.

Vendôme, t., Loir-et-Cher dep., **France**; on R. Loire; leather gds., cottons; mediaeval cas.; p. (1982) 18,218.

Venetia (Veneto), region, N.E. **Italy**; between the Alps and the Adriatic; embraces provs. Vicenza, Verona, Venice, Udine, Treviso, Padua, Belluno, and Rovigo; mtnous. in N., inc. Dolomite Alps; fertile plain of Po R. in S.; intensive arable agr.; ch. c. Venice; a. 18,384 km²; p. (1981) 4,345,047.

Venezia Giulia. See Friuli-Venezia Giulia.

Venezuela, fed. rep., N. cst. **S. America**; wealth derived from long-established but currently stagnant oil ind.; tropical climate, with temper-

ate uplands, tropical forests and tall grass savannah lands (llanos); most economically advanced a. around cap. Carácas and oilfield a. of L. Maracaibo; counter pole of development based on hydroelectric power resources and iron ore in Caroni R. region; growing steel inds., lge. agr. areas economically neglected and socially deprived; coffee from highlands main comm. agr. crop and exp.; a. 912,050 km²; p. (est. 1984) 17,819,000.

Venice (Venezia), c., cap. of V. prov. and ch. c. of Venetia, N.E. **Italy**; built on gr. of islets within lagoon in G. of V., at head of Adriatic; splendid architecture, rich in art treasures and historic associations; extensive canal network, inc. Grand Canal, intensive use leading to erosion of bldgs.; gradually sinking into Adriatic, lge.-scale projects to preserve c.; industl. zone on landward side in subs. of Porto Marghera and Mestre; craft and heavy inds.; p. (1981) 346,146.

Venlo, t., **Neth.**; on R. Maas; agr. mkt. and rly. junc.; chemicals, optical instruments, electric lamps; p. (1982) 62,495.

Ventimiglia, t., Liguria, N.W. **Italy**; on Mediterranean cst. on Fr. border; cath.; flower mkt.; tourism; p. (1981) 26,373.

Ventnor, t., South Wight, I. of Wight, **Eng.**; on S. cst. 18 km S. of Ryde; mild climate, tourist and health resort; p. (1981) 7,941.

Veracruz, st., E. **Mexico**; narrow coastal plain rising to Sierra Madre Oriental; contains volcano Orizaba; recent agr. improvements; growth of petroleum inds.; cap. Jalapa; a. 71,836 km²; p. (1969) 3,629,000.

Veracruz, c., V. st., E. **Mexico**; spt. on G. of Mexico; comm. and industl. ctr. of oil region; nearby Laguna Grande, Mexico's first nuclear power sta. (1984); nr. site where Cortés landed 1519; p. (1979) 306,843.

Vercelli, c., cap. of V. prov., N. **Italy**; in Piedmont, on Sesia R.; rice mkt. for lge. irrigated plain textiles, machin., aircraft parts; p. (1981) 52,488.

Verde, Cape, most W. part of **Africa**; site of Dakar, cap. of Senegal.

Verdun, t., Quebec, **Canada**; sub. of Montreal; p. (1966) 76,832.

Verdun, t., Meuse dep., N.E. **France**; in Lorraine, on R. Meuse; strategic ctr. with varied mnfs.; 12th cent. cath.; scene of famous battle 1916; p. (1982) 24,120.

Vereeniging, c., Transvaal prov., **S. Africa**; on Vaal R.; coal, iron and steel, bricks; Treaty of Vereeniging 1902 ended Boer War; p. (1970) 169,553.

Verkhneudinsk. See Ulan-Ude.

Verkhoyansk, t., Yakutsk ASSR, **RSFSR**; in N.E. Siberia; coldest permanently inhabited place in world; mean Jan. temp. of − 59° F.; ctr. of fur trapping a.; p. c. 2,000.

Vermont, st., New England, **USA**; 'Green Mtn. St.'; admitted to Union 1791; st. flower Red Clover, st. bird Hermitt Thrush; traversed by the Green mtns.; farming, dairying, stock-raising, lumbering, quarrying, machine tool and textile mftg.; traditional inds. revitalised by new inds. coming from neighbouring Quebec; cap. Montpelier; famous for autumn colours; a. 24,887 km²; p. (1980) 511,000.

Verona, c., cap. of V. prov., N.E. **Italy**; on R. Adige; commands route from central Europe to Brenner pass and from Venice to Milan; cath. and notable monuments; active agr. tr. and inds., printing; p. (1982) 265,932.

Versailles, c., cap. of Yvelines dep., N. **France**; S.W. sub. of Paris; famous royal palace; mkt. gardening, distilleries; Treaty of Versailles 1919; p. (1982) 95,240.

Verviers, t., **Belgium**; nr. Liège; ctr. of textile ind. in Ardennes; p. (1982) 54,800.

Vestmannaeyjar or **Westman Is.**, archipelago, S. W. **Iceland**; impt. cod fishing ind. based on Heimaey I; p. (1983) 4,743.

Vesuvius, famous active volcano, S. **Italy**; on shore of Bay of Naples; alt. c. 1,186 m; its eruption in A.D. 79 destroyed Pompeii and Herculaneum, and frequent eruptions have since been recorded; observatory founded 1844; funicular rly. from base of mtn. to rim of crater existed from 1880 to 1944 (destroyed by eruption).

Veszprem, c., **Hungary**; in fruit-growing dist., 96 km S. of Budapest; cath., univ. for chemical ind.; p. (1968) 32,000.

Vevey, t., Vaud can., **Switzerland**; on N. shore of L. Geneva; beautiful situation; chocolate, watches; resort; p. (1970) 17,957.

Viareggio, beach resort, Tuscany, **Italy**; on Tyrrhenian Sea, nr. Pisa; monument to Shelley; p. (1981) 58,136.

Viborg, t., Jutland, **Denmark**; admin. ctr. V. prov.; comm. and route ctr.; anc. cath.; textiles, machin., food processing; p. (est. 1970) 25,468.

Vicenza, c. cap. of V. prov., N.E. **Italy**; in Venetia; mkt. ctr. for surrounding fertile agr. plain; textiles, iron and steel; many examples of Palladian architecture; p. (1981) 114,598.

Vichy, t., Allier dep., **France**; on Allier R.; famous spa; hot mineral springs; lge. exp. of V. water; seat of Pétain govt. during German occupation 1940–3; p. (1982) 63,501 (met. a.).

Vicksburg, t., Miss., **USA**; R. pt., on bluffs of Mississippi at junc. of Yazoo canal; shipping and mftg. ctr. in cotton and timber region; prominent in American Civil War; Confederate surrender 1863; p. (1980) 25,434.

Victoria, st., **Australia**; settled rapidly in 19th century with gold rush; now most densely populated yet smallest mainland st.; Latrobe brown coal, offshore natural gas, hydroelectric power encourage rapid industrialisation; dominated by cap. Melbourne; rural a. of Great Dividing Range produces wheat, sheep and dairy prods.; a. 227,516 km²; p. (1976) 3,646,981.

Victoria, c., cap. of B.C., **Canada**; spt. on Vancouver I.; fishing and fish-processing; sawmills, chemicals, cement; beautiful scenery; tourist ctr.; p. (1979) 224,800 (met. a.).

Victoria, main pt. and harbour between **Hong Kong I.** and Kowloon; built on reclaimed land; admin. ctr. of Hong Kong; p. (1971) 521,612.

Victoria, t., cap. of Labuan I., Sabah, **Malaysia**; fine harbour; p. 3,213.

Victoria, t., cap. of **Seychelles**, Ind. Oc.; harbour on lgst. and most impt. I. of Mahé.

Victoria, t., S. Texas, **USA**; comm. ctr. in prosperous agr. a.; local oilfields; p. (1980) 50,695.

Victoria Falls (Mosi-oa-Toenja), on R. Zambesi, **Zambia**; discovered by Livingstone 1855; falls are 1,674 m wide and broken by islands and rocks.

Victoria, Lake, lgst. L. of **Africa**; bordered by Kenya, Uganda, Tanzania; in depression of Gt. Rift Valley, at alt. 999 m. a. c. 67,340 km²; discharges into Victoria Nile; impt. fisheries; discovered by Speke 1858.

Victoria Land, region, **Antarctica**; discovered by Ross in 1841.

Victoria Nile, R., **Uganda**; E. Africa; name of R. Nile from its source at L. Victoria until it enters L. Mobuto Seso.

Vienna (Wien), c., cap. of **Austria**; R. pt. on branch of Danube; surrounded by Wiener Wald (Vienna forest) and Carpathian foothills; major industl., comm. and transport ctr.; many fine blds., inc. univ., cath., Rathaus, parliament bldgs., magnificent Prater park; influential ctr. of music, cultural and scientific ctr.; home of Haydn, Mozart, Beethoven, Schubert, Mahler, Brahms, and Freud; p. (1978) 1,580,600.

Vienne, dep., W. **France**; drained by R. Vienne; mainly agr. dist.; cap. Poitiers; a. 7,021 km²; p. (1982) 371,428.

Vienne, t., Isère, **France**; nr. Grenoble, on R. Rhône; textiles, metallurgical inds.; Roman remains; overshadowed by Lyons 27 km to N.; p. (1982) 372,000.

Vienne, R., **France**; trib. of the Loire; rises in Massif Central; 354 km long.

Vientiane, admin. cap., Laos; pt. and comm. ctr. on Mekong R.; p. (est. 1966) 132,253 (c.); (est. 1962) 162,297 (met. a.).

Viersen, t., N. Rhine–Westphalia, **W. Germany**; S.W. of Krefeld; textiles, machin., furniture, paper ind.; p. (1983) 79,600.

Vierzon, t., Cher dep., **France**; on R. Cher; bricks, tiles, porcelain from local sands, clay; agr. machin.; p. (1982) 34,886.

Vietnam, Socialist Rep. of, S.E. **Asia**; comprises regions of Cochinchina and Tonkin in former French Indo-China; from 1954–1976 two separate countries, N. and S. Vietnam, based on two rivers, Song-koi and Mekong respectively, and separated by the high Annamite chain of mtns.; long period of civil war resulted in reunification; intensive agr. based on rice cultivation now largely collectivised; monsoon climate and river irrigation aid high yields; coffee, tea, rubber, sugar, main comm. crops but much devastation as result of war; minerals mainly concentrated in the N. with impt. anthracite deposit at Quang-Yen; industl. devel. also mainly in N. around Hanoi and ch. pt. Haiphong; hill tribes practising subsistence agr. inhabit the intervening Annamite mtns.; since reunification ts. declining rapidly; a. 335,724 km²; p. (est. 1984) 58,307,000.

Viet-Tri, t., N. **Vietnam**; 128 km N.W. of Hanoi; chemicals, paper mill, sugar refining.

Vigevano, t., Lombardy, **Italy**; on R. Ticino; impt. agr. and industl. ctr.; footwear, plastics, textiles; cath.; p. (est. 1981) 65,228.

Vigo, spt., **Spain**; transatlantic pt. on V. Bay; processing of imports; oil refining; p. (1981) 261,329.

Vijayanagar, ruined c., S.E. **India**; once cap. c. of Hindu empire in S. Deccan; 96 km in circumference; destroyed by Moslem forces at battle of Talikota 1565.

Vijayavada, t., Andhra Pradesh, **India**; rly. junc., comm. ctr.; irrigation dam, Kistna R.; p. (1971) 317,258 (t.), 344,607 (met. a.).

Vila Real de Santo António, pt., Faro, **Portugal**; on W. bank of Guadiana R.; exp. copper ore, fish, fruit; p. (1981) 7,390.

Villach, t., Carinthia, S. **Austria**; at junc. of Gail and Drava Rs.; impt. route ctr.; tourism; p. (1961) 32,971.

Villahermosa, c., cap. of Tabasco, S.E. **Mexico**; agr. mkt., sugar processing; rich local petroleum deposits; p. (1979) 175,845.

Villa Maria, t., **Argentina**; rly. junc.; ctr. of grain, timber, dairying dist.; p. (1960) 50,000.

Villarrica, t., S.E. **Paraguay**; agr. tr. ctr. for cattle, tobacco, fruit; wines, yerba-maté grown in surrounding a.; p. (est. 1970) 38,052.

Villavicencio, t., E. **Colombia**; in foothills of Andes; comm. ctr. for the *llanos*; cattle tr.; p. (est. 1968) 80,675.

Villaviciosa, t., Oviedo prov., N.W. **Spain**; major fishing pt. on Bay of Biscay; p. (1981) 15,703.

Villeurbanne, t., Rhône dep., **France**; forming part of Lyons agglomeration; metallurgy, chemicals, leather, textiles; p. (1982) 118,330.

Vilna (Lith. **Vilnius**, Pol. **Wilno**), c., cap. of Lithuanian SSR, **USSR**; on Vilija R. (trib. of Niemen); cultural ctr., cath., univ., historic bldgs.; held by Poland 1920–39; lt. inds., food processing; p. (1970) 372,000.

Vilyui, R., Yakut ASSR, **RSFSR**; flows E. from Siberian uplands into Lena R.; R. basin impt. agr. and min. a.; fishing; 2,400 km long.

Vimy, t., Pas-de-Calais dep., N. **France**; nearby Vimy Ridge, site of Allied victory led by Canadians 1915; p. (1982) 3,621.

Viña del Mar, seaside t., central **Chile**, nr. Valparaíso; fashionable S. American resort; oil and sugar refining, textiles; p. (est. 1980) 272,814.

Vincennes, t., Val-de-Marne dep., **France**; sub. of Paris; famous cas. and Bois; industl. and residtl.; p. (1982) 43,068.

Vindhya Hills, mtn. range, central **India**; separating the Deccan from the Ganges basin; c. 640 km long.

Vinnitsa, t., Ukrainian SSR, **USSR**; on R. Bug 192 km S.W. of Kiev; agr. mkt. t.; engin. chemicals, textiles; p. (1980) 323,000.

Virginia, st., **USA**; one of original 13 sts.; 'Old Dominion' St.; admitted to Union 1788; st. flower Dogwood, st. bird Cardinal; wide Atl. coastal plain rising inland to Blue Ridge; famous for high quality "Virginia Leaf" tobacco; industl. ts. of Norfolk, Richmond, Portsmouth and Newport News; cap. Richmond; a. 105,711 km²; p. (1980) 5,346,000.

Virgin Is. (Brit.), W.I.; gr. of Is. E. of Greater Antilles; most impt. Tortola, Virgin Gorda, Anegada; water scarcity, semi-subsistence agr. economy; livestock, fish, fruit, vegetables; a. 153 km²; p. (est. 1976) 12,000.

Virgin Is. (USA), W.I.; external terr. of USA E. of Greater Antilles, 64 km E. of Puerto Rico; 3 main Is., St. Thomas, St. John, St. Croix; bought from Denmark 1917; favourite tourist

a. in Caribbean; cap. Charlotte Amalie on St. Thomas; livestock, sugar; rum distilling; a. 344 km²; p. (est. 1976) 96,000.

Vis (Lissa), I., off Dalmatian cst., Adriatic, **Yugoslavia**; fish-canning ctr.; a. 91 km²; anc. remains; resort; sea battle 1866 between Italian and Austrian ironclads; p. 3,000.

Visby, old spt., **Sweden**; on Gotland I. in Baltic Sea; rich in historic interest; resort; p. (est. 1970) 19,319.

Vishakhapatnam, spt., Andhra Pradesh, **India**; deepwater harbour on Bay of Bengal; exp. manganese and oilseeds from Madhya Pradesh; shipbldg.; p. (1971) 352,504 (t.), 363,467 (met. a.).

Vistula, R., **Poland**; rises in Beskids range of Carpathians, flows through Poland past Krakow to Baltic Sea nr. Gdansk; forms major link in E. European waterway system; coal and timber transport; 1,056 km long.

Vitebsk, c., Belorussian SSR, **USSR**; R. pt. on W. Dvina and impt. rly. junc., in agr. region; textiles, machine tools, food processing; p. (1980) 303,000.

Viterbo, c., cap. of V. prov., **Italy**; N. of Rome; agr. ctr., food-processing; 12th cent. cath. and historic bldgs.; p. (1981) 57,632.

Vitim, R., E. Siberia, **RSFSR**; flows to R. Lena; navigable for 5 months of year; coal and grain tr.; 1,400 km long.

Vitória, spt., Espírito Santo, **Brazil**; new ocean terminal capturing tr. from Rio de Janiero; exp. coffee, cocoa, fruit, iron ore; sugar refining, shoes, textiles, cement; p. (est. 1980) 198,400.

Vitoria, c., cap. of Alava prov., **Spain**; in Basque cty.; stands on hill at 534 m; furniture mnf.; defeat of Fr. by Wellington 1813; p. (1981) 192,773.

Vitry-le-François, t., Marne dep., N.E. **France**; on Marne R.; industl., textiles, earthenware; agr. mkt. for Champagne Pouilleuse; p. (1982) 18,829.

Vitry-sur-Seine, S.E. sub., Paris, **France**; flower growing on sand and gravel terraces of Seine R., acreage being reduced by competition from housing and inds.; p. (1982) 85,820.

Vittoria, t., Sicily, **Italy**; mkt. for wine; p. (1981) 50,220.

Vittorio Veneto, t., **Italy**; N. of Venice; resort; textiles; p. (1981) 30,028.

Vizcaya, Basque prov., N. **Spain**; on Bay of Biscay; iron mng.; iron and steel inds.; dense p.; cap. Bilbao; a. 2,165 km²; p. (1982) 1,188,918.

Vlaardingen, t., S. Holland prov., **Neth.**; 8 km W. of Rotterdam, on Nieuwe Maas; leading fish. pt.; p. (1982) 78,124.

Vladimir, c., cap. of V. oblast, **RSFSR**; between Gorki and Moscow, on trib. of Oka R.; founded 12th cent.; caths., historic bldgs.; machine tools, agr. machin., textiles; p. (1980) 301,000.

Vladimir-Volynski, c., N.W. Ukrainian SSR, **USSR**; one of oldest Ukrainian settlements, founded 9th cent.; agr. mkt. ctr.; p. (est. 1967) 23,000.

Vladivostok, c., spt., **RSFSR**; ch. pt. and naval base on Pac.; terminus of Trans-Siberian rly. and airline from Moscow; ch. cultural ctr. of Far East; shipyards, fisheries, oil refining, engin., chemicals; economic development in hinterland hindered by distance from major ctrs. of p. and ind.; p. (1980) 558,000.

Vlieland, Friesian I., at entrance to IJsselmeer, **Neth.**; resort, nature reserve.

Vlissingen or **Flushing**, spt., Zeeland prov., S.W. **Neth.**; on Walcheren I.; shipyards, oil refining, fishing; resort; birthplace of Admiral de Ruyter; p. (1982) 46,348.

Vlonë, spt., S.W. **Albania**; on Strait of Otranto, Adriatic Sea; salt; oil pipeline connects from Kucovë nr. Berat; p. (1967) 50,000.

Vltava or **Moldau**, R., Bohemia, **ČSSR**; rises in Sumava mtns. (Bohemian Forest) and flows to R. Elbe below Prague; used for hydroelectric power; c. 416 km long.

Voghera, t., Lombardy, **Italy**; rly. junc. and agr. mkt.; textiles, machin. engin.; cas., cath.; p. (1981) 42,639.

Voi, t., **Kenya**, E. Africa; 144 km N.W. of Mombasa on rly. to Nairobi; branch connection with Tanzania rly. system allows agr. prod. from Arusha and Moshi dists. to pass through Mombasa as alternative to Tanga; new shoe factory.

Voiron, t., Isère dep., **France**; on Morge R.,

24 km N.W. of Grenoble; textiles, paper; p. (1982) 19,658.

Vojvodina, aut. prov., N. Serbia, **Yugoslavia**; impt. and fertile agr. dist. crossed by Danube R.; intensive agr., prosperous and dense p.; fruit, vegetables, livestock, food processing; ch. c. Novi Sad; a. 22,489 km²; p. (1971) 1,950,268.

Volcano Is., Japan; 3 volcanic Is. in Pac. Oc., S. of Japan, admin. by USA until 1968, now Japanese.

Volga, R., **USSR**; rises in Valdai hills, flows in serpentine course to Caspian at Astrakhan in wide delta; ch. tribs., Oka, Sura, Vetluga, Kama, Samara; major waterway linked to Baltic Sea, Azov, and Black Seas, and to Moscow; hydroelectric developments reducing sturgeon in Caspian Sea and caviar prod. declining; longest R. in Europe, 3,720 km.

Volga Baltic Waterway (Mariinsk Waterway), **RSFSR**; inland deepwater navigation network linking Black Sea and Caspian Sea in S. with Baltic Sea and White Sea in N.

Volgograd (Stalingrad), c., **RSFSR**; R. pt. on Volga and major rly. ctr.; exp. raw materials, fish; industl. ctr. for steel, engin., chemicals, oil refining; hydroelectric power sta.; fierce siege and successful defence 1942 turning point of second world war; p. (1980) 939,000.

Volhynia, historic region, Ukrainian SSR, **USSR**; on Polish frontier; rich agr. lowland; coal mng. at Novovodinsk; cap. Lutsk.

Volkhov, R., **RSFSR**; flows from L. Ilmen to L. Ladoga; navigable; hydroelectric power sta. and aluminium smelting plant at Volkhov (Leningrad oblast); 208 km long.

Volkingen, t., Saarland, **W. Germany**; on Saar R., 13 km W. of Saarbrücken; coal mng., iron and steel; p. (1983) 44,200.

Vologda, c., **RSFSR**; R. and rly. junc. on upper Sukhona R.; in dairying a.; engin., textiles, sawmilling, paper, dairy inds.; cath., historic bldgs.; p. (1980) 241,000.

Volos, spt., **Greece**; at head of G. of V.; impt. transport, industl., comm. ctr.; exp. agr. prods.; car mnfs.; p. (1981) 71,378.

Volsk, c., **RSFSR**; R. pt. on Volga R.; cement, tanneries, metallurgy, food processing; p. (est. 1969) 71,000.

Volta (White Volta), major R., **W. Africa**; drains extensive terr. in Niger bend, flows S. through Ghana to delta on Guinea cst., 112 km E. of Accra; main means of communication but rapids make through navigation impossible; Volta R. project for industrialisation of Ghana; dam and power plant at Akosombo, aluminium smelter at Tema; 1,520 km long. *See also* **Black Volta**.

Volta Redonda, t., Rio de Janeiro, **Brazil**; state-owned steel plant; p. (est. 1980) 173,000.

Volterra, hill t., Tuscany, **Italy**; Etruscan and mediaeval walls; alabaster, salt; p. (1981) 14,080.

Volzhsky, t., **RSFSR**; new industl. t. on Volga R.; aluminium smelting, chemicals; p. (1980) 214,000.

Voorburg, t., **Neth.**; industl. ctr. E. of the Hague; p. (1982) 43,371.

Vorarlberg, prov., **Austria**; forestry, dairying, tourism; inds. based on hydroelectric power; textiles; cap. Bregenz; a. 2,600 km²; p. (1971) 274,000.

Vorkuta, ctr. of Pechora coal basin, **RSFSR**; beyond Arctic circle, which supplies entire European N. RSFSR; p. (1980) 101,000.

Voronezh, c., **RSFSR**; R. pt. on Voronezh R. nr. junc. with Don; impt. comm. ctr. in fertile agr. dist.; machin., rubber, oil refining, food processing; nuclear power sta.; univ., cath.; p. (1980) 796,000.

Voroshilovgrad. See **Lugansk**.

Voroshilovsk. See **Kommunarsk**.

Vosges, dep., E. **France**; on Franco–German frontier; dairying, vineyards, stone quarrying, textiles; cap. Epinal; a. 5,970 km²; p. (1982) 395,400.

Vosges, highlands, E. **France**; structurally similar to Black Forest, from which they are separated by Rhine rift valley; forested slopes, vineyards; source of Meurthe, Moselle, Sarve, Ill, and Saône Rs.; highest summit Ballon de Guebwiller, 1,425 m.

Voskresensk, t., **RSFSR**; S.E. Moscow; lignite,

chemicals, fertilisers; p. (est. 1969) 61,000.

Votkinsk, t., **RSFSR**; 61 km N.E. of Izhevsk; lge. engin. plant; hydroelectric power sta.; birthplace of Tchaikovsky; p. (est. 1969) 73,000.

Vranja, t., **Yugoslavia**; flax and hemp culture and mnf.; developing industl. ctr. based on handicrafts; p. (est. 1965) 19,000.

Vratsa, t., **Bulgaria**; on R. Vratcanska; jewellery, wine, silk, tanning; p. (est. 1968) 45,232.

Vrsac, t., **Yugoslavia**; milling, wine, brandy; p. (1961) 31,620.

Vulcano, I., Lipari gr., **Italy**; off N.E. cst. Sicily; active volcano; gave its name as generic title for this type of mtn.

Vyatka, R., **RSFSR**; rises in foothills of Urals, flows past Kirov into Kama R.; timber transport, fishing; c. 1,360 km long.

Vyborg (Viipuri), c., **RSFSR**; spt. on G. of Finland, occupies strategic site on Karelian Isthmus, N.W. of Leningrad; Finnish until 1945; exp. timber; shipyards, engin., food processing; p. (est. 1969) 65,000.

Vychegda, R., **RSFSR**; rises in Urals, flows W. to N. Dvina R.; timber transport; 1,120 km long.

Vyrnwy, L., reservoir, Powys, **Wales**; with dam 360 m long supplies water for Liverpool; a. 454 ha.

Vyshni-Volochek, t., **RSFSR**; 118 km N.W. of Kalinin; flour milling, textiles, glass inds.; p. (est. 1969) 73,000.

W

Waal, R., **Neth.**; S. arm of R. Rhine.

Waco, c., Texas, **USA**; in Brazos valley; route ctr., airport; regional cultural ctr.; univ.; textiles, leather; p. (1980) 101,000.

Waddenzee, stretch of shallow water between W. Frisian Is. and **Neth.** mainland.

Wadebridge, spt., Cornwall, **Eng.**; at head of Camel estuary, 10 km N.W. of Bodmin; agr. mkt.

Wadi Halfa, t., **Sudan**; on R. Nile at second cataract; rly. terminus of Sudan rlys.; inundated by Aswan L.; new t. Khashm el Girba for inhabitants.

Wadi Medani, t., cap. of Blue Nile prov., **Sudan**; ctr. of cotton growing dist.; p. (1983) 141,065.

Wagadugu. See **Ouagadougou.**

Wagga Wagga, t., N.S.W., **Australia**; on R. Murrumbidgee; ctr. of agr. and pastoral dist.; p. (1976) 32,984.

Wahiawa, t., Oahu I., **Hawaii**; pineapples; p. (1970) 37,329.

Waikaremoana, L., N.I., **N.Z.**; hydroelectric power.

Waikato, R., N.I., **N.Z.**; rises in L. Taupo and flows N.W. into Tasman Sea; coalfields, hydroelec. power stas.; longest R. of N.Z.; 422 km long.

Wairakei, N.I., **N.Z.**; on L. Taupo; health resort; geothermal power sta.

Waitemata, c., N.I., **N.Z.**; part of Auckland on picturesque inlet; p. (1976) 79,883.

Wakamatsu. See **Kitakyushu.**

Wakatipu, L., Otago, S.I., **N.Z.**; 83 km long, 5 km wide, 360 m deep, 320 m a.s.l.

Wakayama, spt., Honshu, **Japan**; textiles; new iron and steel plant; p. (1979) 400,899.

Wakefield, c., met. dist., West Yorks., **Eng.**; on R. Calder; 13 km S. of Leeds; cath.; ctr. of coal-mng. a.; woollen and worsted gds., chemicals, engin.; p. (1981) 311,787.

Wakefield, t., Va., **USA**; on Potomac R., nr. Fredericksburg; birthplace of George Washington; p. (1980) 1,355.

Wake I., coral atoll, **Pac. Oc.**; between Marianas and Hawaii; comm. and naval base on route to Far East, belonging to USA.

Walachia, region, S. **Romania**; wide plain bounded by Transylvanian Alps and separated from Yugoslavia by Danube; rich agr. a., "the bread-basket of Romania"; Ploiesti oilfields; inds. nr. ch. c. Bucharest; a. 76,563 km²; p. c. 7,500,000.

Walbrzych (Waldenburg), c., S.W. **Poland** (since 1945); formerly in Lower Silesia; industl. and mng. ctr. at 427 m; porcelain, machin., engin.; p. (est. 1983) 137,400.

Walchensee, Lake, Bavaria, **W. Germany**; a. 16 km²; hydroelectric power sta.

Walcheren, I., Zeeland prov., S.W. **Neth.**; in N. Sea at entrance to Scheldt estuary; mainly agr.; ch. ts., Vlissingen, Middelburg; flooded 1944 to stop German advance; tourism.

Waldenburg. See **Walbrzych.**

Wales, principality, **Great Britain**; mostly mtnous.; Cambrian mtns. rise to 1,085 m at Snowdon; contrast betwen N. and Central Wales (pastoral farming, forestry, water supply, tourism, rural depopulation) and S. Wales (coalfield, metal-based inds., lge. ts.); cap. Cardiff; a. 20,761 km²; p. (1981) 2,790,462 (26 per cent Welsh speaking).

Wallasey, t., Wirral, adjoining Birkenhead, Merseyside, **Eng.**; residtl., seaside resort (New Brighton); p. (1981) 90,057.

Wallensee, L., **Switzerland**; 18 km long.

Wallingford, t., South Oxon., **Eng.**; on R. Thames, to N. of its gap between Chilterns and Lambourn Downs; p. (1981) 6,328.

Wallis and Futuna Is., gr. of coral Is., S. **Pac. Oc.**; overseas terr. of France; copra; a. 275 km²; p. (1983) 12,400 (mostly Polynesians).

Wallsend, t., Tyne and Wear, **Eng.**; on N. bank of Tyne, 6 km below Newcastle; Tyne tunnel links with Jarrow; shipbldg., engin., iron, plywood; at end of Hadrian's Wall; p. (1981) 44,699.

Walmer, t., Kent, **Eng.**; 3 km S. of Deal; holiday resort; cas., residence of Warden of Cinque Ports.

Walney, I., off cst. of Cumbria, **Eng.**; opposite Barrow.

Walsall, t., met. dist., West Midlands, **Eng.**; 8 km E. of Wolverhampton; leather and iron gds., engin., steel tubes; p. (1981) 266,128.

Walsingham, v., North Norfolk, **Eng.**; many old bldgs., priory ruins, abbey; mediaeval pilgrimage ctr.

Walsum, t., N. Rhine-Westphalia, **W. Germany**; at confluence of Rhine and Emscher canal; R. pt. for Oberhausen steelwks.; p. (est. 1969) 48,262.

Waltham, c., Mass., **USA**; nr. Boston; science-based inds.; univ.; p. (1980) 58,200.

Waltham Abbey, t., Epping Forest, Essex, **Eng.**; 21 km N.E. London, on edge of Epping Forest; glasshouses (tomatoes); Norman nave of abbey part of parish church; p. (1981) 19,432.

Waltham Forest, outer bor., E. London, **Eng.**; incorporating former bors. of Chingford, Leyton, Walthamstow; industl. and residtl.; p. (1981) 215,092.

Walthamstow. See **Waltham Forest.**

Walton and Weybridge, ts., Elmbridge, Surrey, **Eng.**; on R. Thames, 27 km S.W. of London; eng., aircraft; p. (1981) 49,237.

Walton-le-Dale, t., South Ribble, N.E. Lancs., **Eng.**; on R. Ribble, 3 km E. of Preston; mkt. gardening, cottons, timber; p. (1981) 29,000.

Walvis Bay, spt., **Namibia**; on Walvis Bay, Atl. Oc.; fishing, fish processing; impt. base for S. Africa who wishes to keep it separate from Namibia; p. (1970) 23,461.

Wandsworth, inner bor., S.W. London, **Eng.**; inc. Battersea; on R. Wandle at influx into Thames; oil mills, metal wks., paper, brewing; p. (1981) 255,723.

Wanganui, c., N.I., **N.Z.**; pt. on R. Wanganui; tr. ctr. for wool, grain, meat, dairy prod.; agr. processing, steel-pipes, fertilisers; iron ore deposits; p. (1976) 39,679.

Wanganui, R., N.I., **N.Z.**; famous for its beauty; 265 km long.

Wangaratta, t., Victoria, **Australia**; 232 km from Melbourne; ctr. of varied agr. dist. supplying prods. (milk, wool) for processing; p. (1976) 16,157.

Wankie, t., **Zimbabwe**; site of coal-mng. ind.; 344 km N.W. of Bulawayo; new coal fired power sta.; p. (1982) 39,200.

Wanne-Eickel, t., N. Rhine-Westphalia, **W. Germany**; pt. on Rhine-Herne canal; coal-mng. ctr. of Ruhr; p. (est. 1969) 100,300.

Wansbeck, R., Northumberland, **Eng.**; flows E. from Pennines into N. Sea 5 km N. of Blyth.

Wansbeck, l. gov. dist., Northumberland, **Eng.**; inc. Newbiggin, Ashington and Bedlington; p. (1981) 62,497.

Wansdyke, l. gov. dist., S. Avon, **Eng.**; inland a. inc. Keynsham, Bathavon and Clutton; p. (1981) 76,322.

Wantage, mkt. t., Oxon., **Eng.**; in Vale of the White Horse; birthplace of King Alfred; p. (1981) 8,765.

Wapping, Thames-side dist., London, **Eng.**

Warangal, t., Andhra Pradesh, **India**; textiles, carpets; p. (1971) 207,520.

Ware, mkt. t., East Herts., **Eng.**; on R. Lea; 3 km N.E. of Hertford; p. (1981) 14,203.

Wareham, mkt. t., Purbeck, Dorset, **Eng.**; on R. Frome, on N. of I. of Purbeck, 13 km S.W. of Poole; agr. machin., pipes; p. (1981) 4,577.

Warley, t., Sandwell, West Midlands, **Eng.**; inc. Smethwick, Oldbury and Rowley Regis; varied inds.; p. of dist. (1981) 163,567.

Warminster, t., West Wilts., **Eng.**; on Wylye watershed at edge of Salisbury Plain; agr. mkt., gloves; p. (1981) 15,065.

Warnemünde, spt., **E. Germany**; ferry pt. for rail traffic between Berlin and Copenhagen; shipbldg.; outport for Rostock; resort.

Warrego, R., Queensland, N.S.W., **Australia**; trib. of R. Darling; 640 km long.

Warren, t., Ohio, **USA**; on Mahoning R.; iron and steel mftg.; p. (1980) 56,629.

Warrenpoint, spt., Newry and Mourne, **N. Ireland**; at head of Carlingford Lough; p. (1966) 3,579.

Warrington, t., l. gov. dist., Cheshire, **Eng.**; on R. Mersey and Manchester Ship Canal; metal inds. (wire-drawing), chemicals, brewing, paper; expanded as new c. (to take people from Manchester) with p. (1991) 205,000; attracting high technology inds.; p. (1981) 168,846 (dist.), 134,327 (t.).

Warrnambool, t., spt., Victoria, **Australia**; former pt. on Lady Bay; wool processing, rugs, blankets; p. (1976) 20,195.

Warsaw (Warszawa), c., cap. of **Poland**; on R. Vistula; devastated in second world war; facsimile rebuilding based on Canaletto's paintings; cath., univ.; rly. ctr.; iron, steel, engin., textiles, chemicals; p. (est. 1983) 1,641,300.

Warsop, t., Notts., **Eng.**; 6 km N.E. of Mansfield; limestone, gravel; p. (1981) 13,675.

Warta, R., **Poland**; trib. of R. Oder; connected to R. Vistula by canal; 720 km long.

Warwick, t., Queensland, **Australia**; sawmilling, agr. processing; p. (1966) 10,087.

Warwick, co. t., l. gov. dist., Warwicks., **Eng.**; on R. Avon, 13 km S.W. of Coventry; cas.; agr. implements, brewing, malting; p. (1981) 113,740 (dist.).

Warwick, c., R.I., **USA**; on Narrangansett Bay; textile ctr.; p. (1980) 87,123.

Warwickshire, non-met. co., W. Midlands, **Eng.**; undulating, drained by tribs. of Rs. Severn and Trent, crossed by Cotswolds to S.; sm. coalfield to N.; potential new coalfield in S.; much of industl. N. now inc. in West Midlands met. co.; a. 1,981 km²; p. (1981) 473,620.

Warwickshire, North, l. gov. dist., Warwicks., **Eng.**; close to Midlands conurb., based on Atherstone; p. (1981) 59,808.

Wassatch Mtns., range of Rocky mtns., Utah and Idaho, **USA**; alt. 3,600 m.

Wash, The, bay, N. Sea between Lincs. and Norfolk, **Eng.**; 35 km long, 24 km wide; partly reclaimed to form the Fens; proposed barrage to aid further reclamation and water storage.

Washington, t., Tyne and Wear, **Eng.**; 8 km S.E. of Gateshead; coal, iron and steel, stone quarrying, chemicals; new t. 1964; p. (1981) 47,445.

Washington, c., cap. of **USA**; in Dist. of Columbia on Potomac R.; c. planned as national seat of Government; White House, Capitol, 5 univs.; over half p. Negro; p. (1980) 635,000 (c.), 3,045,000 (met. a.).

Washington, st., **USA**; 'Evergreen St.' admitted to Union 1889; st. flower Western Rhododendron, st bird Willow Goldfinch; in extreme N.W., stretching from Pac. Oc. into Rocky mtns.; over half a. forested; Colombia R. and tribs. provide hydroelectric power; timber, fishing, tourism; cap. Olympia; a. 176,617 km²; p. (1980) 4,130,000.

Wast Water, L. Dist., deepest L. in **Eng.**; 5 km long, 79 m deep.

Watchet, t., West Somerset, **Eng.**; sm. pt. on cst. of Bristol Channel; paper mkg., fishing; p. (1981) 3,050.

Watenstedt-Salzgitter. See Salzgitter.

Waterbury, c., Conn., **USA**; on Naugatuck R.; ctr. of brass ind. and metal gds.; p. (1980) 103,000 (c.), 228,000 (met. a.).

Waterford, co., Munster, **R.o.I.**; mtnous. co. in S.E.; mainly agr., dairying, pigs; fishing; co. t. Waterford; a. 1,867 km²; p. (1981) 38,473.

Waterford, co. t., spt., Waterford, **R.o.I.**; on R. Suir; cath.; brewing, fishing, glass mnfs.; p. (1981) 38,478 (t.).

Waterloo, t., Brabant prov., **Belgium**, nr. Brussels; battle nearby 1815; p. (1982) 24,936.

Waterloo, t., Ont., **Canada**; industl. sub. of Kitchener; p. (1971) 37,245.

Waterloo, c., Iowa, **USA**; on Cedar R.; agr. prod. and tools; p. (1980) 75,985 (c.), 137,961 (met. a.).

Waters of Merom (L. Hula), Upper Galilee, **Israel**; extensive drainage completed 1957; a. 14 km².

Waterton Glacier International Peace Park, Albert and Mont., **Canada** and **USA**; glacial and lake scenery; a. 596 km².

Watertown, t., Mass., **USA**; on Charles R.; textiles, clothing; p. (1980) 34,384.

Watertown, t., N.Y., **USA**; on Black R.; engin., paper; p. (1980) 27,861.

Watford, t., l. gov. dist., Herts., **Eng.**; on R. Colne, 26 km N.W. of London; mkt.; varied inds., inc. lt. and elec. engin., paper, printing; p. (1981) 74,356.

Wattenscheid, t., N. Rhine–Westphalia, **W. Germany**; E. of Essen; coal, metals, footwear; p. (est. 1980) 67,653.

Waukegan, c., Ill., **USA**; on L. Michigan; summer resort; steel, brass, motors, sugar refining; p. (1980) 67,653.

Wauwatosa, t., Wis., **USA**; sub. of Milwaukee; metals, concrete, chemicals; p. (1980) 51,308.

Waveney, R., Norfolk and Suffolk, **Eng.**; 80 km long.

Waveney, l. gov. dist., Suffolk, **Eng.**; based on Lowestoft, Beccles and Bungay; p. (1981) 99,239.

Waverley, l. gov. dist., Surrey, **Eng.**; inc. Farnham, Godalming and Haslemere; p. (1981) 108,901.

Wayatinah, hydroelectric commission v., Tasmania, **Australia**; dam, lagoon and power sta. at confluence of Rs. Nive and Derwent.

Wazirabad (Balkh), t., **Afghanistan**; anc. Bactra, cap. of Bactria, called the "mother of cities", destroyed by Genghiz Khan 1221; textile plant projected; p. c. 13,000.

Weald, The, wooded and pastoral tracts S.E. **Eng.**; extending from Folkestone, Kent, through Surrey, Hants., and Sussex to the sea at Beachy Head; former a. of iron working; name derived from German *Wald* = forest.

Wealden, l. gov. dist., East Sussex, **Eng.**; stretches from Uckfield to S. cst.; p. (1981) 116,498.

Wear, R., Durham/Tyne and Wear, **Eng.**; rises in Pennines, flows through Durham to N. Sea at Sunderland; 96 km long.

Wear Valley, l. gov. dist., Durham, **Eng.**; Pennine a. inc. Bishop Auckland, Crook and Willington; p. (1981) 63,870.

Weaver, R., Cheshire, **Eng.**; industl. trib. of R. Mersey; 72 km long.

Weddell Sea, arm of S. Atl. Oc., **Antarctica**; whaling and sealing.

Wednesfield, t., West Midlands, **Eng.**; metal tubes, materials handling engin.; expanded t.

Wei, R., Shaanxi prov., W. **China**; rises in highlands of Kansu, flows E. between highlands of Shaanxi and Hua Shan to join Yellow R; valley contains very fertile loess soils; formed cradle of Chinese civilisation; c. 800 km long.

Weifang, c., Shandong prov., **China**; coal-mng. ctr.; tobacco processing; p. (est. 1970) 260,000.

Weihai, spt., Shandong prov., **China**; naval base; fishing; vegetable-oil processing, textiles; p. 222,000.

Weimar, t., Erfurt, **E. Germany**; on R. Ilm; ctr. of music and culture in 19th cent., associated with Goethe, Schiller, Nietzsche, Liszt, Herder; scene of establishment of German rep. 1919; elec. and metal inds., textiles, musical instruments, glass; p. (est. 1970) 63,689.

Weipa, Queensland, **Australia**; Aboriginal community t., since 1965 taken over by Queensland to overcome opposition to bldg. of new t., pt., and alumina plant; bauxite nearby at Aurukin; p. (1976) 2,876.

Weisshorn, mtn. peak, **Switzerland**; alt. 4,505 m.

Wejherowo, t., Gdansk, **Poland**; on R. Reda; mediaeval stronghold; palace; p. (1970) 33,700.

Welkom, t., O.F.S., **S. Africa**; ctr. of O.F.S. goldfields; p. (1970) 131,767 (met. a.).

Welland, t., Ont., **Canada**; on Welland Canal; industl. t.; p. (1971) 44,222.

Welland, R., Northants. and Lincs., **Eng.**; rises in Northampton heights and flows N.E. into the Wash; 112 km long.

Welland Ship Canal, Ont., **Canada**; connects Ls. Erie and Ont.; 43 km long; 2-lane waterway.

Wellingborough, t., l. gov. dist., Northants., **Eng.**; on R. Nene, 14 km N.E. of Northampton; mkt.; footwear; expanded t.; p. (1981) 64,147 (dist.).

Wellington, mkt. t., The Wrekin, Shrops., **Eng.**; brewing, sugar refining, timber, toys; name derived from "Watling Town" (stood on Watling Street); with Dawley and Oakengates forms new t. of Telford; p. (1981) 15,699.

Wellington, mkt. t., Somerset, **Eng.**; 10 km S.W. Taunton, anc. woollen ind. still survives; dairy prod.; p. (1981) 10,567.

Wellington, c., spt., N.I., cap. of **N.Z.**; univ.; impt. exp. ctr. for dairy prod., wool, meat; new inds. developing in Hutt valley with vehicle assembly, rubber, oil refineries; p., (est. 1979) 137,600 (c.), 327,000 (met. a.).

Wellington, prov., N.I., **N.Z.**; mtnous., pastoral and dairy farming; a. 28,153 km²; p. (1976) 591,612.

Wells, cath. t., Mendip, Somerset, **Eng.**; on S. flank of Mendip hills; cath., bishop's palace; paper mftg.; tourism; p. (1981) 8,374.

Wels, t., Upper **Austria**; on Traun R.; mkt. for agr. a.; cas.; p. (1961) 41,060.

Welshpool, mkt. t., Powys, **Wales**; on R. Severn; nearby is Powys cas.; p. (1981) 7,030.

Welwyn Garden City, t., Welwyn-Hatfield, Herts., **Eng.**; 34 km N. of London; founded by Sir Ebenezer Howard (1920) as first satellite t. of London; new t. 1948; pharmaceuticals, plastics, radio, and electronics, lt. inds.; p. (1981) 40,496.

Welwyn-Hatfield, l. gov. dist., Herts., **Eng.**; comprises Welwyn Garden City and Hatfield; p. (1981) 93,000.

Wembley, former M.B., Middx., **Eng.**; now inc. in Brent outer bor. Greater London; lt. inds., sports ctr.; British Empire Exhibition 1924-5.

Wenlock Edge, narrow ridge, Shrops., **Eng.**; extends 29 km S.W. from Much Wenlock to Craven Arms; limestone; moorland, mainly above 290 m.

Wensleydale, North Yorks., **Eng.**; valley in N. Pennines drained E. by R. Ure; cattle reared for fattening on lowland farms; some dairying (cheese); length 56 km.

Wenzhou (Wenchow), c., spt., Zhejiang prov., **China**; pt. on estuary of Wu R., E. China Sea; textiles, fishing, coastal tr.; exp. wood, tea, agr. prod.; p. (est. 1970) 250,000.

Wernigerode, t., Magdeburg, **E. Germany**; on N. slopes of Harz mtns.; mediaeval cas.; tourism; p. (est. 1970) 32,662.

Wesel, t., N. Rhine–Westphalia, **W. Germany**; R. pt. at confluence of Rs. Lippe and Rhine, Ruhr conurb.; p. (1983) 55,700.

Weser, R., **W. Germany**; formed by confluence of Fulda and Werra Rs. at Münden; flows N. to N. Sea at Bremerhaven; linked by Mittelland canal to Rhine, Ems, and Elbe; navigable for entire length of 330 m.

Wesermünde. *See* Bremerhaven.

Wessex, anc. kingdom, S. **Eng.**; inc. Berks., Hants., Wilts., Dorset, Somerset and Devon.

West Bengal, st., N.E. **India**; W., mainly Hindu section of former presidency of B. (Muslim E.B. now Bangladesh); on Ganges delta and flood plain; humid sub-tropical climate; very dense p.; rice, jute; ch. c. Calcutta; a. 87,617 km²; p. (1971) 44,440,095.

West Bridgford, t., Rushcliffe, Notts., **Eng.**; at junc. of Grantham canal with R. Trent; residtl. sub. of Nottingham; p. (1981) 28,073.

West Bromwich, t., Sandwell, West Midlands, **Eng.**; on R. Thame, 8 km N.W. of Birmingham; heavy engin. and allied inds., chemicals, springs, oil refining; p. (1981) 154,930.

West Derbyshire, l. gov. dist., Derbys., **Eng.**; Pen-nine a. inc. Matlock, Bakewell and Ashbourne; p. (1981) 66,485.

West Devon, l. gov. dist., Devon, **Eng.**; rural W. of Dartmoor and ts. of Tavistock and Okehampton; p. (1981) 42,996.

West Dorset, l. gov. dist., Dorset, **Eng.**; inc. Lyme Regis, Bridport, Sherborne and Dorchester; p. (1981) 78,337.

Western Australia, st. of the **Australian Commonwealth**; cut off from the rest of A. by desert; lgst. st., nearly a third of continent with only 9 per cent of p. concentrated in S.W. around st. cap. of Perth in fertile Mediterranean-like a.; diversity of relief, Hammersley range in N.W., Kimberley range in N.E., Gibson desert in interior; rich but irregularly distributed mineral deposits; intensive agr. in S.W., wheat and sheep in interior; a. 2,525,500 km²; p. (1976) 1,144,857.

Western Desert, Egypt; part of Libyan Desert; inc. Qattara depression; coastal road from Cairo to Tripoli; fighting in second world war.

Western Isles, l. gov. reg., **Scot.**; remote a. of Outer Hebrides where pastoral farming and fishing have been the traditional livelihood for some time; p. (1981) 31,766.

Western Pacific High Commission Territories, inc. Solomon Is. and Kiribati and Tuvalu Is.

Westernport, inlet, Vic., **Australia**; major heavy industl. a. close to Melbourne, rapidly growing.

Western Sahara (Spanish Sahara), N.W. African cst.; comprising Rio de Oro and Sagui el Hamra; desert; rich phosphate mines at Bou Craa connected to El Aaiun pt. by rly.; upon decolonisation terr. split between Morocco and Mauritania (1976) but declared Saharan Arab Democratic Rep. by Algerians (Polisario) and still disputed; a. 265,993 km², p. largely nomadic (est. 1976) 128,000.

Western Samoa, indep. sov. st., S. **Pac. Oc.**; member of Commonwealth (1970); gained independence from N.Z. 1962; consists of 2 lge ls. (Savai'i, Upolu) and 7 sm. Is.; 70 per cent p. in agr.; c. 30 per cent a. devoted to bananas; exp. bananas, copra, cacao beans; ch. spt. Apia on Upolu I.; a. 2,841 km²; p. (est. 1980) 157,000.

Westerwald, plateau of old volcanic rocks, **W. Germany**; ending in steep slope E. of R. Rhine; fertile soil; pastureland or deciduous woodland; sm. quantities of iron ore in Siegerland.

West Glamorgan, co., S. **Wales**; borders Bristol Channel; inc. Gower Penin. and lge. industl. ts. of Swansea, Neath and Port Talbot; impt. metal refining and engin. inds.; a. 816 km²; p. (1981) 367,194.

West Ham, former C.B., Essex, **Eng.**; sub. to E. of London; bordered by Rs. Thames and Lea; now inc. in Newham bor., Greater London.

West Hartford, t., Conn., **USA**; residtl. sub. of Hartford; metal gds., ctr. for dairying, tobacco-growing dist.; p. (1980) 61,301.

West Indies or **Antilles**, I. grs., **Atl. Oc.**; extend between csts. of Fla. and Venezuela, separating Caribbean Sea and G. of Mexico from Atl.; inc. Cuba, Haiti, Dominican Rep., Bahamas, Barbados, Jamaica, Leeward Is., Trinidad and Tobago, Windward Is., Guadeloupe, Martinique, Curaçao, Puerto Rico, Virgin Is.; mostly volcanic and coral Is.; former colonial terrs. developed for plantation agr. worked by W. African slaves; most of indigenous Indians killed.

West Irian. *See* Irian Jaya.

West Lancashire, l. gov. dist., Lancs., **Eng.**; N. of Merseyside, inc. Skelmersdale and Ormskirk; p. (1981) 106,735.

West Lindsey, l. gov. dist., Lincs., **Eng.**; lge. a. N. of Lincoln and inc. Market Rasen and Gainsborough; p. (1981) 75,859.

West Lothian, l. gov. dist., former co., Lothian Reg., **Scot.**; industl. dist. in Central Lowlands close to Edinburgh; a. 417 km²; p. (1981) 137,773.

Westmeath, co., Leinster, **R.o.I.**; low-lying, drained by R. Shannon, many Ls.; dairying; co. to Mullingar; ch. t. Athlone; a. 1,834 km²; p. (1981) 27,609.

West Mersea, t., Essex, **Eng.**; on Mersea I.; p. (1981) 5,514.

West Midlands, former met. co., **Eng.**; mainly industl. a. centred around Birmingham and the S. Staffs. coalfield (Black Country) and Coventry and the Warwicks. coalfield; many forms of engin. and light inds. inc. vehicle mftg.; p. (1981) 2,355,610.

Westminster, City of, inner bor., London, **Eng.;** on N. bank of R. Thames; W. of City of London; incorporates former bors. of Paddington and St. Marylebone; contains Houses of Parliament, Westminster Abbey, Government offices, Royal Palaces (Buckingham Palace and St. James's); p. (1981) 190,661.

Westmorland, former co., **Eng.;** now part of **Cumbria** non-met. co.

West Norfolk, l. gov. dist., Norfolk, **Eng.;** lge. a. inc. Hunstanton, King's Lynn and Downham Market; p. (1981) 120,754.

Weston-super-Mare, t., Woodspring, Avon, **Eng.;** on Bristol Channel, 32 km S.W. of Bristol; holiday resort; expanded t.; p. (1981) 57,980.

West Orange, t., N.J., **USA;** elec. equipment; home of T. A. Edison; p. (1980) 39,510.

West Oxfordshire, l. gov. dist., Oxon., **Eng.;** in Cotswolds and ts. of Chipping Norton, Witney and Woodstock; p. (1981) 80,266.

West Pakistan. See **Pakistan.**

West Palm Beach, Fla., **USA;** domestic hardware; spt.; tourism; p. (1980) 63,305 (t.), 573,125 (met. a.).

Westphalia. See **North Rhine-Westphalia.**

West Point, military sta., N.Y., **USA;** on Hudson R.; military academy.

Westport, spt., U.D., Mayo, **R.o.I.;** on Clew Bay; fishing; mkt.; p. (1981) 3,379.

Westray, I., Orkney Is., **Scot.;** 16 km long; p. (1971) 841.

West Somerset, l. gov. dist., Somerset, **Eng.;** inc. Exmoor and cstl. ts. of Watchet and Minehead; p. (1981) 32,299.

West Sussex, non-met. co., S.E. **Eng.;** crossed by E.-W. chalk ridge of S. Downs and forested Weald; diverse agr.; dormitory, retirement and tourist ts. on cst. inc. Bognor Regis and Worthing; Crawley new t. in N.; a. 2,015 km²; p. (1981) 658,562

West Virginia, st., **USA;** 'Mountain St.' admitted to Union 1863; st. flower Big Rhododendron, st. bird Cardinal; inc. Allegheny plateau; impt. mng. st. for coal; fruit farming; many industl. ts.; cap. Charleston; a. 62,629 km²; p. (1980) 1,950,000.

Westward Ho!, v., N. Devon, **Eng.;** named after Kingsley's novel.

West Wiltshire, l. gov. dist., Wilts., **Eng.;** stretches from Melksham, Bradford-on-Avon and Trowbridge to Warminster; p. (1981) 99,301.

West Yorkshire, former met. co., **Eng.;** industl. and mainly built-up a. E. of Pennines; traditionally ass. with woollen textile mftg.; inc. major ctrs. of Bradford and Leeds; p. (1981) 2,037,510.

Wetar I., Indonesia; N. of Timor I.; mtns.; underdeveloped; sparse p.; a. 31,080 km².

Wetherby, t., West Yorks., **Eng.;** on R. Wharfe; mkt., t.; racecourse.

Wethersfield, t. Conn., **USA;** oldest settlement (1634) in st.; aircraft parts, agr. implements; p. (1970) 26,662.

Wetterhorn, mtn., **Switzerland;** alt. 3,710 m.

Wetzlar, t., Hesse, **W. Germany;** on R. Lahn; metallurgical and optical inds.; p. (1983) 50,600.

Wexford, coastal co., Leinster, S.E. **R.o.I.;** mixed farming, fishing; cap. Wexford; a. 2,334 km²; p. (1981) 32,237.

Wexford, t., cap. of Wexford; Leinster, S.E. **R.o.I.;** on R. Slaney; agr. processing; outport at Rosslare; p. (1981) 11,417.

Wey, R., Hants., Surrey, **Eng.;** rises in W. Weald, flows N. into R. Thames nr. Weybridge; cuts impt. gap through N. Downs at Guildford; length 56 km.

Weybridge. See **Walton and Weybridge.**

Weymouth and Portland, t., l. gov. dist., Dorset, **Eng.;** on Weymouth Bay, 13 km S. of Dorchester; torpedo and boatbldg., bricks, tiles, engin.; holiday resort; p. (1981) 57,176.

Whaley Bridge, t., High Peak, Derbys., **Eng.;** textile bleaching and finishing; p. (1981) 5,501.

Whangarei, c., N.I., **N.Z.;** deep harbour; oil refining; natural gas pipelines from Kapuni; fertilisers, sheet glass; p. (1976) 39,069.

Wharfe, R., West and North Yorks., **Eng.;** trib. of R. Ouse; 96 km long.

Wheeling, c., W. Va., **USA;** pt. on Ohio R.; comm. and mftg. ctr. in coal and natural gas a.; iron, steel, and metal plants; p. (1970) 46,854 (c.), 180,724 (met. a.).

Whickham, t., Tyne and Wear, **Eng.;** nr. Gateshead; chemicals, paper; p. (1981) 31,543.

Whitburn, burgh, W. Lothian, **Scot.;** 32 km S.W. of Edinburgh; coal, limestone; p. (1981) 12,559.

Whitby, t., North Yorks., **Eng.;** at mouth of R. Esk, 27 km N.W. of Scarborough; anc. spt. and fishing t.; residtl. and coastal resort; abbey; famous for jet ornaments; potash to be mined nearby; p. (1981) 13,763.

Whitchurch, t., Shrops., **Eng.;** 21 km S.W. of Crewe; structural steel, dairy prods.

White, R., Ark. and Mo., **USA;** trib. of Mississippi; hydroelectric power; 1,104 km long.

Whiteadder, R., Berwick, **Scot.;** trib. of R. Tweed; 54 km long.

Whitehaven, spt., Copeland, Cumbria, **Eng.;** on Solway F. 5 km N. of St. Bees Head; coal, methane gas, cement, chemicals; p. (1981) 26,714.

Whitehead, t., Carrickfergus, **N. Ireland;** at entrance to Belfast Lough; seaside resort; p. (1966) 2,740.

Whitehorse, t., cap. of Yukon terr., **Canada;** ctr. coal and copper mng., hunting and fur trapping; once a gold "boom town"; H.Q. Royal Canadian Mounted Police; end of Alaska highway linking Edmonton, Alberta; p. (1966) 4,771.

White Mtns., part. of Appalachian system, N.H., **USA;** highest summit Mt. Washington, 1,918 m.

White Nile (Bahr-el-Abiad), R., **Sudan;** N.E. Africa; strictly, name applied to stretch of R. Nile between L. No and Khartoum; 800 km long.

White Plains, t., N.Y., **USA;** on Bronx R.; residtl.; battle 1776; p. (1980) 46,999.

White Russia. See **Belorussiyan SSR.**

White Sea or G. of Arkangelsk, inlet of Barents Sea, **USSR;** frozen for 6 months of year; connected to Baltic Sea by deep-water canal; impt. fisheries.

Whitley Bay, t., North Tyneside, Northumberland, **Eng.;** 5 km N. of Tynemouth; seaside resort; plastics; p. (1981) 37,079.

Whitstable, spt., Kent, **Eng.;** on Thames estuary 10 km N. of Canterbury; holiday resort, oysters; p. (1981) 27,896.

Whittlesey, t., Fenland, Cambs., **Eng.;** in the Fens, 13 km W. of March; bricks, mkt. gardening; p. (1981) 11,812.

Whyalla, t., spt., S. **Australia;** t. on N.W. shore of Spencer Gulf developed by Broken Hill Co. in 1901 as terminal for Iron Knob iron exp.; major iron and steel wks.; shipbldg. now in difficulties; p. (1976) 33,426.

Wichita, c., Kan., **USA;** in Arkansas valley; rly. wks., oil refineries and equipment, meatpacking ctr. in agr. and stock-raising region; univ.; p. (1980) 279,000 (c.), 411,000 (met. a.).

Wichita Falls, c., Texas, **USA;** oil refining, ctr. in agr. and ranching a.; p. (1980) 94,201 (c.) 130,664 (met. a.).

Wick, spt., sm. burgh, Caithness, **Scot.;** on E. cst., 22 km S. of John O'Groats; airport to Orkneys and Shetlands; herring fishing ctr.; p. (1981) 7,933.

Wicklow, coastal co., Leinster, **R.o.I.;** crossed by Wicklow mtns.; pastoral agr. and tourism; cap. Wicklow; a. 2,033 km²; p. (1981) 45,843.

Wicklow, t., cap. of Wicklow, Leinster, **R.o.I.;** on S.E. cst., 56 km S. of Dublin; mkt.; sm. seaside resort; p. (1966) 3,340.

Wicklow, mtns., Wicklow, **R.o.I.;** highest summit Lugnaquillia, 927 m.

Widecombe, v., Devon, **Eng.;** Dartmoor tourist ctr.; famous through ballad "Widecombe Fair."

Widnes, t., Halton, Cheshire, **Eng.;** on R. Mersey 19 km E. of Liverpool; impt. chemical inds.; expanded t.; p. (1981) 54,411.

Wiener Neustadt, t., Lower **Austria;** rly. and industl. ctr.; heavy machin.; founded 1192; anc. bldgs., cas., cath.; education ctr.; p. (1961) 38,845.

Wieringermeer Polder, reclaimed a., N. Holland, **Neth.;** N.W. of IJsselmeer; a. 202 km².

Wiesbaden, c., cap. of Hesse, **W. Germany;** on Rhine, at S. foot of the Taunus; famous spa.; cas.; ctr. for Rhine wines; chemicals, metal gds.; p. (1983) 272,600.

Wigan, t., met. dist., Gtr. Manchester, **Eng.;** 26 km. N.E. of Liverpool; engin., chemicals, cement, food processing; paper; former coal-mng. ctr.; p. (1981) 308,927.

Wight, I. of, non-met. co., **Eng.;** English Channel,

separated from Hampshire by Spithead and the Solent; crossed by chalk hills, terminating in the Needles; popular holiday resort; ch. ts.; Newport, Ryde, Cowes; a. 381 km²; p. (1981) 118,192.

Wigston, t., Leics., **Eng.**; 6 km S. of Leicester; engin., hosiery; p. (1981) 31,900. *See* **Oadby**.

Wigtown, l. gov. dist., former co., Dumfries and Galloway Reg., **Scot.**; along N. cst. of Solway F.; impt. dairying reg.; a. 1,712 km²; p. (1981) 30,109.

Wigtown, sm. burgh, Wigtown, **Scot.**; on W. Bay, Solway F.; shares admin. with Newton Stewart; p. (1981) 1,015.

Wilhelmshaven, c., Lower Saxony, **W. Germany**; on inlent of N. Sea, 64 km N.W. of Bremen; ch. German naval base until 1945; industl. ctr. with heavy machin., elec. equipment, textiles, furniture; oil pipeline; p. (1983) 99,100.

Wilkes-Barre, c., Penns., **USA**; on Susquehanna R.; industl. ctr. in rich anthracite mng. a.; p. (1980) 51,551.

Wilkes Land, Antarctica; featureless plateau, alt. 2,900 m; immense glaciers; U.S. base taken over by Australia 1959.

Willamette, R., Ore., **USA**; rises in Cascade mtns., flows N. into Columbia R. below Portland; valley gives rich agr. land, wheat, root-crops, dairy prod., hard and soft fruits; ch. ts. Eugene, Salem, Oregon City, Portland; used for hydroelectric power; 480 km long.

Willemstad, pt., cap. of **Neth. Antilles**; on Curaçao I.; oil refining; tourism; p. (1964) 59,586.

Willenhall, t., West Midlands, **Eng.**; locks and keys, drop forgings.

Willesden, former M.B., Middx., **Eng.**; now inc. in Brent under boro; Greater London impt. rly. junc., residtl. and industl.

Williamsburg, c., Va., **USA**; between James and York Rs.; historic t., settled 1632; rebuilt in 1920s to original plan; in Colonial Nat. Historical Park; p. (1980) 9,870.

Williamsport, t., Penns., **USA**; on Susquehanna R.; rly. ctr., timber, machin.; summer resort; p. (1980) 33,401 (t.), 118,416 (met. a.).

Willow South, was to be new cap. (1977), Alaska, **USA**; replacing Juneau; closer to ctr. of p.; lack of finance halted construction.

Wilmington, t., spt., Del., **USA**; on Delaware R.; shipbldg., machin., iron and steel wks.; chemicals; leather, cork, rubber gds.; p. (1980) 523,000 (met. a.).

Wilmington, spt., N.C., **USA**; exp. cotton, tobacco, timber, fertilizers, shipbldg., textiles, chemicals; p. (1980) 44,000 (t.), 139,238 (met. a.).

Wilmslow, t., Cheshire, **Eng.**; on R. Bollen, 10 km S.W. of Stockport; residtl.; pharmaceuticals; p. (1981) 30,207.

Wilton, t., Wilts., **Eng.**; on R. Wylye, 5 km W. of Salisbury; agr. mkt., carpets, felt; anc. cap. of Wessex; many old bldgs.; p. (1981) 4,005.

Wilton, industl. estate, Cleveland, **Eng.**; on S. side of Tees estuary; heavy organic- and petro-chemicals; nylon polymer plant.

Wiltshire, non-met. co., **Eng.**; crossed by chalk downland and Salisbury Plain; barley, wheat, dairying, pigs; co. t. Salisbury; a. 3,484 km²; p. (1981) 518,167.

Wiltshire, North, l. gov. dist., Wilts., **Eng.**; rural a. inc. ts. of Calne, Chippenham and Malmesbury; p. (1981) 102,492.

Wimbledon, dist., London, **Eng.**; lge. open common; site of international tennis tournament; part of London Bor. of Merton.

Wimborne, v., dist., Dorset, **Eng.**; rural a. based on W. Minster; p. (1981) 68,151.

Wimborne Minster, mkt. t., Dorset, **Eng.**; on R. Stour; Roman site and home of Saxon kings; Badbury Rings earthworks nearby; p. (1981) 5,531.

Winchcomb, t., Gloucs., **Eng.**; nr. Cheltenham old mills; pottery, paper; nearby cas.

Winchelsea, anc. t., East Sussex, **Eng.**; 3 km S.W. of Rye; once impt. walled spt. and Cinque port, now 3 km inland.

Winchester, cath. c., l. gov. dist., Hants., **Eng.**; on R. Itchen, 19 km N. of Southampton; anc. Anglo-Saxon cap.; meeting place of parliaments until time of Henry VII; magnificent cath., famous public school; p. (1981) 88,385.

Windermere, lgst. English L., in Cumbria; outlet to Morecambe Bay; supplies water to Manchester; 16 km long, 1·6 km wide.

Windhoek, t., cap. of **Namibia**; in hills at 1,700 m;

comm. ctr., agr. processing; tr. in karakul (Persian lamb); p. (est. 1983) 104,100.

Windrush, R., Oxford, Gloucs., **Eng.**; trib. of R. Thames.

Windscale. *See* **Sellafield**.

Windsor, c., pt., Ont., **Canada**; on Detroit R., linked to Detroit, USA, by tunnel, bridge and ferry; ctr. for car mftg., salt wks., chemicals, paints; univ.; p. (1979) 196,525.

Windsor, New, t., Berks., **Eng.**; on R. Thames, 32 km W. of London; famous royal cas. (founded by William the Conqueror) and park, St. George's Chapel and the Royal Mausoleum; with Maidenhead forms l. gov. dist.; p. (1981) 130,054.

Windward Is., W.I., extend S. from Leeward Is.; consist of Fr. Martinique and former Brit. cols. of Grenada, St. Vincent, St. Lucia and Dominica with their dependencies (the Grenadines divided between Grenada and St. Vincent) which attained associated statehood 1967; sm. limited resources, economically depressed; volcanic; p. (est. 1984) 419,000.

Windward Passage, channel, 96 km wide, between Cuba and Haiti.

Winnebago, L., Wis., **USA**; 43 km long; lgst. L. in Wis.

Winnipeg, c., cap. of Manitoba, **Canada**; at junc. of Red and Assiniboine Rs.; cath., univ.; rly. ctr.; ch. world wheat mkt.; meat packing and food processing; lgst. garment mnf. ctr. in cty.; oil refining; p. (1979) 560,875 (c.), 590,300 (met. a.).

Winnipeg, L., Manitoba, **Canada**; 64 km N. of Winnipeg; 416 km long, 49–96 km wide; contains several lge. Is. (Reindeer, 181 km²; Big I., 155 km²); used for hydroelectric power.

Winnipegosis, L., Manitoba and Saskatchewan, **Canada**; a. (exclusive of Is.) 5,180 km²; 80 km W. of L. Winnipeg, into which it drains.

Winsford, t., Cheshire, **Eng.**; on R. Weaver; 6 km S. of Northwich; ctr. of salt inds., chemicals; expanded t.; computer peripherals; p. (1981) 26,915.

Winston-Salem, t., N.C., **USA**; formed 1913 from union of 2 adjacent ts.; tobacco ctr.; p. (1980) 132,000.

Winterthur, t., Zurich, **Switzerland**; on Eulach R.; rly. ctr., locomotives, machines, cottons; p. (1979) 86,700.

Wirksworth, t., West Derbys., **Eng.**; in Pennines, 8 km S. of Matlock; limestone, fluorspar wks.; ctr. of Derbys. former lead mng.; p. (1981) 5,492.

Wirral, penin., met. dist., Merseyside, **Eng.**; between estuaries of Dee and Mersey; residtl.; comprises Wallasey, Birkenhead, Bebington and Hoylake; p. (1981) 339,488.

Wisbech, t., Fenland, Cambs., **Eng.**; on R. Nene, 18 km from its mouth in the Wash; mkt. gardening, fruit growing and canning, agr. implements; p. (1981) 17,332.

Wisconsin, st., **USA**; 'Badger St.'; admitted to Union 1848; st. flower Wood Violet, st. bird Robin; bounded by Gr. Ls.; lowlying; leading dairying st.; industl. ts. around Gt. Ls.; cap. Madison; ch. t. Milwaukee; a. 145,439 km²; p. (1980) 4,706,000.

Wisconsin, R., Wis., **USA**; trib. of R. Mississippi; used for hydroelectric power; 960 km long.

Wismar, spt., Rostock, **E. Germany**; on Baltic Sea, N. of Schwerin; oil pt. and industl. ctr. with shipyards and food processing inds.; p. (est. 1970) 56,057.

Witbank, t., Transvaal, **S. Africa**; leading coal-mng. dist. with power sta. and carbide and cyanide factories; p. (1970) 50,581.

Witham, t., Essex, **Eng.**; 14 km N.E. of Chelmsford; ctr. of mkt. gardening a.; expanded t.; p. (1981) 25,373.

Witham, R., Leics. and Lincs., **Eng.**; flows into the Wash; cuts impressive gap through Lincoln.

Witney, t., Oxford, Gloucs., **Eng.**; on R. Windrush, 16 km W. of Oxford; woollens, blankets, gloves; p. (1981) 14,109.

Witten, t., N. Rhine–Westphalia, **W. Germany**; on R. Ruhr; glass, machin., metals, chemicals, optical inds.; p. (1983) 104,200.

Wittenberg, t., Halle, **E. Germany**; on R. Elbe; ctr. of Reformation and burial place of Luther (Schlosskirche); cas.; machin., textiles; p. (est. 1970) 47,151.

Wittenberge, t., Schwerin, **E. Germany**; on R. Elbe; rly. junc., repair wkshps., machin.; p. (est. 1970) 33,028.

Witwatersrand, dist., Transvaal, **S. Africa**; gold-mng. dist. producing over quarter of world's gold.

Wivenhoe, t., Essex, **Eng.**; on R. Colne; boat-bldg., oysters, lt. inds.; p. (1981) 6,470.

Włocławek, t., river pt., N. **Poland**; on R. Vistula; impt. paper mnfs., ceramics; p. (est. 1983) 113,400.

Woburn, t., Beds., **Eng.**; 8 km N.E. of Leighton Buzzard; Woburn Abbey (seat of Dukes of Bedford).

Woking, t., l. gov. dist., Surrey, **Eng.**; 6 km N. of Guildford; residtl.; p. (1981) 81,358.

Wokingham, mkt. t., l. gov. dist., Berks., **Eng.**; 8 km S.E. of Reading; agr. tr. and machin., bricks; p. (1981) 113,938.

Wolds, The, chalk downland, Lincs., Humberside, **Eng.**; extend S. to E. Anglian Heights; traditional pastoral agr. changing to extensive arable farming; 72 km long.

Wolfenbüttel, t., Lower Saxony, **W. Germany**; on R. Oker, 11 km S. of Brunswick; noted for ducal library, founded 17th cent., of which Leibnitz and Lessing were librarians; p. (1983) 49,600.

Wolf Rock, isolated rock with lighthouse, at approach to English Channel from Bay of Biscay; 14 km S.W. of Lands End, Cornwall.

Wolfsburg, t., Lower Saxony, **W. Germany**; on R. Aller, N.E. of Brunswick; Volkswagen wks.; p. (1983) 124,000.

Wolin, I., Baltic Sea; off mouth of R. Oder, **Poland**; Nat. Park; fishing, tourism; a. 344 km²; p. (est. 1966) 2,867.

Wollongong Greater, t., N.S.W., **Australia**; 7th c. of A.; heavy inds. attracted by local coal especially at Pt. Kembla; iron, steel, chems.; Australia's only tinplate plant; p. (1976) 197,127.

Wolsingham, t., Durham, **Eng.**; on R. Wear; impt. steel wks.

Wolverhampton, t., met. dist., West Midlands, **Eng.**; heavy and lt. engin., boilers, rayon, elec. engin. and apparatus, iron wks., aircraft and motor components, hollow-ware, tools, strongrooms and safes, paints; p. (1981) 252,447.

Wolverton, t., Bucks., **Eng.**; on R. Ouse, 24 km S.W. of Bedford; rly.-carriage wks.; p. (1981) 22,249.

Wombwell, t., South Yorks., **Eng.**; at E. foot of Pennines, 11 km N. of Sheffield; coal mng., bricks; p. (1981) 16,628.

Wonsan, spt., **N. Korea**; on Sea of Japan; major pt. and rly. ctr.; Japanese naval base in second world war; oil refining; p. (est. 1967) 300,000.

Woodbridge, t., Suffolk Coastal, Suffolk, **Eng.**; on R. Deben; engin., brush mkg.; p. (1981) 7,224.

Wood Green, former M.B., Middx., **Eng.**; now inc. in Haringey outer bor., Greater London.

Woodhall Spa, t., East Lindsey, Lincs., **Eng.**; 6 km S.W. of Horncastle; former spa, bromo-iodine springs; resort; p. (1981) 2,445.

Woodspring, l. gov. dist., Avon, **Eng.**; S. of Bristol and inc. Clevedon, Portishead, and Weston-super-Mare; p. (1981) 162,295.

Woodstock, t., Ont., **Canada**; on R. Thames; ctr. of agr. dist.; lt. mnfs. based on hydroelectric power; p. (1971) 25,559.

Woodstock, t., Oxford, **Eng.**; on Glyme R., 11 km N.W. of Oxford; glove mnfs.; Blenheim Palace; p. (1981) 2,036.

Wookey Hole, cave, Mendip Hills, Somerset, **Eng.**; at foot of limestone hills, 3 km N.W. of Wells; R. Axe emerges from the cave.

Woolwich, dist. former met. bor., London, **Eng.**; on either side of R. Thames; impt. Tudor dockyard, now closed; now part of Greenwich and Newham bors.

Woomera, S. **Australia**; c., 432 km N.W. of Adelaide; base for joint U.K.–Australian guided-weapon testing range extending N.W. across the continent; established 1947.

Woonsocket, t., R.I., **USA**; on Blackstone R.; textiles, rubber gds.; p. (1980) 45,914.

Worcester, l. gov. dist., Hereford and Worcs., **Eng.**; on R. Severn, 38 km N. of Gloucester; cath.; machin., porcelain, glove mkg.; birthplace of Elgar; p. (1981) 74,790.

Worcester, t., Cape Prov., S. **Africa**; viticultural and industl. ctr.; Goudini spa nearby; p. (1980) 162,000 (c.), 373,000 (met. a.).

Worcester, t., Mass., **USA**; univ.; cultural ctr.; machine tools, elec. engin.; p. (1980) 162,000 (c), 373,000 (met. a.).

Worcestershire, former Midland co., **Eng.**; now part of Hereford and Worcs. non-met. co. and West Midlands met. co.

Workington, t., Allerdale, Cumbria, **Eng.**; sm. spt. on Solway F. at mouth of Derwent R., first Bessemer steel plant, heavily dependent upon iron and steel wks. closed (1981), engin.; industl. diversification on nearby industl. estates, inc. bus wks.; p. (1981) 27,581.

Worksop, t., Bassetlaw, Notts., **Eng.**; 24 km S.E. of Sheffield; coal-mng. dist.; brewing, knitwear, glass, flour; p. (1981) 36,893.

Worms, t., Rhineland-Palatinate, **W. Germany**; on left bank of Rhine; historic ctr.; famous imperial diet 1521 when Luther refused to retract; scene of *Nibelungenlied*; ctr. for Liebfraumilch wines; chemical, textile, leather and metal inds.; p. (1983) 73,000.

Worms Head, promontory, on West Glamorgan cst., Gower peninsula, **Wales.**

Worsley, t., Gtr. Manchester, **Eng.**; ctr. of coal-mng. dist.; p. (1981) 49,021.

Worthing, t., l. gov. dist., West Sussex, **Eng.**; on S. cst., 16 km W. of Brighton; holiday resort, retirement ctr. in mkt. gardening dist.; p. (1981) 91,668.

Woy Woy, t., N.S.W., **Australia**; resort and commuter t. for Sydney; clothing; p. inc. in Gosford.

Wrangel I., Arctic Oc., off Khabarovsk terr., **RSFSR**; weather sta.

Wrath, C., N.W. Sutherland, **Scot.**

Wrekin, hill, Shrops., **Eng.**; alt. 403 m.

Wrekin, The, l. gov. dist., Shrops., **Eng.**; inc. Newport, Wellington, Oakengates and Dawley; p. (1981) 123,525.

Wrexham, t., Clwyd, **Wales**; 18 km S.W. Chester; tyres, synthetic fibres, clothing; as **Wrexham Maelor** forms l. gov. dist.; p. (1981) 111,724.

Wrocław (Breslau), c., Silesia, **Poland**; on R. Oder; impt. route ctr. and R. pt.; univ., cath.; rapid industl. development; ctr. of electronics inds.; p. (est. 1983) 631,300.

Wrocław (Breslau), prov., Lower Silesia, **Poland**; until 1945 part of Germany; heavy inds. based on local minerals; cap. Wrocław; a. 24,740 km²; p. (est. 1983) 1,101,000.

Wroxeter, v., Shrops., **Eng.**; on R. Severn, 8 km S.E. Shrewsbury; Roman sta. Uriconium.

Wuchow. See **Wuzhou.**

Wuhan, c., Hubei prov., **China**; formed by union of Hankan, Hanyang and Zhifang; major metropolis on Chang Jiang; integrated iron and steel wks., machine tools, walking tractors, textiles, shipbldg.; univ.; p. (est. 1970) 4,250,000.

Wuhu, c., Anhui prov., **China**; former treaty pt. on Chang Jiang; textiles; p. (est. 1970) 300,000.

Wupper, R., **W. Germany**; trib. of Rhine; industl. concentration along middle course; 64 km long.

Wuppertal, t., N. Rhine–Westphalia, **W. Germany**; formed by amalgamation of Barmen and Elberfeld; textiles, rubber gds., paper, metals, pharmaceuticals; p. (1983) 386,000.

Württemberg-Hohenzollern, former st., **W. Germany**; since 1952 part of Baden–Württemberg.

Würzburg, c., Bavaria, **W. Germany**; on R. Main; univ., cath.; historic bldgs., engin., chemicals, printing; p. (1983) 129,500.

Wurzen, t., Leipzig, **E. Germany**; on R. Mulde; cath., cas.; machin., furniture, leather, foodstuffs; p. (est. 1970) 24,164.

Wuxi (Wusih), c., Jiangsu prov., **China**; on N. shore of Tai L., 120 km W. of Shanghai; univ.; industl. ctr. with cotton mills, chemical wks.; former treaty pt.; p. (est. 1970) 900,000.

Wutongqiao (Wutungkiao), c., Sichuan prov., **China**; S. of Chengdu; p. (1953) 199,000.

Wuzhou (Wuchow), c., R. pt., Guangxi, **China**; on Xijiang; tr. ctr.; exp. tung oil, hides; p. (est. 1970) 150,000.

Wyandotte, t., Mich., **USA**; on Detroit R.; salt deposits; chemical ind.; p. (1980) 34,006.

Wychavon, l. gov. dist., Hereford and Worcs., **Eng.**; inc. Vale of Evesham and Pershore in S. and Droitwich in N.; p. (1981) 95,123.

Wycombe, l. gov. dist., Bucks., **Eng.**; close to Oxon. and inc. High Wycombe and Marlow; p. (1981) 155,591.

Wye, R., Bucks., **Eng.**; rises in Chiltern hills, flows S.E. to R. Thames at Cookham.

Wye, R., **Eng.** and **Wales**; rises in Plynlimmon, flows S.E. into R. Severn at Chepstow; forms deeply incised valley at Symond's Yat; 208 km long.

Wye, t., Kent, **Eng.**; nr. Ashford; impt. agr. college (Univ. of London).

Wylfa Head, Anglesey, Gwynedd, N. **Wales**; nuclear power sta.

Wymondham, t., South Norfolk, **Eng.**; 14 km S.W. of Norwich; mkt.; Benedictine abbey founded 1107; p. (1981) 9,811.

Wyoming, st., **USA**; 'Equality St.'; admitted to Union 1890; st. flower Indian Paintbrush, st. bird Meadowlark; inc. areas of Rocky mtns. and great plains; Yellowstone Nat. Park; scant rainfall; irrigation; cattle and sheep ranching; petroleum; sparse p.; cap. Cheyenne; a. 253,597 km²; p. (1980) 471,000.

Wyre, R., Lancs., **Eng.**; rises in Pennines, flows W. into Lancaster Bay at Fleetwood; 45 km.

Wyre, l. gov. dist., Lancs., **Eng.**; inc. Preesall, Fleetwood and Thornton Cleveleys; p. (1981) 97,721.

Wyre Forest, l. gov. dist., Hereford and Worcester, **Eng.**; inc. Bewdley, Kidderminster and Stourport; p. (1981) 91,474.

X

Xanthi, t., Thrace, **Greece**; on R. Mesta; ctr. of tobacco-growing a.; p. (1981) 88,777.

Xanthus, ruined c., **Turkey**; on R. Xanthus; destroyed 43 B.C.; tourism.

Xauen, t., **Morocco**, N. Africa; holy t. founded 15th cent.; p. (1960) 13,712.

Xiamen (Amoy), c., Fujian, **China**; rail link to Jianxi; tea, fruit, bricks; univ.; formerly treaty pt.; in special Economic Zone to encourage foreign investment; new pt. (1982); 100 factories planned; p. (est. 1970) 400,000.

Xi'an (Sian), cap. of Shaanxi prov., **China**; impt. route and industl. ctr.; food processing and tr.; flour, grain, tea, tobacco, iron and steel, textiles, chemicals; p. (est. 1957) 1,310,000.

Xiangtan (Siangtan), c., Hunan prov., **China**; on navigable Xijiang; regional tr. ctr., tea, cotton, electrical goods, machin., textiles; Mao Tse Tung born nearby; p. (est. 1970) 300,000.

Xi Jiang (Si Kiang), ch. R., S. **China**; headstreams rise in Yunnan plateau, R. then flows E. enters S. China Sea through lge delta nr. Hong Kong; lower valley intensively cultivated, rice, sugar cane, tea; tropical climate permits continuous cultivation of most crops through year; valley densely populated; c. 2,000 km. long.

Xingu, R., Brazil; trib. of Amazon; navigable in its lower course; Nat. Park and Indian reserve threatened by new cattle ranches; 1,920 km long.

Xinhailion. See Lianyungang.

Xining (Sining), cap. of Xining prov., **China**; ctr. of spring wheat a.; woollen mills, iron and steel; new rly. completed to help reduce isolation; p. (est. 1970) 250,000.

Xinjiang Uygur (Sinkiang-Uighur), aut. region, N. W. **China**; borders USSR and Kashmir; very dry climate; remote until new roads and rlys. penetrated a.; ethnic minority p. of Turkish background and Islamic faith; many attempts to develop natural resources and industry by Chinese government; pastoral agr.; sheep, goats; new st. arable farms, wheat, maize, millet; lge. oil reserves; cap. Ürümqi; a. 1,646,800 km²; p. (est. 1968) 8,000,000.

Xinyang (Sinyang), t., S. Henan, **China**; regional ctr. for S. Henan and Hubei; p. c. 75,000.

Xizang Zizhiou. See Tibet.

Xuanhua (Suanhwa), c., Hebei prov., **China**; iron mng.; p. (1953) 114,000.

Y

Yablonovy, mtn. range, Siberia, **RSFSR**; E. of L. Baykal; highest peak, Sokhondo, 2,510 m; crossed by Trans-Siberian rly.

Yaila Mtns., Ukrainian SSR, **USSR**; form S.E. margin of Crimea penin., extend from Sevastopol to

Kerch; form marked climate barrier between Black Sea littoral (Soviet Riviera) and N. part.

Yakima, t., Wash., **USA**; agr. ctr. of irrigated valley, noted for fruit; p. (1980) 49,826 (t.), 172,508 (met. a.).

Yakima, R., Wash., **USA**; trib. of Columbia R.; used for irrigation; 333 km long.

Yakut ASSR, aut. rep., **RSFSR**; borders Arctic Oc.; home of Yakuts; tundra and forest region, isolated; fur trapping, diamond and gold mng., state farms; a. 3,963,355 km²; p. (1970) 664,000.

Yakutsk, t., cap. of Yakut ASSR, **RSFSR**; pt. on Lena R.; univ.; airport; p. (1980) 155,000.

Yallahs Valley, Jamaica; severe soil erosion; govt. improvement scheme of afforestation and new crops; a. 181 km².

Yallourn, t., Victoria, **Australia**; ctr. of lignite mng. a.; Moe serves as residtl. ctr.; p. (1976) 18,710 (inc. Moe).

Yalta, spt., Ukrainian SSR, **USSR**; sub-tropical resort on Black Sea, sheltered by Yaila mtns.; conference between Churchill, Roosevelt, and Stalin 1945; p. (est. 1969) 57,000.

Yalu, R., forms bdy. between N.E. **China**, and N. **Korea**; flows into Yellow Sea; used for hydroelectric power.

Yamagata, t., Honshu, **Japan**; ctr. of rice-growing a.; cas.; p. (1979) 231,848.

Yamaguchi, t., cap. of Y. prov., S.W. Honshu, **Japan**; cas.; comm. ctr., chemicals; p. (1979) 110,134.

Yamal-Nenets National Okrug, RSFSR; inc. Yamal penin.; permafrost; hunting, fishing; cap. Salekhard; lge. natural gas finds; a. 670,810 km²; p. (1970) 80,000.

Yambol, t., **Bulgaria**; on R. Tunja; ruined mosque; agr. ctr.; recent inds. inc. canning, farm machin., textiles, ceramics; p. (est. 1968) 67,941.

Yamethin, dist., Upper **Burma**; teak forests, rice; ch. t. Yamethin; site of irrigation project; p. 9,291.

Yamoussoukra, t., **Ivory Coast**; new cap. replaced Abidjan (1983) to relieve congestion; p. (1983) 70,000.

Yana, R., Siberia, **USSR**; flows into Arctic Sea; navigable; 1,600 km long.

Yangchow. See Yangzhou.

Yangchuan. See Yanqan.

Yangi-yer, t., Uzbek SSR, **USSR**; founded 1957 as ctr. for new irrigated cotton lands of E. Uzbekistan.

Yangtze River. See Chang Jiang.

Yangzhou (Changshu), c., Jiangsu, **China**; in valley of Chang Jiang, N.E. of Shanghai; mkt. for local agr. prods.; p. (est. 1970) 150,000.

Yanqan (Yangchuan), c., Shaanxi prov., **China**; iron working ctr.; p. (1953) 177,000.

Yaoundé, t., cap. of **Cameroon Rep.**, W. **Africa**; lt. inds. inc. beer, cigarettes, textiles; p. (est. 1984) 650,000.

Yapura, R., **Brazil** and **Colombia**, S. **America**; trib. of R. Amazon; length 2,400 km.

Yaracuy, st., **Venezuela**; crossed by Y. valley impt. agr. a. for bananas, coffee, sugar, tobacco; crossed by Pan-American Highway; cap. San Felipe; a. 7,099 km²; p. (est. 1970) 222,241.

Yare, R., Norfolk, **Eng.**; flows E. to N. Sea at Gorleston; forms part of Norfolk Broads navigable waterways; 80 km long.

Yarkand. See Shache.

Yarmouth, spt., Nova Scotia, **Canada**; fisheries; p. (1971) 8,291.

Yarmouth, Great, pt., l. gov. dist., Norfolk, **Eng.**; at mouth of R. Yare; holiday resort; fish and food processing plants; base for N. Sea gas; p. (1981) 80,820 (dist.).

Yaroslavl, c., cap. of Y. oblast, **RSFSR**; on upper Volga in Moscow industl. region; founded 1010; comm. and industl. ctr.; mnfs. inc. textiles, motor vehicles, synthetic rubber, agr. machin.; Volkov theatre, 12th cent. monastery, churches; p. (1980) 603,000.

Yasan, N., **Bulgaria**; lge. refinery and petrochemicals complex.

Yatsushiro, t., Kyushu, **Japan**; p. (1979) 109,251.

Yazd, c., Isfahan prov., **Iran**; in desert a. at 1,190 m; fine silks, carpets; p. (1976) 135,876.

Yazoo, dist., Miss., **USA**; flood plain of R. Mississippi and R. Yazoo; very fertile alluvial soil, but subject to disastrous floods; one of ch. cotton-growing dists. in USA.

Yegoryevsk, t., **RSFSR**; 115 km S.E. of Moscow; lge textile ind.; phosphorite deposits; p. (est. 1969) 65,000.

Yeletz, t., **RSFSR**; on R. Sosna; grain and cattle tr.; cultural ctr.; rly. junc.; p. (1970) 101,000.

Yell, I., Shetlands, **Scot.**; 27 km long; covered in peat moorland; p. (1971) 1,143.

Yellowhead Pass, B.C., Alberta, **Canada**; most N. and lowest of main passes across Rocky mtns.; carries Canadian Nat. rly. on route from Edmonton to Vancouver and Prince Rupert; summit alt. 1,130 m.

Yellowknife, t., N.W. Terr., **Canada**; on N. shore of Gr. Slave L.; ctr. of impt. gold-mng. dist.; linked by air to Edmonton, Alberta; p. (1966) 3,741.

Yellow R. *See* Huang He.

Yellow Sea. *See* Huang Hai.

Yellowstone, L., Wyo., **USA**; 32 km long, 24 km wide; alt. 2,360 m; in Y. Nat. Park.

Yellowstone National Park, N.W. Wyo., **USA**; volcanic scenery, geysers; a. 8,956 km².

Yemen Arab Republic (N. Yemen), S.W. Arabian penin.; climate hot and humid in semi-desert cst. strip; summer rainfall inland on high plateau; land slopes down in E. to desert of Rub'al Khali; agr. basis of economy; irrigated terraced, fertile land in highlands; millet, maize, sorghum, oats, fruits; Mocha coffee main exp.; expanding cotton a. in Tihama cst. a.; first oil fields discovered (1984); severe earthquake (1982); ch. spt. Hodeida; cap. Sana'a; strained relations with S. Yemen; a. 194,250 km²; p. (est. 1984) 6,386,000.

Yemen, People's Democratic Rep. of (S. Yemen), S.W. **Arabia**; comprises strategic pt. of Aden and much desert terr.; independence proclaimed 1967 when Brit. troops withdrawn; hot, dry climate; Brit. withdrawal, decline of tourism and closure of Suez Canal resulted in economic decline; subsistence agr., little comm. exploitation of rich fishing grounds; oil refinery at Aden; cap. Madinat ash Sha'b (N.W. of Aden); strained relations with N. Yemen; a. 290,274 km²; p. (est. 1984) 2,066,000.

Yenangyaung, t., R. pt., **Burma**; on left bank of R. Irrawaddy, 448 km N. of Rangoon; ctr. of Burma oilfields.

Yenisey, R., Siberia, **RSFSR**; rises in Sayan mtns., flows N. into Arctic Oc.; ch. tribs., Angara, Stony Tunguska, Lower Tunguska; hydroelectric power sta. at Krasnoyarsk; linked to Ob R. by canal; middle course navigable; 5,280 km long.

Yentai (Chefoo) c., N. Shandong prov. **China**; pt. on G. of Bo Hai; former treaty pt.; noted for its pongee silk ("Shantung"); p. (est. 1970) 180,000.

Yeo or **Ivel,** R., Dorset, Somerset, **Eng.**; trib. of R. Parrett; 38 km long.

Yeovil, mkt. t., l. gov. dist., Somerset, **Eng.**; on R. Yeo; glove mnf., aero-engin., agr. machin., dairy processing; p. (1981) 130,583 (dist.).

Yerevan or **Erivan,** c., cap. of Armenian SSR, **USSR**; on Zanga R. in deep valley of Caucasus mtns.; founded 8th cent. B.C.; major science-based, industl. ctr.; p. (est. 1980) 1,036,000.

Yes Tor, second highest summit, Dartmoor, Devon, **Eng.**; 618 m.

Yevpatoriya or **Eupatoria,** spt., Crimea, on Black Sea, **USSR**; popular resort; children's sanatoria; chemicals, leather, locks, dried fish; new pt. being built; p. (est. 1969) 75,000.

Yezd. *See* Yazd.

Yibin (Ipin), c., Sichuan prov., **China**, at junction of Chang Jiang and Min Jiang; p. (est. 1970) 275,000.

Yichang (Ichang), c., S.W. Hubei, **China**; on Chang Jiang; site of famous gorges; terminus of lge. vessels from Shanghai.

Yiewsley and West Drayton, former U.D., Middx., **Eng.**; now inc. in Hillingdon outer bor. Greater London; varied lt. inds.

Yingchuan, t., cap. of Ninxia, aut. region, **China**; on Huang He; ctr. of fertile agr. a.; new lt. inds.; p. (est. 1958) 91,000.

Yingkou (Yingkow), c., Liaoning prov., N.E. **China**; 32 km upstream from mouth of Liao R.; soyabean prods.; p. (est. 1970) 215,000.

Yining (Kuldja), c., Xinjiang prov., **China**; on highway to Turkestan; coalfield; recent industl. development inc. iron and steel; p. (est. 1970) 160,000.

Ynys Môn. *See* Anglesey.

Yokkaichi, c., spt., S. Honshu, **Japan**; on Ise Bay, 37 km S. of Nagoya; textiles, petrochemicals, synthetic rubber, porcelain; p. (1979) 252,601.

Yokohama, leading spt., Honshu, **Japan**; on W. shore of Tokyo Bay; steel, chemicals, cars, oil refining, shipyards; univs.; with Tokyo and Kawasaki forms conurb. of Keihin; p. (1979) 2,763,270.

Yokosuka, spt., Honshu, **Japan**; S. of Tokyo; holiday resort; thermal power sta.; p. (est. 1979) 419,779.

Yonkers, c., N.Y., **USA**; on E. bank of Hudson R.; residtl.; lt. inds., textiles; p. (1980) 195,000; part of N.Y. met. a.

Yonne, dep., **France**; in S.E. of Paris basin, inc. Champagne, Burgundy, Orléanais; drained by R. Yonne; cap. Auxerre; agr.; Chablis wines; a. 7,495 km²; p. (1982) 309,500.

Yonne, R., **France**; major trib. of R. Seine; 288 km long.

York, c., co. t., l. gov. dist., North Yorks., **Eng.**; on R. Ouse; in central position in Vale of York; anc. part of c. enclosed by walls; minster, cas., univ.; chocolate, confectionery, rly. wkshps.; p. (1981) 99,787.

York, c., Penn., **USA**; ctr. of fertile agr. region; varied inds., inc. agr. tools, machin., textiles, metal gds.; p. (1980) 381,000 (met. a.).

York, C., Queensland, **Australia**; most N. point on mainland of Australia.

York, Vale of, broad lowland, North Yorks., **Eng.**; between Pennines and N. Yorks. Moors and Yorks. Wolds; drained to Humber by R. Ouse and tribs.; glacial and alluvial soils have required draining; crop farming, wheat, barley, root-crops, associated with fattening of beef cattle; settlement mainly marginal; ch. t. York; length 96 km, width from 16 km in N. to 48 km in S.

Yorke, penin., S. **Australia**; separates Spencer G. and G. of St. Vincent; 160 km long, 48 km wide.

Yorkshire, former co., **Eng.**; formerly divided into 3 separate admin. parts (Ridings) N., E., and W.; now split into 3 non-met. cos., Cleveland, North Yorks., and Humberside and 2 met. cos. West Yorks. and South Yorks.

Yorkshire Moors, hills, North Yorks. and Cleveland, **Eng.**; inc. N. Yorks. Moors, Cleveland hills and Hambleton hills; bounded to N. by Tees valley, S. by vale of Pickering, W. by Swale valley, E. by sea; composed of oolitic limestone; gd. sheep pastures; impt. iron-ore deposits worked in Cleveland hills; max. alt. 454 m.

Yorkshire Wolds, hills, Humberside, **Eng.**; extend N.E. from Humber and terminate in Flamborough Head; chalk; gd. sheep pasture; average alt. 180 m.

Yorktown, v., Va., **USA**; scene of surrender by Lord Cornwallis to Washington 1781.

Yosemite National Park, Cal., **USA**; in Sierra Nevada; contains Yossmite creek and canyon with three famous cataracts.

Yoshkar-Ola, t., Mari ASSR, **RSFSR**; 128 km N.W. of Kazan; cultural ctr.; wood processing, food inds.; p. (1980) 207,000.

Youghal, spt., U.D., Cork, **R.o.I.**; on estuary of the Blackwater; resort; p. (1981) 5,870.

Youngstown, c., Ohio, **USA**; on Mahoning R.; 91 km N.W. of Pittsburgh; ctr. of one of most impt. iron and steel dists. in USA; heavy engin.; univ.; p. (1980) 115,000 (c.), 531,000 (met. a.).

Yoyang. *See* Yueyang.

Ypres (Ieper), t., W. Flanders prov., N.W. Belgium; textiles and textile machin.; ctr. of cloth ind. in middle ages; scene of battles 1914–17; p. (1981) 34,426.

Ypsilanti, t., Mich., **USA**; on Huron R.; residtl., agr. mkt., mnfs.; univ.; p. (1980) 24,031.

Ystwyth, R., Dyfed, **Wales**; flows 40 km to join R. Rheidol at Aberystwyth.

Yuan, R., N.W. Hunan prov., **China**; flows into Dongting Hu and Chang Jiang R.; rapids; 640 km long.

Yucatán, st., S.E. **Mexico**; limestone lowlands poor soils; henequen (sisal hemp), chicle (resin from which chewing gum is made); cap. Mérida; a. 61,968 km²; p. (1969) 817,000.

Yueyang (Yoyang), t., Hunan, **China**; at outlet of Dongting Hu and Chang Jiang; p. 4,800.

Yugoslavia, Socialist Fed. Rep., S.E. **Europe**; comprises reps. of Serbia, Croatia, Macedonia, Montenegro, Slovenia, Bosnia, Hercegovina, and aut. regions of Kosovo and Vojvodina; long W. cst. on Adriatic Sea with well-developed limestone karstic topography; hilly interior; climate Mediterranean on cst., continental in interior; distinctive political development after second world war; refused to accept Soviet hegemony; well-developed links with W.; with major attempts to industrialise, based on energy, heavy and consumer inds. has p. engaged in agr.; economic decision-making increasingly freed from central control; developing tourist ctr., especially with countries of W. Europe, based on climate and attractive Adriatic littoral, with many sm. Is.;

cap. Belgrade; a. 255,698 km²; p. (est. 1984) 23,028,000.

Yukon, R., **Canada** and Alaska, **USA**; flows N.W. and W. into Bering Strait; navigable for 1,920 km; 3,200 km long.

Yukon Territory, prov., N.W. **Canada**; mtnous. (Mt. Logan 6,050 m); gold, silver, lead, zinc; Alaska Highway links with B.C. and Alberta; ch. ts. Dawson, and Whitehorse (cap.); incr. indep. since 1983; a. 536,327 km²; p. (1976) 21,836.

Yuma, t., Arizona, **USA**; at confluence of Rs. Gila and Colorado, nr. Mexican bdr.; ctr. of irrigated agr. region; p. (1980) 42,481.

Yumen, c., N.W. Gansu prov., **China**; leading petroleum ctr.; drilling equipment, precision instruments; on Old Silk Road to Xinjiang; p. (est. 1970) 325,000.

Yunnan, prov., S. **China**; adjoins Burma; mtnous. a. of minority groups; rice, tobacco, tea, cotton; copper, tin; cap. Kunming; a. 420,466 km²; p. (est. 1968) 23,000,000.

Yuzhno-Sakhalinsk, t., **RSFSR**; at S. end of Sakhalin I.; paper, lt. inds.; p. (1980) 143,000.

Yvelines, new dep., **France**; W. of Paris; cap. Versailles; a. 2,271 km²; p. (1982) 1,192,600.

Yverdon, t., Vaud, **Switzerland**; typewriters; p. (1969) 20,700.

Z

Zaandam, t., **Neth.**; industl. dist.; rly. junc.; timber-based inds.; p. (1982) 129,864.

Zabrze, t., Upper Silesia, Katowice, **Poland**; impt. coal-mng. ctr. with associated heavy inds.; cultural ctr.; p. (est. 1983) 196,500.

Zacapa, t., cap. of Z. prov., **Guatemala**; mkt. t. at rly. junc.; tobacco tr. and processing; sulphur springs; p. (1964) 30,187.

Zacatecas, st., **Mexico**; on central plateau at 2,100 m; dry, agr. dist.; sm. mng. ctrs.; a. 72,836 km²; p. (1969) 1,082,000.

Zacatecas, t., cap. of Z. st., **Mexico**; cath.; ctr. of silver mng., pottery, clothing; p. (1970) 56,829.

Zacatecoluca, t., **El Salvador**; cigar mkg., hand looms; coffee, cotton, sugar, vanilla in a.; p. (est. 1968) 15,776.

Zadar (**Zara**), t., **Yugoslavia**; spt. on Croatian cst. of Adriatic Sea; formerly Italian (1920–47); Roman remains; cath.; car ferry to Pesaro (Italy); tourism; p. (est. 1965) 31,000.

Zagan (**Sagan**), t., Zielona Gora, W. **Poland** (since 1945); on R. Bober; cas.; textiles, paper, lignite mines; p. (1970) 21,500.

Zagazig, t., **Egypt**; on Nile Delta; tr. ctr. of fertile agr. a. producing cotton, grains; cotton mills; p. (1976) 202,575.

Zagorsk, c., **RSFSR**; 70 km N.E. of Moscow; woodcarving, toy mkg.; site of famous Troitse-Sergiyeva Lavra monastery, converted into museum 1920; p. (1980) 108,000.

Zagreb, c., **Yugoslavia**; cap. of Croatia; on Sava R.; cath., univ.; tr. fair; many inds., notably petrochemicals based on local petroleum reserves, elec. engin.; airport; second c. of rep.; p. (1981) 768,700.

Zagros, mtns., **Iran**; inc. Iran's major oilfield; highest peak Zardesh Kuh, 4,551 m.

Zahedan, c., **Iran**; cap. of Sistan and Baluchistan prov.; airport; terminus of rly. from Pakistan; p. (1967) 79,257.

Zahle, t., **Lebanon**, S.W. Asia; on slopes of L. mtn.; p. (est. 1964) 57,589.

Zaïre, Rep. of, Central Africa; comprises eight provs. (caps. in brackets): Bas-Zaïre (Matadi), Bandundu (Bandundu), Equateur (Mbandaka), Haut-Zaïre (Kisangani), Kivu (Bukavu), Shaba (Lubumbashi), Kasai Oriental (Mbuji-Mayi), Kasai Occidental (Kananga); lies in vast basin of Zaïre R., mtns. on E. and S. borders; climate equatorial in N., tropical in S.; agr. exp. inc. palm oil, cotton, coffee, but economy based on mng., diamonds (Kasai), cobalt, non-ferrous metals (Shaba), major world producer of copper; radium deposits nr. Lubumbashi; extensive navigation on Zaïre R.; main pt. Matadi on estuary linked by rail to cap. Kinshasa; a. 2,345,457 km²; p. (est. 1984) 32,084,000.

Zaïre, gr. R. of **Equatorial Africa**; numerous tribs., drains 3,885,000 km²; navigable from sea to Matadi for ocean steamers, from Matadi to Pool Malebo interrupted by rapids and falls,

again navigable to Boyoma Falls; proposed power project to be lgst. in Africa; estuary 11–16 km wide; c. 4,800 km long.

Zakinthos (**Zante**), Ionian I., **Greece**; cap. Zakinthos (Zante); devastated by earthquake 1953; currants, wine, olives; a. 717 km²; p. (1971) 30,156.

Zakinthos (**Zante**), t., Zakinthos I., **Greece**; spt. on E. cst.; agr. tr. and processing; p. (1971) 30,156.

Zakopane, t., **Poland**; in High Tatra mtns.; base for mountaineering and winter sports; health resort; tourism; p. (1970) 27,000.

Zalaegerszeg, t., **Hungary**; in Göcsej dist.; oil refining; mkt. t. for grain and livestock; p. (1968) 32,000.

Zambesi, R., S.E. **Africa**; flows E. to Moçambique Channel, Indian Oc.; forms frontier between Zambia and Zimbabwe; inc. Victoria Falls and Kariba and Cabora Bassa dams; navigable but impeded by rapids; 3,520 km long.

Zambia, rep., **Central Africa**; member of Commonwealth; tropical climate, modified by alt.; plateau (1,200 m); subsistence agr.; livestock on uplands free from tsetse fly; mng. basis of economy, especially in copperbelt; world's 4th lgst copper producer; exp. disrupted by Rhodesian U.D.I. (1965); need to develop alternative routes to cst.; pipeline from Ndola to Dar-es-Salaam; construction of Tan-Zam rly. financed by Chinese aid; cap. Lusaka; a. 752,618 km²; p. (est. 1984) 6,445,000.

Zamboanga, t., Mindanao, **Philippines**; spt. on Basilian Strait, exp. prod. timber; p. (1975) 240,066.

Zamora, prov., **Spain**; borders Portugal; drained by R. Duero; cereals, wine, merino sheep; cap. Zamora; a. 10,559 km²; p. (1981) 227,769.

Zamora, t., cap. of Zamora prov., **Spain**; on R. Duero; cath.; agr. tr. and processing ctr.; developing mnfs.; p. (1981) 59,530.

Zamosc, t., Lublin, **Poland**; Renaissance planned t. in valley of Lubianka R.; industl., comm. and cultural ctr. for E. part of Lublin prov.; p. (1970) 34,700.

Zanesville, t., Ohio, **USA**; textiles, pottery, machin.; p. (1980) 28,655.

Zangbo (**Tsangpo**), R., Tibet, **China**; one of headstreams of R. Brahmaputra; 1,350 km. long.

Zanjan, c., **Iran**; cap. of Gilan prov.; cotton, woollen gds.; p. (1966) 82,350 (c.); p. (1967) 461,588 (met. a.).

Zanzibar, terr., E. **Africa**; comprises Is. of Z. and Pemba; joined Tanganyika to form **Tanzania** (1964); major world source of cloves; coconut and coconut prod. major exp. and basis of processing inds.; cap. Zanzibar; a. 2,642 km²; p. (est. 1983) 541,000.

Zanzibar, spt., Zanzibar I., **Tanzania**; on W. cst. 35 km from E. Africa; outlet for clove exp., entrepot tr.; former slave mkt.; p. (1976) 110,669.

Zaporozh'ye, t., Ukrainian SSR, **USSR**; on R. Dnieper, nr. dam and hydroelec. power sta.; metal inds. based on Donets coal and Krivoi Rog iron ore; p. (1980) 799,000.

Zaragoza, prov., **Spain**; largely barren plain suffering from climatic extremes; a. 17,122 km²; cap. Z.; p. (1981) 828,578.

Zaragoza, cap. Z. prov., **Spain**; on R. Ebro; 2 caths., univ.; former cap. of Aragon; rly. junc.; comm. ctr.; p. (1981) 571,846.

Zarate, t., Entre Rios, **Argentina**; paper wks., agr. ctr., meat packing; p. (1960) 52,000.

Zaria, c., N. **Nigeria**; founded 15th cent., old part surrounded by walls; univ., cotton ctr.; rly. ctr., p. (est. 1975) 224,000.

Zary (**Sorau**), t., Zielona Gora, **Poland** (since 1945); textiles; p. (1970) 28,400.

Zawiercie, t., **Poland**; industl. ctr.; coal, iron, textiles, glass; p. (1970) 39,400.

Zdunska Wola, t., **Poland**; nr. Lodz; textiles, engin.; p. (1970) 29,100.

Zealand. *See* **Sjaelland**.

Zeebrugge, spt., **Belgium**; 14 km N. of Bruges; exp. coal, chemicals; oil refining; linked by canal to Bruges.

Zeeland, prov., **Neth.**; a. covering part of Scheldt estuary and Is.; low-lying; dairying; cap. Middelburg; a. 1,787 km²; p. (1983) 354,863.

Zeist, t., Utrecht, **Neth.**; chemicals, toys; p. (1982) 62,055.

Zeitz, t., Halle, **E. Germany**; textiles, chemicals; p. (est. 1970) 46,736.

Zelenodolsk, t., **RSFSR**; on R. Volga, 40 km W. of Kazan; rly. junc.; sawmills; p. (est. 1969) 76,000.

Zelten, Libya, N. Africa; oilfield; 320 km S. of Benghazi; pipeline to Mersa al-Brega.

Zenica, t., Yugoslavia; lge. iron and steel wks.; ctr. of Z. basin; rly. junc.; p. (est. 1965) 54,000.

Zeravshan, R., Tadzhik SSR and Usbek SSR, **USSR;** flows for 736 km before evaporating in desert region N. of Chardzhou.

Zetland. See Shetland.

Zgierz, t., Lodz. prov., central **Poland;** nr. source of R. Bzura; textiles, chemicals, textile machin.; p. (1970) 42,800.

Zhangjiakou (Kalgan), c., Hebei, **China;** nr. Great Wall, 160 km N.W. of Beijing; a main route to Mongolia; tea wool, hides; p. (est. 1970) 1,000,000.

Zhangzhou (Chuangchow), c., Fujian prov., **China;** former pt. now silted up; p. (est. 1970) 130,000.

Zhanjiang (Tsamkong), c., Guandong prov., **China;** spt. on Liuzhou peninsula; cotton , milling, leather mnfs.; p. (est. 1953) 166,000.

Zhdanov (Mariupol), spt., S.E. Ukrainian SSR, **USSR;** on Sea of Azov; metallurgical ctr., chemicals; fishing and fish-processing; p. (1980) 507,000.

Zhangzhou. See Quauzhu.

Zhenjiang (Chinkiang), c., Jiangsu, **China;** former treaty pt. on Chang Jiang, 77 km. below Nanjing; tr. ctr.; p. (est. 1970) 250,000.

Zhijiang (Chekiang), coastal prov., S.E. **China;** cap. Hangzhou; impt. rice growing a.; major natural gas field; a. 102,269 km²; p. (est. 1968) 31,000,000.

Zhitomir, t., Ukrainian SSR, **USSR;** engin., clothing; route ctr.; p. (1980) 250,000.

Zhousan (Chusan), I., and archipelago off E. cst. of **China** and Chang Jiang delta; ch. ctr. Dinghai on Zhousan I.; valuable fishing grounds.

Zhuhai, special economic zone, **China,** N. of Macau; selected (1983) to attract foreign investment; new pt.

Zhujiang (Chukiang or Pearl R.), Guandong, S. **China;** one of most impt. waterways of China; 176 km. long from Guangzhou to Hong Kong; fertile delta known as "land of fish, rice and fruit"; around Guangzhou network of elec., drainage and irrigation stas; built since 1959; estuary now silting.

Zhuzhou (Chuchau), c., Hunan prov., **China;** on Xiang Jiang; rly.; p. (est. 1970) 350,000.

Zibo (Tzepo), c., Shandong, **China;** formed by merging of several coal mng. ts. in the 1950s; p. (1957) 806,000.

Zielona Gora (Grünberg), c., W **Poland** (since 1945); in valley surrounded by wooded hills; admin. and industl. ctr., cap. of Z.G. prov.; textiles, food processing, machin.; viticulture; p. (1970) 73,200.

Zielona Gora, prov., **Poland;** borders E. Germany; glacial sands, wooded; brown coal deposits; cap. Z.G.; a. 14,514 km²; p. (est. 1983) 107,800.

Zigaze (Shigatze), t., Tibet, **China;** on R. Zangbo; tr. ctr. on main caravan routes; p. c. 2,000.

Zigong (Tzekung), c., Sichuan, **China;** petroleum, natural gas, salt wks.; p. (est. 1970) 350,000.

Ziguinchor, t., Senegambia; pt. on R. Casamance; exp. groundnuts; p. (1976) 73,000.

Zilina, t., Slovakia, **ČSSR;** on R. Vah; paper, fertilisers; p. (1967) 39,000.

Zimbabwe, Central Africa; former Brit. col. (Rhodesia), indep rep. 1980; landlocked st.; much of land high veld above 900 m covered in savannah; impressive economic growth with removal of sanctions and end of warfare; manuf. limited by lack of skilled labour; still heavy dependence on agr., maize and tobacco; mng. also impt.; Wankie coal mine lgst. in world; also asbestos, chrome and copper; power from Kariba dam encourages lt. inds.; cap. Harare; a. 389,329 km²; p. (est. 1984) 8,461,000.

Zimbabwe National Park; site nr. Victoria, Mashonaland, of ruined t. built c. 15th cent. A.D. by a Bantu people; discovered 1868.

Zinder, t., Niger, W. Africa; terminus of trans-Saharan motor route; tr. ctr.; former cap.; second t. of Niger; p. (est. 1981) 75,000.

Zion National Park, Utah, **USA;** contains Z. canyon; a. 596 km².

Zipaquirá, t., Colombia; 48 km N. of Bogotá; salt mng., chemicals; cattle-rearing a.; p. (est. 1968) 28,812.

Zistersdorf, t., Lower **Austria;** recently developed oilfields.

Zittau, t., Dresden, **E. Germany;** on R. Mandau; woollens, linens, machin., cars, chemicals; p. (est. 1970) 43,087.

Ziatoust, t., S.W. **RSFSR;** in Ural mtns.; metallurgical ctr.; steel, chemicals, sawmilling; p. (1980) 199,000.

Zletovo, terr., N.E. Macedonia, **Yugoslavia;** oil shales, lead, zinc deposits.

Zlin. See Gottwaldov.

Znojmo or Znaim, t., ČSSR; anc. t., cas.; ctr. of fertile agr. dist.; p. (est. 1968) 25,732.

Zomba, t., former cap. of **Malawi;** 884 m a.s.l. on slopes of Zomba mtn., 67 km N.E. Blantyre; Malawi's univ. t.; p. (est. 1983) 46,000.

Zonguldak, t., Turkey; spt. on Black Sea; coal-mng. a.; p. (1979) 100,436.

Zorita De Los Canes, Guadalajara, **Spain;** on R. Tagus; nuclear power plant.

Zrenjanin, t., Vojvodina, **Yugoslavia;** pt. on R. Begej; ctr. of agr. dist.; agr. processing; p. (1971) 59,580.

Zug, smallest can., **Switzerland;** drained by R. Reuss; contains part of L. Z.; dairying, fruit; cap. Z.; a. 241 km²; p. (1969) 66,700.

Zug, t., cap. of Zug can., **Switzerland;** on L. Z.; elec. engin., printing; p. (1980) 75,930.

Zugspitze, mtn., Bavarian Alps, on Bavarian-Austrian bdr.; highest peak in **Germany,** 2,965 m; connected by rack-and-pinion to Garmisch-Partenkirchen at foot.

Zuider Zee. See IJsselmeer.

Zulia, st., **Venezuela;** centred on L. Maracaibo, producing 70 per cent of Venezuelan oil; timber reserves; cap. Maracaibo; a. 63,902 km²; p. (est. 1970) 1,342,994.

Zululand, Bantu homeland, Natal, **S. Africa;** sugar on coastal plain, livestock on interior plateau; cap. Eshowe; a. 27,006 km²; p. (1970) 2,106,774.

Zürich, c., cap. of Z. can., **Switzerland;** on L. Z. and R. Limmat; cath., univ.; leading world banking ctr.; inds. inc. textiles, paper; p. (1980), 706,170 (met. a.).

Zürich, can., **Switzerland;** forested and agr. a. stretching N. from L. Z.; inds. at cap. Z. and Winterthur; a. 1,728 km²; p. (1980) 1,122,839.

Zürich, L. Z., Switzerland; drained by R. Limmat; length 40 km.

Zutphen, t., Gelderland, **Neth.;** on R. Ijssel; textiles, paper; Sir Philip Sidney died here 1586; p. (1982) 31,919.

Zuetina, oil pt. (1968), **Libya;** pipeline links shore storage sta. with offshore berths.

Zuzhou (Suchow), c., Jiangsu, **China;** at junct. of N. China plain and Chang Jiang basin; impt. rly. junct.; p. (est. 1970) 1,500,000.

Zuzhou (Luchow), c., Sichuan, **China;** coal, iron, kaolin; synthetic ammonia plant; p. (est. 1970) 225,000.

Zweibrücken, t., Rhineland-Palatinate, **W. Germany;** nr. Saarbrücken; cas.; machin., footwear, textiles; p. (1983) 34,100.

Zwickau, c., Karl-Marx-Stadt, **E. Germany;** on R. Mulde; cas.; coal, motors, machin., textiles; birthplace of Schumann; p. (1983) 120,486.

Zwolle, t., Overijssel, **Neth.;** canal ctr.; cattle mkt.; p. (1982) 85,135.

Zyrardow, t., Poland; nr. Warsaw; specialised textile ctr.; p. (1970) 33,200.

Zyryanovsk, t., Kazakh SSR, **USSR;** lead, zinc; p. (est. 1969) 56,090.

GENERAL
INFORMATION

Some three thousand entries, including a number of scientific terms and explanations. Cross references direct the reader to fuller information elsewhere in the book. A list of symbols for correcting proofs will be found at the end of the section.

MEASUREMENTS ARE GIVEN IN METRIC UNITS

Abbreviations

mm	= millimetre	m²	= square metre
cm	= centimetre	km²	= square kilometre
m	= metre	ha	= hectare
km	= kilometre	m³	= cubic metre
km/h	= kilometres per hour	s	= second
g	= gram	min	= minute
kg	= kilogram	h	= hour
tonne	= metric ton		

Equivalents

Length   *Reciprocal*

1 cm	= 0·394 in	2·540
1 m	= 1·094 yd	0·914
1 km	= 0·621 mile	1·609

Area

1 m²	= 1·196 yd²	0·836
1 km²	= 0·386 mile²	2·590
1 hectare	= 2·471 acres	0·405

Volume

1 m³	= 1·308 yd³	0·765
1 litre	= 0·220 gallon	4·546

Mass

1 kg	= 2·205 lb	0·454
1 tonne	= 0·984 ton	1·016

Temperature

$$C = (F - 32) \div 1\cdot8$$
$$F = (1\cdot8 \times C) + 32$$

See also **Metric Equivalents, N8.**

GENERAL INFORMATION

A

Aard-vark (Dutch *aarde* = earth + *vark* = pig), a large nocturnal mammal found only in Africa. It feeds on termites and ants, whose nests it excavates with its enormous claws.

Abacus, a device for making arithmetical calculations, consisting of parallel bars on which are strung movable coloured beads. The earliest form of this instrument was used in Mesopotamia about 3000 B.C., and its use spread westwards throughout the Graeco-Roman world and eastwards to China. An efficient form of the abacus is still used today in parts of Asia.

Abdication. The term usually refers to the renunciation of the royal office by a reigning monarch. Both Edward II (1327) and Richard II (1399) were forced to abdicate, James II left the throne vacant without waiting for a formal deposition, and the abdication of Edward VIII was effected by the Declaration of Abdication Act, 1936. Since 1688 when Parliament declared James II to have abdicated by reason of desertion and subversion of the constitution, no British monarch can abdicate without the consent of Parliament.

Aberration, in astronomy, is the apparent displacement of a star due to the speed of the observer with the earth (*see* **Parallax**). In optics (i) spherical aberration is when there is blurring of the image and fringes of colour at its edges, due to failure of lens to bring light to a single focus; (ii) chromatic aberration is due to the refractive index of glass being different for light of different colours. For instance, violet light is bent more than red.

Abiogenesis, or spontaneous generation; the origination of living from non-living matter. The term is applied to such discredited ideas as that frogs could be generated spontaneously by the action of sunlight on mud, or maggots arise spontaneously in dead meat without any eggs from which the maggots hatch being present. Spallanzani (1729–99) upset the hypothesis of spontaneous generation; Pasteur dealt it a death-blow.

Abominable Snowman. *See* **Yeti.**

Aborigines, a term first applied to an ancient mythical people of central Italy, derives from the Latin *ab origine* = from the beginning. It now signifies the original inhabitants of any country, in particular the aboriginal tribes of Australia. In contrast to their highly complex social and religious customs, the material culture of Australian aboriginals is very low and ill adapted to stand up to contact with European civilisation. Originally estimated at 300,000, their number has dropped in the last 200 years to some 80,000. They have no legal title to their ancient tribal lands, unlike the native people of the USA, Canada, and New Zealand.

Absolute Temperature, Absolute Zero. This is a refined notion requiring some study of thermodynamics for its full understanding. For setting up an absolute temperature scale one must first assign a numerical value to one fixed temperature. For this, the triple point of water has been chosen, *i.e.,* the temperature at which solid, liquid, and gaseous water are all in equilibrium. The triple point is defined to be 273·16 K where K is read for kelvin (after Lord Kelvin). This temperature is 0·01°C on the Celsius scale (*q.v.*) and is thus very close to the melting point of ice. Suppose the pressure and volume of a mass of gas are measured (i) at the triple point of water, giving (pV)tr as the product of the pressure and volume; and (ii) at any unknown temperature T K, giving (pV) as the product. Then the absolute temperature, T K, is defined by

$$T \text{ K} = 273 \cdot 16 \frac{(pV)}{(pV)\text{tr}}$$

It is to be understood that the gas pressure is very low. The nature of the gas is immaterial. More subtly, it can be shown that the temperature so defined is identical with that derived in a rather abstract way in the science of thermodynamics. The absolute scale is therefore also called the thermodynamic scale. Absolute temperatures can be obtained from Celsius temperatures by adding 273·15; thus the absolute temperature of melting ice is 273·15 K. Conversely, absolute zero is a temperature 273·15 K below the temperature of melting ice, *i.e.,* −273·15°C. Theory shows that absolute zero is unattainable, but it has been approached to within about 1 millionth of a degree. Within ten or so degrees of absolute zero, matter develops some remarkable properties. *See* **Kelvin, Cryogenics, Superconductor, Helium.**

Abstract Art, a term applied to 20th cent. plastic arts in which form and colour possess aesthetic value apart from the subject. Usually represented as a modern movement beginning with Cézanne. The idea is ancient, abstract design being found in the Neolithic period, in folk-art, and particularly in Moslem art (which forbids naturalistic representations especially of the human figure). Among those in the tradition are Kandinsky, Braque, Mondrian, Calder.

Acetic Acid, an organic acid produced when ordinary (ethyl) alcohol is fermented by the organism called *Acetobacter aceti*. The same oxidation process yields vinegar: this is a weak and crude solution of acetic acid obtained by trickling dilute alcoholic liquor over beechwood shavings at 35°C. The souring of wine is due to the same process. Acetic acid is used as a food preservative and flavouring material, and in the manufacture of cellulose acetate and white lead.

Acetylene (also called ethyne), a compound of carbon and hydrogen prepared from calcium carbide and water. A very reactive gas, it is used industrially on a large scale to prepare acetaldehyde, chlorohydrocarbon solvents, and many intermediates for plastics manufacture. Burns in air with a highly luminous flame, formerly used for lighting purposes, but is now widely used, with oxygen, in welding. For safe storage and transportation it is dissolved in acetone.

Acid Rain is the name given to rain, snow or sleet contaminated with acid substances so that its acidity is greater than the limit expected by normal concentrations of carbon dioxide dissolving in the rain to give carbonic acid (*pH* 5·5–5·6). The *pH* (*see* **L95**) of acid rain therefore is less than about 5·5. The increased acidity is caused by larger concentrations of a number of contaminants, principally the strong acids, nitric and sulphuric, which arise from industrial effluents containing oxides of nitrogen and sulphur. The European emission of sulphur dioxide doubled between 1940 and 1980. In some European and North American areas such contamination can give a rain *pH* as low as 3 (which is 100 times more acid than *pH* 5). The acid rain can mark fruit and leaves, and adversely affect soil but its main effect is on the aquatic ecosystems especially in regions which cannot naturally buffer acidic inputs such as those with thin soils and granite rocks. It is likely that the disappearance of fish from many Scandinavian lakes has been the result of pollution by acid rain.

Acids, substances having a tendency to lose a positive ion (a proton). This general definition overcomes difficulties of earlier views which merely described their properties and asserted that they are chemically opposite to bases. As a whole acids contain ionisable hydrogen, replaceable by a metal, to form a salt. Inorganic acids are compounds of non-metals or metalloids, *e.g.,* sulphuric, phosphoric acid. Carboxylic acids contain the group –COOH. *See* **F25.**

Actinides, the fourteen metallic elements from thorium (no. 90) to lawrencium (no. 103). All known isotopes of these elements are radioactive and those with atomic number greater than 92 (uranium) have been produced only in significant quantities artificially. Plutonium (no. 94) is obtained from uranium during the course of nuclear reactor operation and the higher transuranic elements can be made from it by the successive capture of neutrons or nuclei of light atoms. The availability of only minute quantities of short-lived isotopes makes the determination of the physical and chemical properties of the higher actinides very difficult. Claims for the discovery of new elements can therefore be controversial and since the discoverers can name the elements their naming is also controversial. There were three different reports for Nobelium (no. 102). Lawrentium (no. 103) is called Joliotium by Russian authors. Element no. 104 was reported in 1964 by a Russian group and called Kurchatovium but is called Rutherfordium (Rf) in the West. Element no. 105 has been named Hahnium (Hn).

Advent, a period devoted to religious preparation for the coming celebration of the Nativity (Christmas). It includes the four Sundays immediately preceding the festival.

Advocatus Diaboli ("the devil's advocate"), a Roman Catholic functionary who presents opposing evidence in regard to the life of any deceased person it may be proposed to canonise.

Aerodynamics, the science of gases (especially air) in motion, particularly in relation to aircraft (aeronautics). The idea of imitating the birds by the use of wings is of ancient origin. Leonardo da Vinci first carried out experiments in a scientific manner. The invention of the balloon in 1783 and the researches of scientists and engineers in the 19th cent. ultimately led to the development of the aeroplane.

Aerolites, the name given to the class of meteorites composed chiefly of heavy silicates. The other two main classes are *siderolites* (nickel–iron and silicates) and *siderites* (nickel–iron).

Aerosol, a suspension of a liquid in a gas; for example, a fog is very small drops of water suspended in air. Formed by spraying the liquid in air, aerosols are used to disperse liquid over a wide area in crop spraying, air freshening and pest control. *See also* **Fluorocarbons.**

Afrikander, type of cattle bred in South Africa.

Afrikaner, an Afrikaans-speaking South African, usually of Dutch descent.

After-damp occurs in a mine after an explosion, causing suffocation. It is composed mainly of carbon dioxide and nitrogen and contains water vapour and carbon monoxide (produced by the burning, in a restricted supply of air, of fine coal dust).

Agaric, large fungi of the family *Agaricaceae,* which includes the mushroom and what are popularly called "toadstools", though the idea that these two lay terms sharply differentiate between edible and poisonous fungi is an incorrect one. Characteristic of the agarics is the presence of a cap or *pileus* (bearing underneath the spore-shedding gills) and a stalk or *stipe.*

Agave, the American aloe or Century Plant which sometimes does not attain to flowering maturity under sixty · or seventy years, and then dies. The flower spray may reach a height of 6 m and in its development the rush of sap is so great that the Mexicans collect for brewing the strong spirit called mescal. 1,000 litres of sap can be obtained from a single plant. Some species of agave yield sisal used for making cord and rope.

Aggression. After many years of consideration a definition of aggression was agreed at the United Nations in 1974. It is the use of armed force by a state against the sovereignty, territorial integrity, or political independence of another state or in any other manner inconsistent with the Charter of the UN.

Air, a mixture of gases in the earth's atmosphere, the main constituents being nitrogen, oxygen and argon. Dry air contains these gases in the following proportions by volume: nitrogen 78·06%, oxygen 21%, argon 0·94%. Other gases are also present in small amounts. Of particular importance are water vapour and carbon dioxide. Water vapour is not only critical for life forms on land but also a major

factor in the behaviour of the atmosphere—weather and climate. Carbon dioxide is utilised by green plants in photosynthesis (**F32**). Air also contains traces of ammonia, nitrogen oxides, hydrogen, sulphur dioxide, ozone, and of the rare gases, helium, krypton, neon and xenon. Near cities and industrial areas there are also large quantities of dust and smoke particles (up to 100,000 particles per cc), and traces of other gases from industrial processes. A litre of air at 0°C and 760 mm pressure weighs 1·2932 g. *See also* **Atmosphere, Pollution.**

Air Glow is the general name given to a large number of relatively weak optical emissions from the earth's upper atmosphere in the height range 70 to 400 km (approx.). It is distinct from the aurora polaris (*q.v.*) which is usually much brighter and normally only observable at high latitudes. Air glow is produced by a combination of photochemical reactions in the upper atmosphere, excitation by photoelectrons, or by solar ultra-violet light. In the latter case it is more correctly called "dayglow." These emissions occur in the ultra-violet and infra-red spectral regions as well as in visible light.

Alabaster, a soft crystalline form of sulphate of lime, or granulated gypsum, easily worked for statuary and other ornamental articles, and capable of being highly polished. Volterra, in Tuscany, yields the finest; that in highest ancient repute came from Alabastron in Egypt, near to the modern Antinoë.

Alb, white vestment reaching to the feet, worn by priests in religious ceremonies.

Albatross, a large sea-bird of almost pure white, black and white, or brown plumage. It nests in colonies on remote islands, but at other times rarely approaches land. Of the thirteen species, nine are found in the southern oceans, one in the tropics, three others in the North Pacific

Albert Memorial, a large Gothic monument designed by Sir George Gilbert Scott, and embellished with sculptures by eminent artists. Erected in memory of Prince Albert in Kensington Gardens at a cost of £120,000.

Alcázar, the palace at Seville, famed for the beauty of; its halls and gardens, in ancient days the residence of the Moorish kings.

Alchemy. *See* **Section J.**

Alcohols. A class of organic compounds of general formula R–OH, where R is an aliphatic radical. "Alcohol" is the name used for ethyl alcohol (ethanol); this is produced by distilling fermented liquors, and synthetically from ethylene, a product of petroleum cracking. Industrially ethyl alcohol is used in the manufacture of chloroform, ether, perfumes, etc. Diluted with wood alcohol or other denaturants ethyl alcohol is called "methylated spirits"; the denaturants are varied according to the industrial purposes for which it is required, the methylated spirits then being largely exempt from duty. Wood alcohol (methyl alcohol or methanol) can be obtained by distilling wood or synthetically from water gas.

Alcoholic Strength. In 1980 Great Britain adopted the OIML (International Organisation of Legal Metrology) system of spirit strength measurement in metric units as required by EEC directive. The alcoholic strength of wine is expressed in percentage volume ("% vol") terms, *i.e.,* the number of volumes of pure alcohol in 100 volumes of the product at 20°C. For spirits the quantity for duty is the litre of alcohol at 20°C. For example, a case of 12 bottles of 75 cl each = 9 litres; at 40% volume 9 litres = 9 × 40% = 3.60 litres of alcohol. The alcoholic strength of spirits and liqueurs appearing on bottle labels is increasingly shown in % vol. terms (*e.g.,* "40.5% vol"). The USA continues to use the US proof gallon (1.37 US proof gallons = 1 British proof gallon).

Aldehyde, the generic term for a class of chemical compounds of general formula R–CHO, where R is an organic radical. Except for formaldehyde, which is a gas, aldehydes are volatile liquids. They are produced by oxidation of primary alcohols. Most important aldehyde is formaldehyde (methanol) used in making the plastics described as formaldehyde resins. Formalin (formaldehyde solution in water) is much used for preserving zoological specimens.

Alder, a river-side tree of the genus *Alnus,* including some 30 species and found in north temperate regions and the Andes. The only species native to Britain is *A. glutinosa*, which has been described as "guardian of river-banks" because of the way its roots bind together the sand and stones, and so slow down erosion. The wood is used for furniture and charcoal.

Aldine Editions are the beautiful books printed in Venice by the Renaissance printer Aldo Pio Manuzio and his family between 1490 and 1597. Italics were first introduced in these books.

Algae, flowerless plants living mostly in water. Seaweeds and the green pond scums are the best known algae. The green powder found on trees is a microscopic alga (*Protococcus*). See **F42**(1).

Algebra, a branch of mathematics in which symbols are used in place of numbers. Sir Isaac Newton styled it the "universal arithmetic". The Chinese were able to solve the quadratic equation before the Christian era but it was Al-Khowarizmi, an Arab mathematician of the early 9th cent., who introduced algebra to Europe.

Alhambra, the ancient palace of the Moorish kings at Granada in Spain, built in the 13th and 14th cent. Though part of the castle was turned into a modern palace under Charles V, the most beautiful parts of the interior are still preserved—the graceful halls and dwelling-rooms grouped round the Court of Alberca and the Court of Lions, with their fountains, arcades, and lovely gardens.

Aliphatic describes derivatives of hydrocarbons having chains of carbon atoms, as distinct from rings of carbon atoms as in benzene (*see* **Aromatic**). The gas butane is aliphatic.

Alkali, the general name given to a number of chemicals which are bases (*q.v.*). The term should be limited to the hydroxides of metals in the first and second group of the periodic table and of ammonia, *e.g.*, NaOH, KOH. They are used commercially in the manufacture of paper, glass, soap, and artificial silk. The word comes from the Arabic *al-kali* meaning calcined wood ashes. Alkalis are extremely soluble in water and neutralise acids to form salts and water.

Alkaloids, a large group of natural products which contain nitrogen; they are usually basic. Isolated from plants and animals, they include some hormones, vitamins, and drugs. Examples are nicotine, adrenalin, and cocaine. Many alkaloids are made synthetically for medicinal use, *e.g.*, morphine, quinine. Their function in plants is not well understood. *See* **Belladonna.**

Alligator, the crocodile of America, found in the lower Mississippi and adjacent lakes and marshes. There is also a Chinese species. Alligators have broader snouts than other crocodiles.

Allotropy. Depending on the temperature, pressure or method of preparation, an element may exist in one of several forms, each having different physical properties (crystal structure, electrical conductivity, melting point, etc.). This is known as allotropy and the different forms of the element are called allotropes. Many elements exhibit allotropy, *e.g.*, sulphur, phosphorus, oxygen, tin and carbon, the most well-known allotropes of carbon being diamond and graphite.

Alloys are combinations of metals made for their valuable special properties, *e.g.*, durability, strength, lightness, magnetism, rust-resistance, etc. Some well-known ones are brass (zinc + copper), coinage bronze (copper + zinc + tin), steels (iron + carbon + various other materials), soft solder (tin + lead), dental fillings (mercury + various ingredients).

All Saints' Day (Nov. 1) is common to both the Anglican and Roman Catholic Churches, and is in commemoration of the saints generally, or such as have no special day set apart for them. Instituted by Pope Boniface IV, early in the 7th cent., this ecclesiastical festival was formerly called "All Hallows".

All Souls' Day (Nov. 2) is a festival of the Roman Church, intended for the mitigation by prayer of the sufferings of souls in purgatory. The commemoration was enjoined by Abbot Odilo of Cluny during the 11th cent. upon the monastic order over which he presided, and was

afterwards adopted generally throughout the Roman Communion.

Allspice, a flavouring obtained from a West Indian tree of the myrtle family, *Pimenta officinalis*, likened to the flavour of cinnamon, nutmeg and cloves combined. The berries resemble peppercorns and are used as a spice in mincemeat, etc.

Alluvium, river transported deposits of sand, mud and gravel which accumulate to form distinctive features such as levées, flood plains and deltas. The frequent renewal of alluvium by flooding causes riverine lands to be some of the most fertile. In Asia alluvial lands support high densities of population, *e.g.*, The Hwang-ho plains and the Ganges delta.

Almond, the fruit of the *Amygdalus communis*, originally indigenous to Persia, Asia Minor and N. Africa; now cultivated in Italy, Spain, France, the USA and Australia. It yields both bitter and sweet oil. Bitter almond oil is obtained by macerating and distilling the ripe seeds; it is used for flavouring and scenting purposes, its fragrant odour being due to the presence of benzaldehyde and hydrogen cyanide. When the seeds are pressed sweet almond oil results: this is used in perfumery, and also as a lubricant for very delicate machinery.

Almuce, a fur stole worn by certain canons.

Aloe, large plants of the lily family, with about 180 species found mainly in the S. African veldt and karroo. The bitter purgative drug (aloes) is prepared by evaporating the plant's sap. *See* **Agave.**

Alpaca, a South American ruminant related to the llama whose long, fine wool is woven into a soft dress fabric known by the same name. Sir Titus Salt first manufactured alpaca cloth (1836). Saltaire, near Bradford, remains to evidence the success which for many years attended the enterprise.

Alpha Particle, or alpha-ray, fast-moving helium nucleus ejected by some radioactive atoms, *e.g.*, polonium. It is a combination of 2 neutrons and 2 protons. *See* **F12.**

Alphabet (so called from the first two letters of the Greek alphabet—alpha, beta) is the term applied to the collection of letters from which the words of a language are made up. It grew out of the knowledge that all words can be expressed by a limited number of sounds arranged in various combinations. The Phoenicians were the first to make use of an alphabetic script derived from an earlier Semitic alphabet (earliest known inscriptions *c.* 1500–950 B.C.) from which all other alphabets have sprung. The stages in the development of the alphabet were mnemonic (memory aids), pictorial (actual pictures), ideographic (symbols), and lastly phonetic. All the ideographic systems died out, with the exception of that of the Chinese.

Altimeter, an instrument used in aircraft to estimate altitude; its usual essential feature is an aneroid barometer which registers the decrease of pressure with height. Roughly 1 millibar corresponds to 9 m. To read an aircraft altimeter correct for its destination, the zero setting must be adjusted for difference of ground height and difference of surface pressure, especially when pressure is falling or when flying towards low pressure.

Altitude, an astronomical term used to signify the angular elevation of a heavenly body; this is measured with a quadrant or sextant. In aeronautics it is the height (in feet or metres) above sea-level.

Alto-Relievo, a term applied to sculptured designs which are depicted in prominent relief on a flat surface, technically signifying that the projections exceeds one-half the true proportions of the objects represented. Basso-relievo is carving kept lower than one-half such projection.

Alum is a compound salt used in various industrial processes, especially dyeing, its constituents being the sulphate of one univalent metal or radical (*e.g.*, potassium, sodium, ammonium, rubidium, caesium, silver, thallium) and the sulphate of a tervalent metal (*e.g.*, aluminium, iron, chromium, manganese), and water of crystallisation.

Alumina is the oxide of aluminium. Very valuable as a refractory material. The ruby is almost 100 per cent. alumina; so also are the emerald, oriental amethyst, etc. An hydrated

aluminium oxide is bauxite, chief ore of aluminium from which the metal is extracted electrolytically.

Aluminium, element no. 13, symbol Al, is a light metal which conducts electricity well. Its specific gravity at 20°C is 2·705. Melting point of aluminium is 660·2°C. It is made commercially by electrolysing bauxite dissolved in cryolite (double fluoride of aluminium and sodium). Aluminium alloys because of their strength and lightness are being increasingly used for construction purposes.

Amadavat, a popular cage bird of the weaver family, mainly crimson with spots, so named because the first specimens came from Ahmadabad in India about 1700.

Amalgam is the term applied to any alloy of which mercury forms a part.

Amber, a brittle resinous substance; in origin, fossilised resin. Obtained mostly from the Baltic coasts, and used for ornaments, pipe mouth-pieces, etc.

Ambergris is a waxy substance produced in the intestines of the sperm whale, and generally found floating on the sea. It is a valuable perfumery material.

Amblyopsis, a species of fish, practically sightless, and with inoperative organs of hearing and feeling, that inhabit the Mammoth Cave of Kentucky. A remarkable illustration of the failure of senses not brought into use.

America's Cup. In 1851 the Royal Yacht Squadron put up for competition a silver cup that has become the most famous trophy in yachting. In that year the New York Y.C. sent the schooner *America* across the Atlantic to compete in a 53-mile (85 km) race round the Isle of Wight; it captured the trophy which now bears its name. Until 1983 none of the many challenges by yachtsmen from Great Britain, Canada, and latterly, Australia, had been successful. In that year, however, in Rhode Island Sound *Australia II*, skippered by John Bertrand, won on the 25th challenge, closing with *Liberty*, skippered by Dennis Connor, in the later stages of the race: after 132 years the silver ewer was handed to the Royal Perth Y.C.

Amethyst, the violet variety of quartz, used as a precious stone, containing traces of manganese, titanium and iron. The finest coloured specimens come from Brazil and the Urals.

Amice, a linen vestment worn about the neck by Roman and many Anglican priests over the alb when officiating at Mass or Holy Eucharist. Formerly worn on the head by priests and pilgrims.

Amines, organic chemicals composed of carbon, hydrogen and nitrogen. They are derived from ammonia, which they resemble in smell and chemical characteristics. The smell of bad fish is due to the presence of amines. Important industrially as intermediates in a wide variety of products, for example, the synthesis of dye-stuffs and man-made fibres such as nylon.

Amino acids, organic compounds containing an amine group and a carboxylic acid group. They are the "building bricks" of proteins (*q.v.*). See **F32(1).**

Ammeter, an instrument for measuring the current flowing in an electric circuit. A contraction of ampere-meter. See **Ampere.**

Ammonia, a colourless gaseous compound comprising three atoms of hydrogen to one of nitrogen. Formerly it was made by heating the horns and hoofs of deer, acquiring the name of spirits of hartshorn. The ammonia of commerce is now procured by coal decomposition in the course of gas-making and by direct synthesis. In the very important Haber process of ammonia production by fixation of atmospheric nitrogen, the nitrogen is made to combine with hydrogen and the ammonia so prepared is converted into nitric acid, ammonium nitrate or ammonium sulphate. The Haber process made Germany self-sufficient in nitrates in the first world war, and was afterwards exploited all over the world.

Ammonites, extinct animals related to the Nautilus. The chambered shell is coiled, usually in a plane spiral, and they are confined to Mesozoic rocks.

Ammonium, the basic radical of ammonium salts. Composed of one atom of nitrogen and four of hydrogen, it behaves chemically like an ion

of a monovalent alkali metal. Ammonium chloride is known as "sal ammoniac". "Sal volatile" is ammonium carbonate.

Amnesty, an act of grace by which a ruler or governing power pardons political offenders.

Amorphous, a term used to indicate the absence of crystalline form in any body or substance.

Ampere, unit of electric current in the SI system of units; named after André Marie Ampère, who in the 1820s helped to lay the foundations of modern electromagnetism. Defined as that constant current which, if maintained in two parallel rectilinear conductors of infinite length, of negligible circular cross section, and placed at a distance of one metre apart in a vacuum, would produce between these conductors a force equal to 2×10^{-7} newton per metre length.

Amphibia. See **F36(2).**

Amphioxus or **Lancelet,** a primitive chordate (**F36(2)**), occurring in sand-banks around British shores and elsewhere.

Anabolism. See **Catabolism.**

Analysis is one of the major branches of modern pure mathematics and includes the theories of differentiation, integration, differential equations and analytic functions.

Anarchism. See **Section J.**

Anchor, an instrument used for keeping ships stationary. Great improvements have been introduced in recent years, stockless anchors being now chiefly used, consisting of a shank and a loose fluke. Lloyd's rules prescribe the number and weight of anchors which must be carried by merchant ships.

Anchorite is a religious person who retires into solitude to employ himself with holy thoughts. Among the early Christians, anchorites were numerous, but in the Western Church they have been few. Their reputation for wisdom and prescience was high, and kings and rulers in olden days would visit their cells for counsel. An anchorite or "ankret" was in mediaeval times a source of fame and profit to the monastic house within which he was voluntarily immured.

Anchovy, a fish of the herring family, distinguished by its large mouth and projecting snout, plentiful in the Mediterranean and much esteemed when cured.

Ancient Lights are rights of light enjoyed by a property owner over adjoining land. Such a right is obtained either by uninterrupted enjoyment for twenty years, or by written authority, and once legally established cannot be upset, no building being permissible that would seriously interfere with the privilege.

Anemometer, an instrument for measuring the strength of the wind. In the most widely used pattern the rotation, about a vertical axis, of a group of hemispherical or conical cups gives a measure of the total flow of air past the cups, various registering devices being employed. The Dines anemograph provides a continuous record of the variation in both velocity and direction; changes of pressure produced in a horizontal tube, kept pointing into the wind by a vane, cause a float, to which a pen is attached, to rise and fall in sympathy with the gusts and lulls. The recently devised hot-wire anemometer, depending upon the change of electrical resistance experienced by a heated wire when cooled, enables very gentle air currents to be investigated.

Aneroid is the kind of barometer which does not depend upon atmospheric support of a mercury (or other liquid) column. It consists of a metallic box, partially exhausted of air, with a corrugated lid which moves with atmospheric changes. A lever system magnifies the lid movements about 200 times and atmospheric pressure is read from a dial. The construction of the vacuum chamber provides automatic compensation for temperature changes. An aneroid barometer is the basic component of an altimeter.

Angelica, an aromatic plant of the Umbelliferae order, *Angelica officinalis,* valuable as a flavouring and possessing medical properties. In olden times supposed to protect against poison.

Angelus, a church bell rung in Roman Catholic countries, at morn, noon, and sunset, to remind the faithful to say their Angelic Salutation.

Angevin Dynasty includes the Plantagenet kings from Henry II to Richard II. The name was derived from Henry II's father, Geoffrey, Count of Anjou.

Angles, a northern tribe originally settled in Schleswig, who with the Saxons and Jutes invaded Britain in the 5th cent.

Angström, a unit of wavelength, named after the Swedish physicist A. J. Angström (1814–74), equal to one hundred-millionth of a centimetre (10^{-8} cm). It is used to measure wavelengths of light, X-rays, etc.

Aniline, a simple aromatic compound ($C_6H_5NH_2$) related to benzene and ammonia. It is obtained from coal-tar. The name recalls the fact that it was first prepared by distilling indigo (*anil* is Portuguese for indigo). In 1856 W. H. Perkin (1838–1907) discovered the first aniline or coal-tar dye, mauve, and thus founded the modern dyestuff industry.

Animal Kingdom. *See* **F36.**

Anise, an umbelliferous plant (*Pimpinella anisum*) found in Egypt and the Levant, and valued for its fruit, aniseed, possessing certain medicinal properties and yielding an aromatic, volatile oil, Also used in cooking. The anise of the Bible is *Anethum graveolens, i.e.,* dill.

Annates were acknowledgments formerly paid to the Popes by way of fee or tax in respect of ecclesiastical preferment and consisted usually of a proportion of the income ("first-fruits") of the office. Introduced into England in the 13th cent.; annexed to the Crown under Henry VIII; transferred to a perpetual fund for the benefit of the poorer clergy in 1704. *See* **Queen Anne's Bounty.**

"Annual Register", a yearly record of political and literary events, founded by Edmund Burke (as editor) in 1759 and Robert Dorsley, the bookseller.

Annunciation, Feast of the (March 25), is a Church festival commemorating the message of the incarnation of Christ brought by the angel Gabriel to the Virgin Mary, hence the title Lady Day.

Anointing is the pouring of consecrated oil upon the body as a mark of supreme honour. In England it is restricted chiefly to the ceremony of the monarch's coronation, and the spoon with which the oil is applied forms part of the English regalia. In the Roman Catholic Church anointing represents the sacrament of extreme unction.

Ant. There are about 6,000 species of ants, which belong to the same order (Hymenoptera) as the bees, wasps and ichneumon flies. They are social in habit, living in communities of varying size and development. There are three basic castes in ants—the females or *queens,* the *males,* and the *workers* (the last-named being neuter), although specialised forms of workers are sometimes found, *e.g.,* the *soldiers* of the harvesting ants. In the communities of those species of ants which evolved most recently there is a highly complex social life and well-developed division of labour. Some species of these ants make slaves of other species, stealing the cocoons before the adult forms emerge. Many ants "milk" green-flies, which they protect for their honey-like secretion, and some ants' nests contain many "guests", such as beetles and silver fish. Some ants harvest grains of corn, and others, from S. America, live on fungi which they cultivate in underground "mushroom beds".

Antarctic Exploration. In earlier centuries it was thought that a great continent must exist in the southern hemisphere, around the South Pole, to balance the known land masses in the north. Its supposed extent was greatly reduced in the 18th cent., particularly when Capt, Cook sailed for the first time south of the Antarctic Circle and reached the edge of the ice-pack. A portion of the ice-covered continent—the coast of Graham Land—was first sighted by Lieut. Edward Bransfield in 1820. Explorers of several other nations sighted portions of the coast-line in other quarters, but the first extensive exploration was made by Capt. James Clarke Ross, who with the *Erebus* and *Terror* penetrated into the Ross Sea in 1841, and discovered the great Ross Ice Barrier in 78° South lat. Interest in the Antarctic did not revive until after 1890, when an international scheme of research was drawn up. A Norwegian, C. E. Borchgrevink, in 1898–1900, was the first to

winter in the Antarctic and to travel on the ice barrier. The British share in this work was carried out by Capt. R. F. Scott's expedition in the *Discovery,* 1901–4. Scott's party sledged across the barrier to 82° 17' South, then a record "farthest south". A little later, Ernest Shackleton beat this by travelling to within 160 km of the South Pole. The Scottish polar explorer William Spiers Bruce led the Scottish national Antarctic Expedition of 1902 in the *Scotia* and discovered Coats Land and founded a meteorological observatory on the South Orkneys. In 1910 Scott organised his second expedition in *Terra Nova,* and became engaged against his will in a "race for the Pole" when, after his departure, the Norwegian Arctic explorer, Roald Amundsen, suddenly announced that he was sailing for the Antarctic. Amundsen set up his base at the eastern end of the Barrier, and, relying on dog teams for hauling his sledges, reached the Pole on 14 December 1911. Meanwhile Scott and his party, their start delayed by adverse weather, were marching southwards, man-hauling their sledges, for Scott was against the use of dogs. After an arduous journey they reached the Pole one month after Amundsen. The return was a struggle against the weather and increasing weakness, probably due to scurvy, until at last they perished within a few kilometres of their base. After the first world war the development of the whaling industry greatly stimulated further exploration. Outstanding expeditions included that of Admiral R. E. Byrd, 1929, when he flew over the South Pole; the British Graham Land expedition, 1934, which carried out the first extensive mapping of any part of the Antarctic continent; and the US Navy's Antarctic Expedition of 1940, when the whole continent was circumnavigated and great areas photographed from the air. In recent years valuable work has been done by the first International expedition, the Norwegian–British–Swedish Expedition to Queen Maud Land, and by the French in Adélie Land. The Falkland Island Dependencies Survey, set up during the war, has continued the scientific exploration of Graham Land. The Antarctic was the scene of high adventure during the International Geophysical Year (1957–58), when scientists from many countries participated in the explorations. The Commonwealth Trans-Antarctic Expedition set out from opposite sides of the continent and met at the South Pole, the UK party, led by Sir Vivian Fuchs, from the Falklands, and Sir Edmund Hillary and his party from New Zealand. The UK party accomplished the first crossing of the White Continent in 99 days. Their scientific work included the marking of seismic and complementary gravimetric studies at frequent intervals along the 3,540 km traverse. Since the Antarctic is becoming important for many reasons, in weather forecasting, in the whaling industry, and as a possible centre for world air routes, the tempo of exploration and research will become even faster in the future.

Anteaters, a small family (the Myrmecophagidae) of mammals from Central and South America. They feed on ants, termites and other insects which they gather with a long tongue covered with sticky saliva.

Antennae, paired feelers of insects and crustaceans. In radio, the term "antenna" is equivalent to "aerial".

Anthem, a choral composition, with or without instrumental accompaniment, usually sung after the third collect in the Church of England services. The words are from the Scriptures, and the composition may be for solo voices only, for full choir, or for both. Among the chief British composers of anthems are Tallis, Purcell, Croft, Boyce, Goss and Stainer.

Anthracite is a black coal with a brilliant lustre. It contains 92 per cent. and over of carbon and burns slowly, without smoke or flame. *See* **Coal.**

Anthropoid, meaning "resembling man", a sub-order of the primate mammals including man and also the gibbon, chimpanzee, orang-utan, and gorilla.

Anthropology. *See* **Section F, Part V.**

Antibiotics, a collective name for any substance

derived from micro-organisms or fungi which is capable of destroying infections, *e.g.*, penicillin. *See* **Section P.**

Anticyclone, a region where barometric pressure is greater than that of its surroundings. Such a system is distinguished on weather charts by a pattern of isobars, usually circular or oval-shaped, enclosing the centre of high pressure where the air is calm. In the remaining areas light or moderately strong winds blow spirally outwards in a clockwise direction in the Northern Hemisphere (and in the reverse direction in the Southern Hemisphere), in accordance with Buys Ballot's law (an observer with back to wind in Northern Hemisphere has lower pressure to left; in Southern to right). Over the British Isles anticyclonic weather is generally quiet and settled, being fair, warm, and sunny in summer and either very cold and often foggy or overcast and gloomy in winter. These systems move slowly and sometimes remain practically stationary for days at a time, that over Siberia being particularly well defined. Extensive belts of almost permanent anti-cyclones occur in latitudes 30° N and 30° S. Persistent anticyclonic weather with easterly winds during the months December to March, 1962–3, brought the coldest and hardest winter to Britain since 1740.

Antimony. Metal element, no. 51, symbol Sb. In group 5 of the periodic table. Exists in various forms, the stable form being a grey metal with a layer structure. The other forms are non-conductors. On being burned, it gives off dense fumes of oxide of antimony. By itself it is not of special utility; but as an alloy for hardening other metals, it is much used. As an alloy with lead for type-metal, and with tin and copper or zinc for Britannia-metal, it is of great value. Most important antimony ore is stibnite (antimony sulphide).

Anti-Pope, one elected in opposition to one held to be canonically chosen; commonly applied to the popes Clement VII and Benedict XIII, who resided at Avignon during the Great Schism (1378–1417).

Anti-proton, the "negative proton", an atomic particle created in high energy collisions of nuclear particles. Its existence was confirmed in Oct. 1955. *See* **Section F.**

Antisemitism. *See* **Section J.**

Antlers are the branched horns of deer, the branches being called tines. Antlers originate as outgrowths of the frontal bone, and are usually shed once a year. Except in the reindeer and caribou they are restricted to the male.

Apartheid. *See* **Section J.**

Ape, a term applied to the gorilla, chimpanzee, orang-utan and gibbon—the anthropoid apes.

Aphelion, the point in the orbit of a planet farthest from the sun; the opposite of perihelion. At aphelion the earth is 1.52×10^8 km from the sun.

Aphids, green-flies or plant lice, a numerous species of destructive insects living on young shoots and foliage, some on roots. Reproduction is by parthenogenesis (virgin birth).

Apis, the sacred bull worshipped by the ancient Egyptians; also the scientific name for the bee.

Apocalyptic writings are those which deal with revelation and prophecy, more especially the Revelation of St. John.

Apocrypha (hidden writings), the books which were included in the Septuagint (Greek) and Vulgate (Latin) versions of the Old Testament but excluded from the sacred canon at the Reformation by the Protestants on the grounds that they were not originally written in Hebrew nor regarded as genuine by the Jews. The books include: 1 and 2 Esdras, Tobit, Judith, additions to Esther, Wisdom of Solomon, Ecclesiasticus, Baruch, Song of the Three Holy Children, History of Susannah, Bel and the Dragon, Prayer of Manasses, 1 and 2 Maccabees. The term is usually applied to the additions to the Old Testament, but there are also numerous Christian writings of the same character. *The New English Bible,* which contains the Apocrypha, was published in 1970.

Apogee, that point in the orbit of a heavenly body which is farthest from the earth; used in relation to the sun, moon and artificial satellites. The sun's apogee corresponds to the earth's aphelion. *See* **Perigee.**

Apostasy is a revolt, by an individual or party, from one form of opinions or doctrinate to another. Julian, the Roman Emperor (331–63), brought up as a Christian, became converted to paganism and on coming to the throne (361), proclaimed religious toleration. Hence his name, Julian the Apostate.

Apostles. The twelve apostles who were disciples of Jesus were: Simon Peter and Andrew (his brother), James and John (sons of Zebedee), Philip, Bartholomew, Thomas, Matthew, James, Thaddaeus, Simon, and Judas Iscariot. After the Ascension Matthias was chosen to take the place of Judas. St. Paul was the leading apostle in the mission to the Gentiles, though he was not one of the twelve. St. Barnabas has also been called an apostle.

Apostles' Creed, the name of the most ancient of the Church's statements of its belief: "I believe in God the Father Almighty; and in Jesus Christ his only Son our Lord, who was born of the Holy Ghost and the Virgin Mary...." A later version is used in the Church of England at morning and evening prayer.

Apostolic Fathers were the immediate disciples or followers of the apostles, especially such as left writings behind. They included Barnabas, Clement of Rome, Ignatius of Antioch, Hermas, Papias of Hieropolis and Polycarp.

Appeasement Policy. The name of the policy during 1937 and 1938 of yielding to the demands of Hitler and Mussolini in the hope that a point would be reached when the dictators would co-operate in the maintenance of peace. The policy culminated in the Munich Agreement (which was the subject of much criticism) after a series of concessions including the recognition of the Italian conquest of Abyssinia and the German annexation of Austria. The policy was finally demonstrated as futile when Hitler seized Czechoslovakia in March 1939.

Appian Way, the oldest and finest of the Roman roads originally laid by Appius Claudius (312 B.C.) from Rome to Capua and thence to Brundisium (Brindisi).

Approved Schools were residential schools, subject to Home Office inspection, for the training of young persons under 17 who, because of disturbed behaviour as a result of unfavourable influences such as bad environment or parental neglect, were guilty of offences or in need of care and protection and had been sent to them by magistrates from juvenile or other courts. The approved school order was abolished by the Children and Young Persons Act 1969. Such young people may now be committed to the care of a local authority and accommodated in a system of community homes ranging from children's homes to borstal type institutions.

April, the fourth month of the year, from the Roman *Aprilis* derived from *aperire* "to open" —the period when the buds begin to open.

Apse is a semicircular recess, arched or dome-roofed, at the end of the choir, aisles, or nave of a church.

Aqueducts are conduits in which water flows or is conveyed from its source to the place where it is to be used. Most famous builders were the Romans and the oldest Roman aqueduct was the Aqua Appia, which dates from about 310 B.C. Among modern aqueducts may be mentioned that of Glasgow, which brings water to that city from Loch Katrine; that of Manchester, which taps Thirlmere; that of Liverpool, with Lake Vyrnwy in North Wales as its source, and the Fron Aqueduct, Powys, which carries water from the Elan Valley to Birmingham.

Arabian Nights Entertainment or **Book of a Thousand and One Nights,** a collection of fascinating tales of the Orient, of mixed Indian, Persian, Arabic, and Egyptian origination, and first made known in Europe by Antoine Galland's French translation (1704–17) from Arabian texts. The "master" tale tells how the princess Shahrazad so beguiles the king through the telling of the tales over one thousand and one nights that her life was spared. English translators include E. W. Lane (1840), Sir Richard Burton (1885–8), John Payne (1882–4).

Arabic Numerals. The modern system of numbering, 0, 1, 2, 3, 4, 5, 6, 7, 8, 9, in which the digits depend on their position for their value is called the Arabic numerical notation. The method is, in fact, of Indian origin. By the 9th cent. Hindu science was available in Arabic, and the Persian mathematician Al-Kwarizimi (c. 830) in his *Arithmetic* used the so-called "Arabic" system of numbering. Gradually the method spread to Europe, taking the place of the Roman system which was useless for calculation. The West is indebted to the Arabs for the zero symbol, the lack of which had been a serious drawback to Greek mathematics. It made the invention of decimal fractions possible.

Aragonite, the unstable form of calcium carbonate found as a mineral in some young deposits. It crystallises in the orthorhombic system but tends to revert to calcite.

Aramaic Languages, the Semitic dialects current in Mesopotamia and the regions extending south-west from the Euphrates to Palestine from about the 12th cent. B.C. until after the rise of Islam, when Aramaic was superseded by Arabic. Both Aramaic and Greek were spoken in Palestine during the time of Christ.

Archaeopteryx, a fossil bird providing a connecting link between reptiles and birds. It had feathers, jaws with teeth, no bill, reptilian bones and skull, a long tail, and it probably used its fore-limbs for gliding flight. The first specimen, found in 1861, in the Solenhofen limestone of Bavaria, is in London's Natural History Museum.

Archbishop, the chief of the bishops of an ecclesiastical province in the Greek, Roman, and Anglican churches. In the Church of England there are two archbishops, the Archbishop of Canterbury, called the Primate of *all* England, and the Archbishop of York, styled the Primate of England.

Archimedes' Principle. When a body is weighed in air and then in any fluid, the apparent loss in weight is equal to the weight of fluid displaced. This scientific fact was noted by the Syracusan philosopher Archimedes (287–212 B.C.) and is frequently used as a basis for density measurements.

Architecture, the art and science of building. The provision of shelter for mankind by the orderly arrangement of materials in a manner which expresses man's attitude to living. The forms which buildings take are the outcome of the function for which they are to be used, of the architect's aesthetic sensibility and the structural method adopted. Until the last hundred years structural methods were limited to timber frames, and columns, lintels, load-bearing walls, arches, vaults, and domes in brick or stone. From these few basic elements have evolved the great variety of historic styles of building to be found throughout the world. To give but one example, the Greeks created those systems of decorated columns and beams, known as the Orders, which were adapted by the Romans, revived decoratively rather than structurally during the Renaissance and are still used in debased form on the more presumptuous type of modern building. In recent years, however, architecture has taken on a new meaning. Once confined to the rich, in the form of Church, State or Commerce, it is now, with the coming of democracy, recognised as an essential social service for all. This, and the development of new structural techniques and materials (steel, aluminium, sheet glass, reinforced concrete, plastics and plywoods, to name a few), have made the interest in historic styles, the mainstay of the older architect, of secondary importance. Modern architecture is the creation of buildings with the highest possible standards of functional performance in terms of efficient planning and structure, good artificial and natural lighting, adequate heating or cooling, and proper acoustic conditions consistent with the price the client can afford to pay. At the same time the architect's task is to design a structure and the spaces the structure delimits, internally and externally which are aesthetically stimulating and satisfying, and well related to the land and buildings around.

Arctic Exploration. Modern exploration of the Arctic begins in the 16th cent. when men sought to reach the East Indies by sailing through the Arctic to the Pacific Ocean. The North-east Passage, via the shores of northern Asia,

was the first attempted. In 1553 and 1554 the English navigators Sir Richard Chancellor and Stephen Burrough sailed into the White Sea, but were prevented by storms and ice from advancing farther eastwards. The project was later revived by the Dutch; Barendts in 1594 discovered Spitsbergen, but also failed to get beyond Novaya Zemlya. It was not, in fact, until 1879 that the Swede, A. E. Nordenskjöld, in the *Vega*, succeeded in reaching the Pacific. The attempts to find a North-west Passage were more numerous and determined. In 1585 John Davis penetrated Davis Strait and coasted along Baffin Island. Hopes ran high when Henry Hudson discovered Hudson Bay in 1610, but a practicable passage continued to elude explorers. The problem was to find a navigable route through the maze of channels in the short summer season, and to avoid being frozen in with supplies exhausted. After the Napoleonic Wars the Admiralty sent out many naval expeditions which culminated in Sir John Franklin's expedition with the *Erebus* and *Terror* in 1845. The ships were beset by ice in Victoria Channel and, after Franklin's death, were abandoned by their crews, who perished from scurvy and starvation on their march southwards. To ascertain their fate, several further expeditions were despatched, and the crew of the *Investigator*, commanded by R. J. M'Clure, sailing eastwards from Bering Strait, were the first to make the Passage, though in doing so they were obliged to abandon their ship. It was thirty years before the Norwegian, Roald Amundsen, succeeded in sailing the *Gjoa* from the east to west. In the meantime, the North Pole had become the goal of explorers. Nansen, in 1893, put the *Fram* into the ice-pack to drift across the Polar basin, and himself made an unsuccessful attempt on the Pole across the pack. This was eventually achieved by the American explorer Robert E. Peary, who after several expeditions in the North Greenland region, sledged to the Pole with Eskimo companions in 1909. The next phase was the employment of airships and aeroplanes in Arctic exploration. In 1926 Admiral Byrd made the first flight over the Pole, and in the same year Amundsen and Lincoln Ellsworth flew the airship *Norge* from Spitsbergern to Point Barrow Alaska. Two years later, the *Italia*, commanded by the Italian, Nobile, was wrecked on a return flight from the Pole, and Amundsen lost his life in an attempt to rescue the survivors. With modern developments in aircraft and navigation, flights over the Polar basin are almost a routine matter. The first voyage under the North Pole was made in August 1958 by the American nuclear-powered submarine *Nautilus*.

Arenaceous Rocks, the rocks composed of grains of sand, chiefly sandstones; quartz is the most abundant mineral in these rocks.

Argillaceous Rocks are a sedimentary group, including the shales and clays.

Argon, chemical element no. 18, symbol A. This was the first of the inert gases (**F14**) to be isolated from air by Rayleigh and Ramsay in 1894. Argon is used for filling gas-filled metal filament electric lamps. In gas discharge tube it gives a blue glow. *See also* **Rare Gases.**

Arithmetic, the branch of mathematics that deals with numerical calculations as in counting, measuring, weighing. The early civilisations used simple arithmetic for commercial purposes, employing symbols and later letters of the alphabet as numerals. When Hindu-Arabic numerals replaced Roman numerals in the Middle Ages it meant a great step forward and led to rapid developments—the invention of logarithms, slide-rule, calculating machines.

Arithmetic Progression, a sequence of numbers in which the successor of each number is obtained by adding or subtracting a fixed number, for example 2, 5, 8, 11, ... or 100, 95, 90, 85. ...

Ark of the Covenant was the sacred chest of the Hebrews and symbolised God's presence. It was overlaid with gold inside and outside. It accompanied the Israelites into battle and was once captured by the Philistines. Eventually it found a resting-place in Solomon's Temple. *See also* **Section S.**

Armada, Spanish, the naval expedition fitted out

by Philip II of Spain in 1588 against England, commanded by the Duke of Medina Sidonia. It comprised 129 ships, was manned by 8,000 sailors and carried 19,000 soldiers and more than 2,000 cannon. Against this formidable force Elizabeth had only 80 ships, manned by 9,000 sailors, under Lord Howard of Effingham, under whom served Drake, Hawkins and Frobisher. The British Fleet awaited the Armada off Plymouth, and at Tilbury there was a considerable defensive land force under the command of the Earl of Leicester. On 19 July the ships of the Armada were sighted off the Lizard, disposed in a crescent 11 km long from horn to horn. The excellent manoeuvring of the English, their fire-ships and a gale from the N.W. combined so effectively to cripple the Spanish ships that the Armada was scattered, only 63 of the original fleet of 129 reaching home via the North of Scotland. It was impossible to embark the army of Parma waiting in the Netherlands. Elizabeth had a medal struck bearing in Latin the inscription, "God blew and they were scattered".

Armadillo, a genus of animals related to the sloths and anteaters, belonging to South America, and carrying a hard bony covering over the back, under which one species (*Tolypeutes*) can completely conceal itself when attacked, rolling itself up like a hedgehog.

Armageddon, according to the Revelation of St. John, the great battle in which the last conflict between good and evil is to be fought.

Armillary Sphere, an early form of astronomical apparatus with a number of circles representing equator, meridian, ecliptic, etc. Used by Hipparchus and Ptolemy and up to the time of Tycho Brahe for determining the position of the stars.

Aromatic. A term used by chemists, originally to describe compounds like benzene, having a characteristic smell. It is a term which implies a collection of chemical characteristics, the salient features being a flat ring structure and a general similarity to benzene.

Arsenic, a metalloid element, no. 33, symbol As in group 5 of the periodic table usually met with as a constituent of other minerals, sometimes by itself. Its compounds are very poisonous. Lead arsenate is a powerful insecticide used for spraying fruit trees. The more stable allotropic form (grey) has a layer structure, and conducts electricity.

Art Deco, the name given by modern collectors to the decorative style of the 1920s and 1930s; it is derived from the long official name of the Paris Exhibition of 1925, which was almost exclusively devoted to "les Arts Décoratifs". Art Deco runs parallel in time with Functionalism (*q.v.*) but unlike that austere and philosophical style, Art Deco is gay, elegant and even frivolous, being a creation of fashionable Paris. It is related superficially to Cubism, using squares, circles and triangles in interesting combinations for ornament. Another popular motif is the modern girl with her shingled head dancing the tango or drinking cocktails. The style is brash and worldly, but in its best expressions full of charm and vitality. Famous names within the style are the glassmaker Rene Lalique (1860–1945), the fashion designers Gabrielle Chanel and Elsa Schiaparelli, and the decorator and illustrator Erte (Roman de Tirtoff, b. 1829). Recently there has been a nostalgic revival of Art Deco, *e.g.*, in films like "Bonny and Clyde" (1967) or "The Great Gatsby" (1974) based on F. Scott Fitzgerald's novel (1925).

Artesian Wells take their name from Artois in France, where the first wells of this kind were constructed in 1126. They are to be found only when a water-bearing bed is sandwiched between two impervious beds. When a boring is made to the lower part of the bed, the pressure of water is sufficient to cause the water to overflow at the surface. Artesian wells were known to ancient Egypt and China, and have existed in the Sahara since the earliest times. The fountains in Trafalgar Square were once fed by artesian wells sunk through the London clay into the chalk about 250 m.

Articles. The *Six Articles* are those contained in an Act of Henry VIII, and were of Roman Catholic origin. The *Thirty-nine Articles* were drawn up for the English church at the Reformation. They are printed at the back of the Prayer Book. Candidates for holy orders in the Church of England are required to subscribe to them, though the form of assent has recently been modified.

Art Nouveau (German *Jugend Stil*) was prevalent in architecture and decoration in Europe and the USA *c*, 1885–1910. It was rooted in the thoughts of Ruskin and William Morris. In reaction against the impersonal uniformity of industrial products which were flooding the market, artists turned to Nature for their inspiration, choosing organically growing forms, flowers or animals, as motifs for decoration or even for shaping whole objects. Another favourite motif was Romantic Woman with long robes and flowing hair, as interpreted so beautifully by Aubrey Beardsley. The sharply undulating line with a whiplash rhythm is a recurring theme. Famous names are the glassmakers Emile Gallé in France and Louis Comfort Tiffany in New York, the English goldsmith Charles Robert Ashbee (1863–1942), Henry Van de Velde (1867–1942) in Belgium and Charles Rennie Mackintosh (1868–1928) in Scotland, both architects and interior decorators, and in pure architecture Antonio Gaudi of Barcelona (1852–1926) and Victor Horta of Brussels (1861–1946).

Arts and Crafts Movement, the English revival of decorative art which began about 1875 as a revolt against the existing vulgarity of internal decoration and furnishings and the pettiness of academic art. Inspired by William Morris and Burne-Jones together with Rossetti, it was strongly influenced by the former's mediaevalism, his hatred of industrialism, and his own version of socialism which included the regeneration of man by handicrafts. His firm of Morris & Co. produced wallpapers, tapestries, furniture, stained-glass windows, carpets and fabrics in a style totally different from that of contemporary Victorian decoration. Morris's Kelmscott Press did much to raise the standards of book design and printing. *See* **Art Nouveau.**

Arum, a genus of plants of the *Araceae* family of which there is but one British species, the wakerobin or cuckoo-pint, sometimes also styled "Lords and Ladies".

Arundel Marbles, a collection of ancient Greek sculptures formed by Thomas Howard, Earl of Arundel in the 17th cent. and presented to Oxford University by his grandson, Henry Howard, who became Duke of Norfolk.

Aryans, nomadic peoples who made their way in successive waves from the Eurasian steppes to the Indus and the Nile during the first half of the 2nd millennium B.C. They crossed the Hindu Kush into N.W. India and settled in the valleys of the Indus and Ganges, where an earlier Indus civilisation had flourished, *c.* 3240–2750 B.C. Their religious ideas are reflected in the Veda (oldest Hindu scriptures, written down many centuries later in Vedic, parent language of Sanskrit). Those who made their way to Syria and Egypt founded the Hyksos empire (*c.* 1720–1550 B.C.). The Aryans introduced the horse-drawn chariot and spoke a language from which the great Indo-European family of languages is derived, with one group in India and Iran, and another in Europe. Because of the misuse of the term by the Nazis, Aryan is now referred to as proto-Indo-European.

Asafoetida, an acrid, strong-smelling gum resin exuded from the stem of umbelliferous plant, *Ferula foetida*, found in Iran and Afghanistan. Formerly used medicinally to treat hysteria; still used in cooking in India, Iran and France.

Ascension Day, or Holy Thursday, is the 40th day after Easter.

Ascot Races are an annual fashionable function dating from 1711 and taking place on Ascot Heath, only 10 km from Windsor, in June. These races have always had royal patronage. The course is *c.* 3 km long.

Ash, a familiar deciduous tree of the genus *Fraxinus*, of over 60 species, native to North temperate regions. The ash held an important place in Norse mythology, as it was supposed to support the heavens with its roots in Hell. The species native to Britain, and to Europe, is *F. excelsior*, a tall tree with compound leaves, greenish flowers, winged seeds, and black buds in winter. It is a valuable timber tree, tough and elastic, and largely used for wheels and handles. The rowan, or mountain ash, *Sorbus aucuparia*, with similar leaves and orange berries, belongs to a different family. *F. pendula* or weeping ash is a strain which makes an ideal natural summer house.

Ashes, The, the symbol which distinguishes the winning cricket team in the Australian Test Matches. In 1882 the Australians won at the Oval by 7 runs. After the match the following epitaph appeared in the *Sporting Times*: "In affectionate remembrance of English Cricket which died at the Oval on 29 Aug. 1882, deeply lamented by a large circle of sorrowing friends and acquaintances. R.I.P. NB. The body will be cremated and the ashes taken to Australia." When the English Eleven went to Australia the same winter it was said that they had come to recover the "ashes". England won two out of three matches, and after the third match the ashes of what is now generally believed to have been a stump were presented in an urn to Ivo Bligh, later Lord Darnley. He bequeathed the urn to the M.C.C., and it now stands in the Memorial Gallery at Lord's.

Ash Wednesday, first day of Lent, the seventh Wednesday before Easter.

Assassination, treacherous murder for political ends, usually of a ruler or distinguished person. Among the most notable: Julius Caesar, 44 B.C.; Thomas Becket, 1170, David Rizzio, 1566; William the Silent, 1584; Henry IV of France, 1610; Jean Paul Marat, 1793; Abraham Lincoln, 1865; Alexander II of Russia, 1881; Archduke Francis Ferdinand of Austria, 1914; Dr. Dollfuss, 1934; King Alexander of Yugoslavia, 1934; Mahatma Gandhi, 1948; King Abdullah of Jordan, 1951; Liaquat Ali Khan, 1951; King Feisal of Iraq, 1958; Mr. Bandaranaike, 1959; President Kennedy, 1963; Malcolm X, 1965; Dr. Verwoerd, 1966; Dr. Martin Luther King, 1968; Senator Robert Kennedy, 1968; Mr. Tom Mboya, 1969; King Faisal of Saudi Arabia, 1975; Lord Mountbatten, 1979; John Lennon, 1980; President Sadat, 1981; Mrs. Indira Gandhi, 1984.

Asteroids or the minor planets are relatively small objects which move in orbits mainly between those of Mars and Jupiter. The first to be discovered (by Piazzi in 1801) was Ceres. Many thousands more have since been discovered, of which nearly 2,000 now have well-determined orbits and have been named. The largest are Ceres (800 km), Pallas (500 km), Vesta (530 km) and Juno (240 km). Few others have diameters of more than 80 km, while those of the majority are less than 5 or 10 km. Of particular interest are the Trojan group, located at the two stable "Lagrangian" points in Jupiter's orbit round the sun, where their locations make isosceles triangles with the sun and Jupiter. Also, a number of asteroids have orbits like that of Icarus which at perigee (*q.v.*) comes close to the sun. The recently discovered Chiron orbits between Saturn and Uranus.

Astrolabe, a mediaeval scientific instrument for taking altitudes, observing the sun by day and the stars by night, and used for telling the time and finding the latitude. Used by the ancient Greeks, later by the Arabs and Persians, and introduced into Europe by way of Spain in the 14th cent. Chaucer is said to have sent his son Lois, a ten-year-old student at Oxford, an astrolabe with a treatise on its use in 1391.

Astrology. *See* **Section J.**

Astronomical Unit, the mean distance between the centres of the sun and earth, or the semimajor axis of the earth's orbit, has a value of about $1 \cdot 495979 \times 10^8$ km (149,597,900 km). This value has been constantly improved over the past 300 years, first using observations of the planets, later transits of Venus across the sun's disc, then observations of minor planets such as Eros as they came near the earth, and now by the transit time of a radar beam bounced off the planet Venus. The astronomical unit is a fundamental quantity for astronomy.

Astronomy. The Pythagoreans believed the stars and planets moved with uniform circular velocity in crystalline spheres, centred round the earth (the "harmony of the spheres"). Hipparchus (190–120 B.C.) made the first star catalogue, discovered the precession of the equinoxes and introduced the idea of epicyclic motion. His planetary system, in the form it was presented by Ptolemy 200 years later, held until the Renaissance when Copernicus revived the heretical view first put forward by Aristarchus of Samos (310–230 B.C.) that the sun and not the earth was at the centre. Galileo, accurate observer and experimenter, went beyond Copernicus; helped by the contributions of Tycho Brahe, Giordano Bruno, Kepler and others, he was able to overthrow the Ptolemaic system of the heavenly spheres and Aristotelian philosophy and pave the way for Newton and modern astronomy. To Galileo we owe the conception of acceleration; to Newton the theory of universal gravitation; they showed that the same laws govern both celestial and terrestrial physics. Three landmarks in more recent times were the discovery of Uranus by Herschel in 1781 which extended the solar system as then recognised; the estimation by Hubble in 1924 of the distance of Andromeda, which showed that our Galaxy was just one of many; and Einstein's theory of relativity which improved on Newton's theory of the solar system by bringing gravitation into the domain of space-time. Today radiotelescopes and space probes are advancing astronomical knowledge and making it possible to explore regions beyond the scope of optical telescopes. The following have held the position of Astronomer Royal (period of office in brackets): John Flamsteed (1675–1719), Edmund Halley (1719–42), James Bradley (1742–62), Nathaniel Bliss (1762–65), Nevil Maskelyne (1765–1811), John Pond (1811–35), Sir George Airy (1835–81), Sir William Christie (1881–1910), Sir Frank Dyson (1910–33), Sir Harold Spencer Jones (1933–55), Sir Richard Woolley (1956–72), Sir Martin Ryle (1972–82), Professor Graham Smith (1982–). *See* **F5–7**, *also* **Radio Astronomy.**

Astrophysics, a branch of astronomy concerned with the physical nature and constitution of the various objects within the universe. Recent developments in radio astronomy and in space research technology, opening up gamma-ray, X-ray, ultra-violet and infra-red parts of the spectrum, have contributed to the major recent advances in this science.

Athanasian Creed, one of the three ancient creeds of the Christian Church, often referred to as the *Quicunque Vult*, is a statement of the doctrine of the Trinity and the Incarnation, and though named after St. Athanasius, it is thought to be the work of St. Ambrose (339–97).

Atmosphere is the gaseous envelope of the earth, and consists of a mixture of gases (*see* **Air**) and water vapour, the variability of the latter being of great importance meteorologically. The ozone layer, which absorbs solar ultra-violet radiation which would be lethal to plant life if it reached the ground lies between 12 to 50 km above the earth. The lower level of the atmosphere up to a height of about 12 km (10 km at the Poles and 16 km at the Equator) is known as the *troposphere*, and it is in this region that nearly all weather phenomena occur. This is the region of most interest to the forecaster studying temperature, humidity, windspeed, and the movement of air masses. Temperature falls with height by about 1°C per 152 m in this layer. The *tropopause* is the boundary between the troposphere and the *stratosphere*. Temperature varies little in the lower levels of this region: it is mainly cloudless, and has no vertical currents. Strangely enough, the lowest temperatures of the atmosphere are to be found not at the Poles, but at about 18 km above the Equator, where a temperature as low as −80°C has been recorded! Temperatures begin to rise about 32 km from the earth's surface at about the same rate as they fall in the troposphere owing to the absorption of solar radiation by the concentration of ozone. The stratospheric air is extremely dry. Near the 100 km level a number of important atmospheric phenomena occur. Above this level the oxygen becomes predominantly monatomic in contrast to the normal diatomic form at lower altitudes. This is the *ionosphere* (q.v.). This layer acts as an electrical radio mirror which makes long-distance radio transmission possible. The region of the Van Allen belts (q.v.) above the earth is called the magnetosphere (q.v.). The auroras are most frequently observed at altitudes between about 100 and 400 km but do extend at times far higher. Many aspects of the upper air can only be studied through space-research techniques. These include the composition and temperature of the charged particles in the ionosphere, the location of the electric currents in the ionosphere which produce the regular variations of the compass needle, as well as those which circulate during magnetic storms, the variation of the intensity of different radiation in the air-glow (q.v.) with height, the composition of the air at heights above 32 km, and so on. In addition, the pressures, density, temperatures, and wind distribution of the neutral atmosphere can be studied more directly, in much greater detail, and up to much greater altitudes than is possible if one is confined to the use of equipment on the ground. Instruments outside the atmosphere can make systematic observations on a world-wide basis of the atmospheric circulation, through observation of cloud cover and of the thermal radiation into space from the atmosphere. Such observations are of great importance for meteorology. *See also* **Ionosphere.**

Atmospherics are electrical impulses which are believed to originate in atmospheric electrical discharges such as lightning. They give rise to crashing background noises in the loudspeakers of radio sets, interfering with reception at distances of up to 6,400 km from the centre of the disturbance. The location of atmospherics with the aid of radio direction-finding methods gives warning of the approach of thunderstorms.

Atom. *See* **F10–17, F23.**

Atomic Pile, an apparatus containing a fissionable element and a moderator, such as heavy water or graphite, in which a self-sustaining fission process proceeds at a controllable rate. The first atomic pile, constructed on a squash court at Chicago, was operated for the first time on 2 December 1942, under the direction of Enrico Fermi. The pile contained 12,400 lb (5,580 kg) of uranium. *See* **Nuclear Reactors.**

Augsburg Confession, name given to the doctrine of faith of the Lutheran churches, drawn up by Melanchthon and endorsed by Luther for the Diet of Augsburg (1530).

August, named after the Emperor Augustus, because it was his "lucky" month.

Auks, duck-like sea-birds, black and white, with short, narrow wings, compact bodies and legs set well back. Breed in colonies on rocky coasts of N. Europe (incl. British Isles) and spend most time in coastal waters. Migrate south in winter. The Auk family includes the Razorbill, Little Auk, Guillemot and Puffin. The Great Auk became extinct in the 19th cent. after ruthless hunting for the sake of its feathers.

Aurora polaris. This wonderful phenomenon of the night sky is a common sight at high northern and southern latitudes, where it is called the aurora borealis and the aurora australis respectively. It is visible less often at temperate latitudes, and only rarely in the tropics. The auroral ovals, or zones of maximum frequency of aurora, surround both of the earth's geomagnetic poles, and the northern auroral oval includes the northern parts of Scandinavia, Canada and Alaska. The aurora is the visible manifestation of complex plasma processes occurring within the earth's magnetosphere (q.v.), whereby streams of high-energy electrons and protons (mainly) are accelerated and dumped via the earth's magnetic field lines into the upper atmosphere. This mechanism produces the light emission of the aurora. The brightest aurora, which may also extend to lower latitudes, occurs during geomagnetic storms, which are complex and large-scale plasma instabilities within the magnetosphere triggered by fluctuations in the solar wind (q.v.) —usually ascribed to "M" regions on the sun

associated with coronal holes, flares and active sunspot groups. Auroral displays may take several forms—a faint glow, a diffuse ribbon of light crossing the heavens, great folded waving curtains or draperies, or the entire sky may be flooded with a rapidly varying brilliant panoply of light. Specially instrumented spacecraft which can directly explore the magnetosphere and high-latitude ionosphere have provided a great deal of our knowledge about this fascinating and complex phenomenon. The aurora is a kind of light essentially different from that of the rainbow which is a partly subjective phenomenon. Each beholder sees his own rainbow, whose light is sunlight refracted and reflected by many raindrops. The raindrops that produce his rainbow depend on his position as well as on the direction of the sun. The aurora, on the contrary, is a light as objective as that of a candle, though produced differently. It is a self-luminescence of the air in particular regions of the atmosphere that lie far above the clouds.

Austerlitz, Battle of, was fought near Brünn, in Moravia, on 2 December 1805, when Napoleon defeated the Russians and Austrians under Kutuzov.

Auto-da-Fé, or Act of Faith, was the ceremony connected with the sentencing of heretics under the Inquisition of Spain and Portugal, the persons found guilty being imprisoned or burned alive. The ceremony took place in some public square, sometimes in the presence of the king and court.

Automation is a modern word used to designate the adoption of methods of automatic control either of manufacturing processes or of any business process involving a large mass of routine work. The word is used in broader and narrower senses. In its broadest sense it covers any form of mechanisation which largely replaces human labour by the work of automatic or semi-automatic machines, such as has been in progress continuously since the Industrial Revolution; but it it better kept to a narrower meaning, in which it is confined to the recent development of electronic or similar devices, involving feedback (automatic detection and correction of malfunction). Human labour is eliminated save for that needed for watching and maintaining the elaborate machines used. In this sense, automation has been spreading rapidly in advanced countries.

Autumn, the third season of the year, begins with the autumnal equinox, and ends with the winter solstice, but the term is generally understood as covering the period from mid-August to mid-November.

Auxins, "plant hormones", organic substances produced by plants to regulate growth. Synthetic auxins are now widely used, *e.g.*, for promotion of root formation in cuttings, differential weed control, prevention of premature dropping of fruit, in storage of potatoes and hard fruit, and to overcome frost damage to fruit buds.

Average is a single number designed to give a typical example of a set of numbers, *e.g.*, a cricketer's batting average for a season gives an idea of his typical score. There are several kinds of average and their uses are studied in the science of statistics (q.v.). A statement that "so and so is the average value" can be misleading if one does not know which average is meant. Three common averages are: the arithmetic average (or mean), the mode, and the median. The arithmetic average of n numbers is found by adding them together and dividing by n; this is a very common method of averaging. The mode of n numbers is the most frequently occurring number. The median is the middle number, *i.e.*, the number which is smaller than just as many of the other numbers as it exceeds. Of the numbers 1, 2, 2, 2, 2, 3, 4, 5, 6, 8, 9, the arithmetic means is 4, the mode is 2, the median is 3.

Avocet, a graceful wading bird related to the stilts, of black-and-white plumage, bluish legs, and slender upturned bill. There are four species. Avocets nest in colonies and there is one in the sanctuary on Havergate Island, Suffolk.

Avogadro's Hypothesis. This is a fundamental concept of chemistry. Equal volumes of all gases under the same conditions of temperature and pressure contain the same number of molecules. This law was instrumental in assigning the formulae of molecules. The hypothesis was put forward in 1811, but was not generally accepted until 1860.

Avogadro's Number. See **F24.**

Aztecs, the name of a native and powerful race found in Mexico when the Spaniards first discovered that country, and with difficulty subdued.

B

Babiroussa, a ferocious, long-legged wild pig, native of Sulawesi, sometimes called the horned-hog, because of the long upper tusks in the male, which are developments of the canine teeth which grow upwards, piercing the upper lip, and curving backwards, often broken in fighting.

Baboon, monkeys belonging to the African genus *Papio.* They are considered the lowest of the Old World (Catarrhine) monkeys, and walk on all fours. In the main terrestrial, but take to trees after food. The mandrill is closely related.

Babylonian Captivity, the period spent by the Jews in Babylon after Jerusalem was captured by Nebuchadnezzar, the Babylonian emperor, in 586 B.C. Traditionally the captivity lasted 70 years, but when Babylon was in turn taken by Cyrus in 538 B.C., the exiles were permitted to return to Jerusalem. The term is also applied in church history to the period 1309–78 when the papacy moved to Avignon, into the control of the French monarchy.

Bacteria. See **F41.**

Bacteriophage (Phage), literally "bacteria eater", *i.e.,* a virus which specifically infects bacteria. In common with viruses which attack animal or plant cells, isolated phages are inert, and can only reproduce by making use of the chemical apparatus of a more sophisticated host cell (in this case a bacterium). However phages may be of two types, virulent or temperate. Virulent phages completely disrupt the normal functioning of the infected bacterium and adapt its reproductive mechanism to produce more phage. This eventually kills the bacterium and the newly assembled phages are released. Temperate phages on the other hand may enter into a remarkable symbiotic relationship with the bacterium, known as lysogeny. The phage genetic material is incorporated into that of the bacterium and is reproduced each time the still functioning bacterium subsequently divides. Furthermore the bacterium is immune from attack by potentially virulent phages of the same type. When such lysogenic bacteria die, phage particles may again be released. Phages carried in lysogenic bacteria are in a state known as prophage and it is often difficult to obtain pure, prophage-free strains of bacteria. Because of their relatively simple structure, phages have been extensively used in research on genetics and molecular biology.

Badger, a carnivorous mammal related to the weasel, of nocturnal and burrowing habits, inoffensive, subsisting chiefly on roots and insects, though sometimes mice, young rabbits and eggs form part of its diet. Badger-baiting was a favourite sport in Britain until it was prohibited in the middle of 19th cent. The badger does little harm and quite a lot of good; badger digging is to be condemned as a cruel sport. In Britain the badger is protected by an Act of Parliament passed in 1973, but the Ministry of Agriculture officials may destroy the animal in areas where bovine tuberculosis has been found.

Bagpipe. Once popular all over Europe, this instrument is still played in Scotland, Ireland, Brittany and elsewhere. The bag acts as a reservoir of air and, when squeezed by the player's arm, forces air through the pipes. One of these, the Chanter pipe, provides the tune and is played by the fingers as in a flageolet. The remainder, the Drone pipes, give a continuous, unvarying note.

Bailey Bridge, invented by Sir Donald Bailey and first used in the N. African campaign 1942–3.

Built up of prefabricated girders, it can be easily transported and erected.

Bailiwick, a feudal term denoting the limits of a bailiff's jurisdiction. The term has survived in the Channel Islands, where Jersey and Guernsey are Bailiwicks.

Balance of Power was the doctrine in British policy whereby European groups should be so balanced as to prevent the emergence of a dominating Power. Thus the balance was maintained between the Triple Alliance (Germany, Austria and Italy) and the Triple Entente (Great Britain, France and Russia) and preserved peace from 1871 to 1914. After the first world war there was tentative support of Germany's recovery to counterweigh the possible French hegemony; but when Germany's power grew under Hitler culminating in the second world war, Britain, France and Russia again became allies. By the end of the war the old system of a balance of power centred upon Europe collapsed to give way to a thermonuclear balance of power between the super-Powers, the Soviet Union (Warsaw Pact) and the United States (Nato alliance). In the future there may be a world of five great Powers—United States, Soviet Union, China, Western Europe, Japan.

Baldachin (It. *Baldachino*), a canopy usually supported by four pillars over throne, altar, or other sacred object. The name is also applied to the silken canopy used in processions and borne by the priest who carries the Host.

Balearic Crane, the crowned crane of the Balearic Islands and the North African mainland, distinguished by its yellowish, black-tipped occipital tuft and by its trumpet note.

Baleen *or* "whalebone" the name given to a series of horny plates growing from the roof of the mouth in those whales classified as Whalebone or Baleen Whales (*Mystacoceti*). There are 300–400 or so plates on each side, and their inner edges are frayed, the whole system constituting a filter for collecting minute organisms used for food. The Baleen Whales include the Right-Whales, the Pacific Grey-Whale and the Rorquals. See **Whales.**

Ballet is a combination of four arts; dancing, music, painting, and drama, each of which is ideally of equal importance. The movement of the individual dancers and the "orchestration" of the whole group is in the hands of the choreographer. The dancer's training follows certain basic rules but save in classical ballet there is considerable freedom of movement. Ballet as we know it today developed professionally at the Court of King Louis XIV of France, though it owes its origins to Italy and in the earliest times to Greece and Rome. Its movements were made up from the dances of courtiers, country folk and tumblers. Technique grew more complex as costume became modified, the body gaining complete freedom with the invention of tights. A succession of great dancers—French, Italian and latterly Russian left their imprint on the art. Contemporary ballet reflects the aesthetics of the Russian, Sergei Diaghilev. In England Dame Ninette de Valois has laid the foundation of a national ballet, at Sadler's Wells and Covent Garden, with a personality that reflects the national character. A Royal Charter was granted in 1957 setting up the Royal Ballet to co-ordinate the activities of the Sadler's Wells group.

Ballistics, the science dealing with the motion of projectiles, especially shells, bombs and rockets. Great advances have been made in this science.

Balloon, the modern balloon consists of a bag of plastic material inflated with a gas lighter than air. The first ascent by man in a hot-air balloon was made on 21 November 1783, and in a hydrogen balloon on 1 December 1783. The most famous of the early scientific flights by manned balloons were those of the Englishmen Coxwell and Glaisher, in 1862, when a height of 11 km was reached. The first aerial crossing of the English Channel by Blanchard and Jeffries was made on 7 January 1785. Piccard's ascent to 16 km, in 1931, marked the conquest of the stratosphere. Four years later the American balloon *Explorer II,* inflated with nearly 112,000 m³ of helium, carried a team of scientists with their floating laboratory to an altitude of 23 km. In 1957 a pressurised balloon carrying an American doctor rose 31 km above the Earth. Captive kite-balloons were widely used in the war as defensive measures against air attack. Meteorologists send their instruments up in balloons to collect data about the upper atmosphere, and of recent years physicists have learned much about cosmic radiation from the study of photographic plates sent to the upper regions in balloons. Ballooning as a hobby is carried on by a number of enthusiasts.

Balsam, a big genus (140 species) of flowering plants. Many species are cultivated for their showy flowers, *e.g., Impatiens noli-me-tangere,* the yellow balsam or "touch-me-not", so called because the fruit explodes when touched, slinging out the seeds. Balsam fir is a conifer (*Abies balsamea*) from which Canada balsam gum is obtained.

Bamboo, a genus of strong grasses, some species growing to over 36 m in height; much used by oriental peoples for all kinds of purposes. The young shoots of some species are tender and esculent.

Banana (family *Musaceae*), a large herbaceous plant cultivated in moist regions of the tropics, and one of the most productive plants known. The main areas of commercial cultivation are in tropical America, the Canary Islands and West Africa. World production is estimated at 20 million tonnes, of which only 3 million are for trade.

Bandicoots, Australasian marsupial mammals, of the size of a large rat or rabbit. They are burrowing animals living largely on insects. The rabbit-eared bandicoot, restricted to Australia, has shrew-like snout, long ears like a rabbit, long crested tail, and a silky coat. The long-nosed bandicoot has a spiny coat and comes from E. Australia. The pig-footed bandicoot h: s two functional toes on the foot, like a pig.

Bank Rate, the rate at which the Bank of England is prepared to lend to the clearing banks. If raised it has the immediate effect of raising the rate of discount on Treasury Bills. Known as the Minimum Lending Rate from Oct. 1972 to Aug. 1981. *See* **Section G.**

Bantu (native word = people), term loosely used for large family of Negro races of Southern Africa.

Baobab, a tropical African tree. The species *Adansonia digitata* is one of the largest trees known, though not the tallest; the trunk can reach 9 m in thickness. The fruit is woody, but its juice provides a cooling beverage. The bark yields a fibre used for making rope and cloth.

Barbary Ape, a large monkey belonging to the genus *Macaca.* It is the only monkey living in relative freedom in Europe, a small colony being found on the Rock of Gibraltar. It has no tail.

Barberry, a genus of berry-producing shrubs containing a hundred species. Several species are cultivated for their flowers and bright berries. Has an interesting pollination mechanism; the base of each stamen is sensitive to touch, and insects probing for nectar cause top of stamen to spring inwards, so dusting visitor's head with pollen which can then be carried to the next flower visited. The common barberry (*Berberis communis*) harbours one stage of the fungus that causes rust of wheat.

Barbican, a fortified entrance to a castle or city, with projecting towers. In the London area called Barbican there was formerly a barbican in front of the city gates.

Barbiturates. A group of drugs derived from a parent compound called barbituric acid; phenobarbitone is the best-known example. They induce sleep and are used in the manufacture of sleeping pills and sometimes as anaesthetics, but they have the disadvantage of being habit forming. *See* **Index to Section P.**

Barbizon School, a school of mid-19th-cent. landscape painters whose main tenet was a return to nature with an exact rendering of peasant life and country scenery painted on the spot. It was named after the village of that name in the Forest of Fontainebleau, where its chief members—Millet, Theodore Rousseau, Daubigny and Diaz—made their home. Their practice of painting direct from nature, which was far from universal at that time, made them the precursors of Impressionism (*q.v.*).

Barcarolle, a Venetian gondolier's song applied to instrumental as well as vocal compositions.

Bard, among the ancient Celts a poet or minstrel whose mission was to sing of heroic deeds. He was supposed to have the gift of prophecy, and was exempt from taxes and military service.

Barilla, soda carbonate or soda ash obtained by burning certain salt-marsh plants (*e.g.,* the saltwort, *Salsola kali*). It used to be in great demand, until the product of the Leblanc and then the Solvay ammonia-soda process was made available by the chemical industry.

Barium, metal element, no. 56, symbol Ba. In group 2 of the periodic table. The metal is soft and easily cut. It occurs as the sulphate and carbonate in nature. It was first prepared by Sir Humphry Davy in 1808, as an amalgam, by electrolysis of barium chloride. The pure metal was not isolated until 1901.

Barium meal. Barium sulphate is opaque to X-rays and before X-ray pictures of the alimentary canal radiologists give a "barium meal" to the patients so that the alimentary canal shows up more clearly.

Barnacles constitute a sub-class (*Cirripedia*) of the Crustacea. The barnacle fouling the bottom of ships is the Goose Barnacle, which has a long muscular stalk and a shell composed of five plates. The Acorn Barnacles, which cover rocks, breakwaters, etc., just below high-water mark are similarly constructed, but have no stalk. The manner of feeding of barnacles was vividly described by T. H. Huxley, who said the barnacle is "a crustacean fixed by its head kicking the food into its mouth with its legs". It was a naval surgeon, J. Vaughan Thompson, who discovered in 1830 that barnacles have a free-swimming larva (or nauplius). In the Middle Ages a curious myth grew up to the effect that the Barnacle changed into a sea-bird called, for that reason, the Barnacle Goose.

Barometer is an instrument for measuring atmospheric pressure, invented at Florence by Torricelli, pupil of Galileo, in 1644. The standard method consists of balancing the air column against a column of mercury, used on account of its high density. The mercury is contained in a long glass tube, closed at one end, and inverted in a cistern also containing mercury. The height of the mercury column, supporting the air column, is taken as the pressure at the time, and can be read off very accurately by means of a vernier scale. Present-day tendency is to express the readings in units of pressure instead of length, the millibar being adopted (1 mb = 1,000 dynes per sq. cm.; 1,000 mb = 75 cm of mercury approx.). The standard instrument is correct for pressures at 0°C in Lat. 45°, so that corrections have to be applied for temperatures and latitudes other than these. Also a correction has to be made for reducing the pressure to mean sea level. *See* **Aneroid.**

Baron, title given in feudal England to a man who held his land directly from the king by military or other honourable service. The first baron created by letters patent was John Beauchamp de Holt, Baron of Kidderminster, in 1387. A baron is a member of the fifth and last grade of the peerage of the United Kingdom and is addressed as "Lord". Life peers and life peeresses rank with hereditary barons and baronesses according to the date of their creation. In Scotland the term baron is used of the possessor of a feudal fief, or the representative by descent of such a fief. The equivalent of the English baron, as a rank of the Scottish peerage, is Lord of Parliament.

Baronet, the lowest hereditary title, instituted by James I to provide funds for the colonisation of Ulster. The first baronet was Sir Nicholas Bacon. Between 1964 and 1983 no recommendations for hereditary honours were made.

Baroque, a term used for the art style of the period *c.* 1600–1720 which was the artistic accompaniment of the Jesuit counter-Reformation. Its most obvious characteristics are: (*a*) its emotional appeal and dramatic intensity both related to its deliberate intention as propaganda ("a good picture makes better religious propaganda than a sermon" said one of its exponents); (*b*) in architecture, a style which is heavily and sometimes almost grotesquely ornate, plentifully covered with voluptuous sculpture on which draperies float rather than hang, with twisted and spiral instead of plain or fluted columns, and unnecessary windows or recesses added for ornament rather than use; (c) its emphasis on the whole at the expense of the parts such that a building's sculpture merges into its architecture and both into its painting (Baroque paintings are as closely knit as a jigsaw puzzle so that one cannot isolate individual figures as would be possible in a Renaissance one). Baroque architecure owing to its origin is found mainly in the Catholic countries; Italy, France, Austria, Bavaria, e.g., the Barberini Palace, Rome, designed by its greatest exponent Bernini and others; the Church of the Invalides, Paris. Baroque artists include Caravaggio, Guido Reni, Murillo and Rubens the greatest Northern Baroque painter. The Baroque style merges gradually into **Rococo** (q.v.).

Barque, a small sailing vessel with three or four masts. A three-masted barque has fore- and mainmasts square-rigged, the mizzenmast fore- and aft-rigged.

Barrow is an ancient artificial mound of earth or stone raised over the site of a burial. In Britain barrows were built from 2500 B.C. until the late Saxon period, but the Egyptian are the earliest barrows known, the great pyramids being a spectacular development of the custom of ceremonial burial. Silbury Hill, south of Avebury, is the biggest artificial mound in Europe, 512 m in circuit at the base, 96 m at top, and 41 m high.

Bartholomew, Massacre of St., occurred in Paris on the night of 24 August 1572, when over two thousand Huguenots were massacred by order of the Catholic French Court.

Baryons, the group of heavier subatomic particles which includes the proton, neutron, lambda and omega-minus particles (and their corresponding anti-particles, called anti-baryons). Baryons interact by means of all the known forces of nature (strong, weak, electromagnetic and gravitational). However, in any closed system the total baryon number (i.e., the number of baryons minus the number of anti-baryons) is constant. This means that the proton, being the lightest known baryon, must be stable against spontaneous decay. Unlike the lighter leptons (q.v.), baryons are now thought to have internal structure reflecting the fact that they are composed of quarks (q.v.). See **F15**.

Basalt Rocks are fine-grained, dark coloured, of igneous origin and occur either as lava flows as in Mull and Staffa, or as intrusive sheets, like the Edinburgh Castle Rock and Salisbury Crags. One of the most noted examples of columnar basalt is that of the Giant's Causeway in Ireland.

Basanite, a smooth black siliceous mineral, or flinty jasper; a crypto-crystalline quartz used as a touchstone for testing the purity of gold, etc., by means of the mark left after rubbing the metal with it. Sometimes styled the Lydian stone.

Base, a substance having a tendency to accept a proton (H+). This is a wide definition and covers unconventional types of compounds. In aqueous solution bases dissolve with formation of hydroxyl ions, and will neutralise an acid to form a salt. In non-aqueous solvents, like liquid ammonia or hydrogen fluoride, compounds classically regarded as salts can be bases, e.g., sodium fluoride is a base in hydrogen fluoride solution.

Basilisk, is a lizard of aquatic habits, with an elevated crest (which it can erect or depress at will) down the centre of its back.

Basques, people of N. Spain and S.W. France, oldest surviving racial group in Europe, who have preserved their ancient language which is unrelated to any other tongue.

Bas-Relief ("low relief"), a term used in sculpture to denote a class of sculptures the figures of which are only slightly raised from the surface of the stone or clay upon which the design is wrought.

Bastille, a castle or fortress in Paris, built in the 14th cent., and used as a state prison, especially for political offenders. Its bad repute as an instrument of despotism excited the hatred of the populace, who stormed and demolished it on 14 July 1789, at the beginning of the Revolution.

Bastinado, an oriental punishment, by beating with a pliable cane on the soles of the feet.

Bats. These mammals fly by means of a membrane stretched between each of the long fingers of the hand and between the fifth finger and the body. Another membrane stretches between the legs and the tail. Most British bats, including the pipistrelle, long-eared bats, noctules, belong to the family Vespertilionidae (with the exception of the horseshoe bats which belong to the family Rhinolophidae). These all feed on insects which they catch on the wing. The problem of how bats can detect their insect prey and avoid obstacles when flying in total darkness has interested zoologists for a very long time. The problem was solved with the advent of sensitive ultrasonic recording devices. Blindness does not affect this ability but deafness leave bats comparatively helpless. One of the most interesting types of bat is the fishing bat (Noctilio) found in central America, which can detect fish by being able to receive echoes from the ripples they make on the water surface. See also **Ultrasonics.**

Bath, Order of the, Britain's second oldest order of knighthood. Exclusive to men since its institution by Henry IV in 1399, women became eligible for admission to the order in 1971. The order has three grades: Knight Grand Cross (G.C.B.), Knight Commander (K.C.B.), and Companion (C.B.). Women members of the order are known as Dame Grand Cross, Dame Commander and Companion.

Battery, Electric, the common term for an electric cell but really meaning a combination of two or more cells. A cell is a device for converting stored chemical energy into electricity which can then be used for heat, light, traction, or any desired purpose. A primary cell will do this until the chemical action is completed and the cell is then useless. In a secondary cell, the chemical actions are reversible and the cell can be returned to its initial condition and used again. This is done by passing an electric current through—a process called recharging. A common primary cell is the Leclanché dry cell; used in torches. This works by the action of sal-ammoniac on electrodes made of zinc and carbon. About a century after it came into common use it is still the chief source of power for portable equipment in armed forces. A common secondary cell is the lead and sulphuric acid accumulator used in cars. Many other types of cell are known and some are under development because the demands of space travel, medicine, warfare, etc., call for batteries of lighter weight, greater reliability, or special properties. See **Fuel Cell, Energy Conversion.**

Bauhaus, a German institution for the training of architects, artists and industrial designers founded in 1919 at Weimar by Walter Gropius (d. 1969). It was closed by Hitler in 1933 and re-opened at Chicago. The Bauhaus doctrine held that there should be no separation between architecture and the fine and applied arts; that art, science and technology should co-operate to create "the compositely inseparable work of art, the great building". Thus it was an organisation with a social purpose. The original institution, at the instigation of Gropius, included on its teaching staff not only architects and technicians but also such noted artists as Paul Klee and Wassily Kandinsky.

Bauxite, the chief ore of aluminium. Chemically it is aluminium oxide. Aluminium metal is made industrially by electrolysing purified bauxite dissolved in fused cryolite. Chief producing areas; Jamaica, Australia, Surinam, USSR, Guyana, France, Greece, Guinea, USA, Hungary, Yugoslavia.

Bayeux Tapestry, a famous tapestry representing the conquest of England by William the Conqueror. It is embroidered on a band of linen 70 m long and 51 cm wide in blue, green, red and yellow, divided into 72 scenes ranging over the whole story of the conquest. The accepted view is that the tapestry was commissioned for Bayeux Cathedral, but a new interpretation is that it is an Anglo-Norman secular work of art, much influenced by the contemporary chansons de geste (songs of deeds), executed by

English embroiderers for a Norman patron. A representation can be seen in the Victoria and Albert Museum in London.

Beagle, a small hound that tracks by scent, and formerly used for hare hunting.

Bears belong to the Ursidae family of the Carnivora. They are plantigrade mammals, walking (like man) on the soles of their feet. Found in most parts of the world except Australia, the common Brown Bear was once spread over the whole of Europe; it became extinct in England about the 11th cent.; 2–2·5 m in length, and stands 1 m or more at the shoulder. The Grizzly Bear of N. America is larger, and the coat is shorter and greyer. The Polar Bear is remarkable in having a white coat all the year round; it spends much time in water, and unlike other bears is entirely carnivorous. Bear-baiting was made illegal in England in 1835.

Beaufort Scale of wind force is used to specify numerically the strength of the wind. Since the introduction of anemometers to measure the actual velocity, equivalent values of the ranges in miles per hour at a standard height in the open have been assigned to the Beaufort numbers. See **Section N.**

Beaver, a genus of mammals of the Rodentia order, with short, scaly ears, webbed hind feet, and a long broad scaly tail. They grow up to 1·2 m long, and live in communities, constructing dams and lodges where they breed. A campaign was launched in 1977 to bring back beavers to Britain where they have been extinct for several hundred years after being mercilessly hunted for their valuable pelt.

Bedlam (a corruption of Bethlehem) was a priory in Bishopsgate, afterwards converted into a hospital for lunatics. The asylum was transferred to St. George's Field, Lambeth, in 1815. The term "bedlamite" came to be applied to any person behaving like a madman.

Beech, a deciduous tree belonging to the genus *Fagus* of some eight or nine species found in north temperate regions. The common beech, *F. sylvatica,* is believed to be native to Britain and is one of our finest trees, with massive trunk, long, pointed winter buds, and smooth, grey bark. There is little undergrowth under its dense shade. It is shorter-lived than the oak taking about 200 years to reach full size and then declining. The timber of beech has a variety of uses, *e.g.,* spoons, handles, tools, and chairs.

Bee-eater, name of a family of brilliantly coloured birds closely related to the rollers and kingfishers inhabiting the tropical and sub-tropical parts of Africa, Asia and Europe. The European species successfully nested in Britain for the first time in 1955 and a pair nested in Alderney in 1956. With their long curved beaks they catch insects on the wing, especially bees and butterflies, and lay their eggs in dark nest tunnels.

Beefeater, *See* **Yeomen of the Guard.**

Beeswax, the secretion of the bee, used for the formation of the cells or honey-comb of the hive; when melted it is what is commercially known as yellow wax, white wax being made by bleaching. Being impervious to water, it acts as a good resistant and is an article of much utility.

Beetles (Coleoptera) constitute one of the biggest orders of insects, numbering over 200,000 species. There are two pairs of wings; the hind pair are used for flight, while the front pair are hardened to form a pair of protective covers (elytra). Some beetles have lost the power of flight and then the elytra are joined together.

Bel and the Dragon is the title of certain supplementary chapters to the "Book of Daniel" of an apocryphal character. First appeared in the Septuagint, but the Jewish Church did not accept it as inspired. In 1546 the Council of Trent declared it to be canonical.

Bell, a hollow body of metal used for making sounds. Bells are usually made from bell-metal, an alloy of copper and tin. Small bells used for interior functions are often made of silver, gold or brass. Ordinary hand-bells are of brass. From the 7th cent. large bells have been used in England in cathedrals, churches and monasteries. The greatest bell in the world is the "King of Bells" in the Kremlin at Moscow which weighs about 198 tonnes, is

627 cm high and 691 cm in diameter. It was cast in 1733 but cracked in the furnace (the broken part weighed 11 tonnes) and is now preserved as a national treasure. Other large bells in Russia include the 171 tonne one at Krasnogvardersk, near Leningrad, and the one of 110 tonnes at Moscow. The Great Bell (Great Paul) at St. Paul's, cast in 1881, weighs nearly 17 tonnes and is the largest in the United Kingdom. Other gigantic bells are the Great Bell at Peking (53 tonnes); Nanking (22 tonnes); Cologne Cathedral (25 tonnes); Big Ben, Westminster (over 13 tonnes); Great Peter, York Minster (10 tonnes). The Curfew Bell is rung in some parts of England to this day, notably at Ripon. The number of changes that can be rung on a peal of bells is the *factorial* of the number of bells. Thus four bells allow 24 and eight bells 40,320.

Belladonna or **Deadly Nightshade** (*Atropa belladonna*), a well-known poisonous wild plant found in Southern Europe and Western Asia. The alkaloid atropine it contains is valuable in medicine, although a large dose is poisonous.

Bell, Book and Candle. To curse by "bell book, and candle" was a form of excommunication in the Roman Church ending with the words: "Close the book, quench the candle, ring the bell".

Benedicite, the canticle in the Book of Common Prayer, known also as "The Song of the Three Holy Children".

Benedictines are monks and nuns of the Benedictine Order who live under the rule of St. Benedict—the monastic code whose influence on the religious and cultural life of the West has been so powerful. The rule is marked by an absence of extravagant asceticism. The greatest of the early Benedictines was Pope Gregory I (590–604) who sent St. Augustine of Canterbury to Anglo-Saxon England. Gregorian plainsong is named after him.

Benzene. An aromatic hydrocarbon obtained from coal tar and some petroleum fractions. It is a volatile inflammable liquid with a characteristic smell. The molecule consists of a flat ring of six carbon atoms, each bound to one hydrogen atom. Benzene is the parent member of many aromatic organic compounds and is widely used in industry to synthesise intermediates for fibres, dyestuffs, explosives and pharmaceutical chemicals.

Beryl, a mineral, of which the emerald is a grass-green variety. Composed of beryllium and aluminium silicates. The pure mineral is colourless; the colour of most beryl comes from traces of impurities, notably iron and chromium. Otherwise it is yellowish, greenish-yellow, or blue, and is found in veins which traverse granite or gneiss, or embedded in granite, and sometimes in alluvial soil formed from such rocks.

Beryllium. Metallic element, no. 4, symbol Be. Very similar to aluminium, it is stronger than steel and only one-quarter its weight. It is not very abundant, its main source is the mineral, beryl. Copper containing 2 per cent. beryllium is used for making springs. Because of its special properties the metal is used as a component in spacecraft, missiles and nuclear reactors. This accounts for its recent development on a technical scale. The metal powder is toxic.

Bessemer Process for making steel depends on the forcing of atmospheric air into molten pig iron to burn out the impurities. Ousted by the oxygen converter. See **Steel.**

Betel, the leaf of an Indian climbing plant, of pungent, narcotic properties. It is destructive to the teeth, and reddens the gums and lips.

Bhang, the Indian name for the hemp plant *Cannabis sativa,* the leaves and seed-capsules of which are chewed or smoked. The potent drug which comes from flowers of the female plant is called hashish in Arabia and marihuana in the United States and Mexico.

Bible (Greek *biblion* = scroll of paper; pl. *biblia* = writings) includes the Hebrew sacred Scriptures (Old Testament) and those held sacred by the Christians (New Testament). The Old Testament—the prehistoric portion—consists of 39 books, and is divided into three parts: (1) the Law, (2) the Prophets, (3) Miscellaneous Writings. The Old Testament was written in Hebrew except for parts of Ezra and Daniel, which were in Aramaic. It was not until the 9th cent. A.D. that a complete Hebrew text was made, the so-called Massoretic text. Before that the main versions were the Alexandrian Greek translation (Septuagint) made in the 2nd cent. B.C. and St. Jerome's Latin Vulgate of the 4th cent. A.D. (It was Jerome who used the Latin word "testament" (formed from *testis* = a witness).) Portions were translated into the Anglo-Saxon in the 8th cent. and the Venerable Bede put the greater part of St. John's gospel into English, but it was not until 1535 that a complete, printed English version appeared—the Coverdale Translation. The Authorised Version dates from 1611 in the reign of James I, and its beautiful phraseology has given it a lasting appeal. The Revised Version dates from 1885. *The New English Bible*, with the Apocrypha, was published in 1970. It is a new translation in plain English prose of the earliest Hebrew, Aramaic, and Greek manuscripts. The finding of the Dead Sea Scrolls (since 1947) has added to our knowledge of Scripture.

Biedermeier, style in interior decoration and the decorative arts developed from Empire (q.v.). It was created in Vienna c. 1815 and the name was derived from a fantasy figure in Viennese writing personifying all that which is sedate and bourgeois. Biedermeier furniture is less austere and grandiose than Empire's predecessors, more intimate and homely. A most important creation is the large circular table on a stem-like foot, which became the centre of family life, around which chairs could be grouped freely, not formally against walls as previously. In Vienna itself the style died out c. 1830, but in other Continental countries it survived well into the second half of the 19th cent. Its English equivalent is Early Victorian.

Billion, formerly in English usage a million million; now a thousand million or 10^9.

Bill of Rights, or Declaration of Rights, was the document setting forth the conditions upon which the British throne was offered to William and Mary in 1688. This was accepted and ultimately became an Act of Parliament.

Binary Notation, for numbers, is a way of representing numbers using only two digits, 0 and 1. Electronic digital computers handle numbers in this form and many people these days are having to learn it. Many school children find it both easy and fascinating—as did the great philosopher and mathematician Leibniz. The ordinary, or decimal numbers, 0, 1, 2, 3, 4, 5, 6, 7, 8, 9, 10 are written in binary notation as follows: 0, 1, 10, 11, 100, 101, 110, 111, 1000, 1001, 1010. The reader might divine the rules from this. The point is you "carry 1", i.e., move the digit 1 a place to the left, when you reach 2. In decimal notation you move 1 a place left when you reach 10. In other words, instead of columns for units, tens, hundreds, thousands, etc., the columns are for units, twos, fours, eights, etc. In binary notation: "1 + 1 = 0 with 1 to carry". Since every digit in binary notation is either 0 or 1 it requires one bit of information to specify a binary digit. *See* Bit and **Computers, Section V.**

Biological Clock. All living organisms undergo cyclical changes in activity of some sort. These are linked to the changes in their environment which are produced by the alternation of night and day, the phases of the moon and the tides, and the cycle of the seasons. These cycles of activity frequently persist if the organism is put into a constant environment in which there appear to be no external clues as to what time or what season it is. A squirrel, for example, wakes up at about the same time each evening even when it is put into constant darkness. It is usual to refer to these activity patterns as being driven by a biological clock inside the organism. But very little is known about how these biological clocks work.

Biological Warfare, is the use for warlike purposes of bacteria, viruses, fungi, or other biological agents. These can be used to spread distress, incapacity, disease or death among the enemy's people or livestock. One of the strange uses to which mankind puts its science is to make naturally infective organisms even more virulent for military use. This sort of research can be done in many countries; it is much cheaper and easier to hide than nuclear weapons development. Secret attack by biological agents is supposed to be easy and it may affect the populations without damaging buildings or bridges. In 1975 the Biological Weapons Convention, 1972, signed by Britain, the United States and Russia, came into force outlawing germ warfare. Any nation suspecting violation may lodge a complaint with the UN Security Council.

Biosphere, that part of the earth in which life exists—a very thin layer near the surface bounded by regions too hostile for life processes to occur. The upper limit is at about 9,000 m above sea level and the lower limit at about 10,000 m in the deep oceans. Ample supplies of solar energy, liquid water and places where liquid, solid and gas all meet seem to be requirements for a biosphere to exist and for all the biological cycles of water, oxygen, mineral, nitrogen, etc., to function.

Birch, a genus of deciduous trees including about 40 species and found only in northern regions. Birches native to Britain, and to Europe generally, are of two species—the silver birch, *Betula pendula*, with its graceful, drooping branches and triangular leaves, and the white birch, *Betula pubescens*, which has erect branches and soft oval leaves. Birch timber is an important plywood timber, the bark is used for tanning leather, and wintergreen oil comes from the bark of black birch, *Betula lenta*, a North American species. The birch is not a long-lived tree, few standing for more than a hundred years. The tallest recorded is at Woburn in Bedfordshire, 31 m high.

Birds, or Aves, are, next to mammals, the highest class of animal life. There are two kinds of modern birds—*Carinatae*, possessing keeled breast-bones and having power of flight; *Ratitae*, having raft-like breast-bones, and incapable of flight; and a sub-class of fossil birds, Archaeornithes, including *Archaeopteryx*. Estimates of the total number of birds breeding in the British Isles vary, but there are 229 breeding species. Of these the commonest are wrens, of which there are 10 million breeding pairs, house sparrows, blackbirds and chaffinches with up to 7 million pairs each, robins with 5 million and starlings with 3·5 million pairs.

The wheatear is usually the first of the migratory birds to return, often reaching Britain at the end of February and always before the middle of March; the sand martin is the first of the "early swallows" to return, followed by the house martin. The first cuckoo arrives about the middle of April, and the whinchat, garden warbler, and sedge warbler during the last week in April. The nightjar, spotted flycatcher, and red-backed shrike are not seen until the first week in May. The swift is among the last to return from Africa and the earliest to depart. Bird-nesting is illegal in Britain. With the passing of the Wildlife and Countryside Act in 1980 the trapping and caging of robins, nightingales, larks, kingfishers, cuckoos, owls, martins, fieldfares, flycatchers, ravens and other birds has been made illegal in Britain. *See also* **F36(2).**

Birds of Paradise, over 40 species of tropical birds inhabiting the dense forests of New Guinea and neighbouring islands. The male birds are remarkable for their brilliant plumage, long tail feathers, and ruffs on wings and neck, which are displayed to advantage during courtship. Related to the Bower Birds of Australia.

Biretta, a four-cornered head-covering worn by ecclesiastics of the Roman Church and varying in colour according to the rank of the wearer. A cardinal's biretta is red, a bishop's purple, a priest's black.

Bise, a keen dry north wind prevalent in Switzerland and South France.

Bishop is a Christian ecclesiastic, a person consecrated for the spiritual government of an area, a diocese or province, to the spiritual oversight of which he has been appointed (diocesan bishops), or to aid a bishop so appointed (suffragan bishops). In the Church of England there are forty-three diocesan bishops, all nominated by the Crown. Two, Canterbury and York, are archbishops having primacy in the respective provinces. The archbishops of Canterbury and York and the bishops of London, Durham and Winchester and twenty-one other diocesan bishops in order of seniority are spiritual peers, and sit in the House of Lords. The (Disestablished) Church of Ireland has two archbishops and twelve bishops; the (Disestablished) Church of Wales an archbishop and five bishops and the Episcopal Church in Scotland seven bishops. *See also* **Cardinal.**

Bismuth, metallic element, no. 83, symbol Bi, in group 5 of the periodic table. Like antimony, the stable form is a grey, brittle, layer structure; electrical conductor. It is readily fusible, melting at 264°C and boiling at about 1420°C. Wood's metal, an alloy with one of the lowest melting points (under 65°C, so that a spoon made of it will melt when placed in a cup of hot tea), contains four parts bismuth, two parts lead, one part tin, one part cadmium.

Bison, a genus of wild cattle, distinguished from the ox by its shorter, wider skull, beard under the chin, high forequarters, and, in winter, a great mane of woolly hair covering head and forequarters. There are two species, the European and the American bison, both now protected in game reserves.

Bit, formerly the word often referred to the metal piece in the mouth of a bridled horse, now more likely to be a technical expression in the mouth of a computer expert. A bit is a unit of information; it is the information that can be conveyed by indicating which of two possibilities obtains. Any object that can be either of two states can therefore store one bit of information. In a technical device, the two states could be the presence or the absence of a magnetic field, or of an electric voltage. Since all numbers can be represented in the binary system (*see* **Binary Notation**) by a row of digits which are *either* 0 *or* 1, it takes one bit of information to specify a binary digit. Bit is short for binary digit.

Bittern, a bird of the heron genus, with long, loose plumage on the front and sides of the neck. It is a solitary bird inhabiting marshes, but rare in Britain.

Bivalves, shell-fish whose shell consists of two hinged valves, lying one on each side of the body, such as mussels, oysters and cockles.

Blackbird, or Merle, a member of the Thrush family, a familiar song bird in Britain. Male is all-black with orange bill; female is mottled brown with brown bill; the young are spotted brown.

Blackcock and Greyhen (as the female is called) are closely related to the Capercaillies but smaller. They nest on the ground and prefer wooded country to open moors. Found in northern half of northern hemisphere. Polygamous, they perform excited courtship dances; the male is a handsome blue-black bird with white undertail, the female dark brown mottled.

Black Death, the plague which swept across Europe in the years 1348–50, beginning in the ports of Italy, brought in by merchant ships from Black Sea ports. It was the worst scourge man has ever known; at least a quarter of the European population was wiped out in the first epidemic of 1348. It reached England in the winter of that year. The disease was transmitted to man by fleas from black rats, though this was not known at the time, the specific organism being *Bacillus pestis.* The disease continued to ravage Europe in recurrent outbreaks up to the late 17th cent. The epidemic which raged in England in 1665 wiped out whole villages and one-tenth of London's population of 460,000. Samuel Pepys wrote a grim account of it in his *Diary. See also* **Labourers, English Statute of.**

Black Hole of Calcutta, the name given to the place where a captured British garrison was confined in 1756, during the struggle for India between the French and British. Into a noisome space, about 6 m square, 146 persons were driven and only 23 were found alive the next morning. The authenticity of the story has been called into question, but after sifting the evidence Professor H. H. Dodwell, in the *Cambridge History of the British Empire,* believes it to be substantially true.

Black Holes. *See* **Astronomy, Section F, Part I.**

Black-letter, the Old English or Gothic type first used in printing blocks.

Black Power. *See* **Section J.**

Black Woodpecker (*Dryocopus martius*), a black

bird about the size of a rook, with slightly crested scarlet crown, found in parts of Europe.

Blenny, a group of marine fishes with spiny rays part of the fin running along the back. Several species are found around the British coast.

Blood Groups. *See* **Index to Section P.**

Bloody Assizes, the assizes conducted in 1685 by George Jeffreys, Lord Chief Justice, at which participants in the Duke of Monmouth's rebellion against King James II were tried. They were marked by relentless cruelty.

Bluebird, a migratory bird of North America, deriving its name from its deep blue plumage, it has a pleasant warbling song and is a familiar sight in the woods from early spring to November. In India and Malaya there is the Fairy Blue-bird; the male is black with shiny blue upper parts. Used as the symbol of happiness by Maeterlinck in his play *The Blue Bird.*

Blue Peter, a blue flag with a white square in the centre, is hoisted 24 hours before a ship leaves harbour (the letter P in the alphabet of the International Code of Signals).

Blue Ribbon, a term in general use to denote the highest honour or prize attainable in any field or competition. Thus the Derby is the blue ribbon of the turf. The expression is derived from the highest Order of Knighthood in the gift of the British Crown, the insignia of which is a garter of blue velvet.

Blue Stocking, a term used to describe a learned or literary woman, particularly if pedantic and undomesticated. It is said that the term derives from the Bas-Bleu club of Paris, which was attended by the literary savantes of the 17th cent. In England a similar literary club was formed about 1780, whose members were distinguished by their blue stockings.

"Blue" Sun, Moon, etc., a phenomenon caused by the scattering of sunlight by transparent particles suspended in the atmosphere, the effect being that blue light is transmitted, and red light extinguished to direct vision. The dust from the Krakatoa eruption in 1883 and the drifting layer of smoke from the forest fires in Alberta, Canada, in September 1950 gave rise to "blue" moons and suns, phenomena sufficiently rare to be described as occurring "once in a blue moon". In the cold climatic conditions of the Pamirs and the far north, vegetation is said to look "blue" on account of the rays of high calorific value (red, yellow, green) being absorbed, while only the blue and violet are transmitted. It was Tyndall who first explained the blue colour of the sky.

Boa, a term applied to a family of snakes of large size, some attaining a length of 9 m. They are not poisonous, but kill their prey by crushing —constriction—hence the name "boa constrictor". They occur both in the Old World and the New, but are more abundant in the latter. Most Boas retain the eggs within the body until young are fully developed, whereas the Pythons almost all lay leather-shelled eggs.

Boar, or Wild Hog, an animal largely distributed over the forest regions of Europe, Asia, Africa and South America. It has a longer snout and shorter ears than its descendant the domestic hog, and is provided with tusks. Having to forage for itself, it is a more active and intelligent animal than the pig of the sty, and offered good sport to the hunter.

Boat, an open vessel, propelled by oars or sails, or both. The boats of a ship of war are the launch, barge, pinnace, yawl, cutters, jolly boat and gig; of a merchant vessel, the launch, skiff, jolly boat or yawl, stern boat, quarter-boat and captain's gig. Every ship is compelled to carry adequate, fully provisioned and equipped life-boats.

Bode's Law, a numerical relationship formulated by Bode in 1772 (though pointed out earlier by J. D. Titius of Wittenberg), which states that the relative mean distances of the planets from the sun are found by adding 4 to each of the terms 0, 3, 6, 12, 24, 48, 96, and dividing each number by 10. The gap between Mars and Jupiter caused Bode to predict the existence of a planet there, which was later confirmed by the discovery of Ceres and other minor planets. The law breaks down however, for Neptune and Pluto.

Boer War lasted from 11 October 1899, when the

Boers invaded Natal, to 31 May 1902, when the Treaty of Vereeniging ended hostilities. At first the operations of the British troops in Cape Colony were unsuccessful and disastrous reverses were sustained. Lord Roberts was then sent out as Commander-in-Chief, with Lord Kitchener as Chief-of-Staff, and from February 1900, when Kimberley was relieved and Cronje was compelled to surrender and Ladysmith and Mafeking were relieved, the struggle was practically over.

Boiling-point is the temperature at which a liquid boils. At that point the pressure of the vapour is equal to the pressure of the atmosphere. Under increased pressure the b.p. rises and under less pressure, as on the top of a mountain, it is lower. At standard atmospheric pressure (760 mm of mercury) the b.p. of water is 100°C; alcohol 78·4°C; ether 35·6°C.

Books, Sizes of. *See* Section N.

Books, Classification of. All libraries are classified to facilitate reference, but the favourite system is the Dewey Decimal System, which divides the whole field of knowledge into ten Main Classes; General Works; Philosophy; Religion; Sociology; Philology; Natural Science; Useful Arts and Applied Science; Fine Arts; Literature; History (including geography and travel and biography). Each of these Main Classes is again subdivided into ten main divisions. As an example: the main class of Sociology receives the number 300. This range 300 to 400 (the next main class) is graduated into tens, and Economics is 330. The range 330 to 340 is again graduated, and the subject of Labour and Capital is 331. This process is carried on by decimals so that 331·2 deals with Remuneration for Work, 331·22 with Wage Scales, and 331·225 with Extra Pay.

Borax (Sodium Pyroborate) is a white, soluble, crystalline salt. It is widely and diversely used, *e.g.*, as a mild antiseptic, in glazing pottery, in soldering, in the making of pyrex glass, as a cleansing agent and sometimes as a food preservative. Borax occurs naturally in the salt lakes of Tibet, where it is called tincal, in California (Borax Lake, Death Valley), and elsewhere.

Bore. In physical geography, an almost vertical wall of water which passes upstream along certain estuaries. Its formation requires special conditions of river flow, incoming high tide, and shape of river channel. It can be spectacular and dangerous on some rivers. In Britain the best known is the Severn bore which can be over a metre high and move at 16–19 km/h. In some parts of Britain the bore is called an eagre.

Boron. A metalloid element, no. 5, symbol B. There are two forms, one crystalline, the other amorphous. It is not very abundant in nature but occurs in concentrated deposits. It is best known in boric acid, which is used as a mild antiseptic (called boracic acid) and borax (*q.v.*). Boron compounds are essential to some plants, *e.g.*, beans. Used in the preparation of various special-purpose alloys, such as impact resistant steel. Compounds of boron and hydrogen are used as rocket fuels.

Borstal, an institution where young offenders between 15 and 21 on conviction may be sent for detention and reform. Emphasis is placed on vocational training in skilled trades. The Children and Young Persons Act 1969 makes provision for the minimum age to be raised to 17, if and when the Home Secretary makes an order to that effect. The first was opened in 1902 at the village of Borstal, near Rochester in Kent.

Boston Tea Party, an incident which occurred on 16 December 1773, on board some tea-ships in Boston Harbour. High taxation imposed by the British Parliament under George III had caused bitter feelings, and instigated by popular meetings, a party of citizens, disguised as Indians, boarded the tea-ships and threw the tea overboard. This incident was a prelude to the American War of Independence (1775–83).

Bounds Beating, an old Anglo-Saxon custom. The parish clergyman and officials go round the parish boundaries accompanied by boys who beat the boundary stones with long sticks

of willow. The ceremony takes place on the Rogation days preceding Ascension Day.

Bourgeoisie, a term used by Marxists to indicate those who do not, like the proletariat, live by the sale of their labour. They include, on the one hand, industrialists and financiers or members of the liberal professions and, on the other, small artisans and shop-keepers who, although their standard of living may not be appreciably higher (and today is often lower) than that of the proletariat, are described as the "petty bourgeoisie". According to the Marxist view of history, the bourgeoisie arose with modern industrialism after it had overthrown the old feudal aristocracy and replaced it as ruling class.

Bow, an instrument for propelling arrows, and, in the days when it was a weapon of war, was usually made of yew or ash, and was about 2 m long, with an arrow *c.* 1 m long. It was the weapon with which Crécy, Poitiers and Agincourt were won. The cross-bow was Italian and was adopted in France, but did not become popular in Britain.

Bow Bells is the peal of the London church of St. Mary-le-Bow, Cheapside, within sound of which one must be born to be entitled to be called a "cockney". Bow Bells had not been heard since 1939, but they once again rang out over the City of London on 20 December 1961.

Bowdlerise, to expurgate a book. Derived from Thomas Bowdler (1754–1825), the editor of the Family Shakespeare, in which "those words and expressions are omitted which cannot with propriety be read aloud in a family". He treated Gibbon's *History of the Decline and Fall of the Roman Empire* in the same way, omitting "all passages of an irreligious and immoral tendency". Such prudery met with ridicule and hence the words "bowdlerism" "bowdlerist", etc.

Bower Bird, native to Australia and New Guinea and related to the Bird of Paradise, though often less striking in appearance. In the mating season the male builds a "bower" of sticks and grasses for courtship displays and as a playground. The Gardener Bower Bird of Papua makes a lawn in front of his bower and adorns it with bright coloured pebbles and flowers which are replaced as they wither. The female builds her nest away from the bower.

Boycott, a term used in connection with a person that the general body of people, or a party or society, refuse to have dealings with. Originally used when Captain Boycott (1832–97) was made the victim of a conspiracy by the Irish Land League which prevented him making any purchases or holding any social intercourse in his district. He had incurred the League's hostility by a number of evictions.

Brass, an exceedingly useful alloy of copper and zinc. Much brass is about two-thirds copper but different proportions give different properties. It is harder than copper and easily worked. Brass in the Bible (Matt. x, 9) probably refers to bronze.

Breadfruit Tree (*Artocarpus altilis*), a native of the South Sea Islands; the fruits are a brownish green, about the size of a melon, and contain a white pulpy substance which is roasted before being eaten. The tree grows 12 m or more. Captain Bligh's ship *Bounty* was on a voyage to Jamaica carrying a cargo of 1,000 breadfruit trees when the mutiny occurred.

Breeder Reactor, a kind of nuclear reactor (*q.v.*) which besides producing energy by the fission process also produces ("breeds") more nuclear fuel at the same time. A typical reaction is: a neutron induces fission of a U-235 nucleus which breaks up into two medium-sized nuclei and some neutrons; one of the latter then enters a U-238 nucleus turning it into U-239 which then decays radioactively *via* neptunium into plutonium which is useful fuel. There are technical problems in breeder reactors which have delayed their practical use but the "breeding" principle is so valuable that experiments have gone on for many years in, *e.g.*, Scotland and Idaho, and breeder reactors will no doubt increase in importance the more the supply of natural nuclear fuel appears to become depleted. *See also* **Nuclear Reactors.**

Breviary (Lat. *breviarium* = abridgment), the short prayer-book of the Roman Catholic Church which gives the Divine Office, *i.e.*, the services to be said daily. The directions for Mass are in the Missal. The current Roman breviary is a simplified version of the one decreed by the Council of Trent, 1568. *See also* Matins.

Bridges are structures for continuing a road, railway, or canal across a river, valley, ravine, or a road or railway at a lower level. From early times bridges were made of timber, stone, or brick, and it was not until the 19th cent. that wrought- and cast-iron were used. Today the materials mostly used are steel and reinforced concrete. Among the most famous of ancient bridges is that of S. Angelo at Rome, built by Hadrian as the Pons Aelius, A.D. 134. The Rialto bridge at Venice dates from 1588. The Ponte Santa Trinita at Florence, one of the finest Renaissance bridges and deemed the most beautiful in the world, was destroyed by German mines in 1944 but has now been reconstructed just as it was before. The first stone bridge across the Thames was begun in 1176. It had 19 arches and was lined with houses and stood until 1831 when it was replaced by the granite bridge designed by Sir John Rennie which stood until 1972. This has been replaced by a three-span concrete bridge with a six-lane carriageway and two footways. The first cast-iron bridge (recently repaired) was built by Abraham Darby at Coalbrookdale, Shropshire, in 1779. Telford's Menai suspension bridge (1825) has since been enlarged, the original design maintained. Another example of Britain's supremacy in constructional iron-work was Robert Stephenson's tubular bridge across the Menai Straits (1850), the prototype of all modern plate girder railway bridges. Other famous bridges are the Niagara (suspension), Forth railway bridge (cantilever), London Tower bridge (suspension), Tay railway bridge, Victoria Jubilee bridge across the St. Lawrence at Montreal (an open steel structure), Sydney Harbour bridge, Lower Zambesi bridge, Storstrom bridge in Denmark, Howrah bridge at Calcutta, Volta bridge of Ghana, Auckland Harbour bridge, Verrazano-Narrows bridge spanning New York's harbour from Brooklyn to Staten I., exceeding by 18 m the centre span of San Francisco's Golden Gate bridge, Rio-Niterói bridge in Brazil. Britain has undertaken in recent years the largest bridge building programme for over a century. The bridges include the road suspension bridge across the Firth of Forth, completed 1964, the Severn suspension bridge (from which the design principles for the new bridge across the Bosporus were taken) and the Tay road bridge, both completed 1966, the Tinsley viaduct, near Sheffield, opened 1968 and the new Humber suspension bridge, linking the ports of Hull and Grimsby, opened in 1981. When completed, it was the longest single-span suspension bridge in the world (1,410 m).

Bridleway. In English law (sec. 27(6) of the National Parks and Access to the Countryside Act 1949) a highway over which the public have the following, but no other, rights of way, that is to say, a right of way on foot and a right of way on horseback or leading a horse, with or without a right to drive animals of any description along the highway.

Britannia Metal, an alloy of tin, antimony and copper, harder than pure tin, corrosion-resistant, used for teapots, jugs (often electroplated).

British Association for the Advancement of Science, The, was founded in 1831 by a group of British scientists under the leadership of Charles Babbage (1792–1871) to stimulate scientific inquiry and promote research in the interest of the nation. Its meetings are held annually in different cities of the United Kingdom.

British Museum, was created by an Act of Parliament in 1753, when the Sir Hans Sloane collection, which the British Government had acquired for £20,000, was added to the Cottonian Library and the Harleian Manuscripts. It was opened to the public in 1759 at Montague House Bloomsbury. The acquisition of the library of George III (known as the King's Library) in 1823 led to the construction of the present building with the new wing (1829), quadrangle (1852), domed reading room (1857), and later additions. The books and the reading room are now part of the British Library (*see* Libraries). The Natural History Department was transferred to South Kensington in the 1880s. As a museum it is perhaps the most famous in the world, since it has many priceless collections of sculptures, antiquities, prints and drawings coins and medals. Its treasures include the Elgin Marbles (*q.v.*), the Rosetta Stone (*q.v.*), the Portland Vase (*q.v.*).

British Rail (British Railways). The name under which the railways of Britain were unified on 1 January 1948. Instead of the former four main railway systems six regions were formed: London Midland region (former L.M.S.R.), Western (former G.W.R.), Southern (formerly S.R.), Eastern (southern area of former L.N.E.R.), N.E. region (N.E. of former L.N.E.R.), Scottish region (Scottish system of the former L.M.S.R. and L.N.E.R.). Under the Transport Act 1962 the British Railways Board was set up to manage railway affairs. The most far-reaching change in the modernisation and re-equipment programme since 1955 has been the replacement of steam traction by electric and diesel locomotives. Under the chairmanship of Lord (then Dr.) Richard Beeching the British Railways Board planned a viable railway system by closing uneconomic branch lines, by developing new services on the liner train principle, and by utilising a more limited trunk route system. Under the Transport Act 1968 some railway passenger services are eligible for grants on social grounds, including urban railways and unprofitable rural services. High-speed inter-city passenger services linking the main centres of Gt. Britain came into operation in 1976 and in 1985 it was announced that the Advanced Passenger Train (the Electra) would go into production. The name was changed to British Rail in 1964. The Serpell Report (1983) has renewed the debate about the future of the railways against a background of competition from road transport.

British Standard Time, The British Standard Time Act of 1968 put Britain an hour ahead of Greenwich Mean Time (GMT) throughout the year for an experimental 3 years. This brought Britain into line with countries in Western Europe where Central European Time is observed. In 1970 Parliament called for the restoration of the previous position—BST in the summer months and GMT in the winter months—as from 31 October 1971.

Brocken-spectre or Glory. The series of coloured rings which an observer sees around the shadow of his own head (or an aeroplane in which he is travelling) as cast upon a bank of mist or thin cloud. This effect is produced by reflection and refraction of sunlight in minute water-droplets in the air just as in a rainbow.

Bromine. A non-metal element, no. 35, symbol Br, member of the halogen family (*q.v.*). It is a red, evil-smelling liquid (Greek *bromos*, a stink). It is an abundant element. In the USA bromide is extracted from sea-water on a large scale. It unites readily with many other elements, the products being termed bromides. Its derivatives with organic compounds are used in synthetic chemistry. Bromoform is a liquid resembling chloroform. Bromides are used in medicine to calm excitement.

Bronze is primarily an alloy of copper and tin, and was one of the earliest alloys known, the Bronze Age (began c. 4,000 B.C. in Middle East) in the evolution of tool-using man coming before the Iron Age (c. 2,000 B.C.) Some modern bronzes contain zinc or lead also, and a trace of phosphorus is present in "Phosphor-bronze".

Bubble Chamber. An instrument used by physicists to reveal the tracks of fast fundamental particles (*e.g.*, those produced in large accelerating machines) in a form suitable for photography; closely related to the Wilson cloud chamber (*q.v.*), but the particles leave trails of small bubbles in a superheated liquid (often liquid hydrogen) instead of droplets of liquid in a supersaturated gas; invented in 1952 by the American physicist, Dr. D. Glaser, Nobel Prizeman, 1960, and developed by Prof. L. W. Alvarez, Univ. of California, Nobel Prizeman, 1968.

Buckingham Palace, London residence of British sovereigns since 1837. Originally built for the Duke of Buckingham (1703); bought by George III in 1762 and remodelled by Nash 1825–36.

Buddhism. See Section J.

Buntings, name of a group of finches, seed-eating birds, usually found in open country. The Yellowhammer, Reed Bunting, Corn Bunting and Cirl Bunting are resident in Britain; the Snow Bunting (which breeds in small numbers in Scotland) and Lapland Bunting are regular winter visitors, and the Ortolan is among the rare visitors.

Butane, a colourless inflammable gas made of carbon and hydrogen; formula C_4H_{10}. Found in natural gas and made as a by-product of oil refining. Butane, like propane (q.v.), can easily be liquefied and moved safely in cans and tanks. It is thus useful as a "portable gas supply"; also used in internal combustion fuels.

Byzantine Art developed in the eastern part of the Roman empire after Constantine founded the city of Constantinople (A.D. 330). It has many sources—Greek, Syrian, Egyptian and Islamic—and reached its zenith in the reign of Justinian (527–65). The major art form was ecclesiastical architecture, the basic plan of which was Roman—either basilican (symmetrical about an axis) or centralised (symmetrical about a point). Arched construction was developed, and the dome became the most typical feature, although, unlike the Roman dome which was placed on a round apartment, the Byzantine dome was placed on a square one on independent pendentives. Frequently small domes were clustered round a large one as in the case of the great church of Santa Sophia (537), the climax of Byzantine architecture. Usually the churches were small and include those of SS. Sergius and Bacchus, Sta. Irene (in Constantinople), S. Vitale in Ravenna, and the much later and larger St. Mark's in Venice. Byzantine art also took the form of miniatures, enamels, jewels, and textiles, but mosaics, frescos and icons (q.v.) are its greatest treasures.

C

Cacao, Theobroma cacao, is an evergreen tree, from 4–6 m high, growing abundantly in tropical America, West Africa, the West Indies, Sri Lanka, etc., yielding seeds, called cocoa beans from which cocoa and chocolate are manufactured. The fruit is 17–25 cm long, hard and ridged; inside are the beans, covered with a reddish-brown skin, which are first fermented, then dried. The trees mature at five to eight years and produce two crops a year.

Cactus, a family of flowering plants numbering about a thousand species adapted to living in very dry situations. The stem is usually fleshy, being composed of succulent tissue, remarkably retentive of water; commonly equipped with sharp thorns which deter animals from eating them. The roots are generally very long, tapping soil water over a large area; a "prickly pear" cactus may have roots covering a circular area 7 m or more in diameter. The leaves are commonly insignificant or absent, and the stem takes over the photosynthetic leaf function and becomes accordingly flattened to expose greater area to sunlight and air. In some kinds of cactus (e.g., Echinocactus) the stem is shaped almost like a sea-urchin.

Cadmium. A metallic element, no. 48, symbol Cd, chemically similar to zinc and mercury. Used in alloys to lower the melting point, as in Wood's metal with bismuth and tin. Alloyed with copper to make electric cables. Like zinc, it is a protective metal and is used in electroplating. The cadmium-vapour lamp gives a characteristic frequency used in measuring wavelength.

Caesium, also spelt **Cesium,** is an alkali metal element, no. 55, symbol Cs, in first group of the periodic table. It resembles rubidium and potassium and was discovered by Bunsen and Kirchoff in 1860. It was the first element whose existence was discovered spectro-

scopically. The caesium atom consists of a heavy nucleus surrounded by 55 electrons, 54 of which are arranged in stable orbits, and one of which, known as the valency electron, in a less stable orbit surrounding them. Used in the construction of photo-electric cells and as an accurate time standard (atomic clock).

Calcium, a silvery-white metallic element, no. 20, symbol Ca. It melts at 810°C and is very reactive. It was discovered by Sir Humphry Davy in 1808, but not until 1898 was it obtained pure, by Moissan. Does not occur as metal in nature, but calcium compounds make up a large part of the earth's crust. Most important calcium sources are marble, limestone, chalk (all three are, chemically, calcium carbonate); dolomite, which is the double carbonate of calcium and magnesium; gypsum, a hydrated calcium sulphate; calcium phosphate and calcium fluoride. Igneous rocks contain much calcium silicate. Calcium compounds are essential to plants and are used in fertilisers. Animals require calcium and phosphorus for bone and teeth formation; deficiency is treated by administration of calcium phosphate. Strontium is chemically similar to calcium, and the radioactive strontium 90 from atomic "fall-out" is therefore easily assimilated by the body.

Calendar, a collection of tables showing the days and months of the year, astronomical recurrences, chronological references, etc. The Julian Calendar, with its leap year, introduced by Julius Caesar, fixed the average length of the year at 365¼ days, which was about 11 minutes too long (the earth completes its orbit in 365 days 5 hours 48 minutes 46 seconds of mean solar time). The cumulative error was rectified by the Gregorian Calendar, introduced in Italy in 1582, whereby century years do not count as leap years unless divisible by 400. This is the rule we now follow. England did not adopt the reformed calendar until 1752, when she found herself 11 days behind the Continent. The Gregorian Calendar did not come into use in Russia until 1918. Old Style and New Style dates are identified as "O.S." "N.S.".

Calends, the first day of the month in the Roman calendar.

Calorie. Unit of quantity of heat. The "small" or fundamental calorie is the amount of heat required to raise the temperature of 1 gram of water from 14·5° to 15·5°C and is equal to 4·185 joules. This is the gram-calorie used in physics and chemistry. The large Calorie (written with a capital C), commonly used in nutritional connotations, is equal to 1000 small calories and is called the kilogram-calorie.

Calvinism. See Section J.

Calypso, West Indian song in the form of a doggerel lampoon composed spontaneously and sung to a guitar. See **E29.**

Cambridge University had a sufficiently good teaching reputation to attract Oxford students in 1209, when lectures at their own university were suspended. In 1226 it had a Chancellor who was recognised by King and Pope. The first college to be founded was Peterhouse in 1284. The university was reorganised and granted a Charter of Incorporation by an act of Elizabeth in 1571. The colleges with their dates of foundation are Christ's (1505), Churchill (1960), Clare (1326), Clare Hall (1966), Corpus Christi (1352), Darwin (1964), Downing (1800), Emmanuel (1584), Fitzwilliam (1966), Gonville and Caius (1348), Jesus (1496), King's (1441), Magdalene (1542), Pembroke (1347), Peterhouse (1284), Queens' (1448), St. Catharine's (1473), St. Edmund's House (1896), St. John's (1511), Selwyn (1882), Sidney Sussex (1596), Trinity (1546), Trinity Hall (1350), Wolfson (1965). The women's colleges are: Girton (1869), Newnham (1871), New Hall (1954), Hughes Hall (formerly Cambridge T. C.) (1885), and Lucy Cavendish Collegiate Society (1965) (for women research students and other graduates; took undergraduates in 1970s). Women were admitted to degrees (though not allowed to sit for examination) in 1920, and to full membership of the University in 1948. Most colleges now admit both men and women students.

Camel, a large ruminant quadruped, inhabiting Asia and Africa, where it is largely used as a beast of burden. There are two species—the

Arabian camel or dromedary, with only one hump; and the Bactrian, or double-humped camel. There are no wild dromedaries, and the only wild bactrians occur in the Gobi Desert. The camel is able to go for long periods without water, not, as was formerly believed, because it stored water in its hump, but because of the unique mechanism of its physiology which enables it to conserve water at the expense of not sweating until 40°C is reached.

Campanile, or bell-tower, is separate from but usually adjoining its parent church. The most famous are in Italy. Giotto's tower at Florence, adjoining the cathedral of Santa Maria del Fiore, is architecturally the finest in the world. Others are at Cremona, the loftiest in Italy (110 m) and Pisa (the leaning tower). The magnificent pointed campanile of St. Mark's, Venice, which collapsed in 1902 and has since been rebuilt in its original form, was begun in 902.

Canal, an artificial watercourse used for navigation which changes its level by means of locks. The completion of the Bridgewater Canal in 1761 to take coal from Worsley to Manchester marked the beginning of canal building in industrial Britain. There are over 4,000 km of navigable inland waterways in Great Britain today, c. 3,200 km of which are under the control of the British Waterways Board set up by the Transport Act 1962. The English network is based on the four great estuaries, Mersey, Humber, Severn and Thames. Under the Transport Act 1968, the Board is enabled to maintain an extensive network of amenity waterways. A number of disused canals are being restored to navigation by the Board in conjuction with local authorities and voluntary societies.

Candela unit of luminous intensity, symbol cd. An idea of the value which this unit represents may be gained from the fact that light obtained from a 40 W filament-type electric lamp or bulb is approximately the same as would be given by a point source of luminous intensity 30 cd. *See* **S.I. units, Section N.**

Candlemas, an English and Roman Church festival in celebration of the Purification of the Virgin Mary. The date is 2 February.

Canon, a term applied to signify a recognised rule for the guide of conduct in matters legal, ecclesiastical and artistic, or an authoritative ordinance: thus we have Canonical Scriptures, Canon Law, etc. A Canon is also a dignitary of the Church, usually a member of a cathedral chapter in the Anglican communion, or in the Roman Church a member of an order standing between regular monks and secular clergy.

Canonical Hours were seven in number in the Western Church; Matins and Lauds, before dawn; Prime, early morning service; Terce, 9 a.m.; Sext, noon; Nones, 3 p.m.; Vespers, 4 p.m.; Compline, bed-time.

Canonisation, the entering of one of the faithful departed on the list of saints of the Roman Catholic Church. The rules governing canonisation were simplified by papal decree in 1969. The forty English martyrs, of whom Edmund Campion was one, executed between 1535 and 1679 and beatified long ago, were canonised in 1970. Beatification, by which a person is called blessed, is usually followed by canonisation, but not necessarily.

Canticles, the name given to the scriptural passages from the Bible sung by the congregation in the various Christian liturgies. They are the *Benedicite, Benedictus, Magnificat, Nunc Dimittis.*

Capercaillie, the largest of the grouse family, found in the Scottish highlands and the pine forests and mountainous regions of Northern and Central Europe and Asia.

Capet, the family name of the royal house of France, founded by Hugh Capet in 987, with its collateral branches. The main line of the dynasty came to an end in 1328 with the death of Charles IV when the throne passed to the related house of Valois. The direct Valois line ended in 1498 with the death of Charles VIII. The first of the Bourbon line was Henry IV whose descendants ruled France (except during the French Revolution and the Napoleonic era) until 1848.

Capitalism. *See* **Section J.**

Capuchins are members of a mendicant order of

Franciscans, founded in the 16th cent. with the aim of restoring the primitive and stricter observance of the rule of St. Francis, so called from the capuce or pointed cowl worn by them.

Carat, a term used in assessing the value of gold and precious stones. In connection with gold, it represents the proportion of pure gold contained in any gold alloy, and for this purpose the metal is divided into 24 parts. Thus 24-carat indicates pure gold, and any lesser number of carats shows the proportion of gold contained in the alloy. The carat as a measure of weight is now obsolete, having been replaced by the *metric carat* of 0·2 grams.

Caravan, a band of travellers or traders journeying together for safety across the Eastern deserts, sometimes numbering many hundreds. There are several allusions to caravans in the Old Testament. The great caravan routes of this period from Egypt to Babylon and from Palestine to Yemen linked up with the Syrian ports and so with Western sea commerce. Many wars have been fought in the past over their control.

Carbohydrates. *See* **Diet, Section P.**

Carbon, a non-metallic chemical element no. 6, symbol C, which occurs in crystalline form as diamonds and graphite; amorphous forms of carbon include charcoal and soot, while coke consists mainly of elementary carbon. The biochemistry of plants and animals largely hinges upon carbon compounds. The study of carbon compounds is called Organic Chemistry. **Carbon 14.** A radioactive isotope of carbon, with a half-life c. 6,000 years, used in following the path of compounds and their assimilation in the body. Also used in determination of the age of carbon-containing materials such as trees, fossils and very old documents.

Carbonari, members of a secret political society originating in Naples, and at one time very numerous. Their chief aim was to free Italy from foreign rule, and they exerted considerable influence in the various revolutionary movements in the first half of the 19th cent. Their name was adopted from the charcoal-burners (*carbonari*), and their passwords, signs, etc., were all in the phraseology of the fraternity.

Carbon dioxide. Commonest of the oxides of carbon. It is formed when carbon and its compounds are burnt with abundant supply of air, and when carbon compounds are oxidised in the respiration process of animals. The atmosphere contains carbon dioxide to the extent of about 325 ppm and is increasing by about 1 ppm per year, principally because of the burning of fossil fuels and possibly because of deforestation which not only leaves more oxidisible material but lowers the amount of carbon dioxide removed by photosynthesis (**F32**).

Carbon monoxide is a colourless gas with no taste or smell. It is formed when coal and coke are burnt with a restricted supply of air; the blue flame to be seen in a coke brazier, for instance, is the flame of carbon monoxide. This gas is very poisonous, forming with the haemoglobin of the blood a compound which is useless for respiration and cherry red in colour, which gives a visible sympton of poisoning by carbon monoxide. With nickel it forms a volatile compound, called nickel carbonyl, and this reaction is the basis of the Mond process for extracting nickel.

Cardinal, one of the chief dignitaries of the Roman Catholic Church who constitute the Pope's council, or Sacred College, and when the papal chair is vacant elect by secret ballot a Pope from among themselves. There are three orders: cardinal bishops, members of the Roman Curia (the central administration of the Church) and bishops of sees near Rome; cardinal deacons, also members of the Curia, holding titular bishoprics; and cardinal priests who exercise pastoral duties over sees removed from Rome, though some are members of the Curia. Pope John Paul I, who had been elected in Aug. 1978 to succeed Pope Paul VI, died suddenly after only 33 days. He was succeeded by Pope John Paul II (Cardinal Karol Wojtyla, Archbishop of Cracow). Pope John Paul II appointed 28 new cardinals in 1985, bringing the total number to 152. Papal insignia were trimmed of embellishment by papal decree in 1969 with the abolition, subsequently revoked, of the famous red hat (the galero) and the shoes with buckles. Cardinals must now retire at 80.

Cardinal Virtues, according to Plato these were justice, prudence, temperance, fortitude—*natural* virtues as distinct from the *theological* virtues of the Roman Catholic Church, faith, hope, charity. The phrase "seven cardinal virtues", combining the two, figures in mediaeval literature. See **Sins, Seven Deadly.**

Carmelites, a body of mendicant friars taking their name from Mount Carmel, where the order was first established in the 12th cent. The original rule of the order required absolute poverty, abstinence from meat and a hermit life. The rigidity of the rule of the order was mitigated by Innocent IV. They wear a brown habit with white mantle, hence their name of White Friars. The order of Carmelite nuns was instituted in the 15th cent.

Carolingians, dynasty of Frankish rulers founded in the 7th cent. The family was at its height when represented by Charlemagne. It ruled, with interruptions, until 987 when the Capetian dynasty succeeded.

Carp, a well-known fresh-water fish, found in plenty in most European and Asiatic still waters; reaches a length of about 60 cm and under favourable conditions lives for about 40 years. Familiar British members of the family are the roach, rudd, dace, chub, gudgeon, tench, minnow, barbel, bream and bleak. The goldfish, popular in ornamental ponds, is the domesticated variety of a Far Eastern member of the carp family.

Carthusians, an order of monks founded in 1084 by St. Bruno at the Grande Chartreuse near Grenoble, and introduced into England about a century later. They built the Charterhouse (corruption of Chartreuse) in London in 1371. The chief characteristics of the order are a separate dwelling-house in the precincts of the charterhouse for each monk, and the general assembly in the Church twice in the day and once at night. They wear a white habit, with white scapular and hood. The liqueur *Chartreuse* was invented by the order and is still their secret. For many years they have derived large revenues from its sale. The order of Carthusian nuns was founded in the 12th cent.

Casein, the chief protein in milk and cheese. It is coagulated by the action of rennet or acid. An important class of plastics ("casein plastics") are produced from it, and these plastics are converted into buttons, kitting-needles, etc. 36,000 litres of milk yield about 1 tonne of casein.

Cassowary, a genus of ostrich-like birds which, together with the emu, forms a separate order found only in Australasia. All species are black, with brightly coloured necks, and with a horny crest on the head. Noted for fleetness.

Castor-oil Plant (*Ricinus communis*), an African shrub now cultivated in most tropical countries. It has broad palmate leaves and bears a spiny fruit containing seeds which when pressed yield the well-known oil.

Cat, the general name for all members of the class *Felidae* of the carnivorous order, from the lion down to the domestic cat. The latter is believed to be descended from the European and African wild cats. Egypt is credited with having been the first country in which the cat was domesticated.

Catabolism, Anabolism, are the terms used to describe the two types of metabolic pathway. Catabolic pathways are routes by which large organic molecules are broken up by enzymes into their simpler constituents *e.g.*, starch into glucose. The anabolic pathways are the routes by which complex molecules are synthesised from simple sub-units, *e.g.*, proteins from amino acids.

Catalyst. A substance which alters the rate of reaction without itself being chemically changed. Various aluminium and titanium compounds are catalysts in the formation of polythene from ethylene. Palladium catalyses the reaction of hydrogen with oxygen (hence its use in gas lighters). Enzymes in the body hasten the breakdown of carbohydrates and proteins by catalytic action. See **F26.**

Cataracts are gigantic waterfalls. The most

famous are those of Niagara in North America, the Orinoco in South America, the Victoria Falls on the Zambesi in Africa, and the Falls of the Rhine at Schaffhausen.

Catechism, an elementary book of principles in any science or art, but more particularly in religion, in the form of questions and answers. There is a great variety of these, including the Lutheran, prepared by Luther in 1529, Calvin's Geneva (in 1536), and the Anglican, in the Book of Common Prayer.

Caterpillar, the larva of a butterfly or moth, worm-like in its segmented body, with 3 pairs of jointed true legs, often curiously marked and coloured, and frequently more or less hairy.

Cathedral, the chief church of a diocese, so called from its containing a Bishop's seat, or episcopal chair. The town in which it is situated is a cathedral city. Some celebrated cathedrals are St. John Lateran of Rome, Notre Dame of Paris, the cathedrals of Cologne and Milan, St. Paul's in London, Canterbury Cathedral, York Minster, and the cathedrals of Durham, Bristol, Gloucester, Peterborough, Exeter, Liverpool, and Coventry (destroyed by bombs, now rebuilt).

Catholicism. See **Section J.**

Cat's eye, a kind of quartz, much valued as a gem, opalescent, and of various shades.

Cavalier, a name adopted during the troubles of the Civil War to designate the Royalist party; it is also used generally in reference to a knightly, gallant or imperious personage.

Caves, natural hollow places in the earth, frequently found in Carboniferous limestone areas. The underground caves are formed by the action of rainwater carrying carbon dioxide, a dilute acid which slowly attacks the limestone rocks. The main caves in the British Isles are in the Mendips, Derbyshire, Yorkshire, S. Wales and in County Clare. Many British inland caves are thought to have been formed at the end of the Ice Age when there was a rise in the water table. The floods of September 1968 moved masses of débris in some of the British caves, redistributing it in a major way; new routes were blocked and old passages reopened. The scientific study of caves is known as spelaeology.

Cedar, a dark-leaved, cone-bearing, horizontal-branched evergreen tree that grows to a considerable height and girth, the best known species in Britain being the Cedar of Lebanon, which was introduced in the 17th cent.

Celluloid, one of the first synthetic thermoplastic materials, discovered by Alexander Parkes in 1865 when he was attempting to produce synthetic horn. It is made by treating cellulose nitrate with camphor and alcohol. Photographic film is made of a similar, but less-inflammable material, formed by the use of cellulose acetate instead of the nitrate.

Cellulose, a carbohydrate, and a constituent of nearly all plants. Cellulose occurs in an almost pure state in the fibres of linen (flax), absorbent cotton, jute, and filter-paper (used in laboratories).

Celsius was an 18th cent. Swedish scientist (**B13**) after whom the modern Celsius temperature scale is named. Since 1954, °C stands for "degree Celsius" instead of "degree Centigrade" but this is only a change in name. Both symbols refer to the temperature scale which calls the melting point of ice 0°C and the boiling point of water at one atmosphere pressure 100°C. See **Absolute Temperature.**

Celts, an ancient race found late in the third millennium B.C. in S.W. Germany, united by a common language and culture, who spread westward into Spain, northward into Britain, eastward to the Black Sea, reaching Galatia in Asia Minor. The "La Tène" iron-age Celts invaded Britain *c.* 250 B.C. After Britain was conquered by the Romans and invaded by the Angles and Saxons there remained as areas of Celtic speech only Wales (Brythonic speakers), Ireland, Scotland, the Isle of Man (Gaelic speakers), and in Cornwall. The late Celtic period in Britain produced a distinctive Christian art (*e.g.*, the Lindisfarne Gospel *c*, 700, and the Irish Book of Kells, dating from about the same time). Surviving Celtic languages are Welsh, Irish, Breton and Scots Gaelic; Cornish survived until the 18th cent. and Manx Gaelic is on the point of extinction.

Centrifuge, a machine which produces large accelerations by utilising the radial force caused by rotating a body about a fixed centre. Centrifuges have found extensive application in modern science. They can be used for the separation of one size of particle from another in biochemistry or in the training of astronauts where the accelerations occurring during rocket lift off can be simulated in a centrifuge on the ground.

Ceramics, are substances in which a combination of one or more metals with oxygen confers special and valuable properties. These include hardness, and resistance to heat and chemicals. Ceramic comes from the Greeek word for pottery, and pottery materials of mud and clay were probably the first man-made ceramics. Nowadays the range is enormous and growing; apart from all the pottery materials, there are firebricks, gems, glasses, concretes, nuclear reactor fuel elements, special materials for electronic devices, coloured pigments, electrical insulators, abrasives, and many other things. The scientific study of ceramics is part of materials science (*see* **Materials Science**). The need to design ceramic objects has inspired great art, and the production of ceramics has become a major industry.

Cerium, a scarce metallic element, no. 58, symbol Ce, discovered by Berzelius in 1803. A mixture of cerium and thorium nitrates is used in the manufacture of gas mantles, which owe their incandescent property to the deposit of cerium and thorium oxide with which they are coated.

Chain reaction. See **F13(1).**

Chalcedony, a mixture of crystalline silica and amorphous hydrated silica, *i.e.*, of quartz and opal. It has a waxy lustre, and is much used by jewellers for necklaces, bracelets, etc. Commonly it is white or creamy. Its bright orange-red variety is called carnelian; its brown variety, sard. Chrysoprase, plasma, bloodstone are varieties which are respectively pale apple-green, dark leek-green, green with red spots.

Chalk, a white limestone, calcium carbonate, found in the Upper Cretaceous deposits (formed from the shells of minute marine organisms). As chalk is porous, few streams form on its surface and consequently it is eroded slowly, although generally speaking it is a soft rock. Its juxaposition with soft impervious clay in some areas results in its forming steep ridges known as escarpments, *e.g.*, N. and S. Downs and Chilterns. In contrast to the dry upland surfaces of chalk, lower levels are frequently saturated with water which emerges as springs.

Chamberlain, Lord, the senior officer of The Royal Household who is responsible for all ceremonial within the palace (levées, courts, garden parties, entertainment of foreign royalties and heads of state) but not the coronation or state opening of parliament. He is also in charge of appointments to The Royal Household. His office as censor of plays was abolished in 1968.

Chamberlain, Lord Great, one of the great officers of state whose duties are now mainly ceremonial. He attends the monarch at the state opening of parliament and at the coronation and is custodian of the Palace of Westminster (Houses of Parliament). The office is hereditary, dating from Norman times, and is held for one reign in turn by the descendants of the De Veres, Earls of Oxford. The present Lord Great Chamberlain is the Marquess of Cholmondeley.

Chameleon, a family of lizards with numerous species. Their ability to change colour is well known, but exaggerated, and is due to the movement of pigment cells beneath the skin. They are slow in movement, arboreal, and mainly insectivorous. Found in Africa, India, Sri Lanka, Madagascar and Arabia.

Chamois, a species of antelope, native of Western Europe and Asia. About the size of a goat, it lives in mountainous regions, and possesses wonderful leaping power, so that it is very difficult to capture. Its flesh is much esteemed, and from its skin chamois leather is made, although today sheep and goat skins are usually substituted. The mating season is October–November and the fawns are born in May or June. Live to be 20–25 years old.

Channel Tunnel, a scheme to bore a tunnel through 32–48 km of chalk under the sea between Dover and Calais has been a subject for discussion ever since Albert Mathieu first conceived the idea as a practical possibility in 1802. In the 1830s proposals for a bridge were made. Investigations have been undertaken from time to time, but on each occasion military doubts or cost, reinforced by the insular feelings of the English, caused the governments of the day to withhold support. In the 1980s plans for a cross channel fixed link began to surface again although it was stated clearly that the project would have to be entirely financed from private capital. The British and French Governments called for the submission of plans for a fixed link by November 1985, stating that the selection of the winning proposal would be made in January 1986.

The announcement in January 1986 of the intention by Britain and France to construct a 31-mile tunnel under the Channel between Cheriton, Kent and Frethun in northern France has brought the idea of a Channel Tunnel very close to realisation. According to the plans by 1993 a direct "fixed link" will be available for travellers to and from the continent.

Chapel Royal, the church dedicated to the use of the Sovereign and Court. There are, among others, chapels royal at St. James's Palace, Buckingham Palace, Windsor, Hampton Court, the Tower, and Holyrood. *See also* **E4(2).**

Charcoal, a term applied to wood that has been subjected to a process of slow smothered combustion. More generally it refers to the carbonaceous remains of vegetable, animal, or combustible mineral substances submitted to a similar process. Charcoal from special woods (in particular buckthorn) is used in making gunpowder. Bone charcoal finds use in sugar refining, as it removes dark colouring matter present in the crude syrup.

Chasuble, a sleeveless vestment worn by ecclesiastics over the alb during the celebration of Mass. It is supposed to symbolise the seamless coat of Christ.

Cheese, an article of food made from the curd of milk, which is separated from the whey and pressed in moulds and gradually dried. There are about 500 varieties differing with method of preparation and quality of milk. They used to be made in the regions after which they are named but nowadays many of them are mass-produced, *e.g.*, Cheddar is made not only in all parts of Britain but in Canada, New Zealand, Australia, Holland and the USA. Cheeses may be divided into 3 main classes: (1) soft, *e.g.*, Camembert, Cambridge, l'Evêque; (2) blue-veined, *e.g.*, Stilton, Gorgonzola, Roquefort (made from ewe's milk), (3) hard-pressed, *e.g.*, Cheddar, Cheshire, Gruyère, Parmesan, Gouda.

Cheetah or "hunting leopard", the large spotted cat of Africa and Southern Asia, the swiftest four-footed animal alive.

Chemical Warfare. This term is usually restricted to mean the use in war of anti-personnel gases, aerosols and smokes, although explosives, napalm, herbicides and defoliants are also chemical agents that are used in war. Anti-personnel chemical weapons may be classified as (*a*) vesicants (agents which produce skin blisters, *e.g.*, mustard gas); (*b*) lacrimators (*e.g.*, the original tear gas, CN, and its British-developed successor CS now preferred for riot control); (*c*) sternutators (sneeze and vomiting agents, usually arsenic compounds, *e.g.*, Adamsite DM); (*d*) nerve gases (extremely lethal agents which incapacitate the nervous system, *e.g.*, the G-agents developed during the second world war and the more powerful **V**-agents developed subsequently); (*e*) lung irritants *e.g.*, phosgene and chlorine). Most of these chemicals can be lethal at sufficiently high concentrations and for this reason it is doubtful whether there exists the "humane" chemical agent which instantly incapacitates but leaves no long-term side effects.

The first occasion when poison gas was used on a large scale was in the first world war; more than 100,000 fatalities resulted from the use of principally chlorine, phosgene and mustard gas. Worldwide revulsion at the hideous effects of chemical weapons and their potential as indiscriminate weapons of mass destruction resulted in the Geneva Protocol of 1925 which prohibited the use of both chemical and bacteriological weapons. It has now been ratified by over 90 nations including all the major powers (although Japan and America are only recent signatories). The Protocol has been generally well observed although notable violations have been by the Italians in Abyssinia (1935–6), the Japanese in China during the second world war and the Americans in South East Asia in the 1960s. It has however failed to prevent the continual development and stock-piling of lethal chemical agents by many nations, although recently there have been moves towards chemical weapons disarmament. *See also* **Biological Warfare.**

Chemistry is the science of the elements and their compounds. It is concerned with the laws of their combination and behaviour under various conditions. It had its roots in alchemy and has gradually developed into a science of vast magnitude and importance. Organic chemistry deals with the chemistry of the compounds of carbon; inorganic chemistry is concerned with the chemistry of the elements; physical chemistry is concerned with the study of chemical reactions and with the theories and laws of chemistry. *See* **F23–8.**

Chernobyl Disaster Site in the Ukraine of 1986 Soviet nuclear disaster. *See* **F71–2.**

Chestnut, the fruit of trees of the genus *Castanea*, members of the family *Fagaceae*. *C. sativa* is the sweet or Spanish chestnut, *C. dentata* the American chestnut and *C. crenata* the Japanese chestnut. The nut is edible. The wood is used in carpentry and fencing. *See also* **Horse Chestnut.**

Chiaroscuro, a term used in painting to denote the disposition of light and shade. Rembrandt is unrivalled as a painter for his contrasts of light and shadows.

Chiltern Hundreds, three hundreds—Stoke, Burnham and Desborough—the stewardship of which is now a nominal office under the Chancellor of the Exchequer. Since about 1750 the nomination to it has been used as a method of enabling a member of Parliament to resign his seat on the plea that he holds an office of honour and profit under the crown. An alternate symbolic post for an M.P. giving up his seat is the stewardship of the Manor of Northstead in Yorkshire which has been used in the same way since 1841.

Chimpanzee, a large anthropoid ape, a native of tropical Africa, of a dark brown colour, with arms reaching to the knee, and capable of walking upright. Its brain is about a third of the weight of the human brain, but is anatomically similar. The animal has considerable intelligence and powers of learning. A suitable subject for space flight experiments.

Chinchilla, a South American burrowing rodent. Grey in colour, and white underneath. Its fur is greatly esteemed for its beautiful fur.

Chippendale Furniture was introduced in the reign of George I by Thomas Chippendale, a cabinet-maker from Yorkshire who migrated to London and set up for himself in St. Martin's Lane, Charing Cross. He was fonder of inventing designs for furniture than of making it, and in 1752 published a book of patterns; the London furniture-makers of the day soon began to model their work upon it.

Chivalry an international brotherhood of knights formed primarily during the 13th cent. to fight against the infidels in the Crusades. For the French the major battle was against the Moslems in the Holy Land and North Africa, the Spaniards fought the same enemy in their own country, and the Germans were concerned with the heathen of Baltic lands, but Chaucer's "very perfect gentle knight" had fought in all these areas. One did not easily become a knight who had to be of noble birth and then pass through a period of probation, beginning as a boy page in the castle of some great lord, serving his elders and betters humbly while he was taught good manners, singing, playing musical instruments, and the composition of verse. Probably he learned Latin, but he certainly learned French, which was the international language of knights as Latin was of scholars. At fourteen he became a squire and learned to fight with sword, battle-axe and lance, and to endure conditions of hard living while carrying out his duties of waiting on his lord, looking after his horses, and in time accompanying him in battle. Only if he showed himself suitable was he finally knighted by a stroke of the hand or sword on the shoulder from the king or lord. Knighthood was an international order and had its special code of behaviour; to honour one's sworn word, to protect the weak, to respect women, and defend the Faith. To some extent it had a civilising effect on the conduct of war (*e.g.* knights of opposing sides might slaughter each other in battle but feast together after), but, since war was regarded as the supreme form of sport, it cannot be said to have contributed to peace.

Chlorine, a gaseous element, no. 17, symbol Cl, of the halogen family, first isolated in 1774 by Scheele by the action of manganese dioxide in hydrochloric acid. It unites easily with many other elements, the compounds resulting being termed chlorides. The gaseous element is greenish-yellow, with a pungent odour. It is a suffocating gas, injuring the lungs at a concentration as low as 1 part in 50,000, and was used during the first world war as a poison gas. Has a powerful bleaching action, usually being used in form of bleaching powder, made by combining lime and chlorine.

Chloroform, a volatile colourless liquid, compounded of carbon, hydrogen, and chlorine. It is a powerful solvent, not naturally occurring but synthesised on a large scale. When the vapour is inhaled it produces unconsciousness and insensibility to pain. It owes its discovery to Liebig, and its first application for medical purposes to Sir James Young Simpson.

Chlorophyll, the green pigment contained in the leaves of plants, first discovered by P. J. Pelletier (1788–1829) and J. B. Caventou (1795–1877) in 1818. Enables the plant to absorb sunlight and so to build up sugar. The total synthesis of chlorophyll was reported in 1960 by Prof. R. B. Woodward. This was an outstanding achievement in the field of organic chemistry. *See* **Photosynthesis, F32(1).**

Chouans, the name given to the band of peasants, mainly smugglers and dealers in contraband salt, who rose in revolt in the west of France in 1793 and joined the royalists of La Vendée. Balzac gives a picture of the people and the country in which they operated in his novel *Les Chouans*. They used the hoot of an owl as a signal—hence the name.

Chough, a member of the crow family, of glossy blue-green-black plumage, whose long curved bill and legs are coral red. It used to be abundant on the cliffs of Cornwall, but its haunts are now restricted to the rocky outcrops of the western coasts and in the mountains near by. It nests in cleft rocks and caves. The Alpine chough with yellow bill inhabits the mountainous districts of Europe and Asia and is not found in Britain. It was found at *c.* 8,200 m on Everest.

Christmas means "mass of Christ" from the old English *Cristes maesse*, which is celebrated by the Western church on 25 December. The actual day on which Christ was born is not known and there is some uncertainty about the year. 25 December as the day of Nativity was not generally observed until the 5th cent. A.D., though, as the winter solstice, it had long been observed as a pagan festival of *sol invictus* (unconquered sun). The first Christmas card dates from about 1843 and the Christmas tree, of pagan origin, was introduced into England from Germany where it had been a tradition since the Middle Ages. Santa Claus is a corruption of Santa Nikolaus (St. Nicholas) patron saint of children, whose feast day properly falls on 6 December.

Chromium, a very hard, bluish-white metal element, no. 24, symbol Cr, melting at very high temperature (above 1,900°C). Its chief ore is chromite or chrome iron-ore (ferrous chromite). "Ferro-chrome" is produced by heating chromite and anthracite in an electric furnace, and chrome steels are prepared by adding the pre-calculated amount of ferro-chrome to melted steel. Best known chrome steel is stainless steel first made by Brearley in 1912 and since then developed greatly at Sheffield. A typical formula is 18 per cent. chromium, 8 per cent. nickel, 74 per cent. iron. Equally important are Stellite alloys, containing chromium, cobalt, tungsten (or molybdenum), which have made possible modern high-speed cutting tools. Dies used in manufacture of plastics are commonly of chrome steel. The elementary metal finds little use alone except in chromium-plating for motor cars, etc.

Chromosomes, the structures contained within the nucleus of every animal and plant cell by which genetic information is transmitted. The chromosome number in somatic (body) cells is constant for each species of plant and animal, e.g., man (46), cat (38), mouse (40) honey bee (16), fruit fly Drosophila (8), potato (48). Chromosomes are long molecules composed of deoxyribonucleoproteins (i.e., proteins and DNA). Human chromosomes have been the subject of much recent research since it has been found that certain disorders are associated with chromosomal aberration, e.g., in Mongolism an extra chromosome is present. See also **Genes, Chromosome Theory (F31), Cell Division (F34).**

Church Commissioners. The Church Commissioners were established in 1948 by the amalgamation of Queen Anne's Bounty (established 1704) and the Ecclesiastical Commissioners (established 1836) to administer Church revenues and to manage Church property generally. The Commissioners control funds of c. £600m.

Cid, El, a famous Spanish hero of the 11th cent., Don Rodrigo Diaz de Vivar, also called Cid Campeador, whose exploits, against Christians and Moors alike, are celebrated in poem, play and romance.

Cilia, minute hair-like projections on the surface of some cells, which beat together in wavelike movements like the wind over a corn-field. These movements can be used as a means of locomotion as in the aquatic organism paramecium. Cilia are also found on the outer layers of the human trachea where they waft particles upwards to the throat, thus protecting the lungs. See **F37, Index to Section P** and **Flagella.**

Cinque Ports, a number of seaport towns on the coast of Kent and Sussex, originally five; Hastings, Romney, Hythe, Dover and Sandwich. Winchelsea and Rye were added later. These ports were required to furnish a certain number of ships, ready for service, and in return they were granted many privileges. The official residence of the Lord Warden is Walmer Castle, near Dover. The present holder of the office is the Queen Mother, the first-ever woman to be appointed.

Cistercians, an order of monks and nuns taking their names from Citeaux, near Dijon, where their first monastery was established in 1098. The order was noted for the severity of its rule. They were famous agriculturists. The habit is white, with a black cowl or hood.

Civil List is the annual sum payable to the Sovereign to maintain the Royal Household and to uphold the dignity of the Crown. The amount is granted by Parliament upon the recommendation of a Select Committee and has to be settled afresh in the first six months of a new reign. The Civil List of Queen Victoria was £385,000; Edward VII and George V, £470,000; Edward VIII and George VI, £410,000; Elizabeth II £475,000. Since 1972 the Civil List allowances have been increased each year to keep pace with inflation. The figures for 1985 are as follows: The Queen's Civil List £3,967,200, Her Majesty Queen Elizabeth The Queen Mother £345,300, HRH The Duke of Edinburgh £192,600, HRH The Princess Anne £120,000, HRH The Prince Andrew £20,000; HRH The Princess Margaret £116,800; and HRH The Prince Edward, £20,000.

The Prince of Wales is entitled to tax-free revenue from the Duchy of Cornwall. Other resources available to the Queen include (1) the sums which Parliament votes to government departments each year, e.g., upkeep of palaces (Dept. of the Environment) royal yacht Britannia and the royal flight (Min. of Defence); (2) privy purse (revenues of the Duchy of Lancaster); (3) personal fortune, the size of which is not disclosed. The Queen pays no direct taxes. 80–100 per cent. of the annuities received by other members of the Royal family are treated

as tax-free expenses. The system under which annual payments are made by the Government to the Queen was changed by the Civil List Act 1975; payments are now included in the annual estimates in the same way as the expenditure of a government department, and subject to scrutiny in the House of Commons. The Civil List now provides only for the Sovereign, the consort of a Sovereign, their children, and the widows of those children.

Cleopatra's Needle on the Thames Embankment is of the time of Tuthmosis III (1500–1450 B.C.). The monolith had nothing to do with Cleopatra, as it only came to Alexandria after her death. It was first erected at the Biblical On (Greek Heliopolis), sacred City of the Sun. It was presented to the British Government by Mehemet Ali in 1819, but not brought to this country until 1878. Weight c. 183 tonnes; height, 20·8 m.

Climate has been defined by Professor H. H. Lamb as the total experience of the weather at any place over some specific period of time. Not only averages but extremes of temperature, variation of humidity, duration of sunshine and cloud cover, amount of rainfall and frequency of snow, frost, gales, etc., are amongst the data normally investigated. The interiors of great land masses are characterised by large ranges of temperature and low rainfall (continental climate), while proximity to oceans has an ameliorating effect with increase in rainfall (oceanic climate). Presence of mountain ranges and lakes and configuration generally produce local modifications of climate, also apparent between the centre and the outlying suburbs of a city. Latitude introduces zones of climate, e.g., tropical rain, subtropical steppe and desert, temperate rain and polar. The climate is always changing in greater or less degree. Every year, every decade, every century brings a somewhat different experience. The recent tendency between 1880 and 1940 for most parts of the world to become warmer has eased off and appears to have given way to a more prolonged cooling tendency.

Clock, a device for measuring the passage of time. The earliest timekeeper was the shadow-clock, a primitive form of sundial, used in Ancient Egypt about 1500 B.C. To find the time at night the water clock or clepsydra was used. The sand-glass dates from the 15th cent. No one knows when the first mechanical clocks were invented, but it is known that a complicated mechanical clock driven by water and controlled by a weighbridge escarpment was built in Peking in 1090. The Dover Clock in the Science Museum is not the earliest surviving clock in England, as was once believed, but early 17th cent. The Salisbury Cathedral clock dates from 1386 and that of Wells Cathedral from 1392. The pendulum clock was invented by the Dutch scientist Christiaan Huygens (1625–95). The first watches were made in Nuremberg shortly after 1500. The marine chronometer is a high-precision timepiece used at sea for giving Greenwich mean time. The quartz-crystal clocks are accurate to one thousandth of a second a day, and the improved atomic clock, developed at the British National Physical Laboratory, which makes use of the natural vibrations of the caesium atom, is an almost absolute measure of time. Its accuracy of 1 sec. in 300 years has been improved to 1 sec. in 1,000 years.

Cloud Chamber, an apparatus invented by C. T. R. Wilson in which the tracks of atomic particles can be made visible. Just as the vapour trails tell of the track of an invisible aircraft high up in the air, so the vapour trails of an unseeable particle can tell of its behaviour. The rays under investigation pass through a chamber containing a gas, e.g., air thoroughly cleansed of dust, supersaturated with water, or alcohol-vapour. As the particle passes through it forms a track of tiny water droplets which can be photographed. After a long and honourable history this wonderful instrument is now virtually obsolete. A later ingenious device for tracking fast fundamental particles is the Bubble chamber (q.v.).

Clouds are formed by the cooling of moist air, the type depending on the way the air cools and the height at which condensation occurs. There are three main classes: (1) high cloud (about 6,100 m)—cirrus (delicate and fibrous), cirrostratus (thin white veil), and cirrocumulus (delicately rippled) consisting of ice crystals; (2) medium cloud (above 2,100 m)—altostratus (dense, greyish veil) and altocumulus (broken flattened cloudlets)—chiefly water particles, often supercooled; (3) low cloud (from near ground to 2,100 m)—cumulus (fair weather, broken, dome-topped), cumulominbus (heavy, towering to great heights), stratocumulus (layer of globular masses or rolls), stratus (like fog but off the ground), nimbostratus (low, rainy cloud). The highest clouds of all, and the rarest, are the noctilucent, seen only on summer nights in high latitudes. They form at about 80 km above the earth and consist of ice-coated dust from meteors.

Clover, plants of the *Trifolium* genus, family *Leguminosae,* with about 250 species. These are "nitrogen fixing" plants and include red clover, white clover, alsike clover and crimson clover. They are of great importance in agriculture because in a good pasture they supply directly or indirectly most of the protein available to the animals. Seed of "wild white" clover has been accepted since about 1939 as the indispensable plant of good United Kingdom grassland, largely through the efforts of pioneers like D. A. Gilchrist (1859–1927).

Coal. Until recently the most important single fuel has been coal. It is a mineral of organic origin, formed from the remains of vegetation which over millions of years has changed to coal by the effects of heat and pressure from overlying rock or water. All coal contains moisture, inflammable volatiles, mineral impurities (some of which remain as coal ash after the coal is burnt), and fixed carbon (the coke that is left after the volatiles have been driven off). The relative proportions vary—from Anthracite, a hard coal containing the highest proportion of fixed carbon, to Lignite or brown coal which is little more than a hard peat. World reserves of bituminous coal have been estimated at 7.5×10^{12} tonnes. If one adds the reserves of brown coal and lignite, this figure is increased by about 15 per cent. The proportion of the reserves that could be economically recovered varies from country to country and estimates vary from 50 to 100 per cent of the reserves. The reserves are highly localised—over half being located in the Soviet Union. In the United Kingdom coal has formed the basis of past industrial prosperity. Peak output occurred in 1913 when 290 million tonnes were mined one third of which was exported. At the end of the second world war production had fallen to 186 million tonnes and was far below demand. In 1947 the British coal industry was brought under public ownership and all its assets were vested in the National Coal Board. During the next ten years great efforts were made to increase coal output but, quite suddenly in 1956, demand for coal fell as oil became a popular fuel and the problem was to cut back the coal industry without causing undue social problems. The fall in demand was accompanied by increasing productivity, both mines and miners having been cut in their numbers by over half. Then as a result of the high cost of oil in 1973 came expansion of the industry with exploration to find new reserves (including offshore drillings). From Spring 1984 the coal industry faced a bitter strike over plans to make large-scale pit closures. In 1983 coal production was 120 million tonnes.

Coat of Arms, in heraldry, a device containing a family's armorial bearings. In mediaeval times an actual coat upon which such device was embroidered; knights wore it over their armour.

Cobalt, element no. 24, symbol Cr, a white metal melting at 1490°C. Two main ores are *cobalt glance* (in which the element is combined with arsenic and sulphur) and *smaltite* (cobalt arsenide). The principal sources are Ontario and Zaïre. Various cobalt alloys are important, *e.g.,* stellite, ferrocobalt and carboloy. Its monoxide is an important colouring medium, and is used for colouring glass and porcelain blue.

Cobra, hooded and very venomous snakes. The best known species are the Indian Cobra, the Egyptian Cobra, and the Black-necked Cobra. Their food consists chiefly of small rodents,

The King Cobra is almost exclusively a snake-eater. "Spitting" Cobras (or Ringhals) of S. Africa are a related genus, capable of spitting their venom several yards.

Coca, a S. American shrub, *Erythroxylon coca,* also cultivated in Java. The leaves yield cocaine, classified as a dangerous drug. When the natives chew the leaves they are enabled to withstand hunger and fatigue, as cocaine acts both as a mental stimulant and as an anaesthetic on the mucous lining of the stomach.

Cochineal *or* **Carmine,** a dyestuff consisting of the dried bodies of the female scale insect (*Dactylopius coccus*) which feeds on cacti. Of ancient origin, the dye was well known to the Aztecs, and was used widely in the Middle Ages. The scarlet tunics worn by the English during the Napoleonic wars owed their colour to carmine.

Cockatoo, a member of the parrot family, bearing a crest of feathers on the head, native to Australia and adjacent regions. Predominant colour is white tinged with yellow or scarlet while some species have dark plumage. The cockatoo of New Guniea is slaty black with pale red cheeks and can crack Kanary nuts which usually require a hammer to break them open.

Cockchafer (*Melolontha*), one of the most destructive of beetles, the larvae feeding on roots. It is about 2.5 cm in length, of a brownish colour, and emits a loud whirring sound when flying.

Cockle, the popular name of the bi-valve shellfish of the genus *Cardium,* found plentifully in sandy bays near low-water line.

Cockroach, inaccurately called the "black beetle"; a pest of bakeries and kitchens. In Britain two species are commonly found; the Common Cockroach (*Blatta orientalis*), resident since the time of Elizabeth I, dark brown, about 2.5 cm long, with the wing covers long in the male and short in the female; and the German Cockroach (*Blatta germanica*), now the most common, half the size, dark yellow, with both sexes fully winged. All species have long antennae and flattened, leathery, shiny bodies. They are nocturnal and omnivorous.

Coconut Palm (*Cocos nucifera*), a tropical tree, growing to a height of 30 m, with a slender trunk surmounted by giant feather-like leaves. One of the most important sources of food and raw material for people living in the tropics. The juice of the fruit, or coconut, is drunk; the kernel is eaten fresh or dried to form copra, which yields animal feeding stuffs and oil, used in the manufacture of soap, margarine, cosmetics, synthetic rubber, etc.; leaves are used for thatching; leaf stalks for canes, fence posts, needles, etc., and the trunk for houses and bridges. Main producing areas: Indonesia, Philippines, Malaysia, Sri Lanka and S. India.

Codes, a term used to designate a system of laws properly classified. The Code of Hammurabi, king of Babylon, *c.* 1751 B.C., had extensive influence over a long period. The Romans formulated several codes of historic importance including the Theodosian Code which summarised the Roman laws from the time of Constantine to 438 A.D. The final codification was made under order of the Emperor Justinian by his chief minister Tribonian and published in 529 with a new edition in 534. The most important of modern codes is the *Code Napoléon,* compiled between 1803 and 1810, and still in force. It has been used as an example for the codification of the laws of a number of countries from America to Japan. Under Frederick the Great the law of Prussia was codified. English law has never been codified, although the law on certain subjects has been gathered up into a single statute. The Law Commission Act, 1965, was passed to consolidate and codify the law.

Codex, a manuscript volume of the Scriptures comprising the Sinaiaticus of the 4th cent., the Vatican codex of the same period, the Alexandrine codex of the 5th cent., and others. The British Museum, in 1933, purchased the *Codex Sinaiticus* from the Soviet Government for £100,000. The Sinaiaticus was written on 347 vellum leaves some fifteen to sixteen hundred years ago and the binding into 2 volumes was completed by Douglas Cockerill and his son in 1936. It was sold to an American in 1981 for $5.2 million.

Coffee, a shrub found originally in Arabia and Ethiopia, but now extensively grown in Brazil, Colombia, Ivory Coast, Uganda, Angola and Central America. It yields a seed or berry which after undergoing the necessary preparation, is ground and used in most countries as a breakfast beverage. The best coffee is the Mocha, an Arabian variety. The stimulating effect of coffee is due to the caffeine, which is also present in tea. The beverage was introduced into Europe in the 16th cent., and the first London coffee shop was opened in 1652.

Coke is the solid residue remaining when coal is carbonised and nearly all the volatile constituents have been driven off. Used as fuel, and as an agent for reducing metallic oxides to metals, *e.g.*, iron ore to iron, in the manufacture of steel.

Colorado Beetle, a serious pest of potato crops. Both adults and larvae feed on the foliage where the orange eggs are laid. The grub is reddish, with two rows of small black spots on each side. The adults are about 1·2 cm long with yellow and black striped wing cases. The beetle is avoided by birds because of its nasty taste, and is controlled by arsenical sprays.

Colosseum, the name of the Flavian amphitheatre at Rome, begun by Vespasian and finished by Titus A.D. 80. In general outline it still remains one of the most magnificent ruins in the world. In the arena of this great building the famous gladiatorial displays and mimic naval battles used to be given, and about 50,000 spectators could be accommodated.

Colossus is the name which the ancients gave to any statue of gigantic size. The Colossus at Rhodes, which was a bronze statue of the sun god, Helios, was the most famous, and reckoned among the seven wonders of the world. It stood over 30 m high at the mouth of the harbour. There is no truth in the legend that ships could pass between its legs. It fell in an earthquake in 224 B.C.

Colugo, also known as "flying lemur", caguan or kubuk, a remarkable mammal which may be regarded as an aberrant insectivore or an aberrant form of the earliest ancestor of the bats. It has nothing to do with lemurs. There are two genera, one inhabiting the Philippines and one inhabiting Malaya. They have a parachute-like membrane which covers them from the neck to the tip of the tail, by means of which they can glide from treetop to ground, a distance of up to 64 m.

Column, in architecture, is an upright solid body serving as a support or decoration to a building. Columns consist of a pedestal, a shaft, and a capital, over which the supported entablature rises. They are named according to the styles of architecture of which they form part, being Doric, Tuscan, Ionic, Corinthian or Composite as the case may be.

Comets are celestial bodies which generally move about the solar system in elongated elliptical or nearly parabolic orbits. Most comets are in the latter category, having extremely long orbital periods, up to millions of years, and have therefore only been seen once in recorded history. They spend most of their lifetimes at extremely large distances from the sun, far outside Pluto's orbit. Those in elliptical orbits appear periodically and a few have been observed regularly. Halley's comet, named after Edmund Halley, who first correctly predicted that this comet would reappear in 1758, was first observed in Roman times and is one of the brightest of the periodic comets. The nucleus of a comet, which appears as a faint star when the comet is very far from the sun, is believed to be a frozen mixture of dust and materials called "ices"— CO_2, H_2O, NH_3 and CH_4, frozen at the low temperatures in the outer solar system. Approaching the sun, the comet is heated by sunlight and the surface "ices" are first vaporised and later photo-dissociated and ionised by sunlight, also freeing the surface dust. The dust, gases and ions produce the fuzzy appearance of the coma of the comet. Under the influence of sunlight acting on dust, and the solar wind and interplanetary field acting on the ions, the cometary tail (often multiple) is produced. This may stretch up to 200 million km, pointing away from the sun. Donati's comet (1858) was possibly the most spectacular of all and was visible even in daylight. Kohoutek's comet (1975) was the first to be observed from space, by the American Skylab and Russian Soyuz, and many exciting new space studies are planned for the next predicted return of Halley's comet in 1985. *See also* **F4(1)**.

Commons are the remnants of the mediaeval open fields round villages in which the villagers had rights in common, *e.g.*, (i) estover—the right of taking wood for house building or firewood; (ii) pasture—the right of grazing beasts; (iii) turbary—the right of digging turf; (iv) piscary—the right to fish. Many of these common lands were enclosed during the agrarian revolution which went on steadily in England from the 15th cent. onwards, and with their enclosure common rights vanished. A Royal Commission on Common Land described the commons in 1965 as the "last reservoir of uncommitted land" which provide, as far as the public is concerned, by far the largest part of the accessible open spaces of the country. Under the Commons Registration Act, 1965, it was the duty of County Councils and County Borough Councils to make a register of all common land and all town and village greens in their areas.

Commons, House of, the Lower House of the British Parliament. *See* **Section D.**

Commune of Paris has twice played a dramatic part in the history of France. In 1792 it was able, through its control of the administrative organisation of Paris, to override the National Assembly. In 1871, after the withdrawal of the Prussian troops, it tried to assert its authority. Public buildings were destroyed by members of the Commune and civil war raged during April and half May, but Government troops savagely suppressed the rising.

Communism. *See* **Section J.**

Compass *or* **Mariner's Compass.** It has been known since very early times that an iron needle, suspended freely to hang horizontally when not magnetised, comes to rest roughly along the geographical north-south line when magnetised. Further, it generally does not hang horizontally. This is the essential behaviour of the *compass*, a navigational instrument whose invention is obscure but which seems to have been known to the Chinese 4,500 years ago. That the behaviour of the compass shows the existence of a *magnetic field* associated with the Earth was first fully recognised by William Gilbert in 1600. Aircraft and ships now largely employ gyrostatic compasses which are not affected by electrical and magnetic disturbances. Sperry, Brown and Anschutz are three important types of gyroscopic compass.

Composite Materials, or more simply composites, are materials which derive useful properties by combining the virtues of two or more components. Combining clay with straw to make tougher bricks is an ancient example in which fibres (straw) are embedded in a matrix or body (the clay). A modern example is fibreglass in which glass fibres are embedded in a plastic matrix. Nature also uses composites as in bamboo in which a lignin matrix binds together the fibres of cellulose to make a light strong structure. Composites may contain flakes or particles embedded in the matrix instead of fibres—it depends on the application. Although the idea is not new composite technology has made rapid strides in the last few decades guided by scientific insight into the nature of solids and the origin of their stengths and weaknesses. The motivation had been that scientifically designed composites offer materials with exceptional strength/weight ratio, desirable magnetic properties and other technological advantages which meet the extreme demands of a variety of industries. For example, composite aluminium containing boron fibres or resin containing graphite fibres can have strength/weight ratios over twice that of high-strength solid aluminium. Composites of many kinds are now widespread in industrial use and are attracting much research and development.

Computer, a technical device for accepting an input of information, processing this information according to some prescribed programme of operations and supplying an output of processed information. Many types of operation can be performed on many types of information and computers are now indispensable in science, business, warfare, government and other activities. Early thinkers in this field were Pascal (17th cent.), Babbage (19th cent.) and Turing (1930s), but electronic computers as we know them appeared during the second world war and the first commercial machine was on sale in 1950. Computers are millions of times faster than human beings at computing; and the introduction of computers into an organisation does more than just speed up the calculations, it tends to transform the whole nature of the organisation. The possibilities for future developments seem enormous. Analogue computers and digital computers are two different kinds stemming from the difference between *measuring* and *counting*. Analogue types handle data that is repeated by physical quantities of continuously variable size such as voltages or lengths. These quantities can be made to vary like the quantities in a problem which the computer is set to solve; the problem is thus solved by analogy. A slide rule is a rudimentary analogue computer in which numbers are represented by lengths of rule. Digital computers handle actual numbers expressed in digits and the quantities in the problem are represented by discrete numbers. These can all be expressed in binary form and thus stored or handled in bits. See **Bit, Binary Notation.**

Conclave, an assembly of Roman Catholic cardinals met together to elect a pope. The last Conclave was held in the Vatican in Oct. 1978 when Cardinal Wojtyla, Archbishop of Cracow, was elected Pope John Paul II.

Concordat, an agreement of convention between the Pope and a secular government regarding ecclesiastical matters. The Concordat of Worms in 1122 between Calixtus II and the Emperor Henry V was famous as deciding a long struggle in regard to investiture. In 1801, Napoleon concluded a concordat with Pius VII defining the restored relations between the head of the Church and the French Roman Catholics.

Condor, a large eagle of brilliant black plumage with a circlet of white feathers round its neck. It is a native of the Andes.

Confederation is a free association of sovereign states united for some common purpose. It is to be distinguished from a Federation, which is a union of states with one central government, each state relinquishing its sovereignty, though retaining some independence in internal affairs.

Confucianism. See **Section J.**

Coniferae are cone-bearing trees, including firs, pines, cedars, cypresses, junipers, yews, etc., and are widely distributed in temperate regions.

Conservatism. See **Section J.**

Constitution, the fundamental organic law or principles of government of a nation, state, society, or other organisation, embodied in written documents, or implied in the institutions and customs of the country or society. The government of the USA, unlike Great Britain, works upon a written Constitution. It was framed when the USA came into existence as a sovereign body, when the Constitution built a republic out of a federation of thirteen states, based on representative government. The constitution was adopted in 1789, and its strength has been tested by the fact that, substantially unchanged, it is the groundwork for a federation which now comprises fifty states. See also **Sections C and D.**

Continent, a word used in physical geography to denote the larger continuous land masses in contrast to the great oceans of the earth. They are: Eurasia (conventionally regarded as 2 continents, Europe and Asia), Africa, North America, South America, Australia and Antarctica. (Australasia is Australia, New Zealand and adjacent islands. Oceania is Australasia and the many islands of the S.W. Pacific.)

Continental Drift. The hypothesis of drifting continents is due to F. B. Taylor, an American geologist who published his theory in 1908, and to the Austrian meteorologist Alfred Wegener in 1910. The latter was impressed by the matching coasts of South America and Africa, which seemed to him to fit together like the pieces of a jigsaw puzzle. Since then many other people have taken up and developed the idea. Acccording to Wegener, at one time there were two primary super-continents. Laurasia and Gondwanaland. The one in the northern hemisphere consisted of North America, Europe, and the northern part of Asia. Its southern counterpart included Antarctica, Australia, India, Africa and South America. These super-continents broke up, and their various bits moved apart. In particular, the southern hemisphere continents drifted radially northwards away from the south pole, and the two Americas shifted westwards from Europe and Africa. What would have been the leading edges of the land masses on this hypothesis, are now heavily buckled up into mountain belts, such as the Cordillera and the Alpine-Himalayan chain. The resistance afforded to drifting by the strong ocean floors may well have been the cause of such structures. Despite the wealth of geological facts which have a bearing on the problem of continental drift, none of these has been able to decide the issue in a conclusive manner. Further studies of rock magnetism (*q.v.*) and of fossil climates should ultimately establish the concept of continental drift on a firm basis. See also **Earth, F8.**

Conurbation, a term used in reference to an extensive and continuous area of urban land-use. Conurbations are frequently formed by the physical coalescence of several formerly free-standing towns. They may themselves coalesce to form a higher order of physical urbanisation, known as a megalopolis. The seven conurbations officially recognised in the UK are Greater London, W. Midlands, S.E. Lancashire, W. Yorkshire, Merseyside, Tyneside and Clydeside, of which the first five are said to form the English megalopolis. In common with other old and well-developed cities throughout the capitalist world, conurbations in Britain show a marked decline in population and employment.

Convention is an assembly of delegates, representatives, members of a party met to accomplish some specific civil, social, political, ecclesiastical or other important object.

Convocation, an assembly called together to deliberate ecclesiastical affairs. In the Church of England the provinces of Canterbury and York each have their convocation. The term is also applied to assemblies of the graduates of certain universities.

Coot. A very widely distributed bird of the rail family and a common resident of the British Isles. The adult is black with a conspicuous white bald shield on the forehead and a white bill. The juvenile is brownish grey with whitish breast and throat. The coot flies heavily, but swims well. It dives frequently and can remain submerged for a considerable time. It is pugnacious and in winter gregarious. The food is chiefly vegetable. The large nest is usually built among aquatic vegetation and the young are fed by both parents. Another species, the Crested Coot, occurs in S. Europe.

Copper, one of the most familiar of metals, element no. 29, symbol Cu, used in ancient times as an alloy with tin in producing bronze, and preceding iron as an industrial material. Copper ores are most abundant in the USA, Chile, Canada, Zambia and Zaire. All copper compounds are poisonous.

Copyright. Under the Copyright Act, 1956, copyright subsists in every original literary, dramatic musical, and artistic work if the author is a British subject or a citizen of the Republic of Ireland or resident in the United Kingdom, or if the work is first published in the United Kingdom. The Act provides that, except in certain special cases, the author of the work shall be the first owner of the copyright, and there are no formalities, such as registration or payment of fees, to be accomplished. Copyright includes the right to reproduce the work in any material form, to perform the work in public, or, if the work is unpublished, to publish the work. The Act also protects sound recordings, films and television and sound broadcasts. Literary, dramatic, musical and artistic works which enjoy the protection of the Act are automatically protected in those countries which are parties to the Berne Copyright Convention or the Universal Copyright Convention. In general, copyright in literary, dramatic, musical and artistic works is vested in the author for the period of his lifetime and 50 years following after which it passes into the public domain and becomes freely available to any who wish to make use of it. The Copyright Libraries, entitled to receive copies of books published in the United Kingdom are given under **Libraries**. The Berne Copyright Convention and the Universal Copyright Convention were revised at a diplomatic conference held in Paris in 1971. The effect of the revisions allows any national of a developing country to obtain, under certain conditions, a compulsory licence to translate and publish a copyright work for the purpose of teaching, scholarship and research, upon payment of compensation to the copyright owner of the original work. The Government Department responsible for matters in connection with copyright is the Industrial Property and Copyright Department, 25 Southampton Buildings, London, WC2A 1AY.

Coral, an order of small marine animals closely related to the sea-anemone, but differing from it in their ability to develop a limy skeleton. They multiply sexually and by budding. The structure of the coral secretions assumes a variety of forms, fan-like, tree-like, mushroom shape, and so forth. Red coral (the skeleton of *Corallium rubrum*) is mainly obtained from the Mediterranean. The coral reefs of the Pacific and Indian Oceans are often many miles in extent. Living corals occur only in warm seas at about 23°C.

Cordite, a smokeless explosive adopted for small arms and heavy artillery by the British Government in the naval and military services in 1889, and composed of 58 parts of nitro-glycerine, 37 of gun-cotton, and 5 of vaseline. It is a jelly or plastic dough, and used in the form of sticks. Invented by Sir Frederick Abel and Sir John Dewar in 1889.

Cork, the bark of a species of oak, *Quercus suber*, grown largely in the South of Europe and North America. The cork tree is said to yield bark every six to ten years for 150 years, and grows to a height of from 6–12 m. Its lightness, impermeability, and elasticity enable it to be used for a variety of commercial purposes, especially for stoppers of bottles.

Cormorant, a large, long-billed water-bird which captures fish by diving. The common cormorant has bronze-black plumage with white cheeks and sides and is found round the sea coasts of most parts of the world, including the British Isles. It nests in colonies on sea cliffs and rocky ledges. The Shag or Green Cormorant is a smaller bird with green-black plumage and a crest.

Corncrake. See **Landrail.**

Corn Laws were statutes intended for the benefit of British agriculture, and restricted import and export of grain. From the 14th to the mid-19th cent. such laws were in force, and were often of a stringent nature. They became so oppressive and caused corn to reach so high a price that the poorer classes were plunged into distress. A powerful anti-corn law agitation was organised of which Cobden, Bright and Villiers were the leaders, and Sir Robert Peel, in 1846, at the time of the Irish potato famine, carried through free trade. The repeal of the Corn Laws marked an important phase in the transformation of an agricultural to an industrial Britain.

Corona or **Solar Corona,** the outer atmosphere of the sun. This glows by virtue of light emitted by the sun and scattered by electrons and dust particles at various heights in the sun's atmosphere and also by light emitted from ionised atoms in the corona itself. Corona light is much fainter than the bright disc of the sun and is invisible against the normal blue of the sky. During total solar eclipses, the corona can be seen by the human eye as a faint glow extending irregularly outwards a few solar diameters from the sun. The sun's atmosphere extends much further than this but is invisible to the eye at large distances from the sun. The corona gases are thought to be very hot (millions of degrees) and in complex violent motion; the gross structure of the corona is connected with the sunspot cycle.

Cortes, the name of the Parliamentary assemblies of Spain and Portugal.

Cosmic Rays are a form of radiation coming from outer space, of deep penetrating power and of great scientific interest. The rays consist of extremely energetic atomic particles—protons, electrons and some heavier nucleons—travelling at speeds very close to that of light. A complex series of events result from their collision with the atmosphere, giving rise to showers of secondary high-energy particles containing many of those listed on **F16**. Cosmic rays are now investigated with instruments buried in deep mines, as well as those in satellites, and the great interest is because we now believe their origin to be in, or associated with, some of the most interesting objects in the universe—supernovae, neutron stars, pulsars and perhaps some gigantic galactic nuclei. See **F3(2)**.

Cosmology is the science which studies the whole universe, its origin, its nature, its size, age and evolution. It is presently a very active science because of many new discoveries of radio astronomy and space astronomy (X-ray, ultraviolet and infra-red) of extremely distant and luminous objects whose radiation has taken many thousands of millions of years to reach us, and whose explanation is taxing many of the world's best theoretical scientists. See **F3–8**.

Cotton, the name of a plant of several species bearing large yellow flowers with purple centres. These centres expand into pods, which at maturity burst and yield the white fibrous substances known as cotton. The raw cotton contains a large proportion of seeds which are removed by "ginning". Long before the Christian era, cotton had been grown and used with great skill in India to make fabrics. The industry was not introduced into England until the middle of the 17th cent. when Protestant refugees from Flanders came to settle in the wool textile districts of East Anglia and Lancashire. With improvements in machinery and expansion of overseas trade in the 18th and 19th cent., Lancashire became the centre of the world's cotton industry but since the second world war man-made fibres have taken the place of cotton. Chief producers: USA, USSR, China, India, Brazil, Mexico, Pakistan, Egypt, Turkey.

Coulomb, a unit of electric charge, named after the French naval engineer, Charles Augustin de Coulomb (1736–1806), equal to the quantity of electricity transferred in one second by a current of one ampere.

County. Since the recent reorganisation of local government in the United Kingdom the distinction between *administrative* counties and *geographical* counties no longer exists. Certain geographical counties have disappeared (e.g., Rutland and Pembroke), new counties have appeared (e.g., Avon and Gwynedd), while former counties have been modified (e.g. Glamorgan and Yorkshire).

Coup d'Etat, a violent change in the government of a state carried out by force or illegally. Examples are the overthrow of the French Republic in 1851 by Louis Napoleon, who then became Emperor, and more recently the military *coups* in the Middle East which brought about the abdication of Farouk of Egypt in 1952 and the assassination of Feisal of Iraq in 1958.

Court Leet, a court of record held annually before the steward of any particular manor or lordship; originally there was only one court for a manor, but in the time of Edward I it branched into two, the court baron and the court leet.

Coypu or **Nutria rat,** a large beaver-like rodent found in S. America; now wild in E. Anglia, where it is causing damage to dykes, reeds, and crops, having escaped from farms where it is bred for its fur.

Crane, a large, graceful wading-bird with elegant long legs and neck, greyish plumage, superficially resembling the heron and related to the bustard. They migrate in V or W formation and have trumpet-like voices. There are several species, found in all continents except S. America, including the Crowned Crane with golden coronet and the Demoiselle with tuftlike crest of white feathers. The Common Crane nested in East Anglia in mediaeval times.

Credit is an advance of money or of goods or services in consideration of a promise of payment later. Trade credit is such an advance from trader to customer; bank credit is an advance of money by a bank to a client, whether a business firm or a private person, in consideration of an interest payment by the borrower.

Creed (Latin *credo* = I believe), a formal statement of belief. The three orthodox Christian creeds are the Apostles' Creed (a summary of their teaching), the Nicene Creed (drawn up by the Church Council at Nicaea in A.D. 325 to define its theological doctrines), and the Athanasian Creed (concerning the nature and divinity of Christ). *See also* under individual headings.

Cremation, the ancient custom, revived in modern times, of burning the dead. Cremation was first legalised in Great Britain in 1885 and the first crematorium opened at Woking in that year. Application for cremation must be accompanied by two medical certificates.

Cricket, a genus of insects of the grasshopper order which move by leaps. The male produces a chirping noise by rubbing its wing-covers together. Just as the males inherit the nerve machinery for emitting the song of the species, so the females receive and respond to that song and to no other.

Crimean War (1853–56). This war between Russia and the allied powers of Turkey, England, France and Sardinia, was connected with the Eastern Question (*q.v.*) and the desire of Russia for a port on the Mediterranean. Chief engagements were the Alma, Balaclava and Inkerman. Fighting virtually ceased with fall of Sevastopol in September 1855. Treaty of Paris signed 30 March 1856.

Crocodiles and their allies (alligators, caimans and gavials) are the largest of modern reptiles. They are well equipped for a predatory life in shallow waters, having powerful tails and strong jaws. Their eggs are laid on land, in sand or decomposing vegetation.

Crow, a family of birds including many well-known species such as the rook, raven, jackdaw, carrion crow, hooded crow, magpie, nutcracker, jay and chough.

Crusades were military expeditions undertaken by some of the Christian nations of Europe with the object of ensuring the safety of pilgrims visiting the Holy Sepulchre and to retain in Christian hands the Holy Places. For two centuries nine crusades were undertaken: First, 1095–99, under Godfrey of Bouillon, which succeeded in capturing Jerusalem; Second, 1147–49, led by Louis VII of France, a dismal failure, which ended with the fall of Jerusalem; Third, 1180–92, in which Richard I of England took part, making a truce with Saladin; Fourth, 1202–4, led by French and Flemish nobles, a shameful expedition, resulting in the founding of a Latin empire in Constantinople; Fifth, 1217–21, led by John of Brienne; Sixth, 1228–29, under the Emperor Frederick II; Seventh, 1248–54, under St. Louis of France; Eighth, 1270, under the same leadership, but cut short by his death on an ill-judged expedition to Tunis; Ninth, 1271–72, led by Prince Edward of England, which accomplished nothing. Millions of lives and an enormous amount of treasure were sacrificed in these enterprises and Jerusalem remained in the possession of the "infidels". The chief material beneficiaries were the Italian maritime cities; the chief spiritual beneficiary was the Pope; but in literature and the arts both Europe and the Levant benefited enormously from the bringing together of the different cultures.

Cryogenics (Greek roots; productive of cold) is the science dealing with the production of very low temperatures and the study of their physical and technological consequences. "Very low" is often taken to mean below about $-150°C$. The growth of cryogenics (essentially a 20th-cent. science) is connected with the discovery of how to liquefy all gases including even helium which resisted liquefaction until 1908. Scientifically, cryogenics is important partly because special phenomena (*e.g.*, superconductivity (*q.v.*)) appear at lower temperatures and partly because more can be learned about ordinary properties by studying them in the absence of heat. Technologically, cryogenics is becoming more and more significant, for example, liquefied gases are rocket propellants, superconductors make valuable magnets, tissue-freezing techniques (using very cold liquids) have been introduced into surgery. *See* **Absolute Temperature.**

Crystal, in everyday usage, a solid chemical substance bounded by plane surfaces which show a regular geometrical arrangement as, *e.g.*, quartz crystals, rock salt, snow flakes. In physics the term means any substances whose atoms are arranged in a regular three-dimensional array. This includes most solids, even those not particularly crystalline in appearance, *e.g.*, a lump of lead. *See also* **Glass** and **Liquid Crystals.**

Cubism, the name of a revolutionary movement in art created in the years 1907-9 by the two painters Picasso and Braque. Rejecting purely visual effects, they approached nature from an intellectual point of view, reducing it to mathematical orderliness. Its respectable grandparent was Cézanne who had once written: "you must see in nature the cylinder, the sphere, and the cone"—a concept which, together with the contemporary interest in Negro sculpture, moved the two founders of the movement to experiment with the reduction of natural forms to their basic geometrical shapes. In practice, this meant combining several views of the object all more or less superimposed in order to express the idea of the object rather than any one view of it. The name Cubism was derisive and the movement aroused the same opposition as Impressionism, Fauvism and the later Futurism. Picasso's *Les Demoiselles d'Avignon* (1907; Museum of Modern Art, New York) was his first Cubist painting. Three phases are recognised: (1) Cubism under the influence of Cézanne; (2) high or analytical Cubism (*c.* 1909–12) concentrating on the breaking-down of form to the exclusion of interest in colour; (3) synthetic Cubism (*c.* 1913) making use of *collage* in which pieces of pasted-on paper (illustrations, wallpaper, newspaper) and other materials were used in addition to paint. Amongst other early cubist painters were Metzinger, Gleizes, Gris and Léger.

Cuckoo, a well-known migratory bird which is found in Great Britain from April to July, hawk-like in shape, with a very characteristic note, uttered during the mating season only by the male. The hen has a soft bubbling call. It lays its eggs in the nests of other birds, *e.g.*, the meadow pipit and hedge sparrow, but only one egg in each nest. Feeds mainly on insects, particularly hairy caterpillars.

Cuneiform, (Latin = *wedge-shaped*), an ancient method of writing by impressing wedge-like strokes into tablets of damp clay which when dried and hardened formed a permanent script. Cuneiform writing developed from its original pictographic form into a phonetic writing and can be traced back to the non-Semitic Sumerians of ancient Mesopotamia, the earliest civilisation known to us. It passed to the Semitic Accadians of Babylonia in the 3rd millennium B.C. who adapted it to their own language. Deciphered by Sir Henry Rawlinson, 1835.

Curfew (Old F. *covre-feu* = cover fire), a regulation common throughout Europe in mediaeval times by which, at a fixed hour in the evening, the church bell was rung as a signal that fires were to be put out and the people were to go to bed. The custom originated in the fear of fire when buildings were built of timber. Nowadays a curfew is imposed by the military in areas where riots or disturbances are expected, compelling the civilian population to remain indoors after nightfall.

Curia, the central government of the Roman Catholic Church. By the reform which came into force on 1 January 1968, its twelve Sacred Congregations or "ministries" were reorganised and reduced to nine. The aim of the reform was to streamline the Curial offices so that the Church's machinery can cope with modern problems, so favouring the desires expressed by the Ecumenical Council convened by Pope John.

Curie, a measure of the rate at which radioactive material emits radiation. One curie is a disintegration rate of 3.7×10^{10} disintegrations per second.

Curlew, a wading-bird of which there are several species. It frequents marshy places, feeds on worms, insects, molluscs and berries and possesses a very long, down-curved bill.

Currency is the name given to the types of cash money—metal or paper—in use in an area (*e.g.* pound, sterling, dollar, franc). It also designates the actual coins or notes issued. Its amount is usually subject to regulation by the Government, or by a Central Bank acting on the Government's behalf. Britain changed over to a £-based decimal currency in February 1971. On 1 January 1985, ½p coins ceased to be legal tender. The old 'halfpenny' first appeared in 1280. *See also* **National Currencies, Section N.**

Cybernetics, the science concerned with the automatic control and communication processes in both animals and machines. Thus it is concerned with brain function, information theory, electronic computers, and automation.

Cyclone, a term usually applied to a tropical revolving storm. Cyclones often occur towards the end of the hot seasons and are mainly confined to tracks in the western areas of the oceans, being known as hurricanes (Caribbean and Pacific), cyclones (Indian Ocean) and typhoons (China Seas). The circulation of air in a cyclone is similar to that in the *depression* of temperate latitudes, but the region of low pressure is much more localised and the pressure gradients steeper. Winds of hurricane strength and torrential rain occur generally, although at the centre of the storm there is a small area, known as the "eye", where fair, calm weather prevails.

Cyclotron, a machine for accelerating charged particles such as protons to very high energies. Devised by E. O. Lawrence in California in 1930, it uses a magnetic field to make the particles traverse nearly circular paths and an electric field to give them an additional pulse of energy each time round. The accelerated particles impinge on targets, and the resulting events are a basic source of information for nuclear physicists. The cyclotron is obsolescent and has led to the development of other machines, *e.g.*, betatrons, synchrotrons. Britain has two major national high-energy machines: a 7 GeV proton synchroton (to be closed and replaced by a "spallation neutron source"), and a 5 GeV electron synchrotron. The European Organisation for Nuclear Research (CERN), to which Britain contributes, carries out research at higher energies.

D

Dactylopterus, a fish of the gurnard family, with wing-like pectoral fins; sometimes known as the flying fish, though that appellation is more generally given to *Exocaetus exiliens*.

Dadaism (French *Dada* = hobby-horse) was a hysterical and nihilistic precursor of **Surrealism** (*q.v.*) resulting from the shock produced by the first world war. Beginning in Zurich about 1915, it spread to other continental cities, such as Berlin and Paris, dying out in 1922. The movement was deliberately anti-art, destructive, and without meaning; it intended to scandalise by such tricks as "compositions" made out of anything that came to hand—buttons, bus tickets, pieces of wire, bits of tin, etc. Other excesses included incoherent poetry, Dada night-clubs, plays, and short-lived newspapers. Many Dadaist painters became Surrealists at a later stage, but where Surrealism is a deliberate attempt to present subconscious and dream-like images, Dadaism was sheer anarchism. Leading Dadaists were Hans Arp, Marcel Duchamp, André Breton, Kurt Schwitters and Max Ernst.

Daddy Longlegs, or **Crane-fly,** a slender long-legged fly of the family Tipulidae. The larvae which do damage to lawns and plants are called leather-jackets. The Americans call Harvestmen (*q.v.*) daddy longlegs.

Daguerreotype, the first practical photographic process, invented in Paris by M. Daguerre during the years 1824–39. The light-sensitive plate was prepared by bringing iodine in contact with a plate of silver. After exposure a positive image came by development of the plate in mercury vapour. Even for open-air scenes the first daguerreotypes involved exposure of 5–10 minutes. The picture came in one copy and the process was therefore of limited use. The wet collodion process (1851)

rendered the technique obsolete.

Dail Eireann, the name of the national parliament of the Irish Republic.

Damaskeening, the art of inlaying one metal upon another, largely practised in the East in mediaeval times, especially in the decoration of sword blades.

Dandies, the name given to a class of exquisites prominent in early Victorian days, and who attracted attention by excessive regard for dress. Their feminine counterparts were the dandizettes.

Danegeld, a tax imposed in England in Anglo-Saxon times to raise funds for resisting the Danes or to buy them off. Edward the Confessor abolished the tax, but it was revived by the Conqueror and subsequently retained, under another name, after the danger from the Danes was past. It is the basis of all taxation in this country. Domesday Book (*q.v.*) was originally drawn up for the purpose of teaching the State how to levy the tax.

Danelaw, the law enforced by the Danes in the kingdoms of Northumbria, East Anglia, and in the districts of the five (Danish) boroughs—lands grouped round Leicester, Nottingham, Derby, Stamford and Lincoln—which they occupied during the Viking invasions of the 9th and 10th cent. The country occupied was also called the Danelaw or Danelagh.

Darter, 1. Snakebirds, a genus of the pelican family, with long, pointed bill and serpent-like neck and resembling cormorants in appearance. There are 5 species. 2. Numerous species of small freshwater fish belonging to the perch family, found in N. America.

Date Palm. *Phoenix dactylifera,* one of the oldest known food plants widely cultivated in N. Africa and W. Asia. It grows to 30 m and continues to bear for 2 or 3 centuries, its fruit being of great value as a food. From the leaves the Africans make roofs for their huts; ropes are made from the fibrous parts of the stalks; and the sap furnishes a stimulating beverage.

Dauphin, the title borne by the eldest sons of the Kings of France from 1349 to 1830.

Day is the most natural unit of time and may be defined as the period of rotation of the earth relative to any selected heavenly body. Relative to the sun it is called the *solar day.* Relative to a fixed star it is called the *sidereal day.* Owing to irregularities in the earth's movements, the time taken for the earth to rotate through 360° relative to the sun is variable, and so the *mean solar day* of 24 hours has been introduced, which is the average throughout the year. The *mean solar day* is our standard, used for purposes of the calendar, and astronomers use *sidereal* clocks to check mean solar time. In practice, for convenience, the sidereal day is determined by the earth's rotation relative to the vernal equinox or first point of Aries, and is equal to 23 hours 56 minutes and 4·091 seconds of mean solar time (*i.e.,* about 4 minutes shorter than a solar day). *See* **Time.**

DDT (dichloro-dephenyl-trichloroethane). A very powerful insecticide which has had wide success in the control of diseases, such as malaria and typhus which are carried by insects. Mosquito swamps are sprayed with DDT to kill the carriers. Because this toxic chemical breaks down very slowly it builds up in birds and animals and its use is now banned in Britain. Its detection in Antarctic wild life confirmed that DDT pollution was virtually world-wide.

Deacon, an ecclesiastical official, who assists in some of the smaller ministerial duties in church or chapel; in the Anglican Church he ranks below a priest.

Dead Languages are such as the ancient Greek and Roman tongues, which are no longer spoken but are preserved in literature.

Dead Sea Scrolls, a group of ancient Jewish documents, consisting of scrolls and fragments which have been recovered since 1947 in the vicinity of Qumran near the Dead Sea and which represent one of the most important finds ever made in the field of biblical archaeology and Christian origins. The scrolls written in Hebrew or Aramaic, were found in caves, the first by chance by an Arab shepherd in 1947. These consisted of biblical texts older by a thousand years than the earliest Hebrew manuscript of the Old Testament (A.D. 895). Many fragments have since been discovered, comprising the whole of the Old Testament with the exception of Esther. In addition there are commentaries and other non-biblical writings, including one called "The War of the Sons of Light with the Sons of Darkness". The writing on the scrolls indicates that they were written over a period of two centuries, the greater proportion before the birth of Christ. A nearby ruin is believed to have been the home of a religious sect called the Essenes (**J18**), to whom the scrolls belonged. By the aid of the latest scientific techniques, including radiocarbon tests, the age of the scrolls is being accurately determined. An account of the scrolls and their implications is given in Edmund Wilson's *The Dead Sea Scrolls: 1947–1969.*

Dean, a Church of England dignitary, ranking below a bishop, and the head of the chapter of a cathedral. A rural Dean supervises a *deanery* or group of parishes. There are also Deans of Faculties in some universities, and at Oxford and Cambridge the *Dean* is in charge of chapel services and disciplinary arrangements.

Death Watch Beetle (*Xextobium rufovillosum*), a wood-boring beetle, larger than the common furniture beetle, found chiefly in the old oak beams of churches and other historic buildings. The grub bores from 4–12 years. The name "death watch" comes from the superstition that the ticking sound, made by the beetle striking its head against the wood, is a sign of approaching death. The death watch beetle in the roof of Westminster Hall was recently smoked out by means of an insecticide called gamma benzine hexachloride. *See also* **Furniture Beetle, Woodworm.**

Decalogue, name given to the Ten Commandments of the Old Testament. There are two versions of them, differing in detail: Exodus xx. 2–17 and Deuteronomy v. 6–21. They are of Hebrew origin and are recognised by Jews and Christians as the divine law given by God to Moses on Mt. Sinai. Most of them are prohibitions in contrast to the beatitudes (pronounced by Christ in the Sermon on the Mount) which are positive, *e.g.,* Blessed are the merciful.

December, the last month of the year in our calendar, and the tenth in the old Roman.

Deciduous Trees are such as shed their leaves at certain seasons as distinguished from evergreens or permanent foliaged trees or shrubs.

Declaration of Independence was an Act by which the American Congress, on 4 July 1776, declared the American colonies to be independent of Great Britain. "Independence Day" is a holiday in the United States.

Defender of the Faith (*Defensor Fidei*), a title conferred upon Henry VIII by Pope Leo X in 1521 for entering the lists against Luther with his pamphlet in defence of the Seven Sacraments. After Henry assumed headship of the Church of England the Pope withdrew the title but it was confirmed to him by Parliament in 1544 and has been used ever since by English monarchs.

Deflation is a policy designed to bring down costs by reducing the supply of means of payment. It is usually advocated as a remedy for inflation, and in this connection is nowadays more often referred to as monetarism. It usually results in a fall in employment. *See* **Section G.**

Dehydrate, to eliminate the water from a substance. The process of dehydration is now used in the food industry, as a result of wartime research, in making such things as dried egg and packet soups. Most vegetables contain over 90 per cent of water, and much of this can be removed under vacuum at low temperatures without appreciably impairing the flavour. The lightness of the dehydrated products is an advantage when supplies have to be transported.

Deliquescence, the process of dissolving by the absorption of moisture from the atmosphere. For instance, chromic acid crystals on exposure to the air quickly deliquesce.

Delta, a triangular tract of land between diverging branches of a river at its mouth, and so called from its general resemblance to the Greek letter Δ *delta.* The best-known examples are the deltas of the Nile, the Ganges, the Niger and the Mississippi.

Deluge, a flood, commonly applied to the story of the Deluge in the Bible, in which Noah and the Ark figure. A similar tradition lingers in the mythologies of all ancient peoples.

Democratic Party, one of the two great American political parties, originated about 1787, advocating restrictions on the federal governments and in opposition to the federalists. It was in 1825 that a group who were in favour of high tariffs seceded, later to become the Republican Party. The Democratic Party was split again over slavery before the Civil War (1861–65), and in the main the southern states have been supporters of the Democrats. The economic depression helped the Democrats to power in 1932 (*see* **New Deal**) and they held office until 1953 when Eisenhower became President. In 1960 Kennedy narrowly won the Presidency and in 1964 Lyndon Johnson swept in with a landslide victory over the Republican candidate. In 1968 and 1972 the Democratic candidates were beaten by Nixon. In 1976 Jimmy Carter won an easy victory over Gerald Ford, but lost in a landslide to Ronald Reagan in 1980. In 1984, the Democratic candidate, Walter Mondale, lost to a triumphant Reagan. The symbol of the party is a donkey, invented, like the Republican's elephant, by the cartoonist Thomas Nast.

Dendrite, a stone or mineral on or in which tree-like tracery appears, the result of the action of the hydrous oxide of manganese.

Density, a measure of the mass per unit volume of a material, usually expressed in grams per cubic centimetre. *Specific gravity* is the ratio of the density of a material at the termperature under consideration to that of water at the temperature of its maximum density ($4°C$). In grams per cubic centimetre the density of gold is $19·3$, silver $10·5$, lead $11·3$, water $0·99997$, air $0·00129$.

Depreciation of a currency is a fall in its relative value in terms of gold or of other currencies. The term is most often used to indicate a fall in the value of one country's money in relation to others. *See* **Section G.**

Depression, a region where barometric pressure is lower than that of its surroundings. These areas of low pressure are usually less extensive than anticyclones (*q.v.*) and may vary from hundreds to thousands of kilometres in diameter. The winds, often of gale force where the depression is deep, blow round the system in an anticlockwise direction in the Northern Hemisphere (in the reverse direction in the Southern Hemisphere). Well above the earth's surface the winds blow along rather than down the pressure gradient but near the surface, friction causes the winds to blow slightly (*c.* 15°) across the isobars. The depression exists only as long as more air diverges out of its upper parts than converges into its lower parts. The majority of depressions which cross the British Isles travel from the Atlantic, sometimes in series or families at rates from a few kilometres to a thousand kilometres a day, bringing their generally unsettled weather with them.

Desalination, the process of removing minerals, chiefly salt, from sea or brackish water to provide pure water for drinking or industry. Small-scale desalinisation by distillation has been practised for many years on ships and small islands. By the 1960s, many large-scale distillation plants were in operation, many of them in hot dry countries as in the Middle East. Kuwait, for example, used oil revenues to buy desalination plant and powers the plant with natural gas. As water for large population centres becomes more precious and desalinisation techniques more efficient, the process may be more and more used though it is expensive in capital outlay and in the cost of heating required to distil the water. Methods other than distillation are under investigation but not as yet much used.

Deserts, vast, barren, stone or sandy wastes where there is almost no rainfall and little or no vegetation. These regions are found in the interior of the continents Africa, Asia and America between 20° and 30° north and south of the equator. Europe is the only continent without deserts. The most famous are the Sahara, the largest in the world, the Gobi desert of central Asia, the Kalahari desert of south-west Africa and the great Australian desert. The marginal extension of deserts (desertification) is a topic of considerable debate. The increasing size of deserts is thought to result from either climatic change or the interference by man.

Detention Centres in Britain are for young people (boys and girls) over 14 but under 21 who have been found guilty of an offence for which an adult could be sent to prison. A rigorous regime of "Short Sharp Shock" was introduced by the Home Sec. in 1980 in some detention centres.

Determinism and Free-will. *See* Section J.

Deuterium or "heavy hydrogen". The second isotope of hydrogen; the third is called tritium. Deuterium atoms have in their nuclei a neutron as well as a proton; tritium nuclei have two neutrons and one proton. In ordinary hydrogen gas about one out of every 5,000 atoms is a deuterium atom. Deuterium was discovered in 1932 by Professor Harold Urey. The oxide of deuterium corresponding to water is called "heavy water". The nucleus of the deuterium atom is called a deuteron. An anti-deuteron consisting of anti-proton and anti-neutron was produced at Brookhaven in 1965, the first compound anti-nucleus ever to be produced.

Devaluation is a definite, official downward valuation of a country's currency in terms of its exchange value with other currencies. The £ was devalued in 1949, when an official exchange rate of £1 = $2.8 was established, and again in 1967, to a rate of £1 = $2.4. Since 1972 there has been greater flexibility in exchange rates and national currencies have been allowed to "float". *See* Section G, Part IV.

Devonian System in geology refers to the strata between the Silurian and the Carboniferous formations. It includes the Old Red Sandstone formation. The fauna of the Devonian include the group of fishes known as the Rhipidistra (on the evolutionary route towards the amphibians), Actinistia (coelacanth), and the Dipnoi or lung fishes. *See* **F48.**

Dew, moisture deposited by condensation of water vapour on exposed objects especially during calm, cloudless nights. The loss of heat from the ground after sunset, by radiation, causes the layer of atmosphere close to the surface to be chilled below the temperature, known as the dew-point, at which the air is saturated with vapour. Part of the vapour condensed may be transpired from blades of grass and foliage of plants.

Dew Pond is a shallow artificial pond which is on high ground and rarely dries up, even during prolonged droughts, despite being used by cattle and sheep as a drinking source. The name arose from the belief that dew deposits at night provided the moisture for replenishment. Drainage of rain-water and mist condensed on neighbouring trees and shrubs are probably more important factors.

Dialectical Materialism. *See* Section J.

Diamond, a mineral, one of the two crystalline forms of the element carbon (the other is graphite), the hardest known substance, used as a gem and in industry. India was the first country to mine diamonds (the Koh-i-noor, which means "mountain of light", known since 1304, came from Golconda near Hyderabad and came into British possession when the Punjab was annexed in 1849). The celebrated diamond mines of South Africa were discovered in the 1870s. Other important diamond producing countries are Zaïre, USSR, Congo, Ghana, Sierra Leone, Namibia, Angola, Tanzania. The world's biggest diamond is the 3,106-carat Cullinan, discovered near Pretoria, South Africa, in 1905. Diamonds can be made artificially by subjecting carbon to very high temperatures and pressures; many industrial diamonds are made this way. Antwerp is the main diamond centre of the world, London the main marketing centre, Amsterdam the main diamond cutting centre.

Diatoms. One-celled algae, common in fresh and salt water. Distinctive feature is the siliceous wall which is in two halves, one fitting over the other like the lid of a box. These walls are often very finely and beautifully sculptured. The diatoms constitute a class of the plant

kingdom known as the Bacillariophyta. *Diatom ooze* is a deep-sea deposit made up of diatom shells. *Diatomite* or *diatomaceous earth* is the mineral form that such diatom oozes assume (sometimes known as kieselguhr which mixed with nitroglycerine yields dynamite).

Diesel Engine, an engine in which the liquid fuel is introduced into a compressed or partially compressed charge of air, and which does not need an extraneous source of ignition. The modern oil engine has been evolved mainly from the principles enunciated by Herbert Akroyd-Stuart in his patent of 1890 and, like the steam and other inventions, represents the improvements achieved by many men, including those by Rudolf Diesel of Germany, in respect of high compression pressures and greater fuel economy.

Diet, in German history, an assembly of dignitaries or delegates called together to debate upon and decide important political or ecclesiastical questions. The most famous imperial Diets were those held at Worms (1521), Speyer (1529), and Augsburg (1530), all of which dealt with matters of religious conflict arising from the Reformation.

Diffusion is the process of mixing which occurs when two liquids or gases are in contact. It is most rapid between gases, and, as laid down by Graham's law, "the rates of diffusion of different gases are in the inverse proportion to the square roots of their relative densities". Diffusion arises through the continual movement of molecules. Even in solids diffusion can occur. If a block of gold and a block of silver are welded together, after some time particles of gold are found in the silver, and *vice versa*.

Dimensions in common speech are the magnitudes of length, breadth and thickness giving, the size of an object, thus a line has only one dimension: length; a plane surface two: length and breadth; and a solid three: length breadth and thickness. In mathematics, hypothetical objects with any number of dimensions are considered. In physics and mechanics, dimensions are numbers which relate the units in which any quantity is measured to the so-called fundamental units. The latter are usually but not necessarily those of length, mass and time. "Dimensional analysis" is an important technique of scientific reasoning.

Dimorphism, the quality of assuming two distinct forms. For instance, carbon, which is graphite in one form, is the diamond in another.

Dinosaur, the name given to a group of extinct reptiles of the Mesozoic period, some of which were of immense size—much larger than crocodiles. *See* **Diplodocus.**

Dip Needle. Instrument for measuring the *dip* or inclination of the earth's magnetic field.

Diplodocus, one of the best known of the extinct mammoth dinosaurs. Fossil remains have been discovered in the Jurassic rocks of the United States. Some reached a length of over 24 m.

Dipnoi *or* **Lung Fishes.** These have the air bladder adapted to function as a lung, and they can remain alive when the stream or marsh in which they live dries up. Species of lung fish occur in Australia, Africa and S. America.

Diptera, an order of insects. Their main characteristic is that they are two-winged, and the common house-fly is the best-known example. There are at least 50,000 species of these insects, including gnats, blow-flies, mosquitoes, tsetses.

Diptych was a folding two-leaved tablet of wood, ivory, or metal, with polished inner surfaces, utilised for writing with the style by the ancient Greeks and Romans. The same term was applied to the tablets on which the names of the persons to be commemorated were inscribed in the early Church. In art any pair of pictures hinged together is styled a diptych, a set of three, a triptych.

Discus, a circular piece of metal or stone about 30 cm in diameter, used in athletic contests by the ancient Greeks and Romans. Throwing the discus was a very favourite game, which was deemed worthy of celebration in Myron's famous *Discobolus* (c. 460 B.C.–450 B.C.), the best copy of which is in Rome.

Disk, an astronomical term denoting the seemingly flat surface of celestial bodies as seen by the eye.

Distillation, a process used to separate liquids of different boiling points. This is effected by placing the mixture in a distillation apparatus and heating. The liquid with the lower boiling point distils over first, the vapour being condensed and collected, forming the first *fraction*. With continued heating the second liquid reaches its boiling point, distils over and the mixture is said to be *fractionated*. Mixtures of liquids with close very high boiling points require more elaborate apparatus. Fractional distillation is a common process in the chemical industry, particularly in the refining of petroleum.

DNA (Deoxyribonucleic acid), a polymer molecule in the form of a double-strand helix containing many thousands of sub-units. Contains the genetic information coded in sequences of sub units called bases. The Nobel Prize for medicine was awarded in 1962 for the discovery of the structure of DNA; that for 1968 for interpreting the genetic code and its function in protein synthesis. See **Nucleic Acids.**

Docks are enclosed water spaces where ships rest while being loaded or unloaded, repaired, or waiting for cargo. There are three main types: the wet dock in which water is maintained at the level of high tide so that vessels remain afloat while loading and unloading; the tidal dock, with open entrance to permit free ebb and flow of tide (*e.g.*, Glasgow, Southampton (which has double tides)); and the dry dock, or graving dock, for overhauling and repairing vessels, so constructed that, after a ship has been docked, the water can be drawn off (*e.g.*, Southampton, Tilbury). The floating dock is a type of dry dock. The Port of London Authority operates four main groups of docks. With the closing of some of the older up-river docks, down-river docks, notably at Tilbury, have been extensively developed. Technological advances in the handling of cargo, *e.g.*, containers (sealed boxes of cargo), have led to modernisation of the docks and labour practices.

Dodo, an extinct bird, giant and flightless, which lived on the island of Mauritius up until 250 years ago. Another species, the white dodo, lived on Réunion. Some reached exceptional sizes. By the end of the 17th cent. Mauritius, Rodriguez, and Réunion had all been colonised, and the dodo along with many other birds vanished forever because of their inability to stand up to man and the animals imported into the islands.

Dog-days, a period of 40 days (3 July–11 August) when Sirius rises and sets with the sun. The ancient superstition, which can be traced back in Greek literature to Hesiod (8th cent. B.C.), was that this star exercised direct influence over the canine race.

Doge, the chief magistrate in the former republics of Venice (697–1797) and Genoa (1339–1797, 1802–5).

Dogfish, a large family of small sharks, seldom more than 1 m in length. The flesh is sold as "rock salmon". The eggs are contained in horny cases called "mermaid's purses". The commonest of the British dogfishes are the spur-dogs.

Doldrums, a nautical term applied to those areas of the Atlantic and Pacific within a few degrees of the Equator towards which the trade winds blow and where the weather is calm, hot and sultry. Pressure is low and the air often rises to produce heavy tropical rainfall and squalls, rendering navigation difficult.

Dolomite, a name applied to a limestone containing appreciable magnesium; also the mineral dolomite, a double carbonate of magnesium and calcium.

Dolphin, a mammal of the whale order, from 2–2·4 m long, with a long, sharp snout, and of an active disposition. They abound in most seas and swim in shoals. A few species live in large rivers (Ganges and Amazon). They can cruise for long periods at around 15 knots and produce bursts of speed in the region of 20 knots, the water apparently flowing smoothly past their bodies. Dolphins are some of the most intelligent of mammals and are currently the subject of scientific experiments in communication. Name also for the fish, dorado.

Domesday Book is the famous register of the lands of England framed by order of William the Conqueror. According to Stowe, the name was derived from *Domus dei*, the name of the place where the book was deposited in Winchester Cathedral; though by others it is connected with doom in the sense of judgment. Its compilation was determined upon in 1085, in order that William might compute what he considered to be due to him in the way of tax from his subjects. William sent into each county commissioners to make survey. They were to inquire the name of each place, the possessor, how many hides of land were in the manor, how many ploughs were in demesne, how many homagers, villeins, cottars, serving men, free tenants, and tenants in soccage; how much wood, meadow, and pasture; the number of mills and fish ponds; what had been added to or taken away from the place; what was the gross value at the time of Edward the Confessor. So minute was the survey that the Saxon chronicler of the time reports "there was not a single hide, nor one virgate of land, nor even, it is shame to tell, though it seemed no shame to do, an ox, nor a cow, nor a swine was left that was not set down". The record, which did not take in Northumberland, Cumberland, Durham and parts of Lancashire and Westmorland, was completed in 1086, and was comprised in two volumes—one a large folio, sometimes called the Little Domesday, which deals with Essex, Norfolk and Suffolk, the other a quarto, sometimes called the Great Domesday. The first is written on 384 double pages of vellum in one and the same hand, and in a small but plain character, each page having a double column. The quarto is written on 450 pages of vellum, but in a single column and in a large, fair character. The original is preserved in the Public Record Office. See also **Danegeld.**

Dominicans, an order of mendicant preaching friars founded by St. Dominic in Languedoc in 1215 and confirmed by the Pope in 1216. The rule of the order was rigorous. The dress was a white habit and scapular with a long black mantle. This gave them the name of Black Friars. Their official name is Friars Preachers.

Donjon, the keep, or inner tower of a castle, and the strongest and most secure portion of the structure. This was the last refuge of the garrison, and there was usually a prison on the lower floor, hence the name *dungeon*.

Don Juan, the legendary hero of many famous works, supposedly based on the life and character of the unscrupulous gallant Don Juan Tenorio of 14th-cent. Seville. The first dramatisation of the legend and the most famous is Tirso de Molina's *El Burlador de Sevilla*. Don Juan was also the subject of Molière's *Le Festin de Pierre*, Mozart's *Don Giovanni*, Byron's *Don Juan*, and José Zorilla's *Don Juan Tenorio*. The latter is played on All Saints' Day throughout Spanish-speaking countries.

Don Quixote, the "knight of the doleful countenance", the hero and title of Cervantes' classic novel of 16th-cent. Spain. Don Quijote de la Mancha, a gentle country gentleman of lofty but unpractical ideals, having read many chivalric romances, believes he is called upon to redress the wrongs of the world. Mounted on his nag Rosinante and accompanied by his companion Sancho Panza, a hard-headed and practical peasant, he sets out on his journeys of knight-errantry.

Dormouse, a family of small, squirrel-like rodents widely distributed throughout Europe and Asia, and living mainly on fruit and nuts. It is of nocturnal habits and sleeps through the winter.

Dot, a French term indicating the property which a wife brings to her husband on marriage and is usually settled on the woman, being her separate property, though the income from it may go towards the general household expenses.

Dotterel, a handsome bird of the plover family found in northern Europe and Siberia. Nests in the Cairngorms, the Grampians and E. Ross. Very tame.

Doukhobors. See **Section J.**

Drachm (or Drachma), an ancient Greek silver coin and weight. One drachma was equivalent to six obols. The word has survived as the name of a weight: Avoirdupois, one-sixteenth part of an ounce; Apothecaries' Weight, one-eighth part of an ounce.

Drag. Term used in mechanics for resistance offered by a fluid to the passage of a body moving through it. When speed of sound is reached drag increases abruptly. The lift/drag ratio gives the aeroplane designer his measure of aerodynamic efficiency.

Dragon, a fabulous monster common to folk-lore in most countries; generally represented as a winged reptile with fiery eyes and breath of flame. A dragon guarded the garden of the Hesperides; in the New Testament there is mention of the "dragon, that old serpent, which is the devil"; St. George, England's patron saint, is supposed to have overcome the dragon; mediaeval legend abounds in dragons; in heraldry the dragon has also a conspicuous place; and in China it was the imperial emblem.

Dragonet, the name of the fish of the *Callionymus* genus, beautifully coloured, and about 30 cm in length. They are common on the British coast and in the Mediterranean.

Dragon Fly, the common name of a well-known order of insects having two pairs of mem-braneous wings, and often of very brilliant colours. They are swift of flight and may be seen hovering over sheets of water in the sun-shine all through the summer. Their chief food is mosquitoes.

Dragon's Blood, a dark-red resinous substance obtained from the fruit of a Malay palm, and possessing medicinal virtues. In a special tech-nique used for making line blocks in printing, dragon's blood is used.

Drawbridge, a bridge that can be lifted up so that no passage can be made across it. It was a usual feature of a fortified castle in the Middle Ages, and was raised or lowered by chains and levers. It spanned the fosse, and on the ap-proach of an attacking party was raised and formed a special barricade to the gate. Modern drawbridges are such as are raised to allow of the passage of boats up and down a river or estuary. The Tower Bridge is a famous London bridge of this type.

Drongo. The King Crow or Indian Black Drongo is frequently seen in India perched on branches or telegraph wires, darting suddenly to catch insects and to attack crows and hawks. Other members of the family are found in Asia, Africa and Australia. Its plumage is black with steel-blue gloss.

Drosophila or **Fruit Fly.** More has been learnt by geneticists from breeding experiments with this insect than with any other.

Dross, the name generally applied to the refuse of molten metal, composed of slag, scales and cinders.

Drought occurs when there has been an absence of rain for a long period or a marked deficiency of precipitation over a much longer period in a climatic zone where precipitation is ordinarily adequate for vegetation or agriculture, river flow and water supplies. It is different from aridity which refers to the extreme dryness of desert or arid regions where rainless periods characterise the climate. Hitherto in the British Isles "an absolute drought" was de-fined as "a period of at least 15 consecutive days without measurable rainfall", but arbitrary definitions of this type are not now normally used. In the British Isles droughts occur from time to time but very long rainless spells at a place are rather rare. The longest recorded spell in the British Isles with no measurable daily rainfall lasted 61 days at Liss (Hants) from 16 March to 15 May 1893. Over the country as a whole the 12-month period beginning 1 May 1975 was the driest such period since records began, with less than 60 per cent. of normal precipitation in parts of the Midlands and S.W. England.

Druidism. *See* **Section J.**

Drupe is the scientific term for stone fruit. The stone forms the inner part (endocarp) of the fruit, and encloses a seed or kernel which is liberated after the flesh part (pericarp) has rotted.

Dry-rot, the term was first used about 1775 to describe the fungal decay of timber in buildings. Creosote distilled from coal tar is the standard material for preservation of timber, and penta-

chlorophenol and copper naphthenate are two compounds now extensively used. Dry wood always escapes dry-rot. Chief fungi causing dry-rot are *Merulius* and *Poria.*

Duck, water bird smaller than the related goose and swan, which together form the family Antidae. Duck refers to the female, drake to the male. The duck family falls into two separate groups: the river or freshwater (surface feeding) ducks, such as the mallard, pintail, wigeon, shoveler, mandarin, teal, garganey; and the sea (diving) ducks, such as the goldeneye, pochard, scoter, eider, and the fish-eating mer-gansers or "sawbills". The ancestor of all domestic breeds, with the exception of the muscovy, is the mallard.

Duckbill, *Ornithorhynchus anatinus,* also duck-billed platypus, a fur-covered, egg-laying, nest-building mammal inhabiting Australia and Tasmania. It has webbed feet and a muzzle like a duck's bill and is about 50 cm long.

Ductility is a property possessed by most metals which renders them capable of being stretched without breaking. Gold is the most, and lead the least ductile of metals, the order being gold, silver, platinum, iron, copper, palladium, alu-minium, zinc, tin, lead. In animated nature the spider and the silkworm produce secretions of notable ductility.

Dugong. A marine mammal, belonging to the order Sirenia (sea-cows). Inhabits Red Sea and Indian Ocean; also found as far East as the Philippines and Australia. Lives on sea-weed. Related to the Manatee.

Duke, the highest rank in the British peerage. Edward, the Black Prince, eldest son of Edward III, who died before his father, was the first English duke, being created Duke of Cornwall in 1337. Since then all Princes of Wales have held that title.

Dukeries, a stretch of English woodland and park country, mainly in Nottinghamshire, comprising the adjacent demesnes of several English dukes and nobles. The Dukeries include Sherwood Forest and the estates of Welbeck Abbey, Clum-ber Park, Worksop Manor and Thoresby Hall.

Dunes. Sand dunes are elliptical or crescent-shaped mounds of loose sand produced by wind action. The dune has a gentle slope on wind-ward side; a steep slope on the leeward side.

Dunlin, very common small wading-bird of the Sandpiper family nesting in Britain. Its range extends to other areas where it also breeds.

Dunmow Flitch, a custom which originated in the parish of Little Dunmow, Essex, in the reign of Henry III, which was that the husband who was prepared to swear before the prior, convent, and townsfolk of Dunmow that he had not re-pented of marriage or quarrelled with his wife for a year and a day, should be rewarded with the gift of a flitch of bacon. The custom has frequently been revived.

Dunnock (*Prunella modularis*), a small bird of rich brown and dark grey plumage common in gardens and hedgerows. Sings a cheerful song all the year round. Called hedge-sparrow in southern England. Another member of the same family, the larger Alpine Accentor (*Pru-nella collaris*), is found on rocky mountain slopes of Europe and Asia.

Duodecimo, a sheet of paper folded into twelve leaves, written "12mo".

Durbar, a term used in India from the Persian word *darbár* meaning "court" or "audience". It may be either a council for administering affairs of state, or a purely ceremonial gather-ing. The word was applied to great ceremonial gatherings like Lord Lytton's durbar for the proclamation of the Queen-Empress in 1877 and the Delhi durbar of 1911.

Dust, solid particles of matter floating in the atmosphere, produced chiefly by volcanic eruptions, sand-storms in desert regions, and industrial and domestic smoke. When the island of Krakatoa erupted in 1883, more than 4 km^2 of dust was thrown into the air and carried three times round the earth by the explosive wave. The particles in dust-storms are much finer than those in sand-storms and are swept up to far greater heights. The local whirlwinds which form over loose dry soils are termed dust-devils.

Dyke. A wall-like intrusion of igneous rock

which cuts across the bedding or other layered structure of the country rock; the word also signifies in alternative usage, a sea-wall and an open drain.

Dynamite, a powerful explosive whose chief element is nitro-glycerine. It was discovered by Nobel in 1867, who absorbed nitro-glycerine in kieselguhr; has a disruptive force of about eight times that of gunpowder.

Dynamo. Machine for transforming mechanical energy into electrical energy. Depends on principle of electromagnetic induction whereby a current is produced in a conductor (e.g., copper wire) traversing a magnetic field. The two essential parts of a dynamo are the conductors or *armature* and the *field magnets*.

Dynasty, a succession of monarchs of the same family, as the Carolingian dynasty, the Bourbon dynasty, the Plantagenet dynasty, etc.

E

Eagle, large bird of prey with huge hooked bill, related to the buzzard, kite, hawk, harrier, falcon and vulture, together forming the family Falconidae. There are many species to be found throughout the world, the Golden, Imperial, Tawny, Spotted and Lesser Spotted being found in Europe. The Golden Eagle, a magnificent-looking bird, nests in the Scottish Highlands, and the White-tailed Sea Eagle, which used to breed in Britain, is now only an occasional visitor. The eagle has been the symbol of royal power since the earliest times, and the American or Bald Eagle is the emblem of the United States.

Earl, a British title of nobility of the third rank, duke and marquis coming first and second. The title dates from Saxon times, and until 1337 ranked highest in our peerage.

Earl-Marshal, in England ranks as the eighth of the great officers of state, is head of the College of Arms, attends the sovereign in opening and closing the session of Parliament, arranges state processions (especially coronations) and assists in introducing newly created peers in the House of Lords. The office is hereditary in the family of the Dukes of Norfolk.

Earth, our habitable globe, is the third of the planets of the solar system in order from the sun and on an average throughout the year takes 24 hours to turn completely round relative to the sun, the whole earth revolving round the sun in a slightly elliptical orbit once in a year of 365·2564 days. The mean distance of the earth from the sun is 149,597,900 km. Recent earth satellite studies have shown that small variations of the surface gravity field (or geoid) occur which are believed to be related more to the structures deep within the earth's mantle than to the location and dimension of crustal features, such as oceans, continents and mountain ranges. The crust consists of a skin, 30 km thick under the continents, but only about 6–8 km thick under the ocean bed, comprised of rocks and sediments or soil. At the base of the crust is a sharp discontinuity (the Mohorovičić Discontinuity) to denser rocks of the mantle. This region, nearly 3,000 km thick, is in a process of slow but inexorable change, one of convection responding to heat sources (due mainly to radioactivity of the materials within the earth). This slow convection is responsible for many changes in the surface of the earth—continental drift (q.v.), earthquakes and volcanic activity. The core is a region of very high density and temperature, comprised of heavy elements such as iron and nickel. The crustal rocks are mainly comprised of oxygen, silicon, aluminium, sodium, potassium, iron, calcium and magnesium, with traces of many other elements. The mass of the earth is about 6,000 million million million tonnes, and it was formed about 4,600 million years ago. The earth has one natural satellite, the moon. See also **F8–10.**

Earthquake, a sudden violent disturbance of the earth's crust; the region of the surface immediately above the "focus", or source where the earthquake originates, is termed the "epi-

centre". On account of their destructive power earthquakes have attracted attention from the earliest times, but accurate study dates only from the last century and the development of a world-wide network of recording stations from the present one. The majority of severe earthquakes result from fractures, usually along existing faults, in underlying rock strata subjected to great strains, the shearing movement sometimes extending to the surface. These dislocations set up vibrations which are propagated as waves throughout the bulk of the earth or round the crust. Frequently the main shock is followed by a series of smaller after-shocks. Minor local earthquakes may be attributed to the effects of volcanic activity, but most of the larger ones originate in non-volcanic regions along well-marked lines of weakness in the earth's crust. Generally the ground is felt to tremble, undergoing oscillations which may gradually or suddenly increase to a maximum and accompanied by sounds. When there is movement of the sea-bed a tsunami (q.v.) may result. One of the greatest of historic times was that which destroyed and flooded Lisbon in 1755. Among the notable shocks of the present century rank those of San Francisco (1906), Messina, Italy (1908), China (1920), Japan (1923), Napier, New Zealand (1931), N.E. Assam (1950), Ionian Is. (1953), Agadir, Morocco (1960), Chile (1960), Iran (1962), Yugoslavia (1963), Alaska (1964), E. Turkey (1966), W. Sicily (1968), Peru (1970), China (1976), S. Italy and North Africa (1980) and N.E. Turkey (1983). See also **Richter Scale** and **F9**(2).

Earthworm, of which there are several species, has a cylindrical body, tapering at both ends and segmented into rings. It moves by contraction of its rings, aided by retractive bristles; is eyeless, but has a mouth, gullet and stomach. Earthworms exist in immense numbers, and perform an important part in the scheme of nature by loosening the soil and rendering it more amenable to tillage. They also form a valuable food for birds and many mammals, and are unequalled as bait for certain kinds of fish.

Earwig, a genus of insects possessing two pairs of wings and anal forceps. It is nocturnal, lives on vegetable matter, and hides by day under stones or in flowers, e.g., dahlias. The old belief that it deliberately creeps into people's ears is altogether unfounded.

Easter, the annual Christian festival in commemoration of the resurrection of Christ, the English name being derived from Eostre, goddess of Spring. The date cannot fall earlier than 22 March nor later than 25 April. Many disputes arose among the early Christians as to the proper time to celebrate this day which governs all other movable feasts. It was eventually ruled at the Council of Nicaea in 325 that Easter Day should be the first Sunday after the full moon following the vernal equinox. If this happens to be a Sunday, then Easter Day is the Sunday after. It should be remembered, however, that this moon is a hypothetical moon of the ecclesiastical calendar, quite imaginary, and generally one or two days later than the real moon we see in the heavens. In fact the reverend fathers at Nicaea did us a bad turn in having anything to do with the moon but then they had no Astronomer Royal to advise them of the complications. See also **Section N.**

Eastern Question, a term formerly applied to the problems arising from the instability of the Mohammedan power of Turkey and its relations with the other nations of Europe. Later connected with other problems of the Near East such as the possession of Constantinople and the position of the Balkan states.

East India Company was incorporated by Elizabeth in 1600. In 1613 the Company set up a factory at Surat, India, and in 1662 Bombay came under the Company's influence and developed into an important trading port. Dupleix wanted to establish French power in India and a struggle for supremacy took place. Clive gained the victory for England and thenceforward British dominion in India remained undisputed except by native princes. In 1772 Warren Hastings was appointed the first Governor-General and in 1784 Pitt's India Act established a Board of Control for the India Company. A great increase of trade resulted, and this rule continued down to 1858, when, as a result of the mutiny, the Crown assumed the sovereignty. With the passing of the Indian Independence Act of 1947, British dominion ended.

Eau-de-Cologne, a popular distilled perfume first manufactured at Cologne in the 18th cent. by Johann Maria Farina, an Italian, and since made in large quantities in Cologne and elsewhere.

Ebony, a name applied to various hard black woods, the best of which are grown in Mauritius and Sri Lanka. There are also Indian and American varieties. Only the inner portions, the heartwood, of the trees are of the necessary hardness and blackness. Ebony is largely used in ornamental cabinet work, for piano keys, canes, etc.

Ecce Homo ("Behold the Man!"), used in reference to the pictures and sculptures representing Christ crowned with thorns.

Ecclesiastical Courts, courts for administering ecclesiastical law and maintaining the discipline of the Church of England. Introduced by the Normans. Originally they had jurisdiction over both clergy and laity.

Eclipse, the partial or complete obscuring of one heavenly body by another. An eclipse of the sun occurs when the moon, which is 1/400th of the diameter of the sun and about 1/390th as far away, obscures some portion of the sun as seen by an observer on the earth. A total eclipse occurs when the whole of the sun's disc is covered by the moon. Astronomers travel many thousands of miles to observe the outer layers of the sun and its corona, which is only possible when the light from the sun is totally obscured by the moon during the few minutes of an eclipse. The total solar eclipse of 7 March 1970, as seen from Mexico, was watched by millions on their television screens. Total solar eclipses have occurred over parts of the British Isles in the years 1424, 1433, 1598, 1652, 1715, 1724, 1927, 1954 (visible from the Shetland Is.), and the next will be seen only from near Land's End on 11 August 1999. *See also* **N11.**

Ecliptic is the sun's apparent path in the sky: the great circle described by the sun from west to east in the course of a year. The sun is exactly on the equator on approx. 21 March, and 23 September, and the points where the celestial equator and ecliptic intersect on these days are called the *equinoctial points.* On approx. 21 June and 22 December the sun reaches its greatest and least midday elevation and its greatest distance north and south of the equator, and the points on the ecliptic on these days are called the *solstices* (*see* **Seasons, Section N**). These four points are equidistant from each other by 90°. The angle of the ecliptic to the earth's equator is called the obliquity of the ecliptic. Due to the gravitational perturbations of the other planets, both the equinoctial point and the obliquity of the ecliptic change with time. The present value of the obliquity is about 23·5.

Ecology, a term first described by the German biologist Haeckel in the 19th cent., is the study of the inter-relationships between living organisms and their environment. **Autecology** is the study of the environmental relationships of *individual* plants and species. **Synecology** is the study of plant and animal *communities* living together as groups and the relationship of these to their environment. Since 1935 the ecosystem has been the major unit of study in synecology. *See also* **F44–7** and **Section Z.**

Ecumenical Council, a general council of the Christian Church summoned when important questions of Church doctrine and policy are to be decided. The early councils were predominantly Greek and convoked by the emperor. Those summoned by the pope when they meet at the Lateran Palace in Rome are called Lateran Councils; others have met at Constance, Florence, Trent and the Vatican. Their decisions are not binding on the rest of Christendom. Only 21 Ecumenical Councils have been held in the history of Christendom. The first was held at Nicaea in 325 when the mystery of the Trinity was defined. The 21st (known as the 2nd Vatican Council), convened by Pope John, opened in October 1962 in St. Peter's, Rome, and ended in December 1965. Two of the principal themes were the reunion of all Christians with the Church of Rome and the Church's place in the modern world. At the last session of the Council the Pope announced his decision to establish for the first time an international synod of bishops in Rome for consultation and collaboration in the government of the Roman Church. This Senate of Bishops provides the balancing factor alongside the Curia, which represents the Papacy and not the episcopacy.

Edda, the name given to two important collections of early Icelandic literature—*the Elder or Poetic Edda,* poems handed down from the 9th and 10th cent., probably Norwegian in origin, and the *Younger* or *Prose Edda* of Snorri Sturluson compiled about 1230. They treat of mythical and religious legends of an early Scandinavian civilisation.

Eddystone Lighthouse, 21 km south of Plymouth, is one of the most isolated in the world. The tower is 51 m high, and its light can be seen for 28 km. The present structure is the fourth that has occupied this dangerous position. The first was of wood, completed by Winstanley in 1698, but it was destroyed by storm in 1703. In 1708 a second and stronger lighthouse was built by Rudyerd. This lasted until 1755, when it was destroyed by fire. Smeaton built the third lighthouse of granite and this withstood storm and tempest for over a hundred years, 1759–1881. The present lighthouse, also of granite, was built 1879–81 on a nearby rock by Sir James Douglass.

Eels, edible fishes of the order Apodes, with snakelike body covered with minute scales embedded in the skin. The common or freshwater eel *Anguilla anguilla* is found in the Atlantic coastal areas of N. America and Europe and in the Mediterranean, and breeds S.E. of Bermuda. The electric eel of S. America is a variety of great interest, being able to cause electric shocks.

Egghead, a term used derogatively to describe the more intelligent and thoughtful people. Frequently applied in USA to the late Adlai Stevenson, who is said to have responded with the appeal: "Eggheads of the world unite. You have nothing to lose but your brains."

Egret, a slender, graceful bird of the heron family, of pure white plumage, famed for its beautiful silky plumes (aigrettes), which appear in the breeding season, and for which it was ruthlessly hunted and would have been exterminated had not international action been taken to protect it. The Little Egret with black bill, black legs, and yellow feet breeds in Mediterranean lands.

Eider, a large diving duck, found along the rocky coasts of northern latitudes, well known for the beautifully warm soft down, called "eider down", which the female bird plucks from her breast to line her nest. In Norway and Iceland the haunts of the eider are preserved and the birds protected by law on account of the much prized "eider down", which is collected from the nests just before the breeding season. "Eider down" is so elastic that a kilogram of it will fill an ordinary bed covering.

Eiffel Tower, built by the French engineer Alexandre Gustave Eiffel (1832–1923) for the Paris Exhibition of 1889. The tower which is made of iron is 300 m high and weighs about 7,000 tonnes.

Eisteddfod (a sitting) was originally a congress of Welsh bards and minstrels, and dates from before the 12th cent. These assemblies, discontinued for a long period, were resumed in 1819, and have been held yearly since, each lasting three or four days. Their object is to foster the Welsh patriotic spirit; they are devoted to orations and competitions in poetry, singing and harp-playing, prizes being awarded to the successful contestants.

Eland, largest species of antelope, native of Africa; large pointed horns, stands 1·5 m high at the withers, and weighs several hundred kg.

Elder, small trees of the *Sambucus* genus, with pinnate leaves, and clusters of white flowers and, later, small purplish-black berries. The black elder, the best known, is common in most parts of Europe, and thrives in Britain. A wine is made from its berries.

El Dorado, a "golden land", was an idea much favoured in the days of the early Spanish explorers. It was believed that somewhere on the South American continent there was a country abounding in gold and precious stones. Many expeditions were fitted out to discover it. Sir Walter Raleigh also went forth on this illusive quest. The term is still used in regard to any place of rich promise.

Eleatics. *See* **Section J.**

Electret, a piece of solid matter which retains a permanent electric polarisation analogous to the magnetic polarisation of a permanent magnet. There are various recipes for making them; carnauba wax is a common constituent.

Electricity. *See* **F21,** *also* **Energy Conversion.**

Electric Telegraph may be said to date from 1836, when Sir Charles Wheatstone and his co-inventor Cooke introduced their Single-Needle instrument, which was soon followed by the Double-Needle apparatus, Morse, in 1837, invented his famous recording instrument. The first electric cable was between Dover and France, and was laid in 1850. The first Atlantic cable was laid in 1858, and the second in 1866. It was in 1899 that the first Marconi wireless telegraph messages were sent between England and France.

Electroencephalograph, an instrument which records the minute voltages produced by the electrical activity of the brain by means of electrodes taped to the scalp. The record of brain waves, known as EEG, shows that there is a general cycle of activity in the brain that underlies both sleep and wakefulness. *See* **Q5(2).**

Electrolysis is the condition established when an electric current passes through a conducting substance, between electrodes, resulting in decomposition and separation into constituents. Water thus becomes decomposed into hydrogen and oxygen.

Electromagnetic waves. *See* **F14.**

Electron. *See* **F11, 16.**

Electronic Music, music composed of electronically generated sound, recorded on tape and played through loudspeakers. Modern technical developments mean that in theory, and to a large extent in practice, a composer can generate and record *any* sequence of sounds he likes, varying at will pitch, intensity, reverberation, rhythm, intervals and all other audible qualities. Such limitless freedom of choice imposes on him severe problems of selection, notation and intellectural and artistic organisation. Though widely composed and performed, *i.e.,* played through loudspeakers or broadcast, electronic music as an art form must still be regarded as experimental and controversial, though its use as incidental or "atmospheric" music in radio and television is well established. Among the well-known composers are Babbitt, Berio, Koenig and Stockhausen.

Electronic News Gathering (ENG), also known in the United States as Electronic Journalism (EJ) or Electronic Camera Coverage (ECC), is a system for obtaining television pictures by means of very lightweight, portable electronic cameras. ENG is highly suited to the coverage of news events. It is usually operated by a crew of two—cameraman and engineer—who are also equipped with a van and field car serving as a mobile base. Pictures from the unit can be used in three ways: they can be transmitted "live", beamed back by radio link to the studio, or recorded on to a videotape cassette on site and taken back to headquarters for editing and transmission. The chief advantage of ENG lies in its speed, as the use of electronic equipment avoids the delay which occurs in the chemical processing of film before it can be transmitted. Wastage is also reduced because new recordings can be made over unwanted or unused material. ENG is in wide use in the USA and in Britain.

Electronics. The science which deals with the behaviour and control of free electrons. It started with the discovery of the electron by Sir J. J. Thomson in 1897. The practical applications, constituting electronic engineering, have given us radio, radar, photo-electric cells, cathode-ray oscillographs, electronic microscopes, television. Nowadays electronics uses devices like transistors such that the electrons move inside solid matter instead of *in vacuo.* This is sometimes referred to as "solid state electronics". *See also* **Microelectronics.**

Electron Microscope. A microscope in which

beams of electrons are focused by magnetic lenses in a manner analogous to the focusing of light beams in the ordinary optical microscope. Modern electron microscopes have very high resolving power and can magnify up to 1,500,000 times, making it possible to explore the cell and the virus. A development of the electron microscope is the scanning electron microscope (stereoscan), developed at Cambridge, which can examine an essentially thick object, giving a very large depth of focus.

Electronvolt, unit of energy used in nuclear physics. It is the amount of energy required to move one electronic charge through a potential difference of one volt. It is very small—$1·6 \times 10^{19}$ joules—and therefore suited to atomic physics. 1 MeV = a million electronvolts; 1 GeV = a thousand million electronvolts; these larger units are used in high energy physics.

Elementary Particle, one of the basic constituents of the material universe. The idea that matter consists of tiny particles goes back to classical times but the modern concept of the atom grew out of the chemistry and physics of the 19th cent. With the discovery of the electron in 1897 and the rise of nuclear physics in the 20th cent., the chemical atom was understood to be a structure built of even more fundamental particles—the electron, the proton and the neutron. In the last few decades, many more particles have been discovered, especially in the study of cosmic rays and by the use of large accelerating machines like those at CERN (Geneva) and Brookhaven National Laboratory (Long Island, New York). Among the later discoveries are the neutrino, the positron, the antiproton, the muon, the pion. These differ in electric charge and mass and other intrinsic properties and many have only a very short lifetime before they change into something else. Whether there is a small number of really elementary particles out of which all the others can be constructed is an unanswered question at the frontier of contemporary physics. *See* **F15–17.**

Elements. In chemistry, substances which cannot be separated into two or more simpler chemical substances. 91 elements are found naturally on the earth, some are observed spectroscopically in the stars and planets, and a further fourteen have been made artificially. Between them these elements can appear in some 1,200 different isotopes, of which 317 occur in Nature. (There are 274 stable isotopes among 81 stable elements.) *See* **F6, F23,** *also* **end Section F.**

Elephant, a proboscidian mammal of which only two species survive—the Asiatic, in India, and the African elephant. No other animals possess a trunk. Both males and females have large ivory tusks, of considerable commercial value. The Indian elephant is usually about 2·7 m high and weighs about 3 tonnes; African elephants are larger, weighing about 6 tonnes, and are usually much fiercer. Several fossil elephants of still larger bulk have been discovered, including the mammoth and the mastodon. The Indian elephant is domesticated and used as a beast of burden, and may live 70 years.

Eleusinian Mysteries, festivals common throughout ancient Greece, agricultural in their symbolism.

Elgin Marbles, a collection of ancient Greek sculptures and architectural fragments got together by the 7th Earl of Elgin and brought to England between 1802 and 1812. These celebrated treasures had originally formed part of the Parthenon at Athens, and were probably carved by pupils of the sculptor Phidias. Lord Elgin expended over £70,000 upon them, and they were purchased for £35,000 for the British Museum, where they can now be seen displayed.

Elk, the largest animal of the deer family, possessing enormous antlers, and standing, when mature, about 2 m high. The American moose is of the same family.

Elm, a stately, wide-spreading tree having some 20 species spread over north-temperate regions, several of which are native and peculiar to Britain. The grandest of the field elms is the English elm, *Ulmus procera,* which may reach a height of *c.* 42 m and a girth of 8 m. The wych elm, *U. glabra,* or Scots elm, is a valuable hardwood and used in boat-building. The fungus that causes Dutch elm disease is carried from tree to tree by a bark beetle. The fungus came from infected veneer logs from central Europe. Ironically the disease was named after the Dutch workers who discovered its cause!

Elzevir, the name of a celebrated family of Dutch printers, who produced editions of Latin, French and German classics, which were highly valued for their beauty of type and accuracy of printing. They flourished in the 17th cent.

Ember-days are set apart for fasting and prayer in the Western Church, at the periods appointed for ordination, viz., the Wednesday, Friday and Saturday after the first Sunday in Lent, Whit-Sunday, 14 September (Holy Cross Day), and 13 December (St. Lucia's Day); of very ancient origin.

Embossing, the art of stamping in relief, letters or designs upon pliant substances.

Emerald. The rich green variety of beryl (beryllium aluminium silicate). The colour is due to the presence of chromium oxide.

Empire, the style created in France during the reign of Napoleon in architecture and all the arts. It is austerely classical, making much use of columns, pediments and the like in buildings as well as furniture, with eagles and sphinxes, reminiscent of Napoleon's campaigns, as ornaments. The style is heavy, grandiose and with a strong element of the heroic. A typical monument is the *Arc de Triomphe* in Paris (begun 1806), almost a repetition of a Roman model. In painting Jacques Louis David interpreted the style with heroic subjects taken from classical mythology or from Napoleon's career. The style was transmitted to the rest of Europe, remaining magnificent and rich at all the Bonaparte courts. In bourgeois surroundings in Germany and Scandinavia it became simple and domesticated but retained its essence of classical dignity.

Encaenia, a festival commemorating a dedication; at Oxford University the annual commemoration of benefactors, accompanied by the conferring of honorary degrees, is held in June.

Encyclical Letters, a term used in reference to letters addressed by the Pope to his bishops upon matters of doctrine or discipline.

Encyclopaedists, a term first applied to the eminent writers who collaborated in the French *Encyclopédie* (1751–65). They included Diderot, D'Alembert, Voltaire, Helvetius; their writings generally were sceptical as to religion, destructive as to politics and had great influence in popularising the social ideas which afterwards resulted in the French Revolution.

Energy. One of the most fundamental concepts of science. A body in motion possesses *kinetic energy* as a result of the *work* done by the forces creating the motion. But a force which does work to stretch a spring does not create motion. Instead, the work is stored up in the spring and is one example of *potential energy.* A raised body also possesses potential energy which turns into kinetic when the body falls. The *heat energy* contained in a body is the sum of the kinetic and potential energy of the constituent atoms which are vibrating all the time. Heat and motion are obtainable from electrical, magnetic, chemical, atomic, and other sources, and physicists therefore define corresponding forms of energy. The vital point is that all forms of energy are transferable into one another *without loss or gain.* This is the Law of Conservation of Energy. It is one of the most fundamental laws of science, and its general validity is the reason why energy is an important idea. Since Einstein, it has been recognised that mass also is interchangeable with energy. *See* **F18,** *also* **Nuclear Energy.**

Energy Conversion. For practical purposes it is frequently necessary to change energy from one into another of its many forms; indeed almost every activity does this in one way or another. The primary sources of energy are the sun, uranium and other elements from which nuclear energy can be drawn, and the tides. The sun is not much used *directly* because its heat is intermittent and not very intense, but solar cookers and refrigerators have been invented and solar batteries (*q.v.*) are used in spacecraft. The sun can be used *indirectly* because it has produced, *via* living processes, fossil fuels like coal and oil and still continues to generate winds, rain and rivers and hence

hydroelectric and wind power. Commonly both fossil fuels and the energy of river or tidal waters are converted into electricity. Windmill type electricity generators are also quite common. The bulk of electricity production is a two-stage process: first fossil or nuclear fuel is used to create heat (*see* **Nuclear Reactors**); then the heat is used to raise steam and drive generators. Efforts are being made to convert heat into electricity more directly, *e.g.,* by using thermoelectric or thermionic effects (*q.v.*), but these have not been used for large-scale production. Once electrical energy is available, factories can make chemical batteries in great numbers and these can then be used as portable energy sources, as can petrol and other refined forms of fossil fuel. *See* **Battery, Fuel Cell, Solar Battery.**

Engraving is the art of cutting or otherwise forming designs of pictures on wood, stone, or metal surfaces for reproduction by some method of printing. Wood-engraving was the earliest in the field, dating from the 15th cent. Later, engraving on steel and copper plates was introduced, and mezzotint, lithography, stipple, aquatint, etc. Most modern methods of reproduction are based on photography.

Entablature, that portion of a building which surmounts the columns and extends to the roof of the tympana of the pediments; it comprises the architrave, the frieze and the cornice.

Enthalpy, another name for the heat content (H) of a system in thermodynamics. If a system generates heat it is presumed that the heat comes from the enthalpy of the system which by the 1st law of thermodynamics (**F20**) thus fails. It can be combined with the entropy (S) in an equation which defines the important thermodynamic quantity called the Gibbs Free Energy: $G = H - TS$ where T is the thermodynamic temperature. G is important in the prediction of chemical change (**F26**).

Entropy, one of the most important quantities in thermodynamics, symbol S. According to Clausius' statement of the Second Law (**F20**) the entropy of an isolated system cannot decrease. Although introduced by Clausius it arose from a consideration of Carnot's studies of the limitation of the convertibility of heat into work. It is most easily viewed as disorder in the statistical approach introduced by Boltzmann. This may be illustrated by considering the separate sets of coloured balls in a box. This is an ordered arrangement (of low entropy). The natural tendency is for the balls to mix and for the colours to become disordered (of higher entropy). We do not expect the opposite process for the balls to spontaneously separate, *i.e.,* we do not expect the entropy to decrease. In the context of energy changes, say in heat engines, the entropy change is equal to the heat change divided by the (thermodynamic) temperature (*see* **L3**).

Enzymes. Organic catalysts which accelerate chemical processes occurring in living organisms. There are a large number present in the cell, and most have a high degree of specificity. Enzyme mechanisms are the key to basic biological processes. See **F32(1).**

Ephemoptera or **May-flies,** an order of insects. In the larval condition they exist from two to three years aquatically, but no sooner do they arrive at maturity than their lives are hurried to a close. They rise up in pyramids on warm summer nights, take no food, propagate and perish. The Latin name expresses the fact that the adults have an ephemeral existence.

Epiphany, a Christian festival celebrated on January 6, originally an old solstice festival, celebrating the birth of light.

Equator, the imaginary great circle of the earth, every point of which is 90 degrees from the earth's poles, and dividing the northern from the southern hemisphere. It is from this circle that the latitude of places north and south is reckoned. The celestial equator is the circle in which the plane of the earth's equator meets the celestial sphere (the imaginary sphere, in which the observer is at the centre, used for representing the apparent positions of the heavenly bodies).

Equinox, the time when the sun crosses the plane of the earth's equator, making day and night of equal length.

Eras are distinctive periods of time associated with some remarkable historical event or personage. *The Christian era* is computed according to a 6th-cent. reckoning to begin with Jesus's birth, AD. 1. The date is placed some years too late. Scholars now believe that Jesus was born *c.* 4 B.C. The *Jewish era* dates from 3761 B.C.; the *Julian era* from the alteration of the calendar by Julius Caesar 45 B.C.; the *Mohammedan era* from the date of the *Hejira*, or the flight of Mohammed from Mecca to Medina, which is A.D.. 622, 16 July, in the Julian Calendar.

Erbium, belongs to the group of rare-earth metals discovered by Mosander in 1842. Element no. 68, symbol Er.

Erg, the unit of work and energy in the centimetre-gram-second system; the energy involved when a force of 1 dyne moves its point of application through a distance of 1 cm.

Ernie, the name given to the "electronic random number indicator equipment", the electronic machine which selected the prizewinning numbers in the first Premium Bond draw, June 1957.

Eros. This asteroid is 24–32 km in diameter. It comes closer to the earth than any other member of the solar system with the exception of the moon and several very small asteroids. Determination of solar parallax based on observations of Eros in 1930–31 yielded until then the most accurate estimate of the distance of the sun from the earth. *See* **Astronomical unit.**

Erse, a term used by Lowland Scottish, and English writers for the Gaelic language spoken in the Highlands of Scotland. Sometimes erroneously applied to Irish, the Gaelic language as spoken in Ireland and revived as an official language in recent times. Dr. Johnson, Sir Walter Scott, and other writers used "Erse" to signify Scottish Gaelic. The language of the Scottish Lowlands (that used by Robert Burns) is related to the English language and not to Gaelic and is variously termed Scots, Braid Scots, the Doric, the Scottish vernacular, and fashionably of late, Lallans.

Escurial or **Escorial,** Spanish monastery built in the mountains near Madrid by Philip II to commemorate the victory over the French at Saint-Quentin (1557). A palace was added later and it also includes a church, library and royal mausoleum. Built in granite in sombre style, it is one of the finest buildings in Europe.

Esperanto, an artificial international language created by L. Zamenhof of Warsaw and first published in 1887. It does not seek to replace national languages but to serve as a second language for international communication. It is based on the internationality of many words in the principal modern languages, and is entirely phonetic in spelling and pronunciation.

Estates of the Realm in Great Britain are the Lords Spiritual, the Lords Temporal and the Commons. They are the great classes invested with distinct political powers, and whose concurrence is necessary to legislation.

Esters. Organic chemicals formed by combining an alcohol with an acid. They have a pleasant smell, and occur naturally in plants as the scent of flowers. Manufactured for use in the perfumery industry, and as flavourings in food. Some esters are used as solvents, notably amyl-acetate ("pear drops") in quick-drying paints. The polymeric fibre "Terylene" consists of chains of molecules containing many ester groups, formed by reacting an alcohol having two alcoholic (OH) groups with an acid having two acid (COOH) groups.

Etching, a technical method for producing graphic work and works of art. A plate, traditionally of copper, is covered with wax; the design or picture desired is drawn with a sharp implement which penetrates the wax. When the plate is exposed to the action of an acid this will etch into the copper where the lines have been drawn. The wax is then removed, ink is applied to the plate with its engraving, and the design or picture can be printed on to paper in many copies. Rembrandt, Goya and others made great and original works of art in the technique, but it was also widely used for reproductive purposes before the invention of photography. Hogarth painted his famous pictures in oil and reproduced them graphically.

Ether, in chemistry, is a volatile inflammable liquid composed of carbon, hydrogen and oxygen. It is a valuable anaesthetic obtained by heating alcohol with sulphuric acid. In physics, in the 19th cent., all space was supposed to be filled with a substance called ether, the chief property of which was to carry light waves, *i.e.*, light was supposed to be waves in this all-pervading medium known as the ether. Speculation and experiment concerned with the ether were very fruitful in advancing physics. Ultimately the attempts by Michelson and Morley to detect the motion of the earth through the ether were unsuccessful in this respect but profoundly successful in stimulating the theory of relativity. The ether concept has now been abandoned. *See also* **F17(2).**

Ethylene (also called ethene). A gas compounded of carbon and hydrogen, it is related to acetylene and ethane. Industrially it is obtained as a by-product in petroleum refining. It has wide uses as a starting material in the industrial manufacture of intermediates, especially alcohol. Its most important application is in the production of polythene (poly-ethylene). *See* **Catalyst.**

Etruscans, people believed to have come from Asia Minor who colonised Italy about 900 B.C., settled in what is now Tuscany and part of Umbria, reached the height of their civilisation about 500 B.C., and were ultimately absorbed by the Romans. They were skilled technicians in bronze, silver and goldwork, and excelled in the art of granular decoration.

Eucalyptus. This genus includes 300 species of evergreen, leathery-leaved trees native to Australia. The oils yielded by different species vary a great deal in their scent and other properties and are chiefly used in pharmacy and perfumery; about 30 species produce oils suitable for medicinal purposes. Various species produce timber.

Euro-dollar Market. An international financial market, located mainly in Britain and Europe, for lending and borrowing dollars, *i.e.*, titles to dollar deposits in United States banks.

Europium, element no. 63, symbol Eu, discovered by Demarcay in 1906. A member of the rare-earth metal group.

Evaporation is the process by which a solid or liquid is resolved into vapour by heat. The opposite process is condensation. Wherever a liquid or solid surface is exposed, evaporation takes place into the space above. If the vapour is continually removed the solid or liquid vanishes into vapour; the higher the temperature the quicker the process. If the vapour is confined, then it collects, getting more concentrated until as many atoms of vapour are condensing as are evaporating. The vapour is then said to be saturated. Evaporation of water from sea, soil, plants, skin, etc., is continuously in progress, so it is a process of fundamental importance to meteorology, botany, physiology, industry, not to speak of human comfort and homely activities such as laundering.

Everest Expeditions. For many years after Mt. Everest had been shown to be the highest mountain in the world, political conditions in Nepal, lying south of the summit, and in Tibet, to the north, prevented mountaineers from attempting an ascent. At last in 1921 the Tibetan authorities gave permission, and the first expedition, organised, as were all subsequent British expeditions, by a joint committee of the Royal Geographical Society and the Alpine Club, and led by Col. C. K. Howard-Bury, was sent out. This was primarily a reconnaissance; besides mapping the northern flanks, it found a practicable route up the mountain. By 1939, six further expeditions had climbed on the northern face. Some were baulked by bad weather, others by problems previously little known, such as the effect of high altitudes on the human body and spirit. Nevertheless, notable climbs were accomplished. In 1924, for example, Col. E. F. Norton reached 8,589 m, and it was on this expedition that G. L. Mallory and Andrew Irvine were seen going well at about the same height. They never returned, however, and what disaster befell them is not known. After the war, political conditions again closed the Tibet route: permission was eventually obtained from the Nepalese Government to make the attempt from the south. In 1951 a reconnaissance expedition under Eric Shipton reached the ice-fall at the exit of the Western Cwm (a high valley lying south-west of the massif), and reported favourably on the prospects for an ascent. The first attempt from this side was made the following year by a Swiss expedition led by Dr. E. Wyss-Dunant, two members of which made an attempt on the summit, but were stopped at approx. 8,601 m by the intense cold and the very strong winds. When the British 1953 Expedition led by Col. John Hunt (now Lord Hunt), was being organised, stress was laid on three main points; proper acclimatisation of the climbers; use of oxygen for the final stages; and the establishment of very high altitude camps, so that the final assault parties would set out fresh and unencumbered. Great attention was also paid to recent developments in diet, clothing and equipment. In all these matters the 1953 expedition was able to draw on the accumulated experience of its predecessors. By the end of April, a base camp had been established below the ice-fall, and with the aid of thirty-four Sherpa porters supplies had been carried up into the Western Cwm. The next critical stage was the ascent of the steep head of the cwm, the Lhotse face, with the threat of avalanches always present. By most strenuous efforts, a camp was established on the South - Col (7,869 m) on 21 May. From this camp on 26 May, T. D. Bourdillon and R. C. Evans climbed the South Peak of Everest (8,760 m), then the highest altitude ever attained. On 28 May Edmund Hillary and the Sherpa leader, Tenzing Norgay, spent the night at the highest camp (8,510 m) and on the following day, 29 May, climbed to the South Summit, negotiated the difficult final ridge, and reached the summit of Everest—the climax of a long, arduous and stirring endeavour.

Evolution, in the words of Sir Julian Huxley (d. 1975), "a natural process of irreversible change which generates novelty, variety and increase of organisation". The theory, as laid down by Darwin, is that all existing species, genera and classes of animals and plants have developed from a few simple forms by processes of change and selection. Up to the time of Darwin a large part of the civilised world believed that life had been created suddenly at the beginning of the world which God had created, according to Archbishop Usher, on 22 October 4004 B.C. The evidence of the rocks, however, has given a more convincing theory of creation, and by studying the fossils preserved in the various layers of the earth's crust the past history of the earth's life has been pieced together. Darwin has been called the Newton of biology. *See* F29–31.

Exchequer, which derives its name from the checkered tablecloth on which accounts were calculated in early Norman times, is a term connected with the revenues of the Crown. In former times it had jurisdiction in all revenue matters. The term Exchequer is now applied to the Governmental department which deals with the public revenues, the working head of which is the Chancellor of the Exchequer.

Existentialism. *See* **Section J.**

Exploration. Modern exploration began in the second half of the 15th cent. with the voyages of the great Portuguese and Spanish discoverers. They were followed by sailors of other European nations, who profited from their developments in navigation and from their charts, and in less than one hundred years the coast-lines of much of the Americas, Africa and South-west Asia had been revealed and the globe circumnavigated. The motives of these early explorers were mixed: they were seeking adventure, trade, plunder, national power and the conversion of the heathen. Few if any were directly interested in advancing scientific knowledge. But from the reports of their voyages and travels, scholars at home compiled descriptions of the strange new world which stimulated their successors to undertake more systematic enquiries. One of the earliest English expeditions to be despatched for scientific research was that of William Dampier on the *Roebuck*, which was sent out by the Admiralty in 1699 to examine the coasts of North-west Australia. In the 18th cent. British explorers were at work mainly in the Pacific Ocean, with the object of breaking the Spanish monopoly of trade. Capt. James Cook sailed thither in 1769 to observe first the transit of Venus at Tahiti, and then to search for the alleged great southern continent. On this voyage he discovered and charted much of the coasts of New Zealand and the east coast of Australia. On his second voyage he was the first to sail across the Antarctic Circle, and he showed that the southern continent was much smaller than had been supposed. By 1800 the general outlines of the continents, except for Antarctica were known, and explorers in the 19th cent. were largely engaged in opening up the interiors. In Africa British explorers solved two problems which had puzzled men for centuries: Mungo Park and Richard Lander established the true course of the River Niger, and Sir Richard Burton, J. H. Speke, Sir Samuel Baker and others revealed the true sources of the Nile. The greatest African explorer of that age was undoubtedly David Livingstone, the missionary, who in three great journeys explored the Zambesi and the region of the Great Lakes, spreading the Gospel, fighting the slave trade, and opening up the interior to settlement and trade. In North America Alexander Mackenzie was the first to cross the main breadth of the continent from sea to sea. In Asia motives were also mixed; men like Charles Doughty, who explored in Arabia, and Sir Francis Younghusband, who journeyed from China to India across the Gobi and the Himalayas, were impelled by a love of adventure and the quest for knowledge, but political considerations were often involved. In recent years, with the main features of the world's surface known, exploration has become more intensive. Teams of scientists go out to study restricted areas in detail. An Antarctic expedition can contribute to our knowledge of world weather, or by biological research into the life history of whales, can help to improve our food supplies. Similarly, expeditions in Africa can help to check the loss of valuable agricultural land through soil erosion, or to develop areas of settlement by schemes for irrigation and power. And there are still great areas to be adequately mapped. All these problems are inter-related, and in solving them the modern explorer can call on many improved techniques and instruments—the aeroplane, the aerial camera, tracked motor vehicles, radio, in fact all the resources of modern science. But the human element is still vital, and for those with the old explorers' spirit there will always be problems left to solve.

Explosives, substances which burn violently to produce gases in such volume that an explosion is induced. Gunpowder was the first explosive to be used; Roger Bacon's powder, consisting of charcoal, sulphur and saltpetre, was the only effective explosive until the 19th cent., but it was difficult to control. Nitroglycerine (glyceryl trinitrate) was first compounded in 1847 by adding glycerine to a mixture of sulphuric acid and nitric acid. In 1866 Alfred Nobel discovered how to make dynamite by absorbing nitroglycerine in the fine sand kieselguhr. Cordite was the joint invention of Sir Frederick Abel and Sir James Dewar (1889). It came into general use as a propellant. High explosives, providing bursting charge for shells and bombs, include TNT (trinitrotoluene), picric acid, cyclonite (RDX) and many others. Slurry explosives can be pumped on to the site and therefore offer advantages in transportation and safety; they are also waterproof. Chemical explosives have been eclipsed by nuclear explosives which have developed from the first atom bomb (dropped on Hiroshima 6 August 1945) to the 100-megaton hydrogen bomb.

Expressionism, a modern art movement confined primarily to the non-Latin countries of Europe which sought to give expression to intimate and personal emotions by means of distortions of line and colour and simplified style which carried a greater impact in terms of feeling. Broadly speaking, this has been characteristic of northern art in general. (*See* **Gothic**.) The term is usually used of the modern movement which influenced the Post-impressionists and subsequent movements in France. Tired of the naturalism of the Impressionists, such artists as van Gogh, Gauguin, Matisse and Rouault, together with the Fauvists (*q.v.*) made use of simple outlines and strong colours. Apart from Toulouse-Lautrec, the principal Expressionists were Norwegian, like Munch, or German, like the painters of *Die Brücke* and *Der Blaue Reiter* groups. Individual artists were Ensor, Kokoschka, Nolde, Rouault and Soutine.

F

Fabian Society. See Section J.

Fables are fictitious narratives intended to enforce some moral precept, and may be either in prose or verse, and deal with personified animals and objects or with human beings. Aesop in ancient times and Hans Christian Andersen and the Brothers Grimm (in many of their stories) must also be made of La Fontaine's and Krylov's fables.

Fairs were established in mediaeval times as a means of bringing traders and customers together at stated periods, and formed the chief means of distribution. The great English fairs of early times were those of Winchester and Stourbridge near Cambridge. Traders from the Netherlands and the Baltic gathered there with the great merchants of London, and goods of every kind, wholesale and retail, were sold. One of the biggest trade fairs was at Nijni-Novgorod, founded in the 17th cent.; other big continental fairs were those of Leipzig (founded in the 12th cent.), Lyons and Prague. Expositions of advanced industrial products are today popular, *e.g.*, Expo 67 held in Montreal.

Fairy Rings are the circles caused in grassland by certain fungi. The circles expand outwards as the fungus spreads, the fruiting bodies being at the periphery. Farther inward where the fungi are decaying the grass grows more strongly, fertilised by the nitrogen released from the rotting fungi. In olden times these rings were held to be the scene of fairy dances.

Falcon, name given to diurnal birds of prey which belong to the same family, *Falconidae*, as the hawk, eagle, buzzard, kite and harrier. They are swift of wing and feed on birds and small mammals. These birds have long, pointed wings, strong, hooked and notched bill, long, curved claws and an eye of great power. Those that breed in Britain are the Kestrel (the most common), Hobby (one of the swiftest of European birds), Merlin and Peregrine, a swift and magnificent bird with slate-grey back, blackish crown, black "moustache" and whitish breast. Other members of the family are the Gyr Falcon from northern latitudes, Iceland and Greenland, which is a winter visitor to Britain, the Lanner, Saker, Eleonora's falcon, Red-footed falcon and the Lesser Kestrel. The Gyr Falcon and the Peregrine were used in the sport of falconry in olden times. Because of its fearlessness and larger size, the female bird was used. When the quarry was sighted, the bird was unhooded, set free, and after mounting high into the air would dart swiftly down to strike the prey. The heron was the usual victim.

Fall-out. Radioactive material produced by nuclear explosions which may cause bodily and genetic damage. (1) *Local fall-out*, due to the return to earth of larger particles, occurs locally, and within a few hours after the explosion; (2) *Tropospheric fall-out*, due to particles which remain in the troposphere and come down within a month or so, possibly all over the world, but within the altitude in which the explosion occurred; (3) *Stratospheric fall-out*, which comes from fragments taken up into the stratosphere and then deposited, in the course of many years, uniformly all over the globe. The two radioactive materials which have given rise to the greatest concern for the health of the individual are strontium-90 and iodine-131.

Both these materials are liable to become concentrated in certain parts of the human body, strontium-90 in bone and iodine-131 in the thyroid gland. Radiation exposure may produce genetic effects, that is effects which may show up in succeeding generations. An extensive survey was carried out by scientists of the US Atomic Energy Commission on the islands of Bikini atoll, site of some 23 nuclear tests, 1946–58. Their records, published in 1969, revealed that the intensity of radioactivity underneath the point of explosion was still exceedingly high. Most of the radiation remaining was due to the radioactive isotope caesium-137. The variation in intensity from one place to another seemed to be correlated with the variations of vegetation: where there was little vegetation weathering had been rapid. (The nuclear test ban treaty, 1963, applies to all nuclear tests except those held underground.)

Fantail, a variety of the domestic pigeon; also a genus of Australian birds of the *Muscicapidae* family. A small New Zealand bird is called a fantail.

Fan Tracery, a complicated style of roof-vaulting, elaborately moulded, in which the lines of the curves in the masonry or other material employed diverge equally in every direction. It is characteristic of the late Perpendicular period of Gothic architecture, and may be seen in St. George's Chapel at Windsor and the Chapel of Henry VII at Westminster Abbey.

Farmer-General, the name given to the financiers who in the days of the old French monarchy farmed certain taxes, contracting to pay the Government a fixed sum yearly, on condition that the unspecified taxes were collected and appropriated by themselves. The revolution of 1789 swept Farmers-General away.

Fascism. See Section J.

Fata Morgana, the name given to a curious mirage often observed over the Straits of Messina, attributed to the magic of the fairy Morgana, half-sister of King Arthur, who was fabled to live in Calabria.

Fathers of the Church were early writers who laid the foundations of Christian ritual and doctrine. The earliest were the Apostolic Fathers (*q.v.*). The Four Fathers of the Latin Church were St. Ambrose, St. Jerome, St. Augustine and St. Gregory the Great. The Four Fathers of the Greek Church were St. Basil, St. Gregory Nazianzen, St. John Chrysostom and St. Athanasius.

Fathom, a nautical measure, the six-foot stretch (1·8 m) of a man's arms. Replaced by the metre on British Admiralty charts, but continued on yachtsmen's coastal charts.

Fatigue, a condition leading to breakage when a solid component, *e.g.*, an axle, is subjected to a large number of fluctuating repetitive stresses. Fatigue is the cause of most failures in service of metal engineering components though fatigue is not confined to metallic materials alone. Fatigue failures result from the *repetition*, not simply from the *size* of the stresses; indeed, fatigue breakage can result from stresses much lower than the material could stand if the load were applied steadily. Fatigue causes minute cracks, usually at the surface, which grow and spread. Early detection is difficult and fatigue, discovered by the railway engineers of the 19th cent., remains a severe engineering problem.

Fats are important foodstuffs. In physiology they constitute a valuable form of reserve food. They contain carbon, hydrogen and oxygen; chemically they are described as esters of glycerol (glycerine). Commonest fats are stearin, palmitin and olein, esters formed by the combination of glycerol with stearic, palmitic and oleic acid respectively. Fats are converted into soap by alkali; this process (saponification) also releases glycerol.

Fault, a term designating a breakage coupled with displacement of geological strata. See **F9**(2).

Fauvism (French *Fauve* = wild beast), a term used, at first contemptuously, to describe the work of a group of French painters who first exhibited at the Salon d'Automne in Paris in 1905. The most prominent among them was Henri Matisse. Forms are freely distorted and colours are selected and applied for their emotive power with no necessary reference to the "real" colour of the object in question. Other famous *Fauves* were Derain, Vlaminck and Rouault. By 1908 the group had lost its cohesion and its members went their separate ways.

February, the second month of the year, contains in ordinary years 28 days, but in leap years 29 days. When first introduced into the Roman calendar by Numa, c. 700 B.C. it was made the last month of the year, preceding January, but in 452 B.C. the position of the two months was changed, February following January.

Federation. See **Confederation.**

Félibrige, a movement founded in 1854 to revive the ancient glories of Provence, initiated by the French poet Frédéric Mistral.

Felspar, the name given to a group of minerals, silicates of aluminium with some calcium and sodium, or potassium, which make up probably more than half of the earth's crust. It is formed in granite and other rocks, both igneous and metamorphic.

Fenestella, the niche set apart on the south side of the altar for the piscina in Roman Catholic churches.

Fermentation, the action of chemical ferments or *enzymes* in bringing about chemical changes in the materials of living animals and plants, *e.g.,* the breaking-down of sugar by yeast into alcohol.

Ferret, a domesticated polecat. It is about half the size of a cat and is bred in captivity to hunt rats and rabbits. It has a long sinuous body and short legs which enable it to enter rabbit and rat holes and chase the quarry out to guns or into nets. Such ferreting is a popular country sport.

Ferrites are compounds containing iron, oxygen, and one or two of a certain range of other possible metallic elements. Ferrites have recently become very important technically, because, unlike ordinary magnetic materials, they combine strong magnetism with electrical insulating properties. Ferrite-rod aerials are now common in portable radios, and ferrite devices are used in radar. See **F22(2).**

Feudalism. See **Section J.**

Fieldfare, the largest member of the thrush family, a regular winter visitor to Britain from Scandinavia. It is brown in colour with a lighter spotted breast and a grey head.

Field-Marshal, the highest ranking title in the British army, and only bestowed on royal personages and generals who have attained great ⏤istinction. The first British Field-Marshal was created in 1736, when John, Duke of Argyll, had the title conferred upon him by George II.

Fifth Column. When Franco, the Spanish dictator, revolted against the Spanish Republic in 1936 and attacked Madrid with four armies, his commander, General Mola declared that a group of fascists within the city was assisting the besiegers. The term is used to describe a body of spies behind a fighting front.

Fighting-Fish, small pugnacious Siamese fish with long caudal and ventral fins. They are kept in glass globes in Siam, and when brought into contact will fight to the death, these encounters being the occasion of much gambling.

Filibuster, a name first given to pirates and buccaneers in the 17th cent. who took possession of small islands or lonely coast lands, and there maintained themselves apart from any governing authority. In later times the term was used to specify men taking part in expeditions whose object was to appropriate tracts of country, and settle upon them in disregard of international law. The most notable expeditions of this kind in modern times were those of Narciso Lopez against Cuba in 1850-51, and of William Walker against Nicaragua, between 1855 and 1860. Both leaders were captured and executed. The term is also used to express the right of a minority in the United States Senate for unlimited debate, which is used on occasions to delay legislation.

Finches, a large family of small birds belonging to the Passerine or perching order of birds. There are about 200 species, including greenfinch, hawfinch, chaffinch, goldfinch, siskin, bullfinch, crossbill, linnet, twite and bunting.

Fir, a cone-bearing tree with small evergreen leaves and of considerable use as timber. There are two types: the Silver Firs and the Douglas Firs numbering about 25 species. All these firs attain to a considerable height, and all yield turpentine or other resinous material.

Fire-damp. See **Methane.**

Fire-Fly, a small winged insect of the *Eleteridae* family, is able to throw out a strong phosphorescent light in the dark. There are some remarkable specimens in tropical countries.

Fire of London, of 1666, extended from East to West, from the Tower to the Temple church, and northward to Holborn Bridge. It broke out in a baker's shop in Pudding Lane, and lasted four days, and destroyed 87 churches, including St. Paul's Cathedral, and many public buildings, among them the Royal Exchange, the Custom House and the Guildhall. In the ruins were 13,200 houses and 400 streets. About 100,000 people were made homeless yet in about 10 years all the houses had been rebuilt. The plague had not disappeared from London when the fire occurred.

Firkin, a former measure of capacity, the fourth part of a barrel, now only used in reference to a small cask or tub for butter, lard, allow, etc.

Fischer-Tropsch Process. A process for making synthetic petrol from carbon monoxide and hydrogen. The synthesis is accelerated by cobalt-thoria and nickel-thoria catalysts.

Fish Louse. Parasitic crustacea found on marine and fresh-water fishes and whales.

Fission, Nuclear. A nuclear reaction in which the nucleus of an atom (*e.g.,* uranium 235, plutonium) captures a neutron, and the unstable nucleus so produced breaks into two nearly equal fragments and throws out several neutrons as well. In biology the term fission is applied to reproduction by fragmentation of a single-cell organism, as in amoeba. See **F13(1).**

Flagella, single hair-like projections found on many micro-organisms. Their sole function is, by complicated motion, to move the organism about. They are longer and less versatile than cilia (*q.v.*).

Flag Officer, a British naval officer who enjoys the right of carrying a flag at the mast-head of his ship, and is of the rank of Admiral of the Fleet, Admiral, Vice-Admiral or Rear-Admiral.

Flagship, the ship that flies the Admiral's flag, and from which orders proceed.

Flamingo, a strangely beautiful, extremely slender wading bird of white and rose-pink plumage with long, slender legs and neck and a long, down-curved bill with which it rakes the mud and obtains its food of worms and molluscs. The wings are bright crimson, bordered with black, and a flock in flight is a picture of singular beauty. There is a large and famous colony in the Camargue, S.E. France.

Flash-Point. This is found by heating an oil in a special cup and taking the temperature at which sufficient vapour is produced to ignite when a small flame is applied. It is an index of the inflammability of oils.

Fleas. Fleas are small parasitic insects belonging to the order *Aphaniptera* (so called because these creatures have no wings). They obtain their food by sucking blood from their host. They are laterally compressed, which immediately distinguishes them from lice. The human flea (*Pulex irritans*) is able to jump vertically a distance of over 18 cm.

Fleet Prison, a noted debtors' prison that stood on the east side of Farringdon Street, London. It was notorious for the cruelties inflicted on prisoners, particularly under the wardenship of Thomas Bainbridge who took charge in 1728. It was pulled down in 1846.

Fleet Street, a famous thoroughfare in London, now the centre of journalism and newspaperdom, though it was long celebrated for its taverns where the literary coteries of the day were wont to meet. It takes its name from the Fleet stream which used to run from Hampstead through Holborn to the Thames at Blackfriars.

Flemings, the Dutch-speaking people of Flanders, whose ancestors of mediaeval times excelled in the textile arts; England owes its early eminence as a manufacturing nation to the migration of numbers of Flemings to this country in the 16th and 17th cent. See also **Walloons.**

Fleur de Lis, the former national emblem of France, the flower of the lily. It was superseded by the Tricolour in 1789, but is still adhered to by the supporters of the old French royalties.

Flint, consists of granular chalcedony with some opaline silica, and occurs as nodules and bands in the Chalk. It is hard and has a conchoidal fracture, so enabling it to be used in making cutting implements in prehistoric times. Before the invention of lucifer matches, it was used along with steel for striking lights.

Flint implements are objects found in the younger geological strata, and constituting evidence of the condition and life of the period. They include knives, clubs, arrow-heads, scrapers, etc., used as weapons, tools and possibly as surgical instruments and in religious ceremonies. Similar to prehistoric specimens are the flint and obsidian implements of some of the primitive peoples of today. Ritual weapons and sacrificial knives continued to be made of stone long after the introduction of metals for practical purposes.

Flounder, one of the most familiar of the smaller flat fishes common round the British coasts, and seldom attaining a weight of over 1·3 kg.

Fluoridation, the process of adding the element fluorine, in the form of suitable compounds, to something deficient in it. Commonly met with as a proposal to add fluorides (fluorine compounds) to drinking water to combat dental decay, especially in children. Some toothpastes are fluoridated and fluoride can also be taken as tablets and in other ways. In 1976 a working party of the Royal College of Physicians recommended that water supplies should be fluoridated when the natural fluoride level is below 1 mg/litre. This recommendation drew on many investigations throughout the world giving evidence for the effectiveness of fluoride in the prevention of decay without harmful side-effects. There is, however, a body of opinion unconvinced by this and opposed to adding fluoride to drinking water, one argument being that to take or not to take fluoride should be a personal decision.

Fluorine, chemical element, no. 9, member of the halogen family, symbol F, it is found in combination with calcium in fluorspar, and occurs in minute quantities in certain other minerals. Discovered by Scheele in 1771, it was first obtained by Moissan in 1886. A pale yellow gas, it is very reactive and combines with most elements except oxygen. Its acid, hydrogen fluoride, etches glass, the fluorine combining with the silicon to form volatile silicon fluoride. Organic fluorine compounds have found use as very stable polymers which resist a wide variety of chemical actions.

Fluorescent Lamp. See **Electric Light and Ultra-Violet Rays.**

Fluorocarbons are hydrocarbons in which some or all of the hydrogen atoms have been replaced by atoms of chlorine or fluorine. They are non-toxic, non-flammable and chemically inert gases or low boiling point liquids. These properties make them very suitable for use as refrigerants, and propellants in fire-extinguishers and aerosols. The most widely used fluorocarbons are the chlorofluoromethanes (CCl_2F_2, CCl_3F and $CHClF_2$). In 1974 it was first suggested that the vast release of fluorocarbons into the atmosphere due to the greatly increased use of aerosols could cause a significant depletion of the protective ozone (q.v.) layer in the upper atmosphere. The mechanism for this involves the decomposition of fluorocarbons at high altitudes as a result of intense solar irradiation. The chlorine atoms so released can then catalyse the conversion of ozone into ordinary molecular oxygen. The degree of ozone depletion that will result is a matter of considerable current controversy. Similarly, opinions differ as to the detrimental effect ozone depletion might have on the incidence of skin cancer and on the climate.

Fluorspar, a mineral; chemically calcium fluoride. Can be colourless, green or yellow, but is most commonly purple. Blue fluorspar under the name of Derbyshire "blue John" has been used for ornamental purposes.

Fly, the popular name for a large number of insects with one pair of wings and a proboscis ter-

minating in a sucker through which fluid substances can be drawn up. The best-known species are the common house-fly, the blue-bottle and the blow-fly. In the larval form flies are maggots, and feed upon decaying substances, animal flesh, etc. Flies are able to walk upon ceilings or upright surfaces by having suckers at the soles of their feet. See **Diptera.**

Flycatcher, name of a large family of small birds, the Muscicapidae. They are insect feeders, catch their food in the air, and are distributed over most countries of the world. The spotted and the pied nest in Britain, which they visit from April to September.

Flying Fish are frequently to be seen in southern waters, and are capable of gliding considerable distances without touching the water. To build up speed for its "take-off" the fish swims rapidly, to break the surface at 24–32 km/h. Maximum air speed is about 64 km/h.

Flying Fox, a member of the bat family, but of much larger size, and confined to the tropical and sub-tropical Old World. Like the bats, it is nocturnal, but it feeds entirely on fruits.

Flying Lemur. See **Colugo.**

Flying Lizard, or *Draco*, an Asiatic lizard, possessing wing-like projections from each side which enable it to make flying leaps through the air, though not sufficient for continuous flight.

Flying Saucers, the name given to certain saucer-like shapes which have on occasion been seen travelling through the atmosphere. For some time speculation was rife, especially in America, but it is now believed that when not hallucinations, meteorological or cosmic-ray balloons, they are nothing more than atmospheric phenomena like mirages or mock suns caused by unusual atmospheric conditions. Described by Dr. Menzel, astrophysics professor at Harvard, "as real as rainbows are real, and no more dangerous". It has been suggested that the study of some of the people who report the sighting of unidentified flying objects (UFOs) would be more rewarding than the investigation of what they saw! See also **Section J.**

Flying Squirrel, rodents of which there are several species in Europe, Asia and America. It possesses a parachute-like fold of skin by means of which it projects itself through the air. In appearance they are much like ordinary squirrels, to which they are related. The African flying squirrels belong to a different family.

Fog is caused by the presence of particles of condensed water vapour or smoke in the surface layers of the atmosphere, the term being applied meteorologically when the resulting obscurity is such as to render objects invisible at distances of up to 1 km. Fogs are frequently formed when the air near the ground is cooled below its dew-point temperature by radiation on a still, cloudless night; by flowing over a relatively cold land or water mass; or by mixing with a colder air stream. An accumulation of smoke over a large city may cause a high fog cutting off the daylight and producing gloom. See **Pollution, Aerosol.**

Foliation, a geological term applied to rocks whose component minerals are arranged in parallel layers as the result of strong metamorphic action.

Folio, a printing term for a sheet of paper folded once, a half sheet constituting a leaf.

Folklore concerns itself with the mental and spiritual life of the people—both civilised and primitive—as expressed in the traditional beliefs, customs, institutions and sayings that have been handed down from generation to generation by word of mouth and with the observation, recording and interpretation of such traditions. (The word *folklore* itself was first suggested and used—as two words *Folk Lore*—by W. J. Thoms in the *Athenaeum* of 22 August 1846, and was at once absorbed into the English language.) Traditional lore of the kind included in the term folklore takes many forms and ranges from omens of good and bad luck (spilling the salt, breaking a mirror, dropping an umbrella, etc.) and the wearing of amulets or the possession of talismans (such as the horse-shoe) as protection against misfortune, to elaborate ceremonial dances such as the Abbots Bromley Horn Dance, the Hobby horses of Padstow and Minehead the Northern sword-dances and the Christmas mummers' plays. Especially important are the beliefs and customs associated with birth, babyhood, marriage and death such being occasions when the individuals concerned require special protection or when unusual happenings can be used for foretelling their future. The child born on a Sunday will be the luckiest; rocking on an empty cradle will ensure the speedy arrival of a new baby; throwing an old shoe after a newly-married couple brings them luck; the bride should be carried over the threshold of the new home; on the sea-coast, death is believed to take place at the ebb-tide; the bees must be told of the death of the master of the house, or they will leave the hive. Another very large section of the subject deals with the traditional sayings and practices associated with particular days and seasons of the year—calendar customs, as they are called. The eating of pancakes on Shrove Tuesday; Mother Sunday customs and the simnel cake; Good Friday as the right day for planting potatoes, but emphatically the wrong day for washing clothes or cutting one's finger-nails; the necessity of wearing something new on Easter Sunday; the children's maypole dances and May garlands; midsummer fires; All Hallowe'en as the most favourable occasion for divining the future—especially in respect of marriage—and for games and sports such as apple-bobbing; the numerous practices accompanying the harvest. All these are examples of calendar customs; their full story would occupy several volumes. Folklorists are interested in all such oral tradition because they think that to a large extent it represents what folk have mentally stored up from the past and transmitted to their descendants throughout the centuries, and because therefore it is able to assist other historic methods—ethnographical, linguistic, archaeological, etc.—in the elucidation of the early story of man. In those countries with a great diversity of peoples in all stages of culture, a knowledge of folklore and what it can teach of the mind of man is of great importance to administrators. The Folk-Lore Society was founded in 1878, and that part of the subject represented by song and dance has now its own organisation in the English Folk Dance and Song Society.

Footpath. In English law a highway over which the public have a right of way on foot only, other than such a highway at the side of a public road.

Force, as a term in physics, signifies an influence or exertion which, when made to act upon a body, tends to move it if at rest, or to affect or stop its progress if it be already in motion. In the c.g.s. system, the unit of force is the dyne; in the foot-pound-second system, the poundal; in the SI system, the newton.

Formaldehyde. Chemically it lies between methyl alcohol and formic acid; oxidation of methyl alcohol yields formaldehyde, and oxidation of formaldehyde produces formic acid. It is used as a disinfectant, in silvering mirrors, and in the manufacture of phenol-formaldehyde plastics (of which bakelite is the best-known example). Solutions of formaldehyde in water, formalin, are used to preserve biological specimens.

Forme, a body of letterpress type, composed and secured for printing from; or a stereotype or electrotype. The former is used more for newspaper formes and the latter in good book work.

Formic Acid can be obtained from a colourless fluid secreted by ants and other insects and plants. It is a strong irritant. Commercially it is obtained from sodium formate, which is synthesised by the absorption of carbon monoxide in caustic soda. It is used in the electroplating, tanning and textile industries.

Fossils. Remains of animals and plants, or direct evidence of their presence, preserved in rocks. They include petrified skeletons and shells, leaf imprints, footprints, etc.

Four Freedoms, a phrase coined by President Roosevelt in January 1941, embodying what should be the goal of the Allies. They were (1) Freedom of speech and expression; (2) Freedom of every person to worship God in his own way; (3) Freedom from want; (4) Freedom from fear.

Fox, carnivorous animal of the canine family, found in considerable numbers in most parts of the world. The common fox *Vulpes vulpes* of Europe is a burrowing animal of nocturnal habits, living upon birds, rabbits and domestic poultry, in the capture of which it displays much cunning. The fox in Britain is preserved from extinction chiefly for hunting pur-poses. Among other notable species are the Arctic fox and the red fox of North America, of which the valuable silver fox, coveted for its fur, is a variety.

Fox-Shark *or* **Thresher Shark,** a large species of shark common in the Atlantic and in the Mediterranean. It is very destructive to small fish, but although it attains a length of 4·5 m it is not dangerous to man.

Franciscans. *See* **Friars.**

Franco-German War (1870–71) was opened by a declaration of war by Napoleon III, but the Germans who were better prepared than the French, won victory after victory. On 12 September Napoleon with 104,000 men were made prisoners at Sedan, a republic was then proclaimed, and Paris sustained a four months' siege. In the end France ceded Alsace and part of Lorraine to Germany, who claimed a war indemnity of £200 million.

Frankincense is of two kinds, one being used as incense in certain religious services and obtained from olibanum, an Eastern shrub, the other is a resinous exudation derived from firs and pines, and largely used in pharmacy.

Franklin, the name given in feudal times to a country landowner who was independent of the territorial lord, and performed many of the minor functions of local government, such as serving as magistrate.

Freeport, a port exempt from customs duties and regulations. The sites chosen by the Government in 1984 for Britain's first freeports are at Belfast, Birmingham, Cardiff, Liverpool and Southampton. When operational, goods can be landed at these ports from outside the Common Market, made into manufactures and re-exported outside the EEC free of duty. The north German towns of the Hanseatic League (**L56**) were among the earliest freeports.

Fresco, a painting executed upon plaster walls or ceilings, a technique which has remained unchanged since it was practised by the great Renaissance artists.

Friars, members of certain mendicant orders of the Roman Catholic Church. The four chief orders are the Franciscans or Grey Friars, the Dominicans or Black Friars, the Carmelites or White Friars and the Augustinians (Austin Friars).

Friday, the 6th day of the week, named after Frigga, the wife of Odin. It is the Mohammedan Sabbath, a general abstinence day of the Roman Catholic Church, and according to popular superstition, an unlucky day.

Friends, The Society of. *See* **Quakers, Section J.**

Frigate-Bird, a web-footed bird widely distributed over tropical latitudes, and deriving its name from its great expanse of wing and forked tail, resembling the shape of a swift vessel. It feeds on flying fish mostly, being unable to dive and also steals from other birds. A frigate-bird was found dying on the Hebridean island of Tiree in July 1953; only twice previously had one been recorded in Europe—the first on the German coast in 1792, and the second on the coast of France in 1902.

Frog, a familiar amphibian, breathing through gills in the earlier (tadpole) part of its existence and through lungs later. It remains three months in the tadpole stage. The frog hibernates underwater in the mud during the winter.

Frost occurs when the temperature falls to, or below, 0°C, which is freezing point. Hoar frost is applied to the needles or feather-like crystals of the ice deposited on the ground, in the same manner as dew. Glazed frost is the clear icy coating which may be formed as a result of rain falling on objects whose temperatures are below the freezing point. These layers of ice, often rendering roads impassable for traffic, damaging overhead power and communication systems and endangering aircraft, can also be caused by condensation from warm, damp winds coming into contact with very cold air and freezing surfaces.

Froth-Hopper *or* **Frog-Hopper.** A family of bugs

(belonging to the insect order *Hemiptera*) which in the larval stage surround themselves with a protective mass of froth ("cuckoo spit"). These insects, which suck the sap of plants, bear a faint resemblance to frogs, and the adults possess great leaping powers.

Fuel Cells. A recent development is a type of battery into which the active chemicals are fed from external fuel tanks. This is the *fuel cell*, which is being developed in a number of versions in several countries. One was demonstrated in action when in 1959 Bacon of Cambridge University used his fuel cell to drive a fork-lift truck and a welding machine. The Bacon fuel cell consists of two electrodes of porous nickel dipping into a solution of caustic potash in water. One electrode is supplied with hydrogen gas from an outside cylinder and the other with oxygen. These gases, forming layers on the nickel, are the active chemicals. The oxygen combines with water to make two negatively charged ions, each consisting of an oxygen and a hydrogen atom joined together (a hydroxyl ion). The hydroxyl ions travel through the solution to the hydrogen electrode, where they combine with hydrogen to form neutral water. Their negative charge (one electron per ion involved) has now arrived at the hydrogen electrode and is ready to flow back to the other electrode through any outside circuit that is provided. This flow constitutes the useful electric current, and it has been provided at the expense of creating water out of the original hydrogen and oxygen. The water can be removed in the form of steam. What is the advantage of all this? In the first place the fuel gases are easy to make and to store in cylinders. Supplying a new gas cylinder is easier and quicker than recharging an ordinary accumulator. Furthermore, a fuel cell is lighter for a given power than an accumulator; satellite designers have found them useful. The fuel cell is not damaged by heavy overloading, and this is valuable for application to vehicle driving. Fuel-cell-driven buses could combine the advantage of diesel buses and trolleybuses. Fuel cells are still in the development stage. It is not certain how they will compete with combustion engines or, in the oil-less future, with improved ordinary batteries.

Fulani, a non-Negro people of Hamitic stock widely distributed in N.W. Africa, chiefly in Nigeria. There are two main branches: the dark-skinned Fulani, settled farmers and city dwellers, Moslem in religion; and the light-coloured Bororo'en who are semi-nomadic herdsmen. The Fulani are different from any tribe in W. Africa though they resemble in some ways the Masai of E. Africa. The Fulani conquered the Hausa states at the beginning of the 19th cent. which passed under British suzerainty after 1903. Sokoto, built in 1810, was capital of the Fulani empire.

Fuller's Earth, a special kind of clay or marl possessing highly absorbent qualities, originally used in the "fulling"—that is, cleansing and felting—of cloth. Now used in clarifying oils. Deposits in America and in south of England.

Function. In mathematics, one quantity y is said to be a function of another quantity x, written $y = f(x)$, if a change in x results in some corresponding change in y. Thus $\sin x$ or $\log x$ are functions of x. If y depends not only on x but on several other quantities as well, y is called a function of many variables.

Functionalism, in architecture, a movement originated by Le Corbusier, Swiss-born French architect and town-planner, who applied the austere principles of the Purist movement in painting to his own art. From about 1924 he designed in concrete, steel and glass, buildings in which every part had a significance in terms of function on the theory that objects created to carry out their particular function to perfection cannot help being beautiful. "A house is a machine for living in." The style was in vogue between the two wars, and although its severity became somewhat modified, it is still the basis of most modern architecture.

Fungi, a class of simple plants, which reproduce from spores and lack the green colouring matter *chlorophyll*. It includes moulds, rusts, mildews, smuts, mushrooms, etc. Potato blight is a fungus disease which caused the failure of the potato crop in Ireland in 1846. 50,000 different fungi are known. *See also* **F42(1), P8(1)**.

Furniture Beetle (*Anobium punctatum*). The common furniture beetle is responsible for 80 per cent of all woodworm damage and is the great pest of the comparatively modern house, causing damage in the main to softwood roofing and flooring timbers. Adults are 3 mm long. The grub tunnels for about 33 months. *See also* **Woodworm, Death Watch Beetle.**

Futurism, an Italian school of art and literature initiated by Marinetti, an Italian writer and mountebank friend of Mussolini at a later period. Its origin took the form of a manifesto published in Paris in 1909 in which Marinetti glorified violence, war and the machine age. In its aggression it favoured the growth of fascism. One of the distinctive features of Futurist art was the use of the principle of "simultaneity" in which the same figure (*e.g.*, a woman descending a flight of stairs) is represented in successive positions like film "stills" superimposed on each other. In spite of two further manifestoes it was not until 1911 that the first examples of Futurist painting and sculpture appeared by the artists Severini, Balla and Boccioni. Apart from the principle of simultaneity, Futurism derived from Cubist and Post-impressionist techniques. The movement faded out early in the first world war.

G

Gabardine, a long, loose, coarse, over-garment, worn by men of the common class in the Middle Ages, and prescribed by law as the distinctive garment of the Jews. The name is now given to a closely woven cloth of wool and cotton used to make raincoats.

Gabbro, a kind of igneous rock, often very coarse-grained, containing a good deal of plagioclase felspar, and monoclinic pyroxene; it may occasionally also include biotite, magnetite, ilmenite and hornblende. A gabbro containing nickel at Sudbury in Canada is one of the richest sources known of that metal.

Gadfly, a widely distributed family of flies with only one pair of wings, including the horse fly. The females are very voracious, being able to bite through the skin and suck the blood of animals. The males are harmless.

Gadolinium. An element, no. 64, symbol Gd, belonging to the rare-earths metals discovered in 1886 by Marignac. It is strongly magnetic.

Gaelic, relating to the Gaels and their language, a term now applied only to the Celtic people inhabiting the Highlands of Scotland, but formerly also to the Celts of Ireland and the Isle of Man.

Galago, "Bush Babies", related to the lemur, native to Africa, large-eyed, in keeping with its nocturnal characteristics.

Galaxy *or* **Milky Way Galaxy** is the huge disk-shaped cloud of gas and stars (some 100,000 million, one of which is the sun) that is turning in space like a great wheel, with a diameter of about 100,000 light years. The Milky Way (that part of the heavens in Milton's words "powdered with stars") is really only a small part of this disk, and every star in the galaxy is moving round the centre under the gravitational control of the whole. The sun and planets lie near the edge of the disk, and it takes them about 250 million years to travel once round. The number of stars that can be seen with the unaided eye is about 3,000, and they all belong to the Milky Way Galaxy, as do most of the stars that can be seen with anything but the greatest telescopes. With the large modern optical and radar telescopes many other systems, similar in size and weight to our galaxy, have been discovered, scattered more or less uniformly through space, and the universe is said to include at least 10,000 million such galaxies. *See also* **F4(2).**

Gale, a high wind now technically defined as one of at least Beaufort force 8. Between thirty and forty gales a year occur on the north and west coasts of the British Isles and only about half of this number in the south-east. At St.

Ann's Head, Dyfed, the anemometer registered a gust of 113 mile/h (182 km/h) on 18 Jan. 1945, which is a record for these islands. Gusts exceeding 113 km/h are rarely experienced in London. Gale warnings are issued for specified areas by the Meteorological Office, the warnings taking the form of radio broadcasts and the hoisting of storm signals at certain points on the coast. *See* **Beaufort Wind Scale, Section N.**

Gall, abnormal vegetable growths caused by insects, mites, bacteria, or fungi, found on all parts of the plant. Oak-apples, Robin's pin-cushion (on wild rose), "witches' brooms" (on trees) are examples. Some are useful com-mercially, *e.g.*, oak apples yield tannic acid and the black oak gall is used in America as animal food.

Galleon, the name given to the old three-decked Spanish treasure vessels employed in conveying the precious minerals from the American colonies to Spain. The term is often applied to any large, especially stately, sailing vessel.

Galley, an oar-propelled sea-boat used by the ancient Greeks and Romans for transport pur-poses, manned by slaves. They were also used as warships from classical to relatively modern times, *e.g.*, Lepanto 1571. When so used the sides were raised to protect the rowers.

Gallic Acid, obtained from gall nuts, sumach, tea, coffee, and the seeds of the mango, is used in the manufacture of inks and as an astringent in medicine. It was discovered by C. W. Scheele (1742–86), a Swedish chemist.

Gallium, metallic element, no. 31, symbol Ga, related to aluminium, but which can be cut with a knife. It was discovered spectroscopically by L. de Boisbaudran in 1875. Long before Mendeleyev had predicted that an element with its properties would be found to fill the then existing gap in the Periodic Table; this gap came immediately below aluminium, so he suggested the name "eka aluminium" for it.

Gallup Poll, a system, introduced by Dr. Gallup in the United States, for testing public opinion on topical subjects by taking a test poll on ques-tions framed to elicit opinions.

Galvanised Iron is iron coated with zinc. The name comes from the fact that such a coat protective against rust could be deposited electrolytically. Electrodeposition is some-times used, but the cheaper and more common process depends on dipping the iron in a bath of molten zinc.

Gamboge, a resinous gum obtained from the sap of *Garcinia morella*, a tree native to Thailand, Cambodia and Sri Lanka, and used as a yellow pigment in paints and also as a purgative.

Game is the term applied to wild animals which are protected from indiscriminate slaughter by Game Laws. In the United Kingdom game comprehends deer, hares, pheasants, partridges, grouse, black game, moor game, woodcocks, bustards and certain other birds and animals of the chase. Game can only be killed (with few exceptions) by persons holding game licences. Occupiers of land and one other person author-ised by them in each case are allowed to kill hares and rabbits on their land without licence. Game cannot be sold except by a person hold-ing a proper licence. There is a "close time" prescribed for the different classes of game; for instance, the selling or exposing for sale of any hare or leveret during March, April, May, June or July is prohibited by law. Grouse cannot be shot between 11 December and 11 August; partridges between 2 February and 31 August; pheasants between 2 February and 30 Septem-ber; and black game between 11 December and 10 August. In regard to foxes and stags, custom prescribes a certain law which sportsmen observe. Game reserves are legally protected areas where natural vegetation and wild life are allowed to remain unmolested by sportsmen or those who might destroy for economic ends.

Gaming, *or* **Gambling**—*i.e.*, staking money on the chances of a game—differs from betting in that it depends upon the result of a trial of skill or a turn of chance. The Betting and Gaming Act of 1959, passed by the Macmillan administra-tion, replaced all the old laws on gaming, which went back to an Act of 1541 entitled "An Acte for Mayntenance of Artyllarie and debarringe

of unlauful games", under which some games were unlawful if played for money in any cir-cumstances. Roulette and any game of dice were among such games. Under the 1959 Act any game was lawful, subject to certain con-ditions. Since then the Betting, Gaming and Lotteries Act, 1963, and the Gaming Act, 1968, have been passed, to deal with unlawful gaming and to prevent the exploitation of gaming by commercial interests. The playing of bingo is now restricted to clubs licensed for bingo only. The Gaming Board in its evidence to the Royal Commission on Gambling (1976) recommended a new Gambling Authority or Commission to ensure that any legalised gambling is not pen-etrated by criminals.

Gammexane, a powerful insecticide, used par-ticularly to kill the tsetse fly and mosquito.

Gangue. Useless minerals associated with metal-lic ores.

Gannet, a fish-eating bird which dives on its prey from a great height, swallowing it under water, is found in large numbers off the coast of Scot-land, and has breeding stations in the Hebrides, St. Kilda, Ailsa Craig, the Bass Rock, Grass-holme Island and on Ortac and Les Etacs (rocks off Alderney). It is a bird of white plumage, black tips to long narrow wings and wedge-shaped tail, and weighs about 3 kg. The gan-net breeds in colonies on ledges of steep, rocky, island cliffs. Related to the cormorants, peli-cans and frigate-birds.

Garden Cities in England were founded by Ebenezer Howard (1850–1928), and his ideas were put forward in his book *Tomorrow—A Peaceful Path to Real Reform* (later re-issued as *Garden Cities of Tomorrow*). New towns should be so placed and planned as to get the best of town and country life, an adaptation of the model villages of certain industrial philan-thropists such as Salt, Richardson, Cadbury, Leverhulme and others. The Garden City Association (later the Town and Country Planning Association) was formed in 1899, and the first garden city was begun at Letchworth in 1903 and successfully established. Welwyn Garden City was also Howard's foundation, established in 1919.

Gardener-Bird, a bird possessing many of the characteristics of the bower bird, and found only in Papua–New Guinea. *See also* **Bower Bird.**

Gargantua, the giant hero of Rabelais' satire, of immense eating and drinking capacity, sym-bolical of an antagonistic ideal of the greed of the Church.

Gargoyle, a projecting spout for carrying off water from the roof gutter of a building. Gargoyles are only found in old structures, modern water-pipe systems having rendered them unnecessary. In Gothic architecture they were turned to architectural account and made to take all kinds of grotesque forms—grinning goblins, hideous monsters, dragons and so forth.

Garlic, a bulbous plant of the same genus as the onion and the leek, and a favourite condiment among the people of Southern Europe. It possesses a very strong odour and pungent taste and its culinary use is agelong.

Garnet, a group of minerals; chemically they are orthosilicates of the metals calcium, mag-nesium, titanium, iron, aluminium. Garnets can be coloured yellow, brown, black, green or red; the blood-red garnet is an important gem-stone.

Garrotte, a method of strangulation used as capital punishment in Spain, and consisting of a collar which is compressed by a screw that causes death by piercing the spinal marrow. Garrot-ting was also applied to a system of highway robbery common in England in 1862–63, the assailants seizing their victims from behind, and by a sudden compression of the windpipe disabling them until the robbery was completed.

Garter. The Most Noble Order of the Garter was founded (c. 1348) by King Edward III, and is the premier order of knighthood in Great Britain. The traditional story associating the garter and the motto with the Countess of Salisbury, who it was said dropped her garter while dancing with the King, who remarked "honi soit qui mal y pense" cannot be ac-cepted. The order was originally limited to the

Sovereign and 25 knights, but the number has been extended, and it may now be bestowed on royal personages and leading representatives of the British peerage. The insignia of the order are the garter of dark-blue velvet with the motto in letters of gold, the mantle of dark-blue velvet lined with white silk, the surcoat and hood, and the gold-and-enamel collar. The garter is worn on the left leg below the knee and by women as a sash over the left shoulder. *See* **Knighthood.**

Gas is an elastic fluid substance, the molecules of which are in constant rapid motion, and exerting pressure. The technique whereby gases are liquefied depends on increasing pressure and diminishing temperature. Each gas has a critical point; unless the temperature is brought down to this point no amountt of pressure will bring about liquefaction. Last gas to be liquefied was helium (1908) which boils at $-209°C$.

Gas from coal was first used as an illuminating agent by William Murdoch towards the end of the 18th cent. in Birmingham, and about 1807 was introduced in London, one side of Pall Mall being lighted with it. It became widely used as an illuminant, and for space heating and cooking. In the U.K. increasing attention has been paid to the use of a primary fuel—natural gas—instead of producing gas from coal or oil. *See* **Gas, Natural.**

Gas, Natural, natural mixture of gases often present with deposits of petroleum, found issuing from the ground in many parts of the world—in the oilfields of Venezuela and the Caucasus, in China, Saudi Arabia, but chiefly in North America. Its chief component is methane. Large industrial centres have made use of this gas since the latter part of the 19th cent., but much of this valuable fuel still goes to waste. Pipelines have been constructed to deliver the gas to where it is wanted. Britain began to ship liquid methane from the Saharan oilfield in 1964. Some of the world's largest natural gas fields have recently been discovered in the North Sea and are being actively exploited. Domestic gas appliances have to be modified if the natural product is substituted for ordinary town gas because the burning characteristics are different. Oil production from the North Sea fields began in 1975 and the main single source of gas in the UK is now natural gas.

Gas Turbine. In this kind of engine mechanical movement is produced by a jet of gas impinging on a turbine wheel; used in aeroplanes, locomotives and ships. These engines are mechanically simple compared with internal combustion engines, and require less maintenance.

Gauge, a standard dimension or measurement, applied in various branches of construction. Thus the standard railway gauge is 4 ft $8\frac{1}{2}$ in (143·5 cm) in the UK, USA and most European countries. The Soviet Union uses the broader gauge of 5 ft (152 cm). Narrow railway gauges of different standards are in use on very steep inclines in various countries. Other standard gauges are fixed in building and gun-boring.

Gauls were inhabitants of ancient Gaul, the country which comprised what is now France, Belgium and parts of the Netherlands, Switzerland and Germany.

Gault, a stratum of blue clay between the Lower Greensand and the Chalk. A typical section of the Gault can be seen at Folkestone.

Gauss, a unit of magnetic induction in the c.g.s. system, named after the great German mathematician and astronomer, K. F. Gauss.

Gavelkind, an old English custom of land tenure in Kent and other places in England, whereby on the death. intestate, of a property owner his property is divided equally among his children and not according to the law of primogeniture. Abolished by the Law of Property Act, 1922, and the Administration of Estates Act, 1925.

Gazelles, a group of small, graceful antelopes which live in the drier regions of Africa and Asia. They can run very fast: speeds of over 64 km/h have been recorded.

Geiger Counter, an electrical device, invented by Geiger, which can detect individual atomic particles, *e.g.*, electrons, protons, etc. It often consists of a tube of gas at a few cm Hg pressure, fitted with two electrodes—a cylinder and an axial wire. A high voltage is kept across the

electrodes, and the passage of a charged particle through the gas releases ions which permit a momentary discharge between the electrodes. Electronic circuits register this discharge as a "count". Geiger counters are used to detect and measure radioactivity and cosmic rays both for technical and research purposes.

Gelatine, a transparent, tasteless, organic substance obtained from animal membranes, bones, tendons, etc., by boiling in water. It is of various kinds, according to the substance used in making it. Isinglass, the purest form of it, is made from air-bladders and other membranes of fish, while the coarser kind—glue—is made from hoofs, skin, hides, etc. Its constituents are carbon, hydrogen, oxygen and nitrogen. Gelatine is applied to an immense variety of purposes, from the making of food jellies to photographic materials.

Gemsbok, a large South African antelope of the open dry plains, sandy coloured with black and white markings on its face, and with long straight horns.

General, a military title next in rank to that of Field-Marshal, the highest officer in the army. Ranking below full General are Lieutenant-General, Major-General and Brigadier.

Generation, a time-measure reckoned at about 30 years when children are ready to replace parents; also the body of persons existing at the same time or period. According to a UN report in 1958 "one can no longer think of generations in traditional terms. Interests and activities are today changing so fast that sets of young people not more than seven or eight years apart in age may be as far apart in their thinking and behaviour as two generations once were." The generation gap is now even fewer years apart.

Generation, Spontaneous. *See* **Abiogenesis.**

Genes, the elementary units of heredity. They exist as highly differentiated regions arranged along the length of the chromosomes which the nuclei of cells carry. A chromosome may carry hundreds or even thousands of genes, each with its own particular structure and specific properties. The position of a particular gene on a chromosome is called its locus. The material of the gene is DNA (*q.v.*). *See* **F34.**

Genesis, the first book of the Pentateuch, compiled in the 5th cent. B.C. from earlier documents, which carries the scriptural narrative from the creation to the death of Joseph. Sometimes there is disagreement, as in the story of the creation, Gen. i and ii. Gen. i reflects the views of the ancient Greek scientist Thales (*c.* 640–546 B.C.) and may be said to be the first scientific account of the creation of the world. The conditions described around the figures of Abraham, Isaac, Jacob and Joseph have a genuine historical basis.

Genetic Code. The elucidation of the structure of DNA (*q.v.*) for which Crick, Wilkins and Watson were jointly awarded the 1962 Nobel Prize for medicine, revealed the code or chemical dictionary out of which messages serving as blueprints for living structures can be made. *See* **Protein synthesis, F34.**

Genetic Engineering is the name given to the introduction of human choice and design criteria into the construction and combination of genes. This refers not to breeding by selection, a traditional process, but to the biochemical alteration of the actual DNA in cells (*see* **Section F, Part IV**) so as to produce novel self-reproducing organisms. Such manipulations became possible when techniques were recently discovered for severing and rejoining DNA molecules and inserting sections into them. Many people regard this development as fraught with enormous significance. Like nuclear power, it can lead to good, to evil, and to accidental hazards, not all of which can be foreseen. Thus when biologists realised they could create new lifeforms, *e.g.*, bacteria, with novel genes, they appreciated that, as well as medically beneficial strains, new virulent forms might by accident be produced and escape into the world. Ultimately, not imminently, men may be able to design the genes of higher animals and even of man himself and thus consciously influence biological evolution. Many scientists have been brought by these possibilities up against an old problem: is science going too far too fast?

Genetics. See **F30(2)**.

Geneva Convention, an agreement made by the European Powers at Geneva in 1864, establishing humane regulations regarding the treatment of the sick and wounded in war and the status of those who minister to them. All persons, hospitals, hospital ships are required to display the Geneva cross—a red cross on a white ground. A second conference held at Geneva in 1868 drew up a supplementary agreement. An important result of this Convention was the establishment of the Red Cross Society in 1870.

Genocide is an international crime, defined by the General Assembly of the United Nations in 1948 as "acts committed with intent to destroy, in whole or in part a national, ethnic, racial or religious group as such". The UN Convention came into force in 1951.

Genus, a term applied in biology to designate a group of similar species. A group of similar genera is called a family. See **F35(2)**.

Geodesy, the science of calculating the configuration and extent of the earth's surface, and determining exact geographical positions and directions, with variations of gravity etc. Land-surveying is a branch of geodesy.

Geography, science concerned with the spatial organisation of natural features and life and man-made artifacts upon and immediately above the surface of the earth. It is increasingly concerned with the processes by which such patterns are generated and this concern is leading to both a greater degree of specialisation within the subject and the merging of its constituent parts with related disciplines of economics, sociology, political science, geology, biology and meteorology.

Geology, the science which deals with the condition and structure of the earth, and the evidence afforded of ancient forms of life. The geological strata are classified in the following categories: *Primary* or *Palaeozoic* (the oldest fossil-bearing rocks including the Cambrian, Ordovician, Silurian, Devonian, Carboniferous, Permian); *Secondary* or *Mesozoic* (Triassic, Jurassic, Cretaceous); *Tertiary* or *Cainozoic* (Eocene, Oligocene, Miocene, Pliocene, Pleistocene); *Post tertiary* (most recent rocks). See **F48**.

Geometrical Progression is a term used to indicate a succession of numbers which increase or decrease at an equal ratio—as 3, 9, 27; or 64, 16, 4.

Geometry is the branch of mathematics which demonstrates the properties of figures, and the distances of points of space from each other by means of deductions. It is a science of reason from fundamental axioms, and was perfected by Euclid about 300 B.C. The books of Euclid contain a full elucidation of the science, though supplemented in modern times by Descartes, Newton and Carnot. Of recent years non-Euclidean geometry has been developed.

Geophysics, the branches of physics which are concerned with the earth and its atmosphere. Meteorology, geomagnetism, aurora and air-glow, ionosphere, solar activity, cosmic rays, glaciology, oceanography, seismology, nuclear radiation in the atmosphere, rockets and satellites—all these are geophysical subjects. The object of the International Geophysical Year, 1957–58, was to investigate the physical phenomena occurring on and around the earth by means of carefully co-ordinated observations made simultaneously all over the globe.

Geothermal Energy. Some of the heavy elements within the earth's crust are radioactive and this gives rise to a temperature rise towards the centre of the earth. The practical exploitation of this geothermal energy comes about when there are hot springs or geysers. It is believed that these are caused by rainwater slowly percolating down to the hot rocks and blowing out as steam. The homes of people living in Reykjavik are heated by geothermal steam and there are a number of small power stations in various parts of the world. Although the costs in the few cases where geothermal power has actually been exploited are remarkably low, the expense of drilling, etc., required when attempting to exploit the heat in the rocks

where surface manifestations do not occur, is likely to limit the use of this source of power.

Geothermal Heating. The earth's interior is hot and in certain localities, often adjacent to volcanic or earthquake-prone regions, reservoirs of hot water or steam exist at accessible depths. Natural hot geysers occur in many such places and people, *e.g.*, the ancient Romans and present-day Japanese, use natural hot water for bathing, cooking and laundry. Occasionally the subterranean reserves permit large-scale power generation by drilling for hot steam and passing it into turbines to produce electricity. Pioneering work on this was done at Lardarello in Italy which can produce hundreds of megawatts. Other sites are in New Zealand, California, Japan and Iceland. There are possibilities in S.W. England.

Germanium. A grey, hard, brittle chemical element, no. 32, symbol Ge, chemically related to silicon and tin. Discovered by Winkler in 1886. Its richest ore is germanite containing 6% of the metal. Coal is also a relatively rich source. Since 1948 it has assumed great importance as a semi-conducting material for making transistors (*q.v.*). Because of this it has been so intensively studied that more is known about its physical properties than about those of any other element.

Gesta Romanorum (Latin = deeds of the Romans), a mediaeval collection of Latin stories of unknown authorship which circulated widely in Europe during the Middle Ages. First printed in the 15th cent. The stories were used by Chaucer, Shakespeare and other writers who found many romantic incidents and legends which they were able to turn to good account.

Gestation, the carrying of young in animals during pregnancy, varies considerably in its length. In the case of an elephant, the period is 21 months; a camel, 12 months; a cow, 9 months; a cat, 8 weeks; a horse, 48 weeks; a dog, 9 weeks; and a pig, 16 weeks. Hens "sit" for 21 days; geese, 30; swans, 42; turkeys, 28; pigeons, 18.

Geysers, hot springs of volcanic origination and action, are remarkable for the fact that they throw out huge streams of boiling water instead of lava as in the case of a volcano. The most famous geysers are those of Iceland, which number over a hundred, the principal one having an opening of 21 m in diameter and discharging a column of water to a height of 61 m. There are also geysers in the Yellowstone region of America, and some in New Zealand.

Ghost-Moth or **Ghost Swift,** an interesting nocturnal insect (*Hepialus humuli*) common in England, possessing in the male a white collar and known for its habit of hovering with a pendulum-like action in the twilight over a particular spot where the female is concealed.

Gibbon, the name of a long-armed ape mainly inhabiting S.E. Asia. It is without tail, and possesses the power of very rapid movement among the trees of the forests.

Gin, a well-known spirit distilled from malt or barley and flavoured with the juniper berry. The principal varieties are the English and American, known as "Gin" or "Dry Gin", and the Dutch, referred to as "jenever" or "Hollandse jenever". In Germany and Austria it is called "Schnapps". The word "Gin" is an abbreviation of "Geneva", both being primarily derived from the French genièvre (juniper).

Giraffe, the tallest of existing animals, reaching a height of from 5–6 m when full grown. Its sloping back and elongated neck seem to be the natural evolution of an animal that has to feed on the branches of trees. It is a native of Africa, is of a light fawn colour marked with darker spots and has a prehensile tongue.

Giralda, a beautiful and remarkable example of Arabian art, erected in 1195 at Seville, still in existence.

Glaciers form in the higher Alpine ranges, and are immense consolidated masses of snow, which are gradually impelled by their force down the mountain-sides until they reach a point where the temperature causes them to melt, and they run off in streams. From such glaciers the five great rivers, the Rhine, the Po, the Rhône, the Inn and the Adige, have their source. The longest of the Swiss glaciers is the Gross Aletsch, which sometimes extends over 16 km. Some of the glaciers of the Himalayas are four times as long. The Muir in Alaska is of enormous magnitude, and that of Justedlals Brae in Norway is the largest in Europe.

Gladiators were professional athletes and combatants in ancient Rome, contesting with each other or with wild beasts. At first they were drawn from the slave and prisoner classes exclusively, but so much were the successful gladiators held in esteem that men came to make a profession of athletics, and gladiatorial training schools were established. When a gladiator was vanquished without being killed in combat, it was left with the spectators to decide his fate, death being voted by holding the hands out with the thumb turned inward, and life by putting forth the hands with the thumb extended. Gladiatorial shows were the chief public displays in Rome from the 3rd to the 4th cent. A.D.

Glass is an amorphous, man-made substance, fluid when hot, solid, though fragile, when cooled. It is made of sand mixed with an alkaline flux, usually soda or potash. While hot, glass can be formed into almost any shape by moulding, blowing or, since the early 19th cent., by machine pressing. Unrefined glass normally has a greenish tinge, due to the iron content of most sands, but it is transparent or at least translucent. To make truly colourless glass is a difficult and expensive process, and such glass resembling the natural mineral, rock crystal, is given the name crystal. Glass can be tinted by the addition of various metallic oxides, cobalt producing blue, manganese mauve, etc. Because it is at once solid and transparent, glass is the perfect material for windows for which it has been used since Roman times. And since it can be made cheaply and is easy to clean, it has been used for containers in homes, shops and pharmacies, again since Roman days. Glass can also be made into things of beauty, by the use of coloured glass and by cutting, engraving, painting and gilding. The earliest vessels of glass so far found come from Egypt and date back to *c.* 1500 B.C. With the invention of glass-blowing in the 1st cent. A.D., the use of glass spread throughout the Roman empire. Many varieties were made, including superb art glass like the Portland vase (*q.v.*) The Arabs were great glassmakers from the 7th to 15th cent. During the Renaissance the Venetians created luxurious art glass, rich in colour and often manipulated into fantastic forms, Bohemia's 17th-cent. glass is wonderfully engraved with pictures and cut into glittering facets. During the 1670s in England George Ravenscroft invented a new, heavy, water-clear crystal, with an addition of lead as the magic ingredient, and English lead glass is still the basis for all modern crystals.

Glass-Snake, genus, *Ophisaurus*, of legless lizards with long fragile tails capable of re-generation when broken. Six species are known; in S.E. Europe, S.W. Asia, Indo-China and N. America. Attains a length of about 60 cm; main colouring, green, with black and yellow markings.

Glauconite. A green mineral, chemically a hydrated silicate of potassium and iron. Commonly found in marine sands (hence these rocks are known as "greensands") and sandstones.

Glaucus is a curious genus of sea slugs often called the Sea Lizard belonging to the molluscs. It is without shell and has a soft body, with horny mouth and four tentacles. It is a native of the Atlantic, and is not more than 30 cm in length.

Glee, an unaccompanied piece for three or more voices. Glee-singing was popular in England during the 18th and early 19th cent. and glee-clubs are still in existence.

Globigerina, an oceanic unicellular animalcule with a perforated shell, and occurring in certain parts of the Atlantic in such vast numbers as to form a bed of chalk ooze with their empty shells.

Glockenspiel, an instrument composed of metal bars each of which is tuned to a note. The bars are struck by hand-hammers and give forth chiming sounds.

Glow-worm, a beetle, possessing the power (much stronger in the female than the male) of emitting phosphorescent light from the hind end of the body. The female is wingless.

Glucinium. See **Beryllium.**

Glucose, Dextrose or **Grape Sugar** is a carbohydrate (*q.v.*). It is produced by hydrolysis from cane sugar, dextrine, starch, cellulose, etc., by the action of reagents. It also occurs in many plants, fruits and honey. For brewing purposes glucose is prepared by the conversion of starch by sulphuric acid. Malt also converts starch into glucose.

Glutton or **Wolverine,** the biggest animal of the weasel family, inhabits the northernmost parts of Europe and America. In build it resembles the bear, and is rather larger than a badger. Its fur is of a brown-black hue, but coarse.

Glycerine or **Glycerol,** occurs in natural fats combined with fatty acids, and is obtained by decomposing those substances with alkalis or by superheated steam. It is colourless and oily and sweet, and is put to a variety of commercial uses, being widely utilised for medicaments, for lubricating purposes, and in the manufacture of nitro-glycerine.

Glycols. Organic compounds containing two alcohol groups. Ethylene glycol is the most widely known example; it is used as an anti-freeze in motor-car radiators on account of its property of greatly reducing the freezing point of water. Also used in the manufacture of "Terylene". See **Esters.**

Glyptodon, an extinct species of gigantic armadillo, fossil remains of which have been discovered in S. America. It was some 2·7 m long, carried a huge tortoise-like shell and had fluted teeth.

Gneiss, a metamorphic rock usually containing quartz, felspar and mica. It is banded, the light-coloured minerals being concentrated apart from the dark minerals.

Gnosticism. See **Section J.**

Gnu or **Wildebeest,** a large antelope from Africa south of the Sahara, distinguished by its excessively short thick neck and large head with a pronounced roman nose. There are two species; the white-tailed gnu is almost extinct, the brindled gnu is still common and migrates in large herds.

Goat-Moth (*Cossus cossus*), a large moth of the *Cossidae* family, common in Britain, evil-smelling and very destructive in the larval stage to trees of the poplar and willow genus, into the wood of which the caterpillar bores during its three years' period of development.

Goats are horned ruminant quadrupeds, indigenous to the Eastern Hemisphere, but now domesticated in all parts of the world. Though related to the sheep, they are a much hardier and more active animal. The male has a tuft of hair under the chin. Many species, including those of Cashmere and Angora, are valuable for their hair, which is used for fine textile fabrics. The milk of the goat is nutritive, and goat-skins are in good demand for leather for gloves, shoes, etc.

God and **Man.** See **Section J.**

Gog and **Magog,** two legendary City of London giants, supposed to be the offspring of certain wicked daughters of the Emperor Diocletian and a band of demons. They were brought captive to London and made to serve as prisoners at the Palace of Brute, which stood on the site of Guildhall. Effigies of the giants have stood in Guildhall since the time of Henry V. They were destroyed in the Great Fire of 1666, replaced in 1672 and used to be carried through the streets of London in the Lord Mayor's Show. The present figures, carved in lime wood by Mr. David Evans, replaced those carved in 1708 by Richard Saunders, which were destroyed in an air raid during the last war.

Gold. Metallic element, no. 79, symbol Au (Latin *Aurum*) related to silver and copper, the coinage metals. The greatest amount of gold is obtained by treating gold-bearing quartz by the cyanide process. The gold is dissolved out by cyanide solution, which is then run into long boxes filled with zinc shavings when the gold is precipitated as a black slime. This is melted with an oxidising agent which removes the zinc.

Gold-Beaters' Skin is the outside membrane of the large intestine of the ox, specially prepared and used by gold-beaters for placing between the leaves of gold while they beat them. Thin membrane is of great tenacity, and gets beaten to such extreme thinness that it is used to put on cuts and bruises.

Gold Standard. Under the gold-standard system which was widely prevalent up to 1941, each gold-standard country fixed the value of its currency in terms of a weight of gold of a certain fineness and was, broadly speaking, ready to exchange its currency freely for gold, which could then be exported without restriction. This involved keeping a gold reserve big enough to meet all likely demands and also to serve as a backing for the issue of notes. The gold standard had to be given up during the first world war; and though it was in substance restored in Great Britain in 1925 (when Churchill was Chancellor), the restoration was never complete, as the gold reserve remained too small for complete freedom to export to be practicable. Sterling had to be devalued in the financial crisis of 1931 (which brought about the fall of the Labour Government) and Great Britain was forced off the gold standard. Imbalance in payments between countries is financed by transfers of gold or foreign exchange. Such reserves are known as international liquidity. *See also* **Section G, Parts II and IV.**

Goldeneye, a species of wild duck, widely distributed over Arctic regions. It is a passage-migrant and winter-visitor to the British Isles. Has nested in Cheshire. Distinguished by a large white spot in front of each eye on a dark ground.

Golden Dawn. *See* **Section J.**

Golden Number, the number of any year in the metonic cycle of 19 years, deriving its name from the fact that in the old calendars it was always printed in gold. It is found by adding 1 to the number of the year A.D. and dividing by 19, the remainder being the Golden Number; or, if no remainder, the Golden Number is 19. The only use to which the Golden Number is put now is in making ecclesiastical calculations for determining movable feasts.

Goldsmiths Company, one of the richest London City Companies; the official assayers of gold and silver, invested with the power of "hall-marking" the quality of objects made from these metals. First charter granted in 1327.

Gondola, the old regulation black boats so common on the canals of Venice, propelled by a gondolier with one oar who stands at the stern. The covered part in the centre (*felze*) is rarely seen nowadays as most passengers are tourists who want to see the city.

Gonfalon, the pennon affixed to a lance, spear or standard, consisting usually of two or three streamers and made to turn like a weather-cock.

Gophers. Rodent mammals. The pocket gophers are stout-bodied burrowers common in the USA. The slender burrowing gophers, also called "ground squirrels", occur in central and western USA. The sisel or suslik is a related European species. They are a great pest among grain crops.

Gordon Riots of 1780 were an anti-popery agitation fomented by Lord George Gordon. Called also "No-Popery Riots".

Gorilla, the largest of the anthropoid apes, found in the forests of Equatorial Africa, and at maturity standing from 1·2–1·5 m high.

Goshawk (*Accipiter gentilis*), a diurnal bird of prey, fearless and extremely agile; loves wooded country and is very destructive of poultry and game-birds. It resembles the peregrine falcon in appearance, but has shorter, rounded wings. This bird was a great favourite of falconers in mediaeval times.

Gospels are those portions of the New Testament which deal with the life, death, resurrection and teachings of Christ. They are the gospels of Matthew, Mark, Luke and John, all compiled in the later part of the 1st cent. The first three are called the *synoptic gospels* because of their general unity of narrative. Mark was the first to be written and John the last, and it is to Mark that one should turn for the most reliable source of knowledge of the life of Jesus. The word *gospel* comes from two Anglo-Saxon words *gode* (good) and *spell* (tidings), a translation of the Greek *evangelion* = evangel, evangelist.

Gothic, the predominant style of architecture in northern Europe from 12th–15th cent. Its most striking characteristic is the extensive use of the pointed arch, but this is really a mere external reflection of the important structural invention of the 12th cent., that of the rib vault, whereby the whole pressure of the stone vaulting is supported on slim ribs which cross each other at a rising centre. On the outside of the building, the pressure from the vaults is caught up and supported by flying buttresses. A complete Gothic construction gives a marvellous effect of airy lightness, also of something striving upwards, towards the heavens, and this is further accentuated when the churches are crowned by lofty towers and spires. The vital structural elements of Gothic architecture were first put into use in the abbey church of St. Denis in Paris *c.* 1140. The style was further developed in a glorious sequence of cathedrals in northern France: Notre Dame in Paris, Rheims, Amiens, Beauvais and others. When, as in Chartres, the windows are filled with stained glass of glowing colours and the doorways flanked with magnificently carved life-size figures of saints and apostles, the whole effect is one of unsurpassed solemnity and grandeur. From France the style spread to other lands in each of which it developed its own characteristics; thus the English churches tended to have massive towers and delicate spires and, as at Salisbury, were often set in open grounds surrounded by lawns; Flemish and Dutch churches were sometimes built of brick as were those in north Germany and Scandinavia; in Spain the Flamboyant style was followed. The main Gothic cathedral in Italy, that of Milan, although begun in 1386 was not completed until the early 19th cent. Late English Gothic is seen, for example, at King's College Chapel, Cambridge, Henry's Chapel at Westminster and St. George's Chapel at Windsor (all *c.* 1500). Gothic is also found in secular buildings, *e.g.*, Little Wenham Hall in Suffolk, the castle at Ghent, the town halls of Louvain and Middelburg and the streets of Gothic houses in Bruges still in use today. Virtually Gothic as a style (excluding the "Gothic revival" of 19th cent. England) ended at the close of the 15th cent. Gothic art is best seen in the illuminated manuscripts of the 13th and 14th cent. and in the church sculpture. Its characteristic is a complete departure from the cool, perfectionist realism of classical times with distortion to produce emotional effects. The human figures are not ideal forms but recognisable as people we might meet in the street: yet there was also the element of wild imagination, intricate design and a wealth of feeling which might be grotesque, humorous, macabre, or even obscene. Gothic style also found expression in the decorative arts, retaining its architectural character even in small-scale works like caskets, chalices and the like in metalwork and ivory.

Goths. A Teutonic people who originally came from southern Sweden (Gotland) and by the 3rd cent. were settled in the region north of the Black Sea. They began to encroach on the Roman Empire and early in the 4th cent. split into two divisions: the "wise" Goths or Visigoths between the Danube and the Dniester (referred to as the West Goths), and the "bright" Goths or Ostrogoths in southern Russia on the Dnieper (referred to as the East Goths). The Ostrogoths were conquered by the Huns *c.* 370, while the Visigoths under Alaric devastated Greece and sacked Rome in 410. Eventually the Visigoths spread to France and Spain and their last king Roderick fell in battle against the Moors in 711. The Ostrogoths regained their independence on the death of Attila in 453 and under their king Theodoric the Great conquered Italy in 493. They lost their identity after Justinian regained Italy, 525–552.

Gourd Family *or* **Cucurbitaceae.** This family of about 650 species of flowering plants includes the gourds, pumpkins, cantaloupes, cucumber, gherkin, water-melon and squashes. Most abundant in the tropics, the cucurbits are mainly climbing annuals with very rapid growth. The bathroom loofah is the skeleton of one cucurbit fruit, *Luffa cylindrica*. The squirting cucumber is another member of the family.

Governor. A device attached to an engine, turbine, compressor, etc., which automatically controls the engine's speed in accordance with power demand. Most governors depend upon the centrifugal action of two or more balls which are thrown outwards as their speed of rotation increases and actuate a throttle valve or cut-off. The centrifugal governor was invented by Thomas Mead, patented by him in 1787. Watt adapted it to the steam engine.

Grail, Legend of the Holy, a tale of Celtic origin which became part of Arthurian legend and the subject of many mediaeval quest-romances. According to the Christian version the grail was the cup which Christ used at the Last Supper, brought to England by St. Joseph of Arimathea.

Grand Prix, the "French Derby" was established by Napoleon III, in 1863. It is the chief French race and is an international competition of three-year-olds.

Granite is a coarsely crystalline igneous rock consisting of quartz and alkali felspars plus mica or hornblende. It is a much used ornamental and building stone; it forms the high ground of Dartmoor and Bodmin Moor.

Graphite or **Plumbago,** commonly called blacklead, is a form of carbon occurring in foliated masses in marble, schist, etc. It is soft, will make black marks on paper or other plain surfaces, and is mainly used for lead pencils. It is also a valuable lubricant. Pure graphite has found a new use with the construction of atomic piles. Important deposits occur in Siberia, Sri Lanka, Malagasy, Canada and USA.

Graptolites, fossil animals confined to Cambrian, Ordovician and Silurian strata. Once classified as hydrazoa but now considered more likely to be hemichordates.

Grasshopper. There are many species of these leaping insects which are related to the locusts and crickets. Most are vegetarians; some eat flies and caterpillars also. The chirping sound they make is made by scraping the hind legs against the wings; in some species a noise is produced by rubbing the wings together.

Gravitation. One of the four, possibly five, types of force known to physics. The others are electromagnetic, nuclear (two types) and colour forces. Gravitational forces are an attraction that one piece of matter has for another; they dominate astronomical phenomena, but inside the atom they are negligible compared with the other types of force. Einstein's General Theory of Relativity is the only theory at present extant which attempts to interpret gravitational forces in terms of more fundamental concepts. See **F15(1), 18(2).**

Graylag, the ordinary wild grey goose of Europe, the species from which domestic geese are derived; frequents fens and marshes; breeds in Iceland, Scandinavia and Scotland; distinguished by pinkish legs and feet and lack of black markings on bill.

Grebe, a diving bird of beautiful plumage found over a great part of the world on lakes and oceans. The two species familiar in Great Britain are the Dabchick or Little Grebe and the large and handsome Great Crested Grebe, which has a feathery tuft, lost in the autumn, on each side of the head. Grebes have remarkable courtship displays. The breast feathers are of a downy softness and silver lustre, for which they were formerly much hunted.

Greek Art. See **Hellenic Art.**

Greek Fire, a combustible supposed to have been composed of sulphur, nitre, naphtha and asphalt, used with destructive effect by the Greeks of the Eastern Empire in their wars.

Greek Kalends, equivalent to never, as only the Romans, not the Greeks, had kalends.

Green Revolution. The "green revolution" is principally due to the American agricultural expert, Dr. Norman Borlaug, who worked in Mexico on the development of new improved strains of wheat, rice, maize and other cereals. The application of new plant varieties transformed the agricultural prospects of India, Pakistan, Sri Lanka, Mexico, the Philippines and other underdeveloped countries; food importers turned into exporters. However of late the inequity in the distribution of fertilisers has affected the grain production of these countries. For his pioneering work Dr. Borlaug was awarded the 1970 Nobel peace prize. See **Section G, Part III.**

Greenwich Mean Time. The first Nautical Almanac, for the use of navigators and astronomers, was published by the Astronomer Royal in 1767. It was based on the meridian at Greenwich, with longitude measured east and west of $0°$. A master clock, which still exists, was built at Greenwich Observatory in 1852 to control the railway station clocks and Greenwich Mean Time, or Railway Time as it was sometimes called, prevailed. In 1884 Greenwich was chosen as the prime meridian of the world and GMT became known as Universal Time. The time-keeping role is now to be done by the International Bureau of Weights and Measures. GMT will become CUT (Coordinated Universal Time) See also **British Standard Time** and **F66.**

Gregorian Calendar. See **Calendar.**

Gresham's Law states that if money, i.e., money with the higher intrinsic value, and bad money are in circulation together, the bad money will tend to drive out the good money from circulation. For instance, the good money is more likely to be melted down or demanded in payment by foreign creditors.

Gretna Green, a celebrated village in Annandale and Eskdale, just over the border from England, where runaway marriages were performed from 1754 to 1856, though only completely stopped during present century.

Griffin, in ancient mythology, a winged creature with an eagle's head and the body of a lion, found in ancient sculptures of Persia and Assyria. Its origin is traced to the Hittites.

Grilse, a young salmon that has only been once to the sea.

Grimm's Law, formulated by Jacob Grimm, an eminent German philologist, lays down a principle of consonantal change in the Germanic languages. For instance, Lat. pater, Eng. father, Ger. Vater; Lat. frater, Eng. brother, Ger. Bruder; Lat. decem, Eng. ten, Ger. zehn.

Grogram (French = gros grain), a kind of rough fabric made of wool and some other fibre, such as silk, mohair or cotton, formerly much used for commoner kinds of wearing apparel.

Grotto, a natural or artificial cave. Among the most famous are the blue grotto of Capri and the grotto of Antiparos (Cyclades, Aegean).

Ground Wave, that part of the energy emitted by a radio transmitter which travels along the ground; as opposed to the sky wave which is reflected back to earth by the ionosphere. With the lower radio-frequencies, the ground wave can be picked up over several thousand miles; in the broadcasting band, over a hundred or so miles; it is virtually useless at high frequencies.

Grouse, game bird of the northern latitudes where some 20 species occur. They are stout, compact, ground-dwelling birds, protectively plumaged (the willow grouse turns white in winter), the male usually being larger and more brightly coloured than the female. The red grouse of the British moorlands has been introduced into Belgium and W. Germany. Of the same family are the blackcock, ptarmigan, capercaillie, American prairie-hen and the partridge. Grouse shooting begins in Britain on Aug. 12.

Guanaco, a large species of llama, common to South America, and utilised as a beast of burden.

Guano, the excrement of sea-birds, found in large quantities on the rocky islands of the western coasts of South America and Nauru Is. It forms a useful fertilising agent, being rich in phosphate and ammonia, and first came into use in 1841, since which time Peruvian guano has been a recognised article of commerce. Beds of guano from 15–18 m in thickness are not uncommon. Fish guano and bat guano from caves in South America and the Bahamas are also used as fertilisers.

Gudgeon, a small fresh-water fish of the carp family with 2 small barbels on the upper lip.

Guelph and Ghibelline, italianised forms of the German words "Welf" and "Waiblingen", the names of two rival princely families whose conflicts made much of the history of Germany and Italy during the Middle Ages. The feuds between these two factions continued in Italy during the campaigns of Emperor Frederick I, and later developed into the fierce struggles of the 13th cent. between emperor and pope. In Italy the Ghibellines supported the side of the German emperors and the Guelphs the cause of the Pope. The present Royal Family of England and other Northern monarchies are descended by different routes from the Guelph George I, Duke of Brunswick-Lüneburg of the House of Hanover.

Guildhall, the place of assembly of the members of a guild, and at one time, when guilds were in full strength, was practically the Town Hall. The London Guildhall is today the hall of meeting for the City of London Corporation.

Guilds for the fostering and protection of various trades have existed in England since Anglo-Saxon times, and from the 12th to the 16th cent. exercised great influence and enjoyed many privileges. There were trades' guilds and craftsmen's guilds, and in all large cities and towns there was a guild hall. Their successes in the Middle Ages led to many monopolistic abuses, and in the end it became necessary to free the country from their restrictive power. The City Guilds (Livery Companies of the City of London) derive their name from the distinctive dress assumed by their members in the 14th cent. There are 84 Guilds in existence.

Guild Socialism. *See* **Section J.**

Guillemot, a genus of sea-birds of the auk family, common in Northern Europe, two species—the Common Guillemot and the Black Guillemot—being natives of our own sea coasts, nesting on the cliffs. Brünnich's Guillemot, an Arctic species, is a rare straggler in the British Isles.

Guinea, an English gold coin of the value of twenty-one shillings, current from 1663-1817, and deriving its name from the first guinea coinage having been struck from gold obtained on the coast of Guinea.

Guinea-Pig, a rodent of the cavy family about 25 cm in length and with a tail so short that it does not project outside the body. It makes an excellent pet, though easily frightened. Its ancestors were species of the wild cavy of S. America said to have been domesticated by the Incas of Peru.

Gules, a heraldic term, denoting a rose of red tincture, indicated by vertical lines drawn or engraved without colour.

Gulf Stream is confined entirely to the western side of the N. Atlantic and is the warm-water current flowing through the Straits of Florida from the Gulf of Mexico parallel to the American coast up as far as Cape Hatteras. From there it continues north-eastwards as a slower, broader, cooler (yet even so, relatively warm) drift of water, merging with the North Atlantic Drift and losing its identity about 40° N. Lat., 60° W. Long. It is a common error to attribute the warmth of the British Isles and Western Europe generally to the Gulf Stream but this has no influence whatever except in so far as it feeds the North Atlantic Drift. Both the Gulf Stream and the North Atlantic Drift owe their movement to the direction of the prevailing winds, and it is the south-westerly airstream coming from warmer regions and passing over the surface waters of the Atlantic Drift that brings the warmth inland to influence the climate of Western Europe.

Gull. An extremely well-known, long-winged sea-bird with rather short legs and webbed feet. In almost all adults the body and tail are white whilst the back and most of the wings are grey or black. In the majority of cases the plumage of juveniles is partly or entirely dusky. Gulls are omnivorous, and are very useful as scavengers. They follow ships and quickly seize upon any refuse which may be thrown overboard. There are 44 species, which vary in size from moderately small to large. With certain exceptions, such as the Kittiwake in the North Atlantic, they are not found very far from land. They are sociable and mostly breed in colonies on cliff-ledges, on islands, beaches and sandhills and among vegetation in swamps, sometimes a long way from the sea. The nest is usually substantial, and the eggs generally number from two to three. Of the 29 species breeding in the northern hemisphere, 14 occur in the British Isles. The pure white Ivory Gull is the most northerly of birds. Sabine's and the Swallow-tailed Gull have forked tails. Ross's Gull has

a black ring round the neck and one species, Franklin's Gull, migrates from the North, where it breeds, to pass the winter in the Southern hemisphere.

Gums are glutinous compounds obtained from vegetable sources, soluble in cold or hot water, but not in alcohol. There are innumerable varieties. Gum Arabic is exuded from a species of acacia grown in Senegal, the Sudan, Arabia, India and other countries, and is a valuable commercial product, used in dyeing, ink-making, as a mucilage, and in medicine. India-rubber is an elastic gum. Gums are also made from starch, potatoes, wheat, etc., from seeds, bark, roots and weeds. Many so-called gums are resins.

Gun-Cotton, a powerful explosive manufactured by subjecting a prepared cotton to the prolonged action of a mixture of three parts sulphuric acid and one part of nitric acid. It burns without explosion on ignition, but by percussion explodes with a force five times greater than gunpowder does.

Gunpowder, also called "black powder", the oldest of explosive mixtures, consists of saltpetre, sulphur and charcoal, intimately mixed, the proportions being varied for different intended uses.

Gunpowder Plot was a conspiracy by a desperate band of Roman Catholics in the reign of James I to avenge the harsh treatment to which Catholics were subjected. Barrels of gunpowder were secreted in the vaults underneath the Houses of Parliament, and it was proposed to fire these when the King and his Ministers assembled on 5 November 1605. The plot was betrayed and Guy Fawkes and his co-conspirators were arrested and executed. The date serves to perpetuate the ancient custom of burning the effigy of Fawkes, a custom in which young people are the most enthusiastic participants, with bonfires, fireworks, etc.

Gurnard, a sea-fish, with large, bony head and diminutive body, of which there are some forty species. They are plentiful in British waters.

Gymnasium, originally the name given in ancient Greece to the public places where Greek youth used to exercise and receive instruction. Plato, Aristotle and other great teachers lectured there. The Greek institution was never very popular with the Romans, and it was not until the 18th and 19th cent. that the cult of combining physical with intellectual activity again found a place in educational systems. In Germany the name was applied to the classical grammar school; in this country and America to the halls where gymnastics were practised.

Gypsies, a nomadic race, believed to be of Indian origin; their language, Romany, is related to the languages of N.W. India. The Rom are spread over many parts of the world, but are most common in Europe where they appeared towards the end of the Middle Ages. The English name *gypsy* comes from the Spanish *gitano* = Egyptian; other European names are *Zigeuner* (Ger.), *zingaro* (It.), *fzigany* (Magyar), all resembling the Persian *singar* = a saddler. Their history has been one of persecution. Hitler treated them like the Jews. In Britain since the war they have been kept increasingly on the move, but in 1968 Parliament passed a Bill to make the provision of sites a duty of local authorities. However, it is likely at the present rate of building to be many years before the 4,500 gypsy households have a site. Economic pressure has largely removed their traditional crafts of tinkering, basket-making, peg-making. The majority now deal in scrap-iron.

Gypsum, a whitish mineral consisting of hydrated sulphate of calcium. The finest gypsum is alabaster. When heated gypsum is converted into the powder called Plaster of Paris; the water it loses can be taken up when the plaster is wetted, and the reconversion of Plaster of Paris into gypsum accounts for the way in which the former sets hard. The name "Plaster of Paris" came from the location of important gypsum quarries in the Montmartre district of Paris. It was found after the flood disasters of January 1953 that gypsum could undo the effect of sea-water. By spreading it for the rain to wash into the soil, thousands of acres of farmland in Holland and Britain were made productive again.

Gyroscope is a symmetrical rapidly rotating object, typically wheel-like, which because of its mass and rotation possesses a lot of the dynamical property known as angular momentum. Basic dynamical laws tell us that angular momentum is conserved and a consequence of this is that the axis of rotation tends to stay pointing in the same direction. Disturbing influences make a gyroscope's motion complicated but the general effect of the presence of a gyroscope attached to any body is to help to stabilise the body's motion. This is made use of in reducing the rocking of ships and in compasses and control systems in aircraft, torpedoes and missiles.

H

Habeas Corpus, the name given to a writ ordering the body of a person under restraint or imprisonment to be brought into court for full inquiry into the legality of the restraint to be made. The first Habeas Corpus Act was passed in 1679, though nominally such a right had existed from Magna Carta, but some of the more despotic kings had disregarded it. In times of public peril the privilege of *habeas corpus* is sometimes temporarily suspended, many instances occurring in the history of Ireland and during the first and second world wars.

Haber Process, the important industrial process for synthesising ammonia from atmospheric nitrogen. Nitrogen and hydrogen are combined at high pressure (*c.* 350 atmospheres) and moderately high temperature (500°C) using a catalyst (made largely of iron). A yield of 30% is obtained. The majority of the world's ammonia is produced in this way or from methods derived from it.

Haddock, one of the best-known fishes abounding in northern seas and averaging about 1·8 kg in weight. Related to the cod. Largely used for curing, and sold as "finnan haddies".

Hade of veins, a mining term indicating the particular inclination that any vein, seam or strata may have from the perpendicular; thus, in Weardale the veins mainly "hade" to the north.

Hadrian's Wall. *See* **Roman walls.**

Haematite, ferric oxide, one of the principal iron ores, containing about 70% of the metal. It is usually found in kidney-shaped masses, and is specular, red or brown, in thin fragments but greyish in bulk.

Haemocyanin, the respiratory pigment of crustaceans and molluscs. It functions like haemoglobin, from which it differs in containing copper instead of iron and being blue when oxidised instead of red. *See* **F39**(1).

Haemoglobin, the pigment containing iron which gives red blood corpuscles their colour. It is a respiratory pigment, having the property of picking up oxygen when the blood passes through the lungs to produce the compound known as oxyhaemoglobin. In other parts of the body the oxyhaemoglobin breaks down, liberating oxygen, which is used in the oxidation process (respiration) that the body tissues carry on. *See* **F38**(2).

Hafiz, besides being the pseudonym of a famous Persian poet, is a title conferred upon any Mohammedan who has committed the whole of the Koran to memory.

Hafnium, a metallic element, no. 72, symbol Hf, discovered by Coster and Hevesy in 1922 and important in the atomic-energy field. It occurs in most zirconium minerals to the extent of about 5%.

Hagiology, a branch of literature that is wholly given up to the history of the saints, and the setting forth of the stories and legends associated with their names.

Hail, hard, roughly spherical balls of ice, consisting of white cores covered by layers of both transparent and opaque ice, frequently falling during thunderstorms. They usually do not exceed 2·5 cm in size, but hailstones as large as tennis balls have been observed. The general theory of a hailstone is that near the top of a cumulonimbus cloud a raindrop becomes frozen,

grows in size by condensation and through collisions with snow particles, and eventually becomes so weighty as to overcome the ascending air currents in the cloud. Falling, it first encounters supercooled water drops, immediately freezing on it, increasing the white core, and then at lower levels ordinary water drops, freezing more slowly, producing a layer of clear ice. Before the hailstone arrives at the ground gusts and lulls may transport it several times up and down both regions, adding alternate coatings of soft white and hard clear ice.

Halcyon, a term associated in olden times with the kingfisher and days of soothing calm, "halcyon days" being a frequently used expression. The legend was that the kingfisher laid its eggs on the surface of the sea at the time of the winter solstice when the sea was unruffled. (Halcyon is the Greek for kingfisher.)

Halibut, one of the largest of the flat fishes, averaging when full grown from 1·2-1·8 m in length, and highly esteemed for the table. Specimens of still larger size occasionally occur. It is plentifully distributed. Its two eyes are on the right side of the head.

Hallmark. A mark or group of marks, impressed by an assay office on gold or silver articles (and on platinum since 1974) guaranteeing the standard of fineness of the precious metal used in them. These marks, which have been applied to silver made in London since the beginning of the 14th cent. and perhaps earlier, make it possible to establish the year and place of assay and also the name of the maker. English pieces of silver usually have not less than four marks, viz., (1) town mark; (2) maker's mark; (3) date letter; (4) sterling mark.

The town mark is rarely changed; in London a crowned leopard's head was used from the earliest days until 1820 with only minor modifications, except for the period 1697–1720 when a lion's head erased was substituted; since 1820 the crown has been omitted.

Until the late 17th cent. a symbol was often used as a maker's mark, from 1696–1720 the first two letters of the maker's surname, and subsequently the maker's initials. Owing to the destruction of the earlier mark plates at Goldsmiths' Hall no maker's name prior to the late 17th cent. can be identified with certainty.

The London date letter is changed at the end of May each year, so each letter covers seven months of one year and five months of the following. The London date cycle has usually consisted of twenty letters: the alphabet of each cycle is of different style, and the letters are enclosed in shields of different shape.

The sterling mark, the lion passant, was introduced in 1544 and continued in use until 1697, when the higher Britannia standard was introduced in order to discourage the practice current amongst goldsmiths of melting down coin of the realm to make plate. The leopard's head crowned and the lion passant were then replaced by a figure of Britannia and a lion's head erased. Though the regulation imposing a higher standard was withdrawn in 1720, a small amount of Britannia standard silver continued to be made and still is made.

From 1784 until 1890 a plate tax was levied on all silver assayed in Great Britain and an additional duty mark, the sovereign's head, was used during this period. A Jubilee mark bearing the head of George V and of Queen Mary was used between the years 1933 and 1935, and in 1953 a coronation mark with the head of Queen Elizabeth was introduced.

Hallmarks giving the London date letter cycles are to be found in **Section U** of the 87th edition. The form of town mark and sterling mark used during each cycle is given at the head of each column. Where a major alteration took place in either of these marks during a date-letter cycle, the alternative forms are also shown. The date of the change can be established by reference to the notes above. At the bottom of each page the marks used by the major provincial, Scottish and Irish assay offices are shown. Owing to lack of space, the complete date-letter cycles are not shown, but two examples only from the 17th, 18th or 19th cent. Where a provincial assay office was established in the 17th cent. or earlier, the marks of one year in the 17th and 18th cent. respectively are shown; where the office was not established until the 18th cent., the marks of one year in the 18th and 19th cent. are given.

Under the Hallmarking Act 1973 the hall-marking of platinum is now compulsory; the hallmark symbol is an orb surmounted by a cross and encompassed by a pentagon; assay offices London and Birmingham.

Halloween (31 October), the eve of All Saints' Day, a time associated, especially in Scotland, with certain pleasing superstitions attractively set forth in Burns's famous poem "Hallowe'en". It is the night when young men and maidens are supposed, by observing certain rites, to have their future wives and husbands disclosed to them.

Hallucinogen, a drug which acts upon the brain to create sensory illusions or hallucinations with a variety of emotional effects. One of the most widely studied is LSD (*q.v.*) which will produce symptoms very similar to those found in some mental disorders.

Halo, a luminous circle usually of 22° radius, surrounding sun or moon, produced by the refraction and reflection of light by ice crystals of high cirrus cloud. It is a very common occurrence, in the British Isles almost one day in three. The inner side is red and the outer a whitish-yellow colour. "Mock suns", *i.e.*, patches of light at the same elevation as the sun are much rarer occurrences, sometimes being of great beauty and brilliance. Halo is the Greek for threshing-floor. *See* **Corona.**

Halogens, the group name for the four non-metallic elements fluorine, chlorine, bromine and iodine. The term "halogen" means "salt-producer".

Halteres, the modified hind-wings of the two-winged flies or *Diptera* (*e.g.*, the house-fly). The equilibrium in flight of these insects depends on the halteres, which are commonly called "balancers".

Hampton Court Conference, presided over at Hampton Court Palace by James I in 1604 and which brought about his authorised translation of the Bible, had an important bearing on the religious differences of the time. James refused to grant tolerations to the Puritans. This sowed the seeds of civil war. Following the conference three hundred English Puritan clergy were ejected from their livings.

Hanaper Office, a former Chancery office, deriving its name from the fact that its writs and papers were kept in a hanaper (hamper). The Chancellor's office thus came to be known as the Hanaper. The Comptrollers of the Hanaper were abolished in England in 1842.

Hand, a measure of 4 in (10 cm), the average size of the palm; used in reckoning height of horses.

Handfasting, an informal marriage custom once prevalent in Scotland, whereby a man and woman bound themselves to cohabit for a year and a day, and at the end of that period either confirmed their contract by a regular marriage or separated.

Hansard, the title given to the official reports of Parliamentary debates, so named after Luke Hansard who in 1774 became partner in a firm of printers to the House of Commons. His son T. C. Hansard was first the printer and then the publisher of an unofficial series of parliamentary debates inaugurated by William Cobbett in 1803. In 1909 production was taken over by H.M. Stationery Office and today's volumes contain full, substantially verbatim, reports of what is said in both Houses of Parliament.

Hanseatic League was a confederation of North German towns established about 1241 for purposes of mutual protection in carrying on international commerce. The League became so powerful that it was able to dominate the foreign trade of Norway, Sweden, Denmark, and even to some extent of London. A branch was established in London and had its guild hall in Cannon Street for hundreds of years. The League existed down to the middle of the 17th cent. Hamburg, Lübeck and Bremen are the only cities which, as free ports, still by commercial courtesy retain the name of Hanse towns. *Hansa* is Old High German for Association or Merchants' Guild. *See also* **Freeport.**

Hapsburg (*Ger.* **Habsburg**), the ruling house

of Austria, 1282–1918; held title of Roman Emperor, 1438–1806, except for 1740–5. The aggrandisement of the Hapsburg family was mainly brought about by a series of fortunate marriages. In 1521 when the Hapsburg power was at its zenith, Charles V divided his dominions into two branches—Austrian Hapsburg and Spanish Hapsburg. The Hapsburg Danubian Monarchy dates from 1526 when the Hungarian and Bohemian crowns were united with the Austrian patrimony of the Hapsburg. The triple union lasted 400 years. The murder of the heir to the Hapsburg thrones, Francis Ferdinand, at Sarajevo in 1914, provoked the outbreak of the first world war. Francis Joseph's great-nephew, Charles, went into exile in 1918. (Prof. C. A. Macartney's authoritative work, *The Habsburg Empire, 1790–1918,* was published in 1969.)

Hara-kiri, the custom of suicide, as formerly practised in Japan, when in disgrace.

Hardware, the electrical, electronic, magnetic and mechanical parts of a computer or data-processing system. *See also* **Software** and **Section V.**

Hare, a rabbit-like animal with longer ears and legs. There are many kinds of hare distributed over the northern hemisphere and in Africa south to the Cape. They do not burrow as do rabbits but rely on camouflage, speed and mobility for safety. *See* **Game.**

Harleian MSS. comprise some thousands of volumes of MSS. and documents, collected by the first Earl of Oxford (1661–1724) and his son Edward. After the death of the latter, his widow handed the MSS. over to the nation for £10,000, and they are deposited in the British Museum.

Harlequin, the buffoon of ancient Italian comedy. As adapted to the British stage, however, harlequin is a pantomime character only, in love with Columbine, appearing in parti-coloured garments and carrying a wand, by which he exercises a magic influence in thwarting the fantastic tricks of the clown and pantaloon.

Harmattan, a dry wind which may blow between January and May across the Sahara to the Gulf of Guinea. Although affording relief from the tropical heat, vegetation withers because of its extreme dryness and much irritation is caused by the clouds of fine dust which it carries.

Harmonic Motion, regular periodic motion of the kind exemplified by a ball bobbing up and down at the end of a spring, and by the piston in a steam engine. It may be simple (simple harmonic motion) or composed of two or more simple harmonic motions. In simple harmonic motion the acceleration is proportional to the distance of the moving body from its original rest position.

Harp-seal, the ordinary Greenland seal, with a dark harp-shaped marking on its back, hence its name. It abounds in Newfoundland waters and further northward towards the Arctic.

Harpy Eagle, a large bird of prey named from the winged monsters of Greek mythology, inhabiting the forest regions of Central and South America. There are eight species, one with handsome grey plumage and large crest which attacks and kills animals much larger than itself, and was called by the Aztecs "winged wolf".

Harrier, a bird of prey of the falcon family; of the various species distributed over the world, three breed in Britain: the moorland Hen harrier, the Marsh harrier and Montagu's harrier. They are large birds with long tails, long legs, long wings and gliding flight. They nest on the ground and eat small mammals, frogs, lizards and small birds.

Hartebeest, common African antelope of a grey-brown colour, with ringed and knotted horns bending backward and tapering to sharp points: gregarious, of large size. There are several species.

Harvest Bug, a very small insect, of a dark red colour, which appears in large numbers in the fields in autumn, and is peculiarly irritating to animals and man by the tenacity with which it attaches itself to the skin and burrows underneath. Probably the larvae of spinning mites (Trombidoids). In the USA they are called "chiggers".

Harvest Moon, the full moon that occurs nearest to the autumn equinox, in September. It rises for several nights running about the same time, and yields an unusually brilliant series of moonlight nights.

Harvestmen are, like spiders, members of the arachnid class but belong to the distinctly different order of Phalangida. They are common in the countryside in autumn and have small oval bodies and eight long slender legs which besides being mere organs of locomotion also act as sense organs. Known as "daddy longlegs" in America and UK.

Hashish, an Arabic word for the narcotic substance prepared from the hemp plant (*Cannabis sativa*). It is known by a variety of names, *e.g.*, bhang in India and marijuana in America.

Hatchment, in heraldry, is a square board, in vertical diagonal position, placed outside a house or on the tomb at the death of a member of a family and so arranged that it indicates the sex and condition of the deceased.

Hawfinch, a well-known European bird of the finch family, having a variegated plumage, a sturdy bill and black-and-white tail. In England it is found in the Midland and Eastern counties, and locally in Scotland.

Hawk. This name is applied to almost any diurnal bird of prey other than eagle, falcon or vulture, but in its strict sense applies only to the *Accipiter* genus—the small Sparrow Hawk and the larger Goshawk, round-winged, long-tailed birds with barred under-parts. They prey upon small birds captured in flight and small mammals.

Hawk-moths, large species of moths, thick of body and strong of wing, which fly with rapid swooping motion, hence the name. There are numerous handsome species in Britain.

Hearth-Money was a tax laid on hearths (in all houses paying the church and poor rates). Charles II introduced it in 1662, and it was repealed in the reign of William and Mary.

Heat, after prolonged controversy over whether or not heat is a "substance" (formerly called "caloric"), it was established in the 19th cent. that heat is a form of energy; it is in fact the combined kinetic and potential energy of the atoms of which a body is composed. Heat can be turned into other forms of energy, *e.g.*, a red hot body loses heat by radiating it in the form of electromagnetic waves ("radiant heat"—chiefly infra-red rays). Heat may also be transferred from one place to another by conduction and, in fluids, by convection. All three processes occur when a glowing fire heats a room. A unit quantity of heat is the calorie, which is the amount of heat sufficient to raise the temperature of 1 g of water by 1°C. In general, adding heat to a body raises its temperature. The number of calories required per gram of material to raise the temperature 1°C is called the *specific heat* of the material. However, adding heat may not raise the temperature-but may instead cause a change of state, *e.g.*, from solid to liquid (melting) or liquid to gas (evaporation). The amount of heat required to melt 1 gram of a solid is called the latent heat of melting. Similarly, there is a latent heat of evaporation. Strictly speaking, the specific and latent heats of a substance depend on how much its pressure and volume are allowed to vary during the measurements. Water has a high specific heat, and this makes the oceans a vast heat reservoir, a factor of great meteorological significance. The science of heat is called thermodynamics, and is of great importance in physics and chemistry. **F20(1).**

Heat Pump, essentially a refrigerator working in reverse, *i.e.*, a device which warms up one place, say, a house by releasing into it heat transferred from another place, say, the air or earth outside the house. The idea is attributed to Lord Kelvin (1852) and later Haldane used a heat pump to heat his house in Scotland. In Summer, a house could be cooled by operating the device in reverse. As in a domestic refrigerator, the heat is transferred by a suitable fluid whose circulation has to be driven by an external supply of energy, *e.g.*, by running a mechanical compressor. With good design and favourable conditions, the energy required to run the heat pump is considerably less than would be required to produce the same warming effect directly. Since the 1930s heat pumps have

been produced commercially for domestic and industrial use but, as always, careful consideration is needed to decide whether in a particular application they are cheaper to run than alternative methods of heating.

Heath, flowering plants of the *Ericaceae* family. Heaths are widely distributed over uncultivated spaces of Europe and Africa. In Britain they are represented by heather (of which there are several species) and ling (*Calluna vulgaris*), which cover thousands of acres of moorland. Some of the African or Cape heaths are very beautiful and much prized by florists. One species of heath (*Erica arborea*) which grows in S. Europe and N. Africa has close-grained woody rootstock used for making briar pipes. In N. Europe acid heathlands, dominated by heather and ling, form one of the most widespread vegetation areas created by man through the destruction of former oak forests, grazing and burning.

Heat Wave is a spell of very hot weather, due chiefly in the British Isles to a warm southerly current of air caused by the presence of an anticyclone over western or central Europe at the same time as a depression is stationary over the Atlantic. High humidity increases the discomfort.

Hegira, an Arab term signifying departure or flight, used in reference to Mohammed's departure from Mecca, A.D. 622, from which date the Mohammedan era is reckoned.

Helicopter, heavier-than-air aircraft which obtains its lifts from blades rotating above the fuselage in windmill-fashion. The first successful helicopters were the Focke-Wulf 61, a German machine (1936), and the VS-300, designed by Igor Sikorsky, flown in 1937. Helicopters can hover, and rise and descend vertically, in addition to being capable of horizontal flight.

Heliotrope, a favourite sweet-scented flowering plant, common in tropical and sub-tropical countries; the Peruvian heliotrope is the "cherry pie" of our summer garden borders.

Helium, a gaseous element, no. 2, symbol He, first discovered by means of the spectroscope in the sun's atmosphere. This discovery, made in 1868 by the astronomer Sir Norman Lockyer, was followed in 1895 by Sir William Ramsay's proof that the element existed on earth. He found it in the uranium ore, clevite. Later it was established that helium is formed by the radioactive decay of many elements which emit *a*-particles (nuclei of helium atoms) and is contained in all radioactive minerals. The largest source of helium is natural gas, the richest in helium being the gas from certain wells in Utah, USA. Next to hydrogen, helium is the lightest gas known, has a lifting power equal to 92% of hydrogen and the advantage that it is inert and non-inflammable. It is used for inflating airships. Ordinary air contains 1 part in 200,000 of helium. It was the last gaseous element to be liquefied, this being achieved by Onnes in 1908 in Leyden. Liquid helium has many remarkable properties only imperfectly understood. As well as being scientifically fascinating it is indispensable in cryogenics (*q.v.*) as a medium for cooling other substances to temperatures near absolute zero. Hydrogen fusion in the "H bomb" produces helium.

Hellebore, a plant of the *Ranunculaceae* (buttercup) family. The best-known British examples are the green and stinking varieties. There is also a garden kind which flowers in December called the Christmas Rose. Hellebore yields a bitter substance which forms a drastic purgative, but is now little used.

Hellenic Art. The art of ancient Greece may be roughly divided into three periods: the prehistoric period (*c.* 1500–1000 B.C.) of the bronze age Mycenaeans; the archaic period (*c.* 600–500 B.C.); and the classical period (*c.* 500–300 B.C.). Of the first period centred on Mycenae in Peloponnesus but extending to the coasts of Asia and the city of Troy we can mention only the massive stone gateways and the shaft graves of Mycenae, where the archaeologist Schliemann discovered painted vases, gold cups, bronze swords and ornaments of what had once been a great, if primitive, civilisation. During the archaic period sculpture was the principal form of art expression. The magnificent male and female figures are reminiscent of Egyptian art, but are distinctive in liveliness of facial expression. The vase-paintings of this period became more elaborate, depicting scenes from mythology or ceremonial events. Typical of classical Greek art is the representation of the beautiful and healthy human body deliberately posed and often carrying out heroic or athletic acts. The vast majority of these statues are known to us only through Roman copies. The *Hermes* of Praxiteles (born *c.* 385 B.C.) is possibly the only existing statue which can be assigned with any degree of certainty to an individual artist. Almost the whole of the Greek genius in architecture was expended on temples which are all basically similar in design—a rectangle with a low-pitched gabled roof resting on side walls. The three orders Doric, Corinthian and Ionic mainly referred to the type of column used, but naturally the whole building was influenced thereby. Some of the main buildings are on the Acropolis, a hill outside Athens, on which stand the Parthenon (from the outer frieze of which the Elgin marbles (*q.v.*), now mostly in the British Museum, were taken), the Erechtheum, famous for its Porch of Maidens, and the gateway known as the Propylaea with its broad flight of marble steps. Apart from that on vases, no Greek painting has come down to us, although Greek painters existed and were noted in their time. All we have are copies in mosaic and fresco made by the Romans, at Naples and Pompeii. Of Greek literature in prose, verse and the drama little can be said here. To the early period (*i.e.*, the archaic age) belong Homer's *Iliad* and *Odyssey*. Hesiod's long poem *Work and Days* and Sappho's love poems, and Pindar's Odes. The period of Pericles in the 5th cent. B.C. produced more great literature than any comparable period in history: the philosophical writings of Plato and Aristotle, the tragedies of Aeschylus, Euripides and Sophocles, the comedies of Aristophanes—all these are still part of the European tradition, and together with Greek architecture played a major part in the Renaissance (*see* **Section J**).

Hellenistic Art, the age of the period of Greek civilisation which began with the conquests of Alexander the Great (356–323 B.C.) and lasted until his former empire (which encompassed most of the Middle East and part of North Africa) was conquered by the Romans in 146 B.C. Culturally it was an important period because it spread Greek culture far beyond its original boundaries—even as far as the north of India, and its centres spread from Athens to the cities of Alexandria in Egypt, Antioch in Syria and Pergamum in Asia Minor. But equally Eastern culture spread to the West: democracy was replaced by absolute monarchy, cosmopolitanism took the place of the Greek tendency to believe that all who were not Greeks were barbarians, and mystical philosophies took the place of Greek rationalism. This was a sensuous, secular, pleasure-loving, rootless society, and these tendencies were reflected in its art. Hellenistic sculpture was sensual, effeminate and violently emotional, depicting individuals and not always noble or beautiful ones. (Classical Greek sculpture was idealistic, showed types rather than individuals and appealed to the intellect rather than the emotions.) Some of the best examples came from the school at Pergamum and later from the island of Rhodes, and the titles themselves speak of their nature: *The Dying Gaul, Gaul Slaying his Wife and Himself* and the famous *Laocoön* (representing Laocoön and his two sons being crushed by two enormous serpents). All these date from about 240 to 50 B.C.—for the culture did not immediately end with the Roman conquest. The enormous frieze of the altar of the temple in Pergamum depicts a battle between gods and giants with tremendous realism and brutal violence far removed from the serene art of classical times. Portrait sculpture is typical of Hellenistic art, where it may almost be said to have been invented, since such ventures in the past had been idealistic rather than realistic. The great Hellenistic cities were geometrically planned and fine public buildings made their appearance in which the slender and graceful Ionic of the ornate Corinthian columns took the place of the more austere and heavy classical ones. Alexandria was celebrated for its vast libraries and was the centre of a brilliant intellectual life (the Septuagint or Greek translation of the Bible was prepared here). Here too worked the mathematicians Euclid and Archimedes, the physicians Erasistratus and Herophilus, and the geographer Pytheas. But Hellenistic literature was a pale reflection of the glories of the past and we mention only the comedies of Menander and the pastoral verse of Theocritus of Syracuse.

Hemiptera, the order of insects to which belong the true bugs. Their wing structure is in most species incomplete, hence the term hemiptera (half-wing). This order includes the familiar water insects, the water boatman and water skater, also the aphids, cicadas, leaf hoppers, scale insects.

Hemlock, a plant of the *Umbelliferae* family, growing in all parts of Britain, and containing a strong alkaline poison. Used medicinally, this alkaline substance is of considerable service, being a powerful sedative. According to Pliny, hemlock was the poison used by the Athenians in putting criminals to death.

Hemp (*Cannabis sativa*), name of a plant native to Asia, now cultivated widely for the valuable fibre contained in the stalk or in some species in the leaves. Hemp fibre has been replaced by cotton for textiles and by jute for sacks and is now chiefly used for cordage and twine. It contains a resinous substance from which the narcotic hashish is made. The seed yields a valuable oil. The term hemp is also used for other fibre plants, including manila hemp from the Philippines, sunn hemp from India, sisal from W. and E. Africa and phormium from New Zealand.

Henbane, a plant found in Britain and other parts of Europe and Northern Asia. It belongs to the potato family *Solanaceae*, grows mostly on waste ground and bears yellow-brown flowers veined with purple. The leaves yield a poisonous alkaloid substance which, medicinally prepared and administered, is of great use. Tincture of henbane is often preferred to laudanum.

Heptarchy, a word derived from the Greek *hepta*, seven, and denoting the seven kingdoms (*archai*) into which Anglo-Saxon England was divided before 900. The seven were Kent, Essex, Sussex, Wessex, Mercia, East Anglia and Northumbria.

Heracleum, a plant of the *Umbelliferae* family, common in southern and central Europe, though only one species, the cow parsnip, grows in England. It has a bitter root, and from the juice of the stem an intoxicating liquor is occasionally prepared.

Herald, an officer of state empowered to make formal proclamations and deliver messages from the sovereign or other high personage whom he serves. In the developments which took place in armorial bearings, the herald was the functionary charged with the duty of their proper depiction.

Heraldry, the knowledge of armorial bearings, was mainly the outcome of the love of outward distinction which prevailed in mediaeval times, "Heraldry," says Stubbs, "became a handmaid of chivalry, and the marshalling of badges, crests, coat-armour, pennons, helmets and other devices of distinction grew into an important branch of knowledge." The *shield*, or *escutcheon*, is the ground upon which armorial signs are traced, the colour of the shield being called the *tincture*, the signs recorded the *charges*. There are seven *tinctures*—*or* (gold), *argent* (silver), *gules* (red), *azure* (blue), *vert* (green), *purpure* (purple) and *sable* (black). The *charges* are classed as "Honourable" and "Subordinate" ordinaries, comprising lines and geometrical forms; and "Common" ordinaries, which latter includes all representations of natural objects. There is also a system of external signs, such as crowns, coronets, mitres, helmets, mantlings, wreaths and crests, each having its distinctive significance. For other distinguishing marks *see* **Hatchment, Quartering, Rampant.**

Heralds' College or College of Arms, was incorporated by Richard III in 1483. Its head is

L59

the Earl Marshal (an office hereditary in the family of the Dukes of Norfolk), and there are three Kings of Arms, six Heralds and four Pursuivants. The business transacted is wholly connected with the tracing of genealogies and the granting of armorial bearings. In Scotland the Heraldic functions are performed by the Lord Lyon King of Arms.

Herbarium, a systematically classified collection of preserved plants. One of the largest in the world is at the Royal Botanic Gardens at Kew.

Heredity is the study of the transmission of physical and mental characteristics from one generation to another. Gregor Mendel (1822–84), a great experimenter in the field of inheritance, established the principle embodied in Mendel's law in his work published in 1866. The ideas which he then put forward were forgotten until the early years of this century, but today they form the basis of the modern study of genetics. Genes are the units of heredity; they are contained in the chromosomes of the cell nucleus. In human cells there are 46 chromosomes—22 pairs of characteristic shape, and a 23rd (the sex chromosomes) similar in women and dissimilar in men, which unite in the process of fertilisation. An individual can only develop, even under the most favourable surroundings, as far as his inherited characteristics, i.e., his genes will allow him to do. It is in the development of personality that the interplay between heredity and environment becomes most apparent. See **Evolution, Section F, Part IV,** also **Q27.**

Hermaphrodite, animals or plants possessing both male and female reproductive organs, e.g., snail, earthworms, most flowering plants.

Hermit Crab, a decapod, with a soft asymmetrical body which it protects by thrusting it into an empty gastropod shell, e.g., whelk, which it carries about, only abandoning it when necessary for a larger one. Found in all seas, many live in commensal relationship with sea anemones etc.

Heron, a large wading bird with long curved neck and pointed bill, is a member of the Ardeidae family, of which there are many species. Egrets and bitterns are included as herons. Herons are to be met with in marsh lands and near rivers and lakes, where they feed on fish and frogs. They nest in trees in large numbers, these colonies being called heronries. The common heron is native to England, and other species from the Continent are frequent visitors.

Herring (Clupes harengus), an important food-fish inhabiting the North Sea which has been subjected to overfishing. In Britain the herring industry is based on the Shetlands and the coastal ports of E. Scotland and N.E. England. Marine biologists have recently reported on its unique structure for hearing which makes it receptive to sound frequencies over a very wide range and able to determine distance, direction and sound of a source of sound.

Hibernation, the dormant condition in which numerous mammals, reptiles, amphibians, insects, plants, etc., pass the winter. The rate of metabolism slows down, and the body temperature drops to that of the surroundings. Work on these low temperatures and their physiological effect has led to improved surgical techniques. Animals of the torrid regions pass through an analogous period (aestivation) during the hot season, when the sources of food are dried up.

Hickory, several species of American tree of the walnut family, remarkable for its very hard, solid, heavy white wood, and bearing an edible, four-lobed nut.

Hieratic Art, a type of art (typified by the major part of the art of ancient Egypt) which is (a) exclusively religious and (b) conventionally based on earlier forms and traditions.

Hieroglyphics are the earliest form of pictured symbolic expression, and are supposed to have been introduced by the ancient Egyptians. They consist of rude depictions of animals, plants, signs and objects, and in their later examples express, in abridged form, ideas and records from which significant historical information has been gleaned. The deciphering of Egyptian hieroglyphics long formed an ardent study, but gradually the key to the riddle was

discovered, and most of the ancient records can now be understood. Besides the Egyptian there are also Hittite, Minoan and Mayan hieroglyphic scripts. See **Rosetta Stone.**

Hi-Fi means high fidelity and refers to gramophones, tape recorders and similar apparatus which will faithfully reproduce sounds. It is not too difficult these days to amplify electrical signals without distorting them much; it is more difficult to turn electrical impulses into exactly equivalent sound waves (with a loudspeaker, for example) or vice versa (with a microphone or gramophone pick-up). Pick-up and loudspeakers are therefore often the weak links in domestic hi-fi and faults in their design, deficiencies in the electronic amplifiers, imperfect gramophone motors can all contribute to audible results ranging from the tolerable to the execrable. Almost perfect sound reproduction is however available to enthusiasts possessing a suitable combination of discrimination, know-how and financial resources. There are periodical magazines which provide guidance.

Hindi, the official language of India.

Hinduism. See **Section J.**

Hindustani, the spoken form of Hindi (written in Devanagari script) and Urdu (written in Arabic characters).

Hippogriff, a fabulous animal like a horse in body, but with the head, wings and front legs and claws of an eagle. The monster frequently appears in the romances of the Middle Ages.

Hippopotamus or "river-horse" the largest living representative of the hog family, widely distributed over Africa, where it lives in herds. It is of immense bulk, attaining a length of 3·6 m and a weight of 4 tonnes and stands about 1·5 m high. Its skin is hairless and about 5 cm thick, and it has a pair of tusks often weighing as much as 2·7 kg. It spends most of its time in the water, and lives entirely on vegetation, both aquatic and terrestrial. The pigmy hippopotamus, which occurs in forests and swamps in W. Africa, is only half the size.

Histology is the study of the structure of plant and animal tissues. These mainly consist of groups of cells with similar functions, e.g., muscle, brain tissue.

Hittites, an ancient race (often mentioned in the Old Testament) who inhabited Cappadocia (region of Eastern Asia Minor) from the third to the first millennium B.C. Excavations have revealed that they attained a high level of civilisation round about 1350 B.C. The Hittites were rivals of Egypt, disputing with the Pharaohs the mastery of the Middle East. They were the first to smelt iron successfully.

Hobby, a bird of the falcon family, 30–35 cm long. Local breeding visitor to England and Wales, April–September; irregular visitor to Scotland and Ireland. They winter in Africa.

Hog, the common name of animals of the Suina family, including the wild boar, pig and sow. The wild boar, Sus scrofa, is the common ancestor. The skin of the hog is covered with bristles, the snout truncated and each foot has four hoofed toes. Hogs are omnivorous feeders and eat almost anything that is given them.

Hogmanay, the Scottish New Year's Eve festival and a national holiday of the country. The custom of demanding Hogmanay bread is still upheld in many parts of Scotland.

Hogshead, a cask of varying capacity, also a specific measure. In the old English measure a hogshead was 63 old gallons of wine (= 52½ imperial gallons = 238·6 litres). Of beer 54 old gallons make a hogshead.

Holly, a hardy evergreen shrub, largely grown in England. Its bright dark green prickly curved leaves and clusters of red berries are familiar in all parts of the country, and used as house decoration between Christmas Eve and Twelfth Night, probably a relic from Roman and Teutonic customs. Its wood is white and hard, valued for carved work, while its bark yields a gummy substance which is converted into bird-lime.

Hologram, a photographic record, taken under special optical conditions, of light reflected from a scene or object. The hologram is typically a piece of film. However it is nothing like a photographic negative of the ordinary kind;

for one thing it will show an unintelligible pattern of light and dark patches. Nevertheless if it is illuminated (again under special optical conditions) the light coming through it will form a *three dimensional* image of the original object. Another radical difference between a hologram and an ordinary film is that if the hologram is cut up, each fragment can be used to construct the entire image. Holography, as a method of recording and reproducing photographic information, was conceived by Gabor in 1947 but was only fully realised in practice after the invention of the laser (*q.v.*), which made available powerful sources of coherent light. The use of laser light is one of the "special conditions" referred to above. Technical applications are being explored in many laboratories. Gabor received the 1971 Nobel prize for his discovery and invention.

Holy Alliance, an alliance ostensibly for conserving religion, justice and peace in Europe, but used for repressing popular tendencies towards constitutional government. Formed by Alexander I of Russia, Francis I of Austria and Frederick William III of Prussia, at Paris on 26 September 1815. Subsequently joined by all the sovereigns of Europe, except the Pope and the King of England. It ended after the 1830 revolution in France.

Holy Coat of Trèves, a garment preserved in the Cathedral of Trèves and said to have been worn by Christ. It was brought from Jerusalem by the Empress Helena in the fourth century.

Holy Roman Empire, the title traditionally given (although the term "Holy" does not appear in a document until 1157) to the revived Empire when the German king Otto I was crowned in Rome by Pope John XII in 962. It endured until Napoleonic times (1806) two years after Francis II had assumed the title of Emperor of Austria.

Holy Rood, an annual Roman Catholic festival held on 14 September to celebrate the Elevation of the Cross in commemoration of its re-erection in Jerusalem by the Emperor Heraclius in 628 after retaking it from the Persians. Also included in the Church of England calendar.

Holyrood, the ancient royal palace at Edinburgh, dating from the 15th cent., and inhabited by many Scottish sovereigns, notably Mary Stuart, the rooms occupied by her (including the one in which Rizzio was murdered) being still shown. It is now known as Holyrood House and is still used as a royal residence.

Holy Water, water blessed by a priest and kept in small fonts at the entrance to Roman Catholic and some Anglican churches, and used by worshippers going in, and out, or by priests in sprinkling.

Holy Week is the week preceding Easter Sunday, and embraces the days of the Sufferings of Christ. It includes Good Friday and Holy Saturday.

Homoeopathy. *See Section J.*

Honey, the sweet syrup formed by bees from the nectar of flower, the sucrose in the nectar being converted into a mixture of the simple sugars, glucose and fructose. Hybla, an ancient town of Sicily, on the southern slope of Mt. Etna, was famous for its honey.

Honey-eater, an Australian bird (of which there are many species) provided with a long curved bill and tufted tongue. It lives by sucking the nectar from the flowers which abound in rural parts of Australia and New Zealand.

Hookah, an Oriental pipe for tobacco smoking, the smoke being drawn through the water of a goblet (commonly a coconut shell) by means of a long flexible tube.

Hoopoe, a remarkably handsome bird with vivid black and white-barred wings and tail and black-tipped crest which opens like a fan. Ranges over Europe, Asia and Africa. It has bred in England and Wales and occurs in the British Isles in small numbers at all seasons. Other species are confined to Africa, Madagascar and India.

Hops, the female "cones" of the hop plant used in brewing; their essential oils give beer an aromatic flavour, and their tannin and resin act as a preservative as well as accounting for the bitter taste desired. The hop is a perennial climber belonging to the mulberry family. The male and female organs are on separate plants; as only the female flower-heads are commercially

useful, female plants predominate in a hop garden, only a very few male plants being grown so that the female flowers can be fertilised.

Horizon, the limit of vision, the apparent line where sea and sky, or land and sky meet. This is termed the visible horizon. An ordinary person at the height of 1·5 m can see for 4·8 km, at 6 m 9·6 km, at 15 m 14·8 km and at 305 m 67·5 km. The figures are approximate.

Hormone, a chemical substance which is released by one part of the body and produces a response in other parts after having been carried there by the bloodstream or some other transport system. Prolactin, for example, is a hormone produced by the pituitary gland of nursing mothers and serves to stimulate and maintain the milk supply.

Horn *or* **French Horn,** a brass instrument of the trumpet family (*i.e.*, played by three valves) whose tube is very thin and long (Horn in F = 12 ft). In consequence the tube is curled in a complicated manner. Owing to the sweet tone it is capable of producing, the Horn sometimes plays as part of the wood-wind.

Hornbill, large bird found in Africa and oriental regions. Some species have a casque or a horny growth above the very powerful beak. It feeds on fruits. When the female has laid her eggs in the hollow of a tree, the male bird stops up the entrance, and keeps her imprisoned until the hatching is completed and the young ones are able to fly. There are about 45 species.

Hornblende, the commonest member of the amphibole group of minerals, a silicate of calcium, magnesium, iron and aluminium, of a dark green colour. It is a constituent of numerous rocks, including diorite, syenite and hornblende schist.

Horned Viper, any of a number of species of African viper which have scales over each eye resembling horns. Their bite is usually very poisonous. The significance of the horns is not known.

Hornet, a general name for many of the bigger wasps. It usually nests in hollow trees, and despite its rather fiercesome appearance does not sting unless unduly provoked.

Horology, the science of time-measurement, including the construction and management of clocks, watches, etc. Instruments of this kind are not known to have existed before the 12th cent. and until the introduction of the pendulum in the 17th cent., clocks were ill-regulated and inaccurate. The time-recording mechanisms of the present day include (*a*) the *clock*, which shows the hours and minutes by hands, and strikes the hours, and sometimes quarters; (*b*) the *timepiece*, which is not generally a fixture and shows the time, but does not strike; (*c*) the *watch*, which is a pocket time-keeper; (*d*) the *chronometer*, which indicates the minutest portions of times; (*e*) electric timepieces, mains electric clocks; (*f*) the highly accurate quartz-crystal and atomic clocks used for astronomical purposes. *See* **Clock.**

Horse Chestnut, one of the large forest trees, with ample branches, and full foliage, and much esteemed for parks and ornamental grounds. The flowers, which appear in May, are white tinged with red and yellow. The tree is native to the mountainous regions of northern Greece. *See also* **Chestnut.**

Horse Guards, the building in Whitehall which until 1872 was the headquarters of the Commander-in-Chief of the British Army. The archway is still sentinelled by mounted guards.

Horse Latitudes, the latitudes of the sub-tropical high pressure systems, between the trade winds and the prevailing westerlies, characterised by light variable winds and low humidity.

Hospitallers, Knights, were of the order of St. John of Jerusalem, at first devoted to the aid of the sick, but afterwards military monks, who became prominent figures in the Crusades of the 12th cent. They adopted the Benedictine black habit with the eight-pointed cross worn by the modern St. John's Ambulance Brigade. In 1309 they took Rhodes, but were expelled by the Ottomans in 1522. In 1530 the emperor Charles V gave them the island of Malta, which as Knights of Malta, they held until 1798, when they were dislodged by Napoleon. The Knights still survive as a sovereign order, with headquarters in Rome. *See* **Templars** and **Teutonic Order.**

Hottentots, name given to certain African natives by Dutch settlers in the 17th cent. They used to occupy the greater part of Cape Colony and though driven out a number still survive in S.W. Africa. Appear to be related to the Bushmen, though their culture is more advanced. In addition to herding, they practise some farming and know how to smelt iron.

Hounds are dogs that were originally bred and trained for hunting, such as the greyhound, foxhound, bloodhound, wolfhound, deerhound, beagle, harrier, etc., but now often kept also as domestic dogs. The greyhound, deerhound and wolfhound hunt by sight, the others, with the bloodhound first in order, track by scent.

House Flies are world-wide and prolific. Their eggs are hatched within 24 hours of being laid, and full maturity is attained in a month. They feed mainly on decayed animals and vegetable matter.

Hovercraft, or air cushion vehicle, is a craft which is lifted on a pad of air underneath it. This pad or cushion must be at a pressure higher than that of the atmosphere and it is made by sucking in air above the craft and ejecting it in a downward stream all round the lower edge. The stream is guided by a flexible skirt and the high pressure air pad is contained partly by the skirt and partly by the air stream itself which forms a continuous air curtain all round the vehicle. Hovercraft are being intensively developed and there are variations in the basic scheme just described and also in the means of propulsion which can be by air or water jets or propellers. Hovercraft were devised by Cockerell in the 1950s and a full-scale example appeared before the British public in June 1959. Craft of over 100 tonnes are made commercially and much bigger ones conceived. The air pad support means that hovercraft can move over land, water or marsh. Cross-Channel hovercraft were introduced in 1966.

Howler Monkey, a genus of South American monkey noted for a laryngeal conformation which enables it to emit a loud reverberant noise something between a yell and a howl, as the name suggests.

Huanuco-bark, a medicinal bark, brought from the Peruvian town of that name, and derived from the *Cinchona micrantha* tree.

Huguenots, a name applied to the French Protestant communities of the 16th and 17th cent. Henry of Navarre, by the Edict of Nantes in 1598, granted them religious freedom, but more than a quarter of a century before—24 August 1572—thousands had been put to death in the massacre of St. Bartholomew. The revocation of the Edict of Nantes by Louis XIV in 1685 drove thousands into exile in England, Holland, Germany and America.

Humanism. *See* **Section J.**

Humble-bee or **Bumble-bee,** the common name of the insects of the genus *bombus,* of the Hymenoptera order. They live in small communities comprising males, females and drones, their habitations being underground. They do not have one queen bee only like the hive bee, but several females occupy the same nest, and these alone live through the winter, breeding and forming new colonies in the spring. Their sting does not have a barb like the honey bee's.

Humidity, the state of the atmosphere with respect to the water-vapour it contains. "Absolute humidity" is defined as the density of the vapour present, while "relative humidity", more frequently employed indicates the degree of saturation, *i.e.,* the ratio of the actual vapour pressure to the saturation vapour pressure at the particular temperature, expressed as a percentage.

Humming Birds are so called because of the humming noise made by the vibration of their wings in flying. They are of radiant plumage, and are among the smallest birds. The smallest bird in the world is the Fairy or Princess Helen's humming bird of Cuba, whose body is only 5·7 cm long. There are from four to five hundred species, and they are confined wholly to North and South America, being most numerous in the tropical latitudes. They have long, slender bills and tubular tongues which reach down

into flowers to suck up the nectar on which they feed.

Hummum, the original name for what is now called the Turkish Bath in this country. One of the first of these baths to be established in London was the Hummums in Covent Garden.

Hundred, the ancient divisonal name given to a portion of a county for administration or military purposes. It is supposed to imply the territory occupied by a hundred families; or the space of a hundred hides of land, or the capacity of providing 100 soldiers. Each hundred had its hundred court, with powers similar to those of a manor court, but this was abolished in 1867 by County Court Act.

Hundred Days, the interval of time between Napoleon Bonaparte's entry into Paris after his escape from Elba and his departure after his abdication, extending from 20 March 1815 to 28 June. During this period occurred the battle of Waterloo, 18 June. *See* **L128.**

Hundred Years' War, a term applied to the almost incessant contest between England and France, lasting from 1338 to 1453, including such famous battles as Crécy, Poitiers and Agincourt, and engaging successively Edward III, Henry V and Henry VI, among English kings.

Huns, a fierce Asiatic race which swept over eastern Europe in the 4th cent. Under Attila about the middle of the 5th cent, they obtained control of a large portion of central and eastern Europe, forcing even Rome to pay tribute. Their defeat at Châlons-sur-Marne in 451 by a mixed army of Romans, Goths and Teutonic tribes, and the death of Attila in 453, terminated their empire.

Hurdy-Gurdy, an Italian rustic musical stringed instrument of the lute order, the sounds of which are produced by the action of a rosined wheel turned by the left hand, the notes being made by the fingering of the right hand.

Hussites. *See* **Section J.**

Hurricane. *See* **Cyclone, Wind.**

Hydra, an aquatic animal of simple structure, whose body is in the form of a cylindrical tube, with a disc-shaped base by which it attaches itself to any shifting substance. Its mouth is surrounded by tentacles by which it catches its food. The Hydra has the power of reproducing lost parts.

Hydrates are compounds containing water of crystallisation.

Hydraulic Ram, a form of automatic pump, used to raise water to a height by the action of its own falling velocity.

Hydraulics, the science of applied hydrodynamics, or water-machine engineering, ranging from pumps to marine engines.

Hydrocarbons are compounds of carbon and hydrogen. They include the *paraffins,* which are saturated compounds (*e.g.,* methane); the ethylene, acetylene and other series which are unsaturated; compounds with ring structures, *e.g.,* benzene, naphthalene and anthracene. Petroleum is composed almost entirely of hydrocarbons.

Hydrochloric Acid, a solution of hydrogen chloride gas in water, and resulting in considerable quantities as a by-product of the soda-ash or salt-cake manufacture. Its solution forms the common hydrochloric or muriatic acid of commerce. It is present to the extent of nearly half a per cent, in the digestive juice secreted by the stomach.

Hydrocyanic Acid, cyanide of hydrogen or prussic acid; very poisonous, and of the odour of bitter almonds. It is formed by the action of acids on sodium or potassium cyanide. Used to kill wasps (and in the gas chamber in the USA). It is a very important chemical on account of the reactions of its derivatives in many synthetic fields. Discovered by Scheele in 1782.

Hydroelectric Schemes. The sun's energy has been indirectly exploited in the past by harnessing the energy of the winds and rain. The climate is due, essentially, to differential heating of the earth. The resulting convection currents in the air (the motion of which is complicated by the rotation of the earth) give rise to winds. Moisture is collected from the sea and deposited high up on mountains as rain. Some of the gravitational energy may be collected as hydropower. Simple windmills or waterwheels are so undependable that they have not been used to any extent since the beginning of the Industrial Revolution. However, the modern form of the waterwheel—the hydroelectric generation plant —is extensively used in mountainous countries and about a third of the world's electricity is produced by this means. The essential requirements for a modern hydroelectric scheme are a river with a sufficient flow of water to provide the required power, a large "head" of water so that a cheap, compact turbine can be used and a dam so that water can be stored until it is required. In some cases a hydroelectric scheme is made economic by being associated with an irrigation or drainage scheme. Such multi-purpose schemes are especially important in India and Pakistan, where most hydro projects are of this type. Other well-known examples include the Snowy Mountains scheme in Australia and the Aswan High Dam in Egypt. Although over 90 per cent of the electricity in certain individual countries, notably Norway, Sweden, Portugal, Switzerland and Uganda is produced from hydroelectric schemes, only a relatively small fraction of the total potential has been exploited. This fraction varies from about a third in Western Europe to a quarter in the United States to a very small fraction in Alaska, Canada, Africa and the hinterland of Asia.

Hydrofluoric Acid is obtained by distillation of fluorspar with sulphuric acid, and is a compound of fluorine and hydrogen. Its action is highly corrosive; a valuable agent in etching on glass, and a rapid decomposer of animal matter.

Hydrogen, symbol H, the simplest element, atomic number (**F11(2)**/) of 1, colourless, and the lightest of all substances. Cavendish in 1766 was the first to recognise that it was an element. It is 14·4 times as light as air, and is found in a free state in volcanic regions. It can be obtained by the action of metals on acids, and forms an explosive mixture with air, burning with oxygen to form water. Commercially it is used to produce the very hot flame of the oxy-hydrogen blowpipe for cutting metals; to fill balloons and airships; to harden certain oils and render them suitable for margarine- and soap-production. The gas can be liquefied, and the presence of the isotope deuterium was detected by Urey in 1931 in the residue of the evaporated liquid. The third isotope, tritium, is very rare. *See also* **Deuterium, Tritium.**

Hydrography, the science of water measurement, as applied to seas, rivers, lakes, currents, rocks, reefs, etc., and embracing the whole art of navigation.

Hydrometer, an instrument for measuring the specific gravity of liquids, especially for ascertaining the strength of spiritous liquors and solutions. It is usually in the form of a glass bulb, to the lower end of which a smaller bulb, containing mercury, is attached which forces the instrument to sink into the liquid which it is to test. The larger bulb has a scale fixed to it, and the indication on this scale of the sinking point shows the specific gravity. There are many varieties: Twaddell's—a pear-shaped bulb containing mercury: Beaumé's, of similar construction, but applicable to liquids both heavier and lighter than water: Sykes', largely employed for determinining the strength of alcohol: and Nicholson's, used for taking the specific gravities of solids.

Hydropathy, the method of treating disease with water, either by bathing or drinking. Natural springs of special chemical and therapeutic properties, such as sulphur springs, and other mineral sources, have been used since prehistoric times for this purpose. It is probably one of the most ancient methods of cure. Recently the beneficial effects of pure water treatment have been advocated. Hydropathic establishments have been set up in many health resorts.

Hydroponics, or soilless growth, is the craft and science of growing plants in liquid nutrients instead of soil. Originally a laboratory technique, hydroponics has become since the 1930s a practical method of vegetable, fruit and flower production on both small and large scale. Basically, the growing plants have their roots in troughs of nutrient solution, either in or out of doors. Advantages include: much higher crop yields; the close control of weeds and diseases; quicker growth; and, very important, the possibilities of growing food in places where ordinary agriculture would be impracticable, *e.g.*, deserts and stony land, city roofs, in houses and in remote situations like Antarctic stations. Hydroponics is widely practised and contributes usefully to agriculture and horticulture in many countries, including the USA, Britain, India and France. Its value in spaceships and planetary colonies has often been pointed out by technological prophets.

Hydrostatics, the science of the pressure and equilibrium of liquids that are non-elastic.

Hydrozoa are a class of water animals of the *Coelenterata* phylum to which hydra (*q.v.*) belongs. In one order of the hydrozoa, free-swimming colonies showing marked division of labour between the individual units occur; this order includes the Portuguese man-of-war.

Hyena, a nocturnal carnivore with powerful jaws. The striped hyenas inhabit N. Africa and S.W. India. The brown hyenas with long shaggy hair are natives of S. Africa. The spotted, or laughing hyena, noted for the peculiar cry from which its name is derived, is also confined to Africa.

Hygrometer, an instrument for measuring the amount of water vapour in the atmosphere. A simple form of hygrometer, known as the wet-and-dry bulb, consists of two vertical thermometers affixed to a frame. One bulb is exposed to the air, and the other is covered with muslin which dips into a water-bath to keep it moist. If the air is saturated, it takes up no moisture from the wet bulb and the two thermometers read the same. If the air is not saturated, evaporation takes place from the wet bulb, latent heat is absorbed from the air and the temperature of the wet bulb is lower than that of the dry bulb. Relative humidity and dew-point of the air can then be derived from suitable tables. Hygrometers depending upon the expansion of human hair and gold-beater's skin and the deposition of dew on a polished surface, when cooled sufficiently, are also in general use. *See* **Humidity.**

Hymenoptera, the order of insects to which bees, wasps, hornets, ants and sawflies belong. They have a well-defined waist, two pairs of membranous wings coupled together, mouth parts modified for biting or sucking; the females possess an ovipositor used for depositing eggs and is sometimes modified for stinging. There are about 70,000 species in this order and many live in highly organised communities. *See also* **Ichneumon Fly.**

Hyperbola. A curve described by certain comets that go round the sun and never return.

Hypsometer, an instrument formerly used by mountaineers to find the height above sea-level by indirectly measuring the atmospheric pressure by determining the boiling point of water at the particular height. Based on the fact that as pressure decreases with height so the boiling point is lowered. Superseded by the aneroid barometer.

I

Ibex, wild goats of several species found in the mountain regions of Europe, Asia and Africa. The male has exceedingly large curved ridged horns. The species that lives in the Alps is called the Steinbock or bouquetin.

Ibis, belongs to a family of birds related to the stork. The sacred ibis of ancient Egypt is now extinct in Egypt but is found in the lakes and swamps of the Sudan near the Upper Nile. It has white and black plumage and a long curved beak. Other species are found elsewhere, the Glossy Ibis (black plumage glossed with purple and green) occasionally visiting England.

Ibo (properly Igbo), a large tribe of S.E. Nigeria, numbering between 5 and 6 million. After the end of British rule they were active in their struggle for national independence and under their leader, Ojukwu, embarked upon the secessionist state of Biafra and the unsuccessful civil war against Federal forces. The Hausa

L63

and the Yoruba are the other main Nigerian groups.

Ice is frozen water. It is a colourless, crystalline and brittle solid. Being only 92% as dense as water, it floats on the latter; the expansion which occurs as water changes into ice causes the fracture of water-pipes, though the fracture only becomes obvious when the ice melts and leaks out through the crack. The temperature at which ice forms is 0°C, 32°F. Ice can be melted by pressure, and the ease and smoothness with which one is able to skate on ice depends on this phenomenon.

Ice Ages. Periods during which the continents were partly or largely covered by ice-sheets and glaciers. The present-day ice-sheets of Greenland and Antarctica are relics of the most recent ice age (one of the eight major ones during the past 700,000 years), which began in the Pleistocene and ended about 10,000 years ago. During this last great glaciation ice sheets covered the northern part of Europe, Asia and North America. There is strong evidence that periodic changes in the earth's orbit around the sun caused the ice ages. The earth is now in one of its warm periods though there are signs that a moderate cooling trend has begun.

Icebergs are detached masses of glacier which subside into the sea and float as wind or current may take them. About one-ninth of an iceberg is above sea-level. The North Atlantic is the chief home of icebergs, which reach the ocean from the ice-clad plateaux of Greenland. Some of these floating masses of ice are of enormous proportions, and constitute in the spring and early summer seasons a great menace to the safety of ships, as was disastrously shown in the *Titanic* catastrophe of 1912. For some years past these menaces to N. Atlantic shipping have been kept under close observation by vessels specially detailed for this work.

Ice-breaker, a special heavy bow-plated ship for forcing a way through ice and used especially at ports of the Baltic Sea and the Great Lakes region of Canada which freeze during the winter months. The Soviet atomic ice-breaker *Lenin*, the first of its kind in the world, launched in December 1957, was designed to cut a channel through ice of any thickness. Her performance allowed the sea-route to the north of Siberia to be kept open throughout the year. Russia has now several nuclear-powered icebreakers.

Icelandic Literature, the old Norse literature, centred about Iceland, which includes numerous works of poetry, mythology and history of interest and importance. Much of this literature is in the saga form. *See also* **Edda.**

Iceland Moss, a kind of lichen (*Cetrario islandica*) which grows in great quantities in the mountain regions of Iceland and other Northern countries. It possesses certain nutritive qualities and is of some value in medicine.

Iceland Spar, a colourless form of calcite (calcium carbonate), frequently found in association with metallic ores; it has the power to produce strong double refraction of light so that two images are seen of an object viewed through a piece of Iceland spar. It was formerly used in optical apparatus for producing polarised light.

Iceni, an ancient British race who in early times lived in Norfolk and other parts of Eastern England. Their most famous ruler was Queen Boadicea, who led her people against the Romans in A.D. 61.

Ice Plant, also called "dew plant" and "diamond plant". A South African mesembryanthemum commonly grown in British gardens. Introduced in 1690.

Ice Saints, St. Mamertus, St. Pancras and St. Servatius, so called because of the legendary cold on these Saints' Days, namely, 11–13 May.

Ichneumon, the Egyptian mongoose, popularly known as "Pharaoh's Rat". It is of great use in checking the multiplication of reptiles. It is frequently domesticated.

Ichneumon Fly, a numerous group of parasitic hymenopterous insects abounding in many lands, and all having the peculiarity of depositing their eggs in the bodies of other insects. It destroys swarms of caterpillars, which become the unwilling hosts of its progeny.

Ichthyology, the natural history of fishes.

Ichthyosaurus was a gigantic marine reptile of the Mesozoic age. The fossils are mostly found in the lias formation. Some were over 9 m.

Icon, an image of a sacred personage used in the home or in churches for devotional purposes by Christians of the Eastern Orthodox faith. Icons can be painted on wood, perhaps with the figures picked out against a golden background, or they can be cast in bronze, in the form of a crucifix, diptych (*q.v.*) or triptych with details in coloured enamels. Subjects are taken from the life of Christ or of the Saints. In churches several icons are sometimes placed together on a screen (the iconostasis, which divides the altar and sanctuary from the main body of the church). The earliest preserved icons date from the 12th cent. Icons were venerated in Russia until the Revolution and remain, still in their archaic stylised form of mediaeval origin, a characteristic feature of the Orthodox Church to this day.

Ides, in the ancient Roman Calendar, the 15th of March, May, July, October, and the 13th of all other months; always the eighth day after the Nones.

Idiom, an expression characteristic of a country, district, dialect or language, which usually gives strength and force to a phrase or sentence. The idioms of a language are its distinctive marks, and the best writers are the most idiomatic.

Idris, a famous giant belonging to the myths of Wales, commemorated by a chair of rock on the top of the Cader Idris mountain in Gwynedd.

Igneous Rocks are such as have been molten under conditions of great heat at some stage in their history: *e.g.*, granite, basalt. *See* **F9(1).**

Ignis Fatuus *or* **"Will-o'-the-wisp",** a phosphorescent light which may often be seen on summer and autumn evenings hovering over marshy ground or graveyards. Its nature is hardly understood, though it is generally believed to be the result of the spontaneous combustion of the gases from decaying organic matter. In olden times when marshy grounds were more common than now, this "dancing light" was very frequently visible and was regarded with superstition.

Iguana, large South American lizard, with a long tail, a scaly back and head, a thick fleshy tongue and a prominent dew-lap in the throat. Specimens of the different species average 1·2–1·5 m in length, and they live mostly in trees, though they are equally at home on land or in the water. The flesh of some species is good eating, as are also the eggs.

Iguanodon, a genus of extinct dinosaurs, whose fossils are found in the Jurassic and Cretaceous rocks. Iguanodons were 4·5–7·6 m long, and walked on their hind legs, the front legs being small and adapted for grasping the branches of trees on the leaves of which they fed.

Ilex, mentioned by classical authors, the holm- or holly-oak, which flourishes round the Mediterranean. To botanists Ilex is the genus to which the holly and maté plant belong.

Iliad, the great epic poem of ancient Greece attributed to Homer (*c.* 700 B.C.). It consists of ancient folk tale and saga, welded into an artistic unity, having as plot the carrying off of Helen by Paris to Troy and the subsequent siege of Troy. *See* **Section I.**

Illuminated MSS. of great value and beauty of decoration exist in most public museums and in many private collections, some of them being of great antiquity, especially those of ancient Egypt executed on papyri. Greek and Latin specimens are also numerous, and the British Museum contains fine examples of all these kinds and also an extensive collection of mediaeval English MSS.

Illuminati. *See* **Section J.**

Ilmenite, a mineral widespread in igneous rocks: chemically it is an oxide of iron and titanium. Rich deposits have recently been found in the Allard Lake area of Quebec: the Travancore sands are also a source of ilmenite.

Immortality. *See* **Section J.**

Immortelles are wreaths, crosses or other designs made from what are called everlasting flowers, which are obtained from certain plants of the Composite order, and retain their colours and compactness for a long time. Immortelles are

L64

largely used as mementoes for decorating graves, especially in France.

Impeachment, a special arraignment, usually before Parliament or other high tribunal, of a person charged with some offence against the State. The custom in England was for the impeachment to be made in the House of Commons, and the trial to be before the House of Lords. The first instance occurred in 1376 when Lord Latimer was impeached. With present parliamentary procedure, impeachment is no longer necessary, since the Cabinet is responsible for the individual actions of its ministers, who, acting as a team, must carry the Commons with them, or resign, when it falls to the Leader of the Opposition to form a new Cabinet. Other famous impeachments were those of the Lord High Chancellor Francis Bacon (1621), Earl of Strafford and Archbishop Laud (1640), Warren Hastings (1788), the last being that of Lord Melville (1805). Under the constitution of the United States public officials may be impeached by the House of Representatives and tried by the Senate. A famous case was that of President Andrew Johnson who was saved from impeachment in 1868 by one vote. Had President Nixon not resigned in 1974 he would have been impeached for the affair of the tapes and his abuse of executive privilege.

Imperialism. *See* **Section J.**

Impressionism, the most important and influential movement in 19th cent. European painting. It gained its name, at first contemptuously, in 1874 from a picture painted by Claude Monet and named by the artist *Impression: soleil levant,* which showed the play of light on water with the observer looking straight into the rising sun. Although intended to be the ultimate form of naturalism the inspiration of the school had been the scientific study of light with an attempt to render the play of light on the surface of objects. Feeling that putting a line around a form was bound to cause it to look unnatural, they used bright colours corresponding to the spectrum and unmixed on the palette, and noted that an object of any given colour casts a shadow tinged with the complementary one (*e.g.*, red-green, yellow-blue). Hence bright sunlight was represented in clear yellows and orange with violet shadows. The first Impressionist exhibition held in Paris in 1874 aroused derision with its paintings by Monet, Renoir, Sisley, Pissaro, Cézanne and Degas among others. Impressionism subsequently led to the entirely artistic and anti-naturalist movement of Post-impressionism. Cézanne, who felt that he wanted to produce "something solid and durable, like the art of the museums" was only dubiously impressionist, as were also Degas and Renoir. Of course, in the wider sense of the word (*i.e.*, the recording of an ephemeral impression of a scene), Whistler, Turner and even Rembrandt used the technique.

Impressment, the forced seizure of persons for military service resorted to by many countries before the establishment of conscription. Press gangs forcibly recruited men for British warships especially during the Napoleonic wars, but such measures were abandoned after about 1850.

Imprimatur, originally an official licence to print and an important formula in the early days of printing. The term is now used in the wider significance of authority, or endorsement.

Incas, an Indian people who inhabited ancient Peru, founded a great empire and reached a high level of civilisation; overthrown by the Spaniards in 1533.

Incense, an aromatic resinous substance which, under combustion, exhales a pungent odour, and is used, mixed with certain fragment perfumes, in the celebration of Mass in Roman Catholic churches. Olibanum or frankincense is ordinarily the leading ingredient.

Incisors, the sharp-edged cutting teeth at the front of mammalian jaws. Rodents have long, sharp incisor teeth. Elephant tusks are modified incisors.

Independence Day, commemorates the adoption of the Declaration of Independence on 4 July 1776. 4 July is celebrated as a holiday in the USA.

Index. The name given to a list of books, prepared by papal authority, which are declared to be dangerous to faith and morals, and therefore forbidden to Roman Catholics, called the *Index librorum prohibitorum.* One of the reforms of the Vatican Council was the closing in 1966 of the Curia office which judged writings for the Church's Index of forbidden books, though the Index itself still remains. The Pope ordered that nothing should be placed on the Index until the author had been given a chance of explaining his views. The first Index was issued by Pope Pius IV, in 1559.

Indian Mutiny. This turning-point in the history of modern India occurred in 1857–58. The ostensible cause was the serving out to the native troops of cartridges greased with animal fat, for contact with this was forbidden both by the Hindu and Mohammedan faiths. A rebellious feeling, however, had long been developing, and when the Sepoys at Meerut in May 1857 refused to obey the English officers, overpowered and put them to death, the mutiny spread like wildfire. The rebels took Delhi and Lucknow, and for many months terrible massacres and atrocities were committed; men, women and children were slain in thousands. Order was re-established in the autumn of 1858 when the governing power was transferred from the East India Company to the Crown.

Indicators, substances which by a marked change in colour are used to indicate the course of a chemical reaction. Litmus paper, for instance, is red with acids and blue with alkalis. In biological work some radioactive substances are used as tracer elements.

Indigo, the substance obtained from the plant *Indigofera tinctoria,* a native of S. Asia, India being the chief producing country. The colouring matter is the result of the decomposition and fermentation of a glucoside contained in the plant. This is afterwards dried and becomes the caked indigo of commerce. Natural indigo has been eclipsed by artificial indigo, a coal-tar dye which came into commercial production at the end of the last century, and which is cheaper and more uniform in quality.

Indium, a scarce lead-coloured metallic element, no. 49, symbol In, found in zinc blende in Saxony and certain other ores. Discovered in 1863 by Reich and Richter. It is an important material in the manufacture of transistors.

Indulgence. In the Roman Catholic Church the remission granted by ecclesiastical authority to a repentant sinner of the temporal punishment still due after the guilt of sin has been forgiven by God. The indiscriminate sale of Indulgences by Tetzel and other Papal agents in the 16th cent. was one of the grievances which led to the Reformation (*see* **Section J**); the Council of Trent made such traffic unlawful.

Indulgence, Declaration of, was the proclamation by which James II suspended the penal laws against Roman Catholics and Dissenters. It was issued in 1688, but the clergy as a body refused to obey, and the trial of the Seven Bishops and their acquittal by a jury followed. An invitation was thereupon sent to William of Orange to become King.

Industrialisation is simply a name for industrial development. It is customarily used in particular to designate the course of events in a hitherto underdeveloped country which is seeking to increase its wealth and productivity by the introduction of more advanced techniques and by the establishment of industries previously not carried on within it. The word usually covers not only the development of modern industrial production but also the provision of electric power-stations, irrigation works and transport and other developments designed to improve production in any field by methods involving large capital investments. The outstanding example in our time of rapid industrialisation has been the Soviet Union, which, unable to get the capital from abroad, had to carry it through by ruthless restriction of the people's consuming power so as to achieve an unprecedentedly high ratio of investment to total production. Industrialisation has in practice meant a high concentration on the expansion of the basic heavy industries and of power supply, coupled with much slower development of the industries supplying consumer goods and of agricultural production; but there is no reason why this should always be the case. It may well be that in most underdeveloped countries development can but be devoted largely to the industries making consumers' goods and to measures designed to increase agricultural production and productivity.

Industrial Revolution. The name, first given by Engels in 1844, to describe the radical changes that took place in Britain during *c.* 1730–1850 to transform a mainly agricultural country into one predominantly industrial. It began with the mechanisation of the textile industry (Hargreave's spinning jenny, 1764, Arkwright's water-frame, 1769, Crompton's mule, 1770, and Watt's steam-engine, 1785), with subsequent major developments in mining, transport and industrial organisation. It was based on Britain's rich mineral resources, particularly coal and iron ore. With the use of the steam-engine as power, industry became concentrated round the coalfields and the great new industrial towns developed—Birmingham, Manchester, Newcastle and Glasgow. Britain became supreme in constructional ironwork (Telford, George and Robert Stephenson). Canals, bridges, railways and ships were built, and great advances were made in the practical application of scientific principles. Aided by colonial exploitation Britain became the most prosperous country in the world. The new industrial capitalists began to replace the country squires as ruling class. But the great accumulation of wealth at one pole of society was matched at the other by poverty and misery, for child labour, long working hours, low wages and slums were features of the industrial revolution in its infancy. As with all great technological developments, the industrial revolution produced related changes in all fields of social life—in politics, art, religion, literature and morals, and with the rise of democracy, social reforms.

Inertia, a term used in mechanics for the property of matter by which it offers resistance to a change in its state of rest or in its state or direction of motion.

Inertial Navigation, an automatic method of dead-reckoning which at present finds its chief application in guided missiles, submarines and aircraft. Navigation by this means is carried out with reference to inertial space (*i.e.,* space which is stationary with respect to the fixed stars) and not to the surface of the earth as in normal navigation (latitude and longitude). This is done by means of high-accuracy gyroscopes combined with highly sensitive accelerometers in an apparatus known as the Ship's Inertial Navigation System. The American nuclear-powered submarine *Nautilus* pioneered the new north-west passage under the polar ice pack by this method of dead-reckoning in August 1958.

Inflorescence, a flowering shoot. Many arrangements of the flowers are possible and there are many kinds of inflorescence; *e.g.,* the spike, catkin, umbel, capitulum (in composites).

Inflation. See **Section G.**

Infra-red Rays *or* **Radiation.** This is the range of rays which come between the visible red rays and the ultra-short Hertzian radiation. The wavelengths involved range between 0·75 micron (0.75×10^{-6}m) and 100 micron (1 millimetre). Infra-red rays penetrate haze; hence landscapes obscured by haze or cloud can be photographed using plates sensitive to infra-red. Many substances strongly absorb these rays and thereby become hot; this happens in toasting bread. Many industries use infra-red lamps for drying paints and lacquers. Very important to chemists, as a tool in the investigation of the structure of compounds, since various groups of elements absorb infra-red radiation at a characteristic frequency. Infra-red astronomy has developed in recent years.

Infula, a sacred fillet, of woollen material, worn on the forehead by priests, magistrates and rulers in Roman times, also by persons fleeing for protection to sanctuary. Later, each of the two lappets of a bishop's mitre.

Ingoldsby Legends, a series of whimsical metrical tales full of droll humour written by the Rev. R. H. Barham, and first published in *Bentley's Miscellany* in 1837. The best known is the *Jackdaw of Rheims.*

Ink, a liquid pigment ordinarily made from an infusion of nut-galls, copperas and gum arabic. Shumac is substituted for nut-galls for inferior inks. An acid is sometimes added to prevent oxidation, and for the blue-black inks a small quantity of solution of indigo serves for colouring. Copying ink contains glycerine or sugar, which keeps the ink moist. Lampblack used to be the leading ingredient in printer's ink but now new methods of manufacturing have been developed. Marking ink is composed of a solution of nitrate of silver, gum, ammonia and carbonate of soda. For red, blue and other coloured inks, colouring solutions are used, for example, Prussian blue. The earliest examples of ink writing (on wooden tablets) ever found in Britain were recovered from the well of a Roman villa (3rd cent. A.D.) during excavations in 1954 at Chew Stoke, Somerset.

Ink Sac, a glandular organ found in squids and other cephalopods which contains an inky solution. When roused the animal discharges the contents of the ink sac into the water, to make a cloud through which its enemies cannot see. The pigment, sepia, comes from the ink sac of the cuttlefish.

Inns of Court, the four bodies in London which enjoy the privilege of calling candidates to the bar after they have studied for a certain number of terms and passed certain examinations. The Inns are: the Inner Temple, the Middle Temple, Lincoln's Inn and Gray's Inn.

Inquisition, a Roman Catholic ecclesiastical court which became a formidable weapon of the Church in the 13th cent. under Pope Innocent III in dealing with charges of heresy. It was effectively set up in the various Catholic countries of the Continent, obtaining its fullest and most sweeping organisation in Spain in the days of Ferdinand and Isabella, when Torquemada was made Grand Inquisitor, and used its powers with terrible severity. See **Auto-da-fé.** In the 18th cent. its influence began to wane, and the jurisdiction of the Congregation of the Holy Office at Rome was limited to the suppression of heretical literature (*see* **Index**). Recently, the Congregation for the Doctrine of Faith (CDF), as it is now called, called into question the orthodoxy of two of the Roman Catholic Church's most respected theologians.

Insectivorous Plants, plants which trap insects with special mechanisms. Plant enzymes or bacteria digest the prey, providing the plants with nitrogen usually scarce in the soil in which they grow. The most common British species are the Sun-dew and the Bladderwort.

Insects. This huge class of invertebrate animals (*see* **Arthropods (F36)**) includes about 100,000 species. Insects are ubiquitous except in the sea, only a very few species being adapted to marine existence. Characteristic features are: the body is divided into three parts, head, thorax and abdomen: the head carries a pair of antennae, the thorax three pairs of legs and usually two pairs of wings. The most primitive insects constituting the sub-class *Apterygota* are wingless. The other sub-class, *Pterygota,* is divided into the *Exopterygota* (*Hemimetabola*), which have a simple metamorphosis, *e.g.,* cockroach, and the *Endopterygota* (*Holometabola*), with a complex metamorphosis, *e.g.,* butterfly, bee. Although many are parasitic on man, animals and plants, innumerable animals and some plants use them as food, and many flowering plants are dependent on a variety of insects for pollination leading to the development of seeds and fruits. See **F36(1), 41(1).**

Insignia, marks or badges of office or honour, such as stars, ribbons, crosses, medallions or other designating objects, worn by members of special Orders or holders of prominent offices.

Instinct. See **F40(2).**

Institut de France was formed in 1795, and after various modifications was in 1832 organised on its present basis. Its five academies are—the Académie Française, Académie des Inscriptions et Belles-Lettres, Académie des Sciences, Académie des Beaux-Arts, Académie des Sciences morales et politiques. It is restricted to 40 members.

Instruments, Musical. Musical instruments may be classified in a number of ways, but in general they fall into one of the three main classes, String, Wind and Percussion, according to how the sound in produced. **Stringed Instruments** are those which produce the sound by the vibration of a string: (*a*) by plucking, as in Harp, Lyre, Psaltery, Zither, Lute, Guitar, Balalaika, Ukelele, Harpsichord; (*b*) by friction (bowed), as in Crwth, Rebec, Viol, Violin, Marine Trumpet, Hurdy-Gurdy; (*c*) by striking (hammered), as in Dulcimer, Pianoforte, Clavichord; (*d*) by wind (blown), as in the Aeolian Harp. **Wind Instruments** are those in which the air in the instruments is set in vibration: (*a*) by blowing into a tube (flue-voiced), as in Recorder, Pandean Pipe, Flute, Organ; (*b*) by means of reeds (reed-voiced), as in Oboe, Clarinet, Saxophone, Bagpipe, Cor Anglais, Bassoon, Organ reed-stops; (*c*) those in which the sound is produced by the vibration of the player's lips against the mouthpiece (lip-voiced), as in Bugle, Horn, Trumpet, Tuba, Trombone, Saxhorn, Flügelhorn, Cornet. In a modern orchestra these are known as the *Brass*; instruments of the flute, oboe and clarinet families as the *Woodwinds*. Then there are the **Percussion Instruments**, which include the Drums, Cymbals, Tambourines, Castenets.

Insulator, a substance that will not conduct electric current. Many solids, liquids and gases are important insulators—rubber, cotton, silk, plastics, porcelain, glass, air, oil. If the applied voltage is too high, all insulators will "break down", *i.e.*, conduct electricity perhaps with resulting breakage, puncture or charring. Thermal insulators will not conduct heat; they are usually the same kinds of substance as electrical insulators.

Insulin is a hormone which controls the supply of sugar from the blood to muscles. The breakdown of sugar provides energy. In diabetes there is a lack of insulin, causing a build-up of blood sugar which can be released by the injection of insulin. It is secreted by the islet tissue of the pancreas, from which it was isolated in 1922 by Banting and Best. Dr. F. Sanger of Cambridge won the 1958 Nobel Prize in Chemistry for isolating and identifying its amino acid components. Prof. Dorothy Hodgkin and her team at the Dept. of Molecular Biophysics at Oxford succeeded in determining the structure of insulin, a task which would not have been possible without the electronic computer. In 1980 insulin became the first product of genetic engineering techniques to reach clinical trials.

Intelligence. Intelligence has been variously defined as the innate potential of a person to learn and understand; to make appropriate judgments; to see the relationships between things; to profit from experience; or to meet adequately new problems and conditions in life. There are many lines of evidence to show that intellectual capacity is closely related to heredity and influenced by environmental factors. The idea of intelligence testing was first devised by the French psychologist Binet at the beginning of this century. He was asked by the French government to invent a test which would weed out backward children in state schools, and thus save public money and avoid holding back the work of the class by teaching children who were incapable of learning at a given standard. Briefly, a series of problems are given to a large number of children and it is thus found out which series can be solved by the average child of a given age-group; if a child of 7 can only pass the tests suitable to the average child of 6, then his mental age is 6. The intelligence quotient or I.Q. is discovered by dividing his mental age by his chronological age and multiplying by 100. A gifted child can usually be spotted at an early age. Although I.Q. tests are the standard method of estimating intelligence, they are not universally accepted as a criterion; a teacher's general judgment may be the best assessment. High intelligence may be inherited, but fail to develop to the full because facilities for education are not available. Recent research suggests that the growth of the brain may be permanently affected by under-nutrition at the time of its fastest growth (the last weeks before birth, and, to a lesser extent, the first weeks after birth). At this vulnerable period even quite minor deprivation can affect the rate and ultimate extent of growth of the brain. This has significance not only for the severely under-nourished babies in the poor parts of the world, but for babies of low birth weight in our own communities. *See also* **Q28.**

Interest is the payment made for the use of borrowed money over time. The rate of interest is the rate per cent per annum charged for such loans. There are many such rates, varying with the plenty or scarcity of borrowable money, with the length of time for which the loans are made, and with the degree of risk, if any, that the loans will not be duly repaid. Short-term loans are usually cheaper than long-term: the lowest rates are usually for "call money" repayable immediately on demand. These are used principally in short-term financial transactions, such as bill discounting. Bank loans, though usually made for fairly short terms, command higher rates. Long-term loans are made chiefly to public authorities, or as bonds or debentures to business concerns. The rates obtained vary with the demand and the supply of such accommodation.

Interferon, identified in 1957 as a defence protein produced in animal cells, is also produced in human immune systems. Its use as a possible anti-cancer agent as well as for other complaints has been limited by extraction problems. Modern production is likely to be by genetic engineering. In 1980 the amino acid sequence was determined for the 150 residues in human interferon.

International Date Line, a line along the 180° meridian marking the difference in time between E. and W. For the westward-bound traveller crossing the line the date would be put forward one day, for the eastward-bound, back one day. To avoid difference of date in adjacent land areas, the line deviates from the 180° meridian where this crosses land.

Introit, the psalm sung by the choir as the priest approaches the altar to celebrate the Eucharist.

Invention of the Cross, a Roman Catholic festival held on 3 May, to celebrate the finding of the alleged True Cross at Calvary by the Empress St. Helena in 326. Also included in the Church of England calendar. *See* **Holy Rood.**

Iodine, a non-metal element, no. 53, symbol I, member of the halogen family (*q.v.*), a substance formerly exclusively obtained from the ribbon-wrack seaweeds. These were burnt and the ashes (kelp) extracted with water. After concentrating the iodides, these were distilled with manganese dioxide and sulphuric acid to yield iodine vapour which was condensed in stoneware bottles. Nearly all iodine now in use is derived from the iodine salt present in Chile saltpetre (natural sodium nitrate). Iodine is used in photography, as an antiseptic solution in alcohol or potassium iodide (tincture of iodine), and in medicine. Discovered by Courtois in 1812.

Ionosphere. Although a certain degree of ionisation occurs at all levels of the atmosphere due to cosmic rays and the radioactivity of rocks, etc., the ionosphere is normally denoted as the region above about 70 km where the ultra-violet component of sunlight is able to ionise a significant fraction of the atoms and molecules present. This ionisation causes the reflection of radio waves by which the ionosphere was initially discovered and for many years, explored. The nomenclature of the ionospheric layers—"D" region up to about 95 km, "E" region 95 km to about 180 km, and "F" region above 180 km—is due to the historical observations of radio wave reflections from "layers". Satellite and rocket observations have shown that the structure is in fact more continuous. Solar flares and aurora cause enhancements of the electron density in the ionosphere, which may result in the disturbance of radio comunications over large distances (radio blackouts). *See also* **Atmosphere, Aurora, Magnetosphere.**

Ions, electrically charged atoms, or groups of atoms. Atoms of the metals lose electrons to become positively charged ions, *e.g.*, the sodium ion (Na^+) has one electron less than the atom. The non-metal ions are negatively charged, *e.g.*, the chloride ion (Cl^-) has one electron more than the atom. Similarly, a group like the sulphate ion ($SO_4{}^{2-}$) has more electrons than the constituent atoms. Thus, the hydrogen atom without its electron is a hydrogen ion or *proton* and the helium atom without its two electrons is a helium ion or *alpha-particle*. When an electric force is applied to certain solutions, the ions into which molecules of the dissolved substance are broken up are attracted to the oppositely charged electrodes, their movements constituting an electric current through the solution. In the same way gases, including air, conduct electricity by virtue of free ions (*see* **F14(1)**). Combustion, radio-activity and ultra-violet and cosmic radiations produce ionisation. *See* **F23**.

Iridium, a white and very hard metallic element, no. 77, symbol Ir, discovered by Tennant in 1804. It occurs naturally as an alloy with platinum or osmium; tips for fountain-pen nibs have been made from the former native alloy. The former standard metre was composed of platinum–iridium alloy (*see* **Metre**) as are parts of scientific apparatus and surgical tools that must be non-corrodible.

Iris, the typical genus of the botanical order *Iridacae*, with tuberous rhizomes and sword-shaped leaves, many of the family having beautiful flowers. About 100 species of Iris are recorded from the northern temperate zone, the most common species wild in Britain being the yellow flag. Orris root, used in perfumery, comes from another iris species.

Iron is a metallic element, no. 53, symbol Fe (Latin *ferrum*), occurring widely in nature in such ores as haematite, loadstone (magnetic iron oxide), spathic ore and iron pyrites. It is extracted by a process known as smelting, with coke and limestone in a furnace. Its many uses are familiar, the most important being in the manufacture of cast- and wrought-iron products and of steels, which are alloys mainly of iron with added carbon and various metals. Iron rust is formed by the action of oxygen and water, and is a coating of iron oxide. *See* **Smelting.**

Ironclads, ships of war cased in iron or steel plates of sufficient thickness to resist projectiles. They were first introduced (1858) in the French Navy, and in 1860 the first British ironclad, the *Warrior*, was launched.

Iron Curtain. In a speech at Fulton, USA, on 5 March 1946, Sir Winston Churchill used this phrase to describe the dividing line behind which, he said, lie all the capitals of the ancient States of Central and Eastern Europe—Warsaw, Berlin, Prague, Vienna, Budapest, Belgrade, Bucharest and Sofia. These famous cities and the populations around them, said Sir Winston, lie in the Soviet sphere and are subject "to a very high and increasing measure of control from Moscow". The phrase is said to have had dining rather than diplomatic origins. The practice of carving at a sideboard behind a screen (an iron curtain) was called dining *à la Russe*.

Ironsides were Cromwell's special troopers, so called because of their solidity and firmness in battle.

Irrational Number, a number such as the square root of two, or pi, which cannot be expressed as the ratio of two whole numbers. *See* **Rational Number,** and *Pi.*

Irredentists, a political party organised in Italy about 1878 with the object of incorporating within Italy neighbouring regions. Also a person, group or party advocating policies for the restoration to their country of territory formerly belonging to it but later lost.

Irrigation, an artificial method of providing water for the growth of plants on lands where the natural supply of water is deficient. For many hundreds of years techniques of irrigation have been slow and primitive (*e.g.*, tanks, inundation canals and the Archimedes screw) and consequent inefficiencies include large water losses by evaporation and seepage, and the watering of only a small area. New developments in perennial irrigation, using barrages, large reservoirs and pumping stations, permit vast tracts of land to be irrigated. Yet these are not without their problems as witnessed after the construction of the Aswan High Dam on the Nile where com-

plex problems of delta erosion and dam lake silting ensued. Irrigation also serves the purpose of supplying *warmth* in winter; *e.g.*, in the English water-meadows, and in the more highly developed Italian *marcite* and winter-meadows, where the water is mostly applied in winter when there is plenty of rain. There are several other functions of irrigation; *e.g.*, washing out of excess salts and the renewing of fertility by the addition of alluvium.

Islam. *See* **Section J.**

Isobars are the lines drawn on charts linking together points of equal barometric pressure.

Isochasms, lines connecting places at which there is an equal probability of seeing an aurora, taking the average over a number of years, based on the auroral catalogue of Fritz.

Isomers are chemical compounds having the same composition but different structural arrangements, and consequently different physical and chemical properties. For example, ethyl alcohol and methyl ether are isomers, since the molecules of both are built up of two atoms of carbon, six of hydrogen and one of oxygen, *viz.*, C_2H_6O; ethyl alcohol, C_2H_5OH; and methyl ether, CH_3OCH_3.

Isotherms are lines drawn on charts through points of equal temperature.

Isotopes. When one talks of an element, say, uranium or lead, the name of the element is a generic name for a collection of uranium species and lead species. The different species are called isotopes. For any particular element, the number and arrangement of electrons around the nucleus are the same in all the isotopes, so all the isotopes have the same chemical properties. Soddy has described isotopes as "elements, the atoms of which have similar outsides but different insides". For example, in the nucleus of the uranium isotopes, U 235, U 238 and U 239, there are respectively 143, 146 and 147 neutrons, but all have 92 protons. The isotopes have different atomic weights, in this instance respectively 235, 238 and 239. But all have the same chemical properties. *See* **F12(1)**.

Ivory, the dentine substance of which the tusks of the elephant, hippopotamus, walrus, etc., are composed. The tusks of the African elephant sometimes weigh as much as 45 kg, and reach a length of 2·4–2·7 m.

Ivory Gull, a small, beautifully shaped sea-bird with striking all-white plumage and black legs which breeds on the rocky shores of the Arctic, being found farther north than any other bird; it occasionally wanders south in the winter.

J

Jabiru, the Brazilian name for the giant stork of South America.

Jacamar, from *Jacameri*, the Brazilian name for a smallish bird with long, sharply pointed bill and brilliant plumage which inhabits the tropical regions of South America east of the Andes. These birds are seen sitting motionless on trees, darting off at intervals, like flycatchers, to catch insects on the wing.

Jacanas, small water birds with immensely long toes which enable them to walk on water lily leaves. They are sometimes called "lily-trotters" and are found in tropical Africa and America. They live in swamps and feed on seeds and insects. Sometimes brilliantly coloured.

Jack, a small schooner-rigged vessel, used in the Newfoundland fisheries; a pike; an oscillating lever; a device used in roasting meat.

Jackal, *Canis aureus*, a small wild dog related to the wolf and resembling a fox. The Common Jackal is found in S.E. Europe, India and Sri Lanka; other species inhabit Africa and Egypt. The jackal is a well-known scavenger. It hunts singly or in pairs, unlike the wolf, which usually hunts in packs.

Jackdaw, one of the smaller members of the Crow family. This European bird is typically black with grey collar. It is easily tamed, makes an amusing pet and delights in making off with and taking to its nest bright objects, such as silverware.

Jacobins, a French revolutionary club or party, formed in 1789, and accustomed to meet at a Jacobin convent, hence the name. It became a controlling force in the Revolution, especially in the movement which led to the Terror. Robespierre was its chief spokesman.

Jacobites, adherents of the Stuart cause after the abdication of James II. First James himself, then his son (the Old Pretender), and later his grandson (the Young Pretender) tried to fan the flame of rebellion in Scotland and Ireland, but after the defeat at Culloden in 1746 the cause was lost. Also the name of the monophysite heretics of Syria, so named after their leader Jacobus Baradaeus in the 6th cent. A.D.

Jade, an exquisite kind of hardstone, ranging in colour from a whitish green to a deep mauvish brown. It can be translucent or opaque and sometimes it is veined. Jade is the common name for two minerals—the rarer *jadeite* (found in Burma, Tibet and China), a sodium-aluminium-silicate, and *nephrite* (found in New Zealand, China, Turkestan and Siberia), a calcium-magnesium silicate. The presence of small quantities of other chemicals accounts for the wide range of shades. In China jade has for centuries been looked upon with great veneration, magical powers have been ascribed to it, and it has been fashioned into ritual objects, also into miniature sculptures of animals or even whole landscapes, charming to look at and incredibly skilfully made. The Chinese word for jade is *yü,* used as a symbol for all that is noble, beautiful and pure.

Jaguar, a South American carnivorous animal resembling the leopard, but larger and more powerful. It preys on other animals but rarely attacks man.

Jainism. *See* **Section J.**

Janeite, a devotee of Jane Austen and her writings.

Janissaries, an élite band of Ottoman foot soldiers who acted as the Sultan's bodyguard. They were conscripts, raised by the "tribute of children" from conquered Christian countries, mainly Serbia and Albania. First recruited under Murad I (14th cent.). They were not allowed to marry. They gained great power under the Ottoman Empire. In 1826 the Sultan Mahmud II had them massacred.

January, the first month of the year, named after Janus, the two-faced god of the Romans. It was the *Wolf monath* and *Aefter Yule* of the Saxons.

Jasmine, a graceful climber belonging to the olive family with odoriferous blossom, originally a Persian plant, but now acclimatised in many varieties in almost all parts of the world. Two species of jasmine (the common jasmine and the Spanish jasmine) yield oils used in perfumery.

Jasper, a precious stone of the chalcedony variety, opaque, and coloured red, brown, yellow and sometimes green. It was greatly esteemed by the ancients, the Bible having numerous allusions to it.

Jay, a gaily-coloured bird of the Crow family, of many species—the Blue jay of N. America, the Canada jay, sometimes called "whisky jack", the Siberian jay and the British jay, fawn-coloured with black and whitish crest and bright blue feathers in the wings. It lives in woods and like the magpie, takes the eggs and young of small nesting birds.

Jazz a rhythmical syncopated music characterised by a strong element of improvisation in the performance, probably originating among the Negro population of the Southern States of the USA. It became popular during the first world war and, in a commercialised form, has held the popular field ever since. Modern dance music and popular songs are based on the jazz idiom, which has also had a profound effect upon more serious contemporary music. *See* **E31.**

Jean, a stout kind of twilled cotton cloth much worn in olden times, and resembling fustian. Blue *jeans,* adopted by American city youngsters from farmworkers, are now the fashion elsewhere and worn not only as overalls by workmen but by both sexes in leisure time.

Jelly-fish. The jelly-fishes, which have gelatinous, translucent bodies fringed at the margin with

delicate tentacles, constitute the coelenterate order *Scyphozoa.* The mouth, with a squarish opening, is seen on the underside, and there are four horseshoe-shaped sex organs.

Jerboa, small jumping mammals of the Rodent order. These mice-like animals have long tufted tails and very long hind legs, the front legs not being used for locomotion.

Jeremiad, any utterance or writing in which sorrow or complaint is the chief characteristic, so named as recalling the style of the "Lamentations of Jeremiah", in the Old Testament.

Jerusalem Chamber, a room in Westminster Abbey, deriving its name from the circumstance of its having originally been decorated with a view of Jerusalem. Henry IV died in this chamber, and the Committee for the Revision of the Bible met there in 1870 and later.

Jesuits, members of the Roman Catholic teaching order founded by Ignatius Loyola in 1534. A long and vigorous course of study is prescribed before they are admitted into the privileges of full membership. They are required to take the vows of voluntary poverty, perfect chastity, perfect obedience and complete submission to the Pope. The Society played an important part in politics.

Jet, a deep black fossil substance admitting of a high polish and much used for jewellery, ornaments and trimming. It is a form of lignite, the most important British deposit being found near Whitby, where jet manufacture has been an established industry for a long period.

Jet Engine, an aeroplane engine which derives its thrust from the high velocity of the gases it ejects. The essential units in a jet engine are a rotary compressor and a gas turbine, the latter driving the compressor. The first reliable, high-performance jet propulsion engine for aircraft was invented by Air Commodore Sir Frank Whittle.

Jet Stream, a meteorological term coined in 1946 to describe the relatively narrow belt of strong winds (160–320 km/h) at levels in the atmosphere from 5–11 km. These winds are important in forecasting weather, and can be a valuable aid to aircraft. From the ground, where there may be little wind, the jet stream can sometimes be seen as high cirrus cloud moving across the sky at high speed.

Jew's Harp. The name is believed to be a corruption of "jaws harp". This instrument consists of a metal frame with a central tongue of spring steel. The frame is pressed against the teeth, and the tongue of the harp is twanged with the finger, the mouth acting as a resonating chamber. By altering the shape of the mouth the resonant frequency and therefore the note can be varied.

Jockey Club, the governing body that, although possessing no legal status, frames rules and laws by which horse-racing and turf matters generally are regulated. The club-house is at Newmarket.

John Bull, the typical figure of an Englishman, bluff, big and burly. Arbuthnot's *History of John Bull* is supposed to have originated the character.

John Dory, a fish found in most temperate seas and common in British waters. It is of a golden-yellow colour (*jaune doré*), has a high dorsal fin with long filaments projecting from the spines, very protractile jaws and is much valued as a table fish. According to legend the dark spot on each side of its body is the thumbprint of St. Peter who took a coin from the fish's mouth (Matt. XVII 24–7).

John o' Groat's House, W. of Duncansby Head, Caithness, popularly named as the northernmost point of Scotland. According to legend the house, which has now disappeared, was built in octagonal form by a Dutchman Jan de Groot who came to live there in the 16th cent. The site is marked and an inn was erected near it in 1876.

Jongleurs were minstrels and jesters who wandered from town to town singing songs, playing musical instruments, dancing and giving entertainments in mediaeval France and Norman England. Jongleurs were low-born in contrast to the Troubadours, who were often of the nobility.

Joule, a unit of energy in the SI system of units,

L69

defined as the work done when the point of application of a force of one newton is displaced through a distance of one metre in the direction of the force. Named after J. P. Joule (1818–89). The relationship between mechanical energy and heat energy is called the mechanical equivalent of heat and was found by Joule to be 778 ft lbf in lb °F units, or 4·18 × 10⁷ ergs in gram °C units, or 1 Nm in SI units. *See* **F20(1).**

Judaism. *See* **Section J.**

Julian Calendar, named after Julius Caesar, who in 46 B.C., finding the Roman year 90 days in advance of the real time, was the first to adopt the calculation of time by the solar year, the average length being fixed at 365¼ days. There was still an overplus of a few minutes every year, and this was rectified by the Gregorian Calendar, introduced in Italy in 1582 and adopted in England in 1752, from which date what is called the "New Style" begins.

July, the seventh month of the year, named after Julius Caesar. It was the *Maed monath* (Mead-month) of the Saxons.

June, the sixth month of the year, containing 30 days and deriving its name from Juno. It was the *Sear* (Dry) *monath* of the Saxons.

Jupiter is the largest of the planets, 11 times the diameter of the earth, 318 times its mass but only one fourth its density. It is the fifth farthest from the sun and is the second brightest. Our knowledge of Jupiter, its fifteen moons, its ring and its magnetosphere was enormously increased in 1979 by data from the Voyager 1 and 2 space-probes which passed the planet at distances of 349,000 km and 722,000 km on March 5 and July 9 respectively. Jupiter is a gaseous planet composed mainly of hydrogen and helium like the sun, possibly with a small molten core of silicates. The centre is presumed to be at a very high temperature (30,000°C) and enormous pressures—a hundred million earth atmospheres—which make hydrogen not only liquid but metallic. This metallic flux leads to intense magnetic fields. Jupiter's large magnetosphere is distorted by the solar wind and contains trapped high energy particles in radiation belts which would be lethal to man. Its existence was first inferred from its radio emissions and was confirmed by Pioneer 11 in 1974. Jupiter's outer gaseous surface is very cold (−120°C) and consists of three layers of crystal clouds (ice ammonium hydrogensulphide and ammonia) interspersed with gaseous hydrogen and helium. It shows massive persistent features like the swirling high pressure Red Spot (larger when first seen in 1664 but which could hold two earths) and the neighbouring white oval formations. All these features are in relative motion, some moving east and others west which account for Jupiter's banded appearance. The persistence of the features arises because Jupiter has no terrain to break them up and because the surface temperature is low. Lightning continuously flashes over the Jovian surface and at the poles there are large auroras caused by an electric current of five million amperes which flows from the poles out to Io, one of the four moons discovered in 1610 by Galileo. The others are Europa, Ganymede and Callisto. The fourteenth moon was discovered in 1979 by Voyager 2 at the outer edge of the thin ring of particles discovered by Voyager 1, which also discovered high plumes due to volcanic activity on Io, the first seen beyond earth (although a recent suggestion is that the plumes are caused by the electric current). Io's sulphurous surface shows no meteoric craters and Europa's smooth ice surface shows only a few impacts and is probably young, unlike the older Ganymede and Callisto whose ice-crust surfaces have many. Ganymede's crust has been reworked, however, by extensive tectonic movements. Ganymede is now known to be the largest moon in the solar system, larger than the planet Mercury. A fifteenth moon was discovered in 1980 by scientists analysing photographs taken by Voyager I in 1979. *See* **F8.**

Jurassic Formation, a series of rocks (the evidences of which are most marked in the Jura Mountains) coming between the Cretaceous and Triassic groups and including the Oolite and the Lias. It is a formation rich in fauna, abounding in echinoids, lamellibranchs, ammonites and belemnites; large reptiles, marine and land, are common, as are the plants called cyads. In Britain the Jurassic outcrop extends from the Dorset coast to the Yorkshire moors. *See* **F48.**

Jury, a body of private citizens chosen and sworn to hear and pass verdict upon evidence brought forward at a trial, inquest or inquiry. The origin of the English jury is obscure but it is thought to have been introduced by the Normans. The jurors are the sole judges of the true facts upon the evidence laid before them. Under the Criminal Justice Act of 1967 their verdicts in criminal courts in England and Wales no longer have to be unanimous but may be by a majority of 10 to 2. The age limit has recently been reduced from 21 to 18 and raised from 60 to 65. In Scotland 45 jurors are summoned in criminal cases, of whom 15 are chosen by ballot, and majority verdicts are accepted: not guilty, not proven and guilty.

Jute, the name given to the fibre of a plant grown largely in Bangladesh in the Ganges delta and used for the manufacture of coarse cloths, cordage and sacks. Calcutta is the biggest jute-manufacturing centre of the world, as Dundee was in the 19th cent.

Jutes, a Low German race who in the 5th cent. invaded the south-eastern part of England, establishing themselves in Kent and making Canterbury their capital.

Juvenile Courts. This is a special kind of Magistrates' Court to deal with accused persons under the age of seventeen. The Magistrates chosen are specially qualified for the work, and where possible a woman is appointed as one of the magistrates who constitute the Court. The Court is held in private away from the ordinary court room. The object of the Juvenile Court is to introduce into the trial a plan to reform the offender by providing for the care and protection which he may need, by removal from undesirable surroundings, and by subsequent education or training. In these objectives the Court has the co-operation of social workers, including Probation Officers (*q.v.*). Radical changes in methods of preventing and treating juvenile delinquency are contained in the Children and Young Persons Act, 1969, the result of the findings of two White Papers, 1965 and 1968. They emphasise the necessity of helping and supporting the child as far as possible in his own family and community, with resort to formal procedures only where he is exposed to moral danger, or control is necessary in the interest of society or of the child. The minimum age for prosecution will be raised from 10 to 12 when the Government is satisfied that "local authorities and other services have the necessary capacity to cope with this change". Children who are below prosecutable age will be dealt with by social casework or by care proceedings.

K

Kangaroo, pouched (marsupial) mammals of Australia and adjacent islands. There are over 20 species, the smaller ones being known as "wallabies". Kangaroos leap in a succession of springy bounds 3–6 m long, the forefeet not touching the ground. They can reach a height of over 2 m and a weight of 90 kg. First seen by white men when Capt. Cook's expedition visited Australia in 1770. Related genera include the tree kangaroos, rat kangaroos and the Tasmanian Jerboa kangaroo.

Kaolin or China Clay is an essential ingredient in hard-paste porcelain (*q.v.*). It results from the decomposition of felspar, and is widely found in China, Japan and the USA. The richest deposits in Europe are in Cornwall, near Limoges in France, and in Czechoslovakia.

Karst, geological formations typical of limestone regions in which the drainage is by underground channels. Rain water carries part of the limestone away in solution, leaving the surface dry and barren and pitted with innumerable hollows. The name comes from the Karst (Slav *Kras*) region of N.W. Yugoslavia where the rocks are massive pure limestone; the barren plateau is characterised by fissures, caves and subterranean rivers.

Kelvin. Lord Kelvin, an important 19th-cent.

physicist, gave his name to the kelvin, symbol K, a measure of temperature on the absolute scale. The Kelvin scale is a development of the scale invented by Celsius (q.v.) for everyday use, long known as the "centigrade" scale; the degree interval on both scales is the same. The conversion formula for the absolute or Kelvin scale is K = C + 273·15. See **Absolute Temperature.**

Kestrel, the most common British falcon, well known for its habit of hovering for minutes at a time with vibrating wings and then swooping down to attack mice and insects. The male has spotted chestnut-brown back, greyish head and tail, which has a broad black band near tip.

Ketones. A class of organic compounds, related to aldehydes, of general formula R_2CO (where R is an organic radical). The simpler ketones, especially acetone, are widely used as solvents for lacquers, synthetic rubber and polymers, such as cellulose acetate and perspex. More complex ketones occur in nature, and some are used in the perfumery industry, muscone (from the musk deer (q.v.)) is an example.

Kew Gardens, officially known as the Royal Botanic gardens, are among the most celebrated gardens in the world. They were started in 1759 by Princess Augusta of Saxe-Gotha, widow of Frederick, Prince of Wales, and mother of George III. They remained private property until 1841, when control passed to the Commissioners of Woods and Forests. They now cover 121 hectares and are administered by the Min. of Agriculture, Fisheries and Food. Since 1841 the gardens have been open to the public, and form one of the most attractive resorts near London.

Keys, House of, is the Manx representative assembly. See **Tynwald.**

Keystone, the stone which occupies the centre and highest point of an arch and is usually the last to be inserted.

Khaki, a clay-coloured cloth adopted for uniforms in the British Army in the time of the war with the Boers, and used in the first and second world wars. First used by Indian regiments.

Kilderkin, once a common liquid measure in England, representing 18 gallons or 82 litres.

Kilogram, unit of mass, defined as the mass of the international prototype kilogram of platinum-iridium kept at the International Bureau of Weights and Measures at Sèvres. A remeasurement of Avogadro's Number (**F24(1)**) may lead to an atomic standard of mass (the second and the metre are already defined in atomic terms), but this will depend on the precision with which atoms can be counted.

Kilowatt. Unit of power, equal to one thousand watts. See **Watt.**

Kinetic Art denotes works of art which actually move or give the illusion of so doing. An early exponent of kinetic art was the American sculptor Alexander Calder (1898–1976) when he launched his famous "mobiles" in the early 1950s. Since then, constructions which rotate, jump, blink with lights, etc. have been made by many artists and the genre is being further elaborated upon today. Kinetic painters give a visual illusion of movement to their pictures by the use of particular colour contrasts or by a skilful play with spirals, squares, etc. in black and white, sometimes with colours blended in. An interesting exponent of the style is the English artist Bridget Riley (b. 1931).

Kinetic Energy, the energy (q.v.) possessed by a particle or body in virtue of its motion. If the motion is destroyed, e.g., by the impact of the body with an obstacle, the kinetic energy vanishes, being turned into some other form of energy such as heat and sound. If the body has mass m and speed v its kinetic energy (leaving out corrections due to relativity) is $\frac{1}{2}mv^2$.

King Crab, remarkable arthropods now classified separately from both Arachnids and Crustacea which they resemble, inhabiting the sea coasts of America, Japan, India and Malay Peninsula, carrying a shield-shaped shell, and having a long pointed spine projecting from the posterior. The body comprises three separate sections articulated together. These crabs—in America known commonly as the horseshoe crab because of their shape—are from 45–60 cm in length.

Fossil king crabs are found as far back as the Silurian. There are about six living species.

Kingfisher, a well-known family of brilliant-plumaged birds, found in all continents, comprising some 250 species and sub-species. The British kingfisher, Aceldo atthis, haunts the rivers and streams, and is one of the most beautiful of native birds, having iridescent blue-green, white and rich chestnut in its plumage and bright-red feet. All kingfishers have long, dagger-shaped bills. In the Malayan region, New Guinea, the Moluccas and Australia, the varieties are very numerous. The quaint Laughing Jackass of Australia is among the largest of the kingfisher family. The European kingfisher is the bird of the Greek legend of the Halcyon.

King-of-Arms, the name of the chief officials of the Heralds' College. There are several in England —the principal being those of the Garter, Norroy and Ulster, Clarenceux. See **Heralds' College.**

Kiosk, a word of Russian or Turkish origin meaning a small open pavilion of light construction much used in Eastern countries as a place of shade and rest. Similar structures are common in the streets of Paris as news and advertisement stands, and in London as telephone boxes.

Kirimon (Kiri no go Mon) and **Kikumon** (Kiki no go Mon), the two Japanese imperial crests, the first a design of leaves, stems and flowers of the Paulownia plant, and the other representing the sixteen-petalled chrysanthemum.

Kite, name of several birds of prey, widely distributed, related to the hawks and eagles, graceful in flight, and distinguished by their long wings and deeply forked tails. The red kite, light chestnut brown, once the most familiar bird of prey in Britain, seen scavenging the streets of London, is now the rarest, and found only in Wales. The Egyptian kite and the pariah kite of India, notorious for their daring thefts, are closely related to the black kite, a smaller European species, with less forked tail and blackish-brown plumage.

Kittiwake, a beautiful white and pearl-grey gull with black legs, dark eyes and greenish-yellow bill. Its range is wide, and includes the British Isles, where it is a local resident. The flight of this only truly oceanic gull, which except in the breeding-season is generally found offshore, is graceful, swift and buoyant. A triangular black patch, noticeable on the ends of the wings when open, is characteristic of the species, as is the call kitti-wake, from which the bird derives its name. It nests in colonies on the ledges of caves and steep cliffs.

Kiwi, flightless, stoutly-built birds of New Zealand now very rare and carefully protected by the Government. They are little larger than a domestic hen, and lay astonishingly large eggs for their size. Incubation and care of chicks fall to the male bird. They have rudimentary wings concealed by the plumage, and the feathers are hair-like. They are nocturnal in habit.

Knighthood is a degree of honour or title common in Europe since the Middle Ages, and was at first exclusively a military order. In Great Britain the four main orders of knighthood are those of the Garter, the Bath, the Thistle and St. Patrick; in addition to which there are several other orders, such as the Order of St. Michael and St. George, the Star of India, etc. There are also Knights Bachelors not associated with any special order. The title is not hereditary, and therefore ranks below that of a baronet, though both are entitled to the prefix "Sir".

Knot, a nautical measure of speed (1 sea mile per hour), and formerly measured by a log-line, divided by knots at equal distances $\frac{1}{120}$ of a geographical mile. The number of knots travelled by the ship in a half a minute corresponded to the numbers of sea miles it travelled per hour. A sea mile is equal to about 1¼ of a statute mile or 1·9 km. Also, a grey and white wading bird, usually a winter visitor to Britain found in flocks on the coast.

Knout, a whip of many thongs, often fatal in its effects, formerly used in Russia for flogging criminals.

Koala, the Australian arboreal marsupial mammal

that looks like a toy teddy-bear, with ashy-grey fur, bushy ears and rudimentary tail. It feeds on the leaves and shoots of certain eucalyptus trees, and is not more than 60 cm in length.

Kohl, a powder prepared from antimony or burnt almond shells, and in common use by the women of the East for darkening the eyelids.

Koto, a musical instrument in general use in Japan consisting of a series of 13 silken strings stretched across a curved wooden surface, and played with the fingers. Each string is 1·5 m long, and has a separate bridge so fixed as to give the vibration necessary for the note it has to produce. It is a sort of horizontal harp, and in the hands of an expert player is capable of giving forth excellent music.

Kremlin, the citadel or walled city within a Russian city which during the Middle Ages served as an administrative and religious centre and offered protection. That of Moscow, now the headquarters of the Russian government, contains the cathedral where the Tsars were crowned, an imperial palace and the "King of Bells" (*see* **Bells**). Its walls which are topped with towers were built in the 15th cent.

Krypton, one of the rare gas elements, no. 36, symbol Kr, occurring in the air to the extent of 1 part in 20 million. It was discovered in 1898 by Ramsay and Travers. It is used in gas-filled electric lamps.

Kusti, the sacred cord or girdle of the Parsees, consisting of 72 threads—the number of the chapters of the *Yasna*—and two branches, each branch containing six knots, together standing for the 12 months of the year.

Kyrie Eleison ("Lord, have mercy"), the name of a common form of prayer in the Anglican, Roman Catholic and Greek Churches; also applied to the English Church responses after the recital of the commandments.

Kyrle Society, named after Pope's "Man of Ross", John Kyrle, founded by Miss Miranda and Miss Octavia Hill in 1875, and having for its object, the decoration of workmen's clubs, hospitals, etc. and the promotion among the poor of a taste for literature, music and outdoor recreation.

L

Labarum, the standard of Constantine the Great, adopted after his conversion to Christianity, marked with his seal and represented upon the coinage.

Labourers, English Statute of, was passed 1350–51, with the object of compelling labourers to accept a certain rate of wages and not leave their employers' service, the Plague having rendered labourers so scarce that they were in great demand and had been insisting on higher pay. These enactments were bitterly opposed and led to the "Peasants' Revolt", headed by Wat Tyler.

Labradorite, a felspar rich in calcium and of a pearly lustre on cleavage, found in masses in igneous rocks, the best samples of which come from Labrador.

Labyrinth, or **Maze,** a combination of roads and passages so constructed as to render it difficult for anyone ignorant of the clue to trace the way to the central part. The Egyptian labyrinth near Lake Moeris had 3,000 rooms, half of them subterranean and the remainder above ground. The labyrinth in Crete, according to Greek myth, was built by Daedalus to house the Minotaur. There was one at Lemnos, renowned for its stalactite columns; and another at Clusium constructed by Porsenna, King of Etruria, about 520 B.C. The labyrinth in which Fair Rosamond was concealed was at Woodstock. Hampton Court maze dates from the 16th cent.

Labyrinthodonts, gigantic fossil amphibians which get their name from the curious labyrinthine structure of their teeth, probably an evolutionary link between fishes and reptiles. They occur in the Carboniferous, Permian and Triassic formations, and remains have been found in Britain and other parts of Europe. Their heads were long, and their footprints, by which they were discovered, closely resemble the prints of the human hand.

Lac, a resinous matter deposited on the branches of a number of tropical trees by the females of the lac insect, the exudation including eggs and a viscous covering. At the gathering time the twigs are broken off and dried in the sun, when the insects die, and the lac that remains is termed *stick-lac*. From this, by the removal of extraneous accretions and dissolving, *seed-lac* is produced. *Shell-lac* is seed-lac after it has been melted and otherwise prepared, and this is the best known of the lacs, being used in printing and the manufacture of varnishes and sealing-wax, and for other commercial purposes.

Lace, a delicate fabric of linen, silk or cotton threads, made by hand or machinery, and worked in various ornamental designs. The kinds of lace are many, deriving their distinctive names either from the method employed in production or from the place where any special variety was originally made. The best-known makes are pillow or bobbin-lace, woven and plaited by hand; needle-point lace, worked by the needle over a traced design; and machine lace, which practically dates from Heathcote's invention of the early part of the 19th cent. Some of the most famed laces are the following: *Alençon*, a needle-point lace; *Brussels*, a very fine kind, with needle-point sprigs and flowers; *Chantilly*, a silk variety with flowers and open-work; *Cluny*, a netlace with darned stitch; *Honiton*, a delicate kind with dainty sprigs and figures; *Mechlin*, generally made in one piece and very varied in design; and *Valenciennes*, or bobbin lace, of great durability, the pattern and ground of which are made at the same time, being one of the best and most costly of laces, now manufactured mainly in Belgium. Nottingham is famous for its lace.

Lace-Wings, insects with frail, transparent and much-veined wings whose grubs eat large numbers of insect pests such as aphids. The eggs are borne at the ends of threads attached to plants.

Ladybird, the common name of a large family of beetles—the *Coccinellidae*. The insect is usually of a red or yellow colour with small black or coloured spots. Ladybirds are of good service to the gardener because their larvae feed on aphids. There are about 2,000 species.

Lady-Day, the day of the festival of the Annunciation of the Virgin Mary, 25 March. One of the four English quarter days.

Lake Dwelling, the name given to certain prehistoric habitations which were thought to have stood on platforms over lakes, like villages in certain Pacific islands. Recent excavations at the Lake of Burgäschi in Switzerland show that the prehistoric Swiss pile dwellings probably stood on the shores of lakes, not on platforms over the water. Also found at Mere and Glastonbury, Somerset.

Lakes are bodies of water collected in depressions of the earth's surface. The most notable lakes are the Great Lake series of North America, including Superior, Michigan, Huron, Erie and Ontario, all discharging into the St. Lawrence River. Africa has an enormous area of lakes, including the Mobutu Seso and the Victoria, forming the sources of the White Nile. Smaller lakes are numerous in other countries—Switzerland, Finland, Italy, England, Ireland, Scotland, all having their lake regions, where the scenery is invariably beautiful and romantic. The Kariba Dam (Zimbabwe–Zambia border) and the Nasser (Egypt) are the largest man-made lakes in the world.

Lake School, the name given, at first in ridicule, to a distinguished trio of poets—Wordsworth, Coleridge and Southey—who made their homes in the English Lake District.

Lamellibranchs (Pelecypods), the class of aquatic, bi-valve molluscs to which the oysters, cockles, mussels, clams and scallops belong. In these animals the body, which is compressed laterally, is enclosed in two hinged shells held together by muscular action. The gills are thin plates hence the name "lamellibranchs". *See* **F36(1),** **41(1).**

Lamination, stratification on a very fine scale, as in shales.

Lammas Day is one of the oldest of the Church festivals, probably derived from the loaf-mass (*hlafmaesse*) of the Anglo-Saxons. It occurs on 1 August. In the olden times it was the day when loaves were given in place of first-fruit offerings.

Lammergeyer, the bearded vulture of alpine regions, resembling an eagle in appearance. It has a white head with black tufts at base of the bill, and its general plumage is dark brown, nearly black. It is found in the remote mountain ranges from southern Spain and parts of Africa to China, and is becoming scarce.

Lampblack, a carboniferous pigment obtained from flame-smoke, and now produced in specially constructed furnaces in which bodies rich in carbon, such as tar, resin, petroleum, etc., are burned. The smoke or soot resulting is collected from the sides of the furnace, and forms lampblack. It finds use in making printer's ink, black paint, etc. Being a very pure form of carbon, it is also utilised in the manufacture of dynamo brushes and arc-lamp carbons.

Lamprey. Eel-like fish having no scales, bones, paired fins or jaws. They attach themselves by their mouths to fish whose blood they suck. Together with the hagfishes, the lampreys are placed in a special class—the Cyclostomes. There are three British lampreys.

"Lancet", the name of a noted English medical journal, established in 1823 by Dr. Wakley.

Land Crab, a family of crabs (*Gecarcinidae*) which live mainly on land, though migrating to the seas to deposit their eggs.

Land League, an association formed in 1879, with Parnell as president, for compelling a reduction in the rents of land, and a reconstruction of the land laws in Ireland, and in case of non-compliance refusing to pay rent. For a time this League exercised great political influence and was an important aid to the Home Rule agitation.

Landrail, popularly known as the Corncrake, was a regular summer visitor to Britain two generations ago, but no longer. Its harsh and piercing note was a familiar sound in English cornfields. It is decreasing almost everywhere.

Landslip, a sudden downward sliding under gravity of large masses of rock, soil, etc.; often set off by earthquake shock or saturation of a particular stratum with water. Many serious landslides have occurred from time to time. In 1618, an earthfall happened at Plurs, on Lake Como, involving the destruction of many buildings and the loss of numerous lives. In 1806 a portion of Rossberg mountain in Switzerland slipped from its position, and falling into the valley below buried many villages and hamlets and over 800 people. A chalk cliff 30–45 m high and 1·2 km long fell at Lyme Regis, in Dorset, in 1839, doing great damage. Over 200 people were killed by a landslip in Naini Tal, in India, in 1880; and at Quebec, in 1889, a rocky eminence called Cape Diamond gave way, many buildings being destroyed and lives lost. Notable landslips in recent times have occurred at Amalfi (Italy) in 1924, at Murchiston (New Zealand) in 1929, at Aberfan (Wales) in 1966 and near St. Gervais (France) in 1970.

Langue d'oc and Langue d'oïl, the two principal mediaeval French dialects, *oc* and *oïl* being their respective words for the affirmative particle (modern French *oui*). *Langue d'oc*, spoken south of the Loire, was the language of the troubadors. Provençal, one of its dialects had a literary revival in the 19th cent. under the influence of the poet Frédéric Mistral. *Langue d'oïl* was spoken in northern France, and it was the dialect of the Paris region which developed into modern French.

Lantern Fly, bugs belonging to the family *Fulgoridae* in which the head is drawn out to form a lantern-like structure. In no instance is the "lantern" luminous, though naturalists used to think it was.

Lanthanides, the fourteen metallic elements following lanthanum in the Periodic Table, *i.e.*, the elements cerium (no. 58) to lutetium (no. 71). They are also known as the rare-earth metals, though they are in fact all more terrestrially abundant than, for instance, mercury or arsenic (with the exception of the unstable radioactive element promethium, no. 61). The lanthanide atoms are distinguished by having an incomplete inner electron sub-shell (the 4f level), this feature giving them interesting magnetic properties. For instance, gadolinium, holmium and dysprosium are ferromagnetic (*see* **F22**) at low temperatures. Chemically, the lanthanides behave similarly, being highly reactive metals usually forming trivalent salts. *See* **Periodic Table, Section F.**

Lapis Lazuli, an azure-blue mineral, being a silicate of aluminium and sodium. The pigment ultramarine is made by grinding it, though artificial ultramarine has largely superseded it. The mineral (also called *lazurite*) has been used as a gemstone since ancient times.

Lapwing *or* **Green Plover**, familiar British bird on moors and marshlands with iridescent greenish-black plumage, white underparts and black crest. Often called "peewit" from its cry. Protected under Protection of Birds Act, 1967.

Larboard is the old nautical term indicating the left-hand side of a ship, and changed by Admiralty order to "port" in 1844. Starboard is the right-hand side.

Larch, a familiar coniferous tree in the mountain regions of northern Europe, and though not native to Britain, the Common Larch is successfully cultivated in various parts of the kingdom. It is one of the best of all turpentine-yielding trees, and the bark is valued for tanning. The larch is an unusual conifer in being deciduous.

Lark, a family of song birds (*Alaudidae*) of many species, some of which—notably the skylark—are famed for their habit of soaring into the air, singing all the while. They build their nests on the ground in the open country and, except for the black lark of Russia, have streaked brown plumage. The skylark and woodlark are the best known British species, while the crested lark and shore lark are among the occasional visitors. Africa has the greatest number of larks; America has only one species, the horned lark.

Larkspur, the common name of the genus *Delphinium*, a favourite flower introduced into British gardens from Switzerland in 1573. The common larkspur is *D. consolida*.

Larva, the undeveloped form of any animal which, before maturity undergoes metamorphosis, usually different from the adult in structure and habits.

Laser. A remarkable kind of light source that was discovered in 1960. With the laser it is possible to probe the behaviour of matter under the influence of enormous energy densities, range and survey vast distances to microscopic accuracy and send millions of telephone and television messages between any two points that can see each other with telescopes. Laser light, in contrast to natural light, is coherent and can be expressed as a regular progression of waves carrying energy along a particular path. Thus the essential difference is that laser light is an orderly sort of wave motion in contrast to ordinary light which is inherently unsteady and therefore an inefficient carrier of information in time. The name *maser*, which is the microwave parent of the laser, derives from the expression "microwave amplification by the stimulated emission of radiation". Upon application to light wavelengths the microwave part of the name lost its meaning and the term maser became generally descriptive of any device in which stimulated emission dominates.

Laser Fusion is a method by which it has been proposed that thermonuclear reactions may be controlled and exploited as a source of energy (*see* **Nuclear Fusion**). The idea is to irradiate a millimetre-sized pellet of a mixture of frozen deuterium and tritium with a short ($\sim 10^{-9}$ s) but very intense pulse of energy in the form of laser light. This has the effect of both compressing the pellet by a factor of at least a thousand and heating it to about 10^8 °C. Under these conditions, thermonuclear reactions—cipally $^2D + {}^3T \rightarrow {}^4He + {}^1n$) proceed sufficiently fast that a net output of energy is obtained before the pellet explosively separates. Formidable technical problems need to be solved before laser fusion can become a practical proposition. These include the development of efficient high-powered lasers and the design of a suitable reactor that can withstand up to 100 micro-hydrogen bomb explosions per second. It is still not clear whether this method of controlling nuclear fusion is more practical than the more conventional approach involving the magnetic confinement of plasmas.

Latent Heat is the quantity of heat required to convert 1 gram of a substance from one form into another. For example, when a solid changes into a liquid or a liquid into a gas, the addition of heat to bring about the change produces no rise in temperature, the energy being absorbed in the form of latent heat. An equal amount is released when the process is reversed. The latent heat of fusion of ice is about 79·6 calories per gram, that of the vaporisation of water about 539 calories per gram.

Lateran Councils were the religious conventions held in the Lateran basilica at Rome for deciding important questions of Church doctrine. The most brilliant was that of 1215 which pronounced in favour of a Crusade. *See* Ecumenical Council.

Lateran Treaty, 1929, between Italy and the Vatican established the Vatican City as an independent sovereign state.

Laterite refers to any tropical soil or soil horizon rich in hydrated ferric and aluminium oxides which harden when exposed to the atmosphere. It is difficult to cultivate and is commonly used for bricks and road metal. Laterite buildings have been known to withstand the weathering for many centuries and a number of fine examples are found in India and S.E. Asia.

Latin America. The Spanish-speaking, Portuguese-speaking and French-speaking countries of N. America, S. America, Central America and the W. Indies. *See* Section K.

Latitude of a point on the earth's surface is its angular distance from the equator, measured on the surface of the earth in degrees, minutes and seconds. Thus the equator is 0° Lat. and the poles 90° Lat. (N. or S.). First determined by Hipparchus of Nicaea about 160 B.C. Latitude introduces zones of climate, *e.g.*, tropical rain, subtropical steppe and desert, temperate rain and polar.

Laughing Gas. *See* Nitrous oxide.

Launce *or* Sand Eel, a family of eel-like sea fishes found in large numbers on the coasts of North America and Europe. There are two species common to British waters. These fishes are of a bright silvery hue, and live much in the sand underneath the water. They are prized as human food and as bait.

Laurentian Shield refers to the Pre-Cambrian rocks in the region of the Upper Lakes of Canada, nearly 5 million sq km in extent. Of enormous importance to Canada on account of the mineral wealth, forests yielding valuable timber and wood-pulp, and water-power.

Lava, the molten rock which is erupted from a volcanic vent or fissure. Also the same material which has cooled and solidified.

Lawn, very fine sun-bleached linen, in olden time called "cloth of Rheims".

Lead, a soft malleable metallic element, no. 82, symbol Pb (Latin *plumbum*), occurring in numerous ores, which are easily smelted. Its most important source is the mineral galena which consists chiefly of lead sulphide; rarely is it found free. Lead is largely used in plumbing on account of its pliability, and in nuclear reactors as a shield against radiation because of its very high density. As an alloy element it combines in the formation of type metal, stereo metal, shot metal, pewter and many other compounds. Oxides of lead are used in some types of glass and in the manufacture of paints (red lead). All lead compounds are poisonous. Leading producers of lead are the United States (Missouri), Australia (Broken Hill) and the Soviet Union.

Leaf Miners, insect larvae which tunnel between the upper and lower skins of leaves. Most leaf miners are caterpillars of tiny moths; some sawfly larvae have the same habit.

Leagues, or combinations of kings, countries, communities, have been frequent since the kings of Canaan united against the Israelites. Among the most famous leagues may be mentioned the Holy or Catholic League, which prevented the recognition of Henry IV as King of France until he became a Roman Catholic; and the League of Augsburg against Louis XIV of France in 1686.

League of Nations, was founded on 10 January 1920, with the object of promoting international peace and security. The original members were the signatories to the Peace Treaties at Versailles, and membership grew to fifty-three as new nations and ex-enemy States were admitted. Two notable absentees were the United States and Soviet Russia, the latter not being represented until 1934. Germany was a member from 1926 to 1933. The League had an Assembly which met at Geneva every year and a Council which met five or six times a year. The Permanent Court of International Justice (now under the UN) sits at The Hague. The League held its last Assembly at Geneva in April 1946. Its place was taken by the United Nations. The International Labour Organisation, set up by the League of Nations, met in April 1944 at Philadelphia and resumed its old quarters at Geneva under the UN in 1946.

Leap Year *or* Bissextile, was fixed by Julius Caesar, 45 B.C., the addition of one day in every four years bringing the measure of the calendar year even with the astronomical year with three minutes per year over. The Gregorian Calendar corrected this by dropping leap year at the centuries not divisible by 400. For instance, 1700, 1800 and 1900 were not leap years.

Learning. *See* F40(2), Q16–20.

Leather was made in ancient Egypt, Greece and Rome, and has through succeeding centuries played an important part in the service of man. It consists of the dressed hides or skins of animals after the process of tanning has been gone through. Untanned skins are known as pelts. Leather is classed either according to the skins from which it is made or the system of preparation employed. The best-known kinds are morocco, kid, Russian, chamois, Cordovan, grained, patent, russet, tan, calf, Hungarian.

Leech, an aquatic blood-sucking worm, mostly found in fresh-water ponds. Each end of the body is provided with a sucker, but that at the head end has jaws and teeth. The medicinal leech has three jaws. The leech attaches itself with avidity to animal bodies and sucks until glutted. Its saliva contains an anti-coagulant.

Leeward, a nautical term, meaning the sheltered side of a vessel—that is, the opposite side to that from which the wind is blowing.

Legion, a body of Roman troops, varying in numbers at different periods. A legion was divided into 10 cohorts, and every cohort into three maniples. Three legions composed the Roman army of occupation in Britain.

Legion of Honour, the French order for distinguished services, military or civil, was instituted by Napoleon I in 1802, and confirmed and modified under later rules. There are five grades—Grands Croix, Grands Officiers, Commandeurs, Officiers and Chevaliers.

Legume, the fruit typical of the pea, bean family, or *Leguminosae.*

Lemming, small light-brown rodents with dark spots, abounding in Scandinavian countries and in Siberia, about 12 cm long, with a short stump of a tail. The migrations of the lemming are famous, probably caused by overbreeding when food is plentiful. So insistent is the urge to keep moving that these animals will march on into the sea in their thousands and be drowned.

Lemur, almost the most primitive member of the primate order of mammals (to which man, apes and monkeys also belong). They are noted for having strong pliant toes enabling them to use their feet as hands, and also well-developed thumbs on the hands. They have long squirrel-like tails, fox-shaped heads and large staring eyes. True lemurs are confined to the Malagasy Rep.; closely related are the "bush-babies" of S. Africa.

Lend-Lease. During the earlier phases of the second world war the bulk of British investments in the USA had to be either sold or pledged to Americans in payment for dollar supplies. After the United States entered the war this drain was stopped by the Lend-Lease arrangement, under which Great Britain met the costs of American consumption in Great Britain, while the United States paid for British supplies from America. This arrangement was abruptly terminated on the ending of hostilities; and Great Britain and other belligerent countries found themselves without means of paying in dollars for indispensable American supplies, including the foodstuffs, materials and capital goods needed for economic reconstruction. In these circumstances Great Britain negotiated with the United States and also with Canada a large loan, which was used for buying dollar supplies and played an inportant part in helping the West European economies to maintain themselves and feed their people while they were carrying through the earlier stages of post-war reconstruction. These loans involved large charges for interest and amortisation in future years, but proved far too small to meet the dollar deficit for more than a short period. In face of this situation the United States launched the Marshall Plan.

Lenses, pieces of transparent material designed to focus an image of an illuminated object. Usually of glass, but plastic lenses are common, and quartz, etc. are used for special purposes. The surfaces of the simplest lenses are parts of spheres. Lenses which are thickest, or thinnest, at the centre are called convex and concave respectively. Lenses of complex shape are often used in microscopes, etc. Electron lenses are arrangements of electric or magnetic fields which focus beams of electrons, e.g., on to T.V. screens.

Lent, the forty days' period of fasting that precedes Easter.

Lepidoptera, the order of insects with scaly wings and bodies, to which the 90,000 butterflies and moths belong.

Leptons. A group of particles which include electrons, neutrinos and muons. All are much lighter than protons or any baryons (q.v.). See **F16.**

Lepus, the constellation of the Hare, situated under the Orion group, and one of the constellations with which the ancients were familiar.

Lettres de Cachet, sealed letters which the kings of France issued to their agents to secure the imprisonment of distrusted or disliked persons without trial. Abolished in 1789.

Levée, a State reception held by the Sovereign or his representative and attended by men only.

Lewis, a contrivance for stone-lifting, the principle of which was known to the ancient Romans; it consists of two dovetail tenons of iron or other metal, expanded by an intervening key in a dovetail-shaped mortice in the stone, and shackled by a ringed bolt to the hoisting chain.

Leyden Jar, the earliest form of electrical condenser. Its invention is usually credited to Muschenbroeck of Leyden (1745). It consisted of a jar coated inside and out with tinfoil for about two-thirds of its height and having its inner coating connected with the top by a brass knob and chain. The jar was charged by connecting it to an electrostatic machine.

Lias, a geological term referring to the lower section of the Jurassic group, and mainly comprising shales and limestones.

Liberalism. See **Section J.**

Libraries, before the invention of printing, were few, and collected together at enormous cost. At Nineveh remains of libraries, consisting of tablets of baked clay, have been discovered. There were two libraries at Alexandria containing a vast collection of rolls or volumes, founded by Ptolemy I Soter (367–382 B.C.) and established by Ptolemy II Philadelphus (309–246 B.C.). Among the great libraries of later times may be mentioned the Vatican Library at Rome, moved to its present premises in 1588; the Royal Library in Paris which later became the Bibliothèque Nationale; the Astor Library, New York; and in England, the Bodleian Library, Oxford, and the British Library (see below). Since 1850 public libraries have been established in all the chief cities and towns of the kingdom. The first lending library was opened in Edinburgh in 1726. In most villages there is a "county library centre" to which collections of books are sent by the County Library. In Great Britain there are 24,000 centres of this kind in village clubs, halls, shops, schools and even homes. In some counties

there is a library van or the bibliobus, as it has been called by a French writer. This travelling library tours on a pre-arranged time-table so that everyone knows exactly when it will arrive. The British Library in London, the National Library of Scotland, in Edinburgh, that of Wales in Aberystwyth, the Bodleian Library of Oxford and the Cambridge University Library comprise the "copyright" libraries, entitled to receive a copy of each new book and journal published in Britain. The British Library Act 1972 brought together into a single organisation (a) the former British Museum Library (the books remaining in the Museum) and the Science Reference Library in Holborn and Bayswater, the whole now being known as the British Library, Reference Division; (b) the former National Lending Library for Science and Technology and its arts and humanities counterpart, the National Central Library, together now known as the British Library, Lending Division, and located at Boston Spa, Yorkshire. It is eventually intended to rehouse Reference Division in a single new building in London, near Euston Station. Lending Division, which has an international reputation for rapid postal lending of journals and photocopies to institutions and libraries remains in Yorkshire.

Libretto (It. booklet), the literary text of an opera or oratorio. Usually the composer and the librettist collaborate in the writing of an opera, but several composers (e.g., Wagner) wrote their own librettos. Boito, librettist to Verdi for Otello and Falstaff, himself composed two operas Mefistofele and Nerone. Most famous of Italian opera librettists was the poet and dramatist Metastasio (1698–1782). His librettos were set to music by many composers, including Gluck, Handel, Mozart, Rossini.

Licence is a permission given to do some act, which without such permission, it would be unlawful to do. Licences are required for keeping dogs, for operating a television receiving set, for driving a motor vehicle, for killing game, for setting up as a bookmaker, for selling beer, wines and spirits, tobacco, etc. and for importing certain items such as arms, ammunition, radioactive materials, animals, plants, drugs and explosives.

Lichens. In every lichen, two plants are associated, one being an alga and the other a fungus. The fungus derives its food from the alga; probably the alga gains too from the association, being protected against desiccation by the fungus (an example of symbiosis). Lichens are the first plants to colonise bare rocks.

Life-Boats were invented by three men, Lionel Lukin who converted a coble into a boat for saving life in 1785; William Wouldhave, who discovered how to make a boat right herself if she capsized; and Henry Greathead, who built a life-boat, partly from Wouldhave's model, in 1789. This boat was stationed at South Shields, which was the first permanent life-boat station to be established. It was not until 1851 that the first life-boat able to self-right was built, and a motor was first installed in a life-boat in 1904. The Arun life-boats, launched in 1971, have twin 460 h.p. diesel engines with a maximum speed of 18.5 knots. All coastal life-boats in this country are maintained by the Royal National Lifeboat Institution founded by Sir William Hillary in 1824. It is supported entirely by voluntary contributions, and has saved over 107,500 people. Its headquarters are in Poole, Dorset. In 1984, it cost over £17m. to maintain the service.

Light, a particular kind of electromagnetic disturbance capable of travelling through space, and some kinds of matter, and of affecting our eyes to cause vision. Its finite speed was first demonstrated by O. Römer, using observations of the eclipses of Jupiter's satellites in 1675. In 1860 Maxwell showed that light waves are electromagnetic. Since Einstein's theory of relativity (1905) it has been generally realised that the speed of light is a fundamental natural constant. Visible light with wavelengths between about 4 and 7×10^{-5} cm is only a small part of the electromagnetic spectrum. The speed of light in vacuum is about $2 \cdot 997925 \times 10^{8}$ m/s.

Light Year, a measure of astronomical distance,

equal to the distance light travels in a period of one year. A light year is 9.463×10^{12} km but the unit parsec is now preferred. (1 pc = 3.2616 l.y.).

Lighthouses, to warn ships of dangerous places and indicate coasts, points, harbours, etc., have existed since the building of the Pharos, a tower of white marble 183 m high, built by Ptolemy II Philadelphus at Alexandria about 280 B.C. In early lighthouses the lights were simple fires. The most famous and one of the earliest British lighthouses is the Eddystone (q.v.). Dungeness lighthouse, opened in 1960, is very modern in design, capable of automatic operation and the first of its kind to incorporate the xenon electric arc lamp as a source of illumination. The electric fog signal consists of sixty loud-speaker units built into the tower just below the lantern, giving a honeycomb effect. The lighthouses of England and Wales, the Channel Islands and Gibraltar are under the control of Trinity House; Commissioners of Northern Lighthouses control those of Scotland; and the Commissioners of Irish Lights control the coasts of Ireland. Particulars of lights in all parts of the world are published for the guidance of navigation in the *Admiralty Lists of Lights*, compiled annually by the British Admiralty.

Lightning, the flash of a discharge of electricity between two clouds, or between a cloud and the earth, when the strength of the electric fields becomes so great as to break down the resistance of the intervening air. With "forked" lightning the actual path, often branched, is visible, while with "sheet" lightning the flash is hidden by the clouds which themselves are illuminated. "Ball" lightning or fireballs is the name given to the luminous balls which have been seen floating in the air during a thunderstorm. The Boys camera has provided much information regarding the sequence of events in a lightning discharge. It is found that a flash consists of a number of separate strokes, usually four or five, and that the discharge of electricity to earth begins with a faintly luminous "leader" moving downwards and branching at intervals. As the ground is approached a much brighter luminosity travels back along the conducting channels, lighting up with several branches. The multiple strokes which follow in fractions of a second have the same "return" nature and are rarely branched. Lightning flashes to earth damage structures, cause loss of life and endanger overhead power systems, often interrupting electricity supply. Such storms generally affect radio transmissions and present hazards to aircraft. Thunderclouds may develop energy far exceeding the capacity of our largest power generating stations.

Lightning Conductor, a metal rod, the upper part of which is of copper with a conical point, the lower portion being iron, which extends into the earth. Its effect is to gather to itself the surrounding electricity and discharge it into the earth, thus preventing its falling upon the protected building. In ships, lightning conductors are fixed to the masts and carried down through the ship's keel-sheathing. Benjamin Franklin was the first to realise the possibilities of lightning protection and, in 1752, carried out his famous experiment of drawing electricity from thunder-clouds, with the aid of a sharp-pointed conductor fixed to a kite.

Lillibulero, an old marching song arranged by Purcell. With words by Wharton, it is said to have "sung James II out of three kingdoms". Used by the B.B.C. during the second world war as a station identification signal preceding news bulletins, and still in use to announce the Overseas Service programmes in English.

Lily Family (Liliaceae), one of the largest families of flowering plants, with 200 genera and 2,500 species. It includes the true lilies (*Lilium*), tulips and hyacinths. Vegetables belonging to the family are the onion and asparagus.

Limes, trees of the genus *Tilia,* including some 30 species spread over north temperate regions. The word is a corruption of "linden". Limes native to Britain are the small-leaved *T. cordata* and the broad-leaved *T. platyphyllos*. The hybrid *T. vulgaris* was introduced into Britain from the Continent during the 17th cent. and is frequently seen in streets and parks. Lime-wood was used by Grinling Gibbons for his fruit, flower and bird decorations.

Limestones, sedimentary rocks composed wholly or largely of calcium carbonate and formed by two main processes, (1) organic (skeletal remains of organisms), e.g., chalk (q.v.) and (2) chemical (precipitation of calcium carbonate), e.g., oolite (q.v.). Marble is limestone that will polish after cutting.

Linen, a textile fabric manufactured from flax fibre, known to the ancient Egyptians, and first manufactured in England under Henry III by Flemish weavers. The greatest linen-manufacturing region in the world is Northern Ireland (largely yarns and the lighter types of fabrics); Scotland produces coarse linens and canvas as well as household linens.

Ling, a sea-fish common on the coasts of Britain, and abounding in more northern waters. It averages about 1 m in length, and is a voracious feeder, living chiefly on small fish. Ling is also the name applied to *Calluna vulgaris,* the plant commonly called "heather".

Linseed, the seed of the flax plant, containing, apart from its fibrous substance, certain oily and nitrogenous matter of considerable commercial value. This yields linseed oil, and some of the residue is used to make cattle food.

Lion, the most impressive of the Cat family. It is chiefly found in open bush country in Africa, being comparatively rare in Asia. Its large square head, its flowing mane (in the males only) and its tufted tail distinguish it. From tip to tip it can reach a length of 3m; a weight of 225 kg.

Lion and Unicorn, the supporting figures of the royal arms of Great Britain, date from the union of Scotland with England (1603) at the accession of James I (James VI of Scotland), the lion representing England and the unicorn Scotland.

Liqueurs are essences combined with alcoholic liquid, and are of many kinds, named according to their flavouring or place of production, and include Maraschino, Chartreuse, Curaçao, Benedictine, Noyau, Kümmel, etc.

Liquid, the name given to matter in such state that it takes its shape from the containing vessel. The volume it occupies is independent of the container, however. See **F20(2)**.

Liquid Crystals form a special class of substance and are true liquids in that they flow easily and can be poured. However, unlike ordinary liquids, liquid crystals have their molecules arranged with geometrical regularity in one or two dimensions, so that they have a certain internal structure similar to that of solid crystals. They are fairly complicated chemicals with somewhat elongated molecules. Liquid crystals are of interest to biologists as well as to chemists and physicists, and not just because they account for the iridescence of beetles. Some body fluids are in fact liquid crystals. There are also technological applications because of their unique electrical and optical properties. They are receiving increasing attention for these reasons.

Litanies were first used in church processions in the 5th cent. The first English litany was commanded to be recited in the Reformed churches by Henry VIII in 1544.

Lithium, a soft metallic element, no. 3, symbol Li, similar to sodium. It is very reactive and is stored under paraffin oil. It is the lightest metal element.

Lithography, the art of drawing on stone and printing therefrom, was discovered by Alois Senefelder about 1796, and was introduced into England a few years later. Many improvements in the art have been made, especially in chrome-lithography and photo-lithography.

Litre, a metric measure, was abolished in 1964 as a scientific unit of volume, but remains as a special name for the cubic decimetre and as an everyday unit, e.g., a litre of petrol.

Liturgy, the name given to the Church ritual, though strictly applying only to the portion used in the celebration of the Eucharist or Lord's Supper. The Anglican liturgy is laid down in the Book of Common Prayer (1662). Temporary powers granted by Parliament in

1965 to the Church to make changes in the form of worship were made permanent in 1974. The Alternative Service Book was introduced in 1980.

Liverworts (Hepatics), a class of simple green plants related to the mosses. Liverworts are most common in damp situations, such as the banks of ditches. The majority of British species are leafy, only some are thalloid.

Lizard, the name given to a diversified order of reptiles, of which there are about 1,600 species. Included among the lizards are the geckos, chameleons, glass snakes, skinks and blind worms.

Llama, mammals related to the camels, from which they differ in small size, absence of the humps, and more woolly coat. The domestic llama of S. America is used as a beast of burden, also providing wool, meat and milk. *See also* **Alpaca, Guanaco.**

Loadstone or **Lodestone,** an oxide of iron, found chiefly in Sweden and Norway. Its scientific name is magnetite. It has the power of attracting pieces of iron and served as the first magnets used in compasses. One of the class of non-metallic magnetic materials nowadays known as "ferrites" (*q.v.*).

Lobby Correspondents are political correspondents of newspapers who do not report the actual proceedings of Parliament—this is done by Parliamentary Correspondents—but interpret political news and events.

Lobsters are marine crustacean animals existing in large numbers in the northern seas of Europe and America and in fair proportion on some parts of the British coasts, especially in the neighbourhood of the Channel Islands.

Locarno, Treaty of, 1925, whereby Germany, France and Belgium undertook to maintain their present frontiers and to abstain from the use of force against each other. Hitler broke the pact by re-occupying the Rhineland, the demilitarisation of which had been recognised by Germany.

Locust, insects of the grasshopper family, but much more powerful. They are inhabitants of hot countries, and often make their appearance in untold millions, like clouds, devastating all the vegetation that comes within their course. The locust-tree (*Ceratonia siliqua*) is supposed to have furnished food to St. John the Baptist in the wilderness, and its "beans" have accordingly been styled "St. John's Bread".

Loess, a deposit of silt or marl laid down by wind action. The biggest loess deposits are in Asia, the source of the dust of which they are composed probably being the deserts of Central Asia. Large deposits in Europe are thought to have originated from the edge of ice sheets during the Ice Age.

Logarithms, a system of calculation invented by John Napier in 1614, and developed by Henry Briggs a few years later. Thus if a number is expressed as the power of another number, *i.e.*, if $a = b^n$, then n is said to be the logarithm of a to base b, written $\log_b a$. Common logs are to base 10 and Napierian to base $2 \cdot 7182818 \ldots$, expressed as e. Their use represents a great saving of time.

Logical Positivism. *See* **Section J.**

Lollards. *See* **Section J.**

Lombards, a German people, originating on the Elber, who settled in Italy in the 6th cent., occupying northern and central regions, and establishing a kingdom with Pavia as capital. They were conquered by Charlemagne in 774, but left their name to the region of Lombardy. Lombard Street, London, takes its name from the Lombard merchants and bankers who came to settle there in the 12th cent.

London Clay, geological stratum which occupies much of the London Basin and part of the Hampshire Basin. It represents the lower stratum of the Eocene. Outside the metropolis, brickfields utilise the clay for brickmaking. Water held down in the Chalk by this impervious stratum is tapped by a number of artesian wells in London. The tunnels of the capital's underground railways run through the London Clay.

London University is recognised as one of the great universities of the world. Originated in the foundation of a non-sectarian college in Gower Street in 1828. Among the chief colleges are:

University College London, King's College, Imperial College of Science and Technology London School of Economics, School of Oriental and African Studies, Queen Mary, Birkbeck. Royal Holloway, Bedford, Westfield and Queen Elizabeth College. London University was the first to throw open all degrees to women (1878). Chancellor, Princess Anne.

Long Distance Walks. The National Parks and Access to the Countryside Act 1949 provided for the establishment in England and Wales of Long Distance Footpaths and Bridleways. The following walks have been opened: Pennine Way (the first long-distance footpath, a magnificent hill walk of 270 miles from Edale in Derbyshire along the Pennines over the Cheviots and the Scottish border); Pembrokeshire Coast Path (from St. Dogmael's to Amroth, 170 miles); Offa's Dyke Path (176 miles along the marches of Wales, one of the most important remaining earthworks of its kind in northwestern Europe); South Downs Way (Beachy Head to Buriton in Hants, 80 miles); South-West Peninsula Coast path (Minehead to Poole Harbour, 520 miles); Coast to Coast Walk from Robin Hood's Bay to St. Bee's (190 miles); Ridgeway (Avebury to Ivinghoe Beacon, 90 miles); Pilgrim's Way (Winchester to Canterbury, 116 miles); Cotswold Way (Bath to Chipping Campden, 95 miles); West Highland Way (Glasgow to Fort William, 100 miles). *See also* **National Parks.**

Longitude of a point on the earth's surface is the angle which the meridian through the poles and that point makes with some standard meridian. The meridian through Greenwich is usually accepted as the standard meridian and the longitude is measured east or west of that line. As the earth revolves through $360°$ in 24 h, $15°$ longitude represent 1 hour's difference in apparent time.

Long Parliament (1640–60), marked the end of Charles I's 11-year attempt to govern without Parliament. It carried through what has come to be called "the English Revolution" and was the parliament of the civil war (1642–49).

Lord Lieutenant is the Queen's representative in the county, and his office is now largely ceremonial. On his recommendation the magistrates or Justices of the Peace are appointed by the Lord Chancellor. The office was created in 1549 to take over the military duties of the sheriff.

Lords, House of, the Upper House of the British Parliament composed of Lords Spiritual and Lords Temporal. The former consist of the two Archbishops and twenty-four English Bishops and the latter of hereditary Peers, Peeresses and Life Peers. The right of the Lords to veto Bills passed by the Commons is restricted by the Parliament Acts of 1911 and 1949. The Lord Chancellor presides over the House of Lords. Under the Peerage Act 1963 a peerage may be disclaimed for life. *See* **Section D.**

Louse, parasitic insect found on the skin of birds and mammals. The two sub-species that parasitise man are the body louse and the head louse. Typhus can be transmitted by lice.

Louvre, one of the old royal palaces of Paris, was built in its present form partly by Francis I and added to by later monarchs, Louis XIV completing the edifice. Napoleon I turned it into a museum and enriched it with the plunder of many foreign art galleries. The great extension to the Louvre building begun by Napoleon I was completed under Napoleon III in 1857. Much injury was done to the building during the Commune of 1871. Amongst other famous treasures it houses the Venus de Milo and Leonardo da Vinci's masterpiece, *La Gioconda.*

LSD (d-lysergic acid diethylamide). This hallucinogenic drug has achieved wide notoriety because of its use by certain people to give themselves abnormal mental experiences. Doctors have frequently warned against the dangers of its use. It is active in extremely small quantities and a dose as small as a fifty-millionth part of a gram can cause marked disturbances of the mental function in man. LSD has been used in the study of mental disease because it produces symptoms very similar to mental disorders such as schizophrenia.

Luddites, a combination of workmen formed in

1811, in a period of great distress, with the object of destroying the new textile machinery then being largely adopted, which they regarded as the cause of their troubles. Their first outbreak was at Nottingham, and was stated to have been started by a young apprentice named Ned Ludd. Afterwards, serious Luddite riots occurred in various parts of the country, especially in West Yorkshire, where many people were killed, mills were destroyed and numbers of rioters were tried and executed. Charlotte Brontë used the period in her novel, *Shirley*.

Lunatic Fringe, term used by Theodore Roosevelt to characterise adherents of reform movements who refuse to recognise difficulty of practical administration and insist upon immediate fulfilment of an extreme programme.

Lutecium, element (no. 71) of the rare-earth metal group discovered in 1907 by Urbain. Symbol Lu.

Lutheranism. *See* Section J.

Lynx, cats of sturdy build, with tufted ears and spotted fur, inhabiting many parts of the world, including Northern and Central Europe. They commit serious ravages among sheep and goats and are very fierce.

Lyon King of Arms, the President of the Scottish Lyon Court, and head of the heraldic organisation for Scotland.

Lyre-Bird, a remarkable family of Australian birds, the males of which possess a beautiful lyre-shaped tail. The bird is not more than 38 cm long, but its tail, displayed during its remarkable courtship dance, is 58 cm in length. There are two species: the Superb and Albert's Lyrebird.

M

Macaque. A family of monkeys which includes the Barbary ape (specimens of which live on Gibraltar), the Rhesus macaque (the organ grinder's monkey and the one used for experimental work in the investigation of disease), the Bonnet monkey of southern India and Sri Lanka, the Crab-eating and the Pig-tailed monkeys of south-eastern Asia.

Macaw, a genus of large parrots with brilliant scarlet and sky-blue plumage, with interminglings of green. Native to South and Central America.

McCarthyism, the term given to the wave of anti-Communist hysteria, associated with the name of Senator McCarthy (1908–57), whose campaign of vilification resulted in the loss of careers and livelihood of many innocent Americans. The campaign lasted from early 1947 to late 1954.

Mace, originally a weapon of offence, now an ensign of authority borne before officers of state and other dignitaries. In the House of Commons the mace is handed to an official of the Crown by the Sergeant-at-Arms at the close of a parliamentary session.

Mach Number. Unit of flight speed. The ratio of speed of flight to speed of sound under same conditions of pressure and density. Speed of sound at sea-level is 762 mile/h (1,226 km/h), so flight speed of 381 mile/h (613 km/h) is equivalent to a Mach Number of ½. At supersonic speeds the Mach Number is greater than 1; subsonic speeds, less than 1.

Mackerel, a sea-fish existing in large numbers in the northern Atlantic off America and Europe. They are beautiful fish with a streamlined body and among the fastest fish in the sea.

Macromolecules are very large molecules about 10,000 times or more as heavy as ordinary small molecules like hydrogen. Most are built up from a large number of simple sub-units, *i.e.*, are polymers (*q.v.*). The term macromolecule is often used in biology, *e.g.*, starch and cellulose are biological macromolecules, both built from glucose sub-units. Other important ones are proteins and nucleic acids. The properties of macromolecules depend on the sub-units of which they are composed.

Madder, one of the most important of dye-stuffs, largely used in producing Turkey-red dye, but now superseded by synthetic alizarin. Natural madder is the root of the *Rubia tinctorum*.

Maelstrom, a great whirlpool. The most famous is that off the coast of Norway, between the islands of Moskenês and Mosken, of the Lofoten group the power of which has been much exaggerated.

Mafia. A term which is connected with Italo-American organised crime. Historically, remoteness from the central government of Italy encouraged the growth in Sicily in the 19th cent. of *mafiosi*, key-men who gained power through fear and violence. Contemporary police records give details of *mafia* behaviour in defending their authority. Emigration of vast numbers of southern Italians to the United States led to a new type of urban *mafioso* who became connected with gangsterism and vice. Sometimes called the *Cosa Nostra*, the organisation has infiltrated city governments and is reputed to be in control of drug smuggling and other illegal operations. In Italy neo-fascist groups have made use of the *mafia* in acts of terrorism, especially in the north.

Magellan, Clouds of, the name given to a pair of small galaxies, satellite systems of our own galaxy, visible only from the southern hemisphere. On account of their relative nearness to the earth (186,000 light-years), they are receiving much attention from astronomers.

Magenta, a blue-red aniline dye discovered in 1859 by Sir W. H. Perkin, and named after the great battle of that year between the French and Austrians.

Magic. *See* Section J.

Magistrates *or* **Justices of the Peace** preside over petty sessional and juvenile courts and are appointed by the Lord Chancellor on the recommendation of the Lord Lieutenant of the County. Most J.P.s are laymen and are unpaid. In certain big towns a legally-qualified, paid, full-time magistrate is appointed, known as a stipendiary magistrate. In London stipendiaries are known as Metropolitan Stipendiary Magistrates. J.P.s are no longer appointed over the age of 60 and they must retire when they reach 70. By the Justices of the Peace Act, 1968, *ex officio* J.P.s are abolished, except for the Lord Mayor and aldermen of the City of London.

Magma, molten rock material rich in volatile constituents prior to its eruption at the surface. With the loss of volatiles it becomes lava.

Magna Carta was sealed by King John at Runnymede on 15 June 1215, in obedience to the insistent demands of the barons and has been confirmed many times by later monarchs. It was not a revolutionary document. It laid down what the barons took to be the recognised and fundamental principles for the government of the realm and bound king and barons alike to maintain them. Its main provisions were that no man should be punished without fair trial, that ancient liberties generally should be preserved, and that no demands should be made by an overlord to his vassal (other than those recognised) without the sanction of the great council of the realm.

Magnesium, a metallic element, no. 12, symbol Mg, first isolated in 1808 by Sir Humphry Davy, who prepared it by electrolysing the chloride. Its chief ores are magnesite and dolomite. Industrially it is obtained by electrolysis. Many important light alloys contain magnesium. The metal burns with a very bright light, and for this reason it is used in photographers' flash bulbs and also in firework manufacture.

Magnetic Storms. These are the effects of magnetospheric storms observed world-wide at ground level as fluctuations of as much as 5% in the earth's magnetic field. The largest effects are observed at high latitudes, in the auroral ovals, and are due to electric currents flowing in the ionosphere and between the ionosphere and the magnetosphere. There may be concurrent disruption of radio communications. *See* **Magnetosphere.**

Magnetism, originally the name given to the quality of attraction for iron possessed by lodestone (*q.v.*). Now known to be a phenomenon inseparably connected with electricity (**F21**). Strong magnetic attraction is possessed by a comparatively small class of substances; iron, nickel and cobalt are the most common elements, but there are several less well known, *e.g.*, gadolinium. Many alloys have valuable magnetic properties which make possible numberless technical devices. New magnetic substances are always being developed (*see* **Ferrites**). The earth acts like a huge magnet with its axis inclined at about 11° to the axis of rotation, the magnetic poles being on the Boothia Peninsula (North Canada) and South Victoria Land (Antarctica). The magnetic field at the surface consists of the regular field of a magnetised sphere with an irregular field superimposed upon it. Variation in the magnetic forces occurs from place to place and from time to time, and maps showing the distribution over the globe of points of the same declination (*i.e.*, the angle which the magnetic meridian makes with the geographical one) are of the utmost importance in navigation. Little is known regarding the origin of the main (regular) field of the earth, but it is believed that the irregularities are due to the presence of intense electric currents in the upper atmosphere and local magnetisation of rock strata. In 1967 the discovery was claimed of isolated magnetic poles, *i.e.*, north and south magnetic poles existing separately, just as positive and negative electrical charges exist separately. If this is confirmed it will probably rank as one of the most important experimental results of the 20th cent., because of its significance for the theory of electromagnetism and fundamental particles. Magnetic field strengths are measured in gauss (c.g.s.) or tesla (S.I.) units.

Magnetohydro-dynamics. A current-carrying wire always experiences a force if it is in a magnetic field. This is the well-known electrodynamic force, and electric motors work because of it. If the current is carried in a fluid, *e.g.*, a liquid metal or a plasma, these forces cause bodily movements to the fluid, which are in general very difficult to calculate. The forces are then called *magnetohydro-dynamic forces*. Now magnetic fields are themselves produced by electric currents; so a current flowing in a fluid produces a magnetic field, which then reacts on the fluid itself by means of the magnetohydro-dynamic forces. In the Harwell machine Zeta, used in studying the technical problems of thermonuclear reactions, this effect acts so as to constrict the electric discharge on to the axis of the tube and thus keeps it away from the walls. This action is assisted by an extra magnetic field produced by a separate current flowing in metallic conductors outside the tube. Thus the hot plasma is contained by magnetohydro-dynamic forces and not at all by the material tube wall. In practical devices of the future magnetic forces may have to sustain plasma pressure of 60 atmospheres—a pressure for which a thick steel wall would normally be used! *See also* **Plasma Physics**.

Magnetosphere. The magnetic field of the earth prevents the plasma of the solar wind from directly impinging on the earth's upper atmosphere and ionosphere. The cavity thus maintained within the solar wind is known as the magnetosphere. The tenuous plasma within this cavity is partly of solar and partly of terrestrial origin, from the solar wind and the ionosphere respectively. These plasmas are subject to large perturbations, known as magnetospheric storms, triggered by fluctuations within the solar wind. These storms generate intense auroral displays, magnetic field fluctuations at ground level, and often major disturbances of the upper atmosphere and ionosphere which may result in disruption of radio communications. The inner parts of the magnetosphere contain the Van Allen radiation belts (*q.v.*). On the sunward side the magnetosphere extends to between 12 and 20 earth radii. However, on the side of the earth away from the sun it extends, like a comet tail, for many millions of km. Jupiter's large magnetic field produces a large magnetosphere, one of the largest features in our planetary system being as large as the sun itself.

Magnificat, the hymn of the Virgin Mary, given in Luke 1, 46 beginning in the Vulgate with the words "Magnificat anima mea Dominum" ("My soul doth magnify the Lord").

Magnitude in astronomy is a measure of the apparent brightness of a star, which is inversely proportional to the square of its distance. A low number indicates a bright star, and a high

one a faint star. The *absolute magnitude* is a measure of *real* brightness, *i.e.*, the brightness a star would have at a standard distance away of 10 parsecs (32·6 light years). The distance can be calculated if the apparent and absolute magnitudes are known.

Magpie, a well-known bird of the crow family, of glossy black and white plumage, famed for its mischievous propensities.

Magyars, the Hungarian race who came to eastern Europe from S.W. Asia and settled in Hungary in the 10th cent. Their language belongs to the Finno-Ugrian group.

Mahdi an Arab leader of great influence, invested with powers akin to those of a Messiah in the Mohammedan mind. The title was taken by Mohammed Ahmed, who overran the Egyptian Sudan, and in 1885 went on to capture Khartoum.

Maidenhair Tree *or* **Ginkgo**. This tree takes its name from the shape of its leaves, which resemble those of the maidenhair fern. Widely cultivated in China and Japan. It is the only survivor of an order of gymnosperms which flourished in Mesozoic times. Botanically interesting because the male gametes are motile.

Malmaison, château at Rueil-Malmaison, a western suburb of Paris. It derives its name from having been inhabited in the 11th cent. by the Norman brigand Odon, and afterwards, according to the tradition, by evil spirits, exorcised by the monks of St. Denis. It was the residence of Napoleon and of the Empress Josephine after her divorce. She died there in 1814 as the result of a chill caught while showing the Russian Emperor round the grounds. In 1900 it was given to the nation.

Mamluks, commonly known as Mameluks, were originally—in the 13th cent.—a bodyguard of Turkish and Circassian slaves in the service of the Sultan of Egypt, and attained such influence that in 1250 they were strong enough to appoint one of their own body to the throne of Egypt. After that a succession of Mamluk Sultans reigned down to 1517. Then the Turks annexed Egypt, and the Mamluks were taken into the service of the Beys. They again came to the front after Napoleon's conquest of Egypt, and for a time resumed governmental sway; but in 1811 they were massacred by order of Mehemet Ali.

Mammoth, extinct elephants of gigantic size. In 1799 the first perfectly preserved specimen was found in Siberia in a block of ice. It was in prehistoric times an inhabitant of Britain and other parts of Europe, as well as of Asia and America.

Mammoth Cave of Kentucky, one of the largest known limestone caverns in the world, with subterranean passages at different levels, lakes and rivers (the Echo R. flows 110 m below the surface); stalactites and stalagmites abound.

Manatee, an aquatic mammal of the sea cow (Sirenia) order of mammals, averaging when full grown from 3–3·6 m in length, with shovel-shaped tail, and forelimbs and nails which almost give the appearance of arms and hands. Gentle and trusting they are under threat from man. Protected in Florida. In spite of their ungainly aspect, they are believed to have given rise to the legend of mermaids.

Manchus, originally nomads inhabiting northern Manchuria who invaded China early in the 17th cent. A Manchu dynasty occupied the imperial throne of China from 1644 to 1911.

Mandarin, the name given to a powerful Chinese official, civil or military, under the old régime, whose rank was shown by the wearing of a button on the cap. Mandarin is the major language of N. China.

Manganese, a metallic element, no. 25, symbol Mn, discovered by Scheele, 1774. It is silver-white, not very hard (it forms a hard alloy with carbon), brittle, and tarnishes when exposed to air. Its chief ore is pyrolusite (manganese dioxide). Steels containing manganese are very tough, used for making machine parts.

Maniple, eucharistic vestment worn over left arm.

Manna, a tree of the ash genus, *Fraxinus ornus*, growing in the South of Europe and in the East and exuding a sweet substance which is gathered, boiled and eaten.

Manometer, instrument used to measure gas

pressure. Usually a U-tube containing water or mercury, one end open to the atmosphere, the other to the gas whose pressure is to be measured. More sensitive for small pressures than the Bourdon gauge.

Mansion House, the official residence of the Lord Mayor of London, stands opposite to the Bank of England, and was erected in 1739–53 from the designs of George Dance.

Mantis. Large insects belonging to the same order as the locusts and grasshoppers. The manner in which the forelegs are held, as though in suppliance, has gained for these insects the common name of "praying mantis". They are distributed throughout the warmer countries of the world.

Manx, the Celtic dialect (Manx Gaelic) of the Isle of Man, now on the point of extinction.

Maoism. See **Section J.**

Maoris, the race living in New Zealand at the time it was first visited by Captain Cook in 1769. They are believed to have migrated from Polynesia about 1350. Up to 1871 they were frequently in arms against the European settlers but their high intelligence and stamina enabled them to adapt themselves and the New Zealand laws have encouraged equal citizenship. They number 270,035 (1976). Today in New Zealand a pure Maori is a rarity.

Maple, trees native to the northern hemisphere. There are over 100 species. The sycamore is the best-known species growing in Britain. The sugar maple abounds in Canada and the eastern parts of the United States. The sugar is tapped by boring holes in the tree in February and March, and the juice that escapes is collected and evaporated. The maple-leaf is the Canadian national emblem.

Maquis, name of the dense scrub in Mediterranean France and Corsica, providing good cover for bandits and outlaws. The French resistance movement adopted the name Maquis during the German Occupation, 1940–45.

Marble is limestone in its hardest and most crystalline form. There are many varieties—33 were used in the building of the Paris Opera House—but white is the purest and rarest. White marble was used by the ancient Greeks for their temples and statues. Among the famous marbles of Italy are the Carrara and Siena marbles, which were used by Renaissance sculptors. Devonshire and Derbyshire yield some beautiful marbles and Connemara furnishes a serpentine-marble.

March, the third month of the year, and the first of the old Roman Calendar. It was named after the god Mars, and was the *Hlyd* (storm) *monath* of the Anglo-Saxons.

Mardi Gras, the last day of the Carnival in France, Shrove Tuesday.

Marionettes are puppets moved by strings. They originated in the *Fantoccini* of the 15th cent. which had such a vogue in Italy and elsewhere on the Continent. The English *Punch and Judy* is a version of Punchinello.

Marmoset, small monkeys confined to the New World. Very squirrel-like in appearance, with long bushy tails, and thick woolly fur, they are pretty little animals and the smallest of all monkeys. There are claws, not nails, on their digits, the big toe excepted.

Marprelate Tracts, seditious pamphlets written with great maliciousness by a group of Elizabethan puritans about 1586, and intended to discredit the episcopacy, caused a great sensation in their time, and led to the execution of their supposed author, John Penry.

Marquess *or* **Marquis,** the title next in precedent to that of duke. The first English marquess was Rovery de Vere, Earl of Oxford, who received the honour from Richard II, in 1385.

Mars, the fourth nearest planet to the sun (*see* **F8**). The enormous amount of new information from the recent visits to Mars, primarily by the US *Mariner* and *Viking* spacecraft, in 1971 and 1976 respectively, has revolutionised our understanding of the planet. Where the brief glimpses of the planet by the early *Mariner 6* and *7* missions showed a dead, barren world, not unlike the moon, the 1971 and 1976 missions showed that the planet's surface displayed many contrasts—the ancient crated terrains glimpsed previously, enormous volcanos, far larger than any on earth, vast wastelands, particularly near the polar regions, scoured by wind-blown dust over many aeons, and most tantalising, in many regions water had set unmistakable marks. We see the plains which have been subject to torrential deluges of rain in, probably, a number of different episodes over hundreds of millions of years. Other regions, extending over hundreds of km, show great gorges and canyons cut by catastrophic floods, when some natural dam has burst, releasing the pent-up waters of a gigantic lake or sea. This pictorial evidence, and more detailed information of the atmosphere and surface obtained from the *Viking* spacecraft tell us that there must have been episodes in the planet's history when its climate was quite different from that observed today. The atmosphere, if only for brief interludes, must have been much denser, and warmer, and rain must have been able to fall. Mars is today too cold and dry for water but there are polar ice caps, and the nature of the meteoric craters suggests that the surface is rock over ice and solid carbon dioxide. The search for life carried out by *Viking* has produced a wealth of new information on the planet, but no traces of organic compounds as evidence, or precursors, of life. Mars has two small moons, Phobos and Deimos, which appear to be asteroidal in nature.

Marseillaise, the French national hymn, written and composed by Rouget de L'Isle, a French engineer officer, who was inspired to write it in 1792 to encourage the Strasburg conscripts. It immediately became popular, and received its name from the fact that it was sung by the Marseillaise troops while marching into Paris.

Marshalsea, a former prison in Southwark, London, closed 1849. It existed as early as Edward III's time and was used as a jail for royal servants convicted of offences. In its later days it became a debtors' prison. Dickens described it in *Little Dorrit.*

Marston Moor, near York, was the scene of the famous battle between Prince Rupert and Cromwell on 2 July 1644. Cromwell's victory was the turning-point in the Civil War.

Marsupials, members of the order of pouched mammals. Except for the opossums of America, all marsupials occur in Australasia, and include the kangaroos, wallabies and wombats.

Martello Towers, circular forts erected on the coasts of England, Ireland and the Channel Isles early in the 19th cent. as defences against the threatened Napoleonic invasion. So called from the circular fort at Mortella (Corsica), which resisted an English sea attack in 1794.

Marten, carnivorous animals of the weasel family; one species (the Pine Marten) was once common in Britain. Most famous for their fur are the Siberian Sable and the American Marten.

Martial Law is a term loosely employed to indicate the suspension of the administration of normal civil law and its replacement by military authority when this is rendered desirable by such circumstances as war or rebellion.

Martin, a well-known bird-visitor to Britain. It belongs to the swallow family, and the two species that spend their summers here are the house-martin, which makes its nest of mud under the eaves of houses, and the sand martin, which builds in sandy banks.

Martinmas *or* **St. Martin's Day,** falls on 11 November, and is one of the Scottish quarter days. St. Martin was a popular Saint with our ancestors and Martinmas was a busy time for the mediaeval housewife. It was the date when "Martlemas Beef" was dried in the chimney, and enough bacon and mutton cured to last until the spring, because, owing to the scarcity of winter fodder, fresh meat could seldom be obtained. This diet of dried meat without vegetables caused scurvy. St. Martin (c. 316–400) was regarded as the patron saint of drinking and jovial meetings, as well as of reformed drunkards. The late spell of fine weather sometimes occurring at Martinmas is called St. Martin's Summer.

Martyrs. People who suffer death in testimony to their faith. Stephen (Acts 6; 7) was the first Christian martyr in 39. The first English martyr was St. Alban, 286, and in Tudor times many eminent churchmen went to the stake. The Smithfield martyrs' memorial church used to be St. Peter's, St. John Street, Clerkenwell. When that church was demolished the memorial moved to the Church of St. James, Clerkenwell Green.

Marxism. *See* **Section J.**

Mason and Dixon Line, boundary line between Pennsylvania and Maryland, for long a source of dispute, drawn up by two English surveyors, Charles Mason and Jeremiah Dixon, between 1763 and 1767. It came to designate the boundary dividing the slave states from the free states of America, and is still used in distinguishing the "North" from the "South".

Masques were light dramatic compositions set to music and performed on special occasions. One of the best-known examples is Milton's "Comus", which was given at Ludlow Castle in 1634.

Mass, the service in the Roman Catholic Church in which are enacted and enshrined Christ's words and actions at the Last Supper. It was first celebrated in Latin in the 4th cent., and was introduced into England in the 7th cent. The use of a vernacular language was sanctioned by the Second Vatican Council (1965).

Mass Spectrograph, an instrument for separating isotopes. It works by sorting electrified particles according to their masses; the particles stream through a magnetic and possibly an electric field, and the lightest particles undergo the greatest deflection.

Massorah, a collection of criticisms on the Hebrew text of the Scriptures, and rules for its correct interpretation.

Mast, a long round piece of timber or tubular steel or iron, standing upright in a vessel, and supporting the yards, sails and rigging in general. The earliest ships had only one mast, carrying a simple sail. The number increased until there were 4 or 5, or even more. Above the lower mast of a sailing-ship comes the topmast, and above that, the topgallantmast and royalmast. The position of each mast is indicated by a prefix, as foremast, foretopmast, foretopgallantmast, foreroyalmast, mainmast, maintopmast, etc. The foremast is in the fore of the ship, the mainmast in the centre and the mizzen nearest the stern. In large vessels nowadays the mast does not extend to the keel, as it formerly did, but is usually stopped at the second deck.

Master of the Revels was an important Court official upon whom devolved the arrangement of Court festivities. The office is at least as old as the time of Edward III. By 1737 it seems to have died.

Master of the Rolls, one of the English judges, formerly a judge of Chancery, but since 1881 a judge of the Court of Appeal only. In addition he has charge of the rolls or records of Chancery and ranks next to the Lord Chancellor and Lord Chief Justice.

Mastodon, an extinct order of quadruped closely resembling the elephant in structure, but is larger.

Materials Science is a blend of science and technology; it is the use of scientific research methods to study and improve materials for practical use. The deeper understanding so obtained enables scientists to design new substances with hitherto unknown combinations of properties that are useful in engineering, aircraft, nuclear power, surgery, etc. Materials science institutes or university departments will usually contain an assortment of chemists, physicists, metallurgists, ceramicists, engineers and others because materials science brings to bear on materials a great many specialised techniques. The scientific study of materials is bringing continual improvement in metals, ceramics, plastics, fibres and many valuable combinations of these.

Mathematics is a body of knowledge expressed in a language of symbols. *Pure* mathematics studies the propositions that can be deduced in this language by applying definite rules of reasoning to sets of axioms. In *Applied* mathematics, the mathematical language is used, often with great effect, to discuss problems of the real world, such as mechanics, statistics and science generally. In range, subtlety, complexity and depth mathematics is unsurpassed among the intellectual disciplines and its study has attracted some of the most brilliant men in history.

Matins, the first of the canonical hours or services of the day in the Roman Catholic Church and Morning Prayer in the Anglican Church. The daily service in the Roman breviary (*q.v.*) used to consist of eight offices or "hours", fixed by canon, for prayer and devotion but since the second Vatican Council the structure has been simplified. Formerly, Matins was recited or sung at midnight, Lauds at sunrise, Prime at 6 a.m., Terce at 9 a.m., Sext at midday, Nones at 3. p.m., Vespers at sunset and Compline before retiring for the night. Lauds are now commonly joined to Matins.

Matrix, a rectangular array of numbers considered as a single mathematical object. There are special rules for multiplying and adding matrices and they are often used in mathematics, physics and elsewhere to simplify calculations and as a notational device.

Mau-Mau, a secret, anti-European, terrorist movement which agitated the Kikuyu tribe of Kenya during the years 1953–57. Mau-mau was a symptom of native insecurity and discontent; emergency powers were lifted in November 1959, and large-scale reforms were instituted. Kenya attained independence in December 1963 with Mr. Jomo Kenyatta as the Prime Minister.

Maundy Thursday, the day before Good Friday, commemorates the Last Supper. "Maundy" derives from Christ's command (mandatum) to his disciples on that day to love one another. It was the custom in the monasteries for the monks to wash the feet of the poor on this day, and for many centuries the sovereigns of England, through their almoners, have distributed money, food and clothing to "as many old men and as many old women as the Sovereign is years of age". The Royal Maundy ceremony is still observed, maundy coins being struck from standard silver.

Mausoleum, a special place of sepulture, generally for the reception of the remains of members of a royal or other family of distinction. The name is derived from the tomb of King Mausolus at Halicarnassus, erected 352 B.C., and forming one of the seven wonders of the ancient world. Another mausoleum of antiquity is that of Hadrian in Rome.

Mauve, a colouring matter produced from lichens by Dr. Stenhouse in 1848, but in 1856 obtained from aniline by William Perkin (1838–1907), who gave it the name Mauveen. This was the first synthetic organic dyestuff ever to be produced, which led to the building up of the great synthetic dyestuffs industry (which Germany dominated before the first world war).

May, the fifth month of the year, but the third of the ancient Roman calendar. Supposed to be named after Maia, the mother of Mercury, to whom sacrifices were offered on the first day of this month. In England in former days May Day was made the occasion of many festivities, including the crowning of the May Queen, dancing round the Maypole, etc.

"Mayflower", the name of the ship which in 1620 conveyed the Pilgrim Fathers, 101 in number, from England to America. *See* **Pilgrim Fathers.**

May Fly. *See* **Ephemeptera.**

Mazarin Bible, an edition of the Latin Vulgate, acknowledged as the masterpiece of the Gutenberg press (1456). It was the first book completely printed from movable types. It is called the Mazarin Bible because the first copy to capture the attention of scholars was found in the library of Cardinal Mazarin, in Paris. Sometimes called the Gutenberg or the 42-line Bible.

Mean. In statistics and mathematics generally understood to be the arithmetic mean. The geometric mean between two quantities is the square root of their product. *See* **Average.**

Mechanical Equivalent of Heat. *See* **Joule.**

Medals, as decorations for military service, were first issued in this country by Charles I, who ordered medals for gallantry to be distributed

L81

to certain soldiers in 1643. Medals were also issued to officers and men who were victorious against the Dutch fleet in 1653. After Lord Howe's victory in 1794 a naval medal was instituted. Medals were also struck for the victory of Waterloo, and since that time special medals have been issued in connection with all our wars. The Victoria Cross, a special reward for personal gallantry, was instituted in 1856. The George Cross for gallantry instituted in 1940 ranks next to the Victoria Cross. The Military Cross was instituted in 1914.

Megalith, a prehistoric monument, consisting of a large single stone or a group of such stones, in a circle as at Stonehenge or in burial chambers as at New Grange, Ireland. Megalithic monuments have been constructed by different peoples in different parts of the world since the third millennium B.C.

Meiosis, special type of cell division by which the gametes or sex cells are generated, resulting in the sperm or ovum receiving only half the number of chromosomes found in a somatic cell. See **Mitosis.**

Mendelian Law. See **F30(2).**

Mendicant Friars, certain religious orders which spread over Europe in the 13th cent., and comprised the Franciscans, Dominicans, Augustines and Carmelites. Originally they depended entirely on alms.

Mercator's Projection, a method of indicating meridians and parallels of latitudes on maps, introduced by Mercator in the 16th cent., and still universally used in navigators' charts.

Mercury, the smallest of the planets (approx. one-twentieth of the earth's mass) is the closest to the sun at a little more than one-third of the earth's average distance. It appears to resemble the earth in its interior and has about the same density but its surface resembles the moon and is heavily cratered. Mercury was visited by Mariner 10 which passed within a few hundred kilometres in March 1974 and which relayed pictures on the two following passes in September 1974 and March 1975 before control of its altitude was lost. It nevertheless continues to revisit Mercury every 176 days (two mercurian years). Mariner 10 was guided to Mercury by the gravitational field of Venus before it became a satellite of the smallest planet. The relayed pictures showed that the planet has an approximately 59-day rotation period exactly twothirds of its orbital period of 88 days. This relationship means that unlike on earth the seasonal variations are with longitude not latitude. Surface temperatures vary from 400°C to −200°C and there is virtually no atmosphere except a thin envelope of helium gas. Mariner 10 measured a small magnetic field at the surface about 1% of the earth's but much stronger than for Venus or Mars.

Mercury or **Quicksilver,** element no. 80, symbol Hg (Latin *hydrargyrum*) is one of the oldest-known metals, whose chief ore is the sulphide, cinnabar, found in certain parts of Spain, China, Japan and South America. It is liquid at ordinary temperature and is used in the construction of barometers and thermometers. Alloys of mercury are called amalgams. It is also of great value in medicine. The metal is used in the mercury-vapour (or "sunlight") lamp, since the vapour gives a bright yellow-white glow in an electric discharge.

Mercy-killing, taking the life of a person suffering from a painful and incurable disease. The killer is often actuated by a good *motive*—the desire to relieve hopeless suffering; but the *intention* is to kill, and the act, in English law, is therefore a crime. (It is not necessary for the prosecution to prove any motive.)

Meridian, an imaginary circle extending through the North and South Poles and any given place. When the sun is at its midday height at any place it is "on the meridian"; hence the terms ante-meridian (a.m.) and post-meridian (p.m.). See also **Greenwich Mean Time.**

Merino Sheep were imported into England from Spain in 1788 and had great influence in improving native breeds, especially in regard to the quality of the wool.

Merit, Order of, founded by King Edward VII in 1902 as a special distinction for eminent men and women without conferring a knighthood

upon them. The Order has twenty-four British companions in addition to foreign honorary members limited in number, as the choice of members is, by the Sovereign's pleasure. Lord Kelvin was the founder companion. Florence Nightingale (1907), Professor Dorothy Hodgkin (1965), Dame Veronica Wedgwood (1969) and Mother Theresa of Calcutta (honorary member, 1983) are the only women to have received this coveted decoration.

Merovingians, the name given to the family that ruled over France from about 500 to 750. Clovis was first of the line and Childeric the last. The "long-haired kings" have become the centre of much recent speculative history.

Mesons (from Greek *meso* = middle), a family of unstable particles of mass between that of an electron and that of a proton. Some are positive, some negative, some neutral. No stable meson is known, the longest-lived particle having a lifetime of only two-millionths of a second. The first of these particles was discovered in cosmic radiation in 1937 and called the mu-meson or *muon.* In 1947 a heavier type was discovered called the pi-meson or *pion* which behaved like the meson predicted on theoretical grounds by Yukawa in 1935. The pion is connected with the theory of nuclear forces. See also **F15, 16.**

Mesozoic. The geological era which includes the Triassic, Jurassic and Cretaceous rocks. See **F48.**

Metamorphic Rocks are such geological deposits as have undergone alterations of structure and mineral reorganisation. The most active agents in producing these metamorphic changes are heat, water and pressure. See **F9(1).**

Metamorphosis, period of development from egg to adult, during which the animals have different forms, as found, *e.g.*, in the life histories of frog and butterfly.

Meteorites are small bodies, asteroids, or fragments of asteroids, which survive their fiery passage through the earth's atmosphere and hit the ground. The present surfaces of the moon, Mars and Mercury tell us that all the planets have been subjected since their formation to bombardment by meteorites. Though some large craters are still to be found on the earth, most have disappeared due to extensive weathering over thousands of millions of years. In some meteorites iron and nickel are the chief metals (siderites), others are like rock (aerolites). The iron meteorites are more common amongst those which have been preserved, but falls of rock-like meteorites occur more frequently. At L'Aigle in France in 1803 from 2000 to 3000 meteorite stones fell; this fall is famous because it convinced scientists that meteorites really came from outside our atmosphere. The largest meteorite stone actually known to have fallen to earth is one which descended in Emmott County, Iowa, in 1870, weighing 197 kg. A meteorite weighing no less than 37 tonnes found in Greenland is now in New York. On 30 June 1908, an enormous object fell in Siberia in a sparsely-inhabited region. A hot blast destoyed all trees within a radius of about 8–16 km, the explosion waves being recorded by barographs as far distant as London, Washington and Batavia. There is still controversy about the nature of the Siberian meteorite, whether it was an asteroid or possibly the nucleus of a small comet.

Meteorology, the science of the atmosphere considered as a heat engine. Deals with weather, climate, optical phenomena, atmospheric electricity, physical processes such as radiation and precipitation, the dynamics and structure of cyclones, anticyclones, etc. Wide application to problems of aviation, agriculture, commerce and shipping. Meteorological observing stations are in operation all over the world, and on the simultaneous or synoptic reports of their instrument readings and estimates of pressure, temperature, humidity, speed and direction of wind, rain, character and amount of cloud, visibility, etc., forecasts, gale, snow and frost warnings are based. Instruments carried by earth satellites (*e.g.*, *Tiros, Nimbus*) outside the atmosphere can make systematic observations on a world-wide basis of the atmospheric circulation, through observation of cloud cover and of the thermal radiation into space from the atmosphere. Such observations together with the use of computers are of great importance for weather analysis and forecasting. The main communications centre for the UK is at the headquarters of the Meteorological Office at Bracknell, Berkshire, where the collection, editing and re-transmission of weather messages continue according to strict schedules day and night throughout the year.

Meteors or more commonly, "shooting stars", are small objects which enter the upper atmosphere to burn up in a bright streak of light. Their origin is mainly in the dust particles ejected in large quantities from comets. Some, particularly the larger and more brilliant ones, called fireballs, or debris of asteroids. Those which reach the earth's surface are called meteorites (q.v.).

Methane. The simplest hydrocarbon, compounded of one carbon atom and four hydrogen atoms. This gas occurs over marshes and swamps, where it is liberated in the decay of vegetable matter. It is the main constituent of natural gas, and also occurs in coal-mines, where it is called "fire-damp" because of the explosive character of its mixture with air. Formerly this natural gas was removed from the coal seams and ran to waste; now in many countries (including Britain) it is being used for commercial purposes.

Methylated Spirit, a mixture of 90 parts by volume ethyl alcohol, 9½ parts wood naphtha (methyl alcohol), ¼ part crude pyridine, together with small amounts of petroleum oil and methyl violet dye. Industrial methylated spirit consists of a mixture of 95 parts by volume ethyl alcohol and 5 parts wood naphtha. It is used as a solvent and a fuel.

Metre, the rhythmical pattern of Verse.

Metre, unit of length in the metric system; since 1983 has been redefined as "the length of the path travelled by light in vacuum during a time interval of 1/299 792 458 of a second". This definition replaces that adopted in 1960 which used the wavelength of the orange-red line of krypton-86. Before that the "international prototype metre" was the distance between marks on the platinum-iridium bar placed at Sèvres in 1889.

Metric System, the system of weights and measures based on the gram and the metre, smaller and larger units being decimals and multiples of the primary units respectively. A decimal currency was adopted in France in 1795 and the metric system of weights and measures in 1799. (In that year the quadrant of the earth was surveyed and the standard metre adopted.) Nevertheless the change was accepted slowly, and as late as 1837 the French Government had to pass a law forbidding the use of the old measures. Since then the metric system has been adopted in most of the continental countries and is used universally in scientific work. Although there have been many attempts to get the system adopted in Britain, it was not until 1965 that the Government encouraged the adoption of the metric system of weights and measures. The changeover to decimal coinage was made in 1971; the system of weights and measures in industry is now mainly metric. See **N7** for **SI** units.

Mezzotint, a technical method for producing graphic work and works of art. A copper plate is made rough by close cross-hatching, so that a print from it produces an even black. When parts of the cross-hatching are scraped away, these areas will come out white when printed. By skilful use of his tools, the artist or technician can produce pictures finely graded from black to white and with a velvety black as background. The principles of the method were known and practised, for instance, by Rembrandt, but mezzotint became most popular for the reproduction of famous paintings from the end of the 18th cent.

Mica. The mica of commerce is a nearly transparent mineral, which has great heat-resisting power, and can be split into thin plates. The most important micas are muscovite (potassium mica), the commoner variety, phlogopite (magnesium mica) and biotite (the magnesium and iron mica).

Michael, St., and George, St., an order of knighthood originally founded for the Ionian Isles and Malta in 1818, and reorganised in 1869, so as to admit Crown servants connected with the Colonies. The Earl of Derby, Earl Russell and Earl Grey were the first of the new knights.

Michaelmas Day, the festival day of St. Michael and All Angels, 29 September, one of the English quarter days.

Microbe, a term proposed by Sédillot in 1878 to denote any microscopic organism, vegetable or animal, or found on the borderland between the two great natural kingdoms. The term is commonly used, but not by scientists.

Microelectronics, a rapidly developing technology of the 1960s which reduces entire electronic circuits to minute size and embeds them in tiny chips of solid material. These are then called integrated circuits. A circuit consisting of, say, a dozen transistors and fifty resistors can be built into a small piece of semiconductor (q.v.) measuring not more than a couple of millimetres in any direction. Hundreds of these circuits can be made simultaneously in penny-size wafers of silicon about one-hundredth of an inch thick. There are great advantages in cheapness, reliability, robustness and speed of electronic performance. The small size is in itself an advantage in space vehicles and medical instruments. Applications to missile control systems, computers and communications equipment are no doubt only the first fruits of this new achievement of the current technological revolution.

Micrometer, an instrument for measuring minute distances; usually attached to the eye-pieces of a microscope or telescope, and consisting of two very fine hairs or wires stretched across the field of view, one fixed, the other movable. It was invented by William Gascoigne in the 17th cent. and improved by later inventors. Sir Joseph Whitworth made one in 1858 to measure the millionth part of an inch.

Micro-organisms, the collective term applied to several types of organism, the most important of which are fungi, viruses, bacteria and protozoa. It is a classification of convenience in biological studies. These organisms are generally simple in their environmental requirements (e.g., have simple nutritional needs) and in cellular organisation. This makes them very suitable for modern biological research. Much of the information on the nature of the genetic code (**F32(2)**) was obtained from experiments on these organisms.

Microphone, device for converting the acoustic energy of sound waves into waves of electrical energy, used in sound amplifying systems. Developed independently by Edison (1877) and Hughes (1878).

Microscope, invented about 1590 by Janssen, and improved by Galileo, Fontana and others, is an instrument which by a lens system magnifies minute objects. Microscopes are simple, compound and binocular. See also **Electron Microscope.**

Middle Ages (c. A.D. 400–1500), usually considered to be the period between the decline and fall of the Western Roman Empire and the fall of Constantinople to the Turks (see **A4-7**). The period covers (a) an earlier part ending with the 12th cent. (sometimes called the Dark Ages) when science was dead, when theology was the main preoccupation, and when the language of the learned West was Latin; and (b) a later age of Arabian influence when alchemy and astrology (at that time indistinguishable from astronomy) were central interests, technology was advancing, and Greek learning was transmitted by Arab scholars. Characteristic features of the mediaeval scene were monasticism (**Sec. J**), the Crusades (q.v.), Gothic art (q.v.), feudalism (**Sec. J**), and the supremacy of Islam in the field of learning. The period came to an end with the general decline of Christendom and the ushering in of the Renaissance (**Sec. J**). The term "Middle Ages" was coined by the 17th-cent. German historian Christoph Keller.

Midrash, name given to the homiletical interpretation of some of the Hebrew Scriptures in which allegory and legendary illustration were freely used. Compiled by Jewish rabbis from c. A.D. 200.

Millenary Petition was presented to James I in 1603, on behalf of nearly 1000 Puritan Ministers against certain of the rites and ceremonies of the Church of England. The Hampton Court Conference was the outcome of this petition.

Millennium, a period of a thousand years. The term is specifically used of the period of a thousand years during which, according to Rev. xx. 1–5, Christ will reign in person on earth. The Millenarians are a sect that interprets the "Millennium" as beginning with the commencement of the 6001st year from the Creation, which, according to Archbishop Ussher (1581–1650), was in 4004 B.C.

Millipede. Arthropods (**F36**) allied to the centipedes, from which they differ in having two pairs of legs to each body segment (except the first three) instead of one pair. Worm-like in shape but with a pair of antennae on the head, they can do much harm to garden plants, unlike centipedes which are beneficial.

Millstone-Grit, a series of grits and sandstones of deltaic origin underlying the coal measures of the Carboniferous system and attaining in England a thickness in parts of 1,525 m. It is from this rock that millstones have been made from time immemorial.

Mimicry, protective similarity of an animal to another animal or to inanimate objects. Examples of the former are the hover flies, which mimic wasps and bees; of the latter, leaf insects, stick insects and caterpillars that look like dead twigs.

Mink. Semi-aquatic mammals closely related to polecats. There is one American species and one European. The fur, which varies light to dark brown, is soft and thick, and is among the most valuable of commercial furs. They now live in the wild in the British Isles.

Minnesingers were minstrel poets of Germany who, during the 12th and 13th cent., composed and sang verses of heroism and love. They were of knightly rank, the counterpart of the French troubadours. See **E3**(2).

Minnow, a small fresh-water fish of the carp family, abounding in all the waters of Europe; it has a mottled back and silvery belly, and forms a popular bait for trout.

Minstrels were originally specially appointed instrumentalists and singers—pipers, harpers and gleemen—engaged by barons and manorial lords to amuse their tenants. Later, minstrels assumed nomadic habits, made their way into the houses of the great and were generally welcome. By Elizabeth's time, however, they were too numerous, and were classed as "rogues and vagabonds", along with actors.

Miracle Plays, mediaeval verse plays, popular in England in the 15th cent., were usually religious in character, representing some of the dramatic incidents of the Bible.

Mirage, an optical illusion caused by unequal temperatures in different layers of the atmosphere near the earth's surface. These temperature variations alter the refracting power of the air and cause light rays to be curved, making the air act as a huge distorting lens. This can happen at sea, in deserts and elsewhere and various types of mirage are known. A common kind in deserts curves light from the sky so that it appears to come from the ground, deceiving the observer into thinking that the sky is reflected in a lake of water. Inverted images of hills, trees, etc. also look as if reflected in the non-existent lake.

Mishna, the first part of the Talmud, setting forth the "Oral Law" of the Jews.

Missal, the name of the mass-book of the Roman Church compiled 492–96 by Pope Gelasius I. The missal used until recently was sanctioned by the Council of Trent, 1546–63, but the current missal was authorised by Pope Paul VI in 1969 following the Second Vatican Council. In the Anglican Communion the Book of Common Prayer superseded the Missal in 1549.

Mistle Thrush receives its name from its partiality to the mistletoe-berry. Larger than the song-thrush, with spotted breast rather than speckled.

Mistletoe, a parasitic evergreen with white berries used as a decoration at Christmas-time. The familiar mistletoe of Europe is the *Viscum album,* which grows on the boughs of lime,

willow, apple, poplar, maple, ash, hawthorn but seldom on oak-trees. It was sacred to the Druids, and in Norse mythology it was a mistletoe dart that killed the god Baldur.

Mistral, a cold, dry, northerly wind peculiar to the French coast of the Mediterranean.

Mitosis, cell division whereby each daughter cell receives the same number of chromosomes as the parent cell. When the gametes (sex cells) are formed a special type of division occurs (meiosis) in which the number of chromosomes is halved. See **F34**(1).

Mitre, the twofold pointed head-dress of bishops and certain abbots of the Western Church and occasionally of other ecclesiastics.

Moa, the name for several species of ostrich-like extinct birds related to the New Zealand kiwi. The largest species, *Diornis maximus,* stood 2·6 m high, the smallest, *Anomalopteryx parva,* was nearer the size of a turkey. This wingless bird became extinct several centuries ago because of hunting by the Maoris from whom the name comes.

Moabite Stone, a stone of the 9th cent. B.C. containing the earliest known inscription in Phoenician characters, and discovered in the highlands of Moab in 1868. It is now in the Louvre, Paris. It records the campaign between Moab and Israel (*c.* 850 B.C.), an account of which is given in the Old Testament (2 Kings 3:27).

Moderator, a material used to slow down neutrons in an atomic pile. Examples of moderators are pure graphite and heavy water. See **Nuclear Reactors.**

Mohole Project, a scheme to bore through the earth's crust to take samples of the mantle rocks beneath. Drilling trials, led by an American team of geophysicists, began in 1961 near the island of Guadalupe off the Mexican coast in the Pacific. The project, however, was cancelled in 1966 on account of the escalating cost. Russian geophysicists started on a similar experiment, boring through land rocks where the digging is much deeper and higher temperatures are met with. The name "Anti-Cosmos" was given to the project. The boundary between the earth's crustal and mantle rocks is known as the Mohorovičić Discontinuity, or, more simply, as the Moho. The technology of deep sea drilling came from this project.

Molasses, sugar-cane juice in its uncrystallised form after boiling. The crystallised part is the raw sugar. Used to make rum.

Mole, a small burrowing animal with long, sensitive nose, about the size of a small rat, with short legs and forefeet armed with strong claws for digging in the earth. Their subterranean dwellings are of curiously ingenious construction, and they do not often leave them except to make raids on mice, frogs, snails, etc. The earth-worm, however, is the mole's chief item of food. Not to be confused with the vole which has a blunt nose.

Mole, or gram molecular weight. See **F24**(1).

Molecular Biology, a rapidly expanding branch of science mainly concerned with cell structure and function at a molecular level, in particular with genes and enzymes and the interaction between the two. Recent work in Britain has led to the unravelling of the structure of DNA, the hereditary substance of the genes, and has played a major part in uncovering the molecular mechanism of the transfer of hereditary information and the nature of the genetic code. Crystallisation of the first enzyme (urease) took place in 1929; the gene as a definite chemical entity was discovered in 1943. See **F29**(1).

Molecule. A group of atoms held together by chemical forces. See **F14, 23,** also **Macromolecule.**

Molybdenum, element no. 42, symbol Mo, a fairly hard white metal with properties resembling those of chromium. Its commonest ore is the sulphide, molybdenite. The chief use of the metals is in the manufacture of alloy steels.

Monasticism. See Section J.

Monazite, a cerium mineral containing some thorium. Occurs as grains, often as sand ("monazite sands"), derived from granites. Deposits occur in India (Travancore), Russia, Norway, Malagasy Rep., S. Africa, Brazil, USA.

Monday, the second day of the week, called by the Anglo-Saxons *Monandaeg* (moon-day).

Mongoose, species of mammals related to the civets, feeding on vermin and reptiles. These animals, which have long tails and short legs, occur in Africa and Asia (especially India). The biggest mongoose is the Egyptian ichneumon, and this has been introduced into the W. Indies because of its ability to kill large poisonous snakes.

Monitor, a family of lizards most resembling dragons. There are about 30 species widely distributed over the tropical parts of Asia, Australia and Africa.

Monroe Doctrine, a principle of American policy declining any European intervention in political affairs of the American continent, outlined by President Monroe in 1823. At the same time interference was disclaimed with existing European colonies in the Western Hemisphere. The American Civil War hampered the application of the doctrine for some time, but afterwards the United States firmly insisted on it. The Doctrine is not international law, but a national policy of the USA.

Monsoons, regular persistent winds which blow at certain seasons in middle latitudes, mainly in South and East Asia. Their occurrence is related to the great changes of pressure which take place between summer and winter over the land mass. In India the south-west monsoon (June–October) is moisture-laden from its long passage over the sea and in the higher regions, especially, there is heavy rainfall. Sudden reversal of the wind results in the cold north-east monsoon (October–March) which is dry on account of the shelter afforded by the mountain ranges to the north. Frequently the term "monsoon" is applied to denote the associated rainfall without reference to the actual winds.

Monstrance, an ornamental transparent receptacle in which the Sacred Host is carried in procession or exposed for adoration.

Month, the 12th part of the calendar year. A lunar month is the interval of new moon to new moon or full moon to full moon; mean length, 29 days, 12 hours, 44 minutes, 2·87 seconds. A sidereal month represents the time of the moon's revolution from a given star back to the same again, 27 days, 7 hours, 43 minutes, 11·5 seconds. In English law, since 1926, a month, unless otherwise expressed, means a calendar month.

Monument of London, a 202 ft (61·6 m) column, overlooking Billingsgate, designed by Wren and erected (1671–77) to mark the starting-point of the Great Fire of London (1666). The original inscription upon it ascribed the fire to "the treachery and malice of the popish faction", which stood until 1831, when the words were erased as objectionable. The black marble staircase has 345 steps (311 to the balcony).

Moon, the earth's satellite, 3,475 km in diameter and 384,400 km distant from the earth. It rotates in the same time as it revolves round the earth (27 days 7 hours 43 minutes), so that the same face is always presented to the earth. The lunar surface is pockmarked by innumerable collisions with solid particles of all sizes. Unlike the earth, it is unprotected by any atmosphere and for aeons of time it has been exposed to every kind of cosmic influence, including the parching effect of solar radiation. All moonlight derives from the sun but on the whole it is a pretty poor reflector. The exploration of the moon by means of rockets began in 1959 when the Russian *Luna 2* crashlanded on the plains of the *Mare Imbrium*. 1969 will be remembered as the year of the U.S. *Apollo* triumphs when man first set foot on the moon. The samples of lunar rock and dust brought back to earth by the *Apollo* astronauts and the Soviet *Luna* unmanned automatic stations are being studied by lunar scientists. Samples date back further than any found on Earth as yet. The most famous, known as the Genesis Rock, is 4,100 million years old. The exploration of the moon at close range by means of spacecraft was made possible only by parallel developments in several branches of technology—rocket propulsion, long-range radio and television transmission, electronic computer control.

Moorhen, a widely distributed bird of the rail family, a common resident in the British Isles.

The adult is blackish with white under tail coverts, a white line on the flanks and a yellow-tipped bill. The frontal shield and the base of the bill are vermilion. It bobs its head, flirts its tail and dives well. The nest is usually placed close to the water's edge or on an overhanging branch. In feeding the young the parents are sometimes helped by their offspring of a previous brood of the season. In N. America the bird is known as the Florida Gallinule.

Moors, the name given to the Moslems who live in N.W. Africa and to those who once lived in Spain. In 711 Moorish Arabs invaded Spain and spread beyond the Pyrenees into France, where they were driven back by the end of the century. Spain, however, remained virtually under Moorish domination until the 11th cent. and during that period was the most civilised and prosperous part of Western Europe. In the arts and sciences the impact of Moorish culture was profound and lasting. Examples of the brilliant splendour of Moorish architecture are still to be seen in Toledo, Córdoba, Seville and Granada. During the long struggle for the Christian reconquest thousands were killed and expelled, and in 1492 Granada, their last remaining kingdom, was forced to surrender. They were virtually exterminated by the Inquisition, and the last were expelled in 1609.

Moose, the largest member of the deer family. The N. American Moose stands 1·6–2 m high, and has huge palmate antlers. There is another New World species, occurring in Alaska. The European species is known as the elk.

Morse Alphabet, a system of dots and dashes intended to be used in combination with the indicator in telegraphy; but usually read by sound, the receiving operator writing down the words in the system as transmitted. This system of signals was invented by the American inventor and artist Samuel Finley Breese Morse (1791–1872) of Charlestown, Massachusetts.

Mosaic, art of arranging small pieces of coloured glass, marble, or other materials in such a fashion as to produce a decorative pattern. Some of the best examples of Byzantine mosaics are to be seen at Ravenna, Rome, Venice and Sicily.

Mosque, a Mohammedan church, the greatest being that of Santa Sophia at Istanbul, now converted into a museum of Byzantine art.

Mosquito, small two-winged flies with long legs and slender body. Their larvae are aquatic. The females of some species are blood-suckers, and thus come to transmit the blood parasites which cause malaria and yellow fever, for example. See **DDT** *and* **Gammexane.**

Mosses. With liverworts, mosses comprise an important group of relatively simple non-vascular land plants, the bryophytes (**F42**). In the main they are small plants, the largest between 30–70 cm high, having been recorded in the Southern Hemisphere. Mosses rarely occur singly, but usually form cushions or small colonies on moist soil, bark, wood, rock or walls. The genus *sphagnum* known as "peat" or "bog mosss" is of commercial value in horticulture. In Lancashire and Cheshire lowland moors in which sphagnum is common are known as "mosses". Reindeer moss is a lichen and Spanish moss a seed plant.

Moths, of the insect order, *Lepidoptera*, differing from butterflies which have clubbed antennae, in having feathery, sometimes thin, pointed antennae, rarely clubbed. Most are nocturnal, and the pupae are usually brown and enclosed in a cocoon unlike those of the butterfly, which are usually naked. See also **Lepidoptera.**

Motion, Laws of. According to Newton: (1) A body continues in its state of rest or uniform motion in a straight line except in so far as it is compelled by external forces to change that state. (2) Rate of change of momentum is proportional to the applied force, and takes place in the direction in which the force acts. (3) To every action there is an equal and opposite reaction. These laws are the basis of almost all engineering and everyday mechanics. Corrections to them have been made by relativity and the quantum theory. See **F17, 19.**

Mule, a cross between a male ass and a horse mare; a hinny is a cross between an ass mare and a horse stallion. Also the name of the spinning machine invented by Crompton in 1779 which combined the principle of Hargreaves' spinning jenny with the machine invented by Arkwright.

Mullions, the vertical bars dividing the lights in a window, forming a highly decorative feature in the Tudor period of English Gothic architecture. The cross-beam or horizontal bar of wood or stone in a mullioned window is styled a transom. See **Windows.**

Munich Agreement. In September 1938 Mr. Neville Chamberlain and M. Daladier, British and French Premiers, reached agreement with Hitler at Munich for the dismemberment of Czechoslovakia, primarily for the benefit of Germany. Czechoslovakia itself was not consulted, nor Russia who with Britain and France had jointly pledged themselves to uphold the independence of Czechoslovakia. Hitler had been threatening that country for some time, but every concession had been met by further demands. After three visits to Germany, during which Hitler raised his demands the British and French statesmen gave way. Mr. Chamberlain declared on return that he had secured "Peace in our Time". The Agreement was the subject of much controversy. Hitler seized Czechoslovakia in March 1939.

Muscles. See **F37(1).**

Musk Deer, a small deer of the Himalayas, standing about 51 cm high. It is grey in colour, slightly brindled, and carries a small pouch in the abdominal region, containing what is commercially known as musk, an article which is of great value in the manufacture of various perfumes. The active constituent of musk, muscone, is now made synthetically. The species has become rare on account of its slaughter for its musk.

Mutton Bird, an Australian name of controversial origin for a shearwater or petrel, *e.g.,* the Short-tailed and Sooty Shearwaters and the Great-winged, Kermadec, and White-headed Petrels. The young are taken by hand from their burrows for human food.

Myrrh, a resinous substance obtained from a tree of the natural order *Amyridaceae,* growing plentifully in Ethiopia and Arabia. Its use for embalming, medical and aromatic purposes may be traced back to the most remote times.

Mysteries, Greek, secret mystic ceremonies of the ancient Greeks, religious drama accompanied by dancing, the most well known being the Eleusinian and Orphic ceremonies.

Mystery Plays were mediaeval religious dramas performed at great ecclesiastical festivals, particularly in France and Bavaria, staging the Nativity, Passion and Resurrection stories from the Gospels.

N

Nadir, one of the two poles of the horizon, the other being the zenith. The nadir is the pole vertically below the observer's feet.

Nahum, one of the books of the Minor Prophets of the Old Testament. It is a prophecy of doom on the approaching sack of Nineveh which fell in 612 B.C. to the Medes and Babylonians.

Nantes, Edict of, was a decree promulgated by Henry IV of France in 1598, giving full freedom of worship to the Protestants of the country. It was the revocation of this edict in 1685 by Louis XIV that drove hundreds of thousands of French Huguenots to this country.

Naphtha, a liquid combustible believed to have been one of the ingredients of "Greek fire". Naphtha is a light, highly inflammable oil obtained by distilling petroleum, shale oil, or coal tar. The petroleum naphtha consists of a mixture of paraffins; that from shale contains olefines as well as paraffins. Coal-tar naphtha contains xylol.

Naphthalene is an aromatic hydrocarbon; it is obtained from coal tar, and its derivatives are much used in the manufactures of colours for dyers and printers. "Moth balls" are made of naphthalene.

Narcotic, a medical dictionary definition is that a

narcotic is a drug that produces stupor; complete insanity or sleep. In terms of drug addiction, a narcotic has been defined as altering and distorting the user's perception of himself and of the external world, being taken primarily for that purpose.

Nardus, a genus of coarse grasses, growing on bleak upland heaths and hill slopes. *Nardus stricta,* known as "mat-weed", is a British species.

Narghile, an oriental tobacco pipe so constructed that smoke passes through water and up a long flexible tube before reaching lips of the smoker.

Narrative Art, a type of art popular during the late 19th cent. based on the principle: "every picture tells a story"—*e.g.,* such paintings as the little Royalist boy surrounded by his anxious family and confronted across a table by the Roundheads bearing the title: "When did you last see your father?" The term, although often applied derisively, suitably describes many works of considerable artistic merit: *e.g.,* Hogarth's *Marriage à la Mode,* his series of eight engravings entitled *A Rake's Progress,* the Bayeux Tapestry, and many Babylonian and Egyptian friezes.

Naseby, Battle of, was fought on 14 June 1645, between the Royalists under the command of Prince Rupert and the King, and the Parliamentarians under Fairfax and Cromwell. Charles I was decisively defeated.

National Anthem, a musical composition with words, officially adopted for ceremonial use as an expression of patriotism and loyalty to a national cause. The national anthem of the United Kingdom, "God save the King (Queen)", probably dates from the late-17th cent, to mid-18th cent. It was sung in 1745, the year of the landing of the Young Pretender. It had no one composer and was probably a recasting of folk-tunes and plainsong. Resemblances can be traced in pieces by Purcell and John Bull.

National Assembly, the name taken by the body responsible for the opening stages of the French Revolution and subsequently by other sovereign bodies in France and elsewhere.

National Covenant, an oath and declaration subscribed to by the Scottish Presbyterians in 1638 to maintain their religion against Charles I's episcopalianising designs.

National Gallery, established in 1824 at Pall Mall, London, with the Angerstein Collection of 38 pictures, purchased for £60,000, as a nucleus. The existing building which was opened in 1838 has been enlarged several times. The National Gallery at Millbank, the Tate Gallery, was given to the nation by Sir Henry Tate in 1897.

Nationalisation is the taking over by the State of the ownership and operation of an industry or service—*e.g.,* coal-mining, railway, transport, gas and electricity. Where this is done without revolution, compensation is usually paid to the previous owners at what is regarded as a fair market price; the compensation is sometimes paid in cash, but more often in fixed-interest-bearing bonds issued either by the State or by the administration of the nationalised service, which is usually a publicly appointed Board or Corporation acting, with greater or lesser autonomy, under the direction of a Minister responsible to Parliament. In some cases the State becomes a partner with private investors in the ownership of a particular enterprise, *e.g.,* oil companies, such as the former Anglo-Iranian and some recent French examples. Nationalisation is usually brought about by a separate Act of Parliament relating to each industry or service taken over. These Acts, in Great Britain, include provision for joint consultation at all levels between the administering boards and the workers employed and their Trade Unions. When, as in the Soviet Union, nationalisation occurs as an outcome of social revolution no compensation is paid to the dispossessed owners.

National Parks. Under the National Parks Act 1949 a National Parks Commission was set up to create National Parks in England and Wales. Ten have been established: Peak District, Lake District, Snowdonia, Yorkshire Dales, Exmoor, Brecon Beacons, Dartmoor, Pembrokeshire Coast, North York Moors and Northumberland. They cover an area of some 13,618 km², or 9 per cent of the total area of England and Wales. It is not intended to change the character of these territories but to control their development so as to harmonise with the two dominant principles: (a) that the characteristic beauty of the landscape within the Park area shall be preserved and (b) that the visiting public shall have ample access and facilities for recreation and enjoyment. The establishment of a new national park has been proposed for mid-Wales. The Commission also has power to designate areas in England and Wales outside the national parks as "areas of outstanding natural beauty". Thirty-three areas had been designated by 1977: Gower, Quantock Hills, Lleyn, Surrey Hills, Dorset, Northumberland Coast, Cannock Chase, Shropshire Hills, Malvern Hills, Cornwall, N. Devon, S. Devon, E. Devon, E. Hampshire, Isle of Wight, Forest of Bowland, Chichester Harbour, Solway Coast, Chilterns, Sussex Downs, Cotswolds, Anglesey, South Hampshire Coast, Kent Downs, Norfolk Coast, Dedham Vale, Suffolk Coast and Heaths, Wye Valley, Arnside and Silverdale, Lincolnshire Wolds, Mendip Hills, North Wessex Downs, Isles of Scilly. Under the Countryside Act, 1968, the National Parks Commission has been reconstituted as the Countryside Commission. *See also* **Long Distance Walks.**

National Physical Laboratory, situated at Teddington, is one of the world's largest and best-equipped laboratories. It conducts research in its three main groups: Measurement, Materials and Engineering Sciences, and maintains British primary standards and physical units. First established in 1900 and managed by the Royal Society, it is now one of the industrial research establishments under the control of the Dept. of Industry.

National Portrait Gallery, established in 1856, and now located in a building in St. Martin's Lane adjoining the National Gallery. Contains portraits of eminent people in British history and a valuable collection of medals and autographs.

National Trust, founded in 1895. "A non-profit-making organisation incorporated by Act of Parliament for the purposes of promoting the permanent preservation of lands and buildings of historic interest or natural beauty for the benefit and access of the people." As a consequence of gifts and public-spirited individuals the Trust now owns many hectares of magnificent scenery and property, including mediaeval castles, bird sanctuaries, ancient monuments, birthplaces and homes of famous men, and classic examples of domestic architecture, preserved for the enjoyment of present and future generations. Since 1946 lands and houses of interest to the nation may be given to the National Trust in lieu of death duties.

Nativity. There are three nativity festivals of the Christian Church: Christmas, 25 December, festival of birth of Christ; the birthday of the Virgin Mary (8 September); and of St. John the Baptist (24 June).

Natterjack, a curious warty, prominent-eyed, brown toad (*Bufo calamita*), having a bright yellow line down the middle of its back. It utters a muttering sort of croak, hence its name.

Natural Law. *See* **Section J.**

Naturalism in painting has been defined as "a direct and spontaneous approach to nature" —to landscape primarily. Constable, Turner and Boudin were among the great naturalist painters of the 19th cent. Naturalistic drama attempts to record as faithfully as possible the actual experiences of life without too much concern for artistic form.

Natural Numbers, the counting numbers 1, 2, 3, 4, 5, . . .

"Nautical Almanac", published under the authority of the Admiralty, is always issued four years in advance, and contains information specially prepared for the use of navigators and astronomers. It first appeared in 1767.

Nautilus, a term now applied only to the pearly-shelled nautilus, the sole surviving example of the four-gilled section of the *Cephalopoda*. Its fossil relatives are called Ammonites. The spiral shell is divided into a number of compartments, the animal living in the last and largest chamber. There are three or four species, all living in tropical seas. The Paper Nautilus is

not related to the Pearly Nautilus, belonging to the same order as the octopus.

Nave is the body or main open portion of a cathedral or church, and extends from the chief entrance to the choir, or chancel, and is usually flanked by aisles. A nave, in mechanics, indicates the "hub" or central part of a wheel.

Neanderthal, the name of the valley lying between Düsseldorf and Wuppertal, where in a limestone cave a now famous skull of a very early species of prehistoric man was discovered in 1856. Fossils of Neanderthal man have been found over a wide area, and from archaeological evidence he began to disappear from Europe during the last Ice Age, about 40,000 B.C.

Nekton, term used to differentiate actively swimming aquatic organisms (*e.g.*, fishes) from the "drifters" or plankton.

Nelson Column, in Trafalgar Square, London, designed by Mr. William Railton, was chosen from among a number of designs—temples, obelisks and various sculptural groups—sent in as a result of a competition held in 1839. The erection of the column was begun in 1840. Twenty-six years later the lions designed by Landseer were set up at the foot of the completed column. The statue of Nelson himself was made by E. H. Bailey and the bronze reliefs at the base executed by Carew, Woodington, Ternouth and Watson, representing the Battles of the Nile, St. Vincent, Copenhagen and Trafalgar. Height 52 m, executed in Portland stone instead of granite, as originally planned, at a cost of £46,000.

Néné *or* **Hawaiian Goose.** At the Severn Wildfowl Trust at Slimbridge Sir Peter Scott saved this bird from extinction.

Neo-Classical Style, term applied to the revival of classical logic and order after the extravagances of Rococo (*q.v.*), beginning in France in the mid-18th cent. and finding expression in architecture and the decorative arts. The style retains some of the daintiness of Rococo, furniture is on a small scale, often gilt, and silks and porcelain favour pastel shades. Straight lines take the place of the wild curvatures of Rococo and classical details like festoons and urn forms are used in many contexts and materials. Its English version is closely associated with the name of the architect Robert Adam whose light and graceful adaptations of Greek and Roman forms were introduced into English country houses. In France the style is sometimes called *Style Louis XVI*, though its dates, c. 1750–c. 1790 do not exactly coincide with the reign of that monarch. Eventually the Neo-Classical style merges into Empire (*q.v.*).

Neodymium, element no. 60, symbol Nd, belonging to the rare earth metal group. Discovered by Welsbach, 1885.

Neo-Impressionism, a development of Impressionism (*q.v.*) by Seurat and Signac during the 1880s who devised the method of painting known as *pointillism* (the application of pure colours in minute touches to form a composite whole, based on a knowledge of the laws of colour and optics). One of the best-known examples of this technique is Seurat's *Sunday Afternoon on the Grand Jatte.*

Neon, inert gas present in air to the extent of about 1 part in 65,000. The crimson glow produced when an electric discharge passes through the gas is familiar in advertising signs. Element no. 10, symbol Ne.

Nepotism, the bestowal of patronage by reason of relationship rather than of merit. It had its origin in the custom of certain Popes to enrich their families out of the offices of the Church.

Neptune. Apart from Pluto this is the most distant of the planets, estimated to be about $4,497 \times 10^6$ km from the sun, and taking about 165 years to revolve around it. Discovered by the German astronomer Galle on 23 September 1846, after its existence had been predicted by Leverrier and Adams. Modern observations coupled with detailed inspection of Galileo's notebook have led to the conclusion that a faint "star" used by Galileo as a reference point for his Jovian observations was Neptune. The planet will be visited by Voyager 2 on 1 September 1989, its last planetary stop. *See* **F8.**

Neptunium, element no. 93, symbol Np, one of the four new elements discovered during the progress of the atomic bomb project in the second world war, Neptunium is formed when a neutron enters nucleus of Uranium 238, and it decays radioactively to yield plutonium.

Neutrino, a neutral particle which carries energy and spin and although possessing little or no mass plays an important part in the interaction of other fundamental particles. The discovery that there are in fact two distinct neutrinos, each with its counterpart, was discovered in 1962 as a result of an experiment made with the 30,000 million-electronvolt proton accelerator at Brookhaven. *See* **F16**.

Neutron, a neutral particle present in all atomic nuclei except the hydrogen nucleus which is a single proton. In the development of nuclear science and technology the neutron has played a most important role and neutrons produce the radioisotopes now widely used in medicine, agriculture and industry. Neutrons and protons are termed nucleons. *See* **F11**(2), **16**.

Neutron Bomb, a thermonuclear fusion weapon which produces increased lethal radiation while the destructive blast and fallout are significantly less than for a fission weapon of equivalent yield; it kills organic life while sparing property, except within a small radius. In 1978 President Carter reserved his decision on production; in 1981 the new Reagan administration decided to go ahead and stockpile the weapon. *See also* **F13**(2).

New Deal. The measures taken by President Roosevelt in USA in 1933 to overcome the great economic crisis which broke out at the end of 1929 and to restore the social security threatened by it. The measures were drawn up by a group of experts called a Brains Trust and they provided for recovery by a programme of public works, including large-scale construction of houses and large-scale assistance to farmers. Loans were granted and authorities formed to stimulate activities which reduced the workless from 17 millions to between 7 and 10 millions. Unemployment relief was regulated and enlarged; and social insurance (which for decades had been a subject of dispute, being held to be contrary to American principles of self-help) was introduced. Many of the changes have become a permanent part of American legislation though some laws were repealed by the US Supreme Court as being unconstitutional.

Newgate Prison was situated at the western end of Newgate Street, opposite the Old Bailey at the site of one of the old London city gates. There is a record of a prison upon this spot in the 13th cent. Later a new one was built by the executors of Richard Whittington, but this was destroyed by the Great Fire in 1666. Still another new prison on this site was erected between 1778 and 1780. In the Gordon Riots of the latter year it was destroyed by fire and re-erected. It was not used as a prison after 1880 and was demolished in 1902–3.

Newspapers. The first news-books to be published at regular intervals in Britain appeared in 1662 with news of what was going on abroad translated from German and Italian news-sheets. Licence to print was obtained from the Star Chamber, which until its abolition in 1641 allowed only the printing of foreign news. With the lifting of the ban on domestic news the Press became free. In the reign of Queen Anne English newspapers employed writers of great intellectual power and versatility. Despite the newspaper tax introduced in 1712, the number of newspapers published in London in 1776 had increased to 53, though the standard of writing was below that of earlier times. The development of the Press was greatly assisted in the 19th cent. by the abolition of the "taxes on knowledge", by the introduction of the cheap postal system and by improvements in printing, distribution, collection of news and advertising. The *London Gazette*, founded in 1665 (and still appearing twice weekly as the official organ of the Government), is the oldest newspaper living. *The Times*, known throughout the world, began as the *Daily Universal Register* in 1785, and adopted its present title in 1788. The *Manchester Guardian* (renamed *Guardian* in 1959), once a provincial but now a national newspaper with a world-wide reputation, began as a weekly in 1821, and became a daily in 1855.

The *Scotsman*, founded as a weekly in 1817 and established as a daily in 1855, and the *Glasgow Herald*, which began as the *Glasgow Advertiser* in 1783, are the leading Scottish newspapers. The London Press, which is national, publishes 10 daily, 1 evening and 7 Sunday newspapers (1985).

Newt, amphibian of lizard shape and mottled markings. There are three British species, the largest being the Great-Crested Newt (*Triturus cristatus*), which attains a length of 15 cm.

Newton, the unit of force in the SI system of units. Under its influence a body with a mass of 1 kilogram will accelerate at a rate of 1 metre per second each second.

Newton's Rings. Concentric circular rings, due to the phenomenon of interference, which are seen around the point of contact of a slightly convex lens with a flat plate of glass.

New Towns. Under the New Town Act 1946 and subsequent Acts 33 new towns have been designated in Britain; 23 are in England and Wales, six in Scotland and four in Northern Ireland. They are: Basildon, Bracknell, Crawley, Harlow, Hatfield, Hemel Hempstead, Milton Keynes, Northampton, Peterborough, Stevenage and Welwyn (to relieve housing problems in the Greater London area); Aycliffe, Corby, Cwmbran, Peterlee and Washington (to serve the special needs of their areas); Newtown (to help stem rural depopulation in mid-Wales); Runcorn and Skelmersdale (to meet the overspill needs of Liverpool and north Merseyside); Telford and Redditch (to take population from Birmingham); Warrington (expanded to take people from Liverpool and Manchester); Central Lancashire New Town (new regional city based on existing towns of Preston, Leyland and Chorley). The six Scottish new towns are Cumbernauld, East Kilbride, Glenrothes, Irvine and Livingston. In Northern Ireland Craigavon is being developed as a new city; Antrim and Ballymena are becoming centres of economic growth; Londonderry and the surrounding district have been designated as an area of special development. The population of the new towns in Great Britain is about 1·7 million. The expansion of large existing towns like Northampton, Peterborough and Warrington means that they are becoming regional centres. A major reversal in Government policy was announced in 1976 to the effect that development resources in future were to be directed towards inner-city areas to halt their decline; the growth of new and expanding towns to be slowed down.

New Year's Day, 1 January. The first New Year's festival of which we have record is that constituted by Numa 713 B.C., and dedicated to Janus.

Nibelungenlied, the German epic of the early 13th cent. comprising numerous mythical poems or sagas. Wagner's *The Ring of the Nibelungs* was based on Norse legends and the Nibelungenlied.

Nicene Creed, a summary of the principles of Christian faith, first issued in 325 by the Council of Nicaea (summoned by the emperor Constantine the Great) for the purpose of thwarting the Arian heresy and asserting the godhead of Christ. Date of Easter fixed at Council of Nicaea.

Nickel, silver-coloured metallic element, no. 28, symbol Ni, fairly soft though harder than iron. Chief source of the metal is the nickel sulphide in iron-copper pyrites deposits in Ontario. Chief uses are: in electroplating, in coins, as an element in alloy steels. A novel method of making pure nickel (by treating the metal with carbon monoxide and heating the resulting liquid, nickel carbonyl) was developed in 1890 by Mond. This discovery led to many technical advances in industrial chemistry, one of which is the production of catalysts.

Night Heron, a stocky, short-legged heron of black and white plumage, red eyes and yellowish legs, crepuscular except in breeding season, and an occasional visitor to Britain.

Nightingale, a familiar singing bird which visits the southern counties of England every summer, and is sometimes found as far north as Yorkshire. It is a shy, brown bird, not often seen, but the song of the male, usually heard in the late evening or at early morn, is of remarkable sweetness and variety. After its wooing period is over its song ceases.

Nightjar, nocturnal, insectivorous bird, owl-like in appearance, with mottled brown plumage of "dead leaf" pattern, and a churring song. It is a common breeding visitor to the British Isles, April to September, and lays its eggs on bare ground.

Niobium is a metal element, no. 41, symbol Nb, related to vanadium. Technical development has been slow because of its rare occurrence, although niobium is now used in ferrous alloys to increase resistance to corrosion and produce steel which can be used at high temperatures.

Nitre or **Saltpetre**, is now mostly manufactured by the double decomposition of sodium nitrate and potassium chloride. Its chief use is the manufacture of gunpowder and fireworks. It has been manufactured in England since 1625.

Nitrogen, a non-combustible gaseous element, no. 7, symbol N, devoid of taste or smell, and constituting nearly four-fifths of the atmospheric air. Nitrogen compounds are essential to plants and animals, and are used in fertilisers.

Nitro-Glycerine, an explosive yellow fluid produced by mixing small quantities of glycerine with a combination of one part of nitric acid and two parts of sulphuric acid. By itself it is a dangerously explosive substance to handle. In 1867, Nobel produced dynamite, a safe explosive made by absorbing nitro-glycerine in kieselguhr.

Nitrous Oxide, a compound of nitrogen and oxygen possessing mild anaesthetic power. Termed "laughing gas" on account of its exhilarating effect. It is still used in dentistry, and for minor operations and has proved useful in a new technique for finding leaks in water mains.

Nobel Prizes. The Nobel Foundation was established at the beginning of the century to give effect to the wishes expressed by Alfred Nobel in his Will. By the terms of the Will the judges are the Swedish Academy of Science, the Caroline Medico-Surgical Institute, the Swedish Academy and five members of the Norwegian Storting. The award of a Nobel Prize is accepted as the highest form of international recognition in the field in which it is given: physics, chemistry, medicine, literature, peace and, since 1969, economics.

Nones were dates of the Roman calendar which fell on the 5th of each month, excepting March, May, July and October, when they fell on the 7th.

Norman Architecture is English Romanesque (q.v.), which flourished from the time of the Norman Conquest and was gradually superseded through a transition period (c. 1175–1200) by the introduction of the pointed arch characteristic of the Early English (first Gothic style). Typical of Norman churches are the round arches, thick walls, massive cylindrical columns, with throughout the basic pattern of the square and the circle. Some churches (e.g., the Temple church in London or the chapel at Ludlow Castle) are wholly circular. Roofs in the early days were flat and towers, usually placed at the "crossing", were square but occasionally round; the spire of all these towers have perished, but it seems likely that they were squat and pyramidal.

North-East Passage, from the North Atlantic to Bering Strait has been rapidly developed by the USSR in recent years as a northern sea route to render accessible vast areas of northern Siberia. Attempts to find a North-East passage were made by Englishmen and Dutchmen in the 16th cent. but they were always defeated by the ice, for the sea is completely frozen for some 4,800 km for 9 months of the year. A Swede succeeded in sailing from Europe to Japan via the Arctic in the late 19th cent. See also **Arctic Exploration.**

North-West Passage, from the Atlantic to the Pacific through the Arctic Seas, has been the dream of navigators for centuries. Attempts to find it were made in the 16th and early 17th cent. by John and Sebastian Cabot, Frobisher, Gilbert, Davis, Hudson and Baffin. Two centuries later Ross, Parry, Franklin and others made the attempt; but it was not until 1903–5 that Amundsen, discoverer of the South Pole, made the complete voyage in the Gjoa. The Canadian icebreaker Labrador was the first deep-draft vessel to traverse the North-West Passage (1954) and the US tanker Manhattan was the first commercial vessel to do so (1969).

Notre Dame, the famous Paris cathedral, was founded in 1163, and is one of the finest specimens of Gothic architecture in Europe. The best descriptions of the buildings are to be found in Victor Hugo's Hunchback of Notre Dame.

November, the 9th month of the year originally, but from c. 700 B.C., when Numa added January and February, it became the 11th month.

Nuclear Energy. Atomic nuclei consist of protons and neutrons joined in various proportions (**F11**). The heaviest naturally occurring nucleus contains 238 particles (92 protons, 146 neutrons) and is uranium 238 (U^{238}); the lightest is hydrogen, which consists of 1 proton. Neutrons and protons attract one another by very strong forces which are not at all well understood; they are called nuclear forces. Consequently it requires energy to be supplied if a nucleus is to be pulled apart into its constituent particles. The energy is required to overcome the attractions of the nuclear forces. Conversely, when the particles rush together to form a nucleus energy is released in the form of heat or radiation. The energy released when protons and neutrons coalesce to form a nucleus is called Binding Energy. The binding energy of a nucleus divided by the number of particles involved is called the binding energy per particle, which we will call B. It is very difficult to overestimate the importance of B to the human race. B varies from nucleus to nucleus, and the exact form of its variation is only roughly understood at the present time. But the most significant thing is that B is greatest for elements of medium atomic weight and lowest at the heavy (uranium) and light (hydrogen) ends of the periodic table. This means that if middleweight nuclei can be formed either from heavy ones or from light ones, B increases and energy is released in either case.

Nuclear Fission. See **F13(1).**

Nuclear Fusion. If light nuclei are hurled at high speeds into intimate contact they sometimes coalesce and release binding energy (see **Nuclear Energy**). This has been studied in laboratories where powerful and energy-consuming machines accelerate small numbers of particles for purely experimental purposes. If useful amounts of energy are to be gained these fusion reactions will have to occur on a bigger scale in an apparatus from which the resulting heat can be extracted in a controlled way. The one "useful" fusion device so far made is the thermonuclear bomb ("H-bomb"). Thermonuclear is the important word. If a suitable gas can be raised to a very high temperature the nuclei are stripped of their electrons and all particles move with very high speeds. The gas is then called a plasma. High enough temperatures will make speeds great enough for fusion reactions to occur and nuclear energy to be released. This is a thermonuclear reaction. For example, in deuterium gas, at temperatures over a million degrees Centigrade, the deuterium nuclei (i.e., heavy hydrogen nuclei consisting of 1 proton joined to 1 neutron) interact to produce helium nuclei. To obtain a net gain in energy from this process, the temperature must be raised to about 100 million degrees C and maintained long enough; otherwise the energy released is less than that required to heat the fuel and to make up for heat losses. Many attempts to study the staggering technical problems are being made, and fusion research is very active in Britain, the USA, Japan and the Soviet Union. The joint European Torus (JET) fusion research project sited at Culham near Oxford aims to develop a new source of energy for the generation of electricity for the 21st cent.

Nuclear Power Stations. Britain generates about 14 per cent of her electricity for public supply in nuclear power stations. There are 11 nuclear power stations which produce electricity for the national grid controlled by the electricity authorities and five controlled by the Atomic Energy Authority or British Nuclear Fuels Ltd. Nine of the 11 nuclear power stations operated by the electricity authorities are at Berkeley, Gloucs. (1962), Bradwell, Essex (1962), Hunterston "A", Scotland (1964), Hinkley Point "A", Somerset (1965), Trawsfynydd, Wales (1966), Dungeness "A", Kent (1966), Sizewell, Suffolk (1966), Oldbury, Avon (1968),

Wylfa, Anglesey (1970). They have all been developed from the classic Calder Hall type, burning natural uranium inserted in a graphite moderator and cooled by carbon dioxide gas. They are called Magnox stations because the fuel elements of natural uranium rods are encased in magnesium alloy cans. A second nuclear power programme is based on the advanced gas cooled reactor (AGR) at Windscale, and include the reactors at Dungeness "B", (1983) and those under construction at Hinkley Point "B", Hunterston "B", Hartlepool (Cleveland) and Heysham (Lancashire). At the time of writing (May 1986) the future programme was still under discussion. The disaster at the Soviet nuclear plant at Chernobyl in the Ukraine (see **F71–2**) has renewed major doubts about safety.

Nuclear Reactors are pieces of apparatus designed to permit nuclear chain reactions to occur under controlled conditions. (Uncontrolled chain reactions are dangerous, *e.g.* atomic bombs.) The success of a reactor depends on the neutrons reaching the U^{235} nuclei to produce more fissions and not being wasted in irrelevant processes or simply escaping through the wall of the apparatus (neutrons are quite difficult to contain). The neutrons leaving the scene of fission are rapidly moving, and they stand more chance of causing another fission if they are slowed down. Consequently a material other than the uranium has to be present to facilitate this, and it is called a moderator. A useful moderator is pure graphite. Thus a reactor may consist of alternate blocks of uranium and graphite. If the reactor is too small so many neutrons escape that there are not enough to keep the chain reaction going. The reactor must therefore be greater than a certain *critical size*. In order to intensify or damp down the chain reaction it is arranged for pieces of neutron-absorbing material, such as cadmium, to be inserted or withdrawn as required. While the chain reaction is proceeding countless numbers of fissions are occurring, each one liberating energy which turns into heat. The temperature therefore increases, and to prevent a catastrophic rise, cooling has to be provided. The reactor therefore has cooling pipes through which a fluid coolant is pumped. The coolant carries the heat away and, in a reactor designed to produce electrical power, the heat is taken to steam-raising boilers and the high-pressure steam is led to turbines which drive the electric generators. What has been briefly described is the type of reactor first used for serious power production at Calder Hall (1956). This is a graphite-moderated, gas-cooled reactor using as fuel natural uranium (*i.e.*, fissile U^{235} greatly diluted with U^{238}). Other thermal types of nuclear reactor are the advanced gas-cooled reactor (AGR), the high temperature reactor (HTR), the steam-generating heavy-water (SGHWR) and the light-water reactor (LWR). It is also possible to make reactors work without slowing the neutrons with a moderator; these are called *fast reactors*. The design of the prototype fast reactor (PFR) at Dounreay is based on experience gained with the Dounreay experimental fast breeder reactor (closed 1977 after 17 years' safe operation) which was the first to produce electricity on a commercial scale (1962) and achieved the highest power output of any of its type in the world. These fast reactors can produce new nuclear fuel in the course of their operation and therefore offer great economies; but they are more difficult to develop than thermal reactors. The fuel is made from the mixed oxides of plutonium and uranium and the coolant is liquid sodium metal. The Government has still to make a crucial decision whether and when to go ahead with a commercial fast breeder reactor.

Environmental considerations are likely to be increasingly topical. Most of the products of the fission process are of necessity radioactive isotopes: they could be gaseous, like krypton, xenon and tritium or solid like strontium, caesium, zirconium and ruthenium. There are also present the new radioactive elements plutonium, curium, actinium, etc. Further, in both the nuclear reactor and in the plant which is used to chemically treat and reprocess the nuclear fuel, radioactivity will be induced in associated structural materials, to varying degrees. In this latter case, unlike the former, the radioactive waste with which one is left can to a great extent be selected and is largely overshadowed in importance by the waste arising from the fission and breeding processes. Even if the whole of the UK electrical power was produced by nuclear means, the volumes of such wastes would be relatively small and need in principle tens of acres of storage area. Much of the activity would decay in a decade, a great deal more in a century, but that associated with the elements bred from uranium, would be present for thousands of years: Pu^{239} has a half-life of 25,000 years. Segregation of the various types of activity is feasible; their incorporation into physically and chemically stable form has received a great deal of study so that storage, readily monitored even for many generations, seems entirely possible. The radioactive properties of these wastes can only be changed by nuclear reactions. Bombardment with neutrons or other highly energetic particles can bring about such reactions so that forms of "nuclear incineration" are feasible but are not yet fully explored. *See also* **F71–2**, for the consequences of the Chernobyl nuclear disaster.

Nucleic Acids. Living matter is built up of cells each of which has a nucleus surrounded by cytoplasm. Cell nuclei are composed chiefly of substances called nucleoproteins, which consist of a protein attached to a nucleic acid (this original name is still used, although nucleic acids are found in the cytoplasm as well as the nucleus). Nucleic acids are complex organic structures made up of chains of compounds called nucleotides (**F32(2)**). Nucleotide molecules have a sugar group attached to a nitrogenous base and a phosphate group. Only two sugar groups are found in the nucleotides, ribose, giving rise to ribonucleic acids (RNAs, found mainly in the cytoplasm) and deoxyribose, which forms deoxyribonucleic acids (DNAs, found mainly in cell nuclei). Seven different nitrogenous bases have been isolated, so that a number of different nucleotides are possible. A repeating, regular pattern of nucleotides is linked by the phosphate groups, forming nucleic acids. The functions of nucleic acids are of fundamental importance. They are concerned in the process of transmission of inherited qualities in reproduction and in building up body proteins. *See* **F34**.

Nuremberg Trial. On 21 November 1945, an International Military Tribunal, consisting of one American, one British, one Russian and one French member, began the trial of twenty-four Nazi leaders. There were four counts: the conspiracy of Nazism; wars of aggression; war crimes; and crimes against humanity. Twelve were condemned to hanging of whom ten were hanged on 16 October 1946. Goering committed suicide; Bormann is now presumed dead; Papen, Schacht and Fritsche were acquitted. The rest received varying terms of imprisonment.

Nuthatch, name of a number of tree-creeping birds, plump, with a short tail, bluish-grey plumage and black stripe under eye. Nest in holes and wedge nuts in bark of trees, hammering them to get a kernel. There are three European species, one, *Sitta europaea*, resident in England.

Nylon, a generic term for any long-chain synthetic polymeric amide which has recurring amide groups as an integral part of the main polymer chain, and which is capable of being formed into a filament in which the structural elements are orientated in the direction of the axis. The first nylon of commercial interest was made in 1935, and the world's first nylon factory—in the United States—began production in 1940.

O

Oak, a tree of the genus *Quercus*, including some 300 species distributed over the northern hemisphere and into the tropics. Two species are native to Britain, where the oak is the commonest tree (1 in 3)—*Q. petraea*, more common in the west and north on shallower, lighter soils, and *Q. robur*, more common in the south on deeper, heavier soils. Oak timber is much prized for its strength and durability, and from the time of the Spanish Armada to Nelson's day was in great demand for naval construction. It has always been used for building, flooring, furniture and cabinet work. The oak is attacked by many insects, the round nut-like oak galls, or oak-apples, being produced by the sting of certain minute gall wasps.

"Oaks", a famous race for three-year-old fillies run at Epsom three days after the "Derby".

Obelisk, a tapering monolithic column, square at the base and pyramidal at the top, regarded by the ancient Egyptians as a sacred stone and usually found at the entrance to the sun temples. Many were transported from Egypt and set up at various times: there is one in the Place de la Concorde in Paris, and one on the Thames Embankment in London—Cleopatra's Needle—originally erected at Heliopolis, centre of the sun-cult, by Tuthmosis III *c.* 1500 B.C.

Observatories. *See* **Astronomy** *and* **Telescope.**

Occam's Razor. *See* **Section J, Q8(1).**

Ocean, comprises the great body of water which covers seven-tenths of the surface of the earth, and has an average depth of 3·2 km. The principal oceans are the Pacific, Atlantic, Indian and Arctic. The greatest ocean depth is in the Pacific, in the Mindanao Deep, 37,782 ft (11,524 m). *See* **F9(2)** *and* **Oceanography.**

Ocean Currents are well-defined streams running over certain portions of the ocean and caused mainly by wind-friction, slope of the sea surface and differences in density of the water, all movements being influenced by the deflective forces due to the earth's rotation. The climatic importance of the great ocean currents is that they constitute one of the means whereby heat is transferred from lower to higher latitudes.

Oceanography is the scientific study of the world ocean, *i.e.*, the single connected body of water that covers 70·8 per cent of the earth's surface. Modern oceanography dates from the voyage of HMS *Challenger* (1872–6) during which wide-ranging observations of the ocean were made, for the first time going well beyond what was directly required to assist shipping. Since then oceanography has matured into a highly technical and interdisciplinary science which may be roughly divided into: biological oceanography (the study of marine organisms and marine ecology); chemical oceanography (concerned with the composition of sea-water); physical oceanography (the study of ocean currents, tides and waves and the role played by the oceans in climate and weather); and geological oceanography (concerned with the formation, composition and evolution of the ocean basins). Oceanographic knowledge is essential to allow exploitation of the enormous food, mineral and energy resources of the ocean with the minimum damage to the ocean environment. However, close international co-operation (through such bodies as the Law of Sea Conference) will also be necessary in order to avoid such hazards as overfishing and marine pollution. By 1982 about one third of the world's oil and gas came from offshore wells and recently vast deposits of metal-rich nodules have been located on the ocean floor. As important future sources of energy, both tidal and wave power have the attractions of being nonpolluting and renewable.

Ocelot, the most common wild cat of S. America. It is about 1·2 m in length, including tail, and of a grey or tawny colour and spotted. Closely related to the Leopard cats.

Octane Number, the index of the knock-rating of petrol. It is based on the arbitrary scale in which iso-octane (which does not cause "knocking") has a value of 100, and normal heptane (which is prone to "knocking") has a value of 0. A good fuel for modern cars must have an octane number greater than 80.

Octarch, the kings of the English heptarchy, Hengist (455) being the first, and Egbert (800) the last.

October, the 10th month, but the 8th in the old Roman calendar. It was held sacred to Mars.

Octopus, a genus of marine molluscs with eight tentacles that bear suckers.

Odyssey, Homer's epic setting forth the incidents of the wanderings of Odysseus on his way back to Ithaca after the Siege of Troy.

Oersted, a unit of magnetic-field intensity in the c.g.s. system.

Offa's Dyke, largest remaining earthwork in Britain, supposed to have been built by Offa (A.D. 757–96) as a defensive boundary line between the English settlers and the dispossessed Welsh of Gwynedd, Powys and Gwent. *See also* **Long Distance Walks.**

Ohm's Law, propounded by G. S. Ohm in 1826, is expressed in the equation: electromotive force (in volts) = current (in amperes) × resistance (in ohms). The ohm is the unit of electrical resistance in the metre-kilogram-second system.

Oil. The great expansion in energy demand over recent years has been met to a large extent by petroleum oil. This contains a wide range of hydrocarbon molecules of varying complexity. The various components are separated from each other by making use of their different boiling points. Crude oil is heated in the base of a fractionating tower; the various components condense at different temperatures in trays at different levels of the tower. The fraction of a given composition can be increased by "cracking" or breaking down the heavier hydrocarbons into lighter ones. The total world reserves of petroleum oil are still uncertain since large parts of the world are still not fully prospected. The cutback and the rise in the price of Middle Eastern oil following the 1973 Arab-Israeli war unleashed a worldwide energy crisis which affected the economies of consumer countries. In 1982, British oil production reached 102·5m tonnes, making her the fifth largest oil producer in the world.

Okapi, nocturnal ruminant mammal, smaller than the giraffe, chestnut brown in colour with zebra-striped legs, native to the African Congo.

Olbers' Comet was discovered in 1815 by Olbers the German astronomer. Olbers also discovered the asteroids Pallas and Vesta (1802–07).

Old Red Sandstone, the continental rocks formed during the Devonian. *See* **F48.**

Olefines, a series of hydrocarbons, in which the hydrogen atoms are double the number of carbon. The first member of the series is ethylene.

Oléron Laws *or* **Judgments**, were a code of maritime laws, introduced into England in the reign of Richard I in the 12th cent. Oléron is an island off the west coast of France, opposite the mouth of the Charente.

Olive. This small tree, whose fruit yields olive oil, is a native of the eastern Mediterranean countries, but has been introduced into cultivation elsewhere. The green unripe fruit is pickled in brine for table olives.

Olympiads were periods of four years which elapsed between each celebration of the Olympic games, held at Olympia in honour of Zeus. These festivals included competitions in literature, art, drama, rhetoric, music and gymnastics, and they were continued, with intervals, from 776 B.C. to A.D. 394. Athletic revivals have taken place at Athens 1896, Paris 1900, St. Louis 1904, London 1908, Stockholm 1912, Antwerp 1920, Paris 1924, Amsterdam 1928, Los Angeles 1932, Berlin 1936, London 1948, Helsinki 1952, Melbourne 1956, Rome 1960, Tokyo 1964, Mexico City 1968, Munich 1972, Montreal 1976, Moscow 1980 and Los Angeles in 1984.

Onomasticians are scientists who study the fascinating subject of names—names of places and names of people—to find out their origins. They tell us, for example, that Cambridge is an Anglo-Norman corruption of *Grantabrycg* = bridge over the Granta; that Harrow-on-the-Hill was an early Anglo-Saxon settlement—"heathen temple on the hill"; that we owe the ridings of Yorkshire to the Vikings (Old Norse *thrithungr* = third part); that in Scotland *-ton* and *-toun* indicate not a town but a hamlet or village. Onomasticians are also concerned with international standardisation of place names.

Onyx *or* **Sardonyx**, a variety of chalcedony built up of different-coloured layers, which are parallel and straight (not curved as in agate).

Oolite, a geological term for the Jurassic oolitic

limestones existing through a long stretch of country extending from Yorkshire to Dorset. It abounds in fossils of molluscs and reptiles. The term "oolite" derives from the fact that these rocks are made of egg-shaped particles of calcium carbonate.

Opal, a mineral consisting of hydrous silica, occurring in numerous varieties and colours. Opals have been prized as gems since at least 400 B.C. but the secret of their unique internal "fire" or opalescence has only recently been learned. It is a result of the diffraction of light by a regular array of tiny silica spheres, about 100 nm in diameter, of which gem opals are now known to be composed. Opal miners are called gougers. Chief source—the Andanooka and Coober Pedy fields of South Australia.

Opera. *See* **Section E.**

Opium was known to the ancients, and used by them as a medicine. It is obtained from the poppy (*Papaver somniferum*), the unripe "head" or seed capsule of that flower yielding a juice which when dried becomes the opium of commerce. The poppy is cultivated in India, Iran, Turkey, Macedonia and China for the sake of this juice, which yields various alkaloids, such as morphine, narcotine, codeine, etc. These days the drug is rarely used medicinally.

Opossum, marsupial mammals found in the more southerly of the United States, South America and Australasia. They are arboreal except for the water-opossum, which eats fish.

Optics, the branch of physics which investigates the nature and properties of light and the phenomena of colour. Burning lenses were known to the ancient Greeks and Ptolemy wrote a treatise on optics A.D. 150. Lenses as visual aids were known in ancient China but eyeglasses were not in use until the 13th cent. Spectacles were in more general use after the invention of printing in the 15th cent. The camera obscura was invented in the 16th cent. and the telescope and microscope at the beginning of the 17th cent.

Oracles were in ancient times supposed to be words spoken by the gods, and it was the custom on important occasions to consult them about the future. The Greeks had the Oracles of Zeus at Dodona, and Apollo at Delphi, while the Romans consulted the Oracles of Mars, Fortune and others.

Orange, a fruit growing in most sub-tropical climates and in universal demand. It is grown on an evergreen tree that attains a height of about 6 m at maturity.

Orang-utan, one of the largest of the anthropoid apes, found only in the swampy forests of Borneo and Sumatra. When full-grown it stands over 1·2 m in height and weighs about 67 kg.

Orchestra, a group of instruments and instrumentalists whose playing is under the direction of a conductor. The composition of a typical symphony orchestra is as follows: STRINGS: 1st Violin (16), 2nd Violin (16), Viola (12), Violoncello (12), Double Bass (8). WOODWIND: Flute (3–4), Piccolo (1), Oboe (3), Cor Anglais (1), Bass Oboe (1), Clarinet (3), Bass Clarinet (1), Bassoon (3), Contra-bassoon (1). BRASS: Horn (6), Trumpet (5), Trombone (3–4), Tuba (2). PERCUSSION: Timpani (3–6), Side Drum (1), Bass Drum (1), Cymbals (1), Harp (2). *See* **E35–38.**

Orders in Council are issued by the sovereign on the advice of a few selected members of the Privy Council. They must not seriously alter the law of the land. Another class of Orders in Council are issued by authority of an Act of Parliament for the carrying out of its provisions.

Ordination, the ceremony of installing ministers or clergymen in clerical offices, has existed from the earliest times. In the Anglican and Roman Catholic Churches the rites of Ordination are performed by bishops; among Nonconformists the power of ordination rests with the governing bodies of the different Churches.

Organ is a musical wind instrument of ancient origin whose tones are produced by the vibrations of air in pipes of varying length. Basically, an organ consists of a number of pipes grouped in rows or ranks according to their special tone-character. The air is fed by

bellows or, in modern organs, by a rotary fan electrically driven. Each rank is controlled by a slider, and the knob that controls the slider is called a stop. The organist pulls out the stops to give the tones he wants, the other pipes being kept out of action by the slider. When a particular note on the keyboard is depressed the player may hear, by pulling out the appropriate stop, not only the normal pitch but the note in several octaves. A stop of which the notes are of normal pitch is called an 8-foot stop, a 16-foot stop would give an octave lower, a 4-foot stop an octave higher and a 2-foot stop two octaves higher. The hand keyboard is called a manual, and the keyboard the pedal board. The basic tone of an organ is its diapason tone, and is normally of 8-foot length and pitch. Most large organs have four manual keyboards and one pedal board. The most important manual is the great organ which comprises the majority of basic stops. The next in importance is the swell organ, so called because the pipes are enclosed in a box fitted with movable shutters operated by a swell-pedal. The effect provides a controlled crescendo or diminuendo. The tone of a typical English swell has a reedy character. The third manual controls the choir organ—a collection of stops suitable for vocal accompaniment. The fourth manual controls the solo organ—a group of stops which, singly or in combination, may provide a solo melody which the remainder of the organ accompanies. The pedal keyboard controls most of the bass stops. In some very large organs there is a fifth manual controlling the echo organ. This is a small group of stops usually set high in the roof of the building to give the effect of distant music. Most church organs have two or three manuals. Modern cinema organs may have some normal stops but rely chiefly on a number of effects unknown to the straight organ.

Organic Chemistry. The chemistry of compounds containing carbon and usually associated with living organisms. *See* **F23.**

Oriel Window is a window projected from the front of a building, rectangular, triangular, or pentagonal. The ordinary bay window and bow window are varieties of Oriel. When an Oriel window does not reach to the ground it usually rests upon moulded sills supported by corbels.

Oriflamme, the name of the original banner of the abbey of St. Denis, and adopted by Louis VI as his standard. It remained the national emblem of France for three centuries. The flag was of red silk, the outer edge being cut in the form of flames.

Original Sin, according to Christian doctrine the corruption that is born with us, as a result of Adam's fall.

Orioles, brilliantly coloured birds, members of the passerine family *Oriolidae*, found in the tropical regions of Asia, Africa and Australia. The golden oriole, perhaps the most beautiful of them all, with brilliant yellow plumage, black wings and tail, winters in Africa, visits England and is known to have nested here.

Orion, a famous constellation of the heavens, comprising nearly a hundred stars, all visible to the naked eye. It contains three stars of the second magnitude in a line, and these are called "Orion's Belt".

Ormer, a shellfish (*Haliotis tuberculata*) which occurs in the Channel Islands and on parts of the French coast. It is considered a great delicacy.

Ornithology, the scientific study of birds.

Ornithorhynchus. *See* **Duckbill.**

Orogeny, large-scale earth movements, including faulting and folding and sometimes igneous activity, which produce a linear belt of mountains, *e.g.*, the Alpine orogeny in Europe which produced the Alps.

Orphism. *See* **Section J.**

Orphrey, the name of an ornamental strip richly embroidered on ecclesiastical vestments.

Orrery, an instrument used in the 18th and early 19th cent. which showed the motions of the planets round the sun and the satellites round their primaries. The first orrery made was named after Charles Boyle, Earl of Orrery.

Orthodox Eastern Church. *See* **Section J.**

Osborne House, near Cowes, in the Isle of Wight. Queen Victoria's favourite winter-residence, and where she died. It was given to the nation by Edward VII, and is now a convalescent home.

Osier, a species of willow growing in damp soils and yielding branches utilised in basket-making.

Osmium, a very hard, bluish-white metallic element, no. 76, symbol Os, of the platinum group and one of the heaviest of known metals. It is obtained from certain sands of South America, California, Australia and Russia. The alloy of osmium and iridium (osmiridium) provides tips for gold fountain-pen nibs.

Osmosis, the process by which absorption of liquids through semi-permeable membranes takes place. A solution exerts osmotic pressure (O.P.) or suction in proportion to concentration but also depending on kind of dissolved substance. The roots of the higher plants are covered with fine root-hairs, within the cell-walls of which the sap is normally of a higher concentration than the dissolved matter in the surrounding soil. The root-hairs, therefore, draw into themselves these weaker salt-solutions. (The explanation of water and salt exchanges is complicated by the selective ability of some cells (*e.g.*, roots) to accept or reject particular dissolved substances along with the water. The absorption of salts by a plant is selective, each plant selecting through the semi-permeable membranes of its root-hairs those substances which are most suited to itself.)

Osprey (*Pandion haliaëtus*), a large and magnificent bird of prey, dark brown above and nearly white below. The head is whitish with a dark band from eye to nape. To the British Isles it is a rare passage migrant. In 1959, thanks to the energy and vigilance of the Royal Society for the Protection of Birds, a pair nested in a Scots pine in Inverness-shire and reared three young. Since then more young ospreys have been safely fledged in this sanctuary. The food consists almost entirely of fish, which the bird seizes with its talons. The so-called osprey plumes do not come from this bird but from the egret.

Ostrich, the largest living bird, related to the rhea, emu and extinct moa, now found only on the sandy plains of Africa and parts of S.W. Asia. The male has beautiful white plumes on wings and tail. The wings are useless in flight, but the birds have a fleetness of foot exceeding that of the swiftest horse. An ostrich's egg weighs 1·3 kg.

Otary, any seal which has external ears (as opposed to the *true seals* which lack them). The eared seals make up the family *Otariidae,* which includes the Sea-lion and the Fur-seal of the N. Pacific.

Otter, an aquatic carnivorous mammal widely distributed over Europe, and at one time very common in England and Wales. The otter averages about 60 cm in length, exclusive of tail, has web-feet and is a very expert swimmer. Otters are harmless and their hunting is a cruel and senseless blood sport. They are now protected in England.

Ounce or **Snow Leopard,** a very beautiful pale spotted cat from the Himalayas about the size of a labrador retriever but with a long furry tail.

Outcrop. Where a bed of rock appears at the surface of the ground, there is an outcrop of the particular rock. The mining of outcrop coal is called open-cast mining.

Oviparous, a zoological term referring to animals which lay eggs to be hatched outside the body of the parent.

Ovipositor, the organ by means of which female insects lay their eggs.

Owls, nocturnal birds of prey, distributed over the greater part of the world. Their forward-looking eyes, embedded in rings of feathers, give them a characteristic "owl-like" appearance, and their plumage, usually a mottled blend of browns and greys, is so soft that their flight is almost noiseless. Owls live on small mammals, reptiles, birds, insects and fish, and are very valuable birds to the farmer. British owls include the barn owl (screech owl), short-eared owl, long-eared owl, tawny owl, little owl. Snowy owls have recently nested in the Shetland Is.

Ox, the popular name of the mammals included in the genus *Bos.* They are hollow-horned ruminants and hoofed quadrupeds, and include the various classes of domestic cattle as well as the different wild species. The adult male is called a bull, the female a cow and the young a calf. The best-known breeds of domesticated cattle are the Durham or Shorthorn, the Angus, the Jersey, Ayrshire, Suffolk and Hereford.

Oxalic Acid, an organic acid obtained from numerous plants, such as sorrel and rhubarb, and produced artificially for commercial purposes from sawdust, treated with caustic potash or caustic soda. It combines with metals to form oxalates; used in the manufacture of ink.

Oxford Clay, a geological formation consisting of a bed of blue clay *c.* 200 m thick, and forming the lower portion of the Upper Jurassic. It makes good bricks.

Oxford Movement. *See* **Tractarianism, Section J.**

Oxford University. The early history of the university is obscure. There was a school at Oxford as early as 1115 and it is known that Robert Pullen, a theologian from Paris, lectured there in 1133. Allusions to Oxford as the most celebrated centre of learning in England occurred in a work of Gerald of Wales in 1184–5. The earliest colleges to be founded were University College (1249), Balliol (about 1263), Merton (1264). In 1571 the university was reorganised and granted a Charter of Incorporation by an Act of Elizabeth. Other colleges and halls with their dates of foundation are: All Souls (1438), Brasenose (1509), Christ Church (1546), Corpus Christi (1517), Exeter (1314), Hertford (1874), Jesus (1571), Keble (1868), Linacre (1962), Lincoln (1427), Magdalen (1458), New College (1379), Nuffield (1937), Oriel (1326), Pembroke (1624), Queen's (1340), St. Anthony's (1950), St. Catherine's (1962), St. Cross (1965), St. Edmund Hall (1270), St. John's (1555), St. Peter's (1929), Trinity (1554), Wadham (1612), Wolfson (1965), Worcester (1714), Campion Hall (1962), St. Benet's Hall (1964), Mansfield (1886), Regent's Park (1958), Greyfriar's Hall (1953). The original women's colleges were:—Lady Margaret Hall (1878), Somerville (1879), St. Hugh's (1886), St. Hilda's (1893), St. Anne's (1952). Women were not admitted to degrees (though allowed to sit for examination) till 1920. Since 1974 almost all colleges have admitted both men and women students.

Oxygen is the most abundant of all terrestrial elements, no. 8, symbol O. In combination, this gaseous element forms about 46% of the earth's crust; one-fifth of the atmosphere; eight-ninths by weight of all water. Discovered independently by Scheele (*c.* 1773) and Priestley (1774). It is colourless, tasteless and odourless, and forms the chief life-supporting element of animal and vegetable life.

Oyster, a bivalve mollusc, of the genus *Ostrea,* having very numerous species and abounding in nearly all seas. The shell is rough and irregular. Oysters are exceedingly prolific, spawning in May and June. In England and Scotland deep-sea oysters are not allowed to be sold between 15 June and 4 August, and other kinds between 14 May and 4 August. In Ireland, no oysters may be taken between 1 May and 1 September, except in certain waters. The Whitstable oyster beds have existed since pre-Roman times; "clocks" are dead oysters.

Oystercatcher, a wading bird with black and white plumage and long, orange bill, inhabiting estuaries and sea-shores. Feeds on mussels, shell fish, etc., but not oysters.

Ozone, a modified form of oxygen, containing three atoms of oxygen per molecule instead of two. It is prepared by passing oxygen through a silent electric discharge. When present in air to the extent of 1 part in 4 million parts of air it kills bacteria, and has been used for this purpose in ventilating systems, *e.g.,* that of underground railways. It is present in extremely small quantities in the lower atmosphere but is comparatively plentiful at heights between 12 and 50 km. As ozone absorbs ultra-violet light of certain wavelengths spectroscopic methods, involving the analysis of sunlight, are chiefly used in ozone determination. *See also* **Atmosphere.**

P

Paca, a genus of large rodents found in Central and South America, and resembling the guinea-pig. It is of nocturnal habits, has streaked and spotted fur and lives on fruits and plants.

Pacific Ocean. The first European to recognise the Pacific as distinct from the Atlantic was the Spanish explorer, Vasco Nuñez de Balboa, who discovered its eastern shore from a peak in Panama in 1513. The first European to sail upon it was Magellan, who entered it by the strait that bears his name in 1520. Sir Francis Drake was the first Englishman to sail upon it in 1577. The world's greatest known ocean depth is in the Mindanao Trench, off the Philippines, 37,782 ft (11,524 m).

Pagan, a person who does not worship God; a heathen. The word is derived from the Latin *paganus* (a countryman or uncultivated person). In the Middle Ages the term was used largely to describe Mohammedans (Moors, Saracens, etc.).

Pagoda, the name given in China, India and other Asiatic countries to a high pyramidal tower, usually, but not necessarily, connected with a temple.

Palaeontology, the science which is devoted to the investigation of fossils: animal (palaeozoology) and plants (palaeobotany). By studying the markings and fossils of living things in the stratified rocks, palaeontologists have been able to establish with astonishing accuracy a record of the evolution of life through geological time. The geologist at the same time with the evidence of the fossils has been able to work out the order and the age of the rocks. *See also* **F48.**

Palatinate, a term formerly applied to two German regions, historically related, the Upper and Lower Palatinates. Now provinces of Bavaria.

Pale, the name given to the part of Ireland colonised by the English and comprising portions of the counties of Louth, Dublin, Meath and Kildare. The Anglo-Norman rulers were styled "Lords of the Pale".

Palimpsests are ancient MSS. or parchments which have been partly effaced and used for fresh writings. Many valuable MSS. were thus lost, but sometimes the second writing has been washed out, enabling the original writings to be deciphered. Among such restorations are a dialogue of Cicero's, a portion of a book of Livy.

Palladium, a scarce metallic element, no. 46, symbol Pd, similar to platinum, with which it is usually found. It is an expensive metal, with desirable properties as a catalyst in reactions involving hydrogen, since it has a remarkable capacity for absorbing this gas; for example, coal gas and air will inflame in the presence of palladium at room temperature. It forms a silver-white alloy with gold, and this is used in some kinds of jewellery. It is used in expensive watches to make non-magnetic springs.

Pallium, a vestmental ornamentation of white wool presented by the Pope to archbishops on their appointment, and the sign of Papal confirmation.

Palm, a large straight-trunked plant or tree common to tropical countries, and usually fruit yielding, such as dates, coconuts, etc. Many commodities useful to man are obtained from plants of the Palm family (*Palmaceae*).

Palm Sunday, the Sunday before Easter, upon which occasion it is customary to carry palms to the churches in some countries, in commemoration of Christ's entry into Jerusalem for the Feast of the Passover, when the people went forth to greet Him with palm branches.

Panama Canal. In 1903 the United States signed a treaty with Panama (which had previously seceded from Columbia) which gave the United States rights in perpetuity over a 16 km-wide strip of land extending across the isthmus for the purposes of building and running the canal. The canal connects the Atlantic and Pacific Oceans, is just over 80 kilometres long (with sea approaches) and the depth varies from 12 to 26 m. It is constructed above sea-level, with locks, and has been available for commercial shipping since 3 August 1914. Agreement was reached in 1978 for the waterway to be turned over to Panama by the end of the century.

Panda, or **Cat-Bear,** is related to the Raccoon. There are two kinds, the Red or True Panda, resembling a large domestic cat, which lives in the eastern Himalayas and S.W. China, and the Giant Panda, which is more like a bear in appearance and inhabits the mountains of western China. Both frequent the dense bamboo forests of those regions.

Pangolin, the scientific name of the "scaly anteater", a toothless mammal, found in W. Africa and S.E. Asia. It has a long extensible tongue which it uses in catching ants and termites, its chief food. When attacked the pangolin rolls itself into a ball, and its scales assume the form of sharp spikes. Pangolins have an Order of their own—the Pholidota, the scale-bearers.

Pantagruel, the leading character in one of the satires of Rabelais.

Pantheon, the famous temple in Rome, originally consecrated to the gods, built by Agrippa in 27 B.C. and rebuilt in the 2nd cent. by Hadrian. Its splendid dome and portico make it one of the most interesting architectural monuments of ancient days. Since the 7th cent. it has been used as a Christian church.

Panther, another name for the leopard, *Panthera pardus,* related to the lion, carnivorous, active climber, found in India, and other parts of Asia, also in Africa.

Papal Infallibility. *See Section J.*

Paper has been known in one form or another from very early times. The papyrus reeds of the Nile swamps served the ancient Egyptians for sheets upon which to inscribe their records. The Chinese and Japanese, centuries later, were using something more akin to modern paper in substance, an Asiatic paper-mulberry, yielding a smooth fibrous material, being utilised. With the spread of learning in Western Europe the necessity of a readier medium made itself felt and paper began to be manufactured from pulped rags and other substances. The first known English paper-mill was Sele mill near Stevenage, built about 1490, which produced the paper for an edition of Chaucer in 1498. Other mills were set up under Elizabeth, using linen and cotton as raw material. Other papermaking staples were later introduced, such as surat, esparto grass and wood-pulp. The chief raw material in the world paper industry is wood-pulp, the main exporters being the timber-growing countries of Canada, Sweden and Finland. Canada is the world's chief producer of newsprint and supplies a large proportion of US requirements.

Papyrus, the earliest known paper made in Egypt at a very remote period from a large species of reed, *Cyperus papyrus.* This plant is to be found all over tropical Africa, especially in the "sudd" region of the White Nile.

Parachute, the umbrella-shaped safety device used in emergency by the crew and passengers of aircraft. The first parachute descent from a great height was made in 1797 by André Garnerin who dropped 915 m from a balloon. Rate of descent for a parachute jump is about 5 m/s.

Paraclete (the Holy Ghost, or Comforter), the name used in the English translations of St. John's Gospel, and adopted by Abelard to designate the convent in Champagne founded by him, of which Héloïse became the abbess.

Paradise, a Persian word used by the translators of the Old Testament to designate the Garden of Eden, and since meaning any place of happiness.

Paraffin, a mixture of hydrocarbons of higher boiling point than petrol. Paraffin was first obtained by distillation of coal, the process being discovered about 1830. About 1848, Mr. James Young procured it from mineral oil, and Irish peat also yielded it. The main source of paraffin supply today is crude petroleum. Used in the manufacture of candles, for waterproofing and numerous other purposes.

Parakeets, various small parrots of vivid plumage native to Australia, Polynesia, Asia and Africa. One of the loveliest of the parakeets is the budgerigar of Australia.

Parallax, the change in direction of a body caused by a change in position of the observer. If the parallax is measured (in degrees of angle) and the distance between the two observation points is known the distance of the observed body can be calculated. The distance of heavenly bodies has been found this way. The first stellar distances were so obtained in 1838 by Henderson, Struve and Bessel. Stellar distances are so great that even when the two observations are made at opposite points of the earth's orbit round the sun, the parallax is always less than $1\cdot0''$ of arc. *See* **Aberration.**

Parameter, a number which is fixed for the application of a theory to one particular situation but may be different for other situations. For example, in a theory of motion near the surface of a planet the acceleration due to gravity may be regarded as a parameter constant for a particular planet but differing from planet to planet. The word is often used in a similar way in discussions of economic affairs.

Parapsychology. *See* **Section J.**

Parchment, made chiefly from the skins of animals, usually of goats and sheep, was employed in olden times before printing was invented and superseded papyrus as writing material. Vegetable parchment, invented by W. E. Gaine in 1853, though not equal in strength and durability to skin parchment, is about five times stronger than ordinary paper. Vellum is parchment made from the skins of young calves or lambs.

Paris University, of which the Sorbonne forms a part was founded in the 12th cent. and is one of the greatest educational institutions of Europe.

Parliament, is the name given to the supreme legislature of the United Kingdom. It consists of the Queen, the Lords spiritual and temporal and the Commons. It meets in two houses: the House of Lords (the Upper or Second Chamber) and the House of Commons. It derives from the Anglo-Saxon *Witans* (*see* **Witan**). The Statute of Westminster (1275) first uses "parlement" of the Great Council in England, which comes from the French word meaning discourse. *See* **Section D.**

Parliamentary Correspondents sit in the Press Gallery of the House of Commons and describe its proceedings for the news media either by impressions or a summary of the debate.

Parquetry, the name of a style of flooring consisting of small rectangular wooden blocks laid down according to geometrical pattern.

Parrot, the popular name of a widely distributed family of tropical birds, including the African grey parrot, the green parrot of South America —both familiar cage pets in this country—and the various parakeets, cockatoos, macaws, lories, etc. Many of these birds possess a remarkable gift of imitating sound, especially that of the human voice.

Parsec, modern unit of astronomical distance, the distance at which the diameter of the earth's orbit subtends an angle of 1 arc second. 1 parsec (pc) = $3\cdot0857 \times 10^{13}$ km.

Parthenogenesis. The development of animals from unfertilised eggs. The drones of the honey bee are parthenogenetic, and the phenomenon is also common among aphids.

Parthenon, the famous Temple of Athena on the Acropolis at Athens, was built under the rule of Pericles between 447 B.C. and 432 B.C. It was made wholly of marble without mortar. The famous sculptured friezes, known as the Elgin Marbles, are now in the British Museum.

Partridge, a well-known British game-bird. Close time: 2 February to 31 August. Two species are common in Britain.

Passport is an official document issued to a person by his own government, certifying to his citizenship and permitting him to travel abroad. Passports to British subjects are granted by the Foreign and Commonwealth Office, authorise bearer to leave the country and guarantee him the state's protection. Passports (1985) cost £15—and are issued for a period of 10 years. Children over 16 require separate passports. Parents of children under 16 who require passports should make application on form (B). A simplified form of travel document (British visitor's passport) is issued for British subjects wishing to pay short visits to certain foreign countries for a fee of £7·50—valid for 12 months. For those making frequent visits abroad a 94-page passport was first issued in 1973, which costs £30 (1985). From 1987, it was planned that British citizens would use a common EEC passport.

Patricians, the aristocracy of ancient Rome.

Paul's Cathedral, St., is the third cathedral church to be built on the site. It was preceded by a Norman building which was practically destroyed by the Great Fire in 1666. This followed a Saxon church which was burnt in 1086. The present building was designed by Sir Christopher Wren. The foundation stone was laid in 1675 and the structure was completed in 1710. It cost a little under £748,000. Its central feature is the dome, crowned by its cupola and lantern with the golden ball and cross. It escaped serious damage during the air raids of the second world war, but many of the surrounding buildings were laid waste.

pC Value, introduced by Dr. C. L. Whittles in 1935 as a measure of salinity of aqueous solutions (soil extract, irrigation water, etc.); defined as the negative logarithm of specific electrical conductivity in reciprocal ohms. Alone or joined with **pH** (*q.v.*) is useful as an index of osmotic pressure (*see* **Osmosis**) and related hindrance to plant growth resulting from excess of fertiliser or soil salts. If manuring is balanced, growth is best about **pC** 3.3.

Peacock, a bird of large size and beautiful plumage, its characteristic feature being a tail of brilliant "eyed" feathers, which it can erect and spread out, the males possessing resplendent feathering to a much greater extent than the females. It is related to the pheasant; one species is found wild in the forests of India, and another inhabits Burma and the Malayan regions, in Africa there is the Congo Peacock.

Peanut, Groundnut *or* **Monkey Nut.** A member of the pea family native to S. America, but now cultivated in many parts of the world. After pollination, the flower stalk bends down and buries the pod containing the peas ("nuts") in the ground. The oil from these "nuts" can be used for margarine manufacture.

Pearl is produced by certain shelled molluscs, chiefly the oyster. The inner surface of the shells of the pearl oyster yield "mother-of-pearl", and distinct pearls are believed to be morbid secretions, caused by some external irritation. Many fine pearls are found in the actual body of the oyster. The Persian Gulf, Sri Lanka, the north-west coast of Western Australia, many Pacific islands and the Gulf of Mexico are among the most productive pearl-fishing grounds. In ancient times Britain was renowned for its pearl fisheries, the pearls being obtained from a species of fresh-water mussel. Western Australia has produced a 40-grain pearl, the finest the world has seen. The largest pearl ever found was the "Beresford-Hope Pearl", which weighed 1,800 grains, over six times as much as the oyster that produced it.

Peat, decayed vegetable matter found mostly in marshy positions, and common in Ireland and Scotland. Peat is coal in its first stage of development; burnt for fuel in many cottage homes.

Peccary, a pig-like animal native to the Americas. There are two species: the collared peccary and the white-lipped peccary, the latter being a vicious and dangerous animal.

Pelican, a genus of bird with long depressed bill pouched underneath, thus able to hold fish in reserve. It has immense wings and webbed feet. Eight species.

Pemmican, venison or other meat, sliced, dried, pounded and made into cakes, used by explorers and others when out of reach of fresh meat.

Penguin, a genus of flightless, fish-eating sea-birds of the southern hemisphere. They are stout-bodied, short-necked and of small, moderate or large size. The Emperor and King Penguins make no nest but protect and incubate the single egg by carrying it in the down feathers between the feet and the body. Other species brood in the usual way and may lay as many as three eggs. Penguins use their flippers for swimming under water. All 17 species are bluish-grey or blackish above and white below. They are very sociable and breed in colonies.

Penicillin. An antibiotic drug produced by the mould *Penicillium notatum*, and discovered by Sir Alexander Fleming in 1928. It is one of the most effective chemotherapeutic agents known.

The mould produces a number of penicillins, all of which are effective antibiotics. See **Index to Section P**.

Peninsular War lasted from 1808 to 1814. Fought in Spain and Portugal (the Iberian peninsula) by the British, Spanish and Portuguese forces, chiefly under Wellington, against the French. The latter were defeated.

Pentagon, government office in Washington (the largest in the world), housing many thousands of military and civilian workers in the War Department of the United States (Army, Navy and Air Force).

Pentateuch, the first five books of the Old Testament—Genesis, Exodus, Leviticus, Numbers and Deuteronomy. Referred to in the Gospel of Mark as "the book of Moses".

Pepys Diary, by Samuel Pepys, was first published in 1825. It gives a picture of the social life of the period 1 January 1660 to 31 May 1669. He bequeathed the manuscript, together with his library, to Magdalene College, Cambridge.

Perch, a well-known family of fresh-water fish, with dark striped sides. The common perch of British rivers and lakes falls an easy prey to the angler because of its voracity.

Perfumes are essences or odours obtained from floral and other substances. The chief flower perfumes are those obtained from rose, jasmine, orange flower, violet and acacia. Heliotrope perfume is largely obtained from vanilla and almonds. Among the aromatic herbs which yield attractive perfumes are the rosemary, thyme, geranium, lavender, etc., while orange peel, citron peel, musk, sandalwood, patchouli and other vegetable products are largely drawn upon. In recent times chemistry has been called into play in aid of the perfumer, and many of the popular perfumes of today are chemically prepared in simulation of the scents of the flowers or other natural substances the names of which they bear. See **Musk Deer**.

Perigee, the closest point of the orbit of an object such as a satellite to the earth. The opposite of apogee (q.v.).

Perihelion. That point in a planet's orbit when it is nearest to the sun; opposite of aphelion. The earth is at perihelion (1.47×10^8 km) in mid-winter, about 3 January.

Peripatus, an animal which stands as a link between the annelid worms and the arthropods. Wormlike with short unjointed legs it breathes by a system of air tubes like those in insects. Certain other points of internal structure point to a relationship with annelid worms. There are some fifty species, the best known being the S. African *Peripatus capensis*.

Perjury, the offence of giving false evidence. The ancient Romans threw the perjurer from the Tarpeian Rock, and after the Empire was Christianised, those who swore falsely upon the Gospel had their tongues cut out. The usual punishment in England from the 16th to the 19th cent. was the pillory, fine and imprisonment.

Permian Formation, a group of rocks lying between the Trias and the Carboniferous strata. It has three subdivisions, Upper, Middle and Lower Permian. See **F48**.

Per Procurationem signature means that the subject of the correspondence has been put into the writer's care by his principal for him to use his personal judgment in the matter, and that he is authorised to sign on behalf of his principal. Normally contracted to *per pro* or *p.p.*

Peruke, the name given to the wigs worn by men in the latter half of the 18th cent. The custom of wearing wigs was gradually superseded by powdering the natural hair. Wigs are still worn by the Speaker of the House of Commons, judges and barristers.

Petrel, the name given to a member of a large, widely-distributed family of sea-birds of great diversity of size and colouring and distinguished by tube-like external nostrils. They usually skim low over the waves, and some, for this reason, are known as shearwaters. The storm petrel or Mother Carey's chicken occasionally patters along the surface, and is often called Little Peter—a reference to St. Peter walking on the water. Except when breeding, petrels are always at sea. They mostly nest in holes and crevices on islands and lay one egg, which is invariably white. The storm petrel, Leach's petrel, Manx shearwater and the fulmar petrel are resident in the British Isles. See also **Mutton Bird**.

Petroleum. See **Oil**.

Pewter, alloy of tin and lead formerly used for making household utensils and ornaments.

pH Value. Introduced in 1909 by the Danish chemist Sørensen to indicate hydrogen-ion concentration on the basis of electrical conductivity and a view of ionisation since discarded; is now taken as a logarithmic scale of acidity or alkalinity of aqueous solutions: acidity 0–7, neutrality at 7·0, alkalinity 7–14. The *pH* of blood is about 7·6 (faintly alkaline).

Phalanger, pouched marsupial mammals. They are arboreal and superficially resemble squirrels. There are two genera of flying phalangers or flying squirrels, which have a remarkable membrane along each side of the body enabling the animals to glide through the air. The members of the phalanger family are confined to the Australasian and oriental regions.

Phalangid, a member of the arachnid family Phalangida: popularly known as "harvesters".

Phalanx, a name applied by the ancient Greeks to a body of pike-men drawn up in close array, with overlapping shields, and eight, ten or more rows deep. The Macedonians stood sixteen rows deep. As many as 500 men could be in the front row.

Pharisees and Sadducees, two ancient Jewish sects. See Judaism, Section J, *also* **Section S**.

Pharmacopoeia, an official publication containing information on the recognised drugs used in medicine. Each country has its own pharmacopoeia. The British Pharmacopoeia (B.P.) is published under the direction of the General Medical Council. The Pharmaceutical Society issues the British Pharmaceutical Codex (B.P.C.); there is also an International Pharmacopoeia (2 vols.) which is issued by the World Health Organisation.

Pharos, the name of the first lighthouse, built by Ptolemy II about 280 B.C., on the Isle of Pharos, at the entrance to the harbour of Alexandria. It was said to be 180 m high but this is doubtful. One of the "seven wonders".

Pheasant, game birds related to the partridges, quails, peacocks, chickens and turkeys, males distinguished by their brilliant plumage and long tapering tail. First found by the Greeks in Georgia where the River Phasis flows through to the Black Sea. Close time: 2 February to 30 September.

Phillippics, the oration delivered by Demosthenes, 352–341 B.C., against Philip of Macedon—remarkable for their acrimonious invective. The word was also used for Cicero's speeches against Antony. In modern use, any impassioned invective.

Philosopher's Stone. See Alchemy, **Section J**.

Phosphorus is a non-metal element, no. 15, symbol P. Most familiar as a waxy, yellow solid which is spontaneously inflammable in air. It has chemical similarities to arsenic, like which it is very poisonous. It was discovered by Brandt in urine in 1669. It is found in most animal and vegetable tissues. It is an essential element of all plants and of the bones of animals. In combination with various metals it forms different phosphates, which are largely utilised as manures. The chief commercial use of phosphorus is in the preparation of matches.

Photoelectric Cell, a device which gives a useful electrical response to light falling on it. There are several kinds depending on the different effects which light may have on a suitably chosen solid (usually a semiconductor), viz., the emission of electrons from the surface ("photo-emissive cell"); change in electrical resistance ("photoconducting cell"); generation of electric current from a specially designed sensitive structure ("barrier layer" or "photovoltaic cell", "solar battery"). Different cells respond differently to lights of various wavelength and must be chosen for each application. See also **Solar Battery**.

Photogrammetry, the science of measurement from photographs taken from an aircraft. Aerial photography has many uses and is of great value to military intelligence and for map-making.

Photon. When light behaves like a stream of discrete particles and not like waves, the particles are called photons. *See* **F14, 16.**

Photosynthesis. *See* **F32(1), 43(2).**

Phrenology. *See* **Section J.**

Phylloxera, a genus of plant-lice related to the aphids, which attacks the grape vine. Many vineyards of France, in common with the rest of Europe, were replanted with native vines grafted on immune stocks from California in 1879 after being ravaged by the insect (which came from America). Curiously enough, the remedy also came from America, the vine stocks there being immune to *phylloxera*.

Pi is the unique number denoted by the Greek letter π and obtained by dividing the length of the circumference of any circle by its diameter. Its value is approximately 3·14159.

Picts, inhabitants of Scotland in pre-Roman times, are held by some historians to be a branch of the old Celtic race, by others to have been of Scythian origin. They occupied the north-eastern portion of Scotland, and were subdued by the Scots in Argyll in the 9th cent., Kenneth MacAlpin becoming king of a united kingdom of the Picts and Scots—the kingdom of Alban.

Pike, a familiar fresh-water fish abundant in the temperate regions of both hemispheres. It forms good sport for the angler in rivers and lakes, and sometimes attains a weight of from 9–13 kg. It is extremely voracious, is covered with small scales and has a ferocious-looking head.

Pilchard, a fish of the herring family, but with smaller scales and more rounded body. It appears off the Cornish coasts in vast shoals every summer.

Pilgrimage. The undertaking of a journey to a distant place or shrine to satisfy a religious vow or secure spiritual benefit, was resorted to in early Christian times. The first recorded pilgrimage is that of the Empress Helena to Jerusalem in 326. In the Middle Ages pilgrimages became common, and were undertaken by monarchs and people of rank in all Christian countries. Moslems have been making pilgrimages to Mecca since the death of the Prophet, such duty being enjoined by the Koran. Among the great centres of Christian pilgrimages are Jerusalem, Rome, the tomb of Becket at Canterbury and the holy places of Lourdes and La Salette in France.

Pilgrimage of Grace (1536), the rising in Lincolnshire and Yorkshire in the reign of Henry VIII against religious innovations and the dissolution of the smaller monasteries, which overlapped with discontents caused by taxation, rising prices, enclosures and land speculation. The insurrection was followed by many executions.

Pilgrim Fathers, the 101 English Puritans, who, after living some years in exile in Holland, to escape persecution in their own country, set sail for America in the *Mayflower*, 6 September 1620, landing at Plymouth, Mass., 4 December. They founded the settlement of Plymouth, and are regarded as the pioneers of American colonisation although 13 years earlier a small Virginian colony had been established.

Pillory, a wooden instrument of punishment in use in England until 1837. It consisted of a pair of movable boards with holes through which the culprit's head and hands were put, and was usually erected on a scaffold. While a person was undergoing this punishment the mob generally pelted him with stones and rubbish, sometimes to his serious injury. People convicted of forgery, perjury or libel were often condemned to the pillory, but from 1816–1837 the only offence for which it could be inflicted was perjury.

Pine, a conifer of the genus *Pinus*, which flourishes all over the northern hemisphere and includes 80–90 species, which afford valuable timber and yield turpentine and tar. The Scots Pine, *Pinus silvestris*, with its blue-green, short needles, set in pairs, and its rosy-orange branches, is native to Britain, as it is to the whole of Europe. It provides the red and yellow deal in everyday use.

Pitcairn Islanders were originally the mutineers of the *Bounty*. They took possession of the island in 1790, and it was not until 1814 that their whereabouts was ascertained, accidentally, by a passing ship. The mutineers, under their leader, Adams, had settled down to a communal existence, married Tahitian women and increased so in numbers that in the course of years they were too many for the island to support, and in 1856 they were removed by the British Government to Norfolk Island. A small number returned to Pitcairn.

Pitchblende or **Uraninite,** a relatively scarce mineral. It is nearly all uranium oxide, but lead, thorium, etc., are also present. Pitchblende from Joachimstal in Czechoslovakia was the material in which radium was discovered by the Curies. Other major sources are the Great Lakes region of Canada and Zaire.

Placebo, medical treatment that the therapist uses deliberately although he knows it is without any specific effect on the condition being treated. There may be various medical reasons for using placebos, *e.g.*, for the beneficial psychological effect on people who like to feel something is being done for them; for differentiating during clinical trials of a new treatment between those persons given the real thing and a control or comparison group of persons given a placebo or inactive imitation.

Plainsong, a style of musical composition sung in unison (all voices singing the same tune without harmony), familiar in the Western Church from very early times and still performed, principally in the Roman Catholic Church. Though restrained and contemplative in spirit, it is capable of expressing deep emotion. *See* **E3(2).**

Planetarium, a complex optical system which projects into the interior of a dome a replica of all the phenomena of the sky that can be seen by the naked eye, *e.g.*, sun, moon, planets, stars, comets, meteors, aurora, eclipses and clouds. There is a planetarium in the Marylebone Road, London, and another (opened in 1966) at Armagh Observatory, N. Ireland.

Planets, the name given to such celestial bodies as revolve round the sun in elliptical orbits. The name was first used by the Greeks to indicate their difference from the fixed stars. There are nine major planets, Mercury, Venus, Earth, Mars, Jupiter, Saturn, Uranus, Neptune and Pluto. There are also a large number of minor planets or asteroids. Saturn, Uranus and Jupiter are ringed. Many important questions can be answered by means of probes sent to the neighbourhood of the planets. These include the measurement of the magnetic field, if any, of the planets, the study of their atmospheres, much of which can be done without actually penetrating to the surface. With instruments landed gently on the surface it is possible to investigate surface conditions and composition by many methods. Even without a soft-landing information on these questions can be obtained by photography and subsequent transmission of the picture back to earth by some form of television scanning. The US Mars probe *Mariner IV* transmitted pictures of the Martian surface in 1965, the Russian *Venus IV* in 1967 made a soft-landing on Venus, and the US *Pioneer 11* came within 43,000 km of Jupiter in December 1974. Two US *Voyager* spacecraft were launched in 1977 flying by Jupiter (1979), Saturn (1980, 1981) and Uranus (1986), sending back exciting new data. *See* under their names, and Special Topic **F69–75.**

Plankton, a word which first came into biological use in 1886 to describe the usually microscopic plants and animals floating, swimming and drifting in the surface waters of the sea. To be distinguished from *nekton* (swimming animals like fishes and squids) and *benthos* (plants and animals living on the sea bottom, like fixed algae, sponges, oysters, crabs, etc.). Of great economic importance, providing food for fish and whales.

Plantagenets, the kings who reigned in England between 1154 and 1485 and included the Houses of Lancaster and York. More correctly they are styled Angevins, from Anjou, of which Geoffrey, father of Henry II, was Count, and whose badge was a sprig of broom (*Planta genista*).

Plasma Physics is the physics of wholly ionised gases, *i.e.*, gases in which the atoms initially present have lost practically the whole of the electrons that usually surround their nuclei, so that the gas consists of a mixture of two components, positively charged ions and negatively charged electrons. The physical properties of a *plasma* are very different from those of an unionised gas. In particular, a plasma has a high electrical conductivity and can carry large currents. *See also* **Nuclear Fusion.**

Plastics, a broad term covering those substances which become plastic when subjected to increased temperatures or pressures. The Plastics Industry is based on synthetic organic examples of this group. There are two classes of plastics: the *thermoplastic,* which become plastic every time they are heated (*e.g.* cellulosic plastics) and *thermosetting,* which undergo chemical change when heated, so that once set they cannot be rendered plastic again (*e.g.,* Bakelite). Plastics are composed of long-chained molecules, *e.g.,* polyethylene.

Plate Tectonics, the contemporary and by now well-developed theory of the movements of the earth's crust. The view is that the surface of the Earth consists of about a dozen rigid plates, some larger than continents, some much smaller, all in ceaseless motion relative to one another. Their separation and approach and their friction and collision are closely related to the evolution of mountain ranges, oceans and rift valleys and to phenomena like earthquakes and volcanoes. *See* **F9.**

Platinum, a metallic element, no. 78, symbol Pt. It is a scarce white metal generally allied with iridium, osmium, ruthenium and palladium. It can only be melted in an oxyhydrogen or electric furnace, but can be rolled out into a film-like sheet, or drawn out to the finest wire; being resistant to acids it is termed a noble metal.

Platonic Solids, five regular solid figures known to the ancient world. They are: the tetrahedron (4 triangular faces), cube (6 square faces), octahedron (8 triangular faces), dodecahedron (12 five-sided faces), icosahedron (20 triangular faces). All the faces and angles of each solid are identical.

Pleiades, famous cluster of stars in the constellation of Taurus. Of the seven principal stars in the group, one is rather faint, and many myths have sprung up about this "lost Pleiad". *See also* **123.**

Pleistocene, the geological period that succeeded the Pliocene. During the Pleistocene, also known as the *Great Ice Age,* there were four cold periods, when the ice sheets covered northern Europe and N. America, separated by warm periods when the glaciers drew back into the mountains. From recent studies based on rock magnetic measurements the transition to Pleistocene took place *c.* 1,850,000 years ago.

Pliocene, the geological period preceding the Pleistocene, and the last major division of the Tertiary strata. It began about fifteen million years ago. *See* **F48.**

Plough Monday, the first Monday after the Epiphany, when in olden times the rustic population returned to work after the Christmas festivities.

Plover, wading birds, widely distributed over marshy places of Europe. Several species occur in Britain, including the Golden-plover, which breeds on the moors of Devon, Somerset, Wales, N.E. Yorkshire and Scotland, and the Ringed plover, Kentish plover and Dotterel.

Pluto, the last planet to be discovered was searched for following the 1914 predictions of P. Lowell and discovered by C. W. Tombaugh at the Flagstaff Observatory in Arizona in January 1930. Generally the most distant of the planets its orbit is much more elliptical than the other planetary orbits and so it sometimes approaches the sun closer than Neptune. It was thought to be different from the other outer Jovian planets which are gaseous and to consist of rock covered in frozen methane gas. Recently the size of Pluto has been revised downwards by interferometric measurement of its diameter. The latest value is between 3,000 and 3,500 km, close to the size of our moon. Pluto's own moon, Charon, was also detected by earth-based telescopes using special photometric measurements. *See* **F8.**

Plutonium, a chemical element, no. 94, symbol Pu, capable of nuclear fission in the same way as Uranium 235. Not until after it had been synthesised in atomic piles during the second world war was it shown to occur in infinitesimally small traces in nature. Its synthesis in the atomic pile depends on the capture by Uranium 238 nuclei of neutrons; immediate product of this reaction is the element neptunium, but this undergoes rapid radioactive disintegration to plutonium.

Poet Laureate is the poet attached to the royal household, an office officially established in 1668, though its origins go back to the early Middle Ages, when minstrels were employed at the courts of English kings. Chaucer, Skelton and Spenser, though not court poets, were all unofficial poets laureate. Ben Jonson has been called the first "official laureate" (1616), but the office was not officially recognised until 1668, when Dryden was formally granted the office. It is customary for the poet laureate to write verse in celebration of events of national importance. Ted Hughes (*see* **B33**) became Poet Laureate in December 1984 after the death of Sir John Betjeman.

Pogrom. Russian word meaning "destruction". First used to describe the Csarist attacks on the Jews in 1881 in Russia. In 1938 Hitler ordered a general pogrom in Germany: all synagogues were destroyed and nearly all Jewish shops and homes, Jewish hospitals and children's homes suffered. During the subsequent war Jews of central Europe were systematically exterminated in cold blood by the Nazis.

Poitiers, Battle of, was fought on 19 September 1356, during the Hundred Years' War, when Edward the Black Prince gained a complete victory over John, King of France, who was taken prisoner and brought to London.

Polecat, an animal of a dark-brown colour, about 46 cm in length, exclusive of tail; the ears and face-markings are white or light brown. It is carnivorous and belongs to the weasel family.

Pole-Star is of the second magnitude, and the last in the tail of the Little Bear constellation. Being near the North pole of the heavens—never more than about one degree from due north—it always remains visible in the Northern hemisphere; hence its use as a guide to seamen.

Police, a regular force established for the preservation of law and order and the prevention and detection of crime. The powers they have vary from country to country and with the type of government; the more civilised and democratic the state, the less police intervention. England, compared with countries abroad, was slow to develop a police force, and it was not until 1829 that Sir Robert Peel's Metropolitan Police Act established a regular force for the metropolis, later legislation establishing county and borough forces maintained by local police authorities throughout England and Wales. Up to that time police duties were discharged by individual constables and watchmen appointed by local areas in England and Wales. The police service in Great Britain today is organised in a number of forces (43 in England and Wales and 6 regional and 2 combined forces in Scotland). In Northern Ireland there is a single force (the Royal Ulster Constabulary). In England and Wales the forces are defined according to area of responsibility:

1. County forces, under a police committee consisting of local councillors and magistrates.

2. Combined forces, covering more than one county, also under a police committee consisting of local councillors and magistrates and representatives from each constituent area.

3. The Metropolitan Police Force, covering an area within a 15-mile (24-km) radius of Charing Cross, but excluding the City of London, under the control of the Home Secretary. Strength *c.* 26,000.

4. The City of London force operating in the area of the city, under the Court of Common Council.

In Scotland the police authority is the regional or island council. Police ranks are: chief constable, assistant chief constable, chief superintendent, superintendent, chief inspector, inspector, sergeant and constable. In the Metropolitan Police area the chief officer is the Commissioner of Police of the Metropolis.

Central authority rests with the Home Secretary in England and Wales and the Secretary of State for Scotland in Scotland. In the present troubles in Northern Ireland responsibility for law and order is retained at Westminster.

Lord Scarman's Report (1981), following the Brixton and Toxteth riots, made radical recommendations for improved police behaviour and policies.

Pollution of the atmosphere is due chiefly to the incomplete combustion of fuels, especially coal, large particles of soot being deposited fairly quickly close to their place of origin and smaller particles (including smoke) remaining suspended in the air for a long time. Invisible air pollutants include sulphur dioxide from power stations and home heating, and carbon monoxide from cars. The introduction of more efficient furnaces, the washing of flue gases and the introduction of smokeless zones have assisted in the abatement of smoke and other forms of pollution. "Smog" (smoke-laden fog) which reduces visibility to zero and affects the respiratory organs, is liable to occur when the air near the earth is cooled below the dew-point temperature by radiation on a still, cloudless night when an accumulation of smoke over a large city cuts off daylight and produces gloom, and absence of wind or vertical currents prevents the lower layers of the air from getting away. Such conditions are associated with the smoke-laden atmosphere of large industrial towns during a winter anticyclone. During the great London smog of 1952 there were 2,000 deaths over and above those expected for the time of year. Since the Clean Air Act of 1956 pollution by smoke and sulphur dioxide has continued to diminish in London, winter sunshine has increased by 70 per cent, and fish now live in the Thames. Some other pollution problems which have been in the public eye are: disposal of nuclear waste (**L89**), acid rain (**L3**), contamination of coastal waters and shores by oil slicks; possibility of depletion of the ozone layer (**L92**). This layer protects us from excessive amounts of ultraviolet radiation and there has been concern that it is being depleted because of pollution with fluorocarbons (**L45**). The carbon dioxide balance is being disturbed by the burning of fossil fuels (**L22**) and it has been calculated that doubling of carbon dioxide concentration would increase earth's surface temperature by 2–3°C.

Polonium, a radioactive element, no. 84, symbol Po, discovered by Madame Curie in 1898, and named after her native land of Poland.

Poltergeist. *See* Section J.

Polymerisation is the linking together of small molecules to make a large long-chain molecule. The general name for polymers of ethylene is Polythene, a wax-like plastic solid which because of its special qualities is used in a variety of ways today.

Polytheism. *See* God and Man, Section J.

Pomology, the science of fruit-growing.

Pontifex, the title assigned in ancient Rome to members of the college of pontifices. "Pontifex maximus" was the official head of Roman religion. It was as "pontifex maximus" that Julius Caesar revised the calendar in 46 B.C., and when after the rise of Christianity the Popes took over the title the revision fell to them.

Pope, The, the head of the Roman Catholic Church, recognised by that Church as the lawful successor of St. Peter. He is elected by the body of Cardinals. Since 1870, when the King of Italy deposed the holder from temporal power, no Pope had left the Vatican between appointment and death until 1929, when peace was made between the Church and State in Italy and compensation was paid to the Holy See for the loss of temporal power. Cardinal Karol Wojtyla, Archbishop of Cracow, was elected Pope John Paul II in 1978, following the sudden death of Pope John Paul I.

Porcelain. The word is thought to be derived from the Italian *porcellana*, indicating the texture of a piglet. The majority of porcelain made on the continent was of "hard-paste", or true porcelain, similar to that discovered by the Chinese as early as the T'ang Dynasty (A.D. 618–907). It was composed of *kaolin* (china-clay) and *petuntse* (china-stone) which when fired in a kiln at a temperature of *c.* 1300°C became an extremely hard and translucent material. The recipe of "hard-paste" porcelain remained a secret of the Chinese until 1709, when it was re-discovered in Europe by Johann Böttger at the Meissen factory (popularly known as Dresden). Aided by disloyal Meissen workmen, factories were later established at Vienna, Venice and in many parts of Germany. Plymouth and Bristol were the only English factories to produce this type of porcelain, from 1768 to 1781. Elsewhere, both in England and France, the material manufactured was known as "soft-paste" or artificial porcelain which was made by blending varying white-firing clays with the ingredients of glass. The French factory of Sèvres began to make some hard-paste porcelain by 1768 and by the 19th cent. such porcelain was the only type being made throughout the whole of the continent. In England Josiah Spode is credited with the introduction of "bone-china" about 1794. This hybrid-paste was quickly adopted by many other factories and today remains the most popular type of English porcelain.

Porphyry, a form of crystalline rock of many varieties that in ancient Egypt was quarried and used for the decorative portions of buildings and vessels. The term is applied generally to the eruptive rocks in which large well-formed crystals of one mineral are set in a matrix of other minerals.

Porpoise, a highly intelligent marine mammal of the dolphin and whale family, and a common inhabitant of northern seas. Porpoises travel in shoals, their progression being marked by constant leapings and plungings. Their average length is from 1·2–1·5 m. There are several species, nearly all being confined to northern oceans.

Port, a special kind of red Portuguese wine, taking its name from Oporto. It was little known in England until the Methuen Treaty of 1703, when it was permitted to be imported at a low duty.

Portland Vase, one of the most renowned specimens of ancient art, long in the possession of the Portland family. In 1810 it was loaned to the British Museum. Here it was shattered in 1845 by a stone from a maniac's hand, but has been skilfully restored. It is said to have been found in the 17th cent. in an ancient tomb near Rome. It was purchased from the Barberini family in 1770 by Sir Wm. Hamilton, subsequently sold to the Duchess of Portland. The vase, which is actually a two-handled urn, stands about 25 cm high, is of transparent dark blue glass, ornamented with figures cut in relief in overlaid white opaque glass. It was purchased by the British Museum in 1945. *See also* Glass.

Portreeve in olden times was an official appointed to superintend a port or harbour, and before the name of mayor was used the chief magistrate of London was styled the Portreeve.

Positivism. *See* Section J.

Positron, the "positive electron", an atomic particle having the same mass but an electric charge equal but opposite to that of an electron. It was discovered in 1932. *See also* **F16**.

Post-Impressionism, a term introduced by Roger Fry to describe the exhibition of paintings sponsored by himself in London (1910–11) officially entitled "Manet and the Post-Impressionists". The exhibition included paintings by Manet, Cézanne, Gauguin, Van Gogh, Seurat, Signac, works by Matisse, Rouault and the *Fauves* (*q.v.*), and sculpture by Maillol. In a second exhibition, held in 1912, Picasso and the Cubists were also represented. The term therefore refers to the movement in modern art which reacted against the transient naturalism of the Impressionists by concerning itself primarily with colour, form and solidity. Most artists today would include Cézanne, Van Gogh and Gauguin as the main Post-Impressionists and maintain that it prepared the way for Fauvism, Cubism and Expressionism.

Potassium, a metal, no. 19, symbol K (German *Kalium*). It is similar to sodium, reacting violently with water. It was discovered by Sir Humphry Davy in 1807, and is now generally obtained by the electrolysis of fused potassium hydroxide or chloride/fluoride mixture. Its principal minerals are caranallite and kainite, and it is relatively common in rocks, accounting for about 2¼% of the earth's crust. An essential element for healthy plant growth; the ashes of plants are relatively rich in potassium.

Potsdam Agreement was signed by Truman, Stalin and Attlee in August 1945. By this Agreement a Council of Foreign Ministers was established, representing the five principal Powers: China, France, Soviet Russia, the United Kingdom and United States of America, with the task of drawing up the peace treaties for submission to the United Nations. It laid down, *inter alia*, that German militarism and Hitlerism should be destroyed; that industrial power should be so reduced that Germany would never again be in a position to wage aggressive war; that surplus equipment should be destroyed or transferred to replace wrecked plant in allied territories; that Germany should be treated as an economic whole; and that local self-government should be restored on democratic lines as rapidly as was consistent with military security. The Potsdam Agreement became a dead letter with the creation of a communist régime in the Russian zone of Germany, and marked the beginning of the "cold war".

Prado Gallery, the great public picture collection of Madrid, containing a superb collection of paintings by Velasquez, Murillo, Raphael, Titian, Dürer, Van Dyck, Rubens and Goya.

Pragmatism. *See* Section J.

Prefect, chief magistrates in ancient Rome. The title is now applied to the chiefs of administration of the departments of France.

Pre-Raphaelite Brotherhood was the name given to their school of thought by three British artists, Dante Gabriel Rossetti, J. E. Millais and W. Holman Hunt, who in 1848 revolted against the academic art of their time and advocated a return to the style of the Italian painters prior to Raphael—the simple naturalism of the Primitives, such as Botticelli, Fra Angelico and Filippo Lippi. Thus they avoided the use of heavy shadows and painted on a white ground in bright colours—a technique which aroused the ire of those used to the dark and murky canvases of the contemporary romantic artists. Although they held these principles in common the three members of the "P.R.B.", as it was popularly called, were really quite different in other respects. Thus Rossetti (who for some reason is always thought of as the typical Pre-Raphaelite) produced works of a highly romanticised mediaevalism which, apart from certain aspects of technique, bear not the slightest resemblance to the sentimental naturalism of Millais or the much more dramatic realism of Holman Hunt (*e.g.*, in *The Scapegoat*). The Brotherhood was later joined by a number of lesser artists, but its works are not commonly accepted with enthusiasm today when the general feeling is that they are sentimental and religiose rather than the product of deeply-felt emotions. Ruskin in his writings defended their work but the movement came to an end in 1853.

Presbyterianism. *See* Section J.

Press-Gang, a body of sailors employed to impress men into naval service, frequently resorted to in England, especially during the war with France in the early 19th cent. Press gangs were not used after about 1850.

Primitive Art. The word "primitive" has a number of different meanings: (1) the art of prehistoric communities (*e.g.*, the famous animal cave-drawings of the Aurignacians, *c.* 25,000 B.C., at Altamira in Spain); (2) the art of modern primitive communities (*e.g.*, Bushman rock-paintings); (3) child art; (4) peasant art which springs from a spontaneous desire to impart beauty to objects of daily use and shows a tendency towards abstraction. Peasant art has many features in common the world over, the woodcarving of the Norsemen being almost indistinguishable from that of the Maoris; (5) the modern school of primitive painting in which naïveté of presentation is either the aim of a highly sophisticated mind (*e.g.*, the self-taught French painter Le Douanier Rousseau (d. 1910), or arises naturally from a simple one (the American "grandma" Moses (d. 1961) who began to paint in her seventies).

Printing by movable types was first used in Europe in 1454 by Johann Gutenberg, a citizen of Mainz. The invention is also claimed for Laurens Koster of Haarlem. It was introduced into England by Caxton, who set up a printing press in Westminster in 1476. Gothic characters were first used, being superseded by Roman letters in 1518. In 1798 Earl Stanhope replaced the wood printing press by one of iron. In 1814 Friedrich Koenig applied the principle of steam power to the press. Mr. John Walter, of *The Times* newspaper, was the first to use the steam press. Improvements were introduced by Applegarth and Cowper in 1828 and great strides were made in 1858 when the Hoe machine was put on the market. Then came the Walter press in 1866 which printed on continuous rolls of paper from curved stereotyped plates. The Monotype machine casts single letters and the Linotype whole lines. The term letterpress is used for all printing methods using plates where the characters stand in *relief*. The other main printing methods are *intaglio* and *planographic*. The development of computer technology using electronic methods has introduced a new era in printing.

The Privy Council is the Sovereign's own council, consisting of about 300 persons who have reached eminence in some branch of public affairs (Cabinet ministers must be Privy Counsellors), on whose advice and through which the Sovereign exercises his or her statutory and a number of prerogative powers. From it have sprung many organs of the constitution and many of our government departments have grown from committees of the Privy Council. For example the Judiciary or courts of justice have grown from the Sovereign's Council sitting as a Court of Justice, and today the Judicial Committee of the Privy Council is a body of distinguished lawyers acting as a Court of Appeal from courts of the Commonwealth.

Probation Officers are attached to particular Courts, sometimes a Magistrates' or a higher court. Sometimes an offender is not sentenced to punishment, but is released "on probation", that is on the condition that he behaves well and follows directions given by the Court or by a probation officer. Such an officer is a trained man (or woman) who advises, assists and befriends people who are placed under his supervision by a court of law. The probation officer, by his assessment of the social background of the offender, can advise the court upon the wisdom of putting the offender on probation. The probation officer by his understanding can so befriend an offender as to provide a basis for his rehabilitation. He undertakes the "after care" of those released from prison or Borstal.

Productivity. Physical productivity is the output of products during a time unit, *e.g.*, so many products per man hour, or day, or year. Total productivity is the sum of all the units of product created during the given time. Labour productivity is the part of the total that is attributed to labour as a factor of production. Productivity of capital is the element attributed to capital as a factor. Productivity of land is the element attributed to the natural powers of the soil, as distinct from what is contributed by the application to it of capital or labour. The term productivity is also used to refer not to the quantity of output, but to its money value.

Propane, a colourless inflammable gas made of carbon and hydrogen; formula C_3H_8. It is easily liquefied and transported liquid in cylinders and tanks. In this form it is familiar as a "portable gas supply" for domestic and industrial uses. It is sometimes mixed with butane (*q.v.*) for this purpose. Propane occurs in natural gas and is a by-product of oil refining.

Proteins are the main chemical substances of living matter: they are a part of every living cell and are found in all animals and plants. All proteins are basically constructed of carbon hydrogen, oxygen and nitrogen, and some contain sulphur, phosphorus (nucleoproteins) and iron (haemoglobin). Proteins are built up of very long chains of amino-acids connected by amide linkages (the synthetic polymers such as "nylon" and casein plastics (from milk) are built up of the same linkages). The structure of protein molecules allows a variety of function. Enzymes, which bring about chemical reactions in living cells, are proteins having specific properties. *See* **F32–3**, *also* **Diet, Section P.**

Proton, a basic constituent of the atomic nucleus, positively charged, having a mass about 1836 times that of the electron. It is a positive hydrogen ion. *See* **F13(2), 16.**

Prout's hypothesis. The English chemist William Prout (1785–1850) advanced the idea that all atoms are made of hydrogen, and their weights are exact multiples of the weight of a hydrogen atom. With the modification that neutrons as well as protons occur in the nucleus, Prout's belief, though rejected for many years, has been substantially vindicated.

Provost, a Scottish official similar in rank to an English mayor. The Provosts of Edinburgh, Glasgow, Aberdeen, Perth and Dundee are styled Lords Provost. The title of provost is also given to the heads of certain colleges.

Prud'hommes (Prudent Men), **Councils of,** were French trade tribunals, of masters and work-men, formed to decide on disputes. Originally a mediaeval institution, they were revived by Napoleon in 1806, and were carried on by the Third Republic.

Psalms, Book of, for many years attributed to David, but present-day scholars are of opinion that the psalms were written by a series of authors at different times and for different purposes, and that few, if any, were written by David. The Holy Scriptures contain 150. *See* **Section S.**

Psychedelism. *See* **Section J.**

Psychic Research. *See* **Section J.**

Psychoanalysis. *See* **Section J.**

Ptarmigan, birds of the grouse family, one species of which inhabits the Scottish Highlands. In the winter the bird assumes a white plumage.

Ptomaines, amino acids produced during the putrefaction of proteins of animal origin. Not a cause of food poisoning, as was once generally supposed, which is almost invariably due to certain specific bacteria.

Publicans, under the Roman Empire, were people who farmed the public taxes. It is this class of officials that is alluded to in the "publicans and sinners" phrase in the New Testament.

Public Corporations, statutory bodies which operate major industries and services in the public interest, *e.g.*, UK Atomic Energy Authority, Bank of England, B.B.C., Electricity Authorities, Gas Council, National Coal Board, British Steel Corporation, British Railways Board, the Post Office, British National Oil Corporation, British Nuclear Fuels Ltd., British Airports Authority. They are account-able to Parliament but their staffs are not civil servants. The present government is pursuing a policy of privatisation of some of these bodies.

Public Schools. The Public Schools Act of 1864 named nine "public" schools: Eton, Harrow, Rugby, Winchester, Westminster, Shrewsbury, Charterhouse, St. Paul's and Merchant Taylors. Today the term embraces many more, and can be applied to all those schools which are financed by bodies other than the State and whose head-masters belong to the Headmasters' Conference as distinct from the Headmasters' Association. There are about 200 such schools in Britain, including among others: Bedford School (founded 1552); Bradfield College, Berks. (1850); Charterhouse, Godalming (1611); Chel-tenham College (1841); Christ's Hospital, Horsham (1553); City of London (1442); Clifton College, Bristol (1862); Dulwich College (1619); Eton College (1440); Felsted, Dunmow, Essex (1564); Haileybury College (1862); Harrow (1571); King Edward's, Birmingham (1552); King's School, Canterbury (600); Malvern College (1865); Manchester Grammar School (1515); Marlborough College (1843); Merchant Taylors' (1561); Mill Hill (1807); Oundle (1556); Radley College, Abingdon (1847); Repton, Derbyshire (1557); Rugby School (1567); St. Albans (948); St. Paul's (1509); Sevenoaks School (1418); Sherborne (1550); Shrewsbury School (1552); Stonyhurst College (1593); Stowe School, Bucks. (1923); Tonbridge (1553); Uppingham, Leics. (1584); Warwick (914); Wellington College (1859); Westminster (1560); Winchester College (1382). Public schools for girls include: Christ's Hos-pital, Hertford (1552), Cheltenham Ladies'

College (founded by Miss Beale in 1853), North London Collegiate School (founded by Miss Buss in 1850), Roedean (1885), Wycombe Abbey (1806). Some public schools are now co-educational.

Pulsars, cosmic objects discovered in 1967 by the Radio Astronomy group at Cambridge; of great scientific interest, since they are probably neutron stars, and extremely dense. Unlike quasars (*q.v.*) they are nearby objects within our own galaxy. *See* **F5.**

Puma, mountain-lion or cougar, a large wild cat found throughout the Americas. It looks like a lean greyish lioness.

Pyramidology. *See* **Section J.**

Pyramids of Egypt, on the west bank of the Nile, are vast stone or brick-built structures with inner chambers and subterranean entrances, built by the Pharaohs as royal tombs and dating from about 3000 B.C. The most celebrated are at Gizeh built during the 4th dynasty. The largest, originally 147 m high, is called the Great Pyramid, one of the seven wonders of the world, built by the Pharaoh Khufu, better known as Cheops, and there he was buried, 100,000 men, according to Herodotus, being employed for 20 years upon it. Chephren, successor of Cheops, erected the second pyramid, and the third was built by Mycerinus, a son of Cheops. The pyramid at Meidum built by King Snefru, founder of the 4th dynasty, is the most imposing of all. American and Egyptian scientists are cooperating in a project to X-ray (by means of cosmic rays) the interior of the Pyramid of Chephren.

Pythons, large snakes, non-poisonous and destroy-ing their prey by crushing it. Some species may reach 9 m in length, and prey upon deer and other small mammals. Found in Asia, Africa and Australia. They lay eggs.

Q

Quadrant, an astronomical instrument for measur-ing altitudes, superseded for navigational pur-poses in modern times by the sextant. It con-sists of a graduated arc of 90° with a movable radius for measuring angles on it.

Quai d'Orsay. An embankment in Paris where the French Foreign Office is situated.

Quail, an edible bird of the partridge family, of which only one species, the Common Quail, is found in England. It is not more than 20 cm long. It is found in most of the warmer regions of the world. In England and Wales the Quail is covered by the Wild Bird Protection Acts.

Quantum Theory. The rapid development of quantum theory has been almost entirely due to the experimental and theoretical study of the interactions between electromagnetic radiation and matter. One of the first steps was taken when it was discovered that the electrons emitted from metals due to the action of ultra-violet radiation have an energy which is not related to the intensity of the incident radiation, but is dependent on its wavelength. Einstein showed in 1905 that this could only be ex-plained on the basis that energy is transferred between radiation and matter in finite amounts, or *quanta*, which are inversely proportional to wavelength. *See* **F17(2).**

Quarks are hypothetical subnuclear particles recently postulated by theoretical physicists concerned with the so-called elementary par-ticles. There may be three kinds, possibly more, all carrying electrical charges which are fractions of those carried by familiar particles like electrons and protons. This and other special properties of quarks make them suitable for explaining the existence of the large number of other particles referred to on **F16–17.** The physical existence of quarks may be demon-strated by experiment at any time and if this happens it will be an exciting triumph for specu-lative theoretical physics. *See* **F15(2).**

Quartering, in heraldry, is the disposition of vari-ous escutcheons or coats of arms in their proper "quarters" of the family shield, in such order as indicates the alliances with other families.

Quartermaster, a military officer charged with the provisioning and superintendence of soldiers in camp or barracks, and holding the equivalent rank to a lieutenant. The Quartermaster-General is an officer who presides over the provisioning department of the whole army. A Quartermaster in the Navy is a petty officer responsible to the Officer of the Watch; at sea for the correct steering of the ship and in harbour for the running of the ship's routine.

Quarto, a sheet of paper folded twice to make four leaves, or eight pages; abbreviated to "4to".

Quartz is a common and usually colourless mineral, occurring both crystallised and massive. In the first form it is in hexagonal prisms, terminating in pyramids. When pure its specific gravity is 2·66. It is one of the constituents of granite, gneiss, etc. Among the quartz varieties are *rock crystal* (colourless), *smoky quartz* (yellow or brown), *amethyst* (purple), *rose quartz* (pink) and *milky quartz* (white). Quartz veins in metamorphic rocks may yield rich deposits of gold. Mining for gold in the rock is termed quartzmining.

Quasars, or in preferred terminology, quasi-stellar radio-sources, form a new class of astronomical objects, first identified in the period 1960 to 1962. They have enormous energy output, and are at vast distances. Many are strong sources of radio waves and fluctuate in intensity. There is still controversy over the nature of these objects. We presently consider that the intense emission comes from a relatively small region at the centre of peculiar galaxies. While a plausible explanation would be the existence of a gigantic black hole formed by the gravitational collapse of the nucleus of the galaxy, dragging in surrounding material, including entire star systems, our information is not yet conclusive. See **F5.**

Queen Anne's Bounty, established by Queen Anne in 1704 for the augmentation of the maintenance of the poor clergy. Since 1 April 1948 Queen Anne's Bounty and the Ecclesiastical Commissioners ceased to exist and became embodied in the Church Commissioners for England.

Queen's (or King's) Speech is the speech prepared by the Government in consultation with the Queen and delivered by Her Majesty in person or by her deputy, at the opening or closing of a Parliamentary session.

Quinine, a vegetable alkaloid obtained from the bark of several trees of the *Cinchona* genus. It is colourless and extremely bitter. The drug, sulphate of quinine, is one of the most valuable medicines, forming a powerful tonic. It is antiperiodic, antipyretic and antineuralgic. In cases of malaria it is the most efficacious remedy of natural origin known.

Quirinal, one of the seven hills of Rome.

Quisling, term which came into use during the second world war to denote traitor, collaborator or fifth-columnist. After Vidkun Quisling, who became head of the puppet government after the German invasion of Norway in 1940.

Quorum, the number of members of any body or company necessary to be present at any meeting or commission before business can be transacted. The House of Commons needs a quorum of 40, the Lords a quorum of 3.

R

Rabbi, a Jewish term applied to specially ordained officials who pronounce upon questions of legal form and ritual, and also generally accorded to any Jewish scholar of eminence.

Raccoon, plantigrade carnivorous mammals common to the American continent. There are several species. The common Raccoon (*Procyon lotor*) is about 60 cm long, with a bush ringed tail and sharp snout. Its skin is valuable.

Race. In the old text-books anthropologists were much concerned with the differences between the various races of Man; they described the Black Man (Negro), the Yellow Man (Mongol), the Red Man (American Indian), the Brown Man (Indian), and the White Man (European). Those who study Man from this point of view further subdivide each group into others. Thus White Man may be divided into

Nordic, Alpine and Mediterranean; Black Man into Hamitic, Bushman and so on. Each of these groups tends to have physical traits which its members hold in common, although, of course, there are no *pure* racial types. All existing races have been fairly thoroughly mixed. What, in view of recent experience, is really important, is that races or even nations do not have psychological traits—at least not *innate* traits. Anthropology dismisses all theories of a superior race as unscientific: there is not the slightest evidence that one race differs in any way from another in its psychological potentialities; Jews, Irish, Scots, Italians do differ (so do the inhabitants of Edinburgh and London): but their differences are due to their situation and not to anything inborn. See **Racism, Section J.**

Raceme, an inflorescence in which the main stem bears stalked flowers, *e.g.*, lupin, foxglove. The youngest flowers at the tip of this axis.

Radar. The basic principle of radar is very similar to that of sight. We switch on a light in the dark, and we *see* an object because the light waves are reflected from it and return to our eye, which is able to detect them. Similarly, the radar station *sees* an object because the invisible radio waves sent out from the transmitter are reflected from it and return to the receiver, which is able to detect them. Thus radar is the use of radio signals that man broadcasts.

The utilisation of radio waves for the detection of reflecting surfaces began with the classical experiment of the late Sir Edward Appleton in 1925, which he conducted in order to demonstrate the existence of the Heaviside layer in the upper atmosphere. During the course of the last war developments took place which tremendously improved the methods and instruments used. As in the case of so many of the inventions primarily developed for the purpose of waging war, many useful applications have been found for radar in times of peace, and, in particular, it has proved of great service as an aid to aerial and marine navigation, and in meteorology and astronomy. Radar astronomy investigates the solar system with the echoes of signals sent out from the Earth.

Radiation, energy emitted in the form of a beam of rays or waves, *e.g.*, acoustic (sound) radiation from a loudspeaker, radiant heat from a fire, β-radiation from a radioactive substance. The radiation of electromagnetic waves from a body depends on its temperature, the amount of energy radiated per second being proportional to the fourth power of the absolute temperature. The hotter the body, the shorter the wavelengths of the radiation; thus the colour of a glowing body depends on its temperature. Of paramount importance to us is radiation from the sun. Amongst other radiations, the sun sends ultra-violet, visible and infra-red (heat) waves. The principal gases of the atmosphere are transparent to practically all of the solar and sky radiation and also that which the earth re-transmits to space. Carbon dioxide and water vapour, however, strongly absorb certain types, the latter, as clouds, playing an important rôle in regulating the temperature of the globe. The cooling of the ground on a clear night is a result of the outgoing long-wave radiation exceeding that coming down from the sky; at sunrise cooling ceases as the incoming radiation becomes sufficient to compensate for the loss of heat.

Radiation, Cosmic. See **F3(2).**

Radio. The theory of electromagnetic waves—of which the radio wave is one—was originated by the British physicist James Clerk Maxwell (**F14**). He showed that both electrical and optical phenomena in space are essentially similar in character, and that the waves if short in wavelength are those of light, and if of longer wavelength those of radio waves. Heinrich Hertz made many useful discoveries about the waves themselves, and about their behaviour under differing conditions, and also about the apparatus for producing them. Marconi developed the use of radio waves as a practical means of communication.

Radio methods are vital for the transmission of observed data from space vehicles back to earth, a process known as "telemetering". This is done by converting the observations into electrical pulses which actuate a suitable radio transmitter so that it radiates a signal, in coded form, which can be received at a ground station and decoded. The transmission of such a signal can also be remotely controlled by means of signals from the earth. Photographic and television techniques may also be employed for obtaining the desired information and sending it back to earth, as in the case of the Russian picture of the reverse side of the moon and the American pictures of the lunar surface. The information may be stored within the spacecraft for a time, and then, upon receipt of a particular radio signal from the earth transmitted by the spacecraft at a time convenient for its reception. Soviet scientists, by a special technique, were able in the case of their *Venus IV* probe (October 1967) to parachute an instrumented canister from the spacecraft so that it could descend slowly to the surface of the planet—a feat described by Sir Bernard Lovell, who was recording the enterprise at Jodrell Bank, as "an experiment of classic elegance". Another breath-taking achievement was the transformation of the faintest of signals from a billion miles away into superb pictures of the planet Saturn and its rings (*see* **Voyagers 1 and 2**). *See also* **Radio Astronomy, Telemetry.**

Radioactivity is the spontaneous transformation of atomic nuclei, accompanied by the emission of ionising radiations. It was discovered in 1896 by Becquerel, who noticed that salts containing uranium sent off radiations which, like X-rays, can blacken a photographic plate. Two years later Marie and Pierre Curie discovered several new chemical elements which possessed the same property, but many times more intense than uranium; the most important of these was radium. Shortly afterwards it was established, mainly by Rutherford, that three types of radiations called α-, β- and γ-rays, are emitted from radioactive substances. It was also Rutherford who, jointly with Soddy, deduced that the emission of the radiations is associated with the spontaneous disintegration of atoms which result in the transformation of one radioactive substance into another. A series of such transformations ends when a stable element is produced. All of the heavy radio-active elements can be arranged in three radio-active series, called, the uranium, thorium and actinium series. Initially, radioactivity was thought to be a property confined only to a few elements occurring in nature. In 1934, however, Irene and Frederick Joliot-Curie dis-covered that ordinary elements can be trans-formed into radioactive forms by subjecting them to bombardment with α-particles. Following this, it was found that beams of other fast particles produced in accelerators can also render ordinary substances radioactive. Nowadays it is known that radioactivity is a general property of matter; any chemical element can be produced in one or more radio-active forms, or isotopes. *See* **F12(1).**

Radio Astronomy. The science of radio astro-nomy makes use of radio apparatus and tech-niques for the observation of events occurring in far distant parts of the universe, and, in so doing, is able to enlarge upon the observational field of optical astronomy in a remarkable way. By means of radio telescopes it is possible to observe parts of the universe so far distant that the radio waves received have taken thousands of millions of years to travel from their source to the earth, and thus to observe happenings which may have occurred near the beginning of the history of the universe. Thus radio astronomy works with signals that are broad-cast by objects in space.

There are two main types of radio telescope. The first, known as the interferometer, uses aerials spaced at large distances to obtain very high angular resolution. Indeed, the so-called very long baseline interferometers (VLBI) use receivers with separations of many thousands of km to obtain higher resolution than any opti-cal telescope. The second, and "steerable", type, is that of the radio telescope at Jodrell Bank, Cheshire, which consists of an enormous concave metal bowl, with the radio aerials at its centre. This, though it has a lower "reso-lution", can be directed or "steered" on to any part of the sky which is above the horizon. The interferometers, particularly the VLBI, have been used to examine the fine structure of many objects, including the nuclei of large and un-usual galaxies. The jet-like structures recently found in several galaxies are of particular in-terest. As well as exploring the structure of gas clouds and clusters in our own galaxy and in more distant ones, several of the large steer-able telescopes have been used as radar anten-nae, for example to explore the surface of the cloud-covered Venus, and to locate suitable landing sites for the *Viking* spacecraft exploring Mars. Increasingly the radio telescope is used as one of an armoury of instruments available to explore the nature of objects of astronomical interest, such as pulsars or quasars.

Radiocarbon Dating is a method of dating the origin of organic materials or objects by observ-ing their radioactivity. It is of great import-ance to archaeology because it enables pre-historic dates back to about 50,000 B.C. to be established for animal and vegetable remains. It works because cosmic rays (*q.v.*) entering the atmosphere create neutrons which convert nitrogen in the air to radioactive carbon. This forms radioactive carbon dioxide and gets in-corporated into animals and vegetables through-out the world along with ordinary carbon di-oxide in a definite ratio, approximately 1 radio carbon atom to 0.8×10^{12} ordinary carbon atoms. When the tissue dies it stops inter-changing its carbon with the atmosphere, *e.g.*, by breathing, and the radioactive carbon in it gradually turns into nitrogen emitting a β-particle (*see* **F12(1)**). The radiocarbon con-tent decreases by about 1% in 88 years. By measuring the proportion of radioactive carbon left in, say, dead wood, and comparing it with living wood, the age of the dead sample can be calculated. This needs careful laboratory experiments. It is now believed that the pro-portion of radioactive carbon in the atmosphere varied from time to time in the past because changes in the earth's magnetic field affected the cosmic rays. This has to be allowed for in calculating the radiocarbon date. One use of radiocarbon dating has been to trace the spread of agriculture through the world from its origin in the Near East *c.* 7000 B.C. *See also* **Tree rings.**

Radiosonde, a weather station in miniature carried aloft by a free balloon to heights normally in the neighbourhood of 16 km. Signals representa-tive of values of atmospheric pressure, tem-perature and humidity are transmitted sim-ultaneously by radio to ground receiving apparatus. The position of the balloon at any instant can be determined by radar, enabling the speed and direction of the upper winds to be deduced.

Radium, a radioactive metallic element, no. 88, symbol Ra, discovered by Marie and Pierre Curie in 1898. Atomic weight 226. Radiotherapy (use of X-rays from radium) is used in the treatment of cancer.

Radon, a radioactive gaseous element, no. 86, symbol Rn, formed by radioactive decay of radium. Its discovery completed the series of ele-ments known as the inert (or rare) gases.

Rain. When moist air rises into lower tempera-tures and becomes saturated, condensation takes place on the numerous hygroscopic par-ticles present in the atmosphere. If the tem-perature is above freezing a cloud of small droplets is formed. These droplets may then grow larger by coalescing with each other as they pass through the cloud until their weight is great enough to make them fall to the earth as rain. In clouds which extend above freezing level, snow and rain both form from the prefer-ential growth of ice crystals at the expense of liquid water droplets. If the resultant ice particle melts as it falls to earth, it gives rain: if not it gives snow. *See also* **Acid Rain.**

Rainbow, a beautiful colour effect visible to an ob-server with back to the sun and facing a rain shower, caused by the refraction and reflection of sunlight in minute water-droplets in the air. From high in the air it would be possible to see a rainbow as a complete circle, but from the ground the most that can be seen is a semi-circle when the sun is just on the horizon; the higher the sun is, the smaller the arc of the rainbow. When conditions are suitable two bows are seen, the secondary with the colours of the spectrum reversed. The colours the rainbow are seven; red, orange, yellow, green, blue, indigo and violet—the colours of the spectrum. See *also* **Aurora.**

Raingauge, an instrument consisting of a deep metal funnel whose stem dips into a graduated glass jar from which the depth of the rain water collected can be read. Continuous records of rainfall are provided by self-registering instruments.

Rain Making is a facility long desired by mankind, especially in the drought-ridden regions, and attempted throughout history by numerous non-scientific means. Since the second world war it has been proved that clouds can sometimes be made to rain or snow by dropping into them from an aeroplane very cold particles of solid carbon dioxide or by burning a solution containing silver iodide. This makes the moisture of the cloud form tiny ice crystals which grow big and finally fall out of the cloud. The process is quite complicated and not fully understood. The practical exploitation is somewhat chancy at present, but experiments have been made in many countries and the United States has a considerable programme of study. As well as scientific there are commercial and legal problems; premature commercial exploitation has resulted in disillusionment in some cases.

Rambouillet, a royal French château (14th cent., rebuilt 18th cent.), near Paris, and the official summer residence of the President of the French Republic. Also the name of the famous literary salon of the Marquise de Rambouillet (1588-1665).

Rampant, in heraldry, is a term applied to the figure of an animal with forelegs elevated, the dexter uppermost. When the animal is shown side-faced it is *rampant displayed*, when full-face, *rampant guardant*; when looking back *rampant reguardant*; and when in sitting position *rampant sejant*.

Rape, a cruciferous plant yielding coleseed or rape-seed, extensively grown in all parts of Europe and India. Rape oil is made from the seeds and as oilcake is a valuable animal feeding-stuff.

Rare Gases (also called **Inert Gases**). These are a group of elements which are chemically inert, comprising helium, neon, argon, krypton, xenon and radon. Cavendish in 1785 noticed that there was in air some gas which was not oxygen, nitrogen or carbon dioxide, but it was not until 1894 that the first of the rare gases was found by Rayleigh and Ramsay. This they called argon (inert). After the discovery of helium in 1895 Kayser, Rayleigh and Travers soon isolated the other gases except radon, which was later detected as a radioactive decay product of radium. Some of these inert gases are used to fill electric-light bulbs, and helium is used in balloons, since it is very light and non-imflammable.

Rat, a well-known group of rodent embracing many species. The *brown rat* appeared in Europe early in the 18th cent., coming from the East and entering by way of Russia; now it is widespread and met with in Britain and all parts of the Continent. The *black rat*, which was the common rat before the arrival of the brown species, is a smaller animal and now comparatively scarce. There are numerous other kinds, all of them gross feeders, and existing in such numbers in many places as to constitute a pest.

Rational Number, a number which can be expressed as a ratio of two whole numbers. Examples are 2, $\frac{1}{4}$, 0·3, − 8. *See* Irrational Number.

Rationalism. *See* Section J.

Rattlesnake, venomous snakes which obtain their name from the possession of a rattle in the end of their tail, consisting of horny pieces so arranged that when vibrated they make a rattling sound. They are only found in N. and S. America.

Raven, a black-plumaged bird of the crow family, with raucous voice and massive bill. Occurs in many parts of Europe, Asia and America. Ravens are easily domesticated and form interesting pets.

Dickens had one which he described in *Barnaby Rudge*.

Ray, fish with a very flat body and broad and fleshy pectoral fins, related to the sharks. There are about 140 species. In Britain they are generally called *skate.*

Razorbill, a sea-bird of the auk family, having a high, furrowed bill and black-and-white plumage. It inhabits rocky cliffs during the breeding season, and at other times is mostly out on the open sea.

Realism is a vague term. As a movement in art it can be said to have started with Gustave Courbet in the mid-19th cent. in his revolt against the classicism of Ingres and the romanticism of Delacroix. He was a man of strong radical views, and like Zola, Balzac and Flaubert in literature, turned to the actuality of everyday life, recording it with frankness and vigour. Some young English painters, notably Bratby, of the "kitchen sink" school, practise what some describe as social realism. In another sense, realism is an attitude concerned with interpreting the essential nature of the subject, revealing truths hidden by the accidentals of ordinary visual appearance. Thus form becomes more significant than content. Beginning with Cézanne and Van Gogh this trend passes on to Cubist and Abstract painting. *See also* **Section J** (philosophy).

Record Office, in Chancery Lane, London, the place where the Public Records of England are preserved, including Domesday Book. More modern records are held at Kew.

Rectifier, an electrical device which will allow electric current to flow in one direction only and can therefore be used for turning alternating current into direct current. Since electricity is usually supplied in alternating form and frequently needed in direct form, rectifiers are of very common use in both industry and the home, for example in radio and television and for battery chargers. Rectifying properties are possessed by a number of different devices, one of which is a thermionic diode (*see* **Valve**). Very large valves filled with mercury vapour are often used for rectifying heavy currents for industrial purposes. Many other rectifiers use semiconductors in close contact with metals or with other semiconductors because such junctions have the property of passing electric current easily only in one direction.

Recusants, people who refused to attend the Anglican Church or to acknowledge the ecclesiastical supremacy of the Crown in the 16th and 17th cent.

Recycling, the process of sorting and re-using waste products. By no means a new idea, and already much used in industry and by the whole community in war-time, recycling assumes prominence when materials are scarce and prices high. There is much evidence from several countries that the public responds well to properly organised schemes for the collection, sorting and re-use of paper, plastic, glass, metals and other waste products common in industrialised countries. An officially commended scheme is operated by the charity Oxfam.

Redstart, a small bird of the Thrush family of handsome plumage and striking song. Two species visit Great Britain: the Common Redstart, with bright chestnut rump and tail, white forehead and black cheeks, favours wooded country, and the Black Redstart, with black breast and throat, chestnut tail and white wing bars, prefers rocky ground or ruins, and breeds in S. England.

Redwing, a bird of the Thrush family which finds its way to this country for the winter. Resembles the song thrush, but distinguished by smaller size, buffish-white eye-stripe, chestnut flanks and underwings. It has bred in Scotland and on Fair Isle.

Redwood *or* **Sequoia.** This genus of coniferous tree comprises two species of Redwoods occuring in N.W. America. Specimens of one species, the Giant Redwood, reach a height of over 90 m and a thickness of 11 m. The age of the largest, the General Sherman tree, is put at 3,500 years.

Referendum and Initiative, two methods by which the wishes of electors may be expressed with regard to proposed legislation. It is developed to the highest extent in Switzerland. In a *Referendum* some specific matter is referred to the electors. The *Initiative* is the means by which electors can compel their representatives to consider a specific issue. Gen. de Gaulle made use of the referendum in seeking the consent of the French nation for his policies. The British Labour Government held a referendum in June 1975, asking voters whether they felt the nation should remain in or withdraw from the European Economic Community. An Act of Parliament was required to authorise the referendum (which was something new in British constitutional history), and a further Act would have been necessary if the majority had been in favour of withdrawal. The result was for continued membership.

Reformation. *See* Section J.

Reform Bills. The principal Bills have been passed for the reform of the Parliamentary franchise. The first was the great Reform Bill of 1832, introduced by Lord John Russell and enacted under the Whig administration of Lord Grey. In addition to a sweeping redistribution of seats, this Act greatly extended the franchise but still left many people without the right to vote. The second Bill, passed by Disraeli in 1867, by giving the vote to workers in towns, established household suffrage. A third Bill, passed in 1884 under a Gladstone ministry, removed the distinction between borough and county franchise, enfranchised agricultural workers, and thus gave the vote to all men over 21. Women had to wait until 1918 to get the vote at the age of 30. The Representation of the People (Equal Franchise) Act, 1928, gave them the right to be registered as Parliamentary electors at the age of 21, thus making England into a true democracy. The Representation of the People Act, 1948, abolished the representation of the universities and the separate representation of the City of London and the business-premises vote. The Representation of the People Act, 1969, reduced the minimum voting age from 21 to 18 at both parliamentary and local government elections.

Refraction. The change of direction which light rays undergo when passing from one medium to another. The phenomenon is due to the fact that in different media light (and other forms of radiation) has different speeds.

Refractory, a substance capable of standing high temperatures and therefore useful for making furnaces and allied apparatus. Some insulating refractories are fire-clay, alumina, porcelain, carborundum, graphite and silica. Some refractory metals are platinum, molybdenum, tungsten, tantalum and the alloys nichrome, chromel, alumel.

Regency Style is the English version of the French Empire *(q.v.)* and approximately covers the period of the regency of Prince George, later George IV, from 1810 to 1820. It is somewhat less austere than the French style, and contains elements of the fantastic and exotic absent from Empire. The most famous monument of Regency style is the Royal Pavilion at Brighton, built for the Prince Regent by John Nash. (Regency style should not be confused with the *Régence* style in France, fashionable during the regency period between the death of Louis XIV in 1715 and the ascent to the throne of Louis XV in 1723. Here the English equivalent is Queen Anne style.)

Reindeer, a genus of deer horned in both sexes, occurring only in northerly regions. It has an average height of 1·3 m, is very fleet of foot and the Laplanders utilise it for draught purposes and for food.

Relativity. The laws of relativity have been substantially proved and have revolutionised our ideas as to the nature of space, time, matter and energy and forced us to think along new lines. In 1949 a new theory by Einstein was announced which sets forth in a series of equations the laws governing both gravitation and electromagnetism, which is said to bridge the gap that separates the universe of the stars and galaxies and the universe of the atom. At present the one is explained by relativity, and the other rests on the quantum theory. *See* **F17–19.**

Relief in sculpture is of three kinds—high relief (*alto-relievo*), in which the figures stand out to the extent of one-half of their natural proportions, low-relief (*basso-relievo*) when the figures project but slightly; and middle-relief (*mezzo-relievo*), when the projection is intermediate.

Renaissance. *See* **Section J.**

Republican Party of the United States was born by the fusion in 1854 of the group who called themselves National Republicans, having split from the Democrats over tariffs in 1825, and the northern Democrats, both of them being opposed to slavery. It came to power when Abraham Lincoln was elected President in 1860 and won 14 of the 18 presidential elections held between 1860 and 1932. It was defeated in 1932 largely as a result of the economic depression and reached its lowest ebb in the years of Roosevelt's New Deal (*q.v.*) The Party went on being defeated every four years until Eisenhower's victory in 1952. Nixon narrowly failed to defeat Kennedy in 1960 and Goldwater was decisively beaten by Lyndon Johnson in 1964. In 1968 and again in 1972 Nixon was successful in winning the Presidency. His fall from power in the aftermath of Watergate made 1974 a bad year for the Republican Party. In 1980 and again in 1984, Ronald Reagan won landslide victories over the Democratic Party. The symbol of the Party is an elephant, the invention of Thomas Nast, a cartoonist, in 1874.

Requiem. Properly a mass for the dead, the term is extended to cover musical settings by Palestrina, Mozart, Verdi and others.

Reredos, the ornamental screen at the back of the altar or communion table. It is often of a highly decorative character and is an architectural feature in many churches in Spain. Other examples are to be found in the following cathedrals in England: Southwark, St. Albans, Winchester, Durham and Liverpool.

Resins, natural resins are vegetable compounds largely employed in the industrial arts. They comprise india-rubber, amber, mastic, copal, etc. "Synthetic resins" is a term sometimes used as a synonym for "plastics".

Reuter, an international news agency, organised since 1941 as a trust and owned by the newspapers of Britain, Australia and New Zealand, founded by Baron J. de Reuter in 1849.

Rhea, a large flightless bird, the "ostrich" of S. America, distinguished from the ostrich proper by smaller size, longer beak, larger wings, no tail and 3 toes instead of 2. There are 2 species.

Rheology, science of flow. *See* **F21(1).**

Rhesus Factor. *See* **Index to Section P.**

Rhinoceros, a large almost hairless animal related to the horse. Two kinds in Africa and several others in Asia. They have a horn, sometimes two, over the snout composed of modified hair. Most are leaf eaters but the largest species, the white rhino of South Africa, is a grazer. Rhinoceroses have been much hunted for their horns, which are reputed to have curative and aphrodisiac properties.

Rhodium, a metallic element, no. 45, symbol Rh, discovered by Wollaston in 1804. It is found in platinum ores in small amounts, generally less than 2 per cent. With platinum it gives a very hard and durable alloy. It is also used, instead of silver, in putting the reflecting layer on a mirror.

Ribbon Fish *or* **Oarfish,** a deep-sea fish, deriving its name from its ribbon-like shape. Though fairly long, it is only a few centimetres thick. The ribbon fish is rarely met with because of its habitat, and most of what is known about it has been learnt from specimens occasionally cast ashore during storms.

Rice, a grain-yielding grass, of which thousands of strains are known today, extensively cultivated in China, India and certain parts of America, and forming the main food of the peoples of China, Japan, India and S.E. Asia. Some 95 per cent. of the world's rice is produced and consumed in the Orient. The grain with the husk is known as "paddy". Arrack, an alcoholic liquor, is made from fermented rice seeds.

Richter Scale, a series of numbers used to record the relative magnitude of earthquakes. Devised by F. Richter of the California Institute of Technology. An earthquake is given a number on the scale by measuring the amplitude of earth movements, *i.e.*, the size of the to and fro motion in an earthquake wave, with a special instrument called a seismometer. The reading is corrected by calculation to allow for the distance of the instrument from the earthquake and the corrected results by observers at different places agree quite well. The scale is logarithmic, *i.e.*, earthquakes differing by one unit on the Richter scale are a factor 10 different in amplitude. An earthquake allotted zero on the scale would give a reading of 10^{-9} m on a standard seismometer 100 km from the centre of the earthquake. Smaller disturbances would have negative values on the scale. The largest known earthquakes had Richter values between $+8$ and $+9$, *i.e.*, they had 10^{+8} to 10^{+9} bigger amplitudes than earthquakes of magnitude zero. It is a widespread misconception that the scale has an upper limit of 10; there are no upper or lower limits to the scale.

Rime, a crystalline deposit of ice formed on objects exposed to wet fog at the same time as frost.

Rinderpest *or* **Cattle Plague,** is a highly contagious disease affecting cattle, sheep and other ruminants. In Europe the disease has been eradicated, but it was formerly very widespread and caused great loss of life among cattle. The disease is caused by a filtrable virus, and is attended by fever and congestion of the mucous membranes.

Ring Dove *or* **Wood Pigeon,** a blue-grey bird, distinguished from other pigeons by larger size (41 cm), white wing-bar, glossy green-and-purple neck and white half-collar. It is very common in Britain.

Rituale, the book of rites used in the Roman Catholic Church for the administration of certain sacraments and other church ceremonies. Like the Roman breviary, it dates in its present form from the Council of Trent.

RNA (Ribonucleic Acid). *See* Nucleic Acids.

Roaring Forties, name applied to the prevailing westerly winds over the oceans in the temperate latitudes of the Southern Hemisphere. Because unimpeded by large land areas the winds are more regular and stronger than the westerlies in the Northern Hemisphere.

Robin (or Redbreast). A small bird with olive-brown upper parts and orange-red forehead, throat and breast; both sexes look alike. The young are speckled, lacking the red breast. Its wide European distribution includes the British Isles, where it is the national bird. It also occurs in N. Africa and W. Asia. The nest is placed in a great variety of situations including holes in banks, trees and walls; in sheds, amongst ivy and sometimes in old tins. Nesting-boxes are readily adopted, but care should be taken to ensure that the entrance-hole is small enough to exclude starlings. Robins are pugnacious and defend their territories with vigour. Their attractive appearance, trustful disposition, engaging ways and sweet song make them extremely popular. The name robin is also applied to a number of very different birds, one of which, the American Robin, occasionally wanders to Europe.

Rock Dove, the grey pigeon *Columbia livia* of Europe and Asia, ancestor of the domestic pigeons as Darwin was the first to show.

Rockets for use in war were first studied by Sir William Congreve early in the 19th cent., and proved very destructive in siege operations. They were invented by the Chinese as long ago as the 11th cent. The Germans devised the huge V2 rocket, carrying a ton of explosive, which was used near the end of the war to bombard London. Rockets are propelled by the burning of fuel (*e.g.*, oxygen or nitric acid), the exhaust, being ejected at high velocity, thrusts the rocket forward. For the study of the properties of the atmosphere vertical sounding rockets are used. Rocket flight in outer space was first presented as practicable by the Russian rocket expert, K. E. Tsiolkovsky, in 1903. The provision of sufficient launching velocity involves the use of rocket motors with adequate thrust. To launch a satellite into an orbit circulating within a few hundred kilometres of the surface a velocity of 29,000 km/h must be imparted. This may be done by using a multi-stage launching system. When the first-stage

motor has burned out it drops off, so that, when the second-stage motor ignites, it does not have to support the weight of the first-stage, and so on. If the launching velocity is increased to 40,000 km/h the vehicle will not return to the neighbourhood of the earth but pass out of the range of the earth's gravitational pull completely. Unless the launching velocity reaches 161,000 km/h it will not escape from the sun and will become an artificial planet. *See also* **Space Research.**

Rock Magnetism. The study of naturally occurring magnetism in rocks is a subject which has gained considerable importance in recent years. There are two principal reasons for this. One is that this so-called "fossilised magnetism" may be able to tell us more about the past history of the earth's magnetic field. The other is that after many years of heated dispute between geologists rock magnetism promises to settle once and for all the controversy as to whether or not the continents have changed their relative positions in past times (continental drift theory (*q.v.*)). This branch of geophysical research, in addition to its academic interest, may well have important economic consequences. It might, for instance, become possible to locate mineral deposits once accumulated under special conditions at certain latitudes but now drifted to other places. Salt and similar deposits formed by the continuous evaporation of solutions in hot countries are one example; oil may well be another. There has been a *steady* change in rock magnetisation direction with geological time. It is now known with some accuracy that the most recent reversal took place 700,000 years ago. It has been found that the older the rock, the farther removed is its fossil magnetisation from the present field.

Rococo, an architectural style which was, in effect, the final stage of **Baroque** (*q.v.*). The name first came into use about 1830 to describe the period 1720-70 and means "shell-shaped" (French *Rocaille*), since the shell was a favourite motif in Rococo ornamentation. At about the beginning of the 18th cent. the heavy older type of Baroque began to show even less restraint than had characterised it in the past; it became still less utilitarian, and showed a kind of playful lighthearted vitality which manifested itself in a wealth of ornamental invention. Baroque was flamboyant and robust, Rococo dainty, graceful and smiling. Its ornaments are frequently asymmetrical, and in this Rococo is unique among the historical styles of Europe. In architecture Rococo is naturally found in those areas where the Baroque had flourished, *i.e.*, Munich, Prague, Vienna and Dresden. In painting, the best expressions of Rococo are to be seen in the works of the French painters Watteau (d. 1721), Boucher (d. 1770), a favourite of Mme de Pompadour, and famous as a decorator of boudoirs, and Fragonard (d. 1806). (As in the case of Baroque, it was typical of Rococo that the sculpture, painting and the decorative arts of a building all expressed the same spirit.)

Roe, popular name given to organs in fish which produce eggs and sperms. "Hard roe" is that of the female and consists of eggs; that of the male is the soft roe or milt.

Roe Deer (*Capreolus capreolus*) deer native to Europe and found in England and Scotland but not Ireland. "Roebuck" is the name of the male adult.

Roller, a tropical Old World bird of the *Coraciidae* family, related to the hoopoe, kingfisher and bee-eater, of strikingly brilliant blue, chestnut, greenish-blue plumage. There are fifteen species, one of which breeds in the far north and visits the British Isles on its migrations to and from its winter quarters in Africa.

Romanesque Architecture, prevailed throughout Europe from the mid-10th to the 13th cent., and implies an art which developed from that of the Romans. Notable in Romanesque style were the rounded arch and masonry vaulting. Romanesque led to the graceful and more complex Gothic (*q.v.*). The Italians never regarded Gothic highly and Romanesque churches, generally based on the basilican plan (oblong with double colonnades and a semi-circular apse at the end), continued to be built there until the beginning of the 15th cent. Some of the best examples can be seen at Pisa (11th cent.), Florence (San Miniato, 1013), Lucca (12th cent.) and Milan (the 12th cent. San Ambrogio, most famous of all). In Germany Romanesque architure flourished longer than in France or England; the most famous churches are in the valley of the Rhine, at Cologne (completely destroyed during the second world war), Mainz and Speyer. In France Romanesque churches are found in Burgundy, Provence and Normandy. For English Romanesque see **Norman Architecture.**

Roman Roads, highways constructed by the Romans. They were of great durability. The best known British roads were Ermine Street (London, Lincoln, York), Fosse Way (Lincoln through Leicester, Cirencester, Bath, Exeter), Watling Street (Channel Ports, London to Shropshire).

Romanticism, a term for a movement in the arts—whether in music, painting, sculpture or literature—which seeks to give expression to the artist's feelings about his subject rather than to be concerned with form or reality. The romantic view is that art is nature seen through a temperament; the realist view is that art is a slice of life. In painting Delacroix (1798–1863) is the romantic artist *par excellence* with his uncontrolled expression of the passions and love of the exotic. In literature the Romantic movement reached its finest form in the works of Goethe, Schiller and Heine; in the poetry of Byron, Keats, Wordsworth, Shelley and Blake; and in the writings of Victor Hugo. Since Romanticism is partly a matter of temperament in the artist just as Classicism is, it may be found at all times and places, although whether or not it becomes predominant depends on contemporary taste. Cubism, for example, with its attention to form is classical whereas Surrealism with its attention to content is romantic. See also **Romantic Movement, Section J.**

Roman Walls were built as frontier barriers under the Emperors Hadrian (76–138) and Antoninus Pius (86–161). Hadrian's works, linking Wall-send-on-Tyne with Bowness-on-Solway, comprised a twenty-foot stone wall, ditches, turrets, "milecastles", fortresses and a double earthen mound, or "Vallum". Impressive ruins are still visible at Chesters and Housesteads. Antoninus Pius, Hadrian's successor, made a further advance, but the turf wall which he built between Forth and Clyde was soon abandoned. Septimius Severus (146–211) restored Hadrian's wall after the assassination of Commodus and the subsequent civil wars. It was finally abandoned between 380 and 390. Archaeologists from Lancaster University have recently excavated the Roman fort of Ravenglass (Roman Glannaventa) on the Cumbrian coast and believe it to have been built as an extension to Hadrian's wall.

Rood Screen, an ornamental partition, separating the choir from the nave in a church, and supporting a crucifix or rood.

Rook, a member of the crow family, abounding in most parts of the British Isles and found in Europe, Asia and N. Africa. It has been introduced into New Zealand. Rooks usually nest in colonies in tall trees. They are highly intelligent birds, and their ways have long been the subject of much careful study.

Rosary, a circular chain of beads, used by Catholics when reciting a particular form of prayer. Each bead represents an entire prayer, and the combined prayers constitute the Rosary.

Roses, Wars of the (1455–85), between the rival houses of York and Lancaster, for the possession of the English crown, began in the reign of Henry VI and ended with the death of Richard III on Bosworth Field. The emblem or badge of the Lancastrians was the red rose and of the Yorkists the white rose. All rivalry between The Roses ended by the marriage of Henry VII, the Lancastrian, with the Princess Elizabeth, daughter of Edward IV, the Yorkist.

Rosetta Stone, discovered in 1799 by the French at Rosetta in Egypt, and deposited in the British Museum. It is a piece of black basalt about 91 cm long, and contains a decree of the Egyptian priests of Ptolemy V Epiphanes (205–181 B.C.)

in (1) hieroglyphics, (2) demotic and (3) Greek characters. It was the three different inscriptions on the same stone that enabled hieroglyphic writing to be deciphered.

Rotten Row, a corruption of *route de roi* (king's drive), the famous riding resort in Hyde Park.

Rouge et Noir, a well-known gambling card game played on a table divided into two sections and marked with two black and two red lozenges. Any number of players can take part, and the money is staked on the red or black spaces. The cards are dealt out, first to Noir, until the pips aggregate more than 30; then in like manner to the Rouge, and the packet coming nearest to 31 wins the stakes.

Roulette, a gambling game played on a table carrying a revolving wheel divided into 37 compartments. Each compartment bears a number, 0 (zero) and 1 to 36. The numbers are mixed and do not follow any particular order. Of these 37 numbers 18 are black and 18 are red, whereas zero is green. The players stake their money on any compartment, colour or combination of numbers they please. The wheel is whirled round and a ball is set rolling in the opposite direction, dropping finally into one of the compartments, thus deciding the winning number and colour.

Roundhead. In the reign of Charles I and later, a Puritan or member of the Parliamentary party who wore his hair cut short. It was originally a term of derision applied by the Royalists, who usually wore ringlets.

Round Towers, high circular towers with conical roof and massive masonry walls, built during the early Middle Ages (c. 10th cent.). It is believed that they served as refuges and lookouts. These buildings are numberous in Ireland, and three remain in Scotland, including that at Brechin which is attached to the church.

Royal Academy of Arts was founded in London in 1768, under the patronage of George III. The early exhibitions of the Academy were held first in Pall Mall, and later in Somerset House where the exhibitions continued to be held until 1836, when the National Gallery being built, the Academy moved its quarters to that building. In 1869 the present Royal Academy at Burlington House was opened. List of presidents: Sir Joshua Reynolds (1768), Benjamin West (1792), James Wyatt (1805), B. West (1806), Sir Thomas Lawrence (1820), Sir M. A. Shee (1830), Sir C. Eastlake (1850), Sir F. Grant (1866), Lord Leighton, (1878), Sir J. E. Millais (1896), Sir E. J. Poynter (1896), Sir Aston Webb (1919), Sir F. Dicksee (1924), Sir William Llewellyn (1928), Sir E. Lutyens (1938), Sir A. J. Munnings (1944), Sir Gerald F. Kelly (1949), Sir A. E. Richardson (1954), Sir Charles Wheeler (1956), Sir Thomas Monnington (1966), Sir Hugh Casson (1976) and Roger de Grey (1984). The Academy holds an exhibition of pictures, statuary and architectural designs every summer.

Royal Hospital, Chelsea, built by Wren, was opened in 1694 as an institution for invalid soldiers.

Royal Institution, established 1799, and incorporated by Royal Charter in 1800 for "the promotion, extension and diffusion of Science and of Useful Knowledge". It was in the building of the Institution that Faraday conducted his experiments. Today it has extensive research laboratories. Famous also for its Christmas lectures designed for a juvenile audience.

Royal Society was founded in 1660 and incorporated by Royal Charter in 1662. Viscount Brouncker being named the first president. Its *Philosophical Transactions* date from 1665. Among those who served as president of the Royal Society are Sir Christopher Wren, Pepys, Sir Isaac Newton, Sir Joseph Banks, Sir Humphry Davy, Prof. T. H. Huxley, Lord Rayleigh, Sir Archibald Geikie, Sir J. J. Thomson, O.M., Prof. Sir C. Sherrington, O.M., G.B.E., Lord Rutherford, O.M., Sir William Henry Bragg, O.M., Sir Henry Dale, O.M., Sir Robert Robinson, O.M., Lord Adrian, O.M., Sir Cyril Hinshelwood, O.M., Lord Florey, O.M., Lord Blackett O.M. (1965), Sir Alan Hodgkin, O.M. (1970), Lord Todd O.M. (1975), Sir Andrew Huxley (1980).

Rubber, substance obtained from the milky juice (latex) exuded by certain tropical trees and shrubs after tapping. Demand spread so rapidly in the 19th cent. that plantations were established wherever the tree would grow. Seeds of the Para rubber tree (*Hevea brasiliensis*) native to the Amazon basin were obtained by Kew, the young plants shipped to Ceylon and it was from these cultivated trees that the vast plantations of Malaysia and Indonesia developed. Recent years have seen great advances in the production of synthetic rubber.

Rubicon, a small river falling into the Adriatic, and forming one of the Italian boundaries, the crossing of which anciently involved decisive action and constituted a declaration of war. Thus the phrase "crossing the Rubicon", denoting an act from which there is no withdrawal.

Rubidium, a metallic element, no. 37, symbol Rb, most closely resembling potassium. It is silver-white and very soft, and was discovered in 1861 by Bunsen and Kirchhoff, using the spectroscope. It is rare, occurring in small amounts in the mica called lepidolite and in potash salts of the Stassfurt deposits in Germany.

Rubrics are instructions in regard to the ceremonies of the Church, appearing in red in the Prayer Book.

Ruby is a deep red variety of Corundum (aluminium oxide); one of the most valued of precious stones. Burma yields some of the finest, and rubies of inferior colour are found in Thailand, Sri Lanka, South Africa and Brazil.

Rudd, a fresh-water fish of wide distribution, plentiful in the rivers of Britain. It is of a reddish-gold colour, with a greenish-blue beard.

Ruff, a bird related to the common sandpiper, at one time common in the Fen districts. The males have a ruff of feathers round the neck in the breeding season. The female is the Reeve.

Ruffe or **Pope,** a small fresh-water fish common in most parts of central Europe, and similar in appearance to the ordinary perch. It is found in British rivers.

"Rule, Britannia!" the national sea-song of England, was written by James Thomson (1700–48), the author of the "Seasons", and set to music by Dr. Arne about 1740. The poet's words were "Britannia, rule the waves!" but it is usually rendered "Britannia rules the waves."

Rum, a ardent spirit distilled from molasses, and containing from 40 to 50 per cent. of alcohol. It is chiefly manufactured in the West Indies, and derives its special flavour from a volatile oil.

Ruminants, animals that chew the cud, being provided with a compartmented stomach, enabling them to swallow food, and later to bring it back to the mouth for mastication; *e.g.*, sheep, goats, oxen, etc. While in the rumen, or storage compartment, some digestion of food, especially cellulose, takes place by bacterial action.

Runcible spoon, a kind of fork used for pickles having three broad prongs. The word was used by Edward Lear about 1870 as a nonsense word and may be derived from *Rouncival* meaning large or huge from the bones said to have been dug up at *Roncesvalles* where Roland fell. Rouncival peas are the large peas called "marrowfats".

Runes, certain characters of an alphabet found in inscriptions in the Germanic languages, found cut into buildings and implements of stone or wood in many parts of northern Europe, including Britain. The runic alphabet originally had 24 letters. Scholars agree that some of the runes derive from Greek and others from Latin.

Ruskin College, the first residential college for working people, founded at Oxford in 1899 by Mr. Walter Vrooman, an American.

Rusts, parasitic fungi, some common species of which have reddish spores which in a mass have a rusty appearance. A well-known species is the Wheat Rust (*Puccinia graminis*), which has an alternative host in the barberry.

Ruthenium, a greyish-white metallic element, no. 44, symbol Ru, discovered by Claus in 1845. It is harder and more brittle than platinum, in whose ores it occurs.

Rutile, mineral titanium dioxide. It is found in many igneous rocks, and in gneisses and schists, Its commonest colour is reddish-brown.

S

Sabaoth, a Hebrew word, meaning an army or host, and applied sometimes to the Supreme Being, *e.g.*, "the Lord of Hosts" (Rom. ix. 29).

Sabbath and Sunday. Sunday, or the Lord's Day, is the first day of the week in the Christian year. It was substituted for the Jewish Sabbath in the 1st cent. A.D. as the Christian day of worship in commemoration of the Resurrection. The Sabbath, in the Jewish system, was the last day of the week (Saturday in the Christian calendar), designated as the day of religious rest in the fourth commandment of the Decalogue. It was the Puritans at the time of the Reformation who applied the term Sabbath to the Christian Sunday and the two terms have been used indiscriminately ever since.

Sabbatical Year was instituted by the Jews in ancient times for the purpose of giving the soil a rest from cultivation. This was every seventh year. In universities a sabbatical year is a year of absence from duty for the purpose of study and travel, granted to professors at certain intervals.

Sable, a furred mammal of the weasel family mainly inhabiting Siberia. It is bright brown in colour, and has a long, bushy tail. American sable is a marten.

Saccharin, a white crystalline solid manufactured from toluene, 550 times as sweet as cane sugar. It is used as a sweetening agent; as a substitute for sugar when sugar is forbidden, as in certain diseases, or when there is a shortage. It has no value as a food.

Safety Lamp, as used in coal-mines, was invented by Sir Humphry Davy in 1816. The flame is enclosed in a cage of fine-meshed wire which allows air to enter and promote burning, but conducts away the heat generated in combustion so that no product of combustion escapes at a temperature high enough to ignite explosive gases in the mine.

Sainfoin, a widely cultivated forage plant, especially adapted for sheep. It is of strong, leafy growth and bears bright red flowers. It belongs to the same family of flowering plants as peas and beans.

St. Elmo's Fire, a glowing brush-like discharge of electricity which takes place from sharp-pointed objects on mountains or the masts of ships exposed to the intense electric fields of thunder-clouds.

Saints' Days. In the liturgy of the Roman Catholic church a saint is commemorated and his intercession sought on a special day (saint's day), usually the anniversary of his death. Pope Paul decreed that from 1 January 1970 the following saints were to be dropped from the calendar; Christopher, Catherine of Alexandria, Alexis, Pudenzia, Susan, Margaret, Viviana, Eustace, Martina, Venantius and Domitilla. Many others, including our own Saint George, and Nicholas (Santa Claus) have been demoted though they may be venerated locally. There are now only 153 saints' days in addition to those in honour of the Apostles, Saint Joseph and the Virgin Mary. The festival of All Saints is on 1 November.

Salamanders are amphibia superficially resembling lizards, from which they differ in having a moist skin and no scales.

Salic Law was probably instituted in France in the 5th cent. for the purpose of excluding females from inheriting the Crown. The Bourbons introduced the same law into Spain, but this was abolished by decree in 1830 to enable Isabella II to succeed.

Salmon, a fish notable for its habit of returning from the sea to spawn in the river where it was itself hatched. Their origin can be inferred from the chemical composition of certain blood proteins. Salmon from the two sides of the Atlantic migrate to communal feeding grounds off Greenland.

Saltpetre. *See* **Nitre.**

Salvarsan, the organic arsenical compound asphenamine, which Ehrlich discovered was able to kill inside the human body the spirochaete germ that causes syphilis. Also known as "606". It has been superseded by neosalvarsan.

Salvation Army. *See* Section J.

Samarium, metallic element, no. 62, symbol Sm, one of the lanthanides (**L72**).

San Andreas Fault, is the dividing line between the North American plate and the North Pacific Ocean plate where "plate" means one of the rigid sections of the earth's crust as conceived in the theory of plate tectonics (*q.v.*). The fault runs roughly north-west-south-east in California passing near San Francisco. The Pacific Ocean bed and the North American continent are sliding past each other along this fault at about 5 cm per year. As at all plate-to-plate boundaries—another is the Western Pacific coast—the San Andreas fault is the scene of great earthquake activity. Between 1934 and 1970 there were over 7,000 earthquakes severer than magnitude 4 on Richter scale (*q.v.*) in and near southern California. Because of large population centres, the activity of San Andreas region is studied with great care and some apprehension about a repeat of the San Francisco earthquake of 1906 which caused displacements of up to 6·4 m along the San Andreas Fault. *See also* **F9**.

Sandering, small wading bird of sandpiper family; breeds in tundra regions of far north, and is seen on sandy beaches of Britain as a winter visitor. Conspicuous white wing stripe and, like Curlew, Sandpiper, Knot, Dunlin and other members of sandpiper family, has marked change of plumage between winter and summer.

Sandpiper, small- to medium-sized wading birds of several species whose migratory powers are so great that they are found in most parts of the world. They include the Common Sandpiper, a bird about 18 cm long, greenish-brown head and back, white under-parts; beak long and slender. Purple, Wood and Curlew-Sandpipers.

Sans-culottes (French = without knee breeches), a term applied by the French aristocrats to the revolutionary leaders during the French Revolution who wore long trousers instead of knee breeches.

Sanskrit is the language of ancient India, spoken by the Brahmins, and existing in early Oriental literature. It was the language of literature and government and is now confined to temples and places of learning. Its relationship to the modern Indian languages is rather like that of Latin and Greek to modern European languages.

Saponin. The term is a generic one applied to a range of organic compounds which produce frothy, soapy solutions. Saponins are extracted from the soapwort root, horse chestnut seeds, etc. Saponin is the basis of the "foam" used for fire fighting; it can be used like soap to make insecticides and fungicides adhere to the leaves of plants. Also used as detergents.

Sapphic Verse, a form of verse said to have been invented by Sappho, the lyric poetess of Lesbos, who flourished about 600 B.C.

Sapphire, a valuable deep blue variety of Corundum (aluminium oxide) found mostly in India, Sri Lanka and Northern Italy. Synthetic sapphire is often used for gramophone styli.

Saracen, the name given in classic times to the Arab tribes of Syria and adjacent territories. In the Middle Ages the current designation among the Christians for their Muslim enemies.

Sarcophagus, the name given to a stone coffin, such as was used by the ancient Egyptians, Greeks, and Romans, for receiving the remains of their famous dead. These sarcophagi were often decorated with rich carvings and sculptures.

Sassanides were a dynasty of Persian rulers descended from Artaxerxes from 226 to 625.

Satellite Communication, the system for transmitting telephone and television signals over long distances. Satellites orbiting the earth at a height of *c.* 35,700 km above the Atlantic, Pacific and Indian oceans provide a global coverage. They take exactly 24 h to complete one orbit and so appear to stay in the same place. *Telstar*, launched in the summer of 1969, took only 2·5 h and was therefore within range of the earth stations on each side of the Atlantic for very short periods. The global satellite system Intelsat (International Telecommunications Satellite Organisation) was founded in 1964 to establish a world-wide system on a commercial basis. The first generation of Intelsat satellites to be launched from Florida was *Early Bird*, which went into service in June 1965. Further series have been introduced since then. For example, in 1981 Intelsat had five satellites covering the Atlantic, Indian and Pacific oceans. The Intelsat 5 type of satellite weighs nearly 2,000 kg and can handle two television channels and 12,000 telephone calls simultaneously. Post may now be sent by satellite through Intelpost which began operating in 1980 and links New York City, Washington D.C., Toronto, Amsterdam, Bonn and London.

Satrap, the name given to the governor of a province (satrapy) in the ancient Persian monarchy.

Saturday, the seventh day of the week (the Jewish Sabbath), derived name from planet Saturn.

Saturn, the sixth planet in order from the sun, from which it is distant 1427×10^6 km and around which it makes a revolution in 29.46 years (**F8**). It is 120,200 km in diameter or 9.42 times as large as the Earth and rotates on its axis in 10h 14 min. Saturn is noted for its magnificent ring system which is composed of myriads of ice-covered particles. Among the planet's 17 moons are Mimas, Enceladus, Tethys, Dione, Titan, Rhea, Hyperion, Iapetus and Phoebe. Titan is the largest (radius 2400 km), being the second largest satellite in the solar system, about the size of the planet Mercury. Galileo was the first to observe that Saturn was ringed; Christiaan Huygens the first to study the nature of the rings; and Jacques Cassini the first to suggest that they were composed of myriads of particles. Our knowledge of the planet and its moons and rings has been greatly increased by the camera observations of the spacecrafts Pioneer 11 (flyby Sept 1979), Voyager 1 (flyby autumn 1980) and Voyager 2 (flyby Aug 1981). *See* **Voyager 1 and 2, L127.**

Saturnalia, festivals held in ancient Rome in honour of the god Saturnus.

Sawfly. These insects are considered to be the most primitive members of the order (*Hymenoptera*) to which the bees and wasps belong. In appearance they resemble somewhat the latter, but there is no waist separating thorax and abdomen. The ovipositor is never used as a sting; usually it is saw-like so that the female can use it to make incisions into tissues of plants where the eggs are laid. The larvae look like caterpillars of butterflies and moths.

Saxons, a Teutonic race originally inhabiting what is now Holstein. By the 7th cent. they had, with the Angles and Jutes, conquered and colonised most of England.

Scallop, marine bivalve molluscs of the genus *Pecten*, which is widely distributed. The scalloped edge to the shell results from a pattern of radiating groves. Related to the oyster.

Scandium, a metallic element, no. 21, symbol Sc. It was discovered in 1879 by Nilson, and occurs in small quantities in certain rarer minerals such as wolframite.

Scarabaeidae, a family of beetles (Scarabs) widely distributed through Africa and Asia and the inner parts of Europe. It is to this genus that the "Sacred Beetle" of the Egyptians belongs, and numerous representations of it are found on ancient monuments.

Sceptre, the staff or rod used since ancient times to symbolise supreme authority. The sceptre used for the coronation of Queen Elizabeth II is the one made for Charles II. It is about 90 cm long and tipped with a jewelled cross.

Schism, an ecclesiastical term for division in a church. The East–West Schism was the separation of the Greek Church from the Latin, finally established in 1054. The Great Schism was the division in the Roman Catholic Church from 1378 to 1415, when there were two lines of popes, one at Rome and one at Avignon. *See* **J11.**

Schist, the geological name of certain metamorphic rocks composed for the most part of mineral with thin plate-like crystals (*e.g.*, mica) so that the layers of a schist are closely parallel. Quartz occurs in schists, and where it preponderates the term "quartz schist" is applied.

Scientific Units. The International Bureau of Weights and Measures at Sèvres near Paris, is the custodian of accurate scientific measurement in terms of internationally agreed units.

Methods of measurement are continually being improved and measurements of new kinds coming into use. In defining units certain principles have evolved which can be expressed as a statement of priorities:

(i) units should be so defined that measurements made in one laboratory should be reproducible in another with as much consistency as possible;

(ii) units of all kinds should, so far as practical, form an interrelated system based on as few fundamental units as possible;

(iii) the fundamental units adopted should have a natural basis, independent of particular man-made objects such as metal bars or weights. An invariable universal natural standard was achieved for the metre in 1958 when it was defined in terms of the wavelength of a line in the spectrum of krypton-86. This was changed in 1983. See **L82** and **S.I. Units.**

Schoolmen, the great scholastic philosophers of the Middle Ages who devoted themselves to the study and exposition of questions of religious inquiry, and attempted to reconcile the teaching of the Church with that of Aristotle. The chief Schoolmen were Archbishop Anselm, Albertus Magnus, Thomas Aquinas, Peter Lombard, Duns Scotus. See also **Section J.**

Scorpion. The scorpions constitute an order of the arthropods. Distinctive features are the pair of powerful claws at the head and a "sting" at the tail, which curves over the back in attack or defence so that it points forwards. The poison injected by the sting is potent, causing instant death in spiders, centipedes, etc., and acute discomfort to humans. The idea that a cornered scorpion can sting itself to death is a myth; scorpions are immune to their own poison.

Scorpion Fly. The scorpion fly, of which there are less than 500 species, constitute a separate order of insects, the *Mecoptera*. They have 2 pairs of membranous wings, and gain their popular name because in some species the end of the abdomen is turned up, though it does not function as a sting.

Scree or **Talus,** the mass of loose, angular rock fragments which accumulate towards the bottom of hill-sides and mountain-sides. These fragments have been detached by weathering processes, in particular frost action.

Scythians, nomadic conquerors and skilled horsemen of ancient times (9th—3rd cent. B.C.) who inhabited much of Southern Europe and Asiatic Russia.

Sea Anemones or **Actinaria,** an order of marine animals of the coelenterate class *Antozia*. They form a large and varied group of about 1,100 species and occur in many beautiful colours, flower-like in form.

Sea Butterfly, marine molluscs which propel themselves by two "wings", or side expansions of the foot. They constitute the order called *Pteropoda*.

Sea Cow. See **Manatee.**

Sea Cucumbers or **Holothurians.** These animals constitute the class of echinoderms called *Holothuroidea*. They are elongated and worm-like, with a ring of about twenty tentacles round the mouth. There are about 500 species.

Sea Eagle, a genus of flesh-eating birds related to the true eagles, kites and other birds of prey. Examples are the Bald Eagle, emblem of the USA, White-tailed Eagle (Grey Sea Eagle), and Steller's Sea Eagle of the Pacific coast of Asia. Last known in Britain in 1911.

Sea Elephant or **Elephant Seal,** a curious genus of seal, the males of which possess a proboscis of *c.* 30 cm in length that suggests an elephant's trunk. They are found on the coast of California and in certain parts of the Southern Ocean; their blubber has a commercial value.

Sea Gravimeter, an instrument to determine the density of the earth's crust beneath the oceans of the world. Designed by Dr. A. Graf of Munich and Dr. J. Lamar Worzel of Columbia University, it can detect changes of one-millionth of the value of gravity at the earth's surface and was used in the oceanographical research programme of the IGY.

Sea Hare, a genus of molluscs (*Aplysia*), so-called because of resemblance to a crouching hare. The shell is thin curved plate largely sunk in the animal's body. They have four tentacles, occur in Britain in the laminaria or ribbon wrack zone, and discharge a purple fluid when molested.

Sea Horse, sea-fish (*Hippocampus*), very numerous in the tropics and comprising some twenty species. Their bodies are ringed and they have prehensile tails. Their heads are horse-shaped, and they swim in a vertical position.

Sea Lily. A class of echinoderms, the sea lilies may be roughly described as "stalked starfishes". There are about 400 living species and several thousand extinct species are known. Otherwise called Crinoids.

Sea Mouse, a genus of marine worms called *Aphrodite*, oval in shape, 20–23 cm long, iridescent, covered with fine bristles.

Seasons comprise the four natural divisions of the year, and are due to the inclinations of the earth's axis to the plane of the ecliptic (*q.v.*). See Section N.

Sea Squirts or **Tunicates.** These animals are placed in the sub-phylum called *Urochorda*; found growing in rounded, jelly-like masses on rocks near low-water level. They get their name through the water jets they discharge.

Sea Urchin, species forming the class *Echinoidae*. The body is globular and covered with spines which may be used for both defence and locomotion. The main organs of locomotion are, however, the tube feet, as in starfishes. Much has been learnt of recent years by marine biologists from experiments with the purple sea urchin *Arbacia*.

Secondary Sexual Characters, characters of animals which are distinctive of sex, but have no direct connection with the reproductive process. Examples are: the mane of the lion and the antlers of some deer.

Secretary Bird, so called because of the quill-like plumes about its ears, is a bird of prey related to the eagles and vultures; common in Africa, and of considerable service as an exterminator of snakes. It is a large bird about 1·2 m in height.

Sedimentary Rocks. See **F9(1).**

Seismology, the branch of geophysics devoted to the study of earthquakes and other earth movements. The instruments used for the registration of earth tremors are termed seismographs and consist in principle of a pendulum system, the supporting framework following the ground movement and the bob remaining at rest, thus setting up a relative movement between two parts. In order to record the displacements completely, at one station, three seismographs are necessary to show the two horizontal and the vertical components of the motion. Apart from detection and study of waves from earthquakes, sensitive seismographs are now widely used in geophysical prospecting, particularly in the search for possible oilfields. See also **Richter Scale.**

Selenium, a non-metallic element, no. 34, symbol Se; related to sulphur it is a dark red colour, and solid, found associated with sulphur, iron, pyrites, etc., though only in small quantities. It is a semiconductor (*q.v.*) and its special electrical properties have led to its use in photoelectric cells and rectifiers. Selenium is widely used in the chemical industry as a catalyst (*q.v.*) in producing aromatic hydrocarbons from less useful hydrocarbons. Also used in making some types of glass.

Semiconductors, substances with numerous special and useful electrical properties a few of which are:

(i) they conduct electricity much better than do insulators, but much less well than metals (hence their name);

(ii) their power to conduct depends strongly on their temperatures—which makes them useful for temperature sensitive devices;

(iii) they are sensitive to light—hence their use in photoelectric cells and solar batteries;

(iv) when in contact with metals, or with other suitable semiconductors, they form a boundary layer which conducts electricity much better one way than the other—this is the basis of many rectifiers some of which, called crystal diodes, are an important component in radios and electronic devices;

(v) their electrical properties can be greatly influenced by putting in minute amounts of impurity, this enables semiconductor devices, especially transistors, to be made with carefully selected properties.

Semiconductors were known to Faraday, but the semiconductor age really arrived with the invention of the transistor (q.v.) in 1947. The ubiquitous transistor is only one of very many semiconductor devices which perform a variety of functions in technical apparatus of all kinds. Semiconductors used in technology are usually small crystals, frequently of germanium or silicon, and their robustness and small power consumption often make them superior to other devices, such as thermionic valves, which they often replace. Other semiconducting materials are cadmium sulphide, selenium lead telluride, indium antimonide. *See also* **F22(1)**.

Senate, the higher governing Assembly of a Legislature. The word, applied primarily to the Roman council, is also used to denote the upper chamber in the legislatures of France, the United States, and other countries. In certain universities the governing body is also called the Senate.

Sensitive Plant. A species of Mimosa (*Mimosa pudica*), whose leaves are extremely sensitive to touch, shaking and burning.

Sepia, the "ink" of the cuttlefish. *See* **Ink Sac.**

September, the ninth month of the year, and the seventh of the old Roman calendar; hence the name, from Septimus. The designation was several times changed by the Emperors, but none of the new names survived for long.

Septuagesima Sunday, the third Sunday before Lent.

Septuagint, the Greek translation of the Old Testament made by Alexandrian Jews between 250 B.C. and 100 B.C. from Hebrew texts now lost. There are many differences between the Septuagint and the Massoretic version (A.D. 900), and therefore it is of great value for textual criticism. The symbol for the Septuagint is LXX.

Serfs, the name given to the peasants formerly existing in Russia, who answered to the condition of the feudal "villeins" of England. They were attached to the soil and were transferred with it in all sales or leases. Serfdom existed in Prussia until 1807 and in Russia until 1861.

Serpentine, a mineral: chemically a hydrous silicate of magnesium. Green serpentine is used as an ornament stone. Fibrous serpentine is called asbestos.

Serval, a collie-dog-sized cat, long-limbed and spotted, from Africa. Preys on a variety of animals, from lizards to small antelope. Black servals occur mainly in mountainous regions.

Set, both in everyday speech (as in tea set, chess set) and in mathematics, a set is a collection of things. The members of the set can be specified by listing them or by describing the properties necessary for membership of the set, *e.g.*, the set of ginger-haired boxers. Set theory is a very important branch of mathematics founded by a great mathematician, Georg Cantor (1845–1918). Its development has influenced many other branches of mathematics. Perhaps one reflection of its fundamental nature is to be found in the fact that many schoolchildren, even of tender age, are now learning set theory and confounding parents who did not hear of it at school when they were there.

Settlement, Act of, passed in 1701, assigned the Crown to the House of Hanover in case of Anne's death without children. The decision represented the determination of the squires and the Anglican Church never again to trust themselves to a Roman Catholic king.

Seven Champions of Christendom, as set forth in mediaeval literature, were St. George of England, St. Andrew of Scotland, St. Patrick of Ireland, St. David of Wales, St. James of Spain, St. Denis of France, and St. Antony of Italy.

Seven Churches of Asia, referred to in the Revelation of St. John, were those of Ephesus, founded by St. Paul in 57, Smyrna, Pergamos, Thyatira, Sardis, Philadelphia (Lydia) and Laodicea (Phrygia), all in W. Asia Minor.

Seven Wonders of the World were: 1. The Pyramids of Egypt; 2. the tomb of Mausolus, King of Caria (hence the word mausoleum); 3. the Temple of Diana at Ephesus; 4. the Walls and Hanging Gardens of Babylon; 5. the Colossus at Rhodes; 6. the Ivory and Gold Statue of Jupiter Olympus; and 7. the Pharos, or Watch Tower, built at Alexandria by Ptolemy Philadelphus, King of Egypt.

Seven Years War was waged by Frederick the Great and England against Austria, France, and Russia, from 1756 to 1763. It resulted in the retention of Silesia by Prussia, the breaking of French power in India and the strengthening of our Indian Empire.

Severn Barrage, a barrier across the River Severn estuary proposed with a view to extracting useful electrical energy from tidal power. Essentially the idea is to let the tidal water flow into a reservoir upstream from the barrage and then to flow seaward under gravity through specially designed hydroelectric generators situated on the barrage. Tidal power has been harnessed in a French project and there is little doubt that the Severn scheme is technically feasible. However, environmental, economic and social factors enter the matter and are influencing consideration of its overall desirability. *See also* **Tidal Power.**

Sexagesima Sunday is the 2nd Sunday before Lent.

Sextant, a reflecting instrument for measuring the angular distances of objects. It is of special importance in navigation and surveying, and contains 60 degrees described on a graduated arc. A small telescope is attached and there are also a couple of mirrors which reflect the distant objects so as to enable them to be accurately observed. The invention is attributed to John Hadley, and to Thomas Godfrey independently, about 1780. The principle had been foreseen, and its application described, at earlier dates by Newton, Halley and Hooke.

Shad, a marine fish belonging to the same genus as the herring. It is found along the Atlantic Coast of the USA, and ascends rivers to spawn.

Shagreen, shark's skin: also untanned leather of peculiar grain made from skins of wild asses, camels and horses.

Shalloon, a kind of cloth manufactured from wool and worsted, and used chiefly for women's dresses and coat linings. It gets its name from the fact that it was originally made at Châlons-sur-Marne. It was called "chalouns" by Chaucer and "shalloons" by Swift.

Shamrock, the three-leaved clover-like plant native to Ireland and its national emblem.

Shark, a large and powerful ocean fish, comprising many species, very widely distributed, but most numerous in tropical seas. They have formidable teeth and are the most carnivorous of all fishes. They usually attain a large size, the whale-shark being often of a length of 15 m. Commercially the shark yields shagreen from its skin, the fins are made into gelatine, and an oil is obtained from the liver.

Sheep, a well-known family of great ruminants of great utility as wool-producers, and for food. From the earliest times sheep have been a source of wealth to England. So much were they valued in the 15th and 16th cent., that their exportation was frequently prohibited. Sheep are classified under (1) longwools; (2) short-wools; and (3) mountain breeds. Most of the longwools carry Leicester blood in their ancestry and the shortwooled Down breeds carry the blood of the Southdown. The Southdown produced the present Suffolk, one of the most popular breeds. Cheviot is an important mountain breed. Of the foreign breeds the most valued are the Merino sheep of Spain, which yield a fine long wool. Australia, USSR, China, New Zealand, India, Argentina, South Africa, Turkey, Iran, UK are the chief wool-producing countries in the world.

Shelduck, a handsome genus of surface-feeding ducks, one of which, the common shelduck, is an inhabitant of Great Britain. It is a beautiful white-and-chestnut plumaged bird with dark-green head and neck and red bill. Another species, the ruddy shelduck, appears in Britain only occasionally.

Shellac. This resin is the secretion of the lac

insect (*Coccus lacca*), which occurs in forests of Assam and Thailand. It is used for making varnish and in the manufacture of gramophone records. *See also* **Lac.**

Sherardizing. Process for coating steel or iron parts with zinc to prevent corrosion; this is done by heating the parts in a closed rotating drum containing zinc dust.

Shilling has been an English coin from Saxon times, but it was not of the value of 12 pence until after the Conquest. It is interchangeable with the 5 new pence decimal piece which came into circulation in 1968.

Ships have existed from prehistoric times. There is mention of one that sailed from Egypt to Greece in 1485 B.C., and in 786 B.C. the Tyrians built a double-decked vessel. No double-decked ship was known in England, however, before the *Royal Harry* was built by Henry VII, and it was not until the 17th cent. that ship-building was carried on in Great Britain as a prominent industry.

Shoddy, the name given to a kind of cloth mainly composed of woollen or worsted rags, torn up and re-fabricated by powerful machinery. It was first made at Batley in Yorkshire about 1813, and became a very important industry employing many thousands of people at Batley and the neighbouring town of Dewsbury.

Shot, the name given to solid projectiles fired from guns. In the time of Henry V stone shot was used, later leaden shot, then iron shot, and finally steel shot, introduced by Sir Joseph Whitworth.

Shrike, a large and varied family of birds of hawk-like behaviour found in all continents except S. America. The Red-backed Shrike, which winters in Africa, is a breeding visitor to England and Wales. It is commonly called the "Butcher Bird" from the way it impales its prey (small birds and insects) on thorn-twigs. The other species on the British list are the Great Grey Shrike, the Lesser Grey Shrike, the Woodchat Shrike, and the Masked Shrike.

Shrove Tuesday, the day before the first day of Lent, receiving its name from the old custom of shriving, or making confession, on that day. In England the day has always been associated with the making of pancakes.

Sicilian Vespers, the term applied to the terrible massacre of French people in Sicily in 1282. The French under Charles of Anjou were then in occupation of the island and had been guilty of many cruelties. It began at Palermo on Easter Monday at the hour of vespers and resulted in the expulsion of the French king and the introduction of Spanish rule.

Silence, Tower of, or *dakhma,* a tower about 8 m high, built by the Parsees for their dead. The corpse is taken inside by professional corpse-bearers and left to be consumed by vultures. Parsees do not burn or bury their dead, and the *dakhma* is to protect the living and the elements from defilement.

Silicon, an important non-metallic element, no. 14, symbol Si, it is related to carbon. Next to oxygen, it is the most abundant constituent of the earth's crust (27% by weight). It occurs in many rocks, and its oxide occurs in many forms (*e.g.* quartz, sand, flint, agate, chalcedony, opal, etc.). Principally used as a semi-conducting material for making transistors and similar devices. The circuitry of the computer is etched on a chip of silicon.

Silicones are synthetic organic derivatives of silicon which because of their high resistance to heat and moisture have special uses, *e.g.*, lubricants, heat-resistant resins and lacquers, and water-repellent finishes. Silicones are compounds in which the molecules consist of chains of atoms of silicon and oxygen alternately. Silicones were developed in the United States from discoveries first made by Prof. F. S. Kipping at Nottingham University. Manufacture began in Britain in 1950, and in the form of fluids, resins, rubbers and greases they find wide use in industry. The largest plant in Europe is in Glamorgan.

Silk, the name given to a soft glossy fabric manufactured from the fine thread produced by the silkworm. It was known to, and highly prized by the ancients, being at one time paid for, weight for weight, with gold. The manufacture of silk was carried on in Sicily in the 12th cent., later spreading to Italy, Spain and France, where Lyons has been the great centre of production from 1450 to this day. It was not manufactured in England before 1604; but when certain French refugees established themselves at Spitalfields in 1688, the industry was developed and became of importance. In the 18th cent. the Lombes of Derby achieved great success in this industry. Japan, China, Italy, Korea and the Soviet Union are the chief silk-producing countries.

Silkworm, the larva of a species of moth, *Bombyx mori.* It is native to China, and has been cultivated with success in India, Iran, Turkey and Italy. The silkworm of commerce feeds on mulberry leaves and produces a cocoon of silk varying in colour from white to orange. The cocoon is the silken habitation constructed by the worm for its entrance upon the pupal condition, and to obtain the silk the pupa is killed by immersing in hot water.

Sill, a sheet-like mass of igneous rock which has been intruded parallel with the stratification of the country rock, cf. a dyke.

Silurian. This geological period is one of the major subdivisions of the Palaeozoic era. Its beginning is estimated at 440 million years ago, and the period lasted about 40 million years. Maximum thickness of the Silurian strata in Britain measures 4,575 m. *See* **F48.**

Silver, a white precious metallic element, no. 47, symbol Ag (Latin *argentum*) found in a free state, also in certain combinations, and in a variety of ores. The chief silver-producing regions are the Andes and Cordilleras. Peru, Bolivia and Mexico have yielded vast supplies of the metal since the 16th century, and Colorado and Nevada in the United States have also been very prolific in silver yield. In England standard silver (that used for coinage) formerly contained 92½ per cent. fine silver and 7½ per cent. alloy, but when the price rose to 89¼d. per oz and the coins became worth more than the face value, the Coinage Act of 1920 was passed, reducing the fineness to half. To provide silver bullion for industry and for a fund towards the redemption of our silver debt to America, it was decided in 1946 to replace the United Kingdom silver coinage by one made of cupro-nickel (75 per cent. copper, 25 per cent. nickel). Maundy money, however, is of the original silver standard. Silver chloride and bromide are light-sensitive compounds and are used in photography.

Simony, the offence of trading in church offices, has been contrary to English law since the time of Edward VI. Elizabeth also promulgated laws against simony. In 1879 a Royal Commission reported on the law and existing practice as to the sale, exchange and resignation of benefices. The position is now controlled by the Benefices Act 1898, the Amendment Measure 1923, and the Benefices Rules 1926.

Sinn Fein (*Irish* = ourselves alone), Irish nationalistic movement founded in 1905 which developed into a mass republican party and triumphed in the establishment of the Irish Free State. An extremist group has survived which represents politically the outlawed IRA. In Northern Ireland *Sinn Fein* was legalized in 1974.

Sins, The Seven Deadly or Capital sins are pride, avarice, lust, anger, gluttony, envy, sloth.

Sirius, the dog-star, so called because of its situation in the mouth of the Dog (Canis Major): it is the brightest star in the sky, and is also one of the nearest to us.

Sirocco, a warm, southerly, often dust-laden, wind blowing across Mediterranean lands from the Sahara, in advance of an eastward-moving depression over the Mediterranean.

Siskin, a small bird of the finch family, common in Northern regions, nesting in Britain. The common Siskin has a yellow-green colour and is a lively, swift-flying bird with a stout bill.

Sistine Chapel, the chapel of the Pope in the Vatican, renowned for its frescoes by Michelangelo.

S.I. Units (Système International d'Unités) form an internationally recognised system of metric units for scientific and technical quantities. The basic units of length, time, mass, electric current, temperature, amount of substance, and luminous intensity are, respectively the metre, second, kilogram, ampere, kelvin (*see* **Absolute Temperature**) mole (*see* **F24**) and candela. The S.I. was recommended for general adoption by a number of international organisations such as the General Conference on Weights and Measures (1960). Many countries have made or are making the S.I. the only legally recognised set of Units. Gt. Britain's decision to "go metric" has brought general use of S.I. units in its train. These units command the widespread though not absolutely unanimous support of industrialists, technologists, and scientists. Many have urged that their adoption will end the confusing multiplicity of units on the world scene. *See* **Section N.**

Six Articles, The Statute of the, was passed in 1539 for compelling adhesion to the chief doctrines of Roman Catholic faith: transubstantiation, communion in one kind only for the laity, vows of chastity, celibacy of the clergy, private masses and auricular confession; those who refused to subscribe to the Articles were treated as heretics. The Act was repealed in 1547.

Skink. The skinks constitute a large family of lizards with large smooth scales, under each of which is a bony plate. The largest species, found in Australia, is about 61 cm long. Some skinks have adopted a burrowing habit and degeneration of the limbs is associated with this. The Common Skink is a small species *c.* 12 cm long, living in deserts of N. Africa.

Skua, falcon-like marine birds related to the gulls found throughout the world. Known as "Robber Birds" because they steal not only the young and eggs of other birds (including penguins) but also their food, which they force them to disgorge in mid-air. The Arctic Skua breeds as far south as Scotland. The Great Skua breeds in both Antarctica and Arctica. Other species are the Pomarine, the Long-tailed, and McCormick's Skua.

Skunk, a North American mammal of the weasel family, with short legs and long bushy tail. All fifteen species are black and white, some being striped and the rest spotted. It secretes and ejects at will a foul-smelling fluid.

Sky. The blue colour of the sky on a summer's day is the result of the scattering of light waves by particles of dust and vapour in the earth's atmosphere. Blue light having almost the smallest wavelength in the visible spectrum (0·00004 cm) is scattered laterally about 10 times as much as the red (0·00007 cm).

Skyscraper. Owing to lack of ground space, increasing cost of land, and growth of modern cities, buildings are being made higher than broader; hence the name. The structures are constructed of steel framework usually clothed in concrete or reinforced concrete. The first modern skyscraper of steel skeletal construction was the Home Insurance Building in Chicago, designed (1883) by William Le Baron. The New York skyscrapers include the World Trade Center building (110 stories), Empire State building (102 stories), Chrysler (77 stories), Rockefeller Center (70 stories), and 60 Wall Tower (67 stories). The tallest building in Britain, recently built, is National Westminster Bank tower, dominating the city skyline (183 m), topping the British Telecom radio tower by 6 m.

Slate, fine-grained clayey rocks which have undergone metamorphism. They cleave easily, and it is this property of cleavage which makes them a valuable source of roofing material. Important quarries producing mainly green slate are in the Coniston–Ambleside area of the Lake District.

Slavery. In its earlier forms, as in the times of ancient Greece and Rome, in the feudal ages, when vassalage and villeinage existed, and in the serfdom of Russia and other northern nations, slavery was attended by many inhumanities and evils; but perhaps in the negro slavery system which prevailed in the British colonies for upwards of 200 years and in certain parts of the United States up to 1865, it attained its highest point of cruelty. In 1833 the Act of Emancipation was passed, emancipating all slaves in British territories, though slavery continued to be tolerated in northern Nigeria, Sierra Leone and in the Anglo-Egyptian Sudan long after that date. Even today slavery and forced labour are still prevalent in some parts of the world.

Slide Rule, an instrument which consists of two logarithmic scales sliding alongside each other. By its use multiplication, division, extraction of roots, etc., are speedily carried out.

Sloth, a curious family of mammals, only found in Central and South America. They dwell almost entirely in the trees, proceeding from branch to branch with their bodies hanging downwards, their weight being supported by their large hook-like claws. They eat foliage.

Slow-Worm, a species of lizard found in Britain which lacks legs. Silver with longitudinal brown stripes, it lives almost entirely on slugs.

Smelting. The process of heating an ore with a reducing agent to convert ore into metal, and with a flux to convert rocky impurities into a slag that will float on top of the molten metal. Slag and metal can then be tapped separately. An example is iron smelting; the reducing agent is coke, and limestone is added as the flux; the smelting is carried out in a blast furnace.

Snake. The snakes constitute the important reptilian order *Ophidia*. Snakes have a scaly, cylindrical, limbless body, lidless eyes, forked tongue, and the upper and lower jaws joined by an elastic ligament. All snakes have teeth used for seizing prey, and the poisonous varieties are furnished with poison fangs in the upper jaw. These fangs are hollow modified teeth and the venom passes into them from a special gland situated behind the angle of the mouth. Some 2,500 species of snakes are known, divided into 13 families. There are 3 British species—the grass-snake, smooth-snake, and adder.

Snipe, a wading bird, long-legged, with long, slender, straight bill, brown plumage, and zig-zag flight. The Common Snipe breeds locally throughout Britain; the Great Snipe and small Jack Snipe are occasional visitors. The close season is February 1 to August 11.

Snow. When water vapour condenses at high levels at a temperature below freezing (sublimation), a cloud of ice particles is formed. If these frozen droplets are small, they fall slowly and gradually assume a feathery crystalline structure, reaching the earth as snowflakes if the temperature remains below freezing.

Socialism. *See* **Section J.**

Soda, carbonate of sodium, is now mainly obtained by certain processes of manufacture from common salt. It was formerly obtained from the ashes of plants. Bicarbonate of sodium is the primary product in the Solvay or Ammonia-soda method for commercial manufacture of soda; it is also formed when carbon dioxide is passed into strong soda solution. The bicarbonate is used in medicine and in the preparation of baking powder.

Sodium, a metallic element, no. 11, symbol Na (Latin *Natrium*), first obtained by Sir Humphry Davy in 1807 from caustic soda by means of the electric battery. Its chloride is *common salt*; the deposits of salt (*e.g.*, in Cheshire and at Stassfurt) have come into existence through the drying up of inland seas. Salt occurs in sea-water to the extent of about 3 per cent.; the Dead Sea contains about 22 per cent. The blood of animals is maintained at a level of about 0·6% sodium chloride. That there is sodium in the sun's atmosphere was confirmed in 1859 by Kirchhoff from his spectroscopic observations. Liquid sodium metal has properties which make it suitable as a coolant in some nuclear reactors; a technique of handling this very reactive liquid has had to be developed.

Software, the internal programmes and operating procedures of a computer as opposed to its hardware. This includes system software designed to make the computer usable as well as programmes intended for particular applications such as commercial or scientific calculations. *See also* **Hardware** and **Section V.**

Soil Erosion occurs when the soil is removed from an area at a faster rate than soil formation. This situation usually occurs as a result of man's interference with the natural balance of the environment by the removal of natural vegetation, overgrazing or by poor farming techniques. Soil thus exposed is then removed by the wind (as in the Dust Bowl in the 1930s) or by rain in the form of gully or sheet erosion (as in the

Tennessee Valley, USA). Methods introduced to stop soil erosion include contour ploughing, afforestation and dry farming techniques.

Solar Battery, one of the innumerable devices made possible by the development of semiconducting materials, notably germanium and silicon. This device creates an electric current from light falling on it. The current can be put to use or stored in storage batteries. The energy of the current is derived from the sunlight, and the solar battery is thus an *energy converting* apparatus. Solar batteries have provided power for the instruments in satellites.

Solar Wind, a continuous stream of electrically charged particles blowing outwards from the sun, supplemented from time to time by intense outbursts from particular regions of the sun's surface. These streams of protons and electrons on encountering the earth's magnetic field distort it and cause magnetic storms (*q.v.*) and aurorae (*q.v.*).

Soldering is a means of joining together two pieces of material, usually metals, by melting a third metal (the solder) into the joint. The solder solidifies in the pores of the other metals and holds them together. The materials to be joined are not themselves melted so the technique requires less heat than welding. Solders are alloys; there are many kinds depending on the materials to be joined and the strength of joint desired. *See* **Welding.**

Solstice, an astronomical term indicating the point at which the sun is most distant from the equator. *See* **Seasons, Section N.**

Soundings at sea, to determine depth at any point, have been taken in all seas, and with considerable accuracy. A deep reading was that of the *Challenger* expedition in 1873, near St. Thomas's in the North Atlantic, when 3,875 fathoms (7,091 m) were sounded. In 1851 H.M.S. *Challenger* recorded the then maximum ocean depth in the Marianas Trench (W. Pacific) by echo-sounding as between 5,882 and 5,950 fathoms (10,764 and 10,80 m). Another deep was located in the S. Pacific in 1952-53 of 5,814 fathoms (10,640 m) in the Tonga Trench, 290 km S. of Tonga Tabu. Since then even greater depths have been recorded, in the Marianas Trench and the Mindanao Deep. *See* **Pacific Ocean.**

Southern Cross, popular name of *Crux*, a constellation of the Southern hemisphere, consisting of four bright stars in the form of a Latin cross. It has been called the pole-star of the south and is indispensable to seafarers.

South Sea Bubble, the name given to a series of financial projects which began with the formation of the South Sea Company in 1711 and ended nine years later in disaster after a mania of speculation. The idea behind the parent scheme was that the state should sell certain trading monopolies in the South seas in return for a sum of money to pay off the National Debt (which stood at £51,300,000 in 1719 when the scheme started). The idea fascinated the public, fabulous profits being dreamt of, and the price of the stock rose out of all proportion to the earnings of the Company. Many dishonest speculative ventures sprang up in imitation with the inevitable result that thousands were ruined. All classes had joined in the gamble and a Committee of Secrecy set up by the House of Commons in December 1720 to investigate the affairs of the Company proved that there had been fraud and corruption on a large scale in the affairs of the Company. Sir Robert Walpole, an opponent of the scheme from the outset, dealt with the crisis.

Space Flight. The Soviet Union was the first country to launch a man into space and bring him safely back to earth. This epoch-making event took place on 12 April 1961, when Yuri Gagarin, tragically killed in an air crash in 1968, circled the earth in a spaceship weighing about 4,826 kg. It was launched by rocket in an elliptical orbit with greatest height 300 km and least 175 km. The inclination of the orbit to the equator was 65° 4′, and the period of revolution was 89 min. 6s. Since then, the Russian *Vostok* cosmonauts Titov (17 orbits), Nikolaev (64 orbits), Popovich (48 orbits), Bykovsky (81 orbits), Tereshkova, the first woman space traveller (48 orbits), the *Voskhod*

cosmonauts Komarov, Feoktistov and Yegorov (16 orbits), Belyaev and Leonov (17 orbits), the American *Mercury* astronauts Glenn (3 orbits), Carpenter (3 orbits), Schirra (6 orbits), Cooper (22 orbits), the *Gemini* astronauts Grissom and Young (3 orbits), McDivitt and White (62 orbits), Cooper and Conrad (120 orbits), Borman and Lovell (206 orbits), Schirra and Stafford (15 orbits), Armstrong and Scott (6·6 orbits), Stafford and Cernan (44 orbits), Young and Collins (43 orbits), Conrad and Gordon (44 orbits), Lovell and Aldrin (60 orbits) were among the first to complete successful missions in space. Leonov was the first to perform the extra-vehicular (EVA) experiment (1965), *i.e.*, to leave an orbiting spaceship and float in space. Russia was the first to achieve an automatic docking (link-up) between two unmanned spacecraft in orbital flight (October 1967), and of two unmanned spacecraft (January 1969). The American *Apollo* mission was accomplished when Armstrong and Aldrin became the first men to set foot on the moon (July 1969). A joint Soviet-American project culminated in a *Soyuz–Apollo* link-up 225 km up on 17 July 1975. On 11 January 1978 two Soviet spacecraft docked with an orbiting laboratory, the first triple link-up in space. The longest endurance record is held by Valentin Lebedev and Anatoly Berezevoy (211 days in space aboard *Salyut 7* in 1982). The first free walk in space was made by two American astronauts on 7 February 1984 from the space shuttle *Challenger*. The *Challenger* disaster in January 1986 has severely disrupted America's space programme.

Space Research. By space research we mean scientific research work which can only be carried to otherwise inaccessible observing locations by rocket propulsion. Such propulsion does not rely on the presence of an atmosphere to provide oxygen so that it is capable in principle of conveying objects to unlimited distances. The subject of space research is, therefore, one which is concerned with scientific applications in various fields of a single highly specialised and powerful technique. It is not a single discipline, but can provide data of great importance for many, such as the physics of the earth, the sun, moon and other bodies of the solar system, astronomy, geodesy and the study of gravitation. The prospect of investigating the biological conditions on different planets such as Mars and Venus is also opened, as well as that of experimental biological studies under conditions of zero gravity. Although the results of many aspects of space research are vital for those concerned with the practical realisation of manned travel in space, space research is largely a branch of pure science, independent of any applications which may stem from it. The major technical problems involved are:

    (*a*) Launching of the instrument-containing vehicle with the necessary velocity.
    (*b*) Guidance and control of the vehicle so it pursues the desired path.
    (*c*) Tracking the vehicle to determine its actual path and the position on the path at any time.
    (*d*) Transmission of the data, recorded by the instruments, back to the earth.
    (*e*) Satisfactory operation of scientific instruments in the environment within the vehicle.
    (*f*) Provision of adequate power supplies to operate the equipment within the vehicle for sufficiently long periods.

It is important to distinguish three distinct types of vehicle—the vertical sounding rocket, the artificial earth satellite, and the deep space probe. The track of a vertical sounding rocket is mainly vertical, and the whole path to the highest point and back is traversed in a few minutes only. An earth satellite circulates in an orbit round the earth in the same way as does our natural satellite, the moon. If it approaches the earth at any point within 160 km of the surface the air resistance causes the path to spiral in so rapidly that the vehicle is eventually burnt up by air friction within the dense atmosphere after an orbital life of a few months only. It follows that artificial satellite vehicles are only useful as instrument containers if the distance of closest approach (the perigee distance) is not much less than 160 km. For the study of the properties of the atmosphere at lower altitudes down to the limit (32 km) attainable by balloons, vertical sounding rockets must be used. It is a great advantage for work at higher altitudes to use satellites, as it is then possible to make systematic observations for months at a time from a great number of positions relative to the earth. During recent years both the American and Russian space programmes have developed the concept of space stations for providing facilities for continuous manned observatories and laboratories in the future. There have now been successful soft landings on Mars and Venus, and "fly by" visits to Jupiter and Saturn. Voyager 2 left Saturn in Aug. 1981 for the outer planets Uranus (1986) and Neptune (1989) and beyond. *See also* **Voyagers 1 and 2.**

Space Shuttle. The first reusable manned space vehicle, *Columbia*, was launched on 12 April 1981 from Cape Canaveral, Florida. It orbited the earth 36 times and returned on 14 April landing in California after a flight of 34 h 22 min with its two crew members controlling its landing. There have been a number of flights since.

Spanish Civil War, 1936 to 1939. The war began with a revolt by the Fascist General Franco against the Republic which had succeeded the Monarchy in 1931. Germany and Italy aided the rebels who besieged Madrid for over 2 years. An International Brigade was formed to help the Republic, but the Spanish Government was faced by the greater part of the Army, and very effective assistance from Italy and Germany. Those powers seized the opportunity to have a curtain-raiser to the world conflict which they intended to precipitate. After a total loss of a million men the Fascists overpowered the Republic.

Sparrow, name given to finch-like birds found in most parts of the world, of which the House Sparrow *Passer domesticus,* is the most familiar of British birds. Also native to Britain is the rural Tree Sparrow, distinguished from the male House Sparrow by its chestnut crown. Other European species are the Italian, Spanish and Rock Sparrows.

Specific Gravity, defined as the ratio of the mass of a particular volume of a substance to the mass of an equal volume of water at 4°C. *See* **Hydrometer.**

Spectroscopy. Newton's arrangement with the prism was the first spectroscope; its function was to separate out the colour components of a source of light. Two hundred years elapsed before this apparatus was developed into a precise scientific instrument, capable of measuring both the wavelength and intensity of each colour component. In this form it is called a spectrometer. All atoms and molecules have well defined characteristic spectra which can be used to recognise them. In order to produce emission spectra it is necessary to energise the material under investigation by some means, such as by heating in a flame. The resulting radiation then consists largely of sharp bright lines, characteristic of the material. Absorption spectra are produced by interposing the experimental material between a white light source and the spectrometer. Then dark lines are seen, corresponding to absorptions of energy, in exactly the same places as the bright lines are observed in the emission spectra. Spectroscopic techniques have now been developed to such an extent that accurate measurements of wavelength and intensity are possible not only in the visible region, but over almost the whole of the electromagnetic spectrum. Two of the most useful types for the chemist are infrared spectroscopy which reveals absorption characteristic of the type of chemical bonds because of their different bond vibration frequencies and nuclear magnetic resonance spectroscopy which operates in the radiofrequency region. It reveals the structure environments of atoms containing particular nuclei. Not only does spectroscopy play an important rôle in probing the structure of matter, but it can be applied in the field of astronomy. The use of radio wave spectroscopy has led to the discovery of several new types of stellar object, and this data is now producing a complete re-

appraisal of our understanding of the universe. *See* **F14(2).**

Sphinx, in Greek mythology, a winged creature with a woman's head and a lion's body. The sphinx of ancient Egypt represented the pharaoh in a divine form.

Spiritualism. *See* **Section J.**

Spirituals, negro melodies with religious inspiration and which are still spontaneously created, but have also passed into art-music.

Sponge. *See* **Porifera, F36(1).**

Spoonbill, a long-legged, marsh bird, closely related to the ibis and stork, remarkable for its snowwhite plumage and broad, flat, spoon-shaped bill. The European species has not bred in England since the beginning of the 17th cent., but is still a regular summer visitor from the Netherlands, where it nests in colonies in reed beds and islets.

Sputniks, the name of the Russian earth satellites first launched during the period of the International Geophysical Year. *Sputnik I,* launched 4 October 1957, became the first man-made earth satellite. *Sputnik II,* launched a month later carried a dog as passenger. *Sputnik III,* launched in May 1958, and weighing well over 2 tonnes, became the first fully-equipped laboratory to operate in space. The father of space travel with rockets was a Russian—Konstantin Eduardovich Tsiolkovsky—the centenary of whose birth practically coincided with the launching of the first earth satellite.

Stalactites are deposits of calcium carbonate formed on the roofs and sides of limestone caves, and in tunnels, under bridges, and other places where the carbonic acid of rain-water percolates through and partly dissolves the limestone, resulting in the growth of icicle-like forms that often assume groupings. The water that drops from these may deposit further calcium carbonate, which accumulates and hardens into sharp mounds or hillocks called stalagmites.

Standard Deviation. In statistics it is often desirable to compare the variability or "spread" of different sets of data. For example, two kinds of light bulb could have the same average life but one kind could be more uniform or consistent than the other. The standard deviation is one of the commonest measures of spread. It is found as follows. If x is one of the data and $\bar{x}$ is the mean of all the x's, then $x - \bar{x}$ is called the deviation. Every deviation is now squared and the average squared deviation calculated. The standard deviation is then the square root of the average squared deviation. The lifetimes of the more uniform kind of light bulb would have a smaller standard deviation than those of the more erratic one.

Star Chamber, an ancient tribunal of state in existence in 1487 and possibly earlier, charged with the duty of trying offences against the government, unfettered by the ordinary rules of law. It was in effect a Privy Council entrusted with judicial functions. Under Charles I the Star Chamber was used by the King and his party to persecute opponents; and in 1641 a Bill carried in both Houses abolished it.

Starling (*Sturnus vulgaris*), a well-known European bird now common in many parts of the world. It has handsome iridescent blackish plumage and nests in holes and crevices. Flocks of starlings are often seen wheeling in the air; thousands roost on buildings in the heart of London. Other European species are the Spotless and Rose-coloured starlings. The latter sometimes wanders to the British Isles.

States-General, national assembly in which the chief estates of the realm were represented as separate bodies. The name, though not the institution, has survived in the Netherlands, where the two houses of parliament are known as states-general. In France the states-general consisted of three orders, clergy, nobility and commons. Philip IV first summoned it in 1302 to support him in his quarrel with Pope Boniface VIII. While absolute monarchy was establishing itself it met rarely, and not at all from 1614 until 1789, when it was convoked as a last resort by Louis XVI. But when it met it declared itself the National Assembly which marked the beginning of the revolution.

Statistics is a science that deals with the collection of numerical facts and the evaluation of their significance. The word is also used to refer to the facts themselves as in "trade statistics". This important science gives precise meanings to words like "average" and to statements like "this set of data is significantly different from that". In a world in which more and more information is becoming available in numerical form (I.Q.s, examination results, tax yields, health records, road accidents, etc.) the proper—as opposed to the misleading—use of statistics cannot be over-emphasised. Many young people can now study statistics at school and college, and governments and industries employ many statisticians. See **Average.**

Statute of Westminster 1931. An Act of parliament which gave a basis of equality to the British Dominions. The Dominions as well as the United Kingdom were defined by the Balfour Memorandum of 1926 as "autonomous communities within the British Empire, equal in status, in no way subordinate one to another in any aspect of their domestic or external affairs, though united by a common allegiance to the Crown, and freely associated as members of the British Commonwealth of Nations". The Statute was the sequel. The Dominions are sovereign States governed solely by their own Parliaments and Governments.

Steam Engine, a machine whereby steam becomes the active agent of the working of machinery, and of very wide application. The leading types of steam engine are: (a) condensing, or low-pressure engines, where the steam is generated by a boiler; (b) non-condensing, in which the cylinder exhausts its steam into the open air. Engines of the latter type are used where portable engines are required.

Steam-hammer, invented (1839) by the Scottish engineer James Nasmyth. Consists basically of a vertical steam cylinder atop two legs with piston-rod passing through cylinder base and attached to a tup (hammer) of from 100 kg to 15 tonnes which rests on an anvil. The tup slides in V grooves on inside of legs. Length of stroke and therefore weight of blow can be accurately controlled from a light tap to a massive punch. It made possible the forging in one piece of multi-throw crankshafts for marine engines, etc. and the mass production of high-class axles and wheels, con rods and buffers, etc. for locomotives and rolling stock.

Stearin is the portion of fatty matters and oils which remains solid at an ordinary temperature, and is a compound of stearic acid with glycerine. It is largely used in the manufacture of candles. With caustic soda stearin forms a soap (sodium stearate), which is present in most commercial soaps which contain sodium palmitate and oleate in addition.

Steel, an alloy of iron and carbon, with varying proportions of other minerals. The famous blades of Damascus and steels of Toledo were made by the cementation and crucible method. The metal produced by the "Bessemer process" (q.v.) is of the highest value for structural purposes, rails, etc. In recent years the technique known as continuous casting has been developed which bypasses some major steps in the conventional process of steel-making.

Stereophonic Broadcasting. A person having normal hearing is able to determine the direction from which a sound reaches him by virtue of the fact that he has two ears, and, therefore, the sound will reach one of them a fraction of a second before it reaches the other. This difference in arrival time allows the brain to calculate direction. It will, therefore, be apparent that if the same person listens to, say, an orchestral concert in a large hall he will be able to determine—even with his eyes shut—the approximate position of a particular instrument with respect to the rest of the orchestra. If, however, he listens at home to a broadcast of the same concert, then, due to the fact that he hears the music after it has been picked up by a single microphone located at one point and radiated over a single-channel transmission system, he will be unable to allocate a definite position to any instrument. The aim of stereophonic broadcasting, or sound reproduction therefore, is to restore the listener's ability to locate the position in space of the various sources of sound and to follow movement. To do this it is necessary to use two microphones in the studio—to

simulate the two human ears—and to transmit their outputs, through two similar, but separate, chains of equipment, to two radio receivers and their two loudspeakers, which must be placed some distance apart, in the listener's home. The fundamental work on two-channel stereophony was done by A. D. Blumlein (1903–42), an electronics engineer and inventor of E.M.I. Ltd., his original patent being dated 1931.

Stereotype, a metal cast taken from movable type which has been set up in the ordinary way. The first to introduce the process in practical form in this country was William Ged, of Edinburgh, who made stereotype plates in 1730. An impression of the type matter is first taken by means of a mould of prepared plaster of Paris or moistened sheets of specially prepared paper and when molten stereo metal is poured upon the mould and allowed to cool and harden, the stereo plate is formed, and can be printed from as a solid block for some time.

Steroids. A class of structurally related compounds, based on a system of condensed rings of carbon and hydrogen, which are widely distributed in animals and plants. Included in the steroid family are sterols, found in all animal cells, vitamin D, sex hormones, bile acids and cortisone, a drug used in the treatment of rheumatic fever.

Stickleback, a family of small spiny-finned fish widely distributed in both fresh and salt water. Male constructs roofed nest held together by sticky secretion from glands near kidneys. Several females deposit eggs therein which he jealously guards until after young are hatched.

Stirrup, a loop of metal U-shaped strap suspended from the sides of the saddle, used for mounting and to support the horseman's foot. Some authorities allege their use as far back as the early Iron Age, and it is generally believed that they were used in battle in A.D. 378, when the Gothic cavalry defeated the legionaries of the Emperor Valens at Adrianople. Stirrups relieved the tension of the rider's knees and so enabled him to be armed from top to toe.

Stoat, a slender, carnivorous mammal with short legs, related to the weasels. The stoat is distinguished from the latter by its longer tail, which has a black tip. The black tip is retained even in the winter when the animal turns white, the fur then being known as "ermine". It is found in northern latitudes, and is abundant in Arctic America.

Stoma (pl. **stomata**), microscopic pores on the surfaces of leaves through which gaseous exchanges take place and water is lost. It has been estimated that a single maize plant bears 200 million stomata, usually closed at night.

Stone-Flies, comprise the order of insects called Plecoptera, which includes some 700 species, of which about thirty occur in Britain. The wings are membranous, and two long, thread-like feelers protrude at the tail end. The larvae are aquatic.

Stonehenge, a remarkable collection of Bronze Age monuments on Salisbury Plain. The site which contains ditches, earthwork-banks and megaliths (large stones) has long been recognised for its architectural innovations (the trilithon or free-standing arch and the circle of dressed and lintelled stone blocks) and for its astronomical, numerical and geometrical properties. The building and rebuilding, according to modern archaeological research, lasted from about 2100 to 1600 B.C.

Stork, a family of heron-like birds with long bills, freely distributed over Europe, Asia, Africa and S. America. The White Stork is an occasional visitor to England, and, more rarely, the Black Stork; these are the only two European storks.

Stratosphere, a layer of the earth's atmosphere which lies between the tropopause (c. 12 km above the earth) and the stratopause (c. 50 km). The ozone layer lies within the stratosphere and is responsible for the relatively high temperature there. The region is less turbulent than the troposphere, and is usually clear of clouds and other "weather", making it attractive for air transport.

Stratum (pl. **strata**), a bed or layer of rock.

Strontium. This silver-white metallic element, no. 38, was discovered by Hope and Klaproth in 1793, and isolated by Sir Humphry Davy in 1808. The chief strontium minerals are celestite (sulphate) and strontianite (carbonate). Compounds of strontium give a brilliant colour to fireworks and signal flares. Radioactive isotopes of strontium (strontium-90) are formed as fission products in nuclear explosions and tend to collect in bone on account of the chemical similarity in strontium and calcium (q.v.). This hazard is a cause of great alarm. See **Fall-out**.

Sturgeon, a large fish found in northern seas and rivers with five rows of bony plates along the back and sides and pointed mouth with four barbels. Caviare is prepared from sturgeon ova. The rights of the Crown to certain wild creatures, including sturgeon, caught off the coasts of Britain and held since the time of Edward II, were abolished in 1970.

Sublimation, when a solid substance is heated and turns into vapour without passing through the liquid stage and then condenses as a solid on a cold surface, it is said to "sublime" and the process is called "sublimation". Iodine behaves in this way, and sublimation is used as a method of purifying it.

Submarine, the first submarine, the *Nautilus*, was designed by Robert Fulton and tried out in the river Seine and in the sea off Brest in 1801. The idea was too revolutionary to find acceptance and it was not until electricity for under-water propulsion became available that the submarine underwent extensive development. Britain became interested about 1900 and the Germans developed it and made it into an instrument of warfare. The first voyage under the North Pole was made in 1958 by the American nuclear-powered submarine *Nautilus* (q.v.). The Royal Navy's nuclear submarine fleet includes 4 Polaris vessels—HMS *Resolution* (1968), *Renown* (1969), *Repulse* (1969), *Revenge* (1970), each armed with 16 missiles with thermonuclear warheads. The Government in March 1982 decided to replace the Polaris force with a new fleet of Trident II submarines at a cost of £7,500m. The Labour Party opposed this decision. Britain's nuclear strategic force is assigned to NATO.

Suez Canal, connecting the Mediterranean and the Red Sea, was built by the French engineer Ferdinand de Lesseps and opened in 1869. An Egyptian company, *Canal Maritime de Suez*, was formed in 1866 with a capital of 200 million francs. The British Government acquired 176,602 shares out of a total of 400,000 for £4 million (value 31 March 1956, £28,982,544). Under the Convention of 1888 all nations were granted freedom of navigation without discrimination in peace or war. The right was recognised by Egypt in the Anglo-Egyptian Agreement of 1954, under which Britain agreed to give up the Suez base. The Suez Canal Company was nationalised by the Egyptian Government without warning in 1956, since when it has been widened and deepened and the average time of transit reduced. The waterway which had been barred to Israeli ships since the creation of the state of Israel in 1948, and to all shipping since the Middle East war of 1967, was reopened in 1975.

Suffragette, member of the Women's Suffrage Movement who in the early part of this century agitated to obtain the parliamentary vote. The movement ended in 1918, when women of 30 were given the vote. In 1928 a Bill was passed which granted equal suffrage to men and women. The leaders of the Women's Suffrage Movement were Mrs. Pankhurst and her two daughters, Sylvia and Dame Christabel, Mrs. Fawcett, Annie Kenney and others.

Sugar, to the chemist the term is a generic one covering a group of carbohydrates, including cane sugar (sucrose), glucose, fructose, and maltose. In ordinary parlance sugar means sucrose, which is obtained from the sugar cane, sugar beet or sugar maple.

Sulphur, element no. 16, is a brittle, crystalline solid, symbol S, abounding in the vicinity of volcanoes. It is yellow in colour. It occurs in combination with other elements, as sulphates and sulphides, and allied with oxygen, hydrogen, chlorine, etc., is of great commercial utility. Used in its pure state it constitutes the inflammable element in gunpowder; it is also used for matches and for making sulphuric acid.

Sulphuric Acid, a compound of great commercial importance, used in a variety of manufactures,

and composed of sulphur, oxygen and hydrogen. Extremely corrosive, and is present in acid rain (q.v.).

Sun, the centre of our solar system, is only one of millions of stars in our galaxy. The earth orbits the sun, which has a diameter of 1·39 million km, at a distance of 149·6 million km. The sun thus has a volume a million times that of the earth. At the surface, the gravitational field is 28 times that at the earth's surface. It rotates on its axis from east to west, though not as a solid, the solar equator turning once in about 25½ days and the poles in about 34 days. Large spots are observed on the sun which form and disappear at irregular intervals. The area of the disc covered by the spots, however, reaches a maximum roughly every 11 years, when the sun's heat seems rather greater than usual and magnetic storms more frequent (sunspot cycle). Spectrum analysis shows that the sun is composed of many elements found in the earth. Its surface temperature is about 6,000°C. Observations made in 1964–65 (Year of the Quiet Sun) complemented those obtained during the International Geophysical Year 1957–58, when the sun was remarkably active. The earth is in the outer atmosphere of the sun and subject to its winds and storms. The apparently inexhaustible heat of the sun, which has maintained life on the earth for millions of years, is derived from the destruction of matter, involved in the transmutation of hydrogen nuclei into helium nuclei, in which process about four million tonnes of matter are destroyed every second. At this rate of conversion the sun will go on radiating for 30,000 million years. The Soviet space rocket *Lunik I*, fired on 2 January 1959, became the first artificial planet of the sun. See also **F8**.

Superconductor, a metal in a state in which its electrical resistance has entirely vanished so that electric currents can flow indefinitely without generating heat or decreasing in strength. The superconducting state of metals was first discovered in mercury by Onnes in Leiden in 1911. There are many magnetic and thermal properties associated with superconductivity and the phenomenon as a whole has proved to be of great scientific interest: it resisted explanation till about 1957. In the meantime many metals and alloys were found to show the property but only at very low temperatures—below $c. -260°C$. There is a growing number of practical applications, e.g., coils of superconducting wire (kept very cold by liquid helium) can be made to carry enough electric current to produce strong magnetic fields. Such fields are very constant and do not require the large supply of electrical power that ordinary electromagnets need.

Supersonic Speed, a speed greater than the speed of sound (in air at sea-level sound waves travel at about 1223 km/h). When a body travels at a speed which is greater than the speed at which disturbances themselves can travel, a mechanism exists for the generation of waves of enhanced intensity. Thus aircraft travelling at supersonic speeds produce shock waves in the air somewhat analogous to the bow waves of fast-moving ships. These shock waves are regions of intensely disturbed air which produce the sonic boom effect so distressing to people living near supersonic routes. *Supersonic* is not to be confused with *ultrasonic* (q.v.).

Surface Tension. The surfaces of fluids behave in some respects as though they were covered by a stretched elastic membrane. This property is called "surface tension". The action of detergents may be attributed in part to a reduction in the surface tension of water, allowing it to wet the surface of dirty articles.

Surrealism. The aim of the Surrealist school of painting and sculpture is to overcome the barriers between conscious and unconscious mind, the real and unreal worlds of waking and dreaming. As such it has a long and respectable ancestry, although the term was not in use until 1922 when it was picked by André Breton from Guillaume Apollinaire who had used it in connection with certain works by Chagall. However, Bosch in the 15th cent., Fuseli and Goya in the 18th, and many other purveyors of the weird and fantastic were the forerunners of modern Surrealism. The modern movement has broadly speaking taken two different directions: the first was towards complete fantasy and absurdity which took the form of "found objects"—*e.g.* a bird-cage filled with sugar-cubes and a thermometer, a bottle-dryer, a bicycle wheel, or abstract works with strange and apparently irrelevant titles such as Paul Klee's *Twittering Machine*; the second towards highly detailed and realistic paintings of objects placed in strange juxtapositions—*e.g.*, Salvador Dali's trees with limp watches drooping over their branches or Georgio de Chirico's deserted and classical-looking streets with long arcaded perspectives and a lone statue or a bunch of bananas in the foreground. On the whole Surrealism has spent its initial force and become almost respectable; its idea of strange juxtapositions, now widely commercialised, finds a place in advertisement illustrations and in the more sophisticated forms of window-dressing.

Swans, large, graceful birds which together with the ducks and geese form the family Anatidae. There are three European species with white plumage; the Mute Swan distinguished by its orange bill with black knob (less prominent in female), a familiar sight on the rivers and ornamental lakes of Great Britain. Two wild swans are winter visitors here, the Whooper and Bewick's Swan. The "pen" (female) and "cob" (male) mate for life and the young swans are called "cygnets".

Swan-upping. The annual marking of the Thames swans which takes place during the third week of July. This ancient ceremony dates back to the 15th cent. when all the Thames swans were declared to be Royal birds owned by the Crown. Two city guilds—the Vintners' and Dyers' Companies—own about a third of the 200 swans now on the Thames. This privilege was granted to them by King Edward IV in return for money grants. Vintners' birds are marked with a nick on each side of the bill, the Dyers' with a nick on the right side only. The Queen's birds are unmarked.

Sweet Potato. This plant (*Ipomoea batatas*), which is a climbing perennial belonging to the convolvulus family, has thick roots that are rich in starch, and are eaten like potatoes. A native of the W. Indies and Central America, new varieties of sweet potato have been bred which stand cooler climates and can be grown as far north as Cape Cod. The sweet potato of New Zealand is called the Kumara.

Swift, a bird so-called from the extreme speed of its flight, resembling a swallow but related to the humming-bird. It has long, scythe-like wings, sooty-black plumage and greyish-white chin. There are several species inhabiting most parts of the world, particularly the tropics. The British breeding bird is among the latest to return from Africa and the earliest to go. Swifts are the only birds to use saliva for their nests. One oriental species builds its nest entirely from saliva.

Sword, hand weapon of metal used in open combat, characterised by a longish blade. During the Middle Ages the most famous blades were those made by the Arabs at Damascus and those made at Toledo.

Symbiosis. When two organisms live together and both derive mutual benefit from the association, the partnership is known as symbiosis. An example is the symbiosis of an alga and a fungus in lichens; another is the ordinary pea plant and the bacteria which live in the nodules on the pea's roots.

Synapse is the point of association between one nerve cell and another. The nervous impulse travelling along one nerve has to be transmitted to the next across a minute gap. This is the synaptic gap. The mode of transmission is chemical though it was at first thought to be electrical. The impulse arriving at the synapse releases a chemical transmitter which diffuses across the gap and stimulates an impulse in the adjacent nerve cell. See **Q5**(2).

Syndicalism. See Section J.

Synod, an assembly of the clergy of a particular church, state, province, or diocese. The Synod of Whitby (664) settled the dispute between the Celtic and the Roman churches in the matter of Easter in favour of the Roman system of reckoning.

Synoptic Charts. These are meteorological charts used in forecasting on which weather conditions at a network of stations, at a standard hour of observation, are recorded, using symbols of the international weather code. Surface weather maps have been drawn regularly for more than a hundred years and the modern advance is the drawing of other maps showing conditions in the upper air. The plotting is done quickly by computer.

Synoptists. The writers of the first three Gospels whose narratives in the main agree, though Matthew and Luke add material not found in Mark (written first); all three differ from John's Gospel.

T

Taiping Rebellion, 1850–64, most famous of China's many peasant uprisings. It took place in Hunan (the province where Mao Tse-Tung was born) and was savagely suppressed with the help of foreign powers.

Taj Mahal, the white marble mausoleum built at Agra by Shah Jehan in memory of his favourite wife who died 1629. Over 20,000 men were occupied for over 20 years in its erection.

Takahe or Notornis, large New Zealand bird of the rail family which for many years was believed to be extinct. Small colony found in 1948 in remote valley of mountainous part of the S. Island. The bird is strictly protected.

Take-Over Bid describes an offer made to all the shareholders of a company to purchase their shares at a named price and conditional upon acceptance by the holders of a named proportion of the total share issue. If accepted the purchaser thus gains control of the company.

Tallage, in Norman times, were taxes levied by the Crown upon lands of the royal demesnes. The levying of tallage was taken away by a statute of 1340 which required the consent of Parliament for all direct taxes.

Tammany, an organisation founded in New York (c. 1786) and formed from a benevolent society named after an Indian chief. It came to exert a powerful influence over political movements in that city. The leaders of the organisation used their power when their party was successful at the polls to appoint their nominee to every prominent office, and exacted bribes for concessions and privileges, and generally Tammany rule has meant wholesale corruption. Of this there was ample evidence in the disclosures of the Tween and other Tammany frauds, and in the fact that the "Boss" usually contrived to make himself wealthy.

Tantalum, a scarce bluish metallic element, no. 73, symbol Ta, discovered by Ekeburg in 1802. Chemically related to vanadium and niobium, it is usually associated with the latter in nature. For several purposes it can be used in place of platinum, and it finds application in the making of surgical instruments. Tantalum is very hard, and resistant to acids (other than hydrofluoric acid); it is used in alloys.

Taoism. See Section J.

Tapestry, a fabric largely used in former times for wall decoration and hangings. It was known to the ancient Greeks, but in its modern form came into prominence in the 15th and 16th cent., when it was manufactured in a marked degree of excellence by the weavers of Flanders, especially those of Arras. The manufacture was introduced into England early in the 17th cent., and was attended by considerable success. At the present day the term is applied to worsted cloths for furniture coverings, and there are also various kinds of tapestry carpets now made. The most famous tapestries of olden times were the Aubusson Tapestry and the Savonnerie. The Gobelin Tapestry factory, originated in Paris in the reign of Francis I, is still a national establishment. *See also* **Bayeux Tapestry.**

Tapirs. The tapirs constitute a family close to the horse family and the rhinoceros in the Ungulate order. They have four toes on the front feet and three on the hind. The snout is drawn out into a short trunk. The largest tapir is the Malayan tapir, which stands 1 m at the shoulder. Four species occur in C. and S. America.

Tar is a dark viscid product obtained from the destructive distillation of wood, coal, peat, etc. Wood tar is acid owing to the presence of acetic acid ("pyroligneous acid"). The highest proportion of coal tar goes into road making. Distillation of coal tar yields many valuable compounds, including benzene, phenol (carbolic acid), naphthalene and creosote; the final residue after distillation is pitch. Based on the chemical manipulation of compounds from coal tar is the preparation of many perfumes, food essences, drugs, antiseptics and plastics.

Tarpeian Rock at Rome received its name from the tradition that Tarpeia, the daughter of the Governor of the Citadel who betrayed the fortress of the Sabines, was crushed to death by their shields and buried beneath the rock. From this height persons guilty of treason were hurled to death.

Tate Gallery, named after its founder, Sir Henry Tate, at Millbank, S.W., was opened in 1897; Sir Henry Tate bore the cost of the building (£80,000) and also contributed the nucleus of the present collection. "The Turner Wing", the gift of Sir Joseph Duveen, was added in 1910.

Tayberry, a high-yielding new fruit, dark red with a strong, sweet flavour, which is a cross between a raspberry and a blackberry.

Tay Bridge spans the Tay at Dundee, opened for rail traffic on 20 June 1887. A previous bridge, completed in 1877, was blown down on 28 December 1879, as a train was passing over it. A new bridge was opened on 18 August 1966 for road traffic, 2,244 m in length, the longest road bridge in Britain.

Tea was introduced into England about the middle of the 17th cent., when it was a great luxury, and fetched from £6 to £10 a pound. It is an Asiatic plant, native properly to China, Japan and India. Up to about 1885 most of the tea imported into this country came from China, the bulk now comes from India and Sri Lanka.

Teal, the smallest of the European ducks and next to the Mallard the commonest British species. It is a handsome bird and a very swift flier, but not as swift as the Garganey or Summer Teal.

Telecommunications. The sending of messages over a distance. The term is generally applied to the sending of messages by telegraph, telephone, radio, television or radar. The first submarine telegraph cable between England and France was laid in 1850 and, following Hertz's investigations into electric waves, Marconi's invention led to Britain being linked with Europe by wireless telegraphy in 1899. The first permanently successful telegraph cable across the Atlantic was laid in 1866. The first telephone service between London and Paris was opened in 1891. The electro-magnetic telephone was invented by Alexander Graham Bell, a Scottish-born American, in 1876. The first submarine telephone cable to span the Atlantic was laid in 1956 connecting Britain with Canada and the United States, and many submarine telephone cables have since been laid including the Commonwealth cable system completed in 1967. The spectacular advances in space research depended on the new tools of work provided by parallel developments in telecommunications, e.g., long-range radio and television transmission, electronic computer control. See also **Satellite Communication, Radar, Radio Television.**

Telemetry, measurement at remote distances by means of a radio-link from the object (missile or satellite) to the ground. The third Russian sputnik, for instance, carried apparatus for measuring, among other things, the pressure and composition of the atmosphere, and the intensity of different kinds of radiation from the sun. Its radio transmitter, powered by solar-energy batteries, sent out the information in coded form by means of uninterrupted signals at 20·005 megacycles with a duration of 150–300 milli-seconds. Radio telemetry from inside the body is increasingly used in medical and biological research; miniature radio transmitters can be swallowed or implanted in man or animal to detect physiological conditions.

Telepathy and **Clairvoyance.** See **Section J.**

Teleprinter, a telegraph transmitter with a typewriter keyboard, by which characters of a message are transmitted electrically in combinations of 5 units, being recorded similarly by the receiving instrument, which then translates the matter mechanically into printed characters. The telex or public teleprinter service provides direct person-to-person transmission of written messages.

Telescope, an optical instrument for viewing objects at a distance, "the astronomer's intelligencer". Lippershey is credited with construction of the first in 1608; Galileo constructed several from 1609 and Newton was the first to construct a reflecting telescope. The ordinary telescope consists of an object-glass and an eye-lens, with two intermediates to bring the object into an erect position. A lens brings it near to us, and the magnifier enlarges it for inspection. A refracting telescope gathers the rays together near the eyepiece and is necessarily limited as to size, but the reflecting telescope collects the rays on a larger mirror, and these are thrown back to the eyepiece. The world's largest reflectors are at Mount Pastukhov, Caucasus (6 m), Mount Palomar, California (200 in), Mount Wilson, California (100 in), the McDonald Observatory at Mount Locke, Texas (82 in), and the Victoria B.C. Observatory (183 cm). The *Hale* 200 in telescope at Mount Palomar has revealed objects never before photographed; it is able to probe space and photograph remote galaxies out to a limiting distance of 2,000 million light years. The *Schmidt* telescope at Mount Palomar has been used to make a huge photographic map of the universe. The 98 in *Isaac Newton* telescope has been moved from the Royal Observatory at Herstmonceux, Sussex, to La Palma, Canary Is. The giant steerable radio telescope built by Manchester University at Jodrell Bank, Cheshire, has a 250 ft reflector. The largest single radio dish in the world is the non-steerable 300 m instrument at Arecibo in Puerto Rico. Another instrument of radio astronomy is the interferometer which consists of spaced aerials. The biggest of these is in New Mexico, the array consisting of 27 steerable parabolic dishes 82 ft in diameter. Recently the technique of linking radio telescopes on different continents has been developed for fine observation. See also **F3, Astronomy, Radio Astronomy.**

Teletext, the system of displaying printed information and simple diagrams on domestic television screens. Two public services are available in Britain—CEEFAX (Seeing Facts), broadcast by the BBC, and ORACLE (Optical Reception of Announcements by Coded Line Electronics), by the Independent Broadcasting Authority. Teletext makes use of some of the spare lines available in the ordinary 625-line television picture, the signals being translated into written display on the screen by means of a special decoding adaptor built into the set or attached to it. User access to the information, broadcast as separate "pages", is obtained by using a pocket calculator-sized keypad. Teletext services in Britain at present offer a wide range of subject material, including weather forecasts, news headlines, sport and financial statistics, in six colours plus white. It is also possible to superimpose news flashes over ordinary programmes. All the information is provided by specially created editorial units and the pages are transmitted in rapid rotation, a one-hundred page "magazine" taking up to 25 seconds in all. CEEFAX and ORACLE pages are made up of a maximum of 24 lines of 40 characters, the same standard format as that of Viewdata. Viewdata links the television set with computerised information via the telephone and is regarded as almost limitless in application as it would be possible to make use of data offered through the global communications satellite system.

Television, or the transmission of images of moving objects by radio. To understand the problems of television it is necessary to consider the action of the human eye. Basically the eye consists of a lens which projects an image of the scene before it upon the retina, a light-sensitive screen at the back of the eye. The retina is made up of several millions of tiny light-sensitive elements, each quite separate and distinct from its neighbours, and each separately connected to the brain by an individual fibre in the optic nerve. Thus the eye is a very complex organ, and it is able to pick out numbers of tiny details from a scene and convey each detail separately and simultaneously to the brain. It does not send a blend of different points of light and shade in the same way that the ear sends a blend of different sounds; if it did the brain would receive a completely unintelligible blur. From this it is clear that a television system which transmitted a mixture of detail would be useless; it must transmit all the details in a scene separately, yet almost simultaneously, and re-assemble them at such a speed that the eye cannot observe the building-up process. A means of doing this was provided by Nipkow in 1884, when he invented his famous scanning disc, and later Weiller invented the mirror drum for the same purpose. Such mechanical devices as these held the field for many years and in 1923 Baird in this country and Jenkins in America were both using them for the experiments which, in 1925, led to the successful transmission of shadows and simple outlines. It was not until 1926, however, that the first practical demonstration of television, as we understand it, took place when Baird transmitted by radio moving pictures of living human faces over a short distance. The B.B.C. began televised broadcasts in 1930; the I.T.A. in 1955. The first television exchange across the Atlantic was made in July 1962 by way of the *Telstar* satellite.

Tellurium, a relatively scarce element, no. 52, symbol Te, discovered in 1782 by von Reichenstein. Chemically it behaves rather like sulphur; its salts are known as tellurides. It occurs chiefly combined with metals in ores of gold, silver, copper and lead. It is a semiconductor, and some of its compounds (also semiconductors) are coming into use in technical devices.

Templars were soldier knights organised in the 12th cent. for the purpose of protecting pilgrims in their journeyings to and from Jerusalem, and obtained their name from having had granted to them by Baldwin II a temple for their accommodation. At first they were non-military, and wore neither crests nor helmets, but a long wide mantle and a red cross on the left shoulder. They were established in England about 1180. During the crusades they rendered valuable service, showing great bravery and devotion. In the 12th cent. they founded numerous religious houses in various parts of Europe and became possessed of considerable wealth. It was this that caused their downfall. Kings and Popes alike grew jealous of their influence, and they were subjected to much persecution, and Pope Clement V abolished the Order in 1312. Edward II in 1308 seized all the property of the English Templars. The English possessions of the Order were transferred to the Hospitallers of St. John, afterwards called the Knights of Malta. *See also* **Hospitallers, Knights, Teutonic Order.**

Temple, a building dedicated to the worship of a deity or deities. Those built by the ancient Greeks at Olympia, Athens and Delphi were the most famous. The Temple of Diana at Ephesus was another. The Temple of Solomon at Jerusalem was destroyed and rebuilt several times; Herod's Temple was destroyed by the Romans in A.D. 70.

Temple Bar, an historic gateway (designed by Sir Christopher Wren in 1672) that until 1877 stood at the junction of the Strand and Fleet Street, London, dividing the City from Westminster. It was re-erected at the entrance to Theobald's Park, near Cheshunt, Herts., in 1888.

Terbium, an element, no. 65, symbol Tb, discovered in 1842 by Mosander, belonging to the group of rare-earth metals.

Teredo, the scientific name of the ship-worm, a peculiar bivalve mollusc, which lodges itself when young on the bottoms of wooden ships and bores its way inwards, causing much injury.

Termites, also known as *While Ants,* though they are not related to the true ants and are placed in an entirely different insect order (*Isoptera*). They abound in the tropics and also occur in temperate countries, though only two species

are common in Europe. There is no British species. They live in colonies and their nests take the form of mounds of earth and wood, cemented together with saliva, and up to 6 m in height. Five separate castes are recognised, three of them being capable of reproduction, and the other two are sterile.

Tern. This slender, gull-like bird has long pointed wings, a deeply-forked tail, pale grey and white plumage, black cap, and is a very graceful flier. There are several species, some of which are summer migrants to Britain. The Arctic tern winters in the Antarctic, returning to find a nesting place in the spring.

Terrapin, a kind of fresh-water tortoise. There are several species widely distributed in the Northern Hemisphere.

Tertiary Rocks, in geology the rocks formed during the Caenozoic era comprising the Eocene, Oligocene, Miocene and Pliocene periods. *See* **F48.**

Teutonic Order, of German military knights, was founded in the Holy Land at the end of the 12th cent. for succouring the wounded of the Christian army before Acre. They were dispersed in the 15th cent. but the Order continued to exist until 1809, when Napoleon I confiscated its properties. In 1840 the order was resuscitated in Austria as a semi-religious knighthood. *See also* **Hospitallers, Knights, Templars.**

Textured Vegetable Protein, often referred to as TVP, is an edible protein material given a fibrous texture in the course of its manufacture from agricultural products. Nutritionally the material resembles meat and the extent to which it also resembles meat in succulence, flavour, feel in the mouth, suitability for chewing, etc. depends on the sophistication of the manufacturing technique and on the skill of the cook. The common starting material is the soya bean which is rich in protein and oil. The latter is removed, also for use in the food industry, and the residue is further processed to concentrate the protein and to remove unwanted flavours. A paste of suitable consistency is then forced under pressure through small holes and solidified as fibres. Bound together with a suitable binder and appropriately flavoured, these fibres form a lump of protein substance analagous to meat. TVP is widely produced, available commercially and used domestically and in the catering industry. Meat products containing it must show it in the list of ingredients.

Thallium, a blue-grey metallic element, no. 81, symbol Tl, discovered by Crookes in 1861. It is obtained from the flue dust resulting from the burning of pyrites for sulphuric acid manufacture.

Thanksgiving Day, a national holiday in the United States, observed on the fourth Thursday in November: instituted by the Pilgrim Fathers in 1621 to celebrate their first successful harvest.

Theodolite. The instrument used by surveyors for measuring angles in the horizontal and vertical planes; also used in meteorology for following balloons to measure the speed and direction of wind.

Therm. The charges for gas for lighting and heating (formerly reckoned at per cubic foot) are now based on the calorific, or heat, value of the gas, and the unit used is termed a therm. The therm is 100,000 British thermal units.

Thermionic Emission is the departure of charged particles from matter under the influence of heat. The higher the temperature the greater the flow of escaping particles. The most common example is the emission of electrons from red-hot electrodes—this is the basic phenomenon made use of in thermionic valves (*see* **Valve**). If the hot electrode (the cathode) is enclosed in an evacuated or gas-filled bulb, the emitted electrons can be collected at another electrode (the anode) and will flow through an external circuit back to the emitter. Thus an electric current has been generated by heat.

Thermodynamics, a term first applied by Joule to designate that branch of physical science which treats of the relations of heat to work. What is called the first law of thermodynamics is thus stated by Clerk Maxwell: "When work is transformed into heat, or heat into work, the quantity of work is mechanically equivalent to the quantity of heat." In one of its many formulations, the second law asserts that "the heat tends to flow from a body of hotter temperature to one that is colder, and will not naturally flow in any other way". *See* **F20.**

Thermo-electric Devices. If two wires of different materials are formed into a loop and if the two joins are kept at different temperatures a current flows in the loop. This was discovered by Seebeck in 1822, and the device is called a thermocouple. The electric current could in principle be made to drive some useful machine, and the energy comes from the heat that is absorbed by the thermocouple—if one part of the thermocouple is not hotter than the others it will not work. It has long been realised that this is a device that converts heat directly into electricity without raising steam and driving dynamos as in a power-station. However, until recently nobody has used thermocouples for much besides temperature measurement, for which they are exceedingly useful. The new development is the manufacture of semiconductors (*q.v.*); for the thermo-electric effects of these new materials are much greater than those of metals. A material much studied in this connection is a compound of bismuth and tellurium, bismuth telluride. It now seems practicable to generate useful electricity from suitably designed thermocouples. For example, the USSR produces a thermo-electric device which uses the heat from the chimney of a domestic oil-lamp to produce enough electricity to work a radio. Presumably this is very useful in remote parts with no electricity supply. But the possibilities do not stop there. Indeed, an eminent Russian authority has stated that thermocouples could produce electricity direct from the warmth of sunlight on a scale and at a cost comparable with conventional fuel-burning power-stations. Even if solar energy cannot be so used, it might be possible to use the heat of nuclear reactors, but this means that the thermo-electric devices would have to stand up to very heavy radioactivity and still work. It is not surprising, however, that many firms are showing great interest in thermo-electricity these days.

Thermometer, an instrument by which the temperature of bodies is ascertained. The most familiar kind of thermometer consists of a glass tube with a very small bore, containing, in general, mercury or alcohol. This expands or contracts with variation in the temperature, and the length of the thread of mercury or alcohol gives the temperature reading on a scale graduated in degrees. Various forms of thermometer are used for particular purposes. *See* **Thermometer Comparisons, Section N.**

Thermonuclear Reactions. *See* **Nuclear Fusion.**

Thirty-nine Articles. *See* **Articles.**

Thistle, Order of. *See* **Knighthood.**

Thorium, a scarce, dark grey, metal element, no. 90, symbol Th, discovered by Berzelius in 1828. All substances containing thorium are radioactive. Chief source of thorium is monazite sand, big deposits of which occur in Travancore (India), Brazil and the USA. Considered important as a potential source of atomic energy since the discovery that it can be transmuted into U^{233}, which is capable of fission like U^{235}.

Thrush, a large family of song-birds of the *Passeriform* order, distributed all over the world. The British species include the robin, redstart, nightingale, song-thrush (or mavis), blackbird, mistle-thrush, ring-ouzel of the mountains and large numbers of migrant fieldfares and redwings from northern Europe are winter visitors.

Thunder, the sound heard after the occurrence of a lightning flash. It is due to vibrations of the air along the path of the flash, which are set up by the sudden heating (and expansion) followed by the rapid cooling (and contraction) to which the air is subjected. It is unusual for thunder to be heard more than 16 km away, the distance being estimated roughly by allowing 1 km for every 3 seconds which elapse between seeing the flash and hearing the thunder. Continued rolling of thunder results from the zig-zag nature of the flash and the multiple strokes of which it is composed, variations in the energy developed along the path, and echo effects. Thunder-

storms are caused by powerful rising currents of air within towering cumulonimbus clouds and are most frequent during the afternoons and evenings of sunny summer days.

Thursday, the 5th day of the week, named after Thor, the Scandinavian deity. To the ancient Romans Thursday was *dies Jovis*, or Jupiter's day.

Tidal Power. The principle of exploiting the energy of the tides is similar to hydro-power since it involves the harnessing of falling water. A barrage across a bay or estuary is filled during flow tide and closed during ebb tide creating a difference in level. When the water is allowed to fall towards the lower side of the barrage it operates a turbine which drives a generator. More sophisticated schemes would incorporate pumped storage facilities. An essential requirement is a large tidal range in order to get a sufficient head of water. Although a 240MW scheme has recently been completed on the River Rance in France, it is believed that the economics of tidal power are generally insufficiently favourable for the method to be widely used. *See also* **Hydroelectric Schemes** and **Severn Barrage.**

Tides, the periodical rise and fall of the waters of the ocean and its arms, are due to the gravitational effect of the moon and sun. Newton was the first to give a general explanation of the phenomenon of the tides. He supposed the ocean to cover the whole earth and to assume at each instant a figure of equilibrium, under the combined gravitational influence of earth, sun and moon, thus making and controlling the tides. At most places there are two tides a day, and the times of high- and low-water vary according to the positions of the sun and moon relative to the earth. When earth, moon and sun are in line (at full moon and new moon) the gravitational pull is greatest and we get "spring" tides. When sun and moon are at right angles (first and third quarters of the moon's phases) we get the smaller "neap" tides.

Tiers Etat, the lowest of the three estates of the realm as reckoned in France—nobility, clergy and commons (*tiers état*)—prior to the Revolution.

Tiger, a powerful carnivorous animal of the cat family, which occurs in India and certain other parts of Asia. Its skin is of a tawny yellow, relieved by black stripings of great beauty of formation. Some tigers attain a length of from 3 to 3·6 m.

Time. The measurement of time has become of increasing importance to man with the advance of civilisation. It was at first almost inevitably based on the succession of night and day, the waxing and the waning of the moon, and on the changing seasons of the year, and the astronomical observation of these three periodic effects has served as the basis of time measurement until recent years. The precision of the observations has continually increased, and clocks have been developed for dividing the day into smaller units. The clocks were adjusted so as to keep in step with the rotation of the earth on its axis, but during recent years an atomic standard of time has been developed, and clocks are now adjusted so as to keep in step with the natural period of an atomic vibration. *See* **Clock, Greenwich Mean Time, British Standard Time** and **N9.**

Tin is a white, metal element, no. 50, symbol Sn (Latin *Stannum*), whose commonest ore is cassiterite (tin oxide), which occurs in Malaya, Indonesia, Bolivia, Zaïre, Nigeria and Cornwall. It protects iron from rusting, and the tin coating on tinplate is applied by dipping the thin steel sheet in molten tin or by electrolysis. Tin alloys of importance include solder, bronze, pewter and Britannia metal.

Tit or **Titmouse,** a small insectivorous bird of the woodlands and forests, bright of plumage and very active and agile, often seen hanging upside down searching for food. There are over fifty species, eight of which occur in Britain: the Great and Blue Tits, familiar in gardens and countryside, the Cole Tit, Marsh Tit, Willow Tit, Bearded Tit, Long-tailed or "Bottle" Tit and the Scottish Crested Tit.

Titanium, a scarce metallic element, no. 22, symbol Ti, difficult to extract from ores, found in association with oxygen in rutile, anatase and brookite, as well as with certain magnetic iron ores. It combines with nitrogen at a high temperature. Discovered by the Rev. William Gregor in 1791. Titanium alloys, being very resistant to stress and corrosion, and combining strength with lightness, and finding wide application not only in marine and chemical engineering but in the building of aircraft, rockets, and the nuclear-energy field. Titanium dioxide is now widely used in making paints.

Tithes, an ecclesiastical tax consisting of a tenth part of the annual produce known to the ancient Jews, and first imposed by Christian authorities in the 4th cent., although not made compulsory in England before the 9th cent. Tithes derived from land are termed "praedial", those derived from cattle being styled "mixed", while others are personal. After the passing of the Tithes' Commutation Act of 1836, tithes were gradually converted into rent charges, and to-day the old form of tithes exists only to a small degree. Consult Tithe Act of 1936.

TNT (Trinitrotoluene). A high explosive formed by the action of a mixture of nitric and sulphuric acids on toluene. Not highly sensitive to shock, it can be used in shells without danger, and is exploded by a time, or detonator, fuse. Apart from wartime applications, it is used in blasting in quarries and mines.

Toad, an amphibian, differing from the frog in having a dry, warty skin, a heavier, squat build and shorter limbs. It has a similar metamorphosis, is largely nocturnal, and will wander far from water after the breeding season. Two toads occur in Britain, the Common Toad and the Natterjack. The latter can be identified by the narrow light stripe running down the middle of the back.

Tobacco is made from the leaves of various narcotic plants of the *Nicotiana* family, which contain a volatile oil and an alkaloid called nicotine. Tobacco is largely grown in America, India, Japan, Turkey, Greece, Canada, Italy, Indonesia, Bulgaria, Philippines, France, Congo, China, Zimbabwe, Zambia, S. Africa, S. America and other countries of a warm climate. It undergoes various processes of preparation. The leaves are first dried, then cut into small pieces, moistened and compressed, and in this form it is known as cut or "shag" tobacco; when moistened with syrup or treacle and pressed into cakes, it is Cavendish; when twisted into string form, it is "twist" or 'pig-tail". For cigars the midribs of the dry leaves are removed, and what is left is moistened and rolled into cylindrical shape. For snuff, the tobacco leaves are moistened and allowed to ferment, then dried, powdered and scented. *See Section P (Respiratory System)* for the connection between tobacco-smoking and lung cancer.

Tolls. Payments for privileges of passage were first exacted in respect of ships passing up rivers, tolls being demanded on the Elbe in 1109. Tolls for land passage are said to have originated in England in 1269, toll-bars being erected at certain distances on the high-roads in the 17th cent., where toll had to be paid for all vehicles passing to and fro. After about 1825 they began to disappear, but still linger on some country roads and bridges. Tolls on London river bridges ceased in 1878-79.

Tonic Sol-Fa, a system of musical notation in which monosyllables are substituted for notes. Thus the major diatonic scale is represented by Doh, Ray, Me, Fah, Soh, La, Te, Doh. The system was invented by a Miss Glover of Norwich in about 1840 and has proved of great assistance in the teaching of music in schools.

Tonsure, the shaven part of the head of a Roman Catholic ecclesiastic, dates from the 5th or 6th cent. In the Roman Catholic Churches only a circle, or a crown, is shaved, while in the Greek Church shaving is forbidden.

Topaz, a transparent mineral gem, being a silicate and fluoride of aluminium and generally found in granite rocks. Its colour is yellow, but it also occurs in pink and blue shades. The best kinds come from Brazil.

Topiary, the art of clipping and trimming trees, shrubs, etc., into ornamental shapes. In Britain this art goes back before Elizabethan times when gardens were formal and the shapes simple and symmetrical. By the end of Queen Anne's reign topiary had become much more elaborate, and all kinds of fanciful shapes were produced. Pliny in his *Letters* tells how box hedges were clipped into different shapes in Roman times.

Topology is a branch of mathematics which studies geometrical objects from the point of view of their general shape rather than their precise measurements. For example, from the point of view of topology a ring doughnut and a picture frame have the same shape because they both have one single hole through them. Topology is used, for example, to deduce geometrical facts about an irregularly shaped object such as the Earth from the geometry of a regular object such as a perfect sphere of the same general shape. In its more formal aspects topology is an important tool in other parts of mathematics.

Tornado, a violent whirlwind, characterised by a black, funnel-shaped cloud hanging from heavy cumulonimbus and travelling at speeds up to 60 km/h. Tornadoes vary in diameter from less than a metre to a kilometre and occur frequently in the Mississippi region of the USA, where it has been estimated that the circling winds of the vortex may reach a velocity of 600 km/h. In West Africa the term is applied to thundery squalls.

Tortoises and Turtles, are cold-blooded reptiles, four-footed and encased in a strong shell protection, the shells of some species being of beautifully horny substance and design, once in much demand for combs, spectacle frames and ornamental work. It is the custom to designate the land species as tortoises and the aquatic kinds as turtles. The green turtle, so called because its fat has a green tinge, is in great demand for soup. Together the tortoises and turtles make up the reptilian order called *Chelonia*, the biggest representatives of which are the giant land tortoises of the Galapagos Islands, reaching a weight of 225 kg and living a century. Some of these giant tortoises are even said to have reached 200 or 300 years of age.

Toucan, a South and Central American family of brilliantly coloured birds, remarkable for their huge bills. Toucans live on fruit, are of arboreal habits, and nest in holes. There are about 37 species.

Touchstone, a kind of jasper called by the ancients "Lydian stone", of economic value in testing the quality of metal alloys, especially gold alloys. The testing process is very simple. The alloy is drawn across the broken surface of the Touchstone, and from the nature of the mark or streak it makes the quality of the alloy can be ascertained.

Tourmaline, a mineral occurring in different colours in prismatic crystals. It is a well-known example of a pyro-electric crystal, *i.e.,* one that has a permanent electric polarisation. A double silicate of aluminium and boron, it occurs in Cornwall, Devon, S. America and Asia.

Tournaments were equestrian contests between military knights and others armed with lances, and frequent in the Middle Ages. The Normans introduced them to England.

Tower of London was built as a fortress by William the Conqueror. It was a royal palace in the Middle Ages and later used as a garrison and prison. Many distinguished prisoners were executed there, or on the neighbouring Tower Hill, including Anne Boleyn, Catherine Howard, Lady Jane Grey, the 2nd Earl of Essex, and the Duke of Monmouth. The Chapel Royal of St. Peter ad Vincula in the Tower was built in 1105 and took its present shape in the reign of Henry VII. The Crown Jewels are kept at the Tower, and in the Armoury a fine collection of armour is preserved. The attendant staff are called Yeomen Warders of the Tower. Their style of dress is of the Tudor period.

Trade-Mark, a mark used in relation to goods for the purpose of indicating a connection in the course of trade between the goods and some person having the right, either as a proprietor or registered user, to use the mark. Trade-marks can be registered, the registration holding good for 7 years and being renewable thereafter indefinitely for periods of 14 years. Infringement of a registered trade-mark renders the infringer liable to damages.

Trade Winds form part of the circulation of air round the great permanent anticyclones of the tropics and blow inwards from north-east (Northern Hemisphere) and south-east (Southern Hemisphere) towards the equatorial region of low pressure. Atlantic trades are more regular than those of the Pacific. The belts may extend over 2,400 km of latitude and, together with the Doldrums, move north and south in sympathy with the seasonal changes in the sun's declination, the average annual range being about 5 degrees of latitude.

Trafalgar, Battle of, was fought off Cape Trafalgar on 21 October 1805, between the British under Nelson and the French and Spanish under Villeneuve and Gravina. It was a complete victory for the British, but Nelson was killed.

Trafalgar Square. The site has often been referred to as the finest in Europe. It was conceived originally as a square by John Nash (1752–1835) when the project was considered of linking Whitehall with Bloomsbury and the British Museum. It was to be named after the new monarch as King William the Fourth's Square but on the suggestion of George Ledwell Taylor (a property owner near the site) alteration to the more popular name Trafalgar Square was agreed to by the King. On the north side the National Gallery was planned by Nash and erected by William Wilkins on the place of the Royal Mews—a work of William Kent a century before. The lay-out was the idea of Charles Barry but he did not approve the erection of the Nelson column (which see). His idea was for the square to have a grand flight of steps from the north side with sculptural figures of Wellington and Nelson but the Commons decided otherwise and the column as designed by William Railton was begun in 1840. The two fountains by Barry were supplanted in 1948 by ones designed (1938) by Sir Edwin Lutyens. Executed in Portland stone they are flanked by some bronze sculptures. In the same year memorial busts of Lords Jellicoe and Beatty were placed by the north wall.

Transept. The cross aisles of a church, projecting at right angles from the nave or choir.

Transistor. An electronic device consisting of a small piece of semiconducting solid (usually germanium or silicon) to which contact is made at appropriate places by three wires. The three parts resemble in function (not construction or behaviour) the cathode, anode, and grid of a thermionic valve, and transistors can perform many of the operations that valves have hitherto been used for in radio, television, etc. They possess several advantages over valves since there is no need for evacuated glass bulbs nor for a heated emitter to give off electrons. This leads to much greater compactness and economy as well as to a much longer life. Nevertheless, there are certain limitations to their use, and they are not yet suitable as substitutes for valves in all cases. The device was invented by the Americans Bardeen, Brattain and Shockley in 1948.

Transubstantiation. See **Section J.**

Treasure-Trove, a legal term applying to treasure (coin, bullion, gold or silver articles) found hidden in the earth or other place, for which no owner can be discovered. The treasure legally belongs to the Crown, but it is the practice to return to the finder all articles not required for national museums and to reward him with the full market value of such as may be retained. It is the duty of the finder to report to the Coroner for the district in which the find is made who holds an inquest to find whether the discovery be treasure-trove or no. In England concealment is a criminal offence. See also **Wreck.**

Tree Frog, occurs most commonly in America and Australasia. The common European tree frog is a brilliant green animal, the adhesive discs at the tips of its fingers and toes enabling it to cling to trees, etc., with ease.

Tree Rings as Natural Calendar. The approximate relationship between radiocarbon dating (q.v.) and true calendar age for the past 7,000 years has been established from measurements on

tree-rings. Because one tree-ring is formed annually and its thickness is characteristic of the climatic conditions during its growth, it is possible, by comparing distinctive groups of rings, to date a series of trees. By using the long-lived Bristle Cone pines, tree-rings dating back to 500 B.C. have been obtained. It has been found that the radiocarbon age around, say, 3000 B.C. is too young by c. 600 years and because of short-term fluctuations near, say, 2000 B.C., a particular radiocarbon age can correspond to more than one true calendar age. These corrections are far less than those proved necessary after the publication of the first radiocarbon dates. Tree-rings (based on the measurement of deuterium in wood) can also show the pattern of temperature fluctuations over hundreds of years and thus make it possible to trace climatic changes before written records began. The term for tree-ring dating is dendrochronology.

Tree Shrew, an arboreal insectivorous mammal of Asia belonging to the family *Tupaiidae.* Tree shrews are related to the shrews, though in appearance they resemble squirrels except for their sharply pointed snout. They occur in Borneo, Thailand, China and Malaya.

Trent, Council of, the longest and one of the most important in the history of the Roman Catholic Church, was convened to combat the doctrines of Martin Luther. It first sat in 1545, the last sitting being in 1563. At this Council the general policy, principles and dogmas of the Roman Catholic Church were settled.

Triassic or **Trias,** the earliest geological period in the Mesozoic era, which began some 225 million years ago. Triassic formations 7,600 m thick occur in the Alps. Modern insects were appearing, and also small reptile-like mammals. Other important Triassic animals were: dinosaurs, ichthyosaurs (marine reptiles), and pterosaurs (flying reptiles). See **F48.**

Tribunes, name assigned to officers of different descriptions in ancient Rome. The original tribunes were the commanders of contingents of cavalry and infantry. The most important tribunes were the tribunes of the plebs, first elected in 494 B.C. as the outcome of the struggle between the patrician and the plebeian orders. They held the power of veto and their persons were sacred.

Trichoptera. This is the insect order comprising the Caddis-flies. These are moth-like insects having hairs on the wings. They are usually found fluttering weakly near water. The larvae are aquatic and are remarkable for the cases (caddis cases) which they build out of sticks, small stones, sand grains, and shells.

Tricolour, the flag of the French Republic since 1789, consisting of three nearly equal vertical bands of blue, white and red (ratio 90:99:111).

Trilobites, extinct marine arthropods, most abundant in the Cambrian and Ordovician systems. Their appearance may be roughly described as resembling that of a woodlouse, and like that animal the trilobites were capable of rolling their bodies up into a ball.

Trinity. The Christian doctrine that God exists in three persons, all co-equal, and indivisible, of the same substance—God the Father, God the Son (who became incarnate as Jesus), begotten of the Father, and God the Holy Ghost, proceeding from Father and Son. The system denying the Trinity is Unitarianism. See **Section J.**

Trinity House, on Tower Hill, London, was incorporated in 1514 as an association for piloting ships, and has ever since been entrusted with various matters connected with the regulation of British navigation. Since 1854 the lighthouses of the country have been under its supervision. The acting Elder Brethren act as Nautical Assessors in Marine cases which are tried by the High Court of Justice. In 1986, it was proposed that Trinity House would lose its responsibility as the principal pilotage authority in Britain to local harbour authorities.

Trireme, an ancient vessel with three rows of oars of great effectuality in early naval warfare. Mentioned by Thucydides. It was a long, narrow vessel propelled by 170 rowers. The Romans copied it from the Greeks.

Tritium, a radioactive isotope of hydrogen which has three times the weight of the ordinary hydrogen atom. It is produced by bombarding an isotope of lithium with neutrons and has a half-life of 12½ years, decaying with the emission of β-particles (electrons).

Triumvirate, a term used to denote a coalition of three persons in the exercise of supreme authority. The first Roman triumvirate was that of Pompey, Julius Caesar, and Crassus, 60 B.C.: the second was that of Mark Antony, Octavus and Lepidus, 43 B.C.

Tropic-Bird, a long-tailed sea bird, of which there are 3 species (the Red-billed, the White-tailed, and the Red-tailed), frequenting the tropical regions of the Atlantic, Pacific and Indian oceans. They are commonly called Bo'sun Birds.

Troposphere. The atmospheric layer which extends from the earth's surface to the stratosphere. As a general rule temperature falls as altitude increases. See **Atmosphere.**

Troubadours, lyric poets who flourished from the 12th to the end of the 13th cent., chiefly in Provence and the north of Italy. They were often knightly amateurs, and cultivated a lyrical poetry intricate in metre and rhyme and usually of a romantic amatory strain, written in the *langue d'oc.* They did much to cultivate the romantic sentiment in days when society was somewhat barbaric and helped considerably in the formation of those unwritten codes of honour which served to mitigate the rudeness of mediaeval days. See also **Jongleurs.**

Trouvère or **Trouveur,** mediaeval poet of northern France, whose compositions were of a more elaborate character—epics, romances, fables, and chansons de geste—than those of the troubadour of the south. The poetry was written in the *langue d'oïl.* Flourished between the 12th and 13th cent.

Truffles are subterranean edible fungi much esteemed for seasoning purposes. There are many species, and they are found in considerable quantities in France and Italy, less commonly in Britain. They are often met with under beech or oak trees, and prefer calcareous soils, but there are no positive indications on the surface to show where they are, and they are not to be cultivated. Hogs, and sometimes dogs, are used to scent them out, the former, by reason of their rooting propensities, being the most successful in the work.

Tsetse, an African dipterous fly belonging to the same family as the house-fly. It is a serious economic pest as it transmits the protozoon causing African sleeping sickness when it pierces human skin in order to suck blood.

Tsunami, a seismic sea wave originating from any one of several submarine geological phenomena such as volcanic explosions, landslides of earth movements. Tsunamis are extremely long wavelength waves which travel in the open ocean at speeds up to 640 km/h. In deep water their height is only barely perceptible, but on reaching shallow coastal water they may attain heights of up to 30 m and can cause devastation to low-lying areas. The Pacific Ocean, whose rim is a seismically active area, is particularly susceptible to tsunamis. Following the damage caused by a tsunami which struck the volcanic islands of Hawaii on 1 April 1946, an early-warning system has been in operation. Tsunamis are often incorrectly referred to as tidal waves.

Tuatara or **Sphenodon,** a reptile of great antiquity, the sole surviving species of the *Rhynchocephalia,* found in New Zealand. It has a rudimentary third eye on the top of the head; this is called the pineal eye and corresponds to tissue which in mammals forms the pineal gland.

Tube Foot, the characteristic organ of locomotion of starfishes and kindred animals. They are arranged in pairs along the underside of the arms, and their sucker-like ends can grip a surface very tightly. The action of the suckers depends on hydraulic pressure.

Tudor Period extends from 1485 to 1603. The first Tudor sovereign was Henry VII, descended from Owen Tudor; then followed Henry VIII, Edward VI, Mary and Elizabeth, the last of the line.

Tuesday, the third day of the week, named from the Saxon deity Tuisto, Tiw or Tuesco. To the Romans it was the day of Mars.

Tuileries, a French royal and imperial palace dating from 1564. It was attacked by insurgents during the outbreaks of 1792, 1830 and 1848, and was burned down during the Commune of Paris in 1871.

Tumulus, a mound of earth raised over the bodies of the dead. The mound of Marathon, enclosing the bodies of the Athenians who were killed in the famous battle with the Persians, is a celebrated tumulus. Such mounds were commonly raised over the tombs of the distinguished dead in ancient times, and sometimes enclosed heavy structures of masonry. The Roman "barrows" were tumuli. Evidence of such mounds are frequent in prehistoric remains.

Tuna or **Tunny,** a large marine fish belonging to the mackerel family, frequenting the warm waters of the Atlantic, Pacific and Mediterranean. Tuna fisheries are an important industry.

Tundra, the vast treeless plains lying in northern N. America and northern USSR where long severe winters and permanently frozen subsoils (permafrost) have resulted in specially adapted plant communities. The summer thaw and impervious permafrost cause waterlogging of lowland areas and marsh plants occur on these sites. In summer the ground cover of lichens and mosses with some flowering plants is distinctive. Stunted willows and birches occur in certain sites.

Tungsten, a hard, brittle metallic element, no. 74, symbol W (it was formerly called wolfram), silver to grey in colour. Its chief ores are wolframite (iron and manganese tungstate) and scheelite (calcium tungstate). Tungsten is alloyed in steel for the manufacture of cutting tools; also in the non-ferrous alloy stellite. Electric lamp filaments are made from tungsten. Tungsten carbide is one of the hardest substances known and is used for tipping tools.

Turbines propelled by steam provide power for the propulsion of many ships, and on land steam turbines are a principal source of power, being used in large central electricity stations, for instance, to convert heat energy into electrical energy. Gas turbines have recently come into use in aeroplanes, and gas-turbine railway locomotives are being developed. The first gas-turbine ship had its trials in 1947, just half a century after the first steam-turbine ship.

Turbot, a large flat fish, highly valued as food. It often attains from 13 to 18 kg in weight. Its flesh is white and firm. It is confined to European waters, and is caught by line or trawl.

Turkey, a fowl of American origin, brought to Europe from America soon after the discovery of that country. It was a domesticated bird in England in the first half of the 16th cent.

Turpentine, an oily substance obtained from coniferous trees, mostly pines and firs. It is widely used especially in making paints and varnishes, and also has medicinal properties.

Turquoise, formerly called Turkey-Stone, is a blue or greenish-blue precious stone, the earliest and best specimens of which came from Persia. It is composed of a phosphate of aluminium, with small proportions of copper and iron. India, Tibet, and Silesia yield turquoises, and a variety is found in New Mexico and Nevada. It derives its name from the fact that the first specimens were imported from Turkey.

Turtle Dove, a summer visitor from Africa to southern England. It is a small, slender bird with reddish-brown upper parts, pinkish throat, black tail with white edges, and a repeated purring note.

Tweed. A rough-surfaced fabric of the twilled type, usually all-wool, though cheaper kinds may include cotton. Of a soft, open, flexible texture, it may have a check, twill or herring-bone pattern. Harris, Lewis, Bannockburn and Donegal tweeds are well known. "Tweeds" is said to have been written in error by a clerk for "twill".

Twelfth Night is the eve of the feast of the Epiphany, and in olden times was made the occasion of many festivities. It was the most popular festival next to Christmas, but is now little observed.

Twilight is the light which is reflected from the upper portion of the earth's atmosphere when the sun is below the horizon (before sunrise or after sunset). The term is most usually understood to refer, however, to the evening light; the morning light we call dawn. The twilight varies in duration in different countries, according to the position of the sun. In tropical countries it is short; in the extreme north it continues through the night.

Tyburn, a former small tributary of the Thames, which gave its name to the district where now stands the Marble Arch, Hyde Park. Here public executions formerly took place.

Tycoon, the title by which the commander-in-chief of the Japanese army (virtually the ruler of Japan) was formerly described by foreigners. (In Japanese *taikun* means great lord or prince.) The term is now applied, usually in a derogatory sense, to an influential business magnate.

Tympanum is, in architectural phraseology, the triangular space at the back of a pediment, or, indeed, any space in a similar position, as over window or between the lintel and the arch of a doorway. In ecclesiastical edifices the tympanum is often adorned with sculpture.

Tynwald, the title given to the Parliament of the Isle of Man, which includes the Governor and Council (the Upper House), and the House of Keys, the representative assembly. This practically constitutes Home Rule, the Acts passed by the Tynwald simply requiring the assent of the Sovereign.

U

Uhlan, a light cavalry soldier armed with lance, pistol, and sabre and employed chiefly as skirmisher or scout. Marshal Saxe had a corps of them in the French Army; and in the Franco-German war of 1870 the Prussian Uhlans won fame.

Ultramarine, a sky-blue pigment obtained from *Lapis lazuli*, a stone found in Tibet, Iran, Siberia and some other countries. A cheaper ultramarine is now produced by grinding and heating a mixture of clay, sulphur, carbonate of soda and resin.

Ultrasonics, sound waves of frequency so high as to be inaudible to humans, *i.e.*, above 15,000 Hz (Hz is SI unit for cycle per sec.). Ultrasonic waves are commonly produced by causing a solid object to vibrate with a suitable high frequency and to impart its vibrations to the air or other fluid. The object may be a quartz or other crystal in which vibrations are excited electrically, or a nickel component which is magnetically energised. There are numerous technical applications, *e.g.* submarine echo soundings, flaw detection in castings, drilling glass and ceramics, emulsification. Ultrasonic waves are an important tool of research in physics. Bats produce very loud sounds when they are flying, but at ultrasonic frequencies (20,000 to 150,000 Hz), so that we cannot ourselves hear them.

Ultra-Violet Rays. These are invisible electromagnetic rays whose wavelengths are less than 3900 Å. (Angstrom = one hundred-millionth of a centimetre.) The sun's radiation is rich in ultra-violet light, but much of it never reaches the earth, being absorbed by molecules of atmospheric gases (in particular, ozone) as well as by soot and smoke particles. One beneficial effect of ultra-violet light on human beings is that it brings about synthesis of vitamin-D from certain fatty substances (called sterols) in the skin. The wavelengths which effect this vitamin synthesis also cause sun tan and sun burn. Ultra-violet lamps (which are mercury-vapour discharge lamps) are also used for sterilising the air inside buildings, their rays being lethal to bacteria. Many substances fluoresce under ultra-violet light; for instance, zinc silicate glows green, while cadmium borate throws out red light. This phenomenon is applied practically in fluorescent lamps, the light of requisite hue being secured by judicious mixture of the fluorescent materials which coat the lamp. *See* **Electric Light.**

Umbra, the full shadow of the earth or moon during an eclipse; the half shadow is called penumbra.

Unciae. The Romans took over the Egyptian cubit and divided it into 16 digits as well as into 12 parts called *unciae*, the *uncia* being the origin of the inch.

Underdeveloped Countries are those in which economic structure and development are held back, or, as some would have it, countries which are underdeveloped in the transitive sense of the word. The causes of the condition of underdevelopment are complex but two opposing sets of theories dominate discussion. On the one hand there are those theories that attribute underdevelopment to the internal characteristics of the underdeveloped countries themselves. This is the doctrine of original underdevelopment as it implies that such countries are responsible for their own underdevelopment. On the other hand there are the theories that ascribe underdevelopment directly to the distortions of economic structure and the exploitation involved in the relations between the developed and underdeveloped countries. The expansion of capitalism from its birthplace in Western Europe has created a world-wide production system and market (*i.e.*, a world economy from which no country is completely isolated) structured and determined by the imperatives of capital accumulation in the developed countries. This view implies that the state and process of underdevelopment in one part of the world is inevitable as long as there is development in another. Development and underdevelopment are then mutually interdependent. *See also* **Section G, Part III.**

Unicorn, a fabulous single-horned animal. In heraldry its form is horse-like, with the tail of a lion and pointed single horn growing out of the forehead. In the Middle Ages the unicorn was a symbol of virginity.

Union of Great Britain and Ireland was proposed in the Irish Parliament in January 1799 after the 1798 Rebellion and came into force on 1 January 1801. The troubled history of Ireland, associated with the question of self-government, nationalism, land and religion, culminated in the Easter revolution of 1916. A treaty giving the 26 southern countries independence in 1921, as the Irish Free State, was followed by a period of internal dissension. In 1937 a new constitution was enacted in Eire in which no reference was made to the Crown. This, however, left in force the External Relations Act of 1936 and with its repeal in 1948, Eire separated itself from the British Crown and thus severed the last constitutional link with the Commonwealth, and became an independent Republic.

Union, Treaty of, was the treaty by which Scotland became formally united to England, the two countries being incorporated as the United Kingdom of Great Britain, the same Parliament to represent both, Scotland electing sixteen peers and forty-five members of the House of Commons. Uniformity of coins, weights, and measures was provided for, Scottish trade laws and customs were assimilated to those of England, and as regards religion and the practices of the law, Scotland was to continue as before. This Act was ratified on 1 May 1707.

Universe in astronomy means not only the star system (of which the sun and planets are a small part) but all the countless star systems or nebulae which may be separated from each other by millions of light-years. *See* **F3–8.**

Universities are institutions of higher education whose principal objects are the increase of knowledge over a wide field through original thought and research and its extension by the teaching of students. Such societies existed in the ancient world, notably in Greece and India, but the origin of the University as we know it today lies in mediaeval Europe, the word *universitas* being a contraction of the Latin term for corporations of teachers and students organised for the promotion of higher learning. The earliest bodies to become recognised under this description were at Bologna and Paris in the first half of the 12th cent.; Oxford was founded by an early migration of scholars from Paris, and Cambridge began with a further migration from Oxford. Other Universities sprang up all over Europe, including three in Scotland—St. Andrews (1411), Glasgow (1451) and Aberdeen (1494)—which were followed by Edinburgh in 1582. These six bodies remained the only Universities in Great Britain until the foundation in 1826–29 of University and King's Colleges in London (resulting in the establishment of the University of London in 1836) and of the University of Durham in 1832. There are (1983) thirty-four Universities in England: Aston, Bath, Birmingham, Bradford, Bristol, Brunel, Buckingham, Cambridge, The City, Durham, East Anglia, Essex, Exeter, Hull, Keele, Kent, Lancaster, Leeds, Leicester, Liverpool, London, Loughborough, Manchester, Newcastle, Nottingham, Oxford, Reading, Salford, Sheffield, Southampton, Surrey, Sussex, Warwick and York. Other institutions of university standard are the University of Manchester Institute of Science and Technology; the Manchester Business School; the London Graduate School of Business Studies; Cranfield Institute of Technology; and the Royal College of Art. Formed from colleges of technology, art and design, commerce and other institutions, thirty polytechnics have been established in England and Wales as centres of higher education. Wales has one University (The University of Wales with colleges at Aberystwyth, Bangor, Cardiff and Swansea) in addition to the Welsh National School of Medicine, the Institute of Science and Technology, and St. David's, Lampeter. Scotland now has eight: Aberdeen, Dundee (1967), Edinburgh, Glasgow, Heriot-Watt (1966), St. Andrews, Stirling (1967), and Strathclyde (1964), Britain's first technological University. Northern Ireland has two: Queen's University, Belfast and the New University of Ulster at Coleraine. The Open University received its charter in 1969; it provides degrees and other courses together with radio and television programmes and began its broadcasts in January 1971. The Republic of Ireland has the University of Dublin (Trinity College, Dublin), and the National University of Ireland with colleges at Dublin, Cork and Galway. In the USA the development of higher education has left the Universities less sharply defined than in Europe and the Commonwealth, among the best known being Harvard (1636), Yale (1701), Princeton (1746), Columbia (1754), Cornell (1865), California (Berkeley), Massachusetts Institute of Technology. In 1973 the United Nations University was established with headquarters in Tokyo. In Britain, Universities receive aid from the State mainly in the form of direct grants from the Treasury made on the advice of the University Grants Committee. But they are selfgoverning institutions free from State control. In 1983, the private institution at Buckingham received its charter.

Uranium, a metallic element, no. 92, symbol U, discovered by Klaproth in 1789 in pitchblende. It is a white metal which tarnishes readily in air. Great developments have followed the discovery that the nucleus of the uranium isotope U^{235} undergoes fission, and uranium minerals have become very important since it was found that atomic energy could be released controllably by taking advantage of fission. Before atomic energy work began to take the major part of the world's output of uranium minerals, the chief users of uranium compounds were the ceramics and textile industries. *See also* **Nuclear Reactors, Nuclear Fission, F13(1).**

Uranus. This planet was discovered by Herschel in 1781. Its diameter is *c.* 51,800 km and its mean distance from the sun is $2,869 \cdot 6 \times 10^6$ km. It has five small satellites and is surrounded by five very thin rings (first seen 1977). Uranus rotates on its side so that each pole faces the sun every half-revolution of the planet round the sun, *i.e.,* every 42 years. Uranus has 5 moons—Miranda, Ariel, Umbriel, Titania and Oberon. Voyager 2 is due to visit Uranus (Jan. 1986) and Neptune (Sept. 1989). *See* **F8 and Voyager.**

Urea, the final product in mammals of the breakdown of nitrogenous waste, *e.g.,* excess aminoacids. It is very soluble in water and is excreted in urine. In 1828 Wohler synthesised urea from inorganic matter. This was the first laboratory synthesis of an organic substance and refuted the idea that living creatures or life force are necessary to create such substances.

Ursa Major and **Ursa Minor** ("Greater Bear" and "Lesser Bear"), two celebrated constellations, each of seven stars, in the northern celestial hemisphere, familiar since ancient times. Ursa Major has also been called "the Plough", "Charles's (Charlemagne's) Wain" or "the Wagon". The "Pointers" in this group of bright stars point to the brightest star in Ursa Minor, the Pole Star. Called the Big Dipper and the Little Dipper in the USA.

V

Valency. A term used by chemists is describe the combining ability of an element with respect to hydrogen. Thus oxygen, which forms water, H_2O, with hydrogen is said to have a valency of two, nitrogen (forms ammonia, NH_3) three, and carbon (forms methane, CH_4) four. Chlorine forms hydrogen chloride, HCl, and is said to be monovalent. This empirical approach cannot account for valency in such compounds as carbon monoxide, CO, which appears to require both elements to have the same valency. With the discovery of the electron it was realised that the concept of valency and chemical bonds is intimately concerned with the electronic structure of atoms, and theories have been advanced to explain why the same element can have different valencies in different compounds. Iron, for example, can have a valency of two ($FeCl_2$, ferrous chloride) or three ($FeCl_3$, ferric chloride). *See* **F11(1), F24(2)** and **Table of Elements.**

Valentine's Day (14 February), is a festival in celebration of St. Valentine, one of the Christian martyrs of the 3rd cent. A sweetheart or Valentine is chosen on that day and letters or tokens sent secretly to the object of affection.

Valhalla, in Scandinavian mythology, is the special Paradise to which the souls of warriors slain in battle were transported.

Valkyries, the chosen handmaidens of Odin, appointed to serve at the Valhalla banquets. Their most important office, however, according to the Norse mythology, was to ride through the air at a time of battle and point out the heroes who were to fall. It is one of these Valkyries who is made the heroine of Wagner's opera "Die Walküre".

Valve, an electronic device consisting of two or more metal plates (electrodes) usually enclosed in an evacuated glass bulb. One of the electrodes is heated causing electrons to be emitted. If a positive voltage is applied to the other electrode, the electrons will move towards it and the valve must conduct electricity. The current will only flow in one direction as the electrons are emitted only from one direction. A valve with two electrodes is called a diode, but by putting in one or more intermediate electrodes the flow of current can be sensitively controlled and the valves are then called triodes, pentodes, etc., according to the total number of electrodes in them. Valves have found extensive applications in amplifiers, rectifiers, oscillators and many electronic devices, but have now been superseded by transistors in many applications where it is advantageous to have greater reliability, smaller power consumption and smaller size.

Vanadium, a scarce metallic element, no. 23, symbol V, whose chief ores are carnotite and patronite. Some iron ores contain it. Most of the vanadium commercially produced finds its way into vanadium steels, which are used for tools and parts of vehicles, being hard, tough and very resistant to shocks. The oxide is used as a catalyst in industry, especially in making sulphuric aicd.

Van Allen Belts. One of the most remarkable discoveries made during the IGY, 1957–58, was that the earth is surrounded by a great belt of radiation. Evidence came from *Sputnik II* (which carried the dog Laika) and from the American satellites, *Explorers I* and *III*. The American scientist, J. A. van Allen, was able to explain the puzzling data collected from these satellites. Subsequent observations with deep space-probes showed that there are in fact two zones of high intensity particle radiation surrounding the earth, one concentrated at a distance of about 1,600 km, the other at about 24,000 km. A close relation exists between the shapes of the zones and the earth's magnetic field. Recent evidence suggests that Jupiter also is surrounded by a dense belt of trapped high-energy particles.

Vatican, the Papal residence at Rome, a famous palace on the hill adjacent to St. Peter's. Its museum is a rich treasure-house of literary and artistic objects. Works of Michelangelo glorify the Sistine Chapel.

Vauxhall Gardens, a famous London pleasure resort from the early part of the 18th to the middle of the 19th cent. It was here that many great singers appeared, where the earliest balloon ascents were made, and where there were fine displays of fireworks.

Venus, the brightest of all the planets, whose orbit lies between the orbits of Mercury and Earth, is second in order from the sun (*see* **F8**). It approaches the earth to within 40 million km. It moves around the sun in the same direction as Earth and the other planets but rotates in the opposite sense. It has been visited by a number of American and Russian probes, some flybys, some soft-landings, others atmospheric probes. Venus has 100 times the atmospheric pressure of the earth and temperatures of 500°C. It is covered in a very thick cloud mainly of carbon dioxide which some scientists believe acts like a greenhouse trapping the heat from the sun. Complex reactions occur in the atmosphere and the rain consists mainly of sulphuric and hydrochloric acid. The cloud rotates about six times faster than Venus rotates and swirls into the polar regions like giant whirlpools. The terrain has been studied by radar, much of it ground-based, but a vast amount of information has come from the Pioneer Venus orbiter which mapped 98 per cent of the surface in two (earth) years. There are two major continents, Aphrodite Terra, about half the size of Africa, and the smaller Ishtar Terra, about the size of Australia, which consists of a very high plateau (c. 3,300 m) and a mountain range dominated by Maxwell Montes (at 10,600 m higher than Everest). Aphrodite Terra has a deep trench 2,900 m below "sea level". Most of the planet (60 per cent) is relatively flat, apparently covered with impact craters.

Venus Fly-trap, a well-known insectivorous plant (*Dionaea muscipula*) occurring in Carolina in damp mossy places. It is related to the Sundew. The leaf is the organ that catches the insects. The leaf blade is in two halves, hinged along the centre line. Each half bears three sensitive hairs called "trigger hairs". When an insect touches a trigger, the two halves of the leaf clap together, trapping the insect between them, when it is digested by a secretion (digestive enzymes) from the leaf, which afterwards absorbs the soluble products.

Vernalization. Seeds which, after being exposed to a low temperature, produce plants that flower earlier than usual are said to have been "vernalized". This technique of seed treatment devised by Lysenko is called vernalization. It is claimed to have been widely used in Russia to obtain cereal crops in places where climatic conditions are favourable for only a short season.

Versailles, Treaty of. The Peace Treaty, 1919, ending the first world war. The first half was devoted to the organisation of the League of Nations. Among the territorial changes Germany ceded Alsace-Lorraine to France, Posen and the Corridor to Poland. Germany undertook to disarm, to abolish universal military service, to keep only a small army of 100,000 and a small navy. Her colonies were to be shared out among the Allies under League Mandates. Reparations were to be paid, but were gradually reduced and entirely ceased in 1932. Hitler took unilateral action against the Treaty especially in regard to rearmament and the annexation of Austria. Hitler's attempt to change the eastern frontiers was the immediate cause of the second world war.

Victoria and Albert Museum, in Kensington, London, was begun in 1852 as the Museum of Ornamental Art at Marlborough House. The present building was completed in 1909. It has the following departments: Architecture and Sculpture, Conservation, Ceramics, Paintings, Prints and Drawings, Oriental Library Metal-

work, Museum Services (inc. Information and Slide Loan Service), Textiles, Furniture and Woodwork. Education (into which the old Circulation Dept., has been absorbed), Theatre Museum. The V. & A. also administers the Wellington Museum (Apsley House, Piccadilly), Ham House (Richmond, Surrey), Osterley Park House (Middx). The Bethnal Green Museum (The Museum of Childhood) is a branch of the V. & A., opened 1872.

Victoria Cross, an order of merit for conspicuous valour, awarded to members of the Army, Navy and Air Force, was established in 1856.

Videotape recording (VTR), technique for recording television programmes on to magnetic tape. The original means of storing programmes for broadcast or library purposes was by filming productions from high-quality monitors, an expensive and slow process, since the film had to be chemically developed and edited in the conventional way. The difficulty in establishing an instant play-back system along the lines of the sound tape recording system lay in the high speed and large amount of tape needed to accommodate the picture signal. The BBC experimented with a machine called VERA (Vision Electronic Recording Apparatus), but it was an American machine, the Ampex VR100, which provided the breakthrough. This recorded the picture across a wider tape rather than along it, and moving at a slower speed. Tapes, in colour or black and white, now run for about 90 minutes and can be used many times by erasing and re-recording, accuracy of editing is achieved to the second by re-recording chosen sequences on to a second machine.

Vienna Congress, sat at Vienna from September 1814 to June 1815, and settled the delineation of the territories of the various European nations after the defeat of Napoleon. The Treaty of Vienna which resulted gave Sri Lanka, Mauritius, Cape Colony, Heligoland, Malta and part of Guyana to England; Belgium, Holland and Luxemburg were united in the Kingdom of the Netherlands; Austria took Lombardy-Venetia; Russia took part of Poland; and Prussia, part of Saxony and the Rhenish province. Except for one or two changes the clauses of the treaty were maintained for over forty years.

Vikings. Scandinavian pirates who from the 8th to the 10th cent. were the terror of northern waters. Sometimes the Viking raids reached south to the Mediterranean and east to the White Sea. Their leader Rurik founded the first Russian kingdom of Novgorod in A.D. 862. The Icelandic Vikings under Eric the Red discovered Greenland in A.D. 982 and a warm period in world climate allowed many to settle there. Their expeditions took them to Labrador and Newfoundland. They excelled in shipbuilding, were fine sailors and craftsmen.

Vinyl Plastics are polymers made from derivatives of ethylene, examples are polyvinyl chloride (PVC), which is used in making plastic pipes and kitchen utensils, among other things; polyvinyl acetate used in the paint industry and in bonding laminated articles like plywood; and polystyrene (poly vinyl benzene) used in making electrical fittings and for lenses.

Viper, a family of poisonous snakes in which the venom-conducting fangs hinge forward when the snake bites. One species is found in Britain, the common viper or adder.

Virus. *See* Index to P, **F31**(2).

Visibility is defined by the distance at which the farthest of a series of objects, specially selected to show against the skyline or in good contrast with their background, can be distinguished. Visibility depends chiefly upon the concentration of water or dust particles suspended in the air. Instruments are available to measure the obscurity of the atmosphere more directly, including that at night. A large lapse rate of temperature and a strong wind are favourable to good visibility; a small lapse rate, calm or light wind favourable to bad visibility. Fog is when the visibility is less than 1,000 m; mist or haze when it is between 1,000 and 2,000 m. *See* **Pollution.**

Viscount, a title of rank coming between that of Earl and Baron. The title originally stood for

deputy-earl. The first English Viscount was Viscount Beaumont, created in 1440.

Vitamins, name of a group of organic substances found in relatively minute amounts in certain foodstuffs, essential for growth and the maintenance of normal bodily structure and function. The Hungarian biochemist Szent-Györgyi, who first isolated vitamin C or ascorbic acid, defined the vitamin as "a substance that makes you ill if your don't eat it!" See **F32(1), Index to P.**

Volcanoes are vents through which magma reaches the surface as lava flows, or as the solid products, *e.g.*, ashes and bombs, of explosive eruption. The vent may be cylindrical or it may be a long fissure. The former type usually builds up cones, *e.g.*, Vesuvius. Notable active volcanoes are Etna, Vesuvius and Stromboli, in Italy; Hekla in Iceland; and Mont Pelée in Martinique. The last-named was in violent eruption in 1902, when the chief town of St. Pierre was completely destroyed. Volcanic eruptions are sometimes linked with brilliant sunset phenomena, *e.g.*, the Indonesian island of Krakatoa (1883), whose atmospheric and tidal effects were recorded all over the world, and Agung on the island of Bali (1963), which had been dormant for 120 years. A new fissure volcano (Surtsey) developed off the coast of Iceland in 1963. Notable was the eruption of Mount St. Helens, Washington state, in 1980.

Vole, a small rodent with blunt nose, round face and short tail. Three kinds occur in Britain: the field, the bank and the water vole.

Volt, the electromotive force unit, named after Alessandro Volta (1745–1827), and defined in terms of the coulomb, the second and the joule.

Voyagers 1 and 2. These spacecraft were launched from Earth on 5 Sept. 1977 and 20 Aug. 1977 respectively as a follow-on mission to the earlier and successful Pioneer 10 and 11 spacecraft. Both were targeted initially to swing by Jupiter (*q.v.*), with Voyager 1 on the faster trajectory, to make the next phase of investigation of Jupiter and its moons, before continuing to Saturn (*q.v.*) and beyond, using the enormous gravitational field of Jupiter to assist them in their journeys. (It was this planet's gravitational field that flung Pioneer 10 (launched 1972) into space in June 1983 to make it the first man-made object to leave the solar system.) Voyager 1, in flying through the Jovian system in 1979, discovered the unique features of Io, the most volcanically active object yet found in the solar system, photographed the ice-covered moons–Europa, Ganymede and Callisto–and made many new discoveries of Jupiter, the largest and most massive planet of the solar system. Voyager 1 began surveying Saturn in Aug. 1980, and continued sending back a vast amount of new data, including some 18,000 pictures of the planet, its moons and, perhaps most spectacularly, its fascinating and complex system of rings. The measurements included infra-red and ultra-violet measurements of the structure of the planet's atmosphere, as well as data on the magnetic field and charged particle environment of the planet. When the spacecraft passed through one of the "gaps" of the ring system on 12 Nov. 1980, it made a series of fascinating revelations.

The flyby of Saturn by Voyager 2 in Aug. 1981 was carefully planned to obtain the maximum of new information to complement that obtained from Voyager 1 to help understand some of the perplexing new phenomena, and revealed even more new features of this beautiful and still enigmatic planet. Even after its Saturn flyby, the work of Voyager 2 will be far from complete: its swing by Saturn will redirect it toward Uranus, on which it will provide our first close-up data in Jan. 1986, and from there it will continue to Neptune (Sept. 1989), taking maximum advantage of a unique arrangement of all four of the outer planets, Jupiter, Saturn, Uranus and Neptune, which only occurs once every 200 years. Voyager 1, which will not pass particularly close to any planet after Saturn, carries a multi-lingual goodwill message as well as musical selections from Beethoven to Rock 'n' Roll to far outside our solar system, although it will take many thousands of years to reach the distances of even the nearest stars.

Vraic, a name for seaweed in the Channel Islands, where it is extensively used as a manure.

Vulgate, a term used to designate the Latin version of the Scriptures sanctioned by the Council of Trent. The work of St. Jerome in the late 4th cent. A.D. still the official Bible of the Roman Catholic Church.

Vulture, a famous bird of prey of two distinctive groups; that of the Old World, whose nostrils are separated by a bony partition, and the New World vulture, which has no such division. Vultures feed on carrion and are the great scavengers of tropical regions. The European species are the Egyptian vulture, Griffon vulture, Black vulture and Bearded vulture. Vultures have no feathers on the head and neck.

W

Wading Birds, *Charadriiformes,* an order of migratory, long-legged, long-billed birds, frequenting marshes and shallow waters. They include the plovers, avocets, stilts, oystercatchers, curlews, phalaropes, godwits, dunlins, sandpipers, redshanks, greenshanks, snipe, woodcocks, the pratincole of the Mediterranean and the sun bittern of tropical America. Many species breed in Britain.

Wagtails, familar long-tailed small birds, the most common British species being the Pied or Water (with sub-species White) Grey and the Yellow (sub-species Blue). Wagtails nest in holes and are active of habit.

Walloons, name given to the French-speaking population of the southern provinces of Belgium, in contrast to the Flemings or Dutch-speaking population of the northern provinces. The Walloon areas contain the mining and heavy industries of the country; the Flemish regions are more agricultural. Walloons number *c.* 3 million. Flemings *c.* 5 million. The *Mouvement Populaire Wallon* desires an autonomous Wallonia within the Belgian state.

Walpurgis Night, the night before 1 May, when witches and creatures of evil are supposed to have liberty to roam. Named after St Walpurgis, an English nun, who went on a mission to Germany in the 8th cent.

Walrus, a very large marine mammal, related to the seals having in the upper jaw two large curved tusks, which average in length from 38 to 60 cm. It lives on bi-valve molluscs, and inhabits the Arctic seas. An adult walrus can exceed 4 m in length and weigh over a tonne.

Wankel Engine *or* **Rotary Engine,** is an internal combustion engine invented by Felix Wankel in the 1930s and greatly developed since by large automobile firms in several countries. The ordinary internal combustion engine has to convert reciprocating motion of the pistons into rotary motion. In the Wankel engine the explosion of the fuel and air mixture drives a moving part (the rotor) directly into rotatory motion, and the rotor itself opens and closes the fuel inlet and exhaust ports. The three spaces between the triangular rotor and its specially shaped housing act successively as intake, compression, explosion and exhaust chambers as the rotor revolves. There are no valves and far fewer moving parts than in an ordinary piston engine. The Wankel engine is claimed to have many advantages in that it is smaller and lighter for a given horse-power, relatively simple, quieter and freer from vibration, and could contribute to pollution control. There are cars now on sale with the Wankel engine and continuous research and development will no doubt test in practice the claim of some protagonists that this engine is the agent of a technological revolution in the automobile.

Wapentake, the ancient name given in the northern countries to territorial divisions corresponding to the Hundreds of southern counties.

Warblers, a family of small, lively song-birds closely related to the flycatchers and thrushes. Represented in Britain by about 36 species, including the chiffchaff, one of the earliest spring visitors, willow-wren, wood-warbler, blackcap, garden-warbler, whitethroat, sedge and grasshopper-warbler.

Water is the simplest compound of hydrogen and oxygen. It is formed when an electric spark is passed through a mixture of the gases, and is a product of combustion of all hydrogen-containing compounds, *e.g.*, petrol, coal, coal gas and wood. Water is essential to living matter, and is the medium which carries food to animals and plants. Salts in hard water may be removed by distillation of the water or by a process known as ion-exchange (water softening). Pure water freezes at 0°C and boils at 100°C and is used as a standard of temperature on this scale. It has a maximum density at 4°C. Heating water above 100°C converts it into steam, which is used under pressure to convert heat energy into useful work, as in electrical power stations and steam engines. Water gas is a mixture mainly of carbon monoxide and hydrogen formed by blowing steam and oxygen through red-hot coke: it is used as a fuel. Water is one of the very few compounds which freezes from the surface down rather than from the bulk of the liquid up. This property has important consequences on the preservation of life in rivers and lakes when they are frozen.

Water Hyacinth (*Eichhornia crassipes*), a beautiful aquatic plant native to Brazil which has spread to other favourable equatorial regions of the world causing havoc on account of its abnormal rate of reproduction away from its natural environment. In recent years it has invaded the Nile and the Zaïre, forming vast floating carpets which block the channels, clog the paddles of river craft and deoxygenate the water, killing the fish. It is being held in check by spraying with the herbicide 2,4-D.

Waterloo, Battle of, was fought on 18 June 1815. The Allies (British, German and Dutch) under Wellington and Blücher defeated the French under Napoleon, ending Napoleon's career.

Waterloo Bridge, crossing the Thames, was built by Rennie, and opened in 1817. It had nine arches, each 120 ft (36 m) span, was built of granite, and had a length (including approaches) of 2,456 ft (749 m). The present bridge, completed in 1942, and formally opened 10 December 1945, is a fine example of reinforced concrete construction. (Architect, Sir Giles Gilbert-Scott.)

Watling Street, the name of the old Roman road which ran from the Channel ports by way of London to Shropshire. *See also* **Roman Roads.**

Watt. A unit of electrical power equivalent to 1 joule of work per second, named after James Watt (1736–1819). *See* **N7.**

Waxbill, a small Oriental and African bird of the *Estrildidae* family, with wax-like bill and beautifully variegated plumage. The Java sparrow, and the Blue-breasted waxbill are attractive, and often find their way into cages.

Wayz-Goose, the name given to a festive gathering of people employed in printing and other works, so called from the fact that in earlier times a goose was the principal dish of the feast.

Weasel. A carnivore mammal found in Britain, smallest member of the group including the Stoat, Polecat, and Pine-marten, about 20 cm long. Its fur is reddish on the upper side of the animal, white on the under side; it may all turn white in winter with the exception of the tail.

Weather is generally accepted as being the current state of the atmosphere, particularly as regards its pressure and temperature, wind, cloud and precipitation. Many other features such as fog, sunshine duration, humidity, pressure tendency, may be added to the list, all items of which are routinely observed by specially instrumented stations usually sponsored by the national meteorological services. Day-to-day changes in the weather as experienced by the individual are due to the passage of circulation systems, many of which bring clearly recognisable areas of "good" (*i.e.*, calm and sunny) weather as frequently occurs in anticyclones and "bad" (*i.e.*, cold, windy, cloudy and rainy) weather. Clearly, the weather in any place at any time is primarily determined by the frequency and intensity of synoptic-scale weather circulation systems (*c.* 3,000 km across). Local weather (over areas of *c.* 100 km) may be heavily influenced by topography, *e.g.*, valley fogs, frost hollows, etc.

Weather Lore. Before instruments were invented to measure atmospheric conditions, man relied on his own observation of wind and sky, behaviour of birds and animals, and came to associate certain phenomena with types of weather. Many popular weather rhymes have survived the centuries, and as long as forecasting is confined to the next 24 hours there is perhaps something to be said for them, particularly those dealing with the winds. What is very unlikely is that next year's summer can be predicted from this year's winter, or that one month's weather is related to that of another. The study of past records reveals too many exceptions for such predictions to be of much use in forecasting.

Weaver Bird, the popular name for a large group of finch-like birds belonging to the family *Ploceidae*, found principally in Africa but also in Southern Asia, Australia, and Europe and remarkable for their habit of building nests formed of blades of grass dexterously interwoven and suspended from the boughs of trees.

Weaving. The interlacing of two or more threads at right angles to form a fabric is a craft that has been practised since ancient times. The main principle of the weaving loom is the same to-day as it was thousands of years ago; a warp extends lengthwise through the loom, the threads being held in separate regular order by being passed through a reed or "slay", while the weft is crossed through alternating threads of the warp by means of a shuttle which holds the weft. Thus the fabric is built up. Weaving was done by hand up to the early part of the 19th cent., when Cartwright's steam-power loom was introduced. The Jacquard loom for weaving figured designs dates from 1801.

Wedding Anniversaries are: first, Paper; second, Cotton; third, Leather; fourth, Fruit and Flower; fifth, Wooden; sixth, Sugar; seventh, Woollen; eighth, Bronze; ninth, Pottery; tenth, Tin; twelfth, Silk and Fine Linen; fifteenth, Crystal; twentieth, China; twenty-fifth, Silver; thirtieth, Pearl; thirty-fifth, Coral; fortieth, Ruby; fiftieth, Golden; fifty-fifth, Emerald; sixtieth, Diamond; sixty-fifth, Blue Sapphire; seventieth, Platinum.

Wednesday, the 4th day of the week, derived its name from Woden or Odin, the Norse god of war.

Weights and Measures. *See* **Section N.**

Welding is a means of joining together two pieces of material, often metals, by heating the joint until the substances melt locally, run together, and then solidify. The heating can be by burning gas (*e.g.*, oxy-acetylene welding) or electric current (electric arc welding). Techniques exist for welding anything from hair-like wires to massive steel plates. *See* **Soldering.**

Werewolf, a man or woman, who according to mediaeval belief, could be turned by witchcraft or magic into a wolf, eat human flesh or drink human blood and turn into himself again. This belief was widely held in Europe, and similar superstitions prevail among most primitive peoples, *e.g.*, the "leopard man" of certain African tribes. Lycanthropy (from Gr. = wolf-man) is a form of madness in which the patient imagines himself a beast. *See* **Section J.**

Westminster Abbey stands on the site of an old church and Benedictine foundation of the 7th cent. It was rebuilt under Edward the Confessor, and again under Henry III, and important additions were made by Edward II, Edward III, Richard II, Richard III and Henry VII, the latter erecting the beautiful eastern chapel in the perpendicular style which bears his name. The west towers and gable were designed by Hawksmoor (1661–1736). The Abbey contains tombs of many sovereigns, of the Unknown Warrior, and many other illustrious men are commemorated by monuments.

Westminster Cathedral, seat of the Roman Catholic Archbishop of Westminster. It was designed by J. F. Bentley and built betwen 1895 and 1910. It is of red brick, in early Christian Byzantine style with a domed campanile, 283 ft (86 m) high, and a decorative interior.

Westminster Hall, adjoining the House of Parliament, was built as a Banqueting Hall by William Rufus, and many courtly festivals were held there in succeeding centuries. King John established the Law Courts there. It now forms a gigantic hallway, leading to the Houses of Parliament. Charles I, Sir Thomas More, and Warren Hastings were tried there.

Whale, a completely aquatic mammal; the fore-limbs are modified to form fin-like paddles and there is virtually no external trace of the hind-limbs. There are two major groups of whales—the *Toothed Whales*, including the Sperm-whale (Cachalot), Dolphin, Killer-whales and Porpoises; and the *Whalebone Whales*. In the latter a series of whalebone plates grow down from the roof of the mouth, and, being frayed at their edges into a hairy fringe, together constitute a filtering mechanism. The animal takes in sea water containing minute organisms on which it feeds; the mouth is then closed and the tongue raised when the water is forced out through the filter, on which is left the food. As the tongue is lowered, the whalebone plates straighten up, flicking the food on to the tongue, which transfers it to the gut. Most whale oil is obtained from the thick layer of fat under the skin (blubber), but in the Sperm-whale there is a large reserve of oil in the head. One of the major users of sperm oil is the leather industry. Ambergris used in perfumery comes from the intestine of whales. The number of whales that may be killed in a season is limited by International Convention. The three main whaling nations are Japan, Norway and the Soviet Union.

Whiskers in physics and materials science (*q.v.*) are tiny rods of crystal, thinner than human hair and perhaps 1 cm long. Their importance lies in the fact that such crystals are free from the defects described in **F21**. They are also free from surface cracks and steps. This means they are immensely strong because failures of strength in ordinary solids are due to imperfections and cracks of one kind or another. Large numbers of whiskers of strong solids like graphite, silicon, or silicon carbide embedded in a matrix of softer matter such as plastic or metal would make a very strong new material. Many laboratories are developing such substances.

White Elephant, a term in common use to designate a gift that causes the recipient more trouble or cost than it is worth; derived from an old-time custom of the Kings of Thailand who presented a white elephant to a courtier whom it was desired to ruin.

Whitehall Palace, built within sight of Westminster by Hubert de Burgh, Earl of Kent, round about 1240, was the residence of the Archbishops of York until Wolsey presented it to Henry VIII in 1530. From then until 1697, when it was burned down, it continued to be the favourite town residence of royalty, and to the Stuarts especially it was a great centre of court festivities. In those days, with its grounds, it extended from the Strand to the river. The only portion of Whitehall Palace now standing is the Banqueting Hall built by Inigo Jones, on a scaffold projected from the front of which Charles I was beheaded. A block of government buildings has been built on part of the site of the old Palace.

White House, the official residence at Washington of the President of the United States.

Whitsuntide, the festival celebrating the descent of the Holy Ghost and occurring seven weeks after Easter.

Widow Bird, certain species of African weaver birds with predominantly black plumage. In the breeding season the male birds are strikingly beautiful, with scarlet and buff markings and long tail feathers. They are social parasites and trick other birds into rearing their young.

Wigeon, a surface-feeding duck of northern Europe, known in Britain more as a winter visitor than a nesting bird. It feeds in flocks in the muddy estuaries and has a characteristic "whee-oo" call.

Willow, a water-side-loving tree of the genus *Salix*, to which the osiers belong. The best cricket-bat blades are made from a white willow, *S. alba* var. *caerulea*, a fine tree with bluish-green leaves, mostly found in Essex. Willow is also used for polo balls. Weeping willow, *S. babylonica*, is native to China and is the willow seen on Old China willow-pattern plates.

Wind, air set in motion by special atmospheric conditions, is of various degrees, from a slight rustling breeze to a hurricane. Winds are *constant*, as in trade winds or anti-trade winds; *periodic*, as in monsoons and other wind-visitations occurring according to influences of season; *cyclonic* and *anti-cyclonic*, when their motion is spiral: *whirlwinds, hurricanes,* and *tornados*, when high temperature and great density induce extreme agitation. Ordinarily, a wind is named from the point of the compass from which it blows, or it may be expressed in degrees from true north. The *sirocco*, the *mistral*, and the *simoom* are local forms of winds of great velocity. A *blizzard* is a biting blast of icy temperature. *See also* **Beaufort Scale, Section N.**

Windmills were in use in the East in ancient times, but were not much seen in Europe before the 13th cent. Wind sawmills were invented by a Dutchman in the 17th cent., and one was erected near the Strand in London in 1633. Great improvements have been made in these mills, especially in the United States, where, by the application of the windshaft principle, much space is saved and the mills can be used for pumping, grinding and other purposes.

Windows (Old Norse *vindauga* = wind-eye), an opening in a wall of a building to admit light and air, and to afford a view of what is outside. In northern Europe windows, as the derivation of the word implies, were first used for ventilation and glass was not used in private houses before the end of the 12th cent. In early Gothic (12th cent.) windows were still small and narrow, with rounded heads. In Early English (13th cent.) they became longer and the heads pointed. In the Decorated period (14th cent.) windows were mullioned (divided by slender bars into panes) and the pointed heads often traceried. In Tudor times when the Renaissance had found its way to England, windows were larger and the bay-window (projecting from the wall) and the oriel window (*q.v.*) were much in vogue; in the late 18th cent. curved bays (called bow-windows) became fashionable. Sash windows (invented by the English) with wooden frames and divided into equal rectangular panes were used in Queen Anne and Georgian houses. Their design was influenced by a passion for symmetry; they were very efficient ventilators. The French window reaches to the floor and has double casements opening as doors. A Dormer window is a vertical window set on the sloping side of a roof. One of the main features of modern architecture is the large area devoted to windows, a development made possible by improved heating systems. Windows are now mass-produced in stock sizes and patterns.

Windsor Castle, the famous British royal residence on the banks of the Thames, as it now stands, was mainly built by Henry III, though a royal residence had existed there from the time of the Conqueror. Additions were made by Henry VIII, Elizabeth and Charles II. Windsor Park and Forest comprise over 5,200 ha.

Wine, the fermented juice of the freshly-gathered grape. There are innumerable varieties, each obtaining its distinctive character from the species of wine producing the grape, the locality of the vineyard, method of cultivation, etc. Wines are of three main kinds: *sparkling,* as in champagne, due to their having been bottled before fermentation is complete; *beverage,* when the must has been fermented out before bottling. Such wines include the famous red and white wines of Burgundy, Bordeaux and the Rhône valley and the white wines of the Rhine, Moselle and Loire valleys. Wines are *fortified* by the addition of alcohol either after fermentation is complete (*e.g.,* Sherry) or during fermentation (*e.g.,* Port). The principal wine-producing countries are: France, Italy, Algeria, Spain, Portugal, Romania, Argentine, Yugoslavia, USA, USSR, Greece, W. Germany, Hungary.

Witan *or* **Witenagemot,** the name given to the king's council of "wise men" in Anglo-Saxon times, composed of the archbishops, bishops, abbots of the greater abbeys, earldormen and influential thanes.

Witchcraft. *See* **Section J.**

Woad, a plant (*Isastis tinctoria*) that in olden days was largely used in England for the blue dye obtained from the leaves. It is a biennial plant belonging to the same family (*Cruciferae*) as the wallflower.

Wolves, well-known carnivorous animals still found in many parts of Europe, but not existing in Britain since the middle of the 17th cent. They usually hunt in packs.

Women's Liberation Movement. *See* **Section J.**

Woodcock, a wading bird, valued for its flesh. It is a member of the snipe family, and breeds in Britain. The parent bird is able to carry its young between its thigh and body when flying to and from the feeding spots. It is one of the birds protected by the Game Laws.

Woodpecker, a familiar tree-climbing, insectivorous bird of conspicuous plumage, of which four species are found in Britain, the green woodpecker or yaffle (because of its harsh cry), the great spotted, the lesser spotted, and the wryneck. They build in the hollows of trees. Yaffle has a long sticky tongue for licking up ground insects, especially ants. The great and lesser woodpeckers obtain insects by digging into tree trunks with strong, chisel-like bills, spearing the insects with a sharp tongue. The metallic drumming sound made by the birds in spring is thought to be caused by their beaks hammering away at some hard resounding substance.

Wood's Metal, an alloy with a very low melting point (65°C, which is under 150°F) so that a spoon made of it will melt when used to stir a cup of tea. Contains bismuth 4 parts, lead 2 parts, tin 1 part, cadmium 1 part. Its use as a heat exchanger has now been largely superseded by silicone oils, which have a wider temperature range.

Woodworm. Four beetles are mainly responsible for woodworm damage: common furniture beetle (*Anobium punctatum*), powder post beetle (*Lyctus brunneus*), death watch beetle (*Xestobium rufovillosum*), and house longhorn beetle (*Hylotrupes bajulus*). Particular attention should be paid to wood in damp, dark and out-of-the-way places, and the backs and under-neaths of furniture. The most frequent cause of woodworm damage is the common furniture beetle (*q.v.*).

Wool is a fibre, made up of very long protein molecules. It has been largely grown and used in the manufacture of cloth in England since before the Roman invasion. It is grown on the backs of sheep, and is of various kinds, according to the breed of sheep from which it is derived. Wool differs from hair in that it has a wavy, serrated fibre, its curl being a notable characteristic, whereas hair has a smooth surface comparatively free from serratures. Long wools are mostly used for the manufacture of worsted goods, and short wools for woollen cloths, though the improvements in machinery in recent years have enabled manufacturers to utilise short wools to a great extent for dress fabrics as well as for woollens. The finest wools are obtained from the fleece of the Spanish merino sheep. Australia, USSR, New Zealand, Argentina and South Africa are the greatest wool-producing countries.

Woolsack, the name given to the seat occupied by the Lord Chancellor in the House of Lords. It is a large square bag of wool, without back or arms, covered with red cloth. At the time when it was first used, in the reign of Edward III, wool was the great staple commodity of the country and, it is said, chosen for the seat of judges as a constant reminder of the main source of the national wealth. The Lord Chancellor is said to be "appointed to the woolsack".

World Population. According to United Nations sources world population in mid-1985 was 5,290 million, an increase of 90 million in one year. More than half the total live in Asia (56·9 per cent). Different countries are at different stages in a demographic transition from the stability provided by a combination of high birth rate and high death rate to that provided by a combination of low birth rate and low death rate. Their recent population history and current trend of growth, the age-structure of their population, and consequently their population potential for the near future are all widely different. Most rapid growth is in Africa with rates of over 3 per cent in some countries. In most European countries the rate is less than 1 per cent. A baby girl born in Norway may expect to live the longest (77·6 years) and a baby boy in Sweden (72·1 years),

but a baby born in some African countries may not live to reach 40 years. It is estimated that about one in 25 of all human beings who have ever lived are alive today. Yves Coppens of the Natural History Museum in Paris writes: "The last million years have seen the birth of Homo sapiens; the last few hundreds of years his alarming proliferation. It took 115 years for the world's population to rise from one to two thousand million; in a further 35 years it rose from two thousand million to three; in the last 15 years from three to four thousand million and the acceleration continues." *See also* **Section G, Part III.**

Wreck, the name given to trove found under water, usually from a maritime wreck. Finds must be brought to the notice of the Official Receiver of Wrecks, an officer of H.M. Customs and Excise.

Wren, a family of small passerine birds possessing upturned tails and most abundant in South America. The British species is an interesting singing bird with a surprising loud note for its size.

X

Xenon a rare gaseous element, no.54, symbol Xe, occurring in minute quantities in the atmosphere, discovered by Sir William Ramsay and M. W. Travers in 1898. *See* **Rare Gases.**

X-Rays were discovered in 1895 by Professor Röntgen, of Wurzburg, while experimenting with a Crookes vacuum tube, when a photographic plate enclosed in a dark box was noticed to have become fogged. X-rays are now commonly used to examine the internal structure of many opaque objects. In medicine, industry and for security, examination may be conducted without physical invasion. X-rays may also be used to probe the structure of matter, for example the atomic structure of crystals. The discovery in the 1960s that cosmic objects emitted intense X-rays has led to many important new astronomical phenomena being discovered. *See* **F12.**

Xylem, the woody tissue of higher plants whose function is to conduct water and mineral salts upwards, and to provide mechanical support.

Y

Yacht, a light vessel now much used for pleasure trips and racing. The first yachting club was the Cork Harbour Club, started about 1720; and in 1812 the Royal Yacht Squadron was founded at Cowes. The Royal Thames Yacht Club dates from 1823. The most famous international yachting trophy is *The America's Cup* (*q.v.*).

Yak, a curious, long-haired ox, found in Tibet used as a beast of burden, and also kept for milk and meat.

Yard, a standard measure of 36 in, the word being derived from the Saxon gryd, or rod. The yard and pound are now defined by reference to the metre and the kilogram: yard = 0·9144 of a metre; pound = 0·45359237 of a kilogram. By international agreement the metre is defined by reference to the wavelength of krypton-86 light.

Yellowhammer, a common British bird of the bunting family, of lemon-yellow and brown plumage. Nests on or near the ground.

Yeomen of the Guard are a body of Foot Guards established in the reign of Henry VII for the protection of the Royal Person. Yeomen are now about 100 in number, and their duties consist in being present on ceremonial State occasions, the yearly distribution of Maundy Money, and the searching of the vaults of the Houses of Parliament on Guy Fawkes' day. "Beefeater" is the nickname of both Yeomen of the Guard and Yeomen Warders of the Tower, and they both wear the style of dress of the

Tudor period, but with one distinction, the Yeomen of the Guard wear a cross belt, the Warders do not.

Yeti, opinions differ as to whether this is a mythical inhabitant of the Himalayas, a primitive primate or bear. Evidence to date is inconclusive.

Yoga. *See* **Section J.**

York Minster, one of the oldest and finest of English cathedrals, is 160 m long, its nave is 73 m broad, and the central tower is 66 m high. The present edifice, in parts, dates back to the 12th cent., but a church stood on the site in the 7th cent. In 1829 it was set on fire by a lunatic named Jonathan Martin. In July 1984, a serious fire caused by lightning wrought severe damage to the south transept.

Ytterbium, a chemical, no.70, symbol Yb, element discovered by Urbain in 1907; one of the group of rare earth metals.

Yttrium, a chemical element, no.39, symbol Y, discovered by Mosander in 1842. It is found in a few rare minerals such as gadolinite, xenotine, fergusonite and euxenite. One of the group of rare earth metals.

Z

Zamboni Pile, a dry galvanic battery, which can provide small amounts of high-voltage current over a very long time. At Oxford a couple of Zamboni piles have kept a bell ringing for over a hundred years. These piles in the second world war were perfected and produced in quantity, being the most convenient source of current for infra-red signalling devices.

Zebra, an African quadruped of whitish-grey colour, with regular black stripings, perhaps the most beautiful member of the Equine family. Rather larger than an ass and smaller than the horse, it has a tufted tail, is of light build, wild and fleet of foot. The Zebra may be threatened with extinction—already the fate of the Quagga species—because of its slaughter by man for its beautiful skin.

Zen Buddhism. *See* **Section J.**

Zenith, the highest point in the heavens above an observer's head, the opposite pole to the nadir.

Zero, the cypher signifying nothing originally came from China. The West is indebted to the Arabs for it, who themselves obtained it from India and passed it to European mathematicians towards the end of the Middle Ages. The zero has also been found in Babylonian cuneiform. The Greeks had no such symbol, which hindered the development of their mathematics. The use of zero led to the invention of decimal fractions and to the later developments in astronomy, physics and chemistry. For absolute zero on the temperature scale *see* **Absolute Temperature.**

Zinc, a familiar metallic element, no.30, symbol Zn, known to the ancients, and used by them in the making of brass. It occurs as the sulphide, carbonate, etc. The ores of zinc are crushed, roasted and reduced with coal. In combination with copper it constitutes the familiar alloy called brass, and zinc itself is much used for roofing and other protective purposes. Zinc ores are mined in Canada, the USA, Mexico, Poland, Australia, Russia, Italy, Spain and many other parts of the world. Zinc smelting is carried on in most industrial countries, including Great Britain.

Zionism. *See* **Section J.**

Zirconium, metallic element, no.40, symbol Zr, was discovered by Klaproth in the sand of the rivers of Sri Lanka in 1789. The crystalline metal is white, soft and ductile; in its amorphous condition it is a blue-black powder. Zirconium is used in atomic reactors as containers for fuel elements, since it does not absorb neutrons.

Zodiac, an imaginary zone or belt of the sky enclosing the circuit over which the principal planets travel. It is divided into 12 equal spaces of 30 degrees each, comprising respectively the 12 signs of the zodiac—Aries, Taurus, Gemini, Cancer, Leo, Virgo, Libra, Scorpio, Sagittarius, Capricornus, Aquarius and Pisces. The idea of the zodiac originated with the Babylonians about 2000 B.C. and passed by way of the Greeks to the Western world.

Zodiacal Light, a faint cone of light occasionally seen stretching along the zodiac from the western horizon after evening twilight or the eastern horizon before morning twilight. It is believed to be due to the scattering of the sun's light by dust particles in orbit round the sun and extending beyond the earth. Recent observations at the high altitudes station at Chacaltaya in the Andes suggest that the dust is travelling round the sun in regular planetary orbits.

Zonda, a warm moist wind in Argentina of great velocity blowing from the north or northwest, and, like the Sirocco in Southern Europe, causes much discomfort. It happens when a depression is moving across the pampas, bringing with it a mass of air from the humid tropics. It is followed by a refreshing wind from the south east.

Zoological Gardens of London were opened in 1828, and belong to the Zoological Society of London. They contain one of the largest and most varied collections of living animals in the world. The Society maintains an open-air zoo at Whipsnade, on the edge of Dunstable Downs; this was opened in 1931.

Zoology, the branch of science concerned with animal life, embracing many aspects such as anatomy, behaviour, classification, distribution and ecology. *See* **Section F, Part IV.**

Zoroastrianism. *See* **Section J.**

Marginal mark	Meaning	Corresponding mark in text
δⁱ *δ*	Delete (take out)	Cross through
	Delete and close-up	Above and below letters to be taken out
stet	Leave as printed (when words have been crossed out by mistake)	. . . . Under letters or words to remain
caps	Change to capital letters	Under letters or words to be altered
s.c.	Change to small capitals	Under letters or words to be altered
caps & s.c.	Use capital letters for initial letters and small capitals for rest of words	Under initial letters and under the rest of the words
l.c.	Change from capitals to lower case	Encircle letters to be altered
bold	Change to bold type	Under letters or words to be altered
ital.	Change to italics	Under letters or words to be altered
rom.	Change to roman type	Encircle words to be altered
w.f.	(Wrong fount.) Replace by letter of correct fount	Encircle letter to be altered
ᘒ	Invert type	Encircle letter to be altered
x	Replace by similar but undamaged character	Encircle letter to be altered
⅄	Insert (or substitute) superior figure or sign	⅄ (Or encircle letters or signs to be altered)
⅄	Insert (or substitute) inferior figure or sign	⅄ (Or encircle letters or signs to be altered)
⌣	Close-up—delete space between letters	Linking words or letters
#	Insert space	∧
eq.#	Make spacing equal	Between words
less#	Reduce space	Between words
trs.	Transpose	Between letters or words, numbered when necessary
centre	Place in centre of line	Indicate position with
⌐	Move to the left	
¬	Move to the right	
n.p.	Begin a new paragraph	Before first word of new paragraph
run on	No fresh paragraph here	Between paragraphs
spell out	The abbreviation or figure to be spelt out in full	Encircle words or figures to be altered
⅄	(Caret mark.) Insert matter indicated in margin	⅄
⅄ ⅄	Insert single quotation marks	⅄ ⅄
⅄ ⅄	Insert double quotation marks	⅄ ⅄

LITERARY COMPANION

This section is arranged in three parts. The first provides a concise yet authoritative introduction to the history of the English novel. The second provides a useful glossary of literary terms. The third consists of special articles, including in this edition a guide to major literary prizes and a discussion of the structuralist debate.

TABLE OF CONTENTS

LITERARY COMPANION

I. THE ENGLISH NOVEL

INTRODUCTION

Definition

A novel is a fictitious prose narrative, usually of more than 50,000 words in length. It often deals with characters and actions that give readers an illusion of reality, but it can also be fanciful or fantastic. Its elements conventionally include a plot or story, personages, dialogue and a setting. Some novels contain such poetic elements as symbol, metaphor and rhythmical construction. Just as the content and general approach of novels show many variations, so the techniques in their writing greatly differ: narratives told in the first or third persons, in the form of letters and from different points of view are amongst the devices of presentation that have been used.

Types

Certain types can be defined, although they cannot always be clearly distinguished from one another.

The *picaresque novel* has a *picaro* (Spanish: "rogue") at the centre of its action, but sometimes this main character is an innocent or foolish person. Many adventures, described comically, satirically or realistically, befall him and influence him. A famous example is Lesage's *Gil Blas* (1715, 1724, 1735). Fielding's *Tom Jones* (1749) and Dickens' *Pickwick Papers* (1836-7) are in this tradition, which has been widely followed in England.

The *Bildungsroman* (German: "formation novel") relates the upbringing and education of the hero, as in Goethe's *Wilhelm Meister's Apprenticeship* (1795-6) and Dickens' *David Copperfield* (1849-50).

Psychological novels, exploring character, motives and relationships, were first established in France, with Madame de La Fayette's *La Princesse de Clèves* (1678) and the Abbé Prévost's *Manon Lescaut* (1731). Richardson's *Pamela* (1740) belongs to this category of fiction, which is often considered the most significant of all the kinds, reaching great profundity in the work of Dostoevsky (1821-81), Tolstoy (1828-1910) and Henry James (1843-1916).

Social novels, with the aim of exposure and reform of abuses and injustice, were prominent in the nineteenth century. Examples are Mrs Gaskell's *Mary Barton* (1848) and Charles Kingsley's *Alton Locke* (1850). Balzac's numerous novels, collected as *La Comédie humaine* (1842-8), and many by Dickens (*e.g. Little Dorrit*, 1855-6) are social novels in a more comprehensive sense, depicting characteristics of French and English society respectively.

The *novel of manners* is a sophisticated presentation of social codes of behaviour, especially amongst the leisured classes. Meredith's *The Egoist* (1878) partly belongs to this type.

Naturalistic novels, like those in Emile Zola's series, *Les Rougon-Macquart* (1871-93), and many by George Gissing (1857-1903), emphasise the power of environment in moulding human character.

Regional novels, by Thomas Hardy (1840-1928) and Arnold Bennett (1867-1931), amongst others, place importance on the traditions and influences of particular areas of a country.

In *adventure* and *detective novels*, the story or plot is a principal feature, as in Wilkie Collins' *The Moonstone* (1868) and Robert Louis Stevenson's *Treasure Island* (1883). The thriller, a variation of this type, is marked by excitement and violence, as in the James Bond novels of Ian Fleming (1908-64).

The *historical novel* deals with the past, sometimes mixing fact and fiction, such as the novels of Sir Walter Scott (1771-1832), Flaubert's *Salammbô* (1862) and Tolstoy's *War and Peace* (1863-9).

Fantasy has become increasingly popular, especially in the form of *science fiction*; Jules Verne (1828-1905) was one of the earliest and most widely read writers of this genre. English writers who have used this kind of fiction include H. G. Wells (1866-1946) and John Wyndham (1903-69). J. R. R. Tolkien (1892-1973) created a new "legendary" world in *The Lord of the Rings* (1954-5).

Purpose

The purpose of a novel varies with its type. Anthony Trollope's statement, made in his study of Thackeray (1879), has a fundamental validity: "the object of a novel should be to instruct in morals while it amuses." At one extreme, some novels are expressly meant to teach, such as some Victorian children's novels and social novels (*e.g.* many written by Charles Kingsley). At the other, some novels are meant simply as entertainment, such as detective stories and much science fiction. Trollope's term, "morals", is difficult to define, but one can say that the aim of most novels is to reveal and stimulate thought about aspects of human behaviour both individually and in personal and social relationships. Apart from these generalisations, the specific purposes of some English novels are described separately in the following survey.

Rise and popularity of the novel

Though stories in verse and prose are as old as human life itself, the novel, as we know it today, became established in the late seventeenth and early eighteenth centuries. Its rise is related to changes in the climate of ideas during that period, with its increasing emphasis on the rational and the actual. Influenced by such thinkers as Sir Isaac Newton (1642-1727) and John Locke (1632-1704), philosophers investigated the ordinary, physical world rather than the world of metaphysical speculation. At the same time, the reading public had increased in numbers, especially amongst the middle classes. This public wanted to read about the behaviour of realistic people in credible surroundings. One result in England was the publication of novels by Defoe, Richardson, Fielding and Smollett in the first half of the eighteenth century.

THE EIGHTEENTH CENTURY

Daniel Defoe

Daniel Defoe (*c.*1661-1731) is regarded as the first notable English novelist. After many years as a political pamphleteer, he published *Robinson Crusoe* (1719), based on accounts of the actual adventures of the mariner, Alexander Selkirk. The book is written with convincing, detailed realism. Robinson Crusoe's practical approach to his predicament and his powerful individualism make him an admirable character who can be seen to have a universal significance. We are shown a man confronted by adversity and yet overcoming it by means of his resourcefulness and holding to his belief in a providential God. The basic idea of a person shipwrecked on an island had a wide appeal, which was reflected in many imitations, including *The Swiss Family Robinson* (1813) by Johann Rudolf Wyss. Defoe's other novels include *Captain Singleton* (1720), *Moll Flanders* (1722), *Colonel Jack* (1722) and *Roxana* (1724). He claimed that *Moll Flanders* had a moral purpose, in that from every part of it "something may be learned, and some just and religious inference is drawn." But it survives because of its lively and uninhibited representation of the personality and doings of its disreputable, resilient heroine, who (like Robinson Crusoe) tells her own story. Formally, Defoe is an unsophisticated writer, who relies mostly on his invention of incident to keep his narrative in motion. His strength lies in his powers of observation and in his rendering of particulars, conveyed in straightforward prose, so that readers feel that they are experiencing things that actually happened.

Richardson, Fielding, Smollett and Sterne

The first great period of the English novel is 1740-71, when four important novelists flourished: Samuel Richardson (1689-1761), Henry Fielding (1707-54), Laurence Sterne (1713-68) and Tobias Smollett (1721-71). George Saintsbury, in *The English Novel* (1913), aptly called them the "remarkable exponents of a new kind of Human Comedy."

Richardson was a printer who was compiling a

collection of model letters to suit various occasions when he thought of writing an epistolary novel. The outcome was *Pamela* (1740), in which the letters reveal the story of Pamela, a servant girl, who resists her master's attempts to seduce her but finally agrees to marry him. *Clarissa* (1747-8), also written in the form of letters, tells of the tragedy of its heroine, who dies after her rape by the libertine, Lovelace. Containing a million words, it is probably the longest novel in English. Richardson's third and last epistolary novel, *Sir Charles Grandison* (1754), centres upon the scrupulously gentlemanly conduct of its hero. These are not novels of external action but are explorations of human psychology, especially of the thoughts and emotions of the young women involved. Their main theme is sexual passion and the moral problems that arise from it. The novels are admired for their sensitive portrayals of emotional and mental processes, realistically presented by means of the letters written by the characters.

Henry Fielding's first novel, *Joseph Andrews* (1742), was conceived partly as a satire on *Pamela*, which he thought hypocritical and sentimental. In picaresque style, he relates the adventures of Joseph Andrews, who is supposedly Pamela's brother, and his companion, Parson Adams. His intention in this "comic epic in prose", as he called it, was to expose the ridiculous. He therefore displays and comments upon hypocritical and affected behaviour in several walks of life. Parson Adams is one of the great humorous characters of English literature and yet he epitomises a true Christian goodness. Fielding's ironic approach reached an extreme in *Jonathan Wild* (1743), in which he treats the villainous thief who is the hero as if he were a great man. *Tom Jones* (1749), his masterpiece, gives us in an ingenious plot the history of a young man of unknown birth: his boyhood in the country, his journey to London and his escapades when he gets there. The book is full of vivid characters and episodes and contains much moral comment from the author himself. *Amelia* (1751) is concerned with the misfortunes of the heroine and her husband and with her patience and virtue. An experienced playwright, Fielding uses dramatic devices and events, sometimes involving physical action. His comedy is occasionally coarse and boisterous but often drily ironical. The reader is frequently aware of his authorial presence and he intervenes directly in the narrative. Like many of his contemporaries, he acknowledges the influence of the classics of Greek and Latin literature and here and there writes in a mock-heroic style. He is the opposite of Richardson, as Dr Johnson said to Boswell: "there was as great a difference between them as between a man who knew how a watch was made (*i.e.* Richardson), and a man who could tell the hour by looking on the dial-plate (*i.e.* Fielding)."

Tobias Smollett is superficially reminiscent of Fielding in his novels: *Roderick Random* (1748), *Peregrine Pickle* (1751), *Ferdinand, Count Fathom* (1753), *Sir Lancelot Greaves* (1760-61) and *Humphry Clinker* (1771). All of them recount the wanderings and adventures of their heroes and can therefore be described as picaresque, although *Humphry Clinker* is an epistolary novel. Smollett depicts an often brutal world with a mixture of relish and repulsion and his novels have a remarkable vivacity of invention. The episodes on board ship in *Roderick Random*, for example, give an unforgettable picture of the cruelties and rigours of eighteenth-century seafaring life.

Laurence Sterne stands apart from the novelists of his time and indeed can still be regarded as unique. *Tristram Shandy* (1760-67) is an eccentric, digressive composition. Chronological order and the sequence of cause and effect do not apply to Sterne's handling of his subject-matter—the hero is not born till half way through the novel, for instance. The personages talk of this and that, the author intervenes at will, a chapter may break off suddenly or may be blank, and so on. Despite this whimsicality and the flux of ideas and impressions, characters, such as My Uncle Toby and the Widow Wadman, are fully realised and an atmosphere of gentle humanity prevails.

Although one cannot draw clear lines of influence, it is possible to see these four novelists—Richardson, Fielding, Smollett and Sterne—as representatives of kinds of approaches to fiction that were apparent in the next two centuries. Richardson displays the interest in psychological introspection characteristic of the work of many twentieth-century writers. The emphasis laid by Fielding and Smollett upon external action has its counterpart in the broad humour and simple characterisation of some nineteenth-century novels. Modern experiments in the form of the novel remind us of Sterne's rejection of the rational development of narrative.

Later Eighteenth-Century Novelists

After the middle of the century, no outstanding English novelist emerged until Scott and Jane Austen started to write fiction at its end. But a few memorable novels appeared, including Oliver Goldsmith's *The Vicar of Wakefield* (1766) and Fanny Burney's *Evelina* (1778). Horace Walpole's *The Castle of Otranto* (1765) is important as the first Gothic novel. This type contained mystery and terror, often associated with the supernatural and a medieval setting. Its famous exponents came later: Mrs Ann Radcliffe, who wrote *The Mysteries of Udolpho* (1794) and Matthew Gregory ("Monk") Lewis, who wrote *The Monk* (1796). The most celebrated is Mary Shelley's *Frankenstein* (1818).

THE EARLY NINETEENTH CENTURY
Sir Walter Scott

The Gothic novels just mentioned are typical of Romantic literature, of whom one of the principal representatives in Britain and Europe in the early years of the nineteenth century was Sir Walter Scott (1771-1832). In his own time and for long afterwards, Scott was regarded as akin to Shakespeare in his comprehensive renderings of human life and his powers of imagination. He was a prolific author, who wrote poems, dramas, short stories, biographies and histories as well as the following novels: *Waverley* (1814), *Guy Mannering* (1815), *The Antiquary* (1816), *The Black Dwarf* (1816), *Old Mortality* (1817), *Rob Roy* (1818), *The Heart of Midlothian* (1818), *The Bride of Lammermoor* (1819), *A Legend of Montrose* (1819), *Ivanhoe* (1820), *The Monastery* (1820), *The Abbot* (1820), *Kenilworth* (1821), *The Pirate* (1822), *The Fortunes of Nigel* (1822), *Peveril of the Peak* (1822), *Quentin Durward* (1823), *Saint Ronan's Well* (1824), *Redgauntlet* (1824), *The Betrothed* (1825), *The Talisman* (1825), *Woodstock* (1826), *The Fair Maid of Perth* (1828), *Anne of Geierstein* (1829), *Count Robert of Paris* (1832) and *Castle Dangerous* (1832). These are historical novels, set in many different places and periods. *Waverley* takes place in Scotland during the 1745 Jacobite Rebellion; *Ivanhoe* in the England of Richard I; and *Quentin Durward* in fifteenth-century France during the reign of Louis XI.

Scott presents a great range of characters, from the lowliest peasants to monarchs, and mingles actual and fictional personages convincingly together. He enables us to see in their adventures, attitudes and relationships the forces of history at work. Their private lives are affected by public events. He imaginatively recreates history in his novels, which also show his sympathy for—and understanding of—all kinds of people, whatever their religious and political beliefs. His narratives are vigorously inventive, with colourful and dramatic scenes, as adaptations for opera, films and television have demonstrated. Having once read them, the reader will recall such things as Waverley's journeyings in the Highlands of Scotland, the battles in *Rob Roy*, Jeanie Deans' interviews with the Duke of Argyll and Queen Caroline in *The Heart of Midlothian*, and Meg Merrilies' roadside curses upon the Laird of Ellangowan in *Guy Mannering*. His memorable characters are often Scots, such as Jeanie Deans, Meg Merrilies, Dominie Sampson (in *Guy Mannering*) and Jonathan Oldbuck (in *The Antiquary*), but also noteworthy are Caleb Balderstone (in *The Bride of Lammermoor*) and Diana Vernon (in *Rob Roy*). His portrait of King James I in *The Fortunes of Nigel* is a remarkably convincing representation of an historical personage. But some of his heroes and women characters tend to be colourless and commonplace. Scott was not greatly concerned with psychological probings or with profound moral or religious issues. He used a huge canvas on which he portrayed the actions of people of every kind and degree in specific places and historical periods. He rendered "the being of the age" (in George Lukács' phrase) and the richness and variety of human life within that age.

Jane Austen

No novelist could be more different from Scott than Jane Austen, as he himself recognised. In an admiring comment on her work, he wrote: "The big bow-wow strain I can do myself like any now going, but the exquisite touch which renders ordinary commonplace things and characters interesting from the truth of the description and sentiment, is denied to me." Jane Austen (1775–1817) wrote only six novels, which were published as follows: *Sense and Sensibility* (1811), *Pride and Prejudice* (1813), *Mansfield Park* (1814), *Emma* (1816), *Northanger Abbey* and *Persuasion* (both 1818). The dates of composition are sometimes different: for example, *Northanger Abbey*, which was published posthumously, was one of her earliest books, begun in 1798. She also wrote shorter stories and fragments, which are conveniently collected in one volume in the *Oxford Jane Austen*.

She based her novels on the people and places with which she was familiar: the upper middle-class society of southern England, particularly Hampshire, the county in which she was born and lived for most of her life. Her work, she modestly wrote, was "that little bit (two inches wide) of ivory, in which I work with so fine a brush as produces little effect after much labour." Her subject-matter is the relationships between men and women, especially those concerned with love and marriage, and she accepts the social code of her class and period. She uses no exciting or ingenious plots, no startlingly dramatic incidents. She ignores doings and people outside the small circle in which her characters move. Yet working within these conventions of subject-matter and social code, she illuminates wider areas of human conduct. In *Persuasion*, for example, she tells the story of Anne Elliot, who had rejected the suit of Captain Wentworth, the man she truly loved, because she yielded to the well-meant advice of Lady Russell, a close friend of her family. Anne and Captain Wentworth, who have met again seven years afterwards, slowly but surely re-establish their loving relationship and eventually marry. Questions raised include the rights and wrongs of persuasion, the place of love and money in marriage, the pressures of family vanity, and motives of men and women respectively when they fall in love. Moral issues like these are treated by Jane Austen with irony and wit as well as sympathy.

Her dialogue and passages of description contain much that is subtle and drily amusing, revealing her as an author who views folly and pretension with amused disfavour and who values the qualities of prudence and tolerance. Elizabeth Bennett in *Pride and Prejudice* comes close to her ideal of what a person should be like and some words that she gives to her can represent the novelist's own approach: "I hope I never ridicule what is wise and good. Follies and nonsense, whims and inconsistencies do divert me, I own, and I laugh at them whenever I can."

Jane Austen's characters come alive through their dialogue and reflections and through the novelist's observations. She constructs her novels neatly and with a feeling of inevitability so that they have an effortless artistic unity. Although she wrote at the time of the Romantic Movement, she remained cool and rational; it is significant that Charlotte Brontë attacked her for lacking warmth and enthusiasm. But her clarity of style and form, her comedy and wit and, above all, her penetrating analyses of behaviour and motive have led to her justifiably being regarded today as one of the greatest of English novelists.

Minor Novelists of the 1820s and 1830s

Between the time of Scott and the time of Dickens, who shot to fame in 1836, there flourished many minor novelists. The most enduring of these is Thomas Love Peacock (1785–1866), who wrote *Headlong Hall* (1816), *Melincourt* (1817), *Nightmare Abbey* (1818), *Maid Marian* (1822), *The Misfortunes of Elphin* (1829), *Crotchet Castle* (1831) and *Gryll Grange* (1860). These were mostly comic, satirical novels of ideas, wittily satirising fashionable thinkers and intellectual tendencies of the age. Peacock's usual device is to place his characters round a dinner-table and to record their conversation. In this way, he could poke fun at the Gothic Novel, Byronic gloom and German romanticism (in *Nightmare Abbey*), modern trends in education and agriculture (in *Crotchet Castle*) and Rousseau's views on natural

man (in *Melincourt*). Some of his characters are caricatures of living people: Scythrop is Shelley (in *Nightmare Abbey*) and Mr Fax is Malthus (in *Melincourt*). His is a rational voice, puncturing what he considered to be the pretensions and affectations of the Romantic Movement. The elegance and polish of his dialogues at the dinner-table make his novels a permanent delight.

Humour of a more obvious sort is present in the once-popular novels of Theodore Hook (1788–1841), such as *Sayings and Doings* (1826–9), but these are now forgotten. They are worth mentioning if only because some critics have seen Hook as a precursor of Dickens. "Fashionable" or "silver-fork" novels, relating the intrigues, customs and speech of high society, were also widely read at this time. Amongst the authors of these were Mrs Catherine Gore (1799–1861) and Edward Bulwer-Lytton (1803–73), whose *Pelham* (1828) still has a little amusing life in it. Bulwer-Lytton achieved fame, too, with his "Newgate Novels", such as *Paul Clifford* (1830) and *Eugene Aram* (1832), which depicted criminal life in a romanticised and even glamorous manner. Scott's prestige and influence led to the production of historical novels. Bulwer-Lytton's *The Last Days of Pompeii* (1834) and some by William Harrison Ainsworth (1805–82)—for example, *The Tower of London* (1840)—are readable, but those by G. P. R. James (1799–1860) have fallen into oblivion. These minor comic, "fashionable", "Newgate" and historical novels have little intrinsic interest for most readers today, although the student of the period will find them valuable for the insights they give, sometimes unwittingly, into the tastes and prejudices of the 1830s.

Undeserving of neglect, however, are the energetic novels of Captain Frederick Marryat (1792–1848). Like several naval officers of the period, he wrote seafaring fiction, beginning with *Frank Mildmay* (1829). *Peter Simple* (1834) and *Mr Midshipman Easy* (1836) were amongst the novels that followed. *Snarleyyow* (1837) is a macabre comedy about an apparently immortal dog. Towards the end of his writing career, Marryat turned to juvenile fiction, which included *Masterman Ready* (1841–2), *The Settlers in Canada* (1844) and *The Children of the New Forest* (1847). His novels are extrovert entertainments, full of vigour and knockabout comedy, written in an unpretentious prose style. Parts of them are reminiscent of Smollett and, more interestingly, of Dickens, who was one of his closest friends.

Some distinctively Scots novels were published at this time. John Galt (1779–1839) wrote *The Annals of the Parish* (1821), which chronicles the doings of a country parish in Scotland, and *The Entail* (1823), a tragicomedy of protracted disputes about an inheritance. Outstandingly original in form and content is *The Private Memoirs and Confessions of a Justified Sinner* (1824) by James Hogg (1770–1835). This story of evil and damnation, a narration followed by a confession, is centred upon the "sinner", who is encouraged in his wickedness by a friend, who—it becomes clear—is the Devil.

This period between Scott and Dickens was therefore productive of novels of great variety. If one had to choose amongst so many writers of fiction (and they have not all been named here), one could point to Peacock, Galt, Hogg and Marryat as novelists worth remembering, with Bulwer-Lytton and Ainsworth not far behind them. All were suddenly outshone, however, in 1836 by the dazzling appearance of Dickens on the scene.

THE EARLY VICTORIAN NOVELISTS

Charles Dickens

Charles Dickens (1812–70), who first came to public notice with sketches and articles in periodicals (collected as *Sketches by Boz* in 1835–6), achieved fame with *Pickwick Papers* (1836–7). This was rapidly followed by *Oliver Twist* (1838), *Nicholas Nickleby* (1838–9), *The Old Curiosity Shop* (1840–41), *Barnaby Rudge* (1841), *A Christmas Carol* (1843) and *Martin Chuzzlewit* (1843–4). These early books were exuberant and original in invention of every kind: colourful characterisation, vivid episodes, extravagant humour, pathos and evocation of the macabre, and an unfailingly fluent, fresh prose style. Many of Dickens' fictional personages immediately became household words: Mr Squeers, Little Nell, Scrooge and Mrs Gamp, to name only four from the books just listed. Similarly, sayings and phrases entered the English language, such as Oliver Twist's asking for more and Mrs Gamp's remarks about her imaginary friend, Mrs Harris. Dickens' tragic powers, especially those displayed in *The Old Curiosity Shop*, were found deeply moving. His evident concern for children, the poor and the deprived appealed to the humanitarian instincts of many of his contemporaries. On the other hand, his comedy made a tremendous impact, as in the *Pickwick Papers*, where Mr Pickwick's adventures and Sam Weller's sayings gave great joy to thousands of readers.

Dombey and Son (1846–8) seems to mark a turning-point in Dickens' career. It is more carefully unified than its predecessors and it relies less on exaggeration of plot and feelings; its central theme of pride is all-important. Dickens' next novel, *David Copperfield* (1849–50), with its suggestions of autobiography, is written in a calmly flowing manner, although it contains characters and incidents as striking as anything he invented: Mr Micawber, Uriah Heep, the storm at Yarmouth. Its subject-matter, concerned chiefly with the private and domestic affections, is, we feel, the product of mature contemplation.

The later novels of Dickens are *Bleak House* (1852–3), *Hard Times* (1854), *Little Dorrit* (1855–7), *A Tale of Two Cities* (1859), *Great Expectations* (1860–61), *Our Mutual Friend* (1864–5) and *The Mystery of Edwin Drood* (unfinished, 1870). They are more sombre than the earlier books. They are constructed with some care and they often deal with specific themes and subjects: the intricacies and deceits of the law (*Bleak House*), the opposition of utilitarian and imaginative values (*Hard Times*), the inefficiencies, irresponsibilities and materialism of mid-Victorian society (*Little Dorrit* and *Our Mutual Friend*) and snobbery (*Great Expectations*).

As we read a Dickens novel, we enter a self-sufficient imaginative world. He has many of the characteristics of a poet. This impression of a fertile, comprehensive imagination is enhanced in his later books by his use of motifs and symbols, such as the fog in *Bleak House*, the prisons in *Little Dorrit* and the dust-heaps and the River Thames in *Our Mutual Friend*. Although he has often been said to draw caricatures rather than characters, the people he creates spring to life on the page. In any case, some of his characters have a convincing truth about them—for example, his self-tormented people, like Miss Wade in *Little Dorrit* and Bradley Headstone in *Our Mutual Friend*. He has an amazing ability to distinguish his numerous characters from one another by their idiosyncrasies of speech. His plots are over-complicated, in a melodramatic mode, but they help to increase the tensions and mysteries that are so important in his stories and also help to hold together the many elements of his complex narratives. It should be remembered that his novels were written and published as serials, which partly accounts for some of his repetitions and exaggerations.

Dickens has astonishing powers of observation, seeing people and things as no one had seen them before, especially their peculiarities and strange resemblances. Allied to these powers is his ability to animate everybody and everything, so that even the furniture in a room can seem to have an active life of its own. He conveys all of this in vital prose, which is capable of expressing a wide range of particulars and moods. His purpose in writing, apart from sheer entertainment, is to put forward a message of hope and love, which he trusts will triumph over evil and over the vices and narrow-mindedness of materialism and a mechanical, uncaring social system.

Dickens' strengths as a novelist include his striking characterisation, his versatile prose, his power to evoke laughter, tears and fears, and his fundamental, positive "message". In the force and extent of his imagination, he stands next to Shakespeare.

William Makepeace Thackeray

William Makepeace Thackeray (1811–63) wrote miscellaneous prose and verse in the 1830s. *Catherine* (1839–40) and *Barry Lyndon* (1844), his first novels, were written partly to satirise the contemporary vogue for "Newgate Novels". *Vanity Fair* (1847–8) established him as major novelist. This book, set in the period of the Regency, tells the related stories of two contrasted women, Amelia Sedley and Becky Sharp. One of its principal purposes is to expose the shams and pretensions of high society, as is indicated by its title, which Thackeray took from Bunyan's *Pilgrim's Progress*. *Pendennis* (1848–50), like *David Copperfield*, is coloured by autobiographical reminiscence. Its eponymous hero encounters temptations during his youth in the country, at Oxbridge and in the London literary world. Thackeray turned to the eighteenth century, his favourite historical period, for the background of *Henry Esmond* (1852), whose melancholy, meditative hero is tormented by his love for Beatrix Esmond and is also active in military and political affairs, including an unsuccessful attempt to put the Old Pretender on the English throne. *The Newcomes* (1853–5) is a chronicle of the loves, intrigues, successes and disappointments of the Newcome family, centred upon Clive and his father, Colonel Newcome. Thackeray's last important novel was *The Virginians* (1857–9), which continues the story of the Esmond family into later generations, set mostly in America during the War of Independence. His career as a novelist ended with *Philip* (1861–2) and the unfinished *Denis Duval* (1864).

During his lifetime and for long afterwards, Thackeray was frequently contrasted with Dickens. Unlike the latter, he avoided complicated plots and caricatures. His narratives flow smoothly from one incident or tableau to another. Thackeray's aim was to be as truthful as possible in his portrayal of people. He disliked the falsities he detected in such novelists as Bulwer-Lytton. His characters, therefore, are often ambiguously conceived, since he refused to simplify what he saw as complexity. A good man like Dobbin in *Vanity Fair* can be ridiculous on occasions; a man as honourable as Henry Esmond can love a woman as fickle and hard-hearted as Beatrix; a schemer like Becky Sharp is sometimes sympathetically described by the author. Like Fielding, whom he admired, Thackeray sought to reveal and mock hypocrisy and cant, especially in the middle and aristocratic classes, from which his fictional personages invariably came. One topic that engaged his attention was snobbery, which he deplored. Yet gentlemanliness was all-important to him, as personified in Colonel Newcome.

Thackeray has been called both cynical and sentimental. On one hand, he shows that conduct is not always what it appears to be; on the other, he depicts some people, especially when they are female, with fulsome affection. In all his work he is a moralist, relating the behaviour, thoughts and motives of his characters to those of his readers and people in general. Commentary, description, dialogue and story-telling are blended in his novels. Furthermore, the novels connect with one another, since characters recur; Pendennis, for example, tells the story of the Newcomes. This fact increases that sense of an actual, fully realised world which many critics have found to be characteristic of Thackeray's fiction.

The Brontës

Charlotte Brontë (1816–55) wrote *Jane Eyre* in 1847. Its second edition, by the way, was dedicated to Thackeray. This novel, which has never lost its power to enthrall the reader, uses a melodramatic plot, coincidence and exaggeration. But these devices, poetically and imaginatively realised by the author, intensify the reality of the passion that informs the book: Jane's sufferings, anger, independent spirit and feelings of love. These are brought close to us by the first-person narration. Her two great temptations, first towards an illicit relationship with Rochester and secondly towards the loveless religious life that St John Rivers offers her, are necessary, we feel, so that she can deserve the final, hard-won happiness that she finds. It is therefore a convincing psychological and moral novel as well as one of dramatic impetus.

Charlotte Brontë's second published novel was *Shirley* (1849), set in the north of England during the Napoleonic Wars and Luddite Riots. In it, we read of the fortunes of Caroline Helstone and Shirley Keeldar. One of its themes is the independence of women, though the book ends conventionally with the happy marriage of each of the heroines. *Villette* (1853) is a strangely-constructed novel, to the point of clumsiness, although its mysterious opening and conclusion are remarkable. But more importantly, its love story of Lucy Snowe, the English teacher in Villette (*i.e.* Brussels), and Paul Emanuel, the

Belgian schoolmaster she meets there, is one of the most sincere and moving in English fiction. *The Professor*, Charlotte Brontë's first novel (written in 1846), was published posthumously in 1857. Basically, it has the same story as *Villette*, though roles and sexes are reversed: an English schoolmaster in Brussels falls in love with a Swiss pupil. It is a novel not to be underrated, since it has a calm air of truthfulness.

Charlotte Brontë was essentially a Romantic novelist, dealing with emotional issues. As already noted, she had a low opinion of Jane Austen's coolness. Her sister, Emily Brontë (1818–48), was even more intense in her treatment of passion. *Wuthering Heights* (1847), her only novel, concerns two generations of the Linton and Earnshaw families in Yorkshire and how they are tormented by the ferocity of Heathcliff, who was brought into their lives as a boy found in the streets of Liverpool. The love between him and Catherine Earnshaw is all-consuming, destructive and yet immortal. *Wuthering Heights*, which has been called a dramatic poem, is full of the most violent emotions, paradoxically made even more intense by the perspective in which they are placed by the various narrators of the story. The construction of the novel—its points of view and its time-shifts—is notable, as are its imagery and passages of poetic description. As in *Jane Eyre*, the settings are important: the interiors of the houses, the Yorkshire moors and the changing seasons.

Anne Brontë (1820–49) echoes some of the themes explored by her sisters. *Agnes Grey* (1847) is about a governess's life and *The Tenant of Wildfell Hall* (1848) is a melodramatic tale of mystery, drunkenness and love.

Anthony Trollope

Anthony Trollope (1815–82) wrote forty-six novels, of which the best-known are contained in two "series". The Barsetshire Novels, dealing with the lives of the clergy and others in a fictional country district, are *The Warden* (1855), *Barchester Towers* (1857), *Doctor Thorne* (1858), *Framley Parsonage* (1861), *The Small House at Allington* (1864) and *The Last Chronicle of Barset* (1867). The Palliser Novels, which are mostly political, are *Can You Forgive Her?* (1864), *Phineas Finn* (1869), *The Eustace Diamonds* (1873), *Phineas Redux* (1874), *The Prime Minister* (1876) and *The Duke's Children* (1880). Other novels worth noting are *The Three Clerks* (1858), *Orley Farm* (1862), *The Vicar of Bullhampton* (1870) and *The Way We Live Now* (1875).

As Trollope himself said in his *Autobiography* (1883), he was a realist and not a sensational novelist. His novels are firmly constructed and written plainly and explicitly, without the poetic imagination of Dickens and the Brontës or the elegant subtlety of Thackeray (whom he admired above all contemporary novelists). Nathaniel Hawthorne, the American novelist, wrote that Trollope's novels were "solid and substantial, written on the strength of beef and the inspiration of ale, and just as real as if some giant had hewn a great lump out of the earth and put it under a glass case, with all its inhabitants going about their daily business, and not suspecting that they were being made a show of." If you want to have an accurate impression of what daily life was like amongst the upper middle-classes of England in the 1850s, then a reading of *Barchester Towers*, for example, will supply you with details of customs, dress, furniture and manner of speech. Apart from this characteristic, Trollope provides the reader with interesting and entertaining plots. The accusations of theft made against the Reverend Josiah Crawley and the ensuing complications make *The Last Chronicle of Barset* a fascinating novel. *The Eustace Diamonds* is another well-constructed tale of intrigue, about Lizzie Greystock's determination to retain an heirloom, a diamond necklace.

Trollope is especially skilful in working out the conflicts between public and private lives, in clerical and political matters above all: the disputes over the wardenship of Hiram's Hospital in *The Warden* and *Barchester Towers* and the jockeyings for power and influence in the Palliser novels. No other English novelist has so comprehensively treated this perpetually relevant subject, though C. P. Snow's *The Masters* (1951) is a modern example influenced by Trollope. He draws his characters with humour and sympathy but he occasionally disconcertingly inter-

rupts his narration with authorial comments, as Henry James noted disapprovingly. He unquestioningly accepts Victorian standards of morality and conduct and sees everything from the standpoint of an upper-middle class English gentleman. Trollope was proud of his craftsmanship and almost without exception his novels are carefully constructed. They remain reliably readable and amusing without being too demanding.

Benjamin Disraeli, Mrs Gaskell and Charles Kingsley

Three novelists who flourished in the mid-nineteenth century were Benjamin Disraeli (1804–81), Mrs Elizabeth Gaskell (1810–65) and Charles Kingsley (1819–75). Like many of their contemporaries, they were perturbed by the social conditions of England brought about by industrialisation. As a result, they wrote influential novels that highlighted the problems of capital and labour and the sufferings of the poor.

Disraeli's first novels (*e.g. Henrietta Temple*, 1837) were of the "fashionable" kind already discussed but in the 1840s he produced three that were concerned with politics and society: *Coningsby* (1844), *Sybil* (1845) and *Tancred* (1847). Disraeli, who at that time was already prominent as a politician, developed his theories of Conservatism in the first of these, using the education, career and ideas of its hero, Coningsby, as the basis of his story. The alternative title of *Sybil* is *The Two Nations*, by which Disraeli denotes the rich and the poor. He dramatises the issues by means of the love between Sybil, the daughter of a Chartist, and Charles Egremont, a member of the aristocracy. In *Tancred*, the eponymous hero, the son of a Duke, journeys to the Holy Land to seek guidance towards true belief and conduct.

Mrs Gaskell's social novels were *Mary Barton* (1848) and *North and South* (1854–5). The first, which is set in Manchester, vividly evokes the appalling conditions of the working class, which Mrs Gaskell knew at first hand. She sensationalises the problem by using a melodramatic plot, involving murder committed by the heroine's father, but there is no escaping the fact that it is a gripping novel that not surprisingly made a considerable impression upon readers in mid-Victorian England. *North and South* contrasts two regions of England, as its title implies, through the medium of its heroine, Margaret Hale, who leaves southern England to live in the industrial north. Mrs Gaskell sympathetically presents a balanced view of social problems, indicating some of the virtues as well as the shortcomings of the employers, personified in John Thornton, with whom Margaret falls in love. Mrs Gaskell's other novels include *Cranford* (1851–3), a quiet and charming account of life amongst genteel middle-class ladies in a northern village in the 1830s; *Ruth* (1853), a harrowing tale of seduction and desertion; and *Wives and Daughters* (1864–6, unfinished), about the characters and family relationships in a provincial town.

Charles Kingsley's interests as a clergyman and Christian Socialist inspired *Alton Locke* (1850), which is about working-class London and Chartism, and *Yeast* (1851), which is concerned with problems of rural England. As in all his books, Kingsley writes with enthusiasm and commitment, not hesitating to preach his social sermons when the occasion prompts. For the student of political and religious ideas of the period, these two novels are valuable sources. Kingsley also wrote historical novels: *Hypatia* (1853), *Westward Ho!* (1855) and *Hereward the Wake* (1866). *The Water Babies* (1863) is a lively, didactic story for children.

George Eliot

George Eliot (the pseudonym of Mary Ann Evans, 1819–80), wrote three long short stories, *Scenes of Clerical Life* (1857) and then the following novels: *Adam Bede* (1859), *The Mill on the Floss* (1860), *Silas Marner* (1861), *Romola* (1862–3), *Felix Holt, the Radical* (1866), *Middlemarch* (1871–2) and *Daniel Deronda* (1876). The first three novels are set in rural England, recalling the Warwickshire where she was born and brought up. *Adam Bede* is the tragic story of Hetty Sorrel, a village girl who is seduced, bears an illegitimate child and is convicted of infanticide. *The Mill on the Floss* is concerned mainly with the life, loves and emotional vicissitudes of Maggie Tulliver, who has some of the characteristics of the author herself. *Silas Marner* tells of an unhappy, miserly weaver, who regains his love of humanity after bringing up a child who has found her way to his cottage door. All, then, are about comparatively humble people and all sympathetically render the seasons, scenes, activities and speech of country life.

For her fourth novel, George Eliot turned to a completely different setting and period, as if to challenge her powers of invention: *Romola* is an historical novel, set in late fifteenth-century Florence, at the time of Machiavelli and Savonarola. It is a moving and exciting account of the conflicts of personal and public issues and of treachery and love. *Felix Holt* has the political events of 1832 as its background, although its principal interest lies in Esther's personal relationships and in the disputes over the ownership of an estate. By general agreement, *Middlemarch* is George Eliot's masterpiece. This long, complex novel has four interwoven plots revealing various themes: love and marriage, ambition, religious hypocrisy and the pressures exerted by a provincial environment. *Daniel Deronda* has two plots and themes, again interrelated: the character and unhappy marriage of Gwendolen Harleth and the revelation of Daniel's Jewish parentage.

George Eliot brought great seriousness of purpose to the novel. Like the other Victorian novelists, she made moral teaching an essential part of her fiction. Although she had lost her belief in orthodox Christianity, she held to the ideals of duty and personal responsibility. She explores these fundamental doctrines of hers through her characters and plots and through much authorial comment. In *Silas Marner*, for example, she shows how Godfrey Cass tries to ignore his past actions that have caused distress to himself and others and how instead he hopes that Chance will come to his aid. To make the point clear to her readers, she writes a long passage, almost like a sermon, on the error of not facing the consequences of one's actions and of trusting to Fortune. Nevertheless, she constantly shows sympathy and tolerance towards her characters. She can express her pity for such people as Casaubon, Rosamond Vincy and Bulstrode in *Middlemarch* whereas a novelist who saw personality in simpler terms would deplore or condemn their faults. Perhaps more than any previous novelist, she describes and analyses the sheer complexity of character, with the result that her portraits, especially of women, have great profundity—Maggie Tulliver in *The Mill on the Floss*, Mrs Transome in *Felix Holt*, Dorothea in *Middlemarch* and Gwendolen Harleth in *Daniel Deronda*. Some of her personages, especially rural folk in her earlier novels, are presented with humour—Mrs Poyser in *Adam Bede* and Maggie's aunts and uncles in *The Mill on the Floss*.

George Eliot was scrupulous in the construction of her novels, allowing few digressions or inessential characters. The villagers' "chorus" in *Silas Marner*, for example, is necessary for our understanding of their opinions of the main characters and of the kind of existence, past and present, amongst which those characters must live. By the standards of the time, she avoids exaggeration and highly coloured incidents. Because of her wise moral concern, her understanding of psychology, and her care over the structure of her novels, George Eliot is regarded nowadays as one of the greatest English novelists.

Charles Reade, Wilkie Collins, and Sensation Novels

From about 1860 onwards, "sensation novels" were enormously popular. Their ingredients could include crime, detection, and passionate and illicit love-affairs; they had, too, a highly emotional atmosphere. Two of the best-known were *Lady Audley's Secret* (1862) by Mary Elizabeth Braddon (1837–1915) and *Uncle Silas* (1864) by J. Sheridan Le Fanu (1814–73).

Dickens, Charles Reade and Wilkie Collins have sometimes been called "sensation novelists" although that is too limiting a description of them. Charles Reade (1814–84), an original and lively author, wrote two famous historical novels: *Peg Woffington* (1853), recounting an episode in the life of the eighteenth-century actress, and *The Cloister and the Hearth* (1861), a romance set in fifteenth-century Europe. His novels dealing with contemporary social abuses include *It is never too late to Mend* (1853), in which he exposes brutalities in the prisons, and *Hard Cash* (1863), in which he describes conditions in a lunatic asylum. Wilkie Collins (1824–89), a friend and associate of Dickens, was a prolific

writer. His most enduring novels, with ingenious plots, are *The Woman in White* (1860), *No Name* (1862) and *The Moonstone* (1868), which is often called the first English detective story.

Victorian Novels: a Summary

The principal early Victorian novelists were therefore Dickens, Thackeray, Charlotte and Emily Brontë, Trollope and George Eliot. Owing partly to the reading public's expectations and partly to such publishing conventions as serialisation and the issue of three-volume novels, their books are lengthy and contain numerous personages and episodes. Sometimes there are digressions and repetitions as well as full, explicit descriptions of places and people. But it can justifiably be argued that in this way an impression of the variety and multifarious nature of human life is successfully conveyed. The novelists' emotional range is wide and often comedy and tragedy co-exist. Sentimentality is found, for example in the presentation of women, children and deathbed scenes. The novelists are moralists, judging behaviour by the standards of the English middle class, who formed the largest part of their reading public. They sometimes intervene in the narrative to make their teaching clear and to involve their readers directly in their fictional worlds. The continuing importance and value of the early Victorian novelists lie in their memorable characters and episodes, the relevant moral themes they develop, their descriptive and poetic uses of language, symbol and imagery, and in general in the many kinds of enjoyments and enrichment they supply so copiously.

THE LATE VICTORIAN PERIOD

George Meredith

George Meredith (1828–1908) was a substantial poet as well as a novelist. After writing an Oriental fantasy, *The Shaving of Shagpat* (1856), he wrote *The Ordeal of Richard Feverel* (1859), *Evan Harrington* (1860), *Emilia in England* (1864, retitled *Sandra Belloni*, 1886), *Rhoda Fleming* (1865), *Vittoria* (1867), *The Adventures of Harry Richmond* (1871), *Beauchamp's Career* (1876), *The Egoist* (1879), *The Tragic Comedians* (1880), *Diana of the Crossways* (1885), *One of our Conquerors* (1891), *Lord Ormont and his Aminta* (1894) and *The Amazing Marriage* (1895). Of these novels, *The Ordeal of Richard Feverel*, *The Egoist* and *Diana of the Crossways* are generally accounted the best.

Richard Feverel is brought up by his father, Sir Austin, according to a System, which should train him to be a perfect English gentleman, who would avoid making the kind of disastrous marriage that the baronet had suffered. The fine plans break down. Richard marries a girl of unsuitable birth and quickly becomes corrupted in London society. Not unexpectedly, there is a tragic end to everything. But the novel is remarkable for its disparate elements: its irony and satire, not only in situation but also in the wry comments of Adrian Harley; its passages of poetic description; the melodramatic turns of the plot; its humour and its pathos. *The Egoist*, in contrast, is perfectly organised, reminiscent of a comedy of manners in the theatre, especially in its denouement. Its comedy lies in the exposure of the egoism of the central character, Sir Willoughby Patterne, but the play of wit is modified by the sympathetic portrayal of Clara Middleton, to whom Sir Willoughby is engaged to be married, and the delightfully fresh portrayal of Crossjay Patterne, a twelve-year-old boy. *Diana of the Crossways* is about a witty, attractive young woman, involved in divorce proceedings and a love affair.

One difficulty in approaching Meredith's novels is his prose style, which is elaborate and allusive and becomes increasingly so in his later work. But it is genuinely witty and poetic. For beauty of detail and evocation of romantic feeling, little in Victorian imaginative prose can rival such passages as the descriptions of the first meetings between Lucy and Richard in *The Ordeal of Richard Feverel* and of Vernon Whitford sleeping under the blossoming cherry tree in *The Egoist*. Like Fielding, Meredith set great store by the ability of comedy to reveal and rectify affectation. "Comedy is the foundation of good sense," he wrote in his *Essay on Comedy* (1877). Another relevant definition comes at the beginning of *The Egoist*: "Comedy is a game played to throw reflections upon social life, and it deals with human nature in the drawing-room of civilized men and women." His theory is brilliantly put into practice in the final chapters of *The Egoist*, when devices and revelations of different kinds bring about Sir Willoughby's humiliation.

Some elements of Meredith's technique are worth remark. He uses recurring motifs and phrases, forming parts of unifying patterns of comment: the ironical quotations from Sir Austin's "Pilgrim's Scrip" and Mrs Mountstewart Jenkinson's phrase about Clara Middleton, "a dainty rogue in porcelain", for example. Allusions can have a poetic resonance, like those he makes to *The Tempest* when describing the young love of Richard and Lucy. He draws significance and beauty from what may seem conventional symbols: the broken porcelain vase in *The Egoist*, for instance. His handling of his characters' psychology is occasionally elusive, but he has meaningful insights to offer and can be seen to be anticipating the "stream of consciousness" in parts of *The Egoist*, notably in "Clara's Meditations". Amongst his main themes are the tensions between appearance and reality (as in Evan Harrington's social position contrasted with his humble birth) and the independence of women (as shown in the fortunes of Clara and Diana).

Meredith was lionised towards the end of his life, but he is unjustly neglected today. At the least, he should be read for the new possibilities he found in the novel-form and for the risks he took. Apart from his importance in the history of the English novel, there is much in his writing that the modern reader will find intrinsically rewarding.

Thomas Hardy

The career of Thomas Hardy (1840–1928) divides into two parts. In the nineteenth century, up to 1896, he published novels. He then abandoned the writing of prose fiction and for the rest of his life concentrated on writing poetry. He divided his novels into three groups. First, there are "Novels of Character and Environment", which comprise *Under the Greenwood Tree* (1872), *Far from the Madding Crowd* (1874), *The Return of the Native* (1878), *The Mayor of Casterbridge* (1886), *The Woodlanders* (1887), *Tess of the Durbervilles* (1891) and *Jude the Obscure* (1896). Secondly, there are the "Romances and Fantasies": *A Pair of Blue Eyes* (1873), *The Trumpet-Major* (1880), *Two on a Tower* (1882) and *The Well-Beloved* (1892). Thirdly, there are the "Novels of Ingenuity": *Desperate Remedies* (1871), *The Hand of Ethelberta* (1876) and *A Laodicean* (1881). Hardy's major works are those in the first of these categories, with the possible additions of *A Pair of Blue Eyes*, *Desperate Remedies* and *The Trumpet-Major*. As well as these novels, Hardy wrote a considerable number of short stories.

His novels are set in Wessex, by which Hardy means Dorset and the adjacent counties of south-west England. This was the region where he was born and where he lived for most of his life. The scenery, occupations, customs, traditions and speech of Wessex all play vital parts in his narratives. One subject of his is the contrast between the rural world and the world outside, seen most dramatically when an outsider comes into the community or a former inhabitant returns. Fancy Day's coming to Mellstock in *Under the Greenwood Tree*, Sergeant Troy's arrival in *Far from the Madding Crowd* and the return of Clym Yeobright and Grace Melbury from the Continent to their native English villages in *The Return of the Native* and *The Woodlanders* respectively are examples of this kind of conflict. Hardy's great respect for traditional custom is evident in his loving rendering of typical country tasks and events: cider-making, tending sheep, felling trees, cutting furze, threshing wheat, lighting bonfires on 5 November, marriage ceremonies, and so on. Following George Eliot's practice, he uses conversation of village people as sources of commentary and local history. A setting can take on a symbolic function, as Egdon Heath does in *The Return of the Native* or the woods do in *The Woodlanders*. A character can become symbolically identified with his occupation and surroundings, like Diggory Venn in *The Return of the Native*.

Hardy's view of life was fatalistic, since he believed that the human situation was, in Lord David Cecil's words, "a struggle between man on the one hand and, on the other, an omnipotent and indifferent fate." One of his most forthright statements of this belief occurs at the end of *Tess of the Durbervilles* when he reports the execution of the heroine: "'Justice' was done, and the President of Immortals, in Aeschylean phrase, had ended his sport with Tess." His novels therefore contain much that is pessimistic and melancholy. The last two, *Tess of the Durbervilles* and *Jude the Obscure*, are the most tragic of all. Jude and Sue Bridehead, the central characters of the last novel, find all their aspirations concerning love, marriage, education and religious belief confounded and defeated and their story ends with the death of Jude and the resignation of Sue to unhappiness.

As an aspect of Hardy's deterministic view of life, he believed in the importance of chance, accident and coincidence. A trivial or thoughtless action, such as Bathsheba Everdene's throwing up a hymn book to see whether it falls open or shut (in *Far from the Madding Crowd*), can have unforeseen, appalling consequences. "Life's Little Ironies" and "Satires of Circumstance", titles of collections of his short stories and verse respectively, can be appropriately applied to much that he wrote. His novels are full of strange, striking episodes, in line with his theory that the artist was justified in using exaggeration and distortion to make his points effectively. Readers of Hardy always remember such things as the slaughter of the pig in *Jude the Obscure*, the sale of Henchard's wife in *The Mayor of Casterbridge*, the death of Mrs Yeobright on the heath in *The Return of the Native* and Sergeant Troy's first encounter with Bathsheba in *Far from the Madding Crowd*. Such scenes and events are there for their emotional impact and for the illumination they shed on key motives and developments in the novels.

Hardy's stories are mostly about the tragedies and disappointments of love between men and women. A favourite plot of his depends on the relationship of a woman with two or three men (e.g. Fancy Day, Eustacia Vye, Anne Garland and Tess). Women play a dominant part in his novels. He draws them with sympathy and understanding and he is especially interested in the personalities and actions of strong-willed women or women striving for independence and a life of their own (Sue Bridehead is a famous example). Amongst his men characters, those who are tortured by misgivings, remorse and disappointment are dramatically presented, as witness Henchard, Boldwood and Jude.

Henry James

The importance of Henry James (1843–1916) in the history of the English and American novel is very great indeed. His practice and the theories he expounded in his essay, "The Art of Fiction", and in the Prefaces to his novels, have been widely influential in this century. An American by birth, James lived and worked in England for most of his life, writing short stories, travel books, essays and numerous novels.

It is convenient to divide the novels into three groups, corresponding to three stages in his career. A favourite theme of his early work is the mutual influences of European and American culture. Principal works of this period are *Roderick Hudson* (1875), *The American* (1877), *The Europeans* (1878), *Daisy Miller* (1879), *Washington Square* (1881), *The Portrait of a Lady* (1881), *The Bostonians* (1886) and *The Princess Casamassima* (1886). His middle period, in which his technique becomes more complex and his subject-matter frequently concerned with English topics, includes *The Tragic Muse* (1890), *The Spoils of Poynton* (1897), *What Maisie Knew* (1897), *The Turn of the Screw* (1898), *The Awkward Age* (1899) and *The Sacred Fount* (1901). James's most difficult novels, which show a return to his interest in the tensions between English and American values, are the final three: *The Wings of a Dove* (1902), *The Ambassadors* (1903) and *The Golden Bowl* (1904).

As a man who had experienced life in the United States and Europe, James was fascinated by the differences in culture between the Old and the New Worlds. On the one hand were the newness, potentiality and democracy of America (wonderfully evoked in the opening chapter of *The Europeans*) and on the other hand were the history and achievements of Europe. In his opinion, expressed in his study of Nathaniel Hawthorne, "it takes a great deal of history to produce a little literature" and "it needs a complex social machinery to set a writer in motion." His most famous treatment of the issues involved in this opposition of two ways of life is *The*

Portrait of a Lady, which many critics think is his most fully accomplished work of fiction. Isabel Archer, an American girl, comes to England and Europe. She is attractive, frank and eager for adventure and experience. Having rejected two suitors and having inherited a fortune from her uncle, she makes a disastrously ill-judged marriage with an expatriate American but finally decides to endure the consequences of her error. The novel is rich in characterisation: apart from Isabel, the most intriguing personages are Ralph Touchett (her cousin, an invalid) and Madame Merle (a cosmopolitan woman, who arranges Isabel's marriage). James reveals, with understanding, tenderness and wit, the virtues and the weaknesses of Isabel. Moreover, he gives a wise and analytical picture of many aspects of human behaviour, relating them where appropriate to the society and culture of the United States, Europe and England. The theme of the young American woman who visits Europe with tragic consequences is repeated in *The Wings of a Dove*, with Milly Theale as the girl in question. *The Europeans*, one of James' earliest books, is a brief, elegant but searching presentation of the same basic subject; in that novel the scene is the United States, which the Europeans visit.

James was also interested in exploring the problems and corruptions of contemporary English society, as embodied in the contents of the house and the avarice for them displayed in *The Spoils of Poynton*. Or there are what the critic F. R. Leavis has called the "egotistic squalors" revealed in the comings and goings of the divorced people and spouses in *What Maisie Knew*. His fascination for observing the effects of corruption of a directly personal kind, irrespective of social pressures, is memorably realised in *The Turn of the Screw*.

He believed intensely in the importance of technique and form for the novelist, who held a "sacred office", in his view. The novelist had a duty, he maintained, to tell the truth and to impart to his fiction an "air of reality". In order to accomplish that aim, the writer had to ensure that the novel was an organic whole, with each of its parts contributing to the totality. James called some nineteenth-century novels "large, loose, baggy monsters" and sought in his own work to practise a strict control over his material. His novels are accordingly tautly constructed and written in the most meticulous prose style. This style in the later novels is difficult and subtle and some critics have thus accused him of sacrificing life and warmth for the sake of brilliant intellectual structures. Meredith and Hardy in their different ways broke with some of the conventions of the Victorian novel; but James departed radically from many of its features and can be regarded as the first of the modern novelists.

Robert Louis Stevenson and the Adventure Novel

Robert Louis Stevenson (1850–94), essayist, poet, travel-writer and novelist, achieved fame with *Treasure Island* (1883) and *Dr Jekyll and Mr Hyde* (1886). His subsequent novels include *Kidnapped* (1886), *The Black Arrow* (1888), *The Master of Ballantrae* (1889), *Catriona* (1893) and *Weir of Hermiston* (unfinished, 1896). With Lloyd Osbourne, his stepson, he wrote *The Wrong Box* (1889), *The Wrecker* (1892) and *The Ebb-Tide* (1894).

Stevenson was as scrupulous a writer as Henry James, one of his friends and correspondents. His novels are precisely and elegantly shaped and are expressed in clear, economical prose. He wrote that the artist's "one main and necessary resource" was his compulsion to "omit what is tedious or irrelevant, and suppress what is tedious and necessary." Action and the revelation of character through action form the main material of his novels. *Treasure Island*, written for boys, is a masterpiece of construction, beginning quietly but ominously, building up suspense with the discovery of Long John Silver's true nature and coming to a climax on the island with the battles between the pirates and Jim Hawkins and his friends. It has incidents and devices that stick in the mind (the black spot, the pirates' chorus) and colourful personages (Long John Silver, Ben Gunn). *Kidnapped* is admirable adventure fiction with an authentic feeling for place and period: Scotland in the years just after the '45 Jacobite Rebellion. Both books gain in immediacy through their first-person narration.

The Master of Ballantrae, set in post-1745 Scotland, is a remarkable tale of evil and persecution,

personified in its leading character, the Master. It has a relentless urgency and a number of unforgettable scenes, such as the duel between the Master of Ballantrae and his brother by candlelight out-of-doors on a frosty night. Although Stevenson emphasised action rather than psychology, at least two of his characters have become household words: Long John Silver and Dr Jekyll, alias Mr Hyde.

The adventure novel or "romance" became popular towards the end of the nineteenth century. With Stevenson's successful *Treasure Island* in mind, Rider Haggard (1856–1925) wrote *King Solomon's Mines* (1885), followed by *She* (1887) and many other books of the same kind. G. A. Henty (1832–1902) wrote prolifically, producing some eighty novels for boys. Other adventures and romances were Conan Doyle's Sherlock Holmes stories (beginning in 1887 with *A Study in Scarlet*) and novels of exciting action, Stanley Weyman's historical novels from 1893 onwards, Anthony Hope Hawkins' *The Prisoner of Zenda* (1894), Bram Stoker's *Dracula* (1897) and E. W. Hornung's Raffles stories from 1899 onwards. The adventure novels of John Buchan (1875–1940) include *Prester John* (1910), *The Thirty-Nine Steps* (1915), *Greenmantle* (1916) and *Mr Standfast* (1919).

Naturalism: Gissing and Moore

Naturalism, which is sometimes used as a synonym for realism, was a literary movement associated mostly with the novels of Emile Zola (1840–1902). Writers who held the doctrine maintained that novels should be as physically detailed as possible, that novelists should use scientific methods of description and analysis and that they should emphasise the importance of environment. The subject-matter of naturalistic novels tended to be about the harsh realities of the lives of the poor and to concentrate on the least ideal aspects of human nature.

George Gissing (1857–1903) was one exponent of naturalism in England, writing about the poverty and miseries of working-class existence in novels such as *The Nether World* (1889). *New Grub Street* (1891) surveys writers' lives, contrasting the success of the unprincipled Jasper Milvain with the wretched life and death of the uncompromising Edwin Reardon. George Moore (1852–1933), strongly influenced by Zola and Maupassant, wrote *Esther Waters* (1894), as well as a variety of other novels. In an objective and yet poignant manner, he relates the hardships suffered by Esther from the time she goes into domestic service as a seventeen-year-old girl.

Naturalism: Arnold Bennett

Arnold Bennett (1867–1931) also modelled his novels on those of the French naturalists. Flaubert, the Goncourt brothers, Zola and Maupassant had established aesthetic ideals for him in their objectivity and precision of language. A writer of dogged productivity, he wrote over thirty novels, beginning with *A Man from the North* (1898). The first of importance was *Anna of the Five Towns* (1902), the title of which makes clear its setting in the Potteries, the midland region of England which is the environment of most of his best fiction. His reputation was established with *The Old Wives' Tale* (1908), a long, detailed study of Sophia and Constance Baines, two sisters, from youth to age. His achievement here is his skilful handling of Time, which E. M. Forster declared was the "real hero" of the book. *Clayhanger* (1910), *Hilda Lessways* (1911) and *These Twain* (1915) are collectively known as *The Clayhanger Family*. Set in the Five Towns, the first two deal respectively with the young lives of Edwin Clayhanger and Hilda Lessways and the third with their married life together. *The Card* (1911) is a lighter story about the agreeable rogue, Denry Machin. *Riceyman Steps* (1923) is a grim novel about a miserly second-hand bookseller in Clerkenwell; it is a tale of meanness, squalor, illness and death and is one of the most powerful of all Bennett's novels.

Bennett is meticulously realistic, supplying explicit details of the environment, thoughts and actions of his characters. He is a regional novelist, who shows us panoramic and close-up pictures of the places where his personages live. *The Old Wives' Tale* opens with a description of the county of Staffordshire, which surrounds his heroines, as he points out. The focus moves to the Five Towns, to St

Luke's Square, to the Baines's shop and finally to the showroom. Bennett slowly completes his picture of the two girls, the shop and the town. Similarly, Edwin at the beginning of *Clayhanger* is shown standing on a canal bridge in a precisely depicted location in the Five Towns. Such accumulation of detail, leaving little to the imagination, was adversely criticised by later novelists, notably Virginia Woolf. But it gives a photographic verisimilitude to Bennett's stories. He is not an idealist or moralist; he is content to display to us his personages and their doings. He is not without sympathy and humour, he is inventive, he can give meaning to trivial and mundane happenings and he constructs his novels solidly.

THE TWENTIETH CENTURY

Rudyard Kipling

Rudyard Kipling (1865–1936) was another author sensitive to the aesthetic shaping of his work. He was primarily a poet and writer of short stories, but two novels of his are *The Light that Failed* (1890) and *Kim* (1901). The former, with its tragic account of the blindness that overcomes Dick Heldar, may be melodramatic and sentimental, but it has a compelling emotional drive that makes it hard to put down. *Kim* evokes the India of the Raj, which Kipling knew intimately as a child and young man. Its central character, the boy Kim, travels through India with a Tibetan lama and becomes involved in espionage organised by the British Secret Service. He is therefore torn between the demands of two ways of life: the contemplative and the active. The novel can be appreciated on several levels: as an adventure story, as an unrivalled description of the peoples, customs and scenes of India, as a glorification as well as a criticism of British imperialism, and as a presentation of conflicts of ideas and loyalties.

H. G. Wells

H. G. Wells (1866–1946) was a prolific and versatile writer whose abiding interests were science and socialist politics. He made his name with scientific romances, which include *The Time Machine* (1895), *The Island of Dr Moreau* (1896), *The Invisible Man* (1897), *The War of the Worlds* (1898) and *The First Men on the Moon* (1901). Although Jules Verne's books were known in England, these were the first thoroughgoing examples of science fiction in English. Based on the sound scientific knowledge he had acquired as a London University student, his stories were daringly imaginative but convincing and still rank among the best of their kind. Their startling subject-matter includes travelling into the future, the coming of Martians to England and journeying to the moon, all realised in credible detail. Wells also wrote social comedies, typically featuring a "little man" of the lower middle class: *Love and Mr Lewisham* (1900), *Kipps* (1905) and *The History of Mr Polly* (1910). He explored social problems in a more serious manner in a third group of novels, including *Tono-Bungay* (1909), *Ann Veronica* (1909) and *The New Machiavelli* (1911). With the exception of *Mr Britling Sees It Through* (1916), his later novels lack the vigour and imagination of his earlier novels and are little read today.

Unlike James, Stevenson, Bennett and Kipling, Wells was impatient with the novel as an art-form, since for him its entertainment value and message were of prime importance. In his science fiction, he wanted to make his readers aware of the potentialities of technological discovery. His social novels had clear lessons to impart. *The History of Mr Polly* is an enjoyable story of the misfortunes and eventual happiness of its hero, with Dickensian humour in its characterisation (*e.g.* Uncle Pentstemon), Mr Polly's pathetically comic aspirations and actions (*e.g.* his conversation with the schoolgirl sitting on a wall and his attempted suicide) and his misuse of language. At the same time, Wells is making serious points about a system of society and education that can starve Mr Polly's imagination and stunt any possibilities of a fulfilled existence for him. The main purpose of *Ann Veronica* is an argument for women's liberation. *Tono-Bungay* is concerned with the world of commerce and *The New Machiavelli* with the world of politics, with relevance to the corruptions which Wells saw in Edwardian England.

Psychological subtlety and experiments with formal techniques have little part in Wells' novels, which succeed in their intention of giving much pleasure blended with instruction. His prose style is spontaneous and lively, sweeping the reader along. His instinctive skills and many-sidedness make him a novelist of considerable achievement.

Joseph Conrad

In contrast to the novels of Bennett and Wells, those by Joseph Conrad (1857–1924) are innovatory in a number of respects. Although he was Polish by birth, he served in the British Merchant Navy for many years and wrote all his novels in English. The principal ones are *Almayer's Folly* (1895), *An Outcast of the Islands* (1896), *The Nigger of the Narcissus* (1897), *Lord Jim* (1900), *The Heart of Darkness* (1902), *Typhoon* (1902), *Nostromo* (1904), *The Secret Agent* (1907), *Under Western Eyes* (1911), *Chance* (1913), *Victory* (1915) and *The Rover* (1923). Conrad also wrote short stories and some books in collaboration with Ford Madox Ford (1873–1939), who was a considerable novelist in his own right.

Conrad's experience as a seaman is reflected in the settings he uses: Malaysia and the Indian Ocean (as in *Lord Jim*), the Congo (*The Heart of Darkness*) and South America (*Nostromo*). London, however, is the setting of *The Secret Agent*. In such places a typical Conrad hero confronts dangers and is compelled to make immediate choices. Conrad concerns himself not so much with the relationships between an individual person and circumstances. Questions of moral decision, heroism and cowardice, loyalty and treachery are therefore basic to his novels. In *Lord Jim*, Jim jumps overboard from the *Patna*, which he mistakenly thinks is about to sink. Tormented by self-accusations of despicable conduct, he seeks to redeem himself. But after achieving a measure of redemption as the respected "Lord Jim", he makes another error of judgment, which brings about his death. Conrad may show us, too, how a sensitive man may be inferior at a moment of crisis to one of little imagination. A solid and stupid man like Captain MacWhirr in *Typhoon* triumphs over the terrible storm and brings his ship to safety.

To demonstrate the complexity of arriving at a true account of happenings and motives, Conrad disrupts chronology and uses various narrators. *Lord Jim* begins with Jim as a water clerk, recounts how the *Patna* hit something below the surface of the sea, and continues with the court of enquiry. At this point, Marlow (a narrator Conrad uses in several books) intervenes. Largely through him, we are given a vivid sense of the way Jim feels defeated and only then do we arrive at the crucial event: the desertion of the *Patna*. Thus chronological order is replaced by a dramatic, significant order. Perspective and shades of meaning are gained by Conrad's using the memories and prejudices of different story-tellers. In *Nostromo*, the events are narrated by the omniscient novelist and also by Captain Mitchell, Decoud (in a letter), Dr Monyghan (in his reflections) and Nostromo. Readers have to work hard at piecing together the mosaic of action and thought and are consequently made aware of the ambiguities and subtleties of human behaviour. Unity is derived from central themes: Jim's agonies of conscience in *Lord Jim*, the storm in *Typhoon* and the silver mine in *Nostromo*.

Conrad's use of English has its awkwardness, especially in colloquial speech, but these are outweighed by the scrupulous way in which he expresses shades of meaning and realises people and things in concrete detail. His novels have great depth and integrity, revealing (in the words of F. R. Leavis) both "keen sensibility" and "exceptional awareness".

John Galsworthy, Hugh Walpole and Somerset Maugham

Three novelists who achieved immense popularity and yet who never rose high in critical esteem (at least in England) were John Galsworthy (1867–1933), Sir Hugh Walpole (1884–1941) and W. Somerset Maugham (1874–1965).

Galsworthy, who was also famous as a playwright, is remembered for *The Forsyte Saga*, which consists of *The Man of Property* (1906), *In Chancery* (1920) and *To Let* (1921). The Forsyte story continues in *A Modern Comedy*, consisting of *The White Monkey* (1924), *The Silver Spoon* (1926) and *Swan Song*

(1928). The substance of these six novels is the relationships and intrigues of a wealthy upper-middle class family from the 1880s to the 1920s. The books have a comforting readability and a documentary value in their charting the outlook, habits and possessions of the family. Galsworthy was awarded the Nobel Prize for Literature in 1932.

Walpole's books have proved to be less durable. *Mr Perrin and Mr Traill* (1911), about the cruel rivalry of two schoolmasters, still has vitality. But the once-favoured novels, such as *Jeremy* (1919), *The Cathedral* (1922) and the four known as *The Herries Chronicle* (1930-33) are little read today.

Somerset Maugham began in naturalistic style with *Liza of Lambeth* (1897). Equally successful as a playwright and a short-story writer, Maugham wrote *Of Human Bondage* (1915), *The Moon and Sixpence* (1919), *Cakes and Ale* (1930), *The Razor's Edge* (1944) and many other novels. His range is wide and he is always a supreme entertainer. His sardonic attitude may disturb some, but most readers find that this gives an edge to his clear, fluent narratives. Although he has been called superficial, no one can deny his sheer readability.

E. M. Forster

Besides Conrad, four novelists of the first half of the twentieth century extended the possibilities of the form: E. M. Forster, Virginia Woolf, James Joyce and D. H. Lawrence.

E. M. Forster (1879-1970) wrote *Where Angels Fear to Tread* (1905), *The Longest Journey* (1907), *A Room with a View* (1908), *Howards End* (1910) and *A Passage to India* (1924). *Maurice* was written in 1914, but because of its homosexual theme was not published till 1971. After 1924, Forster wrote no more novels.

In all his writings, fiction and nonfiction, Forster is liberal and humanist in outlook. He always set great store by loving personal relationships and was suspicious of conceptions of duty, patriotism and imperialism. In a notorious statement in his essay, "What I Believe" (1939), he said: "I hate the idea of causes, and if I had to choose between betraying my country and betraying my friend, I hope I should have the guts to betray my country." Later in the same essay, he declared that he distrusted Great Men and believed in an aristocracy of the "sensitive, the considerate and the plucky".

His novels are elegant, drily humorous and witty, but at the same time they contain elements of the poetical and the mystical. The motto, "Only connect", which appears on the title page of *Howards End*, expresses one of his tenets. To bring out its implications, he will place two sets of ideas in opposition and show the tensions and connections between them. In *Where Angels Fear to Tread*, Lilia, an English girl from the conventional middle-classes, outrages her family when she marries Gino, an Italian dentist. After her death, they make attempts to "rescue" her baby. The comedy and the message of the novel, therefore, derive from the interactions between English and Mediterranean ways of life. The opposition in *Howards End* is between the world of "telegrams and anger" and the world of culture and the finer feelings.

Forster's most ambitious novel, *A Passage to India*, is concerned with the mutual misunderstandings between the Indians and the ruling English in the India of 1910-20. The narrow-minded English community is angered by Dr Aziz' apparent assault on Adela Quested in the Marabar Caves. The principal characters are Fielding, the well-meaning and humane schoolmaster; Dr Aziz, impulsive and warm-hearted; Mrs Moore, the elderly, visionary Englishwoman; and Adela herself, who—like Fielding—has good intentions but is bewildered by her encounter with India. Forster carefully patterns his novel, writes amusing and lively description and dialogue and conveys a sense of the incomprehensibility and fascination of India felt by English people. As always, he seeks to inculcate the truth that love and understanding at the personal level are vital in all circumstances.

In *Aspects of the Novel* (1927), Forster deplored the need to tell a story in the novel. But his novels contain much that is amusing and thought-provoking: surprises in the plot, realistic dialogue, economical but convincing characterisation and unexpected authorial generalisations. Altogether, we get the impression of a sharp but tolerant perception of the virtues and frailties of mankind.

Virginia Woolf

E. M. Forster was associated with the Bloomsbury Group, although he was never a fully committed member of it. The relations and friends who formed the Group between 1905 and the 1930s (Lytton Strachey, Maynard Keynes, Virginia Woolf and her sister Vanessa Bell, Clive Bell, Duncan Grant, Roger Fry and others) saw themselves as rational, enlightened people who rejected the intolerance and narrow-minded morality of the Victorians. They valued love, friendship and the arts.

One of the central figures of the Bloomsbury Group was Virginia Woolf (1882-1941), whose career as a novelist began with two fairly conventional books: *The Voyage Out* (1915) and *Night and Day* (1919). She proceeded to experiment in both form and content and all her subsequent novels are works of originality, breaking with traditional approaches and methods: *Jacob's Room* (1922), *Mrs Dalloway* (1925), *To the Lighthouse* (1927), *Orlando* (1928), *The Waves* (1931), *The Years* (1937) and *Between the Acts* (1941).

Virginia Woolf was opposed to the technique of such Edwardian novelists as Bennett, Wells and Galsworthy. In her opinion, they were materialists, who were "concerned not with the spirit but with the body". Their painstaking renderings of a solid, exterior world meant, she argued, that the inner meaning of life escaped them. What she attempted to do, on the other hand, was to capture the transience and subtlety of experience and thought. In a famous statement, she said that "Life is not a series of gig lamps symmetrically arranged; life is a luminous halo, a semi-transparent envelope surrounding us from the beginning of consciousness to the end." Modern authors should therefore "record the atoms as they fall upon the mind in the order in which they fall" and "trace the pattern, however disconnected and incoherent in appearance, which each sight or incident scores upon the consciousness." To achieve these ends, she uses as a means the "stream of consciousness" technique. She takes us inside her characters' minds, revealing the flow of their thoughts and emotions, past, present and future. The trivial and the grand are fused; the exterior world impinges now and then; repetitions, allusions, memories blend together.

A typical example of this technique is the scene of the dinner-party in *To the Lighthouse*. Outwardly, Mrs Ramsay, the hostess, is serving the food and making unremarkable conversation with her guests. But we are witnesses of the interior lives of these people. The reflections of Mrs Ramsay, Lily Briscoe, Charles Tansley and William Bankes make a delicately woven texture of thoughts and emotions, adding to what we have already learned earlier in the novel.

Realising the difficulty of giving a clear shape to the intangible, Virginia Woolf uses repeated phrases and objects as focal points, such as the royal car in *Mrs Dalloway* and the lighthouse and Lily Briscoe's painting in *To the Lighthouse*. Her prose is supple and quietly rhythmical and contains memorable and beautiful imagery. Her novels have a refined artistry—too rarefied in the opinion of some, who have criticised her for narrowness of social range and sensitivity. But she is one of the most discerning and subtle of psychological novelists.

James Joyce

James Joyce (1882-1941), an exact contemporary of Virginia Woolf, was the most far-reaching innovator in the English novel of this century. His comparatively small output began with a collection of short stories, *Dubliners* (1914), economically realistic evocations of the frustrated lives of ordinary inhabitants of the Irish city. *A Portrait of the Artist as a Young Man* (1916) is an autobiographical novel. This was followed by his masterpiece, *Ulysses* (1922). His last book was *Finnegans Wake* (1939).

Joyce used the stream of consciousness technique, carrying it to greater lengths than Virginia Woolf. It can be seen in its purest form in Molly Bloom's soliloquy at the end of *Ulysses*, where her drifting mental processes as she lies half-asleep are rendered in unpunctuated prose that moves from one apparently disconnected thought to another. His most astonishing innovations were linguistic. *A Portrait of the Artist* begins with childish-sounding language mirroring the boy's immaturity. Throughout the book, his stages of development are recorded in appropriate levels of prose. *Ulysses* is written in widely varied styles of English, most obviously in the scene where Stephen and Bloom await the birth of a baby. The conception and growth of the child are reflected in Joyce's imitations of English prose from Anglo-Saxon times to the end of the nineteenth century. His most extreme linguistic experimentation is in *Finnegans Wake*, a book of such intensive verbal coinage and word-play that it can be said to be written in a new language, for which a key is necessary.

Joyce also employs allusions and symbols, which enrich his meaning once they are interpreted (which again can be a difficult process). *Ulysses* has indirect allegiances to Homer's epic poem, the *Odyssey*, but it is filled with the actuality of one day in Dublin: 16 June 1904. It contains numerous other emblems, references and echoes, making it a fascinatingly complex picture of human experience. His psychological explorations of character are associated with the life and traditions of Ireland, for although Joyce exiled himself from his native country as a young man its politics, religion and customs are inseparable from his work.

Stephen Daedalus, the hero of *A Portrait of the Artist as a Young Man*, is the fictional equivalent of Joyce. His education, temptations and artistic credo make the main subject-matter of the book. Stephen reappears as one of the central characters of *Ulysses*, in which his companion during the day's adventures is a middle-aged Jew, Leopold Bloom. Using their particular situations in early twentieth-century Ireland, Joyce creates a universal impression of the emotions and problems of humanity, by means of interior monologue, sensuous description, individualised dialogue and allusion. In *A Portrait of the Artist*, Stephen said that the highest form of literature is the dramatic. In that form, "the artist, like the God of creation, remains within or behind or beyond or above his handiwork, invisible, refined out of existence, indifferent, paring his fingernails." By fully and uncompromisingly presenting his characters' innermost thoughts and by withholding authorial moral judgement, Joyce aimed to achieve the ideal that Stephen desired.

D. H. Lawrence

D. H. Lawrence (1885–1930) differed in many remarkable aspects from James Joyce and Virginia Woolf in his approach to writing novels. He brought an urgency and spontaneity and, above all, a poetic sense to prose fiction. He was a prolific author, who produced numerous short stories, travel books, poems, plays and essays besides novels. His principal novels are *The White Peacock* (1911), *Sons and Lovers* (1913), *The Rainbow* (1915), *Women in Love* (1920), *The Lost Girl* (1921), *Aaron's Rod* (1922), *Kangaroo* (1923), *The Plumed Serpent* (1926) and *Lady Chatterley's Lover* (1928).

As a novelist, Lawrence considered himself "superior to the saint, the scientist, the philosopher, and the poet", since in his opinion the novel dealt with the complete human being instead of a particular aspect. "The novel," he declared, "is the one bright book of life." His main theme is the tensions, joys and sorrows that exist in personal relationships: those between parents and children, husbands and wives, and other people in love. *Sons and Lovers*, his most famous book, centres upon the semi-autobiographical hero, Paul Morel, whose attachment to his mother inhibits his love for Miriam. The novel is also deeply concerned with the opposition between Paul's sensual coal-mining father and his refined, sensitive mother. *The Rainbow*, to which *Women in Love* is a kind of sequel, shows three generations of the Brangwyn family: the conflict and mutual understanding inherent in passionate marriages and love-affairs and the disputes and reconciliations between parents and children are revealed as repeating themselves through a long period of time. But no summaries can convey the subtleties of Lawrence's handling of the psychological and moral issues involved.

For Lawrence, "blood" and instinct were the dominating forces of life, superior in strength to the dictates of reason, and he saw his task as a novelist to transmit these forces through the medium of words. The result is that his novels lack conventional form. What matters is the internal lives of his characters and not their external actions, except when these actions reveal significant behaviour. He

therefore concentrates on episodes of intensity and he will, where necessary, ignore the reader's expectations of an even time-scale and the clear development of plot and character. "You mustn't look into my novel for the old stable *ego* of character," he wrote. "There is another *ego*, according to whose action the individual is unrecognisable, and passes through, as it were, allotropic states which it needs a deeper sense than any we've been used to exercise, to discover and are states of the same single radically unchanged element." His writing consequently has a great emotional impact and gives the feeling of complete fidelity to life as it actually is, with its contradictions and uncertainties. But Lawrence's uncompromising frankness and refusal to conform to literary and social conventions led to the censorship and banning of some of his books, notably *Lady Chatterley's Lover*, which was too sexually explicit for contemporary English standards—it was not published in Britain in unexpurgated form until 1960.

Lawrence's descriptions of the physical appearance of his characters and their surroundings are direct and sensuous; his prose rhythms and choice of words remind us that he was a poet. Places he lived in inspired many of his settings: the Midlands countryside in *The White Peacock*, Australia in *Kangaroo*, Mexico in *The Plumed Serpent*. His imagery is rich in suggestion and is typically drawn from natural and religious sources. In *The Rainbow*, for example, the rainbow itself, doorways, archways and rural scenery and occupations evoke important aspects of the characters' lives and motives and give unity to the novel.

It has been argued that Lawrence was not always in touch with reality because the intense level at which his personages live lacks credibility. Some critics have deplored his preaching, his lack of humour and his repetitiveness. Some of these criticisms are justified only if the criterion of naturalism is rigorously applied. Most people will agree that his great novels—*Sons and Lovers*, *The Rainbow* and *Women in Love*—are masterpieces of psychological insight and moral profundity.

Other Novelists of the 1920s and 1930s

Although Ronald Firbank (1886–1926) began publishing his work in 1905, his slight, artificial novels seem to represent the frivolous side of the 1920s. Amongst them are *Vainglory* (1915), *Caprice* (1917), *Valmouth* (1919), *The Flower beneath the Foot* (1923), *Prancing Nigger* (1924) and *Concerning the Eccentricities of Cardinal Pirelli* (1926). The wit and fantasy of these books can also be related to the aestheticism of the 1890s.

One of the most influential writers of the two decades was Aldous Huxley (1894–1963). An intellectual and polymath, Huxley wrote satirical, comic novels of ideas, which have affinities with those of Peacock. They include *Crome Yellow* (1921), *Antic Hay* (1923) and *Those Barren Leaves* (1925). *Point Counterpoint* (1928) consists mainly of brilliant conversation pieces, in which the participants (e.g. Rampion, who is based on D. H. Lawrence) exchange ideas on philosophy, politics, religion, the arts and society. Of Huxley's later novels, the most important are *Brave New World* (1932), which is set six hundred years hence, *Eyeless in Gaza* (1936) and *Island* (1962).

Evelyn Waugh (1903–66) made his reputation with comic, witty, mocking novels: *Decline and Fall* (1928), *Vile Bodies* (1930), *Black Mischief* (1932), *A Handful of Dust* (1934), *Scoop* (1938) and *Put Out More Flags* (1942). Waugh's books of this period are characterised by an air of satirical detachment, black comedy and farce, the fertile invention of entertaining personages and episodes and a pointed prose style. They remain freshly amusing, though some readers dislike their apparent heartlessness. *Brideshead Revisited* (1945), with its nostalgic recollections of events centred upon a great country house, is, in contrast, a romantic and even sentimental novel. *The Loved One* (1948), a satire on American funeral customs, marked a return to his earlier manner. Waugh's last considerable work, which some consider to be his masterpiece, was a trilogy: *Men at Arms* (1952), *Officers and Gentlemen* (1955) and *Unconditional Surrender* (1961), later united as *Sword of Honour* (1965). Though this book contains much comedy, it is a sympathetic portrayal of the doubts and anxieties during the Second World War of its central figure, Guy Crouchback, a

Roman Catholic and army officer.

The first novels of George Orwell (pseudonym of Eric Blair, 1903–50) reflect the period: *A Clergyman's Daughter* (1935), *Keep the Aspidistra Flying* (1936) and *Coming up for Air* (1939). His most celebrated were his last two: *Animal Farm* (1945), which is a short fable satirising revolution and dictatorship, and *Nineteen Eighty-Four* (1949), which is a grim picture of a future authoritarian world.

Christopher Isherwood (1904–86) wrote *All the Conspirators* (1928), but made his reputation with the plays he wrote with W. H. Auden in the 1930s and with his two novels about Germany in the last days of the Weimar Republic: *Mr Norris Changes Trains* (1935) and *Goodbye to Berlin* (1939). The narrator of these says "I am a camera" and consequently records his experiences in a spare, objective manner, which nevertheless evokes the emotions of himself and the other characters. Isherwood's other novels, which are varied in content, include *Prater Violet* (1946) and *Down There On A Visit* (1962).

Much of the fiction of Firbank, Huxley, Waugh, Orwell and Isherwood therefore reflects the spirit of the age. But other novelists of the time were free from contemporary preoccupations. The two most famous novels of John Cowper Powys (1872–1963) are *Wolf Solent* (1929) and *A Glastonbury Romance* (1932), which are conceived on a grand scale and are full of a metaphysical awareness of the forces of Nature. His brother, T. F. Powys (1875–1953), is best known for *Mr Weston's Good Wine* (1927). The novels of Ivy Compton-Burnett (1892–1969) are set at the end of the nineteenth century in a stylised world of middle-class families in country houses. Their titles, whose similarities denote the unchanging nature of the novels, include *Pastors and Masters* (1925), *Men and Wives* (1931), *A House and its Head* (1935), *A Family and a Fortune* (1939), *Manservant and Maidservant* (1947), *Two Worlds and their Ways* (1949), *A Father and his Fate* (1957), *The Mighty and their Fall* (1961) and *A God and his Gifts* (1963). Through the medium of mannered conversation, Ivy Compton-Burnett presents stories of wrongdoing, sin and crime. Aspects of evil are coolly and wittily exposed by means of her highly artificial narration.

J. B. Priestley (1894–1984) wrote *The Good Companions* (1929), which was a huge success, and followed this with numerous realistic, entertaining novels, including *Angel Pavement* (1930).

Graham Greene

Graham Greene (b. 1904) has been writing novels for almost sixty years as well as short stories, plays, autobiography, essays and criticism. He began with *The Man Within* (1929) and his subsequent novels are *Stamboul Train* (1932), *It's a Battlefield* (1934), *England Made Me* (1935), *A Gun for Sale* (1936), *Brighton Rock* (1938), *The Confidential Agent* (1939), *The Power and the Glory* (1940), *The Ministry of Fear* (1943), *The Heart of the Matter* (1948), *The Third Man* (1950), *The End of the Affair* (1951), *Loser Takes All* (1955), *The Quiet American* (1955), *Our Man in Havana* (1958), *A Burnt-Out Case* (1961), *The Comedians* (1966), *Travels with my Aunt* (1969), *The Honorary Consul* (1973), *The Human Factor* (1978), *Doctor Fischer of Geneva* (1980), *Monsignor Quixote* (1982) and *The Tenth Man* (1985; written 1944).

Greene's novels are gripping and exciting, since they contain the basic features of such popular fiction as thrillers, adventure stories and spy stories. Their settings are dangerous or exotic places, such as Mexico (*The Power and the Glory*), West Africa (*The Heart of the Matter*), the Congo (*A Burnt-Out Case*), Haiti (*The Comedians*) and Argentina (*The Honorary Consul*). His vivid descriptions of places and people and his fast-moving pace are cinematic and many of his novels have been turned into successful films. Enmeshed in challenging circumstances, his characters are compelled to make moral choices and, in doing so, to face problems of loyalty and faith. As Greene is a Roman Catholic, these problems are generally related to religious belief. Pinkie, the young Roman Catholic criminal in *Brighton Rock*, is dedicated to evil but is opposed by the warm-hearted Ida, who has firm ideas of Right and Wrong, untroubled by theological considerations. Scobie in *The Heart of the Matter*, a self-tormented Catholic, chooses to commit the sin of suicide as a result of his entanglements in unhappy relationships with women. In his novella, *Doctor Fischer of Geneva*, Greene uses memorable, macabre events and strange—even grotesque—characterisation to stimulate thought about profound issues: greed, power, love, revenge and death.

Greene's settings, characters and themes, especially from *Brighton Rock* onwards, are fused into complete statements about the springs of human conduct. The environment, which has sometimes been called "Greeneland", can symbolise and emphasise the dangers experienced by his characters. Because of the quantity and quality of his achievement, Graham Greene is widely considered to be the outstanding English novelist of the past fifty years. This opinion received official recognition when he was appointed a Companion of Honour in 1966 and awarded the O.M. in 1986.

THE NOVEL SINCE 1940

Novelists of the 1940s

Some writers who began their literary careers in the 1930s became more prominent in the war and post-war years. Joyce Cary (1888–1957) began by writing novels set in Nigeria, where he had worked as a government official: *Aissa Saved* (1932), *An American Visitor* (1933), *The African Witch* (1936) and *Mister Johnson* (1939). He followed these with two books about childhood: *Charley is my Darling* (1940) and *A House of Children* (1941). Then there came a trilogy centred upon three characters, Gulley Jimson, Sara Monday and Wilcher: *Herself Surprised* (1941), *To Be a Pilgrim* (1942) and *The Horse's Mouth* (1944), which is generally accounted his best novel. Another trilogy, centred upon Chester Nimmo, was *Prisoner of Grace* (1952), *Except the Lord* (1953) and *Not Honour More* (1955). A further notable novel is *A Fearful Joy* (1949). Cary's most famous works, *Mister Johnson* and *The Horse's Mouth*, are exuberant, inventive and full of *joie de vivre*, largely owing to their central characters, Mister Johnson, an African clerk, and Gulley Jimson, a painter and rogue.

L. P. Hartley (1895–1972) wrote a trilogy dealing with the fortunes of a brother and sister in the early years of this century: *The Shrimp and the Anemone* (1944), *The Sixth Heaven* (1946) and *Eustace and Hilda* (1947). *The Go-Between* (1953) is a vivid, delicate evocation of a boy's being caught up in adult sexual intrigue and of Edwardian country house life.

The sensitive, psychologically penetrating novels of Elizabeth Bowen (1899–1973) include *The House in Paris* (1935), *The Death of the Heart* (1938), *The Heat of the Day* (1949)—usually said to be her greatest achievement, *A World of Love* (1955) and *Eva Trout* (1969).

Henry Green (pseudonym of Henry Yorke, 1905–73) wrote *Blindness* (1926), *Living* (1929), *Party Going* (1939), *Caught* (1943), *Loving* (1945), *Back* (1946), *Concluding* (1948), *Nothing* (1950) and *Doting* (1952). He explores personal relationships in rhythmical prose, much dialogue, imagery and symbols. His novels are some of the most imaginative works of the period.

In contrast, the novels of C. P. Snow (1905–80) are heavily realistic, often dealing with people in the midst of public affairs (in, for example, government and university circles). His best-known novels form the *Strangers and Brothers* sequence: *Strangers and Brothers* (1940), *The Light and the Dark* (1947), *Time of Hope* (1949), *The Masters* (1951), *The New Men* (1954), *Homecomings* (1956), *The Conscience of the Rich* (1958), *The Affair* (1960), *Corridors of Power* (1964), *The Sleep of Reason* (1968) and *Last Things* (1970).

The quiet, perceptive novels of Elizabeth Taylor (1912–75) include *At Mrs Lippincote's* (1945), *A View of the Harbour* (1947), *A Wreath of Roses* (1949), *Angel* (1957) and *Mrs Palfrey at the Claremont* (1971).

Samuel Beckett

As a young man, Samuel Beckett (born 1906) was a friend and associate of James Joyce, whose stream-of-consciousness technique influenced his writing. He first came into prominence in England in 1955 when his English version of his play, *Waiting for Godot*, originally written in French, was performed in London. His novel, *Murphy* (1938), set in London, is written in a fairly traditional manner. *Watt*, completed about 1944, was published in 1953. Three short novels, first written in French and in the form of monologues, comprise a trilogy: *Malone Dies* (1951; English version, 1956), *Molloy* (1951; English version, 1955) and *The Unnamable* (1953; English version, 1958). Like much of Beckett's work, which includes plays, short prose pieces and poems, these three novels are characterised by moods of negation, despair and hopelessness but also by elements of grim humour. Beckett was awarded the Nobel Prize for Literature in 1969.

The 1950s: Anthony Powell, Lawrence Durrell and Angus Wilson

Anthony Powell (b. 1905) wrote some amusing novels in the 1930s, rather like those of Evelyn Waugh: *Afternoon Men* (1931), *Venusberg* (1932), *From a View to a Death* (1933), *Agents and Patients* (1936) and *What's Become of Waring?* (1939). His major work, a sequence called *A Dance to the Music of Time*, began to appear in the 1950s: *A Question of Upbringing* (1951), *A Buyer's Market* (1952), *The Acceptance World* (1955), *At Lady Molly's* (1957), *Casanova's Chinese Restaurant* (1960), *The Kindly Ones* (1962), *The Valley of Bones* (1964), *The Soldier's Art* (1966), *The Military Philosophers* (1968), *Books Do Furnish A Room* (1971), *Temporary Kings* (1973) and *Hearing Secret Harmonies* (1975). Its subject is the relationships of a large circle of friends and acquaintances spanning a period of sixty years and including about three hundred characters. It is written with gentle irony and sharp observation of psychology, manners and social class. Powell has also written *O, How the Wheel Becomes It!* (1983) and *The Fisher King* (1986).

Lawrence Durrell (b. 1912) published his best-known novels in this decade. *The Alexandria Quartet* consists of *Justine* (1957), *Balthazar* (1958), *Mountolive* (1958) and *Clea* (1960). These complex, erotic and exotic novels are notably experimental in their treatment of time. Durrell's other novels include *Tunc* (1968), *Nunquam* (1970), *Monsieur* (1974), *Livia* (1978), *Constance* (1982), *Sebastian* (1983) and *Quinx* (1985).

Angus Wilson (b. 1913) first achieved success with two collections of short stories, *The Wrong Set* (1949) and *Such Darling Dodos* (1952). His novels are *Hemlock and After* (1952), *Anglo-Saxon Attitudes* (1956), *The Middle Age of Mrs Eliot* (1958), *The Old Men at the Zoo* (1961), *Late Call* (1964), *No Laughing Matter* (1967), *As If By Magic* (1973) and *Setting the World on Fire* (1980). An admirer of Dickens, Dostoevsky, Proust and Virginia Woolf, Angus Wilson writes in a realistic, detailed manner with convincing renderings of conversation, although this air of realism does not preclude him from using fantasy and symbolism, especially in his later work. The people and milieux he deals with are predominantly middle-class. His subject-matter is personal relationships, often amongst middle-aged men and women. Class is an important element in some of his work, which is remarkably varied.

Kingsley Amis and John Wain

Other novelists of the 1950s took a disillusioned, ironical look at the postwar world, just as many of the new poets and playwrights of the period did. Distrusting anything grandiose and experimental, they wrote in wryly amusing and observant ways about people of no particular privileges, wealth or pretensions. William Cooper's *Scenes of Provincial Life* (1950), with its significant title, was a forerunner of the disrespectful, non-metropolitan stance which they adopted.

The most accomplished of these writers is Kingsley Amis (b. 1922), whose novels are *Lucky Jim* (1954), *That Uncertain Feeling* (1955), *I Like It Here* (1958), *Take a Girl Like You* (1960), *One Fat Englishman* (1963), *The Anti-Death League* (1966), *I Want It Now* (1968), *The Green Man* (1969), *Girl, 20* (1971), *The Riverside Villas Murder* (1973), *Ending Up* (1974), *The Alteration* (1976), *Jake's Thing* (1978), *Russian Hide-and-Seek* (1980) and *Stanley and the Women* (1984). As a moral novelist, Amis writes with economy, precision, wit and cynical commonsense, constantly puncturing affectations and falsity. *Lucky Jim*, with its account of the fortunes and misfortunes of a provincial university teacher, has become one of the classic comic novels of the past thirty years.

Another versatile novelist is John Wain (b. 1925), whose *Hurry on Down* (1953) achieved the same kind of status and popularity as *Lucky Jim*. His other novels include *Living in the Present* (1955), *The Contenders* (1958), *A Travelling Woman* (1959), *Strike the Father Dead* (1962), *The Young Visitors* (1965), *A Winter in the Hills* (1974) and *Young Shoulders* (1982).

Northern, Working-Class Novelists

Novelists writing of life amongst the working classes, especially in the north of England, also came to the fore in the 1950s. John Braine (b. 1922) wrote *Room at the Top* (1957) about a go-getting young man, Joe Lampton. His subsequent novels, which vary in theme, include *The Vodi* (1959), *Life at the Top* (1962), *The Crying Game* (1964), *Stay With Me Till Morning* (1970), *The Queen of a Distant Country* (1972), *Waiting for Sheila* (1976), *One and Last Love* (1981) *The Two of Us* (1984) and *These Golden Days* (1985). Alan Sillitoe (b. 1928) made his reputation with *Saturday Night and Sunday Morning* (1958) and went on to write novels of different kinds, including *The General* (1960), *Key to the Door* (1961), *The Death of William Posters* (1965), *A Start in Life* (1970), *Travels in Nihilon* (1971), *Raw Material* (1972), *A Flame of Life* (1974), *The Widower's Son* (1976), *The Storyteller* (1979), *The Second Chance* (1981), *Her Victory* (1982), *Down from the Hill* (1984) and *Life Goes On* (1985). Stan Barstow (b. 1928) wrote *A Kind of Loving* (1960); the best-known of his other novels is *A Raging Calm* (1968). The first novel by David Storey (b. 1933) was *This Sporting Life* (1962), about Rugby League football. His other books include *Radcliffe* (1965), *Pasmore* (1972), *Saville* (1976), *A Prodigal Child* (1982) and *Present Times* (1984). *Room at the Top*, *Saturday Night and Sunday Morning*, *A Kind of Loving* and *This Sporting Life*, which were all successfully filmed, stand together as the most famous novels of northern working-class life of the 1950s.

Fantasy and Experiment

Amis, Wain, Braine, Sillitoe, Barstow and Storey are mainly realistic novelists writing without linguistic experimentation or poetic devices. Their subject-matter, point of view and style are down-to-earth. Others of their contemporaries and near-contemporaries used new fictional forms or explored more imaginative areas. J. R. R. Tolkien (1892–1973) wrote *The Lord of the Rings* (1954–5), a trilogy about an imaginary world that for many readers has the power and attraction of genuine mythology. Mervyn Peake (1911–68) created a fantastic, grotesque world in *The Gormenghast Trilogy*: *Titus Groan* (1946), *Gormenghast* (1950) and *Titus Alone* (1959).

William Golding (b. 1911) achieved great success with *Lord of the Flies* (1954), his story of shipwrecked boys who revert to a primitive, savage state. His other novels are *The Inheritors* (1955), *Pincher Martin* (1956), *Free Fall* (1959), *The Spire* (1964), *The Pyramid* (1967), *Darkness Visible* (1979), *Rites of Passage* (1980) and *The Paper Men* (1984). In complex, imaginative ways, Golding explores profound questions of morality, especially the nature of sin and evil. His novels are therefore often difficult but original in technique and content. Golding was awarded the Nobel Prize for Literature in 1983.

Muriel Spark (b. 1918) has written *The Comforters* (1957), *Robinson* (1958), *Memento Mori* (1959), *The Bachelors* (1960), *The Ballad of Peckham Rye* (1960), *The Prime of Miss Jean Brodie* (1961), *The Girls of Slender Means* (1963), *The Mandelbaum Gate* (1965), *The Public Image* (1968), *The Driver's Seat* (1970), *Not to Disturb* (1971), *The Hothouse by the East River* (1973), *The Abbess of Crewe* (1974), *The Takeover* (1976), *Territorial Rights* (1979), *Loitering with Intent* (1981) and *The Only Problem* (1984). Her novels are economically written, witty and sometimes fantastic. With a light touch, she presents the reader with provocative studies of moral and metaphysical issues. Her characterisation is vivid and memorable (*e.g.* Miss Brodie). There is occasionally an element of the fairy tale or myth in her novels (*e.g. The Ballad of Peckham Rye*).

Doris Lessing (b. 1919), a novelist deeply concerned with psychological, political and social tensions (especially in Africa), has also experimented with techniques of fiction. Her novels include *The Grass is Singing* (1950), the *Children of Violence* series (1952–69), *The Golden Notebook* (1962) and *The Good Terrorist* (1985).

One of the most prolific and inventive of postwar English novelists is Iris Murdoch (b. 1919). Her novels are *Under the Net* (1954), *The Flight from the Enchanter* (1956), *The Sandcastle* (1957), *The Bell* (1958), *A Severed Head* (1961), *An Unofficial Rose* (1962), *The Unicorn* (1963), *The Italian Girl* (1964), *The Red and the Green* (1965), *The Time of the Angels* (1966), *The Nice and the Good* (1968), *Bruno's Dream* (1969), *A Fairly Honourable Defeat* (1970), *An Accidental Man* (1971), *The Black Prince* (1973), *The Sacred and Profane Love Machine* (1974), *A Word Child* (1975), *Henry and Cato* (1976), *The Sea, The Sea* (1978), *Nuns and Soldiers* (1980), *The Philosopher's Pupil* (1983) and *The Good Apprentice* (1985). A professional philosopher as well as a novelist, Iris Murdoch raises philosophical issues in her fiction by implication, although she maintains that she writes primarily to entertain her readers. Her books contain numerous characters and incidents and often have complicated plots. Their surface attractions are considerable: narrative pace, lively descriptions of people and places, striking episodes and realistic, entertaining dialogue. She uses symbols (the bell and the sea in the appropriately titled novels, for example) and mysterious happenings and coincidences. She stimulates thought about such problems as intentions, appearance and reality, truth and falsity and the part played in life by contingency and chance.

The 1960s

Anthony Burgess (b. 1917) became well known in this decade with *A Clockwork Orange* (1962). He is a productive, versatile and experimental novelist, whose many other works include *Inside Mr Enderby* (1963), *The Napoleon Symphony* (1974), *Earthly Powers* (1980), *The End of the World News* (1982), *Enderby's Dark Lady* (1984) and *The Kingdom of the Wicked* (1985).

Paul Scott (1920–78) is concerned in his principal novels with the English in India. These are *The Raj Quartet*—which consists of *The Jewel in the Crown* (1966), *The Day of the Scorpion* (1968), *The Tower of Silence* (1971) and *A Division of the Spoils* (1976)— and *Staying On* (1977).

John Fowles (b. 1926) is an ingenious and innovatory novelist, whose books include *The Collector* (1963), *The Magus* (1966, revised 1977), *The French Lieutenant's Woman* (1969), *Daniel Martin* (1977), *Mantissa* (1982) and *A Maggot* (1985).

A number of African and West Indian novelists writing in English established themselves at this time. Chinua Achebe (b. 1930), a Nigerian, wrote *Things Fall Apart* (1958) and followed this with various novels and collections of short stories. V. S. Naipaul (b. 1932), a Trinidadian of Indian descent, became acknowledged as one of the leading novelists of the period. His novels include *The Mystic Masseur* (1957), *A House for Mr Biswas* (1961), *Mr Stone and the Knights Companion* (1963), *The Mimic Men* (1967), *In a Free State* (1971), *Guerrillas* (1975) and *A Bend in the River* (1979).

Edna O'Brien (b. 1932) began her career in this decade with three novels that humorously and poignantly portrayed the lives and loves of young Irish women: *The Country Girls* (1960), *The Lonely Girl* (1962) and *Girls in their Married Bliss* (1964). Her other books include *August is a Wicked Month* (1965) and *Johnny I Hardly Knew You* (1977). After the publication of *Wide Sargasso Sea* (1966), interest revived in the novels of Jean Rhys (1894–1979), including *Good Morning, Midnight* (1939). *Wide Sargasso Sea* is a sympathetic, brilliantly imaginative account of the early life in the West Indies of Mr Rochester's first wife, Charlotte Brontë's fictional character in *Jane Eyre*. The prevalent tone of Jean Rhys's novels is one of sadness and anguish, as experienced and expressed by a lonely suffering woman.

Margaret Drabble (b. 1939) has written novels that subtly explore human relationships, often with women at their centre. Amongst them are *The Garrick Year* (1965), *Jerusalem the Golden* (1967), *The Ice Age* (1977) and *The Middle Ground* (1980).

The 1970s and after

Beryl Bainbridge (b. 1934) is a comically observant, ironical novelist who made her name with *The Bottle Factory Outing* (1974). Her other novels include *Harriet Said* (1972), *Sweet William* (1975), *A Quiet Life* (1976), *Injury Time* (1977), *Young Adolf* (1978), *Another Part of the Wood* (1979), *Winter Garden* (1980) and *Watson's Apology* (1984).

Malcolm Bradbury (b. 1932) and David Lodge (b. 1935), both teachers and critics of literature, became well-known in the 1970s as novelists. They are associated particularly with "campus novels" dealing with the academic life. Bradbury's novels include *Eating People is Wrong* (1959), *Stepping Westward* (1965), *The History Man* (1975) and *Rates of Exchange* (1983). Lodge's include *The British Museum is Falling Down* (1965), *Changing Places* (1975), *How Far Can You Go?* (1980) and *Small World* (1984).

Other novelists who started publishing their work in the 1970s include Martin Amis (b. 1949), William Boyd (b. 1952), Salman Rushdie (b. 1947) and D. M. Thomas (b. 1935).

THE ENGLISH NOVEL IN PERSPECTIVE

This survey has been confined to the English novel, which should be seen in the perspective of the great European and American novels of the past two or three centuries. Its qualities—its particular strengths and weaknesses—can be truly judged only by considering it in relation to the work of such acknowledged masters as Cervantes; Stendhal, Balzac, Flaubert, Zola and Proust; Tolstoy and Dostoevsky; Goethe and Thomas Mann; Hawthorne, Melville and Mark Twain; Manzoni and Svevo. Comparisons are especially important when we look at modern novelists, since much of today's most significant fiction in English comes from the United States. A list of major twentieth-century novelists writing in English would have to include Scott Fitzgerald, Ernest Hemingway, William Faulkner, J. D. Salinger and Norman Mailer, to name only a few. It is necessary, therefore, to realise that this survey of the English novel deals with just one area of an extensive field of literary achievement.

II. GLOSSARY OF LITERARY TERMS

acatalectic. Having the complete number of syllables in a line of verse. *See* **catalectic** *and* **hypercatalectic.**

accentual verse. Verse (like most English verse) which is measured by the number and pattern of stresses in a line and not by the number or quantitative value of syllables. *See* **metre** *and* **syllabic verse.**

act. Principal division of a dramatic work, sometimes subdivided into scenes.

aestheticism. A movement that flourished in the 1880s and 1890s and that considered beauty, not morality, as the most important principle in literary and artistic work. Its key phrase was "Art for art's sake." Two of its chief exponents in England were Walter Pater and Oscar Wilde.

affective fallacy. A phrase coined by M. C. Beardsley and W. K. Wimsatt (1946), who contended that it was false to criticise a poem on the basis of its psychological effects on the reader because as a result "the poem itself, as an object of specifically critical judgement, tends to disappear." *See* **Intentional fallacy** *and* **New Critics.**

alexandrine. A line of verse containing six iambic feet. *See* **metre.**

alienation. The principle, propounded by Bertolt Brecht (1898–1956), that actors and audience should remain detached from a dramatic performance and not become identified with the rôles and action.

allegory. A narrative or description in prose or verse with a hidden meaning or moral message, *e.g.*, Spenser's *Faerie Queene* and Bunyan's *Pilgrim's Progress.*

alliteration. The use of the same consonants in close proximity, often in verse, for the sake of euphony, memorability or emotional effect, *e.g.*,

"the *l*ow *l*ast edge of the *l*ong *l*one *l*and"
(Swinburne, "A Forsaken Garden").

See **assonance.**

ambiguity. Unclear or contradictory meaning. Positively, complexity of meaning and tone, as analysed in William Empson's *Seven Types of Ambiguity* (1930).

amphibrach. *See* **metre**.

anabasis. The progress of an action to a climax, especially in a drama.

anacoluthon. An inconsistency of construction in a sentence, so that the latter part does not grammatically fit with the earlier part, *e.g.*, "One of the prettiest touches was *when*, at the relation of the queen's death . . . *how* attentiveness wounded his daughter" (Shakespeare, *The Winter's Tale*, V, ii).

anacreontic. Applied to light-hearted poetry praising such pleasures as wine, women and song, *e.g.*, Abraham Cowley's *Anacreontics*. (From Anacreon, Greek poet of the sixth century B.C.)

anacrusis. An additional syllable or half-foot at the beginning of a line of verse, *e.g.*,

"Cóld / and cleár- / cŭt faće / whў come / yŏu ̆so
crú- / ĕllў méek?"

(Tennyson, "Maud").

anagnorisis. The discovery or recognition, originally by the protagonist of a Greek tragedy, of a truth that leads to the resolution of the drama, *e.g.*, Othello's discovery of Desdemona's innocence. (Term from Aristotle's *Poetics*.)

anapaest. *See* **metre**.

anaphora. The repetition of a word or phrase at the beginning of consecutive phrases or sentences, *e.g.*,

"*For gold* his sword the hireling ruffian draws,
For gold the hireling judge distorts the laws"
(Johnson, *The Vanity of Human Wishes*).

anti-hero. A principal character who has no traditional heroic qualities but who is diffident, cowardly, foolish and not particularly estimable, *e.g.*, the eponymous hero of Kingsley Amis's *Lucky Jim*.

anti-novel. Loosely used for some twentieth century novels (by Beckett and Robbe-Grillet, for example) with minimal regard for such conventional features as plot and development of character. *See* **nouveau roman**.

antistrophe. In the Greek *chorus* (*q.v.*) and the *Pindaric Ode* (*q.v.*) the response to the *strophe* (*q.v.*), written in the same metrical form.

antithesis. The balanced juxtaposition of words or phrases for the sake of emphasis or contrast, widely used in eighteenth-century prose and verse, *e.g.*,

"But sometimes Virtue starves, while Vice is fed"
(Pope, *Essay on Man*).

apocope. The omission of the final letter, syllable or sound of a word, *e.g.*, the poetic use of "th'" for "the."

aposiopesis. Breaking off a sentence, usually for dramatic effect, *e.g.*,

"I will have such revenges on you both
That all the world shall—I will do such things—
What they are yet I know not"
(Shakespeare, *King Lear*, II, iv).

apostrophe. Address to a person or a personified quality, place or thing, *e.g.*, "Ye distant spires, ye antique towers" (Gray, "Ode on a Distant Prospect of Eton College"); "Stern Daughter of the Voice of God!" (Wordsworth, "Ode to Duty").

apron stage. A stage, like that in the Elizabethan theatre, which projects beyond the proscenium arch into the audience.

art for art's sake. *See* **aestheticism**.

assonance. The use of the same vowel-sounds in close proximity, often in verse, for the sake of euphony, memorability or emotional effect, *e.g.*, 'And deep-asleep he seemed" (Tennyson, "The Lotus-Eaters"). *See* **alliteration**.

asyndeton. The omission of a conjunction between words, phrases or clauses, *e.g.*,

"And dreams of home,
Waving from window, spread of welcome,
Kissing of wife under single sheet"
(W. H. Auden, "The Wanderer").

See **ellipsis**.

Augustan. Referring to the reign of the Emperor Augustus (27 B.C.–14 A.D.), when Virgil, Horace and Ovid wrote, or to the neo-classical period in English literature between *c.* 1670 and 1790, when such writers as Dryden, Addison, Pope, Swift and Johnson conformed to the Augustan principles of reason, order and decorum. *See* **classical** *and* **neo-classicism**.

ballad. A narrative poem (often anonymous) telling of heroic or tragic deeds, typically written in quatrains of alternating four and three stresses and rhyming *abcb* or *abab*, *e.g.*, "Sir Patrick Spens." *See* **quatrain**.

ballade. A poem of three eight-line stanzas (rhyming *ababbcbc*) and one four-line envoi (*bcbc*) with a refrain at the end of each of its four sections, *e.g.*, those written by Hilaire Belloc. *See* **envoi**.

bathos. An anticlimax or sudden descent from the sublime to the commonplace, intentional or unintentional, *e.g.*, the last two lines of Tennyson's "Enoch Arden":

"And when they buried him the little port
Had seldom seen a costlier funeral."

belles-lettres. Elegant, polished prose writing, especially essays, *e.g.*, those written by Max Beerbohm.

Bildungsroman. Literally, "formation novel" (German), *i.e.*, one that relates the upbringing, education and development of its hero, *e.g.*, Goethe's *Wilhelm Meister's Apprenticeship*. *See* **M3**.

black comedy. Comedy that finds amusement in what are conventionally regarded as tragic, sick or pessimistic people and situations, *e.g.*, Joe Orton's *Loot*.

blank verse. Unrhymed iambic pentameter (*see* **metre**), as used in Shakespeare's plays, Milton's *Paradise Lost* and Wordsworth's *Prelude*.

bouts-rimés. Literally, "rhymed ends" (French), *i.e.*, rhyming words supplied in advance to which lines must be fitted.

bowdlerise. To expurgate, from the Rev. Thomas Bowdler (1754–1825), who removed what he considered to be coarse expressions from the plays in his *Family Shakespeare*.

burlesque. A ludicrous, mocking imitation in prose or verse of a literary or dramatic work, *e.g.*, the Duke of Buckingham's *The Rehearsal*, a burlesque of seventeenth-century heroic plays. *See* **heroic tragedy**.

caesura. A break in a line of poetry, often towards the middle, sometimes used to emphasise an antithesis or comparison, *e.g.*,

"Willing to wound, / and yet afraid to strike"
(Pope, *Epistle to Arbuthnot*).

See **antithesis**.

canon. Authentic works of an author or standard works of literature (as studied on academic courses, for example).

canto. A division of a long poem, perhaps consisting of many **stanzas** (*q.v.*), as in Byron's *Don Juan*.

catachresis. A misuse or incorrect application of a word, *e.g.*, "chronic" to mean "severe."

catalectic. Describing a line of verse with one or more syllables missing in the final foot, *e.g.*,

"Rúin / seíze thěe, / rúthlěss / kĭng!"
(Gray, "The Bard").

See **acatalectic**, **hypercatalectic** *and* **metre**.

catalyst. A substance that alters the rate of a chemical reaction but itself remains unchanged. T. S. Eliot used the term as an analogy in his theory of the poet's impersonality: "the more perfect the artist, the more completely separate in him will be the man who suffers and the mind which creates" ("Tradition and the Individual Talent," 1919).

catastrophe. The tragic climax of a drama or narrative.

catharsis. The purgation of pity and terror by means of the representation of those emotions in tragedy (Aristotle, *Poetics*). *See* **tragedy**.

character. A seventeenth-century genre of writing illustrating individual and social human types ("a modest man", "a shopkeeper", *etc.*), *e.g.*, John Earle's *Microcosmography*. More widely, a fictional personage, defined by E. M. Forster in *Aspects of the Novel* (1927) as either "flat" ("constructed round a single idea or quality") or "round" (with the "incalculability of life about it").

chiasmus. A "laying crosswise" of elements in a sentence, *i.e.*, the order of words in one of two parallel clauses or phrases is inverted in the other, *e.g.*,

"Love without end, and without measure grace"
(Milton, *Paradise Lost*).

chorus. A group of actors in Greek drama providing a commentary on the action; a device adapted, for example, by Shakespeare in *King Henry V* and T. S. Eliot in *Murder in the Cathedral*.

classical. Showing a regard for the values and forms of Ancient Greek and Latin literature and so having qualities of order, restraint, reason and precision. *See* **Augustan** *and* **nec-classical**.

clerihew. Comic biographical poem in the form of a *quatrain* (*q.v.*) with lines of various length, rhyming *aabb*, named after its inventor Eric Clerihew Bentley (1875–1956).

comedy. A literary or dramatic work, or aspect of it, that is amusing in various ways. More particularly, a work with a happy ending, *e.g.*, a comedy by Shakespeare. *See* **black comedy**.

comedy of ideas. A play (or novel) that is entertainingly and wittily concerned with ideas, problems and theories, *e.g.*, the novels of Thomas Love Peacock and the plays of Bernard Shaw.

comedy of manners. A play concerned with the behaviour and intrigues of elegant, sophisticated society, *e.g.*, Congreve's *The Way of the World* and Wilde's *The Importance of Being Earnest*.

conceit. An ingenious or highly fanciful example of imagery, perhaps using elaborate figures of speech and word-play, often associated with the *Metaphysical Poets* (*q.v.*), *e.g.*, Donne's comparison of two lovers' souls with a pair of compasses ("A Valediction: Forbidding Mourning").

couplet. Two successive rhyming lines. *See* **heroic couplet** *and* **rhyming couplet**.

dactyl. *See* **metre**.

decasyllable. A line of verse of ten syllables, often synonymous with the iambic pentameter. *See* **metre**.

deconstruction. A theory and method of textual analysis that emphasises the infinite number of uncertainties and ambiguities that exist in any literary work. *See* **post-structuralism** *and also* **M26–30**.

defamiliarisation. A conception of artistic technique held by the Russian Formalist, Victor Shklovsky, who maintained that art enables us to experience the world afresh by means of making things unfamiliar and thus increasing "the difficulty and duration of perception". *See* **formalism** *and also* **M26–30**.

diaeresis. The separation of a diphthong into two sounds, sometimes indicated by a mark (¨) placed over the second vowel, *e.g.*, "Noël".

dialogue. Conversation between two or more people in a literary or dramatic work. Also, a separate genre often used for the discussion of ideas, *e.g.*, Landor's *Imaginary Conversations*.

didactic. Applied to a literary work in prose or verse that aims to instruct the reader lightly or seriously, *e.g.*, Pope's poem, *An Essay on Criticism*.

diegesis. The process of authorial explanations, commentaries and narrative in a fictional work as distinct from the direct display of characters and action by such means as dialogue. Sometimes used in criticism as the opposing term to **mimesis** (*q.v.*). (From Plato's *Republic*.)

dirge. A funeral song or poem, *e.g.*, Shelley's "Autumn: A Dirge". *See* **elegy** *and* **threnody**.

dissociation of sensibility. T. S. Eliot's term (in "The Metaphysical Poets," 1921) to explain the failure of post seventeenth-century poets to amalgamate "disparate experience" to form "new wholes". There was a separation of feeling from thought in their work.

distich. Two lines of verse expressing a complete idea.

dithyramb. A passionate, rapturous poem, *e.g.*, Dryden's "Alexander's Feast".

doggerel. Rough, technically incompetent verse, often comic, vulgar or abusive, *e.g.*, some of the street ballads of the nineteenth century.

donnée. A situation or idea given or suggested to an author, who then bases a literary work on it, *e.g.*, an anecdote at the dinner-table led to Henry James's *The Spoils of Poynton*.

dramatic irony. Words or a situation on the stage understood by the audience in a different way from the way the characters understand them, *e.g.*, Duncan's speech, "This castle hath a pleasant seat . . .", spoken on the eve of his murder there (Shakespeare, *Macbeth*, I, vi).

dramatic monologue. Poem with one speaker addressing a listener or listeners and revealing, knowingly or unknowingly, important aspects of his character and situation, *e.g.*, Browning's "Fra Lippo Lippi."

eclogue. A fairly short pastoral poem often in the form of a dialogue, *e.g.*, the ten *Eclogues* of Virgil.

elegiac stanza. Quatrain of four iambic pentameters rhyming *abab*, as used in Gray's "Elegy in a Country Churchyard".

elegy. A poem of mourning or lament, *e.g.*, Milton's "Lycidas" and Shelley's "Adonais". *See* **dirge** *and* **threnody**.

elision. The suppression of a vowel or syllable in verse for the sake of metrical correctness, *e.g.*, "ta'en" for "taken".

ellipsis. The omission of words, especially in poetry, to achieve compression, complexity or surprise, *e.g.*, in passages of T. S. Eliot's *The Waste Land*. *See* **asyndeton**.

emblem. A symbolic picture with a motto and explanation, associated with allegorical and figurative writing in such seventeenth century works as Francis Quarles' *Emblems*, a collection of religious poems.

end-stopped. Describing a self-contained line of verse that ends with a punctuation mark, *e.g.*,

"Black is the beauty of the brightest day!
The golden ball of Heaven's eternal fire,
That danced with glory on the silver waves,
Now wants the glory that inflamed his beams"
(Marlowe, *Tamburlaine*, 2nd Part, II, iv).

See **enjambment**.

enjambment. The running-on of one line of verse into another without a grammatical break, *e.g.*,

"Nay, but this dotage of our general's
O'er flows the measure . . ."
(Shakespeare, *Antony and Cleopatra*, I, i).

envoi. The short final stanza of a poem, especially a *ballade* (*q.v.*), addressed as parting words to a person or persons, emphasising the subject of the poem.

epic. A long narrative poem in an elevated style celebrating heroic personages and deeds, *e.g.*, Homer's *Iliad* and *Odyssey*.

epic simile. A long, elaborately developed comparison, as found in some epic poems. Sometimes termed *Homeric simile*. *See* **simile**.

epigram. A pointed, witty saying or verse that can be sarcastic, complimentary or amusing, *e.g.*,

"Swans sing before they die; 'twere no bad thing
Did certain persons die before they sing"
(Coleridge).

epigraph. A quotation or motto at the beginning of a work or of a section of it, *e.g.*, 'Mistah Kurtz—he dead" (quotation from Conrad's *Heart of Darkness* prefixed to T. S. Eliot's *The Hollow Men*).

epilogue. The final section of work, serving such purposes as pointing a moral or summarising, *e.g.*, Rosalind's concluding speech in Shakespeare's *As You Like it*.

epiphany. James Joyce's term for a significant moment of revelation that a writer should record: "a sudden spiritual manifestation, whether in the vulgarity of speech or of gesture or in a memorable phase of the mind itself" (Joyce, *Stephen Hero*).

epistolary novel. A novel written in the form of letters, *e.g.*, Samuel Richardson's *Clarissa* and Laclos' *Les Liaisons dangereuses*.

epode. In the Greek *chorus* (*q.v.*) and the *Pindaric Ode* (*q.v.*), the third and last section, coming after the *antistrophe* (*q.v.*).

essay. A fairly short discussion in prose (or, more rarely, in verse) of any topic, light-hearted or serious in tone and formal or informal in style, as written by Bacon, Addison and Lamb.

euphemism The use of a mild, pleasant term to express something disagreeable, harsh or vulgar, *e.g.*, "And lo, he had answered to his name, and stood in the presence of The Master" (Thackeray, *The Newcomes*), meaning "He had died"; "visually challenged" meaning "blind" or "partly blind".

euphony. Agreeable sound in verse or prose achieved by such means as metre, rhyme, alliteration and assonance, enhanced by the meanings and associations of the words chosen, frequently found, for example, in the poems of Tennyson.

euphuism. Highly elaborate, prose style, as found in John Lyly's *Euphues* (1579–80).

eye-rhyme. A rhyme that is visually correct but orally incorrect, *e.g.*, "love" and "rove", though in considering older poetry changes in pronunciation must be borne in mind. Also, Spenser's practice of adjusting spelling to make a rhyme clear to both eye and ear.

fable. A short prose or verse narrative, often with animals as characters, intended to convey a moral lesson, as written, for example, by Aesop, La Fontaine and John Gay.

fabula. In Formalist criticism, a story as it would actually have happened chronologically and objectively, as distinct from its literary treatment in a specific text, which is termed the *sjuzet*. *See* **formalism**.

farce. A comedy of broad, absurd and slapstick humour, often of frantic pace and technical ingenuity, *e.g.*, Ben Travers' *Rookery Nook*.

fashionable novel. A novel about life in high society written in an inflated, sentimental style, popular in the 1820s and 1830s, *e.g.*, Disraeli's *The Young Duke*. *See* **M5**.

foot. *See* **metre**.

foregrounding. Emphasis and prominence achieved in literary work by such means as linguistic deviation from normal usage. *See also* **M26–30**.

formalism. A critical theory and method developed by critics in Russia *c.* 1913–30 (*e.g.*, Shklovsky and Jakobson) that concentrated on the analysis of literary works as self-sufficient structures and paid little or no attention to biographical and social influences. *See also* **M26–30**.

fourteener. A line of verse containing fourteen syllables arranged as seven iambic feet. *See* **metre**.

free verse. Verse with no regular metrical pattern or length of line but with its form sometimes determined by its meaning, *e.g.*, D. H. Lawrence's "Snake". Also known as *vers libre*.

genre. A kind or type of literary work defined by its form and/or its purpose, *e.g.*, comedy, satire, ode.

Georgian poetry. Poetry written between *c.* 1910 and 1925, during the reign of George V, in short, lyrical forms and of easy comprehensibility, typically dealing with English rural subjects in an affectionate and nostalgic manner. The principal poets included W. H. Davies, Walter de la Mare, James Stephens, Edward Thomas and Edmund Blunden.

Gothic novels. Melodramatic novels of the late eighteenth and early nineteenth centuries dealing with terror, mystery and the supernatural, often in medieval settings, *e.g.*, M. G. Lewis's *The Monk*. *See* **M5**.

grand style. A plain, natural and noble style of poetry, as found in Homer (termed thus by Matthew Arnold).

great tradition. Phrase used by the critic F. R. Leavis to denote certain novelists "significant in terms of that human awareness they promote", *i.e.*, Jane Austen, George Eliot, Henry James and Joseph Conrad (*The Great Tradition*, 1948). Leavis would later have added Dickens and D. H. Lawrence to the tradition.

haiku. Japanese verse form of seventeen syllables in three lines of five, seven and five syllables, conveying a single, sharp impression of an image or mood.

half-rhyme. Rhyme in which the consonants are the same but the vowels are different, *e.g.*, "leaves"/"lives", "simmer"/"summer" (taken from Wilfred Owen's "Miners").

hamartia. The flaw or defect in a tragic hero that leads to his downfall (Aristotle, *Poetics*).

hemistich. Half a line of verse, divided at the *caesura* (*q.v.*).

hendecasyllabic. A line of verse of eleven syllables, as used by the Latin poet, Catullus, but rarely found in English.

hendiadys. Expression of a compound notion by two elements co-ordinated by "and" instead of by one element subordinated to the other, *e.g.*, "waving to him *white hands and courtesy*" (Tennyson, "Gareth and Lynette") for "courteous white hands."

heptameter. *See* **metre**.

heroic couplet. A pair of rhyming iambic pentameters, so called because the metre was used in seventeenth century "heroic" plays and poems by Dryden and others. (*See* **heroic tragedy**.) The prevalent metrical form in the eighteenth century. *See* **metre** *and* **rhyming couplet**.

heroic tragedy. Late seventeenth-century type of drama, dealing in an elevated manner with themes of love and honour, written in *heroic couplets* (*q.v.*), *e.g.*, John Dryden's *The Conquest of Granada*.

hexameter. *See* **metre**.

historical novel. A novel set in past times, sometimes mixing fictional and factual characters and events, *e.g.*, Sir Walter Scott's *Ivanhoe*. *See* **M3**.

Homeric simile. *See* epic simile *and* **simile**.

homonym. A word having the same sound and sometimes the same spelling as another but a different meaning, *e.g.*, "fast": "rapid"; "fast": "abstinence"; "fast": "fixed".

homophone. A word having the same pronunciation as another but a different meaning and spelling, *e.g.*, "son" and "sun".

hubris. In Greek tragedy, the arrogance of a hero or heroine who ignores divine commands and who is therefore brought to ruin, *e.g.*, the behaviour of Creon in Sophocles' *Antigone*.

hypallage. Transference of epithet from the normal substantive to an unexpected one, *e.g.*, "Who sees his true love in her *naked bed*" (Shakespeare, *Venus and Adonis*).

hyperbaton. Transposition of words out of normal order or separation of words usually associated together, *e.g.*,

"So much I hate a *breaking* cause to be
Of *heavenly oaths*"
　　　　(Shakespeare, *Love's Labour's Lost*, V, ii).

hyperbole. Exaggeration for the sake of emphasis or comedy, *e.g.*,

"There emerged from scores of by-streets, lanes, and nameless turnings, innumerable people, carrying their dinners to the bakers' shops" (Dickens, *A Christmas Carol*).

hypercatalectic. Describing a line of verse with an extra syllable, *e.g.*,

"Thĕ slīngs / ănd ar̆- / rows ŏf / oūtrage-/ oŭs for̆-/ tūne"
　　　　(Shakespeare, *Hamlet*, III, i).

See **acatalectic, catalectic** *and* **metre**.

hysteron proton. Reversal of normal or temporal order, *e.g.*,

"Take, eat; this is my body"
　　　　(*St. Matthew*, ch. 26)

"Th'Antoniad, the Egyptian admiral,
With all their sixty, fly and turn the rudder"
　　　　(Shakespeare, *Antony and Cleopatra*, III, x).

idyll. A poem, pleasing and contented in tone, on an innocent, rural subject, of the type written by the Ancient Greek poet, Theocritus. More widely, a poem conveying a feeling of calm happiness.

imagery. Figures of speech and other devices of language used to convey sensuous and imaginative impressions to the reader.

Imagism. A poetic movement and theory, flourishing *c.* 1909–14, which emphasised direct treatment of subject-matter, concreteness, extreme economy of language and the rhythm of phrases rather than the rhythm of regular metres. The principal Imagist poets were Richard Aldington, H.D. (*i.e.*, Hilda Doolittle), F. S. Flint, Amy Lowell and Ezra Pound.

imitation. In particular, the practice, commended in the eighteenth century, of copying and adapting classical models (*e.g.*, Pope's *Imitations of Horace*). More generally, synonymous with *mimesis* (*q.v.*).

inscape. Gerard Manley Hopkins' term for the particular, unique, distinctive identity of a thing, an identity which the poet should capture in his work. *See* **instress**.

instress. Hopkins' term for the natural energy that determines an *inscape* (*q.v.*) and that maintains its existence: "the blue [of the sky] was charged with simple instress" (Hopkins' *Journal*, 1871).

intentional fallacy. A phrase coined by M. C. Beardsley and W. K. Wimsatt (1946), who argued that the "design or intention of the author is neither available nor desirable as a standard for judging the success of a work of literary art." *See* **affective fallacy** *and* **New Critics**.

interlude. In the sixteenth century a play performed in the midst of festivities. It could be farcical, romantic or religious and was sometimes indistinguishable from a *morality play* (*q.v.*). John Heywood's interludes are amongst the best-known.

internal rhyme. The rhyming of two or more words within one line of verse, *e.g.*,

"When you're lying *awake* with a dismal *headache*, and repose is taboo'd by anxiety"
　　　　(Gilbert, *Iolanthe*).

See **rhyme**.

inversion. The reversal of normal syntax, usually by putting the verb before the subject, as in poetic language imitating Latin word-order, *e.g.*, the opening six lines of Milton's *Paradise Lost*: "Of Man's first disobedience ... sing heavenly Muse". *See* **Latinism**.

irony. The use of words (verbal irony) or situations (situational irony) to convey the opposite of what is really meant or what might naturally be expected. It can be comic, tragic or satirical, *e.g.*, Fielding's description of Blifil as "this worthy young man" (*Tom Jones*), the remark made by Jane Austen's Mr Bennet about Mr Collins' "talent of flattering with delicacy" (*Pride and Prejudice*) and Thomas Hardy's portrayal of Jude's death in the midst of student festivities at Christminster (*Jude the Obscure*). *See* **dramatic irony**.

Johnsonian. In the literary style and manner of Dr Samuel Johnson (1709–84), *e.g.*, using weighty, well-balanced sentences and a Latinised vocabulary and expressing a pragmatic, common-sense attitude to life and literature.

Lake Poets. The English Romantic poets, Wordsworth, Coleridge and Southey, who lived in the Lake District.

lampoon. A personal satire, often malicious and coarse in tone, *e.g.*, Henry Carey's "Namby-Pamby" (a poem on the poet, Ambrose Philips). *See* **satire**.

langue. A language considered as a whole, abstract system, which all its speakers have in common. (Term used by the linguist, Ferdinand de Saussure.) *See* **parole** *and also* **M26**.

Latinism. Word, phrase, idiom or construction that imitates a Latin one. Characteristics can include sentence-inversion (*see* **inversion**), placing adjectives after and around substantives (see the first example below) and the use of many words (often learned and abstract) derived from Latin (see the second example), *e.g.*,

"I come to pluck your *berries harsh and crude*,
And with *forc'd fingers rude*
Shatter your leaves before the mellowing year"
(Milton, "*Lycidas*").

"A *doctrine* so *extraordinary* and so *sublime* must *inevitably command* the *veneration* of the people" (Gibbon, *Decline and Fall of the Roman Empire*).

lay. A narrative or lyrical poem recounting romantic or adventurous deeds, *e.g.*, Scott's *Lay of the Last Minstrel*.

Leavisite. Pertaining to the ideas and followers of F. R. Leavis (1895–1978), whose rigorous literary criticism was informed by a serious moral concern. *See* **great tradition**.

lexis. The vocabulary of a language, which therefore consists of lexical items (which can include words and brief phrases).

limerick. A comic five-line verse-form in anapaests (*see* **metre**), rhyming *aabba*, ideally with a surprising last line.

litotes. An understatement, particularly one that uses the negative, often made for the purposes of irony or emphasis, *e.g.*, "Mrs Blifil was not over and above pleased with the behaviour of her husband" (Fielding, *Tom Jones*); "No little band of yet remembered names" (Wordsworth, *The Prelude*, I). *See* **meiosis**.

loose sentence. A sentence with the main clause first, followed by subordinate clauses, *e.g.*, "There can be no doubt that this remarkable man owed the vast influence which he exercised over his contemporaries at least as much to his gloomy egotism as to the real power of his poetry" (Macaulay, *Byron*). *See* **periodic sentence**.

lyric. A short poem of a song-like nature, expressing a single—often personal—mood. For numerous examples, *see* Palgrave's *Golden Treasury*.

macaronic. Describing comic or burlesque verse written in mixed languages or languages adapted and distorted, *e.g.*, "Charmer virumque I sing, Jack plumigeramque Arabellam" (first line of "Narrative Macaronic Verses" by Frank Sidgwick).

malapropism. A word used in the wrong sense, sometimes for comic effect, *e.g.*, "I would have her instructed in *geometry*, that she might know something of the *contagious* countries" (Mrs Malaprop in Sheridan's *The Rivals*, I, ii).

masque. A courtly entertainment, popular in the late sixteenth and early seventeenth centuries, consisting of artificial, fantastic dramatic action, dancing, songs, and elaborate costumes and settings, *e.g.*, Ben Jonson's *Masque of Oberon*.

meiosis. An understatement, often used for purposes of emphasis or comedy, *e.g.*,

"A small accident had happened, which somewhat disconcerted them; and this was no other than the thief's escape" (Fielding, *Joseph Andrews*);

"But she is in her grave, and, oh,
The difference to me!"
(Wordsworth, "She dwelt among the untrodden ways").

See **litotes**.

melodrama. Extravagant drama of heightened emotions, characterised by sentimentality and sensationalism, *e.g.*, Leopold Lewis' *The Bells*, in which Henry Irving gave a famous performance.

metaphor. A figure of speech of comparison stating an identity rather than a likeness, *i.e.*, something is said to be that which it only resembles, *e.g.*, "I fall upon the thorns of life" (Shelley, "Ode to the West Wind"); "the very honey of earthly joy" (Cowley, "The Wish").

Metaphysical Poets. Seventeenth century poets, including John Donne, George Herbert, Henry Vaughan, Richard Crashaw and Andrew Marvell, whose subject-matter was usually love or religion. Their poems contain striking imagery, wit, intense passion and powers of argument and persuasion. (Term first used by Dr Johnson, who may have been influenced by a phrase of Dryden's.)

metonymy. The application of the name of an attribute to that of the thing meant, *e.g.*, "Dickens" for "the works of Dickens"; "the Bench" for "the magistrates".

metre. The measure of lines of verse, which in English is basically **accentual** (*q.v.*). Each group of syllables (usually two or three) is a **foot**. These feet of stressed syllables (marked with ´) and unstressed syllables (marked with ˘) are often classified as follows: iambus (˘´); trochee (´˘); spondee (´´); pyrrhic (˘˘); anapaest (˘˘´); dactyl (´˘˘); amphibrach (˘´˘). The number of feet in a line is indicated as follows: monometer (1); dimeter (2); trimeter (3); tetrameter (4); pentameter (5); hexameter (6); heptameter (7). An *iambic pentameter*, for example, is therefore a line of five iambic feet, *e.g.*,

"Bĕlín- / dă smíled, / ănd áll / thĕ wórld / wăs gáy"
(Pope, *The Rape of the Lock*).

Metrical variation, however, is a common feature of English verse.

Miltonic. Pertaining to the work of John Milton (1608–74), with reference to his Latinised syntax and vocabulary, his blank verse, his sonnets and his Protestant theology and outlook.

mimesis. Plato's term for artistic imitation or representation, which he thought necessarily false. Aristotle saw it as a basic function of art, stating that the "objects of imitation are the actions of men". The term can also denote more particularly the direct representation of speech and action in a literary work. *See* **diegesis**.

miracle plays. Fourteenth and fifteenth century plays, sometimes known as Mystery Plays, consisting of dramatised episodes from the Bible, from the Creation to the Day of Judgement, acted by members of trade guilds, usually on Corpus Christi day. Cycles survive from York, Coventry, Wakefield and Chester.

mock heroic. The satirical or comic application of heroic or epic styles, conventions, situations and characters to trivial or vulgar subjects, *e.g.*, Pope's *The Rape of the Lock*.

monodrama. A dramatic work for one character or performer, *e.g.*, Tennyson's poem, "Maud".

monologue. A prose or verse composition spoken by one character or performer, either as a separate work or as part of a work, *e.g.*, Beckett's *Krapp's Last Tape*. *See* **dramatic monologue**, **monodrama** *and* **soliloquy**.

morality plays. Allegorical dramas of the late fifteenth and early sixteenth centuries, in which personified virtues and vices contend for a man's soul, *e.g.*, *Everyman*.

morpheme. The smallest linguistic unit which has a grammatical function and an independent meaning, *e.g.*, sang, bread, -ing, -ed.

mystery plays. *See* **miracle plays**.

myth. Story of unknown origin expressing and explaining universal and religious experience (*e.g.*, fertility and seasonal change) often by means of the deeds of a hero or god. *See* **Section I Classical Mythology**.

Naturalism. Originating in nineteenth century France, a literary movement that aimed at presenting the reality of life, with an emphasis on environment, objectivity and amorality. Prominent naturalistic novelists included Zola, Gissing and Bennett. *See* **realism** *and* **M10**.

negative capability. John Keats' phrase (in a letter, 1817) for the quality, found in such great poets as Shakespeare, "of being in uncertainties, mysteries, doubts, without any irritable reaching after fact and reason".

neo-classicism. The theory and application, particularly in the eighteenth century, of the classical values and rules of reason, order and decorum, as shown in the work of Dryden, Pope and Johnson, who emulated Homer, Virgil, Horace, Juvenal and other writers of Ancient Greece and Rome. *See* **Augustan** *and* **classical**.

neologism. A new word or phrase, or an old word used in a new sense, *e.g.*, "agnostic" (coined by T. H. Huxley) and "prestigious" (meaning "having prestige" instead of "juggling").

New Critics. American group of critics, including Cleanth Brooks, R. P. Blackmur, Robert Penn Warren, John Crowe Ransom and W. K. Wimsatt, who were active in the late 1930s and the 1940s and who advocated close textual analysis, free of biographical and contextual associations. *See* **affective fallacy** *and* **intentional fallacy**.

Newgate novels. Crime novels of the 1820s and 1830s that tended to romanticise criminals and highwaymen, *e.g.*, Bulwer Lytton's *Paul Clifford* and W. H. Ainsworth's *Rookwood*. *See* **M5**.

nouveau roman. Type of French novel that began in the 1950s and that rejected conventional characterisation and plot, as written by Alain Robbe-Grillet. *See* **anti-novel**.

novel. *See* **M1–16** for definitions, types and history.

novella. A short novel, *e.g.*, Conrad's *Typhoon* and D. H. Lawrence's *The Fox*.

objective correlative. T. S. Eliot's term (in his essay on *Hamlet*, 1919) for "a set of objects, a situation, a chain of events which shall be the formula" of a particular emotion expressed in art.

octave. *See* **sonnet**.

ode. A lyrical poem of elaborate structure and elevated diction written to celebrate or commemorate a noble, beautiful or admirable subject or theme, *e.g.*, Keats' "Ode to a Nightingale" and Tennyson's "Ode on the Death of the Duke of Wellington." *See* **Pindaric Ode**.

onomatopoeia. The use or invention of words to imitate sounds, *e.g.*, "buzz", "hiss", "swish", or the imitative effect of such word usage as Tennyson's "murmuring of innumerable bees" ("Come down, O maid").

ottava rima. Eight iambic pentameters (*see* **metre**) rhyming *ababbcc*, as in Byron's *Don Juan*.

oxymoron. Combination of two contradictory terms in one expression, *e.g.*, "fearful joy" (Gray) and "sweet unrest" (Keats).

palindrome. A word, sentence or verse that reads the same backwards or forwards, *e.g.*, "level", "A man, a plan, a canal—Panama."

parable. A short, often realistic story told to exemplify a doctrine or moral, as told by Christ in the New Testament, *e.g.*, "The Sower" and "The Good Samaritan".

paradox. An apparent contradiction or absurdity often designed to upset conventional opinion and to indicate a truth, *e.g.*, G. K. Chesterton's "If we are to be international we must be national" and "The subtle man is always immeasurably easier to understand than the natural man."

parataxis. Arrangement of clauses without conjunctions, *e.g.*, "After a painful struggle I yielded to my fate: I sighed as a lover, I obeyed as a son; my wound was insensibly healed by time, absence, and the habits of a new life" (Gibbon, *Autobiography*).

parody. A comic or satirical imitation of an original work or of the characteristic style of a writer or literary movement, *e.g.*, Max Beerbohm's "Scruts" (a parody of Arnold Bennett) and Henry Reed's "Chard Whitlow" (a parody of T. S. Eliot's *Four Quartets*).

parole. An actual, individual utterance of language, as distinct from *langue* (*q.v.*). (Term used by the linguist, Ferdinand de Saussure.)

paronomasia. A play on words. *See* **pun**.

pastoral poetry. Poetry dealing in an idealised way with rustic life, especially the lives and emotions of shepherds and shepherdesses, *e.g.*, Spenser's *Shepherd's Calendar*.

pathetic fallacy. The false belief that human emotions exist in non-human things and phenomena. Such appearances are "entirely unconnected with any real power or character in the object, and only imputed to it by us", *e.g.*, "the cruel, crawling foam" (Ruskin, *Modern Painters*, where he coined, discussed and illustrated the term, 1856).

pentameter. *See* **metre**.

periodic sentence. A sentence that begins with subordinate clauses and ends with the main clause, *e.g.*, "Since then the imaginary right of vengeance must be at last remitted, because it is impossible to live in perpetual hostility, and equally impossible that of two enemies, either should first think himself obliged by justice to submission, *it is surely eligible to forgive early*" (Samuel Johnson, essay in *The Rambler*). *See* **loose sentence**.

peripeteia. In drama, a sudden change of fortune, "the reverse of what is expected from the circumstances of the action" (Aristotle, *Poetics*), as in Sophocles' *Oedipus Tyrannus*, where the messenger, meaning to make Oedipus happy, reveals the secret of his birth, with tragic consequences.

periphrasis. Roundabout speech or circumlocution, *e.g.*, Mr Micawber's speeches in Dickens' *David Copperfield*.

persona. A character or narrator who can in some cases be thought to be the author in disguise, *e.g.*, Stephen Daedalus in Joyce's *Portrait of the Artist as a Young Man*.

personification. Representation of a thing or quality as a person, *e.g.*, "There Honour comes, a pilgrim grey" (William Collins, "Ode").

Petrarchan sonnet. *See* **sonnet**.

phoneme. The minimum significant sound-unit in language, either consonant-type or vowel-type, *e.g.*, "meat," "boy".

picaresque novel. A novel with a rogue as its hero, undergoing many adventures, *e.g.*, Smollett's *Peregrine Pickle*. *See* **M3**.

Pindaric Ode. An ode modelled on the Greek odes of Pindar (518–438 B.C.) consisting of a **strophe**, **antistrophe** and **epode** (qq.v.) in complex stanzas, this three-part structure often being repeated at least once, *.e.g.*, Thomas Gray's "Progress of Poesy". *See* **ode**.

pleonasm. Using more words than are needed, either unconsciously or deliberately for emphasis, *e.g.*, 'at this moment of time" (for "now") and "most unkindest cut of all" (Shakespeare, *Julius Caesar*).

plot. The sequence or complex of connected events in a fictional narrative or drama, with (in Forster's definition in *Aspects of the Novel*, 1927) "a sense of causality" to distinguish it from *story* (*q.v.*).

poetic diction. Words, phrases and syntax prescribed specifically for poetic use, especially in the eighteenth century, and including *periphrasis* (*q.v.*) (*e.g.*, "the finny tribe" for "fish"), personification and Latinised structures and expressions.

poetic prose. Prose using such devices as rhythm, elaborate imagery, figures of speech and symbols, conventionally associated with poetry, to be found, for example, in some of George Meredith's descriptive passages in his novels.

portmanteau word. One word formed by combining two or more words, *e.g.*, "smog," a combination of "smoke" and "fog". (Term coined by Lewis Carroll in *Through the Looking-Glass*.)

poststructuralism. A development of *structuralism* (*q.v.*), which concentrates on the power of language as a creative force within itself and the indeterminate number of possibilities of meaning and interpretation. *See* **deconstruction** *and* also **M26–30**.

practical criticism. Exercises in the close analysis of texts, as advocated and practised by the critic and teacher I. A. Richards (in *Practical Criticism*, 1929).

prolegomenon. An introduction, sometimes of a learned nature, *e.g.*, R. B. McKerrow's *Prolegomena for the Oxford Shakespeare*.

prolepsis. Anticipatory use of an epithet, *e.g.*, "the two brothers and their murder'd man" (Keats, "Isabella") and " 'I'm killed, Sire!' " (Browning, "Incident in the French Camp").

prologue. The introductory section of a work with such functions as setting the scene, whetting the appetite of audience or reader and giving preliminary explanations, *e.g.*, the opening Chorus of Shakespeare's *Romeo and Juliet*.

prosody. The study of versification, including rhythm, rhyme and stanza forms, as in George Saintsbury's *History of English Prosody*.

pun. A play on words, *e.g.*,

"I cannot say '*whore*':
It does ab*hor* me now I speak the word"
(Shakespeare, *Othello*, IV ii)

"They went and *told* the sexton, and
The sexton *toll'd* the bell"
(Thomas Hood, "Sally Brown").

pyrrhic. *See* **metre**.

quatrain. A four-lined **stanza** (*q.v.*).

realism. In the nineteenth century, the theory and practice of a belief that art (*e.g.*, the novel) should be a precise, truthful representation of life, associated in France with Balzac and the Goncourt brothers, amongst others. Sometimes synonymous with **naturalism** (*q.v.*).

Revenge Tragedy. Popular seventeenth century type of drama, derived from Seneca's plays (1st century A.D.), in which revenge, ghosts and terror are prominent, *e.g.*, Kyd's *The Spanish Tragedy*.

rhetorical question. A question which does not require an answer but which is put for purposes of emphasis, *e.g.*, "Were they again to advance their money on pledges which had been forfeited over and over again?" (Macaulay, "Milton").

rhyme. Identity of sound from the last stressed vowel to the end, sometimes used in conventional patterns, such as **rhyming couplets**, **sonnets** and the **Spenserian stanza** (*qq.v.*).

rhyme royal. A stanza of seven iambic pentameters rhyming *ababbcc*, used, for example, in Chaucer's *Troilus and Criseyde*. *See* **metre**.

rhyming couplet. The same as **heroic couplet** (*q.v.*), but rhyming couplets in iambic tetrameter (*not* known as heroic couplets) are also frequently used, *e.g.*, in Swift's poems. *See* **metre**.

rhythm. Regular recurrence of stress or of long or short sounds, especially in poetry, analysed by the process of **scansion**. *See* **metre**. More widely, patterns of event or motif in various literary compositions, including novels.

roman à clef. A novel about actual people disguised as fictional personages, *e.g.*, Aldous Huxley's *Point Counterpoint*.

roman-fleuve. A long series of inter-related novels, *e.g.*, Proust's *A la Recherche du temps perdu*.

romance. A term of many meanings, including a medieval poetic or prose story of chivalry and love (*e.g.*, Malory's *Morte Darthur*); later, a work dealing with adventures in a fanciful and unrealistic manner (*e.g.*, Shakespeare's *The Winter's Tale*); in modern times, a glamorous, sentimental story of love (*e.g.*, the "romantic novels" published by Mills and Boon).

Romanticism. In literature, the movement at the end of the eighteenth and the beginning of the nineteenth centuries identified with individual expression, sensibility, imagination, emotion, the love of Nature and "simple" people (such as peasants and children) and a wide variety of literary forms. In part the movement was a reaction against **neoclassicism** (*q.v.*). Leading Romantic writers in English literature were Scott, Wordsworth, Coleridge, Byron, Shelley and Keats.

rondeau. A form of verse, originally French, in which lines are repeated at regular intervals. A typical pattern is *aabba*; *aab* and refrain; *aabba* and refrain, all octosyllabic. Written by some minor nineteenth century English poets, *e.g.*, Austin Dobson.

run-on line. *See* **enjambment**.

saga. An ancient Icelandic or Scandinavian prose tale of heroes and great deeds, mostly oral in origin.

samizdat. Self-published, typescript, underground Russian literature expressing opinions and viewpoints unacceptable to the government.

sapphics. A classical, quantitative metre consisting of three longer lines and one shorter.

satire. Prose or verse composition ridiculing and criticising vice and folly by such means as **irony** (*q.v.*), sarcasm, the **mock-heroic** (*q.v.*), **parody** (*q.v.*) and invective. John Dryden said that "the true end of satire is the amendment of vices by correction" (*Absalom and Achitophel*, "To the Reader"). Famous examples include Swift's *Modest Proposal* and Pope's *Dunciad*.

scansion. The process of analysing metre (*q.v.*).

semiology. The science of studying signs, especially those used in systems of communication (including objects, gestures and clothes as well as language). *See* **semiotics** *and also* **Special Topic, M26–30**.

semiotics. The study of patterns of behaviour in communication, particularly through the use of linguistics. More broadly, synonymous with *semiology* (*q.v.*). *See also* **M26–30**.

sensation novel. Mid-nineteenth century English novels of crime, detection and passion, with an atmosphere of excitement, suffering and suspense, *e.g.*, M. E. Braddon's *Lady Audley's Secret*. *See* **M8**.

sestet. *See* **sonnet**.

sestina. Elaborate verse-form of six six-line stanzas ending with a three-line **envoi** (*q.v.*).

Shakespearean sonnet. *See* **sonnet**.

signified and signifier. Saussure's terms for the concept and its oral or written verbal "sound image", indissolubly but arbitrarily connected to each other. *See also* **M26**.

simile. A figure of speech in which two things or actions are likened to each other, usually by means of "as" or "like", *e.g.*,

"Your face, my Thane, is as a book where men
May read strange matters"
(Shakespeare, *Macbeth*, I, v)

"From the earth thou springest
Like a cloud of fire"
(Shelley, "To a Skylark").

sjuzet. *See* **fabula**.

soliloquy. A solo utterance often by a character in a play talking to himself or thinking aloud, as if there were no audience, *e.g.*, Hamlet's "To be or not to be . . .".

sonnet. Poem of fourteen iambic pentameters. The two main forms are the Petrarchan (after Petrarch, 1304–74), consisting of an **octave** (eight lines usually rhyming *abbaabba*) stating the theme and a **sestet** (six lines using different rhymes in various patterns) commenting on the theme or modifying it; the Shakespearean, consisting of three quatrains (usually rhyming *ababcdcdefef*) presenting the theme and a final **rhyming couplet** (*gg*) summarising or clinching the theme. *See* **metre**, **quatrain** *and* **rhyming couplet**.

Spenserian stanza. Eight iambic pentameters followed by one iambic hexameter (or **alexandrine**, *q.v.*) rhyming *ababbcbcc*, as used in Spenser's *Faerie Queene*. *See* **metre**.

spondee. *See* **metre**.

sprung rhythm. Gerard Manley Hopkins' metrical system, dependent on measuring stresses and not on regular numbers of feet or syllables; hence, like the rhythms of common speech, written prose, music and folk poetry.

stanza. A formal arrangement of a group of lines of poetry, usually in a rhyming pattern.

stichomythia. Interchange of short, one-line speeches in dramatic verse, *e.g.*, some of the dialogue between King Richard and Queen Elizabeth in Shakespeare's *King Richard III*, IV, iv.

story. A tale, or the general, complete action of a narrative work, ranging more widely than the **plot** (*q.v.*).

stream of consciousness. Term coined by the philosopher William James (1890) to denote the unending, formless flow of human thoughts and emotions. Some novelists, *e.g.*, James Joyce and Virginia Woolf, have conveyed this "stream" by various techniques (*e.g.*, loose syntax and light punctuation) in order to explore the consciousness of their characters.

strophe. The first section of the Greek **chorus** or the Pindaric **Ode** (*q.v.*).

structuralism. As applied to literature, a complex form of textual analysis concentrating on formal linguistic and thematic patternings, as practised, for example, by Roland Barthes. *See* **Special Topic, M26–30**.

sub-plot. A plot of lesser importance but sometimes used as a parallel or foil to the main plot, *e.g.*, the Falstaff-Prince Hal sub-plot in Shakespeare's *King Henry IV, Part 1*. *See* **plot**.

syllabic verse. Poetry written in metre measured by the number of syllables in each line, *e.g.*, some of W. H. Auden's later verse.

syllepsis. A figure of speech in which one word has the same syntactical relationship to two or more other words but different meanings, *e.g.*, The nymph may "lose her heart, or necklace, at a ball" (Pope, *The Rape of the Lock*). Sometimes synonymous with **zeugma** (*q.v.*).

symbolism. Artistic movement of the 1890s, mostly originating amongst French writers (*e.g.*, Mallarmé and Valéry), using mystical, occult and magical images and musical, evocative language. More widely, the use of objects, actions, scenes and structures to represent or suggest significant themes and ideas in a literary work, *e.g.*, the dust heaps and the Thames in Dickens' *Our Mutual Friend* and the rose, the tower, Troy and swans in Yeats' poetry.

synaesthesia. Combination of sense impressions, as evoked by Keats' "... whose strenuous tongue / Can burst Joy's grape against his palate fine" ("Ode on Melancholy"), which associates tactile, taste, kinetic and possibly visual impressions in one image.

syncope. The cutting short or contraction of a word, especially in poetic usage, *e.g.*, "e'er" for "ever".

synecdoche. A figure of speech in which the part represents the whole or the whole represents the part, *e.g.*, "the multitude of Coketown, generically called 'the Hands' " (*i.e.*, the factory-workers, Dickens, *Hard Times*) and "England" for "the English cricket team".

tercet. A three-lined stanza, particularly as used in **terza rima** (*q.v.*).

terzarima. Verse-form of three-lined stanzas rhyming *aba*, *bcb*, *cdc*, etc., usually iambic pentameters, as used in Shelley's "Ode to the West Wind."

tetrameter. *See* **metre**.

theme. The central idea or topic of a literary work.

threnody. A poem of lamentation. *See* **dirge** *and* **elegy**.

touchstones. Criteria of excellence in poetry provided by the "lines and expressions of the great masters", *e.g.*, Homer, Dante, Shakespeare and Milton (Matthew Arnold's term and definition, "The Study of Poetry," 1880).

tragedy. "An imitation of some action that is important, entire, and of proper magnitude ... effecting through pity and terror the correction and refinement of such passions' (Aristotle, *Poetics*). A drama that ends sadly, especially

with the downfall of a flawed hero. *See* **catharsis**, **hamartia** *and* **peripeteia**.

tragi-comedy. A drama that mixes elements of tragedy and comedy, *e.g.*, Shakespeare's *Measure for Measure*.

trimeter. *See* **metre**.

triolet. Verse-form of eight lines and two rhymes, in which the fourth line repeats the first and the eighth line repeats the second, popular with some late nineteenth century minor poets, including Austin Dobson.

triplet. Three rhyming lines, usually iambic pentameters, sometimes used for variation or emphasis in a poem of **rhyming** or **heroic couplets** (*qq.v.*).

trochee. *See* **metre**.

trope. A figure of speech in general.

unities. Theory partly deriving from Aristotle's *Poetics* and fully formulated by Castelvetro (1505–71) that a drama should conform to the three unities of Action (*i.e.*, there must be no digressions), Time (*i.e.*, the action in performance should correspond as nearly as possible to the duration of the action in real life) and Place (*i.e.*, its scene should not change).

ut pictura poesis. "As a picture, so a poem", *i.e.*, "a poem is like a picture," a much-discussed formulation by the Latin poet, Horace, in his *Art of Poetry*.

vers de société. Light, elegant verse dealing with people and behaviour in polite society, *e.g.*, the poems of W. M. Praed.

vers libre. The same as **free verse** (*q.v.*).

verse. Originally a metrical line; more commonly, a stanza or versification and verse composition in general.

villanelle. Verse-form of five **tercets** (*q.v.*) and one **quatrain** (*q.v.*) with two rhymes. The first line ends the second and fourth tercet; the third line ends the first, third and fifth tercets; the first and third lines then end the final quatrain, *e.g.*, William Empson's "Missing Dates."

zeugma. A figure of speech in which a single epithet or verb is applied to two substantives but is appropriate to only one of them, *e.g.*, "See Pan with flocks, with fruits Pomona crowned" (Pope, *Windsor Forest*). Sometimes used to mean the same as **syllepsis** (*q.v.*).

III. SPECIAL TOPICS

MAJOR LITERARY PRIZES

The following is a selection of major literary prizes awarded since 1970, unless otherwise indicated.

James Tait Black Memorial Prizes (1918)

Two prizes of £1000 each, one for the best biography or work of that nature and the other for the best work of fiction written in English and first published in Britain in the year of the award.

1970	Jasper Ridley—*Lord Palmerston*
	Lily Powell—*The Bird of Paradise*
1971	Julia Namier—*Lewis Namier.*
	Nadine Gordimer—*A Guest of Honour*
1972	Quentin Bell—*Virginia Woolf*
	John Berger—*G*
1973	Robin Lane Fox—*Alexander the Great*
	Iris Murdoch—*The Black Prince*
1974	John Wain—*Samuel Johnson*
	Lawrence Durrell—*Monsieur, or the Prince of Darkness*
1975	Karl Miller—*Cockburn's Millennium*
	Brian Moore—*The Great Victorian Collection*
1976	Ronald Hingley—*A New Life of Chekhov*
	John Banville—*Doctor Copernicus*
1977	George Painter—*Chateaubriand. Volume 1: The Longed-for Tempests*
	John Le Carré—*The Honourable Schoolboy*
1978	Robert Gittings—*The Older Hardy*
	Maurice Gee—*Plumb*
1979	Brian Finney—*Christopher Isherwood: A Critical Biography*
	William Golding—*Darkness Visible*
1980	Robert Bernard Martin—*Tennyson: The Unquiet Heart*
	J. M. Coetzee—*Waiting for the Barbarians*
1981	Victoria Glendinning—*Edith Sitwell: A Unicorn among Lions*
	Salman Rushdie—*Midnight's children*
	Paul Theroux—*The Mosquito Coast*
1982	Richard Ellmann—*James Joyce*
	Bruce Chatwin—*On the Black Hill*
1983	Alan Walker—*Franz Liszt: The Virtuoso Years*
	Jonathan Keates—*Allegro Postillions*
1984	Lyndall Gordon—*Virginia Woolf: a Writer's Life*
	J. G. Ballard—*Empire of the Sun*
	Angela Carter—*Nights at the Circus*
1985	David Nokes—*A Hypocrite Reversed*
	Robert Edric—*Winter Garden*

Booker McConnell Prize for Fiction (1968)

£15,000 for the best full-length novel in English written by a citizen of Britain, the Commonwealth, the Republic of Ireland, Pakistan, or South Africa.

1970	Bernice Rubens, *The Elected Member*
1971	V. S. Naipaul, *In a Free State*
1972	John Berger, *G*
1973	J. G. Farrell, *The Siege of Krishnapur*
1974	Nadine Gordimer, *The Conservationist*
	Stanley Middleton, *Holiday*
1975	Ruth Prawer Jhabvala, *Heat and Dust*
1976	David Storey, *Saville*
1977	Paul Scott, *Staying On*
1978	Iris Murdoch, *The Sea, The Sea*
1979	Penelope Fitzgerald, *Offshore*
1980	William Golding, *Rites of Passage*
1981	Salman Rushdie, *Midnight's Children*
1982	Thomas Keneally, *Schindler's Ark*
1983	J. M. Coetzee, *Life and Times of Michael K*
1984	Anita Brookner, *Hotel du Lac*
1985	Keri Hulme, *The Bone People*

Duff Cooper Memorial Prize (1954)

Approximately £200 and a specially bound copy of Duff Cooper's autobiography, *Old Men Forget*, for a book published in the previous two years on a subject of history, biography, politics or poetry.

1970	Enid McLeod, *Charles of Orleans*

1971	Geoffrey Grigson, *Discoveries of Bones and Stones*
1972	Quentin Bell, *Virginia Woolf*
1973	Robin Lane Fox, *Alexander the Great*
1974	Jon Stallworthy, *Wilfred Owen*
1975	Seamus Heaney, *North*
1976	Denis Mack Smith, *Mussolini's Roman Empire*
1977	E. R. Dodds, *Missing Persons*
1978	Mark Girouard, *Life in the English Country House*
1979	Geoffrey Hill, *Tenebrae*
1980	Robert Bernard Martin, *Tennyson: the Unquiet Heart*
1981	Victoria Glendinning, *Edith Sitwell: a Unicorn among Lions*
1982	Richard Ellmann, *James Joyce*
1983	Peter Porter, *Collected Poems*
1984	Hilary Spurling, *Ivy Compton-Burnett*
1985	Ann Thwaite, *Edmund Gosse: A Literary Landscape*

Prix Goncourt (1903)

Fifty francs for the best prose work in French.

1970	Michel Tournier, *Le Roi des Aulnes*
1971	Jacques Laurent, *Les Bêtises*
1972	Jean Carrière, *L'Epervier de Maheux*
1973	Jacques Chessex, *L'Ogre*
1974	Pascal Lainé, *La Dentellière*
1975	Emile Ajar, *La Vie devant soi*
1976	Patrick Grainville, *Les Flamboyants*
1977	Didier Decoin, *John l'enfer*
1978	Patrick Modiano, *Rue des Boutiques Obscures*
1979	Antoine Maillet, *Pélagie la Charrette*
1980	Yves Navarre, *Le Jardin d'acclimatation*
1981	Lucien Bodard, *Anne-Marie*
1982	Dominique Fernandez, *Dans la main de l'ange*
1983	Frédérick Tristan, *Les Egarés*
1984	Marguerite Duras, *L'Amant*
1985	Yann Queffelec, *Les Noces Barbares*

Hawthornden Prize (1919)

£750 for a work of imaginative literature by an English writer under forty-one years of age.

1970	Piers Paul Read, *Monk Dawson*
1971	No awards
1973	
1974	Oliver Sacks, *Awakenings*
1975	David Lodge, *Changing Places*
1976	Robert Nye, *Falstaff*
1977	Bruce Chatwin, *In Patagonia*
1978	David Cook, *Walter*
1979	P. S. Rushforth, *Kindergarten*
1980	Christopher Reid, *Arcadia*
1981	Douglas Dunn, *St. Kilda's Parliament*
1982	Timothy Mo, *Sour Sweet*
1983	Jonathan Keates, *Allegro Postillions*
1984	No awards
1985	

Somerset Maugham Awards (1947)

£1000–£2000, to be used for a period or periods of foreign travel, for promising authors, British subjects by birth, under 35 years old. Poetry, fiction, criticism, biography, history, philosophy, belles-lettres, and travel books are eligible, but not dramatic works.

1970	Jane Gaskell, *A Sweet Sweet Summer*
	Piers Paul Read, *Monk Dawson*
1971	Susan Hill, *I'm the King of the Castle*
	Richard Barber, *The Knight and Chivalry*
	Michael Hastings, *Tussy is Me*
1972	Gillian Tindall, *Fly Away Home*
	Douglas Dunn, *Terry Street*
1973	Peter Prince, *Play Things*
	Paul Strathern, *A Season in Abyssinia*
	Jonathan Street, *Prudence Dictates*
1974	Martin Amis, *The Rachel Papers*
1975	No award

1976	Dominic Cooper, *The Dead of Winter*
	Ian McEwan, *First Love, Last Rites*
1977	Richard Holmes, *Shelley: the Pursuit*
1978	Tom Paulin, *A State of Justice*
	Nigel Williams, *My Life Closed Twice*
1979	Helen Hodgman, *Jack and Jill*
	Sara Maitland, *Daughter of Jerusalem*
1980	Max Hastings, *Bomber Command*
	Christopher Reid, *Arcadia*
	Humphrey Carpenter, *The Inklings*
1981	Julian Barnes, *Metroland*
	Clive Sinclair, *Hearts of Gold*
	A. N. Wilson, *The Healing Art*
1982	William Boyd, *A Good Man in Africa*
	Adam Mars-Jones, *Lantern Lecture*
1983	Lisa St. Aubin de Teran, *Keepers of the House*
1984	Peter Ackroyd, *The Last Testament of Oscar Wilde*
	Timothy Garton Ash, *The Polish Revolution: Solidarity*
	Sean O'Brien, *The Indoor Park*
1985	Blake Morrison, *Dark Glasses*
	Jeremy Reed, *By the Fisheries*
	Jane Rogers, *Her Living Image*

Nobel Prize for Literature (1901)

The income from the trust fund (approximately £1,750,000) is annually distributed amongst five prizes: Physics, Chemistry, Physiology and Medicine, Literature and Peace.

1970	Alexander Solzhenitsyn
1971	Pablo Neruda
1972	Heinrich Böll
1973	Patrick White
1974	Eyvind Johnson and Harry Martinson
1975	Eugenio Montale
1976	Saul Bellow
1977	Vicente Aleixandre
1978	Isaac Bashevis Singer
1979	Odysseus Elytis
1980	Czeslaw Milosz
1981	Elias Canetti
1982	Gabriel Garcia Márquez
1983	William Golding
1984	Jaroslav Seifert
1985	Claude Simon

Pulitzer Prizes in Letters (1917)

In addition to twelve annual prizes given to journalism, there are awards of $1000 each to American authors in the following six literary categories: (*i*) fiction, (*ii*) plays, (*iii*) history of the United States, (*iv*) biography or autobiography, (*v*) verse, and (*vi*) non-fiction. The six annual winners from 1980 onwards are as follows:

1980	(I)	Norman Mailer, *The Executioner's Song*
	(II)	Langford Wilson, *Talley's Folly*
	(III)	Leon F. Litwack, *Been in the Storm So Long*
	(IV)	Edmund Morris, *The Rise of Theodore Roosevelt*
	(V)	Donald Justice, *Selected Poems*
	(VI)	Douglas R. Hofstadter, *Godel, Escher, Bach: an Eternal Golden Braid*
1981	(I)	John Kennedy Toole, *A Confederacy of Dunces* (posthumous award)
	(II)	Beth Henley, *Crimes of the Heart*
	(III)	Lawrence A. Cremin, *American Education: The Experience, 1783–1876*
	(IV)	Robert K. Massie, *Peter the Great: His Life and World*
	(V)	James Schuyler, *The Morning of the Poem*
	(VI)	Carl E. Schorske, *Fin-de-Siècle Vienna: Politics and Culture*
1982	(I)	John Updike, *Rabbit is Rich*
	(II)	Charles Fuller, *A Soldier's Play*
	(III)	C. Vann Woodward, ed., *Mary Chesnut's Civil War*
	(IV)	William S. McFeely, *Grant: a Biography*
	(V)	Sylvia Plath, *The Collected Poems* (posthumous award)
	(VI)	Tracy Kidder, *The Soul of a New Machine*
1983	(I)	Alice Walker, *The Color Purple*

	(II)	Marsha Norman, '*Night, Mother*
	(III)	Rhys L. Isaac, *The Transformation of Virginia, 1740–1790*
	(IV)	Russell Baher, *Growing Up*
	(V)	Galway Kinnell, *Selected Poems*
	(VI)	Susan Sheehan, *Is There No Place on Earth for Me?*
1984	(I)	William Kennedy, *Ironweed*
	(II)	David Mamet, *Glengarry Glen Ross*
	(III)	No award
	(IV)	Louis R. Harlan, *Booker T. Washington: The Wizard of Tuskegee, 1901–1915*
	(V)	Mary Oliver, *American Primitive*
	(VI)	Paul Starr, *The Social Transformation of American Medicine*
		(*Special Citation*: Theodor Seuss Geisel (known as Dr. Seuss))
1985	(I)	Alison Lurie, *Foreign Affairs*
	(II)	Stephen Sondheim and James Lapine, *Sunday in the Park with George*
	(III)	Thomas K. McCraw, *Prophets of Regulation*
	(IV)	Kenneth Silverman, *The Life and Times of Cotton Mather*
	(V)	Carolyn Kizer, *Yin*
	(VI)	Studs Terkel, *The Good War: An Oral History of World War Two*

John Llewellyn Rhys Memorial Prize (1942)

£500 for a memorable work by a writer under the age of 35 who is a citizen of Britain or the Commonwealth.

1970	Angus Calder, *The People's War*
1971	Shiva Naipaul, *Fireflies*
1972	Susan Hill, *The Albatross*
1973	Peter Smalley, *A Warm Gun*
1974	Hugh Fleetwood, *The Girl who Passed for Normal*
1975	David Hare, *Knuckle*
	Tim Jeal, *Cushing's Crusade*
1976	No award
1977	Richard Cork, *Vorticism and Abstract Art in the First Machine Age*
1978	A. N. Wilson, *The Sweets of Pimlico*
1979	Peter Boardman, *The Shining Mountain*
1980	Desmond Hogan, *The Diamonds at the Bottom of the Sea*
1981	A. N. Wilson, *The Laird of Abbotsford*
1982	William Boyd, *An Ice-Cream War*
1983	Lisa St Aubin de Teran, *The Slow Train to Milan*
1984	Andrew Motion, *Dangerous Play*
1985	John Milne, *Out of the Blue*

W. H. Smith Literary Award (1959)

£4000 for any type of book that has made an outstanding contribution to English Literature, written by a citizen of the U.K. or the Commonwealth.

1970	John Fowles, *The French Lieutenant's Woman*
1971	Nan Fairbrother, *New Lives, New Landscapes*
1972	Kathleen Raine, *The Lost Country*
1973	Brian Moore, *Catholics*
1974	Anthony Powell, *Temporary Kings*
1975	Jon Stallworthy, *Wilfred Owen*
1976	Seamus Heaney, *North*
1977	Ronald Lewin, *Slim: the Standardbearer*
1978	Patrick Leigh Fermor, *A Time of Gifts*
1979	Mark Girouard, *Life in the English Country House*
1980	Thom Gunn, *Selected Poems*
1981	Isabel Colegate, *The Shooting Party*
1982	George Clare, *Last Waltz in Vienna*
1983	A. N. Wilson, *Wise Virgin*
1984	Philip Larkin, *Required Writing*
1985	David Hughes, *The Pork Butcher*
1986	Doris Lessing, *The Good Terrorist*

The Betty Trask Awards (1984)

One main prize of £12,500 and five additional prizes of £1000 each for first novels, published or unpublished, by writers under the age of 35. They are for works of a romantic or traditional—and not experimental—nature.

1984 { Ronald Frame, *Winter Journey*
      Claire Nonhebel, *Cold Showers*
1985   Susan Kay, *Legacy*

Whitbread Literary Awards (1971)

Up to 1985, the awards were given in separate categories as shown below: Novel (N), Biography (B), Poetry (P), Children's Book (CB), First Book (FB), First Novel (FN), Autobiography (A), Short Story (SS).

From 1986, a nomination will go forward from each of the following categories: Novel, First Novel, Children's Novel, Biography or Autobiography, and Poetry. Each nomination will carry an award of £1000. From these, one Book of the Year will be chosen and its author will receive an additional £17,500.

1971	Gerda Charles, *The Destiny Waltz* (N)
	Michael Meyer, *Henrik Ibsen* (B)
	Geoffrey Hill, *Mercian Hymns* (P)
1972	Susan Hill, *The Bird of Night* (N)
	James Pope-Hennessey, *Trollope* (B)
	Rumer Godden, *The Diddakoi* (CB)
1973	Shiva Naipaul, *The Chip Chip Gatherers* (N)
	John Wilson, *CB: A Life of Sir Henry Campbell-Bannerman* (B)
	Alan Aldridge and William Plomer, *The Butterfly Ball and the Grasshopper's Feast* (CB)
1974	Iris Murdoch, *The Sacred and Profane Love Machine* (N)
	Andrew Boyle, *Poor Dear Brendan* (B)
	Russell Hoban and Quentin Blake, *How Tom Beat Captain Najork and His Hired Sportsmen* (CB)
	Jill Paton Walsh, *The Emperor's Winding Sheet* (CB)
	Claire Tomalin, *The Life and Death of Mary Wollstonecraft* (FB)
1975	William McIlvanney, *Docherty* (N)
	Helen Corke, *In Our Infancy* (A)
	Ruth Spalding, *The Improbable Puritan: A Life of Bulstrode Whitelock* (FB)
1976	William Trevor, *The Children of Dynmouth* (N)
	Winifred Gerin, *Elizabeth Gaskell* (B)
	Penelope Lively, *A Stitch in Time* (CB)
1977	Beryl Bainbridge, *Injury Time* (N)
	Nigel Nicolson, *Mary Curzon* (B)
	Shelagh Macdonald, *No End to Yesterday* (CB)
1978	Paul Theroux, *Picture Palace* (N)
	John Grigg, *Lloyd George: The People's Champion* (B)
	Philippa Pearce, *The Battle of Bubble and Squeak* (CB)
1979	Jennifer Johnston, *The Old Jest* (N)
	Penelope Mortimer, *About Time* (A)
	Peter Dickinson, *Tulku* (CB)
1980	David Lodge, *How Far Can You Go?* (N)
	David Newsome, *On the Edge of Paradise: A. C. Benson the Diarist* (B)
	Leon Garfield, *John Diamond* (CB)
	David Lodge, *How Far Can You Go?* (Book of the Year)
1981	Maurice Leitch, *Silver's City* (N)
	Nigel Hamilton, *Monty: The Making of a General* (B)
	Jane Gardam, *The Hollow Land* (CB)
	William Boyd, *A Good Man in Africa* (FN)
1982	John Wain, *Young Shoulders* (N)
	Edward Crankshaw, *Bismarck* (B)
	W. J. Corbett, *The Song of Pentecost* (CB)
	Bruce Chatwin, *On the Black Hill* (FN)
1983	William Trevor, *Fools of Fortune* (N)
	Victoria Glendinning, *Vita* (B)
	Kenneth Rose, *King George V* (B)
	Roald Dahl, *The Witches* (CB)
	John Fuller, *Flying to Nowhere* (FN)
1984/85	Christopher Hope, *Kruger's Alp* (N)
	Peter Ackroyd, *T. S. Eliot* (B)
	Barbara Willard, *The Queen of the Pharisees' Children* (CB)
	James Buchan, *A Parish of Rich Women* (FN)
	Diane Rowe, *Tomorrow is our Permanent Address* (SS)
1985	Douglas Dunn, *Elegies* (Book of the Year).

STRUCTURALISM AND POSTSTRUCTURALISM

I. INTRODUCTION

Literary study in England has traditionally dealt with what it calls "refining the sensibilities" and "enhancing critical awareness". It has stressed the unique, imaginative response of the individual to the organic literary creation. English criticism has been suspicious of theory. T. S. Eliot, an influential critic as well as a major poet, wrote that there was no method "except to be very intelligent". The leading English critic this century, F. R. Leavis, described himself as an 'anti-philosopher' and regarded theory as an intrusion of the abstract into the business of responding flexibly and imaginatively to the "concrete experience" embodied in the literary work.

Since the late 1960s a conflict has been developing in English criticism based on the incursion of French structuralist and poststructuralist critical theory. The hostility this movement has evoked was publicly apparent in 1981 when even Fleet Street became interested in the apparently unwilling departure from Cambridge University of Colin MacCabe, a young, allegedly "structuralist" don. From the traditional point of view, the new theories are an irruption of -isms and pseudo-science into the activity of reading. Poststructuralists, on the other hand, argue that untheorized or antitheoretical forms of analysis introduce unspoken theory by the back door. In the case of established criticism, this would be a traditionally English *empiricism* (see **J17**) coupled with theories of language and the psyche superseded by modern linguistics and psychoanalysis.

An unfamiliar anti-empirical stance and reference to the languages of a wide range of disciplines make structuralism and poststructuralism much more difficult to absorb than the procedures of traditional criticism, which seem "natural", part of the air we breathe. For this reason, and that of space, the following account will deal with a clarification of theory. Some applications to literary texts are recommended in a list of further reading.

II. SAUSSURE

Structuralism and *poststructuralism* derive from the application and critique of a number of concepts advanced by the Swiss linguist Ferdinand de Saussure (1857–1913) in lectures given at the University of Geneva between 1907 and 1911. Students' notes were published after his death as *Course in General Linguistics*.

1. Synchronic and diachronic.

Saussure distinguishes between the *synchronic* description of language, concerned with its structure at a given moment, and the *diachronic*, dealing with its development in time. By concentrating on the *synchronic*, his work sets a pattern for later structuralist accounts of language and other sign systems.

2. Langue and parole.

Langue is the grammatical *system* of a language, *parole* the actual *speech acts* made possible by that system. *Code* and *message* are often used in later structuralist writing to express the same distinction, explained by Saussure as analogous with the rules of chess (*langue*) as opposed to the moves made in particular games or other external factors such as the size and constitution of board and pieces (*parole*).

3. The Sign.

Fig. 1

The key postulate in the *Course* is the *sign*, made up of the *signifier* or "sound image" and *signified* or "concept". Saussure's diagram represents the Latin signifier *'arbor'* ('tree') inextricably bound to its signified concept. Without the concept, "arbor" would be the mere sound it is for one who does not know the language. Similarly the signified exists only because it is attached to a signifier. There is no world of "thoughts" prior to language. The relationship between the two terms of the sign is *arbitrary*, there being no inherent "treeness" in "*arbor*" or its equivalent in any other language, but they are as inseparable as the two sides of a sheet of paper. Each is distinctive only by *differing* from others of its kind—sounds from other sounds, concepts from other concepts. In this process there are no absolutes that permit an ultimate grounding of meaning. "In language", Saussure claims, "there are *only* differences", and these exist "without positive terms".

4. Syntagmatic and associative relations.

The differences in language, through which signs function, are organised by two types of relation. In Nietzsche's statement "I fear we shall never be rid of God, so long as we still believe in grammar", for example, the *syntagmatic* relation is the *linear* combination of the signs in which the meaning of each is never settled until the last link completes the sequence. This line, or *syntagm*, is a chain of differences in which, according to Saussure, "a term acquires its value only because it stands in opposition to everything that precedes or follows it, or both". The *associative* relation is an invisible *vertical* line which attaches each term actually present in the syntagm to every other term that could have been there in its place. "Fear" in Nietzsche's sentence implies many possible alternatives—"hope", "declare", "understand" etc.—and signifies because it differs from each. "God" signifies because it is not "Mr. Smith", "the state" or "the signified"; "grammar" because it is not "cricket", "grandma" and so on. Saussure's analogy is architectural. The spatial arrangement of the column and the architrave it supports suggests the *syntagmatic* relation, but if the column is Doric it implies an *associative* contrast with the Ionic or Corinthian styles. Similarly the *entrée* precedes dessert and follows first course on the menu to constitute a *syntagm*, but the dish served—say rack of lamb—stands in an *associative* relation to other possible *entrées*.

5. Semiology.

Linguistics could, Saussure proposed, eventually take its place in a broader science of signs to be called *semiology* (from the Greek *semeion*, 'sign'). This term remains in use to define an area of theoretical work which developed after Saussure in literary criticism, anthropology and the social sciences generally. *Semiology* can be roughly synonymous with *structuralism*, Saussure's method in linguistics, although the *Course* does not insist on itself as the model for a science of signs. *Semiotics*, a term proposed at about the same time by the American philosopher C. S. Peirce (1839–1914), is sometimes used to mean the same as *semiology* or, on other occasions, to mark a break with Saussure's method.

III. FORMALISM AND STRUCTURALISM

1. Russian Formalism.

The legacy of Saussure is first apparent in the studies of *literary* language carried out by the Russian Formalists. Centred on the Moscow Linguistic Circle (founded 1915) and the Petrograd Society for the Study of Poetic Language *Opoyaz* (1916), this movement included Victor Shklovsky, Boris Eichenbaum, Yuri Tynyanov, Vladimir Propp and Roman Jakobson. Propp attempted to discover the *langue* of the Russian folktale, reducing a variety of character and incident in a hundred stories to combinations of 31 basic "functions". Shklovsky was concerned with the effect of "*defamiliarisation*" or "*estrangement*" (*ostranenie*) in poetry and fiction, where the established codes of a form or genre are stretched to disrupt habitual responses. "As cows eat grass, so literary themes are devoured; devices fray and crumble" says the narrator in Shklovsky's own novel, *Zoo* (1923), which resists the expectations of readers accustomed to fictional realism, self-consciously drawing attention to its own codes and conventions. Jakobson saw this "palpability" of language as the defining characteristic of the poetic, which cuts across the customary, seemingly "natural", functioning of signs by superimposing associative relations on the syntagmatic, making its

own syntax distinctive through effects of balance, opposition and equivalence in sound and grammatical form. A later colleague of Jakobson in the Prague Linguistic Circle, Jan Mukarovsky, coined the term "*foregrounding*" (*aktualisace*) for this process. By holding the foreground, literary language insists on the material, constitutive presence of signs. It resists the illusory passage to a clear, pre-existent signified offered by other, less *openly* "artificial", uses of language.

2. Jakobson.

With the suppression of Formalism in the Soviet Union under Stalin, Roman Jakobson (1896–1982) pursued in Prague, and later in the United States, a range of topics first touched on by Saussure. Analyzing cases of the language disorder *aphasia*, Jakobson noted that it struck either the associative axis or the syntagmatic. Sufferers tended to block on the selection of terms *or* on combining them in sentences, confirming Saussure's insight into the two types of structural relation. Jakobson also proposed a similarity between these two relations and *metaphor* and *metonymy*, adding another key duality to the structuralist lexicon. *Metaphor* works on the *associative* axis by replacing a literal term with an *equivalent* symbolic substitute. In the phrase "the trials and impositions of outrageous fortune", "trials" and "impositions" signify by associative differences with the host of other signs which *could* form that link in the syntagm. Among these are "slings" and "arrows" which Shakespeare makes appear, through metaphor, to replace the original, literal terms. The fact that these "literal" terms are not "original" at all, but supplied *after the event* by hearers who can select any number of "originals" constitutes the particular effect of the metaphoric mode, in which the syntagmatic continually "slides" or "shimmers" across the associative. Metonymy, in contrast, works through the syntagm. Examples of this figure are the use of "Fleet Street" for the British press or "Shakespeare" for the text(s), English language and culture in the sentence "I am reading Shakespeare". In each case, one item from a complex linked *sequence* stands in for the whole. Confronted with the menu, the customer might select one from a number of complete meals on offer by referring metonymically to the *entrée* alone. "I'm for the lamb" could mean the food-syntagm soup, lamb, and rice-pudding as opposed to melon, ham salad and cheese. Metaphorically the same sentence might appear on the lapel-badge of a born-again Christian.

Jakobson observed that the metaphoric (associative) process is primary in Romantic and Symbolist poetry while so-called "realism" is metonymic. This is crucial for the structuralist project in literary criticism as it locates *within language*, and not in some postulated "hard reality", the particular character of "realist" or "naturalist" writing. These forms of signification select metonymic details which evoke whole syntagms of preconstructed meaning that haunt the background and periphery of the text as "experience" or "the world". But the "realistic" is in fact authorized not by the proximity of an extralinguistic "reality" so much as a suppression of the metaphoric and associative in language. Roland Barthes and Christian Metz were to argue later that even such apparently neutral and representational media as the photograph and the film have their own "languages", working either metaphorically or metonymically within sign systems subject to structural analysis.

3. French Structuralism.

With Roland Barthes (1915–80) we arrive at the heyday of French critical theory and the moment of its dissemination into Anglo-American criticism. Barthes brings more coinings into the tradition of Saussure to extend its vocabulary further. *Écrivance* and *écriture* mark the distinction between writing which attempts to make itself transparent, surreptitiously repeating established codes to reproduce as "natural" existing constructions of the real, and writing which foregrounds and fractures traditional forms and the unity of the sign itself. *Écriture* revels in its own materiality and disarticulation to produce in the reader a *jouissance*, a term which enacts the process Barthes describes by refracting an excess of connotative meanings—*play*, *pleasure*, *orgasm*, the *gamble*, *improvisation*, the *incalculable*, *jazz*. *Écri-*

ture, literally "writing", embodies the pleasure of the written word itself, cut off from its origin, neglecting to defend or speak for itself, ultimately "about" nothing but writing. "To write", writes Barthes, is "an intransitive verb". Writing is, at best, an *intertext*, a space in which scraps of other writings, other codes, echo and collide. It is "writable" (*scriptible*), demanding that the reader constitutes meaning(s), unlike the book which is merely "readable" (*lisible*), tying the passive reader to a consumption of preordained sense.

This synopsis necessarily condenses a number of specific lines of attack from different texts by Barthes, incorporating aspects of his earlier, structuralist work and his later writing, which takes poststructuralism into account, particularly the work of Derrida and Lacan. His structuralist position, and its relation to the work of contemporaries in the late 1950s and 1960s, Gérard Genette, A. J. Greimas, Tzvetan Todorov, and Lucien Goldmann, is best understood with reference to that of the anthropologist Claude Lévi-Strauss.

Lévi-Strauss' structural anthropology (*see* **F60–61**) owed a great deal to what he called the "phonological revolution", another aspect of Jakobson's contribution, carried out in conjunction with his Prague associate Nikolay Trubetzkoy. They pointed out that each language employs only a fraction of the full range of human vocal sounds, and that a child, in acquiring its language, drastically *reduces* its infant repertoire. The limited number of sounds, or *phonemes*, that function in a language do so on a principle of difference. *P* is "voiceless", for example, but *B* is "voiced", and this in turn effects difference on the level of the signifier, "*pat*" being different from "*bat*". While *phonetics* deals with actual sounds, used in speech (*parole*), including the idiosyncracies of individual speakers, *phonology* is the study of the limited range of differences in sound which are *functional* in a given language (*langue*). Lévi-Strauss sought, with regard to the superficially disparate data of "savage" cultures, an equivalent for how phonology addressed sound. By establishing basic binary oppositions that held any element of a culture within the differences of a signifying system, he described the structures of, and relationships between, the "languages" of myth, totemism, kinship and food.

The intellectual prestige of structural anthropology lies behind the attempts of structuralist literary theorists to deduce the basic structures of texts, forms, or the *oeuvres* of particular authors. Greimas aims for a refinement of Propp's analysis of the Russian folktale into a "structural semantics" of narrative itself. Barthes and Goldmann, in different ways, describe fundamental oppositions which recur in the plays of Racine. Barthes takes this phase of "scientific" structuralist description beyond literature to offer a general theory of the *semiology* proposed by Saussure and semiological accounts of the associative *paradigms* and combinative *syntagms* of fashion and food in Western societies. *Mythologies* (1957) remains his most telling contribution to cultural criticism. Here he deals with the appropriation of linguistic signs by popular culture and the mass media, in which they become *signifiers* for other, secondary *signifieds* which connote cultural meanings. Thus tree (signifier + signified) might become a signifier of strength, security, continuity, the family or nature in an advertisement. These new "second-order" signs invariably serve the interests of the bourgeoisie, Barthes argues, but are presented as unspoken home truths, bled of their class content and accorded the status of straightforward denotative signs. In analyses of a number of these mythologized phenomena, including wrestling, detergents, Einstein's brain, and a *Paris Match* photograph of a black soldier saluting the French flag, Barthes combines Saussure with the Marx of *The German Ideology* to show how cultural constructs based on changeable historical relations of inequality are transformed into bourgeois ideology into the immutable and perfectly "natural". After *Mythologies*, the self-naturalizing constructions of the mass media, particularly in the production of news and documentaries, remain a central concern of semiotics.

IV. STRUCTURALISM AND MARXISM

In his preface to a new edition of *Mythologies* (1970), Barthes called for a more sophisticated ideological criticism, the need for which was "brutally evident" following the conservative reaction of the French media to the social upheavals of May, 1968, when workers occupied factories and students fought riot police. The answer came in the same year in "Ideology and Ideological State Apparatuses" by Louis Althusser (b. 1918). This essay is a structuralist rereading of Marx on ideology, which attempts an important *rapprochement* between the apparently incompatible ahistorical method of synchronic structuralist description and Marx's dialectical view of history as class-struggle.

Althusser argues that at any historical moment a social formation, in order to perpetuate itself, needs to *produce, reproduce the means of production* (outworn plant, workers *etc.*) and *reproduce the relations of production* (its class system). This third requirement is fulfilled by the *Repressive State Apparatus* of the law, police, army and so forth, which functions ultimately by violence to keep in place the relationship between those who manage and those who are managed. The day-to-day reproduction of these relations, however, is carried out through *ideology* by the *Ideological State Apparatuses* (ISAs), their institutions, discourses and practices. The dominant ISAs under Feudalism were the Family and the Church, under Capitalism the Family and the Educational ISA, which turns out A, B, C, and D people with suitable skills and attitudes for their appropriate slots. Other ISAs are the political, cultural (theatre, publishing, Arts Councils etc.), and of particular interest to semiotics since *Mythologies*, communications.

For Althusser, the only analysis that can locate itself outside ideology issues from the "scientific" Marxist position. This differs from the stance of *Mythologies*, which Barthes describes as *semioclasm*, an ideological act of image-breaking. Althusser does, however, accord a privileged status to "art" in a way which recalls such notions as "foregrounding" and *écriture*. Art, he claims, can partly prise itself away from ideology by an "internal distantiation" which, rather than reproducing the ideological, makes it "visible", as if it were on an agenda. Post-Althusserian Marxist theorists are critical both of this concept of "science" and of Althusser's apparent fetishization of "art". It is, arguably, a *critical practice* which *makes* art work either in the way described by Althusser or in a way more compatible with ideology, and the "artistic" is less an inherent quality of certain types of signification than an ideological category produced within the discourses and institutions theorized by Althusser himself.

V. AFTER STRUCTURALISM

1. Lacan and Derrida.

Althusser's structuralist rereading of Marx puts forward a view of ideology not as "false consciousness" conspiratorially foisted on the populace by the bourgeoisie, but as the "lived relation" of the human subject to the mode of production. Ideology exists for the subject, and the subject only for and in ideology.

A preoccupation with the *subject*, and a concomitant reconsideration of the *sign* are central to *poststructuralism* and mark its main advance on structuralism. Saussure described the structure of language, assuming that it was for the *use* of the various individuals or consciousnesses that made up the language group. Poststructuralism banishes that given pre-existent human consciousness and replaces it with a "subject" which is constructed only as it gains access to language, a "self" which is always other than itself, a process rather than a phenomenon. Saussure's language-user is the metaphysical subject of René Descartes (1596–1650), an absolute which intuitively grasps its own existence. In attempting to move beyond all metaphysical absolutes and push the Saussurean version of constitutive difference a stage further, poststructuralism breaks with Saussure. Whereas the Cartesian subject can say "I think therefore I am", the deconstructed poststructuralist subject might say "'I' is an effect of the signifier, and somehow thinks it thinks".

Althusser's subject, constructed or "interpellated" in ideology for the purposes of "freely" selling his or her labour, is at once active, like the "subject" in grammar, and *subjected*, perpetually acted upon. It is a concept imported directly from the influential rereading of Freud's work in the *Ecrits* (1966) of

Jacques Lacan (1901–1981), for whom "the unconscious is structured like a language" and the basic concepts for describing it are to be drawn from Saussure. Lacan's critical account of Saussure replaces the diagram (*see*, **M26**) in which the tree stands above "arbor", both surrounded by an oval, with the formula s, in which priorities are reversed to give the upper-case *signifier* (S) the upper hand over the signified (s). The enclosing oval which asserts the unified totality of the sign is removed, and the central bar becomes a barrier between signifier and signified. Lacan extrapolates, from the "difference" of structuralism, that if both sounds and concepts signify by their difference from all other sounds and concepts, then before a sound (S) can be linked to a concept (s) to make a sign, it must go through an infinite détour of all other sounds to settle its differences. The concept, meanwhile, is doing roughly the same on its own level. A useful analogy here is the way in which a dictionary, instead of giving a concept for a word, points it in the direction of another word and so *ad infinitum*, "architrave" to "entablature" to "dais" ... In Lacan, signifier and signified would never meet were it not for a form of closure he associates with "upholstery buttons" (*points de capiton*), which pin the two floating masses of S and s together at strategic points. These are certain key signifiers—such as the *Phallus* and "*the Name of the Father*"—which constitute the *Symbolic Order* of meaning in language. The human infant, who has to learn language and gain access to the *Symbolic*, is described as an *hommelette* ("little man", feminized man or broken egg with fluid, ill-defined margins). As s/he enters language, s/he becomes a named, sexed, "unified" subject. The subject exists at the bar between S and s, the sole link between the two, itself constructed only in and for language. At the *Mirror Stage*, when the child recognizes its reflection, the "identity" of the subject is found outside itself, meeting its own gaze, coalescing as something which will always be *other*. The subject maintains its unity and its language precariously as the unconscious signifiers shuttle along axes of metaphor and metonymy, irrupting in the lapse of memory, the unintentional pun, the slip of the tongue to reaffirm that, since Freud, the subject is a *process*, happening in at least two places at once.

The difficulty and complexity of Lacan is matched by that of Jacques Derrida (b. 1930) who, from a basis in philosophy, follows the same drift in taking difference a stage further and undermining all metaphysical absolutes. In *Of Grammatology* (1967), Derrida shows how the work of those conscious of absolutes and devoted to resisting or avoiding them is partially recaptured by metaphysics. He finds in both Saussure and Levi-Strauss a lapse where each states a preference for the spoken over the written word. This apparently marginal concern becomes for Derrida a port of entry for ingenious, *deconstructive* readings. He traces back to Plato a strand in Western thought which sees writing as a secondary adjunct to speech, a decline from its immediacy, and unfolds in this the assumption of a "presence". This *something* which speech is closer to than writing implies a *transcendental signified*, at the *centre* of a structure and outside the play of differences, beyond signification. This return to metaphysics imposes a limit on what seems revolutionary in Saussure or Lévi-Strauss. The "transcendental signified", writes Derrida, has had different names at different times: "essence, existence, substance, subject ... transcendentality, consciousness, God, man ...." In his own writing, these central terms of metaphysics are assiduously avoided, but Derrida acknowledges that the metaphysical permeates language and resorts to a technique of "erasure" in which terms at once unacceptable and unavoidable are crossed out in a way that leaves them visible. Like Lacan, he avoids the clarity of a prose style in which "ideas" take priority over the play of signs, a factor which enhances the problematic aspect of his work. *Sign, signifier* and *signified* are themselves compromised terms for Derrida, who describes what others would call the "play of difference in the signifier" through terms drawn from the scapegoat of metaphysics writing—*gram, trace*, and *grammatology* in place of *semiology*. His coining *différance* compounds Saussurean synchrony and diachrony by combining the spatial dimension of "difference" and the temporal aspect of "deferring" in a wordplay facilitated by the French equivalents of these terms.

2. At close of play.

When Macbeth describes life as "a walking shadow, a poor player / That struts and frets his hour upon the stage", and then as "a tale / Told by an idiot, full of sound and fury, / Signifying nothing", the words can be approached in different ways. We can try to deduce what Shakespeare is telling us about "life", perhaps indirectly through the development of the character "Macbeth". Or we can imagine the actor on stage performing Macbeth, a figure described earlier in the play in terms of bad acting and ill-fitting costume, here drawing attention to his own "sound and fury" as he stands on stage acting. The words too can momentarily be "Signifying nothing" but themselves signifying nothing. This second approach, concerned with undoing the notion that Shakespeare is supplying homilies about "life", will address the signifier and its palpability, the material presence of the actor on stage and the sounds he is making—factors which perpetually outstrip meaning or a Shakespearean *signified*.

Poststructuralist reading devotes itself not to "what the author is trying to say", but to regarding the literary text as a space where both too much and too little are being said simultaneously. Too much for traditional interpretive procedures to be able to establish meaning and thereby transform their literary monuments into repositories of "eternal truth". Too little in the signified to catch up with the unending play of the signifier.

Some literary works may seem to do what the poststructuralist would require of a text without prompting. Surrealism and Symbolism would clearly fall into this category, as would the work of Joyce, Nabokov and many others in modern and contemporary writing. Those works that resist the demands of the signifier and "*textuality*", a term for the qualities of what Barthes calls *écriture*, are "deconstructed" to reveal unsuccessful closures and internal contradictions.

French poststructuralist literary criticism is most often associated with the journal *Tel Quel*, with Barthes's *S/Z* (1970)—a 217-page analysis of a 33-page novella by Balzac, "*Sarrasine*"—and the work of Julia Kristeva. Kristeva's later work, and the essays of Helene Cixous, examine the relationship between poststructuralism and feminism. The most influential poststructuralist readings of English literature are by Americans, most notably members of the "Yale School", Paul de Man, Geoffrey Hartman, Harold Bloom and J. Hillis Miller. In Britain the most illuminating comments on, and applications of, the theory appear in the work of the Marxist critic Terry Eagleton, and volumes in the *New Accents* series of guides by its general editor Terence Hawkes, and by Catherine Belsey and Christopher Norris. Jonathan Culler and David Lodge have both contributed a good deal towards making structuralism accessible in Britain and America but question the more radical implications of poststructuralism, making the movement as a whole, in Eagleton's ironic phrase, "safe for the Free World". In their work the subject, dislodged and left in "process" or "crisis" in the poststructuralist account of "textuality", is firmly reinstated.

The various debates continue and it would be idealistic to assume that they will be resolved on a purely intellectual plane. As Humpty Dumpty, an early poststructuralist celebrated by Lacan says to Alice in *Through the Looking Glass*, what is at stake is not the meanings of words but who is to be master. Friedrich Nietzsche (1844–1900), an earlier critic of metaphysics, makes the point more directly: "the actual causes of a thing's origins and its eventual uses ... are worlds apart ... everything that exists, no matter what its origin, is periodically reinterpreted by those in power in terms of fresh intentions". Michel Foucault (1926–1984) has contributed to contemporary critical theory an account of how the struggle of "ideas" is always contained within a network of "discourses", a term which incorporates what is said or written with the historical system of codes and institution that make it expressible. Here too, all is ultimately determined by the "will to power". In *The Order of Things* (1966), Foucault cites the work of the Argentinian writer Jorge Luis Borges, which opens up in a much less overtly theoretical way an anti-empirical view of the conventional construction of our own world. It is fitting that this} encyclopaedia entry on textuality, difference and related matters should give the last word to Foucault quoting Borges quoting an (imaginary) Chinese encyclopaedia. Here it is written that "animals are divided into: (a) belonging to the Emperor, (b) embalmed, (c) tame, (d) sucking pigs, (e) sirens, (f) fabulous, (g) stray dogs, (h) included in the present classification, (i) frenzied, (j) innumerable, (k) drawn with a very fine camelhair brush, (l) *et cetera*, (m) having just broken the water pitcher, (n) that from a long way off look like flies."

Further Reading

R. Barthes, *Mythologies*, tr. A. Lavers, London: Cape, 1972.

——, *S/Z*, tr. R. Miller, London: Cape, 1975.

C. Belsey, *Critical Practice*, London: Methuen, 1980.

J. Culler, *Structuralist Poetics*, London: Routledge and Kegan Paul, 1975.

J. Derrida, *Of Grammatology*, tr. G. C. Spivak, Baltimore and London: Johns Hopkins University Press, 1976.

T. Eagleton, *Literary Theory*, Oxford: Blackwell, 1983.

V. Erlich, *Russian Formalism*, The Hague: Mouton, 1955.

M. Foucault, *The Order of Things*, London: Tavistock, 1970.

J. V. Harari ed., *Textual Strategies*, London: Methuen, 1980.

T. Hawkes, *Structuralism and Semiotics*, London: Methuen, 1977.

R. Jakobson, *Selected Writings*, The Hague: Mouton, 1962– .

J. Kristeva, *Desire in Language*, tr. T. Gora, A. Jardine, L. S. Roudiez, New York: Columbia University Press, 1980.

J. Lacan, *Ecrits*, tr. A. Sheridan, London: Hogarth Press, 1977.

D. Lodge, *The Modes of Modern Writing*, London: Arnold, 1977.

C. Norris, *Deconstruction*, London: Methuen, 1982.

F. de Saussure, *Course in General Linguistics*, tr. W. Baskin, London: Peter Owen, 1960.

J. Sturrock ed., *Structuralism and Since*. London: Oxford University Press, 1979.

R. Young ed., *Untying the Text*, London: Routledge & Kegan Paul, 1981.

GENERAL COMPENDIUM

A collection of useful tables and data on a variety of unrelated subjects, including the British monarchy, United States Presidents, phases of the moon, sunrise and sunset, eclipses, Roman numerals, foreign phrases, national currencies and the Beaufort wind scale.

TABLE OF CONTENTS

GENERAL COMPENDIUM

ENGLISH MONARCHS
(A.D. 827–1603)

Monarch	Accession	Died	Age	Reigned

I.—BEFORE THE CONQUEST.
SAXONS AND DANES

Monarch	Accession	Died	Age	Reigned
Egbert	827	839	—	12
Ethelwulf	839	858	—	19
Ethelbald	858	860	—	2
Ethelbert	858	865	—	7
Ethelred	865	871	—	6
Alfred the Great	871	899	50	28
Edward the Elder	899	924	54	25
Athelstan	924	939	45	15
Edmund	939	946	25	7
Eadred	946	955	32	9
Eadwig	955	959	18	3
Edgar	959	975	32	17
Edward the Martyr	975	978	17	3
Ethelred II ("the Unready")	978	1016	48	37
Edmund Ironside	1016	1016	27	Apr.–Nov.
Canute the Dane	1017	1035	40	18
Harold I	1035	1040	—	5
Hardicanute	1040	1042	24	2
Edward the Confessor	1042	1066	62	24
Harold II	1066	1066	44	Jan.–Oct.

II.—FROM THE CONQUEST TO THE PRESENT DAY.
NORMANS

Monarch	Accession	Died	Age	Reigned
William I	1066	1087	60	21
William II	1087	1100	43	13
Henry I	1100	1135	67	35
Stephen, Count of Blois	1135	1154	50	19

PLANTAGENETS

Monarch	Accession	Died	Age	Reigned
Henry II	1154	1189	56	35
Richard I	1189	1199	42	10
John	1199	1216	50	17
Henry III	1216	1272	65	56
Edward I	1272	1307	68	35
Edward II	1307	dep. 1327	43	20
Edward III	1327	1377	65	50
Richard II	1377	dep. 1399	34	22
Henry IV ⎫	1399	1413	47	13
Henry V ⎬ Lancaster	1413	1422	34	9
Henry VI ⎭	1422	dep. 1461	49	39
Edward IV ⎫	1461	1483	41	22
Edward V ⎬ York	1483	1483	13	Apr.–June
Richard III ⎭	1483	1485	32	2

TUDORS

Monarch	Accession	Died	Age	Reigned
Henry VII	1485	1509	53	24
Henry VIII	1509	1547	56	38
Edward VI	1547	1553	16	6
Jane	1553	1554	17	9 days
Mary I	1553	1558	43	5
Elizabeth I	1558	1603	69	44

THE BRITISH MONARCHY

(1603 to the Present day)

Monarch	Accession	Died	Age	Reigned
STUARTS				
James I (VI of Scotland)	1603	1625	59	22
Charles I	1625	beh. 1649	48	24
COMMONWEALTH DECLARED, MAY 19, 1649				
Oliver Cromwell, Lord Protector. . . .	1653–8	—	—	—
Richard Cromwell, Lord Protector . . .	1658–9	—	—	—
STUARTS (RESTORATION)				
Charles II	1660	1685	55	25
James II (VII of Scotland)	1685	dep. 1688	68	3
Interregnum Dec. 11, 1688 to Feb. 13, 1689				
William III and Mary II	1689	1702	51	13
		1694	33	6
Anne	1702	1714	49	12
HOUSE OF HANOVER				
George I	1714	1727	67	13
George II	1727	1760	77	33
George III	1760	1820	81	59
George IV	1820	1830	67	10
William IV	1830	1837	71	7
Victoria	1837	1901	81	63
HOUSE OF SAXE-COBURG				
Edward VII	1901	1910	68	9
HOUSE OF WINDSOR				
George V	1910	1936	70	25
Edward VIII	1936	Abd. 1936	—	325 days
George VI	1936	1952	56	15
Elizabeth II	1952			

SCOTTISH MONARCHS

(1034–1603)

	Monarch	Accession	Died
Duncan I	Son of Malcolm II	1034	1040
Macbeth	Slayed Duncan in 1040	1040	1057
Malcolm III (Canmore)	Son of Duncan I	1058	1093
Donald Ban	Brother of Malcolm Canmore	1093	—
Duncan II	Son of Malcolm Canmore, by first marriage	1094	1094
Donald Ban	Restored	1094	1097
Edgar	Son of Malcolm Canmore, by second marriage	1097	1107
Alexander I	Son of Malcolm Canmore	1107	1124
David I	Son of Malcolm Canmore	1124	1153
Malcolm IV (the Maiden)	Son of Henry, eldest son of David I	1153	1165
William I (the Lion)	Brother of Malcolm the Maiden	1165	1214
Alexander II	Son of William the Lion	1214	1249
Alexander III	Son of Alexander II, by second marriage	1249	1286
Margaret, Maid of Norway	Daughter of Eric II of Norway, granddaughter of Alexander III	1286	1290
John Baliol	Grandson of eldest daughter of David, Earl of Huntingdon, brother of William the Lion	1292	1296
Robert I (Bruce)	Great-grandson of 2nd daughter of David, Earl of Huntingdon, brother of William the Lion	1306	1329
David II	Son of Robert I, by second marriage	1329	1371
Robert II (Stewart)	Son of Marjorie, daughter of Robert I by first marriage, and Walter the Steward	1371	1390
Robert III	(John, Earl of Carrick) son of Robert II	1390	1406
James I	Son of Robert III	1406	1437
James II	Son of James I	1437	1460
James III	Eldest son of James II	1460	1488
James IV	Eldest son of James III	1488	1513
James V	Son of James IV	1513	1542
Mary	Daughter of James V, by second marriage	1542	1587
James VI (ascended the Throne of England 1603)	Son of Mary, by second marriage	1567	1625

BRITISH PRIME MINISTERS

	Party	Served
George II, 1727–60		
Sir Robert Walpole	Whig	1721–42
Earl of Wilmington	Whig	1742–3
Henry Pelham	Whig	1743–54
Duke of Newcastle	Whig	1754–6
Duke of Devonshire	Whig	1756–7
Duke of Newcastle	Whig	1757–60
George III, 1760–1820		
Duke of Newcastle	Whig	1760–2
Earl of Bute	Tory	1762–3
George Grenville	Whig	1763–5
Marquis of Rocking-ham	Whig	1766
Earl of Chatham	Tory	1766–8
Duke of Grafton	Whig	1766–9
Lord North	Tory	1770–82
Marquis of Rocking-ham	Whig	1782
Earl of Shelburne	Whig	1782–3
Duke of Portland	Coalition	1783
William Pitt	Tory	1783–1801
Viscount Sidmouth	Tory	1801–4
William Pitt	Tory	1804–6
Lord Grenville	Whig	1806–7
Duke of Portland	Tory	1807–9
Spencer Perceval (assassinated)	Tory	1809–12
George IV, 1820–30		
Earl of Liverpool	Tory	1812–27
George Canning	Tory	1827
Viscount Goderich	Rory	1827
Duke of Wellington	Tory	1827–30
William IV, 1830–7		
Earl Grey	Whig	1830–4
Viscount Melbourne	Whig	1834
Sir Robert Peel	Tory	1834–5
Viscount Melborune	Whig	1835–7
Victoria, 1837–1901		
Viscount Melbourne	Whig	1837–41
Sir Robert Peel	Tory	1841–6
Lord John Russell	Whig	1846–52
Earl of Derby	Tory	1852
Earl of Aberdeen	Peelite	1852–5
Viscount Palmerston	Liberal	1855–8
Earl of Derby	Tory	1858–9
Viscount Palmerston	Liberal	1859–65

	Party	Served
Earl Russell	Liberal	1865–6
Earl of Derby	Conservative	1866–8
B. Disraeli	Conservative	1868
W. E. Gladstone	Liberal	1868–74
B. Disraeli	Conservative	1874–80
W. E. Gladstone	Liberal	1880–5
Marquis of Salisbury	Conservative	1885–6
W. E. Gladstone	Liberal	1886
Marquis of Salisbury	Conservative	1886–92
W. E. Gladstone	Liberal	1892–4
Earl of Rosebury	Liberal	1894–5
Marquis of Salisbury	Conservative	1895–1901
Edward VII, 1901–10		
Marquis of Salisbury	Conservative	1901–2
A. J. Balfour	Conservative	1902–5
Sir H. Campbell-Bannerman	Liberal	1905–8
H. H. Asquith	Liberal	1908–10
George V, 1910–36		
H. H. Asquith	Liberal	1910–15
H. H. Asquith	Coalition	1915–16
D. Lloyd George	Coalition	1916–22
A. Bonar Law	Conservative	1922–3
S. Baldwin	Conservative	1923–4
J. R. MacDonald	Labour	1924
S. Baldwin	Conservative	1924–9
J. R. MacDonald	Labour	1929–31
J. R. MacDonald	National	1931–5
S. Baldwin	National	1935–6
Edward VIII, 1936		
George VI, 1936–52		
S. Baldwin	National	1936–7
N. Chamberlain	National	1937–39
N. Chamberlain	War Cabinet	1939
W. S. Churchill	War Cabinet	1940–45
W. S. Churchill	Caretaker	1945
C. R. Attlee	Labour	1945–51
Sir W. S. Churchill	Conservative	1951–2
Elizabeth II, 1952–		
Sir W. S. Churchill	Conservative	1952–5
Sir A. Eden	Conservative	1955–7
H. Macmillan	Conservative	1957–63
Sir A. Douglas-Home	Conservative	1963–4
H. Wilson	Labour	1964–70
E. Heath	Conservative	1970–4
H. Wilson	Labour	1974–6
J. Callaghan	Labour	1976–9
Mrs. M. Thatcher	Conservative	1979–

PRESIDENTS OF THE UNITED STATES

The terms are for four years; only President F. D. Roosevelt
has served more than two terms.

	Party	Served
1. George Washington	Fed.	1789–97
2. John Adams	Fed.	1797–1801
3. Thomas Jefferson	Rep.	1801–9
4. James Madison	Rep.	1809–17
5. James Monroe	Rep.	1817–25
6. John Quincey Adams	Rep.	1825–9
7. Andrew Jackson	Dem.	1829–37
8. Martin Van Buren	Dem.	1837–41
9. William H. Harrison (died in office)	Whig	1841
10. John Tyler	Whig	1841–5
11. James K. Polk	Dem.	1845–9
12. Zachary Taylor (died in office)	Whig	1849–50
13. Millard Fillmore	Whig	1850–3
14. Franklin Pierce	Dem.	1853–7
15. James Buchanan	Dem.	1857–61
16. Abraham Lincoln (assassinated)	Rep.	1861–5
17. Andrew Johnson	Rep.	1865–9
18. Ulysses S. Grant	Rep.	1869–77
19. Rutherford B. Hayes	Rep.	1877–81
20. James A. Garfield (assassinated)	Rep.	1881
21. Chester A. Arthur	Rep.	1881–5

	Party	Served
22. Grover Cleveland	Dem.	1885–9
23. Benjamin Harrison	Rep.	1889–93
24. Grover Cleveland	Dem.	1893–7
25. William McKinley (assassinated)	Rep.	1897–1901
26. Theodore Roosevelt	Rep.	1901–9
27. Willian Howard Taft	Rep.	1909–13
28. Woodrow Wilson	Dem.	1913–21
29. Warren G. Harding (died in office)	Rep.	1921–3
30. Calvin Coolidge	Rep.	1923–9
31. Herbert C. Hoover	Rep.	1929–33
32. Franklin D. Roosevelt (died in office)	Dem.	1933–45
33. Harry S. Truman	Dem.	1945–53
34. Dwight D. Eisenhower	Rep.	1953–61
35. John F. Kennedy (assassinated)	Dem.	1961–3
36. Lyndon B. Johnson	Dem.	1963–69
37. Richard M. Nixon (resigned)	Rep.	1969–74
38. Gerald R. Ford	Rep.	1974–6
39. James Carter	Dem.	1976–81
40. Ronald Reagan*	Rep.	1981–
*re-elected, November 1984		

FOREIGN PHRASES

Fr., French.   Gr., Greek.   Ger., German.   It., Italian.   L., Latin.   Sp., Spanish

à bas (Fr.), down, down with.

ab extra (L.), from without.

ab incunabilis (L.), from the cradle.

ab initio (L.), from the beginning.

ab intra (L.), from within.

à bon chat, bon rat (Fr.), to be a good cat, a good rat; well attacked and defended; tit for tat; a Rowland for an Oliver.

à bon marche (Fr.), cheap, a good bargain.

à bras ouverts (Fr.), with open arms.

absente reo (L.), the accused being absent.

absit invidia (L.), let there be no ill-will; envy apart.

ab uno disce omnes (L.), from one specimen judge of all the rest; from a single instance infer the whole.

ab urbe condità (L.), from the building of the city; *i.e.,* Rome.

a capite ad calcem (L.) from head to heel.

à chaque saint sa chandelle (Fr.), to each saint his candle; honour where honour is due.

à cheval (Fr.), on horseback.

à compte (Fr.) on account; in part payment.

à corps perdu (Fr.), with might and main.

à couvert (Fr.), under cover; protected; sheltered.

ad astra (L.), to the stars.

ad calendas Græcas (L.), at the Greek calends; *i.e.,* never, as the Greeks had no calends in their mode of reckoning.

à demi (Fr.), by halves; half-way.

a Deo et rege (L.), from God and the king.

ad hoc (L.), arranged for this purpose; special.

ad hominem (L.), to the man; to an individual's interests or passions; personal.

adhuc sub judice lis est (L.), the case has not yet been decided.

a die (L.), from that day.

ad infinitum (L.), to infinity.

ad interim (L.), in the meantime.

ad libitum (L.), at pleasure.

ad modum (L.), after the manner of.

ad nauseam (L.), to disgust or satiety.

ad referendum (L.), for further consideration.

ad rem (L.), to the purpose; to the point.

ad valorem (L.), according to the value.

affaire d'amour (Fr.), a love affair.

affaire d'honneur (Fr.), an affair of honour; a duel.

affaire de cœur (Fr.), an affair of the heart.

a fortiori (L.), with stronger reason.

à gauche (Fr.), to the left.

à genoux (Fr.), on the knees.

à haute voix (Fr.), aloud.

à huis clos (Fr.), with closed doors; secretly.

à belle étoile (Fr.), under the stars; in the open air.

à la bonne heure (Fr.), well timed; all right; very well; as you please.

à l'abri (Fr.), under shelter.

à la mode (Fr.), according to the custom or fashion.

à la Tartuffe (Fr.), like Tartuffe, the hero of a celebrated comedy by Molière; hypocritically.

al fresco (It.), in the open air; out-of-doors.

al più (It.), at most.

alter ego (L.), another self.

à merveille (Fr.), to a wonder; marvellously.

amor patriæ (L.), love of country.

amour-propre (Fr.), self-love, vanity.

ancien régime (Fr.), the ancient or former order of things.

anguis in herba (L.), a snake in the grass.

anno Christi (L.), in the year of Christ.

anno Domini (L.), in the year of our Lord.

anno mundi (L.), in the year of the world.

annus mirabilis (L.), year of wonders; wonderful year.

ante bellum (L.), before the war.

ante lucem (L.), before light.

ante meridiem (L.), before noon.

à outrance (Fr.), to the utmost; to extremities; without sparing.

à pied (Fr.), on foot.

à point (Fr.), to a point, just in time, exactly right.

a posse ad esse (L.), from possibility to reality.

ariston metron (Gr.), the middle course is the best; the golden mean.

arrière-pensé (Fr.), hidden thought; mental reservation.

au courant (Fr.), fully acquainted with.

audi alteram partem (L.), hear the other side.

au fait (Fr.), well acquainted with; expert.

au fond (Fr.), at bottom.

auf Wiedersehen! (Ger.), till we meet again.

au pis aller (Fr.), at the worst.

au revoir (Fr.), adieu; till we meet again.

aut vincere aut mori (L.), either to conquer or to die; death or victory.

a verbis ad verbera (L.), from words to blows.

a vinculo matrimonii (L.), from the bond of matrimony.

à volonté (Fr.), at pleasure.

a vostra salute (It.)

à votre santé (Fr.)   }   to your health.

a vuestra salud (Sp.)

bas bleu (Fr.), a blue-stocking; a literary woman.

beau monde (Fr.), the world of fashion.

beaux esprits (Fr.), men of wit, gay spirits.

beaux yeux (Fr.), fine eyes; good looks.

ben trovato (It.), well or cleverly invented.

bête noire (Fr.), a black beast; a bugbear.

bon gré mal gré (Fr.), with good or ill grace; willing or unwilling.

bonhomie (Fr.), good-nature; artlessness.

bonne bouche (Fr.), a delicate or tasty morsel.

bon vivant (Fr.), a good liver; a gourmand.

brutum fulmen (L.), a harmless thunderbolt.

canaille (Fr.), rabble.

candida Pax (L.), white-robed Peace.

casus belli (L.), that which causes or justifies war.

causa sine qua non (L.), an indispensable cause or condition.

caveat emptor (L.), let the buyer beware (or look after his own interest).

cela va sans dire (Fr.), that goes without saying; needless to say.

ceteris paribus (L.), other things being equal.

chacun à son goût (Fr.), every one to his taste.

cogito, ergo sum (L.), I think, therefore I exist.

comme il faut (Fr.), as it should be.

compos mentis (L.), sound of mind; quite sane.

compte rendu (Fr.), an account rendered; a report or statement drawn up.

conditio sine qua non (L.), a necessary condition.

conseil de famille (Fr.), a family consultation.

consensus facit legem (L.), consent makes the law.

consilio et animis (L.), by wisdom and courage.

consilio et prudentia (L.), by wisdom and prudence.

constantia et virtute (L.), by constancy and virtue.

contra bonos mores (L.), against good manners.

contretemps (Fr.), an unlucky accident; a hitch.

cordon bleu (Fr.), blue ribbon; a cook of the highest class.

cordon sanitaire (Fr.), a line of guards to prevent the spreading of contagion or pestilence.

corpus delicti (L.), the body or substance of a crime or offence.

corrigenda (L.), things to be corrected.

coup de grâce (Fr.), a sudden decisive blow in politics; a stroke of policy.

coup de soleil (Fr.), sunstroke.

credat Judæus Apella (L.), let Apella, the superstitious Jew, believe it (I won't); tell that to the marines.

cucullus non facit monachum (L.), the cowl does not make the friar.

cui bono? (L.), For whose advantage is it? to what end?

culpam pœna premit comes (L.), punishment follows hard upon crime.

cum grano salis (L.), with a grain of salt; with some allowance.

cum privilegio (L.), with privilege.

currente calamo (L.), with a fluent pen.

da locum melioribus (L.), give place to your betters.

damnant quod non intelligunt (L.), they condemn what they do not comprehend.

data et accepta (L.), expenditures and receipts.

de bon augure (Fr.), of good augury or omen.

de bonne grâce (Fr.), with good grace; willingly.

de die in diem (L.), from day to day.

de facto (L.), in point of fact; actual or actually.

dei gratia (L.), by God's grace.

de jure (L.), from the law; by right.

de mal en pis (Fr.), from bad to worse.

de novo (L.), anew.

deo volente (L.), God willing; by God's will.

de profundis (L.), out of the depths.

dernier ressort (Fr.), a last resource.

deus ex machina (L.), one who puts matters right at a critical moment; providential intervention.

dies non (L.), a day on which judges do not sit.

distingué (Fr.), distinguished; of genteel or elegant appearance.

dolce far niente (It.), a sweet doing-nothing; sweet idleness.

double entente (Fr.), a double meaning; a play on words.

dramatis personæ (L.), characters of the drama or play.

dum spiro, spero (L.), while I breathe, I hope.

ecce homo! (L.), behold the man!

eheu! fugaces labuntur anni (L.), alas! the fleeting years glide by.

einmal ist keinmal (Ger.), just once doesn't count.

en avant (Fr.), forward.

en badinant (Fr.), in sport; in jest.

en déshabillé (Fr.), in undress.

en famille (Fr.), with one's family; in a domestic state.

enfant terrible (Fr.), a terrible child, or one that makes disconcerting remarks.

enfin (Fr.), in short; at last; finally.

en passant (Fr.), in passing; by the way.

en plein jour (Fr.), in broad day.

en rapport (Fr.), in harmony; in agreement; in relation.

en règle (Fr.), according to rules; in order.

entente cordiale (Fr.), cordial understanding, especially between two states.

entre nous (Fr.), between ourselves.

en vérité (Fr.), in truth; verily.

e pluribus unum (L.), one out of many; one composed of many.

esprit de corps (Fr.), the animating spirit of a collective body, as a regiment, learned profession or the like.

et sequentes, et sequentia (L.), and those that follow.

et tu, Brute! (L.), and thou also, Brutus!

ex animo (L.), heartily; sincerely.

ex capite (L.), from the head; from memory.

ex cathedra (L.), from the chair or seat of authority, with high authority.

exceptio probat regulam (L.), the exception proves the rule.

ex curia (L.), out of court.

ex dono (L.), by the gift.

exeunt omnes (L.), all go out or retire.

exit (L.), he goes out.

ex mero motu (L.), from his own impulse, from his own free will.

ex nihilo nihil fit (L.), out of nothing, nothing comes; nothing produces nothing.

ex officio (L.), in virtue of his office.

ex post facto (L.), after the deed is done; retrospective.

face à face (Fr.), face to face.

façon de parler (Fr.), manner of speaking.

faire bonne mine (Fr.), to put a good face upon the matter.

fait accompli (Fr.), a thing already done.

fama clamosa (L.), a current scandal; a prevailing report.

faute de mieux (Fr.), for want of better.

faux pas (Fr.), a false step; a slip in behaviour.

festina lente (L.), hasten slowly.

fiat justitia, ruat cœlum (L.), let justice be done though the heavens should fall.

fiat lux (L.), let there be light.

fide et amore (L.), by faith and love.

fide et fiduciâ (L.), by fidelity and confidence.

fide et fortitudine (L.), with faith and fortitude.

fidei defensor (L.), defender of the faith.

fide non armis (L.), by faith, not by arms.

fide, sed cui vide (L.), trust, but see whom.

fides et justitia (L.), fidelity and justice.

fides Punica (L.), Punic faith; treachery.

filius nullius (L.), a son of nobody; a bastard.

finis coronat opus (L.), the end crowns the work.

flagrante bello (L.), during hostilities.

flagrante delicto (L.), in the commission of the crime.

floreat (L.), let it flourish.

fons et origo (L.), the source and origin.

force majeure (Fr.), irresistible compulsion; war, strike, Act of God, etc.

forensis strepitus (L.), the clamour of the forum.

fortuna favet fortibus (L.), fortune favours the bold.

functus officio (L.), having performed one's office or duty; hence, out of office.

gaudeamus igitur (L.), so let us be joyful!

genius loci (L.), the genius or guardian spirit of a place.

gradu diverso, via una (L.), the same road by different steps.

grande parure } (Fr.), full dress.
grande toilette }

guerra al cuchillo (Sp.), war to the knife.

Hannibal ante portas (L.), Hannibal before the gates; the enemy close at hand.

hiatus valde deflendus (L.), a chasm or deficiency much to be regretted.

hic et nunc (L.), here and now.

hic et ubique (L.), here and everywhere.

hic jacet (L.) here lies.

hic labor, hoc opus est (L.), this is a labour, this is a toil.

hic sepultus (L.), here buried.

hoc genus omne (L.), all of this sort or class.

hoi polloi (Gr.), the many; the vulgar; the rabble.

hominis est errare (L.), to err is human.

homme de robe (Fr.), a man in civil office.

homme d'affair (Fr.), a man of business.

homme d'esprit (Fr.), a man of wit or genius.

honi soit qui mal y pense (O. Fr.), evil to him who evil thinks.

honores mutant mores (L.), honours change men's manners or characters.

hors de combat (Fr.), out of condition to fight.

hors de propos (Fr.), not to the point or purpose.

hors d'œuvre (Fr.), out of course; out of order.

ich dien (Ger.), I serve.

idée fixe (Fr.), a fixed idea.

id est (L.), that is.

il a diable au corps (Fr.), the devil is in him.

Ilias malorum (L.), an Iliad of ills; a host of evils.

il penseroso (It.), the pensive man.

il sent le fagot (Fr.), he smells of the faggot; he is suspected of heresy.

imperium in imperio (L.), a state within a state; a government within another.

in actu (L.), in act or reality.

in articulo mortis (L.), at the point of death; in the last struggle.

in capite (L.), in chief.

in curia (L.), in court.

index expurgatorius } (L.), a list of books prohibited
index prohibitorius } to Roman Catholics.

in esse (L.), in being; in actuality.

in extenso (L.), at full length.

in extremis (L.), at the point of death.

in memoriam (L.), to the memory of; in memory.

in nubibus (L.), in the clouds.

in petto (It.), in (my) breast; to one's self.

in re (L.), in the matter of.

in sano sensu (L.), in a proper sense.

in situ (L.), in its original situation.

in vino veritas (L.), there is truth in wine; truth is told under the influence of intoxicants.

ipse dixit (L.), he himself said it; a dogmatic saying or assertion.

ipsissima verba (L.), the very words.

ipso facto (L.), in the fact itself.

ipso jure (L.), by the law itself.

jacta est alea (L.), the die is cast.

je ne sais quoi (Fr.), I know not what.

joci causa (L.), for the sake of a joke.

labor omnia vincit (L.), labour conquers everything.

l'allegro (It.), the merry man.

lapsus linguæ (L.), a slip of the tongue.

lares et penates (L.), household goods.

laus Deo (L.), praise to God.

le beau monde (Fr.), the fashionable world.

lector benevole (L.), kind or gentle reader.

le jeu n'en vaut pas la chandelle (Fr.), the game is not worth the candle; the object is not worth the trouble.

le mot de l'énigme (Fr.), the key to the mystery.

le point du jour (Fr.), daybreak.

lèse-majesté (Fr.), high-treason.

lettre de cachet (Fr.), a sealed letter containing private orders; a royal warrant.

lex loci (L.), the law or custom of the place.

lex non scripta (L.), unwritten law; common law.

lex scripta (L.), written law; statute law.

locum tenens (L.), a deputy.

lucri causa (L.), for the sake of gain.

magnum opus (L.), a great work.

mala fide (L.), with bad faith; treacherously.

mal à propos (L.), ill-timed; out of place.

malgré nous (Fr.), in spite of us.

malheur ne vient jamais seul (Fr.), misfortunes never come singly.

malum in se (L.), evil or an evil in itself.

mardi gras (Fr.), Shrove Tuesday.

mariage de convenance (Fr.), marriage from motives of interest rather than of love.

mauvais goût (Fr.), bad taste.

mauvaise honte (Fr.), false modesty.

mea culpa (L.), my fault; by my fault.

me judice (L.), I being judge; in my opinion.

mens agitat molem (L.), mind moves matter.

mens legis (L.), the spirit of the law.

mens sana in corpore sano (L.), a sound mind in a sound body.

meo periculo (L.), at my own risk.

meo voto (L.), according to my wish.

mise en scène (Fr.), the getting up for the stage, or the putting on the stage.

modus operandi (L.), manner of working.

more suo (L.), in his own way.

motu proprio (L.), of his own accord.

multum in parvo (L.), much in little.

mutatis mutandis (L.), with suitable or necessary alteration.

nervus probandi (L.), the sinews of the argument.

nihil ad rem (L.), irrelevant.

nil desperandum (L.), there is no reason to despair.

noblesse oblige (Fr.), rank imposes obligations; much is expected from one in good position.

nolens volens (L.), willing or unwilling.

nom de guerre (Fr.), a false or assumed name.

non compos mentis (L.), not of sound mind.

non sequitur (L.), it does not follow.

nosce te ipsum (L.), know thyself.

nota bene (L.), mark well.

nudis verbis (L.), in plain words.

obiter dictum (L.), a thing said by the way.

omnia vincit amor (L.), love conquers all things.

ora pro nobis (L.), pray for us.

O tempora! O mores! (L.), O the times! O the manners (or morals)!

oui-dire (Fr.), hearsay.

padrone (It.), a master; a landlord.

par excellence (Fr.), by way of eminence.

pari passu (L.), at an equal pace or rate of progress.

particeps criminis (L.), an accomplice in a crime.

pas de quoi (Fr. abbrev. Il n'y a pas de quoi), don't mention it.

passim (L.), everywhere; in all parts of the book, chapter, etc.

pâté de foie gras (Fr.), goose-liver paté.

pater patriæ (L.), father of his country.

patres conscripti (L.), the conscript fathers; Roman senators.

pax vobiscum (L.), peace be with you.

per ardua ad astra (L.), through rough ways to the stars; through suffering to renown.

per capita (L.), by the head or poll.

per contra (It.), countrariwise.

per diem (L.), by the day; daily.

per se (L.), by itself; considered apart.

pied-à-terre (Fr.), a resting-place; a temporary lodging.

pis aller (Fr.), the worst or last shift.

plebs (L.), the common people.

poco a poco (It.), little by little.

poste restante (Fr.), to remain in the post-office till called for.

prima facie (L.), at first view or consideration.

primus inter pares (L.), first among equals.

pro forma (L.), for the sake of form.

pro patria (L.), for our country.

pro tanto (L.), for so much; for as far as it goes.

pro tempore (L.), for the time being.

quid pro quo (L.), one thing for another; tit for tat; an equivalent.

qui m'aime, aime mon chien (Fr.), love me, love my dog.

qui tacet consentit (L.), he who is silent gives consent.

quod erat demonstrandum (L.), which was to be proved or demonstrated.

quod erat faciendum (L.), which was to be done.

quod vide (L.), which see; refer to the word just mentioned.

quo jure? (L.), by what right?

raison d'être (Fr.), the reason for a thing's existence.

re (L.), in the matter or affair of.

reculer pour mieux sauter (Fr.), to draw back in order to make a better spring.

reductio ad adsurdum (L.), the reducing of a position to a logical absurdity.

requiescat in pace (L.), may he (or she) rest in peace.

respice finem (L.), look to the end.

respublica (L.), the commonwealth.

revenons à nos moutons (Fr.), let us return to our sheep; let us return to our subject.

re vera (L.) in truth.

sans peur et sans reproche (Fr.), without fear and without reproach.

sans rime ni raison (Fr.), without rhyme or reason.

sans souci (Fr.), without care.

sartor resartus (L.), the botcher repatched; the tailor patched or mended.

sauve qui peut (Fr.), let him save himself who can.

savoir-faire (Fr.), the knowing how to act; tact.

savoir-vivre (Fr.), good-breeding; refined manners.

semper idem (L.), always the same.

seriatim (L.), in a series; one by one.

sic passim (L.), so here and there throughout; so everywhere.

sicut ante (L.), as before.

sine die (L.), without a day being appointed.

sine mora (L.), without delay.

sine qua non (L.), without which, not; indispensable condition.

sotto voce (It.), in an undertone.

spirituel (Fr.), intellectual; witty.

stet (L.), let it stand; do not delete.

sub judice (L.), under consideration.

sub poena (L.), under a penalty.

sub rosa (L.), under the rose; privately.

sub voce (L.), under such or such a word.

sui generis (L.), of its own or of a particular kind.

summum bonum (L.), the chief good.

tableau vivant (Fr.), a living picture; the representation of some scene by a group of persons.

tant mieux (Fr.), so much the better.

tant pis (Fr.), so much the worse.

tempora mutantur, nos et mutamur in illis (L.), the times are changing and we with them.

tempus fugit (L.), time flies.

tête-à-tête (Fr.), together in private.

tiers état (Fr.), the third estate; the commons.

to kalon (Gr.), the beautiful; the chief good.

to prepon (Gr.), the becoming or proper.

tour de force (Fr.), a feat of strength or skill.

tout à fait (Fr.), wholly; entirely.

tout à l'heure (Fr.), instantly.

toute de suite (Fr.), immediately.

tu quoque (L.), thou also.

ubique (L.), everywhere.

ubi supra (L.), where above mentioned.

ultra licitum (L.), beyond what is allowable.

ultra vires (L.), beyond powers or rights conferred by law.

urbi et orbi (L.), to the city (Rome), and the world.

utile dulci (L.), the useful with the pleasant.

ut infra (L.), as below.

ut supra (L.), as above stated.

vade in pace (L.), go in peace.

variæ lectiones (L.), various readings.

variorum notæ (L.), the notes of various commentators.

vede et crede (L.), see and believe.

veni, vidi, vici (L.), I came, I saw, I conquered.

verbatim et literatim (L.), word for word and letter for letter.

verbum sat sapienti (L.), a word is enough for a wise man.

ver non semper viret (L.), spring is not always green.

vexata quæstio (L.), a disputed question.

via media (L.), a middle course.

via trita, via tuta (L.), the beaten path is the safe path.

vice versa (L.), the terms of the case being reversed.

videlicet (L.), that is to say; namely.

vi et armis (L.), by force of arms; by main force; by violence.

vigilate et orate (L.), watch and pray.

vita brevis, ars longa (L.), life is short; art is long.

viva regina! (L.), long live the queen!

vivat rex! (L.), long live the king!

viva voce (L.), by the living voice; orally.

voilà (Fr.), behold; there is; there are.

voilà tout (Fr.), that's all.

volo, non valeo (L.), I am willing, but unable.

vox populi, vox Dei (L), the voice of the people is the voice of God.

MAJOR NATIONAL CURRENCIES

Country	Currency
Albania	Lek
Argentina	Austral
Australia	Dollar
Austria	Schilling
Belgium/Lux.	Franc
Belize	Dollar
Bolivia	Peso Boliviano
Brazil	Cruzeiro
Bulgaria	Lev
Burma	Kyat
Canada	Dollar
Chile	Peso
China	Renminbi
Colombia	Peso
Costa Rica	Colón
Cuba	Peso
Czechoslovakia	Koruna
Denmark	Krone
Dominican Republic	Peso
Ecuador	Sucre
Egypt	Pound
El Salvador	Colón
Ethiopia	Dollar
Finland	Markka
France	Franc
Germany (E.)	Mark
Germany (Fed. Rep.)	D. Mark
Greece	Drachma
Guatemala	Quetzal
Guyana	Dollar
Haiti	Gourde
Hong Kong	Dollar
Hungary	Forint
Iceland	Króna
India	Rupee
Indonesia	Rupiah
Iran	Rial
Iraq	Dinar
Israel	Shekel
Italy	New Lira
Jamaica	Dollar
Japan	Yen
Jordan	Dinar
Kenya	K. Shilling
Lebanon	Pound
Malaysia	Ringgit
Mexico	Peso
Morocco	Dirham
Netherlands	Guilder
New Zealand	Dollar
Nicaragua	Córdoba
Nigeria	Naira
Norway	Krone
Pakistan	Rupee
Panama	Balboa
Paraguay	Guarani
Peru	Sol
Philippines	Peso
Poland	Zloty
Portugal	Escudo
Romania	Leu
South Africa	Rand
Spain	Peseta
Sri Lanka	Rupee
Sweden	Krona
Switzerland	Franc
Syria	Pound
Tanzania	T. Shilling
Thailand	Baht
Trinidad and Tobago	T.T. Dollar
Tunisia	Dinar
Turkey	Lira
United Arab Emirates	Dirham
United Kingdom	Pound
U.S.A.	Dollar
U.S.S.R.	Rouble
Uruguay	Peso
Venezuela	Bolivar
Yugoslavia	Dinar
Yemen Arab Rep.	Riyal
Yemen South.	Dinar
Zaïre	Zaïre
Zambia	Kwacha

ROMAN NUMERALS

I	.	1		LXX	.	.	70
II	.	2		LXXX	.	.	80
III	.	3		LXXXVIII	.	88
IV	.	4		XC	.	.	90
V	.	5		XCIX	.	.	99
VI	.	6		C	.	.	100
VII	.	7		CX	.	.	110
VIII	.	8		CXI	.	.	111
IX	.	9		CXX	.	.	120
X	.	10		CC	.	.	200
XI	.	11		CCXX	.	.	220
XII	.	12		CCC	.	.	300
XIII	.	13		CCCXX	.	320
XIV	.	14		CD	.	.	400
XV	.	15		D	.	.	500
XVI	.	16		DC	.	.	600
XVII	.	17		DCC	.	.	700
XVIII	.	18		DCCC	.	800
XIX	.	19		CM	.	.	900
XX	.	20		XM	.	.	990
XXX	.	30		M	.	.	1000
XL	.	40		MD	.	.	1500
L	.	50		MDCCC	.	1800
LV	.	55		MCMLXX	.	1970
LX	.	60		MM	.	.	2000

INTERNATIONAL TIME-TABLE (GMT)

Place	Time h	Place	Time h
Adelaide	21 30	Melbourne	22 00
Amsterdam	13 00	Montreal	07 00
Ankara	14 00	Moscow	15 00
Athens	14 00	Nairobi	15 00
Auckland		New York	07 00
(N.Z.)	24 00	Oslo	13 00
Belgrade	13 00	Ottawa	07 00
Berlin	13 00	Panama	07 00
Bombay	17 30	Paris	13 00
Brisbane	22 00	Peking	20 00
Brussels	13 00	Perth (W.A.)	20 00
Budapest	13 00	Prague	13 00
Buenos Aires	09 00	Quebec	07 00
Cairo	14 00	Rangoon	18 30
Calcutta	17 30	Rio de Janeiro	09 00
Cape Town	14 00	Rome	13 00
Chicago	06 00	San Francisco	04 00
Copenhagen	13 00	St. John's	
Gibraltar	13 00	(N.F.)	08 30
Helsinki	14 00	Singapore	19 30
Hobart	22 00	Stockholm	13 00
Hong Kong	20 00	Sydney	22 00
Istanbul	14 00	Tehran	15 30
Jerusalem	14 00	Tokyo	21 00
London	12 00	Toronto	07 00
Madeira	12 00	Vancouver	04 00
Madrid	13 00	Vienna	13 00
Malta	13 00	Winnipeg	06 00
Mauritius	16 00	Yokohama	21 00

GREEK ALPHABET

A	α	Alpha	N	ν	nu
B	β	beta	Ξ	ξ	xi
Γ	γ	gamma	O	o	omicron
Δ	δ	delta	Π	π	pi
E	ε	epsilon	P	ρ	rho
Z	ζ	zeta	Σ	σ	sigma
H	η	eta	T	τ	tau
Θ	θ	theta	Υ	υ	upsilon
I	ι	iota	Φ	φ	phi
K	κ	kappa	X	χ	chi
Λ	λ	lambda	Ψ	ψ	psi
M	μ	mu	Ω	ω	omega

BANK AND PUBLIC HOLIDAYS

The number of public holidays in England and Wales comprise at present six bank holidays (New Year's Day, Easter Monday, May Day, Spring and Late Summer Holidays at the end of May and August respectively, and Boxing Day), with also two common law holidays (Good Friday and Christmas Day); in Scotland seven bank holidays (New Year's Day, January 3, Good Friday, May Day, Spring and Late Summer Holidays at the beginning of May and August respectively, and Christmas Day); and in Northern Ireland seven bank holidays (New Year's Day, St. Patrick's Day, Easter Monday, May Day, Spring Late Summer Holidays at the end of May and August respectively, and Boxing Day) plus two other public holidays (Easter Tuesday and the anniversary of the Battle of the Boyne).

1987   Bank Holidays in England and Wales—Jan. 1, Apr. 17, Apr. 20, May 4, May 25, Aug. 31, Dec. 25, Dec. 26.
           Northern Ireland—Jan. 1, Mar. 17, Apr. 17, Apr. 20, May 4, May 25, July 13, Aug. 31, Dec. 25, Dec. 26.
           Scotland—Jan. 1, Jan. 2, Apr. 17, May 4, May 25, Aug. 3, Dec. 25, Dec. 26.

Note: There are holidays in lieu of other public holidays which fall at weekends. In Scotland and Northern Ireland a general holiday is not necessarily observed on the same day as a bank holiday.

THE SEASONS

		1986			1987		
		d	h	m		d	h	m
Vernal Equinox—Spring begins	Mar.	20	22	03	Mar.	21	03	52
Summer Solstice—Summer begins	June	21	16	30	June	21	22	11
Autumnal Equinox—Autumn begins	Sept.	23	07	59	Sept.	23	13	45
Winter Solstice—Winter begins	Dec.	22	04	02	Dec.	22	09	46

(All times are in GMT)

THE COUNTRY CODE

GUARD AGAINST THE RISK OF FIRE. Great damage is done every year to crops, plantations, woodlands, and heaths. A match or cigarette thrown away or a pipe carelessly knocked out, picnic fires not properly put out or lighted near dry crops, can quickly start a blaze.

FASTEN ALL GATES. If animals get out of a field they stray. As a result they may do serious damage to crops, suffer injury on the roads, or eat food that is harmful.

KEEP DOGS UNDER CONTROL. Animals are easily frightened, even by small, playful dogs. Stillbirths may be the result.

KEEP TO THE PATHS ACROSS FARM LAND. Crops are damaged by treading; flattened crops are difficult to harvest. Grass is a valuable crop.

AVOID DAMAGING FENCING, HEDGES, AND WALLS. If these are damaged, gaps will be caused. Where a man goes, an animal may follow.

LEAVE NO LITTER. Litter is not just unsightly, but often a danger as well. Broken glass and tins may injure animals and harm machinery.

SAFEGUARD WATER SUPPLIES. Countrymen often depend on wells and streams for water for themselves and for their animals.

PROTECT WILD LIFE, PLANTS, AND TREES. Wild animals should not be disturbed, plants uprooted, or trees treated roughly.

GO CAREFULLY ON COUNTRY ROADS. If there is no footpath, walkers are generally safer on the right, facing on-coming traffic. Care and patience are needed by motorists when passing farm animals.

RESPECT THE LIFE OF THE COUNTRYSIDE. Many of the machines and much of the business stock of which the farmer depends for his livelihood have to be kept in the open. Take care not to damage them.

THE BEAUFORT SCALE OF WIND FORCE

Beaufort number	Wind	Effect on land	Speed	
			mile/h	Knots
0	Calm	Smoke rises vertically	Less than 1	Less than 1
1	Light air	Direction shown by smoke but not by wind vanes	1–3	1–3
2	Light breeze	Wind felt on face; leaves rustle; wind vanes move	4–7	4–6
3	Gentle breeze	Leaves and twigs in motion; wind extends light flag	8–12	7–10
4	Moderate breeze	Raises dust, loose paper and moves small branches	13–18	11–16
5	Fresh breeze	Small trees in leaf begin to sway	19–24	17–21
6	Strong breeze	Large branches in motion; whistling in telegraph wires; difficulty with umbrellas	25–31	22–27
7	Moderate gale	Whole trees in motion; difficult to walk against wind	32–38	28–33
8	Fresh gale	Twigs break off trees; progress impeded	39–46	34–40
9	Strong gale	Slight structural damage occurs; chimney pots and slates blown off	47–54	41–47
10	Whole gale	Trees uprooted and considerable structural damage	55–63	48–56
11	Storm	Widespread damage, seldom experienced in England	64–75	57–65
12	Hurricane	Winds of this force only encountered in tropical revolving storms	Above 75	Above 65

SUNRISE AND SUNSET FOR LONDON, 1987

		Rise	Set			Rise	Set			Rise	Set
		h m	h m			h m	h m			h m	h m
Jan	1	08 06	16 02	May	7	05 23	20 33	September	3	06 15	19 44
	8	08 05	16 10		14	05 11	20 44		10	06 26	19 28
	15	08 00	16 20		21	05 01	20 54		17	06 38	19 12
	22	07 53	16 32		28	04 53	21 03		24	06 49	18 56
	29	07 44	16 44								
Feb	5	07 34	16 56	June	4	04 47	21 11	October	1	07 00	18 40
	12	07 21	17 09		11	04 44	21 17		8	07 12	18 24
	19	07 08	17 22		18	04 43	21 21		15	07 24	18 09
	26	06 54	17 35		25	04 44	21 22		22	07 36	17 54
									29	06 48	16 40
March	5	06 39	17 49	July	2	04 48	21 21	November	5	07 00	16 28
	12	06 23	17 59		9	04 54	21 17		12	07 12	16 16
	19	06 07	18 11		16	05 01	21 11		19	07 24	16 07
	26	05 51	18 23		23	05 10	21 03		26	07 36	15 59
					30	05 20	20 53				
April	2	06 35	19 35					December	3	07 46	15 54
	9	06 20	19 46	August	6	05 31	20 41		10	07 55	15 52
	16	06 04	19 58		13	05 42	20 28		17	08 01	15 52
	23	05 50	20 10		20	05 53	20 14		24	08 05	15 55
	30	05 36	20 21		27	06 04	19 59		31	08 06	16 01

Note: These times are in GMT, except between 0100 on Mar 29 and 0100 on Oct 25 when the times are in BST (1 hour in advance of GMT).

PHASES OF THE MOON, 1987

New Moon				First Quarter				Full Moon				Last Quarter			
	d	h	m		d	h	m		d	h	m		d	h	m
Jan	29	13	44	Jan	6	22	34	Jan	15	02	30	Jan	22	22	45
Feb	28	00	51	Feb	5	16	21	Feb	13	20	58	Feb	21	08	56
Mar	29	12	46	Mar	7	11	58	Mar	15	13	13	Mar	22	16	22
Apr	28	01	34	Apr	6	07	48	Apr	14	02	31	Apr	20	22	15
May	27	15	13	May	6	02	26	May	13	12	50	May	20	04	02
June	26	05	37	June	4	18	53	June	11	20	49	June	18	11	02
July	25	20	37	July	4	08	34	July	11	03	33	July	17	20	17
Aug	24	11	59	Aug	2	19	24	Aug	9	10	17	Aug	16	08	25
Sept	23	03	08	Sept	1	03	48	Sept	7	18	13	Sept	14	23	44
Oct	22	17	28	Sept	30	10	39	Oct	7	04	12	Oct	14	18	06
Nov	21	06	33	Oct	29	17	10	Nov	5	16	46	Nov	13	14	38
Dec	20	18	25	Nov	28	00	37	Dec	5	08	01	Dec	13	11	41
				Dec	27	10	01								

Note: All times are in GMT.

ECLIPSES, 1987

1. An annular-total eclipse of the Sun on March 29. The path of the annular-total phase begins in southern South America, crosses the South Atlantic Ocean, enters Africa near the equator and ends in the Indian Ocean off the horn of Africa. The partial phase is visible from the southern half of South America, the South Atlantic Ocean, part of Antarctica, Africa except the extreme north-western part, the extreme south-eastern part of Europe, the south-western part of Asia and the western part of the Indian Ocean. The

eclipse begins at 10h 03m and ends at 15h 35m; the annular phase begins at 11h 05m and ends at 14h 33m; the total phase begins at 12h 04m and ends at 13h 24m. The maximum duration of the annular phase is 42s; the maximum duration of the total phase is 8s.

2. An annular eclipse of the Sun on September 23 is visible as a partial eclipse from Asia except for the north-eastern and south-western parts, Japan, the Philippine Islands, Indonesia except the south-western part, New Guinea, the north-eastern half of Australia, New Zealand except for the southern part of South Island, and the western part of the Pacific Ocean. The eclipse begins at 00h 15m and ends at 06h 08m; the annular phase begins at 01h 21m and ends at 05h 02m. The maximum duration of the annular phase is 3m 45s.

Source: H.M. Nautical Almanac Office. Reproduced with permission from data supplied to the Science and Engineering Council.

THE COMMONWEALTH

The British Commonwealth of Nations is a free association of independent member nations and their dependencies. The political status of the member nations listed below is clarified and given legal substance in the *Statute of Westminster* drawn up in 1931, before the Commonwealth was founded, by the United Kingdom, Australia and New Zealand.

MEMBERS OF THE COMMONWEALTH, 1986

Country	Capital	Status	Date of Joining	Population
1. Antigua and Barbuda	St. John's	M	1981	100,000 (est. 1980)
2. Australia	Canberra	M	1931	14,800,000 (est. 1981)
3. The Bahamas	Nassau	M	1973	300,000 (est. 1981)
4. Bangladesh	Dhaka	R	1972	92,800,000 (est. 1981)
5. Barbados	Bridgetown	M	1966	300,000 (est. 1981)
6. Belize	Belmopen	M	1981	144,857 (1980)
7. Botswana	Gaborone	R	1966	937,000 (est. 1981)
8. United Kingdom	London	M	1931	55,865,000 (1981)
9. Brunei	Bandar Seri Begawan	M*	1984	200,000 (est. 1981)
10. Canada	Ottawa	M	1931	24,100,000 (1981)
11. Cyprus	Nicosia	R	1961	600,000 (est. 1981)
12. Dominica	Roseau	R	1978	100,000 (est. 1981)
13. Fiji	Suva	M	1970	600,000 (est. 1981)
14. The Gambia	Banjul	R	1965	600,000 (est. 1981)
15. Ghana	Accra	R	1957	12,000,000 (est. 1981)
16. Grenada	St. George's	M	1974	100,000 (est. 1981)
17. Guyana	Georgetown	R	1966	800,000 (est. 1981)
18. India	New Delhi	R	1947	685,200,000 (est. 1981)
19. Jamaica	Kingston	M	1962	2,200,000 (est. 1981)
20. Kenya	Nairobi	R	1963	16,500,000 (est. 1981)
21. Kiribati	Tarawa	R	1979	59,000 (est. 1980)
22. Lesotho	Maseru	M*	1966	1,400,000 (est. 1981)
23. Malawi	Lilongwe	R	1964	6,200,000 (est. 1981)
24. Malaysia	Kuala Lumpur	M*	1957	14,744,000 (est. 1983)
25. Maldives	Male	R	1982(S)	200,000 (est. 1981)
26. Malta	Valletta	R	1964	300,000 (est. 1981)
27. Mauritius	Port Louis	M	1968	960,000 (est. 1983)
28. Nauru	Nauru	R	1968(S)	8,000 (est. 1980)
29. New Zealand	Wellington	M	1931	3,230,000 (est. 1983)
30. Nigeria	Lagos	R	1960	79,700,000 (est. 1981)
31. Papua New Guinea	Port Moresby	M	1975	3,300,000 (est. 1981)
32. St. Kitts and Nevis	Basseterre	M	1983	50,000 (est. 1980)
33. St. Lucia	Castries	M	1979	124,000 (est. 1980)
34. St. Vincent and the Grenadines	Kingstown	M	1979(S)	107,000 (est. 1980)
35. Seychelles	Victoria	R	1976	100,000 (est. 1981)
36. Sierra Leone	Freetown	R	1961	3,600,000 (est. 1981)
37. Singapore	Singapore	R	1965	2,500,000 (est. 1983)
38. Solomon Islands	Honiara	M	1978	200,000 (est. 1981)
39. Sri Lanka	Colombo	R	1948	15,300,000 (est. 1981)
40. Swaziland	Mbabane	M*	1968	600,000 (est. 1981)
41. Tanzania	Dar es Salaam	R	1961	19,200,000 (est. 1981)
42. Tonga	Nuku'Alofa	M*	1970	97,000 (est. 1980)
43. Trinidad and Tobago	Port of Spain	R	1962	1,200,000 (est. 1981)
44. Tuvalu	Funafuti	M	1978(S)	8,000 (est. 1980)
45. Uganda	Kampala	R	1962	14,100,000 (est. 1981)
46. Vanuatu	Port Vila	R	1980	117,000 (est. 1980)
47. Western Samoa	Apia	R	1970	157,000 (est. 1980)
48. Zambia	Lusaka	R	1964	6,000,000 (est. 1981)
49. Zimbabwe	Harare	R	1980	7,600,000 (est. 1981)

M = Monarchy under Queen Elizabeth, represented by Governor-General in all countries except Britain.
M* = Country with its own monarchy.
R = Republic.
(S) = Special Member.

Dependencies of Britain

Anguilla
Bermuda
British Antarctic Territory
British Indian Ocean Territory
British Virgin Isles
Cayman Islands
Falkland Islands and Dependencies
  (South Georgia, South Sandwich Islands)

Gibraltar
Hong Kong
Montserrat
Pitcairn Islands Group
St. Helena and Dependencies (Ascension,
  Tristan da Cunha)
Turks and Caicos Islands

Territories of Member Countries

Australia

Norfolk Island
Heard Island
McDonald Island
Cocos (Keeling) Islands
Christmas Island

New Zealand

Cook Islands
Niue
Tokelau Islands

The Channel Islands and the Isle of Man are dependent territories of the crown and do not form part of the United Kingdom. They have their own legislative assemblies and legal and administrative systems.

MEDICAL MATTERS

Here we give a brief summary of up-to-date medical knowledge, including some recent developments. It must not be allowed to replace your doctor, who should be consulted immediately if you are worried. An index ensures easy reference.

TABLE OF CONTENTS

MEDICAL MATTERS

PART I. INTRODUCTION.

In earlier editions of Pears the Medical Section took the form of a dictionary. More recently we have attempted something different: a small medical textbook for the layman. We have two reasons for this. Firstly, we feel that there are some readers who would like to have an overall picture of modern medicine and learn something of the progress in its various fields. They may like to read the section through as a continuous narrative. Secondly, there are always readers (probably the majority) who simply want to use the section as a ready-reference guide and to that end, rather than have an alphabetically arranged collection of snippets of information (which can be unsatisfying), we have grouped diseases under bodily 'systems'. We have made no attempt to produce a *dictionary* of symptoms because self-diagnosis is foolish. However, we have retained an alphabetical index (Part IV) for easy reference.

The plan in this section is to deal with diseases according to either (a) their cause (*e.g.*, the infections due to bacteria or viruses) or (b) the body system affected (*e.g.*, the nervous system, the heart and blood vessels, the lungs and so on). We cannot emphasise too strongly that this section is not intended as a substitute for seeking medical advice. It is one thing to satisfy curiosity or try and solve a puzzle about a disease, condition or collection of symptoms by "looking it up" but quite another to try and diagnose one's own disease, condition or collection of symptoms in the same way. In other words, this section is no substitute for a doctor and when you are ill, unless you know it to be a trivial, or relatively trivial, self-limiting condition, you must get medical advice. It is easy to listen to and believe unqualified opinions and to take and act on advice from unqualified persons. However, it is unwise to do so because although doctors are sometimes wrong (just as are lawyers, architects, judges and vetinary surgeons) the unqualified are much more likely to be wrong. So choose a doctor you can trust, and then believe what he tells you and carry out his advice. There is no use in complaining about the whole medical profession just because you are dissatisfied with your own G.P. If you are, you should sign on with another.

Of recent years there has been a veritable explosion in medical information for the layman through newspapers, magazines, books, radio and television (collectively referred to as 'the media') and among the more intelligently perceptive of doctors' patients there is now a much greater understanding of "how the body works" and how it can go wrong. Progress in treatment of some diseases has been rapid and, with the more ready access to specialist medical journals in which reports of drug and other trials appear which journalists now have, such news gets into a patient's hands very quickly, albeit often prematurely. The G.P. simply cannot keep up with advances in all fields and is therefore occasionally confronted by a patient who asks him why he cannot have this 'new drug' for his rheumatoid arthritis, for example, a new drug which may not at that stage even have reached the market place.

Modern Medicine

Much in medicine which is now taken for granted (that for the majority of diseases caused by identifiable organisms there is a specific drug treatment, for example) was undreamed of even as recently as 50 years ago. Progress in diagnosis, in preventive medicine and in treatment, both medical and surgical, has been so rapid as to be almost breathtaking. A doctor retiring from active practice in 1985 will have seen smallpox completely eradicated, poliomyelitis practically banished (at least from the U.K.), tuberculosis become curable, coronary artery disease relievable surgically and he will have witnessed the dramatic purge in the field of molecular biology and of the research by immunologists and geneticists into their efforts to control parasitic diseases like bilharzia, malaria and river blindness that affect millions of people in the Third World. One aspect of medicine and medicinal thinking still resistant to progress in understanding in spite of continued research is the effect of mind on body. Many of us still like to think that 'our bodies are just something we have got into, like cars, that ill-health is simply something that has "gone wrong" in one system or another and that therefore provided we find the appropriate expert (a chest physician, a gastro-enterologist or an ophthalmic surgeon, for example) to correct the fault, we will recover. Whereas that idea holds good for a broken leg, for instance, with many diseases the idea that mind can be totally separated from the "defective" part just isn't good enough. You cannot simply divorce your stomach, your bowels, your liver or your heart from your "self". They are all part of you and react, as you yourself react, to all the stresses and anxieties, fears and worries and the hundred and one other factors that are part and parcel of modern living. It is true that most of your stomach can be removed, your gall-bladder entirely so and with the aid of a dialysing machine or a transplant you can get by without your kidneys. As with your car, old or diseased parts can be repaired or totally replaced; even your heart, conventionally the very "seat" of the emotions.

Mens sana in corpore sano—a sound mind in a sound body. Your body and its many parts may be helped to normal function by modern medicines and surgery but, in general, it will only stay that way if you can rid yourself of all those emotional blemishes—anger, frustration, fear, worry and anxiety—which trouble you. Easier said than done, of course, but a good physician can help with good advice, with medicines if necessary—or simply with his ear. Emotional stress can not only inhibit healing of such things as duodenal or gastric ulcers but may even *cause* them. There are many diseases now recognised which are known to be associated with stress factors if not actually caused by them. Mainly these are diseases of the digestive tract or of the heart and blood vessels and you will find some of them discussed in the appropriate sections.

The state of the mind has more influence on bodily functions than you might think and recovery from many serious conditions can be slowed or hastened, depending on your state of mind. Every doctor has had experience of the patient who 'loses the will to live', a situation which is unfortunately commoner than the reverse.

A word about preventive medicine—or helping yourself to health. 'A great deal of nonsense has been talked about the healthy life; at one time we were told to take eighteen chews to each bite, to do deep breathing, to take plenty of exercise, to get lots of fresh air, to eat regularly (or to indulge in peculiar diets). But more recently eminent doctors have cast doubt on most of these fancies. Moderate exercise is necessary to health, but athletes who indulge in violent exercise have not always been noted for longevity. Fresh air is pleasant and stimulating, but, where actual breathing is concerned, it is no better than the air in most rooms. Certainly, one of the problems of our time is air pollution, but at present we are considering ordinary fresh air in comparison with the air indoors, and, in this case, the experts say there is little difference so far as health is concerned.

A balanced diet containing correct amounts of the basic food substances is essential, but there is no evidence that when, or at what intervals, you eat makes the slightest difference—unless you are a sufferer from stomach ulcer, in which case it is necessary that the intervals between meals should not be too long. The whole business of having meals at fixed intervals is nothing but a social convention, and in modern life obviously a matter of convenience. (*See* Diet, **P39**).

Sleep, too, is a necessity. But different people require vastly different amounts of sleep. Some manage on as little as three hours, others seem to believe that they need ten or more. The importance of the dream process is referred to in **Introduction to Psychology, Q15(1)**.

In a number of studies of men and women who lived to a ripe old age it was found that the only factors in common between them were that they had a good balanced diet of healthy food, that they had contented minds, and that they were interested in something which gave them an aim in life. They also came of long-lived families— for living a long and healthy life depends partly upon heredity.

So the main rules of health are:
(1) Don't abuse your body—*i.e.*, exercise it, feed it sensibly and in moderation and don't poison it with cigarette smoke (yours or anyone else's), with alcohol or with other drugs

(2) Think postively about health—make it a purpose for living

(3) Turn your thoughts away from those bodily functions (digestion, circulation, breathing and so on) which can look after themselves. Introspection leads to hypochondriasis, and

(4) Choose your parents for *their* longevity!

The Development of Medicines
A great surgeon, the first of the moderns, was Ambrose Paré, who died in 1590, and one of his best known sayings was: "I apply the dressing, but God heals the wound." He was quite right; for until about sixty years ago, or even less, all the physician could do was to put the patient in as favourable a state as possible to enable his body to cure itself. That is to say, there were hardly any specific drugs—drugs that had a direct effect on the disease. There was quinine, discovered by the Spaniards in America, which was specific for malaria, and there were iron (specific for anaemia) and digitalis (specific for certain types of heart disease), but otherwise nothing until the nineteenth century, when Paul Ehrlich discovered salvarsan, which is specific for syphilis. Ehrlich died in 1914, having conceived the brilliant idea of drugs; which he described as "magic bullets"—*i.e.*, drugs which, like bullets, would be aimed at the real cause of the disease. They would, that is to say, be specific.

Since then a large number of such drugs have been discovered. For example, the antibiotics, such as penicillin, discovered in 1928 by Fleming at St. Mary's Hospital, Paddington. Later, Florey and Chain in Oxford, helped in the war years by the vast resources of the American pharmaceutical industry, were able to make penicillin available to the public in sufficient quantities by new techniques of production. Penicillin is practically non-poisonous (although it is possible to become allergic to it, sometimes with serious results). It can kill some germs in a dilution of one part of penicillin to one hundred million parts of water; it is effective against streptococci, the cause of blood-poisoning, sepsis in wounds, and many other diseases; and also against the germs of anthrax, gonorrhœa, meningitis of some types, syphilis—a whole list of plagues which have troubled man for centuries. Blood-poisoning, whether from wounds or childbirth, used to be almost incurable—now the rate of cure is 80–90 per cent.; anthrax and gonorrhœa have an almost 100 per cent. rate of cure. In pneumonia the rate is about 90 per cent., and early syphilis can be cured in a week, instead of the previous two to three years.

But that was only the beginning. Other antibiotics—streptomycin, tetracycline, erythromycin, and many others—are helping to wipe out the terrible scourges of the human race, in particular, in the case of streptomycin, tuberculosis. The sulpha group of drugs—sulphadiazine, sulphadimidine, etc.—have also proved a great boon. Then there are the new drugs which have created a revolution in psychiatry—the tranquillisers which relieve anxiety, the drugs which clear up certain types of depression, and substances such as chlorpromazine which make it possible to nurse formerly violent patients in the wards of a general hospital. The antihistamine drugs help in allergies, anticoagulants are of value after heart attacks and levodopa mitigates some of the distressing features of Parkinson's Disease.

No drug, old or new, is completely safe—if we define "safe" as meaning having absolutely no potential for harm. The household aspirin, widely used in a variety of conditions for its analgesic (pain-relieving) and antipyretic (fever-reducing) qualities, can cause bleeding from the stomach and small intestine (**P22**). Phenacetin, at one time a component of compound codeine tablets but now withdrawn, can—with prolonged use—damage the kidney. Chloramphenicol, a powerful antibiotic effective in typhoid fever, typhus and whooping cough, can damage the blood-forming cells of the bone marrow producing an agranulocytosis which can be fatal.

Clearly, in any one case, the doctor must weigh up the advantages and disadvantages of this or that drug before prescribing. Minor, self-limiting illnesses do not require potent, potentially toxic remedies. Chloramphenicol is rarely justified in whooping cough, but would never be withheld from a patient with typhoid fever.

Man is a unique species. A new chemical compound promising in animal experiments, for example, as an anti-inflammatory agent, apparently safe when given, say, to mice in a dose 100 times that required to produce that anti-inflammatory effect may, over a long period of time in man, not only have no effect but make his hair fall out or perhaps cause retention of urine. Nevertheless, some animal species do react like man, or vice versa, and it is possible to make reasonably accurate extrapolations from animals to man in terms of drug effect. It is also possible to estimate the toxicity of a drug for man from its toxicity in certain animal species but the ultimate test, both of the effectiveness and the toxicity of a new drug, comes only when it is given to man.

Thalidomide was unique. In every animal test used throughout the drug industry at that time— it was introduced in the late 1950s—it had a clean bill of health. It was chemically related to other drugs which had been in use for a long time. Overdosage with other sedatives such as the barbiturates was common at that time, although less so now. Overdosage with thalidomide was unlikely to prove fatal. It was marketed in Europe and in Britain as a "safe sedative". The tragic results that followed its ingestion by women in the early weeks of pregnancy are now well known. Babies were born with severe deformities of limbs, internal organs or both. That effect could not have been foretold from any animal tests then in use. Since that date new drugs have been subjected to rigorous testing in various animal species to check the effect on foetal development as a statutory requirement, along with the older tests for toxicity which had always been undertaken by reputable drug companies.

The thalidomide disaster of the early 1960s led directly to the setting up of regulatory drug agencies in most countries of the world. In Britain the introduction and clinical testing of new compounds is controlled by the Medicines and Environmental Health Division of the Department of Health and Social Security, statutory machinery set up by the Medicines Act 1968, which followed the purely voluntary scheme of control under what was known as the Dunlop Committee after Sir Derrick Dunlop, its first chairman.

The development and introduction of new drugs is now very strictly controlled. No new drug can be marketed in Britain without the Medicines Commission being satisfied about its efficacy and its safety. We would need space in this edition almost the size of the complete Medical Section to describe fully the workings of the Commission and the limitations that the requirements of the Medicines Act inevitably place on the development and introduction of new remedies. The time from the initial synthesis of a novel compound likely to be of value to its eventual appearance in the pharmacy on prescription is now eight to 10 years. The cost is measured in millions of pounds because, for each successful drug, there will have been many thousands of unsuccessful ones.

Briefly, no new drug or modification of an old one can be sold, whether or not on prescription, unless it has been granted a product licence by the Department of Health and Social Security through its Medicines and Environmental Health Division. Many issues have to be passed to acquire that licence, from the granting of certificates to allow the drug to be tested initially in a limited way in patients in a strictly controlled manner by investigators approved by the Commission, to permission for extension of those trials at a later date to include larger numbers of patients or more investigators, to perhaps a "monitored release"—that is, to enable its use in, say, hospitals only—to the final release on the granting of a full product licence. Thus, the Medicines Commission has control at all stages.

Furthermore, all the stages are dependent on production of evidence relating to the safety and efficacy of the drug, evidence which may take the drug company months, sometimes years, to produce and which, of course, must be acceptable to the Commission. Trials may be stopped at any time, for example, if evidence of side effects of an undesirable nature come to light during clinical testing, or when evidence from some other similar compound indicates a likely risk in the use of the drug in question. Of course, "acceptable" means that the strict criteria which have been laid down by the specialist committees appointed to deal with all the various aspects of drug development, such as toxicology, adverse reactions and so forth, have been met. Experts serve on these committees which meet regularly, but the day-to-day running of the Medicines Commission is in the hands of full-time medically qualified personnel as well as pharmacists, pharmacologists and toxicologists. In addition, outside consultant opinion can be sought.

As well as all these rigid controls on development and testing in the early stages, there is also a scheme of surveillance for untoward side effects. These are the action, or actions, of a drug apart from its main one. Take the well-known side effect of drowsiness which occurs with certain antihistamine drugs: the main action, the one for which the drug is prescribed, is the mitigation of the effects of allergy, such as urticaria. Drowsiness would be an unwanted effect if the patient is not incapacitated and is able to do his usual job. On the other hand, some antihistamines have an appetite-stimulating effect which could, of course, be a useful attribute in certain situations or even allow the drug to be used solely for that purpose, the anti-allergic effect then being incidental.

An adverse reaction is a type of side effect which by definition, is unwanted and potentially harmful. The intestinal bleeding associated with aspirin, or the depressive effects of some of the earlier drugs used to lower blood pressure, such as reserpine and methyldopa, are good examples. When new drugs first become licensed for marketing and are prescribed by doctors on a gradually increasing scale it is important that adverse reactions such as those are reported. Every doctor in the National Health Service, whether in general practice or in hospital, has access to a stock of special record cards on which he can record in a standard way the details of any untoward reaction occurring in his patient during the prescribing of a new or existing drug, and which he has good reason to believe is associated with the taking of that drug. These record cards are posted to the DHSS which has a special unit to deal with them. A doctor noticing, for example that one of his patients developed, say, double vision during treatment with a new antidepressant could not assume in the absence of other firm evidence that the two events were necessarily connected. However, if 100 cards are received by the DHSS reporting the same kind of event, there is good circumstantial evidence that those events are likely to be connected with drug administration. This adverse reaction reporting system, although voluntary, is working well and is an effective "early warning system" for drug toxicity

We have come a long way since thalidomide, but have had to steer between the Scylla of stifling innovation in drug research by excessive control of development and the Charybdis of the free-for-all, profit-motivated bonanzas of the pre-thalidomide era. No system can be perfect, and it is fair to say that had it been necessary, for example, for aspirin, penicillin and streptomycin to be put through the system as we have set it up now they would probably never have reached the market and thence the patient.

Mention must of course be made of the surgical advances and progress in anaesthesia. Hardly a week goes by without operations being undertaken which seemed inconceivable even as short a time as 40 years ago. Transplantation and re-plantation (the re-attachment of severed limbs) are regularly reported; haemodialysis (the 'cleansing' of blood in patients with irreversible kidney disease) is now often undertaken in the patient's own home where, with appropriate adaptation and the modern kidney machine, he or she can run the procedure—single-handed in many instances—and still keep his or her job; and the laser beam is used to deal with detached retinas or to obliterate tiny, microscopic blood vessel 'bubbles' (aneurysms) in the back of the eye while the patient is conscious and cooperative. The list grows daily.

Social Medicine.

Medicine has passed through many phases from the time when disease was regarded as a punishment from the gods or a sign of devil possession to the present era, when increasingly there is a tendency to look on society as the patient. Indeed, one commonly hears doctors and sociologists nowadays talking about "the sick society."

The early primitive stage came to an end—at least in one part of the world—when in Greece, five centuries before Christ, Hippocrates and others began to teach that all diseases were due to natural causes. But after the first ray of hope the outlook began to deteriorate when, during the Middle and Dark Ages (that is, from the fall of the Roman Empire right up to the fifteenth century), there was a return to the belief in devil possession and supernatural causes.

Eighteenth-century medicine in Europe was materialistic, regarding the body as a machine. It was founded upon a sort of pseudo-science—although, of course, there were always individual exceptions, physicians such as Sydenham in England, who, avoiding all theories, based their work on observation of the patient. This mechanistic approach persisted right through the nineteenth century, but medicine became more and more truly scientific, and the century saw the most rapid advances in the field ever known until our own times: the discovery of germs by Pasteur, of antiseptics to combat them by Lister, of vaccination by Jenner and anaesthetics by the American Wells and the Scot Simpson. The use of the microscope by Virchow, who was a German, brought great advances in the understanding of disease and Ehrlich, another German, conceived, as we have already seen, the idea of "magic bullets" which would attack the germs at the root of a disease without harming the patient. But one of the greatest of all these great men is perhaps the least known. His name was Edwin Chadwick.

From the earliest period of recorded history human communities had been constantly ravaged by great plagues which swept over their lands year after year, killing untold millions. The Black Death of 1348-9 wiped out almost half the population of Europe. But, even in the first quarter of the nineteenth century in London, tens of thousands died from typhus, typhoid, and small-pox—and not only these, for periodically cholera would be brought into the country by travellers from abroad.

In the face of these terrible visitations the individual physician was helpless. He could not treat each one of the many sick even had he known how, and Chadwick's claim to fame rests on the fact that he was the first man to think in terms of *social* control of diseases, by so dealing with their causes that they were prevented from arising at all. In order to wipe out typhoid and cholera, he argued, we must ensure clean water supplies; for these diseases are caused by germs carried in polluted water. In order to attack typhus and plague, one must get rid of the lice which carry the germs of typhus and the rat-fleas which carry the germs of plague (including, of course, the rats, which, in turn, carry the fleas).

Chadwick was born in a Lancashire farmhouse where the children were washed every day all over, and he ruthlessly drove an obsession with cleanliness into the heads of his countrymen until, later in the century, it was possible for the German philosopher Treitschke to tell his class in Berlin: "The English think soap is civilisation." Although this remark was meant cynically, there is little doubt that soap, if it is not civilisation in itself, has played a greater part in making civilisation possible than many more elaborate remedies. A population riddled with chronic infectious illness has neither the time nor the energy to apply to the arts or sciences, and soap did a great deal to reduce infection.

One of the first Public Health measures was introduced by Chadwick and others when they brought in legislation to purify the water supply of London. Previously, the citizens had used water from the Thames (they still do, but only after it has been filtered and sterilised at the waterworks!), and from filthy, refuse-laden ponds and springs. Later, Chadwick helped to found the Poor Law Commission, and produced a Report in 1842, the principal suggestions of which were: a municipal water supply for all towns; scientific drainage both in town and country; and an independent health service with large powers for dealing with those who endangered the lives of others by polluting water or causing nuisances. He also proposed a national service for interment of the dead; for in those days bodies often re-mained for days in the overcrowded homes of the poor without burial.

What has the twentieth century contributed to the concept of social health? Well, of course, there has been a great deal of legislation along the lines initiated by Chadwick to control disease, and a great many other measures have been introduced concerned with the idea of positive health—not merely preventing bad health, but trying to bring about the highest possible state of good health.

Orange juice, milk, and good meals for school-children brought about a transformation in child health which became apparent to the least observant. And the National Health service is in the direct line of descent from early nineteenth-century legislation.

But in future years it is probable that the main achievement of the twentieth century will prove to be its extension of the term "social health" to cover every aspect of community life, not only in such subjects as bodily health and its control of social means, but also such problems as mental illness, crime, delinquency, drug addiction, and so on. What we are now asking ourselves is: how far are these problems produced by society itself, and if this is the case, how far can we go in preventing them by social means?

Community medicine takes the view that these problems can never be dealt with solely by moral-ising and retribution, but only by dispassionately analysing causes and dealing with them. In this century we have developed a social con-science. Not always, it is true, a very well-informed social conscience, but at least this is a good beginning. There are organisations for dealing scientifically with delinquency, for dealing with problem children, for spreading knowledge about cancer in order to show people that it can be successfully treated if taken in time. We can well say with John Donne, who died in 1631, that "no man is an island . . . every man's death diminisheth me; for I am involved in mankind." This is the attitude of twentieth-century com-munity medicine.

Summary. Perhaps we can sum up our pro-gress in the past century and a half more dramatically in terms of hard facts.

Before that time a surgical operation was never undertaken except under the gravest circum-stances. There were no anaesthetics and no anti-septics, and the operation was carried out by a surgeon in a filthy tail-coat, stained with the con-gealed blood of countless operations (indeed the surgeons of that time took pride in the dirty condi-tion of their coats as showing how much experience they had previously had). Germs and the part they play in producing disease were unknown, and Paul Ehrlich had not yet been born, so there were no "magic bullets" to attack syphilis, or sera for diphtheria and other diseases. The mentally ill were simply locked up with little treatment and subjected to such indignities as the strait-jacket and the padded cell; now they are given treatment which becomes more effective each year, the padded cell and strait-jacket have gone, and in very few hospitals are the ward doors locked.

In the earlier years of this century you would very likely have died if you had developed pneumonia, "childbed fever" after the birth of a child, men-ingitis, dysentery, typhoid, or tuberculosis. With such infections as blood-poisoning you would have had practically no chance at all. Today, the sulpha drugs and the antibiotics have changed all that. Syphilis and gonorrhoea were lifelong tragedies both to the patient and his family, but now they, too, can be conquered. With scientific research and its application proceeding at a brisk pace many diseases are now being brought under control.

The National Health Service has brought the possibility of good treatment equally to all, and it is up to us to see that all these facilities are used to the full by all who need them.

PART II. DISEASES ARRANGED BY CAUSE OR BODY SYSTEM AFFECTED

THE INFECTIOUS DISEASES.
INTRODUCTION.

INFECTIOUS diseases are those which are caused by an invasion of the body by organisms from outside (the word "organism" simply means other living things, and we are using this word because, as will be seen later, it is not only what are known as

"germs" which can cause infection). We know, too, that what is generally typical about this group is: (*a*) that the disease can be passed on from one person to another, and (*b*) that it is usually accompanied by a raised temperature or fever. Now (*a*), of course, is always true, because the definition of an infectious disease is one that can be passed on to others, but (*b*) is not always true, because a few infections produce little or no temperature, and also because it is possible to have a raised temperature (again in only a few cases) without any infection. For example, certain types of brain injury, tumour, or haemorrhage can produce a raised—or lowered—temperature, and so can the injection of some foreign substance such as milk into the muscles. This is known as "protein shock," and was at one time used in the treatment of certain illnesses. Finally, solutions of dead germs, such as the antityphoid vaccine given to protect troops during the War, may lead when injected to very high temperatures. But, by and large, we are entitled to suppose that the patient with a raised temperature is probably suffering from an infection.

Types of Infection.

As we have seen, it is not only germs which cause infections—so from now on we shall give germs their proper name of "bacteria." Here is a list of the chief offenders which are liable to attack our bodies: bacteria, spirochaetes, viruses, fungi, amoebae, worms and other parasites. Of these, bacteria and viruses are by far the most important, but let us look at them all more closely.

Bacteria are tiny living things which can be seen only under a fairly powerful microscope. Some are grouped like bunches of grapes (staphylococci) or in strings or chains (streptococci). They are given these names because "staphylos" is the Greek word for a bunch of grapes, and "streptos" means a chain. Yet others are comma-shaped (such as the cholera vibrio), or shaped like a drumstick—a rod with a small knob at the end (the tetanus bacillus, which causes lockjaw).

It would be a mistake to think that all bacteria are harmful; for without some species we could not survive for long. Bacteriologists divide them according to their behaviour in the human body into three groups: saprophytic, parasitic or pathogenic, and symbiotic. The *saprophytic* organisms are the bacteria normally found in the skin, mouth, and intestines; they do us neither harm nor good. The *parasitic*, or as they are more usually called, pathogenic (*i.e.*, disease-producing) organisms, are the harmful ones with which we are naturally more concerned. Lastly, there are the *symbiotic* organisms, which, whilst taking something from the body, give something in return. For example, cattle would not be able to digest the cellulose of the grass they eat were it not for helpful bacteria in the lower parts of the intestines, and there are certain bacteria in the large intestine of man which produce vitamins.

Bacteria have two peculiar characteristics: each reproduces by splitting into two separate individuals as often as every twenty minutes in favourable circumstances like an open wound. If no bacterium were destroyed, one individual could produce a mass of bacteria larger than the whole world in a matter of a few weeks (since each of the offspring also divides into two, which in turn divide again—the progression goes: one gives birth to two, these two to four, the four to eight, eight to sixteen, sixteen to thirty-two, and so on—you will see, if you work it out, that in a short period the figure becomes astronomical). Fortunately, many bacteria have accidents, so for the present the world is safe! The other curious thing about bacteria is that, barring accidents, they are potentially immortal. Under ideal conditions in which no bacteria were killed, none would die; for a bacterium there is no death from old age, no corpse except when it is actively destroyed. It simply goes on dividing, dividing, and subdividing for ever.

How, then, are bacteria destroyed? Briefly, the answer is that most are destroyed by the natural defences of the body of whatever host they are preying on; others are destroyed by antiseptics and the new drugs; and many are destroyed when they are excreted from the body in the sputum or through the bowels and land in places where they are dried up and cannot survive —although some bacteria in such circumstances can form what are called "spores," rather like

the seed of plants, so making it possible for them to survive in a state of suspended animation for months on end until picked up accidentally by another unfortunate host. Finally, bacteria, in addition to all these possibilities, face another danger: they may themselves develop disease. This disease is caused by even more minute organisms known as bacteriophages (viruses which affect bacteria), discovered by F. W. Twort in 1915. Attack by bacteriophage causes whole groups of bacteria (known as "colonies") to disintegrate and become harmless.

Although bacteriophage has been used in the treatment of some diseases in human beings, this method has now been largely given up, since the new drugs are infinitely more effective.

Spirochaetes. Spirochaetes, like bacteria, are minute organisms, but differ in being shaped somewhat like a corkscrew and in being able to move (which many bacteria cannot do). Their progress is produced by a sideways wriggling motion. The two main diseases caused by spirochaetes are syphilis and spirochaetal jaundice. Spirochaetal jaundice is carried by rats, and is common in those who work in mines. It is now rare in Britain, but still occurs in Japan, Egypt, and Malaysia; the infection is passed through the skin where the excreta of infected rats mingles with water on damp ground in the mine where miners kneel. Infection may also occur through eating infected food.

Viruses. Unlike bacteria, viruses are too small to be seen under an ordinary microscope. They can, however, be photographed in some cases under an electron microscope, which uses a magnetic field instead of a glass lens and a stream of electrons in place of a beam of light. Viruses cause such diseases as typhus, measles, mumps, poliomyelitis, smallpox, and chickenpox—not to mention such plant and animal diseases as tobacco mosaic disease and foot-and-mouth disease, which often have serious economic consequences. Other virus diseases are psittacosis (an infection of parrots and similar birds which can be transmitted to Man), swine fever in pigs, influenza in Man, and myxomatosis in rabbits. They also cause, it is believed, the common cold.

The main characteristics of viruses are, first, that they can only grow in living cells—unlike bacteria, which readily grow in the laboratory on plates containing a jelly made from meat, broth, gelatin, milk, and other delicacies. The scientist, therefore, must keep them in portions of living tissue kept alive outside the body. Secondly, they are so small that they pass through the pores of the finest filter. Thirdly, a first attack usually produces immunity for life. Second attacks of the common virus diseases mentioned above are very rare; but unfortunately, this rule does not apply to influenza or the common cold. Fourthly, there is reason to believe that viruses represent an extraordinary intermediate stage between the living and non-living; they can, for instance, be produced in crystalline form and yet are just as dangerous when "thawed out." Lastly, the virus diseases have proved for the most part to be little affected by the new antibiotics and other drugs, although vaccination in smallpox and the injection of sera from infected patients in other infections may give immunity for longer or shorter periods.

The two great practical problems that doctors face with viruses are: (i) many viruses are unknown because of the difficulty of growing them outside the body in suitable tissue culture. They cannot therefore be conveniently identified in specimens from the patient, as bacteria can; and (ii) they are unaffected by antibiotics like penicillin. It has been a great step forward to grow viruses artificially in tissue culture, in which they are identified indirectly by the effects they have on the cultural *cells*. But since we do not know exactly how to grow some viruses (like those of infective hepatitis) they have still not been seen.

When we recover from a viral illness like chickenpox, we probably do so by producing virus-killing substances inside our own cells. Scientists are currently searching for these substances in case they can be used, like penicillin, to cure viral disease.

Fungi. Some infections are caused by fungi—that is to say organisms belonging to the same group as moulds, mushrooms, and toadstools. Penicillin and some other antibiotics are produced from moulds, so, as in the case of bacteria, some fungi are helpful; they even help to destroy each other, as bacteria do. For example actinomyces, which can cause infection of the jaw and other tissues, is destroyed by penicillin.

Most fungal infections are trivial and limited to the skin. But, although trivial, they can be unsightly and uncomfortable. Ringworm of the scalp, dhobie itch—an infection of the groin spread by infected underclothing—and so-called "athlete's foot" are caused by a fungus.

Amoebae. Amoebae are small, single-cell organisms, the largest of which (a harmless type found in stagnant ponds in Britain and elsewhere) is just visible to the naked eye. It is about the size of the head of a pin. Amoebae move, in the species which are capable of moving, by pushing forward a part of the cell in the appropriate direction and causing the rest to flow into the advancing portion. Like bacteria, they reproduce by dividing into halves, each of which becomes a new amoeba.

The main human disease caused by amoebae is amoebic dysentery (not to be confused with bacillary dysentery).

Parasites. These may live on the skin like lice (which can carry typhus) or fleas (carriers of plague) or the parasites of scabies which burrow into the skin, or they may live part of their time in the blood or other tissues, like malaria. They often have complicated life-cycles involving other hosts (like mosquitoes) at certain stages of development.

Worms. Worms are intestinal parasites, but the only common types found in Britain are threadworms, the tiny thread-like worms which cause irritability and itching in the skin of children, less often in adults; round-worms, somewhat resembling the ordinary garden earthworm, which seldom lead to symptoms; and tapeworms, which may reach a length of 3 or even 6 m. Many parasitic worms (like parasites elsewhere) lead a double life—they spend part of their life in the human intestine and the other part in the muscles of another animal. The tapeworm, for example, whilst in the human intestine, lays eggs which pass out of the body in the excreta, and are then swallowed by pigs, especially in those parts of the world where human excreta are used as manure in the fields. In the pig, the eggs form cysts in the muscles—meat infected in this way is known as "measly pork"—and when, in turn, the meat is eaten by man, the process in the intestine begins all over again.

Less common types, from our point of view, are the Russian tape-worm (which, as befits a Russian, grows to nearly 9 m!); this type is spread by caviare or undercooked infected fish. The small, leaf-shaped liver fluke lays eggs which are passed into canals or pools in tropical countries in the urine of infected people, hatch out and enter a water snail, and finally leave the snail in the form of small parasites which pierce the skin of bathers, whence they pass to the liver and subsequently the bladder and rectum. This is a serious condition, as is also filariasis (another tropical disease), for which, unlike bilharzia—caused by the liver fluke—no cure is known. The tropical disease known as loa-loa is caused by a variety of filaria.

How the Infection is Spread.

Infection is spread in many ways, some of which have already been mentioned. In the common fevers found in Europe and elsewhere one of the most frequent ways is by *droplet infection*—that is to say, by minute drops carrying the germs which are coughed or sneezed into the air by someone already suffering from the disease. Such droplets can be projected into the air for 3m or more, and when breathed in by someone within range infection may result. Next commonest

mode of spread is perhaps by *infected food, water,* and the dirty hands of those who prepare food: cholera, dysentery, food-poisoning, and typhoid are spread in this way. Spread by *direct contact* is found in the venereal diseases (usually, but not always, spread by sexual intercourse with someone who already has the disease), and, of course, lice, fleas, and other parasites, including the scabies mite, are spread by contact with the infested individual—or sometimes with his clothes or bed linen. Spread through an *intermediary host,* whether it be lice, fleas, or mosquitoes carrying infection, or the various means adopted by worms, has already been described above, so no more need be said. Lastly, the infection may result from *bacteria already within the body;* for example, the bacillus coli which lives in the large intestine is there harmless, but if it gets into the bladder or the ureters (the tubes leading from kidney to bladder) a quite unpleasant result may follow in the form of cystitis or pyelitis.

How the Body Deals with Infection.

The body has many mechanisms of defence against intruders, but suffice it to say here that there are two main ones. First, substances known as antibodies and antitoxins are produced in the blood—the antitoxins to neutralise the poisons produced by the invaders, the antibodies to render them helpless, for example, by causing them to clump together so that they can more easily be dealt with by the second defence mechanism. This second mechanism is provided by the white cells in the blood, some of which (the phagocytes) act like amoebae and swallow up and destroy the germs. Antibodies and antitoxins can be transferred from one individual to another and are used in medicine both to prevent infection and to cure it. This is known as immunisation, and can be active or passive. Active immunisation is produced by injecting either a solution of dead bacteria, as in the case of antityphoid injections, or by injecting live, but weakened, strains of the organism, as in the case of smallpox vaccination. In both cases the body is stimulated to produce its own immune substances. Passive immunisation is used either for people who have been in recent contact with infection or who are already ill, and in this case the antitoxins produced in another person who has had the illness are injected in the form of serum—*i.e.,* the liquid part of the blood without the blood cells. All these natural defences are inefficient in the ill, the underfed, the very young, and the very old.

The mechanisms of the response of the body to infection is the broad field of study of the immunologist.

Antiseptics

The earliest antiseptic was carbolic acid, used by Lister in his operating-theatre in the form of a fine spray directed throughout the operation on the wound, or sometimes in the form of steam from a kettle containing a solution of carbolic. But carbolic is dangerous, and since Lister's time many more useful antiseptics have been discovered. Acriflavine, thymol, and other old favourites have been discarded too. The various forms of carbolic are still used to disinfect drains, but, to tell the truth, the use of antiseptics nowadays is very limited. In surgery the *antiseptic* method has given way to the *aseptic* method—instead of fighting sepsis we see to it that no possibility of sepsis is present before operating; all instruments, the surgeons' and nurses' hands, the skin, are sterilised—the instruments by boiling, the dressings by dry heat, the hands by soap and water, and almost the only antiseptic used is to clean the patient's skin in the area to be operated on.

Antiseptics are used as first-aid treatment for cuts and wounds, but should be applied only once as a general rule—that is, when the wound is first received. The trouble with antiseptics is that as well as killing germs they also kill the surrounding tissues, which antibiotics never do.

Antiseptic sprays to purify the air of a room or to destroy germs lurking in the dust on the sick-room floor—or any other floor—are practically useless. To quote the *British Medical Journal*: "There is no good scientific evidence that any of the chemical air-disinfectants can control the spread of infection in places such as schools, offices, or cinemas. Nor is there any good evidence that any substantial effect on the spread of illness can be obtained by disinfection of dust."

Neither is there any good reason to believe that mouth-washes and gargles have any effect other than making the mouth feel fresher and (temporarily) removing mouth odour—by covering it up with the scent of the antiseptic. Mouth-washes are in contact with the bacteria for far too short a time to have any damaging result, and, in the case of tonsillitis and other diseases, all the important bacteria are hidden far out of any danger from gargles.

Antibiotics.

Some antibiotics—penicillin, streptomycin, erythromycin and so on—have already been mentioned (*see* **P4**). In recent years many others have been introduced—ampicillin, gentamycin, cephalexin. Indiscriminate use of these drugs (*e.g.* for trivial complaints) has led to problems, the most important being the development of resistance by previously sensitive organisms. It is not always convenient or possible to be able to identify the particular germ responsible for an infection and determine to which drug it is sensitive, but if there is an initial clinical response, it can be assumed that the "right" drug has been used. It is important to have a full course of treatment—which usually means ten days minimum.

Other problems are hypersensitivity (allergic) reactions which can take many forms. Once hypersensitivity to one of the antibiotics has been identified (penicillin hypersensitivity is not rare) the patient must be made aware of this, and so protect himself from unwitting prescribing by another doctor. Hospital and GP records are clearly marked in such instances but it is very important that the patient himself knows.

Antibiotics are only available on prescription, at least in the U.K., but medicine cupboards are full of them, accumulated from unfinished courses. Self-prescribing is tempting but ill-advised; antibiotics must always be given under medical supervision. Side effects are common and some are dangerous. Repeated use may lead to rapid overgrowth of fungi *e.g.* thrush (Candida albicans) normally present in harmless numbers in the alimentary tract with serious, sometimes fatal results.

General Treatment of Fevers.

Fevers are ordinarily heralded in by a rise in temperature which is noticeable either by a flushed face or by alternate sensations of heat and cold. A patient with a high temperature may have shivering attacks known as "rigors." Tell the doctor.

A high temperature does not necessarily (especially in a child) mean that the trouble is serious but the lay person should always treat it as such and certainly call a doctor if the patient is a child or an elderly person.

Even the trained physician finds it difficult to tell one fever from another in the early days; for most of the common fevers begin in more or less the same way. It is only when a rash or some other more definite sign becomes evident that a certain diagnosis can be made, and these may not show themselves until the patient has been feeling "run-down" and fevered for some days. Incidentally, although a clinical thermometer is a very useful thing when properly used, many a doctor must feel that, in unskilled hands, it is a menace. The "fussy" type of mother who is constantly taking her child's temperature whenever it looks in the slightest degree different from usual (probably it is simply feeling justifiably bored with its parents), not only causes anxiety to herself but also gives the habit of anxiety to her child. The child is made to feel that the world is a dangerous place, full of germs and all sorts of causes for fear—as indeed it is, but one needs a sense of proportion, and other dangers which we think much less about are at least as frightening and twice as deadly as most germs. Whatever you do, don't get the thermometer habit; your

child, so far as fevers are concerned, is a good deal tougher than you.

Briefly, then, the way to treat a fever in the early stages before the doctor comes, and before one knows exactly what is wrong, is as follows:

(1) Put the patient to bed.

(2) Give little, and easily digested, food; if the patient wants none, give none.

(3) Give plenty to drink—the proprietary preparations containing lemonade and glucose are excellent, but water, weak tea with sugar, or home-made lemonade with squeezed-out lemon juice and sugar, whichever the patient likes best, are at least as good.

(4) Aspirin is useful to relieve headache or other pains and will reduce fever for two or three hours. But it will cure nothing. The patient will be more comfortable, but his illness will not be cured by aspirin except in certain very special cases. Soluble aspirin is best. Do not have special children's aspirins in the house. They are often nicely flavoured, the children are tempted to eat them like sweets, and there have been serious cases of poisoning. For small children, use suitably small quantities of ordinary adult soluble aspirin, having checked the dose with your doctor. Other methods of cooling seriously fevered patients such as bathing, tepid sponging, etc., are strictly for the doctor to prescribe. A patient as hot as that should be in a doctor's hands anyway.

THE INFECTIOUS FEVERS.

The remarks made above apply to the management of *any* fever, and we are now going to discuss particular infectious diseases, beginning with the common childhood fevers, then passing on to less common ones, tropical diseases, and worm and parasitic infestations.

The common infectious fevers are caused by bacteria or viruses, and it is useful to know the meaning of the following terms: *incubation period* is the time which elapses between being infected and developing symptoms; *prodromal period* is the time which elapses between the end of the incubation period and the appearance of a rash; *quarantine period*, the maximum time during which a person who has been in contact with the infection may develop the disease—it is usually two days more than the incubation period; *isolation period* the time a patient is supposed to be isolated.

Views regarding the common infectious fevers have changed a good deal in recent years. Disinfection of rooms is now regarded as almost useless, and more cases are treated at home. Quarantine in the case of the common fevers is thought by a good many doctors to be a waste of time, since all it can do is to postpone infection from early childhood to early adult life, when it is likely to be more serious. For it is a characteristic of these fevers that they affect the adult much more violently than they do the child. However, on this, and all other points, you will have to be guided by the opinion of your family doctor.

Virus Diseases.

First, we shall take the common virus diseases, measles, chickenpox, and rubella or German measles, then the other virus diseases, mumps, infective hepatitis, viral pneumonia, and some less common conditions which do not always produce a typical rash as in the case of the first three.

In nearly all of these fevers there is a long incubation period, and one infection gives immunity for life.

Measles. The incubation period is 10–11 days. The first sign is the appearance of symptoms rather like a severe cold. The eyes become red, and exposure to light is unpleasant, the nose runs, the throat becomes inflamed, and a dry, harsh cough develops. There may be headache and the temperature rises to 39°C or more. Usually the patient is a child, and especially typical is the development of so-called Koplik's spots, which are small, bluish-white, raised spots seen on the inside of the cheek at the back of the mouth. The rash begins on the fourth day of the prodromal period, i.e., 14 days after the initial infection. It shows on the forehead and behind the ears, spreading within a day downwards over the whole body; in another two days it starts to disappear, but often leaves behind a sort of brownish staining which may last for one to two weeks.

Measles can be serious, especially in very young children because of its complications, such as bronchopneumonia and infection of the ear, which can now be treated with antibiotics. These drugs have no effect on the measles virus, but only on the secondarily invading bacteria which have invaded the lungs and ear during the illness. The illness can be attenuated or lessened by injection of antibodies (gamma globulin) from an immune adult, and this is often worth while in the very young. Effective vaccination is now available.

Rubella or German Measles. Incubation period 14–19 days. A mild fever, similar to measles except that the rash is usually the first sign that anything is wrong, and the temperature is rarely above 38°C. The eyes may be pink, and there are enlarged glands at the back of the neck. The rash disappears completely in thirty-six hours. There are no complications.

German measles, in itself, is harmless, but if a woman gets the disease in the early months of pregnancy malformations in the child may appear at birth. Vaccination is advised if a girl has not contracted the disease by the time she reaches puberty. There is no special treatment except the general rules for fevers given above.

Chickenpox. Incubation period 14–15 days, but may be more variable. In children chickenpox is a mild fever which begins with the appearance of tiny blisters on the chest and back. These later spread outwards to the legs, arms and face, and cause itching. Treatment is the general one for fevers already described. Calamine lotion or dusting powder will be helpful for the irritation, and the child's nails should be cut short to prevent scratching and infection of the spots. Whereas children are usually little bothered by chickenpox, young adults may be much more drastically affected—a temperature of 40°C is not uncommon, and then there may be severe headache.

Mumps. Incubation period 17–18 days. Everyone knows the typical appearance of the patient with mumps—the swelling in the salivary glands in front of the ears which makes the face look full. This causes pain later on, and it may be difficult to open the mouth. Temperature is not usually high (about 38°C). Although uncomfortable, mumps is rarely dangerous, but orchitis—swelling of the testicles—is sometimes a complication. Fluid diet should be given if eating is painful, with mouth-washes, and rest in bed.

Infective Hepatitis. "Hepatitis" means inflammation of the liver, and infective hepatitis, which is much the commonest cause of jaundice in young adults, is a viral infection of the liver. The main symptoms are fever, followed by jaundice, which is first noticed in the whites of the eyes as yellow staining, then in the skin. The urine becomes coloured also, and this is most easily noticed if, on shaking in a bottle, the froth shows coloration. If the froth remains white, no jaundice is present. Treatment is a matter for the doctor, but great care should be taken, both by the patient and those in contact with him, to wash the hands thoroughly after urinating or defaecating, after handling utensils from the sickroom, and both before and after eating; for the disease is very infectious.

Viral Pneumonia. Pneumonia is usually caused by bacteria, and when we speak of pneumonia, that is the type we ordinarily refer to. Viral pneumonia is known by doctors as "pneumonitis," and is believed to be closely related to influenza. There is no specific treatment so far, and since diagnosis is a specialist matter little more need be said except that the symptoms in general resemble those of ordinary pneumonia. Psittacosis, another virus disease, can also lead to pneumonia, and although there is no specific treatment for virus infections of the lungs, it is always worth while trying the antibiotics or sulpha drugs in view of the possibility that the lung condition may be caused by a secondary invasion of bacteria.

Influenza. While serious epidemics of influenza take the form of a very dramatic and often fatal disease—for example, the epidemic of "Spanish 'flu" which followed the First World War killed more people than the actual fighting—the milder type more usually seen is difficult to distinguish from the common cold. In fact, many people who complain of "a dose of the 'flu" are suffering from simple colds.

However, a sudden onset, aching in the muscles of the back and legs, and redness of the eyes, would suggest influenza, and especially typical is the depression and weakness which follow influenza but not a cold. The measures suggested above for the general treatment of fever should be applied; but the depression and weakness which follow influenza may need special treatment by the doctor.

Colds. Although everyone thinks he, or she, knows what a "cold" is, the issue is not so simple; for the symptoms of fever, running nose, and a run-down, "headachy" feeling are found in many illnesses. They may be observed, as we have seen, in the early stages of measles before the arrival of the rash, or in a number of other fevers, such as whooping cough. Mild attacks of influenza (see above) may resemble the common cold, and blocking of the nose with discharge and fever may be due to sinusitis—although here there is usually pain above, between, or below the eyes. Colds can be caused by any one of thirty different viruses known as "rhinoviruses" as well as by others which cause influenza, or infect glands (adenoviruses). This is why a single cold does not confer immunity on the sufferer. It is probable that you will not catch a cold from the same virus, at least for the rest of the year, but there are all those others waiting to infect you with other colds in buses, tubes, and other crowded places. Like all infections, do not forget that the best way to avoid them is to keep generally well, and in a good nutritional state. Do not spend money on injections or other vaccines. They do not work, probably because of the multiplicity of viruses involved. It is unlikely that adding vitamins or mineral supplements to normal diet will do any good at all provided you are eating sensibly. The vogue for prophylactic or therapeutic treatment of colds with massive doses of vitamin C has recently received much attention from scientists attempting, with little success, to prove the effect by controlled clinical trial and to find a rational basis for its use.

Poliomyelitis

Polio, or infantile paralysis as it used to be known, is caused by a virus which has a particular affinity for the nerve cells of the spinal cord and which results in paralysis of those muscles under the control of the particular group of cells infected. Rarely, the infection is widespread in the nerve tissue causing paralysis of muscles of swallowing and respiration as well as those of the trunk and limbs. The usual pattern is for a single muscle group to be affected, for example, the muscles controlling the movements of the arm at the shoulder. Such paralysis may be transient with complete recovery, partial with some residual weakness, or total, leaving a "flail limb" which is wasted and powerless.

At one time in this country epidemics of poliomyelitis were common, mainly affecting children and young adults. There is no doubt that mild forms of the disease were always occurring in very young children, forms never diagnosed as such but conferring a natural immunity in later life.

In common with other infections, poliomyelitis begins with a mild or moderate pyrexia, with a sore throat, headache, nausea and perhaps actual vomiting, some five to 10 days after contact with the virus. There may be rigidity of the neck muscles. Paralysis, if it occurs, will become apparent about the second or third day of illness. This stage may last two or three weeks, by which time the temperature will have subsided and the paralysis started to improve. There is no specific treatment and medical care is confined to symptomatic relief. Difficulty with swallowing and breathing calls for special nursing measures. In severe cases, artificial means of maintaining respiration may have to be continued for months, or for the rest of the patient's life. Many severely paralysed polio victims of the post-war epidemics —the self-styled "responauts"—depend for their lives on artificial respirators ("iron lungs").

With the development of the oral vaccine early in the 1960s, and its introduction into the immunisation schedule in this country, the disease has now virtually disappeared from Great Britain.

Smallpox. In previous editions we stated that "since the introduction of vaccination it (smallpox) is comparatively rare in industrialised countries." In the 88th edition we reported that smallpox (*variola major*) had now been eradicated throughout the world. The less serious form of the disease, *variola minor*, is still found in some parts of Africa, but all the signs are that it, too, will soon be eradicated. The last case of *variola major* occurred in Bangladesh in 1975. With the disappearance of the disease vaccination will become unnecessary; however, the World Health Organisation is planning to store vaccine (which can be done almost indefinitely at a temperature of $-20°C$) in sufficient quantities to vaccinate many millions of people should the need ever arise again. We made no excuse therefore for leaving out of that edition of *Pears*, for the first time in its long history, the detailed description of the disease.

Glandular Fever. Sometimes called infectious mononucleosis, since one of its features is an increase in a certain type of white cell—the monocyte—and a change in its microscopic characteristics. It is caused by a virus (the Epstein-Barr), predominantly affects young children and adults and although often taking a protracted course, it is not in itself a serious infection. The main symptoms are fever, enlargement of lymph glands in the neck and a sore throat. A transient body rash may be seen occasionally, particularly during or after the treatment of the sore throat with penicillin or one of its synthetic cousins such as ampicillin. Diagnosis without laboratory tests on the blood (the Paul-Bunnel test) may not be easy although the combination of sore throat, swollen neck glands and a rash is highly suspicious. The disease is self-limiting and there is no treatment.

Typhus. This disease used to be known as "jail fever," because it was frequent in prisons; but overcrowding, poverty, and bad hygienic surroundings anywhere are suitable conditions for epidemics of typhus. Improved conditions in industrialised countries have made it unusual, since typhus is carried from one person to another by infected body lice. It is due to the organism *Rickettsia prowazekii*, which displays both bacterial and viral characteristics.

Typhus comes on suddenly with a rise in temperature to about $39°C$, but within four days it may be as high as $42°C$. There may, or may not, be a rash at this time, and in the second week, when the temperature is at its highest, there is delirium, weakness, and a feeble pulse. The typical typhus rash appears about the fifth day as reddish blotches on the chest, abdomen, and wrists.

Typhus is, needless to say, very serious but responds to modern antibiotics. Preventive measures are directed towards eradicating lice.

Rabies. Finally, we shall deal very briefly with a number of less common virus diseases, beginning, as is appropriate, with *hydrophobia* or *rabies*, since it was in this infection that the great French scientist Louis Pasteur (1822–95) showed the possibility of prevention by vaccination. Unlike Jenner, with his ready-made cowpox virus, which is the virus of smallpox weakened by natural passage through cows, Pasteur had to weaken the rabies virus by passing it through rabbits. The rabbits were infected, and after death the spinal cord was dried and powdered, a solution passed through another rabbit, and so on until the virus was sufficiently weakened.

Rabies is spread by the bite of infected animals, usually dogs, cats, or wolves, who are driven mad by the disease; in Trinidad, however, it has been spread by vampire bats. Those who are bitten usually show no symptoms for six weeks or more, but sooner or later convulsions and delirium arise, which within four to five days are fatal.

There is no cure once the symptoms have developed, but antirabies serum, followed by antirabies innoculation as soon as possible, prevents illness in the majority of cases. Dogs should be muzzled in areas where the disease is common, but quarantining imported dogs has made the infection almost unknown here.

Psittacosis. This is another virus disease which is of interest mainly in that it is spread by birds of the parrot group, such as parrots, lovebirds, macaws, and the rest. It occasionally occurs here in people who have been in contact with birds of this type, and is serious both to the bird and to its owner. Quarantine regulations greatly reduced the risk of infection in Britain. They were lifted a few years ago but concern over recent outbreaks, not only of psittacosis but a number of economically important diseases such as fowl pest, led to their reintroduction in 1976.

The symptoms of psittacosis are fever, cough, and bronchitis. The disease is especially dangerous to old people, but it responds to the same antibiotics as typhus.

Sandfly Fever, or phlebotomus fever, *Dengue*, or breakbone fever, and *Trench Fever* are all somewhat similar conditions in that they resemble influenza and are rarely fatal. They are all due to viruses, spread in the first case by sandflies in tropical climates; in the second by mosquitoes in tropical climates; and in the third by lice in temperate climates. They are all typical "soldiers' diseases"; the first two were common in the Middle East and Far East during the last War, the third during the First World War in France.

Yellow Fever. Of all the virus diseases, seven can now be prevented, or largely prevented, by vaccination—smallpox, measles, German measles, rabies, poliomyelitis (if started early enough), influenza and yellow fever. Yellow fever is carried by a mosquito known as Stegomyia, common in South and Central America and in African ports. For its spread, it therefore needs: a hot climate, the stegomyia mosquito, and an infected person.

In 1898 the United States was at war with Spain in Central America, where yellow fever was a serious problem. Following this war the United States, by this time acutely aware of this terrible disease, asked a Dr. G. E. Waring to deal with it in Havana, where it was rife. But Waring died of yellow fever, as had many millions before him, without knowing its cause, and it was left to Walter Reed, who died in 1902, to prove the connection between the mosquito and yellow fever. By a vigorous war on the mosquito, the disease has been eradicated from Havana and the West Indian islands, and Reed's discovery made possible the building of the Panama Canal.

In yellow fever there is a sudden high temperature, aching of limbs and head, jaundice, and black vomit; the pulse-rate falls as the fever rises. Previous vaccination seems to be preventive if undertaken in time.

Conclusion.

All these virus diseases have this in common: that for many there is no specific cure, although some (see above) can be prevented by vaccination, or by the social control of the creatures carrying the virus. Some of the larger viruses (psittacosis) are destroyed by certain antibiotics. There is usually a long incubation period. Finally the question will sometimes arise of protecting some people from German measles or measles with gamma globulin containing another person's antibodies to the disease. This may be considered for measles in very young patients or to protect the foetus in pregnant mothers in contact with German measles.

Bacterial Diseases.

Bacterial diseases differ from virus infections in a number of respects; their incubation period tends to be shorter: having the disease once does not often confer lifelong protection; and unlike virus diseases, most bacterial diseases respond to one of the antibiotics or sulphonamides. In many cases it is possible to inoculate against the disease to prevent it occurring, as we have seen is possible with only a few of the virus diseases.

Scarlet Fever and Other Streptococcal Infections. In the days, not so long ago, before the arrival of chemotherapy (sulphonamides) and antibiotics, streptococci were very much feared and even caused a high mortality, particularly in such susceptible groups as children, and mothers and babies in maternity hospitals. They are still taken very seriously in the latter and rightly so, although one wonders how much of the mystique is simply a hangover from the days, fifty years ago, when many mothers died from "childbed fever." All signs of infection, such as fever, during the puerperium (the period following childbirth) must be promptly dealt with by a doctor, and only occasionally now is there real cause for anxiety provided treatment is prompt and rigorous.

Scarlet fever is much less common and very much less serious an illness than it used to be, partly because of the effective treatments available today, but also because of a definite but unexplained reduction in its severity. Perhaps the streptococcus has changed, and certainly the improved physical condition of people who are now much better fed and housed than they were, has helped to ward off the terrors of this disease as of so many other infections. The classical picture of signs and symptoms is now so rarely seen that it will not be further described.

The importance of streptococcal infections has shifted from the initial infection, such as a sore throat, to some serious conditions which occasionally arise as a result of some form of delayed sensitivity to the bacteria. Acute rheumatism or rheumatic fever (not to be confused with ordinary aches and pains nor with rheumatoid arthritis) occasionally arise in people who have had a sore throat a few weeks before. Since the streptococcus is not the direct cause of the damage which may consequently occur in the heart or kidney, the antibiotics are no answer except sometimes to keep off further streptococcal invasions.

Diphtheria. This used to be an extremely serious disease, but immunisation has made it almost unknown; it is important, therefore, that all children should be immunised. There are many modern and up-to-date doctors who have qualified since the war who have never seen a case because it has become so rare, and in spite of the propaganda of certain ill-informed people, this saving of children's lives is entirely the result of nationwide inoculation during the war and since. The following description is of historic interest only, and will remain so if a high level of inoculation is kept up by parents.

In a typical case of diphtheria the incubation period is about three days; the patient is a child who becomes ill and pale-looking (*i.e.*, the onset is not sudden, as in many fevers, but insidious); the temperature is only slightly raised to, perhaps, 37° or 38°C, and although there may be no complaint of sore throat, examination will reveal inflammation with—and this is typical of diphtheria —a grey membrane spread over the tonsils, the palate, and the back of the mouth generally. The diphtheria germ does not spread within the body. It stays at the place where it entered (in this case the throat) and sends its toxins throughout the body.

Even after the acute phase is over the patient must not be allowed to walk, because the diphtheria toxin is particularly poisonous to the heart. The ordinary rule is at least one or two months in bed.

Diphtheria also occurs in the larynx—in pre-inoculation days many children choked to death with this form of the infection; in the nose; and, although this is not generally known, wounds can be infected. The so-called "Desert sores" of the North African campaign seem to have been caused by diphtheria-like organisms.

Diphtheria may lead to paralysis of the throat, with difficulty in speaking or swallowing, and paralysis of the eyes or limbs; these are due to neuritis caused by the influence of the toxin on the nerves.

Whooping Cough. For many years whooping cough has been regarded merely as a bother to the patient and a nuisance to others, as, in fact, a trivial disease. Unfortunately, this is not so; because statistics show that it caused more deaths than polio, diphtheria, scarlet fever, and measles put together.

Whooping cough begins in a child as an ordinary cold with cough and slight fever, and this stage lasts for a week or ten days. Then the "paroxysmal stage" begins as a series of coughs following in rapid succession, during which time the patient is unable to breathe. The "whoop" is caused by the noisy indrawing of breath when the fit stops. The face may become blue and congested. Bronchitis is usually present, and bronchopneumonia may result as a complication, so inoculation of all children before the disease has a chance to strike them is most important.

Once whooping cough has begun, there is no specific treatment, although modern drugs can reduce the frequency of the fits of coughing. The antibiotic chloramphenicol has been used for this disease, but the general opinion is that it is ordinarily of little benefit. Chinese physicians once described whooping cough as the "hundred-days cough," and the cough may, indeed, continue for at least a hundred days. There is an effective vaccine.

Food Poisoning Diseases.

Strictly speaking there is no such thing as "food poisoning" if one is thinking of "poisoning" in terms of anything apart from germs. But not so long ago it used to be thought that decomposition of food in itself produced poisons known as "ptomaines" which were deadly to those who swallowed them. All food poisoning is caused by infection of food with bacteria and by no other cause—unless of course, we are thinking of the kind of poisoning which is the concern of the lawyer rather than the medical man.

Here we are considering those diseases which are commonly spread by contaminated food or drink. The classification is not scientific, but then no scientific classification has as yet been devised. First, we shall deal with typhoid, paratyphoid, and dysentery—uncommon here in Britain, although Sonné dysentery is fairly frequent. Then there is gastro-enteritis (which means irritation of the stomach and intestines), which is caused by staphylococci and the germs of the salmonella group, and lastly botulism, which is rare.

Typhoid and Paratyphoid. These diseases are spread by infected water, food, or hands—especially uncooked food, such as milk, salads, oysters, and shellfish. Flies, too, play some part in spreading the disease. Some people are "carriers" and carry and excrete the germs without being themselves affected; for example, "Typhoid Mary," a carrier in the United States in the early years of this century, spent a large part of her life in custody as a public danger, although she did not show any symptoms of typhoid. Nevertheless, this woman caused a great deal of illness in others in her chosen profession of cook.

The influence of Chadwick's propaganda for pure water supplies is shown by the fact that deaths from typhoid, still 332 per 1,000,000 in 1870, fell to 198 per 1,000,000 at the beginning of this century. In the 1920s the death-rate was only 25 per 1,000,000, and now it is even less.

Typhoid fever begins like most fevers with headache, raised temperature, and general feeling of unwellness. This stage lasts about a week, and then the rash appears in the form of rose-red spots on the front of the chest and abdomen and on the back. In the second week there is great weakness, sometimes diarrhoea, flatulence, and mental dullness, together with dry and cracked lips and tongue. The third week is the week, in hopeful cases, of gradual decrease in temperature and other symptoms, and the fourth week is the week of convalescence.

Complications are perforation of the intestine (which needs surgical treatment), delirium, and bronchitis.

Paratyphoid fever is a milder form of typhoid (there are two forms, A and B); ordinarily it can be diagnosed only by scientific tests. The main thing is to inoculate contacts with T.A.B. vaccine and to protect food supplies; treatment is with chloramphenicol.

Dysentery. Dysentery may be caused either by a bacterium or an amoeba; the first type is known as bacillary dysentery, the latter as amoebic dysentery (which is dealt with under tropical diseases). Infection is spread in much the same way as in typhoid. There is high fever, abdominal pain, and diarrhoea, at first consisting of faecal matter, then blood and mucus. In severe cases the death-rate used to be over 20 per cent.

Various bacilli cause dysentery. The common tropical types are the Shiga and Flexner groups, but in this country most epidemics are due to the milder Sonné group.

However, in all these infections sulphaguanidine, ampicillin or tetracycline bring rapid relief, but care must be taken to avoid infection of other people.

Diarrhoea and Vomiting. Leaving out typhoid and paratyphoid fevers and dysentery, there is a group of infections known as "D. and V."—diarrhoea and vomiting. In Britain D. & V. is mostly due to:

(1) Salmonella infection.
(2) Staphylococcal infections.
(3) Other bacteria, ordinarily harmless, such as bacillus coli, when present in sufficient numbers.

Salmonella Infections are the most serious of this group; they affect the small intestine and produce vomiting, severe abdominal pain, and diarrhœa. These symptoms occur about one day after eating infected food and usually clear up within about two weeks, but occasionally death results. Salmonella bacteria are most likely to be found in meat, egg powder, vegetables, and ducks' eggs, but staphylococci are liable to grow in milk products, such as ice-cream and cream buns. Food poisoning from staphylococci is seldom severe, and recovery takes place in about a week. Nevertheless, it is extremely infectious, and causes a great deal of lost time in industry and temporary illness in institutions; for it is in such situations that it is most likely to occur.

Staphylococcal Food Poisoning has greatly increased in recent years, so it is important to know what circumstances are likely to cause it. The reason for its increase has nothing to do, as many people suppose, with the greater use of canned foods, but it has much to do with the greater use of communal feeding and canteen meals. It is

possible for bacterial toxins in infected food to bring about illness even when the canning process has killed the bacteria, but it is certainly extremely rare. Canned foods, in fact, are much safer than so-called "fresh" foods in this respect—except when they have been opened, left about, and then re-heated. The same applies to the re-heating of any kind of food.

The real enemy is the canteen worker with a boil, a discharging nose, dirty hands, or a septic finger. Occasionally food may be infected in the larder by rats or mice, but the sort of canteen or restaurant where this can happen has little to commend it. Frankly, these infections are caused by dirty or stupid people who do not realise that their sore finger or boil can become someone else's diarrhoea and vomiting. Where children are concerned, the outlook is potentially more serious, and in the early part of this century the Summer-time "procession of baby coffins" was all too familiar. Infection is much more common in artificially fed babies or in older children who eat infected ice-cream. However trivial the condition may seem, diarrhoea and vomiting with fever in a child should never be ignored. Those in charge of canteens or restaurants must ensure that staff is supervised, that anyone with a septic infection is put off duty, and that all know about washing after visiting the lavatory and absolute cleanliness.

Bacilli normally present in the intestine, such as bacillus coli, can cause infections if absorbed in large amounts, or if of a different strain from those in the patient's intestine. They are not usually serious.

Botulism. Now uncommon, this is the disease which used to be known as "ptomaine poisoning" on the theory that it was caused by poisons produced by bad food apart from germs. In the 1920s a party of picnickers at Loch Maree in the Scottish Highlands developed botulism and a number died, with the result that the disease attracted much public attention. Botulism is caused by a germ, the bacillus botulinus, which is peculiar in that, like tetanus, its poison attacks the nervous system rather than the intestines, resulting in fits, double vision, paralysis beginning in the face and spreading downwards, and difficulty in swallowing. It is found in tinned fruits or vegetables containing the toxin even when the germ has been killed, but, as we have already seen, the toxin comes from the bacilli, not from decomposition of food as such (in fact, food does not decompose in the absence of germs). Death is common in botulism, but an antitoxin is now available which, if used in time, can cure the disease.

Tuberculosis. No disease causes more public concern, and no disease is more difficult to describe, than tuberculosis; for, like the streptococcus or the staphylococcus, the tubercle germ can attack many different parts of the body and manifest itself in many ways. Furthermore, it is a widely spread disease, infecting not only humans but also cattle, birds and reptiles. But here we shall be concerned with those types common to Man—the human and bovine (*i.e.*, the type occurring in cattle which can be spread to man by infected milk).

The tubercle bacillus is particularly hardy, so that when coughed or spat out on the ground it continues to be infectious for a long time. Infection is therefore caused by: (*a*) drinking infected milk; (*b*) droplet infection through having germs coughed in the face; (*c*) breathing in infected dust. In other words, tuberculosis is caused by absorption through either the lungs or the intestines; the former is common in adults, the latter in children.

But there is a good deal more to the problem than this; we know, for example, that over 90 per cent. of people in industrial countries have been infected with T.B. in early life and have conquered the infection. So the question arises: what conditions predispose to T.B.—why do some people get over the early infection and others not? There are two answers to this question: one is certain—that those who are impoverished and do not get enough food are liable to T.B.; the second is not so certain—that mental stress plays some part. Yet there is reasonably good evidence that such stress as a broken love-affair can cause lowered resistance to breakdown so that when germs are encountered infection will occur.

In children, lung tuberculosis is not common, but tuberculosis of the bones and glands is, as is also infection in the abdomen, the kidney or spine, and, worst of all, tuberculous meningitis. These are often of the bovine type from infected milk. Ordinarily, T.B. in children is less serious than adult infections; but tuberculous meningitis used to be almost invariably fatal until streptomycin was discovered.

Adult tuberculosis usually occurs in the lungs or the pleura—the thin membrane surrounding the lungs. In younger people miliary tuberculosis, which is a form of T.B. blood-poisoning or septicaemia, is a very serious condition, and the infection spreads throughout the whole body in a few weeks.

Lung infection begins gradually in someone who has previously felt unwell. There may be cough, and later blood-stained sputum (although blood which is coughed up does not necessarily prove that T.B. is present). Whatever means of treatment is used, the struggle between disease and patient is likely to be fairly long, but the outlook is now good. The closure of the Swiss sanatoria is due partly to modern disbelief that air in one place is better than that in another, but mainly to improved treatment.

Prevention depends on legal action ensuring tuberculosis-free herds of cattle; on control of spread of the disease by those "open" cases who carry germs in their sputum; on the use of vaccination in childhood with B.C.G. vaccine (which you can ask your doctor about).

Many methods are used in treatment: drugs, such as streptomycin, isoniazid, and P.A.S., lung surgery, rest, and so on. At any rate, tuberculosis is being got under control, but anyone who is worried can get a free X-ray at the nearest Mass Radiography Centre. There are skin tests to show whether there is susceptibility to T.B.

Septicaemia. Commonly known as "blood-poisoning." This is one of those diseases of which textbooks prior to the Second World War used to say: "death usually occurs."

Blood-poisoning occurs generally by spread from some septic area such as a wound (or even a small prick), after childbirth, or any place where certain germs have got admission to the body. The most usual germ is the streptococcus, although the pneumococcus—which ordinarily causes pneumonia—and the staphylococcus may also cause septicaemia.

Fever comes on suddenly and rises rapidly with headaches, sweating, and shivering. The patient is obviously very ill, and later there is wasting and delirium. The white blood cells increase in number. Septicaemia sometimes occurs without any apparent local infection in those who are weak and debilitated.

Pyaemia is a type of septicaemia which leads to the formation of numerous abscesses throughout the body. Its symptoms are the same as described above, except that the causative germ is usually the staphylococcus, and abscesses are found which may need surgical treatment.

However, in both conditions the state of affairs has been revolutionised by the use of the sulpha drugs and antibiotics; cure is now the rule rather than the exception.

Septicaemia should be suspected when any small wound or cut is followed by high temperature and the symptoms described above.

The word *"Toxaemia"* is used when the germs stay in their original position and produce symptoms by spreading their toxins throughout the body. Tetanus, diphtheria, and some kinds of childbirth infection come into this category; the symptoms may vary from mild disturbance to severe illness.

Meningitis means inflammation of the meninges, the covering which, like a layer of plastic, lies over the brain and spinal cord, just as the pleura covers the lungs and the peritoneum covers internal organs in the abdomen. (Hence inflammation of the pleura is known as pleurisy, and inflammation of the peritoneum as peritonitis.)

Various germs may cause meningitis, for example, the bacillus of tuberculosis, the pneumococcus, which ordinarily causes pneumonia, and the streptococcus or staphylococcus, but ordinarily the word refers to *Cerebrospinal Meningitis* or "spotted fever" caused by the meningococcus and occurring at times as an epidemic. It is commonest in the years from infancy to the early twenties, and begins suddenly with headache, vomiting, and fever. The temperature rises quickly, and pain develops in the back and legs; on the second or third day a rash appears on the body, and particularly on the inside of the thighs. Later there is stiffness of the neck, the head may be drawn back, vomiting persists, and the headache can be so severe as to cause the patient to scream with pain.

Fortunately, this type of meningitis (and most of the others) respond to treatment with antibiotics or the sulpha drugs, so the risks are very much less than formerly.

Pneumococcal Meningitis is an unusual complication of pneumonia, and the septic types (*strepto-coccal* or *staphylococcal*) arise either following an infected fracture of the skull or from infection of the ear or mastoid.

Tuberculous Meningitis has already been mentioned; originally always fatal, it is now treatable with streptomycin.

All these diseases are very much a matter for specialist and hospital treatment, but it is worth while mentioning *benign lymphocytic meningitis*, in which, although all the symptoms are present, recovery without specific treatment is invariable. Meningitis, which was during the First World War and after what polio is to us now, is no longer common, and when taken in time is easily treated.

Tetanus is usually known as "lockjaw" because there may be difficulty in opening the mouth, although this is simply part of a spasm of all the muscles of the body. The tetanus bacillus is found in rich soil—hence the disease is less common in desert areas—and tetanus resembles rabies in that: (*a*) it enters at a wound; (*b*) it affects the nervous system; (*c*) it results in fits and ultimately death.

However, active immunisation with T.T. (tetanus toxoid) has resulted in the disease becoming uncommon, and even when developed, treatment with antitoxin, anaesthetics, and curare may lead to cure.

The bacillus is anaerobic (*i.e.*, does not use oxygen) and is most likely to occur in such situations as when a man digging manure or working in his garden sticks a fork through his foot, or, in war-time, when he is wounded in soil contaminated with manure.

Undulant fever, also known as Malta fever or abortus fever, falls into two types: melitensis, which infects goats, and abortus, cattle and pigs. Man gets the disease by reason of close contact with or drinking the milk of infected animals. (The name abortus is given because abortion is produced in cattle and sows.)

In Undulant Fever, as one would suppose, the fever goes up and down for two to three weeks; it may then go down and rise again, persisting for many months. The disease may occur in Britain, but modern drugs are on the whole successful in dealing with it. A striking feature of the disease is the combination of a high temperature with an appearance of relative well-being.

Another disease carried by mammals is *Glanders* or *Farcy*, spread by horses. In glanders there is discharge from the nose and sometimes pneumonia. Occasionally the disease is fatal. In farcy abscesses form, usually along the lymph vessels. Both conditions are very contagious, and treatment is a matter for a specialist; infected horses should be destroyed.

Cholera. Cholera could be classified under the head of food-poisoning, because it is mainly spread by infected water (however, like typhoid, it can also be spread by flies, infected food, and carriers); it could also be classified as a tropical disease, since, although it used to be found in Europe, it is now mainly rife in India.

Also like typhoid, cholera is caused by a bacillus, and can be prevented by early inoculation and care over food supplies—boiling water and milk, washing uncooked foods in chlorinated water, and keeping flies away.

The fever begins in the usual way with a short incubation period, followed by abdominal pain, severe vomiting, and diarrhoea. Later with the loss of fluid from the body there may be cramps in the muscles, diarrhoea increases, and the motions become of the typical "rice-water" type —i.e., there is no solid matter, and the appearance is that of water to which a little milk has been added. This stage is followed by collapse, with low pulse and cold hands and feet. Death, if adequate treatment is not available, results in about 70 per cent. of cases.

Anthrax. The bacillus of anthrax, like that of tuberculosis, can exist outside the body for long periods, and, like that of tetanus, then takes the form of spores or seed-like bodies. It is spread by infected cattle and horses, which get the disease from eating grass containing spores.

In human beings the form the disease takes depends on where the germ alights; sometimes it comes from infected shaving-brushes, when it causes a large sore, like a boil, on the face, known as "malignant pustule"; sometimes it develops in those who inhale the dust from infected hides or wool (hence the name "wool-sorters' disease," which is a form of bronchitis with blood-stained sputum); lastly it may arise through eating infected meat, when the result is intestinal anthrax.

In all cases the outlook is serious. Death is common, preceded by a high temperature, skin symptoms in the first instance, lung symptoms in the second, and food-poisoning symptoms in the third. Penicillin or tetracycline may be effective.

Diseases Caused by Fungi.

There are only two important groups of disease caused by fungus: the serious *actinomycosis* and the relatively harmless, if unpleasant, *ringworm.* Ringworm or tinea will be dealt with later; it affects the hair, the body, the groin (dhobie itch, already referred to), and the feet (athlete's foot). Actinomycosis is spread by a fungus in barley and grasses which may reach the human mouth, settle around bad teeth, and thence pass to the lungs, the bone of the jaw, and even to the intestines or brain. Fortunately, this unpleasant fungus, which was once difficult to eradicate, has proved susceptible to penicillin.

The Venereal Diseases.

The venereal diseases are those caused—or at least that is what the name means—by the goddess of love, Venus. Venus, of course, causes a great deal of trouble, but venereal disease is not necessarily the worst she can do. Venereal disease is spread by sexual intercourse with an infected person.

Gonorrhoea is the result of an infection by the gonococcus (*Neisseria gonorrhoea*) and ordinarily comes on after an incubation period of three to seven days. However, babies can get an infection of the eyes, known as ophthalmia, from their mother if she is infected, and gonorrhoea in young children is often the result of being in contact with infected towels or clothes. The disease in adults is evident when there is a thick, creamy discharge from the sexual organs and sometimes pain on passing water; in infants ophthalmia is prevented by the use of silver nitrate eye-drops at birth. Gonorrhoea is fairly easily cured by the use of sulpha drugs or penicillin; but unfortunately venereal disease is increasing in recent years and drug-resistant forms are becoming more common.

Syphilis is a serious venereal disease caused by a spirochete (*Treponema pallidum*). Stories about lavatory seats are simply stories, although it is occasionally possible to get syphilis by other than sexual means: for example, it has happened that a man playing football has been infected through his hand being grazed by the teeth of someone with syphilis. But this is very unusual, although kissing can spread the disease. Children, too, can be born with syphilis (the so-called congenital syphilis).

Adult syphilis begins with a sore, known as a hard chancre, at the point where the spirochete of syphilis has entered; this may be on the lips, through kissing; on the sexual organs, through intercourse; and very rarely, as explained above, elsewhere. In a short time the chancre disappears and all may seem to be well, but this primary stage is followed by a secondary stage with sore throat, a rash, headache, and enlargement of glands. This, if left alone, also clears up, but is followed by the tertiary stage, in which a chronic infection develops in some part of the body which, presumably, is most susceptible in the particular individual. Thus there may be chronic syphilis of the skin, the bones, the heart, liver, or nervous system.

In the nervous system, the commonest forms are the two diseases of *tabes dorsalis*, in which the spinal cord is infected, and G.P.I. (general paralysis of the insane), in which the brain and mind are affected. These will be discussed under Nervous Diseases.

In congenital syphilis the pregnant mother gives her child syphilis. Such infants are often stillborn or premature, they look wizened, like little old men, and amongst other symptoms are eye disease, "snuffles," a flattened nose, and when the adult teeth appear the front ones may be notched at the biting surface.

The treatment, of course, is very much a matter for a specialist, but diagnosis is usually made through the Wassermann blood test. It was for syphilis that Ehrlich produced his "magic bullet"—an arsenical drug, known as salvarsan, which could attack the organism selectively without harming the body and was the first of the modern specific drugs. Present-day treatment is with penicillin. G.P.I. was once treated with malarial therapy with some success. Penicillin alone is often adequate.

It is important to understand that venereal disease can only be transmitted during sexual intercourse (or with intimate acts associated with it—*e.g.*, "oral sex"), that promiscuity therefore increases the risk, that not all lesions in, on or around the genitals are necessarily venereal disease and that *fear* of contracting it is widespread in many communities. If in doubt consult your own doctor or attend one of the many special clinics which can be found in most cities. Their location is usually advertised in conveniences and other public places. Delay is certainly dangerous.

Chancroid produces small septic ulcers around the sex organs, with swelling of the local glands in the groin, which may suppurate. It is caused by a bacillus, and can usually be cleared up by sulpha drugs within a week. Scabies and lice often pass from one body to another during sexual intercourse, but are not usually thought of as venereal in origin, although in many cases they are.

Tropical Diseases.

Nothing is more difficult than to define the term "tropical diseases." One might define them as the diseases which occur in tropical climates— but then measles occurs there too; and if they are defined as those diseases which are found *only* in the tropics, the solution is no easier, since leprosy, cholera, smallpox, and typhus are usually listed as tropical diseases, yet were found in this country until fairly recently—and the odd case still is.

But what a story could be told about the conquest of those infections which were—and many still are—the scourge of humanity! One day when generals and dictators are forgotten we shall remember that great international army of physicians and bacteriologists who have saved millions of lives and infinitely reduced human suffering: Koch and Ehrlich of Germany, Pasteur and Roux of France, Ross and Jenner of Britain, Reed of America, Noguchi of Japan, and many others. We shall remember how the Jesuit priests brought quinine from Peru to Europe in 1638, the first drug to save people from malaria; how in tropical heat Ronald Ross (1857-1932) peered for hours through his microscope to discover the connection between malaria and the mosquito until the sweat running from his brow rusted the instrument; how Major Walter Reed's work in Havana (1851-1902) made possible the building of the Panama Canal, and think, too, of the American soldiers who died in helping him to find the cause of yellow fever. In mentioning Jenner once more, we should recall Lady Mary Montagu (1689-1762), who brought the practice of vaccination to England from Turkey—or, rather, the practice of "variolation," which meant inoculating with the pus from smallpox cases. This was, of course, a dangerous practice, but the idea was there. Noguchi, one of the great bacteriologists of the nineteenth century, was the son of a poor peasant. He often had to steal to get enough bread even to keep alive, but was later to help in our understanding of syphilis and many tropical diseases.

Yet there is still much to do. Take, for example, the case of Egypt, one of the world's poorest countries, supporting with the help of water from the Nile about 36 million people. But if the river gives food and drink it does other things; for it carries the disease of bilharzia, which kills thousands of peasants yearly. In the villages of Egypt as many as 90–100 per cent. of the population suffer from this terrible disease. The infantile mortality rate is the second highest in the world—29·5 per cent.—seven times higher than that of Holland; the average expectation of life amongst the lower classes is thirty-one years, of the upper classes fifty to sixty years. The country is ridden with bilharzia, ankylostomiasis, malaria, plague, amoebic dysentery, typhus, tuberculosis, and pellagra. Blindness, due to trachoma and other diseases, affects tens of thousands. Such a situation cannot be treated simply by pouring drugs into the country; what is necessary is social control, to enforce purification of the water supplies, the use of insecticides to kill the disease-bearing pests, and removal of the causes of extreme poverty (tuberculosis and vitamin deficiencies which are common in Egypt are diseases of malnutrition).

Relapsing Fever, common in India and Africa, may be louse- or tick-borne; the germ is a spirochaete, similar to that of syphilis, but the disease is non-venereal. Relapsing fever gets its name from the fact that the temperature remains high (39°–41°C) for about a week, returns to normal for a week, and rises again. There may be three to five relapses of this sort. Penicillin is effective; lice or ticks must be eradicated.

Epidemic Jaundice (also known as Weil's disease or—if you prefer it—ictero-haemorrhagica spirochaetosis), is also caused by a spirochaete, and spread by rats. Now it is rarely found in Europe, although it occurred in the trenches during the First World War, in men working in sewers, and in the women who worked in the fish market of Aberdeen, which at one time was rat-infested. It is rarely fatal, but leads to high fever and jaundice. Penicillin in high dosage or tetracycline may help.

Yaws is also a spirochaetal disease, common in the tropics and particularly in children. It is unpleasant, but not serious, and tends to clear up in a year or so. There are raspberry-like growths on the skin, which disappear with the drugs used in syphilis (although the condition is non-venereal). The Wassermann reaction, positive to syphilis, is also positive in yaws.

Leprosy. Whereas syphilis, relapsing fever, epidemic jaundice, and yaws are caused by spirochaetes, leprosy is caused by a bacillus resembling the bacillus of tuberculosis. Leprosy, in fact, should not be included here at all, for it is non-spirochaetal, and not necessarily a tropical infection. Apart from the difficulty of classification, many popular beliefs about the disease are untrue. It is *not* the oldest disease afflicting man; *not* a disease confined to tropical countries; it is *not* very catching; *not* hereditary, *not* incurable; in leprosy the fingers and toes do *not* drop off; it is *not* a divine punishment for wrongdoing. So there are many misunderstandings about this disease, and placing it in the wrong part of the medical section is probably the least.

Leprosy is a serious disease not because of disfiguring light-coloured skin patches and lumps, but because it destroys peripheral nerves. Leprosy may disappear spontaneously, or it may progress until the face is lion-like and the hands and feet wasted and ulcerated. The disease rarely kills, but it is the world's greatest crippler.

Leprosy was once fairly common in colder Western countries, though its extent was exaggerated. The great majority of the 15 million people who suffer from leprosy live in tropical countries, but it still exists in Iceland, Japan, Korea and some of the southern states of the United States. Prolonged and intimate contact with an "open" case is said to be the main mode of infection, but only one infected husband in twenty passes leprosy to his wife.

The sulphone drugs have revolutionised the treatment of leprosy. Given early diagnosis and adequate treatment, the great majority of sufferers could be cured. Established deformity (such as claw hand, drop foot, paralysed eyelids) can be mitigated by reconstructive surgery, although lost sensation cannot be restored.

In the past, only Christian missions were concerned with the plight of the leprosy sufferer. Now, non-sectarian voluntary agencies, Governments and the World Health Organisation have joined in the fight against the disease. Enough is known to control the disease, but not enough is being done, as only one victim in five is at present getting treatment.

Plague is another disease caused by bacteria, common in Europe at one time, but now largely restricted to Asia. Nevertheless, it caused millions of deaths in Europe during the years 1348–49 and 1665 and was the "Black Death," which, indeed, changed the course of history. Interested readers may read Hans Zinnser's *Rats, Lice, and History* about this aspect of the disease. Plague is carried by the bite of the rat flea, but, once people become infected, spread may occur from one to the other by droplet infection—*i.e.*, by coughing and sneezing. After an incubation period of two to ten days, fever develops, rather like severe influenza, and in a day or two the glands in the groin begin to swell, followed perhaps by swelling of the glands elsewhere. This is the usual type of plague, but it is also possible to get disease of the lungs from droplet infection and blood-poisoning from infection of the blood-stream. Both the latter types are almost invariably fatal, and even the glandular type (bubonic plague) has a mortality of about 80 per cent. The vaccine has given place to streptomycin and sulpha drugs which are also used on contacts.

Although we have little space to discuss the subject of plagues and epidemics in general, it is worth noting that serious epidemics have almost always followed wars, revolutions, and economic and political collapse. Thus the Black Death followed the break-up of the Roman Empire, and, in the fourteenth century, accompanied the end of mediaeval civilisation. The Napoleonic wars were followed by other epidemics, and the wars of the 1830s in Europe were followed by influenza. In the most widespread outbreak of influenza after the First World War, more people were killed by the disease than in all the fighting of four years. It is a reflection on the peculiar mentality of Man that this devastating epidemic, which affected almost the whole world, occupies little space in his history books—we still, with few exceptions, regard history as the doings of kings, queens, and generals. Yet, in 1918, 20 million men, and women, and children died from influenza, and no cure has, as yet, been found! Later we shall see that many millions of people die yearly from starvation or vitamin deficiencies. But these facts—the real facts of life—we rarely hear about.

Protozoal Diseases.

Nearly all the diseases caused by protozoa are tropical diseases, although one of the best-known protozoans is the harmless amoeba found in British ponds. Protozoal diseases are caused by these organisms, large in comparison with bacteria, which are really one-celled plants. Viruses are neither animals nor plants, are much smaller than the other two groups, and have some distinctive characteristics described elsewhere.

The only important diseases caused by protozoa are sleeping sickness or trypanosomiasis, malaria, and amoebic dysentery (as contrasted with bacillary dysentery), another disease, leishmaniasis—also known by the numerous names of kala-azar, dum-dum fever, and, in milder form, Delhi boil, Oriental sore, or Baghdad sore—will also be mentioned briefly. These infections are few, but important in their influence on Man; for, as Dr. Clark-Kennedy has pointed out, malaria until recently was responsible for one-fifth of all human sickness, sleeping sickness not so long ago caused a large part of Central Africa to be uninhabitable, and in some areas of the tropics there are probably more people with, than without, amoebic dysentery.

Malaria. The word, of course, means "bad air," just as "influenza" means "influence"—in Italian *influenza di freddo*—the influence of cold. Human beings have a natural tendency to suppose that, when two events occur together, then one must be caused by the other. Yet, although malaria and "bad air" may often go together, and influenza and cold, it does not follow that bad air (whatever that may be) causes malaria nor that cold causes influenza. In fact, the anopheles mosquito carries the amoeba of malaria, and the mosquito prefers climates which some people might describe as "bad," but it is the amoeba, not the air, which causes the disease. Anyhow, the unfortunate mosquito might well use the phrase honoured by many generations of schoolmasters: "It hurts me more than it hurts you!" For the mosquito, too, is sick, and passes on its sickness to the person it bites.

There are several types of plasmodium—which is the scientific name for this amoeba—producing attacks of fever varying in severity and frequency: benign tertian, quartan, and malignant quartan. Entering the body from the mosquito bite, the parasites penetrate the blood cells, multiply there, and finally burst into the blood stream. When this happens the temperature rises, and then they return to the cells to carry out once more the same procedure. Depending on the type, the attacks of fever may be at intervals of three or four days, severe or milder. When someone with malaria is bitten by a mosquito the infection can be transmitted to the next person it meets, but malaria is not infectious from one person to another directly. Quinine, of course, is the time-honoured remedy, but many other drugs are now available: mepacrine, primaquine, chloraquine and some sulpha drugs. The drug must be taken long enough for the infection to die out, otherwise relapses can occur even after leaving a malarial country (but it is only fair to say that, just as some people continue to give themselves the title of "Major" when they have left the army, so others long in Britain continue to describe attacks of cold or 'flu as "my old malaria again," when, to say the least of it, they are exaggerating).

Important as are the drugs used in the treatment of malaria, even more so is the control of the parasite-bearing mosquito. The eggs of mosquitoes hatch in water, and there the young or larval forms can be attacked by pouring oil on the surface of pools so that they are unable to breathe, or by introducing small fish which have a partiality for them. Adult mosquitoes can be killed by insecticides or kept away by repellent creams or nets over beds. Prophylaxis with anti-malaria before entering and while living in known malarial zones is important.

Blackwater Fever is a sequel to malaria in tropical Africa and some parts of India. Rather illogically, it is described as "Blackwater," although the urine is red and the skin is yellow but the result is due to breaking down of the red blood cells by some malarial toxin. Possibly too much quinine may help in producing the illness. Treatment is to give plenty of fluids and no quinine or any other anti-malarial drugs in the early stages. The death-rate is about 25 per cent.

Trypansomiasis or sleeping sickness—not to be confused with *sleepy* sickness—is essentially an African disease (although also found in tropical America) spread by the tsetse fly. Its cause is the type of protozoan known as a trypanosome, almond-shaped with vibrating membranes at the sides which enable it to move through the bloodstream, rather like a flat fish in the water.

There are three stages of the disease: first, the stage of fever with enlarged glands and a rapid pulse; which may continue off and on for three years; secondly, the stage of trembling hands, legs, and tongue, vacant expression, and slow and stumbling speech; thirdly, and lastly, the stage of low temperature, apathy, wasting of the muscles, and possibly death.

Treatment is with pentamidine, suramin or melarsoprol—which give good results in early cases. Preventive measures in infected areas include the destruction of tsetse flies by insecticide, the cutting down of forests near rivers which are inhabited by tsetse flies, and some authorities have suggested the shooting of big game which may form a "reservoir" of the parasites, whence tsetse flies can carry them to human beings. For similar reasons infected people should not be allowed to move to noninfected areas.

Amoebic Dysentery, also known as *Amoebiasis*, is caused by the *Entamoeba histolytica*, an amoeba whose cysts are found in food and water, or spread by infected fingers or flies. There is mild fever and diarrhoea which contains blood. The disease may become chronic, and can cause abscesses, usually in the liver but sometimes in the lungs. Amoebiasis is treated with chloroquine or nitroimidazoles.

Leishmaniasis, kala-azar, or dum-dum fever, is another amoebic disease, probably spread in this instance by the bite of sandflies. It is also known as tropical splenomegaly—enlargement of the spleen in ordinary language—since infection results in enlargement of the spleen and liver, low, irregular fever, and death within a year or so. A milder form, affecting the skin, is known as Delhi boil, Oriental sore, or Baghdad sore, does not lead to kala-azar, and is fairly readily cured. The cure for both conditions is to give injections of antimony compounds which reduce the death-rate from kala-azar from 80 per cent, to about 5 per cent.

Diseases Caused by Parasitic Worms.

Many types of worms infest human beings and other animals. They are interesting for such reasons as their size (which may range from the almost invisible to 9 m or more), their life histories, and their serious or trivial consequences on their hosts. We shall mention only a few groups here, and mainly the ones likely to be met with in Europe—the tapeworms, the roundworms, and the threadworms—although some tropical types will be described briefly.

Tapeworms, as we have seen earlier, like many other types of intestinal worm, lead a double life. What usually happens is that the worm breeds in the human intestine, the eggs pass out in the faeces, and are then swallowed by animals eating contaminated material. In the animal the eggs hatch out into larvae—primitive forms which penetrate the muscle, forming cysts—and Man is infected in turn by eating its meat. Thus *Taenia solium* gets into the flesh of pigs, which, if imperfectly cooked (measly pork), causes infestation of the intestine in Man. It reaches a length of about 3 m. *Taenia saginata*, which reaches a length of about 6 m, is spread in imperfectly cooked beef, and in Baltic countries *Dibothriocephalus latus* gets into the human intestine from caviare or undercooked fish. It reaches the awesome length of 9 m.

Now all the worms we have mentioned so far are found in the human intestine, and the cysts, which are much more dangerous and unpleasant, in the animal's muscles. But in some worms the reverse happens, with the adult in the animal's intestines and the cysts in Man. Thus in Australia the dog tapeworm (*Taenia echinococcus*) produces cysts in both sheep and Man. This is known as hydatid disease, and may remain unsuspected until cysts in the lungs, liver, or elsewhere become infected or rupture. *Trichinella spiralis* is similar in action, being found in the intestines of pigs and getting into the muscles or other organs of Man. The main difference is that this worm migrates from the pig's intestines into its muscles, whence it reaches Man in undercooked pork meat or sausages. The muscular cysts cause swellings and sometimes pain. There are changes in the blood, swelling of the face and leg in the early stages, and fever. A minor epidemic occurred in England in 1941. *Taenia echinococcus* and *Trichinella spiralis* are small—not more than 0·5 cm in length—but are more serious in their consequences than the large worms. Treatment is very difficult, and ordinarily all that can be done is to deal with individual cysts when they make themselves apparent.

The large tapeworms, *Taenia solium* and *saginata* and *Dibothriocephalus latus*, produce varying symptoms or none at all. Usually they are not discovered until some segments of the worm are excreted, but there may be mild indigestion, excessive hunger, and occasionally anaemia. However, when the worm is discovered the patient, not unnaturally, is likely to become anxious and uncomfortable at the thought of "having" a tapeworm; these symptoms are caused by the worry rather than the worm.

Treatment is, of course, a matter for a doctor, who now has a number of very effective drugs to choose from. One has to make sure that the head of the worm has been removed, otherwise it will continue to grow.

Roundworms are similar both in appearance and size to ordinary earth-worms and the eggs reach Man, not from an animal, but from the contaminated fingers of someone else who handles food. They give rise to no symptoms, and are noticed only when discharged in the faeces or occasionally vomited up. Piperazine is an effective treatment.

Threadworms, as the name suggests, are like small 0·5–1 cm long pieces of white thread. They are very common in children, and live mainly in the caecum—*i.e.*, the part of the large intestine near the appendix. The males, which are the smaller ones, remain there, but the females pass down towards the rectum at night-time and lay their eggs in the area around the anus. Infection is by contaminated hands handling food—especially uncooked food—and water. Threadworms are not serious, and cause few symptoms other than itching around the anus and between the legs, but heavily infected children may show symptoms of anaemia. The nervousness often shown by such children is usually the result of the irritation produced by the worms in the anal region. Infection is not common in adults, and in children tends to disappear at puberty.

Treatment is, in theory, simple; for the worms are easily destroyed by a number of drugs, such as piperazine. Ointment is applied to the itching area, and the child should be prevented from scratching. However, since the eggs may lie about the house for some time, reinfection often happens, especially if there are several small children in the home who may pass the disease from one to another.

The idea that intestinal worms in general are likely to cause loss of weight by absorbing food eaten by the patient is largely mistaken; for although it is true that they do live on this food, the amount taken is certainly not enough to be significant.

Tropical Worms. Bilharzia has been mentioned before in connection with its frequency in Egypt, although it is also found in other parts of Africa, Arabia, and Iraq. There are two main types: one infecting the bladder (*Schistosomum haematobium*), the other the rectum (*Schistosomum mansoni*). Bilharzia is more correctly known as schistosomiasis.

The parasite's fantastic life-history begins when a man bathes in infected water, and the small swimming forms known as cercariae pierce and enter his skin—or they may enter the body by drinking infected water. From the skin they pass to the portal vein below the liver, remain there six weeks until they become adult and then swim against the blood-stream down to the pelvis, where the female lays eggs which have a sharp spine. The eggs penetrate into the bladder or rectum—depending on the type of fluke—and pass out in the faeces or urine. If they enter water they hatch out into small moving forms which seek out a water-snail, develop further in its body, and leave it in the form of cercariae ready to find a new human victim. The female fluke is slender and round, about 2·5 cm in length, the male, flat and leaf-shaped, is about 2 cm long, and, as we have seen, their grisly courting takes place in the portal vein, whence the impregnated female passes to the bladder (haematobium) or rectum (mansoni) to lay her eggs.

Infection results in raised temperature and, in the urinary type, blood in the urine; in the intestinal type blood is found in the faeces, and there are symptoms resembling dysentery—*e.g.*, diarrhoea. Treatment in both cases is with antimony tartrate or niridazole. Needless to say, attempts should be made at prevention by telling people to avoid infected canals (usually easier said than done), and by periodically cutting off the water supply to the canals to kill the snails.

Hookworm Disease, or ankylostomiasis, is found in many parts of the world, especially in miners who work on damp ground. The tiny worm enters the body usually through the feet, passes through the blood-stream to the lungs, eats through into one of the bronchial tubes, climbs the windpipe, and passes down the oesophagus into the stomach to end up in the duodenum. It causes anaemia, can be fairly readily cured, but is occasionally fatal.

Elephantiasis. Some types of parasitic worm are spread by insects. Thus in *Filiariasis* mosquitoes inject by their bites the infantile forms of a tiny worm which enters the lymphatic channels; there the blockade they cause leads to the swelling of the legs and the lower part of the body, known as elephantiasis.

PHYSICAL INJURIES.

INTRODUCTION.

In this section we shall inevitably discuss much that could be described as Principles of First Aid. You cannot learn First Aid from a book, even if you read one of the excellent first aid manuals, like those published by the St. John Ambulance Association. The only way is to join one of their many classes of practical and theoretical instruction which are held in all parts of this country and many others.

The most difficult thing to learn is what *not* to do. When a patient is knocked down in the road, people instinctly seem to want to drag him immediately to his feet, or otherwise pull him on to the pavement away from the traffic. Someone will have entered the nearest shop and be emerging with a chair so that the casualty can sit down. Before long a hot strong sweet cup of tea has arrived, and this or some other beverage is being poured into him. All this is instinctive, and all of it is wrong. Do *not* move the patient until you are sure he has no fracture which will be further aggravated by movement. To take an extreme case, a fractured spine clumsily moved may result in permanent widespread paralysis. Guard your patient from the traffic but only move him when you are certain it is safe to do so. If he has any injury which is likely to require a general anaesthetic on arrival in hospital (and this applies to most fractures) do not give anything at all by mouth. No anaesthetic can be given to a patient who has eaten or drunk anything in the previous three hours, in case he vomits while unconscious and dies of obstruction of his airway. Keep your patient warm (do *not* warm him up artificially) keep his head low, and unless he is bleeding severely or has stopped breathing, do nothing but protect him from the ministrations of the uninstructed until the ambulance comes.

Injuries to the Head and Back.

The head contains the brain, an organ with a number of inconvenient properties from the point of view of injury. Its very great importance is matched by its very great vulnerability as a tissue. Its consistency is that of stiff junket. It is quite incapable of repair once damaged and cannot heal by growing new parts in the way that skin and bone can. So it has to be totally enclosed by protective bone which means it cannot swell without compressing itself dangerously within its box—and this not infrequently happens after injury. Furthermore, any bleeding into the interior of the skull can only occur at the expense of compressing the brain, since the brain box is already fully occupied by the brain. There is a story in first aid known as "Concussion and Compression." It begins with a knock-out blow to the head and this is known as concussion. The patient struck a hard enough blow to the head will lose consciousness, if only for a short time, due to the brain being shaken up. Even slight knocks would do this if the brain were not cushioned by a thin layer of cerebrospinal fluid. Most concussed patients quickly regain consciousness, and for the great majority that is the end of the affair except for a sore head and a headache for a few days. Unfortunately for a minority, even though there may have been no fracture, the blow that knocked them out will also have damaged a small blood vessel on the surface of the brain. These patients may be indistinguishable from the luckier ones at first. They may have regained consciousness and will be just as anxious to go home. They will often be quite lucid for some hours. Surgeons call this the "lucid interval." However, when more than a certain amount of blood has accumulated in the head, and the brain is sufficiently compressed by it the patient loses consciousness slowly, for a second time, and from this phase of "compression" he will not recover unless something is done. The lucid interval can last some hours. Brain surgeons can relieve the compression and save the life of the patient only if they have him in their care when it occurs. This is why *all* cases of head injury who have once lost consciousness (concussion), for however short a period of time, and however lucid they may subsequently appear, *all* must be seen by a doctor and, if thought necessary, observed overnight in hospital, in case they are bleeding and proceeding to compression. There is no way of saving these avoidable fatalities other than by treating all cases of concussion seriously. Fractured skull is potentially even more serious, because the blow will have been harder and, the brain is therefore more seriously at risk.

The spinal cord can be regarded as an extension of the brain which runs down the middle of the spinal bones of the vertebral column. It has the same delicate consistency, and the same inability to recover from injury as the brain. Injury is usually the result of a fracture-dislocation of the spine. The consequences of injury are due to a permanent interruption of its two main functions. All movements of the voluntary muscles are only possible if they are connected by nerves to the brain. Except for muscles in the head, all these "motor" nerves run in the spinal cord. The nerve pathways leave the skull through a large hole in its base and run down in the spinal cord to the required level. They then emerge between the spinal bones and travel in bundles to reach the muscles. Motor nerves for the arm leave the cord between the vertebrae of the neck. Those for the leg leave the cord in the lumbar region in the small of the back. If the nerve supply is damaged in any part of its course, the muscles being supplied become paralysed and are unable to move. It follows that if the spinal

cord is damaged, all muscles below the point of damage have been cut off from the brain, and will be paralysed, and this will be permanent because the cord cannot be repaired. Damage to the nerve pathway *after* it has left the cord can often be repaired. Permanent paralysis is only one of the consequences of cord damage, since there is another whole series of nerves running in the cord which carry sensations from all parts of the body to the brain. Therefore there will be loss of sensation as well as paralysis below the point of injury.

It is emphasised that fracture of the spinal bones can occur without damage to the cord taking place. It is when these bones move one over the other, or "dislocate," that permanent cord damage occurs. It is therefore extremely important that cases of back injury be moved very carefully indeed in order to avoid such a disaster, and special ways of moving such patients are taught in First Aid classes.

Haemorrhage and Shock.

Every part of the body must have a blood supply, or else it will die. It is possible to stop the blood supply to a leg, for example, by fastening a wide rubber bandage tightly around the top of the thigh. This so-called "constrictive bandage" is still mentioned in First Aid books as a desperate means of controlling haemorrhage in a limb. It should hardly ever be used, because by stopping all circulation of blood, the entire limb will die in the course of time. Besides, most haemorrhage can be stemmed by direct pressure on the bleeding point. The tissues of the leg, such as its muscle and skin and bone will begin to die in a little more than half an hour after cutting off the blood supply. The brain, however, will begin to suffer within three *seconds* of its blood supply being cut off, and will die in about three minutes. Thus it can be seen that some parts of the body are more susceptible than others to a failure of the blood supply and the brain suffers earliest of all. Since the brain is where most of the vital functions of the body are controlled, it follows that a shortage of blood to the brain is likely to lead to a "depression of the vital functions"—a state of affairs known to First Aiders as "shock."

Shock occurs in a number of conditions, but is always due to a failure of the supply of blood to the vital functions of the brain for one reason or another. Its usual causes are:

(1) haemorrhage, when there is a general shortage, but the brain feels it most;

(2) severe burns, in which much fluid is lost from the blood as will be seen later; and

(3) certain medical conditions causing acute heart failure in which there is a failure to pump blood to the brain because the pump has failed.

The treatment for shock consists basically of restoring the blood supply to the brain, and where it is caused by loss of blood or other fluid, the treatment is transfusion. Finally, it must be emphasised that treatment is always urgent, since the brain cannot function for long without its blood supply, and once damaged by the shortage, can never be repaired. No attempt is made here to describe such treatment completely, but the most important things are to keep the head low so as to reduce the work the heart must do to drive blood to the brain; and to avoid artificial heating of the body by hot water bottles, etc., which only diverts blood away from the brain where it is needed, into the skin where it is not.

The treatment of severe haemorrhage is to stop the bleeding, usually by firm, direct pressure, and then to remember above all things that even though the bleeding has stopped there may be a dangerous state of shock from which the patient could die. This can only be prevented by restoring the circulation to the brain, usually by transfusion; so, having stopped the bleeding drive him fast to hospital for the second part of the treatment which may be as necessary to save his life as the first.

There is great confusion over the use of the word "shock." In the lay mind it is a shake-up of the nervous system caused by a fright, or some bad news, or the sight of something nasty in the woodshed. Even in the medical mind it is sometimes confused, and some of the First Aid books confuse it still further. Too frequently they give the treatment as "loosen all tight clothing from neck, chest, and waist; reassure the casualty and ensure a good supply of air." All this, together with grandmother's hot strong sweet tea is perfectly good enough if the patient is only "shaken-up" by a fright or a fall, but it will be dangerously negligent and time-wasting if he is suffering from true shock due to a failure of blood supply to the brain.

Fainting is a special case which can be prevented by keeping the head low in those who feel faint. It is usually self-curing due to the patient automatically falling into a position in which the head is low. If the faint, however, is due to severe blood loss, this is the same as shock in our proper meaning of the word and must be treated accordingly.

Haemorrhage can therefore be a difficult problem. It is even more so when it is internal. This may be in *medical* cases such as in occasional cases of peptic ulceration in which the blood will be vomited and also passed in the stool. Or it may be *surgical*, in the sense of being caused by injury to internal organs. The blood may emerge from one or other of the various orifices of the body, or it may be entirely concealed within the body. Rupture of internal abdominal organs such as the spleen, kidney and liver can occur with surprisingly little to show in the way of external injury. A fractured thigh bone can pierce the main artery of the leg and cause lethal internal haemorrhage without a drop of blood being visible. In all these cases diagnosis is urgent, followed by emergency blood transfusion if the brain, and hence the patient's life, is to be saved.

Means of detecting the presence of severe haemorrhage without seeing any blood are taught in First Aid Classes as the Signs of Haemorrhage. They are in fact manifestations of the reactions of the body in its attempt to save the failing brain, and are therefore the same as the signs of shock. The main ones are a rapid, feeble pulse, getting more rapid and more feeble as time goes on in a desperate attempt to get the remaining blood to the brain; skin pallor caused by constriction of blood vessels near the surface so that the blood which remains is shunted to the brain away from the less vulnerable skin; and finally, just before death, restlessness and air hunger.

A word of warning about the First Aid treatment of shock due to heart attack (coronary thrombosis). These patients must be transported at complete rest, but many of them react very badly to being made to lie down, since they have great difficulty in breathing in this position. Transport them relaxed, in a sitting position, supported by a large comfortable back rest.

It cannot be too strongly emphasised that with haemorrhage and shock, as with so many First Aid emergencies, the importance of protecting the brain is paramount.

Asphyxia.

The previous section was concerned with maintaining an adequate supply of blood to the brain. This is needed in order to supply the brain's only possible fuel—glucose—and the oxygen with which to burn it. Many different circumstances can conspire to reduce the oxygen content of the blood, and the result in each case is asphyxia. Normally, air is taken into the lungs through the air passages and brought into contact with all the circulating blood. It diffuses from the lungs into the blood, where it enters into a special relationship with the pigment of the red cells—haemoglobin. At the same time, the waste gas carbon dioxide enters the lungs from the blood and is breathed out. The revitalised blood is passed through the heart to build up sufficient pressure to drive it into all the tissues of the body and in particular into the brain. A special system in the brain—the respiratory centre—controls the complicated machinery of respiration and is itself, of course, kept alive by the products of the very mechanism it controls. This mechanism consists of all the muscles of respiration—those which lift the ribs, the diaphragm and many other so-called accessory muscles. They all have to be finely co-ordinated by means of nerve impulses which begin in the brain, pass down the spinal cord and out to the muscles. Information of many kinds comes along sensory nerve pathways to the respiratory centre so that breathing can be automatically adjusted to the changing needs of the moment. In order that life may continue there must be:

   (1) a functioning breathing mechanism to revitalise the blood; and

   (2) a circulation to carry the revitalised blood to the brain and other tissues.

In many cases when breathing stops and unconsciousness supervenes as brain function is depressed, the heart will go on beating for some time longer. The aim of First Aid is to restore the breathing by artificial respiration *before the heart stops*. Once the heart stops—and it eventually does so abruptly and without warning—the brain is dead within the usual few minutes unless *both* the heart and the breathing are restarted; and this is a very much more difficult proposition than artificial respiration alone.

For these reasons, a patient whose breathing has stopped must have it started again without any delay. Here, as in the case of severe haemorrhage, it is no use telephoning the doctor or even putting the patient in an ambulance. The First Aider must act himself, because he is on the spot and the only one in a position to save life. Both actions require elementary First Aid training, and even school children can accomplish them if they have been well taught.

Asphyxia is the name given to a failure of the oxygen supply to the brain and is due to a breakdown in some part of the complicated breathing mechanism outlined above. One of its chief causes is a blockage of the airway by (a) solids or (b) liquids. Any foreign body of the right shape and size will block the airway, as also will the tongue in the unconscious patient. Remember how much more easily the child's airway can become blocked because it is so much smaller. Blockage by a liquid is, of course, drowning. Remember that if a patient drowns in the entire ocean, it is only about half a cupful which is doing him any harm—as it only takes this amount to fill the airway. The same goes for the amount of tea, or vomit, required to kill an unconscious patient if it gets down the "wrong way"—as it will unless someone prevents it.

Another very common cause of asphyxia is carbon monoxide poisoning. Carbon monoxide is a lethal component of car exhaust fumes, incompletely burning and badly ventilated fires and stoves, and domestic coal gas. One of the inconvenient properties of haemoglobin is that it combines with carbon monoxide very much more eagerly than with oxygen. Prolonged contact with even a very slightly contaminated atmosphere can build up a concentration of carbon monoxide in the blood which will prevent the blood from carrying sufficient oxygen—and this is in fact how it kills. It takes a very short time for this to happen if the atmosphere is heavily contaminated. Remember the danger of even a very slight leak of the gas either in the kitchen, or into a car from a faulty exhaust pipe or silencer. Many elderly people die of coal gas poisoning every day because their sense of smell is poor and they do not detect the leak.

Other causes of asphyxia are lack of oxygen in the atmosphere, as occurs at high altitudes; crushing of the chest so that the ribs cannot move; paralysis of the muscles of breathing by interference with their nerve supply, usually in First Aid, as a result of a broken neck and consequent damage to the spinal cord (poliomyelitis can occasionally produce the same effect by attacking the nerves just before they leave the spine); and depressing the respiratory centre in the brain, most commonly nowadays by barbiturate poisoning.

The only really effective method of artificial respiration, which all members of any civilised community should be able to carry out, can be learned in half an hour at a good First Aid class. This is the direct, mouth-to-mouth method, sometimes dramatised by journalists as the "kiss of life." The method is taught with the aid of models and cannot be satisfactorily learned by only reading about it.

In discussing asphyxia, we have again to consider the particularly vulnerable situation of the brain.

Fractures.

Broken bones are not the most serious possible consequences of injuries causing fractures. It is usually more to be feared that further damage will be done by the broken ends of the bones to tissues and organs in the neighbourhood of the fracture. The First Aid treatment of immobilising the part before transporting the casualty is designed to avoid this.

Six types of fracture are commonly taught, but some of them may co-exist in the same injury and the division is only for descriptive purposes. In addition there are two special fractures of the skull.

A "simple" or "closed" fracture is where only the bone is broken, without damage to surrounding tissues and without a wound. A "compound" or "open" fracture is one in which air, and hence germs, can get at the broken bone. This may be through a wound, in whose depths lies the broken bone; or the bone may have been pushed out through the skin; or a bullet track may lead down to the fracture. All these are examples of compound fracture and the great danger is that the bone will become infected. Even now that infections are less feared than before the days of antibiotics, it is still a grave matter for bone to get infected. However the antibiotic is given, we rely on the blood supply to carry it into the infected tissue, and bone has only a very small blood supply. If the infection is not successfully treated it can smoulder for a long time and become a "chronic osteomyelitis" which might ultimately necessitate amputation of the limb—and all because the original fracture was compound or open.

A "complicated" fracture is one in which the broken ends of the bone have damaged some important organ or tissue in the region. For example, a complicated fracture of the ribs is one in which the lung tissue, close behind the inner surface of the rib, has been pierced, and the patient will be coughing up small amounts of bright red, frothy blood. A "comminuted" fracture is one where the bone is broken into several pieces, and an "impacted" fracture is one in which the broken ends have been driven into each other and are firmly impacted. Finally a "greenstick" fracture occurs sometimes in children because their bones are not brittle so do not always break clean across. They partly break like a green stick.

"Depressed" fracture of the skull is where the vault of the skull has been struck and dinted. Many problems arise, since the brain is inevitably compressed and no dressing of the accompanying wound should be allowed to press on the brain. The dangers of infection here are not only to the broken bone, but to the meninges covering the brain, causing meningitis.

Fractured base of skull often passes through that part of the base through which the internal ear channel runs. Thus it frequently results in blood, or cerebrospinal fluid, or a mixture of both, emerging from the ear. The gravity of this fracture lies in the severity of the impact necessary to produce it, which will probably have also caused great destruction of delicate brain tissue. The outlook is usually very poor.

Remember that most casualties with fractures will require a general anaesthetic on arrival in hospital so that their fracture can be set in plaster or otherwise treated. Avoid giving them things by mouth such as drinks, which will mean a three-hour wait before anaesthetic can be administered.

Burns and Scalds.

The severity of burn of scald depends largely on its surface area. If a patient dies of a burn, the cause of death is either infection or shock, the latter being due to fluid loss from the surface. Both hazards depend on surface area, since the bigger the surface the more germs are able to enter, and the more fluid can be lost.

It follows that the small burn on the hand or arm is seldom a threat to life, however deep the injury; and we shall therefore confine our attention to the larger burns of the whole surface of the limb or trunk.

Smaller bodies have a relatively larger surface area, and so a burn of the surface of a child's limb or trunk represents an even greater risk from fluid loss than a corresponding burn in the adult. Everyone has seen the fluid form in the blister of an ordinary small burn. It comes from the fluid part of "plasma" of the blood stream and the loss into such a blister may amount to a thimbleful. This will not hurt anyone. But the loss of similar fluid from the surface of a large burn may amount to many pints. The resultant shock will be partly due to this fluid loss from the blood stream resulting in a reduction in blood supply to the brain. Thus shock from burns has common features with shock from haemorrhage, and it is treated similarly, by transfusion. This time it is not a transfusion of blood but of plasma or some plasma substitute. In practice it is not only water that has been lost but a number of important chemicals dissolved in it as well, so that transfusion solutions have to contain sufficient of each individual substance to restore the deficit.

The arrangements for replacing the lost materials are complex and urgent; every bit as urgent as after a haemorrhage and for the same reason. The brain cannot be left too long in need. In general, the First Aid treatment of burns of large surface area is to keep them clean with a dry dressing and get the patient very quickly to hospital. Life-saving treatment by transfusion cannot start until arrival there. The only permissible delay is in the case of burns caused by corrosive chemicals which must be thoroughly washed off before transport, so that they do not continue to burn the patient on the way.

Unconsciousness.

It is not sufficiently appreciated that the dangers of being unconscious can often far outweigh the dangers from the cause of the unconsciousness. For example it is known that as many as half the deaths from head injuries are due to the airway becoming obstructed and not to the injury itself. The most important thing in managing the unconscious patient from any cause is to preserve an airway. Particularly if the patient is lying on his back it is likely to get blocked:

    (a) by his own tongue as the lower jaw sags backwards;

    (b) by his dentures (so remove them);

    (c) by vomit; and

    (d) by anything anyone may be tempted to give him by mouth.

Nothing whatever should be given by mouth in any circumstances to the unconscious patient, since he cannot swallow and it will inevitably go into his lungs.

Many of these dangers can be very much reduced by not having him on his back. Place him instead in the semi-prone position: half on his side, half on his front, with the upper leg drawn up to prevent him from rolling about. In this position the head will be inclined downwards. The jaw will tend to sag forwards and the tongue with it, away from the back of the throat. Any vomit will also come forwards. If the tongue does get in the way of the breathing the airway can usually be cleared by bending the head backwards as far as it will go and pushing the whole lower jaw forwards, by pushing from behind the angle of the jaw on both sides.

DRUG ABUSE AND DRUG DEPENDENCE.

This section of earlier editions of *Pears* was simply called "Addiction." This word is still much used, but is gradually being replaced by the terms in the present title, because ideas about the nature of the problem and methods of dealing with it are changing. Addiction is a word that conjures up rather 19th century ideas in the minds of readers: opium dens, inscrutable orientals, Sherlock Holmes injecting himself with cocaine—basically a phenomenon of foreign origin, rather frightening if its implications were not literary rather than factual, and not of great significance in Great Britain.

Drug Abuse.

It is now realised by doctors, research scientists, social workers, and the police—if still not by society as a whole—that the truth is quite different. The *abuse* of drugs in this country is at present of large proportions, increasing rapidly and showing no signs of diminishing. It is responsible each year for thousands of deaths by suicide and by accidental overdosage; for an enormous but virtually unmeasurable amount of private suffering; and for the loss to society, in terms of reduced working efficiency, of millions of man-hours every year. It has nothing to do with opium smoking which was never in any case more than the eccentricity of the few. Opium is virtually unused in medicine these days and the amount of smuggling, always small, is now negligible. The problems today arise chiefly from the misuse of drugs given by doctors for their effects on the central nervous system—the pain-killers, sleeping pills, "stimulants," and "tranquillisers."

Drugs and Medicines.

To the doctor, any substance is a drug that can be introduced into the body from outside, and that is capable of producing some detectable effect. Most such substances have a beneficial use. They are "medicines," and as such are given by doctors in suitable cases. Others, for example, nicotine (in cigarettes), alcohol (in beer, wine, or spirits), and carbon monoxide (in coal gas), are of doubtful benefit and of certain harm and are used by doctors, if at all, only under certain very special and usually experimental conditions.

Medicines may be classified under four main headings. First, there are those like quinine, or penicillin and other so-called antibiotics, that actually cure diseases by eradicating the organism (bacteria or other parasites) that cause disturbance of normal bodily function. Second, drugs such as insulin or the steriods overcome in the unhealthy the lack of some necessary substance a healthy body manufactures for itself: they must usually continue to be given for life. Third are the drugs which relieve the signs of disease—for example, there are many new drugs that lower the blood pressure or increase the output of urine—without being able to put right the disturbed basic situation which is the cause of the trouble. Fourth are drugs to relieve the patient's symptoms—which make him feel better, less

breathless, take away his pain, help him to sleep, and so on—although we seldom know why they are able to do this. Indeed, in many cases we suspect that they are acting mainly as a token of help from doctor to patient, and so encouraging his body to fight a more successful battle on its own behalf.

There is no doubt that the genuine advances in beneficial drugs during the last forty years have been enormous; but the very successes of the penicillins, tetracyclines, antimalarials, hormones, and so on have bred in the public and in the medical profession itself an attitude of un-critical wonder. There have been relatively few drugs in the first and second categories mentioned above; and in the field of mental health, the importance of which is now so rightly emphasised, there are virtually none. Yet drugs which act upon the brain are often received as if they were curative although they may pose fresh problems rather than solve the old. Thus, although there are many drugs which act upon the mind, few do this in any fundamental sense; they relieve pain and anxiety, bring sleep and lessening of stress, and may allow the patient to recuperate himself during the relief they provide. But often this deeper change does not occur—sometimes because the doctor has not clearly seen his part in helping to bring it about—and then the sympto-matic relief may come to be sought for its own sake.

Dangers of Long-term Medication with Drugs acting on the Brain.

1. *Toxic effects.* Drugs which act upon the nervous system, like any others, have character-istic toxic or unwanted effects of their own (incidentally, these may become apparent rapidly; even, on rare occasions, after only a single dose). Such effects may have little or nothing to do with the desired effects for which they are being prescribed and taken. For example, it has only come to be realised quite recently that aspirin is liable to cause bleeding, which is occasionally serious, from the lining of the stomach in a large proportion of people who take aspirin regularly; or that phenacetin, another substance very frequently present in analgesics (*i.e.*, pain relievers) that can be bought from chemists without pre-scription, may lead (after prolonged use) to kidney damage. Some drugs may cause rashes and other allergic reactions in susceptible subjects; and jaundice, fainting, tremors, and motor disorders are known to occur in some patients taking a variety of other drugs.

2. *"Rebound."* The body works in such a way, over a variety of its activities, that it tends to return to a "neutral" position after it has departed from this for any reason. For example, over-eating tends to be followed by a lessening of appetite, at least for a time; the runner makes up for his air-deficit during the race by breathing more deeply thereafter; and if, at rest, you breathe for a time more rapidly and deeply than you need, this period will be followed by one in which you breathe *less* often than usual until the balance is restored. These illustrations—and there are others—have nothing to do with drugs; but in a similar way, it seems that if a continued pain, or an unpleasant emotional state such as anxiety or depression is changed into its opposite, or removed altogether by the use of a drug, the prior state may return with increased force when the drug is no longer taken. The "rebound" phenomenon, naturally, encourages the patient to take another dose, and so on.

3. *Habit formation.* This alternation of mood-changed-by-drug with the disturbed mood itself leads to the habit of taking the drug. The patient comes to rely upon it and to take it anyway, even before the unpleasant state has returned. At this stage he is said to be "habituated"; he has a psychological need for the drug, and later may become disturbed at the possibility that it will not be available when he needs it. This might

not matter so greatly, if it were not that continued use of drugs in this way has physical consequences as well.

4. *Tolerance and habituation.* The body also tends to restore its own balance when drugs are given, too. It "learns" surprisingly quickly how to deal with substances with which it has never before been confronted, so that it eliminates subsequent doses more and more quickly and completely. Thus the effect of each successive dose is smaller and lasts for progressively shorter periods of time. To counter this, the patient tends to increase the dose; and the vicious circle continues. At this point he has become physically dependent upon the drug; and he may suffer physically—sometimes so severely that he dies—if supplies are not continued.

As he increases the dose in this way, so his tolerance of its effects increases, to such an extent that after prolonged use he may be taking doses of a drug that are five or ten times greater than those which will kill somebody not dependent upon them in this way. It sometimes happens that a patient develops a renewed craving at some point after a course of treatment, in which the dose of drug has been reduced without removing the underlying cause of his dependence. He may then obtain and use the dose he habitually took before treatment, not knowing that his body will have lost its tolerance of such doses. That dose is now as high for him as for any other person and so may be lethal. There has been a number of deaths for this reason.

Factors in the Causation of Dependence.

The risk of becoming dependent upon a drug is governed by three main factors; the drug itself, the personality of the individual who takes it, and the circumstances in which it is taken. Most adults have taken alcohol at one time or another, unless it is against their code to do so; yet *relatively* few are dependent upon it (relatively few, but many too many; more than half a million in the United Kingdom alone). Many of us have had morphine or some other strong analgesic for medical reasons, without becoming dependent upon it (whatever so-called addicts say, it is extremely rare for anyone to become dependent on an opiate because he was introduced to it in a medical setting). On the other hand, if we start to take such a drug "for kicks"—as more and more people, particularly teen-agers and young adults are doing—it is extremely probable that we shall become dependent upon it, and sooner rather than later at that. It is also probable that each one of us would become dependent, were he obliged to take it regularly, for long enough, and in sufficient dosage. Thus, although there are personalities—psychopathic, immature, or unstable—that are more prone than others to become dependent if they are exposed to the drug, there are also drugs that are more likely than others to cause such dependence no matter to whom they are given. The extent of the dependence will vary; with some, it is never physiological but remains psychological (but not the less real or disturbing for that). Also, the rate at which dependence develops may vary; and the picture presented by the dependent subject—the extent to which his normal life is impaired, or to which he becomes dangerous to himself or others—varies as well. In a very much oversimplified way, some of these relationships will now be summarised for certain substances.

Heroin, morphine and cocaine are usually injected. Barbiturates (sleeping pills) and amphetamines ("Benzedrine") are tablets or capsules, and marihuana ("reefer," hashish) is smoked in cigarettes. Heroin and cocaine are now usually taken together. Combinations of drugs often act differently from their individual constituents and patients dependent upon them are even more difficult to treat. Barbiturate and amphetamine, also, are often mixed (as in "purple hearts"). There is considerable *psychological* dependence on heroin, morphine, cocaine, and amphetamine, but much less with marihuana. *Physiological* dependence is great with heroin and morphine, less with barbiturates, alcohol, and amphetamine in that order, and virtually nil with cocaine and marihuana. Personality plays a greater part in initiating dependence on alcohol, marihuana, and barbiturates than with the others. Heroin, cocaine, and morphine are the cause of more antisocial tendencies in dependent people than alcohol, barbiturates, and amphetamine. The chief danger of marihuana (mere possession of which is illegal) seems to be that the search for it will lead the searcher into localities where his risk of exposure to even more dangerous influences is greatly increased. It is thus sometimes argued that if it were legal to consume marihuana, the number of young people who yearly become dependent upon the other more dangerous drugs would in fact decrease. There is as yet no evidence for or against this proposition. The number of drug dependent people in U.K. is rising fast for heroin and cocaine. This number is very large for alcohol, and is increasing in the case of barbiturates and marihuana. Very few people are dependent on morphine, and the number is not growing.

Treatment.

Exhortations, imprisonment, and other moralistic or legalistic approaches are useless. Treatment of any person dependent upon a drug is a matter for a qualified psychotherapist. It is liable to be time-consuming and frustrating for patient and doctor, and it is frequently unsuccessful. At present, there are too few specialists or centres where treatment can be obtained, although it is to be hoped that this situation will change as the problem is increasingly seen by our society to be of exceptional gravity.

When there is little or no chance of cure, prevention is certainly the best treatment. Drugs should only be taken on the prescription of a doctor; and the patient should remind him from time to time, if this be necessary, that he would like to dispense with his drugs as soon as the doctor thinks it possible. It should also be remembered that there is often no need to reach for the aspirin (or any other drug that anyone can buy from the chemist without prescription) at the first sign of a headache—or to reach for it at all to help one sleep or relax, for which purpose such drugs are in any case pharmacologically useless. A wait for ten minutes is good discipline, and will frequently resolve the problem to an extent that makes a drug unnecessary.

THE BLOOD.

INTRODUCTION.

Doctors who have made a special study of the blood are known as haematologists. Haematology itself is a complex subject because blood itself is complex and its many functions are not easy to describe and only a brief account will be given here. A few basic facts to begin with:

Blood consists of a fluid, called plasma, in which are suspended red and white blood cells and in which are dissolved many substances from the simple ones like glucose to the complex like hormones, proteins and fats. Total blood volume amounts to about five litres; the blood donor gives about half a litre at a session and feels no ill effects. Loss of a litre or more induces surgical shock (*q.v.* First Aid). The cells in blood are either red or white. Red cells are red because they carry a protein called haemoglobin which is capable of carrying oxygen. There are about five million red cells for each cubic millilitre of blood (that is an average sized drop), a total of five thousand million circulating in the body at any one time. The life of a red cell is about six weeks; new ones are constantly replacing old ones which are "buried" by the spleen.

The haemoglobin from dead cells is recycled; new cells are generated in the marrow of bones, including the breast bone, from which samples of marrow can be taken by a technique known as sternal puncture. Such samples are studied with a microscope to establish diagnoses of various blood disorders. White cells are of five basic types, the names of which need not concern us here. Each type has a specific function—some act as bacterial scavengers, some are concerned with antibodies (q.v.) and some with the general defence system of the body which is concerned with the development and maintenance of immunity to various diseases both bactericidal and viral. There are also non-cell particles derived from large cells which the marrow produces. These are platelets, which are concerned with blood clotting. They have the capacity to "stick" to any gaps in blood vessels (such as may be caused by injury or, in the minutest of blood vessels, "wear and tear") and initiate blood clotting. All these types of cells can be studied in the test tube after taking a sample from the patient. This is known as venepuncture, a simple and virtually painless procedure, carried out by doctor or nurse or trained "phlebotomist", by inserting a needle on the end of a syringe into a dilated vein in the crook of the arm. Marrow samples can also be taken, as we have said, from the breast bone—but that is a very different procedure, requiring local anaesthetic and much more skill. For the patient it is not exactly a comfortable procedure either.

The fluid part of the blood, plasma, is more the province of the biochemist than the haematologist. The immunologist is also interested in plasma and all three disciplines tend to overlap to some degree. Plasma can be studied in the same way as whole blood. A venepuncture is carried out, a chemical added to stop clotting and the cells can then be removed in a centrifuge. If blood is allowed to clot in the test tube, the cells are all caught up in the clot and the plasma remains liquid and can be poured off. It is then known as serum. Plasma contains substances which are either dissolved, that is, in solution, or are held "in suspension". By this is meant that the plasma forms an emulsion because protein and fat particles are not soluble and can only form suspensions in this way. The protein and fat particles are in suspension in a like manner. The substances both in solution and in suspension are much too numerous to be dealt with here.

The functions of blood are manifold, but essentially blood is a transport medium, concerned with moving gases (oxygen and carbon dioxide), moving food (protein, carbohydrate, fat, minerals and vitamins) and eliminating waste products (nitrogen, ammonia and other protein breakdown end products).

Red Cell Diseases.

These are of two main groups leading to a shortage of red cells (anaemia), or an excess (polycythaemia). The former is much the more common and there are many different kinds. In all of them the shortage of red cells results in a depletion of the capacity of the blood to carry oxygen. This means that the heart must work harder to send more blood than usual to the tissues, and even so the tissues will often go short. The patient will be persistently tired and listless, and if the anaemia is severe the action of the brain and heart will be seriously impeded, even leading to fainting, cardiac pain, and breathlessness on exertion. All these symptoms, however, can be caused by many other conditions. The only way to be sure they are due to anaemia is by a proper examination of the blood, and even this will not lead to the truth if the picture has been spoilt by the patient taking iron tonics and other remedies of his own accord. Therefore do not dose yourself with tonics, in case you really have anaemia. You may make it impossible to arrive at a proper diagnosis later.

Haemorrhagic Anaemia. Anaemia, a shortage of red cells, may be due to a variety of causes, singly or in combination. One very obvious cause is loss of blood or haemorrhage. Following the sudden loss of a half-litre of blood or more, the red-

cell-producing bone marrow "factory" will step up its production; but even if it is adequately supplied with all the raw materials such as iron, it may well take many weeks to build up the numbers to normal. A very severe degree of haemorrhagic anaemia is usually treated by blood transfusion. Milder degrees can be treated by taking extra iron, often over a long period of time. The supply of iron for making new red-cell pigment is nearly always the bottle-neck which limits production. Haemorrhagic anaemia can commonly occur, however, without a sudden severe haemorrhage. From what has been said about the constant replacement of red cells as they wear out, it must be obvious that even if there is only a slight failure to keep pace with the numbers lost, several months of such a failure can eventually deplete the numbers to the level of very severe anaemia. This situation is common when small amounts of blood are being continuously or repeatedly lost, and here again it is a shortage of dietary iron which is the usual cause of the failure to replace the lost red cells. Normal menstrual loss in women and girls whose diet is on the border-line of iron deficiency is a common cause of progressive tiredness and lack of energy. Where the menstrual flow is heavier than usual, or where it is frankly excessive in older women due to the various common gynaecological disorders, serious anaemia is surprisingly common. During pregnancy a great deal of iron is lost by the mother to the baby, and this, together with the inevitable blood loss at delivery, often makes for a very tired mother indeed, just at the time when there is an enormous amount of work to be done to manufacture milk and attend to all the extra household tasks of baby care. For these reasons it is almost routinely advisable to build up stocks of iron throughout the pregnancy by remembering to take the pills provided. Men as well as women can lose small amounts of blood continuously in later life from gastro-intestinal conditions such as piles, ulcers, and tropical infestations such as hookworm; and here again the anaemia may be just as severe in the long run as that which inevitably follows a sudden, massive haemorrhage. One extra word of warning. Do not assume because you are pale that you are anaemic. Pallor is a very poor guide, because it is dependent on so many other things, like the blood vessels in your skin, and its thickness and translucency. Nothing but a blood test (which is so easy for your doctor to do) can really tell you if you are anaemic. And if your anaemia is due to a blood-losing condition, then that too must be treated. So do not be tempted to treat yourself, and never delay seeing your doctor about any excessive or unexplained bleeding, from any source.

Haemolytic Anaemia occurs when for any reason, there are more blood cells than usual being destroyed in the body. This may be because the cells are abnormally fragile, or because normal cells have been attacked by something to which you are allergic, or rarely because you have become sensitive to your own red cells. Sometimes unborn babies have severe haemolytic anaemia, due to an incompatability of blood group (Rh factor) between the mother and the baby, and the same sort of thing happens if incompatible blood is given by mistake in blood transfusion. Up to a point, in mild haemolytic anaemia, the bone marrow can keep pace with the increased loss of cells, but beyond this point anaemia develops. After incompatible blood transfusions a very dangerous situation results from the effects of the destruction of red cells and the liberation of their products into the blood. One form of jaundice is often produced in haemolytic anaemia, the patient becoming yellow because of the breakdown products of red cells circulating in excess as bile pigments. These latter are normally always present to a small extent due to the normal, comparatively small, rate of destruction of effete red cells.

Aplastic Anaemia is the term given to anaemia due to a virtually total failure of the bone marrow red-cell factory. Sometimes this occurs for no obvious reason. It is sometimes due to a heavy dose of radioactivity or X-rays knocking out the cells of the "factory." It may even be due to cancer cells growing in the bone marrow cavity and not leaving sufficient room for the red marrow cells. It is fortunate that aplastic anaemia is very rare, because it can only be treated by blood transfusions every few weeks for the rest of the patient's life. Very occasionally there have been exceptions to this rule, when the patient's marrow has re-awakened for no apparent reason and suddenly begins to make red cells again. Some marrow diseases have been apparently successfully treated with bone marrow grafts but the technique is of very recent development and it is probably too early for a full assessmant of the potential to be made.

Pernicious Anaemia. This is a fairly uncommon anaemia, which has a very interesting story. The processes by which red cells are manufactured are many and complex, and depend, like so many other bodily activities, on the supply of a vitamin containing cobalt, called vitamin B_{12}. This is nearly always present in more than adequate quantities in the diet, but in order for it to be absorbed from the intestine, there must also be a substance called "intrinsic factor" which is normally made by the lining of the stomach. People with pernicious anaemia have suffered a degeneration of the lining of their stomachs, probably because, for some reason, they have become "sensitive" to this part of their own tissue. This kind of civil war within the body is known as an "auto-immune" disease, and is comparable in type with some forms of haemolytic anaemia. In other words they destroy their own stomach lining, fail to produce "intrinsic factor," and as a result fail to absorb vitamin B_{12} into the body. Faced with a failure in the supply of this essential substance, the bone marrow produces too few red cells, and the few that are produced are deformed, much too large, and very fragile. In addition to its role in blood formation, vitamin B_{12} is essential to the normal functioning of the spinal cord, and in long-standing cases of untreated pernicious anaemia, there is often a resulting neurological disability.

The cure for pernicious anaemia was discovered nearly 60 years ago, and is a triumph for the scientific investigation of the causes of disease. While treating anaemic dogs, an American scientist named Minot discovered that eating raw liver in large quantities produced a tremendous improvement. Patients with pernicious anaemia were then made to eat vast quantities of raw liver—about one or two pounds a day—and were found to get better, whereas previously they had inevitably died. Raw liver is, of course, very unpleasant to eat, and after a few years it was found possible to prepare crude extracts for injection. Injection had the great advantage that no absorption difficulties arose, and much less liver could be used. Biochemists then began the enormous task of trying to find which of the thousands of substances in liver was the vital factor, and after many years of painstaking chemical fractionation of liver and trying out the various fractions as a cure for the disease, vitamin B_{12} was discovered. The pure substance is one of the most powerful substances known, being active in amounts as small as millionths of a gram. Nowadays pernicious anaemia is treated by small occasional injections of the vitamin, whose other name is cyanocobalamin. A similar molecule, without the cobalt atom, is now used. This is called hydroxycobalamin.

Polycythaemia. Too many red cells per cubic millilitre of blood can be found without there being an increase of the total number of red cells in the body. This occurs in dehydration, when there is a loss of plasma without a comparable loss of cells, and is called haemo-concentration. Alternatively, the bone marrow can manufacture more cells than usual as a response to living for long periods at high altitudes. The beneficial result can be that the blood can carry normal amounts of oxygen, even though the supply (in the rarefied air) is reduced. Finally there is a red cell disease in which the bone marrow factory gets out of control and produces too many cells with no beneficial results. The number in the blood can be double the normal and the blood becomes so thick that the heart has difficulty pumping it round the body. This disease (*polycythaemia rubra vera*) used to be treated by repeatedly bleeding the patient to reduce the numbers of cells. It is now treated very successfully with carefully judged amounts of radioactive phosphorus or certain other "antimitotic" chemicals which reduce the rate of multiplication of bone marrow cells.

White Cell Diseases.

Diseases of the white cells are very much less common but when they occur are inevitably serious.

Agranulocytosis. In this condition the number of those white cells which are responsible for phagocytosis of bacteria falls precipitously. The result is that one of the main bodily defences against infection fails, and the patient may die from an overwhelming invasion of germs and the accompanying high fever. The usual cause is abnormal sensitivity to certain drugs, often those which are in widespread use and only give trouble in the occasional case. One example among hundreds is the antibiotic chloramphenicol which specifically kills typhoid bacteria and is used for that purpose. It is believed that about one patient in 60,000 becomes sensitive to it and agranulocytosis often fatally follows. The fact that almost any drug *can* do this to some people and yet be quite safe for the majority, is one good reason not to dose yourself unnecessarily with over-the-counter medicines.

Leukaemia. This is a cancer of the white cells, in which the normal rate of production of any of the white cells gets out of control, leading to a pile-up of abnormal cells at the site of production (bone marrow, lymph nodes, and spleen) or in the blood, or both. In spite of an increase in their numbers, their abnormality renders them unable to combat infection; sepsis and fever result. It is known that this kind of cancer can be caused by the effects of ionizing radiation on the white-cell factory, and it is certain at least in animals, that viruses can also be responsible. Survivors from the atomic explosions in Japan have subsequently suffered from leukaemia far more commonly than the rest of us, as have doctors, nurses, and patients who have been over-exposed to X-rays. At the time of writing, leukaemia is still a uniformly fatal disease, although patients may sometimes survive many years. Their remaining time can nearly always be made more comfortable by various forms of treatment, and one day a cure will be found by the research workers devoting their time to its study. It is difficult not to get very impatient with the slow rate of progress of these studies, particularly when caring for children and young people whose lives are inevitably ended by the disease. The solution, however, as with other forms of cancer, probably depends on the understanding of the nature of life itself, and as long as biological research remains short of the relatively small amounts of money required to tackle these problems at reasonable speed, we have no right to be impatient, except with our elected leaders who spend far more than is needed on less important things.

Hodgkin's disease, Lymphosarcoma and Reticulo acoma. These are diseases which are in some ways akin to *leukaemia.* Abnormal cells are found in the reticulo-edothelial system and proliferate in a disorganised manner, causing enlargement of lymph nodes (glands), spleen and sometimes the liver. Hodgkin's disease, named after a 19th cent. Guy's physician, has been the subject of much research and therapeutic trial. At special centres in London and elsewhere, earlier diagnosis and new methods of ascertaining the extent of the disease process have led to advances in surgical and medical treatment which show much promise. If treated early the disease can be apparently halted or even eradicated.

Hæmorrhagic or Bleeding Diseases.

Whenever blood vessels are damaged by injury, there is a remarkable series of mechanisms which automatically come into operation to stem the flow of blood. There is a constriction of all the smaller vessels in the locality. Platelets stick together and release substances which help the vessels to stay constricted as well as others necessary to blood clotting, and yet others which help to bind the clot tightly together. Later, materials appear to prevent too much clotting, and eventually the clot is removed altogether as healing proceeds. There are some very complicated diseases of this blood-conserving mechanism which can lead to abnormal bleeding, sometimes beneath the skin to produce bruising or even smaller leaks; sometimes leading to a greater loss of blood, particularly following a wound. In some kinds of *purpura* (bleeding tendency) the blood vessels are the cause of the trouble, having become fragile and leaky for a number of reasons. This happens in old age (*senile purpura*), in scurvy, or vitamin C deficiency, as an occasional accompaniment to infective diseases, or as an immunological effect on the lining of blood vessels when the patient becomes sensitised to certain substances (*Schönlein-Henoch* or *anaphylactoid purpura*). The latter often follows a streptococcal sore throat, just as rheumatic fever and acute nephritis do; and as well as the purpura there may be joint pains and nephritis. Just as almost any drug or chemical will cause agranulocytosis in some people, so it can also cause anaphylactoid purpura.

Purpura may also be due to a lack of platelets, known as thrombocytopenia (a shortage of thrombocytes or platelets). This can happen if the bone marrow factory is depressed, since this is where platelets too are made. It is therefore a common accompaniment of leukaemia or aplastic anaemia. Or there can be increased destruction of platelets in some diseases of the spleen. Platelets normally last eight to ten days, but their lifespan can be shortened in heart failure, and following massive transfusions, or often for no apparent reason ("idiopathic" thrombocytopenia), when removal of the spleen can sometimes help.

Finally, defects of the *clotting mechanism* will lead to a bleeding tendency, and since the mechanism itself is very complex, so is the variety of things which can upset it. The liver provides the blood with many of the substances required for clotting, so it is not surprising that a clotting defect commonly accompanies liver disease. One necessary substance for blood clotting is called "antihaemophilic factor" and is missing from people who have inherited the disease *haemophilia*. These unfortunate people may die of haemorrhage from quite small cuts or minor surgical procedures like tooth-extraction, and although it is possible to prepare antihaemophilic factor, it is not yet possible to give continuous, life-long treatment with it. Haemostatic drugs, such as aminocaproic acid, may be used to minimise blood loss during minor operative procedures such as dental extractions.

THE HEART AND BLOOD-VESSELS.

INTRODUCTION.

The heart consists of about 350g of muscle which makes up the walls of its four chambers. Anatomically the human heart closely resembles the sheeps' hearts to be found in a butcher's shop. Indeed it would be an instructive exercise to dissect one of these in the order described below, since there is no other way of properly appreciating what the chambers, valves, etc., are really like. There are two quite separate pumps in the heart—one on the owner's right (or on your *left* if you are looking at the front of someone else) and one on his left. The right heart collects spent, deoxygenated, "venous" blood which returns there from the whole of the body, and gives it the comparatively small push required to drive it through the adjacent lungs. The left heart collects the revitalised, oxygenated "arterial" blood as it trickles away from the lungs, and gives it the enormous push required to build up the arterial blood-pressure, so that it can be forced through all the tissues of the body. As may be expected, the right heart chambers have much thinner walls than the left, since their muscle has less work to do. This will help you get your bearings with the sheep's heart. The tip, or apex, is the lowest part. The thick-feeling side is the left, the thin the right; and the great vessels are at the top.

The upper chamber on the right, or right atrium, has two large openings into it through which all the spent blood arrives from the upper and lower great veins (the superior and inferior venae cavae). Cut open the thin wall of the right atrium with scissors between these two holes to lay open the interior of the chamber, noting the "auricle" or "dog's ear" that forms a small cul-de-sac. The whole chamber is sometimes, inaccurately, called the auricle. You should be able to push a finger downwards into the lower chamber—the right ventricle—through a communicating hole guarded by the three thin cusps of the *tricuspid valve*. These will not obstruct your finger, since they are designed to permit blood flow in the same direction. When the atrium is full of blood, it squeezes its contents through the tricuspid valve into the right ventricle; and when, a split second later, the ventricle is full and contracts, the three cusps come together to prevent the blood from flowing backwards into the atrium again. Instead the spent blood is driven onwards through the *pulmonary valve* (in the upper part of the right ventricle), through the pulmonary artery, to be delivered to the lungs. The pulmonary valve has three very well-defined cusps which prevent blood from coming back into the ventricle as it relaxes to receive more blood from the atrium before the next contraction or beat. It is possible to pass a blade of the scissors from the opened-out right atrium, through the tricuspid valve towards the tip of the heart, and cut along the right border of the heart through the thickness of the ventricular muscle. Then cut upwards again, passing the scissors blade through the pulmonary valve and open up the *pulmonary artery*. If you have done this successfully you will have followed the path taken by the spent blood through the right heart to the lungs. Notice the thick round bands of muscle lining the ventricle, and notice too that you have not entered the left heart, which has no connection with the right except in some congenital malformations (see later). The same dissection can now be made of the left heart. Open up the *left atrium*, noting its "dog's ear" or "auricle," pass the scissors down into the *left ventricle* through the two rather flimsy cusps of the *mitral valve*. Notice how much thicker is the muscle of the left ventricle, and cut upwards through the three well-formed cusps of the *aortic valve* into the main artery of the body—the *aorta*. The aorta as it leaves the left heart is distinguishable from the pulmonary artery as it leaves the right, partly by the extreme toughness of the aortic wall (it has to withstand so much more blood-pressure); and partly by the entrances or orifices of the two small branches given off by the aorta, just beyond the valve cusps, which go to supply the heart muscle itself with blood. These are the *coronary arteries* which are so necessary for the heart's own survival.

The amount of blood pumped in unit time, or the *cardiac output*, can be varied a great deal, according to the needs of the moment. This is accomplished by altering both the heart rate and the stroke volume, the amount expelled per beat. Every minute, the healthy adult man at rest shifts about 5 litres of blood through the heart—an amount equivalent to all the blood he possesses. When exercise is taken, or in response to anxiety or fear, this is stepped up many times, so that the muscles can receive a greatly augmented supply of the materials required for action. The controlling mechanisms which allow these changes to be made automatically are partly organised in the brain by the so-called *cardiac centre*; and partly by local mechanical and chemical stimuli to the heart muscle itself. The cardiac centre is continuously receiving information through nerves about the physical and chemical state of the circulation, and also from the mind; which is partly how certain emotions make the heart beat faster. All the information is integrated, and a cardiac output continuously arranged which is appropriate for current demands.

Cardiac Neurosis. In ordinary circumstances at rest, most healthy people are not conscious of their heart-beat. However, there are many perfectly healthy people whose hearts slip in an extra beat occasionally. Sometimes their owners are aware of this and become unnecessarily alarmed. Their fear causes palpitations (a pounding of the heart) and the tension mounts. An undue anxiety about the tricks played by a healthy heart sometimes leads people to interpret minor pains in the chest, or even indigestion, as grave symptoms of heart disease, and the consequent anxiety leads to still worse symptoms. If you are one of these worried people, take your worries to your doctor, and let him decide for you whether there is anything wrong. A hundred to one there isn't, and then you will have to find something else to worry about, or better still give up the habit altogether. Many people secretly worry about heart disease and high blood-pressure for years, when very often they are worrying unnecessarily. Even if there is cause for worry, so much can be done for these conditions (as it can for cancer) provided medical advice is taken early in the course of the disease. Remember, too, that the slight feeling of giddiness when you get up suddenly from having been lying down, is often experienced by most normal people; but if you get frightened by it you will begin to breathe more quickly and deeply; and this in itself will make you feel even more faint—and so on.

Heart Failure. When the cardiac output of blood is too little for the requirements of the body, a state of *circulatory failure* has arisen, and when this is due primarily to the heart itself being at fault, it is more properly called *heart failure*. As will be seen, heart failure is not a disease, but the common result of a large number of different diseases. The signs and symptoms produced are caused by two sorts of process: (a) tissues of the body have too little blood flow through them and are therefore undersupplied; (b) blood accumulates and stagnates in tissues, causing congestion, since the failing heart cannot move forward the amount of blood presented to it in the great veins. Often the left or right side of the heart fails disproportionately. In *left heart failure* the lungs are congested because they are the territory from which the left heart is failing to move blood. The patient has great difficulty with his breathing, and in advanced cases may not be able to breathe when he lies down, because the lungs become so congested and waterlogged. In *right heart failure* the main veins are congested and the other parts of the body become swollen with excess tissue fluid, mainly in the lower parts such as the legs and ankles. This swelling with fluid is called oedema, and in heart failure is only partly due to the mechanics of the failing heart. It is mainly due to a poorly understood retention of sodium in the body, a situation in which excess water is also retained. Whatever the type of heart failure it is always likely to be a changing condition, since the amount of failure will depend as much on the demands being made as on the state of the heart. For instance, in mild cases at rest when the required cardiac output is small, there may be no signs or symptoms. These may only appear on exertion. Heart failure will be referred to again later under the various conditions which cause it.

Treatment of heart failure is quite logical. It is aimed at correcting the imbalance between supply and demand of blood, and at the removal of the accumulated excess fluid. We can therefore (a) reduce the body's demand for blood; (b) increase the supply or cardiac output; and (c) promote the excretion of sodium and fluid. Demand for blood is reduced by rest, both physical and mental, and by reduction of weight, since obesity (being overweight) is an additional demand on the cardiovascular system. The cardiac output can be increased by administering a "tonic" to the heart muscle in the form of *digitalis*, which is a powerful heart stimulant derived from fox-

glove leaf. Fluid (and hence salt) accumulation can be helped by restricting the intake of salt and by giving drugs which promote its excretion by the kidneys (diuretics). Very occasionally, very large accumulations of fluid in the legs, abdomen, or thorax, are tapped and drained physically, with needles. These remarks on treatment, as elsewhere in the Medical Section, are of course very general and must not encourage anyone to treat himself for such a potentially serious condition as heart failure. Even such a simple measure as doing without salt can be practised quite unnecessarily by many people for years, simply as a result of reading a paragraph like the above. The most they accomplish is to make their food taste horribly dull. If you need to reduce salt intake you should be in your doctor's care, and so please let him decide.

Congenital Heart Disease. It has been estimated that of all the babies born who survive at least one month, there will be about one in every two hundred with some form of congenital heart disease; that is to say that the heart will have failed to develop properly in embryonic life. In some cases this is associated with a virus disease of the mother (commonly rubella, or German measles) or with certain drugs taken by the mother (e.g. thalidomide) at a time, very early in pregnancy, when organs are assuming their adult shape. Parents should see to it that their daughters get German measles before they grow up; and drugs of all kinds should be avoided where possible during early pregnancy. In most cases of congenital heart disease, however, there is no known cause, and it seems that the manner of formation of the embryonic heart is so delicate that it can be thrown out of gear very easily, perhaps even by chance. Scores of different types of defect occur, singly and in combination. Any of the valves may be anatomically defective—either failing to close properly (*incompetence*) or being too tight (*stenosis*); the great vessels (pulmonary artery and aorta) may be switched round, or *transposed*, so that they emerge from the wrong ventricle; there may be defects in the wall (*septum*) which separates the atria or the ventricles on each side (*septal defect*, or "hole in the heart"); or there may be a persistence of the vessel which in the foetus normally by-passes the lungs by joining the pulmonary artery to the aorta (*patent ductus arteriosus*). This vessel normally closes at the time of birth when the first breaths are taken, and subsequently disappears, so that the whole output of the heart is then sent round the lungs. Detecting congenital heart disease early is one of the purposes of routine post-natal check-up examinations of the baby. Exact diagnosis requires very complicated techniques, and sometimes the structural defect can be corrected by surgery, with almost miraculous results.

Rheumatic Heart Disease. Acute rheumatic fever is not to be confused with other forms of rheumatism. Many tissues of the body (particularly the heart) are attacked, as well as the joints, and the trouble is due to a sensitivity which has developed to certain bacteria (*haemolytic streptococci*) which have probably caused a sore throat about three weeks before the onset of the disease. Why acute rheumatism only rarely follows streptococcal sore throat is poorly understood, but this is no consolation to the one per cent or so of the population whose hearts bear its scars. During the acute phase of the illness which usually occurs before the age of fifteen, inflammatory damage occurs to the valves, the heart muscle, and the sac in which the heart lives, the *pericardium*. So there is a *valvulitis* or *endocarditis*, a *myocarditis* and a *pericarditis*. There may be acute heart failure at this stage if the heart is severely affected. The better-known results of rheumatic heart disease, however, are caused in the ensuing years by scarring of the healed valves. The valves are thickened and deformed. They may have lost their elasticity and stretch, so that they do not close properly (*incompetence*); or they may contract and tighten (*stenosis*). In both cases the heart chamber situated next to the affected valve has to work progressively harder, either because it gets no rest in between beats (in *incompetence*); or it has to force the blood through too narrow a hole (in *stenosis*). The end result is some variety of heart failure (P27). Although there are other causes of valvular heart disease which will now be mentioned, rheumatic fever is much the commonest, and much valve trouble can be blamed on rheumatic fever even when the patient has no recollection of ever having suffered from it. The other, much rarer, causes may be syphilis, congenital valvular anomaly, healed bacterial endocarditis, atherosclerosis, and mechanical injury.

The most commonly affected valve is the mitral, usually causing *mitral stenosis*, in which the opening between the left atrium and the left ventricle will sometimes only admit one finger-tip instead of three fingers as it should. In time the left atrium becomes much enlarged as it overworks to force blood through this narrow orifice. Later still a back pressure develops in the lungs causing congestion and breathlessness; and even later the right ventricle is strained as it tries to force blood into the already congested lung. This is a classic example of the march of trouble backwards from the site of the damaged valve involving first the chamber "behind" it (the left atrium), then the territory "behind" that (the lungs), then the pulmonary arteries taking blood to the lungs, and finally the right ventricle trying to send blood to the pulmonary artery. This steady march of events is usually very slow, and can commonly take twenty years or longer from the initial attack of acute rheumatism to the severer symptoms of advanced mitral stenosis. Treatment is both medical and surgical. The heart failure is treated medically as already described. These days surgical reopening of the valve is almost commonplace, either by inserting a finger through the left auricle and breaking down the constriction, or by opening up the heart and re-shaping the valve under direct vision. The latter involves the additional problem of by-passing the heart by the use of some sort of external pump and poses additional problems, even though from other points of view it is obviously more convenient. As always with major surgical procedures much of the problem is in selecting the patients who will benefit from the operation and in whom it is feasible. Quite often there are other valves involved, mainly the aortic or tricuspid or both, and the hydrostatic or "plumbing" problems can be extremely complex. With luck, however, combined with good judgement and good surgery, the lives of incapacitated patients can be transformed by mitral, and other valvular, surgery. Recently a great deal of progress has been made in designing new "ball-in-basket" valves of manmade materials to replace damaged natural valves. The *aortic valve* is stenosed or narrowed by other degenerative processes besides rheumatism. *Tricuspid stenosis* is nearly always rheumatic in origin.

Coronary Heart Disease. This is the term used whenever the blood supply to the heart muscle (through the coronary arteries) is reduced to such an extent that the heart muscle suffers from a lack of supplies. It has a number of causes, but the only really common one is partial obstruction of the coronary arteries by a condition known as *atheroma* or *atherosclerosis*, and sometimes inaccurately called *arteriosclerosis*. This arterial disease is described later (P29). It takes the form of swellings or lumps on the lining of the artery which, if they become large enough to interfere seriously with the flow of blood, produce a blood starvation or *ischaemia* of the tissue being supplied. Obviously, the smaller the artery, the more easily will a lump of given size impede the flow. Equally obviously the greater the demand for blood, as in exercise, the more blood "starvation" there will be. There are two degrees of coronary artery disease: one in which the blood flow is reduced to the point where the increased demands of hard work cannot be met, and this results in *angina pectoris* due to *coronary insufficiency*; the other is when the coronary artery becomes completely blocked, preventing the flow of blood altogether, usually by a *thrombus* or clot of blood, and this is *coronary thrombosis*.

Angina Pectoris. Whenever activity is increased in any muscle, the demands for oxygen and nutriments from the blood-stream increase,

and as these are used up there is an increased production of waste products known as metabolites. To meet the demands for a greater supply and a more efficient waste-disposal, the blood flow through the exercising muscle must always be increased. If sufficient increase does not occur, not only will there be a shortage of supplies, but there will also be a pile-up of metabolites in the muscle which cannot be carried away. It is mainly because of these latter that pain is caused in ischaemic, or blood-starved muscle, and pain is one of the chief symptoms when heart muscle becomes ischaemic. One important mechanism for increasing blood flow normally to exercising muscle is by automatically dilating the vessels concerned. Diseased vessels, such as coronary arteries when they are affected by atheroma, are not so easily dilated, although certain drugs which are powerful dilators of arterioles can accomplish a great deal, albeit temporarily. The measures taken to relieve the pain and blood-starvation of angina are two-fold. The patient can reduce the demands of the heart by a few minutes' rest, and a drug (usually nitroglycerin) can be taken to dilate the coronary vessels of supply. Another obvious long-term way to reduce demands is for the overweight patient to eat less, and reduce the load of extra body weight on his circulation. It is very frustrating, to say the least, that such an incapacitating and often lethal condition should be caused by the narrowing or blockage of only 5 or 8 cm of narrow piping about 3·5 mm wide. It is now possible to treat some forms of coronary artery disease by surgical means.

Heart Attack or *Coronary Thrombosis.* It should readily be understood from the above description that heart attacks will vary in their severity according to the amount of heart muscle deprived of blood; and this in turn will depend on where in the coronary artery the obstruction occurs. Most usually it is the left ventricular muscle which is cut off from supplies and dies, either in part or in all of its thickness. Since it is the left ventricle which does most of the work of pumping blood to the body, serious heart failure (P27) is to be expected. If too much muscle is killed, the heart will simply stop, and the patient will suddenly die. It is much more usual, however, for enough muscle to be left for survival, albeit with a greatly reduced cardiac efficiency. A heart attack is usually accompanied by severe pain, similar to the pain of angina but more severe, and unrelieved by rest or by the patient's usual drugs. Very occasionally the event occurs apparently without pain, or with so little that it is ignored. These so-called "silent" coronary attacks can make diagnosis extremely difficult. Since the doctor depends very considerably with heart attacks on an exact, spontaneous description of symptoms for his diagnosis, no description will be given here. There are many over-anxious people who will read these words and could be misled into an unspontaneous description of their own symptoms, and this could make the task of treating them such a problem that they could even be mis-diagnosed as a result. If you have the smallest worry that your chest pain is due to your heart, take your anxiety to your doctor without delay. He will almost certainly be able to re-assure you; and if it happens to be your heart after all, you will have taken the first sensible step towards proper treatment. Dangerous as heart attacks are, they are by no means the death warrant that many lay people think, any more than cancer is. The treatment for a true heart attack is urgent and prolonged. Patients must be at complete rest and their pain relieved quickly. The area of heart muscle they have lost must be allowed to heal with a good, firm scar, and this can take three months of rest, often in hospital.

You can help to avoid a heart attack by not smoking, avoiding obesity and living a physically active life. Avoid sudden exercise, however, when you are not in training. Surgeons are able to replace diseased coronary arteries in some patients with small veins taken from other parts of the body.

Blood-pressure. The blood is normally under great pressure in the arterial system, since it is this which forces it into all the tissues of the body.

It is therefore no more meaningful to say you have "blood-pressure" than to say you have a temperature. You would be very badly off without. Blood-pressure which is too high, however, can give rise to problems, though not always. It is another of those conditions like angina and cancer, which engender much anxiety among people even when they do not suffer from them. For this reason doctors are often unwilling to disclose a patient's blood-pressure and because of this they unjustifiably earn a reputation for unreasonable secrecy. They are themselves to blame for the general public anxiety as the following true story shows. Some years ago a lady in her fifties wished to accompany her husband to a post abroad which was to last four years. All arrangements had been made—the husband resigned his previous job, sold the house, etc.—when it was discovered at a routine medical examination that she had a high blood-pressure, and she was very solemnly advised by the rather elderly doctor not to go. There was great consternation and emotional upheaval, not least because of the inconvenience involved. Eventually she was allowed to go at her own risk. The husband's job lasted eight years instead of four, during which the lady was in no way inconvenienced by her blood-pressure; except that she worried interminably about it. On returning home to retire she began to think she had angina, and elaborate hospital investigation revealed that, as might be expected, her arteries were not as young as they used to be. She was undoubtedly suffering from mild angina, but not as badly as she thought. The opportunity then arose, in her late sixties, to go abroad yet again, and this she did, living a quite strenuous life, and one which she enjoyed. She returned home again, twenty years after she had gone abroad for the first time, able to run a home and still with very little inconvenience from her blood-pressure. There is no doubt that it had been very high all that time, and it is also certain that she will one day die, although it may well not be of her blood-pressure. How much better it would have been for her not to have been told it was high in the first place and to have avoided all these years of anxiety. It is not being suggested here that high blood-pressure is a trivial condition, but that it is for doctors to worry about rather than patients! If you ever find out your own blood-pressure, never try to work out for yourself what the figures mean. It is much too complicated. Finally, it should be mentioned that high blood-pressure may occasionally be associated with, or "secondary to," certain kidney diseases (*nephritis*) including a strange condition known as *toxaemia of pregnancy*, which lasts only as long as the pregnancy, provided great care is taken. Most high blood-pressure is, however, "primary", and without any known association or cause.

Low Blood-pressure. Some people seem normally to have surprisingly low blood-pressure all the time. There is nothing whatever wrong with this; indeed it may even be beneficial. At least they are unlikely ever to suffer the effects of high blood-pressure. The sudden low blood-pressure of circulatory failure or shock (**P27**) is another matter and must be urgently treated.

Irregularities of the Heart-beat. How quickly or how slowly the heart beats is largely under the control of the cardiac centre in the brain and the level of certain hormones in the blood. The *regularity* of the beat, however, is controlled by the so-called pace-maker in the wall of the right atrium, and by the way impulses from the pacemaker travel through specialised conducting heart cells (the bundle of His and its branches) to the ventricles. When any part of this elaborate mechanism is upset, either by altering the biochemical or electrical conditions of these specialised tissues, or by killing some of them off by deprivation of blood supply in the course of a heart attack, disordered rhythm can result. Increase (*tachycardia*) or decrease (*bradycardia*) in rate is nearly always a normal response to exercise, or anxiety. Very occasional irregularity, such as the mis-timing of an occasional beat is also quite normal in some people, although many are alarmed by it. Persistent irregularity, however, is abnormal. Its true nature can usually be elucidated by making an electrical record of the heart-beat—

an electro-cardiogram. The commonest causes are varieties of coronary artery diseases or rheumatic heart disease.

Pericarditis. The heart beats inside a bag or sac. At every beat its outer surface slides against the lining of the sac, lubricated by a small amount of fluid. This is the pericardial sac, the *pericardium* being strictly the lubricated membrane which lines the sac and which also covers the outer surface of the heart. Sometimes inflammation occurs—*pericarditis*—and the sliding surfaces become roughened and even separated by a fluid effusion. Very occasionally, so much fluid accumulates that the heart's action is seriously impeded. Pericarditis may be due to infection or to rheumatic fever, and it usually overlies the area of damaged muscle after a heart attack. This illustrates something which people rarely appreciate—that inflammation is not by any means always due to infection by bacteria. The last two varieties of pericarditis are quite free from germs (sterile).

Myocarditis. A term loosely applied to disorders affecting the heart muscle. There are lots of very rare causes. The really common ones are due to acute or chronic rheumatic causes or to coronary artery disease, both of which are described above.

Endocarditis or inflammation of the lining of the heart is a term loosely applied to any disorder of the valves or heart lining. All varieties of rheumatic valvular disease (**P27**) are included. Bacterial endocarditis in its several forms usually involves valves already damaged by rheumatic disease. It is a complication which is still much to be feared, though somewhat less so now that antibiotic drugs are available.

Atheroma or *Atherosclerosis.* This is the condition referred to above in which lumps arise on the lining of arterial blood-vessels. Although it is therefore a disease of the arteries, its importance lies in the way blood flow is held up, either by the lumps themselves, or by thrombosis ultimately blocking the narrowed portion of the pipework. The effects on the body are therefore those of depriving the tissues of blood. It is an astonishing fact that in England and America, more people die of the consequences of atheroma than of any other single disease, including all forms of cancer put together. Furthermore, cancer is mainly a disease of old age, whereas many of the effects of atheroma on men occur in early middle age. If narrowing of the artery is going to do significant harm it is easy to see that it will be of more consequence in those parts of the body where small-bore vessels are supplying tissues whose functions are necessary for life. Exactly such a situation exists in the heart and in the brain. An additional factor is that the arrangement of the blood supply in these tissues is such that any particular area has only one vessel leading to it. This is unusual among the tissues generally, where several alternative, or "collateral" vessels usually supply an area, and where others can take over if one becomes obstructed. We have, therefore, a situation in which perhaps the most important tissues —the heart and the brain—run the greatest risk of deprivation, and this leads to angina and coronary thrombosis on the one hand, and cerebral thrombosis and haemorrhage ("stroke illness") on the other, accounting jointly for about one death in every five. In addition, the effects of atheromatous narrowing are often felt in the legs, where the blood supply to the muscles is inadequate for exercise, leading to intermittent pain comparable with that in the heart in similar circumstances. This is called *intermittent claudication*, or intermittent closing of the leg arteries. In its most severe forms, it leads to the need for amputation, although in most cases early treatment can avoid this. It is small wonder that there is intensive research into the causes of atheroma, as with cancer, but it is probably true to say that we still know rather more about cancer. A lot of attention has been given to the amounts of certain fats in the circulating blood, particularly cholesterol. This fat is found in larger amounts in the blood of sufferers from atheroma, and is also found in the arterial lumps themselves.

Efforts have therefore been made to reduce blood cholesterol by modifications of the diet, but it has been extremely difficult to prove that this has done any good. Many other factors are known to contribute to atheroma, and hence to heart attacks and strokes, some of which can be reduced and others not. Such factors are age, obesity, high blood-pressure, and smoking cigarettes. People who lead an active life, like bus conductors, seem to have less trouble than others who are less active, like bus drivers. Sudden severe exercise, however, is bad if you are not used to it. It is better, and life saving, to take regular, moderate exercise. Women have less atheroma than men, until the menopause when they begin to catch up, so that hormones have something to do with it. Serious starvation, such as occurred in the German-occupied territories of Holland and Scandinavia and in the concentration camps conferred one benefit—a freedom from atheroma, but obviously we cannot all starve, and the puzzle remains. Like many of the more important outstanding medical puzzles, there is no single factor responsible, and this is what makes it difficult to solve.

Aortic Disease. The aorta, the main artery of the body, running from the left ventricle down through the chest and abdomen, also suffers from atheroma, but is too wide (about 2·5 cm across) to become obstructed. However, weaknesses occur in the thickness of its wall, sometimes due to syphilis but nowadays much more usually due to atheroma, which results in a ballooning out of a part of the vessel, rather like you sometimes see in an old bicycle inner tube. In days gone by these *aneurysms,* as the dilations are called, reached an enormous size, and would wear away the breastbone and ribs, to appear as large pulsating masses on the chest. Now that advanced syphilis is less common, atheromatous aneurysm, with a predilection for the abdominal aorta, is the one most commonly seen; and these days it is treated by replacement of the diseased portion of vessel. *Dissecting aneurysms* of the aorta are another variety in which the blood, under high pressure, somehow finds its way in between the layers of the aortic wall and then suddenly rips up and down the whole length of the vessel, separating (or dissecting) one layer from another in its path. Sometimes it tracks back towards the heart and suddenly fills the pericardium with blood to stop the heart's action altogether.

Embolism. This term refers to any foreign object travelling in the circulation and becoming impacted when it reaches a vessel too small for it to pass through. It may be a thrombus (**P30**), a collection of cancer cells, a group of bacteria, a chunk of infected pus from an abscess, a collection of fat droplets or even a bubble of air. If it originates in a vein it travels to the right heart and to the lungs. If it comes from the left heart or an artery, it will impact in any part of the arterial tree. Reasonably enough an arterial embolus will commonly end up in those parts of the body with the richest blood supply, like the brain, the kidneys, the liver or the bone marrow. A thrombotic embolus will cause death of the tissue in the area previously supplied by the blocked vessel, a condition known as *infarction.* Perhaps the commonest source of thrombotic embolism is the lining of the heart chambers where a thrombus has occurred at the site of muscle damaged by a heart attack. Massive pulmonary (lung) embolism is usually the result of the thrombosis of the leg veins in people kept immobile following surgery or childbirth. That is why postoperative patients are got out of bed for a while as soon as the first day after the operation. The cells of a cancer embolus usually die; but if they survive, a new cancer deposit begins to grow where the embolus impacts, and this is one of the ways cancer may spread. An infected embolus may infect the vessel wall when it impacts, producing a weakness which may give way. Air embolism, if enough insoluble gas enters the circulation, can kill by making so much froth in the heart chambers as to impede the normal pumping action. If bubbles pass the lungs and enter the brain, all sorts of neurological disorders like scores of tiny strokes arise. The same sort of thing happens all over the body in the "bends" or "caisson" disease,

in which the blood literally boils. It is due to a too rapid return to normal pressure from regions of high pressure at great depths or from pressurised chambers. Fat embolism sometimes occurs after fractures, due to marrow fat entering damaged veins and being carried away to the lungs.

Thrombosis. This is not quite the same as clotting. It is the mass which arises when platelets adhere to the lining of blood-vessels or heart chambers. Blood clot accumulates among layers of deposited platelets and the thrombus therefore has structure, unlike pure blood clot. Thrombosis usually occurs when the lining of the vessel or chamber is damaged by atheroma or inflammation, or when the circulation becomes very stagnant. One danger is that it will become dislodged and travel as an embolus during the first week or ten days of its existence. After this time it is usually firmly incorporated into the vessel walls by cells which migrate into it from the surrounding tissue. The other danger is, of course, that the tissue previously supplied by the blocked vessel will die before a collateral circulation can be established. As previously explained, this is called infarction. All the technical terms in this section are used elsewhere and can be looked up.

Varicose Veins. When veins become swollen they also often become tortuous (wriggly), and particularly on the surface of the leg look very unsightly. They are, however, a sign of a sluggish circulation, and are often due to disease in small valves within the veins which normally prevent the blood from pooling backwards, down towards the feet. They are often a normal maternal accompaniment of pregnancy and disappear after the child is born. If allowed to persist, the sluggish circulation allows the formation of unpleasant ulcers, mainly in elderly people. Treatment is according to severity. In the early stages they are helped by supportive stockings. Later, often as an out-patient, the sufferer may have to have them removed or obliterated by a surgeon.

Raynaud's Disease. This is a strange condition in which the finger tips and in severe cases all the fingers or the whole hand respond in an exaggerated way to cold. The vessels supplying the hand are constricted and the fingers go white as the blood drains from them. Then the capillaries dilate and become distended and filled with blood. But owing to stagnation it is venous and blue, and the fingers are therefore blue. Now we have all experienced this in very cold weather, but sufferers from Raynaud's disease, nearly always women, respond even to very slight cold, like putting their hands into cold water. Even emotional stress will start the process off. In very severe cases the fingers will be so deprived of blood for so long, that sores will develop and fingers can even be lost, but this is very rare, and can be avoided by an operation to cut the nerves which supply the circular muscle of the vessels concerned. In most cases it is sufficient to avoid getting the hands cold.

Frostbite. Strictly speaking, this is literally a freezing of the tissues. Although their freezing point might be expected to be close to that of water, it usually only occurs at temperatures below $-13°$ C. The patient may feel a pricking feeling at first, and feel an area of firmer, pale skin on the cheeks, nose, ears, fingers, or toes. If these parts are numb with cold, the onset of frostbite may not be felt, and will often only be noticed by others. In countries where extreme cold is prevalent, it is usual for complete strangers to stop each other in the street and point it out when they see it. It is important not to rub the affected part nor to apply direct heat in any form. Rapid warming can be harmful; re-warming by close application of body temperature is good treatment, *e.g.,* fingers can be firmly held in the armpit or a warm hand closely applied to an ear or a nose.

THE RESPIRATORY SYSTEM.

INTRODUCTION.

When air is drawn in during the process of breathing, it is brought into very close contact with the blood passing through the lungs. In this way the air we breathe in, which contains 20 per cent oxygen, is confronted with "spent" blood returning from the tissues which contains much less, and oxygen therefore diffuses into the blood from the air. At the same time, the waste gas, carbon dioxide, passes by diffusion in the reverse direction from the blood into the air, because there is much more carbon dioxide in the returning "spent" blood than the tiny amount in the air we breathe. The blood is therefore continually circulating through the lungs and exchanging carbon dioxide for oxygen from the air we breathe in. When we breathe out, we disperse the carbon dioxide into the atmosphere.

When the air enters the nose or mouth, it passes into the windpipe or *trachea*, through the vocal cords in the pharynx. The trachea is held open all the time by rings of cartilage and is lined by a mucus-secreting membrane covered by millions of tiny "hairs" or cilia. These continuously waft a sheet of sticky mucus upwards, which traps any dust or other small particles we may have inhaled, until a collection of this material in the pharynx stimulates us to cough and expel the phlegm, usually to be swallowed. At its lower end, the trachea or windpipe divides into two, the right and left main *bronchus*. Each main bronchial tube enters a lung, one on each side, and proceeds to divide repeatedly within the lung until the air is being carried by more and more smaller and ever smaller tubes called *bronchioles*. There are many millions of these on each side, and each one ends in a collection of very small balloon-like structures —the air sacs or *alveoli*. If you were to cut across a lung and examine the cut surface in a good light, you would see that it is a spongy tissue, with many millions of tiny holes, each one just visible to the naked eye. These are the air sacs. In their walls run the blood capillaries, each one of which is a branch of the vessels carrying "spent" blood from the right side of the heart. At this stage, the blood is only separated from the air in the sacs by the walls of the capillaries and of the air sacs themselves. Both structures are extremely thin, making for easy diffusion of the gases between blood and air.

The action of breathing is accomplished by two muscular mechanisms. One is by the muscles which move the ribs, and the other by the diaphragm, a sheet of muscle which runs across the body, separating the chest cavity from the abdominal cavity. These muscles are all actuated by nerves, just as all other muscles are. Those running to the muscles of breathing are organised by a mechanism in the brain known as the *respiratory centre*. It is this centre—one of the so-called vital centres of the brain—which receives information from many different sources, and translates it into instructions for the breathing mechanism. Thus, when you run for a bus, you will automatically breathe more deeply and more quickly because the respiratory centre has been informed about all the extra carbon dioxide in your blood which has been produced by the exercising leg muscles. Even the conscious instructions involved when you blow a trumpet, inflate a balloon, or during speaking, all pass first to the respiratory centre. It is the death of the cells of this and other vital centres of the brain that is the ultimate cause of death in everyone who dies.

Bronchitis may be acute or chronic. It is an inflammation of the lining mucous membrane of the larger air passages or bronchi, and results in much more secretion than the amount normally produced, mixed with some pus. The acute form is often caused by viruses, with "secondary" infection from bacteria. It may sometimes be caused by irritant gases, like the sulphur dioxide in smog. The chronic, or long-standing form of bronchitis is often associated with *emphysema*, in which the small air sacs of the lung architecture are destroyed or distorted, leaving larger spaces than normal, often surrounded by fibrous scar tissue. Such an arrangement makes the normal gaseous exchange difficult between air and blood. While the exact cause of chronic bronchitis is difficult to discover, because it is such a mixture of causes, it is mainly associated with older age

groups, particularly men, in damp foggy climates like ours in Britain, with polluted town air and especially with smoking. Smoking also makes any existing bronchitis much worse. Bronchitis can cause even more trouble than lung cancer, since instead of dying in a short time, the bronchitic lives for many years in chronic sickness. About 30,000 people die of bronchitis each year. It isn't smart to smoke. Patients cough, and produce varying amounts of sputum, or phlegm. They often wheeze like asthmatics. This may go on for many years before the right side of the heart begins to fail (P27). Gradually, during this time, the chest tends to become barrel-shaped. Treatment consists of getting the patient to stop smoking or otherwise contaminating his lungs, preventing infection, particularly during winter months, with germ-killing antibiotics, and breathing exercises. The outlook for chronic bronchitis and emphysema is nevertheless not good, although many patients continue with their disease for many years, provided they take constant care to obey instructions and stop smoking.

Bronchial Asthma is a condition in which the finer air passages become constricted due to an allergic response. In addition, an increased secretion tends to obstruct them and the patient wheezes. In many cases it can be shown that he is allergic to a particular component of dust, or, less commonly, a foodstuff. This is the same sort of thing as occurs in the upper respiratory passages in hay fever, but the effect is on a different, lower part of the respiratory system. Many other cases are due to respiratory infection of some sort, probably combined with an allergy to the bacteria causing it. A predisposition to asthma is often inherited. Once a patient has become asthmatic, his attacks may be triggered off by such additional things as emotional stress, changes in temperature (particularly sudden cold), irritating fumes or smoke, and physical exertion. These are secondary factors, and although much of the treatment is concerned with them, it is unlikely that any of them is a sole cause of the condition. Treatment is directed at the relief of the breathing difficulty and of the wheezing, as well as the control of the causative factors. Many useful drugs are available to dilate the contracted air passages and reduce the obstructing secretions. Asthma in children often gets better as the patient grows up. Asthma is another condition made much worse by smoking. Patients should avoid extremes of cold and humidity particularly out-door exertion in cold, damp weather. They should also avoid exposure to respiratory infection.

A tiny living mite about 0·3 millimetres long exists in large numbers in nearly all mattress and floor dust. This is the cause of much asthma, and in such cases it is often very helpful to vacuum-clean mattresses and floors frequently.

Bronchiectasis. In this condition the bronchial air passages are abnormally and permanently dilated, and the normal structure of the walls destroyed. It is thought to be caused by obstructions of the tubes which lead to dilatation of the parts beyond. Secretions accumulate, and since they cannot easily drain away, they become infected. The infection helps to complete the process of destruction of structures in the bronchial wall. The patient has a chronic cough which often produces large quantities of purulent sputum, and there are often recurrent episodes of pneumonia. Diagnosis is made by a special X-ray examination—a bronchogram—in which a material, opaque to X-rays, is dropped into the air passages. This shows up the dilated and distorted tubes. In some cases, where the disease is localised to one part of the lung, it is often a good idea to cut out that portion, and this is particularly true in young people. Vigorous physiotherapy, involving drainage of the lungs by placing the patient in a suitable posture, together with antibiotic drugs for the infection, are other forms of treatment.

Cystic Fibrosis is an inborn disease which affects chiefly the lungs and the digestive system. It is sometimes called *Fibrocystic disease of the Pan-*

creas, and sometimes "Mucoviscidosis". Until it was medically recognised forty years ago, children affected usually died from pneumonia in the first year of life. This, of course, was before antibiotics were available for the treatment of infections. Today, cystic fibrosis is known to be the commonest genetically determined disorder affecting children in Britain. One child in 2,000 receives one of the abnormal genes from each parent. Such a child therefore has a double dose of the harmful gene, and will have the disease from birth. One person in 25 of the general population carries only one of these abnormal genes, and such an individual will not have the disease, but will be a carrier of the abnormal gene. If such a seemingly normal carrier marries another carrier, there is a one in four chance of each of their children being affected. The children, therefore, who actually develop cystic fibrosis have inherited the disease *equally* from both parents, who are carriers, but are themselves unaffected by the disease. Although much has been learned about cystic fibrosis in the past forty years, there remain many unsolved problems, and we still cannot define precisely the biochemical fault which causes it. The prospects for survival into reasonably healthy adult life are steadily improving, but they depend upon early diagnosis and careful management through childhood. In cystic fibrosis most of the damage is caused by the excessive viscidity, or stickiness, of the mucus which is produced in the breathing tubes as a lubricant, and also in the ducts of the pancreatic gland which provides enzymes to help digestion. Being thick and sticky, instead of thin and slimy as in the normal, this mucus tends to block the passages instead of keeping them clear. The pancreatic cells are permanently destroyed. The gland cannot secrete pancreatic enzymes, and the food, especially protein and fat, is not properly absorbed. This deficiency can be compensated fairly well by giving pancreatic extract by mouth with every meal, and by dietary care.

The major clinical problem is in the lungs. The lung passages normally have a thin coating of mucus which is propelled steadily upwards, and is completely renewed in less than one hour. It moves more suddenly on coughing. In cystic fibrosis this upward movement is slowed down and interrupted. There is difficulty in keeping the passages clear, especially when infection with bacteria or viruses greatly increases the amount of mucus. This results in intermittent blocking of the air passages, difficulty in breathing, incomplete use of the lungs, and persistent local pockets of infection. If such infectious processes are not controlled, areas of lung will be destroyed, chronic infection will persist, and multiple lung cavities will develop. These predispose to further infection, interfering with the natural development of the lung—a process not normally complete until halfway through childhood—thus adding to the respiratory problems which the child will face in later life. Unless a correct diagnosis is made and proper treatment instituted before the first serious lung infection has occurred, the resulting lung damage may well be permanent.

Pneumonia. This is an infection of the lung tissue, rather than of the air passages. The lung is the only internal organ which is directly exposed to the air, and since there are germs of all kinds in the air, it is a source of surprise that pneumonia is not a much more common event in all of us. The answer lies, as with all infections, in the fact that it is not simply (or even mainly) bacteria which cause disease, but our own lack of resistance to them. If we allow germs to thrive and multiply by being unhealthy or run down or undernourished, infective disease will occur. If we are fit, the entry of those same harmful germs into the body causes us no inconvenience, unless we are very young, or very old, or unless the invasion of germs is abnormally overwhelming. This helps to explain why pneumonia is so often quoted as a cause of death. In most cases it is merely a terminal event occurring in the elderly sick, whose normal resistance is so far reduced by their illness that they succumb to an invasion which they would normally not notice. There are two main kinds of pneumonia, and in both the air sacs

become filled with inflammatory secretions, making the normally porous lung tissue as solid as liver. In *lobar pneumonia*, a whole segment (or lobe) of the lung becomes solid. In *bronchopneumonia*, areas of lung tissue surrounding the smaller bronchioles become consolidated, leaving normal porous lung tissue in between. Bronchopneumonia is the one which occurs in the rather stagnant lungs of people who are already ill or bedridden. Both forms respond to treatment with the appropriate antibiotics, provided any underlying debility does not interfere with the patient's own resistance. In the terminal bronchopneumonia of fatal illness, it is sometimes considered kinder not to treat the additional pneumonia. *Pleurisy* is a natural complication, and before the days of antibiotic drugs *lung abscess* was very much feared. Another form of pneumonia—*viral pneumonia*—is referred to in **P9**(2).

Pneumoconiosis. This is a term which refers to a large group of different diseases, all of which are caused by breathing in some form of dust over a very long period of time. It is therefore an occupational hazard of certain trades. We have already mentioned the mechanisms of mucus secretion in the air passages which normally trap small particles from the air, and prevent them reaching the lung. However, in some occupations there is so much dust breathed in over the months and years that these normal barriers are defeated. About a quarter of the earth's crust consists of silicon, in quartz, flint, or sand. *Silicosis* occurs in people who have worked for many years in trades like mining, stone crushing, sandblasting, or metal grinding, who are often breathing silicon dust in high concentration. When the particles arrive in the air sacs, they set up an irritant chemical reaction which produces nodules of scar tissue. Silicosis for some reason predisposes to tuberculosis. Emphysema also occurs and there is a general impairment of respiratory function. Coalminer's pneumoconiosis is similar to silicosis but not identical with it. It is more prevalent in some coalfields than others, owing to the different composition of the dust to which these unfortunate men are daily exposed. It is hoped that modern mining methods will help to reduce this dread disease. Asbestos is a complex silicate of magnesium, calcium, and iron. *Asbestosis* is caused by inhaling its fine fibres. *Berylliosis* is caused by compounds of beryllium, used in the manufacture of fluorescent lamps. *Farmer's lung* is a pneumoconiosis caused by inhaling hay and grain dust, and is similar to *bagassosis* and *byssinosis* caused by sugar cane and cotton dust respectively. The newest pneumoconiosis to be reported is *mushroom worker's lung*, caused by something in the compost in which mushrooms are commercially grown.

Pulmonary Embolism. This catastrophic, yet quite common condition has already been briefly referred to (**P30**(1)). It is a cause of tragic, sudden death in people who have had operations or have given birth to babies some days previously, or who have been bedridden for any other cause. The first event is that the blood in the veins of the legs becomes stagnant, due to the lack of exercise; and together with the tendency to clot which often follows surgery or childbirth, the whole length of a leg vein may be obstructed for twelve inches or more by an elongated clot of blood. This does little harm to the circulation of the leg, since there are plenty of other veins for returning blood to the heart. The danger is that the clot will become dislodged and be swept upwards towards the heart by the flow of returning blood. When this happens it is carried by way of the right auricle and ventricle into the pulmonary vessels which normally carry spent blood to the lungs. Here, for the first time, it enters vessels which are getting smaller as they divide, and it then impacts in the main pulmonary artery. The patient, who may have been recovering very well, suddenly collapses and not unusually dies there and then. At autopsy a long coiled-up mass of clot is found obstructing the pulmonary vessels. It often can be seen to form a cast of the leg vein and even bears the marks of the small venous valves which are present at its site of origin. With the dramatic advances being made in chest surgery, it is now sometimes possible in selected cases to operate to remove the clot. Success clearly depends on the patient's surviving long enough to be taken to the operating theatre for the major operation of *pulmonary embolectomy*. Three quarters of all cases of pulmonary embolism die within two hours, and therefore the best hope would be to prevent the occurrence altogether. This is not at present possible, but clotting in leg veins can be discouraged by early exercise following surgery and childbirth. Patients often resent having to get up the next day because it is so uncomfortable. Herein, however, lies their best hope of avoiding pulmonary embolism.

Haemoptysis. This means coughing up blood or blood-stained material. It must be distinguished from *haematemesis*, in which the blood is vomited from the stomach. It must always be taken seriously because of the underlying lung disease which may be present. No one who coughs up blood, in however small a quantity, should neglect to inform their doctor so that its source can be determined. Haemoptysis occurs in a variety of lung disease, some of which is not serious but much of which must be treated immediately if it is not to become so. This is a suitable place to repeat our general rule that you should see your doctor without delay if you have any unexplained bleeding from any part of the body, however well you feel. And this includes haemoptysis.

Fat Embolism. Liquid fat sometimes enters the bloodstream following extensive crush injuries to soft tissue and bone. It splits up into millions of small globules which are carried to the lungs, and impact in small blood vessels there, producing obstruction of the lung circulation and consequent difficulties in breathing.

Lung Cancer. This is one of the commonest, nastiest and most incurable forms of cancer which can occur. It is also probably the easiest to prevent. Each year over 32,000 people die of lung cancer in Great Britain, all but 5,000 of them men. Every year the toll goes on. There has been no reasonable doubt for several years now that it is associated with cigarette smoking, and the evidence is overwhelming. However, in spite of this certain knowledge, smoking continues to increase, and every year there are more and more people dying unpleasantly of lung cancer. It seems that nothing the health authorities can do is able to stop it. Intensive campaigns of public advertising of the dangers, and well organised instruction in schools have so far made no impression whatever on the smoking habits even of people who accept the evidence. The only group of people who are known to have stopped smoking are British doctors, very many of whom have given it up, and it is easy to show that giving it up has saved them from the disease. Their colleagues who have not done so have continued to die. Undoubtedly a large factor contributing to the failure of anti-smoking propaganda is the enormous expenditure by the tobacco manufacturers on very clever advertising, amounting to many millions of pounds each year. Moreover they spend a pitiful fraction of this amount on their own research into the harmful effects of their own product, which has so far discovered nothing which was not already known by research doctors many years ago. Another problem is that it takes a number of years to get cancer. It is not like an infectious disease which is caught a few days after exposure to the bacteria concerned. It may be fifteen or twenty years before the cancer begins, and many smokers are apparently unwilling to look so far ahead. Furthermore, not everyone who smokes dies this way; and so a smoker can gamble with his life and hope it will not be him. The present writer once had to perform a series of post-mortem examinations on people who died of lung cancer, and this helped him to stop smoking completely, having smoked more than twenty cigarettes a day for several years. Not everyone can have this incentive. The main

encouragement to smoke probably comes from other people. Schoolboys are easily impressed when their teachers and parents stop smoking. They are not likely to fear the habit when these same people smoke openly. The smoking doctor is also a powerful stimulus to people to carry on smoking.

Lung cancer grows in the wall of a main bronchial air passage. If it grows inwards it can obstruct the air way, choking that part of the lung it is supplying with air. This causes collapse and infection of the lung and may lead to *lung abscess*. The patient will then cough up blood-stained infected and purulent material. Such a case is comparatively lucky, since the disease declares itself early by producing symptoms. In others, the lump may grow outwards into the surrounding lung and produce no symptoms at all in the early stages. Indeed, it may spread to other parts of the body, like brain or bone or liver before causing any trouble to the patient. If this happens he may go to his doctor because of fits, changes of personality, or fracture, only to discover that the origin of the trouble is in the lung.

The chances of cure are negligible, although much can be done to relieve the pain and suffering of the last stages of the illness. Not more than one in twenty patients is alive two years after it is first diagnosed. Surgery, by removing the lung, and irradiation of the growth are the standard palliative treatment. It is not the practice of the Medical Section to alarm the reader unnecessarily, but if only a few are induced to stop giving themselves such a horrible disease, then writing in this way will have been justified.

Secondary Cancer of the Lung. In nearly all forms of cancer, the big problem is that it spreads to other parts of the body. If this were not so it could be eradicated by surgical removal more often than it is. One common way in which it spreads from any part of the body is by entering the bloodstream and being carried as clumps of living cancer cells to distant parts. When these come to rest in smaller blood vessels, they begin to grow and colonise the new environment. Such new colonies are called *secondary deposits* or *metastases*. It so happens that all veins (except portal veins of the liver) lead to the right heart and thence directly to the lungs, and for this reason the lungs are a very common site of *secondary* cancer, which may have begun in the bowel, or breast, or indeed anywhere else in the body. Other common sites of secondary, blood-borne cancer are the brain, liver, bone marrow, and kidney, since all of them have an abundant blood supply, and there is therefore a high chance of the travelling cells arriving there. Secondary cancer of the lung usually consists of several lumps scattered throughout the lung. Lung cancer itself is usually only one growth. One of the main reasons for the success of early diagnosis is that treatment may be possible before blood-borne and other means of spread have occurred. Unfortunately, in the case of primary cancer of the lung, even early diagnosis is of little avail, but in many other common cancers permanent cure is possible if treatment is begun early enough.

Pleurisy. The chest is lined by one layer of a thin membrane called the *pleura*. The lungs are covered and enclosed by a second, continuous layer of this same membrane. When the lungs move during respiration, the pleura covering the lungs rubs against the pleura lining the chest, lubricated by a very thin layer of pleural fluid separating the two pleura. Whenever the pleural surface becomes inflamed, this is known as *pleurisy*. It is nearly always due to inflammatory disease of the adjoining lung, and is therefore not strictly a disease in its own right. For example, pneumonia, tuberculosis, lung cancer, or a lung infarct (**P30**(2)) will produce a pleurisy if the area of diseased lung adjoins the lung surface. Sometimes the area of inflamed inner pleura will tend to stick to its outer layer or rub painfully against it, producing a sharp pain when the patient breathes. Sometimes a large effusion of fluid is produced which separates the two layers and collapses the lung by occupying space in the chest which the lung should be occupying. This latter is more usual in tuberculosis or cancer.

The lung can be collapsed by the entry of anything between the normally adjacent layers of pleura. For example, air can be introduced, either deliberately to rest the lung in tuberculosis, or by accidental penetrating wounds of the chest wall, or by accidental rupture of the emphysematous lung (q.v.). This condition is called *pneumothorax* or "air in the chest." Bleeding into the cavity between the pleura is called *haemothorax*.

THE DIGESTIVE TRACT AND LARGE INTESTINE.

INTRODUCTION.

The digestive tract consists of the mouth, pharynx, oesophagus (or gullet), stomach, small intestine, large intestine (or colon), rectum, and anus. The small intestine is very long, and is subdivided into the duodenum, jejunum, and ileum. It ends at the junction of the ileum with the caecum, where there is a small blind side-tube, the appendix. The caecum leads into the colon. The whole tract has two main mechanical functions and two main biochemical ones. Mechanically, food has to be chewed in the mouth and further minced up by muscular squeezing, mainly by the stomach. It has also to be propelled along by an orderly series of squeezing movements known as *peristalsis*. While it is still in the digestive tract, food has to be digested. That is to say, it has to be broken down chemically into suitable materials for absorption into the system, and secondly, it has to be absorbed across the wall of the intestine into the blood stream, itself a highly complex biochemical process. The blood stream it now enters is a special part of the circulation, the "portal" system, which travels directly to the liver without first passing to the heart. In the liver the broken-down foods are processed and issued in their new form into the general, or "systemic" circulation, by which they are finally carried to all the tissues of the body.

As the food passes along the digestive tract (or, as it is sometimes called, the alimentary canal), it is mixed with various secretions which are either made in the wall of the tract, or by organs outside the wall connected to the main pathway by small tubes. Examples of the latter are bile, manufactured by the liver and sent into the duodenum through the bile ducts; and pancreatic juice, which comes from the pancreas down the pancreatic ducts, also into the duodenum. These secretions are either digestive juices concerned with splitting up the foodstuffs so that they can be absorbed, or they have a lubricant so that the gut contents slide along easily under the influence of peristalsis. Roughly speaking, it may be said that digestive juices give place to lubricant secretions at the junction between the small and large intestine.

The constituents of the diet are dealt with in a later section. The principal classes with whose digestion we are now concerned are carbohydrates, proteins, and fats.

Carbohydrates are sugars and starches. There are many sugars, which may exist alone, in pairs, or with lots of them stuck together. Alone they are such things as glucose or fructose. Common table sugar is a substance called sucrose, formed by sticking one glucose molecule to one fructose molecule. Starch is lots of glucose molecules all stuck together. Digestion of carbohydrates consists of splitting up sugars and starch into single sugars like glucose, since only single sugars can be absorbed into the system. The splitting is done by digestive *enzymes* which are found in the juices secreted into the digestive tract. Sugar-splitters are found in the saliva of the mouth, in the pancreatic juice of the duodenum, and in the duodenum's own juice from its own wall. On the face of it, you might think it would be better to eat glucose which needs no digestion and can be absorbed in

this form, than to eat starch which has first to be split; and so a lot of money has been made out of a gullible public by the sale of glucose drinks and powder. In fact digesting starch is no problem whatever, even for the sick, who can obtain their carbohydrate energy just as easily (and much more cheaply) from potatoes as from expensive glucose. The end result of eating both is the same. The starch-splitting enzyme in saliva is mixed with the food as it is chewed, and it is therefore probably a good idea to chew it well. However, even if the food is bolted it does not seem to matter very much. People without teeth (neither their own nor dentures) seem to digest their carbohydrate quite well, presumably by means of their pancreatic juice at a later stage.

Proteins, which are found in meat, cheese, and eggs, have very large molecules consisting of lots of small ones strung together. Unlike starch, in which all the component glucose molecules are identical, the amino acids of which proteins are composed come in many different types. They all contain nitrogen, and there are about twenty-seven varieties. One protein differs from another in the proportions of the mixture and the order in which they are stuck together. Only single amino acids can be absorbed from the food, and so protein digestion again consists of splitting the material down into its building bricks. There is a strong protein splitting enzyme in the gastric (or stomach) juice called pepsin, whose job it is to split the long amino-acid chains into shorter chains. Several other protein-splitters in the duodenal and pancreatic juice contrive to break the smaller chains into individual amino acids which are then absorbed and sent to the liver for processing.

Fats mainly consist of glycerol to which are attached three fatty acid molecules for each molecule of glycerol. An enzyme in pancreatic juice splits the fatty acids off the glycerol, but would have some difficulty penetrating the globules of fat without the help of bile. One of the constituents of bile (bile salts) has detergent properties like washing-up powder and breaks the fat globules up into a very fine suspension so that the enzyme can get at the fat. Some fat particles of this size can even be absorbed as such, without preliminary splitting.

The processes by which all these enzymic secretions are produced are very finely controlled. They are very expensive to make in terms of energy and raw materials, and so it would be very wasteful to produce them all the time, even when there was no food to digest. And so the body has some very well designed automatic arrangements for sampling the foods as they are eaten and passed on, which ensure that exactly the right kind of juice is waiting in every part of the digestive tract for whatever food arrives. As soon as the food is digested the supply of enzymes is automatically switched off, so that there is very little waste of precious materials. It is, of course, beyond the scope of this account to describe the control mechanisms. Suffice it to say that they are operated partly by nerve reflexes which signal the imminent arrival of food, and partly by special hormones produced in various parts of the gut wall. The best secretion is affected even by psychological factors, so that pleasant company and surroundings, attractive appearance of the food, and an eager anticipation of it all make for good digestion and good health. These psychological factors are all capable of proper scientific investigation and proof. The poor health of those who habitually and irregularly bolt unpalatable food is probably due to such factors as these. So is the failure of appetite in the depressed, the anxious adult, or the scolded child.

Nearly all the digestion which has been described occurs in the stomach and upper part of the small intestine (the duodenum, jejunum, and upper ileum). Almost all absorption of the products of digestion occurs in the small intestine which is long and intricately folded to give it a large surface area for this purpose. The colon, or large intestine, is adapted for conserving water, by removing it from the residual waste material. This has then to be eliminated, and being rather dry its passage has to be lubricated by suitable secretions of mucus.

Constipation. Here, perhaps we had better mention the morbid question of constipation, about which so many people are obsessed and hold such pronounced views. First of all, what is it? For some people it is entirely normal only to pass motions about once or twice a week. For others the normal frequency is once or twice a day. What is abnormal? The answer is that the only thing worth worrying about is only pronounced change of bowel habit, particularly in middle-aged and older people. By a change is meant a change from that individual person's normal routine. Such a pronounced change—either in the direction of constipation or diarrhoea—is worth consulting your doctor about if it persists for more than a week or two. Otherwise, forget your bowels and leave them to work naturally as they know best. Many believe that constipation is the root of all evil, that it causes a mysterious condition known to them (although, alas, not to doctors) as "auto-intoxication." Sedulously fostered by the manufacturers of patent medicines, their beliefs range from the notion that headaches, spotty skin, muddy skin, and tiredness are caused by constipation, to the more extreme idea that the whole system is being poisoned and that, if the bowels do not work, the individual will shortly die. Of course, all this is the merest rubbish; for, as Professor Samson Wright, whose *Applied Physiology* is one of the most famous of medical text-books, has pointed out, there is no such thing as absorption of poisonous products from the bowel. There is no such thing as "auto-intoxication." "The symptoms of constipation," he writes, "are largely due to distension and mechanical irritation of the rectum." It has been shown that an enema removes these symptoms *immediately*, which would not be the case if they were due to poisons in the blood, and exactly the same symptoms can be produced by packing the rectum with cotton-wool. Wright mentions the case of a man who went for just over a year without bowel motion, and at the end of that time, although his abdomen was distended and he felt some discomfort, he was not noticeably ill. Needless to say, telling these facts to the purgative addict will only make him annoyed, but it is as well to note that if no known diseases are due to constipation (although constipation may be a symptom of another disease), the regular use of purgatives *can* cause disease.

Constipation should be treated first by diet containing plenty of roughage—bran and oatmeal are excellent—plenty of stewed and fresh fruits, and at least 1½ litres of fluid should be taken daily. Failing that, one of the best things to take is a proprietary product prepared from senna pods. Never to be taken regularly are liquid paraffin, castor oil, preparations of aloes, Epsom salts, and all the other dreadful stuff that people swill down.

Oesophagus.

The oesophagus, or gullet, is more than a simple tube for taking the food from the mouth to the stomach. It is normally closed except when swallowing, and the act of swallowing is very complicated. When the material to be swallowed arrives in the back of the throat there is an automatic mechanism which opens the top end of the oesophagus to receive it, and from then onwards everything happens automatically. The next portion of the tube opens and the top closes strongly, so that the food (or drink) is propelled forcibly down the next segment. Then the part below this relaxes and the material is squeezed further downwards and so on until it arrives in the stomach. This squeezing (or milking) action is akin to the action known as peristalsis which propels contents in other parts of the gut. Thus when you see someone swallowing a glass of beer very quickly in warm weather, it is not going "down the hatch" under the influence of gravity, however much it may look like it. It is perfectly possible to swallow the same, or any other liquid, standing on your head. Getting into that position

is the only difficult part. Sometimes this complicated swallowing mechanism gets out of order, leading to difficulties of swallowing, or *dysphagia*. Another disorder known as *hiatus hernia* occurs at the lower end of the oesophagus as it meets the stomach. At this point the oesophagus has to pass through the diaphragm, the sheet of muscle which separates the chest from the abdomen. The muscular fibres of the diaphragm are normally arranged in a ring around the oesophagus. These help to keep the lower end shut, so that the acid contents of the stomach do not regurgitate upwards, causing inflammation (*oesophagitis*) or heartburn. A hiatus hernia is when muscle fibres get slack, and the upper end of the stomach can even slide upwards into the chest. People with hiatus hernia get heartburn after meals, and particularly when they bend down or lie down. Except for very severe forms, which need surgical repair, the treatment is to eat less at a time, reduce the acidity with a suitable antacid and reduce weight so that the weight of the abdomen does not press upwards so much. The other disease of the oesophagus, quite unrelated to the above, is *cancer of the oesophagus*, the cause of which is still unknown in most cases. When cancer occurs in the wall of any tube, it will often encircle the tube and gradually narrow the way through. This is what happens in the oesophagus, leading to difficulty in swallowing, particularly solids. It is a condition usually, of rather elderly men, although it is sometimes associated with a special form of severe anaemia in women. Treatment is in some way to keep the passage open, either by transplanting a new tube, or more usually, by removing the constricted piece and joining up the remainder.

The Stomach and Duodenum.

By far the commonest diseases of the stomach and duodenum are *gastric ulcer* and *duodenal ulcer*. They are actually the same condition in two different sites and are often classed together as *peptic ulcer* or *acid-peptic disease*. The ulcers, which are rather like sores on the lining of the stomach or duodenum, may be "acute" or "chronic." Acute ulcers tend to be small and there are often several of them. Chronic ulcers are usually single. They may be small, or they may be several centimetres across. Chronic ulcers smoulder for months and even years, like a sore which will not heal, and a great deal of scar tissue forms in their depths. Thus they may in time erode their way right through the wall of the stomach, destroying all its layers, and begin to eat into surrounding structures like the pancreas or liver. The fact that they do not perforate more frequently is due to all the fibrous scar tissue which is formed during the slow eroding process. Healing of such a destructive ulcer is nevertheless common, and the great problem is how to help the natural healing process to win against the ulcer's tendency to erode. Better still would be to discover the cause, and prevent it happening in the first place. This extremely common affliction is confined to the human species and has been known since the earliest times. It does not vary very much with diet or with social class. Although occurring at all ages, it usually begins between the ages of twenty and forty, and is most commonly found in men between forty-five and fifty-five. Gastric ulcer is four times, and duodenal ulcer ten times more common in men than in women. It is always due to an inability of the lining to stand up to the normal digestive activity of the stomach contents. These are normally acid and contain a powerful enzyme for digesting proteins. Again it is perhaps more surprising that we all do not digest our own stomachs, rather than that some unfortunate people do digest small areas slowly. In certain abnormal conditions when the stomach stops making acid, ulcers always heal. However, some ulcers occur without excessive secretion of acid and many heal without the acid being neutralised with antacids. All this points to the main trouble being in the response of the lining to acid rather than to the acid itself. Nevertheless, the most effective treatment at present known involves regulating gastric secretion, and particularly its acidity. It is also known that peptic ulcers are more common in people whose occupations involve administrative and professional responsibility, competitive effort and nervous tension, long periods of anxiety or frustration. Presumably the higher nervous system influences these events by the same nerves, which normally help to control secretion.

The main symptom of peptic ulcer is pain, and this usually responds well to proper doses of antacids. Many different varieties are available and a lot of money is made from selling them. When indigestion persists for longer than a few days it is always better to see your doctor so that a proper diagnosis can be made and the best remedies begun. Many other causes exist for similar pains, and you should not try to make the diagnosis yourself. It may be necessary to analyse your gastric secretions in the hospital laboratory. Almost certainly you will have a special X-ray examination, and since the stomach cannot easily be seen on a normal X-ray, they will have to show it up by making you drink a white material containing barium. This will be seen as a silhouette of the stomach and duodenal contents. Searching for an ulcer this way is a highly skilled matter and is performed by doctors specially trained in radiology.

Until recently, no drugs capable of influencing the course of peptic ulcer in any significant manner were available and the physician had to rely on general measures, such as rest, diet and the administration of antacids to relieve pain and discomfort: episodes of acute haemorrhage were not uncommon and required surgical intervention if life were threatened.

However, recent advances in our knowledge of gastric and duodenal pathology have led to the development of at least two therapeutic agents of which the newest, *cimetidine*, is highly effective. Developments in fibre-optic technology have contributed greatly to progress in peptic ulcer treatment. The gastro-enterologist can now pass a *flexible* instrument, the *gastroduodenal endoscope* (the gastroscope is a *rigid* tube), under mild sedation through the patient's gullet and into the stomach and duodenum and view the lesions directly. Once an ulcer is diagnosed, the time has come to stop treating yourself with antacids from the chemist's counter, and to take the ones your doctor decides are best. Smoking should be stopped by ulcer patients (as, indeed, by everyone else, but that is another matter) because it inhibits healing. Alcohol tends to increase acid secretion and should be avoided. It is also *extremely important* to avoid taking any form of aspirin, even in quite small amounts, since this can lead to very serious bleeding from the ulcer. The ulcer patient should be warned that hundreds of proprietary preparations contain aspirin and all of them are dangerous for him. Search for the formula in small print on the label before taking any remedy, looking particularly for acetyl salicylic acid—the correct name for aspirin. Even some widely sold "hang-over" remedies which are sold for "upset-stomach" contain large quantities of aspirin. Some of the patients with "upset stomach" are, of course, ulcer patients, and some even die of haemorrhage following the ingestion of aspirin.

The main complications of peptic ulcer are bleeding, perforation, and a narrowing of the pylorus, or lower part, known as *pyloric stenosis*. Bleeding is caused by the eroding ulcer eating away at one of the many blood vessels in the stomach or duodenal wall. It leads to the passing of "altered" blood in the stool (*melaena*), or to the vomiting of blood (*haematemesis*). When the initial bleeding occurs, the patient may feel suddenly faint, and a little later will notice the black, tarry colour of his stool. This is sometimes confused with a similiar colour when the patient is taking iron. Peptic ulcer is not the only cause of this very serious haemorrhage, which constitutes a hospital emergency whatever its cause. The treatment, like that of every large haemorrhage, is blood transfusion which must be continued until the bleeding stops, or until the patient is sufficiently fit for surgery, should that be deemed necessary. Perforation is perhaps the most serious complication of peptic ulcer, leading to the spilling of stomach contents within the abdominal cavity. Treatment is invariably surgical, either the closure of the perforation or the partial removal of the stomach.

Surgical removal of part of the stomach is often the only way to treat a peptic ulcer which has had its chance to heal in other ways. It is tempting for the patient to "have it out and done with," but the time for surgery is a matter of fine judgment. So many ulcers heal by medical means if you give them a chance, and operations are for those which persistently refuse, or which become complicated.

Stomach Cancer. The stomach is a fairly common site for primary cancer. There is no known reason for this, and it is particularly important to stress that we know of no connection whatever between the peptic ulcers which have just been discussed and cancer. Stomach cancer used to be the commonest cancer of men, but the current rise of lung cancer has pushed it into second place. There are some strange geographical differences in its distribution. For example, it is much commoner in Japan and Scandinavia than in England or the U.S.A. It is difficult to see any reason for this in dietary habits. In Wales it causes three times as many deaths as in South-East England. All this is very puzzling, as is so much of our information about cancer generally. One of the main problems with stomach cancer is that it often causes the patient no inconvenience and thus produces no symptoms of note until the disease is far advanced and it is difficult to do much. Treatment is by surgical removal of the growth, and even in the most advanced cases a great deal can often be done to make the patient more comfortable.

The Small Intestine.

The small intestine runs from the stomach to the caecum and comprises the duodenum, jejunum, and ileum in that order. On a more cheerful note it may be remarked that it is very rarely the site of cancer. Its main problems arise in connection with defects in absorption mechanisms, with obstructions, and with a strange inflammatory condition known as *regional enteritis*. Most obstructions are due not to blockages of the tube, but to failures of peristaltic propulsion, the process which is briefly described above under "oesophagus." Such a failure is called *ileus*. When peristalsis stops for any reason, the result is severe dehydration and loss of important chemicals like sodium and chloride from the body. This is because about 9 litres of fluid enter the small intestine each day in the form of digestive juices, and all of this has to be pushed onwards to be reabsorbed into the system at lower levels. If peristalsis fails, this bulk of fluid remains in the small intestine, or is vomited. In both cases it is lost to the body itself, leading to serious dehydration and illness. Treatment is by very careful replacement by transfusion of the fluid and the chemicals lost, and by removal of the trapped fluid within the intestine through a tube threaded down through the mouth.

Regional enteritis or *ileitis* is sometimes known as *Crohn's disease*. It is a very mysterious condition in which the normally supple wall of the small intestine becomes inflamed and gradually replaced by thick fibrous scar tissue, so that it looks and feels like a thick garden hose. Loops of inflamed gut stick together, and channels open between them, and if the disease progresses a mass of adherent, thickened intestine results to which everything in the neighbourhood also adheres. However, for some unknown reason some cases do not progress downhill in this way and get better spontaneously. Surgical treatment is necessary for the majority, however, particularly those with advanced disease leading to complications such as obstruction or perforation. Sometimes an early case can be resolved by cutting out the length of affected gut, although recurrences are unfortunately common.

Appendicitis. This must be one of the best-known surgical diseases of the intestinal tract.

The appendix is a narrow, blind-ended side tube attached to the caecum near the end of the small intestine. Appendicitis is when it becomes obstructed, or infected, or both. From its position it is almost predictable that it will get obstructed sooner or later by pieces of faecal matter which pass its entrance and which are normally infected. The surprising thing is that it does not happen more often. Once this has occurred, however, a closed abscess forms, and as the abscess distends the appendix, it first weakens its wall, making it gangrenous, and then bursts into the abdominal cavity causing *peritonitis* (see later). It would be useless and misleading to describe the symptoms of acute appendicitis in detail, since it is difficult even for experienced doctors to distinguish them from those of several other conditions. Suffice it to say that any severe, persisting pain in the abdomen, whether continuous or intermittent, whether associated with diarrhoea or not, should lead the sufferer to a doctor for a quick diagnosis. Germ-killing antibiotics are useless against appendicitis, and any laxative is extremely dangerous as it may cause an acutely inflamed appendix to perforate.

The Large Intestine or Colon.

The two main serious diseases of the colon are ulcerative colitis and cancer in its various forms. *Ulcerative colitis* is yet another mysterious disease in which severe ulceration of the lining of the colon gives rise most frequently to diarrhoea with the passage of blood and mucus. In fact it can be like dysentery, and it has often been considered to be due to some form of infection. Unfortunately no particular germ can routinely be found in these cases, and the situation is endlessly confused by the presence in the normal bowel of lots of different germs anyway. Nevertheless the ulcerated lining of the bowel certainly does get infected by the germs normally present, and this makes the disease worse. Therefore germ-killing antibiotics are often helpful in alleviating symptoms and can lead to an earlier settling down of the condition, although not to a cure. It has long been known that certain kinds of psychological upset are often associated, but here again the disease is so unpleasant for the sufferer that he is to be forgiven some despondency as a result of, rather than as a cause of, his troubles. It is also suspected that ulcerative colitis may be an auto-immune disease; that is it may represent rejection by the patient of his own colonic lining in a manner somewhat comparable to the tissue rejection which often follows organ transplantation. Some of the more alarming complications are perforation through the wall of the ulcerated bowel, and sometimes massive haemorrhage occurs. The mainstay of medical treatment is the drug *sulphasalazine* together with dietary measures and the occasional use of other drugs to minimise symptoms. Surgery may be required to relieve obstruction, deal with perforation, remove chronically affected parts of the bowel, etc.

Cancer of the Colon and Rectum. This is another very common form of cancer, which can often be completely cured by surgical removal of the growth provided it is caught in the early stages before it has spread. The commonest symptom is a change in bowel habit, either towards constipation or, more often, towards diarrhoea, in the second half of life. There may be rectal bleeding, or the passage of mucus, and there may be abdominal pain. We cannot too often repeat that any such change of bowel habit, or any unexplained bleeding from any site should lead the patient promptly to his doctor.

Diverticulitis. Some people have small pockets or sacs in the wall of the colon known as diverticula. A minority of these sometimes get inflamed, and this is *diverticulitis.* Occasionally perforation occurs.

Hernia or Rupture. This is a condition in which abdominal contents, usually a loop of intestine, protrude forwards through the muscular wall of the abdomen. The wall consists of a sheet of muscle fibres running in several directions. They normally become tense when we cough, or strain, or in getting up from a recumbent position. There are places in the groin on each side where there is a way through the muscle for the spermatic cord in the male. In many men a weakness can arise at this point, and if it persists, the way through may enlarge and allow loops of bowel to emerge from behind the muscle sheet to appear as a lump under the skin of the groin. On relaxation the lump can be made to disappear by pushing the contents back the way they came; and they will re-emerge when the patient strains. This is an extremely common complaint in men, and it should be treated by an operation in which the muscle wall is repaired. Some men, however, neglect to have their rupture treated until one day it proceeds to "strangulate." This is the term used when the muscle tightens around the neck of the protruding loop of bowel, cutting off its blood supply. From then onwards the loop becomes gangrenous and the intestine is obstructed by having a part of itself nipped outside the abdominal wall. The patient is in severe pain, vomits continuously, and quickly is liable to get into such a poor condition that surgical relief is difficult. It is therefore a surgical emergency, and it would have been better to have had the relatively simple repair operation earlier and at leisure. Hernia in the region of the groin is of two types: *inguinal hernia* and *femoral hernia*, the difference between them being technical and of no consequence to the patient. They nearly always occur in men. Other types of hernia less frequently occur in both sexes. *Incisional hernia* is when the muscle wall has been weakened at the site of an old abdominal operation and has failed to heal properly. *Umbilical hernia* occurs owing to the natural weakness of the abdominal wall at the navel, and is so common in babies as to be almost normal. When a baby cries and thereby puts a strain on his abdominal wall, a lump often appears in the region of the navel, and this can be very alarming for the parents. They should of course show it to their doctor who will nearly always be able to reassure them. It is self-healing without operation in the majority of cases.

Peritonitis. The cavity of the abdomen in which the intestines and other organs lie is called the peritoneal cavity, and it is lined by a thin membrane called the peritoneum. When this becomes inflamed the condition is a serious one and is called *peritonitis.* Inflammation may be bacterial, as occurs following a burst appendix and the spillage of bacteria and pus in the cavity. It may be a sterile peritonitis as often follows perforation of a peptic ulcer, when the inflammation is caused by the acid contents of the stomach. It is always very dangerous, probably because of the large surface area afforded by the peritoneum for the absorption of inflammatory toxins.

Haemorrhoids are simply varicose veins in the rectal and anal regions. They are very common, and are caused probably in about equal degrees by inherited weakness of the veins, strain such as heavy lifting, and constipation (this is one of the very few conditions in which constipation may do some damage, due to the mechanical pressure of hardened faeces in the rectum on the veins). Pregnant women are liable to develop haemorrhoids or "*piles*," as they are commonly called, owing to the pressure of the baby's head in the pelvis. Haemorrhoids may be external or internal, the former being in the anal region below the sphincter, the latter in the rectum; the two usually go together. There may be no symptoms, but the veins are liable to bleed, to get thrombosed (*i.e.*, a clot forms within) or to become infected. When clotting or infection occurs the piles enlarge and tend to be pushed out through the anus during defaecation, when they form extremely painful external swellings. Treatment in simple cases may be by the use of suppositories—cones of a firm grease containing suitable medicaments which are inserted in the rectum—in other cases the veins may be injected, as with varicose veins of the leg, in order to close them, but when there is much bleeding, thrombosis, infection, or interference with bowel movements they should be removed surgically.

THE LIVER.

The liver is the largest organ and has such a wide variety of known functions (to say nothing of the unknown) that it is also one of the most complicated. Nearly all of its functions are biochemical, and it is often called the laboratory of the body. Medical students, when asked to enumerate the functions of the liver, usually stick at about twenty-five, nearly all of them to do with general metabolism: that is the biochemical processing of substances taking part in structure or as body fuel. For example, the liver makes proteins from the amino-acids absorbed from the gut, and breaks down amino-acids and manufactures a waste product (urea) from them. It stores carbohydrates as glycogen, and conducts many of the processes necessary to turn carbohydrates into energy. It manufactures prothrombin with the help of vitamin K, and this is essential for blood clotting. It makes bile and secretes it into the gall bladder and bile ducts (see later). The three main constituents of bile (cholesterol, bile pigment or bilirubin, and bile acids) all have to be processed, or metabolised, in the liver during the production of bile. Vitamin B_{12} and iron are also stored and dealt with there, and these are involved in preventing various forms of anæmia (q.v.); and in addition to all these things the liver is the place where harmful substances, both from within the body and from outside it, are dealt with and rendered harmless. This last function of "detoxication" is often accomplished by making the offending molecules suitable for rapid excretion by the kidneys, or by altering their chemical shape to make them harmless.

Nearly all of these very different things are done by one single type of cell: the liver cell, and it is one of the remarkable features of the design that this cell can be so versatile. There also have to be some very efficient transport systems in the liver, in addition to the usual blood supply and venous drainage possessed by all other tissues.

One of these is the "portal venous system." Whenever a substance is absorbed across the gut wall from any part of the intestine into the interior of the body it enters the special draining blood vessels of the portal system, which are arranged throughout the length of the digestive tract. All these veins eventually unite in the main portal vein which enters the liver. Everything absorbed from the gut is therefore taken first to the liver to be processed. After this the products are carried away from the liver in the ordinary veins to the heart, and are distributed to the rest of the body by the arterial system. The liver has arteries of its own by which it receives oxygen and nutriment like any other tissue. The fourth transport system collects the bile as it is formed within the liver and delivers it to the gall bladder and bile ducts, which eventually drain it into the duodenum.

Portal Hypertension means high blood pressure in the portal venous system, and is the usual accompaniment to cirrhosis (see later). When the terminations of the portal veins in the liver are strangled and obstructed by cirrhotic disease, this tends to blow them up, or dilate them with blood. There is a natural escape route for the portal blood where the lower end of the oesophagus or gullet joins the upper end of the stomach. At this place some of the portal veins draining the stomach are connected with the ordinary veins draining the oesophagus so that when pressure rises in the portal system, blood tends to be diverted into these connecting veins, and they in turn become dilated, or varicose. Trouble begins when these dilated connecting veins, which bulge inwards into the oesophagus, are damaged by food particles passing across them and bleed severely into the stomach. The patient vomits large quantities of blood (haemalemesis) or passes tarry altered blood in the stool

(melaena). The other main cause of these is the bleeding which occasionally accompanies peptic ulcer (q.v.).

A second complication of portal hypertension (and hence of cirrhosis) is ascites, in which large amounts of a lymph-like fluid accumulate in the abdominal cavity. The fluid contains a great deal of precious protein and salt which is lost to the body economy. Ascites also sometimes accompanies cancerous deposits in the abdomen.

Jaundice means being yellow because there is too much yellow bile pigment circulating in the blood, and there are three main possible causes for this. The term "yellow jaundice," like "gastric stomach" is therefore unnecessarily redundant: there is no other kind.

Bile pigment comes from broken-down red blood cells, which normally come to the end of their time after existing for about 120 days. The breakdown products of red cells can always be found in the blood of normal people, but there is normally insufficient colour to show. Abnormal amounts of colour build up quite logically in any of the following three circumstances:

(1) If too many red cells are being destroyed and even the normal liver cannot deal with the amount of bile pigment produced, it piles up in the blood, and haemolytic jaundice is the result. The expression simply means jaundice due to (abnormally large) red-cell destruction.

(2) If the liver cells are themselves sick and unable to cope even with the normal amounts of pigment from normal red-cell destruction. Here too the pigment will pile up and cause hepatocellular jaundice, or liver-cell jaundice.

(3) If the bile ducts carrying bile away from the liver are blocked, then bile will pile up behind the blockage and re-enter the blood stream, causing obstructive jaundice. In this case the rate of red-cell breakdown is normal, and the liver cells are normal: at least for a time.

It is enormously important for the treatment of jaundice for the doctor to diagnose its type correctly, since the treatment varies from surgical relief of obstruction to the medical treatment of viral infection or of excess red-cell destruction.

The so-called differential diagnosis of jaundice is often exceptionally difficult, and sometimes requires some very sophisticated laboratory tests and X-rays. At other times it is extremely easy and is obvious from a cursory glance at the urine and the stool. In any case all jaundice is a highly technical matter for the doctor who must be consulted early.

There is a special jaundice of newborn babies which resembles haemolytic jaundice and can occasionally have serious consequences for the developing brain (kernicterus) if it is allowed to become too severe. When this is threatened, steps are taken to reduce the level of circulating bile pigment by replacement of the baby's blood or by other means.

The commonest cause of hepatocellular jaundice is infective or viral hepatitis. Obstructive jaundice is usually due either to blockage by gallstones (q.v.) or by a lump pressing on the bile ducts from an adjacent cancer. This can often be quite satisfactorily relieved by surgery.

Infective Hepatitis. There is a group of disorders affecting the liver which are caused by viruses. The incubation period is often very long, and the sickness and other debility caused is often quite severe and prolonged. One variety, known as serum sickness, is now much less common than a few years ago. It used to be transmitted by using the same needle for injections into several different people, or from transfusing contaminated blood. A greater awareness of the problem, and the use of disposable needles and syringes has cut down the incidence.

Cirrhosis. There are many different kinds of cirrhosis, the commonest of which has already been mentioned under *portal hypertension* above. In all cases, liver cells are slowly poisoned and are killed off over a long period of time. In response to this, the surviving liver cells undergo cell division, trying to make good the numbers lost, and at the same time fibrous scar tissue replaces the damaged tissue throughout the organ. The result is a hard, knobbly liver. The many "knobs" are spherical areas of regenerated new cells, and they are separated by thickened bands of scar tissue. All of this destroys the normal architecture and leads to the portal hypertension and ascites mentioned above. In some countries (*e.g.*, France and the United States) excessive alcohol is the main cause of the original liver damage which starts it all off. In others (*e.g.*, Bantu South Africa) it seems to be nutritional starvation of the liver. In England much less than half the cases are due to alcohol, and many are thought to be due to a previous episode of infective hepatitis (*q.v.*), but this is not certain. Infective hepatitis is quite common but cirrhosis is comparatively rare. So that the great majority of people do not progress from one to the other. One day soon the treatment for advanced cirrhosis will be to replace the liver by transplantation, but there are still many problems to overcome before this can become routine.

Cancer of the Liver. Cancer of the liver is quite common, but it is nearly always cancer which has spread in the blood stream from other parts of the body. The liver is a favourite site for such secondary deposits, since it has a large blood supply and will receive a generous helping of anything being carried. It is also a very "fertile soil" for the cancer seedlings to grow in. Primary cancer of the liver is uncommon, and only occurs in a few cases of pre-existing cirrhosis.

Gallstones. These are "stones" formed by some of the major constituents of bile coming out of solution and forming solid bodies. They are very common, and often cause no trouble at all. When they do, it is usually a colicky intermittent severe pain. This is due to the muscular walls of the bile passages contracting in an effort to expel an obstructing stone into the duodenum. The second common trouble arising from gallstones is obstructive jaundice, described above. It is small consolation to gallstone sufferers that the stones are often very pretty, often being composed of beautiful cholesterol crystals coloured by varying shades of bile. If they contain calcium they will be visible on an X-ray. Otherwise they are not seen. Stones often occur in conjunction with inflammation of the gall bladder, known as *cholecystitis.* The treatment for gallstones is to remove them surgically together with the gall bladder if they are causing persistent symptoms. Ways of avoiding surgery by dissolving them in substances taken by mouth are under investigation.

The Pancreas.

This is a soft, elongated gland lying behind the stomach; it is about 12·5 cm long and 5 cm wide. Within its tissues lies the duct, which, when it leaves the pancreas, passes into the duodenum near the point of entry of the bile-duct. This duct transmits the juices containing enzymes which aid in the digestion in the small intestine. The pancreas, however, has two main functions: not only does it manufacture these important digestive juices, but in certain specialised areas, known as the islets of Langerhans, it manufactures insulin, the hormone which makes it possible for the body to utilise sugar. *Diabetes mellitus* or ordinary diabetes is a chronic disorder usually caused by a deficient secretion of insulin. The unused sugar accumulates in the blood and acts as a poison, which, in extreme cases, sends the patient into coma and may—indeed, in former times, usually did—result in death. The treatment of diabetes was revolutionised by the discovery of the hormone insulin by Banting and Best in 1921. On the whole, diabetes is more severe in young people than in the elderly, but with correct treatment it is possible for all cases to lead a perfectly normal life except for dietary restrictions and insulin injections. Not to be confused with *Diabetes insipidus* (**P43**(**1**)).

DIET.

When considering diet, and the effect it has on our health and well-being, there is more to it than just the things we eat. We must also know about what our body does with the food, and it would be unscientific not to acknowledge the effects of our psychological make-up and our nutritional beliefs on what we eat, what we do with it, and how well (or ill) we feel as a result.

For example, a deep-rooted conviction that brown eggs or free-range poultry are better for us than white eggs or intensively reared birds is entirely unsupported by any evidence. However, if we believe such a thing sufficiently, we will not only eat the "better" ones, but we will feel happier and more secure afterwards, and this is likely to make us healthier. Food fads can occasionally be dangerous, as when extreme vegetarians become ill through lack of certain vitamins (*e.g.* B$_{12}$) which are present only in the foods they exclude. But this is so rare, even among strict vegetarians, that such danger can virtually be ignored. On the whole (and vegetarianism is probably a good example of this) food faddism often leads to a sense of health and well-being in the believer, and should not be attacked by the rest of us for that. It is an accepted fact that personal misfortune, even when it is severe, is more easily withstood by those with strong religious conviction than by others. In the same way, a firm attachment to a theory of what is good for you can produce a feeling of well-being and genuine good health, when another person on exactly the same food intake will not feel so fit. These factors—religious belief, food faddism, or the bedside manner of a kind or persuasive doctor —are commonly dismissed by free-thinking people because they are not "true" or "real." All three, however, can materially affect our health just as can a shock, a personal tragedy or being in love. The trouble starts, and the magic ceases to work, when adherents declaim their beliefs as *ex cathedra* truths and expect the rest of us to swallow them as wholly (or holy) as they do.

Thus there are genuine *facts* about food, and fallacies too; and as well as these there is a no-man's-land between in which one man's fact is another man's fallacy.

The basic constituents of any diet are protein, fats, carbohydrates, water, vitamins, minerals, salts, and indigestible roughage. All are chemicals whose structure and function are reasonably well understood. Even the mystical differences between fine table wines, so beloved of the connoisseur and gourmet, are reasonably well understood in chemical terms. Perhaps that is a pity.

Much nonsense is talked, especially by nutritionists, about minimal daily requirements. In general terms, however, requirements can be described in terms of how many calories there are in the total intake of proteins, fats, and carbohydrates per day, and how these are distributed between the three classes of food. The other substances mentioned above are only required in trace or small amounts except for water; and roughage is only required as a mechanical stimulus to bowel movement.

During the process of digestion (described on **P34–5**) all proteins are split into their constituent amino acids; all carbohydrates are split into their constituent simple sugars and most fats are converted into fatty acids and glycerol. At this stage, and not until this stage, all these simpler building bricks derived from the three classes of food are absorbed into the body proper, and taken to the liver and other tissues. Here they are "metabolised." That is to say they are either burned as fuel for the various processes of the body; or they are built up again into proteins, fats, and carbohydrates of the special kinds the body needs. They will either be used to rebuild structures suffering ordinary wear and tear or they will be stored. Many of them will be converted into a different class from the one they came from when they entered the body. For example, excess carbohydrate is converted into fat; or if there is a shortage of carbohydrate, some will be made out of the protein amino-acids which would normally have been used for tissue growth and repair. Thus it is only a generalisation to say that dietary carbohydrates are fuel and proteins are for building bodily structure. The body can convert one into the other, and spoil the calculation.

There is a great deal of confusion in people's minds about *energy*, and that is why the word *fuel* has been used above in connection with carbohydrates. The lay person uses energy as a term meaning something which allows us to leap about, running and jumping and skipping and dancing, and which keeps us from getting tired and run down. Thus, the food industry tells us, we need potatoes or breakfast cereals for these activities or for a hard day's work. This is a deliberate commercial confidence trick, and the scientist is largely to blame. He originally handed out the word energy to an eager food industry and an unsuspecting public, forgetting to explain that he meant it in the strictly scientific sense of fuel for bodily processes. It simply is not true that more potatoes, or more cornflakes will make you more active. Indeed the reverse is the case, and after a certain point they will only be converted into fat and reduce your activity. The nutritionist measures energy as calories, which are units of heat, and it is certainly true that you must eat enough of these each day if you wish to remain alive, let alone active.

All the three main classes of food provide calories, and in an ordinary well-balanced diet about 15% are provided by protein. Carbohydrates produce most of the remainder. Each gram of fat contains about twice the calories of a similar quantity of carbohydrate. We simply eat less fat than carbohydrate, because fat has a "high satiety value." It takes away the appetite for more. Proteins are mostly found in meat, fish, eggs, cheese, and milk. However, there is quite a lot of protein in many predominantly starchy foods like bread, and such grains as wheat, rice, and corn. Carbohydrates are mainly found in bread, potatoes, sugar, pastry, sweets, and so forth. That is one of the words which fortunately seems to be used by both scientists and laymen in much the same sense.

Some substances are absolutely essential to the body if life is to continue, even if they are only needed in trace amounts. These are substances which the body's own factories (like the liver) cannot make for themselves, even if they are provided with the correct ingredients.

One group of such substances are the *vitamins.* Some of these are found in predominantly fatty foods (milk, butter, cheese and so on) and are known as the fat-soluble vitamins—Vitamins A, D, E and K; the others are water-soluble—the Vitamin B group and Vitamin C. All have now been chemically identified, are manufactured and can be bought over a pharmacist's counter. The myth has grown up that if a little is good for one then a lot more will be better and there are a great many vitamin enthusiasts who consume vast quantities of such manufactured products in the belief that by doing so they will induce extra vitality and energy. Unless your diet is unbalanced in some way (a vegetarian diet may be grossly deficient in Vitamin B_{12}) you will not need extra vitamins.

Fortunately, most people buy food because they like it, not because it does them good; and provided they have normal dietary tastes they will usually get a perfectly adequate selection of the things we have spoken of as necessary for good health. The main danger in England is to have a surfeit and become overweight. In addition there are certain times of life when conscious attention should be paid to what is necessary. For example babies and nursing mothers have special dietary needs and will hear about them from their Health Visitor or from their Welfare Clinic or Doctor. Elderly people living alone are also prone to dietary deficiencies for reasons ranging from poverty to loss of appetite or inability to look after themselves properly.

Recent surveys have revealed some interesting facts about people's attitude to food and their knowledge of it. For example, half the people asked knew that meat was a source of protein, a third mentioned eggs and a fifth cheese, fish, and milk. But practically no one knew there was protein in bread. Yet in England about a fifth of our daily protein intake comes from bread, and nearly a third from cereals as a whole. Fish is well known as a source of protein, but did you know that on average we only obtain 4% of our daily protein from fish—less than we get from

potatoes (5%)? No one seems to know that potatoes are an important source of vitamin C, although fruit and vegetables are well-known sources. Calcium is recognised in milk, but most people forget its presence in cheese. Most people are very confused about iron. Why does everyone think it is mainly in green vegetables, when these are really such a poor source? For our daily requirement of iron we would each have to eat 1 kg. spring greens or peas; or 2 kg. of sprouts! In fact meat provides one of our best sources, and one-fifth of our daily needs is contained in bread.

Since most of the people who read *Pears* live in England let us return finally to our commonest nutritional disease, or our commonest form of malnutrition in these islands: obesity. Call it "being overweight" if you like, but acknowledge that it means being fat. Being fat is not only unattractive and unsightly but it is dangerous to health and carries a high mortality. Ask any life insurance company how they view your chances if you are overweight and you will find they are as worried about it as if you had high blood pressure, or smoke heavily. It is a particularly important cause of heart disease. However, it is very important to know exactly what we mean by fatness. Many girls who are not at all fat think they are, and this leads them to diet unnecessarily. On the other hand there are people who do not appreciate they are overweight. Here is a table which shows what your weight should be according to your height.

DESIRABLE WEIGHTS FOR MEN AND WOMEN ACCORDING TO HEIGHT AND FRAME, AGES 25 AND OVER

Men Height (in shoes 2·5 cm heels)	Weight in kilograms (in indoor clothing)		
	Small frame	Medium frame	Large frame
157	51–54·5	53·5–59	57–64
160	52–56	55–60·5	59–65·5
162	53·5–57	56–62	60–67
165	55–59	58–63	61–69
167	56–60·5	59–65	63–71
170	58–62	61–67	64·5–73
172	60–64	63–69	67–75·5
175	62–66	64·5–71	68·5–77
177	63·5–68	66–72·5	70·5–79
180	65·5–70	68–75	72–81
183	67–72	70–77	74–83·5
185	69–73·5	72–79·5	76–86
188	71–76	73·5–82	78·5–88
190	72·5–77·5	76–84	81–90·5
193	74·5–79·5	78–86	82·5–93

Women Height (in shoes 5 cm heels)	Weight in kilograms (in indoor clothing)		
	Small frame	Medium frame	Large frame
147	42–44·5	43·5–48·5	47–54
150	43–46	44·5–50	48–55·5
152	43·5–47	46–51	49·5–57
155	45–48·5	47–53	51–58
157	46–50	48·5–54	52–59·5
160	48–51	50–55·5	53·5–61
162	49–53	51–57	55–63
165	50·5–54	53–59	57–64·5
167	52–56	54·5–61	59–66
170	53·5–58	56–63	60·5–68
172	55·5–59·5	58–65	62–70
175	57–61	60–67	64–72
177	59–63·5	62–68·5	66–74
180	61–65·5	63·5–70·5	68–76
183	63–67	65·5–72	69·5–78·5

If you are overweight according to these tables you need to slim, and the question is how? Answer: by will-power. There is no other satisfactory method than to decide to eat less, and to eat as little carbohydrate as possible. For the time being eat as much meat, fruit, green vegetables, and as much fat as you like, but no sugar, starch, sweets, cakes, pastry, or biscuits, and no eating between meals. And cut down on beer and other alcoholic drinks. In case you are tempted to eat "slimming" foods, be aware that there is no such thing. There is nothing you can eat which will cause you to lose weight, in spite of what the advertisement says. In special cases doctors will prescribe tablets to suppress appetite, but they are too dangerous for general use without supervision, and they do not work as well as will-power. At the same time take more exercise. Walk to work. If you make a real and genuine effort for three months without success, you should ask your doctor for advice. Almost certainly you will have to admit you have not really tried. Good luck!

NUTRITIONAL DISORDERS.

Nutritional Deficiency and Malnutrition.—Until quite recently a consideration of malnutrition would have merely led to an account of how too little food, or a deficiency of certain articles in the diet, produced deficiency diseases at the time of the restriction. For example lack of vitamins of various kinds gives rise to such diseases as rickets, scurvy, beri-beri, and pellagra; and an overall shortage of food to general starvation. These may be considered the immediate or concurrent effects of a poor diet. Modern nutritionists, however, are beginning to be concerned with two more kinds of nutritional disorders; and although the study of both kinds is in its infancy, both will be introduced in this account.

The first deals with the effects of comparatively small amounts of harmful constituents in our diet, introduced either voluntarily or involuntarily, and consumed for a long period of time; and the second with the lasting effects on our adult well-being of nutritional deficiencies in early life even though they have long since been corrected.

When viewed in this light, one or other of these three kinds of nutritional disorder may at this moment be affecting almost every individual in every part of the world, "privileged" or "underprivileged." Let us first define some terms.

Undernutrition, strictly speaking, means a state of affairs in which the quality of the diet is perfectly good. There is the correct balance of the various dietary constituents and all the necessary components are present: but there is simply too little of it. Many hundreds of millions of people throughout the underprivileged world are suffering and dying from this kind of undernutrition, and the simplicity of the problem must be appreciated: they simply need more food of the kind they are at present getting, and which can often be produced locally.

Malnutrition means an imbalance of the various constituents: a relative lack or excess of one or more of them. It usually leads to conditions which are, from the point of view of medical treatment, much more difficult to deal with. And therefore doctors often class them as "more serious."

The diseases of malnutrition range from the widespread protein deficiencies in other parts of the underprivileged world to *obesity* in our own better-off industrial countries, which is usually due to excess carbohydrate. Make no mistake about it: obesity (or being overweight) is a widespread disease of nutritional imbalance, and it kills. It is the commonest form of malnutrition in (for example) England and America today, and is a consequence of the sophistication of our diet in modern times. Between one-fifth and one-tenth of the population of the United States is more than 20% overweight, and to be 10% or 15% overweight is almost the rule nowadays in people over thirty. There are high authorities in the world of nutritional science who attribute all this overfed malnutrition to the consumption of refined sugar, or sucrose. They say it is not only the amount of refined sugar we put in our tea or on our breakfast cereals, but also the amount in sweet cakes, biscuits, drinks, chocolates and sweets, and so forth. For some people it adds up to a phenomenal quantity each day. According to this school of thought we are not so

much suffering from a surfeit of carbohydrates or starches, but from this single sugar, sucrose. It is interesting to reflect on the recent banning of the artificial sweetener, cyclamate, by many governments. This substance, having been used extensively throughout the world as an apparently harmless non-fattening substitute for sugar, was suddenly banned in America because in very large doses (equivalent to the amount taken in hundreds of cups of coffee per day for a long time) it was found to produce cancer in rats. It has never been shown to do humans any harm, whereas the effects of sugar in producing an overweight population, thereby indirectly kill tens of thousands of British people each year. This is a fascinating example of the difficulties confronting our legislators in making balanced judgments when deciding to ban a foodstuff, a drug, or an artificial fertiliser.

Much the most widespread form of malnutrition, however, is a variety protein-lack which is part of a collection of nutritional diseases known as *Protein-Calorie Deficiency*. In very large underprivileged areas of the world, the childhood population receives such an inadequate diet that children live continuously on the brink of nutritional disaster. It only requires a small extra restriction or stress to topple them over into one of the clinical conditions to be described. At this stage they cease to be merely hungry. They become nutritionally ill. Sometimes the force which produces the disaster is a community catastrophe like a famine, an earthquake, or a war. Sometimes it is a family catastrophe like the loss of a lactating mother or a parental delinquency. Parents abandon young children as often in Africa as anywhere else. Sometimes the clinical nutritional disease is unmasked by a common childhood illness like measles, or gastro-enteritis which the well-fed child would have overcome. The starved child reveals his malnutrition instead and frequently dies. When the precipitating cause of the "epidemic" of malnutrition is a war or other national calamity, our newspapers and television screens carry distressing pictures of thin skeletal, pot-bellied children, and the conscience of a few is touched. It is insufficiently realised that these scenes can be witnessed anywhere in the continents of Africa and Asia, and in large parts of Central and South America any day of the week in normal times. The war has not been the cause, but is only the precipitating factor which has revealed the chronic malnutrition in more children than would normally exhibit it openly.

Protein-Calorie Deficiency is a collection of different kinds of childhood malnutrition. Some are due predominantly to deficiency of protein and are collectively called Kwashiorkor, a West African word meaning "red-haired boy" (see below). Others are mainly due to a severe deficiency of overall foodstuffs and are called *Marasmus*. But in any real-life situation the severe *mal*nutrition of Kwashiorkor exists side-by-side with all gradations between itself and the severe *under*nutrition of Marasmus, so that many intermediate forms of "marasmic kwashiorkor" are described. In Kwashiorkor the child is typically listless, apathetic, whining, with a reddish discoloration of the hair, a peeling, scaly skin, and with much extra fluid in his tissues causing oedema. He is so listless as not even to be hungry. In marasmus the child is ravenously hungry. He is extremely thin and "starved" looking and is quite a different picture.

There is good reason to believe that even when protein-calorie deficiency is successfully treated, there will always be some lasting restriction of mental function, particularly if the malnutrition occurred as early as the first year of life. This is especially true in situations of appalling poverty in towns, where thousands of babies are not breastfed because their mothers are at work. Many of them die. Some of them are no heavier than their birth weight at one year of age. Breast feeding in an underprivileged community is an essential insurance for childhood health and survival.

Two new avenues of nutritional inquiry were mentioned at the beginning of this section. The impact of very long continued intake of refined sugar over many years on our bodily health is an example of one of them. Scientists and others are also becoming alarmed at the effects of modern food additives when taken, even in small amounts, over a long period. These additives include colouring matter, decolorising chemicals, taste "enhancers," and so forth, which are present in everyone's diet in a "civilised community." We are as unable to avoid a constant dosage with them as if they had been added to our water supply. It is, however, difficult to strike a balanced attitude. It is one thing to suspect that these additives are harmful and quite another to prove it. Naturally if any of them are shown to produce harm in animals given reasonable quantities they are invariably withdrawn. But in practice it is extremely difficult for animal experiments to mimic the conditions of human intake, especially as the human life span involves eating the substance concerned in small quantities for several decades. Thus it is easy to postulate the harmful effects of monosodium glutamate (a very common taste enhancer) but practically impossible to prove the question either way. It is not sufficient to condemn "chemicals." All natural foods consist of chemicals, and so do we.

The other new topic in nutrition is more soundly based on animal experiment. It has been repeatedly found that if animals do not grow quickly enough at certain early periods of life, they not only become small, but they remain smaller than they should be even when they are subsequently given as much as they like to eat. This is true of all animals and birds so far studied. For example, if rats are suckled in large families it is found that they are smaller by the time they are weaned (3 weeks of age) than those suckled in small families. The interesting thing is that if they are then given as much as they want to eat for the rest of their lives, the small animals from the larger families never catch up to the others. Whereas if their growth is not restricted until later in their "childhood," full "catch-up" is possible soon after normal diet is resumed. In other words there is a critical time in early life when growth can be permanently affected. At the moment it is difficult to know whether the same is true of humans and, if so, when is our period of vulnerability. There is some suggestion that the corresponding critical period in humans is during the last part of gestation in the uterus, and the first year or so of postnatal life. This new idea may turn out to be very important for world nutrition. Since there will not be enough food for all the children all the time, it may become important to concentrate our aid to underprivileged countries on certain sections of the population only. It may be a good idea to see that pregnant mothers and small babies are specially fed. In this way we may be able to put off the periods of inevitable malnutrition until a time of life when it is recoverable. Such a plan would also go a long way to safeguarding the development of the brain which also occurs mostly at the same early time of life.

We shall now describe some of the better-known nutritional deficiencies, bearing in mind that vitamin deficiencies are virtually unknown in the better-off countries. No one in England need spend money buying vitamins, as has been emphasised in the preceding section. Vitamin deficiency can still occur, however, in elderly people living alone and not having a well-balanced diet. It also occurs for similar reasons in alcoholics, vagrants, etc., and very occasionally in small children.

Beri-beri is a group of diseases usually confined to the Far East where a diet of polished rice results in a poor intake of vitamin B₁ (thiamine). In one form there is oedema (q.v.); in another the peripheral nerves are affected leading to tingling and numbness. A similar condition is occasionally seen in alcoholics and diabetics. Treatment is with thiamine, and with other vitamins too, since most sufferers are going short of more than one.

Pellagra is found among maize-eating populations and is due to a deficiency of several vitamins including niacin, another member of the B group of vitamins. There is dermatitis on exposed skin, and soreness of the mouth and tongue, with gastro-enteritis.

Scurvy is due to vitamin C deficiency. In children bone growth is affected. At all ages there is bleeding into the skin (bruising), impaired wound healing, mental depression, and anaemia. Most fresh fruit and vegetables contain vitamin C and a diet containing these prevents the disease.

Vitamin A deficiency is commonly found in children in some underprivileged countries. It causes permanent blindness, with thickening opacity and dryness of the whites of the eyes leading to ulceration of the eye. Beyond a certain stage, therefore, a child's sight cannot be saved. The only real hope is prevention, with an adequate diet.

Rickets, another disease of early childhood, is caused by deficiency of vitamin D. Bones are not properly calcified, and their softness leads to deformities of the legs and many other bones. Vitamin D can either be eaten in the diet or produced under the skin under the influence of sunlight. Therefore rickets commonly occurs when both the diet and the sunlight are inadequate. It was once very common in industrial England, and is still to be seen very occasionally there and in impoverished urban communities in the United States.

THE ENDOCRINE GLANDS.

Glands are structures or organs which manufacture secretions (except for *lymph glands* which are not glands at all and should be called *lymph nodes*). The secretions are of two main kinds. The first are passed down tubes, or ducts, or are secreted directly into the hollow organs, and act locally. Good examples are the salivary glands which make saliva and pass it down ducts into the mouth for digestion of its contents and lubrication. These are *exocrine glands*. The second kind have no ducts, and secrete their product straight into the blood stream. This secretion is called a *hormone* and it is carried to all parts of the body by the blood where it acts at a distance on some remote part. These are the *endocrine glands* or *ductless glands*, and a number of them will be discussed in this section.

The first hormone, or "chemical messenger," was discovered by the British physiologist Starling in 1904, but the effects of removing some of the endocrine glands were known centuries before when removal of the male testes (castration) was practised to procure a form of manpower safe for the harem, to salvage a good male alto voice for the church choir, or to convert a rooster into a more eatable capon.

Anterior Pituitary.—Many of the endocrine glands do not act as separate autonomous organs in spite of their great differences. They are organised into a well-disciplined band by a "master-gland" called the anterior pituitary. Somebody once called it the "conductor of the endocrine orchestra" and the phrase is still repeated *ad nauseam* in students' examination papers. The pituitary, consisting of its two parts, anterior and posterior, is not much bigger than a pea and it sits right in the middle of the skull, centrally beneath the brain and joined to the brain by a short stalk. This astonishing tiny nodule of tissue produces at least eight important hormones.

One of these is *growth hormone*, which is necessary for normal growth, and also has an influence on insulin. An excess causes *gigantism* and *acromegaly*, often coinciding with diabetes, and too little results in a form of dwarfism. Three others, known as *gonadotrophic hormones* regulate the cyclical and other activities of the reproductive organs and lactating breast. Another, *thyrotrophic hormone*, regulates thyroid activity, *Adrenocorticotrophic hormone*, or *ACTH*, as its name implies, looks after the activities of another important endocrine gland, the adrenal cortex. And there are several others.

Hypopituitarism, including *Simmonds' disease* and *Sheehan's disease*, results from destruction of the anterior pituitary. It is extremely rare, and is usually associated with difficult childbirth involving very severe bleeding. There are disturbances of all the functions mentioned above, particularly thyroid and adrenal failure (q.v.) with upset sexual function. Treatment is by replacing the lost hormones.

Hyperpituitarism, including *gigantism* and *acromegaly*, results from over-activity of the anterior pituitary, and is usually due to a tumour or overgrowth of the gland. In acromegaly the growth hormone is produced in excess over a long period of time in an adult. This results in overgrowth of all the organs except the brain, and it is characteristic to find enlarged extremities—feet, hands, and jaw. In gigantism the same has occurred during childhood before the bones have stopped growing and the result is a person who may be 2 m tall or more.

Posterior Pituitary. The posterior part of the gland is really a quite separate gland. The main hormone it produces is concerned with the excretion of urine by the kidney (antidiuretic hormone). Deficiency of the hormone results in *Diabetes Insipidus*, not to be confused with *Diabetes Mellitus* or "sugar diabetes." In diabetes insipidus, the patient produces enormous quantities of dilute urine. He consequently has a prodigious thirst and consumes astonishing quantities of fluids. Treatment is by replacing the missing hormone.

Thyroid. The thyroid gland in the neck secretes an iodine containing hormone called thyroxine. Excess of it causes *hyperthyroidism*, *thyrotoxicosis*, or *Graves' disease*. Lack of it produces *cretinism* in the growing child or *myxodoema* in the adult. Thyroxine is concerned with the metabolic rate of cells throughout the body, or the rate at which they work, as well as with the proper growth of developing tissues, especially the brain. Too much thyroxine as in thyrotoxicosis leads to over-activity, warm sweatiness in an over-excitable patient whose pulse is rapid and who is eating ravenously to try to replace the wasted energy. In spite of his appetite he is very thin, and he often has bulging eyes for a reason not understood. Treatment is by drugs which neutralise the thyroxine or by cutting out some of the gland. A *cretin* is a child usually born with insufficient thyroid. He is destined to grow poorly, and to mental subnormality of a permanent and distressing kind. If the condition is diagnosed soon after birth treatment with thyroxine can avert most of the trouble. In myxoedema, thyroxine is deficient in an adult. They become slow in all their bodily processes, the hair thins and their flesh is puffy with a dry, wrinkled skin. Treatment is by thyroid replacement. *Goitre* simply means enlargement of the gland. It may be accompanied by overactivity or underactivity, or with little functional change. One variety (Derbyshire neck) occurs in areas short of iodine in the soil and drinking water.

Adrenal Cortex. The adrenal or suprarenal glands sit, as the name implies, one on top of each kidney. There are two distinct parts: the cortex or outside which secretes steroid hormones, and the *adrenal medulla*, or core, which secretes adrenalin. There are many different steroid hormones in the adrenal cortical secretion, which look after such divers matters as sodium and potassium balance, sexual function, the reaction of the body to stress, and the regulation of sugar levels. *Addison's disease* (not to be confused with Addisonian anaemia) results from adrenal cortical insufficiency, and is often due to destruction of the gland by tuberculosis. There is weariness, malaise, pigmentation of skin creases and mucous membranes. They are short of sodium and have excess potassium. Treatment is with cortisone (replacement of the missing hormone) and by extra salt by mouth for the lack of sodium. *Cushing's* disease is due to excessive adrenal cortical function, and sometimes also occurs in patients treated with cortisone for other purposes. They have a striking redistribution of fat in the face, neck, and trunk, with stretch marks similar to those acquired by most women during pregnancy. The facial obesity makes them "moon-faced," and female patients may suffer masculinisation with deepening of the voice and hirsutism.

Testis. The male testes, as well as producing sperm are also endocrine glands producing steroid hormones known as androgens. They are mainly concerned with maintaining secondary sex characteristics. At the time of puberty the controlling secretions from the anterior pituitary begin to appear and androgens are produced. There is a whole range of rare disorders, resulting in everything from precocious puberty to delayed puberty. It should be borne in mind that the normal time of puberty can vary by several years from one boy to another.

Ovary. The human ovary has two functions: to produce ova, or eggs; and to produce two hormones, oestrogen and progesterone. These functions begin at puberty, one of whose features in the female is the onset of menstruation, or menarche. Just as in boys, the timing of normal puberty is very variable, but on the average, girls achieve puberty before boys. As social conditions improve, the age of menarche is getting younger generation by generation. All the secondary sex characteristics are under the control of the ovarian hormones which are released in response to the appropriate anterior pituitary hormones. The changes which occur in the womb and elsewhere in the intervals between menstrual periods and the periods themselves are controlled by a cyclical or rhythmic secretion, first of oestrogen and then of progesterone, by the ovary. This cycle is upset by pregnancy to allow the development of the embryo. It can also be upset by taking certain combinations of the two hormones by mouth. These can prevent the formation of ova, and are a popular form of contraception. In late middle age, the ovaries lose their function, the menstrual cycles cease to occur, and reproductive life is at an end. This is called the *menopause* or "change of life," and is sometimes accompanied for a time by distressing symptoms due to a temporary imbalance between oestrogen and progesterone. Many sexual functions, however, continue well after the menopause into old age, and these can include a continuing libido or sexual desire.

Parathyroid. Four tiny parathyroid glands are buried behind the thyroid gland and are responsible for regulating the body calcium and phosphate. They are therefore particularly important for the building and maintenance of bones and teeth. Since a proper calcium level in the blood is necessary for muscle (including heart muscle) contraction, and for correct functioning of nerves, disorders of the parathyroids can give rise to muscular spasms as well as loss of bone calcium. The latter can result in fragility and fractures. Overactivity of the glands leads to too much calcium and the formation of stones especially in the kidney.

Pineal. We end this section with a mystery gland. Like the pituitary it is small—about the size of a pea—and sits well back at the base of the brain. It was endowed in ancient times with metaphysical properties all of which remain speculative. In fish and lizards and certain lower vertebrates it is a kind of third eye, and receives light. In higher mammals, like ourselves, it is so far from any source of light that it could scarcely do so. It can be removed without harm. Indeed it normally becomes calcified and inactive about the time of puberty, and its position seen on X-rays of the skull can be a good guide to whether the brain is being pushed to one side by an abnormal mass.

THE URINARY SYSTEM.

Everyone knows what kidneys look like—in fact, the term "kidney-shaped" is used to describe other objects. Within the kidneys the blood-vessels carrying waste materials subdivide and finally end up in little coils or glomeruli through which waste products are filtered into the other system, the system of tubes which, beginning as tiny cups around the glomeruli, become larger and larger until they join the ureter passing out at the foot of the kidney, the hilum, a point at which both the veins and tubes enter and leave. The kidneys, of course, lie one on each side in the loins, so that if one puts one's hands on the hips and then slides them farther back they will cover the area over the left and right kidney. The ureters pass down on each side to the bladder, which is the storage tank of the products excreted by the kidneys, and lies in the mid-line down low in the abdomen; it is somewhat pear-shaped, and at its base in men there lies the prostate gland— a gland which apparently has few functions but can be a nuisance. Its only known function is that it adds something to the semen from the testes without which the semen would be sterile. Then, from the base of the bladder a single tube, the urethra, passes to the outside. One can, in fact, visualise the urinary system as a capital Y, in which the two upper limbs are the ureters, the place where they meet is the bladder, and the single limb at the foot is the urethra. Clearly, then, there may be diseases of the kidneys, of the ureters, of the bladder, of the prostate gland, or of the urethra.

The amount of urine may be increased or diminished. It is *increased* in the following conditions: after drinking excess of fluids; after taking drugs (known as *diuretics*) which are given to increase the flow; in diabetes of both types—mellitus and insipidus; in some types of chronic kidney disease; and finally, in emotional states of excitement. It is *decreased* in the following conditions: acute nephritis; any disease in which fluid is being lost in other ways, such as diarrhoea or sweating in fevers; when the fluid intake is small; and when both ureters are blocked by stones. Passing a great deal of urine is known as *polyuria*, passing very little as *oliguria*, passing frequent small amounts is simply called *frequency*. Normally, the urine is acid, but in infections of the bladder it may become alkaline owing to decomposition by bacteria. Abnormal substances, or normal substances in abnormal quantities, may occur in the urine and give the doctor an indication of what is wrong. In fact, urine analysis is a very important part of medical diagnosis. Thus urea is a normal content of urine which is increased in fevers, wasting diseases, or diabetes; the amount of urea is to some extent a measure of the degree of tissue breakdown. Uric acid is found in small quantities in normal urine, but the amount is increased in fevers and after an attack of gout (uric acid is important in the causation of gout, but has nothing at all to do with rheumatism in general, so one may disregard the advertisements in the popular Press showing unpleasant pictures of joints with sharp crystals of uric acid which are alleged to cause the pain of rheumatic disease). Oxalates are not ordinarily found in urine, but, since they occur in such foods as rhubarb and strawberries, and some people are unable to deal with them, such individuals may develop stones or have pain on passing urine after eating oxalate-containing fruits.

Two very important substances which ought not to be in normal urine are albumen and sugar. Albumen is a protein, and its presence in the urine indicates that the filters of the kidney are leaking —they are allowing protein to pass out which ought to remain in the body. Albumen is easily tested for, and its presence may indicate kidney disease or nephritis as it is usually called by doctors. On the other hand, small amounts of albumen occur in fevers and in nervous conditions —*functional albuminuria*. Sugar, too, should not be present, but its presence does not necessarily indicate diabetes; for small amounts may occur in nervous conditions or in some people after taking large quantities of carbohydrate.

Blood in the urine may give it an appearance which varies from bright red to a dark, smoky colour. It is found in many diseases: acute nephritis, stone, tumours, poisoning by certain drugs, infections such as bilharzia or malaria, papilloma (*i.e.*, non-malignant tumour of the bladder), after injury, in high blood-pressure,

scurvy, and blood diseases. Sometimes it occurs for no known reason at all.

It will be remembered (or if it is not, you can look it up on **P27 (2)**) that streptococcal infection of the throat may cause in some people disease of the valves in the heart or endocarditis. In such cases, although the germ is found in the throat, it is not found in the heart or indeed anywhere else in the body. *Acute nephritis* occurs in the same circumstances, with the sole difference that the kidneys instead of the heart are affected. The disease appears to be an allergic reaction to the toxins of the streptococcus. The patient, often a child, has a sore throat (and even this may be absent or fail to be noticed) or sometimes the infection may arise in other sites: after scarlet fever, erysipelas, burns, and disease of the ear. A few days later there is headache, vomiting, pain in the loins, slight rise in temperature, and especially typical is *dropsy* or oedema. This begins in the face, first around the eyelids, and then affects the ankles; later it may become more general and affect the rest of the body. Blood and albumen are found in the urine, and the blood-pressure is slightly raised. The outlook is usually good if the kidneys are rested by reducing the amount of protein taken in and also the amounts of salt and water. When this is done, the inflammation soon goes and no permanent harm results. In other cases, however, if treatment is inadequate or the condition severe, the symptoms may go, but the albumen found in the urine persists. This means that permanent damage has been done, and although there may be nothing else to show for many years, *chronic nephritis* develops. In this case, the blood-pressure continues to rise, and since the filters of the kidneys no longer work efficiently, urea, the principal waste-product of the body to be excreted in the urine, is retained in the blood and only small amounts escape from the system. Hence chronic nephritis sooner or later leads to heart failure or haemorrhage in the brain from the rising blood-pressure, or to the form of poisoning known as *uraemia* which results from the retention of urea in the blood. Uraemia may come on suddenly or gradually, but ends in progressive coma, drowsiness, and unconsciousness. There may be convulsions similar to those of epilepsy, high fever, and difficulty in breathing to complicate the picture.

Another type of nephritis which seems to have nothing at all to do with streptococcal infections, and the cause of which is completely unknown, is *nephrosis*. Developing in early adult life, its onset is insidious, and the patient first shows signs of oedema in his white and puffy face and the swelling of his legs. (It should be said here that if you have swelling of the ankles or elsewhere, you would be foolish to jump to conclusions; for such swelling is common in many diseases—in heart disease, in allergic conditions, in neurotic illness, and even just from hot weather.) When the urine is examined in a case of nephrosis it is found to be full of albumen and, as in chronic nephritis, the blood urea starts to rise. The end-results of nephrosis are the same as those of chronic nephritis and depend upon the damage originally done.

The modern diuretics of the thiazide group help to control the oedema and, provided enough healthy tissue remains, remove both the fluid and the waste-products.

In recent years there have been considerable advances in the development of the artificial kidney. Once only used within hospital, artificial kidneys or dialysers as they are known, can now be used in patients' own homes, thus obviating in some cases long journeys to hospital twice a week for treatment. Dialysis is a relatively temporary measure; renal transplants now offer real hope to many sufferers although there are far more suitable recipients than there are potential donors.

Pyelitis is an infection of the pelvis of the kidney, that is to say, of the part where the ureter leaves the kidney. It is usually caused by the bacillus coli, which is normally present in the body, or by the streptococcus. These germs may reach the ureter through the blood-stream or may pass upwards from the bladder. Obstruction anywhere in the urinary tract which causes the urine to stagnate is liable to cause pyelitis. Symptoms come on suddenly, with high fever, pain in the loin (the infection is usually on one side only, and is commoner in women), and pain in the abdomen. When urine is passed there is a burning sensation, and it is passed frequently and in small amounts. On examination, the urine is found to be highly acid and full of bacillus coli or whatever the causative germ may be. Pyelitis is fairly readily treated by the antibiotics or sulpha drugs. Plenty of fluids should be given and the urine made alkaline by administration of alkalis.

Cystitis means inflammation of the bladder, either acute or chronic, and its causes are much the same as in the case of pyelitis. There is pain over the lower abdomen, frequency, and sometimes slight fever. The treatment is as for pyelitis. *Urethritis* is an inflammation of the urethra, with burning pain on passing water and frequency. The most serious cause (although it can usually be easily dealt with now) is gonorrhoea. But non-specific urethritis is common, and in this case various germs or none may bring about pain and frequency; there is often a large neurotic element. Urethritis should be regarded as probably due to gonorrhoea, which has already been discussed elsewhere, when there is a thick, creamy discharge from the penis or discharge in women following sexual intercourse with an infected person.

Kidney stones or Renal calculi sometimes form, and, as in the case of gall-stones, what causes them is not certain. They may be caused by disorders of metabolism—that is, in the inability of the body to deal with calcium, proteins, uric acid, and other products; or by vitamin deficiency, obstruction in the urinary tract, and urinary infections. But when a stone or stones are formed various events may occur: thus it may remain in the kidney and cause no symptoms; or it may cause repeated attacks of pain, infection, and blood in the urine (haematuria); or it may completely block the passage of urine from the kidney to such a degree that it degenerates and becomes useless; or, lastly, it may pass into the ureter, and when this occurs very severe pain, known as *renal colic*, will occur. A stone passing down the ureter into the bladder may become stuck in the urethra, although this is uncommon, since a stone small enough to get down the ureters is likely to be capable of manoeuvring through the rest of the tract. In fact, about 80–90 per cent. of stones are passed spontaneously. Stones not passed spontaneously may have to be removed by operation, but whether this is undertaken or not depends on various factors, such as the general health of the patient, the amount of trouble caused by the stone, and the health of the other kidney —for it is dangerous to operate on one kidney unless one is sure that the other is functioning efficiently.

If a stone blocks the passage of urine on one side for any length of time *hydronephrosis* may result, in which the part where the ureter enters the kidney swells with the retained urine. Ultimately much of the kidney may be destroyed by the back-pressure. The same effect may be produced by kinking of the ureter or anything else which causes obstruction. Sometimes children are born with hydronephrosis, and when the dilation is due to kinking of the tube the condition may be intermittent, with attacks of renal colic during which only small amounts of urine are passed; this is followed with relief and the passage of large quantities.

Tumours and Cysts. The kidney may also be the site of tumours and cysts which produce pain in the loins, sometimes a lump over the kidney which can be felt, and blood in the urine. Cancer of the bladder is a serious condition in which the bladder may have to be removed, so the urinary flow has then to be directed elsewhere. Either the ureters are brought out on to the skin surface, a procedure known as *cutaneous ureterostomy*, or they are implanted in the large bowel, so that the urine flows out with the faeces. This is described as *uretero-colostomy*.

There may also be benign tumours of the bladder or *papillomas*, which are soft and bleed easily; a great deal of blood is passed, but there is usually little or no pain. In this, and similar, diseases of the bladder examination of the inside of the organ is carried out by means of a cystoscope, a thin tube which is passed up the urethra and has a small electric light at the end which enables the surgeon to see what is going on. Instruments may also be passed through the tube, and simple papillomas can be cauterised. Similar instruments are used in the examination of the stomach (gastroscope) and the bronchial tubes (bronchoscope). When some obstruction in the outlet of the bladder or in the urethra occurs the bladder, of course, fills with urine, which cannot be passed, and very painful dilation occurs. In this case an attempt may be made to pass a catheter, a thin rubber tube, into the bladder to relieve the tension, or if this fails a *suprapubic cystotomy* is performed—an incision is made in the abdomen over the bladder and a tube inserted into it, through which the urine escapes. This is ordinarily a temporary expedient, and later when the patient's health has improved an attempt will be made to remove the cause of obstruction. The most common cause of such obstruction is *enlargement of the prostate gland* at the base of the bladder, which surrounds this area and the beginning of the ureter. About 40 per cent. of men over sixty have some degree of obstruction due to this cause, and about 20 per cent. of these require operation. The gland is about the size of a walnut, and, as we have seen, its function is to supply part of the fluid which makes up the semen, the male sex secretion. Enlargement of the prostate may be benign or malignant, and, although nobody knows just why, such benign enlargement tends to occur in most men in later life. There may be no symptoms, but characteristically there is frequency during the day and the need to get up at night to pass water. The flow of urine being impeded by constriction of the urethra, the passage is less forceful than normal, and there is a tendency for dribbling to occur. If the obstruction is severe and not relieved the back-pressure may be transmitted to the ureters and kidneys, resulting finally in kidney failure and uraemia. The prostate, except in cases of very mild enlargement, has to be removed either through the abdomen or through the perineum (the part of the body lying between the sex organs and the anus). Sometimes, in less serious cases, it is possible without an incision to cut away the obstructing part by an electrocautery inserted, as is a cystoscope, through the urethra. Prostatectomy was once a serious operation, all the more so because the patient was usually elderly and not in good condition, but new techniques and the use of antibiotics have greatly improved the outlook.

Cancer of the Prostate is always serious, but if discovered in time it can be operated on successfully. The gland, of course, has to be completely removed; in inoperable cases, or in patients unfit to stand operation, the tumour may be treated by means of female sex hormones, which cause it to shrink and may prolong life by some years.

THE NERVOUS SYSTEM.

The nervous system consists of the Central Nervous System and the Peripheral Nervous System. The brain and spinal cord make up the former. The latter consists of the nerve fibres by which the Central Nervous System is connected to all parts of the body. Human beings have a more complicated brain than any other animal species, but it is only its complexity which makes it different from the brains of other mammals like rats and pigs and cows. We do not have the largest brains, since whales, for example, have much larger ones. Ours is not even the largest for the size of the body. Mice and dolphins and several other creatures have relatively larger brains when compared with body weight. Furthermore the cells and materials of which our brain is composed are virtually identical with those in other mammals, and its living properties are also the same.

Before describing some of the diseases of the nervous system it will be helpful to say a little about how it is made and how it works. Each human brain probably contains about ten thousand million (10,000,000,000) nerve cells and perhaps four or five times this number of supporting "glial" cells. Each nerve cell has many long thin branching projections, called dendrites, rather like the branches of a tree, leading to many thousands of "twigs" for each single nerve cell. At the end of each "twig" there is a special structure called a *synapse* by which contact is made with other nerve cells. It is through these connections that very large numbers of nerve cells give information (or send impulses) to each other so that they can be co-ordinated. As well as these dendritic branches, each nerve cell gives off one large trunk called the *axon*, down which final messages are sent as the result of all the information it receives from its dendrites. Some axons are many feet long. Some end in another synapse, by which the outgoing message is passed to yet another nerve cell. Some axons, those of the peripheral nerves, end directly on organs like muscles or glands, instructing them and making them work.

Messages are passed along dendrites and axons as electrical impulses. These are generated in the nerve cell "body." They are modified according to information received from other nerve cells and propagated down the axon. It is this superficial resemblance to a series of electrical cables which has given rise to comparisons of the brain with a telephone system or a computer, and as long as it is realised how infinitely more complicated each brain is than any known computer, the comparison is not a bad one. However, the brain generates its own electric power from the fuel brought in its own blood supply; and no spare parts or spare cables are available if the originals should get damaged, except in peripheral nerves. Furthermore the contact of one nerve cell with another through a synapse is not an electrical contact, and neither is the contact between a nerve and the muscle or other organ it is controlling. In both cases the connection is chemical. Thus when an electrical impulse arrives at the end of the nerve fibre, a chemical is released into the gap between it and the next nerve or organ, and it is this chemical which carries the stimulus forward. There is also an arrangement to neutralise the chemical transmitter when the impulse has been transmitted. So the resemblance to a telephone exchange or computer can sometimes be misleading.

Many of the nerve axons which transmit electrical impulses are clothed in fatty *myelin sheaths*, a little like the plastic insulation around an electric wire. Here again the resemblance is only partial, since the myelin sheaths are interrupted at regular intervals and these gaps in the insulation play an important role in transmitting the impulse. One of the important functions of the non-nervous *glial* cells of the brain is to manufacture and maintain the myelin sheaths.

Most of the functions of the brain are quite unknown, and even the ones we know about are very poorly understood. It is assumed to be the organ of higher mental function, of the mind and intellect; but there is surprisingly little evidence for this, and no one has any idea what physical structures or mechanisms subserve these functions. The brain is known to control all bodily functions by means of *motor* and other nerves which carry impulses from the brain outwards to all parts of the body. Sometimes these are under our voluntary control; mostly they are involuntary, reflex or automatic. Reflex actions are the result of impulses passed inwards from the body towards the brain by means of sensory nerves. Information arriving in the brain about the various sensations like heat, pain, touch, position, the need for saliva or gastric juice or even the thought or smell of food, are acted on in the various "centres" in the brain. These send out instructions down the "motor" or "secretary" nerves which instruct the muscles or glands to take appropriate action. Thus a *reflex* has a "sensory ending" which appreciates some sort of sensation. This is converted into an electrical impulse which is sent towards the brain or spinal cord along a sensory or "afferent" nerve. The impulse arrives at a "centre" in the central nervous system which co-ordinates all the relevant information and issues instructions. These travel as impulses outwards, along "efferent" nerves towards "effector" organs like muscles or glands, and an appropriate action occurs automatically. The pathway from sensory ending to effector organ is called a *reflex arc*. Many reflex activities are partly under voluntary control, although

mainly automatic. If you touch something hot you will automatically withdraw your hand. But if it is a hot china cup which has cost you a lot of money, you are capable of overriding the tendency to drop it, at least for a time. Breathing is automatic, but it can also be controlled, again at least for a time.

Clearly the brain is a very delicately organised piece of machinery, and its cells are extremely specialised for their job. Achieving this kind of specialised perfection brings many difficulties, however, and the brain cells have become highly dependent on the proper functioning of the other body systems, especially the blood circulation, the respiratory system, and the systems regulating the detailed nutrient composition of the blood. Failure of these systems, even for a very short time, can damage the nerve cells. Nearly all death, from whatever original cause, is produced this way, by an ultimate interference with nerve cell function.

We have already mentioned that the brain and spinal cord are unable to repair or replace any components which get damaged. The vulnerability of the brain is even more obvious when it is realised how easily damage and destruction can occur. For example, unless a rich supply of oxygen and glucose is continuously arriving in the blood stream, brain cells will cease to function in a few seconds and will die in a few minutes, and they can never be replaced. This is in marked contrast to other tissues of the body. The leg, for example, may carry on for over half an hour without any blood at all because the muscle and other cells can find other ways of surviving. Thus the brain can be permanently damaged if the blood contains insufficient oxygen (through asphyxia), insufficient glucose, or if the blood supply is blocked or if the blood pressure falls. All these are likely to happen to any of us at any time, and so there are elaborate mechanisms trying to prevent them occurring. Most of the subject of physiology is concerned with the mechanisms designed to protect the brain, and most of us ultimately die because they eventually fail. One of the clever features of the body design is that all the mechanisms which protect the brain from a supply failure are controlled by the brain itself. Thus the brain has itself been made to control the heart beat and the breathing and the many other systems which are needed for its own survival.

In all that follows concerning disease of the nervous system it will be seen that the effects of neurological disease on the patient are the direct result of something going wrong with one of the structures or mechanisms we have described.

Diagnostic Techniques in Neurology. The doctor has many ways of testing the nervous system, most of which test its various functions as outlined in the introduction. Thus tests of sensation, muscular movement and reflexes of all kinds as well as the special functions of taste, smell, vision, hearing, speech and intellect play a part. A great deal can be learned about the brain by *arteriography*. In this test a radio opaque substance is put into the arteries supplying the brain, and an X-ray picture taken immediately afterwards shows up all the blood vessels. *Ventriculography* is an X-ray examination after gas has been introduced into the brain cavities or ventricles which are normally filled with *cerebrospinal fluid*; *myelography* is an X-ray of the spinal cord after a radio-opaque substance has been injected into the space between the spinal cord and the bony vertebral canal which houses it.

The development of the EMI Scanner, a relatively new concept in diagnostic radiology, has now made most of those "invasive" diagnostic techniques unnecessary. The equipment needed is expensive and is presently only available at a very few centres. Sometimes *radioactive isotopes* are put into the blood stream and carried into the brain where they can be detected from outside the skull by counters. *Electroencephalography* measures the electrical waves generated by the brain by placing electrodes on the scalp. *Electromyography* does the same for muscles.

Consciousness and Unconsciousness (Coma). Everyone knows what consciousness is until he tries to define it. Full consciousness is generally taken to imply not only wakefulness but the total complement of human mental faculties. In clinical medicine, however, something less than this is usually meant. For example a demented person, or one whose memory is lost (*amnesia*), or one whose powers of speech are lost (*aphasia*) may still be "conscious." There is really a continuous gradation between full consciousness and coma, passing through drowsiness and even "stupor" in which condition a patient can be aroused from coma but sinks back into it when left alone. Many different things can cause coma ranging from swelling of the brain, compressing it in its rigid box of bone, to disorders in other body systems resulting in a failure to provide for the brain's needs. Examples of the first are bleeding within the brain or *brain tumours*, both of which occupy space and can only do so by producing compression. In the second category are asphyxia preventing oxygen from reaching the brain, lack of glucose in the blood, circulatory failure in which there is insufficient blood, or insufficient blood pressure. Fainting is a comparatively minor example.

Sleep and Insomnia. Nobody knows what causes sleep, why it is necessary, and how it helps. It is quite different from coma or even stupor, since as much oxygen and glucose is necessary asleep as awake. Insomnia is experienced by everyone at some time, and for some reason is very distressing if it persists. There are three forms: failing to get to sleep, intermittent wakefulness, and awaking early. Nearly all insomniacs sleep more than they think. They should eat light evening meals and avoid stimulants like tea and coffee after mid-day. Elderly people should realise they need less sleep. Being cold or having a full bladder can be a cause. Or simply not being tired. Sedative drugs are a last resort, but they can be useful in "breaking the habit" of wakefulness. Obviously there may be psychological factors such as anxiety and excitement. *Narcolepsy*, or a true inability to keep awake is comparatively rare. Both narcolepsy and insomnia are really extreme examples of what all normal people suffer from occasionally.

Headache is man's most common pain. Here again we must distinguish between the very common varieties of comparatively trivial significance and the rare ones due to serious causes. Some headaches are due to continuous tightness in muscles of the scalp, and are often "nervous" or psychological in origin. Others result from nose blockage and congestion, sinus problems, eye strain, toothache, etc. Migraine is a special kind and will be described below. Very occasionally indeed headache is due to serious disease like brain tumour. Most headache results from "living it up" or being "run down," or both. The headache of alcoholic hangover is probably due to dehydration. It can often be avoided by consuming a great quantity of water (a half litre or so, before going to bed), but few people are prepared to do this in the circumstances. Be careful when using aspirin, which is a useful remedy for headache, since it is very dangerous for people with stomach complaints like gastritis or gastric or duodenal ulcer. Occasionally aspirin makes the stomach bleed, and this can be so severe as to kill. A safer pain killer is paracetamol. Be particularly careful in treating "hang-over" headaches by patent fizzy remedies. They are very effective, but often contain large quantities of aspirin described in small print by its proper name as acetyl salicylic acid.

Migraine. This is a very special variety of "sick headache" and requires special treatment under medical supervision. It has many different forms, but usually there is a definite sequence of events. An attack often starts with some alteration of vision. The patient has shimmering blind spots or other visual disorders. This is followed by a well localised severe headache which may end in nausea or vomiting. The whole thing is caused by a poorly understood disorder of the blood vessels. There are special drugs, mostly derivatives of ergot, which are effective, especially if used when the first signs of an attack appear. Although there is a direct physical cause for an

attack, it is also certain that some of the trouble is psychological tenseness. People with migraine are often rather anxious, striving and perfectionist people. Also it has been noticed that attacks are much less frequent when the necessary pills are being carried available for use. However, as with all other conditions which are partly "psychological" in origin they are none the less distressing for the patient. It simply means that the treatment is also partly psychological in encouraging him to come to terms with his problems.

Ménière's Disease is one of the conditions in which the organ of balance in the middle ear is affected, giving rise to *vertigo*, a form of giddiness. It usually begins in middle life in the same sort of person who sometimes has migraine. There is buzzing in the ears and some intermittent loss of hearing as well as vertigo. During an attack the patient may be unable to walk because of his loss of balance, and nausea and vomiting are common. Treatment is by special drugs, and occasionally an operation on the ear is necessary.

Epilepsy is a symptom, not a disease, which is common at all ages but especially children. It has been attributed to St. Paul, Julius Caesar, Napoleon, and (with more justice perhaps) to Dostoyevsky. Many varieties of attack occur often in the same patient, the commonest and best known being the *grand mal* or major seizure. In this the patient falls down unconscious and rigid and the jaw is clenched, so that there is danger of the tongue being bitten. This so-called tonic phase is followed, within a minute or so, by a clonic phase in which the limbs contract rhythmically. The attack ends with the patient going limp and gradually recovering consciousness, a process which may take up to an hour. Occasionally the patient has a brief warning, most often an indescribable feeling in the stomach. There are two common forms of minor seizure, one occurring mainly in children and the other more often in adults. The common minor attacks in children are often called *petit mal* or *absence*, which well describes the instantaneous and brief loss of consciousness often unaccompanied by any change in posture. Recovery is equally instantaneous. On the other hand, in the other forms of epilepsy which arise from various parts of the brain, but especially from the lobe under the temporal region, there is often a warning similar to that which may precede a major seizure. In these cases the patient shows only confusion, no definite loss of posture, but automatic activity such as fumbling with buttons, muttering, and grimacing. Following these attacks there may be a quite prolonged period of confusion in which the patient may wander away and occasionally may be violent. Criminal acts are very rarely carried out in this state.

A large number of people have had one or two fits in their lives, particularly at times of physical or psychological stress. "Fever" or "Febrile" convulsions (often called teething fits in the past) are extremely common in young children and are often thought of as something different from epilepsy since the attacks rarely continue in later years. This form of epilepsy and some cases of *petit mal* are the only forms in which hereditary factors are important in the causation, and these are the least serious forms of epilepsy. They are very rarely associated with serious physical or psychological disturbances. Most other forms of epilepsy are due to a scar or other area of brain damage. It is a proportion of these cases which develop the psychological disturbances that are occasionally very serious.

Not every patient who has had one or two fits need necessarily take regular anticonvulsant drugs; that is drugs which damp down the abnormal excessive activity of the brain that leads to the attacks. Many drugs are available of which the most important are phenobarbitone, phenytoin and clonazepam. The succinimides and troxidones are effective only against minor seizures. The choice is a matter of skilled medical judgment. Patients often find it difficult to get work because of the reluctance of employers to take on someone who may be more prone to accidents and whose fits may distress other workers. Obviously there are some jobs which epilepsy sufferers should not do because of the danger involved (from for example, moving machinery), and they should not drive a car. A few cases are so severe that work is almost impossible, but employers have a duty whenever possible to employ these people whose mental health may suffer greatly if they are made to feel outcasts and who ordinarily are as efficient, or even more so, as the next man. It is also hoped that employees will become less prejudiced about epilepsy as the general public become less ignorant about medical matters.

Congenital Malformations. The proper shape of the brain and spinal cord is achieved quite early in development by about the thirteenth week after conception. During this time very slight changes in the foetal environment can produce disastrous malformations. The drug thalidomide, for example, operated on other body systems while they were passing through this phase of construction. Some viruses can do the same thing. Most malformations are without known cause, but it is certain that something went wrong at this very early stage, and it only needs a very minor interference with the normal process to do the permanent damage. At about this time the bones of the spine are beginning to enclose, or form a roof over the developing spinal cord. Sometimes they fail to complete the process, resulting in *spina bifida.* If the coverings of the cord protrude through the defect, this is a *meningocele,* and if the cord itself protrudes it is a *meningomyelocele.* The whole protrusion may be covered with skin, but if it is not, the cord soon becomes infected. The effect on the patient is variable, according to the amount of damage to the nerve fibres in the cord, and there are varying degrees of paralysis and loss of sensation below the area involved together with loss of bowel and bladder control. Much help is often obtained from surgical repair, but many cases remain in a distressing condition always, and the only really useful attack on the problem is research to find the cause and prevent it happening. The same is true of the *malformations of the brain.* In one of these, hydrocephaly, the narrow channel is blocked which transmits the cerebrospinal fluid from the chambers within the brain where it is secreted to the outer coverings to be taken back into the blood stream. Blockage of the channel (or aqueduct) results in distension of the brain by fluid, enlargement of the head, and mental retardation. Sometimes a by-pass valve can be inserted to restore normal fluid circulation with very gratifying results.

Cerebral Palsy is a physically disabling condition of impaired muscle co-ordination caused before, during or shortly after birth by damage to or maldevelopment in the portion of the brain which controls movement. There are 3 main types: *spasticity, athetosis,* and *ataxia* depending on what area of the brain has been affected. Inherited defects do not play a large part in cerebral palsy. The general incidence of the disorder is thought to be 2.5 per 1,000 births. To make a donation or for further information and advice contact: the Spastics Society, 12 Park Crescent, London W1N 4EQ.

Motor Neurone Disease. This is a group of distressing diseases usually occurring in people over 40, in whom the parts of the brain and spinal cord which look after muscular movement degenerate. The group includes *Amyotrophic Lateral Sclerosis, Progressive Muscular Atrophy, Progressive Bulbar Palsy,* and *Primary Lateral Sclerosis.* The results are paralysis or weakness with wasting of the muscles of the body, including those concerned with arms, legs, breathing, speaking, etc. Nothing whatever is known of the cause. It is uncommon, but this is little comfort to the sufferer.

Parkinson's Disease, formerly known as The Shaking Palsy, derives its present name from the London physician James Parkinson (1755–1824) whose description established it as a clinical entity. It is one of the commonest illnesses to affect the human brain with more than one in 1,000 of the population as a whole (though one in 100 of those above 60 years of age) suffering from it. The average age of onset is about 55 though one in seven contract it in their thirties or forties. It has three classical features: shaking (or tremor), muscular rigidity and poverty of movement. A stooping, shuffling gait and a mask-

like loss of facial expression are common. It is a progressive disease affecting patients in variable degrees of severity and different degrees of progression. A good deal can now be done to help these patients with drugs and since the condition results from a malfunctioning of brain cells which produce a chemical 'messenger' known as dopamine replacement of this substance by the drug levodopa (often accompanied by an additive in a combined preparation) is often the first line of treatment. Occasionally younger patients have benefited from surgical destruction of small areas of diseased brain. It is important to remember that many elderly people have some tremor of the head or hands called *Senile Tremor* and this is *not* Parkinson's Disease. It is merely one of the features of achieving advanced seniority as a citizen. The Parkinson's Disease Society of 36 Portland Place, London W1N 3DG sponsors, from monies raised, medical research as well as promoting patient welfare.

Chorea. This is a group of diseases in which there is involuntary muscle movement, weakness, and emotional instability. There will be clumsiness, awkward gait, twitching of limbs, face, hands, trunk, or tongue. They include *Acute Chorea* or *St. Vitus' Dance* occurring in children from 5 to 15, *Hereditary* or *Huntington's Chorea* occurring in a well-defined genetic pattern and beginning later, between 35 and 50. *Tics* or habit spasms are not part of these diseases but are often of psychological origin. They are usually eye blinking, head shaking.

Stroke Illness or Cerebrovascular Diseases. Strokes are due to diseases of the brain's blood vessels which either burst or get blocked. The same blood-vessel disorders cause heart attacks by blocking the coronary arteries supplying the heart. Strokes and heart attacks together kill more people than any other single cause including cancer. They account for one death in every five. Perhaps less is known of the cause of this disease than is known about cancer, and much more research is needed to find out if it is to be prevented. The cause of the commonest cancer (of the lung) is now known and it can be prevented by stopping smoking. Perhaps the prevention of strokes and heart attacks will mean an equally difficult abstinence from all those foods which make us fat. At least it is known that being overweight leads to death from these causes, just as smoking may lead to death from lung cancer.

If any artery supplying blood to any part of the brain is blocked, the territory supplied will die; and the bodily functions for which that part of the brain is responsible will cease. The process is called *infarction* of the brain, the dead area being an *infarct.* The blockage is usually due to thrombosis (see **P30**) of the blood within a vessel, a *thrombus* being a rather complicated clot with a structure of its own. The underlying cause is the arterial disease, atheroma (see **P29**) together with stagnation of the circulation. About one blockage in ten is due to a small piece of a much larger thrombus in the heart chambers being flung into the blood stream and impacting in the distant vessel in the brain. This is *cerebral embolism* (see **P30**). If the area of dead or infarcted brain is not too large the patient will recover from his unconsciousness, but will be left with permanent loss of function (paralysis, etc.) related to that part of the brain.

When a blood vessel supplying the brain bursts, this causes *cerebral haemorrhage* or apoplexy. The vessel may be on the surface (*subarachnoid haemorrhage*) or in the depths of the tissue (*intracerebral haemorrhage*). Strokes tend to occur in older people, because the associated arterial disease is a product of age and high blood pressure. Occasionally a subarachnoid haemorrhage occurs in a younger person with an unsuspected malformation of the arteries of the base of the brain known as a *berry aneurysm.* This is a small berry-sized blown-out balloon due to a defect in the wall of the vessel. Berry aneurysms can often be treated surgically. Intracerebral haemorrhage carries a very poor outlook, however, since much brain tissue is often destroyed by the escaping blood, especially the deep tissues responsible for the vital functions. Haemorrhage within the brain cavity can also be caused by injury (see *concussion and compression,* **P19**).

Inflammatory Diseases of the Nervous System. The membranes covering the brain are called the meninges. Inflammation of these, nearly always by blood-borne infection or infection following injury, is called *meningitis*. Cerebrospinal and spotted fever which used to be common and very much feared was only one variety caused by a germ called "meningococcus." It is now rare. Almost any other germ may cause meningitis, and when the germ is susceptible to one of the antibiotics it is usually treatable. It will usually be necessary to identify the germ by taking a sample of cerebrospinal fluid from a convenient space around the spinal cord in the lower back. When the disease is caused by the tubercle bacillus (*tuberculous meningitis*) the problem is more difficult because the patient is often not so obviously ill until the later, less treatable stages. *Cerebral abscess*, or abscess of the brain is very serious because it occupies space in the closed box of the skull and compresses the brain, as well as being a destructive process. It may arise due to an infected piece of tissue or pus being carried to the brain in the blood stream from a distant site in the lungs or heart. When the brain or cord tissue is itself inflamed it is called *encephalitis* (brain) or *myelitis* (cord) or *encephalo-myelitis* (both). These conditions are comparatively uncommon.

Herpes zoster (Shingles) is a common viral infection of the nervous system which affects sensory nerve roots where they enter the spinal cord. The initial symptoms are of pain in the area supplied by the affected nerves—commonly one side of the trunk, the buttock or the face—followed by the appearance of blisters. Treatment is symptomatic, as there is no specific remedy. Soothing lotions may be applied to the blisters and analgesics given for the pain. The disease is fairly short-lived, but neuralgia may persist for weeks after the blisters have healed.

Shingles is interesting in that it is not a *primary* viral infection, but the result of reactivation of the varicella/zoster virus (so called because it causes *either* chicken pox or shingles) which has lain dormant in nerve root cells, probably since childhood. Primary infection with the virus at whatever age causes chicken pox, not shingles; if an adult who has never had chicken pox or shingles comes into contact with a child with chicken pox or an adult with shingles, he is likely to contract the former but not the latter.

Shingles is infectious from the time the blisters appear until they have crusted over and healed. However, it is not as infectious as chicken pox.

Multiple sclerosis is the most important of the *demyelinating diseases* in which the myelin or "fatty" sheaths which insulate nerve fibres appear to disintegrate. This occurs patchily and seemingly randomly throughout the central nervous system (*i.e.* the brain and spinal cord) and results in interference with the passage of impulses through the affected nerves. Changes in sensation, balance or muscular co-ordination occur at varying intervals of time and spaced out over months or years in such a way as to appear unconnected. There is at present no reliable, objective diagnostic test for multiple sclerosis and diagnosis has to be made from the history of such episodic symptoms. The cause is unknown, but from various pieces of evidence such as the odd distribution of the disease in the world (the incidence is very much higher in Scandinavia and Scotland than on the Equator) one theory is that multiple sclerosis is the result of a recrudescence of a dormant viral infection which may be picked up during the teenage years. It is commonly held that once diagnosis of MS is made it means a sentence of years of increasingly severe disablement which will progress relentlessly and inexorably and reduce the patient to a helpless vegetable state in twenty or thirty years. That may be the case, but in fact such a gloomy picture is very uncommon. Much research has gone into the natural history of MS and it is clear that there are seven distinct patterns of the disease. These cover a wide range of symptom patterns from that characterised by a sudden onset of symptoms with relatively few relapses after the first year, to that manifested by sudden onset followed by unremitting relapses causing progressively greater degrees of physical impairment which may indeed lead to

much distressing disability and relatively early death. But between these two extremes, of which the first is far the commonest form for the disease to take and the latter relatively infrequent, there lies a whole range of disease patterns and prediction is difficult.

The Multiple Sclerosis Society exists to sponsor research, to care for patients and to give advice and support to friends and relatives. For more information write to them at their offices at 286 Munster Road, Fulham, London, SW6 6BE.

Brain Tumours. The brain is no exception to the rule that any cell in any tissue of the body can suddenly begin to disobey the body's rules regarding its growth and multiplication. A totally unknown mechanism governs how many cells of a certain type there ought to be and calls a halt to cell multiplication when this number is reached. Every now and then one of them turns a blind eye and goes on dividing, and the result is a tumour, or lump, of anarchic cells which obey no rules. Tumours are commonest in cells which normally go on dividing throughout life, in order to replace those lost by wear and tear. Examples are the cells lining the air passages in the lung, or the alimentary tract in the stomach or large bowel. Fortunately for the brain there is little cell division once it has grown. Nerve cells cannot divide at all in adult life, and the supporting glial cells only do so in response to injury. Therefore primary brain tumours are much less common than those elsewhere. Also many brain tumours like many of those elsewhere, are benign or "innocent" tumours. They are not cancerous, and need only be removed for the patient to be completely cured. The brain, however, is at two major disadvantages compared with other tissues when it comes to tumours. One is that all tumours as they grow take up space, and space in the skull is already fully occupied. Thus even an innocent tumour can compress the brain within its rigid box of bone and become most dangerous until it is removed. The second disadvantage is due to the very large blood supply of the brain. Cancer in other parts of the body spreads partly by sending small pieces of itself to other tissues by way of the blood stream, and those tissues like liver, lung, kidney, and brain which have a big blood supply naturally receive more than their share of other tissues' tumour. These secondary deposits, or *metastases*, cause compression and other trouble in the brain much more frequently than the brain's own primary tumours. Indeed convulsions or other signs of brain disorder may be the first indication that there is a primary tumour in the lung or breast or elsewhere.

Diseases of Peripheral Nerves. Compared with the nerves of the central nervous system (brain and spinal cord), the peripheral nerves are comparatively rarely affected by disease. They have some similarities of structure with central nerve fibres in that their fibres are often covered with myelin sheaths and are arranged in bundles. A special feature, however, is that they are enclosed by connective tissue sheaths and it is probably these which allow a peripheral nerve to grow again, or regenerate, after it has been cut or damaged. Central nerve fibres are unable to do this. After *injury of a peripheral nerve* the part away from the centre is cut off from its parent cell body and it dies. All function, whether motor or sensory, is lost. But in the course of many months the central surviving part grows into the connective tissue sheaths which act like tubes to guide the new nerve to its destination. Provided the cut ends are close enough together and correctly aligned, and provided enough fibres reach their correct destination, good functional recovery is possible.

A disorder of a peripheral nerve is called a *neuropathy* and means nothing more than that. There are many kinds. One of the most distressing is *trigeminal neuralgia*, again fortunately rare. The trigeminal or fifth cranial nerve has a motor and sensory territory on the face. In this condition there are paroxysmal episodes of extremely severe pain which may resist all treatment except destruction of the nerve itself with consequent facial paralysis and loss of sensation. At the other more trivial extreme are the occasions when a leg "goes to sleep" or gets "pins and needles" after crossing it and pressing on a nerve for too long. *Bell's Palsy* is sudden loss of function of the seventh cranial nerve and there is again paralysis on one side of the face which usually recovers in time. Some bacterial diseases, especially leprosy, invade the nerves themselves. Chronic alcoholism may affect the nerves, as may diabetes, probably by interfering with the nutrition of the nerve cell. So may exposure to arsenic or lead or an unpleasant nerve poison which may contaminate cooking oil known as TOCP, or triorthocresylphosphate.

Muscular Dystrophies. These are a series of diseases of muscle in which there is progressive wasting and weakness of muscle, the causes of which are entirely unknown. They are divided up according to the age of onset and the muscles involved. *Duchenne's muscular dystrophy* occurs in the first decade of life. It affects most of the muscles eventually, including the heart muscle and those concerned with breathing, and so the outlook is not good. Other forms are inherited. The Muscular Dystrophy Group (Nattrass House, 35 Macaulay Rd. London SW4 0QP) gives great assistance to sufferers.

Myasthenia Gravis. This is a strange disorder of the mechanism which transmits instructions from nerve to muscle at the "neuromuscular junction," leading to extreme weakness.

MENTAL ILLNESS

Conventionally mental illness is divided into two categories, psychosis (madness), and neurosis (exaggerated symptoms of commonly experienced states). The dividing line is not a clear one though, since even the acts of a madman are understandable if you accept his view of the world. Psychoses are themselves divided into: *organic*, implying that we can identify a physical cause, and *functional*, where the brain structure appears to be intact but its performance is abnormal. This division is now seen to be very blurred since there are physical diseases and drugs which can lower the threshold for response, or alter a person's perceptions so that he appears to be mad, albeit temporarily. The more research is done, the more organic causes are found for abnormal behaviour, and the more hope is raised for successful medical intervention.

Organic Psychoses.

The organic psychoses result from actual damage to the brain. This damage can be caused by disease, as in syphilis; by tumours; by dietary deficiencies, as in inadequate vitamin B12 absorption; by poisons such as alcohol and lead; by drugs such as LSD or amphetamine; by problems of blood circulation such as heart failure or atheroma; and by genetic inheritance. The onset of illness can be either an acute confusional state or a chronic reaction known as *dementia.* The acute episode is characterised by an impairment of consciousness which may vary from difficulty in holding on to the point of a story, to actual coma. The chronic reaction, on the other hand, does not affect consciousness but intellect, memory and personality. Characteristically, memory for recent events is lost, while that for remote ones is preserved. About one in ten men and women over the age of 65 is likely to be affected. Since it is the most commonly and voluntarily ingested poison, it is worth giving a special mention to alcohol. It is hard to define what is meant by the term 'alcoholic', but anyone whose daily intake of alcohol exceeds 5 units is generally agreed to qualify. (A unit of alcohol is a half pint of beer, or a single measure of spirits, or a glass of wine). Alcohol-related disabilities can be classed as social, psychological and physical. Social problems are often noticed first, and include failure to perform an expected role as parent or spouse or at work, or breaking social rules as in driving offences. Psychological difficulties include increased depression and personality deterioration. *Delerium Tremens*, (DTs), is an acute confusional state involving intense fear and restlessness with hallucinations. Most alcoholics experience blackouts ranging from momentary lapses to memory loss involving several hours. Intellectual impairment can occur and may be permanent, even after alcohol is abandoned.

Other physical problems associated with alcoholism include a doubled death rate, liver damage, gastritis, anaemia, increased rates of cancer, and infections such as TB. Sexual incompetence is common. The children of alcoholic mothers are at increased risk of deformity and growth retardation.

Functional Psychoses.

Functional psychoses broadly fall into two categories: *Schizophrenia* and *Manic Depressive Psychosis*. Schizophrenia was a term introduced by Eugene Bleuler in 1911 to describe a group of illnesses in which there was a splitting of the psychic functioning so that the association between two ideas was bizarre, and mood seemed inappropriate to the circumstances. Nowadays schizophrenia is diagnosed on the presence of certain accepted symptoms such as a lack of insight, auditory hallucinations especially of voices discussing the patient in derogatory terms, the idea that radio and TV programmes refer to him directly, unreasonable suspicions, or a flatness of response. However, the concept has been challenged by workers such as Thomas Szasz, who regards it as a medical fiction, and Scheff, who believed that many of the symptoms arose from being labelled 'Mad'. It seems that schizophrenia occurs in all societies, but in less developed countries appears to be more acute yet to offer better prospects for recovery. About one person in a hundred will develop the condition, and there is an increased risk where close relations are affected. There are many theories of causation though an inheritance factor is clear, but there is argument about what this factor might be, and the extent to which its influence is affected by life events. Theories invoking abnormalities in the substances responsible for the transmission of signals within the brain itself are supported by the fact that some symptoms of schizophrenia can be induced experimentally. But as yet the physical theories are not wholly proven. The concept of the 'Schizophrenogenic' mother who causes illness in her child, and the theory that abnormal dominance patterns in the family are the cause have proved equally hard to verify. The 'Double Bind' hypothesis of Bateson, that an emotionally disturbed parent, who says one thing to a child but at the same time suggests a deeper, contradictory, message will eventually cause the child to withdraw into a fantasy world, is another explanation. The Personal Construct Theory of Bannister and Fransella says that we build up constructs and relationships between them in order to understand our world. In this theory if the construct of Generous-Mean is linked with those of Honest–Dishonest and Gentle–Violent, then we expect someone we know to be generous to be also honest and gentle. If these associations are weak or inconsistent, then the world is a chaotic and fearful place. Whatever the role of early experience in the causation of schizophrenia it is clear that current stress brings on an attack.

The treatment of schizophrenia was revolutionised by the introduction in the 1950s of phenothiazine drugs which not only tranquillise but also have specific anti-psychotic effects. The fact that schizophrenic patients are increasingly returned to their community, able to function, is due in large part to these pharmacological advances, and to the concept of 'milieu therapy' involving group activities, recreation and occupational therapies.

Manic Depressive Psychosis is characterised by swings of mood between depression and elation without apparent cause, and in this form is called the *bipolar* state. More frequently, the disease is *unipolar*, showing only periods of depression interspersed with periods of normality. The difficulty in defining depression as an illness is firstly to distinguish it from a symptom, and secondly to make a distinction between normal and morbid depression which is depression of greater severity and duration than would be expected in a given population from the apparent cause. This last is a very subjective rating and this makes depression a difficult subject for research. The expectancy that one will suffer a depressive illness in one's lifetime is about one to three per cent, with females more likely than males. Generally it is accepted as a phenomenon of later life, but can occur at any age. In depression the major symptom is of a persisting sad, despairing mood, especially severe on waking up. Agitation or marked slowing down may be present, and hallucinations are not uncommon.

Ideas of unworthiness, guilt and persecution are frequent, loss of appetite, loss of weight, loss of sexual drive and loss of menstruation are also common. The causation of depressive illness is another area where authorities are in dispute, and theories abound. Seligman points to learned helplessness as a cause. In his experiments animals exposed to repeated stresses beyond their control, exhibited apathy, difficulty in accepting that they could do anything to help themselves, loss of appetite, and reduced sociability. The idea that depression is the result of aggressive feelings which cannot be channelled out and so are turned in on oneself, is a simplified view of what Freud said. Some support is lent to this idea by the fact that depressive illness is less common in time of war. Certain biochemical changes have been found in the brains of depressed patients, and the anti-depressant drugs work in ways to correct these imbalances, but whether these intra-cellular changes are cause or effect, and how this comes about, is still not entirely clear. Treatment is by specific anti-depressant drugs of which there are now many, by psychotherapy of various kinds, and much more rarely now by Electro-convulsive therapy (ECT) which can be life-saving in very severe cases. Treatment with lithium is often successful in reducing the severity of mood swings.

Mania is a state of elation, hurried speech, and physical overactivity. Irritability is common if the patient is frustrated. Grandiose plans are made and money can be lavishly spent. Gradually as the illness progresses the sufferer becomes confused, angry, hallucinated, incoherent and exhausted. Treatment is usually by tranquillising drugs.

Neurosis.

Neurosis as we now understand it is a concept we owe to Freud, and to him, too, we owe the distinction between the neurotic disorders of *hysteria*, *anxiety* and *obsessionality*, and the disorders of *personality*. Those in the latter category, while having no detectable disease, are treated by psychiatrists as if they had, and this is a decision of society as a whole since the alternative is to refer such people to the legal or social services. Because the category of neurosis is so vague, it is hard to put a figure on how many people may be affected, but researchers in General Practice consultations estimate about one in ten women, and half that many men are at risk. The reason for this disparity is not clear, but may be due to factors such as the greater freedom for expression of frustration enjoyed by men in our society than women. The majority of neurotic illnesses clear up, and may do so spontaneously, although obsessional and hypochondriacal symptoms are more persistent than others. Obsessional neurotics display recurring ruminations and rituals. Obsessional ruminations are thoughts which are felt to be foreign, yet cannot be denied, they give rise to uncomfortable tension and anxiety, and often the rituals are designed to combat and control the symptoms in a magical way. Frequent hand washing to allay fears of contamination is an example. Indecisiveness is another symptom which may be crippling, as in the case of a gardener who, asked to weed out weak seedlings, could only progress a few inches down the first row because he could not decide what to do about a medium-sized plant. Compulsive checking that the gas taps are off, or the doors locked, may lead in extreme cases to an inability to leave the house. Treatment is difficult, the present approach being behaviour modification techniques such as *modelling*, where the therapist shows by example that there is no danger in a feared situation; Flooding, where the patient is, so to speak, thrown in at the deep end and shown that he can in fact swim when he thought that he could not; Thought Stopping; and Relaxation techniques.

Anxiety neurosis as a pathological state where anxiety is either unrelated to a recognisable threat, or the degree of anxiety is out of proportion to the threat. The mechanism of our response to a threat appears to depend on the level at which the threat is perceived, if at a conscious level, the response is fear, if at an unconscious level, the response is anxiety. Symptoms include weakness, dizziness, sweating and tiredness. The physical symptoms are themselves unpleasant and increase the feelings of being threatened. Treatment may be by reassurance and explanation, by psychotherapy aimed at bringing the threat into conscious appraisal, or by drugs which are now widely, and often inappropriately, prescribed. Phobic anxiety occurs when unreasonable fear is focused on a particular object or situation, and leads to avoidance, Agoraphobia, literally a fear of the Market Place, claustrophobia, fear of enclosed spaces, and animal phobias are well recognised. Social phobias, such as fear of eating in public or fear of vomiting are often harder for the sufferer to acknowledge. Phobic states are often associated with a traumatic event in the past, and avoidance through fear leads to a form of conditioning which reinforces the fear. Gradually the sufferer extends the range of feared and avoided stimuli. Behavioural therapy offers the chance to reverse this process.

Much is made of the manipulative nature of neurotics, and the idea of secondary gain, where the neurotic is perceived as getting the better of those around him by organising his, and other people's, lives to fit in with his symptoms. Certainly neurotic people can be very irritating in their demands and social failings, but their conscious experience is of personal suffering, their gains are at an unconscious level, and one cannot but be saddened by the waste their lives represent.

Suicide as a completed act is on the decline, but the rate of attempted suicide is rising. Most attempts are preceded by a warning of intention, often quite explicit. Men, especially alcoholic or physically ill men, are more likely to complete the attempt than are women for whom the attempt itself, rather than the ending of life, seems to be the important feature.

Mental Illness in Childhood.

Mental illness in childhood refers to psychoses specific to children such as autism, to emotional disorders, and to disorders of conduct. Because children are dependent on their families, much interest has centred on relationships within the family and on maternal deprivation as factors in the creation of childhood difficulties. The work of Bowlby highlighted problems consequent on the infant's need for attachment being denied, and he expressed the view that poor early experiences led to failures in later life to develop social relationships. Autism is a state where the child displays abnormalities of language, indifference to people, and ritual behaviour. Autistic children do not grow into schizophrenics, they grow up into autistic adults, and most remain severely handicapped. Phobias and obsessional behaviour are common in children and usually appear and disappear rapidly, especially with prompt intervention. Depressive illness is rare before puberty and where depressive features are seen it is usually in response to environment.

Conduct disorders include persistent lying, stealing, disobeying, truanting, fighting or setting fires. The distinction from delinquency is important since the latter implies breaking the law which is quite common in adolescence. There is a high correlation between these behaviours and difficulty in reading, though whether this is because of a shared impairment or the result of educational frustration is not clear. Treatment is by careful assessment of the family situation, and by social and educational intervention. The future is not rosy though, since about half the antisocial boys in one long-term study went on to be antisocial men in later life.

Anorexia Nervosa is usually a disorder of adolescent girls in which food avoidance, weight loss, failure of menstruation and overactivity predominate. Anorexics often display a distorted view of their own bodies, being unable to see how thin they have become. The underlying difficulty may be a need to control something in their life at a time of actual dependence on parents, or an attempt to avoid the challenge of puberty and the demands, particularly of sexuality, that adulthood makes. Treatment is by behaviour modification, supervised weight gain, and psychotherapy. Bulimia Nervosa is a variant in which meals, often very large meals, are eaten and then vomiting is induced to get rid of them.

THE SKIN.

The skin in the course of development before birth is particularly closely associated with the nervous system. It is therefore not surprising that so many skin diseases are influenced by emotional states. Other causes of skin disease are infectious, glandular disorders, vitamin deficiencies, and the numerous conditions for which no cause has been discovered, but which presumably are due to metabolic disorders.

One of the commonest skin symptoms is *itching* or *pruritus*. It may accompany many different general diseases, for example diabetes and jaundice. It may also be troublesome during the menopause (the change of life in women), in old age, or in nervous conditions. Sedatives and sex hormones sometimes help the itching during the menopause, and there are ointments which may be useful.

Itching in the region of the anus and genital organs is relatively common. It may be caused by worms, by irritating vaginal discharge, or by sugar in the urine, as in diabetes. The alteration in the normal bacteria of the bowel which follows treatment with various antibiotics also often causes anal pruritus and soreness. In many cases however the itching has some psychological cause. In treatment it is important to avoid ointments and creams which contain a local anaesthetic, because these substances can cause severe allergic reactions if used for longer than a few days, and may thus make the condition much worse. Treatment with a local corticosteroid application is more effective and safer.

Parasites, such as the *scabies* mite or *lice* can cause severe and persistent itching. The scabies mite is very small, and since it burrows under the skin surface, is unlikely to be seen; it is the cause of itching most commonly between the fingers and on the front of the wrists. The itching is worst when the body becomes heated, as in bed. Treatment consists of painting the body from head to foot with benzyl benzoate application, followed the next day by a hot bath. Since scabies is contracted through close personal contact with an infested person it is often desirable for several or all members of a family to be treated at the same time, even though only one of them may be affected. Lice are specialists, one type of which affects the scalp, another the body, and a third the genital area. Head lice are destroyed by lethane, body lice by insecticides and genital (pubic) lice by shaving off hair and washing. Obviously, the clothes, especially in the case of body lice, should be disinfested, by using a hot iron particularly over the seams, which lice (for some inexplicable reason) seem to favour. Apart from the discomfort they cause, lice are dangerous as potential carriers of typhus fever.

Baldness, or *Alopecia*, is a very common condition, as is manifested by the extraordinary number of preparations advertised as curing it. When many preparations are offered for the treatment of one condition it is a fair judgment to assume that none of them is likely to be effective. There are, in fact, two types of baldness; one, which is much the commoner, is hereditary, and cannot be influenced in the slightest by any treatment, the other, *alopecia areata*, is caused by nervous stress, and would recover in most cases by itself, whether one used a solution of soot and water or the most expensive "hair food." There is no such thing as a hair food, any more than there is such a thing as a nerve food, and although it is probable that hair hygiene may delay baldness, it certainly cannot prevent it. All hair tonics and "foods" are useless, and their uselessness is only equalled by their costliness. Those who have lost their hair and find it growing again after using some alleged tonic are people who have had *alopecia areata* and whose hair would have grown back anyhow. In women the hair often thins out soon after a pregnancy, but a few months later it usually returns to normal.

Seborrhoea is a condition in which there is over-activity of the sebaceous glands. The most usual form it takes is *dandruff*. However, it takes other forms, and those who have dandruff may also have rashes on the face, shoulders, and chest. In these areas there is a patchy, greasy, and often itchy, rash which does not clear up until the primary condition in the scalp is dealt with. The scalp should be washed with one of the modern sulphur-containing shampoos at least twice a week, and the affected parts on the face and chest can be dealt with by the use of a sulphur lotion (*not* on any account by greasy ointments). Seborrhoea is not in itself difficult to treat, but since the condition depends on over-secretion of sebum, the skin lubricant, treatment may have to be persisted in during the years of early adulthood, when it is most active.

Erythema Intertrigo is, quite simply, the sort of irritation which occurs usually from excessive sweating under the armpits, between the legs, and under the breasts in women. All that need be done is to wash frequently and to dust the affected areas after washing with powder. This is the condition which, in the tropics, is known as "prickly heat" and elsewhere as a "sweat rash." In some people *hyperhidrosis* or *excessive sweating* is a problem, especially when the sweating is accompanied with body odour—the sort of thing that, according to the advertisements, "even your best friends won't tell you." There is little need for anyone in these days to suffer in this way: for the cosmetic firms have produced many highly efficient deodorants which not only control odour but also control the amount of sweating. Chlorophyll, which has been much advertised as removing odours, is effective when applied directly to surfaces which give off an unpleasant smell. It is however ineffective when taken by mouth, and does not prevent body odours. Stale sweat smells bad because it is decomposed by bacteria, and this type of body odour can be largely prevented by preparations containing harmless antiseptic and anti-perspirants.

Erysipelas is an infection of the skin caused by the haemolytic streptococcus. It begins as a red, raised area anywhere on the body where the germs have been able to enter through a small crack or cut in the skin. The red area advances and spreads over the body until the disease is got under control. Erysipelas is very infectious, and those who look after the patient should wash their hands thoroughly after contact. At one time the disease used to spread as an epidemic throughout the hospital wards, but this is very rare nowadays. Treatment is, of course, a matter for the doctor.

Chilblains are common in cold weather, especially in those with poor circulation. Ordinarily they occur in the toes and fingers, but may appear on the nose and ears. The part affected becomes swollen, dusky, and there is pain and itching, sometimes leading to ulceration. Protection of the body, especially the hands and feet, from cold is the best and the only really effective way of preventing chilblains. Warm lined gloves and footwear, and arm stockings or trousers should be worn outdoors. Adequate heating of rooms is essential: a temperature between 18° and 21°C is recommended. Most tablets, medicines, ointment, or creams for chilblains are useless. A skin affection caused by heat is rather grandiosely described as *crythema ab igne*, and used frequently to be seen on the legs of ladies addicted to roasting their legs before the fire. It takes the form of red patches on the front of the legs and can be removed only by avoiding the cause.

Dermatitis means "inflammation of the skin," and therefore the word could be, strictly speaking, applied to any skin disease. In fact the term is used almost interchangeably with the term *eczema*. There are three main types of dermatitis or eczema. The first, *primary irritant dermatitis* results from injury of the skin by some powerful chemical, such as strong alkali or turpentine. The second, *contact dermatitis* is due to sensitisation of the skin to some substance which is normally liable to cause this type of allergic sensitivity; examples are nickel (in jewellery and suspender buckles), epoxy resins, rubber additives, primulas and chrysanthemums, and even ingredients of cosmetics. Contact dermatitis may continue for a long time, even after the patient is no longer in contact with the offending material. The third type is often called *constitutional eczema*. Although the skin is apt to react adversely to various irritants and sensitisers the major part is played by the personality, and there is often a history of eczema, hay fever or asthma in the family. Treatment is more difficult, but local corticosteroids and tar, sedatives and psychological treatment can be of great help. Infantile eczema also belongs in this category, but in most patients it disappears as the child grows up.

Impetigo is an infectious skin disease caused primarily by the streptococcus, but later often infected with staphylococci. It usually occurs on the face, and takes the form of blisters filled with pus on a red base; when the blisters burst their place is taken by yellow crusts. Impetigo is very infectious and easily spread by the fingers, dirty towels, or cloths; therefore, one of the first necessities is to prevent infection of others or reinfection of oneself by avoiding scratching and using a different towel each day, which must on no account be used by anyone else. Treatment is simple with an antibacterial ointment, so the main issue is prevention of contamination.

Urticaria or *Nettlerash* is a familiar skin disease in which itching weals appear on the skin, usually for no obvious reason. It is not infectious, and can be caused by nervous stress, certain drugs, allergy to some foods, or even exposure of the skin to cold. In some people it is possible to write on the skin with a fingernail: the "writing" appears in the form of weals. This is known as *dermographism*; it occurs in many normal persons as well as in many patients with urticaria. The antihistamine drugs are the most useful in the treatment of urticaria. Urticarial swelling of the tongue or throat requires urgent medical attention.

Acne, or *"Blackheads,"* is a condition found on the face and shoulders; its appearance is so familiar that no description is necessary. Acne is one of those conditions which is the end result of many factors. There is, first, a greasy skin, the result of glandular upset (which is why the disease usually occurs in adolescence); secondly, there is infection of the skin; and thirdly, there is blockage of the sebaceous ducts, which ordinarily allow the grease from the skin to pass out on to the surface. Since the condition starts with excess secretion of grease, ointments should never be used, and probably the best applications are drying lotions containing some sulphur preparation which inhibits secretion of grease. The face should be frequently washed, and it is possible now to obtain detergent solutions which are both antiseptic and prevent grease formation. In severe cases ultraviolet ray treatment may be necessary.

Rosacea. As has already been implied elsewhere, although the wages of sin may be extremely unpleasant, the wages of extreme virtue may be no less troublesome. Thus *rosacea*, in which the nose and cheeks become red and greasy and the skin coarsened, occurs alike to chronic alcoholics and elderly ladies with no vices other than a preference for strong tea. Both cases are associated with indigestion, since, regrettable as it may seem, strong tea and alcohol are about equally liable to cause the gastritis which may be at the root of this complaint. However, in many patients the chronic flushing is caused in other ways and psychological factors are important.

Lichen Planus is one of the numerous skin diseases which seem to be due to nervous states of tension. It may occur on any part of the body, but is most common on the front of the forearms and legs. The rash takes the form of nodules which are lilac in colour and have a dent on the top; when these disappear a stain is left behind. There is severe itching. Treatment is a matter for a doctor, as it also is in the case of *psoriasis*, a very common disease of largely unknown origin, which is extremely resistant to treatment. It tends to run in families. It takes the form of slightly raised papules, usually on the elbows and knees; typically the papules are covered with dry, silvery-looking scales. Apart from the rash, the patient is usually in perfectly good health and there is no itching. Many drugs have been used in psoriasis, notably chrysarobin, and while it is not difficult to cause the rash (which may occur anywhere on the body) to disappear in one area or even in all areas for a time it has a strong tendency to return.

Warts, or *Verrucae* are familiar enough. They are caused by a virus, and are, theoretically at least, contagious (although having removed many warts, the writer has never found them contagious). Most frequently they are found on the hands, but may occur elsewhere. Treatment is best carried out by a doctor, who will use a cautery, a caustic carbon dioxide frozen into "snow." A curious feature of the common wart is that it can sometimes be caused to disappear by suggestion, which is presumably why so many old wives charms are not necessarily without effect. Different altogether from the common wart is the *plantar wart*, which occurs on the soles of the feet and often causes a good deal of discomfort. It is best dealt with by a chiropodist or in bad cases by a skin specialist since it is highly infectious.

Ichthyosis is a disorder of skin formation with which some unfortunate people are born. The oil and sweat-producing glands do not function well and the skin is dry and scaly like the skin of a fish. It is, however, possible to help the condition, which does not affect the general health, by frequent alkaline baths to wash off the scales, and the subsequent use of lanolin to replace the lacking oil. Large doses of vitamin A seem to help in some cases, and there have been reports in the medical Press of cases being helped by hypnosis; this, however, is very much a matter for speculation.

Cancer, Rodent Ulcer, and Cysts. Cancer of the skin occurs mostly in old people, and takes the form of what is described as an *epithelioma*. It is most common on the face and hands, and usually appears as a nodule which breaks down and produces an ulcer. The glands may later be affected, but such cancers can almost invariably be cured unless a considerable time has elapsed during which they have been neglected. *Rodent ulcer* is a form of ulcer which appears on the inner corner of the eye or the side of the nose in old people. It does not spread over the body, but acts by eating into the tissues in the area where it has started. X-ray or operation is necessary, but the outlook is good. *Cysts* on the skin are due to blockage of the sebaceous glands. They may become very large, and are best removed, as they may become infected. They do not turn into cancer, and there is no such thing as "male" and "female" cysts. It does sometimes happen that moles, especially of the bluish-black type, may become malignant, so it is perhaps best to have them removed surgically when they exist. *All moles which change in appearance or size should be at once referred to a doctor.*

Skin Grafts.

These are a very complex subject which can be only briefly discussed here. They are used basically for a number of conditions in which large areas of skin have been removed from the body, as in burns or serious accidents. In other cases, as in plastic surgery, grafts may be used to make a new nose, eyelids, and so on. The following are the main types:

Pinch Grafts are small, circular pieces of skin cut from some other part of the body. (The former method of using grafts from another person has been given up almost completely, since such grafts—except in the case of identical twins—never "take.") The small pieces are laid on the area without skin and gradually grow together. *Split-thickness grafts* are grafts removed from another part of the body by an instrument known as a dermatome, which cuts sections about 10 by 20 cm. containing part of the deep layers of the skin.

In *Full-thickness Grafts*, on the other hand, the whole thickness of the skin is removed from elsewhere and applied to an area which has to bear friction or heavy weights, such as the hand or the foot. Lastly, and this is largely used in plastic surgery, there is the *Pedicle graft*, which, unfortunately, although it is certainly the most exciting type, is rather difficult to describe. Briefly, if one, for example, wants to make a new nose, one cuts an area of skin and underlying fat about 5 cm wide and 12·5–15 cm long in the abdomen. One end, however, remains attached so that it gets adequate blood-supply. The problem is how to get this tissue to the nose, and this is done by a complicated process of leap-frog. First, the free end of the graft is attached to the forearm, whilst its "root" remains in the original site, and when it begins to grow and get its blood-supply from the arm, the original "root" is cut. So we now have a "sausage" of tissue attached to the arm. The arm is then lifted to the face and kept firmly in position there until the new free part becomes attached. It is then detached from the arm, modelled to the correct shape, and grows where the nose used to be!

THE JOINTS.

Rheumatism is a word most doctors wish did not exist. This is partly because they do not understand it, but mainly because it is a condition which strictly does not exist: which is small comfort to the many millions of people who are more or less totally incapacitated by it. The truth is it is used for a hotch-potch of very real diseases, in all of which there is pain and stiffness of what is called the musculo-skeletal system, *i.e.*, the muscles and the joints. It may mainly involve the joints, in which case it should have been called arthritis; or it may involve other structures near the joints like tendons, muscles and fibrous tissue. Joints may either suffer from inflammation or degeneration or both, and the trouble may be acute or chronic or both; so it is easy to see what a mix-up the subject becomes, especially when we must include the joints of the spine as well as the limbs, feet and hands.

A good deal of arthritis used to be due to various germs, but these types are much less common now that the infections causing them have become rarer or better treated. They used to include gonorrhoea, tuberculosis, septic joints, syphilis, brucellosis, typhoid fever, dysentery and so on. The importance of *Rheumatic fever*, which is a reaction to an infection (streptococcal sore throat) rather than being actually caused by the streptococcus, is not because it involves the joints. This arthritis quickly clears up, but there may also be disease of the heart which may be serious and has been described on **P27**.

Rheumatoid arthritis is a completely different condition in which there is non-infective inflammation of connective tissues throughout the body. In the joints, the normally smooth, lubricated synovial membrane lining the joint cavity becomes scarred, leading to distortion, especially of small joints like those of the hand. Another characteristic feature is its capacity to vary in severity from time to time, with a strong tendency to unexplainable periods when it gets better or worse. This makes it extremely difficult to know whether any form of treatment is being useful, since any response may have occurred in any case. As in all diseases which behave like this, especially those in which medical men are also baffled, there

are almost as many theories and treatments as there are doctors. It has never been satisfactorily shown to be caused by infection, faulty nutrition, "glands," emotions or personality disturbance, nor is it convincingly inherited. The best current theory links it with an increased sensitivity reaction, perhaps to the body's own tissues, known as "autoimmunity." From the patient's point of view there is swelling and deformity of the joints with tenderness on pressure and pain on movement. Treatment involves a lengthy and complicated regime of rest, relief of pain with aspirin, exercises and the application of heat, with attention to general physical and mental health. At some stage adrenal corticosteroids (cortisone and its derivatives) are often tried, but although these can give great relief they have to be very carefully used to avoid very unpleasant side-effects.

Osteoarthritis is another completely different condition closely related to the normal processes of ageing. Therefore it occurs in older people and tends to be in larger, weight-bearing joints of the spine, hips and knees rather than in the hand; although the end joint of the fingers is commonly affected. Hard wear and tear, especially that caused by overweight, or injury may be the beginning of it. It is *not* due to diet, and dieting has no part in treatment except in those who need to slim. Physiotherapy, including heat, is helpful. It is not such a relentless condition as rheumatoid arthritis and patients should be reassured about this.

Fibrositis and other vague forms of "rheumatism" are very often manifestations of psychological problems. This does not make them any less real, but it directs treatment towards the mental state rather than to the joints and muscles.

EYES, EARS, NOSE AND THROAT.

Diseases of the *eyes* are very specialised and only very general information can be given here. The most common is inflammation of the conjunctiva causing redness and usually due to infection or some irritant substance or dust. If it persists and leads to hard crusts of yellow pus on waking in the morning, get it seen by a doctor for treatment probably with antibiotics. First-aiders are usually instructed how to remove small particles of grit from under the lids. It is important that these should not scratch the front of the eye—your window on the world—as this may lead to scarring and poor vision. So, above all, do not rub them in. Also, if you are fishing one out of someone else's eye, see it before removing it. Do not have a general sweep round in vague hopes of finding it. If in any doubts, obtain skilled help. Remember the eyes are part of the brain: the only visible part. Perhaps this is why people's eyes are so revealing.

Conditions such as glaucoma, cataract and disorders of vision are beyond the scope of this section.

Foreign bodies in the ears and nose are a constant minor problem with children. In these cases, whether they be peas, beads or peanuts, do *not* attempt to fish them out. They are doing no harm where they are, provided the child can be prevented from fiddling with them. Get him to a doctor who knows far better than you do about the delicate structures of the ear drum or the internal nose just behind the object, and has the proper gadget to get it out.

Sore throats are a nuisance we all have to put up with from time to time. If they last more than a few days they should be treated professionally. Persistent or recurrent sore throats are often due to over-eager treatment with antibiotics not allowing the body to learn how to fight the germs itself. Never prescribe antibiotics for yourself, especially in lozenge form, and only expect your doctor to give them when other measures have failed.

Tonsils and their inflammation may be a problem. It is comparatively rarely that they should be removed, yet every year hundreds of thousands of innocent children are subjected to this ritual cruelty to satisfy the misconceptions of their parents and the greed (or ignorance) of some surgeons. Of course there are many children who benefit so much from having tonsils out that the operation (which has real dangers) is worth doing. But please allow your doctor to decide if it is necessary, and do not pressurise him into recommending it. (The same is true of *circumcision*, for which there are no hygienic, and practically no medical indications. If your reasons for inflicting this cruel assault on your little boy are religious or emotional, then please admit it: but do not pretend it is "necessary" or even medically helpful.)

DISEASES OF WOMEN.

The *internal sexual organs* of a woman, like the urinary system, can best be described as shaped like a capital Y. At the tips of the arms of the Y are the female sex glands, the ovaries: the two arms running downwards are the Fallopian tubes: the point where the arms meet is the womb or uterus: the single leg of the Y is the vagina. These are the *primary sexual organs* of a woman and they undergo regular cyclical changes in response to the control exercised over them by the pituitary gland, situated in the base of the skull. This control is mediated by chemical messengers (hormones) secreted into the circulation. The ovaries also secrete hormones, oestrogen, and progesterone, and a delicate hormonal balance is maintained between the pituitary gland and the ovaries. Each month an egg cell (ovum) matures and is released from the ovary, usually midway between two menstrual periods: the ovum is wafted along the Fallopian tubes by waves of contraction and if fertilised embeds in the lining of the uterus which has been conditioned to nourish it by the ovarian hormones. If it is not fertilised the ovum escapes from the uterus, altered hormone levels then cause the lining of the uterus to be shed (this is menstruation), usually about 14 days after ovulation. After menstruation a new cycle begins; another ovum matures and a fresh lining grows in the uterus. These cyclical changes recur from puberty to the menopause. Menstruation does not occur during pregnancy, of which a missed period is often the first sign. However, women do miss periods even though they are not pregnant, and this usually means that some minor and temporary change has occurred in the hormone balance. If three consecutive periods are missed it is wise to consult a doctor.

The *breasts* are called *secondary sexual organs* and are also under the influence of the ovarian hormones. Two conditions which need treatment are *mastitis* and *cancer of the breast*, both of which are characterised by lumps within the breast tissue. Mastitis may be uncomfortable but is not dangerous and can be treated medically, whereas cancer is more serious. The distinction between mastitis and cancer can only be made by a doctor and any woman who discovers a lump in her breast must seek medical aid *at once*.

Abscesses also occur in the breast, nearly always when the mother is feeding her child. Here again, a lump appears, the breast becomes red and very tender, and the woman may be feverish. Treatment with antibiotics is sometimes successful, especially if the mother consults her doctor quickly, otherwise treatment is by a small operation.

The Ovaries. The two commonest diseases of the ovaries are cysts and disorders arising from hormonal imbalance. The symptoms of ovarian disease are usually abdominal or low back pains, and heavy and painful loss during the periods, which may become irregular. These signs should be taken as a warning to consult a doctor.

The Fallopian Tubes. Infection of the Fallopian tubes is called salpingitis. The membrane lining the tubes is continuous with the lining of the uterus, hence an infection is rarely confined to a circumscribed area in either the tubes or the uterus, and pelvic inflammatory disease is a better name for this condition. Pelvic inflammatory disease often follows an abortion, or childbirth where part of the afterbirth (placenta) has been retained, or can spread from an infection in a nearby organ, for example the appendix. Infection is sometimes conveyed by the blood from another septic source in the body. The gonococcus is another cause of infection. The disease is characterised by pain and tenderness in the lower part of the abdomen, accompanied by fever, general malaise and frequently (but not invariably) a vaginal discharge. The treatment of pelvic inflammatory disease is usually medical and is the same irrespective of the primary site of infection. Before the introduction of antibiotics the disease often became chronic and the Fallopian tubes were frequently blocked by a cicatrising scar, a cause of subsequent sterility.

The Uterus. This is a hollow muscular organ and both its musculature and its lining membrane can be the site of disease. *Fibroids* are non-malignant muscular tumours which develop in many women. The main symptom is a heavy menstrual loss and surgical removal of the uterus (hysterectomy) is often necessary. This is a major operation, but modern anaesthesia and operative techniques minimise the discomfort. Hysterectomy does not impair sexual pleasure, but no more babies can be conceived. Infection of the lining of the uterus is usually part of a generalised pelvic inflammatory disease (*see* Fallopian tubes).

Cancer of the Uterus and Cervical Smears. The uterus is pear-shaped and consists of a body and neck. The wide end is uppermost (the body) and the narrow neck (cervix) projects into the top of the vagina. Cancer of the cervix is commonest in middle-aged women who have married young and have had a large family; cancer of the body of the uterus usually occurs after the menopause and is more common in nulliparous women. The symptoms are variable and it is sufficient to emphasise that any woman who has unexpected bleeding, especially after intercourse, whether her periods have stopped or not, *must* see her doctor at once. The treatment depends on individual circumstances, but is usually by operation. It is now possible to detect cancer of the cervix long before symptoms develop and at a stage when the disease can be eradicated by a relatively small operation. This early detection has been made possible by the development of exfoliative cytology. Cells taken from the cervix (without discomfort to the woman) are examined under a microscope. This test is popularly known as the "cancer test" or "cervical smear." A cervical smear is often taken as part of the routine gynaecological examination by consultants, general practitioners, and family planning doctors, and is also being included in some population screening programmes. It is a big step forward in preventive medicine and may ultimately solve the problem of cancer of the cervix. Every woman between the ages of 25 and 60 should seize any chance to have this test done.

Prolapse means a sagging down of the uterus into the vagina and the cervix may even appear at the outside. It is a result of frequent childbirth and laxness of the ligaments which support the uterus: weakness of the vaginal walls often occurs at the same time. The symptoms of uterine prolapse are low back pain and a heavy dragging feeling in the lower abdomen: these are often overshadowed by the distressingly embarrassing incontinence which results from lax vaginal walls. The stress of only a sneeze, a cough, or a giggle often causes the involuntary escape of urine. The cure is operative and very rewarding.

Dysmenorrhoea or pain with the periods, is very common and most women experience this symptom at some time or another. Very often a girl's first periods are troublesome, but dysmenorrhoea develops after a year or two: this suggests that a psychological element is involved. Dysmenorrhoea is a symptom which has many varying causes, and the sensible thing to do, if pain is troublesome, is to see a doctor.

Amenorrhoea means stopping of the periods in a young woman. It may signify pregnancy or glandular disease or it can be purely psychological.

Abortion means the death and expulsion of a foetus before the 28th week of pregnancy. Abortion may happen spontaneously (*i.e.* naturally) or be deliberately induced. If deliberate, it may be legal or illegal (although a woman who aborts herself commits no offence) and the Abortion Act 1967 defines those conditions in which abortion is legal. The two main symptoms of abortion are bleeding and abdominal pain. Any bleeding occurring during pregnancy ought to be reported at once. Pain starts in the back and lower abdomen and is usually spasmodic in character, and like colic it works up to a peak and then temporarily passes off. Any pregnant woman with pain and bleeding should go to bed at once and send for her doctor. When doctors are convinced that a pregnancy should be terminated then an abortion by safe surgical means may be performed in hospital.

FAMILY PLANNING

The Family Planning Service.

In Britain a service of *free* family planning advice and supplies is in operation, that is, *free* to the consumer. The service is the responsibility of the Department of Health and Social Security which delegates its running mainly to Area Health Authorities and Family Doctors. The service is available to men and women irrespective of age, marital status and nationality.

Sources of the Service.

1. *Area Health Authorities:* provide Family Planning Clinics in local Health Centres and sometimes in other buildings—*e.g.*, those taken over from the Family Planning Association. Some require an appointment but others provide a "walk-in" service at certain specified times.
2. *Family Doctors:* 90% of doctors in the Health Service primary care sector (GPs) have contracted to supply family planning to women *either* (a) just for their own patients *or* (b) for any woman who wishes to consult them. This service may be either (i) methods excluding the intra-uterine device ("IUCD" or "coil") or (ii) methods including the provison of IUCDs.
3. *Hospitals:* supply the service mainly
   (a) for the patients of that hospital referred from other departments and
   (b) for patients referred to their family planning clinics by the patients' own doctors (usually for IUCDs).
4. *Private Sector:*
   1. The Family Planning Association still provides clinics in some areas, including some special vasectomy clinics.
   2. Brook Advisory Centres operate in certain places and tend to specialise in advising the young.
   3. The Marie Stopes Clinic is in London (and advertises in the press).
   4. The British Pregnancy Advisory Service provides a pregnancy advisory service in some areas.
   5. Some Family Practitioners undertake vasectomies.
   6. Some hospital consultant surgeons do private vasectomies, female sterilisations and reversals of sterilisation operations.

How to find out about the Family Planning Service in your area.

Anyone wishing to use the service can obtain the address of a clinic or a family doctor from any one of a number of sources.

1. *The Citizens Advice Bureau:* the address is in the telephone directory.
2. *The telephone directory:* Area Health Authority clinics are usually under the heading Health and subheading Clinic for each Health Authority. Private clinics will be under their own names.
3. *Area Health Authorities:* (H.Q. telephone number usually in Directory) Health Centres; Health Visitors; Nurses; Midwives; Family Doctors;* Any clinic (baby, dental etc.)
4. *Family doctors' surgeries.*
5. *School nurses, school teachers, school counsellors.*
6. *Social workers.*

N.B. If a person goes to a family doctor she may be required to sign a form to the effect that the doctor has undertaken to provide her with contraception for the following 12 months. This is not binding on her and if for any reason she is unable to return to that doctor, or does not wish to, she may still obtain help elsewhere, *e.g.*, at a clinic or from another doctor. The patient has the choice.

At most, but not all, family planning clinics an appointment system operates.

* The list of Family Doctors issued by the Family Practitioners Committees is available in Public Libraries and Post Offices. Doctors in the list who offer Family Planning Services have "C" or "C+" after their names.

METHODS OF FAMILY PLANNING

Methods Used by the Woman.

"The pill" ("combined oral contraceptive pill").

This consists of two female type hormones, oestrogen (usually pronounced as if the first "o" were another "e", that is eestrogen), and progestogen.

Preparations:

Many different combinations of these two hormones are marketed. Nowadays most formulae contain 30–50 units (micrograms) of oestrogen, whereas twelve years ago most contained 100 units. Even the amount of progestogen has been reduced to the bare minimum which is effective. Most pills have the same amount of hormone throughout the course but some recently produced pills have differing amounts of progestogen during the course, giving the lowest total amount of hormone per month.

Mode of action:

The pill works by stopping the egg cell from being shed from the ovary, and if no egg cell is shed, no fertilisation can take place. They are thus virtually 100% effective as a contraceptive, the tiny proportion of failure which occurs being almost invariably due to human error, *e.g.*, forgetting to take the pill.

The Menstrual Cycle.

Some people may like to have a more detailed description of the way in which the pill affects the normal menstrual cycle.

The menstrual cycle begins thus: A tiny part of the base of the brain (the *hypothalamus*) sends out a hormone called Releasing Factor (R.F.) which stimulates the pituitary gland to release a hormone called follicle stimulating hormone (F.S.H.). This in turn stimulates a group of follicles or egg sacs in the ovary. Each egg sac is a small fluid-filled bubble lined with special cells and containing an immature egg cell. The lining cells are stimulated to produce oestrogen and more and more of this accumulates in the blood stream. Eventually by "negative feed back" the oestrogen causes the pituitary gland to decrease the production of F.S.H. (*i.e.* high level of oestrogen → low level F.S.H.), and by "positive feedback" causes the pituitary gland to produce a sudden surge of another hormone called luteinising hormone, L.H. (*i.e.*, high level oestrogen → high level of L.H.). This L.H. causes the largest egg sac bubble to burst, releasing the egg cell, which is caught by the fringe at the free end of the uterine tube and wafted down the tube into the uterus, during which time it can be fertilised. Meanwhile the burst bubble in the ovary turns yellow and is called the "yellow body" (or *corpus luteum*). This produces both oestrogen and another hormone progesterone which are both vital for the continuation and promotion of any pregnancy. If no pregnancy occurs the yellow body collapses after 14 days, the lining of the uterus is shed in menstruation, the level of oestrogen (and progesterone) in the blood drops, and this causes the pituitary gland to step up the output of F.S.H. again.

The combined pill consists of oestrogen and progestogen, similar to those hormones produced by the "yellow body". These act on the pituitary gland as they would in a pregnancy and prevent the release of F.S.H. and L.H., so that egg cells are neither prepared nor released. Thus, taking the pill is in some ways like being constantly pregnant, which until the present century was probably the most natural and likely way for a woman in the fertile age group to be.

Method of taking the pill.

A woman starts to take the pill initially on the 1st day of a normal period, or on the 5th day of a normal period, depending on the particular pill. If she starts on the first day, she is protected from risk of pregnancy immediately. If she starts on the fifth day she is not protected until she has taken 14 pills. The pill is taken for 21 days followed by a rest interval of 7 days and this pattern is repeated indefinitely. The pills are provided in packets of 21. (There is one pill which is supplied in packs of 22 and a rest interval of only 6 days is required.) During the seven days without the pill the "pill period" comes. This is not a true period, but is simply due to stopping the pill, when such lining of the womb as has been allowed to form, is shed.

Protection from pregnancy is maintained unless:

she is more than 4–12 hours late in taking a pill (depending on the pill dosage)
she misses a pill
she has diarrhoea or vomiting so that the pill is lost before it can be absorbed.

If protection is lost she should continue to take the pills in the ordinary way but use other contraceptives, *e.g.*, the sheath, as well until the end of that packet of pills.

A few pills are put up in packets with 7 inactive tablets as well as 21 active tablets, so that a pill is taken every day. These are useful for people who find the "on–off" regime difficult to remember.

Other drugs and the pill.

A few drugs hasten the breakdown of the pill in the body and so make it less effective. Such drugs include some of those used to treat epilepsy and some, but not by any means all, antibiotics, some drugs for treating rheumatism and one or two other drugs more rarely used. Conversely, the pill is suspected of making some other drugs less effective, for example some drugs for treating depression. It is always advisable for a woman to remind any doctor who is prescribing for her that she is taking the pill.

The pill is the commonest method of birth control being used in Britain. 28% of the 11 million women in the fertile age group 15–44 use it, according to the Family Planning Association estimate 1979. In the under-30 age group, recent estimates are that about 70% are using it. In spite of the fact that the pill affects in some degree, usually slight or moderate, much body chemistry and therefore many body systems, rather as pregnancy does, most people feel no different on the pill.

Pill problems and side-effects

Connected with "pill period".

Occasionally slight bleeding happens during the days when pills are being taken, particularly when a woman first starts to take the pill. If it is very slight it is called "spotting", if rather heavier, *i.e.*, necessitating the wearing of some sort of protection, it is referred to as "breakthrough bleeding". If this is in the first month or two of pill-taking it usually settles down spontaneously. If later on, a change of pill may be indicated. It can be due to erratic pill-taking, *i.e.*, being late taking a pill, or forgetting to

take a pill, or it can be caused by having to take one of a very few other drugs which have the effect of hastening the breakdown of the pill in the body so that it does not have time to be effective. It is best to consult your doctor if bleeding happens, particularly if it happens when drug treatment is given. To be absolutely safe in those circumstances it is wise to use other contraceptives, *e.g.*, sheaths, as well until the end of that packet of pills.

Other side effects.

Occasionally, and usually in the early weeks of pill-taking, other side effects are experienced such as nausea, breast tenderness, headaches or weight gain. If these are troublesome and do not settle the pill may have to be changed or even, rarely, stopped. Some symptoms such as depression, general leg aches, and decreased interest in sex, are more doubtfully attributable to the pill and may have some quite other cause, but all these problems should be discussed with the doctor.

Headaches: Migraine headaches are usually one-sided, often associated with feeling sick or with actual vomiting and sometimes with disturbances of vision. Sometimes these headaches seem to improve when a woman takes the pill, but more often they seem to become more frequent. Sometimes they come only in the pill-free week. Often a change to a pill with a lower dose of oestrogen, or even to a progestogen-only pill, will eliminate such headaches.

It is advisable to stop taking the pill if

(a) *migraine occurs for the first time* when the pill is taken or
(b) migraine becomes "focal".

By "focal" is meant that other localised symptoms are experienced such as attacks of tingling or weakness on one side of the body, brief episodes of difficulty in speaking or visual disturbances such as transient loss of part of the field of vision. This might be a sign of a brief loss of blood supply to a part of the brain and a warning of the danger of stroke.

Headaches other than migraine: these are of course not uncommon in women who are not taking the pill. They are not uncommon in men. If they should increase when the pill is taken then changing the pill to one with a lower dose of oestrogen, or with a different progestogen (or even to one containing progestogen only) will help.

Blood pressure: In most women the blood pressure rises very slightly on the pill. In a few, it rises to above the normal level. Having a blood pressure higher than normal over a period of time renders a person more liable to diseases of the circulation. Fortunately the blood pressure is easy to monitor regularly.

Blood clotting: Blood clotting is a normal function of the body and is the body's way of sealing a cut or otherwise injured blood vessel. In women who take the pill various factors which influence blood clotting both in the blood itself and in the blood vessel wall, are altered, so that although the blood is slightly more liable to clot, the clot is more liable to be dissolved. The net result is still a slightly increased tendency to blood clotting (thrombosis).

Blood clotting or thrombosis can occur in a vein, or in an artery.

In a vein: It can extremely rarely occur in a normal vein in a person who is not taking the pill. It is only about four times more likely (or four times less unlikely) in a person taking the pill. If it occurs, it is usually in the deep veins of the leg, mainly because blood flow tends to be slowest there. It usually causes relatively little localised damage but very occasionally a piece of the blood clot can break off and be swept in the blood stream through the heart and into the lungs where it can block a blood vessel and even occasionally prove fatal.

N.B. Moderate varicose veins with no evidence of any past thrombosis are not reasons for not taking the pill.

In an artery (thrombosis) is due to the fact that "hardening of the arteries" (atherosclerosis) affects almost everyone and in the developed world has usually begun by the age of 20. Roughened patches on the artery wall allow blood clots to form on them and occasionally to block them. The pill slightly increases the risk of this happening, again by about 4–5 times. Other factors which more strongly increase the likelihood of this happening are smoking, which at less than 15 cigarettes/day increases the risk by 5 times and at more than 20 cigarettes/day increases the risk by 10 times,

increasing age, particularly the age of 35 years and older,

high blood pressure and

abnormal blood fats. A few people have these from birth, but this is a disorder which runs in families and can be detected by a blood test.

Clotting in an artery of the heart muscle is called coronary thrombosis. Clotting in an artery of the brain, and bleeding from an artery of the brain, which can result from a weak patch in a blood vessel and/or high blood pressure, are known as cerebral thrombosis or a stroke.

In October 1983 the results of one American and one British study of cancer among women using oral contraceptives were published in the medical press. The first of these appeared to suggest that long-term use of certain types of pill by younger women (under 25) may be associated with an increased risk of breast cancer; other previously published studies had shown no such connection. The British study showed that a group of women who had chosen to take a combined oral contraceptive had an increased incidence of cancer of the neck of the womb (cervical cancer) in comparison with a similar group of women who had elected to use intra-uterine contraceptive devices (*e.g.,* the coil). Both studies suggested that the progestogen content of mixed pills could be implicated. All the women in the pill group who had been found to have invasive cervical cancer were treated effectively.

The Committee on Safety of Medicines considered both these studies very carefully and concluded that women should be prescribed pills which had the lowest progestogen content but that there was no need for any woman to make an immediate change. Furthermore, the Committee endorsed the British study authors' recommendation that all long-term users of oral contraceptives should have regular cervical cytology examinations ("smears"). Of course, your family or clinic doctor will have all the Committee of Safety of Medicine's information and will know which pill to recommend.

Helpful side effects: the pill almost always prevents period pains. It also frequently reduces the unpleasant effects of "premenstrual tension" which some women experience, including feelings of depression, irritability and tenseness.

The Progestogen-only pill.

This pill, as its name implies, contains only one hormone, progestogen. It is sometimes called the mini-pill but as this name is also occasionally used for very low dose combined pills, it will be better to call it the progestogen-only pill, or P-O-P.

Until the past year or two this pill was used mainly by women who were breast feeding as it is 98 per cent effective as a contraceptive, but does not diminish the milk flow. A very small amount of the hormone does get into the milk; it is not known whether this can affect the baby but it is thought that it does not.

Recently the P-O-P is being more widely used, particularly by women over the age of 35, and also by younger women. It is probably the next most effective method of birth control to the combined pill, having a failure rate of rather less than 2 pregnancies among 100 women taking it for a year.

Mode of action: The P-O-P works mainly by making the secretion from the neck of the womb (the cervix) scanty and thick so that the sperms do not get through. The pill does not as a rule stop the egg cell from being shed, so that the periods which come are natural periods, though they may be lighter than usual because the pill does make the lining of the uterus thinner and less suitable for a fertilised egg cell to settle in. It also probably slows down the transporting of the egg cell in the uterine tubes by diminishing the waves of movement in them which normally help to get the egg cell into the uterus.

Side effects: There are two slight risks with the P-O-P. One is the slight risk of unwanted pregnancy. The other is the risk of the nuisance of irregular bleeding.

The irregular bleeding may take the form of more frequent, usually slight, bleeding or less frequent bleeding. Sometimes the periods cease altogether, or become extremely infrequent. This means that the very small amount of hormone in the pill is having a similar effect on the pituitary gland to that of the combined pill, so that it does not stimulate egg release in the ovaries. Provided it is ascertained that the pill-taker is not pregnant, the contraceptive effect is excellent in these people, and probably because the dose of hormone is so small the pituitary gland seems to recover its normal functions very rapidly when this pill is stopped. In general tests have shown that the P-O-P has far less effect on body chemistry than has the combined pill. Blood clotting and blood pressure seem to be little affected.

Method of taking the P-O-P.

The P-O-P is taken continuously and without breaks. Starting on the first day of a period it is taken every day. Because the effect on the secretion from the neck of the womb is greatest for the first six hours after taking it, it is advisable for it to be taken about six or seven o'clock in the evening, so that protection is high at bed time when intercourse is most likely. Because the effect rapidly declines after 24 hours it should be taken at the same time every day and not more than 2 hours late, otherwise the protection is broken. It takes about 2 weeks for the protection to build up initially, and the same after any break in protection due, for example, to being late taking a pill, missing a pill or pills or having a stomach upset.

The Coil or Intra Uterine Contraceptive Device (I.U.C.D.).

Coils are devices which are inserted into the uterus and remain there until a pregnancy is desired. All are made of plastic, some have very fine copper wire wound round them to increase their effectiveness. They are all highly effective, having a failure rate of about 2 pregnancies per 100 women using it for a year.

Various shapes of coils are used. The copper wire covered ones are the Copper 7, Gravgard, the Copper 1 and the Multiload. The plastic only ones are the Lippes loop and the Saf-T coil.

Each device has a thread attached to it which passes through the neck of the womb into the vagina. This can be pulled by the doctor when the coil is to be removed. A woman should never try to remove her coil herself.

The mode of action is not entirely clear, but the coil seems to prevent the fertilised egg cell from embedding in the uterus.

The method is generally considered to be more suitable for women who have had a baby than for those who have not, because in the latter the very slight risk of an infection ensuing is 7 times greater. An infection could occasionally, if untreated, proceed to involve the uterine tubes, even rarely sealing them. A woman fitted with a coil not infrequently has slightly longer and heavier and occasionally more painful periods than were usual for her.

The coil is used by about 5% of the 11 million women in the fertile age group 15–44 (F.P.A. estimate 1979).

The Cap or Diaphragm.

The cap or diaphragm is a circle of soft rubber with a firm rim which is inserted by the woman into the vagina so that it covers the neck of the womb (the cervix) and so physically prevents sperms from entering it. It is always used with a sperm-killing jelly or cream. There are a few different shapes of cap. Most are flat, but some are variations on a thimble shape and fit closely over the cervix. One of these is also made in plastic and can be used by a person who is allergic to rubber. The suitable cap size has to be estimated and the cap first fitted by a doctor (or nurse).

Method of use:

The cap can be put in anything up to 3 hours before intercourse, or longer if more sperm-killing preparation (spermicide) is inserted. The cap should be left in for 6–8 hours after intercourse, and if this happens again before 6 hours have elapsed, more spermicide is inserted and the cap is left in for a further 6 hours. It is then removed, washed with soft soap and water and stored in its box.

The cap has the advantage of being absolutely harmless to health. It does not affect the periods or the body systems or chemistry in any way.

It is slightly less effective than either pill or coil. The failure rate has been estimated variously as 2–8 per 100 women using it for a year, probably varying with the conscientiousness of the user.

It is used by about 3% of women in the fertile age group (F.P.A. estimate 1979).

Method Used by the Man.

The sheath (or condom or French letter or "Durex"). The sheath is made of very fine rubber, nowadays almost always including a lubricant and sometimes including a spermicide. Most have a teat-shaped end to receive the semen.

Method of use: The air should be squeezed out of the teat end before the sheath is put on so that there is room for the semen and the sheath will not burst. The sheath should then be unrolled on to the erect penis before the penis makes any contact with the woman, as there can be a drop of fluid which contains sperms and is quite sufficient to make her pregnant. The man should hold the sheath in place when he withdraws. Unless the sheath contains spermicide the woman should always use a spermicidal pessary or foam in addition.

Advantages: Sheaths are completely harmless and in fact can give some protection against sexually transmitted diseases ("V.D.") They are readily available—*free* (when *prescribed* by the doctor) from all Area Health Authority Family Planning Clinics and on payment from chemists' shops and from slot machines which are found mainly in public houses, hotels, garages and service stations and sometimes in clubs, restaurants and holiday camps.

The failure rate is variously estimated at between 0·4 and 6 per 100 couples using it for a year and can be very low if the method is conscientiously used. The method is second only to the pill in the number of people using it—25 per cent of couples where the woman is in the fertile age-group (F.P.A. estimate 1979).

Natural Methods of Birth Control.

These unfortunately are not very reliable. They are all based on the woman finding out when her egg cell is shed, *i.e.,* her "ovulation time", and avoiding intercourse around that time. Sperms can live in the vagina for up to 3 days and the egg cell lives for at least 48 hours after it is shed.

There are two methods of detecting ovulation time. The *Calendar method* involves the woman in recording the length of her menstrual cycle for *at least* 6 months before it can any way be relied on. The woman must make a note of the first day of bleeding of each cycle. The last day of the cycle is the day before the next onset of bleeding. The calculation of the "safe period" is made by deducting 18 from the shortest cycle and 11 from the longest. For example, with a shortest cycle of 25 days and a longest of 31 the safe period would be *before* day 7 and *after* day 20 $(25 - 18 = 7; 31 - 11 = 20)$. If only the safe period around day 20 is used the method is considerrably more reliable.

The *Temperature method* is based on the fact that immediately after ovulation there is a distinct rise in body temperature which persists until the next period starts. The method involves taking the temperature first thing every morning *before* eating, drinking or smoking and plotting it on a chart each day. The safe period begins about four days *after* ovulation (as detected by the rise in temperature) and continues until the next menstrual period begins.

Other more accurate home-methods of finding the moment of ovulation are being explored, including tests on the mucus from the cervix, which becomes thin, clear and "stringy" at ovulation times; tests on vaginal enzymes; and even urine tests, but no simple test requiring no expertise is yet available.

Coitus interruptus, withdrawal or "being careful".

This should be mentioned in this section on "natural methods" because it is probably used at some time by many couples, though less than a

generation ago. It means that the man withdraws his penis before climax or ejaculation. This requires great will-power at the height of sexual excitation. Even if withdrawal is achieved, it may be too late. There are enough sperms in the drop of fluid which emerges from the penis in the early stages of sexual stimulation to cause a pregnancy. The method is therefore highly fallible, frustrating and often futile—akin to "shutting the stable door . . ." Although it cannot be recommended, it is a method requiring no expert help or artificial equipment, and is better than nothing. The failure rate is at least 17%.

Sterilisation.

Sterilisation of the woman. Tubal tie or tubal ligation.

This means cutting the tubes which carry the egg cells from the ovary to the uterus. Although this is not a major operation it may involve a general anaesthetic and an abdominal operation. It can now sometimes be done through a very small cut under a local anaesthetic with an instrument called a laparascope, which can shine a light into the abdomen through a quite narrow tube. At operation the uterine tubes are cut and a piece taken out before each end is sealed. In addition the cut end nearest the uterus may also be embedded in the uterine wall to make doubly sure that the two ends do not rejoin. Sometimes the tubes are not cut but gold clips are put on to close the lumens of the tubes.

The operation must be regarded as irreversible as it is extremely rarely possible to reverse it.

Sterilisation of the man. Vasectomy.

Vasectomy means cutting the tubes which carry the sperms into the semen or seminal fluid, which is the fluid produced during intercourse.

The testicles have two functions. One is to produce sperms. The other is to produce the hormone testosterone which gives a man his maleness, for example his deep voice and his beard, and his sex drive. The hormone is carried in the blood stream. The sperms are carried in special tubes called the *vas deferens* which run under the skin of the scrotum. Thus the tubes are easily accessible to the surgeon. At operation the tube on each side is cut and a small piece is removed. This is to leave a gap to prevent the cut ends from re-uniting. The cut ends are sealed and the skin cut closed. The operation takes 15–20 minutes, can be done under general or local anaesthetic, and causes minimal discomfort afterwards. The result of the operation is that the sperms formed in the testicle do not get through to the penis. They go on being formed, but are gradually broken down again and reabsorbed by the blood stream. The sperms which are already in the *vas* beyond the cut end will still go into the seminal fluid, and it may be 3 months before they have all been ejected. A sample of fluid is usually checked about 2 months after the operation, and another 2 weeks later. There is no visible change in the fluid, only under the microscope it can be seen that there are no sperms in it. Nor is there any change in a man's virility, potency or sex drive. A man should have the operation only if he is sure he will not wish for further children. Although in some cases it may be possible to reverse the operation and give him back his fertility this can never be certain. He should be prepared to accept that it is irreversible.

THE NATIONAL HEALTH SERVICE

The National Health Service was reorganised in 1974 but as a result of the recommendations of the Royal Commission (under Sir Alec Merrison) some further reorganisation is being carried out. As patients, we are really only interested in the kind of service we get from the NHS, not so much how it is actually run. Nevertheless, it is useful to know something about NHS organisation, particularly when we feel that as consumers we may sometimes be getting a raw deal. This account is not comprehensive and is intended only as a guide to the way things are organised at the present time.

The General Practitioner.

Let us begin with the *general practitioner* (GP)— or *family doctor* or *primary care physician*—and go back along the administrative lines to the man whose ultimate responsibility the NHS is, the Secretary of State for Social Services (at present, Mr. Norman Fowler). The GP is *not* a salaried official, an employee of the Department of Health and Social Security (DHSS) although it is quite commonly believed that he is. In fact he is self-employed, working under contract to a committee which has a salaried administrator and appropriate full-time secretarial and administrative staff. This is the *Family Practitioner Committee* (FPC) which replaced the "Executive Councils" in 1974.

What are they and what do they do? They are statutory bodies under the National Health Service Acts which administer the contracts of the four health professions—doctors, dentists, pharmacists and opticians—in their areas. Their members are nominated on the one hand by the professions themselves and on the other by the Area Health Authorities and other bodies such as Local Authorities and Community Health Councils (*q.v.*). They do not have direct responsibility to those Authorities although they work very closely with them, but to the DHSS which is the funding body. The FPCs use the money allocated to them by the DHSS out of which they pay the doctors, dentists, pharmacists and opticians and the administrative costs of the Committee itself. They are pretty efficient NHS bodies, using only about 1½% of their annual budget allocation for administrative purposes. Meetings are held six or seven times a year, some in public, some in private. Members are only paid their expenses for attending.

Capitation Fee

A doctor on contract to the FPC gets a fixed annual fee for each patient on his NHS 'list'. This is the *capitation fee*, currently (1986) between £6·45 and £10·30 according to the age of his patients. A dentist is paid for each "item of service" and pharmacists and opticians are paid for each prescription dispensed and, in the latter's case, for each eye test carried out. As far as the NHS doctor is concerned, his income is derived mainly from capitation fees but he also gets a number of other special fees and some allowances for expenses, the details of which need not concern us here. In general, there are supplementary fees for *night visits*, for *midwifery*, for *elderly patients*, for *vaccinations* and so on. As far as expenses are concerned, the GP can claim up to 70% of the wages of his ancillary staff unless one of them happens to be his wife. He must provide, equip and maintain his own consulting room and buy, maintain and run his own car.

Dentists claim for each piece of work they carry out—inspections, fillings, denture fitting and so on. Unlike the doctors they don't have *lists* of patients. Likewise the pharmacists and opticians. The NHS doctor is responsible to the FPC for every patient on his list. Patients are free to come and go as they like but the choice of doctor will obviously be limited in relatively sparsely populated areas. "Responsible" means 24 hours a day, seven days a week and 52 weeks a year. In practice of course, a doctor will arrange for an assistant or a partner in a practice, or a *locum tenens* to act for him at times when he cannot be available himself. Nevertheless, by the terms of his FPC contract it is up to him to provide full cover. The growth of medical deputising services in certain areas, notably the large cities, has helped the single-handed doctor considerably; he can now at least have some nights and weekends off though he must pay for the service himself. Where difficulties arise—sudden illness or death for example—the FPC may arrange for cover.

A patient has a statutory right to be seen by the doctor with whom he or she has registered (*i.e.*, on whose list he is) either at his surgery or at home and of course would have reasonable grounds for complaint if he or she never, or hardly ever, found that particular doctor available. If a patient has trouble finding a doctor with whom to register the FPC can often help.

The sale of medical practices (other than private practices) was abolished in 1948 at the start of the Health Service. It is now the responsibility of the FPC to allocate the list of the deceased practitioner to a suitable successor. This is done by advertising the vacancy in the medical press,

interviewing applicants and then making the appointment. A doctor cannot start a practice (other than a private one) just anywhere he pleases; he needs the permission of the FPC to do so. Some areas are under-doctored (known officially as "designated") and permission is often a formality but some already have a full quota ("restricted") and permission may not be given at all.

As the NHS doctor is first and foremost responsible to his FPC it is to that Committee that you must address yourself if you have a query, a doubt, an actual complaint or simply want a list of the doctors avilable in the area so that you can register with one or change from one to another. The FPC's address is in the telephone directory although the Post Office, library or police station will also have it, as well as the FPC list of NHS doctors practising in your area.

The Complaints Procedure.

If you have a complaint then you should take it up in the first instance with the Administrator of the FPC—not with the British Medical Association (BMA), the General Medical Council (GMC), the Department of Health (DHSS) or the Secretary of State himself (although you are perfectly entitled to do so). If the complaint is about *service* (e.g. you could not get hold of your doctor at a certain time or that repeated requests for visits were apparently ignored) then it need go no further than the FPC. There is an established procedure for dealing with such matters. The FPC, as we have seen, is the contractual body vis-à-vis the doctors, dentists, pharmacists and opticians and is therefore fully competent to deal with those complaints relevant to their respective *Terms of Service*. FPCs will also handle complaints of a purely medical nature (at least initially) such as allegations of wrongful diagnosis or inappropriate treatment; these are dealt with through specially appointed sub-committees ("*Service Committees*") by a recognised *service case procedure*.

If the complaint is fairly straightforward the Administrator of the FPC (or the Chairman himself) may be able to deal with it quite informally between complainant and doctor. If not, the relevant Service Committee will handle it; there will be a formal hearing, with witnesses giving evidence for both sides. Should the complaint be upheld, the FPC has the authority to reprimand or even fine the doctor (or pharmacist, optician or dentist) concerned.

The FPCs look after the profession on the one hand and their patients on the other—these are their direct responsibilities. At the *District* level, *Management Teams* (DMTs) are responsible for the services in a section or District of their AHA. Not all AHAs have District subdivisions, by the way, but those that have (some 60 of them) will have between two to six Districts according of course to size and services available. The DMTs are made up of AHA members and are responsible for the hospital, community and administrative services of the District. There are also District Management committees which are made up of doctors from local practices, from the hospital services and from *Community Medicine* (sometimes known as Medical Officers of Health). Their job is to discuss policies for their District and make recommendations to the DMT.

Community Health Councils.

Concerned more directly with Health Service consumer interests are the *Community Health Councils* (CHCs). These are statutory bodies set up at the time of the 1974 reorganisation and there is one for each District (or Area if there are no District divisions). Their task is to "represent the local communities' interests in the health services to those responsible for managing them".

The CHCs are made up of part-time voluntary workers, half of whom are appointed by the Local Authority (a Borough Council, for example) and half by the local voluntary organisations such as the Association for the Disabled, the WVS and so on, and the Regional Health Authority. The average size is about 30. Each Council has two, occasionally three, full-time salaried administrators—a secretary and a deputy or assistant—whose job it is to run the day-to-day business, to act as public relations officers and to undertake research into various problem areas.

Full meetings of a Council will usually take place monthly and such meetings are open to the public. There will be discussion of local issues which can be anything from deficiencies in the ambulance services to a proposal to close down a wing of the local hospital. CHCs have no powers to do anything about such things but their opinions are listened to and their recommendations sometimes acted upon. Each Area Health Authority is obliged to meet its FPCs at least once a year and *must consult* with them over planning proposals. Area Health Authorities must also consult CHCs about proposals to close hospitals or other health buildings. If the CHC opposes such closures the matter can be referred to the Secretary of State. In practice, however, the Secretary has usually confirmed the closures.

CHCs produce reports on vital issues and are obliged to prepare an annual report for the AHA. Their supplementary reports—on abortion facili-

ties, ante-natal care, services for the elderly, hospital catering and so on—are normally sent to the AHA, the FPC, community organisations and the newspapers. Some CHCs have been very active in resisting hospital or ward closures and in some cases successful in preventing them. To a certain extent (limited by their terms of reference) CHCs can set about their tasks just how they please and no two CHCs probably work in the same way. Some run health courses for old age pensioners for example. Others may find themselves bogged down for months with fact finding when hospital closure is threatened.

With the abolition of AHAs and transfer of their responsibilities to a more local level (*i.e.* District level), the Government did suggest that separate consumer representation would be unnecessary.

However, CHCs will stay and you should get to know about your local branch and what it is doing. Your views about local health services will be welcomed. The address should be in the telephone directory—or you can find out from the library, post office or indeed your own GP.

PART III. SPECIAL TOPICS

HEALTH HAZARDS FROM ABROAD

Introduction.

The demise of most lethal infectious diseases in Britain has been the result firstly of the vast improvements in sanitation and nutrition since the latter half of the 19th cent., plus, more recently, the effective deployment of immunisation. We were also protected to some extent by our relative isolation. The long sea voyage from tropical countries where these diseases persisted far exceeded the incubation period for most infections and the chances of unsuspected cases being imported were relatively small.

Cheap air travel has changed the situation in two ways. First, there has been a vast escalation in the numbers of people travelling to and from Britain. In 1946 200,000 tourists arrived in Britain; in 1980 there were over 12 million visitors to Britain and over 17 million visits abroad by UK residents. Many of these people were travelling to or from warm climate countries where serious infectious diseases are still common and nearly all such persons now travel by air. The second effect of air travel is the shortened duration of the journey. It is now possible to reach Britain within 24 hours from any part of the globe. People who have been infected abroad, therefore, may have been in this country for days, perhaps weeks, before they become ill. They will have dispersed to many destinations in Britain and may have travelled extensively within this country and have come into contact with many persons known and unknown during the incubation period and early symptomatic stage of their illness. Few doctors in Britain are familiar with the early manifestations of infections common in warm climate countries and may not immediately recognise the cause. It is, therefore, extremely important that returning travellers who become ill within a month or two of going abroad tell their doctor where they have been.

In this situation it is not surprising that the numbers of cases of imported infectious diseases reported in Britain in recent years have gone up and that the possibility of this happening sometimes causes public alarm, particularly when the more exotic and lethal infections are involved.

It would be wrong to convey the impression that once we leave the safe confines of "this sceptred isle" we step into a jungle of hazards from which we shall be lucky to escape unscathed, or that those who arrive here from abroad are a potential menace to our communal health. The risks must not be underestimated, but they are often exaggerated. They can certainly be reduced if travellers understand the dangers and take sensible and simple precautions which need not mar their holiday pleasure or unduly hamper their business activities. This article sets out to help travellers by explaining some of the hazards

and how they can be avoided or the risks minimised.

The Traveller and the Country.

Travellers can be categorised by their lifestyle. At one extreme is the high-powered executive or diplomat who is whisked by limousine from airport to air-conditioned super luxury hotel where he is cocooned in comfort with Western-style food prepared under careful hygienic conditions. He is a spectator of the real life of the countries he visits, living in an imported habitat and scarcely exposed to more risks than he would be at home, though he would be naive to suppose that he is totally safe. At the other extreme is the adventure-seeking young man or woman who roams through Asia or Africa, seeking the meaning of life or just "an experience," living "native," eating and sleeping in the villages under indigenous conditions. In doing so the adventurer exposes himself to all manner of serious risks, to which the native survivors of childhood are long since immune, for which, if he survives, he may pay for the rest of his life. Most of us who travel can neither afford the insulated environment of super luxury, nor perhaps would wish to isolate ourselves from the life of the countries we visit. Equally we have neither the desire nor perhaps the courage, some would call it foolhardiness, to go to the extreme of totally abandoning the comforts and standards of hygiene to which we are accustomed.

Countries too can be categorised. Clearly, when travelling in most countries in Northern Europe or North America the risks to our health are not dissimilar to those we encounter at home. In tropical and sub-tropical countries, by contrast, we are liable to meet totally unfamiliar hazards. These can be divided into two groups. First, there are many diseases associated with poor hygiene due to the inadequate application of available and effective public health measures, which derive more from the intractable poverty of many countries in these parts of the world rather than their climate. Second, there are those infections which are largely confined to these parts of the world because the ecological conditions required for their survival exist only in warm climates and not in more temperate zones. This applies mainly where the lifecycle of the agent responsible for the disease involves complex relationships with non-human hosts as well as with man himself. More details of these two groups of diseases will be given later in this article.

High Risk Travellers.

For the reasons given above most business travellers visiting the major commercial centres are relatively safe, while those who travel rough are extremely vulnerable, but the numbers in both groups are comparatively small. It is rather the enormously expanding tourist trade which constitutes a far greater potential problem. This is partly because of the huge numbers of people involved and partly the poor conditions under which they often travel and are accommodated and the fact that they are going to ever more remote places. Unfortunately, in their desire to contain costs, carriers and hoteliers may be tempted to cut corners with hygiene standards, thereby exposing their clients to avoidable risks, while for commercial reasons they do not wish to advertise the unavoidable health risks that exist in the remoter parts of the world where they invite people to go. Reports of outbreaks of infectious diseases among holiday makers are a regular occurrence and almost certainly many more isolated cases never come to notice. Few people are aware of the medical risks which they run on their travels and even fewer are informed on the simple precautions they can take to avoid or at least minimise these. But, unless legally required to do so, it is doubtful whether many travel agents will routinely take the necessary steps to warn and inform their clients.

Two other groups of travellers deserve special mention. These are students coming to Britain for further education and immigrant workers and their families, many of whom come from poor countries in tropical regions. Some of them may have contracted an infection in their home country before departure but only develop symptoms after their arrival. They and their doctors must be alert to this possibility if they fall ill. The conditions required for the spread of most such diseases do not exist in Britain so there is little risk that they will spread. However, these same people, when they return home for a visit after many years absence, are themselves again at special risk having lost much of the immunity to local infections they acquired in childhood. Not realising this they may act as if they had never been away, neglecting to take the necessary precautions. The group at greatest risk of all, however, are the children of immigrants who visit their parents' country of origin. As family visitors, they are drawn into local life and exposed to its hazards in ways that other visitors usually would not. Brought up in ignorance of the particular hazards of such countries and with no more immunity to them than any other Briton, they are very vulnerable.

Specific Infections.

These will be considered in three groups: those associated with poor hygiene, those that are ecologically likely to remain confined to warm climate countries and a small miscellaneous group.

Diseases associated with poor hygiene.

Cholera. Historically this is by far the most important member of this group. It used to have a high fatality rate but, thanks to modern methods of treatment, this has been much reduced. The infection is essentially waterborne and is acquired by drinking water polluted with sewage or by eating salads or fruit washed in contaminated water. During the last 100 years the disease had become progressively controlled until it was more or less confined to countries bordering on the Bay of Bengal. Then in 1961 a new type of cholera appeared in Indonesia. Since then the disease has flared up again and has spread to many countries of South East Asia, Central and West Africa, with outbreaks also in the Middle East and North Africa. General advice on precautions for travellers in these areas are detailed below. Travellers to and from endemic areas are usually required to have been vaccinated and to possess a valid international certificate in an approved form. The vaccine, however, is only moderately effective and protection lasts no more than six months.

Typhoid fevers. Typhoid and paratyphoid fevers are usually contracted from eating food or drinking water that has become contaminated by the excreta of a carrier. Occasionally large outbreaks occur. For example, in 1963 an outbreak occurred in the Swiss ski resort of Zermatt when over 400 residents and tourists, including some Britons, were affected. In this case the infection was thought to be waterborne. The next year there was a large outbreak in Aberdeen that probably arose from a contaminated tin of corned beef from the Argentine. Most cases of typhoid seen in Britain nowadays, however, are in people who have picked up the infection abroad, commonly in Asian immigrants who have been on visits to their countries of origin or in holidaymakers to some Mediterranean countries. General advice on precautions to reduce risks to the traveller are detailed below. Immunisation offers some protection against typhoid and can be advised for those visiting high risk countries but its efficacy against paratyphoid is unknown.

Diarrhoea and dysentery. Attacks of "travellers' diarrhoea" are common in people who visit warm climate countries. In the great majority no specific cause is found, though some cases may be due to viruses and some to bacteria, most commonly bacillary dysentery or salmonella food poisoning. The condition in most people is self-limiting and requires only symptomatic treatment with anti-diarrhoeal drugs and plenty of fluids. Antibiotics are of no value in treating the majority of cases and can be positively harmful. They should certainly not be taken without medical advice. A more serious form of dysentery is *amoebic dysentery* which may lead much later to the formation of liver abscesses. This requires specialist treatment.

Food and water precautions. The germs responsible for cholera, typhoid fever, "travellers' diarrhoea" and dysentery usually come from contaminated food and water. The golden rule, therefore, for travellers in countries where these infections are prevalent and where standards of hygiene in respect of sewage disposal or food production and preparation are in question is to eat only food that has been cooked and is still hot, to avoid milk (unless boiled) and milk products (*e.g.* cheese and yoghurt) and not to drink water that has not been boiled or otherwise sterilised. Fruit should be washed in water containing sterilising tablets and peeled by the traveller himself and he should not be tempted by the delicious looking cut fruits and vegetables or uncooked delicacies that are often displayed on street stalls, or even served in respectable restaurants. It is wise to drink only beverages such as tea and coffee made with boiled water, canned or bottled carbonated drinks, and beer or wine and not to add ice unless certain that it has been made from boiled water. Tap water should be regarded as unsafe and water used for brushing teeth, therefore, should be boiled or sterilised chemically (*e.g.* with chlorine tablets or iodine). Simple precautions such as these will help to reduce substantially the risks of unpleasant and debilitating gastrointestinal illnesses.

Hepatitis. Infectious hepatitis is caused by a virus of which there are two main types, A and B. Both can be equally serious but they behave in different ways. Type A occurs in epidemics or in isolated cases. It is spread usually by the faecal contamination of food or water supplies, in much the same way as the diarrhoeal diseases described above, and can be avoided by taking the same precautions as with other food and water-borne infections. In addition, partial and short-lived protection can be given by an injection of immunoglobin (a protective protein extracted from the blood of people who have had the infection and recovered). But this is only recommended for people going to places where the risk of exposure to infection is high and hygiene is poor. Type B hepatitis is usually only passed on through contact with the blood of a carrier. In practice the commonest non-accidental ways in which this happens are by the shared use of contaminated needles by drug takers, by ear-piercing or tatooing where aseptic precautions are not taken and sometimes in homosexual relationships.

Poliomyelitis. Polio is largely a disease of the past in Britain and people have forgotten how devastating it can be, with permanent crippling a common result. In the last few years nearly all cases reported in Britain have been in people who have travelled to countries where the disease is still endemic and who failed to be immunised before departure. Immunisation with three doses of oral (sugar lump) vaccine, or a booster dose if previously immunised, is simple, safe and effective. It is an essential precaution for all travellers to warm climate countries.

Leprosy. This is mentioned only to reassure travellers that the possibility of contracting the infection is extremely remote, even in countries where leprosy is common, since infection is usually only transmitted under conditions of prolonged and close household contact. The small number of known cases in Britain are in people who have lived abroad for prolonged periods.

Diseases confined to warm climate countries.

Some infections flourish in warm countries which are not found in more temperate zones because the life cycle of the organism concerned depends on intermediate hosts or vectors which exist only in the tropics. Some of these, such as malaria and plague, once did have a wider distribution but control of the vectors has ensured not only their disappearance but also that even if they are imported by a returning traveller they could not be spread. The majority of infections in this group have only local importance and are unlikely to be encountered by travellers unless they visit remote rural areas in endemic zones. Only those few infections that ordinary travellers need to guard against are described here, together with Lassa fever which is included because, though it is exceedingly rare, it causes great alarm in the public mind.

Malaria. Malaria is still to be found in most tropical and sub-tropical parts of the world. It remains a major cause of illness and death among people living in these areas and is the chief threat to the health of visitors from non-malarious countries. The disease is caused by a parasite which is transmitted from man to man through the bite of certain species of mosquito. The lifecycle of the parasite is completed partly in the human host and partly in the mosquito. The control of malaria, therefore, depends on either destroying the vector mosquitoes or by the suppression of malaria in infected people. A great deal of progress was made along both these lines during the 1950s and 1960s, but since then increasing resistance of the mosquito to insecticides and of the parasite to the drugs used to treat and prevent the disease has retarded progress. In some areas, particularly in the Indian subcontinent and South East Asia, there has been a resurgence of the disease.

There are several types of malaria which vary in frequency from one part of the world to another, as does the extent of drug resistance. It is important, therefore, for the traveller to obtain reliable information on the local malarial hazard and on the appropriate prophylactic (preventive) drug for the places he intends to visit. It must be stressed that prophylaxis is vital for *all* travellers to malarious regions, *however brief their stay*. It is an advantage to start taking the drug a few days before arrival and *essential to continue taking it regularly throughout the stay and for at least a month after leaving the area*. Apart from taking the appropriate drugs it is also prudent to wear protective clothing, especially between dusk and dawn, together with an insect repellant on exposed parts; a mosquito bed net is also essential in an unscreened bedroom.

The extent of the risk is brought out by the statistics of cases reported in Britain. In the 1960s only 100–200 cases of malaria were notified each year, but during the 1970s the number rocketed to over 2,000 per annum. The largest proportion of these cases were in tourists, including former immigrants returning home and children born in Britain of immigrant parents, but a substantial number were in new immigrants. The time interval after arrival in Britain before onset can be many months in certain forms of malaria and this must be suspected as the cause of any febrile illness within 12 months of arrival in people who may have been exposed.

Yellow Fever. The virus which causes yellow fever has its main reservoir in monkeys in the forests of central Africa and the northern part of South America and is transmitted among them and to man by the bite of certain species of mosquitoes. In the 19th cent. large urban epidemics took place and the building of the Panama Canal was interrupted after 35,000 workers died of the disease. Anti-mosquito measures and mass vaccination have greatly reduced the problem. Now the risks are very small for travellers who visit only urban areas. However, because of the seriousness of the disease, and to help prevent spread of the virus, International Health Regulations require the vaccination of all those proposing to reside in or travel through endemic zones. In order to obtain the required international certificate vaccination must be carried out in a recognised centre.

Schistosomiasis. Unlike many diseases of warm climates schistosomiasis continues to flourish and to spread. It is found in many countries of the Middle East, Africa, South America and the Far East. It is caused by a parasite that has a lifecycle involving a number of mammalian hosts and certain species of fresh water snails. Man becomes infected through the skin when bathing or paddling in water inhabited by these snails. The incubation period can be very long, extending to weeks or months. The effects are varied depending on the species concerned, but can involve chronic disease of the bowel, liver and bladder in particular. Control programmes which combine the use of moluscicides, drug treatment of cases, improved sanitation and education, particularly of children concerning indiscriminate excretory habits, are making only slow progress. The visitor to endemic zones is strongly advised to avoid paddling or swimming in fresh water channels, rivers or pools (unless properly chlorinated).

Lassa Fever. This disease was first recognised in West Africa in 1969 when three missionary nurses working in Lassa became ill with a mysterious infection and two died. It was later shown to be due to a previously unrecognised virus. Since then a number of localised outbreaks have been notified in several countries in West Africa. Cases have also occurred among medical and nursing staff tending patients with the disease and in laboratory workers handling specimens from them. The only natural reservoir of infection so far identified is a species of rat which sheds the virus in urine and saliva. Transmission to man probably occurs through the contamination of food, dust and air. However, it is clear that direct person-to-person transmission *can* occur, though probably only by close contact as in personal nursing. For this reason and because of the lethal nature of the infection patients with suspected Lassa fever are nursed in stringent isolation in special units. The risks to travellers in West Africa and casual contacts of cases, however, are considered to be extremely small.

Other infections related to travel.

Smallpox. Once a real hazard to travellers, against which vaccination was routinely required, smallpox is mentioned here only to be dismissed. It is now several years since the last naturally acquired case of smallpox was reported in Somaliland and in May 1980 the World Health Organisation declared smallpox to have been eradicated from the world. This magnificent achievement means that smallpox vaccination has been abandoned by almost all countries and WHO recommends that vaccination certificates should no longer be required for travel anywhere in the world.

Rabies. This is a very frightening disease because once symptoms develop it is always fatal. The disease is caused by a virus and it affects many species of animals, particularly dogs, jackals, foxes and bats. The infection is transmitted in the saliva of rabid animals through a bite or lick on a scratch or abrasion (it does not penetrate intact skin). In Britain no indigenous case of human rabies has been reported since 1902 but it is endemic among animals in most parts of the world. Unfortunately in the last 30 years the disease has been spreading across Europe from the East, especially in foxes, and has now reached Northern France. For this reason strict animal quarantine laws are in force in Britain and it is rightly regarded as a serious offence to attempt to evade them. Fortunately human rabies is relatively rare. Not all those exposed to infection acquire the disease and man appears not to be highly susceptible. Nevertheless any traveller who is licked or bitten by an animal which it is suspected may have rabies (including stray or wild animals where proof may be impossible unless the animal is caught) should immediately wash the wound thoroughly and urgently seek medical advice. Prompt treatment can prevent the onset of the disease. Prophylactic vaccination before travel is not routinely recommended except in special circumstances, for example in those working in remote rural areas where there is a high risk.

Sexually transmitted diseases. Most countries have experienced a very great increase in the incidence of sexually transmitted diseases in recent years. Obviously changes in sexual behaviour have played a part in this but there is evidence of a definite relationship between the numbers of tourists, the extent of their travels and the incidence of these diseases. Those travellers who, under a liberating sense of anonymity when away from home, perhaps encouraged by the influence of alcohol, are tempted into casual sexual encounters should be aware of the considerable risks they run.

Conclusion.

This account of some of the hazards to health associated with travel is by no means comprehensive and focuses only on the more common and dangerous infections. The most important precautions that the traveller should observe are, first, well before departure to check on what immunisations may be required or desirable for visits to their intended ports of call and, if the area is malarious, which anti-malarial drugs are advised. Second, if visiting areas where standards of hygiene or sanitation are suspect, to regard no source of water (including ice) as safe to drink, unless known to have been boiled or adequately treated to ensure its purity, and to be circumspect about foods consumed, particularly those that are uncooked or cold and milk or milk products. Third, he should protect himself from insect bites, avoid swimming except in properly chlorinated pools, and, most important, be sure to take his anti-malarial drugs regularly where indicated and to continue for a month after leaving the area. Beyond this, the exercise of common sense and restraint will reduce the risks to a low level. Finally, and most important, if he falls ill on return home he should be sure to inform his doctor of his travels so that he can take this into consideration in reaching a diagnosis and deciding on treatment.

Further Reading.

Health on Holiday and Other Travels by Professor George Dick, A Family Doctor booklet, published by the British Medical Association.

THE TRAGEDY OF COT DEATHS

Introduction.

There surely cannot be a greater family disaster than the sudden, unexpected death of one of the children, particularly when it happens to an apparently normal healthy infant last seen alive tucked up and sleeping peacefully in his cot. Yet such a devastating event occurs to some 2,000 families a year in Britain alone—that means about one baby for every 500 live births. Such unexpected deaths make up about half of all the deaths in the age group 1 week to 2 years; the problem is worldwide and research is being actively pursued in many countries, especially in Europe and Australia.

There are, of course, many reasons for such "unexpected" deaths. Nine out of ten occur in children under the age of 8 months and in some instances (about one in three) a cause can be definitely established at the post-mortem examination. There may have been an unsuspected physical abnormality or an acute and overwhelming infection undiagnosed in life because the symptoms were nothing more than a snuffle or a slight cough. But in most instances of unexpected death, particularly among the age group 2 to 5 months, no cause of death can be found at post mortem; such deaths are then registered as "cot deaths" or, more recently, as *"sudden infant death syndrome"* (SIDS).

The Scale of the Problem.

The sudden infant death syndrome accounts for roughly one third of all deaths occurring in children between the ages of 2 weeks to 1 year with the highest number of deaths occurring among the 3- and 4-month-old infants. It is more likely to happen to a boy than a girl and to a premature infant of either sex. There are more SIDS deaths in the winter than the summer, among non-whites than whites and among poor families rather than in the better-off; and the bottle-fed baby is more at risk than the breast-fed. In most instances, death occurs in sleep, without any apparent impairment of health when the child is put to bed. The disease remains a blight throughout the world and continues to defeat the researchers.

A family stricken in this way is not just bereaved, it is shattered; the need for help and support from the moment of the poignant discovery is desperate. The sheer suddenness of the event aggravates normal grief, compounded by the fact that the victim was apparently normal and healthy when he or she went to sleep. Invariably parents are assailed by feelings of guilt. What did we do wrong?—Could we have foreseen or prevented this?—Didn't we notice he wasn't well when we tucked him up last night? These are the kind of thoughts that run through distracted parents' minds at times such as these but, over the years, groups of such bereaved parents who have come through the SIDS experience have come together to offer their support and help to the newly stricken.

Tackling the Problem: The Foundation for the Study of Infant Deaths.

What is being done to try and unravel this fortunately uncommon yet devastating disease—if indeed it turns out to be a disease at all? In 1953, the then Ministry of Health (now the Department of Health and Social Security) set up a Steering Committee to enquire into "sudden death in infancy" and investigations set in motion at that time went on for some 5 years. The Medical Research Council were invited by the Ministry to consider the first interim report and on their recommendation the study was enlarged and the work continued until 1964. The Committee was unable to reach any firm conclusion but 10 years of careful study and enquiry had at least produced pointers to further research in the areas which seemed most likely to produce meaningful answers.

It was thought at that time that "unexpected deaths" might probably be a combination of a number of factors such as acute hypersensitivity to cows' milk protein, respiratory infection and unsuitable (*i.e.* oversoft) bedding. The investigation also brought together a number of paediatricians (child specialists), pathologists, family doctors, statisticians and others who were interested in the subject. Many of them had been pursuing their own independent researches rather unbeknown to each other. One such pathologist, the late Professor Francis Camps, set up a Symposium in 1970 with the help of a generous donation from a relative of a couple who had lost their first son in this tragic way. At that Symposium, which was held in Cambridge, the idea of establishing a fund for research into SIDS was mooted and the following year the Foundation for the Study of Infant Deaths was born. It is a registered charity, sponsoring research into the causes and the prevention of sudden infant death and encouraging support for affected families. Based in London, it also acts as a collecting point for information which is made available both to the medical profession and to parents who have suffered the tragedy.

The Work of the Foundation.

As far as research is concerned, the Foundation has in the first 10 years of its life allocated over £500,000 to numerous research programmes at centres throughout the United Kingdom. Along what lines does such research run? Have we any clues to follow? Indeed we have, and the first and foremost has always been the question of "hidden" bacterial or viral infections which may affect the respiratory or nervous system in a sudden and overwhelming way. But it is one thing to find a particular bacterium or virus at post-mortem but quite another to show that it was the cause of death. Other clues lie in the area of nutrition (cows' milk protein allergies), in environmental and sociological factors and in breathing patterns. A *single* cause is unlikely—several factors may play a part in such deaths.

Medical research is always made just that little less complex if the relevant disease or condition can be reproduced in animals. The early unravelling of vitamin deficiencies—scurvy, beri-beri, rickets and pellagra—was possible because the effect of dietary changes on experimental small animals like the guinea pig, rat and chicken could be so easily studied. As far as we know, nothing quite akin to SIDS occurs in the animal world (although cat and dog breeders are familiar with the unexplained isolated litter death) but much interest in the last year or two has been focused on the possible role that biotin deficiency may play. Biotin (sometimes known as vitamin H) is a relatively simple chemical substance found in liver, kidneys, eggs and milk. It is also produced in the lower bowel by harmless bacteria although how much this contributes to our daily requirement for the vitamin isn't known.

Biotin Research.

The broiler chicken breeder runs the risk of losing some of his brood unexpectedly if he doesn't supplement their feed with this important vitamin, for without it they develop a deficiency disease which renders them fatally susceptible to "stress" (such as a sudden night noise). In the late 1970s a group of Australian workers suggested that similar "stress deaths" might occur in other biotin-dependent species, even the human infant. Certainly the bottle-fed infant was at theoretical risk of biotin-deficiency because the manufacture of artificial feeds (from cows' or goats' milk) is incompatible with the preservation of that particular vitamin. However, in recent years, the manufacturers have taken steps to ensure that the vitamin content generally—not only biotin—of their products is made up to the proper nutritional level and certainly most, if not all, infant foods in the UK now have been so fortified.

The earlier findings from post-mortem examinations that infants who had died inexplicably had low levels of biotin in their livers compared with those who had died from overt and explainable causes led to a further careful collaborative research between the Australian doctors and those in England who were also interested in the problem. As in the earlier pilot studies, the livers of SIDS infants were found to be much less well stocked with biotin than those of infants who had died from known causes, the lowest values being found among the still-born and in infants dying in the first week of life. Biotin reaches the infant while it is in the uterus as the vitamin readily crosses the placenta from the maternal to the infant bloodstream. However, infants born prematurely may not have had time to absorb sufficient of the vitamin. Levels of biotin in colostrum, which is the very first secretion from the maternal breast and which precedes the appearance of full-blown breast milk, are low and breast milk itself varies greatly in its biotin content.

But if the analogy with the broiler chick is valid then there has to be still a stress factor which, in the biotin-depleted infant, actually triggers the process—whatever it is—that causes the sudden death. Such stress could in fact be a mild, in itself non-fatal illness. It could be a missed meal or a sudden temperature change. We just do not know. Further research is needed to find out how normal infants get their biotin and whether some need more than others.

What else is being done? The Foundation for the Study of Infant Deaths, as has been mentioned, sponsors research, supports bereaved families and acts as an information centre. What research is it currently sponsoring?

Current Areas of Research.

In the first place, most attention is being focused on breathing patterns and heart rhythms in full-term and premature infants and those born to families who have previously suffered cot deaths. The hope is, of course, that abnormal breathing patterns may be identified and some way found to screen healthy infants for cot death potential and thus take steps to protect such "at risk" babies.

The Apnoea Alarm.

One ingenious idea is the use of an *apnoea alarm*. It is known that some healthy infants make natural pauses in their breathing while asleep. These are transient periods of apnoea—which simply means "no breathing." Could it be that something goes awry with the apparently normal mechanism (the physiological purpose of which seems obscure) causing the apnoea period to be prolonged, with subsequent sudden death? If such a period could be recognised—and electronic gadgetry to detect apnoea and set off an alarm system has been devised—then in some instances it might be possible to prevent untimely death. Such alarms are programmed only to function if an apnoeic period exceeds 20 seconds. In practice there are snags with using such equipment in the home and their value as preventers of cot deaths is unestablished at present. The idea is, of course, that prompt action by a parent or nurse on hearing the alarm may enable an infant who might otherwise be going to die to be resuscitated. There may well be a place for such apnoea alarms in certain clearly defined situations such as:

(1) Premature infants who seem especially susceptible to prolonged periods of apnoea and whose breathing may still be irregular in spite of their appearing generally well.

(2) The so-called "near-miss" SIDS infant—the baby who has been found apnoeic and blue-looking (cyanotic)—although in many instances there are definite causes found, e.g. pneumonia, breathholding attacks and obstruction of air passages by partly regurgitated food.

(3) Some brothers and sisters of previous cot death victims whose parents may need the extra support that the provision of an apnoea alarm may give.

The problem is complicated because it is known that some apparently normal infants have "natural" pauses in breathing while asleep, breathing again quite spontaneously. An apnoea alarm would of course pick this up and in turn wake the infant which in itself might so adversely influence this normal rhythm. The alarms themselves depend on detecting temporary cessation of chest muscle activity and would not therefore detect a sudden obstruction in the throat during which chest muscles are still active although no air is actually getting down into the lungs. Furthermore, as with any sensitive equipment, false alarms can occur. The idea is potentially sound but the value of using such sensitive equipment has yet to be proved and at the present time the evidence of the value of these alarms for preventing cot death by their widespread use among normal infants is totally lacking.

Advice from the Foundation.

As long as funds can be raised, research will continue to be sponsored and supported by the Foundation. In the meantime it gives informed support to bereaved families by letter or telephone, offering to put them in touch with others who have come through a similar tragedy and are willing to help. It also has a number of informative leaflets for parents, health visitors and doctors. A Newsletter is also regularly published. All these are available from their headquarters at: 5th Floor, 4 Grosvenor Place, London SW1X 7HD (Tel: 01-235 1721 or 01-245 9421).

Although initially only concerned in this way with disseminating information relevant to the immediate problems facing families and their medical advisers when cot deaths have occurred, the Foundation has responded to many requests for advice on *infant care* generally by producing a "green card" giving valuable advice on certain aspects of such care and setting out guidelines for all parents on "When to consult a Doctor about your baby". This is an important contribution to infant care and is reproduced in full below, with permission.

Infant Care Guidance.

Feeding:

Breast feeding is the natural and the best way to feed your baby. Coughs, colds and tummy upsets are less frequent in breast fed babies because breast milk helps them to resist and recover from infection. The early months of breast feeding are the most valuable. You and your baby will succeed best if you are quiet and undisturbed when feeding.

If you cannot breast feed or if you decide at some time to change to bottle feeding, keep the bottles and teats sterilised. Use a recommended baby milk up to the age of 6 months. Follow the instructions for making up the feeds accurately and carefully. If your bottle-fed baby appears hungry, the amount given at each feed and/or the number of feeds can be increased, but do not strengthen the mixture by adding extra milk powder. Never leave a baby sucking at this bottle on his own. Very few babies need solid foods before the age of 3 months, but most want a mixed diet as well as milk feeds by the age of 6 months. Consult your health visitor or doctor about feeding and vitamin supplements.

Babies aged over 1 month are sometimes thirsty and want a drink of water (without sugar), which has been boiled once only and cooled. This is especially important if they are feverish or have a cold, a chest infection, diarrhoea or vomiting. Illness is hardly ever caused by teething.

Crying:

All healthy babies cry from time to time; some babies cry much more than others; and some babies cry regularly at a certain time of day. If crying continues and is not due to the usual causes—hunger, thirst, discomfort, wet or soiled nappies, tiredness, loneliness or being too hot or cold—and gentle rocking of the pram or cot or cuddling does not settle the baby, then see your doctor or health visitor.

Sleeping Position:

Select a cot with a firm, well-fitting mattress; a baby does not need a pillow. Traditionally, newborn babies were put on their side to sleep with the lower elbow a little in front of the body, and put down on the opposite side after the next feed; this is still good practice. A rolled nappy placed by the back will prevent the baby rolling onto his back. Some babies like to sleep on their tummy, with the face turned to one side. As the baby grows the position in which he or she settles happily is probably the best.

Temperature:

Keep your young baby's room at an even temperature of about 65°F (19°C) both day and night. Newborn babies need to be well wrapped until about one month old after which they are better at keeping themselves warm. Protect your baby including his head from draughts and use the pram hood in chill winds. In cold weather a baby can lose heat quickly even in his cot or pram. To check whether your baby is warm enough put your hand beneath the covers to feel his body. If the room is too warm or the baby overclothed, a baby can get too hot; he will feel hot or sweaty to touch and may be thirsty. Fresh air is good for a healthy baby, but not when he has a cold, or in foggy or cold weather. In hot weather keep the pram hood down and shade your sleeping baby from direct sunlight with a sun canopy.

Some Suggestions When to Consult a Doctor About Your Baby

IF YOU THINK your baby is ill even without any obvious symptoms *CONTACT YOUR DOCTOR.*
IF YOUR BABY shows any of the following symptoms especially if he has more than one *YOUR DOCTOR* would expect you to ask for advice.

Always Urgent

A fit or convulsion, or turns blue or very pale.
Quick, difficult or grunting breathing.
Exceptionally hard to wake or unusually drowsy or does not seem to know you.

Sometimes Serious

Croup or a hoarse cough with noisy breathing.
Cannot breathe freely through his nose.
Cries in an unusual way or for an unusually long time or you think your baby is in severe pain.
Refuses feeds repeatedly, especially if unusually quiet.
Vomits repeatedly.
Frequent loose motions especially if watery (diarrhoea). Vomiting and diarrhoea together can lead to excessive loss of fluid from the body and this may need urgent treatment.
Unusually hot or cold or floppy.

*Even if you have consulted a doctor, health visitor or nurse, IF BABY is not improving or is getting worse, TELL YOUR DOCTOR AGAIN THE SAME DAY.

EMERGENCY ACTION
GET MEDICAL HELP IMMEDIATELY
Contact your DOCTOR.
Telephone for an AMBULANCE (dial 999) or take baby to a Hospital ACCIDENT or CASUALTY department.

While waiting for a doctor or ambulance to arrive:

If Baby is Not Breathing

Stimulate baby by flicking the soles of his feet or picking him up. If no response, begin RE-SUSCITATION through his mouth-and-nose.
Place baby on his back on a table or other firm surface.
Suck the baby's nose clear.

If baby does not grasp or breathe:

Support the back of his neck, tilt his head backwards and hold his chin upwards.
Open your mouth wide and breathe in.
Seal your lips round his nose and mouth.
Breathe GENTLY into his lungs until his chest rises.
Remove your mouth to allow the air to come out and let his chest fall.
Repeat gentle inflations a little faster than your normal breathing rate, removing your mouth after each breath.
Baby should begin to breathe within a minute or so.

For a Fit or Convulsion

Lay your baby on his tummy with his head low and turned to one side.
Clear his mouth and nose of any sick or froth.
If he is hot, cool by sponging his head with tepid water (just warm).

For a Burn or Scald

Put the burnt or scalded part immediately in clean cold water.
Lightly cover the part with a very clean cloth or sterile dressing.
Do not apply oil or ointments; do not prick blisters.

For an Accident

Give *FIRST AID* if you know how.
If your baby has swallowed pills, medicines or household liquids, *TAKE THE BOTTLE TO HOSPITAL AS WELL.*

FIRST AID

This section which lists emergencies in alphabetical order is designed for rapid reference. Yet it would be wise to make sure now of knowing very thoroughly the parts dealing with Bleeding, Burns, Resuscitation, Shock and Unconsciousness, situations which are immediately life threatening.

Nothing can teach first aid as effectively as attending one of the many courses organised by the three main organisations:

St. John's Ambulance Association, 1, Grosvenor Crescent, London, S.W.1.
British Red Cross Society, 9, Grosvenor Crescent, London, S.W.1.
St. Andrew's Ambulance Association, Milton Street, Glasgow, C.4.

Their local addresses are in the telephone directory; enquiry will get details of classes held at various hours of the day.

Purpose of First Aid.

First aid is not treatment proper (which is "Second Aid"). It aims to save life, to prevent further harm or suffering and to keep the victim in the best condition until taken over by a doctor or a nurse.

Under ordinary circumstances attempts to do more can be detrimental. If you limit your help to what is outlined here you cannot go wrong.

General Principles.

There are two priorities:

1. That the patient must breathe.
   (—see Choking, Resuscitation, Unconsciousness)
2. That severe bleeding is controlled.
   (—see Bleeding)

In any accident scene try to judge quickly which

person most needs immediate attention. Treat a victim where he is; do not move him unless the surroundings suggest immediate danger (*e.g.*, fire, fumes, collapsing building).

Handle the patient with gentleness and sympathy yet achieve an atmosphere of reassurance and confidence by firm instructions and methodical actions.

Clear away a crowd (always demoralising to the victim) and use likely bystanders to telephone for an ambulance when necessary. Let your message be clear and written if possible. Let it clearly state the exact locality, the number of patients and the nature of their troubles. Always guard against shock (*q.v.*).

Asthma Attacks.

Breathing becomes very difficult, harsh and wheezing, fighting against air passages narrowed in spasm. Fear aggravates and relaxation relieves spasm. Show calm confidence.

1. Allow fresh air ventilation. Loosen tight clothes.
2. Help the mechanics of breathing by telling the patient
to sit upright with a straight back but all the rest of the body relaxed;
to direct breathing movements from the lower part of the chest.
3. Give him medicines he has prescribed for the emergency but avoid overdose.

Bleeding.

Treat mild bleeding as for wounds (*q.v.*).
For severe bleeding aim to let the blood clot by stopping or slowing the flow.

1. Immediately firmly press the edges of the wound together between fingers and thumb or press the palm of the hand hard down on it. (Maintain this at least ten minutes.)
2. Lie the patient down: elevate a bleeding limb (unless you suspect it to be fractured).
3. Slip a thick pad (handkerchief, gauze, wool) under your hand. Replace the hand pressure with a firmly bound bandage (stocking, belt, scarf).
4. If blood still leaks out add another pad and bandage.
5. Protect against shock (*q.v.*).

Nose Bleeding.

1. Have the patient sit up.
2. Get him to pinch between finger and thumb the whole lower half of the nose and maintain this for at least ten minutes. Repeat another ten minutes if necessary.
3. Tell him not to sniff or blow his nose.

Ear Bleeding.

1. Bandage or tape a loosely covering dressing (gauze, handkerchief) over the ear.
2. Lie the patient down towards the injured side.—*Nose or ear bleeding which follows a blow to the head may signify a fractured skull which needs immediate medical attention.*

Tooth Socket Bleeding.

This may follow after a dental extraction. Get the patient to bite hard on to a big pad (gauze, bunched-up handkerchief) placed over the bleeding area. He maintains pressure at least ten minutes sitting with a hand under his chin and the elbow on a table.

Blood Vomited.

This could appear black due to the effect of stomach acids.

1. Lie the patient down, on his side, with his head low.
2. Give him nothing to eat or drink.
3. Get a doctor or ambulance.
4. Guard against shock (*q.v.*).

Blood Coughed Up (see also Chest Injury).
Blood from the Back Passage.
Blood in the Urine.

However slight and brief the loss, always seek a doctor's opinion.

Blisters

Leave them intact and protect them with a simple dressing. But if they are so big as to be in the way and need flattening:—

1. Boil a needle for ten minutes: leave it in the water until needed.
2. Wash the blister area with soap and water.
3. Holding the needle by one end pierce the blister at two opposite points. Press down with clean cloth to squeeze the fluid out.
4. Dress it like a wound (*q.v.*).

Burns (*see also* Chemical Burns).

1. Put out flames the quickest way: a douche of water; smothering with cloth (rug, coat, blanket).
2. Remove burnt clothes, but leave on what is adherent to the skin.
3. Cool the burnt part with cold water for at least ten minutes, longer if pain persists. Plunge a limb in a bucket or sink. Cover other parts with a thick cloth soaked in water; renew it if it dries.
4. Lie the patient down; keep a burnt limb elevated; remove possibly constricting things (rings, bracelets) from a burnt region before it swells.
5. Dress the burn as a wound (*q.v.*).
6. Guard against shock (*q.v.*).—in severe burns give to drink half a cupful of tepid water with a pinch of salt and sugar every ten or fifteen minutes.

Car Accidents.

1. Urgently stop severe bleeding (*q.v.*) or give resuscitation (*q.v.*) where this is needed; treat choking (*q.v.*). Unless they are at risk from fire or fumes leave the injured where they are. Look for victims thrown into ditches or over walls and hedges.
2. Minimise risks by forbidding smoking (petrol leak), by switching off the ignition and applying the brakes.
3. Set your own car off the road if possible; at night have its light shining on the scene.
4. Detail bystanders (wearing or carrying white objects at night) to stop approaching traffic some 200 yards on either side.
5. Send a message for help (written down) detailing the exact place, the number injured and the injuries.
6. Give other first aid to those in the cars without trying to move them: attempts to pull them out, especially from a distorted car, can do great harm. Leave to the rescue services.

Chemical Burns.

Rapidly wash away the chemical with copious free-flowing water. Remove any contaminated clothing.
The contaminated eye, closed in painful spasm, may need gently forcing open; let the water flow on it without force and bend the patient towards the affected side so that the washings flow off at once.

Chest Injury.

Where there has been a severe blow or deep wound to the chest, possibly followed by blood being coughed up:

1. Clear the mouth of any obstruction (blood, vomit, dentures).
2. If there is an open wound at once close it with the palm of your hand firmly applied. While you keep it there, improvise a thick pad (towel, cloth, handkerchief, sock) to replace your hand. Tape or bandage it securely to make an air-tight seal.
3. Loosen tight clothing.
4. Lie the patient down *towards* the injured side. If he has difficulty in breathing have him half propped up with head and shoulders raised.
5. Cover him loosely.
6. Get ambulance urgently.

Choking.

1. With your fingers try to clear any obstruction (food, toy, dentures) from the back of the throat.

2. If this fails the patient to relax, to bend well forward; give a hard slap between the shoulder blades. This may loosen the obstruction so that the patient can cough it out. A small child you place head down over your arm or your bent knee. Try up to four separate slaps.

If back slapping fails try to force the matter out by pressure:

1. Patient standing: stand behind him; put both your arms round his waist. Patient lying: turn him on his back; kneel astride him.

2. Place your fist (thumb side first) on his abdomen *between his navel and the lower end of his breast bone*; cover your fist with your other hand.

3. Make firm thrust inwards and upwards. This may propel the obstruction out of his windpipe. Try up to four separate thrusts. If these fail continue alternating four slaps and four thrusts. After each of these be ready to remove immediately any matter propelled into the mouth.

After receiving thrusts the patient must be checked by a doctor lest internal damage has occured.

If an obstruction is not cleared and the patient ceases breathing and collapses begin resuscitation (*q.v.*).

Always remember that in the unconscious the tongue may fall back and be an obstruction. *See* Unconsciousness.

Cold Effects. *See* **Exposure and Hypothermia.**

Cramp.

Cramps may follow severe loss of body fluid and minerals—as with severe repeated diarrhoea, vomiting or sweating. Slowly give tepid drinks containing a small pinch of table salt to each cupful or with diluted meat or yeast extracts.

Sudden cramp in a single muscle can be stopped by having the patient strongly stretch the muscle. In the front of the arm: straighten the elbow and swing the arm back. In the front of the thigh bend the knee and swing the leg back. In the back of the thigh: straighten the knee and swing the leg forward. In the calf: bend the foot up at the ankle while straightening the leg.

Diabetes.

Under certain circumstances a diabetic treated with insulin may suddenly collapse through sugar deficiency. Passing through phases of weakness, vagueness, sweating, tremor, uncoordinated actions and slurred speech he may go into a coma.

If he is conscious give him two teaspoonfuls (or lumps) of glucose or sugar in water. Failing this, give anything sweet; jam, honey, chocolate. This should clear him rapidly but repeat the dose after ten minutes.

If he is unconscious send for medical help urgently. Give nothing by mouth and put the patient in the recovery position (*q.v.*).

Ear—object in.

Do not try to poke it out.

A small object (*e.g.*, insect) can sometimes be floated out and out by lying the patient down with the ear uppermost and pouring in a little water or olive oil. But do not try this if the ear drum is possibly damaged or the ear is painful.

Electric Shock.

At once disconnect the current (at the switch or by pulling a plug out). If you cannot do this do not touch the patient but knock him away from his contact with any non-conducting material; wooden stick, light furniture, folded thick garment.

He may need resuscitation (*q.v.*). He may have sustained a fracture (*q.v.*) or a burn. He may recover, only to collapse later; keep watch and send him to hospital.

Beware of very high voltage currents, as from wires of electric pylons: keep at least 20 feet away and do not try to rescue until the electricity authority has cut the current.

Epileptic Attack.

The patient may suddenly become unconscious, fall and soon begin convulsive jerkings, and sometimes frothing at the mouth.

1. Do not try to stop the jerking, but protect him from banging against furniture. Move the furniture or push cloth in position as buffer.

2. Clear froth from the mouth.

3. Once the convulsions stop put him in the recovery position (*q.v.*)—but beware lest he sustained a fracture (*q.v.*) in falling.

A succession of closely following attacks is dangerous: get medical aid at once.

Exposure.

A hill climber or a worker inadequately dressed against cold weather becomes slow, inefficient, clumsy, drowsy. Eventually he collapses and if not properly treated may die.

1. Put him to rest.

2. If you can, get him into a warm shelter. Otherwise protect him with screens of clothes or blankets and poles.

3. If he is conscious give warm drinks (cocoa, chocolate, tea). On no account give alcohol.

4. Get wet cold clothes off him if possible and put him in warm dry covers (sleeping bag, blankets). A plastic sheet over those helps to retain heat. Include the head, leaving only the face free.

See also **Hypothermia.**

Gradual rewarming is given when the patient has become cold gradually. However, when exposure has been sudden, as with falling in extremely cold water, you can warm up fast by putting the patient in a bath at about 40° C. (103° F.).

Eye Injury.

Fix a loosely covering pad over the eye and get medical aid.—Do NOT use drops or ointments.—If the wound is severe and painful keep the patient on his back and cover both eyes (since movement of the good eye entails that of the injured one).

Eye—Object In.

Have the patient seated in a good light and stand behind him. If you can see the object on the white of the eye try to lift it off gently with the rolled-up and moistened twist of a handkerchief. If it does not come easily it may be embedded; leave it alone.

If it is within the coloured part of the eye leave it for a doctor to treat.

If you cannot see it look under the lids. The lower lid you pull down as he looks upwards. The upper lid you must evert as he looks down; lay a matchstick along the "hinge" of the lid; firmly grasp the edge of the lid and roll it up over the matchstick.

Fainting.

Lie the patient down with his legs higher than his head (if this is not possible, get him seated with his head bent low between his knees); loosen any tight clothes: tell him to breathe deeply and slowly. He should soon recover. A drink of water (provided he is conscious) will help.

If he has fainted fully treat as for unconsciousness (*q.v.*).

Fractures.

Always suspect a broken bone where a blow or crush near a bone is followed by pain, swelling, deformity, weakened or restricted movement. Not all these features are always present: sometimes relatively slight pain is the only one.

Your task is to prevent movement which could worsen the condition by shifting a broken edge of bone into an important organ, or by making it pierce hitherto unbroken skin (with a risk of infection). No one will blame you for undue caution—but all will hold you responsible if you allow a fractured bone to do more damage by movement which could have been avoided.

When a fracture is suspected:—

    1. Warn the patient not to move and bystanders not to try to lift him.

    2. At once control any severe bleeding (q.v.). Dress any wound (q.v.) temporarily.

    3. Now immobilise the fractured area including the joint at either end. The best splint is the patient's own body; e.g., injured arm secured against chest, injured leg against good leg (move the good leg up to the injured one). Or a thin board or rolled-up newspaper, well buffered with cloths and towels tied round it can be slipped under a fore-arm and wrist. Between the injured part and the splinting surface fill any hollows with firm padding of wool, or bunched-up cloth, socks, handkerchiefs. Tie the whole firmly with bandages (or stocking, thin towels) making the knots over the splint (not the hurt part) and avoiding bandage directly over the level at which you suspect the fracture. Work gently; do not lift or move the injured part.

    4. Help to reduce shock (q.v.).

These are the general principles. How best to apply them for individual fractures you can learn from first aid courses.

If you expect expert help (doctor, nurse, ambulance) to arrive soon, then omit step 3 above and keep the patient lying still.

The fractured spine. When a blow or fall gives a painful back or neck, the vertebral column may be fractured. Inexpert moving may possibly drive a bone fragment into the spinal cord of nerves, causing paralysis or loss of feeling. It is most important to let the patient lie still until experienced first aiders take over. Keep him warm with a loose covering of blanket or coat.

Frostbite.

Do not heat the area directly or put it in hot water. Do not rub it.

    1. Remove any wet cover (e.g., glove).

    2. Remove any tight object (garter, ring, bracelet).

    3. Cover the area loosely with dry material and let it warm up slowly. Fingers can be tucked under clothes into the opposite armpit. Nose, chin or ear can be covered with a dry hand.

Hanging.

Support the victim by his legs. Get the cord cut and be prepared to receive his weight as he falls. Loosen the cord round the neck. Act fast. Get medical help.

See also **Choking** *and* **Resuscitation.**

Head Injuries.

Blows to the head can cause fracture of the skull and also brain damage.

Fracture of the skull is not always obvious. Skin may swell over the site. Sometimes a fracture of the base of the skull (the body platform within the head at eye and ear level which supports the brain) may show up by bruising round an eye or by blood loss from ear or nose (see **Bleeding**).

Brain Damage may be of two kinds:—

Concussion, a temporary "shaking up" of brain tissue causing immediate "knock-out" unconsciousness. Recovery is in anything from a few seconds to several hours.

Compression of the brain develops from bleeding within the skull, from displacement of a fractured bone or from general swelling of the damaged brain tissues within the hard unyielding skull. The patient gradually (minutes or hours) becomes comatose and perhaps unconscious. This condition is dangerous.

The patient is unconscious—see unconsciousness.

The patient is dazed: put him in the recovery position (q.v.) and watch him closely while awaiting help.

The patient recovers after a knock-out (concussion). He may yet develop features of compression as well. However much he wants to carry on, keep him at rest, under observation and get medical advice.

In all cases remember that head injuries are often accompanied by injuries to other parts of the body.

Heart Attack.

Sudden heart attacks may produce:—

    severe gripping pain in the centre of the chest, sometimes spreading to the neck, shoulder or arm; fast weak pulse; breathlessness; pallor and blueness; sweating.

    or sudden painless breathlessness with slight cough and very wet bubbly breathing.

In either case send urgently for medical help. Get the patient to rest (in bed if possible). If he is very breathless it will be easier for him to be in a sitting position, against banked-up pillows. Otherwise have him lying down.

Loosen tight clothes. Keep him warmly but loosely covered. Mop any sweat from the face.

Heat Effects.

Heat Exhaustion. Anyone working in an unusually hot atmosphere is helped to remain cool by copious sweating which extracts heat from the body as it evaporates off the skin. But this loss of fluid also carries with it essential minerals from the body. The patient may collapse with his temperature normal or just a little raised; his skin is pale, moist and sunken, his pulse fast and weak. Muscles depleted of minerals go into cramp.

Let him rest in a cool place and give him (slowly) fruit juices or water with half a teaspoonful of salt added to each pint.

Heat Stroke happens in unusually hot and moist areas in rare industrial circumstances and in some tropical zones. Evaporation of sweat cannot take place in an atmosphere already saturated with water vapour. The patient becomes burning hot with a red dry skin and a fast forceful pulse. He may suddenly collapse and go into coma.

He must rest, have his clothes removed and be fanned or sponged down with cold (but not iced) water. The condition is dangerous and needs medical help.

Hypothermia.

Small babies and the elderly are specially susceptible to cold, e.g., overnight in a poorly heated bedroom. They become lethargic, comatose and then unconscious. Extremely cold to touch, even under bedclothes, the skin is white (though in babies it may be deceptively pink). Death may follow.

Cover the patient well including the head, leaving the face free. Put him in the recovery position (q.v.). Warm him GRADUALLY by warming the whole room and by giving slowly warm (not hot) drinks. Do NOT give alcohol. Do NOT use electric blankets or hot-water bottles.

Insect Bites.

Cool with water or (better) smooth in anti-histamine cream.

If a bee sting has been left in the skin pull it out with fine tweezers; apply these well down near the skin so that they do not squeeze in any venom left at the free top of the sting.

Lightning.

As for electric shock (q.v.) except that the patient can be touched at once as he bears no electric charge. Put a dry dressing over any skin burns.

Nose Bleed. *See* Bleeding.

Nose—Object in.

Do not try to probe it. Unless GENTLE nose blowing gets it out consult a doctor.

Poisoning.

Do not try to administer antidotes. Do not give salt solutions.

If the patient is unconscious.
Treat as for unconsciousness (q.v.).

If he is conscious.
Give, slowly, soothing drinks to dilute the poison (water, barley water, milk and water).

Put him in the recovery position (q.v.) while awaiting the ambulance. He may lose consciousness.

In all cases.

Get the patient urgently to hospital.

Send with him any remaining poison or empty container and a sample of any vomit.

Keep a close watch on him all the time you are with him.

Poisoning by pesticides (weed or insect killers).

The patient must be at complete rest. If his clothes and skin are contaminated with the poison (splashes, spray droplets) remove clothes and wash the skin copiously with water (avoid contaminating yourself). If he is conscious give sweetened drinks.

Poisoning by gases.

Get the victim rapidly out of the contaminated atmosphere, but do not venture within this unless you have a lifeline and respirator, with others to safeguard you.

Recovery Position.

This safeguards the patient's comfort and breathing if he is unconscious, or comatose, or likely to lose consciousness. It consists in having him—

lying on his side;
with lower arm and leg stretched out straight behind him;
upper leg and arm bent forward at right angles at hip, knee, shoulder, elbow;
face tilted slightly downwards and head bent backwards (NO pillow).

This ensures a clear airway and lets any fluid in the mouth (saliva, blood, vomit) flow out and not choke the patient.

To get him in position:

1. Empty his pockets; remove items like bracelet or wrist watch. Put his belongings away safely. Loosen tight clothing.
2. Kneel alongside him.
3. Straighten his arms alongside his body; tuck the nearer hand below his hip.
4. Put one of your hands under his face to protect it as your other hand pulls him at the hip over towards you, on his side.
5. Adjust the limbs.
6. Cover him with a blanket or coat.

However, do not move the patient if circumstances suggest he received a heavy blow to the backbone. In that case ensure free breathing by keeping his head bent well back (never sideways). Be ready to clear immediately any vomit from his mouth.

Resuscitation.

This is the attempt to restore life to someone who has stopped breathing. NEVER try it unless this really is the case; you will do harm if the patient has collapsed but is still breathing. Do not try it if the problem is that of fighting against choking (q.v.).

In cases of drowning do not try to tip the patient up to drain out water; this wastes valuable time.

(It is best to have learnt the technique in organised first aid classes, practising only on a manikin.)

Artificial Respiration.

Act very quickly:—

1. Get the patient on his back.
2. Bend his head fully backwards and keep it thus all the time.
3. With fingers rapidly clear out any obstructing matter from mouth and throat.
4. Hold his mouth open (keep your fingers clear of his lips) and pinch his nose shut.
5. Take a deep breath in: open your mouth wide and seal your lips round his mouth: breathe firmly into his mouth. The air going in should make his chest rise. Do not blow more forcibly than is needed to achieve this.
6. Lift your mouth off. His chest will now sink as air comes out. Meantime you take another breath in.
7. Continue by repeating the breathing processes of steps 5 and 6.

The first four breaths you give quickly. Thereafter time yourself by the rise and the natural fall of the patient's chest.

With small children you need not pinch the nose, but let your mouth seal over both the nose and mouth of the patient. Much gentler blowing is needed, and quite small puffs are right for babies.

Keep on until medical authority takes over.

If patient vomits turn his head to one side and clear out the mouth. Then resume artificial respiration, with the first four breaths quick ones.

Successful artificial respiration should soon improve the patient's colour, and later you may find he begins to breathe for himself, even if only weakly. Watch this closely, for he may cease again.

Heart Compression.

If there is no improvement it may be necessary to add heart compression to artificial respiration. This, however, cannot be safely learnt except from first aid class teaching and demonstration. (See the Introduction to this section.)

Shock.

Failure of the heart and of the circulation of the blood may follow any serious injury (bleeding, wounds, burns, fractures). This can happen in minutes or hours according to the severity of the lesion.

In first aid terms this dangerous physical condition is called Shock. The patient is pale, cold, sweating, faint or comatose, with weak and fast pulse and breathing.

Try to prevent or to minimise the development of shock before it appears by applying the following simple but valuable measures to every badly hurt patient.

1. At once stop severe bleeding (q.v.).
2. Treat the patient where he is (unless you both are in an area of danger).
3. Lie him down: keep his head low and his legs raised (but avoid movement where a fracture is suspected).
4. Loosen tight clothing.
5. Keep him warm by covering below and loosely above him—but do not use hot-water bottles.
6. Gently dress any wounds—with the minimum of disturbance.
7. Guard his mental state. Be sympathetic but as optimistically reassuring as possible. Never whisper to others. Never assume that because the patient appears unconscious he cannot hear and understand what is said near him.

Do not give the badly injured patient anything to drink. This could worsen his condition and risk vomiting and choking, especially if he becomes unconscious or needs an anaesthetic. If he is very thirsty let him refresh himself by sucking a moistened handkerchief.

Snake Bite.

The adder is the only dangerous snake in Britain. Its bite can cause collapse and great pain, but only very rarely is it fatal.

1. Lie the patient down.
2. Wipe or wash the bite area. Put on a dry dressing.
3. Cover the area with a thick pad and bandage it in position so that it presses down very firmly.
4. Immobilise the bitten part as if it were a fracture (q.v.).
5. Get the patient rapidly to hospital.
6. Reassure him about his recovery. Give aspirin or paracetamol to minimise pain.

You NEVER cut or suck the bite, or apply chemicals. You NEVER use a tourniquet.

Sprains.

These are stretched and torn ligaments at a joint.

Immediately after it happens you can reduce the swelling and pain which will follow by applying a cold compress—a cloth soaked in cold water and then wrung out to be just moist. Keep it in position half an hour, and renew it if it gets dry.

Otherwise support the joint firmly with layers of cotton wool interleaved between turns of crepe bandaging. Beware of making it so tight that it interferes with circulation in the limb.

A severe sprain may be difficult to distinguish from a fracture. If in doubt treat as for the latter.

Strains.

A strain is an overstretching of muscle fibres, and is very like a sprain except that it does not necessarily happen at a joint. Treat it as a sprain.

Strokes.

Some part of the brain has sudden damage of its blood supply. The results are as variable as are the functions of the brain: e.g., poor feeling or power in hand, arm or leg, altered speech, loss of bladder control, paralysis of one side, or unconsciousness.

A mild effect may be the forerunner of more serious damage. Get the patient to bed, if necessary in the recovery position (q.v.), and keep him under observation until the doctor arrives.

Unconsciousness.

In first aid finding the cause of unconsciousness is less important than protecting the patient's breathing. The unconscious patient lying on his back and with head straight or bent towards the chest is at risk of choking from his lax tongue, flopping against and obstructing his throat. Correct positioning prevents this. Act methodically:—

1. Has the patient stopped breathing? He will urgently need resuscitation (q.v.).
2. Is his airway blocked making breathing difficult? Clear any material from his mouth. Bend his head straight back at the neck (but do not twist or turn it), and keep it there (see Choking).
3. Arrest any severe bleeding (q.v.).
4. Dress any wounds (q.v.).
5. Consider the possibilities of fractures (q.v.). If you suspect they might be present do not move him (specially important if he might have injured the backbone); stay by his head to ensure its proper position and to clear out immediately any fluid (saliva, blood, vomit) which threatens to choke.

If he can be moved:—

6. Turn him into the recovery position (q.v.)

Two other important points are that you NEVER try to give anything by mouth to the unconscious or comatose, and that you realise how much you must guard your speech, since these patients may overhear and understand what is spoken near them.

Wounds.

The general treatment is simple, and should avoid the use of antiseptics or ointments.

1. At once control any severe bleeding (q.v.).
2. Sit or lie the patient down.
3. Put a clean temporary dressing on the wound.
4. Wash your hands. Prepare dressings and bandages.
5. Wash *around* the wound (but not the open wound itself) with swabs or clean material moistened with soap and water. Use a fresh swab or material area for each stroke.
6. Cover the wound with a large dry dressing. Over this place a thick soft pad. Bandage firmly.
7. Put the injured part at rest.
8. Take measures against shock (q.v.).

Dressings. Gauze from freshly opened pack. Or improvise from clean handkerchief or small towel, held by corners, allowed to fall open and then refolded so that inside surface comes to outside. A leg or arm can be slipped inside a pillow-case.

Padding. Cotton wool. Or improvise from bunched clean handkerchief, sock.

Bandages can be improvised from stockings, necktie, belt.

Object embedded in wound. Do not try to remove it. Cover it with a clean dressing and over this place a "frame" of padding to surround the side of the object and protect above it. You can now apply further padding and bandages without pressing on the object.

Tetanus (lockjaw) is a risk in wounds contaminated with soil or from animals or thorns. Get medical advice.

THE BACK—AND ITS PROBLEMS

The backbone is of course not a single bone at all but is made up of small bones known as vertebrae (single, vertebra) which together form a column— the *spinal column.* There are twentynine vertebrae, all basically having the same structure and shape but differing each one from the other, markedly in some parts of the spine but only slightly in others. There are seven in the neck (cervical), the first two being called the atlas and the axis, their relationship one to the other being unique in the whole column, twelve in the chest (thoracic) to which the ribs are attached, and five in the abdomen (lumbar). The remaining five (sacral) are fused together and are wedged into the bony pelvic girdle.

The basic structure and shape of a vertebra is that of a section of round column made up of vertebral *bodies,* each of which has side pieces extending from it, meeting at the back and having off-shoots at the sides which form joints with the vertebrae above and below each bone. The side pieces form a bony canal through which runs the spinal cord in its protective sheath, an extension of the brain containing nerve trunks serving to convey "messages" to and from the brain centres. The cord has branches which supply the trunk and limbs; these branches make their exits through gaps between the side pieces at each vertebral junction. The cord itself ends at the junction between the first and second of the lumbar vertebrae and beyond that there is no nerve tissue as such, only a thin filament which runs down almost to the last bone of the column, the *coccyx.* The coverings of the brain which enclose the fluid which bathes it (cerebro-spinal fluid) continue down the spinal column covering the cord and likewise protect it. It is possible to sample the fluid by passing a hollow needle through the back between the spines of the lower lumbar vertebrae and this procedure (the lumbar puncture) has been and indeed still is a very important diagnostic aid in the interpretation of various neurological problems.

The side pieces which form the canal meet at the back, and it is these that can be felt as knobbles up and down the whole spinal column—these are the vertebral *spines* and are useful anatomical landmarks being easily identified and numbered accordingly. Thus doctors speak of "C5 & 6" for the fifth and sixth cervical vertebra (counting always from above downwards) or "L4 & 5" for the fourth and fifth lumbar. Usually the knobbles—the spines of the vertebrae—can be seen or felt running straight down the middle from neck to small of the back, but it is quite normal to find one, sometimes two, which are slightly out of line, especially in the upper part or the thoracic region. It does not mean that your back is "out of place", although fractures and displacements can and do occur, of course, but usually not without symptoms.

Each vertebra is separated from its neighbour (with the exception of the five fused ones in the sacrum) by a firm ring of fibrous tissue and cartilage (gristle) in the centre of which is a soft, pulpy but highly elastic blob of material. The whole structure forms an integral part of adjoining vertebral body surfaces and is attached to the strong ligaments which run up and down the length of the column and which, with the spinal muscles, are responsible for the relative rigidity of the whole backbone. These structures are the *intervertebral discs* and they are not just cushions sitting precariously between the vertebral bodies ready to slip out from one side to another, forward or backward. They are the chief connecting bonds of the vertebrae. But more about "discs" later.

The backbone is not a rigid rod. It has natural

curves which make the whole column look from the side rather like a slightly flattened and elongated S, with a tail. The neck region is slightly convex forward, the chest backward, the lumbar area forward again (much more so in women) and the pelvic area backward, with the concavity somewhat downward.

The complex ligamentous and muscular structures surrounding the backbone are responsible for maintaining the natural curves which are produced in the first place by slight differences in height between the front and back of the vertebral bodies.

There is sometimes a slight *sideways* curvature in the chest region—convex to the right in the right-handed and to the left in the left-handed. Such a sideways curve is called a scoliosis.

The natural curves are not rigidly held and it is possible to straighten the back a little more by hanging from a horizontal bar and letting the arms take the whole body weight. This is a form of traction, a technique used by physiotherapists and manipulators in certain circumstances. A totally rigid rod for a backbone would be impossible to tolerate. Every step would jar the base of the skull and even a small jump would probably result in concussion, if not actual unconsciousness. Some of the day-to-day jarring of this sort is absorbed by the curves and some by the intervertebral discs which in this instance certainly exert a shock absorbing effect. The discs are very much part of the mechanism and account for no less than a quarter of the total spinal length. Some of the lessening of height with age is due to shrinkage of the discs although actual collapse of a vertebral body can produce a more dramatic shortening.

The musculature of the back is complicated and the details need not concern us. The most well-developed muscles are those which act to keep the column erect. You can feel them come into action as you straighten up or, even better, as you lean backwards, pointing your chest upwards; they can then be felt as hard masses each side of the bony spines, especially in the small of the back. Control of back movement is complex and actions such as bending (forwards or backwards or sideways) and twisting are the result of intricate and coordinated muscle actions. The back is really like a series of short levers joined together; movement of one vertebra upon another is controlled by short muscles and allows appropriate movement to be carried out as a whole (and controlled by the long muscles extending nearly all the way up the back) without the whole thing buckling. Backs do buckle, and one of the common causes used to be tuberculosis. An abnormal bend produced by disease such as tuberculosis or poliomyelitis (or by bad posture in childhood) is known as a kyphosis. This is usually convex backward (hunchback) but if it is a sideways bend it is, as has been mentioned, scoliosis. Often the two deformities are present together when it is known as kypho-scoliosis.

With such a complicated structure it is not surprising that things can go wrong. Back problems are very common, ranging from simple back strain to the "slipped disc". Advertisements for orthopaedic beds appear in the press and sufferers are exhorted to put firm boards or even complete doors under mattresses which are allegedly too soft and therefore "bad for the back". Some ten percent of hospital out-patients in an orthodaedic department are there because of back problems. Why should this be so? Is it because we have over the millennia adopted an upright stance? Would we have been any better off going on all fours? Animal evidence suggest that in fact we might not, for long backed animals—the bacon pig or the dachshund for example—also suffer back troubles. Is it because we abuse the superbly architectured structure of the spinal column with its intricate pattern of ligaments, muscles and discs? We do not honestly know, but there are undoubtedly clearly defined predisposing tendencies to back troubles, many if not all of which are avoidable. What sort of things can go wrong? Perhaps the commonest mishap is not peculiar to the back at all but it is much more inconvenient when it affects the back rather than any other part. This is simple *muscle strain*, a vague term which is used to describe the painful few days or even weeks which may follow an unusual effort such as forking or digging in the garden for the first time in the season or lifting heavy objects in the wrong way. Because the strain in this case is usually on the lumbar group of the spinal muscles, the pain is felt in the small of the back and is called lumbago, a term which simply means *low back pain*. Treatment is essentially avoidance of the kind of activity that triggered off the incident. That doesn't necessarily mean absolute rest although that may well be ideal. Local heat may help, although the ointments which claim to induce the extra heat deep in the muscles and infra-red lamps are probably no better than the humble hot water bottle. Certainly locally applied heat does bring transient relief but probably does nothing to accelerate a return to normal. It is quite likely that such strains rupture small muscle fibres, with consequent effusion of tissue fluid into the muscle sheath which leads to swelling and pain which is felt in the muscle group as a whole.

Lumbago is very common and in nine out of ten instances, it is a simple self-limiting condition which means it will get better whatever you do or don't do. Lumbago is of course a symptom, not a disease in itself, and rarely it may have other serious causes than simple strain. Low back pian occurring without any apparent precipitating act of the kind mentioned needs medical advice. Any of the triggering factors which cause an attack of lumbago may produce the condition commonly known as the "slipped disc". As mentioned earlier, each vertebra is separated from its neighbour by the intervertebral disc which, because of its intimate attachment to the ligaments which run up and down the spinal column cannot slip. A disc can however "prolapse" that is to say a portion of it may protrude through the fibres of the ligaments in places where for some reason or another those ligaments may be readily separated or otherwise weakened. The discs are quite thick, especially in the lumbar region, and in old age, they shrink and become rather less elastic; in that state they are less likely to prolapse, "slipped discs" being in fact much more common in the younger person.

Just what makes a disc prolapse with its accompanying acute pain which although felt in the small of the back may run into one or another buttock and down the back and side of the leg (a condition called *sciatica*) is not known. Prolapse may be likened to the bursting of a car inner tube through a slit in the outer cover. The intervertebral discs are under a good deal of pressure while we are sitting or standing, but even more so when we bend or lift. If a disc has prolapsed while it is under pressure, the protrusion is usually backwards and there is the danger that it may press on one or other of the nerves and cause severe pain. As the common site for a disc prolapse is in the lumbar region where the roots of the sciatic nerve arise, sciatica is likely to occur. However, it must be remembered that the disc lesions are not confined to the lower back but can sometimes also arise in the neck.

When the pressure on the prolapsed disc is lessened, by resting with the backbone more or less horizontal, the extruded part may resume its normal position although if the ligament through which it protruded in the first place remains weakened or torn, then recurrence is very likely. It is this tendency to recur which makes the condition so difficult to cope with. Although rest is the prime requirement in an initial treatment of prolapsed intervertebral disc there is a place for immediate manipulation. The aim of this kind of treatment is to manipulate the spine and reduce the intervertebral pressure and relax the ligament enough to permit reduction of the protrusion. Having done that the next problem is to prevent an immediate or later recurrence. Clearly, manipulation of this kind requires a specialist skill. Sometimes the simple home remedy of hanging by the hands from the top of a convenient doorway, a form of natural traction which allows the intervertebral pressure to fall and give the disc a chance to recover its normal contour, may be effective. On the other hand, more prolonged traction sessions in the hands of a physiotherapist may be required.

Unfortunately, any treatment of a recurring disc lesion is time-consuming and considerable discomfort and disability has to be suffered meanwhile. Sometimes interference with the sciatic nerve roots not only causes severe and intractible pain but may indeed affect the proper functioning of the leg muscle with weakness and sometimes actual paralysis. Chronic sciatic nerve irritation may lead to muscle wasting and a consequent limp. Surgery certainly has a place in the treatment of chronic, recurring prolapsed disc and one of the techniques used aims at removing a piece of the bony arch against which the root of the sciatic nerve is being pressed, an operation known as laminectomy. This in itself may have to be combined with spinal fusion, a more extensive operation in which bone taken from a hip can be grafted on to two or three adjacent vertebrae and thus prevent their movement in any direction. Pressure on the discs is relieved in the area so treated and the risk of recurrence is virtually nil.

There are of course other ways of preventing undue movement and recurrence of disc protrusions without actually undergoing surgery. There are specially designed corsets, but these should always be prescribed and made to measure for you and not bought from surgical appliance shops where there may be no qualified surgical appliance fitter. Earlier it was suggested that there are ways of avoiding back trouble—or at least minimising one's chances of falling victim to some of the ills that have been discussed. As most if not all of these are due to strain or other abuse it makes sense to avoid them. One of the most important things is to see that the muscles which are responsible for maintaining the upright posture are kept in trim. This can be done by indulging in general sporting activities, particularly swimming, horse riding, walking or playing golf. If you are not able to do any of these things, then simple bedroom floor exercises can go a long way to keeping your back muscles in good shape. Just lying supine—i.e. flat on your back—and then rhythmically arching the spine between the shoulders and buttocks then relaxing is an excellent way to strengthen the all-important muscle groups. There are many good books available describing other exercises.

The other important part of general back care is to avoid too much sitting in easy chairs or indeed on any piece of furniture which allows the natural forward curvature of the lumbar area to slump backwards which while letting your vertebral muscles off a good deal of work, does little to keep them in trim for the routine job of maintaining the proper vertebral postures. The design of car seats, at least in the more popular models, leaves a lot to be desired and the aim should be to choose a car with a seat which does more than allow one simply to slump at the wheel. There are various gadgets which can be fixed to the back of most such seats to give that very necessary lumbar support but it is of course far better to have a properly designed seat in the first place.

It must be remembered that pain may be felt in the back which arises from other general causes. Perhaps the commonest of these are anxiety and depression; indeed these prime examples of the group of psychoneurotic illnesses can cause aching and pain in almost any part of the body. The headache is a common manifestation of anxiety, phobia or depression but such "neurotic" pain may cause a backache as severe and disabling as the severest muscle strain. Organic disease can also be responsible for back pain. Inflammation of abdominal contents—colitis, ileitis, pancreatis and so on—and disease of structures such as the kidneys, bladder and rectum can all produce low back pain. But other symptoms appear with most of such illnesses and backache as the only symptom of these abdominal or pelvic diseases is rare.

What of disease of the back itself? Ankylosing spondylitis should be mentioned as should spondylolysthesis, Paget's disease, tuberculosis, osteoporosis and osteomalacia. *Ankylosing spondylitis* affects relatively young adults and produces a slow progressive stiffening of the back over a long period of time, leading to a generalised forward curvature of the spine and a typical gait. Although a history of increasing stiffness, usually starting in the neck, is typical, diagnosis can only be made for certain by an x-ray examination. No accepted treatment is known, but in spite of its potential danger (damage to the bone marrow) irradiation with x-rays can be helpful.

Spondylolysthesis may give rise to no symptoms at all. It is a displacement forward of one of the vertebral bodies, usually the fifth lumbar.

Paget's disease (osteitis deformans) may affect any bone. It is a localised thickening of the hard part of the bone of unknown cause, commoner in women than men and essentially a disease of the older person. The predominant symptom is deformity and pain.

Osteoporosis may occur at any age but commonly affects women after the menopause. Essentially it is a relative loss of bone mineral content with weakening of the bone structure. There is a tendency to fracture, particularly the wrist and neck of the femur. Pain is the predominant symptom, and height may be lost as vertebral bodies crumble.

Osteomalacia is a softening of bone with a tendency to deformity, caused by lack of vitamin D. It is not uncommon among the Asian immigrant population. When it occurs in children it is known as rickets. Treatment with vitamin D is curative—indeed adequate vitamin D either in the diet or produced in the body by adequate exposure to sunlight will prevent the disease occurring at all. Lastly, one should mention *tuberculosis* but this is now very rare except in some areas of high immigrant population.

THE PROBLEM OF AIDS

AIDS, the Acquired Immune Deficiency Syndrome, is the result of infection by a virus known in the English-speaking world as the Human T-cell Lymphotropic Virus type III, (HTLV III), and in France, where it was independently discovered, as the Lymphadenopathy Associated Virus (LAV).

History.

No one knows how the infection spread to man but it seems to have occurred in Africa in the area south of the Sahara desert, and its spread to the rest of the world was probably via Haiti and thence carried by holidaymakers to the USA in the 1970s. As with any viral illness in an unprotected population the disease has spread rapidly and fatally. In the summer of 1981 the Centre for Disease Control in Atlanta, USA, noticed that there was a sudden and unexplained increase in illnesses which rarely affect American men. The realisation dawned that a new illness had emerged whose effect was to reduce drastically a person's ability to fight off infection or malignancy. By September 1983 there were 2,259 known cases of whom 917 had died of the condition; the disease had spread from three major urban centres to involve most states of the USA. By June 1985 the number of recorded cases had risen to 12,067 in the USA alone, and of these more than 6,000 had died. In the UK the first AIDS case was reported in December 1981, and by February 1985 there were 132 cases known with 58 deaths attributed to AIDS. World wide figures are not available but the disease is not contained by national boundaries and the problem is fast becoming a global one.

At first it seemed that the disease was confined to homosexual men (they account for 72% of cases in the USA, 89% of those in the UK), intravenous drug abusers (17% in the USA, less in the UK), and men with Caribbean connections, principally Haitians. More recently patients receiving blood transfusions, the children of affected mothers, and even the heterosexual partners of affected men have been found to have the disease, though these last groups account for only 3% of the total.

The spread of HTLV III appears to be primarily by semen and blood. In the USA and in the UK this is usually during homosexual intercourse though the pattern in Africa, where men and women are almost equally affected, appears to indicate spread by heterosexual contact is also possible. This variation in the pattern of disease is unexplained. The main risk factors amongst homosexual men are receptive anal intercourse and multiple sexual partners. The insertive partner does not appear to be at risk and spread from an infected female to her male partner is exceptional.

Transmission of AIDS has occurred during blood transfusion and in the treatment of haemophiliac patients with concentrated blood products. However, this problem is being brought under control by heat-treating supplies and by screening blood donations. Careful studies have shown that vaccination and immunisation are not involved in disease spread. In children the syndrome probably occurs because there has been a mingling of blood in the placenta or during the birth process. Though the virus has been isolated in saliva and tears, there is no evidence that these fluids are involved in infecting others. The disease is not highly infectious and its startling increase is due to the long latency period between infection and the emergence of symptoms, a latency period during which the unwitting victim is himself infectious.

The Reaction to Infection.

After infection with HTLV a person may react within a few days with a glandular fever type response, showing a raised temperature, rash and tender enlarged lymph glands; more usually there is no response at all. The incubation period between infection and the appearance of symptoms varies from 15 to 58 months. A blood test can show the presence of the virus but cannot predict who will go on to develop the full syndrome. About 10% of homosexual men who have had the virus for more than 3 years will go on to develop AIDS. In fact there is a wide spread of response to infection, by far the greatest number having no symptoms at all. Some develop the so called Progressive Lymphadenopathy Syndrome and of these some recover and some go on to AIDS proper. Several other factors may be implicated in the development of AIDS but we do not have much clear knowledge yet. One factor contributing to infection appears to be the presence of other viral infections at the time of exposure; the first virus may render the body's defences more vulnerable to attack by HTLV. Other factors such as genetic endowment, good general health and good nutrition may protect from infection or prevent the development of AIDS.

Some of the lymphocytes, or white cells, circulating in the bloodstream are classified as T helper cells and others as T suppressor cells. The T helper cells stimulate the body's defence mechanisms whilst the suppressor cells shut down the mechanisms when they are no longer needed. The action of HTLV III is to injure the T helper cells, altering the ratio of helper to suppressor cells in the blood so diminishing the body's ability to fight off disease or the growth of abnormal cells. Indeed it is the supresion of this normal immune defence system which leads to the AIDS victim being struck down by diseases which rarely affect man, or by diseases which we can normally throw off quite easily. A distressing aspect of AIDS is that in many cases patients develop such severe reactions to the antibiotics prescribed to treat these illnesses that the treatment has to be abandoned, and this is a contributory factor to the high death rate from the condition. Although AIDS has a slow onset, once symptoms appear the downward course of the illness can be very rapid, and urgent hospital treatment may be needed. At present there is no cure for AIDS and the death rate is high at about 50%. Much research is being done with the dual aims of destroying the virus particles and restoring the body's defences. HTLV multiplies inside the T helper cells and the treatment strategies are aimed firstly at preventing the virus from gaining entry to the cell. A vaccine would do this, but so far a satisfactory one has not been developed. This is because HTLV III is constantly changing its outer coating so preventing recognition by particles designed to attack it. The second measure of defence is to prevent the virus from multiplying once it is inside the T cell, and here there is good news. Several drugs will do this in the laboratory situation and these are now being tested in human trials. Once destruction of the virus has been achieved restoration of the body's defences may occur spontaneously or be stimulated by bone marrow transplants. The results of work now being done are encouraging.

Meanwhile, known risk factors should be avoided. Sexual partners should, where possible, be restricted to established relationships. The efficiency of condoms in limiting disease spread is not established but would probably help. Devices which pierce the skin such as hypodermic needles, razors and toothbrushes should not be shared. Intimate kissing is probably best avoided with strangers, but there is no evidence that coughing or sneezing spreads the disease nor that there is any risk involved in sharing washing, eating or cooking utensils or toilet facilities. Infection has not spread within families apart from sexual contact or to the newborn of infected mothers.

AIDS is a serious condition but there is no justification for panic reaction.

LEGIONNAIRE'S DISEASE

The name was given to commemorate the members of the American Legion who contracted a severe form of pneumonia while attending a conference in Philadelphia in 1976. Pontiac fever is a milder form of the same infection.

The disease is responsible for about 2% of cases of severe pneumonia, occurs more often in August and September and most seriously affects smokers, males and persons over the age of 40. Children appear to be only mildly affected but in the elderly, or those who already have chronic illnesses the death rate may rise to 10 or 15%. The incubation period is on average 7 days but may be as little as 2 days. Symptoms suggest a viral chest infection, though in fact the organism responsible is a bacterium. Three types of bacteria have so far been implicated but Legionella is the most important.

Legionella has been found in natural and artificial collections of fresh water, and epidemics have arisen from hospital and hotel ventilation systems. Chlorination of water tanks appears to help in limiting the spread of infection but attempts to eradicate the bacteria have proved disappointing. Treatment is usually effective if the condition is recognised in good time.

PART IV. INDEX AND GLOSSARY

Cretin, 43 (1).

Cretinism, 43 (1).

C.S.F. (*i.e.* cerebrospinal fluid), 46 (2)

Cushing's disease, 43 (1).

Cutaneous ureterostomy, 45 (1).

Cystic fibrosis, 31 (2).

Cystitis, 45 (1).

Dandruff. *See* Seborrhoea, 52 (1).

Deficiency diseases, 41–2.

Dementia, 50 (1).

Demyelinating diseases, 49 (1).

Dengue, 11 (2).

Dermatitis, 52 (2).

Dhobie itch, 8 (1), 15 (1).

Diabetes insipidus, 43 (1).

Diabetes mellitus, 39 (1).

Diarrhoea, and vomiting, 13 (1), 62 (2).

Diet, 39–41.

Digestive tract, 34–38.

Diphtheria, 12 (1).

Diverticulitis, 37 (1).

Dropsy, 44 (2).

Duchenne's muscular dystrophy, 50 (1).

Ductless glands, 42 (2).

Duodenal ulcer, 35 (2).

Duodenum, 35 (2).

Dysentery, 13 (1), 62 (2).

Dysmenorrhoea, 55 (2).

E.C.T. The abbreviated form of the name for a modern type of treatment for certain psychiatric disorders—electro-convulsive-therapy. *See under* Psychosis, 50 (1).

Eczema, 52(2).

Ehrlich, Paul (1854–1915). German bacteriologist, 4 (1), 5 (2), 15 (2).

Electrocardiogram, (E.C.G.), 29 (2).

Electroencephalography, (E.E.G.), 46 (2).

Electromyography, (E.M.G.), 46 (2).

Elephantiasis, 18 (2).

Embolism, 30 (1), 32 (2).

Emphysema, 31 (1).

Empyema. A collection of pus in the lung (usually a complication of other diseases).

Encephalitis, 49 (1).

Encephalo-myelitis, 49 (1).

Endemic. Referring to a disease, means prevalent in a particular area.

Endocarditis. Disease of the valves of the heart, 29 (2).

Endocrine glands, 42–3.

Enzymes, 34 (1).

Epidemic jaundice. 16 (1).

Epilepsy, 47 (2).

Epithelioma (cancer of the skin), 54 (1).

Erysipelas, 52 (2).

Exocrine glands, 42 (2).

Eye, disease of the, 54 (2).

Fallopian tubes, 55 (1).

Family Planning, 56–59.

Farcy, 14 (2).

Fat embolism, 33 (1).

Fats. *See* Diet.

Fevers, general treatment of, 9.

Fibroids, 55 (2).

Fibrositis, 54 (2).

Fits. *See* Epilepsy.

Fleming, Sir Alexander (1881–1955). Scottish bacteriologist, discoverer of penicillin, 4 (1).

Food poisoning diseases, 12–15.

Fractures, 21 (2). *See also First Aid*, 66.

Frostbite, 30 (2).

Fungi, diseases caused by, 8 (1), 15 (1).

Gall-bladder, 38 (1).

Gallstones, 39 (1).

Ganglion. A small cystic swelling, usually on the wrist, dealt with by simple surgical treatment.

Gastric ulcer, 35 (2).

Geriatrics. The medical study of old age.

German Measles, 10 (1).

Gigantism, 43 (1).

Gingivitis. Inflammation of the gums due to infection and requiring treatment by a dentist.

Glanders, 14 (2).

Glandular diseases, 42–3.

Glandular fever, 11 (1).

Glaucoma, 54 (2).

Glial cells of the brain, 46 (1).

Goitre, 43 (1).

Gonadotrophic hormones, 42 (2).

Gonorrhoea, 15 (1).

Grand mal. *See* Epilepsy, 47 (2).

Graves' disease, 43 (1).

Growth hormone, 42 (2).

Gynaecology. The study of the diseases of women, 55–56.

Haematemesis. Vomiting of blood, 33 (1), 36 (1).

Haematuria. The passing of blood in the urine, 44 (1).

Haemoglobin. The red pigment in the blood.

Haemolytic anaemia, 24 (2).

Haemophilia, 26 (1).

Haemoptysis. The spitting-up of blood, 33 (1).

Haemorrhage anaemia, 24 (1).

Haemorrhagic diseases, 26 (1).

Haemorrhage of the brain, 48 (2).

Haemorrhoids, 37 (2).

Hair. *See* Alopecia, 52 (1).

Headache, 47 (1). *See also* Migraine.

Head injuries, 19 (1).

Health: general principles, 3 (2).

Heart attack, 28 (2).

Heart beat, 29 (1).

Heart, 26.

Heart failure, 27 (1).

Heart: how it works, 26–7.

Hepatic. Concerning the liver.

Hepatitis, infective, 10 (1), 38 (2), 62 (1).

Hereditary or Huntington's chorea, 48 (2).

Hernia, 37 (1).

Heroin, 23 (1).

Herpes zoster, 49 (1).

Hiatus hernia, 35 (2).

Hodgkin's disease, 25 (2).

Hookworm disease, 18 (2).

Hormones. *See* Endocrine glands.

Hydrocephaly, 48 (1).

Hydronephrosis, 45 (1).

Hyperpituitarism, 43 (1).

Hypochondriasis, the unfounded belief that one is suffering from a serious disease.

Hysteria, 51 (1).

Ichthyosis, 53 (2).

Immunity, 8 (2).

Impetigo, 53 (1).

Incubation period. *See* Infectious Fevers, 9 (2).

Infantile paralysis. *See* Poliomyelitis, 10 (2), 62 (2).

Infarction, 30 (1), 48 (2).

Infection, how spread, 8 (1).

Infectious diseases, 6–18.

Infective hepatitis, 10 (1), 38 (2).

Infectious mononucleosis, 11 (1).

Inflammatory diseases of the nervous system, 49 (1).

Influenza, 10 (2).

AN INTRODUCTION TO PSYCHOLOGY

This section is concerned with the science and study of the human mind, a territory rich in mystery, a glimpse of which we catch through the enigma of memory, and in the misty drama of our dreams. It represents a unique guide to one of the most exciting experimental sciences of today.

TABLE OF CONTENTS

AN INTRODUCTION TO PSYCHOLOGY

The purpose of this section is to provide a general introduction to the young but expanding science of psychology. The topic itself is of course enormously broad and can only be summarised at best. However, it is hoped it will serve to give some idea of the fascinating material that psychologists study and also of their occasionally remarkable, and always interesting findings. The section also aims to dispel some of the illusions that have surrounded the subject and to define its boundaries to the extent that the reader will not only begin to understand what psychology is, but also what it isn't!

I. INTRODUCTION.

What is a Psychologist?

The popular image of a psychologist is a fairly well-defined one—he is a man who treats mental illness in the way that a doctor treats physical ones. His principal equipment, apart from a well-furnished "consulting room," is a leather couch for patients to lie on, a well-stocked library, and a cabinet of mysterious drugs of one kind or another to send them off to sleep. He is particularly interested in the dreams of his clients and may use some form of hypnosis to study their "repressed" thoughts and secret emotions. He is probably very wealthy, because of the enormous fees he charges, and may speak with a central European accent.

Silly though the above description may sound, it is nevertheless unfortunately true that it corresponds pretty closely to the kind of picture that most people have of a psychologist and of the kind of work he does. Remote though this description is from the truth—at least as far as the vast majority of psychologists is concerned—the average person can be forgiven for having it firmly lodged in his mind, for in literally hundreds of movies, TV and radio plays, books and novels this is the picture that has been painted. One of the first tasks of this section will be to attempt to straighten out some of these misconceptions so that a clearer idea of the nature of psychology can be given. While the mysterious and, unfortunately, rather glamorous aspect of psychology that concerns itself with mental illness and its treatment is certainly one facet of the topic, there is a good deal more to it than that. Furthermore, the part of psychology which deals not with the abnormal but with the strictly *normal* brain is the area which has best repaid scientific study and, as we hope to show, which has uncovered the most exciting raw material.

This section, therefore, begins with a clarification of the role of the psychologist, and continues with a brief introduction to his principal fields of study—the brain and human behaviour. After this we take in turn the four main areas of study which assist him in his quest for an understanding of human nature. These are Perception, Learning and Memory, Motivation, and finally Personality and Thinking.

One of the main sources of confusion in people's minds arises from puzzlement over the distinction between four commonly used words which, while differing in meaning in important respects, are almost invariably lumped together as one. These are (1) Psychiatry, (2) Psychoanalysis, (3) Psychotherapy, and (4) Psychology. The words do look and sound rather similar but it is not difficult, once the right definitions have been given, to sort the four clearly out in one's mind. Let's take psychiatry first.

(1) **Psychiatry** is the art of *treating* mental diseases or illnesses by medical means and it is a specialist branch of medicine, entered through the medical profession and taught at hospitals or universities. A psychiatrist therefore is quite invariably a doctor of medicine with ordinary medical degrees but with a postgraduate training in mental illness and its treatment. No one may call himself a psychiatrist unless so qualified, and no one may prescribe drugs or surgery in treating mentally sick individuals unless he is medically qualified. There is an important point of issue here, for in England, and many other countries, people not trained as psychiatrists may nevertheless diagnose and treat mental illnesses—provided that they do not use drugs or surgery to do so.

(2) **Psychoanalysis** is a particular form of examination or diagnosis of an individual's mental state based on the theories of the mind and personality advanced by Sigmund Freud and his colleagues or followers, and the reader may like to turn to the entry on the subject in **Section J**. An interesting feature of psychoanalysis is that, unlike psychiatry, it may be practised without medical or academic qualifications on the part of the analyst. A special training analysis at a recognised institute is normally undertaken by the would-be practitioner, however this is not normally made available to individuals unqualified in medicine or psychology.

(3) **Psychotherapy** is the practice of treating mental diseases or illnesses by more or less *any* means. Thus, strictly speaking, both the psychiatrist and the psychoanalyst are psychotherapists—as are any other individuals using reputable methods who offer therapy for the mind. Once again notice that this implies that one may call oneself a psychotherapist irrespective of whether one has medical or academic qualifications, and it is a word that tends to be adopted, with impunity, by a good many "quacks" and charlatans who can of course do fearful damage in this tricky area.

(4) **Psychology** is literally the study of the mind (or soul) but its area has broadened somewhat in the last century as we have learned that one cannot consider the mind as totally isolated from the body, and it now includes the study of human personality and behaviour. Psychologists also study the behaviour and brain of animals wherever such studies throw light on human behaviour. It is important to realise that psychologists are first and foremost trained as scientists rather than as medical experts and do not necessarily take much interest in abnormalities of the brain and mental processes. Those who do, tend to take postgraduate training in what is known as "clinical psychology," and may add to their knowledge by undergoing training in psychoanalysis.

It is obvious that there is a good deal of overlap between these four aspects of the topic and in the following section we shall be entering the territory of psychiatry and psychoanalysis to some extent, but mainly concerning ourselves with psychology —the science and study of the human mind, personality, and behaviour.

1. The Brain.

From the moment of our birth and emergence from the security of the womb our body is controlled and dominated by a single but complex organ, a library, switchboard, signal-box, computer, and many other things all rolled into one—the brain (see **F40(1)**, **P46**). Very properly encased in a hard shell of bone and equipped with instruments for detecting food or danger at a distance—eyes, ears, etc.—the brain matures slowly, unlike other bodily organs, reaching its peak of efficiency and potential approximately 18 years after birth. From then onwards, slowly and almost immeasurably at first but with remorseless steadiness, it slides into decline. Its proper functioning determines the "normality" of the behaviour of the individual and the part he can play in society, its efficiency determines to some extent his intelligence and his ability to compete, its storage capacity and information retrieval system, his potential to learn and remember. In addition its computing power determines his creativity and is the primary function which distinguishes between the mature human being and the other animals on earth. No organ or complex of organs is guarded and shielded so carefully.

The brain is the main focus of interest for the psychologist, for there can be little doubt that the key to the understanding of human personality and behaviour lies locked up within it. Its complexity of course is daunting, but thanks to physiological and anatomical studies it is possible to get at least a general idea of what's going on. In the first place the brain acts as the principal co-ordinator of messages coming in from the various sense organs, and then as the dispatch point for the appropriate responses. This co-ordinating centre is easily best developed in man, and is present in most of the "higher" animals. Simpler creatures, however, such as amoeba and certain tiny worms, get along without any important co-ordinator of nervous impulses and respond diffusely to changes in the environment—moving vaguely away from things that "annoy" or damage them and towards food or other "pleasant" things. Such animals are literally the slaves of their environment, incapable of setting up goals to achieve and with no facility for computing the sequences of any action. One important branch of the evolutionary tree shows a steady trend towards increasing brain size and, with it, freedom from this slavery.

In the second place the brain acts as the storehouse of information which the senses have gathered at some time in the individual's life. To us it may seem "obvious" that we have a memory—a device for looking at things that took place in the past—and indeed it is hard to imagine ourselves without one. However, a large number of creatures get by with only the most limited of memory systems, and some with none at all. Clearly a good deal must depend upon how long an animal is to live. If its life-span is to be brief, then it need not set aside much room to store information from its past. If it is to live for many years, survive in a changing and generally rather dangerous environment, and learn by its mistakes and its previous achievements, then this ability to refer back to the past is obviously essential. In human beings mechanisms of learning and memory are of vital importance and we will devote a good deal of this section to discussing the way in which psychologists study these.

The third primary function of the brain is to provide the computing and decision-making processes which dictate so much of human and higher animal behaviour. It is also, in the case of man, the centre of consciousness and at the same time that elusive faculty we call personality.

2. How Does the Brain Divide up its Functions?

Nowadays we rather take for granted that important things such as thinking, remembering, etc., are mediated through the brain and it comes as something of a shock to recall that early philosophers located the majority of such processes in the heart or the stomach! Even today, a good deal of controversy exists over exactly which part of the brain does what and, as we shall see when we discuss the contradictory experimental evidence later, there is even a suggestion that certain processes are dealt with by the brain *as a whole* rather than by some specific part. However, the picture is reasonably clear.

In the first place the brain is composed of a vast number of cells—the building blocks of all living systems—which in this case have become highly specialised and stretched out, rather like telephone lines. These are known as nerve or neural cells or, yet again, as neurones. They act as communication units, receiving electrical signals from other parts of the body. Comparative anatomists are able to trace the routes of whole chains of cells starting at, say, the finger tips and finishing up in a particular slab of the brain where such tactile messages are gathered and interpreted. On the whole messages from the eyes tend to finish up in the back of the brain, or occipital lobes; messages from the ears, nose, etc., on the side, or temporal lobes. In the front exists a large chunk of nervous tissue with a rather mysterious function inasmuch as it seems to be more directly related to the personality and mood of its owner than to any of his senses. In addition there are parts of the brain concerned more with output than input—the so-called motor areas which dispatch the signals commanding various parts of the body to move. Finally there are the parts principally involved in the storage of information, memory, etc.

All these areas we have been talking about up till now are known as the cerebral cortex and they are located on the outer surface of the brain itself —i.e., right up against the inside of the skull. You should by now have gathered that the cortex deals largely with psychological factors closely tied up with consciousness and awareness—seeing, hearing, thinking, remembering, etc. This ties in rather nicely with its alternative name, the neo-cortex (or new tissue), for in evolutionary terms this part of the brain is "new." In general, the closer that an animal species approximates to man, the greater the proportion of its brain is assigned to neocortex, and the more the particular animal is capable of independent, deliberate and purposeful activity.

Tucked in beneath the cerebral cortex, growing out of the spinal cord, are the so-called lower centres—the old brain. Here in a number of specialised blocks are located the control centres which deal with the most automatic (but no less important) bodily functions such as cardiac activity, respiration, temperature, etc., and which it is unnecessary or inconvenient to keep under conscious control. Damage or injury to these centres is generally very serious, whereas damage to the outer layer of the brain, even when extensive, can have surprisingly little effect on the individual's way of life.

To sum up, we note that the brain is divided into two major functional areas in evolutionary terms—the old and the new. The former largely deals with the vital automatic processes, and the latter with the receiving and interpreting of sensory input and the decision-making processes which guide our interaction with the outside world. Clearly this is an enormously simplified picture (specific aspects of this topic are dealt with in greater detail later) and the brain and central nervous system (CNS) is complicated almost beyond description, with much of its mechanics and rules of operation still poorly understood. How then can one set out to study it properly and unravel its secrets?

3. Methods of Studying the Brain.

Psychologists and physiologists favour many approaches to finding out how the brain works, and while it won't be possible to look at them all in this section it will be worthwhile spending a bit of time on some of the most important lines of attack. These can be classed under the headings (1) comparative anatomy, (2) surgical tissue destruction, (3) electro-encephalography, (4) microelectrode recording, (5) biochemical analysis, (6) behavioural research, and (7) introspection. Some of these are really only possible with animals as the experimental subjects, and others are more suited for research on human beings.

(1) *Comparative Anatomy.*

This is perhaps the most obvious and logical method of all, but it has one serious and insurmountable drawback. Suppose that one wanted to find out how a motor-car engine worked and that one had no prior knowledge of its operation but knew what one looked like from the outside. Failing instruction booklets or advice from motor mechanics, the best method might seem to be to get hold of a complete engine and take it apart to examine its components. Given enough skill one might even be able to put it back together again. The chances are that with a relatively simple device, such as an automobile engine, an intelligent person would begin to see the principles of operation. However, until he had actually watched it at work and studied the effect of, say, depressing the accelerator or pulling out the choke, his comprehension of the device might be limited and he could well come to some funny conclusions about its function and operating habits. This approach is essentially that of the comparative anatomist who sets out to study the brain by examining a dead specimen, peering at it through a microscope, cutting out bits here and there and hoping to work out what each section contributes to the whole. Unfortunately, whereas the average motor-car engine probably contains a maximum of about 1,000 discrete and separate components, some of which are rather large and "obvious," the brain contains a conservative minimum of *ten thousand million* neurones or nerve cells and no large obvious "moving parts" to give the anatomist useful clues. It is little wonder therefore that while students of the brain adopting post mortem dissection have, in the course of the last few centuries, acquired a pretty clear picture of the way in which the brain is laid out—an anatomical atlas so to speak—most of the principles of cerebral operation are still more or less unknown. One of the great drawbacks of this system, as you will probably have guessed, is the fact that anatomical dissection and analysis can only be done in the dead animal.

(2) Surgical Tissue Destruction.

To return to our rather inexact analogy with the motor-car engine, let us assume that our investigator finds himself with a working, running engine to play with. Let us also assume that he has already made himself pretty familiar with the anatomy of the "dead" engine and has perhaps formed some hypotheses as to what certain parts of it do. For example, he might have a suspicion that the carburettor and the sparking plugs were particularly important, or that a key to the complete device working was that the pistons should move up and down in the cylinders. One of the first things he might do would be to systematically remove what he considered to be important parts of the engine and note how its performance was affected. Using this technique of selective removal he might soon begin to confirm or reject his hunches and a gradual comprehension of the function and capabilities of the engine would build up in his mind. He might find that whereas the removal of one sparking plug did not stop the engine, it would lower its pulling power. Removal of the carburettor in toto would be calamitous, while twiddling with it might have unpredictable effects, making it run better or worse. On the other hand, filing bits off the iron cylinder block would make no difference whatsoever. Once again the psychophysiologist is faced with something immensely more complex when he studies the brain, but there is nevertheless obviously something to be gained by adopting a similar procedure with the working or living system. The systematic removal or destruction of parts of cerebral tissue has, in fact, been one of the most rewarding approaches adopted by brain scientists, though there are naturally severe limitations to the technique. In the first place such surgery cannot be performed on human beings, except where it is a necessary feature of therapeutic brain surgery (*e.g.*, as when removing a brain tumour) and can only be justified in living animals in the interest of serious and clearly defined scientific research. (Despite the assumptions of anti-vivisectionists, no reputable scientist enjoys performing experimental surgery on living animals and these are always conducted in such a way as to cause the creature as little distress and suffering as possible.) In the second place, the very act of surgery itself probably introduces side-effects which serve to complicate the picture. However, this technique, when skilfully used, has led to some informative experiments.

(3) Electroencephalography.

As we have said earlier, the principal building blocks of the brain are the neurones, specialised cells devoted to the transmission of information from one part of the body to the other. This transmission is effected by a change in the electrical potential of the cell along its long stem. The main bodies of cells tend to be pressed up against one another and when a change in potential occurs in one, this tends to trigger off a similar response in a neighbouring cell at a junction point known as a *synapse*. Incidentally, the long stems of the cells (which may be a yard or more in length in certain parts of the body) are covered by an insulating sheath which prevents the electrical "message" leaking out en route and which makes them strangely similar to the kind of electrical wires and cables we use in telecommunications. With a thousand million cells jammed up together in the head, all of them propagating electrical signals in one way or another, it should not surprise anyone to learn that sensitive recording devices can be used to get a picture of the overall electrical activity going on in the brain. Studies of this type (electroencephalography, or EEG for short) couldn't begin until suitable recording machines had been developed and thus, although scientists had been pretty confident that the brain was a potent source of electrical energy since the middle of the 19th cent., it wasn't until the 1920s that anyone was able to get a readable picture of this. The pioneers in this technique were the physiologists Berger and Adrian, who attached little electrodes to the outside of the human scalp and by hooking these up to amplifiers and then to special recording pens were able to get a kind of plot of the electrical activity going on within. To their surprise what emerged was not just a meaningless hodge-podge of electrical "noise" but rather a series of precise and elegant rhythms, the frequency and amplitude of these depending upon the part of the brain where the electrodes were applied, and also—most excitingly —on the individual's mental state at the time of the recording. As time has passed and recording technology has advanced, an immense amount of data has been gathered on these so-called brain waves, and while it is true to say that the high hopes of the pioneers who believed that they were about to unravel the brain's mysteries almost overnight with this technique have not been realised, the EEG has proved its worth in more ways than one. In medicine, for example, certain disruptions of the "normal" brain wave pattern can give clear indications to the expert of the presence of epilepsy or determine the site of otherwise totally inaccessible brain tumours. The EEG can also be enormously useful in evaluating the effectiveness and mode of operation of new drugs and is helping in our understanding of the nature of sleep—the EEG of a sleeping person differs significantly from that of a waking one. Curiously one of the most promising-looking of the many rhythms which the brain emits—and one of the first discovered by the English scientist Adrian, the so-called alpha rhythm, has turned out to be one of the most disappointing. The alpha rhythm, which is generally picked up by electrodes attached to the back of the head (over the occipital or visual cortex), is a beautifully neat and stable wave of about 14 cycles per second frequency. It is present when the individual is relaxed and has his eyes closed. Opening the eyes and looking around, or alternatively keeping them closed and doing a bit of mental arithmetic, causes the rhythm to disappear, and the hypothesis was soon advanced that alpha was a reliable index of the rather abstract mental state known as "attention." Unfortunately for this convenient idea, on further study it was found that the rhythm did not always behave as it should, sometimes doing exactly the opposite to what was expected of it. Furthermore about one in ten otherwise normal individuals show no alpha rhythm at all. The picture has been complicated even further by the publication in 1973 of a book *The Origin of the Alpha Rhythm*. In this the author, Dr. Olof Lippold of University College, London, advances the argument that alpha rhythm in fact reflects physiological tremor of the eye muscles, and therefore has very little to do with internal cerebral states. The presence of abundant alpha in the EEG, Lippold argues, is more likely to be evidence of poor vision than any special capacity to control one's attention. It's fair to say that Lippold's views are still highly controversial, but it should equally be clear that the simple view that brain waves denote complex internal processes is by no means established. All these drawbacks aside the EEG is still one of the best ways of getting some kind of index as to what is going on inside the head of a human or animal, without resorting to surgery or interfering seriously with normal thought processes.

(4) Microelectrode Recording.

For all practical purposes the record obtained by the EEG is a gross, overall view of the brain at work. The waves and rhythms encountered must, at the least, represent the sum of the activity of literally hundreds of thousands of neural cells, presumably firing more or less in synchrony. Going back once more to the motor-car analogy, the EEG could be likened to a garage mechanic listening with a stethoscope to the pulsing of an engine when running at high speed. Changes of speed, adjustments in carburation of timing, etc., would give characteristically different running sounds, but little if anything could be deduced about the state of activity of an individual component unless it were a very large one. Much the same limitations, only on a gigantic scale, surround the use of the EEG as a device for measuring specific aspects of brain activity. Quite recently, however, an interesting technological development has occurred which allows a more precise and delicate analysis of cortical cell firing to be undertaken—in fact to allow even the output from a single neural cell to be monitored. This technique involves the use of what are known as microelectrodes, tiny slivers of metal, thousandths of an inch in diameter, which when in contact with an electrical source—in this instance the body of a nerve cell or neurone—transmit a pulse of electricity to an amplifier and recording apparatus. We shall discuss the remarkable findings which have come from experiments of this kind later in the section on "Perception." Microelectrode techniques, incidentally, can on occasions be used with human subjects. In such cases, naturally the opportunity arises when an individual is undergoing brain surgery for, say, the removal of a cerebral tumour. In these circumstances with the patient's permission, the surgeon may perform experiments to study single cell responses with results which have been of great interest.

(5) Biochemical Analysis.

Scientists have recently shown increasing interest in the microstructure of cerebral tissue, not just the neural cell but in its basic constituents—in other words at the molecular level. Clearly there is not much hope or point in trying to record the behaviour of molecules by electrode recording or even by microscopic visual analysis, so some other method must be found if one is concerned with this level of analysis at all. This is where the psychologist teams with the biochemist—an example of the kind of interdisciplinary approach which is becoming common in brain research. As with much of the chemical analysis performed in other fields, scientists discover the nature of the substance they are examining by observing its behaviour when mixed with other chemicals or compounds. Crudely speaking, one mixes the unknown substance with some known chemical and simply watches what happens, the reaction which follows giving clues as to the nature of the chemical under study. Now in the case of the brain or the constituents of neurones, it is obvious that one is dealing with more than one single substance so the first problem is how to separate the constituents in order to study them individually. To achieve this biochemists use a number of techniques such as

chemical separation, simple heating, and even whirling the material round at great speeds in centrifuges. The biochemical approach to brain research is a bit too complicated to deal with in detail here, but in the view of many it is one of the most promising avenues in this field.

(6) Behavioural Research.

Psychologists are interested not merely in the structure of the brain of humans and animals but also of course in their behaviour. By behaviour one means the way in which the individual interacts with its environment and its reasons for doing so. A study of what, when, and how a creature does something can tell one a good deal about the rules that govern behaviour. The way in which a bird builds its nest, a cat rears its kittens, a dog threatens another dog, frequently follow set patterns and presumably have something to do with the way in which at least a part of its brain is organised. Careful study of such behavioural patterns even allows one to make certain predictions about what an animal will do next in a given set of circumstances—and once one is able to predict accurately one has generally discovered something important. Studying animals (or people) "in the wild" is easier said than done and tends to be frustrating because of their tendency to do unpredictable things and their general disinclination to perform to order. Furthermore the range of behaviour that one can study by such methods is limited to the so-called "instinctive" actions which are frequently simple in function and execution. The alternative is to confine the animal in a laboratory and observe its reactions to an experimentally controlled environment. In this way one can study its learning and memory processes, its sensory mechanisms, its intelligence and capacity to "reason," its behaviour under conditions of stress, its preference for various foods, etc., etc. Behavioural research of this kind has turned out to be almost the most important method employed by psychologists in their attempt to understand the brain.

(7) Introspection.

The oldest and perhaps most obvious method of studying the brain was simply to think about it! This was the method adopted by early philosophers who believed that if one was sufficiently logical and intelligent one could work out the solution to practically anything. Unfortunately, while the brain, mind, etc., might seem to be an ideal subject for its own thought process, this method of analysis—known as introspection—just doesn't seem to work in the way that it should. The principal problem is that much of the brain's activities are exceedingly rapid and automatic, as anyone can demonstrate for themselves. For example, turn your head and look at an object on the wall. It will be "perceived" and recognised apparently instantaneously. Even if you can detect a faint lag between the act of inspection and the act of perception, it is quite impossible to describe the steps or stages in the process. Much the same applies to other important mental faculties. One cannot, merely by thinking about it, say how one actually learns something, or how one calls an item up from memory. It was realising the relative hopelessness of this quest which led philosophers interested in the brain to convert themselves in the middle part of the 19th cent., into psychologists and adopt an experimental rather than an intellectual approach to the problem. However, it should be equally clear (though many psychologists seem to have forgotten this) that there is a whole world of material which does not seem to make itself available to any of the experimental approaches (1–6) which we have described above. The study of language itself is a good example, being part of our mental life and thus of great interest. Similarly certain features of abnormal psychology ranging from the bizarre thought processes of schizophrenics to the near-mystical states of mind reported by artists and poets, or the distortions of perception and personality induced by the hallucinogenic drugs, are central to the topic of psychology and are clearly only approached in the first instance through some measure of introspection. What too of the raw material of psychoanalysis and the rich glimpse of the interior of our minds granted us through our dreams? These are merely a few examples to highlight a single point that—when studying the brain we should not ignore the mind's power to look in on itself.

This concludes our condensed survey of some of the principal methods used by psychologists and their colleagues in attempting to get to grips with their exciting and challenging field. The reader may have been surprised by a number of things, one of which must surely be how very much wider is the territory covered by psychology than is commonly believed.

4. What do Psychologists Study?

We now come to examine the main areas making up the subject matter of psychology. There are all kinds of ways of breaking this material down and as the topic is so immense (and enlarging quite rapidly) one or two important aspects will have to be left aside. We shall only refer in passing, for example, to the important sub-sections of Child Psychology, Industrial Psychology, and Ergonomics, for these need to be treated separately if they are to be properly understood. Furthermore, much of the material inherent in Sociology will have to be passed over for similar reasons. The reader will also notice some overlap between the various headings which merely confirms what one ought to suspect—that in studying human beings or living animals, it is really impossible to segment the approach completely. A person is an entity and something more than the sum of his various parts.

For the purposes of this Introduction we will consider Psychology as constituting principally the study of four major factors—

(1) Perception, which includes the study of the way information is gathered by the brain and how it is interpreted;

(2) Learning and Memory, which deals with the way the information is stored once it has been gathered and, subsequently, how it is retrieved when wanted;

(3) Motivation, which includes the vital topic of why a human or animal interacts with its environment and why it does one thing rather than another; and

(4) Personality and Thinking, which tackles the abstruse problems concerned with consciousness, self-awareness, and, naturally, disorders of both.

Anyone reading this Introduction seriously will find that in acquiring his first formal background in Psychology he will also have to think at times like a physiologist, a philosopher, an anthropologist, and a good experimental scientist, all rolled into one. This will turn out to be less complicated than one might imagine.

II. PERCEPTION.

(a) Information Gathering and Information Decoding.

The topic of perception itself breaks down into two significantly different headings and it is very important to comprehend the distinction between the two before going any further. These are the processes of *information gathering* and *information decoding*. If these words seem a bit bothersome, they need not be. Information has a meaning in science rather broader than details of train times or facts from history, and it really deals with the influence of one object, person, or thing, on another. For example, when you look at the sun or a bright light, photons from the luminous object strike the retina or sensitive layer at the back of the eye. As the result of this the retina changes its state slightly and in due course passes signals back to the brain. Now the interaction between the sun and the retina, odd though it may seem at first, constitutes an exchange of information, and when the message finally reaches the

brain and the sun is recognised for what it is, the information has flowed all the way from sun to brain. If this appears to be an odd use of the word "information," then this is probably because one has tended to think that information can only be conveyed through words or numbers and "meaningful" conversations. The more one considers this limited point of view, however, the less reasonable it seems. If one looks at a painting, which contains neither numbers nor words, but a picture of, say, a ship at sea, then most people will agree that it is conveying information (the artist originating it whenever he painted the picture). In fact we can use this analogy to add that the painting itself can be looked upon as a kind of information store since the artist who set the whole process going could easily be dead and gone, and yet his message continues to be conveyed. If one no longer feels it inappropriate to talk of the sun as an emitter of information to the eye, then we have made a major advance and can move on into the meat of this sub-section. It is really important to get some grasp of the scientific use of words like information and information storage for they will pop up time and time again and one can make nothing of modern psychology without them. Incidentally, when we spoke of the retina sending signals up to the brain where the sun was "recognised," it should be remembered that what reaches the brain is not a kind of miniature sun but rather a pattern of impulses which need to be interpreted. This interpretation we call information decoding and it is the second important factor in perception which we will come to shortly. But first, how is the information received and gathered?

(b) The Five Senses.

Simple creatures, such as amoeba, react in a vague, generalised way to objects in their environment. The reason for this is that they have no specialised equipment to allow them to detect what is taking place, or about to take place, around them, and no computing centre capable of selecting alternative modes of behaviour. As we ascend the evolutionary scale from jellyfish to worms and up through reptiles, mammals, birds, etc., we note increasing specialisation of the body's cells, the development of devices capable of scanning the external environment and increasingly complex co-ordinating nervous centres (brains). By the time we reach Man and other advanced animals, the individual is not merely reacting to his environment but consciously aware of its flux, able to predict many of its changes before they can effect his body physically, and frequently manipulating it significantly to suit his own ends. This immense versatility is dependent upon information from the environment being fed into the nervous system for processing, and the devices which the body has developed to gather this information are known as the senses—vision, hearing, touch, taste, and smell—roughly in order of importance. Without these senses, the interface between the central nervous system and the world outside, a living creature is nothing more than a helpless vegetable, incapable of survival. For this reason if we are to get anywhere with understanding the operation of the brain we will need to know a fair bit about the sense organs that feed it. We shall spend most time on the two most important—vision and audition.

(c) The Eye.

Perhaps the most useful information from the brain's point of view would be that which concerns the detection of food or a mate at a distance or, of course, the presence of danger in the form of a predator. Consequently, the most vital and remarkably developed of our sense organs are our eyes, which are geared to detecting radiation over a frequency range which we call "light." For those who like this kind of detail, the actual spectrum detected by the eye covers light frequencies whose wavelengths range from about 380 nm to about 720 nm (1 nm $= 10^{-9}$m). All this means is that the distance from peak to peak of the waves which constitute the light is a very small amount indeed—far less than a thousandth of a millimetre in fact. Note, however, that not only can the eye detect the 380 nm and the 720 nm waves quite easily but it can also discriminate between them and a whole lot of other wavelengths in between as well. In fact we call the 380 nm waves "violet," the 720 nm "red," those of about 500 nm "green," etc. Remember the minute wavelengths involved and you will appreciate that whichever part of the eye handles this kind of information must be very sensitive indeed. This fabulous bit of equipment, one of the most remarkable of all biological systems, is called the retina.

The Retina.

Situated in a layer at the back of the eye the retina is a kind of screen on to which rays of light are focused by the lens after having passed through a window at the front, which is called the cornea. The question now arises as to how the retina detects the light rays and how it then signals the relevant information on to the brain. There are two ways of answering this question, one very complicated and reasonably accurate, the other quite simple and slightly less accurate. We'll choose the simpler and lose a bit of accuracy without worrying too much.

The principle employed is that of energy absorption. The retina is a densely packed mass of neural cells whose speciality is that they contain light-sensitive substances known as "pigments." These substances change their state rapidly when the photons from a light source strike them, and this change, which is really a high-speed chemical reaction, acts as the trigger which "fires" the cell. This in turn sends a pulse of electrical activity up the neurone's long stem in the direction of the brain. After it has fired, the cell then requires a brief period to recover its normal state and for the minute portion of bleached pigment to regenerate, during which time (known as the refractory period) it will not fire again. Multiply all this by one hundred million, which is the approximate number of cells in the retina, and you will get some idea of the frenzied activity contributing to the process of vision. To complicate matters there are at least two major types of visual receptors, the cones and the rods. To go into their infrastructure in detail is really the province of physiology, but it is necessary to know something about their prime function, which is that the cones tend to handle the higher levels of luminance met in daytime and also mediate colour vision, while the rods, which are far more sensitive, tend to come into life in the dusk or dark. The shift from cone to rod vision, which, like most of the body's basic functions, is entirely automatic, is something we all experience regularly in our daily life. Walk out of the sun into a dark room and for a moment one is "blinded." Walk out of a dark room into the sun and again one is "blinded." Actually all that is happening is that the visual system is having to shift from one set of receptors to another and when the change is extreme and rapid, the lag in the switchover is dramatically apparent.

Colour Vision

Psychologists have known for a long time that the cones, which tend to be packed in the centre or "more useful" part of the retina, have something to do with colour vision, but just how they do this job has been a matter of much debate and argument. One of the most likely bets would seem to be that particular types of cone are equipped with particular types of pigment, one sensitive to light in the "red" range, another to light in the "yellow," another in the "blue," etc. But how many types of cone would one need, therefore, to get the kind of colour vision we enjoy? Would one have a separate type for each subtle shade of hue for example? When thinking such things out scientists always try to see first if they can get by with the smallest possible number of hypothetical elements, and only bring in extra mechanisms when they are absolutely stumped—a principle known as "Occam's razor" and one universally revered in science and philosophy. With this in mind and with a bit of ingenuity, the general view at the moment is that

three separate types of colour receptor are all that are needed to account for human colour vision; this is known as the trichromatic theory, which is all we need to know about it for the purposes of this article. But just to show how complicated things are, and yet how interesting for this very reason, we will pause to look at some experiments in human colour vision which show that no matter how neat and simple an explanation is in psychology, there is always a joker hiding in the pack.

Some Experiments in Colour Vision.

To understand these experiments, which were performed by a Swiss psychologist, Dr. Ivo Kohler, we need to know a little bit about the phenomena known as after-images. This information will come in handy again a little later on when we talk about after-images in a slightly different context. You may have observed that if you look at a bright light for longer than a second or two, when you close your eyes you see a continuing image of the object which may persist for quite a while and exhibit a nice range of rather bright colour changes. If you haven't observed this, then you can experiment yourself by just fixing with one eye on the filament of an electric light bulb—not too close to the eye. Count five slowly as you do so, then close your eyes and observe. (Don't do this with the sun, by the way, as it could be dangerous.) Now the important point at this stage is the changes in colour you will see taking place, which are generally believed to occur because the bright light has slightly overbleached the retinal pigments and they are taking longer than usual to recover. In the process of recovering they continue to send signals to the brain, which interprets this information as if there was still a light source present and thus the bulb filament is "seen" long after it has really gone. The colour changes themselves are probably due to the fact that some pigments regenerate a bit more quickly than others and thus a sequence of colours is perceived. All this involves lights of greater than average intensity and the question is whether one could get "after-images" with low intensity objects looked at for a long time. The answer is yes, and for anyone who hasn't noticed this before, another simple experiment can be tried. Take a book with a brightish colour binding—say red. Fix on it with one eye, trying to keep your head and eye as still as possible and hold it for about one minute. Now, turn the head away from the book and look at a blank, light wall or other flat surface. What one will see is a rather amorphous image of the book, but coloured green, which will linger for about half a minute before it fades away. This is another version of the first trick, with the after-image being due to the bleaching of the red pigment, and to various other changes that follow in its wake. Now the after-image, as we have noted, soon fades away and no doubt this has something to do with the intensity of the original stimulus. But what would happen if, instead of merely exposing oneself to the colour for a minute or two, one extended the time period to an hour, or a day, or a week, or even longer? This is exactly the question that Kohler set out to answer. To get over the problem of how one could possibly go on looking at something for hours or days on end, he decided on the simple expedient of wearing tinted spectacles and going about his business as usual. For the first experiment, using pink spectacles, he made a number of interesting discoveries. Number one was that although for the first few hours in his experiment the world took on a rosy hue, before the first day was over things were nearly back to normal. After a few days there was no longer any suggestion of a more than normal amount of pink about and his vision appeared to be unaffected—even though, of course, all light was being filtered through the red lenses and thus inevitably tinted. Discovery number two came when he finally took the lenses off to find the whole world tinged with green—the so-called complementary colour of red—a tint which remained for days! His next experiment, apart from doing the whole thing over again with a different set of colours—blue lenses providing a yellow world, green a red one, etc.—was to wear spectacles with one lens red and the other green. This time the position was more complicated. If he closed his right eye, which had the red filter in front of it, then he saw green through the other lens and vice versa. With both eyes open, however, the two colours would "mix" in his brain and the world appeared through a kind of bluey haze. At this point you might care to try to predict what the scientist found when, after a few weeks of this and after all the colour had washed out, he finally removed the spectacles. In the first place, if he looked at the world through both eyes he saw the complementary to blue (which is yellow) but if he looked through either of his eyes singly he saw the world tinted with the appropriate complementary colour, red or green. Once again the new tints took some time to disperse. All this of course, while exceedingly interesting, could still be reasonably explained on the theory of pigments bleaching away due to long exposure and taking some time to regenerate. Unfortunately for this simple idea, but fortunately for people who like problems, Kohler's next experiment produced a surprise result. For this he had the ingenious idea of segmenting his spectacles so that the right half of each lens was tinted red, the left half green. The position now was that if the wearer looked to the *right* with *both* eyes he saw a red-tinted world, if to the *left* a green-tinted one. Looking straight ahead produced a muddling fusion of both colours. In due course, as one might predict, all spurious colours washed out wherever one was looking. Now came the surprise. On removal of the spectacles Kohler found that when he looked ahead he saw the complementary "fused" colour, but when he looked to the right he saw the complementary of red, which was green. When he looked to the left he saw the complementary of green, which was red. To work out why this was surprising one must think about what was happening in the retina. In the early experiments, with the whole of the right visual field tinted red, say, the persisting perception of the green after-image was felt to be due to some changes in the pigmentation of the cells in the retina. But clearly this will not do in the final experiment, for in this case the same areas of retina seem to be doing two different things. After the glasses had been removed, when the subject gazed to the right he saw a green field and one might assume that this was because the pigment had been changed by overstimulation. But how could this account for the fact that when the subject turned his eyes to the left there was a change of perceived colour to red? Clearly the pigment itself couldn't have changed in that time nor could it change back when the eyes reverted to the left. Obviously, quite contrary to what one might expect, the colour changes were dependent, in this case, not on the state of the retina but rather on the direction of gaze!

No one has satisfactorily explained Kohler's intriguing results to date, but they do suggest one important point which one is always in danger of neglecting in psychology—that a living organism is not just a collection of parts acting independently of each other. In the drastic situation of wearing tinted lenses for days, or even weeks, changes were evidently taking place not just in the retina of the eye, but also in higher centres of the brain.

More About the Rods and Cones.

Returning briefly to the retina and its constituent cells we might just take a closer look at the rods which, you will recall, come largely into play in conditions of poor luminance.

The extraordinary sensitivity of the rods is the most interesting thing about them. Unlike the cones, which need the brightness of daylight to do them justice, one single rod will be triggered into action by light whose energy is as low as 100 aJ ($1\ aJ = 10^{-18}$ J), and if that is a value which has no meaning one can get a graphic idea of this sensitivity when one learns that in total blackness the eye could detect the light of a single candle five miles away! Put another way, the amount of kinetic energy used in lifting a pea only two cm would, if converted to light energy, be enough to give a brief sensation of light to every person that has ever lived on earth! The clustering of

cones in the centre of the retina, the fovea, has been mentioned and the rods consequently tend to be scattered around in the periphery. You can detect this geographical distribution yourself by noticing that whereas in daytime your vision is much better directly in front of you, in very dim light you will be able to see objects on the edge of your visual field rather better. You might also care to note how the periphery of the retina, populated largely by rods and devoid of cones, is remarkably insensitive to colour. Offhand one gets the impression that the whole of one's visual field is richly endowed with colour, but this is far from true. A simple experiment will demonstrate this. Fix, with one eye closed, on a predetermined spot—a mark on a piece of paper will do. Then, slowly bring into your field of vision from the side a small piece of coloured paper drawing it closer and closer to the central spot. Now if you can manage to keep your eye really still and maintain fixation despite the tendency to peek at the incoming paper, you will be surprised how far in the latter will have to be before you can detect its colour with certainty. Try the experiment again with another colour and note that it may be recognised earlier or later. In this way it is possible to plot a simple map of one's own retina, defining the boundaries of the colour sensitive areas and nicely illustrating the division of retinal receptors into two distinct types with different jobs to do—the rods and the cones.

(d) Perception as a Dynamic Process.

Everything we have said in this particular section has reinforced the idea that creatures with complex brains are something far more than automata responding blindly to changes in the environment. Information fed in through the eyes, etc., is processed in some way by the brain, or "decoded," as we put it earlier. In fact it is this business of decoding and the possible mechanisms which help to achieve it that interest psychologists more than the raw details as to how the senses actually gather the information in the first place. Nevertheless until relatively recently there was a school of thought in psychology that made desperate attempts to deny, or at least reduce, the role of a central integrating process, implying that animal and human behaviour could ultimately be reduced to a great mass of stimulus-response networks, triggering each other into action in a totally mechanical fashion. This "Behaviourist" school, as it was known, had more impact on theories of learning and we shall look at it more closely when we come to the appropriate section, but it also influenced the thinking of psychologists interested in perception. The trouble with this point of view is that it is so obviously inadequate to explain the rich material of perceptual experience. One has only to think of the visual illusions that are experienced when information "correctly" relayed from the eye is "misunderstood" or incorrectly "decoded" in the brain itself. Clearly it is enormously interesting that all human beings fall prey to illusions, for it suggests that some common mechanism exists which is causing them.

The Gestalt Approach to Perception.

Among the first people to take this up as a general principle and use it as a frontal assault on the Behaviourist view was the so-called "Gestalt school" of psychology, founded in the early part of the century by three talented psychologists, Kurt Koffka, Wolfgang Kohler and Max Wertheimer. In point of fact they looked more closely at other common features or anomalies of perception than at visual illusions, for they believed that the introspective and experimental analysis of human perceptual experience allowed one to deduce the "laws of perceptual organisation" and that these laws must throw light on the fundamental operating procedures of the brain itself. A simple introduction to Gestalt theory is given in Section J so we will confine ourselves here to looking at a few of their more important ideas, most of which are still valid in modern psychology. The first was their insightful statement that in perception *the whole is something more than the sum of its parts.* This principle is nicely illustrated by the fact that a series of dots drawn fairly close together in the shape of a ring are perceived as having a very definite "form"— *i.e.,* that of a circle—despite the fact that all one has actually put on a paper is a collection of dots. Dots are all that are perceived by the retina, and the signals passed up to the brain can only be those arising as the result of the dot stimuli. Look at such a picture, however, and one sees a circle. But where does this come from? From the brain say the Gestalt psychologists, pointing out that the whole (*i.e.* the perception of the circle) is something over and above the sum of its parts (*i.e.* a collection of points or dots). The same thing can be applied to lines, or practically any other shape, and can even apply in the auditory sense (a "tune" is something over and above a collection of separate notes played in sequence).

Gestalt Laws of Perceptual Organisation.

The Gestalt school argued that this was clear evidence for the existence of dynamic forces in the brain whose function was to mould or *structure* the information as it was fed in by the senses. Further examples of this structuring could be seen in other types of visual phenomena, and Koffka and his colleagues formulated a number of "laws of perceptual organisation" which they held were universal and also, probably, innate or "built into" the brain at birth. These laws are a bit too involved for us to discuss in detail but one or two are worth mentioning because the reader can conduct simple experiments for himself. The first, known as "Continuity," is a rather obvious one and similar to the example of a dotted circle that we had earlier. This states that a collection of dots arranged so that they form a "continuous" line, whether straight or curved, would tend to be perceived *as a unit.* In other words, structuring forces within the brain tend to act upon such dots causing them to be perceptually linked despite the fact that they have no true continuity in the physical sense. The age-old perception of the constellations in the sky, formed out of near random stellar patterns, is a good example of the law of "Continuity" in action. Another important law is that of "Similarity." To observe this in operation, scribble on a sheet of paper about twenty small crosses at random. Now, among these crosses again scribble down about 10 small circles. Look at the composite picture and you will probably note that the circles, more or less wherever they are, tend to stand out in isolation from the crosses—the law of "Similarity" in operation. Obvious? Maybe—but why *should* similar things stand out against a dissimilar background? Obviously some important factor in perception must be at work. Yet one more Gestalt "law," that of "Closure," is worth mentioning because its operation is easy to observe experimentally. Koffka and his colleagues believed that the perceptual organising system tended to dislike incomplete or partial figures and where possible would "close" them. This was particularly true, they argued, with neat, simple figures such as circles, triangles, etc. To illustrate this, draw a small neat circle on a piece of paper but leave a small gap in it, say about a tenth of its circumference. Now close your eyes and open them very briefly to give yourself a fleeting glimpse of the figure you have drawn. The chances are that what you will see is a circle—without the gap. Try this on someone else who doesn't know that there is a gap present and it will work even better. Now one might reasonably argue that one has missed the gap because one didn't have time to see it, but that's really no explanation as to why one should see a *complete* circle. The Gestalt argument is that in such fleeting glimpses, the law of Closure within the brain overrides the rather feeble information about the gap that comes up from the retina and the result is the gap just never gets perceived. The effect, incidentally, works for longer looks at patterns viewed in dim light.

A good deal of controversy surrounded the Gestalt approach to perception, much of which has died down in recent years as the Gestalt point of view has gradually fallen out of favour. One of the most controversial facets of the theory was the belief that the so-called laws were innate, or

present at birth. In other words if one could somehow question a new-born baby and get a sensible answer out of it we would find that it too had its perceptions modified according to the Gestalt laws of Continuity, Closure, etc. And this brings us to the very interesting question of just what it is that babies can see at birth—if anything.

(e) **Learning to See.**

Anyone who has spent any time with very young babies will realise that their powers of perception are at best poorly developed. The mother may feel greatly flattered at being "recognised" with a smile, but the harsh facts are that a young baby will produce a charming smile for practically anything—even an absolutely horrific mask—that's placed in front of it. The psychologist William James (brother of the novelist Henry James) actually stated that the world of the newborn baby was a "buzzing, booming confusion"—in other words a mass of sensory data rushing up to the brain with nothing up there to interpret it. This is probably close to the truth—at least as far as human babies are concerned, for there is very good evidence that babies do not come into the world equipped with the ability to perceive the environment in the orderly, clear-cut way that adults do. Incidentally, this is not due to any deficiency in their visual system for the new-born eyes are physiologically mature with at least the *potential* for detailed colour and pattern vision. What seems to be happening is that in the first few months, perhaps years of life, young humans literally have to *learn to perceive,* as the brain gradually acquires the power to integrate the information sent up by the senses, into a meaningful picture of the environment. There can be no better illustration of the vital distinction psychologists draw between vision (or audition for that matter) and the act of *perception.* One concerns itself with input, the other with its interpretation. Now with animals it is a different story—somewhat. Among the primates, chimpanzees, monkeys, etc., perception at birth is better than with humans but still pretty uncertain and the lower down the animal kingdom (this is called the phylogenetic scale) one goes, in general, the better the creature is equipped at its birth to perceive the environment. Look at it another way and say that the simpler the creature and the less well equipped with cerebral cortex, the more wiring or circuitry is built into it and carried over to every member of the species. This of course is what is meant by instinct—an inherited behaviour pattern or function of some kind which appears in every member of a species at birth. *See also* **F40**(2).

Instincts are very useful in one sense since the creature endowed with them doesn't have to learn the instinctive task and can perform it at birth (suckling is one of the few human instinctive reflexes). On the debit side, however, is the fact that one can't *unlearn* the instincts either, so that the more of them one has, the more likely they are to get one into trouble if one is a creature likely to change its environment in any radical way. Think, for example, how powerless human beings would be if they were subject to an instinctive desire to hibernate for six months at the onset of each winter. Clearly instincts are good for creatures with limited cerebral capacity, but a big handicap if one wants to respond in a flexible way to the world around one. The big question now is, does the ability to perceive develop as a natural consequence of the maturing brain, or is it dependent upon practice and experience?

Some Investigations.

If one takes kittens and brings them up in total darkness for, say, a month, on being subjected to the light they seem to have normal perception—pretty well equivalent to that of kittens normally brought up. However, if one extends the rearing-in-the-dark for a much longer period, say a year, then the young cat never seems to achieve normal vision on its introduction to a lighted world. Post mortem examination of the brain reveals that certain parts of the visual system seem to have failed to develop in the normal way. Evidently there is a critical period, which when exceeded without visual experience, stultifies the brain so that normal perception can never be achieved. But what of humans? This may seem an impossible question to answer for how could one conduct the necessary experiment—*i.e.*, deprive new-born babies of light for up to a year—without outraging all moral and ethical values? In fact, by an odd and fortunate twist, the necessary data has come to us without the need to perform an impossible experiment. In the 1930s new techniques of surgery allowed the performance for the first time of an operation to graft the human cornea. This, you will recall, is the transparent window on the front of the eye which can, with age or disease, become clouded and opaque. Occasionally the cornea may be opaque at birth with the result that the individual can never achieve the perception of patterns or shapes. Because some light is getting through the milky window, however, he may be able to tell the difference between, say, periods of light and dark. Prior to the 1930s people afflicted with clouded corneas were consigned to a life of effective blindness—the more tragic because in all essentials they were frequently equipped with perfectly operating retinae, optic nerve, etc. With the development of corneal transplant surgery the picture dramatically changed and, while the operation is now usually performed at a relatively early age, there was an initial group of people in middle-age waiting to be treated who had *never had normal vision*. Realising that this provided a unique opportunity for an interesting observational study, the German psychologist Von Senden arranged to follow the progress of the patients with new corneas and record their reactions to the sight of objects which they had hitherto only heard described. Von Senden was set for some surprises—but nothing like the ones that he got. In the first place the newly-sighted patients, far from gazing round in wonder at the marvels of the visual world, were apparently totally incapable of making any sense out of it! This was not, incidentally, a mere failure to recognise subtle differences such as exist between people but a totally inability to tell the difference between most common, everyday objects. Showing the patients large simple drawings, such as a triangle and a square, naming them and then switching their relative position would totally confuse the patients. In order to tell the difference they would have to laboriously trace the outlines of each figure, carefully counting the corners. Notice that they could *see* the outlines, corners, etc.—their eyes were functioning properly—but they were unable to perceive the pattern. Their brains were simply not equipped to recognise shapes and, like young babies, they had to learn the whole process slowly and laboriously. Von Senden's second surprise came when he found that few of the patients seemed to find, at least in the early stages, the gift of sight at all welcome. Some, in fact, literally begged the doctors in the hospital to replace the bandages over their eyes! As with young babies, their visual world was indeed one of "buzzing, booming confusion" and it took some getting used to. There's a happy ending to Von Senden's story. All patients in due course acquired the ability to perceive, slowly at first but with increasing speed and confidence.

The moral of all this is clear, and once again emphasises all the points we have been trying to make about perception. The brain is a device designed to integrate information fed into it by its senses. In due course this integration becomes almost automatic, but this is reached only after a long period of training, which in humans occupies the greater part of infancy and early childhood. How much is actually "built into" human brains at birth in the field of perception? Probably very little, if Von Senden's work is accepted without reservation. Unfortunately there's some curious contradictory work to muddle the issue (as usual) and it concerns experiments with young babies performed by the psychologist J. J. Gibson. His strategy was to take infants and get them to crawl towards what he termed a "visual cliff." This consisted of a sheet of strong glass placed across a kind of trench or ditch in the laboratory, the bottom of which was lined with a chequer

pattern. The children were tempted to cross the trench to come to their mother, this of course involving their venturing out over the glass sheet. Adults might naturally hesitate slightly, pondering perhaps the strength of the glass and the depth of the pit below it. Young babies would of course know nothing of the fragile nature of glass so should not be worried by that. Nor, if they were not equipped with proper pattern recognition mechanisms, should they be able to appreciate the "depth" of the pit or the nature of the visual "cliff" they would have to cross. Gibson found, however, that all children showed exceptional caution when reaching the "cliff" point, and many could not be tempted into apparently empty space. Common sense? Perhaps, but either they have the perceptual mechanism or they don't, and in this case it looks as though the perception of depth, and even some kind of appreciation of the gradients involved in the cliff were at least present in the babies capable of crawling. Does this contradict the work of Von Senden? Not necessarily—perhaps certain vital things (such as the ability to recognise a steep slope) are "instinctive" in humans, while matters such as the perception of patterns like faces, triangles, squares, etc., need to be learned.

(f) The Building Blocks of Perception.

To this point we have been considering (i) how the information is fed into the brain; and (ii) the evidence for the fact that dynamic integrating forces act on this information to mould it in specialised ways. We must now try to consider how this processing might take place. In other words what actually happens inside the brain when a particular pattern or shape is recognised?

Investigation of Individual Nerve Cells.

To get some insight into this we need to take a closer look at one of the latest techniques for studying the brain which we referred to earlier and which is known as microelectrode recording. The principle here is to insert an exceptionally fine electrode into the cortex of an anaesthetised animal, endeavour to place it against the body of a single neural cell and then, via a suitable amplifying system, record the pattern of electrical activity given off by the cell. This technique, which was developed in the 1950s, represents a significant advance over that of electroencephalography (the recording of brain waves from outside the head) inasmuch as instead of being faced with a rather vague pool of electrical activity, possibly coming from numerous cerebral sources, one is able to study the responses of what must surely be the brain's fundamental unit, the neural cell. Studied in this way the activity of a single cell is very interesting. Firstly cells appear to have no period of total inactivity—whether the creature is sleeping or waking and whether stimulated or not, single cells keep up a steady, periodic burst of firing at an average frequency of one burst every few seconds. This has acquired the name of "spontaneous activity," which is another way for saying that psychologists and physiologists don't know what causes it. In the normal, living brain therefore, even when the creature is in a totally relaxed state, millions of cells are bursting periodically into action, a continuous background of electrical noise. This presumably signals the presence of life itself for only with the death of the individual do the brain's cells cease their restless firing. When the animal is stimulated in some way, by light, noise, heat, cold, etc., then measurable changes take place. If the stimulus is visual, cells in the visual cortex of the brain burst into life, while those in areas subserving other senses remain at their spontaneous level. Introduce auditory stimuli, or mixtures of other stimuli and cells perk up in the appropriate areas of the brain. All this is very much as one might expect, backing up our knowledge that different sections of the cortex handle different tasks. But can one focus down rather more sharply? What happens if one studies the behaviour of cells within only one area of the cortex when different stimuli mediated by the same sense are fed in?

This experiment was first performed by the American physiologists, Hubel and Wiesel, with remarkable results. First, they located a cell in the visual cortex of the cat and began to record the output from it when the cat was shown a variety of visual patterns. At first the cell merely exhibited the normal background firing, but when the cat was shown a luminous vertical line, the cell suddenly burst into frenzied life. In the meanwhile other cells in different parts of the visual cortex continued with only background firing. When the vertical bar was slowly rotated so that it was tilted on to the diagonal, the first cell gradually relapsed into background firing but in the meanwhile, another cell began to increase its firing rate. This too "switched off" when the bar was rotated again to a new angle, while yet another cell sprang to life. In this way Hubel and Wiesel, in a memorable series of experiments in the 50s and 60s, began to systematically plot the cat's visual cortex, noting over and over again the fact that individual cells seemed to be specially "labelled" to respond only to specific stimuli. The same applied to cells in the auditory cortex and even—though these were much harder to track down—in other sensory areas. In homely terms what the two Americans had done was to isolate the building blocks of perception, the terminal points in the brain where information being fed in was categorised or classified and where the amazing process of pattern recognition was actually taking place. Similar experiments were soon being performed with a variety of animal species, and also with a range of ages from the infant animal to the totally mature. Here again evidence seemed to imply that with animals higher up the phylogenetic scale, these "perceptual units" tended to be learnt rather than built in, for they were rarely present in the very young animal or the mature animal which had been experimentally deprived of normal environment.

Recent Experiments on the Human Perceptual System.

All this tells one a good deal about the animal brain, but can one make the bald assumption that a recognition system of this kind exists in humans as well? Microelectrode recording with living humans is probably out, except in certain rare surgical cases, so one might expect this to remain an academic question for all time. However, by one of those happy chances which favour scientists from time to time, some recent experiments performed in England suggest that the human perceptual system *does* work along lines similar to that of the animals. These experiments involve a technique which has the rather daunting name of the "stabilised retinal image," but which is a good deal simpler than it sounds at first.

To see the significance of this one needs first to appreciate the relationship between movements of the eyes and the image projected on to the retina. Looking directly at a pattern of some kind, as we have learnt, leads to an image being focused on the retina at the back of the eye, much as an image is projected on to the film at the back of a camera. Now, suppose that the pattern, instead of remaining stationary, moves across the visual field, then clearly the image moves correspondingly across the retina. Conversely, if the object remains fixed, but one moves one's eyes, then the image is again displaced across the retina. Well, what happens if the object remains absolutely stationary and one keeps one's eyes fixed carefully on it? Does the projected image then lock solidly on to the retina? The answer is actually, no, but for no reason more peculiar than that it happens to be physically impossible to keep one's eyes absolutely still. No matter how hard one tries, the eyes continue to move in a fine, trembling motion, barely detectable without specialised instruments. Inevitably the image of any object in the visual field trembles rapidly on the retina at the same time. This might seem to make vision rather imprecise and blurry, but for reasons we haven't the space to go into, this tremor actually serves to *improve* vision—in particular the kind of super-detailed vision which allows us to see minute specks or very fine lines such as spiders' cobwebs. For some time psychologists have been curious about what would

happen to vision if these fine eye movements did not exist, but since they are quite involuntary and automatic the task seemed pretty hopeless. Then someone—the physicist R. W. Ditchburn—had the bright idea of tackling the problem from a different viewpoint. He simply wore a contact lens (which of course acts like a new outer layer to the eye) with a short stalk sticking out of the front of it. On the end of this stalk he fastened a little photograph and a lens to focus the image sharply on the retina. By this trick he had effectively cut out the effect of all movement made by the eye, great or small, because wherever the eye moved now, so the contact lens followed it, and the stalk and photograph followed it too. If you think for a moment you will realise that this means that the projected image of the pattern remains in one position on the retina—the stabilised retinal image. (If you find this difficult to visualise, try sketching the system on a bit of paper—eye, contact lens, stalk, pattern, and of course image on the retina. The logic will immediately be apparent.)

With this system Ditchburn made two very interesting observations. Firstly, the "stabilised" pattern disappeared, thus suggesting that the fine eye movements were essential to visual perception. Secondly, he reported that when a pattern disappeared it frequently did so *in part*, rather than washing out as a whole as one would rather expect. Furthermore, the parts that came and went tended to be neat, even sections of a pattern. For example, a cross would alternate between the vertical and horizontal bars, a triangle would break up into one or other of its three sides, etc. A number of experiments have since been performed with human subjects using this ingenious and unusual apparatus, with results which suggest to psychologists that they are dealing with the same kind of perceptual units Hubel and Wiesel found in the cat. The tendency of the lines to appear and disappear as units when viewed as stabilised images seems to imply that basic "line units" are also present in the human brain—the building blocks of perception again.

It so happens that these fascinating fragmentation effects can be observed by a simple experimental method which does not involve wearing specially fitted contact lenses. You will recall that we spoke earlier of after-images, which are temporary changes in the state of the retina caused by a bright light and these are, of course, perfectly stabilised images since they are part of the retina itself. To observe them oneself the best trick is to sit in a rather dark room and stare at the window-frame against the bright sky outside. Do this, keeping one eye closed and the other as still as you can manage, for about thirty seconds. Then close both eyes and *keep them closed*. After a second or so you will see a vivid after-image of the cross-pieces of the window frame and you will note that the vertical and horizontal bars of which it is composed come and go independently of each other. This is something far more than a trick incidentally—as you do it you will be watching your own brain at work processing the pattern locked on to the retina.

We have spent a good deal of time on vision and visual perception because (a) it is easily the most important of the sensory channels, and (b) because it is the area of perception best charted by psychologists and physiologists. We will now take a less detailed look at the other senses.

(g) The Ear.

The eyes, as we have learnt, are equipped to detect visual radiations within a fantastically fine range of wavelength—less than a thousandth of a millimetre. From the brain's point of view this takes care of a good slab of some of the most important sources of energy and radiation within the universe, but a brain equipped only with eyes would be "blind" to a good deal of important information. Therefore we find a complete set of specialised receptors handling other areas of interest, of which by far the most important are the ears. These are tuned to pick up waves and vibrations too, but of air waves rather than light, and in an entirely different range. The absolute spectrum to which the human ear responds is between 20 and 15–18,000 Hz (waves per second), with a peak sensitivity between about 1,000 and 6,000 Hz. All sounds we can hear, therefore, consist ultimately of vibrations of the air occurring within this frequency range, and in the case of human speech we are dealing with a complex pattern of such vibrations. The ear's method of detecting these and translating them into an electrical code is ingenious and enormously efficient.

Auditory Perception.

The process begins with the outer ears (the flaps of skin on the side of your head!) which serve to catch sound waves coming from the most important direction, which in the case of human beings is in front of them. The importance of these directional indicators is considerable and you can note how strikingly you can change your own auditory perception by flexing the ears with your hand, or cupping your hands so that the "directional indicators" point backwards. Once channelled into the innards of the system, the sound waves are forced down an ever-narrowing tube where they come up against something called the tympanic membrane which is better known as the eardrum. Popular belief seems to be that the auditory process stops here, but from what you have learnt already you can work out that there will need to be much more than this. The translation of the physical vibration of the eardrum into electrical signals will have to take place. In fact the vibrating drum itself sets into motion a beautiful percussive machine in miniature, three tiny and elegant bones known as the hammer, anvil, and stirrup, which carry the message deeper into the ear where they come up against yet another "drum." This is the gateway to a spiral tube called the cochlea, which is filled with a densely packed fluid, and the walls of which are lined with hundreds of thousands of tiny hairs. As the last of the bones in the tiny percussive link beats up against the fluid inside the cochlea, it sets up a series of rapid shock waves which in turn induce complex patterns and rhythms of movement in the hairs linking the cochlear wall—rather like the shifting waves of motion that the sea induces in forests of sea-weeds, only on a faster time-scale. These hairs are themselves hooked up to auditory nerve cells and in some way, at present uncertain to psychologists and physiologists, specific movements of the hairs tend to activate specific cells, the end product being that a series of complex but significantly different patterns of electrical activity make their way up the brain. Here the auditory centres get down to the business of interpreting these electrical signals into "meaningful" sounds.

Thinking of the immense sensitivity of the hairs in the cochlear fluid, it may have occurred to you that it ought to be possible to set them in motion by almost any kind of external vibration—and thus hear without vibrating air waves having moved into the ear. This is quite true. Sound waves can be transmitted through other media than air, including bone, and thus even if the ears are blocked one can hear certain sounds remarkably well. Try it for yourself and you will note that the quality of your hearing changes markedly —your own voice, for example, will sound deeper and barely less loud, yet if you whisper you will not hear yourself at all. The reason for this is that with ears blocked, the sound is being propagated to the cochlea by bone conduction and this acts as a filter, cutting out the high-frequency components almost totally but letting in the lower notes without too much trouble. This is why earplugs are disappointingly ineffective.

This is probably enough about the ear which, if the truth is known, is rather less well understood by psychologists than the eye. Only one major point might be briefly touched on. Why do we have two ears rather than, say, one large one at the top of our head? The answer is that a binaural system allows us to locate sounds rather better; slight differences in the time it takes for sounds to reach each ear (as when one ear is slightly closer to a sound source) cause fractional delays in the arrival of the respective signals to the brain—enough for the magnificent computer there to deduce the sound source's rough location.

(h) Smell, Taste, and Touch.

Olfaction.

Of the remaining three senses, only one is concerned with detecting objects at a distance after the fashion of vision and audition. This is olfaction or, as we generally call it, the sense of smell. Olfaction is particularly interesting because it is concerned with the detection of chemical substances in the air, rather than with wave or vibration analysis. Animals of all kinds make much use of their ability to recognise the chemical changes taking place in plants, other animals, etc., which serve to indicate "good" (*i.e.* necessary for survival) or "bad" (*i.e.* dangerous) objects. These may range from the sweet smell of edible fruit, the characteristic odour of a mate in a sexually receptive state, or the nauseous smell of rotting flesh, riddled with dangerous bacteria. Unlike vision and audition, the olfactory sense mechanism is relatively simple in form, consisting of two small patches of cells situated rather high up in the nasal passages and not in the main line of breathing. This accounts for the animal habit of sniffing to detect smells better, the sniff being a method of pushing air up into the rather inaccessible smell receptors. As with pretty well everything else in the body the olfactory receptors are specialised nerve cells, immune of course to light or air vibration, but incredibly quick to react to a wide range of airborne molecules. The presence of particular molecules on a receptor causes a chemical change to take place in the cell, this in turn inducing an electrical signal to pass up the olfactory nerve. Psychologists have not spent too much time on this sense for it seems to be of relatively low importance to modern man, but have pondered the interesting question as to just how many different kinds of smells human beings can detect. You might try to think about this for yourself and before you say hundreds, you should realise that most smells, like most colours, are complex mixtures of a relatively small number of primaries. There is, as it happens, no definite agreement as there is on the seven colours of the visual spectrum, but an early classification by the psychologist Findley in 1924 has probably not been bettered. His "smell prism" listed six primaries which you may like to compare with your own choice. Each smell is identified with a substance which Findley thought was a typical generator of the odour. (1) fragrant (oil of jasmine), (2) etherial (oil of lemon), (3) resinous (turpentine), (4) spicy (cinnamon), (5) putrid (hydrogen sulphide or rotten eggs) and (6) burned (oil of tar).

Taste.

We now move from the distance senses to the so-called "proprioceptors" which is the name psychologists give to the senses concerned with the detection of things actually in contact with the body. Although it is not classed in this way the logical one to look at next is taste, which has much more in common with smell than most people imagine. Taste in itself is a rather feeble sense, mediated by a number of chemically sensitive receptors on the back and sides of the tongue, and the relative overemphasis of its importance is due to the fact that when people talk about great subtleties of taste they are generally talking about great subtleties of smell, for the latter is vital in any gastronomic treat. The simplest test of this is to sample some particularly good tasting substance, savour its flavour and then hold one's nose. The reduction in taste is dramatic, and one can soon realise how a bad head cold can have such drastic effects on the enjoyment of food and drink. One other remarkable feature of the sense of taste is how quickly it adapts out— a drink which tastes sweet or sour at the first taste, slips into bland neutrality before the glass is emptied. This is another experiment the reader can surprise himself with, particularly if he holds his nose while drinking, thus eliminating the vital smell component. The classification of tastes is somewhat easier it seems than that of smell, with most psychologists settling for four primaries, with which you will probably find yourself agreeing—sour, salt, sweet, and bitter. Anyway the plain fact is that the gustatory sense is a very limited tool in mankind's sensory workshop and poses few experimental questions.

Touch and Sensitivity to Pain.

The remaining sense, that of touch, includes under its heading a good deal of sub-senses such as the detection of pressure, heat, cold, and the highly enigmatic pain. Pressure, heat, and cold are fairly well-understood, probably being mediated by a number of different types of specialised cells embedded in the skin. Much controversy surrounds the number of different types of receptors involved and the matter is complicated by the fact that no one has positively identified a "pain" receptor—*i.e.* one which fires only when a potentially dangerous stimulus contacts the body. An early view held that pain was simply the signal the brain received when any kind of stimulus was excessive, but for a number of reasons this will not do. There are also some peculiar factors such as the observation that it is not all that easy for a person, without any other cues, to tell the difference between hot and cold objects. Immersing a finger in icy cold water and in very hot water briefly provokes a generally unpleasant sensation, but it is hard to tell with the eyes closed and without prior knowledge which end of the temperature spectrum is being experienced. Pain itself, the scourge of mankind (and yet his saviour in cases where it keeps him out of danger) is an incredibly mysterious phenomenon and we will not be able to say much about it here except to point out that much of its operation is determined by processes going on in the brain rather than in peripheral parts of the body. Human sensitivity to pain also varies enormously. Among certain rather neurotic people intense pain may be felt at relatively minor physical afflictions, while other people may bear (or learn to bear?) what would generally be accounted as gross physical discomfort with equanimity. The action of pain-killing or analgesic drugs is also very poorly understood. Some recent exciting studies by the physiologist, P. D. Wall, suggest however that we may be on the edge of a major advance in our understanding of pain. He has shown that in certain cases of otherwise intractable pain —following, say, serious limb injury—great relief can be achieved by the electrical stimulation of certain "inhibiting nerves" *in the site of the wound itself.* This is not counter irritation but somehow bringing into action a "damping" or inhibiting system which in the area of the wound had ceased to function properly. In extraordinary experiments patients have been taught literally to switch off their pain by stimulating these inhibitory nerves with a small electrical device at the side of their bed. Other experiments along these lines are presently taking place in various parts of the world, and brain scientists are watching their outcome with the greatest interest.

(i) **Are there any Other Senses?**

If we take pleasure and pain as separate senses, which might seem reasonable, then even forgetting about all other possible sub-divisions of sensory detection the traditional five senses are not enough. Most psychologists, however, are content with the traditional categorisation. One important area not particularly well covered by the present human sensory range is that of high energy radiation beyond the ultra-violet. It so happens that until quite recently few living things came much into contact with radiation of this kind—the odd cosmic particles bursting through the earth's envelope of air, while dangerous, are too rare to be worth developing special receptors for. Within the past century, however, man has begun to work regularly with high-energy radiation sources and has suffered a good deal as a consequence. X-rays, for example, were grossly misused in the early days after their discovery, and similarly numerous deaths have been caused by the misapplication of nuclear fission devices. The problem is simply that although the radiation

is doing our body mortal harm, we expose ourselves to it because we are not equipped with "radiation detectors" to warn us. Once the pain arising from tissue damage arrives—it may take decades for the damage to become apparent—it is too late to do anything about the original stimulus. This apparent digression is merely to remind one of the tremendous role the senses play in our lives, and how brief our span of life in this dangerous universe would be without them. But what of other senses? A frequently used term is that of the "sixth sense," and many people believe that humans and animals are equipped with some other major sense which allows the creature either to detect some danger at a vast distance— way beyond the range of vision or audition—or alternatively to allow one mind to communicate with another mind. We discuss this problem briefly in the section on Ideas and Beliefs, but it also has a place here since many people believe that the study of extra-sensory perception is a legitimate branch of modern psychology. The first argument against the idea of ESP (you may not feel it is particularly convincing) is that no one has been able to detect any mechanism in any part of the brain which could possibly be transmitting or receiving the messages conveyed by the sixth sense. Believers in ESP reply (a) that one might be discovered at any time, and (b) that perhaps no transmitter or receiver is necessary anyhow. The first point is of course irrefutable, but the second raises a different question and suggests that whatever mind-to-mind contact is, it cannot be looked on in the way we have been attempting to look at either sensation or its necessary complement, perception. There is an even more cogent argument, however, which the vast majority of psychologists today adopt—that there is simply no experimental evidence for the existence of telepathy anyhow. In this case it is quite unnecessary to start looking for mechanisms to mediate it. In experiments conducted to sort out the ESP controversy, psychologists *have* found that people are very much better at gathering information from each other without the use of speech than had hitherto been realised. Tiny changes in facial expression, nervous movements, shifts of eyes, even long periods of unusual silence can all serve to give the trained observer important clues as to what is going on in another person's head. Fortune tellers, detectives, and expert card players have known this for years and are only too aware that they are getting their information by clever and insightful use of their normal senses, but rely on other people's ignorance of just how good these mechanisms really are.

(j) **Sensory Deprivation.**

Any individual, human or animal, born without a reasonably complete complement of senses would almost certainly be doomed to an early death or a life of relying on other humans for assistance. A few startling souls, such as the late Helen Keller, fought their way out of the solitude of total blindness and deafness to lead full and useful lives, but these are golden exceptions to a fairly inflexible rule. Miss Keller in her autobiography tells of her gradually emerging realisation that the universe consisted of "other things" outside herself and states that it was only through an understanding of this that she began to form the concept of herself as an individual personality. This serves to reinforce the point of view stressed by modern psychology that the individual is a mesh between himself and his environment. True personality has no reality without constant and evolving interplay with the external world. But what would be the effect on the normal personality of inducing enforced perceptual isolation? In the early 1950s, as scientists began to see that man would soon be able to make voyages into space, the psychologists began to ponder how well human beings could stand up to the physical and psychological isolation of a space capsule. Man is gregarious, naturally at ease among his fellows, and tends to become eccentric and unbalanced when separated from other humans for any length of time. What, they asked, would be the effect of the extended and rather dramatic isolation imposed on the astronauts of the future? To test this a number of experiments were set up in which people were isolated in sealed chambers under conditions of greatly reduced sensory input for lengthy periods. Initial studies seemed to show that the experience was unexpectedly unpleasant, and, sensing that they were on to something significant, psychologists at McGill University in Montreal, where the pioneering work was done, decided to tighten up their experimental situation. Students were hired at the relatively princely sum (for students) of a dollar an hour and told that they could spend as many hours in isolation as they pleased. They were then placed in stuffed clothing rather like divers' suits, and lowered into chambers of water maintained at body temperature. The helmets of their suits were lightproof and the chamber was sealed and covered to be soundproof. The outcome of all this was that even if the student made a body movement he would feel no apparent response as his body, encased in the bulky clothing, would merely float around in the unresisting water. External vision and sound being eliminated, and with ears plugged to prevent him hearing his own breathing, the subject was in a state of almost total sensory deprivation. His only link with the outside world was a "panic button," which he could press to alert the experimenters if for some reason he wanted to terminate the experiment. What did the psychologists expect? That most students would like nothing better than to do nothing for weeks on end and get paid a solid wage for doing so? The results surprised everyone. Most subjects had had more than enough after only a few hours, and only one stuck it out for more than a day and he suffered a neurotic hangover for his pains. For human beings, total isolation from sensory input is evidently one of the most unpleasant experiences imaginable.

The experiments caused a surge of controversy and a good deal of speculation as to what the results implied. The students' principal objection was that they became oppressed with vivid and bizarre hallucinations, both visual and auditory, apparently comparable in strength and unpleasantness to the hallucinations reported by alcoholics suffering from *delirium tremens* or (more fashionable today) the worst excesses of an LSD trip. These vanished as soon as the subject was removed from the chamber and apparently did not occur again. The first hypothesis advanced was interesting—that living things have a hunger or need for sensory input, comparable to, but of greater strength than, the need for food. Furthermore, when the sensory appetite was not assuaged, the brain began in desperation to create its own sensory material, hence the hallucinations. This hypothesis was unchallenged at first, but an alternative point of view has recently been put forward based on the recent discoveries in the field of sleep and dream research. Many psychologists now believe that humans need to dream and that one of the principal functions of sleep is to allow our brains to undergo a kind of sort-out of the programmes which control the central computer. In this view the hallucinations occurring during sensory deprivation would really be an example of the individual dreaming *while he was awake*, the subject's brain having been fooled into "thinking" that it was asleep by the sharp reduction in sensory input which had occurred. For various reasons the human brain carefully keeps the important process of dreaming separate from the waking state and there is some suggestion that to fully experience our dreams would be a psychologically intolerable experience. If this is correct then the McGill experiments and their successors show not a need for sensory input with consequent hallucinations to feed the sensory appetite, but rather the effects of allowing human beings a glimpse of the "inner space" of their minds. Similarly, incidentally, one can look upon both the LSD trip and the alcoholic hallucinations as examples of the same process occurring—except that the tripper has stimulated his dreaming mechanism into action through the drug, while in the case of the alcoholic, his excessive intake of alcohol has led to an inhibition of the normal dream process which bursts into activity when he is awake. Whatever the explanation for the strange experiences of the isolated students, there is no doubt that the human being is not psychologically equipped to face up to total loss of sensory

inflow for any sustained period. The adventures of the astronaut have in fact taken place in relatively richly-endowed sensory environments and so the expected problems have not arisen. But what of space voyages lasting for months, or even years?

(k) The Problem of Attention.

We have now really finished with the senses and perception as such, but before moving on to our section on Learning and Information storage, we need to think a little bit about the problems which are posed by the great influx of information to the brain, how it sets about coping with this and how it assigns priorities to the multitude of signals it is faced with. This involves the process which we know as Attention. To get some idea of the task facing the brain, let us take up another simple analogy, even if it isn't 100 per cent accurate to the purist's eye.

The brain can be likened to a complex communications centre, sorting vital information, rather like an air traffic control at an international airport. Information floods in from various sources, with the controller paying attention to the scene through the windows, to radio calls, to messages coming by teleprinter and by hand, etc. One way to sort out the muddle might to be assign one mode of messages to one controller, the second to another, etc., but the problem of co-ordination remains. At some stage the senior controller must select which set of signals he is to work on, switching when appropriate to other sets, and issuing instructions to the aircraft waiting to take off and land. Now there are two ways in which he might select the information. The first would be to cut off the unwanted signals at his desk by refusing to allow the stimuli to reach him, a strategy which might lead to a jam of information such as messengers, bits of paper, telephones off the hook, etc., cluttering up the control room. A second strategy would be to staunch the flow of information in the unwanted channels closer to their source, in this case at the point where they first come into the control tower. Real air traffic centres, fortunately, never get into the kind of muddle we are implying here, and nor, in most cases, does the brain. But which of the above strategies is the closest to that adopted by the brain in attending to one particular set out of a vast pool of competitive information? Until about 10 years ago psychologists tended to favour the idea that the first of the two systems was in operation with every sensory stimulus making its way to the brain to contribute to some great tangle in need of constant sorting out. Confusion and uncertainty under stress were considered to be an example of the tangle getting momentarily too complicated.

This view has now been largely rejected thanks to some brilliant experiments by the outstanding young Mexican psychologist, Raul Hernandez-Peon, who was later tragically killed in a car crash. Hernandez-Peon's experiment, which many people consider to be the first big breakthrough in the psychological study of attention, was performed first on that most useful of laboratory animals, the cat, but later repeated on other creatures. The first stage was to implant a microelectrode into the cat's brain, specifically in an area known as the cochlear nucleus. You will recall the word cochlea from our section on audition, as being the seat of the translation of the incoming sound waves into electrical signals. Now the cochlear nucleus is the first major junction box at which auditory signals meet before beginning their ascent to the brain. Prior to this there is only the network of neurones springing directly from the tiny hairs in the cochlea itself. By attaching the electrode to an amplifier and looking at the output on a TV screen, the experimenter could watch the electrical impulses from the ear as they passed through the big nucleus. The ticking of a metronome, for example, could be seen as a regular beat in time with the tick. Hernandez-Peon then set about trying to attract the cat's attention away from the metronome and did so by showing it a mouse. The cat, as predicted, gazed with interest at the mouse whereupon—the electrical signal indicating the still-ticking metronome vanished from the TV screen! This is odder than one thinks at first. Remember that the electrode was planted in the nucleus in the region of the ear, and yet the electrical signals were no longer passing this point. If the metronome was still ticking, then its sound waves should still be activating the ear and should still be trying to send their impulses up the auditory nerve. Clearly then, a gate was being closed not in the brain but right down at the level of the ear—the message to close it, however, presumably being sent down from the brain. How could this gate-shutting message get down to the ear? Evidently there must be neural fibres which send their messages downwards from brain to receptor and not just in the other direction as had hitherto been believed. These corticifugal fibres, as they are called, are now believed to run to other sensory areas, including the retina in animals and humans, and while they are very difficult to track down by anatomical analysis they are thought to serve a very important function. The facts of the case seem to be that Hernandez-Peon had discovered one of the basic mechanisms of attention, the ability of a creature to filter relevant from irrelevant information. Thanks to his work it now looks as though the brain prevents itself from having to face a muddle of conflicting information by cutting off the unwanted signals actually at the level of the receptor, thus preventing a press of confusing and irrelevant information from flooding in. Once attention shifts again, then the appropriate gates are opened and information flows as before. If this tells us something about the selective filtering of important as against useless information, does it also say something about the way a mother will be undisturbed in the night by the flight of a jet plane and yet wake to her child's slightest cry? Perhaps this is an area which mothers know more about than psychologists ever will.

III. LEARNING AND MEMORY.

(a) How is the Information Stored?

Earlier we discussed the specialist use of the word information that psychologists and other scientists employ and remarked how important it is for an understanding of current work on the brain that one rids oneself of the idea that information can only be conveyed in the form of spoken or written messages. We now need to consider the general problem of the *storage* of information, a concept fundamental to the interesting topics of learning and memory. Most people can readily accept the idea that a book is a store of verbal information as, in a different way, is a gramophone record. In reality in neither case are words actually stored. In books the information is held in the form of coded marks, called printing, which need to be decoded by the reader before he can understand the original message. Similarly in the case of the gramophone record the information, which might be the sound of a pop star singing, is coded into the form of a series of ridges on a plastic, the decoding being done by a needle plus amplifying equipment, speakers, etc. Using devices like books, films, and records, information can be held in store for very considerable periods of time, the original message sitting around more or less indefinitely until someone gets down to decoding it. Messages written on the walls of prehistoric caves by our dim and distant ancestors are still passing their information across today, and even the fossils we find in Cambrian rock formations are messages of a kind, though the senders did not consciously originate the signals. In essence then a message consists of an information source, some kind of transmitting medium and a receiver. There may also be a delay built in—storage—in which case some kind of encoding and decoding process will be added to get the message in and out of store. All this preamble leads us now to the point where, having in the previous section considered the information gathering and decoding processes in the brain, we can now consider its role as a storage device. Unlike books and records, which operate on fairly simple lines, the brain chooses immensely complicated and still rather mysterious techniques to do its job.

First, perhaps we should clear up a small point which otherwise will cause confusion—the fact that psychologists distinguish clearly between the two processes, learning and memory. In fact the distinction is simple, particularly in the light of the principles we have just been considering. Learning is the process of feeding information into store, and memory (or remembering) the process of extracting it once again. The next question is the really big one—in the case of the brain just how is this done?

Returning momentarily to gramophone records and books we can see that the process of information storage implies that the incoming signal has changed the state of the storage device, book, record, or whatever, in some way, either by covering it with marks, ridges, or, in the case of magnetic tape, altering the electrical properties of its surface. Something similar must happen in the brain. Information flows up from the receptors, is processed or interpreted by the perceptual mechanism, and then, depending upon circumstances, fed into some store where it is held until required. What kind of changes could be taking place in the neural circuitry of the brain to constitute the laying down of a memory? Psychologists have been divided on this question for decades, and there are three fairly separate competitive approaches. Without giving too much away we shall probably end up feeling that the true explanation will turn out to be some kind of mixture of all three. The three main suggestions can be summarised as (1) the neurological, (2) the biochemical, and (3) the electrical.

The first suggests that as information is fed in, causing certain patterns of brain cells to be activated, minor changes take place on the structure of these cells, modifying them in a rather gross, physical way. This would be similar in a sense to the changes that take place in the surface of a gramophone record when it is first made. The second argues that such gross changes are unlikely and that the storage must take the form of modification of the biochemical or even molecular structure of the brain, changes taking place *within* rather than on the surface of individual cells. The third view advances the hypothesis that since the brain is a mass of electrical energy, and electricity is the basis of neural activity, then the psychologist should look for changes in the electrical patterns of the brain as an index of the fact that something has been stored. We will look at each point of view in greater detail shortly, but first it will be useful to study the experimental evidence.

(b) Early Studies of Learning.

Experimental psychology started in the latter part of the 19th cent. largely as the result of pioneering work of the German physiologist and psychologist Wilhelm Wundt. No one today gets greatly excited at Wundt's experiments nor at his writings, but he was one of the first people in the world to realise that one could actually subject the raw material of mental activity to the experimental method and in this way he is memorable. Wundt concentrated on perception and similar topics and also conducted the first studies of reaction time—the delays humans make between being given the signal to start a task and actually beginning it. He had little to say about the matter of learning and memory, leaving it to a successor, Hermann Ebbinghaus, to get the ball rolling in this area.

Ebbinghaus's experiments were beautifully simple. He took human beings into his laboratory and set out to teach them lists of words, plotting the success rate (number of words in a sequence remembered) against the number of repetitions that had been given. This may all seem fright fully obvious, particularly when we say tha. Ebbinghaus found that the more repetitions, the better the list of words were learned. This is exactly what one would expect now, a century later, but at that time things weren't so clear cut. Furthermore, Ebbinghaus showed that when you plotted the rate of learning on a graph, a very characteristic curve emerged, common to all his normal subjects, which indicated a gentle improvement in learning with the first few repetitions of the list, followed in due course by a sharply accelerating rise which in turn tapered off. Finally a point came when the list was either completely learned, or no further improvement was made. The important factor was that while there were individual differences in the final level of achievement, and also in the time taken before the main surge of learning took place, the shape of the curve was very similar for all subjects. In other words, while there were significant differences in the ability of subjects to learn his word lists, the nature of the learning process seemed to be interestingly similar. Ebbinghaus's findings are as valid today as they were then and his learning curve fits rather well to the overall pattern of animal learning as well.

In his quest for objectivity he produced another interesting idea. It seemed to him that if one were to compare the performance of two different people in a learning task, one couldn't deduce much about their respective talents by examining the slope of the learning curve unless one knew something about their previous experience with the subject matter. For example, one person might, because of his job or something, simply have been more frequently exposed to the material featured and this would give him a built-in advantage which confused the issue. How about using foreign languages? Again Ebbinghaus felt that to get absolutely pure learning curves one would have to be certain that the subjects had not received prior exposure to the languages in question, a task almost impossible in principle. This led to his invention of a curious tool in the psychologist's workbox, the nonsense syllable, which is still used today as the standard material for many tests of learning ability. It consists of a word with a meaningful sound and look to it, but which is almost complete nonsense inasmuch as it has no obvious meaningful association. ZAT, BOK, FID, BIJ, HAB are a few examples of this strange vocabulary. Ebbinghaus-type experiments are, as you can believe, immensely boring to perform and subjects today normally have to be paid in order to persuade them to take part! However, his realisation that human learning processes could be brought into a real, if rather dull, laboratory setting was a big step forward. Furthermore he had realised the necessity of separating out performance in one task from the background of past experience, an idea which has had far-reaching consequences on the design of all psychological experiments since and which even touches on the important question of the interplay between heredity and environment which we shall look at in the final section.

(c) Learning Experiments with Animals.

The use of nonsense syllables gets over the problem of past experience in one limited area of experimental psychology only, and if one really wants to know something about the formation of the learning process from scratch then one either has to start with very young babies, or use laboratory animals. One psychologist went so far as to read aloud lengthy passages of Greek prose to his infant son at an age when the baby couldn't even understand English. Years later the psychologist gave his son, by now a young man, a number of passages of Greek prose to learn, among which were the sections the baby had previously heard. The outcome was that the sections to which the child had been exposed as a baby were found to be significantly easier than the fresh material. This odd and very tedious experiment has never been repeated, though it is generally rejected by psychologists today as having been imperfectly controlled. For example, who can say for certain what the young man had or had not learnt in the period between the two phases of the experiment? It nevertheless remains as one of a few heroic efforts to use young babies as subjects in learning experiments and it also highlights some of the great difficulties involved.

By the turn of the century more and more psychologists were beginning to follow the lead given by their physiological cousins in bringing animals into the research laboratory. One of the first and most important figures to do so was the American Edward Thorndike, who began to look at the behaviour of specially bred white rats in laboratory learning experiments. Now with humans the problem of how to get the subject to do what one wants him to—learn nonsense syllables or whatever—is met by simply speaking to him about it. With animals this won't work, so Thorndike decided that they would have to be rewarded in some way if they were to learn anything. Reward can be any one of a lot of things, and for an animal it can be getting out of a situation it doesn't like, such as some kind of maze or puzzle box in which a number of specific moves have to be made in sequence before it can get out. Thorndike found that most animals make strenuous and fairly determined efforts to get out of boxes, mazes, etc., and can follow a fairly elaborate sequence of moves in order to reach their goal. Rats, for example, will learn to press a series of levers in the right order if they will open the door to a box, and they will gradually get better and better with practice. Similarly, when placed in a complicated maze, provided they are rewarded with food or escape at the end, they will soon find their way round it. The crucial point here seemed to be the reward, and while pet owners have known for centuries that a piece of sugar presented at the proper time will make a pet do tricks, it is really not clear why it should. To say that it is because the animal "wants the sugar" is no explanation as to why this trick should be learnt rather than some other pattern of behaviour. But Thorndike found without doubt that an animal would learn a maze or similar task far better if it were rewarded in some way at the completion of the task, and he too couldn't see just why, in physiological terms, the neural events which made up the correct performance of the task should be "built in" simply because the animal was rewarded, while incorrect patterns of behaviour were rejected. Ebbinghaus had come to the conclusion that successful learning was a function of the number of times the task was repeated. Thorndike argued that while practice helped to make perfect, it needed something else as well—i.e. the successful completion of the act. How would one measure success? Well, getting out of a maze or finding sugar at the other end would presumably count, and Thorndike described this principle as the "Law of Effect," believing that he had discovered two factors necessary for learning to be successful (for the information to be placed into the store), one being *frequency*, the other being *effect*. Psychologists at the time carefully sidestepped the niggling question of how *effect* (something happening at the end of a sequence) could work back in time to establish the sequence in memory by arguing that the reward or reinforcement did not itself cause the sequence to be stored in the memory system. It simply made that sequence more likely to be called up on some future occasion. But, replied the critics, wouldn't that imply that all sequences were stored with both right and wrong behaviour lodged equally firmly in memory? This question is still being hotly debated today, and we will shortly be taking a look at the evidence concerning what is and isn't learnt in an experimental situation. But first a word about one of the most important concepts not only in modern psychology, but also in 20th cent. science—the conditioned reflex.

(d) Pavlov and the Conditioned Reflex.

The great Russian physiologist Pavlov reached the peak of his scientific genius in the early years following the Communist revolution in Russia, where his very physical approach to psychological phenomena found favour with his country's leaders. The reasons were ideological. To many it seemed that Pavlov could explain all behaviour in purely mechanistic terms and thus do away with mystical, metaphysical, and, to Communist thinking, totally out-of-date views of Man's nature. Pavlov, it was felt, was at last exorcising the Ghost out of the Machine. His findings in fact sent ripples across the world, and the face of psychology was changed by them—notably in injecting into it the realisation that a good psychologist must think like a physiologist at least as often as he thinks like a philosopher. On the other hand, his naïvely simple view of the machinery of mind and brain was bound sooner or later to be exposed as only partially adequate, missing many of the richly complicated facets of human behaviour which must be faced up to and not denied. What was Pavlov really saying? At rock bottom his ideas revolved around the notion of the conditioned reflex arc, a concept that all wishing to understand modern psychology must get clear in their minds sooner or later.

The experiments in question were exceedingly simple inasmuch as they confined an animal to a rather limited environment and studied its behaviour in the most fundamental kind of learning situation. Pavlov, who was enormously interested in gastric and salivary secretion, had noticed that some of the animals in his laboratory would respond to the presence of food with copious flows of saliva, while others would not. Some would even respond excitedly when a particular food pan appeared while others again would not. He reasoned that these differences were in some way a function of the particular animal's past experience and set out to study this in detail. Firstly, he devised a method of measuring saliva flow, which would normally be copious when an animal was presented with its food bowl. He then introduced, just prior to the presentation of the food, a buzzer, bell, light, or some other similar stimulus. Initially the preliminary stimulus would yield no salivary response, but after a while, provided that the pairing of the presentations was kept up, the first traces of saliva would begin to appear upon the sound of the bell. If this were reliably followed by food, soon the saliva would appear in full flood to bell alone. Failure to offer up the food, however, if persistent, would lead to a gradual falling off in the amount of saliva until it ultimately dwindled away. Pavlov declared that this must imply that a probably instinctive reflex—salivating to food—had become linked in neural terms with a stimulus which had at first been totally irrelevant, the sounding of a bell. The more frequently the two events were linked and the more closely they were associated in time, the stronger the new reflex arc would be. Lack of association between bell and food would lead to the extinction of the reflex arc. The fact that extinction was not total could be nicely shown by introducing the food again, whereupon things would come rapidly back to normal with the bell producing copious flows of saliva once more. Today this seems a fairly trivial observation, but at the time Pavlov, his co-workers, and psychologists all over the world became immensely excited about the conditioned reflex. The reason was that there seemed to be no reason in principle why the whole of an animal's behavioural responses had not been acquired in just this simple way with the same argument applying with equal force to humans. At the root of all behaviour lay a simple physiological principle. By employing this properly, all living things could have their behaviour patterns moulded in whatever direction was felt to be appropriate, all psychological malfunctions could be corrected, education made simple, the wild beast tamed, the workings of the brain fully described and comprehended. This, for a brief period, was the golden goal (if one likes to think of it in that way) of the new science of psychology—to see man for what he really was: a complex mass of inherited and conditioned reflex arcs.

If Pavlov and his followers in Russia clung to this dream for decades longer than did less politically committed scientists in other parts of the world, then this is understandable. One of the goals of scientific endeavour is simplification and an explanation of human behaviour in terms of stimulus-response units would certainly meet part of that goal. But on the other hand part of the goal of science is also objectivity—even at the risk of complicating explanations—and before long it became obvious that the animal in the experimental Pavlovian set up was *not* behaving as a complicated automaton. For example, it is possible to condition an animal to lift its foot to avoid an electric shock if a bell reliably signals the imminence of the shock. Now place the animal on its side, ring the bell and—will the animal lift its foot? Yes—but not before getting up to the standing position first. But if the animal is blindly responding to the firing of a neuro-muscular reflex arc, why does it not simply raise its foot while lying down? And how does the standing up act become incorporated into the

reflex sequence without prior training? Such experiments were simply discounted at first as being too inconvenient for the theory, but as time went on the immense oversimplification of the stimulus-response theory of behaviour became obvious. But not before a major movement sprang up in the United States which attempted to make dynamic and imaginative use of Pavlov's findings in an attempt at an all-embracing psychological theory. We now turn to look at this, the so-called Behaviourist School.

(e) The Rise of Behaviourism.

Sometime before Pavlov's ideas began to have impact in the West, a spontaneous movement had been developing among psychologists to reject the traditional methods of introspection in experimental research. The interplay of conscious thought and mental activity was felt inevitably to confuse the issue, and workers were urged wherever possible to make objective rather than subjective judgments. One of the hardest advocates of this line was J. B. Watson, who even went so far as to argue that introspective studies of consciousness, etc., were not merely misleading, but positively useless. In principle, Watson proposed, it should be possible to give a total explanation of the subject matter of psychology—whether human or animal—in descriptive, mechanical terms concerning the outward manifestations of behaviour. This implied ultimately taking such extreme points of view as declaring thinking to be merely "sub-verbal speaking," better described in terms of minor twitches of the throat, mouth, and tongue muscles than in patterns of electrical activity in the higher centres of the brain. All that was needed to give the Behaviourist school impetus was Pavlov's discovery of the conditioned reflex, and when this was published it was eagerly incorporated as the prop of Watson's argument. To Watson and his colleagues the only realistic and profitable way to look at human and animal behaviour was in terms of a strictly mechanistic model, the conditioned reflex arcs serving as the vital links in the creature's chain of activity. Now many people might agree that an animal in a highly restricted laboratory situation, trained to salivate to bells, raise its paw to avoid an electric shock, etc., might well be coming as close to a biological machine as one could imagine, but was this a really adequate way of describing its behaviour "in the wild"? Critics of Behaviourism were quick to point out certain peculiarities that they felt could not be handled by Watson's simple system. Take a dog, for example, and face it with a series of doors, behind one of which is to be found food, sometimes one door, sometimes another. Now train the dog to respond to a light switched on briefly as signalling food. Now indicate the door which has food by switching on a light above it, and the dog will soon learn to trot up reliably to the appropriate door. What has happened? Easy, say the Behaviourists —the dog has been conditioned to approach a light for food, and the reflex carries over to a light above a door. The dog is not really responding to the door, but to the light which sets the appropriate reflex arc in motion, just as pushing a button can cause a car to start. But what, the critics argued, about the fact that the light is switched on for only a few seconds, and yet even after it is off the dog still moves towards the door? Watson replied that the light caused the animal to look towards the door and it immediately adopted a particular posture, setting its musculature up so that it would set off in the appropriate direction, no longer needing the light for a guide. This might seem fair enough, but for the fact that if, just as the animal is about to set off for the door, you hold it, refusing to allow it to move, it still "shows interest" in the door. Furthermore, if you let go in five minutes time, the chances are that the animal will set off to the correct door—a bit long one would have thought for the reflex arc to have been maintained in suspended animation. Was it not simpler, Watson's critics replied, to face up to the fact that the animal was using the light as a signal and was holding the door in some mental form as a kind of goal to which it could make a delayed response if necessary? So adamant were the Behaviourists that all behaviour could be explained in terms of sequences of conditioned muscular movements that they strove to argue that even during the delay the animal was still maintaining a muscular posture—rather in the way that a hunting dog freezes to point to prey. Furthermore, Watson produced what he believed to be irrefutable evidence for the dominance of the muscular activity, even on a task as complex as learning to run a maze. In this rather cruel-sounding experiment he trained a whole lot of rats to find their way through a rather detailed maze. He then proceeded to eliminate by surgery all normal sensory equipment—eyes, ears, smell, etc., leaving only the kinaesthetic, or touch, sense. These grossly deprived animals nevertheless still managed to find their way through the maze, allowing him to conclude that in line with the conditioned-reflex notion, the animals were relying predominantly on a chain of muscle reflexes. For a brief period this dramatic experiment seemed to clinch the Behaviourist case. But then came a counter-experiment, even more drastic. A psychologist called Lashley repeated Watson's experiment, but this time also removed the sense of touch by spinal surgery. The wretched creatures even now managed to stagger through the maze—though they were certainly no longer equipped with proper muscular responses. Lashley, correctly, felt this dealt with the ultra-simple Behaviourist argument and that somehow or other the animals must be retaining some kind of general directional sense, a sort of "notion" as to where the exit lay. At about this time more attacks on Behaviourism came from a rival point of view—the Gestalt school. Watson himself shortly afterwards became involved in a sensational divorce case which forced him, in those less permissive times, to resign from academic life. He ended his brilliant career in, of all things, the advertising profession.

(f) Gestalt Psychologists and Learning.

With its emphasis on such ideas as "the whole is something more than the sum of its parts" and its insistence on the idea that the brain has dynamic organising powers which serve to modify input and intervene between stimulus and response, the Gestalt point of view was clearly about as far removed from the naïve Behaviourist viewpoint as was possible. One of the principal allies of the Gestaltists in its early days was K. S. Lashley, referred to above, a brilliant experimentalist with an eye for the essentials of the problem. Throughout his long research life he remained open-minded about various schools of psychology and unconvinced on the various rival theories concerning the physiological basis of memory. He was, however, quick to see the basic weaknesses in the various brain models that fellow psychologists were always confidently erecting, and the first to feel the sharpness of his attack were the Behaviourists. Lashley swiftly realised that the attractive simplicity of the Pavlov/Watson argument was that the basic unit in learning consisted of a fundamentally simple physiological system, a neural reflex arc. In ordinary terms this could be looked on as a chain of cells connecting from, say, the retina through the higher centres of the brain (where the chain would be forged) down to the muscle or set of muscles which constituted motor output. In other words, a light would strike the retina, a number of cells would fire. These in turn would excite cortical cells which had, by prior conditioning, become linked into a reflex arc. Finally these would, quite mechanically, induce the appropriate muscular response. The memory itself constituted the connecting cells in the cortex, and this memory had been established by the learning or conditioning process. Lashley then realised that a memory unit, or an engram as he named it, must be represented by a particular set of cells in a particular part of the brain. In principle, therefore, one should be able to discover these sets of cells and find out what kind of memory is located in what part of the brain.

Lashley's technique was again that of surgical destruction of tissue and using this he performed one of the most remarkable experiments in the history of modern psychology and physiology. His findings created a shock of disbelief and con-troversy, and their full implications are still not fully understood today—over 50 years after he performed the experiment. Taking a large number of rats, he trained them until they were highly familiar with a complicated maze. He then proceeded to remove from each rat a small portion of cortical tissue, taking a different area but an equivalent amount from each rat. In due course he had removed from his collection of rats the equivalent of one complete brain, though no individual animal had had more than 5 per cent of its cortical tissue destroyed. He then took another set of rats, trained them in the maze, and again removed the equivalent of a brain, but this time taking 10 per cent from each rat. With a further sample he went through the procedure again, but removed a quarter of each rat's brain, and in his final group he had a limited number of animals, each of which had had half its cortex removed. See if you can work out what he found. Remember that if the memory or engram consisted of a series of linked cells then one might expect that these would be found in one relatively small segment of the brain. Interrupting the chain at any point should presumably destroy or grossly handicap memory. Now from the simple behaviourist point of view, most people would have to predict that one or two rats whose hunk of cortex removed had featured the conditioned reflexes involving the maze, would be completely clueless when placed in it. The engram would have been removed. This would then tell the experimenter, as Lashley had hoped, which part of the brain dealt with such tasks as maze learning. Other animals, who had not lost their maze engram would show no detriment in their performance of this task. To his amazement, and to everyone else's for that matter, Lashley found that his first group of rats, each of whom had lost about 5 per cent of cortical tissue, were apparently totally unaffected by the surgery, running the maze just as well as they did before! The rat with bigger chunks of tissue removed were slightly more affected, but even those with only half a brain left were still able to run the maze fairly competently. The loss of memory seemed to be somewhat proportional to the amount of tissue removed, but *not in any way to the area removed*! In other words, the mysterious engram did not seem to be located in any single spot, and Lashley was forced to conclude that it looked as though learning and memory were a function of the whole brain rather than just part of it.

As could be imagined, these findings were not well received by the conditioned reflex advocates and numerous attempts made to repeat them merely served to support these first findings. They were received enthusiastically by the Gestalt psychologists, who saw them as another example of their argument that the brain must be considered as an integrated whole and not as simply a bundle of conditioned reflexes.

The next strong—perhaps the strongest—anti-Behaviourist argument came from one of the Gestalt school founders, Wolfgang Kohler. His findings were disclosed in his important book, *The Mentality of Apes*, which can be bought in paperback and which everyone interested in psychology should read. Kohler, who was one of those clever scientists who manage to find themselves work in exotic parts of the world, conducted his critical experiments at the Primate Research Station in the Canary Islands. Here he watched with great interest the considerable learning skills of the higher apes, such as chimpanzees, and quickly arrived at the conclusion that conditioned reflex theory was not adequate to explain the scope of their intellectual behaviour. His most famous observation concerned the never-to-be-forgotten chimpanzee, Sultan. Kohler had noticed that chimpanzees will play about with sticks and similar devices in their cage, which they seem to use as toys. He then began to wonder whether the monkeys could ever be induced to use them as tools, so after placing potential implements inside Sultan's cage he then put a banana on the other side of the bars just outside its reach. After a bit of fruitless stretching the ape took one of the sticks and pulled the banana in. Now this in itself is a remarkable achievement, and if the ape had actually "worked out" the solution then it would have been suggestive of very much higher thought processes in the animal than had hitherto been believed possible. However, it could be reasonably argued that the chimpanzee had seen some other person or animal using the stick as a tool and was therefore merely imitating, an action which could, with a bit of latitude, be thought of in behaviouristic terms. Kohler's next step put paid to that point of view. He placed in the cage several sticks of various lengths which could be fitted together to form a longer one, and, taking care not to show this technique to the monkey, again set a banana outside the bars but out of reach of any one single stick. After scratching round fruitlessly with various sticks and making aggrieved noises, Sultan began to play rather aimlessly with the sticks, occasionally fitting them together by chance. Suddenly Kohler, who was watching, saw the chimpanzee fit two sticks together, stare at them for a moment and then, as if making a decision, walk rapidly to the side of the cage and with this new long pole pull the banana in. The moment of comprehension when the ape "realised" what he could do Kohler wittily termed the "ah-ha reflex," a phrase which sums up beautifully a sensation we all understand and which was totally unaccounted for by the Pavlovian approach to the problem.

(g) Later Developments in Learning Theory.

You may have the feeling that Behaviourism, conditioned reflex theory, and its attendant experimental studies are more or less worthless and a hindrance rather than a help to the development of modern psychology. This is far from the truth. The point is that despite its vigorous self-confidence and contempt for "introspective" approaches to psychology, Behaviourism really only falls down through its pretensions to providing a *complete* theory of mind and brain. The Behaviourist experiments still work, and there is undoubtedly such a thing as the conditioned reflex, though one has next to no idea, from the physiological point of view, how it is laid down. Throughought the 1930s and beyond, psychologists supporting the Behaviourist position performed thousands of ingenious and often highly imaginative experiments to back up their ideas, these always being subject to counter-attack from the opposition, most of whom were followers of the Gestalt school. For years arguments raged over Kohler's "insight" study with the chimpanzees, and became even hotter when experiments claiming to demonstrate "insight" in lesser creatures, such as rats, were performed. Gradually, under intense pressure, the Behaviourist hard-line softened, the pretence that animals were no more than bundles of totally automatic reflexes was quietly abandoned. Once this occurred, and the Behaviourist method was put to work studying the functioning of living systems, then experimental psychology was set for a boom. One of the most significant features of the conditioned-reflex method, as exemplified by Pavlov's original experiments, was its usefulness for examining the nature of animal perception. Offhand one might wonder how it could be possible to tell what an animal sees, or more exactly, how fine is its capacity for perceptual discrimination. How could one find out whether a rat could tell the difference between a triangle and a square and between one colour and another? One can ask humans, but rats ...? In the case of colours, what one could do would be to train the creature to respond to a red light, and then gradually alter its hue in the direction of another colour, say blue. If, before one had made much of a change in hue, the animal was ceasing to respond then one would know that it was detecting the change of hue. As for shape perception, the problem is even easier. In the very early days Pavlov conditioned his dogs to respond positively (*i.e.*, with saliva) to a circle, and negatively (*i.e.*, raising paw to avoid shock) when a rather angular ellipse was shown to it. Then he gradually made the circle more and more like an ellipse, and the ellipse more and more like a circle. Up to a point he got clear-cut appropriate responses, until the pattern lay somewhere in between. At this point the dog, poor creature, had a nervous breakdown, which wasn't too nice for it, but which told Pavlov a lot about its sensory and perceptual

processes. While on these slightly macabre topics it might be worth mentioning that today dogs and rats have largely been supplanted for behaviouristic studies by a rather quaint choice of animal—the pigeon. The fact is that pigeons have been found to have quite remarkable powers of sensory discrimination and will peck away at buttons to get food or avoid electric shocks for hours on end. So good is the pigeon at telling the difference between patterns that it was even once proposed for a fantastic rôle in modern warfare—not its traditional job of carrying messages from spies but, believe it or not, as the control centre for a flying bomb! In the early days of guided missiles the kind of electrical equipment available was too bulky, cumbersome and unreliable to be easily put into flying bombs. This was particularly true about the equipment necessary to allow the bomb to select the correct target at the other end. One bright psychologist argued that the pigeon would be an inexpensive, compact, and reliable "pilot" for a flying bomb. The device, complete with pigeon in a little cabin, could be launched off on course and when the bird spotted the target (say an enemy battleship) which it had been previously trained to recognise, it would peck at the appropriate button and that would be that! So far as one can tell the idea was never implemented, which is probably a good thing for us humans—to say nothing of the pigeons. The idea might be described as one of the less fruitful to come from Pavlov's original idea and serves to remind us that psychology, just as any other science, can be properly or improperly used, depending upon circumstances and the individuals involved. But let us now return to the basic question—what is the actual nature of the learning process or the memory trace?

(h) The Nature of the Engram.

Earlier we said that there were three broad approaches to the problem of the memory trace, the neurological, the electrical, and the biochemical.

(1) *The Neurological.*

This is probably the kind of model that Pavlov would put forward today if he were alive. To understand it, remember that the conditioned reflex is essentially a chain of cells running from sense organ to motor-output (finger, paw, eyeblink, whatever). The cells of course were there in the first place, built into the animal from birth. It is the connections between cells, the links in the chain that are forged in the learning process. Fine, but how *are* the connections formed? Why one chain rather than another? A number of attempts have been made to solve this one, perhaps the most ingenious in recent years coming from the Canadian psychologist D. O. Hebb, an architect incidentally of the sensory deprivation experiments, and one of the first psychologists to be elected as a Fellow of the Royal Society. Hebb had been impressed by the discovery that nerve cells were frequently adorned with tiny bumps or knobs which tended to cluster at the points where the cell made contact with other cells—the *synapse*. There was even some suggestion from microscopic studies that these synaptic knobs tended to become larger and more profuse in the brains of more mature animals. Suppose, Hebb argued, that when a nerve cell was fired, it made contact with another via a synaptic knob and thus triggered the second cell into action. Suppose also that each time a synapse was bridged via a contact knob, this knob grew a little, as though through exercise, and thus made better contact. This, as time went on, would significantly raise the likelihood of a nervous impulse crossing at this point. If one can imagine the process repeated with a whole series of cells, then one can see that repeated firings would also increase the likelihood of particular chains of cells being activated, thus wearing a kind of path through the nervous system down which the neural impulse would "prefer" to travel. This, Hebb suggested, could be the basis of the conditioned reflex—simply a connection made progressively easier each time the route was travelled.

Hebb's theory attracted a good deal of attention when it was first published over 20 years ago, first because it seemed to fit the known physiological facts (such as they were) and second because it seemed to get over one of the awful difficulties facing any neurological theory of learning—the experiments of Lashley. Recapping briefly, these showed that the memory trace or engram for a particular task was not located in any one small section of the brain. Now Hebb's synaptic knob model implied that the initial path followed by a nervous impulse might be pretty random throughout the cortex, wandering here and there until, with repeated firings, it became established. This would quite possibly be a rather straggly chain and not necessarily the shortest distance between two points. Add to this the fact that the acquisition of a complex habit, such as learning a maze, would obviously depend upon thousands, possibly hundreds of thousands, of these neural links being established, and one can begin to see that Lashley's experimental results no longer seem to fly in the face of reason. Removal of any single chunk of cortical tissue would simply serve to remove a more or less random selection of the neural chains serving as the maze-memory. The more one took out, the worse the memory of the maze would be, but no single piece removed would ever eliminate the whole of the memory! To many people Hebb's theory, crude though it might be, fairly tackles the apparent paradox of Lashley's results. Others are not so sure. Its main default, the intervening years have shown, is that his nice ideas about the growth of synaptic knobs and their significance as contact points between cells are probably no longer valid. Today their function, and even their existence in the form that Hebb discussed, is questioned by many physiologists. Furthermore, for various reasons, there has been a strong shift towards the point of view that whatever form the learning process takes it is unlikely to involve changes in neural tissue—at least of such magnitude. To many psychologists and their colleagues, changes in the molecular structure of the cell must be involved. Before considering the evidence for this hypothesis, we need to examine briefly the Gestalt psychologists' attempt to account for learning and memory.

(2) Electrical Field Theory.

We have been talking of the Gestalt psychologists without pointing out an interesting fact—that the two principal founders were first trained as physicists! Jumping the broad gap between physics and psychology might seem a bit much, but Wolfgang Kohler was one who did it, and in doing so he injected into his theorising some of the ideas basic to his native topic. In the main this involved the concepts of electrical field theory. Without going into this in boring detail, it so happens that an electrical source, either in the form of a battery, a current flowing down a wire or whatever, spouts electrons in its immediate neighbourhood and these constitute an electromagnetic field. As the name implies, the most striking example of such a field is to be seen in the ordinary common-or-garden magnet, and the structure of the field can be observed by placing the magnet in a large mass of iron filings. Now Kohler and his friends argued that the brain was a potent source of electromagnetic energy and ought, therefore, to create a field within and around its tissue. The field would be powerful enough to modify incoming electrical input from the senses and to some extent impose its own pattern on it. Hence the Gestalt "laws" of perceptual organisation. This would be a two-way process, however, for sensory input, no matter how feeble, would impose at least minor changes on the structure of the cerebral field. Such changes, the Gestaltists argued, would constitute the basis of learning. It was a bold, if somewhat implausible point of view, and was treated as a serious alternative to the Pavlovian conditioned reflex ideas for at least a period. It had one or two gross defects, however, which even the Gestalt psychologists found worrying. In the

first place, no kind of recording device seemed able to pick up any signs of permanent or semipermanent electrical fields surrounding the brain. The EEG seemed to be a rhythmic picture of electrical change within, rather than of a static, powerful field highly resistant to change. Secondly, there is the odd data from electro-shock therapy. This much-maligned method of treating highly-depressed psychiatric patients relies on jolting the brain with a powerful electric shock, a not particularly pleasant process which nevertheless generally brings a notable remission in patients' symptoms. The point here is not to argue the pros and cons of ECT, as it is called, but to indicate that such tremendous shocks should be enough to seriously disturb any electrical fields, no matter how well-established, with presumably drastic effects on memory. In fact long-term memory is today unaffected by ECT, though, as the Gestalt supporters were quick to point out, there is short-term amnesia for events immediately preceding the electric shock. Thirdly, and finally, as it happens, there is the clinching experimental work of Lashley—not his tissue-removal experiment, but yet another in the catalogue of his remarkable repertoire. Lashley's procedure was as follows. He first taught a large number of rats a particular maze. Then he inserted in their cortex very fine sheets of gold leaf—a notorious destroyer of electrical fields. He then ran the rats through the same maze again, and found no evidence of any detriment in their performance. He also taught other rats the maze after they had had the gold leaf implanted, and found that they learnt it with no undue difficulty. After this work the Gestalt battle cry never seemed so loud or so convincing again. It is doubtful, actually, whether they ever really believed the electrical field theory, but it was a nice idea while it lasted.

(3) The Biochemical Argument: Some Fresh Surprises.

The memory capacity of the human brain is absolutely enormous. It has been calculated that it is quite capable of storing all the information ever fed into it—in other words there is no need for anything ever to be thrown out of store to make room for fresh material. The real problem in this case is not finding enough room to pump in information, but in finding a sufficiently efficient system to pull it out rapidly. Not only do psychologists believe that the brain has this almost limitless storage capacity, but they also have some evidence that all the information fed in, no matter how trivial, actually *is* stored! Some of the most exciting evidence to back up this belief has come from studies made during human brain surgery. These studies are a trifle gruesome and the squeamish might like to jump a paragraph or two here.

For a particular type of surgery—such as the excision of a brain tumour—it is necessary to remove a portion of the cranium and for various reasons it is advisable to perform the entire operation with the patient fully conscious. This is not so horrific as all that, for the brain itself has no pain-detecting cells and the initial opening can be made with a local anaesthetic. One or two scientifically-minded surgeons, notably Dr. Wilder Penfield, have taken the opportunity presented by this surgical requirement to perform certain experiments which have turned out to be of immense interest. With the patient's permission and co-operation, Penfield stimulated selected exposed portions of their cortex with tiny electric currents. Moving round from sensory area to sensory area he found that his tiny electrical stimuli provoked characteristic sensations from the patients. In the visual areas they might "see" lights, colours, etc., in the auditory areas "hear" sounds, and in the temporal lobes, get impressions of smells, taste, etc. Stranger still, Penfield found that certain parts of the so-called association areas of cortex, when stimulated, led to the patient recalling specific memories, often of apparently forgotten items. One woman got a vivid impression of herself in a kitchen of a former home and hearing the voice of her mother, long since dead. Others reported equally specific memories, sometimes with fragments of speech or conversation attached, quite often of items which the patients reported they "hadn't thought of for years." One possible implication of this exciting work is, as we have said, that *all* information that has ever been put into the brain is stored as memory just in case it should ever be needed again. If this is so, then to most psychologists the idea that the memory trace is laid down in the form of major structural changes in the cell body (such as with synaptic knobs) is no longer tenable. There simply aren't enough cells to cope. But suppose that the engram is laid down *within* the cell, at sub-microscopic level in the form of, perhaps, the rearrangement of the specialised molecular structure. Since no one has ever got a really good look at a molecule, either in the nervous system or out of it, this might seem to be a bit of optimistic guesswork, but there is in fact some strange evidence to back the idea up. To consider this we must acquaint ourselves with one of the lowliest creatures capable of learning— the little flatworm, planaria. There is a good deal of argument about how far down the animal kingdom some form of learning can take place. Some workers even claim to have demonstrated memory mechanism in tiny single-celled creatures such as amoeba or its hairy cousin, paramecia, but you can be sure that any information stored was of the simplest and most rudimentary kind. It is when we get to the simplest form of worms, and planaria is one of these, that something closer to memory in the real sense can be clearly demonstrated. Typical of the kind of task which planaria manage, albeit with a good deal of intellectual effort, is to turn right rather than left at a little junction in order to get food or avoid an electric shock. They can also be conditioned to wince to a light being switched on when this is always followed by an electric shock— rather like Pavlov's dogs. Now planaria has the most rudimentary, almost non-existent central nervous system. It has a front end, shaped rather like an arrow with tiny light-sensitive organs in it, and which is clearly its head. It also has a back end which the charitable would call a tail. The question now is—in what part of the tiny body are memories laid down? The head would seem to be the most likely bet, though you might feel it would be hard to tell for sure. At this point the psychologist makes use of another of planaria's interesting features—its ability to regenerate tissue with ease. Take a knife and slice off planaria's tail and both ends swim away, one rather more efficiently than the other. Now in due course the head section will produce a new tail and—rather fantastically—the tail will produce a new head! Planaria can do other odd things too. Cut down the centre of its head without actually removing any tissue and in due course the two half-heads will regenerate into two full heads, producing a peculiar but rather neat looking creature. If one makes several flaps, instead of just two, you end up with lots and lots of heads on one body and get a very odd-looking planaria indeed. All this is very interesting, but the exercise has more point than this. In the first case, ask yourself a question; suppose you teach planaria a little maze and then slice the head into two. Now, of the regenerating heads, which has got the "memory" of the maze stored in it? Left; right; both; neither? Actually, the answer is both, and this should give some clue as to the answer to the next question. Cut a maze-trained planaria in half (head and tail) and let the respective sections develop again into a full creature. One would certainly expect that the head part plus its new tail would be able to perform its little task without much trouble, but what about the tail with its new head? The answer is that this too can "run" the maze. If this seems to be contradicting everything we've said about learning and the brain in general up to now, then in a way it is. We must remember that planaria is an exceedingly simple creature with no CNS to speak of and no nerve cells of the kind found in higher animals. The engram, wherever it is, is certainly not formed by the development of synaptic knobs or by the modification of complex electrical fields. Furthermore, as it is evidently stored in tail as well as head section, then it must presumably be laid down in most, if not necessarily all, of the animal's body cells. This is the point where the biochemists step in

and argue that it is not the outside but rather the interior structure of the cell that is modified through learning. Odd indeed, but there is odder yet to come. Researchers got a collection of planaria and taught them a particular task— turning right in a simple maze—and then took an equivalent number of planaria with no experience of this kind. They then collected the first group and whirled them round in a mixing bowl until all that was left was a homogeneous planaria soup, and repeated the process with the other, untrained group. They now fed the two kinds of soup (planaria will eat more or less anything that's hanging round) to different groups of totally untrained planaria and subsequently trained these in the original right-turn task. This produced an extraordinary result. The planaria who had been fed the soup consisting of trained planaria seemed to learn the maze task significantly quicker than those who had been fed the untrained soup! You will know enough about experimental psychology by now to realise that these results caused immense controversy, and a series of experiments were immediately launched by workers who had found the first result incredible. The controversy, incidentally, still rages as many of the attempts to repeat the experiments have not worked, but the original protagonists still maintain the validity of their results. It is not hard to see why the critics got so hot under the collar, for the implications of the findings, if valid, will throw into question just about every theoretical approach to learning to date. Since the planaria were thoroughly mashed up, no neural connections or even any formal kind of organisation within the system would remain to carry the maze information across to the cannibal planaria. Furthermore, one would have thought that the digestive processes of the cannibals would have completed the process of destruction. How then could the original maze habit, or traces of it, be possibly preserved and carried over? No one on either side of the argument has been able to offer up any convincing explanation, except that if the results are valid, then the maze habit, in the case of planaria at any rate, must be stored right down at molecular level—in other words at such a microscopic level that any mixing and digestion could have little or no effect on it. But even if the planaria results *are* valid, would the same thing necessarily apply to humans? Not necessarily, but if a process works for one living system it could in principle work for another, and we must remember our conclusion that the brain's enormous memory store suggests that modification of the neurone itself would be at too gross a level. It may well be we shall find the brain puts down information in more than one way. There is reasonable evidence, for example, that many animals and humans are equipped with two kinds of memory store—a short-term, and possibly highly unstable one, and a long-term, more or less perpetual system. Information fed into our brains might go initially to the short-term store where it is filtered for relevance or general usefulness. If unwanted for some reason it might be eliminated, but if wanted, passed on to the longer-term system. Perhaps the short-term memory (the kind that allows you to "momentarily" remember a new telephone number) is electrical and the long-term biochemical, neurological or both. At this moment psychologists and physiologists across the world are concentrating on these exciting problems and perhaps, within the next few years, we shall have some new answers and, quite certainly, some fresh surprises.

(i) Unsolved Problems.

This section has attempted to raise some of the issues confronting psychologists in their attempt to solve one of the main mysteries of the brain— how information is stored and processed within it. Although a fair bit has been learned in the past decades, it has really served to show that the problem is much more complicated than the earlier workers ever imagined. Furthermore, you will have noticed that precious little has been said about how the information is extracted, for the very good reason that precious little is known about this. Curiously some interesting clues are beginning to come from the study of computers, man's own specially-created slave brains. These are already capable of storing quite immense quantities of information, and engineers have been working steadily at improving methods of storing information and of getting it out in a hurry. In recent years the computer engineers and the psychologists have been tending to get together and pool their ideas—with some interesting results. To more and more scientists it has become increasingly obvious that the study of the brain is real ground for interdisciplinary contact, and that contributions to its study can come equally from psychologists, physiologists, physicists, engineers, mathematicians, educationalists, and so on. The highly successful Brain Research Association, for example, is composed of scientists from practically every discipline, with psychologists and physiologists, who are traditionally the kingpins in brain science, making up no more than 25 per cent of its ranks. Perhaps the really big problems in brain research will only come from multi-disciplinary teams of this kind. But this is something of a digression and we must now pass on from learning and memory to the lesser, but no less interesting problem of motivation.

IV. MOTIVATION.

(1) Why Does an Animal Do One Thing Rather Than Another?

This question aptly sums up the problem of animal and human motivation, an important facet of modern psychological research. As is always the case with psychology, perhaps more so than with other fields of science, what initially seem to be straightforward questions, designed to elicit straightforward answers, become steadily more complicated on close inspection. The odd, almost philosophical difficulties surrounding motivation are a good example. Why *does* an animal do one thing rather than another? Because it wants to, is the stock reply—a reply which actually doesn't get anywhere at all. To say that the reason for doing something is because the doer *likes it* is no explanation, merely renaming the problem so that it comes up in a different guise. It so happens that we tend to like doing the things we do, though of course this doesn't always apply. We certainly like to eat, but do we eat principally because we like it or because the food is essential to our survival? Perhaps the key is tied up here somewhere, and the rock-bottom cause for all animal and human behaviour lies in the need to keep the individual creature alive. Well, that will certainly do for food and water, but it clearly doesn't work for other common activities, such as sex. In the long term the survival of all living things depends upon sexual activity but animals certainly don't understand this and humans only found out the link between the sexual act and conception a millennium or so ago. And anyone who believes that people indulge in sex solely to allow the human species to survive is very naïve indeed. Now the situation gets even more complicated. It seems as if we make love because we like it, with the long-term result being that the species survives. But what can be the link, in physiological terms, between liking something and it "doing us good"? And just to complicate matters even more, supposing that we accept this link, how do we explain other common patterns of human behaviour? Why do some people like going to football matches or art galleries? Why don't they go there to eat the footballers or the paintings, and how is the survival of the human species helped by such practices anyway? Having muddled the issue thoroughly—or, rather, showed it up in its true light—we can now go on to see how psychologists have set to work to try to unravel it. They have not got very far, but they have got somewhere.

(2) The Mechanical Tortoise.

The first people to face up to the problems raised above were the Behaviourists. In their gallant attempt to explain human and animal behaviour in mechanistic terms they realised that

they would have to account for the tendency of animals to set out to do things rather than simply engage in random, diffuse activity, and they thought this could be fairly simply handled. They were most anxious, of course, to avoid explaining different types of behaviour in terms of different goals—to suggest that an animal had got a goal in mind was to imply that it had a mind and furthermore some kind of "picture of the future" in it. To begin with they took the simplest possible form of mechanical analogy. Imagine a clockwork mouse, which when wound up runs across the floor. What caused it to do so? The clockwork and the energy tied up in the spring, of course, with its direction determined by such matters as the orientation of its wheels, the angle of the floor, etc. Anyone saying that the toy crossed the floor because it wanted to would be being silly. Similarly, the Behaviourists stated, one should be able to avoid the same kind of inference when observing the movements of a real mouse. If the response is that the real mouse can do a good deal more than just run across a floor—can squeak, change direction, avoid cats and eat cheese—then the reply in essence is that one could build a mechanical mouse to do that as well, provided one had the time and ingenuity. The more complicated and versatile the mechanical mouse the harder it would become to tell the difference between the two, and when one had two apparently identical mice, would one still talk about one "wanting" to cross a floor and the other doing it purely automatically? Was there an important difference anyway? Critics of Behaviourism argued that indeed there was a difference. The "real" mouse ate the cheese because it satisfied a need for the food, whereas the mechanical mouse, no matter how many bogus sounds of enjoyment it made as it munched the food, was merely going through an essentially meaningless mechanical process. This is a dangerous argument, for suppose that one decided to power the artificial mouse not by clockwork but by the combustion of cheese and made it so that it would stop when its inner store of cheese ran out ... one would now have an artificial mouse with a "need" for cheese as great as that of its biological counterpart. If this seems an unlikely step to take, consider the case of Grey Walter's mechanical tortoise. In an effort to replicate some of the conditions of behaviour, the great English psychologist, Dr. Grey Walter of the Burden Neurological Institute, constructed a tortoise which exhibited some of the paramount properties of living creatures. His tortoise—a shell on wheels with no pretensions to looking like an animal—was powered by storage batteries which drove a motor allowing it to run around on the floor. Its movements were far from aimless, for it was also equipped with photocells in its head capable of detecting areas of light or dark. A series of simple switches inside were arranged so that when the tortoise's batteries were fully charged, the device would move towards dark areas of a room, finding its way underneath chairs and tables, carefully working its way round books, human feet, etc., placed in its way. With batteries low, a different switching arrangement would come into operation and the device would now tend to avoid dark areas and seek out light ones—in particular the light inside its "hutch" where a battery charge was conveniently situated. Once inside the hutch Grey Walter's tortoise would connect up to the battery charger, later emerging "replenished" to set out for dark places again! Here the Behaviourist argument emerges most strongly. It is not, of course, that Grey Walter had manufactured a living thing—no one is making that claim—but rather a matter of whether the tortoise's tendency to seek out its battery for recharging, etc., constituted a need in the same sense as does the real mouse's need for cheese. This is a big question which you will probably have to think out for yourself. In the meanwhile let's see how the Behaviourists attempted to translate animal behaviour into similar terms.

(3) Drives and Needs.

The Behaviourist position can be summed up as an attempt at describing animal behaviour in the simplest possible way, and to do this they evolved the concept of "Drive." A drive is described as something which causes an animal to perform a particular act, and the ideal position, from the behaviouristic viewpoint, would be to find that all animal activity could be explained in terms of a limited number of drives. To begin with things looked simple and promising, for it appeared as if a drive could be thought of as something that promoted bodily well-being. For example, when an animal is short of food it is running out of power. This causes a sensation known as "hunger" which signals a bodily "need" and this in turn sets in motion a chain of activity which culminates in eating. When the food has been ingested, the need is satisfied, the hunger vanishes and the drive is reduced. The same argument applies to thirst and, with a bit of modification, to sex. In the latter case if an animal does not engage in sexual activity for a given period of time certain substances build up in the body, the hormonal system becomes unbalanced, etc., and a need builds up in the body, which gives rise to a drive. This in turn pushes the creature towards sexual activity with a suitable mate. Carry this on just a bit more and include a "need" to escape painful situations and you've practically got the whole of animal behaviour sewn up. What's more it is sewn up in a very convincing way because the needs and drives are not vague and ambiguous, but relate directly to vital bodily processes which if not operating properly will cause the animal's death. All animal behaviour could be explained in terms of a drive to (i) reduce hunger, (ii) reduce thirst, (iii) reduce pain, and (iv) achieve sex. To those who didn't want to talk about "achievement," which seemed to imply that an animal was actually setting out to do something, then the final one could be rephrased (iv) to reduce sexual tension. An animal in a state of need would be activated by some or all of these drives and would continue to "behave" until all drives were reduced. Protagonists of this delightfully simple point of view even showed how learning theory could benefit from drive-reduction ideas; a pattern of behaviour or conditioned reflex would be established, they claimed, if at its conclusion a drive was reduced. If no drive-reduction took place, then the behaviour pattern would not be learned. In the 'thirties and 'forties a number of mathematically inclined psychologists even attempted to express this in the form of sets of equations which looked enormously impressive on paper but which, alas, bore little relationship in practice to the way living animals actually behaved. For example, people soon realised that a bit of a problem emerged for an animal if all its drives were set at maximum, as it were, and all the appropriate drive-reducing stimuli were at hand. Take a rat, severely deprived of food and water, and place it in a cage with both available. What is it going to do first, eat or drink? Presumably it will be pushed in the direction suggested by the strongest drive. Using this as an idea it was decided that it ought to be possible to rank animal drives in order of strength by a simple test. Place a rat deprived of either food, water, or sexual activity in a box facing the necessary drive-reduction stimulus across an electrified grid. Now, how strong an electric shock is the rat prepared to put up with in order to fulfil its need? Experimenters found that thirst was the most effective stimulus, food next, and sex third. This was all fine until they found that rats satisfied in all three modes would still occasionally cross the grid even when there was nothing on the other side! Now what kind of drive could be operating here? Furthermore, they found that an animal, again supplied with plenty of food, water, etc., would still run through a complicated maze and learn it pretty well, despite the lack of drive-reduction at the other end! Before long the theorists found themselves rather glumly proposing "exploration" or curiosity-reducing drives to account for the well-known fact that animals like to roam about all over the place. This, naturally, allows one to have a completely comprehensive theory of behaviour and learning in drive-reduction terms, but with the penalty of converting a simple, fairly sharply defined theory, tied closely to described bodily requirements, into a complicated, diffuse, and far less convincing one. If any activity not explained in terms of the original drives can now be accounted for in terms of a reduction of an exploratory drive, then one has an "explanation" of the behaviour. But to many people's minds it is no better than those around before the whole concept of drives and needs was introduced. Similarly, there was a certain neatness and utility to the idea that a pattern of behaviour could be learned if at its conclusion a drive such as hunger or thirst was reduced. This neatness vanishes when we are told that an animal has learnt something else because its curiosity was satisfied, or the opposite, that it was not learnt because its curiosity drive was *not* reduced! Clearly the root of all these difficulties lies in the refusal of many psychologists to admit that a creature or a person does something or learns something because it likes it. Fair enough. We have already pointed out how subjective is the idea of an animal doing something because it "wants to," and the job of the psychologist is to try to define behaviour objectively rather than subjectively. What was clearly needed was some definable describable physiological process which could correspond to "pleasure," and until this was found psychologists could proceed no further in the field of motivation. In 1954 experiments were published which gave them the green light.

(4) The Pleasure Centre.

The arrival of microelectrode recording techniques allowed numerous experimental studies of the animal and even, occasionally, the human brain in action to be made. In a prolonged assault on the inner intricacies of the cerebral cortex and lower control centres psychologists and physiologists began the elaborate job of mapping the brain, defining as rigidly as they could which areas were devoted to what function. In many cases the areas they stimulated seemed to be "silent," *i.e.*, provoking no obvious response from the animal. Others however were more dramatically active. In 1956 the American James Olds and the Englishman Peter Milner were studying the responses of rats with electrodes implanted in what is known as the septal area of the brain, a spot beneath a body known as the corpus callosum. Animals stimulated with low voltage electric currents in this area seemed to behave in an odd way—almost as if they were enjoying the experience. For many years it had been known that stimulating the area known as the hypothalamus could produce symptoms of rage in animals, the creatures responding as though angered or threatened, the "sham rage" switching off immediately the electric stimulus ceased. Similarly areas had been found which when stimulated would cause dozy, apparently sleepy behaviour. Now here was something very different and Olds and Milner began to suspect that they had hit on something akin to a "pleasure" centre. To test this they designed a weird electrical circuit, surely one of the oddest ever to be seen in a laboratory. From the electrode in the rat's septal region a wire ran to the battery providing the electrical stimulus. In the rat's cage they placed a lever, and connected this to the battery in such a way that when the lever was pressed the battery emitted a single pulse, thus allowing the rat—if it wanted to—to stimulate this particular area of the brain. Although they had half suspected that the rats might occasionally give themselves a jolt in this "pleasure area," no one had anticipated the extent of the rats' involvement. All animals, once they had discovered the trick of pushing the lever, went into a sustained surge of lever pressing, keeping the activity up for literally hours on end. In fact there was some suggestion that they might have kept it up for ever, had not physical exhaustion sooner or later intervened. Given the choice of alternative levers providing food, water, or the chance to stimulate their septal regions, all rats reliably chose the latter, even those who had been substantially deprived of opportunities to eat or drink for some time. The lack of apparent satiation of the effect was one of the really odd things about the discovery. No human or animal appetite has ever been found which cannot be satisfied, if only for short periods. Only where some severe pathology is involved, such as with a disease or brain tumour, do the normal appetites remain unquenched. But here was something quite different—an appetite which seemed to have boundless depths and which outrode any of the other paramount needs of tha animal. It was for this reason that Olds and Milner hypothesised that they had hit on the centre in the brain which mediates the sensation which we humans know of as "pleasure." How surprising is it that some such centre exists? Not very. When we do something we like, be it eating, drinking, or even going to a football match, then the feeling of pleasure that we get must be matched by some parallel process in the brain, and it could well be that this is located in some convenient but specific centre. Olds and Milner, incidentally, found that their animals would very swiftly learn a task if they were rewarded by a session on the pleasure centre, and here perhaps another important point emerges. There has always been some evidence, though the matter is by no means settled, that learning was somehow improved if following the performance of the desired task, a "reward" such as food, drink, sex, etc., was given. The big question is, what kind of signal is given to the memory system to denote when something is to be permanently laid down? Olds and Milner appeared to have provided one possible answer, and one that would have greatly satisfied Pavlov, Watson, and their immediate successors, the reinforcing stimulus—the message that declares that something will be learnt—is a message that has passed through the pleasure centre. The validity of this idea is still uncertain, but it has the merit of answering an age-old question in reasonably simple fashion, and also of helping us towards the solution of an even more venerable philosophical one—the nature of pleasure itself.

(5) Emotion.

This is one of the most misunderstood words in the psychologist's vocabulary and is a source of endless confusion. The trouble is it means so many things to so many different people. To the psychologist, however, it has a fairly specific meaning and we must try to get some idea of what this is. Only by doing so can we avoid falling into such traps as to say. "Animals cannot feel emotions," or "Computers can never think because they have no emotions." First let's attempt to nail the word "emotion" to the wall and try to analyse it. When we talk of people being emotional, what exactly do we mean? That they tend to weep a lot, get easily angered? Sorrow and anger are emotions, that is clear. But is not love an emotion too? Do we mean that emotional people tend to fall in love a good deal? Or do we mean that their love is deeper than others—or perhaps shallower? Already some confusion is creeping in. Let's ask now how we know that someone is emotional, or in an emotional state. The answer is probably that they exhibit a characteristic behaviour pattern which allows us to judge. If they wave their fists, go red in the face and shout, then we might infer that they were angry. Of course they could be acting and merely pretending to be angry, in which case what is the dividing line between the real and the simulated emotion? The answer would seem to be that the latter was not accompanied by an internal *feeling* of a special kind, and this now tells us that there are at least two sides to emotion—subjective psychological state and an external, physiological one. In fact, psychologists find it convenient to consider three aspects. The first is the *behavioural—i.e.* the kind of activity in which the angry or otherwise emotional person engages. This is generally easily detected and is of the waving-arms-around variety. The second is the *physiological*, which consists of considerably more discrete behavioural signs, not always obvious to the observer but which may be detected by suitably sensitive instruments. The third is the *psychological* or introspective and this refers to the "state or mind" of the individual when he is angry or whatever. This of course cannot be directly sensed by other individuals who rely on the angry person reporting to them "how he feels." How are these linked together, and what function do they serve?

(a) *The Behavioural.*

If you fire a pistol behind someone's back they exhibit a very characteristic response, the most common feature of which is that they jump some distance into the air. This may seem desperately obvious, but actually there is a good deal more to the response than that. High speed photography shows that all human beings respond to sudden loud noises by a highly predictable behavioural sequence, of which the jump is just one part, and which bears the name "the startle pattern." It includes a marked hunching of the shoulders, closing the eyes, baring the teeth, raising the hands in the direction of the face. It doesn't take long to see that these actions, which occur reliably in all human beings, are not random and pointless but serve to help the individual respond rapidly to a dangerous situation. The jump is an alerting response, the eyes are closed to protect them, the hands raised in defence or perhaps to strike, the teeth bared possibly as a threatening or warning sign. Similarly, at a more common emotional level, the waving fists and loud voice of an angry man equip him to some extent for battle. And what of the tears and the cowering posture of a thoroughly frightened individual? Well, these in some way suggest to the aggressor that the battle is over and are signals to him to stop fighting. Men, being natural fighters, tend to do little in the way of crying and will generally scrap on until they are physically incapable of continuing. Women, on the other hand, who are not particularly strong or well-equipped to fight, tend to slip into weeping and submission, although far less easily than used to be the case before the Women's Liberation Movement removed the dominant role of the male from our society. The very obvious facial expressions made by people in various emotional states led the great Charles Darwin to the view that the type of face made was a good index of what emotion the individual was in the grips of. To test this idea, psychologists took photographs of the facial expressions of people in various emotional states and then asked other people to try to name them. The results were poor, with few people doing better than chance. The only expression reliably recognised and correctly assigned to an emotion was a smile, and even this was occasionally confused with other emotional states such as pain, or even fear. The same experiment performed with movies yielded somewhat better results, and when sound was added results were again improved. The clinching thing, however, seems to be the setting in which the behaviour takes place, for people become very accurate at judging emotions when they see the surroundings in which the other people are behaving. Clearly the external signs of emotion, despite their immediate and rather obvious manifestations, are an unreliable guide to what is going on inside the individual's head. The same argument, incidentally, applies to animals, though somewhat less forcefully. Most animals give pretty explicit signs when they are angry or when they are afraid. One can even detect something suspiciously like guilt in the general pattern of behaviour of a dog which has done something it shouldn't. But can one really talk of a dog "feeling guilty"? If not—why not? Whatever answer you give will be quite as valid as any given by a psychologist.

(b) *The Physiological.*

The signs and signals we talked about above were all grossly obvious, and yet, as we pointed out, somewhat unreliable. To a large part they seem to be the outward manifestations of an internal process which at the same time serve a useful purpose, as when the startle pattern alerts the individual into a posture suitable for defensive or aggressive action. But what are the finer, physiological manifestations of emotion? These must obviously involve changes in the state of bodily and cerebral activity. Psychologists have pinned down no fewer than 11 distinct facets of human and animal behaviour which give a clear index of changes in emotional states. To give some idea of the complexity of emotional behaviour we will look at each of these briefly.

(1) The first, and perhaps the most obvious, is heart-rate. The heart's job is to pump blood around the body and the blood provides the vital organ supply to the brain. The more intense the activity, the more oxygen is consumed and the more the blood needs to be circulated. It should be no surprise therefore to anyone to learn that as activity is stepped up, so heart-rate increases and vice versa. Furthermore, heart-rate tends to accelerate just prior to some important or exciting piece of activity, or even on merely thinking about it, and this means that we have here one index of emotional state. A device known as the electrocardiogram (ECG) can give a very precise picture of heart fluctuations and represents one objective way of plotting this information.

(2) We have already implied another measure, respiration. This increases more or less alongside heart-rate, and is a pretty good index of most emotions. Irregularities of breathing, including variations in the depth of breaths, are a particularly good index of nervousness as most people know and all this can be detected by a suitable instrument.

(3) More or less hand-in-hand with the above come changes in local blood pressure and volume, the facial accompaniments of which—blanching or blushing—are only too obvious. These can be measured by a device known as the plethysmograph, which is merely a version of the kind of device a doctor uses to measure your blood pressure in a routine medical examination.

(4) A somewhat harder emotional symptom to measure, but very characteristic of most emotional states, is muscle tension and its associate, tremor. In anger, rage, and other aggressive states muscles become tensed to be ready for rapid action and if this is carried too far we get trembling of the limbs—a familiar accompaniment of great nervousness or fright.

All the above are easily discernible indices, amenable to instrumentation but not depending upon it. The remaining manifestations are harder to detect, though just as valuable once one has caught them. Beginning with the most obvious we have:

(5) The pilomotor response, which is a hangover from the days when our ancestors had a good deal more hair than we do today, and which can be seen when a cat's fur fluffs out in rage or fear. In humans today we call it goose-pimples and it is often a precursor to the feeling of full-blooded fear.

(6) Even harder to measure is salivary secretion which is the kind of response Pavlov studied with his dogs. In anxiety or fear the saliva flow tends to be inhibited and we find ourselves with "dry mouths."

(7) An index of emotion which is particularly obvious to the individual is the change in gastrointestinal motility. Movements of the stomach and intestine are brought to a brief but definite halt in strong emotional states with a complementary, and often rather dramatic, surge back to action shortly afterwards. There are plenty of homely and slightly vulgar expressions to describe the consequences of this.

(8) There has been a recent rise of interest in the pupillary response as an index of certain types of emotion. The pupil of the eye tends to dilate in moments of anger or pain with slight dilation occurring during periods of "interest" in something. This has led some clever psychologists who work in the advertising profession to use this as an index of the relative effectiveness of different types of advertisement. All the subjects have to do is look at the subject matter while a recording camera photographs the pupils of their eyes from a distance!

(9) Because the endocrine or glandular system is active in emotional states the chemical constitution of the blood changes markedly as the hormones flow within it, but this index, while potentially useful, is of course abnormally hard to measure directly.

(10) Next we come to the so-called galvanic skin response (GSR) which is in fact nothing more than the electrical resistance of the skin. For various reasons, not properly understood, the resistance of the skin to an electrical current changes with most emotional states, tending to decrease as a function of the intensity of the emotion. This can be detected with a suitable instrument and meter and is perhaps particularly interesting because it is an automatic response which the individual is not consciously aware of. Connect someone up to a GSR meter, tell him that you are going to stick a pin in him and the needle will swing wildly. It is a very effective demonstration of an entirely involuntary response and is generally one of the first experiments that fledgling psychologists perform on each other in their laboratory classes.

(11) Finally there is the EEG, which we referred to earlier on (see Q5). The electrical activity of the brain does change with varying degrees of bodily activity, though what these changes mean is a matter for skilled interpretation.

(c) *The Psychological.*

You will have noticed that many of the above indices—stomach motility, muscle tension, etc.—have definite physical accompaniments which are only too obvious to the individual experiencing the emotion and it should not be too surprising in the light of all this that an emotional state markedly alters our physical and psychological feelings and sensations. But is this all there is to emotion? Can the age-old human passions of love and hate be reduced to permutations of salivary secretion, blood pressure, pilomotor response and electro-cortical activity? Put so baldly of course the answer is no. Love demands a partner, a setting, a trigger and some temporal span—as does hate. In humans these require the active participation of the complex computer we call the brain, and a background of education, social activity, and some awareness of goals other than the immediate. Nevertheless, the intense physiological and psychological changes which envelop us when we are in love, or when we fight in passion, contribute the better part of the powerful sensations we feel. But which of the three faces of emotion, the behavioural, the physiological, or the psychological is the real or most significant one?

The answer is that no single one predominates for emotion is a complex of all three. When the object of our emotion, be it love, hate, or whatever, is first encountered then mind and body combine to set the individual up for the optimum pattern of responses. This involves some permutation of physical change which, naturally, is reflected in psychological changes of mood. These in turn provoke outward changes on a larger scale which may involve combat or the ritual of love. If this description seems to debase the concept of human emotional response then this is a pity for there is no reason why it should. The powerful forces that thrust men into the numerous passions of the world would have no meaning were they not accompanied by potent changes in bodily state. The artistry that springs from these passions is no fraction diminished because we can identify the physiological and psychological changes that accompany and, to some extent, determine them.

It will have occurred to you that in this section on motivation we have drifted closer and closer to another of the critical areas that psychologists study—the nature of human personality. Psychologists know far less about this area than they would like to, but their century of scientific activity (a small span compared with the history of the more traditional sciences, such as physics) has begun to pay off. In the next and final section we will take a look at what they have done, or have tried to do, in this most fascinating of areas.

V. PERSONALITY AND THINKING.

(1) What Constitutes a Person?

To many people this is the most important single question in psychology and indeed, perhaps, in the combined fields of science and philosophy. What is it that makes up that unique blend of psychological and physiological factors we call "personality"? The answer is, predictably, complicated and before we can even begin to consider it we must attempt to define the problems in the field. In the first place let's consider the most venerable and apparently simplest answer—a person is that thing in the head which thinks, feels, is aware of itself as an individual entity, and which controls a brain and body. This is the answer which probably fits best with the non-technical philosophy of the man-in-the-street and which matches also with a long-standing traditional view fostered by the majority of systems of religious belief. Put another way, it states that human beings are composed of essentially two parts. One of these is physical and consists of the body and its control centre, the brain. The second is non-physical, and is called the mind, soul, spirit, or some similar name. This is a separate entity which controls the body through its brain and while involved in this way must obey the laws of the physical world. It may, however, survive the death of its body (one of the most widespread of religious views of personality) and occasionally, as with telepathy, precognition, etc., may step outside to contact other similar minds in other parts of the world or even take a peek into the future. As we have said, this is an exceedingly widespread view of the nature of personality and it will be the one held by many who read this article. This is now the point where you could ask whether this view is acceptable to psychologists, and that is a fair and proper question. It requires, however, two separate answers. In the first place some psychologists, though certainly not the majority, accept this or some very similar view, but on an entirely personal plane. When they think as scientists, however, most are inclined to disagree with it. Nothing that has been uncovered in the history of experimental psychology, with the possible exception of the very dubious evidence for telepathy, suggests that the human personality is a separate entity to be considered in isolation from brain and body. Psychologists who choose to believe otherwise frankly admit that they do so on the basis of faith or hunch, and argue that even though the scientific facts appear to contradict their beliefs at the moment, perhaps in due course experimental psychology will uncover fresh new material to change the whole picture.

Does "Mind" Exist?

An increasing number of psychologists and brain scientists today take a hard-line on the "spiritual" view of personality, but does this mean that mind does not exist, as the Behaviourists strove so hard to prove? Certainly not. There is clearly a whole range of rich psychological activity which cannot be explained simply in terms of bundles of conditioned reflexes and the like. What seems to have happened in fact is that as animals have evolved via the remorseless processes of evolution, so more and more "power" has been given to the cerebral control centres. At some stage in the evolutionary ladder—it is very hard to say exactly where—the brain ceased to be a purely automatic device and some glimmerings of what we call consciousness began to appear. In the early stages, this probably merely took the form of a "switch" in the brain which allowed the creature to select from one or two alternative modes of action. This capacity would imply some system within the brain capable of making a "comparison" of the two modes and thus of "standing back from itself." Increase the complexity of the brain and its capacity to select, predict, and determine and you will see that the evolution of a higher control centre capable of

"inspecting" ongoing activity will emerge. Thus could the thing we know of as consciousness develop. Incidentally, if you feel that such an abstracting, self-inspecting system could not be conceived in purely mechanical terms then you are wrong, for the latest developments in computer technology have been devoted to achieving this. But before getting caught up in arguments about whether computers could "think" (we'll tackle this briefly later on) let us just summarise the current approach to the problem that most psychologists accept today. Mind is a phenomenon which has arisen almost inevitably as brain complexity and power have increased, and its function is to select alternative activities and compute the consequences. Just as human bodies and brains differ in countless ways, so human minds, subtly moulded over the years from infancy to adulthood, differ too. The result is that the world is populated with a large number of human beings, united as a species, but each one an individual entity, compounded of body, brain, and mind. All three are equally real, equally important—and equally helpless without each other's company. Let us now take a look at the principal forces which serve to mould these individual entities we call people, and some of the essential ways in which they differ.

(2) Interplay of Heredity and Environment.

People and animals differ in a large number of ways, and are alike in others. We share certain features—upright posture, well-developed brains, etc.—with other primates, such as chimpanzees. We also share certain features—binocular vision, mammalian reproduction techniques, etc.—with white rats. We even have a limited amount in common—respiratory systems depending upon oxygen, need to ingest some kind of food, etc.—with creatures as lowly as the earwig, but nothing with cabbages or oak trees, except perhaps a dependence upon sunlight. Now what is it that determines these similarities and differences? The answer is summed up in the word heredity. Creatures of particular species mate with each other and hand on to their offspring, via the genes and chromosomes, the physical characteristics of the species (see **F31**). They may even hand on certain predetermined patterns of behaviour, which we have earlier referred to as instinct (see also **F40**). Broadly speaking, the lower down the phylogenetic scale, the more behavioural information is carried over via the genes, and the less flexible is the creature's ultimate behaviour pattern. Earwigs, for example, come into the world fully equipped to go about their simple business on this planet. They present almost identical faces to the world around them, and taking it all in all they change little from birth to death. Earwigs are largely the product of heredity, the principal forces which mould them lying in the genes of their parents and the incredibly long history of their species stretching back for hundreds of millions of years. At the other end of the continuum we have human beings whose physical characteristics and a very limited number of behaviour patterns are inherited, but whose "personalities" and individualities (unlike the earwigs) change significantly throughout the span of their lives. These changes are the consequence of the impact of the environment on the flexible human brain, a flexibility which allows human beings to respond swiftly and intelligently to the changing hazards and opportunities of the world. It should be clear, therefore, that the basic differences that so obviously exist between the personalities of different people, reflect the experiences that each individual has had in his or her lifetime. See a newborn child and search for signs of its personality. You will look for a long time to no avail. But watch a child grow from infancy to adolescence and you will see the personality slowly building and emerging—more or less hand-in-hand with the young person's growing awareness of his own individuality, his strengths and his weaknesses.

Twin Studies.

Striking evidence of the immense influence that the environment has on us comes from the famous studies of identical twins performed in America by Newman in the 1930s. There is a bit of confusion in most people's minds about what actually are "identical" twins as opposed to the ordinary, born-on-the-same-day variety. In the case of the latter—known as fraternal twins—what has happened to produce the happy event is that during conception two of the eggs in the mother have been fertilised and thus two babies are born. Without going into too much detail this means that two quite separate creatures develop, each being equipped with the random genetic mix that follows the meeting of the father's sperm with the mother's egg. The children, when born, may be of different sex, different colour hair, eyes, etc., and are likely to be no more alike than would be brothers or sisters born in different years or even decades. Each, therefore, begins with a different hereditary pattern, as determined by the genes. With identical twins a curious fluke occurs. By some process, *after* conception and *after* gene mixing has taken place, the fertilised egg splits, amoeba fashion, and two babies begin to develop—but both have identical gene patterns and thus, up to the moment of birth, can be looked upon as totally identical human beings. This weird identity is, we all know, frequently carried on throughout the twins' lifetime, even though it is generally noticeable that the similarities become less marked with age. Now to return to Newman's experiment. Nineteen pairs of identical twins were found (a good deal of research was needed) who had for one reason or another been reared apart from an early age and had grown up in different environments. Newman found that while the adult twins maintained a striking physical resemblance, the personalities of the pairs seemed in many cases to have moved apart. In one case, the first of the pair had been successful in worldly terms, had acquired a college education, and was happily married with a stable family, while the second had been less fortunate and was leading a rather unsatisfactory life in an unskilled job in a working-class neighbourhood. Twin "A" seemed optimistic, good-humoured, and more dominant a personality, while twin "B" was morose, lethargic, and lacking in self-confidence. Similar observations were in general noted with other twins, particularly in cases where one of the pair had been reared in a more stable and economically more satisfactory environment. No better illustration of the relative influence of heredity and environment on human personality can be found than in studies of this kind. But is it only physical characteristics that are genetically determined? Is none of the psychological make-up of the individual "built-in" to him at birth? We can answer this by saying that twin-studies have shown that while personality is certainly modified by the environment, there is a good deal of evidence that intelligence is relatively untouched by normal environmental differences. Newman and his colleagues, for example, found that there was a higher correlation between the IQ test scores of *identical twins reared apart* than there was between *fraternal twins reared together*—a finding which suggests that intelligence may be largely inherited. The great British psychologist, Sir Cyril Burt, also produced what seemed to be striking evidence of the inheritability of intelligence with studies made of schoolchildren in the 1930s and the 1940s. In 1976, however, Burt's work came under severe and unexpected criticism, and this led to a reopening of the whole question of the relative importance of genetic as opposed to cultural factors in determining intelligence. Part of the problem, of course, is that there is often confusion over the meaning of the word "intelligence," and for this reason it is perhaps worth looking closer at it.

(3) Intelligence and IQ Testing.

Psychologists have spent a good deal of time arguing about what exactly is meant by intelligence and it is not worth covering this battle-scarred ground again. One definition which makes a good deal of sense is "versatility of adjustment" which is another way of talking about the kind of flexible response to the environment which is so characteristic of humans. This of course means that we can talk of animals having some degree of intelligence, and most psychologists nowadays would agree that this makes sense. The only problem arises if one considers intelligence to be inextricably tied up with consciousness, thought, language, etc., which of course it is not. Certainly the ability to communicate in linguistic terms and to think in abstract modes are signs of a highly intelligent creature, but some degree of intelligence may be present without those traits. Probably one could even talk of intelligence being present in any animal that could modify its behaviour in response to the environment and repeat this behavioural response at some later date. This means, as you will have gathered, that intelligence is present in any creature that can learn, including our little friend planaria. It is of course a *very* limited form of intelligence and planaria would not come out with much of an IQ (intelligence quotient) if submitted to human IQ tests. The structure of these tests, incidentally, becomes comprehensible if one sees them as measures of human flexibility rather than of knowledge. The standard IQ test, which formed the basis of the much-reviled 11-plus exam, is an attempt at getting some idea of an individual's general flexibility rather than how much information is actually crammed into his head. Without getting involved in the educational argument here, the point is that a test of the child's inherent capability is more likely to give some index of his fitness for higher education than is a test of his knowledge, and this is what the IQ test attempts to sort out. Hence the relative uselessness of "cramming" to prepare for the 11-plus and the surprise results it sometimes produced. You may think you see a bit of a contradiction here. On the one hand we have said that intelligence, whatever it is, seems to be built in the individual and is something to do with his basic brain power. In this case why are new-born babies not fully intelligent at birth? The paradox is solved by saying that the peak of intelligence is not reached until the brain is fully mature (at about 18 years of age in homo sapiens) after which it begins to decline remorselessly with increasing age. Thus you will find that scores on IQ tests are "weighted" according to age. For very young children considerable allowance is made for age and their "raw" score is upgraded according to a standard scale. So too is the score for older people who inevitably score lower in IQ tests than do 18-year-olds. Thus we find that a university professor aged 60 would produce a far lower raw score than a young student of equivalent intelligence—even though the venerable professor's head contains far more knowledge! If this seems odd, remember that it is the individual's potential and general flexibility that the tests are all about and not the depth of his fund of knowledge. The IQ test itself is a rather arbitrary affair and was arrived at in the first place by a group of psychologists selecting a bunch of questions which they felt best tested this rather elusive faculty of flexibility. They then arrived at a scoring system which achieved the result that if you tested a large number of people, drawn randomly from the population, their average score would equal 100. In fact this is exactly what an IQ of 100 means—it is the average score of the population at large. This has led to the sarcastic observation of one psychologist that intelligence was "that faculty that is measured by intelligence tests"! This is a witticism with some truth in it, but nevertheless the IQ has a practical value, notably as a sorter out of the bright from the dull in a situation where environmental or social backgrounds might have intervened to cloud the issue. The 11-plus is one such example, as is the fact that the IQ test taken prior to university entrance is the best-known predictor of success in final degree examinations—at least in the USA. On the other hand, as you may have suspected, social and cultural factors can influence IQ scores, thus suggesting that they are not as pure as might have been hoped. Tests conducted on white and black children in America in the 1930s, for example, showed a marked difference in IQ between the two racial groups—the whites coming out pretty clearly ahead. This was greedily seized on by racialists as demonstrating the innate superiority of the white children until it was pointed out that the selection of the two samples was faulty, the black children had been drawn from rural parts of the south while the whites came from the urban north. When a repeat experiment was performed, drawing the whites from the rustic south and the blacks from the northern cities, exactly the reverse finding emerged, killing one age-old notion and at the same time highlighting the fact that IQ tests were vulnerable to social and cultural factors. Incidentally, for those who like to pursue racial arguments, it is interesting to note that the highest IQ ever recorded by standard tests, shattering 200, was scored by—a young Negro girl. When considering the world as a whole, however, the fact remains that humans are very heavily divided from each other by a barrier potentially more difficult to surmount than those of race, class, or creed—intelligence. Furthermore the gulf is one that is particularly difficult to bridge because of lack of incentive on either side. A highly intelligent person generally finds the company of a rather dull person quite unacceptable, and the reverse is also true. Also, the differences between high and low IQs are likely to become more apparent in the coming decades as the old barriers of class, etc., which used to mask intelligence, dissolve. From this important aspect of human personality we now move on to consider the nature of one of the processes most characteristic of human brains—thought.

(4) Thinking.

We have suggested that personality is an amalgam of the various faculties which are associated with cerebral activity, and that variations in personality reflect variations in the individual's environmental history. Any creature with a reasonably flexible set of responses to its environment can therefore be said to have some rudimentary personality, and many of us can detect this in our domestic pets. If this seems a peculiar notion then this is only because we have erroneously tended to think of personality as being a solely human trait, rather in the way that people dismiss animals in general as having no intelligence. But what is it that does distinguish us from other animals—do we differ merely in terms of the capacity and computing power of our brains? Probably the answer is yes, though it has to be recognised that the gulf is pretty wide. Yet if one looks at the cerebral equipment of, say, a chimpanzee one gets the feeling that there shouldn't be all *that* difference! Furthermore, if one comes closer to home and looks at some of our ancestors such as Neanderthal or Cro-Magnon Man, it is hard to account for the differences between their primitive lives and ours today. Certainly we exist 100,000 years later in time and it would be a bit pathetic if we hadn't progressed since then. But the same argument surely should apply to chimpanzees who do not seem to have developed much in the same period, and the whole thing seems even odder when we learn that the now extinct Neanderthal Man had a cranial capacity (brain size) greater than that of modern man. One might explain the vast difference between Man and his rivals on the ground that he was the possessor of an immortal soul or divine spirit. Leaving this rather unsatisfactory explanation aside, let us try to find some other approach. The key lies in the capacity of humans for abstract thought—taking a step back in their minds and "introspecting." With this marvellous facility comes a natural talent to convert the results of these introspections into a code and communicate them to other members of the species. The communicating code is what we call language, and the introspective process, with or without a linguistic component, is known as thinking. Thinking of a kind probably comes in a good deal lower down, at the level where individual animals make "decisions," such as when a dog, faced with a fence blocking it from its food ultimately gives up trying to climb over it and simply walks round it! Kohler's chimpanzee Sultan was certainly indulging in something pretty close to thought when he fitted two sticks together to reach a banana. Nevertheless, there is rather good evidence that the development of a spoken language, such as only humans have, is the trigger which allows a kind of detached, abstract processing to go on and which has allowed us to build up an immense cultural heritage over the past 10,000 years.

(a) *Thought and Language.*

How much is thought tied in with speech? You will remember that Watson liked to call thought "sub-verbal speech" and there is some truth in this. Open your mouth and think the word "bubble." You will probably notice a kind of catch in your throat—which shows how the two processes are tied together. On the other hand, think of some visual scene—say a polar bear sitting on an iceberg. Most people can conjure up a pretty reasonable mental picture of scenes like this without too much trouble and certainly without saying vocally or sub-vocally, either the word bear or iceberg! Incidentally, if you *can't* get a mental image of this kind, don't worry, for about a third of the world's population can't either. This facility for producing "pictures in the mind" has puzzled psychologists for a century—in particular those who can't manage the images themselves, who are inclined to be a bit sceptical about the whole thing. Twist the topic round and consider the case of visual illusions and other perceptual anomalies. For example, take the kind where two lines, objectively the same, look to be of different length. No matter how much measuring with a ruler and how much you tell yourself that the lines are similar, your erroneous percept remains. Here perception and thought are *not* inextricably tied, which disposes of any lingering arguments that thinking was merely a consequence of visual, auditory, or some other input. Incidentally, the link between thought and language is suddenly coming under close study again, some 50 years after Watson had originally tried to explain one in terms of the other. This arises from the young sub-science known as psycholinguistics, the founder of which is the American mathematician, Noam Chomsky. His thesis, rather seriously over-simplified, is that the structure of language can be used to give us a valuable key to the inner logic of the brain's operation. We can never hope to know directly how the inner mechanics of the brain work, he says, so we must look to find them reflected in some more directly observable process. Chomsky and his followers argue that in addition to its "surface" grammar (the kind of grammar we learn at school) all human languages have a deeper set of rules, closely tied in with the programmes which handle the deepest and most fundamental thought processes. Look closely at language, state and define the logic of the "deep grammar" and you have taken a peek at the brain's deepest secrets. It is an interesting idea, shared by many scientists who hold that similar clues can come from a study of dreams, but it suggests that the problem of defining thinking is even harder than we at first imagined.

(b) *Can a Machine Think?*

Yet another approach comes from computer scientists, who, concerned with devising computers capable of communicating in linguistic terms with human beings, have been taking a close look at these problems. From one of the pioneers of computer science, the late British Alan Turing, came a penetrating analysis of the philosophical problems of thought which reopens the discussion again from an entirely fresh angle. He did this by posing the question. "Can a machine think?" Turing pointed out that the almost universal response to this question was "No," but while people felt pretty confident in their opinion, they were seldom able to give a really good reason for it. Typical responses, when they were asked why a machine couldn't think, included, "because you can never get more out a machine than you put into it," "because machines have no souls," and "because only people can think." None of these arguments is valid. In the first place, it is only partly true to say that you can get no more out of a machine than you put in it, and in any case what has that to do with thinking? The second and third points are equally dubious. However, Turing realised that people had a built-in inclination to assume that thinking was a property of humans only, and as a computer engineer who hoped ultimately to see "thinking computers" developed, he was anxious to correct this impression. To do so he rephrased the question this way: "Supposing that you continually built ever more clever computers, how would you know whether one had begun to think or not?" Pointing out that the only evidence we have about whether humans can think (apart from taking their word for it) is the nature of the conversation they have with us, he suggested that one would base one's decision on how well the computer was able to communicate and discourse. Assuming that the fact that the computer was a large metal object with glowing lights, reams of paper tape, etc., would bias people in their judgment of whether it was thinking or not, he proposed that the decision should be based on a simple game. Take one very clever computer which you have reason to suppose may be capable of thought and place it in a room "A." Now take a person in a room "B," and a third in a room "C." Connect up computer "A" and person "B" to person "C" by wires connected to teletypes (special typewriters which allow one to feed information into computers and allow them to respond). Person "C" doesn't know who is on the end of either teletype, "B" or the computer, but he proceeds to try to find out by asking them questions through their respective teletypes. Now if the computer was really dim it would soon give itself away by its dim answers, but if it was really clever it might easily fool "C" into thinking it was the person "B." One important rule of the game, incidentally, is that both "B" and the computer were attempting to fool "C," the object being not to be identified correctly as either human or machine. Now, said Turing, if the point comes where "C" cannot reliably and certainly decide which of his two communicators is which, then to all intents and purposes the computer "A" must be said to be capable of thought! This is really a brilliant approach to the problem even if it seems to be a bit obscure at first. What Turing was really saying was that the *real* evidence that thinking is taking place is evidenced by what the individual, be it human, animal, or computer, actually does, and not what it looks like.

Before leaving this enigmatic topic, consider two recent developments in this area:

(1) In at least two centres in the United States psychologists are engaged in dramatic and apparently successful attempts at "conversational" communication with chimpanzees. The husband and wife team of the Gardners at the State University in Reno, Nevada, have taught a chimpanzee to communicate using American sign language—a series of gestures with hand and arm. Their animals apparently are able to converse in sentences at about the level of communication of a three-year-old human child. Another researcher, David Premack at the University of California, has been teaching his chimpanzees to understand the meaning of special plastic symbols or "words." Using these the chimpanzees form sentences by placing the symbols on a magnetised blackboard, and have built up a substantial working vocabulary. They have even got to the stage of understanding and creating sentences featuring the conditional, for example "pick up the red cup *if* blue light is on," etc. Some of Premack's brightest animals are actually using a specially modified typewriter to generate their messages.

(2) Many psychologists and computer scientists believe that a breakthrough in the field of artificial intelligence—the creation of a robot or computer capable of "reason"—is imminent. Developments in this field, which have been painfully slow since the first major computers were constructed in the 1940s, have been accelerating in the last decade. To take one example—computers can now be programmed to play really good games of chess and can beat top-ranking club players—if not world masters yet. A game played between a Russian and an American computer for the computer chess championship of the world in Stockholm in 1974 was described as "startling" by one chess expert who watched it. The Russian computer won incidentally. The distinguished philosopher and statistician, Professor I. J. Good, himself an outstanding chess player, has evolved the concept of what he calls the "ultra-intelligent machine" (UIM). This he defines as a computer capable of performing every intellectual function at least as well as a human being. Professor Good believes that one of the first tasks that scientists will give to the UIMs to perform will be to set about finding ways of making themselves even more intelligent. This no doubt would rapidly solve all mankind's problems, though it might mean that the UIMs will decide that man is redundant. And a species that becomes redundant, Professor Good reminds us, tends to wither away.

(5) The World of Inner Space.

We have constantly indicated that psychology is the study of behaviour—the activities of living creatures which respond in a meaningful nonrandom way to the vagaries of their environment. The key to understanding these patterns of behaviour is of course the brain, and within the brain itself the programmes which control and determine its actions. One important point which all who study the brain swiftly come to realise, and one which this section has attempted to emphasise, is that no living system can be considered as a mechanical assembly of different parts. Each, whether earwig, cat, or human being, is a complex, integrated system functioning as a unit. The further up the phylogenetic scale one rises, the more complex the system and the more sophisticated and elegant its mechanics. At the human level with mental activities and consciousness emerging as super-control systems, the study of psychology reaches its most fascinating point. Here too, it must be admitted, as a science it has made least headway. There are probably good reasons for this, some related to the intrinsically complicated nature of the mind, others to the attitude of the psychologists themselves. The early pioneering work of Wundt, Ebbinghaus, and others seemed to be setting psychology on course as a science in its own right. The work of Pavlov, immensely important and relevant as it was, served to weaken psychology as a discipline and shift its bias drastically in the direction of physiology. Psychologists themselves ceased to think like psychologists and instead attempted to convert themselves into second-hand physiologists, part-time mathematicians, and indifferent clinicians. This trend, which gathered strength in the 1930s, has persisted until quite recently when a growing disenchantment with the relatively meagre results stemming from the millions of behaviouristic experiments involving pigeons, monkeys, and rats has led to an inevitable swing of the pendulum. More now than at any time in this century is the principal creature for psychological study acknowledged to be man himself. Freud's fabulous and enduring insight—that the mind itself has two vitally important parts, the conscious and the unconscious, each integrated and yet strangely autonomous—is being treated with ever greater respect and understanding today. The realisation that human beings are controlled not merely by their conscious thoughts, wishes, and desires but also by dynamic forces of great power which are *not* under conscious control and barely available to linguistic analysis, is at last becoming a part of even the layman's view of mental life. The tip of the iceberg above the sea, as Freud pointed out, is that part of the mind which is under conscious control. Below the sea, massively enigmatic, lies the great bulk of the unconscious, the repository of the programmes which largely determine the behaviour of man. This is the zone, rich in mystery, which must ultimately be plotted by psychology and its researchers. This is the territory, glimpses of which we catch through the enigma of memory, the hallucinations of dementia, and in the misty drama of our dreams. The controversial English author J. G. Ballard has christened this territory "inner space," in contrast with the vast reaches of outer space that the first human astronauts are today beginning to explore.

SPORTING COMPANION

Association Football, Athletics, Badminton, Baseball, Basketball, Billiards, Bowls, Cricket, Golf, Greyhound Racing, Gymnastics, Hockey, Horse Racing, Lawn Tennis, Motor Racing, Rifle Shooting, Rowing and Sculling, Rugby League, Rugby Union, Show Jumping, Snooker, Speedway, Squash Rackets, Swimming & Diving, Table Tennis. A special topic in this edition looks at the history of The Ashes, the cricket battle between England and Australia.

SPORTING COMPANION

ASSOCIATION FOOTBALL

FOOTBALL LEAGUE CHAMPIONS

1950–1	Tottenham H	1962–3	Everton	1974–5	Derby C
1951–2	Manchester U	1963–4	Liverpool	1975–6	Liverpool
1952–3	Arsenal	1964–5	Manchester U	1976–7	Liverpool
1953–4	Wolverhampton W	1965–6	Liverpool	1977–8	Nottingham F
1954–5	Chelsea	1966–7	Manchester U	1978–9	Liverpool
1955–6	Manchester U	1967–8	Manchester C	1979–80	Liverpool
1956–7	Manchester U	1968–9	Leeds U	1980–1	Aston Villa
1957–8	Wolverhampton W	1969–70	Everton	1981–2	Liverpool
1958–9	Wolverhampton W	1970–1	Arsenal	1982–3	Liverpool
1959–60	Burnley	1971–2	Derby C	1983–4	Liverpool
1960–1	Tottenham H	1972–3	Liverpool	1984–5	Everton
1961–2	Ipswich T	1973–4	Leeds U	1985–6	Liverpool

FOOTBALL ASSOCIATION CHALLENGE CUP WINNERS

1950–1	Newcastle U	1962–3	Manchester U	1974–5	West Ham U
1951–2	Newcastle U	1963–4	West Ham U	1975–6	Southampton
1952–3	Blackpool	1964–5	Liverpool	1976–7	Manchester U
1953–4	West Bromwich A	1965–6	Everton	1977–8	Ipswich T
1954–5	Newcastle U	1966–7	Tottenham H	1978–9	Arsenal
1955–6	Manchester C	1967–8	West Bromwich A	1979–80	West Ham U
1956–7	Aston Villa	1968–9	Manchester C	1980–1	Tottenham H
1957–8	Bolton W	1969–70	Chelsea	1981–2	Tottenham H
1958–9	Nottingham F	1970–1	Arsenal	1982–3	Manchester U
1959–60	Wolverhampton W	1971–2	Leeds U	1983–4	Everton
1960–1	Tottenham H	1972–3	Sunderland	1984–5	Manchester U
1961–2	Tottenham H	1973–4	Liverpool	1985–6	Liverpool

FOOTBALL LEAGUE MILK CUP WINNERS

1960–1	Aston V	1969–70	Manchester C	1978–9	Nottingham F
1961–2	Norwich C	1970–1	Tottenham H	1979–80	Wolverhampton W
1962–3	Birmingham C	1971–2	Stoke C	1980–1	Liverpool
1963–4	Leicester C	1972–3	Tottenham H	1981–2	Liverpool
1964–5	Chelsea	1973–4	Wolverhampton W	1982–3	Liverpool
1965–6	West Bromwich A	1974–5	Aston V	1983–4	Liverpool
1966–7	Queen's Park R	1975–6	Manchester C	1984–5	Norwich C
1967–8	Leeds U	1976–7	Aston V	1985–6	Oxford U
1968–9	Swindon T	1977–8	Nottingham F		

SCOTTISH LEAGUE CHAMPIONS

1950–1	Hibernian	1962–3	Rangers	1974–5	Rangers
1951–2	Hibernian	1963–4	Rangers	1975–6	Rangers
1952–3	Rangers	1964–5	Kilmarnock	1976–7	Celtic
1953–4	Celtic	1965–6	Celtic	1977–8	Rangers
1954–5	Aberdeen	1966–7	Celtic	1978–9	Celtic
1955–6	Rangers	1967–8	Celtic	1979–80	Aberdeen
1956–7	Rangers	1968–9	Celtic	1980–1	Celtic
1957–8	Hearts	1969–70	Celtic	1981–2	Celtic
1958–9	Rangers	1970–1	Celtic	1982–3	Dundee U
1959–60	Hearts	1971–2	Celtic	1983–4	Aberdeen
1960–1	Rangers	1972–3	Celtic	1984–5	Aberdeen
1961–2	Dundee	1973–4	Celtic	1985–6	Celtic

SCOTTISH FOOTBALL ASSOCIATION CUP WINNERS

1950–1	Celtic	1962–3	Rangers	1974–5	Celtic
1951–2	Motherwell	1963–4	Rangers	1975–6	Rangers
1952–3	Rangers	1964–5	Celtic	1976–7	Celtic
1953–4	Celtic	1965–6	Rangers	1977–8	Rangers
1954–5	Clyde	1966–7	Celtic	1978–9	Rangers
1955–6	Hearts	1967–8	Dunfermline A	1979–80	Celtic
1956–7	Falkirk	1968–9	Celtic	1980–1	Rangers
1957–8	Clyde	1969–70	Aberdeen	1981–2	Aberdeen
1958–9	St Mirren	1970–1	Celtic	1982–3	Aberdeen
1959–60	Rangers	1971–2	Celtic	1983–4	Aberdeen
1960–1	Dunfermline A	1972–3	Rangers	1984–5	Celtic
1961–2	Rangers	1973–4	Celtic	1985–6	Aberdeen

SCOTTISH LEAGUE CUP WINNERS

1950–1	Motherwell	1962–3	Hearts	1974–5	Celtic
1951–2	Dundee	1963–4	Rangers	1975–6	Rangers
1952–3	Dundee	1964–5	Rangers	1976–7	Aberdeen
1953–4	East Fife	1965–6	Celtic	1977–8	Rangers
1954–5	Hearts	1966–7	Celtic	1978–9	Rangers
1955–6	Aberdeen	1967–8	Celtic	1979–80	Dundee U
1956–7	Celtic	1968–9	Celtic	1980–1	Dundee U
1957–8	Celtic	1969–70	Celtic	1981–2	Rangers
1958–9	Hearts	1970–1	Rangers	1982–3	Celtic
1959–60	Hearts	1971–2	Partick T	1983–4	Rangers
1960–1	Rangers	1972–3	Hibernian	1984–5	Rangers
1961–2	Rangers	1973–4	Dundee	1985–6	Aberdeen

WORLD CUP WINNERS

1930	Uruguay	1958	Brazil	1974	W Germany
1934	Italy	1962	Brazil	1978	Argentina
1938	Italy	1966	England	1982	Italy
1950	Uruguay	1970	Brazil	1986	Argentina
1954	W Germany				

EUROPEAN CHAMPIONS' CUP WINNERS

1955–6	Real Madrid	1965–6	Real Madrid	1975–6	Bayern Munich
1956–7	Real Madrid	1966–7	Glasgow C	1976–7	Liverpool
1957–8	Real Madrid	1967–8	Manchester U	1977–8	Liverpool
1958–9	Real Madrid	1968–9	A C Milan	1978–9	Nottingham F
1959–60	Real Madrid	1969–70	Feyenoord	1979–80	Nottingham F
1960–1	Benfica	1970–1	Ajax	1980–1	Liverpool
1961–2	Benfica	1971–2	Ajax	1981–2	Aston V
1962–3	A C Milan	1972–3	Ajax	1982–3	Hamburg SV
1963–4	Inter Milan	1973–4	Bayern Munich	1983–4	Liverpool
1964–5	Inter Milan	1974–5	Bayern Munich	1984–5	Juventus
				1985–6	Steaua Bucharest

EUROPEAN NATIONAL CUP–WINNERS' CUP

1961	Florentina	1970	Manchester C	1979	Barcelona
1962	Atletico Madrid	1971	Chelsea	1980	Valencia
1963	Tottenham H	1972	Glasgow R	1981	Dynamo Tbilisi
1964	Sporting Lisbon	1973	A C Milan	1982	Barcelona
1965	West Ham U	1974	Magdeburg	1983	Aberdeen
1966	Borussia Dortmund	1975	Dynamo Kiev	1984	Juventus
1967	Bayern Munich	1976	Anderlecht	1985	Everton
1968	A C Milan	1977	Hamburg SV	1986	Dynamo Kiev
1969	Sl Bratislava	1978	Anderlecht		

UEFA CUP WINNERS

1958	Barcelona	1969	Newcastle U	1979	Borussia M
1960	Barcelona	1970	Arsenal	1980	Eintracht F
1961	A S Roma	1971	Leeds U	1981	Ipswich T
1962	Valencia	1972	Tottenham H	1982	Gothenburg
1963	Valencia	1973	Liverpool	1983	Anderlecht
1964	Real Zaragossa	1974	Feyenoord	1984	Tottenham H
1965	Ferencvaros	1975	Borussia M	1985	Real Madrid
1966	Barcelona	1976	Liverpool	1986	Real Madrid
1967	Dynamo Zagreb	1977	Juventus		
1968	Leeds U	1978	PSV Eindhoven		

EUROPEAN NATIONS COMPETITION

1960	USSR	1972	W Germany	1980	W Germany
1964	Spain	1976	Czechoslovakia	1984	France
1968	Italy				

ATHLETICS

1984 OLYMPIC GAMES (LOS ANGELES)

Men

100 metres C Lewis US 9·99s
200 metres C Lewis US 19·80s
400 metres A Babers US 44·27s
800 metres J Cruz Brazil 1 min 43s
1,500 metres S Coe GB 3 min 32·53s
5,000 metres S Aouita Morocco 13 min 5.59s
10,000 metres A Cova Italy 27 min 51·1s
Marathon C Lopes Portugal 2h 9 min 21s
4 × 100 metres relay US 37·83s
4 × 400 metres relay US 2 min 57·91s
110 metres hurdles R Kingdom US 13·20s
400 metres hurdles E Moses US 47·75s

3,000 metres steeplechase J Korir Kenya 8 min 11·8s
20 kilometres walk E Canto Mexico 1h 23 min 13s
50 kilometres walk R Gonzalez Mex 3h 47 min 26s
High jump D Moegenburg W Ger 2·35m
Long jump C Lewis US 8·54m
Triple jump A Joyner US 17·26m
Pole vault P Quinon France 5·75m
Shot put A Andrei Italy 21·26m
Discus throw R Dannenberg W Ger 66·6m
Javelin throw A Haerkoenen Fin 86·76m
Hammer throw J Tiainen Fin 78·08m
Decathlon D Thompson GB 8,797 pts

Women

100 metres E Ashford US 10·97s
200 metres V Brisco-Hooks US 21·81s
400 metres V Brisco-Hooks US 48·83s
800 metres D Melinte Romania 1 min 57.6s
1,500 metres G Dorio Italy 4 min 3·25s
3,000 metres M Puica Romania 8 min 35.96s
Marathon J Benoit US 2h 24 min 52s
4 × 100 metres relay US 41·65s
4 × 400 metres relay US 3 min 18·29s

100 metres hurdles B Fitzgerald Brown US 12.84s
400 metres hurdles N El Moutawakeled Morocco 54·61s
High jump U Meyfarth W Ger 2·02m
Long jump A Stanciu Romania 6.96 m
Shot put C Losch W Ger 20.48m
Discus throw R Stalman Neth 65.36m
Javelin throw T Sanderson GB 69·56m
Heptathlon G Nunn Australia 6,390 pts

OLYMPIC RECORDS

Men

100 metres 9.95 J Hines US 1968 Mex C
200 metres 19.80s C Lewis US 1984 Los A
400 metres 43.86s L Evans US 1968 Mex C
800 metres 1 min 43s J Cruz Brazil 1984 Los A
1,500 metres 3 min 32·53s S Coe GB 1984 Los A
5,000 metres 13 min 5.59s S Aouita Mor 1984 Los A
10,000 metres 27 min 38·35s L Viren Fin 1972 Mun
Marathon 2h 9 min 21s C Lopes Por 1984 Los A
4 × 100 metres relay 37·83s US 1984 Los A
4 × 400 metres relay 2 min 56·16s US 1968 Mex C
110 metres hurdles 13·2s R Kingdom US 1984 Los A
400 metres hurdles 47.64s E Moses US 1976 Mont
3,000 metres steeplechase 8 min 8·02s A Garderud Swe 1976 Mont

20 kilometres walk 1h 23 min 13s E Canto Mexico 1984 Los A
50 kilometres walk 3h 47 min 26s R Gonzalez Mex 1984 Los A
High jump 2·36m G Wessig E Ger 1980 Mos
Long jump 8·90m R Beamon US 1968 Mex C
Triple jump 17·35m J Undmae USSR 1980 Mos
Pole vault 5·78m W Kozakiewicz Pol 1980 Mos
Shot put 21·35m V Kiselyou USSR 1980 Mos
Discus throw 68·28m M Wilkins US 1976 Mont
Javelin throw 94·58m M Nemeth Hun 1976 Mont
Hammer throw 81·8m Y Sedykh USSR 1980 Mos
Decathlon 8,797 pts D Thompson GB 1984 Los A

Women

100 metres 10·97s E Ashford US 1984 Los A
200 metres 21·81s V Brisco-Hooks US 1984 Los A
400 metres 48·83s V Brisco-Hooks US 1984 Los A
800 metres 1 min 53·43s N Olizarenko USSR 1980 Mos
1,500 metres 3 min 56·58s T Kazankina USSR 1980 Mos
3,000 metres 8 min 35.96s M Puica Rom 1984 Los A
Marathon 2h 24 min 52s J Benoit US 1984 Los A
4 × 100 metres relay 41·60s E Ger 1980 Mos
4 × 400 metres relay 3 min 18·29s US 1984 Los A
100 metres hurdles 12·56s V Komisova USSR 1980 Mos

High jump 2·70m U Meyfarth W Ger 1984 Los A
Long jump 7·06m T Kolpakova USSR 1980 Mos
Shot put 22·41m I Slupianek E Ger 1980 Mos
Discus throw 69·96m E Jahl E Ger 1980 Mos
Javelin throw 69·56m T Sanderson GB 1984 Los A
Heptathlon 6,390 pts G Nunn Australia 1984 Los A

1982 EUROPEAN CHAMPIONSHIPS (ATHENS)

Men

100 metres F Emmelmann E Ger 10·21s
200 metres O Prenzier E Ger 20·46s
400 metres H Weber W Ger 44·72s
800 metres H-P Ferner W Ger 1 min 46·33s
1,500 metres S Cram GB 3 min 36·49s
5,000 metres T Wessinghage W Ger 13 min 28·90s
10,000 metres A Coya Italy 27 min 41·03s
Marathon G Nijboer Holland 2h 15 min 16·00s
4 × 100 metres relay USSR 38·60s
4 × 400 metres relay W Ger 3 min 00·51s
110 metres hurdles T Munkelt E Ger 13·41s
400 metres hurdles H Schmid W Ger 47·48s
3,000 metres steeplechase P Ilg W Ger 8 min 18·52s

20 kilometres walk J Marin Spain 1h 23 min 43·00s
50 kilometres walk R Salonen Finland 3h 55 min 29·00s
High jump D Mogenburg W Ger 2·30m
Long jump L Dombrowski E Ger 8·41m
Triple jump K Conner GB 17·29m
Pole vault A Krupsky USSR 5·60m
Shot put U Beyer E Ger 21·50m
Discus throw I Bugar Czech 66·64m
Javelin throw U Höhn E Ger 91·34m
Hammer throw Y Sedykh USSR 81·66m
Decathlon D Thompson GB 8,744 pts

Women

100 metres M Göhr E Ger 11·01s
200 metres B Wöckel E Ger 22·04s
400 metres M Koch E Ger 48·15s
800 metres O Mineyeva USSR 1 min 55·41s
1,500 metres O Dvirna USSR 3 min 57·80s
3,000 metres S Ulmasova USSR 8 min 30·28s
Marathon R Mota Portugal 2h 36m 04·00s
100 metres hurdles L Kalek Poland 12·45s

400 metres hurdles A-L Skoglund Sweden 54·58s
High jump U Meyfarth W Ger 2·02m
Long jump V Ionescu Rom 6·79m
Shot put I Slupianek E Ger 21·59m
Discus throw T Hristova Bul 68·34m
Javelin throw A Verouli Greece 70·02m
Heptathlon R Neubert E Ger 6,622 pts

1982 COMMONWEALTH GAMES (BRISBANE)

Men

100 metres A Wells Scot 10·02s
200 metres M McFarlane Eng & A Wells Scot 20·43s
400 metres B Cameron Jamaica 45·89s
800 metres P Bourke Aus 1 min 45·18s
1,500 metres S Cram Eng 3 min 42·37s
5,000 metres D Moorcroft Eng 13 min 33·00s
10,000 metres G Shahanga Tanz 28 min 10·20s
Marathon R de Castella Aus 2h 9 min 18·00s
4 × 100 metres relay Nigeria 39·15s
4 × 400 metres relay England 3 min 05·45s
110 metres hurdles M McCoy Can 13·37s
400 metres hurdles G Brown Aus 49·37s

3,000 metres steeplechase J Korir Kenya 8 min 23·94s
30 kilometres walk S Barry Wales 2h 10 min 16·00s
High jump M Ottey Can 2·31m
Long jump G Honey Aus 8·13m
Triple jump K Connor Eng 17·81m
Pole vault R Boyd Aus 5·20m
Shot put B Pauletto Can 19·55m
Discus throw B Cooper Bahamas 64·04m
Javelin throw M O'Rourke NZ 89·48m
Hammer throw R Weir Eng 75·08m
Decathlon D Thompson Eng 8,410 pts

Women

100 metres A Taylor Can 11·00s	100 metres hurdles S Strong Eng 12·78s
200 metres M Ottey Jamaica 22·19s	400 metres hurdles D Flintoff Aus 55·89s
400 metres R Boyle Aus 51·26s	High jump D Brill Can 1·88m
800 metres K McDermott Wales 2 min 01·31s	Long jump S Ferguson Bahamas 6·91m
1,500 metres C Boxer Eng 4 min 08·28s	Shot put J Oakes Eng 17·92m
3,000 metres A Audain NZ 8 min 45·53s	Discus throw M Ritchie Scot 62·98m
4 × 100 metres relay England 43·15s	Javelin throw S Howland Aus 64·46m
4 × 400 metres relay Canada 3 min 27·70s	Heptathlon G Nunn Aus 6,282 pts

BADMINTON

ALL ENGLAND CHAMPIONSHIPS

Men's singles

1950–2	W P Soon (Malaya)	1975	S Pri (Denmark)
1953–4	E B Choong (Malaya)	1976	R Hartono (Indonesia)
1955	W P Soon (Malaya)	1977	F Delfs (Denmark)
1956–7	E B Choong (Malaya)	1978	L S King (Indonesia)
1958	E Kops (Denmark)	1979	L S King (Indonesia)
1959	T J Hok (Indonesia)	1980	P Padukone (India)
1960–3	E Kops (Denmark)	1981	L S King (Indonesia)
1964	K A Nielsen (Denmark)	1982	M Frost (Denmark)
1965	E Kops (Denmark)	1983	L Jin (China)
1966	T A Huang (Malaya)	1984	M Frost (Denmark)
1967	E Kops (Denmark)	1985	Z Jianhua (China)
1968–74	R Hartono (Indonesia)	1986	M Frost (Denmark)

Women's singles

1950	T Ahm (Denmark)	1972	N Nakayama (Japan)
1951	A S Jacobsen (Denmark)	1973	M Beck (GB)
1952	T Ahm (Denmark)	1974	H Yuki (Japan)
1953	M Ussing (Denmark)	1975	H Yuki (Japan)
1954	J Devlin (US)	1976	G Gilks (GB)
1955–6	M Varner (US)	1977	H Yuki (Japan)
1957–8	J Devlin (US)	1978	G Gilks (GB)
1959	H M Ward (GB)	1979	L Koppen (Denmark)
1960	J Devlin (US)	1980	L Koppen (Denmark)
1961–4	G C K Hashman (US)	1981	S A Hwang (Korea)
1965	U H Smith (GB)	1982	Z Ailing (China)
1966–7	G C K Hashman (US)	1983	Z Ailing (China)
1968	E Twedberg (Sweden)	1984	L Lingwei (China)
1969	H Yuki (Japan)	1985	H Aiping (China)
1970	E Takenaka (Japan)	1986	Kim Yun Ja (Korea)
1971	E Twedberg (Sweden)		

BASEBALL (US)

WORLD SERIES WINNERS

1958	New York Yankees	1968	Detroit Tigers	1978	New York Yankees
1959	Los Angeles Dodgers	1969	New York Mets	1979	Pittsburgh Pirates
1960	Pittsburgh Pirates	1970	Baltimore Orioles	1980	Philadelphia Phillies
1961	New York Yankees	1971	Pittsburgh Pirates	1981	Los Angeles Dodgers
1962	New York Yankees	1972	Oakland Athletics	1982	St Louis Cardinals
1963	Los Angeles Dodgers	1973	Oakland Athletics	1983	Baltimore Orioles
1964	St Louis Cardinals	1974	Oakland Athletics	1984	Detroit Tigers
1965	Los Angeles Dodgers	1975	Cincinnati Reds	1985	Kansas City Royals
1966	Baltimore Orioles	1976	Cincinnati Reds		
1967	St Louis Cardinals	1977	New York Yankees		

BASKETBALL

OLYMPIC CHAMPIONS

Men		Women	
1936–48–52–56			
–60–64–68	USA	—	
1972	USSR		
1976	USA	USSR	
1980	Yugoslavia	USSR	
1984	USA		

WORLD CHAMPIONS

	Men				
1950	Argentina	1963	Brazil	1974	USSR
1954	USA	1967	USSR	1978	Yugoslavia
1959	Brazil	1970	Yugoslavia	1982	USSR

	Women				
1953	USA	1964	USSR	1975	USSR
1957	USA	1967	USSR	1979	USA
1959	USSR	1971	USSR	1983	USSR

ASDA NATIONAL CUP

1979	Doncaster	1983	Solent	1986	Kingston
1980–1	C Palace	1984	Solent		
1982	Solent	1985	Kingston		

NATIONAL CHAMPIONSHIP

1973	London ESK	1981	Sunderland	1985	Manchester
1974	C Palace	1982	C Palace	1986	Kingston
1975	EAS Islington	1983	Sunderland		
1976–7–8		1984	Solent		
–9–80	C Palace				

NATIONAL LEAGUE

1973	Avenue (Leyton)	1979	Doncaster	1985	Kingston
1974	C Palace	1980	C Palace	1986	Manchester U
1975	EAS Islington	1981	Birmingham		
1976–7		1982–3	C Palace		
–8	C Palace	1984	Solent		

BILLIARDS

WORLD CHAMPIONS (professional)

1951	C McConachy (NZ)	1974	R Williams (W)	1983	R Williams (W)
1968	R Williams (W)	1976	R Williams (W)	1984	M Wildman (E)
1971	R Williams (W)	1980	F Davis (E)	1985	R Edmonds (E)
1973	R Williams (W)	1982	R Williams (W)	1986	R Foldvari (A)

UNITED KINGDOM CHAMPIONS (professional)

1947	J Davis	1951	F Davis	1981	R. Williams
1948	S Smith	1979	R Williams	1983	F Davis
1950	J Barrie	1980	J Karnehem		

BOWLS

EBA NATIONAL CHAMPIONSHIPS
Single-handed

1960	D J Bryant	1969	J Davidson	1978	C Burch
1961	P A Line	1970	H Kershaw	1979	D J Cutler
1962	C Mercer	1971	D J Bryant	1980	T Buller
1963	C S Graham	1972	D J Bryant	1981	A Thompson
1964	P A Line	1973	D J Bryant	1982	C Ward
1965	R E Lewis	1974	W C Irish	1983	J Bell
1966	D J Bryant	1975	D J Bryant	1984	W Richards
1967	W C Irish	1976	A O'Connell	1985	R Keating
1968	N R Groves	1977	C Ward		

CRICKET

TEST MATCHES

England v. Australia
(first played 1876)
Won: England 86 Australia 96 Drawn: 75
England v. South Africa
(first played 1888)
Won: England 46 South Africa 18 Drawn: 38
England v. West Indies
(first played 1928)
Won: England 21 West Indies 35 Drawn: 34
England v. New Zealand
(first played 1929)
Won: England 30 New Zealand 3 Drawn: 27
England v. India
(first played 1932)
Won: England 30 India 9 Drawn: 33
England v. Pakistan
(first played 1954)
Won: England 13 Pakistan 3 Drawn: 23
England v Sri Lanka
(first played 1982)
Won: England 1 Sri Lanka 0 Drawn: 1

SCHWEPPES (now BRITTANIC) COUNTY CHAMPIONSHIP

1950	Lancashire	1962	Yorkshire	1975	Leicestershire
	Surrey	1963	Yorkshire	1976	Middlesex
1951	Warwickshire	1964	Worcestershire	1977	Kent
1952	Surrey	1965	Worcestershire		Middlesex
1953	Surrey	1966	Yorkshire	1978	Kent
1954	Surrey	1967	Yorkshire	1979	Essex
1955	Surrey	1968	Yorkshire	1980	Middlesex
1956	Surrey	1969	Glamorgan	1981	Nottinghamshire
1957	Surrey	1970	Kent	1982	Middlesex
1958	Surrey	1971	Surrey	1983	Essex
1959	Yorkshire	1972	Warwickshire	1984	Essex
1960	Yorkshire	1973	Hampshire	1985	Middlesex
1961	Hampshire	1974	Worcestershire		

GILLETTE (now NATWEST) CUP

1963	Sussex	1971	Lancashire	1979	Somerset
1964	Sussex	1972	Lancashire	1980	Middlesex
1965	Yorkshire	1973	Gloucestershire	1981	Derbyshire
1966	Warwickshire	1974	Kent	1982	Surrey
1967	Kent	1975	Lancashire	1983	Somerset
1968	Warwickshire	1976	Northamptonshire	1984	Middlesex
1969	Yorkshire	1977	Middlesex	1985	Essex
1970	Lancashire	1978	Sussex		

JOHN PLAYER LEAGUE

1969	Lancashire	1975	Hampshire	1981	Essex
1970	Lancashire	1976	Kent	1982	Sussex
1971	Worcestershire	1977	Leicestershire	1983	Yorkshire
1972	Kent	1978	Hampshire	1984	Essex
1973	Kent	1979	Somerset	1985	Essex
1974	Leicestershire	1980	Warwickshire		

BENSON & HEDGES CUP

1972	Leicestershire	1977	Gloucestershire	1982	Somerset
1973	Kent	1978	Kent	1983	Middlesex
1974	Surrey	1979	Essex	1984	Lancashire
1975	Leicestershire	1980	Northamptonshire	1985	Leicestershire
1976	Kent	1981	Somerset		

PRUDENTIAL WORLD CUP

1975	West Indies
1979	West Indies
1983	India

GOLF

OPEN CHAMPIONSHIP

1950	A D Locke (SA)	1962	A Palmer (US)	1974	G J Player (SA)
1951	M Faulkner (GB)	1963	R J Charles (NZ)	1975	T Watson (US)
1952	A D Locke (SA)	1964	A Lema (US)	1976	J Miller (US)
1953	B Hogan (US)	1965	P W Thomson (Aus)	1977	T Watson (US)
1954	P W Thomson (Aus)	1966	J Nicklaus (US)	1978	J Nicklaus (US)
1955	P W Thomson (Aus)	1967	R de Vicenzo (Arg)	1979	S Ballesteros (Spain)
1956	P W Thomson (Aus)	1968	G J Player (SA)	1980	T Watson (US)
1957	A D Locke (SA)	1969	A Jacklin (GB)	1981	W Rogers (US)
1958	P W Thomson (Aus)	1970	J Nicklaus (US)	1982	T Watson (US)
1959	G J Player (SA)	1971	L Trevino (US)	1983	T Watson (US)
1960	K D G Nagle (Aus)	1972	L Trevino (US)	1984	S Ballesteros (Spain)
1961	A Palmer (US)	1973	T Weiskopf (US)	1985	S Lyle (GB)

GREYHOUND RACING

THE DERBY
(All races photo-timed since 1953 and run over 500 metres from 1975)

	Owner	Greyhound	Trainer	Time(s)
1960	Mrs B J Dash's	Duleek Dandy	W H Dash, Private	29·15
1961	Mr D Heale's	Palm's Printer	P J McEvoy, Clapton	28·84
1962	Mr P J Dunphy's	The Grand Canal	P J Dunphy, Ireland	29·09
1963	Mr S J Barrett's	Lucky Boy Boy	J Bassett, Clapton	29·00
1964	Mr S Donohue's	Hack Up Chieftain	P Stagg, Belle Vue	28·92
1965	Messrs V R & P V Leah's	Chittering Clapton	A Jackson, Clapton	28·82
1966	Miss P Wallis & Sir R Adeane's	Faithful Hope	P Keane, Clapton	28·52
1967	Mr N Finson's	Tric-Trac	R Hookway, Owlerton	29·00
1968	HRH The Duke of Edinburgh's	Camira Flash	R Singleton, White City	28·69
1969	Mr H Orr's	Sand Star	H Orr, Ireland	28·76
1970	Mr R A Young's	John Silver	B Tompkins, Private	29·01
1971	Mr H G White's	Dolores Rocket	H G White, Private	28·74
1972	Messrs B Stanley & G & B Marks'	Patricia's Hope	A Jackson, Clapton	28·55
1973	Messrs G & B Marks & J O'Connor's	Patricia's Hope	J O'Connor, Ireland	28.66
1974	Mr J DeMulder & Miss L Walker's	Jimsun	G DeMulder, Hall Green	28·76
1975	Mr D M Law's	Tartan Khan	G Lynds, Bletchley	29.57
1976	Mr R H Lancaster's	Mutts Silver	P Rees, Wimbledon	29·38
1977	Mr R Bacci's	Balliniska Band	E Moore, Belle Vue	29·16
1978	Mrs S Pearce's	Lacca Champion	P Mullins, Private	29·42
1979	Mr R H Hadley's	Sarah's Bunny	G DeMulder, Hall Green	29·53
1980	Mr A McLean's	Indian Joe	J Hayes, Ireland	29·69
1981	Mr S Barnett's	Parkdown Jet	G McKenna, Ireland	29·57
1982	Mr L James'	Laurie's Panther	T Duggan, Romford	29·60
1983	Mr J J Quinn's	I'm Slippy	Mrs B Tompkins, Coventry	29·40
1984	Mr J Duffy's	Whisper Wishes	C Coyle, Maidstone	29.43
1985	Mr D J Hawthorn	Pagan Swallow	P Rees, Wimbledon	29.04

GYMNASTICS

1984 OLYMPIC GAMES (LOS ANGELES)

Men

Combined exercises (team) US
Floor exercises Li Ning China
Horizontal bar S Morisue Japan
Parallel bars B Conner US

Horse vault Yun Lou China
Pommel horse Li Ning China
Rings K Gushiken Japan &
  Li Ning China

Women

Combined exercises (team) Romania
Individual overall M L Retton US
Balance beam S Pauca Romania
Floor exercises E Szabo Romania

Uneven bars Yanhong Ma China &
  J McNamara US
Horse vault E Szabo Romania
Rhythmic L Fung Canada

HOCKEY

OLYMPIC CHAMPIONS

1908	England	1952	India	1976	New Zealand
1920	Gt Britain	1956	India	1980	India
1928	India	1960	Pakistan	1984	Pakistan
1932	India	1964	India		
1936	India	1968	Pakistan		
1948	India	1972	W Germany		

HORSE RACING

THE DERBY

	Horse	Jockey	Owner
1950	Galcador	W Johnstone	M Boussac
1951	Arctic Prince	C Spares	Mr J McGrath
1952	Tulyar	C Smirke	The Aga Khan
1953	Pinza	G Richards	Sir V Sassoon
1954	Never Say Die	L Piggott	Mr R S Clark
1955	Phil Drake	F Palmer	Mme Volterra
1956	Lavandin	W Johnstone	M Wertheimer
1957	Crepello	L Piggott	Sir V Sassoon
1958	Hard Ridden	C Smirke	Sir V Sassoon
1959	Parthia	W H Carr	Sir H de Trafford
1960	St Paddy	L Piggott	Sir V Sassoon
1961	Psidium	R Poincelet	Mrs Arpad Plesch
1962	Larkspur	N Sellwood	Mr R Guest
1963	Relko	Y Saint-Martin	M F Dupré
1964	Santa Claus	A Breasley	Mr J Ismay
1965	Sea Bird II	T P Glennon	Mr M J Ternynck
1966	Charlottown	A Breasley	Lady Z Wernher
1967	Royal Palace	G Moore	Mr H J Joel
1968	Sir Ivor	L Piggott	Mr R R Guest
1969	Blakeney	E Johnson	Mr A Budgett
1970	Nijinsky	L Piggott	Mr C W Engelhard
1971	Mill Reef	G Lewis	Mr P Mellon
1972	Roberto	L Piggott	Mr J Galbreath
1973	Morston	E Hide	Mr A Budgett
1974	Snow Knight	B Taylor	Mrs N Philips
1975	Grundy	P Eddery	Dr C Vittadini
1976	Empery	L Piggott	Mr B Hunt
1977	The Minstrel	L Piggott	Mr R Sangster
1978	Shirley Heights	G Starkey	Lord Halifax
1979	Troy	W Carson	Sir M Sobell
1980	Henbit	W Carson	Mrs A Plesch
1981	Shergar	W R Swinburn	The Aga Khan
1982	Golden Fleece	P Eddery	Mr R Sangster
1983	Teenoso	L Piggott	Mr E Moller
1984	Secreto	C Roche	Mr L Miglitti
1985	Slip Anchor	S Cauthen	Lord Howard de Walden
1986	Shahrastani	W. R. Swinburn	The Aga Khan

THE GRAND NATIONAL

	Horse	Jockey	Owner
1950	Freebooter	J Power	Mrs L Brotherton
1951	Nickel Coin	J A Bullock	Mr J Royle
1952	Teal	A P Thompson	Mr H Lane
1953	Early Mist	B Marshall	Mr J H Griffin
1954	Royal Tan	B Marshall	Mr J H Griffin
1955	Quare Times	P Taffe	Mrs W H E Welman
1956	ESB	D Dick	Mrs L Carver
1957	Sundew	F Winter	Mrs G Kohn
1958	Mr What	A Freeman	Mr D Coughlan
1959	Oxo	M Scudamore	Mr J E Bigg
1960	Merryman II	G Scott	Miss W H S Wallace
1961	Nicolaus Silver	H Beasley	Mr C Vaughan
1962	Kilmore	F Winter	Mr N Cohen
1963	Ayala	P Buckley	Mr P B Raymond
1964	Team Spirit	G W Robinson	Mr J Goodman
1965	Jay Trump	C Smith	Mrs M Stephenson
1966	Anglo	T Norman	Mr S Levy
1967	Foinavon	J Buckingham	Mr C P T Watkins
1968	Red Alligator	B Fletcher	Mr J Manners
1969	Highland Wedding	E Harty	Mr T H McKay, jun.
1970	Gay Trip	P Taaffe	Mr A Chambers
1971	Specify	J Cook	Mr F W Pontin
1972	Well to Do	G Thorner	Capt T Forster
1973	Red Rum	B Fletcher	Mr N Le Mare
1974	Red Rum	B Fletcher	Mr N Le Mare
1975	L'Escargot	T Carberry	Mr R Guest
1976	Rag Trade	J Burke	Mr P Raymond
1977	Red Rum	T Stack	Mr N Le Mare
1978	Lucius	B R Davis	Mrs D Whitaker
1979	Rubstic	M Barnes	Mr J Douglas
1980	Ben Nevis	C Fenwick	Mr R Stewart, jun.
1981	Aldaniti	R Champion	Mrs V Embericos
1982	Grittar	C Saunders	Mr F Gilman
1983	Corbiere	B de Haan	Mr B Burrough
1984	Hallo Dandy	N Doughty	Mr R Shaw
1985	Last Suspect	H Davies	Anne, Duchess of Westminster
1986	West Tip	R Dunwoody	Mr P Luff

LAWN TENNIS

DAVIS CUP

1950–3	Australia	1973	Australia	1980	Czechoslovakia
1954	USA	1974	South Africa	1981	USA
1955–7	Australia	1975	Sweden	1982	USA
1958	USA	1976	Italy	1983	Australia
1959–62	Australia	1977	Australia	1984	Sweden
1963	USA	1978–9	USA	1985	Sweden
1964–7	Australia				
1968–72	USA				

WIMBLEDON CHAMPIONSHIPS

Men's Singles

1950	J E Patty (US)	1962	R Laver (Aus)	1974	J Connors (US)
1951	R Savitt (US)	1963	C R McKinley (US)	1975	A R Ashe (US)
1952	F A Sedgman (Aus)	1964	R Emerson (Aus)	1976	B Borg (Sweden)
1953	E V Seixas (US)	1965	R Emerson (Aus)	1977	B Borg (Sweden)
1954	J Drobny (Egypt)	1966	M Santana (Spain)	1978	B Borg (Sweden)
1955	M A Trabert (US)	1967	J D Newcombe (Aus)	1979	B Borg (Sweden)
1956	L A Hoad (Aus)	1968	R Laver (Aus)	1980	B Borg (Sweden)
1957	L A Hoad (Aus)	1969	R Laver (Aus)	1981	J P McEnroe (US)
1958	A J Cooper (Aus)	1970	J D Newcombe (Aus)	1982	J Connors (US)
1959	A Olmedo (Peru)	1971	J D Newcombe (Aus)	1983	J P McEnroe (US)
1960	N A Fraser (Aus)	1972	S R Smith (US)	1984	J P McEnroe (US)
1961	R Laver (Aus)	1973	J Kodes (Czech)	1985	B Becker (WG)

Women's Singles

1950	A L Brough (US)	1962	J R Susman (US)	1974	C Evert (US)
1951	D J Hart (US)	1963	M Smith (Aus)	1975	B-J King (US)
1952	M Connolly (US)	1964	M E Bueno (Braz)	1976	C Evert (US)
1953	M Connolly (US)	1965	M Smith (Aus)	1977	S V Wade (GB)
1954	M Connolly (US)	1966	B-J King (US)	1978	M Navratilova (Czech)
1955	L Brough (US)	1967	B-J King (US)	1979	M Navratilova (US)
1956	S J Fry (US)	1968	B-J King (US)	1980	E F Cawley (Aus)
1957	A Gibson (US)	1969	A Jones (GB)	1981	C Lloyd (US)
1958	A Gibson (US)	1970	M Court (Aus)	1982	M Navratilova (US)
1959	M E Bueno (Braz)	1971	E F Goolagong (Aus)	1983	M Navratilova (US)
1960	M E Bueno (Braz)	1972	B-J King (US)	1984	M Navratilova (US)
1961	A Mortimer (GB)	1973	B-J King (US)	1985	M Navratilova (US)

Men's Doubles

1950	J E Bromwich & A K Quist	1969	J D Newcombe & A D Roche
1951	K McGregor & F A Sedgman	1970	J D Newcombe & A D Roche
1952	K McGregor & F A Sedgman	1971	R Emerson & R Laver
1953	L A Hoad & K R Rosewall	1972	R A Hewitt & F D McMillan
1954	R N Hartwig & M G Rose	1973	J S Connors & I Nastase
1955	R N Hartwig & L A Hoad	1974	J D Newcombe & A D Roche
1956	L A Hoad & K R Rosewall	1975	V Gerulaitis & A Mayer
1957	G Mulloy & J E Patty	1976	B E Gottfried & R Ramirez
1958	S Davidson & U Schmidt	1977	R L Case & G Masters
1959	R Emerson & N A Fraser	1978	R A Hewitt & F D McMillan
1960	R H Osuna & R D Ralston	1979	P Fleming & J P McEnroe
1961	R Emerson & N A Fraser	1980	P McNamara & P McNamee
1962	R A Hewitt & F S Stolle	1981	P Fleming & J P McEnroe
1963	R H Osuna & A Palafox	1982	P McNamara & P McNamee
1964	R A Hewitt & F S Stolle	1983	P Fleming & J P McEnroe
1965	J D Newcombe & A D Roche	1984	P Fleming & J P McEnroe
1966	K N Fletcher & J D Newcombe	1985	H P Gunthardt & B Taroczy
1967	R A Hewitt & F D McMillan		
1968	J D Newcombe & A D Roche		

Women's Doubles

1950	A L Brough & W Dupont	1969	M Court & J A Tegart
1951	S J Fry & D J Hart	1970	R Casals & B-J King
1952	S J Fry & D J Hart	1971	R Casals & B-J King
1953	S J Fry & D J Hart	1972	B-J King & B Stove
1954	A L Brough & W Dupont	1973	R Casals & B-J King
1955	A Mortimer & J A Shilcock	1974	E Goolagong & P Michel
1956	A Buxton & A Gibson	1975	A K Kiyomura & K Sawamatsu
1957	A Gibson & D R Hard	1976	C Evert & M Navratilova
1958	M E Bueno & A Gibson	1977	R L Cawley & J C Russell
1959	J Arth & D R Hard	1978	G E Reid & W M Turnbull
1960	M E Bueno & D R Hard	1979	B-J King & M Navratilova
1961	K Hantze & B-J Moffitt	1980	K Jordan & A Smith
1962	B-J Moffitt & J R Susman	1981	M Navratilova & P H Shriver
1963	M E Bueno & D R Hard	1982	M Navratilova & P H Shriver
1964	M Smith & L R Turner	1983	M Navratilova & P H Shriver
1965	M E Bueno & B-J Moffitt	1984	M Navratilova & P H Shriver
1966	M E Bueno & N Richey	1985	K Jordan & P D Smylie
1967	R Casals & B-J King		
1968	R Casals & B-J King		

WIMBLEDON CHAMPIONSHIPS

Mixed Doubles

1950 E W Sturgess & A L Brough	1969 F Stolle & A Jones
1951 F A Sedgman & D J Hart	1970 I Nastase & R Casals
1952 F A Sedgman & D J Hart	1971 O K Davidson & B-J King
1953 E V Seixas & D J Hart	1972 I Nastase & R Casals
1954 E V Seixas & D J Hart	1973 O K Davidson & B-J King
1955 E V Seixas & D J Hart	1974 O K Davidson & B-J King
1956 E V Seixas & S J Fry	1975 M C Riessen & B M Court
1957 M G Rose & D R Hard	1976 A D Roche & F Durr
1958 R N Howe & L Coghlan	1977 R A J Hewitt & G R Stevens
1959 R Laver & D R Hard	1978 F D McMillan & B F Stove
1960 R Laver & D R Hard	1979 R A J Hewitt & G R Stevens
1961 F Stolle & L R Turner	1980 J R Austin & T Austin
1962 N A Fraser & W Dupont	1981 F D McMillan & B F Stove
1963 K N Fletcher & M Smith	1982 K Curren & A E Smith
1964 F Stolle & L R Turner	1983 J M Lloyd & W Turnbull
1965 K N Fletcher & M Smith	1984 J M Lloyd & W Turnbull
1966 K N Fletcher & M Smith	1985 P McNamee & M Navratilova
1967 O K Davidson & B-J King	
1968 K N Fletcher & M Court	

MOTOR RACING

World Champion Drivers

1950 G Farina (It)	1962 G Hill (GB)	1974 E Fittipaldi (Braz)
1951 J M Fangio (Arg)	1963 J Clark (GB)	1975 N Lauda (Austria)
1952 A Ascari (It)	1964 J Surtees (GB)	1976 J Hunt (GB)
1953 A Ascari (It)	1965 J Clark (GB)	1977 N Lauda (Austria)
1954 J M Fangio (Arg)	1966 J Brabham (Aus)	1978 M Andretti (US)
1955 J M Fangio (Arg)	1967 D Hulme (NZ)	1979 J Scheckter (SA)
1956 J M Fangio (Arg)	1968 G Hill (GB)	1980 A Jones (Aus)
1957 J M Fangio (Arg)	1969 J Stewart (GB)	1981 N Piquet (Braz)
1958 M Hawthorn (GB)	1970 J Rindt (Austria)	1982 K Rosberg (Fin)
1959 J Brabham (Aus)	1971 J Stewart (GB)	1983 N Piquet (Braz)
1960 J Brabham (Aus)	1972 E Fittipaldi (Braz)	1984 N Lauda (Austria)
1961 P Hill (US)	1973 J Stewart (GB)	1985 A Prost (Fr)

RIFLE SHOOTING

Queen's/King's Prize Winners

1950 R Greig	1962 P Hall	1974 F Harris
1951 G Boa	1963 K Pilcher	1975 C M Y Trotter
1952 A Kinnier-Wilson	1964 A Harris	1976 W H Magnay
1953 N McCaw	1965 J Allen	1977 D A Friend
1954 G Twine	1966 R Hampton	1978 G R Graham
1955 L Fenwick	1967 J Powell	1979 A St G Tucker
1956 G Twine	1968 A Parke	1980 A Marion
1957 J Love	1969 F Little	1981 G M Ayling
1958 R Fulton	1970 G F Arnold	1982 L Peden
1959 I Mallabar	1971 R M Stevens	1983 A Marion
1960 G Westling	1972 R P Rosling	1984 D Richards
1961 N Beckett	1973 K M Pilcher	1985 J Bloomfield

ROWING AND SCULLING

1984 OLYMPIC GAMES (LOS ANGELES)

Men

Single sculls P Karppinen Finland 7 min 24s	Coxless fours NZ 6 min 3.48s
Double sculls US 6 min 36.87s	Coxed fours GB 6 min 18.64s
Coxless pairs Romania 6 min 45.39s	Coxless quadruple sculls W Ger 5 min 57.55s
Coxed pairs Italy 7 min 5.99s	Eights Canada 5 min 41.32s

Women

Single sculls V Racila Romania 3 min 40.68s	Coxed fours Romania 3 min 19.3s
Double sculls Romania 3 min 26.75s	Coxed quadruple sculls Romania 3 min 14.11s
Coxless pairs Romania 3 min 32.6s	Eights US 2 min 59.8s

THE UNIVERSITY BOAT RACE

		min	s	lengths
1952	Oxford	20	23	canvas
1953	Cambridge	19	54	8
1954	Oxford	20	23	4½
1955	Cambridge	19	10	16
1956	Cambridge	18	36	1¼
1957	Cambridge	19	1	2
1958	Cambridge	18	15	3½
1959	Oxford	18	52	6
1960	Oxford	18	59	1
1961	Cambridge	19	22	4¼
1962	Cambridge	19	46	5
1963	Oxford	20	47	5
1964	Cambridge	19	18	6½
1965	Oxford	18	17	4
1966	Oxford	19	12	3½
1967	Oxford	18	52	3½
1968	Cambridge	18	22	3½
1969	Cambridge	18	4	4
1970	Cambridge	20	22	3
1971	Cambridge	17	58	10
1972	Cambridge	18	36	9½
1973	Cambridge	19	21	13
1974	Oxford	17	35	5½
1975	Cambridge	19	27	3¾
1976	Oxford	16	58	6½
1977	Oxford	19	28	7
1978	Oxford	19	00	†
1979	Oxford	20	33	3½
1980	Oxford	19	20	canvas
1981	Oxford	18	11	8
1982	Oxford	18	21	3¼
1983	Oxford	19	7	4½
1984	Oxford	16	45*	3¾
1985	Oxford	17	11	4¾
1986	Cambridge	17	58	7

*Record time †Cambridge sank

Won: Cambridge 69 Oxford 61

RUGBY LEAGUE

LEAGUE CHAMPIONS

1950–1	Workington T
1951–2	Wigan
1952–3	St Helens
1953–4	Warrington
1954–5	Warrington
1955–6	Hull
1956–7	Oldham
1957–8	Hull
1958–9	St Helens
1959–60	Wigan
1960–1	Leeds
1961–2	Huddersfield
1962–3	Swinton/Hunslet
1963–4	Swinton/Oldham
1964–5	Halifax
1965–6	St Helens
1966–7	Wakefield T
1967–8	Wakefield T
1968–9	Leeds
1969–70	St Helens
1970–1	St Helens
1971–2	Leeds
1972–3	Dewsbury
1973–4	Salford
1974–5	St Helens
1975–6	Salford
1976–7	Featherstone R
1977–8	Widnes
1978–9	Hull K R
1979–80	Bradford N
1980–1	Bradford N
1981–2	Leigh
1982–3	Hull
1983–4	Hull K R
1984–5	Hull K R
1985–6	Halifax

CHALLENGE CUP WINNERS

1950	Warrington
1951	Wigan
1952	Workington T
1953	Huddersfield
1954	Warrington
1955	Barrow
1956	St Helens
1957	Leeds
1958	Wigan
1959	Wigan
1960	Wakefield T
1961	St Helens
1962	Wakefield T
1963	Wakefield T
1964	Widnes
1965	Wigan
1966	St Helens
1967	Featherstone R
1968	Leeds
1969	Castleford
1970	Castleford
1971	Leigh
1972	St Helens
1973	Featherstone R
1974	Warrington
1975	Widnes
1976	St Helens
1977	Leeds
1978	Leeds
1979	Widnes
1980	Hull K R
1981	Widnes
1982	Hull
1983	Featherstone R
1984	Widnes
1985	Wigan
1986	Castleford

RUGBY UNION

THORN-EMI COUNTY CHAMPIONS

1950	Cheshire
1951	E Midlands
1952	Middlesex
1953	Yorkshire
1954	Middlesex
1955	Lancashire
1956	Middlesex
1957	Devon
1958	Warwickshire
1959	Warwickshire
1960	Warwickshire
1961	Cheshire
1962	Warwickshire
1963	Warwickshire
1964	Warwickshire
1965	Warwickshire
1966	Middlesex
1967	Durham/Surrey
1968	Middlesex
1969	Lancashire
1970	Staffordshire
1971	Surrey
1972	Gloucestershire
1973	Lancashire
1974	Gloucestershire
1975	Gloucestershire
1976	Gloucestershire
1977	Lancashire
1978	Gloucestershire
1979	Middlesex
1980	Lancashire
1981	Northumberland
1982	Lancashire
1983	Gloucestershire
1984	Gloucestershire
1985	Middlesex
1986	Warwickshire

INTERNATIONAL CHAMPIONS

1950–1	Ireland	1963–4	Scotland	1973–4	Ireland
1951–2	Wales		Wales	1974–5	Wales
1952–3	England	1964–5	Wales	1975–6	Wales
1953–4	England	1965–6	Wales	1976–7	France
	Wales	1966–7	France	1977–8	Wales
	France	1967–8	France	1978–9	Wales
1954–5	France	1968–9	Wales	1979–80	England
	Wales	1969–70	France	1980–1	France
1955–6	Wales		Wales	1981–2	Ireland
1956–7	England	1970–1	Wales	1982–3	France
1957–8	England	1971–2	Wales		Ireland
1958–9	France	1972–3	England	1983–4	Scotland
1959–60	England		France	1984–5	Ireland
	France		Ireland	1985–6	France
1960–1	France		Scotland		Scotland
1961–2	France		Wales		
1962–3	England				

SHOW JUMPING

OLYMPIC TEAM CHAMPIONS (NATION'S CUP)

1912	Sweden	1952	Gt Britain	1976	France
1920	Sweden	1956	Germany	1980	Canada (Sub. Olympic
1924	Sweden	1960	Germany		Games, Rotterdam)
1928	Spain	1964	Germany	1984	USA
1936	Germany	1968	Canada		
1948	Mexico	1972	W Germany		

ROYAL INTERNATIONAL HORSE SHOW 1985

Class	Country	Rider	Horse
King George V			
Gold Cup	Gt Britain	Malcolm Pyrah	Towerlands Anglezarke
Q Elizabeth Cup	Gt Britain	Sue Pountain	Ned Kelly VI
Grand Prix	Gt Britain	Peter Charles	April Sun

HICKSTEAD DERBY 1985

	W Germany	Paul Schockemohle	Lorenzo

HORSE OF THE YEAR SHOW 1985

Leading Show			
Jumper '85	Gt Britain	Nick Skelton	St James
Everest Double Glazing			
Championship	Gt Britain	David Bowen	Boysie

OLYMPIA INTERNATIONAL SHOW 1985

Crosse & Blackwell			
Grand Prix	Gt Britain	Malcolm Pyrah	Towerlands Anglezarke

SNOOKER

WORLD CHAMPIONS

1927–46	J Davis (E)	1970	R Reardon (W)	1981	S Davis (E)
1947	W Donaldson (S)	1971	J Spencer (E)	1982	A Higgins (I)
1948–9	F Davis (E)	1972	A Higgins (I)	1983	S Davis (E)
1950	W Donaldson (S)	1973–6	R Reardon (W)	1984	S Davis (E)
1951	F Davis (E)	1977	J Spencer (E)	1985	D Taylor (I)
1952	H Lindrum (Aus)	1978	R Reardon (W)	1986	J Johnson (E)
1964–8	J Pulman (E)	1979	T Griffiths (W)		
1969	J Spencer (E)	1980	C Thorburn (Can)		

CORAL UNITED KINGDOM CHAMPIONS

1977	P Fagan	1980	S Davis	1983	A Higgins
1978	D Mountjoy	1981	S Davis	1984	S Davis
1979	J Virgo	1982	T Griffiths	1985	S Davis

MERCANTILE CREDIT CLASSIC CHAMPIONS

1982	T Griffiths	1985	W Thorne
1983	S Davis	1986	J White
1984	S Davis		

ROTHMANS GRAND PRIX CHAMPIONS

1982	R Reardon	1985	S Davis
1983	T Knowles		
1984	D Taylor		

JAMESON INTERNATIONAL CHAMPIONS

1981	S Davis	1984	S Davis
1982	T Knowles		
1983	S Davis		

BENSON & HEDGES MASTERS

1978	A Higgins	1981	A Higgins	1984	J White
1979	P Mans	1982	S Davis	1985	C Thorburn
1980	T Griffiths	1983	C Thorburn	1986	C Thorburn

DULUX BRITISH OPEN CHAMPIONS

1985	S Francisco
1986	S Davis

CAR CARE WORLD TEAM CUP

1979	Wales	1983	England
1980	Wales	1985	Ireland
1981	England	1986	Ireland
1982	Canada		

SPEEDWAY

WORLD CHAMPIONS

1950	F Williams (W)	1962	P Craven (E)	1974	A Michanek (Sw)
1951	J Young (Aus)	1963	O Fundin (Sw)	1975	O Olsen (Denmark)
1952	J Young (Aus)	1964	B Briggs (NZ)	1976	P Collins (E)
1953	F Williams (W)	1965	B Knutsson (Sw)	1977	I Mauger (NZ)
1954	R Moore (NZ)	1966	B Briggs (NZ)	1978	O Olsen (Denmark)
1955	P Craven (E)	1967	O Fundin (Sw)	1979	I Mauger (NZ)
1956	O Fundin (Sw)	1968	I Mauger (NZ)	1980	M Lee (E)
1957	B Briggs (NZ)	1969	I Mauger (NZ)	1981	B Penhall (US)
1958	B Briggs (NZ)	1970	I Mauger (NZ)	1982	B Penhall (US)
1959	R Moore (NZ)	1971	O Olsen (Den)	1983	E Muller (W. Ger)
1960	O Fundin (Sw)	1972	I Mauger (NZ)	1984	E Gundersen (Den)
1961	O Fundin (Sw)	1973	J Szczakiel (Pol)	1985	E Gundersen (Den)

SQUASH RACKETS

DAVIES & TATE BRITISH OPEN CHAMPIONSHIP

1950–5	Hashim Khan (Pak)	1966–7	J P Barrington (Ire)	1982	Jahangir Khan (Pak)
1956	Roshan Khan (Pak)	1968	G B Hunt (Aus)	1983	Jahangir Khan (Pak)
1957	Hashim Khan (Pak)	1969–72	J P Barrington (Ire)	1984	Jahangir Khan (Pak)
1958–61	Azam Khan (Pak)	1973	G B Hunt (Aus)	1985	Jahangir Khan (Pak)
1962	Mohibullah Khan (Pak)	1974	Q Zaman (Pak)	1986	Jahangir Khan (Pak)
1963–5	A A AbouTaleb (UAR)	1975–81	G B Hunt (Aus)		

SWIMMING AND DIVING

1984 OLYMPIC GAMES (LOS ANGELES)

Men

100 metres freestyle A Gaines US 49·8s
200 metres freestyle M Gross W Ger 1 min 47·44s
400 metres freestyle G Dicarlo US 3 min 51·23s
1,500 metres freestyle M O'Brien US 15 min 5·2s
100 metres backstroke R Carey US 55·79s
200 metres backstroke R Carey US 2 min 0·23s
100 metres breaststroke S Lundquist US 1 min 1·65s
200 metres breaststroke V Davis Can 2 min 13·34s
100 metres butterfly M Gross W Ger 53·08s

200 metres butterfly J Sieben Aus 1 min 57·04s
200 metres individual medley A Baumann Can 2 min 1·42s
400 metres individual medley A Baumann Can 4 min 17·41s
4 × 100 metres freestyle relay US 3 min 19·03s
4 × 100 metres medley relay US 3 min 39·3s
4 × 200 metres freestyle relay US 7 min 15·69s
Highboard diving G Loughanis US 710·91 pts
Springboard diving G Loughanis US 754·41 pts
Water polo Yugoslavia

Women

100 metres freestyle C Steinseifer & N Hogshead US (tie) 55·92s
200 metres freestyle M Wayte US 1 min 59·23s
400 metres freestyle T Cohen US 4 min 7·1s
800 metres freestyle T Cohen US 8 min 24·95s
100 metres backstroke T Andrews US 1 min 2·55s
200 metres backstroke J de Rover Neth 2 min 12·38s
100 metres breaststroke S Lundquist US 1 min 1·65s
200 metres breaststroke A Ottenbrite Can 2 min 30·38s

100 metres butterfly M Meagher US 59·76s
200 metres butterfly M Meagher US 2 min 6·9s
200 metres individual medley T Caulkins US 2 min 12·64s
400 metres individual medley T Caulkins US 4 min 39·24s
4 × 100 metres relay US 3 min 43·43s
4 × 100 metres medley relay US 4 min 8·34s
Highboard diving Z Jihong China 435·51 pts
Springboard diving S Bernier Canada 530·70 pts

TABLE TENNIS

WORLD CHAMPIONSHIP

Men

1950	R Bergmann (Eng)	1959	Jung Kuo-Tuan (China)	1975	I Jonyer (Hungary)
1951	J Leach (Eng)	1961	Chuang Tse-Tung (China)	1977	M Kohno (Japan)
1952	H Satoh (Japan)	1963	Chuang Tse-Tung (China)	1979	S Ono (Japan)
1953	F Sido (Hungary)	1965	Chuang Tse-Tung (China)	1981	Guo Yuehua (China)
1954	I Ogimura (Japan)	1967	N Hasegawa (Japan)	1983	Guo Yuehua (China)
1955	T Tanaka (Japan)	1969	S Itoh (Japan)	1985	Jiang Jialing (China)
1956	I Ogimura (Japan)	1971	S Bengtsson (Sweden)		
1957	T Tanaka (Japan)	1973	Hsi En-Ting (China)		

Women

1950–5	A Rozeanu (Romania)	1967	S Morisawa (Japan)	1977	Pak Yung Sun (Korea DPR)
1956	T Okawa (Japan)	1969	T Kowada (Japan)		
1957	F Eguchi (Japan)	1971	Lin Hui-Ching (China)	1979	Ge Xinai (China)
1959	K Matsuzaki (Japan)	1973	Hu Yu-Lang (China)	1981	Tong Ling (China)
1961	Chiu Chung-Hui (China)	1974	M Alexandra (Romania)	1983	Cao Yanhua (China)
1963	K Matsuzaki (Japan)	1975	Pak Yung Sun (Korea DPR)	1985	Cao Yanhua (China)
1965	N Fukazu (Japan)				

SPECIAL TOPICS

GALLERY OF SPORTING CHAMPIONS

Banks, Gordon (b. 1937). In soccer most of the glory goes to goal-scorers but the men who save goals are just as important. Gordon Banks was playing for Leicester City—previously he had been with Chesterfield and was later to join Stoke City—when he was selected to play for England against Scotland at Wembley in 1963. After his great performances for his country in the 1966 World Cup, which culminated in England beating West Germany in the final in extra-time, he was recognised as the world's best goalkeeper. He also helped Stoke to win the Football League (now the Milk) Cup in 1972. Seven months later, in a car accident, he suffered bad eye injuries and was forced to retire from the game.

Barna, Victor (1911–72). A Hungarian master of table tennis who later came to Britain via France and adopted British nationality. Predominantly a close-to-the-table player with strong wrist action and a match-winning backhand, he led Hungary to the forefront of the sport, with 22 gold medals to his credit. He won five singles world championships, four in succession, and was equally as prominent in the doubles and mixed doubles, all in the 1930s. And he played in seven winning Swathling Cup teams. Founder of the Swathling Club for ex-international table tennis players.

Blankers-Koen, Mrs. Fanny (b. 1918). This Dutch lady came to London at the age of 30 to astonish the crowds at the White City by winning Olympic gold medals for the 100 and 200 metre sprints and the 80 metre hurdles, also inspiring the Netherlands to snatch the 4 × 100 metres relay from Australia. In all she competed in 11 races and won them all. During her career she set world records for many track and field events including 11·3s for 100 metres, 11·00s for 80 metre hurdles and for 100 metres, and 1·71 metres for the high jump. She was one of the greatest women pentathletes.

Bradman, Sir Donald (b. 1908). The first Australian cricketer to be knighted, he was a remarkable, not to say indomitable batsman. In his youth he practised with a stump to hit a golf ball thrown repeatedly against a fence, thus acquiring his incredibly sharp eye for the pitch of a cricket ball however fast it was bowled at him. He played for New South Wales, South Australia and his country, for which, as captain, he never lost a Test rubber. His first-class career, which began at the age of 19 and ended in 1948 with the Australians' tour of England, produced over 28,000 runs at an average of 95·14 and included 117 centuries. When Douglas Jardine, the England captain, tried to restrain his incredible run-getting in the so-called "body-line" series of 1932–3, Sir Donald, adapting his style to the short-pitched, rising ball aimed, optimistically, at his leg stump, still averaged 56·57 in four Tests. Since his retirement he has given invaluable service to Australian cricket as an administrator.

Burton, Mrs. Beryl (b. 1937). An amateur cyclist of much distinction, she excelled particularly in time-trial events. In a 12-hour time-trial in 1967 she covered 277½ miles, which was five miles more than the British men's record. A year later she cycled 100 miles in just under four hours, again bettering the best existing male performance. She was also the holder of national women's records for the 10, 25 and 50 miles on road, besides other records. And from 1959 she held the British Women's Best All-Rounder title for a quarter of a century.

Charlton, Bobby, CBE (b. 1937). Although from 1958 to 1970 he made 106 appearances for England and was a member of the 1966 side that, by beating West Germany 4–2 in extra-time, brought the World Cup to this country for the first time, possibly the peak of Bobby Charlton's career—both for himself and for his many thousands of admirers—occurred in another Wembley final. On 29 May 1968 Manchester United won the European Champion Clubs' Cup by 4–1 against the redoubtable Portuguese club, Benefica. United—Bobby's *only* club and the one to which he had given such loyal service—were the first English club to take this coveted trophy. One of the sur-

vivors of the tragic Munich air disaster of 1958, in which seven of his team-mates—"the Busby Babes"—were killed, Bobby was noted for his acute positional sense, his powerful and accurate shooting and, not least, for his unfailing good sportsmanship. He retired in 1973 and had a brief spell in football management but is now one of our best-known soccer panellists.

Chichester, Sir Francis (1901–72). Six years after winning the first *Observer* single-handed transatlantic yacht race in 1960, Sir Francis set out in his ketch, Gipsy Moth IV, a 53-footer, to sail round the world. He made only one stop—at Sydney, Australia—and arrived back at Plymouth nine months later to a rapturous welcome. It was a tremendous feat for a man who was combating what he knew would prove a terminal illness. He was knighted by Queen Elizabeth II later that year.

Connolly, Maureen (1934–69). In a short career and, sadly, a short life. "Little Mo" quickly established herself as one of the greats of lawn tennis. She was only 16, a disarming little figure barely five feet tall, when she first won the United States singles title but with her quick reactions and abounding energy she commanded the court in all her matches. Wimbledon had begun to look like Louise Brough's province until 1952 when, in the singles final, her teenage compatriot beat her 7–5, 6–3—and again two years later in a 20-game battle. In between Maureen had retained her title by overcoming Doris Hart and 1953 was also the year when she became the first woman to make tennis's Grand Slam—winning the United States, the English, the French and the Australian singles titles. She retired from the tennis circuit in 1959, having broken a leg, married, and devoted herself to coaching until becoming incapacitated.

Corbett, J. J. (1886–1933). "Gentleman Jim", a San Franciscan bank clerk, became the first heavyweight boxer to win the world championship under the Queensberry Rules when he knocked out James L. Sullivan in 1892. The bout lasted 22 rounds. Corbett acquired his sobriquet not only for his classical style but for his popularity outside the ring. He held his title for five years but lost it to 34-year-old British champion Bob Fitzsimmons on a punch that, today, might be reckoned as below the belt. In all he won 20 of his 31 fights, losing only five.

Dempsey, Jack (1895–1983). A rugged, two-fisted croucher, sometimes known as the Manassa Mauler, ex-hobo and lumberjack, who fought his way through the boxing booths and saloons of the Middle West to become heavyweight champion of the world. He took the title in 1919 by beating the massive Jess Willard whom he knocked down seven times. He was successful in defending his title in five bouts, only to lose it on points to the upstanding Gene Tunney. In the return match at Soldiers' Field, Chicago in 1927, which Dempsey also lost, his opponent was on the floor for 14 seconds—it has become known as the Battle of the Long Count—but Dempsey was to blame for his slowness in finding a neutral corner. In his later years he squired a fashionable restaurant in Manhattan.

Finney, Tom, OBE (b. 1922). Born in Preston, Lancashire and signing professional forms for Preston North End at the age of 18, after three years as an amateur, Tom Finney's illustrious career, which included the honour of twice being elected "Footballer of the Year", began. For his club he made more than 430 appearances and scored 187 goals. As a winger he had much in common with Stanley Matthews. His attitude to soccer was Corinthian. He was too adept, too thoughtful a footballer to need unfair methods to succeed. With his speed and footwork he could dazzle any defence. The difference between them was that in his 76 matches for England Tom Finney played in four different positions for he was as useful as a deep-lying striker as on the wing. Unlike most modern forwards he had the ability to dribble and twist his way to the bye-line and pass low across the goal—a gift to a waiting attacker.

Fry, Charles B. (1872–1956). Surely a champion by virtue of his extraordinary versatility. "C.B." not only played cricket for Oxford University, Surrey, Sussex, Hampshire and England but was also an England soccer international, a long-jumper (he once shared the world record for this event) and played a good game of rugby. As a cricketer he scored 30,886 runs, including 94 centuries, and topped the batting averages six times. He captained England against Australia in the home series of 1912, the third and final Test, in which The Ashes were successfully defended, being the first "timeless" Test in England. He was a man of considerable scholarship and was respected as one of the most informed journalists of his time.

Grace, Dr. W. G. (1848–1915). Best known as a batsman for Gloucestershire and England—his total of over 54,000 runs in first-class cricket included 126 centuries—he was also a formidable all-rounder. As a bowler he gathered nearly 2,900 wickets; as a fieldsman he took over 870 catches. Twenty-eight times he scored 1,000 runs or more in a season; and in 1895, at the age of 46 he scored that number in the month of May. And he captained England in five series against Australia. The bearded doctor, an amateur cricketer who nevertheless profited from the game, was so compelling an attraction that when it was known in the City of London he had come to the wicket at Lord's or the Oval, the streets became jammed with hansom cabs. He played Test cricket until he was 50, then displayed his talents for the short-lived London County.

Hashman, Mrs. Judy (b. 1935). Perhaps better known as Judy Devlin (her maiden name) she completely dominated the All England badminton championship in the 1950s and 1960s, winning the singles ten times, the doubles seven times. And she helped the United States win the Uber Cup three times. Also to her credit: 12 US singles titles, 10 doubles and six mixed doubles. Always in complete command of the court, her style, anticipation and athleticism have been an object lesson to junior players. Married to G. C. K. Hashman, she has lived in England for the past 26 years.

Hobbs, Sir J. B. (1882–1963). A quiet and modest man whose mastery of the technique of batting is still unequalled, Hobbs exchanged Parker's Piece, Cambridge, where he played cricket as a boy, for the Oval in his early 'twenties. The great Tom Hayward was his first opening partner for Surrey, to be followed by Andy Sandham, but the famous England partnership was Hobbs and Sutcliffe, though earlier Sir Jack had shared in profitable opening stands with another Yorkshireman—Wilf Rhodes. They notched up a record 323 against Australia. Although Hobbs had little interest in the mere amassing of runs he scored 61,237, including 197 centuries, 98 of them when he was over forty, during his 30-year career. In each of 26 seasons he topped 1,000 runs.

Lenglen, Suzanne (1899–1938). Born in Compiegne, Suzanne was competing in the French hard court singles at the age of fifteen. In 1919 she made her first appearance at Wimbledon and although it was the first time she had played on grass, beat the experienced Mrs. Lambert Chambers. The French girl's grace, agility and devastating accuracy astonished everyone. The new short-sleeved, short-skirted champion was acknowledged as a star almost overnight. Triple champion in France from 1919 to 1923, 1925 and 1926, she also won the Wimbledon singles title another five times. She had such a strong will to win, plus a fiery Gallic temperament, it was difficult for tournament organisers and spectators to accept that she had a delicate constitution but in fact as her tennis became more and more in demand she suffered increasingly from asthma. In 1926, after a tiff with the referee—much less common in those days than now—she withdrew from Wimbledon and soon turned professional, starting a tennis school. There was nothing dull about Mlle Lenglen and she, as much as any other player, made Wimbledon the magnetic tournament it has now become.

Matthews, Sir Stanley, CBE (b. 1915). The first footballer to be knighted, Sir Stanley joined Stoke City's ground staff at the age of fourteen. An outside-right whose ball control and zig-zag dribbling baffled a host of defenders, he helped the Potteries club to the First Division of the Football League.

Eighteen years later he was transferred to Blackpool and it was the famous forward line of Matthews, Mudie, Mortensen, Slater and Parry which enabled the club to beat Bolton Wanderers 4–3 in the FA Cup Final of 1953. In 1961, when he was 46, Sir Stanley rejoined Stoke and it was in their colours he played his last Football League game, against Fulham. He had made some 880 first-class appearances, including 54 games for England.

Owens, Jesse (b. 1913). Amid all the Swastika banners and Nazi salutes at the 1936 Olympic Games in Berlin the performances of a black athlete from Cleveland, Ohio outshone anything the much-vaunted Aryan race could produce. Jesse Owens won four gold medals—for the 100 and 200 metres, the long jump and as a member of the United States team in the 4 × 100 metres relay. This was on top of his feats the previous year when, in under an hour at one meeting, he had equalled or broken six world records in the sprints, hurdles and long jump. A man with the iron determination, dignity and poise of the true champion.

Puskas, Ferenc (b. 1927). Will always be remembered as the "Galloping Major" of Hungary, the first foreign soccer team to vanquish England in England. This was in 1953 at Wembley. The home country, captained by Billy Wright, fielded such talented players as Alf Ramsey (later England team manager), Matthews and Mortensen, but as a side were completely dazzled by the individual skills and revolutionary tactics of the Hungarians. Backed up by skilful midfield players like Zakarias and Bozsik, and with Hidegkuti as a deep-lying centre-forward, Puskas was always the kingpin of every move and one of his two goals was quite unforgettable. With a back flip to avoid Wright's tackle he swivelled round and his left-foot shot was low and deadly. Hungary won 6–3 and six months later, in Budapest, by 7–1—a further tribute to Puskas's astute captaincy and supreme individual skill.

Rhodes, Wilfred (1877–1973). Starting with Yorkshire at the age of 21, Rhodes played first-class cricket for the next 32 years. For more than a score of seasons he took his 100 wickets—4,187 in all—and scored nearly 40,000 runs. A slow left-arm bowler he regularly batted as a tail-ender in the days of C. B. Fry, A. C. Maclaren and "Plum" Warner. At Melbourne in the 1903–4 series he opened the innings for England with Tom Hayward of Surrey but scored only 3 and 16 not out. Down the batting order he went until five years later at the Oval when at No. 3, in the final Test against Australia, he contributed 66 and 54, and in 1910, against South Africa at Johannesburg, and this time opening the innings with Jack Hobbs, made another 66. He played in 58 Tests, made 2,325 runs, including two centuries, and took 127 wickets. Steeped in the game, he was still a familiar figure at the Test grounds even in his nineties, though by that time he was blind. He always played for his county or his country, never for himself.

Richards, Sir Gordon (b. 1904). Confident, quick off the mark and one of the most popular figures on the course, Sir Gordon, knighted in 1953, the year he won the Epsom Derby on Pinza, was the most successful flat-race jockey of our times, possibly for all time. In only three of the 29 years spanning his riding career did he fail to rank as champion jockey. He rode 4,870 winners, and his 259 in 1933 beat Fred Archer's long-standing record for a season of 249. Fourteen years later he did even better, with 269.

Ruth, "Babe" (1895–1948). A baseball batter whose remarkable ability for hitting home runs gained him a reputation even in countries like Britain where big-time baseball did not exist. At the start of his professional career with Boston Red Sox in 1914 he was mainly a pitcher and in this role helped his club to win the World Series three times in four years. But when, in 1919, he established a major league home run record with 29 he was transferred to New York Yankees and celebrated by more than doubling that number. He held the overall record of 714 home runs until Hank Aaron topped it by one nearly 40 years later. Since he was also a brilliant outfielder George Herman Ruth must be reckoned one of the best all-rounders in first-class sport.

Sailer, Toni (b. 1935). This young Austrian skier rocketed through the 1956 Winter Olympic Games at Cortina, Italy with such speed, style and intelligent pre-planning that he achieved what no Alpine expert had thought possible. In far from perfect conditions Toni won the downhill, the slalom and the giant slalom events, collecting three gold medals. Moreover, he won them by conclusive margins—by 3, 4 and 6·2 seconds. Twelve years later Jean-Claude Killy of France also triumphed in the triple runs but, as distinct from Sailer's, they were split-second victories. Sailer's racing career was short but he was a world champion for four seasons and dominated the scene.

Spitz, Mark (b. 1950). Swimming for the United States in the 1972 Olympic Games at Munich, this fierce competitor won a record seven gold medals. These were for the 100 and 200 metres free-style, the 100 and 200 butterfly, and in his country's two free-style relays and the 4 × 100 metres medley relay—all in world record time. It was also a record bag for any Olympic competitor. Judged by his own high standards he had been a relative failure in the previous Games in Mexico—of his

four medals there only two were gold—but in Munich his naturally aggressive style, allied to incredible stamina, unquestionably made him Lord of the Pool.

Tilden, W. T. (1893–1953). "Big Bill", born in Philadelphia, achieved world fame for his ferocious and commanding tennis. Apart from his mighty service he was a master of stroke play which he executed with theatrical panache. He was the first American to win the singles title at Wimbledon (1920), and retained it the following year. The United States singles title was also his—from 1920 to 1925 and he was a member of the US Davis Cup team which held the trophy for six successive years. In 1930, at the age of 37 he not only collared the British and Italian singles titles but was once again the American champion. And he was equally effective in winning many doubles and mixed doubles titles over the years. He wrote many books, mostly instructional, some plays and tried his hand at acting. One of the most colourful characters of this century.

FAMOUS SOCCER CLUBS

Arsenal. *Founded:* 1886 at Woolwich. Became a professional club five years later as Royal Arsenal competing in Div. II of the Football League. Known as Woolwich Arsenal from 1896 to 1913 when they moved to Highbury in N. London. Still called "The Gunners". *Ground:* Highbury Stadium. *Colours:* red and white shirts, white shorts. *Manager:* George Graham. *Previous managers:* include Herbert Chapman, George Allison, Tom Whittaker, George Swindin and Don Howe. *Honours:* include seven times Football League champions between 1930 and 1953, again in 1970–71. FA Cup-winners 1929–30, 1935–6, 1949–50, 1970–71, 1978–9; runners-up six times. Fairs Cup-winners 1963–4; UEFA Cup-winners 1969–70. *Best win:* 12–0 *v.* Loughborough Town, Div. II, 1900, avenging a record 0–8 defeat against the same club five years earlier. *Record gate:* 73,295 *v.* Sunderland, Div. I, 1935. *Highest league scorer:* Ted Drake 42, 1934–5. *Noted players past and present:* W. Barnes, C. Bastin, D. Bowen, D. Compton, L. Compton, R. Daniel, T. Docherty, E. Drake, E. Hapgood, J. Hulme, D. Jack, A. James, B. Joy, A. Kelsey, P. Jennings, A. Macaulay, M. Macdonald, T. Neill, S. Nelson, L. O'Brady, D. O'Leary, P. Rice, J. Roberts, G. Swindin.

Aston Villa. *Founded:* 1874. One of the 12 original members of the Football League 1888, the founder of the League, William McGregor, being a club official. Known as "The Villans". First played at Perry Bar. *Ground:* Villa Park, Aston, Birmingham. *Colours:* claret and blue shirts, white shorts. *Manager:* Graham Turner. *Previous managers:* include Joe Mercer and Ron Saunders. *Honours:* include Football League champions six times between 1888 and 1910, again 1980–81, runners-up eight times. FA Cup-winners: 1886–7, 1894–5, 1896–7, 1904–5, 1912–13, 1919–20, 1956–7; runners-up twice. Football League Cup-winners: 1960–61, 1974–5, 1976–7, runners-up twice. European Champions' Cup-winners; 1981–2. *Best win:* 13–0 *v.* Wednesbury OA, FA Cup 1886, *Worst defeat:* 1–8 *v.* Blackburn R., FA Cup, 1888–9. *Record Gate:* 76,588 *v.* Derby C., FA Cup, 1945–6. *Highest league scorer:* T. Waring 49, 1930–31. *Noted players past and present:* J. Bache, D. Blanchflower, G. Cowans, A. Ducat, T. Ford, H. Hampton, W. Houghton, P. McParland, T. Morley, F. Moss, C. Nicholl, I. Powell, G. Shaw, T. Smart, P. Withe.

Cardiff City. *Founded:* 1899 as Riverside, turned professional in 1910. Played in the Southern League until 1920 when they were elected to the Football League, Div. II, achieving immediate promotion to Div. I and the folowing season gaining fourth place. *Ground:* Ninian Park. *Colours:* blue shirts, white shorts and known as "The Blues". *Manager:* Alan Durban. *Previous managers:* include Trevor Morris, Cyril Spiers, Jimmy Andrews, George Swindin, Frank O'Farrell, Jimmy Scoular. *Honours:* Football League runners-up—to Huddersfield T., 1923–4. FA Cup-winners 1926–7, runners-up once. Many times winners of the Welsh Cup. *Best win:* 9–2 *v.* Thames, Div. III(S),—1932. *Worst defeat:* 2–11 *v.* Sheffield U., Div. II, 1925–6. *Record gate:* 61,566 Wales *v.* England, 1961. *Highest league scorer:*

S. Richards 31, Div. III(S) 1936–7. *Noted players past and present:* C. Baker, J. Blair, E. Curtis, L. Davies, W. Davies, P. Dwyer, J. Evans, T. Farquharson, T. Ford, H. Hardy, A. Harrington, B. Hole, F. Keenor, J. Nelson, L. Phillips, K. Pontin, G. Reece, S. Richards, A. Sherwood, D. Sullivan.

Celtic. *Founded:* 1887. *Ground:* Celtic Park, Glasgow. *Colours:* green and white hooped shirts, white shorts. *Manager:* David Hay. *Honours:* from 1892, as one of the original members of the Scottish Football League, 20 times champions of Div. I and 17 times runners-up. Premier Div. champions 1976–7, 1978–9, 1980–1, 81–2, 85–6; three times runners-up. Scottish Cup-winners: 28 times, 15 times runners-up. Scottish League Cup-winners: nine times, including five years in succession (1966–70), runners-up eight times. First British club to win the European Champions' Cup (1966–7); runners-up in 1970. *Best win:* 11–0 *v.* Dundee, Div. I, 1895. *Worst defeat:* 0–8 *v.* Motherwell, Div. I, 1895. *Record gate:* 92,000 *v.* Rangers, Div. I, 1938. *Highest league scorer:* J. McGrory 50, Div. I, 1935–6. *Noted players past and present:* A. Bennett, T. Burns, J. Campbell, R. Collins, P. Crerand, K. Dalglish, J. Delaney, E. Doyle, R. Evans, J. Fernie, A. Gemmill, D. Hay, J. Hay, J. Johnstone, D. McGrain, J. McGrory, D. Mackay, J. McMenemy, W. McNeill, J. Quinn.

Chelsea. *Founded:* 1905 and elected to the Football League, Div. II. *Ground:* Stamford Bridge, Fulham Road, London SW. *Colours:* royal blue with white pinstripe shirts, blue shorts and known as "The Pensioners". *Manager:* John Hollins. *Previous managers:* include Ted Drake, Tommy Docherty, Dave Sexton. *Honours:* Football League champions 1954–5; runners-up 1906–7, 1911–12, 1929–30, 1962–3, 1976–7. FA Cup-winners 1969–70 and runners-up 1914–15, 1966–7. Football League Cup-winners 1964–5, runners-up 1971–2. Winners of the European Cup-winners' Cup 1970–71. *Best win:* 13–0 *v.* J. Hautcharage, European NC Cup, 1971. *Worst defeat:* 1–8 *v.* Wolverhampton W., Div. I, 1953. *Record gate:* 82,905 *v.* Arsenal, Div. I, 1935. *Highest league scorer:* J. Greaves 41, 1960–61. *Noted players past and present:* K. Armstrong, H. Baker, R. Bentley, P. Bonetti, F. Blunstone, P. Brabrook, J. Cock, W. Dickson, A. Ducat, H. Gallacher, J. Greaves, R. Harris, J. Kirwan, T. Law, T. Lawton, E. McCreadie, W. Mitchell, P. Osgood, R. Tambling, T. Venables, C. Viljoen, R. Wilkins, A. Wilson, V. Woodward.

Everton. *Founded:* 1878 as St. Domingo and played at Stanley Park. Turned professional 1885. One of the original members of the Football League. *Ground:* Goodison Park, Liverpool. *Colours:* royal blue shirts, white shorts and known as "The Toffees". *Manager:* Howard Kendall. *Previous managers:* include Cliff Britton, John Carey and Harry Catterick. *Honours:* Football League champions 1890–91, 1914–15, 1927–8, 1931–2, 1938–9, 1962–3, 1969–70, 1984–5 and runners-up seven times. FA Cup-winners 1905–6, 1932–3, 1965–6, 1984; six times runners-up. Runners-up to Aston V. in the 1962–3 Football League Cup final. *Best win:* 11–2 *v.* Derby C., FA Cup 1889–90.

Worst defeat: 4–10 *v.* Tottenham H., Div. I, 1958. *Record gate:* 78,299 *v.* Liverpool, Div. I, 1948. *Highest league scorer:* W. Dean 60, Div. I, 1927–8. *Noted players past and present:* W. Balmer, W. Bingham, C. Britton, W. Cresswell, D. Davies, W. Dean, T. Eglington, P. Farrell, T. P. Griffiths, E. Hughes, B. Labone, R. Latchford, T. Lawton, H. Makepeace, J. Mercer, E. Sagar, J. Sharp, N. Southall, R. Vernon.

Leeds United. *Founded:* 1904 as Leeds City playing in Div. II of the Football League. Re-formed in 1919 under present name. *Ground:* Elland Road. *Colours:* blue and yellow pinstripes on white shirts, white shorts and known as "The Peacocks". *Manager:* Eddie Gray. *Previous managers:* include Brian Clough, Jimmy Armfield, Allan Clarke. *Honours:* Football League champions 1968–9, 1973–4 and runners-up 1964–5, 1965–6, 1969–70, 1970–71, 1971–2. FA Cup-winners 1971–2 and runners up 1964–5, 1969–70, 1972–3. Football League Cup-winners 1967–8. UEFA Cup-winners 1967–8, 1970–1. *Best win:* 10–0 *v.* Lynoslo, European Champions' Cup, 1969. *Worst defeat:* 1–8 *v.* Stoke C., Div. I, 1934. *Record gate:* 57,892 *v.* Sunderland, FA Cup, 1967. *Highest league scorer:* J. Charles 42, Div. II, 1953–4. *Noted players past and present:* W. Bremner, K. Burns, J. Charles, T. Cherry, D. Cochrane, R. Collins, T. Cooper, W. Copping, H. Duggan, W. Edwards, B. Flynn, E. Gray, E. Hart, N. Hunter, P. Lorimer, P. Madeley, A. Powell, G. Sprake, B. Sproston, J. Stephenson, B. Stevenson, F. Worthington, T. Yorath.

Liverpool. *Founded:* 1892 and elected to Div. II of the Football League the following year. *Ground:* Anfield Road. *Colours:* all red, hence "The Reds". *Manager:* Kenny Dalglish, in succession to Joe Fagan, Bob Paisley, Bill Shankly etc. *Honours:* Football League champions 1900–1, 1905–6, 1921–2, 1922–3, 1946–7, 1963–4, 1965–6, 1972–3, 1975–6, 1976–7, 1978–9, 1981–2–3–4, 1985–6. A record number of 16 times (seven times runners-up). FA Cup-winners 1964–5, 1973–4, 1985–6 (4 times runners-up). Football League Cup-winners in four successive years—1980–81, 1981–2, 1982–3—and again in 1983–4. European Champions' Cup-winners 1976–7, 1977–8, 1980–81. UEFA Cup-winners 1972–3, 1975–6. *Best win:* 10–1 *v.* Rotherham U., Div. II, 1896. *Worst defeat:* 1–9 *v.* Birmingham C., Div. II, 1954. *Record gate:* 61,905 *v.* Wolverhampton W., FA Cup, 1952. *Highest league scorer:* R. Hunt 41, Div. II, 1961–2. *Noted players past and present:* J. Bamber, H. Chambers, R. Clemence, K. Dalglish, S. Hardy, E. Hughes, R. Hunt, J. Jones, K. Keegan, G. Lathom, W. Liddell, E. Longworth, T. McDermott, D. McMullen, P. Neal, M. Parry, A. Raisbeck, I. Rush. I. St. John, E. Scott, C. Sidlow, G. Souness, P. Thompson, J. Toshack.

Manchester City. *Founded:* 1887 as Ardwick (an amalgamation of West Gorton and Gorton Athletic) under which name they were one of the original members of Div. II of the Football League, 1892. *Ground:* Maine Road, Moss Side. *Colours:* all sky blue. Known as "The Citizens". *Manager:* Billy McNeill, following John Bond, Malcolm Allison, Joe Mercer and John Hart, among others. *Honours:* Football League champions 1936–7, 1967–8, and three times runners-up. FA Cup-winners 1903–4, 1933–4, 1955–6, 1968–9 and four times runners-up. Football League Cup-winners 1969–70, 1975–6 and once runners-up. Winners of European Cup-winners Cup 1069–70. *Best win:* 11–3 *v.* Lincoln C., Div. II, 1895. *Worst defeat:* 1–9 *v.* Everton, Div. I, 1906. *Record gate:* 84,569 *v.* Stoke C., FA Cup, 1934. *Highest league scorer:* T. Johnson 38, Div. I, 1928–9. *Noted players past and present:* S. Barkas, C. Bell, I. Broadis, E. Brook, M. Busby, R. Clarke, J. Corrigan, S. Cowan, P. Doherty, W. Donachie, A. Hartford, W. Jones, D. Law, J. McMullen, W. Meredith, R. Paul, D. Revie, F. Swift, M. Woosnam.

Manchester United: *Founded:* 1878 by railwaymen and as Newton Heath were elected in 1892 to Div. I of the Football League. Adopted their present name in 1910 on moving from Bank Street. *Ground:* Old Trafford. *Colours:* red shirts with white trim, white shorts. Known as "The Reds". *Manager:* Ron Atkinson. *Previous managers:* include Sir Matt Busby, Frank O'Farrell, Wilf Guiness and Dave Sexton. *Honours:* Football League champions 1907–8, 1910–11, 1951–2, 1955–6, 1956–7, 1964–5, 1966–7 and nine times runners-

up. FA Cup-winners 1908–9, 1947–8, 1962–3, 1976–7, 1982–3, 1984–5; runners-up three times. European Champions' Cup-winners 1967–8 (first English club to win the trophy). *Best win:* 10–1 *v.* Wolverhampton W., Div. I, 1892–3. *Worst defeat:* 0–7 *v.* Aston V., Div. I, 1930. *Record gate:* 76,962 *v.* Grimsby T., FA Cup semi-final, 1939. *Highest league scorer:* D. Viollet 32, Div. I, 1959–60. *Some noted players past and present:* T. Aston, J. Blanchflower, R. Bryne, J. Carey, R. Charlton, J. Delaney, D. Edwards, W. Foulkes, H. Gregg, N. McBain, C. McGarth, S. McIlroy, W. McMullen, W. Meredith, T. Miller, J. Nicholl, J. Nicholson, S. Pearson, D. Pegg, B. Robson, J. Rowley, T. Taylor, D. Viollet, W. Whelan, N. Whiteside, R. Wilkins, R. Williams.

Newcastle United. *Founded:* 1882, "West End" linking with "East End" to become United. Elected to Div. II of the Football League in 1893. *Ground:* St. James' Park. *Colours:* black and white striped shirts, black shorts and known as "The Magpies". *Manager:* Jack Charlton. *Previous managers:* include Gordon Lee, Joe Harvey and Charlie Mitten. *Honours:* Football League champions 1904–5, 1906–7, 1908–9, 1926–7. FA Cup-winners 1909–10, 1923–4, 1931–2, 1950–51, 1951–2, 1954–5 and runners-up four times. European Fairs Cup-winners 1968–9. *Best win:* 13–0 *v.* Newport C., Div. II, 1946. *Worst defeat:* 0–9 *v.* Burton W., Div. II, 1895. *Record gate:* 68,386 *v.* Chelsea, Div. I, 1930. *Highest league scorer:* H. Gallacher 36, Div. I, 1926–7. *Some noted players past and present:* I. Allchurch, F. Brennan, I. Broadis, T. Casey, E. Davies, W. Foulkes, H. Gallacher, K. Keegan, W. Low, W. McCracken, T. McDermott, M. Macdonald, R. Mackay, A. McMichael, P. McWilliam, J. Milburn, J. Richardson, J. Rutherford, C. Spencer, C. Veitch, S. Weaver.

Nottingham Forest: *Founded:* 1865 and elected to Div. I of the Football League 1892, its fifth season. *Ground:* City Ground, Trent Bridge. *Colours:* red shirts with white pinstripe, white shorts. Known as "the Foresters". *Manager:* Brian Clough. *Previous managers:* include Billy Walker, John Carey, Dave Mackay, Allan Brown. *Honours:* Football League champions 1977–8 and twice runners-up. FA Cup-winners 1897–8, 1958–9, runners-up once. European Champions' Cup-winners 1978–9, 1979–80. *Best win:* 14–0 *v.* Clapton, FA Cup 1890–91. *Worst defeat:* 1–9 *v.* Blackburn R., Div. II, 1937. *Record gate:* 49,945 *v.* Manchester U., Div. I, 1967. *Highest league scorer:* W. Ardron 36, Div. III(S), 1950–51. *Some noted players past and present:* V. Anderson, G. Birtles, I. Bowyer, K. Burns, F. Forman, A. Gemmill, J. Hanna, W. Hennessey, E. Hughes, J. Iremonger, T. Jackson, N. Linacre, T. Lindley, F. Morgan, M. O'Neill, J. Robertson, P. Shilton, C. Todd, T. Woodcock.

Portsmouth. *Founded:* 1899 from the Royal Artillery Club of the Southern League and themselves competed in that competition until 1920. Elected to the new Third Division of the Football League. As champions of the southern section 1923–4, promoted to Div. II, reaching Div. I three years later. *Ground:* Fratton Park. *Colours:* royal blue shirts, white shorts and known as "Pompey". *Manager:* Alan Ball jnr. *Previous managers:* include Jimmy Dickinson, MBE, who, as a player, made 764 appearances for the club and collected 48 England caps; Ian St. John, John Mortimer, Freddie Cox, Jack Tinn, George Smith. *Honours:* Football League champions 1948–9, 1949–50. FA Cup-winners 1938–9, twice runners-up. *Best win:* 9–1 *v.* Notts C., Div. II, 1926–7. *Worst defeat:* 0–10 *v.* Leicester C., Div. I, 1928. *Record gate:* 51,385 *v.* Derby C., FA Cup, 1949. *Highest league scorer:* W. Haines 40, Div. II, 1926–7. *Some noted players past and present:* J. Allen, J. Dickinson, D. Dougan, R. Flewin, J. Froggatt, W. Haines, P. Harris, J. Henderson, R. Irvine, J. McAlinden, J. Mackie, J. Mansell, L. Phillips, J. Scoular, J. Smith, N. Uprichard, A. Wilson, F. Worrall.

Preston North End. Founded 1880 by the cricket club of the same name. Another original member of the Football League, 1888, and its first champions, hence "The Old Invincibles" and "Proud Preston" by which they were hailed. Also known as "The Lilywhites". *Ground:* Deepdale Road. *Colours:* white shirts with blue trim, blue shorts. *Manager:* Brian Kidd, succeeding Alan Kelly, Harry Catterick, Tommy Docherty, Bobby Charlton, Alan Ball snr., Cliff Britton, Jimmy

Milne among others. *Honours:* Football League champions 1888-9, 1889-90 and six times runners-up. FA Cup-winners 1888-9, 1937-8; five times runners-up. *Best win:* 26-0 *v.* Hyde, FA Cup 1887. *Worst defeat:* 0-7 *v.* Blackpool, Div. I, 1948. *Record gate:* 42,684 *v.* Arsenal, Div. I, 1938. *Highest league scorer:* E. Harper 37, Div. II, 1932-3. *Some noted players past and present:* A. Beattie, R. Beattie, W. Cunningham, S. Davies, T. Docherty, T. Finney, J. Goodall, E. Harper, R. Howarth, A. James, W. John, R. Langton, J. McCall, A. Maclaren, F. O'Farrell, W. Roberts, E. Quigley, T. Thompson.

Rangers. *Founded:* 1873, one of the original members of the Scottish League, 1890. *Ground:* Ibrox Stadium, Glasgow. *Colours:* royal blue shirts, white shorts and known as "The Blues". *Manager:* Graeme Souness. *Honours:* 35 times champions of the Scottish League, Div. I and runners-up 21 times. Twice champions in the eight seasons of the Premier Division, and twice runners-up. Scottish Cup-winners 24 times, runners-up 14 times. Scottish League Cup-winners 11 times and five times runners-up. *Best win:* 14-2 *v.* Whitehill 1883 and Blairgowrie 1934, both in the Scottish FA Cup. *Worst defeat:* 1-7 *v.* Celtic, Scottish League Cup final, 1957. *Highest league scorer:* S. English 44, Div. I, 1931-2. *Some noted players past and present:* A. Archibald, J. Baxter, G. Brown, E. Caldow, S. Cox, A. Cunningham, J. Dawson, J. Drummond, N. Gibson, J. Greig, R. C. Hamilton, W. Henderson, S. Jardine, D. Johnstone, W. Johnston, I. McColl, R. McKinnon, R. McPhail, D. Meiklejohn, T. Muirhead, W. Reid, A. Smellie, A. Smith, N. Smith, C. Stein, D. Wilson, G. Young.

Sheffield Wednesday. *Founded:* 1866 by a local cricket club and known as "The Wednesday" until 1929, having been elected to the Football League, Div. I in 1892. *Ground:* Hillsborough. *Colours:* wide blue and white stripes, blue shorts and known as "The Owls". *Manager:* Howard Wilkinson in succession to Jack Charlton, Len Ashurst, Alan Brown, Derek Dooley, Vic Buckingham and Steve Burtenshaw among others. *Honours:* Football League champions 1902-3, 1903-4, 1928-9, 1929-30 and once runners-up. FA Cup-winners 1895-6, 1906-7, 1934-5 and twice runners-up. *Best win:* 12-0 *v.* Halliwell, FA Cup, 1891. *Worst defeat:* 0-10 *v.* Aston V., Div. I, 1912. *Record gate:* 72,841 *v.* Manchester C., FA Cup, 1934. *Highest league scorer:* D. Dooley 46, Div. II, 1951-2. *Some noted players past and present:* J. Blair, E. Blenkinsopp, E. Burgin, T. Crawshaw, J. Fantham, R. Froggatt, F. Kean, J. McCalliog, E. McConnell, A. Quixall, E. Rimmer, P. Rodrigues, J. Sewell, R. Springett, G. Stephenson, A. Strange.

Sunderland. *Founded:* 1879 as a district teachers' amateur club. Became Sunderland 1881 and in 1890 were elected to the Football League in place of Stoke C. *Ground:* Roker Park. *Colours:* red and black stripe on white shirts, red shorts. Known as "The Rokerites". *Manager:* Lawrie McMenemy. *Managers* have included; Len Ashurst, Ian McColl, Alan Durban, Alan Brown. *Honours:* Football League champions 1891-2, 1892-3, 1894-5, 1901-2, 1912-13, 1935-6 and five times runners-up. FA Cup-winners 1936-7, 1972-3, once runners-up. *Best win:* 11-1 *v.* Fairfield, FA Cup, 1895. *Worst defeat:* 0-8 *v.* West Ham U., Div. I, 1968. *Record gate:* 75,118 *v.* Derby C., FA Cup 1933. *Highest league scorer:* D. Halliday 43, Div. I, 1928-9. *Some noted players past and present:* G. Aitken, J. Baxter, W. Bingham, A. Bridgett, C. Buchan, H. Carter, W. Cresswell, J. Crossan, R. Daniel, J. Doig, W. Elliott, T. Ford, R. Gurney, D. Halliday, G. Holley, C. Hurley, I. Lawther, R. Lee, L. Roose, D. Tueart, D. Watson, W. Watson.

Tottenham Hotspur. *Founded:* 1882 as "Hotspur". Became a professional club in 1895 and moved from Northumberland Park to their present ground three years later. Members of the Southern League until 1908 when elected to Div. II of the Football League. *Ground:* White Hart Lane, London N. *Colours:* white shirts, navy blue shorts and known as "Spurs" or "The Lilywhites". *Manager:* David Pleat. *Previous managers:* include Peter Shreeves, K. Burkinshaw, Arthur

Rowe, J. Hulme, Peter McWilliam, W. Nicholson. *Honours:* Football League champions 1950-51, 1960-61 (season of League and FA Cup "Double") and four times runners-up. FA Cup-winners 1900-1, 1920-21, 1960-61, 1961-2, 1966-7, 1980-1, 1981-2. Football League Cup-winners 1970-71, 1972-3. Winners of European Cup-winners' Cup 1962-3. UEFA Cup-winners 1971, 1984. *Best win:* 13-2 *v.* Crewe Alexandra, FA Cup, 1960. *Worst defeat:* 2-8 *v.* Derby C., Div. I, 1976. *Record gate:* 75,038 *v.* Sunderland, FA Cup, 1938. *Highest league scorer:* J. Greaves 37, Div. I, 1962-3. *Some noted players past and present:* S. Archibald, O. Ardiles, G. Armstrong, E. Baily, D. Blanchflower, A. Brazil, W. Brown, R. Burgess, M. Chivers, T. Clay, J. Dimmock, M. England, W. Evans, J. Greaves, A. Grimsdell, G. Hoddle, P. Jennings, D. Mackay, G. Mabbutt, L. Medley, A. Mullery, M. Norman, E. O'Callaghan, S. Perryman, A. Ramsey, R. Smith, G. Roberts, J. Seed, F. Walden, J. White, V. Woodward.

West Bromwich Albion. *Founded:* 1879 as West Bromwich Strollers. One of the 12 original members of the Football League, 1888. *Ground:* The Hawthorns. *Colours:* navy blue and white striped shirts, white shorts and known as "The Throstles". *Manager:* Ron Saunders. *Previous managers:* include Ron Wylie, Don Howe, Alan Ashman, Vic Buckingham, John Giles. *Honours:* Football League champions 1919-20 and twice runners-up. FA Cup-winners 1887-8, 1891-2, 1930-31, 1953-4, 1967-8 and five times runners-up. Football League Cup-winners 1965-6, twice runners-up. *Best win:* 12-0 *v.* Darwen, Div. I, 1892. *Worst defeat:* 3-10 *v.* Stoke C., Div. I, 1937. *Record gate:* 64,815 *v.* Arsenal, FA Cup, 1937. *Highest league scorer:* W. Richardson 39, Div. I, 1935-6. *Some noted players past and present:* R. Allen, J. Astle, P. Barnes, W. Bassett, A. Brown, A. Hartford, D. Kevan, A. Millington, F. Morris, J. Murphy, G. Owen, J. Pennington, C. Regis, J. Reynolds, W. Richardson, A. Robertson, B. Robson, R. Robson, D. Statham, J. Vernon, G. Williams, S. Williams, W. Williams.

West Ham United. *Founded:* 1895 as Thames Ironworks, adopted present name while competing in the Southern League; elected to the Football League, Div. II in 1919. *Ground:* Upton Park, London E. *Colours:* claret and blue shirts, white shorts and known as "The Hammers". *Manager:* John Lyall. *Previous managers:* include Ron Greenwood, Ted Fenton, Charlie Paynter. *Honours:* FA Cup-winners 1963-4, 1974-5, 1979-80; lost to Bolton W. in the first Wembley Cup final, 1923, when more than 120,000 people were in the ground. Football League Cup runners-up 1965-6, 1980-81. Winners of European Cup-winners' Cup 1964-5; runners-up 1975-6. *Best win:* 10-0 *v.* Bury, FL Cup, 1983. *Worst defeat:* 2-8 *v.* Blackburn R., Div. I, 1963. *Record gate:* 42,322 *v.* Tottenham H., Div. I, 1970. *Highest league scorer:* V. Watson 41, Div. I, 1929-30. *Some noted players past and present:* J. Bond, W. Bonds, T. Brooking, J. Byrne, N. Cantwell, A. Devonshire, A. Hufton, G. Hurst, F. Lampard, T. MacDougall, A. Martin, R. Moore, F. O'Farrell, M. Peters, S. Puddefoot, J. Ruffell, J. Tresadern, V. Watson.

Wolverhampton Wanderers. *Founded:* 1877, elected 1888 to the Football League as one of the 12 original members. Known as "Wolves". *Ground:* Molineux Grounds. *Colours:* old gold shirts, black shorts. *Managers* have included Tommy Docherty. John Barnwell, Sammy Chung, Bill McGarry, Andy Beattie, Ted Vizard, Stan Cullis. *Honours:* Football League champions 1953-4, 1957-8, 1958-9, runners-up five times. FA Cup-winners 1892-3, 1907-8, 1948-9, 1959-60 and four times runners-up. Football League Cup-winners 1973-4, 1979-80. *Best win:* 14-0 *v.* Crosswell's Brewery, FA Cup, 1886-7. *Worst defeat:* 1-10 *v.* Newton Heath, Div. I, 1892. *Record gate:* 61,315 *v.* Liverpool, FA Cup, 1939. *Highest league scorer:* D. Westcott 37, Div. I, 1946-7. *Some noted players past and present:* H. Allen, P. Broadbent, S. Cullis, D. Dougan, R. Flowers, A. Gray, J. Hancocks, K. Hibbitt, A. Hinton, E. Hughes, J. Mullen, E. Peers, C. Phillips, W. Slater, S. Smyth, R. Thompson, D. Westcott, B. Williams, D. Wilshaw, W. Wright.

THE BATTLE FOR THE ASHES

ENGLAND v. AUSTRALIA 1876–1985

Introduction

When the England players strolled off the field on that early September day at the Oval, easy winners of the sixth and final Test match of the 1985 series, they knew that the Ashes had once again been wrested from Australia. And it showed in their faces. It was England's third win against Australia's one, with two matches drawn.

Yet those same Ashes, the traditional symbol of victory of one country over the other, had been a comparative latecomer in the most famous of all cricket contests. They had met 11 times before that. It was the Hon. Ivo Bligh, England captain on his country's fourth visit to Australia, who was the first to be presented with the urn containing the Ashes, said to be those of a stump used in the match, after he had led his side to a 69 run victory in the third Test, which secured the rubber, at Sydney in January 1883.

The previous year, at the Oval, a strong England side, including such doughty characters as W. G. Grace, Barnes, Hornby and Lyttleton, had lost the only Test match played. Needing only 85 runs to win they had suffered a middle-order collapse with Australia's "demon" bowler, Fred Spofforth, taking seven wickets for 44. This induced the *Sporting Times* to publish an obituary notice: "In affectionate remembrance of English Cricket which died on the Oval, on August 29th, 1882." It ended with the announcement: "The body will be cremated and the Ashes taken to Australia." And so they were.

A remarkable doctor

Along with George Parr of Nottinghamshire, who took only the second English touring team to Australia, Gloucestershire's Dr. William Gilbert Grace, then only 25 years old, must be given much of the credit for establishing the close ties between cricketers of both countries which led to Test match competition. Invited to Australia by members of the Melbourne Cricket Club in 1873, Grace and his party had to undertake a seven weeks' voyage. But it must have been some compensation for them to find that the hallowed English game was already popular enough to draw a crowd of several thousand to a match on the South Melbourne ground which they watched soon after their arrival. Their own tour involved travelling up to 100 miles from one venue to another—and this by horse-drawn coach over rough tracks. The cricketers of those days must have been tough characters indeed.

W. G. Grace first appeared for England in a Test match in 1880. Just the one match was played—at the Oval—and, opening the innings with his brother, E.M., he scored 152. England made 420, enforced the follow-on and beat Australia by five wickets.

The doctor was not a member of the touring party to Australia the following year but again opened for England in the single Test at the Oval played in August 1882. It was all over in two days, the Aussies, surprisingly perhaps, benefitting from the rain-affected wicket and winning by 7 runs.

Again England were without him in Australia in 1882–3, a drawn series, but be played in each of the three home Tests of 1884. In the first, at Manchester, he batted stolidly to stave off a possible innings defeat for England; contributed to a victory by an innings and 5 runs at Lord's; and was run out for 19 in the final Test at the Oval, a drawn game in which over 900 runs were scored. And he was still the bulwark of the side in the winning series of 1886, 1888 and 1890. He made his first (and last) Test appearances in Australia in 1891–2 and was still at his peak though the Aussies took the series by two wins to one. He played in only two of the three home Tests in 1893 but was captain in the only decisive match of that series.

England, without Grace, still held the Ashes after their tour of 1894–5 but, once again, he was appointed to lead his country when Australia came over the following year. And at the Oval England won the rubber by 66 runs. It was three years later at Trent Bridge on Australia's next tour that the famous bearded figure, towering over the stumps,

was to be seen as an England cricketer for the last time. Although his contribution with the bat was modest, as captain he steered his side to a draw, considerably helped, one should add, by the stylish Ranjitsinhji's 93 not out in the second innings. England, without Grace, lost by ten wickets in the second Test at Lord's and the remaining three Tests were drawn.

So that year England lost, not only the Ashes, but a giant of a cricketer whose very presence on the field, history tells us, suggested to the opposition that all their strategems would avail them nothing. In that span of 15 years his country won 11 series of Test matches, Australia only three, one being drawn. Altogether, in first-class cricket, W. G. Grace made 54,896 runs but, perhaps, even more remarkably, also took 2,876 wickets.

An historic hundred

It was an Australian, opening batsman Charles Bannerman, who scored the first Test century. He was on 165 in the first Test of the 1876–7 series when a hand injury forced him to retire. But it was a Surrey player, G. A. Lohmann, who provided the peak Test bowling performance of the Victorian era, taking eight wickets for 35 when Australia were dismissed for 84 at Sydney in 1887. In the previous Test of the two-match series England had come out for only 45, their lowest against Australia to date. Until 1902, when England skittled them out for 36 at Birmingham, Australia's lowest total had been their 42 at Sydney in 1888, Lohmann and Yorkshire's Robert Peel taking four and five wickets respectively. An Australian who played in 18 Tests from 1877–90 and as captain in all but three of them was W. L. Murdoch, his highest scores being 211 and 153 not out.

In all the 19th century saw England win 26 matches, Australia 20; 10 were drawn. England also led in the 19 series—11–6. Two were drawn. In the last series of that era, played in England in 1899, only one of the five Tests proved decisive, the Aussies winning the second Test at Lord's by 10 wickets. This was mainly achieved by the superb batting of Clem Hill of South Australia (135) and Victor Trumper of New South Wales (135 not out) which gave their side a lead of 215 on the first innings. Archie MacLaren, the Lancashire and England captain, carried his bat for 88 in the second innings and Tom Hayward of Surrey scored 77, but the tourists had little difficulty in getting the 28 runs needed for victory.

The struggle for supremacy

England's failure to regain the Ashes in the first Test series of the twentieth century must have been due, in some measure, to Sydney Barnes's leg injury in the third Test. Barnes, an enthusiastic league cricketer who, in his time, played for Warwickshire, Lancashire and Staffordshire, bowled fast-medium with occasional devastating spin. He was still playing in his sixties and, in fact, lived to the age of ninety-four.

Barnes's five wickets for 65 had accelerated England to win by an innings and 124 runs in the first Test at Sydney. And the 13 wickets he took at Melbourne should have put him on the winning side again, but the England batsmen, formidable on paper, crumpled to the bowling of Monty Noble and Hugh Trumble. He broke down after bowling only seven overs in the next Test, nor was he able to bat in the second innings, and, Australia, winning that one by four wickets, went on to grab the fourth and fifth Tests.

When one considers the undoubted strength of the England team both on that tour of 1901–2 and the home series that followed it seems incredible that Australia should have contrived to hold the Ashes. Among the batsmen were A. C. MacLaren, C. B. Fry, the great stylist K. S. Ranjitsinhji, F. S. Jackson, J. T. Tyldesley, Gilbert Jessop and Wilfred Rhodes, who made 1,000 runs over 20 times for Yorkshire, often at No. 11.

Certainly they shattered Australia in the first Test at Edgbaston in 1902, declaring at 376 for nine, then tumbling out their opponents for 36 (Rhodes taking seven for 17 with his slow left-arm spinners). But Black Country rain came to the aid of the tourists when, following on, they had lost two wickets for 46. Rain practically wiped out the second Test at Lord's and by taking the next two Australia were comfortably home with the Ashes still in their keeping.

For the 1903–4 series England had a new leader in "Plum" Warner of Middlesex while, for the opposition, Monty Noble took over from Darling. Despite the presence of Victor Trumper with two centuries to his name, and good all-round performances from the Australian captain, England, 3–1, had made sure of regaining the Ashes by the time they came to Melbourne to draw the fifth Test which the host country won by 218 runs. B. J. T. Bosanquet, who fathered the "Bosie" or googly, took 16 wickets for England in this series.

Bosanquet made his mark again as England's chief wicket-taker, with eight for 107, in Australia's defeat in the first Test at Nottingham in 1905, A. C. MacLaren's 140 being the highest individual innings. Heavy rain accompanied the Aussies to Lord's and the sides could only draw. At Leeds, too, it was the same result. But at Old Trafford England were on top again, great all-round batting and eight wickets for 126 in the match from W. Brearley giving them a win by an innings and 80 runs. Although the final Test at the Oval was drawn the spectators were given a feast of centuries—144 by C. B. Fry, 112 n.o. by J. T. Tyldesley and 146 from R. A. Duff, Australia's greater.

However, the 1907–8 series saw the barometer swing Australia's way once again. They took it by four Tests to one. Jack Hobbs, who was to score a record 12 centuries against the "Old Enemy", was a member of the touring party but not selected for the first Test. And George Gunn, whose name still has a magic ring in Nottingham, only just scraped into the side. He scored 119 and 74.

In this country the following year Australia rallied after losing the first Test by ten wickets to take the Lord's and Headingley Tests and hold England to a draw both at Old Trafford and the Oval. These were fairly low-scoring matches but in the final Test W. Bardsley made a century in each innings and F. Lever's eight for 31 in the fourth Test was the best bowling performance of the series.

Jack Hobbs—"the Master"

Although, by this time, England could call on such accomplished batsmen as George Gunn, Frank Woolley and J. W. Hearne, it was the prime craftsmanship of Jack Hobbs that, to a great extent, stemmed the flow of Australia's supremacy. In the first Test at Sydney in the 1911–12 series Hobbs had to bow to Victor Trumper, whose 113 put Australia on the path to victory. But from his 126 not out at Melbourne which gave England the second Test, Hobbs went on to score 187 at Adelaide and 178 at Melbourne again, while in the final Test Woolley, unbeaten on 133, clinched the series at 4–1.

When England took the 1912 series as well by winning the final Test at the Oval (the first "timeless" Test in this country) with Hobbs contributing 66 and 32, Frank Woolley 62 and Barnes, Dean and Woolley (10 for 49) snatching most of the wickets, England held the Ashes and had won four of the post-1900 series, Australia likewise, and the match results since 1876–7 stood at: England 40, Australia 35, drawn 19.

Between the wars

Both Warwick Armstrong of Australia and J.W.H.T. ("Johnny-Won't-Hit-Today") Douglas of England had led their countries before the 1914–18 War and were at the helm once more for the 1920–1 series. But whereas England had a nucleus of seven from the pre-war Test side, only Macartney, Bardsley and Kelleway, besides Armstrong, were tried and tested players for Australia. Nevertheless, Australia won each of the five Tests—convincingly, too. Hobbs made 122 at Melbourne and 123 at Adelaide (after A. C. Russell's 135 not out in the first innings) and Harry Makepeace of Lancashire scored 117 at Melbourne, despite spinner Mailey's impressive haul of 13 wickets in the match. However, for Australia not only did Collins, Kelleway, Armstrong (two),

Pellew and Macartney record centuries but their bowlers were the more effective, a menacing combination of speed and spin.

Armstrong captained Australia for the last time on their 1921 tour. And in the first two Tests, at Trent Bridge and Lord's, J. W. H. T. Douglas was at the helm for England. But these matches were lost by ten-and eight-wicket margins and at Leeds the 32-year-old Hon. Lionel Tennyson took over. Australia won, just the same. The Old Trafford and Oval Tests being drawn, largely because of the weather, England had gone for ten Test matches without a win.

It was timely that in a home series against South Africa a polished batsman from Yorkshire should join Hobbs to form one of the most famous opening partnerships in the history of cricket. When Hobbs and Sutcliffe opened against Australia at Sydney in the first Test of the 1924–5 series they put up 157. Despite this, however, and with the great-hearted Hampshire bowler, Maurice Tate, among the wickets, England lost by 193 runs, Collins, Ponsford and Taylor the century-makers and Gregory, Mailey and Kelleway taking out the bulk of England's batting. Australia won four matches of that series, England one.

Following four drawn games, the Oval Test of 1926, the year of Britain's General Strike—a class war of some bitterness—saw two distinguished elevens fighting it out to a finish. Percy Chapman of Kent had replaced A. W. Carr as England captain and Wilfred Rhodes, now 49 years old, joined Tate, Larwood and George Geary in the bowling attack. The renowned firm of Hobbs, Sutcliffe, Woolley and Hendren were there to get the runs.

Australia topped England's first innings total of 280 by 22 runs. But Hobb's 100 and Sutcliffe's 161 in the second innings helped the home country to a forbidding total of 436 and with a thunderstorm drenching the uncovered wicket on the third day Australia were put out for a mere 125. Chapman's team did even better on the 1928–9 tour, winning the series 4–1, with Wally Hammond scoring 251, 200, 177 and 119 not out on the way. Hobbs, Hendren, Sutcliffe and Leyland were also centurymakers. So England held the Ashes they had snatched away from Australia on those soggy August days of 1926 and, to that date, were only two matches behind their rivals—46 wins to 48, with 25 drawn.

The inimitable Don

The first Test of the 1930 series, at Nottingham, was also Don Bradman's first Test match in this country. When Tate bowled him for 8 in the first innings the spectators must have wondered what all the fuss had been about. But they were soon to discover that the pre-tour publicity had not erred in praising the remarkable ability of the lad from Cootamundra. His second knock of 131 was an innings against the odds: he held out for over four hours against fine bowling by Tate, Tyldesley and Robins (Larwood was taken ill on the last day of the match). England took the match by 93 runs.

At Lord's, and facing an England total of 425 (Duleepsinhji 173), Woodfull, the Australian captain, and Bradman made 409 between them—155 and 254 respectively—and the tourists declared at 729 for six. England replied with 375, thanks to a lusty 121 from Chapman, but it was not enough to redress the balance and the sides were all-square in the series.

The next two Tests were drawn despite Bradman's 334 in an Australian total of 566 at Leeds and rain decided the issue at Manchester. But in the final Test at the Oval yet another double-century from Bradman took his side to 695 against England's 405 (Sutcliffe 161) and, bowling out R. E. W. Wyatt's team for 251 in the second innings Australia took the honours by an innings and 39 runs and returned home with the Ashes.

From 1924 to 1930 Hobbs and Sutcliffe shared 15 century opening stands for England, while in the 1930 series alone Don Bradman scored 974 runs.

The "body-line" tour

After the Australian film in which the more sensational episodes of the 1932–3 series were re-enacted, the leading "characters" are now legendary. Douglas Jardine, of Oxford University and Surrey, the sometime wearer of a Harlequin cap which particularly annoyed sections of the Australian cricketing public, and a captain with a firm belief in the efficacy of pre-match tactics, was determined to recapture the Ashes by reducing the scoring power of the Australian batsmen—particularly Bradman's.

England were two up in the series when they came to Adelaide. They lost four quick wickets and were largely indebted to Leyland (83), Wyatt (87) and Paynter (77) for a first innings total of 341, but Jardine knew that he must strike early at the Australian batting strength if victory was to be on. Using his pacemen—Larwood, Bill Voce and "Gubby" Allen—he positioned at least five or six fielders close on the leg side and instructed the bowler to pitch short-length balls in line with the leg stump. Impossibly cramped in their stroke-play, the batsmen, in trying unorthodox methods of getting the ball away from the leg-trap, were often badly hit on the body. Oldfield, in fact, trying to take evasive action, edged the ball into his own face. Bradman, temporarily at a loss, was caught off Larwood for 8.

England won that Test by 338 runs, by six wickets in the next and by eight wickets in the final Test. They had recaptured the Ashes by four matches to one—but for the first time in 57 years of sporting rivalry those ashes were bitter to the taste.

Australia's revenge

Although England, holders of the Ashes, were in the driving seat with such experienced Test batsmen as Sutcliffe, Hammond, Leyland and Hendren, and an artful attack including Yorkshire's Hedley Verity, they were by no means as strong as they might have been when the 1934 series started at Trent Bridge. Where were Larwood and Voce, the deadly home-ground bowlers? Selectors and players alike must have had nightmares thinking of ways to circumvent Bradman's inexorable run-rate—already, in 23 Test innings against England, he had amassed 1,838 runs for an average of 87.52. As it turned out, Chipperfield was the highest scorer for Australia with 99 but their ace spinners, Grimmett and O'Reilly, won the match for them, taking 19 wickets between them.

In the second Test England turned the tables on the visitors by an innings and 38 runs, Verity taking 15 for 104 in the match. Both the third and fourth Tests were drawn, despite Bradman's 304 at Leeds, so the teams came to the Oval for the final Test with everything to fight for. England had a sorry match. Leyland's 110 helped them to score 321 in reply to the tourists' impressive 701 (Ponsford 266, Bradman 244) but England's 'keeper, Leslie Ames, retired hurt and Bowes was too ill to bat. They lost the match by 562 runs and surrendered the Ashes to one of the strongest Australian sides they had ever had to face.

Under the captaincy of Don Bradman Australia took the 1936-7 series by three matches to two. Allen's side had resounding victories at Brisbane and Sydney—by 322 runs and an innings and 22 respectively, Leyland scoring 126 in the first Test, Hammond 231 in the second. But the full power of Australian batting made itself felt in the following Tests, with the Don notching 270, 212 and 169 and with centuries from Fingleton, McCabe and Badcock. England's best bowling performances were Bill Voce's six for 41 and Farnes's six for 96.

Hutton's marathon innings

Only four Tests were played in 1938. After two draws, Australia won at Leeds and England at the Oval. The tourists kept the Ashes but Len Hutton of Yorkshire, batting for over 13 hours, at that time the longest individual Test innings in history, scored 364—30 runs more than Bradman's great innings at Leeds in 1930. Neither Bradman nor Fingleton batted in either innings for Australia, both nursing injuries incurred while fielding.

A. G. Moyes, writing in his *Australian Cricket* on England's 1946-7 tour, considered that "from the English standpoint, the resumption was rather too soon after the war" but praised the MCC for thinking "first of the good of the game". In the first Test at Brisbane England, under Wally Hammond, faced not only a formidable Australian total of 645 but wet-wicket conditions. They could muster only 141 and, following on, 172. At Sydney, too, the Australians, in reply to England's 255, amassed 659 for

eight, declared. Even Bill Edrich's 119 in the second innings could not prevent another innings defeat. The third and fourth Tests were drawn but the final Test again went to the home country. Len Hutton scored 122 in England's first innings but then was too ill to continue, nor could he come to the crease in the second innings. So Australia, three up with two drawn, still held the Ashes.

A year later, on their tour of England, the Australians not only won four of the five Tests but were unbeaten in all matches. It was Don Bradman's final tour and he made the most of it. Norman Yardley, the Yorkshire captain, led England and his side included men of the calibre of Hutton, Washbrook, Bill Edrich, Denis Compton, Alec Bedser and Jim Laker, but besides their powerful batting the Aussies had the incomparable bowling partnership of Keith Miller and Ray Lindwall, plus Bill Johnston whose own tally of English wickets was 27.

Bradman came out for a duck in his last Test innings—bowled by Eric Hollies of Warwickshire—but in Test matches against *all* countries, over 50 of them, he had scored close on 7,000 runs and his average was 99.94.

Picking up the pieces

Australia were again triumphant in the 1950-1 series, and again won four Tests, though this time England did manage to snatch one. Lindsay Hassett had succeeded Bradman as captain, his opposite number being Freddie Brown who, first playing for Surrey, had then revived one of the lowliest English counties—Northamptonshire. And it was his five wickets for 49 which had enabled England to win the final Test.

Celebrating Coronation Year

Having held the Ashes for 19 years and with their latest four-Tests' victory still fresh in their minds, Hassett's men must have felt confident of further conquest in England in 1953, the Coronation Year. Of course Bradman would be missed but even before the first Test the irrepressible Keith Miller, at Worcester, and young Neil Harvey, at Leicester, had scored double centuries, the latter going on to collect centuries at Manchester, Hove and Southampton. And in the forefront of the attack would be Miller, fast-left-arm Bill Johnston and the promising young leg-spinner, Richie Benaud.

The first Test at Nottingham fell to bad weather, with Hutton, the skipper, and Reg Simpson, the local hero, well set to get the 229 needed to win. Alec Bedser had distinguished himself by taking 14 for 99 in Australia's two innings. The Lord's Test, also drawn, featured the incredible last-ditch partnership of Willie Watson of Yorkshire and Trevor Bailey of Essex, who stayed together for over five hours withstanding everything Lindwall, Johnston, Miller and the spinners could hurl at them. Old Trafford, true to its woeful reputation, produced rain that cost the third Test nearly 16 playing hours and, not surprisingly, the game petered out to a draw. The Leeds Test, too, was drawn but much stirring cricket over the five days attracted some 150,000 spectators. They saw Australia score 266 against England's 167, then an England revival built on a fighting third-wicket stand by Bill Edrich (64) and Denis Compton (61), while Jim Laker, at No. 9, missed his half-century by only two runs. Australia fought hard to get the necessary 177 runs to win but lost four wickets and were 30 runs short at the end of the match.

And so to the Oval for the final Test. It was here that England clearly out-played the Aussies. For the fifth time Hutton had lost the toss and the tourists batted. Against Fred Trueman at his deadliest, Alec Bedser and Bailey their batting, apart from Hassett (53) and Lindwall (a late 62), crumbled. They were all out on the first day for 275. However, England's batsmen were equally troubled by Lindwall and Johnston, though Hutton's 82 and Bailey's 64 bumped up the total to 306. It was England's spinners—Lock and Laker—who, making full use of a sticky wicket, bagged the honours in the visitors' second innings, taking five for 45 and four for 75 respectively. But that popular Middlesex pair, Edrich and Compton, record-breakers six seasons before with 7,355 runs between them, had the honour of clinching the match, the series and the Ashes on the fourth day.

Nevertheless, Australia could still claim that in

the 49th year of Test rivalry they had won 69 matches to England's 61, with 38 drawn.

The "Typhoon" hits Australia

Although informed critics gave most of the credit for a successful defence of the Ashes in 1954–5 to Len Hutton, who had never captained England more astutely, and indeed it was a fitting curtain to the Yorkshireman's brilliant career, undoubtedly his pace attack of Bailey, Bedser, Loader, Statham and Tyson, buttressed by the guile of spinners Wardle and Appleyard, turned the scales in England's favour.

Handicapped by the injury to Denis Compton, who broke a bone in his hand when running full-tilt into the boundary pickets, England lost the first Test at Brisbane by an innings and 154 runs, Australia having declared at the formidable total of 601. But at Sydney six wickets for 85 from Frank Tyson (soon named the "Typhoon") and Brian Statham's three for 45 gave England victory by 38 runs. Peter May's 104 and Neil Harvey's 92 not out were the best batting performances.

Again England were on top at Melbourne, Colin Cowdrey's 102 in the first innings and May's 91 in the second giving heart to their bowlers. In the event Tyson took nine for 95 and Statham seven for 98. Tyson had a run-up to the bowling crease of some 30 yards and not a yard of it was wasted. He must have cut a truly fearsome figure to the unfortunate batsmen. And Statham's untiring accuracy was to be encountered from the other end. England tied up the series at Adelaide and the final Test was drawn, no play being possible for more than three of the scheduled six days. Three Tests to England, one to Australia, one drawn.

Jim Laker's harvest

The English summer of 1956 was no summer at all. It was one of the wettest for many years. Ian Johnson was Australia's captain for his second series but it was Peter May's baptism in the post. The first Test at Trent Bridge was a low-scoring match conducted, due to frequent showers, in fits and starts and May declared twice in an effort to force a decision. However, Burke and Burge held out for the tourists with 137 still needed to win. At Lord's, in the second Test, Johnson won the toss and his openers, McDonald and Burke, put on 137. In reply to Australia's total of 285, England could only scrape up 171, the captain supplying 63 of them. Richie Benaud's bold second-innings knock of 97 went a long way to winning the match for the visitors; again, it was only May (53) who looked at all comfortable against the bowling of Miller, five for 80 and ten wickets in the match, and Ron Archer, four for 71.

The greatest pre-match talking point of the third Test at Leeds was the selection of Cyril Washbrook of Lancashire, 42 years old and Hutton's opening partner on the 1950–1 tour. But the selectors' reliance on experience was certainly vindicated when, batting at No. 5, Washbrook helped May to put on 187 for the fourth wicket. Godfrey Evans and Trevor Bailey made the tail wag and England's 325 dwarfed the Australian innings of 143 and 140. The triumphant bowlers were the Surrey "twins", Laker and Lock, with figures of 11 for 113 and seven for 81 respectively.

Old Trafford witnessed another home victory, this time by an innings and 170 runs, a match in which all first-class bowling records were shattered when, after taking nine for 37 in Australia's first innings, Laker took all ten wickets in the second.

England's long dark tunnel of the 'sixties

Not for the first time England's delight at having retained the Ashes was short-lived—and their suffering prolonged. Australia were now to be dominant for more than a decade. England's 1958–9 tour was initially beset by injuries with replacements having to be found at short notice; and there were also accusations that Australian umpires were condoning "chucking" and "dragging" by some of the home side's bowlers. According to reports the England players condemned Meckiff for throwing and Rorke for throwing *and* dragging. (This was under the old law which stated that at the instant of delivery the bowler had to have "at least some part of

one foot behind the bowling crease".) England lost four Tests and one was drawn.

Australia's "suspect" bowlers were missing from their 1961 touring party, cooling the temperature all round, and with Australia led by Richie Benaud five Test matches were played in an excellent spirit.

At Edgbaston in the first Test the England bowling was hammered after their batsmen had managed only 195 runs. Australia declared at 516 for nine, Neil Harvey having scored 114, the baseball-loving Norman O'Neill 82, Simpson 76 and Mackay 64. But in England's second innings the tourists' attack was equally unsuccessful. Ted Dexter hit 180 and Subba Row, 112. England were 401 at the close.

In the second Test at Lord's, with Australia coasting to victory, Trueman and Statham took five quick wickets and only Peter Burge's sturdy 37, with Davidson blocking at the other end, put their side one up in the series. At Headingley, however, England made it all square, Trueman taking five for 58 and six for 30.

Previously Old Trafford had never been a lucky ground for the Aussies—they had not won there since 1902. But although they were 177 runs behind on the first innings, Lawry's century urged them on to a winning total of 432 second time round. Benaud's six for 70 was the deciding factor and ensured that Australia retained the Ashes.

Ted Dexter, taking over the captaincy from Peter May, did well to hold the Australians to a drawn series in 1962–3, especially as the England fielding was reported to be below Test standard. After a drawn game at Brisbane, England won at Melbourne by seven wickets, with centuries from Cowdrey and Sheppard, and Titmus and Trueman each taking five wickets. But Australia took the next Test by much the same margin and the last two Tests were drawn. At no time, however, did England look like bearing off the Ashes and the following year, at home, Australia were the only winners of a Test, the other four being drawn.

Yet there were some outstanding individual performances in that 1964 series. At Lord's, in the second Test, John Edrich's 120 deserved better support. At Old Trafford Ted Dexter's 174 and Ken Barrington's 256 were the chief factors in England's total of 611—this in reply to Australia's 656 for eight, declared (Simpson 311, Lawrie 106). And in the final Test at the Oval Geoff Boycott's 113 was buttressed by an undefeated stand between Cowdrey (93) and Barrington (54).

Mike Smith of Warwickshire led the England party to Australia in 1965–6 while Bobby Simpson and Brian Booth captained the host country in three and two Tests respectively. Again drawn matches predominated. In the first Test at Brisbane young Doug Walters, hailed as another Bradman, batted for more than five hours for his 322, though this was an hour less than Lawry took to score 166. England, bent on saving the match, depended on the stoicism of Boycott, Edrich and Barrington. It was much the same at Melbourne in the second Test, Burge and Walters making centuries for Australia and Edrich and Cowdrey for England. Big totals to little result.

At Sydney England really got on top, forcing the home country to follow on—this for the first time since "Laker's Test" in 1956. Barber made 185, Edrich 103 and Boycott 84 toward a total of 488; Titmus, David Allen and David Brown collected the wickets. Australia took their revenge at Adelaide, England's two innings failing to match the home side's 516, of which Bobby Simpson made 225, Bill Lawry 119. Rain curtailed the final Test at Melbourne but again over 1,000 runs were scored, Bob Cowper making 307 and Lawry 108 for Australia, Ken Barrington 115 for England.

Colin Cowdrey captained England in all but one of the five Tests of 1968 but the drawn series was bedevilled by rain. However, the final Test at the Oval, which England started still one down, provided some excitement, Basil D'Oliveira's 158 and John Edrich's 164 being the major contributions to a total of 494. The visitors battled manfully to match it, skipper Lawry making 135, but fell short by 170 runs. When England came out for 181 in their second innings Australian hopes revived—until Derek Underwood of Kent wrecked their innings by taking seven for 70.

So the series was saved. But for the sixth series running Australia had had a firm grasp on the Ashes. And since 1876–7 Australia had won 80 Tests, England 66, with 74 drawn.

Illingworth's triumph

Ray Illingworth, an astute and solid all-rounder who, in 1969, had left Yorkshire, his native county, to captain Leicestershire, was appointed to lead his country in the 1970–1 series. Some voices had been raised in favour of Colin Cowdrey but they were soon silenced when "Illy's team", after drawing the Tests at Brisbane and Perth, won at Sydney by 299 runs. This was the fourth Test, the third, at Melbourne, having been abandoned without a ball being bowled.

Steady batting by England (Boycott 77 and 142 n.o.) produced totals of 332 and 319 for five, declared, while Australia, 236 in their first innings, slumped to 116 in the second, England's pace attack of Bob Willis and John Snow—seven for 40—building on what Illingworth, Underwood and D'Oliveira had accomplished earlier. England also won the final Test, though more narrowly. The fifth and sixth Tests had been drawn.

It was the first time in 16 years that England had proved resolute enough to regain the Ashes, and to accomplish it abroad, denying Australia a single victory, was particularly rewarding.

Moreover, in 1972, and despite Bob Massie's incredible fast spell at Lord's, when he followed his eight wickets for 84 in England's first innings with eight for 53 in the second, Illingworth's side still contrived to win two of the five Tests against the two of Australia and thus retain the Ashes. Besides Massie, the tourists had that ferocious bowler, Dennis Lillee and, in the batting line-up, the abrasive Chappell brothers, Ian and Greg.

The Chappells call the tune

England's 1974–5 tourists, led by Mike Denness of Kent, met the full force of Australia's determination to show that their failure to regain the Ashes two years before had been a mere slip-up. At Brisbane they won by 166 runs, the Chappell brothers forcing the pace and Jeff Thomson, powerfully fast, taking six for 46 in England's second innings. They also won at Perth, Edwards and Walters scoring centuries and Thomson claiming five for 93.

At Melbourne in the third Test, England did well to draw, their opponents being only eight runs off victory when stumps were drawn. Dennis Amiss made 90 and Tony Greig, the South African who played for Sussex and was later to succeed to the captaincy, following his 110 at Brisbane with a cavalier 60.

However, Australia still looked the stronger combination and proved it by winning at Sydney by 171 runs and by 163 at Adelaide. England's consolation prize was the final Test at Melbourne in which they made 529 (Denness 188, Fletcher 146) and won by an innings. But the Ashes had already been surrendered.

By winning the first Test at Edgbaston later in the year, the other three Tests being drawn, captain Ian Chappell must have felt he had done much to restore his country's supremacy in the battle for the Ashes.

Mike Brearley, captain of Middlesex, joint county champions and winners of the Gillette Cup that year, was appointed to lead England in the 1977 home series. Greig had captained England in the Centenary Test match at Melbourne in March, Brearley being one of his opening bats, but the South African had become too deeply involved in the Packer Deal for the commercialization of one-day cricket in Australia for the selectors' liking.

The Australians sent a moderate side and their ace bowler, Jeff Thomson, obviously felt the lack of Dennis Lillee to bowl at the opposite end. After a drawn game at Lord's, England won the next three Test matches, the final Test at the Oval resulting in another draw. Boycott made two centuries in the series, Woolmer and Knott one each. In the Lord's match Bob Willis took seven wickets for 78.

Nor did Brearley's team have any trouble in defending the Ashes in Australia in 1978–9, winning by five Tests to one. On a short tour in 1979–80 England had to bow to Greg Chappell's men in each of the three matches played but the Ashes were not at stake. The result of a single encounter in 1980, with the home side under Ian Botham, was a draw but again the Ashes were not up for grabs.

Botham's comings and goings

The next Ashes series was in 1981. Nottingham's long-held reputation for providing "featherbed" pitches being in the past, a low-scoring match was no great surprise, though perhaps few cricket followers would have laid a bet on neither side touching 200. Ian Botham of Somerset, destined to become one of the greatest all-rounders Test cricket has known, and who had captained England against West Indies the previous summer, was bowled by Terry Alderman for a single in the first innings but a stand between Gatting and Dilley hoisted England's total to 185. But it was Botham who caught and bowled Alan Border, Australia's highest scorer with 63. The match-winners were bowlers Alderman (four for 68 and five for 62) and Lillee (three for 34 and five for 46).

The second Test at Lord's having ended disappointingly for England, Botham gave up the captaincy and at Leeds it was Mike Brearley, once more, who led England on to the field. Botham, obviously relieved to have cast off the extra burden of leadership, took six wickets for 95. But Australia still made 401 for nine, declared, Dyson and Hughes being responsible for nearly half that total. England were dismissed for 174 but Bob Willis shrugged this off and bowling with tremendous verve, proceeded to take eight Australian wickets for 43—they were all out for 111. And Botham, the batsman, scoring 149 not out, won the match for England by 18 runs.

At Edgbaston, for the fourth Test, the match appeared to be going Australia's way. They needed only 151 to win, having shot England out for 189 and 219. But along came Botham, suddenly quicker than ever, to rattle out five batsmen at the cost of only one run. It was inspired captaincy by Brearley to give the ball to Botham when he did. John Emburey's off-spin had removed four Australian batsmen in the first innings but Brearley knew, and he was proved to be right, that when the boat needed to be rocked the Somerset all-rounder was the man to do it.

At one point in the final Test at Old Trafford it looked as if Australia, although they had no hope of regaining the Ashes, might square the series. They were 101 down on the first innings but with England at the crease again Alderman and Lillee cut down the early batting power, only Boycott and Tavare giving them much trouble. When Botham strode out, flailing his bat as usual, five wickets had gone for 104. Hitting mightily—88 of his 118 runs came from boundaries—he turned the game completely in England's favour. With Knott and Emburey also notching 50's, the total rocketed to 404.

The second innings of Yallop (114) and Border (123 n.o.) were a brave attempt to counteract the Botham explosion but England, with three Tests to their credit, were worthy winners by 103 runs. They had now triumphed in three successive series and their hold on the Ashes seemed fast.

In the interim, however, England were denied the services of several men of proved Test class due to their having played in South Africa early in the spring of 1982—Gooch, the opening bat, and Emburey, our best off-spinner, amongst them—so that for the 1982–3 tour under Bob Willis there were some new faces, new, at least, to the Ashes series.

The first Test at Perth was a high-scoring draw. Both teams scored over 400 in their first innings, Greg Chappell's 117 being the highest individual effort. Derek Randall's 115 lifted England's second innings and Australia were set 340 to win in a couple of hours. Willis bagged the wickets of both openers but that was the end of the excitement.

But Brisbane did produce a result, Australia winning by seven wickets. Only Alan Lamb and Botham seemed at all settled against the bowling of Geoff Lawson (11 for 34 in the match) and Jeff Thomson (five for 73). At Adelaide, too, in the third Test, England were outclassed, losing by eight wickets after being asked to follow on, though David Gower's 114 matched Greg Chappell's 115 for stroke-making.

The fourth Test at Melbourne was as thrilling as any match in the history of the struggle for the Ashes. In reply to England's 284 (Tavare 89, Lamb 83) the Aussies scored 287 (Hughes 66). Graeme Fowler's 65 was the best individual innings in England's second knock—all out for 294. Australia needed 292 to win. Eventually it rested on Alan Border, coming in at No. 6, and the last man,

Thomson, to take the match. And they came within four runs of doing it. Most of the batsmen had gone to the bowling of Cowans, the Middlesex pace bowler, who took six for 92, but with Border by now looking unbeatable Willis brought Botham back. In one delivery Botham managed to bend the ball wickedly, Thomson got a touch and Geoff Miller of Derbyshire took the slip catch.

England produced a great effort to win or draw the final Test at Sydney and retain the Ashes but the Aussies were just too much for them. Kim Hughes scored 137, Border a couple of 80's and although in England's second innings Eddie Hemmings of Notts struggled to 95, batting at No. 9, and everyone but Geoff Cook got double figures, the match and the series still went to Australia.

After holding the Ashes over two well-fought series, England had now relinquished them.

Good for Gower

The auguries for England's chances of regaining the Ashes in 1985 were quite promising. At home the previous summer, and with a new skipper in David Gower of Leicestershire, England had lost all five Test matches to West Indies. But on the credit side Alan Lamb had made three centuries, Graeme Fowler one; and in one innings Botham had taken eight wickets. Also, Australia had done little better in the West Indies in the spring, losing three Tests, drawing two.

At Headingley in the first Test, under overcast skies, Australia elected to bat and, against lacklustre bowling, made 331 of which Andrew Hilditch, opening with Graeme Wood, scored 119. The tourists, handicapped by Geoff Lawson suffering a throat infection, had to rely heavily on 20-year-old McDermott and he did get rid of Gooch and Gower cheaply. But Robinson, the Notts opener, batted with extraordinary aplomb for his 175 and with fifties from Gatting, Botham and the wicketkeeper, Downton, England put 533 on the board. Wayne Phillips, the visitor's keeper, came up with a brave 91, backed by 80 from Hilditch and 64 from Wessels in Australia's second innings but England still had no difficulty in winning by five wickets.

Six days of rain preceded the Lord's Test, indeed the month was bidding fair to become the wettest June on record, so when Alan Border won the toss he had no hesitation in asking England to bat. McDermott removed Gooch, Robinson and Gatting before three figures were on the board but Gower, although eventually another victim of McDermott, played a captain's innings of 86 and gritty knocks by Lamb, Downton and Emburey brought the total to 290, McDermott having taken six for 70. As ever, Botham was among the wickets when Australia batted, taking five for 109, but Border (196) and Ritchie (94) hoisted the tourists to 425 and England's 261 in their second innings seemed scarcely enough to trouble their opponents. It wasn't. Before lunch on the final day Australia had collected the 127 runs needed and won by four wickets.

After the rain-affected third Test at Trent Bridge, which ended in a draw but was enhanced by centuries from Gower for England and from Wood and Ritchie for Australia, the countries were still on level terms in the series. Nor did the fourth Test at Old Trafford change the situation. Rain interfered with several sessions of play and particularly thwarted England who, in reply to the tourists' 257, had made 482 for nine, declared, Mike Gatting scoring 160. Border saved the Australians, being unbeaten on 146.

Although it also rained at Edgbaston during the fifth Test, England went two up in the series by declaring at 595 for five, in response to Australia's 335. Gower made a splendid 215, Tim Robinson 148 and Mike Gatting, reliable as always, 100 not out. They did not have to bat again, dismissing Australia for 142, Richard Ellison of Kent following his seven for 77 with four for 27, in each innings taking the invaluable wicket of Alan Border.

At the Oval, in the sixth and final Test, Border, dismissed by leg-breaker Phil Edmonds for 38 in the first innings, battled stoutly to save his side when they followed on from England's 464 but he simply ran out of partners, wickets falling like ninepins to the bowling of Ellison and Botham. And the Ashes had shuttled England's way again.

Australia's only consolation—and one doubts whether they set much store by it—was that on the overall count of 257 Test matches played since 1882–3, the first series in which they competed for the Ashes, Australia had won 96, England 86, with 75 drawn.

BIBLICAL
GLOSSARY

This section provides an easy to
use treasure-house of information
about the biblical world. It presents
a concise and valuable guide to
the people, places and events which
have had so much influence on the
course of history. A special article
in this issue provides an outline
survey of biblical history from the
time of Abraham to the Christian
era.

THE LAND OF PALESTINE

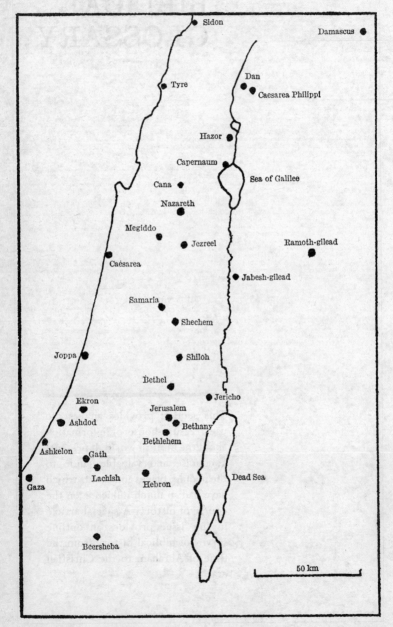

N.B. This map does not represent Palestine as it was at any one period of history. It shows most of the Palestinian locations mentioned in the text from whatever period.

BIBLICAL GLOSSARY

INTRODUCTION

There is a sense in which the Bible is part of every person's heritage. Though it is sometimes claimed that we are now living in a post-Christian era, the marks of a Christian culture are part of our everyday experience: the great cathedrals of our cities, the parish churches and village chapels of our countryside, the frequent allusions to biblical ideas or symbols in the works of many of our novelists, poets and playwrights, even the appearance of a Christian hymn, *Amazing Grace*, in the "pop" charts. At the root of this culture is the revelation of God offered by the Bible.

Even to those who do not accept the faith it proclaims, the Bible has much to commend it. It contains some fine poetry, vivid story-telling, deep insights into the human condition and moral guidance which has stood the test of time. It is also of enormous value simply as a historical resource. For Christians, of course, it is much more than this, a unique revelation of God.

It is not, however, an easy book. The modern British reader has to bridge a time-gap of at least 2,000 years (often much more) and enter into an alien culture if he is to become familiar with the biblical world. It is astonishing how many Christians have succeeded in making this transition with little or no help, and found that the Bible can still speak across the barriers of time and space. But today it should not be necessary for anyone to read the Bible unaided. Within the last century our understanding of the way the biblical writers worked, of the cultural background against which their lives were set, and of the wider historical and religious background of the surrounding nations have all increased enormously.

Much of this new knowledge is now available in large, definitive dictionaries of the Bible and in detailed commentaries on individual books. The reader who wishes seriously to improve his understanding of the Bible must consult such works. This section, however, is intended to offer assistance to those who do not possess more specialised works of reference, with information which is simply presented but does not gloss over the complexity of the issues, and which is based on the consensus of modern scholarly opinion.

ABBREVIATIONS USED IN GIVING BIBLICAL REFERENCES

Acts	Acts	Isaiah	Is	Nehemiah	Neh
Amos	Amos	James	Jas	Numbers	Num
Chronicles	Chr	Jeremiah	Jer	Obadiah	Obad
Colossians	Col	Job	Job	Peter	Pet
Corinthians	Cor	Joel	Joel	Philemon	Phlm
Daniel	Dan	John	Jn	Philippians	Phil
Deuteronomy	Deut	Jonah	Jon	Proverbs	Prov
Ecclesiastes	Ecc	Joshua	Josh	Psalms	Ps
Ephesians	Eph	Jude	Jude	Revelation	Rev
Esther	Esth	Judges	Judg	Romans	Rom
Exodus	Ex	Kings	Kgs	Ruth	Ruth
Ezekiel	Ezek	Lamentations	Lam	Samuel	Sam
Ezra	Ezra	Leviticus	Lev	Song of Songs	Song
Galatians	Gal	Luke	Lk	Thessalonians	Thes
Genesis	Gen	Malachi	Mal	Timothy	Tim
Habakkuk	Hab	Mark	Mk	Titus	Tit
Haggai	Hag	Matthew	Mt	Zechariah	Zech
Hebrews	Heb	Micah	Mic	Zephaniah	Zeph
Hosea	Hos	Nahum	Nah		

S4

A

Aaron. The elder brother of Moses, he was appointed by God to be Moses' spokesman in the negotiations with the Egyptian Pharaoh for the release of the Jews (Ex 4:14). After the exodus, in Moses' absence, he made a golden calf for the people to worship (Ex 32:1-6). In spite of this lapse, tradition regards him as Israel's first High Priest (Ex 29:1-7).

Abednego. One of three young men who, according to the book of Daniel, survived being thrown into a blazing furnace for refusing to worship a gold statue set up by King Nebuchadnezzar (Dan 3:1-27).

Abel. The second son of Adam and Eve, he was killed by his elder brother Cain out of jealousy because God found Abel's offering of a lamb more acceptable than his offering of grain (Gen 4:1-8). The story probably reflects a feeling among traditionalists that the Jews had been corrupted by the agricultural civilisation of Canaan, and were less acceptable to God than when they had been shepherds.

Abiathar. When his father Ahimelech was killed by Saul for his unwitting involvement in David's escape, Abiathar fled to join David's outlaw band (1 Sam 22:16-23). He subsequently became David's High Priest, but was banished by Solomon because he supported Adonijah in the struggle for succession to the throne (1 Kgs 1:5-7, 26-27).

Abijah. King of Judah (915-913 B.C.).

Abner. Saul's commander-in-chief. After Saul's death he supported Ishbosheth, his only surviving son, as king of Israel, but soon became disenchanted with him. He was negotiating with David to transfer the allegiance of the northern tribes to him when he was murdered by David's commander, Joab, in pursuance of a family quarrel (2 Sam 3:6-27).

Abraham. Abraham, originally known as Abram, is regarded as the father of the Jewish people. While there are doubtless legendary elements in the stories told of him, there is no reason to question his historical existence, probably in the period 2000-1800 B.C. Through the stories of Abraham run two complementary themes: God's promises and Abraham's faith. God promises to Abraham that he will have numerous descendants, that they will occupy the land of Canaan and that they will be a source of blessing to all mankind (Gen 12:1-3). Abraham responds to these promises with faith, shown in his willingness to set out for the promised land not knowing where he is being led, and to sacrifice his son Isaac when he thinks that this is what God requires. Neighbouring peoples (e.g. the Moabites) still practised child sacrifice a thousand years later, and this story, as well as indicating Abraham's faith, reflects the early understanding of the Jews that God did not require human sacrifice.

Absalom. David's third son. After his sister Tamar had been raped by his elder half-brother Amnon, he plotted revenge and eventually had Amnon killed (2 Sam 13). As a result he had to flee to the small state of Geshur which his grandfather ruled. After three years he was permitted to return at the instigation of David's general, Joab, who probably felt that Ammon had only got his due punishment. He then proceeded to plot against his father, sowing seeds of discontent among the northern tribes especially (2 Sam 15:1-6) and finally raised an army to march on Jerusalem. David withdrew across the Jordan, gained time to organise loyal forces and crushed the rebels. In the decisive battle Absalom was killed by Joab, even though David had expressly instructed that he should not be harmed (2 Sam 18:6-15).

Acts of the Apostles. The book is clearly a sequel to Luke's gospel, being addressed to the same person, Theophilus, and referring to an earlier work which described "the things that Jesus did and taught from the time he began his work until the day when he was taken up to heaven." It is invaluable for the insight it gives into the first thirty years of the Christian church. Peter and Paul are the leading personalities in the book, yet the theme is not one of human heroes but of God at work among the community of believers through the gift of the Holy Spirit.

The somewhat surprising ending, with Paul under house arrest in Rome, has led many to wonder whether the work was unfinished or a third volume planned, yet in some ways this is a most fitting conclusion—Paul in spite of everything proclaiming the good news at the very heart of the Roman empire.

Adam. The name is simply the Hebrew for "man". Adam is therefore to be thought of not as the first man in a historical sense but as the symbolic prototype of all mankind.

Adonijah. The fourth son of David. As the eldest surviving son by the time his father reached old age, he expected to succeed to the throne and had himself declared king by Abiathar and Joab before David's death. David, however, nominated Solomon to succeed him and Solomon soon found occasion to accuse Adonijah of treachery and have him put to death (1 Kgs 1:5-53, 2:13-25).

Agrippa, see **Herod Family.**

Ahab. King of Israel (869-850 B.C.). The son of Omri, who arranged his marriage to Jezebel, daughter of the king of Tyre, as part of his policy of friendly relations with Phoenicia. His chief fault was his failure to curb the excesses of his wife, who was determined to supplant the worship of Yahweh with the worship of her own god, Baal Melkart. He ignored the advice of the prophet Micaiah to go to battle against the Syrians at Ramoth-Gilead, where he was fatally wounded by an arrow.

Ahaz. King of Judah (735-715 B.C.). Ahaz came to the throne at a moment of crisis. King Pekah of Israel and King Rezin of Damascus had formed an alliengiance against the powerful Assyrians, and were threatening to attack Judah if she did not join them. In desperation, and against the advice of Isaiah, he appealed to the Assyrians for help. This he received, but at the cost of becoming an Assyrian vassal. He is criticised by the biblical historians for taking part in idolatrous practices, and is even said to have sacrificed his own son (2 Kgs 16:1-4).

Ahaziah. (1) King of Israel (850-849 B.C.). The son of Ahab, within two years of coming to the throne he fell from a balcony and never recovered from his injuries (2 Kgs 1:2).
  (2) King of Judah (842 B.C.). The son of Jehoram, he had the misfortune to be visiting his father's namesake, Jehoram king of Israel, at the time of Jehu's rebellion in which he was killed (2 Kgs 9:27-28).

Ahijah. A prophet from Shiloh who predicted the division of the kingdom after Solomon's death by tearing his robe into twelve pieces and giving ten of them (representing ten tribes) to Jeroboam, later to be the first king of the breakaway state of Israel (1 Kgs 11:29-40).

Ahimelech. The priest at Nob who unwittingly assisted David's escape from Saul by giving him food and a sword. He was subsequently killed by Saul together with all the other priests at Nob (1 Sam 21:1-9).

Alexandria. Though only mentioned four times in the Bible (all the references being in Acts), Alexandria had a large Jewish community almost from its foundation in 332 B.C. by Alexander the Great, and it was here that the Septuagint, the Greek translation of the Old Testament, was made during the third and second centuries B.C.

Amalekites. A nomadic people who lived in the desert regions to the south of Israel. They attacked the Israelites during their march from Egypt to the promised land, and were later attacked and defeated by both Saul and David (1 Sam 15:1-9, 30:1-20).

Amaziah. King of Judah (800-783 B.C.). After succeeding in regaining territory earlier lost to the Edomites, Amaziah got into an unnecessary and disastrous quarrel with King Jehoash of Israel from which he emerged the clear loser. He was eventually assassinated at Lachish, whence he had fled, having heard of a plot against his life (2 Kgs 14:1-19).

Ammonites. A trans-Jordanian tribe frequently at war with the Israelites. It was in action against the Ammonites that Saul proved his powers of leadership (1 Sam 11:1-15), and although David seems to have established good relations with King Nahash of Ammon, his son insulted David's envoys and bitter hostilities ensued. David ultimately took the Ammonite crown, but only after a long struggle (1 Sam 10:1–11:1, 13:26–31).

Amon. King of Judah (642–640 B.C.). The son of the hated Manasseh, he was soon assassinated because he continued in his father's idolatrous ways.

Amos. The first of the great reforming prophets of the eighth century B.C., we know relatively little about the man himself as opposed to what he taught. A herdsman and grower of figs from Tekoa in Judah, he prophesied in the cities of Israel to which he perhaps travelled to sell his produce. His prophetic career may have lasted as little as a few months sometime during the period 760–750 B.C.

Amos was appalled by a society in which an affluent minority exploited the poverty-stricken majority. Loans would be made to the poor, and when they were unable to repay them, their houses and land would be seized, or their children sold into slavery to pay off the debt. The use of false weights and measures by the merchants was commonplace, and bribery in the courts ensured that no case against them would ever succeed. Yet these same merchants made lavish sacrifices to God at the national shrines of Gilgal and Bethel.

Amos believed in a God of righteousness who demanded right living from his people. Furthermore, he was a God of limitless power who controlled the forces of the universe and directed the course of human history. If his people failed to see the evil of their ways he would use a foreign power as the instrument of his judgement upon them. The fact that they were a chosen people would not prevent this: indeed they, more than any other nation, should know what God required and their failure to meet his standards was all the more blameworthy.

The message of Amos is uncompromising, and needs to be balanced by the words of later prophets who saw the possibility of redemption as well as judgement. Nevertheless his importance is immense, as the man who proclaimed with a new clarity the incompatibility of worshipping God and exploiting one's fellow men.

Ananias. (1) A member of the early church who sold some property and gave part of the proceeds to the church, but claimed to have given all. Peter accused him of lying to God, and he fell down dead (Acts 5:1–6).

(2) A Christian in Damascus who, in response to a vision, went and baptised Saul following his conversion (Acts 9:10–19).

(3) The Jewish High Priest before whom Paul appeared after his arrest - in the temple at Jerusalem (Acts 23:1–5).

Andrew. The brother of Simon Peter and one of the first disciples.

Annas. Though he had retired from the High Priesthood before the time of Jesus' trial, Annas continued to exercise influence through his son-in-law and successor, Caiaphas.

Antioch. (1) The capital of the Roman province of Syria and an important centre of early Christianity. It was here that disciples were first called Christians, and it was this church that sent Paul and Barnabas out on the first missionary journey (Acts 13:1–3).

(2) A city in Pisidia (part of Asia Minor) visited by Paul on his first missionary journey (Acts 13:13–52).

Apocalypse. Prophetic description of the end of the world from the Greek word meaning "revelation".

Apollos. A Jew from Alexandria who proclaimed the gospel in Ephesus but only knew about John's baptism as opposed to Christian baptism in the Holy Spirit. After Prisca and Aquila had explained Christianity more fully to him he went on to Corinth where, unfortunately, opposing factions developed according to whether they "followed" Apollos or other teachers (Acts 18:24–28, 1 Cor 1:12–13).

Aquila. A Jew who, with his wife Prisca, was expelled from Rome by an edict of Claudius and settled in Corinth. Here they welcomed Paul, and later worked with him in Ephesus (Acts 18:1–4, 24–26).

Aramaeans, see **Syrians.**

Areopagus. An open space in Athens, often used for public debates, and where Paul addressed the Athenians (Acts 17:16–34).

Ark of the Covenant. An ornate wooden chest believed to contain the stone tablets on which the ten commandments were written. It accompanied the Israelites throughout their nomadic wanderings and was then kept at Shiloh during the early years of the occupation of Palestine. Brought by the Israelites to encourage them in battle against the Philistines at Aphek, it was in fact captured, but the Philistines soon returned it, attributing a series of disasters to its presence. David brought it to Jerusalem, where Solomon eventually enshrined it in the temple. It is presumed to have remained there until the temple was destroyed by the Babylonians in 586 B.C.

Artemis. A Greek goddess identified with the Roman Diana. Her temple at Ephesus was famous, though the worship there seems to have been based on an earlier fertility cult.

Asa. King of Judah (913–873 B.C.).

Ascension. Although this is the word normally used to describe Jesus' departure from the earth, its significance is metaphorical rather than literal. It signifies the return of Jesus to God, and the taking up again of the power and authority he voluntarily laid down in order to share the human experience (Acts 1:6–11).

Ashdod. One of the five Philistine city-states.

Asher. (1) The eighth son of Jacob, his second by Zilpah, Leah's slave-girl.

(2) The tribe of Asher which occupied fertile land along the coastal plain north of Mount Carmel.

Ashkelon. One of the five Philistine city-states.

Assyria. A major power to the north-east of Israel for over two centuries. As early as 853 B.C. Ahab had to meet the threat of an Assyrian invasion, though it was not until the accession of Tiglath-pileser III to the Assyrian throne in 745 B.C. that Assyria took a dominating role in the affairs of Palestine. By 721 B.C. the northern kingdom of Israel had become an Assyrian province and the southern kingdom of Judah was paying heavy tribute. An attempt by Hezekiah to become independent from Assyria in 705 B.C. was punished by an invasion in which all the fortified cities of Judah except for Jerusalem itself were taken and destroyed. Judah remained subservient to Assyria until the Assyrian empire began to break up under pressure from the Medes and the Babylonians about 630 B.C.

Athaliah. Queen of Judah (842–837 B.C.). The wife of Jehoram, king of Judah and mother of Ahaziah, who succeeded him. When Ahaziah lost his life in Jehu's rebellion, Athaliah seized the throne and put to death all male members of the royal family except for Joash, one of Ahaziah's sons who was hidden by his aunt. After six years in hiding he was proclaimed king by members of the forces acting on the instructions of Jehoiada the priest, and Athaliah was killed.

Athens. Visited by Paul on his second missionary journey. The sermon he preached there (Acts 17:16–34) is notable for its attempt to speak to Greek thinkers in terms they would find familiar, but his success appears to have been slight and Athens was never an important centre of Christianity.

Atonement, Day of. The most solemn day of fasting in the Jewish calendar. The High Priest went into the most sacred part of the temple (the only day of the year on which this was permitted) to make a special offering in expiation of the sins of the people. These sins were symbolically transferred to a goat (the "scape-goat") which was then driven out into the wilderness (Lev 16:20–34).

B

Baal. The Hebrew word means simply "master", "owner" or "husband", and it was used as a general term for foreign gods, but especially for the Canaanite fertility god. Although the debased sexual practices associated with the worship of this god were fiercely condemned by Hebrew writers, it was probably through contact with Canaanite religion that the people of Israel came to view their own God as creator and lord of the world of nature.

Baasha. King of Israel (900–877 B.C.), and involved in a border dispute with Asa, king of Judah.

Babel, Tower of. The significance of the story is mythological rather than historical. Partly it is an attempt to explain the variety of human languages, but it also reflects a view long held in certain sectors of Israelite society that man's close relationship with God was broken once he began to build cities and become, in his own eyes, self-sufficient. Like the story of Adam's disobedience it regards human greed and arrogance as the root causes of his estrangement from God.

Babylonians. When the Babylonians and Medes destroyed Assyria they divided their empire between them, with the Babylonians taking the southern portion. They therefore took over from the Assyrians the dominating role in Palestinian affairs from 605 B.C. Rebellions against Babylonian overlordship in 598 B.C. and 589 B.C. were disastrously unsuccessful, the latter resulting in the destruction of Jerusalem and its temple and the exile of many of its people in 586 B.C.

Baptism. The origins of baptism are obscure. John the Baptist baptised as a sign of repentance (Mk 1:4–5), and the Jews are known to have used a form of baptism as a means of entry to the Jewish faith for non-Jews, though it is uncertain whether or not this custom was established before John started baptising. There is no record of Jesus baptising anyone, yet it seems to have been established as the mode of entry into the Christian church from earliest times (Acts 1:38). Baptism was first administered to adult believers, or sometimes to whole families on the conversion of the head of household (Acts 16:33), and from this seems to have sprung the practice of baptising infants of Christian parents.

Barabbas. According to an established custom of releasing a prisoner at Passover time, Pilate set free Barabbas in preference to Jesus on the insistence of the crowd (Jn 18:38–40).

Barnabas. A prominent member of the early church, invariably exerting an influence for good at crucial moments. He was the first to befriend Paul in Jerusalem after his conversion (Acts 9:26–27). Sent by the Jerusalem church to report on work among the Gentiles which had begun in Syrian Antioch, he made a favourable recommendation, remained himself to continue the work and brought Paul to join him (Acts 11:19–26). He was Paul's companion on the first missionary journey (Acts 13:1–3), but did not accompany him on the second journey for characteristic reasons. Paul did not want to take John Mark, who had failed them on the first journey, while Barnabas wanted to give him a second chance. Significantly Paul was later to become reconciled to John Mark, thus confirming Barnabas' judgement (2 Tim 4:11).

Bartholomew. One of the twelve disciples. *See* **Nathaniel.**

Baruch. Acted as scribe to Jeremiah and read out a message from Jeremiah in the temple precincts at a time when Jeremiah himself had been banned from speaking there (Jer 36:1–8).

Bathsheba. The wife of Uriah, an officer in King David's army. Because she was expecting a child by David, he gave orders that Uriah be left in an exposed position during the fighting against the Ammonites, and he was killed. Bathsheba's child died in infancy, but she subsequently bore Solomon (2 Sam 11:2–12:25).

Beersheba. A town on the southernmost border of Judah: hence the expression "from Dan to Beersheba" to mean the whole of Israel.

Belshazzar. The last king of Babylon before its capture by the Persian monarch Cyrus in 539 B.C. Mentioned in the Bible only in the book of Daniel, particularly in the dramatic story of his downfall recorded in the fifth chapter.

Benjamin. (1) The twelfth son of Jacob, his second by Rachel, who died in giving birth to him (Gen 35:16–18).

(2) The tribe of Benjamin, occupying a relatively small area just north of Judah.

Bernice. The sister of Herod Agrippa II, she

heard with him Paul's defence of his conduct before the Roman governor Festus (Acts 25:13–26:31).

Bethany. A village just outside Jerusalem, the home of Lazarus, Martha and Mary. It was here that Jesus stayed on his final visit to Jerusalem.

Bethesda. A pool in Jerusalem believed to have healing properties, particularly when the waters were disturbed. The scene of one of Jesus' healing miracles in John 5:1–9.

Bethlehem. A town in Judaea some five miles south of Jerusalem and known from before King David's time. Chiefly famous as the birthplace of Jesus, although some scholars now believe it more likely he was born in or near Nazareth which was in Galilee.

Bildad. The second of Job's three "comforters" (Job 8).

Booths, *see* **Tabernacles.**

C

Caesarea. A city on the Palestinian coast built by Herod the Great and named after Caesar Augustus. The Roman governors of Palestine had their residence in Caesarea, and it was here that Paul was tried before Felix and Festus, spending the intervening two years under arrest (Acts 24:1–26:32).

Caiaphas. The High Priest during the time of Jesus' ministry, who presided at his examination before the Jewish Council.

Cain, *see* **Abel.**

Cana. A village in Galilee where Jesus attended a wedding celebration and, according to John 2:1–11, turned water into wine.

Canaanites. The people who occupied the territory subsequently taken over by the people of Israel. Their civilisation was materially more advanced than that of the people of Israel, but morally they lagged far behind and their cultic practices are frequently condemned by biblical writers.

Capernaum. A little frontier town by the Sea of Galilee which for a time was the centre of Jesus' ministry. It was here that he called Matthew (Mt 9:9) and performed a number of healings including that of the centurion's servant (Lk 7:1–9).

Carmel. The culmination of a spur branching westwards from the main north-south mountain range of Palestine and almost reaching the coast. It was the scene of Elijah's confrontation with the prophets of Baal (1 Kgs 18:19–40).

Chaldeans, *see* **Babylonians.**

Christ, *see* **Jesus** and **Messiah.**

Christian. A nickname, first used in Syrian Antioch (Acts 11:26), which gradually became the normal way of describing a follower of Christ. Elsewhere in the New Testament, Christians are referred to as followers of "the Way", Nazarenes or simply the saints.

Chronicles, Books of. These books give an account of the history of the Jews from the death of Saul to the return from the exile. They are therefore largely a retelling of events already recorded by earlier authors in the books of Samuel and Kings. The purpose of the chroniclers seems to have been to reassure their people of God's care for them in spite of the adversities recently suffered, and this leads them to present an unjustifiably rosy view of Israel's history (*e.g.* glorifying David's reign and glossing over his weaknesses). Consequently most scholars prefer to rely on the earlier and more sober accounts in Samuel and Kings, but, treated with caution, the information in Chronicles provides a useful supplement to the earlier records.

Colossians, Letter to the. As far as is known, Paul himself never visited Colossae, but the church there had been founded by Epaphras, a close associate of Paul (Col 1:7). Perhaps he felt some responsibility for the Colossian Christians because of this. The letter was probably written during Paul's imprisonment in Rome and appears to be a response to reports of false teachers in Colossae. These teachers suggest that there is a special kind of knowledge (over and above the knowledge of Christ) which is necessary for salvation, and they advocate an ascetic way of life. Paul's reply stresses that Christ alone is all-sufficient for the needs of his readers.

Commandments. There are, of course, many commandments in the Bible, but the ten commandments which God is said to have given to Moses on Mount Sinai have a special place. They are seen as the basis of God's agreement with the people of Israel and, significantly, combine religious and social obligations. In Israel's religion true worship and right living are not to be separated (Ex 20:1–17).

Corinth. Strategically situated at a major junction of trading routes, Corinth in New Testament times was a wealthy city which not even Athens could match in importance among the cities of Greece. It also had an evil reputation, however, because of its notoriously lax moral standards. Both its importance and its depravity may have commended it to Paul as a place to preach the Christian gospel. He spent 18 months here about A.D. 50 (Acts 18:1–18), and made at least one further visit, possibly two. His letters to the church at Corinth show that he was passionately concerned about its welfare.

Corinthians, Letters to the. Although Paul's correspondence with the Corinthians is collected into two letters in the New Testament, most scholars are agreed that they include parts of four separate communications summarised below:

(1) A letter of warning against pagan influences, a fragment of which appears in 2 Corinthians 6:14–7:1 and which is referred to in 1 Corinthians 5:9–13.

(2) The letter now known as 1 Corinthians.

(3) An extremely severe letter partly preserved in 2 Corinthians 10–13.

(4) A much more relaxed letter, perhaps showing relief that the severe letter had had the desired effect, and preserved in 2 Corinthians 1–9.

The letters afford valuable insights into the problems which faced a small Christian community set in a pagan environment, and into the relationship between Paul and a church which nearly drove him to distraction because of its waywardness and the depth of his concern for it.

Cornelius. A Roman centurion whose baptism by Peter represented an important step in the progress of the Christian church from a Jewish sect to a universal faith (Acts 10).

Covenant. The concept of the covenant—an agreement between God and man—is implicit throughout the Old Testament. The first explicit reference comes in the story of Noah where God makes a covenant to save Noah and his family from the impending flood and subsequently agrees never again to send such a flood upon the earth. God then makes a covenant with Abraham to establish his descendants as a chosen people, though it should be noted that they are chosen to bring God's blessing to all nations (Gen 12:3). It is however, the covenant made at Sinai after the exodus that is regarded as the most important. In this covenant God offers the people of Israel a special place in his plans if they will serve him alone and obey his commandments (Ex 19:5–6). Again it is noteworthy that the people of Israel are to serve God as priests, i.e. as people who mediate the knowledge of God to others.

Covenant, Book of the. In 622 B.C. during the course of repairs on the temple, a scroll was discovered which is described as the Book of the Covenant. When this was brought to King Josiah he realised that his people had failed to live up to God's demands, and set in motion the most far-reaching religious reforms ever known in Judah. These included the suppression of all pagan cults, an edict that in future sacrifice could only take place in the temple in Jerusalem, and the re-institution of the Passover which had apparently not been celebrated for many years (2 Kgs 22:3–23:23). The close similarities between these measures and instructions contained in the book of Deuteronomy suggest that the Book of the Covenant was in fact the first edition of Deuteronomy. It is thought to have been written by pious Jews during the long and evil reign of Manasseh (687–642 B.C.) as a re-statement and amplification of the covenant with Moses. Not daring to publish it openly at the time, they hid it in the temple, hoping that it would later be discovered and acted upon.

Creation. There are two creation stories in the Old Testament, a primitive version which nevertheless has considerable charm starting at Genesis 2:4, and the more familiar version with which Genesis begins, but which is actually later in origin. See also **Genesis**.

Cross. The supreme symbol of the Christian faith because it represents the depths of suffering Jesus was prepared to embrace in order to save mankind by inaugurating God's Kingdom upon earth. Crucifixion was the normal method of execution for those who did not possess Roman citizenship, and because the wounds inflicted were not in themselves very serious, a strong man could take days to die. According to Mark 15:44, Pilate was surprised that Jesus had died within hours.

Cyrus (c. 559–530 B.C.). The Persian king who overthrew the Babylonian empire and allowed the exiled Jews to return to their homeland.

D

Damascus. An ancient city, the capital of Syria. In the Old Testament, in fact, Damascus and Syria are synonymous. It was on his way to Damascus to persecute the Christian community there that Paul had his conversion experience.

Dan. (1) The fifth son of Jacob, his first by Bilhah, Rachel's slave-girl.

(2) The tribe of Dan, occupying a small area north of Judah and west of Benjamin.

(3) The city of Dan in the far north of Israel: hence the expression "from Dan to Beersheba" meaning the whole of Israel.

Daniel. Almost certainly written between 167 and 164 B.C., Daniel is one of the last of the books of the Old Testament chronologically. At this time the Greek ruler Antiochus Epiphanes was attempting systematically to destroy the Jewish religion. The book was written to encourage the resistance movement with stories of Daniel and his friends, who refused to compromise in religious matters during the Babylonian captivity some four hundred years earlier. The second half of the book contains obscure visions which appear to predict the ultimate downfall of pagan empires and the triumph of the people of God.

David. King of Israel from about 1000 to about 960 B.C. It is not clear whether David first came to Saul's attention as a skilled musician able to soothe him in his depressions (1 Sam 16:17–23) or as the shepherd boy who killed the Philistine champion Goliath (1 Sam 17:12–51). In either case he soon showed his military skill, and before long was receiving adulation greater than Saul himself (1 Sam 18:7). Saul's insane jealousy forced David to flee from his court and become an outlaw, eventually offering his services, and those of the 600 men who had joined him, to the Philistines as a way of keeping out of Saul's clutches (1 Sam 27:1–4).

Whilst nominally a Philistine vassal, David attacked traditional enemies of Israel such as the Amalekites, and distributed his booty among the tribe of Judah, thus indicating that his change of allegiance was a temporary expedient (1 Sam 30:1–31). When Saul was killed in battle David was immediately accepted as king of Judah (2 Sam 2:4), but the northern tribes were ruled by Saul's son, Ishbosheth, until he was assassinated by two of his officers (2 Sam 4:5–8).

As king of all Israel David rapidly subdued the Philistines (2 Sam 5:17–25), and soon turned his attention to the Ammonites, who had insulted his ambassadors (2 Sam 10:1–5). During the Ammonite war he successfully beat off a Syrian attack and subsequently annexed much Syrian territory. He also conquered the Moabites and the Edomites east of the Jordan. In the end he ruled an empire stretching some 725 kilometres from north to south and 185 kilometres from east to west.

David was not just a brilliant military tactician however. He was a statesman who understood the need for national unity and the crucial part to be played by his people's religion in achieving this. He established his capital in Jerusalem because it was close to the boundary between Judah and the northern tribes, and did not actually belong to any of the tribes, being still in the hands of the Jebusites. This was presumably to avoid inter-tribal jealousy. Although he did not build a temple, he brought the ark of the covenant to Jerusalem, thus establishing it as a religious centre and not just an administrative capital.

David's later years were marred by struggles among his sons to gain the throne, and he seems to have been uncharacteristically weak and indecisive in dealing with them.

Deborah, Song of. If this hymn of triumph over the enemy commander, Sisera, was composed at the time of the events, as seems likely, it dates from before 1100 B.C. and is therefore one of the oldest fragments of literature in the Old Testament (Judg 5:2–31).

Dedication, Feast of. A feast to commemorate the rededication of the temple following its desecration by the Greek ruler Antiochus Epiphanes in 168 B.C.

Demetrius. A silversmith of Ephesus who stirred up trouble for the Christian community because the success of Christianity was affecting the trade of those who made silver models of the temple of Artemis (or Diana), the local goddess (Acts 19:23–41).

Deuteronomy, *see* **Covenant, Book of the.**

Devil. Contrary to popular opinion, the devil has a very minor role in the biblical writings. In the book of Job, Satan is counsel for the prosecution at the court of God, and therefore not a figure of evil as such. At the beginning of Jesus' ministry the devil appears in the role of tempter (Lk 4:1–13) and elsewhere as the adversary of God (1 Jn 3:8). Strictly, Jewish and Christian monotheism seems to offer no place for a devil except as a subordinate of God, and perhaps he is best regarded as a valuable, but mythological expression of the reality of evil.

Diana, *see* **Artemis.**

Dispersion (Greek Diaspora). Over a period of centuries many Jews left Palestine for a variety of reasons. Some left in times of famine to seek food elsewhere, some fled from invading armies or were forcibly exiled, others went voluntarily to set up business in the major centres of commerce. By New Testament times these Jews of the Dispersion outnumbered those in Palestine, and there were few cities round the eastern Mediterranean without a sizeable Jewish colony. It is no accident that some of the most important figures in the early church—Stephen, Philip, Barnabas and Paul, for example—were Jews of the Dispersion, for their circumstances made them less fettered by tradition and more open to new thinking.

Dorcas. A Christian woman who lived in Joppa and was renowned for her good deeds among the poor. According to Acts 9:36–42 Peter restored her to life after she had died.

E

Ecclesiastes. A strange book to find in the Bible because of its apparently unrelenting pessimism. The burden of the author's message seems to be that there is no fulfilment to be found in human existence. Man's life on earth is governed by the endless cycle of the seasons, all too soon to be ended by death, beyond which there is no certainty of anything. Some commentators suggest that the author was simply exposing the limitations of a purely rational approach and thereby demonstrating the need for a wider view of human life based on trust in God, but if this was the author's intention he fails to make it at all explicit.

Edomites. Recognised as relations of the Jews because of their alleged descent from Esau, the Edomites were nevertheless often in conflict with the people of Israel. Their territory extended from the southern end of the Dead Sea to the Gulf of Aqaba, and was of importance

because of its copper mines and because it afforded access to African trade routes via the Red Sea. David conquered the Edomites and Solomon made full use of the strategic advantages thus gained, but they gradually reasserted their independence and were never again completely subjugated by the people of Israel.

Egypt. Although the influence of Egypt on Palestinian affairs was less dramatic than that of the Mesopotamian empires of Assyria and Babylonia, it was far more persistent. From very early times the story of the Jews is linked with Egypt, and the great event of Jewish history is the escape from Egyptian captivity. During the period when Assyria and Babylon were at the height of their power, Egypt used the Palestinian states to foment trouble against them, promising assistance if they rebelled against their Mesopotamian overlords. The promised assistance did not always materialise, however, and when it did it was inadequate. After the destruction of the temple by the Babylonians in 586 B.C. a considerable number of Jews sought refuge in Egypt, and it was in Egypt during the third and second centuries B.C. that the Greek translation of the Old Testament was made. References to Egypt in the New Testament are far fewer, though Joseph and Mary are said to have fled there to protect their child from the wrath of Herod.

Ekron. One of the five Philistine city-states.

Elah. King of Israel (877–876 B.C.).

Eli. The priest who brought up Samuel (1 Sam 2:11).

Elihu. A young man who, after Job's three "comforters" had failed to persuade him of the error of his ways, made another attempt to do so (Job 32).

Elijah. A prophet from Tishbe in Gilead, Elijah is rightly considered one of the great figures of the Old Testament. He was the supreme champion of Israel's God at a time when Jezebel was trying to substitute the worship of her own god, Baal Melkart. This epic struggle is epitomised by the confrontation between Elijah and the prophets of Baal on Mount Carmel (1 Kgs 18:19–40). While many different interpretations of this story have been offered, ranging from the absolutely literal to the purely legendary, there can be no doubt whatever that the conflict it represents was real. Apart from this, however, the Elijah stories contain many pointers towards a more complete understanding of God. On Mount Horeb (Sinai) he realised that God was to be found in quiet reflection rather than in dramatic natural events, and the instructions he received there showed that God's power extended beyond Israel to the surrounding nations (1 Kgs 19:8–16). The encounter with King Ahab over Naboth's vineyard (1 Kgs 21:1–24), while not proclaiming anything new, is a forceful restatement of God's concern with social justice, and clearly anticipates the work of Amos.

Eliphaz. The first of Job's three "comforters" (Job 4).

Elisha. Though he is inevitably linked with his master and predecessor Elijah, Elisha is a very different character. More miraculous incidents are recorded about Elisha, yet many of them are trivial, e.g. recovering an axe-head from the river Jordan (2 Kgs 6:1–7), and the effect is to diminish rather than enhance his stature. Whereas Elijah was a largely solitary figure spending long periods in the wilderness, Elisha associated freely with the communities of prophets and lived in the capital city, Samaria, for at least part of his career. Though not always in sympathy with the kings of Israel, he advised them in military matters. He added little or nothing to the understanding of God achieved by Elijah, but some of the ways in which he exemplified that understanding are notable, e.g. the breadth of concern shown in the healing of Naaman, the commander of the Syrian army (2 Kgs 5:1–19).

Elizabeth. The mother of John the Baptist and a relative of Mary, mother of Jesus.

Emmanuel. The name, meaning "God with us", is in fact used in a prophecy of Isaiah to King Ahaz during a time of crisis. Isaiah says that a young woman will conceive and bring forth a son, whom she will name Emmanuel. He is saying, in effect, that in nine months' time the situation will have improved so much that parents will give their children a name expressive of God's care for his people. Though the immediate prophecy, therefore, refers to events in the immediate future, it is not surprising that Christians should have seen in these words the foreshadowing of God's presence with his people in Christ (Mt 1:22–23).

Epaphras. An associate of Paul who founded the church at Colossae (Col 1:7).

Epaphroditus. A Christian from Philippi who was sent by the Philippian church to render assistance to Paul during imprisonment, probably in Rome. While with Paul he had a serious illness and Paul thought it best to send him back home possibly taking the letter to the Philippians with him (Phil 2:25–30).

Ephesians, Letter to the. Although apparently written by Paul, there is considerable doubt as to the authorship of this letter. It was not uncommon in those times for a follower of a great teacher to write in the teacher's name and, far from being considered fraudulent, this was regarded as a mark of respect. The style of writing is not quite as in Paul's other letters, themes are introduced which appear nowhere else in his correspondence, and there is a remarkable absence of personal greetings considering that Paul had spent two years in Ephesus. If the author were not Paul, however, he was clearly well acquainted with Paul's writings, especially the letter to the Colossians, parts of which are quoted almost verbatim. The first part of the letter emphasises the unity of Christian believers, whose common life in Christ overrides all human distinctions, and the glory of the church which, whatever its human weaknesses, is Christ's body. The second part of the letter draws out the implications of this view of the church for practical living.

Ephesus (in Asia Minor). The capital of the Roman province of Asia and an important trading centre, Ephesus was famous for its temple of Artemis (Diana). It had a substantial Jewish population, and soon became an important centre of Christianity. Paul visited Ephesus as he returned from his second missionary journey (Acts 18:19–21) and subsequently spent two years there (Acts 19:1–10).

Ephraim. (1) Although he was Joseph's second son, he received from Jacob his grandfather the blessing normally due to the eldest, and established an important tribe (Gen 48:17–19).

(2) It appears that Joseph never had a tribe named after him, but he gave rise to two of the tribes of Israel, named after his sons Manasseh and Ephraim. The tribe of Ephraim occupied fertile land running down to the Mediterranean coast north of Dan and Benjamin and south of Manasseh. Its significance in the affairs of Israel was such that the northern kingdom was often referred to as Ephraim.

Epicureans. A school of Greek philosophers with whom Paul debated in Athens (Acts 17:18).

Esau. The first-born son of Isaac, he sold the birthright which was his by tradition to his younger brother, Jacob, for a bowl of soup (Gen 25:27–34). He is regarded as the ancestor of the Edomites.

Esther. Dated between 150 and 100 B.C., the book of Esther describes how a Jewish heroine of that name became queen to the Persian king, Xerxes, and was able to save her people from the evil plotting of one Haman. The book makes no mention of God at all, and it appears to have gained its place in the Old Testament purely as an expression of nationalist sentiments. The deliverance from Haman is still celebrated by Jews in the feast of Purim.

Eve. Adam's partner (Gen 2:21–24, 3:20). As Adam should be thought of as a symbolic prototype of mankind, so is Eve the typical woman rather than the first woman.

Exile. The term usually refers to the exile of the leading Jewish people in Babylon between 586 and 538 B.C., though there had been an earlier deportation in 597 B.C. This experience was of great importance to the Jews for a number of reasons. They had to learn how to worship God without the temple and without sacrifice, and so it was here that forms of worship developed which were based on the recollection of the

way God had led them throughout their history. This in turn stimulated interest in writing down their history, and it was during the exile that much of the editorial work on the historical books of the Old Testament was done. On the negative side, the Jews became more exclusive during the exile because of fears that intermarriage would result in the loss of their religious and national identity. The Jews, therefore, emerged from the exile purified but also hardened in a way that was not entirely to the good.

Exodus. The name given to the escape of the people of Israel from Egypt, an escape always seen as the supreme symbol of God's concern for them and an event still celebrated annually by Jews in the feast of the Passover. While some allowance has to be made for exaggeration of the incidents leading up to the escape, there is no reason to doubt the essential historical truth of the account. It appears that, originally having gone to Egypt because of famine in Palestine, the Jews had become slave-labourers working on Egyptian building projects. They were freed from this oppression about 1250 B.C. under the leadership of Moses with the assistance of a remarkable sequence of events known as the plagues of Egypt (Ex 7:14–12:36). The pursuing Egyptian army fell into a panic as their chariots sank in the waters of a shallow swamp, successfully crossed on foot by the Israelites, in the area of the Suez canal today. Whatever our interpretation of these events, the people of Israel had no hesitation in ascribing them to God.

Exodus, Book of. As its name implies the book of Exodus tells the story of the Jews' escape from Egypt, but it contains much else of importance besides. It includes the account of God's covenant with the people of Israel at Sinai based on the ten commandments, and goes on to give instructions about the construction of the ark and of the tent in which it is to be housed, as well as directions concerning worship.

Ezekiel. Ezekiel is probably the most difficult of the major prophets for the modern reader to come to grips with. Among the Jews deported to Babylon in the first exile of 597 B.C., his call to be a prophet came in Babylon and the whole of his prophetic ministry was carried out there, though his prophecies are directed to his people in Jerusalem as well as to the exiles. Many of the messages of Ezekiel are in the form of symbolic visions of great complexity; in fact, Ezekiel has been called "the father of apocalyptic", a kind of visionary writing represented elsewhere in the Bible by the books of Daniel and Revelation. The Old Testament book stresses the responsibility of the individual before God, rather than the people as a corporate body (Ezek 18:1–4), looks forward to the restoration of his people (Ezek 37:1–14) and presents a vision of the future temple and its worship (chapter 40 onwards). This interest in ritual, the result of his priestly status (Ezek 1:1) is in sharp contrast to earlier prophets who tend to condemn ritual, or at least the insincerity of ritual without righteousness.

Ezra. A lawyer who led a party of exiles to Jerusalem from Babylon about 460 B.C. (Ezra 7:1–9) and played a major role in the re-establishment of the worship of the temple. Unfortunately he shows the hard-line tendencies some of the Jews developed in exile, to the extent of insisting that Jews who had married foreign wives should get rid of them and their children. The book of Ezra relates events from the first return of exiles in 538 B.C. up to those in which Ezra himself was involved. It is not clear how much of the book is the work of Ezra and how much the work of later editors.

F

Felix. The Roman governor of Judaea from about A.D. 52 to 58, he had a Jewish wife and was apparently well informed about the Christian way (Acts 24:22–25). He kept Paul in custody for two years, having no cause to condemn him but unwilling to release him for fear of opposition from the Jewish leaders (Acts 24:27).

Festivals, *see* separate entries under **Dedication, Feast of; New Year; Passover; Tabernacles, Feast of; Weeks, Feast of.**

Festus. The Roman governor of Judaea who succeeded Felix about A.D. 58. He seems to have behaved with absolute correctness in his dealings with Paul, and would probably have set him free had not Paul taken the matter out of his hands by appealing to Caesar (Acts 25:1-12, 26:30-32).

G

Gabriel. The literal meaning of the name is simply "man of God". In Jewish tradition one of seven archangels, he is said to have announced the birth of John the Baptist to Zechariah (Lk 1:5-20) and of Jesus to Mary (Lk 1:26-38).

Gad. (1) Jacob's seventh son, his first by Zilpah, Leah's slave-girl.
  (2) The tribe of Gad, holding territory east of the Jordan to the north of that occupied by Reuben.

Galatia. The ancient kingdon of Galatia was in central Asia Minor, but the Roman province of the same name included a much larger area reaching down to the Mediterranean coast. Paul visited several towns within the Roman province on his first missionary journey.

Galatians, Letter to. One of the earliest of Paul's letters, probably written in *c.* A.D. 54, though some scholars would date it to A.D. 49, making it the first of all his surviving letters. It was written, almost certainly, to the churches Paul founded in the Roman province of Galatia on his first missionary journey, and is unusual in being addressed to a group of churches rather than a single church. The purpose in writing is very clear: Paul has been told that there are people going round the churches claiming that circumcision and the acceptance of the Jewish law is a necessary part of Christianity. Paul writes with the utmost urgency and vigour to refute these claims. He himself had been a Pharisee and knew that the attempt to satisfy God by perfect obedience to the law was impossible. It was faith in Christ which had liberated him from that futile pursuit, and the last thing he wanted was to see anyone persuaded into taking up something he had only discovered by long and painful experience to be of no value. The letter gives some useful autobiographical information as Paul recounts the way in which he became an apostle, and lays the foundations for the more fully developed statement of his theology in the letter to the Romans some years later.

Galilee. The area west of the Sea of Galilee (actually an inland lake some 20 km long) where Jesus was brought up and spent the greater part of his ministry. In the time of Jesus it formed the northern part of the Roman province of Galilee and Peraea, governed by Herod Antipas.

Gallio. The proconsul of the Roman province of Achaia before whom Paul was accused during his eighteen-month stay at Corinth (Acts 18:12-17). An inscription from Delphi establishes that Gallio was in Corinth by A.D. 52, probably having been appointed the previous year. It is implied (though not definitely stated) in Acts that Paul's trial took place soon after Gallio's arrival, and if this is accepted it fixes Paul's ministry in Corinth within a year or so, providing a useful fixed point in the chronology of the early church.

Gamaliel. A well-known Jewish teacher who numbered Paul among his pupils (Acts 22:3), and who argued in the Jewish Council against trying to stamp out Christianity on the grounds that history would show whether it was a movement from God or a worthless novelty (Acts 5:34-40).

Gath. One of the five Philistine city-states.

Gaza. The southernmost of the five Philistine city-states.

Gedaliah. When Zedekiah, the last king of

Judah, was taken in chains to Babylon in 586 B.C., the Babylonians appointed Gedaliah as governor. Though in his brief spell of office he seems to have acted with wisdom and humanity, he was soon assassinated by supporters of the royal house who regarded him as a traitor (2 Kgs 25:22-26).

Gehazi. Elisha's servant, condemned by Elisha for accepting gifts against his instructions from the healed Syrian commander, Naaman (2 Kgs 5:19-27).

Genesis. As the name implies, the first book of the Bible. Chapters 1-11 contain the acounts of the creation and the stories of Adam and Eve, Cain and Abel, Noah and the tower of Babel. These stories, though they may have some basis in historical fact, are important mainly for their mythological value. They are to be seen as parables, conveying in a vivid and often entertaining way, the convictions of their authors on immensely important matters—the nature of God, the nature of the universe and the nature of man. From chapter 12 onwards, with the entrance of Abraham into the story, the book is dealing with historical figures, however much allowance may have to be made for the inevitable legendary accretions acquired during centuries of handing down by word of mouth. Whatever their degree of historical accuracy, these stories of the early ancestors of the Jewish people are richly perceptive in their observations of human life and, above all, man's religious quest.

Gentiles. The word usually translated as Gentiles means literally "the peoples" or "the nations", i.e. the peoples other than the people of Israel. The Bible shows ambivalent attitudes among the Jews towards Gentiles. The covenants with Abraham and Moses both stress that the people of Israel are to be a blessing to "the nations", but during and following the exile the fear of religious and ethnic absorption made the Jews increasingly exclusive. Even in the early church there was a long and sometimes acrimonious debate before the mission to the Gentiles was accepted by all as an inevitable implication of Christian belief. It was this crucial decision which made Christianity a universal faith and no longer just a sect within Judaism.

Gethsemane. An olive grove on the western slopes of the Mount of Olives, facing Jerusalem across the Kidron valley, it was apparently Jesus' custom to go here with his disciples to avoid the crowds, and it was here that he was arrested (Mk 14:32-52).

Gibeah. A town some 7 km north of Jerusalem which was Saul's capital throughout his reign.

Gideon. Before the monarchy was established, the people of Israel relied on inspired leaders, known as judges, to raise armies and cope with enemy aggression as the need arose. Gideon was one such leader, renowned for his victory over the Midianites (Judg 7:1-22).

Gilgal. (1) A town on the west bank of the Jordan, just north of the Dead Sea, where the people of Israel first entered the "promised land" and Saul was later proclaimed king.
  (2) A settlement north of Bethel where there was a community of prophets in the time of Elijah and Elisha (2 Kgs 2:1, 4:38).

God. The existence of God is never discussed in the Bible; it is simply assumed from start to finish. But if the biblical authors never question God's existence, they do question what sort of God he is and, as one would expect of a varied group of writers working over a period of many centuries, they do not all arrive at the same conclusion. Samuel believed that God demanded the total destruction of Israel's ancient enemy the Amalekites, severely criticised Saul because he had spared the life of Agag the Amalekite king, and himself cut him to pieces (1 Sam 15:1-33). The writer of 2 Kings 2:23-24 believed that God had punished some boys who had made fun of Elisha by causing them to be mauled by bears. Clearly these are primitive views of God which cannot be reconciled with the God revealed by Jesus.

In spite of these relics of primitive religion, however, the Bible as a whole presents a remarkably unified view of God, with most of the key concepts established at quite an early date in

Israel's history. The "otherness" of God is expressed in the idea that no man could look upon the face of God and live (Ex 33:20) or that anyone who touched the ark, representing God's presence, would be struck dead (2 Sam 6:6–8). Later on these primitive attempts to express belief in a God whose ways are unsearchable, whose powers are unlimited, whose holiness is literally aweful, and who is as far removed from man as the heavens are from the earth, find nobler expression in such passages as the call vision of Isaiah (Is 6:1–8) and many of the Psalms. But the God of the Bible, though far removed from man in his wisdom, power and purity, is never remote. From the very earliest stories in the Bible he is a God who involves himself in the life of men, both making demands on them and caring for them. What he demands from men is justice in their dealings with each other. The ten commandments (Ex 20:1–17) form the basis of the moral code by which men are to live, and it is significant that even the king is subject to these demands and open to criticism for failure (1 Kgs 21:17–19) unlike other monarchs of the day who were a law unto themselves. What he offers men is a constant concern for their welfare, seen at an early stage in the exodus and expressed most movingly among Old Testament writers by the prophet Hosea, who daringly compares God to a faithful husband whose love for his wife does not waver in spite of her infidelity. So the thinkers of the Old Testament prepared the way for one whose moral demands reached new and frightening heights in the commandment to "love your enemies and do good to those who hate you", but who offered men the means to reach these heights by their response to a God who "so loved the world that he sent his only begotten son".

Golgotha. The name of the place where Jesus was crucified, the word means "skull". Whether this is a reference to the shape of the hill or an indication that executions had long been carried out there is uncertain, as is the location.

Goliath. A Philistine warrior of enormous stature supposedly killed by David, though 2 Samuel 21:19 says that it was Elhaman who killed Goliath, and it seems possible that tradition transferred this exploit to the more famous David.

Gomorrah. One of five cities described in Genesis 14:3 as occupying the valley of Siddim. The location is not quite certain, but is thought to be covered now by the southern part of the Dead Sea. Notorious for its wickedness, the city was destroyed by burning sulphur according to Genesis 19:24–25.

Greeks. Apart from its literal meaning, the word is often used in the New Testament as a general word for non-Jews. Thus in Romans 1:16 Paul says that the gospel is the saving power of God for "the Jew first but the Greek also". Some modern versions use the translation "Gentile" when this is the sense intended.

H

Habakkuk. A prophet whose ministry coincided with the rise to power of the Babylonians in the closing years of the seventh century B.C. The Old Testament book views the ascendency of the Babylonians as an act of God, but nevertheless questions how God can countenance such ruthless people, and declares that they are doomed, whereas "the righteous shall live by faith" (Hab 2:4).

Hagar. The slave-girl of Abraham's wife Sarah. When it seemed that Sarah would never have a child, Hagar was given to him to bear his children, and gave birth to Ishmael (Gen 16:1–4, 15). After the birth of Sarah's own son, Isaac, she sent Hagar and Ishmael away, but God promised Abraham that Ishmael would become the father of a nation (Gen 21:9–20).

Haggai. A prophet who prophesied about 520 B.C. some twenty years after the first Jews had returned from the exile to Jerusalem. He said that the reason for the poor harvests the people were getting was their failure to make a start on rebuilding the temple, and encouraged them to begin the rebuilding programme.

Haman. The villain of the book of Esther, an official at the Persian court who schemed to bring about the destruction of the Jews.

Hannah. The mother of Samuel, she was childless for many years and therefore considered to be out of favour with God. She made a promise that if God granted her a son she would dedicate him to the service of his sanctuary at Shiloh (1 Sam 1:1–28).

Hazael. An army officer who came to the Syrian throne shortly before 840 B.C. by suffocating the ruling monarch, Benhadad, in his bed. Elijah had been instructed to anoint Hazael king of Syria, but had not been able to do so before his death. Elisha is said to have told Hazael that he would become king, though he did not apparently anoint him (2 Kgs 8:7–15). Hazael was to be a scourge to Israel throughout his long reign, and it is significant that the people of Israel were prepared to see even an enemy who oppressed them as God's appointed agent.

Hazor. A large town in the far north of Israel, one of those which Solomon specially fortified and made into a garrison town for his chariot forces (1 Kgs 9:15–19).

Hebrew. The language in which the Old Testament was written. Over the last fifty years, archaeological work has brought to light a vast quantity of texts in Hebrew or closely related Semitic languages, and this has greatly increased our knowledge, making accurate translation possible where previously it was necessary to resort to conjecture.

Hebrews, Letter to the. Although traditionally ascribed to Paul, it has long been recognised that this is not one of Paul's letters, being quite unlike Paul's writing in both style and content. The main theme of the letter is an interpretation of the significance of Jesus' life and teaching based on the concept of priesthood—Jesus as the supreme mediator between God and man. It is most famous for its eleventh chapter on the nature of faith. The obviously Jewish outlook of the writer has led most commentators to assume that the letter was destined for a community of Jewish Christians, as the title implies, but even this has been questioned and it has to be said that authorship, destination and circumstances of writing remain conjectural.

Hebron. A city in the territory of Judah, it was David's capital for a time before the northern tribes accepted him as king and he established Jerusalem as the new religious and administrative centre. It had, however, been a city of importance for centuries before the Jews occupied Palestine.

Hermon. At over 2,800 m., Mt Hermon is the highest point in Palestine and also represents the far north-eastern frontier of Israel at the height of her power. It is considered by some to be the scene of the transfiguration because of its proximity to Caesarea Philippi.

Herod Family. Four Herods of four different generations are mentioned in the New Testament, in addition to Philip, who was also a member of the family. Herod the Great ruled the whole of the territory of the Jews (under Roman authority) from 40 to 4 B.C. He was the Herod ruling at the time of the birth of Jesus (which was incorrectly calculated when the Christian calendar was established: hence the anomaly of Jesus' birth taking place "before Christ"). Although suspicious and intolerant by nature, he kept his country free from conflict for 35 years, which was no mean achievement. On his death, his kingdom was divided between his three sons, Archelaus, Herod Antipas and Philip. Archelaus, however, was deposed in A.D. 6 and his territory came under the direct rule of a Roman governor. Herod Antipas, the Herod who had John the Baptist killed and before whom Jesus was tried, continued to rule Galilee and Peraea until his banishment in A.D. 39. Philip ruled Ituraea and Trachonitis until his death in A.D. 34. The territories of both Herod Antipas and Philip passed to Herod Agrippa I, who persecuted the Church and had James put to death (Acts 12:2). He himself died in A.D. 44 and was succeeded by

Herod Agrippa II, the king before whom Paul appeared in Acts 25.

Herod the Great

Aristobulus   Antipas   Archelaus   Philip
            (tetrarch of Galilee)   (tetrarch of
                Mk 6:14   Decapolis)

Herod Agrippa I   Herodias
    Acts 12:1   Mk 6:17

Herod Agrippa II   Bernice   Drusilla
    Acts 25:13   Acts 25:13   Acts 24:24

Herodias. Originally the wife of Philip (not the tetrarch), she was subsequently married to his half-brother Antipas. It was John the Baptist's objection to this marriage which brought about his imprisonment and eventual death (Mk 6:14–29).

Hezekiah. King of Judah (715–687 B.C.). Hezekiah came to the throne as a vassal of Assyria as his father, Ahaz, had been. The Assyrian ruler, Sargon II, was having difficulties elsewhere in his empire, however, and Hezekiah soon removed Assyrian religious objects from the temple, a step he might have hesitated to take but for the temporary Assyrian weakness. He also attacked the old Canaanite places of worship which were still used, and broke a bronze serpent allegedly made by Moses before which incense was burned. The exact extent of his religious reforms is uncertain, but it is clear that they were far-reaching. In spite of his removal of Assyrian cult objects from the temple, Hezekiah did not join other small Palestinian states, led by the Philistine city of Ashdod, in rebellion against the Assyrians in 713 B.C., perhaps because Isaiah opposed the enterprise. In 705 B.C., however, when Sargon II died, Hezekiah did refuse tribute to Assyria. Facing troubles elsewhere, it was 701 B.C. before the new king Sennacherib was able to move against Judah. When he did, he devastated 46 of Judah's fortresses and, in the words of his own inscription, shut up Hezekiah in Jerusalem "like a bird in a cage". What happened at this point is not clear. 2 Kings 18:14–16 says that Sennacherib demanded vastly increased tribute and Hezekiah meekly agreed. 2 Kings 18:17–19:37, however, relates how Hezekiah defied Sennacherib and the Assyrian had to return home after his army had been struck down by some mysterious agency. No attempt to reconcile these conflicting statements is entirely satisfactory, and this has led some scholars to suggest that the account of Hezekiah's successful defiance relates to a second invasion about 688 B.C. There is no corroborative evidence for this however.

Hinnom. A deep valley south-west of Jerusalem where child sacrifice was carried out according to Jeremiah 7:30–34. It is not clear from Jeremiah when this occurred (at no time was it a normal feature of Jewish religion), but it may have been during the long and evil reign of Manasseh (687–642 B.C.).

Hittites. A people referred to many times in the early period of Old Testament history from the time of the patriarchs to the establishment of the monarchy. It is now known that they ruled a considerable empire, centred on Asia Minor and achieving its maximum influence between 1400 and 1200 B.C.

Hosea. Hosea prophesied in the northern kingdom of Israel shortly after Amos (i.e. from about 750 B.C. onwards) during a period of political anarchy which was eventually to lead to the end of Israel as an independent kingdom in 721 B.C. His prophetic message is coloured throughout by his own experience of marriage, though the facts about his marriage are disputed, the evidence being ambiguous on many points. The most commonly accepted view is that his wife Gomer was unfaithful to him and eventually left him to become a prostitute. Falling upon hard times, she was sold into slavery, from which Hosea bought her back,

attempting to reform her by keeping her in seclusion for a period of time. Such a view certainly accords well with Hosea's daring portrayal of God as the faithful and persistent lover who will not abandon his faithless wife Israel. Although Hosea's message is therefore supremely hopeful, being based on the constant love of God for his people, it is not lacking in stern warnings of judgement, for the concept of God's love does not exclude the possibility of corrective punishment and Hosea is utterly appalled by the idolatry and unrighteousness of his people. Yet even God's judgement is seen as something positive, as a necessary step towards the re-establishment of a relationship between God and his people which is based on faithfulness on both sides.

Hoshea. King of Israel (732–724 B.C.). The last king of Israel, Hoshea came to the throne by the assassination of his predecessor Pekah. It was a period of Assyrian domination and for a while Hoshea wisely remained subservient to his Assyrian masters. When the capable Assyrian ruler Tiglath-pileser III died in 727 B.C., however, Hoshea made an alliance with Egypt and withheld tribute. The new Assyrian king Shalmaneser V, attacked and overran Israel, taking Hoshea captive in 724 B.C., though the capital city, Samaria, held out against the Assyrians until 721 B.C. Thereafter Israel was an Assyrian province.

I

Iconium. A city in the Roman province of Galatia visited by Paul and Barnabas on Paul's first missionary journey (Acts 13:51–14:6).

Immanuel, see **Emmanuel.**

Isaac. The son of Abraham and Sarah, he was nearly sacrificed to God until God showed Abraham that he did not require child sacrifice (Gen 22:1–14). His wife Rebecca bore him twin sons, Esau and Jacob, whose descendants became the Edomites and the people of Israel respectively.

Isaiah. It has long been recognised that the book of Isaiah is the work of three major prophets, often known for convenience as first, second and third Isaiah.

First Isaiah, also sometimes called Isaiah of Jerusalem, prophesied from "the year that King Uzziah died" (i.e. 742 B.C.) until at least the end of the eighth century B.C., and his work occupies chapters 1–39 of the book which bears his name. It has been said that Isaiah was more of a statesman than a prophet because of the close interest he took in Judah's affairs, and especially her foreign policy. Thus, when King Ahaz was threatened by Pekah of Israel and Rezin of Syria, Isaiah advised against taking panic measures because he believed the threat would be short-lived. Ahaz, however, ignored his advice, appealed to Assyria for help and became an Assyrian vassal for the remainder of his reign. Later Isaiah warned King Hezekiah against becoming involved in rebellion against Assyria led by the Philistine city-state of Ashdod, and this time his advice was heeded. He also constantly spoke out against reliance on Egyptian help against the Assyrians. But to call Isaiah a statesman rather than a prophet is to ignore the religious foundations of his political advice. He believed in a God whose control of history was absolute. He also believed that his people's difficulties were the result of their failure to put their trust in God and to meet his moral demands in their social life. For him, therefore, the way to solve their problems was to put these things right. Political intrigues and alliances with foreign nations were not only worthless but diverted attention from the real issues. For much of his career Isaiah regarded the Assyrians as instruments of God's judgement, and consequently argued that resistance to them was futile, but towards the end of his life he encouraged King Hezekiah in defying them, perhaps feeling that his people had now received sufficient punishment and certainly believing that the arrogance of the

Assyrians must in its own time come under God's judgement.

Second Isaiah, the author of chapters 40–55 of the prophetic book, was a prophet of the exile. Like the earlier Isaiah he had a profound belief in the utter sovereignty of God, and expresses this in some of the most beautiful and exalted language in the Old Testament. His most important contribution to religious thought, however, comes in the sections which speak of a suffering servant of the Lord. These passages are enigmatic, and it is not clear whether Isaiah was speaking of a past, present or future figure. What is important is the insight—quite astonishing in his time—that a man who set himself to serve God faithfully might be despised, reviled and rejected and that God might somehow bring healing to his people through such a person. Whatever Isaiah himself intended, it is hardly surprising that Christians equate the suffering servant with Christ.

Third Isaiah, responsible for chapters 56–66, mostly addresses people back in Jerusalem after the exile, offering them encouragement through his belief in a God who keeps his promises. It may seem strange to us that the work of three different prophets, living at different times, should have been combined in this way in one book under one name, yet the book does show a fundamental unity of outlook, especially in its proclamation of God's sovereignty. It seems possible that the first Isaiah left behind a group of disciples which continued in existence long after his death, a group which included the two later authors and which was responsible for the editing of the book of Isaiah as we know it.

Ishbosheth. The only one of Saul's four sons to survive his final tragic battle against the Philistines, Ishbosheth was accepted as king by the northern tribes while Judah proclaimed David as its king (2 Sam 2:8–11). David carefully avoided open confrontation with Ishbosheth while constantly weakening his position by diplomatic pressure. Abner, Saul's general, soon defected and Ishbosheth was eventually murdered in his bed by two of his officers (2 Sam 4:5–7).

Ishmael. The son Abraham had by Hagar, Sarah's slave-girl, when it seemed that Sarah herself would have no children (Gen 16:1–4, 15). After Sarah had Isaac, Hagar and Ishmael were driven out (Gen 21:9–20).

Israel. In the first instance this is the name given to Jacob by his mysterious opponent in the wrestling match at Peniel (Gen 32:22–28). His descendants therefore became the children of Israel, or simply Israel. When, after Solomon's reign, the northern tribes rebelled against his son Rehoboam, the term was reserved for the northern kingdom as opposed to the southern kingdom of Judah. Sometimes the term "all Israel" is used of the undivided kingdom to distinguish this usage from the later use for the northern kingdom only.

Issachar. (1) The ninth son of Jacob, his fifth by Leah.

(2) The tribe of Issachar which occupied a fairly small area west of the Jordan and south of the Sea of Galilee.

J

Jabesh-Gilead. A town just east of the Jordan which Saul delivered from the Ammonites (1 Sam 11:1–11). In gratitude the men of Jabesh-Gilead rescued the bodies of Saul and his sons from the Philistines and took them back to give them a decent burial (1 Sam 31:11–13).

Jacob. One of twin brothers, Jacob nevertheless had no claim on his father's property or the special blessing reserved for the eldest son because he was the second from his mother's womb. However, he first got his brother, Esau, to agree to sell his birthright (Gen 25:29–33) and then tricked his blind father Isaac into giving him the blessing (Gen 27:1–29). He fled from his father's wrath to his uncle Laban, in whom he met someone almost as crafty as himself. He served Laban for seven years for his

younger daughter Rachel, only to find after his marriage that he had been given the elder daughter Leah (Gen 29:15–26). He then had to serve another seven years for Rachel. Nevertheless, Jacob prospered with Laban and returned a wealthy man to be reconciled with Esau (Gen 33:1–4). He ended his days in Egypt as the guest of his eleventh son, Joseph (Gen 47:11–12). The stories of Jacob which do not gloss over his failings, show a man who is often self-centred and careless about God in his early years, but who comes to see that God has plans for him and has in fact been caring for him throughout his life.

Jahweh, see Yahweh.

James. (1) One of the three disciples who were with Jesus on the mount of transfiguration (Mk 9:2–9). The brother of John and a son of Zebedee, he was later killed by Herod Agrippa I (Acts 12:1–2).

(2) Another disciple, the son of Alphaeus, of whom nothing more is known (Mk 4:18).

(3) The brother of Jesus who apparently became an apostle after a special resurrection appearance to him (1 Cor 15:7, Gal 1:19) and subsequently became leader of the Jerusalem church (Acts 15:13–21).

James, Letter of. Though some have identified the author as James the brother of Jesus, this can only be speculation, nor is there any clear indication to whom the letter was first addressed. It is a set of practical instructions on how to live the Christian life, and its emphasis on deeds (as opposed to Paul's emphasis on faith) led Luther to dismiss it as "a letter of straw". In reality, however, there is no conflict; for both James and Paul righteousness is a product of faith.

Jebusites. The original inhabitants of Jerusalem, they were not conquered by the people of Israel when they occupied Canaan but remained as an independent city-state. David took the city, however, by sending his men along a water tunnel, and established his capital there (2 Sam 5:6–10).

Jehoahaz. (1) King of Israel (815–801 B.C.). The son of Jehu, Jehoahaz was an ineffective ruler and spent the whole of his reign under Syrian domination.

(2) King of Judah (609 B.C.). The unfortunate Jehoahaz succeeded his father Josiah who had been killed in battle with the Egyptians. He was almost immediately deposed by the Egyptians in favour of his brother Eliakim, who took the throne-name Jehoiakim.

Jehoash. King of Israel (801–786 B.C.). A strong ruler who regained from Syria all the territory lost by his father Jehoahaz, and who also defeated King Amaziah of Judah after being provoked into a quarrel he did not seek.

Jehoiachin. King of Judah (598–597 B.C.). Jehoiachin came to the throne when a Babylonian army was already on the march against Jerusalem because of his father Jehoiakim's rebellion. Within three months he surrendered the city and was taken into exile where he spent the rest of his life.

Jehoiakim. King of Judah (609–598 B.C.). Placed on the throne by the Egyptians after they had killed his father Josiah in battle and deposed his elder brother Jehoahaz, Jehoiakim remained a vassal of Egypt until 605 B.C. when the Egyptians were routed by the Babylonians. He transferred his allegiance to Babylon, but in 601 B.C. another battle between the Egyptians and Babylonians on the Egyptian frontier resulted in the withdrawal of the Babylonian armies to reorganise. Interpreting this as weakness, Jehoiakim rebelled. In December 598 the Babylonians marched against him, and in the same month Jehoiakim died, possibly by assassination (this may be implied by Jeremiah 22:18, 36:30). Jeremiah, himself forced into hiding by Jehoiakim, is scathing in his criticism of the king as one who callously exploited the people and shed much innocent blood.

Jehoram. (1) King of Israel (849–842 B.C.). A son of Ahab, he actually succeeded his brother Ahaziah, who died after a short reign leaving no sons. During his reign the Moabites successfully rebelled against him, and the war against Syria, in which Ahab had lost his life, dragged on. It was while recovering from wounds received in the Syrian war that he was killed in Jehu's coup.

(2) King of Judah (849–842 B.C.). Like his contemporary and namesake in Israel, Jehoram of Judah lost territory to his enemies in Edom and also on the Philistine frontier. He was married to Ahab's sister (or possibly daughter) Athaliah, who was to seize the throne after the death of their son Ahaziah.

Jehosphaphat. King of Judah (873–849 B.C.). A capable ruler who allied himself with Omri and Ahab, his contemporaries in Israel, to subjugate enemies across the Jordan and, with rather less success, keep the Syrians at bay. In 2 Chronicles 19:4–11 we are told of a reform of the judicial system he carried out, and it seems from 2 Kings 3:14 that Elisha held him in considerable respect.

Jehu. Jehu was anointed king while serving as commander of Jehoram's army by one of the prophets acting on Elisha's instructions (2 Kgs 9:1–10). He promptly killed Jehoram, who was recovering from wounds in Jezreel, King Ahaziah of Judah who had the misfortune to be visiting him at the time, and the evil Jezebel who, as queen mother, still exercised considerable influence. He went on to exterminate every surviving member of the royal family and the worshippers of Baal. In so doing he broke the alliance with Judah, on which Israel's defence against her enemies largely depended, and deprived the nation of many of its leading figures. In spite of the ferocity of his coup, he was unable to withstand the aggression of Hazael, king of Syria, and lost all his territory across the Jordan.

Jephthah. One of the inspired leaders of Israel known as judges, before the days of the monarchy. He defeated the Ammonites, having made a vow to sacrifice the first living thing he met on his return if God gave him victory. In consequence he was compelled to sacrifice his own daughter (Judg 11:1–39).

Jeremiah. Jeremiah was called to be a prophet as a young man about 630 B.C. and prophesied until after the fall of Jerusalem to the Babylonians in 586 B.C. His long prophetic ministry therefore spanned the last years of Judah as an independent kingdom. His early prophecies paint a terrifying picture of impending disaster (Jer 5:23–31) which, in the short term at least, never materialised and made Jeremiah feel that God had made a laughing stock of him (Jer 20:7). Among the many fascinations of the book of Jeremiah are the frankness of the prophet's conversations with God and his reflections on how to distinguish true prophecy from false. When Josiah carried out his great religious reforms in 622 B.C. Jeremiah supported them and thus aroused the anger of his family, who were priests at Anathoth just outside Jerusalem and probably objected to the ban on sacrificial worship except in the temple (Jer 11:1–8,21). Although a supporter of the reforms initially, Jeremiah soon saw their limitations or even dangers: because the external forms of Judah's religion had been regularised people might become complacent, failing to realise that what God really required was a change of heart. It was this that led Jeremiah to speak of a new covenant written in men's hearts (Jer 31:31–34). From Jehoiakim's time onwards Jeremiah became increasingly unpopular because of his insistence that the presence of the temple would not save the Jews from the Babylonians, contrary to the accepted doctrine that God would never permit his city to be taken or his temple destroyed (Jer 26:1–11). During the siege of Jerusalem he was imprisoned and nearly killed as a traitor because he constantly advocated surrender and was suspected of deserting to the Babylonians (Jer 37:11–38:13). When Jerusalem finally fell, Jeremiah was permitted to remain rather than being taken into exile on the express instructions of King Nebuchadnezzar (Jer 39:11–14). After the murder of the newly appointed governor, Gedaliah, Jeremiah was taken against his will to Egypt by the remaining officials who fled there. Here he ended his days. In spite of the almost unrelieved tragedy of his life, Jeremiah was not without hope. At the height of the siege of Jerusalem he bought a plot of land from a kinsman as a symbol that people would one day have the confidence to engage in business again (Jer 32:1–15), and he wrote a letter to the first group of exiles, taken to Babylon in 597 B.C., declaring that the future of the nation was in their hands and that God had plans for their welfare (Jer 29:1–14).

Jericho. A very ancient city a few miles west of the Jordan, it was the first stronghold to be captured by Joshua after crossing the river. In Elijah's time it was the home of a company of prophets (2 Kgs 2:4–5), and in the gospels it is the setting for the healing of blind Bartimaeus and the rehabilitation of Zacchaeus (Lk 18:35–19:9).

Jeroboam I. King of Israel (922–901 B.C.). Jeroboam first appears as one of Solomon's officials in charge of forced labour. Told by the prophet Ahijah that he would receive ten of the twelve tribes of Israel, he became a marked man and had to flee to Egypt to escape Solomon's wrath (1 Kgs 11:26–40). After Solomon's death he returned to lead the northern tribes in their revolt against Rehoboam, and became the first king of the northern kingdom (1 Kgs 12:1–20). He established a capital at Shechem initially, but later moved to Tirzah, which remained the capital until the reign of Omri. Clearly he could not have his people going to the Jerusalem temple to worship, since the cult there celebrated amongst other things, God's eternal covenant with the house of David. He therefore established two rival centres at the ancient shrines of Dan and Bethel, and in each of them placed a golden calf. The significance of these animals is not in fact clear, but the biblical writers assume that they were idols and the name of Jeroboam is always associated by them with idolatry (1 Kgs 12:26–30).

Jeroboam II. King of Israel (786–746 B.C.). Long-lived and capable, in human terms Jeroboam II must be judged one of the most successful kings the northern kingdom ever had. The biblical record gives few details but states that he "restored the border of Israel from the entrance to Hamath as far as the Sea of Arabah" (2 Kgs 14:25). It appears from this that his northeastern border stood where it had been in Solomon's time. The books of Amos and Hosea give a vivid picture of social conditions during Jeroboam's reign, a picture of great prosperity, but prosperity confined to a fortunate minority who cared little for the fate of the masses.

Jerusalem. An ancient city originally occupied by the Jebusites but captured from them by David. It made an ideal capital because of its military strength, because it was near the border between Judah and the northern tribes who were now being brought together again under David's rule, and because it did not actually belong to any of the tribes, having remained as an independent enclave until David took it. As time went on it acquired a mystical significance as the city of God, with the temple as his dwelling-place. This mystique was partly, though not entirely, destroyed by the experience of the exile, which showed that Israel's faith could survive without Jerusalem and its temple.

Jesse. The father of David (1 Sam 16:1).

Jesus. Without doubt more words have been written about Jesus than any other figure in history, and the debate still continues, not only about the historical facts but about their significance. It is impossible in a short article to do justice to the complexity of the issues arising from the life of this man, but the main facts of his public ministry may be stated with some certainty.

The existence of Jesus, as a religious leader put to death by the Romans at the instigation of the Jewish authorities, is attested by the contemporary Jewish historian Josephus. For the details of his life and teaching we have to rely mainly on the four gospels written some 35 to 65 years after his death. The earliest of these, Mark, does not record the birth of Jesus and the birth stories contained in Luke and Matthew are important more for their symbolic value than for their contribution to our historical knowledge. They do establish the date of Jesus' birth as about 4 B.C. (the obvious anomaly is due to the fact that when the

Christian calendar was established much later the date of Jesus' birth was miscalculated). Virtually nothing is known about his life until he was nearly thirty when he received baptism from John the Baptist and was confirmed in his conviction that God had entrusted him with a special mission and he retired to the wilderness to reflect upon it (Lk 3:21–22, 4:1–13). When he returned he declared his manifesto in the synagogue at Nazareth using some words of Isaiah, "to bring good news to the poor, to proclaim liberty to the captive and recovery of sight to the blind, to set free the oppressed, and to announce that the time has come when God will save his people". He proceeded to put this manifesto into practice in both words and actions. Jesus believed that the Kingdom of God foreshadowed in the Old Testament was about to be realised and his teaching was to prepare people for that Kingdom which he described in his parables. "Unless a man has been born again he cannot see the Kingdom of God" (Jn 3:3). Wherever he went he healed the sick. Whether these were miracles in the sense that normal physical laws were set aside is, of course, open to question, but they are such an integral part of the gospel records that they cannot be ignored. It seems clear that Jesus was able to heal people who could not otherwise be healed in his day, and drove himself to exhaustion in doing so, thus demonstrating in practice the love of God he preached. Inevitably this made him popular, in the end embarrassingly so, for the people came to have expectations of him which he had no intention of fulfilling (Jn 6:14–15). As it became clear that he was not going to lead his countrymen in throwing off the the yoke of Roman rule, disillusionment set in. It had also become clear that alongside the tremendous assurance of God's unwavering love Jesus set demands far harder to meet than those of the Old Testament. What other teacher had ever required that they should love their enemies and do good to those who hated them (Mt 5:43–48)? The religious authorities had never shared the popular enthusiasm for Jesus, partly because of his disregard for sabbath rules (Mk 2:23–3:6) but even more so because the note of authority in his teaching put them to shame and seemed to imply a special relationship with God (Mk 2:1–12). Jesus, well aware that their net was closing in around him, set out for Jerusalem for the final confrontation (Lk 9:51). Here, having failed to trap him by any legal method the authorities arrested him by night with the connivance of Judas (Mk 14:43–46), condemned him in their own court on the charge of blasphemy (Mk 14:55–64) and rushed him before the Roman governor on charges of political subversion (Mk 15:1–5). Within hours he was dead, executed by crucifixion (Mk 15:24–37). Yet not long afterwards his followers, who had gone to ground after his arrest, were boldly proclaiming his message regardless of the risks and declaring that death had been unable to hold him fast (Acts 2:22–24). In all the inevitable questioning over the resurrection of Jesus one fact seems beyond dispute: that his disciples were prepared to stake their lives on its reality.

Jethro. A Midianite priest whose daughter Zipporah was married to Moses (Ex 2:16–22). He also advised Moses on the setting up of a judicial system after the exodus (Ex 18:13–26).

Jezebel. A Phoenician princess who was married to Ahab, probably as part of his father Omri's policy of friendly relations with the Phoenicians for trade purposes. She was a fanatical devotee of the Phoenician Baal Melkart and made strenuous efforts to introduce his worship to Israel, equally strenuously opposed by Elijah (1 Kgs 18:19–40). Her involvement in Naboth's unjust execution (1 Kgs 21:1–15) shows a completely despotic view of the king's rights. She outlived Ahab and continued to exercise an evil influence as queen mother during the reigns of his sons Ahaziah and Jehoram until killed in Jehu's rebellion.

Jezreel. A city which seems to have been used as a second capital by the kings of Israel about the time of Ahab. It was here that Jehoram

went to recover from his wounds received in the Syrian wars and where he was killed, together with Jezebel, in Jehu's coup (2 Kgs 9:14–35). Hosea named his first child Jezreel as a symbol of judgement on the house of Jehu for its unnecessary brutality (Hos 1:3–4).

Joab. David's commander-in-chief and a considerable influence upon him. It was he who persuaded David to accept Absalom back from exile (2 Sam 14:1–24), though after Absalom's death he took David to task for showing excessive grief over his rebellious son rather than gratitude to those who had been loyal to him (2 Sam 19:1–8). As David's life drew to a close Joab backed Adonijah as his successor, but David nominated Solomon, who subsequently had Joab killed (1 Kgs 1:5–6, 2:28–34).

Joash. King of Judah (837–800 B.C.). The only son of Ahaziah to escape Athaliah's slaughter, he was kept in hiding for six years and then proclaimed king at the age of seven on the instructions of Jehoiada the priest (2 Kgs 11:1–11). Under Jehoiada's influence he made repairs to the temple, but according to Chronicles 24:17–22 he showed a very different character once Jehoiada was dead. Certainly he must have aroused the hatred of his subjects, as he was eventually assassinated.

Job. The book of Job is a protest against the commonly accepted view that God rewards the good with prosperity and punishes the wicked with suffering. It postulates the case of a man who had led a blameless life (Job's personal code of conduct described in chapter 31 is astonishing in its closeness to the ideals later proclaimed by Jesus) who nevertheless suffers every conceivable disaster from the death of his children to painful and disfiguring illness. The major part of the book consists of dialogue between Job and three of his friends (later joined by a fourth). The friends try to convince Job that he must have done something to deserve his misfortunes, while Job continues to protest his innocence and cannot accept this explanation of his suffering. The book does not arrive at any specific answer to the problem of innocent suffering but rejects facile solutions, declaring in majestic poetry that God is far greater than human understanding can encompass.

Joel. The book of Joel tells us nothing about the author except his father's name, and there is no clear indication when he lived, though a date in the fifth or fourth century B.C. is likely. The prophet regards a severe infestation of locusts as a sign of God's judgement on his people, and calls them to repent. He looks forward to a time when God will pour out his spirit on everyone, men and women, young and old alike, a passage quoted by Peter on the first Whit Sunday.

John. (1) John the Baptist. A kinsman of Jesus, he was also his forerunner, preaching repentance to all who would listen and baptising them in the Jordan as a symbol of the new way of life to which they committed themselves (Lk 3:3–14). Jesus accepted baptism from John but then embarked on a very different kind of ministry. It is clear, however, that the two men regarded each other with the greatest respect (Lk 7:18–28). John was imprisoned by Herod Antipas for criticising his marriage to his half-brother's wife Herodias, and it was Herodias who eventually engineered his execution (Mk 6:17–28).

(2) The brother of James, a son of Zebedee and one of the inner group of disciples who were with Jesus on the mount of transfiguration. Though the identification between John and "the disciple whom Jesus loved" in John's gospel is not certain, it is widely assumed. In the early days of the Christian church he was a prominent leader with Peter (Acts 3:1–10, 4:1–21) but we hear relatively little of him afterwards. His connection with the writing of the fourth gospel is problematic (see next entry).

John, Gospel of. The fourth gospel is clearly different from the other three even to the casual reader. To name only the most obvious difference, whereas the teaching of Jesus in the first three gospels is in the form of short pithy sayings or vivid parables, in John it appears as long philosophical discourses. The gospel is not therefore so much an account of the life of Jesus as an interpretation of its significance. But although the author has deliberately and freely recast the teaching of Jesus into a more explicitly theological form, this does not mean that he is not concerned with the historical truth; indeed, the leading British New Testament scholar of recent times has argued that in some respects the historical information in the fourth gospel is superior to that in the other three. The author then was a man of great intellectual stature who had long reflected on the significance of Jesus, and was capable of expressing his conclusions in a form more akin to Greek philosophical writing than traditional Jewish teaching, but who was also in contact with a good historical source independent of the other three gospels. John the disciple of Jesus, with his humble background as a Galilean fisherman, seems an unlikely author, but may well have been the source of the author's historical information.

John, Letters of. The three letters of John show many similarities with the fourth gospel in their vocabulary, style and thematic content, but there are some difficulties in ascribing them to the same author. If they were not by the author of the fourth gospel they were certainly written by someone thoroughly steeped in his way of thinking. The first letter is concerned with a form of false teaching which claims that there is a special way of knowing God open only to the initiated, that Jesus was not truly a physical person and that morality, having nothing to do with actions in the physical world has nothing to do with religion. In opposing this heresy John insists on the physical reality of Jesus and declares that knowing God is inseparable from loving others. Whereas the first letter appears to be a "circular" for general dissemination among the churches, the second is addressed to "the dear lady and her children"—probably a local church. It is much shorter but deals with the same false teaching. The third letter is addressed to an individual, Gaius, encouraging him and warning him against one Diotrephes.

Jonadab. The son of Rechab, he seems to have been the real founder of the Rechabites who tried to maintain the way of life of their forefathers, living in tents rather than houses and not planting crops or vineyards or drinking wine. Apart from this the only information we have on Jonadab is that he helped Jehu in his seizure of the throne (2 Kgs 10:15–17).

Jonah. The book of Jonah is in effect a short story, making a very important point in a humorous way. The essence of the story is Jonah's reluctance to preach to the people of Nineveh, the Assyrian capital, in case they listen to him and consequently enjoy the benefits of God's favour! His attempt to flee to a distant place out of God's reach is foiled by a storm and the great fish which conveniently deposits him on the Palestinian shore once more. Realising that he has no option but to do as God has told him, he goes and preaches to the people of Nineveh, who, as he had feared, repent of their evil and turn to God. Jonah consequently sulks over God's failure to punish them for their previous sins until God shows him how unreasonable his attitude is. The book is thus a witty but serious appeal to the Jews to broaden their conception of God and to rejoice in his concern for other nations. In spirit it comes close to several of the parables of Jesus, e.g. the parable of the prodigal son and his elder brother who refuses to rejoice over the return of the lost one.

Jonathan. One of the four sons of Saul whose reckless daring was largely responsible for a victory over the Philistines at the pass of Michmash (1 Sam 14:1–23). He is best known, however, for his unwavering friendship with David which survived his father's intense jealousy and David's ultimate exile (1 Sam 19:1–7, 20:1–42). He was killed, together with his father and two other brothers, in battle against the Philistines (1 Sam 31:1–4).

Joppa. A port on the Palestinian coast where Peter was staying when he had his vision showing him that there was no distinction between Jew and Gentile in God's sight (Acts 10:9–23).

Joram, see Jehoram.

Jordan. The river Jordan runs north-south from the foot of Mount Hermon to the Dead Sea through a rift valley which is below sea level for the greater part of its length. It forms a natural division between the central highlands of Palestine to the west and the plateau of the Transjordanian desert to the east. As well as being a natural barrier it is also a psychological one, the crossing of the Jordan having the same sort of significance for the people of Israel as the crossing of the Rubicon for Julius Caesar—a decisive step on the road to conquest.

Joseph. (1) The eleventh son of Jacob, his first by Rachel. A precocious child who provoked the enmity of his brothers, he was taken and sold as a slave in Egypt by Ishmaelite or Midianite traders. Not only is the story confused on this point but also as to whether he was sold to the traders by his brothers or rescued by the traders from a pit where his brothers had left him (Gen 37:12–35). After various vicissitudes in Egypt he gained high office by his power to interpret dreams, and in this position he was able both to help and test his brothers incognito when they came seeking corn in time of famine (Gen 41:1–45:14). Eventually he brought his father and brothers to live in Egypt (Gen 47:11–12). While there is no reason to doubt that the Joseph stories have a historical basis, they may well have been embellished in order to drive home the theological point made in Joseph's words to his brothers when he revealed his identity: "so it was not really you who sent me here but God" (Gen 45:8). Joseph gave rise to two of the tribes of Israel named after his sons Ephraim and Manasseh.

(2) The husband of Mary. Information on Joseph is sparse. He was a descendant of David (Mt 1:20), and worked as a village carpenter in Nazareth (Mt 13:55). He is not mentioned after the visit to Jerusalem when Jesus was twelve (Lk 2:41–51), and it seems a reasonable supposition that he had died before Jesus began his public ministry. This has led to the tradition, not necessarily true, that he was much older than Mary.

(3) Joseph of Arimathea. A rich Jew who was a member of the Jewish Council but who sympathised with Jesus and his cause. After Jesus' execution he requested the body from Pilate and had it buried in his own rock-hewn tomb (Mk 15:42–46).

Joshua. The book of Joshua takes its name from Moses' successor and records the invasion and settlement of Canaan by the people of Israel under his leadership. While it includes some very early material, the book has been extensively edited and did not reach its final form until centuries after the events it describes. It is generally considered that the picture it presents is a simplified one, representing the invasion of Canaan as a single co-ordinated campaign with Joshua as commander-in-chief. In fact, the likelihood is that the occupation was far more haphazard, with some of the tribes at least acting independently and Joshua commanding only the most successful part of the invasion forces. In particular there are indications in Joshua 15:13–14 and Judges 1:11–21 that the southern tribes of Judah, Simeon and Benjamin may have operated in isolation from the main body with a man called Caleb as their leader. The most famous incident in the conquest is undoubtedly the battle of Jericho, and controversy still rages on what actually happened on this occasion (Josh 6:1–20). In spite of the unresolved historical questions, the character of Joshua emerges clearly—a man of simple faith who believed that God had given the land of Canaan to the people of Israel and would continue to support them if they remained true to him.

Josiah. King of Judah (640–609 B.C.). Josiah is chiefly remembered for the great religious reform he carried out in 622 B.C. following the discovery in the temple of a Book of the Covenant which made him realise how far short his people had fallen from the standards God demanded. He closed down all pagan altars and, in order to prevent irregularities, decreed that sacrifice could only be offered in the temple in Jerusalem. These measures were extended even to parts of the old northern kingdom of

Israel, indicating the degree of freedom Josiah enjoyed due to the preoccupation of the Assyrians with survival against the Medes and Babylonians. He also reinstated the celebration of the Passover which had apparently lapsed (2 Kgs 23:1–23). In 609 B.C. the Egyptians marched through Judah on their way to render assistance to the beleaguered Assyrians, preferring to maintain a weakened Assyria in power than to face a strong Babylon. Josiah tried to stop them and was killed in battle at Megiddo.

Jotham. King of Judah (742–735 B.C.). The son of Uzziah, Jotham ruled as co-regent with his father for some years as his father had contracted "leprosy" (i.e. a disfiguring skin disease, not necessarily leprosy as it is known today), and could not carry out public duties. Little is said about Jotham except that he continued the good work of his father, building the upper gate of the temple. At the end of his reign he was under pressure from Pekah of Israel and Rezin of Syria to join an anti-Assyrian coalition, but this problem was left to his successor Ahaz.

Judaea. Like many names which denote an area, the term Judaea is used differently at different times. Its most common usage, however, is to denote the Roman province of Judaea, the area of southern Palestine which from A.D. 6 onwards came under the rule of a Roman governor rather than a member of the Herod family. It was this province which was governed by Pontius Pilate and later by Felix and Festus.

Judah. (1) The fourth son of both Jacob and Leah.
(2) The tribe of Judah which occupied a large area to the west of the Dead Sea and as far as the Egyptian frontier.
(3) The name of the southern kingdom after the northern tribes had broken away under Jeroboam I. While its boundaries coincided roughly with the old tribal area of Judah, it also included most of the territory of Benjamin.

Judas. (1) Judas, son of James, a disciple of Jesus about whom nothing else is known.
(2) Judas Iscariot, the disciple of Jesus who betrayed him. John 12:4–6 states that he was in charge of the common purse used by the disciples and stole from it, but apart from that there is little information on him prior to his act of betrayal. After betraying Jesus for 30 pieces of silver (Mt 26:14–16) he returned the money and committed suicide (Mt 27:3–5). His motives will always remain a matter of speculation. The most charitable view is that he was trying to force Jesus into a position where he would have to perform a dramatic miracle to save himself, thus convincing the sceptics, and he never anticipated that Jesus would let himself be killed.

Jude, Letter of. A short letter warning of the dangers of false teaching and the judgement which will befall those who distort the Christian message. Though it has been suggested on the basis of Mark 6:3 that the author was one of the brothers of Jesus, this is by no means certain, nor is there any clear indication to whom the letter was addressed.

Judge. The term is used in several senses in the Old Testament, including the modern sense of one who arbitrates in a legal dispute or enforces the law. There is, however, an important special use of the term to describe men like Gideon, Jephthah and Samson who exercised leadership among the tribes of Israel, especially in times of danger, during the period between the settlement of Canaan and the establishment of the monarchy. Their authority was regarded as God-given and was entirely personal, i.e. it did not extend to their sons. In many ways they acted as kings, but for a long time the establishment of a recognised monarchy was resisted on the grounds that it would be a denial of God's sovereignty (Judg 8:22–23).

Judges, Book of. This book deals with the history of the people of Israel during the period of the Judges, i.e. from the death of Joshua until shortly before the anointing of Saul as Israel's first king. It contains some material (e.g. the song of Deborah in chapter five) which is contemporaneous with the events described, and therefore of enormous historical value, though

like all the historical books of the Old Testament it was not edited into its final form until centuries later. Much of the book is concerned with the battles for survival against hostile tribes, but as in all the writings of the Old Testament the uniting theme is a theological one, tracing in Israel's history a recurring cycle of disobedience, oppression, repentance, deliverance leading after a time to forgetfulness, further disobedience and so on.

K

Kenites. A tribe which lived in southern Palestine and, unlike many of the surrounding tribes enjoyed friendly relations with the people of Israel, perhaps because they had religious affinities with them. Moses' father-in-law, Jethro, was a Kenite (Judg 1:16) and the Rechabites who long persisted as an ascetic group among the people of Israel appear to have been closely connected with the Kenites (1 Chr 2:55).

Kidron. A stream running through a deep valley to the east of Jerusalem and separating the city from the Mount of Olives.

Kings, Books of. The two books of Kings are the major source for nearly 400 years of the history of the people of Israel, from the accession of Solomon around 960 B.C., through the division of the kingdom on Solomon's death and the end of the northern kingdom after the fall of Samaria in 721 B.C., to the destruction of Jerusalem and the exile of the leading people by the Babylonians in 586 B.C. Like all the historical books of the Old Testament, it is a composite work containing material of different ages and not reaching its final form until centuries after some of the incidents described. Many of the major events recorded, however, can be confirmed by archaeological evidence from other sources, e.g. the Moabite stone, an inscription of Mesha, king of Moab, which describes relations between his people and the northern kingdom of Israel about the time of Jehoram and, except in minor details, agrees with the biblical record. The interest of the authors of Kings was not in history as an academic exercise, however, but history as it revealed the hand of God, and the kings of Israel and Judah are therefore judged by their loyalty to Yahweh, and the fortunes of their people are related to this. On this criterion all the kings of Israel are judged to have failed, but among the kings of Judah, Uzziah, Hezekiah and Josiah especially are regarded as good kings.

L

Laban. Jacob's uncle and the father of Leah and Rachel.

Lachish. An important city and stronghold about 50 km south-west of Jerusalem. Against both the Assyrians in 701 B.C. and the Babylonians in 587 B.C. it proved its defensive strength, in the latter campaign holding out longer than any other city except Jerusalem itself. Important archaeological finds have been made there, including the Lachish letters written in the heat of the Babylonian invasion.

Lamentations, Book of. Traditionally known as the Lamentations of Jeremiah, there is in fact no evidence to connect them with the prophet. The book is a collection of fine poems mourning the devastation of Jerusalem in 586 B.C. The third chapter expressed hope for the future, however, and the fifth is a prayer for mercy.

Laodicea. A city of Asia Minor near Colossae. The church there is referred to in Revelation 3:14–22 and criticised for its lukewarmness. There is particular irony in the author's claim that the church is blind, for Laodicea was famed for an eye ointment made there. It appears from Colossians 4:16 that Paul wrote a letter to Laodicea, though he never visited it as far as is known.

Last Supper, see **Lord's Supper.**

Lazarus. (1) The brother of Martha and Mary whom, according to John 11:17–44, Jesus raised to life again.

(2) The poor beggar in Jesus' parable of the rich man and Lazarus (Lk 16:19–31).

Leah. The elder daughter of Laban and first wife of Jacob. She bore six of Jacob's twelve sons (Gen 29:31–30:20).

Levi. (1) The third son of both Jacob and Leah.
(2) *See* **Matthew**.

Levites. It appears that the descendants of Levi never possessed any tribal territory of their own but were dispersed among the other tribes. At an early stage, by a process which is far from clear, they were associated with the priesthood, and it became the custom that only Levites could be priests, although not all Levites were. Later the term was used for an order of temple assistants with lower status than priests, as in the parable of the good Samaritan.

Leviticus. As the name of the book implies it is almost entirely concerned with Levitical or priestly duties (*see* above), the offering of worship and sacrifice, the maintenance of ritual purity and the proper response to God's holiness. To the modern reader who does not accept the need for physical sacrifice as part of worship, much of it may appear irrelevant or even repugnant, yet it represents a real desire to give to God the respect properly due to him, and it is not completely taken up with obscure ritual instructions, for it includes the words quoted with approval by Jesus, "love your neighbour as you love yourself" (Lev 19:18).

Lord's Prayer. This brief prayer, given by Jesus in response to a request from his disciples (Lk 11:1), is highly characteristic of his thought. It first places God at the centre of the worshipper's life and only then concerns itself with human needs, asking only for the basic physical requirements of food from day to day and the spiritual necessities of forgiveness and strength under testing.

Lord's Supper. The name given both to the last meal Jesus had with his disciples and to its re-enactment by the Christian community subsequently. The earliest account of the meal occurs in 1 Corinthians 11:23–26, and it is clear from the fact that Paul was instructing the Corinthian church in the proper celebration of the Lord's Supper that it was an established part of Christian worship by the mid-fifties A.D. Accounts are also given in the first three gospels. While John does not describe the meal itself, his treatment of the feeding of the five thousand is given strong sacramental overtones (Jn 6:25–58) which suggest a knowledge of the Lord's Supper. It is impossible to reconstruct with certainty the exact words of Jesus on this occasion, but it seems clear that he linked the breaking of bread and sharing of wine with his approaching sacrifice and ultimate triumph, and also with the new covenant (or new relationship) between God and man foreseen by Jeremiah (Mk 14:22–25).

Lot. A nephew of Abraham who journeyed with him to Canaan. Eventually they had to separate because their herds were too big to remain together, and Lot chose the plain of the Jordan near the Dead Sea as his territory. When escaping from the destruction of Sodom and Gomorrah his wife is said to have looked back and been turned into a pillar of salt (Gen 19:26).

Luke. Luke is referred to only three times in the New Testament, but is of special interest as being almost certainly the author of the third gospel and the book of Acts (*see* below). Only one of the references, that in Colossians 4:14, gives any information other than his name. Here he is spoken of as "our dear doctor", and since Paul has earlier named three people as the "only Jewish converts who work with me" it follows that Luke was a Gentile.

Luke, Gospel of. The question of the authorship of this gospel is closely linked to that of Acts, which is clearly a sequel to the gospel, being addressed to the same person Theophilus. The author of Acts sometimes uses the first person plural, showing that he was present himself for certain parts of the story, including Paul's crossing from Troas to Philippi on his second missionary journey and his voyage to Rome as a prisoner. It seems likely, therefore, that he would be among the people Paul names as his co-workers in his letters and, by a process of

elimination, Luke emerges as the strongest candidate. Since there is also a tradition going back to the second century that Luke was the author of the third gospel this seems a near certainty. About half the material in Luke's gospel comes from Mark (in those days copying another author's work, far from being considered unethical, was regarded a mark of respect), and some of the remainder comes from a collection of the sayings of Jesus which Matthew evidently used as well. Luke had other sources of his own, however, and it is to him that we owe the preservation of some of Jesus' best-loved parables including those of the good Samaritan and the prodigal son. He also gives us the delightful story of Zacchaeus and the account of the two disciples on the road to Emmaus. He lays special emphasis on Jesus' concern for Gentiles and outcasts, emphasises the role of women in his ministry and shows the importance of prayer in his life.

Lydia. A resident of Philippi and dealer in the purple-dyed cloth for which that area was famous, she was Paul's first convert there and opened her house to him and his companions (Acts 16:13–15).

Lystra. A city in the Roman province of Galatia visited by Paul during his first missionary journey (Acts 14:6–19).

M

Macedonia. A Roman province including parts of northern Greece, Albania and Yugoslavia with Philippi as its chief city. It was here that Paul first preached in Europe (as opposed to Asia Minor) in response to a vision of a man of Macedonia asking for his help (Acts 16:9–12).

Malachi. The book of Malachi clearly comes from some time after the reconstruction of the temple following the Babylonian exile. A probable date would be the first half of the fifth century B.C. The prophet takes his people to task for their laxity in the worship of God and their failure to obey the terms of God's covenant. He warns of God's judgement but also speaks of his saving power (Mal 4:2–3).

Malta. Paul was shipwrecked and spent the rest of the winter here on his journey to Rome (Acts 27:39–28:11).

Manasseh. (1) The elder of Joseph's two sons.
(2) The tribe of Manasseh, which occupied a large area on both banks of the Jordan to the north of Ephraim.
(3) King of Judah (687–642 B.C.). Regarded as the worst king in Judah's history, he actively promoted Assyrian and other pagan religious practices, sacrificed his own son and "killed so many innocent people that the streets of Jerusalem were flowing with blood" (2 Kgs 21:16).

Manna. The name of the food which God is said to have provided for the people of Israel during their wanderings in the wilderness (Ex 16:1–31). It is thought to have been a secretion formed by insects feeding on the scrublands of the desert.

Mark. The house of John Mark's mother, Mary, appears to have been the headquarters of the Jerusalem church (Acts 12:12). Paul and Barnabas took him to work with them in Antioch (Acts 12:25) and subsequently on the first missionary journey (Acts 13:5). He left them at Perga to return to Jerusalem, however, and this led to Paul refusing to take him on his second journey, with the consequence that Barnabas took him to Cyprus instead (Acts 15:36–40). It is clear from Colossians 4:10 and other references that Mark later became a close associate of Paul, and we are also told here that he was Barnabas' cousin. For his connection with the second gospel see below.

Mark, Gospel of. There is a tradition dating back to A.D. 135 that the second gospel was written by Mark on the basis of Peter's memories of the life and teaching of Jesus. It seems probable that Mark collected these reminiscences shortly before Peter's death in Nero's persecution of A.D. 64 and published his gospel in Rome soon afterwards. While the identification of this Mark with John Mark cannot be absolutely certain, it seems highly likely, since John Mark knew Peter from the early days in Jerusalem. The view that the gospel is based on the first-hand information of an eye-witness is borne out by the many vivid details it contains—details often omitted by Luke and Matthew when they later used Mark's work as a basis for their own. They had other material to include and economised on unnecessary detail. Mark's gospel is of special value, therefore, as the one with most direct links with the events described.

Martha. The sister of Mary and Lazarus, who gave Jesus hospitality at her home in Bethany just outside Jerusalem (Lk 10:38–41, Jn 11:1).

Mary. (1) The mother of Jesus. Our knowledge of Jesus' mother is very limited. The birth stories present her as a pious girl, open to God's bidding. Luke's account of the visit to Jerusalem when Jesus was twelve shows her anxious and somewhat uncomprehending of her unusual son (Lk 2:41–51), and it is later suggested (Mk 3:21) that she may have attempted to restrain Jesus in his public ministry. John records that she was present at the crucifixion, and that Jesus entrusted her to the "beloved disciple". By this time she must have been old by current standards and may well have died soon after.

(2) The sister of Martha and Lazarus, who was praised for her sense of priorities in listening to Jesus (Lk 10:38–41).

(3) Mary Magdalene. A woman whom Jesus cured of "seven demons" (Lk 8:2), and who became one of those who travelled with Jesus and his disciples ministering to their needs. She was present at the crucifixion, was among a group which discovered the empty tomb and was a witness of the resurrection (Mk 15:40, 16:1, Jn 20:11–18). The tradition which identifies her with the sinful woman of Luke 7:37 is wholly without foundation.

(4) The mother of James and Joseph. Another woman who followed Jesus to Jerusalem, witnessed his crucifixion and saw the empty tomb (Mk 15:40, 47, 16:1).

(5) The mother of John Mark (Acts 12:12).

Matthew. Also called Levi, Matthew was a tax collector before becoming one of the twelve disciples (Mt 9:9–13, cf. Mk 2:13–17).

Matthew, Gospel of. It is highly unlikely that the author of the gospel was the disciple Matthew, since he draws heavily on Mark for much of his material, and this would have been unnecessary for an eyewitness of the events. Like Luke, he also uses a collection of the sayings of Jesus in addition to some material of his own (*e.g.* the parable of the sheep and the goats). It is clear that the author was a Jewish Christian who was concerned among other things to stress the continuity between the Christian church and the old community of the people of Israel. Significantly, Matthew traces the ancestors of Jesus back to Abraham, whereas Luke traces them back to Adam, the symbolic father of the whole human race, and Matthew frequently states that events occurred in order to fulfil Old Testament prophecies. He arranges most of his material in five sections, possibly a conscious imitation of the Pentateuch (the five books of teaching which begin the Old Testament and have a special status among the Old Testament writings for Jews). Each section begins with a narrative and continues with the teaching of Jesus. It is the teaching of the first main sections in chapters 5–7 which constitutes the so-called Sermon on the Mount.

Megiddo. A city of strategic importance controlling the pass through the Carmel ridge from the coastal plain on the south to the Plain of Esdraelon on the north side. It was fortified by Solomon, and it was here that King Josiah lost his life in battle against the Egyptians. It is an important archaeological site.

Melchizedek. A king and priest who gave hospitality to Abraham (Gen 14:18–20) and who is referred to by the author of Hebrews as a forerunner of Christ, himself a priest-king (Heb 7:1–8:2).

Menahem. King of Israel (745–738 B.C.). Menahem secured the throne by the murder of his predecessor Shallum and a bloody struggle against his opponents. He gave tribute to the Assyrian ruler Tiglath-pileser III, hoping both to forestall any Assyrian designs on his territory and gain support to keep him in power. He raised the money by taxation, for which he was not popular.

Mephibosheth. A crippled son of Jonathan who was befriended by David (2 Sam 9:1–13), though he later entertained hopes of gaining the throne as the only remaining descendant of Saul (2 Sam 16:3). Perhaps because this was by now a totally unrealistic hope, David chose to overlook the matter (Sam 19:24–30).

Mesha. The king of Moab during Jehoram's reign, he succeeded in regaining much territory from Israel, according to an ancient inscribed stone known as the Moabite stone. This is consistent with 2 Kings 3:27, which implies that after a highly successful campaign against Mesha, the Israelite forces were unnerved by Mesha's sacrifice of his son and withdrew, having failed to bring the rebel into subjection.

Meshach. One of the three young men who, according to the book of Daniel, survived being thrown into a blazing furnace for refusing to worship a gold statue set up by King Nebuchadnezzar (Dan 3:1–27).

Mesopotamia. The fertile area between the rivers Tigris and Euphrates. It was from this land that Abraham came, and it was also the land of the Assyrians and Babylonians who had such an influence on the history of the people of Israel.

Messiah. The Hebrew word means "anointed one" and therefore implies kingship. "Christ" is the Greek equivalent. The concept of a Messiah has a complex background, but essentially it was born out of Israel's calamitous history and a sense of disillusionment with her leaders. As a result of these factors the hope grew up of a future leader who would truly be God's representative and would consequently restore his people to the position of power and prosperity they enjoyed under David and Solomon. The balance between his spiritual and political functions seems to have been viewed differently by different groups, however, which may well explain why Jesus was apparently prepared to accept the title from his disciples (in a spiritual sense) while forbidding its general use for fear of misunderstanding (Mk 8:27–30).

Micah. A contemporary of Isaiah prophesying in the southern kingdom of Judah towards the end of the eighth century B.C., Micah pronounces God's judgement on his people for their failure to establish a just society and declares that not even the temple will be spared in the general destruction (Mic 3:12). His book is best known for its simple but searching statement of God's requirements: to do what is just, to show constant love and to walk in humble fellowship with God (Mic 6:8). Many scholars consider that the more hopeful elements in the book of Micah are later editorial insertions, and on this view Micah must be considered primarily as a prophet of judgement like Amos before him in the northern kingdom.

Micaiah. A prophet who, in contrast to the 400 court prophets, predicted disaster for King Ahab if he went to take Ramoth-Gilead from the Syrians (1 Kgs 22:1–35).

Miletus. A port near Ephesus. Paul called the leaders of the Ephesian church to meet him here on his last journey to Jerusalem, and warned them against false teachers (Acts 20:17–38).

Miriam. The elder sister of Moses, she is referred to as a prophetess when she leads the women of Israel in a song and dance of triumph after the crossing of the sea on the escape from Egypt (Ex 15:20–21).

Moabites. Occupying land east of the Dead Sea, the Moabites were generally hostile to the people of Israel. David conquered them, but they reasserted their independence in the period of weakness after the division of the kingdom, only to be subjugated again later by Omri. They were finally led to independence by Mesha while Jehoram was king of Israel.

Molech. A Canaanite god whose worship involved child-sacrifice. King Manasseh apparently worshipped him (2 Kgs 21:6), but Josiah desecrated the site of these sacrifices to prevent them happening again (2 Kgs 23:10).

Mordecai. The cousin and foster-father of Queen Esther (Esth 2:6–7).

Moses. If Abraham is the father of the Jewish race, Moses is the founder of Jewish religion. This does not mean, however, that the religion he established had no antecedents, but it was under Moses that it achieved its definitive form. While it is admittedly difficult to disentangle fact from legend in many of the stories of Moses, there is no reason to doubt their essential historical basis as recollections of the great leader who took the people of Israel from slavery in Egypt to the threshold of the promised land, and in the process firmly established their religious traditions. At the centre of Moses' religion is the concept of the covenant, an agreement between God and the people of Israel whereby God gives them a special position of responsibility in his plans and they pledge him their loyalty and obedience. This obedience is to be expressed not only in worship but also in behaviour towards others as laid down in the ten commandments. It is, in essence, a joyful religion because it springs from a sense of gratitude for what God has done, and in this respect as in many others, it is a precursor of Christianity.

N

Naaman. Commander of the Syrian army, cured of "leprosy" (*i.e.* a disfiguring skin disease) by Elisha (2 Kgs 5:1–19).

Naboth. Owner of a vineyard adjoining King Ahab's palace, he was put to death on false evidence at Jezebel's instigation so that Ahab could take the property in the absence of an heir (1 Kgs 21:1–16).

Nadab. King of Israel (901–900 B.C.). Assassinated within two years of his accession by Baasha whilst fighting the Philistines at Gibbethon (1 Kgs 15:27).

Nahum. The book is a poem exulting in the fall of the Assyrian capital Nineveh, which is seen as an example of God's judgement on a nation which had long taken for granted its dominant position and gave no thought to the suffering of its subject peoples. Nineveh fell in 612 B.C., and the poem appears to be contemporary with the event.

Naphtali. (1) The sixth son of Jacob, his second by Bilhah, Rachel's slave-girl.
(2) The tribe of Naphtali, occupying territory to the north and west of the Sea of Galilee.

Nathan. A prophet who advised David not to build a permanent temple in Jerusalem and rebuked him for his misconduct with Bathsheba. Nevertheless, he backed Bathsheba's son, Solomon, in the struggle for succession. It was largely through him that David was eventually persuaded to declare himself in Solomon's favour (1 Kgs 1:11–40).

Nathanael. Often identified with Bartholomew, since John omits all mention of Bartholomew but names Nathanael as one of the disciples. Brought to Jesus by Philip (who is linked with Bartholomew in the other gospels), Jesus referred to him as "a true Israelite in whom there is nothing false" (Jn 1:47).

Nazareth. The home of Joseph and Mary, and the place where Jesus lived until he began his itinerant ministry. Until then this small Galilean town was of no importance and is not even mentioned in the Old Testament.

Nazirite. A person dedicated to God's service and following an ascetic rule of life involving abstinence from alcohol and refusal to cut hair amongst other things. Samson was a Nazirite (Judg 13:2–24) and John the Baptist may have been (Lk 1:15).

Nebuchadnezzar. The Babylonian ruler (605–562 B.C.) under whose orders Jerusalem was taken and destroyed and the people exiled in 586 B.C. By the standards of his day he was not excessively ruthless, and it could be argued that only the intransigence of the Jews compelled him to treat them with severity.

Nehemiah. A Jewish exile who became cupbearer to the Persian king Artaxerxes and was allowed by him to go to Jerusalem as governor about 445 B.C. in order to accelerate reconstruction of the nation's life. The book of Nehemiah relates how he overcame opposition to get the walls of Jerusalem rebuilt. It also tells how Ezra read the law aloud to the people and got them to enter into an agreement to keep it. While it seems that the two men worked to-

gether on the re-establishment of the nation's religious and economic life, the relationship between them is not entirely clear.

New Year. Originally the Jewish New Year began in the autumn, but during the exile the Babylonian New Year starting in the spring was adopted. The autumn New Year was still maintained for cultic purposes, however, and there has been much speculation, based on strong but circumstantial evidence mainly from the Psalms, over the possibility that the autumn New Year was the occasion of a major religious festival celebrating and renewing the covenant.

Nicodemus. A member of the Jewish Council who sympathised with Jesus and came to see him by night—presumably fearful of associating with him openly (Jn 3:1–12). He objected to the Council condemning Jesus without giving him a chance to defend himself (Jn 7:50–51) and helped Joseph of Arimathea to give Jesus a decent burial (Jn 19:39–42).

Nineveh. The capital of Assyria until its destruction by the combined forces of the Medes and Babylonians in 612 B.C. Among the people of Israel it was legendary for its size and sinfulness (Jon 1:2).

Noah. While the story of Noah may have a historical basis, its primary value lies in what it says about God. It shows God as one who does not fully carry out the judgement which man's sinfulness deserves, but in his generosity makes a new start possible.

Numbers, Book of. The name of the book refers to two censuses of the people of Israel recorded in it, one just before they left Mount Sinai and the other about a generation later. The book covers the history of the people of Israel from the exodus until just before the crossing of the Jordan and lays down various rules for everyday life and worship.

O

Obadiah. (1) A high official under King Ahab who tried to protect loyal worshippers of Yahweh against the persecution of Queen Jezebel (1 Kgs 18:2–15).
(2) A prophet who wrote sometime after the fall of Jerusalem in 586 B.C., condemning the Edomites for taking advantage of Judah's plight to settle old scores, and predicting final victory for the people of Israel.

Omri. King of Israel (876–869 B.C.). Although Omri is only given six verses in the books of Kings (1 Kgs 16:23–28), and is condemned for leading his people into idolatry, he was a capable ruler who in a relatively short reign established good relations with both Judah and the Phoenician states, subjugated enemies east of the Jordan and built a new capital, Samaria.

Onesimus. A runaway slave who was converted by Paul and eventually sent back to his master Philemon, bearing with him the letter of that name.

P

Palestine. Derived from "Philistine", the name originally referred only to the southern part of the coastal plain around the Philistine cities, but it came to be used for the whole of the area bordering the eastern Mediterranean from the Lebanon southwards to the Egyptian frontier and across to the desert land of Transjordan.

Passover. A festival celebrated in spring by a special meal. Originally it probably derived from a custom of sacrificing the first lamb of the new season, but it became associated with the deliverance from slavery in Egypt, and it is as a way of remembering this that it has been celebrated ever since. It is followed by a week of eating unleavened bread, also in memory of the escape from Egypt.

Paul. We know more about Paul than about any other leader of the early church, our information coming both from Acts and his own letters. Born in Tarsus in Asia Minor, he was brought up in strictest Jewish tradition and studied under the renowned teacher, Gamaliel. He considered it his duty to persecute the Christian community, and was present at the stoning of Stephen, whose saintly behaviour towards his executioners almost certainly sowed the first seeds of doubt in his mind. These doubts culminated in a shattering conversion experience as he travelled to Damascus to continue his persecution of the Christians there. It was not until many years had elapsed, however, that Paul emerged as the leading figure in the mission to the Gentiles, and he did so at the instigation of Barnabas, who sent for him to help in the work at Antioch. Soon the church decided to send Paul and Barnabas on a missionary journey which took them first to Cyprus and then into the Roman province of Galatia. By this time some of the Jewish Christians were becoming alarmed at the large number of Gentile converts, and on their return they went to a gathering in Jerusalem to thrash out questions of policy with regard to the admission of Gentiles to the church. Here, Paul, more aware than anyone else of the futility of the Jewish law, strongly resisted the imposition of Jewish customs on Gentile converts, and appears to have won, though the argument was to rumble on for many years. Soon he undertook a second missionary journey with Silas, in the course of which he founded the first church in Europe at Philippi and stayed for eighteen months in Corinth. On a third journey he spent two years in Ephesus before revisiting the churches founded earlier during his second journey. On a visit to Jerusalem at the end of his third journey he was arrested by Roman guards during a disturbance in the temple courtyard when Jews alleged that he had taken Trophimus, a Gentile from Ephesus, into the temple. After two years' imprisonment during which he was neither condemned nor declared innocent, Paul appealed to Caesar and was duly sent to Rome. We are told in Acts 28:30 that he was there for two years, presumably waiting for his accusers to present a case against him, and this may imply that he was then released, since the rule was that a case must be presented within two years. However, this is not certain, and tradition has it that he died, together with Peter, in Nero's persecution of A.D. 64. From about A.D. 50 onwards Paul wrote numerous letters, mainly to churches he had founded, but occasionally to churches he had not visited himself, and some of these letters form a substantial part of the New Testament. Some have accused Paul of complicating the simple gospel preached by Jesus, yet the church today may owe its very existence to Paul's clear understanding that Christianity could not just remain an offshoot of Judaism, but must become a universal religion.

Pekah. King of Israel (737–732 B.C.). Seizing the throne by assassinating his predecessor, Pekah immediately entered an anti-Assyrian coalition with his Syrian neighbour Rezin. Together they made threats against Ahaz, king of Judah, who soon appealed to the Assyrians for help. In 733 B.C. Tiglath-pileser III attacked Israel, capturing many cities and deporting much of the population. It was possibly only Pekah's assassination by Hoshea, who promptly surrendered, which saved Israel from further destruction.

Pekahiah. King of Israel (738–737 B.C.). Assassinated after a short period by Pekah, probably because of discontent with his policy of submission to Assyria.

Pentateuch. The first five books of the Old Testament, having special significance for the Jews as the Torah, the basis of Jewish law.

Pentecost, *see* **Weeks, Feast of.**

Peter. The undisputed leader of the disciples, and of the Christian church during its earliest days. A Galilean fisherman, he was brought to Jesus by his brother Andrew and quickly became one of the inner group of disciples. He showed his leadership in his declaration of faith in Jesus as the Christ at Caesarea Philippi, and it was here that Jesus added the name Peter (the rock) to his original name Simon. After Jesus' arrest he denied all knowledge of him, but it could be argued that he was only exposed to this temptation because he had had the courage to follow Jesus to the High Priest's house. He was the first disciple to enter the empty tomb and preached the first Christian sermon on the day of Pente-

cost. He was also instrumental in paving the way for Gentiles to enter the church through the baptism of the Roman centurion Cornelius and his subsequent defence of this action (Acts 10:1–11:18). It is unfortunate, though understandable, that the emphasis in the second half of Acts on the work of Paul leave us in ignorance as to the subsequent development of Peter's ministry. Tradition has it that he founded the church in Rome, and died there in Nero's persecution of A.D. 64.

Peter, Letters of. There is considerable doubt whether either of these letters is by the disciple Peter, or indeed whether they are by the same author. The first letter is written to encourage Christians in Asia Minor who are suffering or are likely to suffer, for their Christian faith. If this were written during a specific period of persecution it would almost certainly have been that under the Roman emperor Domitian (A.D. 81–96), since Nero's persecution does not appear to have extended far beyond the capital, and this would rule out authorship by Peter if he had died in A.D. 64. The second letter, which shows a detailed knowledge of the letter of Jude, is a general warning against false teachers. Many scholars regard it as the latest document in the New Testament, with a date in the second century.

Pharaoh. The title of the kings of Egypt. The Pharaohs under whom the people of Israel served as forced labourers have not been identified with certainty, but the likelihood is that the Pharaoh at the time of the exodus was Rameses II (reigned 1304–1237 B.C.).

Pharisees. One of the chief sects within Judaism at the time of Jesus. The movement started as an attempt to bring everyday life more closely into conformity with the law of Judaism, so that religious observance became an integral part of daily living. Jesus would hardly have quarrelled with this aim, but the effect had been to emphasise trivial details and lose sight of basic principles. It was this, and the sense of self-righteousness so often engendered, that Jesus criticised in the Pharisees.

Philemon, Letter to. A short personal letter from Paul to a member of the church at Colossae. Onesimus, Philemon's slave, had run away to Rome, where he came into contact with Paul. Paul would have liked to keep him as he was proving so useful, but felt bound to return him to Philemon, begging Philemon to welcome him back not just as a slave but as a Christian brother.

Philip. (1) Ruler of Ituraea and Trachonitis (4 B.C.–A.D. 34), *see* **Herod family.**

(2) One of the twelve disciples about whom little is known, although John's gospel gives him slightly greater prominence than the other three (Jn 1:43–46, 12:20–22, 14:8–9).

(3) One of the seven deacons appointed to organise the distribution of resources in the system of sharing goods adopted by the early church in Jerusalem (Acts 6:1–6). In fact, he quickly became a notable evangelist, working among the Samaritans and also in southern Palestine, where he converted an Ethiopian official travelling home, before settling in Caesarea, where he still lived nearby thirty years later (Acts 8:4–40, 21:8).

Philippi. A city of Macedonia where Paul first preached in Europe (Acts 16:12).

Philippians, Letter to the. Unlike many of Paul's letters, the letter to the church at Philippi does not seem to have been written with any particular object in mind—to combat false teaching (Galatians) or pave the way for a possible future visit (Romans). It is simply keeping in touch with old friends, for the church at Philippi had apparently been the first to give Paul financial support so that he could be a full-time missionary without the necessity of plying a trade (Phil 4:15–16). Although he warns the Philippian Christians to be on their guard against any attempt to impose Jewish customs on them (Phil 3:2–7), he seems confident of their ability to maintain their Christian life against any opposition it encounters. The whole atmosphere of the letter is one of gratitude, joy and peace, all the more remarkable as Paul was in prison and possibly close to death as he wrote (Phil 1:20–24).

Philistines. A people who came from Crete or the Aegean islands to settle on the coastal plain of Palestine about the same time that the people of Israel were entering Canaan from the east. They were organised in five main city-states and were a serious threat to the Israelites because of their iron weapons (Israel being still in the Bronze Age), their use of chariots and their military form of government. After the period of acute antagonism which was brought to a close by David's unchallengeable superiority, they lived relatively peacefully apart from occasional incidents until, sometime after the exile, the Philistines disappeared as an independent entity.

Phoenicia. A term used to describe the coastal area north of Mount Carmel which is now the Lebanon. It was never a kingdom as such, but included a number of city-states, of which Tyre was the most important. The Phoenicians were seafarers and traders and times of prosperity in Israel often hinged upon good relations with Phoenicia, as in Solomon's reign.

Pilate, Pontius. The Roman governor of Judaea at the time of Jesus' execution, he does not seem to have handled the admittedly difficult task of governing the Jews particularly well. All the gospels represent him as resisting the death sentence on Jesus, however, and only passing it under Jewish pressure. John implies that the Jews had some kind of hold over Pilate: possibly because of previous blunders he could not afford to antagonise the Jews again. In fact, he was recalled to Rome c. A.D. 36, tried and imprisoned.

Priest. In the early period of Jewish religion there were no priests. The head of the family would perform any religious functions necessary. Samuel, however, is said to have condemned Saul for offering sacrifice, thereby usurping his proper function (1 Sam 13:8–14). This suggests that by now a specific priestly role was recognised. It was with the construction of the temple and the development of more elaborate rituals that a priesthood became essential, though it was the offering of sacrifice which remained the primary function.

Prisca, *see* Aquila.

Prophet. What marks a person out as a prophet has been much debated. The prophets of Baal on Mount Carmel present an extremely unedifying spectacle as they dance and cut themselves to invoke the power of their god (1 Kgs 18:26–29), yet there were prophets in Israel whose behaviour was not dissimilar (1 Sam: 10:10–13). There is clearly a vast gulf between such people and men of the calibre of Amos, Hosea or Jeremiah. The one thing they have in common is their enthusiasm for God. It is possible to trace the gradual transition from these primitive prophets who expressed themselves in emotional outbursts to the great religious thinkers of later times but to sum up the difference in terms of emotions against intellect (or any other pair of contrasting qualities) is an over-simplification. Possibly the best short definition of a prophet is "one who is convinced that God has something to say through him". Note that, although prophets were generally expected to have knowledge of future events, this is not an essential part of the Hebrew concept of prophecy.

Proselyte. One who was not a Jew by birth but who, by circumcision and a form of baptism, had become a Jew by faith. Acts 2:11 refers to the presence of proselytes in Jerusalem for the day of Pentecost.

Proverbs, Book of. This is basically a collection of short sayings offering advice on how to act in everyday situations, but, as with all the biblical writings, it emphasises an important theological belief—that all true wisdom comes from God and is based on respect for him. The sayings are traditionally ascribed to Solomon, who may indeed be responsible for some of them, but the compilation of the book certainly took place centuries after his death and incorporated much later material.

Psalms. It is a truism to say that the Psalms are the hymn book of the Old Testament, yet it is only recently that the implications of this obvious truth have been explored. If the Psalms were collected for use in corporate worship, we need to ask for each Psalm, "On what sort of occasion would these have been appropriate sentiments to express?" In recent years this approach has led to some interesting conclusions about the worship of the people of Israel, and greatly illuminated the Psalms themselves. For the ordinary reader, however, the attraction of these poems remains what it has always been—their expression of a very wide range of human emotions within an overall context of faith in God.

Publius. The chief official (his exact status is unclear) on Malta when Paul was shipwrecked there. Paul cured his father of a fever (Acts 28:7–10).

Q

Qirinius. Described by Luke as the governor of Syria at the time of Jesus' birth, though if this took place in the reign of Herod the Great, Luke is wrong on this point. He later had two terms of office as governor of Syria, but at this time commanded the Roman army there.

R

Rabbah. The Ammonite capital, captured by David. It was during the siege of Rabbah that David arranged for Uriah to be left exposed to the enemy, in order to marry his wife Bathsheba (2 Sam 11:14–17).

Rabbi. Sometimes translated "teacher", but implying rather more than this. It is a respectful title, suggesting that the one who uses it accepts the authority of the one to whom it is used. In John's gospel Jesus is addressed in this manner several times.

Rachel. Laban's younger daughter and Jacob's second wife, though she was his first choice (Gen 29:18–28). She bore him Joseph and Benjamin.

Rahab. A prostitute of Jericho who concealed two spies sent by Joshua, and was subsequently spared when the other inhabitants were slaughtered (Josh 1:1–21, 6:22–25).

Rameses. An Egyptian city where Israelite slave labour was used, and from which the people of Israel started out on the exodus. It was on the eastern edge of the Nile delta, and is generally identified with a city earlier known as Avaris and later as Tanis.

Ramoth-Gilead. A town on the border between Israel and Syria which was the scene of bitter fighting between these traditional enemies. It was here that Ahab died, and that Jehoram received the wounds from which he was recovering at the time of Jehu's coup.

Rebecca. The sister of Laban, wife of Isaac, and mother of the twins Esau and Jacob.

Rechabites. The descendants of Rechab, about whom we know nothing except that he was the father of Jonadab, who laid down the rules of the Rechabite community. He insisted that they lived in tents and refrained from alcohol, thus trying to protect them against the corrupting influences of Canaanite civilisation. Jeremiah commends the Rechabites for their faithfulness to these principles, in contrast to the lack of faithfulness found elsewhere among the people of Israel (Jer 35:1–17).

Red Sea. The name translated as "Red Sea" in older versions of the Bible is not always to be equated with the Red Sea as known today. References in the exodus story may be to a shallow inland lake in the region now cut through by the Suez Canal, and in 1 Kings 9:26 the reference is to the Gulf of Aqaba, the eastern limb of the Red Sea, rather than the Red Sea itself.

Rehoboam. King of Judah (922–915 B.C.). The son of Solomon, Rehoboam refused to listen to the grievances of his people at the beginning of his reign and as a consequence was faced with rebellion by the ten northern tribes under Jeroboam's leadership. Rehoboam was unable to prevent the division and soon gave up any attempt to reassert his authority over Israel. He lost nearly all his foreign territory, was invaded by the Egyptians and had to ransack his treasury to pay the tribute demanded (1 Kgs 12:1–24, 14:25–26).

Resurrection. It is quite clear from the book of Acts that the resurrection of Jesus was the central theme of early Christian preaching. It is equally clear that those who proclaimed the resurrection in this way stood a considerable risk of sharing the fate of their leader. It follows that they must have been absolutely certain in their own minds of the truth and importance of their claims. Because these claims are admittedly extraordinary, it is natural that people should have sought explanations in terms of natural causes, but no such explanation has proved entirely satisfactory. In any case, an extraordinary event is needed to explain the transformation in the behaviour of the disciples. Among those who believe in the resurrection it is, of course, possible to find a wide variety of interpretations as to what exactly took place.

Reuben. (1) The first-born son of both Jacob and Leah.

(2) The tribe of Reuben, which occupied an area on the eastern shore of the Dead Sea between Ammonite and Moabite territory.

Revelation, Book of. Without doubt the most difficult book in the New Testament for modern readers because its thought-forms and imagery are so remote from those to which we are accustomed. Written during a time of persecution, probably that of the emperor Domitian in the last decade of the first century, it declares in highly metaphorical language that the stage of human history is set in the context of an eternal scheme of things, in which God reigns supreme. Whatever their present sufferings, ultimate victory is assured to those who put their trust in Jesus. The writer describes himself as John, and some scholars have identified him with the disciple John, but there is no solid evidence for this. There is no question of the writer being the author of John's gospel or the letters of John.

Rezin. King of Syria (about 740–732 B.C.). An ally of Pekah, king of Israel, against the Assyrians. Together they threatened to attack Judah if King Ahaz would not join their coalition. Rezin was killed by the Assyrians when they finally took his capital, Damascus.

Romans. The Roman empire provides the context in which the events of the New Testament took place. Many Jews hated the Romans, and there were frequent misguided attempts at rebellion which culminated in the revolt of A.D. 66 and the eventual destruction of Jerusalem by the Romans in A.D. 70. In spite of occasional persecution, Roman rule was generally helpful to the spread of Christianity through its maintenance of political stability and good communications.

Romans, Letters to the. Paul's letter to the Romans was written to an already flourishing church which he did not know personally. Its purpose was apparently to pave the way for further missionary work in the western Mediterranean, using Rome as a base. Paul seems to feel it necessary to lay before the Roman church the gospel that he preaches, and this letter provides the most coherent statement of his theology that we possess. Its great emphasis is on faith in Jesus as the sole necessity for reconciliation with God, and the inadequacy of legalistic forms of religion where the follower's relationship with God depends on his having met God's demands in every detail.

Rome. The capital of the Roman empire, a church seems to have been established there at an early but unknown date. Tradition says it was founded by Peter, but there is no biblical evidence for this. Paul spent two years there under arrest and, again according to tradition, died there with Peter in Nero's persecution.

Ruth. The book of Ruth is one of the gems of the Old Testament. It tells how Ruth, the Moabite widow of an Israelite husband, decides to accompany her widowed mother-in-law, Naomi, back to her home town of Bethlehem. In so doing Ruth accepts Israel's God as her own. Boaz, a kinsman of Naomi, notices Ruth gleaning the remains of his barley field and ultimately marries her, and they give birth to Obed, David's grandfather. The story is a parable (as is suggested by the names of the chief characters, all of them symbolic), but may rest on a historical fact, for much of the point of the story depends on Ruth being David's great-grandmother, and if this were made up the point would be lost. The book is essentially a plea for tolerance of mixed marriages, and as such it shows a liberality of outlook matched in the Old Testament only by the book of Jonah. Attempts to date the book have proved very difficult, but the most likely period is shortly after the exile, when the Jewish community was becoming more exclusive.

S

Sabbath. The observance of the sabbath as a day of rest and worship goes back at least to the time of Moses, yet it was only during the exile that it came to assume the importance it has had ever since for Jews. Deprived of temple worship, and living among aliens, strict sabbath observance became the identifying characteristic of a good Jew. By Jesus' time the number of rules about the sabbath was enormous, and while Jesus clearly supported the principle of the sabbath, he would not let his work be hindered by such petty rules. This became one of the major sources of friction between him and the Pharisees.

Sacrifice. Although the Jews came to realise at an early stage that God did not require human sacrifice (Gen 22:9–14), animal sacrifice continued to be part of their worship until the destruction of Herod's temple by the Romans. Many of the prophets questioned the value of the practice, however, declaring that what God really wanted was justice and compassion in all men's dealings with their fellows.

Sadducees. A major party within Judaism at the time of Jesus. They were mainly of priestly background and, because many of them occupied positions which depended on the good will of the Romans, they generally favoured a conciliatory approach. Unlike the Pharisees, many of whom commanded respect by their conscientiousness, the Sadducees were liked by no one.

Salome. One of the women who had followed Jesus from Galilee to Jerusalem, watched the crucifixion and saw the empty tomb.

Samaria. Originally the name referred to the new capital city built by Omri, king of Israel. It was increasingly used, however, as another term for the northern kingdom as a whole. After the kingdom had ceased to exist it denoted an area corresponding to the central part of the old kingdom.

Samaritan. An inhabitant of Samaria. The Jews considered Samaritans to be excluded from their ranks because, following the deportation of many Samaritan citizens by the Assyrians in 721 B.C. and the establishment of people from other parts of the Assyrian empire on their soil, many mixed marriages had taken place. Since the northern kingdom had always been considered idolatrous by southern Jews, this put them both religiously and socially beyond the pale.

Samson. A Nazirite, and one of the most famous of the judges. He seems to have had more valour than discretion, however, and provoked the Philistines needlessly (Judg 15:1–6). He paid for this unnecessary bravado with his life (Judg 16:4–30).

Samuel. Samuel was the last great leader of Israel before the establishment of the monarchy, and a unique figure combining the functions of prophet, priest, judge and even ruler. Undoubtedly the most significant part of his work was the creation of the monarchy, but unfortunately the role he played in this is far from clear. There are two conflicting accounts interwoven in 1 Samuel. One represents Samuel privately anointing Saul as king on God's instructions, and later arranging for a public acclamation of his kingship when he has proved himself in battle. The other suggests that the people demanded a king against Samuel's advice and that only under protest did he arrange a system for choosing a king by lots. Whatever his initial attitude, his support for Saul was soon withdrawn when Saul offered sacrifice instead of waiting for Samuel to do it (1 Sam 13:8–14) and failed to destroy totally the Amalekites according to Samuel's instructions (1 Sam 15:13–23). It seems clear that Samuel came to regard Saul as one who was usurping God's position, and his hostility did much to break the man who, willingly or otherwise, he had created king.

Samuel, Books of. The two books of Samuel cover an epoch-making period in Israel's history. They trace the development of a loose confederation of tribes, without any established form of government, into a considerable empire under a dynastic ruler. Like all the historical books, they contain material from a variety of sources, some much closer to the events than others. We are fortunate, however, to have in 2 Samuel 9–20 (and continuing in 1 Kings 1–2) a continuous source which is widely recognised as the finest piece of history writing of its time from anywhere in the world. The author deals with the reign of David in such a way that he can only have been a close associate of the king himself. Not only does he describe in detail David's conversations with his advisers, but he does it so vividly that the characters of the major participants are laid open to scrutiny. He is quite remarkable in his absence of bias. He paints a sympathetic portrait of David but does not gloss over his failings, and neither condemns nor attempts to justify his more questionable activities. About no other king in the history of the monarchy is our information so reliable.

Sanhedrin. A council meeting under the High Priest at Jerusalem which had ultimate authority in religious and legal matters except for the power to pass the death penalty. This was why the Jews had to take Jesus before Pilate. The stoning of Stephen appears to have been a flagrant violation of this restriction. How and when the Sanhedrin was established is uncertain, but it came to an end with the destruction of Jerusalem in A.D. 70.

Sarah. Wife of Abraham and mother of Isaac. One of a number of women in the Bible whose child was seen as a special mark of God's favour because it came late in life.

Saul. (1) As the first king of Israel shortly before 1000 B.C., Saul faced a near impossible task, and his undoubted courage in battle was not an adequate qualification. The people of Israel wanted a king to defend them from their enemies, especially the Philistines, but they were not yet ready to give up their tribal independence, or support a permanent army as opposed to a constantly changing collection of volunteers. So he occupied an uncomfortable position in which more was expected of him than of the judges of old, but without any constitutional means of exercising his authority. When Samuel, a powerful influence on public opinion, withdrew his support, Saul clearly felt exposed and vulnerable, and the popularity of the young hero David increased his sense of insecurity. When David fled from his jealousy, helped unwittingly by the priest Ahimelech, Saul's slaughter of Ahimelech and his household was widely regarded as unjust, and must have alienated the priesthood. Thereafter much of his time and energy was diverted into hunting down David when it could have been more usefully employed in other ways. His final battle was an act of desperation, meeting the Philistines on level ground at the foot of Mount Gilboa, where their chariots gave them a decisive advantage. In the early years of his reign he seems to have enjoyed success, however, ejecting the Philistines from the central mountain range and, temporarily at least, being sufficiently free from the Philistine threat to strike at other enemies across the Jordan and far to the south. When he died there seems to have been no move to dispense with a king, so in spite of his ultimate failure, he seems to have achieved the acceptance of the monarchy by his people and thus paved the way for his successors.

(2) The Hebrew name by which Paul was known before his conversion. He may have taken the Roman form of his name to signify that he was "a new man in Christ", or possibly in order to identify himself with the Gentiles.

Scapegoat. A goat on which the sins of all the people were symbolically laid before driving it out into the wilderness. This happened annually on the Day of Atonement (Lev 16:20–22).

Scribes. The scribes were the professional interpreters of the law from the exile onwards. Many of them were also Pharisees, and the two are often linked in the New Testament.

Scripture. The term can be applied to any body of writings, but in the New Testament (where it is sometimes used in the plural) it invariably refers to the Old Testament. The use of the term by Christians to signify the Bible as a whole naturally came later.

Scrolls, Dead Sea. A collection of about 500 documents, the first of them discovered in 1947, from caves near the Dead Sea. Written between 170 B.C. and A.D. 70, some of them relate to the life of the ascetic community to which they belonged and others are parts of the Old Testament. Surprisingly the most ancient manuscripts of the Old Testament previously known were mediaeval, yet the differences in the text are mostly insignificant.

Sennacherib. The king of Assyria who invaded Judah in 701 B.C., destroyed 46 of its fortified cities and shut up Hezekiah "like a bird in a cage" (to use the words of his own inscription). He did not take Jerusalem, but it is not clear whether this was because of a disaster in the Assyrian camp or because Hezekiah accepted his punitive terms of surrender.

Septuagint. The Greek translation of the Old Testament, so called because of a tradition that it was made by 72 scribes. The latin septuaginta actually means 70, and hence the use of LXX as an abbreviation.

Shadrach. One of three young men, who according to the book of Daniel, survived being thrown into a blazing furnace for refusing to worship a gold statue set up by King Nebuchadnezzar (Dan 3:1–27).

Shallum. King of Israel (745 B.C.). He came to the throne by assassinating his predecessor and died in the same manner a month later.

Shaphan. The high official of King Josiah who took the Book of the Covenant from the temple and read it to him (2 Kgs 22:3–10). His family later protected Jeremiah, particularly during Jehoiakim's reign.

Sheba, Queen of. Sheba, in the Arabian peninsula, was a trading nation. The visit of the Queen of Sheba to Solomon (1 Kgs 10:1–10, 13) was probably what would now be called a trade mission, with Solomon offering copper in exchange for spices.

Shechem. A town with ancient religious connections, since Jacob is said to have built an altar there (Gen 33:18–20). Centrally situated on the borders of Ephraim and Manasseh, it became the first capital of the northern kingdom.

Shiloh. A town where the tabernacle was taken after the occupation of Canaan and which became the site for a permanent temple, the central sanctuary for the confederation of Israelite tribes before the monarchy (1 Sam 1:3). Jeremiah refers to the destruction of this temple, most probably by the Philistines (Jer 7:12).

Sidon. Next to Tyre, the most important city of Phoenicia and a good port. Jesus passed through its territory on at least one occasion (Mk 7:31).

Silas. Sent with Paul and Barnabas to present the findings of the Council of Jerusalem to the church at Antioch, he subsequently became Paul's companion on the second missionary journey (Acts 16:22–41). Probably to be identified with the Silvanus mentioned in some of Paul's letters.

Siloam. The name of a pool within the city walls of Jerusalem, fed from a spring outside by a tunnel some 620 m long. The tunnel was cut by Hezekiah (2 Chr 32:30) and can still be seen today.

Simeon. (1) The second son of Jacob and Leah.
(2) The tribe of Simeon which originally possessed territory south of Judah but was then absorbed into its neighbour.

Simon. (1) see Peter.
(2) Simon the Zealot, one of the twelve disciples, whose name suggests that he started at

least with very different political ideals from Jesus (Mk 3:18).

(3) **Simon the Pharisee.** The man with whom Jesus was eating when a sinful woman anointed him (Lk 7:36–47).

(4) **Simon of Cyrene.** The man who was compelled to carry Jesus' cross (Mk 15:21).

(5) **Simon Magus.** A miracle-worker in Samaria who, when he saw the effects of the Holy Spirit on a group of converts Peter and John had laid hands on, tried to buy this power from them (Acts 8:9–24).

Sinai. The peninsula between the Gulf of Suez and the Gulf of Aqaba which was the first objective on the exodus from Egypt. Mount Sinai (also called Horeb) has not been identified with certainty. If the giving of the law was accompanied by volcanic activity, as certain elements of the account suggest, a site on the eastern side of the Gulf of Aqaba (and therefore not on the Sinai peninsula at all) would be preferable on geological grounds.

Smyrna. An important city on the Aegean coastline of Asia Minor. The book of Revelation (Rev 2:8–11) refers sympathetically to the church there and its steadfastness under persecution, but we know little else about it.

Sodom. A city of evil reputation, probably to be located in an area now covered by the southern part of the Dead Sea. The city was destroyed by burning sulphur (presumably a volcanic disturbance) according to Genesis 19:24–25.

Solomon. King of Israel (c. 960–922 B.C.). Solomon is traditionally regarded as a wise king, yet by the end of his reign his subjects were seething with discontent, and it would have taken a man of exceptional ability to win back their loyalty. Rehoboam, his son, was not such a man, and so the great empire of Solomon was reduced almost overnight to two insignificant states. For this Solomon must take much of the blame. His reputation for wisdom is not without foundation, however. Inheriting a large and relatively peaceful empire from his father, David, he was never in serious danger from enemies, though he strengthened his defences and added chariots to his army just in case. He was thus able to concentrate on economic policy and proved a genius at exploiting his position across a number of major trade routes as well as developing the copper mines south of the Dead Sea. The wealth generated by this economic development went into building his own palace and its ancillary buildings and the first temple. He allowed himself to get carried away by the splendour of his own designs, however, and got into such debts that not even heavy taxation could pay them and he had to give away territory to his neighbour Hiram, king of Tyre, in payment for the supply of cedar wood (1 Kgs 9:10–11). These measures, together with the system of forced labour introduced to man the copper mines and the building projects, were exceedingly unpopular. So was his marriage to foreign wives (often in pursuance of trade agreements) and his tolerance of their pagan religions. Less obviously the reign of Solomon saw the beginnings of an insidious trend towards the concentration of power in the hands of a small number of people, which led ultimately to the kind of social injustice so fiercely condemned by the prophets. That Solomon was clever is beyond dispute; whether he was wise may be debated.

Sosthenes. The leader of the synagogue at Corinth who was beaten by the Jews (Acts 18:17). The reason for this is not stated. Possibly he had shown sympathy towards Christianity, since a Sosthenes is associated with Paul in the writing of 1 Corinthians (1 Cor 1:1).

Stephen. Appointed originally as one of the seven administrators of the charitable work of the Jerusalem church (Acts 6:1–6), Stephen soon showed himself a powerful advocate of the Christian faith. He was brought before the Jewish Council on charges of denigrating the temple and denying the necessity for the law of Moses, and was illegally executed by stoning, the traditional Jewish method (Acts 6:8–60).

Stoics. Members of a Greek school of philosophers who believed in the suppression of the emotions so as to remain unaffected by life's adversities. Paul debated with the Stoics in Athens (Acts 17:18).

Stoning. The method of execution among the Jews, and the prescribed penalty for 18 crimes. The accusers were required to throw the first stone (Deu 17:5–7, see John 8:7 for Jesus' reaction to this rule).

Sychar. According to John 4:5–6 the site of Jacob's well. Usually identified with Shechem.

Synagogue. The development of synagogue worship was a response to three things: the law forbidding sacrifice except in the Jerusalem temple, the destruction of the temple in 586 B.C. and the dispersion of the Jews. As a result, the offering of sacrifice could no longer be a regular way of worship and a non-sacrificial form of worship had to be developed. This was based on the reading and exposition of the Law, interspersed with psalms and prayers, and it set the pattern for later Christian worship.

Syrians. Also known as Aramaeans, these people were Israel's immediate north-eastern neighbours. At one time forming several small kingdoms, they gradually coalesced into a single state which was frequently at war with Israel. Syria became a province of Assyria following the destruction of Damascus, the capital, in 732 B.C.

T

Tabernacle. The name given to the "tent of meeting", the place where Moses met with God and which represented God's presence among his people. An elaborate structure, it was in effect a travelling temple.

Tabernacles, Feast of. Known also as the Feast of Booths, the festival was both a celebration of the grape harvest and a recollection of the wilderness wanderings, symbolised by people living in temporary shelters (booths) throughout the week.

Tarsus. A city in Asia Minor which was the home of Paul. It had a large Jewish population, but was also noted for its Greek philosophers, and it was this dual background that equipped Paul especially to be a missionary to the Gentiles.

Temple. There were three successive temples in Jerusalem. Solomon's temple, the first, was destroyed by the Babylonians in 586 B.C. After the exile a second temple was built, but due to the circumstances of the time this seems to have been a relatively poor affair. Then in 19 B.C. Herod the Great began work on the third temple, a large and imposing structure in every way. Though substantially complete by Jesus' time the finishing touches were not added until about A.D. 60. Ten years later it was destroyed by the Romans.

Ten Commandments, see **Commandments.**

Tertullus. A Roman or Romano-Jewish lawyer whom the Jewish Council employed to present the case against Paul before Felix (Acts 24:1–9).

Tetrarch. Both Herod Antipas and Philip were known as tetrarchs because they each received roughly a quarter of Herod the Great's kingdom (the other half going to Archelaus).

Thaddeus. One of the twelve disciples (Mk 3:18), known in Luke as Judas, son of James (Lk 6:16).

Thessalonians, Letters to the. The two letters of Paul to the Thessalonians are the earliest writings in the New Testament unless, as some scholars think, Galatians came earlier. They were written from Corinth, within a short time of each other, about A.D. 52. Amongst other things they show that the church at that time still expected the second coming of Christ in a literal form quite shortly, and that this expectation had led to undesirable behaviour such as refusal to work any more. Although Paul's correspondence with the Corinthians two to three years later shows that he still thought in terms of a second coming then, it is not a theme which occurs in his later letters.

Thessalonica. The capital of Macedonia in northern Greece, the city was visited by Paul during his second missionary journey (Acts 17:1–9) and presumably on the short tour he made of the Greek churches following his ministry in Ephesus (Acts 20:1–6).

Thomas. One of the twelve disciples well characterised in John's gospel, where he appears as loyal but slow to learn. His confession of Jesus as "My Lord and my God" after the resurrection identifies Jesus with God more clearly than any other statement in the gospels, however (Jn 20:28).

Tiglath-pileser III. King of Assyria (745–727 B.C.). It was Tiglath-pileser who established the Assyrian dominance of Palestine which was to last well over a century. It was to him that Ahaz of Judah appealed for help against Israel and Syria, both of which were invaded and devastated.

Timothy. Born of a Jewish mother and Greek father, Timothy was a native of Lystra. When Paul revisited the city at the start of his second missionary journey he asked Timothy to join him. From this time onwards he was constantly with Paul, or working elsewhere under Paul's oversight, and only three of the letters ascribed to Paul do not mention him.

Timothy, Letters to. There are difficulties in ascribing to Paul the two letters to Timothy. The style is not quite like Paul's, and the more formal organisation of the church suggests a later period. The most probable view is that they do contain fragments of personal notes written by Paul to Timothy, but that these have been used by a later author as the basis for general advice to church leaders. Similar considerations apply to the letter to Titus, which is often linked with the two letters to Timothy under the title of the Pastoral Letters.

Titus. A companion and co-worker of Paul, he seems to have been particularly involved in Paul's correspondence with Corinth, carrying his letters and acting as his representative (2 Cor 7:7, 8:16–17).

Titus, Letter to, *see* **Timothy, Letters to.**

Tongues, Speaking with. An outpouring of incomprehensible sounds which often accompanied a state of religious excitement in New Testament times, and still occurs in some churches today. The implication that the disciples actually spoke in foreign languages on the day of Pentecost is probably intended as a way of symbolising the universal relevance of the gospel. Paul warned against giving undue emphasis to this gift of the Spirit (1 Cor 14).

Tribes of Israel. Traditionally descended from the twelve sons of Jacob, the number remained twelve in spite of some changes. The descendants of Joseph in fact formed two tribes, named after his sons Ephraim and Manasseh, whereas Simeon fairly quickly became absorbed into Judah.

Tyre. The principal city of Phoenicia, and the centre of a city-state. The kings of Tyre were often on good terms with the kings of Israel, and the two nations traded to their mutual advantage (1 Kgs 5:1–11).

U

Unclean Foods. By long established tradition the Jews did not eat (and still do not eat) certain foods which were ritually unclean. This, and the fact that every meal was seen as a family religious occasion, meant that Jews rarely sat down at table with Gentiles. When Jewish and Gentile Christians began to associate with one another this was one of the difficulties they had to face (Rom 14:14–15).

Unleavened Bread, *see* **Passover.**

Ur. The home town of Abraham, sited in the southern part of the fertile flood-plain of the Tigris-Euphrates river system.

Urim and Thummim. Two objects used by a priest to determine God's will. It is not known how they were used, but the technique was probably to ask specific questions, to which the objects, on being thrown like dice, would then give a "yes" or "no" answer (1 Sam 14:41).

Uzziah. King of Judah (783–742 B.C.). Long-lived, capable and with the welfare of his people at heart, Uzziah was one of the better kings of Judah. He repaired and strengthened the defences of Jerusalem, re-equipped his army (with slings for hurling stones among other things), attacked the Philistine cities and recaptured from the Edomites the important port of Elath on the Gulf of Aqaba (2 Chr 26:1–15). Towards the end of his reign he was stricken by a skin disease and his public duties were taken over by his son Jotham.

W

Weeks, Feast of. Also known as Pentecost, the feast came at the end of the wheat harvest and later was associated with the giving of the Law on Sinai. It was during this feast that the apostles received the gift of the Holy Spirit (Acts 2:1–4).

Wisdom Literature. A name applied to books such as Proverbs, Job and Ecclesiastes which discuss philosophical issues or offer practical advice for living. There is a parallel literature from other middle-eastern civilisations, but the Hebrew literature is unique in its emphasis on the knowledge of God (and not merely academic knowledge but the knowing that comes from a relationship) as the basis of all wisdom.

Y

Yahweh. The proper name of the God of Israel was written as YHWH, there being no vowels in Hebrew. How it would have been pronounced (in fact it was considered too sacred ever to be spoken aloud) is a matter of speculation, but modern opinion favours Yahweh. Jehovah is an earlier and now outmoded attempt to render the same name.

Z

Zacchaeus. A tax collector of Jericho who became a follower of Jesus and generously compensated all those he had previously cheated (Lk 19:1–10).

Zadok. He appears to have been High Priest jointly with Abiathar during David's reign, but when Abiathar was banished by Solomon for supporting Adonijah in the struggle for succession, Zadok became the sole High Priest.

Zebulum. (1) The tenth son of Jacob, his sixth by Leah.
(2) The tribe of Zebulum which occupied a fairly small area of northern Israel surrounded by Manasseh, Issachar, Naphtali and Asher.

Zechariah. (1) King of Israel (746–745 B.C.). The son of Jeroboam II, he was assassinated by Shallum.
(2) A prophet who wrote chapters 1–8 of the book of Zechariah about 520 B.C. His prophecies look forward to the restoration of the temple and the new age about to dawn. Chapters 9–14 are from a later date.
(3) The father of John the Baptist.

Zedekiah. King of Judah (597–586 B.C.). The uncle of his predecessor Jehoiachin, he was placed on the throne by the Babylonians when Jehoiachin surrendered to them in 597 B.C. and was deported. In 589 B.C. Zedekiah himself rebelled and so precipitated the final crisis in the history of Judah. After Jerusalem fell in 586 B.C. he fled, but was captured, and after watching all his sons killed he was blinded and taken in chains to Babylon.

Zephaniah. A contemporary of Jeremiah, Zephaniah threatened a day of judgement against his people, primarily because of their unfaithfulness in worshipping other gods, but also he looked forward to repentance and restoration.

Zimri. King of Israel (876 B.C.). After assassinating his predecessor Elah, Zimri ruled for only seven days before committing suicide in order to avoid being murdered by Omri.

Zion. Originally just the name of one of the hills on which Jerusalem is built, it came to be a symbolic term indicating the dwelling-place of God and associated with the belief that he would always protect Jerusalem.

Zophar. The third of Job's "friends" (Job 11).

SPECIAL TOPIC

SURVEY OF BIBLICAL HISTORY

The Earliest Beginnings

Biblical history begins with Abraham. To say this is not to suggest that the characters in the first ten chapters of Genesis are entirely un-historical, but the stories about them are told for their universal significance rather than their historical importance. The question we need to ask about them is not "Did this really happen?" but "What does this really mean?"

When we come to Abraham, however, the situation is different. It is still true that the stories about him were related for their religious significance rather than an academic interest in history for its own sake. It is also true that none of the stories of Abraham can be verified from any other source, nor would we expect to find such verification. Yet these stories present us with a credible historical figure living within a geographical, social and cultural context of which we do have some information from other sources. Archaeological and documentary evidence from Mesopotamia shows that nomadic herdsmen lived very much the kind of life depicted in the Abraham stories in the period of history about 1500 years before Christ. Nor can the constant witness of the Jews throughout their history to Abraham as the founding forefather of their faith be dismissed, Whatever the bare facts may have been and whatever the distortions introduced by particular theological interpretations of the facts, from this point onwards we are dealing with a historical record open to the techniques of historical investigation.

Exodus

If Abraham was the founder of the Jewish faith, Moses was the architect of the Jewish nation even though the fruits of his work were not to reach fulfilment until two hundred years or so after his death. At some point in their history the descendants of Abraham became slave labourers working for the Egyptians and it was Moses who led them to independence. Clearly there must be room for doubt as to whether the events of the exodus happened exactly as they are described in the Bible but there is no reason to doubt the basic fact of slavery followed by liberation. The situation depicted in the biblical account of the Egyptians using foreign slave populations on their ambitious building works is known to correspond to events during the reign of Rameses II who came to the throne in 1304 B.C. The exodus may well have taken place some time during the next thirty years or so.

Occupying Canaan

According to tradition the people of Israel spent forty years in the wilderness between the escape from Egypt and the conquest of Canaan. In fact the picture pieced together by the biblical historians is a little more complex. We are not to think of the people of Israel all entering the promised land together as a single army under a unified command at one particular moment. Rather we must envisage a gradual infiltration, in which particular parts of Canaan were occupied by different tribes over a period of time with varying degrees of help from the other tribes.

Whatever the precise details of this process of occupation, by about 1100 B.C. the people of Israel were well established in Canaan though they were not yet a nation in the modern sense. They had no king, no machinery of government and no permanent army. What held them together was a common religious heritage which laid down rules for the regulation of daily life, and within the context of this religious tradition it was possible for most decisions, e.g. judicial matters, to be dealt with locally by a meeting of the elders of the community.

When danger threatened, as it often did, was met by improvisation. A charismatic leader, a Samson or a Gideon, would raise the rallying cry and envoys would be sent to all the tribes to drum up support. A volunteer army would be gathered and once the danger was over it would just as quickly disperse. It was the Philistines who finally made this kind of improvisation inadequate.

Establishing a Kingdom

The Philistines were originally seafarers from the Aegean islands who settled on the coastal plains of Palestine about the same time as the tribes of Israel occupied the central mountain core. They were a more formidable threat than any of the other enemies of Israel because they had iron weapons rather than bronze and because they were well organised under a military form of government. It was to meet this threat that Saul was anointed as Israel's first king. This move was not made without opposition, however, and the internal conflicts surrounding the establishment of the monarchy are clearly revealed in the biblical narrative.

Close study of the story of the anointing of Saul in I Samuel shows that it is in fact a conflation of two incompatible accounts. In one, Samuel takes the initiative and anoints Saul according to God's instructions. In the other it is the people who demand a king and Samuel seeks to dissuade them, telling them that they have no need of any king other than God himself. Only under pressure does he eventually give in and agree to their demands, making it clear that he will not be responsible for the consequences. Whatever the truth about the way Saul came to the throne it is certain that Samuel soon opposed him and this, combined with the growing adulation of the young David, led to a deep sense of insecurity in him not actual paranoia. Of Saul's courage there was never any doubt but after some early victories over the Philistines he did not succeed in the purpose for which he had been anointed. When he and all but one of his sons lost their lives in a desperate last bid to break Philistine domination, the threat remained as potent as when he ascended the throne.

David

The reign of David, spanning the forty years or so from about 1000 B.C. onwards, is the best documented of any of the Old Testament monarchs. A large part of II Samuel was evidently written by a very close associate of David and the picture he paints is quite remarkable both for its literary merit and its lack of bias. We have here something akin to the modern historical biography, a work at once sympathetic to its subject yet quite objective in recording his failings.

Though there were obviously many in Israel who looked to David as the natural leader of the nation following Saul's death, his succession to the throne was not straightforward. Ishbaal, the one surviving son of Saul, had been declared king by Abner, Saul's general-in-chief. David, while avoiding any open conflict with Ishbaal, exerted subtle diplomatic pressure to isolate him and gradually swung even Saul's former supporters behind him. Eventually Ishbaal was assassinated but David, possibly genuinely outraged by this action and certainly wanting to make sure that he could not be accused of complicity in the crime, had the assassins executed.

Having thus secured sole claim to the throne with the minimum of strife and bitterness he first set about the Philistines and then subjugated Israel's enemies on every side, establishing a substantial empire. He took the old Jebusite city of Jerusalem and made it his capital for both strategic and diplomatic reasons. It was a readily defended site and it had been an enclave within the territory of Israel not belonging to any tribe. Thus David hoped to minimise inter-tribal jealousies. He established the machinery of government and a permanent highly skilled army in a way that Saul had never been able to do and it is scarcely surprising that the reign of David was always remembered with nostalgia as the ideal period of Israel's history. His reign was not a total success however. In particular he never seems to have exercised much control over his sons, who engaged in constant conspiracies against each other and against David himself in his later years in order to secure the succession to the throne.

Solomon

When David died it was Solomon who succeeded in establishing himself as his successor but only by ruthlessly suppressing all opposition. He brought the empire established by David to new heights of prosperity by the careful cultivation of diplomatic and trade relations with his neighbours, exploiting Israel's position as the land "bridge" between Europe, Asia and Africa. But the fruits of this new prosperity were not evenly distributed and the demands he made upon his people were much resented. In the end he overreached himself to the extent that he had to trade off small parts of his territory to pay his debts.

When he died, his son Rehoboam (922–915 B.C.) promised a continuation and intensification of his policies and ten of the twelve tribes responded by rebelling under the leadership of Jeroboam. Rehoboam was unable to quell the revolt and was left as ruler of the much diminished kingdom of Judah while Jeroboam established a new kingdom of Israel which he ruled until 901 B.C.

Division and weakness

The southern kingdom of Judah, with Jerusalem as its capital, was always the more stable of the two and the more firmly attached to the distinctive religious traditions of the Jewish people. The northern kingdom of Israel, having been born out of revolution, suffered several further violent changes of dynasty in the two hundred years of its existence. Without the stabilising influence of the Jerusalem temple it was also more wayward in its religious affairs, frequently flirting with pagan religious practices. Initially it had no permanent capital but eventually the new city of Samaria was established for this purpose.

The division of Solomon's empire naturally led to a period of weakness during which most of the territorial gains made by David and consolidated under Solomon were lost. Although a full-scale civil war between the two kingdoms was avoided, relations were uneasy and there were sporadic border skirmishes for many years until both sides came to accept the status quo.

They did not only have each other to contend with however. Rehoboam had to raise a considerable sum in tribute to the Egyptians in order to forestall an invasion by Shishak which is documented in Egyptian sources as well as the Bible. In the northern kingdom Baasha (900–877 B.C.) was harried by Syrian forces and thus we begin to see the emergence of a pattern which was to recur frequently over the next three centuries. Sandwiched between Egypt to the south-west and first Syria, then Assyria and later Babylon to the north-east, Israel and Judah were often buffer states between two great powers and consequently enjoyed only limited independence.

Resurgence

The periods of greatest security were generally those when both kingdoms had able rulers who were willing to co-operate with each other, e.g. Jehoshaphat (873–849 B.C.) in Judah with Omri (876–869 B.C.) and Ahab (869–850 B.C.) in Israel. Ahab, however, aroused the wrath of the prophets, especially Elijah, by embracing the religion of his Phoenician wife Jezebel and the discontent thus aroused finally boiled over in Jehu's bloody rebellion against Ahab's son Jehoram.

The most successful period of the two kingdoms came during the reigns of Uzziah (783–742 B.C.) in Judah and Jeroboam II (786–746 B.C.) in Israel. Taking advantage of temporary weaknesses among their neighbours, they succeeded in expanding their joint territories to cover an area nearly as large as the empire of David and Solomon. Like Solomon they used their geographical position to develop trade and thus were able to experience a life of luxury hitherto unknown. But as in Solomon's time this prosperity was unevenly distributed for the wealth of the few was gained through the exploitation of the many. Amos in the south and Hosea in the north raged against the repression of the poor and weak and the abandonment of fundamental religious principles. They foresaw that such a society contained the seeds of its own destruction and indeed within twenty-five years of Jeroboam's death the northern kingdom had ceased to exist as an independent political entity.

Assyrian supremacy

The immediate cause of Israel's downfall was the rise of Assyria under Tiglath-pileser III (745–727 B.C.), Shalmaneser V (727–722 B.C.) and Sargon II (722–705 B.C.) but it is possible that she could at least have survived under Assyrian overlordship had it not been for her own bitter internal wrangles. In her last twenty years Israel had six kings and four of them died by assassination. The final mistake was that of Hoshea (732–724 B.C.) who thought that he could throw off the Assyrian yoke when Tiglath-pileser III died in 727 B.C. Although Shalmaneser V was busy for a time with uprisings elsewhere in his empire, in 724 B.C. he struck Israel with devastating force, capturing Hoshea and deporting a large proportion of the population. The capital, Samaria, held out until 721 B.C. but its eventual fall to the Assyrians signalled the end of the northern kingdom which became an Assyrian province.

Meanwhile in Judah King Ahaz (735–715 B.C.) had followed a policy of submission to the Assyrians. In fact he went much further than he need have done, apparently actively embracing Assyrian gods and religious practices. When Hezekiah succeeded him in 715 B.C. he put his father's policies into reverse, carrying out a widespread religious reform which involved the removal of Assyrian cult objects from the temple and the closing down of pagan altars where the old Canaanite religion was still practised. When Sargon II died in 705 B.C. Hezekiah openly rebelled against his successor Sennacherib. It was some time before Sennacherib was able to respond but in 701 B.C. he launched a devastating attack. Excavations at Lachish, one of the most strongly defended cities in Judah, have unearthed a pit containing 1500 skeletons from this time. Soon only Jerusalem remained defiant.

What happened next is not clear. The Assyrian records state that Hezekiah paid a vastly increased tribute to the Assyrians in return for the withdrawal of their forces. The biblical account of the events in II Kings 18 appears to contradict itself. At one point it corroborates the Assyrian view yet at another it says that disaster (plague?) struck the besieging forces and they fled. Some scholars therefore take the view that there were two campaigns against Judah, one in which Hezekiah was humiliated and another some years later in which he was successful in defying the Assyrians.

Throughout these turbulent years the first Isaiah (i.e. the prophet who wrote Isaiah 1–39) was active. He is sometimes referred to as a prophet-statesman because his utterances often contained quite specific advice on how to respond to the current political situation. In truth, however, his political views cannot be separated from his religious insights. He advocated the avoidance of any direct challenge to Assyria and denounced alliances with neighbouring countries for that purpose. On the other hand he did not favour Ahaz's abject acceptance of Assyrian customs. In his view it was Judah's business to follow God's laws and let God deal with the Assyrians. If, however, the people of Judah failed to obey God's laws then he would use the Assyrians as an instrument of judgement against them.

Hezekiah's successor, Manasseh (687–642 B.C.), is regarded by the religious historians of the Old Testament as the worst king ever to occupy the throne of Judah. Admittedly he had the misfortune to reign at the very zenith of Assyrian power and had little option but to remain subservient, but he had no need to rebuild the old Canaanite places of worship. He is also said to have burned one of his sons as a sacrifice and to have shed much innocent blood. When his son Amon (642–640 B.C.) seemed set to continue his policies he was soon assassinated, a rare occurrence in Judah and indicative of the strength of feeling against him. This brought the eight-year-old Josiah to the throne.

Assyrian decline and the rise of Babylon

Josiah (640–609 B.C.) was the last king of Judah to have a significant degree of independence. The Assyrian empire, which had seemed unassailable during Manasseh's reign, began to crumble after the death of Asshurbanapal in 633 B.C. under the attacks of the Medes and the Babylonians and this left Josiah with a relatively free hand. In 622 B.C. during restoration work on the Temple, a Book of the Covenant was discovered which set out the terms of God's agreement with Israel and the laws he expected his people to follow. This document is generally identified with the book of Deuteronomy and it is thought to have been written in secret during Manasseh's savage reign by devout followers of the traditional Jewish faith as a way of ensuring that their traditions survived. Josiah took its message seriously and carried out the most thorough reform of Judah's religion ever known.

By 609 B.C. Assyrian forces were making their last stand against the Medes and Babylonians. At this point they gained an unexpected ally in the form of their old enemy Egypt. The Egyptians calculated that it was better to prop up a weakened Assyria than face a rampant Babylon. They marched through Judah to Assyria's assistance and were intercepted at Megiddo by Josiah who lost his life in the ensuing battle.

The Egyptians were unsuccessful in their bid to save the Assyrians but brought Judah under their control until they were driven back by the Babylonians in 605 B.C. Thus Jehoiakim (609–598 B.C.) passed from Egyptian to Babylonian overlordship. Trying to exploit their advantage the Babylonians fought a pitched battle with the Egyptians on the very frontier of Egypt in 601 B.C. but the outcome was indecisive and both sides suffered heavy losses. The Babylonians returned home to reorganise and, interpreting this as a sign of weakness, Jehoiakim rebelled. In December 598 B.C. a Babylonian army marched against Jerusalem and in the same month Jehoiakim died. His son surrendered within three months and was deported, together with many others among the leaders of the people.

Incredibly Zedekiah (597–587 B.C.) did not learn from the mistakes of his predecessors. Probably as early as 594/593 B.C. he was consulting with envoys from surrounding states about the possibility of further rebellion and in 589 B.C. he openly rebelled. This time the Babylonians had no intention of permitting any further insubordination and after a long and terrible siege Jerusalem was taken, its temple destroyed and its walls broken down. The fleeing Zedekiah was caught near the Jordan and witnessed the execution of his sons before being blinded and led in chains to Babylon. A massive deportation of the population took place and Judah became a Babylonian province ruled by a governor.

Jeremiah, possibly the most remarkable of all the Old Testament prophets, lived throughout the last forty years of the kingdom of Judah and constantly offered deeply perceptive comments on its affairs. The call to be a prophet came to him about the year 627 B.C. and he initially welcomed Josiah's reforms following the discovery of the Book of the Covenant. This apparently made him enemies among some of his own family who were provincial priests and therefore bitterly opposed to the edict which made Jerusalem the only legitimate place for sacrificial worship. But Jeremiah quickly saw that reforming the institutions of religion was not enough; indeed it could have an undesirable effect if people thought that it was the only step necessary. There had to be an inner revolution within the hearts of individuals.

The false dependence of his people upon the outward trappings of religion was a constant theme in Jeremiah's preaching. Unlike nearly all his contemporaries, he did not accept that God would protect the temple in Jerusalem at all costs and that therefore those who lived in the shadow of its walls need never fear anything. Indeed he saw the attacks of the Babylonians as God's judgement on a hypocritical people and declared that surrender to the Babylonian forces was the only sensible course of action to avoid further unnecessary suffering. For these seditious statements he was imprisoned and very nearly killed. Yet Jeremiah laid the foundations for the re-thinking of Israel's faith that had to take place during the Babylonian exile for he had learned to see the hand of God in suffering and humiliation as well as in triumph, in the failures of his people as well as their successes. It was on such foundations that the later Isaiahs (the authors of Isaiah 40–55 and 55–66 respectively) were able to build.

After the exile

The books of Ezra and Nehemiah record the

return of the exiles following the overthrow of the Babylonian empire by the Persian monarch Cyrus in 539 B.C. but the Bible is largely silent about Jewish history from this point onwards until the New Testament takes up the story with the birth of Jesus. Initially under the overlordship of Persia, Palestine then became part of the Greek empire of Alexander the Great and finally passed into the hands of the Romans. There was a brief period of virtual independence following the overthrow of the last of the Greek rulers, Antiochus Epiphanes, in 164 B.C. The descendants of the Maccabean family which had led the revolt ruled as high priests for a time and even began to call themselves kings, but they depended on the goodwill of Rome. By New Testament times Palestine was part of the Roman province of Syria and the Jewish kings mentioned in the New Testament were Roman puppets.

If the political affairs of the Jewish nation during this period are of little interest to the student of the Bible, there are however important religious, social and cultural developments. The effect of the Babylonian exile on Jewish religion was to make it more legalistic. Before the exile the chief expression of religious faith had been the sacrificial worship carried out in the temple at Jerusalem. With sacrificial worship anywhere except the temple forbidden, this form of religious expression was now denied to them. So the Jews came to emphasise scrupulous observance of the laws laid down in the Pentateuch (the first five books of the Old Testament) as the best form of witness to their faith and the best way of maintaining their separateness from the Babylonians among whom they had to live. This also explains the growing exclusiveness of the Jewish faith for devout Jews were anxious to avoid the dilution of their faith by foreign practices.

The exile was also responsible for the development of the synagogue. With sacrifice no longer possible, a form of worship evolved which was based on the recitation and exposition of God's acts in history. The synagogue, then, provided a place of worship and teaching for the many hundreds of Jewish communities which became established throughout the eastern Mediterranean as a result of Jews fleeing from famine or invasion or being forcibly deported. The existence of these Jewish communities in almost every city was to be crucial to the spread of Christianity, and synagogue worship was to provide the basic pattern for Christian worship.

A further factor of considerable significance was the establishment of Greek as the common language of trade and commerce following Alexander's conquests. By the time of Jesus many Jews outside Palestine spoke only Greek and it was for this reason that a Greek translation of the Old Testament had been completed in Alexandria by about 150 B.C. Jesus, then, was born into a world unified as never before, and perhaps never since, by Roman rule and Greek language.

The Christian era

When we come to consider the chronology of the New Testament period there are surprisingly few events that we can date with absolute confidence. Yet by using these few fixed points together with the internal evidence of the New Testament itself we can put dates to most events within a year or two either way.

Luke tells us that Jesus was born during the reign of Herod the Great who is known to have died in 4 B.C. We can therefore say with certainty that the calculation on which the Christian calendar is based is wrong. If, as Matthew implies, Herod lived for some time after the birth of Jesus, we may suggest a tentative date around 6 B.C. Apart from the incident in the temple when Jesus was twelve, the gospels record nothing more of him until the start of his public ministry which Luke dates as during the fifteenth year of the reign of Tiberius. Unfortunately the Jews and the Romans had different ways of calculating the years of a monarch's reign but this makes the likely date A.D. 27. The date of the crucifixion is generally accepted as A.D. 30 though A.D. 29 is possible.

For the dates of events in the early years of the Christian church we have to work backwards from two known dates: the famine which occurred in A.D. 46 during the reign of Claudius and the arrival in Corinth in the summer of A.D. 51 of the Roman proconsul Gallio. Since Paul was tried before Gallio shortly after his arrival and Paul himself had been in the city eighteen months at the time, this gives us a fixed point in Paul's career from which we can work both backwards and forwards. Nevertheless there are difficulties in establishing the dates of some events. Paul says, for example, that he went to Jerusalem to meet the apostles three years after his conversion and again fourteen years later. Does this mean fourteen years after the first visit or fourteen years after his conversion? The first meaning seems the most natural interpretation of the words yet this would involve putting his conversion in A.D. 31 which is earlier than might reasonably be supposed granted that one has to allow time for the growing church to seem a real threat to the Jewish authorities, for Paul to have become involved in the persecution of Christians and subsequently to have seen the error of his ways.

However, points of uncertainty such as this do not greatly affect the overall picture. Even if we place Paul's conversion in A.D. 34, which most scholars would regard as the latest possible date, it is a strong indication of the astonishing vitality and rapid growth of the early church that the Jewish authorities should perceive it as such a threat so soon after the death of Jesus. That Jewish persecution of Christians did not cease with the conversion of Paul is evident from the fact that Herod Agrippa I was engaged in such a persecution at the time of his death in A.D. 44.

We may link the famine during the reign of Claudius, known to have taken place in A.D. 46, with the visit of Barnabas and Paul to Jerusalem bearing famine relief gifts from Antioch (Acts 11: 25–30). Paul's first missionary journey can then be placed during the years A.D. 47–48, and the Council of Jerusalem to discuss the admission of gentiles to the church in A.D. 49 (Acts 15). Immediately after this Paul set out on his second missionary journey, arriving in Corinth in A.D. 50 and remaining there until after his appearance before Gallio in the summer or autumn of A.D. 51. It was while he was at Corinth that he wrote the two letters to the Thessalonian Church, which makes them the earliest documents in the New Testament.

After a brief visit to Jerusalem and Antioch Paul was off again on his third missionary journey, arriving in Ephesus during A.D. 52 or 53 and remaining there for three years. After leaving Ephesus he did a quick tour of the churches in Greece and then travelled to Jerusalem, arriving in time for the feast of Pentecost in A.D. 56 or 57. During the period of the third missionary journey he had written letters to the Corinthians, the Galatians and the Romans. The letter to the Romans was probably intended to pave the way for a visit to Rome. It is unique among Paul's letters in addressing a church he did not already know.

While in Jerusalem Paul was arrested and brought before the Roman governor Felix who found him not guilty but kept him in custody to appease the Jewish authorities. When Felix was replaced by Festus in A.D. 59 (or possibly A.D. 58) Paul appealed to Caesar. He would therefore have arrived in Rome in the spring of A.D. 60 in all probability, having wintered in Malta following his shipwreck there.

At the end of Acts Paul is still under house arrest in Rome and we have no certain knowledge of what happened next. Roman law stated that if a man had appealed to Caesar and his accusers did not appear to present their case within two years he must be set free. Since the Jewish authorities would be unlikely to pursue their case in Rome, knowing that they would have little chance of success in a Roman court which had no interest in the religious arguments of the Jews, it seems probable that Paul was free again by A.D. 62. Since he had been making plans to visit Rome in any case, he may well have stayed there, in which case it seems likely that he was one of the martyrs of Nero's persecution two years later, but this must remain a conjecture.

The New Testament provides no account of events beyond Paul's Roman imprisonment some thirty years after the death of Jesus. To conclude a survey of biblical history at this point would be highly unsatisfactory, however, for most of the New Testament documents had still to be written.

The first of the gospels was that of John Mark, written in Rome and based on the reminiscences of Peter shortly before his death in Nero's persecution. Admittedly the only evidence for this is tradition, but it is an ancient tradition and entirely plausible. Similarly there is no reason to doubt that Luke and its sequel Acts were written by the doctor of that name who accompanied Paul on certain stages of his missionary journeys (hence the parts of Acts which are written in the first person plural, the so-called "we" passages). Both Luke and Matthew had copies of Mark and incorporated most of his material into their own gospels. They also used another written source which no longer exists as a separate document and which consisted of a collection of the sayings of Jesus. Finally they had their own sources which provide us with stories exclusive to either Luke or Matthew.

Clearly, then, Luke and Matthew were written at a later date than Mark. Given that every copy of Mark's work had to be made by hand and that widespread distribution would take several years to achieve, it is unlikely that either Luke or Matthew could have been completed much before A.D. 75 and Matthew may well have been rather later. Though his gospel is the most Jewish in its outlook it is also the most critical of the scribes and pharisees and this may reflect the increasingly bitter relations between church and synagogue in the period after A.D. 80. It is clear that the author of Matthew is not the disciple of that name for an eyewitness of the events would hardly rely so much on other sources.

John's gospel shows all the signs of long and mature theological reflection on the life and teaching of Jesus by someone who was as familiar with the abstract concepts of Greek philosophy as with the more concrete ways of expression characteristic of Hebrew thought. Such an integration of two essentially different ways of thinking does not happen overnight and this makes it unlikely that the fourth gospel was written before the last decade of the first century.

So we reach the end of biblical history a century or so after the birth of Jesus with the church under threat, certainly, from both Jewish and Roman authorities but growing in numbers daily and equipped with a body of writings which were to become the fundamental basis of its faith and life.

AN INTRODUCTION TO COMPUTING

This section in *Pears* provides a concise yet wide-ranging introduction to the world of computing. It provides not only a guide to the key terms and vocabulary but looks also at the practical applications of one of the most important technological features of the 1980s. A special topic in this edition looks at the growing use of microcomputers.

TABLE OF CONTENTS

INTRODUCTION TO COMPUTING

This article is in five parts with illustrations:

I. Introduction
II. Historical Background
III. Hardware: the actual components which comprise a computer
IV. Software: the programs which control the computer and enable the user to obtain results in a form that he can readily understand
V. Future developments
VI. Special Topic: Microcomputers

I. INTRODUCTION.

Computers have brought about a greater change in our society in the last twenty years than any other force and are likely to continue to do so until the next century. The industry surrounding computers is growing rapidly, providing employment for many but at the same time making others redundant. Jobs which computers can do far more reliably, faster and cheaper are lost. The redeployment of labour and the prospect of increased leisure are causing social upheavals which require new ideas and significant changes of attitude.

The Application of Computers.

Computers can store vast amounts of information in a very small space and are used by the banks to keep accounts, print out statements and control transactions. They are also used by the police to keep personal records, fingerprints and other details. In the rapidly developing field of *robotics* computers are now being used to control manual operations done by machines. These too are taking over work, previously done by people, in the manufacture of cars, in weaving and other industries. Computers play an important role in controlling artificial satellites, decoding information and communications generally. They are used to predict the weather with increasing accuracy. On the debit side, however, they play an important role in the development of weapons, being used to control missiles and to design ever bigger and better bombs.

Programmed Learning.

This article deals mainly with the large computer whose power seems to double every two years. The small computer, however, is no less important and an increasing number of homes nowadays have some electronic device to do simple arithmetic. Programmable computers, which are no longer expensive, are increasingly used at home and in schools to perform calculations and to teach computing. Small computers are also used to teach other subjects in *programmed learning*. Here the pupil is confronted by the computer with a question and a set of possible answers. If he makes the right choice the computer simply passes on to the next step but if he makes a wrong choice he is supplied with further information or asked further questions in order to help him realise his error. Not until he fully understands the answer does the computer pass on to the next step. Programmed learning is nowadays the subject of quite a lot of research.

Servomechanisms.

Many computers are designed for a single purpose only, such as controlling a robot on a car assembly line. The robot can place the cylinder block in the correct position, spray the bodywork with paint or do up nuts without human aid. Advanced machine tools are often controlled by computer so that the position of holes drilled in a block of metal or the shape into which it is cut depends on a set of punched cards given to the tool. Heat-seeking missiles are designed to attack enemy aircraft and missiles by detecting and being attracted to their hot exhausts. They are examples of *servomechanisms* controlled by computers because as soon as the enemy aircraft deviates from its predicted course the missile's computer has to make a fresh set of calculations to direct the missile towards it. Computers are also used in industry to control the manufacture of chemicals. For example, when the temperature of the reactor vessel becomes too hot or the concentration of one chemical becomes too high the computer immediately calculates and causes the correct action to be taken.

II. HISTORICAL DEVELOPMENT OF COMPUTERS.

One of the simplest devices to aid arithmetic is the *abacus* (**L3**), devised by the Chinese. There is more than one type of abacus, but basically it is a frame with several wires across it, on each of which are strung a number of beads. Each wire represents a digit of a number and the position of the beads on that wire tells the operator what that digit is. The abacus is still widely used in the East and a skilled operator can do calculations on it faster than an electronic calculator. However it takes far longer to acquire the necessary skill and so it is little used in the West.

The first fully mechanical device was made by Pascal in 1642 to help his father, a tax collector, keep accounts. Numbers were represented by the rotation of wheels which were geared together in order to represent carry digits. Leibnitz in 1694 created a more sophisticated device which could also multiply and divide, but this proved less reliable than Pascal's machine. The first example of a robot controlled machine was Jacquard's loom in 1801. This machine was capable of weaving complicated patterns which depended on the position of holes in punched cards that were supplied to the machine.

The Contribution of Babbage.

Charles Babbage (1791–1871), was probably the person who contributed more ideas than anyone else to the development of the computer. He was paid large sums of money by the British Government to develop his *difference engine*, a machine designed to calculate tables by the method of differences. He abandoned this project ten years later in order to work on a more advanced machine, the *analytical engine*. Although he was always far too ambitious for the technology available to him and the machine he designed was never completed, it incorporated many of the ideas that are used in modern computers. It was to be capable of reading instructions and data from punched cards which were examined for holes by moving rods. These instructions could include *loops*, which meant the same set of instructions could be repeated over and over again without having to write them down each time. In this way, for example, the square of each integer between one and a million could be calculated with very few instructions. Because the machine could be made to obey different sets of instructions it was *programmable*. It had a *memory* which could be used for storing data or numbers created in the course of executing the instructions. The results were printed out automatically instead of having to be read and written down by the operator, a process Babbage considered to be unreliable. The machine that Babbage designed therefore had an *input device* for reading in instructions and data, an *output device* for printing numbers, a *memory* for remembering numbers and an *arithmetic unit* for actually performing the calculations. These are the essential ingredients of a modern computer.

The First Electronic Computers.

Up to 1946 all computers used the movements of mechanical parts to perform their operations and store their numbers, but in that year the first electronic computer, called ENIAC, was built which only used the movements of electrons to do its calculations. Because pulses of electrons can be made to move much faster than mechanical parts electronic computers operate much faster than mechanical ones. This computer stored numbers in *denary* form (numbers with digits from 0 to 9) and had to be programmed by pulling switches. In 1949 there followed EDSAC and later EDVAC, electronic computers using *binary* numbers (**L17**), which were fully programmable. The early electronic computers used valves to do the necessary switching, while nowadays transistors are used because they are much faster, more compact and produce far less heat. The memory devices in the earliest electronic computers were columns of mercury in which were created square wave pulses of sound. These travel from one end of the column to the other where they are converted into electrical pulses. These in turn are amplified and used to create fresh pulses of sound at the beginning of the column. Thus a stored number exists as a set of pulses which go round and round a column of mercury until the number is changed. Nowadays far more efficient memory devices are used.

III. HARDWARE.

The Basic Ingredients of a Computer.

There are basically two sorts of computers, the digital computer and the analogue computer, although there are hybrid types. The digital computer represents numbers and other information by discrete states so that it is not possible to go continuously from the number 1.5 to 1.6. The analogue computer represents numbers by physical quantities which it can measure, such as voltage or current and it is quite possible for a number to change continuously. For example, a watch with hands is an analogue device for the position of the hands may change continuously but a watch with numbers that change every second is a digital device because there is no state between these numbers. Digital computers are in wider use for general problems, being more versatile and having the advantage that they do not make mistakes so that the same calculation, when repeated, will always produce an identical result. They can also produce results correct to twelve or more significant figures while results from analogue computers may only be correct to two or three significant figures. However, it is often possible to set up electrical circuits consisting of resistors, capacitors, inductors, transistors and other devices which are equivalent to various physical problems and by measuring the currents and voltages in these circuits obtain numerical answers to certain problems which would require far more time on a digital computer.

This article will deal mainly with large digital computers and it is first necessary to see what the vital ingredients of such computers are. The basic function of the computer is to read in data which may be in the form of numbers or letters, to process this data in the manner required by the user, and output the results in a convenient form. In order to do this an *input device* for reading in data is required. To process the data the computer requires a set of instructions called a *program* which also must be read in by an input device. An output device is required to output the results. The computer will also require a *memory* in which to store the data and instructions. Instructions are stored in the same parts of the memory as the data. The actual calculations and manipulation of the data are performed in the *arithmetic unit* which is capable of addition, multiplication, etc. and various logical operations. Finally the *control unit* gives the necessary orders to the other units. It tells the memory which numbers to send to the arithmetic unit, brings instructions from the memory, orders the arithmetic unit to carry out these instructions and arranges for the results to be stored in the memory. This is illustrated in Fig. 1. The control unit and the arithmetic unit together comprise the *central processor* which is the heart of the computer. The running of the computer is controlled by a control switchboard called the *console*. The console, main memory and central processor form the *main frame* of the computer. The main memory does not have sufficient capacity for the computer's requirements and additional slower forms of memory are required whose contents can be transferred to the main memory when needed. The additional memories comprise the *backing store* and an example of such a *storage device* is a reel of magnetic tape. Just as a magnetic tape can be used to store the notes of a symphony and then played back at home on a hi-fi set so it can be used to store numbers. The backing store together with the input and output devices comprise the *peripherals*. Fig. 2 (**V5**) illustrates the basic ingredients of a computer.

The main frame of the computer has a number of input and output channels to which peripherals may be connected. Between the computer and each peri-

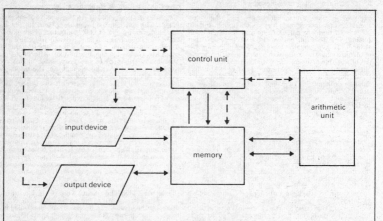

Fig. 1 Diagram illustrating flow of control instructions and information on a computer.

- - - represents path of control information

—— represents path of data and program instructions

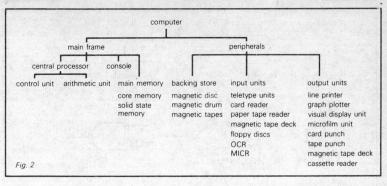

Fig. 2

pheral there has to be a small computer called an *interface* in order to match the coded electrical impulses that the computer understands with those that the peripheral understands.

Input and Output Units.

A large computer has many different kinds of input units, some of which are described below. Nowadays programs are often typed directly into the computer's memory at a *teletype unit* and its replies to the user are either typed back automatically through the same typewriter or displayed on a television screen which is part of the teletype unit. A large computer may well have over a hundred users connected to it simultaneously, each one expecting a reply from the computer within a few seconds, and their programs simultaneously stored within its memory. Anyone connected to the computer in this way is said to be *on-line*. Although feeding in information in this way is more expensive than by other means it is very convenient because typing and programming mistakes can easily be corrected by means of the excellent *editing programs* now available. Keeping the program stored within the computer's memory saves the user having to carry a hard copy of the program around with him, which in the case of a large program could be very bulky.

A cheaper way of feeding in data or a program is to type it in on a microcomputer and store it on a floppy disc (*see Part VI*) which can then be read in by a main frame. Alternatively they can be typed in on a *card* or *tape punch* causing holes representing the data to be punched on cards or paper tape. However, this method is becoming obsolescent. If paper sheets are typed using a font which the computer can recognise (Optical Character Recognition or OCR) they may be fed into the computer directly using a *document reader*. Merchandise at supermarkets usually has an optical bar code on its cover which can be recognised by a detector at the checkout. This conveys information to a central computer. OCR has the disadvantage that a blot or stain can prevent correct reading. Magnetic Ink Character Recognition (MICR) is used on bank cheques and by the Post Office for automatic sorting of letters.

Most of these forms of input must also be a form of output. For example, a program on cards which has been fed in and corrected may need to be output on cards. If a program generates a very large number of numbers which are stored on magnetic tape these numbers will have to be read in by some other program as data. In addition to these forms of output a device capable of printing out results is needed. The most commonly used such device is called the *line printer* because it prints out a complete line of about 140 characters at a time. For each character position there is a wheel which is rotated until the correct character is opposite the paper. The row of wheels is then pressed into the paper and a complete line is printed. Another output device is the *graph plotter*, capable of drawing graphs on paper. Graphs can also be displayed on a television screen and photographed or xeroxed directly. This means that the result can be obtained more quickly but the quality

of output may be less good than that from the graph plotter.

Buffers.

Buffers are memory devices which are used solely to store information which is being transmitted from one part of the computer to another. For example, the time taken to read in numbers from punched cards is limited by the speed of the card reader which is far slower than the rate at which the central processor can handle information. In order to prevent the inefficiency of having the main frame of the computer held up by the card reader the information is first transferred to a buffer which can then pass it on to the central processor at high speed. All input and output devices are slow compared with the central processor and require buffers for efficient operation. Buffers may also be inserted in other parts of the computer to allow one part of the computer to catch up with another part.

A large computer does much of its work in a *time sharing* mode. Here a large number of programs are stored simultaneously within the memory and the computer will work for a few seconds on one program and then start working on another program before execution of the first program is complete. Another reason why time sharing is so important nowadays is because so much work is done on line with many users working simultaneously at teletype units connected to the computer and expecting results while they wait.

Binary Arithmetic.

When people do arithmetic they represent numbers by a string of digits where each digit can take one of 10 values, 0, 1, 2, ... 7, 8, 9. This is known as the *denary representation* and as an example 47239 represents the number equal to $9 + 3 \times 10 + 2 \times 10 \times 10 + 7 \times 10 \times 10 \times 10 + 4 \times 10 \times 10 \times 10 \times 10$. Computers, on the other hand, use the *binary representation* of numbers where each digit can only be 0 or 1. For example, 11101 in binary representation means $1 + 0 \times 2 + 1 \times 2 \times 2 + 1 \times 2 \times 2 \times 2 + 1 \times 2 \times 2 \times 2 \times 2$ which is 29 in denary. Binary representation is inconvenient for people to use because it requires too many digits. 8 in denary is 1000 in binary and 47239 in denary is 1011100010000111 in binary. In order to do arithmetic in denary however, people have to remember their multiplication and addition tables. In binary representation the tables are much simpler and are shown below:

	0	1			0	1
0	0	0		0	0	1
1	0	1		1	1	0 + carry

Binary multiplication   Binary addition

For example, the binary addition table shows that $1 + 1 = 0 + carry$ and the binary multiplication table shows that $1 \times 0 = 0$. The greater simplicity of the

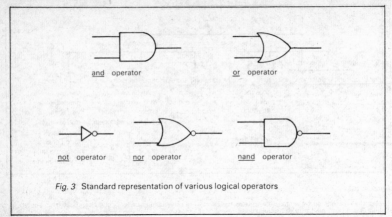

Fig. 3 Standard representation of various logical operators

binary multiplication and addition tables allows the computer to work faster.

A still more important advantage of binary representation to the computer is that most physical objects have just two well defined states. For example, a ring of magnetic material may be magnetised in either the clockwise or the anticlockwise direction. Since binary digits can only be *either* 0 or 1, the digit 0 can be represented in the memory of the computer by magnetising a ring in the clockwise direction and the digit 1 by magnetising a ring in the anticlockwise direction. There are 2^5 ($2 \times 2 \times 2 \times 2 \times 2$) ways of magnetising a set of 5 magnetic rings and consequently 5 magnetic rings can be used to remember every integer between 1 and 2^5. In order to remember longer numbers more rings are required.

Units of Information.

We have just seen how 5 magnetic rings can be used to say which value a number takes out of 2^5 possible values. It is said that 5 magnetic rings can store 5 *bits* of information. "Bit" is an acronym for "binary digit" (**L18**). A number with 5 binary digits contains 5 bits of information and requires at least 5 magnetic rings to store it. In general n rings can store n bits of information. When the computer calculates $x \times y$ it does not send the first "bit" of x to the arithmetic unit and then the second bit and so on. This would be very inefficient. Instead several bits are put together forming a *word*, the *word length* being the number of bits in the word. When a computer transmits information from one part to another it transmits a whole word at a time. All words in a particular computer are of the same length although the word length may vary from computer to computer. The greater the word length of a computer the greater the accuracy of its calculations. The amount of information a large computer can store in its main memory may typically be one million 64 bit words which is equivalent to 64 million bits. Each word is stored in a *storage register* which may comprise 64 magnetic rings. The electrical circuitry is such that when that word is required to do a calculation the content of each ring is sent simultaneously to the arithmetic unit.

Computers are normally designed so that they can remember numbers in basically two different ways. If a number is an *integer*, such as 67, without a fractional part, it can be remembered as an integer. However this representation is no good if the number is 67.321 for the .321 will be lost. 67.321 can however be represented in the form $\pm .xyz \times 10^{\pm ab}$ in denary. Suppose we were to try to represent every number in denary in the form $\pm .xyz \times 10^{\pm ab}$ for any $x \geq 1$ and any y, z, a, b. It would be possible to represent every positive and negative number whose magnitude lies between 10^{-100} and 10^{99} in this way with three figure accuracy. If, on the other hand, they could be represented in the form $\pm .xyzw \times 10^{\pm abc}$

a greater range of numbers could be represented with greater accuracy. $\pm .xyzw$ is called the *mantissa* and $\pm abc$ is the *exponent part*.

In binary 67.321 is approximately 100011.0101 or $.1000110101 \times 2^{+110}$. If a computer had a word length of 64 bits the designers would decide how many bits, 16 say, would be used to remember the exponent and how many bits, 48 say, for the mantissa. A number remembered in this way would be said to be in *floating point* form. The arithmetical operations that the computer has to perform on floating point numbers are of course completely different from those on numbers which are remembered as integers.

Logical Operations.

When we say $7 \times 9 = 63$ we can think of the multiplication sign $\times$ as an operator which acts on two inputs, seven and nine, to produce one output which is sixty-three. In the table for binary multiplication it can be seen that when both inputs are 1 the output is 1, otherwise the output is 0. If we suppose that 1 corresponds to "true" and 0 to "false" the output is "true," *i.e.* is 1, only if both inputs are also "true." For this reason the binary multiplication operator is equivalent to the logical *and* operator because (A and B) is only true when both A and B are true. The standard representation for the operator is drawn in Fig. 3. If the designer of the computer chooses to make a positive voltage represent the value 1 and a zero voltage represent the value 0 then by means of transistors or other devices he has to invent a circuit which will give a positive output voltage when both input voltages are positive and zero voltage otherwise.

Another important logical operator is the *or* operator which gives output 0 only when both inputs are zero. This is because (A or B) is true if A is true or B is true or both are true. The *not* operator has only one input and its output is 1 when the input is 0 and its output is 0 when the input is 1. The *nor* operator is equivalent to applying an or operator and then applying a not operator so that the output is only 1 when all the inputs are 0. The *nand* operator is equivalent to applying an and and then applying a not. The standard representation for all these operators is drawn in Fig. 3. A nor operator with only one input is equivalent to a not operator and it can be shown that any logical operator can be constructed just out of nor operators. The circuit in Fig. 4 is equivalent to an and operator. In some computers the only logical operators used are nor operators in order to reduce the variety of components. Such a computer is said to use *nor logic*.

The action of a computer in processing data and producing output can be regarded as a sequence of logical operations and an electronic circuit equivalent to a nor operator is shown later. It has already been shown how a multiplication between two

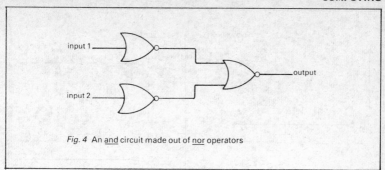

Fig. 4 An <u>and</u> circuit made out of <u>nor</u> operators

binary digits is equivalent to an and operation. An addition between two binary digits has two outputs, a sum and a carry and can be represented by the logical diagram in Fig. 5. The carry is 1 only when both inputs are 1. The sum is 1 when either of the two inputs is 1 and the other is 0. This circuit is known as a *half adder*. A *full adder* is a circuit which has two outputs, a sum and a carry, and has three inputs, input A, input B and a carry from a previous digit. It can be made out of two half adders. Two binary numbers consisting of several binary digits can be added together by a succession of additions. All other operations such as multiplication and division can be carried out in the same way that people carry them out when they do arithmetic, by a succession of logical operations, although they are more complicated than addition.

Transistors.

The logical operators just described may be thought of as switches which allow a current to pass when the output is one and no current to pass when the output is zero. Although transistors are not the only devices which can do this they are the devices most commonly used in computers today and are described below. Silicon is the most widely used material in transistors today and operates well at the temperatures in which we live. Extremely pure silicon can be prepared quite cheaply and ways have been found of making very complicated devices out of it. Silicon is known as a *semiconductor* because

unlike most materials which are either good conductors of electricity or good insulators silicon is only a moderately good insulator and its conductivity increases with temperature and amount of impurity.

Many materials behave as though they create an enormous number of *states*, each state having a particular energy. Each electron has to go into some particular state but no more than one electron can enter any one state. In other words no state may have two electrons in it. In metals and semiconductors these states can be divided into two bands, the *valence band* and the *conduction band* as illustrated in Fig. 6. The conduction band states have higher energies than the valence band states and for silicon this difference corresponds to about 1 volt. The electrons prefer to lie in low energy states so that the probability that a state is filled gets smaller as the energy of the state increases. The energy level at which the probability that a state is filled is exactly one half is called the *Fermi level*. If a state is a long way below the Fermi level it will almost certainly be filled and if it is a long way above the Fermi level it will almost certainly be empty.

An electric current occurs when electrons move from one state to another travelling in one general direction. The amount of current is the rate at which positive charge flows past some point. Since an electron carries a negative charge the current flows in the opposite direction to the electrons. If a band is completely empty of electrons it does not conduct

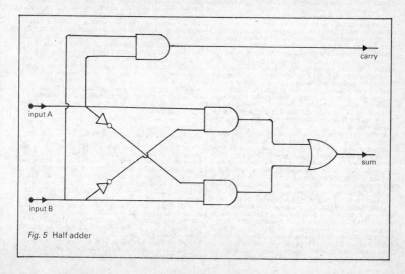

Fig. 5 Half adder

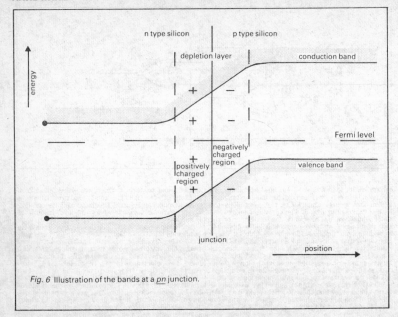

Fig. 6 Illustration of the bands at a *pn* junction.

any electricity but if a band is completely full it does not conduct electricity either, because there is no empty new state for an electron to move into. The conduction of electricity therefore depends on having either the conduction band or the valence band partly full and partly empty. Metals which are good conductors have their valence bands virtually completely filled, but electrons can travel along their conduction bands because they are only partially filled. Pure silicon is not a good conductor because the valence band is nearly filled and the conduction band is nearly empty so that neither band is a good conductor. In pure semiconductors like silicon the Fermi level is nearly half way between the valence and the conduction band states.

It is possible however to add impurities to the silicon which cause the Fermi level to move towards either the conduction or the valence band, so that either the conduction or the valence band becomes conducting. If *donor* impurities such as arsenic or phosphorus are added the material is called an *n*-type semiconductor and some of the conduction band states are filled allowing the conduction band to conduct electricity. If, on the other hand, *acceptor* impurities such as indium or gallium are added some of the valence band states are unfilled and this type of material is called *p*-type semiconductor. These unfilled states are called *holes* and a hole may be thought of as a positively charged particle capable of travelling through the semiconductor along the valence band.

The operation of a transistor depends on having a junction between an *n*-type and a *p*-type semiconductor. Fig. 6 illustrates what happens at such a junction when there is no current. Because there is no current the system is in equilibrium and fundamental theory of physics can show that for a system in equilibrium the Fermi level is the same throughout the transistor. The conduction band in the *n*-type silicon on the left has to join up with the conduction band in the *p*-type silicon on the right and similarly for the valence band. In order for this to occur there has to be a positively charged region on the left of the interface and a negatively charged region on the right-hand side. In the region close to the interface on both sides neither the conduction nor the valence band is very close to the Fermi level. This means there are not many electrons in the conduction band or holes in the valence band to con-

duct electricity. This region is therefore called the *depletion layer* and is an insulator.

In order that a current passes from left to right holes have to pass from left to right in the valence band or electrons must pass from right to left in the conduction band. The position of the Fermi level (*see* Fig. 6) shows there are very few holes on the left-hand side of the junction and very few electrons on the right-hand side. This means that a positive current can not flow from left to right. It is possible for current to pass from right to left however because there are holes on the right-hand side which can go to the left-hand side and electrons on the left-hand side which can travel to the right. Because of the way the conduction band and the valence band slope however, the electrons and holes require additional energy in order to climb a potential barrier on crossing the junction. This means a potential difference greater than about 0·6 volts is required before a significant amount of current flows. After the electrons have crossed from the *n*-type material to the *p*-type material they can fall from the conduction band into the valence band where they cancel some of the holes. Similarly holes which have passed from the *p*-type to the *n*-type material are cancelled by electrons falling from the conduction to the valence band. The transistor just described is called a *diode* because it only permits current to flow in one direction.

The Bipolar Transistor.

The *bipolar transistor*, invented in about 1950, can be either of the *npn* or the *pnp* type. An *npn* transistor is illustrated in Fig. 7 and consists of two *n*-type regions called the *emitter* and the *collector* with a narrow layer of *p*-type semiconductor sandwiched between, called the *base*. The collector is put at positive potential relative to the emitter causing electrons to flow from the emitter to the collector and this current is controlled by adjusting the potential of the base. If the base is made negative relative to the emitter current tries to flow from the emitter to the base which is not allowed and so no current flows. If however the base is made positive relative to the emitter, electrons flow from the emitter to the base and continue to flow towards the collector because the collector is positive relative to the base.

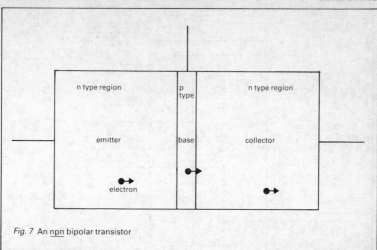

Fig. 7 An npn bipolar transistor

Because the base is deliberately made very thin electrons do not have time to fall from the conduction band to the valence band before they reach the collector. In this way electrons can flow from the emitter to the collector and small changes in current through the base cause large changes in the current through the collector. The transistor therefore acts as an *amplifier* turning small signals into large signals.

Field Effect Transistors.

Another important type of transistor is the *field effect transistor* known as the *FET*. An *n-channel FET* is illustrated in Fig. 8. It has three electrodes, the *source*, the *drain* and the *gate*. Between the source and the drain is a long channel of *n*-type material but there is a region of *p*-type semiconductor near the surface and to this region is attached the gate. Near the interface between the *n*-type and *p*-type semiconductor is the depletion layer which, as already discussed, is an insulator. When the drain is at positive potential relative to the source, electrons are attracted from the source to the drain. The number of electrons which pass depends on the thickness of the depletion layer. When the gate is made negative relative to the source current tries to pass in the forbidden direc-

tion between the *n*-type material and the *p*-type and this causes the depletion layer to become thicker and electrons are prevented from passing from the source to the drain. This means that when the gate is made negative the current from the source to the drain becomes smaller. This effect makes it possible to use the FET as an amplifier.

The Manufacture of Transistors.

Silicon transistors have to be made from extremely pure silicon with impurities not exceeding one part in a thousand million. This is achieved by the method of zone refining (Fig. 9). A silicon rod is held in a vacuum and a heater coil is placed round it. An A.C. current of very high frequency is passed through the coil and this induces electric currents in the silicon rod. The energy of these currents turns into heat causing the silicon to melt in the region of the coil. The heater coil is slowly moved down the rod and the molten region moves along with it. Most of the impurities are swept along in front of the molten region leaving relatively pure silicon behind. By making several passes with the heater coil extremely pure silicon can be obtained. However it does not yet have crystalline structure.

The next stage is to produce a silicon crystal by melting pure silicon in a crucible, dipping a small

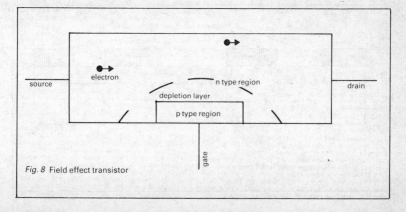

Fig. 8 Field effect transistor

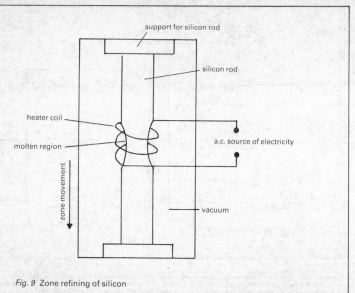

Fig. 9 Zone refining of silicon

seed crystal into the melt and slowly drawing it out. The molten silicon attaches itself to the seed crystal and is drawn out as a long rod. Its atoms are now arranged in layers in a perfectly regular structure. If *n*-type or *p*-type silicon is required the correct amount of impurity is added to the melt. The crystalline rod is now cut into narrow slabs called *wafers* about half a millimetre thick.

Each of these wafers can be converted into hundreds of silicon chips each containing thousands of transistors, resistors and capacitors. Although the method of making *integrated circuits* on silicon chips need not be dealt with in detail, the principle behind making *pn* junctions and *npn* junctions is fairly simple. Suppose some acceptor impurity is added to the melt when the silicon crystal is drawn so that each wafer is of *p*-type material. The wafer is heated in an oven containing phosphrous vapour. The phosphorus diffuses very slowly through the layers of solid silicon and causes those parts near the surface exposed to the phosphorus to change from *p*-type to *n*-type silicon. In this way a simple *pn* junction can be made and used as a diode.

When making a more complicated circuit not all the surface is exposed to the phosphorus vapour. The wafer is previously heated in a furnace containing oxygen causing a protective layer of silicon dioxide to be formed on the surface. Part of this silicon dioxide can be etched away leaving complicated patterns of exposed silicon surface. The phosphorus vapour can not pass through the silicon dioxide so that a pattern of *n*-type and *p*-type silicon is produced as shown (Fig. 10). Techniques exist for making very complicated integrated circuits on a silicon chip of size $\frac{1}{2}$ cm $\times$ $\frac{1}{2}$ cm $\times$ $\frac{1}{2}$ mm and terms such as LSI (large scale integration) and VLSI (very large scale integration) have come into being. Chips with over 100,000 transistors on them are now being produced commercially and the number is increasing all the time.

Various Circuits.

Using the symbols illustrated in Fig. 11 on the right, a *nor* circuit is illustrated in Fig. 12 and is discussed below.

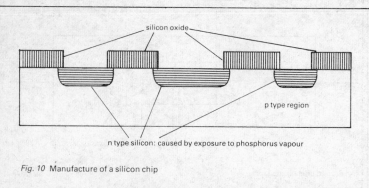

Fig. 10 Manufacture of a silicon chip

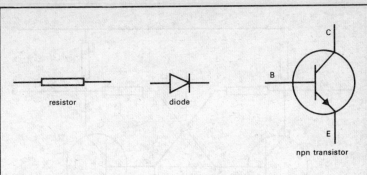

Fig. 11 Standard representation of some electronic components

The emitter, E is held at zero potential and Y is held at a potential of about 6 volts. Suppose all three inputs are zero so that the electric potential at the base, B is zero. Since there is no potential difference between E and B the transistor does not conduct electricity and the current passing through C and the resistor R is small. Ohm's law tells us that because the current passing through the resistor is small there is very little potential difference across it and the potential of the output is nearly 6 volts.

Now suppose one or more of the inputs is positive. If input 1 is positive current can flow from input 1 towards B across diode D1. This current can not flow out through inputs 2 or 3 because of diodes D2 and D3 which only allow current to flow one way. B is therefore at positive potential relative to E and therefore the transistor becomes conducting. Because the transistor has very little resistance to the current which flows through it, the output is at very nearly zero potential.

The results can be summarised as follows: If all three inputs are zero the output is positive. If one or more of the inputs is positive the output is zero. This is equivalent to a nor operator with three inputs. There is no reason why there should not be as many inputs as one likes but in the case where there is only one input the circuit is equivalent to a not operator.

The Bistable Circuit.

Another very useful circuit is the *bistable circuit* which contains two *npn* transistors (*see* Fig. 13). It is designed to have two stable states, one in which the left-hand transistor conducts electricity and the right-hand does not and the other which is the other way round. The state of the circuit represents the number 0 or 1 according to which transistor is conducting. When a positive pulse is applied to input 2 the right transistor becomes conducting and when a positive pulse is applied to input 1 the left transistor becomes conducting.

The circuit works as follows: If the left transistor T_1 is conducting Q and B_2 are at nearly zero po-

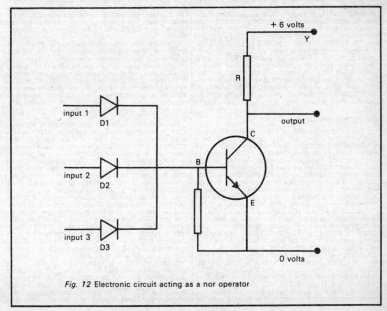

Fig. 12 Electronic circuit acting as a nor operator

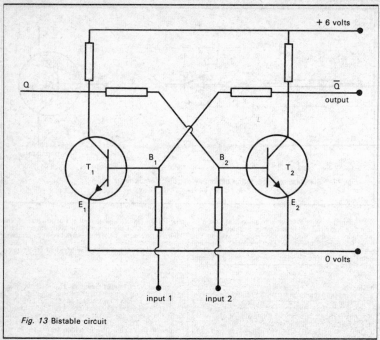

Fig. 13 Bistable circuit

tential. Since B_2 is at zero potential no current flows through the right transistor T_2 and therefore $\bar{Q}$ is positive. Since Q is positive B_1 is also positive since it is connected to Q by a resistor through which only a small current flows. Since B_1 is positive T_1 remains conducting. This state of affairs continues until a positive voltage impulse in applied to input 2. When this happens B_2 becomes positive, T_2 becomes conducting and the potential at Q and $\bar{B}_1$ falls to zero. This causes T_1 to stop conducting so that the potential at Q becomes positive. This means the potential at B_2 remains positive and T_2 remains conducting until a positive voltage impulse is sent to input 1. In short, the bistable circuit can be used as a memory device.

Various Memory Devices.

A large computer will use many different ways of "remembering" numbers each with its own particular advantages and disadvantages. In the last section a *solid state memory* device using transistors was described. Solid state memory has the advantage of very short *access* and *write times*, that is the time that is required to make a copy in the arithmetic unit of the contents of the memory or write the contents of the arithmetic unit into the memory. Now that it is possible to get an enormous number of transistors on to a single chip solid state memory is also very compact and becoming much cheaper. It does however have the disadvantages that it is more expensive at present than other memories and that it is *volatile*, which means that if the electric power were switched off due to some failure the contents of the memory would be lost.

Another solid state memory device that is often used is a MOS capacitor attached to a MOS transistor (MOS = "metal oxide semiconductor"). The memory holds the value 1 or 0 according to whether the capacitor is charged or not. Since the charge leaks away the capacitor has to be recharged every few thousandths of a second and so this form of

memory is called *dynamic* solid state as opposed to *static* solid state like the bistable circuit. Although the dynamic memory is somewhat slower than the static memory it is cheaper and uses less power and therefore creates fewer cooling problems (*see* **Part V**).

Until recently computers used to store bits of information by magnetising magnetic rings in either a clockwise or anti clockwise direction, corresponding to value 0 or 1, say. This method has the advantage of being *non-volatile* so that the values are retained if the power were switched off. Magnetic bubble memories (*see* **Part V**) are coming into use but they have slow access times. There is some interest in using Josephson devices at liquid helium temperature but this technology has not yet arrived and belongs to the future.

The main memory of most computers is nowadays entirely solid state memory. Although a large computer may have a main memory of a million 64 bit words it needs a much larger memory than this so that other, cheaper forms of memory have to be found. A very commonly used way of storing information is on a magnetic disk. This actually consists of many disks rigidly attached to a spindle which is made to rotate at high speed. Each disk is coated with magnetic material, the principle being the same as that of a tape recorder. For each disk there are a number of reading and writing heads that are capable of reading information from the disk or writing information on to it. These heads can move radially towards or away from the spindle so that any part of the disk can be reached. A large magnetic disk may store over one hundred million numbers and have an access time of about 20 milliseconds.

Instead of a disk, a drum coated on the outside with magnetic material and rotating at high speed can be used. The way in which a read/write head is capable of reading or recording information is illustrated in Fig. 14. When information is being recorded the input current causes a magnetic field

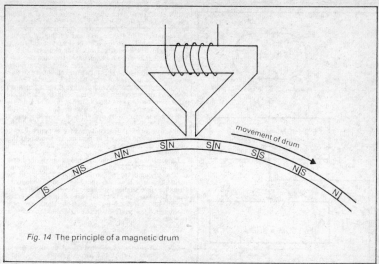

Fig. 14 The principle of a magnetic drum

across the open ends of the iron core. Since the moving drum is just under this gap some of the magnetic field magnetises the magnetic surface. As the input current varies a sequence of north and south poles on the drum are produced. When information is being read from the drum the north and south poles induce changes of magnetic flux in the head as they pass under the gap. This in turn produces electric currents in the coil which can be interpreted as information that can be stored elsewhere.

Tape Decks.

In addition to a magnetic disk or drum a large computer will have several tape decks for reading and writing information on to magnetic tape. This form of memory is much more troublesome than the disk since a tape has to be obtained from the computer library by the computer operators and mounted on a deck. Each tape contains about five million numbers and there is no limit to the amount of information which can be stored in this way. Computer users may have their own magnetic tape in the library on which they have stored their own programs or data, to be fed into the computer when required.

The solid state memory, core memory, magnetic disk and drum are all forms of *random access memory* since a number can be read from any of these devices without having to read all the numbers before it. It is however very inefficient to read from the disk or drum a single number at a time because of the time required to move the read/write head to the required position and wait for the disk or drum to rotate to the required position. Instead a whole block of numbers recorded in succession on the disk is read. For this reason the disk and drum are known as *block access memories*, suitable for storing blocks of numbers or other information. A magnetic tape is known as a *serial memory* because numbers have to be read in the order in which they are stored on the tape. The disk, drum and tapes are not part of the main memory, being too slow but comprise the *backing store*.

IV. SOFTWARE.

Flow Charts.

To do a useful job a computer normally needs two forms of input, data and a set of instructions. A set of instructions expressed in a way that the computer

can understand is called a *program*. Programs have to be written in languages especially invented for the purpose of instructing computers and enabling the *programmer* to tell the computer the various operations it must perform in the correct sequence.

Before writing a program a programmer must decide on the logical order of a number of operations and to do this he often uses a *flow chart*. Fig. 15 illustrates a flow chart for a simple program to calculate $1/1 + 1/2 + 1/3 + \ldots + 1/900$. Instructions are often called *statements* and in this particular diagram they are labelled S1, S2, ... S8 although this is not usual. Control passes from one statement to the next, *e.g.* from S4 to S5, unless there is a statement saying control must pass to some other statement. S6 is a conditional statement, placed in a different shaped box, which says control must pass back to S4 unless $I = 900$ in which case control passes to S7. Because control passes back from S6 to S4 there is a *loop*. Control passes round this loop 900 times as I goes from 1, 2, 3, ... to 900 and each time this happens $1/I$ is added to SUM. When $I = 900$ SUM has the right value and so control passes to S7. The result is printed out and execution terminates.

If this program were written in the language called BASIC it might look like this:

```
10   LET SUM = 0
20   LET I = 0
30   LET I = I + 1
40   LET SUM = SUM + 1.0 / I
50   IF I ≠ 900 THEN 30
60   PRINT SUM
```

Machine Language.

Each type of computer has its own language called *machine language* which is different from the machine language of another make of computer. Because a computer can only understand its own language a program written in another language such as BASIC must be converted into an equivalent program written in machine language. This conversion is done by a special program called a *compiler* which accepts the program in BASIC as data and produces a program in machine language as output.

Each storage register of a computer has an *address* so that, for example, variable I in the program just considered may be in the storage register with address 507 say, while variable, SUM is stored at address 403 say. Any storage register can be used for storing an instruction. The instructions are usually stored in sequence so that if one instruction

This will be illustrated by an example later. Computer operations take place in cycles called *machine cycles* which are alternately *instruction cycles* and *execution cycles*. Suppose the instruction register contains word p. In the first step of the instruction cycle the word q, say, which is stored at address p, is brought to the control unit. This word consists of two parts, the *operation part* and the *operand part*. The operation part specifies the next operation to be performed by the computer and the operand part specifies the address of some storage register. In the second step of the instruction cycle both parts are decoded and placed in the operation register and the address register repectively. In the final step of the instruction cycle the number in the instruction register is increased by one. This is because the next instruction to be carried out is held at this address unless the present instruction causes control to be passed to some other instruction. In the execution cycle the operation held in the operation register is executed.

Let us imagine the machine language of our hypothetical computer is sufficient to read three numbers a, b, c, to calculate $(a \times b) + c$ and to print out the result. Assume that each machine language instruction has five digits, the first two digits being the operation part and the final three being the operand part. For simplicity let us assume there are only eight basic instructions in the machine language as follows:

00000	stop further processing
01xyz	read the next word from the input device and store it at address xyz
02xyz	output the word stored at address xyz
03xyz	copy the word stored at address xyz into the accumulator
04xyz	copy the contents of the accumulator into address xyz
05xyz	multiply the number stored in the accumulator by the number stored at address xyz and keep the result in the accumulator
06xyz	add the number stored at address xyz to the number stored in the accumulator and keep the result in the accumulator
07xyz	put xyz in the instruction register. This means the next instruction to be executed is at address xyz.

When stored in the computer these instructions would of course be in binary representation. The program to evaluate $a \times b + c$ in machine language might look like this:

01157	read a and store it at address 157
01231	read b and store it at address 231
01161	read c and store it at address 161
03157	put a in the accumulator
05231	the contents of the accumulator become $a \times b$
06161	the contents of the accumulator become $(a \times b) + c$
04157	the contents of address 157 are erased and replaced by $(a \times b) + c$
02157	$(a \times b) + c$ is output
00000	execution ceases.

The program itself would not include the explanations but just consist of the 9 five-digit numbers, one after the other. The addresses 157, 231, 161 could be replaced by any other addresses and the result would be the same.

A computer with so few machine language instructions as that described above would not be able to do many types of calculations. It cannot divide, subtract, do conditional statements, read from and output to different devices, edit text, choose the format for numbers that are output, etc. In order to perform the variety of operations expected of a modern computer it must have a far greater number of basic operations than the computer just described.

Assembly Language.

Assembly language is the next language higher than machine language. The programmer does not have to remember the address of each variable he uses but instead will give the variable a name such as V1, V2, V3, etc. The language will be made easier

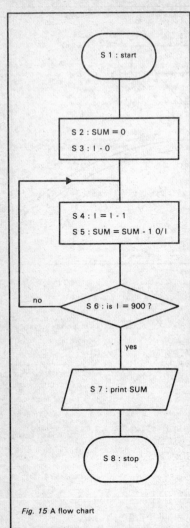

Fig. 15 A flow chart

The flow chart shows:

- S 1 : start
- S 2 : SUM = 0
- S 3 : I - 0
- S 4 : I = I - 1
- S 5 : SUM = SUM - 1 0/I
- S 6 : is I = 900 ? (no / yes)
- S 7 : print SUM
- S 8 : stop

is held at address 114 the next instruction is stored at address 115. The control unit will probably have a special register called an *instruction register* which holds the address of the next instruction. It will also require an *operation register* to specify the next operation that the arithmetic unit must do, such as multiplication or addition. This operation must be performed on a word called the *operand* which may be a number or a string of letters. The address of the next operand required is held at the *address register*. The address register may alternatively hold the address where the result of a calculation is to be sent for storage. When a word is sent from a storage register to the arithmetic unit it is stored in a special register called an *accumulator* or simply a *register*. An arithmetic unit may have several accumulators depending on its complexity.

Let us take a very simple hypothetical computer and consider how it performs some basic operations.

to remember by the use of mnemonics so that instead of the machine language instruction "06161" which means "add the contents of address 161 to the accumulator" he may have to write "ADD V3," meaning "add V3 to the contents of the accumulator." Another important difference is that instead of having to write "07043" meaning "transfer control to the instruction stored at address 043" he can use a *label*. He could write "GOTO L2" and before the appropriate instruction insert "L2," L2 being a label. This facility makes it much easier to amend programs because when instructions are added to or removed from a program in machine language the address of each instruction is also changed. This causes control to pass to the wrong instruction unless the programmer has made changes in the goto instructions. Assembly language is like machine language because to every instruction in assembly language there is a single corresponding instruction in machine language.

Assembly languages are difficult to use but are nevertheless used extensively because they are very powerful. They enable the programmer to exercise complete control over the way in which his program is executed and obtain greater efficiency. They have the disadvantage that like machine languages, the assembly language of one make of computer is different from that of another make. Consequently a program written in assembly language for one computer cannot be used for any other computer.

The Use of High Level Languages.

Most programming nowadays is done in a high level language as this saves the programmer's time and means that the program can be used on more than one computer. A high level language is a language where a single statement may correspond to several instructions in machine language. For example, "10 LET A = (B/C + 3/D)/E + 1" is a statement in BASIC telling the computer to calculate A. This would require at least seven machine language instructions. The statement above involves working out an *arithmetic expression* and putting the result into A but there are many other kinds of statements. "IF X = Y THEN GOTO L1;" is a *conditional statement* in ALGOL, telling the computer to go to the point in the program labelled L1 if X = Y, otherwise carry straight on. "121 FORMAT (15H YOUR SALARY IS, F10.2)" is a *format statement* in FORTRAN. If at some other point in the program the statement "PRINT 121, X" occurs, the computer will first print out "YOUR SALARY IS" and then the value of X. The value of X is printed out in a format defined by F10.2, requiring 10 spaces in all, having 2 digits behind the decimal point and seven in front. High level languages also allow the use of *subscripted variables*. Thus in ALGOL instead of saying "X[1] : = 1;   X[2] : = 2;   ...   X[1000] : = 1000;", which would be very tedious one can say "FOR I : = 1 STEP 1 UNTIL 1000 DO X [I] : = I;". X[1], X[2] etc. are subscripted variables. X is called an *array* and its size, in this case a thousand, has to be specified somewhere in the program.

Another powerful facility in high level languages is the use of subroutines which are like complete programs in themselves. For example, after the main body of a FORTRAN program there may occur a set of statements like this:

```
S1:   SUBROUTINE ALPHA(U, V)
S2:   U = U + 1
S3:   V = V + U * U
S4:   RETURN
S5:   END
```

This is a very simple example of a subroutine with two *formal parameters*, U and V. Somewhere in the main body of the program or in some other subroutine there will be at least one statement such as "CALL ALPHA(X, Y)." When the computer reaches a statement like this during execution, control passes to statement S1 and statements S2 and S3 are executed. When the statement "RETURN" is reached during execution of the subroutine, control is passed back to the statement immediately following the "CALL ALPHA(X, Y)" statement which caused the subroutine to be entered. When the statement "CALL ALPHA(X, Y)" occurs X, Y are called the *actual parameters*. X has to be matched with U and Y with V as U, V are the *formal parameters* which occur in statement S1.

What happens is best illustrated by an example. Suppose that at a place where a statement "CALL ALPHA(X, Y)" occurs X has the value 4, Y is 50, U is 100 and V is 200. Control passes to statement S1 and new *local* variables, U and V, say, are set up within the subroutine. These are not the same as U and V outside the subroutine which remain 100 and 200. U is matched with X and becomes 4 and V is matched with Y and becomes 50. In statement S2 U becomes 5 and in statement S3 V becomes 75. At statement S4 control passes to the statement immediately following the "CALL ALPHA(X, Y)" statement and X becomes U and Y becomes V. After the statement "CALL ALPHA(X, Y)" has been executed, X has become 5, Y is 75, U is 100 and V is 200. Because the subroutine does not interfere with the main program or other subroutines in any way it can be written by someone who knows nothing about the rest of the program. Large libraries of subroutines are available to do special calculations such as integration, for example. These can be inserted by programmers into their programs.

Comparison between High Level Languages.

Nowadays there are at least ten major high level languages, each developed with some particular purpose in mind. Some sample programs are shown at the end of this subsection. FORTRAN is the earliest such language and was developed in 1954 by IBM (International Business Machines), the largest company making computers. It has undergone many changes and improvements since then and now exists in several *dialects*. It was originally developed for doing scientific problems but is also quite widely used in accounting and business. Although it is unsatisfactory in certain respects it is still the language used more than any other, partly because of the enormous number of programs and subroutines that have already been written in it.

ALGOL60 was developed in 1960 and is a more precisely defined language than FORTRAN and more elegant. Although it is considerably used in Europe it has not achieved the wide use of FORTRAN. It is nevertheless an important step in language development and several new languages are derived from it, in particular PASCAL. ALGOL68 is probably the most sophisticated language yet developed. It is designed to match our own thought processes and as we use very sophisticated concepts, ALGOL68 is correspondingly difficult to learn. It is also difficult to write an efficient compiler for it. PL/1 is a language containing ingredients from both ALGOL and FORTRAN and is gaining in popularity.

BASIC was developed in 1965 and is intended to be easy to learn and is very suitable for beginners. Although somewhat less powerful than FORTRAN or ALGOL it is nevertheless convenient for dealing with complicated problems. It is the main language for microcomputers.

The languages just mentioned are mainly intended for use in scientific or mathematical problems. COBOL is a language intended for use in business and not for scientific programming. Although it is not a language that is particularly easy to learn, it is designed so that a person who is not a programmer can find a COBOL program easy to understand. In addition to COBOL there are other languages designed for specialised uses. SNOBOL, for example, is designed to process strings of characters and do pattern matching. Although it can do arithmetical operations it is less efficient at this than other languages. There are also languages which are especially designed for *real time* computing, that is obtaining results while connected to the computer.

Overleaf there is an example of the same program written in BASIC, FORTRAN and ALGOL. It is designed to read the income of twelve people as data, work out the average income, the spread of their incomes and print out the results.

Compilers.

In order to be able to use a language on a particular computer there must be a compiler available that will translate a program written in that language into a machine language program for that computer. There may be more than one compiler available for a particular language. One compiler is

First the program is written in BASIC:

```
00100 REM INCOMES ANALYSIS PROGRAM
00110 DIM A(12)
00120 LET N = 12
00130 LET S = 0
00140 LET V = 0
00150 FOR I = 1 TO N
00160 INPUT X
00170 LET A(I) = X
00180 LET S = S + X
00190 LET V = V + X * X
00200 NEXT I
00210 LET S = S / N
00220 LET T = SQR( V / N - S * S )
00230 PRINT "AVERAGE INCOME =", S, "STANDARD DEVIATION =", T
```

Next the program is written in FORTRAN:

```
      PROGRAM EARN(INPUT,OUTPUT,TAPE5=INPUT,TAPE6=OUTPUT)
C INCOMES ANALYSIS PROGRAM
      N = 12
      SUM1 = 0.0
      SUM2 = 0.0
      DO 10 1 = 1, N
    1 FORMAT( F8.2 )
      READ( 5, 1 ) X
      SUM1 = SUM1 + X
      SUM2 = SUM2 + X * X
   10 CONTINUE
      AVERAG = SUM1 / FLOAT( N)
      VAR = SUM2 / FLOAT(N) - AVERAG ** 2
      STD = SQRT(VAR)
    2 FORMAT( 22H  AVERAGE EARNINGS = , F10.4,
     +        34H STANDARD DEVIATION OF EARNINGS = , F 10.2 )
      WRITE( 6, 2 ) AVERAG, STD
      STOP
      END
```

Below the program is written in ALGOL 60:

```
EARN:
BEGIN
  INTEGER I, N;
  REAL SUM1, SUM2, AVERAGE, STD, VAR, X;
  COMMENT  INCOMES ANALYSIS PROGRAM;
  N := 12;
  COMMENT N IS NUMBER OF PEOPLE AND CAN BE CHANGED IF NECESSARY ;
  SUM1 := SUM2 := 0.0;
  FOR I := 1 STEP 1 UNTIL N DO
  BEGIN
    INPUT( 50, "(" DDDDDD.DD ")" , X );
    SUM1 := SUM1 + X;
    SUM2 := SUM2 + X * X;
  END;
  AVERAGE := SUM1 / N;
  VAR := SUM2 / N - AVERAGE ** 2;
  STD := VAR ** 0.5;
  OUTPUT( 51, "(" "(" AVERAGE EARNINGS = ")", DDDDDD.DD,
      "(" STANDARD DEVIATION OF EARNINGS = ")", DDDDDD.DD ")" ,
      AVERAGE, STD ) ;
END
```

designed not to use too much computer time to translate a program and to have good *diagnostics*. This means that when things go wrong the computer is able to diagnose the error and give the user plenty of information which he can use to correct the program. A compiler like this is used for *debugging* programs, that is removing errors from them. However this sort of compiler may not produce a very efficient *object program*. In other words, the machine code program that is produced by this compiler takes more computer time to do a calculation than is necessary. For this reason another compiler which may take longer to translate a program but which produces an efficient object program may be needed for programs which have been debugged.

Some compilers are better than others depending on the amount of effort that has been put into making them. A compiler is usually a very large program, using up a large part of the main memory and consequently leaving less memory space available for the program which has been compiled. The size and efficiency of a compiler may depend on the language it has to translate, the more sophisticated the language, the more difficult it is to translate it.

Graphics.

Although it is not difficult for a large computer to calculate a million numbers it is very difficult for a person to absorb all this information. One way of making it easy for people to understand results is to display them in the form of a graph. Packages of subroutines have been developed for this purpose. The graphs produced can be drawn with a pen on paper, produced on microfilm or displayed on a television screen. It is quite easy, in principle, to display a function of one variable on a screen as a curve, but the problem of displaying a function of several variables is more difficult. In a map temperature as a function of position on the earth's surface can be displayed by making high temperature red and low temperature blue, with colours in between representing temperatures in between. The same principle can be used to display any function of two variables on a colour television set. Another way of representing functions of two variables or three dimensional objects is by the use of lines as illustrated in Fig. 16. Routines exist for displaying functions in this way and showing them from different angles.

Networks.

The computer that is used does not have to be close to the user and may be hundreds of miles away connected to the user by telephone. For example, much of the computing done by the Home Office in London is performed by a computer near Liverpool. Computer *networks* have been set up which make this possible. The computer which does the work is called the *host computer* but there have to be other computers called *nodes* which are used to transmit information from the place of origin to the host and back again. A network may have several host computers. Any one of the computers may carry out the task required unless the user specifies which computer is to be used.

To illustrate the use of a network, London University consists of several separate colleges, many of which have their own computers. However the University has its own computer centre with some of the most powerful computers that have ever been built. These computers are linked together by a network called METRONET which enables someone at Imperial College, say, to use either an Imperial College computer, a London University computer or a Queen Mary College computer. Several universities in the south west of England have computers which are linked together by a network called SWUCN. SWUCN in turn is linked to METRONET enabling someone at Bristol University to use the powerful Cray 1 computer at the London University Computer Centre. Many networks like this exist in this country.

V. FUTURE DEVELOPMENTS.

Recently two new computers, the Cray 1 and the Cyber 205 have appeared costing about £7 million each. They are far more powerful than any other computers on the market and have been labelled "supercomputers," being able to do up to 100 million calculations per second. One reason why they can achieve such speeds is that they can do several calculations simultaneously. This is achieved by *pipelining*. For example, adding two numbers together requires several operations. These two numbers enter a *pipe* and several stages later the result emerges. Before the final result appears however another pair of numbers can enter the pipe. One can think of the pipe therefore as containing several cal-

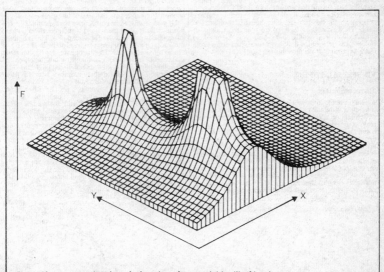

Fig. 16 A computer drawing of a function of two variables like f (x, y)

culations each passing forward through it and carried out in successive stages. Such computers may also have several pipes. The operations on all computers are synchronised by a *clock* which emits pulses. Each stage in the execution of a program corresponds to a pulse and in the Cray 1 and Cyber 205 there are about 100 million pulses a second. New computers are being designed to do calculations faster by doing several calculations simultaneously and this means that the *architecture* of computers is becoming more sophisticated. It is likely that in the future new languages will be required which can exploit the ability of future computers to do several operations simultaneously.

The speed of a computer is limited by two things, the switching time and the time taken by an electric pulse to go from one part of the computer to another. The switching time may be thought of as the time a transistor takes to go from a conducting state to a non-conducting state or vice versa. Since the switching time is now only of the order of one thousand millionth of a second the time an electric pulse takes to travel from one part of the computer to another is becoming a more serious limitation. Nothing can travel faster than the speed of light and light can only travel one foot in a thousand millionth of a second. It is very important that everything is made as small as possible and the memory does not require too much space. The latest computers have silicon chip memories and since a memory of several million words is required it is necessary to have a very large number of transistors on a silicon chip. The Cray 1 and Cyber 205 use chips with about 4,000 transistors on them but now chips are available with nearly a million transistors on them, known as VLSI.

One of the problems with packing a very large number of silicon chips into a small space is that they use power and this means a lot of heat is generated in this space. An elaborate cooling system is a very important part of a supercomputer. Silicon may be replaced in the future by Gallium Arsenide which is over ten times faster. It is less affected than Silicon by radiation caused by an atomic bomb so military establishments are interested in developing it. Another important development in computers which may occur in the future is the use of *bubble memories*. If the surface of a non-magnetic material is coated with a thin layer of magnetic material which is magnetised in a small magnetic field towards the surface, small regions in the material, called magnetic bubbles are magnetised in the opposite direction, away from the surface. These bubbles can be moved around and used to represent binary digits. Bubble memories cannot replace transistors in the main memory because they are too slow. However they can contain a great deal of information in a small space and may be used to replace the magnetic disk eventually, as they have the advantage of no moving parts.

VI. SPECIAL TOPIC.

Microcomputers.

The increase in power of computers has been such that it is nowadays possible to build a computer which sits on a desk top and which has more power than a computer needing a large, air-conditioned room twenty years ago. A computer like this, which does all its processing on a single chip, is called a *microcomputer*. Because they are able to perform tasks which would have required a main frame computer several years ago, microcomputers are replacing main frames for many purposes which do not require a large memory and this section of the market is expanding rapidly. Such a computer can vary in price from £10 for a programmable pocket

calculator to more than £2,000 for an IBM personal computer.

Any sophisticated computer needs some way of storing information in permanent form, *e.g.* programs for later use, and the method of permanent storage which is most used with microcomputers is on floppy disks. A typical floppy disk consists of a disk of diameter 5¼ inches coated with magnetic material which remains permanently within a special envelope. For use this must be placed inside a disk drive unit. When information is read from or written onto the disk the disk is made to rotate rapidly inside the envelope and the transfer of information is complete within a few seconds. The envelope, which does not rotate, has special slots cut in it which allow the read/write head belonging to the disk drive to lie very close to the surface of the disk. A disk can typically store from 60K to 1¼M bytes of information, depending on the quality of the disk drive. A byte is eight bits and corresponds to about one character, such as a letter, digit or space. Here K stands for about a thousand and M for a million. Since *Pears Cyclopaedia* contains about eight million letters about eight floppy disks would be required to store all the text in *Pears*. Recently Winchester disks have been developed which can hold over 50M bytes of information and are far more reliable.

The use of microcomputers in the office is likely to expand rapidly in the next few years. Information and text stored on disks is more compact and often more retrievable than the same information stored in a filing cabinet. Such a collection of information forms a *data base* or *data bank* and the management and updating of data bases is an important branch of computing. Perhaps the most important office use, however is word processing. Typically a word processing program, stored on a disk, usually developed by a software company and sold for two or three hundred pounds is fed into the memory of the computer. The text to be edited is either typed directly into the computer or fed in from another disk. The word processing program can be used to correct typing errors, adjust the line width, spacing, number of lines to a page, right justify, insert text, delete text, replace one word by another whenever it occurs, *etc.* The results are either stored on disk or typed out. Word processors are often used to type out automatically circular letters, sent to different people at different addresses. Some microcomputers are designed to perform no other task than word processing and are called *dedicated word processors*. Accounting is another important use for microcomputers and accounting programs can easily be purchased.

Microcomputers have become very popular in the home where they are used for recreation (video games), education and office purposes. The language normally used by home programmers is BASIC or an extension of it. The program for converting statements in BASIC into machine language, called an *interpreter*, is usually stored in ROM (read only memory). ROM is solid state memory which is filled at the time of manufacture and can not be changed. RAM (random access memory), on the other hand, is solid state memory whose contents can be changed at will by the user and forms the main memory of a microcomputer. A typical amount of RAM is 64K bytes although many microcomputers have provision for buying more memory and extending it. A cheaper form of permanent memory than disks is cassettes, played on an ordinary cassette deck. However, since access times may be of the order of several minutes instead of a few seconds they are less used. Typical costs for a home computing outfit are £100 to £400 for the computer, including keyboard, a television set to provide the screen, £200 to £800 for a disk drive unit, if required, and £200 to £500 for a printer, if required.

INDEX

Each section has a letter and, where appropriate, the column is given in brackets after the page number, *e.g.*, F8(1), G25(2). Some of the sections are alphabetically arranged and index themselves. Their contents are not included here except where it is anticipated some special difficulty may arise. The sections "Medical Matters" and "The World of Music" have each a separate index and glossary.

E

F

G

V

X

Y

W

Z